THE DALAI LAMA

ALSO BY ALEXANDER NORMAN

Secret Lives of the Dalai Lama:
The Untold Story of the Holy Men Who Shaped Tibet,
from Pre-History to the Present Day

THE DALAI LAMA

An Extraordinary Life

✷

ALEXANDER NORMAN

RIDER
LONDON • SYDNEY • AUCKLAND • JOHANNESBURG

1 3 5 7 9 10 8 6 4 2

Rider, an imprint of Ebury Publishing,
20 Vauxhall Bridge Road,
London SW1V 2SA

Rider is part of the Penguin Random House group of companies
whose addresses can be found at global.penguinrandomhouse.com

First published in Great Britain by Rider in 2020
Published in the United States by Houghton Mifflin Harcourt Publishing Company

www.penguin.co.uk

A CIP catalogue record for this book is available from the British Library

Hardback ISBN: 9781846044663
Trade paperback ISBN: 9781846044670

Printed and bound in Great Britain by Clays Ltd, Elcograf S.p.A.

Book design by Greta D. Sibley

Map by Mapping Specialists, Ltd.

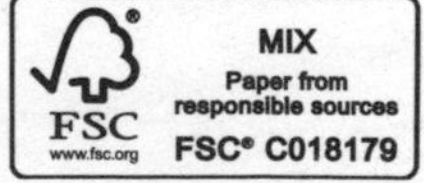

Penguin Random House is committed to a sustainable future for our business, our readers and our planet. This book is made from Forest Stewardship Council® certified paper.

For my children:

M.R.N.

E.A.N.

T.F.H.N.

CONTENTS

A Note on Language and Spelling

Most would agree that the Tibetan alphabet, in each of its forms, is highly attractive on the page. Its use in a nonspecialist book such as this is out of the question, however. Moreover, the standard (Wylie) method of transcription into European characters, although it renders the Tibetan accurately, produces almost equally baffling results for the general reader. Who would guess that *bstan 'dzin rgya mthso* (the name of the present Dalai Lama) is pronounced "Tenzin Gyatso"?

In view of this difficulty, I have given phonetics (often my own) for all Tibetan words and names. Where they occur more than once, I have—in most cases—included them in the glossary at the end, together with the correct Wylie transliteration.

It is also worth noting that Tibetan uses different tones, so words that are phonetically similar may have an entirely different meaning. Notoriously, the words for "ice," "shit," and "fat" are pronounced exactly alike, save for tonal register.

Political Tibet Today
KAZAKHSTAN
MONGOLIA
Area enlarged
QINGHAI PROVINCE
GANSU PROVINCE
Xining
Lanzhou
CHINA
PAKISTAN
Dharamsala
TIBET AUTONOMOUS REGION
Chengdu
Mussoorie
New Delhi
Lhasa
NEPAL
BHUTAN
SICHUAN PROVINCE
INDIA
N
KUNLUN MO
KASHMIR
Gartok
Ü-TSANG
HIMALAYAN MOU
Tashilhunpo Monastery
Shigatse
Gyantse
DROMO (YATUNG)
Mount Everest
NEPAL
Kathmandu
SIKKIM
Gangtok
Thimphu
Kalimpong
INDIA
0 100 mi
0 100 km

Cultural Tibet

INTRODUCTION

Waldorf Astoria Hotel, New York, August 1989

Striding up to Reception, I announce my purpose.

"I am looking for Mr. Tenzin Tethong, private secretary to His Holiness the Dalai Lama."

Under my arm I am carrying the draft manuscript of the Dalai Lama's autobiography, *Freedom in Exile,* on which I have been working for the past several months.

The receptionist stares at me blankly. Perhaps it is my strong English accent.

"Mr. De Whaaat?" she demands in a slow drawl.

Three decades later, such a response is unimaginable. One of the world's most instantly recognizable people, the Dalai Lama sells out sports stadiums from Sydney to São Paolo, from Oslo to Johannesburg. With around 20 million Twitter followers, the Dalai Lama has more than the pope, and his online presence continues to grow. He is a recipient of the Nobel Peace Prize, the Congressional Gold Medal, and the richest award of them all, the Templeton Prize for spiritual progress. He holds the freedom of cities and honorary degrees too numerous to list. His image adorns wristwatches and screensavers, while his Amazon page gives details of more than two hundred books crediting him as author. Sales of several individual titles run into the millions. Unquestionably, the Dalai Lama is one of the best-known and best-loved public figures of modern times.

Yet for all his latter-day superstardom, few know much about the Dalai Lama or about the culture he embodies. And of what is known, a great deal is misunderstood. For example, many people suppose that the Dalai Lama is a religious leader—a sort of Buddhist pope. But unlike the pope, who claims authority over every priest and prelate in Christendom, the Dalai Lama has no jurisdiction over any other lama or monk. Neither is he the head of his own particular faith tradition, nor is he the leader of any of the subgroups within that tradition. In fact, he is not even abbot of the monastery of which he is a member. So when he says, as he often does, that he is "just a simple Buddhist monk," the Dalai Lama is not just being characteristically modest. He is straightforwardly telling the truth. The Dalai Lamas—of which the present one is the fourteenth—have only ever been simple Buddhist monks, even though the Great Fifth Dalai Lama was one of the most powerful men in Asia, and even though the Dalai Lamas have always been venerated by people far beyond the Land of Snows (as Tibetans often refer to their country).

From a political perspective, however, the Dalai Lamas have been anything but ordinary. Beginning with the Great Fifth, they have been—in theory at least—temporal leaders of a people whose country is the size of western Europe, spanning over fifteen hundred miles from a border with Pakistan in the west to China in the east, and almost a thousand miles from Mongolia in the north to India, Nepal, and Burma in the south. But it is little known that in 2011, the present Dalai Lama renounced his claim to lead his people as head of state in favor of a democratically elected layman. As a result, the office of Dalai Lama is now purely a teaching office. This makes perfect sense, however: the word *lama* is the Tibetan translation of the Sanskrit word *guru*—a spiritual guide.

Together with these misunderstandings, the Dalai Lama's image as smiling saint for all seasons fails to do justice either to the Dalai Lama as a person or to the tradition he represents. It neglects his extraordinary achievements in settling a diaspora community now a quarter of a million strong. It neglects how he has unified a people previously sharply divided along geographical, tribal, and sectarian lines. It neglects how, in so doing, he has opened up the institution of the Dalai Lama to all Tibetans in a way that it never was before. It neglects his political reforms. It neglects his remarkable attainments as a scholar-practitioner: he is unquestionably one of the most accomplished and learned masters of Vajrayana Buddhism to have emerged within the past century. It neglects the astonishing impact the Dalai Lama has had on the shape of the modern world. Above all, it neglects one of the most extraordinary cultures ever to have evolved on the face of the earth and the complex, often turbulent history that brought it into being.

In writing this book, therefore, I have sought above all to set the Dalai Lama's deeds in the context of the history and culture of the Tibetan tradition, and it is for this reason that I have shown in some detail the circumstances of how the regency that governed Tibet until the Dalai Lama was of age both came into being and came to an end. Without some understanding of what and where the Dalai Lama comes from, we are likely both to miss the scale of his accomplishments and to misconstrue the enormity of the challenges he has faced.

I hope particularly to show how the Dalai Lama's motivations have caused him to act in the way he has acted—these motivations being themselves determined by his understanding of the Tibetan tradition. I take as my starting point the fact that what has chiefly inspired him is the bodhisattva vow he took at the age of fifteen. Out of compassion, he committed himself to direct his every thought, word, and deed to the benefit of all sentient beings in their quest to overcome suffering. The Dalai Lama's life story can thus be understood as a teaching that shows, from the perspective of the tradition, what compassion really is and how this construal of compassion plays out in the everyday world.

Here, though, I should say something about the words "tradition" and, especially, "Tibetan tradition" as I use them in this book. When I claim that the Dalai Lama exemplifies the Tibetan tradition, I take the term to denote that which is handed down, or handed over, from one generation to another —not just the habitual practices of many Tibetans over time but also the body of ideas and beliefs that attach to these practices. When, for example, I say that, according to Tibetan tradition, there are many hells, some hot, some frozen, I am saying that according to the understanding of most orthodox believers within the tradition, this is the case. I don't mean to claim that all Tibetans everywhere have always believed this, only that most have and do.

At the same time as making this point about tradition, I should also emphasize that, so far as the Tibetan *religious* tradition is concerned, there is Buddhism with, so to speak, local accents but no such thing as a specifically

Tibetan Buddhism. From the Tibetan point of view, the Buddhism preserved within this tradition is the highest, most complete form of Buddhism—even if some of its teachings and practices are regarded as heterodox by others.

Because of my interest in setting the Dalai Lama in the context of Tibetan culture and history and presenting his biography as a lived lesson in what, from the perspective of his tradition, it is to be truly compassionate, I have been less interested in recounting what the Dalai Lama says. Both his spiritual teachings and his political views are recorded in the hundreds of books and many thousands of hours of video and voice recordings that have been made over the sixty years since he came into exile. It is to these sources that those interested in the Dalai Lama's spiritual and political philosophy should turn.

As to what the Dalai Lama is actually *like,* I regard this question as secondary to the question of what the Dalai Lama *means*—not merely by what he says but also by what he does. There is something to be said for personal detail, but in my opinion this tells us much less about the man than that, for example, his religious commitments include some that a number of authorities even within his own Gelug school consider to be dangerously mistaken. How the Dalai Lama interprets and shapes the Tibetan tradition, and, especially, where he departs from it, are in my view more telling and, from a historical perspective, more significant than what his favorite television program is or what his hobbies are. For the record, his preferred viewing is nature programs—he is a fan of David Attenborough—while for hobbies, though he is less active than formerly, he has been an enthusiastic amateur horologist, and he continues to take a keen interest in the garden surrounding his residence.

Having said this, given that I have had the enormous privilege of working with the Dalai Lama on three of his most important books, including his (second) autobiography, I should at least attempt an answer to the question of what he is like as a person.* The best way I can think of doing so is by recounting the beginning of a conversation I had with him some years ago. I told him how my wife had recently chided me that it was a disgrace how, after knowing His

---

* I once calculated that these books alone entailed spending in excess of 250 hours working alone, or in narrowly restricted company, with the Dalai Lama.

Holiness for then more than a quarter century, I still could not hold a proper conversation with him in his own language. I had to admit she was right, I said, and for that, I told him, I ought to apologize.

"Well, if it comes to that," he replied in his familiar heavily accented English, "it is me who should apologize. I have been learning your language since nineteen forty-seven!"

In those few words are summed up the grace, the humility, and the kindness of the man.

I first met the Dalai Lama in Dharamsala, his exile home in India, during March 1988, when I went to interview him on behalf of the London *Spectator*. There was one thing about that first encounter that struck me at the time as slightly strange and has since come to seem prophetic. When I was shown into his audience chamber, I had just enough time to register that the room was empty before I realized the Dalai Lama was standing almost directly in front of me. It was not as if he had been there all along and I suddenly noticed him; rather my impression was that he literally appeared out of nowhere.

Something similar occurred a year or so later—but this is supposed to be a biography, not autobiography. Suffice it instead to say that quite a lot of our work that followed over the years since then was undertaken while the Dalai Lama was away from his exile home and on the road—in the United States, Denmark, Italy, Germany, France, the UK, and elsewhere in India. This has allowed me to see him in a variety of different settings, from which I have gleaned some observations perhaps worth relating.

I know him, for example, to be fastidious—his nails are always neatly trimmed—though he is not the least showy as to dress. His clothing is of good quality but not the finest. His shoes are sturdy and well polished, but of respectable and not high-end provenance. Rupert Murdoch—a media tycoon and not a moralist—once called the Dalai Lama a "canny old monk in Gucci loafers." He was wrong. The Dalai Lama wears Hush Puppies as a rule, never Gucci. At home he wears flip-flops.

It is true that the Dalai Lama has a fondness for good timepieces, but he does not have a collection. He wears an unornamented gold Rolex. Invariably he gives away any he no longer has use for. In fact, I have one of them (gifted by him first to someone else). It is a plain stainless steel Jaeger-LeCoultre

Memovox with a mechanical alarm (which would no doubt have appealed to him) that he wore for a time during the 1960s.

Although quite the opposite of extravagant in terms of possessions, the Dalai Lama has admitted to having a somewhat "free-spending" nature. When he was a child, he would buy as many animals destined for slaughter as he could—to the point where his officials ran out of room to keep them. As an adult, on more than one occasion he visited shopping malls during his first trip to the United States in 1979. His tutor Ling Rinpoché cautioned him against making unnecessary purchases, however, and so far as I know, he has rarely been seen in any sort of retail outlet since. He does not use a computer, so he is not an online shopper. Instead his extravagance—if such it is—is limited nowadays to giving away money, mainly to humanitarian causes. When he won the Templeton Prize in 2012, he immediately donated the great majority of its almost $2 million award to the Save the Children Fund.* This was in honor of the charity's generosity to Tibetan refugees in the early days of exile.

In private, the Dalai Lama is attentive to others' needs and will, for example, ask if you prefer coffee if only tea has been served. He will ensure that there are nuts or cookies available alongside the *dri churra* (a molar-cracking dried cheese from Tibet) of which he is fond. He will adjust the blinds so the sun is not in your eyes. He may ask whether you find it too hot or too cold and have the heating or air-conditioning adjusted. If it seems to him that the room layout for an audience could be improved, he will have his staff move furniture around until he finds it satisfactory. I recall one occasion during the early days of our acquaintance when I came across him moving chairs in his hotel room in preparation for a press conference.

The Dalai Lama is a hearty eater, though this is in part because, as an ordained monk, he may eat only twice a day, and never after noon—though he might choose to do so if he is a guest at a luncheon while abroad, and he may also take a cookie or two during the course of the afternoon if he has had a particularly arduous day. As to diet, he is not fussy. He leans toward vegetarianism in principle but, on account of illness and doctors' advice, he eats meat

---

* He also gave $200,000 to the Mind and Life Institute and the remainder, approximately $75,000, for science education within the Tibetan monasteries in exile.

without scruple—though one need have no doubt he prays for the postmortem well-being of each creature that he consumes.

As for looking after his own needs, he sometimes jokes that he would not know how to make a cup of tea. Nor does he cook and, aside from helping make *khabse* (New Year's cookies) in the kitchens of the Potala Palace when very young, he has rarely seen the inside of a kitchen. At least when younger, however, he would happily build a fire. But he has always been restricted in what he has done for himself, having been surrounded with staff and attendants since very early childhood. Of these he retains a small community. Within his household, there are around ten, including cooks and orderlies. He has four or five personal attendants, all of them monks, as well as a number of retainers who, because of their age, have only the lightest duties and who remain with him simply as friends. It is to this little community that he turns for conversation and respite at the end of the day. In terms of office staff, they are divided into Tibetan and English sections, most, though not all, of whom are laymen. He employs four (up from only two until comparatively recently) principal private secretaries, who are in turn supported by a small number of subordinates. Although the Dalai Lama appoints these men himself (and, out of consideration for his monastic state, they are all men), their names are submitted to him by the Central Tibetan Administration. Together they constitute his eyes and ears beyond the confines of the Ganden Phodrang, as his home headquarters is known (much as the administration in Washington is known as "the White House"). To be sure, he also listens carefully to what visitors tell him, and he has family and friends from whom he gains intelligence.

If he is less well informed than he should be on a given topic, it will be because the people surrounding him have failed, for whatever reason, to brief him as fully as they ought. Perhaps inevitably, given the small pool of people on whom he has to rely, this does sometimes happen.

Besides his permanent staff, there are larger numbers of bodyguards. At home, the Dalai Lama is watched over by a contingent from the Indian army in addition to his Tibetan security. As to his relations with these, he maintains a certain formality except with the most senior of them, but he is considerate of their needs too. He always has a friendly word for those who keep watch at night when he goes for his early morning walk. (He is in the habit of strolling outside, or along hotel corridors, as soon as he has completed his first prayers.) And when traveling, he invariably takes time out to talk to those who serve him.

Much is made of the Dalai Lama's sense of humor. I have often thought that Tibetan humor generally is quite similar to the English: ready, often earthy, and with a love of irony and absurdity. The best success I have had with a joke was a very innocent one about a mouse. I would not tell him a vulgar story, however. He would likely think it odd that anyone other than his closest family or colleagues would do such a thing. But he is no spoilsport. He once asked me about the wedding of a young Tibetan official that I had attended—whether anyone had gotten tipsy? When I said yes, he was not at all disapproving. When I learned that, besides nature programs, he would sometimes watch an episode of the perennial English comedy series *Dad's Army,* I once sent him a box set, but I do not know whether he ever saw it. I also included a *Mr. Bean* film, as I thought this would appeal to him.

Although he does not stand on ceremony—he actively dislikes formality and any sort of pretense—the Dalai Lama is conscious of the dignity of his office. On one occasion when I failed to produce a *kathag,* the silk offering scarf it is customary to present on meeting, he did not hesitate to reprimand me. On another occasion, I committed one of those faux pas that seemed innocuous to me as a foreigner but which must have caused serious offense. Again, he made me aware of my mistake, but kindly. I do not believe he would have done so if he had not known me as well as he does, however. He is sensitive to others' feelings. That said, he does sometimes make an artless remark that takes people aback. I recall hearing that he laughingly scolded a fellow writer for having fingernails "that looked like claws."

The Dalai Lama is also both affectionate by nature and often tactile. He will pretend to give friends a playful slap on the back of the head. He may clasp your hand and hold it, or nuzzle his cheek against yours, or stroke your beard. Being tactile is a characteristic he shares with his predecessor the Great Thirteenth Dalai Lama, who, having evaded a pursuing Chinese army by fleeing over the mountains into neighboring Sikkim, was rapturously received by the people each according to his or her custom. Some bowed, some offered salaams, some prostrated themselves, but there were three little Scottish girls on ponies—their father was a local missionary—who insinuated themselves into the procession right behind behind him. When he slowed to acknowledge the crowd, they jumped down and ran ahead to await the Dalai Lama at the government guesthouse where he would be staying. As he walked up to it, the Great Thirteenth paused unspeaking to run his fingers through Isa Graham's flaxen locks, "feeling it between finger and thumb, as one feels silken threads to test their quality and texture." Disappearing into the building, he came out only a few moments later to feel her hair again while the crowd gasped.

In considering these personal characteristics, it is vital we do not lose sight of the fact that the Dalai Lama is a monk before he is anything else—and a monk with enormous ritual responsibilities. A weakness of a biography like this is that it cannot avoid giving the impression that the subject's life is all about his public deeds. In the case of the Dalai Lama, however, it is actually his interior life that is the more important. It is therefore essential that the reader bear in mind the Dalai Lama's total commitment to his monastic calling. Every day on rising, without fail, he begins with at least three hours of prayer and meditation. Every evening, without fail, he concludes with an hour or more of the same. And during the day, he will pray and study to the extent his schedule allows, very often including when eating. When on retreat, which he undertakes for extended periods of up to three weeks at least once a year, but also for shorter periods of a few days multiple times during the course of the year, he increases his commitment (by rising at 3 a.m. instead of 4:30) and limits his involvement with worldly affairs to an hour or two per day whenever possible.

I have already mentioned my deficiency in spoken Tibetan. Though functionally literate in the language, I am also reliant on a dictionary or the good offices of some kind person save for the shortest and most basic texts. In some ways, though, this has been a blessing. It has meant that I have come closer to a number of Tibetan friends than might have been the case if I were more self-sufficient. It has also been a constant reminder that I write as an outsider, as an observer, looking in.

It is arguably less of a failing that I am not a Buddhist. It has enabled me to ask questions and think thoughts that would otherwise have been more difficult, if not impossible. But for this same reason, I have no doubt that some of what I say here will seem to some impertinent and possibly even disrespectful, even though I mean neither impertinence nor disrespect. It is also possible that some of the material may be painful to some of my readers. With respect to this, I take encouragement from the Dalai Lama himself, who, on many occasions, has spoken of the need for fair and balanced assessment of the facts. I trust that I have succeeded; certainly this has been my aim at all times.

PART I

✷

A Prophecy Fulfilled

I

The Travails of the Great Thirteenth

It is tempting to begin our story with the first Saturday in July 1935, when, by the Gregorian calendar, the present Dalai Lama was born. And yet to do so would be to ignore the context of that birth. In a way, it would be more accurate to begin with the evening of the seventeenth of December 1933, and the circumstances surrounding it, when the Great Thirteenth Dalai Lama "withdrew his spirit to the Tushita paradise"—where dwell all those on the point of Enlightenment—as pious tradition expresses the matter. The death of the previous Dalai Lama is what precipitates the birth of the next —even if, as in this case, it happens that more than nine months elapse between the two events.

Yet there is also a case for beginning with the birth of the First Dalai Lama, since, after all, each incarnation is considered to share the same mental continuum. But besides necessitating a long digression into history, this would be problematic. It turns out that the First Dalai Lama was in fact the Third. What happened was that a lama by the name of Sonam Gyatso was summoned by

Altan Khan (a descendant of Genghis) to Mongolia, where they met in 1578. Altan, the new strongman of Central Asia, was looking for a way to legitimize his rule, and Sonam Gyatso, as one of the most renowned lamas of the day, looked to be just the person to lend him respectability. Accordingly, Altan, in the idiom of that time, conferred on the Tibetan a number of high-flown titles, one of which pronounced him Dalai Lama. The word *dalai* is simply a Tibetanization of the Mongolian word for "ocean," which in turn translates the second half of Sonam Gyatso's name. Yet because Sonam Gyatso was in fact the third incarnation of a lineage connected with Drepung, Tibet's largest monastery, it followed that he must, in fact, be the Third Dalai Lama.

There is an added complication, however. Besides being the third exemplar of the Drepung line, Sonam Gyatso is also considered to have been forty-second in an unbroken lineage going back to the time of the historical Buddha, who lived during the fifth century BCE. It is this lineage that associates the Dalai Lamas with Chenresig, the Bodhisattva of Compassion, whom they are understood to manifest on earth. And yet this lineage is itself antedated by yet another that connects Chenresig with a young prince who lived 990 eons ago. How long is an eon? A disciple is said once to have asked the Buddha the same question. He replied with an analogy: Suppose there were a great mountain of rock, seven miles across and seven miles high, a solid mass without any cracks. At the end of every hundred years, a man might brush it with a fine Benares cloth. That great mountain would be worn away and come to an end sooner than ever an eon. It becomes apparent that, as soon as we start delving into the history of the Dalai Lama, we are faced with the most profound of questions. Indeed, it turns out that, so far as the present Dalai Lama is concerned, we have before us not merely the biography of one man but the story of a being who, from the perspective of his tradition, has been perfected and purified of all defilements through the performance of unnumbered good deeds over countless lifetimes and who manifests here on earth not for his own good but for that of all others. This is, moreover, a story in which the remote past is just the other day and matters supernatural are as real as the natural and as close as right next door.

To understand the Dalai Lama, therefore, we need to try to catch a glimpse of the world as Tibetan tradition sees it: not as one that began with a single moment of Creation, nor as one where everything might ultimately be expressed as a string of mathematical formulae—a world of atoms and electrons, protons and neutrons. We should not even think of it as a world explicable in terms of quanta and probability. The world as it is understood through the lens of Tibetan tradition did not begin with a big bang which sent the Earth spinning among galaxies and solar systems and ever-expanding space. The world according to Tibetan tradition has no beginning at all. Indeed, the world we see around us exists not on account of atomic or subatomic particles but on account of the accumulated karma of numberless sentient beings over eons of time.

So let us begin our story not with the birth of the present Dalai Lama, or Lhamo Thondup (the *h* in Lhamo and in Thondup can both be safely ignored, while the *T* in Thondup is hard, almost a *D*), as the infant Fourteenth was known at birth, nor with the death of his predecessor. Let us ignore convention and begin instead with a homely snapshot of the visit of the Thirteenth Dalai Lama to a village in far eastern Tibet one fine day during the spring of 1907.

Returning from the small monastery of Shartsong, the Precious Protector—this being one of the epithets by which all Dalai Lamas are commonly known by Tibetans—repaired to the grassy summit of a nearby hill together with his companion for the day, Taktser Rinpoché. (Taktser is pronounced roughly *Taksé*. It means, literally, the Place where the Tiger Roared. Rinpoché, an honorific applied to the highest class of monk, but also to certain places and objects, means something like Precious One.) The Rinpoché, who took his name from the village that stood beneath them, was the most important lama of the local area, which lay at the farthest extreme of the northeastern province of their country, known to Tibetans as Amdo.

We have grown used to the idea of nation-states with clearly defined borders, but for most of history the demarcation between peoples—even those of different ethnicity—was never so sharply drawn. From the Chinese perspective, at that time Taktser and its environs lay firmly within Qinghai province. But from the Tibetan perspective, for the best part of a millennium (roughly from the seventh to the seventeenth century), the village had been unambiguously part of Tibet. And although at the time of the Great Thirteenth's visit the Chinese had reasserted their control over the area, the majority of the local population remained Tibetan.

After commenting favorably on the natural beauty of the landscape, the Dalai Lama expressed his desire to visit Taktser village. So it was that, following a picnic lunch, the Great Thirteenth personally visited each homestead. There, we are told, he delighted the householders by engaging them in conversation and asking innumerable questions about their lives. So moved was one villager that she subsequently took a scoop of ashes from the fire on which the Dalai Lama's lunch was cooked and buried them in the courtyard in front of the family home.

At the conclusion of his visit, the Precious Protector announced that he had fallen in love with this pretty little valley and promised one day to return. Alas, he never did. Or at least he did not do so in his guise as Thirteenth Dalai Lama. But it was here that twenty-eight years later the present Dalai Lama was born—into the family in front of whose house those ashes lay buried.

The circumstances of that fateful picnic back in 1907 were hardly propitious. This was a moment of history when the Chinese empire of the Qing dynasty was tottering toward extinction while the British Empire, although at its peak in terms of power and prosperity, was soon to fade after the maelstrom of the First World War, creating a vacuum that would be filled by the twin terrors of fascistic nationalism and communism. At this moment, the Tibetan leader was in exile from Lhasa, his capital. Three years previously, British troops under the command of Colonel Francis Younghusband had Gatling-gunned their way into central Tibet, causing the Dalai Lama to flee north to Mongolia. This invasion, arguably one of the least glorious feats of arms in the long history of the British Empire, had come about ostensibly as a result of the Dalai Lama's government refusing to recognize Britain's protectorate over Sikkim, a small Buddhist kingdom sandwiched between Tibet and India. In fact, it had more to do with British paranoia about the rising power of Russia. That, and the dream one of the Great Thirteenth's closest advisers had of a pan-Buddhist federation in Central Asia uniting Mongolia, Tibet, and other Buddhist lands under the spiritual leadership of the Dalai Lama and the military protection of the Russian Empire.

This adviser was Agvan Dorjieff, whose unfamiliar name must have sounded thrillingly sinister to contemporary British ears. When, around the turn of the century, it became clear to Queen Victoria's ministers that Dorjieff had personal links with the tsar himself, there grew a conviction that Something Must Be Done. Questions were asked in Parliament.* People wrote to newspapers demanding action, while Lord Curzon, viceroy of India, began to plot. For him it was essential that Tibet remain a neutral buffer between the Russian Empire and the northern borders of the British Empire.

The military campaign that ensued was as swift as it was brutal. The first action occurred on March 31, 1904, and resulted in the expenditure by the British of fifty shrapnel shells, fourteen hundred machine-gun rounds, and 14,351 rounds of rifle shot for no loss of life on the British side but 628 Tibetans slain. Among the dead were two generals and two monk-officials. Even Younghusband admitted it was a massacre. He did, however, admire the Tibetans' calmness and tenacity under fire. For their part, the Tibetans were astonished not just by the firepower of the *inji* invaders but also by their code of conduct in war. Never before had they seen their wounded treated in enemy field hospitals and those taken prisoner merely disarmed and given cigarettes and a small sum of money before being set free.

Less than a fortnight later, Younghusband was camped outside the vast fortress of Gyantse, which lay just a few days' march from Lhasa. From there he issued an ultimatum to the Dalai Lama, giving the Tibetan leader until June 12 to send competent negotiators or he would resume his march. While they had no interest in conquest, what the British wanted, aside from favorable trading rights, was to compel the Tibetans to accept a British presence in Tibet so that they could monitor and, if necessary, check developments that might prove harmful to India, the jewel in the crown of their empire.

As for the Dalai Lama, he and his council of ministers, the Kashag, were determined to refuse any contact until the invading army withdrew. Younghusband's letter, sealed and beribboned in best imperial fashion and carried to Lhasa by a newly released prisoner, came back unopened several days later. The Tibetans calculated that, however mighty the British, they would never

*Whether by spooky coincidence or as evidence of some strange karmic link, the first of these was put by my great-grandfather Sir Henry Norman, Baronet (then plain Mr.).

be able to take Gyantse fort. The wrathful protectors of the Buddhadharma (the doctrine or Way of the Buddha) would see to that. But Gyantse fell in no time, and Younghusband resumed his march. Hastily appointing a senior monastic official as regent, the Dalai Lama fled north in the direction of Mongolia. He could at least be sure that his co-religionist there, the Jetsundamba Lama, would offer him sanctuary and protection until the British could be got rid of.

The Dalai Lama's welcome by the senior-most religious figure in Mongolia was less than generous, however. The Great Thirteenth's official biography notes a dispute over the relative height of the two men's thrones when they met, but it is also recorded that the Dalai Lama was appalled to discover that the Mongolian, against the rules of monastic tradition, had taken a wife and was both given to drink and addicted to tobacco. He even had the temerity to smoke in the Dalai Lama's presence.* This was a major insult. Nonetheless, the Dalai Lama was compelled to remain at the Mongolian hierarch's headquarters in Urgya (modern-day Ulaanbaatar) for the time being.

When, in September of that year, Younghusband withdrew from Lhasa, the Tibetans were as amazed as they were relieved. It seems they fully expected a wholesale British takeover on the model of previous invasions of Tibet by Mongolians and Manchus in turn.† But relief turned to dismay when it became clear the British were adamant that the Dalai Lama must remain in exile.

The Great Thirteenth therefore stayed in Urgya another year. One of the few Europeans who had an audience with him at this time was a Russian explorer, who gives us a description of the Dalai Lama's demeanor during their conversation. It was, he declares, "one of great calmness." The Dalai Lama "often looked me straight in the eye, and each time our glances met, he smiled slightly and with great dignity." When, however, "the matter of the English and their military expedition was touched upon, his expression changed. His face clouded with sorrow, his gaze fell and his voice broke with emotion."

Meanwhile in China, Cixi, the Dowager Empress, was similarly devastated

* From the perspective of the tradition, tobacco is an intoxicant and is therefore prohibited.

† From the Chinese perspective, the Manchus themselves were, like the Tibetans, a "barbarian" race—in contrast to the "civilized" Han over whom they ruled from 1644 to 1912.

by the British seizure of Lhasa. "Tibet," she wrote, "has belonged to our dynasty for two hundred years. This is a vast area, rich in resources, which has always been coveted by foreigners. Recently, British troops entered it and coerced the Tibetans to sign a treaty. This is a most sinister development . . . [W]e must prevent further damage and salvage the present situation." When, a year later, rebellion, led by the monks of Batang Monastery, broke out against the Chinese presence in Kham, the second of Tibet's two eastern provinces, she took this as her cue and dispatched an army under one of her generals, Zhao Erfeng. This was to prove the last major undertaking of the now exhausted Qing dynasty, in power since the mid-seventeenth century.

The Khampa rebellion took place in 1905, two years before the Precious Protector's visit to Shartsong. There was at the time a small Chinese outpost in the township of Batang, which stands amid fertile plains irrigated by the upper Yangtze River. This had been established following the invasion of central Tibet, by Mongol descendants of Genghis Khan, when the Manchu emperor of China was called on for help by the Tibetans. The unintended but inevitable consequence of this was that Tibet fell under the sway of the Qing empire.

From the perspective of the Tibetans, however, the relationship between themselves and the Qing dynasty was to be regarded in terms of the relationship between the Dalai Lama and the reigning emperor. In Tibetan eyes, the arrangement was not a political one. It was, rather, a spiritual relationship whereby the Tibetan hierarch and the Chinese emperor were respectively priest and patron. This was seen in the association between Rolpai Dorje, a high lama close to the Seventh Dalai Lama, and the then emperor, to whom he gave spiritual teachings. (The emperor and the Dalai Lama never met; the relationship was thus enacted by proxy.)

Understanding how this priest-patron relationship works from the Tibetan point of view is crucial to understanding how Tibetans conceive of what at first glance looks like a straightforward surrender of sovereignty to the Chinese, first under the Yuan dynasty and then again under the Qing. To do so, it is important to realize that from its earliest days, Buddhism has been a religion of renunciation. To begin with, its teachings were preserved and propagated by celibate men, and latterly women, living in forest-based communities away from "civilization." The Buddha specified that his followers were to be mendicants, to beg their bread rather than to bake it. This meant they were dependent on others for their survival, a dependency that, as the religion spread and the tradition of communal living in monasteries developed, led to the need for patronage on a large scale. This came to be provided by those princely families that had awakened to the truth of the Buddhist teachings. But while the *sangha,* or monastic community, was materially dependent on this patronage, it was understood that those providing it were similarly dependent on the *sangha* for their spiritual well-being. And since, according to the Buddhist analysis, spiritual well-being takes precedence over material well-being, the *sangha* took at least theoretical precedence over the royal house—even if, of course, the religious community could not survive without its patronage.

When today the Chinese government points to the historic ties between China and Tibet and claims that these show that Tibet is, and has long been, an "inalienable part" of China, it sees only the political arrangement whereby, among other things, the emperor stationed his troops there. It ignores totally the spiritual dimension, which for Tibetans is of far greater importance.

This said, when the monks of Batang Monastery rose up against the Chinese troops in 1905, they could well have been accused of forsaking their own side of the bargain by taking the lead in a ferocious bloodletting. Indeed, so grotesque are the accounts of the atrocities they committed that it seems hard to believe they are not exaggerated. The sources, though varied, are in such agreement, however, that it is clear they are not.

The uprising targeted not only the Chinese but also a small mission operated by two French priests of the Roman Catholic Church. The priests and their converts were all murdered. Subsequently thc unrest spread across the neighboring countryside. This included a small Sino-Tibetan trading station where another missionary community had taken root and which was at the time served by two more French priests. Staying with "the hospitable and venerable" chief of the mission at the time was the renowned Scottish botanist and plant hunter George Forrest. On hearing that the Chinese garrison stationed nearby had been "wiped out almost to a man," the three foreigners, together with their small community of converts, fled by moonlight. The next day, one of the priests was shot, "riddled with poisoned arrows . . . the Tibetans immediately rushing up and finishing him off with their huge double-handed swords." The remainder of the "little band, numbering about 80, were picked off one by one, or captured, only 14 escaping." One who almost succeeded in evading their attackers, a band of some thirty monks, was Père Dubernard, the other priest, but he was

> eventually run to ground in a cave . . . His captors broke both arms above and below the elbow, tied his hands behind his back, and in this condition forced him to walk back to the blackened site of [the mission]. There they fastened him to a post and subjected him to the most brutal humiliation; amongst the least of his injuries being the extraction of his tongue and eyes and the cutting off of his ears and nose. In this horrible condition he remained for the space of three days, in the course of which his torturers cut a joint off his fingers and toes each day. When on the point of death, he was treated in the same manner as [his fellow priest], the portions of the bodies being distributed amongst the various lamaseries [monasteries] in the region, whilst the two heads were stuck on spears over the lamaserie of the town.

Those in charge of the Catholic mission believed that the atrocities followed specific instructions by the Dalai Lama himself, but this seems unlikely in the extreme, given what we know of the Great Thirteenth's attitude toward both capital punishment and the practice of mutilation. He accepted that capital punishment was in certain circumstances a regrettable necessity, but in one of his earliest decrees he had reserved it for crimes of treason alone. He also decreed the abolition of mutilation, and while he permitted flogging, he much preferred restorative justice where possible. On one occasion he ordered a disgraced official to plant a thousand willow trees, on another that the guilty party should repair a stretch of road.

What the destruction of the Catholic mission and the attempt to kill Forrest tells us, therefore, is that the monasteries were often a law unto themselves. It also tells us that if our image of pre-Communist Tibet is one of monks serenely meditating in the mystic fastness of their mountain retreats, we must revise it. But the monks' uprising also highlights graphically the intense feeling that Tibetans had toward outside interference, whether it came from missionaries wanting to preach the gospel or from Chinese wanting to "pacify" them. All and any intruders were unwelcome. Their overriding motive was to protect the Buddhadharma, which they feared—rightly as it turned out—would be harmed if outsiders (that is, non-Buddhists) gained admittance to their country. Indeed, when the first Christian missionaries came to Lhasa back in the eighteenth century, they had been warmly welcomed. Their personal morality and keen interest in Buddhism recommended them as worthy spiritual seekers. It was only gradually that the *sangha* came to realize that despite their friendliness, their high culture, and their manifest sympathy for the poor, these foreigners were not merely interested in learning about Buddhism but were in fact intent on destroying it through conversion.

In Batang, the Chinese *amban,* or governor, met a fate similar to the missionaries'. The monks of a nearby monastery succeeded in capturing him and, having flayed his skin, they stuffed it with grass and paraded it around town, subsequently using this disgusting image first in a ritual for banishing evil and then for target practice within the monastery, before finally trampling it underfoot.

When the Dowager Empress's general arrived in the local area, the reprisals began at once. Desiring to make himself feared by the Tibetans, he immediately ordered three prisoners to be placed in a cauldron of "cold water, tied hand and foot, but with their heads propped up." A fire was then "built under the cauldron and slowly the water was brought to a boil." Some prisoners "had oil poured upon them and [were] burned alive. Others had their hands cut off and sent back as a warning to those from whom they came. Others [were] taken and, with a yak hitched to each arm and each leg . . . torn in pieces."

Informing the populace that henceforth they should consider themselves subjects of the Qing emperor, General Zhao ordered not only that they were to wear Chinese dress, but also that the men should adopt the hated Manchu queue (pigtail) and desist from sporting the traditional Khampa topknot. This, often dashingly threaded with strands of red-dyed wool, made them "resemble living demons" according to him. The presence of Butcher Zhao, as he was quickly named, "only made confusion worse confounded," in Forrest's account, and it took almost a year and many more atrocities before Zhao succeeded in forcing a peace. It took him all that time to starve into submission the three thousand monks of Chatreng Sampeling Monastery, who had taken to arms with especial ferocity. But when they finally surrendered, he had no compunction in executing every last one of them.

Unexpectedly, Zhao was not without his allies among the local Tibetan population. According to one witness, "in order to curry favour with the Chinese," members of the local Tibetan population brought numbers of their own countrymen in to be beheaded. "Heads fell every day, and so many bodies lay in the streets of Batang that at times the dogs feasted. No one dared touch or bury them, for fear they would be considered friends of the dead and in turn suffer the death penalty."

By the time Zhao had completed his "pacification" of Kham, the Dalai Lama, much disturbed by the news reaching him from the south, especially the suggestion that the general had soled his soldiers' boots with pages of scripture torn from the monasteries' holy books, had left his unwelcoming host in Urgya and relocated to Kumbum Monastery some five hundred miles to the north of Batang and its environs. Kumbum was especially important to the Precious Protector because of its association with Je Tsongkhapa. It was he who had been the progenitor of the reformed Gelug school of Buddhism to which the Dalai Lamas have all belonged. Kumbum was also, as it remains, Amdo's most important religious center, housing in its heyday several thousand monks.

By remarkable coincidence, John Weston Brooke, an English explorer, and the Reverend Ridley, yet another missionary, were present at Kumbum on the day in late October 1906 when the Dalai Lama arrived there. Describing the occasion, they inform us that the Dalai Lama's entourage was preceded by a Chinese band which made a "shrieking" and "diabolical" noise on the approach to Kumbum, "five or six men . . . shuffling along in a gait that was neither a walk nor a run. They were dressed as they liked, played as they liked, and shuffled as they liked." Behind these musicians came the imperial standard bearers, in the same disorder, followed by Tibetan outriders "dressed in wonderful long yellow coats and curious hats made of gilded wood, riding rough, high-spirited ponies . . . Suddenly," they report, "a distinguished-looking Tibetan galloped out of the crowd and shouted to the onlookers to '*koutou*.'"

The Englishmen dismounted from their ponies but "refused to do more, so [the Tibetan official] left us to harangue the Chinese, who were quite indifferent and only laughed and said rude things."

Ridley and Brooke were subsequently granted an audience with the Precious Protector, though it could hardly be counted a success. They found themselves quite unable to persuade him that the British were, as Ridley claimed, "a kind people," still less that if he "would come to India and meet with them and learn to know them, he would not mind their coming to his country." Instead, Brooke claimed that he had "never seen such a hard, expressionless face as that of the Dalai Lama."

The description seems unfair. It was too much to have expected the Precious Protector to be wholly gracious, given that, as Englishmen, the two visitors stood for the enemy who had deprived the Tibetan hierarch of his throne. Besides, we have it on the authority of several other European visitors that the Great Thirteenth was by no means wholly unbending. Years later he formed an unlikely friendship with the British political officer for Sikkim, Sir Charles Bell, who confirms the Dalai Lama's habitually stern expression but notes also the "welcoming smile that softened his features" whenever they met for talks.

The Dalai Lama remained at Kumbum for more than a year. As if the horrific news of Zhao's scripture-trampling marauders in the south were not enough, the Great Thirteenth also had to contend with the lack of discipline he found among the monastic community at Kumbum itself. "Many monks," we are told, "had taken to drinking, smoking and gambling." He therefore made it his business to renew respect for the *vinaya,* the monastic code that regulates both the spiritual and the administrative life of the *sangha.* The Dalai Lama also reinvigorated the academic side of Kumbum's monastic life, paying particular attention to the monks' proficiency in debate. This might have caused resentment as, typically, the monasteries firmly resisted any interference, no matter from whom. But such was the Tibetan leader's prestige, and such his personal magnetism, that he succeeded without alienating his hosts. Indeed, so deeply venerated was he that, day after day throughout his stay at Kumbum, he received countless pilgrims from far and wide, all seeking audiences with him. He would frequently bestow his blessing on crowds of thousands, while to visiting monks he gave spiritual teachings and initiations, ordaining many hundreds. Though it is true that some of Kumbum's officials grumbled at the expense of maintaining him, for as long as he remained with them, the Great Thirteenth enjoyed the highest esteem of the local people.

To be sure, the Dalai Lama's time at this, the greatest of Amdo's religious foundations, was not all gloom. In any case, it is pleasant to think of him enjoying at least some respite from his many difficulties when he went on pilgrimage that fine spring day to Shartsong Monastery and stopped on his way back to give his blessing to the little village of Taktser.

2

A Mystic and a Seer: The Regency Established

The Great Thirteenth's promise to return one day to Taktser was duly recorded by his officials and then, no doubt, completely forgotten. Something of his relationship with the village was preserved when, in middle age, the Precious Protector was asked to confirm the identity of the new incarnation of his friend Taktser Rinpoché, who had recently died. This he did, and the boy entered the monastery at Shartsong. But the time that elapsed between the Great Thirteenth's visit to Taktser in 1907 and his rebirth there in 1935 was so full of incident it is hardly surprising that it was not until long afterwards that anyone noticed the significance of his promise to return.

It was similarly not until many years later that anyone saw the significance of another seemingly trivial deed of the Great Thirteenth. Sometime during 1920, when repair work to the eastern wing of the Potala Palace—the magnificent thousand-chambered seat of government and principal residence of the Dalai Lamas—was being undertaken, the Great Thirteenth gave instructions for a blue bird to be painted on the wall of a staircase that led to the north side of the West Chamber on the floor above. He also called for a white dragon to be painted on its eastern wall. This, it is said, perplexed everyone because there was neither scriptural nor iconographic warrant for such images in these locations. A strict canon governed all forms of representation and their placement, although of course the authority of the Dalai Lama would certainly trump such considerations. It was not until long after that anyone realized the significance of the images. The blue bird represented the year (that of the Water Bird) during which the Great Thirteenth would depart this life (1933). The white dragon indicated the year of the Iron Dragon (1940), in which his successor would be enthroned.

It is notable that high lamas sometimes furnish explicit details of both their death and their next incarnation, including when and where they will be reborn. Occasionally the most highly evolved masters go so far as to give not only the name of the infant into which their stream of consciousness will pass but also those of its parents. But that level of detail is usually available only after intensive investigation, while here, the choice of imagery at the Potala sounds more spontaneous.

Other than these, the Great Thirteenth gave few indications of his intention to withdraw his mind from earthly existence. Ordinarily, high lamas can be expected to do so. But the only other sign the Great Thirteenth vouchsafed was his recent summoning of a Nepalese photographer operating in Lhasa at that time to come and take his portrait, a gesture in which some saw significance. His passing was therefore as great a shock to his attendants as it was to the general populace. So swift was his decline that there were even whisperings of foul play.*

His portrait was taken at the Norbulingka Palace in November 1933. A few weeks later, the Precious Protector developed a cough, though he continued to work as usual. After about a week without improvement, the Great Thirteenth failed to appear at the public audience scheduled at the Upper Tantric College on the twelfth of December. By now he had developed a high fever. Then,

---

*Remarkably, this allegation found its way onto the front page of the *Daily Illini,* the student newspaper of the University of Illinois, on December 20, 1933. Presumably the story was picked up from a British source.

on the sixteenth, the Precious Protector broke with his usual routine of letter writing in the morning and took first to his chair and then to his couch. That night he refused the two bowls of soup he normally took before going to bed.

Sometime after 10 that night, the Lord Chamberlain sounded the alarm. Summoning the other attendants, he instructed them to call the three senior-most members of the court, including the chief secretary and the treasurer. Not having been informed of the Dalai Lama's illness before this moment, they were surprised to learn that the Precious Protector was suddenly very unwell. On arrival, they immediately prostrated themselves and, as is customary whenever a high lama falls ill, begged the Dalai Lama to remain in his body. It is believed that this is under his control and that how and when he dies is a matter of his choosing.

An hour later, the Nechung oracle was ordered to attend—this being the state oracle and the government's go-to supernatural counsel and support. The medium arrived in such a hurry that one account claims he did not even have time to dress properly. He subsequently went into a trance, during which he administered some medicine. It seems that the Dalai Lama tried to refuse this, but the medium forced it on him.

When Nechung came out of his trance, the Precious Protector's doctor contended that the "Seventeen Heroes for Subduing Colds" that the oracle had administered was far too strong for the Dalai Lama's present condition, which, as if in direct confirmation, worsened immediately. By noon the following day, he was unconscious.

A deputation of high lamas was now admitted to the Presence to entreat him further to remain in the body. But he opened his eyes only briefly, breathing his last sometime around 6:30 p.m.

The first that most people knew of the Dalai Lama's passing was when butter lamps were lit on the roofs of the Potala Palace and of nearby Sera Monastery. It was many more days before the news made its way to the farthest reaches of Tibet. Meanwhile, it became incumbent on the government to appoint a regent who would steer the ship of state on a steady course until the new Dalai Lama could be found and educated to the point where he was able to take over the helm. In light of the degree to which the Great Thirteenth had centralized power into his own hands, and the level of involvement he maintained in all aspects of both spiritual and temporal affairs, it is at first sight remarkable that he seems not to have given much thought to his own succession. One might even argue that such negligence is evidence of a certain megalomania. The devout would simply counter that, foreseeing all things, the Dalai Lama merely withdrew his spirit for a brief period in order that he be young and vigorous when it came to meeting the challenges that lay ahead.

Besides, the Dalai Lama did leave a final testament as a guide to those responsible for selecting the regent and looking after the welfare of the Tibetan people until the moment when his successor would reach his majority. It is remarkable for its prescience. Isolated from the world he might be, but the Great Thirteenth had a firm grasp of the great movements of the day. He understood clearly the danger communism spelled to the free practice of religion. Despite the deep misgivings of the monasteries, which were hostile to the notion of a standing army (when necessary they would supply armed monks), he was adamant that Tibet needed a strong and independent military establishment:

> If we are not able to protect our own country, then everyone . . . will be wiped out so completely that not even their names will remain. The estates and property of the monasteries and monks will be annihilated . . . [and] we will be forced to wander the land as servants of our enemies. Everyone will be subjected to torture, and both day and night will be an unending round of fear and suffering. Such a time as this will come for sure!

His words fell on deaf ears, however, and, within a matter of days, a bitter struggle for power broke out.

Ordinarily the regent was chosen from among the high lamas of four particular monasteries, but the Great Thirteenth had caused one of these to be destroyed for its treachery during the recent occupation of Lhasa by a Chinese army. Furthermore, any one of the three most powerful men in Tibet at the time of the Great Thirteenth's demise was in a strong position to seize power from the monasteries. These were Kumbela, the Lord Chamberlain; Tsarong, the former army commander; and Lungshar, an ambitious aristocrat with modernizing tendencies who was Tsarong's implacable foe. Langduen, the ultraconservative but ineffectual chief minister, was not one of them. There was, however, one entity still more powerful than these three men: the combined influence of the three great monasteries in the Lhasa region—those of Ganden, Drepung, and Sera—also known as the Three Seats. As it happened, Tsarong was absent from Lhasa at this time and, not desiring to join the fray, played no part in the events that followed.

It was thus a straightforward contest between Kumbela and Lungshar, with the Three Seats casting the deciding vote. Lungshar's strongest suit in this regard was his professed hostility to the idea of an independent army. At first, however, Kumbela's position looked impregnable. During the last years of the Dalai Lama's life, his authority had been supreme, and for the few days after the Precious Protector "withdrew his spirit," most seem to have anticipated that Kumbela would assume the regency. Besides being the Great Thirteenth's most trusted servant, to whom was delegated the day-to-day running of the household, Kumbela was de facto commander in chief of the *tongdra,* the Dalai Lama's personal bodyguard, which he had formed just a few years previously.

In recruiting the rank and file of this bodyguard, Kumbela's strategy had been to do so solely from among the gentry. His thinking was that, having a better education than the lower orders, they would make better soldiers. Kumbela saw to it that they were well fed and wore specially tailored uniforms, paying for their gold-embroidered insignia out of his own pocket and personally ordering the officers' uniforms from Calcutta. The officers (themselves all members of the aristocracy) even went for training in machine gunnery at the British garrison still stationed at Gyantse. When the Dalai Lama died, it thus seemed certain that Kumbela would exploit his position. Yet for reasons that are not at all clear, he made no attempt to do so. Perhaps he saw his appointment as regent as a foregone conclusion.

Lungshar was quick to exploit this inaction.

Of all the high officials within the late Dalai Lama's government, Lungshar was the most worldly wise, having traveled widely outside Tibet. When the Great Thirteenth came up with a scheme whereby five boys from the gentry class were sent to England for schooling, it was Lungshar who accompanied them. He subsequently visited several European countries, taking careful note of the political systems of each. What seems particularly to have impressed him was the way in which Britain had managed to avoid the violent revolutions against monarchy that had afflicted Europe during the course of the previous century. On returning to Tibet, he therefore set about gathering support for a constitutional settlement that would see some of the Dalai Lama's temporal power vested in a secular authority organized according to democratic principles.

But if his sympathies were for government elected by popular vote, Lungshar's methods were decidedly Machiavellian. When the National Assembly took up the question of Kumbela's culpability in the Precious Protector's unexpected demise, Lungshar cleverly used the occasion to instigate revolt among the Dalai Lama's bodyguard.

In the end, the erstwhile Lord Chamberlain was charged not with murder but with the lesser crime of failing to keep the National Assembly informed of the Dalai Lama's health. For this he was stripped of office, relieved of all his property, and banished to a remote district far from the capital.

With Kumbela out of the way, Lungshar and his supporters could argue for a regency by a council made up of the existing prime minister and two more officials, one monastic and one lay—the layman in question being Lungshar himself. The National Assembly was, however, dominated by the abbots of the Three Seats. While there was considerable support for Lungshar's idea among the more progressive elements of the aristocracy, the conservative faction was bound to take sides with the religious authorities. The result was a stalemate. This in itself was a victory for the conservatives since the inevitable outcome was recourse to the deities. The matter of who should be appointed regent would be decided by divination, while each of the candidates would be a leading figure within the monastic community.

A grand religious ceremony was duly held, which the entire government of several hundred officials attended. Presiding was the ex-abbot of Ganden Monastery. From a total of three possibilities, the name that emerged was that of the youngest, the twenty-four-year-old Reting Rinpoché.

Of all the candidates for regent, Reting Rinpoché was unquestionably the most charismatic. Born to a humble family in central Tibet, he had quickly displayed signs of exceptional ability. It is held that, when he was around five years of age, the young prodigy became angry with his elder sister, stamping his right foot on the ground with such force that it imprinted itself on the very rock on which he was standing. A second indication of genius came not long afterwards, when his mother left him to watch over a pot of *thukpa* (meat broth with noodles) while she went to milk the family cow. After some time, the little boy came running and announced that it was about to boil over so he had closed up the pot. When she came back, his mother saw that he had taken off one of his bootlaces and used it to tie off the neck of the earthenware vessel. A third sign of the boy's high spiritual attainment came on an occasion when he drove a wooden peg into solid rock. He explained that this was to tie his horse to—even though his family did not then own one. This must therefore be a portent, since only the aristocracy and high lamas had horses. The boy had subsequently been recognized by the Great Thirteenth himself as the authentic reincarnation of one of his foremost teachers.

As to the character of the Rinpoché, as a young man he was—according to the testimony of one of his nieces—kind, playful, and solicitous. She also attests to a characteristic of his that many took to be a sign of the highest spiritual attainment, a "delicate fragrance about his person."

Some of the foreigners who met Reting Rinpoché, a man slightly below average height, with enormous protruding ears and a perpetual frown, were less than favorably impressed. Hugh Richardson, then British political officer for Tibet, described him as "gauche," "self-centred," and "immature," while General Sir Philip Neame, who undertook a military inspection of the Tibetan army (at the request of the Tibetan government itself) in 1936, described him as "a very mediocre personage of little personality, brains, or education, and of no particular family, chosen . . . [for] being a nonentity."

Whatever his true qualities, the new regent had been selected by the gods themselves. It might have seemed to some of Lungshar's supporters, therefore, that nothing was to be done. But Reting was young and Langduen, the chief minister, who continued in office, was weak and indecisive. Commenting on the recent installation of electric light in the capital's more important houses (including his own), Langduen timorously remarked that "new things only bring misfortune." If Lungshar acted fast enough, there remained a good chance that he could seize the initiative and achieve the end he desired.

Today, the more secular-minded remember Lungshar as power-hungry and self-serving. To the more pious, he is simply seen as wicked and to have gotten the fate he deserved. What tends to be overlooked is the fact that he seems genuinely to have taken to heart the late Dalai Lama's concerns for the fate of Tibet. Like the Dalai Lama himself, he had acquired from his travels a sense of the momentous events taking place elsewhere in the world. To the east, the Chinese were attempting to reunify following a disastrous civil war and invasion by the Japanese. To the west, Russia, having overthrown dynastic rule by the tsars, was in the process of a violent collectivization of agriculture and industry. To the south, Indian opposition to British rule was increasingly forthright. To the north, Inner Mongolia, although nominally independent, was effectively under Russian control. It was clear to Lungshar that if Tibet were to survive as an independent state in the modern era, it would need to concern itself with the modern world.

The reforms Lungshar had in mind would see the power of the great landed families redistributed among the more numerous (and more progressive) minor aristocracy. This was revolutionary in itself. But what made his ambition especially dangerous from the point of view of the monasteries was the implicit threat to them implied by his intended greater role for the National Assembly. That of the Kashag, the council of ministers, would thereby be downgraded. This would have, as a further consequence, a diminution of the prospective new Dalai Lama's political power when eventually he reached his majority. While at first the monasteries were reassured by Lungshar's professed anti-military stance, gradually the ramifications of his scheme began to dawn on them.

A month after his selection, Reting Rinpoché was formally installed as regent. Meanwhile, Lungshar worked hard to secure support. By mid-March 1934 he felt confident enough to hold his first open meeting. With roughly a quarter of the National Assembly declaring for him, his position was by no means secure, but it was adequate for his purposes at this stage. For now, Lungshar's aim was simply to put a petition to the Kashag. This was designed to undermine the position of its most powerful member, Trimon Shapé.

Lungshar intended to present this petition on May 10, the timing of his submission known to only a few. One of these, an early ally, had by this time decided that his own career prospects were in fact best served by throwing his support behind Trimon. He therefore sent a warning to Trimon that Lungshar was poised to make a move against him. While Lungshar's intentions were almost certainly peaceful, the warning clearly implied that Trimon's life was in danger. Early on the morning of the tenth, therefore, Trimon left his house with several servants and sought an immediate meeting with the regent and the chief minister. Together they decided that Trimon should flee to Drepung Monastery while orders were issued for Lungshar's arrest.

The petition was duly presented to the remaining three members of the Kashag later that morning. In the afternoon, Lungshar was summoned to a meeting of the government department of which he was a member. At first undecided whether to attend or not, he seems to have determined to go on the grounds that he had done nothing illegal and there was some chance that the officials he was to meet with could be brought into the fold. This was a major miscalculation. He was met at the Potala Palace with an arrest order accusing him of serious crimes, including, disastrously, failure to appreciate the kindness of the late Dalai Lama. While waiting for the official who should at this point have ceremonially removed his topknot and robe of office, Lungshar made a bid to escape. He had left the servant to whom he had entrusted his pistol just outside in the corridor. As ill luck would have it, the servant was at that moment on his way back from the latrines downstairs. Recognizing Lungshar's plight, he held out the weapon toward him as his master ran down the stairs. But just as the two men met, the servant was seized by several janitors while Lungshar was overpowered by a palace guard. He was forcibly escorted back to the regent's office.

Having undone Lungshar's topknot and taken his government robe from his back, the official and his assistants began to remove his footwear. As they did so, Lungshar managed to break free and swallow a piece of paper that had fallen out of the first boot. But he was unable to do so a second time as another piece of paper fell out of his other boot when it was removed. On inspection, this had written on it, next to an occult symbol, the fateful words *Do harm to Minister Trimon.*

This was black magic.

Or so the story goes. The alternative version is that the black magic component was a later invention to justify Lungshar's punishment. Trampling on a person's name would, with the aid of a wrathful deity, bring about the violent demise of the victim. A similar tactic had been employed in an attempt on the life of the Great Thirteenth some four decades previously—not so long ago that the event should have been forgotten. On that occasion, the young Dalai Lama, having suffered several bouts of illness, summoned the oracle in an attempt to discover the cause. It transpired that a pair of boots belonging to one of his teachers was implicated. On questioning, the reverend teacher agreed that there did seem to be something strange about the boots: every time he wore them, he suffered a nosebleed. When they were examined, it was found that the sole of one of them contained a piece of paper on which the Dalai Lama's name was written adjacent to the symbol for *shinje she,* Lord of Death*. Again this was black magic, and in this case it was being employed in the most heinous of crimes—there being none greater than the attempted killing of the Precious Protector. As a result, the ex-regent, who was behind the plot, and three accomplices—including the then chief minister—were arrested, charged with treason, and sentenced to death. The Dalai Lama intervened and the death penalty was rescinded, but the ex-regent nonetheless died in mysterious circumstances, apparently drowned in a vat of water. Meanwhile his co-conspirators all had bamboo driven under their nails and received a hundred lashes before being sent into exile. Even the chief minister's wife was forced to wear for a week the *cangue* (a portable pillory consisting of a wooden collar, worn around the neck, to which the victim's hands were shackled).

In Lungshar's case, his crime seemed to his enemies to warrant the severest penalty. Not only had he tried to undermine the position of the Kashag by introducing reforms that must harm religion itself, but also he had resorted to the dark arts. It was thus decided that he should have his eyes put out.

It is arguably a favorable sign that this punishment had not been handed down for so long that no one could be found who had experience of carrying it out. Members of the butcher caste tasked with the operation were forced to rely on the folk memory of their clan. Involving the application of yak knuckles to each temple and a tourniquet tightened until the eyeballs popped out,

* Also known as Yamantaka.

the technique proved successful on one side only. Eventually, the recalcitrant globe was simply gouged out with a knife and the sockets cauterized with boiling oil.

The humiliation of Lungshar (who, though he survived the experience, unsurprisingly lived only a year longer, incarcerated in a dungeon of the Potala Palace) meant that the government of Tibet during the regency period remained, on the one hand, rigidly conservative and, on the other, indecisive with respect to any serious issue with which it was confronted. But what the incident tells us about the politics of Tibet at the time is of considerably less significance than what it tells us about the Tibetan tradition itself. Lungshar's proposed reforms were both moderate and reasonable. Full democracy and the accountability of government to the Tibetan people were not in question, though his plans were a step in that direction. The mere fact that Lungshar could be accused of black magic suggests that the tradition itself rendered Tibet completely unready to take its place in the modern world.

3

A Child Is Born

While Lungshar was in the process of discovering just how premature was his vision of a new Tibet, the search for the new incarnation of the Dalai Lama began in earnest. Following his enthronement as regent in 1934, Reting Rinpoché's primary task was to sift and assess the various signs and portents brought to his attention. An early event concerned the embalmed body of the lately departed Precious Protector. It had been seated, wrapped in gauze, facing south in its burial chamber. But when after some time the embalmers came to put in fresh salt, they found the head inclined toward the east. This they took to be significant, and when it happened again, there could be no doubting its importance.

The utterances of the various oracles associated with the Dalai Lama were also of the greatest interest at this time, and not just what they said but their actions, too. When three of them all turned to the east and threw offering scarves—again not once but twice—this was of clear significance.

Further help came from signs in nature. Among those noted by the monastic officials charged with collating evidence were some curious cloud formations that appeared on the northeastern horizon. There were also some unusual botanical indications. It came to the attention of the authorities that snapdragons had bloomed unexpectedly underneath the stairs that stood at the eastern end of the public discourse area adjacent to the Jokhang, the most important temple in Lhasa. And then there was the matter of the strange star-shaped fungi that appeared at the base of a wooden pillar standing to the northeast of the shrine where the late Dalai Lama had been entombed.

It was concluded that, taken together, all these signs indicated that the search for the new incarnation should be conducted in the east. What was needed now was greater precision. More than a thousand miles separated Lhasa from what was then considered to be the border with China. It was in hopes of getting a more fine-grained answer that, during the summer of 1935, the regent traveled to the monastery founded and consecrated by the Second Dalai Lama during the first decade of the sixteenth century. This was Chokor Gyal in southern Tibet. Situated at a remarkable fifteen thousand feet, the monastery is overlooked by three mountains, each regarded as the abode of a different tutelary, or guardian, deity.

Of still greater significance, however, is the lake that lay half a day's journey away, Lhamo Lhatso. This is held by tradition to be the dwelling place of Palden Lhamo—the Glorious Goddess—the protector deity most closely associated with the Dalai Lamas. These protector deities (of whom somewhere between fifteen and twenty are fully attested) are central to the Tibetan tradition. They are quite distinct from the tutelary deities; their chief characteristic being to channel the "wrathful," or negative, aspects of particular fully enlightened beings. This wrath is deployed to guard both the doctrine itself and the community of practitioners. It can also be made available to communities and individuals as an aid to overcoming obstacles. In the case of some protectors, for example Yamantaka (Lord of Death), they may also be taken as meditational deities, whereby the form and attributes of the deity are (imaginatively) assumed by individual practitioners as a means to overcome their own negative thoughts and emotions in the quest for Enlightenment. But these are specialist practices; on the whole, the protectors are treated with great caution. It is well understood that, misdirected, their fearsome energy can cause untold harm.

The power of the protectors can be appreciated in their iconography: the Glorious Goddess, Palden Lhamo, is described as having a dark blue body—

> in her right hand she brandishes a club over the brains of those who have broken their promises to her; in her left hand, on a level with her heart, she holds a skull-cup filled with blood and other substances used in exorcism. Her mouth is open and between her sharp teeth she gnaws on a human corpse. As she does so, her joyous yelps resemble roaring thunder. She has three red, round eyes, which gleam like lightning. Her yellowing hair stands on end and her eyelashes and beard blaze like the fire which flames up at the end of cosmic eons. In her right ear she wears a lion, in her left, a snake. On her head she wears a diadem of five skulls, while round her neck is draped a garland of fifteen freshly severed heads, dripping blood.

Small wonder that, faced with depictions of these extraordinary beings for the first time, the Victorian explorers of Tibet were convinced that the Buddhism they found practiced there was a debased form of the religion, which, cut off from its original sources, had degenerated into mere devil worship. (One wonders what the first Buddhists to travel in the West made of Christians praying to a deity disfigured and nailed to a cross.) In any case, what those explorers failed to realize was that, from the Tibetan perspective, the protector deities, for all their gruesome attributes, are ultimately agents of compassion.

Following his retreat at the Second Dalai Lama's monastery, and after conducting the appropriate *sadhanas* (rituals) to propitiate the Glorious Goddess, the young regent did indeed experience a detailed vision in the waters of the lake. First, he saw three letters of the alphabet (actually syllables), *Ah, Ka*, and *Ma*. There followed a vision of a three-storied monastery with three distinguishing features: its second story was painted the color of turquoise, its top story was adorned with a golden roof, and there was a "thread-like" path leading east from the monastery to a hill, on top of which stood a single-story building with a blue roof.

Having noted down the contents of his vision, the Rinpoché took these details as the object of further meditative investigation. On returning to Lhasa, he also consulted with Nechung and other oracles over the course of a full year. At the end of this time, he ordained three search parties. Each headed by a *tulku* (a reincarnate lama) and assisted by three senior monks, these search parties were to conduct investigations in three far eastern districts. One search party was dispatched to the southeast, another went roughly due east, while the third went to the northeast.

Not that Reting Rinpoché's instructions went entirely unopposed. There were those who were skeptical that the Dalai Lama would take rebirth so far from Lhasa: Would there not be a danger that if he was from some remote part of the borderlands, he might fall into Chinese hands? Surely the gods would not take that risk? Furthermore, there was a promising local candidate, a boy born into the family of the Great Thirteenth Dalai Lama. Soon after his birth, a horse from the Dalai Lama's stables had broken loose and run straight to the infant's house, a credible indication that there was a connection between the Precious Protector and the baby boy. But Reting was adamant that the first symbol he had seen in the waters of the lake referred to Amdo, the eastern province. In clear confirmation, the oracle of Samye Monastery took off his breastplate and gave it to Kewtsang Rinpoché, the *tulku* appointed to lead the party that would go to Amdo.

The three teams left Lhasa during the autumn of 1936. As it turned out, the two that went east and southeast found not a single plausible candidate, while even the one that was sent to Amdo did not at first find any that seemed promising. Nevertheless, one significant early event was a meeting between Kewtsang Rinpoché and the Panchen Lama—after the Dalai Lama, the second-most-important and powerful *tulku* in the land—who was then residing at Riwoche.

The Ninth Panchen Lama was at this time living in self-imposed exile. He had fled his monastery at Tashilhunpo in protest at the Great Thirteenth's imposition of new taxes to fund the army. When the Dalai Lama found out, he had been outraged, sending an armed party to apprehend him. It arrived too late, however, and the Panchen made good his departure, first to Mongolia and then to China. "It is not known why you have left your monastery," wrote the Precious Protector subsequently, "in which you should now be sitting in meditation. You seem to have forgotten the sacred history of your predecessors and wandered away to a desert . . . like a moth attracted by lamplight."

Traditionally, the Panchen and Dalai Lamas serve each other as religious teachers in successive incarnations, the older one acting as mentor to the younger. This was most famously the case when the Fourth Panchen Lama tutored both the Fourth and the Great Fifth Dalai Lamas (there have so far been two Dalai Lamas acclaimed as Great, the Fifth and the Thirteenth, though it is whispered already of the present incarnation). It is also true that there are some who point to the fact that—at least according to one way of reckoning—the Panchen Lama lineage is the senior lineage. And it is indisputable that, considered as a spiritual master, the First Panchen was more highly accomplished than the First Dalai Lama. There had thus always been rivalry, not so much between the individuals themselves as between their respective *labrangs,* or estates. In this instance, it is generally believed that the Panchen Lama, a man of "singular sweetness and charm," according to Sir Charles Bell, had been put up to his eastern escapade by the men surrounding him.

That the Panchen Lama's animosity was not personal is attested to by the fact that, when he met with the search party leader, the Panchen Lama gave Kewtsang Rinpoché a list of candidates whose names had been brought to his attention and whom he had investigated by the usual methods of meditative inquiry. It included the name of Lhamo Thondup, the boy who would eventually be proclaimed Dalai Lama.

Thus equipped, the search party made its way to Kumbum Monastery, arriving in the spring of 1937, where it was greeted by a large number of local dignitaries, both monastic and lay.

Not until winter did Kewtsang Rinpoché and his men finally reach the village of Taktser, however. Perhaps one reason for their slowness to investigate the boy there was the fact that the family into which the candidate had been born had already yielded an important incarnation—that of the Taktser Rinpoché, his older brother, and reincarnation of the man with whom the Great Thirteenth had enjoyed a picnic lunch three decades previously. By now, the new Taktser Rinpoché, thirteen years older than Lhamo Thondup, was a novice at Shartsong Monastery. It must have seemed highly unlikely that the same family could harbor one still greater. Besides, it was not as if the parents were particularly distinguished. They didn't even speak proper Tibetan but a kind of hybrid language known as *siling ke,* which necessitated that the team take an interpreter with them.

Yet the search party was startled to realize that the architectural features of the birthplace of the child matched precisely the details provided by Reting Rinpoché on the basis of his vision. And they were immediately impressed with the now two-year-old boy they met. A member of the party later recalled how he went straight up to Kewtsang Rinpoché and "pulled the rosary [he] wore round his neck and said, 'give me this!'

"'Tell me who I am and then I will give it to you,' replied Kewtsang Rinpoché.

"'You are an *Aka** from Sera. *Mani, mani,*'† the boy replied spontaneously.

"'Who is the man [next door]?' asked Kewtsang Rinpoché, and the boy replied, 'Tsedrung Lobsang!'"

Then he pointed to the interpreter and gave his name too. According to the official account, he gave all this information spontaneously and "without any hesitation or doubt." The members of the search party also noted that his mannerisms were "extraordinarily profound for his age."

Such were the first miracles. For his own part, the Dalai Lama himself remembers almost nothing of this first interview, save for the piercing eyes of the man who subsequently became his senior personal assistant. As the search party went to leave Taktser the following day, they did so with heavy hearts; they longed to stay and bask in his presence. When the boy "firmly insisted" they take him with them, it was only by his parents' playing a trick on little Lhamo Thondup that they were able to prevent the boy from following after.

So as not to arouse the suspicions—or, presumably, the hopes—of the

---

* Probably meaning "uncle" but used by children to refer to any authority figure.

† *Mani* probably refers either to a *mani* stone—a stone with a prayer inscribed on it—or the prayer (mantra) itself.

family, Kewtsang Rinpoché had disguised himself as a servant during this first visit to the boy's house. The search party had portrayed itself as a group of pilgrims en route to nearby Shartsong. After a brief return to Kumbum Monastery, however, in order to confer with his colleagues (and, we may assume, with the deities), and to send a message to the government back in Lhasa, Kewtsang Rinpoché together with his team returned to Taktser a few weeks later.

On this occasion he did so in his official capacity as head of one of the search parties looking for the new Dalai Lama and warranted to thoroughly examine the child. Along the way, the search party met with a number of auspicious signs, faithfully recorded. First, they encountered several people carrying barrels of curd, milk, and water. Second, they met with a young Chinese close to the house who suggested a route that took them to the front door of the boy's house rather than the more usual direct route which led to the back door. Third, just as they reached the door, they heard the sound of a conch shell being blown from the top of Kumbum Monastery, calling the monks to assembly. Finally, on entering the house, they heard a cuckoo—the first, they noted, of spring.

It was teatime when they arrived, and while refreshments were being served, the boy appeared. Wearing a kind of "jump-suit," he had a "look of joy on his face."

With the usual courtesies discharged, now came the moment of truth. Could the child recognize what had belonged to him in his former life from among other objects that did not? Kewtsang Rinpoché began by holding up two dark-colored rosaries and asking which one the little boy wanted. The right one, as it turned out. The same happened with a pair of yellow rosaries: the boy correctly chose the one that had belonged to the Great Thirteenth. There followed a near disaster. On being shown two canes and pausing for a while, the little boy picked out the wrong one. But after a moment, he picked them both up again and examined "the handle and the tip of each with concentration." They were both of the same design, the only difference being in the tip, one of which was made of bronze, the other of plain iron. This time, he held on to the correct one, "holding it straight with its tip to the floor." In itself, this near mistake was a most auspicious sign: it was later recalled that the Great Thirteenth had in fact given away the first cane to a colleague. That must be why the child had picked it up and then put it down.

There followed a test involving three lengths of fabric which the boy had to identify from among others before he was presented with the final two objects. These were a small hand drum made of ivory, and another, larger *damaru,* a drum with two faces. The first the Great Thirteenth had used for summoning his attendants; the second was a more elaborate instrument furnished with a "golden belt and [a] brocade handle." Most children would no doubt have selected the larger, gaudier of the two instruments, but without hesitation, the small boy chose correctly and, "holding it in his right hand, he played it with a big smile on his face; moving around so that his eyes could look at each of us from close up. Thus, the boy displayed his occult powers." The four members of the search party were left spellbound.

That night, staying with the family, Kewtsang Rinpoché made further inquiries. The test had been highly persuasive but was by no means the end of the matter. It must therefore have been somewhat disconcerting when he asked the child's parents whether any auspicious signs had accompanied the birth of their son. "No," they replied, "nothing of that kind." From some of the local people, however, they learned that there had been, among other indications, a rainbow directly over the house at around the time of the birth. Also, the boy's father had been seriously ill and in fact had nearly died. But when the child was born, the father had enjoyed a miraculous recovery. And it was remembered that in the past, whenever a great lama had been reborn in the locality, it had been presaged by a series of natural calamities. In this case, there had been four years of successive crop failures, and the boy's family had themselves lost some of their most valuable livestock. Five of their best horses bolted one day and leaped over a cliff to their deaths below. Then seven of their mules sickened and died, one by one. Thus encouraged, when they finally turned in that night, the members of the search party were so excited that none of them could sleep, "even for a moment."

The skeptical reader will doubtless see this whole account as a classic example of myth-making. There is even some support for this view from within the tradition itself. The Great Fifth Dalai Lama—whose birth is said to have been accompanied by a rain of flower-shaped snowflakes—wrote disparagingly in his autobiography about the selection procedure he himself underwent. In his case it was less formal, with only his teacher present. When he was shown the "images and rosaries," he could, by his own account, "utter no words" of recognition. Nonetheless, when his teacher went out of the room, the Dalai Lama heard him say, "'I am absolutely convinced he recognised the objects.'" To be fair, the present Dalai Lama disputes a straightforward reading of this passage, cautioning that the Great Fifth had a "very sarcastic" style of writing which ought not to be taken at face value.

We should remember, however, that the word "myth" has come to denote something that "didn't really happen" and has thus become a generally pejorative term. Yet this development rests on the assumption that the only events that can be securely known to be true are those that can be verified empirically. The point to be borne in mind is that from the Buddhist perspective, the way things *really* are is quite different from the way science tells us they are. Science leaves out karma (the fruit, or consequences to us and to our future selves, of our actions), and it leaves out the supernatural. What looks, from a modern perspective, to be "mythological" and therefore not actually or even possibly true is considered by the tradition to be both possibly and in many cases actually true.*

---

*It is also worth remembering that the dominance of this impoverished view of what is possibly true is a very recent development in the history of thought. Most people, most of the time, have taken the larger view that our senses are not the only source of reliable evidence—even if the contrary idea has been around as far back as we can see. In the West, the ancient Greek philosopher Democritus, a contemporary of Gautama Buddha, is associated with this position.

4

The View from the Place of the Roaring Tiger: Tibet's Nameless Religion

It is often said that the present Dalai Lama comes from a humble peasant background, but this is not strictly accurate. According to family legend, his ancestors served as soldiers in the army of Tibet's greatest monarch, the seventh-century King Songtsen Gampo. Subsequently, they lived for many generations as nomads, herding their flocks from place to place before eventually settling in the region of Taktser. By the time of the Manchu conquest of China and the Tibetan borderlands in the mid-seventeenth century, the family had become relatively prosperous, and for the next two hundred years that remained the case. But then, toward the end of the nineteenth century, disaster struck. The village was destroyed during a rebellion against Manchu rule, and the family, made destitute, was reduced to living in "grinding poverty" in the caves of the surrounding hills.

It was not until one of its members was recognized as the reincarnation of a famous lama that the family's fortunes revived. This was Taktser Rinpoché, the man with whom the Great Thirteenth shared the picnic. (He was also the great-uncle of the present Dalai Lama.) Because of the continued danger, the young prodigy was taken as a child to Mongolia to be educated. There he gained a reputation as a great teacher and, returning home in middle age, is said to have brought with him a vast fortune, including ten thousand camels. This is surely an exaggeration, but as a result of their now famous scion's generosity, the lama's relatives were able to buy back the land they had lost and to build a house that, in the words of one of the Dalai Lama's older brothers, was "one of the best in the village . . . a new Chinese style home that was large and spacious." The family into which the present Dalai Lama was born was thus one of petty landowners. They were not aristocrats to be sure, but neither were they members of the very large class of people that was directly dependent on the monastic or aristocratic estates. Employing three servants (one of them Chinese, another a Hui Muslim), they owned "over fifty sheep, a number of yaks, and several *dzomo*" (a female cross between a yak and a cow).

Entered from the lee side, the new Dalai Lama's family home was a miniature fortress built around all four sides of its internal courtyards, at the center of which stood a pole hung with prayer flags bleached by the sun and torn by the constant breeze blowing in off the nearby mountain range. There were no windows in the outer walls, however, and the few internal openings were covered with rice paper, not glass. The southern wing of the house included a dog kennel and a sheep pen, while the northern wing contained the family chapel next to the best room—the room in which visitors were received—and the main bedroom. The east wing was taken up by the kitchen, which was divided into two equal halves, and included the main living space. There was a large stove and a tub for water; one side of the space had a wooden floor while the other was of compacted earth. The west wing served as a cow barn and stable, with a storeroom and a guest room adjacent. Yet it was not in the guest room but in the stable, alongside the cattle, that the children were brought into the world. The first to survive was Tsering Dolma, a daughter born in 1917. She was followed by three sons—Taktser Rinpoché (1922), Gyalo Thondup (1928), and Lobsang Samten (1933)—before the Precious Protector, who was born, according to the Tibetan (lunar) calendar, on the fifth day of the fifth month in the (female) Wood Pig year of the sixteenth Rabjung calendrical cycle—or July 6, 1935, according to the Western calendar.

Up at cockcrow in the dark hour before dawn, mother to light the fire, father to take the horses to water, the family lived, until they moved to Lhasa when Lhamo Thondup was officially acclaimed, the rugged but satisfying life of pastoralists everywhere. At the time of the boy's birth, the village comprised some thirty homesteads and so, we can assume, had a population approaching two hundred. Because children in such communities were seen as a boon, not a burden, families tended to be large—while there was no question of grandparents moving out. Yet childhood was something of a contest with nature, and life tended not to be long. With no doctors within many days' walk, still less a hospital, it is little wonder that of the sixteen children the Dalai Lama's mother bore, only seven survived into adulthood. Nonetheless, the eldest recalled in his autobiography that he and his siblings lived a "happy and contented life in our remote village," adding that they "found it strange when the occasional travellers passing through found it necessary to express sympathy with us on account of what they perceived to be our hard lot."

For food, the main staple was *tsampa,* roasted barley flour made edible by adding either tea, milk, or *chang* (barley beer) and kneaded into small balls in a bowl. Another staple was potato, which featured at most meals, but legumes were scarce except in their brief season. There was fresh meat, though in the autumn months only, this being the time when the animals were ready for slaughter. For the rest of the year, dried meat had to suffice. The only exception to this rule was if a beast died unexpectedly. When an animal was brought to the table, it was honored by being consumed in its entirety. Everything that could be eaten was eaten; anything not edible was put to use. The intestines, carefully drawn, were used as casings for sausage and stuffed with congealed blood and gobbets of fat, and *tsampa* flour. Brains and brawn, tripe, liver, and lights (or lungs) were all washed, seasoned, and roasted. The lights were considered a special delicacy, while some of the tripe was set aside and used for storing butter. The kidneys, nestled in sheaths of fat, were cooked in the glowing embers of the hearth. The trotters too made good eating, while the horn was used for making glue.

In the summer, raspberries and strawberries and bilberries could be picked wild in the woods nearby, while from the family vegetable plot came radishes and other salad foods and wheat for milling. Peas were grown for fodder, and there was dairy produce aplenty. But above all, in this household there were baked goods in abundance: deep-fried *khabse* cookies and plump loaves of bread, rolls fat with butter and sugar and raisins, and sticky dumplings soft as pillows, all made in the Amdo style. Even today, family members recall with wistful pride the delicious confections of the *gyalyum chenmo* (literally, the Great Royal Mother).

Because the household economy depended for its health on the produce grown and the livestock reared, with the occasional sale or purchase of a horse, every storm rolling in from Kyeri, the mountain in the shadow of which the village stood, was watched with apprehension. A single hailstorm could destroy the labor of many weeks, and the house had to be battened down every time. Yet in spite of the frequent violence of the climate, sheep and goats, pigs, yaks, *dri* (the female counterpart of a yak), and *dzo* lived alongside the horses and the human folk in symbiotic kinship. Apart from the weather (the winters were bitter, and snow came often), the only natural enemies universally acknowledged were the wolf and the *hu-hu*—bands of marauding men of the local Hui population.

Though wolves rarely attacked people, a wolf pack could easily carry off a flock of sheep or, on occasion, bring down cattle and sometimes even horses. No surprise, then, that the man who came home with a wolf carcass was considered a hero, and wolf hunting was an important activity, though other predators—mainly foxes and lynx—were hunted as well.

But the *hu-hu* were more to be feared than any wolf pack. Descendants of Central Asian traders who had settled in China during the Middle Ages, the Hui constituted the principal ethnic group, other than the Tibetans, settled in the region. Every so often they would conduct raids among the Tibetan community, scouring the countryside for plunder. Then as now, the Tibetans lived mostly in the more remote areas, while the Hui—still for the most part traders—were found in and around the larger settlements, notably Siling, where there was a large mosque. And while on the whole the Tibetans lived quietly off the land, the Hui, who were more directly exposed to the greater Chinese economy, were more restive. Especially during the declining years of the Qing dynasty and then, more recently, during the Chinese civil war which broke out during the late 1920s, conditions were harsh, and from time to time unrest led to looting. The situation was complicated by the fact that, following the fall of the Qing, the Hui elite had joined forces with the Chinese Nationalist Guomindang party. The Hui leader Ma Bufang was one of their number, and it was his soldiers who, not long before the birth of the Dalai Lama, had fought a battle with the Tibetans and slaughtered not only the combatants but their children too. Joseph Rock, the Austro-American explorer, writing in *National Geographic,* described how their little heads were "strung about the walls of the Moslem [Hui] garrison like a garland of flowers."

Yet if wolves and marauding gangs were a perennial threat to the family's security, a threat in many ways still more serious was that posed by entities of quite a different order. This threat was described by the Dalai Lama's mother in her autobiography, where she speaks of the visits of a *kyirong,* a type of ghost that can change its form at will. The first haunting the Great Mother recalls occurred when she lay gravely ill. On this occasion, the *kyirong* manifested as a young girl who appeared in a dream, but who remained visible after the Great Mother awoke. The dream girl held out a bowl of what at first sight seemed to be Chinese tea, but which turned out to be blood. As the patient tried to sit up in bed, the ghost "slipped to the door, laughing all the while, and disappeared."

On another occasion, the Dalai Lama's mother was sitting beside her ailing newborn. All of a sudden, she heard first the heavy footsteps of the *kyirong* on the roof of the house, then the sound of it descending to the door and unlatching it. The *kyirong,* she wrote, came in "and stood beside me." Thinking that the ghost—the appearance of which is not described—could not harm her child, the *gyalyum chenmo* took the baby up in her arms. But then the lamps, which she had just lit, flickered and went out. The next thing she knew, the child was crying on the floor ten feet away, though the "lamps were once more lit, and I was still sitting upright. I was not aware how my child had got to the floor." For the next fourteen days, the baby was severely ill, "his eyes swollen out of all proportion. He cried constantly, and nothing I could do would comfort him. In the mornings I would notice bloody scratch marks in and around his eyes, and there were bloodstains on his cheeks. Three weeks later his crying ceased, but he seemed lifeless. When he could finally open his eyes, to my horror [they] had turned from brown to blue. He had become blind."

The *kyirong* was not finished with the family yet, however, and appeared some time later in the form of an old man. After this visit, her baby's eyes became swollen again while an older daughter's eyes also became infected. This time, the son's illness was fatal; he died just past his first birthday.

These stories are worth relating, as they give a clear picture of the world into which the Dalai Lama was born. It was a world enchanted. Not enchanted in the optimistic Disney sense of frolicking fairy princes and princesses, but in the darker sense of the visible world possessed by a realm of beings only rarely seen. In this conception of nature, humans are largely unwelcome intruders on earth, who must contend with a hidden host, the jealous guardians of territory considered by these entities as theirs by right. It was a world that would have been familiar to countless millions of people elsewhere at this time. Among the country dwellers of Ireland, for example, the *aes sidhe,* the "Fair Folk," were still well attested, and even today we hear of Laplanders sure that their farms are guarded by trolls.

If there is a major difference between the folk beliefs of Tibetans and those of other peoples, it is only the strength of the hold they had—and to some extent continue to have—over the popular imagination. Many scholars speak of these folk beliefs in terms of Tibet's "nameless religion." It is not just that houses are haunted by shape-shifting ghosts. Every feature of the landscape and every creature dwelling within it falls under the aegis of some sprite or spirit or deity. Even the bolts of lightning in a storm were said to issue from the mouths of celestial dragons. Every mountain, every lake, every river, every stream and waterfall, the forests, the wildernesses, even each individual tree and shrub belongs in some sense to one or more god or godling. So too does every valley, field, and pathway, not to mention every town, village, and even monastery. If that were not enough, the very stars and planets above have their attendant deity. Father Desideri, an eighteenth-century Jesuit missionary to Tibet, wrote of the "dreadful and tedious solitude" of the territory he crossed on his way to Lhasa. He was quite wrong. For Tibetans, their country, so barren and empty to the European eye, positively brims with life unseen. There are minor deities (known as *lha*) in every strange rock formation, every cave, and every cavern. Even the tools of agriculture, the implements of the kitchen, the saddles and tack of horses, the harness of yak, *dri,* and mule have their presiding spirits. And woe betide anyone who neglects to appease the hearth gods. For the nomadic population of Tibet (much smaller in size today than it used to be, but perhaps great enough to account for half the country's total population* during the period in question), these hearth gods are of particular importance. They are "strange jealous creatures [that] swarm at the rising of the smoke in a new tent, and take proprietary though at times perverse interest in the new hearth. Because of their displeasure, children die or are born dead. Their frightful blows bring blindness, strange swellings and the swift rotting of anthrax . . . What tent can hope for peace if the hearthstone spirits are angry?"

There is, then, no place or object that does not fall within the purview of some unseen being which, like the *kyirong,* may take on outward form from time to time and as occasion demands—with which human beings must contend: entities like the *shi dre,* the *gson dre,* and the *rollang.* The *shi dre* is the form most often assumed by victims of calamity such as violent death—whether by rockfall or by murder. In the latter case, the deceased may pursue the perpetrator of the crime relentlessly until he too comes to a hideous end. The *gson dre* are, by contrast, a kind of spirit whose interest is restricted to women, mainly at night, whose bodies they inhabit and whose actions they control. This demon's hapless victims become its plaything, bringing misfortune and lingering disease—no doubt often venereal—to those women it possesses. The *rollang* are similar to the zombies and undead familiar to the Western imagination. These take possession of a corpse at the very moment when the spirit animating it departs and, having done so, wreak havoc among the living.

Some of these unseen beings are more powerful than others. The mountain gods, for example, are of great importance in that they command the loyalty of many, while the influence of the hearth gods extends only to those who come into contact with the hearth's fire. The influence of the *lu,* or *naga,* is restricted to bodies of water. Nonetheless, in every case, because of their nature, anyone wishing to live in peace must perforce enter into relationship

---

*It is impossible to give an accurate number for the total population of Tibet. Even today, no reliable numbers exist. Suffice it to say that Tibetans have traditionally claimed around 6 million, while the Chinese offer a figure around half this.

with these beings. Similarly, anyone wishing to embark on some enterprise, whether it be a journey by land or a river crossing or the building of a house or the pitching of a tent, must take care to identify on whose territory they will be encroaching and take appropriate measures to appease and propitiate them.

In most cases, offerings are made—whether of food, money, or prayer. For propitiation of the mountain gods, it is usual to build cairns—sometimes made of animal horns and generally adorned with prayer flags—and, one day in the year, to offer weapons. To the hearth deities are made daily offerings of *tsampa* flour. In the past, some of the more powerful deities would demand blood sacrifice, though since the advent of the Buddhadharma, superior methods using only symbolic sacrifice are now employed—and to better effect. A highly trained adept may call on the gods to produce rain or to avert hailstorms. But some of the more troublesome minor beings, such as the *kyirong,* can be extremely difficult to deal with. Certain kinds of wood smoke can be helpful, especially that of the juniper tree or of particular types of rhododendron. In some circumstances, the performance of meritorious deeds, such as redeeming animals destined for slaughter, may prove effective. In others, a scapegoat may be required. Tibet's first Western-trained physician, Dr. T. Y. Pemba, describes in his autobiography how, when he fell sick with a mysterious illness at the age of around thirteen, his family called on the services of some monks from their local monastery. For several days they recited prayers and chanted, but when the boy's condition continued to deteriorate, his parents resorted to more drastic measures. They bought a sheep that was destined for slaughter—the choice of animal being determined by the fact that the boy had been born in a Sheep year, reckoned according to the Tibetan lunar calendar. It was then painted and kept "almost as a pet." When this, too, failed to bring about any improvement, a ritual using a human scapegoat was performed. This entailed finding another youth to participate, since, Dr. Pemba explains, "it was believed that in this ritual, my disease would be transferred to the other boy." For this reason, "only a very poor family was likely to allow one of its children to take part."

Unfortunately for Dr. Pemba (but presumably to the relief of the scapegoat), the ritual did not work. At first, everyone was perplexed. But when Dr. Pemba's family "found out that, the day before [I fell sick], I had been awful enough to urinate in the stream where a fierce deity was believed to live, they were sure this had brought on my illness." They began to leave offerings of food at the water's edge and begged the deity to relent. "I suppose he forgave me because in a few days I became much better," he wrote, though he later concluded that the illness was meningitis.

Dr. Pemba takes a thoroughly modern view of his illness. What this viewpoint lacks from the traditional perspective is a plausible account of *why* these events occurred in the first place. Why did Dr. Pemba fall ill? Why did the Great Mother find her infant suddenly on the floor? To say simply that the one acquired an infection and that the other merely imagined that she had not fallen asleep lacks the explanatory power of a supernatural cause. And for all the Dalai Lama's interest in contemporary scientific endeavor, this world in which human beings must contend with supernatural beings was the one into which he was born and the existence of which, to this day, he does not disavow.

5

"Lonely and somewhat unhappy": A Hostage in All but Name

Although Kewtsang Rinpoché was certain he had found the authentic reincarnation of the Great Thirteenth, there remained two other candidates on the Panchen Lama's list to examine. The first child the search party interviewed after returning from Taktser turned out to be more promising than any other they had seen so far, apart from Lhamo Thondup. But this one was too shy even to touch any of the objects that had belonged to the Great Thirteenth. He was subsequently identified as the reincarnation of a lesser figure. The other child unfortunately discounted himself in the most comprehensive manner by dying before he could be examined. This brought to an end the Rinpoché's work, and he submitted his report to the government in a coded telegram as well as by messenger traveling on horseback. It was now left to the regent to look at the evidence supplied by all three search parties and to consult with the oracles. Why it took several months for his reply to come back is not clear, but among the reasons must have been the fraught political situation prevailing in the Amdo area at that time.

Following the fall of the Manchu dynasty, the Nationalist government, now under the leadership of Chiang Kai-shek, had come to power in China. But already its authority was being seriously challenged by Mao Zedong's Communists, and civil war had broken out. Crucial to the Nationalists' campaign to hold off a Communist army that crossed the Yellow River in 1936 was the Hui Muslim warlord Ma Bufang. By annihilating the Communists in a fierce battle, he succeeded in establishing himself as governor of Qinghai, the western Chinese province that claimed much of Amdo as its own territory. This he ruled with little regard for the central government.

Kewtsang Rinpoché realized correctly that if Ma came to know of the strong likelihood that the infant Dalai Lama was under his jurisdiction, there was every chance that not only would he seek to extort large sums of money from the Tibetans, but also that he might try to send a military escort with the boy to Lhasa. If this happened, it would give the Chinese government the opportunity to claim a presence in the Tibetan capital. The search party leader thus determined to keep the child's identity secret and announce only that he was one of several promising candidates.

In the meantime, the infant prodigy was taken by his parents in the fall of 1937 to Kumbum Monastery, where he would reside until his final confirmation by the authorities in Lhasa. There was nothing unusual in this: boys would be "given" to a monastery, often at an early age—though it was rare for one quite so young. In the case of the Dalai Lama, his parents decided that Lobsang Samten, his next elder brother, should also enter the *sangha* at this time so that at least little Lhamo Thondup would have a companion close to his own age. That their eldest son, the sixteen-year-old Taktser Rinpoché, was already studying at the monastery must have given them further comfort at the thought of leaving their youngest child there. Yet despite the fact that the three brothers would be together, the little boy was distraught when he realized that his mother meant to leave him at the monastery, and he begged to be taken home. In his autobiography, Taktser Rinpoché wrote how Lhamo Thondup was soon joined in his lamentation by Lobsang Samten, and recalled how, "a last attempt to distract my little brother by getting him to look at the dancing snowflakes outside the window . . . failed, and then we were all three in floods of tears."

Thus began what, as the Dalai Lama later wrote—with how much understatement we can only guess—was "a lonely" and "somewhat unhappy period of my life." Having two brothers as companions hardly made up for the separation from his mother, from whom he was barely weaned. By way of compensation, he quickly formed a close attachment to the man he called Ponpo, the monk attendant who was his principal caregiver. The memory of time spent enfolded in the warmth of this monk's robes never left him, and he has spoken of how, for comfort, he would sometimes suck a mole on the man's face "until it became red." Indeed, he became so attached to Ponpo that he could not bear to lose sight of his robe. Even when his attendant was in the kitchen, the little boy would watch the hem of his garment through the curtain that separated the cooking area from his living quarters, lying on the floor to do so. Yet although the outsider is horrified at the thought of a child barely out of infancy being torn from its mother's breast and handed over to unknown male caretakers, the Dalai Lama himself feels no animosity either toward his parents or toward the system that dealt the blow.

Kumbum turned out to be a decidedly bracing environment. While his brother Lobsang Samten was having lessons, the Dalai Lama "had no one to play with," and he remembers "peering round the curtain in the doorway to try to attract his attention without letting his tutor see me." On one occasion, the four-year-old Dalai Lama watched horrified as a young monk was beaten for some failure in his studies, though he also remembered that the teacher who beat the boy "was very nice to me, and . . . would give me peaches as I sat inside his robe." And yet while it might look as though there were advantages in being a candidate for the highest office in the land, these were unevenly granted. The future Dalai Lama and his two brothers also had an uncle—a brother of their father—at the monastery, to whom the younger ones took "a childish dislike," partly on account of the mustache of which he was unbecomingly proud, and partly on account of the fact that he was often cross with them. On one never-to-be-forgotten occasion, the little boy muddled the pages of scripture his uncle was reading, at which he "picked me up and slapped me hard. He was extremely angry and I was terrified. For literally years afterwards I was haunted by his very dark pockmarked face and fierce moustache. Thereafter, whenever I caught sight of him, I became very frightened."

As the Dalai Lama confessed later, "for the most part" he was "quite unhappy" during his time at Kumbum. The fact that he was considered possibly to be the earthly manifestation of Chenresig counted for little. "As far as I knew, I was just one small boy among many."

While waiting for word to come back from the regent, and hoping to fool the governor, Ma Bufang, Kewtsang Rinpoché requested permission to test an additional ten boys at Kumbum Monastery. The governor objected to the venue and proposed another, which the Tibetans were compelled to accept. When Ma Bufang was informed that the boy from Taktser had performed more successfully than the other candidates and that the search party was requesting permission to take him to Lhasa for further tests, the governor's interest was aroused and he ordered that all the candidates be brought to his headquarters in Xining so he could conduct his own examination. More dangerous still, the child who had so impressed the search party also made the greatest impression on the governor. Ma Bufang advised the Tibetans that this was undoubtedly the one they were looking for. It was now inevitable that he would use the child as a bargaining chip.

Several months after this event, the Lhasa authorities delivered the momentous news that the boy from Taktser was indeed the authentic rebirth of the Great Thirteenth. Reting Rinpoché, having deliberated with the utmost care and consulted with all the relevant supernatural authorities, was entirely confident in the matter. The child should be brought to Lhasa as soon as possible. Predictably enough, as soon as word got out, and despite the fact that, officially, the Tibetans continued to insist that the boy from Taktser was but one of several candidates, no one was taken in.

Finding the reincarnation of the Great Thirteenth was something to be shouted from the rooftops. This brought more than mere honor to Taktser and its environs. This was more even than a blessing. This was the earthly manifestation of Chenresig, Bodhisattva of Compassion, erupting into the human realm right here on this piece of now-and-always-to-be-hallowed ground. This was a theogony—the coming of a god.

There followed what proved to be a lengthy wrangle, which escalated from a straightforward demand from the governor for payment of 100,000 silver dollars (equivalent to somewhere between $15,000 and $20,000 at the time, an enormous sum in those days) to negotiations that involved not only Ma Bufang's administration but also the Chinese central government, the (British) government of India, and the Tibetan government.

Furthermore, as soon as Reting Rinpoché's confirmation was received from Lhasa, the monastic authorities at Kumbum announced that every monastery in the area and all the local people must be given the opportunity to receive the Precious One's blessing. It was inconceivable that he should be among them and that for mere reasons of worldly affairs people should be prevented from enjoying his benediction. When Kewtsang Rinpoché demurred, there was even a moment when some of the younger monks at Kumbum threatened the search party with violence.

Ma Bufang's demand for an initial payment of 100,000 silver dollars was soon followed by one for a further 300,000 in cash to be paid to the governor's office. In addition, the authorities at Kumbum themselves put in a demand for a full set of the late Dalai Lama's ceremonial robes and a throne plus a set of the Great Thirteenth's two-hundred-volume edition of the scriptures, all to be written in gold. This, they argued, was fair recompense for the costs associated with looking after the child and his family, which had by now moved nearby, and in any case an appropriate acknowledgment of the monastery's role in his discovery.

Not having the funds available, the Tibetans turned in desperation to the Chinese Nationalist (Guomindang) government for help—with predictable results. The Chinese set their own—unacceptable—conditions, the most troubling of which was their insistence that an escort of the Nationalist army go with the boy to Lhasa. They also wanted the Tibetan government to declare publicly whether or not the boy from Taktser was in fact the new Dalai Lama. The Tibetans prevaricated but in the end agreed to a representative of the Guomindang traveling to Lhasa—though he had to do so via India. Still, however, the Tibetans insisted that the child was only one of two candidates. An official announcement would not be made before the boy could be examined alongside the Lhasa candidate—the boy whose connection with the Great Thirteenth had been indicated by the horse escaping its stable (but who, in reality, had already been ruled out).

By this time, Lhamo Thondup was almost four years old and had been at

Kumbum for over a year and a half. It was clear to all that he was an exceptional child, whatever Lhasa might finally decide. Some photographs taken by an American journalist* who visited Kumbum in early 1939 show the alert, curious, self-assured features still recognizable more than eighty years later. We glimpse, too, a trace of authority in his bearing. This is a child who looks more than equal to the task that lay in front of him. Though his time at Kumbum may not have been a happy one, it is clear from these images that it had not defeated him.

It was a matter of great satisfaction to the child Dalai Lama when, finally, word came that he was to leave for Lhasa. As he later put it, he "began to look to the future with more enthusiasm." Although he realized he would not be returned to his mother, at least he had the prospect of seeing her every day: his parents, now elevated to the rank of the highest nobility in the land, were to join him on the journey. The family party also comprised his maternal grandmother; the terrifying monk uncle; his older sister, Tsering Dolma, and her husband; his second-eldest brother, Gyalo Thondup, together with —though he was only eleven years old—the boy's fiancée, a "strikingly pretty girl" in the estimation of one European who saw her in Lhasa soon after their arrival; Lobsang Samten; and their younger sister, just born, Jetsun Pema.

Traveling in a caravan that took almost three months to cover the distance —there were at the time no roads and, apart from three cars, since abandoned, which the Great Thirteenth had imported to Lhasa, and a bicycle belonging to the British mission, no wheeled vehicles of any sort in Tibet—the Precious Protector was conveyed, together with Lobsang Samten, in a sort of palanquin carried on the backs of a pair of mules. According to the Dalai Lama himself, the journey was by no means an entirely serene progress through the vastness of the Tibetan landscape: "We spent a great deal of the time squabbling and arguing, as small children do, and often came to blows. This put our conveyance in danger of overbalancing. At that point our driver would stop the animals and summon my mother . . . When she looked inside, she always found the same thing: Lobsang Samten in tears and me sitting there with a look of triumph on my face. For despite his greater age, I was the more forthright."

---

*This was Archibald Steele, a reporter for the *Chicago Daily News.*

For two months the caravan made its way slowly from east to west without passing a single settlement. Typically, each day's journey covered no more than ten miles, and at the end of each stage a tented encampment would accommodate the travelers. What most impressed little Lhamo Thondup was the wildlife, which in those days remained in great abundance, among them "the vast herds of *drong* [wild yaks] ranging across the plains, the smaller groups of *kyang* [wild asses] and occasionally a shimmer of *gowa* and *nawa,* small deer which were so light and fast they might have been ghosts." Gyalo Thondup, the second-eldest brother, recalled how, when they reached the shores of the Kokonor, the huge (2,600 square mile) lake that divides historic Tibet from Mongolia, they saw "thousands of red tufted cranes and wild geese," which they all chased but could never catch.

What the Dalai Lama does not mention, because for him as a Tibetan it is unremarkable, is the vividness of the landscape through which they traveled: the sharp clarity of outline afforded by the atmosphere at high altitude. By day, the eye can see mountains on the horizon more than a hundred miles away; at night, the intensity of light when the sky is cloudless is scarcely to be imagined. You have never truly seen the stars nor had any inkling of their number until you have seen them in the pristine night skies of Tibet. Yet when there is cloud cover, and there is only the struggling flame of candles, the black of night takes on new meaning. And both by day and by night, the traveler must at all times be alert to sudden changes in the weather and the hazards they bring: the storms appearing as if by malevolent miracle from an empty sky, every cloud presaging torrential rain that turns placid mountain streams into raging torrents in a matter of minutes, or hailstones the size of golf balls that destroy crops in an instant, or blankets of snow that scar the retina when the sun shines on it. So too with the wind: one moment the breeze is soft as the caress of gossamer, a moment later someone descries a huddle of black hurtling forward like a posse of wild horsemen, and before there is time to take cover, a choking dust blizzard is upon you and a marrow-freezing wind tears at your clothing. This was an environment in which merely to stay alive was, for many, an ordeal—an ordeal that had to be confronted on a poor diet and was fraught with the ever present danger of brigandage on the one hand and, on the other, the onset of disease against which there was no remedy save the chanting of prayers and the casting out of spirits. And in spite of the extraordinary abundance of wildlife, here too there was serious danger. From the wolf packs that would carry off livestock to the cobras that infested the lower-lying regions, from the rabid dogs roaming village and countryside alike to the delicate but deadly monkshood, a species of wildflower that can kill without leaving a trace in a matter of hours, hidden menace lurked everywhere. As for the terrain itself, beyond the plains stood the looming mountains with their giddying ravines, plunging waterfalls, and the breathless passes between them, while to the north lay the upland desert where all was barren and desolate, save perhaps for a huddle of black horsehair tents far in the distance betokening a lonely nomad settlement.

At last, three months after setting out and ten days' journey from Lhasa, the caravan was met by a government official bringing the formal proclamation that the boy from Taktser had indeed been declared the authentic incarnation of the Great Thirteenth.

It was here that, a few days later, the regent came to prostrate himself before the Dalai Lama as the child presided over the first of many religious ceremonies that would culminate in his ascension to the Lion Throne early the following year. Recalling the days spent at the encampment, the Dalai Lama's second eldest brother, Gyalo Thondup, speaks in his autobiography of the comings and goings of "the officials, secretaries and monks" who made up the senior echelons of government and the "processions going on for hours; the food; the tea; the incense; the drums; the horns; the cymbals; the huge masks; the colourful costumes; the dancing and dramatic re-enactments" of historical events. It was at once a celebration, a pageant, a medieval fair, and a religious festival.

After several days of ceremonies, what had begun as a caravan and was now a cavalcade many thousands strong moved off. The next stop was Reting Monastery, from which the regent hailed. Dating from the tenth century, the foundation boasted a cedar forest said to have sprung from the hairs on the head of Atisha, the great Indian scholar saint to whose memory the monastery was dedicated. Here, the regent and the Dalai Lama's father discovered their common love of horses. Already there was magnificent stabling for dozens of splendid animals. It would not be long before these horses were joined by many more from the trading caravans brought from Amdo to Lhasa by the *yabshi kung,* as the Dalai Lama's father was now known. As was his right, the regent was invariably offered the pick of the crop among the horses the *yabshi kung* subsequently imported from the eastern breeding grounds, while the *kung* was often invited to elaborate picnic parties and horse gymkhanas arranged for the mutual gratification of the two enthusiasts.

It was also at Reting Monastery that the regent briefed the Dalai Lama's parents as to what they could expect in Lhasa. They would find many flatterers, and some people would certainly try to harm them. In particular, he warned the *gyalyum chenmo* never to accept food that had not been cooked in her own kitchen, "as it might be poisoned."

Leaving Reting Monastery for Lhasa, a week's journey distant, the caravan made its way to the environs of the small monastery of Rigya just outside the city. Here, on the plain below, a huge tented encampment had been erected. At its center stood the Macha Chenmo—the Great Peacock—a splendid blue-and-white construction that was only ever used to welcome the new Dalai Lama back to his temporal home. A poetic description of the return of the Sixth Dalai Lama gives some idea of the splendor of the occasion. At night it was said to have seemed that all "the stars of heaven [had] come down to earth." Then when the newly recognized Dalai Lama resumed his journey for the short distance to Lhasa, it caused "such a thunder of hooves as had never before been heard."

No film of the event—which took place on October 8, 1939—survives, though there are still photographs, and we know enough about Tibetan ceremony to have a good sense of what it must have been like: the sumptuous silk brocade of the lay officials, the ladies' magnificent jewelry of silver and turquoise and coral, the impossible headdress of even humble womenfolk—strange lattices of wood, adorned with precious stones, beneath which the hair was braided and strung like so much wash hung out to dry. And alongside them, the grave countenances of the solemn but inwardly exultant clergy, the eager bustling of the crowd seeking a place to stand, the longing expressed in the torrent of mantras recited, the smoke of incense burning, the reverent hush and humble obeisance of the common people as the procession drew close. But one has to think past these outer manifestations of gladness to recognize the true—the inner—and spiritual significance of the occasion. The profundity of the emotional connection Tibetans have with the Dalai Lama is beyond anything others can easily imagine. It was with a mixture of awe, reverence, and yearning, coupled with the tenderest feelings of possession, blessedness, and good fortune, that the whole population turned out to greet their beloved. That he was a somewhat unruly child who pulled away from the regent to get back to his mother and, to his terror, had to be manhandled back to his place by a bodyguard "with big bulging eyes" was nothing to them. The one in whom the *bodhi*—the awakened mind of the Buddha—resides is not merely a monarch. He is someone who connects, in himself, the seen world with that unseen.

PART II

✷

The Lion Throne

6

Homecoming: Lhasa, 1940

To those for whom the city represented what its etymology suggests—*lha,* "gods," *sa,* "earth," and hence "the gods' dwelling place on earth"—we can suppose that what occurred on that day when the Fourteenth Dalai Lama came home to Lhasa must have seemed a glimpse into the very mysteries of existence. To Tibetans generally, a visit to the holy city was the fulfillment of a lifelong ambition. It had then, as it still does, the same draw as Jerusalem, Rome, and Mecca have for followers of the Abrahamic religions. Merely to visit its shrines and holy places is to acquire spiritual merit. To such people, the mystical aura of this, the place to which the earthly manifestation of Chenresig, Bodhisattva of Compassion, was now returning, would render invisible the squalor and deprivation that might be the first thing to have struck a time traveler from the modern age.

According to Alexandra David-Néel, the fearless and indefatigable French explorer who reached the capital during the 1920s, Lhasa was "a town full of animation, inhabited by jolly people whose greatest pleasure is to loiter and chat out-of-doors." A less flattering picture is presented by the Japanese pilgrim Ekai Kawaguchi, who visited some years earlier. Describing the city as a "metropolis of filth," he recoiled in horror at the puddles of water into which people would openly defecate. In contrast to the broad squares where the great dramas of the liturgical year were enacted, there lay alleyways "narrow and devious," crowded, and "obscured by tumbledown buildings whose mud and stone walls were forever disintegrating and collapsing," the paths between them potholed with "pools of sludge." William Stanley Morgan, the Welsh-born doctor attached to the 1936–37 British mission to Lhasa, was appalled by the beggars he encountered "squatting or lying in the dust by the roadside." They were, he wrote, "mainly old and infirm—some blind and others lame or deformed. Many had huge goiters [from] long standing thyroid deficiency. Clad in sheepskin chubas [the traditional Tibetan gown] or bundled up in a mass of rags, they hung with dirt." He blanched, too, at the sight of the city's communal garbage dump, consisting of "great piles of offal eight and ten feet high" and surrounded "with a black and slimy ooze." His traveling companion, Freddy Spencer Chapman, a future jungle war hero, was particularly distraught over the dogs swarming around the refuse. "They were at once a revolting and pathetic sight—bodies bared with skin disease, huge suppurating sores covered with flies, lamed, often dragging a . . . useless leg, eyes gouged out, ears torn off . . . Nothing I had ever seen could compare with them."

To a Tibetan out-of-town visitor such as T. Y. Pemba, however, Lhasa was a place of wonder and delight. "The ordinary residents," he wrote, "were gay, witty, sharp and flamboyant . . . [and] Lhasa prided itself on having the gayest, prettiest and perhaps the 'loosest' women in Tibet." The city was divided into several different communities: there was a Muslim quarter, a small Nepalese quarter, and a quarter where the *ragyabas* lived—the butcher caste who also took the dead to the places of sky-burial, where the corpse was dismembered and fed to the ever-hovering vultures. The houses of these *ragyabas* were made almost entirely of animal horn. There were particular places where criminals would gather, too, some yoked together in pairs and shackled at the feet, others handless, having been mutilated for their misdeeds, the stumps "immersed . . . in boiling oil to arrest the bleeding." Although the Great Thirteenth had not approved of the practice, there is reason to suppose that it was carried out at least until the end of the regency period, and it remains a familiar trope of propaganda put out by the Chinese that it was they who outlawed such barbarism.

Owing to the absence of roads, let alone modern methods of communication (save for the telegraph line up from India that the British had installed for their own benefit), the city was one where rumor and counter-rumor were a continuous feature of life. Once, at around this time, the people were struck with terror when a story began to circulate that an army of Kazakhs was approaching, led by "an Amazon with breasts that hung to her waist." Her army was reputed to be so huge that it took a whole day to review it, while it was said to be "armed with strange secret weapons of immense power." It turned out the "army" was a ragged band of starving men, women, and children who had fled Sinkiang province and were on their way to seek asylum in India.

Lhasa was at this time a city with a settled population of probably no more than ten thousand. This might double or even triple during the most important annual festivals or, as in this case, at the Dalai Lama's homecoming. Within a few hours' walk stood the three largest monasteries in Tibet: Sera, with seven thousand monks, at around five miles distant; Drepung, with perhaps as many as ten thousand, around seven miles away; and Ganden, the third-largest monastery with a population of around three thousand monks, which was just under twenty miles from the capital. Almost every able-bodied monk would decamp and make his way to the city on great occasions such as this, crowding the streets "from sunrise to sunset," while at night, visitors slept crammed in stables and camped in courtyards.

In marked contrast to the squalor of large parts of the city stood the Dalai Lama's two palaces, the Potala and the Norbulingka, and the mansions of the aristocracy. It was the Norbulingka to which, with his next-elder brother, Lobsang Samten, the Dalai Lama was taken on this joyous occasion. Built as a summer retreat for the Seventh Dalai Lama at around a mile and a half to the southwest of Lhasa, the palace was topped with a golden roof and fronted with pillars, its windows glazed and protected from the sun by awnings decorated with auspicious symbols rendered in appliqué. Altogether more homelike than the Potala, it was surrounded by leafy parkland and several well-tended gardens that provided sanctuary to a menagerie of animals, including variously "a herd of tame musk deer; at least six enormous Tibetan mastiffs which acted as guard dogs . . . a few mountain goats; a monkey; a handful of camels; two leopards and a very old and rather sad tiger," and a large number of birds, including "several parrots; half a dozen peacocks; some cranes; a pair of golden geese and about thirty very unhappy Canada geese whose wings had been clipped."

It was at the Norbulingka that the Precious Protector had his first presentiment that he might indeed have some special connection with the Great Thirteenth. Up until that moment he had merely accepted what he had been told. But on this occasion, or so his mother informed him later, he announced that he would like to go to the Chensalingka. This was a building erected in the grounds of the Norbulingka by the Great Thirteenth. "She told me that we entered one room and I pointed to [a] box and said to open it. My teeth would be there." Sure enough, it was found to contain teeth that had belonged to his predecessor.

The Dalai Lama's parents had, in the meantime, taken up residence in a mansion situated beneath the northern wall of the Potala. This was to be their home until a new, more modern dwelling could be built for them. Although family photographs of this time show happy faces, the installation of the newcomers from Taktser was not entirely to the satisfaction of Lhasa's leading families. Some clearly still felt that the relative of the Great Thirteenth was a more suitable candidate, given his better connections.* Not only were the new Dalai Lama's family uneducated commoners (his mother was illiterate), but also they spoke a dialect that marked them as being from a part of Tibet hardly known in Lhasa.

Himself of lowly birth, the regent was attuned to the difficulties the family faced and arranged for the government to grant several landed estates to them, to ensure their independence. Even so, it takes little imagination to see what an ordeal those first few months must have been for the new arrivals, plunged into the round of formal entertaining that is the lot of the families of high officials everywhere. The fact that they needed an interpreter to begin with (the

---

*This was Ditru Rinpoché, still alive at the time of writing and a respected lama in his own right.

Amdo dialect they spoke was sufficiently different from the high-flown locutions of Lhasa as to need translating) was no doubt difficulty enough.* The records of the British officials who knew them well show the Lhasa aristocracy to have been little different from aristocracies anywhere else—fond of flummery and elaborate etiquette. The leading ladies were no doubt quick to share their opinions of the manners and comportment of the *gyalyum chenmo,* while the men (a lot of them idly rich and not a few of them habitual opium smokers) would have been eager to take the measure of the *yabshi kung.* Many aristocrats had by now been exposed to polite British society in places like Kalimpong and Darjeeling, and the disparity between their level of sophistication and that of the new Dalai Lama's family would have been immediately apparent. But while the *yabshi kung* received mixed reviews, the *gyalyum chenmo* captivated the hearts of prince and pauper alike with her simple, unaffected charm. Legendarily generous, she was humble, kindly, and warmly affectionate.

The new Dalai Lama's first public engagement after his homecoming was the tonsuring ceremony at which both he and the now eight-year-old Lobsang Samten were inducted as novice monks. As was his right, and only fitting, the regent himself performed the ritual haircutting that marked the Dalai Lama's entry into the monastic novitiate and gave the young hierarch his new name: Jamphel Ngawang Lobsang Yeshe Tenzin Gyatso.

When at last the proceedings were over, the child returned to the small building within the grounds of the Norbulingka which was to be his home for the first year in Lhasa. To begin with, the Dalai Lama's mother had right of access to him, and they saw each other regularly, if not every day. And though life promised to be lonely for one so young, the following days were enlivened by the New Year festival which began shortly afterwards, commencing with the ceremony of the Priest's New Year and ending on the twenty-seventh day with the "Sky Archery" ceremony. Strolling minstrels and wandering friars frequented every street, while the more pious, clad in leather knee and elbow

* Still in common use today, honorific Tibetan is almost an entirely different language from colloquial Tibetan.

pads, circumambulated the Jokhang Temple, measuring their body length on the ground. "One saw many of these people, their faces dusty and bruised, their eyes tight with pain and [their] mouths set hard," noted an observer. Above all, though, this was a time of rejoicing, a time for families to come together, for old friendships to be rekindled and new ones formed. There was street theater and music and dance. Two perennial favorites were the lion and peacock dances, the former featuring an imp who tries to tame the beast, succeeding at last, to the delight of the crowd.

Unfortunately for the young Dalai Lama, he was forbidden to participate in the celebrations. From his point of view, the most important element of the proceedings was the Monlam Chenmo, the Great Prayer Festival, which began on the sixth day of the New Year. A central feature of Monlam, the Brilliant Invocation of the Glorious Goddess, necessitated that he move to a suite of rooms at the top of the Jokhang Temple, where he would reside until the final day of the festival. Preceded by ranks of soldiers with bayonets fixed, the boy was carried in a palanquin whose bearers marched with a peculiar gait so as to minimize its swaying. Once the Precious One was safely within the temple, the carousing could resume once more, whereupon "the crowd really let themselves go . . . [T]here was great merrymaking that night."

Dating back to the eighth century, the Jokhang is considered the most important temple in all Tibet and is a place of pilgrimage sacred to each of the different traditions within Tibetan Buddhism. There are four principal schools, or sects, within the Tibetan tradition: the Nyingma (literally the "Old Ones," who are associated with the seventh-century sage Padmasambhava, the Lotus-Born One), the Sakya (dating from the eleventh century and associated with the Kon clan of central Tibet), the Kargyu (dating from the twelfth century and associated chiefly with Karma Pakshi and Milarepa), and the Gelug (founded by Tsongkhapa in the fifteenth century and the only one to require celibacy of its monks). Here, despite his tender years, the boy was to preside over a ceremony at which incense was offered to Palden Lhamo, the Glorious Goddess and protector deity (the one invoked by the regent at the lake called Lhamo Lhatso), in whose spiritual care the Dalai Lamas subsist.

Several days later followed the most spectacular of all the New Year public ceremonies. This was the Casting-Out of the Votive Offering, and it was only on the eve of this event that the young Precious Protector was permitted to come down and walk among the crowds. It was, as he recalled in his autobiography, "one of the best moments in the Dalai Lama's year." This was the one day, he wrote, when "I was allowed outside to walk round the streets so that I could see the *torma,* the huge, gaily coloured butter sculptures traditionally offered to the Buddhas on this day. There were also puppet shows and music played by military bands and an atmosphere of tremendous happiness amongst the people."

With its strong military character, the ceremony that followed was notable for its displays of martial prowess. Soldiers sang war songs in honor of the Glorious Goddess as they brandished their bows and arrows and fenced with swords. Part of the proceedings enacted a standoff where men armed with guns would aim at an opposing rank and shout abuse at them, taunting them in an episode known as "the Incitement." This culminated in a series of flashes and bangs as firecrackers exploded. The foot soldiers departing, a detachment of cavalry then appeared, riding slowly beneath the Dalai Lama's window while he remained sequestered inside. On reaching the entrance to the temple forecourt, the riders would dismount and prostrate themselves before him, though to his intense frustration, the Dalai Lama could only peep through a yellow curtain. It was then the turn of the monks of Namgyal Monastery, who appeared in their finest vestments, carrying on their heads the tall, curved yellow felt hat characteristic of the Gelug order, some censing the air with sweet-smelling herbs, others carrying musical instruments. There was also a contingent carrying the *shinyen* cymbals, the purpose of which was to drive out evil.

After preliminary invocations, the assembled religious began a ceremony to welcome the *torma,* which were now brought forward, accompanied by a phalanx of monks. Consisting of "wooden frames bound with leather on which stood various images and decorations, all made of butter" brightly dyed, the sculptures were a most impressive sight, standing up to thirty feet tall. The images having earlier been ritually infused with the evil of the past year, the Namgyal choir now began chanting the liturgy of exorcism. When this was complete, the sculptures were taken out of the courtyard and carried in procession to an open space on the southern side of the city while the monastic orchestra continued to play. This, though, was but the prelude to the grand finale of the day's proceedings, the arrival of the Nechung oracle, possessed already by the spirit of Dorje Drakden.

Some silent film shot by an aristocratic cineaste at the 1959 Monlam Chenmo gives us a glimpse of the oracle in action. Bursting forth from within the temple itself, the medium—his trance fully developed—rushes out clasping a sword in one hand and a bow and arrow in the other. The crowd visibly gasps. Golden and shot through with flaming color, the oracle's tunic is adorned with a breastplate of polished silver that radiates light at his every move. On his head he wears a vast crown—said to have weighed more than eighty pounds—decked with peacock feathers, studded with precious stones, and trailing plumes of white horsehair. As the musicians urge him on with a giddy rhythm that mounts faster and faster, the oracle, holding his weapons aloft, begins to dance. Lifting his legs high, he whirls around and around in a crescendo of color, the sunlight flashing off his breastplate as if it were on fire. After several breathtaking gyrations, Nechung* leaves the courtyard and, now supported by two attendants and accompanied by the monastic orchestra, heads off down the road in the direction taken by the party bearing the *torma*.

When at last the oracle reaches the place where the *torma* now lie on a mass of brushwood, he fires an arrow toward them and, to the intense satisfaction of all present, the pyre erupts in butter-fueled flames to the screams and yells of the crowd, heard above the still chanting monks. This signifies the destruction of the old year's evil, wiping the slate clean at the dawn of the new. Finally, three ancient cannon—known respectively as the Idiot, the Old She-Demon, and the Young She-Demon—are fired. Their reports could be heard by the Dalai Lama, who, to his continued frustration, remained in his apartment in the Jokhang. There he had to await the final procession, which would wend its way slowly back from the site of immolation, so all those participating could abase themselves beneath his window.

The next day was the last of the Great Prayer Festival. A procession of monks, including the Ganden Throne Holder—technically the most senior religious authority in the land—followed an image of Maitreya, the Buddha

* Although, strictly speaking, one should say "the medium of the Nechung oracle," it is simpler to refer to him as Nechung or "the oracle."

to come, around a circuit which brought them to a halt in front of the chamber where the Dalai Lama remained hidden behind his gauze curtain. Again, the Nechung oracle appeared in a trance, and, following his ritual dance and presentation of an offering scarf to the image, all would prostrate themselves beneath the youngster's window.

But what of the little boy himself? While we might prefer to imagine the holy child rewarding these supplications with inward grace and outward benediction, by his own account he behaved no better—and possibly even a little worse—than the majority of small boys might in his position. "The sight of all those people down there was too much for me," he wrote. "I boldly poked my head through the curtain. But, as if this were not bad enough, I remember blowing bubbles of spit which fell on people's heads as they threw themselves down to the ground far below!"

During the time of the Great Thirteenth, Maitreya's procession was followed by an appearance of the Dalai Lama's elephant. After forcing its way through the crush of maroon-clad monastics, it would kneel at the foot of the building and trumpet its salute before leading the procession out of the courtyard. This was the moment for the cannon to be fired once more, at which the religious ceremony would conclude and the secular entertainments begin. Its report signaled the start of a horse race. Surprisingly for a people who made so much use of the animal, these horses were riderless. Urged on by the crowds of spectators that lined the route from Drepung Monastery to the center of town, they were joined at the halfway mark by human athletes, who, at the sound of a second gunshot, would take off, competitors of both species occupying the same space on the road. As the Dalai Lama put the matter, "This tended to result in enjoyable confusion as both arrived simultaneously."

Shortly after the conclusion of the New Year festivities, the young leader's formal enthronement ceremony was held in the Potala.* According to witnesses, the child could not have conducted himself more perfectly. A "solid, solemn but very wide-awake boy, red-cheeked and closely shorn," he "sat quietly and with great dignity, completely at ease in these strange surroundings, giving the proper blessing to each person."

---

*On February 22, 1940, to be precise.

But if the people were thus reassured, the ceremony was of little consequence to the boy himself. He was more eager to get his hands on the gifts the British delegation had brought for him. These included a Meccano construction set, a pedal car, a tricycle, a "nightingale clock," and, most exciting of all, a pair of parakeets. Of the two brothers, however, only Lobsang Samten was permitted to attend the children's party given at the Dekyi Lingka—literally, the Garden of Happiness—which housed the British mission. The Dalai Lama's monk caretakers deemed it unsuitable for him to go. This was cruelty enough, but when the head of the British mission, Sir Basil Gould, explained to Lobsang Samten that it would be better if the birds could remain at the Dekyi Lingka until they had acclimatized properly following their journey over the mountains, the Dalai Lama was distraught. Unable to bear the wait, the young hierarch sent a messenger to the British two days later requesting that the birds be sent at once. They were duly dispatched, together with detailed instructions for their care. Another two days followed before, to their surprise, the British received the birds back. It transpired that the Precious Protector was persuaded that perhaps the sahibs should after all be responsible for the creatures until they had adjusted to the Lhasa climate.

The parakeets were doubtless the source of many moments of welcome distraction during that first year. When, however, the New Year festival inaugurating the subsequent (Iron Snake) year—1941—came to an end, what had amounted to a honeymoon period for the young Dalai Lama also came to a close. During the past year, his duties had been minimal, but from now on he would have to participate in the daily tea ceremony in the Great Hall—a magnificent, somewhat low-ceilinged chamber, its walls covered with frescoes topped with gilded stucco. This was a formal gathering of senior government figures over which the boy Dalai Lama presided while affairs of state were discussed, but in which he played no part. More onerously, it was at this moment that he, together with Lobsang Samten, now began their formal education as novice monks. This entailed shifting his quarters from the Norbulingka Palace to his new residence in the penthouse on the top floor of the Potala, again with Lobsang Samten for company, where he occupied the same suite of rooms that both the Great Fifth and the Great Thirteenth had occupied. Besides a bedroom, this comprised a small private chapel and several large anterooms, though, unlike accommodations in one or two of the aristocratic mansions, it did not have a bathroom.*

Rising miraculously from the Marpo Ri, the Red Hill, the Potala is unquestionably one of the architectural wonders of the world, wholly dominating the Lhasa townscape even today. (In 1994 it was added to the UNESCO World Heritage list.) And as anyone who has set eyes on it will testify, it is an extraordinary feat of human ingenuity. "The contrasts and rhythms of different materials, of solids and voids, of heavy and light, of monochrome and intense colour, are startling, subtle and pleasing at the same time," according to one guide to Tibetan architecture, while the "seemingly floating golden roofs are ethereal forms in contrast to their solid substructure." In all, the building covers around 1.3 million square feet (more than half again as large as Buckingham Palace) and stands nearly four hundred feet high. It has, moreover, fully a thousand rooms, the largest of which, the West Main Hall, has a floor area covering some 7,250 square feet.

Dating back to the mid-seventeenth century, though the site was originally built on much earlier—certainly no later than the seventh century and very likely long before that—the building consists of two separate but connected palaces, the White and the Red. Inaugurated by the Great Fifth Dalai Lama's teacher of the magical arts, who drew a sacred mandala at its heart, the Potala took half a century to complete—though even this seems too short a time when one considers not just the size of the structure but also its incredible complexity. Stonemasons, carpenters, woodcarvers, and artists came from all over Tibet as well as from among Nepal's Buddhist community.

Besides quartering the Dalai Lamas—year round before the Norbulingka was built—the Potala was home both to a large community of monks and to a small number of laymen. Namgyal Monastery, the foundation to which the Dalai Lama himself belonged, and which existed primarily to serve him through its prayer and liturgy, was situated within its precincts and numbered up to two hundred monastics. The Potala was, furthermore, the seat of Tibet's religio-political government.† This was the institution, inaugurated by the

---

*The Tsarong mansion already had two.

†I use this term to translate *chos srid zung 'brel.*

Great Fifth, that united the spiritual and temporal realms under the leadership of the Dalai Lama. For this reason, besides the monks of Namgyal, thirty or so highborn monastic officials who composed the upper echelons of the civil service were also in residence, plus another large contingent of monk clerks, not to mention serving staff, kitchen staff, and the guardians of the various storerooms, as well as resident tailors, prison guards, and inmates of the palace dungeons. In addition there was a garrison of soldiers, together with a contingent of grooms for the Dalai Lama's and government officials' horses stabled within the Potala's many-storied splendor.

Yet for all its magnificence, few would deny that the Potala is also somber in the extreme. Outside it looks more like a military fortress than the palace of the Bodhisattva of Compassion, while inside it feels more like a giant sepulcher than anyone's home.

The military character of the building is by no means as inappropriate as it might at first seem, however. It was built with an eye both to withstanding a lengthy siege such as the Mongols might have undertaken and to the often overlooked martial aspect of the Dalai Lama institution. It is hardly surprising, then, that, like his predecessor, the present Dalai Lama came to prefer the Norbulingka as a place to live.

With respect to these military overtones, it is vital to recognize that quite as important as the Dalai Lama's authority over the temporal realm is his authority over the unseen forces of the Tibetan Buddhist pantheon—not just the minor deities of home and hearth but also the protector deities of the Buddhadharma. Many of these protectors are conceived of as warriors, masters of their own fortresses with retinues of armored minions. Besides being an impregnable redoubt to protect the Dalai Lama and his government against their earthly enemies, the Potala is thus also a visible symbol of his role as one whose power extends to the realm of the gods. Not merely an earthly protector of his people, he is their supernatural protector as well. He guards his country and his subjects against the unseen hosts in thrall to the cravings of untamed desire and the karmic consequences of unexpiated sin.

The funerary aspect of the Potala's interior has much to do with the fact that it also functions partly as a giant mausoleum. The reliquary stupas, or tombs, of the Fifth, Seventh, Eighth, Ninth, and Thirteenth Dalai Lamas are all contained within its walls. Those of the Great Fifth and the Great Thirteenth are particularly splendid, as befits the achievements of those two incarnations. Indeed, the tomb of the Great Thirteenth stands three stories high and necessitated considerable structural alteration to the palace to accommodate it. Smothered in gold and set with thousands of precious stones, it faces an altar on which stands an offering mandala composed, it is said, of 200,000 pearls. But for all the magnificence of the carvings, the statuary, the mural paintings, the *thangkas,** and other products of the Tibetan artistic genius, as the Dalai Lama himself would be the first to admit, the place was hardly suited to the five-year-old boy whose home it now was.

Placed under the care of three principal attendants, the Master of the Ritual (*choepon khenpo*), the Master of the Kitchen (*soelpon khenpo*), and the Master of the Wardrobe (*simpon khenpo*), the Dalai Lama was looked after with, according to one British official, a "devotion and love, almost surpassing the love of women." But this can hardly have been adequate recompense for the lack of a mother's love from the point of view of one so young. Moreover, the rooms he occupied were as dismal as they were disastrously ill-kept. "Everything . . . was ancient and decrepit," he later recalled, "and behind the drapes that hung across each of the four walls lay deposits of centuries-old dust." The rooms were also pitifully cold and dimly lit, and so badly infested with mice that the curtains surrounding the little boy's bed ran with urine.

The environment in which the young Dalai Lama began his academic career was decidedly austere. Yet, in the Tibetan tradition, the emphasis placed on learning is such that, for the Gelugpas at least, scholarship and sanctity are almost synonymous. The boy's education was thus of crucial importance for, unless he could command the respect of the monastic community, he could not hope to govern effectively. To understand why this is so, we need to have some idea of the way in which the monasteries functioned—and to

* A *thangka* is a religious painting executed on a scroll that is generally bordered with silk brocade. The most important contain paint infused with the powdered relics of one or more high masters.

a large extent continue to function—within Tibetan society. The main purpose of the monasteries is twofold. They exist, first, to furnish their members with an environment conducive to private spiritual practice and to provide a superlative education such that the more able of them can become teachers of the dharma. The Three Seats of Ganden, Drepung, and Sera (the Harvard, Yale, and Princeton of Tibet) are in this respect very much like the medieval universities of Europe, which grew out of the teaching faculties of the various Christian religious orders. While the different halls or colleges of the Christian universities, like the Tibetan monasteries, fulfilled the liturgical practices—the masses and devotions—of their particular order, there are important differences between the ancient European universities and their Tibetan counterparts. This was reflected in the other principal function of the monasteries, which was to mediate between the seen world and the unseen.

It is in this second function that the major differences lie. For Christians, God is transcendent. That is to say, God exists independently of the world, even if He pervades it. In Buddhism, there is no such transcendent realm; the world is unbounded, so although there are levels of being that start with the gross and ascend through different strata to the most refined state, the realms of the Buddhas, these realms are not considered to exist "outside" or "beyond" the totality of all that there is. The monasteries are thus deeply concerned with "this-worldly" matters, even though this concern is principally focused on the gods and godlings of the supernatural realm. They are not only seats of learning, then, but also fortresses from which spiritual armies are mustered through ceremonies—lasting sometimes whole days and nights, during which millions of mantras may be recited, tens or even hundreds of thousands of liturgical texts chanted, and thousands of pages of scripture read—which are then sent forth to do battle with the enemies of the Buddhadharma.

Of course, as is the case with every institution, even in their heyday there were few really excellent monks and many who were "lazy, stupid and mere parasites." For those whose intellectual gifts did not mark them out as future scholars (the majority), the daily ceremonies were largely what monastic life consisted of. As to their other duties, some were designated as traders and bankers, undertaking business on behalf of the monasteries, chiefly through selling and bartering the produce of the landed estates that supported them. But monastic officials would also make loans and collect taxes on lands the monastery owned. Others would work in the monastery administration, while still others, because of their artistic skill, would be employed in the workshops as painters and sculptors. Those suited to more menial tasks might work in the kitchens or perhaps as tailors. Up until 1959, there also existed a distinct subclass of monks known as the *dob dob.* These were fraternities of monks whose principal concerns were sport, fighting, and to some extent sexual adventure. These, according to one observer, were "tough looking characters, with dirty greasy clothes[,] their faces painted with black streaks." With regard to their sporting activities, these were generally conducted off-site and might include running or weightlifting, while their fighting often involved wielding the heavy keys that were typically worn on a chain around the waist. Latterly they had taken to practicing with firearms as well. As for their sexual exploits, they would sometimes lie in wait around Lhasa in the evening in the hope of capturing young aristocratic boys, on whom they would take their pleasure. Yet if the *dob dob* were feared by both layman and monastic alike, they were also very often the ones who would nurse the sick and dying. The *dob dob* should not, however, be confused with the monastic proctors and disciplinarians, who would keep order with whip and staves during the great liturgical ceremonies, prodding those who fell asleep and lashing those who were unruly. These were monks of good reputation who, together with the abbot and chant master (the *umze*), comprised the leadership of the monasteries. The more physically imposing of their number made up the monastery police force. Padding their shoulders to look still more fearsome, they would patrol the monastic precincts carrying an elaborately decorated mace as a sign of office.

Although there was a sharp division between the different activities of the monks, the larger monasteries were made up of two or more colleges, or *dra tsang.* These were further subdivided into *khang tsen*, or "houses" (rather like Griffindor and other houses in the Harry Potter novels). These *khang tsen* had strong local affiliations, so that monks from Kham were likely to join one, monks from Amdo another, those from Mongolia still another, and monks from central or western Tibet another again. Similarly, each college was generally home to one or more incarnation lineages. But although some colleges were inevitably wealthier than others, and although the monasteries themselves had their own landed estates, almost without exception, anyone joining had to have at least some independent source of income. This would usually come from the individual monk's own family or from a wealthy patron, but in any case, lack of funds could be a major source of difficulty for even the most able scholars. It was only when such individuals graduated and were able to teach in their own right that they could hope to become self-sufficient.

In the case of the Three Seats, besides the heads of each college, there were also various senior monastic appointments. Yet while these senior lamas, all of whom had come up through the ranks, were acclaimed teachers, the system of recognizing reincarnate lamas (or *tulkus*) meant that immense prestige also attached to this other class of monks—whether or not they were themselves notable scholars. And it was these *tulkus,* a sort of monastic aristocracy, who played a key role not only in the religious life of Tibet but also in its political life.

The development of the *tulku* system, which finds its apotheosis in the institution of the Dalai Lamas, was in fact unknown until the thirteenth century. Its first instantiation came when a widely admired teacher and thaumaturge gave directions that enabled his reincarnation to be identified.* Here, though, it is important to be clear about what is being claimed when a child is identified as a reincarnation of a high lama.† It is not that the soul, or even the essence, of the deceased passes into the body of his successor. As we shall see, it is a fundamental claim of Buddhist thinkers that there is no substantial self. It is rather the accumulated karma attaching to the stream of consciousness that manifests through one individual which is passed on to, or made manifest in, another sentient being. That said, to the uneducated peasantry of Tibet, reincarnation is understood very much along the lines of a soul entering a new body, even if it is doctrinally incorrect.

It is also important to realize that a clear distinction is drawn between *re-*

---

*This was Karma Pakshi, ca. 1204–1283.

†All lamas who reincarnate in this way enjoy the highest status: there are no low-status or minor reincarnate lamas.

birth and *reincarnation.* In essence, while rebirth is what befalls all sentient beings, reincarnation is open only to those far advanced along the path to Enlightenment. The difference lies in the ability of those who reincarnate to be able to choose the timing and manner of their rebirth. This reflects the notion that all reincarnates are understood to manifest the boundless compassion of one or more bodhisattvas—beings who stand on the verge of Enlightenment and thus have most of the attributes of one who is fully enlightened, including, for example, omniscience, yet who choose to remain among sentient beings in order to help them on their way to Enlightenment.

No reliable figures exist as to the number of reincarnate lamas scattered throughout the Tibetan Buddhist world at the time of the Dalai Lama's boyhood, but certainly many hundred and very likely more than a thousand seems plausible. It was, in any case, the most important of them who ruled Tibet at this time, alongside the senior-most monastic officials and the aristocracy. How this played out in the years immediately prior to Tibet's "liberation" by Communist China will be seen in the catastrophic clash that broke out between two of the most important *tulkus* after the Dalai Lama himself.

7

Boyhood: Two Cane-Handled Horsewhips

The Dalai Lama is, from the perspective of the Tibetan tradition, both an object of worship and a source of merit. By worshipping him, and even more by giving materially to him, one acquires merit—merit that, one hopes, will contribute to a favorable birth in the next life. From his very first days in Lhasa, therefore, the young Dalai Lama attended ceremonies and functions at which he received not just the occasional foreign delegation but the much more numerous pilgrims, whether lay or monastic, for whom merely to be touched on the head with the red cotton tassel at the end of a short wooden stick, which was the Dalai Lama's means of blessing them, was the crowning moment of their lives. Thereafter, "death held no fears." One young visitor who joined the waiting line at this time noted, however, that, "surrounded by several elderly monks who now and then bent down and whispered to him," the boy himself looked "no different from our urchin friends."

But if his public duties were vital to maintaining a connection with his people, from a personal perspective it was the Dalai Lama's formation as a monk that took precedence over all. We might ask why this was so, why he needed educating at all, given that one of the chief characteristics of bodhisattvas is omniscience. It is true that, from the perspective of Buddhist tradition, learning for the Dalai Lama and other high incarnations is to a large extent a question of relearning. But though Chenresig himself is all-knowing, it does not follow that his earthly manifestations are not subject to the usual constraints of embodied existence. Together with Lobsang Samten, the Precious Protector therefore began his day in just the same way as any other novice monk.

Having risen at dawn, they would set about their first task, which was to prepare the room in which their teacher would join them. Then, while awaiting his arrival, the boys would begin performing the preliminary invocation to Manjushri, Bodhisattva of Wisdom. This prayer ends with the syllable *dhih,* pronunciation of which is thought to sharpen one's faculties. The boys would repeat it as many times as possible in a single breath: *dhih, dhih, dhih, dhih, dhih, dhih, dhih, dhih* . . . This done, they would start reciting the lines they had memorized the previous day, chanting at the top of their voices for maximum impact, and rocking their small bodies rhythmically back and forth. No doubt there was often more laughter than industry, but on hearing the footsteps of the Dalai Lama's tutor, they would fall silent.

Describing these early days, the Dalai Lama recounts how, as the tutor took his seat, one of two cane-handled horsewhips that hung on a pillar in the room would be taken down by an attendant and placed beside his teacher, who sat opposite the little boy's throne on a "raised seat with no supporting cushions or backboard." The teacher in question was Ling Rinpoché. Appointed as assistant tutor alongside the regent, who acted as senior tutor, Ling Rinpoché came to be the single most important person in the Dalai Lama's life. A man with incredible powers of recall and an acknowledged clairvoyant, he also had a reputation for being a stern disciplinarian. In the biography he later wrote in homage to his tutor, the Dalai Lama tells, approvingly, the story of how, as deputy abbot of Gyuto Monastery, Ling Rinpoché punished some monks for not knowing the words to a particular series of chants. Ordering them to collect sand in sacks, he paraded them for inspection in the monastery courtyard. For reasons that are unclear, he further ordered that one of them be flogged. This caused a number of monks to grumble about Ling Rinpoché. Yet the

Dalai Lama commends the punishment as a good deed, noting that when a smallpox epidemic struck soon after, "it is said that those monks who had to ferry bags of sand, apart from one or two, recovered from the disease," this at a time when the fatality rate following infection was somewhere between a third and half of all cases.

According to the Dalai Lama, Ling Rinpoché was one of those rare beings who could manifest the *siddhi*—the magical powers—of the most advanced yogins. On one occasion during a divination ritual he threw a stick that landed upright, an event that "everyone present regarded . . . with astonishment." The Dalai Lama also notes uncritically the story that a particular statue in his tutor's monastery would change its appearance according to whether Ling Rinpoché was in good health or not. When he was, it would turn its face to the sky. When not, it would be downcast.

If the fact of corporal punishment was very much present, even for one so exalted as the Dalai Lama, so too was that other staple of a traditional education: learning by rote. Even today, the novice studying in a Tibetan Buddhist monastery dedicates much of his first ten years as a monk to memorizing the most important texts and rituals of his craft. This he does by chanting out loud—itself held to be a meritorious act because it benefits the many supernatural beings that surround humans at all times, who may not have had the opportunity to study the dharma for themselves. Although rote learning has become unfashionable in modern schools, one reason for the high value placed on memorization of texts in the Buddhist tradition is that, in order to understand a text, it is considered essential to have the words available for instant recall. What is known darkly becomes illumined when the meaning is expounded by the teacher.

Helpfully, the majority of texts that the novice is required to commit to memory are written in verse form. Pass by a monastery when the youngsters are studying and you might think the whole place is in an uproar as they fight to make their voices heard. This is encouraged as, in so doing, they learn to concentrate to the point where nothing can distract them—for which reason a teacher will sometimes deliberately try to throw them off. A relatively recent story is told of how one of the novices at Namgyal Monastery was reciting a text when the Dalai Lama himself entered the room and proceeded to scratch him on the back. It was bad enough that anyone should do this, but that it was the Dalai Lama himself must have produced extraordinary emotion on the part of the young monk. It is to his great credit that history relates a successful outcome: he got to the end of the piece without fault or stumble.

The first text the Dalai Lama learned was one known as the Ganden Lha Gya Ma: the Hundred Deities of Ganden. Composed in honor of the fourteenth-century Gelug master Je (Lord) Tsongkhapa, this is a short devotional practice that calls on the master and his two chief disciples:

> From your place at the heart of the One Who Is to Come—
> Guardian of those hundreds of the blessed in the Joyful Land—
> Come! Reposing on a cloud white as the freshest curd,
> Come! All-knowing Lobsang Drakpa,
> Come! And bring your two heart disciples:
> Take your places before me,
> And seat yourselves on lion throne, lotus, and moon

Although the Dalai Lama often says he was a poor student, he is widely acknowledged as having the ability not just to quote verbatim from all the root texts but also, in his teachings, to be able to quote lengthy passages from the prose commentaries. It is evident he did not waste all his time.

The Dalai Lama also has a fine hand. Within the tradition, penmanship is regarded as an art in itself, and he was taught calligraphy from the beginning. This was in marked contrast to the education of most other novices, among whom the ability to write was rare. Remarkably, it was not uncommon for even the most proficient scholars to be unable to write even their own names. There were several reasons for this. Writing was regarded as the province of monastery administrators and, as such, a less important occupation than the study and mastery of the sacred texts. Partly, too, the denigration of writing reflected the innate conservatism of the monasteries. Writing was the source of innovation and therefore should be taught only to those who could be trusted. It was also regarded as unnecessary: there was little if anything that had been left unsaid. Above all, however, at least within the major monastic institutions of Ganden, Drepung, and Sera, skill in debate was regarded as a greater accomplishment.

For those who did learn to write, the task was complicated by the fact that there were three major scripts to master: one (*u chen*) is used for the printed word; a second (*u me*), a more cursive script, is used for everyday correspondence, note taking, essay writing, and so forth; and a third (*chu yig*) is a highly stylized cursive script used in formal correspondence and legal documents. Possibly in a dissenting move on the part of his writing tutor, for practice in the third, and most demanding, script, the boy Dalai Lama was given the text of the Great Thirteenth's final testament, with its dire warnings of ruin if the Tibetan government did not set aside its habitual infighting. As a result, not only did the Dalai Lama develop an elegant hand, but also, from an early age, he was aware of the disastrous extent to which his predecessor's recommendations were being neglected.

By the time of the Precious Protector's homecoming, many influential Lhasans had grown to dislike the regent, Reting Rinpoché, intensely. Personally, he was known to be fond of soccer and marksmanship; he was in fact something of a crack shot. It is said he once persuaded a young associate to allow him to shoot an egg from his outstretched hand. When, afterwards, Reting asked what had given him the confidence to do so, the monk replied that he had taken the view that if the shot had killed him, he would have died at the hand of a high lama and would therefore be assured of a favorable rebirth. But if these eccentricities could perhaps be overlooked, the venality of the Reting *labrang* (or household) could not.*

As was customary, following the new Dalai Lama's arrival in Lhasa, the National Assembly met to discuss an appropriate reward to be bestowed on the regent for successfully identifying and repatriating the rightful occupant of the Lion Throne. While there was general agreement that a reward of sev-

---

*Roughly equivalent to a modern-day personal trust, the *labrang* is the legal owner of the estates and other property attaching to the *tulku* who becomes its life tenant. When he "manifests the act of passing away," the assets of the *labrang* pass to his successor. Much like a modern-day trust, the *labrang* may well have a trading arm, and it will also have a household which it maintains. At that time, the *labrang* manager of Reting was a notably grasping character, a man completely unable to resist an opportunity to make money, whether by extortion, taxation, or pushing the boundaries of trade agreements entered into innocently by others.

eral landed estates would be suitable, one of the regent's placemen announced that fifty or even sixty estates would be inadequate to express the gratitude the government should properly feel toward him. This prompted an argument in the course of which one of the more outspoken ministers repeated a proverb:

> After eating the mountain, hunger is not satisfied,
> After drinking the ocean, thirst is not slaked.

This was interpreted by the regent's party as an open insult, and the minister in question was forced to resign. Shortly afterwards, Reting moved to reward the monk who had spoken in his favor by making him abbot of an important college. This incensed the college members, all of whom remained loyal to the present incumbent. A standoff ensued and resulted in the regent's finally having to back down. But before he did so, his support within government circles had largely evaporated. Not long afterwards, rumors began to circulate about the regent's sexual indiscretions.

It seems inescapable that these rumors were grounded in fact and that not only did Reting have a male lover but also he had also fathered a child by a relative's wife. And whereas a blind eye could be turned to the one (indeed, homosexual relationships were nothing unusual within the monasteries and were condemned only if the parties engaged in penetrative sex), to the other no leniency could be shown. A monk who had broken one of his root precepts* was no longer a monk. It was for this reason that posters began to appear in Lhasa asserting Reting's unfitness to administer vows to the young Dalai Lama. Within the Tibetan tradition, vows are not sworn by the one who will keep them but are "administered," or "conferred," by someone who already maintains the precepts the novice vows to keep. In this case, the regent was due to confer the thirty-six preliminary monastic precepts on the Dalai Lama as part of the *getsul* ceremony, at which the boy would formally embark on the path to full ordination as a *bikshu* (the title given to one who is so ordained) in the

---

*Besides chastity, these included vows not to kill, not to steal, and not to boast about one's spiritual attainments.

Mahayana* tradition—the Mahayana being the more recent of the two great schools within Buddhism taken as a whole.

This was a scandal of the most serious import. Of course, the Regent could simply deny the rumors—as many advised that he should. But for all his faults, it is clear that Reting Rinpoché took his vocation seriously. He had offended against the precepts of his calling, and he could not and would not try to pretend otherwise. He therefore announced that various spiritual and oracular sources had given strong presentiments of danger to his life if he did not at once resign his position and undertake a lengthy retreat.

Who, then, should take his place as regent? It is clear that Reting saw resignation as only a temporary measure. He would indeed undertake a lengthy retreat, but once the *getsul* ceremony was out of the way, and when the scandal had died down, he would reassume his position until the Dalai Lama came of age. With this in mind, he would ask his own teacher, the elderly Taktra (pronounced, roughly, "Ta-tag") Rinpoché, to stand in for him.

Many of those closest to Reting urged him to reconsider. He could avoid the *getsul* ceremony by claiming illness. But Reting refused. In that case, at least one of his advisers urged, he should make sure not actually to relinquish power. Taktra should act only in matters of minor importance. Reting must not make the mistake of letting go of "the orphan's box of brick tea."

The story of the orphan's box of brick tea (the tea that Tibetans generally drink is made from leaves compressed into bricks for ease of transport) perfectly illustrates the thought processes of a traditionally educated Tibetan. Once there was a child who became orphaned. Being in need, he went at once in search of his uncles and aunts. On asking succor of them, he was serially rebuffed. "I'm not your uncle." "I'm not your aunt." Alone and distraught, the orphan went on his way, when, as great good luck would have it, he came across an abandoned box of brick tea. These were riches indeed! It was a time

---

*Mahayana means literally the Great Vehicle, in contrast to Hinayana, meaning, pejoratively, the Lesser Vehicle, though this usage is less usual today. Instead, Theravada is preferred. This—earlier—tradition rejects (generally speaking) as spurious the Mahayana scriptures, which only began to emerge at the beginning of the first millennium, some five hundred years after the death of the historical Buddha.

when tea was in great scarcity. All of a sudden, he found himself besieged by people claiming to be his relatives. At this he bowed down before the box: "Because of you, I have found uncles. Because of you, I have found aunts." It is, of course, a version of the story of the goose that laid the golden egg.

Reting is said to have laughed on being reminded of the story, knowing full well that in his case the box of brick tea symbolized his power as regent. But still he would not budge.

The first the now seven-year-old Dalai Lama knew of the matter was when asked who he thought should replace Reting as his senior tutor. It is likely that the question was posed in such a way that the only answer was Taktra. In any case, the appointment suited the boy, who considered the elderly Taktra "a very gentle man." But though Taktra may have been gentle in person, and apt to fall asleep on those occasions when he came to conduct a lesson with the Precious Protector, it turned out that in his dealings with others, he was as stern and unyielding as his politics were dictatorial and his religion was reactionary.

Right away the new regent, installed in early 1941, determined that Reting should have nothing further to do with the young Dalai Lama. Partly this was due to Reting's behavior. But one thing that seems particularly to have concerned the new regent was his former student's dabbling in Nyingma teachings and practice.

Since the demise of the Great Thirteenth, a major development within Gelug circles was the increased popularity of devotion to the protector deity Dorje Shugden, claimed guardian of the legacy of Tsongkhapa. It was held that Shugden took severe exception to anyone belonging to the Gelug school who took Nyingma teachings, and Reting had done just that. In 1937 he had sought out a reclusive Nyingma hermit* to initiate him into the mysteries of *dzogchen,* a set of esoteric practices said to have been brought to Tibet by Padmasambhava, the eighth-century wonder-worker and saint known as the Lotus-Born. The new regent was, by contrast, determined that the young Dalai

---

*This was Chatral Rinpoché (1913–2015). Note that it is not enough merely to read and accept the validity of a body of scripture. The seeker must receive them in a transmission from a suitably qualified master.

Lama should not be exposed to heresy of this sort. He therefore appointed as assistant tutor, alongside himself as senior tutor and Ling Rinpoché as junior tutor, the charismatic young Trijang Rinpoché, an aristocrat with fine manners and a large following among the upper echelons of Lhasan society. In common with both regents and with Ling Rinpoché, the new assistant tutor was a student of the most renowned lama of the early twentieth century, Phabongka Rinpoché, and of them all, none guarded his legacy so zealously. The reason this was so significant is that Phabongka Rinpoché was the deity's chief advocate and cheerleader.

Whereas Ling Rinpoché, who came from a humble background, was distinctly otherworldly, Trijang Rinpoché was more outgoing, with a much-admired talent for his ability simultaneously to compose and recite religious verse—a kind of spiritual rap, if that is not too profane an analogy. And he too was an accomplished mystic. A somewhat alarming example of his powers is seen in his foreknowledge of the death of those with "perverted intentions": whenever he dreamed of yaks, sheep, or some other living creature being killed in connection with a given individual, it was a sure sign of that person's imminent demise. This he attributed to "the wrathful assistance of the protector," Dorje Shugden, to whom he was especially close. In another dream, he "saw a platter with many frogs on it." Two of these jumped out from under the cloth covering the platter, and, he recalled, "I could see fresh red sores on their backs," while the rest of the frogs became "soft and mushy." This he understood as a sure sign that he would soon recover from a severe illness. But an even more remarkable sign of Trijang's spiritual attainments was his ability to influence the weather. In his autobiography he records how on one occasion, after he had given a short teaching while traveling, a black cloud suddenly formed, and his party was caught in a hailstorm that hurled down particles of ice "the size of dried apricots." The thunder and lightning were so violent that it felt as if the sky and earth were being rent asunder. Inside the tents, sparks of fire and a smell like gunpowder seemed to presage a thunderbolt. At once the Rinpoché made an offering to the local spirits and sought the aid of the protector deities by making a tea offering to them. But though he recited the prescribed mantras and undertook the requisite visualizations as best he could, nothing had any effect. It was only when he burned some fresh excrement (presumably his own) that the gods relented. "Immediately the sky above became clear, like the opening of a skylight."

Unfortunately for the young Dalai Lama, this new appointment served only to increase the burdens he faced. As Trijang Rinpoché recalled in his autobiography, "His Holiness seemed a bit shy on my first visit, as his personal attendants had apparently mentioned that Trijang Tulku had a short temper." It seems indeed that Taktra Rinpoché was concerned at the boy's tendency to misbehave. "On the advice of the precious regent . . . I maintained a serious expression and did not smile." Yet he was even colder toward Lobsang Samten, whom he would scold "with a grave countenance, chiding him for distracting his younger brother."

This was evidently the beginning of a somewhat irksome period in the young boys' lives, though from his autobiography, *Freedom in Exile,* we gather that the Precious Protector's natural ebullience prevented him from ever falling into despondency. Clearly one who enjoyed the rough-and-tumble of boyhood play, the Dalai Lama relates a forbidden game that involved placing a wooden board at an angle and running at it as fast as possible to see how far he and Lobsang Samten could jump. He was also fond of soccer, despite this too being forbidden out of religious scruple. When the British mission had introduced the sport to Lhasa some years previously, the monasteries, seeing the enthusiasm that Tibetans quickly developed for the game, were appalled. Correctly seeing it as an agent of foreign influence and change, they likened it to "kicking the Buddha's head," and soon after, the civil authorities instituted a public ban.

If the Precious Protector was at times a somewhat unruly student, he could, as we have seen, conduct himself with becoming gravity. In December 1942, a pair of American spies from the Office of Strategic Services (one of the organizations out of which the CIA was subsequently created) paid the Dalai Lama a visit in the Potala. Disappointingly for them, the protocol of the day demanded that the Precious Protector receive them in silence and that they leave him in silence—though this was clearly not the case when Thomas Manning met the six-year-old Ninth Dalai Lama in 1811. As Captain Ilya Tolstoy (a grandson of the great Leo) wrote, he and his companion were "immediately impressed by his young but stern face and not at all frail constitution."

Tolstoy and his companion, a Captain Dolan, had come to Tibet in the hope of surveying an overland route between India and China that could be used to supply the Chinese Nationalists against the Japanese, who had recently invaded large parts of China. The usual route across Burma had been cut when the Japanese ousted the British from that country. The Tibetan route was never used, but the connection thereby established with the United States came soon enough to have important consequences for the Dalai Lama. In the meantime, however, it was the gifts the Americans brought that were of most interest to the boy. Alongside a signed photograph of President Truman, a model of a nineteenth-century sailing ship executed in silver, and several pieces of glass, it was the multi-movement Patek Philippe pocket watch that pleased him the most. (By chance he had sent it for repair in Switzerland at the time of his flight into exile in 1959 and still has it in his possession.)

In fact, the two OSS men were not the only Americans in Lhasa during this period. The photographer Archibald Steele, who had happened to be in Kumbum at the time of the Dalai Lama's discovery, visited in 1944 on assignment for the *Chicago Daily News.* From his reports it is clear that, outwardly at least, an atmosphere of calm prevailed in the Tibetan capital while the Second World War raged far away. Noting that when an enterprising trader brought a consignment of motorcycles to Lhasa, it took only one incident of a government minister's horse being frightened for a ban to be proclaimed, Steele had no reason to doubt the senior government minister's claim that, really, "nothing ever happens here." Events such as the Dalai Lama's removal from the Potala to the Norbulingka Palace on the eighth day of the third month, the Festival of Mahakala, were in any case of far greater import to Tibetans than what was going on in the world on the other side of the Himalayas. For the Dalai Lama, too, the weeks that followed were most enjoyable. It was during this time that he had the pleasure of watching the theatricals that were held outside the palace grounds. Besides operas and *cham,* the religious dances famed for the acrobatic whirling and leaping of the performers, there were also satires in which the players dressed up as members of the aristocracy and lampooned them. "It was," as the Dalai Lama recalled in his autobiography, "such a happy time!"

Yet beneath Lhasa's calm exterior, an explosive confrontation was brewing. At the beginning of the Dalai Lama's ninth year (1944), the Nechung oracle had warned of looming obstacles that could harm the Precious Protector. In the Buddhist view, an "obstacle" is a spiritual circumstance likely to produce a negative impact on one or more individuals if not cleared by means of appropriate action. In the case of a high lama, this would normally take the form of a long-life ceremony, during the course of which the protector deities are besought to intervene on his behalf to clear away accretions of negative karma. It might be thought that as a manifestation of a bodhisattva, the Dalai Lama would be impervious to such hindrances, but that is not the case. Because of his exalted position, he is in fact especially vulnerable. Moreover, the greater the perceived danger, the greater the spiritual firepower that needs to be deployed in his defense. It was at this moment that, sensing an opportunity, the self-exiled Reting made a move. Given the nature of their deep spiritual connection, he could plausibly advance himself as the right person to intercede on the Dalai Lama's behalf. It was now three years since he had given up the regency, and this being the standard length of time for an important retreat, his reappearance in Lhasa should cause no surprise. Taktra, however, suspecting correctly that Reting was hoping to reassume the regency, did not respond to his overtures.

The reason for Taktra's silence is not hard to determine. Not only was he intent on keeping his position for personal reasons, but also Reting had further alienated himself from the government by maintaining independent contact with Shen Zonglian, the suave Harvard-educated representative of the Chinese Nationalists who had been stationed in Lhasa since 1937. Reting's continued closeness to the Dalai Lama's family was a further source of dismay. The *yabshi kung* had by this time also become deeply unpopular. Keenly aware of his status, the Dalai Lama's father never failed to exercise the privilege of having people on horseback dismount when they encountered him in the street. On one occasion when someone failed to do so, he had the man flogged. On another, he confiscated the rider's horse (even though the man was sick and unable to walk). He had, as a result, recently been publicly censured by the National Assembly for bad manners.

Most concerning of all was the confluence of these two associations. Following private discussions between Reting and the Chinese representative, arrangements had been made for Gyalo Thondup, the Dalai Lama's second-eldest brother, now seventeen years of age, to be sent to China to be educated. And not only that, but also he would be enrolled in Nanking University as a special student under the direct sponsorship of Generalissimo Chiang Kai-shek himself. Astonishingly, this meant that the Dalai Lama's brother would become the houseguest of the president of China.

Gyalo Thondup first met the Generalissimo and his American-educated wife soon after arriving in Nanking. Thereafter he was a frequent guest at their house. "They came to treat me as a son," he wrote many years later. Finding them "unfailingly warm and gracious hosts," he "visited their home frequently and often dined with them on the weekends." What especially impressed him about the couple was how well they treated their staff and how austerely they lived. "Dinner at the home of President and Madam Chiang was," he recounted, "invariably simple."

Given this level of intimacy, it is clear that the Generalissimo had marked Gyalo Thondup as an important future ally. No doubt when the Dalai Lama attained his majority, Gyalo Thondup would have been put forward as the Chinese president's personal representative in Tibet, responsible for seeing to the implementation of the Nationalists' five-races policy, *zhonghua minzu,* whereby the Han, Manchu, Tibetan, Hui, and Mongol peoples would unite to form the Chinese nation.

Taktra could do nothing about Reting's arrangement with the Chinese on Gyalo Thondup's behalf, but he could continue to ignore Reting's pleas for a meeting, while the ex-regent himself fretted and began to plot.

Meanwhile, the young Dalai Lama continued his education and attended the daily tea ceremony. Then at night, he and Lobsang Samten would listen in gleeful terror to the ghost stories told by the "sweepers"—the serving staff—in the Potala. And he would count down the days to his mother's next visit.

8

Trouble in Shangri-La: Devilry and Intrigue on the Roof of the World

When Reting resigned the regency, Taktra had wasted no time in eliminating his predecessor's allies in government. Nonetheless, Reting still had powerful supporters. In the eyes of the people, nothing could detract from the fact of his childhood miracles, nor from his gift of the return of the Dalai Lama. When he finally reappeared in Lhasa in December 1944 in the company of a large and splendid retinue, it was only a matter of time before open confrontation would break out between the present regent and his predecessor. For his part, Taktra Rinpoché had no intention of relinquishing his position.

As for any opinion the Dalai Lama might have had, he was not consulted. Although he was required to attend the morning tea ceremony that brought together all the government's senior members, his role in affairs of state at this stage was minimal and purely formal. All that was demanded of him was that he be a good pupil and study hard. And this, indeed, was a matter of some concern to Taktra. The reports reaching him from the Dalai Lama's tutors were far from encouraging. It was therefore decided that the boy must be separated from his brother, Lobsang Samten, who was instead enrolled in one of Lhasa's few (private) schools.

This was a serious blow. Now the two brothers saw each other only once a month. "When he left after each visit," the Dalai Lama wrote in adulthood, "I remember standing at the window watching, my heart full of sorrow, as he disappeared into the distance." In place of his brother, his serving staff—the monk "sweepers" who cleaned the rooms and served as waiters—became the Dalai Lama's playmates. These uneducated men from lowly backgrounds were his constant companions, and it is largely thanks to them that the Dalai Lama can look back fondly on this period of his childhood. "They were full of fun and joy . . . always joking," he declared. Somewhat unexpectedly, the games they played mostly involved pretending to be soldiers. It turns out that many of the men had been recruits in their youth and had trained in British army drill. They taught the Precious Protector how to stand to attention and present arms using pieces of wood for guns. Then "we would march [around] the gardens." They would also fight mock battles in the Norbulingka park, while back at the Potala, where to go outside meant only to go out onto the roof, the young Dalai Lama would spend hours engrossed in copies of *Life* magazine, with their dramatic pictures of the world war just concluded, and fashioning squadrons of tanks out of *tsampa* dough.

The sweepers were also an inexhaustible source of stories and folktales, of which Tibet has a generous supply. Popular motifs include shape shifters and talking animals, wicked stepmothers and benevolent strangers, scurrilous monks and beautiful goddesses, hermits in caves and wandering minstrels, foolish girls and fortune-tellers, not to mention the ghosts and demons whose capricious nature is the bane of Everyman's life. There were also stories concerning the Potala itself—about the great birds that would come and carry off small boys, and about Arko Lhamo, the merest mention of which occasioned terror in the boy's innermost being. This was a demon spirit said to occupy a storeroom in the dungeons below.

The looming dispute between the Taktra government and the former regent came a step closer when Reting called on the government to drop charges against some monks from his alma mater, Sera Che, one of the colleges at Sera

Monastery.* They had been accused of beating a government debt collector—with, among other weapons, a leg of dried mutton—so badly that he died of his wounds.

Here it is important to say something about loyalty in traditional Tibetan culture. As in medieval Europe, ties between individuals as well as with the institutions that gave them a home were sacrosanct. Not only were ex-students morally obliged later in life to contribute materially to their monastery, but also they had an obligation to defend its honor as staunchly as if it were their own family. In the traditional view, this extended to the shedding of blood where necessary.

Even though the Sera monks were charged with manslaughter, Reting Rinpoché was determined that Sera Che should not lose face and be forced to hand the accused over for questioning. Had he been successful in reclaiming the regency, this would have been a relatively easy matter to arrange. But the fact that he had failed to do so did not lessen the obligation he felt, and he continued to support the Sera authorities in what became a trial of strength with the government.

The standoff continued throughout the whole of 1945, coming to a head only as the Great Prayer Festival of the following year approached. This was to be the first in which the young Dalai Lama would act in an official capacity. It was therefore essential that there be no disruption or break with protocol. Knowing this, the abbots of Sera announced that the monastery would not participate in the forthcoming ceremonies unless the charges against their monks were dropped. At the same time, weapons were distributed throughout the monastery in case the government should decide to try to apprehend the presumed culprits by brute force. The monastery leadership was convinced that the case did not lie within the government's jurisdiction and was a matter for themselves alone. In other words, what lay at the heart of the dispute was the question of the central government's right, and indeed its ability, to impose its authority on individual monasteries.

---

*Che was one of the two *khang tsen,* or colleges, that made up Sera Monastery, the other being Sera Mey.

The government, for its part, refused to budge. As a result, none of Sera's monks were present at the opening ceremonies of the New Year festival. When the government subsequently announced that the case could be postponed if the monks attended as usual, the Sera abbots interpreted this move to mean that the case would now be settled in their favor. The monks duly came to Lhasa and were present at all the remaining New Year ceremonies.

Ultimately the disastrous standoff between Sera Che and the government had no impact on ensuing events, and it is doubtful whether the Dalai Lama was even informed. For him, the most important aspect of this New Year festival was his induction at Drepung Monastery, which marked his formal entry into the course of learning that would culminate in the award of the *geshe* degree. Something like a doctorate in the modern Western university curriculum, it is this that qualifies a monk to take students and to be a teacher of the Buddhadharma.

The Dalai Lama's junior tutor, Trijang Rinpoché, records a lighthearted moment during a rehearsal for his young student's debut at Drepung when all those present had a fit of the giggles as the preliminary prayers were being chanted. First Ling Rinpoché burst out laughing, then the boy, then the abbot of Namgyal Monastery, the Lord Chamberlain, the chief attendant, and, finally, the junior tutor all "laughed uncontrollably." Everyone, that is except Taktra Rinpoché, the regent, who looked on sternly.

In the event, the Dalai Lama gave an impressive demonstration of his abilities, to the great satisfaction of his tutors. But with the 1946 New Year festival concluded, events in Lhasa took a turn for the worse. The agreement to postpone the case against the Sera monks turned out to be nothing more than that. The regent had no intention of dropping the charges. Instead he planned to arrest the abbot of Sera Che when he came to the Norbulingka later in the year for the traditional reception of the monastery leadership by the Dalai Lama. Perhaps warned, the abbot avoided the ceremony, claiming ill health. He then called on his monks to join him in open revolt against the government. But in another twist, part of the college refused to support him. Realizing that without their full backing there was no chance of facing down the government, the abbot resigned on the spot and, together with his closest supporters, fled in the direction of his native place.

The government, alerted to what had happened, immediately sent troops to apprehend the abbot, dead or alive. But while he himself escaped, disguised as a beggar, his brother, who was with him, was mortally wounded in an engagement to the east of Lhasa. Because of their strong family resemblance, the soldiers mistakenly assumed that they had killed the abbot. Only when his head and hands arrived back in Lhasa, sent as proof of mission accomplished, was it realized that the intended target had escaped. He, meanwhile, sought refuge with the Chinese, who gave him a warm welcome. At last, however, the government was able to prosecute the monks it had sought for so long. They were all duly flogged.

Reting Rinpoché, now returned to his own monastery and following events from afar, was incensed. At first he wanted to go to Sera Che and lead a rebellion against the government in person, lamenting that it was he himself who had given Taktra his position first as assistant tutor to the Dalai Lama, then as senior tutor, and finally as regent. And although he was eventually dissuaded from taking so drastic a course of action, Reting's next move could only be interpreted by the government as a staggering betrayal. Writing directly to Chiang Kai-shek, he asked for Chinese support against the Tibetan government on the grounds that the regent was pro-British. If the Nationalists would send troops to enable him to take back the regency, he, Reting, would cooperate fully with the Chinese.

As if this were not enough, the ex-regent's closest advisers urged immediate action. Reting Rinpoché argued that his people should wait until the Chinese responded. But those surrounding him were desperate men, and while he might be a Buddhist practitioner gifted with extraordinary insight, Reting's judgment in temporal matters was decidedly poor. To their continued entreaties, he replied that he would support them in whatever they decided was necessary, adding only that they should be careful. Rashly, they decided that what was needed was Taktra's liberation from earthly existence. The problem they now faced was that the regent rarely ventured out in public. Two possibilities were considered. One was to ambush him as he returned to Lhasa from his hermitage later in the year. This would enable the attack to take place at night, far from the city. Ultimately this plan was abandoned. Instead he was to be hit with hand grenades during his inspection of the butter sculptures at the conclusion of the next Great Prayer Festival.

As it happened, Taktra did not venture out on the evening to inspect the *torma.* At this time another political faction, the Tibet Improvement Party, had begun recruiting members. Founded by a group of dissident monks—which included Kumbela, Lord Chamberlain to the Great Thirteenth, exiled following the latter's death—and supported by a wealthy trader from the eastern province of Kham, the group was allied to the Chinese Nationalists and committed to the overthrow of the government, by revolutionary means if necessary. Aware of its existence, and recognizing his own unpopularity with many who felt that, when it came to graft, he was no better than his predecessor, Taktra remained out of sight. He did, however, move to ensure that the Dalai Lama himself was further isolated from the looming crisis by curtailing his mother's access to him. His concern was that she was "misinforming" her son. As a result, not only did she have to arrange her visits in advance, but also she needed to be accompanied by an official.

Whether or not Taktra Rinpoché had anything to do with the death of the Dalai Lama's father shortly after the Great Prayer Festival of 1947 is a matter for conjecture. What is known is that the *yabshi kung* became ill soon after eating a large amount of a pork, a meat of which he was particularly fond. It is plausible that trichinosis was the cause of death, given that he was ill for almost three weeks. But many say that he was poisoned. He was, after all, deeply unpopular with large numbers of the aristocracy and, from the regent's point of view, immensely dangerous: he remained close to Reting, his eldest son was being touted as the next abbot of Kumbum Monastery, and his second son was a personal guest of President Chiang Kai-shek in China, not to mention that his fourth son was Dalai Lama. A family legend contends that the poisoner was the manager of the *yabshi kung*'s country estate outside Lhasa. But whether or not the accusation is true—and the Dalai Lama himself retains an open mind on the matter—it was certainly to the regent's advantage for this increasingly well-connected ally of Reting's to be taken out of the picture at this time.

One might expect the death of his father to have had a considerable impact on the Dalai Lama, but in fact they rarely saw each other, and in contrast to his reaction to the deaths of others close to him, the Dalai Lama has never made much of this loss.

Meanwhile, given that the regent had no scheduled public appearance before mid-April, the Reting plotters, impatient to act, turned to still more desperate measures. They devised a package bomb consisting of a wooden box concealing a standard Mills bomb of British manufacture. Once the firing pin was withdrawn, a sliding lid held the trigger in place. The device was delivered to the regent's secretary with a message identifying the contents as a secret report from the governor of Kham. Since it was usual for important missives to contain a gift, the size and weight of the box would not have aroused suspicion.

Unfortunately for the plotters, their plans fell victim to the traditional Tibetan habit of interpreting the word "urgent" to mean something other than a requirement for immediate action. The package was placed in a drawer, where it sat for several weeks. After some time, one of Reting's associates threw an anonymous note through the window of Taktra's residence suggesting that important information was being withheld from him. This, however, was seen as nothing more than a crude attempt to sow discord and was ignored by Taktra's household. A servant of the regent's secretary became curious about the package, however, thinking it might contain something valuable, and decided to see for himself. Carefully opening the box, he heard a hissing sound and, judging it possessed, ran from the room, narrowly escaping injury when it exploded.

News of the assassination attempt was passed back from the British mission to London, where the story found its way into the newspapers. The *Daily Mail* published a report under the headline "Trouble in Shangri La." But although the regent's office was unable to trace the individual who had delivered either the bomb or the later message, the regent was now alert to the serious danger in which he stood.

Two weeks passed before Taktra hit back. When he did so, it was on the basis of a top-secret telegraph message received in Lhasa from the Tibetan representative in Nanjing (the Nationalists' capital, also known as Nanking). His contacts had obtained direct proof of Reting Rinpoché's request for urgent military assistance from the Chinese. This was incontrovertible evidence of the ex-regent's treachery. Taktra moved with unusual haste. That very night he dispatched two ministers and a detachment of two hundred troops to Reting

Monastery. Meanwhile, orders were given for Reting Rinpoché's Lhasa residence to be sealed and searched. As Taktra hoped, this yielded plenty of incriminating evidence, including at least one grenade wrapped in silk brocade. But some of Reting's men, apprised of the impending raid, escaped in the direction of Reting Monastery, hoping to alert the ex-regent to the danger he faced.

When, the following week, soldiers arrived at his monastery, they discovered Reting Rinpoché innocently feeding birds on the roof of his house. Although this was an arrest, it was conducted with the full formality that was the ex-regent's due; the officers all prostrated themselves three times and offered a *kathag*. He gave them his blessing in return. They then "invited" him to go with them back to Lhasa. But of course it was on their terms, not his. He was compelled to ride a mule rather than his usual mount, a horse called Yudrug, which they dared not let him ride, as it was well known to possess supernatural powers.

As soon as news of Reting's arrest reached the monks of Sera Che, an angry mob demanded that the senior monk scholars compel the abbot to intercede with the government. But although they tried, the abbot was an appointee of Taktra's and not inclined to act. On realizing that the scholars had been rebuffed, the mob immediately stormed the abbot's house. They were met by his chief steward, who, fearing for his master's life, pulled out a revolver and shot the ringleader and wounded another of the rebels. Unluckily for him, his revolver then jammed and he was in turn cut down with a sword, along with two of his servants. Meanwhile, the abbot, who lived upstairs, ran onto the roof and tried to make good his escape. But coming to a gap between buildings, he hesitated to jump and was slain by the monks pursuing him.

Sera Che was now in open rebellion against the government in support of their beloved brother, the ex-regent. One of the college's incarnate lamas declared himself "war leader" and set about organizing troop dispositions. A plea to negotiate with the government was swiftly rejected; instead, a group hastened to Lhasa with the intention of breaking into Reting's house to retrieve the weapons locked inside. They were prevented from carrying out their plans, though they did inflict a number of casualties in the attempt.

Undaunted, the Sera monks, correctly assuming that the party escorting Reting back to Lhasa would pass in front of the monastery, lay in wait. When the posse appeared, the monks unleashed what fire they could muster from their depleted armory. The government's forces fully anticipated this, however, and, as soon as the monks appeared, began to shoot. One eyewitness described how a stream of monks burst from the monastery precincts, only to be driven back by the weight of fire. Many died that day, while Reting himself was duly incarcerated.

Another eyewitness to this dreadful scene was the young Dalai Lama, watching events unfold from the roof of the Potala. With his telescope he had a good view of Sera Monastery a mile distant. For him, the spectacle was first and foremost a matter of wonder and excitement. "At last," he recalled, "this was some proper work for my telescope to do." But we do not get any sense that he was alert to the danger he himself was now in. With Reting out of the way, the only limit to the regent's power would be the person of the Dalai Lama, who, as a twelve-year-old boy cut off from his family, would be in no position to fight his own battle, should that prove necessary.

Next day, the Sera monks launched another attack on Lhasa to try to seize some weapons kept in a house belonging to a trading partner of the Reting estate. Fearing just such an attempt, the government had already sealed the house, but this time the monks were successful. With the loss of only three of their number, they managed to make off with a large consignment of matériel. In response, the army was ordered to deploy the artillery. The first attempts to shell the rebel monastery later in the day were unsuccessful, however. To the jeering of the monks, the army commander sent urgently for J. T. Taring, one of the officers who had trained with the British in India. Describing how he was summoned during the night, Taring subsequently recalled how, as if in presentiment of what was to follow, he and many others heard a loud moaning sound "like the call of the guardian deity of the cremation ground."

Re-sighting the guns, Taring scored a direct hit on one of the buildings where the monks were suspected of hiding. But even though it was by now clear to the rebels that the government was prepared for all-out war, they refused negotiations. They would back down only if the government released the ex-regent, fully restored his rights and property, and dropped all charges against the bomb plotters. Short of that, they announced, they would have no regrets even if Sera Che were reduced to rubble.

By the time the crisis had fully played out, at least two hundred monks would die, though some estimates put the eventual death toll at nearer three hundred. Around thirty government soldiers were also killed.

When the monks finally gave in, they put down their weapons, returned to their cells, and resumed their prayers as if nothing had happened. The five ringleaders were immediately seized and thrown in jail, there to spend the rest of their lives. A minority continued to defy the government, and it would be several more weeks before they were captured. They were all flogged, with between one and two hundred lashes apiece, before being put in irons and having the cangue fastened around their necks.

While the siege of Reting Rinpoché's alma mater was moving toward its bloody conclusion, the ex-regent himself remained in custody. Because the government now had in its possession not only copies of the letters he had sent to the Chinese but also a clear instruction to kill Taktra, he had no room to maneuver. His only real hope was to appeal personally to Taktra Rinpoché in his capacity as the regent's *chela,* or spiritual son. This bond is regarded as sacred and therefore impossible to abrogate. But his captors ensured that the appeal was not heard. In the meantime, Reting faced calls for various torments, including that his eyes be put out, as Lungshar's had been, or that he be sewn inside an animal hide and thrown off a high cliff in accordance with a seventh-century edict of King Songtsen Gampo.

For more than a week the government ministers deliberated over what punishment should be meted out to the ex-regent. At one point, the Precious Protector was approached (it is not clear by whom) to intervene on Reting's behalf while the ex-regent lay incarcerated in the dungeons below the Potala. But as he explained later, "my position was hopeless." With his father dead and himself isolated not just from Lobsang Samten but also, lately, from his mother, the future ruler was given no opportunity to express any opinion he might have, let alone influence proceedings at this critical moment. Then, on May 8, Reting suddenly died. He had recently complained of a headache and asked that he be moved to a brighter, less cramped cell. This request was refused, but he was permitted a visit by a doctor, who prescribed medicine. It is said that around midnight, piercing screams could be heard coming from the area of the Potala where Reting was imprisoned.

Immediately rumors began to spread. According to one, the ex-regent had died from having his testicles crushed, supposedly in punishment for having broken his vow of celibacy. Another, more plausible, held that the medicine he had been given was in fact poison. Still another charged that he had been strangled. But whatever the cause, all Lhasa was in shock. In spite of his many faults, Reting Rinpoché was held in highest regard for his spiritual accomplishments, and his popularity among the laity was immense. Loud were the shouts of sorrow that went up when mourners came to view his body, displayed in the temple at his Lhasa residence.

No sooner was Reting out of the way than the regent took the opportunity to revisit the question of the identity of the Dalai Lama himself. Support for Ditru Rinpoché, the nephew of the Great Thirteenth, still remained strong in certain circles. It would be hugely advantageous to Taktra if he could show that Reting had made a mistake in the selection process. The prestige Reting had enjoyed as the one who had found the Dalai Lama would then be his. Accordingly, with the connivance of the National Assembly, it was agreed to put the question to the deities once more, and Nechung was publicly invoked in a trance.

This was a startling development. It amounted to an attempted coup d'état, though in the face of Taktra's disloyalty to the young Dalai Lama, the deities made it resoundingly clear that the current occupant of the Lion Throne had been correctly identified. Yet this was still not enough for the Dalai Lama's detractors, and, astonishingly, the matter was put to the deities one more time. And even when this additional investigation came down clearly in favor of Tenzin Gyatso, there was a move—unsuccessful—to question them yet again.

Humiliatingly, Taktra had been publicly rebuked by the deities. It is hardly surprising, therefore, that from this point on, though he had defeated his opponent, the regent found himself completely isolated. His plan to keep the Dalai Lama in a similar state of isolation became increasingly ineffective. Showing considerable initiative, the Precious Protector used his close relations with the sweepers to maximum effect. From them he learned not only about the petty injustices they had to face on a daily basis but also about the inequity of the taxes imposed on the lower classes. On one occasion, with their help, he eavesdropped outside the door when the regent and other high officials were hearing a complaint brought by a peasant. "The officials started bullying him, and they just would not allow him to talk," he recalled. Gradually, the young Dalai Lama began to get a sense that social and political reform was urgently needed.

The Dalai Lama was also keenly aware of Tibet's backwardness with respect to modern technology. By this time he had discovered the Great Thirteenth's cars lying neglected at the Norbulingka and was eager to see them running again. Together with the Great Thirteenth's driver, he started working on them, cannibalizing parts from one for the benefit of the other. Meeting eventually with success, he made his first attempt at driving, which ended in an embarrassing shunt, the effects of which he did his best to disguise. Seeking as much information about the outside world as possible, he also began taking his first English lessons from one of the four young men who had been sent to England for education by the Great Thirteenth.* But it was not until 1949, when he was fourteen, that he was finally able to free himself completely from the regent's control.

---

*This was Chang Ngopa Rinzin Dorje, also known as Kusho Ringang.

9

The Perfection of Wisdom: The Higher Education of a Tibetan Buddhist Monk

Without question, the person who had the greatest impact on the Dalai Lama as he grew to maturity was Ling Rinpoché. Although his senior tutor was a strict disciplinarian, the Tibetan hierarch feels only gratitude for the way he "did his best to instil good qualities in me" and continues to hold him in the highest regard. The growing awareness of his responsibilities not just to the Tibetan people but to all sentient beings was evidently almost overwhelming at times. The Dalai Lama speaks of having felt like a boat cut adrift, imperiled on the one hand by whirlpools and waterfalls, and running aground on the other, but it was Ling Rinpoché who helped stabilize the craft. By others, the Precious Protector's senior tutor is remembered as a man with little in the way of small talk, reserved—though not without a keen sense of humor—and a monk whose conduct was in every way exemplary. Later, the two men developed a firm friendship, marked by deep respect on both sides.

It was Ling Rinpoché who first introduced the young Dalai Lama to the discipline of *tsoe pa* (generally translated as debate but more accurately as dialectics). This was, as it remains, the cornerstone of the education of a novice monk in the Tibetan tradition.

As anyone who has witnessed a monastery courtyard during a debating session will be aware, it is also one of its chief glories. Observing the shouting, the laughter, the jeering, the foot-stamping, and the flourishing of rosary with which the challenger belabors his adversary, you could be forgiven for thinking you were watching a prizefight. It is only the figure of the defender sitting rock-like and imperturbable that reminds you this is a scholarly rather than a pugilistic contest. It was this practice that lay at the heart of the young Dalai Lama's education: his prowess as a debater would determine his reputation as a scholar.

We would have to go back to the Middle Ages in Europe to find anything close to what remains a vital element of Tibetan culture. But while debate in the Tibetan tradition strongly resembles the Western Socratic method, it differs from it in one crucial respect. Whereas the Socratic method is a free inquiry into the truth or falsity of a given proposition, Tibetan debate is principally concerned with clarifying that which is already known: *the way things really are.* If this sounds like a travesty of what dialectics ought to be, that is to miss the point. Although debate in the Tibetan tradition may approach its subject matter with forensic precision, it is not an inquiry. It is, first, a method of sharpening the logical reasoning skills of the practitioner and, second, a discipline that aims to reinforce what the Buddha* revealed when he proclaimed the Four Noble Truths, namely:

1. The truth of suffering
2. The truth of the cause of suffering
3. The truth of the cessation of suffering
4. The truth of the Path to the cessation of suffering

We might paraphrase this by saying, first, that, contrary to what the Christian Bible tells us, the world is not "good." It is unsatisfactory. When we are in it, we suffer. Moreover, all those things of the world that we think will make

---

*The word "Buddha" may be translated as "one who is awakened."

us happy or bring us satisfaction are in fact only causes of further suffering. To put the matter in Judeo-Christian terms, the world itself is, in a sense, the Fall. Second, suffering is not gratuitous; it is caused—by our karma coming to fruition.* This includes not only moral suffering (the suffering attendant on negative acts, whether done by us or against us) but also natural suffering, like illness, old age, and death. Third, there is, fortunately, a way to overcome suffering (this could be called the gospel—the "good news" of Buddhism) through eliminating the causes of suffering. Fourth, the way to eliminate the causes of suffering is to follow the Path, indicated by the Buddha, to its final end, which is liberation from suffering, or nirvana.†

The basic handbooks of debate, the *Collected Topics,* were, for the Dalai Lama, as for every student entering a Gelug monastery, the principal object of study from the moment he was introduced to them. It was these that set out what it was that must be learned, while debate was the means by which the young scholar learned first to internalize and then to defend, through logical argument, what he had learned.

Because the principles around which Tibetan debate is structured are universal, anyone familiar with the basics of Aristotelian logic will have no trouble following those of the Indo-Tibetan tradition. Both trade on the inadmissibility of contradiction, and both recognize argument as requiring one or more premises to reach a conclusion. Like Aristotelian logic, Indo-Tibetan logic is essentially syllogistic and thus does not attain the mathematical precision of modern predicate logic. Yet adherents of both systems uphold their ultimate superiority even in the face of modern advances.

---

* It is important to realize that the doctrine of karma is by no means deterministic. The most highly realized practitioners may in certain circumstances be immune to its effects. Moreover, the present moment is precisely an opportunity to effect a transformation of one's accumulated karma. For example, when a negative memory (itself a karmic residue) is correctly contextualized, it may go from being a negative to a positive imprint. My memory of an accident or mishap may continue to distress me until I understand it as a timely warning to change my behavior.

† Such liberation is often termed "Enlightenment," but this can be misleading. It suggests a moment of epiphany. From the Buddhist perspective, one who is enlightened is straightforwardly one who has passed beyond suffering into nirvana.

Where the Indo-Tibetan philosophical tradition differs from the classical Western philosophical tradition is in its assumptions about the way the world really is. For Aristotle and his successors, the world is on its way to its final consummation in perfection. In the Indo-Tibetan system, the basic premise is that the world is chiefly characterized by suffering and that the cause of suffering is ignorance. Ignorance of what? Ignorance of the way things really are. The purpose of logical analysis is thus, in the Buddhist view, to dispel ignorance. As we come truly to understand the nature of things, so we will understand the need to become truly and limitlessly compassionate as a means to final liberation. What is it to be truly and limitlessly compassionate? Above all, being compassionate entails desiring that others cease to suffer and thus doing all we can to aid them in their quest to overcome suffering. Since the path elaborated by the Buddha is the sole means of overcoming suffering, the best help we can give others is guidance along that path. The better qualified we are, through our mastery of the teachings and practices that lead to liberation, the better equipped we will be to exercise compassion. And such mastery, it is held by the Gelug school, is best achieved through proficiency in debate, by means of which the practitioner develops his or her understanding of the great classics of Buddhist literature.

It was essential that the young Dalai Lama be accomplished in the art not just because of this, however. At the end of his formal education as a monk there would be no final written examinations, just keenly observed public debates. Although, as Dalai Lama, the Precious Protector was spared the rough-and-tumble of the courtyard (though one suspects he would have relished it) and instead had the advantage of being assigned a number of sparring partners (or *tsenshab*) with whom he would debate under the direction of his tutors, his eventual graduation was not a mere formality. He would have to earn the monastic community's respect just like any other prospective teacher.*

---

*Not all the Dalai Lamas have been great scholars. The Fourth, a Mongolian descendant of Genghis Khan, never learned Tibetan to an adequate degree and was likened, somewhat uncharitably, to an "empty box" (by Desi Sangye Gyatso in his biography of the Great Fifth); the Sixth refused to take holy orders, preferring instead to write love poetry and go on adventures with the more louche among the aristocratic youth of his day; the Eighth, a sickly young man,

But there was another—vital—element in the education of the Dalai Lama. His inner development as a meditator was of equal if not greater importance, and here too Ling Rinpoché's influence was paramount.

At the beginning of the meditator's training, the mind is likened to a rampaging elephant which it is his business to subdue, just as the mahout subdues the elephant. This is done in thirty-three carefully programmed stages. To begin, the elephant runs away from the mahout. But with persistence and gentleness, the beast is brought to the point where it will accept a rope. In the diagrams used in Buddhist textbooks to depict the process, the elephant is shown at the beginning as black in color and led by a black monkey. The monkey symbolizes distraction, while black symbolizes lethargy—the two great obstacles to taming the mind. When, at around the halfway mark, the mahout at last takes charge of the elephant, he finds it reluctant to move. But gradually, with persistence and kindness, the elephant is persuaded to follow its master. Eventually, trust is built up and the elephant does its tamer's bidding until eventually it no longer needs the rope. First it follows, then it allows itself to be mounted. The monkey is similarly tamed before being sent on its way. Finally, at the thirty-third stage, the mahout and the elephant become friends and the animal does whatever it is bidden.

Many today are somewhat familiar with Buddhist meditation thanks to the popularity of mindfulness. But within the Tibetan tradition, mindfulness is only one of a wide range of techniques. Moreover, it is almost invariably practiced alongside "insight," or single-pointed meditation—and always within the ethical and spiritual framework of Buddhism. Insight meditation aims at increasing the practitioner's ability to concentrate, single-pointedly, and with the mind fully alert, on a given object, whether this object be physical, such as a statue or a *thangka,* or visualized, such as a meditation deity—for hours on end in the case of the most accomplished practitioners. But there are many other techniques as well, some involving breathing and others physical exercises, while still others involve practitioners visualizing themselves as

---

showed little aptitude for philosophy and spent most of his time sunning himself on the veranda.

deities. All aim at the eventual goal of complete mastery of the practitioner's mental states.

It is also important to understand that these practices are, from the point of view of the tradition, in no sense a turning away, or a tuning out, from the world. The Tibetan word for meditation, *gom,* means, literally, familiarization. Thus, for example, in "exchanging self for other," the meditator becomes familiar with the emotional states attendant on visualizing a friend, a random individual toward whom one has no particular feelings, and an enemy. Having identified the positive, neutral, and negative emotional states that these different visualizations arouse, the meditator becomes thoroughly acquainted with the first emotion—with the intention of developing the very same feeling toward the enemy as the yoga progresses.

The Buddhist theory of mind expounded in the *Collected Topics* entails that each of the senses constitutes a distinct consciousness. Something seen is thus an object of eye-consciousness, something heard is an object of ear-consciousness, something smelled is an object of olfactory consciousness. And yet, most important of all, and most radical, is the further understanding that ultimately there is no substantive self that bears these different aspects of consciousness, or in which mind itself may be said to reside. Buddhism teaches that what we mistakenly suppose to be our "self" is precisely the cause of the suffering we endure.

But if the self is ultimately illusory, what of physical objects? According to some thinkers, matter is a karmic effect of beings existing (where karma is the imprint on the individual mental continuum, or stream of consciousness, of a being's actions, whether positive, negative, or neutral). Physical objects (including rocks, rivers, and oceans) are held to be the fruit of the deeds of sentient beings over limitless time. Furthermore, the universe we see around us is not made up of vanishingly small non-physical particles out of which first matter, then life, then consciousness emerge. Other Buddhist thinkers are agnostic as to the origins of matter, saying only that the existence of physical objects is just an aspect of the way things are. Generally speaking, however, in Buddhism mind precedes matter. Does this then mean that consciousness itself is what reality ultimately consists in? In fact, although there is a Buddhist school of thought that holds this to be the case, the Gelug tradition, following Nagarjuna's Middle Way approach, speaks of two truths, "conventional" and "ultimate."* Traditionally taught only to those deemed capable of hearing it without misunderstanding, the doctrine maintains that what we take to be real is illusory: no more substantial than the foam that appears on a fast-flowing stream, or the reflection of the moon in a pool of water, or a flash of lightning in the dark of night. The ultimate nature of reality is empty—indeed, it is emptiness itself.

Here is not the place for a discussion of the merits of this claim. Suffice it to say that it has found support among contemporary anti-realist philosophers worldwide. It is also important to understand that, at least for Tsongkhapa (founder of the Dalai Lamas' Gelugpa sect and Tibet's most subtle philosopher), the doctrine is not, as is sometimes maintained, the nihilistic claim that ultimately nothing at all exists. It is instead a claim about how things exist: they exist, but only dependently—hence the further claim that all phenomena are interdependent. There is no first cause, and nothing that exists does so essentially. This should not be taken to mean that the Buddhist tradition as handed on to the Dalai Lama was without a clear picture of how the world we inhabit came into being. On the contrary, Buddhism has a detailed theory of both the natural and the supernatural realms, and cosmology was a major component of the curriculum set out in the *Collected Topics.*

In brief, the traditional scheme envisages a great four-sided world mountain, Meru, which rises out of a vast ocean.† To north, south, east, and west are grouped a number of islands. One of these islands, Dzambu Ling, the Rose Garden, is the one we humans inhabit. In other words, our world is flat. Why do we not see Mount Meru? Because the side toward which we face is composed of lapis lazuli—the color of the sky. And what of the sun and the moon? These are held aloft by cosmic winds which carry them in an orbit around the mountain. Beneath the earth lies, first, the realm of the *yidag,* the hungry ghosts, then the hell regions, eight of them cold and eight of them hot.

---

*Nagarjuna (ca. 150–250 CE), arguably the greatest Buddhist philosopher, is most widely known for his Mulamadhyamakarika, or *Verses on the Fundamental Wisdom of the Middle Way.*

† Saint Isidore of Seville, the late-antique encyclopedist, also places a great mountain at the center of the world.

Altogether there are six realms that together make up samsara, the always unsatisfactory state in which all sentient beings subsist until they attain Enlightenment. At the top there is the realm of the blissful gods; beneath this comes that of the demigods. Third comes the human realm. Beneath the human realm is the animal realm. Next comes the realm of hungry ghosts and finally the realm of the various hells. Yet, although the human realm is not at the top of this hierarchy, it is only as a human that a being has the opportunity to become enlightened during this very life.

The blissful gods are held to reside on the summit of Mount Meru, while the demigods live at different levels, according to status and spiritual development. The human and animal realms need no explanation, but that of the hungry ghosts demands one. A being (whether god, demigod, human, or animal) who in this life is gluttonous and driven by the desire for food is in danger of being reborn as a "hungry ghost," or *yidag*. These piteous creatures have enormous bellies, absurdly long and thin necks, eyes that emit pestiferous and fiery gases that dry up everything their gaze alights on, and mouths the size of the eye of a needle. Subsisting in the underworld, not far below the surface of the earth, they are perpetually tormented by their inability to satisfy their hunger.

As for the hell realms, as one might expect, these increase in severity the further down one goes; by the time we reach the sixth hell, the custodians of this realm seize the damned, throw them into large cauldrons, and boil them like fish before impaling them on red-hot iron stakes until their intestines obtrude and flames burst forth from every orifice.

With respect to the realm of the demigods, although their conditions are far superior to those on earth (there are no food shortages or natural disasters to worry about), the inhabitants are not to be envied. They spend their time fighting and are almost invariably reborn in the lower realms. Even those who attain the highest heavens and experience bliss to a degree we humans cannot imagine are not immune to suffering and death, nor from the possibility of sliding back into one of the other realms through the accumulation of negative karma. They remain within samsara.

Although today the Dalai Lama rejects a literal reading of this cosmology, nonetheless, in just the same way that the Genesis story lies behind Big Bang theory and continues to haunt the Western imagination, the traditional picture of the world elaborated in the scriptures grounds the Mahayana worldview and continues to haunt the Tibetan imagination. It is also true that, by the time of the Dalai Lama's boyhood, this traditional Tibetan view of the universe was under pressure. Children of the aristocracy and merchant classes educated by the British in India already had a very different picture of the world—which is undoubtedly part of the reason why the English language school in Lhasa that opened in 1947 was shut down after only one term. The monasteries were opposed on the grounds that its presence would harm the Buddhadharma.

It was for similar reasons that the young Dalai Lama was forbidden to speak to Lowell Thomas, the legendary American journalist and broadcaster, who visited Lhasa in 1949. During his audience, the fourteen-year-old Dalai Lama "smiled when asked and agreeably changed position for our cameras," Thomas noted. But that was all. It was not until late in 1949 that the teenager at last contrived a meeting at which he could actually speak with a foreigner. This was the thirty-three-year-old Austrian mountaineer and, notoriously, former SS Oberscharführer and Nazi Party member Heinrich Harrer, one of Lhasa's six resident Westerners.* There might have been one more—a Catholic missionary based at Yerkalo. But soon after setting out for Lhasa, where he intended to implore the Dalai Lama's protection, he was shot by monks from a nearby monastery.

Much has been made of Harrer's dubious past (which forced a re-edit of the film based on his travelogue of the same name, *Seven Years in Tibet*). That he was not a dedicated Nazi (he claimed to have worn his uniform only once, on the day he married his first wife) is attested to by the fact that, having escaped from a British internment camp at Dehra Dun in northern India together with fellow Austrian Peter Aufschnaiter, he decided to try for Lhasa rather than proceed to Japan (Germany's ally at the time). He was an adventurer, not an ideologue. A stronger case can be made for a link between the

---

* Apart from Harrer and his fellow Austrian Peter Aufschnaiter, the others were Hugh Richardson, the British political officer; Reginald Fox and Robert Ford, both of them British radio operators; and a White Russian refugee by the name of Nedbailof who helped electrify the capital.

Nazis and Reting Rinpoché, at least when he was regent. During the 1930s, the Ahnenerbe, the institute founded by Heinrich Himmler to give academic respectability to the party's racial ideology, sent a total of three expeditions to Tibet, the last of them attending the 1939 New Year celebrations in Lhasa. The purpose of their visit was to determine the truth of a claim that the Tibetans were in fact descendants of a lost Aryan tribe. Reting Rinpoché was on good terms with the expedition leader, Ernst Schaefer, who was well liked by Himmler. All five members of his team were Nazi ideologues, and one was subsequently convicted of being an accessory to the murder of eighty-six Jews at Auschwitz. A famous photograph shows Schaefer and his men posing with senior Tibetan officials in front of a swastika flag and two SS pennants they had put on display at a dinner party in Lhasa. Some see in this evidence of an unambiguous link between esoteric Vajrayana Buddhism and Nazism.

After several unsuccessful attempts, Harrer, together with Aufschnaiter, had reached Lhasa during the middle of January 1946 following two years of grueling travel.* Given that the prohibition against foreigners entering Tibet without government permission was rigorously enforced, this was a very considerable feat.

En route, the two of them had passed themselves off variously as itinerant dentists, as traders, and as the advance party of an important foreign dignitary. Having survived more than one serious attempt on their lives, they were given a cordial welcome in Lhasa by the aristocratic family whose house they chanced to enter on their arrival in the capital. Eight days later, by which time they had been visited by many of the highest-ranking laity—including an army general eager to learn all he could about the German tank commander Erwin Rommel—they received word that the Dalai Lama's family wished to meet them. But it was to be more than three years before Harrer's first meeting with the Dalai Lama himself. In the meantime, he and Aufschnaiter had to apply for asylum. At first their application was refused, and it was only thanks to Aufschnaiter's engineering skills that they were eventually allowed to stay. Subsequently Auf-

---

*In fact, they had four other companions to start with, of whom two made it into Tibet, but they split into separate parties. The others turned back before reaching Lhasa.

schnaiter worked on a hydroelectric power project and helped plan the city's first sewage works, while Harrer, who had good English and was an accomplished lensman, soon found himself in demand as a translator and occasional court photographer.

Eventually, Harrer was approached by Lobsang Samten—by this time serving as Lord Chamberlain—with a request to build a movie theater for the Dalai Lama in the grounds of the Norbulingka Palace. As the Dalai Lama recounts in his autobiography, one of the things he had found among the belongings of the Great Thirteenth was an old film projector, which, astonishingly, by taking it apart and carefully reassembling it, he had returned to working order. He was now eager to put it to use.

When Harrer and the Dalai Lama did finally make each other's acquaintance in the second half of 1949, it was clearly only after a carefully orchestrated campaign. Harrer reports of their first meeting that the hurried blessing the Dalai Lama bestowed on him "seemed less like the ceremonial laying-on of hands than an impetuous expression of feeling on the part of a boy who had at last got his way." This enthusiasm was in marked contrast to the coldness with which the monastic officials surrounding the Precious Protector acknowledged Harrer's greeting.

In his travelogue *Seven Years in Tibet,* Harrer includes a chapter portentously titled "Tutor to the Dalai Lama." This is an overstatement of their relationship. Although Harrer and the teenaged Dalai Lama met more or less weekly over a period of a little more than six months, their time together was entirely informal. It was a friendly, sometimes joshing relationship—the Dalai Lama nicknamed Harrer *gopse,* or "straw head"—albeit one they both took seriously. They remained friends until the end of Harrer's long life.

It was helpful that Harrer was as down-to-earth as his protégé. The Dalai Lama, impatient with the protocol that surrounded him, and already conscious that the religious education he was getting was inadequate to the political role he must soon undertake, was eager to learn as much as he could from his new friend. "He seemed to me like a person who for years brooded in solitude over different problems," Harrer recalled, "and now that he at last had someone to talk to, wanted to know all the answers at once."

Harrer quickly found that, besides being boundlessly curious, the youngster was also intensely serious. The Dalai Lama soon sorted the eighty films in his collection into those that were educational in some way and those that were mere entertainment. The former he watched more than once—a documentary about Mahatma Gandhi being a favorite—while the others he set aside. And when he asked a question, he expected a full and reasoned answer, such that Harrer had to take "the utmost trouble to treat every [one of them] seriously and scientifically." Yet it was always clear where the Dalai Lama's true priorities lay. He would invariably break off their conversations in plenty of time for his official studies, as he did not like to keep his real tutors waiting—any more than he liked to be kept waiting himself. On one occasion Harrer was ten minutes late for an appointment and was scolded for his temerity.

The picture of the young Dalai Lama that emerges from Harrer's account is one of a highly intelligent, inquisitive, studious, serious-minded yet good-humored young man with a keen sense of his responsibilities and a nature as affectionate as his mind was open and eager. "Sometimes," recounts Harrer, "he came running across the garden to meet me, beaming with happiness and holding out his hand." Regarding Harrer himself, despite the strange irony that the incarnation of the Bodhisattva of Compassion was tutored by a former SS man, we have no reason to suppose that Hugh Richardson spoke in bad faith when giving his assessment of Harrer, even if it does seem somewhat extravagant. He once said* that, if there was only one other person left on earth, he would have wanted that person to be Harrer. As for the thought that Harrer must have known about the Holocaust, we have similarly no reason to suppose he had any inkling of it until after the war. He left Germany in 1939, while the Wannsee Conference that inaugurated the Final Solution did not take place until January 1942. This does not touch the question of whether the Dalai Lama's friend was an anti-Semite, surely a precondition of membership in the SS. It seems that, at the very least, he must have been when he joined, even if fellow

---

* He said this to me, in a (filmed) interview at his home in St. Andrews, Scotland, in 1994. Richardson, having been the British political officer resident in Lhasa, subsequently worked—in an identical role—for the Nehru government until 1950.

mountaineer Reinhold Messner is right in believing that Harrer's experiences in Tibet caused him to change his mind. It is also undeniable that Tibet's esoteric Buddhism speaks loudly to the romantic strain in fascist ideology. And if what chiefly motivated Harrer was curiosity and love of adventure, it is difficult to imagine that his dream of reaching Lhasa was not partly inspired by fantasies about what he would find there.

When, at the Dalai Lama's request, Harrer began to teach him English, the Austrian was surprised to discover that the youngster had already taught himself the Roman alphabet and would transcribe the pronunciation of words "in elegant Tibetan characters." Harrer was duly impressed. "What versatility!" exclaimed the Austrian. "Strenuous religious studies, tinkering with complicated mechanical appliances, and now modern languages!" Together they would "listen to the English news on a portable radio and [take] advantage of the passages that were spoken at dictation speed."

As well as wanting to learn English from him, the Dalai Lama tasked Harrer with teaching him the rudiments of arithmetic and geography (his favorite subject, though even more than classroom study, he enjoyed working on mechanical devices). Math he did not take to, but he was astonished, Harrer tells us—just as many Westerners today are astonished—to hear that Tibet was as large as it is. And he was delighted to discover that the highest mountain in all the world rose on its southern extremity. Besides instruction in these subjects, the young man was also eager to learn about current affairs and modern developments like the jet engine and the atom bomb. It turned out that the Dalai Lama was familiar with all the different types of aircraft and armored vehicles used by the various powers in the recently concluded war. He was also familiar with the names of the great men of the day—Churchill, Eisenhower, Molotov. Yet it was apparent that he often "did not know how persons and events were connected with each other." As to any concerns the Austrian may have had about his young friend's capacity to absorb all this new information, "he continually astonished me," Harrer recalled, "by his powers of comprehension, his pertinacity and his industry."

If Harrer's picture of the young Dalai Lama shows him not to have been so very different from any other highly intelligent teenager of his time—or indeed of any time—there was one thing that might at first strike us as unusual: the Precious Protector had not a trace of skepticism with respect to the religion he was being brought up in. Not for him the wrestling with faith of Saint Augustine. According to Harrer, the Dalai Lama was, for example, "convinced that by virtue of his faith and by performing the prescribed rites he would be able to make things happen in faraway places." Moreover, "when he had made sufficient progress, he would send me there and direct me from Lhasa" by means of telepathy. As we shall see, the Dalai Lama's conviction that the supernatural realm is not imaginary is one that he maintains to this day.

10

"Shit on their picnic!": China Invades, 1949–50

While the young Dalai Lama was learning all he could about the modern world from Harrer, following the end of the world war, events within it were reaching a climax. In China, the Communists were moving ever closer to victory. When Ma Bufang, the Muslim warlord who had demanded ransom for the Dalai Lama's release, lost his headquarters to the Reds during the summer of 1949, it was clear to Tibetans that China's capital must soon fall. It remained only for Chiang Kai-shek to withdraw to Taiwan before, on October 1, Chairman Mao declared the founding of the People's Republic of China. This brought to an end more than twenty years of strife, during the course of which countless millions had died. But while the Communists' victory caused deep uneasiness on the part of the Tibetan government, the regent, Taktra Rinpoché, offered no response beyond ordering the Three Seats to begin the ritual chanting of the scriptures.

For his part, the young Dalai Lama still played no active role in government affairs. During the winter of that year, he did, however, instruct his junior tutor,

Trijang Rinpoché, to renew the protector support substances in the Potala. This entailed reconsecrating various ritual objects so as to ensure the constant presence and protection of the wrathful protector deities. According to Trijang, the substances used included such items as "double-edged steel swords with scorpion hilts tempered in blood and poison . . . [a] bow made from the horn of an uncastrated ox . . . [b]lack banners with mantras and figures drawn on them with weapon-spilled blood . . . the skull of an illegitimate child filled with charmed substances . . . a corpse shroud around which the long mantras of calling, expelling and slaying . . . had been written," and an image of Palden Lhamo on which "were smeared the juices of sexual union."

Meanwhile, Tibetan government officials did eventually dispatch a letter to their Chinese counterparts acknowledging the Communists' victory. Addressed to "the honourable Mr. Mao Tse Tung," it began by explaining that "Tibet is a peculiar country where the Buddhist religion is widely flourishing and which is predestined to be ruled by the Living Buddha of Mercy or Chenrezig. As such, Tibet has from the earliest times up to now, been an Independent Country whose Political administration had never been taken over by any Foreign Country." The letter ended, one short paragraph later, with the demand that "those Tibetan territories annexed as part of Chinese territories some years back should now be returned to their rightful jurisdiction."

To the Chinese, who had a lively sense of history, the claim that Tibet had "always been independent" can only have seemed nonsensical. What was the office of Imperial Preceptor, created in the thirteenth century by the Yuan emperor Kublai Khan, if it was not an office for the governance of Tibet? And had not the Qiangxi emperor sent troops to aid Tibet in expelling the Nepalese incursion in the seventeenth century? Indeed, had not the Dalai Lamas' very recognition been subject to ratification by the Qing throne? What was this if not subjection? And as to foreign interference, China was no foreign country—though Britain was, and so was India.

In fact, Tibetans do not deny any of these claims. But they interpret them very differently. Furthermore, Tibetans cannot forget that, for almost three hundred years from the middle of the seventh century, Tibet was the center of a great trading empire, controlling what came to be known as the Silk Road linking Rome in the west with China in the east. Tibet was at the time also the major military power of Central and Southeast Asia. Frequent were the defeats dealt China by Tibetan armies in the Tarim Basin and elsewhere. There was even a thrilling moment—in 763 CE—when Tibetan forces deposed the T'ang emperor and, if only for three weeks, set up their own in his place. This was an extraordinary feat of arms: Chang'an, seat of the T'ang empire, was at the time a city of a million people, one of the greatest the world had ever seen—rivaled only by ancient Rome in terms of size and sophistication. By the end of the eighth century, the Tibetan emperor controlled territory stretching as far as Persia in the west, to the Bay of Bengal in the south, to within striking distance of Chang'an in the east, and up to the Pamirs (in modern-day Tajikistan) in the north.

In 821 the two emperors entered into a treaty, the terms of which were inscribed on three stone stele, or pillars, in both Chinese and Tibetan script, and erected one on the border itself and one each in the respective capitals, "in order that it may never be changed [and] so that it may be celebrated in every age and every generation." The one in Lhasa still exists for all to see. It stands near the base of the Potala, albeit partially shielded from view by its "protective" covering, still proclaiming that "both Tibet and China shall keep the country and frontiers of which they are now in possession," and that

> the whole region to the east of that being the country of Great China, and all to the west is, without question Great Tibet . . . from either side of that frontier there shall be no warfare, no hostile invasions, and no seizure of territory. There shall be no sudden alarms and the word "enemy" shall not be spoken . . . Between the two countries no smoke or dust shall appear . . . Tibetans shall be happy in Tibet and Chinese shall be happy in China.

From the Tibetan perspective, the treaty between the emperor and his Chinese counterpart has never been abrogated.

What happened when the thirteenth-century Yuan emperor Kublai Khan summoned Phagpa, head of the Sakya sect, which was then the most prominent in Tibet, to the imperial court was not, for Tibetans, the political subjugation of one country by another but rather the establishment of a spiritual relationship between two individuals. In exchange for religious instruction granted by Phagpa at Kublai's request, the Khan entered into a priest-patron (*cho yon*) relationship, whereby the Khan gained spiritual merit through taking religious teachings and the lama gained the emperor's material support. And whatever the political ramifications of such a relationship, they did not change the terms of the earlier treaty. The same applies with respect to the relationship between the Dalai Lamas and the Qing emperors of the eighteenth to the twentieth centuries. Again, theirs was a personal, spiritual relationship that conferred obligations on both parties. Crudely put, the priest prayed for the emperor and the emperor paid for the priest—and paid not just in terms of treasure but in blood, too. It became a royal duty for the emperor to protect his guru.

From the Chinese perspective, the spiritual teachings of the priest were an offering of tribute to the emperor. Once tribute had been paid, the emperor would graciously provide his protection on the grounds that the tribute payer had rendered himself a vassal. So whereas the ancient treaty spoke of an alliance between the two thrones, the new dispensation understood the relationship as one in which the one summoned was subordinate to the will of the one summoning.

In January 1950, Mao announced the return of Tibet to the Chinese Motherland as one of the Communist Party's top priorities for the year. Soon after, he called on the Tibetan government to send representatives to Beijing to discuss how they wished to facilitate this "liberation." For many weeks, his communiqué went unanswered.

Eventually the Tibetan government stirred itself to appeal to the British and American governments and, in spite of its tardy recognition of Indian independence, to the nonaligned Indian government as well. But although the Indians (albeit with American and British connivance) did agree to supply arms (including mortar bombs but not antiaircraft shells as requested), it was far too little to make a difference and at least ten years too late, given the training that would be required. Although, on the back of this gesture, the bodyguard regiment, which had disbanded itself on the demise of the Great Thirteenth, was hastily revived, there was never a realistic chance that it could be made battle-ready in time. One thing the Tibetan government did do was to send Robert Ford, a British radio operator it had employed to instruct a small cadre of officials in the use of telecommunications, together with two radio sets, out to Chamdo in the east. Understanding that, if the Communists were to take Lhasa, they must first take Chamdo, the Tibetans reckoned that posting Ford there with his radios would at least give the government some warning in the event of disaster.

The new technology brought with it a number of problems, however. When Lhalu, the outgoing governor of Chamdo, had occasion to speak with Trijang Rinpoché over the air, he was nearly undone by the novelty of the experience. Before beginning the call, he "approached the microphone reverently and placed a ceremonial white scarf . . . in front of it [and] bowed his head as if to receive a blessing." Although his replacement, Ngabo (the *g* can safely be ignored), a young reform-minded aristocrat, was less troubled by etiquette, the new governor was so afraid of its breaking down that he refused to allow the second set out of his sight. Any chance he had of early warning about hostile troop movements from sending it out closer to where the Chinese were likely to approach from was thereby lost.

The spring and summer months of 1949 passed with a heightening sense that something immense was about to happen. One day a comet appeared in the dawn sky to the south of Lhasa, followed on August 15 by a massive earthquake (measuring 8.6 on the Richter scale) in the southeast, technically just inside India, though in an area settled by Tibetans. This, Harrer reports, was accompanied by "thirty or forty" dull explosions and a strange glow visible in the sky to the east. Though Harrer assured the Dalai Lama these were nothing more than physical events, for the Dalai Lama—to this day—they were clearly more than that. When the capital of a stone pillar at the Potala was found lying on the ground and a gargoyle on the roof of the Jokhang started gushing water, despite the "blazing summer weather," it was taken as conclusive proof, if further evidence were needed, that the deities were mightily perturbed.

Not long afterwards, a series of posters appeared on the walls along the street leading to the Norbulingka Palace bearing the slogan "Give the Dalai Lama the Power," and rumors began to sweep Lhasa that the oracles were urging the regent to step down. There was by this time a general feeling that only the Precious Protector could save his people from looming catastrophe. For the time being, however, he remained sequestered within the Norbulingka, his only real contact with events in the outside world coming from Harrer's weekly visits.

The Chinese government meanwhile stepped up pressure on the regency, calling on it to send competent negotiators at once. Initially the proposed talks were to have taken place in Hong Kong, but the British, who administered the territory at the time, not wishing to become involved, demurred. The venue was then shifted to New Delhi. At the same time, the Chinese sent an emissary (actually a monk volunteer) to Chamdo with a series of demands. Conveniently for the Tibetans, he died soon after his arrival—of poison, according to the Chinese, who were furious. Finally, the Communist leadership announced in September that if it wanted to avoid war, the Tibetan government should immediately acknowledge that Tibet was part of China, that the People's Liberation Army (PLA) now be deployed on Tibet's international borders, and that Tibet immediately cut all ties with the "imperialist powers."

For the Tibetans, this was completely unacceptable. Yet the prospect of war was equally untenable. Unable to see a way out of the conundrum, the government did what it always did when faced with a dilemma. It stalled. Accordingly, on October 5, 1950, Mao, his patience spent, ordered the PLA to attack multiple Tibetan positions in the eastern province of Kham.

Ngabo's defense plan amounted to little more than hoping that the mere presence of his troops, together with reinforcements on their way from Lhasa, would be sufficient to give the PLA pause. Then, if the negotiations taking place in Delhi could just be put off a little longer, winter would intervene, and the gods would have more time to work a miracle.

This was hopelessly optimistic. The Chinese were perfectly capable of launching an attack in winter. As for the thought that the battle-hardened PLA would be put off by the arrival of a few hundred reinforcements from Lhasa, that too was a vain hope. It is true that the PLA was far from home, with a long and vulnerable supply chain. But the Chinese army command was well aware that the Khampas, in whose province Chamdo lay, were hardly less hostile to the Lhasa government than they were to the Chinese themselves. As recently as 1934, a Khampa warlord had made a serious bid to wrest control of the region from Lhasa. Ngabo could not count on anything more than minimal support from the local tribespeople.

On October 7 the Chinese struck again, this time cutting off Chamdo's southern escape route. The local army commander responded by surrendering his entire force without a fight, leaving the town at the mercy of the PLA. Because of his refusal to deploy the second radio set, news of this catastrophe did not reach Ngabo for several days, however. It has been argued that Ngabo willfully betrayed Chamdo into the hands of the Chinese, a charge that his subsequent collaboration with the Communists supports. But the fact is, even if he had been able to stall the PLA's advance, the outcome was inevitable. Nonetheless, he did not wish to surrender without being ordered to do so. He therefore contacted his opposite number in Lhasa in order to ascertain the instructions of the Kashag, the regent's four-man cabinet. There was no reply. On the third attempt, Lhasa was finally goaded into responding.

"Right now," Ngabo was told, "it is the period of the Kashag's picnic and they are all participating in this. Your telegrams are being decoded and then we will send you a reply."

At this he exploded.

"Shit on their picnic! Though we are blocked here, and the nation is threatened and every minute may make a difference to our fate, you talk about that shit picnic!"

There was no further contact with Lhasa that day. This was the time of year when almost the entirety of the populace took themselves off to the parkland outside the city for a week of relaxation (not to say drinking and gambling), the wealthy in their tents, the poor camped al fresco. Ngabo thus had no orders as to whether he should try to hold Chamdo or whether he should withdraw. Already convinced that resistance to the Chinese would be futile, the governor determined that, in the absence of clear directions from Lhasa, he would simply await the arrival of the Chinese and hope to effect an escape at the last moment.

The next day, news of the loss of another town to the south of Chamdo came in, followed that evening by a message from Riwoche in the southeast that the PLA were now in occupation of that town as well. Chamdo was surrounded. Without telling anyone, Ngabo abandoned his post that night.

At seven o'clock the following morning, Ford, the British radio operator, realized something was amiss. Having woken to the sound of bells ringing and horses' hooves on the street outside, he looked out to see "people . . . running in all directions." His immediate concern was the reaction of the local Khampa population. Realizing that the government forces were in full retreat, they wasted no time in looting what possessions and weaponry the Lhasans had left behind. And beyond that, it was clear that they were intent on killing any remaining government officials they could lay their hands on.

Showing rather greater initiative than Ngabo, Ford made his way to the radio station and disabled the transmitters before heading south in the hope of reaching the Indian border. Unfortunately for him, the earthquake two months earlier had rendered this impossible and he was forced to follow the retreating governor in the direction of Lhasa. Managing to evade hostile Khampas, he caught up with Ngabo later that same day. But they could go no farther and were both taken into Chinese custody. While Ngabo and his entourage were treated to a hearty meal and his soldiers each given a silver coin and told to return home, Ford was taken back to Chamdo, where he was interrogated and charged with being a British spy.*

With Kham now lost, it could be only a matter of time before Lhasa followed. Having no other option, Taktra therefore instructed the government's

---

*For the next five months, Ford was held in solitary confinement in a rat-infested cell, forced on many occasions to sit motionless for sixteen hours at a time. "I was never struck a single blow," he later recalled, "but mentally it was no holds barred." Over the subsequent three years, he was subject to relentless interrogation and "re-education" before finally signing a false confession in May 1954. He was sentenced to ten years in prison. No sooner had this sentence been pronounced than he was told that he was to be deported. Whether this was true or another attempt to break him he did not know for another six months until, eventually, he was taken across China to one of the railway bridges that led into Hong Kong and told to walk across, not knowing "whether I would get a bullet in my back." Phodo, as he was affectionately known by Tibetans, subsequently became a vocal supporter of the Tibetan cause and was invariably called on by the Dalai Lama whenever the Precious Protector visited Britain. In 2011 he was honored by the Tibetan community in exile, who symbolically handed over a one-hundred-sang note by way of back pay, together with an apology for the delay "due to extenuating circumstances." He died in 2013 at the age of ninety. I had the privilege of meeting him twice. He was as courteous and self-effacing an individual as ever to have been the partial cause of an invasion of one country by another.

chief negotiator to inform the Chinese ambassador that the Tibetan government was now willing to accept Chairman Mao's terms. The Dalai Lama, following events as best he could, was devastated. Instinctively he knew that he must act. While the news that Chamdo had fallen was grave, the regent's decision to surrender seemed to him utter folly. Surely, he argued, the correct thing to do was to consult with the deities before taking such a large step as to surrender sovereignty. That the regent did not face down the fifteen-year-old Dalai Lama shows how uncertain of his own position he now was. He agreed to a divination at which the Dalai Lama and the highest-ranking members of the government would be present. This would take place in the Mahakala chapel at the Norbulingka, where the protectors Mahakala and the Glorious Goddess would both be invoked to give their opinion.

With respect to the Dalai Lamas personally, after the Glorious Goddess, Mahakala is the second-most important of the protectors. Recognized within the Hindu tradition as a consort of Kali, the Destroyer, Mahakala is held to have shown his care for the Dalai Lama institution when the first Dalai Lama (Gendun Drub, 1391–1474) was an infant. One night, bandits attacked the encampment where his family was settled. Fearing for her baby's life, the future Dalai Lama's mother took the child and hid him in the cleft of a rock before fleeing. When she returned the next morning, trembling for his safety, she found a raven protecting the little boy. This, it was later understood, was Mahakala in earthly form. To commemorate the episode, the protector is often shown in *thangkas* and sculpture with a raven's head.

The result of the divination showed that the protectors were of the firm opinion that no such concession should be made to the Chinese, and an order countermanding the original directive was immediately sent to the government's negotiators in Delhi. It came too late, however. The Chinese were already pressing for a date for formal negotiations to begin in Beijing. Chairman Mao was determined that Tibet should come into the fold, and to be seen to come into the fold voluntarily rather than be forced to accept terms. But he had made it abundantly clear that if Tibet did not come willingly, he was prepared to order the PLA to move on Lhasa.

The Tibetan negotiators understood that the only hope for Tibet was full-throated support from any one of either the Republic of India, Great Britain, or the United States—and preferably from all three. But the Indian government of Jawaharlal Nehru was determined not to be drawn into a conflict which it had neither the resources nor the will to prosecute. Rather, Nehru dreamed of a new world order in which both China and India could participate on an equal footing with Britain, America, Russia, and the great powers of Europe.

The British, for their part, made clear that they did not wish to become involved and merely reiterated their policy of recognizing Chinese "suzerainty" over Tibet—though without ever defining precisely what they meant by the term.

As for the United States, it had begun to take an interest in Tibet, seeing there an opportunity for opposing the spread of communism in the East. Overt support was not in question, however, and even America said that it would not back the appeal that the Tibetans, acting on the secret advice of the Indian political officer resident in Lhasa (no longer Richardson), now sought to have heard by the United Nations.

In the meantime, following the divination in the Mahakala chapel, the Tibetan government held a further audience with the deities, this time consulting the Nechung and Gadong oracles for their advice on what action should now be taken. At first the deities were less than forthcoming. Nechung said only, "If you don't make good offerings, I cannot protect religion and the welfare of the people." The Gadong oracle likewise said nothing of consequence. Exasperated, one of the ministers in attendance pleaded with Nechung: "While we [humans] are dull and stupid, you are the one who has brilliant wisdom and knowledge of things. You also have the special responsibility for Buddhism in general and Tibet in particular. You should not be behaving like an ordinary human being, so give us a proper prophecy."

At this, the medium (still in a trance) began dancing. When he came directly in front of the Dalai Lama, he prostrated himself three times and, with tears streaming down his face, proclaimed that power should at once be transferred to the Dalai Lama. Taktra Rinpoché now had no option other than to resign. All that remained was for an auspicious day for the formal handover ceremony to be chosen. The date settled on was November 17, 1950—a scant four months after the Precious Protector's fifteenth birthday.* From now on, all important decisions would be referred to him.

Yet if this was a moment of immense significance both to the Dalai Lama personally and to the history of these times, it was the Dalai Lama's adoption of the sacred bodhisattva vow at just this moment that was, from his own point of view, still more important. With this he pledged to serve others with every fiber of his being unceasingly until such time as they should all become enlightened. It is a commitment that he has often commemorated since by quoting the prayer of the revered eighth-century monk Shantideva:

For as long as space endures
And for as long as living beings remain,
Until then, may I too abide
To dispel the misery of the world.

A week after the Dalai Lama's assumption of temporal power, Tibet's appeal to the United Nations was heard. But given India's desire not to antagonize the Chinese, and given that both Britain and the United States were content to follow India's lead, it was inevitable that this would not amount to anything. For the Tibetans, there was nothing to do but accept the Chinese demand and send a delegation to Beijing, no matter what the Dalai Lama's or the deities' feelings on the matter might be.

The most pressing question to be answered now was whether the Dalai Lama should remain in Lhasa or leave. When the British invaded in 1904, the Great Thirteenth had fled north to Urgya. This time, however, the only plausible destination outside Tibet was Sikkim to the south, and perhaps from there into India. In 1950 Sikkim was still an independent state, ruled by a Tibetan prince, or Chögyal, with a predominantly Tibetan population. Again this question was not one that could be decided by earthly opinion alone, so the deities were consulted. Their verdict was that, for safety's sake, the Dalai

---

*The Dalai Lama thought of himself as sixteen, however. According to the Tibetan way of reckoning, sentience begins at conception and a child is a year old at birth.

Lama should quit the capital. It was decided, however, that rather than head straight into exile, he should take refuge in the village of Dromo (known locally as Yatung) on the Tibetan side of the border. There he could be in close proximity to Dungkhar, a monastery with which Taktra Rinpoché and the Dalai Lama's two tutors all had close connections. This was an early-sixteenth-century Gelugpa foundation and seat of a famous oracle. It was also home to a large number of hermits. These hermits would in some cases withdraw from the world until the end of their natural life and have themselves immured in their cells in the hills surrounding the monastery with only a small aperture, closed up by a brick, through which to receive food once daily.

The plan was for the Dalai Lama to quit Lhasa in secret, accompanied by his court and senior members of the government, while two *tsit tsab,* or chief ministers, appointed by the Precious Protector would remain behind in Lhasa to deal with the Chinese as and when they arrived. It was, however, clear to the local populace that something significant was afoot because of the number of heavily laden mules seen leaving the Potala. These carried the contents of the Dalai Lama's treasury, which the Chögyal had kindly agreed to keep in his strong rooms until the crisis was resolved.

According to Harrer, outwardly life in Lhasa "followed its normal course." But inwardly people were terrified. Despite the stories that had begun to circulate of heroic actions by individual soldiers, it was well understood that the army at Chamdo had been routed. And people had a keen memory of the plunder and arson of the last Chinese army to descend on the holy city when it had chased the Great Thirteenth out four decades earlier.

It was therefore a considerable surprise when it became apparent that the People's Liberation Army was showing exemplary restraint in Chamdo. Prisoners were well treated, rations were paid for, and, crucially, respect was being shown to the *sangha.* Not only had there been no looting, but also the soldiers were treating the local population in Chamdo with courtesy. Clearly they were obeying their orders to the letter: "You are not allowed to propagandize against superstition . . . [W]hen visiting monasteries, you should make contact first. And when you go on a visit, you are not allowed to touch the images. Also you should not spit or fart in the vicinity of the monastery."

It is often forgotten that in its early days, the leadership of the Chinese Communist Party genuinely believed it possible to bring about a more just and equitable society for all peoples by putting into practice Karl Marx's political philosophy. Liberation was not just about China securing its borders but about sharing the benefits of revolution. This entailed the abolition of feudalism and, with this, the implementation of true justice. As in China, so it would be in Tibet: the land would be taken from the hands of the aristocracy, the monasteries, and the gentry and distributed among the people. No longer would one small group of individuals lord it over a vastly larger group purely on account of an accident of birth.

Of course, Tibetans saw matters quite differently. They understood well enough that theirs was a backward country. Doubtless there was a minority that would have welcomed the overthrow of the feudal system. But for the majority, what Marxist theory understood to be a socioeconomic system was simply the Tibetan way of life. Whether your position in life was high or low, it reflected the karma accumulated during former lives. If you were treated harshly by your landlord, you could at least be certain that he would suffer in a future life. The way to mitigate your own suffering was through spiritual practice and the accumulation of merit. For the majority, therefore, all talk of reform was met with outright hostility. For now, however, Mao let it be known that there was no question of actually implementing change before the Tibetans were ready for it.

The sincerity of this reassuring pledge was sharply contradicted by the Dalai Lama's eldest brother, who made a sudden appearance in the capital just before the Precious Protector left for the south. Following his election as abbot of Kumbum Monastery a year earlier, Taktser Rinpoché had observed at first hand the behavior of the Communists in Amdo. It had quickly become apparent that, whatever the Communists might say about leaving people free to practice their faith, the reality was quite different. He had found himself dogged by a pair of party officials delegated to accompany him everywhere and harangue him at every turn: the monks of Kumbum must be integrated into the labor force; the practice of using butter to fuel the thousands of lamps should cease at once. Why were the monasteries' resources frittered away on incense and silk offering scarves? And when had prayer "ever filled a man's belly"? Did he not have to admit that religion stood in the way of progress?

It did not take the Rinpoché long to conclude that he could better serve his people by resigning the abbacy and using his position as brother of the Dalai Lama to try to win support for Tibet among the countries of the free world. In the meantime, he advised the Precious Protector to go into exile without delay. The Communists would show their true colors before long, and it was essential that the Dalai Lama be out of harm's way. They had even suggested that he, Taktser Rinpoché, should kill the Dalai Lama if he showed signs of resisting Tibet's liberation! With these shocking words, the Dalai Lama's eldest brother left Lhasa for Dromo accompanied by their mother.

Following a few days later, the newly enthroned leader made it his business to talk to as many ordinary people as he could. Passing himself off as a young official, the Dalai Lama succeeded in having a number of eye-opening conversations. Because he was a member of a large caravan, there was no danger to his person, but for ordinary people, traveling in Tibet was fraught with danger, not just from the elements, which might at any moment unleash their fury, but from bandits who would often attack smaller parties. These conversations, he noted later, gave him further insight into the "petty injustices of life suffered by my people," and he "resolved as soon as [he] could to set about making changes to help them."

If the Dalai Lama himself found reasons to be grateful for this unsought departure from his capital, many of those whom his traveling party encountered en route were distraught. On one occasion they passed by a large group of young monks. The Dalai Lama, dressed in layman's clothes, went unnoticed, but his tutors following behind were besieged. As Trijang Rinpoché recalled: "It was heartbreaking . . . The monks surrounded us on all sides, throwing scarves and money left and right. Openly weeping, they held onto the reins of our horses and would not let us go."

The Precious Protector arrived at Dungkar Monastery on January 2, 1951. Dromo, lying some three hundred miles southwest of Lhasa and situated in the valley said by locals to be the most beautiful in all Tibet, was famous for its wildflowers and gurgling mountain streams—and for the bears that roamed its forests; many of the region's woodcutters were horribly disfigured from encounters with them. The Dalai Lama's stay there offered welcome respite from the tense atmosphere prevailing in Lhasa, and he quickly resumed his "usual routine of prayers, meditation, retreats and study." This included "retreats on single-deity Vajrabhairava, Eleven-Face Avalokiteśvara, and the inner practice of protector Kālarūpa," all of them meditation yogas* associated with the Diamond Path of Anuttara tantra, into which the Dalai Lama had recently been initiated.

According to its proponents, the Diamond Path originates with what is known as the Third Turning of the Wheel, which the Buddha is said to have enacted when he preached to an audience of bodhisattvas. Some say this occurred during his earthly ministry, others that it took place in one of the Buddha realms. It was not, however, until the eighth century that any historical evidence for the tradition begins to emerge. This takes the form of a body of esoteric literature emphasizing the individual practitioner's inward Buddha nature. Crudely put, the path to Enlightenment becomes primarily a matter of clearing away the accretions and obstructions of accumulated karma to reveal the already enlightened state in which, in fact, all sentient beings subsist.

With their emphasis on elaborate ritual and on highly structured meditative practices, the tantras are considered the most powerful weapons in the spiritual practitioner's armory. They are also the most controversial. Many —including the majority who follow the Theravada tradition—do not accept the tantras at all, arguing that they are pseudepigrapha: writings that falsely claim authority. Nonetheless, they are central to Buddhism in the Tibetan tradition and were by now part of the Dalai Lama's daily practice. They are held by their proponents to be a method of transmuting the mind in such a way as to realize the innate (already enlightened) Buddha mind that all beings have seeded within them—though it is also well understood that they should be taught only by appropriately qualified teachers, and then only to a minority of students. It is often said that tantra is akin to the kiss of a beautiful woman with teeth like the fangs of a snake.

* The word *yoga* means discipline. A *yogi* or *yogin* is one who engages in a given discipline or practice.

If the tantras are controversial within some Buddhist circles, another matter of controversy among Tibetans more generally also dates from this time at Dromo. It was here that the Dalai Lama formed a close connection with Dorje Shugden, the deity popularized by Phabongka Rinpoché during the time of the Great Thirteenth. At the deity's request (speaking through an oracle), the Precious Protector composed a prayer in his honor titled "Melody of the Unceasing Vajra." Structured as a classical "seven-limbed" invocation, the "Melody" pays homage, makes verbal offerings, confesses the supplicant's faults, rejoices, requests the deity to turn the wheel of the dharma, requests that the upholders of the dharma not pass into nirvana before all sentient beings pass beyond suffering, and ends, finally, with a dedication. As it turned out, in forming this connection with Dorje Shugden, the young Dalai Lama unwittingly implicated himself in a contest that was to explode violently more than four decades later.

In the meantime, the Dalai Lama's most pressing task was to respond to the Chinese demand that he send negotiators to Beijing to ratify an agreement for the "peaceful liberation of Tibet." It was finally decided that Ngabo, the former governor of Chamdo, together with a small delegation that included the Dalai Lama's brother-in-law, should proceed to the Chinese capital.

Arriving toward the end of April 1951, the Tibetans were met at the railway station by Zhou Enlai, Mao's second in command, amid great fanfare. The result of the ensuing negotiations over the future status of Tibet was, of course, a foregone conclusion. The Communists had already prepared the document they wanted the Tibetans to accept. In response, the Tibetans presented a list of points they wished to discuss with their counterparts. The first point they took issue with, against the Communists' claim, was the suggestion that the Dalai Lama was under the heel of foreign imperialists. Whatever the Chinese might suppose, there was no imperialist influence or power in Tibet. Harrer and Aufschnaiter were by now gone; Richardson was back in Scotland; Ford was a prisoner of the PLA; and Reginald Fox, also a radio operator, had gone with his Sikkimese wife to India.

The Chinese stood firm. It was made clear to the Tibetans, as one delegate expressed the matter, "that if they were so arrogant as to refuse to accept that Tibet was part of China, then they could all go back home any time they pleased."In that case, a single wireless message would be sent to the PLA and it would advance immediately on Lhasa. Responsibility for any loss of life that occurred would be on the Tibetans' shoulders and theirs alone.

Could the Tibetans have called the Communists' bluff? Perhaps. On the one hand, had they done so, there could have been no pretense that what followed was a "peaceful liberation." On the other hand, Mao had made clear that Tibet must be taken whatever the price in diplomatic terms, and Ngabo and the other members of the delegation were well aware of the fact. They concluded that they had no option but to accept. The Seventeen Point Agreement for the Peaceful Liberation of Tibet was signed and sealed* in the Great Hall of the People in Beijing on May 23, 1951.

Throughout the discussions leading up to the signing of the agreement (which many Tibetans maintain is no such thing because it was signed under duress), the Tibetan delegation was in radio contact with the Dalai Lama's court in Dromo, so the outcome cannot have come as a surprise to them. Yet in his autobiography the Dalai Lama recounts that the first he knew of the provisions of the seventeen points was when he listened to the Tibetan-language news broadcast on Chinese radio that evening. From this it is obvious that, as still only a fifteen-year-old boy, he was not informed of every detail of what was being said and done in his name. It is also a reminder that even in those most difficult days, the Dalai Lama's spiritual life took priority over his worldly responsibilities.†

The question that faced the Dalai Lama and his court now was whether they should return to Lhasa or cross over the border into Sikkim and from there to India. It was a relatively easy journey, a matter of a few days only. For the time being, there was no way the Chinese could prevent such a move. But

---

*When Ngabo objected that he had not brought the official government seal with him, the Chinese provided him with one of their own devising.

†I recall being astounded when, during one of our first meetings, the Dalai Lama told me that, as a rule, he devoted more than 80 percent of his time to spiritual matters, and less than a fifth to worldly matters. He confirmed this during an interview on April 2, 2019.

although the government of India had begun by saying that it would grant the Dalai Lama asylum if requested, by this time it was much less clear that he would be welcome on Indian soil.

To add to the young leader's dilemma, a meeting between his minister for foreign affairs and an American government official had yielded the information that if the Dalai Lama would publicly repudiate the Seventeen Point Agreement, the United States would be sympathetic to the idea of supplying armaments to oppose by force the Chinese occupation of Tibet.

While the representatives of the Three Seats present in Dromo were united in their wish to see the Dalai Lama return to Lhasa, many of the government's lay officials were of the view that he should seek exile, if not in India, then elsewhere. Both Sri Lanka (then Ceylon), because it was a Buddhist country, and America, because the Dalai Lama seemed likely to be welcome there, were discussed as possibilities. In his absence, once a suitable place in exile could be determined, a military campaign would be fought with such assistance as might be forthcoming from the United States and from the Chinese Nationalists in Taiwan, who had also indicated their interest.

Among supporters of this view were the recently laicized Taktser Rinpoché (known henceforth as Jigme Norbu) and the Dalai Lama's second-eldest brother, Gyalo Thondup, who had just returned from China to Tibet. Perhaps the most surprising advocate of armed struggle was, however, the Lord Chamberlain, Phala, recently appointed after Lobsang Samten's retirement on health grounds following a stress-induced breakdown.*

On the one hand, the Dalai Lama believed what his eldest brother told him about the Chinese in Amdo and could see the imminent fulfillment of his predecessor the Great Thirteenth's prophecy. On the other hand, he was mindful of China's proximity and vast superiority in terms of numbers and military might, no matter that, as Gyalo Thondup later wrote, "the US [seemed] so great and powerful that it could make almost anything happen." Without firmer assurances of help from outside, the Precious Protector concluded that he had better return to Lhasa. The deities concurred, though to the consternation of many who felt certain that for the Dalai Lama to return

---

*According to Harrer, he suffered a heart attack.

to Lhasa would be to walk straight into a trap. Appalled, one minister even demanded to see inside the second dough ball used in the divination to ensure that it didn't have the same answer written inside.

It remained only for the Precious Protector to meet with General Zhang Zhinwu, Mao's personal emissary, who arrived in Dromo shortly afterward. In his autobiography the Dalai Lama describes watching the general and two aides-de-camp approach the monastery through his binoculars: "three men in drab grey suits." Their meeting was, he notes, "coldly civil."

11

Into the Dragon's Lair: The Dalai Lama in China, July 1954–July 1955

Just before his departure from Dromo, the Dalai Lama received a secret letter from Heinrich Harrer. The Austrian had been in contact with the American embassy in Delhi. The United States government had confirmed that it wished to assist the Dalai Lama, and Harrer urged his young friend to abscond to India. This, he suggested, might be done by adopting any one of three possible stratagems. The Dalai Lama could choose a small group and leave unannounced at night; Harrer himself could come to Dromo in disguise to escort him; the third alternative was to rendezvous at a designated spot where a light aircraft would pick him up. But although they were given due consideration, none of Harrer's proposals was adopted. This assurance of American support was welcome, but too much was uncertain and there was little concrete to go on. The Dalai Lama thus departed Dromo for Lhasa on July 22, 1951.

En route to the capital, the Precious Protector stopped several times to give teachings. When, at one of these, the *vajra* (a ritual hand implement symbolizing the irresistible force of a thunderbolt) that he was holding slipped from his fingers and fell into the folds of Ling Rinpoché's robes, "many present remarked that this was an extraordinary thing to happen and were convinced that it was a very auspicious sign," he later recalled. It demonstrated clearly the depth of the link between *guru* and *chela,* between teacher and pupil. And in the light of this happy event, there can be little doubt that all were convinced the decision not to go into exile had been the right one.

The Dalai Lama returned home to an emotional welcome. Only the presence of the PLA's General Zhang and his staff marred the occasion. When, however, an advance guard of six hundred Chinese troops arrived two weeks later, people began to grow seriously alarmed. A rumor flew around that the soldiers wearing gauze face masks, of which there were a number, were human flesh eaters. The subsequent arrival of the main body of troops—more than seven thousand—precipitated a complete collapse of morale. There could no longer be any doubt that Tibet was lost. Almost overnight the population of the capital increased by 50 percent, though no provision had been made for them. Also, while the soldiers camped outside the city, many of the senior ranks, together with party officials, demanded rooms and offices within Lhasa itself. At once the price of both food and accommodation rocketed, to the grievous discomfort of the poor—though to the private satisfaction of the aristocracy, who were quick to seize the opportunity for profit. By releasing small quantities of grain at a time, local landowners, who had ample supplies (grain kept for many years in the Tibetan climate), were able to ensure that prices remained high. The Chinese were nonetheless "incredibly over-generous," according to the resident Indian mission officer, and, paying in silver with dayan (the old Nationalist currency), "in a short time . . . spent prodigal sums."

To be fair to them, the Chinese were well aware of the need not to overburden the populace and immediately began planting underutilized land outside Lhasa. But if this was in itself objectionable to Lhasans, what made it vastly more so was the use of "nightsoil"—human feces—to fertilize the crop. To the Tibetans, this was an abomination.

The first concern of the Chinese was to build a garrison for their army and, at the same time, to establish a supply chain that would enable it to be provisioned with men and matériel from army headquarters in southwestern China. This required a road link to Chengdu, work on which began at once.

As for governance, Tibet's new masters were content to allow the Tibetan National Assembly to continue to function. With regard to the Dalai Lama, he would continue to be recognized as head of state. But, understanding that his chief responsibility was to continue his education and deepen his spiritual practice, the Precious Protector himself played little direct part in the drama unfolding beneath the steep walls of the Potala.

Another communication addressed to the Dalai Lama personally and sent indirectly from the US embassy in India declared that America was "willing to help Tibet now" and would welcome a public repudiation of the Seventeen Point Agreement, in which case it would support an appeal to the United Nations and both assist with any application for asylum and help arm a resistance movement. But while this was taken as evidence of America's continued goodwill, the offer was not acted on. From his own perspective, if he was to lead his people, the Dalai Lama must first earn their respect in his capacity as a lama, and the best place for him to do that was in Tibet. To this end, rather than immersing himself in any kind of political resistance to the Chinese, he requested instead that his senior tutor initiate him into the mysteries of the Kalachakra, considered by many to be the most powerful of all the tantras. This required that Ling Rinpoché undertake a qualifying retreat during the winter in preparation for conferral during the forthcoming New Year of the Water Dragon (1952).

The Dalai Lama's political role was in the meantime delegated to the two *tsit tsab* he had appointed the previous year. This did not prove a very satisfactory arrangement. As one aristocrat recalled many years later, the two chief ministers "refused to respond positively to the Chinese" no matter what the circumstances and instead invariably "challenged and confronted them in an angry and adversarial manner." For several months, General Zhang put up with this, mindful that his main responsibility was to "make harmonious relations and eliminate hatred between nationalities." But the formation of a grassroots opposition movement, the Tibetan People's Association (TPA), which began to demonstrate publicly against the Chinese presence, meant it was only a matter of time before the general lost patience. When he finally did so, it was for the surprising reason that the two *tsit tsab* had taken the side of the TPA against the Tibetan government. If there was one thing still less pleasing than the presence of the Chinese to most of the aristocracy, it was expressions of dissent against themselves by the masses. The TPA's demonstrations amounted to a repudiation of the government's policy of appeasement and (profitable) collaboration with the Chinese. Moreover, to the aristocracy, the TPA's agitation seemed guaranteed to provoke the Chinese, to say nothing of the danger of harm to their own interests. For its part, the main concern of the TPA itself was the likely injury to religion if the Chinese remained. Yet paradoxically, it did not have the support of the monasteries, which were also nervous about antagonizing the Chinese. When, therefore, an angry General Zhang demanded that the *tsit tsab* be dismissed and the TPA proscribed, the two chief ministers had no one to speak for them.

In this, the first decisive moment of his career as political leader, the Dalai Lama chose not to back his two ministers, even though he had appointed them, and even though they stood clearly on the side of the people. Instead, he reluctantly accepted their resignation. Although Tibetan history has its share of warrior leaders, the tradition expects the Dalai Lama to be a spiritual, not an earthly, hero, and his acquiescence in the Chinese demand is early evidence of the Dalai Lama's understanding that his political vocation was to be a keeper of the peace and a seeker of dialogue rather than one who confronts and faces down an overwhelmingly superior foe. One consequence of this acquiescence was, however, that the hundred or so members of the Tibetan People's Association were sent for "reeducation."

Another difficulty the young leader faced at this time was how to manage relations with Tashilhunpo Monastery and the young Panchen Lama. Following the death in 1937 of the Ninth Panchen Lama, still in exile from his headquarters at Tashilhunpo, two rival candidates had emerged. Just as was the case when the Panchen Lama was consulted during the search for the Dalai Lama, so tradition held that the Dalai Lama be consulted during the selection of the new Panchen Lama. In this instance the Dalai Lama was too young to play a meaningful role in the procedure, so it was the regent who had taken it on. Given residual tensions between the two sees (in the original sense of the word "see," meaning a seat of authority), it was perhaps inevitable that they should opt for different candidates. One consequence of this was to bind Tashilhunpo more firmly first to the Chinese Nationalists, to whom it turned for support against the Ganden Phodrang (the Dalai Lama's government), and then to the Communists. When Mao came to power, the young Tashilhunpo-approved candidate sent a congratulatory telegram praising the Communists for completing the "grand salvation of the country and the people"—or, rather, his closest advisers did. He himself was only eleven years old at the time. When the Chinese came to Lhasa, they thus had a powerful ally whose own followers could be relied on to support them against the Dalai Lama. It was therefore incumbent on the Dalai Lama to forge a new relationship with Tashilhunpo. But when the young Panchen Lama was brought to Lhasa in 1952, it was clear that whatever good personal qualities he may have had, the Chinese were unwilling to allow him to develop any sort of friendship with the Dalai Lama.

Meanwhile, the inflation that had beset the Lhasa economy eased later that year when the PLA's first crop was harvested, and an atmosphere of uneasy peace took hold. This was helped by the fact that, although some in the Communist Party leadership were impatient to begin implementing socialism in Tibet, Chairman Mao continued to insist on gradual integration. He was encouraged in this by General Zhang's early assessment of the Tibetan religious hierarchy. Zhang believed that the Panchen Lama definitely remained favorable to Beijing, while the "Dalai Lama belongs to the middle but may possibly turn left."

One of the things that may have encouraged Zhang in this view was the creation by the Dalai Lama of a Reform Bureau within the nominally still functioning Tibetan government. This office called for a series of reforms that sought, on the one hand, to bring about genuine improvement in the lives of ordinary people and, on the other, to preempt the Communists' program. Among other initiatives, these reforms required that all civil servants, whether lay or monastic, become paid employees of the government. This was intended to put a stop to the graft—the bribery, extortion, and selling of favors—by means of which those in public office had, in place of any salary, traditionally looked after their own interests. Another initiative of the bureau was a program of land reform, which called for the voluntary distribution among the landless of some of the aristocracy's manorial possessions. If the introduction of salaries was not universally welcomed, this proposal was even more unpopular. The aristocrats protested that "if you take away the pastures, you lose the flowers too"—the flowers being the taxes and interest that the government itself received from these holdings. Events soon overtook the work of the bureau, but its very existence shows that from the beginning, the Dalai Lama saw no contradiction between his religious faith and social and economic reform.

In the meantime, the Precious Protector's eldest brother, Jigme Norbu (formerly Taktser Rinpoché, abbot of Kumbum), had arrived in the United States and made contact with officials from the State Department. The Dalai Lama, communicating with him via letter carried by trusted intermediaries to India, and from there to America, instructed him to hold off on requesting direct support for the time being. From the Precious Protector's point of view, following his initiation into the Kalachakra tantra earlier in the year, the most important thing for him to do was to master it.

In the decades since, the Dalai Lama has made the rites of the Kalachakra tantra a central feature of his public ministry and, at the time of writing, has conferred it thirty-four times, many in the West. As he explains it, the tantra is a powerful support to the cause of world peace. Involving the creation of an astonishingly intricate mandala using individual grains of colored sand (a mandala is a two-dimensional symbolic representation of some aspect of the world, in this case the palace of Kalachakra, Lord of Time), the tantra includes elaborate rituals, accompanied by complex hand movements known as *mudras,* during which initiates visualize themselves in a variety of different settings, culminating in entry to the palace. By way of preliminaries, participants meditate on the miseries of samsara—the otherwise endless series of births and deaths to which all beings are bound until they become enlightened—recognizing it for what it is: "an ocean fraught with frightful sea monsters . . . the crocodiles of birth, ageing and death."

With regard to the visualizations, these are, again, directed toward familiarizing the mind with particular mental states. One of them involves imagining oneself being born as a child and entering the body of Kalachakra through his mouth. Once inside, the practitioner melts in a single drop of *bodhichitta* (the aspiration to seek liberation for all sentient beings) and descends through the deity's body via its energy centers, before exiting via the tip of his erect penis and entering, through the "lotus" of her vagina, the womb of Kalachakra's sexual consort, Vishvamata. If this were not startling enough, we discover that the Kalachakra texts also give detailed information about building trebuchets —a kind of oversized catapult, used as a siege engine in medieval times—and flamethrowers. It turns out that an important aspect of the tantra is that it is held to have been taught initially to the king of Shambala, a hidden land from which, at the end of our present era, he will lead an invincible army in airborne ships to defeat the barbarians who have taken over the world.

As the Dalai Lama is now at pains to stress, these martial aspects of the tantra are to be understood symbolically, not literally. The real enemy is not the barbarian horde but the ignorance that gives rise to the afflictive emotions of anger, greed, strife, and so forth.* It is nevertheless clearly more than a coincidence that the Dalai Lama's focus at this time was on a set of practices the character of which is both apocalyptic and concerned with deliverance from evil.

Likewise, it cannot be mere coincidence that, during the winter of 1952, Trijang Rinpoché was to be found again restoring a number of *thangkas* depicting the protectors. It might be that the collective karma of Tibetans was such that the protector deities had been unable to keep the Chinese at bay, but it did not follow that the deities should be abandoned. On the contrary, they must be encouraged to redouble their efforts on behalf of the people.

The Chinese, having by this time completed the garrisoning of their troops in a new barrack complex in Lhasa, turned their attention to building the infrastructure for their future administration of Tibet. This included a new hospital and a school open to all. There were also party initiatives aimed at recruiting cadres to work for the implementation of socialism. Not everything the Chinese did in this regard was unpopular. As Lobsang Samten's future wife recalled: "When we passed fourteen, we became members of the Youth Organisation. Actually although our parents were not very keen, many of us were really enthusiastic for this new order of things . . . [W]e did a lot of good work,

---

*Remarkably, although the texts do not specify precisely who these symbolic barbarians are, it is clear from the fact that their religion is founded in a place called Mecca, their men circumcised, and their women veiled that it is Islam that the tantra has in mind. The first textual evidence of the Kalachakra tantra dates from the tenth century—a time when Buddhist northern India was being invaded by Muslims.

social work, planting trees, cleaning the main street outside our school. It was fun too, there were lots of social gatherings and dances. We enjoyed the freedom . . . a freedom we'd never had before the Chinese came." It was, however, mainly the aristocrats, and particularly the children of the aristocracy, who benefited from these innovations. They were the ones who could afford to patronize the teashops and restaurants that sprang up to cater to the Chinese. And they were the ones who had previously been most constrained by social convention. The Precious Protector was, of course, removed from all such activities. In effect, he was now little more than a figurehead whose official role in government was occasionally to dignify meetings with his presence. This does not mean that he was not keenly interested in every development, but his primary focus remained his education.

An important milestone in the Dalai Lama's life occurred during the New Year festival of 1954, when, now eighteen, he received full ordination as a priest, or *bikshu,* at which point he accepted the full 253 precepts of monkhood.* His ordination was itself preliminary to the Dalai Lama's first conferral of the Kalachakra initiation, to an audience said to have been a hundred thousand strong, in the grounds of the Norbulingka. Such a figure sounds implausibly high, but we can be confident that it would have been in the tens of thousands. The initiation, with its evocation of a world on the brink of destruction, was a dramatic event on many levels, not least that it occurred in the context of discussions over whether or not he should accept an invitation to travel to Beijing. Chairman Mao wanted the Dalai Lama to attend the inaugural meeting of the National People's Congress that autumn. This was to mark the formal adoption of China's new constitution. The Three Seats and the majority of senior government officials were vehemently opposed, while only a few—including Ngabo—were in favor. There were many concerns, not least the proposed methods of transport. The plan was to go via road, rail, and air, none of which appealed to his advisers—least of all the flying component. As one official explained to his Chinese counterpart: "The aeroplane is linked neither to the heavens, nor does it touch the earth . . . [W]e cannot risk it."

* In contrast, nuns maintain a whopping 364.

There was also serious concern that, having gone to China, the Precious Protector might not be permitted to return. This had happened to an earlier incarnation of Chenresig, who was more or less held hostage by Kublai Khan.* More pressing still was the perceived risk that the Dalai Lama, being young and impressionable, might have his head turned. Given his enthusiasm both for the Reform Bureau and for all things mechanical, this seemed eminently possible. In the event, however, the Dalai Lama, having consulted the great protector Mahakala, declared that he would go in spite of the objections expressed not only by Tibetan officialdom but also by a resurgent Tibetan People's Association.

It turned out that the airplane journey should have been the least of anyone's worries. Much more dangerous was the section where the road ran out and the travelers were forced to walk. Trijang Rinpoché wrote in his autobiography: "We were terrified of the possibility of boulders hurtling down on us in landslides, or of [ourselves] falling thousands of feet into deep gorges [as we made] our way falteringly across makeshift wooden bridges built over torrents swollen by the heavy rains, their spray filling the air."

With the Chinese in charge of the arrangements, the Tibetans were compelled to accept a very different alternative to the elaborate manner of traveling to which they were accustomed. In between settlements, they slept in "shabby tents" and were required to share the PLA's mess arrangements. The Dalai Lama was somewhat aghast at being offered a spittle-smeared mug of tea by a soldier, though, being thirsty, he noticed its condition only after drinking from it. The whole experience was humbling, and yet, as Trijang Rinpoché remarked in connection with a tantric practice that speaks of "Brahmins, outcasts and pigs all sharing without division," they treated the experience as "an observance of pious practice."

On his arrival in Chamdo, on August 19, the Dalai Lama was welcomed by

---

*This was Phagpa Lodro Gyaltsen (1235–1280), who became Imperial Preceptor for Tibet in the court of the Yuan emperor Kublai Khan, a fact that supplies one of the arguments the Chinese government makes in connection with Tibet's claimed status as a vassal state since the thirteenth century.

a large crowd of local Tibetans and two Czech nationals,* one a photographer, the other a journalist. Having been carefully briefed by their Chinese minders—not to wear anything made of metal, not to cross his shadow, not to get too close—they were surprised by the Dalai Lama's informality and approachability. When they began taking photographs of him, the Precious Protector instructed his own photographer to take photographs of them. Subsequently, he suspended a prayer ceremony in order that the Westerner might be able to take up the optimum position for his shot.

When the Dalai Lama finally took to the skies for one leg of the journey, in the Chinese premier's private aircraft, he was not much impressed, remarking, "The craft in which we flew was very old and even I could tell it had seen better days."

Completing the last leg by train in the company of the Panchen Lama and his entourage, the Dalai Lama was met on arrival in Beijing by Zhou Enlai, second in the Communist Party hierarchy after Mao Zedong, and Zhu De, head of the PLA. The Tibetans were then taken to a house previously owned by the Japanese mission, a sizable three-story mansion, the top floor of which was given over to the Dalai Lama and his two tutors, while his family occupied the remainder. Among these were his mother, his eldest sister and her husband (who was head of the Precious Protector's bodyguard), Lobsang Samten, their younger sister, and their six-year-old youngest brother, Ngari Rinpoché.

Almost at once the Tibetans were plunged into a program that was to occupy them often from early morning until late at night. The very next day there was a welcoming banquet in Zhongnanhai's great Pavilion of Purple Light; then, according to the Dalai Lama's mother, the day after that, "with no rest," they were "required to attend" a political meeting.

Presumably because he wanted to create a sense of anticipation, Mao did not schedule a meeting with the Dalai Lama until the following week. In the meantime, everything was done to reassure the young leader that China was the future and that future was bright. A major role in this was played by a

---

*These were Josef Kolmas and Jan Vanis. The story is from Vanis, via his nephew, also Jan, who kindly shared with me the transcript of his uncle's recollection.

young Khampa by the name of Phuntsog (pronounced something like "Pun-sock," where the *u* is as in "put") Wangyal, but generally referred to as Phun-wang (similarly pronounced "Punwang").* Originally from Batang, where the Catholic missionaries were murdered, Phunwang had attended a Chinese school, which by that time was one of several foreign establishments in the town, including a revived Catholic mission school and an American mission school and orphanage (each of which continued in existence right up until the Communists came to power). His best friend was a student at the American mission school, and through him, Phunwang came under the influence of the missionaries, whose ideals of brotherly love made a lasting impression on him.

While still a teenager, Phunwang began reading works by Lenin and Mao and became a founding member of the Tibetan Communist Revolutionary Group. As with many revolutionaries, a major spur to Phunwang's political zeal was the hypocrisy he witnessed around him. He once saw a young woman being viciously beaten by a monk. Her crime was to have brewed beer for the monastery. Seizing the whip, Phunwang demanded to know why the monks who drank the beer were not being punished instead. On another occasion, he was disgusted to see a number of freshly severed human ears nailed to the gates of a local magistrate's headquarters.

Phunwang also deplored the burden on the common people of the corvée system. This was the rule that officials on government duty could commandeer transport, fodder, food, and accommodation. While some aristocrats were open to the idea of change, most were, he wrote later, "elegantly dressed, sophisticated socially, completely out of touch with the ordinary people, ripe for revolution."

A major component of Phunwang's thinking was the notion that Khampas must set aside their traditional hostility to central Tibet and recognize that, ethnically, they were the same. But while many were sympathetic to the

*It is common practice for family and friends to abbreviate names to the first syllable (though in fact any combination of syllables can be used) of the two given names. Aside from aristocratic or otherwise well-known families and some lamas, it is unusual for Tibetans to have or to use surnames, or family names.

idea of throwing off the Chinese yoke, and some even saw the need for social reform, the thought of making common cause with the central Tibetan government was anathema to most, who took the view that the Chinese were better masters than their own central government. As he recalled in his autobiography, the Tibetan government exerted high taxes and flogged "anyone who couldn't pay." while, although "the Chinese acted as our lords . . . they didn't steal things from the people." He did not confine his hostility to the ruling class of his own government, however. He was even more horrified at the treatment inflicted by the Chinese Nationalist soldiery, recounting with distaste one occasion when they "tied a prisoner to a wooden post in the centre of their garrison's courtyard and systematically began to stab him with their bayonets. When their victim's screams became too distressing, they gagged him. They stabbed him everywhere, but not too deeply, because the idea was to allow each of the hundreds of Chinese soldiers to wet his bayonet with the blood of a living enemy. This, they believed, would bring them luck."

By the time of the Dalai Lama's visit, Phunwang was a trusted member of the Communist Party and self-evidently the ideal liaison officer. It was he who accompanied the Precious Protector to each of his meetings with Mao and he who interpreted between them. As events would prove, Phunwang was disastrously naïve about the Communists, yet it is important to acknowledge the genuineness of his idealism—which appealed enormously to his young charge.

When the Dalai Lama finally met the Great Helmsman, as Mao was also known, the Chinese leader "did not," in the estimation of Phunwang, "act like the great leader he was, but spoke informally, [as if to] a friend." For his part, the Dalai Lama "spoke well, without any nervousness." The conversation lasted around an hour, with Mao doing much of the talking. When it was over, the Chinese leader escorted the Dalai Lama to his car and opened the door for him. "Your coming to Beijing was like coming back to your own home," said Mao, shaking the Dalai Lama's hand. "Whenever you come to Beijing, you can call me. You can come to my place whenever you want to. Don't be shy." The meeting was a splendid success. The Dalai Lama, thrilled to meet the man he had heard so much about, could hardly contain his delight. "He was so excited," Phunwang recalled, that "he hugged me," exclaiming: "Phunwang-la,* today things went very well. Mao is a great person who is unlike others."

The party leadership could hardly have dared hope for such an outcome, and when the Dalai Lama applied to join the Communist Party, it must have seemed that the ultimate prize was within its grasp. (In the end, though, nothing came of his request.)

A week later, the Chinese were given further encouragement in their thinking that the Dalai Lama might become an ally. At a speech to the first National People's Congress, on September 16, 1954, the Precious Protector announced that "one of the main fabrications of the enemy for sowing discord is that the Communist Party and the People's Government destroy religion . . . But these pernicious rumours . . . have been utterly exploded. The Tibetan people have learned from their own experience that they have freedom of religious belief." This is a startling statement. It is true that freedom of religious belief was enshrined in the new constitution. It is also certain that Phunwang would have had a hand in writing this speech. But did it represent the Dalai Lama's honest opinion?

It was now four years since his elder brother had resigned the abbacy of Kumbum Monastery, yet the Tibetan leader could hardly have forgotten Jigme Norbu's account of Chinese heavy-handedness. He had by this time also heard reports of similar behavior elsewhere in Kham and Amdo. In a speech made during the 1990s, the Dalai Lama admitted that "when dealing with the Chinese, you have no choice but to be conciliatory . . . On those occasions when I met Mao Zedong, I flattered him a little." It seems possible, therefore, that the Dalai Lama was calculating that his best hope of keeping religion safe was to amplify Mao's words, and so hold him to them. It seems that both men had similar opinions of each other as key players in their respective domains. Mao saw the Dalai Lama as crucial to winning over the Tibetans. The Dalai Lama, having seen how Mao was regarded by his deputies, understood that his strategy should be to develop a strong personal relationship with the Chinese leader.

---

*The suffix *–la* (correctly *lags*) denotes an honorific. It is used as a mark of respect: the Dalai Lama does not place himself above such considerations.

In the days following, the Tibetan leader, though not accepted as a full member of the party, was appointed a deputy chairman of the Standing Committee of the National People's Congress. This was a wordy title for a position that carried neither weight nor responsibility, but it did show that the Dalai Lama had won approval from the party leadership. A week later, Chairman Mao made an unexpected announcement. In place of the planned Military-Administrative Committee that was intended to manage the transition between the "liberation" of Tibet and the full implementation of socialism, the party would create a new Tibet Autonomous Region (TAR) with the Dalai Lama as its chairman and the Panchen Lama as his deputy. This was a pleasant surprise to the Tibetans. The word "autonomous" was extremely heartening, even though it soon became clear that the proposed TAR would not include Kham or Amdo. Nevertheless, with strong support from the Dalai Lama, the proposal was officially accepted by the Tibetan delegation.

In between the formal engagements at which affairs of state were discussed, the Dalai Lama and his entourage were frequently invited to evening entertainments. On one occasion he attended a performance of the Chinese state opera. There were also dance parties in the evening, which occasionally he and the Panchen Lama attended. At these it was common for girls from the state dance troupe to go up to guests and invite them to dance. Though Mao himself was an avid consumer of lissome females, and though Zhou is known also to have taken mistresses from among the dancers, the Chinese premier gave strict instructions "not to let the lamas dance even if they wanted to."

These parties were not wholly wasted on the Precious Protector. He was, wrote Phunwang, "extremely alert, and he liked to observe people and size them up. He noticed right away that Zhou was a very good dancer and told me that the way Zhou danced made him appear youthful . . . By contrast when Mao and Zhu De danced, they showed their age."

Phunwang was similarly observant. "Meeting often with the Dalai Lama made me realise that he was not in good physical condition. In fact," he wrote, "it worried me enough that I suggested he start doing exercises to radio music every morning." Phunwang was also surprised to learn from the Dalai Lama of the spartan nature of his life and concluded that the food he ate was considerably inferior to that enjoyed by most aristocrats in Lhasa.

Another of Phunwang's observations was that the Precious Protector was not an enthusiastic small talker. Such conversation he declared to be "silly. Wasteful." Yet on the subject of socialism for Tibet, he was "extremely interested, and asked many questions." Tibet was, "he openly agreed, backward and had to be reformed. Without reforms, he said, there was no hope for Tibetans to progress."

Early the following year, the new arrangements regarding the administration of Tibet were signed into law and the political component of the visit was concluded. The remainder of the Dalai Lama's sojourn in China was to be spent on the road, as both he and the Panchen Lama were taken on (largely separate) tours of the country. Some remarkable film footage survives. There are vignettes of the Precious Protector, well wrapped up in a smart overcoat, visiting a steelworks. We see him waving to crowds from a jeep. There is a moment when, saying good-bye at a train station, the Panchen Lama suddenly remembers his manners and, removing his hat to touch foreheads, gives his senior a cheeky grin. The two had been kept largely apart by their respective (Tibetan) courts, and while officially relations between them were cordial at best, a glimpse of warmth is evident.

The tour itself was a partial success. The Dalai Lama showed himself "eager to learn about all aspects of Communism," wrote Phunwang. But his friends and family were less so. The tour was highly regimented. "From morning till evening there was some programme," his mother recalled. "On some days we had to get up at four in the morning, and we would not return until seven in the evening." At the beginning of every meal a bell would sound, and when it was over, the bell would ring again. In the industrial centers, they found the cities "clogged with pollution and smoke," while, apart from in Shanghai, where "traces of the old gaiety" could still be seen, "the uniformity" of the blue shirts and trousers and blue serge hats of the people they met depressed the Tibetans. They themselves still wore the dazzling silks that were now made only for the export market. But more than anything else, they were struck by the poverty of the peasantry in the countryside, where, for lack of livestock, ploughs were yoked to human beings.

According to one young Tibetan official, it was clear that the Dalai Lama and his party were "never taken to any place that would give us adverse opinions." Furthermore, the Communists habitually claimed more than was their due for the improvements they showed to their guests. "Our guides [said] that all the machinery in the plants had been manufactured by the Chinese themselves," and since most of the Tibetans present could not read English, they didn't doubt it. "However," as the British-educated official wrote later, "I could plainly read the words, 'made in U.K.' or 'made in U.S.A.' on most of the machinery . . . We had a good laugh about Chinese attempts to fool us."

None of this is to say that the Tibetans were wholly unimpressed by what they saw in China. Many of the lay contingent could recognize the advantages of modern transport. Nor were they unappreciative of the efforts to ensure their material comfort. Most were delighted with the food —though not Ling Rinpoché, who preferred to rely on the bag of *tsampa* he carried with him everywhere. Nonetheless, all were mightily relieved when it was announced that they would be returning to Tibet following a modest celebration of Losar, the Tibetan New Year, in Beijing.

At a banquet the Dalai Lama hosted to mark the event, the Chinese leader again impressed the Precious Protector with his charm. Picking up morsels with his own chopsticks, Mao even shared food from his plate—to the horror of the Dalai Lama, who was all too aware of the Great Helmsman's stinking breath and rotten teeth. A slightly sour note was struck when the Dalai Lama explained to Mao that it was customary to toss a pinch of *tsampa* in the air as an offering to the gods. The Communist leader did so, but then threw a second pinch to the ground, "with a mischievous expression" on his face. This bad impression was drastically reinforced when Mao escorted the Dalai Lama to his car. Having asked the Tibetan leader whether there was anyone in Lhasa who could send a telegram, and having spoken of the need for continual direct contact with him, he praised the Dalai Lama for his scientific cast of mind, adding conspiratorially that, really, "religion is poison." It was at that moment when the young leader realized that Mao had completely misjudged him. He had mistaken the Dalai Lama's scientific turn of mind for skepticism about spiritual matters. For his part, the Dalai Lama had wanted to believe Mao when he said that religion had nothing to fear from communism. Now he saw that the Chinese leader was "the destroyer of the Dharma after all."

12

The Land of the Gods: India, November 1956–March 1957

The Dalai Lama's first important stopover on returning to Tibet was Kumbum Monastery, his temporary home in infancy. Having presided over several great ceremonies, albeit with a reduction in the number of monks in attendance, he traveled with his entourage from there to Taktser, his birthplace. To his mother's dismay, as she recalled in later life, the place "had become wretched. We saw signs of poverty everywhere; peasants wore tattered clothes and lived in a scene of total destitution." Worse, the local population was prevented from even seeing the Dalai Lama.

Matters improved somewhat as the Dalai Lama traveled west, making a slow and prayerful progress from shrine to shrine and from monastery to monastery. But many people had shocking stories of Chinese brutality to tell. In the end these were so numerous, and so clearly evidence of bad faith on the part of the self-styled liberators, that what little of the Dalai Lama's optimism had survived his final encounter with Chairman Mao had all but evaporated by the time he reached Lhasa on June 30, 1955, just one day short of a year since he'd left and a week before his twentieth birthday.

And there were not only temporal but also spiritual portents of impending disaster. The Dalai Lama's junior tutor, Trijang Rinpoché, who for the first part of the return journey had traveled separately via Kham, recounts how the contents of a magical box he encountered en route which had hitherto provided an inexhaustible supply of "miraculous iron pills" had recently dwindled to nothing. Then on the last leg from Chamdo, an event occurred that could only be interpreted as highly inauspicious. Hardly had the Dalai Lama and his two tutors crossed a bridge on foot—damaged by a wild torrent, it was deemed too dangerous to drive on—than it split in half and went crashing into the ravine, leaving all their luggage on the other side. Heavy rain also affected the Dalai Lama's procession into the Norbulingka, forcing all who took part to wear protective clothing over their ceremonial attire, and "it occurred to many," Trijang Rinpoché recalled, "that this was not a good omen."

Yet at a religious teaching he gave soon after, the Dalai Lama articulated a positive view of Sino-Tibetan relations. China had not come to be "lord" over Tibet, he explained, but had instead come as an equal partner to assist the Tibetans in the secular development of their country. Recognizing that the Communists' claims to friendship and fraternal concern were the only weapons that could be used against them, he began—as he had clearly intended following his first meeting with Mao—pursuing a strategy of taking the word of the Chinese leader at face value. The autonomy for Tibet promised at the party conference and the religious freedom guaranteed in the constitution were both plainly stated. It was therefore a matter of holding the Chinese to their commitments.

Almost no sooner had the Dalai Lama given his speech than news started to circulate of the arrest not only of several Khampa chieftains but also of a number of lamas in Kham for resisting Chinese interference. This was shocking. Even so, when he met Alan Winnington, the British communist writer and Beijing correspondent for the *Daily Worker,* the Dalai Lama was in an extremely cautious mood. When asked what had happened in Tibet since the signing of the Seventeen Point Agreement, the Dalai Lama replied dutifully that before "liberation, Tibet could see no way ahead. Since [then], Tibet has left the old way that led to darkness and has taken a new way leading to a bright future of development." Here was a young man evidently resigned to economies of truth because he dared not tell the whole.

In fact, on the way back from Beijing, the Dalai Lama had confided in Trijang Rinpoché his belief that, from his way of speaking, Mao "harboured a low opinion of Tibetans," as well as "many other things that [Trijang Rinpoché] must keep secret within the innermost core of [his] heart." The reality was that the Dalai Lama was keenly aware of the disastrous position he was in.

An early test of how genuine the Chinese commitment was to true autonomy for Tibet came with the formation of a new Tibetan People's Association. Ostensibly a charitable organization founded to distribute alms for the poor of Lhasa (whose condition communism had manifestly not succeeded in abolishing), its first thought was to submit a petition to the Chinese requesting the withdrawal of all their troops from Tibet. On the advice of the Nechung oracle, this petition was put to the cabinet in advance of the first meeting of the Preparatory Committee of the Tibet Autonomous Region. Of course, no petition was ever going to make a positive impression on the Chinese, and the petitioners understood this. But at the time they hoped that submitting it would encourage the Kashag to cease appeasing the Chinese and take a firmer stand. Instead, the petition's main effect was to give the Communists the opportunity to test the Dalai Lama's loyalty to the Motherland.

It took two months for the Kashag to respond. In the meantime, the Tibetan government was caught in an agony of indecision. The Chinese were adamant that the "fake Tibetan People's Association" must be disbanded. The ministers, however, feared that if they went head-to-head with the TPA, there would be trouble.

The outcome was inevitable. The Dalai Lama himself would have to step into the breach. Only he, not the Kashag, had the authority to take on the TPA. An edict, signed by the Precious Protector, was drawn up and published by tacking up a poster in several public places. It began by referring to the unhappiness of the people on account of the Five Poisons—ignorance, attachment, aversion, pride, and envy—as a result of which "even the insects living under the earth have not been happy." It went on to remind the reader that in Tibet, "there is no custom of a few people from the masses calling a people's meeting and interfering in the work of the government." Such meetings were "a very serious error." Research, it said, had shown how "most of the people in this Association had sincere thoughts," but they "had been deceived by bad leaders" who "wanted to uproot the good laws of old Tibet" and "wanted to do bad deeds." The TPA must be disbanded at once, and the leaders were to "confess their errors." Concluding on a threatening note, it warned that "if there are some thoughtless people who don't listen and continue to do this, we will apply strong punishments."

The Tibetan People's Association duly disbanded, and its leader subsequently went into exile in India with a view to making contact with the Dalai Lama's brother, Gyalo Thondup. For his part, GT, as he was known, had formed a small group of émigrés determined to do whatever they could from outside Tibet to resist the Chinese. This included renewing contact with the American embassy in Delhi and cultivating those members of the Indian government who were sympathetic to the plight of Tibet and nervous about China's designs both on the disputed Northeast and on large swaths of territory in Kashmir to which the Communists laid claim. Despite the recent 1954 Panchsheel (Five Principles of Coexistence) Accord between India and China, there was still a significant number of Indian politicians who fell into this category.

Among them was Apa Pant, the Oxford-educated prince turned Gandhian freedom fighter, by whom Gyalo Thondup was approached on behalf of the government about a possible invitation to the Dalai Lama to visit India. Jawaharlal Nehru, the Indian prime minister (who had briefly met the Tibetan leader in Beijing), sought the Dalai Lama's attendance at the Buddhajyanti celebrations scheduled for the end of 1956 to commemorate the 2,500th anniversary of the birth of the Buddha. Nehru's purpose in this seems to have been mainly to test China's commitment to the Sino-Indian accord. The Dalai Lama's appearance would also lend prestige to the event and show India's Buddhists that the government was mindful of their interests.

News of the invitation was hugely exciting to the Precious Protector. Not only would it be the fulfillment of a religious aspiration—for Tibetans, India is *arya bhumi,* the land of the gods—but also it would give him the opportunity to speak with the heirs of Mahatma Gandhi, whose successful campaign to rid India of the all-powerful British was such an inspiration to him.

The Dalai Lama was also clearly aware of the mounting opposition to the Chinese occupation in Kham and Amdo. Although Mao had promised gradual reform, and although he had agreed to autonomy for central Tibet, in the eastern provinces feudalism was being brought to an abrupt and bewildering end with the collectivization of farmland. This ought, perhaps, to have been expected, given Mao's recent remark: "On this matter Marxism is indeed cruel and has little mercy."

Although the Chinese understood that the imposition of reform was likely to provoke revolt, especially in Kham, the initial response on the part of the peasantry, the *mi ser* (literally, and for no clear reason, the golden-headed ones), was in fact sullen acceptance. No doubt it was a boon to them, on the one hand, to be relieved of their debts and the obligations of the old system. On the other hand, the psychological impact was immense: a whole layer of meaning had been torn from the world. Despite the hardship, there had been a sense of worth in the fulfillment of one's obligations and the promise of recompense in future lives. Nonetheless, there was little direct resistance and no uprising until the PLA demanded that the Khampa people hand in their guns. It was this, and not the land reforms, that initially precipitated open rebellion.

Matters came to a head when the Chinese demanded that the monks of Lithang Monastery in Kham, together with the local nomad population, surrender their weapons. At this time the monastery held around six thousand monks, most of whom were armed, as was the entirety of the surrounding population, said to have constituted a hundred thousand households. Both the nomad chieftain and the monks agreed that under no circumstance were they prepared to do so. It was indeed the monks who were foremost among the volunteers when the decision was subsequently made to attack the Chinese administrative office adjacent to the monastery. On a snowy day in March 1956, the assault began with the Khampas charging the Communist Party headquarters and setting it on fire. Somewhere between two and three hundred party workers, including a number of local recruits, were killed in the ensuing battle.

Many similar outbreaks of violence occurred elsewhere in the district, with hundreds killed and wounded and terrible revenge exacted against collaborators. According to a Chinese report (doubtless somewhat exaggerated but nonetheless not wholly implausible, given the fate of the Christian missionaries): "If someone supported the CCP [the Chinese Communist Party] . . . with their heart, they would cut out his heart. If someone read materials distributed by the CCP, they would cut out his eyes. If someone listened to the CCP, they would cut off his ears. If someone raised his hand to support the CCP, they would cut off his hand." With surprising ease the Khampas took control not just of Lithang but of a large number of Chinese outposts in the region. It could not be long before the Chinese counterattacked, but, being more familiar with banditry than with conventional warfare, the Khampas in the meanwhile confined themselves to looting whatever arms and armaments they could lay their hands on. When the counteroffensive came twelve days later, the insurgents were quickly driven back. Most made straight for the monastery, which, with its high defensive wall, did at least offer some protection.

Rather than engage in a lengthy siege, the Chinese began tunneling underneath the monastery. Unfortunately for them, the tunnel was discovered. As the Chinese emerged from it, they were "stabbed to death before they even had time to take out their guns."

How the Buddhist tradition, as it developed in Tibet, regards warfare and other forms of violence is not widely understood. It is a given that all intentional killing is wrong, and there is no Buddhist just war theory as such. But one of the Jataka Tales, a compendium of stories about the previous lives of the Buddha, tells how once he was traveling in a boat when he discovered that a crew member intended to kill all five hundred passengers. Because the passengers were all holy men on the verge of Enlightenment, the Buddha foresaw that the killer, if successful, would incur the penalty of 100,000 eons in hell. He therefore killed the man to spare him this fate, at the same time facilitating the Enlightenment of the five hundred. The moral here is that in extreme circumstances, violence may be justifiable in defense of the Buddhadharma. The proviso is that the one engaging in violence must do so out of correct motivation. As the Dalai Lama has said, where this obtains, and "where the motive is good and there are no other possibilities, then seen most deeply it [violence] is non-violence, because the aim is to help others." Remarkably, in certain circumstances, killing, from the Buddhist perspective, can be seen as an act of compassion.

From this, it becomes clearer why the Dalai Lama was taught not to oppose physical force actively in all circumstances. It also goes some way toward contextualizing the fact that, within the monasteries, breaking the vow of celibacy was considered a graver sin than killing a Chinese.

Following the Lithang uprising, the Chinese army command made known that it was nonetheless prepared to offer a negotiated settlement. If the rebels surrendered and handed over their weapons, there would be no reprisals. While discussions over this proposal were taking place, two aircraft dropped bombs on the mountainside adjacent to the monastery. This was to alert the rebels to what would happen if they rejected the offer. Though determined not to surrender, the Khampas could see that holding out against aerial bombardment was out of the question. They decided therefore to take their chances and flee during the night. The first few parties of escapees were successful in breaking out undetected, but it was not long before the Chinese realized what was happening. According to one Tibetan survivor, by this time "the Tibetans were going out like sheep and goats; and the Chinese had automatic weapons, so they killed a large number of people." Even so, a few, including the young Khampa chieftain, held out to the bitter end. Carrying his weapon above his head, he finally surrendered to the Chinese commander, only to draw a pistol from his *chuba* and shoot the man dead before being killed himself.

When news of the carnage reached Lhasa, the Dalai Lama was appalled beyond words. What upset him most was a photograph of the damage to Lithang Monastery. That anyone would resort to aerial bombardment against people who could not defend themselves defied belief. Aside from harming the combatants, what about the collateral damage to innocent people—to elderly monks, to animals and other sentient beings, and to precious religious artifacts? The very idea was beyond comprehension. Realizing what had happened, he later wrote, "I cried."

The Dalai Lama's immediate response to the catastrophe of Lithang was to demand a meeting with the senior Chinese general resident in Lhasa at the time, telling him, "How are Tibetans supposed to trust the Chinese if this is how you behave?" At the same time, he sent first one, then another personal letter to Chairman Mao. That these went unanswered told him all he needed to know about the reality of the assurances Mao had given in Beijing. The letters do not survive, and it is not clear that they were even delivered. In desperation, he entrusted yet another letter to Phunwang, who was to deliver it by his own hand. This too was similarly unacknowledged.

A second offering of the Kalachakra tantra, timed to coincide with the opening sessions of the Preparatory Committee, may have relieved the gloom to some extent. It certainly provided a morale boost for the audience, whose faces were "filled with awe" and "shone with happiness," as one official recalled half a century later. But it was the unexpected news, brought by the maharajah of Sikkim, that Nehru himself had followed up on his plan and written to the Chinese government on behalf of the Dalai Lama to invite him to attend the forthcoming Buddhjyanti celebrations, which really lifted his spirits. The maharajah found the Dalai Lama "anxious to leave," while the invitation had put the Chinese in a quandary. The danger on one side was that the Dalai Lama would become a powerful spokesman for Tibet abroad. On the other, preventing him from going might endanger the nonaggression pact assuring "cooperation for mutual benefit" into which China and India had entered in 1954. In the end, they responded by saying that he was too busy to accept.

Deeply disappointed, the Dalai Lama left Lhasa to pay a visit to Reting Monastery, where, accompanied by his two tutors, he conferred novice vows on the young reincarnation of his former senior tutor, Reting Rinpoché. At the time, Reting Monastery was the repository for some famous relics, including its founder's robes and the Indian texts he had used over nine hundred years ago. There were also some letters written in the great Tsongkhapa's own hand. As the founder of the Gelug school, Tsongkhapa had a special place in the Dalai Lama's heart. Yet while the visitors were delighted to find these relics still intact, they were dismayed to discover that the monastery was in large part ruined. Atisha's reliquary stupa had been robbed of its gilding and precious stones, there were bullet holes in many of the statues, and piles of rubble lay all around. Evidently no attempt had been made to clear up the debris from the destruction wrought during an attack on government troops following the ex-regent's arrest ten years earlier.

On returning to Lhasa from Reting, the Dalai Lama learned of an unexpected development. Following Nehru's intervention, Mao had executed a U-turn on the proposed trip to India, and the Dalai Lama was informed that he would be permitted to go after all. Although Mao took the precaution of scheduling two consecutive visits to India by Zhou Enlai during the time the Dalai Lama was to be in the country, the Chinese made the further decision not to send a large delegation to accompany the Precious Protector. As Deng Xiaoping—later to emerge as Mao's successor—wrote, this was to be "a test" for the Dalai Lama. Mao meanwhile spoke candidly of the risks this entailed at a meeting of the Communist Party Central Committee: "It must be anticipated that the Dalai Lama may not come back, and that in addition, he may abuse us every day, making allegations such as 'the Communists have invaded Tibet,' and that he may go so far as to declare the 'independence of Tibet.'" Yet the prospect held no terror for Mao: "Shall I feel aggrieved at the desertion of one Dalai? Not at all . . . What harm will his departure do to us? None whatsoever. He can't do more than curse us."

Traveling overland by car via Shigatse, where he joined up with the Panchen Lama, the Precious Protector spent a short time at Dromo, the border town he had last seen in 1951, before continuing the journey on horseback, up the steep track that led to the Nathu Pass, before it plunged down into Sikkim on the other side. The carcasses of mules that had "probably perished from exhaustion" and "clusters of sinister-looking vultures" hopping among them that were a perennial feature of the Tibetan trade routes might have served as a prophetic warning of the fate that was to befall Tibet.

India was a revelation, however. "People," the Dalai Lama immediately saw, "expressed their real feelings and did not just say what they thought they ought to say." The arrangements were, from his perspective, rather chaotic compared with the regimentation in China, but the enthusiasm of the people won him over. Everywhere he went, he was greeted by huge crowds of well-wishers, many of whom had traveled long distances just to get a glimpse of him.

From the Indian point of view, the Tibetan delegation was something of a revelation too. The task of hosting them "was not made easier by the fact that the Lamas' followers were explosively sensitive to the smallest niceties of protocol and were ready to draw daggers at the merest suspicion of a slight," according to one Indian official. Another challenge was the Indians' awareness that any "accident" that might befall the Dalai Lama would be hugely advantageous to the Chinese—a mishap that would be relatively easy to arrange and then to lay at the door of the Indian government. His security was thus a constant source of anxiety, exacerbated by the tumultuous enthusiasm shown for the Tibetan leader whenever he appeared in public. A glimpse of this can be seen in the newsreels shot during his visit and in the recollections of some of those delegated to look after him.

Describing an occasion when he escorted the Panchen Lama to his quarters in Gangtok, Nari Rustomji* wrote:

> We had hardly passed the Palace gates before a crowd that seemed like the entire population of Sikkim lunged madly forward, man, woman and child, with arms vainly outstretched, for a touch of the vehicle we were travelling in. I seriously feared our station wagon would be overturned, but there was no remedy as the police, themselves devout Buddhists, were too overawed by the Presence [a common epithet used by Tibetans both for the Dalai and the Panchen Lamas] to dream of controlling the crowds. Coins, currency notes, ceremonial scarves, amulets came whirring through the windows . . . until at last we were compelled to close them in self-defence. Our security arrangements might have served well enough for common or garden mortals, but certainly not for the Living God, whose only protection now was his own divinity.

With respect to the two lamas' personalities, Rustomji, himself a Parsi (an adherent of Zoroastrianism), recalled his impressions in his autobiography: "I have often been asked whether I was ever aware of supernatural forces emanating from the Lamas' presence. I have to confess that, for all the eager and excited anticipation of their divine immanence, they remained, for me, two very

*Rustomji was the epitome of an official from the latter days of the British Raj: a Cambridge-educated classicist, violin player, and prizewinning gymnast.

charming and sensible young men, of gentle and considerate manner, inquiring and vigorous mind and irresistibly attractive personality."

This attractiveness was, he also noted, not lost on some of their young female devotees, perhaps inspired by folk memories of the dissolute Sixth Dalai Lama. "It was," he wrote, "evident from the homely talk" of some of his Sikkimese friends that

> there were many in Lhasa who were as carried away by the youthful charm of the Lamas as by their divinity, and they told us tales of some of their more passionate young friends whose secret purpose in seeking the Dalai Lama's blessing was that they might be nearer the object of desire . . . Could it really be, wondered the belles of Lhasa, that the Dalai Lama could be utterly immune to feminine allure? It was a challenge to Venus which provoked them to higher endeavours. The Panchen, too, was not without his admirers. And wicked gossip whispered that the chinks in his armour were already showing through.

But while the Panchen Lama's susceptibility to female charms struck Rustomji, he noted that, though the Dalai Lama "had a delightful sense of fun . . . there was something not of this world, ethereal and ageless, in [his] expression that moved me the more deeply."

From the moment he set foot in the country until the day he left, eleven weeks later, the question at the forefront of the Dalai Lama's mind was whether to return to Tibet, or was now the moment to seek asylum abroad? There were strong feelings in both directions among those closest to him. In favor of staying in India were his older brothers Gyalo Thondup and Jigme Norbu—the first already based in India, the second having flown in specially from America. Sitting up with them until midnight, the Dalai Lama recalled, "Their views really shook me." Phala, too, the Lord Chamberlain, together with one of the former *tsit tsab*, took a similar line. On the other side were the four members of the Kashag and, less vociferously, the two tutors, while the representatives of the Three Seats were firmly in favor of returning to Tibet. Also of importance was the opinion of the people of Tibet, who could be assumed to favor his return. For them to be without the Dalai Lama was to be bereaved.

From Sikkim, the Precious Protector flew to Delhi, where his first engagement was to lay flowers and a *kathag* at Rajghat, in honor of Mahatma Gandhi, whose memorial stands there. The experience affected him profoundly. "It was a calm and beautiful spot," he later wrote, "and I felt very grateful to be there, the guest of a people like mine who had endured foreign domination."

The next few days in Delhi were occupied with official receptions at which he was greeted by almost every dignitary in the capital. Not only was the Dalai Lama still nominally a head of state, but also the Tibetan leader was something more than a mere political figure. For many Indians he was an avatar, a holy man without compare. Though they did not share his religion, they nonetheless eagerly sought *darshan* of him: a blessing and a glimpse of the divine.

While he was in Delhi, the Dalai Lama met with Zhou Enlai, the Chinese premier, who was en route to a number of other Asian countries. As the Dalai Lama wrote in his autobiography, he found Zhou "as full of charm, smiles and deceit as ever." Besides telling the Tibetan leader of Mao's recent decision to delay reforms indefinitely in the Tibet Autonomous Region, Zhou assured him that if the Dalai Lama would care to accompany him back to Beijing, Chairman Mao would be glad to see the Precious Protector again and to allay in person any fears he might have. As for Gyalo Thondup and Jigme Norbu (both of whom Zhou clearly suspected of agitating for the Dalai Lama to seek asylum abroad), should they happen to be short of funds, the Chinese embassy would be happy to supply the Dalai Lama with money to give them—though it would be better if he did not disclose its source. This last was a strange remark. For all his guile, it is clear that Zhou was a less astute judge of character than his adversary.

Notwithstanding Zhou's assurance that there would be no reforms in the Tibet Autonomous Region, it left untouched the question of what was to happen in Kham and Amdo. The violent struggle now firmly under way there was certain to continue.

From Delhi, the Precious Protector traveled to Bodh Gaya, where, to his delight, he was able to spend several days conducting ceremonies at this, the most sacred of all Buddhist pilgrimage sites. A speech he made at this time is remarkable for its prescience. Noting that in one of the sutras, or scriptures, there is a prophecy made by the Buddha that 2,500 years after his *parinirvana*

—or passing beyond suffering—the dharma would flourish in the land of the red-faced people, he explained that some held this to refer to its spread in Tibet, "but one scholar has interpreted otherwise. According to him the prediction refers to Europe." What the Dalai Lama could not have imagined at the time was that it would be he, more than anyone else, who would bring this about. Instead, his attention was focused when, on the last day of his stay at Bodh Gaya, unexpected news came that Zhou would be returning to Delhi the following day and sought an urgent meeting with the Tibetan leader.

At once the Dalai Lama sent a message to one of the young Tibetan government officials who had remained behind in Delhi. He was to leave immediately for the northeastern hill town of Kalimpong, where he was to discharge the medium of the Nechung oracle from his Scottish mission hospital bed, where he was being treated for arthritis, and bring him to Delhi the very next day. This was a tall order, given the distances involved and the as yet underdeveloped state of regional air links. Nonetheless, in spite of delays necessitating some frantic negotiation with airline officials and a frosty reception from the other passengers when they finally took their seats two hours after the scheduled departure, the Nechung medium and his two attendants successfully made it back to Delhi on time. It subsequently emerged that his advice was that the Precious Protector should now seek asylum.

Meanwhile, the Dalai Lama himself had fared less well. Arriving in Delhi by train earlier that evening, he had been hijacked by the Chinese ambassador. Without informing his Indian counterparts, the ambassador met the Dalai Lama at the train station and escorted him to his own car, which drove directly to the Chinese embassy. Meanwhile the rest of the Tibetan entourage took their seats in cars provided by the Indian government. The Tibetans arrived back at Hyderabad House, where they were quartered, aghast to find that they had mislaid their precious cargo. Only after frantic telephoning was the Dalai Lama finally located and retrieved from the Chinese embassy, where he had already had the first of what was to be several meetings with Zhou Enlai. It was a stunning diplomatic coup on the part of the Chinese.

These encounters with Zhou surrounded a critical meeting with Nehru at which the Precious Protector sought to determine the prime minister's attitude toward a formal request for asylum. The Indian leader made clear his determination not to make any commitments that would harm India's relationship with China. Indeed, so fully was his mind made up that he barely attended to what the Precious Protector had to say: "At first he listened and nodded politely. But . . . after a while he appeared to lose concentration as if he were about to [fall asleep]." The Dalai Lama explained that he had done all in his power to make the relationship with China work, but that he was now beginning to think it might be better to remain in India rather than return to Tibet. This evidently brought Nehru to his senses. He understood what the Tibetan was saying, he assured him, "but you must realise . . . that India cannot support you." His advice was rather that the Dalai Lama should hold the Chinese to the terms of the Seventeen Point Agreement and speak out forcefully when they failed to do so.

At his subsequent meetings with Zhou, the Dalai Lama gave no indication that he was considering applying for political asylum. Indeed, the (Chinese) transcripts of the meetings have him dutifully speaking in the first-person plural when referring to Chinese government policy in Tibet. Yet it is clear also that the Chinese premier was well aware that the Tibetan leader had been making inquiries. He cautioned the Dalai Lama that, if he stayed in India, he would be in political exile. "At first when you say something bad against us as strongly as possible, you will get some money. The second and third time, when you do not have much to say against us, you will get small sums of money, and in the end they will not have money to give you."

The opposing voices of the Nechung oracle and the Chinese premier were deeply unsettling, and when he left Delhi a few days later in the company of the Panchen Lama for a month-long tour of the country, the Dalai Lama was still in a quandary.

His schedule over the next few weeks consisted of visits to various important Buddhist pilgrimage sites, interspersed with sightseeing trips to several cities including Bombay, Calcutta, Bangalore, and Mysore. These visits to places connected with the founder of Buddhism had a profound impact on the Dalai Lama—none more so than at Vulture Peak in northeastern India, where the Buddha is believed to have preached the Mahayana, or Great Vehicle, for the first time. Here—possibly in prophetic anticipation of the thousands of monks he was himself to ordain over subsequent decades—the Dalai Lama enjoyed a vision during meditation of hosts of monks reciting the Wisdom Mantra: "*Om Ga-te Ga-te, Paraga-te, Bodhi Svaha.*"

The visits to India's industrial centers were of less interest. In news footage shot during this part of the visit, we see the Dalai Lama being shown around an industrial engineering project. He adjusts repeatedly an obviously uncomfortable workman's safety helmet, and it is clear he is not enjoying the experience. Trijang Rinpoché, too, was completely underwhelmed. The factories with their swirling rivers of molten lead reminded him only of the "hell realms."

Doubtless the Indians' intentions were to show the Tibetans that China had nothing on them in terms of material progress, but what impressed the Dalai Lama most was the enthusiasm of the people for their young democracy. The viewer of the contemporary footage is struck by the self-confidence of the crowds that attended the Precious Protector's every public appearance. (Pilgrims could travel at half price on the railways.) On each arrival, the Dalai Lama is garlanded and presented with bouquets of flowers as the press fight for photographs and crowds cheer. In contrast, faithful Tibetans stand meekly patient in hope of catching a glimpse of the Precious One. Yet it is also instructive to look at the demeanor of the Dalai Lama himself. The pressure he felt himself under is palpable. At the Dehra Dun Military Academy he sits, evidently somewhat reluctantly, next to a copiously beribboned general, doubtless comparing the military might on display with what he had seen in China. As the presidential steam train lent to him for his journey draws slowly away from the station, he can be seen smiling and waving somewhat awkwardly in unfamiliar Western style. Following a visit to the Taj Mahal, he takes his place uncertainly behind Nehru on an elephant's back. At the Air Force Academy he follows a more obviously eager Panchen Lama in taking a turn sitting in a training aircraft. In Calcutta he is taken to watch —without very much enthusiasm—the horseracing at the anachronistically named Royal Calcutta Turf Club. It is a relief to see him riding a miniature train with a delight exceeded only by that of the Panchen Lama, who altogether forgets the dignity of his office, veritably whooping with joy. One has a sense that here is a young man embattled, overburdened even, yet also someone determined to do his best whatever the circumstances.

The India trip ended, as it had begun, in Kalimpong. The Dalai Lama took up residence in the very same house as that occupied by the Great Thirteenth in 1911, following his own flight to exile in India when the Chinese sent an army into Lhasa. As it had long been, the town was a nest of spies (to use Nehru's own words). To add to its febrile atmosphere was the presence of hundreds of refugees, mainly from Kham, desperate for the Dalai Lama to call them to arms. Prominent among these refugees was Gyalo Thondup, who had by now come to terms with John Hoskins, the twenty-nine-year-old head of the CIA's Far East Division. America was by now very interested in Tibet as a way to cause trouble for the Chinese Communists. Hoskins, who was based at America's Calcutta consulate, did not have a very favorable first impression of GT. "There was a lot of submissiveness rather than dynamism," he noted. Yet in spite of this poor initial impression, Washington decided the CIA should support the training, equipping, and insertion of an initial eight (later reduced to six) Tibetan agents. Hoskins gave Gyalo Thondup the task of recruiting the men, and he in turn involved his elder brother, Jigme Norbu. The six recruits were all Khampas, of whom four were ex-monks, one of these former ecclesiastics an especially fiery character by the name of Wangdu, who in his youth had shot a man dead for that age-old crime of "disrespect." The agency's estimation of GT changed over time. When eventually the CIA program came to an end, its then operations director requested that Gyalo Thondup "please arrange for your next incarnation to be Prime Minister of a country where we can do more to help you!," noting that he had been extraordinarily successful in obtaining both material and political support from the United States.

It is certain that by now the Dalai Lama knew something of the CIA's interest in supporting a resistance movement in Tibet. But Washington had not been unequivocal in championing the Tibetan cause, having failed in recent communications to make clear that it would back a resolution at the United Nations calling for Tibetan independence. Nor was it certain that the United States would recognize a Tibetan government in exile. Had Washington's assurances been more explicit, it seems possible the Dalai Lama would have ignored the majority of his advisers, who favored returning, risked Nehru's ire, and formally requested asylum. But in the absence of such assurances, the Tibetan leader remained uncertain.

While still considering his options, the Dalai Lama met with several senior government officials who had come from Lhasa ostensibly to escort him on the last leg of his journey back home. In fact, their purpose in coming was to brief the Precious Protector on the continuing deterioration of relations with the Chinese and to implore him to seek asylum.

Inevitably the matter was put, once more, to the oracles—this time not only that of Nechung but also that of Gadong, another highly regarded source of spiritual counsel. When both declared in favor of a return to Tibet, those opposed were appalled. It was well known that Nechung's earlier advice had been to stay in India. Many were doubtful of the new result. Yet when questioned on this very point, Nechung replied that he knew that he would not have been believed if he had spoken in favor of return any earlier. He had therefore adopted "skillful" means. This is the practice whereby a teacher adapts his discourse to the capacity of his audience.

In order to verify that the deities had been interpreted correctly, their pronouncements were also made the subject of a *mo**—a dough ball divination—in front of the *thangka* of the Glorious Goddess by the Dalai Lama himself, but with the same result. This caused further dismay among those pressing for him to remain. "When men become desperate they consult the gods," declared one minister. "When the gods become desperate, they tell lies."

This divination finally decided the matter. Yet although the Dalai Lama was now committed to returning, it was, he announced, with several important provisos. One was that, from now on, taking Nehru's advice, he and the Kashag would vigorously protest any Chinese measures they deemed unacceptable. Another was that, henceforth, the people—that is, the represen-

---

*Among many other forms of divination practiced by Tibetans, that of *mo* is widely used. Preceded by a period of meditation and accompanied by appropriate prayers and invocations, this is performed by placing in a vessel two or more balls, traditionally of barley dough, distinguished from one another sometimes with dye, but more usually by pieces of paper with possible answers written on them and concealed inside. The balls are then rotated ever more swiftly until one flies out, propelled by centrifugal force. Though simple enough in operation, conducting a *mo* is a grave and serious business. The correct spiritual outlook and motivation are essential if it is to be accurate. And the more spiritually advanced the questioner, the more reliable will be the answer.

tatives of the Tibetan People's Association—would be consulted. But most important, some officials would remain behind in India with responsibility for maintaining links with the Indian State Department as well as the American officials with whom the Dalai Lama's brothers were in contact. And in order to facilitate this, a secret codebook was drawn up and distributed among select members of both the government and the stay-behind party.

But while the Dalai Lama had made up his mind to return, those wishing him to remain had other ideas and immediately set about formulating audacious plans to prevent him from going.

Despite the Precious Protector trying to persuade the Panchen Lama to accompany him to Sikkim, the younger man elected to return directly to Tibet from Calcutta. On his return, he was greeted effusively by the PLA's General Fan Ming. Instead of staying in the capital as planned, however, the Panchen Lama left suddenly for his headquarters at Shigatse. It seems that he had become aware of credible evidence of a scheme to assassinate him. And the putative assassins were not Chinese but Tibetan.

This is astonishing. Most Tibetans could not conceive of such an idea. But given lingering doubts as to the Pachen Lama's authenticity—for a long time, it will be recalled, there were two official candidates—and the serious ill-feeling toward him for his staunchly pro-Chinese stance, the existence of such a plot seems not implausible. Presumably the thought was that if the Panchen Lama was killed, the Dalai Lama would be forced to change his mind and stay in India out of fear for his own safety.

Another scheme called for simultaneous attacks on the Chinese to be carried out in Lhasa and Dromo. Orders were dispatched to the leadership of Tibet's burgeoning resistance movement to foment rebellion in alliance with the recently revived bodyguard regiment. Unfortunately for the plotters, the bodyguard resisted, and the plan came to nothing. Meanwhile, heavy snowfall blocked the Nathu Pass. For two more weeks the Dalai Lama remained in Sikkim. When eventually his party was able to cross the pass, it felt, as Trijang Rinpoché put it, like "being returned to prison."

13

"Don't sell the Dalai Lama for silver dollars!": Lhasa, 1957–1959

The Dalai Lama's first stop on his return to Tibet was Dromo. There, taking Nehru's advice to be more assertive, he told Chinese officials that, rather than focus on any good that had been done, it was important now to discuss openly the failings of the Communist Party's intervention in Tibet. For their part, the Chinese convened a meeting of the Tibet Work Committee. This was the organization that actually implemented Chinese government policy in Tibet. Remarkably, it was decreed that the majority of party cadres then working the country should be returned to China, with only a small percentage remaining. Similarly, many locally recruited (that is, Tibetan) cadres were to lose their positions while the various offices of the Preparatory Committee were either to close or to be greatly reduced in size. It seemed that Chairman Mao was determined to make good on Zhou Enlai's promises to the Dalai Lama. But while the directives were plain, the reality on the ground was very different. The numbers of Chinese actually withdrawn were far fewer than the central government called for. And though reform in central Tibet could wait, there was to be no letup in Kham and Amdo.

There was further bad news for the Dalai Lama when, moving on from Dromo, he went to pay a visit to the Panchen Lama at the junior man's headquarters at Tashilhunpo. It quickly became clear that the Panchen Lama's circle had a message for him. Instead of offering the Dalai Lama accommodation within the monastery itself, they had made arrangements for him to stay within the great fort. But then rumors of a far greater insult reached the Dalai Lama's ears: that the Tashilhunpo monks were performing the ritual for dispersing evil spirits, the implication being that he himself was the evil spirit. Credence was lent to this rumor when news came that an important Rinpoché close to the Dalai Lama had died suddenly—suggesting that the ritual had only narrowly missed its target.

Insult piling on insult, when he went to teach within Tashilhunpo itself, he found that only "torn and inferior" furnishings had been put out for his use, and the throne he was seated on was old and shabby and set up "in a dilapidated room" that was filled not with the Tashilhunpo monastic community but only with monks from neighboring monasteries. Arrangements had been made for the Tashilhunpo monks to receive their grain ration that same day, so that any who sought an audience with the Dalai Lama would miss out. It was, in the Dalai Lama's view, "a very bad show." Taken in isolation, this deliberate snubbing of the Dalai Lama would seem gratuitous. In the context of the rumored attempt on the life of the Panchen Lama, it becomes more understandable. As a result, relations between the two sees fell to a low unknown since the time of their predecessors.

Returning to Lhasa, the Dalai Lama reassumed his position as chairman of the Preparatory Committee for the Autonomous Region of Tibet, but thanks to Mao delaying the implementation of reform, his duties were not onerous. He could thus turn his attention to what was, from his perspective, the most important matter at hand, the Geshe Lharampa examinations marking the end of his formal education. These were now scheduled to take place during the Monlam celebrations two years hence.

A moment of respite that occurred in the meantime was his visit to Ling Rinpoché's hermitage at Gerpa. So thoroughly destroyed in the 1960s that today it is scarcely possible to discern where the building stood, then it was large enough to accommodate a sizable community of monks. At a long-life *puja** performed for the Dalai Lama's benefit, the Precious Tutor spoke movingly of how Chenresig, Boddhisattva of Compassion, had worked tirelessly to help sentient beings free themselves from the wretchedness of samsara. Years later, the Dalai Lama recalled how, "with tears filling my eyes, I prayed that I would indeed, as my root [principal] lama was so fervently wishing, live a long life and accomplish great things for living beings and the Buddha's teachings."

During the summer of that year, 1957, two major events occurred that would have far-reaching consequences. The first concerned the dedication of a "golden throne" to the Dalai Lama. The second, related event was the infiltration of the first CIA-trained agents back into Tibet.

The "golden throne" was an initiative of a wealthy Khampa trader named Gonpo Tashi Andrugtsang, who, at the time of the previous year's Kalachakra initiation, had thrown his weight behind a project to make a symbolic offering to the Dalai Lama of a jewel-studded golden throne as a gift from the people of eastern Tibet. The work of forty-nine goldsmiths, nineteen engravers, five silversmiths, six painters, eight tailors (who worked the brocade), six carpenters, three blacksmiths, and three welders, and containing more than 1,500 ounces of gold—worth something like $2 million in today's money, to say nothing of the value of the lapis, coral, turquoise, and other precious stones—it was almost certainly the most valuable single gift to any Dalai Lama from the laity. Yet while the throne, unprecedented in its extravagance, was an important expression of (mainly) Khampa devotion, its deeper significance lay in the network of communities and individuals the project drew together: it was, in fact, a cover for the recruitment of a rebel army, the Volunteer Force for the Protection of the Dharma, known as Chushi Gangdruk. To begin with, the majority of those it recruited were Khampas, with Amdowas making up the second-largest grouping; it was these who had so far borne the brunt of Chinese "reform." And though the Khampas in particular were traditionally hostile to the Lhasa government, there was not a man among them who would not sooner die than see the Dalai Lama harmed. Of the relationships established between the rebels and Lhasa officialdom at this time, none were more momentous than those

---

*An act of worship, a ceremony.

with the Lord Chamberlain and with Trijang Rinpoché (whose monastery was in Kham). It was he who became the army's de facto spiritual mentor.

This extraordinary development meant that two of the individuals closest to the Dalai Lama were complicit in what, in the Chinese view, was the establishment of a treasonous organization that went against the Tibetan leader's publicly proclaimed policy of cooperation with China. It also meant that the Lord Chamberlain had a link, via the rebels who were in regular contact with Gyalo Thondup in Kalimpong, to the CIA itself.

By early summer, the agency had taken charge of the six Tibetans recruited by Gyalo Thondup. Following a suitably cloak-and-dagger journey via Bangladesh (then East Pakistan), the six men were delivered to the Japanese island of Saipan. There, to their collective astonishment, they were met by the Dalai Lama's eldest brother, Jigme Norbu, and a Kalmyk lama by the name of Geshe Wangyal, together with a small team of CIA instructors.*

Their leader was Roger McCarthy, a gregarious thirty-year-old whose previous assignment had been to train Lao intelligence service personnel for operations in North Vietnam. He was delighted to be able to report to his seniors that, whereas the Lao had a disturbing tendency to hold hands when frightened, the Tibetans were "brave, honest and strong . . . Basically, everything we respect in a man." Fearless of heights, the trainees quickly gained proficiency as parachutists. It was mastering the complexities of Morse code that was to prove the more challenging component of the training program. They would have to transmit using a script devised by Geshe Wangyal. Since none of the trainees were strong writers even in their native language, the results were never very satisfactory.

By late autumn, the six men were judged ready for infiltration. They would operate as three two-man teams, dropped in different locations, each team equipped with a cache of weapons and supplies. The air drops were successful (though one of the Khampas was unable to jump and had to enter overland), and by December, two of the agents had reached Lhasa, where they obtained an audience with the Lord Chamberlain. He took a close interest in the two

---

*Geshe Ngawang Wangyal (1901–1983) was a protégé of Agvan Dorjieff, the Tibeto-Buryat confidant of the Great Thirteenth.

men's stories, but when they asked for a message from the Dalai Lama formally requesting assistance from America, he demurred in the idiom characteristic of Tibetan protocol and was "completely non-committal."

It seems not unlikely that the Dalai Lama was informed of the CIA's direct involvement in Tibet toward the end of that year but, for fear of implicating him, only in the most general terms. We might nonetheless ask whether, if a workable military solution had been available, the Dalai Lama would have supported it. Yet even had the United States decided to intervene on a massive scale, as it had in Korea and would in Vietnam, it is hard to see him being more than a bystander in any event.

Following successful insertion of its first batch of agents, whose chief task was to establish communications with Chushi Gangdruk, the CIA elected to step up its support. This was in spite of an inauspicious start. When some subordinates went to brief John Foster Dulles, the agency director, he began by asking where Tibet was, "gesturing in the direction of Hungary" on his wall map. It was decided, nonetheless, that the agency would no longer train agents—of whom there were to be more than 250 by the time the program was closed down a decade later—in Japan. Instead, there was to be a dedicated facility in the United States, close to the unprepossessingly named town of Leadville, Colorado. Formerly a prisoner of war camp for German soldiers captured in Africa, Camp Hale was chosen both for its remoteness and for its harsh climate. It was snow-covered for much of the year, while its mountainous terrain and its altitude, at over nine thousand feet, was ideally suited to the Tibetan training program, code-named "ST CIRCUS."

At this point, the Dalai Lama's eldest brother left the program and took up a teaching post at Columbia University, while Geshe Wangyal returned to his home in New Jersey, where he set up America's first Tibetan Buddhist center in a converted garage. But while Jigme Norbu no longer played an active role in the program, the venerable prelate remained on the books, taking a weekly train to Washington. There, in an agency safe house, its refrigerator well stocked with beer (which Geshe-la, as he was known, drank "to ward off colds"), he would attempt to decipher the often garbled Morse code messages received, via a rebroadcast station on Okinawa, from the teams on the ground in Tibet.

By 1958, while the Precious Protector redoubled his efforts to master the scholastic curriculum, and while the Chinese kept as low a profile in Lhasa as was consistent with having around ten thousand troops in the vicinity, Kham was in open revolt. How bad things were can be seen in what came to be known as the Xunhua Incident of spring 1958, when seventeen PLA soldiers were killed and, in reprisal, 435 rebels, with a further 2,499 taken prisoner. In the crackdown that followed, many "monastery religious personnel" were targeted for especially harsh treatment and "paraded before the masses as living teaching materials." This was just one incident among hundreds that occurred throughout Kham and Amdo during this period.

To make matters worse for the Khampas and Amdowas, the collectivization of farming was so ineptly handled that food shortages became increasingly serious. Recently released records give some indication of the severity of the situation, in which, for instance, fully a third of the population of Namthang township died of starvation at this time, while another third fled. The party officials responsible for implementing reform made sure not to reveal the severity either of the famine or of local resistance, instead sending reports that grossly distorted the picture of what was actually happening. Thus, one local party secretary could report to Beijing that, during 1958, "we took a great leap forward in all aspects of socialist construction" even while many herdsmen were reduced to scavenging for edible plants.

The Chinese were beginning to be alarmed at the levels of local resistance. Already there had been a (staggering, considering the small size of the population) total of 235,000 troop deployments across the three provinces since the PLA's arrival in Lhasa in 1951. The realization, from captured matériel, that the rebels had foreign backing was further disquieting. And while the Chinese could be confident in their overwhelming numerical superiority, Mao was concerned that if control of the eastern provinces was lost, even temporarily, his policy of gradual reform in central Tibet would become unworkable. He therefore hailed the opportunity that rebellion afforded, declaring the news of its outbreak "excellent . . . the greater the disturbance the better." This was all that was needed to justify a merciless campaign against the resistance movement.

Following the CIA's supply drops, Chushi Gangdruk began to show its potential, producing a significant number of small tactical wins over the PLA—an outpost overrun here, a convoy attacked and halted there. But when Gompo Tashi, the Chushi Gangdruk leader, took his men into central Tibet on an ambitious raid against Damshung Airport to the north of Lhasa, they were forced back when the Chinese deployed spotter planes and field artillery against them. Besides lack of arms—there were more volunteers than rifles to go around, and many were armed with nothing more than knives, swords, and ancient flintlocks—the rebels suffered from poor communications and ineffective leadership. At least half of their number had been recruited from the monasteries, and few had any concept of military discipline. Moreover, here in central Tibet the terrain was against them. Forced onto the open plains, they were easy targets from the air.

With rebellion now spreading out of Kham and into the so-called Tibet Autonomous Region, the National Assembly looked on in growing dismay. So long as their collaboration with the Chinese continued, they were secure. What little support they had from the people depended on being able to claim that, without their protection, things would be worse. Yet many, especially the junior members, felt that the Khampas were showing the way.

It was precisely at this moment of escalating violence that, at the end of the year, the Dalai Lama quit the Norbulingka for a tour of the Three Seats. At each of them in turn he would be publicly examined by way of preliminary to the final debates for the award of his *geshe* degree. These final debates were scheduled to take place at the Jokhang during the forthcoming Monlam Great Prayer Festival. His first stop was at Drepung, where the Precious Protector led a prayer assembly to which the monastery responded by offering him a long-life *puja*. Just as this was about to begin, a monk fell into a spontaneous trance, channeling one of the protector deities, and made an offering of *mendel trensum*, a most auspicious occurrence.* Having debated with Drepung's most able scholars and satisfied the community as to his proficiency, the Dalai Lama progressed to Sera, where he was challenged on Nagarjuna's famously difficult text *Verses on the Fundamental Wisdom of the Middle Way.*

---

*A symbolic offering of the world and all that is in it.

The final stop was Ganden. Remarkably, a short film showing highlights of the Dalai Lama's performance there may be found on the Internet. In crackling black and white, the footage can only gesture toward the magnificence and solemnity of the occasion. Notice the entrance of the Dalai Lama into the monastery, flanked by two men, one lay, the other monastic. See how, in holding their hands, he holds also one end of the offering scarves draped around their necks. In being supported by them, he also leads them: they are bound to him as if by a silken yoke. We do not need to know the precise meaning of this to understand that something of great profundity is being enacted here.

From Ganden, the Precious Protector moved to Tsal Gungthang, a small monastery built in the twelfth century which lay on his way back to Lhasa. Though it would be completely destroyed within a few years, his stop there provided an opportunity for the Dalai Lama to take a few days' rest before returning to the pressure cooker that the capital had become. No sooner had he settled in than word came from the Chinese that Chushi Gangdruk had struck again. Many PLA soldiers had been killed. If the Dalai Lama and his government did not accept responsibility for ensuring that the attacks ceased forthwith, the Chinese would take forceful action. As Trijang Rinpoché noted in his autobiography, the news disturbed the Dalai Lama greatly and he returned to the Norbulingka in a "troubled state of mind." It is testimony to the efficacy of the young leader's meditation practice that, in spite of the mounting pressure on him to act, he was able nonetheless to concentrate on preparing for the final element of his *geshe* exams. The Panchen Lama meanwhile cabled a message to Chairman Mao assuring the Great Helmsman of his own best endeavors to suppress the rebels.

The Dalai Lama's final examination was to take place during early March 1959. As usual, the monks of Drepung assumed responsibility for civil obedience, and the entirety of the local population was involved in the great liturgical events that would culminate on March 10 by the Western calendar. More than ever before, the Lhasa valley was full of tents, with tens of thousands of visitors coming from near and far. News of the rebels' successes contributed to the febrile atmosphere, with the crowds partly festive and partly terrified of what might happen next.

The Dalai Lama's chief of security concluded that with tensions running at such a level, it would take little to spark a riot. Accordingly, it was announced that the Dalai Lama was feeling a little unwell and the public talk that, by tradition, he gave on the first day of the festival had been canceled, along with the customary evening procession to view the butter sculptures. This had an electrifying effect—precisely the opposite of what was intended. People began to fear for the Dalai Lama's safety. It was at this time, during the Gutor festival marking the close of the year, that the Chinese issued him an invitation to attend a performance of a visiting dance troupe as soon as his examinations were over. Without giving the matter much thought, he accepted.

The Precious Protector had something very different on his mind than entertainment. He had performed well at the Three Seats, but what lay before him was an event at which he would contend with more than a dozen specially chosen scholars representing different monasteries throughout Tibet for almost ten hours in four different locations within the Jokhang Temple precincts. This was no mere formality. His reputation as an academic would depend on his performance that day.

When it came, he defended his understanding of Pramana in the morning, of Madhyamaka and Prajnaparamita in the afternoon, and of Vinaya and Abhidharma in the evening. There is no record of the exact questions put to him, but they would have covered all the basics—colors, definitions, comparisons, existents versus nonexistents, and the like—as well as more abstruse subjects pertaining to dependent origination and the two truths. What is on record, though, is that the Dalai Lama did not merely acquit himself well; he established himself—magnificently—as one of the finest debaters of his generation, a reputation that underpins his authority in monastic circles to this day.

Recalling the event years later, the Dalai Lama noted, in splendidly ornate prose, how the "cream of scholars" debated with him on "the difficult points in the vast and profound classical texts," while Ling Rinpoché, to whose credit the Dalai Lama's performance would redound, watched "with close attention." Subsequently, recalled the Dalai Lama, "the nectar of [the Precious Tutor's] words in expressing his pleasure . . . developed in me a great youthful fountain of joy." Similarly, Trijang Rinpoché noted his deep satisfaction at watching the Precious Protector "wither the creeping vine of audacity of those who were so arrogantly proud of their learning." It was, all agreed, a most praiseworthy performance.

The Dalai Lama was now free to enjoy the remainder of the Great Prayer Festival. Yet it was becoming increasingly obvious that something momentous was in the offing. The Chinese thought so too. They were convinced the government was "hatching a plot."

The festival concluded on March 4, and the next day the Dalai Lama left his rooms at the Jokhang to return to the Norbulingka. Back home, there were two immediate items on his agenda. The more important was a proposed visit to Beijing in the spring. It was rumored (correctly as it turned out) that Mao was planning to step down as president, and the Precious Protector was concerned about what the implications for Tibet might be. More immediately, there was the matter of his promised attendance at the performance of the Chinese dance troupe. When two Chinese officials came to offer congratulations to the Dalai Lama on attaining his Geshe Lharampa degree, they asked him to confirm a date. He suggested that either the tenth or eleventh of March would suit.

In the meantime, in an outburst that further heightened the tension, a furious General Tan Guansen (temporarily in command of the PLA in Lhasa) addressed the Tibetan Women's Association, shaking his fist and declaring that unless the Khampas ceased their rebellion, the PLA would "make short work of smashing all their monasteries to smithereens," adding, threateningly: "There's a piece of rotten meat here in Lhasa, and flies have been swarming in. We'll have to dispose of the meat to get rid of the flies."

On the ninth, a Chinese official presented himself at the Norbulingka with a draft protocol for the events of the following day. Unusually, it did not mention arrangements for the entourage that invariably attended the Dalai Lama. Instead, those who were invited (including members of the Dalai Lama's family) received individual invitations. But if this was arguably an excusable departure from established procedure, what followed was not. The Chinese declared that, since the venue was within the Lhasa garrison, there would be no need for the Precious Protector to be accompanied by his bodyguards. If the Dalai Lama must be accompanied, the Tibetans could send two or three personnel. They were to be unarmed, however. The choice, therefore, was whether the Precious Protector would travel from the Norbulingka by car, which the PLA would supply, along a route protected all the way into the headquarters by the PLA, or whether he would bring his own vehicle along a route protected by Tibetan security as far as the river crossing, at the other side of which lay the garrison, where the PLA would take over responsibility for the Dalai Lama's security.

Neither suggestion was acceptable. It was well known that the Chinese had abducted a number of high lamas and government officials in Kham following their attendance at some high-level event. Even if there was no intention to do so on the Chinese side—and there is no credible evidence of such a plan—there was no way that the people would let the Tibetan government run such a risk.

The chief of security returned to the Norbulingka, where he put the dilemma to the Lord Chamberlain and another official. Unable to decide what to do, they sought an audience with the Dalai Lama himself. In his autobiography, the Lord Chamberlain recounted how the Precious Protector responded. "Maybe this isn't as serious as it sounds," he said pensively. "Everything's set for tomorrow, and it seems like a bad idea to cancel."

The three officials demurred. But the Dalai Lama insisted that it would be all right.

There was nothing to be done now except carry out the Precious Protector's wishes. In the first instance, orders were given for a hundred plainclothes security to mingle with the crowd the following day. Yet when word of the impending visit became more generally known, there was resistance from all quarters. Had not the Nechung oracle recently advised that the "all-knowing Guru" be told not to venture outside?

The Lord Chamberlain sought another audience, this time to try to dissuade him from going; but the Dalai Lama insisted. It was too late, he said, to back out now.

Faced with the Dalai Lama's determination, a number of officials decided that it was their responsibility to stop him. When they left the Norbulingka that evening, they began spreading word that the Chinese intended to kidnap the Precious Protector. To this rumor was added the news that there had recently been increased activity at Damshung Airport. Also, a convoy of trucks was reported to have arrived recently at the Chinese garrison. It was obvious that these were going to be used to transport the Dalai Lama to the airport, and he would then be taken captive to Beijing—led off in chains, just as the Sixth Dalai Lama had been.*

The following morning, crowds of people began streaming out of Lhasa in the direction of the Norbulingka. Government officials arriving for work found the road blocked and their way barred. By mid-morning thousands had gathered, and still they kept coming. It was believed by some that the Precious Protector had already been abducted, and rumor and counter-rumor only served to fuel the people's passion. Whenever a minister's vehicle left the compound, it was searched lest the Dalai Lama should be hidden inside by some traitor abducting him. Though clearly the crowd's intention at the outset was simply to protect the Dalai Lama, as the day wore on, its mood turned to anger and bitterness. Cries of "Don't sell the Dalai Lama for *da yuan*" (Chinese silver dollars) filled the air.

Inside the palace grounds, government officials began to fear that the people would attack the Chinese. Yet it was not so much the Chinese who were the object of the crowd's wrath as it was themselves: the ruling class.

No one remembers at what point violence erupted, or what tipped the people over the edge, but the first sign of serious trouble came when a Tibetan official wearing a PLA uniform arrived in a Chinese jeep and sought entry to the palace compound. Knocked unconscious by a flying projectile, he escaped being stoned to death only by the reaction of his driver, who swung the vehicle around and took him straight to the Indian medical mission for treatment. But then, when a group recognized a junior monastic official who, having arrived that morning wearing his monk's robes, was now observing the crowd dressed in white shirt, slacks, a Chinese hat, and a white face mask of the sort often worn by the enemy, they lost all restraint. Some said that he was carrying a pistol, others a hand grenade. He probably wasn't, but they beat him to death all the same.

---

*Back in 1706.

Just as Mao had predicted, the masses were at last revolting violently against the reactionary upper strata, albeit not for oppressing them. It was because they were seen to have betrayed the Dalai Lama.

Even as the crowd exploded with bloodlust, many of the highest-ranking members of the government were at that very moment being sumptuously entertained within the Chinese barracks. As planned, they had gone independently in the expectation of the Dalai Lama's joining them later. After a splendid meal, those present, including the two tutors, were entertained with a film while the laymen played mahjong and the youngsters took to the dance floor.

The Kashag meanwhile, realizing that they had lost control, were concerned above all that the Chinese should not become involved. As soon as it became clear that the Dalai Lama could not safely leave the palace, it was agreed that three senior ministers would present themselves to the Chinese leadership and explain the situation. On arrival, they were met by children lined up along the path into the camp holding greeting scarves and flowers. Clearly the Chinese were unaware of the gravity of the situation and were still expecting the Dalai Lama. On hearing the news, the general exploded with rage, accusing the ministers of orchestrating the uprising themselves. He then warned them that there was no point in pinning their hopes on the Khampa rebels: "Don't forget that we beat the Guomindang, who had an army eight million strong! The Party is showing forbearance. Think it over carefully!" He finished by telling them they must keep the Dalai Lama safe, track down the conspirators, compensate the dead official's family, and bring the murderers to justice.

In the meantime, a group of representatives of the crowd was admitted to the Ceremonial Hall of the Norbulingka. Some called noisily for independence; others wanted to negotiate a new agreement with the Chinese; all were concerned for the Dalai Lama's safety. No clear leaders came forward, and the meeting broke up in disarray.

By 4 p.m., most of the demonstrators had left the precincts of the Norbulingka and were now marching through the Barkor, the pilgrim's route that circumambulates the Jokhang Temple, chanting and shouting variously:

Tibet has always been free!
Chinese Communists out of Tibet!
Down with the Seventeen Point Agreement!
Tibet for Tibetans!

That evening, General Tan sent the Precious Protector a personal letter advising him to stay where he was — presumably so that he could claim that the PLA had been in charge of the situation all along. When the messenger arrived with the letter, he found the Dalai Lama "sitting anguished, with his head in his hands." The Tibetan leader replied apologetically the following day to the effect that he would have liked to have attended the show but had been prevented by "reactionary, evil elements" who were "carrying out activities endangering me under the pretext of ensuring my safety," adding that he was "taking measures to calm things down."

But if the Dalai Lama was genuinely hopeful that these "reactionary, evil elements" were going to return to their homes and continue life as normal, it was a forlorn hope. The next day, armed militia began to build barricades along the road leading to the palace. Machine-gun posts were erected and manned not just by the Khampa militiamen but also by members of the Tibetan army who had taken off their PLA uniforms and insignia. In addition, armed volunteers congregated at the main gate of the Norbulingka to augment the official guard. The Chinese, meanwhile, deployed extra troops along the main road.

Though the crowd outside the Norbulingka on the eleventh was not so large as it had been the previous day, inside there was turmoil, with the people's representatives again gathering. Like them, most of the younger government officials were in favor of repudiating the Seventeen Point Agreement and demanding the restoration of Tibetan independence. At this point, however, the Dalai Lama himself intervened, summoning the entire group of about seventy. The Chinese general had not, he explained, compelled him to accept the invitation to the dance performance. Moreover, he was "not in any fear of personal danger from the Chinese." They should, therefore, "stop holding these meaningless gatherings, which would only bring trouble." In view of this unexpected intervention, it was agreed that the protests should from now on be conducted not outside the Norbulingka but at Shol, the settlement at the foot of the Potala.

A second, more threatening letter from General Tan reached the Dalai Lama later that day. "The reactionaries have now become so audacious that they have openly and arrogantly engaged in military provocations," he declared. "The Tibet Military Command has sent letters, therefore," to the Kashag, "telling them to remove all the fortifications . . . immediately. Otherwise they will have to take full responsibility themselves for the evil consequences." The Dalai Lama duly ordered his ministers to ensure that the fortifications were removed, with the—perhaps predictable—result that they were instead strengthened. In his reply to General Tan on the twelfth, the Dalai Lama could nonetheless claim that he had ordered "the immediate dissolution of the illegal people's conference and the immediate withdrawal of the reactionaries, who arrogantly moved into the Norbulingka under the pretext of protecting me."

Meanwhile, the Tibetan Work Committee cabled Beijing to say that "the Tibetan people had formally arisen and severed ties with our Party leadership and would henceforth strive for 'Tibetan Independence.'" It went on to claim that a "reactionary plot" was afoot to abduct the Dalai Lama. Although Mao himself was out of the capital on a visit to Wuhan, Beijing replied immediately to the effect that it was "a very good thing" that "the Tibetan elite has revealed its treasonous, reactionary nature. Our policy should be to let them run rampant, encouraging them to expose themselves even further. This will justify our subsequent pacification." Accordingly, the committee should "gather every available scrap of evidence of our adversaries' reactionary, treasonous activities" while continuing to court the Dalai Lama himself. Mao was clearly aware of a plan whereby the Precious Protector might withdraw from Lhasa. Nonetheless, he took the view that his departure would do "no harm."

Following this directive, the PLA began to reinforce their positions in and around the city and to obtain accurate ranges for their artillery—all this against the moment when orders came from Beijing to suppress the rebellion. But no special preventive measures were put in place to thwart any possible withdrawal of the Dalai Lama.

On the twelfth, the protesters duly moved to Shol, where, in an event that has been commemorated annually ever since, the women of Lhasa—under the leadership of an aristocratic mother of six who, for her crime, was subsequently executed by firing squad—had already gathered in the thousands to stage their own demonstration in favor of independence. Several ministers attended the people's representatives meeting that also took place that day, cautioning them that the Dalai Lama was suffering from the turmoil: "He looked haggard and was refusing to eat or speak, and kept sighing to himself." Again, no consensus was reached. The crowds of armed militia remained in place outside the Norbulingka, while inside, in fulfillment of Mao's suspicion, a plan to "snatch the egg without frightening the hen" (that is, to extract the Dalai Lama without alerting either the protesters or the Chinese) began to be put together by Phala, the Lord Chamberlain. This had long been contemplated as a possibility but, following the advice of the oracles, now became a reality. As a first step, Phala dispatched messengers to the two CIA operatives whom he had spurned earlier, calling them urgently to Lhasa.

On March 14, the Kashag issued an order for businesses to reopen and for the people to lay down their arms and to desist from drinking alcohol and from quarreling with the Chinese. Although this edict was ignored, it does seem to have contributed to a slight easing of tension in the city. The situation down at the Norbulingka remained chaotic, however, with large numbers of Khampa militia still in place, though they remained without any clear leadership.

Later that day the Dalai Lama again consulted Nechung. The deity counseled him to try to "keep open the dialogue with the Chinese." Presumably this was what lay behind the Precious Protector's careful reply to General Tan's third letter, received on the fifteenth. The general (actually the letter was drafted by Deng Xiaoping in Beijing) suggested, "If you think it necessary and possible to extract yourself from your present dangerous position of being held by traitors, we cordially welcome you and your entourage to come and stay for a short time in the Military Area Command." The Dalai Lama responded by thanking him for his concern and accepting the offer: "In a few days from now when there are enough forces I can trust I shall make my way in secret to the Military Area Command. When that time comes, I shall first send you a letter."

It could easily be argued that the Dalai Lama was being disingenuous here, but the truth is that, even now, he had not yet fully made up his mind what to do. One might also argue that this was the moment for the young Dalai Lama to exercise true leadership, to set aside his own safety and take charge of the situation himself. Yet this would be to misconstrue the whole Tibetan tradition. As we have seen already, the celebrated figures of Tibetan history are not those who renounce their own safety and take on the external enemy. Rather, they are spiritual heroes who renounce the world in order to take on the internal enemy: ignorance. Those who look within the Tibetan tradition for a Saint Louis of France or a Richard Coeur de Lion will do so in vain. Caught between the Scylla of taking the rebel side and facing down the might of the Chinese and the Charybdis of taking the Chinese side and facing down the ire of his own people, the Dalai Lama did precisely what the tradition expected of him. He did nothing. Instead, he continued his practice as usual. He had to wait until either the situation resolved itself or the deities instructed him clearly on what he should do.

This they did, perhaps as late as the fifteenth or even the sixteenth when, having consulted with the Kashag, the Dalai Lama again sought their advice. This time, besides Nechung, the oracles of Gadong, Shinjachen, and Shugden were invoked too. Not in person, to be sure: apart from the medium of the Nechung oracle, who had come to the Norbulingka, the others remained in their own residences. A trusted intermediary was sent in each case. The answer was unanimous. The Dalai Lama should leave as soon as possible. In the case of the Shugden oracle, there was, in addition, an explicit instruction as to which route to take out of Lhasa. If the Dalai Lama followed this instruction, he was promised that neither he nor anyone else in his entourage would come to the least harm. The oracle gave one further stipulation: "Someone bearing the name of Dorje must travel at the head of the victor's party, confidently wielding this sword." Having uttered these words, the medium faced in the direction of Ramagang to the southwest, loosed an arrow, and performed a ritual dance, gesturing with the sword. For his own part, the Dalai Lama himself performed a divination in front of the miraculous speaking image of the Glorious Goddess, Palden Lhamo, who duly concurred.

By now all arrangements were in place: horses had been dispatched to the other side of the Kyichu River, which stood a little over a mile away; food had been prepared by a team of monks from Sera working under canvas in the palace grounds; the Khampa militia had been alerted; the CIA agents had been found and briefed. Within the palace itself, the gate security was warned that a truck might at some point need to go out to the Potala in order to collect ammunition from the armory. If that happened, it was to be let straight through; no need to check inside.

When, on the afternoon of the seventeenth, two loud explosions rent the air within the palace grounds, there was a moment of panic. It was too late! The Chinese were already attacking! But when nothing further was heard, and there was no sign of enemy activity, the consensus of the security detail was that these must be ranging shots. An attack might not have begun, but it was surely imminent. There was no time to lose. The Lord Chamberlain sent an official to the Indian consulate to inquire whether Nehru would grant the Dalai Lama asylum should the need arise. Concurrently, a party of officials was dispatched to the treasury, where, we are told, they withdrew a large gold brick, fifty gold elephant coins, forty gold Tibetan coins, two golden crab figurines, a golden goblet, and 141,267 Indian rupees for immediate expenses. The overture to the consulate was less immediately fruitful. By the time the answer from India came back in the affirmative, the Precious Protector had been gone forty-eight hours.

As soon as darkness fell, the Lord Chamberlain's plan was put into action. At approximately eight o'clock that evening, the Dalai Lama's family—that is, his mother, his elder sister, and his younger brother—left the palace by the southern exit and made their way to the rendezvous on the south side of the Kyichu River. (His grandmother, aged over eighty, had to remain behind.) They were followed by the two tutors, who, together with the four members of the Kashag, lay down under a tarpaulin in the truck, which was supposedly on its way to collect ammunition from the Potala armory. The Dalai Lama himself was to leave on foot, accompanied by the Lord Chamberlain.

The Precious Protector in the meantime explained the situation to a group of the people's representatives, assuring them that his withdrawal was a temporary measure. He then wrote a brief letter to the Panchen Lama before making a final visit to the Mahakala chapel. Already the deity's protection was being invoked by a group of chanting monks. As the Dalai Lama recalled later, "no one looked up although I knew my presence must have been noticed." He then went forward and presented a *khatag,* a gesture that implied not just farewell but the intention to return. "Before leaving," he added, "I sat down for a few minutes and read from the Buddha's sutras," stopping at a passage that spoke of the need to "develop confidence and courage . . . A few minutes before ten o'clock, now wearing unfamiliar trousers and a long, black coat, I threw a rifle over my right shoulder and, rolled up, an old *thangka* that had belonged to the second Dalai Lama over my left." This was the image of the Glorious Goddess That Had Spoken. Then, slipping his glasses into his pocket, he stepped into the chill night air. Met by two soldiers, he was escorted to the main gate in the inner wall, where he was met by the head of the bodyguard. By his own admission, he was extremely scared.

PART III

✷

Freedom in Exile

14

On the Back of a Dzo: *The Flight to Freedom*

It turns out that the Dalai Lama need not have been so frightened, at least with respect to the Chinese. Only days earlier, Chairman Mao had decreed that, should the Dalai Lama "and his cohorts" attempt to leave, "we should not attempt to stop them . . . We should just let them go, no matter where they are headed." It is true that, earlier on the very day when he left, the Politburo, several of whose members had just returned from Wuhan, where Mao was quartered at that moment, had taken a different line—presumably on Mao's orders. In an instruction communicated to General Tan, they called on him to "do everything possible to prevent the Dalai Lama from fleeing," though this was qualified with the injunction that "should he succeed in doing so, it doesn't matter." Unfortunately for the Chinese, even if they wanted to fulfill the order to prevent the escape, it is clear that this latter instruction was not immediately acted on and, just as the deity had said, the Precious Protector did not encounter "the least harm."

The first leg of the journey was on foot to the stream that lay a hundred yards or so beyond the Norbulingka's walls. This was crossed by means of steppingstones, which, the Dalai Lama recalled, "I found it extremely difficult to negotiate without my glasses. More than once I almost lost my balance." On the far side, the Precious Protector was met by a contingent of heavily armed soldiers bringing with them a horse, which he mounted for the mile-and-a-bit ride to the Tsangpo River. At one point the Dalai Lama took a wrong turn in the dark, only realizing his mistake when he found himself alone. Thereafter, the Lord Chamberlain personally led his horse and did not let go of its bridle until it was light the next morning.

At the river, the ferry stood waiting, a cumbersome raft with minimal steering which relied chiefly on the current to get across. While the horses and the majority of the militiamen boarded, the Dalai Lama and a smaller number of companions crossed in a yak hide coracle. On the other side, the rest of his party—numbering around eighty in all—were waiting. Fortunately, the night was moonless with low clouds and poor visibility, but even so, the escapees were terrified to see the flash of torchlight from the Chinese garrison only a few hundred yards away. At first sight, it seems remarkable that the Ramagang ferry, by which the Dalai Lama and his entourage made good their escape, was not patrolled by the PLA, even if the Chinese were not intent on preventing the Precious Protector from fleeing Lhasa. Yet, given their policy of allowing the Tibetan rebels free access to the city, the better to target them later, it is not so surprising.

After crossing the river and traversing the plain that lay between it and the mountains, the party faced a steep climb. At about three o'clock the following morning, the Dalai Lama and his companions took a short rest at a small farm, where they drank tea and regrouped. After little more than an hour, they pressed on. Just as dawn broke, they approached the crossing point between the Tsangpo and the next valley. It was at this point that they noticed how, in the confusion of the night, the horses' tack had been mixed up. The finest saddles and bridles were worn by the shaggiest ponies, while the best horses were adorned with the meanest of harnesses. This provided a welcome opportunity for some hearty laughter as they toiled the remainder of the distance to the pass, reaching it at around eight o'clock in the morning. The Dalai Lama recalls how, at the top, he turned around and looked at Lhasa, praying for a few minutes that he would one day return.

Shortly after the Precious Protector and his companions had begun their descent into the next valley, all those government officials who had not left with the Dalai Lama arrived at the Norbulingka for the customary morning tea ceremony. It was only then that the majority learned of the Precious Protector's escape. The news was received with a mixture of shock and relief that the Dalai Lama was out of immediate danger. In the letter he had written, the young leader put four junior ministers in charge of the army, giving them the task of negotiating with the Chinese. Should they refuse to do so, the ministers "must deliberate profoundly amongst [themselves] and come to an agreement about whether to fight or to use other methods of resistance." No immediate decision was reached, however. Some called for war at once. Others, equally overoptimistic, advocated talking with the Chinese while overseas assistance was sought. In any case, it was decided not to release the news of the Dalai Lama's departure for the time being, as the day was astrologically inauspicious.*

The Chinese meanwhile acted on the new orders from Beijing and moved to seal off the Ramagang ferry. But this was their only important military initiative of the day. Even on the morning of the nineteenth, General Tan can be seen cautioning his commanders to maintain a defensive posture. "We should not be the ones to fire the first shot," he declared. It was only in the evening that he decided on battle. Having contacted Beijing to confirm definitively that the Dalai Lama had fled, Tan issued a warning to his troops that a rebel attack was likely to occur at any moment. In fact, what actually happened was, when a PLA patrol ignored a challenge by rebels stationed close to the ferry, the Khampas opened fire. It was this that gave the Chinese the pretext they

---

*Right up until this time, the government of Tibet published an astrological almanac which identified days that were or were not auspicious for certain types of government business. A late example can be seen in the museum of the Tibetan Medical and Astrological Institute in Dharamsala.

were looking for. At just after three o'clock on the morning of March 20, the "pacification" of Lhasa began.

Among the targets was the Norbulingka, which came under fire from "countless guns and cannons." The devastation was wholesale. As the day dawned, "from left to right one saw nothing but the bodies of animals and people . . . Throughout the city, Tibetans gave their lives—soldiers and civilians alike." The resistance coalesced around the now seventy-one-year-old Tsarong, a war hero during the time of the Great Thirteenth. His headquarters, set up at the base of the Potala, was well defended, but was no match for the heavy guns that the Chinese quickly brought to bear. After bombarding the palace, Chinese troops soon overwhelmed the assortment of militiamen and their leader.*

How severe the bombardment really was is hard to determine. Tibetan eyewitnesses suggest that it was prolonged and indiscriminate, killing many thousands. Inevitably Chinese reports say that the "rebellion" was put down at the cost of very few lives. Two Communist-sympathizing English journalists who visited Lhasa three and a half years later claimed to have seen no evidence of any damage to the Norbulingka.† It was what followed the crushing of the rebellion that was in many ways more significant. And about this, there is much less doubt.

The Dalai Lama was completely unaware of what was happening. For his part, he hoped that, when it became known that he had left, the crowds would disperse and life in Lhasa would return to normal. The Chinese would have no reason to attack. In the meantime, having walked for the better part of twenty-four hours, the Precious Protector and his party had by now spent the night in a small monastery, where he and his senior advisers held the first of what were to become nightly meetings.

Although the evacuation of the Norbulingka had been several days in the planning, the exact route taken—one of dozens possible—was determined

---

* It was during this bombardment that the college of traditional Tibetan medicine at the top of Chakpori, previously a striking feature of the Lhasa skyline, was destroyed. In its place today stands an array of communications towers.

† These were Stuart and Roma Gelder of the British daily *News Chronicle*.

only at the last minute and on an ad hoc basis. To begin with, rather than head due south, taking the shortest route, they followed the Shugden oracle's injunction to head in a southwesterly direction. Not only did this take the escape party through country that was impassable to motor vehicles, but also it kept them in territory that was entirely under partisan control. The PLA had concentrated its forces at the main strategic settlements and on the roads running between them. Yet although Chushi Gangdruk forces held the countryside, there was concern about possible attacks from the air. It was reassuring, then, that the weather at this time of year made aviation challenging while the mountainous terrain further increased the level of difficulty for aerial pursuit. Mercifully, too, the Chinese had very limited air assets at this time, and it was not until they were almost at the Indian border that the refugees saw an aircraft at all.

The fact that the Precious Protector had left before word came back from the Indian consulate that he and his entourage would be welcome in India meant that the Dalai Lama was uncertain whether Nehru would permit them to enter the country. One alternative they considered was the state of Kachin in northern Burma (today's Myanmar), where a small community of Tibetan villages stood high up in the borderlands. If, however, he was to proceed to India, there was also some doubt as to whether to take the shorter route via Bhutan or to go directly. But for the time being, the priority was to get as far from Lhasa as possible.

According to some accounts, the fighting in the capital continued for a full six days. The Chinese claimed the rebellion, as they characterized it, was suppressed much more quickly, after which it was only a matter of determining who the ringleaders were. All those deemed to have taken part in the uprising were taken prisoner—certainly many thousands of individuals, of whom large numbers were later to die in custody. Of those who survived, those labeled class enemies remained in prison at least until the death of Mao in 1976, while those judged to have committed crimes against the party and the Motherland were transported to the provinces, where they were enrolled in forced-labor gangs. Their task: the construction of the Workers' Paradise that Tibet was destined to become.

For all who were not known to support the Chinese, the next decade and more was a time of unremitting hardship, pitiful rations, hard labor with inadequate clothing and minimal rest, and repeated *thamzing,* or "struggle sessions."

This was a form of public humiliation during which the accused were forced to confess to crimes in front of an audience who would then abuse them verbally, and sometimes physically. This served as a prelude to punishment and "reform." In addition, victims were sometimes dressed in the most ludicrous attire. A famous photograph shows an aristocrat dressed in ceremonial brocades further adorned with women's underwear and topped with a dunce cap on which the various charges against him were written. Typically, too, the accused would have their hands tied behind their back in such a way as to force them to bend double with their arms straight out behind in a position known as "the airplane." By day, teams of prisoners were forced to compete with one another, singing "patriotic" songs extolling the virtues of Chairman Mao and the Communist Party. In the evening there were interminable classes devoted to the exposition of socialist doctrine. For those who showed a lack of enthusiasm, further torments were meted out through either solitary confinement or other struggles. To make matters worse, there was the ever-present danger of other prisoners, intent on improving their own lot, making accusations against their fellows.

Especially harsh treatment was reserved for the *sangha,* whether as members of the government or simply as people who had taken up arms against the Chinese. Though religion was tolerated while the Dalai Lama remained nominal head of the Tibetan administration, now it was held in official derision. Prisoners caught saying prayers were routinely beaten. The dire prophecy given by the Great Thirteenth had begun to be amply fulfilled.

But this was not yet an understood reality for the Dalai Lama. Five days out from Lhasa (though still little more than sixty miles), the Precious Protector was intercepted by the two CIA agents for whom the Lord Chamberlain had sent, bringing with them a radio, a mortar, and a consignment of rifles, handguns, and ammunition; their arrival was a welcome boon. There had been an American airdrop within the last month, and the Khampa fighters could now be equipped with weapons adequate to their determination to protect the Dalai Lama. Most of these were natives of the area surrounding Trijang Rinpoché's monastery. It was the monks of this foundation who had dealt so harshly with the Catholic missionaries earlier in the century. Fiercely loyal to their homeland—which for them was Kham and not Tibet—most would perish in subsequent fighting with the Chinese. But although their natural suspicion of the Lhasa government—intense to the point of hatred, easily aroused—remained intact, it counted for nothing now that the Dalai Lama himself was in danger. Fortified by their belief in the protection of Dorje Shugden, they ate little, slept little, and lived in daily peril not just from the enemy but also from the weather, often with nothing but the rough sheepskin clothes they stood up in as protection against the elements. These were hard men who lived hard lives.

Yet it can also be said that the Dalai Lama and all those traveling with him showed their hardiness. Although the distance from Lhasa to the Indian border where they crossed is only around a hundred miles as the crow flies, the route they ended up taking was a particularly arduous one, with a large number of mountain passes. There were frequent snowfalls, and for most of the time, temperatures were well below zero. Given that the Precious Protector's habitual exercise was little more than the occasional stroll through the park surrounding the Norbulingka, it was a considerable achievement.

At this juncture, the Dalai Lama hoped that he might still be able to establish a headquarters somewhere inside Tibet that was close enough to the border in case of dire need. But when his party was intercepted by a posse of horsemen who brought news of the bombardment of Lhasa, it became obvious that exile was the only plausible option. In direct confirmation of this, a letter from one of the Dalai Lama's secretaries in Lhasa followed soon after. This made plain the full extent of the horror that had befallen the capital. Evidently the hoped-for negotiations were mere wishful thinking. Plans were immediately put in hand for a formal repudiation of the infamous Seventeen Point Agreement. This, it was decided, would take place at Lhuntse Fort several days hence. Accordingly, it was there, on March 26, 1959, and in a grand ceremony attended not only by the governor, the abbots of eight local monasteries, and the Dalai Lama's entire entourage but also by several thousand people from the local area, that the Dalai Lama, having metaphorically torn up the treaty, reestablished his own independent government with the fortress as its temporary capital.

The fact that the fort was actually situated in eastern Bhutan meant that the proclamation of the Dalai Lama's new government here would cause diplomatic difficulties in the future. The Indian border official who later received the Dalai Lama was certainly most surprised to hear of this excursion into Bhutanese territory, for although ethnically Tibetan, Bhutan was, as it remains, an independent sovereign state,* its borders protected by the Indian government.

Diplomatic niceties notwithstanding, on hearing of the Dalai Lama's proclamation from a report sent over the radio by the two CIA operatives that evening, American officialdom sent its congratulations together with the offer of help should the Tibetans have any specific requests. Told this, the Lord Chamberlain instructed the radio operator to ask whether an airplane might be sent in case of difficulty. Also, could the Americans kindly use their good offices to request asylum for His Holiness in India? A possible landing strip had in fact already been identified, as had a drop zone for supplies. As for the possibility of asylum, Nehru had already signaled his approval via the consulate in Lhasa, though neither the Americans nor the Tibetans were aware of this.

After spending a second night in Bhutan, the Dalai Lama and his entourage rose before dawn on March 27 in order to tackle the steep track that would take them to the last Tibetan villages before the border with India. Disastrously, they soon became lost in a snowstorm. Having no goggles, they wasted several hours as they traveled in the wrong direction before they realized their mistake and were forced to retrace their steps. Once they were over the next pass, however, the weather improved, and they reached a small settlement where they halted in the late afternoon.

The next day there was yet another pass to cross, and it was here that the Tibetans received the biggest fright of their journey. Just as they reached the saddle between the two valleys, they spotted a large aircraft flying at (relatively speaking) low altitude nearby. Though it was too far away to be certain of the type, according to subsequent analysis by CIA officers it was indeed "Chicom"—a Chinese Communist airplane. The Dalai Lama's then twelve-year-old brother, Ngari Rinpoché, is, however, convinced that, given it had no markings, it must have been Indian, though there remains a strong possibility that it was in fact American. In any case, after a few fear-inducing seconds it flew off, leaving the Tibetans in enough doubt to ensure that they kept up the pace as they approached the last leg of their journey. Two days later they reached the

*To the envy of every Tibetan, Bhutan became a member of the UN in 1971.

village of Mang Mang, the last Tibetan settlement before the border. There, for the first time on the journey, and for his penultimate night in Tibet, the Dalai Lama slept under canvas, in a tent that leaked copiously from the rain that began to fall almost at once. After a damp and sleepless night, the Precious Protector contracted a fever, and it was decided he should remain in situ for one more day at least. Moving to the upper floor of a small farmhouse, he passed his last night in Tibet with, as he later recalled, cockerels crowing in the rafters above and cattle lowing in the stable below. On the thirty-first, he made the decision to press on. Too ill to ride a horse, the Dalai Lama mounted instead a more placid animal, a *dzo,* a cross between a yak and a cow. And it was on this humble form of transport that the Precious Protector, the Victor, Lion Among Men, Wish-Fulfilling Jewel, Ocean of Wisdom, earthly manifestation of Chenresig, Bodhisattva of Compassion, quit his homeland and crossed the border with India at two o'clock in the afternoon.

15

Opening the Eye of New Awareness: Allen Ginsberg and the Beats

Word of the Precious Protector's escape spread swiftly around the world, but for want of information, the many news agencies taking an interest in the story were compelled to hold their breath. Ten days after the Dalai Lama disappeared from Lhasa, the Indian president sent an urgent letter to Nehru asking for a report. The prime minister replied, saying, "We do not yet know where the Dalai Lama is." He was being decidedly economical with the truth. Thanks to the presence of the American-trained radio operators among the escapees, Washington—with the help of Geshe Wangyal—was able to monitor the party's progress almost the entire way along its route. Nehru, second only to President Eisenhower, was informed the day before writing to the Indian president that the escape party had arrived safely at the border. But it would not do to broadcast the government's intelligence capability owing to its links with the CIA.

As for the press, there were slim pickings for the hundreds of reporters who converged on the remote tea-growing settlement of Tezpur in far northeastern India. It was here, after resting a week in a remote town close to where he crossed the border, that the Dalai Lama was welcomed by the mayor and a large crowd of well-wishers immediately prior to entraining for Mussoorie, a further two days' journey to the west. There were no interviews, not even for old friends like Heinrich Harrer, who had made a special journey. All that was to be granted him and others was a short, moderately worded statement from the Dalai Lama (the text agreed to in advance with the Indian government) explaining briefly the circumstances leading up to his request for political asylum and thanking the people and government of India "for their spontaneous and generous welcome." Following lunch with local dignitaries, the Dalai Lama and his entourage left for the station without further word. Despite the Tibetan leader's temperate language, his words were immediately denounced by the Chinese. "The so-called statement of the Dalai Lama . . . is a crude document, lame in reasoning, full of lies and loopholes," thundered the *People's Daily*.

Two days after leaving Tezpur, the Precious Protector reached Mussoorie, where Nehru had arranged for the Tibetan leader to stay at Birla House, the splendid country retreat of a family of wealthy industrialists close to the prime minister. On arrival, as indeed he had been all along the way, he was given an exuberant welcome by the local people.

Almost the Dalai Lama's first act on arrival was to preside over the requisite rituals "to invoke the commitment of the Dharma Protectors who had vowed to guard the teachings of the Buddha, in order to quickly pacify these troubling times in the world at large and specifically in . . . Tibet." The deities had not been able to save Tibet, but at least they had kept the Dalai Lama safe.

The very next day, Nehru himself arrived. At first, the Indian prime minister had granted asylum only to the Tibetan leader and his immediate entourage, unaware—as was the Dalai Lama at the time—that there would be a mass exodus of refugees from Lhasa and its environs following in the Precious Protector's wake. But when reports reached Nehru of the fighting in Lhasa, he relented. Now all were welcome, provided they gave up their arms. For Nehru, the whole affair was deeply troubling. As he explained to the Dalai Lama, his "being in India [kept] alive the question of Tibet in the world," which for China was "immediately one of irritation and suspicion." On the one hand, he had hoped that with the mutual accord treaty signed in 1954, there might be permanently friendly relations between China and India. The presence of the Dalai Lama and his followers threatened this. On the other hand, he clearly felt some responsibility for having insisted on the Precious Protector's return to Tibet three years earlier. In their four hours of talks, Nehru assured the Tibetan leader of his welcome, but at the same time emphasized that the Indian government would not support his claim to Tibetan independence. The prime minister's plain speaking on the subject caused the Dalai Lama later to recall that Nehru could be something of a bully. For his part, though, it is clear the prime minister found the young Tibetan leader exasperatingly naïve. When the Dalai Lama told him of his determination both to win back independence for Tibet and to avoid any further bloodshed, Nehru exploded, "his lower lip quivering with anger . . . 'That is not possible!'"

The twenty-four-year-old Dalai Lama may have been politically naïve, but he was well aware that he and his fellow refugees faced a decidedly uncertain future. Many Tibetans, including senior members of the Dalai Lama's entourage, assumed it was simply a matter of time before their return would be negotiated. America and the other great powers would surely support Tibet as soon as they understood the reality of the situation. The Dalai Lama himself had no such illusions. Furthermore, it soon became clear that, while Mussoorie was a congenial place to stay, it was remote both physically and psychologically from the political hub of New Delhi. That the resort retained—as it does to this day—an air of colonial gentility with several once grand hotels and a number of prestigious English-style private schools was small recompense.*

There were some advantages to these new circumstances, however. Left entirely to their own devices, and having few demands on their time, to their satisfaction the monastic element within the Dalai Lama's household was able, as Trijang Rinpoché later wrote, to "focus . . . on religious practice" and "observe the discipline of renunciates."

While life in Mussoorie settled soon enough into quiet routine, one of the most trying aspects of exile quickly became apparent. Information about

---

* Among them was Doon School, where Nehru's grandson and future prime minister Rajiv Gandhi was educated.

what was happening at home, still more so of what had become of individual people, was almost impossible to come by. The Chinese said only what they wanted to say and refused entry to all foreigners. And such news as did reach the Precious Protector's ears was uniformly bad. The refugees who followed in his wake brought with them shocking tales of Chinese brutality. But then as the springtime heat gave way to the summer's monsoon rain, another, more pressing problem made itself felt. Most of those arriving had nothing but the heavy clothing suitable to the Tibetan climate and were completely ignorant of conditions in India. Worse, they had little resistance to the tropical illnesses that quickly broke out among them. During a visit to Delhi in June 1959, the Dalai Lama therefore urged the Indian government to move them to camps on higher ground.*

By this time a number of international relief agencies were working with the refugees, who continued to arrive in large numbers until, by the end of the year, they were estimated to total around eighty thousand, including many children. In the beginning they were placed in camps close to the border, where the agencies, notable among them the Save the Children Fund and the Swiss Agency for Development and Cooperation, first encountered them. Meanwhile, the Dalai Lama's American friends had also not been slow to act. That summer the CIA was instrumental in obtaining for the Dalai Lama both the recently instituted Ramon Magsaysay Award for Community Leadership and, somewhat improbably, the Admiral Richard E. Byrd Memorial Award for International Rescue. The one commemorated a Philippine politician, the other an American explorer. But together these awards went a good way toward meeting the need for funds for the time being. The agency was also responsible for an investigation of the legal status of Tibet, undertaken by the International Commission of Jurists, whose personnel arrived among the refugees during the summer. The commission subsequently published a report, based on interviews and bolstered by historical research, which argued that Tibet had been, de facto, an independent sovereign state from the mo-

---

*Many of the refugees, children included, were subsequently drafted to build roads in some of India's most remote areas. This was their chief — often dangerous — employment for many years.

ment when the Great Thirteenth expelled the Qing garrison from Lhasa in 1912. This would form the basis of the legal case for subsequent appeals to the United Nations.

It seems certain that the CIA, acting in concert with sympathetic members of the Indian government, also had a hand in the new statement the Dalai Lama released at this time. Speaking of the "tyranny and oppression" of the Chinese authorities, the Precious Protector said that he would welcome "change and progress," but that the Chinese had "put every obstacle in the way of carrying out . . . reform." Instead, "forced labour and compulsory exactions, a systematic persecution of the people, plunder and confiscation of property belonging to individuals and monasteries and execution of leading men" were "the glorious achievements of the Chinese rule in Tibet."

The public repudiation of the Seventeen Point Agreement that followed (and here one might be forgiven for supposing that the twenty-four-year-old leader had been writing political speeches all his life) was precisely the justification the CIA needed for its continued support of the resistance movement. But while the Dalai Lama's clearly ghostwritten speech was enough for Washington, the Tibetan resistance still hoped for something more. To this end, Gonpo Tashi, the rebel leader, paid an early visit to Mussoorie. There he learned that although the Precious Protector supported the aims of the movement—a Tibet free of Chinese interference—and was full of admiration for the bravery and determination of the rebels, and accepted that there were times when the Buddhadharma must be defended by all means, including violence, giving his support was a step he could not in good conscience take. Besides, the government in exile's impending appeal to the United Nations—which the Dalai Lama was determined to lodge in spite of Nehru's stated opposition—would lose much of its force if Tibet could not present itself as a peaceful victim of China's aggression.

This was a huge personal disappointment to Gonpo Tashi, described by his CIA handler, Roger McCarthy, as "one of the most impressive figures I . . . ever met." Nonetheless, the Tibetan rebel leader played a leading role in planning a major operation scheduled for the coming winter.

In September, eighteen men (the first batch from Camp Hale) were parachuted into Pemba, a district approximately two hundred miles northeast of

Lhasa, where the rebels were jointly led by a layman and a young reincarnate lama. The agents were accompanied by an extremely generous supply of war matériel: 126 pallets of arms and armaments, together with first aid and food supplies, dropped in three separate sorties. Altogether this was adequate to equip something like five thousand men.

Though properly armed for the first time, the rebels proved unable to capitalize on the munificence of their backers. While the CIA envisaged a classic, highly mobile guerrilla operation, with the rebel force taking to the hills and coming down in small numbers to attack the Chinese at moments and in places of weakness before disappearing back to the mountain trails they knew so well, the reality was very different. The Tibetans' modus operandi was, as it had always been, to fight in large, loose, mainly mounted formations. This could be effective when they had numerical superiority on open ground but was much less so in the face of even small numbers of a well-armed enemy properly dug in. More significant still was the Tibetan fighters' vulnerability to air strikes. The result was a foregone conclusion.

Recounting the CIA's reaction to the debacle years later, Roger McCarthy, the director of operations, recalled: "At first we didn't believe the reports coming in. We thought it was an exaggeration, an error. But it wasn't." The Chinese attacked the rebel encampment—home not just to the soldiers but also to their wives and children—with aircraft and long-range artillery. "It was genocide, pure and simple."

One might have expected the experience at Pemba to cause the Americans to lose faith in the ability of Tibetans to wage effective war against the Chinese. That it did not suggests the CIA hoped that, with more rigorous training in guerrilla tactics, Chushi Gangdruk could yet become a serious threat to the Chinese. The Tibetans knew their terrain and could survive the harshest conditions; they just needed to learn to fight in small detachments. This now became the focus of their training in the United States.

While the CIA was hopeful of modernizing Tibetan tactics through its training program, the agency also supported a more traditional force that had gathered at Mustang, a remote ethnically Tibetan province in northern Nepal. With arms and funding channeled through India, several thousand men gathered here to form what was intended as a reinvasion force. To keep morale up and to test the force's readiness to fight, the Mustang guerrillas launched periodic raids into southern Tibet—scoring, on occasion, what has been described as "one of the greatest intelligence hauls in the history of the agency." This was the acquisition, following a raid on a transport convoy, of a blue satchel containing detailed information about PLA troop dispositions and intentions, along with the first confirmed reports of famine and unrest in China during the Great Leap Forward. This was at a time when almost nothing was known either about the internal workings of the Chinese military or about conditions in China itself.

It remains open to speculation how fully aware the Dalai Lama was of the enormous scale of the operations both in Pemba and in Mustang, but there is room for supposing that he did indeed have a clear idea of what was going on, even if he did not know every detail. From the memoir of John Kenneth Knaus, the CIA's director of operations in India, who met the Dalai Lama in 1964, it is evident that the Tibetan leader knew exactly who Knaus was. It is also clear that the Dalai Lama was profoundly ambivalent about the whole business. One side of him, the merely human, wished Knaus and his team every success. The other side, the religious, forbade him to do so. Knaus recalled how, as a result, the Precious Protector imposed "a remarkably effective, though invisible, barrier between us" when the American entered the audience chamber.

For the Dalai Lama, perhaps the only positive thing to emerge from the CIA program was its effect on people's thinking. Knaus reports him allowing that "Tibet had been made up of many tribes who would not co-operate with one another. Now our common enemy—the Communists—had united us . . . as never before."

In April 1960 the Dalai Lama and his entourage moved out of their temporary accommodations in Mussoorie. Early on, Nehru had instructed his officials to find a more permanent base for the Tibetan leader. When the village of McLeod Ganj, a small hill station above Dharamsala, was put forward as a possible solution, the Dalai Lama and his advisers were skeptical. Lying 250 miles due north of Delhi, it was even more remote from the capital than their present quarters. It looked to the Tibetans as if their hosts wanted them as far away as possible. Yet when the Tibetan minister dispatched to assess the offered

A demeanor of "great calmness" in the eyes of some, "such a hard, expressionless face" in the eyes of others: the Great Thirteenth Dalai Lama, Calcutta, circa 1907. *Courtesy of Dominic Winter Auctioneers*

A. T. Steele, 1939

"No different from our urchin friends": one of the earliest known images of the Fourteenth Dalai Lama, Kumbum Monastery, 1939. *Courtesy of the Center for Asian Studies at Arizona State University*

Brother and sister (Gyalo Thondup and Jetsun Pema) with their mother and father, the *gyalyum chenmo* and the *yabshi kung*, 1939. *Courtesy of the Center for Asian Studies at Arizona State University*

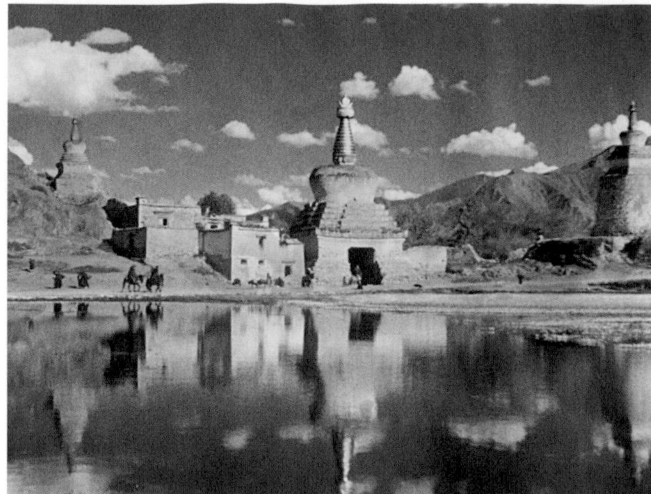

Lhasa's western gate, photographed in 1938. *Royal Geographical Society (with IBG)*

Fond of dogs and horses, the regent, Reting Rinpoché, in a serious mood following a reception at the British mission in Lhasa, 1940. *© Pitt Rivers Museum, University of Oxford*

The Norbulingka Palace, 1938. *Royal Geographical Society (with IBG)*

A "solid, solemn . . . very wide-awake boy, red-cheeked and closely shorn." Lhasa, 1944. *Courtesy of the Center for Asian Studies at Arizona State University*

Aged eighteen, photographed in Chamdo en route to Beijing, 1953. *Jan Vanis*

View of the Potala Palace from Chakpori, Lhasa, 1936. *© Pitt Rivers Museum, University of Oxford*

At an entertainment in Chamdo, 1953. Note the People's Liberation Army personnel in the background.
Jan Vanis

Exchanging pleasantries at the Tibetan delegation's farewell banquet in Beijing, 1955. From left to right: Zhou Enlai, the Panchen Lama, Mao, the Dalai Lama, Liu Shaoqi. *Keystone-France/Alamy*

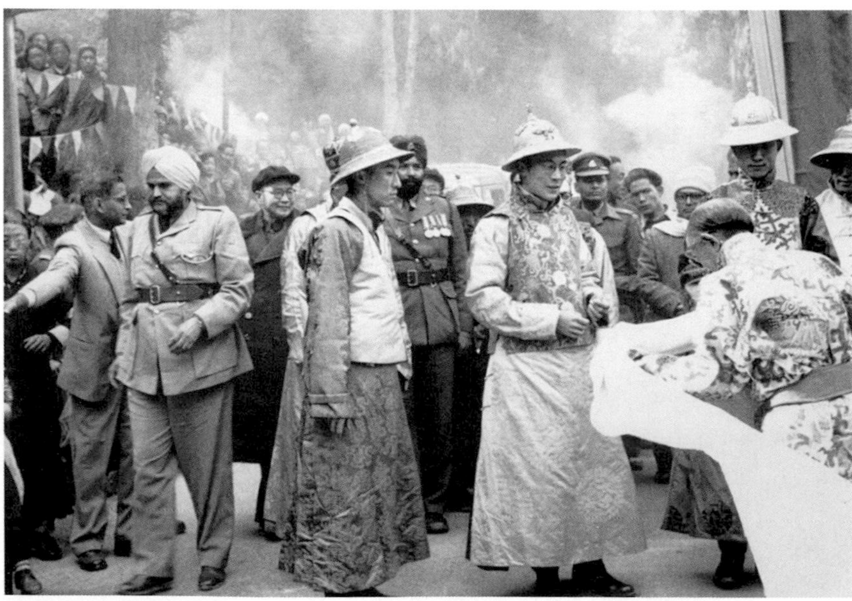

Being received by the Chögyal of Sikkim while the Panchen Lama, seen here to the left of the Dalai Lama, looks on. Gangtok, 1956. *Office of His Holiness the Dalai Lama*

With the two tutors: Ling Rinpoché (left) and Trijang Rinpoché. India, 1956. *Courtesy of the Office of H.E. Kyabje Ling Rinpoché*

Into exile: a moment of respite, 1959. *Office of His Holiness the Dalai Lama*

How the tradition sees him: detail from a fresco in the Potala Palace, 1956. *Photo © by Thomas Laird, 2018, "Murals of Tibet, TASCHEN"*

With schoolchildren, Mussoorie, late 1959 or early 1960. *© Tibet Documentation/ Tibetan Children's Village School*

With a local family in Dharamsala, 1960. The Dalai Lama is wearing the "well-pressed" trousers that he donned occasionally in the early days of exile. *Courtesy of Tibet Documentation*

With Lhasa apsos. On the left is Tashi, a gift of Tenzing Norgay, the Everest mountaineer. On the right is Senge, noted for his huge appetite. Actually, though, the Dalai Lama prefers cats. Dharamsala, 1970s. *Office of His Holiness the Dalai Lama*

A cruel irony of history: inspecting the secret Tibetan troops of India's Special Frontier Force, Establishment 22, in Chakrata, 1972. The photograph, rumored to have been taken by a Chinese spy, in fact originates from General Uban's personal collection. He stands to the left of the Dalai Lama. *© Ken Conboy*

Receiving the 1989 Nobel Peace Prize in Oslo. *Eystein Hanssen/ Scanpix Norway/PA Images*

"Look, no hands!" Getting ideas for a future free Tibet. Santa Fe, 1991. *Photo by Bob Shaw, courtesy of Project Tibet*

How the West sees the Dalai Lama, complete with badly photoshopped teeth, on the cover of *Vogue,* winter 1992–93. *© Vogue Paris*

What a coincidence! "Interrupted" by President Bill Clinton at the White House, April 1994. *Courtesy of the Clinton Presidential Library*

An "old ham," or a genuine sense of fun? With students attending a Tibetan medicine course. Dharamsala, 2014. *Office of His Holiness the Dalai Lama*

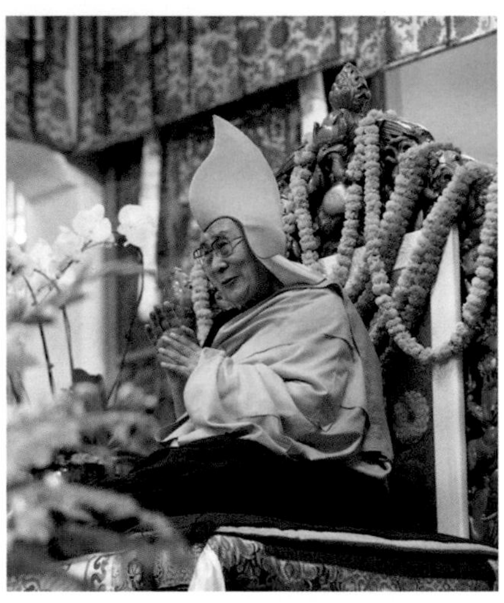

Precious Protector, the Victor, Lion Among Men, Wish-Fulfilling Jewel, Ocean of Wisdom, earthly manifestation of Chenresig, Bodhisattva of Compassion. Dharamsala, 2018. *Office of His Holiness the Dalai Lama*

land and accommodations returned proclaiming that "Dharamsala water is better than Mussoorie milk," with no alternative on offer, a decision was made to accept and move.

On their arrival, a question quickly arose over whether the Tibetan official had been offered an inducement. The monsoon in McLeod Ganj is frequently the most severe in the whole of the Indian subcontinent; it is nothing for forty inches of rain to fall in a month and not unheard of for five inches to fall in a single day. As well as remote, the village was run-down and furnished with only the most basic facilities. The road up was scarcely drivable, and the housing was cramped and dilapidated, while the landowner to whom it belonged still lamented the day when "the Britishers" had left. This was Nauzer Nowrojee, whose family had grown prosperous trading with India's late colonial masters.* Their family's general store was by now as much a museum as it was a business, and the faded pictures of British royalty that jostled with advertisements for forgotten luxuries like Pears soap and the *Illustrated London News* only increased the sense of desolation. By the time of the Tibetans' move, apart from the local Gadi tribespeople who farmed the steep hillsides, the population of this once wealthy resort consisted mainly of a handful of retirees from the Indian civil service and a single English family who had stayed on after Indian independence.

Little more than a year after he quit the splendors of the Norbulingka, the Dalai Lama thus found himself sharing the former district commissioner's residence with "his mother, his two sisters, his brother-in-law . . . the Masters of Robes, Ceremonies and Food, his Lord Chamberlain, and an assortment of secretaries and translators," not to mention several personal attendants. This was a considerable population for a house that had been built for a single family and its staff. It was in poor repair, too: the roof leaked, and during the monsoon, rainwater filled several buckets in the Dalai Lama's bedroom most days for two months and more, while in winter, the only heat came from a handful of small fireplaces scattered throughout the building. True, the winters in Lhasa were colder, but in Dharamsala the damp made it feel colder

---

*Nauzer Nowrojee was subsequently to find fame as the prototype of the uncle in Rohinton Mistry's novel *A Fine Balance.*

still. At least, though, the Dalai Lama was better off than several senior ministers who found themselves sharing an abandoned cowshed—though by all accounts they did so without complaint, their good humor and dignity intact, despite the lost opulence of the life they had known in Tibet.

If his accommodations left something to be desired, and if the situation in which the Tibetans now found themselves was utterly disorienting, the Precious Protector himself wasted no time taking advantage of the leisure he was suddenly able to enjoy. A Ping-Pong table was installed in one of the reception rooms, and that first winter of 1960–61 there were snowmen and snowball fights, while during the succeeding warmer months, and to the dismay of some of those closest to him, the Precious Protector took pleasure in making excursions among the surrounding hills. Climbing as high as the sixteen-thousand-foot pass below Mun Peak, he and a handful of companions would occasionally spend the night in a small trekkers' hut.

While the Dalai Lama was now able to enjoy personal freedom to an extent that would have been impossible in Tibet, there was no denying that he and his court had effectively been released to a backwater. Nonetheless, he was pleased also to have more time for study and for spiritual practice, and he was glad, too, to have the opportunity to set about bringing real reform to the way the Tibetan government functioned. For a start, he decided—against the advice of Hugh Richardson, the last British political officer in Tibet, who had made an early visit to Dharamsala to offer his services—that a minimum of protocol should be observed toward himself, outside the religious sphere. People to whom he gave audiences were not to be required to sit on chairs lower than his, nor would guests be encouraged to prostrate themselves before him. More controversial still, Tibetans themselves would no longer be required to do so. And from the outset he made it clear that he wished to be accessible to all comers, most especially to any from overseas who asked to see him. Tibet had been isolated from the world for far too long.

Visiting Delhi in 1960, the Precious Protector granted his first televised interviews. One of these was with the director of the World Council of Churches. In it the Dalai Lama comes across as a remarkably grounded and clear-sighted young man. Speaking of the prospects for the Tibetan refugee children, he admits, "We are still backward in the field of education, and we suffer for it," adding: "At the same time, we cannot ignore our own, ancient culture. This must be taught side by side with modern education." Asked in the second interview, with Prince Panu of Thailand, whether his resistance to the Chinese could simply be a cover for the "desire for power and riches," he turns the question around adroitly: "How can that be? If I desired power and wealth, I could surely obtain them by forfeiting the right of my people to resist the invaders . . . I did not become Dalai Lama by use of force and power. Why then should I try to gain [these things]?"

This clarity of vision found its most powerful expression in the political field. Toward the end of 1960, barely eighteen months after arriving in India and only twenty-five years of age, the Precious Protector gave the first of a remarkable series of speeches. "We exiled Tibetans living in free India must exert our fullest effort," he declared, "for the benefit of those who remained behind," forced to work like "beasts of burden," with limited food, "like hungry-ghosts," and experiencing "tremendous fear and agony like hell beings." It was the responsibility of the exile community to do all it could to prepare a better society for the future. They could not and should not "retain all the ancient systems of Tibet," he announced to civil servants in November 1960. "We must have change in the future. As the world is changing rapidly, we should also move together with the rest of the world." Yet while some understood the need for reform, others evidently did not. There were those who "genuinely [strove] hard through many challenges," but also "some people who do not take responsibility according to their . . . abilities," for which failing the Dalai Lama was quick to admonish them. "I am greatly disappointed with some officials, especially some senior officials," he declared.

Evidently aware of the Precious Protector's dissatisfaction at the lack of progress, a group of officials called for a "written oath" of allegiance to him. But he was unimpressed. "The 'written oath' was taken repeatedly in Tibet. And it was again taken as soon as we arrived in Mussoorie . . . A 'stronger written oath' was taken at Bodhgaya. What benefit have these 'written oaths' given? Yet again, today you are taking another 'written oath.' I cannot give credit to these attractive documents, empty words and talks. I believe in facts . . . Attractive paperwork and pretentious speeches are useless." Similarly, repeated offerings of "long-life" religious ceremonies for his benefit only exasperated him. For the Dalai Lama, it was abundantly clear how and why Tibet had been lost. What had happened was due primarily to "our many years of negligence in the past."

Although many were still hopeful that the Dalai Lama, by virtue of his relationship with Chenresig and the protectors, could perform miracles, he did not share this view. As Tibetans, they would have to pay the karmic debt themselves. Moreover, he was all too keenly aware that the charity extended by organizations such as the Save the Children Fund, and covertly by the United States, could not be counted on indefinitely. "Our foreign aid and assistance will eventually be terminated," he noted in a speech in March 1961. "We must be very careful." He was equally clear-sighted about putting excessive faith in diplomatic initiatives. "We should not," he warned, "place too much importance on my brother Gyalo Thondup's attendance at the United Nations Organisation's meeting," which was scheduled for the fall. This was a reference to ongoing attempts to have the issue of Tibet's right to independence raised at the highest level within the international community.

The Dalai Lama also understood the vital importance of recruiting new staff from the younger generation. "They are, by nature, physically stronger," he argued, "more [alert], more creative, and more aware of international events." From now on, therefore, all government appointments would be on merit, not on seniority or birth or status. As for monastic appointments in government, whereby in former times many positions were held jointly by both a monk and a layman, these would cease forthwith. He was quick, too, to take advantage of political trends. Reminding his audience that "Buddha, the compassionate one, has given equal right for both *Bikshu* [monks] and *Bikshuni* [nuns]," he argued that it was appropriate to give "equal opportunity to both men and to women to practice religion." The Dalai Lama also called on Tibetan women to participate in all areas of life in exile, including government.

Not all the young leader's innovations met with approval. His plan to raise revenue through taxation was resisted by some influential Khampas, known as the Group of Thirteen, who claimed that the government in exile was ignoring Khampa needs. This provoked immense resentment on behalf of those loyal to the Dalai Lama, and when one of the thirteen was murdered, a close relative of the Dalai Lama's was accused of being responsible. By no means did the Precious Protector have the unwavering support of all his people even in these days of direst need.

Yet notwithstanding the immense difficulties he faced, for the Dalai Lama, the catastrophe of exile was also an opportunity. He had understood from his discussions with Harrer as a teenager eager to learn about the world that Tibet could not afford to remain in psychological isolation. It was, he later said, "our worst mistake, our greatest mistake." For him, the material benefits of the modern world should not be refused simply on the grounds that they were foreign, and certainly not on the grounds that they were somehow "unnecessary," as some of the more conservative members of the establishment thought. In the Dalai Lama's view, it was a question of navigating a middle way between the outright forsaking of tradition and a complete rejection of novelty.

Again and again in his speeches to members of the Tibetan government in exile, we find the Dalai Lama exhorting, cajoling, encouraging, and imploring his fellow exiles to abandon any thoughts of Tibetan superiority and to embrace modern methods. At times it seems as if he alone saw the reality of the situation the refugees now faced. "We still have faults of delaying and being careless in our actions," he exclaimed, evidently exasperated. "Others set specific times and finish their work ahead of schedule. In our case, forget about completing the work ahead of time; we cannot even complete our work in the specified time."

One of the first tasks he set for the civil service was to develop a constitution that could be tested in exile and taken back to Tibet on their presumed return. A newly created Commission of Tibetan People's Deputies was assisted in this by a member of the Indian Supreme Court, Purushottam Trikamdas, also a member of the International Commission of Jurists. Former president of India Rajendra Prasad was enlisted as well, though he died before he was able to produce his comments. A controversial element of the proposed constitution was a clause providing that the Dalai Lama himself could be impeached if a two-thirds majority insisted on it. Most Tibetans were appalled that such an idea could be conceived, let alone committed to print. To their way of thinking, the logic of democracy demanded that still more power be granted to the Dalai Lama, not less. Yet the Dalai Lama himself insisted on the impeachment clause.

If the Dalai Lama's role was pivotal in the reform process, it was no less so in the practical sphere of resettling the eighty thousand refugees who managed to escape Tibet before the Chinese fully sealed the border. The Nehru government made clear that it would not permit large numbers of potentially restive Tibetans anywhere nearby, and instead granted the refugees land far to the south, in the region of the then minor provincial city of Bangalore—its future status as tech powerhouse not even a wild dream. It was here, on virgin ground, that some fifty-eight villages were established. Arriving at the camps, "many of the Tibetans broke down [and wept] on seeing the thick forest filled with wild animals and the work that lay before them." Yet, in a remarkably short time, the majority became flourishing communities. It was among these that, in due course, the Three Seats of Ganden, Drepung, and Sera were eventually refounded. But first, as the Dalai Lama later explained, "we considered setting up schools to be more important." Accordingly, using English as their primary language, several schools, generously staffed and subsidized by the Indian government, were quickly built, while most of the monastic community remained in the north, quartered in an old prison camp that had at different times held both Mahatma Gandhi and Nehru himself.

Besides overseeing establishment of the refugee villages, the Dalai Lama was also instrumental in bringing into being several institutions intended to help safeguard Tibet's cultural heritage. The first of these was an opera company, the Tibetan Institute of Performing Arts. Another was the Library of Tibetan Works and Archives, which, besides housing a considerable collection of *pecha*—printed religious works in loose-leaf format—also began publishing works relating to Tibetan history and culture, the majority of them in English.

It goes without saying that all this enterprise came at a cost, and, especially in the early years, funding was a major difficulty. At his second meeting with Nehru after coming into exile, the Dalai Lama raised the question of taking out a loan from the Indian government. Could the Tibetan government in exile possibly borrow 200 million rupees (just under $4 million) from the Indian exchequer? Presumably this was to be secured against the eventuality of the Dalai Lama's resuming his position in Tibet. In reply, Nehru expostulated that the Indian government itself did not have such a large sum, let alone such a surplus available to loan. When the Tibetan leader, greatly embarrassed, explained that this was what he had been advised to ask for, Nehru warned him "to be cautious about listening to such advice from his ministers." It was a point well taken.

Soon after, the Tibetan leader decided that the treasure still under the care of the maharajah of Sikkim should be sold. First by mule, then by car, and finally by a specially chartered aircraft, it was transported to Calcutta, where it was melted down, graded, and hallmarked before sale, eventually raising approximately $2 million on the bullion market, or around 26 million rupees. It was clear that there should have been quite a bit more, however. To this day, the disbursement of the Dalai Lama's treasure remains a source of controversy among Tibetans. Several people besides Gyalo Thondup, not all of them Tibetan, were involved in the operation, and each, at one time or another, has been accused of malfeasance. The funds that did become available were used to make a number of investments, apparently at the suggestion of Nehru himself. Besides various pieces of real estate, these included holdings in a paper mill in Bhopal and, by way of an unsecured loan, one in the Calcutta-based Gayday Iron and Steel Company. Only four years later, when the investments were transferred into the Dalai Lama Charitable Trust, the total value had fallen to a mere 8.2 million rupees, less than a third of the original sum.

Another early undertaking, and one that in the future provided significant revenue, was publication of the first of the Dalai Lama's two autobiographies. At the suggestion of Hugh Richardson, David Howarth, an English ex–Royal Navy officer turned popular historian, was commissioned to produce a book that drew on a text dictated by the Dalai Lama and subsequently translated into English. Published in London by Weidenfeld and Nicolson in 1962 under the title *My Land and My People*, it was well reviewed though it enjoyed only modest sales. Nonetheless, the book became essential reading for the increasing numbers of foreigners who began to make their way to Dharamsala. The Dalai Lama also authored at this time the only book ever published under his name to have been entirely written by himself, *Opening the Eye of New Awareness*, a basic introduction to Buddhism in the Tibetan tradition.

Apart from Harrer, Richardson, and Howarth, among the Precious Protector's first overseas visitors were four members of America's avant-garde literary scene, poets Allen Ginsberg and his lover Peter Orlovsky, together with Gary Snyder and his wife, Joanne Kyger, who arrived together at Swarg Ashram (the name of the Dalai Lama's residence) in early 1962. A record of the meeting, which arguably says more about the Beats than it does about the Dalai Lama, is given in Kyger's journal:

> We met the Dalai Lama last week right after he had been talking with the King of Sikkim, the one who is going to marry an American college girl. The Dali [*sic*] is 27 and lounged on a velvet couch like a gawky adolescent in red robes. I was trying very hard to say witty things to him, but Allen Ginsberg kept hogging the conversation by describing his experiments on drugs and asking the Dalai Lama if he would like to take some magic mushroom pills and were his drug experiences of a religious nature, until Gary said really Allen the inside of your mind is just as boring and just the same as everyone elses is it necessary to go on; and that little trauma was eased over by Gary and the Dalai talking guru to guru like about which positions to take when doing meditation and how to breathe and what to do with your hands, yes yes that's right says the Dalai Lama. And then Allen Ginsberg says to him how many hours do you meditate a day, and he says me? Why I never meditate, I don't have to. Then Ginsberg is very happy because he wants to get instantly enlightened and can't stand sitting down or discipline of the body.

The suggestion that the Dalai Lama did not meditate because he "did not have to" is certainly a mistake on the author's part. Nonetheless, Kyger's journal entry is valuable as an example of the blithe arrogance of some of the Dalai Lama's Western visitors in the early days of exile.* But if it is evident that the audience was no great success on either side, the Tibetan leader's meeting with the poets was the first of many encounters with exponents of the West's counterculture.

---

*I cannot entirely exclude at least my younger self from this accusation.

In an unsettling juxtaposition, Ginsberg's visit took place at almost exactly the same time that the Panchen Lama submitted to the Chinese Politburo what became known as his seventy-thousand-character petition, a document that paved the way for his downfall and subsequent imprisonment. When the Dalai Lama fled Lhasa in 1959, the Panchen Lama was quick to assure the Chinese of his own continuing loyalty. For this he was rewarded with leadership of the Preparatory Committee for the Tibet Autonomous Region, of which position the Dalai Lama was summarily stripped.

For the next two years the Panchen Lama was successfully used by the Communists as their chief collaborator. In 1962 he was presented to a visiting English journalist, to whom he dutifully explained how, as "a cadre of the People's Republic of China, [he was] performing [his] duties in accordance with the policies of the Chinese Communist Party." Yet in fact he had by this time undergone a remarkable transformation. Having witnessed the aftermath of the suppression of revolt in Lhasa at first hand in 1959, and then, in 1960, having toured Amdo province and again seen for himself the abuses inflicted on Tibetans in the name of education and reform, he began to voice criticisms of the party. A year later he took the opportunity to visit his home village while returning to Lhasa from Beijing. Seeing with his own eyes the abject poverty to which his kinsmen had been reduced—all their metal cooking utensils had been confiscated in the local commune's drive to make steel—he declared that now, "in the socialist paradise, unlike in feudal times, beggars did not even have a begging bowl."

The experience persuaded him that he should prepare a formal report to the leadership declaring the many "errors" he had witnessed in the party's imposition of reform in Tibet. Over a period of several months during the early part of 1962, he began work on a petition. Written in Tibetan, it was subsequently rendered into Chinese and submitted during the summer of the same year. One of those he asked to work on the translation refused on the grounds that the criticisms voiced were too dangerous. Some of the statements were indeed toned down on the advice of Ngabo, the man who had lost Chamdo and who was now a senior collaborator with the Chinese, who also suggested that the document include a preamble praising the party for the good it had also wrought in Tibet. In spite of these changes, it remained an extraordinarily courageous undertaking. The Panchen Lama's teacher is said to have prostrated himself and, with tears running down his face, begged the Precious One not to go ahead. He had consulted the oracles and they had indicated clearly that inauspicious consequences would follow. But with astonishing determination, the twenty-four-year-old Panchen Lama ignored all advice.

Although at first the petition was received with little comment, Mao denounced it soon enough as a "poisoned arrow aimed at the Party by reactionary feudal overlords." For his remarkable bravery, the Panchen Lama was arrested and "struggled against" for fifty consecutive days. He was then thrown into prison. From time to time he would be dragged from his cell and subjected to further *thamzing* in front of large crowds. One infamous event that occurred during the Cultural Revolution is said to have "wounded him more than any other." At a public meeting, his sister-in-law was persuaded to accuse him from the podium of having raped her, following which his younger brother beat him on stage for the alleged crime. Afterwards he was put in solitary confinement, and for the next decade, it was unknown whether he was alive or dead.

The Dalai Lama's meeting with Ginsberg thus stands in stark contrast to the reality of life in Tibet, even if it gave an indication of how things presently stood in the West. Indeed, from the Dalai Lama's own perspective, a much more important encounter than his meeting with the Beats was his meeting with the lineage holder of Shantideva's *tong len* practice. Kunu Lama, a Tibetan layman living anonymously in Varanasi, was the recipient of the actual teaching that Shantideva himself had conferred on one of his students and which had subsequently been passed down, teacher to student, in an unbroken stream from generation to generation. To receive a teaching in this way is to hear the very words of the Master as if from his own lips.

Shantideva himself, author of the *Guide to the Bodhisattva's Way of Life,* is one of the Dalai Lama's favorite authors and a great spiritual hero of the Tibetan tradition, while the practice of *tong len,* today popular with many advanced mindfulness enthusiasts and even taught as part of social and emotional learning programs in increasing numbers of schools in the West, entails the meditative exchange of "self for other." The meditator calls to mind someone toward whom he or she feels negatively and imagines exchanging his or her own good qualities for the other's negative qualities. Of course, most who adopt the practice do not have the privilege of direct transmission.

In order to track down the lama, the young aspirant ordered his chauffeur to drive around Varanasi in monsoon rains until, by good luck, he saw the reclusive yogin in the street. To the consternation of those with him, he ordered the car to stop, jumped out, and humbly offered a *kathag* to the teacher, beseeching him for initiation into the practice. At first the lama tried to refuse, saying he was not worthy to teach it to the Dalai Lama. When, however, the Precious Protector followed him into his own home, despite his protestations, he finally consented.

Meanwhile, the fact that Nehru had made it clear to the Dalai Lama that the Indian government would not support any request for him to travel abroad was at the time a source of frustration to the Dalai Lama. The Indian leader did not wish to antagonize the Chinese further than he already had in granting the Dalai Lama asylum. Yet in later years, the Dalai Lama credited his enforced grounding with giving him the opportunity to further his spiritual practice in a way that might not otherwise have been possible—even if it is true that his temporal duties have to this day prevented him from undertaking the three-year, three-month, three-day retreat that every serious practitioner aspires to make at least once in his or her lifetime. When he was finally granted leave to travel, eight years after arriving in exile, his first overseas visit was to Japan, followed three months later by a trip to Thailand, in both cases to participate in Buddhist conferences.

The restrictions Nehru's government continued to place on the Dalai Lama did not prevent Mao from administering a sudden and completely unanticipated reminder of China's territorial ambitions when, following a number of skirmishes with Indian troops, the PLA mounted an incursion across the so-called McMahon line, the border with Tibet bequeathed by the British which the Dalai Lama had crossed two years earlier. Striking precisely at the moment when the world's attention was diverted by the Cuban Missile Crisis (in the fall of 1962), the Chinese outgunned, outmaneuvered, and quickly outfought the Indians, who were ill-prepared and ill-led. Remarkably, the PLA withdrew after barely a month. But the episode left Nehru humiliated and utterly demoralized, his dream of uniting India and China in fraternal cooperation against the old world colonial powers turned to nightmare.

There was, however, an important development in the Indian government's relationship with the Tibetan government in exile that came as a direct outcome of the debacle. In its wake, at the suggestion of hawks in the Foreign Ministry, Nehru consented to the founding of a secret military unit, Establishment 22. Under command of the Intelligence Bureau, and as such directly controlled by his own office, the Special Frontier Force (SFF), as it was also known, would be a specialist mountain warfare unit recruited, except for its senior-most officers, entirely from among the Tibetan refugee community. Though it was originally planned to have a strength of six thousand men under arms, its immediate success saw its numbers double within a short time. The chance to join what Gyalo Thondup, the unit's chief recruiting officer, advertised as an army that would one day retake Tibet was irresistible to many young Tibetan men. Once more the Dalai Lama found himself in the invidious position of feeling admiration at the enthusiasm of the recruits, gratitude to the Indians (and, of course, the Americans) for supporting the venture, and dismay at the violation of the Gandhian commitment to nonviolence with which increasingly he identified. This did not prevent him from presiding over a ceremony at which protective talismans for the troops were consecrated. But it certainly did fuel Chinese mistrust of the Precious Protector's subsequent identification as a leading figure in the world peace movement.

16

"We cannot compel you": Cultural Revolution in Tibet, Harsh Realities in India

The trickle of news coming out of Tibet during this period was, for the Dalai Lama, saddening in the extreme. As for himself, having been stripped of his position as head of the Preparatory Committee for the Autonomous Region of Tibet, he was now officially an outcast, a "villain," a "liar," a "murderer," a "wolf in monk's robes." The worst of criminals, he had pretended loyalty to the Motherland while seeking its destruction all along. His duplicitous letters to General Tan Guansen were all the proof needed. It was pointless therefore to pray to him. More troubling still, the dharma itself was portrayed as nothing more than an elaborate system of exploitation created for the sole purpose of maintaining the power and status of an unproductive elite. If the protectors were real, would they not have protected? They were nothing more than idols made of clay. The reincarnation system was a hoax connived in by the powerful to enslave the ignorant poor. Such was the relentless message of the propaganda sessions to which the populace was subjected on a daily basis. In addition, thousands of monks and nuns were forcibly laicized. Paraded in front of large gatherings of the masses, they were issued with raffle tickets and deemed to have married the person found to have the corresponding ticket.

As for prison life, the cruelty Tibetans encountered can scarcely be imagined. One former inmate explained how

> as the disparity between labour and sustenance widened, our physical strength weakened day by day, the quality of the materials worsened, the hardship increased, and by midday two or three members of each group would be laid out with exhaustion . . . But in spite of such grave hardship, at the nightly group or general meetings, many of the weaker workers were said to be "resisting about reform" and subjected to struggle. There were those who passed away the same night after undergoing the torture of struggle.

Even for those not held prisoner, because of food shortages and lack of money, many of the better-off families were reduced to bartering their treasures for a minute fraction of their true value: priceless jewelry exchanged for a few pounds of butter or sacks of grain. As for the monasteries, their lands were requisitioned without compensation. By the time Stuart and Roma Gelder, two communist-sympathizing British journalists, visited Lhasa in late 1962, the Three Seats were near-empty shells, their populations reduced by 90 percent or more—a fact of which husband and wife wrote approvingly. These were "the last priests of the last and strangest theocracy in human history . . . In a few years, when they would all be dead, none would come here to take their places."

For anyone fortunate enough to have grown up in a genuinely democratic country, the treatment meted out to the Tibetans in the weeks, months, and years following the Dalai Lama's flight seems scarcely imaginable. Merely expressing doubt as to the efficacy of communist methods was enough to endanger one's life. As for religion, any teaching was, of course, forbidden, and any perceived sympathy for the Dalai Lama was severely punished. But what made the Tibetan experience so pernicious was the vindictiveness with which "reform" was forced upon the people, to say nothing of the systematized attacks on their most deeply held convictions. Yet it must be remembered that what took place in Tibet during the early sixties was to a large degree simply a reflection of what was happening in China itself. The "Hundred Flowers" campaign of 1957, when, over the course of several weeks, Mao invited criticism of the party, was followed swiftly by the "Anti-Rightist" movement, when those "snakes" (Mao's word) who had taken the bait were charged with crimes against the party. Soon anyone who was deemed merely to hold "rightist" opinions became a legitimate target. As a result, at least half a million people—many of them from minority groups—were imprisoned, transported to labor camps, or liquidated over the next three years. Among those imprisoned and brutally treated was Phunwang, the Dalai Lama's Communist Party mentor during his 1954 trip to Beijing, convicted of politically incorrect thought. Held for two years in detention with frequent interrogations and humiliations during which, "because they knew I worried about my children, they sometimes let a baby cry outside my cell late at night," he was eventually sentenced to solitary confinement for nine years, by the end of which he had lost the power of speech. This was succeeded by another nine years in the mental patients' wing of Beijing's notorious Qincheng Prison for political prisoners before he was finally released and rehabilitated in 1978.* It took him another two years before he could speak properly again.

To make matters even worse, the Anti-Rightist movement coincided with Mao's Great Leap Forward, an economic campaign designed to transform China from an agrarian society to an industrial society. This initiated a period of extreme hardship for the entire population of the Chinese empire during which tens of millions died through starvation. The inability, already manifest, of agricultural collectivism to deliver reliable food supplies was tragically underscored by three successive years of crop failure, exacerbating an already

* Astonishingly he lived another thirty-six years until his death in 2014, aged ninety-two, having fully recovered and authored several books, one of them a remarkable exercise in Hegelian dialectics intended to demonstrate that, of necessity, *Liquid Water Does Exist on the Moon* (the book's title).

dire situation. The Great Leap was not, of course, a leap forward but a leap into darkness and despair.

Inevitably, those who felt the effects of famine the most acutely were the inmates of the gulags. "During [those] three years [1960–1963]," recalls a Tibetan who lived through the ordeal, "thousands quickly starved to death. In every prison camp horse carts were constantly pulling out loads of dead bodies." One former Tibetan government official recounted how, during those years,

> we began to look for . . . nourishment wherever we could find it. If we saw a worm all the prisoners would run for it and if you got it you immediately popped it in your mouth, otherwise it would be taken away . . . The livestock was also fed on grain, and in their excrement undigested grains of wheat would come out. We would pick these grains out of the manure pile and eat them . . . Sometimes, digging away in the fields, we would find bones. Human bones or animal bones. We would eat this too . . . Even if we knew it was human bone, still we would eat it.

The failure of the Great Leap Forward greatly diminished Mao's authority within the Communist Party, and for a time it looked as if he would lose control altogether. In what must surely rank as one of the most brazen acts of cynicism in history, the Great Helmsman responded in 1966 by unleashing the Cultural Revolution. This was characterized by a vicious hostility to the "Four Olds": old customs, old culture, old habits, old ideas. By attacking tradition itself and going over the heads of the political establishment to appeal directly to the country's youth, Mao, promoting a cult of himself, succeeded in bringing about a destructive furor that for almost a decade teetered on the verge of anarchy. Significantly, though, it secured his position as paramount leader. It is not clear how many died as a consequence of this tactic, but the toll is widely believed to be in the tens of millions. Yet, although it is sometimes alleged that the destruction of Tibet occurred as a result of the "excesses" of the Cultural Revolution, in fact its true destruction had occurred during the years immediately following the Dalai Lama's exile. The main effect of the Cultural Revolution in Tibet was to make the lives of the people even less bearable.

Compelled to work sixteen-hour days, anyone caught merely cooking at home would be severely punished. And now, not only was the Dalai Lama not to be prayed to; he was to be ritually denounced by the masses.

As for the Dalai Lama himself, if, in the wake of Allen Ginsberg's visit, there was a steady trickle of Beats and hippies who sought him out in Dharamsala throughout the 1960s, there were also increasing numbers of more serious seekers. One of these was Robert Thurman, then a student of the CIA's translator monk Geshe Wangyal, but today doubtless most famous for being the father of the actress Uma Thurman. At the time, Thurman, recently divorced, was a young Harvard BA on a spiritual quest. Meeting the Dalai Lama at Sarnath in eastern India when both were attending a conference of the World Fellowship of Buddhists in November 1964, Thurman recalled how he sensed a certain "guardedness" about the Tibetan, while the speech the Dalai Lama gave "sounded strained and formal." There was "a sense of him being from far away and high above and not quite relaxed in his surroundings." Nonetheless, when Thurman expressed interest in monkhood, the Dalai Lama invited him to visit Dharamsala, where he assigned him to the care of Ling Rinpoché.

The two young men (the Dalai Lama was not quite thirty, while the American was still in his early twenties) subsequently met on a regular basis at the Precious Protector's house. It turned out that the Dalai Lama was as keen as ever to learn about the outside world. After discussing the dharma, "he would invariably begin asking me questions about the many things he was wondering about," wrote Thurman, "Freud, Einstein and Thomas Jefferson, life in the Americas and Europe . . . the subconscious, relativity and natural selection." Yet for all the evident pleasure the Dalai Lama took in their meetings, "though basically energetic and cheery . . . [h]e seemed slightly stressed, lonely, a little sad."

Thurman was subsequently ordained by the Dalai Lama, the first Westerner to attain that dignity, though to the Precious Protector's "strong" disappointment ("which lasted quite a while"), the American went barely a year before disrobing and marrying model-turned-psychotherapist Nena von Schlebrügge, the ex-wife of countercultural luminary Timothy Leary, in 1967.

Another important visitor at this time was Thomas Merton. The (by adoption) American Roman Catholic monk of the Cistercian Order of Strict Observance came to Dharamsala in November 1968, en route to Thailand, where he was to die, electrocuted as he stepped out of the shower, just a few weeks later.* His appearance among the Tibetan community seems almost providential, given the recent embassy of Trijang Rinpoché to the Vatican, where he obtained an audience with Pope Paul VI. This was evidently more of a diplomatic success than it was a meeting of minds, however. Neither thought it worthwhile to leave a written record of the event, although Trijang Rinpoché subsequently reported to the Dalai Lama his dismay at the lack of "spiritual depth" of the Europeans: "They are concerned with this life only and have a strong sense of grasping after permanence in all things . . . [T]hey are preoccupied with indulging the mere illusion of joy and happiness."

The Dalai Lama's meeting with Merton took place at a moment remarkable both in the history of Buddhism in Tibet and in that of the Roman Catholic Church. The one faced the catastrophe of invasion by an external enemy committed to the ideology of modern materialism. The other was itself fighting a spiritual war with the same enemy. In a way, therefore, both the Dalai Lama and the pope faced a similar dilemma.

Because so many of the Tibetan rites were specific to particular shrines and temples in Tibet, and because most of the important festivals—especially those pertaining to the New Year—were peculiar to particular buildings and locations within Lhasa, rupture was unavoidable for the Tibetans. No longer would the cavalry assemble in their ancient chain mail in the courtyard of the Jokhang; no longer would the sound of the Old She-Demon, the Young She-Demon, and the Idiot boom to signal the immolation of the evils of the year past; no longer would the ministers in all their medieval finery prostrate themselves beneath the main temple at the close of the last day. All that would have to be let go. But what else could be safely consigned to the past, and what must be preserved at all costs? Together with his two tutors and other high ecclesiastics, the Dalai Lama was compelled to make many hard decisions. "We divided our culture into two types," he explained. "In the first category, we placed that which, we determined, needed to be retained only in books as past

*The last of his three meetings with the Dalai Lama took place on November 8, 1968. Merton died on December 10.

history. The second category included whatever could bring actual benefit in the present . . . Therefore many of our old ceremonial traditions I discarded—no matter, I decided. Let them go." Yet there was no attempt to modernize the liturgy itself. The wording and procedures of all the rituals went untouched, nor was there any move to bring the language or indeed the ceremonial—the vestments, the gestures, or the objects employed—up to date, no thought of *aggiornamento,* of making the faith less mysterious or more readily comprehensible.

The pope jumped the other way. Retaining most of the ceremony and outer trappings of the church, he radically attenuated the liturgy through the adoption of a new Mass, dropping Latin and many other elements of tradition.* Only in their commitment to the supernatural were both leaders in complete agreement.

Thomas Merton was in a way emblematic of this "renewed" Catholic Church. One of the most influential Christian writers of the twentieth century, he had by now become deeply interested in Buddhism, causing some to believe that, had he lived, he would have converted. For the first of his three meetings with the Precious Protector, the conversation, according to Merton, was all about "religion and philosophy and especially ways of meditation." The Dalai Lama was, he wrote, "most impressive . . . strong and alert, bigger than I expected . . . A very solid, energetic, generous and warm person."

For his part, the Dalai Lama records his gratitude to Merton for introducing him to "the real meaning of the word Christian." The fifty-three-year old Westerner was, he found, a "truly humble and deeply spiritual man," a view that will not surprise any of Merton's many admirers. Yet one wonders what the Dalai Lama would have thought of Merton had he known of the Catholic's recent liaison with a woman three decades his junior. By the same token, one wonders what Merton, a peace activist and critic of the Vietnam War, would have made of the CIA's involvement in Tibet at the time. There is reason to think both would have been horrified.

---

*To be fair to Paul VI, he had inherited most of these reforms from his predecessor, John XXIII. Paul was the one who implemented them.

Merton's journal record of his conversations over several days with the Tibetan monk gives a penetrating insight into the Dalai Lama's real preoccupations. Politics seems to have been mentioned hardly at all, except in relation to the putative compatibility of Marxism and monasticism, the topic of Merton's forthcoming conference contribution: only if Marxism was confined to "the establishment of an equitable economic and social structure," in the Dalai Lama's view. Of greater interest to the Dalai Lama was the question of the stages of the spiritual path within the Catholic tradition. "Having made vows, did the monks continue to progress along a spiritual way, toward an eventual illumination, and what were the degrees of that progress?" Merton does not record his answer, but doubtless would have referred to the writings of mystics such as Saints Teresa of Ávila and Bonaventure. Both describe a seven-stage journey of spiritual development by means of service to others, and prayer. Merton's visit thus alerted the Dalai Lama to the depth of Christian culture in a way that, perhaps, the brisk Anglicanism of some of his other Western visitors had not.

Merton's visit was also significant for the welcome news it brought of the Catholic Church's change in attitude toward mission. Whereas in the past the emphasis had been on obtaining converts, now it was on witness. The issue of conversion is one that still rankles for the Dalai Lama and for Tibetans generally. Buddhism does not seek converts. (When, as has occasionally happened, some of the Dalai Lama's Christian visitors have let their enthusiasm get the better of their good manners and sought to make a convert of him, the insult is thus doubly felt.) The guru teaches only when asked—and asked again. As for mission, the assumption is that as non-Buddhists* come to have a better understanding of what Buddhism is, and in particular when they come to have a better understanding of how things really are, they will naturally seek instruction from a spiritual guide and, in due course, will enter the path to liberation themselves.

It was around the time of Merton's visit that the Dalai Lama and his inner circle had the first indication that the CIA's Tibet program would soon be

* In Tibetan, *phyi rol pa,* literally, outsiders—in contrast to *Nang pa,* meaning insiders (where *nang* means "home").

drawing to a close. Gyalo Thondup was alerted by the head of the Russian news agency in Delhi to the fact that moves were afoot in Washington to reach out to the Chinese. As a presidential candidate, Richard Nixon had argued that China could not be kept outside the family of nations, nurturing fantasies in "angry isolation." Now that he was in power, it was clear that President Nixon intended to follow up on his pledge.

To the Dalai Lama personally these developments were not wholly unwelcome. At least, fewer people stood to be killed by the rebels or in retaliation for their attacks. But when it emerged that the CIA's funding of the Tibetan government in exile itself was also under threat, he was persuaded by the more hawkish of his advisers to make loud protestations of commitment to the quest to regain Tibet's independence. In an early speech to mark the anniversary of the "Tibetan National Uprising Day," the Dalai Lama had decried the "inhuman treatment and persecution" of his people at the hands of the Chinese. He had also spoken of their "passive struggle against tyranny and oppression." More recently, the temperature had risen sharply. Speaking of the "naked horror, sufferings and nightmarish hardships" endured by his countrymen in Tibet, he characterized the Chinese as "alien rulers," adding that "not to speak of fundamental human rights, a Tibetan is denied even the right to exist as a human being." Now it was the "great and sacred responsibility" of all Tibetans to commit to the "unmitigated continuation of the national struggle." The Dalai Lama called on his countrymen to "rededicate themselves to this sacred task."

Whether or not this fiery rhetoric had a direct impact on those setting the State Department's budget, we do not know. Nonetheless, for a little while longer, the funding was maintained—as indeed was the rhetoric. In 1971 we find the Dalai Lama speaking of "Tibetan courage" and the people's "determination never to live under alien rule." There should be no doubt that they would "carry on the struggle till we see Tibet once again in its rightful place among the nations of the world." This overt championing of independence for Tibet did not go down well with the Indian administration, for which, as the Dalai Lama reported subsequently to the government in exile, it caused significant "problems."

At this time, Prime Minister Indira Gandhi was in danger of losing control of her Congress Party.* For ideological reasons, Congress retained an instinctive sympathy for the Chinese Communist Party as overthrowers of colonialism—despite the fact that the Communists had shown themselves to be avid colonists. As a result, Mrs. Gandhi could do without further problems stirred up by her country's Tibetan guests. In response to the Dalai Lama's renewed stridency, she let it be known that the future of the Tibetan Special Frontier Force, which, it will be recalled, had been set up following the Sino-Indian War of 1962 and now gainfully employed fully twelve thousand of the refugees, was in the balance.

This was deeply unwelcome news. If both American funding and funding of the SFF were to be withdrawn simultaneously, the viability of the whole community would be threatened. To compound the Dalai Lama's worries, the news from Tibet was deeply concerning. In 1969 and 1970, a wave of revolts and protests had broken out, with significant numbers of casualties inflicted on the Chinese. In retaliation, there had been mass arrests and public executions.

Yet remarkably, in spite of the many obstacles he faced within the temporal realm, on the spiritual plane this was an especially fruitful period for the Dalai Lama. Robert Thurman, with wife and two children in tow, visiting the Dalai Lama in 1971, noticed "an astonishing, exciting change in him . . . He had come alive philosophically." In particular, Thurman noticed, the Dalai Lama "no longer referred every question" to his teachers. Instead, he gave his own "lucid and lyrical explanations of difficult texts." Exactly what spiritual realizations he attained during this period remain secret in accordance with every initiate's vow of silence, but a number of hints suggestive of the Precious Protector's growing stature as a yogin can be gleaned both from his biography of Ling Rinpoché and from the autobiography of Trijang Rinpoché.

From Trijang Rinpoché we gather that toward the end of 1969 the Dalai Lama had a number of auspicious dreams, and that, during a subsequent retreat, he consecrated some long-life pills—"and other substances"—which

*Indira Gandhi, Nehru's daughter; in office 1966–1977 and again from 1980 until her assassination in 1984.

he presented to the junior tutor. The importance of dreams within tantric practice would be hard to overestimate. Because physical sensation is absent in dreams, the practitioner's mental states are considered to be more immediately available, and more readily open to manipulation, during sleep. The majority of dream yoga teachings are "ear-whispered," and therefore secret. But we do know that this remarkable set of practices aims to further the initiate's quest for Enlightenment. To induce lucid dreaming, the practitioner lies on his right side, the right hand cupping the cheek with the thumb pressing a nerve by the cheekbone. The left arm is extended and rests on the left hip. Once the dream is established, there are four principal steps: first, the sleeper, realizing he (or she) is dreaming, takes control of the dream; second, the dreamer "re-describes" the dream such that it becomes a form of spiritual practice; third, the dreamer "multiplies" the dream, imagining himself or herself in a variety of different situations; fourth, the dreamer dissolves the dream into the clear light of mere awareness—one of the features of which is non-duality. Once mastery of the technique is gained, it is said to be possible to travel not just around the terrestrial world but into different worlds, or *loka,* to meet with other spiritual practitioners and to converse with and even take teachings from them. In the Dalai Lama's own case, he has on occasion been able to reconnect with his past lives and has spoken of dreaming that he was once a slave in an ancient Egyptian pharaoh's court.

The Dalai Lama attained another important milestone in his spiritual development toward the end of the following year when he began the completion stage of an advanced tantric practice called *tum mo*—literally, Fierce Woman—yoga. Ordinarily the training involved takes a little over two years, though it may take much longer, depending on aptitude and the ability of the individual to devote himself or herself wholeheartedly to the regime. This includes a requirement to undertake a minimum of 100,000 prostrations, in which the practitioner lays himself or herself down at full stretch, arms out, on the ground while reciting the "refuge" formula (a short prayer to the deity being invoked). An additional ten thousand prostrations are undertaken in case of errors during the practice, plus another thousand in case of further mistakes. It is not surprising to learn that, for best results, besides conducting these exercises very early in the morning (though not before half light, on account of the harmful influences that may beset the practitioner when it is dark), the yogin is advised to adopt meat in his or her diet.* Later in the training, *tum mo* yogins visualize themselves as deities coupled with a consort in the "union of bliss and emptiness." This entails the repetition of 400,000 mantras for the male and 200,000 mantras for the female deity, plus a further 100,000 mantras for the *dakinis* in their retinue. (A *dakini* may be understood most simply as a female spiritual being.)

Of all tantric practices, *tum mo* yoga is capable of producing the most spectacular empirically demonstrable results—results of which the Dalai Lama himself was skeptical at the outset. Though only a byproduct of the training, which is chiefly concerned with pacifying the initiate's afflictive emotions in preparation for experiencing the "union of bliss and emptiness" at which all tantric practice aims, the physical effect of *tum mo* is to raise the body temperature to extraordinary levels. This occurs as a result of the "vase" breathing exercises that form part of the discipline. At the invitation of the Dalai Lama during the early 1980s, a team from the Harvard Medical School led by Dr. Herbert Benson visited Dharamsala to conduct experiments on some adepts. They found that the most proficient meditators could raise their core temperature by up to fifteen degrees Fahrenheit, while in specific areas of the body it went even higher. A popular event, first described by Alexandra David-Néel, the French traveler and religious seeker, is the annual competition held today by hermits high above the snow line in the mountains above Dharamsala. The one who wins is the yogin who can dry out the largest number of sheets soaked in freezing water and draped about his naked torso. Yet when the Americans came to do their research, they "found that without gloves their fingers became numb so quickly that they could not fix the electrodes to the body to obtain their readings. The tests had to be done indoors."

Another feature of *tum mo* yoga is the "levitation" that forms a standard part of the practice, whereby "the practitioner sits in full lotus posture and by means of a downward flip of the legs propels himself upwards in a jump which may reach several feet." When Alexandra David-Néel witnessed the

---

*This may well be a reason why the Dalai Lama is not wholly vegetarian. The yogas he practices can be very demanding physically.

spectacle for the first time, she was somewhat disappointed, having hoped that she would see something that defied physical laws. Nonetheless, it is startling enough. And while the temptation is to take these remarkable physiological effects as an end in themselves, it is vital to remember that their whole purpose is to enable the yogin to attain direct insight of the nature of mind, which, when undistracted by thought, is seen, according to the tradition, to be clear and limpid as a still lake. When the practitioner attains this level of clarity, the mind is found to be empty of self. What remains is mere awareness.*

The context of this spiritual progress on the part of the Dalai Lama included two conferrals of the Kalachakra initiation, one in Dharamsala in 1970 and the other at one of the south Indian settlements early the following year. Apart from his initiation into Shantideva's *tong len* lineage, one of the most important teachings the Dalai Lama had taken since coming into exile included further initiation into the mysteries of the apocalyptic Kalachakra tantra by its greatest contemporary exponent, the Eleventh Kirti Rinpoché (1926–2006). In a notably vivid dream of Kalachakra's female consort, the Dalai Lama received clear encouragement to spread the peacemaking power of the tantra throughout the world. Accordingly, he made a commitment to serve as the bodhisattva's principal advocate and to offer the Kalachakra initiation as frequently as possible. This was validated during a subsequent retreat when, in a vision he had of Kalachakra in wrathful form, the bodhisattva indicated to the Dalai Lama that he had his full support in this.

How these spiritual events tie in with developments in the temporal sphere can only be guessed at, but it is a fact that the Kalachakra initiation the Dalai Lama conferred in 1971 preceded by only a few months one of the least known but most devastating episodes in the history of his life in exile.

The decade had begun with the worst weather ever recorded on the eastern coast of the Indian subcontinent. A disastrous cyclone killed up to a quarter of a million people in East Pakistan (present-day Bangladesh), flooding huge areas and forcing millions from their homes. The Pakistani government's

*There is an interesting argument to be had here about whether the yogin's experience is merely a psychological state induced by self-hypnosis. Yet for the one who attains such experience, it is evident that there is an attendant indubitability that defies such an easy reduction.

inept handling of the crisis precipitated a level of civil unrest that began to threaten its existence. Following the violent partition of India after independence from Britain in 1947, the predominantly Muslim territories had formed the Islamic Republic of Pakistan, which, at the time, was subdivided into two administrative regions, both governed from Islamabad but separated by more than a thousand miles. By mid-1971, opposition to the Pakistan government had grown to such an extent that civil war began to look likely. Now, millions of refugees from East Pakistan started streaming west toward India, and disease and starvation threatened on an epic scale. To compound the horror, the central government of Pakistan ordered its army to quell the protests in an operation that saw perhaps another quarter of a million—mostly Bengali civilians—dead.

Prime Minister Gandhi meanwhile, seeing both a welcome distraction from her domestic difficulties and an opportunity to seriously weaken India's traditional foe, called in her generals. Among these was S. S. Uban, head of special forces and commander of Establishment 22, the Tibetan Special Frontier Force. Already famous for his alleged exploits as a scout commander in David Stirling's Long Range Desert Patrol (forerunners of Britain's special forces regiment, 22 Special Air Service) during the Second World War, Uban was one of those military men, by no means rare, who manage to combine their commitment to kill when called on with a strong religious faith. Ordering him to "carry out reconnaissance and conduct whatever unconventional warfare [he] deemed necessary," the prime minister made clear to General Uban that she wanted a decisive result in East Pakistan. He in turn asked for an entirely free hand. "Will you allow me to take all my men with me, Tibetans and all?" he demanded. "Tibetans?" she replied. "Goodness! Will you be able to control them?"

"Yes, leave that to me," he replied. "They [will] do anything I ask of them."

Meanwhile, as the world looked on appalled, the tragedy unfolding in East Pakistan inspired what *Rolling Stone* magazine hailed as a "brief incandescent revival of all that was best about the Sixties," the Concert for Bangladesh organized by ex-Beatle George Harrison and featuring many of the artists associated with that decade's counterculture. It is thus one of those cruel ironies of history that, almost at the very moment when forty thousand of New

York's emancipated youth descended on Madison Square Garden for Harrison's concert, Establishment 22's two senior-most Tibetan officers appeared in Dharamsala, carrying with them a letter from the prime minister herself. This, though not addressed personally to the Dalai Lama, set out the Indian position. "We cannot compel you to fight a war for us," Mrs. Gandhi wrote, "but the fact is that General A A K Niazi [the Pakistan army commander in East Pakistan] is treating the people of East Pakistan very badly. India has to do something about it. In a way, it is similar to the way the Chinese are treating the Tibetans in Tibet . . . It would be appreciated if you could help us fight the war for liberating the people of Bangladesh."

There was some force in the Indian argument that Pakistan's suppression of the Bengalis was analogous to Chinese suppression of the Tibetans. There was also no denying that the Pakistani junta's methods were outrageous. But in reality, the Dalai Lama had no option. This was a test of loyalty. It was a test that, should he fail it, could have disastrous consequences, the least of which would be disbandment of the SFF itself. With the greatest reluctance he therefore acquiesced in what can only be described as India's dirty war. Regretfully giving the soldiers his blessing, he consented with only the forlorn caution that they should spare as many lives as possible.

The move was not wholly unsupported by the Dalai Lama's inner circle. Moreover, Trijang Rinpoché had close relations with many in the SFF. During the summer of 1970, he was to be found visiting the soldiers in Chakrata at the invitation of their commander. On succeeding days with the soldiers, the junior tutor granted them a number of tantric permissions—that is, permission to undertake specific practices—as well as a long-life initiation. Thereafter, he gave teachings, transmissions, and advice to individual companies and their commanders according to need.*

By mid-November 1971, and three weeks before hostilities were formally declared, the Tibetans were airlifted to Assam. From there they were infiltrated by canoe into the jungle-covered Chittagong Hills. The plan, known as

---

*Remarkably enough, the British army retains, at least at the time of this writing, at least one Tibetan Buddhist monk on strength as chaplain to its Gurkha regiments. More than half of all Gurkhas are Buddhist.

Operation Eagle, was that they would outflank Pakistan's own special forces and head for the coast, ready to cut off any attempted retreat in the direction of Burma. Wearing unmarked uniforms and armed with Bulgarian assault rifles—this partly to disguise who they really were and partly to confuse the enemy—the Tibetans quickly overran the Pakistani position. "After that," recalled Uban, "they were unstoppable." It was for this action that they earned themselves the sobriquet "the Phantoms of Chittagong."*

On December 3, the Pakistani air force launched what was billed as a preemptive strike against India, as a result of which, as Trijang Rinpoché noted, for the next two weeks "everyone lived in a state of anxiety." In retaliation, India officially declared war. By the sixteenth it was all over thanks largely to the SFF: the Pakistani army was routed, and General Uban was a national hero. "And do you know why Unit 22 was so successful?" he asked afterwards. "Their reputation preceded them. The very idea of Tibetans struck terror in the hearts of the Pakistanis. They heard Unit 22, and the whole bloody world was running away!" As for the Tibetans themselves, "their morale—you should have seen—sky high! They felt they could take back Tibet tomorrow." When he came subsequently to write a memoir of the campaign, Uban dedicated his book to "the gallant officers and men of the SPECIAL FRONTIER FORCE, who made the supreme sacrifice of their lives, braving dangers beyond the call of duty and blazing immortal trails in the history of righteous wars waged against oppression and for the freedom of all mankind."

Victory in Bangladesh was a massive boost to morale for the Indian army generally, and hugely important for the SFF as a demonstration of both its effectiveness and the loyalty of the Tibetan refugees to India. It also demonstrated that, well-armed, well-trained, and well-led, India's clandestine Tibetan army was an extremely potent force. Unfortunately for the Tibetans, because their participation in the war was unofficial—so secret, in fact, that most of the Indian Eastern Army command was unaware that they had already been operating behind enemy lines for three weeks when the war began—there could be no official recognition of their contribution. Instead, all who participated received a bounty of around 500 rupees, but there were to be no

* Uban published a memoir of the same name.

medals, nor any commendations for bravery. When the impossibility of official acclaim became apparent, there was immense disappointment in the ranks. Fearing, perhaps, that dismay at being overlooked might lead to disaffection and from there to open dissent, Uban contacted Dharamsala. The outcome was as welcome as it was unprecedented. The Dalai Lama announced to a parade of the entire unit that, having a few days to himself, he wanted to pay them a personal visit. It was he himself who led the inspection at their base in Chakrata in June 1972.

Although this is the only time that the Dalai Lama is known to have visited the soldiers, that he did not disapprove of the Special Frontier Force is suggested by the fact that his younger brother subsequently became one of its officers.

Back in Dharamsala, the Precious Protector was quick to resume his spiritual training under the direction of the two tutors. From Trijang Rinpoché, he received a number of permissions, "starting with the common torma initiation and the exclusive Cittamani Tara, together with the most secret Heart Absorption Permission," in return for which the Dalai Lama offered his junior tutor "the permissions of the seventeen emanations of Four-Faced Mahakala, Robber of Strength . . . including Split Faces, Striking the Vital Point and Secret Accomplishment," but excluding, for reasons not specified, the "Entrusted Black Brahman." From Ling Rinpoché, too, the Dalai Lama received, "a very special Cittamani initiation."

A year later, the Precious Protector was finally permitted by the Indian government to undertake a six-week, eleven-country tour of Europe during the autumn. This was a welcome development. Not that it was a wholly altruistic move on the part of Prime Minister Gandhi. Against the background of America's thawing relations with the PRC, we might reasonably suspect that unleashing the Dalai Lama was her way of reminding the world that India should not be forgotten amidst the euphoria of rapprochement between the superpowers. It can also be read as a reward for the Dalai Lama's cooperation in the Bangladesh war.

17

"Something beyond the comprehension of the Tibetan people": The Yellow Book *and the Glorious Goddess*

The prospect of his forthcoming trip to the West was a matter of great encouragement not just for the Dalai Lama but for Tibetans generally. Yet while arrangements were being put in place for the now thirty-eight-year-old Dalai Lama's eleven-country itinerary, there occurred a series of events that were to have shattering repercussions both within the exile community and in Tibet.

The first indication of trouble came on the day when the Dalai Lama arrived to consecrate a new statue in the main temple in Dharamsala. To the contemporary reader, the consecration of a statue might seem an unremarkable event, but that would be to ignore the central place that iconography occupies within the Buddhist tradition—as indeed it does in non-secular traditions generally. Gombojav Tsybikov, the Buryato-Russian explorer who visited Lhasa on the cusp of the twentieth century, described how pilgrims would pay a fee to place their own images in the presence of the Jowo, the "self-arisen" statue of the Buddha brought to Tibet in the seventh century by King Songtsen Gampo's Chinese princess bride. Its monk attendants would also sell the bodies of mice that, having gorged themselves on the barley offering made to the statute, had died in its presence. Their meat was considered especially efficacious for expectant mothers facing difficult births. On the occasion in question, the statue was of Padmasambhava, the Lotus-Born—one of the greatest spiritual heroes of the Tibetan Buddhist tradition and, furthermore, the key figure within the Nyingma tradition.

An initiative of the Dalai Lama himself, this project was intended by him to rectify a mistake made during the 1950s. At that time a leading Nyingma master had petitioned the Kashag to have a statue of the Lotus-Born consecrated in the Jokhang Temple as a defense against the Chinese. Significantly, this statue was to portray the sage in the form of Nangsi Zilnon, Overcomer of Obstacles, and it was to be positioned facing east. Although the Kashag accepted the proposal for a statue, when it was erected it was not in the correct form, and it faced south. The dedication now of a statue in the correct form and facing in the right direction in Dharamsala would thus correct the earlier failure.* Another aspect of the undertaking was the Dalai Lama's wish to foster unity among the different schools within the Tibetan tradition. The Lotus-Born is venerated by a large percentage of Tibetans, irrespective of sectarian affiliation, and is thus a unifying figure. Right from the beginning of the exile period, it had been clear to the Precious Protector that the survival of the Tibetan people depended on their coming together as a community. One of his first acts on arrival in Dharamsala had been to convene a meeting of the senior-most representatives of each of the different Tibetan religious traditions. Urging them "to fulfil the . . . welfare of all Tibetans," the Dalai Lama set the tone for increased cooperation among the different schools. Similarly, his founding of the Institute of Buddhist Dialectics in 1973 was another major initiative designed to further his ecumenical vision. Open to students of all backgrounds, the institute sent a clear signal that it was the Mahayana tradition in general, rather than any particular school within it, that was important.

When the day of consecration of the new statue arrived, the Dalai Lama was surprised to see far fewer monks and nuns attending than he would have expected. On making inquiries, he learned that a recently published book had

---

*It can be safely assumed that the Dalai Lama was encouraged in this project by Nechung.

caused many to boycott the ceremony for fear of supernatural consequences. The book, *An Account of the Protective Deity Dorje Shugden, Chief Guardian of the Gelug Order, and of the Punishments Meted Out to Religious and Lay Leaders Who Incurred His Wrath,* better known simply as *The Yellow Book,* had been written by a well-regarded student of Trijang Rinpoché. Little more than a pamphlet —it was originally intended as a supplement to a longer work by Trijang himself—the book opened with an ominous dedication: "Praise to you, Protector of the Yellow Hat tradition, you who grind to dust great adepts, high officials and laymen alike." There followed a list of well-known individuals who had allegedly incurred the wrath of the protector Dorje Shugden for having polluted the pure teachings of the Gelug tradition by venerating objects and individuals associated with other schools or by adopting their practices—particularly those of the Nyingma sect. Among these were many familiar figures of the regency period, including Reting Rinpoché, the former regent, along with Lungshar, whose eyes were put out, and Trimon, a chief minister who lost his mind toward the end of his life.

The word Nyingma means simply "ancient" and is applied to those teachings, lineages, and practices that came to Tibet with the first diffusion of Buddhism, roughly from the seventh to the ninth centuries. This was the time of the religious kings, of whom there were three, each considered a manifestation of Chenresig. Following the apostasy of a later monarch, who persecuted Buddhism to the brink of extinction, Tibet endured a Dark Age for two hundred years before a second diffusion of Buddhism began during the eleventh century. This revival was undertaken by a number of sages working independently of one another and to whom can be traced the later different traditions—the Kadam (from which the Dalai Lama's Gelug school is derived), Sakya, Kargyu, and Jonang traditions.

Within the Buddhist tradition generally, the authority of a given lineage—the lineage being the teacher-to-student relation through which a set of teachings and practices is transmitted—is derived from the ability to trace it back to its origin with the Buddha. This is complicated, particularly in the Mahayana tradition, by the fact that certain of the most highly accomplished masters are said to have received a particular teaching or practice directly, often in a vision of the Buddha, even though they were not his contemporaries. Suffice it to say that some purists hold that all those lineages that claim to derive from the Lotus-Born and the first diffusion of Buddhism in Tibet were in fact broken during the Dark Age and subsequently corrupted. The Lotus-Born's devotees (who make up perhaps a third of the monastic community and an even higher percentage among the laity, for whom adherence to a single sect is less important) believe, however, that many of the lineages brought to Tibet by the Lotus-Born did in fact survive. They hold, moreover, that the Lotus-Born is a manifestation of a fully enlightened being, a "second Buddha."

What is known about the Lotus-Born apart from what the Nyingma tradition says about him is scant. Contemporary records show only that he came to Tibet during the reign of Tibet's second Dharma King and that he was involved with the foundation of Samye, the country's first monastery, toward the end of the eighth century CE. They also tell us that he was expelled from Tibet on the orders of the king and, moreover, that the Lotus-Born foiled an attempt to murder him as he left the court. But the records have nothing to say about his real importance. They do not tell us about the prophecy he uttered on his banishment, to the effect that, in future, the divisions in Tibet would be not between believer and nonbeliever but between the followers of the doctrine themselves. As to the fifty-six years some say that he spent in Tibet following his official banishment, the contemporary records are completely silent. Yet it is to these years that his most important work is said to belong. Secretly, silently, the Lotus-Born waged war on Tibet's indigenous deities, subduing them and binding them over as protectors of the faith. These he put under the command of a certain Pehar, a deity whom he persuaded to leave his abode on the Mongolian steppes to take up residence as the chief protector of Samye Monastery.

Why this is so significant is that it is Pehar who speaks through Dorje Drakden, muse of the Nechung oracle. Pehar himself is a fallen angel. Many eons ago, during an incarnation as a Brahmin priest, he succumbed to the charms of a beautiful girl. For seven days and seven nights they made love in the temple where he lived. Outcast thereafter, Pehar was reborn first in the hell realms, then again as a human being, destined to wander the world homeless until he died. He was then reborn the son of a minor deity, and it was in this incarnation that he took up his vocation as a local god among the Uighur peoples of Central Asia. Why precisely Pehar was chosen by the Lotus-Born to come to Tibet is unclear. But he later emerged as the most important of the dharma protectors. How this came about is significant to our story because it connects the time of the Great Fifth Dalai Lama to the present day.

During the sixteenth century, Pehar had a disagreement with the abbot of Samye Monastery. As a result, the abbot decreed that there was no need for the deity to be depicted in a new chapel then under construction. Incensed, the deity retaliated by manifesting as a boy who came to offer his services as a fresco painter. As recompense for his work, the boy asked only that he be permitted to paint a small monkey holding a stick of incense somewhere on one of the walls. The abbot agreed, the chapel was adorned with the customary religious scenes, and the boy departed. That night, however, Pehar slipped into the image of the monkey and, using the stick of incense, set the building ablaze.

Realizing he had been tricked, the abbot had a demon trap constructed. These devices, still very much a feature of Tibetan Buddhist practice, consist of lengths of yarn stretched in an intricate geometrical pattern over a wooden frame, somewhat in the manner of a giant cat's cradle. The demon is lured in by means of offerings and invocations, and then is unable to find a way out. The deity was subsequently caught, placed in a casket, and pitched into the river. Sometime later, the box washed up on the banks of the Kyichu about half a day's journey from Lhasa, where it was seen by the Great Fifth —though whether in a dream or whether he was alerted to its presence by a third party is obscure. In any case, he ordered the box to be brought ashore, adding that on no account should it be opened. Remarkably, the farther the box was carried from its resting place, the heavier it became, until the monk deputed to the task could carry it no longer. Puzzled, he ignored the instruction not to look inside and opened it up. To his surprise, a pigeon emerged and flew into the branches of a nearby tree. Hearing of this, the Great Fifth admonished the monk and ordered that a shrine be built at the base of the tree. The shrine subsequently became incorporated into Nechung Monastery, and it was among the monks of this foundation that Pehar's oracle began once more to manifest itself. The most important of the dharma protectors can thus be traced unambiguously back to the ministry of the Lotus-Born.

On hearing of the existence of *The Yellow Book* on that day in Dharamsala, the Dalai Lama was deeply affected. Not only was this a public rebuke, and not only did it clearly insinuate that evil would befall him if he continued along his chosen path of rapprochement between the different traditions, but also it was an insult to Nechung, who had sanctioned the admission of the Lotus-Born (in statue form) to the temple. It was one thing to hold reservations about the Dalai Lama's policy of openness to the non-Gelug traditions—he was well aware that some did—but to publish what amounted to a loaded personal criticism without informing him in advance was an insult. The fact that the author was a member of the Dalai Lama's inner circle and a heart disciple of Trijang Rinpoché and could therefore be assumed to have done so with the junior tutor's full knowledge only made matters worse. Nor was this a trivial issue of dharma politics, as the violent events that ensued would show.

The Dalai Lama thus had much on his mind when, during the fall of that year, he embarked on his trip to Europe.

Apart from being an eye-opener, allowing the Dalai Lama to experience what, up until then, he had only heard about, the visit to Europe seems to have had less impact than might have been expected. The Dalai Lama quickly realized that the two hemispheres, East and West, were "not so different after all." From contemporary media coverage of the visit, we learn that the Dalai Lama had been well briefed by the Indian government, which made clear that he was not permitted to engage in political activities but should confine himself strictly to religious matters. An interview on Dutch television shows him laughing at the questions of an interviewer trying to maneuver him into being indiscreet. Since his trip was entirely nonpolitical, he explained, he did "not want to spoil" it. In spite of this, he was nonetheless received by a number of political leaders, including both the president and the prime minister of Ireland. Among senior religious figures, he met with Pope Paul VI, the Archbishop of Canterbury, and the Aga Khan. And in London he was delighted to find a number of elderly ex-officials who had actually served in Tibet during the time of the British Empire and could speak Tibetan. But perhaps most important for the Dalai Lama personally was his meeting with the two hundred Tibetan children who had been adopted post-exile into Swiss families, though he was disappointed to find that most had lost their mother tongue. In view of this, he encouraged monks at the recently founded Rikon Monastery in nearby Zell to provide language classes for them.

On his return to Dharamsala, it was not long before the Dalai Lama was plunged back into the intricacies of supernatural politics. Early in 1974, during the government's annual invocation of the Nechung oracle, the deity handed down a prophecy that shook the Dalai Lama to the core. Something, declared the deity, had upset the mind of Palden Lhamo. As the Precious Protector wrote subsequently, "This was something beyond the comprehension of the Tibetan people." So serious was the matter that "on the following day it was decided it would be right to perform an effective *tsok** ritual propitiation of Palden Lhamo and the five king emanations, to be followed by an invitation to Nechung . . . during which confessions and apologies would be made to Palden Lhamo and Nechung would be asked to clarify what we had done wrong."

The difficulty here was that the Glorious Goddess is far too exalted a being to be contactable by straightforward means. She does not speak through an oracle in the way Pehar speaks through the Nechung oracle. Nor does Dorje Drakden, through whom Pehar speaks, have the right of access to her. He can help in the process, but other than in the most exceptional cases—such as when, during the reign of the Great Fifth, she spoke directly from her *thangka*—Palden Lhamo is accessible only through dream, divination, and inference following careful preparation. The Dalai Lama would have to inquire—something that would take time (months rather than weeks, possibly even years rather than just months) and great diligence. Nonetheless, the importance of the pronouncement cannot be overstated, and investigation of its meaning became a central focus of the Dalai Lama's spiritual practice.

In the meantime, there were important developments on the earthly plane. Now that the CIA had withdrawn all its funding of the Tibetan resistance, the situation with respect to the guerrilla camp in Mustang in northern Nepal came quickly to a head. The guerrillas themselves had declared that they would never give up. But then a new king ascended the throne in Nepal in early 1972. It soon became clear that this monarch would not, as his father had

*A *tsok* offering is a highly charged ritual practice that involves the offering of both material and spiritual substances to the tantric deities as a means to gaining wisdom and merit.

done, simply turn a blind eye to the antics of the Tibetan freedom fighters in Mustang. It was, after all, a province of Nepal, however remote. Following a visit by the new king to Beijing during the autumn of 1973, the Nepalese issued an ultimatum. The camp must either disband voluntarily or face a military contest—with either the Nepalese army, the Chinese, or both.

The terms were generous nonetheless: if the freedom fighters went quietly, the Nepalese government would provide a million dollars (presumably supplied by the Americans) to help resettle the troops. In return, the Nepalese would acquire the Tibetans' weapons. But while the majority of camp residents saw the futility of trying to carry on under these circumstances, a minority still refused to lay down their arms.

Watching with mounting concern over the prospect of an international incident with potentially embarrassing consequences, given that the rebels' financial and other support was being channeled through India, the Indian government contacted the Dalai Lama, requesting that he intervene. It was decided that he should make a voice recording to be played to the diehards. This was duly conveyed to the rebel camp—with disastrous results. On hearing the Dalai Lama's words, the soldiers felt as if the world had been cut from beneath them. For them, the Dalai Lama was their reason for sacrificing not just family but all worldly ambition in the "sacred cause" of which he had spoken so eloquently in his March 10 statement just recently. The tape recording asking the rebels to lay down their arms seemed nothing less than betrayal. Several took their own lives on the spot—one of the commanders slashing so vigorously at his own throat that he completely decapitated himself. Another soldier threw himself wordlessly from the top of a cliff. Others were so dazed that "they wandered around crying, like they didn't even know where they were." It was a tragic end to a project that was, in reality, doomed from the outset.

While on the earthly plane the disbanding of the Mustang guerrilla camp brought to a close Tibetan dreams of an armed liberation of Tibet, on the spiritual plane a similar sundering occurred soon after. During his investigations of the Glorious Goddess's terrifying pronouncement, the Dalai Lama encountered both the Great Fifth and the Great Thirteenth in dreams, and both former incarnations advised him to cease propitiating Dorje Shugden. It emerged that what had upset the mind of the Glorious Goddess two years previously was in fact Shugden's behavior. This was a very serious development, yet it was subsequently given supernatural approval not once but three times when the Dalai Lama conducted separate divinations in front of the Great Fifth's *thangka* of the Glorious Goddess, which, on that never-to-be-forgotten occasion, had spoken directly. The advice was the same in every case: not only should he cease propitiating Shugden in public, but also he should cease doing so in private, too. In fact, as far back as the late 1960s, Pehar, speaking through Nechung, had warned the Dalai Lama and the government that they should beware of the deity. But on that occasion the Dalai Lama had rebuked him for openly criticizing an important fellow protector. After all, had not Shugden played a vital role in the escape into exile? And was he not the guardian of the Gelugpa tradition itself? How could Pehar presume to speak against a colleague in this way?

In the fall of 1976, the Dalai Lama conferred his sixth Kalachakra initiation on a large audience just outside Leh in Ladakh, a remote, ethnically Tibetan province of northern India. Formerly a tributary principality of the Tibetan government, today Ladakh has a Muslim population approaching that of the Buddhist population. But while traditionally Islam is hostile to polytheism, of which Buddhism is considered an example, the Tibetan lamas of the region are widely respected—and the Dalai Lama himself is a popular figure among the Muslim community. On this occasion, it is said that the young daughter of a local mullah, who was taking his family to see the Tibetan holy man, was jokingly told by the grown-ups that she would see that he had four arms like the figures in many of the Buddhists statues. When, however, they asked her afterwards whether she had seen them for herself, she replied that he didn't have four arms. He had a thousand. This was reckoned a marvelous event by Tibetans when they came to hear of it. Chenresig is often depicted as having a thousand arms.

It was on the second day of this Kalachakra initiation that news came of the death of Chairman Mao at the age of eighty-two. The Dalai Lama, greatly moved at the passing of the man he had once admired so greatly, immediately led prayers for him.

No one supposed that this single event would change conditions in Tibet overnight. It was, however, an occasion for hope that life might improve. Credible reports (since corroborated) that a number of Tibetans were executed for showing inadequate remorse at the news of Mao's death quickly dampened expectations. Yet soon after, very different signals began to emerge from Beijing. An early indication of change came when, that same year, a senior American official was invited to visit Tibet. Six months later, Ngabo —the former governor turned collaborator and now a senior government official in Tibet—announced that the Precious Protector would be welcome to return home, "so long as he stood on the side of the people." Both were promising developments. The sudden reappearance of the Panchen Lama at a political conference was yet another hopeful sign. It seemed that the reformers were now in the ascendant, and while open dissent remained impermissible, gradually it became clear that China was seriously intent on liberalization.

As the Dalai Lama watched developments with keen interest, matters relating to the dharma protectors came to a head, culminating in a ceremony at which he summoned Nechung in front of a gathering of high lamas to confirm in public what he had told the Precious Protector in private. Now that he had broken with Shugden, "it would be excellent," proclaimed Nechung, "if the Dalai Lama . . . could receive as many initiations, transmissions and core teachings as possible from all the Tibetan traditions." This meant that, apart from taking Nyingma teachings, the Dalai Lama should also take teachings from masters representing each of the other traditions: Sakya, Kargyu, and Jonang. The Dalai Lama could now consider his determination to help preserve the Tibetan Buddhist tradition in its entirety by taking teachings from each of the different schools as having the approbation of the protectors themselves.

From the Dalai Lama's perspective, the loss of many lineages due to the destruction of the dharma in Tibet had to be limited to the extent possible. One way of helping to do so was for him to take initiations as widely as he was able. This was in keeping with the high lamas' traditional role as custodians of the teaching lineages. Broadening his remit to do so beyond his own school meant that he would be free to explore large areas of the tradition that would otherwise be off limits to him. Among these were the *dzogchen* teachings of the Nyingmapa and the *mahamudra* teachings of the Kargyupa. These *dzogchen* teachings, of which the most well known are to be found in the *Tibetan Book of the Dead,* describe a method of attaining Enlightenment in a single lifetime. In fact, similar methods are also described within the Gelug tradition, but proponents of *dzogchen* claim they are less efficacious than those described in this, arguably the most important of the Treasure Texts. A Treasure is a text, or sometimes an object, believed to have been hidden by the Lotus-Born (though other great masters are also associated with the practice) during his sojourn in Tibet and revealed by a qualified yogin when karmic conditions ripen suitably.

Similarly, *mahamudra** teachings are also to be found within the Gelug corpus, but the Kargyu tradition has a special focus on them and presents them in a unique form that the Dalai Lama was keen to help maintain. This new openness would also allow the Dalai Lama to be initiated into lineages that preserved variations on those maintained by the Gelug school, for example the extraordinary Chod† tradition that is again practiced by both Nyingma and Kargyu, as well as by Gelug yogins. These practices are attributed to an eleventh-century female practitioner by the name of Ma Chig Labdron. When only a girl, and despite her protests that she wanted to become a renunciate, her parents married her off. But so determined was Ma Chig to practice the dharma that she first burned her hands and feet and then, when that did not persuade her husband and parents to let her go, she cut off her own thumbs. Eventually they realized there was no stopping her and she finally had her way. So severe was her asceticism that her hair turned yellow and her eyebrows red, and yet still she was not taken seriously. It was only when the abbot of the monastery close to where she lived came and saw for himself not just these outward signs but signs of her inward realizations that she was accepted as one worthy of the highest respect. As for the Chod teachings, these include a set of visualizations whereby the meditator takes on a series of identities, becoming, among others, a wrathful goddess, a calm purifying god, and finally a fearless yogi, all of whom offer their own flesh and blood as food for the demons. For best results, these visualizations are conducted in a graveyard, or cremation ground, at night. Again, these practices are not unknown within

---

*The term refers to the union of wisdom and emptiness.

†Correctly *gcod,* which means "cutting through" or "severing" and refers to the hindrances or obstacles that stand in the yogin's way on the path to Enlightenment.

the Gelug tradition, while the habit of practicing among the recently dead is a well-known trope within the tradition as a whole. The Dalai Lama's spiritual lineage includes an incarnation known as the Yogin of the Burning Ground. Prior to his manifestation as King Songtsen Gampo, the first of the religious kings, Chenresig manifested as one known for his habit of frequenting cremation grounds, wearing the shrouds of the deceased, dancing, lying on top of corpses, and eating food left in offering for the dead.

Nechung's approbation of the Dalai Lama's desire to be initiated into practices from across the whole of the Tibetan tradition, not just by Gelug masters, but by other lamas, may seem unremarkable, but it is important to understand the radical nature of this development. One might think of the head of one of the most austere evangelical churches suddenly coming out in favor of inviting Catholic priests to bring their incense, Gregorian chant, communion rails, and confession into church on Sunday. For the majority of Tibetans, it was nonetheless a welcome move. It underlined the fact that this was a Dalai Lama whose wish was to serve all, irrespective of their religious commitments. Yet the change was also to have devastating consequences within the refugee community.

In the meantime, however, the Chinese government began to make overtures to a number of individuals who they thought might be able to influence the Dalai Lama. Among these were Heinrich Harrer and Prince Peter of Denmark and Greece. Having written *Seven Years in Tibet,* Harrer had gone on to make several other notable expeditions. The prince was less well known but had been an important figure in Kalimpong during the 1950s. An anthropologist by training, he had made a special study of the widespread practice of polyandry among Tibetans.* While both Harrer and Prince Peter eventually took up the invitation to revisit Tibet, they found no miraculous transformation for the better under the new regime—quite the contrary in fact—and neither was able to recommend that the Dalai Lama should ask to return, though the Chinese clearly hoped they would.

---

*His own marital arrangements were much more traditional, except that his marriage to a Russian divorcee four years his senior prevented him from sustaining his claim to the Greek throne.

The Dalai Lama's initial response to China's newfound commitment to openness and reform was muted, therefore. After so many years of the harshest treatment for any Tibetans who resisted Chinese rule, he and the Kashag were skeptical that any fundamental change had occurred. After all, despite some economic liberalization, the basic commitments to communism, to one-party rule, and to the occupation of Tibet were not in question. When, however, Gyalo Thondup—now living in Hong Kong—was approached by some officials of Xinhua, the Chinese state news agency, it became clear that Beijing was in earnest. This was the first contact, if indirect, between the Dalai Lama and the Chinese government in almost twenty years. The party leadership wanted to open a dialogue. With his brother's approval, Gyalo Thondup met with officials in Beijing in March 1979 and, on the twelfth, with Deng Xiaoping himself.

To his surprise, the Chinese leader—whom the Dalai Lama had met when, during the 1950s, Deng was political commissar for the southwestern military district—told Gyalo Thondup that, apart from independence, there was nothing that could not be discussed. And lest the Dalai Lama doubt what he was saying, he should send trusted emissaries to Tibet to investigate the situation for themselves: "Better to see with one's own eyes than to hear something a hundred times from other people."

For his part, Gyalo Thondup, deeply suspicious of Deng—mainly on account of documents he claimed to have seen suggesting that Deng, whom he nicknamed "the Dwarf," had been the very person who authorized the destruction of monasteries in Tibet—put forward three proposals on behalf of the Dalai Lama. The first was that Deng make good on his recent promise that contact between Tibetans inside Tibet and those in exile could be permitted. The second, taking up Deng's offer, was that the exile community be allowed to send representatives to investigate the "new Tibet." Third, the Dalai Lama would like to send some newly qualified teachers to Tibet. To all three proposals Deng responded enthusiastically, asking at once how many teachers were available. When Gyalo Thondup suggested Dharamsala might send "fifty for a start," the Chinese leader complained that was "no good. We need at least one thousand!"

From this encounter was born a plan whereby the Dalai Lama would send a series of fact-finding missions to Tibet to assess the situation on the ground. Should their reports concur with the Panchen Lama's recent speech declaring that "the present standard of living in Tibet is many times better than that of the 'old society,'" the Precious Protector might then accept Deng's further proposal—that he himself return for a visit.

This turn of events was as welcome to the exile community as it was unexpected. Many had given up hope of ever hearing what happened to loved ones who had stayed behind. Yet it was a moment of optimism tempered by dreadful anxiety; much of the news would surely be bad. The Dalai Lama nonetheless instructed his immediate elder brother, Lobsang Samten, recently returned from America, where he had been working anonymously for several years as a janitor at a school in Scotch Plains, New Jersey, to lead the first delegation.* He himself meanwhile set out on a trip to Moscow, the Buryat Republic, and Mongolia. In 1979 Russia still looked like a world superpower, and there was clear merit in developing relations with other players to the greatest extent possible in the field of global politics.

On his arrival in Moscow, the Dalai Lama discovered that Marxist tyranny remained alive and well in Russia. Describing a visit to Lenin's study at the Kremlin, he was later to recall the absurdity of being "watched over by an unsmiling plain-clothes security man who was clearly ready to shoot" at the least provocation. He also noted how out of touch the Russian Communist Party was with the common people. His aides reported how, after he had thanked a doorman in the Kremlin, the man announced that this was the first time in twenty-five years of service that anyone had uttered a word of gratitude. But while the trip to the USSR both sent a signal to China that he was not without friends even in the communist bloc and was a great encouragement to the Buddhists of the Soviet Republics, the trip the Dalai Lama took to the United States in the fall of 1979 was of far greater significance.

---

*Lobsang Samten was, by all accounts that I have heard, the most gentle of souls and his mother's admitted favorite. His decision to return to India may have been influenced by his recent discovery and exposure in the local press.

18

From Rangzen *to* Umaylam: *Independence and the Middle Way Approach*

For several years now, the Dalai Lama's representatives in America had been in touch with sympathetic political figures in Washington, notably Joel McCleary, a student of Geshe Wangyal and then deputy assistant for political affairs at the White House. Although President Ford had regarded the Dalai Lama primarily as the Indian government's "burden," President Carter understood, and was sympathetic to, the human rights angle of the Tibetan issue. The Dalai Lama would be welcome in the United States provided, as usual, that he kept to religious themes.

Arriving on September 3, 1979, the now forty-four-year-old Dalai Lama maintained a schedule that took him on a hectic tour of twenty-two cities over seven short weeks, starting with New York and ending with Washington, DC. Prophetically, the first word uttered in public by the Dalai Lama was "compassion." This was in answer to a question posed at a press conference asking whether he had a message for the United States. Subsequently mixing general talks on spirituality with more-technical discourses on Buddhist philosophy, the Dalai Lama was an immediate hit. Robert Thurman, by now a college professor, later recalled how, on reconnecting with the Dalai Lama, he "almost keeled over." Noting that the Tibetan leader had "always been charming and interesting and very witty," he saw that since their last meeting in 1971, the Dalai Lama had again increased markedly in stature and "opened up some inner wellspring of energy and attention and intelligence," adding, "He was glorious." It seems certain that the Dalai Lama's spiritual progress during the intervening years had given him a powerful self-assurance. Though his life had been—and would continue to be—a struggle in the face of overwhelming odds, nonetheless, sustained by his ever-increasing accomplishments as a yogin, he had grown in confidence and authority. Thurman noticed this, and increasing numbers of people who came into his presence noticed it too. Here was a man who, faced with almost unbearable responsibility from a young age and forced to confront a world for which he had been completely unprepared, nevertheless remained faithful to the spiritual tradition in which he had been raised. In so doing, he found a strength more than equal to the demands of the world in which he now began to move.

That said, this first visit to the United States was a low-key affair, its organization sometimes verging on the chaotic, the flights mostly economy class and the security arrangements less than confidence inspiring. To the alarm of one volunteer, the notional commander of the security detail at one event "intimated that he would be 'packing heat' . . . To call him amateurish would have been a compliment."

Besides visiting many of the country's most famous landmarks, including Thomas Jefferson's Monticello estate, the Dalai Lama also gave teachings at the Buddhist center established by Geshe Wangyal, the CIA's interpreter monk. Among his academic engagements were talks at both Amherst College and Harvard University, where he disarmed and delighted his audiences as he apologized for needing "a walking stick for [his] broken English." Only at the University of Washington did he encounter any opposition, when a number of Maoist students in the audience started yelling at the Dalai Lama.

An important follow-up to this first trip to the United States was the subsequent issue of a compilation of several of the Dalai Lama's talks, published under the title *Kindness, Clarity, and Insight,* edited by Jeffrey Hopkins, who had translated for the Dalai Lama throughout the visit. This was to become the first of dozens of such books. More than anything else, though, the American visit showed the Dalai Lama that while his audiences were sympathetic to the Tibetan cause, they were hungry above all for spiritual and moral guidance. Understanding what Trijang Rinpoché had described as the "lack of spiritual depth" of most Westerners, the Dalai Lama was struck by the climate of "competitiveness" and "insecurity," in which "many people appear[ed] able to show their true feelings only to their cats and dogs." He was also struck by the enthusiasm of the young for what he had to say on a wide variety of topics, not just Buddhism but also "cosmology and modern physics" and questions having to do with "sex and morality." He began to see that, quite apart from acting as a "free spokesman" for Tibet, he might have something to contribute to a people grown apart from their own religious tradition.

The enthusiasm shown toward the exiled Tibetan leader both in the United States and in the USSR's Buddhist territories was not lost on the Chinese, yet it seems they were genuinely confident that what the exile community's missions—which had meanwhile left for Tibet—discovered would persuade the Dalai Lama to go back and, in due course, take up a position within the Chinese administration of his country. It is conceivable that Deng saw the Precious Protector as a future ally in the quest for China's emergence on the world stage. Yet on his return from Tibet, Lobsang Samten could report nothing to assuage the Dalai Lama's fear that, should he go back, he would again be a mere puppet of the central government, while his people continued to suffer discrimination and harassment, their religion disastrously curtailed by the state. Recalling the conditions the first delegation found, Lobsang Samten spoke of the team's intense sorrow: "We were very upset. We were so proud of our people . . . their strength was so encouraging. But it was also very sad. Their poverty was extreme. Most were just in rags, like beggars."

On returning to Dharamsala, carrying many hundreds of letters, the team members were able to give the first comprehensive review of conditions in "China's Tibet." Everywhere they traveled they were greeted by crowds of people, many of them in tears, lamenting their miserable conditions and asking for news of the Dalai Lama. It was clear that Tibetans had become second-class citizens in their own country, that education and health care for Tibetans was poor or nonexistent, and, worst of all, that religion had been all but destroyed. Hardly a single monastery, out of a total estimated at around six thousand, had escaped unscathed. The Three Seats stood in utter ruination, Ganden reduced to a bombed-out hulk.* The Jokhang too had been despoiled.† Both the Potala and the Norbulingka had been robbed of many of their treasures—even though the Potala was protected during the Cultural Revolution, allegedly on the orders of Zhou Enlai. The entire religious establishment had been laid waste, while many structures bore evidence of desecration, the better to inflame the people: temples used in some cases for storing grain, in others even as slaughterhouses.

It was true that some new towns had been erected—consisting almost entirely of Brutalist block buildings—but these were in any case mostly occupied by Chinese settlers. In Tashikiel, for example, the quarter where the Tibetans lived was "little better than an open grave. Its buildings were in total disrepair, its streets muddy and impassable." The people lived in "dark, decaying rooms with barely any furniture or utensils and no running water and only intermittent electricity."

The Dalai Lama was horrified. This was even worse than he had feared. And yet, rather than publicize the delegation's findings, he concluded that the government in exile should continue with plans already in hand to send a further four teams into Tibet.

As it turned out, the second delegation arrived in Tibet shortly before the arrival of Chinese Communist Party secretary general Hu Yaobang, who headed the highest-ranking central government delegation Tibet had seen in thirty years. Evidently he was himself disturbed by what he found. "We feel that our Party has let the Tibetan people down. We feel bad!" he exclaimed,

---

*It was not aerial bomb damage, however, but destruction by artillery fire.

†I saw evidence of this with my own eyes when visiting the Jokhang in April 1988. Giving my tour party's guide the slip, I wandered through its chambers. All were completely empty, their floors swept clean, and on the wall of an upstairs chapel I saw a large hammer and sickle, quite well executed in red paint, superimposed on an ancient fresco.

apparently weeping, in a major speech. Following this, and presumably as a gesture of good faith, the local leader of the Tibet Autonomous Region's Revolutionary Workers' Committee (effectively the party-appointed governor) was removed from his post. Furthermore, it was announced that a large percentage of government cadres would be returned home. Hu subsequently promulgated a new six-point plan for the development of Tibet, which included a tax holiday for farmers and disbanding of the hated (and woefully inefficient) farm collectives. But though welcomed by the people, Hu's initiative was resented by many party cadres. As a result, its implementation was slow and patchy. Tibet was seen as a punishment posting with little attraction for Chinese government officials. As a result, those who took positions there tended to be the less able, the less well educated, and the most open to financial inducement. It is not hard to imagine that more than a few were tyrants in their particular locale. In any case, Hu's proposed reforms threatened them all and were deeply resented.

It has often been suggested that hosting these delegations from the exile community was a public relations disaster for the Chinese, but this is not straightforwardly true. It is clear that the Chinese were hopeful that, after being shown the advances made in Tibet over the past two decades, as well as the irreversibility of the changes, the delegates would advise the Dalai Lama that he should return. Indeed, it seems the Chinese were genuinely concerned that the Dalai Lama's delegates, whom they saw as former "feudal overlords," might be given a hostile reception by the masses. But while it was true that people climbed on the roofs of the cars in which the delegates traveled, this was in hope not of visiting physical violence on them but of obtaining a vicarious blessing from the Dalai Lama.

The fact that what each of the delegations found was a deeply traumatized and largely impoverished people watching helplessly as the large majority of jobs went to Chinese immigrants, while Tibetan children were not even allowed to learn their own language in such schools as there were, suggested to the Dalai Lama that what Mao had ultimately intended was the complete destruction of Tibetan identity. Yet China's apparent willingness to break with the past and to improve the lot of its people, including the Tibetans, presented the Precious Protector with a genuine dilemma. It seemed indeed that the Beijing government had been kept largely ignorant of what had been going on in Tibet these past twenty years, relying to a large degree on inaccurate and self-serving reports. Now, however, it looked as if there was a willingness to treat Tibet more fairly. Given this, and given his wish, deeply felt, to visit his people, the Dalai Lama announced that, all being well, he would do so sometime in 1985.

In the meantime, a second long visit to the United States, during the summer of 1981, further underscored the Dalai Lama's estimation of the spiritual crisis in the West. Besides teaching at a number of different Buddhist centers, the Dalai Lama conferred his first Kalachakra initiation in America on 1,200 mostly young seekers in a field outside Madison, Wisconsin. This was only appropriate, given that the Dalai Lama "had immersed himself in the study and practise of [the] visionary world" of the Kalachakra tantra for a great many years now. Notwithstanding its apocalyptic imagery, he was convinced that promulgating the tantra worldwide could have a positive impact on the cause of universal peace.

The event in Madison caused some local officials to fear they might end up with a Woodstock-style hippie free-for-all on their hands. And it did indeed inspire some responses (for example, June Millington's jazz-funk composition "When Wrong Is Right") that might have raised eyebrows among the more conservative authorities. But on the whole, the event was well received. Attendees appreciated the fact that, while those wishing to take up Kalachakra practice seriously were now initiated into a system that might take half a lifetime of assiduous practice to master, the Dalai Lama made available a daily "six session yoga" for those who could not fit the full practice into their schedule. And for those who merely wanted to attend out of curiosity, there was no obligation to undertake any of the practices at all. This is not always the case. On some occasions the obligations imposed on initiates are quite onerous. The requirement to recite a given mantra one hundred thousand times is by no means rare.

The other major event of this visit to the United States was a series of talks the Dalai Lama gave at Harvard University, subsequently published as *The Buddhist Path to Peace.* Although to some, the Dalai Lama seemed, in the words of Pico Iyer, "like a figure from another planet," and the complexity of his exposition of basic Buddhist principles consisted largely of "philosophical discourses almost none . . . could follow," the main message of the talks —that there can be no world peace in the absence of inner peace—struck a chord. On the one hand, the Dalai Lama showed that peace is the responsibility not so much of governments as of individuals. On the other, he made clear that those who perpetrate violence must take responsibility for their actions, a message that resonated powerfully with his audience.

There was, however, a moment during this trip when the Dalai Lama might have seemed to court controversy. One of the Buddhist centers at which he gave teachings was the Naropa Institute at Boulder, Colorado, the foundation of the popular but eccentric Chogyam Trungpa. Although he doubtless knew that Trungpa had his critics, it is uncertain whether the Dalai Lama was aware of the recent scandal at Naropa. As a self-proclaimed practitioner of so-called Crazy Wisdom, Trungpa modeled his teaching style on the fifteenth-century Kagyu master Drukpa Kunley. Besides having, like Trijang Rinpoché, a genius for spontaneous religious poetry, Drukpa Kunley was also an enthusiastic flute player, *chang* drinker, and fornicator who fathered many children, one of them on a fifteen-year-old nun. But while such behavior may seem extraordinary to the outsider, the antinomian antics of some of the greatest tantric adepts, or *mahasiddi,* are an important and cherished part of the Tibetan tradition. Correctly understood, the shocking behavior of these holy madmen is but the illusory sport, designed to instruct, of a fully enlightened being.

Trungpa had a devoted following, which included, among other well-known figures, Allen Ginsberg. With Trungpa's encouragement, Ginsberg had been a co-founder of the Jack Kerouac School of Disembodied Poetics, whose creative writing program was—as it remains—a key part of the Naropa curriculum.

Ginsberg himself was away when the incident—memorialized in a private-circulation book, *The Great Naropa Poetry Wars*—occurred. At a Halloween party, Trungpa, drunk, ordered all present to strip naked. When W. S. Merwin, a visiting poet, and his new wife refused to join in and returned to their room, the master ordered his bodyguards to bring them back. The guards began to batter the door down. As Merwin recalled: "I was not going to go peacefully. I started hitting people with beer bottles . . . It was a very violent scene." But the bodyguards were too much for him, and the reluctant couple were led back and forcibly undressed.

The incident came to the attention of the national press. One commentator claimed to see an incipient fascism not just in the guru's leadership but in the dharma generally. Coming to Trungpa's defense, Ginsberg argued that the Tibetan teacher was infallible and that this was a lesson whose meaning had not yet become clear.*

The fact that the Dalai Lama visited only a year after the scandal broke suggests either that he was ignorant of what had occurred or that he knew and was prepared to lend his name to Trungpa's center nonetheless. There is no record of any kind of public reprimand from the Dalai Lama. Yet to look for such a reprimand would be to misunderstand the tradition. Because the individual lama is under no authority but his own, a public rebuke by another lama would be an unjustifiable assumption of superiority. Furthermore, given that teachers' spiritual attainments are known only to themselves, to rebuke would be to call these attainments into question. Within the spiritual sphere, the Dalai Lama's authority is moral rather than juridical. That his personal fidelity to the *vinaya,* or monastic code, is exemplary is itself a rebuke to those who flout it. And while not denying the possibility of genuine *siddi*—the exercise of magical power—the Dalai Lama has often referred to the standard test for determining whether an individual lama is sufficiently qualified to engage in these practices: such a person should be able to eat a portion of wholesome food or a portion of excrement with equal indifference. When asked how many people there might be capable of passing this test, he invariably replies by saying that, to the best of his knowledge, at present there are "none."

It was during this, his second long visit to America, that the Dalai Lama began to articulate some of his most appealing insights. Declaring that "happiness comes from within" and that "the purpose of religion is not for arguing," he explained that, beyond any considerations of creed or philosophy, ultimately his religion was "kindness." This resonated powerfully with the many

---

*The late Sogyal Rinpoché, putative author of the multimillion-selling *Tibetan Art of Living and Dying,* is a more recent example of a popular lama falling afoul of that prejudice which favors outward behavior measuring up to claimed inner disposition.

who sought a meaningful inner life without the trappings or commitments of religion, and from now on, the Dalai Lama's simple message of dogma-free spirituality was to be the cornerstone of his ministry to the wider world.

Returning from America to India, the Dalai Lama traveled immediately to Dharamsala to see his mother. The *gyalyum chenmo* had been in slow decline following a stroke several years earlier and was clearly nearing the end of her life. As his sister recalled, on a visit to his mother's bedside, the Dalai Lama "talked to her, just like a little boy coming home . . . He gently told her not to be afraid of dying, but to concentrate on the *thangkas* and say the *mani* prayers." It cannot have been a surprise when, just a short while later in Bodh Gaya, news reached him of her death. Naturally it saddened him. Apart from brief separations, they had been close throughout his adult life, and until recently, she would often send bread and pastry, baked in the Amdo style, up to the Dalai Lama's residence. Yet as he himself admitted, it was the death later that same year of his attendant, Ponpo*, that affected him the more deeply. It was Ponpo whose mole the infant Dalai Lama had sucked for comfort and who had mothered him, during his time at Kumbum, in a way more tenderly than even the *gyalyum chenmo* had been able to —even if, as he so often tells audiences, it was his mother who first introduced him to the meaning of the word "compassion."

As was only to be expected, middle age brought with it increasing numbers of separations. A third came right at the end of 1981, when Trijang Rinpoché also "manifested the act of passing away." Although, following the break with Shugden, the Dalai Lama was not as close to his junior tutor as he had been, the bond between them was by no means broken. When the Dalai Lama heard of his guru's illness, his first act on returning home from giving teachings in Sikkim was to pay the sick man a visit and to ask him "to remain in this world for the welfare of living beings." The Precious Protector was again among the first to pay his respects when, having spent two days in meditation on the "clear light of death," the master abandoned earthly life.

If the passing of his mother, Lobsang Jinpa, and Trijang Rinpoché signaled the beginning of the end of an era, the continued liberalization taking place in

---

*His real name was Lobsang Jinpa. Ponpo, his nickname, means "the Boss."

Communist China just as clearly signaled the start of a new one. When, during the spring of 1982, a quartet of high-ranking Tibetan government in exile officials traveled to Beijing for what promised to be substantive discussions, all realized that they would soon know how far the party's commitment to reform would go with respect to the Land of Snows.

In accordance with the Dalai Lama's wishes, the officials boldly proposed that from now on, Tibet, as an administrative entity, should include not just the so-called Tibet Autonomous Region but also Kham and Amdo. Second, they proposed that Tibet be granted equivalent status to that proposed for Hong Kong, which would return to Beijing's control when its lease to Great Britain expired in 1997. Tibet would thereby enjoy genuine autonomy through the principle of "one country, two systems."*

The Chinese flatly rejected both proposals. The first, they said, was unrealistic, given that Kham and Amdo had long been subsumed variously within Sichuan, Qinghai, Gansu, and Yunnan provinces. The second suggestion implied a much higher status for Tibet than was plausible, given the fact that it was an economic backwater. Hong Kong was a major trading entity in its own right. Instead the delegation should refer to the five-point plan issued earlier by Hu Yaobang as the basis for any discussion.

Clearly, the Chinese had no interest in any claims made by or on behalf of the government in exile. Only the Dalai Lama's status and future role were up for discussion. It is true that, in former times, a key aspect of the question of Tibet's status with respect to China was the question of the Dalai Lama's status with respect to the emperor. Would the emperor leave his throne and greet the Dalai Lama outside the palace? Must the Dalai Lama kowtow to the emperor? Did the emperor treat the Dalai Lama as a vassal or recognize his authority? Yet having already abandoned any thought of restoring the old system and by fully embracing democracy, the Precious Protector conceived of his role quite differently. Above all, his concern was to serve the Tibetan people as a whole,

*This is the constitutional principle formulated by Deng Xiaoping whereby the former independent Chinese polities (Hong Kong, Macao, and, it was assumed, in due course Taiwan) would retain a large measure of independence following reunification with the Motherland.

not just those living in what China called the Tibet Autonomous Region—effectively just the central and western provinces.

It was this re-envisioning of the role of the Dalai Lama that lay behind his insistence that, henceforth, the three provinces be treated as a single entity. Historically, Lhasa's ability to assert control over and raise taxes from the provinces was distinctly limited. By embracing the non-Gelug schools, however, he had created the conceptual space for a type of leadership that transcended the divisions of the past. The recent exaltation of the Lotus-Born and repudiation of Shugden by the Dalai Lama should thus not be seen as an eccentric throwback to an arcane and irrelevant aspect of Tibetan culture. Instead it was a bold move to break with a narrow, inward-looking metaphysics of government and repurpose it to serve all Tibetans, irrespective of region or religious affiliation. The Dalai Lama had instigated a revolution of his own.

It was during the impasse that followed the meeting of the Dalai Lama's embassy to Beijing that Ling Rinpoché suffered a serious stroke. The previous year, the Precious Tutor had undertaken an arduous tour of America and Europe. Exhorting his Tibetan audiences to remain united in friendship, regardless of regional or doctrinal differences, Ling Rinpoché had used his own—immense—prestige to consolidate this reorientation of the Dalai Lama's role away from narrow concern for the Gelug tradition and its government of Tibet toward a much wider role.

News of Ling Rinpoché's illness reached the Precious Protector while he was on a trip to Switzerland. As he wrote later, the Dalai Lama was at first "tormented with fear" that he would not be able to cope should "the Precious Tutor [show] the act of entering nirvana." On his return to Dharamsala, the Dalai Lama's first act was to visit Ling Rinpoché. He went back many times over the next three months. Sometimes the Precious Tutor showed signs of improvement, and sometimes he appeared to get worse. By the time the Dalai Lama left for Bodh Gaya in December, he was "almost . . . used to this awful situation." Thus, when he heard that Ling Rinpoché had entered *tukdam* on December 25, "the earlier fear of not being able to bear the separation was not so strong." In retrospect, the Dalai Lama was convinced that this "taking on" of illness was a deliberate act of generosity on the part of the Precious Tutor, to enable his pupil to become used to the idea of being without the "rock" on which he had leaned his whole adult life.

Clinically speaking, Ling Rinpoché was dead. Yet from the perspective of the Tibetan tradition, the mind stream of the most advanced practitioners does not leave the body at once. Sensing the approach of death, the master begins the prescribed meditation practices and enters a state of mental equipoise such that when the body ceases to function, the mind is absorbed in the clear light held to be the most subtle level of consciousness. This is *tukdam,* wherein the practitioner passes from the earthly realm in what the Western tradition describes as "the odor of sanctity." At the moment of death, the room may be filled with a pleasant smell, sometimes lingering for days, while the body remains for a time incorrupt.* In Ling Rinpoché's case, at precisely the moment when he entered *tukdam,* his attendant and several others also clearly heard the sound of bells and a *damaru* drum.

It was not until half past six in the morning of the eighth day that definitive signs of the Precious Tutor's final passing announced themselves. According to the Dalai Lama's own account, there was a snowstorm with snowflakes in the shape of flowers, and much thunder. During this time the Precious Tutor left his meditation.

> As a sign of this a little urine seeped from his *vajra,* and his complexion changed. However, there was still some warmth on his vest around the chest area, and so the ceremonial washing of the body was postponed for that day. On the seventh at around eleven o'clock, more urine was emitted, and a few tears came from his eyes. At four o'clock the washing ceremony was performed.

The Dalai Lama does not mention post-mortem practices other than the washing and then the salting rituals. Partaking of the body of those masters considered to be enlightened beings who have taken earthly form seven times

---

* Saints Teresa of Ávila (1515–1582) and, more recently, Thérèse of Lisieux (1873–1897) are well-attested examples.

is held to be effective means of attaining higher realization. To this end, bodily matter may be cut from the corpse for later consumption in the form of so-called "precious pills."* Some of the liquid in which the corpse is washed may also be drunk as a sacrament.

That Ling Rinpoché was a master in the highest degree is in no doubt from the perspective of those closest to him. A fellow adept spoke of how on occasion the Precious Tutor appeared to him in a vision "with a head, nose and so forth that was extraordinarily bright," adding that "behind his ears [were] two small horns radiating blue light . . . with decorations [of] small tongue-like wall hangings." And it was noted by the Dalai Lama himself that "even Palden Lhamo, mistress of the desire realm, could not compete with this great master and had to comply with his wishes." Ling Rinpoché was, or so it seemed to those who knew him best, the veritable manifestation of a fully enlightened being.

Whether or not we accept the truth of this claim, it is undeniable that the senior tutor was the handmaid of the Dalai Lama's role as global teacher of the Buddhadharma. It was out of gratitude to his guru that the Dalai Lama would use his position to make available what he himself had been taught to all who sought it.

If, in fulfilling this role bequeathed to him by Ling Rinpoché, the Dalai Lama was able also to act as a "free spokesman," as he put it, for the people of Tibet, that was to be welcomed. But his reading of the global situation persuaded him that confronting China directly would not succeed. Still less was violence a plausible solution. In view of this, he became increasingly convinced that Tibetans should abandon their claim to complete independence. What mattered was the welfare and happiness of all Tibetans. If his people's happiness could be secured with Tibet as an administrative entity within the People's Republic of China—if, that is, they could enjoy freedom of religion,

---

*This practice is *sKye bdun sgrub pa,* literally "accumulating for the seventh rebirth." While at first sight shocking, it is important to recognize that theophagy—the sacramental eating of a god—lies at the heart of Christian practice: Catholic Christians believe that, in Holy Communion, they too are actually eating the very flesh and drinking the very blood of Jesus, albeit that their outward form of body and blood has changed to those of bread and wine.

association, and speech, and if their material needs were met—he would, as he put it, have "no point to argue." It made sense, therefore, to ignore China's recent rebuff and take Deng Xiaoping at his word. If "anything" could be discussed except independence, he would drop the call for *rangzen* (independence) and adopt instead *umaylam*—a middle-way approach between reaction and surrender.

PART IV

✷

Bodhisattva of Compassion

19

Cutting Off the Serpent's Head: Reaction and Repression in Tibet

Over the decades since the Dalai Lama's first trip to America in 1979, he has made well over four hundred separate visits to foreign countries to teach, to lecture, and to preach. Despite this, only occasionally has he visited a country more than once during the course of a year. What is more, almost invariably these trips have been undertaken at the invitation of a third party, usually a Buddhist group. The only exceptions to this rule have been the occasional private visits for medical purposes or to collect an award. Similarly, he has rarely stayed as a guest in a private house, though he describes one exception in his book *Ethics for the New Millennium.* On this occasion, as he discloses in a disarming confession, he learned an important lesson when, as he was visiting the bathroom, his curiosity got the better of him. Peeking inside a cupboard, he looked through the medicines he found there. To his surprise, he saw that these included antidepressants—and yet this was the house of an exceptionally wealthy family. Evidently wealth and well-being did not always go hand in hand.

When the Dalai Lama makes an overseas trip, it is usual for his hosts to be instructed to book modest accommodations, and, certainly during the earlier visits, this was the rule. During the 1980s, he would travel with a considerably smaller entourage than later, perhaps half a dozen strong, compared with a dozen more recently. Typically this would include two personal attendants, a secretary, two or three security men, and one or two government in exile officials. In recent years, more security has been involved and, on longer trips, more personal attendants. Often, of late, he has also been accompanied by a diarist, the Englishman Jeremy Russell; it is he who compiles the daily reports for the Dalai Lama's (English-language) website.

Of all these overseas trips, only one could be described as a vacation in the accepted sense of the word. This was a ten-day trip to Austria and Switzerland in 1983. After meeting with a small group of scientists in the Tyrolean mountain resort of Alpbach, the Dalai Lama was persuaded to spend a few days sightseeing in Switzerland. It is worth mentioning in this context Trijang Rinpoché's delight on a trip of his own to Switzerland when he witnessed a fireworks display over Lake Geneva. He wrote subsequently that "seeing flowers of every colour appear and fall like sparkling rain from space really helped improve the way I visualized the emission and dissolution of light and the purifying rain of nectar during my daily practices." There is no record of the Dalai Lama's seeing fireworks at Lake Geneva, but it is certain that he himself undertakes just such visualization practices on a daily basis, even when traveling.*

The visit to Alpbach itself brought the Dalai Lama together for the first time with the Chilean biologist and philosopher Francisco Varela. A student of the wayward lama Choegyam Trungpa, Varela was subsequently credited with being the founding father of neuro-phenomenology, a branch of science he described as taking a pragmatic approach to the "hard question" of consciousness. They became friends at once, both agreeing that science and Buddhism were, in essence, entirely compatible methodologies designed to solve the same problem of improving the quality of life for all beings. Before

*I have often thought that a biopic—possibly even an autobiopic—using computer-generated imagery to re-create some of these experiences would be an outstanding way to gain insight of the Dalai Lama's spiritual life.

the gathering was over, the forty-eight-year-old Tibetan, as eager as ever to learn, invited Varela to Dharamsala to initiate him into the mysteries of neuroscience, then Varela's principal area of research. The two subsequently met on many occasions through the Mind and Life Institute, which they co-founded in 1991. Varela died in 2001, but the Dalai Lama keeps a photograph of him on his desk to this day, while the institute itself has become a flourishing multinational forum. Bringing scientists and meditators ("contemplatives") together to study, it researches, among other things, whether Buddhist meditation techniques could benefit society as a whole and, if so, how they might be taught in a secular environment. A major component of the Dalai Lama's efforts to reach out to the scientific community, the Mind and Life Institute has attracted some of the great names in science, including two Nobel laureates: Daniel Kahneman, the Israeli economist and psychologist, and Yuan Tseh Lee, the Taiwanese chemist. Also associated with the institute are world-renowned psychologists Jon Kabat Zin and Daniel Goleman, both of them leaders in the field, who have contributed significantly to the exponential growth of interest in secularized Buddhist meditation techniques associated with the mindfulness movement. The work of neuroscientist Richie Davidson should also be mentioned in this context. Indeed, there have been rich collaborations for many, even if one skeptical early participant quipped that "Buddhist psychology takes people who think they're somebody and helps them understand they're nobody; Western psychology takes people who think they are nobody and helps them understand they're somebody."

From the start, the Dalai Lama found it easier to meet with scientists sympathetic to his ideas than to meet with sympathetic politicians. Although he personally made no special effort to do so, his various representatives abroad did their utmost to develop support for the Tibetan claim to independence—despite the fact that the Dalai Lama himself was moving away from this as a goal. One regular attendee at the press conferences his representatives invariably organized when he arrived in a foreign country recalled how, even in New York City, these were "almost deserted" during the 1980s. And on those occasions when meetings with journalists and others were well attended, there were some embarrassing misconceptions about what the Dalai Lama actually stood for. On an early visit to the United States, a business CEO asked him whether he felt "closer to John Lennon the dreamer, or to Gandhi the politician." The Dalai Lama had never heard of Lennon, and as for dreaming, for him this was not something one did to little or no purpose. More than once, too, he was brought to tears by someone in the audience asking him what was the "quickest, easiest, cheapest" way to attain Enlightenment.

Nonetheless, in spite of these occasional misunderstandings, and in spite of the lack of overt interest in Tibet among politicians, small coalitions of influential supporters did begin to emerge in America and in Europe. At this stage, few people outside Buddhist circles knew much about Tibet. Political support in America at first came as much from Republicans, such as the notoriously right-wing Jesse Helms, and social conservatives, such as *New York Times* editor turned columnist Abe Rosenthal (whose epitaph proclaims that "he kept the paper straight"), as from Democrats. For the right, Tibet was a stick with which to beat the Communist Chinese, a popular stance under the Reagan administration. The Dalai Lama's hoped-for 1985 visit to Tibet not having taken place, that summer ninety-one members of the U.S. Congress wrote an open letter to the Chinese president urging the Communist Party to enter into meaningful negotiations with the Tibetan government in exile. When the Chinese denounced the letter, it was this disparate group of supporters who encouraged the Dalai Lama to follow up their initiative with what became known as his "Five Point Peace Plan for the Future of Tibet."

Invited to address the Congressional Human Rights Caucus in Washington during the fall of 1987, coincidentally at the very moment when Gyalo Thondup arrived in Beijing on business, the Dalai Lama called first for the transformation of the whole of Tibet into what he described as a "zone of peace," whereby his homeland would be completely demilitarized. The Dalai Lama's second proposal was that the Chinese government halt its population transfer policy, whereby large numbers of non-Tibetans were "threatening the very existence of the Tibetans as a distinct people." Instead, his third point, their fundamental human rights should be respected and democratic freedom for Tibetans implemented. Fourth, the natural environment of Tibet—devastated since the Chinese occupation—should be restored, and in particular, the Chinese should desist both from developing nuclear weapons and from dumping nuclear waste in Tibet. Finally, he said, now was the time for "earnest negotiations" on the future status of Tibet and of "relations between the Tibetan and Chinese peoples."

Significantly, there was no mention of independence. Nonetheless, as the Dalai Lama must have feared, the party leadership in Beijing immediately rejected the plan. The Chinese were also pained that Gyalo Thondup had informed them that the Dalai Lama's visit to Washington would be of no importance. Either he had lied, or, if he had been telling the truth and had no foreknowledge of the speech to Congress, he must not be as close to the Dalai Lama and the exile government as he claimed.

But what shocked both sides was the violent protest that erupted in Lhasa the following week. On September 27, a party of monks from one of the Three Seats appeared in Lhasa carrying a Tibetan flag and proceeded to circumambulate the Jokhang Temple, shouting slogans and calling for self-rule (*rangzen* in Tibetan). The monks were quickly arrested and beaten. Four days later—significantly, on China's national day—another group of monks from Sera staged a second demonstration. This was joined by a number of laypeople. Again the demonstrators were rounded up and beaten by police. But as the morning wore on, a large crowd gathered outside the police station where the demonstrators had been detained, demanding their release. A confrontation developed, the outcome of which was that the crowd stormed the station, setting it on fire and freeing the detainees. One of the monk protesters, badly burned in the flames, was carried aloft in front of the crowd, which, further enraged, began pelting the police with stones. In response, law enforcement officers now in position on the roofs of adjacent buildings began to shoot. Up to ten demonstrators were killed.

The Chinese immediately claimed that the Dalai Lama personally was behind the protests. It is conceivable that Dharamsala had alerted some of its contacts inside Tibet that the Dalai Lama would deliver an important speech during his trip to the United States. It seems likely that the Indian government had been informed that something was in the offing, given that, whereas up until now an Indian official had always accompanied the Dalai Lama on his trips abroad, on this occasion he went unaccompanied. So at least some people knew in advance that the Dalai Lama was poised to make an important declaration. Yet, given his attitude toward violence, and in light of the certainty that any protest, however peaceful, would itself be met with violence, it is not credible that he would have issued any such orders.

International coverage of the event nonetheless meant that China was forced to take seriously the resentment to which the riots bore testimony. At once a split arose between those party officials who felt that liberalization in Tibet had gone too far and those who countered that the authorities had "divorced [them]selves from the masses and harmed them." There were calls by the conservative faction to cancel the Great Prayer Festival due to be held the following March, its revival having been recently permitted by the Chinese. Surprisingly, these calls were met with support among the older monks at the Three Seats, fearful that they would not be able to control the younger generation. Yet it was the Chinese head of the Tibet Autonomous Region who insisted that, just as he had attended the previous festival—wearing Tibetan dress—he would do so again. Foreign journalists had been invited, and it would be an embarrassing admission that he was not in control of the situation if the event were to be canceled. In the meantime, as a gesture of reconciliation, the Panchen Lama was sent on a mission to the three major monasteries with news of a generous benefaction from the government. Furthermore, all but a handful of those detained following the late September disturbances were released.

Realizing that the Chinese planned to use the 1988 Monlam Festival in Lhasa as propaganda to demonstrate that local reforms were working, many monks boycotted the proceedings. It was not until the last day that there was any trouble. When the statue of Maitreya, the Buddha to come, was being paraded around the Barkor (the pilgrim's route around the Jokhang Temple), there was a sudden call from one of the participating monks for the release of the remainder of his colleagues still being held since the demonstration the previous fall. When ordered to desist, he was immediately joined by others who shouted pro-independence slogans. Within minutes, a riot was in full swing. The disturbance, involving several thousand people, both lay and monastic, lasted the whole day. A number of police vehicles were overturned and set ablaze, and several shops were set on fire, while the crowd pelted the police with stones. The day ended when security forces stormed the Jokhang Temple, killing, according to Tibetan and foreign eyewitnesses, more than twenty unarmed demonstrators, including a twelve-year-old boy. (Chinese sources claim there were just three casualties—one of them a policeman who had been hiding in a toilet and whose killing in cold blood was independently verified.) The scale of the rioting far exceeded anything that had been seen the previous year.

It was against this background of unrest that the Dalai Lama delivered a second public and again overtly political message to China from another foreign capital. In his "Strasbourg Statement" of June 1988, he gave a clarification and reaffirmation of the Five Point Peace Plan but this time with what appeared to be an explicit modification of his earlier position with regard to independence. Now, he declared, "the whole of Tibet . . . should become a self-governing democratic entity . . . in association with the People's Republic of China."

At first sight, inclusion of the phrase "in association with the People's Republic of China" looked intended to reassure Beijing that the Dalai Lama was willing not merely to pay lip service to giving up the idea of Tibet as an independent country, but actually to give China a recognized role in the governance of Tibet. This time, the Dalai Lama's initiative was not rejected out of hand—at least not by the Chinese. Instead, it provoked a hostile reaction within some Tibetan circles. The Dalai Lama's own eldest brother, Jigme Norbu, by now a respected academic at Indiana University, circulated a letter among the exile community urging his fellow exiles to reject the proposal. The head of the refugee Tibetan Youth Congress likewise denounced the proposal—though he later claimed that he had been encouraged to do so by the Dalai Lama himself. Some have taken this to mean that the Dalai Lama wanted to show the Chinese that he was willing to take on the hardliners within his own community. In any case, the Tibetan Youth Congress remains to this day opposed to the Dalai Lama's policy of not seeking independence for Tibet. If, therefore, there is doubt as to how hostile some of the reaction really was, there can be no doubt that a great many did see the Strasbourg Statement as a sellout.

When, after some weeks' deliberation, the Chinese again rejected the Dalai Lama's proposal, it was on the grounds that the statement was simply a covert bid for independence: the word "association" did, after all, clearly imply co-equal status. Beijing was also displeased at the inclusion of a foreign legal expert as a member of the proposed Tibetan negotiating team.* Yet it seems that what was really at issue was the Dalai Lama's continued insistence that "Tibet" included both Kham and Amdo, and, moreover, that its people must be accorded freedoms and privileges that were not even in prospect for the domestic population of China. From the Chinese perspective, neither demand seemed remotely realistic.

News of this latest rejection only added to the resentment that had manifested itself in the violent demonstrations of the preceding two years. On International Human Rights Day in December 1988, a demonstration led by monks won immediate support from bystanders in Lhasa. Despite the fact that the demonstrators were unarmed and orderly, two were summarily shot, while a European bystander was also injured. Subsequently, a trial of those deemed to have been the ringleaders was swiftly arranged and deterrent sentences were handed out, including several for life imprisonment and more than one of execution (though in fact no execution took place). In this heightened atmosphere, many Tibetans viewed the sudden and unexpected death of the Panchen Lama just seven weeks later as a politically motivated assassination. Tibet's second-most widely revered incarnation had recently given several speeches openly critical of Beijing, and it seemed certain to many that his death had been ordered as a warning to those who would deviate from the party line. It is hard to see what Beijing would gain by such a move, however. The fact that the Panchen Lama had been cruelly treated following his earlier criticism of Mao seems a far more plausible cause of his premature death aged only fifty. He was by then considerably overweight and was known to have diabetes and high blood pressure.

While Tibetans everywhere remained shocked and in sorrow, an invitation to the Dalai Lama from the official Buddhist Association of China to attend the Panchen Lama's funeral presented him with a troubling dilemma. The invitation could only have come from the very highest level of government. Moreover, it provided both sides with an uncontroversial opportunity

*This was Michael van Walt van Praag, a Belgian-born, US-based international jurist.

to meet which might otherwise have taken years of diplomacy to achieve, even if both sides were willing. And yet the Dalai Lama refused.

In his second autobiography, *Freedom in Exile,* the Dalai Lama makes clear that "personally" speaking, he "wanted to go." Whether his refusal was the decision of the Kashag—perhaps fearing that if he went he would be kidnapped or forced into making some public concession, just as Ngabo had been thirty years before—or whether it was on the advice of Nechung, or perhaps because of an intervention on the part of the Indian government, we do not know.

Yet more unrest in Lhasa broke out a few weeks later, at the turn of the Tibetan New Year, causing the authorities to ban the official celebration of the Great Prayer Festival. In spite of this, large crowds gathered on the day that Monlam was to have been celebrated, and a further three days of rioting ensued. It is unknown how many died in the subsequent crackdown, although one report puts the figure as high as several hundred, including almost a hundred monks. Then, on March 7, 1989, the Chinese authorities decreed that all foreigners residing in Lhasa must leave. The following day, martial law was enacted. It was lifted formally a year later, though it is questionable whether in any meaningful sense it has ever been lifted.

The Dalai Lama was devastated, yet he was impotent to do anything other than pray and protest to the Chinese while reminding Tibetans that any protests must be strictly nonviolent.

If the Panchen Lama's death was arguably a contributory factor in the March riots, the death a month later of Hu Yaobang led to an upheaval in China that made the Lhasa disturbances seem trivial in comparison. One of the more liberal members of the Politburo, Hu had been forced to take responsibility and resign following the anti-CCP student protests that erupted in China during 1985–86. For the six weeks following his demise, Tiananmen Square became the focus of pro-democracy/anti-government demonstrations which, at their height, attracted over a million people. At first the party leadership could come to no decision; but, fearful of the growing unrest in eastern Europe which Soviet Russia was doing nothing to combat, when the protests began to spread outside Beijing and across the whole of China, Deng finally ordered in the military on June 4. Hundreds, possibly thousands, were killed and the protest leaders arrested in a crackdown that drew fierce condemnation from around the world.

It was against this backdrop that, in October, the committee of Norwegian dignitaries responsible for the Nobel Peace Prize selected the Dalai Lama to be the recipient of the 1989 award. When the news broke, it was a joyous moment for Tibetans at home and abroad—a shaft of sunlight illuminating their benighted land, a vindication of their story, a harbinger of the restoration they so earnestly longed for. It was, too, a matter of intense pride that *their* guru, *their* leader, *their* kinsman had been publicly acknowledged in this way. Surely China must now accept democracy, grant the Tibetan people freedom, or remain forever beyond the pale. For the Dalai Lama himself, at that moment traveling in the United States, a report broadcast on the radio suggesting he had won did, he admitted later, excite him a little. But with no further mention on the evening news, he assumed that it had been nothing more than a rumor. When the award was confirmed early the following morning, his attendants waited until after he had completed his meditation before telling him, by which time he was, he said, "no longer excited." He was, however, both surprised and pleased to hear that the prize came with some money. There was a leper colony in India to which he had long wanted to make a donation. He would also use some of the prize money to set up the Foundation for Universal Responsibility, a Delhi-based charity working mainly in education and in interfaith and peace-building projects.

With the award of the Nobel Prize, the "Tibetan issue" became, at a stroke, a global issue, and from this moment on, the Dalai Lama began his ascent to superstardom. Yet as the brutal suppression of the Tiananmen protests made clear, the conservatives within the Politburo had by now reasserted their authority. A siege mentality prevailed, and the government quickly announced its "extreme regret and indignation" concerning the award. For the Chinese, the Nobel committee selection constituted "open support for the Dalai Lama and the Tibetan separatists in their activities to undermine national unity and split China." This was nothing but a collaboration between the Dalai Lama and "hostile foreign forces."

The fall of the Berlin Wall a month later served only to deepen Chinese paranoia. In contrast, it gave the Dalai Lama an opportunity to underscore his status as a world figure by visiting the wall just days after its dismantling. It was a poignant moment for him. "As I stood there," he recalled, "in full view of a still-manned security post, an old lady silently handed me a red candle. With some emotion, I lit it, and held it up. For a moment the tiny dancing flame threatened to go out, but it held and, while a crowd pressed round me, touching my hands, I prayed that the light of compassion and awareness would fill the world and dispel the darkness of fear and oppression."

Returning home to Dharamsala, the fifty-five-year-old Dalai Lama received a rapturous welcome. Yet for him personally, perhaps an even more pleasing event at this time was news of the discovery of the reincarnation of his senior tutor, Ling Rinpoché. When, early the following year, the five-year-old came for a visit, the Dalai Lama was visibly moved. An observer noted how, as the little boy stood to leave the audience chamber, the Dalai Lama "bent down to adjust [Ling Rinpoché's] shoestrap, then stayed down, waving, smiling and blowing kisses like a loving father till the boy was out of sight."

In spite of all the publicity in the immediate aftermath of the award of the Nobel Prize, the Dalai Lama remained at this time relatively unknown both in America and beyond, at least outside Buddhist circles and human rights advocacy groups. His press conferences were better attended than they had been, but as one journalist noted, even now he had "no handlers, advance men, interpreters, press people, or travel coordinators," and he continued to be largely reliant on volunteers when overseas. As a result, the arrangements made on his behalf remained somewhat haphazard. This gave the Dalai Lama the opportunity occasionally to make impromptu changes to his schedule such as one occasion in 1991, while staying in Santa Fe. Having met with a succession of interested people, including "politicians, movie stars, New Age gurus, billionaires and Pueblo Indian leaders," the Dalai Lama announced that he would like to go up into the mountains to watch the skiing. To the consternation of those accompanying him, he insisted on taking a chairlift so that he could get as close to the action as possible. The story is recounted in a delightful article by the writer Douglas Preston.

Sitting quite relaxed, with nothing to hold onto (there was no safety bar), the Dalai Lama "spoke animatedly about everything he saw on the slopes. As he pointed and leaned forward into space [his assistant], who was gripping the arm of the chair with whitened knuckles, kept admonishing him in Tibetan . . . begging His Holiness to please sit back, hold the seat, and not lean out so much."

But the Dalai Lama would not listen.

"How fast they go!" he exclaimed. "And *children* skiing! Look at [that] little boy!" In fact, the slope in question was just a "bunny slope and the skiers weren't moving fast at all. Just then, an expert skier entered from a higher slope, whipping along. The Dalai Lama saw him and said, 'Look—too fast! He [is] going to hit [the] post!' He cupped his hands, shouting down to the oblivious skier, 'Look out for post!' He waved frantically. 'Look out for post!' The skier, who had no idea that the incarnation of the Bodhisattva of Compassion was crying out to save his life, made a crisp little check as he approached the pylon, altering his line of descent, and continued expertly down the hill. With an expostulation of wonder, the Dalai Lama sat back and clasped his hands together . . . 'Ah! This [is] a *wonderful* sport!'" adding that, in a future free Tibet, he was sure that there would be plenty of good skiing to be had.

Many of those who have had the good fortune to travel with the Dalai Lama on his overseas trips have commented on the keen interest he takes in his surroundings, the torrent of questions, his openness to talking to whosoever comes his way, the jokes—often at his own expense—the laughter and his concern for others, especially those in distress. On hearing this, it is all too easy to forget that, throughout it all, his spiritual practice—the three to four hours of meditation he engages in every morning without fail and the hour and more in the evening—remains the most important part of the Dalai Lama's day. But doubtless this is precisely what enables him both to deal with the frequent trials he has to face and to move seamlessly among the vast array of people he encounters, giving each his full attention, "as if," in Preston's words, "he shut out the rest of the world to focus his entire sympathy . . . care and interest on you" alone.* And perhaps this is the secret of his appeal. Here is someone who is manifestly authentic, someone who does exactly and in all circumstances precisely what he urges others to do—and with joy, not gravity, with generosity, never rancor, and all in a spirit of forgiveness of failure.

---

*Queen Elizabeth II is said to have the same ability.

From Santa Fe the Dalai Lama traveled to Washington, where, in April 1991, he was received for the first time by a serving president of the United States—at that time the elder George Bush. Significantly, their meeting did not take place in the White House itself. It nonetheless provoked a furious response from Beijing. But for the Dalai Lama, an American president was only a warm-up. Among the other world leaders he met in the afterglow of the Nobel award were Pope (now Saint) John Paul II (again), the king of Sweden, Prince Charles of the United Kingdom, and then the presidents of Ireland, Lithuania, Estonia, Bulgaria, Poland, Argentina, and Chile, followed by the prime ministers of Great Britain, Norway, Cambodia, Australia, and New Zealand. Having been a political nonentity up until that moment, with Bush's endorsement he was suddenly the man of the hour. These were heady times both for the Dalai Lama and his growing band of followers—mainly the idealistic young but also many older people who were beginning to wake to a political cause that seemed unarguable. Here was the Tibetan David standing up to the Chinese Goliath, armed only with the rhetoric of nonviolence and compassion.

Later that same year the Dalai Lama returned to New York to confer the Kalachakra initiation on a large audience in an event cosponsored by the actor Richard Gere and Tibet House.* Whether or not there was any direct causal connection between this and the momentum that now gathered behind the movement for a free Tibet is of course impossible to say. Nonetheless, there is little doubt that when he met with President Bill Clinton two years later, the Dalai Lama's campaign on behalf of the Tibetan people had reached a new phase. It was Clinton, perhaps sensing a cause that covered all the bases, who subsequently did the most of any international statesman to make the Tibetan issue a genuine matter of government policy. Indicating support for an earlier State Department report to Congress concerning the forthcoming review of China's most favored nation status, the Clinton administration moved toward endorsing "dialogue with the Dalai Lama or his representatives" as a condition of its extension.

Spiritually, too, the years immediately following the Nobel award were frenetic. There was a total of nine Kalachakra conferrals between 1989 and 1995,

*The event was held at Madison Square Garden.

and there were many interfaith encounters besides. In 1994, at the invitation of the World Community for Christian Meditation, the Dalai Lama spoke at a conference dedicated to the dialogue between Buddhism and Christianity. Commenting on passages drawn from the four Christian gospels, the Dalai Lama discussed both similarities and dissimilarities between the two religions. In one memorable analogy he reminded his audience that, in the quest to find common ground, it was important to bear in mind the danger of, as the Tibetan saying has it, "trying to put a yak's head on a sheep's body." Nonetheless, many people present were touched by the manifest humility of the Dalai Lama engaging with a faith tradition other than his own.

But the Chinese know, as the Romans knew, that *cunctando regior mundus:* delay rules the world. Although then less than half a century old, the Communist Party's rule draws on ancient tradition. Its leadership thinks in decades rather than in terms of the few years between presidential elections. If they were successful in turning China into an economic superpower, they understood that it would be only a matter of time before the Dalai Lama became an irrelevance. The Western powers would certainly prioritize trade over human rights. Thus, even as Tibet support groups began to spring up on university campuses around the world, and as increasing numbers of A-listers came forward to support the Dalai Lama's cause—Richard Gere had long been known for his support, but he was now joined by others such as actors Goldie Hawn and Sharon Stone, composer Philip Glass, and hip-hop artist Adam Yauch—the Politburo began planning the Third National Forum for Work in Tibet. This was a conference to be held in Beijing in July 1994 which would review policy and set out strategy into the new millennium. Its main emphasis, at least in the documents made available to the public, was economic: Tibet was a provincial dead end that must be developed. Its real focus, however, centered on fostering the "unity of the nationalities" and the territorial integrity of the Motherland. Not only was there to be no letup in the campaign to identify and root out groups and individuals with "splittist" sympathies, but now the Dalai Lama himself was to be held personally culpable for any challenges to China's claims over Tibet. The Third Forum was thus characterized above all by its unprecedented emphasis on explicitly attacking the Precious Protector, which all officials in Tibet were required to repeat whenever called upon to do so. He was not seeking justice for his people; he was intent on destroying China's territorial integrity and national unity. By internationalizing the Tibetan question, he had "bartered away his honour for Western hostile forces' patronage." People should be in no doubt: "Although sometimes Dalai speaks softly and says nice things to deceive the masses, he has never ceased his splittist activities." For this reason, the "Dalai clique" must be attacked unremittingly: "To kill a serpent, we must first cut off its head."

A further feature of the Third Forum was its focus on religion. This was in response to the fact that it was overwhelmingly members of the *sangha* who had led each of the recent protests. Of those detained following the disturbances, only a third were laypeople—doubly remarkable given the small numbers of monks and nuns now remaining in the population. This observation elicited a response typical of the secular state when confronted with religiously motivated dissent: "The purpose of Buddhism is to deliver all living creatures in a peaceful manner," but "the Dalai and his clique" had "violated the religious doctrine . . . to fool and incite one people against the other," using "godly strength to poison and bewitch the masses," incorporating "Tibetan independence" in his sermons. "Such flagrant deceptiveness and demagoguery constitute a blasphemy to Buddhism."

To counter the Dalai Lama's subversive message, it would be necessary to ensure that all those in positions of authority in Tibet disavow the Precious Protector. All political figures and dignitaries, and all monks and nuns, had to repeat or endorse in writing four sentences explicitly denouncing "the Dalai." No one in public employment could any longer erect an altar in their home, and, within two years, there was a ban on displaying or even possessing pictures of the Dalai Lama, while all Tibetan students were prohibited from visiting monasteries or attending any kind of religious ceremony. It was vital that young people should keep before them a proper understanding of the misery of the masses before liberation. They should be in no doubt about the sources of past suffering and the conditions of present happiness.

The immediate consequence of these new policies announced by the Third Forum was another wave of protests that erupted over the winter of 1994–95.

In that they were again largely led by members of the *sangha,* these were similar to those that had occurred earlier. But there were two important differences. Whereas before the protests were confined to Lhasa, now they spread to outlying regions. And while earlier the monasteries involved in dissent were invariably Gelugpa foundations, now it was evident that the other sects were also involved. This made clear that the Dalai Lama's own policy of openness to all schools within the Tibetan tradition had found support outside circles habitually loyal to him. In the past, the Chinese might have expected the non-Gelug monasteries not to follow the Precious Protector's lead. But no longer.

Further confirmation of the success of the Dalai Lama's efforts at conciliation between the different elements of Tibetan society came during the selection process of the new Panchen Lama. By convention it falls to the Dalai Lama to oversee the procedure, should he be of age. Similarly, the Panchen Rinpoché is, theoretically at least, consulted during the selection of the Dalai Lama (as indeed happened during the search for the present incarnation, although in this case his involvement was limited—on account of the fact that the Panchen Lama died before the process was complete). Selection of the new Panchen Lama (whom the Chinese would doubtless seek to influence) was of critical importance given there was every likelihood that he would play a major role in the selection of the next Dalai Lama.

In light of the historic rivalry between the two sees, it would not have been wholly surprising if the authorities at Tashilhunpo had turned to the Chinese (who had lately provided the monastery with a generous benefaction), rather than to Dharamsala, for assistance in the process. For their part, the Chinese had their own understanding of correct procedure. This involved deployment of the *ser bumba,* the hated Golden Urn. Imposed on Tibet by Qianlong, Qing emperor of China during the late eighteenth century, this was the protocol whereby the final selection of the highest incarnations was to be confirmed by a so-called Divine Lottery whereby the names of rival candidates were to be written on ivory tablets in Tibetan, Manchu, and Mandarin, placed in the urn, and drawn out under supervision of the local Chinese *amban,* or governor. Because of the situation then prevailing, the Golden Urn's use had been dispensed with at the time of both the present Dalai Lama's and the late Panchen Lama's selection: the Chinese were unable to enforce its use. But now the Chinese were certain to insist on its deployment.

In what some Tibetan officials saw as a gesture of conciliation, the Chinese authorities permitted Chadrel Rinpoché, abbot of Tashilhunpo, and as such the person in overall charge of the search, to put a letter seeking the Dalai Lama's guidance into Gyalo Thondup's hands during a visit by the Dalai Lama's brother to Beijing in July 1993. At that moment, it even seemed possible that the authorities might be willing to dispense with use of the Golden Urn. In the end, Chadrel Rinpoché, who had in the meantime had secret word from the Dalai Lama which of the candidates was the authentic reincarnation, was unable to secure dispensation before the day deemed by the Dalai Lama to be the most auspicious on which to make his choice known publicly. To Chadrel Rinpoché's embarrassment and to the fury of the Chinese authorities, the Dalai Lama preempted them by making his own announcement.

It was an extremely risky move, and one that the Dalai Lama must have known would bring serious repercussions. It cannot have come as any great surprise to him when Chadrel Rinpoché was subsequently arrested, along with his chief assistant. What may have caught him by surprise, however, was the speed with which the Chinese authorities detained the little boy declared by the Dalai Lama to be the authentic incarnation and announced another candidate as the "official" Panchen Lama. The Precious Protector's own choice, just six years old, thus became one of the youngest political prisoners in the world. His whereabouts remain unknown.

Why would the Dalai Lama have risked such an outcome? We can but speculate. The only thing we can be certain of is that he did not make the decision lightly. He would, moreover, have consulted closely with Nechung and the other dharma protector, and indeed it is almost certain that their counsel was what clinched the matter.

Whatever the Dalai Lama's intentions, the Panchen Lama controversy clearly impacted the thinking of the Chinese authorities. There was to be no letup in their campaign against the Precious Protector. Those who held the view that the outbreaks of unrest in Tibet were directly attributable to the liberalization of the 1980s were firmly in the ascendant—a position consolidated by further outbreaks of unrest later in the year. To the dismay of the Dalai Lama, who continued to assert the importance of all protest being peaceful, this culminated, in December 1996, with the explosion of a bomb in Lhasa, injuring five people and damaging two hotels and a government building.

Although it was evidently not intended to cause massive loss of life—the device was remotely detonated in the early hours of the morning—this was a shocking development. Up until now, violence, when it had broken out, had done so in the context of civil unrest. But this was malice aforethought. It was now but a short distance to premeditated acts of mass murder. Unless, of course, this was a false flag operation. It is not impossible to imagine that the bomb—much more sophisticated than anything seen thus far in Tibet—was in fact planted and exploded by the authorities themselves. It would be naïve to suppose that a regime capable of administering beatings and electric shocks to detainees as a matter of routine would never undertakc such operations.

As a result of both the Panchen Lama debacle and continued unrest in Tibet, one decade removed from the time when a visit to Tibet by the Dalai Lama had seemed a genuine possibility, the political situation was now almost as bad as it had been before Deng's overtures and certainly at any time since Hu Yaobang's intervention in the early 1980s. Given the enormous popularity the Dalai Lama was starting to enjoy on the international scene, and given too the seriousness with which his efforts to bring the situation in Tibet to the attention of political leaders worldwide was being met, this seems cruelly ironic. But the devastating turn that events in the exile community took over the next twelve months was a tragic reminder of the epic scale of the difficulties that the Dalai Lama has faced since the day the search party came knocking at his parents' farmstead door.

20

"An oath-breaking spirit born of perverse prayers": The Murder of Lobsang Gyatso

At the beginning of every year, the Dalai Lama grants a general audience at the main temple in Dharamsala, where he delivers a quasi–State of the Union Address. There follows, soon after, the Precious Protector's spring teachings. During those of 1996, the Dalai Lama surprised his audience by speaking in unusually forceful terms about Dorje Shugden. Over the years since his first public repudiation of him, the Dalai Lama had often repeated his view that the deity was unreliable. Increasingly he had suggested that monks in particular should not have recourse to Shugden. He had, in addition, requested (and requests of the Dalai Lama have the authority of orders within the Tibetan community) that certain statues of Shugden in prominent settings within the major monasteries be removed and, in some cases, replaced with statues of Nechung. On this occasion he issued for the first time a forthright condemnation of Shugden practice, saying that anyone who wished to continue it should no longer consider the Dalai Lama to be their guru. Those in this category should neither attend his teachings nor take any empowerments from him. Beyond this, he made it clear that, on account of the regrettable persistence of Shugden practice, there would, if necessary, have to be follow-up. The matter had reached the point where, if nothing was done, there was danger of harm not just to the Ganden Phodrang government but to his own life, which could be shortened as a result.

The speech was greeted with general dismay. Shugden remained a popular figure, especially among Khampas and traders as well as with the late Trijang Rinpoché's many followers. Of all the supernatural beings venerated by Tibetans, he is the one to whom ordinary people can most easily relate. Besides his claimed role as principal protector of the Gelug school, Shugden is also known for facilitating the prosperity of his followers. But to many, the most shocking aspect of all was the fact of Shugden's perceived pivotal role in the successful escape of the Dalai Lama from Lhasa in 1959.

The dismay was not just on the part of Shugden devotees, however. People were also appalled that there were some within the community who would disregard the Dalai Lama's requests with respect to the practice. It was well understood that the Dalai Lama would not speak out without just cause, and since nothing is more precious than the life of the Precious Protector, if it was the case that his life was endangered, those who continued to defy him were guilty of serious wrongdoing. With this in mind, some reacted with zealous indiscretion. Taking advantage of the absence of the abbess, they threw out as rubbish the Shugden statue kept in Dharamsala's Ganden Choeling Nunnery. Later, a number of departments within the Tibetan exile administration took it on themselves to mount a campaign to root out from government employ any who maintained a connection with the deity—even if this amounted to no more than the usual monthly ritual offering. The Department of Health, among others, circulated a notice requiring all employees and their families to sign a letter of abjuration. At the same time, representatives of the Dalai Lama visited the monasteries in southern India to apprise them of the Precious Protector's directive. Worrying reports began to spread that those who refused to sign or comply were beaten up. By early summer, resistance groups started to emerge, and demonstrations against the Dalai Lama's proclamation were held at both the Ganden and Sera Monasteries.

As tensions began to mount, a number of devotees found their businesses boycotted, while signs began to appear in shop windows announcing that Shugden supporters would not be welcome. The question of loyalty was on everyone's lips.

No doubt part of the government in exile's zeal can be attributed to the desire to be seen to be doing something. Recent events in Dharamsala had already heightened tensions within the exile community. Not long before, a man had been found working in the Dalai Lama's kitchen who had links with the Chinese government. In the previous two years, a total of five spies had allegedly been uncovered in Dharamsala by Indian intelligence. There was also a rumor that the Tibetan administration's internal security had recently foiled a plot that called for a female agent, posing as a new arrival from Tibet, to put nerve agent in her hair so that when the Dalai Lama touched her in blessing, he would be poisoned. On top of this, following the recent fatal stabbing of a young Indian by a Tibetan youth, relations between Dharamsala's immigrant and resident Gaddi communities had fallen to a disastrous low.* There was even talk of the Indian government's relocating the entire Tibetan population to an area south of Delhi, while the Dalai Lama himself had declared that he would move to southern India if his continued presence in Dharamsala was inconvenient.

The possibility of another move was hugely unsettling to the exile community, and there can be little doubt that the McCarthyite paranoia that gripped many of those in authority can be attributed to the tense atmosphere then prevailing. But what was most toxic of all was the response of a small but well-organized cell of Shugden devotees within the Gelugpa establishment. Posters denouncing the Dalai Lama's declaration appeared in Dharamsala and elsewhere, and a court case was brought in the wake of the government's campaign, while Amnesty International was appealed to on the grounds that Shugden's devotees were being denied the right to freedom of religious belief.

As the crisis worsened, an anonymous letter circulated in Dharamsala

---

*The Gaddi are an Indian hill tribe of pastoralists who have farmed the foothills of the Himalayas since time immemorial.

threatening the Dalai Lama with a "bloodbath." At the same time, death threats were issued against the young incarnation of Trijang Rinpoché and another senior Shugden lineage holder, Song Rinpoché. Simultaneously, an attempt was made on the life of a former abbot of one of the Ganden colleges by Shugden supporters. Then, at a séance during which the Dalai Lama invoked Nechung and several other oracles, one of the mediums (in a trance) accused a lama in attendance of being an unrepentant Shugden devotee and attacked him. A fracas broke out, and the lama subsequently threatened to sue, until the Dalai Lama personally intervened. In January 1997 a respected *geshe* was beaten up in Delhi.

But even the best-informed observer could not have predicted what would happen next. The Venerable Lobsang Gyatso was a close associate of the Dalai Lama. It was he whom the Tibetan leader had chosen to be founder-director of the School of Buddhist Dialectics when it was inaugurated in 1973. An example of one of the Dalai Lama's many forward-looking initiatives, the school (now Institute) was set up with the purpose of offering an advanced education grounded in Buddhism's ancient Nalanda tradition but outside the traditional monastic setting. By this time, it had integrated modern science and English language classes into the curriculum, alongside courses designed to introduce students to the full range of the Tibetan Buddhist tradition. With a towering reputation as a scholar-practitioner, Lobsang Gyatso—invariably referred to as Gen-la (honorable teacher)—was known as a kind but strict disciplinarian whose way of life was as austere as it was exemplary. Notoriously outspoken, somewhat rough in his diction and combative in his manner, he nevertheless inspired the greatest loyalty among his students. To the fury of some, he was also a notable supporter of the Dalai Lama's pronouncements on Shugden.

On a bitter cold night right at the end of the Tibetan year (in 1997 it fell during February), at the very moment when it is traditional to banish ritually the evils and spiritual defilements of the past twelve months before welcoming in the next, four visitors called at Gen-la's room. Earlier in the day he had met with the Dalai Lama, and now he was working with two students who were translating a religious text into Chinese. Situated within the precincts of the main temple, his room was within earshot of the Dalai Lama's private compound—though no one reported hearing anything. When the visitors left a short while later, Lobsang Gyatso and his two companions lay dead or dying with multiple knife wounds. Renowned as a fighter in his youth, he must have put up a struggle. There was blood high up the walls. But his assailants had stabbed him in the eye, slashed him in the throat, and plunged a blade deep into his heart. His companions fared no better, though one survived to gasp his life away soon after arriving at the Delek Hospital, half a mile down the hill, where he was taken as soon as the alarm was raised. From there he was sent to the Chandigarh hospital, but he died en route.

The whole of Dharamsala reeled in shock. Among foreign residents and local journalists, rumors began to circulate to the effect that Lobsang Gyatso had been murdered for the large amount of cash he had brought back with him from a recent fund-raising trip to Hong Kong. Another story was that a drunken brawl in the basement of the building (where there was a small restaurant) had somehow spun out of control. But the truth is, most Tibetans knew perfectly well what lay behind the tragedy. This was an attempt by the deity's supporters to intimidate the Dalai Lama into dropping his policy on Shugden practice. By way of confirmation, an open letter to the Dalai Lama published in the name of the Delhi-based Shugden Supporters Society which circulated a few days later issued a stark warning: "We have already offered you three corpses, you will find others if you continue with your approach."

Ultimately, the controversy over Shugden's status is a theological one. Within Buddhism, "church" and state, or rather *sangha* and state, have not come apart as they have in the West. As a result, theological controversy very quickly finds its way out of the monastery and into the political arena, often with immediate and far-reaching consequences. In the case of Shugden, what was at stake was not merely the question of what status should correctly be assigned to a certain deity—in particular whether he is simply a minor being or one of the protector deities, as his followers proposed. It was also the question of who should govern Tibet. According to devotees of Dorje Shugden, the present Dalai Lama had shown by his actions that he himself was unqualified to occupy the Lion Throne.

In the immediate aftermath of the murder, confusion reigned. It was several hours before the police were called—long enough for the killers to make good their escape. The Indian criminal investigation concluded eventually that the suspects had fled abroad. For months afterwards, Dharamsala remained paralyzed. The Dalai Lama, however, maintained his position regarding the Shugden issue. On his behalf the letter-writing campaigns continued, and both monks and laymen were required to sign a statement declaring that they had no connection with Shugden.

During the fall of that same year (1997), the Dalai Lama gave a long and careful explanation, subsequently published, justifying his position. Its main thrust was to argue that it was not Shugden the practitioner should worry about offending, but the Buddha. To the outsider, the speech gives a moderately worded and clear exposition of the Dalai Lama's thinking behind his injunction. To Shugden's devotees, it was a tissue of falsehoods and outright lies. For them, the crux of the matter was as much the purity of the Gelugpa teachings that, in their view, the Dalai Lama's advocacy of Padmasambhava, the Lotus-Born, and the Nyingma tradition generally, threatened, as it was the insult to the deity himself that upset them. For devotees of Shugden, a powerful minority of the Gelug school, the teachings of their founder, Tsongkhapa, were to be practiced and preserved without taint. For the Dalai Lama, Shugden threatened the ecumenical approach he wanted to take toward the other Tibetan schools.

Yet far more was at issue here than the "lama politics" of which the Dalai Lama sometimes speaks. For the tradition, and hence for him, the gods and protectors are not mere fictions. They are both real and powerful. While the gods have limited abilities, the dharma protectors are vastly more capable and can influence events not only in the world but within other realms too. The protectors are considered to be manifestations of different bodhisattvas, just as the Dalai Lama himself is a manifestation of Chenresig, and their main function is to keep the dharma itself from harm. And while the Dalai Lama characterizes Shugden as nothing but the lowest form of godling, to Shugden devotees he is the wrathful manifestation of Manjushri, Bodhisattva of Wisdom.

We can understand the Dalai Lama's insistence that worship of Shugden cease only when we see that for him, Shugden, like Nechung (the great rival of Shugden), is not merely a projection or imaginative construct but as real as the flesh and blood in which human beings manifest. It is precisely this construal of the deities and the protectors as real that lies behind the Dalai Lama's relationship with Nechung. As he recounts in his autobiography: "When I was small, it was touching. Nechung liked me a lot and always took great care of me. For example, if he noticed I had dressed carelessly or improperly, he would come over and rearrange my shirt, adjust my robe and so on." As to his character, "he is very reserved and austere, just as you would imagine a grand old man of ancient times to be." To be clear, the Dalai Lama is referring not to the medium through whom Dorje Drakden manifests but to Dorje Drakden himself.

As a rule, the Dalai Lama consults with Nechung formally only once or twice a year, always during the Great Prayer Festival and sometimes on other important occasions. But he also consults with him privately on a more frequent basis. When he does so informally, the medium does not wear the full regalia of his office, which is reserved for the great occasions of state. Although there exist a number of YouTube videos of Nechung and other oracles in a trance, to appreciate fully their importance to the tradition, it is necessary to witness the phenomenon at first hand, a privilege granted to few outsiders.

The Dalai Lama, sumptuously clad in yellow silk over his habitual maroon robe, sits on an elaborately decorated throne while he presides over the entirety of the Namgyal monastic community. It will be recalled that Namgyal is the monastery that exists to serve the Dalai Lama and to conduct rituals on behalf of the Tibetan government. This community is divided into the choir, made up of a majority of the monks—perhaps forty of them—and the orchestra, which comprises perhaps a dozen. Many are, like the Dalai Lama, swaddled in the yellow outer robe of the Gelug school, while the more senior wear the tall, forward-curving headdress that is adopted only for the most important liturgies.

Before the ceremony begins, the medium looks small and vulnerable, clearly conscious that what he is about to undertake will test him to the utmost limits of his strength. His ordeal begins with the impossible bass of the *umze*, the cantor, who leads the monastic choir and whose voice is joined shortly by the steady beat of a pair of drums. These drums are of shallow construction and are held vertical on a short pole and struck with a curved stick. In response, there is an immediate contraction around the medium's jaw, and it is clear the possession is already beginning. The look of vulnerability is gone, and now, after another minute and to a sudden trembling of cymbals and oboes thrilling, two attendants come forward and proceed to fasten in place a breastplate of burnished silver about the size of a small salver. As they do so, the *kuten,* or medium, tries to help, but he fumbles ineffectually, no longer in full control of his limbs.

The Dalai Lama, meanwhile, has withdrawn his attention inward and his demeanor has become more serious. Rocking gently back and forth, he joins in the chant, as the orchestra beseeches the presence of the deity with mounting insistence. But again, after a clamoring crescendo, the monks fall silent before the chant begins anew to the tap of the drums and a slow rumble of voices following the cantor's lead.

All at once there is a palpable sense—of what?—that something momentous is under way. But more than that—of a *mysterium et tremendum fascinans,* a mystery before which the onlooker stands in awe, both fearful and fascinated.

The chant starts to swell once more. The medium, now fully dressed, remains seated as the Dalai Lama looks on. One senses a definite rapport between him and Nechung—the deity, though, not the medium. This is evidently a meeting of familiars. Indeed, there is nothing to suggest that, for the Precious Protector, anything untoward or remarkable is about to take place. The same may be said of the congregation as a whole: many people are quietly chatting to one another, even as they tell their rosaries. The medium sits quite peacefully now, his eyes closed and his hands upon his knees. But again there is a sudden increase in the tempo of the drums and an outburst of oboe—and trumpet, the famed *gang ling,* crafted from human femur, which accompanies first a quivering, then a clashing of the cymbals in climax. The Precious Protector, eyes cast down, rocks forward and back faster and with shorter, more abrupt movements.

Without any sign from the medium himself, two attendants bring the oracle's headdress. This consists of a huge helmet, its wide brim supporting a superstructure of intricate religious symbols, each of these studded with precious stones, while sprays of what look like horsehair burst from the crown, falling at least the length of a man's arm behind. It is hard to believe anyone could wear such a thing unsupported. To an observer it looks as if it must weigh thirty pounds or more—though it is said that, in former times, it was more than twice as heavy. Once it is tied in place, an improbably thin strap passing under his chin, the *kuten* stops grimacing, and his expression assumes a look of deep serenity as the next cycle of invocations begins. It is indeed so hypnotic, this sound, its strong, steady, rhythmic flow so overwhelming, that it seems surprising that more people do not succumb. And in fact, they sometimes do. What is more, the tempo of chant and music has a profound impact on the experience of the medium himself, who must visualize, while it progresses, first the mandala—the symbolic representation of his dwelling place—corresponding to the deity and then the arrival of the deity as he steps out of his mandala. On this occasion, evidently attuned to the least sign that all is not as it must be, one of the attendants—there are four altogether—comes forward and reties the headdress.

After the five minutes or so that the chant cycle takes, yet another begins. Now the medium begins to jerk spasmodically, his whole body quaking. The Dalai Lama, who has been following this part of the proceedings silently, joins in the chant briefly. The *kuten* is leaning back, his mouth forced wide, his breathing stentorian, as oboe, horn, and cymbal combine once more in clashing crescendo. An attendant now brings what looks as if it must be a sword, covered with a red cloth, together with a bow but no arrows. In times past, when the ceremony took place outside, the oracle would generally loose off several. He did so when indicating the direction in which the search parties looking for the present incarnation of the Dalai Lama should conduct their search. And it is said that, once, long ago, one struck and killed a child.

The timbre and tempo of the chant change. One of the trumpeters keeps time by tapping his finger on his instrument, while the oracle, still seated and partially screened by a ministering attendant, continues to tremble and twitch. The Dalai Lama, hitherto bareheaded, dons a tall, forward-curving yellow headpiece with long silken earflaps reaching to his shoulders, and at that moment there is a faint sound of tinkling bells. Could this be the deity announcing himself?

The *kuten* remains seated, clutching his weapons, one leg trembling with increasing violence. All of a sudden he begins to emit short, sobbing grunts

—"ah-ah-ah"—as the orchestra rises once more in a crescendo. And now, taking his accoutrements firmly in hand, Nechung rises from his throne, its tiger-skin covering visible for the first time. As he does so, the whole congregation—though not the choir and not the Dalai Lama—stands too.

The Precious Protector, eyes cast down, sways gently in silent prayer.

With Dorje Drakden clearly in full possession of the medium, the first part of the ceremony is over. It is now for individual members of the government to greet him, each rising in turn to go forward and present a *kathag,* a white silk scarf representing an offering of one subordinate to his or her superior.

It is only when the last *kathag* has been presented that Nechung turns to the Dalai Lama. There is something matter-of-fact about the manner in which he responds to the oracle. The choir continues its chant, and after this brief acknowledgment, it is the turn of three successive monastic officials to speak with Dorje Drakden. Bending low toward the *kuten,* they put their questions to him, and he replies in a voice unexpectedly high-pitched and sobbing almost as if he were on the verge of tears, like a coerced child. It is impossible not to feel enormous concern for the human being thus used. The observer has the impression that he can barely contain the enormous force to which he has granted temporary residence. Small wonder these men do not often survive beyond middle age.

After the last question, the *kuten* resumes his throne but continues to quake and to emit a curious hissing sound while the officials confer with one another. Occasionally it looks as if the oracle wishes to stand but is unable to, the vast headdress turning from side to side as he twists his neck, his lower lip pulled down in rictus gape. And every so often he speaks, apparently repeating himself as if frustrated that he has not been properly understood. The officials, having spoken among themselves, now return, evidently seeking further clarification.

At last the interviews are complete. Dorje Drakden has imparted his augury of the year ahead, and the oracle gesticulates with his hand, stabbing the air with an index finger. He stands once more as oboe, trumpet, and cymbal rise again. Turning to the Dalai Lama, he takes a pace or two forward, with his sword in one hand and, in the other, a peacock feather—a symbol of purity—

which he proceeds to offer to the Precious Protector. The exchange is perfunctory and yet unaccountably moving.

Only now does the Dalai Lama himself rise. He places a *kathag* around the oracle's neck before they consult together privately for perhaps a minute, after which the Precious Protector reassumes his throne. Almost at once the deity abandons its earthly confinement, and the medium falls back into the arms of his waiting attendants. Deftly they untie the enormous headdress before carrying out the medium's inert and rigid body.

In any consideration of the Shugden controversy, it is thus essential to keep in mind the intimate relationships that the protectors have with earthbound mortals, relationships that we see most vividly as they are played out in these consultations with the oracles. For not only do Nechung and Shugden speak through mediums, but also there are many other deities that speak through oracles besides these two. Even today, there are many mediums who channel deities, both within Tibet and in exile, though only a handful are conduits for the supra-mundane protectors. The remainder give voices to more minor beings. But they are by no means rare.

Aside from the question of the reality of the protectors and their communications with human beings, with respect to the issue of Shugden himself, we also need to understand something of the role that Tsongkhapa—whose teachings it is allegedly Shugden's special responsibility to protect—plays within the Gelug tradition, at the pinnacle of which the Dalai Lama stands.

The fourteenth-century founder of the Dalai Lama's own Gelug tradition, Tsongkhapa (literally, and somewhat deflatingly, the Man from the Land of Onions) is unquestionably the most important figure to have emerged in Tibet in the past six hundred years. He was, most educated Tibetans would agree, Aristotle, Shakespeare, Saint Francis, and Einstein all rolled into one. Showing early signs of brilliance, Tsongkhapa began his monastic career in a small monastery close to the present Dalai Lama's birthplace in Amdo. As a child, he was said to be capable of memorizing seventeen folios of scripture a day—approximately fifteen hundred words—and to have perfect recall ever after. Once ordained, he adopted the life of a wandering hermit, taking teachings from many different masters—though none of them Nyingma. One of his early devotions was to recite the mantra of his principal meditational deity a hundred million times. Gifted with a laser-sharp intelligence, he was able at once to grasp the most abstruse arguments in metaphysics and to reconcile apparently contradictory theses. He was a poetic genius, too, with an extraordinary facility with words. Much of his most important and difficult philosophy is framed in perfectly metered verse, while his spiritual songs and praises are said to be without compare for their ability to move the heart of the one who recites them. If, though, he had one virtue that crowned all others, it was his proficiency in the meditative practices of a yogin. He was a visionary whose personal relationship with Manjushri, Bodhisattva of Wisdom, would mark him as the outstanding practitioner of the Buddhadharma of his—and, many would argue, of any—age since that of the Buddha Shakyamuni himself.

As well as being a stickler for the rules of personal conduct, Tsongkapa brought to the monastic movement itself a renewed emphasis on the life and works of the historical Buddha. The annual celebration of the Great Prayer Festival in Lhasa was one of his key innovations. He also established Ganden Monastery, which—together with its sister foundations at Drepung and Sera—came to be the single most important religious foundation in Tibet. From his own time up to the present, Tsongkhapa continues to inspire not only young Tibetans but also, increasingly, people from all over to renounce the world and dedicate themselves to the monastic life. Yet Tsongkhapa is not without his critics. There are those who question the authenticity of his self-proclaimed relationship with the bodhisattva Manjushri. Others are suspicious of the way in which he totally ignored the earlier Tibetan tradition of which the Lotus-Born is the key figure. Yet for the present Dalai Lama himself, Tsongkhapa is the scholar-saint of the Tibetan tradition to whom he feels closest, and he regularly gives teachings on the master's Great Treatise on the Stages of the Path to Enlightenment.

With respect to Shugden, as the Dalai Lama explained in his 1997 talk, the origins of the deity's cult lie in the seventeenth century, during the lifetime of the Great Fifth Dalai Lama. It was this incarnation—the one to whom the present Dalai Lama has often said he identifies with most closely—who acquired for the Dalai Lama institution its temporal power. Until his alliance with Gushri Khan, the Mongolian warlord who became chief patron of the

Gelugpas, the Dalai Lamas were merely one among several reincarnation lineages renowned for their spiritual attainments. His predecessor the Fourth Dalai Lama, Yonten Gyatso, can, by virtue of his Mongolian princely ancestry, be regarded as an earlier attempt at gaining political power for the (still relatively young) Gelugpa sect. But the Fourth Dalai Lama died a failure, unimpressive in either the temporal or the spiritual realm. As a result, during the interregnum that followed his death, the Gelugpas, having no reliable backing, struggled for survival "like a butter lamp flickering in a raging storm." It was only when, through the diplomacy of his chamberlain, the (not yet deemed Great) Fifth Dalai Lama forged an alliance with Gushri Khan, head of the Qoshot Mongols, that Gelug fortunes were transformed. Sweeping all before them, the Mongolians destroyed first the resurgent Bonpos of the kingdom of Beri in eastern Tibet. It is the Bonpos who claim to be the guardians of the original religion of Tibet (though they have adopted many Buddhist practices). Then, despite the Dalai Lama's deep misgivings, and after a lengthy siege, the Mongolians toppled the Kargyu-supporting king of Tsang in central Tibet.

When, subsequently, the Dalai Lama established his headquarters in Lhasa, he oversaw a major expansion of the Gelug establishment. Yet for all his dedication to the legacy of Tsongkhapa, and despite being the incarnation of its most important lineage, he was himself a master of the Nyingma tradition and an initiate of many of its most secret and occult practices, notably the art of war magic.

Even in the seventeenth century, there was considerable opposition within Gelug circles to the Dalai Lama's enthusiasm for the Nyingma tradition. This opposition coalesced around a gifted lama by the name of Drakpa Gyaltsen, who had in fact been a candidate when the Fifth Dalai Lama was being searched for. Both sides agree that matters eventually came to a head when Drakpa Gyaltsen died, though how he did so is a matter of dispute. According to devotees of Shugden, the two met in a debate, which, humiliatingly, the Dalai Lama lost. The following day, the victor was found dead with the silk offering scarf the Dalai Lama had been compelled to present to him in recognition of his triumph rammed down his throat. Exactly what happened next is also a matter of controversy, although there is broad agreement at least as to the outcome.

As we saw earlier, it is well understood that victims of violent crime are likely to be reborn as *shi dre,* a kind of ghost that often causes harm to those with whom it comes into contact. Something similar seems to have happened with Drakpa Gyaltsen. When his remains came to be cremated, it is said that a thick pall of black smoke rose from the pyre, assuming the shape of an open hand, which hung suspended in the air. Soon after, strange events began to be reported in central Tibet: the silver casket into which his ashes had been deposited started to emit a buzzing sound; animals became unaccountably sick and many died; crops failed. More troubling still, the dishes on which the Dalai Lama's food was set overturned themselves spontaneously, and there came the sound of stones crashing onto the roof of the Potala. The noise could be drowned out only by monks blowing on the huge *dung chen* horns normally used to summon the faithful to prayer. Exasperated, the Dalai Lama summoned the abbot of the recently founded Mindroling Monastery (a Nyingma foundation), who presided over construction of a demon trap. On this occasion, however, the abbot was distracted at a critical moment during the ritual, enabling the spirit to escape. In the end, the best that could be done was to lure it to a lonely spot where a small shrine was built in its honor.*

Shugden devotees claim that, at this point, the Dalai Lama was forced to accept that this was no ordinary spirit but that Drakpa Gyaltsen, having been reborn in a heavenly realm, was revealed to be a dharma protector, whose real name was Dorje Shugden.† It is even alleged that the Great Fifth wrote prayers in his honor, though, as the present Dalai Lama pointed out in his 1997 speech, there is no evidence for this in any of the eighteen volumes of the collected works. On the contrary, these make clear that, far from settling at the shrine, Shugden's "harmful activities only intensified." In response, the Great Fifth ordered a huge ritual onslaught, culminating in a fire ceremony during which ef-

* This was at the Trode Khangsar, which still stands in Lhasa today.

† There is, however, another tradition, which holds that the real origins of Shugden lie with the maleficent activity of a seventeenth-century Kargyu lama. It is alleged that, owing to friction between the Gelug and Kargyu schools at that time, this lama succeeded in "hacking" Drakpa Gyaltsen's spirit, then sending him off to another realm and substituting an evil spirit in its place to masquerade as a dharma protector but in fact to do maximum harm to the Gelugpas.

figies of the "perfidious interfering spirit" and his entourage were burnt. A sign of success was "the smell of burning flesh that everybody witnessed."

Unfortunately for the Dalai Lama, despite this promising sign, ultimately his campaign failed and the spirit survived. By the time of the Great Thirteenth Dalai Lama, Shugden's cult had spread to Kham, where, thanks to the enthusiastic advocacy of one of the greatest and most famous lamas of this time, Phabongka Rinpoché, guru to both Ling Rinpoché and Trijang Rinpoché and a teacher of legendary charisma, he acquired an enormous following. This was further bolstered by Shugden's spectacular manifestation through the Panglung oracle. Joseph Rock, the Austro-American botanist and explorer who reported on the massacre of Tibetan children by Hui bandits, recounted in *National Geographic* how, during a séance he witnessed in 1928, the oracle "took a sword handed to him, a strong Mongolian steel blade . . . [and] [i]n the twinkling of an eye . . . twisted it with his naked hands into several loops and knots!"

The Great Thirteenth likewise had severe reservations about the deity. Formally reprimanding Phabongka, he required him to desist from spreading the practice. But by now it was too late. So when the Great Thirteenth Dalai Lama died in 1933, some said that Shugden had a hand in his demise. In spite of this, the cult of the deity continued to spread, especially among the laity in Kham. So powerful did he become that it is said the western gate of Nechung Monastery was kept permanently locked, as it was there that Shugden waited, poised to move in the moment Pehar attained final liberation.

Part of the discomfort Shugden's devotees feel about the present Dalai Lama's attempted proscription of his cult is the thought that he is calling the commitment of many great masters of the Gelug tradition into question. Also, by implication, that he is willing to abrogate the *samaya*—the sacred bond established when a pupil takes a teaching from a lama—that exists between himself and those Shugden devotees, notably Trijang Rinpoché and the regent Taktra Rinpoché, whose student he was. The bond further requires that the student sees the teacher as the actual embodiment of the Buddha. This means that to criticize the teacher in any way is to criticize the Buddha himself. Yet the Dalai Lama is quick to point out that while he had just such a relationship with Reting Rinpoché, no one argues that Reting did not make mistakes. For him to deny these would be to contradict the evidence—the letters the ex-regent wrote asking for Chinese support—that he saw with his own eyes. Furthermore, just because he has come to the conclusion that Trijang Rinpoché's Shugden practice was mistaken, he emphasizes that this should in no way be seen as disrespecting either the high spiritual attainments or the great contribution of his junior tutor. He even confided that his regard for Trijang Rinpoché remains so deep that, on one occasion, he even dreamt of "lapping up" his teacher's urine as the junior tutor relieved himself. To the outsider this seems a surprising—even shocking—anecdote to share, but to a monastic audience, it will have put them in mind of a relatively common practice whereby small quantities of the bodily waste of high lamas are ritually imbibed as a means to furthering one's own spiritual progress.*

Over the years since his 1997 address, the Dalai Lama has maintained his position on Shugden (whom he refers to as *dolgyal*—the king demon) with consistency, explaining that, when it comes to matters of such importance, "being a fairly forthright person, I just don't know how to be courteous and discreet." Fortunately, there have been no more killings, though there is anecdotal evidence of continuing friction between the two factions. More destructive has been the internationalization of the issue. This has been seen in protests, such as those that occurred during high-profile visits by the Dalai Lama to the University of Oxford in 2008 and, in 2015, to the University of Cambridge. Organized by an alliance of Shugden groups in the West, these incidents bear eloquent testimony to the power of metaphysics to move human beings; this is, after all, a deity that, until at most a century ago, had not been heard of beyond the reaches of a relatively small number of Himalayan communities. Yet it is in Tibet that the greatest damage has been done. The controversy has not gone unnoticed by the Chinese authorities, and it is unsurprising

---

*When Father Johannes Grueber, the first European known to have visited Lhasa, reached the capital in 1661, he was scandalized to discover that the most highly prized remedy in the Tibetan pharmacopoeia was the Dalai Lama's and other high lamas' excrement, desiccated and incorporated into "Precious Pills." While Precious Pills continue to be manufactured, it is remarkable to see that medical opinion has lately turned in favor of a similar practice (fecal microbiota transplant) for treatment of certain intestinal conditions.

to learn that a number of Shugden-supporting monasteries have been, in recent years, recipients of generous funding from Chinese government sources.

Without question, the Shugden controversy highlights the single most challenging aspect of the encounter between Tibetan tradition and contemporary secular society. The Dalai Lama is fully committed to introducing the natural sciences not only into the ordinary school curriculum but into the monastic curriculum as well. He is similarly committed to the advancement of women, to full democracy, and to institutional transparency.* At the same time, it is clear that the Dalai Lama remains fully immersed in the traditional Buddhist worldview—even if he regards the cosmological texts as needing interpretation—and to the dharma protectors and their supernatural enemies central to that worldview.

At the time of writing, there appears to be an uneasy truce between declared Shugden supporters and those who follow the Dalai Lama on the issue. Among the exile population, anecdotal evidence suggests that the proportion of Shugdenpa is unlikely to be more than 10 to 15 percent at the most. A similar figure is probably true of Tibetans in Tibet itself. Nevertheless, both Ganden and Sera Monasteries in exile have seen breakaway groups opening separate Shugden monasteries, and there are several other, smaller monasteries in exile that have opened separate Shugden houses too. It is thus not impossible that Shugden numbers could grow during a future regency period. From the Precious Protector's point of view, it is fortunate that the one person who might have emerged to take on leadership of the pro-Shugden faction, the new Trijang Rinpoché, has shown no inclination to do so. Indeed, the young man discovered himself to be at the center of a plot to discredit the Precious Protector. It emerged that a group of Shugden devotees planned to murder his chief assistant with the intention of laying the blame on Dalai Lama loyalists. Even so, there are signs that such leadership could yet emerge.

When the 101st Ganden Throne Holder, the highest authority within the Gelug establishment, retired in 2009, observers were stunned when news

---

* It is true that the government in exile (the Central Tibetan Administration) has some quite obvious shortcomings in both respects, but this is a very young institution as well as a very new idea in terms of the tradition.

emerged that he had joined the breakaway Shugden-supporting Shar Ganden Monastery in southern India. If true, this meant that, throughout his six-year incumbency, he had been in undeclared opposition to the Dalai Lama all along—a revelation made all the more remarkable for his impeccable scholarly and spiritual conduct. This defiance of the Dalai Lama at the very highest level suggests that there might be other, similarly highly placed opponents of the Precious Protector waiting for a safe moment to declare themselves. At the very least, it suggests that there is likely to be further turmoil in the community when the Dalai Lama chooses to manifest the act of passing away.

21

Tibet in Flames: The Beijing Olympics and Their Aftermath

If the violence of the Shugden controversy has to some extent overshadowed the latter years of the Dalai Lama's biography, it has had little impact on his reputation internationally. Following the award of the Nobel Peace Prize, public recognition of the Precious Protector has continued to grow —as has appreciation of his message of universal compassion.

One moment when this surging popularity might have suffered came in 1997, when the Dalai Lama's private office received an open letter from a prominent gay activist seeking clarification over some remarks the Precious Protector had recently made. The Dalai Lama had given an interview during which he had expounded the classical Buddhist view of active same-sex relationships —that they are impermissible—apparently contradicting a more liberal stance he had taken earlier. In response, the Dalai Lama agreed to meet a small group of gay and lesbian Buddhists in San Francisco during the summer of that year. Later, one of the participants wrote of how, "stepping into the June sunlight [afterward, he] felt tired, calm, enormously grateful—and disappointed." The

Dalai Lama had explained that, while for non-Buddhists the strictures did not apply, for followers of the Buddhadharma, certain sexual practices were indeed forbidden. He explained further that the prohibition against these activities applied equally to non-same-sex couples. It followed, therefore, that it was not same-sex relationships themselves that were proscribed but only the physical expression of them. He added, however, that the matter was one of tradition and that this tradition reflected the moral codes of the time, allowing the possibility that change could come about "in response to science, modern social history and discussion within the various Buddhist *sanghas*." As for himself, while he was open to the possibility of such change, he had no authority to bring it about single-handedly even if he wanted to. The activists should therefore advocate for their interests according to the Buddhist principles of "rigorous investigation and non-violence"—presumably remaining chaste while doing so.

The notion that the Dalai Lama could be persuaded to change his mind if the tradition itself changed its mind, while not quite what the group was looking for, was enough to satisfy most people that the highest Tibetan spiritual authority was not closed to the possibility of a development of doctrine—even if this was an example, noted by one commentator, of how the Dalai Lama "delights listeners everywhere by being the rare spiritual figure who says there is no need for temples or scripture" but then "disappoints them, often, by suggesting that there is a need for old-fashioned ethics and all the things your grandmother told you were good for you." Yet it is clear that this tendency to disappoint does not diminish the Dalai Lama's appeal to those attracted to his identification with nonviolence and compassion, and to his insistence that warmheartedness is of greater value than which religious tradition people do or do not adhere to. This, surely, is what is behind his emergence, during the closing years of the twentieth century, as a universal "doctor of the soul"—Pico Iyer's evocative soubriquet—even though it is also true that Buddhism explicitly denies the existence of the soul.

At the close of the twentieth century, this growing appreciation of the Dalai Lama was augmented by high-profile appearances at events such as a rock concert celebrating the fiftieth anniversary of the Universal Declaration of Human Rights. Here, alongside the likes of Bruce Springsteen and the surviving members of Led Zeppelin, the Dalai Lama took to the stage in Paris to declare his own commitment to human rights—infuriating the Shugden devotees who were, at that moment, making a case to Amnesty International that he had infringed theirs by proscribing worship of the deity.

Arguably the most important element in securing the Dalai Lama's reputation as a "doctor of the soul" was the publication in 1998 of *The Art of Happiness.* Marketed as being jointly authored by the Dalai Lama, the book was based on a series of interviews granted to the American psychiatrist Dr. Howard Cutler. In presenting and interpreting the Dalai Lama's outlook to Westerners educated in the norms of contemporary society, the work succeeded brilliantly in presenting not so much the profundity of its subject's thinking as the notion that happiness (admittedly never precisely defined) could be attained by "assembling" the causes and conditions of happiness—which, the book further suggested, did not necessarily include the strict discipline of the religious life. The book was an immediate—and enduring—success, selling more than a million copies in its first year of publication in America alone.

With the Dalai Lama's increasing popularity came increasing requests for talks and teachings. Most continued to be at the invitation of different Buddhist groups around the world. In fulfilling these, the Dalai Lama would often drive himself so hard that he would return to Dharamsala utterly exhausted. Although his public talks are generally given extemporaneously, he prepares meticulously for every teaching he gives. His principal translator, the brilliant Cambridge-educated (now former) monk Thupten Jinpa, recalls once catching sight of the Dalai Lama's heavily annotated copy of a notoriously abstruse text. Jinpa later noticed that, during an enforced wait at the airport, he "delved into his small shoulder bag and . . . launched into deep study," approaching the text almost like a young student.

Not all invitations came from Buddhist groups, however. In 2000 the Dalai Lama visited Northern Ireland to participate in, among other events, one billed as "testimonials from victims of sectarian violence." This was organized by the Catholic monk Father Laurence Freeman, who had also organized the Good Heart conference where the Dalai Lama commented on the Christian gospels. Besides meeting, and being photographed with, Gerry Adams, the Irish Sinn Fein leader whom many believe to have been a senior member of the terrorist Irish Republican Army, the Dalai Lama also met with the man he has since described as his "hero," Richard Moore. One of three speakers to give their testimonial, Moore had been blinded as a ten-year-old boy by a rubber bullet fired by a British soldier, which hit him between the eyes. Prior to the event, the Dalai Lama placed Moore's hand on his head and face, inviting him to picture what he felt. A few years afterwards, Moore met with his assailant and made an unlikely friend of him. At the Dalai Lama's invitation, the two men then traveled to Dharamsala, where the Tibetan leader presented them to a large audience of refugee schoolchildren, explaining that their story exemplified what he meant by compassion, reconciliation, and forgiveness.*

There were some light moments, such as when, having been gifted a "vineyard"—claimed to be the smallest in the world, and consisting of precisely four vines—the Dalai Lama was invited in front of a crowd of a thousand onlookers to fire a pistol in the air, as tradition demanded, on completion of the "harvest." He took the gun from the previous owner (a Catholic monk), looked at it, hesitated for a moment, then kissed it and handed it back.

By now, the Dalai Lama's popularity was such that, shortly after the two-year anniversary of 9/11, a crowd of 65,000 came to Central Park to hear him declare that "the very concept of war is out of date." And as an example of the seriousness with which Buddhist thought is now beginning to be taken by the scientific community, during the winter of 2005 the Dalai Lama was invited to address the American Society for Neuroscience. The invitation to do so was not without controversy. A five-hundred-signature petition (largely, it seems, from among scientists with a connection to China) urged the organizers to withdraw it, on the grounds that his proposed lecture on the value of meditation "is of poor scientific taste because it will highlight hyperbolic claims, limited research and compromised scientific rigour." One delegate was critical of the Dalai Lama's belief that the mind and the body are separable and that, moreover, it is possible for the consciousness of one individual to be trans-

* Moore founded the charity Children in Crossfire, of which the Dalai Lama is now patron. He is a gifted musician and as a young man played lead guitar in the musical *Jesus Christ Superstar* when it opened in Dublin. He often jokes that in holding him up as any kind of hero, the Dalai Lama shows that he is a terrible judge of character.

ferred into the body of another. The reference here is to the Buddhist practice of *phowa,* whereby the practitioner transfers his or her consciousness into the body of another, either recently deceased or who desires to practice the dharma in another realm.*

The Dalai Lama's lecture was well received nonetheless, even if many remained skeptical of some of his claims about the benefits of meditation. But few would have wished to argue with the Dalai Lama's further claim that, while countless billions of dollars were spent annually on exploring outer space, it was time to devote proper resources to probing the "inner space" of consciousness.

If these examples of the Dalai Lama's mounting stature throughout the world are impressive, the devotion he continues to inspire among Tibetans in Tibet is arguably even more so. A striking instance of this occurred in 2006, when a comment, picked up from a speech he gave in Bodh Gaya, electrified the whole country when word of it was somehow circulated in Tibet. In view of the threat to the long-term survival of several rare species indigenous to Tibet, the Dalai Lama had suggested that it would be a good idea if Tibetans ceased to wear or to use animal fur. They responded by the hundreds and thousands. Himalayan tiger and leopard skin, otter pelts, sable and bear skin, all highly prized both as clothing and as furnishings in religious ceremonies, were brought from their places of safekeeping and publicly burned. Had the Chinese doubted for a moment where the loyalty of the vast majority of Tibetans lay, this was a forceful reminder of how things stood. In vain did they try to halt the bonfires; to no effect were the arrests of the organizers.

Between 1995 and 2002, from the disappearance of the Panchen Lama until the time of Beijing's confirmation as the venue for the Games, there had been no official contact between the Chinese authorities and the Tibetan government in exile, recently recast as the Central Tibetan Administration. This was despite—perhaps even because of—America's enthusiastic advocacy of dialogue between the two sides. In October 1997, Bill Clinton had urged his Chinese counterpart, Jiang Zemin, to initiate meaningful talks with the Dalai

---

*The sign of successful transference is said to be the appearance of a small hole at the crown of the head, into which it is traditional to push a blade of kusha grass.

Lama, and on a visit to Beijing the following year, the American president confronted Jiang during a live press conference, saying of the Dalai Lama, "I believe him to be an honest man, and I believe that if he had a conversation with President Jiang, they would like each other very much." Whether the laughter from the audience that followed was generous or nervous is unclear.

Nonetheless, with the Olympics looming, and perhaps due to China's concern following more than one visit by the Dalai Lama to Taiwan, contact between Beijing and Dharamsala was reestablished, and one or more government-level meetings took place each year from 2002 in the run-up to the Games, with increasing signs of progress. These followed a potentially difficult moment occasioned, during 2000, by the dramatic flight from Tibet of the fourteen-year-old Ogyen Trinley Dorje, head of the Karma Kargyu tradition, who, having walked from his monastery in Tibet to the Nepalese border and subsequently flown to Kathmandu by helicopter, arrived in Dharamsala in early January. Rumors that he was a spy were put about by those whom his presence in exile threatened. In particular this included a rival to his leadership position who already occupied substantial property assets belonging to the Kargyu in India. For his part, however, the Dalai Lama recognizes the "Tibetan" candidate and has since taken a close, even avuncular interest in the young man's education and welfare, saying more than once that he expected the Karmapa to play an important role in the future of the refugee community.

When the controversy occasioned by this unexpected arrival had abated, and following successive rounds of talks between officials from Dharamsala and Beijing, in 2007 the Dalai Lama's chief negotiator announced that, although the differences in viewpoint on the question of the Tibetan issue were "numerous," they had, he said, "reached the stage where, if there is political will on both sides, we have an opportunity to finally resolve this issue." This was an extraordinary development, and even though the Chinese responded to the Dalai Lama's Congressional Gold Medal, awarded that year by the Bush administration, by describing it as a "farce," optimism within the exile community rose to its highest since the Deng era. In fact, the award, made by an act of Congress, which must be cosponsored by two-thirds of the membership of both the House of Representatives and the Senate, was a matter of immense significance not only for the Tibetan exile leadership but also for the Chinese, to whom it looked like a major upgrading of the Dalai Lama's political status by the United States. The perception was further reinforced when Congress authorized the president to confer the award on the Dalai Lama in person.

In Tibet, meanwhile, China's denunciation of the award, along with, for example, continued restrictions on display of photographs of the Dalai Lama, caused serious resentment. If anyone expected the Tibetan masses to turn the other cheek to this latest insult following the Congressional award, and to the continued demonization of the Dalai Lama in the months leading up to the Beijing Olympics, they were tragically disappointed. Once more, Tibet erupted in flames and in fury.

On March 10, 2008, monks staged a protest against Chinese rule that centered on the Ramoche Temple in Lhasa. Here it needs to be understood that, besides this date being significant as the one on which the Dalai Lama fled Tibet, it also falls during the first month of the Tibetan New Year, which itself commemorates *chorul dawa:* the Month of Miracles. These signs were performed by the Buddha in answer to the gibes and abuse of nonbelieving heretical teachers before a crowd of more than ninety thousand. Making the miracles of Christ look like the trivial deeds of a minor *siddha,* the Buddha began by flying through the air. He then produced a stunning display of fire and water emanating from his body. Next, he planted his toothpick in the ground and it grew into a vast tree, laden with fruit and fragrant flowers. On the following day, he "manifested" two mountains made of the most precious stones. Thereafter, he produced a lake. Next he manifested a voice that sounded throughout the world, expounding the dharma. The day after, he radiated a light which filled the universe. On the penultimate day, he made his patrons world rulers. On the last day, the Buddha pressed down on his seat with the fingers of his right hand, and from beneath arose Vajrapani, a wrathful bodhisattva, who scattered the heretics and smashed their thrones. Then the Buddha radiated eighty-four thousand beams of light from each pore of his skin. On the tip of each ray reposed a lotus, on which was seated another Buddha preaching the dharma. Given the resonance of these events and of this time in the Buddhist psyche, it is hardly surprising that the New Year is a time of heightened emotion for Tibetans, especially within the monasteries.

Also, it is important to remember that the Dalai Lama's identification with Chenresig is not, for Tibetans, merely an abstract theological proposition. It is built into their self-understanding. As every child knows, Chenresig is the father of the Tibetan race, first manifesting in the guise of a monkey. One day he was importuned by an ogress who lived among the mountains and was at that moment mourning the death of all her children. Moved by pity, the monkey accepted the ogress's request to become her mate. It was their offspring who were the first Tibetans. Thus it stands to reason that Chenresig, as his name implies—translated literally it means the One Who Looks Down with Compassion—takes special care of the successors of his own progeny. Moreover, that he has since taken human form in the Dalai Lamas and their predecessors is only to be expected, given the bodhisattva's relationship with the Tibetan people. The relationship between Chenresig and the Tibetan people is thus a feature of the way the world is.

When we understand how the tradition conceives the Dalai Lama, we begin to see why it is so hard for Tibetans to hear him slandered. We also see why it is so hard for communism to make real converts among the Tibetan people. And indeed why, six decades since his flight into exile, the Dalai Lama's picture still cannot be shown in his homeland.

The forced dispersal of the demonstration at the Ramoche Temple in March 2008 was the trigger of a disastrous riot. Many in the crowd, including a number of monks, went on a rampage. Over a period of several days, mobs of Tibetans attacked both ethnic Chinese and Hui Muslims, killing, it is thought, up to eighteen innocent civilians. At one point an attempt was made to storm the Lhasa mosque, the rioters setting its gate ablaze, while large numbers of businesses owned both by Han Chinese and the Hui minority were torched. Foreign eyewitnesses spoke of stabbings and stonings as shops burned and were looted, and several non-Tibetan hotels were also set ablaze and vandalized. Not only were men involved but women and children, too. There were dozens of police injuries, and large numbers of vehicles—including a fire engine—were destroyed. In all, the number of separate incidents ran into the dozens, possibly hundreds, as the city erupted. Among other measures, the Chinese authorities responded by cutting off the water supply to the Three Seats, whose personnel were implicated in the disturbances, preventing food and medical deliveries to the monasteries. But news of the unrest spread quickly and was followed by riots in Kham and Amdo, a number of them turning violent and resulting in several deaths, both of Chinese and Tibetans, and the destruction of property.

It seems hard to deny that the viciousness of the 2008 uprising harmed the Tibetan cause in the eyes of the world. Yet it is true that claims about video shot in various locations during the protests suggested that some of the rioters were operating under a false flag as *agents provocateurs.* That the weapons and dress of a number of the individuals involved did not correspond to the area in which the incidents took place is taken as evidence they were planted by the Chinese. And it is indeed also true that it would have been extremely helpful to the central government if the rioters could be portrayed as racist thugs. Nevertheless, even if some of these accusations of deception on the part of the Chinese are correct, it seems unlikely that they could account for all the violence. Nor can we say that the memory of those little Tibetan boys and girls, their heads strung like a garland of flowers about the Hui military garrison eighty years earlier, nor even the memory of the casual brutality of the Cultural Revolution forty years before, could possibly justify what occurred, even if it does contextualize it.

For most people worldwide, Tibet was hardly a major issue. Many had heard of the Dalai Lama, but few know much about his homeland. It was therefore a matter of deepest regret to the Tibetan leader that, when news of the Land of Snows did finally make headlines, the picture it presented should be so dismal. Nevertheless, at the time, it did not prevent the Chinese president from announcing to international media just before the Olympics: "Our attitude towards contacts and consultation with the Dalai Lama is serious." This was taken by sympathizers as a sign that the main effect of the riots was to show the Chinese the strength of Tibetan discontent. While it certainly did that, once the Games safely passed without major protest—despite earlier suggestions, no head of state apart from Poland's stayed away in solidarity with the Tibetan people—Tibet abruptly vanished from the world's consciousness. A proposal on autonomy presented by negotiators from Dharamsala that autumn met with nothing more than derision. By the end of the year, the Dalai Lama was admitting that all his efforts of the past thirty years to find a political solution agreeable both to Tibet and to the Chinese had failed.

Since then, the Dalai Lama has made repeated admissions of the failure of his policy of rapprochement with China. From his perspective, his determination to meet Beijing halfway by demanding autonomy but not independence for Tibet has resulted in nothing other than cynical maneuvering on the part of the Chinese government. When the spotlight was on China at the time of the Olympics, its officials let drop one or two hopeful remarks for the benefit of those listening but then failed to act on them. And yet, in admitting the failure of his Middle Way policy, the Dalai Lama did not disavow it. Instead, he immediately responded with a plan to call a referendum to learn the will of the people. Did they or did they not want to continue with the policy in spite of its manifest failure? At first the vote was to have included all Tibetans, but the impracticality of a full plebiscite meant that, in the end, it was confined only to the diaspora. Unsurprisingly, it was found that the vast majority were indeed in favor of accepting the Dalai Lama's views and continuing with the policy.

Of course, such a referendum was only ever going to yield one result, given that the Middle Way was still the Dalai Lama's preferred option. But it is important to recognize here the Dalai Lama's openness to dissent. To the dismay of many, some Tibetans in exile even had the temerity to do so. Both the Tibetan Youth Congress, long a source of rumblings in favor of direct, even violent action, and Amnye Machen (a Dharamsala-based research institute) made clear their rejection of the Dalai Lama's policy, albeit expressing full confidence in his spiritual authority. A small number of elected politicians also broke ranks. To this, traditionalists reacted with outrage at what they saw as open expressions of disloyalty, some even calling for violence to be visited on the offenders.

It is often imagined that genuine democracy, once established, must, by virtue of its own internal logic, succeed as soon as it is implemented. That this view is naïve is shown by several recent attempts to initiate rule by the people, for the people, in countries where, historically, other systems have traditionally prevailed. In the case of the Tibetan diaspora (as no doubt would also be the case if ever democracy came to Tibet itself), loyalty to the Precious Protector is seen—even by many educated young people—as having greater value than the free expression of opinion. Yet for all this, most recognize the wisdom of the Dalai Lama's position. To make violence a component of policy is unthinkable for him. But beyond this, it is obvious that, even if every man, woman, and child were to take up arms, a few million Tibetans could not possibly succeed against the might of all China. The effect of conflict would only be more pain and more suffering for more people. The Dalai Lama's Middle Way policy thus prevails.

And yet, tragically, a new and still more desperate expression of discontent erupted among Tibetans just a few months after the Beijing Olympics as a young monk from Kirti Monastery in Kham poured gasoline over himself and lit a match. When, in 1963, a Vietnamese monk had done the same in protest against the Diem government, President John F. Kennedy said of the Pulitzer Prize–winning photograph of the event that no other news picture in history had aroused such emotion around the world. But though also photographed, the incident in Tibet was barely remarked on by the world's media.

Although at first this looked like an isolated incident, it was followed by a shocking spate of fourteen more self-immolations in 2011 and a staggering eighty-six in 2012. The figure dropped to twenty-eight the year after and eleven the year after that, and, since then, only a handful more have been recorded. But just when it seems the last flames have died down, more leap into Tibetans' collective consciousness as some (usually) young man or some young woman undertakes the ultimate protest and another name is added to the martyrs' memorial in Dharamsala. At the time of writing, more than 150 cases have been recorded.

The statistics are as sorrowful as they are startling. But it is the Dalai Lama's reaction to them that seems to many to be almost as remarkable, if differently so. While one might expect him firmly to oppose such horror, at no point has he come forward categorically to condemn the practice. In fact, self-sacrifice, usually by burning but also by other methods, such as starvation, is an attested component of Buddhist tradition with scriptural warrant—in both the Jataka Tales and the Lotus Sutra, for example. When, therefore, the Dalai Lama is called upon by the Chinese to repudiate self-immolation, it is actually not surprising that he refrains from doing so definitively—even though he discourages it. For him, the question is one of motivation. To the extent that the act is motivated by compassion (a motivation that the Dalai Lama has said would be extremely hard to maintain in the circumstances), it may be considered licit nonetheless. We should also remember that, from the point of view of the families and loved ones of those who have made what they see as the ultimate sacrifice, an edict from the Precious Protector condemning the practice would seem a cruel repudiation.

For an outsider, it is almost impossible to imagine the depths of despair, coupled with love for the Dalai Lama, that, even after all these years, a majority of Tibetans continue to feel in the depths of their hearts. If, though, we look at some of the photographs taken during the first half of the twentieth century—or, better still, some of the silent film shot by Sir Basil Gould on his 1940 expedition to Lhasa for the enthronement of the Dalai Lama—perhaps we can attain an inkling of it. Though somewhat grainy, the best frames give a vivid sense of the tradition that still has such a grip on the Tibetan imagination. There we catch a glimpse of the culture before the ill winds of industrialism blasted the country's fragile landscape. There we see the world ordered aright: the high-ranking members of the Ganden Phodrang government, the length of pendant in their left ear denoting their rank, standing swathed in delicious golden brocade shot with turquoise and green, vermillion and violet, the womenfolk adorned with fabulous headdresses on which are displayed lapis, coral, and jade, while around their necks they sport strings of *gzi,* the strange "heaven pearls" said to have been made by the gods themselves.* There we see the leading lamas of the day, likewise sumptuously clad, as befits their status, and the serried ranks of religious—testimony to the indispensability of the *sangha* in public life—while we can almost hear the whirl of prayer wheels spinning in the hands of the faithful to affirm the primacy of religion in the lives of the laypeople. But we note, too, signs of the feudal character of the old society: the grooms trotting alongside their masters' palfreys, the servants standing mutely expectant at their beck and call.

If it is true that in this film and in old photographs we get an inkling of what has been lost, it would be quite wrong to suppose that it is the outward

*Though these have been identified as a form of agate, there has been no definitive classification of the natural bead that I am aware of. Genuine stones now change hands for thousands of dollars apiece.

expression of this loss that people mourn. The often opium-addicted, often weak, conniving, and morally corrupt aristocrats are not missed. Still less does anyone regret the abolition of the feudal system, the exploitation of the many by the few, and the lifelong obligations to monastic and manorial estates. No, it is neither the pomp nor the circumstance of the old days that is regretted. Rather, it is the right-ordering of the world—a world where the Potala's Lion Throne is occupied by the Precious Protector and in which the rites and remembrances of religion occupy their proper place at the heart of public life—that is so keenly lamented.

Very likely those young men and women who sacrifice themselves have little idea what the return of the Dalai Lama would entail; they merely sense that it would be enough. And they would be right. The fact is, it is unthinkable that he would do so without some guarantee of basic liberties for his people: education in their own language, freedom of association, equality of opportunity, and, above all, the lifting of restrictions on religious practice. Of course, no such rights were recognized in the old Tibet. Outside the monasteries there was little, if any, education available, and none for free. There was no freedom of association or opinion, as Lungshar learned to his terrible cost. As for equality of opportunity, the concept had no meaning—even if it was true that a good number of lamas, such as Reting Rinpoché himself, were of humble background and that one or two who came to the Dalai Lama's attention were promoted to the aristocracy. In general, if you were born to a low estate, that was your karma. If, then, you ran away from a master, you were justly liable to punishment—even though you had no means of paying debts incurred by your forebears many generations ago. Far from bringing about a return to the old ways, the Dalai Lama's reinstallation at the Potala would signify a radical departure from the past. Yet while all this would of course be welcome, it is the mere fact of Chenresig residing among his people for which most Tibetans yearn before all else.

22

The Magical Play of Illusion

In April 2011 the Dalai Lama announced his full retirement from office as leader of the Tibetan government in exile.* Henceforth it would be headed by a democratically elected first minister. In thus handing over political power, the Precious Protector brought to an end three and a half centuries of theocratic rule—albeit that power had for long periods been vested in regents acting in the name of the Dalai Lama. It was a reform not universally applauded by Tibetans, but it had clearly been among the Precious Protector's plans from the moment he decided in favor of democracy on first coming into exile.

The Dalai Lama effected extraordinary change with this move. When Altan Khan, the Mongol strongman of sixteenth-century Central Asia, proclaimed Sonam Gyatso, abbot of Drepung, to be Taleh (the Mongolian term

* By chance, I happened to be in audience with the Dalai Lama when the document enacting his resignation was brought for signature. He left the room for a few minutes and returned with the air of a man in whom relief mingled with awe at what he had wrought.

for ocean, from which the word "Dalai" is derived) Lama, the Tibetan was head of a monastery comprising several thousand monks. But although this conferred immense prestige and great wealth, the direct political power attaching to him personally was limited to the sway he held over the Gelug establishment in general and over Drepung and its sister monasteries and their estates in particular. It was not until the Great Fifth secured the patronage of another of the Khans that the institution of the Dalai Lama attained such prestige that, in combination with his viceroy and backed by the military might of the Mongols, he could exercise political power across the Tibetan Buddhist world as a whole. In so doing, the Great Fifth forged the Tibetan people into a broadly harmonious society in a way that had not been seen since the fall of the religious kings in the ninth century. Moreover, his imaginative recapitulation of the Tibetan empire brought the spiritual realm of gods, demons, and protectors together with the earthly realm of human beings, their landed property, and their possessions, and made both answerable to a single authority.

What the present Dalai Lama brought about with his retirement was thus not just his withdrawal from politics but the end of the dispensation whereby, in effect, the Dalai Lama united within himself the functions of both priest and patron. This, it will be remembered, was the paradigmatic relationship whereby the priest, or lama, guaranteed the legitimacy of the king, while the king in turn supported the lama temporally. Under the new dispensation, the Dalai Lama continues to rule the supernatural realm while earthly matters are placed under the authority of a secular establishment. What is especially innovative about this maneuver is the elevation of the people themselves to the role of patron.

The withdrawal of the Dalai Lama's authority from the temporal realm was almost as important for its psychological as for its political value. No longer should Tibetans look to the Dalai Lama for answers to every question of a practical nature that, in theory at least, they had hitherto been free to put to him. Instead, they would stand on their own feet. The Dalai Lama and his successors could thus concern themselves with what they are actually trained for, namely, spiritual direction, even if, to the end of this life, he would remain a symbolic figurehead for his people.

Given that the Precious Protector's every word is held by most of his people to have divine authority, it presumably takes considerable restraint on his part not to speak out on earthly matters from time to time. But save for his handling of the Shugden controversy, insofar as it is a political matter, the Dalai Lama has so far shown little inclination to intervene in affairs of state. Instead, the former leader has dedicated himself to fulfilling what he describes as his three "main commitments." These are, first, as a human being, by helping others to be happy; second, as a Buddhist monk, by working to bring about harmony among the world's various religious traditions; and third, as a Tibetan, by helping to preserve his country's unique language and culture. In this last, he emphasizes the enormous debt the Tibetan tradition owes to what it inherited from the Indian scholar-saints of Nalanda, the Buddhist monastic university that flourished from the fifth to the twelfth century and provided the blueprint for the monastic universities of Tibet.

A major component of these commitments is the Dalai Lama's dedication to the environmentalist cause. The destruction of wildlife in Tibet since 1950 is a continuing sorrow to him, though his attitude toward the environment generally is neither sentimental nor a function of his religiosity. There is nothing "sacred or holy" about nature, he writes in his autobiography; rather, "taking care of our planet is like taking care of our houses." Similarly, while he is a ready advocate of compassion in farming and has said on occasion that he would like to be the "world spokesman for fish," he does not go so far as to deny categorically the possibility that animal experimentation might, in certain circumstances, be justifiable—provided that the motive in doing so is altruistic. It is characteristic of the Buddhist approach to avoid absolutes. Also to the dismay of some, the Dalai Lama, though he has often spoken in favor of vegetarianism, is, as we have seen, not a vegetarian himself. Moreover, he recognizes the difficulty of living in an environmentally responsible way and does not make a fetish of doing so. While eschewing baths, he admits that, in taking a shower morning and evening, there might be little difference in his water consumption.

With respect to his commitment to helping others find happiness, the Dalai Lama includes scientific research as an important component in the human search for felicity. To this end, he continues to meet and to engage in dialogue with scientists from around the world. Whether a consequence of this is that he has himself "become one of the world's greatest scientists," as

Robert Thurman has suggested, may be open to question. It is certainly not a claim he would make for himself. But his patronage of a compendium of Buddhist scientific texts demonstrates his wish to see Buddhist inquiry, especially into the nature of consciousness, given serious consideration by outsiders. Noting the congruence between the Buddhist and the scientific worldviews, the Dalai Lama wonders why "the impulse for helping and kindness are not recognized as drivers for human behaviour and . . . flourishing?" If scientists were to ask these questions honestly, he believes that they would find the answers provided by Buddhist thinkers compelling.

In the field of interreligious dialogue, the Dalai Lama has, since retiring from office, continued to meet and to pray with religious leaders and prominent spiritual figures from around the world. Setting aside his vow to refrain from intoxicating beverages, he once partook of Holy Communion administered by Archbishop Desmond Tutu. On another occasion, he donned an apron to serve food in a church-run homeless shelter in Australia. Despite hostility from some quarters, the Dalai Lama has visited Israel more than once; in 2006, he met with both the Sephardi and Ashkenazi chief rabbis. He has also visited several Islamic countries, notably Jordan, again more than once, meeting with Prince Ghazi bin Mohammed, a leading figure in Islamic interfaith dialogue, later that same year.

Besides advocating pluralism with respect to other religions, it is evident that the Dalai Lama also wishes to strengthen his followers in their faith. As a rule, he counsels people to remain within their own faith tradition, remarking that if a person is a poor practitioner of one, changing to another will do nothing to improve matters. Referring to his visit to the monastery of Le Grand Chartreuse, where he noticed the monks' feet cracked with cold from wearing only sandals, he praises the dedication of followers of non-Buddhist religions. At the same time, he speaks of his concern about Tibetan teachers abroad who live luxuriously or flout their vows. Yet his concern about behavior inappropriate to prelates is not confined to Buddhists. When Pope Francis removed a German ecclesiastic for the ostentatious restoration of his residence, the Dalai Lama wrote to congratulate the Roman pontiff.* Whether or not it is true

*This was Franz-Peter Tebartz-van Elst, the so-called "Bishop of Bling."

that, of all the other religions, the Dalai Lama feels closest to Catholicism is an open question. On the one hand, for him it is given a priori that there is no Creator. On the other hand, the superficial similarities between many of the liturgical practices of Rome and Lhasa cause him to wonder if there was not earlier contact between the two traditions. Both religions practice ritual eating and drinking, and both venerate the relics of saints. It is also true that the Dalai Lama has been hosted many times by ecumenically minded Catholic organizations, and if he is not mistaken, the Dalai Lama enjoys divine approval for fostering links with the Catholic Church. On a visit to Fatima in 2001, he experienced a vision of the Virgin Mary, whose statue turned and smiled at him. In this context, it is not entirely clear how we are to interpret his remark that one of the biggest surprises of his life came when Pope Benedict XVI proclaimed the indispensability of reason to religious faith. In the Dalai Lama's view, if people would only think hard enough, they would come to see the truth of *how things really are*—and thus the falsity of the pope's position and the correctness of his own.

The Dalai Lama's dedication to these three main commitments has meant that his retirement from politics has not resulted in any more leisure than before. He continues to receive dozens of invitations to talk or teach even though, when his office accepts any of these on his behalf nowadays, it is on the proviso that the Dalai Lama's public appearances are limited to two hours a day. Meanwhile, he continues to take spiritual teachings and instruction from other lamas as often as his schedule permits, while he maintains rigorously his own practice and study. When traveling abroad, he makes no concession to jet lag and always rises at the same time of day. His one real recreation is to attend monastic debates and follow the progress of the rising generation of scholars, particularly on his visits to the great monastic universities refounded in the south of India. A particular source of joy to him on such occasions is that he is able to do so not, as is generally supposed by non-monastics, as a "great authority" but rather as a supremely well-informed student eager to learn from those who, unlike him, have been able to devote their whole lives to study.

He continues to take the opportunity while traveling to visit places of interest or special significance. He prayed at the site of Martin Luther King's assassination on one trip to America. On another, he announced his wish to visit an active volcano. As a bonus, on that particular occasion he was delighted to spot a plant species that he had cultivated at home in Dharamsala. "Suddenly," recalls Thurman, "with a whoop of glee, he leaped off the roadway and across a ditch . . . and clambered up the opposite embankment . . . He then asked to be photographed holding out a leaf . . . He stood there in his goofy hat, grinning from ear to ear . . . 'Next life,' he announced, 'I will be a naturalist!'"

Since retiring, the Dalai Lama has continued to confer the Kalachakra initiation—both at home in India and abroad. In 2014 he did so for the third time in Ladakh, where a new palace was built for him toward the end of the last century, onto a crowd estimated at a quarter of a million. At the time of writing, he has conducted the Kalachakra ceremonies thirty-four times since his initiation into the practice.

With regard to those invitations to speak in public that the Dalai Lama accepts, it is of course true that they are the ones that his closest advisers deem suitable to recommend to him. Any that are proposed directly may be lobbied against by the same individuals. It is also natural that, sometimes, personal connections and preferences on their part come into play. And it is true that, over the years, there have been a number of missteps. One of the most embarrassing was the series of audiences granted in the late 1980s to Shoko Asahara, the Japanese cult leader and future mass murderer. Since Asahara's emergence as the mastermind of the gas attack on a Tokyo subway station, the Dalai Lama has often pointed out that, if he was, as a manifestation of a bodhisattva, perfectly omniscient, he would not have been hoodwinked by the cult leader.

A more recent embarrassment was the Dalai Lama's public talk in Albany, New York, partially sponsored by the controversial group known as NXIVM (pronounced Nexium). It was alleged that the organization, besides conducting dubious financial activities, was also a sex cult, an allegation that has since been proven correct. It has also been claimed that, as a condition of the Dalai Lama's participation in the event, a large sum of money changed hands. The Dalai Lama's office was quick to point out that the Dalai Lama never charges a fee for appearing, a fact attested to by many who have organized events at which he has been featured.* It should also be said that the Dalai Lama mentioned in his talk that he was aware that there was controversy about NXIVM, which, he suggested, should be investigated properly. Nonetheless, it is apparent that there was a link between the Dalai Lama and the Tibetan monk working in a semiofficial capacity, subsequently removed from office, who had facilitated his appearance. This individual was subsequently reinstated and exonerated, although his position was then almost immediately abolished by the Dalai Lama, suggesting some uncomfortable behind-the-scenes maneuvering. It has struck some that the Precious Protector may not always be well served by those closest to him.

There have also been several occasions when a portion of the Dalai Lama's supporters have been disappointed by the choice of events that his advisers have arranged for or encouraged him to attend. His appearance on the Australian *Master Chef* TV show was a case in point. Another was his appearance at Glastonbury Festival in Britain. In the latter case, however, the Dalai Lama did say that he had enjoyed himself—despite being kissed on stage by singer Patti Smith, to the outrage of many Tibetans. Unless, however, we are prepared to say (as indeed the Chinese do say) that the approbation of dozens of world leaders who have welcomed him, numerous chancellors of universities who have conferred honorary degrees on him, and each of the (certainly hundreds and probably thousands of) mayors and community leaders who have made civic awards to the Dalai Lama—to say nothing of the millions of ordinary people who have been encouraged by and have drawn inspiration from the Dalai Lama—has been, in every single case, misinformed and misguided, it would be hard to argue that these occasional lapses tell us more about the man than his many successes. And even those who do hold a negative view must acknowledge the Dalai Lama's fidelity to his role. After all, what was to stop him as a young man from forsaking his robes and gravitating to the fleshpots of the free world?

It is true nonetheless that the Dalai Lama has attracted the ire of some

---

*I am one of them. The rule explained at the outset was that organizers could charge to cover the costs of hosting the Dalai Lama and his entourage. Any surplus should be donated to one or more local charities.

commentators in the Western media. One such was Christopher Hitchens, who criticized him for, among other reasons, seeming to support India's testing of thermonuclear weapons. Furthermore, he has drawn dismay in some quarters for suggesting that Europe is for Europeans and that, while migrants should be welcomed, they should plan to return home to build their countries as soon as they are in a position to do so. Some have accused him of exploiting his audiences, of being a "ham," as one put it, and the "crowd-pleaser to end all crowd-pleasers." Against this, others have noted that he often makes a point of addressing and embracing the mentally disturbed, including those who seem likely to be violent, who attend events at which he appears. Besides, the Dalai Lama has been known to make artless remarks that have, on occasion, deeply offended people. On a visit to Norway, he once pointed to a teenaged girl and told her, giggling, that she was "too fat." These are hardly the actions of a "ham." The Dalai Lama has also been criticized for some of his friendships. His affection for George W. Bush (who painted the Dalai Lama's portrait) causes difficulty for some. His personal regard for Nancy Pelosi perhaps causes difficulty for others. Yet his unaffected charm and evident humanity have won him countless admirers.

As to the future, while it is clear that, functionally, the Dalai Lama's retirement from his leadership role is genuine, it remains to be seen whether his reforms will survive him. It is not impossible to imagine an ambitious future incumbent of the office—or, perhaps more likely, a weak successor manipulated by ambitious staff—re-appropriating political power. This is a particular danger should the Precious Protector "manifest the act of passing away" sooner rather than later. It would be surprising to learn that he has not had exactly the same thought, however. From what he has said about his succession, besides repeating that there will be a Fifteenth Dalai Lama only if that is the wish of the Tibetan people as a whole (which, undoubtedly, it will be), he has made clear that, as one of a number of options, he is already considering the possibility of appointing a successor while still living, by identifying a *ma de tulku.* This is an incarnation appointed when the previous incumbent remains alive.

Usually the procedure for anointing such an incarnation entails an elderly lama declaring that the *bodhi* which resides with himself has been identified as residing with someone younger, usually a disciple or spiritual friend, though sometimes an assistant or even (somewhat less plausibly) a relative. The one so named then occupies the lama's position within both the spiritual and the temporal realms, taking on all property, tithes, and title of the one making the appointment while the incumbent himself retires, often moving to a hermitage and going on permanent retreat. One huge advantage of success in identifying and confirming the new Dalai Lama in this way is that it would greatly complicate any attempt on the part of the Chinese authorities to interfere in the succession. Should this not come to pass, however, and should the Dalai Lama not appoint his successor personally, it is certain that the traditional methods of identification will be used, and in anticipation of his death outside Tibet, the Dalai Lama has made clear that his incarnation should also be sought outside Tibet. It is even rumored that Palden Lhamo, the Glorious Goddess, has been invited to move her residence from the visionary lake in Tibet to another lake, somewhere in Ladakh.*

But if the Precious Protector has, potentially, settled the question of what form the Dalai Lama institution will take in the future, and if he finds a way to finesse the succession problem (though understanding full well that the Chinese are sure to anoint their own "official" candidate), there remains at least one important obstacle to securing his ultimate vision. While he wishes the Dalai Lama to be an inclusive figure, able to speak for all Tibetans irrespective of their regional origin (whether they hail from Ü-Tsang, Kham, or Amdo), and irrespective of which denomination they belong to, the Shugden challenge remains. What this amounts to, practically speaking, is the age-old question faced by all ancient institutions under pressure from events in the world: whether to turn toward it and risk annihilation, or whether to turn away and retreat to first principles, or some version thereof, in the hope of weathering the storm until a full-scale revival can be brought about. As we have seen, the

*When I put this to the Dalai Lama in April 2019, he did not answer directly but conceded that, on a recent visit to Ladakh, many had observed an unusual cloud formation roll over the mountains from Tibet during a teaching he was giving. As soon as the ceremonies were concluded, the cloud went back the way it came, leaving a rainbow in its wake. "So, something mysterious," he said.

outcome of the contest between these two impulses, the one represented by Shugden, the other by Nechung, has yet to be finally settled, and the problem remains a thorn in the Precious Protector's flesh.

Let us suppose, however, that the present Dalai Lama lives, as he has suggested he might, to be well over a hundred, and that he succeeds both in implementing his vision of the Dalai Lama institution as a unifying force for all and in settling the question of his succession. What are the prospects for his people?

It is difficult to be optimistic. The Chinese Communist Party's policy of economic expansion as a means of preserving its position has been an outstanding success. It has shown that liberal democracy is by no means an inevitable entailment of capitalism. On the contrary, the panoptico-Leviathan state the party has created looks very much able to face down any merely ideological challenge to its existence. What it cannot assimilate, it will surely destroy. Thus China's ascent as a world superpower looks set to continue into the foreseeable future, while, just as the party's planners forecast long ago, fewer and fewer countries will dare risk their trading relations with China for the sake of a few million Tibetans.

Indeed, this is already happening. The Dalai Lama has been refused visas to South Africa and Botswana. As early as 2008 the British Foreign Office ceased (after more than a century) to recognize China's suzerainty over Tibet and instead acknowledged Tibet as an "integral part of China." For the foreseeable future, and assuming no radical change in attitude on the part of Beijing, it looks certain, therefore, that Tibetans will continue to face political and cultural subjugation in their own homeland. It is an open question how long this can be sustained before the notion that the Tibetan people might one day be emancipated ceases to have real meaning. It might well have passed already. If this is true, the further question is whether the culture can survive. This is really the question of whether Tibetan Buddhism is able to do so. Here, too, the signs are not all encouraging. The religious impulse among Tibetans in Tibet seems undeniably to be declining as young people concern themselves more with this life than the next. Although the combined population of the Three Seats in exile today is said to equal their historic numbers, with upwards of twenty thousand monks in residence, numbers are down from their peak a decade or so ago, partly a result of the fact that China now prevents easy migration from Tibet, but partly because it is less and less usual for families to send children to the monasteries as a matter of course. A further worry is whether the tradition can again produce individual practitioners of the stature of, for example, the Dalai Lama's tutors.

As for the prospects of a full restoration of religion in Tibet under Chinese rule, unquestionably the biggest impediment to this is the tradition's association with the idea of Tibetan independence. For the Precious Protector, however, the survival of the Buddhadharma in Tibet is more important than nationhood. He clearly hopes that with the Dalai Lama institution decoupled from government, it will cease to be a focal point for nationalism. Whether or not this translates into a less political *sangha* within Tibet remains to be seen. But there are reasons to be cautiously optimistic for the survival of the tradition on other grounds. The growth of interest in religion generally, and in Buddhism in particular, is one of the most important, if also one of the least documented, features of modern China. We are compelled to rely on anecdotal evidence, but it seems clear that a major revival is under way. To take one example, the mixed-sex monastic settlement at Larung Gar in a remote part of Kham was home, until recently, to around forty thousand monks and nuns living consecrated lives. In 2016 the authorities ordered that this be reduced to just two thousand nuns and fifteen hundred monks (the disparity in numbers being perhaps a reflection of the perception that women religious are less likely to cause trouble than their male counterparts), and demolition of many dwellings began soon after. At the time of writing, the exact status of Larung Gar is unclear. But what is known is that, both at its height and now, approximately half the numbers were, as they remain, made up by ethnic Chinese.

Religious revivals are one thing of which, historically, the Chinese authorities have been extremely wary. The White Lotus Rebellion, followed by the Taiping Rebellion—both of them inspired by charismatic religious leaders—were important factors in the demise of the Qing dynasty. Given this, the likelihood is that there will continue to be friction between state and *sangha* in both Tibetan- and Han-dominated territories. Already recognition of new incarnations is technically forbidden, and at the time of writing, there are severe restrictions on the activities of the monasteries generally.

As for the thought that the present, or a future, Chinese leader might experience a Constantinian-style spiritual conversion (Constantine being the fourth-century Roman Emperor who became a Christian): while intriguing, the reality is that such a turn of events would be unlikely to have much impact. Even Chairman Mao was unable invariably to dictate terms to the Politburo. And while it is not impossible that the party could tolerate a Buddhist premier, what it could not tolerate is any move that threatened its grip on Tibet. It is, therefore, hard to imagine a Chinese president inviting the Dalai Lama even for a short visit to his homeland. That said, there does appear to have been a moment (though later denied) in 2014 when the Dalai Lama and the general secretary of the Chinese Communist Party (and thus paramount leader of China), Xi Xinping, might have met. It is believed by many Tibetans that Xi's wife is a practicing Buddhist and that he himself is personally sympathetic toward both Buddhism and the Dalai Lama, perhaps on account of the fact that his father was stationed in Tibet during the 1950s. While the Chinese leader was on a visit to Delhi, the Dalai Lama's office contacted the Chinese embassy to see whether a personal meeting between the two men might arranged. It transpired that Xi was willing. But, allegedly after an intervention by the Indian government, the meeting did not in fact take place. Yet even had it done so, it is difficult to imagine any radical change of policy on China's part.

If it is true that China is unlikely to make political concessions with respect to Tibet, the question that must be faced is whether there is any realistic hope for the survival of a distinct Tibetan identity. Of course, dynasties come and go, but so too do whole peoples. The Celts dominated western and central Europe for perhaps a thousand years before the coming of the Romans. The Phoenicians were earlier and lasted longer. The Aztecs are a more recent people that once flourished and have since disappeared. It is not wrong to fear, as the Dalai Lama fears, for the long-term future of the Tibetan people under such a regime as the Chinese have brought into being. There is nevertheless one entity that has shown itself consistently able to endure harassment, persecution, and even genocidal hatred: the human spirit itself. Here we might think of that of the Jewish people, who for so much of their history have been persecuted. If the experience of the Jews, whose endurance has been underpinned by religious faith, is anything to go by, the prospects for survival of the Tibetan people look more secure, especially given leadership by an individual who eschews the ordinary inducements of the world—the fame (which the present Dalai Lama has shown himself entirely willing to give up over the Shugden controversy) and the fortune (there is little doubt the Dalai Lama would be content with nothing more than a room in which to meditate) which are the perennial temptations of those in power. Indeed, the Dalai Lama's own spirit—his life-force, his character, his resolve in the face of overwhelming odds—shows that where unshakeable faith meets with wholehearted renunciation of self, human beings are capable of surmounting even the most abject circumstances. (This, surely, is the secret of the Dalai Lama's personal magnetism: the aura that he exudes, at all times and in every circumstance, of an absolute conviction, rooted deep within a tradition that is itself both rich and profound, a conviction that is yet worn lightly and grounded in a generous—and palpable—good-naturedness.)

The greatest threat to the Tibetan people is thus the same as the threat to the Dalai Lama institution itself: that the onslaught of the contemporary world proves too much for the individual who takes up the present incarnation's mantle. So intimately connected is the Dalai Lama institution with Tibetan identity that it is impossible to think of this identity surviving long should the Dalai Lama himself (or, less plausibly but, according to the present incarnation, possible, herself) be less than fully rooted in the tradition and less than wholly committed to the role. Already there are signs of weakening within the Karmapa institution. One of the claimants to the title of Karmapa, in defiance of tradition, has married. The other has spoken of his battle with depression. And while the Dalai Lama institution has shown itself capable of enduring wayward behavior, as in the case of the lovelorn Sixth Dalai Lama, and even lack of direction over long periods, such as the century and more that elapsed between the demise of the Seventh and the coming of age of the Great Thirteenth Dalai Lama, it is doubtful it could survive a thoroughgoing apostasy—either of an individual Dalai Lama or of the people themselves.

And yet, all this being said, even if there are just a few families surviving on the Himalayan plateau in the days and years following the collapse of the present Chinese empire—which, if history is any guide, must surely come—it is almost impossible to imagine them forgetting the One Who Looked

Down with Compassion on their forefathers. Remembering this, will they not look for signs and wonders in nature and go searching for his face among the newborn children in their black horsehair tents, those miraculous emblems of human endurance against the wind and the cold and the depredations of ghost and demon, in the harsh uplands of the Land of Snows? This could happen after a lengthy hiatus and seems all the more likely when we consider the myth that is sure to be woven out of the achievements of the present incarnation.

Consider the extraordinary reversal of ill fortune that the Fourteenth has brought about. When he was followed into exile by eighty thousand destitute refugees, one might have hoped, at best, for their rapid absorption into Indian society while the Dalai Lama himself went on to establish one or more small Buddhist centers either in India or elsewhere. For him to have presided over the establishment of a widely successful, broadly cohesive diaspora that numbers now perhaps a quarter of a million individuals scattered across the world, and besides this to have won for Buddhism in the Tibetan tradition a following numbering in the millions worldwide, is quite astonishing and certainly without parallel in the modern world.*

Whereas fifty years ago the number of Tibetan Buddhist centers outside Tibet —the first of them set up by the amiable beer-drinking CIA translator Geshe Wangyal—could be counted on the fingers of one hand, today there are certainly thousands. The present Dalai Lama has also established close links with Buddhist communities outside his own tradition such that his counsel and benediction are frequently sought by monks and nuns from Korea, Vietnam, Taiwan, Mongolia, Thailand, Japan, and even mainland China itself. Absent the leadership of the farmer's son from Taktser, it is almost impossible to imagine such a state of affairs.

It is arguably true that the upsurge of interest in Buddhism generally is only partly due to the Dalai Lama, and that it might have occurred anyway, but it seems overwhelmingly unlikely that it would have done so to the extent it has without the tireless work of the Precious Protector. It seems indeed, just

---

*To this achievement might also be added the extraordinary success of Tibetan studies as an academic discipline. From this has come a vast literature of translations and other secondary literature.

as he foresaw, the Buddha's prophecy that, two and a half millennia after his parinirvana, the teachings would flourish in the land of the red-faced people has been fulfilled, in large part through his own efforts. Beyond this, though, we can consider the contribution by the Dalai Lama to humanity's growing familiarity with the concept of compassion. It is remarkable that, on the best measure available, the frequency of usage of the word "compassion" during the past half century has increased more than 200 percent in English, while in some European languages (German, for example) the increase has been substantially greater. In a way that was certainly not true half a century ago, compassion is now seen as a cornerstone of health care, as a goal of education, as a precondition of peace, and as of significance to the world of business. It is increasingly accepted that even prisoners merit being shown compassion. It is hard to imagine the preeminent position the virtue of compassion has come to occupy within public discourse without the Dalai Lama's advocacy. This, too, is a towering achievement that will surely animate his memory within the tradition.

What, though, of his legacy to the world itself? Arguably his most significant contribution has yet to be widely appreciated. For many, if not most, the word "compassion" is synonymous with empathy. If, however, the Dalai Lama's relationship with Chenresig, Bodhisattva of Compassion, is to be taken seriously, it surely follows that the Precious Protector's whole life is, in an important sense, an object lesson in the meaning of compassion. And it turns out that, on this view, there is more to being compassionate than is ordinarily supposed.

Considering his life's work, we see that, for the Dalai Lama, compassion consists first and foremost in generosity—not just generosity in the sense of gift giving, though even in this sense he is generous to a fault. His immediate gift of the prize money that accompanied both the Nobel and the Templeton awards is testimony to this. It should also be mentioned that he has made numerous—often substantial—donations to charities around the world for such causes as disaster relief. All royalties from his many books (over two hundred separate titles in all, several of them million-sellers) are paid directly into one of several charitable foundations that he has caused to be set up. Beyond this, he is also personally generous. He recycles gifts as a matter of course, but has been known to make cash gifts and interest-free loans to family and friends—and not exclusively to Tibetans. When the New Zealand–born Theosophist known throughout Dharamsala affectionately (if also somewhat fearfully) as Auntie Joyce needed full-time care at the end of her life, having for decades volunteered her secretarial service to the government in exile, it was the Dalai Lama who, hearing that she was in want, settled her bills. He is also notoriously generous with his time, often inconveniencing himself by extending both public talks and private audiences in order to answer questions. Yet from a Buddhist perspective, his generosity is made manifest most forcefully and most valuably through his service to the Buddhadharma: the countless talks he has given, the thousands of teachings and initiations he has granted, the tens of thousands of rituals in which he has participated and ordinations he has conferred.

While generosity in this sense of serving others through furthering appreciation and understanding of the Buddhadharma represents the full flowering of the Dalai Lama's compassion, it is also important to recognize that there are other—indispensable—aspects to his exemplification of the virtue of compassion. If it is right to say that the Precious Protector's whole life can be seen as living out what it means to be compassionate, we see that it also embraces the virtue of prudence in practical matters. Looking back on his life, we see that it meant, for example, not becoming involved either in the CIA's operations in Tibet or in the Chushi Gangdruk resistance during the 1950s and 1960s. At the same time, his living out of compassion did not cause him categorically to prohibit their endeavors. Similarly, it has not precluded a certain pragmatism, as, for example, when he acquiesced in India's request to send Establishment 22 to war in Bangladesh—however much it pained him to do so.

It is also clear from the Dalai Lama's biography that compassion entails a willingness both to compromise and, where appropriate, to exercise resolve. Giving up the quest for independence for Tibet is an obvious example of a judicious compromise, while his fidelity to Buddhist doctrine is testament to his resolve. The Four Noble Truths are not open to negotiation. Nor are the basic Buddhist insights into the ultimate nature of reality: the doctrines of karma, of dependent origination, of emptiness, and, as a corollary of these, of no-self. But if defending what is a priori may not demand much in the way of effort, there are times when being compassionate entails holding the line in the face of determined opposition. Thus compassion is clearly related to courage. With respect to the Shugden controversy, it would have been easy to make concessions. Instead, the Precious Protector has risked his entire reputation in defending what he judges to be the correct position in regard to the deity—not for his own good, but for the good of all. Less obviously, but just as important, the Dalai Lama also shows, in his dealings with the protectors, that being compassionate means upholding the truth of the supernatural realm. It is not the case, in his view, that Buddhism can be stripped of the supernatural or that the protectors can be dispensed with. The Buddhadharma cannot simply be reduced to ethics and mindfulness meditation, notwithstanding the paramount importance of both right conduct and inner calm. Helping others to see this is, again, part of what it means to be compassionate—even if it is true that the Dalai Lama does not emphasize protector practice among neophyte Buddhists.

When we take seriously the claim that the Precious Protector is the earthly manifestation of Chenresig, we see also that compassion is, in many respects, a conservative virtue. Not that the Dalai Lama himself can be pigeonholed as a conservative. His advocacy of democracy in the political sphere and his ecumenism in the religious sphere make this plain. So too does his consideration of women. The Dalai Lama has been a staunch supporter of the recent introduction of the *geshema* degree for nuns, even though he has made clear that the tradition is such that women cannot actually be ordained. It is also true that some lighthearted comments about the need for a possibly female future Dalai Lama (not ruled out entirely, although a necessary condition of full Enlightenment is that the individual is male) to be attractive caused disappointment in some areas. Similarly, the Dalai Lama's encouragement of science as part of the monastic curriculum shows his commitment to the betterment of the world through technology. He has often said that if he had had to choose a career other than monasticism, he would have wanted to be an engineer.

Another vital feature of the Precious Protector's exposition of compassion is his insistence that it is not pompous. As anyone who has had the privilege of meeting him knows, the ever present smiles and the irrepressible laughter are wholly unforced. One is reminded of Chesterton's remark about there being "some one thing that was too great for God to show us when he walked upon our earth and I have sometimes fancied that it was his mirth." In contrast, the Dalai Lama, having plumbed the depths of consciousness through his daily meditation practice, shows no such restraint.

But if there is one thing above all that the Dalai Lama shows, it is that compassion is the fruit of *bodhichitta,* the determination to work unstintingly for the Enlightenment of all sentient beings—all humans, gods, demigods, animals, hungry ghosts, and denizens of the hell realms. It is this aspiration that finally determines the Dalai Lama's conduct: his every thought, word, and deed. All his teaching, all his writings, all his public talks, all his media appearances and interviews with journalists, all his charitable works, all the rituals in which he participates, all the divinations he undertakes, all his private prayer and meditation, even all his political endeavors are expressions of this single aim. By teaching and by example, his ultimate goal is to help others understand the way things really are and thus to set them on the path to liberation. It turns out that, in this, his wish to help people overcome ignorance and to cease grasping at the existence of a substantial self, the Dalai Lama is a much more radical figure than is generally supposed. And yet to miss this is to miss the whole point of his ministry. Unlike the Christ who taught selflessness, the Buddha taught self-lessness. The Dalai Lama wants us to understand that, ultimately, there is no self and no other, indeed no Dalai Lama, no Precious Protector, no Tibet—that in the end there is only the magical play of illusion.

AFTERWORD AND ACKNOWLEDGMENTS

One of the biggest challenges in writing this book was having to confront the yawning gap between the Tibet of historical record and what might be called the Facebook image of Tibet. What strikes us most forcibly about the Tibet of historical record is, echoing the words of Johan Huizinga, the great Dutch historian, writing of the European Middle Ages, the "violent tenor of life" that characterizes it. As we have seen, justice was often summary and, by modern standards, cruel. Offense was easily given and easily taken, meeting all too often with revenge, while grudges might be borne for centuries, given new life every so often by a ferment of religious belief. Yet the fact is there have always been two Tibets. On the one hand, there is Tibet as it is perceived by the tradition, a tradition expressed in the culture and customs of the people but also grounded in the landscape, the flora and fauna of the roof of the world. On the other, there is Tibet as it is perceived from outside the tradition.

The Tibet that tradition sees is one where, whatever the failings of individual men and women—and none would wish to say that the blinding of Lungshar or the murder of Reting Rinpoché was anything but iniquitous—theirs was a society that nonetheless prized and often practiced compassion. From the perspective of the tradition, the existence of the monasteries and the dedication of the people to their religion is all the proof that is needed, since to practice the Buddhadharma *is* to be compassionate. With respect to Tibet as it is seen from outside, there is a greater variety of opinion. To some, Tibet before the Chinese takeover of the middle years of the twentieth century was the "wisdom heart of the world," its emptiness was "sacred space," its people were "guardians of a storehouse of spiritual treasures" whose religion was an "inner science" while they, as its practitioners, were "exponents of sacred technology." To others, it was simply and without remainder a "hell on earth" where the masses "groaned under the tyranny of serfdom."

If, at first sight, the tradition's view of itself is unjustifiably optimistic, neither of these outside perspectives stands up to scrutiny either. Although doubtless many suffered at the whims of their masters, there is scant evidence that the majority considered their way of life hellish. What came afterwards was more nearly hell. Furthermore, it is clear that the Dalai Lama, the very personification of the Tibetan tradition, was himself intent on the abolition of feudalism from early on. Equally, the historical record shows that the two-dimensional characterization of Tibet as a land of monks meditating in the mystic fastness of the Himalayan Mountains while the laity lived in serene harmony with one another and with nature is completely untenable. Neither extreme serves the cause of the Tibetan people, who, if they are to be served at all, would profit most from a sober analysis of their grievances and sufferings.

Moreover, if we content ourselves with saying that the truth lies somewhere in between, there is a danger of overlooking the way in which both the Tibetan tradition and the Dalai Lama himself radically challenge contemporary society. In a way, we could call this the challenge of the natural world to the scientific world. From the perspective of the tradition, the existence—and willingness to use—not just weapons of mass destruction but weapons that kill indiscriminately seems a disastrous state of affairs. A society that would permit, let alone condone, such a thing must be barbarous in the extreme. Similarly, the fact of what, from the perspective of the tradition, is nothing less than infanticide being practiced on an industrial scale (the millions of abortions carried out annually) seems atrocious beyond imagining, while, at the other end of life, the treatment of the elderly and infirm, abandoned in nursing homes outside the family, seems heartless and ungrateful. And the mechanized slaughter of untold numbers of animals on a daily basis looks obscene. From a contemporary standpoint, these seem normal and rational solutions to the challenges of modern living. Yet against these features of the modern world, the occasional and always to be regretted failings of individuals in the history of Tibet look, from the perspective of the tradition, altogether easier to forgive.

. . .

I have to thank a large number of people for their help over the years that this project has been under way. First and foremost, I would like to thank His Holiness the Dalai Lama himself for kindly inviting me to stay at the SOS Tibetan Youth Hostel during December 2014 so that he might be available to answer the great many questions I had for him at the outset of this work. Subsequently, the Dalai Lama generously met with me on several occasions, culminating in a lengthy interview granted on what was supposed to be a day of complete rest in April 2019. This should not be taken to imply that I had the opportunity to clear up every doubt or query, or that this is in any sense an authorized biography. Nevertheless, I can claim to have had well in excess of my fair share of access to the Dalai Lama during the writing and research of this book.

Ippolite Desideri, the eighteenth-century missionary to Tibet, notes that, as a generality, the Tibetans he met with were "kindly, clever, and courteous by nature." This is certainly true of all those of the Dalai Lama's compatriots who so generously gave of their time to help me with this project. In particular, I should like to mention and thank Mr. Tendzin Choegyal (Ngari Rinpoché), Yangten Rinpoché, Mrs. Rinchen Khando, Mr. Tenzin Geyche Tethong, Dr. Thupten Jinpa (who read and commented on parts of the manuscript: I was especially gratified that he "really enjoyed" the last chapter), Mrs. Namgyal Taklha, the late Mr. Rinchen Sadutsang, Mrs. Sadutsang, the late Mr. Tsering Gongkatsang, the late Mr. Tsewang Norbu, Professor Samten Karmay, Mr. Paljor Tsarong, Mr. Tenzin Namgyal Tethong, Mr. Jamyang Choegyal Kasho, and, especially, Mr. Tenzin Choepel—each of whom gave invaluable support and generously helped whenever asked.

I also thank Mr. Jeremy Russell for answering questions and pointing the way whenever I asked; Mr. Aniket Mandavagane for his insights from his position as Indian government liaison officer to the Dalai Lama; Dr. Jianglin Li for sharing unpublished material and entering into a lengthy correspondence about the Chinese occupation of Tibet during the 1950s; Mr. Ralf Kramer for many discussions, for sharing his encyclopedic knowledge of sources and where to find them, for his help with obtaining many of the images in this book, and for his work on the bibliography and notes; Dr. George FitzHerbert, in particular for sharing his paper on Tibetan war magic; Professor Ulrike Roesler for several introductions; Professor Mel Goldstein for sharing sources and unpublished material relating to the Dalai Lama's escape from Lhasa and kindly entering into a lengthy correspondence about these; and Dr. Jan Westerhoff for an illuminating discussion about Indo-Tibetan logic. From within the walls of academia, I am indebted above all to Professor Robbie Barnett for his acute reading of, and corrections to, substantial parts of the text. He saved me from many mistakes.

There are many other people who have, over many years, helped shape my thinking on Tibet's history and culture, but for more general discussions of a philosophical nature, I wish to thank in particular Mr. Stephen Priest; Dr. Ralph Weir (who was good enough to read and comment on the manuscript); Dr. Samuel Hughes; and Professor Benedikt Goecke. For his theological reading of the manuscript, I thank Mr. Nikolas Prassas.

Despite all this help, I am quite certain that there remain many errors. These I claim as my own.

Finally, for her assistance in sourcing photographs, I thank Ms. Jane Moore, while, for his readiness to share unpublished manuscripts, I am especially indebted to Mr. David Kittlestrom of Wisdom Books. For her unfailing and sorely tested patience, and for her critical acumen, I should like to thank my editor at Houghton Mifflin Harcourt, Ms. Deanne Urmy.

For their patience I would also like to thank my wife and my children, Rosie, Edward, and Theo. Finally, I must single out my daughter for the insight expressed in the penultimate sentence of the last chapter.

THE FOURTEEN DALAI LAMAS

The First Dalai Lama: Gendun Drub (1391–1474) Posthumously recognized, he was one of the "heart disciples" of Tsongkhapa. Especially esteemed for his writings on the *vinaya,* he is nonetheless not so highly regarded as his contemporary Khedrup Je, who is associated with the Panchen Lama lineage.

The Second Dalai Lama: Gendun Gyatso (1475–1542) Noted especially for his spiritual songs, he referred to himself as a "mad beggar monk" and became abbot first of Tashilhunpo and then of Drepung Monastery. In terms of spiritual attainment, he is regarded as one of the most accomplished of the Dalai Lamas.

The Third Dalai Lama: Sonam Gyatso (1543–1588) The first Dalai Lama to be recognized in his lifetime but, because he was considered the reincarnation of Gendun Gyatso, who was himself accepted as the reincarnation of Gendun Drup, it followed that when Altan Khan bestowed on him the title Dalai Lama, he must in fact be the Third. It is largely thanks to his efforts that Mongolia became a major component of the Gelug establishment.

The Fourth Dalai Lama: Yonten Gyatso (1589–1617) A direct descendant of Genghis Khan, the Fourth is regarded as one of the least successful Dalai Lamas. He never learned to speak Tibetan well, and his spiritual attainments were negligible. According to a story heard by Tsybikov, the Russo-Buryat explorer, he died from poisoning.

The Great Fifth: Nawang Lobsang Gyatso (1617–1682) Unifier of Tibet under the government of the Ganden Phodrang thanks to the patronage of the Mongolian warlord Gushri Khan. An ecumenist who sought to engage each of the different schools within the Tibetan tradition, the Great Fifth was an initiate of many Nyingma practices, a matter of controversy during his lifetime and later. When he died, the event was concealed from the public for almost fifteen years while the Sixth Dalai Lama grew to maturity. It was the Great Fifth who established Nechung as state oracle.

The Sixth Dalai Lama: Tsangyang Gyatso (1683–1706) Refused to take monastic vows and lived as a layman. He is chiefly remembered for his love songs—and for bedding the daughters of most of the aristocratic houses of his day.

The Seventh Dalai Lama: Kelzang Gyatso (1708–1757) Criticized by the Fourteenth Dalai Lama for his narrowly sectarian bias, the Seventh Dalai Lama is nonetheless highly regarded both for his writings and for his spiritual attainments. It was during his reign that a relationship was forged with the Qing emperors.

The Eighth Dalai Lama: Jamphel Gyatso (1758–1804) Although fully ordained, the Eighth Dalai Lama was reluctant to assume temporal power, relying instead on his regent even when he came of age. It was during his reign that Tibet fought, and lost, a disastrous war against the Gorkhas of Nepal.

The Ninth Dalai Lama: Lungtok Gyatso (1805–1815) The first Dalai Lama known to have contact with a European, he was visited by the eccentric British traveler Thomas Manning. He showed signs of great promise as a spiritual practitioner. There is some suspicion that he was murdered.

The Tenth Dalai Lama: Tsultrim Gyatso (1816–1837) Plagued with ill health, he seems not to have assumed temporal power and in any case died before having any impact. Some believe that he was slowly poisoned at the behest of the Chinese *amban.*

The Eleventh Dalai Lama: Khedrup Gyatso (1838–1856) A promising scholar, he was invested with temporal power at the age of seventeen. His death just three years later is believed by many to have been orchestrated by his ex-regent.

The Twelfth Dalai Lama: Trinley Gyatso (1857–1875) Invested with temporal power as an infant following a coup against the regent, he ruled for only a short time and showed little promise as a scholar before his demise—many believe at the hands of two of his attendants, who in any case were arrested, tortured, and exiled.

The Great Thirteenth: Thubten Gyatso (1876–1933) The Great Thirteenth was the first Dalai Lama since the Eighth to dodge the machinations of his regent and of the Qing *ambans* and attain both spiritual and temporal power. He was forced to flee Lhasa for exile, first in Mongolia and then in China, by a British military expedition under Colonel Younghusband (see Glossary). Almost no sooner had he returned than he was pushed out by Qing military forces. This time he fled south to British-controlled India. On the fall of the Qing dynasty in 1912, he returned and set about restoring his authority. Opposition from the Three Seats thwarted his plans to establish an independent military.

The Fourteenth Dalai Lama: Tenzin Gyatso (b. 1935) The subject of this book.

GLOSSARY OF NAMES AND KEY TERMS

Here I give brief definitions of some key terms alongside thumbnails of leading figures in the story. While I give Tibetan both phonetically and in Wylie, the Sanskrit terms are given only phonetically. Note that in the text itself, I have also used phonetics for most Tibetan words.

Amdo (A mDo) The eastern province of historical Tibet. Since 1950 absorbed variously into Sichuan, Qinghai, Gansu, and Yunnan provinces of the People's Republic of China.

Amdowa (A mdo ba) One who hails from Amdo (such as the present Dalai Lama).

bodhichitta The spontaneous wish, rising out of Great Compassion, to attain Enlightenment for the benefit of all sentient beings.

bodhisattva A being with the wish to facilitate the liberation of all other sentient beings before taking Enlightenment; more generally, anyone who has generated *bodhichitta.*

Buddha Literally, one who is awakened; one who knows the Truth (of the way things really are).

Buddhadharma The path to liberation taught by the Buddha.

CCP Chinese Communist Party.

Chiang Kai-shek (1887–1975) Leader of the Chinese Nationalists (Guomindang), president of the Republic of China 1928–1975, from 1928 to 1949 within China proper, latterly on the island of Taiwan. Raised a Buddhist, he converted to Christianity on marrying his fourth wife, Soong Mei-ling

(Madame Chiang, ca. 1898–2003). Inheriting the ideology of Sun Yat-sen, he saw Tibetans as a minority Chinese ethnic group.

Chenresig (sPyan ras gzigs) (in Sanskrit, Avalokitesvara) Bodhisattva of Compassion.

Chushi Gangdruk (Chu bzhi sgang drug) The Kham Four Rivers, Six Ranges Tibetan Defenders of the Faith Volunteer Army.

Cultural Revolution (1966–1969) Motivated by Mao's desire to restore his own power following the Great Leap Forward, and to secure his legacy, the Great Proletarian Cultural Revolution was a period of violent class struggle during which the "bourgeoisie," allegedly intent on restoring capitalism, were to be eliminated. In Tibet, not only was all private property confiscated, but also it was impermissible even to cook at home. Arguably its chief achievement was the destruction of many monuments and artifacts held to symbolize the "four olds": old customs, old culture, old habits, and old ideas.

dharma A Sanskrit term meaning, literally, "the way": Buddhism in particular; religion more generally.

dob dob (rDob rdob) Fraternities of monks from whose ranks were drawn the monastery "police," noted also for their sporting, fighting, and homosexual activities.

Dorje Drakden (rDo rje grags ldan) A deity who is a minister in the retinue of the dharma protector Pehar, and who communicates with the Dalai Lama and members of the Ganden Phodrang via the medium of the Nechung oracle.

Dorje Shugden (rDo rje shugs ldan) His proponents hold him to be a wrathful emanation of Manjushri, Bodhisattva of Wisdom, and as such a dharma protector; his opponents maintain that he is merely a worldly spirit.

Enlightenment The state attained by one who has achieved liberation from samsara and is thus fully awakened as to the way things really are.

emptiness (sTong pa nyid) The ultimate nature of reality.

Four Noble Truths

1. The truth of suffering

2. The truth of the cause of suffering
3. The truth of the cessation of suffering
4. The truth of the Path to the cessation of suffering

Gadong (dGa' gdong) One of the oracles consulted by the Dalai Lama and members of the Ganden Phodrang for auguries of the future. A recent medium was mute when in trance. He could only simper.

Ganden (dGa' ldan) Monastery founded by Tsongkhapa in 1409; mother house of the Gelug school.

Ganden Phodrang (dGa' ldan pho brang) Name used to refer to the government of the Dalai Lamas.

Ganden Throne Holder The senior-most position within the Gelug school.

Gelug (dGe lugs) Literally, the Way of Virtue. Sometimes known as the New Kadam tradition, also as the Yellow Hat sect; the Gelug tradition, to which all Dalai Lamas have belonged, was founded by Tsongkhapa in the fifteenth century.

Gelugpa One who follows the Gelug tradition.

geshe (dGe bshes) An academic degree awarded to monks.

geshema (dGe bshes ma) An academic degree awarded to nuns (an innovation of the current Dalai Lama).

Geshe Wangyal (dGe bshes Ngag dbang dbang rgyal) (1901–1983) The Kalmykian monk student of the Great Thirteenth's favorite, Agvan Dorjieff, Geseh Wangyal founded the first Tibetan Buddhist center in America while working as a CIA agent.

Glorious Goddess (dPal ldan lha mo) Palden Lhamo, one of the most powerful protector deities, closely associated both with Tibet in general and the Dalai Lama lineage in particular.

Gonpo Tashi Andrugtsang (A 'brugs mgon po bkra shis) (1905–1964) Freedom fighter and founder of Chushi Gangdruk.

Gould, Sir Basil (1883–1956) British political officer of Sikkim, Bhutan, and Tibet. Attended the enthronement of the present Dalai Lama as representative of the viceroy of India and of the British Crown.

Great Compassion (sNying rje chen po) The wish or aspiration to facilitate the liberation of all sentient beings from samsara (*see* samsara).

guru A spiritual guide or teacher (*see* lama).

Gyalo Thondup (rGya lo don 'grub) (b. 1928) Second-eldest brother of the present Dalai Lama, protégé of Chiang Kai-shek, and a CIA agent.

gyalyum chenmo (rgyal yum chen mo) Title of the Dalai Lama's mother.

Harrer, Heinrich (1912–2006) Austrian-born mountaineer, student ski champion, and adventurer. His BA was in geography, and he qualified as a teacher before becoming a member of the SS and subsequently joining the Nazi Party. He saw the Dalai Lama regularly during the first half of 1950 and wrote about his experiences in the classic travelogue *Seven Years in Tibet.*

Hinayana Literally "Lesser Vehicle" in contrast to Mahayana "Great Vehicle" Buddhism; arguably a derogatory term for non-Mahayana Buddhism.

hungry ghost or ***yidag*** (Yi dwags) A being belonging to the realm below that of animals and insects but above that of hell beings.

Jetsun Pema (rJe btsun pad ma) (b. 1940) Younger sister of the Dalai Lama. For over four decades she served as president of the Tibetan Children's Villages, the school system founded by the Dalai Lama for the education of Tibetan refugee children.

Jokhang (Jo khang) The most important temple in Tibet, it stands at the eastern end of Lhasa and is sacred to each of the different Buddhist traditions indigenous to Tibet.

Kalachakra tantra Literally the "Wheel of Time" tantra, known since the eleventh century, this is a complex system of practices claimed by the Dalai Lama to be beneficial to the cause of world peace. It features explicit sexual imagery and an apocalyptic "theology" in which barbarian hordes are put to the sword by an invincible army emanating from Shambala, a hidden kingdom located within the Himalayas.

Kargyu (bKa' brgyud) Founded in the eleventh century, the tradition is particularly associated with Marpa and his famous disciple Milarepa. It split subsequently into several different schools centered on different incarnation lineages.

karma (Kar ma) Its literal meaning is "action," and it refers to the positive, negative, or neutral imprint of a given action on the actor's mental continuum. It is the sentient being's negative karma that keeps it within samsara.

Kashag (bKa' shag) The four-member council of ministers, or cabinet, of the Dalai Lamas and their regents. Traditionally, two members were monks. In recent times there have also been women Kashag members.

kathag (kha dags) A length of (generally) white silk offered to a person or object (such as an image) to whom respect is due. These are of varying lengths and quality. The method of offering is to drape the *kathag*, which resembles a scarf, over the wrists with the arms outstretched, the hands open, and the palms turned upward.

khabse (Kham zas) Traditional New Year cookies.

Kham (Khams) Eastern province of historical Tibet, presently absorbed variously into the PRC's Tibet Autonomous Region and its Sichuan, Qinghai, Gansu, and Yunnan provinces.

Khampa (Khams pa) One who hails from Kham, such as Gonpo Tashi Andrugtsang (*see* Gonpo Tashi Andrugtsang).

kuten (sku rten) Literally, the basis. A medium through whom one or more deities may speak.

lama (bLa ma) A teacher or spiritual guide (the word translates the Sanskrit term *guru*).

liberation

1. From samsara, the necessary condition of Enlightenment
2. From the "living hell" of serfdom by the Chinese Communist Party

Ling Rinpoché (Gling rin po che) (1903–1983) Ninety-seventh Ganden Throne holder and senior tutor to the Fourteenth Dalai Lama.

Lobsang Samten (bLo bsang bsam gtan) (1933–1985) Immediate elder brother of the Fourteenth Dalai Lama. Educated with the Dalai Lama, 1940–1945; Lord Chamberlain; school janitor in Scotch Plains, New Jersey; leader of first delegation to Tibet.

Losar (Lo sar) Tibetan New Year (calculated according to the lunar calendar).

Lotus-Born, The (Sanskrit: Padmasambhava) Eighth-century Kashmiri-born sage and thaumaturge. He was present at the founding of Samye, Tibet's first monastery, but was subsequently banished from the kingdom. Surviving an assassination attempt, he is said to have spent the next fifty-six years in Tibet subduing its indigenous deities and binding them over to serve the Buddhadharma.

Mahakala (Ma ha ka la) Protector deity, considered a wrathful emanation of Chenresig. He is closely associated with the Dalai Lamas, having protected the infant First Dalai Lama in the form of a raven.

Mahayana Literally "Great Vehicle" (in contrast to "Lesser Vehicle" Buddhism); the earliest Mahayana teachings, which propound the way of the bodhisattvas, have been dated to around the first century CE.

Maitreya The Buddha to come.

Manchu The "barbarian" race of Manchuria, now subsumed as part of the People's Republic of China, from which originated the Qing dynasty.

mandala A two- or sometimes three-dimensional symbolic representation of the cosmos, or some part of it.

Manjushri The Bodhisattva of Wisdom.

Mao Zedong (1893–1976) Popularly known as the Great Helmsman, he was a Communist revolutionary and guerrilla leader who became the founding father of the People's Republic of China. The Fourteenth Dalai Lama once composed a prayer in his honor.

mo (Mo) Common form of divination that may use, for example, dough balls, inside of which paper with different possible answers are concealed, or dice.

Monlam Chenmo (sMon lam chen mo) The Great Prayer Festival that celebrates the Month of Miracles of the Buddha, held at the beginning of the Tibetan New Year.

National Assembly Traditionally comprising the aristocratic families of Tibet.

Nechung (gNas chung) A monastery situated outside Lhasa and close to Drepung where resides the medium who channels Dorje Drakden. Also an alternative name for the deity himself.

Nehru, Jawaharlal (1889–1964) According to the sometime US ambassador to India Loy Henderson, he was the "vain, sensitive, emotional, and complicated" ex-British public schoolboy and Cambridge-educated lawyer who became prime minister of India from independence in 1947 until his death in 1964.

Ngabo, Nawang Jigme (Nga phod gnag dbang 'jigs med) (1910–2009) Tibetan aristocrat and former governor of Chamdo, he was a member of the delegation that signed the Seventeen Point Agreement. According to Gyalo

Thondup, he was the "biggest traitor of all time," but Ngabo was nonetheless trusted by the Dalai Lama, who often sought his opinion and advice.

nirvana The state beyond suffering in which all those who have attained final liberation subsist.

Norbulingka (Nor bu ling kha) Literally the Jewel Park, founded by the Seventh Dalai Lama in the mid-eighteenth century, it became the summer retreat of subsequent Dalai Lamas, although both the Great Thirteenth and the Fourteenth both based themselves there permanently.

Nyingma (rNying ma) Literally the "old" or "ancient" tradition, associated with the Lotus-Born during the first diffusion of Buddhism to Tibet.

Nyingmapa (rNying ma) A follower of the Nyingma tradition.

oracle There were many oracles in Tibet, those of Nechung Monastery and Panglung Hermitage being only the most famous. Most monasteries and most villages had their own medium who would channel one or more deities.

Padmasambhava *See* Lotus-Born.

Palden Lhamo (dPal ldan lha mo) *See* Glorious Goddess.

Panchen Lama (Pan chen la ma) The second-most important reincarnation lineage within the Gelug tradition, centered on Tashilhunpo Monastery in southern Tibet.

Pehar (Pe har) More correctly Gyalpo Pehar, the protector deity of the Tibetan government who communicates with Dorje Drakden (*see* Dorje Drakden).

Phabongka Rinpoché (Pha bong rin po che) (1878–1941) Guru to Taktra Rinpoché, Ling Rinpoché, and Trijang Rinpoché, among others, Phabongka Rinpoché was a charismatic teacher and is credited with popularizing the cult of Dorje Shugden as protector of the Gelug tradition.

Phuntsog Wangyal (Phun tsogs dbang rgyal) (1922–2014) An early member of the CCP, Phunwang, as he was known, interpreted for the Dalai Lama during his visit to China. He was subsequently purged following the One Hundred Flowers campaign, spending nineteen years in prison.

PLA The People's Liberation Army, the standing army of the People's Republic of China.

Potala (Po ta la) Palace built during the seventeenth century to house the Dalai Lama and the government of Tibet.

Preparatory Committee for the Autonomous Region of Tibet This was the precursor to the modern-day Tibet Autonomous Region. Its nominal head was the Dalai Lama, who was succeeded in 1959 by the Tenth Panchen Lama.

protector deity (Srung ma) Of these there are two classes: the worldly protectors and the dharma protectors.

Qing dynasty (1644–1912) Established by the Manchu Aisin Gioru clan, it revived the empire of the earlier T'ang dynasty.

rebirth The doctrine of transmigration. When a sentient being dies, it is reborn in one of the Six Realms unless it has succeeded in attaining Enlightenment. When first encountered by the Jesuit missionaries in Tibet, it was castigated for justifying infanticide: if a child was unwanted (usually because it was female), it might be exposed and left to die in the pious hope that it would obtain a more favorable rebirth.

reincarnation The means by which the most highly evolved spiritual masters are able to choose the manner and timing of their rebirth.

Religious Kings (Chos rgyal) Of these there were three. First, **Songtsen Gampo** (Srong btsan sgam po) (604–649/50). Though he was a warrior chieftain, it is he who is credited with bringing Buddhism to Tibet. Famously, he married both Chinese and Nepalese princesses. Second, **Trisong Detsen** (Khri srong lde'u btsan) (742–797), who oversaw expansion of the Tibetan empire to its greatest extent and was on the throne when Tibetan forces briefly toppled the T'ang emperor. Third, **Rapalchen** (Ral pa can) (802–836), whose piety was such that he is said to wear woven hair extensions which his monastic advisers would sit on when in his presence. It is related that he was murdered by having his head twisted until his neck broke.

Reting (Rwa sgreng) Monastery founded by Drom Thonpa, an earlier incarnation of Chenresig, in the eleventh century, as headquarters of the Kadam tradition.

Reting Rinpoché (Rwa sgreng rin po che) (1912–1947) The Dalai Lama's root guru and first regent, regarded as a great mystic and seer, he was almost certainly murdered.

Richardson, Hugh (1905–2000) The last British political officer to serve in Tibet, he was both an outstanding scholar and an accomplished linguist, said to have spoken impeccable Lhasa Tibetan with the slight trace of an Oxford accent.

Rinpoché (Rin po che) An honorific title meaning, literally, "Precious One," generally reserved for reincarnate lamas.

samaya May either refer to the commitment of an initiate or to the sacred bond established between master and pupil wherein the master is seen as an embodiment of the Buddha himself.

samsara Or cyclic existence, the always unsatisfactory state in which all sentient beings suffer and remain until they attain Enlightenment, at which point they are liberated from samsara.

sangha The monastic community.

Shakyamuni Literally the sage of the Shakyas, ca. fifth-century BCE historical Buddha, born Prince Gautama in present-day Nepal and also known as Siddhartha (the one who accomplishes).

shi dre (Shi "dre) A type of ghost into which victims of violent death may transform.

Six Realms In descending order:

1. The heavenly realm (within which there are many heavens or grades of heaven)
2. The realm of demigods or demons
3. The human realm
4. The animal realm
5. The realm of hungry ghosts
6. The hell realm (within which there are many hells or grades of hell)

skillful means (Thabs; *upaya* in Sanskrit) The practice whereby a teacher adapts his words and deeds to the level of spiritual attainment of his audience.

Songtsen Gampo (Srong btsan sgam po) *See under* Religious Kings.

tantra A set of esoteric practices intended to speed the initiate's progress on the path to full Enlightenment.

Tashilhunpo (bKra shis lhun po) Monastery in southern Tibet, seat of the Panchen Lama, founded in 1447 by the First Dalai Lama.

Taktra Rinpoché (sTag brag rin po che) (1874–1952) Regent of Tibet, 1941–51.

thangka A religious painting on a scroll, usually framed with silk brocade, that may contain relics and/or other ritually consecrated substances.

Theravada Tradition regarded by its proponents as authentically preserving the original teachings of the Buddha. In general, Theravadins do not accept the Mahayana scriptures. The tradition remains dominant in Southeast Asia and Sri Lanka.

Three Seats (gDan sa gsum) Ganden, Drepung, and Sera Monasteries: the Harvard, Princeton, and Yale of Tibet.

torma (gTor ma) Butter sculpture: at Losar, different monasteries would compete with one another to produce the finest examples. Up to thirty feet high, they were paraded around the Barkhor on the last day of the Monlam Chenmo.

TPA Tibetan People's Association, a grassroots movement that grew up in opposition to the Chinese during the 1950s.

Trijang Rinpoché (Khri byang rin po che) (1901–1981) Junior tutor to the Dalai Lama and leading advocate of Dorje Shugden.

tsampa Roasted barley flour, a staple of the Tibetan diet.

Tsongkhapa (Tsong kha pa) (1357–1419) Also known as Je Rinpoché, founder of the Gelug school.

tukdam (Thugs dam) The meditative state whereby the most accomplished practitioners attain the clear light (*od gsal*) of primordial consciousness as they transition from embodied life to the heavenly realms from which they will again take rebirth for the benefit of sentient beings.

tulku (sPrul sku) Literally "emanation body," the technical term for a reincarnate lama.

TWC Tibet Work Committee, front of the Chinese central government that carries out its policies in Tibet.

Ü-Tsang (dBus gTsang) The combined southern provinces of Tibet.

Vajryana The Diamond Path. Some scholars regard Vajryana Buddhism as a distinct tradition, alongside the Theravada and Mahayana traditions, others hold simply that it is the apotheosis of the Mahayana tradition.

vinaya ("Dul ba) The monastic code or set of precepts by which the renunciate lives. For monks there are 253, for nuns 364.

yabshi (Yab gzhis) Term referring to the Dalai Lama's household, including his family.

yabshi kung (Yab gzhis khang) The Dalai Lama's father, in which *kung* is a title roughly equivalent to duke.

yoga Perhaps best translated as "discipline," yoga denotes both the practice and the set of practices whereby the yogin/yogini trains the mind in the quest for Enlightenment.

yogin Male practitioner of yoga.

yogini Female practitioner of yoga.

Younghusband, Colonel Sir Francis (1863–1942) British army officer and explorer turned mystical writer who led the expedition that captured Lhasa in 1904.

Zhou Enlai (1989–1976) Premier of the People's Republic of China from its inception until his death, Zhou was the famously suave diplomat who managed affairs of state, including foreign affairs, while Mao struggled against perceived enemies of the Revolution.

NOTES

Introduction: Waldorf Astoria Hotel, New York, August 1989

page

xx *Tibetan humor:* Sir Basil Gould, the political officer for Sikkim, Bhutan, and Tibet, thought the same thing. See Basil Gould, *The Jewel in the Lotus: Recollections of an Indian Political* (London: Chatto & Windus, 1957), p. 207: "Tibetans laugh at the same things and in the same tone, and appreciate beauty in just the same things as Englishmen."

xxi *"feeling it between finger and thumb":* Charles Bell, *Portrait of the Dalai Lama* (London: Collins, 1946), p. 88.

1. The Travails of the Great Thirteenth

7 *fifty shrapnel shells:* Patrick French, *Younghusband: The Last Great Imperial Adventurer* (London: HarperCollins, 1995), p. 224.

those taken prisoner: Tsepon W. D. Shakabpa, *Tibet: A Political History* (New Haven: Yale University Press, 1967), p. 212.

8 *"one of great calmness":* Petr Kuz'mich Kozlov, *Tibet I Dalai Lama* (St. Petersburg, 1920). I have changed the last word of Mark Belcher's translation of this passage from "nervousness" to "emotion," which seems more apt.

9 *"Tibet," she wrote:* First Historical Archives of China, vol. 30 (1996), quoted in Jung Chang, *Empress Dowager Cixi: The Concubine Who Launched Modern China* (London: Jonathan Cape, 2013), p. 366.

10 *"the hospitable and venerable":* Philip Short, *In Pursuit of Plants: Experiences of Nineteenth and Early Twentieth Century Plant Collectors* (Portland, OR: 2004), p. 108. Forrest's account was originally told in his paper, its title splendidly understated, "The Perils of Plant Hunting" in the *Gardeners' Chronicle* of May 1910.

11 *"eventually run to ground":* Short, *In Pursuit of Plants,* p. 114. Forrest himself only just survived. At one point in the course of his three-week ordeal, much of it passed at 16–17,000 feet, he trod on an inch-wide spike in a booby trap, which, "passing through the bones of my foot," protruded "half a hand's width" from the other side.

He accepted that capital punishment: Charles Bell, *Portrait of the Dalai Lama* (London: Collins, 1946), p. 157.

12 *The Chinese* amban*:* Xiuyu Wang, *China's Last Imperial Frontier: Late Qing Expansion in Sichuan's Tibetan Borderlands* (Lanham, MD: Lexington Books, 2011), p. 124.

in a cauldron of "cold water": Albert Leroy Shelton, *Pioneering in Tibet: A Personal Record of Life and Experience in Mission Fields* (New York: F. H. Revell Company, 1921), pp. 93–94. See also Eric Teichman, *Travels of a Consular Officer in North-west China* (Cambridge: Cambridge University Press, 1921), p. 228.

"resemble living demons": Sam van Schaik, *Tibet: A History* (New Haven: Yale University Press, 2011), p. 84.

"only made confusion worse": Short, *In Pursuit of Plants,* p. 108.

13 *"in order to curry favour":* Flora Beal Shelton, *Shelton of Tibet* (New York: George H. Doran, 1923), 171–72.

a "shrieking" and "diabolical" noise: W. N. Fergusson, *Adventure, Sport and Travel on the Tibetan Steppes* (New York: Charles Scribner's Sons, 1911), pp. 2–3.

14 *"a kind people":* Fergusson, *Adventure, Sport and Travel,* p. 3.

"welcoming smile ": Bell, *Portrait,* p. 103.

"Many monks": Gyalo Thondup with Anne F. Thurston, *The Noodle Maker of Kalimpong: The Untold Story of My Struggle for Tibet* (London: Rider, 2015), p. 7.

2. A Mystic and a Seer

17 *a white dragon:* Khemey Sonam Wangdu, Basil J. Gould, and Hugh E. Richardson, *Discovery, Recognition and Enthronement of the 14th Dalai Lama: A Collection of Accounts* (Dharamsala: Library of Tibetan Works and Archives, 2000), p. 3.

18 *forced it on him:* Melvyn C. Goldstein, *A History of Modern Tibet: 1913–1951,* vol. 1, *The Demise of the Lamaist State* (Berkeley: University of California Press, 1989), p. 141. See also the account in Charles Bell, *Portrait of the Dalai Lama* (London: Collins, 1946), chap. 68.

19 *If we are not able:* Sam van Schaik, *Tibet: A History* (New Haven: Yale University Press, 2011), p. 204.

22 *stamping his right foot:* Lest anyone doubt the veracity of this story, one can, according to the regent's niece, who visited his monastery in 2006, still see the imprint carefully preserved in a chapel. Tseyang Sadutshang, *My Youth in Tibet: Recollections of a Tibetan Woman* (Dharamsala: Library of Tibetan Works and Archives, 2012), p. 37.

one of his nieces: His niece remembers him at the start of an important religious ceremony smiling and waving at her and then, during an interval, toying with her fingers. When a smallpox epidemic broke out in the region of Reting Monastery, she was taken to see the Rinpoché while he undertook a spiritual retreat at a hermitage in the mountains. There he gave her some powder which included the desiccated skin of a cousin who had contracted and survived the disease. This, the great lama explained, was to be inhaled up the nose like snuff. When she did so and duly sneezed, he "very kindly let down the folded sleeve of his yellow silk shirt" and allowed her to blow her nose on it.

Sadutshang, *My Youth in Tibet,* pp. 37, 45. A delicate fragrance is a well-attested characteristic of Christian holy men too: Saint Philip Neri was one of them, Saint Pio of Pietrelcina another.
"gauche," "self centred," and "immature": Hugh E. Richardson, *High Peaks, Pure Earth: Collected Writings on Tibetan History and Culture* (London: Serindia, 1998), p. 715.
"a very mediocre personage": Philip Neame, *Playing with Strife: The Autobiography of a Soldier* (London: George G. Harrap, 1947), p. 159. See also Philip Neame, "Tibet and the 1936 Lhasa Mission," *Journal of the Royal Central Asian Society* 26 (April 1939): 234–46.
"new things": Isrun Engelhardt, *Tibet in 1938–1939: Photographs from the Ernst Schäfer Expedition to Tibet* (Chicago: Serindia, 2007), p. 29.

25 *chief minister's wife:* Bell, *Portrait,* p. 54. The full story of Lungshar's fall is given in chap. 6 of Melvyn C. Goldstein, *A History of Modern Tibet: 1913–1951,* vol. 1, *The Demise of the Lamaist State* (Berkeley: University of California Press, 1989), chap. 6. Apparently Lungshar did not resent his punishment. He took it as karmic retribution for having once blinded a sheep with a nonfatal shot from his sling.

3. A Child Is Born

27 *took to be significant:* The most authoritative account of the events described in this chapter is to be found in Khemey Sonam Wangdu, Basil J. Gould, and Hugh E. Richardson, *Discovery, Recognition and Enthronement of the 14th Dalai Lama: A Collection of Accounts* (Dharamsala: Library of Tibetan Works and Archives, 2000).

28 *strange star-shaped fungi:* See the account in Mary Taring, *Daughter of Tibet* (London: John Murray, 1970). Basil Gould visited Lhasa in August 1936, so it seems possible he actually saw the fungi. But he says they looked more like antlers; see his *Jewel in the Lotus: Recollections of an Indian Political* (London: Chatto & Windus, 1957).

29 *in her right hand:* Adapted from Réne de Nebesky-Wojkowitz, *Oracles and Demons of Tibet* (Delhi: Book Faith India), p. 22.

30 *"It is not known":* The story is told in more detail in Alexander Norman, *Secret Lives of the Dalai Lama* (New York: Random House, 2008), p. 352.

31 *"singular sweetness":* Charles Bell, *Portrait of the Dalai Lama* (London: Collins, 1946).

32 *the search party:*The full account of the search party is given in Wangdu, Gould, and Richardson, *Discovery, Recognition and Enthronement,* pp. 14–15.

33 *" a kind of "jump-suit":* Wangdu, Gould, and Richardson, *Discovery, Recognition and Enthronement,* p. 15.

34 *"No," they replied:* Robert Thurman recounts a story about the Dalai Lama's mother having a dream about a bright blue dragon escorted by two playful green snow lions, but I have not seen this corroborated anywhere. Robert Thurman, *Why the Dalai Lama Matters* (New York: Atria, 2008), p. 14.
"even for a moment": Gyalo Thondup with Anne F. Thurston, *The Noodle Maker of Kalimpong: The Untold Story of My Struggle for Tibet* (London: Rider, 2015), pp. 15, 19.

35 *"utter no words":* Quoted in Françoise Pommaret, *Lhasa in the Seventeenth Century: The*

Capital of the Dalai Lama, trans. Howard Solverson (Leiden: Brill, 2003), p. 69. See also Samten Karmay's translation of the relevant passage in the Great Fifth's autobiography, *The Illusive Play* (Chicago: Serindia, 2014).

"very sarcastic": Personal interview.

4. The View from the Place of the Roaring Tiger

36 *"grinding poverty":* Gyalo Thondup with Anne F. Thurston, *The Noodle Maker of Kalimpong: The Untold Story of My Struggle for Tibet* (London: Rider, 2015), p. 4.

37 *"one of the best":* Thondup, *Noodle Maker,* pp. 6–13. The Dalai Lama's extended family owned forty-five acres, while his parents owned approximately six and a half acres of land themselves—enough to be classified as landlords, and therefore "class enemies" by the Communists. Jianglin Li, "When the Iron Bird Flies: The 1956–1962 Secret War on the Tibetan Plateau," unpublished ms., trans. Stacey Mosher.

38 *"happy and contented life":* Adapted from Thubten Jigme Norbu, *Tibet Is My Country* (London: Rupert Hart Davis, 1960), p. 51.

40 *"strung about the walls":* Gary Geddes, *Kingdom of Ten Thousand Things: An Impossible Journey from Kabul to Chiapas,* illustrated ed. (New York: Sterling Publishing Company, 2008), p. 175.

"slipped to the door": Diki Tsering, *Dalai Lama, My Son: A Mother's Story* (London: Virgin, 2000), pp. 37–38. Although the provenance of this work might cause the strictest biographers to raise their eyebrows, it was first taken down in note form by one grandchild as a series of stories and subsequently turned into a continuous narrative by another before it received the ministrations of its English editor. The book's artlessness and charm nonetheless give it the ring of authenticity.

"and stood beside me": Tsering, *Dalai Lama, My Son,* pp. 40–41.

41 *guarded by trolls:* With respect to Laplanders, see, for example, Andrew Brown, "Gods and Fairytales," *The Spectator,* February 14, 2015.

"nameless religion": Starting with the great French Tibetologist R. A. Stein. See his *Tibetan Civilisation,* trans. J. E. Stapleton Driver (London: Faber and Faber, 1972).

celestial dragons: Tsewang Y. Pemba, *Young Days in Tibet* (London: Jonathan Cape, 1957), p. 146. For a useful Tibetan account, see Norbu Chophel, *Folk Culture of Tibet* (Dharamsala: Library of Tibetan Works and Archives, 1983); for a scholarly analysis of the different classes, see Geoffrey Samuel, *Civilized Shamans: Buddhism in Tibetan Societies* (Washington, DC: Smithsonian Institution Press, 1993).

"dreadful and tedious solitude": Although he was wrong on this point, Desideri's *relazione* of his seven-year sojourn in Tibet (available in *Mission to Tibet: The Extraordinary Eighteenth-Century Account of Father Ippolito Desideri SJ,* ed. L. Zwilling, trans. M. Sweet [Somerville, MA: Wisdom Publications, 2010]) is extremely valuable for its many insights of the time. The quotation is from the earlier translation of Desideri's *relazione, An Account of Tibet: The Travels of Ippolite Desideri di Pistoia, SJ, 1712–1727,* ed. Filippo de Filippi, rev. ed. (London: G. Routledge, 1937), p. 353; the whole of his "Report on Tibet and Its Routes" gives an extraordinary perspective on both eighteenth-century

Tibet and Counter-Reformation Europe. Desideri himself was a linguistic genius. It took him less than two years to master the language sufficiently well to write the first of his three books in Tibetan (one of them a catechism of the Christian faith, two of them philosophical works designed to refute Buddhism). See Donald S. Lopez and Thupten Jinpa, *Dispelling the Darkness: A Jesuit's Quest for the Soul of Tibet* (Cambridge: Harvard University Press, 2017).

42 *"strange jealous creatures":* Robert B. Ekvall, *Tents Against the Sky* (London: Gollancz, 1954), p. 188.

43 *"almost as a pet":* The full story is told in Pemba, *Young Days in Tibet,* pp. 148–50.
human scapegoat: Practices such as these were not confined to treatment of the sick. It is said that at the great Nyingma foundation at Samye there was "a special room where the bodies that get lost in the Bardo, the realm between successive lives, were chopped up and [in which] the weighing of souls for punishment occurred . . . [O] ccasionally it became politically necessary for a man to be put in this room as a ransom for the sins of Tibet." John Crook and James Low, *The Yogins of Ladakh: A Pilgrimage Among the Hermits of the Buddhist Himalayas* (1997; repr., Delhi: Motilal Banarsidass, 2012), p. 199 and n. 65.

44 *"found out that":* Pemba, *Young Days in Tibet,* p. 149.

5. "Lonely and somewhat unhappy"

46 *"A last attempt":* Thubten Jigme Norbu, *Tibet Is My Country* (London: Rupert Hart Davis, 1960), p. 128.

47 *"lonely" and "somewhat unhappy":* Dalai Lama, *Freedom in Exile: The Autobiography of His Holiness the Dalai Lama of Tibet* (London: Hodder & Stoughton, 1990), p. 12.
suck a mole: Raimondo Bultrini, *The Dalai Lama and the King Demon,* trans. Maria Simmons (New York: Tibet House US, 2013), p. 338.
"no one to play with": My Land and My People: The Autobiography of His Holiness the Dalai Lama (London: Weidenfeld and Nicolson, 1962), p. 27.
"a childish dislike": Dalai Lama, *Freedom in Exile,* p. 14.

48 *"for the most part":* Dalai Lama, *Freedom in Exile,* p. 14.
Ma Bufang: Neither the Tibetan nor the Chinese historians have been kind to Ma. To the Tibetans he was "so devious and scandalous in his behaviour that it was beyond description." The Dalai Lama's elder brother recalled how, on tax-collecting missions, Ma's officials would hunt down the local people, string them up by the ankles, and beat them with bamboo sticks if they tried to evade payment. Gyalo Thondup with Anne F. Thurston, *The Noodle Maker of Kalimpong: The Untold Story of My Struggle for Tibet* (London: Rider, 2015), p. 26. To the victorious Communists, Ma, as a supporter of the Nationalist Guomindang, was a counterrevolutionary and a traitor to the nation. But anecdotal evidence suggests that he was affable, good-humored, and forward-thinking. An American government official visiting Qinghai province praised his leadership as one of the most efficient in China, and one of the most energetic. Ma was particularly concerned with reforestation and gave free seeds and instructions for planting to the

peasantry, saying that the tree was the "salvation of the desert." As onetime leader of the great mosque of Xining, he might be expected to have been socially conservative, but in fact Ma Bufang set up a modern school for girls that provided a secular education. On the Communists' accession to power, ostensibly on pilgrimage to Mecca, he fled to Saudi Arabia, where he died in 1975.

49 *100,000 silver dollars:* Melvyn C. Goldstein, *A History of Modern Tibet: 1913–1951,* vol. 1, *The Demise of the Lamaist State* (Berkeley: University of California Press, 1989), p. 321.

via India: See Goldstein, *History of Modern Tibet,* 1:323. This fact shows that, while Amdo itself was outside Lhasa's control, the Chinese government could not dictate terms to the Tibetans with respect to central Tibet.

50 *"began to look":* Dalai Lama, *Freedom in Exile,* p. 14.

"a strikingly pretty girl": Heinrich Harrer, *Seven Years in Tibet* (London: R. Hart-Davis, 1953), p. 205.

"We spent a great deal": Dalai Lama, *Freedom in Exile,* p. 15.

51 *"the vast herds":* Dalai Lama, *Freedom in Exile,* p. 15.

"thousands of": Thondup, *Noodle Maker,* p. 33.

52 *"the officials, secretaries and monks":* Thondup, *Noodle Maker,* p. 35.

53 *"as it might be poisoned":* Diki Tsering, *The Dalai Lama, My Son: A Mother's Story* (London: Virgin, 2000), p. 93.

"the stars of heaven": Michael Aris, *Hidden Treasures and Secret Lives: A Study of Pemalingpa (1450–1521) and the Sixth Dalai Lama (1683–1706)* (London: Kegan Paul International, 1989), p. 149.

54 *these outer manifestations:* One of the best single collections of photographs of premodern Tibet can be seen at the Pitt Rivers Museum in Oxford. This is viewable in its entirety online at http://tibet.prm.ox.ac.uk/tibet_project_summary.html.

"with big bulging eyes": Thomas Laird, *The Story of Tibet: Conversations with the Dalai Lama* (London: Atlantic, 2006), pp. 269–70.

6. Homecoming

57 *"a town full of animation":* Alexandra David-Néel, *My Journey to Lhasa* (Harmondsworth: Allen Lane, Penguin Books, 1940), p. 273.

58 *"metropolis of filth":* Ekai Kawaguchi, *Three Years in Tibet* (London: Theosophical Publishing Society, 1909), p. 407. Though he was a devout pilgrim, the city evidently disgusted Kawaguchi. He spoke of "the filth, the stench, the utter abomination of the streets."

"squatting or lying": William Stanley Morgan, *Amchi Sahib: A British Doctor in Tibet, 1936–37* (Charlestown, MA: Acme Bookbinding, 2007), p. 73. Dr. Morgan was attached to the 1936–37 British mission to Lhasa under Sir Basil Gould. His lively memoir is notable for its description of the syphilis clinic he ran. Monks from the local monasteries made up a large percentage of his patients. On venereal disease among Tibetans, see also Harrer, *Seven Years,* p. 176.

"They were at once": Frederick Spencer Chapman, *Lhasa: The Holy City* (London: Chatto & Windus, 1938), p. 148.
"The ordinary residents": Tsewang Y. Pemba, *Young Days in Tibet* (London: Jonathan Cape, 1957), p. 76.
stumps "immersed": Pemba, *Young Days in Tibet,* p. 86.

59 *"an Amazon with breasts":* Pemba, *Young Days in Tibet,* p. 109.
settled population: Estimates vary, but most agree that the population was around ten thousand. W. S. Morgan puts it at a mere eight thousand (*Amchi Sahib,* p. 86).
Within a few hours' walk: Remarkably enough, a common way of measuring both time and distance was to give the number of cups of tea that could be drunk over the course of a given interval. Tibetans at this time drank spectacular quantities. Charles Bell reports that many people he knew would consume "sixty or seventy cups daily," though the Great Thirteenth limited himself to "about forty cups, of ordinary tea cup size, each day." Charles Bell, *Portrait of the Dalai Lama* (London: Collins, 1946), p. 303.
"from sunrise to sunset": David-Néel, *My Journey to Lhasa,* p. 273.

60 *"a herd of tame musk deer":* Dalai Lama, *Freedom in Exile: The Autobiography of His Holiness the Dalai Lama of Tibet* (London: Hodder & Stoughton, 1990), p. 38.
until that moment: Thomas Laird, *The Story of Tibet: Conversations with the Dalai Lama* (London: Atlantic, 2006), p. 271.

61 *habitual opium smokers:* See Henrich Harrer's foreword in Dorje Yudon Yuthok, *House of the Turquoise Roof* (Ithaca: Snow Lion Publications, 1990), p. 12.
take the measure: Sir Basil Gould, in *Jewel in the Lotus: Recollections of an Indian Political* (London: Chatto & Windus, 1957), p. 220, described him as "a man of quiet and gentle poise." Hugh Richardson once described him to me as "a dreadful old horse coper."
warmly affectionate: Describing her to me, Tenzin Geyche Tethong, scion of an old and senior aristocratic family, asserted that the *gyalyum chenmo* was "really something . . . quite a remarkable person." Similarly, Gould described her as "surely one in a million, the worthy mother of a Dalai Lama" (*Jewel in the Lotus,* p. 220). Heinrich Harrer also has many good things to say of her.

62 "*One saw many of these people":* Pemba, *Young Days in Tibet,* p. 84.
marched with a peculiar gait: Pemba, *Young Days in Tibet,* p. 98.
"really let themselves go": Pemba, *Young Days in Tibet,* p. 115.

63 *"one of the best moments":* Dalai Lama, *Freedom in Exile,* p. 45. The Casting-Out *(smon lam gdor rgyag)* was celebrated on February 7 in 1940, the year in question. For a full description, see Hugh Richardson, *Ceremonies of the Lhasa Year* (London: Serindia Publications, 1993).
Consisting of "wooden frames": Pemba, *Young Days in Tibet,* p. 114.

65 *"The sight of all those people":* Dalai Lama, *Freedom in Exile,* p. 48.
"This tended to result": Dalai Lama, *Freedom in Exile,* p. 49. See also Alexandra David-Néel's account in *My Journey to Lhasa,* chap. 8. She adds that most of the spectators were drunk by this time.
A "solid, solemn": Gould, *Jewel in the Lotus,* p. 218.

66 *He was more eager:* Gould, *Jewel in the Lotus,* p. 231.

67 *"The contrasts and rhythms":* Knud Larsen and Amund Sinding-Larsen, *The Lhasa Atlas: Traditional Tibetan Architecture and Townscape* (London: Serindia, 2001), p. 104.
around 1.3 million square feet: Gyurme Dorje, *Tibet Handbook,* 4th ed. (Bath: Footprint, 2008), p. 97.

69 *200,000 pearls:* Dorje, *Tibet Handbook,* p. 102. I wonder who counted them.
"devotion and love": Khemey Sonam Wangdu, Basil J. Gould, and Hugh E. Richardson, *Discovery, Recognition and Enthronement of the 14th Dalai Lama: A Collection of Accounts* (Dharamsala: Library of Tibetan Works and Archives, 2000), p. 79.
"ancient and decrepit": Dalai Lama, *Freedom in Exile,* p. 22.
ran with urine: Dalai Lama, *Freedom in Exile,* p. 23.

70 *millions of mantras:* When, for example, the Great Fifth Dalai Lama fell ill in 1681, the monks of Doenye Ling Monastery recited the *mig tse ma* no fewer than 21,750,000 times. This was followed by a complete recitation of the 108 volumes of the *kangyur* a total of 108 times by thousands of novice monks throughout the country, recitation of the Perfection of Wisdom in Eight Thousand Lines three times, the *bhadracari* 199,500 times, the *namasangiti* 59,300 times, the Sadhana of the Goddess of the White Umbrella 105,500 times, the Heart of the Perfection of Wisdom 149,300 times, the Hymn to Tara 1,043,600 times, and the Life Dharani 9,533,000 times. See *Sans-rgyas rgya-mtsho: Life of the Fifth Dalai Lama,* trans. Ahmed Zahiruddin (New Delhi: Academy of Indian Culture, 1999). According to Georges Dreyfus, the monasteries are indeed "first and foremost ritual communities." Georges B. J. Dreyfus, *The Sound of Two Hands Clapping: The Education of a Tibetan Buddhist Monk* (Berkeley: University of California Press, 2003), p. 44.
"lazy, stupid": Pemba, *Young Days in Tibet,* p. 80.

71 dob dob: The best descriptions of *dob dob* culture are to be found in Tashi Khedrup, *Adventures of a Tibetan Fighting Monk,* ed. Hugh Richardson (Bangkok: Orchid Press, 2003). See also Melvyn C. Goldstein, "A Study of the Ldab Ldob," *Central Asiatic Journal* 9, no. 2 (1964): pp. 123–41; and Kawaguchi, *Three Years in Tibet,* esp. the chapter titled "Warrior Priests of Sera." According to Kawaguchi, "the beauty of young boys was a frequent cause" of fighting, "and the theft of a boy [would] often lead to a duel"
(p. 292). Kawaguchi, himself an ordained *bhikku,* speaks of "nights . . . abused as occasions for indulging in fearful malpractices. They [the *dob dob*] really seem to be the descendants of the men of Sodom and Gomorrah mentioned in the bible" (p. 470).
tough looking: Pemba, *Young Days in Tibet,* pp. 80–81. According to Dreyfus, *dob dob* are forbidden in the monasteries in exile (*Two Hands Clapping,* p. 345, n. 25).

7. Boyhood

74 *"death held no fears":* Tsewang Y. Pemba, *Young Days in Tibet* (London: Jonathan Cape, 1957), pp. 112, 113.

75 *a "raised seat":* The account of Ling Rinpoché is drawn from Dalai Lama, *The Life of My*

Teacher: A Biography of Kyabje Ling Rinpoché (Somerville, MA: Wisdom Publications, 2017), pp. 147–48, 371, 129, 101, 120.

76 *A relatively recent:* I do not remember who told me this story, but I have no difficulty believing it. Georges B. J. Dreyfus, *The Sound of Two Hands Clapping: The Education of a Tibetan Buddhist Monk* (Berkeley: University of California Press, 2003), provides the best account of the life and culture of a modern Tibetan monastery.

77 *From your place:* Free translation by the author, with acknowledgments to Dr. T. J. Langri.

78 *the hand of a high lama:* Melvyn C. Goldstein, *A History of Modern Tibet: 1913–1951,* vol. 1, *The Demise of the Lamaist State* (Berkeley: University of California Press, 1991), p. 465. The Dalai Lama is himself an accomplished marksman. In days gone by, he would use an air rifle to scare any cats he caught stalking birds.

79 *After eating:* Goldstein, *History of Modern Tibet,* 1:344.
these rumors: See Goldstein, *History of Modern Tibet,* vol. 1, chap. 9. Further details are supplied in Jamyang Choegyal Kasho, *In the Service of the 13th and 14th Dalai Lamas* (Frankfurt am Main, Tibethaus Deutschland, 2015), chap. 10.
homosexual relationships: When one is considering the issue of homosexuality within the monasteries, it is important to be clear that traditional Tibetan culture does not recognize homosexuality either as an identity or as a category of human nature. It is only homosexual acts that are acknowledged. Similarly, so far as the *vinaya,* or code of conduct for monastics, is concerned, only those acts involving penetration are actually considered an infraction of the root vow of chastity. Non-penetrative acts are considered lesser infractions and were generally overlooked. It was by no means unusual for older monks to take younger monks as sexual consorts. But while this was generally consensual it need not imply that the passive partner regarded the activity as anything more than a duty. The authoritative account is in Melvyn C. Goldstein, *The Struggle for Modern Tibet: The Autobiography of Tashi Tsering* (London: Routledge, 1997), pp. 28–29. See also Heinrich Harrer, *Seven Years in Tibet* (London: R. Hart-Davis, 1953), p. 194; and Tashi Khedrup, *Adventures of a Tibetan Fighting Monk,* ed. Hugh Richardson (Bangkok: Orchid Press, 2003), p. 50.

80 *"the orphan's box":* Kasho, *In the Service,* p. 118.

81 *"a very gentle man":* Dalai Lama, *Freedom in Exile: The Autobiography of His Holiness the Dalai Lama of Tibet* (London: Hodder & Stoughton, 1990), p. 19.
dictatorial: See, for example, Thomas Laird, *The Story of Tibet: Conversations with the Dalai Lama* (London: Atlantic, 2006), p. 277. Archibald Steele, *In the Kingdom of the Dalai Lama* (Sedona, AZ: In Print Publishing, 1993), p. 60, describes him as "a paragon of conservatism."

82 *"perverted intentions": The Magical Play of Illusion: The Autobiography of Trijang Rinpoche,* trans. Sharpa Tulku Tenzin Trinley (Somerville, MA: Wisdom Publications, 2018), pp. 100, 114, 91.

83 *"His Holiness seemed":* Trijang, *The Magical Play of Illusion,* p. 148.

introduced the sport: Basil Gould, *Jewel in the Lotus: Recollections of an Indian Political* (London: Chatto & Windus, 1957), p. 207.
Thomas Manning: For his remarkable story, see my *Secret Lives of the Dalai Lama* (New York: Random House, 2008), pp. 318–21.
"immediately impressed": Ilia Tolstoy, "Across Tibet from India to China," *National Geographic* 90, no. 2 (1946): 169–222.
84 *"such a happy time":* Dalai Lama, *Freedom in Exile,* p. 51.
85 *publicly censured:* The edict was seen and included in translation by the British mission in its weekly dispatch to India. Goldstein, *History of Modern Tibet,* 1:373.
86 *"They came to treat me":* Gyalo Thondup with Anne F. Thurston, *The Noodle Maker of Kalimpong: The Untold Story of My Struggle for Tibet* (London: Rider, 2015), p. 73. Madam Chiang seems to have been genuinely solicitous of Gyalo Thondup. It was apparently she who, following the death of the *yabshi kung,* arranged for a private aircraft to fly the brothers' grandmother and sister to India. See Diki Tsering, *The Dalai Lama, My Son: A Mother's Story* (London: Virgin, 2000), p. 127.

8. Trouble in Shangri-La

88 *"When he left":* Dalai Lama, *Freedom in Exile: The Autobiography of His Holiness the Dalai Lama of Tibet* (London: Hodder & Stoughton, 1990), p. 21.
"They were full of fun": Thomas Laird, *The Story of Tibet: Conversations with the Dalai Lama* (London: Atlantic, 2006), pp. 277, 274.
Arko Lhamo: Laird, *The Story of Tibet,* p. 278.
90 *"laughed uncontrollably": The Magical Play of Illusion: The Autobiography of Trijang Rinpoche,* trans. Sharpa Tulku Tenzin Trinley (Somerville, MA: Wisdom Publications, 2018), p. 163.
91 *gave him a warm welcome:* Melvyn C. Goldstein, *A History of Modern Tibet: 1913–1951,* vol. 1, *The Demise of the Lamaist State* (Berkeley: University of California Press, 1991), pp. 441–42. The abbot eventually returned to Tibet as a collaborator of the Communists.
he would support them: Goldstein, *History of Modern Tibet,* 1:466.
92 *"misinforming" her son:* Diki Tsering, *The Dalai Lama, My Son: A Mother's Story* (London: Virgin, 2000), p. 120.
whether or not the accusation: Jamyang Norbu, for one, disputes it. See his "Shadow Tibet" blog post for June 29, 2016, "Untangling a Mess of Petrified Noodles," jamyang norbu.com.
93 *incontrovertible evidence:* See the section of a speech where the Dalai Lama mentions Reting Rinpoché at https://www.dalailama.com/messages/dolgyal-shugden/speeches-by-his-holiness-the-dalai-lama/dharamsala-teaching. I discussed the Reting episode at length with H. E. Richardson, British political officer for Tibet at the time, at his home in St. Andrews, Scotland. He admitted that he had absolutely no inkling of what was going on in government circles before the affair erupted.
94 *a horse called Yudrug:* Goldstein, *History of Modern Tibet,* 1:486.

he hesitated: Goldstein, *History of Modern Tibet,* 1:488.

95 *"At last":* Dalai Lama, *Freedom in Exile,* p. 33.

alert to the danger: Laird, *The Story of Tibet,* p. 185.

"like the call": Goldstein, *History of Modern Tibet,* 1:499.

96 *Around thirty:* Goldstein, *History of Modern Tibet,* 1:505. With respect to the government's losses, I include the sixteen soldiers subsequently killed at Reting. See also the account in Jamyang Choegyal Kasho, *In the Service of the 13th and 14th Dalai Lamas* (Frankfurt am Main: Tibethaus Deutschland, 2015), chap. 10.

no room to maneuver: Goldstein, *History of Modern Tibet,* 1:505. See also Laird, *The Story of Tibet,* p. 287.

"my position was hopeless": Laird, *The Story of Tibet,* p. 287.

98 *"The officials started bullying him":* Laird, *The Story of Tibet,* p. 279.

his first attempt at driving: The story is charmingly told by the Dalai Lama in *Freedom in Exile,* pp. 42–43.

9. The Perfection of Wisdom

99 *"did his best":* Dalai Lama, *The Life of My Teacher: A Biography of Kyabje Ling Rinpoché* (Somerville, MA: Wisdom Publications, 2017), p. 153. I think it fair to assume that in likening himself to a boat cut adrift, the Dalai Lama has in mind the perils of a Himalayan torrent.

107 *"smiled when asked":* Lowell Thomas, *Out of This World* (London: Macdonald and Co., 1951), p. 155.

a Catholic missionary: This was Father Maurice Tournay, a Swiss priest later declared Blessed by Pope John Paul II for having died "in odium fidei"—at the hand of one motivated by hatred of the faith. His story is told in Robert Loup, *Martyr in Tibet* (Philadelphia: D. McKay and Co., 1956). The actual date of his martyrdom was August 11, 1949.

a link between the Nazis: An entertaining account may be found in Mark Hale, *Himmler's Crusade: The True Story of the Nazis' 1938 Expedition into Tibet* (London: Bantam Books, 2003).

108 *Schaefer and his men:* One of these was Bruno Beger, convicted in 1974 of having helped select a group of Jews whose skulls were to form the basis of a collection designed to show the subhuman characteristics of their possessors. An anthropologist by training, Beger was sentenced to a mere three years in prison, which in fact he never served. He subsequently became a regular, if embarrassing, attendee at Tibet-related events in Germany and abroad. I met him at a luncheon given by the Dalai Lama at London's five-star Grosvenor House Hotel in 1992. Although this was before the age of Wikipedia, it is nonetheless somewhat surprising that Beger should have been invited. I remember being told that he had been a Nazi, but presumably the details of his service were unknown to the organizers of the event, which was designed to bring together all those surviving Europeans who had visited Tibet prior to 1949. In retrospect, Beger struck me in conversation as both shamefaced about his past and unrepentant. Subsequent research shows

him to have been a deeply unpleasant character; see Heather Pringle's excellent and disturbing book *The Master Plan: Himmler's Scholars and the Holocaust* (London: Fourth Estate, 2006), pp. 260–62. Also present at the luncheon was Archie Jack, who as a young man had been a competitor at Hitler's Olympics and subsequently visited Lhasa. It was Jack who was responsible for setting free the flock of doves that the Führer was to have released at the opening ceremony. Furiously anti-Nazi, he told me later that at dinner with Tsarong Shapé, the Great Thirteenth's favorite, they had discussed the possibility of assassinating Hitler. Tsarong told him that if he could procure a lock of the German leader's hair, the matter could easily be arranged by monks adept at black magic.

an unambiguous link: See a useful article by Kalachakra scholar Alexander Berzin at https://studybuddhism.com/en/advanced-studies/history-culture/shambhala/the-nazi-connection-with-shambhala-and-tibet.

109 *"seemed less like":* Heinrich Harrer, *Seven Years in Tibet* (London: R. Hart-Davis, 1953), p. 248. The book was a huge best-seller when first published and has been continuously in print ever since. Harrer was modest and generous enough to point out that it was vastly more successful in English than in any other of the more than fifty languages into which it was translated, a success he attributed to his translator, Richard Graves —brother of the poet Robert Graves. It is certainly true that *Return to Tibet,* the book he published three decades later, reads as if written by somebody else entirely, and with greatly inferior literary talent.

"He seemed to me": Harrer, *Seven Years,* p. 249. Harrer was of humble background. Although he was university educated himself, his father had been a postal worker. I met Harrer on a number of occasions. Though well into his eighties by then, he was still full of life and interested in all matters Tibetan and struck me as down-to-earth and affable, just as the Dalai Lama describes him.

110 *"the utmost trouble":* Harrer, *Seven Years,* p. 249.

"he came running": Harrer, *Seven Years,* p. 257.

111 *caused him to change his mind:* This is the opinion expressed by Messner, the great Italian mountaineer, who knew Harrer. In an interview with *Die Welt,* he speaks of how Harrer's conduct after the war was quite different from his conduct before the war. See https://www.welt.de/print-welt/article189698/Einer-der-Zaehesten-seiner-Generation.html.

the romantic strain in fascist ideology: See Nicholas Goodrick-Clarke, *Black Sun: Aryan Cults, Esoteric Nazism, and the Politics of Identity* (New York: NYU Press, 2001), p. 4.

"elegant Tibetan characters": Harrer, *Seven Years,* pp. 253, 258.

mechanical devices: Harrer, *Seven Years.* p. 249.

"did not know": Harrer, *Seven Years,* pp. 253, 258.

112 *"convinced that by virtue":* Harrer, *Seven Years,* p. 255.

10. "Shit on their picnic!"

114 *"double-edged steel":* *The Magical Play of Illusion: The Autobiography of Trijang Rinpoche,* trans. Sharpa Tulku Tenzin Trinley (Somerville, MA: Wisdom Publications, 2018),

pp. 187–88. A highly placed source assures me that these "support substances" would have been actual rather than merely symbolic.

"the honourable": India Office Records quoted in Melvyn C. Goldstein, *A History of Modern Tibet: 1913–1951,* vol. 1, *The Demise of the Lamaist State* (Berkeley: University of California Press, 1991), p. 624.

115 *"in order that":* There are various translations. The earliest known is into Russian, dating from 1827; the earliest in English dates from 1880 (that of S. W. Bushell in *The Early History of Tibet from Chinese Sources*).

117 *"approached the microphone reverently":* Robert Ford, *Captured in Tibet* (London: G. Harrap and Co., 1957), p. 64.

"thirty or forty" dull explosions: See Heinrich Harrer, *Seven Years in Tibet* (London: R. Hart-Davis, 1953), p. 259; Dalai Lama, *Freedom in Exile: The Autobiography of His Holiness the Dalai Lama of Tibet* (London: Hodder & Stoughton, 1990), p. 55.

"blazing summer weather": Harrer, *Seven Years,* p. 260.

"Give the Dalai Lama": Harrer, *Seven Years,* p. 263.

119 *"Right now":* Goldstein, *History of Modern Tibet,* 1:692.

120 *"people . . . running"*: Ford, *Captured,* p. 127.

charged with being a British spy: All quotations are drawn from his obituary in the *Daily Telegraph,* October 6, 2016; but see also his memoir *Captured in Tibet* (London: G. Harrap and Co., 1957).

122 *"If you don't make good offerings":* Goldstein, *History of Modern Tibet,* 1:705.

123 *For as long:* Dalai Lama, *Freedom in Exile,* p. 314.

124 *a famous oracle:* The story of how the oracle was (quite recently) identified is instructive. The phenomenon of people—not just monks—falling into a trance during religious ceremonies is common, but not all of them communicate intelligibly. I recall hearing someone do so during a dawn ceremony on the roof of the Tsuglhakang in Dharamsala. It sounded like the hoarse barking of a fox. Nor is it the case that when they do communicate intelligibly they are channeling anyone important. It could be just a ghost impersonating one of the protector deities. In the case of the Dungkhar oracle, it is said that a pilgrim who had traveled all the way from Mongolia asked for admittance at the monastery but was refused. Not only was he thrown out by one monk, but also he was abused and beaten by four others from whom he implored help. At this he left, uttering a curse that the five monks who had ill-treated him would all be dead within a year. Sure enough this came to pass, but not before another monk had fallen into a trance and begun "to jump about, beating his breast and making weird noises through clenched teeth." It was not until the five were dead that the deity could be understood. It turned out to be the spirit of the Mongolian pilgrim, through which no fewer than six different deities subsequently manifested. See Tsewang Y. Pemba, *Young Days in Tibet* (London: Jonathan Cape, 1957), p. 40.

the end of their natural life: The Second Dalai Lama's mother, Ma Cig Kinga, a famous renunciate, is an example. He kept her skull for use as a ritual chalice. See

Alexander Norman, *Secret Lives of the Dalai Lama* (New York: Random House, 2008), p. 173.

"followed its normal course": Harrer, *Seven Years,* p. 275.

"You are not allowed": Adapted from Melvyn C. Goldstein, *A History of Modern Tibet,* vol. 2, *The Calm Before the Storm, 1951–1955* (Berkeley: University of California Press, 2007), p. 182.

126 *"ever filled a man's belly":* Thubten Jigme Norbu, *Tibet Is My Country* (London: Rupert Hart Davis, 1960), p. 211.

bandits: Almost every European traveler mentions these, but so too does Dr. Pemba; see *Young Days in Tibet,* p. 51.

"petty injustices": Dalai Lama, *Freedom in Exile,* p. 64.

"It was heartbreaking": Trijang, *Magical Play,* p. 181.

Dungkar Monastery: When Archie Jack visited the monastery en route to Gyantse and then Lhasa just over a decade earlier, it had left a poor impression: "The monks were suspicious, filthy dirty (many of the young boys covered in large running sores). No photographs could be taken and altogether one had a very unpleasant, unclean, nauseating feeling on emerging from the place." Archibald Jack, unpublished Tibet journal, Royal Geographical Society, London. Against this, traveling the same route, Robert Byron, his near contemporary, wrote in his *First Russia, Then Tibet* (London: Macmillan, 1933), p. 206, that "from the monks we received nothing but hospitality and smiles," although it is clear that Byron did not actually visit Dungkar Monastery itself.

127 *horribly disfigured:* Pemba, *Young Days in Tibet,* p. 58.

"usual routine": Dalai Lama, *Freedom in Exile,* p. 65.

tantras are considered: The tantras are also associated with a system of sexual practices, their centrality to the tradition attested in the frequent depictions of the protectors united in sexual congress with a consort. Unsurprisingly, these practices are the source of much misunderstanding, but it is important to acknowledge that the Dalai Lama asserts their validity, going so far as to say that undertaking them physically during at least one lifetime is necessary for Enlightenment. Within the Gelug tradition generally, however, the practices are confined to the mental, not the physical plane.

The theory behind the sexual practices owes much to how the human being is conceived in relation to the cosmos. The tantras envisage a correspondence between the two such that the mind-body composite is in fact a microcosm of the universe itself. And just as the sun and the moon, the planets and the stars are held aloft by cosmic winds, so too the mind is held to be sustained by infinitesimally subtle internal winds that pass along the body's "wind channels." These winds are held to carry "drops" or seeds of potential, which, correctly utilized, enable the practitioner to have direct experience of non-duality. This in itself is an essential preparation for the ultimate attainment of full Enlightenment.

In mundane terms, what is required for the sexual practices actually to contribute toward the individual's spiritual progress is that one be able to engage in the most advanced meditative techniques. Without such ability, it will not be possible to exercise the necessary control over the body. It is not enough for the male merely to be able to prevent the release of seminal fluid, nor for the female to be able to control her climax. To obtain the highest spiritual insights, the practitioner must be in full control of the subtlest energies that are activated during sexual congress. Of the males, it is said that the most accomplished are able actually to reverse the flow of semen from the tip of the sex organ and withdraw it back down the shaft.

For an account by June Campbell of her experiences as a consort, see *Traveller in Space: Gender, Identity and Tibetan Buddhism* (London: Athlone, 1996). From Campbell's perspective, her relationship with Kalu Rinpoché, the Kagyu master, was ultimately exploitative. It is remarkable to learn that Kalu Rinpiche's reincarnation reports that he himself was sexually abused when a minor.

the kiss of a beautiful woman: John Crook and James Low, *The Yogins of Ladakh: A Pilgrimage Among the Hermits of the Buddhist Himalayas* (1997; Delhi: Motilal Banarsidass, 2012), p. 279.

128 *"that if they were so arrogant":* Rinchen Sadutshang, *A Life Unforeseen: A Memoir of Service to Tibet* (Somerville, MA: Wisdom Publications, 2016), p. 144.

129 *in radio contact:* Sadutshang, *A Life Unforeseen,* p. 145.

130 *"so great and powerful":* Gyalo Thondup with Anne F. Thurston, *The Noodle Maker of Kalimpong: The Untold Story of My Struggle for Tibet* (London: Rider, 2015), p. 146.

131 *"three men":* Dalai Lama, *Freedom in Exile,* p. 72.

11. Into the Dragon's Lair

133 *"many present":* Dalai Lama, *The Life of My Teacher: A Biography of Kyabje Ling Rinpoché* (Somerville, MA: Wisdom Publications, 2017), p. 163.

human flesh eaters: Melvyn C. Goldstein, *A History of Modern Tibet,* vol. 2, *The Calm Before the Storm, 1951–1955* (Berkeley: University of California Press, 2007), p. 206.

"in a short time": Goldstein, *History of Modern Tibet,* 2:206.

134 *"willing to help":* Goldstein, *History of Modern Tibet,* 2:149.

"challenged and confronted": Goldstein, *History of Modern Tibet,* 2:188 (quoting Lhalu), 181.

136 *"grand salvation":* Melvyn C. Goldstein, *A History of Modern Tibet: 1913–1951,* vol. 1, *The Demise of the Lamaist State* (Berkeley: University of California Press, 1989), p. 684.

unwilling to allow: Dalai Lama, *Freedom in Exile: The Autobiography of His Holiness the Dalai Lama of Tibet* (London: Hodder & Stoughton, 1990), p. 84.

"the Dalai Lama belongs": Goldstein, *History of Modern Tibet,* 2:442.

"if you take away the pastures": Jianglin Li, *Tibet in Agony: Lhasa, 1959* (Cambridge: Harvard University Press, 2016), p. 73.

137 *hold off:* Goldstein, *History of Modern Tibet,* 2:370.

"an ocean fraught": Dalai Lama, *Kalachakra Tantra: Rite of Initiation,* trans., ed., and with an introduction by Geoffrey Hopkins, enlarged ed. (Somerville, MA: Wisdom Publications, 1999), p. 178.

"lotus": Dalai Lama, *Kalachakra Tantra,* p. 95.

138 *"When we passed fourteen":* Mary Craig, *Kundun: A Biography of the Family of the Dalai Lama* (London: HarperCollins, 1997), pp. 184–85.

139 *social convention:* Jamyang Choegyal Kasho, *In the Service of the 13th and 14th Dalai Lamas* (Frankfurt am Main, Tibethaus Deutschland, 2015), p. 193.

"The aeroplane": Goldstein, *History of Modern Tibet,* 2:482.

140 *"shabby tents":* Trijang, *Magical Play,* p. 204.

spittle-smeared: Dalai Lama, *Freedom in Exile,* p. 93.

"Brahmins, outcasts and pigs": Trijang, *Magical Play,* p. 318.

141 *"The craft":* Dalai Lama, *Freedom in Exile,* p. 94.

taken to a house: Diki Tsering, *The Dalai Lama, My Son: A Mother's Story* (London: Virgin, 2000), p. 140.

"required to attend": Diki Tsering, *The Dalai Lama, My Son,* p. 140.

142 *the hypocrisy he witnessed:* Melvyn C. Goldstein, Dawei Sherap, and William R. Siebenschuh, *A Tibetan Revolutionary: The Political Life and Times of Bapa Phüntso Wangye* (Berkeley: University of California Press, 2004), pp. 53, 90.

"elegantly dressed": Goldstein, Sherap, and Siebenschuh, *A Tibetan Revolutionary,* p. 72.

143 *"anyone who couldn't pay":* Goldstein, Sherap, and Siebenschuh, *A Tibetan Revolutionary,* pp. 72, 55.

"act like the great leader": Goldstein, Sherap, and Siebenschuh, *A Tibetan Revolutionary,* p. 191.

144 *"one of the main fabrications":* Goldstein, *History of Modern Tibet,* 2:494–95.

"when dealing with": https://www.dalailama.com/messages/dolgyal-shugden/speeches-by-his-holiness-the-dalai-lama/dharamsala-teaching (accessed March 21, 2019).

145 *"not to let the lamas dance":* Goldstein, Sherap, and Siebenschuh, *A Tibetan Revolutionary,* p. 191.

"extremely alert": Goldstein, Sherap, and Siebenschuh, *A Tibetan Revolutionary,* p. 191.

"Meeting often": Goldstein, Sherap, and Siebenschuh, *A Tibetan Revolutionary,* pp. 191, 193.

146 *"silly. Wasteful":* Goldstein, *History of Modern Tibet,* 2:504.

"extremely interested": Goldstein, Sherap, and Siebenschuh, *A Tibetan Revolutionary,* p. 192.

film footage: It is easily found on YouTube; see www.youtube.com.

"eager to learn": Goldstein, Sherap, and Siebenschuh, *A Tibetan Revolutionary,* p. 192.

"From morning till evening": Diki Tsering, *The Dalai Lama, My Son,* p. 140.

147 *"I could plainly read":* Rinchen Sadutshang, *A Life Unforeseen: A Memoir of Service to Tibet* (Somerville, MA: Wisdom Publications, 2016), p. 180.

bag of tsampa*:* Sadutshang, *A Life Unforeseen,* p. 182.

"with a mischievous expression": Dalai Lama, *Freedom in Exile,* pp. 107, 108.

12. The Land of the Gods

148 *"had become wretched":* Diki Tsering, *The Dalai Lama, My Son: A Mother's Story* (London: Virgin, 2000), p. 145.

149 *June 30, 1955:* Several different dates have been proposed for the Dalai Lama's homecoming. I use the one he himself gives in *The Life of My Teacher: A Biography of Kyabje Ling Rinpoché* (Somerville, MA: Wisdom Publications, 2017), p. 191.

"miraculous iron pills": *The Magical Play of Illusion: The Autobiography of Trijang Rinpoche*, trans. Sharpa Tulku Tenzin Trinley (Somerville, MA: Wisdom Publications, 2018), pp. 336, 343.

"lord": Melvyn C. Goldstein, *A History of Modern Tibet,* vol. 3, *The Storm Clouds Descend, 1955–1957* (Berkeley: University of California Press, 2014), p. 31.

news started: Rinchen Sadutshang, *A Life Unforeseen: A Memoir of Service to Tibet* (Somerville, MA: Wisdom Publications, 2016), p. 189.

150 *"liberation, Tibet could see":* Alan Winnington, *Tibet: Record of a Journey* (London: Lawrence and Wishart, 1957), p. 132.

"harboured a low opinion": Trijang, *Magical Play,* p. 340.

"even the insects": Goldstein, *History of Modern Tibet,* 3:71–72.

152 *the all-powerful British:* While there was undoubtedly much to draw inspiration from, remarkably, the British population of India, including wives, children, and traders, along with government and military personnel, was only around 150,000 at the end of the nineteenth century, while the general population approached 300 million. The British population may have increased somewhat during the early twentieth century, but it seems never to have risen above 250,000. See, e.g., https://history.stackexchange.com/questions/15298/how-many-britons-lived-in-india-during-the-british-raj-1858-1947. The skill of the British had been to flatter the Indian princes and play the different states off against one another with minimal effort on their part. The other crucial ingredient for Mahatma Gandhi's success was, arguably, the conquerors' residual allegiance to the teachings of Christ's Sermon on the Mount, which the Mahatma had made central to his political philosophy.

"On this matter": Goldstein, *History of Modern Tibet,* 3:95.

the nomad chieftain: The chieftain's name was Yoenrupoen. See Goldstein, *History of Modern Tibet,* 3:133ff.

153 *"If someone supported the CCP":* Goldstein, *History of Modern Tibet,* 3:139.

"stabbed to death": Goldstein, *History of Modern Tibet,* 3:230.

correct motivation: There are other supports for compassionately motivated violence; see, for example, Jacob Dalton, *Taming the Demons* (New Haven: Yale University Press, 2011).

"where the motive is good": Roger Hicks and Chogyam Ngakpa, *Great Ocean, an Authorised Biography: The Dalai Lama* (Shaftesbury, Dorset: Element Books, 1984), p. 162.

154 *"the Tibetans were going out":* Goldstein, *History of Modern Tibet,* 3:234.
the damage: Incorrectly, it was inferred that this had been inflicted by the bombers, mentioned in the article accompanying the photograph. This was further conflated with rumors (which turned out to be true) that Batang Monastery had also been bombed. Melvyn C. Goldstein, *A History of Modern Tibet,* vol. 2, *The Calm Before the Storm, 1951–1955* (Berkeley: University of California Press, 2007), p. 238.
"I cried": Dalai Lama, *Freedom in Exile: The Autobiography of His Holiness the Dalai Lama of Tibet* (London: Hodder & Stoughton, 1990), p. 121.

155 *"How are Tibetans":* Dalai Lama, *Freedom in Exile,* pp. 121–22.
"filled with awe": Sadutshang, *A Life Unforeseen,* p. 159.
"anxious to leave": John Kenneth Knaus, *Orphans of the Cold War: America and the Tibetan Struggle for Survival* (New York: PublicAffairs, 1999), p. 131.

156 *no attempt had been made:* See the description in Trijang, *Magical Play,* p. 351.
"It must be anticipated": Goldstein, *History of Modern Tibet,* 3:338–39.
"probably perished": Tsewang Y. Pemba, *Young Days in Tibet* (London: Jonathan Cape, 1957), p. 131.
"their real feelings": Dalai Lama, *Freedom in Exile,* p. 127.
"was not made easier": Nari Rustomji, *Enchanted Frontiers: Sikkim, Bhutan and India's North-Eastern Borderlands* (Oxford: Oxford University Press, 1971), pp. 123, 215.

157 *We had hardly passed:* Rustomji, *Enchanted Frontiers,* pp. 215, 216.

158 *"It was evident":* Rustomi's observation regarding the Panchen Lama was perceptive. The lama subsequently married the daughter of a senior Chinese Nationalist army officer. I had the honor once of meeting the Panchen Lama's daughter, whose business card, printed on pink stock, identified her unexpectedly as a princess.
"Their views": Goldstein, *History of Modern Tibet,* 3:343.

159 *"It was a calm and beautiful":* Dalai Lama, *Freedom in Exile,* p. 127.
did not share: That said, there were undoubtedly some modernists within the Nehru government who thought Tibetan Buddhism was a hilarious concoction of falsehoods. See the remarks of Apa Pant quoted in Goldstein, *History of Modern Tibet,* 3:364.
"as full of charm": Dalai Lama, *Freedom in Exile,* p. 129.
happy to supply: Goldstein, *History of Modern Tibet,* 3:377.

160 *"but one scholar": The Political Philosophy of the XIVth Dalai Lama: Selected Speeches and Writings* (Delhi: Tibetan Parliamentary and Policy Research Centre, 1998), p. 5.
made it back: Sadutshang, *A Life Unforeseen,* pp. 196–97.

161 *"At first he listened":* Dalai Lama, *Freedom in Exile,* pp. 128, 129. As I recall, the Dalai Lama originally said in his book that Nehru did in fact drift off briefly, but it was decided during the editing process to spare the blushes of his Indian readers. Ted Heath, the former British prime minister, whom he met during the early 1980s, likewise fell asleep during a meeting with the Dalai Lama.
the (Chinese) transcripts: See Goldstein, *History of Modern Tibet,* vol. 2, chap. 11, "The Dalai Lama Visits India."

"At first when you say": Goldstein, 3:422.

162 *enjoyed a vision:* William Meyers, Robert Thurman, and Michael G. Burbank, *Man of Peace: The Illustrated Life Story of the Dalai Lama of Tibet* (New York: Tibet House, 2016), p. 84. I am assuming he saw this vision while meditating.

"hell realms": Trijang, *Magical Play,* pp. 355–56.

163 *"There was a lot of submissiveness":* Kenneth Conboy and James Morrison, *The CIA's Secret War in Tibet* (Lawrence: University Press of Kansas, 2002), p. 33.

"please arrange": Knaus, *Orphans of the Cold War,* p. 297.

164 *"When men become desperate":* Dalai Lama, *Freedom in Exile,* p. 132.

165 *such a plot:* Goldstein, *History of Modern Tibet,* 3:431. The only written account is that of General Fan Ming himself in his autobiography.

"being returned to prison": Trijang, *Magical Play,* p. 218.

13. "Don't sell the Dalai Lama for silver dollars!"

166 *Zhou Enlai's promises:* Melvyn C. Goldstein, *A History of Modern Tibet,* vol. 3, *The Storm Clouds Descend, 1955–1957* (Berkeley: University of California Press, 2014), pp. 445–51.

far fewer: see Jianglin Li, "When the Iron Bird Flies: The 1956–1962 Secret War on the Tibetan Plateau," unpublished ms., trans. Stacey Mosher, p. 117.

167 *performing the ritual:* Goldstein, *History of Modern Tibet,* 3:44. See also *The Magical Play of Illusion: The Autobiography of Trijang Rinpoche*, trans. Sharpa Tulku Tenzin Trinley (Somerville, MA: Wisdom Publications, 2018), p. 359.

"a very bad show": Goldstein, *History of Modern Tibet,* 3:44. In fact, many Tashilhunpo monks did attend in the end, but that was clearly not the monastery authorities' intention.

168 *"with tears filling my eyes":* Dalai Lama, *The Life of My Teacher: A Biography of Kyabje Ling Rinpoché* (Somerville, MA: Wisdom Publications, 2017), p. 189.

The work of: See http://www.jamyangnorbu.com/blog/2014/09/27/the-political-vision-of-andrugtsang-gompo-tashi/ (accessed November 1, 2017).

169 *"brave, honest and strong":* Kenneth Conboy and James Morrison, *The CIA's Secret War in Tibet* (Lawrence: University Press of Kansas, 2002), p. 55.

170 *"completely non-committal":* Conboy and Morrison, *Secret War,* p. 69.

"gesturing in the direction": See opening sequence of the documentary *The Shadow Circus: The CIA in Tibet.*

"to ward off colds": Conboy and Morrison, *Secret War,* p. 81.

171 *"monastery religious personnel":* Jianglin Li, *Tibet in Agony: Lhasa, 1959* (Cambridge: Harvard University Press, 2016), p. 50.

"we took a great leap": Li, *Tibet in Agony,* p. 55. The original population of Namthang township was just under two thousand.

"excellent": Li, "When the Iron Bird Flies," pp. 377, 164.

172 *an ambitious raid:* Conboy and Morrison, *Secret War,* p. 78.

progressed to Sera: See Dalai Lama, *Life of My Teacher,* pp. 190–91.

173 *"troubled state of mind":* Trijang, *Magical Play,* p. 228. Here I prefer the more literal translation of the first redaction.

geshe *exams:* For a description of the final examination of a Gelug monk, see Georges B. J. Dreyfus, *The Sound of Two Hands Clapping: The Education of a Tibetan Buddhist Monk* (Berkeley: University of California Press, 2003), pp. 256–59.

cabled a message: International Commission of Jurists, *The Question of Tibet and the Rule of Law* (Geneva, 1959), p. 9.

174 *had been canceled:* Here I follow Li, *Tibet in Agony,* pp. 100–101.

"cream of scholars": Dalai Lama, *Life of My Teacher,* p. 193.

175 *"hatching a plot":* Li, *Tibet in Agony,* p. 101.

"make short work": Li, *Tibet in Agony,* p. 105.

176 *"Maybe this isn't":* The autobiography of Phuntsog Tashi Taklha, the Dalai Lama's chief of security, quoted in Li, *Tibet in Agony,* p. 111. I had the honor of knowing Phuntsog Tashi when he lived in London. He was not a man of obvious military bearing.

"all-knowing Guru": Li, *Tibet in Agony,* p. 112. One might object here that if the Dalai Lama really was all-knowing, he would not need this or indeed any advice from the oracle. But actually the epithet "all-knowing" or "omniscient" is a common one used of high lamas to refer rather to their mastery of the doctrine.

177 *already been abducted:* Tsering Shakya, *The Dragon in the Land of Snows: A History of Modern Tibet Since 1947* (New York: Columbia University Press, 1999), p. 192.

beat him to death: Shakya, *Dragon in the Land of Snows,* p. 192. Goldstein also covers the incident in detail.

178 *"Don't forget":* Li, *Tibet in Agony,* p. 129.

179 *Tibet has always been free!:* Li, *Tibet in Agony,* p. 157.

"sitting anguished": Li, *Tibet in Agony,* pp. 135, 177.

volunteers congregated: Tubten Khetsun, *Memories of Life in Lhasa Under Chinese Rule,* trans. Matthew Akester (Delhi: Penguin for Columbia University Press, 2009), p. 29.

"not in any fear": My Land and My People: The Autobiography of His Holiness the Dalai Lama (London: Weidenfeld and Nicolson, 1962), p. 189.

"stop holding": Phuntsog Tashi Takhla, quoted in Li, *Tibet in Agony,* p. 150.

180 *"The reactionaries":* Li, *Tibet in Agony,* p. 178.

"the Tibetan people": Li, *Tibet in Agony,* pp. 162, 163.

181 *"He looked haggard":* Li, *Tibet in Agony,* pp. 179, 157.

"snatch the egg": From my conversations with Tenzin Geyche Tethong and Tendzin Choegyal, November 2018.

issued an order: Li, *Tibet in Agony,* p. 159.

"keep open the dialogue": Dalai Lama, *Freedom in Exile: The Autobiography of His Holiness the Dalai Lama of Tibet* (London: Hodder & Stoughton, 1990), p. 148.

"If you think it necessary": Li, *Tibet in Agony,* p. 184.

182 *"Someone bearing the name":* Trijang, *Magical Play,* p. 245.

183 *"a large gold brick":* Li, *Tibet in Agony,* p. 200.

184 *"no one looked up":* Dalai Lama, *Freedom in Exile,* p. 151.

14. On the Back of a *Dzo*

187 *It turns out:* I am immensely grateful to Dr. Jianglin Li and to Professor Melvyn Goldstein, both of whom not only shared much unpublished material with me but also took the trouble to enter into lengthy discussions with respect to the question as to whether, as some have claimed, the Chinese deliberately allowed the Dalai Lama to escape. Professor Goldstein inclines to this view; Dr. Li inclines the other way.

Both, surely, are right, albeit in different ways. It is true, as Professor Goldstein points out, that Mao made clear as early as 1956 that he was not worried about the Dalai Lama quitting Lhasa to live abroad. Mao maintained this position consistently, at least until March 16. As Dr. Li points out, however, it is evident that, at the Politburo meeting on March 17, the day the Dalai Lama fled the Norbulingka, this policy had changed. In essence, now it was "best to try to keep the Dalai Lama in Lhasa. *However, if he leaves, it is not a big deal*" (Wen Feng, "Tan Guansan Jiangjun Zhihui Lasa Pingpan Shimo" [The Complete Story of How General Tan Guansan Put Down the Rebellion], *Wenshi Jinghua* 228 [May 2009]: 4–13). No minutes of this meeting have been published, but the three accounts of it that we do have all concur on this point. What is not entirely clear is whether this was Mao's directive, communicated to Zhang Jingwu, Zhang Guohua, and Huang Kecheng, whom he had summoned to his temporary headquarters at Wuhan, and who had arrived back in Beijing on the train that day, or whether this was the Politburo's collective view. Either way, it is clear that there had been a change of plan. What we also do not know is when General Tan was made aware of this change. There is no paper trail. The Politburo meeting took place during the afternoon of March 17. It could be that its instructions were communicated immediately afterwards via telephone. It could also be that a cable was sent either on the evening of the same day or sometime the following day. What is clear is that if Tan did receive the instruction on the seventeenth, he did nothing about it. Although he would have had only a few hours to act, he could at least have sent out one or more night patrols that evening; he could have alerted the informants he would certainly have had on the ground to look out for and report any suspicious movements around the Norbulingka; he could have ordered one or more checkpoints to be established on the road leading away from the Norbulingka. It is evident that he did not.

It is thus correct to say that the Chinese allowed the Dalai Lama to escape, but this was rather an act of omission than an act of commission. They were clearly aware that he might attempt to withdraw from Lhasa, but they did not knowingly permit him to do so—unless we accept at face value the anecdote supplied by Professor Goldstein's interviewee Li Zuomin, who recounted that an official at the Norbulingka, Goshampa, had contacted Ngabo (by what means is not stated) on the seventeenth to inform him that the Dalai Lama planned to leave that night. Ngabo is said to have passed the message by telephone to Li, who in turn informed General Tan. Tan then called Beijing for instructions. He was told to let the Dalai Lama go.

The trouble here is that for this to be correct, Tan's interlocutor in Beijing would have had to ignore the Politburo's instruction issued earlier that day. This seems implausible. From other evidence, it also clear that Tan did not, in fact, learn until the nineteenth that the Dalai Lama had fled, and indeed it was not until that day that he informed Beijing. There is also no other evidence to corroborate Li Zuomin's claim. Could he have been lying? It is certainly not unknown even for retired officials to fabricate evidence to save face for the institution they served.

To me, the most likely sequence is that the Chinese maintained a permissive policy toward the possibility of the Dalai Lama's withdrawing right up until the seventeenth, changing it only on that day. Very likely General Tan was made aware of this change in the early evening of the same day, but, following receipt of the Dalai Lama's letter saying that he would like to take up the general's offer to come to the PLA for safety, Tan did not act on his new instructions immediately.

Subsequently no effort was made to capture the Precious Protector on account of the instruction "not to worry" should he in fact succeed in getting away. But with the caveat regarding the putative evidence supplied by Li Zuomin, this does not amount to the Chinese leadership knowingly permitting the Dalai Lama to leave. If Li Zuomin's evidence is true, why have the Chinese not published the communiqués between Lhasa and Beijing that were sent on March 18? The reason is surely that it would be embarrassing to do so.

"and his cohorts": Mao's cable of March 12 has not been published in its entirety, but a summary is quoted in Jianglin Li, *Tibet in Agony: Lhasa, 1959* (Cambridge: Harvard University Press, 2016), p. 167.

"do everything possible": Jianglin Li, "When the Iron Bird Flies: The 1956–1962 Secret War on the Tibetan Plateau," unpublished ms., trans. Stacey Mosher, p. 264.

"the least harm": The Magical Play of Illusion: The Autobiography of Trijang Rinpoche, trans. Sharpa Tulku Tenzin Trinley (Somerville, MA: Wisdom Publications, 2018), p. 245.

188 *"I found it extremely difficult":* Dalai Lama, *Freedom in Exile: The Autobiography of His Holiness the Dalai Lama of Tibet* (London: Hodder & Stoughton, 1990), p. 152.

mixed up: This story is told by Trijang Rinpoché in his autobiography but not in the published English-language version, *Magical Play.*

189 *"must deliberate profoundly":* See Sumner Carnahan and Lama Kunga Rinpoche, *In the Presence of My Enemies: Memoirs of Tibetan Nobleman Tsipon Shuguba* (Santa Fe, NM: Heartsfire Books, 1998), p. 4.

seal off: Li, *Tibet in Agony,* pp. 234, 243, 235.

190 *"countless guns":* Carnahan and Lama Kunga Rinpoche, *In the Presence,* p. 4.

191 *One alternative they considered:* http://www.atimes.com/article/dalai-lama-prefer-exile-myanmar-india/ (accessed December 10, 2018).
a full six days: Carnahan and Lama Kunga Rinpoche, *In the Presence of My Enemies,* pp. 4–5.
192 *A famous photograph:* See Jamyang Choegyal Kasho, *In the Service of the 13th and 14th Dalai Lamas* (Frankfurt am Main: Tibethaus Deutschland, 2015), p. 205.
Prisoners caught saying prayers: Besides the oral histories collected by various organizations, such as the International Commission of Jurists and the Library of Tibetan Works and Archives, there are several good firsthand accounts of the period available in English. One of the most thorough is that of Tubten Khetsun (*Memories of Life in Lhasa Under Chinese Rule,* trans. Matthew Akester [Delhi: Penguin for Columbia University Press, 2009]), a minor aristocrat who served in the Dalai Lama's administration. Also useful is the biography of Kabshoba, a minister, by his son Jamyang Choegyal Kasho (*In the Service*). The autobiographies of Phuntsog Wangyal and Tashi Tsering give a flavor of the miseries of life in prison in Beijing. Probably the most famous is that of Palden Gyatso (*Fire Under the Snow: The True Story of a Tibetan Monk* [London: Harvill Press, 1997]), kept a prisoner for three decades, but other useful accounts are given in Shuguba (Carnahan and Lama Kunga Rinpoche, *In the Presence of My Enemies*) and Khetsun. David Patt, *A Strange Liberation: Tibetan Lives in Chinese Hands* (Ithaca: Snow Lion Publications, 1993), provides the stories of Ama Adhe, a nomad woman and mother of two incarcerated for over twenty years, and Tenpa Soepa, a government official jailed for a similar period. Of course, these should all be read with a critical eye, but the increasing availability of Chinese sources, especially those provided by Jianglin Li (*Tibet in Agony* and "When the Iron Bird Flies"), goes a long way toward substantiating even the more horrific of the claims made.
193 *This made plain:* See Li, *Tibet in Agony,* p. 301.
194 *most surprised:* See the report for April 5, 1959, of Har Mander Singh, the Indian political officer based at Tawang, http://www.claudearpi.net/wp-content/uploads/2018/03/April-5-Report-on-the-entry-of-His-Holiness-the-Dalai-Lama-into-India.pdf (accessed December 11, 2018).
an airplane might be sent: Li, *Tibet in Agony,* p. 304.
the last Tibetan villages: This second night was in fact passed at a monastery a short distance away from the fortress. Li, *Tibet in Agony,* p. 305.
a large aircraft: Amazingly, the moment was captured on film. It can be seen near the beginning of the documentary *The Shadow Circus,* part 3.
no markings: Dr. Jianglin Li concurs that the lack of markings means that it could not have been Chinese.

15. Opening the Eye of New Awareness

196 *"We do not yet know":* http://www.archieve.claudearpi.net/maintenance/uploaded_pics/590330_Nehru_to_Rajedra_Prasad.pdf (accessed November 21, 2018).

197 *no interviews: Time* nonetheless put the story on its cover for April 15, 1959, under the headline "THE ESCAPE THAT ROCKED THE REDS." An early account can be found in Noel Barber, *The Flight of the Dalai Lama* (London: Hodder & Stoughton, 1960).
"for their spontaneous": The full text may be read in *The Political Philosophy of the Dalai Lama: Selected Speeches and Writings,* ed. Dr. Subash C. Kashyap (New Delhi: Rupa, 2014), pp. 3–5.
"The so-called statement": Dalai Lama, *My Land and My People: The Autobiography of His Holiness the Dalai Lama* (London: Weidenfeld and Nicolson, 1962), p. 218.
"to invoke the commitment": Dalai Lama, *The Life of My Teacher: A Biography of Kyabje Ling Rinpoché* (Somerville, MA: Wisdom Publications, 2017), p. 200.
"immediately one of irritation": Quoted in Lobsang Gyatso Sither, *Exile: A Photo Journal, 1959–1989* (Dharamsala: Tibet Documentation, 2017), p. 15.

198 *"his lower lip":* Dalai Lama, *Freedom in Exile: The Autobiography of His Holiness the Dalai Lama of Tibet* (London: Hodder & Stoughton, 1990), p. 161.
"focus . . . on religious practice": The Magical Play of Illusion: The Autobiography of Trijang Rinpoche, trans. Sharpa Tulku Tenzin Trinley (Somerville, MA: Wisdom Publications, 2018), p. 253.

200 *"tyranny and oppression":* International Commission of Jurists, *The Question of Tibet and the Rule of Law* (Geneva, 1959), pp. 197–98.
"one of the most impressive": Mikel Dunham, *Buddha's Warriors: The Story of the CIA-Backed Tibetan Freedom Fighters, the Chinese Invasion, and the Ultimate Fall of Tibet* (New York: Jeremy P. Tarcher/Penguin, 2004), p. 332. For an unexpected account of the resistance fighters, see also Chris Mullin, *Hinterland* (London: Profile Books, 2017).

201 *generous supply of war matériel:* Among the supplies were 370 M1 rifles with 192 rounds for each one, four machine guns with a thousand rounds apiece, and two radio sets. A month later, a second drop delivered a similar quantity of weapons, including this time three recoilless rifles (or bazookas). A third delivery, on the night of the next full moon, comprised 226 pallets with eight hundred rifles, twenty cases of hand grenades, 113 carbines (presumably M4 close-quarter rifles), and two hundred cases of ammunition, each containing ten thousand rounds. A final drop onto Pemba in January 1960 was the largest of all. Three aircraft dropped a total of 657 pallets, which, in addition to a proportionately similar number of arms as the previous three drops, also included thirty cases of various first aid items, a dozen crates of food, and a mimeograph machine for producing propaganda. Among the food rations was a special *tsampa,* formulated for mountain warfare by Kellogg's. John Kenneth Knaus, *Orphans of the Cold War: America and the Tibetan Struggle for Survival* (New York: PublicAffairs, 1999), p. 280.
"At first we didn't believe": Dunham, *Buddha's Warriors,* p. 339.

202 *"one of the greatest intelligence hauls":* John Kenneth Knaus, speaking in the documentary *The Shadow Circus.*
"a remarkably effective": Knaus, *Orphans of the Cold War,* p. 2.
"Tibet had been": Knaus, *Orphans of the Cold War,* p. 330.

203 *"Dharamsala water":* Dalai Lama, *Freedom in Exile,* p. 173.
"his mother, his two sisters": John F. Avedon, *In Exile from the Land of Snows* (London: Michael Joseph, 1984), p. 86.

204 *suddenly able to enjoy:* Although rumors that he occasionally listened to Beatles records and that he wore jeans in private are false, it is true that he would sometimes forsake monastic robes and don a pair of "well-pressed" (as he once mentioned to me) trousers.
a small trekkers' hut: Avedon, *In Exile from the Land of Snows,* p. 86.
televised interviews: Both may be found on the Internet.

205 *"We exiled Tibetans": Speeches of His Holiness the XIVth Dalai Lama (1959–1989),* trans. Sonam Gyatso, vol. 1 (Dharamsala: Library of Tibetan Works and Archives, 2011), pp. 7–8, 3.
"The 'written oath'": Speeches of His Holiness, 1:14–15, 118.

206 *"Our foreign": Speeches of His Holiness,* 1:29, 31.
"They are, by nature": Speeches of His Holiness, 1:9, 36.

207 *"our worst mistake":* Pico Iyer, *The Open Road* (London: Bloomsbury, 2008), p. 228.
"We still have faults": Speeches of His Holiness.

208 *fifty-eight villages:* The number I use is that provided by the Central Tibetan Administration; see its Department of Home website, https://tibet.net/department/home/.
"many of the Tibetans": Avedon, *In Exile from the Land of Snows,* pp. 67, 85.

209 *"to be cautious":* Gyalo Thondup with Anne F. Thurston, *The Noodle Maker of Kalimpong: The Untold Story of My Struggle for Tibet* (London: Rider, 2015), p. 213.
less than a third: See Rinchen Sadutshang, *A Life Unforeseen: A Memoir of Service to Tibet* (Somerville, MA: Wisdom Publications, 2016), p. 241.

210 *four members:* Ginsberg, author of *Howl,* both the most celebrated and the most widely excoriated American poem of the 1950s, was a self-confessed pederast and early member of the North American Man/Boy Love Association. He later became a prominent member of the Buddhist community associated with Chogyam Trungpa. Orlovsky is probably best remembered, if indeed he is remembered at all, other than for his association with Ginsberg, for his strikingly titled collection *Clean Asshole Poems and Smiling Vegetable Songs.* Snyder gained a reputation as the poetic voice of Deep Ecology. Kyger, also a poet, taught for many years at Trungpa's Naropa community. It is not entirely clear whether Orlovsky was in fact present at the audience, as he was in the habit of "lock[ing] himself in the bathroom all night and smok[ing] opium" preparatory to vomiting "all the next morning." Joanne Kyger, *The Japan and India Journals, 1960–1964* (New York: Tombouctou Books, 1981), p. 193.
We met the Dalai Lama: Kyger, *The Japan and India Journals,* entry for April 11, 1962; letter to Nemi April 10, 1962, pp. 193–96.

211 *"a cadre of":* Stuart Gelder and Roma Gelder, *The Timely Rain* (London: Hutchinson and Co., 1964), p. 61.
"in the socialist paradise": A Poisoned Arrow: The Secret Report of the 10th Panchen Lama (London: Tibet Information Network, 1997), p. xvii.

212 *"poisoned arrow": A Poisoned Arrow,* pp. xx–xxi.
214 *protective talismans:* Trijang, *Magical Play,* p. 260.

16. "We cannot compel you"

215 *a "villain," a "liar":* Dalai Lama, *Freedom in Exile: The Autobiography of His Holiness the Dalai Lama of Tibet* (London: Hodder & Stoughton, 1990), pp. 199–200.

216 *deemed to have married:* Tubten Khetsun, *Memories of Life in Lhasa Under Chinese Rule,* trans. Matthew Akester (Delhi: Penguin for Columbia University Press, 2009), p. 138.

as the disparity: Khetsun, *Memories,* p. 107.

"the last priests": Stuart Gelder and Roma Gelder, *The Timely Rain* (London: Hutchinson and Co., 1964), p. 50. One wonders what the Gelders would have made of Drepung today, with its ten thousand mostly young monks.

217 *"because they knew":* Melvyn C. Goldstein, Dawei Sherap, and William R. Siebenschuh, *A Tibetan Revolutionary: The Political Life and Times of Bapa Phünto Wangye* (Berkeley: University of California Press 2004), p. 245.

tens of millions died: Today, the Chinese government admits to around 15 million, though, for example, Frank Dikotter in *Mao's Great Famine: The History of China's Most Devastating Catastrophe, 1958–1962* (London: Bloomsbury, 2010) argues for a figure three times higher.

218 *"three years":* Sumner Carnahan and Lama Kunga Rinpoche, *In the Presence of My Enemies: Memoirs of Tibetan Nobleman Tsipon Shuguba* (Santa Fe, NM: Heartsfire Books, 1998), p. 162.

we began to look for: David Patt, *A Strange Liberation: Tibetan Lives in Chinese Hands* (Ithaca: Snow Lion, 1993), p. 182.

Great Leap: Another story from this time that deserves to be better known is that of Tashi Tsering. Born into a polyandrous peasant farming family in 1929, Tashi Tsering was sent off at the age of ten as a candidate for the Dalai Lama's personal dance troupe. His district was one of those obliged to supply young boys as a sort of tax. But although this tax was hugely resented, a position in the troupe was a sure way of entering government service once the term of engagement was up, even if conditions were harsh. As he explained, "the teachers' idea of providing incentives was to punish us swiftly and severely for each mistake. They constantly hit us on the faces, arms and legs." As a way both to escape these harsh conditions and to further improve his prospects, Tashi Tsering accepted the offer of becoming a senior monk official's *drombo,* or catamite.

This relationship enabled him to obtain an education that would not otherwise have been available to him, such that, when his term in the dance troupe came to an end on passing his eighteenth birthday, he was able to obtain a good job as a clerk in the Potala treasury. Subsequently, he married then divorced before traveling to India during the 1950s with the intention of learning English. There he came into contact with Gyalo Thondup and, through him, became involved in the oral histories project of the

International Commission of Jurists. As a result of this work, Tashi Tsering came to know a wealthy young American who agreed to help him continue his education in America.

Although he did well in his studies, Tashi Tsering decided that above all he wanted to serve his people in their hour of need. He dreamed of setting up a kindergarten for his home village. Deciding that he must return to Tibet, he relinquished a comfortable academic's life in America in exchange for a place at the Chinese-run Tibetan Minority Institute, not far from the Dalai Lama's birthplace in Amdo. Subsequently he taught at a remote provincial school before falling under suspicion of being a spy. In 1970 he was denounced as a counterrevolutionary and imprisoned.

Writing of his experiences later, he recounted how he was interrogated "day after day" before being compelled to write and rewrite accounts of his life in America, of his relationship with Gyalo Thondup, and of his reason for wanting to return to Tibet. When finally sentenced, he was transferred to a prison for political prisoners. "Our daily routine was rigorous," he recalled. "We were made to get up early in the morning, given some watery rice soup, and then sent to the fields to do intentionally demeaning manual labour. We worked in the pig pens or carried human excrement or urine . . . to the fields, where it was used as fertiliser. We also, of course, were still subject to relentless and systematic indoctrination to correct our thinking." This entailed giving an account of their "daily, hourly and minute-by-minute mental activities." Small wonder that many broke under the strain. Tashi Tsering's story is told in Melvyn C. Goldstein, William Siebenschuh, and Tashi Tsering, *The Struggle for Modern Tibet: The Autobiography of Tashi Tsering* (New York: M. E. Sharpe, 1997), p. 121. Finally released, Tashi Tsering went on to found more than seventy schools in central Tibet.

219 *a certain "guardedness":* Robert Thurman, *Why the Dalai Lama Matters* (New York: Atria, 2008), p. 5.

"he would invariably": Thurman, *Why the Dalai Lama Matters,* p. 6.

"strong" disappointment: Robert A. F. Thurman, "The Dalai Lama's Roles and Teaching," in *Understanding the Dalai Lama,* ed. Rajiv Mehrotra (Delhi: Viking India, 2004), p. 12. Leary himself had been briefly encountered by some of the CIA's Tibetan recruits. Recognizing that "one of the most serious problems facing the Tibetans [was] a lack of trained officials equipped with linguistic and administrative abilities," the agency funded a program whereby selected candidates were enrolled at Cornell University. On one occasion they attended a seminar given by Leary, a psychologist and advocate of hallucinogenic drug use, during which he "raced around a darkened auditorium chanting and beating drums." This, we are told, left his Tibetan audience "completely baffled." See John Kenneth Knaus, *Orphans of the Cold War: America and the Tibetan Struggle for Survival* (New York: PublicAffairs, 1999), p. 285.

220 *lack of "spiritual depth": The Magical Play of Illusion: The Autobiography of Trijang Rinpoche,* trans. Sharpa Tulku Tenzin Trinley (Somerville, MA: Wisdom Publications, 2018), p. 292.

"We divided our culture": John F. Avedon, *In Exile from the Land of Snows* (London: Michael Joseph, 1984), p. 92.

221 *"religion and philosophy":* Thomas Merton, *The Asian Journals* (London: Sheldon Press, 1974), pp. 100–101.
"the real meaning": Dalai Lama, *Freedom in Exile,* p. 207.
recent liaison: See Mark Shaw, *Beneath the Mask of Holiness* (New York: St. Martin's Press, 2009).
222 *"the establishment":* Merton, *The Asian Journals,* pp. 125, 124.
223 *"inhuman treatment":* Speech of March 10, 1962, https://www.dalailama.com/messages/Tibet.
"passive struggle": Speech of March 10, 1963, https://www.dalailama.com/messages/Tibet.
"naked horror": Speech of March 10, 1969, https://www.dalailama.com/messages/Tibet.
"Tibetan courage": Speech of March 10, 1971, https://www.dalailama.com/messages/Tibet.
significant "problems": Speeches of His Holiness the XIVth Dalai Lama (1959–1989), trans. Sonam Gyatso, vol. 1 (Dharamsala: Library of Tibetan Works and Archives, 2011), p. 65.
224 *casualties inflicted on the Chinese:* The March 10 statement for 1971 claims at least a thousand; https://www.dalailama.com/messages/Tibet.
"an astonishing, exciting": Thurman, *Why the Dalai Lama Matters,* p. 7.
"lucid and lyrical": Thurman, "The Dalai Lama's Roles and Teaching," p. 12.
"and other substances": Trijang, *Magical Play,* p. 336.
225 *To induce lucid dreaming:* John Crook and James Low, *The Yogins of Ladakh: A Pilgrimage Among the Hermits of the Buddhist Himalayas* (1997; repr., Delhi: Motilal Banarsidass, 2012), p. 196.
226 *coupled in the "union of bliss":* Crook and Low, *The Yogins of Ladakh,* p. 196.
skeptical at the outset: Crook and Low, *The Yogins of Ladakh,* p. 69.
raise their core temperature: Herbert Benson, *Your Maximum Mind* (New York: Avon Books, 1991), pp. 16–22.
"found that without gloves": Crook and Low, *The Yogins of Ladakh,* p. 90. What "amused the monks very much was that the Americans . . . never asked them how to do it!" It should be noted that a later study by other scientists found that heat gains could be produced by non-meditators just using the breathing exercises. It was found that the main effect of meditation was to prolong the effects of the exercises. See https://www.ncbi.nlm.nih.gov/pmc/articles/PMC3612090/.
"the practitioner sits": Crook and Low, *The Yogins of Ladakh,* p. 220.
227 *startling enough:* See, for example, https://www.youtube.com/watch?v=Kelb5IGbLXM.
in a vision: William Meyers, Robert Thurman, and Michael G. Burbank, *Man of Peace: The Illustrated Life Story of the Dalai Lama of Tibet* (New York: Tibet House, 2016), pp. 135, 161–65. Each bodhisattva is considered to have one or more wrathful forms. These they manifest when required to clear accretions of karmic negativity.
228 *one of those military men:* When he met the Dalai Lama for the first time, General Uban touched the monk's feet and ever afterwards wore a ring that the Dalai Lama gave him;

https://talesfromanoasis.wordpress.com/2014/09/08/indias-phantom-warriors-part-ii-maj-gen-uban-and-his-beloved-two-twos/. The centurion mentioned in chapter 7 of the Gospel of Luke and chapter 8 of the Gospel of Mark was presumably another such soldier. Yet although Uban's career with the Special Air Service is widely cited, the archivist of 22 SAS regiment informs me that no one of this name is known to have served either in the regiment or in its predecessor, the Long Range Desert Group.
"carry out reconnaissance": Adapted from Mikel Dunham, *Buddha's Warriors: The Story of the CIA-Backed Tibetan Freedom Fighters, the Chinese Invasion, and the Ultimate Fall of Tibet* (New York: Jeremy P. Tarcher/Penguin, 2004), p. 385. See also Claude Arpi, "A Two Two as Army Chief," *Indian Defence Review,* http://www.indiandefencereview.com/news/a-two-two-as-army-chief/ (accessed March 28, 2019).

229 *"We cannot compel you":* http://tibetwrites.in/index.html%3FNot-their-own-wars.html (accessed January 24, 2018).
Regretfully giving: See *The Autobiography of Dasur Ratruk Ngawang of Lithang,* vol. 2 (Dharamsala: Amnye Machen Institute, 2008), p. 131.

230 *"After that":* Kenneth Conboy and James Morrison, *The CIA's Secret War in Tibet* (Lawrence: University Press of Kansas, 2002), pp. 244–45.
"everyone lived": Trijang, *Magical Play,* p. 341.
"And do you know why": Dunham, *Buddha's Warriors,* pp. 385–86.
"the gallant officers": Sujan Singh Uban, *Phantoms of Chittagong* (New Delhi: Allied Publishers, 1985), p. iv.

231 *From Trijang Rinpoché:* Trijang, *Magical Play,* pp. 345, 346.
"a very special Cittamani initiation": Dalai Lama, *The Life of My Teacher: A Biography of Kyabje Ling Rinpoché* (Somerville, MA: Wisdom Publications, 2017), p. 275.

17. "Something beyond the comprehension of the Tibetan people"

232 *the Buryato-Russian explorer:* Tsybikov is quoted in Isabelle Charleux, *Nomads on Pilgrimage: Mongols on Wutaishan (China), 1800–1940* (Leiden: Brill, 2015), p. 36.

233 *"to fulfil":* *Speeches of His Holiness the XIVth Dalai Lama (1959–1989),* trans. Sonam Gyatso, vol. 1 (Dharamsala: Library of Tibetan Works and Archives, 2011), p. 3.

234 *The book:* See Raimondo Bultrini, *The Dalai Lama and the King Demon* (New York: Tibet House US, 2013), p. 122.

237 *"not so different":* Dalai Lama, *Freedom in Exile: The Autobiography of His Holiness the Dalai Lama of Tibet* (London: Hodder & Stoughton, 1990), p. 215.
"not want to spoil": https://www.youtube.com/watch?v=Qwwfj_5A3S8.

238 *upset the mind:* Dalai Lama, *The Life of My Teacher: A Biography of Kyabje Ling Rinpoché* (Somerville, MA: Wisdom Publications, 2017), p. 298.

239 *"they wandered around crying":* Mikel Dunham, *Buddha's Warriors: The Story of the CIA-Backed Tibetan Freedom Fighters, the Chinese Invasion, and the Ultimate Fall of Tibet* (New York: Jeremy P. Tarcher/Penguin, 2004), pp. 388–89, tells the story, which the Dalai Lama partially corroborates in *Freedom in Exile,* p. 211.
advised him to cease: William Meyers, Robert Thurman, and Michael G. Burbank, *Man*

of Peace: The Illustrated Life Story of the Dalai Lama of Tibet (New York: Tibet House, 2016), p. 138.

241 *"so long as he stood":* Quoted in Tsering Shakya, *The Dragon in the Land of Snows: A History of Modern Tibet Since 1947* (New York: Columbia University Press, 1999), p. 370.

"it would be excellent": Dalai Lama, *Life of My Teacher,* p. 310. In so doing, the protector was encouraging the Dalai Lama to align himself with the *ris med,* or nonsectarian, movement, which had flourished during the first third of the twentieth century.

242 *Ma Chig Labdron:* Her story is told in, e.g., John Crook and James Low, *The Yogins of Ladakh: A Pilgrimage Among the Hermits of the Buddhist Himalayas* (1997; Delhi: Motilal Banarsidass, 2012), chap. 15.

244 *"Better to see":* Shakya, *Dragon in the Land of Snows,* p. 376.

"fifty for a start": Mary Craig, *Kundun: A Biography of the Family of the Dalai Lama* (London: HarperCollins, 1997), pp. 308.

245 *"the present standard":* Craig, *Kundun,* p. 306.

"watched over": Dalai Lama, *Freedom in Exile,* p. 296.

His aides reported: Daniel Goleman, *A Force for Good: The Dalai Lama's Vision for Our World* (London: Bloomsbury, 2015), p. 56.

18. From Rangzen to Umaylam

246 *"burden":* See John Kenneth Knaus, https://case.edu/affil/tibet/tibetanSociety/documents/usstuff.PDF, p. 78 (accessed March 28, 2019).

a message for the United States: Marcia Keegan, *The Dalai Lama's Historic Visit to North America* (New York: Clear Light Publications, 1981), unpaginated.

247 *"almost keeled over":* Pico Iyer quoting Thurman in "Making Kindness Stand to Reason," in *Understanding the Dalai Lama,* ed. Rajiv Mehrotra (Delhi: Viking India, 2004), p. 54.

"intimated that he": Barry Boyce, *The Many Faces of the Dalai Lama,* https://www.lionsroar.com/the-many-faces-of-the-dalai-lama/ (accessed March 28, 2019).

"a walking stick": Pico Iyer, *The Open Road* (London: Bloomsbury, 2008), p. 66.

248 *spiritual and moral guidance:* Iyer, *The Open Road,* pp. 75, 219, 220.

"We were very upset": John F. Avedon, *In Exile from the Land of Snows* (London: Michael Joseph, 1984), p. 333.

249 *bombed-out hulk:* Avedon, *In Exile from the Land of Snows,* p. 349.

"little better than": William Meyers, Robert Thurman, and Michael G. Burbank, *Man of Peace: The Illustrated Life Story of the Dalai Lama of Tibet* (New York: Tibet House, 2016), p. 189.

"We feel that our Party": Tsering Shakya, *The Dragon in the Land of Snows: A History of Modern Tibet Since 1947* (New York: Columbia University Press, 1999), pp. 381, 382.

251 *"had immersed himself":* Meyers, Thurman, and Brinkman, *Man of Peace,* p. 162.

"six session yoga": Dalai Lama, *Kalachakra Tantra: Rite of Initiation,* trans., ed., and intro. by Geoffrey Hopkins, enlarged ed. (Somerville, MA: Wisdom Publications, 1999), p. 382.

subsequently published: The Dalai Lama at Harvard: Lectures on the Buddhist Path to Peace (Ithaca: Snow Lion, 1988).

"like a figure": Iyer, *The Open Road,* p. 74. This is a somewhat surprising admission from someone who won a Congratulatory Double First from the University of Oxford.

252 *a private-circulation book:* Tom Clark, *The Great Naropa Poetry Wars* (Santa Barbara: Cadmus Editions, 1980). Trungpa can be seen in action in a number of films on YouTube. See, for example, https://www.youtube.com/watch?v=YgviVWanZgc.

"I was not going": https://archive.nytimes.com/www/nytimes.com/books.99/04/04/specials/merwin-own.html?_r=1 (accessed May 14, 2018).

253 *incipient fascism:* https://www.cadmuseditions.com/naropa.html (accessed May 14, 2018).

there are "none": For one instance, see https://www.youtube.com/watch?v=owP4rsM7AZQ.

254 *dogma-free spirituality:* For his message more generally, see, for example, his book *Beyond Dogma: The Challenge of the Modern World* (London: Souvenir Press, 1996).

"talked to her": Mary Craig, *Kundun: A Biography of the Family of the Dalai Lama* (London: HarperCollins, 1997), p. 323.

"manifested the act": The Magical Play of Illusion: The Autobiography of Trijang Rinpoche, trans. Sharpa Tulku Tenzin Trinley (Somerville, MA: Wisdom Publications, 2018), p. 376.

255 *five-point plan:* See Shakya, *Dragon in the Land of Snows,* p. 384, for details.

256 *Exhorting his Tibetan audiences:* See Dalai Lama, *The Life of My Teacher: A Biography of Kyabje Ling Rinpoché* (Somerville, MA: Wisdom Publications, 2017), p. 328.

"tormented with fear": Dalai Lama, *Life of My Teacher,* p. 363.

257 *absorbed in the clear light:* A clear and detailed account of the process is given in the hagiography of the Ninth Dalai Lama. See Glenn H. Mullin, *The Fourteen Dalai Lamas: A Sacred Legacy of Reincarnation* (Santa Fe, NM: Clear Light Books, 2000).

clearly heard: Dalai Lama, *Life of My Teacher,* p. 364.

As a sign of this: Dalai Lama, *Life of My Teacher,* p. 364.

258 *may also be drunk:* For an account of the practice, see Nyoshul Khenpo, *A Marvelous Garland of Rare Gems: Biographies of Masters of Awareness in the Dzogchen Lineage* (Junction City, CA: Padma Publishing, 2005), pp. 211–12. Somewhat hair-raisingly, it describes an occasion when some visitors were so enthusiastic for spiritual nourishment that they literally tore at the flesh of a recently deceased high master.

"with a head": Dalai Lama, *Life of My Teacher,* p. 299.

"free spokesman": Speech of March 10, 1980.

19. Cutting Off the Serpent's Head

263 *one exception:* See Dalai Lama, *Ethics for the New Millennium* (New York: Riverhead Books, 2000), p. 7.

264 *"Seeing flowers of every colour": The Magical Play of Illusion: The Autobiography of*

Trijang Rinpoche, trans. Sharpa Tulku Tenzin Trinley (Somerville, MA: Wisdom Publications, 2018), p. 291.

265 *"Buddhist psychology takes people.":* William Meyers, Robert Thurman, and Michael G. Burbank, *Man of Peace: The Illustrated Life Story of the Dalai Lama of Tibet* (New York: Tibet House, 2016), p. 197.

"almost deserted": Pico Iyer, "Making Kindness Stand to Reason," in *Understanding the Dalai Lama,* ed. Rajiv Mehrotra (Delhi: Viking India, 2004), p. 53.

266 *"closer to John Lennon":* Pico Iyer, *The Open Road* (London: Bloomsbury, 2008), pp. 75, 158.

"zone of peace": The speech was delivered on September 21, 1987. The full text may be found at https://www.dalailama.com/messages/tibet/five-point-peace-plan.

267 *In response:* This was witnessed by several foreigners. Various contemporary accounts of these events exist, of which the reports in the *New York Times* are the most comprehensive.

It seems likely: An overview of events may be found in Tsering Shakya, *The Dragon in the Land of Snows: A History of Modern Tibet Since 1947* (New York: Columbia University Press, 1999), pp. 414–16.

268 *"divorced":* Chinese source quoted in Shakya, *Dragon in the Land of Snows,* p. 422.

Within minutes: See Melvyn C. Goldstein, *The Snow Lion and the Dragon,* new ed. (Berkeley: University of California Press, 1999), p. 83.

269 *one of them a policeman*: I am grateful to Professor Robbie Barnett for drawing this incident to my attention.

"the whole of Tibet": The full text of the Strasbourg Statement is available on the Dalai Lama's official website at https://www.dalailama.com/messages/tibet/strasbourg-proposal-1988.

later claimed: See Goldstein, *The Snow Lion and the Dragon,* p. 139, n. 24. For others openly critical of the Dalai Lama, see Shakya, *Dragon in the Land of Snows,* p. 524, n. 88.

271 *"personally" speaking:* Dalai Lama, *Freedom in Exile: The Autobiography of His Holiness the Dalai Lama of Tibet* (London: Hodder & Stoughton, 1990), p. 287.

unknown how many died: https://www.nytimes/com/1990/08/14/world/chinese-said-to-kill-450-tibetans-in-1989.html (accessed May 24, 2018).

272 *"no longer excited":* Adapted from Mary Craig, "A Very Human Being," in *Understanding the Dalai Lama,* ed. Rajiv Mehrotra (Delhi: Viking India, 2004), p. 72. His actual words were "no more excited."

Nobel Prize: One pleasing bonus of his subsequent visit to Norway to attend the award ceremony was the opportunity it afforded the Dalai Lama to fulfill a lifelong wish to ride in a reindeer sleigh when he visited the Sami people in Lapland. Meyers, Thurman, and Burbank, *Man of Peace,* p. 219.

"extreme regret": See *Christian Science Monitor,* October 10, 1989, https://www.csmonitor.com/1989/1010/odali.html (accessed February 7, 2019).

273 *"As I stood there":* Dalai Lama, *Freedom in Exile,* p. 290.

"bent down to adjust": Craig, "A Very Human Being," p. 72.

"no handlers, advance men": Douglas Preston's article about the Dalai Lama's visit to Santa Fe in April 1991, from which this account is drawn, is widely available on the Internet; see, e.g., "The Dalai Lama's Ski Trip," Slate.com.

275 *"dialogue with the Dalai Lama":* A May 28, 1993, White House report to Congress on China's most favored nation status extension lists "seeking to resume dialogue with the Dalai Lama or his representatives" as a favorable step China should take to ensure MFN renewal. See https://www.savetibet.org/policy-center/chronology-of-tibetan-chinese-relations-1979-to-2013/ (accessed April 29, 2019).

276 *manifest humility:* I was one of them. See Dalai Lama, *The Good Heart: A Buddhist Perspective on the Teachings of Jesus* (London: Rider, 1996).

277 *"bartered away his honour":* Article by Li Bing in *Tibet Daily,* quoted in *Cutting Off the Serpent's Head: Tightening Control in Tibet, 1994–1995* (New York: Human Rights Watch, March 1996), p. 18.

"To kill a serpent": This saying was the inspiration for the title of a 1996 report published jointly by the Tibet Information Network and Human Rights Watch, Asia. Its author (now Professor), Robbie Barnett, kindly drew my attention to weaknesses in an earlier version of this paragraph.

"The purpose of Buddhism": Cutting Off the Serpent's Head, p. 18.

279 *an extremely risky move:* The story is told variously in Dalai Lama, *Freedom in Exile; Cutting Off the Serpent's Head;* Goldstein, *The Snow Lion and the Dragon;* and, most authoritatively, in Isabel Hilton, *The Search for the Panchen Lama* (New York: W. W. Norton, 2000). Chadrel Rinpoché was sentenced to six years in prison.

280 *explosion of a bomb:* https://www.nytimes.com/1996/12/30/world/bomb-at-government-offices-wounds-5-in-tibetan-capital.html. See also the relevant Tibet Information Network reports.

beatings and electric shocks: For firsthand accounts, see "Torture," section 2 of part 2, in *Cutting Off the Serpent's Head.* See also Palden Gyatso, *Fire Under the Snow: The True Story of a Tibetan Monk* (London: Harvill Press, 1997).

20. "An oath-breaking spirit born of perverse prayers"

282 *threw out as rubbish:* Raimondo Bultrini, *The Dalai Lama and the King Demon* (New York: Tibet House US, 2013), p. 198.

283 *by Indian intelligence:* Bultrini, *The Dalai Lama and the King Demon,* p. 242.

284 *"bloodbath":* Bultrini, *The Dalai Lama and the King Demon,* pp. 201, 292–93.

A fracas broke out: Bultrini, *The Dalai Lama and the King Demon,* p. 201.

285 *"We have already offered":* Bultrini, *The Dalai Lama and the King Demon,* p. 352.

286 *justifying his position:* See https://www.dalailama.com/messages/dolgyal-shugden/speeches-by-his-holiness-the-dalai-lama/dharamsala-teaching.

287 *"When I was small":* Dalai Lama, *Freedom in Exile: The Autobiography of His Holiness the Dalai Lama of Tibet* (London: Hodder & Stoughton, 1990), p. 234.

292 *a hundred million times:* If, as seems plausible, he was able to do so at a speed of one hundred recitations per minute, this would have taken a little under seventeen thousand

hours—two entire years of his life. For an authoritative biography, see Thupten Jinpa, *Tsongkhapa: A Buddha in the Land of Snows* (Boulder: Shambala, 2019).

294 *"harmful activities":* http://www.dalailama.com/messages/dolgyal-shugden/historical-references-historical-references-fifth-dalai-lama. See also the relevant section in Samten Karmay, *The Illusive Play: The Autobiography of the Fifth Dalai Lama* (Chicago: Serindia Publications, 2014).

295 *"took a sword":* Joseph F. Sungmas Rock, "The Living Oracles of the Tibetan Church," *National Geographic* 68 (1935): 475–86. In the article, Rock uses his own phonetics and a Sinicized version of his name, but it is clear that he is referring to the Shugden oracle. He refers to the gurgling sound, said to represent the *kathag* stuffed down Drakpa Gyaltsen's throat, that the medium emitted. Rock published photographic evidence of several knotted swords in the magazine.

poised to move in: René von Nebesky-Wojkowitz, *Where the Gods Are Mountains* (London: Weidenfeld and Nicholson, 1956), p. 210.

296 *"lapping up" his teacher's urine:* https://www.dalailama.com/messages/dolgyal-shugden/speeches-by-his-holiness-the-dalai-lama/dharamsala-teaching. See also the quotation in Georges B. J. Dreyfus, *The Sound of Two Hands Clapping: The Education of a Tibetan Buddhist Monk* (Berkeley: University of California Press, 2003), p. 62, where the anecdote is mentioned of a high lama drinking from his guru's chamber pot.

unsurprising to learn: A Reuters report published in December 2015 offers hard evidence of China's involvement in the Shugden controversy: https://www.reuters.com/investigates/special-report/china-dalailama.

297 *planned to murder:* Bultrini, *The Dalai Lama and the King Demon,* pp. 310–12.

21. Tibet in Flames

299 *"stepping into":* https://www.lionsroar.com/gays-lesbians-and-the-definition-of-sexual-misconduct/ (accessed March 29, 2019).

300 *"delights listeners":* Pico Iyer, *The Open Road* (London: Bloomsbury, 2008), p. 146.

301 *making a case:* Amnesty subsequently found that the issue fell outside its purview of "grave violations of fundamental human rights." See https://www.amnesty.org/download/Documents/152000/asa170141998en.pdf (accessed April 29, 2019).

"delved into his small shoulder bag": Thupten Jinpa, "The Dalai Lama and the Tibetan Monastic Academia," in *Understanding the Dalai Lama,* ed. Rajiv Mehrotra (Delhi: Viking India, 2004), p. 200.

302 *some light moments:* The story is told at https://www.nzz.ch/schweiz/warum-der-dalai-lama-einen-weinberg-im-wallis-besitzt-ld.1397292 and https://www.deutschlandfunk.de/schweizer-wallis-der-weinberg-des-dalai-lama.1242.de.html?dram:article_id=336905.

"is of poor scientific taste": https://www.theguardian.com/world/2005/jul/27/research.highereducation (accessed February 21, 2019).

303 *"inner space":* Yudhijit Bhattacharjee, "Neuroscientists Welcome Dalai Lama with Mostly Open Arms," *Science* 310 (November 18, 2005).

304 *"I believe him to be":* https://www.nytimes.com/1998/06/28/world/clinton-china-overview-clinton-jiang-debate-views-live-tv-clashing-rights.html (accessed April 13, 2019).
a rival: The story of the two rival candidacies is well told in Mick Brown, *The Dance of Seventeen Lives: The Incredible Story of Tibet's 17th Karmapa* (London: Bloomsbury, 2005). Arguably there is room for a second edition, given that the "Tibetan" Karmapa has acquired a Dominican passport, to the evident annoyance of the Indian government, while the "Indian" Karmapa, in defiance of tradition, has taken a wife. The controversy over who should inherit the previous Karmapa's wealth continues at this writing.
"numerous": https://www.savetibet.org/policy-center/chronology-of-tibetan-chinese-relations-1979-to-2013/.

306 *the Lhasa mosque*: See *The Economist,* March 19, 2008.

307 *claims about video*: I recall the Dalai Lama himself telling me about this at the time, though whether he had seen them himself is not clear.
it seems unlikely: The best account of the unrest available in English, which is also a political manifesto, is *The Division of Heaven and Earth: On Tibet's Peaceful Revolution* by Shokdung, trans. Matthew Akester (London: C Hurst Publishers, 2017). There are also several authoritative eyewitness accounts in contemporary newspapers, notably the *New York Times*, *The Guardian,* and *The Economist.*
the Dalai Lama was admitting: See the *Daily Telegraph,* November 3, 2008.

310 *extremely hard to maintain:* I am grateful to Professor Robbie Barnett for drawing this remark to my attention.
the silent film: The Gould film is accessible on YouTube.

22. The Magical Play of Illusion

313 *his viceroy:* Widely believed to have been the Great Fifth's natural son, Desi Sangye Gyatso, known to his contemporaries as Flat-Head, was a great figure in his own right. Formerly a monk, he was a polymath and a lifelong scholar. He was also an accomplished athlete and archer. It is further reported that "of the noble ladies of Lhasa and those who came there from the provinces, there was not a single one whom [he] did not take to bed." Michael Aris, *Hidden Treasures and Secret Lives: A Study of Pemalingpa (1450–1521) and the Sixth Dalai Lama (1683–1706)* (London: Kegan Paul International, 1989), p. 123.

314 *"sacred or holy":* Dalai Lama, *Freedom in Exile: The Autobiography of His Holiness the Dalai Lama of Tibet* (London: Hodder & Stoughton, 1990), p. 296.
not a vegetarian himself: He explains that this is on advice of doctors, following a bout of hepatitis. His continued meat eating may also have something to do with the fact that it is recommended for those engaging in the practices of highest yoga tantra. See John Crook and James Low, *The Yogins of Ladakh: A Pilgrimage Among the Hermits of the Buddhist Himalayas* (1997; repr., Delhi: Motilal Banarsidass, 2012), p. 89.
he admits that: Daniel Goleman, *A Force for Good: The Dalai Lama's Vision for Our World* (London: Bloomsbury, 2015), p. 146.

"become one of": Robert Thurman, *Why the Dalai Lama Matters* (New York: Atria, 2008), p. 57.

315 *"the impulse for helping":* Dalai Lama, *Science and Philosophy in the Indian Buddhist Classics,* ed. Thupten Jinpa (Somerville, MA: Wisdom Publications, 2017), p. 16.

partook of Holy Communion: Dalai Lama and Desmond Tutu with Douglas Abrams, *The Book of Joy: Lasting Happiness in a Changing World* (London: Hutchinson, 2016), p. 182.

homeless shelter: Goleman, *Force for Good,* p. 146.

changing to another: See Dalai Lama, *Ethics for the New Millennium* (New York: Riverhead Books, 2000), p. 238.

316 *contact between the two traditions:* It is well known that there were Christian communities living in both China and Central Asia during the first millennium. There is also written evidence of a Christian mission to Tibet as early as the eighth century. The Chaldean Christian patriarch Timothy I, writing to his friend Severus, mentions that he is preparing to anoint a metropolitan for the "Land of the Tibetans." See Alexander Norman, *Secret Lives of the Dalai Lama* (New York: Random House, 2008), p. 30 and note.

smiled at him: Personal communication.

one of the biggest surprises: Pico Iyer, *The Open Road* (London: Bloomsbury 2008), p. 77.

"great authority": Thupten Jinpa, "The Dalai Lama and the Tibetan Monastic Academia," in *Understanding the Dalai Lama,* ed. Rajiv Mehrotra (Delhi: Viking India, 2004), p. 205.

317 *"Suddenly":* Thurman, *Why the Dalai Lama Matters,* p. 189.

319 *Christopher Hitchens:* In *Salon* magazine (https://www.salon.com), July 1998.

Europe is for Europeans: https://www.independent.co.uk/news/world/europe/dalai-lama-europe-refugee-crisis-immigration-eu-racism-tibet-buddhist-a8537221.html. His saying so recalls the seventh-century stone pillar in Lhasa which claims that China is for the Chinese and Tibet for the Tibetans, as well as the slogan "Tibet is for Tibetans" chanted outside the Norbulingka in March 1959.

being a "ham": Ann Treneman, writing in *The Times* of London, May 23, 2008. See also the summary at the end of a Xinhua News Agency article referencing the *Daily Mail,* http://www.gov.cn/english/2008-12/12/content_1176383.htm.

mentally disturbed: Iyer, *Open Road,* p. 238; Thupten Jinpa, *A Fearless Heart: Why Compassion Is the Key to Greater Wellbeing* (London: Piatkus, 2015), p. 44.

320 *It is even rumored*: I am grateful to Professor Robbie Barnett for drawing this to my attention.

323 *might have met:* See https://www.ndtv.com/book-excerpts/president-xi-was-to-meet-me-in-delhi-in-2014-but-dalai-lama-exclusive-2037863?fbclid=IwAR1vEKVngMFlEKdsjTIzUkOTr-D2FwazSohTo6d4eejvifu8gWmiVI6I-H8. It should be noted that the Dalai Lama's office has since downplayed the significance of the story.

326 *the best measure available:* See https://books.google.com/ngrams and search under

"compassion." If one further analyzes the number of references to the Dalai Lama in relation to the number of references to Buddhism and compassion, it is notable that the references that associate him with compassion amount to a full 50 percent of the number of references that associate Buddhism with compassion.

329 *"some one thing":* This is the last sentence of G. K. Chesterton's *Orthodoxy* (1908).

BIBLIOGRAPHY

(A more comprehensive bibliography providing background and history may be found in my *Secret Lives of the Dalai Lama.*)

An Account of Tibet: The Travels of Ippolito Desideri di Pistoia, SJ, 1712–1727. Edited by Filippo de Filippi, revised ed. London: G. Routledge, 1937.

Aris, Michael. *Hidden Treasures and Secret Lives: A Study of Pemalingpa (1450–1521) and the Sixth Dalai Lama (1683–1706).* London: Kegan Paul International, 1989.

Avedon, John F. *In Exile from the Land of Snows.* London: Michael Joseph, 1984.

Barber, Noel. *The Flight of the Dalai Lama.* London: Hodder & Stoughton, 1960.

Bell, Charles. *Portrait of the Dalai Lama.* London: Collins, 1946.

Benson, Herbert, *Your Maximum Mind.* New York: Avon Books, 1991.

Brown, Mick. *The Dance of Seventeen Lives: The Incredible Story of Tibet's 17th Karmapa.* London: Bloomsbury, 2005.

Bultrini, Raimondo. *The Dalai Lama and the King Demon.* New York: Tibet House US, 2013.

Byron, Robert. *First Russia, Then Tibet.* London: Macmillan, 1933.

Carnahan, Sumner, and Lama Kunga Rinpoche. *In the Presence of My Enemies: Memoirs of Tibetan Nobleman Tsipon Shuguba.* Sante Fe, NM: Heartsfire Books, 1998.

Chang, Jung. *Empress Dowager Cixi: The Concubine Who Launched Modern China.* London: Jonathan Cape, 2013.

Chapman, Frederick Spencer. *Lhasa: The Holy City.* London: Chatto & Windus, 1938.

Charleux, Isabelle. *Nomads on Pilgrimage: Mongols on Wutaishan (China), 1800–1940.* Leiden: Brill, 2015.

Chophel, Norbu. *Folk Culture of Tibet.* Dharamsala: Library of Tibetan Works and Archives, 1983.

Conboy, Kenneth, and James Morrison. *The CIA's Secret War in Tibet.* Lawrence: University Press of Kansas, 2002.

Craig, Mary. *Kundun: A Biography of the Family of the Dalai Lama.* London: HarperCollins, 1997.

Crook, John, and James Low. *The Yogins of Ladakh: A Pilgrimage Among the Hermits of the Buddhist Himalayas.* 1997. Reprint. Delhi: Motilal Banarsidass, 2012.

Cutting Off the Serpent's Head: Tightening Control in Tibet, 1994–1995. New York: Human Rights Watch, March 1996.

Dalai Lama XIV. *My Land and My People: The Autobiography of His Holiness the Dalai Lama.* London: Weidenfeld and Nicolson, 1962.

———. *Freedom in Exile: The Autobiography of His Holiness the Dalai Lama of Tibet.* London: Hodder & Stoughton, 1990.

———. *The Good Heart: A Buddhist Perspective on the Teachings of Jesus.* London: Rider, 1996.

———. *Kalachakra Tantra: Rite of Initiation.* Translated, edited, and introduced by Geoffrey Hopkins. Enlarged edition. Somerville, MA: Wisdom Publications, 1999.

———. *Ethics for the New Millennium.* New York: Riverhead Books, 2000.

———. *Speeches of His Holiness the XIVth Dalai Lama (1959–1989).* Translated by Sonam Gyatso. Dharamsala: Library of Tibetan Works and Archives, 2011.

———. *The Political Philosophy of the Dalai Lama: Selected Speeches and Writings.* Edited by Dr. Subash C. Kashyap. New Delhi: Rupa, 2014.

———. *The Life of My Teacher: A Biography of Kyabje Ling Rinpoché.* Somerville, MA: Wisdom Publications, 2017.

———. *Science and Philosophy in the Indian Buddhist Classics.* Edited by Thupten Jinpa. Vol. 1. *The Physical World.* Somerville, MA: Wisdom Publications, 2017.

Dalai Lama and Desmond Tutu with Douglas Abrams. *The Book of Joy: Lasting Happiness in a Changing World.* London: Hutchinson, 2016.

Dalton, Jacob. *Taming the Demons.* New Haven: Yale University Press, 2011.

David-Néel, Alexandra. *My Journey to Lhasa.* Harmondsworth: Allen Lane, Penguin Books, 1940.

Dikotter, Frank. *Mao's Great Famine: The History of China's Most Devastating Catastrophe, 1958–1962.* London: Bloomsbury, 2010.

Dorje, Gyurme. *Tibet Handbook.* 4th edition. Bath: Footprint, 2008.

Dreyfus, Georges B. J. *The Sound of Two Hands Clapping: The Education of a Tibetan Buddhist Monk.* Berkeley: University of California Press, 2003.

Dunham, Mikel. *Buddha's Warriors: The Story of the CIA-Backed Tibetan Freedom Fighters, the Chinese Invasion, and the Ultimate Fall of Tibet.* New York: Jeremy P. Tarcher/Penguin, 2004.

Ekvall, Robert B. *Tents Against the Sky.* London: Gollancz, 1954.

Engelhardt, Isrun. *Tibet in 1938–1939: Photographs from the Ernst Schäfer Expedition to Tibet.* Chicago: Serindia, 2007.

Fergusson, W. N. *Adventure, Sport and Travel on the Tibetan Steppes.* New York: Charles Scribner's Sons, 1911.

FitzHerbert, S. G. "Rituals as War Propaganda in the Establishment of the Ganden Phodrang State." *Cahiers d'Extrême Asie,* EFEO, 27 (2018): 49–119.

Ford, Robert. *Captured in Tibet.* London: G. Harrap and Co., 1957.

French, Patrick. *Younghusband: The Last Great Imperial Adventurer.* London: HarperCollins, 1995.

Gelder, Stuart, and Roma Gelder. *The Timely Rain.* London: Hutchinson and Co., 1964.

Goldstein, Melvyn C. *A History of Modern Tibet: 1913–1951.* Vol. 1. *The Demise of the Lamaist State.* Berkeley: University of California Press, 1989.

———. *A History of Modern Tibet.* Vol. 2. *The Calm Before the Storm, 1951–55.* Berkeley: University of California Press, 2007.

———. *A History of Modern Tibet.* Vol. 3. *The Storm Clouds Descend, 1955–57.* Berkeley: University of California Press, 2014.

Goldstein, Melvyn C., Dawei Sherap, and William R. Siebenschuh. *A Tibetan Revolutionary: The Political Life and Times of Bapa Phüntso Wangye.* Berkeley: University of California Press, 2004.

Goleman, Daniel. *A Force for Good: The Dalai Lama's Vision for Our World.* London: Bloomsbury, 2015.

Goodrick-Clarke, Nicholas. *Black Sun: Aryan Cults, Esoteric Nazism, and the Politics of Identity.* New York: NYU Press, 2001.

Gould, Basil J. *The Jewel in the Lotus: Recollections of an Indian Political.* London: Chatto & Windus, 1957.

Gyatso, Palden. *Fire Under the Snow: The True Story of a Tibetan Monk.* London: Harvill Press, 1997.

Hale, Mark. *Himmler's Crusade: The True Story of the Nazis' 1938 Expedition into Tibet.* London: Bantam Books, 2003.

Harrer, Heinrich. *Seven Years in Tibet.* London: R. Hart-Davis, 1953.

———. *Return to Tibet.* London: Penguin, 1985.

Hicks, Roger, and Chogyam Ngakpa. *Great Ocean, an Authorised Biography: The Dalai Lama.* Shaftesbury, Dorset: Element Books, 1984.

Hilton, Isabel. *The Search for the Panchen Lama.* New York: W. W. Norton, 2000.

Iyer, Pico. *The Open Road.* London: Bloomsbury, 2008.

Jinpa, Thupten. *A Fearless Heart: Why Compassion Is the Key to Greater Wellbeing.* London: Piatkus, 2015.

———. *Self, Reason and Reality in Tibetan Philosophy: Tsongkhapa's Quest for the Middle Way.* London: Routledge Curzon, 2002.

———. *Tsongkhapa: A Buddha in the Land of Snows.* Boulder: Shambala, 2019.

Karmay, Samten. *The Illusive Play: The Autobiography of the Fifth Dalai Lama.* Chicago: Serindia Publications, 2014.

Kasho, Jamyang Choegyal. *In the Service of the 13th and 14th Dalai Lamas.* Frankfurt am Main: Tibethaus Deutschland, 2015.

Kashyap, Dr. Subash C., ed. *The Political Philosophy of the Dalai Lama: Selected Speeches and Writings.* New Delhi: Rupa, 2014.

Kawaguchi, Ekai. *Three Years in Tibet.* London: Theosophical Publishing Society, 1909.

Keegan, Marcia. *The Dalai Lama's Historic Visit to North America.* New York: Clear Light Publications, 1981.

Khedrup, Tashi. *Adventures of a Tibetan Fighting Monk.* Edited by Hugh Richardson. Bangkok: Orchid Press, 2003.

Khetsun, Tubten. *Memories of Life in Lhasa Under Chinese Rule.* Translated by Matthew Akester. Delhi: Penguin for Columbia University Press, 2009.

Kilty, Gavin. *The Case against Shukden: The History of a Contested Tibetan Practice.* Somerville, MA: Wisdom Publications, 2019.

Knaus, John Kenneth. *Orphans of the Cold War: America and the Tibetan Struggle for Survival.* New York: PublicAffairs, 1999.

Kyger, Joanne. *The Japan and India Journals, 1960–1964.* New York: Tombouctou Books, 1981.

Laird, Thomas. *The Story of Tibet: Conversations with the Dalai Lama.* London: Atlantic, 2006.

Larsen, Knud, and Amund Sinding-Larsen. *The Lhasa Atlas: Traditional Tibetan Architecture and Townscape.* London: Serindia, 2001.

Li, Jianglin. *Tibet in Agony: Lhasa, 1959.* Translated by Susan Wilf. Cambridge: Harvard University Press, 2016.

———. "When the Iron Bird Flies: The 1956–1962 Secret War on the Tibetan Plateau." Unpublished manuscript. Translated by Stacey Mosher.

Loup, Robert. *Martyr in Tibet.* Philadelphia: D. McKay and Co., 1956.

Mehrotra, Rajiv, ed. *Understanding the Dalai Lama.* Delhi: Viking India, 2004.

Merton, Thomas. *The Asian Journals.* London: Sheldon Press, 1974.

Meyers, William, Robert Thurman, and Michael G. Burbank. *Man of Peace: The Illustrated Life Story of the Dalai Lama of Tibet.* New York: Tibet House, 2016.

Mission to Tibet: The Extraordinary Eighteenth-Century Account of Father Desideri SJ. Translated by M. Sweet. Edited by L. Zwilling. Somerville, MA: Wisdom Publications, 2010.

Morgan, William Stanley. *Amchi Sahib: A British Doctor in Tibet, 1936–37.* Charlestown, MA: Acme Bookbinding, 2007.

Mullin, Glenn H. *Path of the Bodhisattva Warrior: The Life and Teachings of the Thirteenth Dalai Lama.* Ithaca: Snow Lion Publications, 1988.

———. *The Fourteen Dalai Lamas: A Sacred Legacy of Reincarnation.* Santa Fe, NM: Clear Light Books, 2000.

Neame, Philip. *Playing with Strife: The Autobiography of a Soldier.* London: George G. Harrap, 1947.

Nebesky-Wojkowitz, René de. *Oracles and Demons of Tibet.* Delhi: Book Faith India, 1993.

Nebesky-Wojkowitz, René von. *Where the Gods Are Mountains.* London: Weidenfeld and Nicholson, 1956.

Norbu, Thubten Jigme. *Tibet Is My Country.* London: Rupert Hart Davis, 1960.

Norman, Alexander. *Secret Lives of the Dalai Lama.* New York: Random House, 2008. (Published in the UK as *Holder of the White Lotus.* London: Little, Brown, 2008.)

Nyoshul Khenpo. *A Marvelous Garland of Rare Gems: Biographies of Masters of Awareness in the Dzogchen Lineage.* Junction City, CO: Padma Publishing, 2005.

Patt, David. *A Strange Liberation: Tibetan Lives in Chinese Hands.* Ithaca: Snow Lion Publications, 1993.

Pemba, Tsewang Y. *Young Days in Tibet.* London: Jonathan Cape, 1957.

A Poisoned Arrow: The Secret Report of the 10th Panchen Lama. London: Tibet Information Network, 1997.

Pringle, Heather. *The Master Plan: Himmler's Scholars and the Holocaust.* London: Fourth Estate, 2006.

The Question of Tibet and the Rule of Law. Geneva: International Commission of Jurists, 1959.

Rahula, Walpola Sri. *What the Buddha Taught.* 1959. Reprint. Oxford: One World Publications, 2008.

Richardson, Hugh. *Ceremonies of the Lhasa Year.* London: Serindia Publications, 1993.

Rustomji, Nari. *Enchanted Frontiers: Sikkim, Bhutan and India's North-Eastern Borderlands.* Oxford: Oxford University Press, 1971.

Sadutshang, Tseyang. *My Youth in Tibet: Recollections of a Tibetan Woman.* Dharamsala: Library of Tibetan Works and Archives, 2012.

Samuel, Geoffrey. *Civilized Shamans: Buddhism in Tibetan Societies.* Washington, DC: Smithsonian Institution Press, 1993.

Sans-rgyas rgya-mtsho: Life of the Fifth Dalai Lama. Translated by Ahmed Zahiruddin. New Delhi: Academy of Indian Culture, 1999.

Santideva. *The Bodhischaryavatara.* Translated with an introduction and notes by Kate Crosby and Andrew Skilton. Oxford: Oxford University Press, 1995.

Schaeffer, Kurtis, and Matthew Kapstein. *Sources of Tibetan Tradition.* New York: Columbia University Press, 2013.

Shakabpa, Tsepon W. D. *Tibet: A Political History.* New Haven: Yale University Press, 1967.

Shakya, Tsering. *The Dragon in the Land of Snows: A History of Modern Tibet Since 1947.* New York: Columbia University Press, 1999.

Shelton, Albert Leroy. *Pioneering in Tibet: A Personal Record of Life and Experience in Mission Fields.* New York: F. H. Revell Company, 1921.

Shelton, Flora Beal. *Shelton of Tibet.* New York: George H. Doran, 1923.

Shokdung. *The Division of Heaven and Earth: On Tibet's Peaceful Revolution.* Translated by Matthew Akester. London: C. Hurst Publishers, 2017.

Short, Philip. *In Pursuit of Plants: Experiences of Nineteenth and Early Twentieth Century Plant Collectors.* Portland, OR: Timber Press, 2004.

Sither, Lobsang Gyatso. *Exile: A Photo Journal, 1959–1989.* Dharamsala: Tibet Documentation, 2017.

Steele, Archibald. *In the Kingdom of the Dalai Lama.* Sedona, AZ: In Print Publishing, 1993.

Stein, R. A. *Tibetan Civilisation.* Translated by J. E. Stapleton Driver. London: Faber and Faber, 1972.

Strong, Anna Louise. *When Serfs Stood Up in Tibet.* Peking: New World Press, 1960.

Teichman, Eric. *Travels of a Consular Officer in North-west China.* Cambridge: Cambridge University Press, 1921.

Thomas, Lowell. *Out of This World.* London: Macdonald and Co., 1951.

Thondup, Gyalo, with Anne F. Thurston. *The Noodle Maker of Kalimpong: The Untold Story of My Struggle for Tibet.* London: Rider, 2015.

Thurman, Robert. *Why the Dalai Lama Matters.* New York: Atria, 2008.

Trijang Rinpoche. *The Magical Play of Illusion: The Autobiography of Trijang Rinpoche.* Translated by Sharpa Tulku Tenzin Trinley. Somerville, MA: Wisdom Publications, 2018.

Tsering, Diki. *The Dalai Lama, My Son: A Mother's Story.* London: Virgin, 2000.

Uban, Sujan Singh. *Phantoms of Chittagong.* New Delhi: Allied Publishers, 1985.

van Schaik, Sam. *Tibet: A History.* New Haven: Yale University Press, 2011.

Wang, Xiuyu. *China's Last Imperial Frontier: Late Qing Expansion in Sichuan's Tibetan Borderlands.* Lanham, MD: Lexington Books, 2011.

Wangdu, Khemey Sonam, Basil J. Gould, and Hugh E. Richardson. *Discovery, Recognition and Enthronement of the 14th Dalai Lama: A Collection of Accounts.* Dharamsala: Library of Tibetan Works and Archives, 2000.

Williams, Paul. *Mahayana Buddhism: The Doctrinal Foundations.* 2nd ed. London: Routledge, 2009.

INDEX

Stanley Gibbons Simplified Catalogue

Stamps of the World 5

2015 Edition

Countries **New South Wales – Singapore**

Stanley Gibbons Ltd
London and Ringwood

BY APPOINTMENT TO
HER MAJESTY THE QUEEN
PHILATELISTS
STANLEY GIBBONS LTD
LONDON

1914 - 2014

80th Edition
Published in Great Britain by
Stanley Gibbons Ltd
Publications Editorial, Sales Offices and Distribution Centre
7, Parkside, Christchurch Road,
Ringwood, Hampshire BH24 3SH
Telephone +44 (0) 1425 472363

British Library Cataloguing in
Publication Data.
A catalogue record for this book is available
from the British Library.

Volume 5
ISBN 10: 0-85259-933-1
ISBN 13: 978-0-85259-933-4

Boxed Set
ISBN 10: 0-85259-936-6
ISBN 13: 978-0-85259-936-5

Published as Stanley Gibbons Simplified Catalogue from 1934 to 1970, renamed Stamps of the World in 1971, and produced in two (1982-88), three (1989-2001), four (2002-2005) five (2006-2010) and six from 2011 volumes as Stanley Gibbons Simplified Catalogue of Stamps of the World.

Item No. 2881– Set15

Printed and bound in Wales by Stephens & George

Contents – Volume 5

Introduction

The ultimate reference work for all stamps issued around the world since the very first Penny Black of 1840, now with an improved layout.

Stamps of the World provides a comprehensive, illustrated, priced guide to postage stamps, and is the standard reference tool for every collector. It will help you to identify those elusive stamps, to value your collection, and to learn more about the background to issues. *Stamps of the World* was first published in 1934 and has been updated every year since 1950.

Included is a guide to stamp identification so that you can easily discover which country issued your stamp.

Re-designed to provide more colourful, clearer, and easy-to-navigate listings, these volumes continue to present you with a wealth of information to enhance your enjoyment of stamp collecting.

Features:

- Current values for every stamp in the world
- Easy-to-use simplified listings
- World-recognised Stanley Gibbons catalogue numbers
- A wealth of historical, geographical and currency information
- Indexing and cross-referencing throughout the volumes
- Worldwide miniature sheets listed and priced
- Thousands of new issues since the last edition

For this edition, prices have been thoroughly reviewed for Great Britain and the Channel Islands up to date, and all Commonwealth countries up to 1970, with further updates for Commonwealth countries which have appeared in our recently-published or forthcoming comprehensive catalogues under the titles *Brunei, Malaysia and Singapore, Falkland Islands, Western Pacific, St Helena and Dependencies, New Zealand and Canada*. Other countries with complete price updates from the following comprehensive catalogues are: *Italy and Switzerland, Russia* and *China*. New issues received from all other countries have been listed and priced. The first *Gibbons Stamp Monthly* Catalogue Supplement to this edition is September 2014.

Information for users

Scope of the Catalogue

Stamps of the World contains listings of postage stamps only. Apart from the ordinary definitive, commemorative and air-mail stamps of each country there are sections for the following, where appropriate. Noted below are the Prefixes used for each section (see Guide to Entries for further information):

- postage due stamps – Prefix in listing D
- parcel post or postcard stamps – Prefix P
- official stamps – Prefix O
- express and special delivery stamps - Prefix E
- frank stamps – Prefix F
- charity tax stamps – Prefix J
- newspaper and journal stamps – Prefix N
- printed matter stamps – Prefix P
- registration stamps - Prefix R
- acknowledgement of receipt stamps – Prefix AR
- late fee and too late stamps – Prefix L
- military post stamps- Prefix M
- recorded message stamps – Prefix RM
- personal delivery stamps – Prefix P
- concessional letter post – Prefix CL
- concessional parcel post – Prefix CP
- pneumatic post stamps – Prefix PE
- publicity envelope stamps – Prefix B
- bulk mail stamps – Prefix BP
- telegraph stamps used for postage – Prefix PT
- telegraph stamps (Commonwealth Countries) – Prefix T
- obligatory tax – Prefix T

As this is a simplified listing, the following are NOT included:

Fiscal or revenue stamps: stamps used solely in collecting taxes or fees for non-postal purposes. For example, stamps which pay a tax on a receipt, represent the stamp duty on a contract, or frank a customs document. Common inscriptions found include: Documentary, Proprietary, Internal Revenue and Contract Note.

Local stamps: postage stamps whose validity and use are limited in area to a prescribed district, town or country, or on certain routes where there is no government postal service. They may be issued by private carriers and freight companies, municipal authorities or private individuals.

Local carriage labels and Private local issues: many labels exist ostensibly to cover the cost of ferrying mail from one of Great Britain's offshore islands to the nearest mainland post office. They are not recognised as valid for national or international mail. Examples: Calf of Man, Davaar, Herm, Lundy, Pabay, Stroma.

Telegraph stamps: stamps intended solely for the prepayment of telegraphic communication.

Bogus or "phantom" stamps: labels from mythical places or non-existent administrations. Examples in the classical period were Sedang, Counani, Clipperton Island and in modern times Thomond and Monte Bello Islands. Numerous labels have also appeared since the War from dissident groups as propaganda for their claims and without authority from the home governments. Common examples are the numerous issues for Nagaland.

Railway letter fee stamps: special stamps issued by railway companies for the conveyance of letters by rail. Example: Talyllyn Railway. Similar services are now offered by some bus companies and the labels they issue likewise do not qualify for inclusion in the catalogue.

Perfins ("perforated initials"): stamps perforated with the initials or emblems of firms as a security measure to prevent pilferage by office staff.

Labels: Slips of paper with an adhesive backing. Collectors tend to make a distinction between stamps, which have postal validity and anything else, which has not.

Cut-outs: Embossed or impressed stamps found on postal stationery, which are cut out if the stationery has been ruined and re-used as adhesives.

Further information on a wealth of terms is in *Philatelic Terms Illustrated*, published by Stanley Gibbons, details are listed under Stanley Gibbons Publications. There is also a priced listing of the postal fiscals of Great Britain in our *Commonwealth & British Empire Stamps 1840-1970* Catalogue and in Volume 1 of the *Great Britain Specialised Catalogue* (5th and later editions). A full list of our current publications is given on page xiv

Organisation of the Catalogue

The catalogue lists countries in alphabetical order with country headers on each page and extra introductory information such as philatelic historical background at the beginning of each section. The Contents list provides a detailed guide to each volume, and the Index has full cross-referencing to locate each country in each volume.

Each country lists postage stamps in order of date of issue, from earliest to most recent, followed by separate sections for categories such as postage due stamps, express stamps, official stamps, and so on (see above for a complete listing).

"Appendix" Countries

Since 1968 Stanley Gibbons has listed in an appendix stamps which are judged to be in excess of true postal needs. The appendix also contains stamps which have not fulfilled all the normal conditions for full catalogue listing. Full catalogue listing requires a stamp to be:

- issued by a legitimate postal authority
- recognised by the government concerned
- adhesive
- valid for proper postal use in the class of service for which they are inscribed
- available to the general public at face value with no artificial restrictions being imposed on their distribution (with the exception of categories such as postage dues and officials)

Only stamps issued from component parts of otherwise united territories which represent a genuine political, historical or postal division within the country concerned have a full catalogue listing. Any such issues which do not fulfil this stipulation will be recorded in the Catalogue Appendix only.

Stamps listed in the Appendix are constantly under review in light of newly acquired information about them. If we are satisfied that a stamp qualifies for proper listing in the body of the catalogue it will be moved in the next edition.

"Undesirable Issues"

The rules governing many competitive exhibitions are set by the Federation Internationale de Philatelie and stipulate a downgrading of marks for stamps classed as "undesirable issues".

This catalogue can be taken as a guide to status. All stamps in the main listings are acceptable. Stamps in the Appendix are considered, "undesirable issues" and should not be entered for competition.

Correspondence

We welcome information and suggestions but we must ask correspondents to include the cost of postage for the return of any materials, plus registration where appropriate. Letters and emails should be addressed to Lorraine Holcombe, 7 Parkside, Christchurch Road, Ringwood, Hampshire BH24 3SH, UK. lholcombe@stanleygibbons.co.uk. Where information is solicited purely for the benefit of the enquirer we regret we are seldom able to reply.

Identification of Stamps

We regret we do not give opinion on the authenticity of stamps, nor do we identify stamps or number them by our Catalogue.

Thematic Collectors

Stanley Gibbons publishes a range of thematic catalogues (see page xiv for details) and *Stamps of the World* is ideal to use with these titles, as it supplements those listings with extra information.

Type numbers

Type numbers (in bold) refer to illustrations, and are not the Stanley Gibbons Catalogue numbers.

A brief description of the stamp design subject is given below or beside the illustrations, or close by in the entry, where needed. Where a design is not illustrated, it is usually the same shape and size as a related design, unless otherwise indicated.

Watermarks

Watermarks are not covered in this catalogue. Stamps of the same issue with differing watermarks are not listed separately.

Perforations

Perforations – all stamps are perforated unless otherwise stated. No distinction is made between the various gauges of perforation but early stamp issues which exist both imperforate and perforated are usually listed separately. Where a heading states, "Imperf or perf"or "Perf. or rouletted" this does not necessarily mean that all values of the issue are found in both conditions

Se-tenant Pairs

Se-tenant Pairs – Many modern issues are printed in sheets containing different designs or face values. Such pairs, blocks, strips or sheets are described as being "*se-tenant*" and they are outside the scope of this catalogue, although reference to them may occur in instances where they form a composite design.

Miniature Sheets are now fully listed.

Guide to Entries

A Country of Issue

B Part Number – shows where to find more detailed listings in the Stanley Gibbons Comprehensive Catalogue. Part 6 refers to France and so on – see p. li for further information on the breakdown of the Catalogue.

C Country Information – Brief geographical and historical details for the issuing country.

D Currency – Details of the currency, and dates of earliest use where applicable, on the face value of the stamps. Where a Colony has the same currency as the Mother Country, see the details given in that country.

E Year Date – When a set of definitive stamps has been issued over several years the Year Date given is for the earliest issue, commeorative sets are listed in chronological order. As stamps of the same design or issue are usually grouped together, a list of King George VI stamps, for example, headed "1938" may include stamps issued from 1938 to the end of the reign.

F Stanley Gibbons Catalogue number – This is a unique number for each stamp to help the collector identify stamps in the listing. The Stanley Gibbons numbering system is universally recognized as definitive. The majority of listings are in chronological order, but where a definitive set of stamps has been re-issued with a new watermark, perforation change or imprint date, the cheapest example is given; in such cases catalogue numbers may not be in numerical order.

Where insufficient numbers have been left to provide for additional stamps to a listing, some stamps will have a suffix letter after the catalogue number. If numbers have been left for additions to a set and not used they will be left vacant.

The separate type numbers (in bold) refer to illustrations (see M).

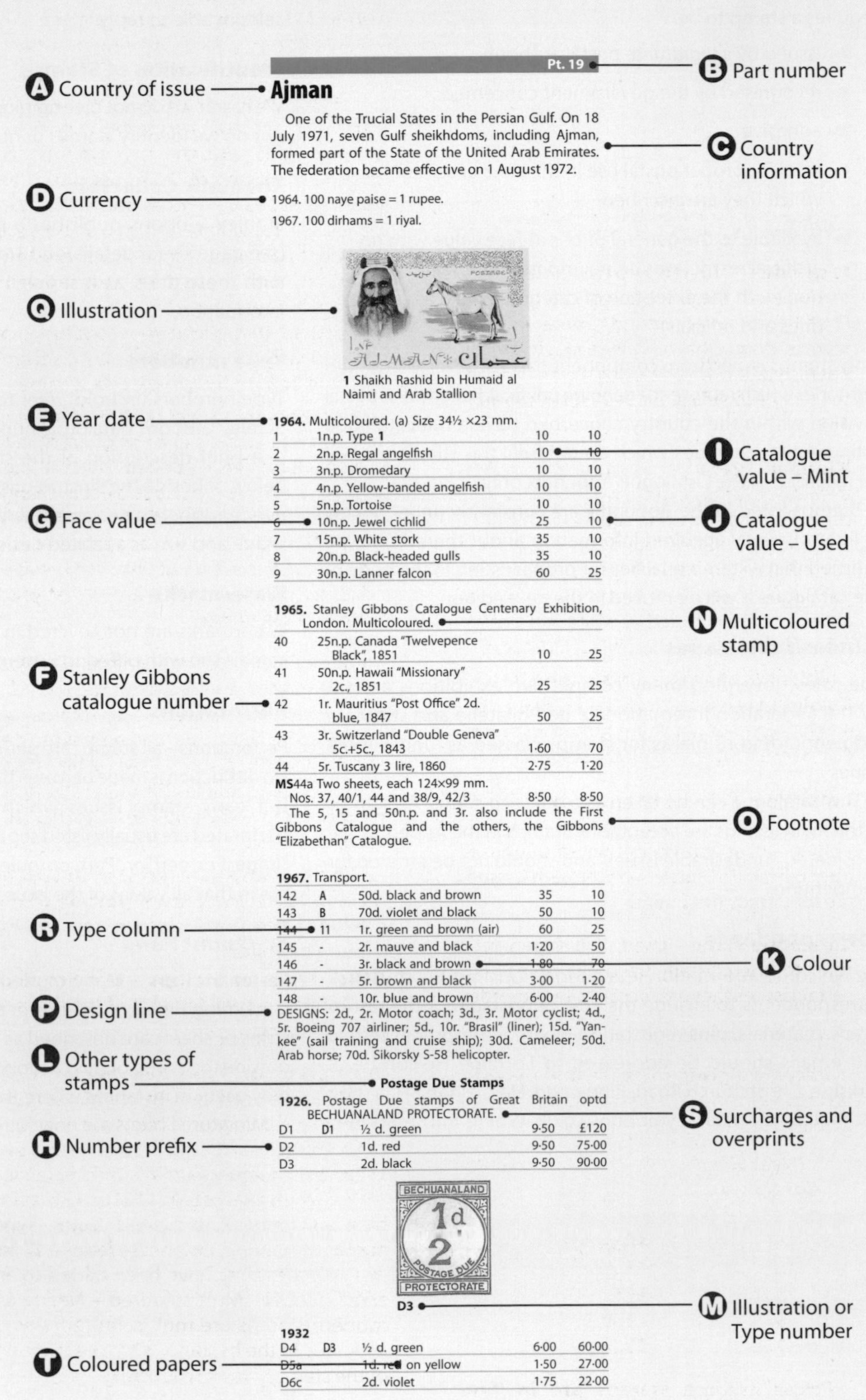

Pt. 19

Ajman

One of the Trucial States in the Persian Gulf. On 18 July 1971, seven Gulf sheikhdoms, including Ajman, formed part of the State of the United Arab Emirates. The federation became effective on 1 August 1972.

1964. 100 naye paise = 1 rupee.
1967. 100 dirhams = 1 riyal.

1 Shaikh Rashid bin Humaid al Naimi and Arab Stallion

1964. Multicoloured. (a) Size 34½ ×23 mm.

1	1n.p. Type **1**	10	10
2	2n.p. Regal angelfish	10	10
3	3n.p. Dromedary	10	10
4	4n.p. Yellow-banded angelfish	10	10
5	5n.p. Tortoise	10	10
6	10n.p. Jewel cichlid	25	10
7	15n.p. White stork	35	10
8	20n.p. Black-headed gulls	35	10
9	30n.p. Lanner falcon	60	25

1965. Stanley Gibbons Catalogue Centenary Exhibition, London. Multicoloured.

40	25n.p. Canada "Twelvepence Black", 1851	10	25
41	50n.p. Hawaii "Missionary" 2c., 1851	25	25
42	1r. Mauritius "Post Office" 2d. blue, 1847	50	25
43	3r. Switzerland "Double Geneva" 5c.+5c., 1843	1·60	70
44	5r. Tuscany 3 lire, 1860	2·75	1·20

MS44a Two sheets, each 124×99 mm. Nos. 37, 40/1, 44 and 38/9, 42/3 — 8·50 8·50

The 5, 15 and 50n.p. and 3r. also include the First Gibbons Catalogue and the others, the Gibbons "Elizabethan" Catalogue.

1967. Transport.

142	A	50d. black and brown	35	10
143	B	70d. violet and black	50	10
144	11	1r. green and brown (air)	60	25
145	-	2r. mauve and black	1·20	50
146	-	3r. black and brown	1·80	70
147	-	5r. brown and black	3·00	1·20
148	-	10r. blue and brown	6·00	2·40

DESIGNS: 2d., 2r. Motor coach; 3d., 3r. Motor cyclist; 4d., 5r. Boeing 707 airliner; 5d., 10r. "Brasil" (liner); 15d. "Yankee" (sail training and cruise ship); 30d. Cameleer; 50d. Arab horse; 70d. Sikorsky S-58 helicopter.

Postage Due Stamps

1926. Postage Due stamps of Great Britain optd BECHUANALAND PROTECTORATE.

D1	D1	½ d. green	9·50	£120
D2		1d. red	9·50	75·00
D3		2d. black	9·50	90·00

D3

1932

D4	D3	½ d. green	6·00	60·00
D5a		1d. red on yellow	1·50	27·00
D6c		2d. violet	1·75	22·00

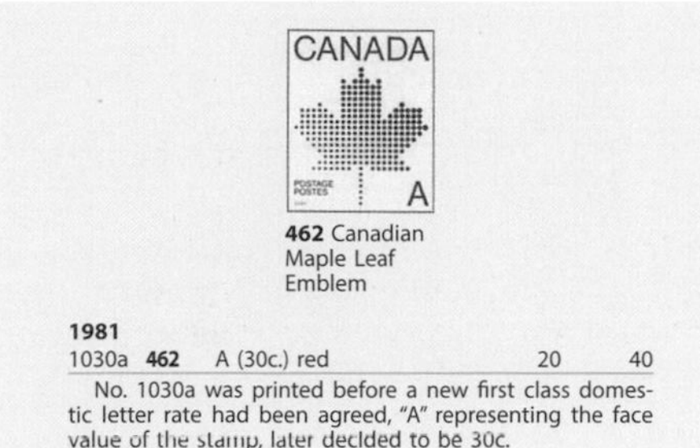

462 Canadian Maple Leaf Emblem

1981
1030a **462** A (30c.) red 20 40

No. 1030a was printed before a new first class domestic letter rate had been agreed, "A" representing the face value of the stamp, later decided to be 30c.

(G) **Face value** – This refers to the value of each stamp and is the price it was sold for at the Post Office when issued. Some modern stamps do not have their values in figures but instead shown as a letter, see for example the entry above for Canada 1030a/Illustration 462.

(H) **Number Prefix** – Stamps other than definitives and commemoratives have a prefix letter before the catalogue number. Such stamps may be found at the end of the normal listing for each country. (See Scope of the Catalogue p.viii for a list of other types of stamps covered, together with the list of the main abbreviations used in the Catalogue).

Other prefixes are also used in the Catalogue. Their use is explained in the text: some examples are A for airmail, E for East Germany or Express Delivery stamps.

(I) **Catalogue Value** – Mint/Unused. Prices quoted for pre-1945 stamps are for lightly hinged examples. Prices quoted of unused King Edward VIII to Queen Elizabeth II issues are for unmounted mint.

(J) **Catalogue Value** – Used. Prices generally refer to fine postally used examples. For certain issues they are for cancelled-to-order.

Prices

Prices are given in pence and pounds. Stamps worth £100 and over are shown in whole pounds:

Shown in Catalogue as	
10	10 pence
1.75	£1.75
15.00	£15
£150	£150
£2300	£2300

Prices assume stamps are in 'fine condition'; we may ask more for superb and less for those of lower quality. The minimum catalogue price quoted is 10p and is intended as a guide for catalogue users. The lowest price for individual stamps purchased from Stanley Gibbons is £1.

Prices quoted are for the cheapest variety of that particular stamp. Differences of watermark, perforation, or other details, outside the scope of this catalogue, often increase the value. Prices quoted for mint issues are for single examples. Those in *se-tenant* pairs, strips, blocks or sheets may be worth more. Where no prices are listed it is either because the stamps are not known to exist in that particular condition, or, more usually, because there is no reliable information on which to base their value.

All prices are subject to change without prior notice and we cannot guarantee to supply all stamps as priced. Prices quoted in advertisements are also subject to change without prior notice. Due to differing production schedules it is possible that new editions of Parts 2 to 22 will show revised prices which are not included in that year's Stamps of the World.

(K) **Colour** – Colour of stamp (if fewer than four colours, otherwise noted as "multicoloured" – see N below). Colour descriptions are simple in this catalogue, and only expanded to aid identification – see other more comprehensive Stanley Gibbons catalogues for more detailed colour descriptions (see p.xxxix).

Where stamps are printed in two or more colours, the central portion of the design is the first colour given, unless otherwise stated.

(L) **Other Types of Stamps** – See Scope of the Catalogue p.viii for a list of the types of stamps included.

(M) **Illustration or Type Number** – These numbers are used to help identify stamps, either in the listing, type column, design line or footnote, usually the first value in a set. These type numbers are in a bold type face – **123**; when bracketed (**123**) an overprint or a surcharge is indicated. Some type numbers include a lower-case letter – **123a**, this indicates they have been added to an existing set. N Multicoloured – Nearly all modern stamps are multicoloured; this is indicated in the heading, with a description of the stamp given in the listing.

(O) **Footnote** – further information on background or key facts on issues

(P) **Design line** – Further details on design variations

(Q) **Illustration** – Generally, the first stamp in the set. Stamp illustrations are reduced to 60%, with overprints and surcharges shown actual size.

(R) **Key Type** – indicates a design type (see p. xii for further details) on which the stamp is based. These are the bold figures found below each illustration. The type numbers are also given in bold in the second column of figures alongside the stamp description to indicate the design of each stamp. Where an issue comprises stamps of similar design, the corresponding type number should be taken as indicating the general design. Where there are blanks in the type number column it means that the type of the corresponding stamp is that shown by the number in the type column of the same issue. A dash (–) in the type column means that the stamp is not illustrated. Where type numbers refer to stamps of another country, e.g. where stamps of one country are overprinted for use in another, this is always made clear in the text.

(S) **Surcharges and Overprints** – usually described in the headings. Any actual wordings are shown in bold type. Descriptions clarify words and figures used in the overprint. Stamps with the same overprints in different colours are not listed separately. Numbers in brackets after the descriptions are the catalogue numbers of the non-overprinted stamps. The words "inscribed" or "inscription" refer to the wording incorporated in the design of a stamp and not surcharges or overprints.

(T) **Coloured Papers** – stamps printed on coloured paper are shown – e.g. "brn on yell" indicates brown printed on yellow paper. No information on the texture of paper, e.g. laid or wove, is provided in this catalogue.

Key-Types

Standard designs frequently occuring on the stamps of the French, German, Portuguese and Spanish colonies are illustrated below together with the descriptive names and letters by which they are referred to in the lists to avoid repetition. Please see the Guide to Entries for further information.

French Group

A "Blanc" B "Mouchon" C "Merson" D "Tablet"

INTERNATIONAL COLONIAL EXHIBITION

E F " G H

I "Faidherbe" J "Palms" K "Balay" L "Natives" M "Figure"

German Group

N "Yacht" O "Yacht"

Spanish Group

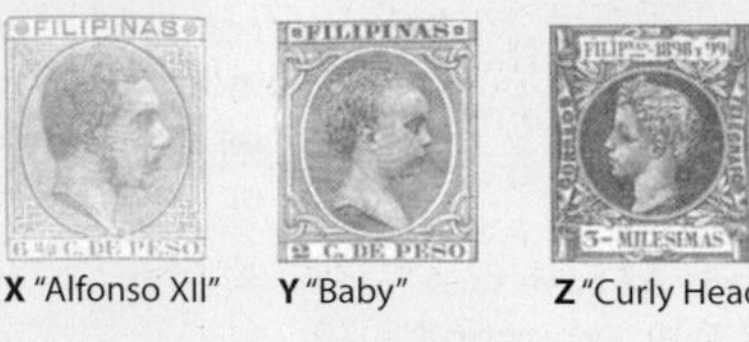

X "Alfonso XII" Y "Baby" Z "Curly Head"

Portuguese Group

P "Crown" Q "Embossed" R "Figures" S "Carlos" T "Manoel" U Ceres" V "Newspaper" W "Due"

Selling Your Stamps?

Summary Tip #22:
5 Different Ways to Sell your Stamps: Selling via on-line Auction.

Dear Collector,

In Parts 1 to 4 of 'Selling your Stamps' we discussed the advantages and disadvantages of 4 different ways to sell your stamps. In all of these there were the common threads of best methodology of selling to dealers and what to avoid if you are thinking of consigning your stamps for sale by public stamp auction.

Here in Part 5 we discuss the merits and demerits of 'DIY' - do-it-yourself - i.e. you selling your stamps direct to collectors. Ultimately - apart from selling to colleagues or members of your stamp club/ circuit … there are really only 2 ways - the 1st of which - placing advertisements in Stamp Magazines to sell direct to collectors - (please take our word for it) - does not bear thinking about for collectors.

Let me explain: advertising in Stamp Magazines is expensive. In some monthly magazines it can cost the best part of £1,000= (US$1,600=) pro-rata per page to advertise. It can take years to 'build' trust and 20+ years to build databases of over 20,000 collectors. In the same way that one 'swallow does not make a summer' - one advertisement costing many hundreds of pounds/dollars will not usually 'yield' more than 20 responses from collectors, often less … and that may be for a 'free offer' in the first place. Philatelic advertising 'pays' as part of an overall marketing campaign - not 'stand-alone'.

You must be a committed seller offering superb service … depending upon what you are selling it can take months to build up sufficient high rated 'feedback' to build client 'trust'.

No. The answer to your quest to sell direct to collectors lies on the internet. This is where you employ the might of 'eBay/Amazon/ delcampe' to locate your clients for you. Naturally you pay a commission to do so when you 'list' an item for sale and a commission when you sell it … but these represent a fraction of your selling price and your items for sale are found directly by buyers who are likely to be collectors.

Of course this sounds like 'manna from heaven' and in many ways it is; but nothing is that simple in life otherwise we would all be millionaires. Take eBay - it is hard to imagine a more demanding taskmaster/environment. If you are not serious about selling on-line - take our advice - don't bother … the 'learning curve' is steep. You won't be successful without opening a 'Paypal' account and if you are dilatory about photographing / describing stamps, answering queries, posting the goods and accepting returns you will be severely punished by your clients - who 'expect' to buy one evening, pay on-line and have their stamps delivered all within a few days at most …

…. remember your eBay clients have the power to 'rate' you and all others can see. Internet auctions are transparent - and certainly on eBay you cannot 'rate' your clients or retaliate. You must be a committed seller offering superb service … depending upon what you are selling it can take months to build up sufficient high rated 'feedback' to build client 'trust'.

We often purchase collections from 'eBayers' who have literally given up …. but if this has not deterred you … you will be hard pressed to find a better avenue to 'reach' collectors directly … but be prepared - some items will sell for more than you expect … whilst others will sell for far less. 'On-line' price comparisons are easy and unscrupulous/naive sellers (often still with high feedback ratings) are commonly seen selling mutton dressed as lamb which easily undermines the price of similar high quality items you may be selling.

To read the rest of this series 'SELLING YOUR STAMPS?' see the relevant pages in each volume:

Summary Tip 18 – Volume 1 (opposite Key Types)
Summary Tip 19 – Volume 2 (opposite Key Types)
Summary Tip 20 – Volume 3 (opposite Key Types)
Summary Tip 21 – Volume 4 (opposite Key Types)
Summary Tip 22 – Volume 5 (opposite Key Types)

Please go to Volume 6 (opposite Key Types) to see how UPA can pay you up to 36% more for your collection.

So this brings us to the end of our 'Selling Your Stamps' series of 5 articles. The purpose has been to cogently 'inform' collectors of the variety of options open to them when disposing of their collections. If you have any further selling query please contact the writer. In our next 'tip #23' we'll further discuss the relationship of 'catalogue value' to real value..

Happy collecting from us all,

PS. If you find this 'tip' interesting please forward it to a philatelic friend.

Andrew McGavin

Managing Director: Universal Philatelic Auctions, Omniphil & Avon Approvals, Avon Mixtures, Universal Philatelic (Ebay)

ANDREW PROMOTING PHILATELY ON THE ALAN TITCHMARSH SHOW ITV

STAMPS! WE LOVE THEM! Buying or selling your stamps? Collectors – we have four different departments that can help you fi nd all the stamps you want.
Our Auctions have up to 20,671 lots in our famous quarterly auctions.
Visit **www.upastampauctions.co.uk** when you want to buy or sell stamps.
If you'd like to receive the rest of the series, why not sign up for our FREE Stamp Tips of The Trade via our website

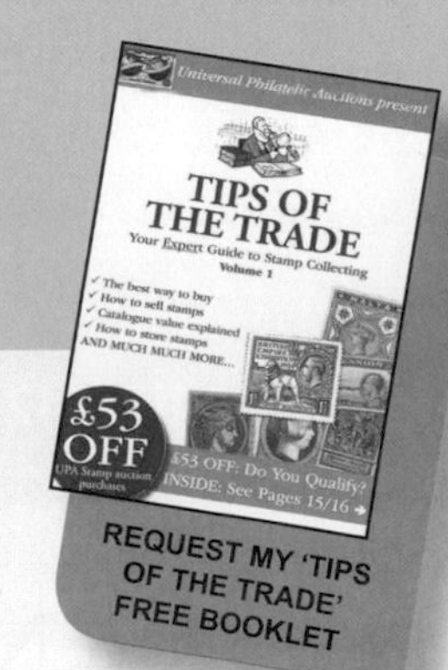

REQUEST MY 'TIPS OF THE TRADE' FREE BOOKLET

If you'd like to discuss the sale of your collection please contact Elaine or Andrew on 01451 861111

UNIVERSAL PHILATELIC AUCTIONS, 4 The Old Coalyard, West End
Northleach, Glos. GL54 3HE UK
Tel: 01451 861111 • Fax: 01451 861297
www.upastampauctions.co.uk • sellSG@upastampauctions.co.uk

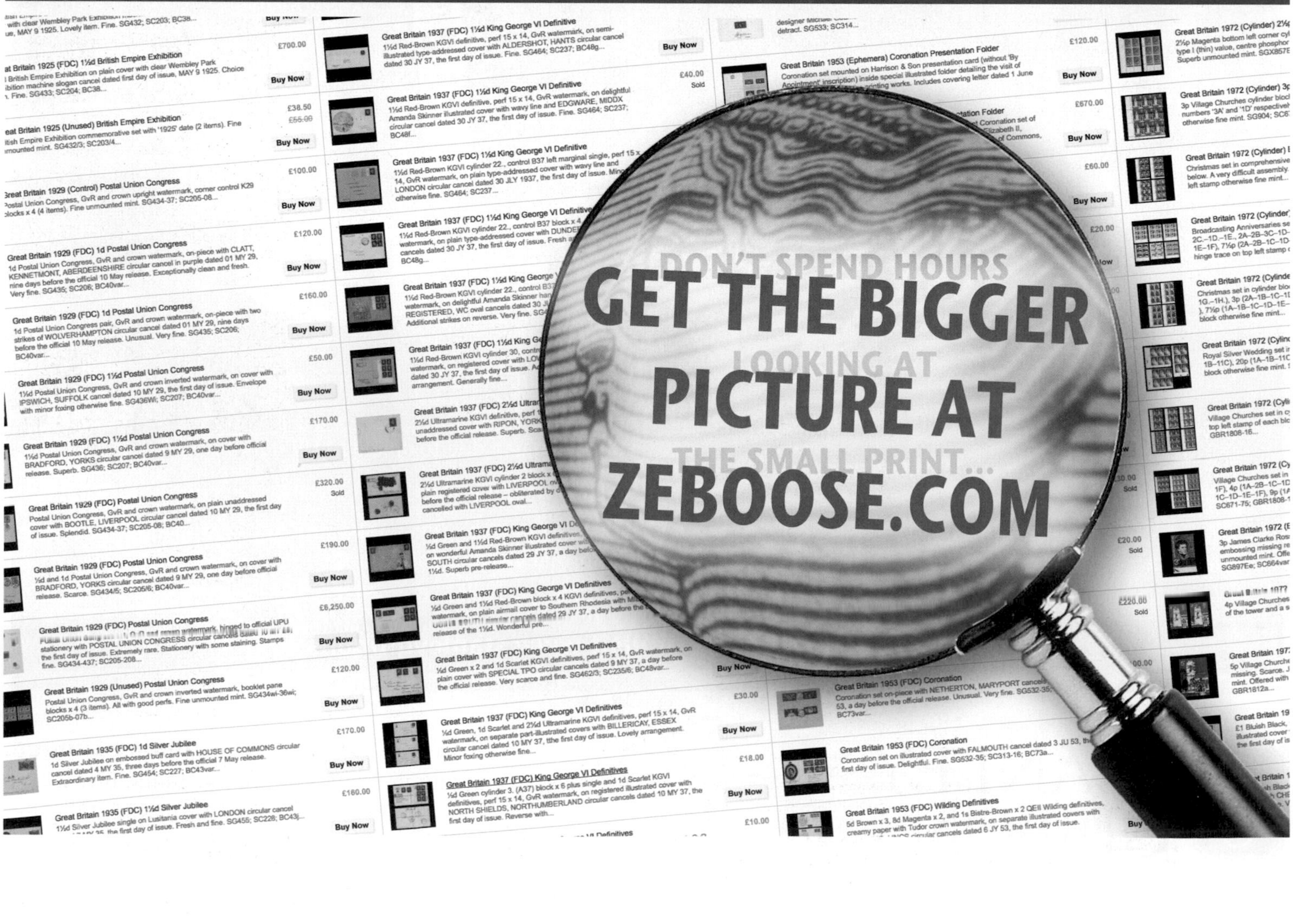

Pt. 1

NEW SOUTH WALES

A S.E. state of the Australian Commonwealth, whose stamps it now uses.

12 pence = 1 shilling; 20 shillings = 1 pound.

1 Seal of the Colony

1850. Imperf.

11		1d. red	£8000	£375
25		2d. blue	£6500	£160
42		3d. green	£8000	£250

8

1851. Imperf

47	**8**	1d. red	£1700	£140
83	**8**	1d. orange	£400	30·00
86	**8**	2d. blue	£300	12·00
87	**8**	3d. green	£500	42·00
76	**8**	6d. brown	£3250	£250
79	**8**	8d. yellow	£11000	£600

11

16

1854

109	**16**	1d. red	£275	24·00
112	**16**	2d. blue	£250	14·00
115	**16**	3d. green	£1300	90·00
88	**11**	5d. green	£1200	£650
90	**11**	6d. grey	£1400	35·00
96	**11**	6d. brown	£1400	35·00
98	**11**	8d. orange	£15000	£1300
100	**11**	1s. red	£2250	70·00

For these stamps perforated, see No. 134 etc.

24

1860. Perf

195	**16**	1d. red	£100	45·00
134		2d. blue	£200	13·00
226e	**16**	3d. green	6·00	1·00
233d	**11**	5d. green	11·00	1·25
143	**11**	6d. brown	£650	65·00
165	**11**	6d. violet	£130	4·75
236	**11**	8d. yellow	£190	19·00
170	**11**	1s. red	£225	8·00
297c	**24**	5s. purple	48·00	13·00

26

28

1862. Queen Victoria. Various frames.

223f	**26**	1d. red	9·00	1.25
225g	**28**	2d. blue	13·00	1·00
230c		4d. brown	75·00	2·75
234	-	6d. lilac	95·00	1·50
346a	-	10d. lilac	13·00	5.00
237	**11**	1s. black	£130	7·00

1871. As No. 346a, surch **NINEPENCE**.

322		9d. on 10d. brown	10·00	4·25

42

1885

238b	**42**	5s. green and lilac	£700	£110
275	**42**	10s. red and violet	£250	50·00
242	**42**	£1 red and lilac	£8000	£4250

45 View of Sydney

46 Emu

52 Capt. Arthur Phillip, 1st Governor, and Lord Carrington, Governor in 1888

1888. Centenary of New South Wales.

253	**45**	1d. mauve	13·00	1·00
254e	**46**	2d. blue	15·00	40
338	-	4d. brown	10·00	4·00
256	-	6d. red	32·00	4·50
297ffb	-	6d. green	26·00	16·00
306	-	6d. yellow	14·00	8·00
257	-	8d. purple	25·00	8·50
347	-	1s. brown	27·00	1·75
263	-	5s. violet	£225	32·00
350b	**52**	20s. blue	£325	65·00

DESIGNS—As Type **45**: 4d. Capt. Cook; 6d. Queen Victoria and Arms; 8d. Superb lyrebird; 1s. Kangaroo. As Type **52**: 5s. Map of Australia.

55 Allegorical Figure of Australia

1890

265	**55**	2½d. blue	13·00	60

1891. Types as 1862, but new value and colours, surch in words.

266	**26**	½d. on 1d. grey	4·50	5·00
267a	-	7½d. on 6d. brown	5·00	3.25
268c	-	12½d. on 1s. red	14·00	16.00

58

62

63

64

66 Superb Lyrebird

67

1892

272	**58**	½d. grey	4·50	40
298	**58**	½d. green	3·50	1·50
300	**62**	1d. red	5·00	70
335	**63**	2d. blue	2·25	35
296b	**64**	2½d. violet	26·00	2·00
303	**64**	2½d. blue	8·00	1·00
352	**67**	9d. brown and blue	16·00	1·75
349b	**66**	2s.6d. green	42·00	22·00

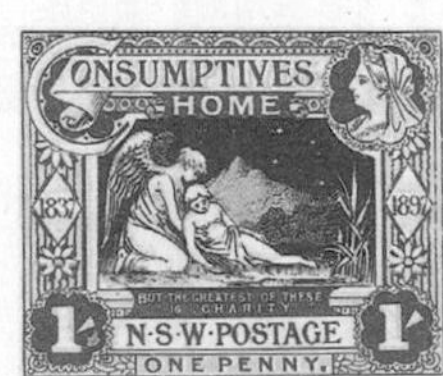
60

1897. Diamond Jubilee and Hospital Charity.

280	**60**	1d. (1s.) green and brown	48·00	50·00
281	-	2½d. (2s.6d.) gold & blue	£225	£225

DESIGN—VERT: 2½d. Two female figures.

OFFICIAL STAMPS

1879. Various issues optd **O. S.**

O20b	**26**	1d. red	13·00	1·40
O21c	**28**	2d. blue	9·00	1·00
O25c	**16**	3d. green	5·00	4·25
O26a	-	4d. brown (No. 230c)	17·00	4.00
O29b	**11**	5d. green	15·00	18.00
O31b	-	6d. lilac (No. 234)	22·00	6·50
O32	**11**	8d. orange	26·00	11·00
O11		9d. on 10d. (No. 322)	£850	£800
O18a	-	10d. lilac (No. 346a)	£375	£110
O33b	-	1s. black (No. 237)	29·00	8·00
O18	**24**	5s. purple	£400	90·00

1885. B. Fiscal stamps of 1885

O37	**24**	10s. red and violet	£5000	£1200
O38	**24**	£1 red and violet	£30000	£15000

1888. C. Issue of 1888 (Nos. 253/350b)

O39*b*	1d. mauve	3·00	75
O40	2d. blue	4·50	40
O41	4d. brown	11·00	4·25
O42	6d. red	8·50	8·50
O43	8d. purple	23·00	12·00
O44b	1s. brown	32·00	4·75
O49*a*	5s. violet	£350	£100
O48	20s. blue	£15000	£1000

1890. D. Issues of 1890 and 1892.

O55	**26**	½d. on 1d. grey	65·00	80·00
O58b	**58**	½d. grey	8·50	11·00
O54	**55**	2½d. blue	11·00	10·00
O56	-	7½d. on 6d. (No. 283)	45·00	70·00
O57	-	12½d. on 1s. (No. 284c)	65·00	£110

POSTAGE DUE STAMPS

D1

1891

D1	**D 1**	½d. green	11·00	6·50
D2b	**D 1**	1d. green	18·00	3·25
D3e	**D 1**	2d. green	22·00	3·75
D4	**D 1**	3d. green	60·00	11·00
D5b	**D 1**	4d. green	42·00	3·75
D6	**D 1**	6d. green	55·00	14·00
D7	**D 1**	8d. green	£110	26·00
D8	**D 1**	5s. green	£250	50·00
D9	**D 1**	10s. green	£650	70·00
D10b	**D 1**	20s. green	£600	

REGISTRATION STAMPS

15

1856

102	**15**	(6d.) red and blue (Imp)	£1600	£170
105	**15**	(6d.) orange and blue (Imp)	£1500	£200
119	**15**	(6d.) orange and blue (Perf)	£850	65·00
127	**15**	(6d.) red and blue (Perf)	£200	22·00

Pt. 1

NEW ZEALAND

A group of islands in the south Pacific Ocean. A Commonwealth Dominion.

1855. 12 pence = 1 shilling; 20 shillings = 1 pound.
1967. 100 cents = 1 dollar.

1

1855. Imperf.

34	**1**	1d. orange	£700	£275
35	**1**	1d. red	£450	£300
39	**1**	2d. blue	£700	90·00
40	**1**	3d. lilac	£600	£160
43	**1**	6d. brown	£1600	£110
45	**1**	1s. green	£1600	£350

1862. Perf.

110	**1**	1d. orange	£225	42·00
132	**1**	1d. brown	£250	48·00
114	**1**	2d. blue	£225	22·00
133	**1**	2d. orange	£170	29·00
117	**1**	3d. lilac	£160	35·00
119	**1**	4d. rose	£3250	£250
120	**1**	4d. yellow	£250	£120
122	**1**	6d. brown	£325	28·00
136	**1**	6d. blue	£225	55·00
125	**1**	1s. green	£325	£120

3

1873

151	**3**	½d. pink	14·00	2·00

5 **6** **7** **8** **9** **10** **11**

1874. Inscr "POSTAGE".

180	**5**	1d. lilac	60·00	8·00
181	**6**	2d. red	65·00	7·00
154	**7**	3d. brown	£170	80·00
182	**8**	4d. purple	£190	55·00
183	**9**	6d. blue	£130	12·00
184	**10**	1s. green	£200	50·00
185	**11**	2s. red	£375	£300
186	**11**	5s. grey	£375	£300

13 **16** **19**

1882. Inscr "POSTAGE & REVENUE".

227	**13**	½d. black	4·75	60
237	**10**	1d. red	5·00	10
238	**9**	2d. mauve	16·00	1·00
239	**16**	2½d. blue	55·00	4·00
240	**10**	3d. yellow	55·00	8·50
223	**19**	5d. black	65·00	27·00
243	**8**	6d. brown	70·00	6·00
244	**9**	8d. blue	80·00	60·00
245	**7**	1s. brown	£100	7·00

23 Mount Cook or Aorangi

24 Lake Taupo and Mount Ruapehu

25 Pembroke Peak, Milford Sound

26 Lake Wakatipu and Mount Earnslaw

28 Sacred Huia Birds

29 White Terrace, Rotomahana

30 Otira Gorge and Mount Ruapehu

31 Brown Kiwi

32 Maori War Canoe

33 Pink Terrace, Rotomahana

34 Kea and Kaka

35 Milford Sound

1898

246	**23**	½d. purple	8·50	1·50
302	**23**	½d. green	9·00	1·25
247	**24**	1d. blue and brown	6·00	60
248	**25**	2d. red	38·00	25
249	**26**	2½d. blue (A)*	11·00	50·00
320	**26**	2½d. blue (B)*	27·00	5·00
261	**28**	3d. brown	24·00	2·25

252	**29**	4d. red	17·00	19·00
263	**30**	5d. brown	42·00	5·00
254	**31**	6d. green	65·00	45·00
312	**31**	6d. red	40·00	7·50
325	**32**	8d. blue	48·00	11·00
326	**33**	9d. purple	40·00	8·50
268*a*	**34**	1s. orange	70·00	5·00
328	**35**	2s. green	£130	32·00
329*b*		5s. red	£225	£300

*Type A of 2½d. is inscr "WAKITIPU", Type B "WAKATIPU".

40 Commemorative of the New Zealand Contingent in the South African War

1900

274	**29**	1d. red	13·00	20
275*b*	**40**	1½d. brown	10·00	4·00
319	**25**	2d. purple	5·50	2·50
322*d*	**24**	4d. blue and brown	4·00	3·25

The 1d., 2d. and 4d. are smaller than the illustrations of their respective types.

42

1901

303	**42**	1d. red	3·00	10

44 Maori Canoe "Te Arawa"

1906. New Zealand Exhibition, Christchurch. Inscr "COMMEMORATIVE SERIES OF 1906".

370	**44**	½d. green	38·00	35·00
371	-	1d. red	16·00	16·00
372	-	3d. brown and blue	55·00	85·00
373	-	6d. red and green	£200	£275

DESIGNS: 1d. Maori art; 3d. Landing of Cook; 6d. Annexation of New Zealand.

50

1907

386	**50**	1d. red	23·00	3·00
383	**28**	3d. brown	50·00	15·00
376	**31**	6d. red	45·00	10·00
385	**34**	1s. orange	£110	24·00

These are smaller in size than the 1898 and 1901 issues. Type **50** also differs from Type **42** in the corner ornaments.

50 **51** King Edward VII **53** Dominion

1907

387	**51**	½d. green	5·00	50
405	**53**	1d. red	1·75	10
388	**51**	2d. mauve	9·50	6·50
389	**51**	3d. brown	23·00	1·25
390a	**51**	4d. yellow	6·00	9·50
396	**51**	4d. orange	20·00	15·00
391	**51**	5d. brown	17·00	5·00
392	**51**	6d. red	40·00	2·00
393	**51**	8d. blue	13·00	3·50
394	**51**	1s. red	50·00	5·00

These are smaller in size than the 1898 and 1901 issues. Type **50** also differs from Type **42** in the corner ornaments.

1913. Auckland Industrial Exhibition. Optd **AUCKLAND EXHIBITION, 1913.**

412	**51**	½d. green	21·00	55·00
413	**53**	1d. red	27·00	50·00
414	**51**	3d. brown	£130	£250
415	**51**	6d. red	£160	£300

62 King George V

1915

435	**62**	½d. green	1·50	20
416	**62**	1½d. grey	3·25	2·50
438	**62**	1½d. brown	2·25	20
417a	**62**	2d. violet	7·00	50·00
439	**62**	2d. yellow	2·25	20
419	**62**	2½d. blue	3·25	7·00
440	**62**	3d. brown	7·00	75
421	**62**	4d. yellow	4·25	60·00
422e	**62**	4d. violet	7·00	50
423	**62**	4½d. green	17·00	28·00
424	**62**	5d. blue	7·00	1·00
425	**62**	6d. red	9·00	50
426	**62**	7½d. brown	14·00	28·00
427a	**62**	8d. blue	8·50	55·00
428	**62**	8d. brown	30·00	1·50
429	**62**	9d. green	17·00	2·75
430c	**62**	1s. orange	14·00	50

1915. No. 446 optd **WAR STAMP** and stars.

452	½d. green	2·25	50

64 "Peace" and Lion **65** "Peace" and Lion

1920. Victory. Inscr "VICTORY" or dated "1914 1919" (6d.).

453	**64**	½d. green	3·00	2·50
454	**65**	1d. red	4·50	60
455	-	1½d. orange	3·00	50
456	-	3d. brown	12·00	14·00
457	-	6d. violet	14·00	17·00
458	-	1s. orange	23·00	50·00

DESIGNS—HORIZ (As Type **65**): 1½d. Maori chief. (As Type **64**): 3d. Lion; 1s. King George V. VERT (As Type **64**): 6d. "Peace" and "Progress".

1922. No. 453 surch **2d. 2d. TWOPENCE**.

459	**64**	2d. on ½d. green	4·75	1·40

69 New Zealand

1923. Restoration of Penny Postage.

460	**69**	1d. red	4·00	60

70 Exhibition Buildings

1925. Dunedin Exhibition.

463	**70**	½d. green on green	3·00	15·00
464	**70**	1d. red on rose	4·25	7·00
465	**70**	4d. mauve on mauve	30·00	75·00

71

1926

468	**71**	1d. red	75	20
469	-	2s. blue	75·00	29·00
467	-	3s. mauve	£110	£200

The 2s. and 3s. are larger, 21×25 mm.

73 Nurse

1929. Anti-T.B. Fund.

(a) Inscribed "HELP STAMP OUT TUBERCULOSIS"

544	**73**	1d. +1d. red	11·00	18·00

(b) Inscribed "HELP PROMOTE HEALTH"

545	1d. +1d. red	20·00	45·00

74 Smiling Boy

1931. Health Stamps.

546	**74**	1d.+1d. +1d. red	75·00	75·00
547	**74**	2d.+1d. +1d. blue	75·00	60·00

75 New Zealand Lake Scenery

1931. Air.

548	**75**	3d. brown	22·00	16·00
549	**75**	4d. purple	22·00	22·00
550	**75**	7d. orange	22·00	9·00

1931. Air. Surch **FIVE PENCE**.

551	5d. on 3d. green	10·00	10·00

77 Hygeia Goddess of Health

1932. Health Stamp.

552	**77**	1d. +1d. red	24·00	30·00

78 The Path to Health

1933. Health Stamp.

553	**78**	1d. +1d. red	15·00	20·00

1934. Air. Optd **TRANS-TASMAN AIR MAIL "FAITH IN AUSTRALIA."**

554	**75**	7d. blue	35·00	50·00

80 Crusader

1934. Health Stamp.

555	**80**	1d. +1d. red	11·00	17·00

81 Collared Grey Fantail **83** Maori Woman **85** Mt. Cook

86 Maori Girl **87** Mitre Peak **89** Harvesting

91 Maori Panel **93** Capt. Cook at Poverty Bay

1935

556	**81**	½d. green	3·25	1·50
578	-	1d. red	4·50	10
558a	**83**	1½d. brown	6·50	13·00
580	-	2d. orange	30	10
581c	**85**	2½d. brown and grey	1·00	5·50
561	**86**	3d. brown	12·00	3·75
583d	**87**	4d. black and brown	1·00	20
584c		5d. blue	2·00	2·25
585c	**89**	6d. red	1·25	20
586d		8d. brown	4·00	1·50
631	**91**	9d. red and black	3·00	5·00
588	-	1s. green	2·50	1·25
590c		3s. chocolate and brown	3·25	3·25

DESIGNS—As Type **81**: 1d. Brown kiwi; 2d. Maori carved house; 1s. Parson bird. As Type **87**: 8d. Tuatara lizard. As Type **85**: 5d. Swordfish; 3s. Mt. Egmont.

95 Bell Block Aerodrome

1935. Air.

570	**95**	1d. red	1·00	70
571	**95**	3d. violet	5·00	3·00
572	**95**	6d. blue	9·50	3·00

96 King George V and Queen Mary

1935. Silver Jubilee.

573	**96**	½d. green	75	1·00
574	**96**	1d. red	1·00	80
575	**96**	6d. orange	20·00	32·00

97 "The Key to Health"

1935. Health Stamp.

576	**97**	1d. +1d. red	2·50	3·75

99 N.Z. Soldier at Anzac Cove

1936. Charity. 21st Anniv of "Anzac" Landing at Gallipoli.

591	**99**	½d. +½d. green	75	1·75
592	**99**	1d. +1d. red	1·25	1·40

100 Wool

1936. Congress of British Empire Chambers of Commerce, Wellington. Inscr as in T **100**.

593	**100**	½d. green	30	30
594	-	1d. red (Butter)	30	20
595	-	2½d. blue (Sheep)	1·50	8·00
596	-	4d. violet (Apples)	1·25	5·50
597	-	6d. brown (Exports)	4·00	6·50

105 Health Camp

1936. Health Stamp.

598	**105**	1d. +1d. red	2·75	3·75

106 King George VI and Queen Elizabeth

1937. Coronation.

599	**106**	1d. red	30	10
600	**106**	2½d. blue	[illegible]	[illegible]
601	**106**	6d. orange	1·10	2·25

107 Rock climbing

1937. Health Stamp.

602	**107**	1d. +1d. red	3·75	3·75

108 King George VI

1938

603	**108**	½d. green	8·50	10
604	**108**	½d. brown	20	40
605	**108**	1d. red	5·00	10
606	**108**	1d. green	20	10
607	**108**	1½d. brown	26·00	3·25
608	**108**	1½d. red	20	80
680	**108**	2d. orange	30	10
609	**108**	3d. blue	20	10
681	**108**	4d. purple	80	1·00
682	**108**	5d. grey	1·00	1·00
683	**108**	6d. red	1·00	10
684	**108**	8d. violet	1·00	1·25
685	**108**	9d. brown	2·00	60
686b	-	1s. brown and red	60	80
687	-	1s.3d. brown and blue	2·50	1·25
688	-	2s. orange and green	8·00	2·50
689	-	3s. brown and grey	4·50	3·50

The shilling values are larger, 22×25½ mm, and "NEW ZEALAND" appears at the top.

109 Children playing

1938. Health Stamp.

610	**109**	1d. +1d. red	9·00	3·25

110 Beach Ball

1939. Health Stamps. Surch.

611	**110**	1d. on ½d. green	4·75	6·00
612	**110**	2d. on 1d.+1d. red	5·50	6·00

112 "Endeavour", Chart of N.Z. and Captain Cook

1940. Centenary of Proclamation of British Sovereignty. Inscr "CENTENNIAL OF NEW ZEALAND 1840 1940".

613	-	½d. green	50	10
614	**112**	1d. brown and red	4·00	10
615	-	1½d. blue and mauve	30	60
616	-	2d. green and brown	1·50	10
617	-	2½d. green and blue	2·00	1·00
618	-	3d. purple and red	4·00	1·25
619	-	4d. brown and red	14·00	1·50
620	-	5d. blue and brown	10·00	3·75
621	-	6d. green and violet	11·00	1·25
622	-	7d. black and red	1·75	4·00
623	-	8d. black and red	11·00	6·00
624	-	9d. green and orange	7·50	2·00
625	-	1s. green and deep green	13·00	4·00

DESIGNS—HORIZ (as T **112**): ½d. Arrival of the Maoris, 1350; 1½d. British Monarchs; 2d. Abel Tasman with "Heemskerk" and chart; 3d. Landing of immigrants, 1840; 4d. Road, rail, ocean and air transport; 6d. "Dunedin" and "frozen mutton" sea route to London; 7, 8d. Maori council; 9d. Gold mining methods, 1861 and 1940. (25×21 mm): 5d. H.M.S. "Britomart" at Akaroa, 1840. VERT (21×25 mm): 2½d. Treaty of Waitangi. (As T **112**): 1s. Giant kauri tree.

1940. Health Stamps.

626	**110**	1d. +½d. green	11·00	14·00
627	**110**	2d. +1d. orange	11·00	14·00

1941. Surch.

628	**108**	1d. on ½d. green	1·75	10
629	**108**	2d. on 1½d. brown	1·75	10

1941. Health Stamps. Optd **1941**.

632	**110**	1d. +½d. green	50	2·25
633	**110**	2d. +1d. orange	50	2·25

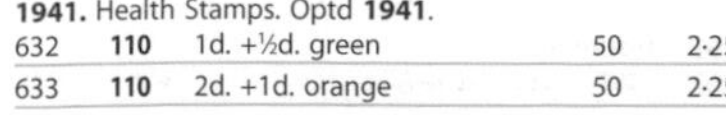

125 Boy and Girl on Swing

1942. Health Stamps.

634	**125**	1d. +½d. green	30	1·25
635	**125**	2d. +1d. orange	30	1·25

126 Princess Margaret

1943. Health Stamps.

636	**126**	1d. +½d. green	20	1·50
637	-	2d. +1d. brown	20	25

DESIGN: 2d. Queen Elizabeth II as Princess.

1944. Surch **TENPENCE** between crosses.

662		10d. on 1½d. blue and mauve (No. 615)	15	30

129 Queen Elizabeth II as Princess and Princess Margaret

1944. Health Stamps.

663	**129**	1d. +½d. green	30	40
664	**129**	2d. +1d. blue	30	30

130 Peter Pan Statue, Kensington Gardens

1945. Health Stamps.

665	**130**	1d. +½d. green and buff	15	20
666	**130**	2d. +1d. red and buff	15	20

131 Lake Matheson

132 King George VI and Parliament House, Wellington

133 St. Paul's Cathedral

139 "St. George" (Wellington College War Memorial window)

1946. Peace Issue.

667	**131**	½d. green and brown	20	65
668	**132**	1d. green	10	10
669	**133**	1½d. red	10	50
670	-	2d. purple	15	10
671	-	3d. blue and grey	45	15
672	-	4d. green and orange	50	20
673	-	5d. green and blue	1·25	1·75
674	-	6d. brown and red	20	30
675	**139**	8d. black and red	20	30
676	-	9d. blue and black	20	30
677	-	1s. grey	1·00	40

DESIGNS—As Type **132**: 2d. The Royal Family. As Type **131**: 3d. R.N.Z.A.F. badge and airplanes; 4d. Army badge, tank and plough; 5d. Navy badge, H.M.N.Z.S. "Achilles" (cruiser) and "Dominion Monarch" (liner); 6d. N.Z. coat of arms, foundry and farm; 9d. Southern Alps and Franz Josef Glacier. As T **139**: 1s. National Memorial campanile.

142 Soldier helping Child over Stile

1946. Health Stamps.

678	**142**	1d. +½d. green and orange	15	15
679	**142**	2d. +1d. brown & orange	15	15

145 Statue of Eros

1947. Health Stamps.

690	**145**	1d. +½d. green	15	15
691	**145**	2d. +1d. red	15	15

146 Port Chalmers, 1848

1948. Centenary of Otago. Various designs inscr "CENTENNIAL OF OTAGO".

692	**146**	1d. blue and green	25	35
693	-	2d. green and brown	25	35
694	-	3d. purple	30	60
695	-	6d. black and red	30	60

DESIGNS—HORIZ: 2d. Cromwell, Otago; 6d. Otago University. VERT: 3d. First Church, Dune-din.

150 Boy sunbathing and Children playing

1948. Health Stamps.

696	**150**	1d. +½d. blue and green	15	20
697	**150**	2d. +1d. purple and red	15	20

151 Nurse and Child

1949. Health Stamps.

698	**151**	1d. +½d. green	25	20
699	**151**	2d. +1d. blue	25	20

1950. As Type **F6**, but without value, surch **1½d. POSTAGE**.

700		1½d. red	40	30

Type **F6** is illustrated at end of New Zealand

153 Queen Elizabeth II and Prince Charles

1950. Health Stamps.

701	**153**	1d. +½d. green	25	20
702	**153**	2d. +1d. purple	25	20

155 Cairn on Lyttleton Hills

1950. Centenary of Canterbury, N.Z.

703	-	1d. green and blue	60	85
704	**155**	2d. red and orange	60	85
705	-	3d. deep blue and blue	60	1·25
706	-	6d. brown and blue	75	1·00
707	-	1s. purple and blue	75	1·60

DESIGNS—VERT: 1d. Christchurch Cathedral; 3d. John Robert Godley. HORIZ: 6d. Canterbury University College; 1s. Aerial view of Timaru.

159 "Takapuna" class Yachts

1951. Health Stamps.

708	**159**	1½d. +½d. red and yellow	50	1·00
709	**159**	2d. +1d. green and yellow	50	25

160 Princess Anne

161 Prince Charles

1952. Health Stamps.

710	**160**	1½d. +½d. red	15	30
711	**161**	2d. +1d. brown	15	20

1952. Surch in figures.

712	**108**	1d. on ½d. orange	30	1·00
713	**108**	3d. on 1d. green	10	10

164 Queen Elizabeth II

165 Coronation State Coach

166 Westminster Abbey

1953. Coronation.

714	-	2d. blue	40	30
715	**164**	3d. brown	30	10
716	**165**	4d. red	1·40	2·50
717	**166**	8d. grey	1·00	1·60
718	-	1s.6d. purple and blue	2·75	3·25

DESIGNS—As Type **165**: 2d. Queen Elizabeth II and Buckingham Palace; 1s.6d. St. Edward's Crown and Royal Sceptre.

168 Girl Guides

169 Boy Scouts

1953. Health Stamps.

719	**168**	1½d. +½d. blue	15	10
720	**169**	2d. +1d. green	15	40

170 Queen Elizabeth II

171 Queen Elizabeth II and Duke of Edinburgh

1953. Royal Visit.

721	**170**	3d. purple	15	10
722	**171**	4d. blue	15	60

172

173

174 Queen Elizabeth II

1953. Small figures of value.

723	**172**	½d. black	15	30
724	**172**	1d. orange	15	10

725	**172**	1½d. brown	20	10
726	**172**	2d. green	20	10
727	**172**	3d. red	20	10
728	**172**	4d. blue	40	50
729	**172**	6d. purple	70	1·60
730	**172**	8d. red	60	60
731	**173**	9d. brown and green	60	60
732	**173**	1s. black and red	65	10
733	**173**	1s.6d. black and blue	1·50	60
733bc	**173**	1s.9d. black and orange	4·00	1·50
733d	**174**	2s.6d. brown	13·00	8·00
734	**174**	3s. green	14·00	50
735	**174**	5s. red	30·00	4·50
736	**174**	10s. blue	50·00	19·00

175 Young Climber and Mts. Aspiring and Everest

1954. Health Stamps.

737	**175**	1½d. +½d. brown and violet	15	30
738	**175**	2d. +1d. brown and blue	15	30

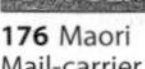

176 Maori Mail-carrier **177** Queen Elizabeth II

1955. Centenary of First New Zealand Stamps. Inscr "**1855–1955**".

739	**176**	2d. brown and green	10	10
740	**177**	3d. red	10	10
741	-	4d. black and blue	70	1·00

DESIGN—HORIZ (As Type **176**): 4d. Douglas DC-3 airliner.

179 Children's Health Camps Federation Emblem

1955. Health Stamps.

742	**179**	1½d. +½d. brown and chestnut	10	60
743	**179**	2d. +1d. red and green	10	35
744	**179**	3d. +1d. brown and red	15	15

180

1955. As 1953 but larger figures of value and stars omitted from lower right corner.

745	**180**	1d. orange	50	10
746	**180**	1½d. brown	60	60
747	**180**	2d. green	40	10
748b	**180**	3d. red	30	10
749	**180**	4d. blue	1·00	80
750	**180**	6d. purple	8·00	20
751	**180**	8d. brown	3·50	4·25

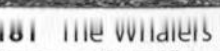

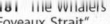

181 "The Whalers of Foveaux Strait" **183** Takahe

1956. Southland Centennial.

752	**181**	2d. green	30	15
753	-	3d. brown	10	10
754	**183**	8d. violet and red	1·25	1·75

DESIGN—As Type **181**: 3d. Allegory of farming.

184 Children picking Apples

1956. Health Stamps.

755	**184**	1½d. +½d. brown	15	70
756	**184**	2d. +1d. green	15	55
757	**184**	3d. +1d. red	15	15

185 New Zealand Lamb and Map

1957. 75th Anniv of First Export of N.Z. Lamb.

758	**185**	4d. blue	50	1·00
759	-	8d. red	75	1·25

DESIGN—HORIZ: 8d. Lamb, sailing ship "Dunedin" and "Port Brisbane" (refrigerated freighter).

187 Sir Truby King

1957. 50th Anniv of Plunket Society.

760	**187**	3d. red	10	10

188 Life-savers in Action

1957. Health Stamps.

761	**188**	2d. +1d. black and green	15	70
762	-	3d. +1d. blue and red	15	10
MS762b Two sheets, each 112×96 mm, with Nos. 761 and 762 in blocks of 6 (2×3) Per pair			7·00	25·00

DESIGN: 3d. Children on seashore.

1958. Surch

763a	**180**	2d. on 1½d. brown	15	10
808a	**180**	2½d. on 3d. red	15	30

192 Boys' Brigade Bugler

1958. Health Stamps.

764	-	2d. +1d. green	20	40
765	**192**	3d. +1d. blue	20	40
MS765a Two sheets, each 104×124 mm, with Nos. 764/5 in blocks of 6 (3×2) Per pair			10·00	22·00

DESIGN: 2d. Girls' Life Brigade cadet.

193 Sir Charles Kingsford-Smith and Fokker F.IIa/3m Southern Cross

1958. 30th Anniv of First Air Crossing of Tasman Sea.

766	**193**	6d. blue	50	75

194 Seal of Nelson

1958. Centenary of City of Nelson.

767	**194**	3d. red	10	10

195 "Pania" Statue, Napier **196** Australian Gannets on Cape Kidnappers

1958. Centenary of Hawke's Bay Province.

768	**195**	2d. green	10	10
769	**196**	3d. blue	30	10
770	-	8d. brown	70	1·50

DESIGN—As Type **195**: 8d. Maori sheep-shearer.

197 "Kiwi", Jamboree Badge

1959. Pan-Pacific Scout Jamboree, Auckland.

771	**197**	3d. brown and red	30	10

198 Careening H.M.S. "Endeavour" at Ship Cove

1959. Centenary of Marlborough Province. Inscr as in T **198**.

772	**198**	2d. green	30	10
773	-	3d. blue	30	10
774	-	8d. brown	1·40	2·00

DESIGNS: 3d. Shipping wool, Wairau Bar, 1857; 8d. Salt industry, Grassmere.

201 Red Cross Flag

1959. Red Cross Commemoration.

775	**201**	3d.+1d. +1d. red and blue	20	10

202 Grey Teal

1959. Health Stamps.

776	**202**	2d. +1d. yellow, olive and red	50	65
777	-	3d. +1d. black, pink and blue	50	65
MS777c Two sheets, each 95×109 mm, with Nos. 776/7 in blocks of 6 (3×2) Per pair			9·00	26·00

DESIGN: 3d. New Zealand stilt.

204 "The Explorer"

1960. Centenary of Westland Province.

778	**204**	2d. green	20	10
779	-	3d. salmon	30	10
780	-	8d. black	90	3·00

DESIGNS: 3d. "The Gold Digger"; 8d. "The Pioneer Woman".

207 Manuka (Tea Tree) **215** Timber Industry **219** Taniwha (Maori Rock Drawing)

1960

781	**207**	½d. green and red	10	10
782	-	1d. multicoloured	10	10
783	-	2d. multicoloured	10	10
784	-	2½d. multicoloured	1·00	10
785	-	3d. multicoloured	30	10
786	-	4d. multicoloured	40	10
787	-	5d. multicoloured	1·25	10
788	-	6d. lilac, green and turquoise	50	10
788d	-	7d. red, green and yellow	65	4·50
789	-	8d. multicoloured	40	10
790	-	9d. red and blue	40	10
791	**215**	1s. brown and green	30	10
792*b*	-	1s.3d. red, sepia and blue	2·00	25
793	-	1s.6d. olive and brown	75	10
794	-	1s.9d. brown	15·00	15
795	-	1s.9d. multicoloured	2·50	1·00
796	**219**	2s. black and buff	2·50	10
797	-	2s.6d. yellow and brown	1·50	1·00
798	-	3s. sepia	17·00	1·00
799	-	3s. bistre, blue and green	2·00	1·75
800	-	5s. myrtle	2·00	80
801	-	10s. blue	4·00	3·25
802	-	£1 mauve	10·00	8·00

DESIGNS—VERT (as Type **207**): 1d. Karaka; 2d. Kowhai Ngutu-kaka (Kaka Beak); 2½d. Titoki (plant); 3d. Kowhai; 4d. Puarangi (Hibiscus); 5d. Matua tikumu (Mountain daisy); 6d. Pikiarero (Clematis); 7d. Koromiko; 8d. Rata. (As T **215**): 1s.3d. Rainbow trout; 1s.6d. Tiki. (As T **219**): 5s. Sutherland Falls; £1 Potutu Geyser. HORIZ (as T **215**): 9d. National flag; 1s.9d. Aerial top- dressing. (As Type **219**): 2s.6d. Butter-making; 3s. Tongariro National Park and Chateau; 10s. Tasman Glacier.

225 Sacred Kingfisher

1960. Health Stamps.

803	**225**	2d. +1d. sepia and blue	50	75
804	-	3d. +1d. purple & orange	50	75
MS804b Two sheets, each 95×107 mm, with Nos. 803/4 in blocks of 6 Per pair			27·00	38·00

DESIGN: 3d. New Zealand pigeon.

227 "The Adoration of the Shepherds" (Rembrandt)

1960. Christmas.

805	**227**	2d. red & brown on cream	15	10

228 Great Egret

1961. Health Stamps.

806	**228**	2d. +1d. black and purple	50	70
807	-	3d. +1d. sepia and green	50	70
MS807a Two sheets, each 97×121 mm, with Nos. 806/7 in blocks of 6 (3×2) Per pair			27·00	35·00

DESIGN: 3d. New Zealand falcon.

232 "Adoration of the Magi" (Durer)

1961. Christmas.

809	**232**	2½d. multicoloured	10	10

233 Morse Key and Port Hills, Lyttleton

1962. Telegraph Centenary.

No.	Type	Description	Unused	Used
810	**233**	3d. sepia and green	10	10
811	-	8d. black and red	90	90

DESIGN: 8d. Modern teleprinter.

236 Tieke Saddleback

1962. Health Stamps.

No.	Type	Description	Unused	Used
812		2½d. +1d. multicoloured	50	70
813	**236**	3d. +1d. multicoloured	50	70
MS813b		Two sheets, each 96×101 mm, with Nos. 812/13 in blocks of 6 (3×2) Per pair	40·00	50·00

DESIGN: 2½d. Red-fronted parakeet.

237 "Madonna in Prayer" (Sassoferrato)

1962. Christmas.

No.	Type	Description	Unused	Used
814	**237**	2½d. multicoloured	10	10

238 Prince Andrew

1963. Health Stamps.

No.	Type	Description	Unused	Used
815*b*	**238**	2½d. +1d. blue	30	40
816	-	3d. +1d. red	30	10
MS816b		Two sheets, each 93×100 mm, with Nos. 815/16 in blocks of 6 (3×2) Per pair	25·00	40·00

DESIGN: 3d. Prince Andrew (different).

240 "The Holy Family" (Titian)

1963. Christmas.

No.	Type	Description	Unused	Used
817	**240**	2½d. multicoloured	10	10

241 Steam Locomotive "Pilgrim" (1863) and Class DG Diesel Locomotive

1963. Centenary of New Zealand Railway. Inscr as in T **241**. Multicoloured.

No.	Type	Description	Unused	Used
818		3d. Type **241**	40	10
819		1s.9d. Diesel express and Mt. Ruapehu	1·75	1·25

243 "Commonwealth Cable"

1963. Opening of COMPAC (Trans-Pacific Telephone Cable).

No.	Type	Description	Unused	Used
820	**243**	8d. multicoloured	50	1·00

244 Road Map and Car Steering-wheel

1964. Road Safety Campaign.

No.	Type	Description	Unused	Used
821	**244**	3d. black, yellow and blue	30	10

245 Silver Gulls

1964. Health Stamps. Multicoloured.

No.	Type	Description	Unused	Used
822		2½d. +1d. Type **245**	40	50
823		3d. +1d. Little penguin	40	50
MS823b		Two sheets, each 171×84 mm, with Nos. 822/3 in blocks of 8 (4×2) Per pair	48·00	65·00

246 Rev. S. Marsden taking first Christian Service at Rangihoua Bay, 1814

1964. Christmas.

No.	Type	Description	Unused	Used
824	**246**	2½d. multicoloured	10	10

1964. Surch **7D POSTAGE**.

No.	Type	Description	Unused	Used
825	**F6**	7d. on (-) red	50	1·50

248 Anzac Cove

1965. 50th Anniv of Gallipoli Landing.

No.	Type	Description	Unused	Used
826	**248**	4d. brown	10	10
827	-	5d. green and red	10	60

DESIGN: 5d. Anzac Cove and poppy.

249 I.T.U. Emblem and Symbols

1965. Centenary of I.T.U.

No.	Type	Description	Unused	Used
828	**249**	9d. blue and brown	55	35

250 Sir Winston Churchill

1965. Churchill Commemoration.

No.	Type	Description	Unused	Used
829	**250**	7d. black, grey and blue	30	50

251 Wellington Provincial Council Building

1965. Centenary of Government in Wellington.

No.	Type	Description	Unused	Used
830	**251**	4d. multicoloured	10	10

252 Kaka

1965. Health Stamps. Multicoloured.

No.	Type	Description	Unused	Used
831		3d. +1d. Type **252**	40	65
832		4d. +1d. Collared grey fantail	40	65
MS832c		Two sheets, each 100×109 mm, with Nos. 831/2 in blocks of 6 (3×2) Per pair	38·00	48·00

254 I.C.Y. Emblem

1965. International Co-operation Year.

No.	Type	Description	Unused	Used
833	**254**	4d. red and olive	20	10

255 "The Two Trinities" (Murillo)

1965. Christmas.

No.	Type	Description	Unused	Used
834	**255**	3d. multicoloured	10	10

256 Arms of New Zealand

1965. 11th Commonwealth Parliamentary Conf. Multicoloured.

No.	Type	Description	Unused	Used
835		4d. Type **256**	20	10
836		9d. Parliament House, Wellington, and Badge	40	45
837		2s. Wellington from Mt. Victoria	2·75	4·00

259 "Progress" Arrowhead

1966. Fourth National Scout Jamboree, Trentham.

No.	Type	Description	Unused	Used
838	**259**	4d. gold and green	15	10

260 New Zealand Bell Bird

1966. Health Stamps. Multicoloured.

No.	Type	Description	Unused	Used
839		3d. +1d. Type **260**	50	75
840		4d. +1d. Weka rail	50	75
MS841		Two sheets, each 107×91 mm. Nos. 839/40 in blocks of 6 (3×2) Per pair	20·00	50·00

262 "The Virgin with Child" (Maratta)

1966. Christmas.

No.	Type	Description	Unused	Used
842	**262**	3d. multicoloured	10	10

263 Queen Victoria and Queen Elizabeth II

1967. Centenary of New Zealand Post Office Savings Bank.

No.	Type	Description	Unused	Used
843	**263**	4d. black, gold and purple	10	10
844	-	9d. multicoloured	10	20

DESIGN: 9d. Half-sovereign of 1867 and commemorative dollar coin.

265 Manuka (Tea Tree)

1967. Decimal Currency. Designs as earlier issues, but with values inscr in decimal currency as T **265**.

No.	Type	Description	Unused	Used
845	**265**	½c. blue, green and red	10	10
846	-	1c. mult (No. 782)	10	10
847	-	2c. mult (No. 783)	10	10
848	-	2½c. mult (No. 785)	10	10
849	-	3c. mult (No. 786)	10	10
850	-	4c. mult (No. 787)	30	10
851	-	5c. lilac, olive and green (No. 788)	50	1·00
852	-	6c. mult (No. 788d)	50	1·00
853	-	7c. mult (No. 789)	60	1·50
854	-	8c. red and blue (No. 790)	60	60
855	**215**	10c. brown and green	60	1·00
856	-	15c. green and brown (No. 793)	2·25	2·25
857	**219**	20c. black and buff	1·00	20
858	-	25c. yellow and brown (No. 797)	1·25	2·00
859	-	30c. yellow, green and blue (No. 799)	1·25	25
860	-	50c. green (No. 800)	1·75	50
861	-	$1 blue (No. 801)	9·00	1·00
862	-	$2 mauve (No. 802)	4·00	6·00
F219a	**F6**	$4 violet	2·50	1·50
F220a	**F6**	$6 green	3·00	3·25
F221a	**F6**	$8 blue	3·00	4·50
F222a	**F6**	$10 blue	3·00	3·75

For 15c. in different colours, see No. 874.

268 Running with Ball

1967. Health Stamps. Rugby Football.

No.	Type	Description	Unused	Used
867	**268**	2½c. +1c. multicoloured	15	15
868	-	3c. +1c. multicoloured	15	15
MS869		Two sheets. (a) 76×130 mm (867). (b) 130×76 mm (868). Containing blocks of six Per pair	20·00	38·00

DESIGN—HORIZ: 3c. Positioning for place-kick.

271 Brown Trout

273 Forest and Timber

1967

No.	Type	Description	Unused	Used
870		7c. multicoloured	1·00	1·00
871	**271**	7½c. multicoloured	50	70
872	-	8c. multicoloured	75	70
873	**273**	10c. multicoloured	50	10
874	-	15c. green, deep green and red (as No. 793)	1·00	1·00
875	-	18c. multicoloured	1·00	55
876	-	20c. multicoloured	1·00	20
877	-	25c. multicoloured	1·75	2·00
878	-	28c. multicoloured	60	10
879	-	$2 black, ochre and blue (as No. 802)	13·00	13·00

DESIGNS: 7c. "Kaitia" (trawler) and catch; 8c. Apples and orchard; 18c. Sheep and the "Woolmark"; 20c. Consignments of beef and herd of cattle; 25c. Dairy farm, Mt. Egmont and butter consignment. VERT: 28c. Fox Glacier, Westland National Park.

No. 871 was originally issued to commemorate the introduction of the brown trout into New Zealand.

No. 874 is slightly larger than No. 793, measuring 21×25 mm, and the inscr and numerals differ in size.

278 "The Adoration of the Shepherds" (Poussin)

1967. Christmas.

No.	Type	Description	Unused	Used
880	**278**	2½c. multicoloured	10	10

279 Mount Aspiring, Aurora Australis and Southern Cross

1967. Centenary of Royal Society of New Zealand.

881	**279**	4c. multicoloured	25	20
882	-	8c. multicoloured	25	80

DESIGN: 8c. Sir James Hector (founder).

281 Open Bible

1968. Centenary of Maori Bible.

883	**281**	3c. multicoloured	10	10

282 Soldiers and Tank

1968. New Zealand Armed Forces. Multicoloured.

884	4c. Type **282**	25	10
885	10c. Airmen, Fairey Firefly and English Electric Canberra aircraft	40	50
886	28c. Sailors and H.M.N.Z.S. "Achilles", 1939, and H.M.N.Z.S. "Waikato", 1968	70	1·60

285 Boy breasting Tape and Olympic Rings

1968. Health Stamps. Multicoloured.

887	2½c. +1c. Type **285**	20	15
888	3c. +1c. Girl swimming and Olympic rings	20	15
MS889	Two sheets, each 145×95 mm. Nos. 887/8 in blocks of 6 Per pair	16·00	45·00

287 Placing Votes in Ballot Box

1968. 75th Anniv of Universal Suffrage in New Zealand.

890	**287**	3c. ochre, green and blue	10	10

288 Human Rights Emblem

1968. Human Rights Year.

891	**288**	10c. red, yellow and green	10	30

289 "Adoration of the Holy Child" (G. van Honthorst)

1968. Christmas.

892	**289**	2½c. multicoloured	10	10

290 I.L.O. Emblem

1969. 50th Anniv of Int Labour Organization.

893	**290**	7c. black and red	15	30

291 Supreme Court Building, Auckland

1969. Centenary of New Zealand Law Society.

894	**291**	3c. multicoloured	10	10
895	-	10c. multicoloured	20	35
896	-	18c. multicoloured	30	95

DESIGNS—VERT: 10c. Law Society's coat of arms; 18c. "Justice" (from Memorial Window in University of Canterbury, Christchurch).

295 Student being conferred with Degree

1969. Centenary of Otago University. Multicoloured.

897	3c. Otago University (vert)	15	10
898	10c. Type **295**	30	25

296 Boys playing Cricket

1969. Health Stamps.

899	**296**	2½c. +1c. multicoloured	40	65
900	-	3c. +1c. multicoloured	40	65
901	-	4c. +1c. brown and ultramarine	40	2·00
MS902		Two sheets, each 144×84 mm. Nos. 899/900 in blocks of 6 Per pair	16·00	50·00

DESIGNS—HORIZ: 3c. Girls playing cricket. VERT: 4c. Dr. Elizabeth Gunn (founder of first Children's Health Camp).

299 Oldest existing House in New Zealand, and Old Stone Mission Store, Kerikeri

1969. Early European Settlement in New Zealand, and 150th Anniv of Kerikeri. Multicoloured.

903	4c. Type **299**	20	25
904	6c. View of Bay of Islands	30	1·75

301 "The Nativity" (Federico Fiori Barocci)

1969. Christmas.

905	**301**	2½c. multicoloured	10	10

302 Captain Cook, Transit of Venus and "Octant"

1969. Bicentenary of Captain Cook's Landing in New Zealand.

906	**302**	4c. black, red and blue	40	15
907	-	6c. green, brown and black	55	1·00
908	-	18c. brown, green and black	70	50
909	-	28c. red, black and blue	1·10	1·75
MS910		109×90 mm. Nos. 906/9	14·00	30·00

DESIGNS: 6c. Sir Joseph Banks (naturalist) and outline of H.M.S. "Endeavour"; 18c. Dr. Daniel Solander (botanist) and his plant; 28c. Queen Elizabeth II and Cook's chart, 1769.

306 Girl, Wheat Field and C.O.R.S.O. Emblem

1969. 25th Anniv of C.O.R.S.O. (Council of Organizations for Relief Services Overseas). Multicoloured.

911	7c. Type **306**	35	85
912	8c. Mother feeding her child, dairy herd and C.O.R.S.O. emblem (horiz)	35	90

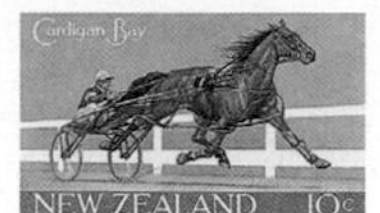

308 "Cardigan Bay" (champion trotter)

1970. Return of "Cardigan Bay" to New Zealand.

913	**308**	10c. multicoloured	30	30

309 "Vanessa gonerilla" (butterfly)

310 Queen Elizabeth II and New Zealand Coat of Arms

1970

(a) Size as T **309**

914	-	½c. multicoloured	10	20
915	**309**	1c. multicoloured	10	10
916	-	2c. multicoloured	10	10
917	-	2½c. multicoloured	30	20
918	-	3c. multicoloured	15	10
919	-	4c. multicoloured	15	10
920	-	5c. multicoloured	30	10
921	-	6c. black, green and red	30	1·00
922	-	7c. multicoloured	50	1·00
923	-	7½c. multicoloured	75	2·00
924	-	8c. multicoloured	50	1·00

(b) Size as T **310**

925	**310**	10c. multicoloured	50	15
926	-	15c. black, flesh and brown	75	50
927	-	18c. green, brown & black	75	50
928	-	20c. black and brown	75	15
929	-	23c. multicoloured	60	30
930b	-	25c. multicoloured	50	75
931	-	30c. multicoloured	50	15
932	-	50c. multicoloured	50	20
933	-	$1 multicoloured	1·00	1·00
934	-	$2 multicoloured	2·50	1·00

DESIGNS—VERT (as T **309**): ½c. "Lycaena salustius" (butterfly); 2c. "Argyrophenga antipodum" (butterfly); 2½c. "Nyctemera annulata (moth); 3c. "Detunda egregia" (moth); 4c. Charagia virescens" (moth); 5c. Scarlet wrasse ("Scarlet parrot fish"); 6c. Big-bellied sea horses; 7c. Leather-jacket (fish); 7½c. Intermediate halfbeak ("Garfish"); 8c. John Dory (fish). (As T **310**): 18c. Maori club; 25c. Hauraki Gulf Maritime Park; 30c. Mt. Cook National Park. HORIZ (as T **310**): 15c. Maori fish hook; 20c. Maori tattoo pattern; 23c. Egmont National Park; 50c. Abel Tasman National Park; $1 Geothermal power; $2 Agricultural technology.

311 Geyser Restaurant

1970. World Fair, Osaka. Multicoloured.

935	7c. Type **311**	20	75
936	8c. New Zealand Pavilion	20	75
937	18c. Bush Walk	40	75

312 U.N. H.Q. Building

1970. 25th Anniv of United Nations.

938	**312**	3c. multicoloured	10	10
939	-	10c. red and yellow	20	20

DESIGN: 10c. Tractor on horizon.

313 Soccer

1970. Health Stamps. Multicoloured.

940	2½c. +1c. Netball (vert)	25	70
941	3c. +1c. Type **313**	25	70
MS942	Two sheets. (a) 102×125 mm (940). (b) 125×102 mm (941). Containing blocks of six Per pair	16·00	50·00

314 "The Virgin adoring the Child" (Correggio)

1970. Christmas.

943	**314**	2½c. multicoloured	10	10
944	-	3c. multicoloured	10	10
945	-	10c. black, orange & silver	30	75

DESIGNS—VERT: 3c. Stained glass window, Invercargill Presbyterian Church "The Holy Family". HORIZ: 10c. Tower of Roman Catholic Church, Seckburn.

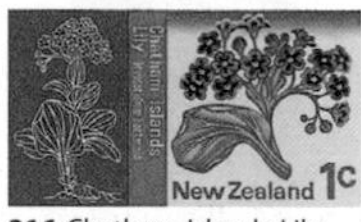

316 Chatham Islands Lily

1970. Chatham Islands. Multicoloured.

946	1c. Type **316**	10	35
947	2c. Shy albatross	30	40

317 Country Women's Institute Emblem

1971. 50th Annivs of Country Women's Institutes and Rotary International in New Zealand. Multicoloured.

948	4c. Type **317**	10	10
949	10c. Rotary emblem and map of New Zealand	20	60

318 "Rainbow II" (yacht)

1971. One Ton Cup Racing Trophy. Multicoloured.

950	5c. Type **318**	25	25
951	8c. One Ton Cup	25	1·50

319 Civic Arms of Palmerston North

1971. City Centenaries. Multicoloured.

952	3c. Type **319**	10	10
953	4c. Arms of Auckland	10	15
954	5c. Arms of Invercargill	15	1·10

320 Antarctica on Globe

1971. Tenth Anniv of Antarctic Treaty.

955	**320**	6c. multicoloured	1·00	1·75

321 Child on Swing

1971. 25th Anniv of UNICEF.

956	**321**	7c. multicoloured	50	1·25

1971. No. 917 surch **4c**.

957	4c. on 2½c. multicoloured	15	10

323 Satellite-tracking Aerial

1971. Opening of Satellite Earth Station.

958	**323**	8c. black, grey and red	50	1·50
959	-	10c. black, green and violet	50	1·00

DESIGN: 10c. Satellite.

324 Girls playing Hockey

1971. Health Stamps. Multicoloured.

960	3c. +1c. Type **324**	40	65
961	4c. +1c. Boys playing hockey	40	65
962	5c. +1c. Dental health	60	2·00
MS963	Two sheets, each 122×96 mm. Nos. 960/1 in blocks of six Per pair	16·00	45·00

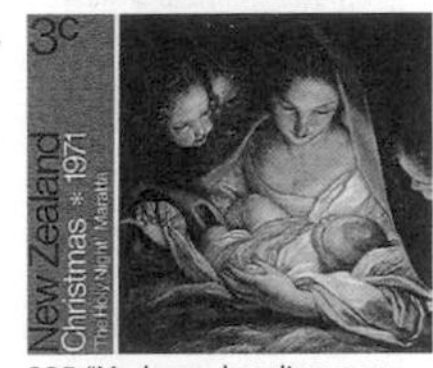

325 "Madonna bending over the Crib" (Maratta)

1971. Christmas. Multicoloured.

964	3c. Type **325**	10	10
965	4c. "The Annunciation" (stained-glass window)	10	10
966	10c. "The Three Kings"	50	1·25

Nos. 965/6 are smaller, size 21½×38 mm.

326 "Tiffany" Rose

1971. First World Rose Convention, Hamilton. Multicoloured.

967	2c. Type **326**	15	90
968	5c. "Peace"	35	25
969	8c. "Chrysler Imperial"	60	1·10

327 Lord Rutherford and Alpha Particles

1971. Birth Centenary of Lord Rutherford (scientist). Multicoloured.

970	1c. Type **327**	20	50
971	7c. Lord Rutherford and formula	55	1·75

328 Benz (1895)

1972. International Vintage Car Rally. Multicoloured.

972	3c. Type **328**	20	10
973	4c. Oldsmobile (1904)	20	10
974	5c. Ford "Model T" (1914)	20	10
975	6c. Cadillac Service car (1915)	25	45
976	8c. Chrysler (1924)	40	1·75
977	10c. Austin "7" (1923)	40	1·25

329 Coat of Arms of Wanganui

1972. Anniversaries.

978	**329**	3c. multicoloured	15	10
979	-	4c. orange, brown & black	15	10
980	-	5c. multicoloured	25	10
981	-	8c. multicoloured	40	1·25
982	-	10c. multicoloured	40	1·25

DESIGNS AND EVENTS—VERT: 3c. Type **329** (centenary of Wanganui Council); 5c. De Havilland D.H.89 Dragon Rapide and Boeing 737 (25th anniv of National Airways Corp); 8c. French frigate and Maori palisade (bicentenary of landing by Marion du Fresne). HORIZ: 4c. Postal Union symbol (10th anniv of Asian–Oceanic Postal Union); 10c. Stone cairn (150th anniv of New Zealand Methodist Church).

330 Black Scree Cotula

1972. Alpine Plants. Multicoloured.

983	4c. Type **330**	20	10
984	6c. North Island edelweiss	25	35
985	8c. Haast's buttercup	35	70
986	10c. Brown Mountain daisy	45	1·20

331 Boy playing Tennis

1972. Health Stamps.

987	**331**	3c. +1c. grey and brown	30	65
988	-	4c. +1c. brown, grey and yellow	30	65
MS989		Two sheets, each 107×123 mm. Nos. 987/8 in blocks of six Per pair	15·00	40·00

DESIGN: No. 988, Girl playing tennis.

332 "Madonna with Child" (Murillo)

1972. Christmas. Multicoloured.

990	3c. Type **332**	10	10
991	5c. "The Last Supper" (stained-glass window, St. John's Church, Levin)	15	10
992	10c. Pohutukawa flower	35	70

333 Lake Waikaremoana

1972. Lake Scenes. Multicoloured.

993	6c. Type **333**	60	1·00
994	8c. Lake Hayes	70	1·00
995	18c. Lake Wakatipu	1·00	1·50
996	23c. Lake Rotomahana	1·10	2·00

No. 995 is inscribed "Lake Wakatipu", but actually shows Kawarau River, which flows out of the lake.

334 Old Pollen Street

1973. Commemorations.

997	**334**	3c. multicoloured	10	10
998	-	4c. multicoloured	15	10
999	-	5c. multicoloured	15	15
1000	-	6c. multicoloured	40	50
1001	-	8c. grey, blue and gold	25	50
1002	-	10c. multicoloured	40	80

DESIGNS AND EVENTS: 3c. (centenary of Thames Borough); 4c. Coalmining and pasture (centenary of Westport Borough); 5c. Cloister (centenary of Canterbury University); 6c. Forest, birds and lake (50th anniv of Royal Forest and Bird Protection Society); 8c. Rowers (Success of N.Z. rowers in 1972 Olympics); 10c. Graph and people (25th anniv of E.C.A.F.E.).

335 Class W Locomotive

1973. New Zealand Steam Locomotives. Multicoloured.

1003	3c. Type **335**	20	10
1004	4c. Class X	20	10
1005	5c. Class Ab	20	10
1006	10c. Class Ja No. 1274	75	1·40

336 "Maori Woman and Child"

1973. Paintings by Frances Hodgkins. Multicoloured.

1027	5c. Type **336**	20	15
1028	8c. "Hilltop"	30	80
1029	10c. "Barn in Picardy"	30	65
1030	18c. "Self-portrait Still Life"	70	1·75

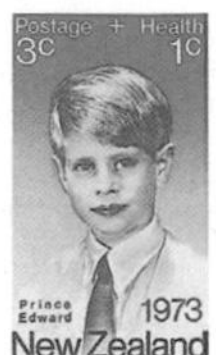

337 Prince Edward

1973. Health Stamps.

1031	**337**	3c. +1c. green & brown	30	50
1032	**337**	4c. +1c. red and brown	30	50
MS1033		Two sheets, each 96×121 mm, with Nos. 1031/2 in blocks of 6 (3×2) Per pair	14·00	40·00

338 "Tempi Madonna" (Raphael)

1973. Christmas. Multicoloured.

1034	3c. Type **338**	10	10
1035	5c. "Three Kings" (stained- glass window, St. Theresa's Church, Auckland)	10	10
1036	10c. Family entering church	25	50

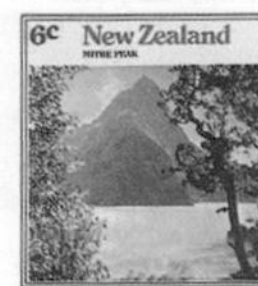

339 Mitre Peak

1973. Mountain Scenery. Multicoloured.

1037	6c. Type **339**	30	70
1038	8c. Mt. Ngauruhoe	40	1·00
1039	18c. Mt. Sefton (horiz)	60	1·75
1040	23c. Burnett Range (horiz)	70	2·25

340 Hurdling

1974. Tenth British Commonwealth Games, Christchurch.

1041	**340**	4c. multicoloured	10	10
1042	-	5c. black and violet	10	10
1043	-	10c. multicoloured	60	15
1044	-	18c. multicoloured	15	50
1045	-	23c. multicoloured	20	80

DESIGNS: 5c. Ball-player (4th Paraplegic Games, Dunedin); 10c. Cycling; 18c. Rifle-shooting; 23c. Bowls.

341 Queen Elizabeth II

1974. New Zealand Day. Sheet 131×74 mm, containing T **341** and similar horiz designs, size 37×20 mm. Multicoloured.

MS1046	4c.×5 Treaty House, Waitangi; Signing Waitangi Treaty; Type **341**; Parliament Buildings extensions; Children in class	70	2·50

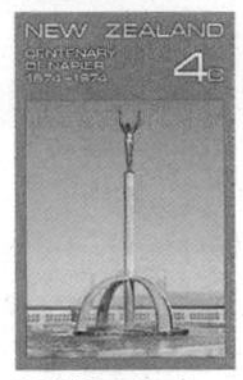

342 "Spirit of Napier" Fountain

1974. Centenaries of Napier and U.P.U. Multicoloured.

1047	4c. Type **342**	10	10
1048	5c. Clock Tower, Berne	20	30
1049	8c. U.P.U. Monument, Berne	55	1·60

343 Boeing Seaplane, 1919

1974. History of New Zealand Airmail Transport. Multicoloured.

1050	3c. Type **343**	20	10
1051	4c. Lockheed 10 Electra "Kauha", 1937	25	10
1052	5c. Bristol Type 170 Freighter Mk 31, 1958	25	30
1053	23c. Short S.30 modified "G" Class flying boat "Aotearoa", 1940	1·10	2·00

344 Children, Cat and Dog

1974. Health Stamps.

1054	**344**	3c. +1c. multicoloured	20	50
1055	-	4c. +1c. multicoloured	25	50
1056	-	5c. +1c. multicoloured	70	1·50
MS1057		145×123 mm. No. 1055 in block of ten	14·00	40·00

Nos. 1055/6 are similar to Type **344**, showing children with pets.

345 "The Adoration of the Magi" (Konrad Witz)

1974. Christmas. Multicoloured.

1058	3c. Type **345**	10	10

1059	5c. "The Angel Window" (stained glass window, Old St. Pauls Church, Wellington)	10	10
1060	10c. Madonna lily	30	90

346 Great Barrier Island

1974. Offshore Islands. Multicoloured.

1061	6c. Type **346**	20	30
1062	8c. Stewart Island	30	1·00
1063	18c. White Island	40	1·25
1064	23c. The Brothers	50	1·40

347 Crippled Child

1975. Anniversaries and Events. Multicoloured.

1065	3c. Type **347**	10	10
1066	5c. Farming family	10	10
1067	10c. I.W.Y. symbols	15	65
1068	18c. Medical School Building, Otago University	40	1·75

COMMEMORATIONS: 3c. 40th anniv of New Zealand Crippled Children Society; 5c. 50th anniv of Women's Division, Federated Farmers of New Zealand; 10c. International Women's Year; 18c. Centenary of Otago Medical School.

348 Scow "Lake Erie"

1975. Historic Sailing Ships.

1069	**348**	4c. black and red	25	10
1070	-	5c. black and blue	25	10
1071	-	8c. black and yellow	30	50
1072	-	10c. black and yellow	30	50
1073	-	18c. black and brown	50	1·75
1074	-	23c. black and lilac	60	1·75

SHIPS: 5c. Schooner "Herald"; 8c. Brigantine "New Zealander"; 10c. Topsail schooner "Jessie Kelly"; 18c. Barque "Tory"; 23c. Full-rigged clipper "Rangitiki".

349 Lake Sumner Forest Park

1975. Forest Park Scenes. Multicoloured.

1075	6c. Type **349**	25	40
1076	8c. North-west Nelson	30	70
1077	18c. Kaweka	50	1·25
1078	23c. Coromandel	70	1·40

350 Girl feeding Lamb

1975. Health Stamps. Multicoloured.

1079	3c. +1c. Type **350**	15	30
1080	4c. +1c. Boy with hen and chicks	15	30
1081	5c. +1c. Boy with duck and duckling	40	1·50
MS1082	123×146 mm. No. 1080×10	11·00	40·00

351 "Virgin and Child" (Zanobi Machiavelli)

1975. Christmas. Multicoloured.

1083	3c. Type **351**	10	10
1084	5c. "Cross in Landscape" (stained-glass window, Greendale Church) (horiz)	10	10
1085	10c. "I saw three ships" (carol) (horiz)	35	65

352 "Sterling Silver"

353 Queen Elizabeth II (photograph by W. Harrison)

353a Maripi (knife)

353b Rainbow Abalone or Paua

1975. Multicoloured

(a) Garden Roses

1086	1c. Type **352**	10	10
1087	2c. "Lilli Marlene"	10	20
1088	3c. "Queen Elizabeth"	60	10
1089	4c. "Super Star"	10	60
1090	5c. "Diamond Jubilee"	10	10
1091a	6c. "Cresset"	40	1·00
1092a	7c. "Michele Meilland"	40	10
1093a	8c. "Josephine Bruce"	30	10
1094	9c. "Iceberg"	40	60

(b) Type **353**

1094aab	10c. multicoloured	30	10

(c) Maori Artefacts.

1095	**353a**	11c. brown, yellow & black	30	80
1096	-	12c. brown, yellow & black	30	50
1097	-	13c. brown, mauve & black	40	1·00
1098	-	14c. brown, yellow & black	30	20

DESIGNS: 12c. Putorino (flute); 13c. Wahaika (club); 14c. Kotiate (club).

(d) Sea Shells. Multicoloured.

1099	20c. Type **353b**	15	20
1100	30c. Toheroa clam	25	50
1101	40c. Old woman or coarse dosinia	30	45
1102	50c. New Zealand or spiny murex	40	45
1103	$1 New Zealand scallop	70	1·00
1104	$2 Circular saw	1·00	1·75

(e) Building. Multicoloured.

1105	$5 "Beehive" (section of Parliamentary Buildings, Wellington) (22×26 mm)	1·75	1·50

354 Family and League of Mothers Badge

1976. Anniversaries and Metrication. Multicoloured.

1110	6c. Type **354**	10	10
1111	7c. Weight, temperature, linear measure and capacity	10	10
1112	8c. "William Bryon" (immigrant ship), mountain and New Plymouth	15	10
1113	10c. Two women shaking hands and Y.W.C.A. badge	15	60
1114	25c. Map of the world showing cable links	30	1·25

ANNIVERSARIES: 6c. 50th anniv of League of Mothers; 7c. Metrication; 8c. Centenary of New Plymouth; 10c. 50th anniv of New Zealand Y.W.C.A.; 25c. Link with International Telecommunications Network.

355 Gig

1976. Vintage Farm Transport. Multicoloured.

1115	6c. Type **355**	15	40
1116	7c. Thornycroft lorry	15	10
1117	8c. Scandi wagon	20	15
1118	9c. Traction engine	15	30
1119	10c. Wool wagon	15	30
1120	25c. Cart	40	1·75

356 Purakaunui Falls

1976. Waterfalls. Multicoloured.

1121	10c. Type **356**	25	10
1122	14c. Marakopa Falls	40	95
1123	15c. Bridal Veil Falls	45	1·10
1124	16c. Papakorito Falls	55	1·25

357 Boy and Pony

1976. Health Stamps. Multicoloured.

1125	7c. +1c. Type **357**	20	40
1126	8c. +1c. Girl and calf	20	40
1127	10c. +1c. Girls and bird	40	1·00
MS1128	96×121 mm. Nos. 1125/7×2	2·50	6·00

358 "Nativity" (Spanish carving)

1976. Christmas. Multicoloured.

1129	7c. Type **358**	15	10
1130	11c. "Resurrection" (stained-glass window, St. Joseph's Catholic Church, Grey Lynn) (horiz)	25	30
1131	18c. Angels (horiz)	40	1·00

359 Arms of Hamilton

1977. Anniversaries. Multicoloured.

1132	8c. Type **359**	15	35
1133	8c. Arms of Gisborne	15	35
1134	8c. Arms of Masterton	15	35
1135	10c. A.A. emblem	15	50
1136	10c. Arms of the Royal Australasian College of Surgeons	15	50

ANNIVERSARIES: No. 1132, Cent of Hamilton; 1133, Cent of Gisborne; 1134, Cent of Masterton; 1135, 75th anniv of Automobile Association in New Zealand; 1136, 50th anniv of R.A.C.S.

360 Queen Elizabeth II

1977. Silver Jubilee. Sheet 178×82 mm, containing T **360** and similar vert designs showing different portraits.

MS1137	8c.×5 multicoloured	65	1·60

361 Physical Education and Maori Culture

1977. Education. Multicoloured.

1138	8c. Type **361**	30	60
1139	8c. Geography, science and woodwork	30	60
1140	8c. Teaching the deaf, kindergarten and woodwork	30	60
1141	8c. Tertiary and language classes	30	60
1142	8c. Home science, correspondence school and teacher training	30	60

1977. Nos. 918/19 surch.

1143	7c. on 3c. "Detunda egregia" (moth)	40	70
1144	8c. on 4c. "Charagia virescens" (moth)	40	70

363 Karitane Beach

1977. Seascapes. Multicoloured.

1145	10c. Type **363**	15	10
1146	16c. Ocean Beach, Mount Maunganui	30	30
1147	18c. Piha Beach	30	30
1148	30c. Kaikoura Coast	35	40

364 Girl with Pigeon

1977. Health Stamps. Multicoloured.

1149	7c. +2c. Type **364**	20	50
1150	8c. +2c. Boy with frog	20	55
1151	10c. +2c. Girl with butterfly	40	1·00
MS1152	97×120 mm. Nos. 1149/51×2	1·40	6·50

Stamps from No. **MS**1152 are without white border and together form a composite design.

365 "The Holy Family" (Correggio)

1977. Christmas. Multicoloured.

1153	7c. Type **365**	15	10
1154	16c. "Madonna and Child" (stained-glass window, St. Michael's and All Angels, Dunedin) (vert)	25	25
1155	23c. "Partridge in a Pear Tree" (vert)	40	1·25

366 Merryweather Manual Pump, 1860

1977. Fire Fighting Appliances. Multicoloured.

1156	10c. Type **366**	15	10
1157	11c. 2-wheel hose, reel and ladder, 1880	15	25
1158	12c. Shand Mason steam fire engine, 1873	20	30
1159	23c. Chemical fire engine, 1888	30	90

367 Town Clock and Coat of Arms, Ashburton

1978. Centenaries.

1160	**367**	10c. multicoloured	15	25
1161	-	10c. multicoloured	15	25
1162	-	12c. red, yellow and black	15	15
1163	-	20c. multicoloured	20	30

DESIGNS—VERT: No. 1161, Mount Egmont (cent of Stratford); 1162, Early telephone (cent of telephone in New Zealand). HORIZ: No. 1163, Aerial view of Bay of Islands (cent of Bay of Islands County).

368 Students and Ivey Hall, Lincoln College

1978. Land Resources and Centenary of Lincoln College of Agriculture. Multicoloured.
1164 10c. Type **368** 15 10
1165 12c. Sheep grazing 15 30
1166 15c. Fertiliser ground spreading 15 30
1167 16c. Agricultural Field Days 15 40
1168 20c. Harvesting grain 20 40
1169 30c. Dairy farming 30 90

369

1978. Coil Stamps.
1170 **369** 1c. purple 10 65
1171 **369** 2c. orange 10 65
1172 **369** 5c. brown 10 65
1173 **369** 10c. blue 30 80

370 Maui Gas Drilling Platform

1978. Resources of the Sea. Multicoloured.
1174 12c. Type **370** 15 15
1175 15c. Trawler 15 20
1176 20c. Map of 200 mile fishing limit 20 30
1177 23c. Humpback whale and bottle-nosed dolphins 25 35
1178 35c. Kingfish, snapper, grouper and squid 40 60

371 First Health Charity Stamp

1978. Health Stamps.
1179 **371** 10c. +2c. black, red and gold 20 35
1180 - 12c. +2c. multicoloured 20 40
MS1181 97×124 mm. Nos. 1179/80×3 1·00 4·00
DESIGNS: 10c. Type **371** (50th anniv of Health Stamps); 12c. Heart Operation (National Heart Foundation).

372 "The Holy Family" (El Greco)

1978. Christmas. Multicoloured.
1182 7c. Type **372** 10 10
1183 16c. All Saint's Church, Howick (horiz) 25 35
1184 23c. Beach scene (horiz) 30 50

373 Sir Julius Vogel

1979. Statesmen. Designs each brown and drab.
1185 10c. Type **373** 25 50
1186 10c. Sir George Grey 25 50
1187 10c. Richard John Seddon 25 50

374 Riverlands Cottage, Blenheim

1979. Architecture (1st series).
1188 **374** 10c. black, light blue and blue 10 10
1189 - 12c. black, light green and green 15 40
1190 - 15c. black and grey 20 45
1191 - 20c. black, brown and sepia 25 45
DESIGNS: 12c. The Mission House, Waimate North; 15c. "The Elms", Tauranga; 20c. Provincial Council Buildings, Christchurch.
See also Nos. 1217/20 and 1262/5.

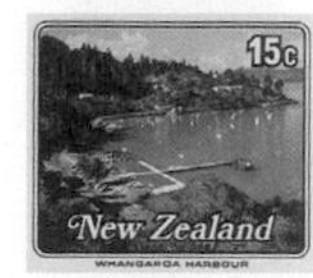

375 Whangaroa Harbour

1979. Small Harbours. Multicoloured.
1192 15c. Type **375** 15 10
1193 20c. Kawau Island 20 40
1194 23c. Akaroa Harbour (vert) 20 65
1195 35c. Picton Harbour (vert) 30 85

376 Children with Building Bricks

1979. International Year of the Child.
1196 **376** 10c. multicoloured 15 10

377 Two-spotted Chromis

1979. Health Stamps. Marine Life. Multicoloured.
1197 10c. +2c. Type **377** 20 50
1198 10c. +2c. Sea urchin 20 50
1199 12c. +2c. Red goatfish and underwater cameraman (vert) 20 50
MS1200 144×72 mm. Nos. 1197/9, each×2 1·00 2·75

1979. Nos. 1091a/3a and 1094ab surch.
1201 4c. on 8c. "Josephine Bruce" 10 50
1202 14c. on 10c. Type **353** 20 10
1203 17c. on 6c. "Cresset" 25 1·00
1203b 20c. on 7c. "Michele Meilland" 25 10

379 "Madonna and Child" (sculpture, Ghiberti)

1979. Christmas. Multicoloured.
1204 10c. Type **379** 15 10
1205 25c. Christ Church, Russell 30 50
1206 35c. Pohutukawa (tree) 40 70

380 Chamber, House of Representatives

1979. 25th Commonwealth Parliamentary Conf, Wellington. Multicoloured.
1207 14c. Type **380** 15 10
1208 20c. Mace and Black Rod 20 30
1209 30c. "Beehive" wall hanging 30 75

381 1855 1d. Stamp

1980. Anniversaries and Events.
1210 **381** 14c. black, red and yellow 20 30
1211 - 14c. black, blue & yellow 20 30
1212 - 14c. black, green & yellow 20 30
1213 - 17c. multicoloured 20 30
1214 - 25c. multicoloured 25 35
1215 - 30c. multicoloured 25 40
MS1216 146×96 mm. Nos. 1210/12 (as horiz strip) (sold at 52c.) 1·00 4·00
DESIGNS: No. 1211, 1855 2d. stamp; 1212, 1855 1s. stamp (125th anniv of New Zealand stamps); 1213, Geyser, wood-carving and building (Centenary of Rotorua (town)); 1214, "Earina autumnalis" and "Thelymitra venosa" (International Orchid Conference, Auckland); 1215, Ploughing and Golden Plough Trophy (World Ploughing Championships, Christchurch).

382 Ewelme Cottage, Parnell

1980. Architecture (2nd series). Multicoloured.
1217 14c. Type **382** 15 10
1218 17c. Broadgreen, Nelson 15 25
1219 25c. Courthouse, Oamaru 20 35
1220 30c. Government Buildings, Wellington 25 40

383 Auckland Harbour

1980. Large Harbours. Multicoloured.
1221 25c. Type **383** 20 20
1222 30c. Wellington Harbour 25 30
1223 35c. Lyttelton Harbour 25 35
1224 50c. Port Chalmers 40 1·10

384 Surf-fishing

1980. Health Stamps. Fishing. Multicoloured.
1225 14c. +2c. Type **384** 25 85
1226 14c. +2c. Wharf-fishing 25 85
1227 17c. +2c. Spear-fishing 25 55
MS1228 148×75 mm. Nos. 1225/7, each×2 1·25 3·25

385 "Madonna and Child with Cherubim" (sculpture, Andrea della Robbia)

1980. Christmas. Multicoloured.
1229 10c. Type **385** 15 10
1230 25c. St. Mary's Church, New Plymouth 25 25
1231 35c. Picnic scene 40 1·00

386 Te Heu Heu (chief)

1980. Maori Personalities. Multicoloured.
1232 15c. Type **386** 15 10
1233 25c. Te Hau (chief) 15 20
1234 35c. Te Puea (princess) 20 10
1235 45c. Ngata (politician) 30 30
1236 60c. Te Ata-O-Tu (warrior) 30 50

387 Lt. Col. the Hon. W. H. A. Feilding and Borough of Feilding Crest (cent)

1981. Commemorations.
1237 **387** 20c. multicoloured 20 20
1238 - 25c. orange and black 25 25
DESIGN AND COMMEMORATION: 25c. I.Y.D. emblem and cupped hands (International Year of the Disabled).

388 The Family at Play

1981. "Family Life". Multicoloured.
1239 20c. Type **388** 15 10
1240 25c. The family young and old 20 20
1241 30c. The family at home 20 35
1242 35c. The family at church 25 45

389 Kaiauai River

1981. River Scenes. Multicoloured.
1243 30c. Type **389** 20 25
1244 35c. Mangahao 20 30
1245 40c. Shotover (horiz) 25 40
1246 60c. Cleddau (horiz) 45 65

390 St. Paul's Cathedral

1981. Royal Wedding. Multicoloured.
1247 20c. Type **390** 30 30
1248 20c. Prince Charles and Lady Diana Spencer 30 30

391 Girl with Starfish

1981. Health Stamps. Children playing by the Sea. Multicoloured.
1249 20c. +2c. Type **391** 20 65
1250 20c. +2c. Boy fishing 20 65
1251 25c. +2c. Children exploring rock pool 20 35
MS1252 100×125 mm. Nos. 1249/51, each×2 1·00 3·00
Nos. 1249/50 were printed together, *se-tenant*, forming a composite design.
The stamps from No. **MS**1252 were printed together, se-tenant, in horizontal strips, each forming a composite design.

392 "Madonna suckling the Child" (painting, d'Oggiono)

1981. Christmas. Multicoloured.
1253 14c. Type **392** 15 10
1254 30c. St. John's Church, Wakefield 20 25
1255 40c. Golden tainui (flower) 35 35

393 Tauranga Mission House

1981. Commemorations. Multicoloured.

1256	20c. Type **393**	20	10
1257	20c. Water tower, Hawera	20	10
1258	25c. Cat	25	35
1259	30c. "Dunedin" (refrigerated sailing ship)	25	40
1260	35c. Scientific research equipment	25	45

COMMEMORATIONS: No. 1256, Centenary of Tauranga (town); 1257, Centenary of Hawera (town); 1258, Centenary of S.P.C.A. (Society for the Prevention of Cruelty to Animals in New Zealand); 1259, Centenary of frozen meat exports; 1260, International Year of Science.

394 Map of New Zealand

1982

1261	**394**	24c. green and blue	30	10

395 Alberton, Auckland

1982. Architecture (3rd series). Multicoloured.

1262	20c. Type **395**	15	15
1263	25c. Caccia Birch, Palmerston North	15	25
1264	30c. Railway station, Dunedin	40	30
1265	35c. Post Office, Ophir	25	40

396 Kaiteriteri Beach, Nelson (Summer)

1982. New Zealand Scenes. Multicoloured.

1266	35c. Type **396**	20	30
1267	40c. St. Omer Park, Queenstown (Autumn)	25	35
1268	45c. Mt. Ngauruhoe, Tongariro National Park (Winter)	25	40
1269	70c. Wairarapa farm (Spring)	40	60

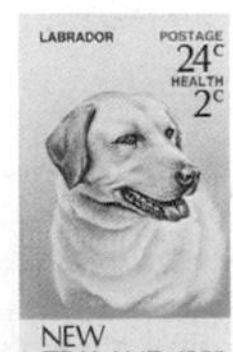

397 Labrador

1982. Health Stamps. Dogs. Multicoloured.

1270	24c. +2c. Type **397**	65	1·00
1271	24c. +2c. Border collie	65	1·00
1272	30c. +2c. Cocker spaniel	65	1·00
MS1273	98×125 mm. Nos. 1270/2, each×2	3·25	6·50

398 "Madonna with Child and Two Angels" (painting by Piero di Cosimo)

1982. Christmas. Multicoloured.

1274	18c. Type **398**	15	10
1275	35c. Rangiatea Maori Church, Otaki	25	30
1276	45c. Surf life-saving	40	40

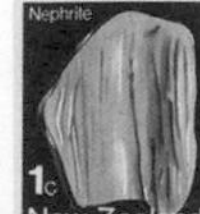

399 Nephrite **399a** Grapes

399b Kokako

1982. Multicoloured.

(a) Minerals

1277	1c. Type **399**	10	10
1278	2c. Agate	10	10
1279	3c. Iron pyrites	10	10
1280	4c. Amethyst	15	10
1281	5c. Carnelian	15	10
1282	9c. Native sulphur	20	10

(b) Fruits. Multicoloured.

1283	10c. Type **399a**	50	10
1284	20c. Citrus fruit	35	10
1285	30c. Nectarines	35	10
1286	40c. Apples	35	10
1287	50c. Kiwifruit	40	10

(c) Native Birds. Multicoloured.

1288	30c. Kakapo	60	25
1289	40c. Mountain ("Blue") duck	60	35
1290	45c. New Zealand falcon	1·25	35
1291	60c. New Zealand teal	2·25	2·00
1292	$1 Type **399b**	1·00	30
1293	$2 Chatham Island robin	1·00	50
1294	$3 Stitchbird	1·25	1·40
1295	$4 Saddleback	1·50	2·00
1296	$5 Takahe	3·75	3·25
1297	$10 Little spotted kiwi	4·00	5·00

400 Old Arts Building, Auckland University

1983. Commemorations. Multicoloured.

1303	24c. Salvation Army Centenary logo	20	10
1304	30c. Type **400**	20	40
1305	35c. Stylized kangaroo and kiwi	20	40
1306	40c. Rainbow trout	25	55
1307	45c. Satellite over Earth	25	55

COMMEMORATIONS: 24c. Salvation Army centenary; 30c. Auckland University centenary; 35c. Closer Economic Relationship agreement with Australia; 40c. Centenary of introduction of rainbow trout into New Zealand; 45c. World Communications Year.

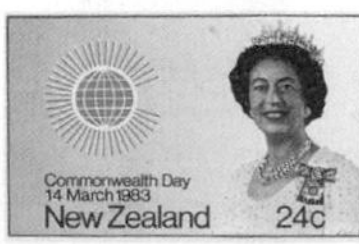

401 Queen Elizabeth II

1983. Commonwealth Day. Multicoloured.

1308	24c. Type **401**	20	10
1309	35c. Maori rock drawing	30	50
1310	40c. Woolmark and woolscouring symbols	30	80
1311	45c. Coat of arms	30	80

402 "Boats, Island Bay" (Rita Angus)

1983. Paintings by Rita Angus. Multicoloured.

1312	24c. Type **402**	20	10
1313	30c. "Central Otago Landscape"	25	45
1314	35c. "Wanaka Landscape"	30	50
1315	45c. "Tree"	35	70

403 Mt. Egmont

1983. Beautiful New Zealand. Multicoloured.

1316	35c. Type **403**	20	35
1317	40c. Cooks Bay	25	40
1318	45c. Lake Matheson (horiz)	25	45
1319	70c. Lake Alexandrina (horiz)	40	70

404 Tabby

1983. Health Stamps. Cats. Multicoloured.

1320	24c. +2c. Type **404**	35	90
1321	24c. +2c. Siamese	35	90
1322	30c. +2c. Persian	50	1·00
MS1323	100×126 mm. Nos. 1320/2, each×2	1·75	3·00

405 "The Family of the Holy Oak Tree" (Raphael)

1983. Christmas. Multicoloured.

1324	18c. Type **405**	15	10
1325	35c. St. Patrick's Church, Greymouth	30	45
1326	45c. "The Glory of Christmas"	35	80

406 Geology

1984. Antarctic Research. Multicoloured.

1327	24c. Type **406**	25	10
1328	40c. Biology	30	40
1329	58c. Glaciology	40	1·60
1330	70c. Meteorology	45	90
MS1331	126×110 mm. Nos. 1327/30	1·25	3·50

407 "Mountaineer", Lake Wakatipu

1984. New Zealand Ferry Boats. Multicoloured.

1332	24c. Type **407**	20	10
1333	40c. "Waikana", Otago	25	45
1334	58c. "Britannia", Waitemata	30	1·60
1335	70c. "Wakatere", Firth of Thames	45	85

408 Mount Hutt

1984. Ski-slope Scenery. Multicoloured.

1336	35c. Type **408**	20	25
1337	40c. Coronet Park	25	30
1338	45c. Turoa	25	30
1339	70c. Whakapapa	40	75

409 Hamilton's Frog

1984. Amphibians and Reptiles. Multicoloured.

1340	24c. Type **409**	20	45
1341	24c. Great Barrier skink	20	45
1342	30c. Harlequin gecko	20	35
1343	58c. Otago skink	30	80
1344	70c. Gold-striped gecko	40	75

410 Clydesdales ploughing

1984. Health Stamps. Horses. Multicoloured.

1345	24c. +2c. Type **410**	40	90
1346	24c. +2c. Shetland ponies	40	90
1347	30c. +2c. Thoroughbreds	40	90
MS1348	148×75 mm. Nos. 1345/7, each×2	1·75	3·25

411 "Adoration of the Shepherds" (Lorenzo di Credi)

1984. Christmas. Multicoloured.

1349	18c. Type **411**	15	10
1350	35c. Old St. Paul's, Wellington (vert)	20	30
1351	45c. "The Joy of Christmas" (vert)	30	70

412 Mounted Riflemen, South Africa, 1901

1984. New Zealand Military History. Multicoloured.

1352	24c. Type **412**	20	10
1353	40c. Engineers, France, 1917	30	45
1354	58c. Tanks of 2nd N.Z. Divisional Cavalry, North Africa, 1942	40	1·50
1355	70c. Infantryman in jungle kit, and 25-pounder gun, Korea and South-East Asia, 1950–72	45	90
MS1356	122×106 mm. Nos. 1352/5	1·00	2·25

413 St. John Ambulance Badge

1985. Centenary of St. John Ambulance in New Zealand.

1357	**413**	24c. black, gold and red	20	15
1358	**413**	30c. black, silver and blue	25	45
1359	**413**	40c. black and grey	30	1·10

The colours of the badge depicted are those for Bailiffs and Dames Grand Cross (24c.), Knights and Dames of Grace (30c.) and Commanders, Officer Brothers and Sisters (40c.).

414 Nelson Horse Tram, 1862

1985. Vintage Trams. Multicoloured.

1360	24c. Type **414**	20	10
1361	30c. Graham's Town steam tram, 1871	25	50
1362	35c. Dunedin cable car, 1881	25	55
1363	40c. Auckland electric tram, 1902	25	55
1364	45c. Wellington electric tram, 1904	25	65
1365	58c. Christchurch electric tram, 1905	35	1·75

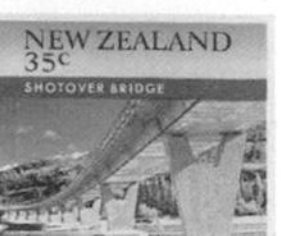

415 Shotover Bridge

1985. Bridges of New Zealand. Multicoloured.

1366	35c. Type **415**	25	45

1367	40c. Alexandra Bridge	25	45
1368	45c. South Rangitikei Railway Bridge (vert)	30	1·00
1369	70c. Twin Bridges (vert)	40	1·00

416 Queen Elizabeth II (from photo by Camera Press)

1985. Multicoloured, background colours given.

1370	**416**	25c. red	35	10
1371	**416**	35c. blue	65	10

417 Princess of Wales and Prince William

1985. Health Stamps. Designs showing photographs by Lord Snowdon. Multicoloured.

1372	25c. +2c. Type **417**	90	1·25
1373	25c. +2c. Princess of Wales and Prince Henry	90	1·25
1374	35c. +2c. Prince and Princess of Wales with Princes William and Henry	90	1·25
MS1375	118×84 mm. Nos. 1372/4, each×2	4·25	6·00

418 The Holy Family in the Stable

1985. Christmas. Multicoloured.

1376	18c. Type **418**	20	10
1377	40c. The shepherds	45	85
1378	50c. The angels	45	1·00

419 H.M.N.Z.S. "Philomel" (1914–47)

1985. New Zealand Naval History. Multicoloured.

1379	25c. Type **419**	50	15
1380	45c. H.M.N.Z.S. "Achilles" (1936–46)	70	1·40
1381	60c. H.M.N.Z.S. "Rotoiti" (1949–65)	90	2·00
1382	75c. H.M.N.Z.S. "Canterbury" (from 1971)	1·25	2·25
MS1383	124×108 mm. Nos. 1379/82	3·00	5·25

420 Police Computer Operator

1986. Centenary of New Zealand Police. Designs showing historical aspects above modern police activities. Multicoloured.

1384	25c. Type **420**	35	55
1385	25c. Detective and mobile control room	35	55
1386	25c. Policewoman and badge	35	55
1387	25c. Forensic scientist, patrol car and policeman with child	35	55
1388	25c. Police College, Porirua, "Lady Elizabeth II" (patrol boat) and dog handler	35	55

421 Indian "Power Plus" 1000cc Motor Cycle (1920)

1986. Vintage Motor Cycles. Multicoloured.

1389	35c. Type **421**	30	35
1390	45c. Norton "CS1" 500cc (1927)	30	50
1391	60c. B.S.A. "Sloper". 500cc (1930)	40	1·50
1392	75c. Triumph "Model H" 550cc (1915)	50	1·60

422 Tree of Life

1986. International Peace Year. Multicoloured.

1393	25c. Type **422**	30	30
1394	25c. Peace dove	30	30

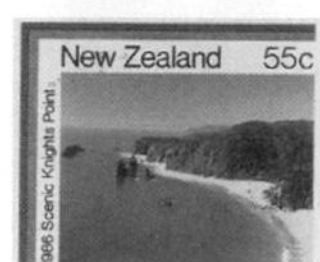

423 Knights Point

1986. Coastal Scenery. Multicoloured.

1395	55c. Type **423**	35	55
1396	60c. Becks Bay	35	70
1397	65c. Doubtless Bay	40	1·00
1398	80c. Wainui Bay	50	1·00
MS1399	124×99 mm. No. 1398 (sold at $1.20)	1·40	1·25

424 "Football" (Kylie Epapara)

1986. Health Stamps. Children's Paintings (1st series). Multicoloured.

1400	30c. +3c. Type **424**	40	75
1401	30c. +3c. "Children at Play" (Philip Kata)	40	75
1402	45c. +3c. "Children Skipping" (Mia Flannery) (horiz)	50	75
MS1403	144×81 mm. Nos. 1400/2, each×2	2·25	2·00

See also Nos. 1433/5.

425 "A Partridge in a Pear Tree"

1986. Christmas. "The Twelve Days of Christmas" (carol). Multicoloured.

1404	25c. Type **425**	20	10
1405	55c. "Two turtle doves"	45	55
1406	65c. "Three French hens"	50	1·00

426 Conductor and Orchestra

1986. Music in New Zealand.

1407	**426**	30c. multicoloured	20	10
1408	-	60c. black, blue & orange	35	60
1409	-	80c. multicoloured	45	1·50
1410	-	$1 multicoloured	55	1·00

DESIGNS: 60c. Cornet and brass band; 80c. Piper and Highland pipe band; $1 Guitar and country music group.

427 Jetboating

1987. Tourism. Multicoloured.

1411	60c. Type **427**	50	50
1412	70c. Sightseeing flights	60	75
1413	80c. Camping	70	75
1414	85c. Windsurfing	70	1·00
1415	$1.05 Mountaineering	90	1·40
1416	$1.30 River rafting	1·10	1·50

428 Southern Cross Cup

1987. Yachting Events. Designs showing yachts. Multicoloured.

1417	40c. Type **428**	20	15
1418	80c. Admiral's Cup	35	80
1419	$1.05 Kenwood Cup	45	1·25
1420	$1.30 America's Cup	55	1·40

429 Hand writing Letter and Postal Transport

1987. New Zealand Post Ltd Vesting Day. Multicoloured.

1421	40c. Type **429**	1·00	1·50
1422	40c. Posting letter, train and mailbox	1·00	1·50

430 Avro Type 626 and Wigram Airfield, 1937

1987. 50th Anniv of Royal New Zealand Air Force. Multicoloured.

1423	40c. Type **430**	55	15
1424	70c. Curtiss Kittyhawk I over World War II Pacific airstrip	80	1·75
1425	80c. Short S25 Sunderland flying boat and Pacific lagoon	90	1·75
1426	85c. Douglas A-4F Skyhawk and Mt. Ruapehu	90	1·60
MS1427	115×105 mm. Nos. 1423/6	5·50	6·50

431 Urewera National Park and Fern Leaf

1987. Centenary of National Parks Movement. Multicoloured.

1428	70c. Type **431**	40	45
1429	80c. Mt. Cook and buttercup	40	45
1430	85c. Fiordland and pineapple shrub	40	55
1431	$1.30 Tongariro and tussock	60	80
MS1432	123×99 mm. No. 1431 (sold at $1.70)	1·60	2·00

432 "Kite Flying" (Lauren Baldwin)

1987. Health Stamps. Children's Paintings (2nd series). Multicoloured.

1433	40c. +3c. Type **432**	80	1·50
1434	40c. +3c. "Swimming" (Ineke Schoneveld)	80	1·50
1435	60c. +3c. "Horse Riding" (Aaron Tylee) (vert)	1·25	1·50
MS1436	100×117 mm. Nos. 1433/5, each×2	5·00	7·00

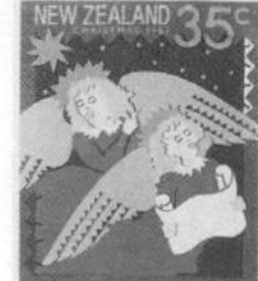

433 "Hark the Herald Angels Sing"

1987. Christmas. Multicoloured.

1437	35c. Type **433**	30	10
1438	70c. "Away in a Manger"	65	70
1439	85c. "We Three Kings of Orient Are"	80	85

434 Knot ("Pona")

1987. Maori Fibre-work. Multicoloured.

1440	40c. Type **434**	20	10
1441	60c. Binding ("Herehere")	30	50
1442	80c. Plait ("Whiri")	40	1·25
1443	85c. Cloak weaving ("Korowai") with flax fibre ("Whitau")	40	1·25

435 "Geothermal"

1988. Centenary of Electricity. Each shows radiating concentric circles representing energy generation.

1444	**435**	40c. multicoloured	20	10
1445	-	60c. black, red and brown	30	45
1446	-	70c. multicoloured	30	75
1447	-	80c. multicoloured	30	65

DESIGNS: 60c. "Thermal"; 70c. "Gas"; 80c. "Hydro".

436 Queen Elizabeth II and 1882 Queen Victoria 1d. Stamp

1988. Centenary of Royal Philatelic Society of New Zealand. Multicoloured.

1448	40c. Type **436**	35	75
1449	40c. As Type **436**, but 1882 Queen Victoria 2d.	35	75
MS1450	107×160 mm. $1 "Queen Victoria" (Chalon) (vert)	3·00	3·50

437 "Mangopare"

1988. Maori Rafter Paintings. Multicoloured.

1451	40c. Type **437**	25	45
1452	40c. "Koru"	25	45
1453	40c. "Raupunga"	25	45
1454	60c. "Koiri"	35	75

438 "Good Luck"

1988. Greetings Stamps. Multicoloured.

1455	40c. Type **438**	85	1·00
1456	40c. "Keeping in touch"	85	1·00
1457	40c. "Happy birthday"	85	1·00
1458	40c. "Congratulations" (41×27 mm)	85	1·00
1459	40c. "Get well soon" (41×27 mm)	85	1·00

439 Paradise Shelduck

1988. Native Birds. Multicoloured.

1459a	5c. Sooty crake	15	65
1460	10c. Double-banded plover	20	40
1461	20c. Yellowhead	30	40
1462	30c. Grey-backed white-eye ("Silvereye")	40	30
1463	40c. Brown kiwi	45	20
1463b	45c. Rock wren	50	60
1464	50c. Sacred kingfisher	60	70
1465	60c. Spotted cormorant ("Spotted shag")	60	80
1466	70c. Type **439**	1·00	1·50
1467	80c. Victoria penguin ("Fiordland Crested Penguin")	1·00	1·50
1467a	80c. New Zealand falcon	2·00	2·00
1468	90c. New Zealand robin	1·25	1·50

The 40 and 45c. also exist self-adhesive.

440 Milford Track

1988. Scenic Walking Trails. Multicoloured.

1469	70c. Type **440**	25	50
1470	80c. Heaphy Track	30	55
1471	85c. Copland Track	30	65
1472	$1.30 Routeburn Track	50	1·00
MS1473	124×99 mm. No. 1472 (sold at $1.70)	1·25	1·50

441 Kiwi and Koala at Campfire

1988. Bicentenary of Australian Settlement.

1474	**441**	40c. multicoloured	40	50

A stamp in a similar design was also issued by Australia.

442 Swimming

1988. Health Stamps. Olympic Games, Seoul. Multicoloured.

1475	40c. +3c. Type **442**	40	75
1476	60c. +3c. Athletics	60	1·25
1477	70c. +3c. Canoeing	70	1·25
1478	80c. +3c. Show-jumping	90	1·40
MS1479	120×90 mm. Nos. 1475/8	3·25	4·25

443 "O Come All Ye Faithful"

1988. Christmas. Carols. Designs showing illuminated verses. Multicoloured.

1480	35c. Type **443**	30	15
1481	70c. "Hark the Herald Angels Sing"	50	65
1482	80c. "Ding Dong Merrily on High"	50	90
1483	85c. "The First Nowell"	55	1·10

444 "Lake Pukaki" (John Gully)

1988. New Zealand Heritage (1st issue). "The Land". Designs showing 19th-century paintings. Multicoloured.

1484	40c. Type **444**	20	10
1485	60c. "On the Grass Plain below Lake Arthur" (William Fox)	30	35
1486	70c. "View of Auckland" (John Hoyte)	35	65
1487	80c. "Mt. Egmont from the Southward" (Charles Heaphy)	40	65
1488	$1.05 "Anakiwa, Queen Charlotte Sound" (John Kinder)	50	1·40
1489	$1.30 "White Terraces, Lake Rotomahana", (Charles Barraud)	50	1·40

See also Nos. 1505/10, 1524/9, 1541/6, 1548/53 and 1562/7.

445 Brown Kiwi

1988

1490	**445**	$1 green	2·00	3·75
1490b	**445**	$1 red	2·25	3·25
1490c	**445**	$1 blue	1·00	2·00
2090	**445**	$1 violet	1·00	1·00
2090a	**445**	$1.10 gold	1·00	1·90
2090b	**445**	£1.50 brown	1·10	1·25

See also Nos. **MS**1745, **MS**1786 and **MS**2342.

446 Humpback Whale and Calf

1988. Whales. Multicoloured.

1491	60c. Type **446**	65	70
1492	70c. Killer whales	70	90
1493	80c. Southern right whale	70	1·00
1494	85c. Blue whale	75	1·50
1495	$1.05 Southern bottlenose whale and calf	1·00	2·00
1496	$1.30 Sperm whale	1·10	2·00

Although inscribed "ROSS DEPENDENCY" Nos. 1491/6 were available from post offices throughout New Zealand.

447 Clover

1989. Wild Flowers. Multicoloured.

1497	40c. Type **447**	40	20
1498	60c. Lotus	50	65
1499	70c. Montbretia	60	1·25
1500	80c. Wild ginger	70	1·25

448 Katherine Mansfield

1989. New Zealand Authors. Multicoloured.

1501	40c. Type **448**	25	15
1502	60c. James K. Baxter	35	50
1503	70c. Bruce Mason	40	70
1504	80c. Ngaio Marsh	40	75

449 Moriori Man and Map of Chatham Islands

1989. New Zealand Heritage (2nd issue). The People.

1505	**449**	40c. multicoloured	60	15
1506	-	60c. brown, grey and deep brown	1·00	75
1507	-	70c. green, grey and deep green	60	90
1508	-	80c. blue, grey and deep blue	1·50	90
1509	-	$1.05 grey, light grey and black	75	1·75
1510	-	$1.30 red, grey and brown	90	2·00

DESIGNS: 60c. Gold prospector; 70c. Settler ploughing; 80c. Whaling; $1.05, Missionary preaching to Maoris; $1.30, Maori village.

450 White Pine (Kahikatea)

1989. Native Trees. Multicoloured.

1511	80c. Type **450**	35	45
1512	85c. Red pine (Rimu)	35	55
1513	$1.05 Totara	50	1·10
1514	$1.30 Kauri	55	1·10
MS1515	102×125 mm. No. 1514 (sold at $1.80)	1·50	1·75

451 Duke and Duchess of York with Princess Beatrice

1989. Health Stamps. Multicoloured.

1516	40c. +3c. Type **451**	80	1·50
1517	40c. +3c. Duchess of York with Princess Beatrice	80	1·50
1518	80c. +3c. Princess Beatrice	1·40	1·75
MS1519	120×89 mm. Nos. 1516/18, each×2	5·50	7·50

452 One Tree Hill, Auckland through Bedroom Window

1989. Christmas. Designs showing Star of Bethlehem. Multicoloured.

1520	35c. Type **452**	20	10
1521	65c. Shepherd and dog in mountain valley	50	50
1522	80c. Star over harbour	55	65
1523	$1 Star over globe	75	1·00

453 Windsurfing

1989. New Zealand Heritage (3rd issue). The Sea. Multicoloured.

1524	40c. Type **453**	50	15
1525	60c. Fishes of many species	85	90
1526	65c. Striped marlin and game fishing launch	90	1·00
1527	80c. Rowing boat and yachts in harbour	1·00	1·00
1528	$1 Coastal scene	1·25	1·10
1529	$1.50 "Rotoiti" (container ship) and tug	1·90	3·25

454 Games Logo

1989. 14th Commonwealth Games, Auckland. Multicoloured.

1530	40c. Type **454**	25	30
1531	40c. Goldie (games kiwi mascot)	25	30
1532	40c. Gymnastics	25	30
1533	50c. Weightlifting	30	35
1534	65c. Swimming	35	45
1535	80c. Cycling	80	70
1536	$1 Lawn bowling	60	70
1537	$1.80 Hurdling	80	1·75
MS1538	Two sheets, each 105×92 mm, with different margin designs. (a) Nos. 1530/1 (horiz pair). (b) Nos. 1530/1 (vert pair) Set of 2 sheets	5·00	5·50

455 Short S.30 modified "G" Class Flying Boat "Aotearoa" and Boeing 747-200

1990. 50th Anniv of Air New Zealand.

1539	**455**	80c. multicoloured	1·40	1·10

456 Chief Kawiti signing Treaty

1990. 150th Anniv of Treaty of Waitangi. Sheet 80×118 mm, containing T **456** and similar multicoloured design.

MS1540	40c. Type **456**; 40c. Chief Hone Heke (first signatory) and Lieut-Governor Hobson (horiz)	2·00	3·50

457 Maori Voyaging Canoe

1990. New Zealand Heritage (4th issue). The Ships. Multicoloured.

1541	40c. Type **457**	60	15
1542	50c. H.M.S. "Endeavour" (Cook), 1769	1·00	80
1543	60c. "Tory" (barque), 1839	1·00	1·00
1544	80c. "Crusader" (full-rigged immigrant ship), 1871	1·50	1·50
1545	$1 "Edwin Fox" (full-rigged immigrant ship), 1873	1·75	1·50
1546	$1.50 "Arawa" (steamer), 1884	2·00	3·25

458 *Thelymitra pulchella*

1990. "New Zealand 1990" International Stamp Exhibition, Auckland. Native Orchids. Sheet 179×80 mm, containing T **458** and similar vert designs. Multicoloured.

MS1547	40c. Type **458**; 40c. "Corybas macranthus"; 40c. "Dendrobium cunninghamii"; 40c. "Pterostylis banksii"; 80c. "Aporostylis bifolia" (sold at $4.90)	4·50	4·50

The stamps in No. **MS**1547 form a composite design.

459 Grace Neill (social reformer) and Maternity Hospital, Wellington

1990. New Zealand Heritage (5th issue). Famous New Zealanders. Multicoloured.

1548	40c. Type **459**	45	10
1549	50c. Jean Batten (pilot) and Percival P.3 Gull Six aircraft	65	85
1550	60c. Katherine Sheppard (suffragette) and 19th-century women	60	1·50
1551	80c. Richard Pearse (inventor) and early flying machine	90	1·50
1552	$1 Lt.-Gen. Sir Bernard Freyberg and tank	1·10	1·50
1553	$1.50 Peter Buck (politician) and Maori pattern	1·00	2·50

460 Akaroa

1990. 150th Anniv of European Settlements. Multicoloured.

1554	80c. Type **460**	55	70
1555	$1 Wanganui	70	75
1556	$1.50 Wellington	1·10	2·25
1557	$1.80 Takapuna Beach, Auckland	1·25	2·25
MS1558	125×100 mm. No. 1557 (sold at $2.30)	3·50	3·50

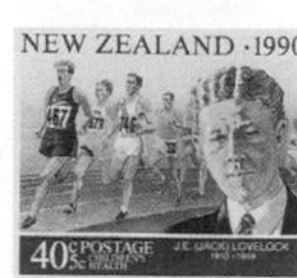

461 Jack Lovelock (athlete) and Race

1990. Health Stamps. Sportsmen (1st series). Multicoloured.

1559	40c. +5c. Type **461**	70	1·00
1560	80c. +5c. George Nepia (rugby player) and match	90	1·75
MS1561	115×96 mm. Nos. 1559/60, each×2	3·25	5·00

See also Nos. 1687/8.

462 Creation Legend of Rangi and Papa

1990. New Zealand Heritage (6th issue). The Maori. Multicoloured.

1562	40c. Type **462**	25	10
1563	50c. Pattern from Maori feather cloak	35	55
1564	60c. Maori women's choir	40	60
1565	80c. Maori facial tattoos	45	80
1566	$1 War canoe prow (detail)	50	1·00
1567	$1.50 Maori haka	75	2·75

463 Queen Victoria

1990. 150th Anniv of the Penny Black. Sheet 169×70 mm, containing T **463** and similar vert designs.

MS1568	40c.×6 blue (Type **463**, King Edward VII, King George V, King Edward VIII, King George VI, Queen Elizabeth II)	4·50	6·00

464 Angel

1990. Christmas.

1569	**464**	40c. purple, blue & brn	20	10
1570	-	$1 purple, green & brown	55	30
1571	-	$1.50 purple, red & brown	80	2·25
1572	-	$1.80 purple, red & brown	1·00	2·25

DESIGNS: $1 to $1.80, Different angels.

465 Antarctic Petrel

1990. Antarctic Birds. Multicoloured.

1573	40c. Type **465**	80	30
1574	50c. Wilson's storm petrel	90	75
1575	60c. Snow petrel	1·10	1·25
1576	80c. Southern fulmar	1·25	1·25
1577	$1 Bearded penguin ("Chinstrap Penguin")	1·40	1·25
1578	$1.50 Emperor penguin	1·60	4·00

Although inscribed "Ross Dependency" Nos. 1573/8 were available from post offices throughout New Zealand.

466 Coopworth Ewe and Lambs

1991. New Zealand Farming and Agriculture. Sheep Breeds. Multicoloured.

1579	40c. Type **466**	35	20
1580	60c. Perendale	45	60
1581	80c. Corriedale	60	70
1582	$1 Drysdale	75	75
1583	$1.50 South Suffolk	1·00	2·75
1584	$1.80 Romney	1·25	2·75

467 Moriori, Royal Albatross, Nikau Palm and Artefacts

1991. Bicentenary of Discovery of Chatham Islands. Multicoloured.

1585	40c. Type **467**	75	50
1586	80c. Carvings, H.M.S. "Chatham", Moriori house of 1870, and Tommy Solomon	1·50	2·25

468 Goal and Footballers

1991. Centenary of New Zealand Football Association. Multicoloured.

1587	80c. Type **468**	75	1·75
1588	80c. Five footballers and referee	75	1·75

Nos. 1587/8 were printed together, *se-tenant*, forming a composite design.

469 Tuatara on Rocks

1991. Endangered Species. The Tuatara. Multicoloured.

1590	40c. Type **469**	40	60
1591	40c. Tuatara in crevice	40	60
1592	40c. Tuatara with foliage	40	60
1593	40c. Tuatara in dead leaves	40	60

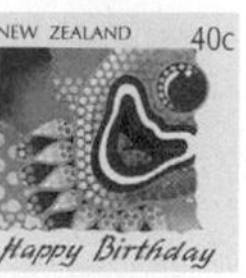

470 Clown

1991. "Happy Birthday". Multicoloured.

1594	40c. Type **470**	75	85
1595	40c. Balloons	75	85
1596	40c. Party hat	75	85
1597	40c. Birthday present (41×27 mm)	75	85
1598	40c. Birthday cake (41×27 mm)	75	85
1599	45c. Type **470**	75	85
1600	45c. As No. 1595	75	85
1601	45c. As No. 1596	75	85
1602	45c. As No. 1597	75	85
1603	45c. As No. 1598	75	85

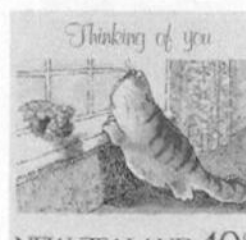

471 Cat at Window

1991. "Thinking of You". Multicoloured.

1604	40c. Type **471**	75	85
1605	40c. Cat playing with slippers	75	85
1606	40c. Cat with alarm clock	75	85
1607	40c. Cat in window (41×27 mm)	75	85
1608	40c. Cat at door (41×27 mm)	75	85
1609	45c. Type **471**	75	85
1610	45c. As No. 1605	75	85
1611	45c. As No. 1606	75	85
1612	45c. As No. 1607	75	85
1613	45c. As No. 1608	75	85

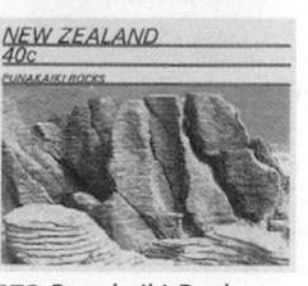

472 Punakaiki Rocks

1991. Scenic Landmarks. Multicoloured.

1614	40c. Type **472**	30	10
1615	50c. Moeraki Boulders	40	35
1616	80c. Organ Pipes	70	60
1617	$1 Castle Hill	80	70
1618	$1.50 Te Kaukau Point	1·25	1·60
1619	$1.80 Ahuriri River Clay Cliffs	1·50	1·90

473 Dolphins Underwater

1991. Health Stamps. Hector's Dolphin. Multicoloured.

1620	45c. +5c. Type **473**	90	1·25
1621	80c. +5c. Dolphins leaping	1·25	2·00
MS1622	115×100 mm. Nos. 1620/1, each×2	4·50	6·50

474 Children's Rugby

1991. World Cup Rugby Championship. Multicoloured.

1623	80c. Type **474**	55	80
1624	$1 Women's rugby	60	60
1625	$1.50 Senior rugby	1·10	2·50
1626	$1.80 "All Blacks" (national team)	1·25	2·50
MS1627	113×90 mm. No. 1626 (sold at $2.40)	2·75	5·00

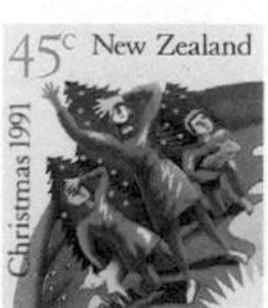

475 "Three Shepherds"

1991. Christmas. Multicoloured.

1628	45c. Type **475**	45	80
1629	45c. Two Kings on camels	45	80
1630	45c. Mary and Baby Jesus	45	80
1631	45c. King with gift	45	80
1632	65c. Star of Bethlehem	60	80
1633	$1 Crown	70	95
1634	$1.50 Angel	1·10	2·25

476 *Dodonidia helmsii*

1991. Butterflies. Multicoloured.

1635	$1 Type **476**	1·00	60
1641	$2 "Zizina otis oxleyi"	2·50	1·75
1642	$3 "Vanessa itea"	3·25	3·00
1643	$4 "Lycaena salustius"	2·50	3·00
1644	$5 "Bassaris gonerilla"	7·00	5·50

479 Yacht "Kiwi Magic", 1987

1992. New Zealand Challenge for America's Cup. Multicoloured.

1655	45c. Type **479**	35	10
1656	80c. Yacht "New Zealand", 1988	60	70
1657	$1 Yacht "America", 1851	80	85
1658	$1.50 "America's Cup" Class yacht, 1992	1·25	1·75

480 "Heemskerk"

1992. Great Voyages of Discovery. Multicoloured.

1659	45c. Type **480**	55	25
1660	80c. "Zeehan"	90	1·10
1661	$1 "Santa Maria"	1·25	1·10
1662	$1.50 "Pinta" and "Nina"	1·50	2·50

Nos. 1659/60 commemorate the 350th anniv of Tasman's discovery of New Zealand and Nos. 1661/2 the 500th anniv of discovery of America by Columbus.

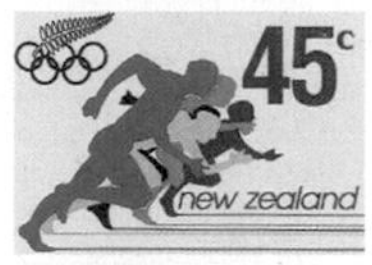

481 Sprinters

1992. Olympic Games, Barcelona (1st issue).

1663	**481** 45c. multicoloured	50	50

See also Nos. 1670/3.

482 Weddell Seal and Pup

1992. Antarctic Seals. Multicoloured.

1664	45c. Type **482**	60	15
1665	50c. Crabeater seals swimming	70	60
1666	65c. Leopard seal and Adelie penguins	90	1·50
1667	80c. Ross seal	1·00	1·25
1668	$1 Southern elephant seal and harem	1·10	1·25
1669	$1.80 Hooker's sea lion and pup	1·75	4·25

Although inscribed "ROSS DEPENDENCY" Nos. 1664/9 were available from post offices throughout New Zealand.

483 Cycling

1992. Olympic Games, Barcelona (2nd issue). Multicoloured.

1670	45c. Type **483**	65	20
1671	80c. Archery	70	70
1672	$1 Equestrian three-day eventing	75	85
1673	$1.50 Sailboarding	1·00	1·60
MS1674	125×100 mm. Nos. 1670/3	4·00	5·00

484 Ice Pinnacles, Franz Josef Glacier

1992. Glaciers. Multicoloured.

1675	45c. Type **484**	30	10
1676	50c. Tasman Glacier	40	35
1677	80c. Snowball Glacier, Marion Plateau	60	70
1678	$1 Brewster Glacier	70	85
1679	$1.50 Fox Glacier	1·10	1·60
1680	$1.80 Franz Josef Glacier	1·25	1·60

485 "Grand Finale" Camellia

1992. Camellias. Multicoloured.

1681	45c. Type **485**	45	10

1682	50c. "Showa-No-Sakae"	50	40
1683	80c. "Sugar Dream"	65	60
1684	$1 "Night Rider"	75	70
1685	$1.50 "E.G. Waterhouse"	1·25	2·75
1686	$1.80 "Dr. Clifford Parks"	1·50	3·00

1992. Health Stamps. Sportsmen (2nd series). As T **461**. Multicoloured.

1687	45c. +5c. Anthony Wilding (tennis player) and match	1·00	1·25
1688	80c. +5c. Stewie Dempster (cricketer) and batsman	1·00	1·50
MS1689	115×96 mm. Nos. 1687/8, each×2	5·00	6·50

486 Tree and Hills

1992. Landscapes. Multicoloured.

1690	45c. Type **486**	60	65
1691	45c. River and hills	60	65
1692	45c. Hills and mountain	60	65
1693	45c. Glacier	60	65
1694	45c. Hills and waterfall	60	65
1695	45c. Tree and beach	60	65
1696	45c. Estuary and cliffs	60	65
1697	45c. Fjord	60	65
1698	45c. River delta	60	65
1699	45c. Ferns and beach	60	65

487 Reindeer over Houses

1992. Christmas. Multicoloured.

1700	45c. Type **487**	90	1·25
1701	45c. Santa Claus on sleigh over houses	90	1·25
1702	45c. Christmas tree in window	90	1·25
1703	45c. Christmas wreath and children at window	90	1·25
1704	65c. Candles and fireplace	1·10	90
1705	$1 Family going to church	1·40	1·00
1706	$1.50 Picnic under Pohutukawa tree	2·00	3·50

488 1920s Fashions

1992. New Zealand in the 1920s. Multicoloured.

1707	45c. Type **488**	50	15
1708	50c. Dr. Robert Jack and early radio announcer	55	65
1709	80c. "All Blacks" rugby player, 1924	85	1·00
1710	$1 Swaggie and dog	95	1·00
1711	$1.50 Ford "Model A" car and young couple	1·75	2·25
1712	$1.80 Amateur aviators and biplane	2·00	2·75

489 "Old Charley" Toby Jug

1993. Royal Doulton Ceramics Exhibition, New Zealand. Multicoloured.

1713	45c. Type **489**	30	10
1714	50c. "Bunnykins" nursery plate	35	35
1715	80c. "Maori Art" tea set	55	60
1716	$1 "Ophelia" handpainted plate	65	75
1717	$1.50 "St. George" figurine	1·00	2·50
1718	$1.80 "Lambeth" salt-glazed stoneware vase	1·25	2·50
MS1719	125×100 mm. No. 1718	1·60	2·50

490 Women's Fashions of the 1930s

1993. New Zealand in the 1930s. Multicoloured.

1720	45c. Type **490**	40	10
1721	50c. Unemployed protest march	45	40
1722	80c. "Phar Lap" (racehorse)	85	70
1723	$1 State housing project	65	65
1724	$1.50 Boys drinking free school milk	1·25	3·00
1725	$1.80 Cinema queue	1·25	2·50

491 Women signing Petition

1993. Centenary of Women's Suffrage. Multicoloured.

1726	45c. Type **491**	30	10
1727	80c. Aircraft propeller and woman on tractor	55	75
1728	$1 Housewife with children	60	75
1729	$1.50 Modern women	90	2·25

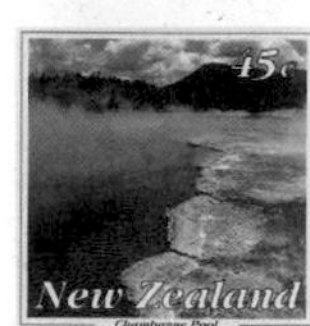

492 Champagne Pool

1993. Thermal Wonders, Rotorua. Multicoloured.

1730	45c. Type **492**	50	10
1731	50c. Boiling mud	50	40
1732	80c. Emerald pool	65	70
1733	$1 Hakereteke Falls	70	80
1734	$1.50 Warbrick Terrace	1·25	1·75
1735	$1.80 Pohutu Geyser	1·25	1·75

See also No. **MS**1770.

493 Yellow-eyed Penguin, Hector's Dolphin and New Zealand Fur Seal

1993. Endangered Species Conservation. Multicoloured.

1736	45c. Type **493**	85	1·25
1737	45c. Taiko (bird), Mount Cook lily and mountain duck ("Blue Duck")	85	1·25
1738	45c. Giant snail, rock wren and Hamilton's frog	85	1·25
1739	45c. Kaka (bird), New Zealand pigeon and giant weta	85	1·25
1740	45c. Tusked weta (23×28 mm)	85	1·00

494 Boy with Puppy

1993. Health Stamps. Children's Pets. Multicoloured.

1741	45c. +5c. Type **494**	60	90
1742	80c. +5c. Girl with kitten	90	1·50
MS1743	115×96 mm. Nos. 1741/2, each×2	3·00	4·50

1993. "Taipei '93" Asian International Stamp Exhibition, Taiwan. Multicoloured.

(a) No. **MS**1743 optd **TAIPEI '93** and emblem on sheet margin

MS1744	Nos. 1741/2, each×2	18·00	22·00

(b) Sheet 125×100 mm, containing Nos. 1490/c.

MS1745	**445** $1 green, $1 blue, $1 red	6·50	8·50

495 Christmas Decorations (value at left)

1993. Christmas. Multicoloured.

1746	45c. Type **495**	45	85
1747	45c. Christmas decorations (value at right)	45	85
1748	45c. Sailboards, gifts and Christmas pudding (value at left)	45	85
1749	45c. Sailboards, gifts and Christmas pudding (value at right)	45	85
1750	$1 Sailboards, baubles and Christmas cracker	1·00	1·25
1751	$1.50 Sailboards, present and wreath	1·50	3·25

496 Rainbow Abalone or Paua

1993. Marine Life. Multicoloured.

1752	45c. Type **496**	1·25	1·25
1753	45c. Green mussels	1·25	1·25
1754	45c. Tarakihi	1·25	1·25
1755	45c. Salmon	1·25	1·25
1756	45c. Southern blue-finned tuna, yellow-finned tuna and kahawai	1·25	1·25
1757	45c. Rock lobster	1·25	1·25
1758	45c. Snapper	1·25	1·25
1759	45c. Grouper	1·25	1·25
1760	45c. Orange roughy	1·25	1·25
1761	45c. Squid, hoki and black oreo	1·25	1·25

497 Sauropod

1993. Prehistoric Animals. Multicoloured.

1762	45c. Type **497**	50	15
1763	45c. Carnosaur and sauropod (30×25 mm)	75	90
1764	80c. Pterosaur	75	85
1765	$1 Ankylosaur	80	95
1766	$1.20 Mauisaurus	1·10	2·50
1767	$1.50 Carnosaur	1·25	2·50
MS1768	125×100 mm. $1.50 No. 1767	2·00	2·00

1993. "Bangkok '93" International Stamp Exhibition, Thailand. Multicoloured.

(a) No. **MS**1768 optd **BANGKOK '93** and emblem on sheet margin

MS1769	$1.50 No. 1767	1·60	2·00

(b) Sheet 115×100 mm, containing No. 1735.

MS1770	$1.80 multicoloured	2·75	3·75

498 Soldiers, National Flag and Pyramids

1993. New Zealand in the 1940s. Multicoloured.

1771	45c. Type **498**	80	25
1772	50c. Aerial crop spraying	85	60
1773	80c. Hydro-electric scheme	1·10	80
1774	$1 Marching majorettes	1·40	90
1775	$1.50 American troops	1·90	2·50
1776	$1.80 Crowd celebrating victory	2·00	2·50

499 Bungy Jumping

1994. Tourism. Multicoloured.

1777	45c. Type **499**	30	10
1778	45c. White water rafting (25×25 mm)	40	55
1779	80c. Trout fishing	50	70
1780	$1 Jet boating (horiz)	60	80
1781	$1.50 Tramping	1·00	2·00
1782	$1.80 Heli-skiing	1·25	2·00

See also No. **MS**1785.

500 "New Zealand Endeavour" (yacht)

1994. Round the World Yacht Race.

1783	**500**	$1 multicoloured	1·00	1·75

501 Mt. Cook and New Zealand Symbols

1994

1784	**501**	$20 blue and gold	13·00	15·00

1994. "Hong Kong '94" International Stamp Exhibition. Multicoloured.

MS1785	95×115 mm. $1.80 No. 1782	3·50	3·50
MS1786	100×125 mm. $1×3 As Nos. 1490/c	4·50	5·00

503 Rock and Roll Dancers

1994. New Zealand in the 1950s. Multicoloured.

1787	45c. Type **503**	35	10
1788	80c. Sir Edmund Hillary on Mt. Everest	75	55
1789	$1 Aunt Daisy (radio personality)	65	65
1790	$1.20 Queen Elizabeth II during 1953 royal visit	1·25	1·25
1791	$1.50 Children playing with Opo the dolphin	1·25	1·75
1792	$1.80 Auckland Harbour Bridge	1·40	1·75

504 Mt. Cook and Mt. Cook Lily ("Winter")

1994. The Four Seasons. Multicoloured.

1793	45c. Type **504**	30	10
1794	70c. Lake Hawea and Kowhai ("Spring")	45	45
1795	$1.50 Opononi Beach and Pohutukawa ("Summer")	80	1·00
1796	$1.80 Lake Pukaki and Puriri ("Autumn")	1·10	1·25

505 Rainbow Abalone or Paua Shell

1994. New Zealand Life. Multicoloured.

1797	45c. Type **505** (25×20 mm)	30	45

1798	45c. Pavlova dessert (35×20 mm)	30	45
1799	45c. Hokey pokey ice cream (25×20 mm)	30	45
1800	45c. Fish and chips (35×20 mm)	30	45
1801	45c. Jandals (30×20 mm)	30	45
1802	45c. Bush shirt (25×30½ mm)	30	45
1803	45c. Buzzy Bee (toy) (35×30½ mm)	30	45
1804	45c. Gumboots and black singlet (25×30½ mm)	30	45
1805	45c. Rugby boots and ball (35×30½ mm)	30	45
1806	45c. Kiwifruit (30×30½ mm)	30	45

See also Nos. 2318/27.

506 Maui pulls up Te Ika

1994. Maori Myths. Multicoloured.

1807	45c. Type **506**	30	45
1808	80c. Rona snatched up by Marama	45	40
1809	$1 Maui attacking Tuna	50	50
1810	$1.20 Tane separating Rangi and Papa	75	1·50
1811	$1.50 Matakauri slaying the Giant of Wakatipu	80	1·50
1812	$1.80 Panenehu showing crayfish to Tangaroa	90	1·50

507 1939 2d. on 1d.+1d. Health Stamp and Children playing with Ball

1994. Health Stamps. 75th Anniv of Children's Health Camps. Multicoloured.

1813	45c. +5c. Type **507**	50	80
1814	45c. +5c. 1949 1d.+½d. stamp and nurse holding child	50	80
1815	45c. +5c. 1969 4c.+1c. stamp and children reading	50	80
1816	80c. +5c. 1931 2d.+1d. stamp and child in cap	75	1·00
MS1817	130×90 mm. Nos. 1813/16	2·00	3·25

508 Astronaut on Moon (hologram)

1994. 25th Anniv of First Manned Moon Landing.

1818	**508** $1.50 multicoloured	2·25	2·75

509 "people reaching people"

1994. Self-adhesive.

1818ab	**509** 40c. multicoloured	75	55
1819	**509** 45c. multicoloured	1·00	65

510 African Elephants

1994. Stamp Month. Wild Animals. Multicoloured.

1820	45c. Type **510**	90	1·10
1821	45c. White rhinoceros	80	1·10
1822	45c. Lions	90	1·10
1823	45c. Common zebras	90	1·10
1824	45c. Giraffe and calf	90	1·10
1825	45c. Siberian tiger	90	1·10
1826	45c. Hippopotamuses	90	1·10
1827	45c. Spider monkey	90	1·10
1828	45c. Giant panda	90	1·10
1829	45c. Polar bear and cub	90	1·10

1994. "Philakorea '94" International Stamp Exhibition, Seoul. Multicoloured.

MS1830	125×100 mm. Nos. 1459a/65	6·50	6·00
MS1831	125×100 mm. Nos. 1820, 1822, 1824/5 and 1828/9	3·25	4·50

511 Children with Crib

1994. Christmas. Multicoloured.

1832	45c. Father Christmas and children (30×25 mm)	40	40
1833	45c. Type **511**	30	10
1834	70c. Man and toddler with crib	50	60
1835	80c. Three carol singers	55	65
1836	$1 Five carol singers	60	65
1837	$1.50 Children and candles	85	2·25
1838	$1.80 Parents with child	1·00	2·25
MS1839	125×100 mm. Nos. 1833/6	2·00	2·75

512 Batsman

1994. Centenary of New Zealand Cricket Council. Multicoloured.

(a) Horiz designs, each 30×25 mm

1840	45c. Bathers catching balls	75	90
1841	45c. Child on surf board at top	75	90
1842	45c. Young child with rubber ring at top	75	90
1843	45c. Man with beach ball at top	75	90
1844	45c. Woman with cricket bat at right	75	90
1845	45c. Boy in green cap with bat	75	90
1846	45c. Man in spotted shirt running	75	90
1847	45c. Woman in striped shorts with bat	75	90
1848	45c. Boy in wet suit with surf board at right	75	90
1849	45c. Sunbather with newspaper at right	75	90

(b) T **512** and similar vert designs. Multicoloured.

1850	45c. Type **512**	85	40
1851	80c. Bowler	1·50	1·00
1852	$1 Wicket keeper	1·75	1·00
1853	$1.80 Fielder	2·75	3·00

1995. "POST X '95" Postal History Exhibition, Auckland. Sheet 130×90 mm, containing No. 1297 and a reproduction of No. 557 optd "**SPECIMEN**".

MS1854	$10 multicoloured	18·00	18·00

513 Auckland

1995. New Zealand by Night. Multicoloured.

1855	45c. Type **513**	45	10
1856	80c. Wellington	70	45
1857	$1 Christchurch	80	60
1858	$1.20 Dunedin	1·10	1·50
1859	$1.50 Rotorua	1·25	1·90
1860	$1.80 Queenstown	1·40	1·90

See also No. **MS**1915.

514 The 15th Hole, Waitangi

1995. New Zealand Golf Courses. Multicoloured.

1861	45c. Type **514**	65	30
1862	80c. The 6th hole, New Plymouth	1·00	90
1863	$1.20 The 9th hole, Rotorua	1·50	2·50
1864	$1.80 The 5th hole, Queenstown	2·40	3·00

515 New Zealand Pigeon and Nest

1995. Environment. Multicoloured.

1865	45c. Type **515**	65	65
1866	45c. Planting sapling	65	65
1867	45c. Dolphins and whales	65	65
1868	45c. Thunderstorm	65	65
1869	45c. Backpackers	65	65
1870	45c. Animal pests	65	65
1871	45c. Noxious plants	65	65
1872	45c. Undersized fish and shellfish	65	65
1873	45c. Pollution from factories	65	65
1874	45c. Family at picnic site	65	65

516 Teacher with Guitar and Children

1995. Maori Language Year. Multicoloured.

1875	45c. Type **516**	30	10
1876	70c. Singing group	45	55
1877	80c. Mother and baby	50	60
1878	$1 Women performing traditional welcome	60	75
1879	$1.50 Grandfather reciting family genealogy	1·00	2·00
1880	$1.80 Tribal orator	1·10	2·00

517 Map of Australasia and Asia

1995. Meetings of Asian Development Bank Board of Governors and International Pacific Basin Economic Council, Auckland. Multicoloured.

1881	$1 Type **517**	1·00	1·00
1882	$1.50 Map of Australasia and Pacific	1·50	2·75

518 "Black Magic" (yacht)

1995. New Zealand's Victory in 1995 America's Cup.

1883	**518** 45c. multicoloured	55	55

519 Boy on Skateboard

1995. Health Stamps. Children's Sports. Multicoloured.

1884	45c. +5c. Type **519**	75	1·50
1885	80c. +5c. Girl on bicyle	1·75	2·00
MS1886	130×90 mm. Nos. 1884/5, each×2	5·00	6·50

1995. "Stampex '95" National Stamp Exhibition, Wellington. No. **MS**1886 additionally inscr with "Stampex '95" and emblem on sheet margin. Multicoloured.

MS1887	130×90 mm. Nos. 1884/5, each×2	6·00	7·00

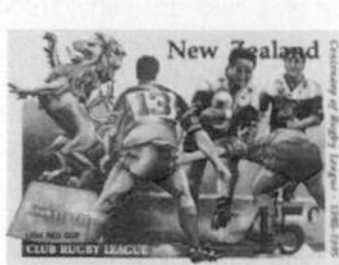

520 Lion Red Cup and Players

1995. Centenary of Rugby League. Multicoloured.

1888	45c. Trans Tasman test match (30×25 mm)	50	60
1889	45c. Type **520**	35	10
1890	$1 Children's rugby and mascot	80	1·10
1891	$1.50 George Smith, Albert Baskerville and early match	1·40	2·75
1892	$1.80 Courtney Goodwill Trophy and match against Great Britain	1·50	2·50
MS1893	125×100 mm. No. 1892	2·50	3·00

521 Sheep and Lamb

1995. Farmyard Animals. Multicoloured.

1894	40c. Type **521**	75	75
1895	40c. Deer	75	75
1896	40c. Mare and foal	75	75
1897	40c. Cow with calf	75	75
1898	40c. Goats and kid	75	75
1899	40c. Common turkey	75	75
1900	40c. Ducks	75	75
1901	40c. Red junglefowl	75	75
1902	40c. Sow with piglets	75	75
1903	40c. Border collie	75	75
1904	45c. As Type **521**	75	75
1905	45c. As No. 1895	75	75
1906	45c. As No. 1896	75	75
1907	45c. As No. 1897	75	75
1908	45c. As No. 1898	75	75
1909	45c. As No. 1899	75	75
1910	45c. As No. 1900	75	75
1911	45c. As No. 1901	75	75
1912	45c. As No. 1902	75	75
1913	45c. As No. 1903	75	75

1995. "Singapore '95" International Stamp Exhibition. Multicoloured.

MS1914	170×70 mm. Nos. 1909/13	3·25	4·00
MS1915	148×210 mm. Nos. 1855/60	11·00	15·00

No. **MS**1915 also includes the "JAKARTA '95" logo.

522 Archangel Gabriel

1995. Christmas. Stained Glass Windows from St. Mary's Anglican Church, Merivale (Nos. 1916/18), The Lady Chapel of St. Luke's Anglican Church, Christchurch (Nos. 1919/22) or St. John the Evangelist Church, Cheviot (No. 1923). Multicoloured

(a) As T **522**

1916	40c. Type **522**	70	25
1917	45c. Type **522**	70	25
1918	70c. Virgin Mary	1·00	90
1919	80c. Shepherds	1·10	1·00
1920	$1 Virgin and Child	1·40	1·10
1921	$1.50 Two Wise Men	2·25	2·75
1922	$1.80 Wise Man kneeling	2·50	2·75

(b) Smaller design, 25×30 mm.

1923	40c. Angel with trumpet	50	50

523 Face and Nuclear Disarmament Symbol

1995. Nuclear Disarmament.

1924	**523** $1 multicoloured	1·00	1·25

524 Mt. Cook

1995. New Zealand Scenery. Multicoloured.

1925	5c. Type **524**	10	50
1926	10c. Champagne Pool	10	10
1927	20c. Cape Reinga	15	20
1928	30c. Mackenzie Country	20	25
1929	40c. Mitre Peak (vert)	30	35
1930	50c. Mt. Ngauruhoe	35	40
1931	60c. Lake Wanaka (vert)	45	50

1932 70c. Giant kauri tree (vert) 50 55
1933 80c. Doubtful Sound (vert) 60 65
1934 90c. Waitomo Limestone Cave (vert) 65 70
1934a 90c. Rangitoto Island 3·00 70
1934b $1 Taiaroa Head (27×22 mm) 1·00 80
1934c $1.10 Kaikoura Coast (27×22 mm) 1·00 85
1934d $1.30 Lake Camp, South Canterbury (27×22 mm) 5·00 2·00
1934e $2 Great Barrier Island (27×22 mm) 1·50 1·60
1934f $3 Cape Kidnappers (27×22 mm) 2·25 2·40
1935 $10 Mt. Ruapehu (38×32 mm) 7·50 7·75

For similar self-adhesive designs see Nos. 1983a/91b.

For miniature sheets containing some of these designs see Nos. **MS**1978, **MS**1998, **MS**2005, **MS**2328 and **MS**2401.

525 Dame Kiri te Kanawa (opera singer)

1995. Famous New Zealanders. Multicoloured.

1936 40c. Type **525** 1·00 40
1937 80c. Charles Upham, V.C. (war hero) 1·00 85
1938 $1 Barry Crump (author) 1·25 1·00
1939 $1.20 Sir Brian Barratt-Boyes (surgeon) 1·75 1·50
1940 $1.50 Dame Whina Cooper (Maori leader) 1·75 2·00
1941 $1.80 Sir Richard Hadlee (cricketer) 3·00 2·25

526 National Flags, Peace Dove and "50"

1995. 50th Anniv of United Nations.

1942 **526** $1.80 multicoloured 2·25 3·00

527 Fern and Globe

1995. Commonwealth Heads of Government Meeting, Auckland. Multicoloured.

1943 40c. Type **527** 50 25
1944 $1.80 Fern and New Zealand flag 2·50 3·00

528 "Kiwi"

1996. Famous Racehorses. Multicoloured.

1945 40c. Type **528** 55 10
1946 80c. "Rough Habit" 85 55
1947 $1 "Blossom Lady" 1·00 65
1948 $1.20 "Il Vicolo" 1·40 1·60
1949 $1.50 "Horlicks" 1·50 2·00
1950 $1.80 "Bonecrusher" 2·00 2·50
MS1951 Seven sheets, each 162×110 mm. (a) No. 1945. (b) No. 1946. (c) No. 1947. (d) No. 1948. (e) No. 1949. (f) No. 1950. (g) Nos. 1945/50 Set of 7 sheets 16·00 19·00

529 Kete (basket)

1996. Maori Crafts. Multicoloured.

1952 40c. Type **529** 25 10
1953 80c. Head of Taiaha (spear) 45 40
1954 $1 Taniko (embroidery) 55 50
1955 $1.20 Pounamu (greenstone) 70 1·25
1956 $1.50 Hue (gourd) 75 1·75
1957 $1.80 Korowai (feather cloak) 90 1·75

See also No. **MS**2049.

530 Southern Black-backed Gulls

1996. Seaside Environment

1968 40c. Type **530** 55 60
1969 40c. Children, sea cucumber and spiny starfish 55 60
1970 40c. Yacht, gull and common shrimps 55 60
1971 40c. Gaudy nudibranch 55 60
1972 40c. Large rock crab and clingfish 55 60
1973 40c. Snake skin chiton and red rock crab 55 60
1974 40c. Estuarine triplefin and cat's-eye shell 55 60
1975 40c. Cushion star and sea horses 55 60
1976 40c. Blue-eyed triplefin and Yaldwyn's triplefin 55 60
1977 40c. Common octopus 55 60

1996. "SOUTHPEX '96" Stamp Show, Invercargill. Sheet 100×215 mm, containing No. 1929×10.

MS1978 40c.×10 multicoloured 5·50 5·50

531 Fire and Ambulance Services

1996. Rescue Services. Multicoloured.

1979 40c. Type **531** 50 20
1980 80c. Civil Defence 90 90
1981 $1 Air-sea rescue 1·10 1·10
1982 $1.50 Air ambulance and rescue helicopter 1·60 2·75
1983 $1.80 Mountain rescue and Red Cross 2·25 2·50

532 Mt. Egmont, Taranaki

1996. New Zealand Scenery. Self-adhesive. Multicoloured.

1983a 10c. Champagne Pool 1·00 1·25
1984b 40c. Type **532** 35 40
1985 40c. Piercy Island, Bay of Islands 55 55
1986b 40c. Tory Channel, Marlborough Sounds 35 40
1987 40c. "Earnslaw" (ferry), Lake Wakatipu 55 55
1988b 40c. Lake Matheson 35 40
1989b 40c. Fox Glacier 35 40
1990 80c. Doubtful Sound (as No. 1933) 90 90
1990b 90c. Rangitoto Island (as No. 1934a) 90 90
1991 $1 Pohutukawa tree (33×22 mm) 1·00 1·00
1991b $1.10 Kaikoura Coast 1·00 1·25

533 Yellow-eyed Penguin

1996. Marine Wildlife. Multicoloured.

1992 40c. Type **533** 35 25
1993 80c. Royal albatross (horiz) 70 60
1994 $1 Great egret (horiz) 75 70
1995 $1.20 Flukes of sperm whale (horiz) 80 1·60
1996 $1.50 Fur seals 90 2·00
1997 $1.80 Bottlenose dolphin 1·10 2·00

See also Nos. **MS**1999 and **MS**2037.

1996. "CHINA '96" Ninth International Stamp Exhibition, Peking. Multicoloured.

MS1998 180×80 mm. Nos. 1926/8 and 1930 1·50 2·00
MS1999 140×90 mm. Nos. 1994 and 1996 2·25 3·00

No. **MS**1999 also shows designs as Nos. 1992/3, 1995 and 1997, but without face values.

534 Baby in Car Seat

1996. Health Stamps. Child Safety. Multicoloured

Stamps from No. **MS**2002 are slightly larger with "NEW ZEALAND" and the face values redrawn.

(a) Ordinary gum

2000 40c. +5c. Type **534** 50 75
2001 80c. +5c. Child and adult on zebra crossing 90 1·50
MS2002 130×90 mm. Nos. 2000/1, each×2 2·75 2·75

(b) Self-adhesive

2003 40c. +5c. Type **534** (21½×38 mm) 50 75

1996. "CAPEX '96" International Stamp Exhibition, Toronto. Multicoloured.

(a) No. **MS**2002 optd **CAPEX '96** and emblem on sheet margin

MS2004 Nos. 2000/1, each×2 3·25 2·75

(b) Sheet 180×80 mm, containing Nos. 1931/4.

MS2005 $3 multicoloured 3·25 3·25

535 Violin

1996. 50th Anniv of New Zealand Symphony Orchestra. Multicoloured.

2006 40c. Type **535** 30 30
2007 80c. French horn 80 1·50

536 Swimming

1996. Centennial Olympic Games, Atlanta. Multicoloured.

2008 40c. Type **536** 40 15
2009 80c. Cycling 1·25 80
2010 $1 Running 80 80
2011 $1.50 Rowing 1·00 2·75
2012 $1.80 Dinghy racing 1·00 2·75
MS2013 120×80 mm. Nos. 2008/12 4·00 6·50

537 "Hinemoa"

1996. Centenary of New Zealand Cinema. Multicoloured.

2014 40c. Type **537** 30 15
2015 80c. "Broken Barrier" 60 60
2016 $1.50 "Goodbye Pork Pie" 1·00 2·25
2017 $1.80 "Once Were Warriors" 1·10 2·25

538 Danyon Loader (swimmer) and Blyth Tait (horseman)

1996. New Zealand Olympic Gold Medal Winners, Atlanta.

2018 **538** 40c. multicoloured 50 50

539 Beehive Ballot Box

1996. New Zealand's First Mixed Member Proportional Representation Election.

2019 **539** 40c. black, red and yellow 30 40

540 King following Star

1996. Christmas. Multicoloured

(a) Size 35×35 mm

2020 40c. Type **540** 30 10
2021 70c. Shepherd and Baby Jesus 50 40
2022 80c. Angel and shepherd 55 40
2023 $1 Mary, Joseph and Baby Jesus 70 50
2024 $1.50 Mary and Joseph with donkey 1·25 2·75
2025 $1.80 The Annunciation 1·25 2·50

(b) Size 30×24 mm. Self-adhesive.

2026 40c. Angels with trumpets 50 75
2027 40c. King with gift 50 50

541 Adzebill

1996. Extinct Birds. Multicoloured

(a) Size 40×28 mm

2028 40c. Type **541** 60 40
2029 80c. South Island whekau ("Laughing Owl") 1·25 1·25
2030 $1 Piopio 1·25 1·10
2031 $1.20 Huia 1·50 1·75
2032 $1.50 Giant eagle 1·75 2·50
2033 $1.80 Giant moa 2·00 2·50
MS2034 105×92 mm. No. 2033 2·00 2·00

(b) Size 30×24 mm. Self-adhesive.

2035 40c. Stout-legged wren 60 60

1996. "TAIPEI '96" Tenth Asian International Stamp Exhibition, Taiwan. Multicoloured.

(a) No. **MS**2034 overprinted with "**TAIPEI '96**" logo on sheet margin

MS2036 105×92 mm. No. 2033 2·75 2·75

(b) Sheet 140×90 mm, containing Nos. 1993 and 1997. Multicoloured.

MS2037 Nos. 1993 and 1997 2·75 2·75

No. **MS**2037 also shows designs as Nos. 1992 and 1994/6, but without face values.

542 Seymour Square, Blenheim

1996. Scenic Gardens. Multicoloured.

2038 40c. Type **542** 30 10
2039 80c. Pukekura Park, New Plymouth 60 60
2040 $1 Wintergarden, Auckland 70 70
2041 $1.50 Botanic Garden, Christchurch 1·10 2·50
2042 $1.80 Marine Parade Gardens, Napier 1·25 2·50

543 Holstein Friesian Cattle

1997. Cattle Breeds. Multicoloured.

2043	40c. Type **543**	50	10
2044	80c. Jersey	1·10	70
2045	$1 Simmental	1·25	75
2046	$1.20 Ayrshire	1·60	1·60
2047	$1.50 Angus	1·60	2·25
2048	$1.80 Hereford	1·75	2·00

1997. "HONG KONG '97" International Stamp Exhibition. Multicoloured.

MS2049 130×110 mm. Nos. 1952/3 and 1956	2·00	2·50
MS2050 101×134 mm. Nos. 2044/5 and 2047	2·25	2·75

No. **MS**2050 is also inscribed for the Chinese New Year ("Year of the Ox").

544 James Cook and Sextant

1997. Millennium Series (1st issue). Discoverers of New Zealand. Multicoloured.

2051	40c. Type **544**	80	45
2052	80c. Kupe and ocean-going canoe	1·00	90
2053	$1 Carved panel depicting Maui (vert)	1·25	1·00
2054	$1.20 Anchor and "St. Jean Baptiste" (Jean de Surville) (vert)	1·75	1·60
2055	$1.50 Dumont d'Urville, crab and "Lastrolabe"	2·00	2·00
2056	$1.80 Abel Tasman and illustration from journal	2·00	2·00

See also Nos. 2140/5, 2216/21, 2239/44, 2304/9 and 2310.

545 Rippon Vineyard, Central Otago

1997. New Zealand Vineyards. Multicoloured.

2057	40c. Type **545**	30	10
2058	80c. Te Mata Estate, Hawke's Bay	60	60
2059	$1 Cloudy Bay Vineyard, Marlborough	70	70
2060	$1.20 Pegasus Bay Vineyard, Waipara	85	1·75
2061	$1.50 Milton Vineyard, Gisborne	1·25	2·75
2062	$1.80 Goldwater Estate, Waiheke Island	1·25	2·50
MS2063	Seven sheets, each 150×110 mm. (a) No. 2057. (b) No. 2058. (c) No. 2059. (d) No. 2060. (e) No. 2061. (f) No. 2062. (g) Nos. 2057/62 Set of 7 sheets	11·00	15·00

See also No. **MS**2081.

546 Cottage Letterbox

1997. Curious Letterboxes. Multicoloured. Self-adhesive.

2064	40c. Type **546**	50	50
2065	40c. Owl letterbox	50	50
2066	40c. Blue whale letterbox	50	50
2067	40c. "Kilroy is Back" letterbox	50	50
2068	40c. Nesting box letterbox	50	50
2069	40c. Piper letterbox	50	50
2070	40c. Diver's helmet letterbox	50	50
2071	40c. Aircraft letterbox	50	50
2072	40c. Water tap letterbox	50	50
2073	40c. Indian palace letterbox	50	50

547 "The Promised Land", 1948 (Colin McCahon)

1997. Contemporary Paintings by Colin McCahon. Multicoloured.

2074	40c. Type **547**	30	10
2075	$1 "Six Days in Nelson and Canterbury", 1950	65	60
2076	$1.50 "Northland Panels" (detail), 1958	1·00	2·00
2077	$1.80 "Moby Dick is sighted off Muriwai Beach", 1972	1·10	2·00

548 Carrier Pigeon (based on 1899 "Pigeon-gram" local stamp)

1997. Centenary of Great Barrier Island Pigeon Post.

2078	**548**	40c. red	50	75
2079	**548**	80c. blue	90	1·50

See also Nos. **MS**2080 and **MS**2122.

1997. "Pacific '97" International Stamp Exhibition, San Francisco. Multicoloured.

MS2080 137×120 mm. Nos. 2078/9, each×2	2·50	2·50
MS2081 140×100 mm. Nos. 2057, 2059 and 2061	3·00	3·00

No. **MS**2080 is in a triangular format.

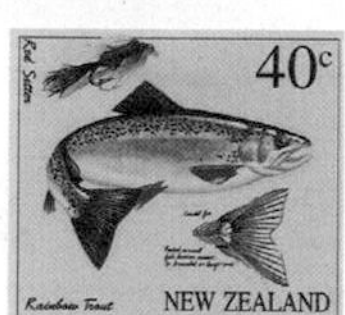

549 Rainbow Trout and Red Setter Fly

1997. Fly Fishing. Multicoloured.

2082	40c. Type **549**	30	10
2083	$1 Sea-run brown trout and grey ghost fly	70	60
2084	$1.50 Brook charr and twilight beauty fly	1·10	2·25
2085	$1.80 Brown trout and Hare and Cooper fly	1·25	2·25

See also No. **MS**2172.

550 "Beach Scene" (Fern Petrie)

1997. Children's Health. Children's paintings. Multicoloured

(a) Ordinary gum

2086	40c. +5c. Type **550**	45	75
2087	80c. +5c. "Horse-riding on the Waterfront" (Georgia Dumergue)	80	1·25
MS2088	130×90 mm. Nos. 2086/7 and 40c.+5c. As No. 2089 (25×36 mm)	1·75	1·75

(b) Self-adhesive.

2089	40c. +5c. "Picking Fruit" (Anita Pitcher)	70	60

551 The "Overlander" at Paremata, Wellington

1997. Scenic Railway Services. Multicoloured.

2091	40c. Type **551**	50	20
2092	80c. The "Tranz Alpine" in the Southern Alps	90	80
2093	$1 The "Southener" at Canterbury	1·00	90
2094	$1.20 The "Coastal Pacific" on the Kaikoura Coast	1·40	2·00
2095	$1.50 The "Bay Express" at Central Hawke's Bay	1·60	2·50
2096	$1.80 The "Kaimai Express" at Tauranga Harbour	1·75	2·25

See also No. **MS**2173.

552 Samuel Marsden's "Active", Bay of Islands

1997. Christmas. Multicoloured

(a) Ordinary gum

2097	40c. Type **552**	30	10
2098	70c. Revd. Marsden preaching	50	50
2099	80c. Marsden and Maori chiefs	60	50
2100	$1 Maori family	70	70
2101	$1.50 Handshake and cross	1·00	1·75
2102	$1.80 Pohutukawa (flower) and Rangihoua Bay	1·10	1·75

(b) Smaller design, 29×24 mm. Self-adhesive.

2103	40c. Memorial cross, Pohutukawa and Bay of Islands	40	40

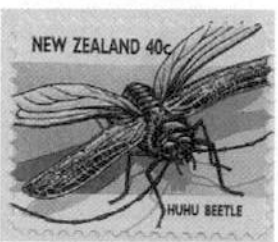

553 Huhu Beetle

1997. Insects. Multicoloured. Self-adhesive.

2104	40c. Type **553**	50	50
2105	40c. Giant land snail	50	50
2106	40c. Giant weta	50	50
2107	40c. Giant dragonfly	50	50
2108	40c. Peripatus	50	50
2109	40c. Cicada	50	50
2110	40c. Puriri moth	50	50
2111	40c. Veined slug	50	50
2112	40c. Katipo	50	50
2113	40c. Flax weevil	50	50

554 "Rosa rugosa"

1997. New Zealand–China Joint Issue. Roses. Multicoloured.

2114	40c. Type **554**	50	50
2115	40c. "Aotearoa"	50	50
MS2116	115×95 mm. 80c. Nos. 2114/15	1·00	1·00

555 Queen Elizabeth II and Prince Philip

1997. Golden Wedding of Queen Elizabeth and Prince Philip.

2117	**555**	40c. multicoloured	50	75

556 Cartoon Kiwi on Busy-bee

1997. New Zealand Cartoons. "Kiwis Taking on the World". Multicoloured.

2118	40c. Type **556**	40	10
2119	$1 "Let's have 'em for Breakfast"	70	55
2120	$1.50 Kiwi dinghy winning race	1·10	1·50
2121	$1.80 "CND" emblem cut in forest	1·25	1·50

1997. "Aupex '97" National Stamp Exhibtion, Auckland. Sheet 140×120 mm. Multicoloured.

MS2122 Nos. 2078/9, each×2	2·10	2·10

No. **MS**2122 is in a triangular format.

1997. International Stamp and Coin Exhibition 1997, Shanghai. Sheet as No. **MS**2116, but redrawn to include "Issued by New Zealand Post to commemorate the International Stamp and Coin Expo. Shanghai, China. 19–23 November 1997" inscr in English and Chinese with additional die-stamped gold frame and logo.

MS2123 115×95 mm. Nos. 2114/15	1·00	1·00

557 Modern Dancer

1998. Performing Arts. Multicoloured.

2124	40c. Type **557**	25	10
2125	80c. Trombone player	55	55
2126	$1 Opera singer	1·25	75
2127	$1.20 Actor	80	1·25
2128	$1.50 Singer	1·00	2·00
2129	$1.80 Ballet dancer	1·25	2·00
MS2130	Seven sheets, each 150×110 mm. (a) No. 2124. (b) No. 2125. (c) No. 2126. (d) No. 2127. (e) No. 2128. (f) No. 2129. (g) Nos. 2124/9 Set of 7 sheets	12·00	17·00

558 Museum of New Zealand

1998. Opening of Museum of New Zealand, Wellington. Multicoloured.

2131	40c. Type **558**	30	35
2132	$1.80 Museum, spotted cormorant and silver gull	1·40	1·40

559 Domestic Cat

1998. Cats. Multicoloured.

2133	40c. Type **559**	30	10
2134	80c. Burmese	60	60
2135	$1 Birman	65	65
2136	$1.20 British blue	70	1·25
2137	$1.50 Persian	90	2·25
2138	$1.80 Siamese	1·10	2·00

1998. Chinese New Year ("Year of the Tiger"). Multicoloured.

MS2139 100×135 mm. Nos. 2133, 2135 and 2138	2·00	3·00

560 Maoris and Canoe

1998. Millennium Series (2nd issue). Immigrants. Multicoloured.

2140	40c. Type **560**	35	15
2141	80c. 19th-century European settlers and immigrant ship	75	65
2142	$1 Gold miners and mine	1·00	80
2143	$1.20 Post 1945 European migrants and liner	1·25	1·10
2144	$1.50 Pacific islanders and church	1·40	1·75
2145	$1.80 Asian migrant and jumbo jet	1·60	1·60

561 "With Great Respect to the Mehmetcik" Statue, Gallipoli

1998. Joint Issue New Zealand–Turkey. Memorial Statues. Multicoloured.

2146	40c. Type **561**	40	35
2147	$1.80 "Mother with Children", National War Memorial, Wellington	1·25	1·40

562 Mother and Son Hugging

1998. "Stay in Touch" Greetings Stamps. Multicoloured. Self-adhesive.

2148	40c. Type **562**	35	35
2149	40c. Couple on beach	35	35
2150	40c. Boys striking hands	35	35
2151	40c. Grandmother and grandson	35	35
2152	40c. Young boys in pool (horiz)	35	35
2153	40c. "I'LL MISS YOU ... PLEASE WRITE" (horiz)	35	35
2154	40c. Symbolic couple and clouds (horiz)	35	35
2155	40c. Young couple kissing (horiz)	35	35
2156	40c. Couple sat on sofa (horiz)	35	35
2157	40c. Maoris rubbing noses (horiz)	35	35

563 Mount Cook or Aorangi

1998. Centenary of 1898 Pictorial Stamps. Designs as T **23/26** and **28/35** with modern face values as T **563**.

2158	**563**	40c. brown	30	50
2159	**24**	40c. blue and brown	30	50
2160	**25**	40c. brown	30	50
2161	**28**	40c. brown	30	50
2162	**29**	40c. red	30	50
2163	**31**	40c. green	30	50
2164	**32**	40c. blue	30	50
2165	**34**	40c. orange	30	50
2166	**26**	80c. blue (inscr "LAKE WAKITIPU") (35×23 mm)	60	75
2167	**26**	80c. blue (inscr "LAKE WAKATIPU") (35×23 mm)	60	75
2168	**30**	$1 brown (23×35 mm)	70	85
2169	**33**	$1.20 brown (35×23 mm)	85	1·60
2170	**35**	$1.50 green (35×23 mm)	1·00	1·75
2171	-	$1.80 red (as No. 329) (23×35 mm)	1·25	1·75

See also Nos. **MS**2188 and **MS**2214.

1998. "Israel '98" World Stamp Exhibition, Tel Aviv. Multicoloured.

MS2172 112×90 mm. Nos. 2082 and 2085	2·50	2·75
MS2173 125×100 mm. Nos. 2092/3 and 2095	4·00	4·00

564 "Wounded at Cassino"

1998. Paintings by Peter McIntyre. Multicoloured.

2174	40c. Type **564**	20	10
2175	$1 "The Cliffs of Rangitikei"	60	55
2176	$1.50 "Maori Children, King Country"	80	1·10
2177	$1.80 "The Anglican Church, Kakahi"	1·00	1·10

See also No. **MS**2215.

565 Girl wearing Lifejacket

1998. Children's Health. Water Safety. Multicoloured

(a) Ordinary gum

2178	40c. +5c. Type **565**	40	60
2179	80c. +5c. Boy learning to swim	60	90
MS2180	125×90 mm. Nos. 2178/9, each×2	2·00	2·00

(b) Smaller design, 25×37 mm. Self-adhesive.

2181	40c. +5c. Type **565**	30	50

566 Sunrise near Cambridge

1998. Scenic Skies. Multicoloured.

2182	40c. Type **566**	30	10
2183	80c. Clouds over Lake Wanaka	60	50
2184	$1 Sunset over Mount Maunganui	70	55
2185	$1.20 Rain clouds over South Bay, Kaikoura	80	1·10
2186	$1.50 Sunset near Statue of Wairaka, Whakatane Harbour	1·10	1·25
2187	$1.80 Cloud formation above Lindis Pass	1·25	1·50

See also No. **MS**2245.

1998. "TARAPEX '98" National Stamp Exhibition, New Plymouth.

MS2188 90×80 mm. Nos. 2166/7	1·60	1·75

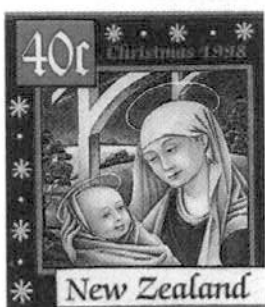

567 Virgin Mary and Christ Child

1998. Christmas. Multicoloured

(a) Ordinary gum

2189	40c. Type **567**	25	10
2190	70c. Shepherds approaching the stable	40	30
2191	80c. Virgin Mary, Joseph and Christ Child	50	35
2192	$1 Magi with gift of gold	60	40
2193	$1.50 Three magi	1·10	1·75
2194	$1.80 Angel and shepherds	1·25	1·75

(b) Smaller design, 24×29 mm. Self-adhesive.

2195	40c. Type **567**	35	30

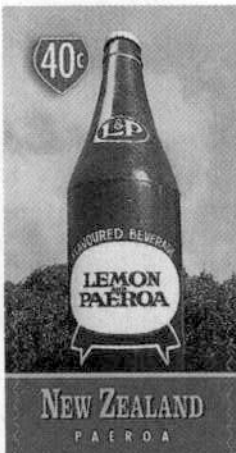

568 Lemon and Mineral Water Bottle, Paeroa

1998. Town Icons. Multicoloured. Self-adhesive.

2196	40c. Type **568**	40	40
2197	40c. Carrot, Ohakune	40	40
2198	40c. Brown Trout, Gore (25×36 mm)	40	40
2199	40c. Crayfish, Kaikoura (25×36 mm)	40	40
2200	40c. Sheep-shearer, Te Kuiti (25×36 mm)	40	40
2201	40c. "Pania of the Reef" (Maori legend), Napier (25×36 mm)	40	40
2202	40c. Paua Shell, Riverton (24×29 mm)	40	40
2203	40c. Kiwifruit, Te Puke (24×29 mm)	40	40
2204	40c. Border Collie, Lake Tekapo (24×29 mm)	40	40
2205	40c. "Big Cow", Hawera (24×29 mm)	40	40

569 Moonfish

1998. International Year of the Ocean. Multicoloured.

2206	40c. Type **569**	35	50
2207	40c. Mako shark	35	50
2208	40c. Yellowfin tuna	35	50
2209	40c. Giant squid	35	50
2210	80c. Striped marlin	50	70
2211	80c. Porcupine fish	50	70
2212	80c. Eagle ray	50	70
2213	80c. Sandager's wrasse	50	70

Nos. 2206/9 and 2210/13 respectively were printed together, *se-tenant*, forming composite designs.

See also Nos. **MS**2246 and **MS**2277.

1998. "Italia '98" International Philatelic Exhibition, Milan. Multicoloured.

MS2214 90×80 mm. Nos. 2167 and 2170	3·00	3·25
MS2215 112×90 mm. Nos. 2176/7	2·00	2·25

570 Wellington in 1841 and 1998

1998. Millennium Series (3rd issue). Urban Transformations. Multicoloured.

2216	40c. Type **570**	30	10
2217	80c. Auckland in 1852 and 1998	50	40
2218	$1 Christchurch in 1851 and 1998	55	50
2219	$1.20 Westport in 1919 and 1998	70	1·25
2220	$1.50 Tauranga in 1880 and 1998	80	1·50
2221	$1.80 Dunedin in 1862 and 1998	1·00	1·50

571 "Fuchsia excorticata"

1999. Flowering Trees of New Zealand. Multicoloured.

2222	40c. Type **571**	25	10
2223	80c. "Solanum laciniatum"	40	35
2224	$1 "Sophora tetraptera"	50	50
2225	$1.20 "Carmichaelia stevensonii"	60	1·00
2226	$1.50 "Olearia angustfolia"	80	1·50
2227	$1.80 "Metrosideros umbellata"	90	1·50

See also No. **MS**2286.

572 Civic Theatre, Auckland

1999. Art Deco Architecture. Multicoloured.

2228	40c. Type **572**	30	10
2229	$1 Masonic Hotel, Napier	2·00	80
2230	$1.50 Medical and Dental Chambers, Hastings	80	1·40
2231	$1.80 Buller County Chambers, Westport	90	1·40

573 Labrador Puppy and Netherland Dwarf Rabbit

1999. Popular Pets. Multicoloured.

2232	40c. Type **573**	40	20
2233	80c. Netherland dwarf rabbit	60	40
2234	$1 Tabby kitten and Netherland dwarf rabbit	70	50
2235	$1.20 Lamb	85	1·25
2236	$1.50 Welsh pony	1·25	1·50
2237	$1.80 Two budgerigars	1·25	1·50
MS2238	100×135 mm. Nos. 2232/4	1·75	1·75

No. **MS**2238 also commemorates the Chinese New Year ("Year of the Rabbit").

See also No. **MS**2287.

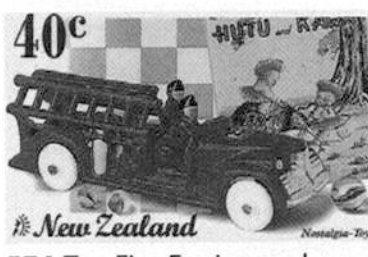

574 Toy Fire Engine and Marbles

1999. Millennium Series (4th issue). Nostalgia. Multicoloured.

2239	40c. Type **574**	30	10
2240	80c. Commemorative tin of biscuits and cereal packet	40	40
2241	$1 Tram, tickets and railway crockery	60	50
2242	$1.20 Radio and "Woman's Weekly" magazine	70	1·25
2243	$1.50 Coins, postcards and stamps	80	1·60
2244	$1.80 Lawn mower and seed packets	90	1·60

1999. "Australia '99" World Stamp Exhibition, Melbourne. Multicoloured.

MS2245 130×70 mm. Nos. 2182 and 2187	1·90	1·90
MS2246 130×90 mm. Nos. 2206/7 and 2210/11	2·00	2·00

575 Hunter Building, Victoria University

1999. Centenary of Victoria University, Wellington.

2247	**575**	40c. multicoloured	30	30

576 Auckland Blues Player kicking Ball

1999. New Zealand U-Bix Rugby Super 12 Championship. Multicoloured. Ordinary or self-adhesive gum.

2248	40c. Type **576**	30	40
2249	40c. Auckland Blues player being tackled	30	40
2250	40c. Chiefs player being tackled	30	40
2251	40c. Chiefs lineout jump	30	40
2252	40c. Wellington Hurricanes player being tackled	30	40
2253	40c. Wellington Hurricanes player passing ball	30	40
2254	40c. Canterbury Crusaders lineout jump	30	40
2255	40c. Canterbury Crusaders player kicking ball	30	40
2256	40c. Otago Highlanders player diving for try	30	40
2257	40c. Otago Highlanders player running with ball	30	40

577 "The Lake, Tuai"

1999. Paintings by Doris Lusk. Multicoloured.

2268	40c. Type **577**	30	10
2269	$1 "The Pumping Station"	70	50
2270	$1.50 "Arcade Awning, St. Mark's Square, Venice (2)"	90	1·60
2271	$1.80 "Tuam St. II"	1·10	1·40

See also No. **MS**2276.

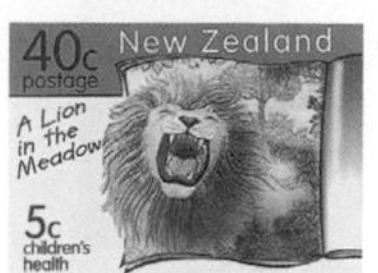

578 "A Lion in the Meadow" (Margaret Mahy)

1999. Children's Health. Children's Books. Multicoloured

(a) Ordinary gum

2272	40c. +5c. Type **578**	55	55
2273	80c. +5c. "Greedy Cat" (Joy Cowley)	70	70
MS2274	130×90 mm. 40c. + 5c. Type **578**; 40c. + 5c. As No. 2275 (37×25 mm); 80c. + 5c. No. 2273	1·40	1·40

(b) Smaller design, 37×25 mm. Self-adhesive.

2275	40c. +5c. "Hairy Maclary's Bone" (Lynley Dodd) (37×25 mm)	50	50

1999. "PhilexFrance '99" International Stamp Exhibiton, Paris. Multicoloured.

MS2276	112×90 mm. Nos. 2268 and 2271	1·75	1·75
MS2277	130×90 mm. Nos. 2208/9 and 2212/13	2·00	2·00

579 "APEC"

1999. Tenth Asia-Pacific Economic Co-operation Meeting, New Zealand.

2278	**579** 40c. multicoloured	30	30

580 West Ruggedy Beach, Stewart Island

1999. Scenic Walks. Multicoloured.

2279	40c. Type **580**	30	10
2280	80c. Ice lake, Butler Valley, Westland	50	40
2281	$1 Tonga Bay, Abel Tasman National Park	65	65
2282	$1.20 East Matakitaki Valley, Nelson Lakes National Park	75	90
2283	$1.50 Great Barrier Island	90	1·60
2284	$1.80 Mt. Egmont, Taranaki	1·10	1·40
MS2285	Seven sheets, each 150×110 mm. (a) No. 2279. (b) No. 2280. (c) No. 2281. (d) No. 2282. (e) No. 2283. (f) No. 2284. (g) Nos. 2279/84 Set of 7 sheets	11·00	13·00

See also No. **MS**2295.

1999. "China '99" International Stamp Exhibition, Peking. Multicoloured.

MS2286	112×90 mm. Nos. 2222/3	1·00	1·00
MS2287	100×135 mm. Nos. 2232 and 2234	1·00	1·00

581 Baby Jesus with Animals

1999. Christmas. Multicoloured

(a) Ordinary gum

2288	40c. Type **581**	20	10
2289	80c. Virgin Mary praying	40	30
2290	$1.10 Mary and Joseph on way to Bethlehem	55	50
2291	$1.20 Angel playing harp	60	80
2292	$1.50 Three shepherds	75	1·25
2293	$1.80 Three wise men with gifts	90	1·25

(b) Smaller design, 23×28 mm. Self-adhesive.

2294	40c. Type **581**	30	30

1999. "Palmpex '99" National Stamp Exhibition, Palmerston North. Sheet 130×90 mm, containing No. 2284. Multicoloured.

MS2295	$1.80, Mt. Egmont, Taranaki	1·40	1·40

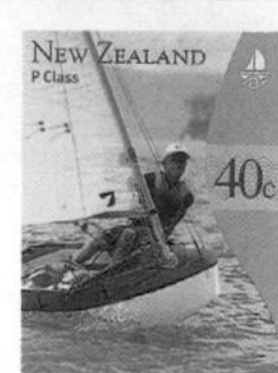

582 "P" Class Dinghy

1999. Yachting. Multicoloured

(a) Size 28×39 mm. Ordinary gum

2296	40c. Type **582**	25	10
2297	80c. Laser dinghy	45	35
2298	$1.10 18ft skiff	60	60
2299	$1.20 Hobie catamaran	60	75
2300	$1.50 Racing yacht	75	1·25
2301	$1.80 Cruising yacht	90	1·25
MS2302	125×100 mm. Nos. 2296/301	3·25	3·75

(b) Size 23×28 mm. Self-adhesive.

2303	40c. Optimist dinghy	30	30

583 Group of Victorian Women (female suffrage, 1893)

1999. Millenium Series (5th issue). New Zealand Achievements. Multicoloured.

2304	40c. Type **583**	30	15
2305	80c. Richard Pearse's aircraft (powered flight, 1903)	75	55
2306	$1.10 Lord Rutherford (splitting the atom, 1919)	80	85
2307	$1.20 Boat on lake (invention of jet boat, 1953)	80	90
2308	$1.50 Sir Edmund Hillary (conquest of Everest, 1953)	1·10	1·50
2309	$1.80 Protesters and warship (nuclear free zone, 1987)	1·10	1·60

584 Sunrise and World Map

2000. Millennium Series (6th issue).

2310	**584** 40c. multicoloured	65	30

585 Araiteuru (North Island sea guardian)

2000. Chinese New Year ("Year of the Dragon"). Maori Spirits and Guardians. Multicoloured.

2311	40c. Type **585**	20	10
2312	80c. Kurangaituku (giant bird woman)	35	25
2313	$1.10 Te Hoata and Te Pupu (volcanic taniwha sisters)	50	45
2314	$1.20 Patupaiarehe (mountain fairy tribe)	55	70
2315	$1.50 Te Ngarara-huarau (giant first lizard)	60	1·00
2316	$1.80 Tuhirangi (South Island sea guardian)	70	1·00
MS2317	125×90 mm. Nos. 2315/16	2·00	2·00

586 Chilly Bin (cool box)

2000. New Zealand Life (2nd series). Each including a cartoon kiwi. Multicoloured. Self-adhesive.

2318	40c. Type **586**	35	45
2319	40c. Pipis (seafood delicacy)	35	45
2320	40c. "Lilo"	35	45
2321	40c. Chocolate fish	35	45
2322	40c. Bach or Crib (holiday home)	35	45
2323	40c. Barbeque	35	45
2324	40c. Ug (fur-lined) boots	35	45
2325	40c. Anzac biscuits	35	45
2326	40c. Hot dog	35	45
2327	40c. Meat pie	35	45

2000. "The Stamp Show 2000" International Stamp Exhibition, London. Sheet 110×80 mm, containing Nos. 1934b and 1934e/f. Multicoloured.

MS2328	$1 Taiaroa Head; $2 Great Barrier Island; $3 Cape kidnappers	4·00	4·50

587 Volkswagen Beetle

2000. "On The Road". Motor Cars.

2329	**587**	40c. brown and black	25	10
2330	-	80c. blue and black	45	35
2331	-	$1.10 brown and black	65	60
2332	-	$1.20 green and black	70	75
2333	-	$1.50 brown and black	80	1·25
2334	-	$1.80 lilac and black	90	1·25

DESIGNS: 80c. Ford Zephyr Mk I; $1.10, Morris Mini Mk II; $1.20, Holden HQ Kingswood; $1.50, Honda Civic; $1.80, Toyota Corolla.

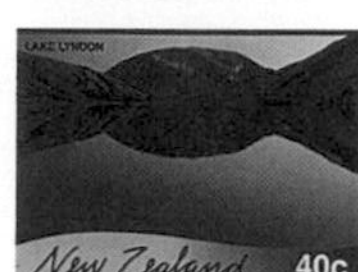

588 Lake Lyndon, Canterbury

2000. Scenic Reflections. Multicoloured.

2336	40c. Type **588**	50	20
2337	80c. Lion (cruising launch) on Lake Wakatipu	85	40
2338	$1.10 Eruption of Mount Ruapehu	1·00	70
2339	$1.20 Rainbow Mountain Scenic Reserve, Rotorua	1·00	1·90
2340	$1.50 Tairua Harbour, Coromandel Peninsula	1·10	1·75
2341	$1.80 Lake Alexandrina	1·25	1·60

See also No. **MS**2368.

2000. "EXPO 2000" World Stamp Exhibition, Anaheim, U.S.A. Sheet 132×78 mm, containing Nos. 1490, 1490b/c and 2090/a.

MS2342	$1 red; $1 blue; $1 violet; $1 green; $1.10 gold	3·25	4·00

589 Lady Elizabeth Bowes-Lyon and Glamis Castle, 1907

2000. Queen Elizabeth the Queen Mother's 100th Birthday. Multicoloured.

2343	40c. Type **589**	60	30
2344	$1.10 Fishing in New Zealand, 1966	1·10	70
2345	$1.80 Holding bunch of daisies, 1997	1·75	1·60
MS2346	115×60 mm. Nos. 2343/5	3·00	2·75

590 Rowing

2000. Olympic Games, Sydney, and other Sporting Events. Multicoloured.

2347	40c. Type **590**	30	10
2348	80c. Show jumping	65	40
2349	$1.10 Cycling	1·25	80
2350	$1.20 Triathlon	75	85
2351	$1.50 Bowling	90	1·40
2352	$1.80 Netball	90	1·40

Nos. 2351/2 omit the Olympic logo.

591 Virgin Mary and Baby Jesus

2000. Christmas. Multicoloured

(a) Ordinary gum

2353	40c. Type **591**	35	10
2354	80c. Mary and Joseph on way to Bethlehem	60	25
2355	$1.10 Baby Jesus in manger	85	60
2356	$1.20 Archangel Gabriel	95	90
2357	$1.50 Shepherd with lamb	1·25	1·90
2358	$1.80 Three Wise Men	1·40	1·75

(b) Self-adhesive. Size 30×25 mm.

2359	40c. Type **591**	35	30

592 Geronimo (teddy bear)

2000. Children's Health. Teddy Bears and Dolls. Multicoloured

(a) Ordinary gum

2360	40c. +5c. Type **592**	35	50
2361	80c. +5c. Antique French doll and wooden Schoenhut doll	55	70
2362	$1.10 Chad Valley bear	60	50
2363	$1.20 Poppy (doll)	65	80
2364	$1.50 Swanni (large bear) and Dear John (small bear)	70	1·00
2365	$1.80 Lia (doll) and bear	90	1·00
MS2366	100×60 mm. 40c. + 5c. Type **592**; 80c. + 5c. As No. 2361	1·00	1·00

(b) Self-adhesive. Size 29×24 mm.

2367	40c.+5c. +5c. Type **592**	35	40

2000. "CANPEX 2000" National Stamp Exhibition, Christchurch. Sheet 95×80 mm, containing Nos. 2336 and 2341. Multicoloured.

MS2368	40c. Type **588**; $1.80 Lake Alexandrina	1·60	1·75

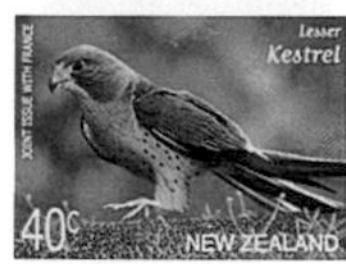

593 Lesser Kestrel

2000. Threatened Birds. Multicoloured.

2369	40c. Type **593**	50	30
2370	40c. Yellow-fronted parakeet	50	30
2371	80c. New Zealand stilt ("Black Stilt")	70	55
2372	$1.10 Fernbird ("Stewart Island Fernbird")	75	70
2373	$1.20 Kakapo	90	1·00
2374	$1.50 Weka rail ("North Island Weka")	1·10	1·25
2375	$1.80 Brown kiwi ("Okarito Brown Kiwi")	1·25	1·25

Nos. 2369 and 2375 form a joint issue with France.

See also No. **MS**2393.

594 *Sonoma* (mail ship) at Quay

2001. Moving the Mail in the 20th Century.

2376	**594**	40c. purple and red	35	35
2377	-	40c. green	35	35
2378	-	40c. agate	35	35
2379	-	40c. blue	35	35
2380	-	40c. brown	35	35
2381	-	40c. purple	35	35
2382	-	40c. black and cinnamon	35	35
2383	-	40c. multicoloured	35	35
2384	-	40c. mauve	35	35
2385	-	40c. multicoloured	35	35

DESIGNS: No. 2377, Stagecoach crossing river; 2378, Early postal lorry; 2379, Paddle steamer on River Wanganui; 2380, Railway T.P.O.; 2381, Loading mail through nose door of aircraft; 2382, Postwoman with bicycle; 2383, Loading lorry by fork-lift truck; 2384, Aircraft at night; 2385, Computer mouse.

See also No. **MS**2424.

595 Green Turtle

2001. Chinese New Year ("Year of the Snake"). Marine Reptiles. Multicoloured.

2386	40c. Type **595**	35	10
2387	80c. Leathery turtle	50	30

2388 90c. Loggerhead turtle 60 50
2389 $1.30 Hawksbill turtle 85 1·10
2390 $1.50 Banded sea-snake 1·00 1·40
2391 $2 Yellow-bellied sea-snake 1·25 1·40
MS2392 125×90 mm. Nos. 2390/1 2·50 3·00

2001. "Hong Kong 2001" Stamp Exhibition. Sheet 100×80 mm, containing Nos. 2374/5. Multicoloured.
MS2393 $1.50, North Island weka; $1.80, Okarito brown kiwi 2·50 2·50

596 Camellia

2001. Garden Flowers. Multicoloured.
2394 40c. Type **596** 20 10
2395 80c. Siberian iris 40 30
2396 90c. Daffodil 50 50
2397 $1.30 Chrysanthemum 75 1·10
2398 $1.50 Sweet pea 80 1·25
2399 $2 Petunia 1·00 1·25
MS2400 95×125 mm. Nos. 2394/9 3·25 4·25

2001. Invercargill "Stamp Odyssey 2001" National Stamp Exhibition. Sheet 133×81 mm, containing Nos. 1934a/d. Multicoloured.
MS2401 90c. Rangitoto Island; $1 Taiaroa Head; $1.10, Kaikoura Coast; $1.30, Lake Camp, South Canterbury 2·75 3·00

597 Greenstone Amulet

2001. Art from Nature. Multicoloured.
2402 40c. Type **597** 20 10
2403 80c. Oamaru stone sculpture 40 30
2404 90c. Paua ornament 50 50
2405 $1.30 Kauri ornament 75 1·10
2406 $1.50 Flax basket 80 1·25
2407 $2 Silver-dipped fern frond 1·00 1·25

Nos. 2402/7 were each printed in sheets of 25 (5×5) in which the stamps were included in four different orientations so that four blocks of 4 in each sheet showed the complete work of art.

598 Douglas DC-3

2001. Aircraft. Multicoloured.
2408 40c. Type **598** 35 15
2409 80c. Fletcher FU24 Topdresser 65 35
2410 90c. de Havilland DH.82A Tiger Moth 70 60
2411 $1.30 Fokker FVIIb/3m Southern Cross 90 1·10
2412 $1.50 de Havilland DH.100 Vampire 1·00 1·40
2413 $2 Boeing & Westervelt seaplane 1·25 1·40

599 Parcel

2001. Greetings Stamps. Multicoloured.
2414 40c. Type **599** 35 45
2415 40c. Trumpet 35 45
2416 40c. Heart and ribbon 35 45
2417 40c. Balloons 35 45
2418 40c. Flower 35 45
2419 90c. Photo frame 65 80
2420 90c. Fountain pen and letter 65 80
2421 90c. Candles on cake 65 80
2422 90c. Star biscuits 65 80
2423 90c. Candle and flowers 65 80

2001. "Belgica 2001" International Stamp Exhibition, Brussels. Sheet 180×90 mm, containing Nos. 2376/85. Multicoloured.

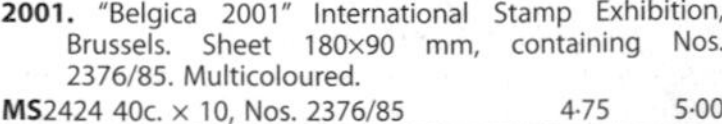

MS2424 40c. × 10, Nos. 2376/85 4·75 5·00

600 Bungy Jumping, Queenstown

2001. Tourism Centenary. Multicoloured

(a) Size 38×32 mm. Ordinary gum
2425 40c. Type **600** 25 10
2426 80c. Maori Canoe on Lake Rotoiti 45 30
2427 90c. Sightseeing from Mount Alfred 55 60
2428 $1.30 Fishing on Glenorchy river 75 80
2429 $1.50 Sea-kayaking in Abel Tasman National Park 85 1·25
2430 $2 Fiordland National Park 1·10 1·40

(b) Size 30×25 mm. Self-adhesive.
2431 40c. Type **600** 45 45
2432 90c. Sightseeing from Mount Alfred 80 85
2433 $1.50 Sea-kayaking in Abel Tasman National Park 1·25 1·40

2001. "Philanippon '01" International Stamp Exhibition, Tokyo. Sheet 90×82 mm, containing Nos. 2429/30. Multicoloured.
MS2434 $1.50 Sea-kayaking in Abel Tasman National Park; $2 Fiordland National Park 2·25 3·00

601 Family cycling

2001. Children's Health. Cycling. Multicoloured

(a) Size 39×29 mm. Ordinary gum
2435 40c. +5c. Type **601** 50 35
2436 90c. +5c. Mountain bike stunt 85 75
MS2437 Circular, 100 mm diameter. Nos. 2435/6 1·25 1·10

(b) Size 29×231/2. Self-adhesive.
2438 40c. +5c. Boy on bike 40 30

602 "When Christ was born of Mary free"

2001. Christmas. Carols. Multicoloured

(a) Size 29×34 mm. Ordinary gum
2439 40c. Type **602** 25 10
2440 80c. "Away in a manger" 45 20
2441 90c. "Joy to the world" 50 35
2442 $1.30 "Angels we have heard on high" 75 80
2443 $1.50 "O holy night" 85 1·00
2444 $2 "While shepherds watched" 1·10 1·50

(b) Size 21×26 mm. Self-adhesive.
2445 40c. Type **602** 40 30

603 Queen Elizabeth II at State Opening of Parliament, 1954

2001. Queen Elizabeth II's 75th Birthday. Multicoloured (except 40c.).
2446 40c. Type **603** (black and silver) 50 30
2447 80c. Queen Elizabeth II on walkabout, 1970 80 50
2448 90c. Queen Elizabeth II wearing Maori cloak, 1977 90 55
2449 $1.30 Queen Elizabeth II with bouquet, 1986 1·25 80
2450 $1.50 Queen Elizabeth II at Commonwealth Games, 1990 1·40 90
2451 $2 Queen Elizabeth II, 1997 1·60 1·25

604 Rockhopper Penguins

2001. New Zealand Penguins. Multicoloured.
2452 40c. Type **604** 50 30
2453 80c. Little penguin ("Little Blue Penguin") 75 50
2454 90c. Snares Island penguins ("Snares Crested Penguins") 85 60
2455 $1.30 Big-crested penguins ("Erect-crested Penguins") 1·10 85
2456 $1.50 Victoria penguins ("Fiordland Crested Penguins") 1·25 1·10
2457 $2 Yellow-eyed penguins 1·60 1·40

605 Gandalf (Sir Ian McKellen) and Saruman (Christopher Lee)

2001. Making of The Lord of the Rings Film Trilogy (1st issue): *The Fellowship of the Ring*. Multicoloured

(a) Designs 24×50 mm or 50×24 mm.
2458 40c. Type **605** 60 30
2459 80c. The Lady Galadriel (Cate Blanchett) 1·10 60
2460 90c. Sam Gamgee (Sean Austin) and Frodo Baggins (Elijah Wood) (horiz) 1·10 75
2461 $1.30 Guardian of Rivendell 1·60 2·00
2462 $1.50 Strider (Viggo Mortensen) 1·75 2·50
2463 $2 Boromir (Sean Bean) (horiz) 2·25 3·50

(b) Designs 26×37 mm or 37×26 mm. Self-adhesive.
2464 40c. Type **605** 40 35
2465 80c. The Lady Galadriel (Cate Blanchett) 60 60
2466 90c. Sam Gamgee (Sean Austin) and Frodo Baggins (Elijah Wood) (horiz) 75 80
2467 $1.30 Guardian of Rivendell 1·25 1·75
2468 $1.50 Strider (Viggo Mortensen) 1·50 2·00
2469 $2 Boromir (Sean Bean) (horiz) 1·60 2·50

See also No. **MS**2490, 2652/63 and 2713/25.

606 "Christian Cullen" (harness racing)

2002. Chinese New Year ("Year of the Horse"). New Zealand Racehorses. Multicoloured.
2470 40c. Type **606** 30 15
2471 80c. "Lyell Creek" (harness racing) 50 25
2472 90c. "Yulestar" (harness racing) 55 50
2473 $1.30 "Sunline" 80 80
2474 $1.50 "Ethereal" 90 1·40
2475 $2 "Zabeel" 1·25 1·40
MS2476 127×90 mm. Nos. 2473/4 3·75 4·25

607 *Hygrocybe rubrocarnosa*

2002. Fungi. Multicoloured.
2477 40c. Type **607** 35 10
2478 80c. *Entoloma hochstetteri* 55 30
2479 90c. *Aseroe rubra* 65 50
2480 $1.30 *Hericium coralloides* 80 1·10
2481 $1.50 *Thaxterogaster porphyreus* 90 1·40
2482 $2 *Ramaria aureorhiza* 1·25 1·60
MS2483 114×104 mm. Nos. 2477/82 5·50 5·50

608 War Memorial Museum, Auckland

2002. Architectural Heritage. Multicoloured.
2484 40c. Type **608** 25 10
2485 80c. Stone Store, Kerikeri (25×30 mm) 45 40
2486 90c. Arts Centre, Christchurch (50×30 mm) 50 50
2487 $1.30 Government Buildings, Wellington (50×30 mm) 75 80
2488 $1.50 Dunedin Railway Station (25×30 mm) 80 1·00
2489 $2 Sky Tower, Auckland 1·00 1·25

2002. "Northpex 2002" Stamp Exhibition. Sheet 130×95 mm, containing Nos. 2458, 2461 and 2463. Multicoloured.
MS2490 40c. Gandalf (Sir Ian Mckellen) and Saruman (Christopher Lee); $1.30 Guardian of Rivendell; $2 Boromir (Sean Bean) (horiz) 6·50 6·50

No. **MS**2490 was sold at face value.

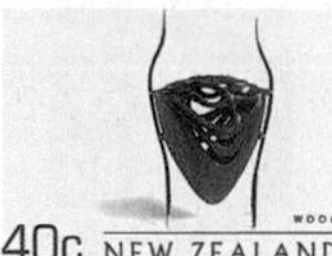

609 "Starfish Vessel" (wood sculpture) (Graeme Priddle)

2002. Artistic Crafts. Joint Issue with Sweden. Multicoloured.
2491 40c. Type **609** 25 25
2492 40c. Flax basket (Willa Rogers) (37×29 mm) 25 25
2493 80c. "Catch II" (clay bowl) (Raewyn Atkinson) 40 40
2494 90c. "Vessel Form" (silver brooch) (Gavin Hitchings) 50 50
2495 $1.30 Glass towers from "Immigration" series (Emma Camden) 75 85
2496 $1.50 "Pacific Rim" (clay vessel) (Merilyn Wiseman) 80 1·40
2497 $2 Glass vase (Ola and Maria Höglund) (37×29 mm) 1·00 1·40

Nos. 2492 and 2497 are additionally inscribed "JOINT ISSUE WITH SWEDEN".

610 *Brodie* (Anna Poland, Cardinal McKeefry School) (National Winner)

2002. Children's Book Festival. Stamp Design Competition. Designs illustrating books. Multicoloured.
2498 40c. Type **610** 30 35
2499 40c. *The Last Whale* (Hee Su Kim, Glendowie Primary School) 30 35
2500 40c. *Scarface Claw* (Jayne Bruce, Rangiora Borough School) 30 35
2501 40c. *Which New Zealand Bird?* (Teigan Stafford-Bush, Ararimu School) 30 35
2502 40c. *Which New Zealand Bird?* (Hazel Gilbert, Gonville School) 30 35
2503 40c. *The Plight of the Penguin* (Gerard Mackle, Temuka High School) 30 35
2504 40c. *Scarface Claw* (Maria Rodgers, Salford School) 30 35
2505 40c. *Knocked for Six* (Paul Read, Ararimu School) 30 35
2506 40c. *Grandpa's Shorts* (Jessica Hitchings, Ashleigh Bree, Malyna Sengdara and Aniva Kini, Glendene Primary School) 30 35
2507 40c. *Which New Zealand Bird?* (Olivia Duncan, Takapuna Intermediate School) 30 35
MS2508 230×90 mm. Nos. 2498/507 4·25 4·50

611 Queen Elizabeth the Queen Mother, 1992

2002. Queen Elizabeth the Queen Mother Commemoration.
2509 **611** $2 multicoloured 2·00 1·60

612 Tongaporutu Cliffs, Taranaki

2002. Coastlines. Multicoloured

(a) Size 38×29 mm. Ordinary gum
2510 40c. Type **612** 25 20
2511 80c. Lottin Point, East Cape 50 55
2512 90c. Curio Bay, Catlins 60 65
2513 $1.30 Kaikoura Coast 85 1·00
2514 $1.50 Meybille Bay, West Coast 95 1·75
2515 $2 Papanui Point, Raglan 1·25 1·75

(b) Size 28×21 mm. Self-adhesive.
2516 40c. Type **612** 35 30
2517 90c. Curio Bay, Catlins 85 1·10
2518 $1.50 Meybille Bay, West Coast 1·50 1·75

613 Basket of Fruit

2002. Children's Health. Healthy Eating. Multicoloured

(a) Ordinary gum
2519 40c. +5c. Type **613** 50 55
2520 90c. +5c. Selection of vegetables 75 80
MS2521 90×75 mm. Nos. 2519/20 and as No. 2522 (22×26 mm) 1·75 2·00

(b) Self-adhesive.
2522 40c. +5c. Fruit and vegetables (22×26 mm) 30 35

2002. "Amphilex 2002" International Stamp Exhibition, Amsterdam. Sheet 130×95 mm, containing Nos. 2462/3. Multicoloured.
MS2523 $1.50 Strider (Viggo Mortensen); $2 Boromir (Sean Bean) (horiz) 2·50 2·00
No. **MS**2523 was sold at face value.

614 St. Werenfried, Tokaanu

2002. Christmas. Church Interiors. Multicoloured

(a) Size 35×35 mm. Ordinary gum
2524 40c. Type **614** 25 10
2525 80c. St. David's, Christchurch 50 25
2526 90c. Orthodox Church of Transfiguration of Our Lord, Masterton 60 50
2527 $1.30 Cathedral of the Holy Spirit, Palmerston North 85 75
2528 $1.50 St. Paul's Cathedral, Wellington 95 1·10
2529 $2 Cathedral of the Blessed Sacrament, Christchurch 1·25 1·60

(b) Size 25×30 mm. Self-adhesive.
2530 40c. St. Werenfried, Tokaanu 30 30

615 *KZ 1* (racing yacht)

2002. Racing and Leisure Craft. Multicoloured.
2531 40c. Type **615** 35 30
2532 80c. *High 5* (ocean racing yacht) 65 55
2533 90c. *Gentle Spirit* (sports fishing and diving boat) 75 70
2534 $1.30 *North Star* (luxury motor cruiser) 1·00 1·00
2535 $1.50 *Ocean Runner* (powerboat) 1·25 1·40
2536 $2 *Salperton* (ocean-going yacht) 1·40 1·60
MS2537 140×80 mm. Nos. 2531/6 4·75 5·00

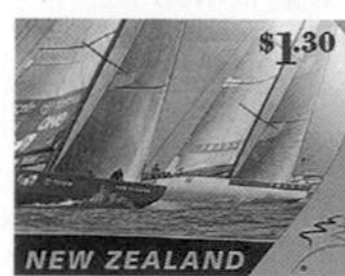

616 *Black Magic* (New Zealand) and *Luna Rossa* (Italy)

2002. America's Cup, 2003 (1st issue). Scenes from 2000 final, between New Zealand and Italy. Multicoloured.
2538 $1.30 Type **616** 95 90
2539 $1.50 Aerial view of race 1·00 1·00
2540 $2 Yachts turning 1·40 1·60
MS2541 140×80 mm. Nos. 2538/40 3·75 4·25
See also Nos. 2562/5.

2002. "Stampshow 02" International Stamp Exhibition, Melbourne. No. **MS**2541 with "Stampshow 02" emblem and inscription on the margin. Multicoloured.
MS2542 140×80 mm. Nos. 2538/40 3·00 3·25

617 Green-roofed Holiday Cottage and Paua Shell

2002. Holiday Homes. Multicoloured.
2543 40c. Type **617** 30 35
2544 40c. Red-roofed cottage and sunflower 30 35
2545 40c. White-roofed cottage and life-belt 30 35
2546 40c. Cottage with orange door, boat and fishing fly 30 35
2547 40c. Blue-roofed cottage and fish 30 35
2548 40c. Cottage and caravan 30 35

618 "The Nativity" (15th-cent painting in style of Di Baldese)

2002. New Zealand–Vatican City Joint Issue.
2549 **618** $1.50 multicoloured 1·25 1·40

2002. Making of The Lord of the Rings Film Trilogy (2nd issue): *The Two Towers*. As T **605**. Multicoloured

(a) Designs 50×24 mm or 24×50 mm. Ordinary gum
2550 40c. Aragorn (Viggo Mortenson) and Eowyn (Miranda Otto) (horiz) 60 20
2551 80c. Orc raider (horiz) 1·00 40
2552 90c. Gandalf the White (Sir Ian McKellen) 1·10 70
2553 $1.30 Easterling warriors (horiz) 1·40 1·25
2554 $1.50 Frodo (Elijah Wood) 1·60 2·00
2555 $2 Eowyn, Shield Maiden of Rohan (Miranda Otto) (horiz) 1·90 2·25

(b) Designs 37×26 mm or 26×37 mm. Self-adhesive.
2556 40c. Strider (Viggo Mortenson) and Eowyn (Miranda Otto) (horiz) 25 30
2557 80c. Orc raider (horiz) 80 50
2558 90c. Gandalf the White (Sir Ian McKellen) 70 65
2559 $1.30 Easterling warriors (horiz) 1·10 1·10
2560 $1.50 Frodo (Elijah Wood) 1·25 1·25
2561 $2 Eowyn, Shield Maiden of Rohan (Miranda Otto) (horiz) 1·40 1·75

2003. America's Cup (2nd issue). The Defence. As T **616**. Multicoloured.
2562 40c. Aerial view of Team New Zealand yacht 25 30
2563 80c. Two Team New Zealand yachts 50 55
2564 90c. Team New Zealand yacht tacking 60 65
MS2565 140×80 mm. Nos. 2562/4 1·75 1·75

619 Shepherd with Flock in High Country

2003. Chinese New Year ("Year of the Sheep"). Sheep Farming. Multicoloured.
2566 40c. Type **619** 30 15
2567 90c. Mustering the sheep 50 35
2568 $1.30 Sheep in pen with sheep dog 80 70
2569 $1.50 Sheep shearing 1·00 1·25
2570 $2 Sheep shearing (different) 1·25 1·40
MS2571 125×85 mm. Nos. 2568 and 2570 2·25 2·25

620 Jon Trimmer in *Carmina Burana*

2003. 50th Anniv of Royal New Zealand Ballet. Scenes from past productions. Multicoloured.
2572 40c. Type **620** 30 15
2573 90c. *Papillon* (horiz) 50 35
2574 $1.30 *Cinderella* 80 70
2575 $1.50 *FrENZy* 1·00 1·25
2576 $2 *Swan Lake* (horiz) 1·25 1·40

621 Officer, Forest Rangers, 1860s

2003. New Zealand Military Uniforms. Multicoloured.
2577 40c. Type **621** 45 45
2578 40c. Lieutenant, Napier Naval Artillery Volunteers, 1890s 45 45
2579 40c. Officer, 2nd Regt, North Canterbury Mounted Rifles, 1900–10 45 45
2580 40c. Mounted Trooper, New Zealand Mounted Rifles, South Africa 1899–1902 45 45
2581 40c. Staff Officer, New Zealand Division, France, 1918 45 45
2582 40c. Petty Officer, Royal New Zealand Navy, 1914–18 45 45
2583 40c. Rifleman, New Zealand Rifle Brigade, France, 1916–18 45 45
2584 40c. Sergeant, New Zealand Engineers, 1939–45 45 45
2585 40c. Matron, Royal New Zealand Navy Hospital, 1940s 45 45
2586 40c. Private, New Zealand Women's Auxiliary Army Corps, Egypt, 1942 45 45
2587 40c. Pilot serving with R.A.F. Bomber Command, Europe, 1943 45 45
2588 40c. Fighter Pilot, No. 1 (Islands) Group, Royal New Zealand Air Force, Pacific, 1943 45 45
2589 40c. Driver, Women's Auxiliary Air Force, 1943 45 45
2590 40c. Gunner, 16th Field Regt, Royal New Zealand Artillery, Korea, 1950–53 45 45
2591 40c. Acting Petty Officer, H.M.N.Z.S. *Tamaki*, 1957 45 45
2592 40c. Scouts, New Zealand Special Air Service, Malaya, 1955–57 45 45
2593 40c. Canberra Pilot serving with R.A.F. Far East Command, Malaya, 1960 45 45
2594 40c. Infantrymen, 1st Bn, Royal New Zealand Infantry Regt, South Vietnam, 1960s 45 45
2595 40c. Infantryman, New Zealand Bn, UNTAET, East Timor, 2000 45 45
2596 40c. Monitor, Peace Monitoring Group, Bougainville, 2001 45 45
Nos. 2577/96 were printed together, *se-tenant*, with detailed descriptions of the designs printed on the reverse.

622 Ailsa Mountains

2003. New Zealand Landscapes. Each including the fern symbol after the country inscr. Multicoloured.
2597 5c. Geyser, Whakarewarewa, Rotorua 10 10
2598 10c. Central Otago 15 10
2599 20c. Rainbow Falls, Northland 25 20
2600 45c. Kaikoura 55 35
2601 50c. Type **622** 55 35
2602 50c. Lake Coleridge, Canterbury 55 35
2603 $1 Coromandel 1·00 65
2604 $1 Rangitoto Island, Auckland 1·60 1·50
2605 $1.35 Church of the Good Shepherd, Lake Tekapo 1·75 1·75
2606 $1.50 Arrowtown 2·00 1·00
2607 $2 Tongariro National Park 2·25 1·40
2608 $2.50 Abel Tasman National Park 2·50 1·60
2609 $3 Tongaporutu, Taranaki 3·00 2·50
2610 $5 Castlepoint Lighthouse 4·50 3·75
Nos. 2600, 2602, 2604 and 2606 also come self-adhesive.

623 Sir Edmund Hillary and Mount Everest

2003. 50th Anniv of Conquest of Everest. Multicoloured.
2616 40c. Type **623** 75 90
2617 40c. Climbers reaching summit and Tenzing Norgay 75 90

624 Buckingham Palace

2003. 50th Anniv of Coronation. As Nos. 714/18 (Coronation issue of 1953) but face values in decimal currency as T **624**.
2618 **624** 40c. ultramarine 45 25
2619 - 90c. brown 80 70
2620 - $1.30 red 1·25 1·25
2621 - $1.50 blue 1·40 1·50
2622 - $2 violet and ultramarine 1·60 1·60
DESIGNS—VERT: (as T **164**)—90c. Queen Elizabeth II; $1.50, Westminster Abbey. HORIZ: (as T **624**)—$1.30, Coronation State Coach; $2 St. Edward's Crown and Royal Sceptre.

625 New Zealand vs. South Africa Match, 1937

2003. Centenary of New Zealand Test Rugby. Multicoloured.
2623 40c. Type **625** 35 15
2624 90c. New Zealand vs. Wales match, 1963 55 45
2625 $1.30 New Zealand vs. Australia, 1985 80 70
2626 $1.50 New Zealand vs. France, 1986 90 1·40
2627 $1.50 All Blacks jersey 90 1·40
2628 $2 New Zealand vs. England, 1997 1·25 1·50
MS2629 100×180 mm. Nos. 2623/8 4·50 5·00

626 Papaaroha, Coromandel Peninsula

2003. New Zealand Waterways. Multicoloured.
2630 40c. Type **626** 45 25
2631 90c. Waimahana Creek, Chatham Islands 75 70
2632 $1.30 Blue Lake, Central Otago 1·25 1·25
2633 $1.50 Waikato River 1·40 1·50
2634 $2 Hooker River, Canterbury 1·60 1·75

627 Boy on Swing

2003. Children's Health. Playgrounds. Multicoloured

(a) Size 39×29 mm. Ordinary gum

2635	40c.+5c. +5c. Type **627**	50	60
2636	90c.+5c. +5c. Girls playing hopscotch	90	1·00
MS2637	88×90 mm. Nos. 2635/6 and 40c.+5c. Girl on climbing frame	2·00	2·00

(b) Size 24×29 mm. Self-adhesive.

2638	40c.+5c. +5c. Girl on climbing frame	60	40

628 Benz Velo (1895)

2003. Veteran Vehicles. Multicoloured.

2639	40c. Type **628**	45	25
2640	90c. Oldsmobile (1903)	75	70
2641	$1.30 Wolseley (1911)	1·25	1·25
2642	$1.50 Talbot (1915)	1·40	1·50
2643	$2 Model T Ford (1915)	1·60	1·75

629 Christ Child in Crib

2003. Christmas Decorations. Multicoloured

(a) Size 30×30 mm. Ordinary gum

2644	40c. Type **629**	35	10
2645	90c. Silver and gold bird	65	30
2646	$1.30 Silver candle	90	70
2647	$1.50 Bells	1·00	1·40
2648	$2 Angel	1·25	1·60

(b) Size 21×26 mm. Self-adhesive.

2649	40c. Type **629**	45	35
2650	$1 Filigree metalwork decoration with baubles	1·00	1·00

2003. "Bangkok 2003" World Philatelic Exhibition. Sheet, 110×80 mm, containing Nos. 2572/3 and 2576.

MS2651	40c. Type **620**; 90c. *Papillon* (horiz); $2 *Swan Lake* (horiz)	3·00	3·00

2003. Making of The Lord of the Rings Film Trilogy (3rd issue): *The Return of the King*. As T **605**. Multicoloured

(a) Designs 24×49 mm or 49×50 mm. Ordinary gum

2652	40c. Legolas	50	35
2653	80c. Frodo Baggins	85	70
2654	90c. Merry and Pippin (horiz)	95	75
2655	$1.30 Aragorn	1·25	1·25
2656	$1.50 Gandalf the White	1·50	1·50
2657	$2 Gollum (horiz)	2·00	2·75

(b) Designs 24×35 mm or 35×24 mm. Self-adhesive.

2658	40c. Legolas	50	35
2659	80c. Frodo Baggins	85	70
2660	90c. Merry and Pippin (horiz)	95	75
2661	$1.30 Aragorn	1·25	1·25
2662	$1.50 Gandalf the White	1·50	1·50
2663	$2 Gollum (horiz)	2·00	2·75

2003. "Welpex 2003" National Stamp Exhibition, Wellington. Sheet 120×100 mm, containing Nos. 2626/8.

MS2664	$1.50 New Zealand vs. France, 1986; $1.50 All Blacks jersey; $2 New Zealand vs. England, 1997	5·50	5·50

630 Hamadryas Baboon

2004. New Zealand Zoo Animals. Multicoloured

(a) Ordinary gum. Size 29×39 mm

2665	40c. Type **630**	45	25
2666	90c. Malayan sun bear	85	70
2667	$1.30 Red panda	1·25	1·25
2668	$1.50 Ring-tailed lemur	1·40	1·50
2669	$2 Spider monkey	1·60	1·75
MS2670	125×90 mm. Nos. 2668/9	3·00	3·00

(b) Self-adhesive. Size 24×29 mm.

2671	40c. Type **631**	45	35

No. **MS**2670 commemorates Chinese New Year, "Year of the Monkey".

2004. Hong Kong 2004 International Stamp Exhibition. Sheet, 110×80 mm, containing Nos. 2627/8.

MS2672	$1.50 All Blacks jersey; $2 New Zealand vs. England, 1997	3·50	3·50

631 New Zealand Team

2004. Rugby Sevens. Multicoloured.

2673	40c. Type **631**	45	25
2674	90c. Hong Kong team	85	70
2675	$1.50 Hong Kong Stadium	1·40	1·50
2676	$2 Westpac Stadium, Wellington	1·75	2·00
MS2677	125×85 mm. Nos. 2673/6	4·00	4·00

Stamps of the same design were issued by Hong Kong.

632 Parliament Building, Auckland, 1854

2004. 150th Anniv of First Official Parliament in New Zealand.

2678	**632**	40c. purple and black	45	35
2679	-	45c. purple and black	55	60
2680	-	90c. lilac and black	85	70
2681	-	$1.30 grey and black	1·25	1·25
2682	-	$1.50 blue and black	1·40	1·40
2683	-	$2 green and black	1·60	1·75
MS2684		186×65 mm. Nos. 2678/82	5·00	5·00

DESIGNS:45c. As No. 2678; 90c. Parliament Buildings, Wellington, 1865; $1.30 Parliament Buildings, Wellington, 1899; $1.50 Parliament House, Wellington, 1918; $2 The Beehive, Wellington, 1977.

633

2004. "Draw it Yourself" Postcard Labels. Multicoloured. Self-adhesive.

2685	$1.50 Type **633**	3·00	3·75
2686	$1.50 Rosine with "New Zealand Post" at bottom left	3·00	3·75
2687	$1.50 As Type **633** but emerald	3·00	3·75
2688	$1.50 Reddish violet with "New Zealand Post" at bottom left	3·00	3·75

634 Mountain Oysters

2004. Wild Food Postcard Labels. Multicoloured. Self-adhesive.

2689	$1.50 Type **634**	3·00	3·75
2690	$1.50 Huhu grubs	3·00	3·75
2691	$1.50 Possum pate	3·00	3·75

635 Local Man outside Post Office on Tractor

2004. Kiwi Characters Postcard Labels. Multicoloured. Self-adhesive.

2692	$1.50 Type **635**	3·75	4·75
2693	$1.50 Children on horseback	3·75	4·75
2694	$1.50 Elderly couple outside their home	3·75	4·75

636 Kinnard Haines Tractor

2004. Historic Farm Equipment. Multicoloured.

2695	45c. Type **636**	45	25
2696	90c. Fordson F tractor with plough	80	65
2697	$1.35 Burrell traction engine	1·25	1·40
2698	$1.50 Threshing mill	1·25	1·60
2699	$2 Duncan's Seed Drill	1·60	1·75

637 "Dragon Fish"

2004. World of Wearable Arts. Multicoloured.

2701	45c. Type **637**	45	25
2702	90c. "Persephone's Descent" (man in armour costume)	80	65
2703	$1.35 "Meridian" (woman in silk costume)	1·25	1·40
2704	$1.50 "Taunga Ika" (woman in net costume)	1·25	1·60
2705	$2 "Cailleach Na Mara" (woman in sea witch costume)	1·60	1·75

638 Magnolia

2004. Garden Flowers. Multicoloured.

2706	45c. Type **638**	45	25
2707	90c. Helleborus	80	65
2708	$1.35 Nerine	1·25	1·40
2709	$1.50 Rhododendron	1·25	1·60
2710	$2 Delphinium	1·60	1·75
MS2711	160×65 mm. Nos. 2706/2710	4·75	5·00

The 45c. stamp in No. **MS**2711 was impregnated with the fragrance of Magnolia.

2004. Salon du Timbre International Stamp Exhibition, Paris. Sheet 125×95 mm, containing designs from **MS**2664 and No. 2676.

MS2712	$1.50 New Zealand vs. France 1986, $1.50 All Blacks jersey; $2 Westpac Stradium	3·50	3·75

639

2004. Emergency 5c. Provisional Stamp.

2713	**639** 5c. blue and vermilion	1·75	2·00

640 Skippers Canyon (The Ford of Bruinen)

2004. Making of The Lord of the Rings Film Trilogy (4th issue): Home of Middle Earth. Multicoloured. Designs 40×30 mm

(a) Ordinary gum.

2714	45c. Type **640**	35	40
2715	45c. Arwen facing Black Riders	35	40
2716	90c. Mount Olympus (South of Rivendell)	65	70
2717	90c. Gimli and Legolas	65	70
2718	$1.50 Erewhon (Edoras)	1·10	1·25
2719	$1.50 Gandalf the White, Legolas, Gimli and Aragorn riding to Rohan	1·10	1·25
2720	$2 Tongariro (Emyn Muil, Mordor)	1·50	1·60
2721	$2 Frodo and Sam	1·50	1·60
MS2722	100×180 mm. Nos. 2714/21	7·25	7·50

(b) Designs 29×24 mm. Self-adhesive.

2723	45c. Skippers Canyon (The Ford of Bruinen)	45	45
2724	45c. Arwen facing Black Riders	45	45
2725	90c. Mount Olympus (South of Rivendell)	65	80
2726	90c. Gimli and Legolas	65	80

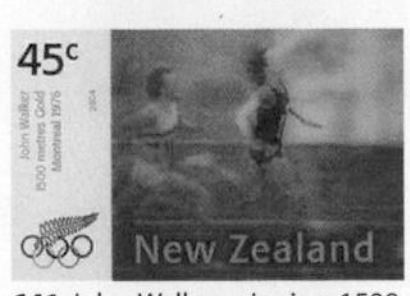

641 John Walker winning 1500 Metre Race

2004. Olympic Games, Athens. Gold Medal Winners. Multicoloured. Self-adhesive.

2727	45c. Type **641**	60	40
2728	90c. Yvette Williams (long jump)	95	85
2729	$1.50 Ian Ferguson and Paul MacDonald (kayaking)	1·60	1·75
2730	$2 Peter Snell (800 metre race)	1·75	1·75

2004. World Stamp Exhibition, Singapore. Sheet 125×95 mm containing Nos. 2717/19. Multicoloured.

MS2731	90c. Gimley and Legolas; 90c. Mount Olympus (South of Rivendell); $1.50 Gandalf the White, Legolas, Gimley and Aragorn riding to Rohan; $1.50 Erewhon (Edoras)	3·50	4·00

2004. Tourism (1st series). As T **622**. Multicoloured.

2732	$1.50 The Bath House, Rotorua	1·25	1·40
2733	$1.50 Pohutu Geyser, Rotorua	1·25	1·40
2734	$1.50 Hawke's Bay	1·25	1·40
2735	$1.50 Lake Wakatipu, Queenstown	1·25	1·40
2736	$1.50 Mitre Peak, Milford Sound	1·25	1·40
2737	$1.50 Kaikoura	1·25	1·40

See also Nos. 2868/73.

642 Children playing in the Sea

2004. Children's Health. A Day at the Beach. Multicoloured

(a) Size 30×40 mm. Ordinary gum

2738	45c.+5c. +5c. Type **642**	35	40
2739	90c.+5c. +5c. People in dinghy and swimmer	65	70
MS2740	102×90 mm. Nos. 2738/9 and 45c.+5c. Children fishing (25×30 mm)	1·40	1·50

(b) Size 24×29 mm. Self-adhesive.

2741	45c.+5c. +5c. Children fishing	35	40

643 Christmas Dinner

644 Christmas Dinner

2004. Christmas. Multicoloured. Designs 49×49 mm

(a) Ordinary gum

2742	45c. Type **643**	40	10
2743	90c. Traditional Maori meal	65	25
2744	$1.35 Barbecued prawns and salmon	95	80
2745	$1.50 Pie and salad	1·00	1·50
2746	$2 Plum pudding and pavlova	1·40	1·75

(b) Vert designs as T **644**. Self-adhesive.

2747	45c. Type **644**	45	40
2748	90c. Traditional Maori meal	80	70
2749	$1 Christmas cake and cards	95	1·00

2004. "Baypex 2004 Hawke's Bay Stamp Show". Sheet 130×70 mm, containing Nos. 1934f and 2733. Multicoloured.

MS2750	$1.50 Hawke's Bay, $3 Cape Kidnappers	4·00	4·75

645 Whitewater Rafting

2004. Extreme Sports. Multicoloured.

2751	45c. Type **645**	50	25

2752	90c. Snowsports	80	65
2753	$1.35 Skydiving	1·25	1·25
2754	$1.50 Jet boating	1·25	1·60
2755	$2 Bungy jumping	1·60	1·75

646 Sheep

2005. Farmyard Animals and Chinese New Year ("Year of the Rooster"). Multicoloured

(a) Ordinary gum

2757	45c. Type **646**	45	40
2758	90c. Dogs	80	70
2759	$1.35 Pigs	1·25	1·25
2760	$1.50 Rooster	1·25	1·40
2761	$2 Rooster perched on farm equipment	1·60	1·75
MS2762	126×90 mm. Nos. 2760/2761	3·50	4·25

(b) Size 24×30 mm. Self-adhesive.

2763	45c. Sheep	45	40

647 Beneficiaries (Centenary of Rotary International)

2005. Anniversaries of Organisations. Multicoloured.

2764	45c. Type **647**	45	40
2765	45c. Rural development (50th Anniv of the Lions)	45	40
2766	45c. Canoeists (150th Anniv of YMCA)	45	40
2767	$1.50 Building development (Centenary of Rotary International)	1·25	1·50
2768	$1.50 Miniature train (50th Anniv of the Lions)	1·25	1·50
2769	$1.50 Beneficiaries jumping (150th Anniv of YMCA)	1·25	1·50
MS2770	130×100 mm. Nos. 2764/9 and central gutter	4·50	5·25

648 1855 Full Face Queen, London Print (No. 1)

2005. 150th Anniv of New Zealand Stamps (1st issue). Stamps of 1855–1905. Multicoloured.

2771	45c. Type **648**	45	25
2772	90c. 1873 Newspaper (Nos. 143/5)	80	70
2773	$1.35 1891 Government Life (No. L 5)	1·25	1·10
2774	$1.50 1989 Pictorial, Mt. Cook (No. 259)	1·40	1·75
2775	$2 1901 Universal Postage (No. 277)	1·60	1·75
MS2776	160×80 mm. Nos. 2771/75	5·00	5·50

See also Nos. 2777/2781 and 2791/**MS**2796.

2005. 150th Anniv of New Zealand Stamps (2nd issue). Stamps of 1905–1955. As T **648**. Multicoloured

(a) Ordinary gum

2777	45c. 1906 New Zealand Exhibition (No. 371)	45	25
2778	90c. 1931 Health (No. 546)	80	70
2779	$1.35 1935 Airmail (No. 571)	1·25	1·10
2780	$1.50 1946 Peace (No. 676)	1·40	1·75
2781	$2 1954 Queen Elizabeth II (No. 736)	1·60	1·75
MS2782	160×80 mm. Nos. 2766/70	5·00	5·50

(b) Designs 25×30 mm. Self-adhesive.

2783	45c. As No. 2777	50	65
2784	90c. As No. 2778	75	85

2005. Pacific Explorer World Stamp Exhibition, Sydney.

MS2785	109×90 mm. Nos. 2775 and 2780	3·25	3·50

649 Cafe, 1910s

2005. Cafe Culture. Multicoloured. Self-adhesive.

2786	45c. Type **649**	45	30
2787	90c. Cafe, 1940s	80	70
2788	$1.35 Cafe, 1970s	1·25	1·25
2789	$1.50 Tables outside cafe on pavement, 1990s	1·25	1·40
2790	$2 Internet cafe, 2005	1·60	1·75

2005. 150th Anniv of New Zealand Stamps (3rd issue). Stamps of 1955—2005. As T **648**. Multicoloured.

2791	45c. 1965 50th Anniversary of the Gallipoli Landing (No. 827)	45	25
2792	90c. 1988 Round Kiwi (No. 1490)	80	70
2793	$1.35 1990 The Achievers Katherine Sheppard (No. 1550)	1·25	1·25
2794	$1.50 1994 Maori Myths Maui (No. 1807)	1·40	1·60
2795	$2 2003 Centenary of New Zealand Test Rugby (No. 2627)	1·60	1·75
MS2796	160×80 mm. Nos. 2791/5	5·00	5·50

650 All Blacks Jersey

2005. DHL New Zealand Lions Rugby Series. Self-adhesive.

2797	**650** 45c. black and grey	55	65
2798	- 45c. multicoloured	55	65
2799	- $1.50 black and grey	1·25	1·50
2800	- $1.50 multicoloured	1·25	1·50

DESIGNS: No. 2797, Type **650**; 2798, Red Lions jersey; 2799, As No. 2797; No. 2800, As No. 2798.

651 Kiwi

2005. Personalised Stamps. Multicoloured.

2801	45c. Type **651**	45	55
2802	45c. Pohutukawa (native Christmas tree)	45	55
2803	45c. Champagne glasses	45	55
2804	45c. Balloons	45	55
2805	45c. Wedding bands	45	55
2806	45c. Gift box	45	55
2807	45c. Baby's hand	45	55
2808	$1.50 Globe	1·25	1·40
2809	$2 As Type **651**	1·60	1·75
2810	$2 Fern	1·60	1·75

652 Kakapo ("Relies heavily on camouflage for defence")

2005. Endangered Species. Kakapo. Designs showing the Kakapo with different facts inscribed. Multicoloured.

2811	45c. Type **652**	70	60
2812	45c. "Night Parrot unique to New Zealand"	70	60
2813	45c. "Nocturnal bird living on the forest floor"	70	60
2814	45c. "Endangered – only 86 known surviving"	70	60

653 Child and Horse

2005. Children's Health. Pets. Multicoloured

2815	45c.+5c. +5c. Type **653**	55	55
2816	90c.+5c. +5c. Child holding rabbit	90	95
MS2817	100×90 mm. Nos. 2815/16 and 45c.+5c. Children and dog (25×30 mm)	2·50	2·50

(b) Size 25×30 mm. Self-adhesive.

2818	45c.+5c. +5c. Children and dog	50	55

2005. Taipei 2005 International Stamp Exhibition. Sheet, 110×90 mm, containing Nos. 2733 and 2737.

MS2819	$1.50 Kaikoura; $1.50 Pohutu Geyser, Rotorua	2·50	2·75

654 Baby Jesus

2005. Christmas. Multicoloured

(a) 35×35 mm. Ordinary gum

2820	45c. Type **654**	40	15
2821	90c. Mary and Joseph	75	55
2822	$1.35 Shepherd	1·25	1·10
2823	$1.50 Wise Men	1·40	1·50
2824	$2 Star	1·60	2·00

(b) Size 24×29 mm. Self-adhesive.

2825	45c. Type **654**	45	35
2826	$1 Gifts on straw	85	85

655 King Kong

2005. *King Kong* (film). Multicoloured.

2827	45c. Type **655**	40	35
2828	90c. Carl Denham	75	70
2829	$1.35 Ann Darrow	1·25	1·10
2830	$1.50 Jack Driscoll	1·40	1·50
2831	$2 Ann Darrow and Jack Driscoll	1·60	1·75
MS2832	180×65 mm. Nos. 2827/31	4·75	5·50

2005. National Stamp Show, Auckland. Sheet, 120×90 mm, containing Nos. 2774, 2780 and 2794.

MS2833	$1.50 1989 Pictorial, Mt Cook (No. 259); $1.50 1946 Peace (No. 676); $1.50 1994 Maori Myths – Maui (No. 1807)	4·75	5·50

656 Lucy opening the Wardrobe

2005. Making of The Chronicles of Narnia: *The Lion the Witch and the Wardrobe* (film). Multicoloured

(a) Ordinary gum

2834	45c. Type **656**	40	25
2835	90c. Lucy, Edmund, Peter and Susan in snowy forest (horiz)	75	70
2836	$1.35 The White Witch tempting Edmund with Turkish delight (horiz)	1·25	1·10
2837	$1.50 Dissenters turned to stone statues in courtyard of White Witch's castle	1·40	1·60
2838	$2 Lucy and body of Aslan (horiz)	1·60	1·75

(b) As Nos. 2834/8 but smaller. Self-adhesive.

MS2839	200×70 mm. 45c. Type **656** (25×35 mm); 90c. As No. 2835 (35×25 mm); $1.35 As No. 2836 (35×25 mm); $1.50 As No. 2837 (25×35 mm); $2 As No. 2838 (35×25 mm)	6·00	7·00

657 Labrador Retriever Guide Dog

2006. Chinese New Year ("Year of the Dog"). Multicoloured

(a) Ordinary gum

2840	45c. Type **657**	50	25
2841	90c. German Shepherd Dog	90	70
2842	$1.35 Jack Russell Terrier	1·40	1·25
2843	$1.50 Golden Retriever	1·50	1·90
2844	$2 Huntaway (New Zealand Sheepdog)	1·75	2·00
MS2845	124×89 mm. Nos. 2843/4	5·50	6·00

(b) Size 25×30 mm. Self-adhesive.

2846	45c. Type **657**	50	45

658 Street Scene, c. 1930

2006. 75th Anniv of Hawke's Bay Earthquake. Multicoloured.

2848	45c. Type **658**	60	55
2849	45c. Aerial view of devastated city of Napier	60	55
2850	45c. Aerial view with roofless church and intact Public Trust Building, Napier	60	55
2851	45c. Fire engine and crew	60	55
2852	45c. HMS *Veronica*	60	55
2853	45c. Sailors from HMS *Veronica* clearing debris	60	55
2854	45c. Red Cross nurses with hospital patient	60	55
2855	45c. Rescue services	60	55
2856	45c. Abandoned vehicles on broken road ("Devastation")	60	55
2857	45c. Outdoor hospital ward, Botanical Gardens, Napier ("Medical services")	60	55
2858	45c. Emergency mail plane	60	55
2859	45c. Refugees on road	60	55
2860	45c. Refugee tents, Nelson Park	60	55
2861	45c. Makeshift cooking facilities, Hastings	60	55
2862	45c. Maori women ("Community spirit")	60	55
2863	45c. Refugees boarding train	60	55
2864	45c. Reconstruction work ("Building industry")	60	55
2865	45c. Hastings Street rebuilt in Art Deco style, 1933	60	55
2866	45c. Carnival procession ("Celebrations")	60	55
2867	45c. Entrance to National Tobacco Company building, Ahuriri, 2005	60	55

Nos. 2849/50 form a composite design showing an aerial view of Napier after the earthquake.

2006. Tourism (2nd series). As T **622**. Multicoloured.

2868	$1.50 Lake Wanaka	1·40	1·60
2869	$1.50 Mount Taranaki	1·40	1·60
2870	$1.50 Halfmoon Bay, Stewart Island	1·40	1·60
2871	$1.50 Franz Josef Glacier, West Coast	1·40	1·60
2872	$1.50 Huka Falls, Taupo	1·40	1·60
2873	$1.50 Cathedral Cove, Coromandel	1·40	1·60

659 Queen Elizabeth II

2006. 80th Birthday of Queen Elizabeth II.

2874	**659** $5 multicoloured	5·00	5·00
MS2875	105×100 mm. No. 1272 of Jersey; $5 Type **659** (sold at $17.50)	13·00	15·00

No. **MS**2875 is identical to **MS**1273 of Jersey.

660 Champagne Glasses

2006. Personalised Stamps. Multicoloured.

No.	Description		
2876	45c. Type **660**	45	50
2877	45c. Buzzy Bee (toy)	45	50
2878	45c. Silver fern	45	50
2879	45c. Pohutukawa flower	45	50
2880	45c. Christmas star decorations	45	50
2881	45c. Engagement and wedding rings	45	50
2882	45c. Red rose	45	50
2883	$1.50 As No. 2878	1·25	1·40
2884	$2 As No. 2879	1·60	1·75
2885	$2 As No. 2880	1·60	1·75

2006. Washington 2006 World Philatelic Exhibition. Sheet, 120×80 mm containing designs as Nos. 2809/10 but without imprint date.

No.	Description		
MS2886	$2 Fern; $2 Type **651**	4·50	4·50

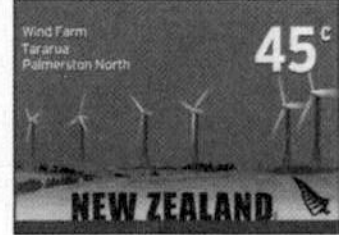

661 Wind Farm, Tararua, Palmerston North

2006. Renewable Energy. Multicoloured.

No.	Description		
2887	45c. Type **661**	75	25
2888	90c. Roxburgh Dam, Central Otago (hydro)	1·25	90
2889	$1.35 Biogas production, Waikato	1·75	1·50
2890	$1.50 Wairakei Geothermal Power Station	2·00	2·50
2891	$2 Solar-powered lighthouse, Cape Reinga (vert)	2·75	3·00

662 "5" and Tomatoes

2006. Children's Health. "5+ A Day" Healthy Eating Campaign. Multicoloured

(a) Ordinary gum

No.	Description		
2892	45c. +5c. Type **662** (30×40 mm)	85	70
2893	90c. +10c. "+" and oranges (30×40 mm)	1·50	1·50
2894	$1.35 "a" and garlic (30×30 mm)	1·75	1·60
2895	$1.50 "DAY" and kiwi fruit (40×30 mm)	2·25	2·75
2896	$2 Hand silhouette and red cabbage (30×40 mm)	2·50	3·00
MS2897	120×90 mm. Nos. 2892/6	9·00	10·00

(b) Self-adhesive.

No.	Description		
2898	45c. +5c. Type **662** (25×30 mm)	1·25	1·25

663 Gold Panning, c. 1880s

2006. Gold Rush. Multicoloured.

No.	Description		
2899	45c. Type **663**	75	25
2900	90c. Settlement at Kurunui Creek, Thames, c. 1868 (horiz)	1·40	90
2901	$1.35 Chinese prospectors at Tuapeka, Otago, c. 1900s (horiz)	1·75	1·50
2902	$1.50 Last Otago gold escort at Roxburgh, 1901 (horiz)	1·90	2·50
2903	$2 Waterfront at Dunedin, c. 1900s (horiz)	2·25	3·00
MS2904	125×90 mm. As Nos. 2899/903 but "NEW ZEALAND" on stamp and fern symbol in gold	9·50	11·00

664 Decorated Silver Fern (Hanna McLachlan)

2006. Christmas. Designs showing winning entries in children's stamp design competition "What Christmas Means to Me". Multicoloured. Size 34×34 mm

(a) Ordinary gum

No.	Description		
2905	45c. Type **664**	60	15
2906	45c. Angel appearing to shepherds and magi (Isla Hewitt)	60	60
2907	45c. Extended family around Christmas tree (Caitlin Davidson)	60	60
2908	45c. Virgin Mary and baby Jesus (Maria Petersen)	60	60
2909	45c. Beach and pohutakawa tree (Deborah Yoon)	60	60
2910	45c. New Zealand wood pigeon and Christmas star (Hannah Webster)	60	60
2911	90c. Santa hat on kiwi fruit (Pierce Higginson)	1·00	60
2912	$1.35 Kiwiana Christmas trees (Rosa Tucker)	1·25	1·00
2913	$1.50 Pattern of four pohutukawa flowers (Sylvie Webby)	1·40	1·75
2914	$2 Camping at Christmas (Gemma Baldock)	1·75	2·00

(b) Size 24×29 mm. Self-adhesive.

No.	Description		
2915	45c. Type **664**	50	25
2916	$1.50 As No. 2913	1·40	1·50

665 Dragon Boat Festival

2006. Summer Festivals. Multicoloured.

No.	Description		
2917	45c. Type **665**	75	40
2918	90c. Race day	1·40	90
2919	$1.35 Teddy bears' picnic	1·75	1·50
2920	$1.50 Outdoor concert	1·90	2·50
2921	$2 Jazz festival	2·25	2·75
MS2922	185×80 mm. Nos. 2917/21	9·00	9·00

2006. Kiwipex 2006 National Stamp Exhibition, Christchurch. Sheet 120×90 mm.

No.	Description		
MS2923	As Nos. 2809/10 but without imprint date (sold at $5)	6·50	7·50

This sheet was sold at $5, a premium of $1 above the face value. The premium funded the NZ Philatelic Trust.

2006. Belgica '06 International Stamp Exhibition, Brussels. Sheet 120×90 mm.

No.	Description		
MS2924	Nos. 2883×2 and 2884	6·50	7·50

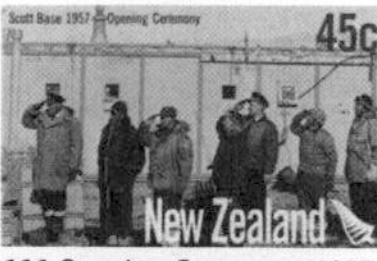

666 Opening Ceremony, 1957

2007. 50th Anniv of Scott Base, Antarctica. Multicoloured.

No.	Description		
2925	45c. Type **666**	1·50	40
2926	90c. Scott Base, 1990	2·50	1·10
2927	$1.35 Aerial view of Scott Base, 2000	3·00	2·00
2928	$1.50 "SCOTT BASE" sign	3·50	4·50
2929	$2 Scott Base, 2005	3·50	4·50

667 Kunekune Piglet

2007. Chinese New Year ("Year of the Pig"). Multicoloured.

No.	Description		
2930	45c. Type **667**	75	25
2931	90c. Kunekune pig	1·40	90
2932	$1.35 Arapawa pig	1·75	1·60
2933	$1.50 Auckland Island pig	1·90	3·00
2934	$2 Kunekune pig, young sow "Ruby"	2·25	3·00
MS2935	125×90 mm. Nos. 2932/3	4·25	4·75

668 Tuatara

2007. Native Wildlife. Multicoloured. Phosphorised frame. Self-adhesive.

No.	Description		
2936	45c. Type **668**	75	40
2937	90c. Kiwi	1·40	90
2938	$1.35 Hamilton's frog	1·75	1·60
2939	$1.50 Yellow-eyed penguin	2·50	3·00
2940	$2 Hector's dolphin	2·50	3·00

2007. Northland 2007 National Stamp Exhibition, Whangarei. Sheet 119×80 mm.

No.	Description		
MS2941	Nos. 2884 and 2891	7·00	8·00

669 Scouts of 1908 and Lt. Col. David Cossgrove (NZ Scouts founder)

2007. Centenaries. Multicoloured.

No.	Description		
2942	50c. Type **669**	1·25	1·40
2943	50c. Dr.Truby King (founder of Plunket Society) and nurse with baby, 1920s	1·25	1·40
2944	50c. All Golds, first New Zealand rugby league team, 1907	1·25	1·40
2945	50c. Sister Suzanne Aubert (founder) and classroom at Home of Compassion, 1907	1·00	1·00
2946	$1 Parents with baby, 2007 (Plunket Society)	2·00	90
2947	$1.50 Elderly lady and carer, 2007 (Home of Compassion)	2·50	2·75
2948	$2 Kiwi rugby league team, 2007	3·50	4·75
2949	$2 Scouts abseiling, 2007	3·50	4·75

Centenaries: Nos. 2942, 2949 World Scout Movement; 2943, 2946 Plunket Society; 2944, 2948 Rugby League in New Zealand; 2945, 2947 Home of Compassion.

2007. Personalised Stamps. As Nos. 2876/82 but new values. Multicoloured.

No.	Description		
2950	50c. Buzzy Bee (toy)	70	70
2951	50c. Pohutukawa flower	70	70
2952	50c. Engagement and wedding rings	70	70
2953	50c. Silver fern	70	70
2954	50c. Type **660**	70	70
2955	50c. Red rose	70	70
2956	50c. Christmas star decorations	70	70

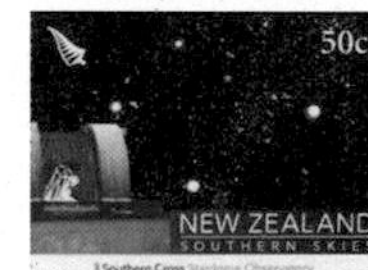

670 Southern Cross and 0.5m Zeiss Telescope at Stardome Observatory, Auckland

2007. Southern Skies. Multicoloured.

No.	Description		
2957	50c. Type **670**	1·50	45
2958	$1 Pleiades and 1m McLellan telescope, Mt. John Observatory, Tekapo	2·00	1·00
2959	$1.50 Trifid Nebula and 24cm telescope, Ward Observatory, Wanganui	2·75	2·25
2960	$2 Southern Pinwheel and 1.8m MOA telescope, Mt. John Observatory	3·25	4·00
2961	$2.50 Large Magellanic Cloud and 11m Southern African large telescope	4·00	4·50

671 "good as gold"

2007. Classic Kiwi

No.	Description		
2962	50c. Type **671**	70	70
2963	50c. "sweet as"	70	70
2964	50c. "she'll be right"	70	70
2965	50c. "hissy fit"	70	70
2966	50c. "sparrow fart"	70	70
2967	50c. Kiwi and "cuz"	70	70
2968	50c. "away laughing"	70	70
2969	50c. "tiki tour"	70	70
2970	50c. "away with the fairies"	70	70
2971	50c. "wop-wops"	70	70
2972	50c. "hard yakka"	70	70
2973	50c. "cods wallop"	70	70
2974	50c. "boots and all"	70	70
2975	50c. "shark and taties"	70	70
2976	50c. "knackered"	70	70
2977	50c. "laughing gear"	70	70
2978	50c. "everyman and his dog"	70	70
2979	50c. "bit of a dag"	70	70
2980	50c. "dreaded lurgy"	70	70
2981	50c. "rark up"	70	70

The shiny black portions at the right of Nos. 2962/81 are printed in thermochromic ink which fades temporarily when exposed to heat, revealing translations of the Kiwi slang on the stamps.

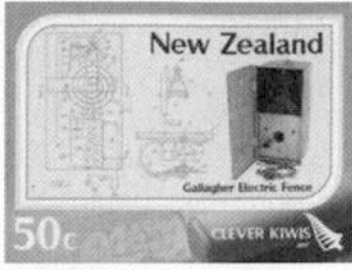

672 Electric Fence (Bill Gallagher), 1969

2007. "Clever Kiwis". New Zealand Inventions. Multicoloured.

No.	Description		
2982	50c. Type **672**	60	30
2983	$1 Spreadable butter (Norris and Illingworth)	1·25	1·10
2984	$1.50 Mountain buggy, 1992	2·00	2·00
2985	$2 Jet boat (Bill Hamilton)	3·25	3·75
2986	$2.50 Tranquilliser gun (Colin Murdoch), 1950s	3·75	4·00

2007. Bangkok 2007 20th Asian International Stamp Exhibition. Sheet 80×70 mm.

No.	Description		
MS2987	Nos. 2735/6	4·00	4·00

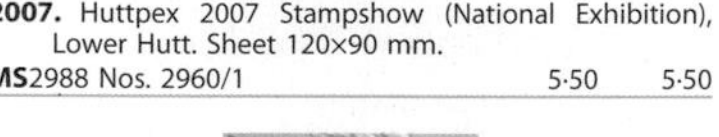

2007. Huttpex 2007 Stampshow (National Exhibition), Lower Hutt. Sheet 120×90 mm.

No.	Description		
MS2988	Nos. 2960/1	5·50	5·50

673 Girl releasing Peace Dove

2007. Children's Health. Peaceful World. Multicoloured.

(a) Size 30×40 mm

No.	Description		
2989	50c.+10c. +10c. Type **673**	1·00	1·00
2990	$1+10c. +10c.	1·75	1·75
MS2991	100×90 mm. 50c.+10c. Girls with peace lily (24×29 mm) and Nos. 2989/90	3·00	3·00

(b) Size 24×29 mm. Self-adhesive.

No.	Description		
2992	50c.+10c. +10c. Girls with peace lily	1·50	1·50

674 Queen Elizabeth II and Prince Philip, c. 2007

2007. Diamond Wedding of Queen Elizabeth II and Prince Philip. Multicoloured.

No.	Description		
2993	50c. Type **674**	50	50
2994	$2 On their wedding day, 1947	2·75	2·75
MS2995	110×90 mm. Nos. 2993/4	3·25	3·25

675 Christmas Symbols (Sione Vao)

2007. Christmas. Showing winning entries in children's stamp design competition 'Christmas Symbols'. Multicoloured

(a) Ordinary gum

No.	Description		
2996	50c. Type **675**	60	10
2997	$1 Robin wearing Santa hat (Reece Cateley)	1·10	40
2998	$1.50 Baby Jesus (Emily Wang)	2·25	2·00
2999	$2 Beach cricket (Alexandra Eathorne)	3·00	3·50
3000	$2.50 Fantail (Jake Hooper)	3·75	4·50

(b) Self-adhesive. Size 24×29 mm.

3001	50c. As Type **675**	60	50
3002	$1.50 As No. 2997	1·75	1·75

676 'GO YOU GOOD THING'

2007. Personalised Stamps. Multicoloured.

3003	50c. Type **676**	75	75
3004	50c. 'Look Who it is!'	75	75
3005	50c. 'Love Always'	75	75
3006	50c. 'THANKS A MILLION'	75	75
3007	50c. 'WE'VE GOT NEWS'	75	75
3008	50c. 'Wish you were here'	75	75
3009	$1 'Time to Celebrate'	1·40	1·40
3010	$1 'Kia Ora'	1·40	1·40
3011	$1.50 'You gotta love Christmas'	2·25	2·25
3012	$2 Chinese inscription	3·00	3·00

677 Dusky Sound, Fiordland

2008. Underwater Reefs. Multicoloured

(a) Ordinary gum. Designs 39×29 mm

3013	50c. Type **677**	75	30
3014	$1 *Callanthias australis* (splendid perch) and *Ecklonia radiata* (common kelp), Mayor Island, Bay of Plenty	1·50	1·25
3015	$1.50 Hydrocoral *Errina novaezelandiae* (red coral), Fiordland	2·25	2·50
3016	$2 *Diadema palmeri* (diadema urchin), Volkner Rocks, White Island, Bay of Plenty	3·00	3·50
MS3017	120×80 mm. Nos. 3013/16	11·00	11·00

(b) Self-adhesive. Size 29×24 mm.

3018	50c. Type **677**	75	75
3019	$1 As No. 3014	1·40	1·40

678 Rabbits

2008. Chinese New Year ('Year of the Rat'). Pocket Pets. Multicoloured.

3020	50c. Type **678**	1·00	30
3021	$1 Guinea pigs	1·75	1·25
3022	$1.50 Rats	2·50	3·00
3023	$2 Mice	3·25	3·50
MS3024	125×90 mm. Nos. 3022/3	6·50	7·50

679 Drought, 1997–98

2008. Weather Extremes. Multicoloured.

3025	50c. Type **679**	1·00	75
3026	50c. Pedestrians in gale, Auckland, March 2007	1·00	75
3027	$1 Storm waves, Evans Bay, Wellington, January 2001	1·60	1·40
3028	$1.50 Flooded farmland, Hikurangi, 2007	2·50	2·25
3029	$2 Snow storm, Ohai, Southland, May 2001	3·00	3·50
3030	$2.50 Heat, Matarangi beach, Coromandel, 2005	4·00	3·75

2008. Taipei 2008 21st Asian International Stamp Exhibition. Sheet 120×90 mm.

MS3031	No. 3012 and as No. 3023	5·75	5·75

680 Sapper John Luamanu and Baby Daughter, ANZAC Day Parade, 2007

2008. ANZAC (1st series). Multicoloured.

3032	50c. Type **680**	1·00	75
3033	50c. Auckland Infantry Battalion landing at Gallipoli, 25 April 1915	1·00	75
3034	$1 New Zealand soldiers on Western Front, April 1918	1·75	1·40
3035	$1.50 Sling Camp and chalk kiwi on Salisbury Plain, England, 1919	2·75	2·50
3036	$2 Maori Battalion performing haka, Helwan, Egypt, June 1941	3·50	3·25
3037	$2.50 161 Battery, Nui Dat, Vietnam, 1965–71	4·25	4·25

681 *Miro Whero, Miro Ma, Miro Pango*

2008. 150 Years of Kingitanga (Maori King) Movement. Designs showing art by Fred Graham. Multicoloured.

3038	50c. Type **681**	75	40
3039	$1.50 *He Piko He Taniwha*	2·00	2·25
3040	$2.50 *Kia Mau* (horiz)	3·75	4·00

682 The Pevensie Children playing in the Surf

2008. Making of The Chronicles of Narnia: *Prince Caspian* (film). Multicoloured.

3041	50c. Type **682**	1·25	45
3042	$1 Queen Susan	2·00	1·25
3043	$1.50 High King Peter	3·25	3·50
3044	$2 Prince Caspian	4·00	4·00

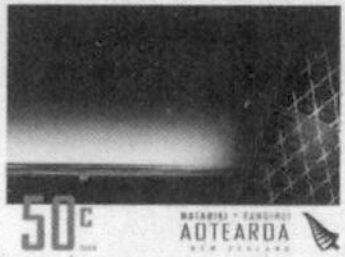

683 'Ranginui' (sky)

2008. Matariki (Maori New Year). Multicoloured.

3045	50c. Type **683**	75	60
3046	50c. Te Moana Nui A Kiwa	75	60
3047	$1 Papatuanuku	1·50	1·10
3048	$1.50 Whakapapa	2·50	2·25
3049	$2 Takoha	3·00	3·50
3050	$2.50 Te Tau Hou	4·00	4·50
MS3051	150×90 mm. Nos. 3045/50	10·50	10·50

684 Girl riding Bicycle ('INSPIRE')

2008. Children's Health. Multicoloured

(a) Ordinary gum

3052	50c.+10c. +10c. Type **684**	1·25	1·25
3053	$1+10c. +10c. Boy kayaking ('PASSION')	1·60	1·75
MS3054	140×90 mm. 50c. +10c. Boy with arms outstretched in triumph (34×32 mm) and Nos. 3052/3	3·00	3·00

(b) Self-adhesive.

3055	50c.+10c. +10c. Boy with arms outstretched in triumph ('EXCEL') (34×32 mm)	1·00	1·00

685 Rower ('CELEBRATE')

2008. Olympic Games, Beijing. Multicoloured.

3056	50c. Type **685**	1·25	1·00
3057	50c. Cyclist ('PASSION')	2·00	1·25
3058	$1 Kayaker ('SUCCEED')	2·00	1·50
3059	$2 Athlete ('MOTIVATE')	3·25	4·00

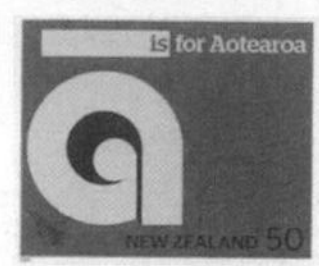

686 'a' is for Aotearoa

2008. The A to Z of New Zealand. Multicoloured.

3060	50c. Type **686**	80	80
3061	50c. B is for Beehive (Parliament House, Wellington)	80	80
3062	50c. C is for Cook (Captain Cook)	80	80
3063	50c. D is for Dog (from Footrot Flats cartoon strip)	80	80
3064	50c. E is for Edmonds (Thomas Edmonds)	80	80
3065	50c. F is for Fantail (bird)	80	80
3066	50c. G is for Goodnight Kiwi (TV cartoon)	80	80
3067	50c. H is for Haka	80	80
3068	50c. I is for Interislander (ferry)	80	80
3069	50c. J is for Jelly Tip (ice cream)	80	80
3070	50c. K is for Kia Ora	80	80
3071	50c. L is for log o'wood (Ranfurly Shield rugby trophy)	80	80
3072	50c. M is for Mudpools	80	80
3073	50c. N is for Nuclear Free	80	80
3074	50c. O is for O.E. (overseas experience)	80	80
3075	50c. P is for Pinetree (All Black player Colin Meads)	80	80
3076	50c. Q is for Quake (earthquakes)	80	80
3077	50c. R is for Rutherford (nuclear physicist Sir Ernest Rutherford)	80	80
3078	50c. S is for Southern Cross	80	80
3079	50c. T is for Tiki (carved by Lewis Gardiner)	80	80
3080	50c. U is for Upham (Captain Charles Upham's Victoria Cross)	80	80
3081	50c. V is for Vote (suffragette Kate Sheppard)	80	80
3082	50c. W is for Weta (model of insect)	80	80
3083	50c. X is for x-treme sports	80	80
3084	50c. Y is for Yarn	80	80
3085	50c. Z is for Zeeland (explorer Abel Tasman)	80	80

687 Last Spike Ceremony, Manganui-o-te-Ao, 1908

2008. Centenary of the North Island Main Trunk Railway Line. Multicoloured.

3086	50c. Type **687**	1·00	40
3087	$1 KA 947 class steam locomotive on display at Taumarunui, 1958	1·75	1·10
3088	$1.50 Steam hauled goods train on Makatote Viaduct, 1963	2·25	2·00
3089	$2 Steam hauled goods train climbing the Raurimu Spiral, 1964	3·00	3·75
3090	$2.50 EF powered 'Overlander' crossing Hapuawhenua Viaduct, 2003	4·00	4·50

2008. WIPA08 International Stamp Exhibition, Vienna. Sheet 121×85 mm.

MS3091	Nos. 3046 and 3048/9	4·50	4·75

688 Nativity

2008. Christmas (1st issue). Multicoloured

(a) Ordinary gum

3092	50c. Type **688**	60	10
3093	$1 Holy Family	1·10	40
3094	$1.50 Mary and baby Jesus	1·75	2·25

(b) Self-adhesive. Size 24×29 mm.

3095	50c. As Type **688**	60	50
3096	$1.50 As No. 3094	1·60	1·60

689 Sheep wearing Santa Hat and Jandals (Kirsten Fisher-Marsters)

2008. Christmas (2nd issue). T **689** and similar square designs showing winning entries in children's stamp design competition 'Kiwi Christmas'. Multicoloured.

3097	50c. Type **689**	60	10
3098	$2 Pohutukawa flowers and koru (Tamara Jenkin)	2·25	2·75
3099	$2.50 Kiwi wearing Santa hat (Molly Bruhns)	2·50	2·75

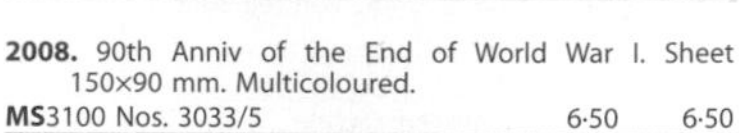

2008. 90th Anniv of the End of World War I. Sheet 150×90 mm. Multicoloured.

MS3100	Nos. 3033/5	6·50	6·50

690 Sir Edmund Hillary

2008. Sir Edmund Hillary Commemoration. Multicoloured.

3101	50c. Type **690**	1·00	40
3102	$1 Edmund Hillary and Tenzing Norgay during first ascent of Mt. Everest, 1953	1·75	1·10
3103	$1.50 On tracked vehicle, Trans-Antarctic Expedition, 1955–8	2·50	2·25
3104	$2 Sir Edmund Hillary (founder of Himalayan Trust, 1960) with Nepalese children	3·00	3·50
3105	$2.50 Appointed to the Order of the Garter, 1995	3·00	3·50

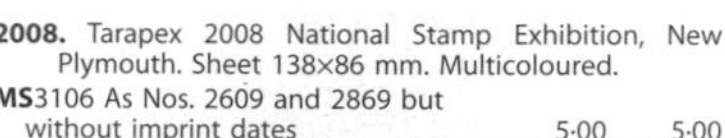

2008. Tarapex 2008 National Stamp Exhibition, New Plymouth. Sheet 138×86 mm. Multicoloured.

MS3106	As Nos. 2609 and 2869 but without imprint dates	5·00	5·00

691 Pencarrow Lighthouse

2009. Lighthouses of New Zealand. Multicoloured.

3107	50c. Type **691**	1·00	45
3108	$1 Dog Island Lighthouse	1·75	1·00
3109	$1.50 Cape Brett Lighthouse	2·50	2·50
3110	$2 Cape Egmont Lighthouse	3·50	4·00
3111	$2.50 Cape Reinga Lighthouse	3·75	1·25

Nos. 3107/11 commemorate the 150th anniversary of New Zealand's first lighthouse (Pencarrow Head).

692 Lunar Ox Symbol

2009. Chinese New Year ('Year of the Ox'). Multicoloured.

3112	50c. Type **692**	80	65
3113	$1 Ox	1·40	1·40
3114	$2 Chinese lanterns and Auckland Harbour Bridge	2·75	3·50
MS3115	Nos. 3112/14	4·50	5·00

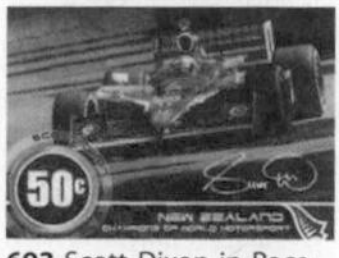

693 Scott Dixon in Race Car

2009. New Zealand Champions of Motorsport

(a) Ordinary gum

3116	50c. Type **693**	1·25	45
3117	$1 Bruce McLaren in Formula One race car	2·00	1·25
3118	$1.50 Ivan Mauger on speedway motorcycle	2·75	2·50

3119 $2 Denny Hulme in race car 3·50 3·50
3120 $2.50 Hugh Anderson on Grand Prix motorcycle 4·00 4·25
MS3121 Nos. 3116×20 12·00 11·00

3122 50c. As Type **693** 1·00 1·00
3123 $1 As No. 3117 1·50 1·50

694 Giant Moa

2009. Giants of New Zealand. Multicoloured.
3124 50c. Type **694** 1·50 65
3125 $1 Colossal squid 2·25 1·25
3126 $1.50 Southern right whale 3·50 2·75
3127 $2 Giant eagle 4·25 4·50
3128 $2.50 Giant weta 4·50 4·75
MS3129 179×90 mm. Nos. 3124/8 14·50 13·50

2009. International Polar Year 2007–2009. Sheet 120×80 mm. Multicoloured.
MS3130 As No. 2871×2 but without imprint dates 7·50 7·50

695 Funeral Procession of the Unknown Warrior, Wellington, 2004

2009. ANZAC (2nd series). 'Comrades in Arms'. Multicoloured.
3131 50c. Type **695** 1·40 1·00
3132 50c. NZ (Maori) Pioneer Battalion on break from trench improvement, World War I 1·40 1·00
3133 $1 No. 75 (NZ) Squadron RAF and Wellington bomber, World War II 2·75 1·75
3134 $1.50 HMS *Achilles* (Leander class cruiser), World War II 3·00 2·50
3135 $2 Kayforce gun crew in action, Korea, 1 April 1952 3·75 4·00
3136 $2.50 Soldiers of ANZAC Battalion boarding RAAF Iroquois helicopter, Vietnam, 23 March 1968 4·00 4·25

2009. China 2009 World Stamp Exhibition, Luoyang, China. Sheet 95×90 mm. Multicoloured.
MS3137 Nos. 3010, 3012 and 3113 5·25 5·50

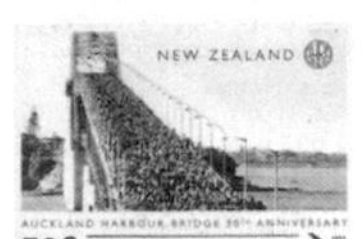

696 Pedestrians crossing Bridge before its opening to Traffic, 1959

2009. 50th Anniv of Auckland Harbour Bridge. Multicoloured.
3138 50c. Type **696** 1·00 40
3139 $1 Auckland Harbour Bridge (with two extra lanes) in 2009 1·50 1·10
3140 $1.50 Auckland Harbour Bridge in 1961 2·50 3·00
3141 $2 Auckland Harbour Bridge at night, 2009 3·00 3·25

697 Heitiki from 'Te Maori' Exhibition, 1984

2009. Matariki (Maori New Year). Multicoloured

(a) Self-adhesive
3143 50c. Type **697** 75 45
3144 $1 Heitiki by Raponi 1·40 1·10
3145 $1.50 Heitiki made from corian by Rangi Kipa 2·25 2·25
3146 $1.80 Female heitiki made from greenstone 2·50 2·50
3147 $2 Female heitiki, c. 1849, from the Museum of New Zealand 3·00 3·25
3148 $2.30 Heitiki made from paraoa by Rangi Hetet, 1991 3·50 3·75

(b) Ordinary gum.
MS3149 150×90 mm. As Nos. 3143/8 12·00 12·00

2009. New Zealand Landscapes (2nd series). As T **622**. Multicoloured

(a) Ordinary gum
3150 30c. Tolaga Bay 75 45
3151 $1.80 Russell 3·00 3·00
3152 $2.30 Lake Wanaka 3·50 3·50
3153 $2.80 Auckland 3·75 3·75
3154 $3.30 Rakaia River 4·25 4·25
3155 $4 Wellington 5·50 6·00

(b) Self-adhesive.
3156 $1.80 As No. 3151 2·75 3·00

698 Lighthouse (Cape Reinga) and Angler

2009. A Tiki Tour of New Zealand. Sheet 99×280 mm containing T **698** and similar square designs. Multicoloured.
MS3157 Type **698**; Hole in the Rock Tour (Cape Brett); Maui snaring the sun (Maori legend); Yachting; Sky Tower (Auckland) and surf boat; Marlin fishing; Waikato rugby (Mooloos); Rower, statue of shearer and Maori carving; Pohutukawa tree, east coast style whare (meeting house), surfing and horse-riding; Mt. Taranaki; Gumboot and wind turbines; Gannet (Cape Kidnappers); Tribute state (Greymouth) and Municipal Building (Westport); Grapes, fly-fishing and glass blowing; Richard Seddon statue (Parliament) and windsurfer; Mount Cook lily and statue of Mackenzie's dog (Lake Tekapo); Roadside crayfish caravan (Kaikoura) and Neil Dawson's Chalice sculpture (Christchurch); Whale watching; Crayfish, black robin and fishing boat (Chatham Islands); Milford Sound and jetboat (Shotover river); 'Wings over Wanaka' (biplane); Kakapo; Curling; Stewart Island shag and chain sculpture (Rakiura track, Oban) 20·00 22·00

No. **MS**3157 contains 24 stamps and one stamp-size label, the backgrounds forming a composite design of a map of New Zealand.

699 1996 Child Safety 40c.+5c. Stamp

2009. 80th Anniv of Children's Health Stamps. Multicoloured. (a) Ordinary gum.

(a) Ordinary gum
3158 50c. +10c. Type **699** 1·75 1·75
3159 $1 +10c. 1932 Hygeia 1d.+1d. Health stamp 2·25 2·25
MS3160 100×90 mm. 50c.+10c. 1943 Princess Elizabeth 2d.+1d. Health stamp (25×30 mm) (p 14×14½) and as Nos. 3158/9 (p 14) 3·25 3·25

(b) Self-adhesive
3161 50c. +10c. 1943 Princess Elizabeth 2d.+1d. Health stamp (25×30 mm) 1·75 1·75

700 Beach Cricket

2009. KiwiStamps. Multicoloured. Self-adhesive.
3162 (–) Type **700** 1·00 1·00
3163 (–) Kiwi fruit 1·00 1·00
3164 (–) State Highway 1 road sign 1·00 1·00
3165 (–) Windfarm and umbrella blown inside out 1·00 1·00
3166 (–) Lawnmower 1·00 1·00
3167 (–) Caravan 1·00 1·00
3168 (–) Flying duck wall ornaments 1·00 1·00
3169 (–) Fish and chips at the beach 1·00 1·00
3170 (–) Swanndri jacket on barbed wire fence 1·00 1·00
3171 (–) Sausage on fork and barbecue 1·00 1·00

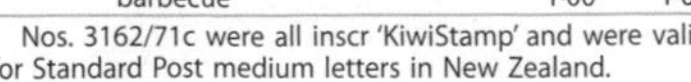
Nos. 3162/71c were all inscr 'KiwiStamp' and were valid for Standard Post medium letters in New Zealand.

701 Three Shepherds

2009. Christmas (1st issue). Multicoloured.

(a) Ordinary gum
3172 50c. Type **701** 75 10
3173 $1 Mary, Joseph and Infant Jesus 1·50 60
3174 $1.80 Three magi with gifts 2·50 3·50

(b) Self-adhesive. Size 30×25 mm.
3175 50c. As Type **701** 75 75
3176 $1.80 As No. 3174 2·25 2·25

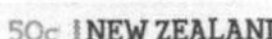

702 Seaside Chair and Pohutukawa Tree (Felix Wang)

2009. Christmas (2nd issue). T **702** and similar square designs showing winning entries in children's stamp design competition 'What do you love about Christmas?'. Multicoloured.
3177 50c. Type **702** 75 10
3178 $2.30 New Zealand pigeon wearing Christmas hat (Danielle Aldworth) 3·00 3·75
3179 $2.80 Christmas presents (Apun Bakshi) 4·25 4·50

2009. Timpex 2009 National Stamp Exhibition, Timaru. Sheet 170×92 mm. Multicoloured.
MS3180 As Nos. 3101/2 and 3105 (all p 14) and specimen stamp as Type **501** (p 14½×15) 6·50 6·50

No. **MS**3180 was sold for $6.50, with a $2.50 surcharge to fund the Philatelic Trust.

703 Sir Peter Blake ('Inspirational Leader')

2009. Sir Peter Blake (yachtsman) Commemoration. Multicoloured.
3181 50c. Type **703** 1·00 45
3182 $1 Sir Peter Blake at wheel and yacht ('Whitbread Round the World Yachtsman') 1·75 1·25
3183 $1.80 Sir Peter Blake using winch and catamaran ('Jules Verne Trophy Record Breaker') 3·00 2·75
3184 $2.30 Sir Peter Blake, Americas Cup trophy and yacht *New Zealand* ('Passionate Kiwi') 4·00 4·50
3185 $2.80 Sir Peter Blake and yacht *Seamaster* on expedition in Antarctica ('Environmentalist') 4·50 4·75
MS3186 160×58 mm. Nos. 3181/5 13·00 13·00

704 Lunar Tiger Symbol

2010. Chinese New Year. Year of the Tiger. Multicoloured
3187 50c. Type **704** 1·00 75
3188 $1 Tiger 1·90 1·90
3189 $1.80 Head of tiger 2·75 2·75
3190 $2.30 Beehive (Parliament House, Wellington) 3·75 4·00
MS3191 150×90 mm. Nos. 3187/90 8·50 8·50

705 Heitiki

2010. Personalised Stamps. Sheet 94x82 mm. Multicoloured.
MS3192 $1.80 Type **705**; $2.30 As Type **660**; $2.30 Engagement and wedding rings; $2.30 Pohtukawa flower 13·00 14·00

706 Allosaurus

2010. Dinosaurs of New Zealand. Multicoloured

(a) Ordinary gum
3193 50c. Type **706** 95 85
3194 $1 Anhanguera 2·25 2·25
3195 $1.80 Titanosaurus 3·00 3·00
3196 $2.30 Moanasaurus 3·75 3·75
3197 $2.80 Mauisaurus 4·50 4·50

(b) Self-adhesive. Sheet 230×200 mm.
MS3198 As Nos. 3193/7 13·00 13·00

707 ANZAC Soldier

2010. ANZAC (3rd series). Remembrance. Multicoloured.
3199 50c. Type **707** 1·50 1·25
3200 50c. Gallipoli veterans marching, ANZAC Day, 1958 1·50 1·25
3201 $1 Posthumous VC Award Ceremony for Second Lieutenant Te Moana-Nui-a-Kiwa Ngarimu, Ruatoria, 1943 2·50 1·75
3202 $1.80 Nurses laying wreath, Cairo Cemetery, ANZAC Day, 1940 3·50 3·00
3203 $2.30 ANZAC War Memorial, Port Said, Egypt, 1932 4·50 5·00
3204 $2.80 Veteran at Sangro War Cemetery, Italy, 2004 4·50 5·00

708 Peony and Pohutukawa Flowers

2010. Expo 2010, Shanghai, China. Multicoloured.
3205 50c. Type **708** 95 95
3206 $1 Maori Kaitiaki (carved by Lyonel Grant for New Zealand pavilion) and Chinese Fu Dog 1·75 1·75
3207 $1.80 Pan Gu (Chinese creation story) and Tane creating world of light (Maori legend) 2·25 2·25
3208 $2.30 Shanghai and Auckland skylines 2·50 2·50
3209 $2.80 Jade cong (Chinese good luck symbol) and jade heitiki 2·75 2·75
MS3210 180×140 mm. As Nos. 3205/9 9·00 9·50

Nos. 3205/9 have text in English and Chinese printed on the back of the stamps.

Stamps from **MS**3210 do not have text printed on the reverse.

2010. London 2010 Festival of Stamps. Sheet 130×90 mm. Multicoloured.
MS3211 Nos. 3199 and 3203/4 9·00 9·00

709 Manu Aute

2010. Matariki
3212 50c. Type **709** 1·00 80
3213 $1 Manu patiki (vert) 1·75 1·75
3214 $1.80 Manu taratahi (vert) 3·00 3·00

3215 $2.30 Upoko tangata 3·75 4·00
MS3216 150×90 mm. Nos. 3215/18 8·75 8·75

710 Centenary Series Jersey

2010. Centenary of Maori Rugby. Multicoloured.
3217 50c. Type **710** 1·25 80
3218 $1.80 Centenary logo 3·00 3·00
MS3219 160×90 mm. Nos. 3220/1 3·50 3·50

711 Monarch Butterfly

2010. Children's Health. Butterflies

(a) Ordinary gum
3220 50c.+10c. +10c. Type **711** 1·50 1·50
3221 $1+10c. +10c. Tussock butterfly 2·00 2·00
MS3222 166×95 mm. 50c.+10c. Boulder copper butterfly (26×30 mm) and Nos. 3220/1 3·25 3·25

(b) Self-adhesive. Size 25x30 mm. Die-cut perf 9½x10
3223 +10c. Boulder copper butterfly 1·50 1·50

712 Silver Fern (All Blacks emblem)

2010. All Blacks (national rugby team)
3224 **712** 60c. black 1·00 80
3225 **712** $1.90 black 3·00 3·00
MS3226 90×78 mm. As Nos. 3224/5 but 35×20 mm (p 15×14½) and Nos. 3224/5 4·00 4·00

2010. New Zealand Landscapes (3rd series). Multicoloured.

(a) Ordinary gum. Phosphorised paper
3227 $1.20 Mitre Peak, Milford Sound 1·60 1·60
3228 $1.90 Queenstown 2·75 2·75
3229 $2.40 Lake Rotorua 3·75 3·75
3230 $2.90 Kaikoura 4·50 4·50
3231 $3.40 River Avon at Christchurch 5·50 5·50

(b) Self-adhesive. Phosphor frame
3232 $1.20 As No. 3227 1·75 1·75
3233 $1.90 As No. 3228 3·00 3·00
3233b $2.40 As No. 3229 (1.2.12) 3·75 3·75

713 Emblem

2010. Rugby World Cup, New Zealand (2011)
3234 **713** 60c. multicoloured 1·00 1·00
3235 **713** $1.90 multicoloured 3·00 3·00
MS3236 91×79 mm. As Nos. 3234/5 but 35×20 mm (p 15×14½) and Nos. 3234/5 7·75 7·75

2010. Personalised Stamps. Multicoloured.
MS3237 165×82 mm. 60c.×8 As Type **660**; Buzzy Bee (toy); Silver fern; Pohutukawa flower; Engagement and wedding rings; Red rose; As Type **705**; Teddy bear 7·50 7·50
MS3238 94×82 mm. $1.90 As Type **705**; $2.40 As Type **660**; $2.40 Engagement and wedding rings; $2.40 Pohutukawa fllower 18·00 19·00

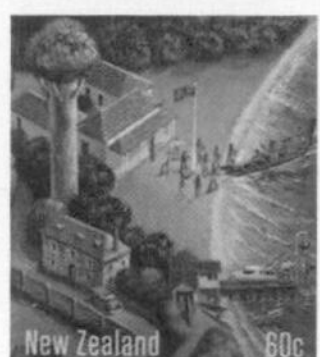

714 Tane Mahuta (oldest tree), Kerikeri Stone Store and Treaty House at Waitangi

2010. 'New Zealand A Slice of Heaven'. Multicoloured.
MS3239 60c.×25 Type **714**; Fountain and waterfront, Oriental Bay, Wellington; Octagon Plaza with Dunedin Cathedral and St. Paul's Church, Dunedin; Auckland Ferry Terminal; The Beehive, Wellington; Sky Tower, Auckland; One Tree Hill, Auckland; Mt. Ruapehu and Waikato River; Hot air balloons shaped as sheep, cow's head and kiwi; Christchurch Cathedral and River Avon; Horse race; Rural garage, coffee shop and church; Mt. Cook, helicopter and plane; War memorial, ploughed field and lake shore; Lake Taupo, Huka Falls and bridge; Champagne Pool, geysers, mud pools and marae; Rugby match; Queenstown, Lake Wakatipu and the Remarkables Range; Skiers, biplane, glider and golf course; Shotover River and Skippers Suspension Bridge; Seaside caravan park; Titahi Bay boatsheds; Hawke's Bay vineyard; Farm with sheep in pens; Nugget Point 27·00 28·00

The stamps and margins of No. **MS**3239 form a composite design.

715 1960 2d. 'The Adoration of the Shepherds' (Rembrandt) Stamp

2010. Christmas. 50th Anniv of New Zealand Christmas Stamps. Multicoloured.

(a) Phosphorised paper.
3240 60c. Type **715** 1·00 30
3241 $1.20 1970 3c. stamp showing 'The Holy Family' stained glass window from Invercargill Presbyterian Church 2·75 1·50
3242 $1.90 1979 35c. Pohutukawa tree stamp 3·00 3·00
3243 $2.40 1983 45c. 'The Glory of Christmas' stamp showing star and flowers 4·00 4·75
3244 $2.90 2000 40c. Virgin Mary and Baby Jesus stamp 4·75 5·00

(b) Self-adhesive. Size 25x30 mm
3245 60c. As Type **715** 1·00 1·00
3246 $1.90 As No. 3242 2·75 3·00

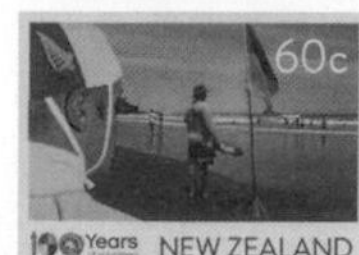

716 Surf Lifeguard with Rescue Tube

2010. Centenary of Surf Life Saving. Multicoloured.
3247 60c. Type **716** 1·10 60
3248 $1.20 Lifeguards in inflatable rescue boat (IRB) 2·25 1·40
3249 $1.90 Ski paddlers in Surf Life Saving Championships 2·75 2·75
3250 $2.40 Surf boat 3·75 4·25
3251 $2.90 March past of lifeguards in 1930s surf carnival 5·00 5·00

2010. Palmpex 2010 National Stamp Exhibition, Palmerston North. Sheet 150×90 mm
MS3252 No. 2090b×3 7·50 7·50

717 Rabbit Symbol

2011. Chinese New Year. Year of the Rabbit. Multicoloured.
3253 60c. Type **717** 1·10 60
3254 $1.20 Chinese style rabbit 1·90 1·50
3255 $1.90 Leaping rabbit 3·25 3·50
3256 $2.40 Christchurch Cathedral and Chinese kite 3·75 4·25
MS3257 150×90 mm. Nos. 3253/6 10·00 10·00

2011. INDIPEX 2011 World Philatelic Exhibition, New Delhi. Multicoloured.
MS3258 Nos. 3227/9 9·00 9·00

718 Whakaeke (choreographed entrance)

2011. Kapa Haka (Maori performing arts). Multicoloured.

(a) Self-adhesive
3259 60c. Type **718** 1·10 1·10
3260 60c. Poi (dancer swinging taupo ball on flax cord) 1·10 1·10
3261 $1.20 Waiata-a-ringa (action songs) 2·25 2·25
3262 $1.90 Haka 3·25 3·25
3263 $2.40 Whakawatea (choreographed exit) 3·75 3·75
3264 $2.90 Moteatea (traditional chant) 4·50 4·50

(b) Ordinary gum
MS3265 150×90 mm. As Nos. 3259/64 16·00 16·00

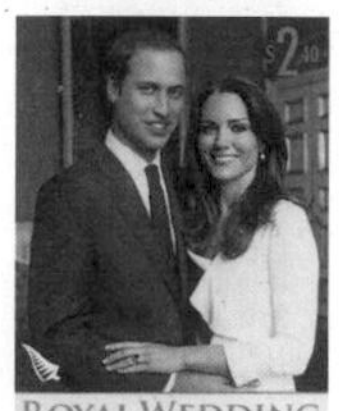

719 Prince William and Miss Catherine Middleton

2011. Royal Wedding. Multicoloured.
3266 $2.40 Type **719** 4·00 4·00
3267 $2.40 Prince William and Miss Catherine Middleton embracing 4·00 4·00
MS3268 135×91 mm. Nos. 3266/7 8·00 8·00

720 Hokey Pokey (vanilla and crunchy toffee ice cream)

2011. KiwiStamps (2nd issue). Multicoloured.
3269 (–) Type **720** 95 95
3270 (–) Kiwi road sign 95 95
3271 (–) Beach 95 95
3272 (–) Trout fishing 95 95
3273 (–) Mountain biking 95 95

721 Charles Heaphy, 11 February 1864, Waikato, New Zealand

2011. Victoria Cross. The New Zealand Story. Multicoloured.
3274 60c. Type **721** 1·25 1·25
3275 60c. William James Hardham, 28 January 1901, South Africa 1·25 1·25
3276 60c. Cyril Royston Guyton Bassett, 7 August 1915, Gallipoli 1·25 1·25
3277 60c. Donald Forrester Brown, 15 September 1916, High Wood, France 1·25 1·25
3278 60c. Samuel Frickleton, 7 June 1917, Messines, Belgium 1·25 1·25
3279 60c. Leslie Wilton Andrew, 31 July 1917, La Basse Ville, France 1·25 1·25
3280 60c. Henry James Nicholas, 3 December 1917, Polderboek, Belgium 1·25 1·25
3281 60c. Richard Charles Travis, 24 July 1918, Hébuterne, France 1·25 1·25
3282 60c. Samuel Forsyth, 24 August 1918, Grévillers, France 1·25 1·25
3283 60c. Reginald Stanley Judson, 26 August 1918, Bapaume, France 1·25 1·25
3284 60c. Harry John Laurent, 12 September 1918, Gouzeaucourt Wood, France 1·25 1·25
3285 60c. James Crichton, 30 September 1918, Crevecoeur, France 1·25 1·25
3286 60c. John Gildroy Grant, 1 September 1918, Bancourt, France 1·25 1·25
3287 60c. James Edward Allen Ward, 7 July 1941, on operations over Holland 1·25 1·25
3288 60c. Charles Hazlitt Upham, 22–30 May 1941, Crete and 14–15 July 1942, Western Desert 1·25 1·25
3289 60c. Alfred Clive Hulme, 20–28 May 1941, Crete 1·25 1·25
3290 60c. John Daniel Hinton, 28–19 April 1941, Greece 1·25 1·25
3291 60c. Keith Elliott, 15 July 1942, Western Desert 1·25 1·25
3292 60c. Moana-Nui-a-Kiwa Ngarimu, 26–27 March 1943, Tunisia 1·25 1·25
3293 60c. Lloyd Allen Trigg, 11 August 1943, sea patrol, Atlantic Ocean 1·25 1·25
3294 60c. Leonard Henry Trent, 3 May 1943, on operation over Holland 1·25 1·25
3295 60c. Victoria Cross of New Zealand (awarded to Bill Henry Apiata, 2004, Afghanistan) 1·25 1·25

722 Humpback Whale

2011. 'Beyond the Coast'. Multicoloured.
MS3296 60c.×10 Type **722**; White-faced storm petrel (horiz); John dory (horiz); Yellowfin tuna (horiz); Hammerhead shark (horiz); Kingfish (horiz); Lord Howe coralfish; Snapper (horiz); Arrow squid (horiz); Orange roughy (horiz) $1.90 Yellow moray eel (horiz); $1.90 King crab 17·00 18·00

The stamps and margins of No. **MS**3296 form a composite design showing marine life from the surface to the sea bed.

723 Modern Greenstone He Matau by Lewis Gardiner

2011. Matariki. Hei Matau. Multicoloured.

(a) Self-adhesive
3297 60c. Type **723** 1·00 1·00
3298 60c. Functional whalebone fish hook, 1500-1800 1·00 1·00
3299 $1.20 Inanga greenstone hei matau, c. 1800 2·25 2·25
3300 $1.90 Modern hei matau in multiple materials by Lewis Gardiner 3·25 3·25
3301 $2.40 Wooden hei matau with bone barb, c. 1800 3·75 3·75
3302 $2.90 Symbolic Maui's hook made from whalebone, 1750-1850 5·00 5·00

(b) Ordinary paper
MS3303 150×90 mm. As Nos. 3297/3302 16·00 16·00

724 Kiwi

2011. Children's Health. Flightless Birds. Multicoloured.

(a) Ordinary gum

3304	60c. +10c. Type **724**	1·75	1·75
3305	$1.20 +10c. Kakapo	2·75	3·00
MS3306	130×90 mm. 60c.+10c. Takahe (26×30 mm) and Nos. 3304/5	4·75	4·75

(b) Self-adhesive. Size 26×30 mm

3307	60c. +10c. Takahe	1·25	1·25

The upper and left portions of No. **MS**3306 are cut around in the shape of a takahe

2011. Round Kiwi Stamps

3308	**445**	$1.20 black	3·25	3·25
3309	**445**	$1.90 silver	3·75	4·00
3310	**445**	$2.40 blue	4·00	4·50

2011. Philanippon 2011 World Stamp Exhibition, Yokohama, Japan. Sheet 130×90 mm

MS3311	No. 3225×2 and No. 3309	10·50	10·50

725 1 State Highway

2011. Counting in Kiwi. Sheet 190×226 mm containing T **725** and similar vert designs. Multicoloured.

MS3312	60c.×21 Type **725**; 2 jandals; 3 hour ferry ride across Cook Strait (seagull and ferry); 4 stars of Southern Cross; 5 year old starting school; 6 runs in cricket - out of the park; 7 players in netball team (ball landing in net); Number 8 wire; 9 dressed to the nines; 10 guitar; First 11; 12 Bluff oysters; 13 lamingtons (cakes); 14 national parks (fish and lake); 15 players in rugby team; 16 driving age (car mirror and dice); 17 Captain Cook's landing, 1769; 18 voting age; 19 protected surf breaks (surfboard and wave); 20 bucks (parrot wearing crown); 21 key to the door	23·00	23·00

726 Webb Ellis Cup

2011. Webb Ellis Cup (World Cup Rugby, New Zealand)

3313	**726**	$15 gold, black and grey	27·00	30·00

No. 3313 was produced using Motionstamp technology, giving a three dimensional effect to the trophy.

No. 3313 was only available mounted in a display card or as a first day cover.

727 Hiker

2011. 'The New Zealand Experience'. Multicoloured.

3314	60c. Type **727**	1·40	1·10
3315	60c. Sailing dinghy, motor boat and windsurfer	1·40	1·10
3316	$1.20 Fishing	2·25	1·90
3317	$1.90 Maori man performing kapa haka and marae	3·50	3·50
3318	$2.40 Skiier and helicopter	4·00	4·50
3319	$2.90 Bungy jumping	5·00	5·50
MS3320	160×90 mm. Nos. 3314/19	16·00	16·00

728 Baby Jesus in Manger

2011. Christmas. Multicoloured.

(a) Ordinary paper

3321	60c. Type **728**	1·90	60
3322	$1.20 Angel appearing to shepherds	2·75	1·75
3323	$1.90 Mary, Joseph and baby Jesus	3·25	3·25
3324	$2.40 Shepherds with baby Jesus	3·75	4·25
3325	$2.90 Wise men with baby Jesus	5·00	5·50

(b) Self-adhesive. Size 25×30 mm

3326	60c. As Type **728**	1·60	1·00
3327	$1.90 As No. 3323	3·25	3·50
3328	$2.40 As No. 3324	4·25	4·50

2011. China 2011 27th Asian International Stamp Exhibition, Wuxi, China. Sheet 130×90 mm.. Multicoloured.

MS3329	Nos. 3308/10	9·25	9·25

729 Chinese Character for Dragon

2012. Chinese New Year. Year of the Dragon. Multicoloured.

3330	60c. Type **729**	1·25	60
3331	$1.20 Paper-cut dragon	2·00	1·50
3332	$1.90 Dragon lantern	2·50	2·50
3333	$2.40 Dunedin Railway Station and pair of swallows	6·00	6·00
MS3334	150×90 mm. Nos. 3330/3	10·75	10·75

730 Pohutukawa (*Metrosideros exselsa*)

2012. Native Trees. Multicoloured.

3335	60c. Type **730**	1·50	60
3336	$1.20 Cabbage tree (*Cordyline australis*)	2·50	2·00
3337	$1.90 Kowhai (*Sophora microphylla*)	3·25	2·75
3338	$2.40 Nikau (*Rhopalostylis sapida*)	4·75	5·00
3339	$2.90 Manuka (*Leptospermum scoparium*)	5·50	6·00
MS3340	160×90 mm. Nos. 3335/9	16·00	16·00

731 Tiger Moth ('The Beginning')

2012. 75th Anniv of the RNZAF (Royal New Zealand Air Force). Multicoloured.

3341	60c. Type **731**	1·75	1·75
3342	60c. Air Training Corps cadets	1·75	1·75
3343	60c. Pilot and navigator in cockpit of Wellington bomber ('WWII Europe')	1·75	1·75
3344	60c. Women's Auxiliary Air Force members in front of de Havilland Express aircraft	1·75	1·75
3345	60c. Servicing Unit aircraft maintenance area, Ondonga, New Georgia, 1943 ('WWII Pacific')	1·75	1·75
3346	60c. Loading hopper into modified bomb bay of Avenger NZ2504 for aerial topdressing trials, Masterton Aerodrome, 1949	1·75	1·75
3347	60c. Territorial Air Force No. 3 (Canterbury) Squadron	1·75	1·75
3348	60c. de Havilland Venom WK428 of 14 Squadron over RAF Station, Changi, Singapore ('South East Asia')	1·75	1·75
3349	60c. RNZAF A-4 Skyhawk and HMAS *Adelaide* off Perth, 1996 ('ANZAC')	1·75	1·75
3350	60c. Super Sea Sprite helicopter SH-2G taking off from flight deck of Anzac-class ship HMNZS *Te-Mana* ('Naval Support')	1·75	1·75
3351	60c. RNZAF Hercules at McMurdo Base, Antarctica ('Transport')	1·75	1·75
3352	60c. Three 'Huey' Iroquois helicopters, Timor, 2001 ('Peacekeeping')	1·75	1·75
3353	60c. Search and rescue training and RNZAF Iroquois helicopter	1·75	1·75
3354	60c. Aircraft flying in 'missing man' formation ('Remembrance')	1·75	1·75
3355	60c. NH90 advance medium utility helicopter ('The Future')	1·75	1·75

732 Official New Zealand Portrait of Queen Elizabeth II

2012. Diamond Jubilee. Multicoloured.

3356	70c. Type **732**	1·75	1·75
3357	70c. Official New Zealand portrait of Queen Elizabeth II and Duke of Edinburgh	1·75	1·75
3358	$1.40 Queen Elizabeth II and Duke of Edinburgh wearing ceremonial cloaks for Maori reception, Hastings, New Zealand, 1986	3·25	3·25
3359	$1.90 Queen Elizabeth II and Duke of Edinburgh waving from car, Wellington, 1981	4·50	4·50
3360	$2.40 Queen Elizabeth II and Duke of Edinburgh on Silver Jubilee tour, Wellington, 1981	5·00	5·50
3361	$2.90 Queen Elizabeth II giving Christmas broadcast from Government House, Auckland, 1953	6·00	6·50
MS3362	101×97 mm. Nos. 3356/61	20·00	21·00

2012. New Zealand Landscapes (4th series). Multicoloured.

(a) Ordinary gum

3363	$1.40 Cape Reinga	2·50	2·50
3364	$2.10 Stewart Island	3·75	3·75
3365	$3.50 Lake Matheson	6·25	6·25

(b) Self-adhesive

3366	$1.40 As No. 3363	2·50	2·50
3367	$2.10 As No. 3364	3·75	3·75

2012. All Blacks (national rugby team). As Nos. 3224 and **MS**3226 with new face value

3368	**712** 70c. black	1·75	1·75
MS3369	90×61 mm. As No. 3368 but 35×20 mm (p 15×14½) and No. 3368	2·50	2·50

733 Pouakai (birdman), Pareora

2012. Matariki. Maori Rock Art. Multicoloured.

(a) Self-adhesive

3370	70c. Type **733**	1·25	1·25
3371	70c. Seated tiki figure on ceiling of shelter, Maerewhenua	1·25	1·25
3372	$1.40 Two people on mokihi (bulrush water craft), Opihi	2·50	2·50
3373	$1.90 Te Puawaitanga, Waitaki	3·50	3·50
3374	$2.40 Tiki figure, Te Ana a Wai	4·25	4·25
3375	$2.90 Taniwha on ceiling of shelter, Opihi	5·25	5·25

(b) Ordinary gum

MS3376	150×91 mm. As Nos. 3370/5	16·00	16·00

2012. Personalised Stamps. As No. **MS**3237 with new face values. Multicoloured.

MS3377	70c.×8 As Type **660**; Buzzy Bee (toy); Silver fern; Pohutukawa flower; Engagement and wedding rings; Red rose; As Type **705**; Teddy bear	9·00	9·00

2012. Indonesia 2012 World Stamp Championship and Exhibition, Jakarta. Sheet 120×90 mm containing Nos. 3335 and 3337/8

MS3378	Nos. 3335 and 3337/8	8·00	8·00

734 Cape Reinga and Kaitaia

2012. Tiki Tour of New Zealand (2nd issue). Multicoloured.

MS3379	70c.×20 Type **734**; Whangarei and Bay of Islands; Cape Brett; Lion Rock; Auckland, Hamilton and Tauranga; White Island and East Cape; Mt. Taranaki, New Plymouth and Hawera; Rotorua, Taupo and Palmerston North; Napier and Gisborne; Fish and boat; Westport and Greymouth; Nelson and Kaikoura; Wellington; Chatham Islands; Milford Sound and Mitre Peak; Mt. Cook, Queenstown and Timaru; Christchurch; Invercargill, Gore and Stewart Island; Dunedin; Taiaroa Head	29·00	30·00

735 Selu Tuiga depicting Samoan Parliament and Beehive, Wellington

2012. 50th Anniv of Treaty of Friendship between New Zealand and Samoa. Selu Tuiga (Samoan head comb in shape of traditional tuiga headdress). Multicoloured.

3380	70c. Type **735**	1·25	1·25
3381	$1.40 Tuiga with niu (coconut tree) design	2·50	2·50
3382	$1.90 Selu Tuiga depicting Maota Fa'amasino (Courthouse, Apia)	3·50	3·50
3383	$2.40 Selu Tuiga with tatau (tattoo) motifs and patterns	4·25	4·25
3384	$2.90 Selu Tuiga depicting Immaculate Conception of Mary Cathedral, Mulivai	5·25	5·25
MS3385	150×90 mm. Nos. 3380/4	15·00	15·00

736 Sea Lion Pup

2012. Children's Health. New Zealand Sea Lion (*Phocarctos hookeri*)

(a) Ordinary gum

3386	70c. +10c. Type **736**	1·75	1·75
3387	$1.40 +10c. Sub-adult male	3·00	3·25
MS3388	147×91 mm. 70c.+10c. Sea lion pup (head) (26×30 mm) and Nos. 3386/7	7·00	7·50

(b) Self-adhesive. Size 26×30 mm

3389	70c. +10c. Sea lion pup (head)	1·25	1·25

737 *Aramoana* (Picton to Wellington ferry, 1962-84)

2012. Great Voyages of New Zealand. Multicoloured.

3390	70c. Type **737**	1·75	1·25
3391	$1.40 Waka (Maori canoe) crossing Cook Strait	2·75	2·50
3392	$1.90 *Earnslaw* (Kingston - Queenstown - Glenorchy steamer), Lake Wakatipu	4·00	3·50
3393	$2.40 *Dunedin* (Port Chalmers to London, 1874-90)	4·75	5·50
3394	$2.90 *Rotomahana* (Wellington to Lyttelton, Australia), 1870s-1925	6·00	6·50
MS3395	136mm x 75mm. Nos. 3390/4	15·00	15·00

738 Mary, Joseph and Baby Jesus

2012. Christmas. Multicoloured.

(a) Ordinary gum

3396	70c. Type **738**	1·25	60
3397	$1.40 Shepherds	2·50	1·25
3398	$1.90 Angel	3·50	3·25
3399	$2.40 Three Wise Men offering gifts	4·25	4·75

3400 $2.90 Journey of the Three Wise Men 5·25 5·75

(b) Self-adhesive. Size 25×30 mm

3401 70c. As Type **738** 1·25 1·25
3402 $1.90 As No. 3398 3·50 3·50
3403 $2.40 As No. 3399 4·25 4·25

2012. Blenpex 2012 National Stamp Exhibition, Marlborough. Sheet 131×91 mm

MS3404 Nos. 3356, 3359 and 3361 9·00 9·00

739 Bilbo Baggins

2012. *The Hobbit* (film trilogy): *An Unexpected Journey* (1st issue)

(a) Ordinary gum. Phosphorised paper

3405 70c. Type **739** 1·25 60
3406 $1.40 Gollum (Andy Serkis) 2·50 1·50
3407 $1.90 Gandalf (Ian McKellen) (horiz) 3·50 3·50
3408 $2.10 Thorin Oakenshield (Richard Armitage) (horiz) 3·75 4·00
3409 $2.40 Radagast (Sylvester McCoy) 4·25 4·75
3410 $2.90 Elrond (Hugo Weaving) 5·25 5·75
MS3411 111×66 mm. 70c. Type **739** 1·25 1·25
MS3412 111×66 mm. $1.40 No. 3406 2·50 2·50
MS3413 111×66 mm. $1.90 No. 3407 3·50 3·50
MS3414 111×66 mm. $2.10 No. 3408 3·75 3·75
MS3415 111×66 mm. $2.40 No. 3409 4·25 4·25
MS3416 111×66 mm. $2.90 No. 3410 5·25 5·25

(b) Self-adhesive. Size 26x37 mm or 37x26 mm

3417 70c. As Type **739** 1·25 1·25
3418 $1.40 As No. 3406 2·50 2·50
3419 $1.90 As No. 3407 3·50 3·50
3420 $2.10 As No. 3408 3·75 3·75
3421 $2.40 As No. 3409 4·25 4·25
3422 $2.90 As No. 3410 5·25 5·25

2012. Beijing 2012 International Stamp and Coin Expo. Sheet 121×90 mm

MS3423 As Nos. 3330 and 3332/3 7·00 7·00

740 Calligraphic Snake by Zhao Meng-fu (1254-1322)

2013. Chinese New Year. Year of the Snake. Multicoloured.

3424 70c. Type **740** 1·25 60
3425 $1.40 Paper-cut greeting snake patterned with silver ferns and pomegranates 2·50 1·50
3426 $1.90 Lantern with koru-shaped snake design 3·50 4·00
3427 $2.40 Koru-snake lanterns on Skyline Gondola, Queenstown 4·25 4·75
MS3428 150×90 mm. Nos. 3424/7 10·50 10·50

741 Hen and Chickens Fern (*Asplenium bulbiferum*)

2013. Native Ferns. Multicoloured.

3429 70c. Type **741** 1·25 60
3430 $1.40 Kidney Fern (*Cardiomanes reniforme*) 2·50 1·50
3431 $1.90 Colenso's Hard Fern (*Blechnum colensoi*) 3·50 3·50
3432 $2.40 Umbrella Fern (*Sticherus cunninghamii*) 4·25 4·75
3433 $2.90 Silver Fern (*Cyathea dealbata*) 5·25 5·75
MS3434 160×90 mm. Nos. 3429/33 15·00 15·00

742 *A Lion in the Meadow*

2013. Margaret Mahy (children's writer) Commemoration. Multicoloured.

3435 70c. Type **742** 1·25 60
3436 $1.40 *A Summery Saturday Morning* 2·50 1·50
3437 $1.90 *The Word Witch* 3·50 3·50
3438 $2.40 *The Great White Man-eating Shark* 4·25 4·75
3439 $2.90 *The Changeover* 5·25 5·75
MS3440 140×85 mm. Nos. 3435/9 15·00 15·00

743 Kiwi Team One on Patrol, North-east Bamyan, Afghanistan, 2011

2013. ANZAC (4th series). New Zealanders serving Abroad. Multicoloured.

3441 70c. Type **743** 1·25 1·25
3442 70c. RNZAF Iroquois helicopter carrying Australian troops, Dili, Timor-Leste, 2008 1·25 1·25
3443 $1.40 Territorial Army members performing haka, Honiara, Solomon Islands, 2009 2·50 2·50
3444 $1.90 M113A1 tank of Queen Alexandra's Mounted Rifles on checkpoint duty, Bosnia-Herzegovina, 2007 3·50 3·50
3445 $2.40 ANZAC class frigate *Te Kaha* on patrol off Antarctica, 1999 4·25 4·25
3446 $2.90 Kiwi symbol on hillside at post Armistice Korean headquarters of 16th Field Regiment, Royal New Zealand Artillery, 1953 5·25 5·25
MS3447 Seven sheets, each 155×110 mm. (a) No. 3441. (b) No. 3442. (c) No. 3443. (d) No. 3444. (e) No. 3445. (f) No. 3446. (g) Nos. 3441/6 32·00 32·00

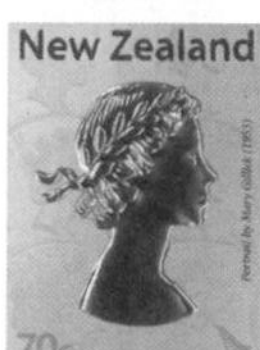

744 Portrait by Mary Gillick, 1953

2013. 60th Anniv of the Coronation. Portraits of Queen Elizabeth II from New Zealand Coins. Multicoloured.

3448 70c. Type **744** 1·75 1·50
3449 70c. Re-engraved portrait by Mary Gillick, 1956 1·75 1·50
3450 $1.40 Portrait by Arnold Machin, 1967 3·00 2·50
3451 $1.90 Portrait by James Berry, 1979 4·00 3·75
3452 $2.40 Portrait by Raphael Maklouf, 1986 4·75 5·50
3453 $2.90 Portrait by Ian Rank-Broadley, 1999 5·50 6·00
MS3454 150×90 mm. Nos. 3448/53 19·00 19·00

2013. Australia 2013 World Stamp Exhibition, Melbourne. Sheet 150×91 mm

MS3455 Nos. 3448, 3450 and 3453 9·00 9·00

745 Piko (silver fern) and Tane Mahuta (God of the Forest)

2013. Matariki. Koru (pattern derived from silver fern frond, symbolising renewal). Multicoloured.

(a) Self-adhesive

3456 70c. Type **745** 1·25 1·25
3457 70c. Manu Tukutuku (kite) and koru pattern symbolising wind 1·25 1·25
3458 $1.40 Nguru (flute) and Hine Raukatauri (Goddess of Flute Music) 2·50 2·50
3459 $1.90 Pataka (storehouse) covered in Koru 3·50 3·50
3460 $2.40 Kotiate (club) and Mangopare design representing hammerhead shark 4·25 4·25
3461 $2.90 Patiki (flounder) design symbolising hospitality 5·25 5·25

(b) Ordinary gum

MS3462 151×91 mm. Nos. 3456/61 16·00 16·00

746 Bee gathering Nectar

2013. Honey Bees. Multicoloured.

3463 70c. Type **746** 1·00 1·50
3464 $1.40 Bees returning to hive 1·75 1·50
3465 $1.90 Worker bees transferring nectar to honey storage area of hive 2·50 2·50
3466 $2.40 Beekeeper removing honeycomb 3·75 4·25
3467 $2.90 Honey 4·50 4·75
MS3468 137×81 mm. Nos. 3463/7 12·00 12·00

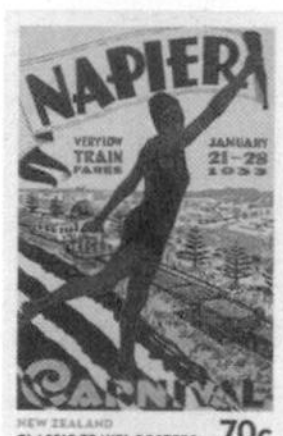

747 Napier, 1933

2013. Classic Travel Posters. Multicoloured.

3469 70c. Type **747** 1·00 1·00
3470 70c. New Zealand The Sportsman's Paradise (game fishing - hooked marlin) 1·00 1·00
3471 70c. Tree Fern 1·00 1·00
3472 70c. Rata Blossom Franz Josef Glacier 1·00 1·00
3473 70c. For the Worlds Best Sport (angler) 1·00 1·00
3474 70c. Cities of New Zealand Wellington 1·00 1·00
3475 70c. Your New Zealand Holiday Fly Teal (carved Maori figure, Arthur Thompson), 1950s 1·00 1·00
3476 70c. Get in the Queue for Queenstown 1·00 1·00
3477 70c. Timaru by the Sea 1·00 1·00
3478 70c. New Zealand (lake and mountains) 1·00 1·00
3479 70c. Tauranga for Winter Sunshine 1·00 1·00
3480 70c. Kea (Alpine Parrot) 1·00 1·00
3481 70c. Southern Alps Travel the Mount Cook way! 1·00 1·00
3482 70c. Marlborough Sounds 1·00 1·00
3483 70c. Sheep Droving in New Zealand 1·00 1·00
3484 70c. New Zealand for your next holiday (Maori woman) 1·00 1·00
3485 70c. For Winter Thrills Mt. Cook Train to Timaru (skiier) 1·00 1·00
3486 70c. Mt. Egmont 8,260 ft 1·00 1·00
3487 70c. Fly Teal to nearby New Zealand (Maori figures, geyser and Mt. Cook) 1·00 1·00
3488 70c. Blue Baths, Rotorua 1·00 1·00

748 Castlepoint (centenary of lighthouse), Wairarapa Coast

2013. Coastlines. Multicoloured.

3489 70c. Type **748** 1·00 50
3490 $1.40 Nugget Point 1·75 1·50
3491 $1.90 East Cape 2·50 2·50
3492 $2.40 Pencarrow Head, near Wellington 3·75 4·25
3493 $2.90 Cape Campbell 4·50 4·75
MS3494 160×91 mm. Nos. 3489/93 12·00 12·00

749 Boy with Pet Lamb

2013. Children's Health. Country Pets. Multicoloured.

(a) Ordinary gum

3495 70c. +10c. Type **749** 1·25 1·25
3496 $1.40 +10c. Girl with piglet 1·75 2·00
MS3497 140×90 mm. Nos. 3495/6 and 70c.+10c. Boy with goat on school Pet Day (25x30 mm) 4·00 4·25

(b) Self-adhesive. Size 25×30 mm

3498 70c. +10c. Boy with goat on school Pet Day 1·25 1·25

750 Duke and Duchess of Cambridge with Prince George outside St. Mary's Hospital, 22 July 2013

2013. Birth of Prince George of Cambridge. Multicoloured.

3499 70c. Type **750** 1·50 1·50
3500 $1.90 Prince William holding Prince George 2·75 3·00
3501 $2.40 Duke and Duchess of Cambridge, Duchess holding Prince George 3·75 4·25
3502 $2.90 Catherine, Duchess of Cambridge holding Prince George 4·50 4·75

2013. Upper Hutt 2013 National Stamp Show. Sheet 141×80 mm

MS3503 As Nos. 3432/3 9·50 10·50

751 Giving Christmas Present

2013. Christmas. Multicoloured.

(a) Ordinary gum

3504 70c. Type **751** 1·00 50
3505 $1.40 Christmas lunch 1·75 1·10
3506 $1.90 Decorating the tree 2·50 2·50
3507 $2.40 Cricket on the beach 3·75 4·25
3508 $2.90 Carol singing 4·50 4·75

(b) Self-adhesive. Size 25×30 mm. (i) Domestic mail

3509 70c. As Type **751** 1·00 70

(ii) International Post

3510 $1.90 As No. 3506 2·50 2·75
3511 $2.40 As No. 3507 3·75 4·25

2013. *The Hobbit* (film trilogy): *The Desolation of Smaug* (2nd issue)

(a) Ordinary gum

3512 70c. Thorin Oakenshield (Richard Armitage) 1·00 60
3513 $1.40 Gandalf (Ian McKellen) 1·75 1·25
3514 $1.90 Tauriel (Evangeline Lilly) (horiz) 2·50 2·25
3515 $2.10 Bilbo Baggins (Martin Freeman) (horiz) 2·75 2·75
3516 $2.40 Legolas Greenleaf (Orlando Bloom) 3·75 4·25
3517 $2.90 Bard the Bowman (Luke Evans) 4·50 4·75

(b) Self-adhesive. Size 26x37 mm or 37x26 mm

3518 70c. As No. 3512 1·00 1·00
3519 $1.40 As No. 3513 1·75 1·75
3520 $1.90 As No. 3514 2·50 2·50
3521 $2.10 As No. 3515 2·75 3·00
3522 $2.40 As No. 3516 3·75 4·50
3523 $2.90 As No. 3517 4·50 5·00

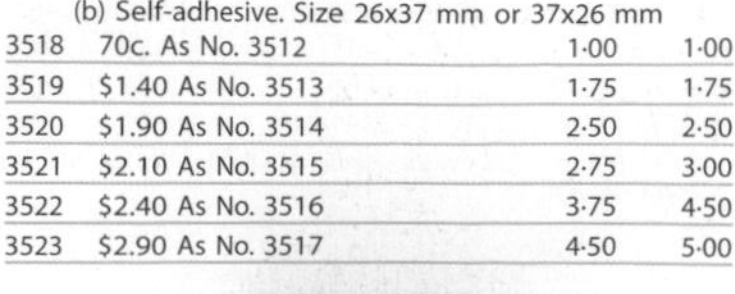

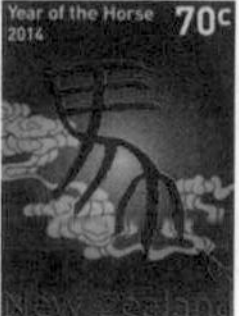

752 Horse Pictogram

2014. Chinese New Year. Year of the Horse. Multicoloured.

3524 70c. Type **752** 1·25 1·25
3525 $1.40 Paper-cut horse 2·50 2·50

3526 $1.90 Show-jumping 3·50 3·50
3527 $2.40 Rotorua Museum of Art and History 4·25 4·25
MS3528 150×90 mm. Nos. 3524/7 10·50 10·50

753 *Hormosira banksii* (Neptune's Necklace)

2014. Native Seaweeds. Multicoloured.
3529 70c. Type **753** 1·25 1·25
3530 $1.40 *Landsburgia quercifolia* 2·50 2·50
3531 $1.90 *Caulerpa brownii* (sea rimu) 3·50 3·50
3532 $2.40 *Marginariella boryana* 4·25 4·25
3533 $2.90 *Pterocladia lucida* (agar weed) 5·25 5·25
MS3534 160×90 mm. Nos. 3529/33 16·00 16·00

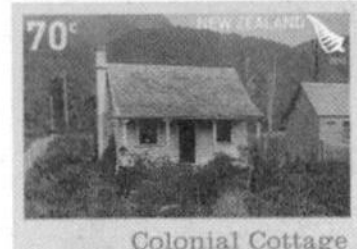

754 Colonial Cottage

2014. Construction of a Nation. Multicoloured.
3535 70c. Type **754** 1·25 1·25
3536 $1.40 Villa 2·50 2·50
3537 $1.90 Californian bungalow 3·50 3·50
3538 $2.40 Art Deco house 4·25 4·25
3539 $2.90 State House 5·25 5·25
MS3540 130×89 mm. Nos. 3535/9 15·00 15·00

The top margin of No. **MS**3540 is cut around in the shape of a house roof.

755 Recruitment Poster for Air Training Corps, 1942

2014. ANZAC (5th series). World War II Poster Art. Multicoloured.
3541 70c. Type **755** 1·25 1·25
3542 70c. Woman driving tractor ('HELP FARM FOR VICTORY', Women's Land Service), October 1943 1·25 1·25
3543 $1.40 Pilot ('THE AIR FORCE NEEDS MEN!', Royal New Zealand Air Force), February 1941 2·50 2·50
3544 $1.90 Warship ('NAVY WEEK') on fund raising poster for 3rd Liberty Loan, June 1943 3·50 3·50
3545 $2.40 Soldier throwing grenade ('ARMY WEEK' on fund raising poster for 3rd Liberty Loan, June 1943 4·25 4·25
3546 $2.90 Maori soldier and fund raising poster in Maori language ('TARINGA WHAKARONGO!'), 1941 5·25 5·25
MS3547 165×110 mm. No. 3541 1·25 1·25
MS3548 165×110 mm. No. 3542 1·25 1·25
MS3549 165×110 mm. No. 3543 2·50 2·50
MS3550 165×110 mm. No. 3544 3·50 3·50
MS3551 165×110 mm. No. 3545 4·25 4·25
MS3552 165×110 mm. No. 3546 5·25 5·25
MS3553 165×110 mm. No. 3541/6 16·00 16·00

Nos. **MS**3547/53 were only available from $19.90 stamp booklets.

756 Duke and Duchess of Cambridge with Prince George, August 2013

2014. Visit of Duke and Duchess of Cambridge to New Zealand, April 2014. Multicoloured.
3554 70c. Type **756** 1·25 1·25
3555 $2.40 Official Christening photograph, Clarence House, London 4·25 4·25

757 Franz Josef Glacier

2014. New Zealand Landscapes (5th series). Multicoloured.

(a) Ordinary gum
3556 60c. Type **757** 1·10 1·10
3557 $1.60 Moeraki Boulders 3·00 3·00
3558 $2.50 Pancake Rocks 4·50 4·50
3559 $3.60 Waikato River 6·50 6·50

(b) Self-adhesive
3560 $2 Mount Taranaki 3·50 3·50
3561 $2.50 As No. 3558 4·50 4·50

2014. All Blacks (national rugby team). As Nos. 3224/**MS**3226 with new face values
3562 **712** 80c. black 1·40 1·40
3563 $2.50 black 4·50 4·50
MS3564 90×80 mm. As Nos. 3562/3 but 35×19 mm (p 15×14½) and Nos. 3562/3 11·00 11·00

EXPRESS DELIVERY STAMPS

E1

1903
E1 **E1** 6d. red and violet 38·00 23·00

E2 Express Mail Delivery Van

1939
E6 **E2** 6d. violet 1·50 1·75

LIFE INSURANCE DEPARTMENT

L1

1891
L13 **L1** ½d. purple 90·00 4·00
L14 **L1** 1d. blue 90·00 75
L9 **L1** 2d. brown £140 3·75
L4 **L1** 3d. brown £325 35·00
L5 **L1** 6d. green £400 80·00
L6 **L1** 1s. pink £600 £150

1905. Similar type but "V.R." omitted.
L37 ½d. green 8·00 9·00
L22 1d. blue £275 30·00
L38 1d. red 3·25 2·00
L26 1½d. black 50·00 8·50
L27 1½d. brown 1·50 3·00
L21 2d. brown £1500 £130
L28 2d. purple 60·00 35·00
L29 2d. yellow 12·00 4·00
L30 3d. brown 55·00 38·00
L35 3d. red 16·00 24·00
L41 6d. pink 20·00 42·00

L3 Castlepoint Lighthouse

1947. Lighthouses.
L42 **L3** ½d. green and orange 2·25 70
L43 - 1d. olive and blue 1·75 1·25
L44 - 2d. blue and black 3·50 1·00
L45 - 2½d. black and blue 9·50 13·00
L46 - 3d. mauve and blue 4·25 1·00
L47 - 4d. brown and orange 4·25 1·75
L48 - 6d. brown and blue 4·50 2·75
L49 - 1s. brown and blue 4·50 3·75

LIGHTHOUSES—HORIZ: 1d. Taiaroa; 2d. Cape Palliser; 6d. The Brothers. VERT: 2½d. Cape Campbell; 3d. Eddystone; 4d. Stephens Island; 1s. Cape Brett.

1967. Decimal currency. Stamps of 1947–65 surch.
L50a 1c. on 1d. (No. L43) 1·00 6·50
L51 2c. on 2½d. on 2½d. (No. L45) 8·00 14·00
L52 2½c. on 3d. on 3d. (No. L46) 1·25 4·00
L53 3c. on 4d. on 4d. (No. L47) 2·75 5·00
L54 5c. on 6d. on 6d. (No. L48) 75 6·50
L55a 10c. on 1s. (No. L49) 75 4·00

L13 Moeraki Point Lighthouse

1969
L56 **L 13** ½c. yellow, red and violet 65 1·50
L57 - 2½c. blue, green and buff 50 1·00
L58 - 3c. stone, yellow & brn 50 60
L59 - 4c. green, ochre and blue 50 75
L60 - 8c. multicoloured 40 2·00
L61 - 10c. multicoloured 40 2·00
L62 - 15c. multicoloured 40 1·25

DESIGNS—HORIZ: 2½c. Puysegur Point Lighthouse; 4c. Cape Egmont Lighthouse. VERT: 3c. Baring Head Lighthouse; 8c. East Cape; 10c. Farewell Spit; 15c. Dog Island Lighthouse.

1978. No. L57 surch **25c**.
L63 25c. on 2½c. blue, green and buff 75 1·75

L17

1981
L64 **L17** 5c. multicoloured 10 10
L65 **L17** 10c. multicoloured 10 10
L66 **L17** 20c. multicoloured 15 15
L67 **L17** 30c. multicoloured 25 25
L68 **L17** 40c. multicoloured 30 30
L69 **L17** 50c. multicoloured 30 35

OFFICIAL STAMPS

1891. Optd **O.P.S.O.**
O1 **3** ½d. pink — £1400
O2 **13** ½d. black — £900
O13 **23** ½d. green — £850
O4 **10** 1d. pink — £800
O19 **42** 1d. red — £1100
O6 **9** 2d. mauve —
O8 **16** 2½d. blue — £850
O14 **26** 2½d. blue (A) — £1100
O21 **26** 2½d. blue (B) — £1300
O22 **28** 3d. brown — £2500
O16 **24** 4d. blue and brown — £800
O11 **19** 5d. black — £850
O20a **30** 5d. brown —
O12 **8** 6d. brown (No. 224b) — £850
O18 **32** 8d. blue — £950
O23 **34** 1s. red —
O24 **35** 2s. green — £850

Optd OFFICIAL

1907. Pictorials.
O59 **23** ½d. green 17·00 75
O60b **42** 1d. red 27·00 70
O61*a* 2d. purple 8·50 1·60
O63 **28** 3d. brown 50·00 1·75
O64 **31** 6d. red £250 25·00
O65 **34** 1s. orange £110 22·00
O66 **35** 2s. green 85·00 £140
O67 - 5s. red (No. 329) £170 £190

1908
O70 **50** 1d. red 70·00 5·00
O72 **31** 6d. red (No. 254) £225 35·00

1910. King Edward VII etc.
O73 **51** ½d. green 16·00 40
O78 **53** 1d. red 5·50 10
O74 **51** 3d. brown 14·00 80
O75 **51** 6d. red 19·00 5·50
O76 **51** 8d. blue 12·00 29·00
O77 **51** 1s. orange 55·00 20·00

1913. Queen Victoria.
O82 **F4** 2s. blue 65·00 60·00
O83 **F4** 5s. green 90·00 £130
O84 **F4** £1 red £650 £550

1915. King George V.
O88 **62** ½d. green 1·25 20
O90 **62** 1½d. grey 5·50 1·00
O91 **62** 1½d. brown 5·00 30
O98 **62** 2d. yellow 2·50 50
O99 **62** 3d. brown 7·00 70
O101 **62** 4d. violet 14·00 7·00
O102 **62** 6d. red 5·00 75
O103 **62** 8d. brown 65·00 £190
O104 **62** 9d. green 42·00 38·00
O105b **62** 1s. orange 7·00 2·00

1933. "Arms".
O111 **71** 1d. red 2·00 20
O112 **71** 2s. blue 85·00 £130
O113 **F6** 5s. green £325 £375

Optd Official

1936. "Arms"
O133aw 5s. green 40·00 6·00

1936. As 1935.
O120 **81** ½d. green 7·50 4·50
O115 - 1d. red (No. 557) 10·00 1·25
O122 **83** 1½d. brown 48·00 4·75
O123 - 2d. orange (No. 580) 12·00 10
O124a **85** 2½d. brown and grey 14·00 21·00
O125 **86** 3d. brown 48·00 3·50
O126c **87** 4d. black and brown 9·00 1·00
O127c **89** 4d. red 16·00 40
O128a 8d. brown 8·50 16·00
O130 **91** 9d. red and black 20·00 22·00
O131b 1s. green (No. 588) 40·00 3·00
O132d **93** 2s. olive 50·00 11·00

1938. King George VI.
O134 **108** ½d. green 28·00 2·25
O135 **108** ½d. orange 2·75 4·25
O136 **108** 1d. red 35·00 15
O137 **108** 1d. green 7·00 10
O138 **108** 1½d. brown 75·00 23·00
O139 **108** 1½d. red 17·00 12·00
O152 **108** 2d. orange 6·00 10
O140 **108** 3d. blue 7·00 10
O153 **108** 4d. purple 4·75 3·75
O154 **108** 6d. red 20·00 50
O155 **108** 8d. violet 8·00 7·50
O156 **108** 9d. brown 9·00 6·50
O157a - 1s. brown and red (No. 686b) 8·50 12·00
O158 - 2s. orange and green (No. 688) 40·00 16·00

1940. Centenary stamps.
O141 ½d. green 3·00 35
O142 1d. brown and red 7·50 10
O143 1½d. blue and mauve 6·50 2·00
O144 2d. green and brown 9·00 10
O145 2½d. green and blue 5·00 2·75
O146 3d. purple and red 8·00 1·00
O147 4d. brown and red 42·00 1·50
O148 6d. green and violet 35·00 1·50
O149 8d. black and red 35·00 17·00
O150 9d. olive and red 14·00 4·00
O151 1s. green 50·00 3·00

O6 Queen Elizabeth II

1954
O159a **O6** 1d. orange 50 75
O160 **O6** 1½d. brown 3·75 5·50
O161a **O6** 2d. green 40 60
O162 **O6** 2½d. olive 3·00 1·50
O163a **O6** 3d. red 40 10
O164b **O6** 4d. blue 1·00 50
O165 **O6** 9d. red 9·50 3·25
O166 **O6** 1s. purple 1·25 30
O167 **O6** 3s. slate 22·00 40·00

1959. Surch.
O169 2½d. on 2d. on 2d. green 1·25 2·50
O168 6d. on 1½d. on 1½d. brown 50 1·10

POSTAGE DUE STAMPS

D1

1899
D9 **D1** ½d. red and green 4·00 16·00
D14 **D1** 1d. red and green 20·00 3·75
D15 **D1** 2d. red and green 55·00 9·50
D12 **D1** 3d. red and green 17·00 6·50
D16 **D1** 4d. red and green 40·00 20·00

D6	D1	5d. red and green	32·00	50·00
D7	D1	6d. red and green	45·00	48·00
D2	D1	8d. red and green	60·00	85·00
D8	D1	10d. red and green	75·00	£100
D3	D1	1s. red and green	70·00	95·00
D4	D1	2s. red and green	£120	£150

D2

1902

D18	D2	½d. red and green	2·75	3·00
D30	D2	1d. red and green	3·75	80
D22*a*	D2	2d. red and green	7·50	3·00
D36	D2	3d. red and green	15·00	50·00

D3

1939

D41	D3	½d. green	5·00	5·00
D42	D3	1d. red	3·50	3·75
D43	D3	2d. blue	6·00	2·75
D47aw	D3	3d. brown	9·00	21·00

POSTAL FISCAL STAMPS

F4

1882

F98	F4	2s. blue	65·00	8·00
F99	F4	2s.6d. brown	80·00	9·00
F100	F4	3s. mauve	£160	12·00
F102	F4	5s. green	£170	15·00
F108	F4	10s. brown	£300	27·00
F123	F4	£1 red	£400	90·00

The above are revenue stamps authorised for use as postage stamps as there were no other postage stamps available in these denominations. Other values in this and similar types were mainly used for revenue purposes.

F6 "Arms" Type

1931. Various frames.

F191	F6	1s.3d. yellow	25·00	4·25
F192	F6	1s.3d. yellow and black	9·00	4·25
F193	F6	2s.6d. brown	16·00	1·40
F194	F6	4s. red	35·00	2·00
F195	F6	5s. green	24·00	1·25
F196	F6	6s. red	55·00	3·25
F197	F6	7s. blue	55·00	6·00
F198	F6	7s.6d. grey	85·00	95·00
F153	F6	8s. violet	32·00	35·00
F154	F6	9s. orange	32·00	29·00
F155	F6	10s. red	24·00	10·00
F156	F6	12s.6d. purple	£170	£170
F202	F6	15s. green	80·00	24·00
F203	F6	£1 pink	32·00	3·75
F159	F6	25s. blue	£650	£900
F160	F6	30s. brown	£400	£250
F161	F6	35s. yellow	£5000	£6500
F206w	F6	£2 violet	£180	22·00
F207	F6	£2 10s. red	£450	£475
F208w	F6	£3 green	£250	65·00
F165	F6	£3 10s. red	£2250	£2750
F210	F6	£4 blue	£325	£200
F167	F6	£4 10s. grey	£1800	£2000
F211w	F6	£5 blue	£375	70·00

1939. Surch in bold figures.

F216b		£10 on £10 blue	£1400	£425
F212	F6	3/6 on 3s.6d. green	21·00	8·00
F214	F6	5/6 on 5s.6d. lilac	70·00	27·00
F215	F6	11/- on 11s. yellow	£100	48·00
F216	F6	22/- on 22s. red	£450	£200
F186	F6	35/- on 35s. orange	£800	£400

Pt. 15

NICARAGUA

A republic of Central America, independent since 1821.

1862. 100 centavos = 1 peso (paper currency).
1912. 100 centavos de cordoba = 1 peso de cordoba (gold currency).
1925. 100 centavos = 1 cordoba.
1990. Currency Reform. 150000 (old) cordoba = 1 (new) cordoba

2 Volcanoes

1862. Perf or roul.

13	2	1c. brown	1·80	1·40
4	2	2c. blue	4·00	1·50
14	2	5c. black	3·25	2·00
18	2	10c. red	3·50	2·50
19	2	25c. green	3·50	3·50

5

1882

20	5	1c. green	25	30
21	5	2c. red	25	30
22	5	5c. blue	25	30
23	5	10c. violet	30	85
24	5	15c. yellow	65	17·00
25	5	20c. grey	1·00	4·50
26	5	50c. violet	1·30	9·25

6 Steam Locomotive and Telegraph Key

1890

27	6	1c. brown	20	30
28	6	2c. red	20	30
29	6	5c. blue	20	25
30	6	10c. grey	20	30
31	6	20c. red	20	1·90
32	6	50c. violet	20	5·25
33	6	1p. brown	30	8·00
34	6	2p. green	30	
35	6	5p. red	30	
36	6	10p. orange	30	

7

1891

37	7	1c. brown	35	40
38	7	2c. red	35	40
39	7	5c. blue	35	30
40	7	10c. grey	35	50
41	7	20c. lake	35	2·75
42	7	50c. violet	35	5·25
43	7	1p. sepia	35	5·25
44	7	2p. green	35	9·25
45	7	5p. red	35	
46	7	10p. orange	35	

8 First Sight of the New World

1892. Discovery of America.

47	8	1c. brown	35	40
48	8	2c. red	35	30
49	8	5c. blue	35	30
50	8	10c. grey	35	30
51	8	20c. red	35	3·00
52	8	50c. violet	35	7·75
53	8	1p. brown	35	7·75
54	8	2p. green	35	9·25
55	8	5p. red	35	
56	8	10p. orange	35	

9 Volcanoes

1893

57	9	1c. brown	35	30
58	9	2c. red	35	30
59	9	5c. blue	35	30
60	9	10c. grey	35	30
61	9	20c. brown	35	2·40
62	9	50c. violet	35	4·75
63	9	1p. brown	35	7·25
64	9	2p. green	35	9·25
65	9	5p. red	35	
66	9	10p. orange	35	

10

1894

67	10	1c. brown	35	20
68	10	2c. red	35	30
69	10	5c. blue	35	20
70	10	10c. grey	35	30
71	10	20c. red	35	2·50
72	10	50c. violet	35	5·00
73	10	1p. brown	35	7·25
74	10	2p. green	35	13·00
75	10	5p. brown	35	16·00
76	10	10p. orange	35	

11

1895

77	11	1c. brown	25	30
78	11	2c. red	25	30
79	11	5c. blue	25	30
80	11	10c. grey	25	30
81	11	20c. red	25	3·25
82	11	50c. violet	25	5·25
83	11	1p. brown	25	5·25
84	11	2p. green	25	8·25
85	11	5p. red	25	11·50
86	11	10p. orange	25	

12 Map of Nicaragua

1896. Date "1896".

90A	12	1c. violet	35	1·00
91A	12	2c. green	35	50
92A	12	5c. red	35	30
93A	12	10c. blue	60	50
94A	12	20c. brown	3·50	4·25
95A	12	50c. grey	70	8·25
96A	12	1p. black	95	11·50
97A	12	2p. red	95	16·00
98A	12	5p. blue	1·10	18·00

1897. As T **12**, dated "1897".

99A		1c. violet	60	50
100A		2c. green	60	50
101A		5c. red	60	30
102A		10c. blue	6·75	85
103A		20c. brown	3·00	4·00
104A		50c. grey	9·50	9·75
105A		1p. black	9·50	14·00
106A		2p. red	21·00	20·00
107A		5p. blue	21·00	43·00

13 Arms of Republic of Central America

1898

108	13	1c. brown	30	40
109	13	2c. grey	30	40
110	13	4c. lake	30	50
122	13	5c. olive	26·00	50
112	13	10c. purple	16·00	60
113	13	15c. blue	40	1·50
114	13	20c. blue	10·50	2·00
115	13	50c. yellow	10·50	10·00
116	13	1p. blue	40	16·00
117	13	2p. brown	20·00	22·00
118	13	5p. orange	26·00	32·00

14

1899

126	14	1c. green	20	40
127	14	2c. brown	20	30
128	14	4c. red	40	40
129	14	5c. blue	20	30
130	14	10c. orange	20	30
131	14	15c. brown	20	70
132	14	20c. green	40	80
133	14	50c. red	20	3·00
134	14	1p. orange	30	9·00
135	14	2p. violet	30	20·00
136	14	5p. blue	30	25·00

15 Mt. Momotombo

1900

137	15	1c. red	50	20
138	15	2c. orange	50	20
139	15	3c. green	85	30
140	15	4c. olive	1·00	30
184	15	5c. red	50	25
185	15	5c. blue	50	25
142	15	6c. red	14·50	5·00
186	15	10c. mauve	1·60	20
144	15	15c. blue	8·25	70
145	15	20c. brown	8·25	70
146	15	50c. lake	7·25	1·10
147	15	1p. yellow	12·50	4·00
148	15	2p. red	10·50	2·40
149	15	5p. black	10·50	3·00

1901. Surch **1901** and value.

151	15	2c. on 1p. yellow	5·25	3·00
169	15	3c. on 6c. red	6·25	4·50
163	15	4c. on 6c. red	5·25	4·00
173	15	5c. on 1p. yellow	7·75	6·50
152	15	10c. on 5p. black	6·75	4·50
168	15	10c. on 2p. red	5·75	4·00
153	15	20c. on 2p. red	7·75	7·50
176	15	20c. on 5p. black	5·25	3·50

1901. Postage Due stamps of 1900 optd **1901 Correos.**

177	D16	1c. red	1·00	40
178	D16	2c. orange	85	40
179	D16	5c. blue	1·00	60
180	D16	10c. violet	1·30	1·10
181	D16	20c. brown	1·30	1·30
182	D16	30c. green	1·00	1·10
183	D16	50c. lake	1·00	1·10

1902. Surch **1902** and value.

187	15	15c. on 2c. orange	2·10	80
188	15	30c. on 1c. red	1·00	2·20

27 Pres. Santos Zelaya

1903. Tenth Anniv of Revolution against Sacaza and First election of Pres. Zelaya.

189	27	1c. black and green	40	50
190	27	2c. black and red	70	50
191	27	5c. black and blue	40	50
192	27	10c. black and orange	40	90
193	27	15c. black and lake	60	2·00
194	27	20c. black and violet	60	2·00
195	27	50c. black and olive	60	5·00
196	27	1p. black and brown	60	6·00

1904. Surch **15 Centavos.**

200	15	15c. on 10c. mauve	4·25	2·50

1904. Surch **Vale**, value and wavy lines.

203	15	5c. on 10c. mauve	1·90	30
204		15c. on 10c. mauve	30	30

1905. No. 186 surch **5 CENTS**.

205	5c. on 10c. mauve	60	40

37 Arms

1905

206	**37**	1c. green	30	20
207	**37**	2c. red	30	20
208	**37**	3c. violet	40	30
280	**37**	3c. orange	40	20
209	**37**	4c. orange	40	30
281	**37**	4c. violet	40	20
282	**37**	5c. blue	40	20
211	**37**	6c. grey	60	40
283	**37**	6c. brown	3·00	1·50
212	**37**	10c. brown	95	30
284	**37**	10c. lake	95	20
213	**37**	15c. olive	85	40
285	**37**	15c. black	95	20
214	**37**	20c. lake	60	40
286	**37**	20c. olive	95	20
215	**37**	50c. orange	3·00	1·50
287	**37**	50c. green	1·30	40
216	**37**	1p. black	1·60	1·50
288	**37**	1p. yellow	1·30	40
217	**37**	2p. green	1·60	2·00
289	**37**	2p. red	1·30	40
218	**37**	5p. violet	1·90	2·50

1906. Surch **Vale** (or **VALE**) and value in one line.

292	2c. on 3c. orange	1·60	1·30
293	5c. on 20c. olive	40	30
247A	10c. on 2c. red	1·60	50
223B	10c. on 3c. violet	4·75	4·50
248A	10c. on 4c. orange	1·60	30
291B	10c. on 15c. black	1·30	30
250B	10c. on 20c. lake	2·40	90
252A	10c. on 50c. orange	2·10	1·60
234	10c. on 2p. green	21·00	13·00
235	10c. on 5p. violet	£100	70·00
226B	15c. on 1c. green	30	20
229A	20c. on 2c. red	60	30
230A	20c. on 5c. blue	70	50
236	35c. on 6c. grey	3·00	2·20
232A	50c. on 6c. grey	30	50
238	1p. on 5p. violet	43·00	25·00

51

1908. Fiscal stamps as T **51** optd **CORREO–1908** or surch **VALE** and value also.

260	**51**	1c. on 5c. yellow	40	30
261	**51**	2c. on 5c. yellow	50	30
262	**51**	4c. on 5c. yellow	70	40
256	**51**	5c. yellow	60	40
257	**51**	10c. blue	50	30
263	**51**	15c. on 50c. green	60	40
264	**51**	35c. on 50c. green	4·25	1·00
258	**51**	1p. brown	50	2·00
259	**51**	2p. grey	50	2·50

50

1908. Fiscal stamps as T **50** optd **CORREOS–1908** or surch **VALE** and value also.

268	**50**	2c. orange	3·50	2·00
269	**50**	4c. on 2c. orange	1·90	90
270	**50**	5c. on 2c. orange	1·60	60
271	**50**	10c. on 2c. orange	1·60	30

1909. Surch **CORREOS–1909 VALE** and value.

273	**51**	1c. on 50c. green	4·25	1·60
274	**51**	2c. on 50c. green	7·25	3·00
275	**51**	4c. on 50c. green	7·25	3·00
276	**51**	5c. on 50c. green	4·25	1·80
277	**51**	10c. on 50c. green	1·10	80

1910. Surch **Vale** and value in two lines.

296	**37**	2c. on 3c. orange	95	50
300	**37**	2c. on 4c. violet	30	20
301	**37**	5c. on 20c. olive	30	20
302	**37**	10c. on 15c. black	40	20
303	**37**	10c. on 50c. green	30	20
299	**37**	10c. on 1p. yellow	95	40
305	**37**	10c. on 2p. red	60	50

1911. Surch **Correos 1911** (or **CORREOS 1911**) and value.

307	**51**	2c. on 5p. blue	40	40
312	**51**	5c. on 2p. grey	1·60	1·00
308	**51**	5c. on 10p. pink	85	40
309	**51**	10c. on 25c. lilac	40	30
310	**51**	10c. on 2p. grey	40	30
311	**51**	35c. on 1p. brown	40	30

1911. Surch **VALE POSTAL de 1911** and value.

313	5c. on 25c. lilac	1·60	1·30
314	5c. on 50c. green	5·25	5·00
315	5c. on 5p. blue	7·25	7·00
317	5c. on 50p. red	5·25	5·00
318	10c. on 50c. green	1·60	50

64

1911. Railway tickets as T **64**, with fiscal surch on the front, further surch for postal use. (a) Surch **vale CORREO DE 1911** and value on back.

319	**64**	2c. on 5c. on 2nd class blue	30	30
320	**64**	05c. on 5c. on 2nd class blue	30	30
321	**64**	10c. on 5c. on 2nd class blue	30	30
322	**64**	15c. on 10c. on 1st class red	40	40

(b) Surch vale **CORREO DE 1911** and value on front.

322c	2c. on 5c. on 2nd class blue	6·25	6·00
322d	05c. on 5c. on 2nd class blue	£160	£160
322e	10c. on 5c. on 2nd class blue	60·00	80·00
322f	15c. on 10c. on 1st class red	16·00	16·00

(c) Surch **CORREO** and value on front.

323	2c. on 10c. on 1st class red	1·60	1·50
324	20c. on 10c. on 1st class red	5·75	5·00
325	50c. on 10c. on 1st class red	10·50	10·00

(d) Surch **Correo Vale 1911** and value on front.

326	2c. on 10c. on 1st class red	30	30
328	5c. on 5c. on 2nd class blue	1·40	1·30
327	5c. on 10c. on 1st class red	30	30
330	10c. on 10c. on 1st class red	1·60	1·20

(e) Surch Vale **CORREO DE 1911** and value on back.

331a	5c. on 10c. on 1st class red	21·00	
332	10c. on 10c. on 1st class red	13·50	

(f) Surch **CORREO Vale 10 cts. 1911** and bar obliterating oficial on front.

333	10c. on 10c. on 1st class red	1·20	1·00

70

71

1912

337	**70**	1c. green	40	20
338	**70**	2c. red	50	20
339	**70**	3c. brown	40	20
340	**70**	4c. purple	40	20
341	**70**	5c. black and blue	30	20
342	**70**	6c. brown	40	1·20
343	**70**	10c. brown	30	20
344	**70**	15c. violet	30	20
345	**70**	20c. brown	30	20
346	**70**	25c. black and green	40	20
347	**71**	35c. brown and green	2·50	1·80
348	**70**	50c. blue	1·30	50
349	**70**	1p. orange	1·80	2·50
350	**70**	2p. green	1·90	3·00
351	**70**	5p. black	4·75	4·50

1913. Surch **Vale 15 cts Correos 1913**.

352	**71**	15c. on 35c. brown & green	40	30

1913. Surch **VALE 1913** and value in "centavos de cordoba". A. On stamps of 1912 issue.

353	**70**	½c. on 3c. brown	50	40
354	**70**	½c. on 15c. violet	30	20
355	**70**	½c. on 1p. orange	30	30
356	**70**	1c. on 3c. brown	85	60
357	**70**	1c. on 4c. purple	30	20
358	**70**	1c. on 50c. blue	30	20
359	**70**	1c. on 5p. black	30	20
360	**70**	2c. on 4c. purple	40	30
361	**70**	2c. on 20c. brown	4·25	5·00
362	**70**	2c. on 25c. black & green	40	20
363	**71**	2c. on 35c. brown & green	30	50
364	**70**	2c. on 50c. blue	30	20
365	**70**	2c. on 2p. green	20	20
366	**70**	3c. on 6c. brown	20	20

B. On Silver Currency stamps of 1912 (Locomotive type).

367	**Z1**	½c. on 2c. red	60	50
368	**Z1**	1c. on 3c. brown	50	30
369	**Z1**	1c. on 4c. red	50	30
370	**Z1**	1c. on 6c. red	40	20
371	**Z1**	1c. on 20c. blue	50	20
372	**Z1**	1c. on 25c. black & green	50	30
384	**Z1**	2c. on 1c. green	7·75	1·50
373	**Z1**	2c. on 25c. black & green	4·00	5·00
374	**Z1**	5c. on 35c. black & green	50	40
375	**Z1**	5c. on 50c. olive	50	40
376	**Z1**	6c. on 1p. orange	50	20
377	**Z1**	10c. on 2p. brown	50	40
378	**Z1**	1p. on 5p. green	40	40

1914. No. 352 surch with new value and Cordoba and thick bar over old surch.

385	**71**	½c. on 15c. on 35c.	30	20
386	**71**	1c. on 15c. on 35c.	30	20

1914. Official stamps of 1913 surch with new value and thick bar through "OFICIAL".

387	**70**	1c. on 25c. blue	50	30
388	**71**	1c. on 35c. blue	40	30
389	**70**	1c. on 1p. blue	30	20
391	**70**	2c. on 50c. blue	40	20
392	**70**	2c. on 2p. blue	40	20
393	**70**	5c. on 5p. blue	30	20

79 National Palace, Managua

80 Leon Cathedral

1914. Various frames.

394	**79**	½c. blue	85	20
395	**79**	1c. green	85	20
396	**80**	2c. orange	85	20
397	**79**	3c. brown	1·30	30
398	**80**	4c. red	1·30	40
399	**79**	5c. grey	50	20
400	**80**	6c. sepia	9·25	6·00
401	**80**	10c. yellow	95	20
402	**79**	15c. violet	6·25	2·00
403	**80**	20c. grey	11·50	6·00
404	**79**	25c. orange	1·60	50
405	**80**	50c. blue	1·40	40

See also Nos. 465/72, 617/27 and 912/24.

1915. Surch **VALE 5 cts. de Cordoba 1915**.

406	5c. on 6c. sepia	1·60	40

1918. Stamps of 1914 surch **Vale centavos de cordoba**.

407	**80**	½c. on 6c. sepia	4·25	1·50
408	**80**	½c. on 10c. yellow	2·50	30
409	**79**	½c. on 15c. violet	2·50	60
410	**79**	½c. on 25c. orange	5·25	2·00
411	**80**	½c. on 50c. blue	2·50	30
440	**80**	1c. on 2c. orange	1·60	30
413	**79**	1c. on 3c. brown	3·00	30
414	**80**	1c. on 6c. sepia	13·50	5·00
415	**80**	1c. on 10c. yellow	25·00	8·00
416	**79**	1c. on 15c. violet	4·75	80
418	**80**	1c. on 20c. grey	2·50	30
420	**79**	1c. on 25c. orange	4·75	1·00
421	**80**	1c. on 50c. blue	14·50	4·50
422	**80**	2c. on 4c. red	2·50	30
423	**80**	2c. on 6c. sepia	25·00	8·00
424	**80**	2c. on 10c. yellow	25·00	5·00
425	**80**	2c. on 20c. grey	13·50	3·50
426	**79**	2c. on 25c. orange	5·75	40
427	**80**	5c. on 6c. sepia	10·50	4·50
428	**79**	5c. on 15c. violet	3·50	60

1919. Official stamps of 1915 surch **Vale centavo de cordoba** and with bar through "OFICIAL".

444	**80**	½c. on 2c. blue	50	20
445	**80**	½c. on 4c. blue	1·30	20
446	**79**	1c. on 3c. blue	1·30	30
432	**79**	1c. on 25c. blue	1·60	30
433	**80**	2c. on 50c. blue	1·60	30
443a	**80**	10c. on 20c. blue	1·40	40

1921. Official stamps of 1913 optd **Particular** and wavy lines through "OFICIAL".

441	**70**	1c. blue	1·60	60
442	**70**	5c. blue	1·60	40

1921. No. 399 surch **Vale medio centavo**.

447	**79**	½c. on 5c. black	85	80

1921. Official stamp of 1915 optd **Particular R de C** and bars.

448	**79**	1c. blue	6·75	3·00

1921. Official stamps of 1915 surch **Vale un centavo R de C** and bars.

449	**79**	1c. on 5c. blue	1·80	70
450	**80**	1c. on 6c. blue	85	30
451	**80**	1c. on 10c. blue	1·20	30
452	**79**	1c. on 15c. blue	2·10	30

90

1921. Fiscal stamps as T **23** surch **R de C Vale** and new value.

453	**90**	1c. on 1c. red and black	20	20
454	**90**	1c. on 2c. green and black	20	20
455	**90**	1c. on 4c. orange and black	20	20
456	**90**	1c. on 15c. blue and black	20	20

No. 456 is inscr "TIMBRE TELEGRAFICO".

1921. Independence Centenary.

457	-	½c. black and blue	1·00	1·00
458	**91**	1c. black and green	1·00	1·00
459	-	2c. black and red	1·00	1·00
460	-	5c. black and violet	1·00	1·00
461	-	10c. black and orange	1·00	1·00
462	-	25c. black and yellow	1·00	1·00
463	-	50c. black and violet	1·00	1·00

DESIGNS: ½c. Arce; 2c. Larreinaga; 5c. F. Chamorro; 10c. Jerez; 25c. J. P. Chamorro; 50c. Dario.

1922. Surch **Vale un centavo R. de C.**

464	**80**	1c. on 10c. yellow	30	30

1922. As Nos. 394, etc, but colours changed.

465	**79**	½c. green	20	20
466	**79**	1c. violet	20	20
467	**80**	2c. red	20	20
468	**79**	3c. olive	20	20
469	**80**	6c. brown	20	20
470	**79**	15c. brown	50	20
471	**80**	20c. brown	70	20
472	**80**	1cor. brown	1·20	50

Nos. 465/72 are size 27×22¾ mm.

For later issues of these types, see Nos. 617/27 and 912/24.

1922. Optd **R. de C.**

473	**79**	1c. violet	30	20

91 Jose C. del Valle

1922. Independence issue of 1921 surch **R. de C. Vale un centavo**.

474	**91**	1c. on 1c. black and green	1·00	1·00
475	-	1c. on 5c. black and violet	1·00	1·00
476	-	1c. on 10c. black and orange	1·00	60
477	-	1c. on 25c. black and yellow	1·00	50
478	-	1c. on 50c. black and violet	50	30

94

1922. Surch **Nicaragua R. de C. Vale un cent.**

479	**94**	1c. yellow	20	20
480	**94**	1c. mauve	20	20
481	**94**	1c. blue	20	20

1922. Surch **Vale 0.01 de Cordoba** in two lines.

482	**80**	1c. on 10c. yellow	1·00	40
483	**80**	2c. on 10c. yellow	1·00	30

1923. Surch **Vale 2 centavos de cordoba** in three lines.

484	**79**	1c. on 5c. black	1·30	20
485	**80**	2c. on 10c. yellow	1·30	20

1923. Optd **Sello Postal**.

486	-	½c. black and blue (No. 457)	7·75	7·50
487	**91**	1c. black and green	2·50	90

1923. Independence issue of 1921 surch **R. de C. Vale un centavo de cordoba**.

488	1c. on 2c. black and red	70	70
489	1c. on 5c. black and violet	85	20

No.	Type	Description	Unused	Used
490		1c. on 10c. black and orange	30	30
491		1c. on 25c. black and yellow	40	40
492		1c. on 50c. black and violet	30	20

1923. Fiscal stamp optd **R. de C.**

No.	Type	Description	Unused	Used
493	90	1c. red and black	20	20

1924. Optd **R. de C. 1924** in two lines.

No.	Type	Description	Unused	Used
494	79	1c. violet	20	20

99 F. Hernandez de Cordoba

1924. 400th Anniv of Foundation of Leon and Granada.

No.	Type	Description	Unused	Used
495	99	1c. green	1·60	30
496	99	2c. red	1·60	30
497	99	5c. blue	1·00	30
498	99	10c. brown	1·00	40

1925. Optd **R. de C. 1925** in two lines.

No.	Type	Description	Unused	Used
499	79	1c. violet	30	30

1927. Optd **Resello 1927**.

No.	Type	Description	Unused	Used
525	79	½c. green	30	20
528	79	1c. violet (No. 466)	20	20
555	79	1c. violet (No. 473)	30	30
532	80	2c. red	20	20
533	79	3c. green	30	20
537	80	4c. red	32·00	23·00
539	79	5c. grey	1·00	30
542	80	6c. brown	13·50	11·00
543	80	10c. yellow	30	20
545	79	15c. brown	85	30
547	80	20c. brown	50	30
549	79	25c. orange	85	30
551	80	50c. blue	40	20
553	80	1cor. brown	1·30	40

1928. Optd **Resello 1928**.

No.	Type	Description	Unused	Used
559	79	½c. green	30	20
560	79	1c. violet	20	20
561	80	2c. red	20	20
562	79	3c. green	40	15
563	80	4c. red	40	20
564	79	5c. grey	20	20
565	80	6c. brown	20	20
566	80	10c. yellow	30	20
567	79	15c. brown	40	20
568	80	20c. brown	50	30
569	79	25c. orange	85	30
570	80	50c. blue	1·30	20
571	80	1cor. brown	1·30	40

1928. Optd **Correos 1928**.

No.	Type	Description	Unused	Used
574	79	½c. green	30	20
575	79	1c. violet	20	10
576	79	3c. olive	75	25
577	80	4c. red	35	20
578	79	5c. grey	30	20
579	80	6c. brown	45	20
580	80	10c. yellow	55	25
581	79	15c. brown	1·80	25
582	80	20c. brown	1·90	25
583	79	25c. orange	1·90	25
584	80	50c. blue	1·90	25
585	80	1cor. brown	4·75	2·20

1928. No. 577 surch **Vale 2 cts.**

No.	Type	Description	Unused	Used
586		2c. on 4c. red	1·20	35

1928. Fiscal stamp as T 90, but inscr "TIMBRE TELEGRAFICO" and surch **Correos 1928 Vale** and new value.

No.	Type	Description	Unused	Used
587	90	1c. on 5c. blue and black	30	20
588	90	2c. on 5c. blue and black	30	20
589	90	3c. on 5c. blue and black	30	20

1928. Obligatory Tax. No. 587 additionally optd **R. de T.**

No.	Type	Description	Unused	Used
590		1c. on 5c. blue and black	65	25

1928. As Nos. 465/72 but colours changed.

No.	Type	Description	Unused	Used
591	79	½c. red	40	20
592	79	1c. orange	40	20
593	80	2c. green	40	20
594	79	3c. purple	40	25
595	80	4c. brown	40	25
596	79	5c. yellow	40	20
597	80	6c. blue	40	25
598	80	10c. blue	85	25
599	79	15c. red	1·30	45
600	80	20c. green	1·30	45
601	79	25c. purple	26·00	5·50
602	80	50c. brown	3·25	90
603	80	1cor. violet	6·00	2·75

See also Nos. 617/27 and 912/24.

106

1928

No.	Type	Description	Unused	Used
604	106	1c. purple	35	25
647	106	1c. red	35	25

For 1c. green see No. 925.

1929. Optd **R. de C.**

No.	Type	Description	Unused	Used
605	79	1c. orange	30	20
628	79	1c. olive	30	20

1929. Optd **Correos 1929**.

No.	Type	Description	Unused	Used
606		½c. green	30	20

1929. Optd **Correos 1928.**

No.	Type	Description	Unused	Used
607	99	10c. brown	75	55

1929. Fiscal stamps as T 90, but inscr **"TIMBRE TELEGRAFICO"**. A. Surch **Correos 1929 R. de C. C$ 0.01** vert.

No.	Type	Description	Unused	Used
613	90	1c. on 5c. blue and black	30	20

B. Surch **Correos 1929** and value.

No.	Type	Description	Unused	Used
611		1c. on 10c. green and black	30	20
612		2c. on 5c. blue and black	30	20

C. Surch **Correos 1929** and value vert and **R. de C. or R. de T.** horiz.

No.	Type	Description	Unused	Used
608		1c. on 5c. blue and black (R. de T.)	30	20
609		2c. on 5c. blue and black (R. de T.)	20	20
610		2c. on 5c. blue and black (R. de C.)	23·00	1·30

1929. Air. Optd **Correo Aereo 1929. P.A.A.**

No.	Type	Description	Unused	Used
614	79	25c. sepia	2·00	2·00
615	79	25c. orange	1·70	1·60
616	79	25c. violet	1·20	70

1929. As Nos. 591/603 but colours changed.

No.	Type	Description	Unused	Used
617	79	1c. green	20	20
618	79	3c. blue	30	20
619	80	4c. blue	35	20
620	79	5c. brown	35	20
621	80	6c. drab	50	35
622	80	10c. brown	55	20
623	79	15c. red	90	25
624	80	20c. orange	1·40	45
625	79	25c. violet	30	20
626	80	50c. green	50	20
627	80	1cor. yellow	4·00	1·20

See also Nos. 912/24.

112 Mt. Momotombo

1929. Air.

No.	Type	Description	Unused	Used
629	112	15c. purple	20	20
630	112	20c. green	35	35
631	112	25c. olive	45	35
632	112	50c. sepia	75	70
633	112	1cor. red	95	90

See also Nos. 926/30.

1930. Air. Surch **Vale** and value.

No.	Type	Description	Unused	Used
634		15c. on 25c. olive	45	35
635		20c. on 25c. olive	75	70

114 G.P.O. Managua

1930. Opening of the G.P.O., Managua.

No.	Type	Description	Unused	Used
636	114	½c. sepia	1·40	1·30
637	114	1c. red	1·40	1·30
638	114	2c. orange	95	90
639	114	3c. orange	1·90	1·80
640	114	4c. yellow	1·90	1·80
641	114	5c. olive	2·75	2·75
642	114	6c. green	2·75	2·75
643	114	10c. black	3·00	2·75
644	114	25c. blue	6·00	5·75
645	114	50c. blue	9·25	9·00
646	114	1cor. violet	28·00	27·00

1931. Optd **1931** and thick bar obliterating old overprint "1928".

No.	Type	Description	Unused	Used
648	99	10c. brown (No. 607)	75	1·80

1931. No. 607 surch **C$ 0.02.**

No.	Type	Description	Unused	Used
649		2c. on 10c. brown	60	1·10

1931. Optd **1931** and thick bar.

No.	Type	Description	Unused	Used
650		2c. on 10c. brown (No. 498)	75	2·10

1931. Air. Nos. 614/16 surch **1931** Vale and value.

No.	Type	Description	Unused	Used
651	79	15c. on 25c. sepia	£160	£150
652	79	15c. on 25c. orange	60·00	60·00
653	79	15c. on 25c. violet	16·00	16·00
654	79	20c. on 25c. violet	9·25	9·00

1931. Optd **1931.**

No.	Type	Description	Unused	Used
656	79	½c. green	35	20
657	79	1c. olive	35	20
665	79	1c. orange (No. 605)	30	20
658	80	2c. red	35	20
659	79	3c. blue	35	20
660	79	5c. yellow	3·75	2·75
661	79	5c. sepia	1·20	45
662	79	15c. orange	1·30	55
663	79	25c. sepia	12·00	7·25
664	79	25c. violet	4·50	3·00

1931. Air. Surch **1931** and value.

No.	Type	Description	Unused	Used
666	80	15c. on 20c. on 25c. olive (No. 635)	9·75	9·25
667	80	15c. on 25c. olive	6·25	6·00
668	80	15c. on 50c. sepia	55·00	55·00
669	80	15c. on 1cor. red	95·00	90·00

120 G.P.O. before and after the Earthquake

1932. G.P.O. Reconstruction Fund.

No.	Type	Description	Unused	Used
670	120	½c. green (postage)	1·80	1·70
671	120	1c. brown	2·20	2·10
672	120	2c. red	1·80	1·70
673	120	3c. blue	1·80	1·70
674	120	4c. blue	1·80	1·70
675	120	5c. brown	2·20	2·10
676	120	6c. brown	2·20	2·10
677	120	10c. brown	3·75	2·75
678	120	15c. red	5·25	3·00
679	120	20c. orange	3·75	3·75
680	120	25c. violet	3·75	3·75
681	120	50c. green	3·75	3·75
682	120	1cor. yellow	7·50	7·25
683	120	15c. mauve (air)	1·80	1·70
684	120	20c. green	2·00	2·00
685	120	25c. brown	7·00	6·75
686	120	50c. brown	9·25	8·75
687	120	1cor. red	14·50	14·00

1932. Air. Surch **Vale** and value.

No.	Type	Description	Unused	Used
688	112	30c. on 50c. sepia	1·50	1·50
689	112	35c. on 50c. sepia	1·50	1·50
690	112	40c. on 1cor. red	1·70	1·60
691	112	55c. on 1cor. red	1·70	1·60

For similar surcharges on these stamps in different colours see Nos. 791/4 and 931/4.

1932. Air. International Air Mail Week. Optd **Semana Correo Aereo Internacional 11–17 Septiembre 1932.**

No.	Type	Description	Unused	Used
692		15c. violet	75·00	70·00

1932. Air. Inauguration of Inland Airmail Service. Surch **Inauguracion Interior 12 Octubre 1932 Vale C$0.08.**

No.	Type	Description	Unused	Used
693		8c. on 1cor. red	20·00	20·00

1932. Air. Optd **Interior–1932** or surch **Vale** and value also.

No.	Type	Description	Unused	Used
705	120	25c. brown	9·25	9·00
706	120	32c. on 50c. brown	9·25	9·00
707	120	40c. on 1cor. red	7·50	7·25

1932. Air. Nos. 671, etc, optd **Correo Aereo Interior** in one line and **1932**, or surch **Vale** and value also.

No.	Type	Description	Unused	Used
694		1c. brown	21·00	20·00
695		2c. red	19·00	18·00
696		3c. blue	9·25	9·00
697		4c. blue	10·00	9·75
698		5c. brown	9·25	9·00
699		6c. brown	9·25	9·00
700		8c. on 10c. brown	9·25	9·00
701		16c. on 20c. orange	9·25	9·00
702		24c. on 25c. violet	9·25	9·00
703		50c. green	9·25	9·00
704		1cor. yellow	9·25	9·00

1932. Air. Surch **Correo Aereo Interior–1932** in two lines and **Vale** and value below.

No.	Type	Description	Unused	Used
710	80	1c. on 2c. red	2·30	2·20
711	79	2c. on 3c. blue	2·30	2·20
712	80	3c. on 4c. blue	2·30	2·20
713	79	4c. on 5c. sepia	2·30	2·20
714	80	5c. on 6c. brown	2·30	2·20
715	80	6c. on 10c. brown	2·30	2·20
716	79	8c. on 15c. orange	2·30	2·20
717	80	16c. on 20c. orange	2·30	2·20
718	79	24c. on 25c. violet	4·75	4·50
719	79	25c. on 25c. violet	4·75	4·50
720	80	32c. on 50c. green	4·75	4·50
721	80	40c. on 50c. green	4·75	4·50
722	80	50c. on 1cor. yellow	1·60	1·60
723	80	100c. on 1cor. yellow	2·30	2·20

127 Wharf, Port San Jorge

128 La Chocolata Cutting

1932. Opening of Rivas Railway.

No.	Type	Description	Unused	Used
726	127	1c. yellow (postage)	15·00	
727	-	2c. red	15·00	
728	-	5c. sepia	15·00	
729	-	10c. brown	15·00	
730	-	15c. yellow	15·00	
731	128	15c. violet (air)	19·00	
732	-	20c. green	19·00	
733	-	25c. brown	19·00	
734	-	50c. sepia	19·00	
735	-	1cor. red	19·00	

DESIGNS—HORIZ: 2c. El Nacascolo Halt; 5c. Rivas Station; 10c. San Juan del Sur; 15c. (No. 730), Arrival platform at Rivas; 20c. El Nacascolo; 25c. La Cuesta cutting; 50c. San Juan del Sur quay; 1cor. El Estero.

1932. Surch **Vale** and value in words.

No.	Type	Description	Unused	Used
736	79	1c. on 3c. blue	35	15
737	80	2c. on 4c. blue	30	15

130 Railway Construction

1932. Opening of Leon–Sauce Railway.

No.	Type	Description	Unused	Used
739	-	1c. yellow (postage)	15·00	
740	-	2c. red	15·00	
741	-	5c. sepia	15·00	
742	130	10c. brown	15·00	
743	-	15c. yellow	15·00	
744	-	15c. violet (air)	19·00	
745	-	20c. green	19·00	
746	-	25c. brown	19·00	
747	-	50c. sepia	19·00	
748	-	1cor. red	19·00	

DESIGNS—HORIZ: 1c. El Sauce; 2c., 15c. (No. 744), Bridge at Santa Lucia; 5c. Santa Lucia; 15c. (No. 743), Santa Lucia cutting; 20c. Santa Lucia River Halt; 25c. Malpaicillo Station; 50c. Railway panorama; 1cor. San Andres.

1933. Surch **Resello 1933 Vale** and value in words.

No.	Type	Description	Unused	Used
749	79	1c. on 3c. blue	20	20
750	79	1c. on 5c. sepia	20	20
751	80	2c. on 10c. brown	20	20

133 Flag of the Race

1933. 441st Anniv of Columbus' Departure from Palos. Roul.

No.	Type	Description	Unused	Used
753	133	½c. green (postage)	1·70	1·60
754	133	1c. green	1·40	1·30
755	133	2c. red	1·40	1·30
756	133	3c. red	1·40	1·30
757	133	4c. orange	1·40	1·30
758	133	5c. yellow	1·70	1·60
759	133	10c. brown	1·90	1·80
760	133	15c. brown	1·90	1·80
761	133	20c. blue	1·90	1·80
762	133	25c. blue	1·90	1·80
763	133	30c. violet	4·75	4·50
764	133	50c. purple	4·75	4·50
765	133	1cor. brown	4·75	4·50
766	133	1c. brown (air)	1·40	1·30
767	133	2c. purple	1·40	1·30

768	133	4c. violet	2·30	2·20
769	133	5c. blue	2·30	2·20
770	133	6c. blue	2·30	2·20
771	133	8c. brown	1·10	1·10
772	133	15c. brown	1·10	1·10
773	133	20c. yellow	2·30	2·20
774	133	25c. orange	2·30	2·20
775	133	50c. red	2·30	2·20
776	133	1cor. green	11·00	11·00

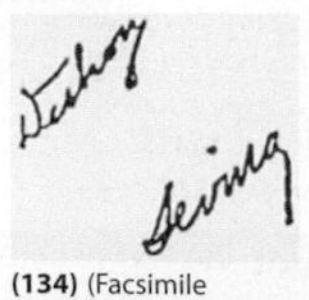

(134) (Facsimile signatures of R. E. Deshon, Minister of Transport and J. R. Sevilla, P.M.G.)

1933. Optd with T **134**.

777	**79**	½c. green	45	20
778	**79**	1c. green	20	10
779	**80**	2c. red	65	20
780	**79**	3c. blue	20	10
781	**80**	4c. blue	30	20
782	**79**	5c. brown	30	10
783	**80**	6c. drab	35	25
784	**80**	10c. brown	35	20
785	**79**	15c. red	45	25
786	**80**	20c. orange	65	45
787	**79**	25c. violet	75	35
788	**80**	50c. green	1·20	70
789	**80**	1cor. yellow	6·50	2·30

1933. No. 605 optd with T **134**.

790	**79**	1c. orange	35	20

1933. Air. Surch **Vale** and value.

791	**112**	30c. on 50c. orange	30	20
792	**112**	35c. on 50c. blue	45	20
793	**112**	40c. on 1cor. yellow	45	20
794	**112**	55c. on 1cor. green	55	20

135 Lake Xolotlan

1933. Air. International Airmail Week.

795	**135**	10c. brown	1·40	1·30
796	**135**	15c. violet	1·40	1·30
797	**135**	25c. red	1·40	1·30
798	**135**	50c. blue	1·40	1·30

(136)

1933. Air. Inland service. Colours changed. Surch as T **136** and optd with T **134**.

799	**80**	1c. on 2c. green	20	10
800	**79**	2c. on 3c. olive	20	10
801	**80**	3c. on 4c. red	20	10
802	**79**	4c. on 5c. blue	20	10
803	**80**	5c. on 6c. blue	20	10
804	**80**	6c. on 10c. sepia	20	10
805	**79**	8c. on 15c. brown	20	20
806	**80**	16c. on 20c. brown	20	20
807	**79**	24c. on 25c. red	20	20
808	**79**	25c. on 25c. orange	20	20
809	**80**	32c. on 50c. violet	20	20
810	**80**	40c. on 50c. green	30	20
811	**80**	50c. on 1cor. yellow	30	20
812	**80**	1cor. on 1cor. red	1·20	90

1933. Obligatory Tax. As No. 647 optd with T **134**. Colour changed.

813	**106**	1c. orange	35	20

1934. Air. Surch **Servicio Centroamericano Vale 10 centavos**.

814	**112**	10c. on 20c. green	35	25
815	**112**	10c. on 25c. olive	30	25

See also No. 872.

1935. Optd **Resello 1935**. (a) Nos. 778/9.

816	**79**	1c. green	20	20
817	**80**	2c. red	20	20

(b) No. 813 but without T **134** opt.

818	**106**	1c. orange	30	20

1935. No. 783 surch **Vale Medio Centavo**.

819	**80**	½c. on 6c. brown	35	20

1935. Optd with T **134** and **RESELLO – 1935** in a box.

820	**79**	½c. green	20	20
821	**80**	½c. on 6c. brown (No. 819)	20	20
822	**79**	1c. green	30	20
823	**80**	2c. red	65	20
824	**80**	2c. red (No. 817)	30	20
825	**79**	3c. blue	30	20
826	**80**	4c. blue	30	20
827	**79**	5c. brown	30	20
828	**80**	6c. drab	30	20
829	**80**	10c. brown	75	20
830	**79**	15c. red	20	20
831	**80**	20c. orange	1·20	20
832	**79**	25c. violet	45	20
833	**80**	50c. green	55	20
834	**80**	1cor. yellow	65	20

1935. Obligatory Tax. No. 605 optd with **RESELLO – 1935** in a box.

835	**79**	1c. orange	95·00	

1935. Obligatory Tax. Optd **RESELLO – 1935** in a box. (a) No. 813 without T **134** opt.

836	**106**	1c. orange	35	20

(b) No. 818.

868		1c. orange	30	20

1935. Air. Nos. 799/812 optd with **RESELLO – 1935** in a box.

839	**80**	1c. on 2c. green	20	20
840	**79**	2c. on 3c. olive	20	20
879	**80**	3c. on 4c. red	20	20
880	**79**	4c. on 5c. blue	20	20
881	**80**	5c. on 6c. blue	20	20
882	**80**	6c. on 10c. sepia	20	20
883	**79**	8c. on 15c. brown	20	20
884	**80**	16c. on 20c. brown	20	20
847	**79**	24c. on 25c. red	45	25
848	**79**	25c. on 25c. orange	30	25
849	**80**	32c. on 50c. violet	20	20
850	**80**	40c. on 50c. green	95	65
851	**80**	50c. on 1cor. yellow	65	25
852	**80**	1cor. on 1cor. red	1·50	90

1935. Air. Optd with **RESELLO – 1935** in a box. (a) Nos. 629/33.

853A	**112**	15c. purple	55	20
873	**112**	20c. green	35	25
855A	**112**	25c. green	65	55
856A	**112**	50c. sepia	65	55
857A	**112**	1cor. red	55	55

(b) Nos. 791/4.

858A		30c. on 50c. orange	65	55
859A		35c. on 50c. blue	65	55
860A		40c. on 1cor. yellow	65	55
861A		55c. on 1cor. green	65	55

(c) Nos. 814/5.

862A		10c. on 20c. green	£550	£500
863A		10c. on 25c. olive	55	45

1935. Optd with **RESELLO – 1935** in a box.

864	**79**	½c. green (No. 465)	20	20
865	**79**	1c. green (No. 617)	20	20
866	**80**	2c. red (No. 467)	60	20
867	**79**	3c. blue (No. 618)	20	20

1936. Surch **Resello 1936 Vale** and value.

869		1c. on 3c. blue (No. 618)	20	20
870		2c. on 5c. brown (No. 620)	20	20

1936. Air. Surch **Servicio Centroamericano Vale diez centavos and RESELLO – 1935** in a box.

871	**112**	10c. on 25c. olive	30	25

1936. Obligatory Tax. No. 818 optd **1936**.

874	**106**	1c. orange	75	25

1936. Obligatory Tax. No. 605 optd with T **134** and **1936**.

875	**79**	1c. orange	75	25

1936. Air. No. 622 optd **Correo Aereo Centro-Americano Resello 1936**.

876	**80**	10c. brown	30	25

1936. Air. Nos. 799/800 and 805 optd **Resello 1936**.

885		1c. on 2c. green	20	20
886	**79**	2c. on 3c. olive	20	20
887	**79**	8c. on 15c. brown	30	25

1936. Optd with or without T **37**, surch **1936 Vale** and value.

888		½c. on 15c. red	20	20
889	**80**	1c. on 4c. blue	30	20
890	**79**	1c. on 5c. brown	30	20
891	**80**	1c. on 6c. drab	35	20
892	**79**	1c. on 15c. red	30	20
893	**80**	1c. on 20c. orange	20	20
895	**80**	2c. on 10c. brown	30	20
896	**79**	2c. on 15c. red	95	70
897	**80**	2c. on 20c. orange	45	25
898	**79**	2c. on 25c. violet	35	20
900	**80**	2c. on 50c. green	35	25
901	**80**	2c. on 1cor. yellow	35	20
902	**80**	3c. on 4c. blue	65	45

1936. Optd **Resello 1936**.

903	**79**	3c. blue (No. 618)	35	20
904	**79**	5c. brown (No. 620)	30	20
905	**80**	10c. brown (No. 784)	45	35

1936. Air. Surch **1936 Vale** and value.

906	**112**	15c. on 50c. brown	20	20
907	**112**	15c. on 1cor. red	20	20

1936. Fiscal stamps surch **RECONSTRUCCION COMUNICACIONES 5 CENTAVOS DE CORDOBA** and further surch **Vale dos centavos Resello 1936**.

908	**90**	1c. on 5c. green	35	20
909	**90**	2c. on 5c. green	35	20

1936. Obligatory Tax. Fiscal stamps surch **RECONSTRUCCION COMUNICACIONES 5 CENTAVOS DE CORDOBA** and further surch. (a) **1936 R. de C. Vale Un Centavo**.

910		1c. on 5c. green	35	25

(b) **Vale un centavo R. de C. 1936**.

911		1c. on 5c. green	45	25

1937. Colours changed. Size 27×22¾ mm.

912	**79**	½c. black	20	20
913	**79**	1c. red	20	20
914	**80**	2c. blue	20	20
915	**79**	3c. brown	20	20
916	**80**	4c. yellow	20	20
917	**79**	5c. red	20	20
918	**80**	6c. violet	20	20
919	**80**	10c. green	20	20
920	**79**	15c. green	20	20
921	**80**	20c. brown	45	20
922	**79**	25c. orange	45	20
923	**80**	50c. brown	45	20
924	**80**	1cor. blue	65	25

1937. Obligatory Tax. Colour changed.

925	**106**	1c. green	30	20

1937. Air. Colours changed.

926	**112**	15c. orange	20	20
927	**112**	20c. red	20	20
928	**112**	25c. black	30	20
929	**112**	50c. violet	30	20
930	**112**	1cor. orange	65	25

1937. Air. Surch **Vale** and value. Colours changed.

931		30c. on 50c. red	30	20
932		35c. on 50c. olive	30	20
933		40c. on 1cor. green	30	20
934		55c. on 1cor. blue	30	20

1937. Air. Surch **Servicio Centroamericano Vale Diez Centavos**.

949		10c. on 1cor. red	30	20

1937. Air. No. 805 (without T **134**) **optd 1937**.

950	**79**	8c. on 15c. brown	45	25

142 Baseball Player

1937. Obligatory Tax. For 1937 Central American Olympic Games. Optd with ball in red under "OLIMPICO".

951	**142**	1c. red	45	20
952	**142**	1c. yellow	45	20
953	**142**	1c. blue	45	20
953a	**142**	1c. green	45	20
MS953b		134×90 mm. Nos. 951/3a	4·75	4·50

1937. Nos. 799/809 optd **Habilitado 1937**.

954	**80**	1c. on 2c. green	20	20
955	**79**	2c. on 3c. olive	20	20
956	**80**	3c. on 4c. red	20	20
957	**79**	4c. on 5c. blue	20	20
958	**80**	5c. on 6c. blue	20	20
959	**80**	6c. on 10c. brown	20	20
960	**79**	8c. on 15c. brown	20	20
961	**80**	16c. on 20c. brown	20	20
962	**79**	24c. on 25c. red	20	20
963	**79**	25c. on 25c. orange	30	20
964	**80**	32c. on 50c. violet	30	25

144 Presidential Palace, Managua

1937. Air. Inland.

965	**144**	1c. red	20	20
966	**144**	2c. blue	20	20
967	**144**	3c. olive	20	20
968	**144**	4c. black	20	20
969	**144**	5c. purple	20	20
970	**144**	6c. brown	20	20
971	**144**	8c. violet	20	20
972	**144**	16c. orange	20	20
973	**144**	24c. yellow	20	20
974	**144**	25c. green	30	20

145 Nicaragua

1937. Air. Abroad.

975	**145**	10c. green	20	20
976	**145**	15c. blue	20	20
977	**145**	20c. yellow	20	20
978	**145**	25c. violet	20	20
979	**145**	30c. red	30	20
980	**145**	50c. orange	35	20
981	**145**	1cor. olive	70	55

146 Presidential Palace

1937. Air. Abroad. 150th Anniv of U.S. Constitution.

982	-	10c. blue and green	1·90	1·10
983	**146**	15c. blue and orange	1·90	1·30
984	-	20c. blue and red	1·10	1·10
985	-	25c. blue and brown	1·10	1·10
986	-	30c. blue and green	1·10	1·10
987	-	35c. blue and yellow	60	60
988	-	40c. blue and green	50	50
989	-	45c. blue and purple	50	45
990	-	50c. blue and mauve	50	45
991	-	55c. blue and green	50	45
992	-	75c. blue and green	50	45
993	-	1cor. red and blue	1·10	60

DESIGNS: 10c. Children's Park, Managua; 20c. S. America; 25c. C. America; 30c. N. America; 35c. Lake Tiscapa; 40c. Pan-American motor-road; 45c. Priniomi Park; 50c. Piedrecitas Park; 55c. San Juan del Sur; 75c Rio Tipitapa; 1cor. Granade landscape.

146b Diriangen

1937. Air. Day of the Race.

993a	**146b**	1c. green (inland)	20	20
993b	**146b**	4c. lake	20	20
993c	**146b**	5c. violet	30	25
993d	**146b**	8c. blue	30	25
993e	**146b**	10c. brown (abroad)	20	20
993f	**146b**	15c. blue	20	20
993g	**146b**	20c. pink	30	25

147 Letter Carrier

1937. 75th Anniv of Postal Administration.

994	**147**	½c. green	20	20
995	-	1c. mauve	20	20
996	-	2c. brown	20	20
997	-	3c. violet	20	20
998	-	5c. blue	20	20
999	-	7½c. red	55	35

DESIGNS: 1c. Mule transport; 2c. Diligence; 3c. Yacht; 5c. Packet steamer; 7½c. Steam mail train.

147a Gen. Tomas Martinez

1938. Air. 75th Anniv of Postal Administration.

999a	**147a**	1c. blk & orge (inland)	25	25
999b	**147a**	5c. black and violet	25	25
999c	**147a**	8c. black and blue	35	35
999d	**147a**	16c. black and brown	35	35
999e	-	10c. blk & grn (abroad)	35	25
999f	-	15c. black and blue	35	35
999g	-	25c. black and violet	50	50
999h	-	50c. black and red	60	60

DESIGNS: 10c. to 50c. Gen. Anastasio Somoza.

1938. Surch **1938 and Vale**, new value in words and Centavos.

1000	79	3c. on 25c. orange	25	25
1001	80	5c. on 50c. brown	35	25
1002	80	6c. on 1 cor. blue	25	25

149 Dario Park

150 Lake Managua

151 President Somoza

1939

1003	149	1½c. green (postage)	25	10
1004	149	2c. red	25	10
1005	149	3c. blue	25	10
1006	149	6c. brown	25	10
1007	149	7½c. green	25	10
1008	149	10c. brown	35	25
1009	149	15c. orange	35	25
1010	149	25c. violet	35	25
1011	149	50c. green	35	35
1012	149	1cor. yellow	75	50
1013	150	2c. blue (air: inland)	25	25
1014	150	3c. olive	25	25
1015	150	8c. mauve	25	25
1016	150	16c. orange	25	25
1017	150	24c. yellow	25	25
1018	150	32c. green	25	25
1019	150	50c. red	25	25
1020	151	10c. brown (air: abroad)	25	25
1021	151	15c. blue	25	25
1022	151	20c. yellow	25	25
1023	151	25c. violet	25	25
1024	151	30c. red	25	25
1025	151	50c. orange	35	25
1026	151	1cor. olive	45	45

1939. Nos. 920/1. Surch **Vale un Centavo 1939**.

1027	79	1c. on 15c. green	25	25
1028	80	1c. on 20c. brown	25	25

153 Will Rogers and Managua Airport

1939. Air. Will Rogers Commemorative. Inscr "WILL ROGERS/1931/1939".

1029	153	1c. green	25	25
1030	-	2c. red	25	25
1031	-	3c. blue	25	25
1032	-	4c. blue	25	25
1033	-	5c. red	25	25

DESIGNS: 2c. Rogers at Managua; 3c. Rogers in P.A.A. hut; 4c. Rogers and U.S. Marines; 5c. Rogers and street in Managua.

156 Senate House and Pres. Somoza

1940. Air. President's Visit to U.S.A. (a) Inscr "AEREO INTERIOR".

1034		4c. brown	25	25
1035	156	8c. brown	25	25
1036	-	16c. green	25	25
1037	156	20c. mauve	60	35
1038	-	32c. red	25	25

(b) Inscr "CORREO AEREO INTERNACIONAL".

1039		25c. blue	25	25
1040		30c. black	25	25
1041	156	50c. red	60	45
1042	-	60c. green	60	35
1043	-	65c. brown	60	35
1044	-	90c. olive	80	35
1045	-	1cor. violet	1·20	70

DESIGNS: 4c., 16c., 25c., 30c., 65c., 90c. Pres. Somoza addressing Senate; 32c., 60c., 1cor. Portrait of Pres. Somoza between symbols of Nicaragua and New York World's Fair.

158 L. S. Rowe, Statue of Liberty and Union Flags

1940. Air. 50th Anniv of Pan-American Union.

1046	158	1cor.25 multicoloured	95	80

159 First Issue of Nicaragua and Sir Rowland Hill

1941. Air. Centenary of First Adhesive Postage stamps.

1047	159	2cor. brown	3·00	1·10
1048	159	3cor. blue	10·00	1·70
1049	159	5cor. red	28·00	4·00

1941. Surch **Servicio ordinario Vale Diez Centavos de Cordoba**.

1050	153	10c. on 1c. green	25	25

161 Rube Dario

1941. 25th Death Anniv of Ruben Dario (poet).

1051	161	10c. red (postage)	45	20
1052	161	20c. mauve (air)	35	20
1053	161	35c. green	40	25
1054	161	40c. orange	45	25
1055	161	60c. blue	80	35

1943. Surch **Servicio Ordinario Vale Diez Centavos**.

1056	153	10c. on 1c. green	4·75	25

162 "V" for Victory

1943. Victory.

1057	162	10c. red and violet (postage)	25	25
1058	162	30c. red and brown	25	25
1059	162	40c. red and green (air)	35	25
1060	162	60c. red and blue	35	25

163 Red Cross

164 Red Cross Workers and Wounded

1944. Air. 80th Anniv of Int Red Cross Society.

1061	163	25c. red	95	45
1062	-	50c. bistre	1·20	70
1063	164	1cor. green	2·30	2·00

DESIGN—VERT: 50c. Two Hemispheres.

165 Columbus and Lighthouse

166 Columbus's Fleet and Lighthouse

1945. Honouring Columbus's Discovery of America and Erection of Columbus Lighthouse near Trujillo City, Dominican Republic.

1064	165	4c. black & green (postage)	25	20
1065	165	6c. black and orange	35	30
1066	165	8c. black and red	45	40
1067	165	10c. black and blue	55	45
1068	166	20c. grey and green (air)	25	20
1069	166	35c. black and red	40	30
1070	166	75c. pink and green	60	45
1071	166	90c. blue and red	95	80
1072	166	1cor. blue and black	1·00	40
1073	166	2cor.50 red and blue	2·40	2·40

168 Roosevelt as a Stamp Collector

1946. President Roosevelt Commemorative Inscr "HOMENAJE A ROOSEVELT".

1074	168	4c. green & black (postage)	20	20
1075	-	8c. violet and black	30	30
1076	-	10c. blue and black	40	40
1077	-	16c. red and black	50	50
1078	-	32c. brown and black	40	40
1079	-	50c. grey and black	40	40
1080	-	25c. orange & black (air)	30	20
1081	-	75c. red and black	40	30
1082	-	1cor. green and black	50	50
1083	-	3cor. violet and black	4·25	4·00
1084	-	5cor. blue and black	6·25	6·00

DESIGNS—portraying Roosevelt. HORIZ: 8c., 25c. with Churchill at the Atlantic Conference; 16c., 1cor. with Churchill, De Gaulle and Giraud at the Casablanca Conference; 32c., 3cor. with Churchill and Stalin at the Teheran Conference. VERT: 10c., 75c. Signing Declaration of War against Japan; 50c., 5cor. Head of Roosevelt.

171 Managua Cathedral

172 G.P.O., Managua

1947. Managua Centenary. Frames in black.

1085	171	4c. red (postage)	20	20
1086	-	5c. blue	30	20
1087	-	6c. green	30	20
1088	-	10c. olive	30	20
1089	-	75c. brown	30	30
1090	-	5c. violet (air)	20	20
1091	172	20c. green	20	20
1092	-	35c. orange	20	20
1093	-	90c. purple	40	30
1094	-	1cor. brown	60	50
1095	-	2cor.50 purple	1·70	1·50

DESIGNS—POSTAGE (as Type **171**): 5c. Health Ministry; 6c. Municipal Building; 10c. College; 75c. G.P.O., Managua. AIR (as Type **172**): 5c. College; 35c. Health Ministry; 90c. National Bank; 1cor. Municipal Building; 2cor.50, National Palace.

173 San Cristobal Volcano

174 Ruben Dario Monument, Managua

1947. (a) Postage.

1096	173	2c. orange and black	20	20
1097	-	3c. violet and black	20	20
1098	-	4c. grey and black	30	20
1099	-	5c. red and black	60	30
1100	-	6c. green and black	30	20
1101	-	8c. brown and black	40	20
1102	-	10c. red and black	60	30
1103	-	20c. blue and black	2·10	50
1104	-	30c. purple and black	1·60	50
1105	-	50c. red and black	3·50	1·00
1106	-	1cor. brown and black	1·20	60

DESIGNS—as Type **173**: 3c. Lion on Ruben Dario's tomb, Leon Cathedral; 4c. Race stand; 5c. Soldiers' Monument; 6c. Sugar cane; 8c. Tropical fruits; 10c. Cotton; 20c. Horses; 30c. Coffee plant; 50c. Prize bullock; 1cor. Agricultural landscape.

(b) Air.

1107	174	5c. red and green	20	20
1108	-	6c. orange and black	20	20
1109	-	8c. brown and red	20	20
1110	-	10c. blue and brown	20	20
1111	-	20c. orange and blue	30	30
1112	-	25c. green and red	40	40
1113	-	35c. brown and black	30	30
1114	-	50c. black and violet	40	30
1115	-	1cor. red and black	85	80
1116	-	1cor.50 green and red	85	80
1117	-	5cor. red and brown	6·75	6·50
1118	-	10cor. brown and violet	5·25	5·00
1119	-	25cor. yellow and green	10·50	10·00

DESIGNS—As Type **174**: 6c. Baird's tapir; 8c. Highway and Lake Managua; 10c. Genizaro Dam; 20c. Ruben Dario Monument, Managua; 25c. Sulphur Lagoon, Nejapa; 35c. Managua Airport; 50c. Mouth of Rio Prinzapolka; 1cor. Thermal Baths, Tipitapa; 1cor.50, Rio Tipitapa; 5cor. Embassy building; 10cor. Girl carrying basket of fruit; 2cor. Franklin D. Roosevelt Monument, Managua.

175 Softball

176 Pole-vaulting

177 Tennis

1949. Tenth World Amateur Baseball Championships. (a) Postage as T **175/6**.

1120	175	1c. brown	20	20
1121	-	2c. blue	85	20
1122	176	3c. green	30	20
1123	-	4c. purple	20	20
1124	-	5c. orange	50	20
1125	-	10c. green	50	20
1126	-	15c. red	85	20
1127	-	25c. blue	85	20
1128	-	35c. green	1·30	30
1129	-	40c. violet	1·90	30
1130	-	60c. black	2·10	40
1131	-	1cor. red	2·50	1·30
1132	-	2cor. purple	4·75	2·50
MS1132a		Thirteen sheets 140×105 or 105×140 mm (vert designs). Nos. 1120/32 in blocks of four	£120	£120

DESIGNS—VERT: 2c. Scout; 5c. Cycling; 25c. Boxing; 35c. Basketball. HORIZ: 4c. Diving; 10c. Stadium; 15c. Baseball; 40c. Yachting; 60c. Table tennis; 1cor. Football; 2cor. Tennis.

(b) Air as T **177**.

1133	177	1c. red	20	20
1134	-	2c. black	20	20
1135	-	3c. red	20	20
1136	-	4c. black	20	20
1137	-	5c. blue	30	20
1138	-	15c. green	95	20
1139	-	25c. purple	2·10	30
1140	-	30c. brown	1·90	30
1141	-	40c. violet	50	30
1142	-	75c. mauve	4·75	2·75
1143	-	1cor. blue	5·25	1·50
1144	-	2cor. olive	2·10	1·80
1145	-	5cor. green	2·50	2·40
MS1145a		Thirteen sheets each 125×115 mm. Nos. 1133/45 in blocks of four	£200	£200

DESIGNS—SQUARE: 2c. Football; 3c. Table tennis; 4c. Stadium; 5c. Yachting; 15c. Basketball; 25c. Boxing; 30c. Baseball; 40c. Cycling; 75c. Diving; 1cor. Pole-vaulting; 2cor. Scout; 5cor. Softball.

178 National Stadium, Managua

1949. Obligatory Tax stamps. Stadium Construction Fund.

1146	178	5c. blue	40	20
1146a	178	5c. red	40	20
MS1146b		87×97 mm. No. 1146 in block of four	5·25	5·00

179 Rowland Hill

180 Heinrich von Stephan

1950. 75th Anniv of U.P.U. Frames in black.
1147 **179** 20c. red (postage) 20 20
1148 - 25c. green 30 20
1149 - 75c. blue 50 30
1150 - 80c. green 30 30
1151 - 4cor. blue 1·00 90
MS1151a Five sheets each 114×126 mm. Nos. 1147/51 in blocks of four 36·00 35·00
DESIGNS—VERT: 25c. Portrait as Type **180**; 75c. Monument, Berne; 80c., 4cor. Obverse and reverse of Congress Medal.

1152 16c. red (air) 20 20
1153 **180** 20c. orange 20 20
1154 - 25c. black 30 30
1155 - 30c. red 40 30
1156 - 85c. green 60 50
1157 - 1cor.10 brown 60 50
1158 - 2cor.14 green 2·50 2·40
MS1158a Seven sheets each 126×114 mm. Nos. 1152/8 in blocks of four 41·00 40·00
DESIGNS—HORIZ: 16c. Rowland Hill; 25, 30c. U.P.U. Offices, Berne; 85c. Monument, Berne; 1cor.10 and 2cor.14, Obverse and reverse of Congress Medal.

181 Queen Isabella and Columbus's Fleet

182 Isabella the Catholic

1952. 500th Birth Anniv of Isabella the Catholic.
1159 10c. mauve (postage) 20 20
1160 **181** 96c. blue 85 80
1161 - 98c. red 85 80
1162 - 1cor.20 brown 1·00 1·00
1163 **182** 1cor.76 purple 1·30 1·30
MS1163a 160×128 mm. Nos. 1159/63 4·25 4·00

1164 2cor.30 red (air) 2·30 2·20
1165 - 2cor.80 orange 2·10 2·00
1166 - 3cor. green 2·30 2·20
1167 **181** 3cor.30 blue 2·30 2·20
1168 - 3cor.60 green 2·75 2·50
MS1168a 160×128 mm. Nos. 1164/8 11·50 11·00
DESIGNS—VERT: 10c., 3cor.60, Queen facing right; 98c., 3cor. Queen and "Santa Maria"; 1cor.20, 2cor.80, Queen and Map of Americas.

183 O.D.E.C.A. Flag

1953. Foundation of Organization of Central American States.
1169 **183** 4c. blue (postage) 20 20
1170 - 5c. green 20 20
1171 - 6c. brown 20 20
1172 - 15c. olive 30 20
1173 - 50c. sepia 30 30
1174 - 20c. red (air) 20 20
1175 **183** 25c. blue 20 20
1176 - 30c. brown 20 20
1177 - 60c. green 30 30
1178 - 1cor. purple 70 70
DESIGNS: 5c., 1cor. Map of C. America; 6c., 20c. Hands holding O.D.E.C.A. arms; 15c., 30c. Five presidents of C. America; 50c., 60c. Charter and flags.

184 Pres. Solorzano

185 Pres. Arguello

1953. Presidential Series. Portraits in black. (a) Postage. As T **184**.
1179 **184** 4c. red 20 20
1180 - 6c. blue (D. M. Chamorro) 20 20
1181 - 8c. brown (Diaz) 20 20
1182 - 15c. red (Somoza) 20 20
1183 - 50c. green (E. Chamorro) 20 20

(b) Air. As T **185**.
1184 **185** 4c. red 20 20
1185 - 5c. orange (Moncada) 20 20
1186 - 20c. blue (J. B. Sacasa) 20 20
1187 - 25c. blue (Zelaya) 20 20
1188 - 30c. lake (Somoza) 20 20
1189 - 35c. green (Martinez) 20 20
1190 - 40c. plum (Guzman) 30 20
1191 - 45c. olive (Cuadra) 30 30
1192 - 50c. red (P. J. Chamorro) 30 20
1193 - 60c. blue (Zavala) 30 30
1194 - 85c. brown (Cardenas) 40 40
1195 - 1cor.10 purple (Carazo) 50 50
1196 - 1cor.20 bistre (R. Sacasa) 50 50

186 Sculptor and U.N. Emblem

1954. U.N.O. Inscr "HOMENAJE A LA ONU".
1197 **186** 3c. drab (postage) 20 20
1198 **A** 4c. green 20 20
1199 **B** 5c. green 20 20
1200 **C** 15c. green 95 20
1201 **D** 1cor. turquoise 85 30
1202 **E** 3c. red (air) 20 20
1203 **F** 4c. orange 20 20
1204 **C** 5c. red 20 20
1205 **D** 30c. pink 1·00 30
1206 **B** 2cor. red 1·70 1·00
1207 **A** 3cor. brown 2·50 1·80
1208 **186** 5cor. purple 3·00 2·40
DESIGNS: A, Detail from Nicaragua's coat of arms; B, Globe; C, Candle and Nicaragua's Charter; D, Flags of Nicaragua and U.N.; E, Torch; F, Trusting hands.

187 Capt. D. L. Ray

188 North American Sabre

1954. National Air Force. Frames in black. (a) Postage. Frames as T **187**.
1209 **187** 1c. black 20 20
1210 - 2c. black 20 20
1211 - 3c. myrtle 20 20
1212 - 4c. orange 20 20
1213 - 5c. green 20 20
1214 - 15c. turquoise 20 20
1215 - 1cor. violet 20 20

(b) Air. Frames as T **188**.
1216 10c. black 20 20
1217 **188** 15c. black 20 20
1218 - 20c. mauve 20 20
1219 - 25c. red 20 20
1220 - 30c. blue 20 20
1221 - 50c. blue 50 50
1222 - 1cor. green 40 30
DESIGNS—POSTAGE: 2c. North American Sabre; 3c. Douglas Boston; 4c. Consolidated Liberator; 5c. North American Texan trainer; 15c. Pres. Somoza; 1cor. Emblem. AIR: 10c. D. L. Ray; 20c. Emblem; 25c. Hangars; 30c. Pres. Somoza; 50c. North American Texan trainers; 1cor. Lockheed Lightning airplanes.

189 Rotary Slogans

1955. 50th Anniv of Rotary International.
1223 **189** 15c. orange (postage) 20 20
1224 **A** 20c. olive 20 20
1225 **B** 35c. violet 30 20
1226 **C** 40c. red 30 20
1227 **D** 90c. black 50 40
MS1227a 127×102 mm. Nos. 1223/7 5·25 5·00

1228 1c. red (air) 20 20
1229 **A** 2c. blue 20 20
1230 **C** 3c. green 20 20
1231 **189** 4c. violet 20 20
1232 **B** 5c. brown 20 20
1233 **B** 25c. turquoise 20 20
1234 **189** 30c. black 20 20
1235 **C** 45c. mauve 40 30
1236 **A** 50c. green 40 30
1237 **D** 1cor. blue 50 40
MS1237a 127×102 mm. Nos. 1233/7 10·50 10·00
DESIGNS—VERT: A, Clasped hands; B, Rotarian and Nicaraguan flags; D, Paul P. Harris. HORIZ: C, World map and winged emblem.

1956. National Exhibition. Surch Conmemoracion Exposicion Nacional Febrero 4-16, 1956 and value.
1238 5c. on 6c. brown (No. 1171) (postage) 20 20
1239 5c. on 6c. black & bl (No. 1180) 20 20
1240 5c. on 8c. brn & blk (No. 1101) 20 20
1241 15c. on 35c. violet (No. 1225) 20 20
1242 15c. on 80c. grn & blk (No. 1150) 20 20
1243 15c. on 90c. black (No. 1227) 20 20
1244 30c. on 35c. black and green (No. 1189) (air) 20 20
1245 30c. on 45c. blk & ol (No. 1191) 20 20
1246 30c. on 45c. mauve (No. 1235) 20 20
1247 2cor. on 5cor. purple (No. 1208) 1·00 1·00

190a

1956. Obligatory Tax. Social Welfare Fund.
1247a **190a** 5c. blue 20 20

191 Gen. J. Dolores Estrada

1956. Cent of War of 1856. Inscr as in T **191**.
1248 - 5c. brown (postage) 20 20
1249 - 10c. lake 20 20
1250 - 15c. grey 20 20
1251 - 25c. red 20 20
1252 - 50c. purple 40 20
1253 **191** 30c. red (air) 20 20
1254 - 60c. brown 20 20
1255 - 1cor.50 green 30 30
1256 - 2cor.50 blue 40 40
1257 - 10cor. orange 2·50 2·00
DESIGNS—VERT: 5c. Gen. M. Jerez; 10c. Gen. F. Chamorro; 50c. Gen. J. D. Estrada; 1cor.50, E. Mangalo; 10cor. Commodore H. Paulding. HORIZ: 15c. Battle of San Jacinto; 25c. Granada in flames; 60c. Bas-relief; 2cor.50, Battle of Rivas.

192 President Somoza

1957. Air. National Mourning for Pres. G. A. Somoza. Various frames. Inscr as in T **192**. Centres in black.
1258 15c. black 20 20
1259 30c. blue 30 30
1260 **192** 2cor. violet 1·00 1·00
1261 - 3cor. olive 2·10 2·00
1262 - 5cor. sepia 3·50 3·50

193 Scout and Badge

194 Clasped Hands, Badge and Globe

1957. Birth Centenary of Lord Baden-Powell.
1263 **193** 10c. olive & vio (postage) 20 20
1264 - 15c. sepia and purple 20 20
1265 - 20c. brown and blue 20 20
1266 - 25c. brown and turquoise 30 20
1267 - 50c. olive and red 40 40
MS1267a 127×102 mm. Nos. 1263/7. Imperf 3·00 3·00

1268 **194** 3c. olive and red (air) 20 20
1269 - 4c. blue and brown 20 20
1270 - 5c. brown and green 20 20
1271 - 6c. drab and violet 20 20
1272 - 8c. red and black 20 20
1273 - 30c. black and green 30 30
1274 - 40c. black and blue 30 30
1275 - 75c. sepia and purple 30 30
1276 - 85c. grey and red 40 40
1277 - 1cor. brown and green 50 50
MS1277a 127×102 mm. Nos. 1273/7. Imperf 5·25 5·00
DESIGNS—VERT: 4c. Scout badge; 5c., 15c. Wolf cub; 6c. Badge and flags; 8c. Badge and emblems of scouting 20c. Scout; 25., 1cor. Lord Baden-Powell; 30., 50c. Joseph A. Harrison; 75c. Rover Scout; 85c. Scout. HORIZ: 40c. Presentation to Pres. Somoza.

195 Pres. Luis Somoza

1957. Election of Pres. Somoza. Portrait in brown. (a) Postage. Oval frame.
1278 **195** 10c. red 20 20
1279 **195** 15c. blue 20 20
1280 **195** 35c. purple 30 20
1281 **195** 50c. brown 40 20
1282 **195** 75c. green 70 60

(b) Air. Rectangular frame.
1283 20c. blue 20 20
1284 25c. mauve 20 20
1285 30c. sepia 20 20
1286 40c. turquoise 30 30
1287 2cor. violet 1·30 1·30

197 Archbishop of Managua

196 Managua Cathedral

1957. Churches and Priests. Centres in olive.
1288 **196** 5c. green (postage) 20 20
1289 - 10c. purple 20 20
1290 **197** 15c. blue 20 20
1291 - 20c. sepia 20 20
1292 - 50c. green 20 20
1293 - 1cor. violet 30 30
1294 **197** 30c. green (air) 20 20
1295 **196** 60c. brown 20 20
1296 - 75c. blue 20 20
1297 - 90c. red 30 30
1298 - 1cor.50 turquoise 50 50
1299 - 2cor. purple 70 70
DESIGNS—HORIZ: As Type **196**: 20, 90c. Leon Cathedral; 50c., 1cor.50, La Merced, Granada Church. VERT: As Type **197**: 10, 75c. Bishop of Nicaragua; 1, 2cor. Father Mariano Dubon.

198 "Honduras" (freighter)

1957. Nicaraguan Merchant Marine Commemoration. Inscr as in T **198**.
1300 **198** 4c. black, blue and myrtle (postage) 25 15
1301 - 5c. violet, blue and brown 25 15
1302 - 6c. black, blue and red 25 15
1303 - 10c. black, green and sepia 25 15
1304 - 15c. brown, blue and red 30 20
1305 - 50c. brown, blue and violet 40 30
1306 - 25c. purple, blue and ultramarine (air) 25 20
1307 - 30c. grey, buff and brown 25 20
1308 - 50c. bistre, blue and violet 35 25
1309 - 60c. black, turquoise and purple 40 35
1310 - 1cor. black, blue and red 50 45
1311 - 2cor.50 brown, blue and black 1·60 1·50
DESIGNS: 5c. Gen. A. Somoza, founder of Mamenic (National) Shipping Line, and "Guatemala" (freighter); 6c. "Guatemala"; 10c. "Salvador" (freighter); 15c. Freighter between hemispheres; 25c. "Managua" (freighter); 30c. Ship's wheel and world map; 50c. (No. 1305), Hemispheres and ship; 50c. (No. 1308), Mamenic Shipping Line flag; 60c. "Costa Rica" (freighter); 1cor. "Nicarao" (freighter); 2cor.50, Map, freighter and flag.

199 Exhibition Emblem

1958. Air. Brussels International Exn. Inscr "EXPOSICION MUNDIAL DE BELGICA 1958".
1312 **199** 25c. black, yellow & green 20 20
1313 - 30c. multicoloured 20 20

1314	-	45c. black, ochre and blue	25	20
1315	199	1cor. black, blue and dull purple	30	30
1316	-	2cor. multicoloured	40	40
1317	-	10cor. sepia, purple and blue	1·90	1·80
MS1317a		130×119 mm. Nos. 1312/17	14·50	14·00

DESIGNS: As Type **199**: 30c., 20cor. Arms of Nicaragua; 45c., 10cor. Nicaraguan pavilion.

200 Emblems of C. American Republics

1958. 17th Central American Lions Convention. Inscr as in T **200**. Emblems (5c., 60c.) multicoloured; Lions badge (others) in blue, red, yellow (or orange and buff).

1318	200	5c. blue (postage)	20	20
1319	-	10c. blue and orange	20	20
1320	-	20c. blue and green	20	20
1321	-	50c. blue and purple	30	30
1322	-	75c. blue and mauve	50	40
1323	-	1cor.50 blue, salmon and drab	70	60
MS1323a		157×90 mm. Nos. 1318/23	3·00	3·00
1324		30c. blue and orange (air)	20	20
1325	200	60c. blue and pink	30	30
1326	-	90c. blue	40	30
1327	-	1cor.25 blue and olive	50	40
1328	-	2cor. blue and green	85	70
1329	-	3cor. blue, red and violet	1·20	1·20
MS1329a		157×90 mm. Nos. 1324/9	4·75	4·50

DESIGNS—HORIZ: 10c., 1cor.25, Melvin Jones; 20, 30c. Dr. T. A. Arias; 50, 90c. Edward G. Barry; 75c., 2cor. Lions emblem; 1cor.50, 3cor. Map of C. American Isthmus.

201 Arms of La Salle

1958. Brothers of the Nicaraguan Christian Schools Commemoration. Inscr as in T **201**.

1330	201	5c. red, blue and yellow (postage)	20	20
1331	-	10c. sepia, blue and green	20	20
1332	-	15c. sepia, brown & bistre	20	20
1333	-	20c. black, red and bistre	20	20
1334	-	50c. sepia, orange & bis	20	20
1335	-	75c. sepia, turquoise & green	30	30
1336	-	1cor. black, violet & bis	40	40
1337	201	30c. blue, red & yellow (air)	20	20
1338	-	60c. sepia, purple & grey	30	30
1339	-	85c. black, red and blue	30	30
1340	-	90c. black, green & ochre	40	40
1341	-	1cor.25 black, red and ochre	60	50
1342	-	1cor.50 sepia, green and grey	70	60
1343	-	1cor.75 black, brn & bl	85	70
1344	-	2cor. sepia, green & grey	1·00	1·00

DESIGNS—HORIZ: 10, 60c. Managua Teachers Institute. VERT: 15, 85c. De La Salle (founder); 20, 90c. Brother Carlos; 50c., 1cor.50, Brother Antonio; 75c., 1cor.25, Brother Julio; 1cor., 1cor.75, Brother Argeo; 2cor. Brother Eugenio.

202 U.N. Emblem

1958. Inauguration of UNESCO Headquarters Building, Paris. Inscr as in T **202**.

1345	202	10c. blue & mauve (postage)	20	20
1346	-	15c. mauve and blue	20	20
1347	-	25c. brown and green	20	20
1348	-	40c. black and red	20	20
1349	-	45c. mauve and blue	20	20
1350	202	50c. green and brown	20	20
MS1350a		85×103 mm. Nos. 1345/50	1·00	1·00
1351		60c. blue and mauve (air)	20	20
1352		75c. brown and green	30	30
1353		90c. green and brown	30	30
1354		1cor. mauve and blue	30	30
1355		3cor. red and black	75	75
1356		5cor. blue and mauve	1·20	1·10
MS1356a		85×103 mm. Nos. 1351/6	4·25	4·00

DESIGNS—VERT: 15c. Aerial view of H.Q. 25, 45c. Facade composed of letters "UNESCO"; 40c. H.Q. and Eiffel Tower. In oval vignettes—60c. As 15c.; 75c., 5cor. As 25c.; 90c., 3cor. As 40c.; 1cor. As Type **202**.

203 **204**

1959. Obligatory Tax. Consular Fiscal stamps surch. Serial Nos. in red.

1357	203	5c. on 50c. blue	30	20
1358	204	5c. on 50c. blue	30	20

205

1959. Obligatory Tax.

1359	205	5c. blue	30	20

206 Cardinal Spellman with Pope John XXIII

1959. Cardinal Spellman Commemoration.

1360	206	5c. flesh & green (postage)	20	20
1361	A	10c. multicoloured	20	20
1362	B	15c. red, black and green	20	20
1363	C	20c. yellow and blue	20	20
1364	D	25c. red and blue	20	20
MS1364a		116×128 mm. Nos. 1360/4	70	70
1365	E	30c. blue, red & yell (air)	20	20
1366	206	35c. bronze and orange	20	20
1367	A	1cor. multicoloured	30	30
1368	B	1cor.5 red and black	30	30
1369	C	1cor.50 yellow and blue	30	30
1370	D	2cor. blue, violet and red	50	50
1371	E	5cor. multicoloured	1·40	1·00
MS1371a		116×128 mm. Nos. 1365/71. Perf or imperf	4·25	4·00

DESIGNS—VERT: A, Cardinal's Arms; B, Cardinal; D, Cardinal wearing sash. HORIZ: C, Cardinal and Cross; E, Flags of Nicaragua, Vatican City and U.S.A.

207 Abraham Lincoln

1960. 150th Birth Anniv of Abraham Lincoln. Portrait in black.

1372	207	5c. red (postage)	20	20
1373	207	10c. green	20	20
1374	207	15c. orange	20	20
1375	207	1cor. purple	30	30
1376	207	2cor. blue	40	30
MS1376a		152×116 mm. Nos. 1372/6. Imperf	1·20	1·20
1377		30c. blue (air)	20	20
1378		35c. red	20	20
1379		70c. purple	20	20
1380		1cor.5 green	30	30
1381		1cor.50 violet	40	40
1382	-	5cor. ochre and black	1·30	1·30
MS1382a		152×116 mm. Nos. 1377/82. Imperf	3·75	3·75

DESIGN—HORIZ: 5cor. Scroll inscr "Dar al que necesite—A. Lincoln".

1960. Air. Tenth Anniv of San Jose (Costa Rica) Philatelic Society. Optd **X Aniversario Club FilatelicoS. J.—C. R.**

1383		2cor. red (No. 1206)	85	80
1384		2cor.50 blue (No. 1256)	85	80
1385		3cor. green (No. 1166)	1·10	1·10

1960. Red Cross Fund for Chilean Earthquake Relief. Nos. 1372/82 optd **Resello** and Maltese Cross. Portrait in black.

1386	207	5c. red (postage)	20	20
1387	207	10c. green	20	20
1388	207	15c. orange	20	20
1389	207	1cor. purple	30	20
1390	207	2cor. blue	50	40
1391	207	30c. blue (air)	20	20
1392	207	35c. red	20	20
1393	207	70c. purple	20	20
1394	207	1cor.5 green	30	30
1395	207	1cor.50 violet	40	40
1396	-	5cor. ochre and black	1·30	1·20

210

1961. Air. World Refugee Year. Inscr "ANO MUNDIAL DEL REFUGIADO".

1397		2cor. multicoloured	50	40
1398	210	5cor. ochre, blue & green	1·00	80
MS1398a		100×70 mm. Nos. 1397/8	3·00	3·00

DESIGN: 2cor. Procession of refugees.

211 Pres. Roosevelt, Pres. Somoza and Officer

1961. Air. 20th Anniv of Nicaraguan Military Academy.

1399	211	20c. multicoloured	20	20
1400	-	25c. red, blue and black	20	20
1401	-	30c. multicoloured	20	20
1402	-	35c. multicoloured	20	20
1403	-	40c. multicoloured	20	20
1404	-	45c. black, flesh and red	20	20
1405	211	60c. multicoloured	20	20
1406	-	70c. multicoloured	20	20
1407	-	1cor.5 multicoloured	30	30
1408	-	1cor.50 multicoloured	30	30
1409	-	2cor. multicoloured	40	40
1410	-	5cor. black, flesh & grey	90	85
MS1410a		Two sheets each 160×100 mm. Nos. 1399/1404 and 1405/10. Imperf	3·75	3·50

DESIGNS—VERT: 25, 70c. Flags; 35c., 1cor.50, Standard bearers; 40c., 2cor. Pennant and emblem. HORIZ: 30c., 1cor.5 Group of officers; 45c., 5cor. Pres. Somoza and Director of Academy.

1961. Air. Consular Fiscal stamps as T **203/4** with serial Nos. in red, surch **Correo Aereo** and value.

1411		20c. on 50c. blue	20	20
1412		20c. on 1cor. olive	20	20
1413		20c. on 2cor. green	20	20
1414		20c. on 3cor. red	20	20
1415		20c. on 5cor. red	20	20
1416		20c. on 10cor. violet	20	20
1417		20c. on 20cor. brown	20	20
1418		20c. on 50cor. brown	20	20
1419		20c. on 100cor. lake	20	20

213 I.J.C. Emblem and Global Map of the Americas

1961. Air. Junior Chamber of Commerce Congress.

1420		2c. multicoloured	20	20
1421		3c. black and yellow	20	20
1422		4c. multicoloured	20	20
1423		5c. black and red	20	20
1424		6c. multicoloured	20	20
1425		10c. multicoloured	20	20
1426		15c. black, green and blue	20	20
1427		30c. black and blue	20	20
1428		35c. multicoloured	20	20
1429		70c. black, red and yellow	20	20
1430		1cor.5 multicoloured	30	30
1431		5cor. multicoloured	85	85

DESIGNS—HORIZ: 2c., 15c. Type **213**; 4c., 35c. "J.C.I." upon Globe. VERT: 3c., 30c. I.J.C. emblem; 5c., 70c. Scroll; 6c., 1cor.5, Handclasp; 10c., 5cor. Regional map of Nicaragua.

1961. Air. First Central American Philatelic Convention, San Salvador. Optd **Convencion Filatelica–Centro–America–Panama–San Salvador–27 Julio 1961**.

1432	158	1cor.25 multicoloured	50	50

215 R. Cabezas

1961. Air. Birth Centenary of Cabezas.

1433	215	20c. blue and orange	20	20
1434	-	40c. purple and blue	20	20
1435	-	45c. sepia and green	20	20
1436	-	70c. green and brown	30	20
1437	-	2cor. blue and pink	30	30
1438	-	10cor. purple and turquoise	1·70	1·30

DESIGNS—HORIZ: 40c. Map and view of Cartago; 45c. 1884 newspaper; 70c. Assembly outside building; 2cor. Scroll; 10cor. Map and view of Masaya.

216 Official Gazettes

1961. Centenary of Regulation of Postal Rates.

1439	216	5c. brown and turquoise	20	20
1440	-	10c. brown and green	20	20
1441	-	15c. brown and red	20	20

DESIGNS: 10c. Envelopes and postmarks; 15c. Martinez and Somoza.

1961. Air. Dag Hammarskjold Commemoration. Nos. 1351/6 optd **Homenaje a Hammarskjold Sept. 18-1961**.

1442		60c. blue and mauve	30	30
1443		75c. brown and green	30	30
1444		90c. green and brown	30	30
1445		1cor. mauve and blue	30	30
1446		3cor. red and black	85	80
1447		5cor. blue and mauve	1·90	1·80

1962. Air. Surch **RESELLO C$ 1.00**.

1449	207	1cor. on 1cor.5 black and green	20	20
1448	-	1cor. on 1cor.10 brown (No. 1157)	20	20

See also Nos. 1498/1500a, 1569/70, 1608/14, 1669/76 and 1748/62.

219 "Cattleya skinneri"

1962. Obligatory Tax. Nicaraguan Orchids. Multicoloured.

1450		5c. Type **219**	30	30
1451		5c. "Bletia roezlii"	30	30
1452		5c. "Sobralia pleiantha"	30	30
1453		5c. "Lycaste macrophylla"	30	30
1454		5c. "Schomburgkia tibicinus"	30	30
1455		5c. "Maxillaria tenuifolia"	30	30
1456		5c. "Stanhopea ecornuta"	30	30
1457		5c. "Oncidium ascendens" and "O. cebolleta"	30	30
1458		5c. "Cycnoches egertonianum"	30	30
1459		5c. "Hexisia bidentata"	30	30

220 UNESCO "Audience"

1962. Air. 15th Anniv of UNESCO.

1460	220	2cor. multicoloured	40	30
1461	-	5cor. multicoloured	85	80
MS1461a		90×65 mm. Nos. 1460/1. Imperf	1·60	1·50

DESIGN: 5cor. U.N. and UNESCO emblems.

1962. Air. Malaria Eradication. Nos. 1425, 1428/31 optd with mosquito surrounded by **LUCHA CONTRA LA MALARIA**.

1462		10c.	30	30
1463		35c.	40	30

1464	70c.	50	40
1465	1cor.5	60	50
1466	5cor.	1·20	1·50

221a Reproduction of Nos. 1/2 and Early Postmarks

1962. Air. Centenary of First Nicaraguan Postage Stamps. Sheet 85×95 mm. Imperf.

MS1466a **221a** 7cor. multicoloured 3·00 3·00

222 Arms of Nueva Segovia

1962. Urban and Provincial Arms. Arms multicoloured; inscr black; background colours below.

1467	**222**	2c. mauve (postage)	20	20
1468	-	3c. blue	20	20
1469	-	4c. lilac	20	20
1470	-	5c. yellow	20	20
1471	-	6c. brown	20	20
1472	**222**	30c. red (air)	20	20
1473	-	50c. orange	20	20
1474	-	1cor. green	20	20
1475	-	2cor. grey	40	40
1476	-	5cor. blue	1·00	1·00

ARMS: 3c., 50c. Leon; 4c., 1cor. Managua; 5c., 2cor. Granada; 6c., 5cor. Rivas.

223 Liberty Bell

1963. Air. 150th Anniv of Independence.

1477	**223**	30c. drab, blue & black	25	20

224 Blessing

1963. Air. Death Tercentenary of St. Vincent de Paul and St. Louise de Marillac.

1478	-	60c. black and orange	20	20
1479	**224**	1cor. olive and orange	30	20
1480	-	2cor. black and red	60	50

DESIGNS—VERT: 60c. "Comfort" (St. Louise and woman). HORIZ: 2cor. St. Vincent and St. Louise.

226 Cross on Globe

1963. Air. Ecumenical Council, Vatican City.

1482	**226**	20c. red and yellow	20	20

227 Ears of Wheat

1963. Air. Freedom from Hunger.

1483	**227**	10c. green and light green	20	20
1484	-	25c. sepia and yellow	30	20

DESIGN: 25c. Barren tree and campaign emblem.

228 Boxing

1963. Air. Sports. Multicoloured.

1485	2c. Type **228**	20	20
1486	3c. Running	20	20
1487	4c. Underwater harpooning	20	20
1488	5c. Football	20	20
1489	6c. Baseball	20	20
1490	10c. Tennis	30	20
1491	15c. Cycling	30	20
1492	20c. Motor-cycling	30	20
1493	35c. Chess	40	30
1494	60c. Angling	50	30
1495	1cor. Table-tennis	60	40
1496	2cor. Basketball	85	90
1497	5cor. Golf	2·50	2·00

1964. Air. Surch **Resello** or **RESELLO** (**1500a**) and value.

1498	-	5c. on 6c. (No. 1424)	30	20
1499	-	10c. on 30c. (No. 1365)	50	20
1500	**207**	15c. on 30c.	70	30
1500a	**201**	20c. on 30c.	20	20

See also Nos. 1448/9, 1569/70, 1608/14 and 1669/76.

1964. Optd **CORREOS**.

1501	5c. multicoloured (No. 1451)	20	20

231 Flags

1964. Air. "Centro America".

1502	**231**	40c. multicoloured	30	30

232 "Alliance Emblem"

1964. Air. "Alliance for Progress". Multicoloured.

1503	5c. Type **232**	20	20
1504	10c. Red Cross post (horiz)	20	20
1505	15c. Highway (horiz)	20	20
1506	20c. Ploughing (horiz)	20	20
1507	25c. Housing (horiz)	20	20
1508	30c. Presidents Somoza and Kennedy and Eugene Black (World Bank) (horiz)	20	20
1509	35c. School and adults (horiz)	20	20
1510	40c. Chimneys (horiz)	30	20

233 Map of Member Countries

1964. Air. Central American "Common Market". Multicoloured.

1511	15c. Type **233**	20	20
1512	25c. Ears of wheat	20	20
1513	40c. Cogwheels	20	20
1514	50c. Heads of cattle	20	20

1964. Air. Olympic Games, Tokyo. Nos. 1485/7, 1489 and 1495/6 optd **OLIMPIADAS TOKYO - 1964**.

1515	2c. Type **108**	20	20
1516	3c. Running	20	20
1517	4c. Underwater harpooning	20	20
1518	6c. Baseball	20	20
1519	1cor. Table-tennis	2·30	2·20
1520	2cor. Basketball	3·00	3·00

235 Rescue of Wounded Soldier

1965. Air. Red Cross Centenary. Multicoloured.

1521	20c. Type **235**	20	20
1522	25c. Blood transfusion	20	20
1523	40c. Red Cross and snowbound town	30	20
1524	10cor. Red Cross and map of Nicaragua	2·30	1·60

236 Statuettes

1965. Air. Nicaraguan Antiquities. Multicoloured.

1525	5c. Type **236**	30	25
1526	10c. Totem	30	25
1527	15c. Carved dog (horiz)	30	25
1528	20c. Composition of "objets d'art"	30	25
1529	25c. Dish and vase (horiz)	30	25
1530	30c. Pestle and mortar	30	25
1531	35c. Statuettes (different) (horiz)	30	25
1532	40c. Deity	30	25
1533	50c. Wine vessel and dish	30	25
1534	60c. Bowl and dish (horiz)	30	25
1535	1cor. Urn	50	30

237 Pres. Kennedy

1965. Air. Pres. Kennedy Commemorative.

1536	**237**	35c. black and green	25	20
1537	**237**	75c. black and mauve	40	25
1538	**237**	1cor.10 black and blue	50	35
1539	**237**	2cor. black and brown	1·30	90

MS1539a Four sheets each 90×116 mm. Nos. 1536/9 in blocks of four. Imperf 8·75 8·50

238 A. Bello

1965. Air. Death Centenary of Andres Bello (poet and writer).

1540	**238**	10c. black and brown	20	20
1541	**238**	15c. black and blue	20	20
1542	**238**	45c. black and purple	20	20
1543	**238**	80c. black and green	20	20
1544	**238**	1cor. black and yellow	30	30
1545	**238**	2cor. black and grey	50	50

1965. Ninth Central American Scout Camporee. Nos. 1450/9 optd with scout badge and **CAMPOREE SCOUT 1965**.

1546	5c. multicoloured	40	40
1547	5c. multicoloured	40	40
1548	5c. multicoloured	40	40
1549	5c. multicoloured	40	40
1550	5c. multicoloured	40	40
1551	5c. multicoloured	40	40
1552	5c. multicoloured	40	40
1553	5c. multicoloured	40	40
1554	5c. multicoloured	40	40
1555	5c. multicoloured	40	40

MS1555a 127×102 mm. Sheet No. **MS**1277a optd **CAMPOREE SCOUT 1965** on each stamp 12·00 12·00

240 Sir Winston Churchill

1966. Air. Churchill Commemorative.

1556	**240**	20c. mauve and black	20	20
1557	-	35c. green and black	20	20
1558	-	60c. ochre and black	20	20
1559	-	75c. red	30	30
1560	-	1cor. purple	50	40
1561	**240**	2cor. violet, lilac & black	70	60
1562	-	3cor. blue and black	1·00	90

MS1563 99×95 mm. Nos. 1558/61. Imperf 2·10 2·00

DESIGNS—HORIZ: 35c., 1cor. Churchill broadcasting. VERT: 60c., 3cor. Churchill crossing the Rhine; 75c. Churchill in Hussars' uniform.

241 Pope John XXIII

1966. Air. Closure of Vatican Ecumenical Council. Multicoloured.

1564	20c. Type **241**	20	20
1565	35c. Pope Paul VI	20	20
1566	1cor. Archbishop Gonzalez y Robleto	30	20
1567	2cor. St. Peter's, Rome	40	30
1568	3cor. Papal arms	70	60

1967. Air. Nos. 1533/4 surch **RESELLO** and value.

1569	10c. on 50c. multicoloured	20	20
1570	15c. on 60c. multicoloured	20	20

See also Nos. 1448/9, 1498/1500a, 1608/14 and 1669/76.

243 Dario and Birthplace

1967. Air. Birth Centenary of Ruben Dario (poet). Designs showing Dario and view. Multicoloured.

1571	5c. Type **243**	20	20
1572	10c. Monument, Managua	20	20
1573	20c. Leon Cathedral (site of Dario's tomb)	20	20
1574	40c. Allegory of the centaurs	20	20
1575	75c. Allegory of the mute swans	30	20
1576	1cor. Roman triumphal march	30	20
1577	2cor. St. Francis and the wolf	40	30
1578	5cor. "Faith" opposing "Death"	1·00	95

MS1579 Two sheets each 130×107 mm. Nos. 1571/4 and 1575/8 5·75 5·50

244 *Megalura peleus*

1967. Air. Butterflies. Multicoloured.

1580	5c. *Heliconius petiveranua* (vert)	30	20
1581	10c. "Colaenis julia" (vert)	30	20
1582	15c. Type **244**	30	20
1583	20c. "Aneyluris jurgensii"	40	30
1584	25c. "Thecla regalis"	40	30

225 "Map Stamp"

1963. Air. Central American Philatelic Societies Federation Commemoration.

1481	**225**	1cor. blue and yellow	30	20

1585	30c. "Doriana thia" (vert)	40	30
1586	35c. "Lymnias pixae" (vert)	50	40
1587	40c. "Metamorpho dido"	50	40
1588	50c. "Papilio arcas" (vert)	50	40
1589	60c. "Ananea cleomestra"	60	50
1590	1cor. "Victorina epaphaus" (vert)	85	60
1591	2cor. "Prepona demophon"	1·00	80

245 McDivitt and White

1967. Air. Space Flight of McDivitt and White. Multicoloured.

1592	5c. Type **245**	30	30
1593	10c. Astronauts and "Gemini 5" on launching pad	30	30
1594	15c. "Gemini 5" and White in Space	30	30
1595	20c. Recovery operation at sea	30	30
1596	35c. Type **245**	30	30
1597	40c. As 10c.	30	30
1598	75c. As 15c.	30	30
1599	1cor. As 20c.	40	40

246 National Flower of Costa Rica

1967. Air. Fifth Year of Central American Economic Integration. Designs showing national flowers of Central American countries. Multicoloured.

1600	40c. Type **246**	30	20
1601	40c. Guatemala	30	20
1602	40c. Honduras	30	20
1603	40c. Nicaragua	30	20
1604	40c. El Salvador	30	20

247 Presidents Diaz and Somoza

1968. Air. Visit of Pres. Diaz of Mexico.

1605	-	20c. black	20	20
1606	**247**	40c. olive	30	20
1607	-	1cor. brown	40	20

DESIGNS—VERT: 20c. Pres. Somoza greeting Pres. Diaz; 1cor. Pres. Diaz of Mexico.

1968. Surch **RESELLO** and value.

1608		5c. on 6c. (No. 1180) (postage)	60	60
1609		5c. on 6c. (No. 1471)	60	60
1610		5c. on 6c. (No. 1424) (air)	30	20
1611		5c. on 6c. (No. 1489)	30	20
1612	**156**	5c. on 8c. (No. 1035)	30	20
1614	-	1cor. on 1cor.50 (No. 1369)	30	20

See also Nos. 1448/9, 1498/1500a, 1569/70 and 1669/76.

249 Mangoes

1968. Air. Nicaraguan Fruits. Multicoloured.

1615	5c. Type **249**	30	20
1616	10c. Pineapples	30	20
1617	15c. Oranges	30	20
1618	20c. Pawpaws	30	20
1619	30c. Bananas	30	20
1620	35c. Avocado pears	30	20
1621	50c. Water-melons	30	20
1622	75c. Cashews	30	20
1623	1cor. Sapodilla plums	50	30
1624	2cor. Cocoa beans	85	50

250 "The Crucifixion" (Fra Angelico)

1968. Air. Religious Paintings. Multicoloured.

1625	10c. Type **250**	20	20
1626	15c. "The Last Judgement" (Michelangelo) (vert)	20	20
1627	35c. "The Beautiful Gardener" (Raphael) (vert)	20	20
1628	2cor. "The Spoliation of Christ" (El Greco) (vert)	60	50
1629	3cor. "The Conception" (Murillo) (vert)	85	60
MS1630	100×80 mm. 5cor. "The Crucifixion" (Dali)	3·50	3·50

1968. Air. Pope Paul's Visit to Bogota. Nos. 1625/8 optd **Visita de S. S. Paulo VI C. E. de Bogota 1968.**

1631	**250**	10c. multicoloured	20	20
1632	-	15c. multicoloured	20	20
1633	-	35c. multicoloured	30	30
1634	-	2cor. multicoloured	60	50

252 Basketball

1969. Air. Olympic Games, Mexico. Multicoloured.

1635	10c. Type **252**	20	20
1636	15c. Fencing (horiz)	20	20
1637	20c. High-diving	20	20
1638	35c. Running	20	20
1639	50c. Hurdling (horiz)	30	30
1640	75c. Weightlifting	30	30
1641	1cor. Boxing (horiz)	40	40
1642	2cor. Football	1·00	80
MS1643	100×120 mm. Nos. 1639/42	2·50	2·50

253 Midas Cichlid

1969. Air. Fish. Multicoloured.

1644	10c. Type **253**	30	20
1645	15c. Moga cichlid	30	20
1646	20c. Common carp	30	20
1647	30c. Tropical gar	30	20
1648	35c. Swordfish	30	20
1649	50c. Big-mouthed sleeper	30	20
1650	75c. Atlantic tarpon	30	20
1651	1cor. Lake Nicaragua shark	40	30
1652	2cor. Sailfish	60	40
1653	3cor. Small-toothed sawfish	1·00	65
MS1654	83×137 mm. Nos. 1650/3	4·25	4·00

1969. Air. Various stamps surch **RESELLO** and value.

1655	10c. on 25c. (No. 1507)	20	20
1656	10c. on 25c. (No. 1512)	20	20
1657	15c. on 25c. (No. 1529)	20	20
1658	50c. on 70c. (No. 1379)	20	20

255 Scenery, Tower and Emblem

1969. Air. "Hemisfair" (1968) Exhibition.

1659	**255**	30c. blue and red	20	20
1660	**255**	35c. purple and red	20	20
1661	**255**	75c. red and blue	20	20
1662	**255**	1cor. purple and black	30	25
1663	**255**	2cor. purple and green	55	50
MS1664		75×111 mm. Nos. 1659/60, 1662/3. Perf or imperf	1·60	1·50

1969. Various stamps surch. (a) Optd **CORREO**.

1665	5c. (No. 1450)	60	60
1666	5c. (No. 1453)	60	60
1667	5c. (No. 1454)	60	60
1668	5c. (No. 1459)	60	60

(b) Optd **RESELLO** and surch.

1669	10c. on 25c. (No. 1529)	20	20
1670	10c. on 30c. (No. 1324)	20	20
1671	10c. on 30c. (No. 1427)	20	20
1672	10c. on 30c. (No. 1530)	20	20
1673	15c. on 35c. (No. 1531)	20	20
1674	20c. on 30c. (No. 1307)	20	20
1675	20c. on 30c. (No. 1401)	20	20
1676	20c. on 35c. (No. 1509)	20	20

258 "Minerals"

1969. Air. Nicaraguan Products. Multicoloured.

1677	5c. Type **258**	20	20
1678	10c. "Fish"	20	20
1679	15c. "Bananas"	20	20
1680	20c. "Timber"	20	20
1681	35c. "Coffee"	30	20
1682	40c. "Sugar-cane"	30	20
1683	60c. "Cotton"	30	20
1684	75c. "Rice and Maize"	30	20
1685	1cor. "Tobacco"	40	25
1686	2cor. "Meat"	65	45

1969. 50th Anniv of I.L.O. Obligatory tax stamps. Nos. 1450/9, optd **O.I.T. 1919-1969.**

1687	5c. multicoloured	30	30
1688	5c. multicoloured	30	30
1689	5c. multicoloured	30	30
1690	5c. multicoloured	30	30
1691	5c. multicoloured	30	30
1692	5c. multicoloured	30	30
1693	5c. multicoloured	30	30
1694	5c. multicoloured	30	30
1695	5c. multicoloured	30	30
1696	5c. multicoloured	30	30

260 Girl carrying Tinaja

1970. Air. Eighth Inter-American Savings and Loans Conference, Managua.

1697	**260**	10c. multicoloured	20	20
1698	**260**	15c. multicoloured	20	20
1699	**260**	20c. multicoloured	20	20
1700	**260**	35c. multicoloured	20	20
1701	**260**	50c. multicoloured	20	20
1702	**260**	75c. multicoloured	30	20
1703	**260**	1cor. multicoloured	50	30
1704	**260**	2cor. multicoloured	85	50

261 Pele (Brazil)

1970. World Football "Hall of Fame" Poll-winners. Multicoloured.

1705	5c. Type **261** (postage)	30	30
1706	10c. Puskas (Hungary)	30	30
1707	15c. Matthews (England)	30	30
1708	40c. Di Stefano (Argentina)	30	30
1709	2cor. Facchetti (Italy)	1·00	80
1710	3cor. Yashin (Russia)	1·30	1·00
1711	5cor. Beckenbauer (West Germany)	1·60	1·30
1712	20c. Santos (Brazil) (air)	30	30
1713	80c. Wright (England)	40	30
1714	1cor. Flags of 16 World Cup finalists	50	40
1715	4cor. Bozsik (Hungary)	1·40	1·00
1716	5cor. Charlton (England)	1·60	1·30

262 Torii (Gate)

1970. Air. EXPO 70, World Fair, Osaka, Japan.

1717	**262**	25c. multicoloured	20	20
1718	**262**	30c. multicoloured	20	20
1719	**262**	35c. multicoloured	20	20
1720	**262**	75c. multicoloured	30	20
1721	**262**	1cor.50 multicoloured	50	30
1722	**262**	3cor. multicoloured	85	80
MS1723		108×78 mm. Nos. 1720/2. Imperf	1·90	1·50

263 Module and Astronauts on Moon

1970. Air. "Apollo 11" Moon Landing (1969). Multicoloured.

1724	35c. Type **263**	20	20
1725	40c. Module landing on Moon	20	20
1726	60c. Astronauts with U.S. flag	20	20
1727	75c. As 40c.	30	20
1728	1cor. As 60c.	40	20
1729	2cor. Type **263**	70	40

264 F. D. Roosevelt

1970. Air. 25th Death Anniv of Franklin D. Roosevelt.

1730	**264**	10c. black	20	20
1731	-	15c. brown and black	20	20
1732	-	20c. green and black	20	20
1733	**264**	35c. purple and black	20	20
1734	-	50c. brown	20	20
1735	**264**	75c. blue	20	20
1736	-	1cor. red	30	20
1737	-	2cor. black	60	40

PORTRAITS: 15c., 1cor. Roosevelt with stamp collection; 20c., 50c., 2cor. Roosevelt (full-face).

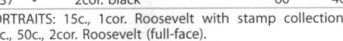

265 "The Annunciation" (Grunewald)

1970. Air. Christmas. Paintings. Multicoloured.

1738	10c. Type **265**	15	15
1739	10c. "The Nativity" (detail, El Greco)	15	15
1740	10c. "The Adoration of the Magi" (detail, Durer)	15	15
1741	10c. "Virgin and Child" (J. van Hemessen)	15	15
1742	10c. "The Holy Shepherd" (Portuguese School, 16th cent)	15	15
1743	15c. Type **265**	15	15
1744	20c. As No. 1739	15	15
1745	35c. As No. 1740	20	20
1746	75c. As No. 1741	25	20
1747	1cor. As No. 1742	30	25

1971. Surch **RESELLO** and new value.

1748	30c. on 90c. black (No. 1227) (postage)	21·00	20·00
1749	10c. on 1cor.5 red, black & red (No. 1368) (air)	30	30
1750	10c. on 1cor.5 mult (No. 1407)	30	30
1751	10c. on 1cor.5 mult (No. 1430)	30	30
1752	15c. on 1cor.50 green and red (No. 1116)	40	40
1753	15c. on 1cor.50 green (No. 1255)	40	40
1754	15c. on 1cor.50 yellow and blue (No. 1369)	40	40
1755	15c. on 1cor.50 black and violet (No. 1381)	40	40
1756	20c. on 85c. black and red (No. 1276)	50	50

1757 20c. on 85c. black, red and blue (No. 1339) 50 50
1758 25c. on 90c. black, green and ochre (No. 1440) 70 70
1759 30c. on 1cor.10 black and purple (No. 1195) 95 90
1760 40c. on 1cor.10 brown and black (No. 1157) 1·10 1·10
1761 40c. on 1cor.50 mult (No. 1408) 1·10 1·10
1762 1cor. on 1cor.10 black and blue (No. 1538) 3·00 2·75

266 Basic Mathematical Equation

1971. Scientific Formulae. "The Ten Mathematical Equations that changed the Face of the Earth". Multicoloured.
1763 10c. Type **266** (postage) 15 15
1764 15c. Newton's Law 15 15
1765 20c. Einstein's Law 30 25
1766 1cor. Tsiolkovsky's Law 1·00 60
1767 2cor. Maxwell's Law 2·10 1·30
1768 25c. Napier's Law (air) 20 15
1769 30c. Pythagoras' Law 30 20
1770 40c. Boltzmann's Law 40 20
1771 1cor. Broglie's Law 95 40
1772 2cor. Archimedes' Law 1·60 80

267 Peace Emblem

1971. "Is There a Formula for Peace?".
1773 **267** 10c. blue and black 15 15
1774 **267** 15c. blue, black and violet 15 15
1775 **267** 20c. blue, black & brown 15 15
1776 **267** 40c. blue, black and green 30 25
1777 **267** 50c. blue, black & purple 40 40
1778 **267** 80c. blue, black and red 60 60
1779 **267** 1cor. blue, black & green 85 80
1780 **267** 2cor. blue, black & violet 1·60 1·50

268 Montezuma Oropendola

1971. Air. Nicaraguan Birds. Multicoloured.
1781 10c. Type **268** 30 20
1782 15c. Turquoise-browed motmot 30 20
1783 20c. White-throated magpie-jay 30 20
1784 25c. Scissor-tailed flycatcher 30 20
1785 30c. Spotted-breasted oriole (horiz) 30 20
1786 35c. Rufous-naped wren 30 20
1787 40c. Great kiskadee 40 30
1788 75c. Red-legged honeycreeper (horiz) 50 30
1789 1cor. Great-tailed grackle (horiz) 60 30
1790 2cor. Belted kingfisher 1·00 40

269 "Moses with the Tablets of the Law" (Rembrandt)

1971. "The Ten Commandments". Paintings. Multicoloured.
1791 10c. Type **269** (postage) 15 15
1792 15c. "Moses and the Burning Bush" (Botticelli) (1st Commandment) 15 15
1793 20c. "Jepthah's Daughter" (Degas) (2nd Commandment) (horiz) 15 15
1794 30c. "St. Vincent Ferrer preaching in Verona" (Morone) (3rd Commandment) (horiz) 15 15
1795 35c. "Noah's Drunkenness" (Michelangelo) (4th Commandment) (horiz) 25 20
1796 40c. "Cain and Abel" (Trevisani) (5th Commandment) (horiz) 25 25
1797 50c. "Joseph accused by Potiphar's Wife" (Rembrandt) (6th Commandment) 35 30
1798 60c. "Isaac blessing Jacob" (Eeckhout) (7th Commandment) (horiz) 50 50
1799 75c. "Susannah and the Elders" (Rubens) (8th Commandment) (horiz) 85 80
1800 1cor. "Bathsheba after her Bath" (Rembrandt) (9th Commandment) (air) 1·00 50
1801 2cor. "Naboth's Vineyard" (Smetham) (10th Commandment) 1·60 80

270 U Thant and Pres. Somoza

1971. Air. 25th Anniv of U.N.O.
1802 **270** 10c. brown and red 15 15
1803 **270** 15c. green and emerald 15 15
1804 **270** 20c. blue and light blue 15 15
1805 **270** 25c. red and purple 20 15
1806 **270** 30c. brown and orange 20 15
1807 **270** 40c. green and grey 20 20
1808 **270** 1cor. green and sage 30 25
1809 **270** 2cor. brown & light brown 75 45

1972. Olympic Games, Munich. Nos. 1709, 1711, 1713 and 1716 surch **OLIMPIADAS MUNICH 1972**, emblem and value or optd only (5cor.).
1810 40c. on 2cor. multicoloured (postage) 15 15
1811 50c. on 3cor. multicoloured 20 15
1812 20c. on 80c. mult (air) 15 15
1813 60c. on 4cor. multicoloured 20 15
1814 5cor. multicoloured 1·20 1·00

272 Figurine and Apoyo Site on Map

1972. Air. Pre-Columbian Art. A. H. Heller's Pottery Discoveries. Multicoloured.
1815 10c. Type **272** 15 15
1816 15c. Cana Castilla 15 15
1817 20c. Catarina 15 15
1818 25c. Santa Helena 15 15
1819 30c. Mombacho 15 15
1820 35c. Tisma 15 15
1821 40c. El Menco 15 15
1822 50c. Los Placeres 20 15
1823 60c. Masaya 20 20
1824 80c. Granada 25 20
1825 1cor. Las Mercedes 35 25
1826 2cor. Nindiri 65 45

273 "Lord Peter Wimsey" (Dorothy Sayers)

1972. Air. 50th Anniv of International Criminal Police Organization (INTERPOL). Famous Fictional Detectives. Multicoloured.
1827 5c. Type **273** 20 15
1828 10c. "Philip Marlowe" (Raymond Chandler) 20 15
1829 15c. "Sam Spade" (D. Hammett) 30 15
1830 20c. "Perry Mason" (Erle Stanley Gardner) 30 15
1831 25c. "Nero Wolfe" (Rex Stout) 30 15
1832 35c. "C. Auguste Dupin" (Edgar Allan Poe) 35 20
1833 40c. "Ellery Queen" (F. Dannay and M. Lee) 35 25
1834 50c. "Father Brown" (G. K. Chesterton) 45 25
1835 60c. "Charlie Chan" (Earl D. Biggers) 55 40
1836 80c. "Inspector Maigret" (Georges Simenon) 65 50
1837 1cor. "Hercule Poirot" (Agatha Christie) 95 70
1838 2cor. "Sherlock Holmes" (A. Conan Doyle) 1·70 1·30

274 "The Shepherdess and her Brothers"

1972. Air. Christmas. Scenes from Legend of the Christmas Rose. Multicoloured.
1839 10c. Type **274** 15 15
1840 15c. Adoration of the Wise Men 15 15
1841 20c. Shepherdess crying 15 15
1842 35c. Angel appears to Shepherdess 15 15
1843 40c. Christmas Rose 15 15
1844 60c. Shepherdess thanks angel for roses 20 20
1845 80c. Shepherdess takes roses to Holy Child 20 20
1846 1cor. Holy Child receiving roses 30 20
1847 2cor. Nativity scene 50 45
MS1848 132×132 mm. Nos. 1839/47 2·30 2·20

275 Sir Walter Raleigh and Elizabethan Galleon

1973. Air. Causes of the American Revolution. Multicoloured.
1849 10c. Type **275** 15 15
1850 15c. Signing "Mayflower Compact" 15 15
1851 20c. Acquittal of Peter Zenger (vert) 15 15
1852 25c. Acclaiming American resistance (vert) 15 15
1853 30c. Revenue stamp (vert) 15 15
1854 35c. "Serpent" slogan—"Join or die" 40 20
1855 40c. Boston Massacre (vert) 40 20
1856 50c. Boston Tea-party 40 40
1857 60c. Patrick Henry on trial (vert) 40 40
1858 75c. Battle of Bunker Hill 50 40
1859 80c. Declaration of Independence 60 40
1860 1cor. Liberty Bell 85 50
1861 2cor. US seal (vert) 1·60 1·00

1973. Nos. 1450/54, 1456 and 1458/9 optd **CORREO**.
1862 **219** 5c. multicoloured 30 25
1863 - 5c. multicoloured 30 25
1864 - 5c. multicoloured 30 25
1865 - 5c. multicoloured 30 25
1866 - 5c. multicoloured 30 25
1867 - 5c. multicoloured 30 25
1868 - 5c. multicoloured 30 25
1869 - 5c. multicoloured 30 25

277 Baseball, Player and Map

1973. Air. 20th International Baseball Championships, Managua (1972).
1870 **277** 15c. multicoloured 25 15
1871 **277** 20c. multicoloured 25 15
1872 **277** 40c. multicoloured 25 20
1873 **277** 10cor. multicoloured 2·10 1·80
MS1874 105×134 mm. Nos. 1870/3 3·00 3·00

278 Givenchy, Paris

1973. World-famous Couturiers. Mannequins. Multicoloured.
1875 1cor. Type **278** (postage) 30 30
1876 2cor. Hartnell, London 60 50
1877 5cor. Balmain, Paris 1·60 1·20
1878 10c. Lourdes, Nicaragua (air) 20 15
1879 15c. Halston, New York 20 15
1880 20c. Pino Lancetti, Rome 20 15
1881 35c. Madame Gres, Paris 20 15
1882 40c. Irene Galitzine, Rome 20 15
1883 80c. Pedro Rodriguez, Barcelona 30 20
MS1884 170×170 mm. Nos. 1875/82 4·25 4·00

279 Diet Chart

1973. Air. Child Welfare. Multicoloured.
1885 5c.+5c. Type **279** 15 15
1886 10c.+5c. Senora Samoza with baby, and Children's Hospital 15 15
1887 15c.+5c. "Childbirth" 15 15
1888 20c.+5c. "Immunization" 15 15
1889 30c.+5c. Water purification 15 15
1890 35c.+5c. As No. 1886 15 15
1891 50c.+10c. Alexander Fleming and "Antibiotics" 20 20
1892 60c.+15c. Malaria control 20 20
1893 70c.+10c. Laboratory analysis 20 20
1894 80c.+20c. Gastroenteritis 30 30
1895 1cor.+50c. As No. 1886 40 40
1896 2cor. Pediatric surgery 50 50

280 Virginia and Father

1973. Christmas. "Does Santa Claus exist?" (Virginia O'Hanlon's letter to American "Sun" newspaper). Multicoloured.
1897 2c. Type **280** (postage) 15 15
1898 3c. Text of letter 15 15
1899 4c. Reading the reply 15 15
1900 5c. Type **280** 15 15
1901 15c. As 3c. 15 15
1902 20c. As 4c. 15 15
1903 1cor. Type **280** (air) 30 30
1904 2cor. As 3c. 60 60
1905 4cor. As 4c. 1·10 1·10
MS1906 197×143 mm. Nos. 1903/5 4·25 4·00

No **MS**1906 has an inscription in English on the reverse.

281 Churchill making Speech, 1936

1974. Birth Cent of Sir Winston Churchill.
1907 **281** 2c. multicoloured (postage) 15 15
1908 - 3c. black, blue and brown 15 15
1909 - 4c. multicoloured 15 15
1910 - 5c. multicoloured 15 15
1911 - 10c. brown, green & blue 15 15
1912 - 5cor. multicoloured (air) 1·40 1·40
1913 - 6cor. black, brown & bl 1·90 1·80
MS1914 Two sheets each 85×64 mm. (a) 4cor. black, yellow and green; (b) 4cor. multicoloured 3·00 3·00

DESIGNS: 3c. "The Four Churchills" (wartime cartoon); 4c. Candle, cigar and "Action" stickers; 5c. Churchill, Roosevelt and Stalin at Yalta; 10c. Churchill landing in Normandy, 1944; 5cor. Churchill giving "V" sign; 6cor. "Bulldog Churchill" (cartoon); **MS**1914 (a) Churchill and 10 Downing Street; (b) Churchill House of Parliament.

282 Presentation of World Cup to Uruguay, 1930

1974. World Cup Football Championship. Multicoloured.
1915 1c. Type **282** (postage) 15 15
1916 2c. Victorious Italian team, 1934 15 15

1917	3c. Presentation of World Cup to Italy, 1938	15	15
1918	4c. Uruguay's winning goal, 1950	15	15
1919	5c. Victorious West Germany, 1954	15	15
1920	10c. Rejoicing Brazilian players, 1958	15	15
1921	15c. Brazilian player holding World Cup, 1962	15	15
1922	20c. Queen Elizabeth II presenting Cup to Bobby Moore, 1966	15	15
1923	25c. Victorious Brazilian players, 1970	15	15
1924	10cor. Football and flags of participating countries, 1974 (air)	3·00	2·75

MS1925 Two sheets each 115×112 mm. (a) 4cor. As 10c.; (b) 5cor. As 20c — 3·50 — 3·50

283 *Malachra* sp.

1974. Wild Flowers and Cacti. Multicoloured.

1926	2c. Type **283** (postage)	15	15
1927	3c. *Paguira insignis*	15	15
1928	4c. *Convolvulus* sp.	15	15
1929	5c. *Pereschia autumnalis*	15	15
1930	10c. *Ipomea tuberosa*	15	15
1931	15c. *Hibiscus elatus*	15	15
1932	20c. *Plumeria acutifolia*	15	15
1933	1cor. *Centrosema* sp. (air)	30	30
1934	3cor. *Hylocereus undatus*	70	60

284 Nicaraguan 7½c. Stamp of 1937

1974. Centenary of U.P.U.

1935	**284**	2c. red, green & blk (postage)	15	15
1936	-	3c. blue, green and black	15	15
1937	-	4c. multicoloured	15	15
1938	-	5c. brown, mauve & blk	15	15
1939	-	10c. red, brown and black	15	15
1940	-	20c. green, blue and black	15	15
1941	-	40c. multicoloured (air)	20	20
1942	-	3cor. green, black & pink	95	90
1943	-	5cor. blue, black and lilac	1·40	1·40

MS1944 108×128 mm. 1cor. As 20c.; 2cor. As 4c.; 4cor. Jet Airliner over Globe (horiz). Imperf — 3·00 — 3·00

DESIGNS—VERT: 3c. 5c. stamp of 1937; 5c. 2c. stamp of 1937; 10c. 1c. stamp of 1937; 20c. ½c. stamp of 1937; 40c. 10c. stamp of 1961; 5cor. 4cor. U.P.U. stamp of 1950. HORIZ: 4c. 10c. air stamp of 1934; 3cor. 85c. U.P.U. air stamp of 1950.

1974. Air West Germany's Victory in World Cup Football Championships. Nos. 1924 and **MS**1925 optd **TRIUMFADOR ALEMMANIA OCCIDENTAL**.

1945	10cr. multicoloured	3·00	2·50
MS1946	Two sheets each 115×112 mm	4·00	4·00

286 Tamandua

1974. Nicaraguan Fauna. Multicoloured.

1947	1c. Type **286** (postage)	15	15
1948	2c. Puma	15	15
1949	3c. Common raccoon	15	15
1950	4c. Ocelot	15	15
1951	5c. Kinkajou	15	15
1952	10c. Coypu	15	15
1953	15c. Collared peccary	15	15
1954	20c. Baird's tapir	15	15
1955	3cor. Red brocket (air)	1·00	80
1956	5cor. Jaguar	1·60	1·00

287 "Prophet Zacharias"

1975. Christmas. 500th Birth Anniv of Michelangelo. Multicoloured.

1957	1c. Type **287** (postage)	15	15
1958	2c. "Christ amongst the Jews"	15	15
1959	3c. "The Creation of Man" (horiz)	15	15
1960	4c. Interior of Sistine Chapel, Rome	15	15
1961	5c. "Moses"	15	15
1962	10c. "Mouscron Madonna"	15	15
1963	15c. "David"	15	15
1964	20c. "Doni Madonna"	15	15
1965	40c. "Madonna of the Steps" (air)	15	15
1966	80c. "Pitti Madonna"	20	20
1967	2cor. "Christ and Virgin Mary"	40	40
1968	5cor. "Michelangelo" (self-portrait)	1·20	1·00

MS1969 101×87 mm. Nos. 1967/8. Imperf — 3·00 — 3·00

288 Giovanni Martinelli ("Othello")

1975. Great Opera Singers. Multicoloured.

1970	1c. Type **288** (postage)	15	15
1971	2c. Tito Gobbi ("Simone Boccanegra")	15	15
1972	3c. Lotte Lehmann ("Der Rosenkavalier")	15	15
1973	4c. Lauritz Melchior ("Parsifal")	15	15
1974	5c. Nellie Melba ("La Traviata")	15	15
1975	15c. Jussi Bjoerling ("La Boheme")	15	15
1976	20c. Birgit Nilsson ("Turandot")	15	15
1977	25c. Rosa Ponselle ("Norma") (air)	15	15
1978	35c. Guiseppe de Luca ("Rigoletto")	15	15
1979	40c. Joan Sutherland ("La Figlia del Reggimiento")	15	15
1980	50c. Enzio Pinza ("Don Giovanni")	15	15
1981	60c. Kirsten Flagstad ("Tristan and Isolde")	30	20
1982	80c. Maria Callas ("Tosca")	40	25
1983	2cor. Fyodor Chaliapin ("Boris Godunov")	85	45
1984	5cor. Enrico Caruso ("La Juive")	2·00	1·00

MS1985 137×119 mm. 1cor. As 80c.; Nos. 1983/4. Perf or imperf — 4·25 — 4·00

289 The First Station

1975. Easter. The 14 Stations of the Cross.

1986	**289**	1c. multicoloured (postage)	15	15
1987	-	2c. multicoloured	15	15
1988	-	3c. multicoloured	15	15
1989	-	4c. multicoloured	15	15
1990	-	5c. multicoloured	15	15
1991	-	15c. multicoloured	15	15
1992	-	20c. multicoloured	15	15
1993	-	25c. multicoloured	15	15
1994	-	35c. multicoloured	15	15
1995	-	40c. multicoloured (air)	15	15
1996	-	50c. multicoloured	15	15
1997	-	80c. multicoloured	20	20
1998	-	1cor. multicoloured	25	20
1999	-	5cor. multicoloured	1·20	1·00

DESIGNS: 2c. to 5cor. Different Stations of the Cross.

290 "The Spirit of 76"

1975. Bicentenary of American Independence (1st series). Multicoloured.

2000	1c. Type **290** (postage)	15	15
2001	2c. Pitt addressing Parliament	15	15
2002	3c. Paul Revere's Ride (horiz)	15	15
2003	4c. Demolishing statue of George III (horiz)	15	15
2004	5c. Boston Massacre	15	15
2005	10c. Tax stamp and George III 3d. coin (horiz)	15	15
2006	15c. Boston Tea Party (horiz)	15	15
2007	20c. Thomas Jefferson	15	15
2008	25c. Benjamin Franklin	15	15
2009	30c. Signing of Declaration of Independence (horiz)	15	15
2010	35c. Surrender of Cornwallis at Yorktown (horiz)	20	20
2011	40c. Washington's Farewell (horiz) (air)	20	15
2012	50c. Washington addressing Congress (horiz)	25	15
2013	2cor. Washington arriving for Presidential Inauguration (horiz)	1·00	80
2014	5cor. Statue of Liberty and flags	2·10	1·90

MS2015 133×128 mm. 7cor. As 1c. Perf or imperf — 3·00 — 3·00

See also Nos. 2506/**MS**2072.

291 Saluting the Flag

1975. "Nordjamb 75" World Scout Jamboree, Norway. Multicoloured.

2016	1c. Type **291** (postage)	10	10
2017	2c. Scout canoe	10	10
2018	3c. Scouts shaking hands	10	10
2019	4c. Scout preparing meal	10	10
2020	5c. Entrance to Nicaraguan camp	10	10
2021	20c. Scouts meeting	20	20
2022	35c. Aerial view of camp (air)	20	20
2023	40c. Scouts making music	20	20
2024	1cor. Camp-fire	50	20
2025	10cor. Lord Baden-Powell	2·20	1·70

MS2026 Two sheets each 126×112 mm. (a) 2cor. as 4c. and 3cor. as 2c. (Perf); (b) 2cor. as 5c. and 3cor. as 1cor. (Imperf) — 3·00 — 3·00

292 President Somoza

1975. President Somoza's New Term of Office, 1974–81.

2027	**292**	20c. multicoloured (postage)	15	15
2028	**292**	40c. multicoloured	15	15
2029	**292**	1cor. multicoloured (air)	30	30
2030	**292**	10cor. multicoloured	2·10	1·90
2031	**292**	20cor. multicoloured	4·25	3·50

293 "Chess Players" (L. Carracci)

1975. Chess. Multicoloured.

2032	1c. Type **293** (postage)	15	15
2033	2c. "Arabs playing Chess" (Delacroix)	15	15
2034	3c. "Cardinals playing Chess" (V. Marais-Milton)	15	15
2035	4c. "Duke Albrecht V of Bavaria and Anna of Austria at Chess" (H. Muelich) (vert)	15	15
2036	5c. "Chess game" (14th-century Persian manuscript)	15	15
2037	10c. "Origins of Chess" (India, 1602)	15	15
2038	15c. "Napoleon playing Chess in Schonbrunn Palace in 1809" (A. Uniechowski) (vert)	15	15
2039	20c. "The Chess Game in the House of Count Ingenheim" (J.E. Hummel)	15	15
2040	40c. "The Chess-players" (T. Eakins) (air)	20	15
2041	2cor. Fischer v Spassky match, Reykjavik, 1972	1·00	60
2042	5cor. "William Shakespeare and Ben Jonson playing Chess" (K. van Mander)	1·90	1·30

MS2043 142×67 mm. Nos. 2041/2 Perf or imperf — 4·25 — 4·00

294 Choir of King's College, Cambridge

1975. Christmas. Famous Choirs. Multicoloured.

2044	1c. Type **294** (postage)	15	15
2045	2c. Abbey Choir, Einsiedeln	15	15
2046	3c. Regensburg Cathedral choir	15	15
2047	4c. Vienna Boys' choir	15	15
2048	5c. Sistine Chapel choir	15	15
2049	15c. Westminster Cathedral choir	15	15
2050	20c. Mormon Tabernacle choir	15	15
2051	50c. School choir, Montserrat (air)	15	15
2052	1cor. St. Florian children's choir	30	20
2053	2cor. "Little Singers of the Wooden Cross" (vert)	40	30
2054	5cor. Pope with choristers of Pueri Cantores	1·20	1·00

MS2055 163×127 mm. 10cor. First performance of "Stille Nacht", Obendorf Church, Austria, 1818 (40×47 mm). Imperf — 11·50 — 11·00

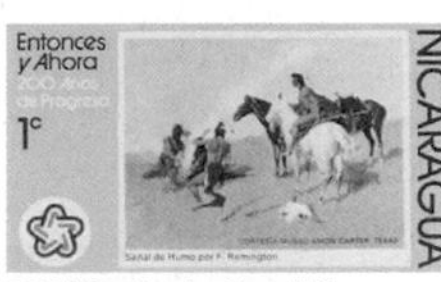

295 "The Smoke Signal" (F. Remington)

1976. Bicent of American Revolution (2nd series). "200 Years of Progress". Multicoloured.

2056	1c. Type **295** (postage)	10	10
2057	1c. Houston Space Centre	10	10
2058	2c. Lighting candelabra, 1976	10	10
2059	2c. Edison's lamp and houses	10	10
2060	3c. "Agriculture 1776"	10	10
2061	3c. "Agriculture 1976"	10	10
2062	4c. Harvard College, 1776	10	10
2063	4c. Harvard University, 1976	10	10
2064	5c. Horse and carriage	10	10
2065	5c. Boeing 747-100 airliner	10	10
2066	80c. Philadelphia, 1776 (air)	20	20
2067	80c. Washington, 1976	20	20
2068	2cor.75 "Bonhomme Richard" (American frigate) (John Paul Jones's flagship) and H.M.S. "Seraphis" (frigate), Battle of Flamborough Head	85	60
2069	2cor.75 U.S.S. "Glenard Phipscomp" (nuclear submarine)	85	60
2070	4cor. Wagon train	1·00	75
2071	4cor. Amtrak gas turbine train, 1973	1·00	75

MS2072 140×111 mm. 10cor. George Washington and Family; 10cor. President Ford and Family — 6·25 — 6·00

296 Italy, 1968

1976. Olympic Games, Victors in Rowing and Sculling. Multicoloured.

2073	1c. Denmark 1964 (postage)	10	10
2074	2c. East Germany 1972	10	10
2075	3c. Type **296**	10	10
2076	4c. Great Britain 1936	10	10
2077	5c. France 1952 (vert)	10	10
2078	35c. U.S.A. 1920 (vert)	20	10
2079	55c. Russia 1956 (vert) (air)	20	20
2080	70c. New Zealand 1972 (vert)	20	20
2081	90c. New Zealand 1968	30	20
2082	20cor. U.S.A. 1956	4·75	4·00

MS2083	157×109 mm. 10cor. First Women's Rowing "Eights" Event; part of U.S.A. crew, 1976 (39×52 mm)	3·25	3·00

1976. Air. East Germany Victory in Rowing Event at Montreal Olympics. Nos. 2082 and **MS**2083 optd **REPUBLICA DEMOCRATIC ALEMANA VENCEDOR EN. 1976.**

2084	20cor. multicoloured	5·25	3·50
MS2085	157×109 mm. 10cor. multicoloured	2·50	2·00

298 Buce Jenner

1976. Air. Decathlon Winner at Montreal Olympics.

MS2086 **298**	165×165 mm. 25cor. multicoloured	6·25	6·00

299 Mauritius 1847 2d. "Post Office"

1976. Rare and Famous Stamps. Multicoloured.

2087	1c. Type **299** (postage)	10	10
2088	2c. Western Australia 1854 "Inverted Mute Swan"	10	10
2089	3c. Mauritius 1847 1d. "Post Office"	10	10
2090	4c. Jamaica 1920 1s. inverted frame	10	10
2091	5c. U.S 1918 24c. inverted aircraft	10	10
2092	10c. Swiss 1845 Basel "Dove"	20	10
2093	25c. Canada 1959 Seaway inverted centre	20	10
2094	40c. Hawaiian 1851 2c. "Missionary" (air)	20	20
2095	1cor. G.B. 1840 "Penny Black"	20	20
2096	2cor. British Guiana 1850 1c. black on magenta	40	40
2097	5cor. Honduras 1925 airmail 25c. on 10c.	1·10	95
2098	10cor. Newfoundland 1919 "Hawker" airmail stamp	2·00	1·80
MS2099	140×101 mm. 4cor. Nicaragua 1881 "Grey-town" cover with G.B./ Nicaragua stamps	2·10	2·00

300 Olga Nunez de Saballos (Member of Parliament)

1977. Air. International Women's Year. Multicoloured.

2100	35c. Type **300**	15	15
2101	1cor. Josefa Toledo de Aguerri (educator)	30	30
2102	10cor. Hope Portocarreo de Samoza (President's wife)	2·30	2·00

1977. 50th Anniv of National Guard. Designs as **MS**1410a with revised inscription "1927–1977 Aniversario Guardia Nacional de Nicaragua".

MS2103	Two sheets each 160×100 mm. Nos. 1399/1404 and 1405/10. Imperf	4·00	3·75

301 "Graf Zeppelin" in Hangar

1977. 75th Anniv of First Zeppelin Flight. Multicoloured.

2104	1c. Type **301** (postage)	15	15
2105	2c. "Graf Zeppelin" in flight	15	15
2106	3c. Giffard's steam-powered dirigible airship, 1852	15	15
2107	4c. "Graf Zeppelin" in mooring hangar	15	15
2108	5c. "Graf Zeppelin" on ground	15	15
2109	35c. Astra airship "Ville de Paris" (air)	20	20
2110	70c. "Schwaben"	30	20
2111	3cor. "Graf Zeppelin" over Lake Constance	1·00	80
2112	10cor. LZ-2 on Lake Constance	3·25	2·50
MS2113	101×65 mm. 20cor. Mooring crew handling "Graf Zeppelin". Perf or imperf	7·25	5·00

302 Lindbergh and Map

1977. 50th Anniv of Lindbergh's Transatlantic Flight. Multicoloured.

2114	1c. Type **302** (postage)	15	15
2115	2c. Map and "Spirit of St. Louis"	15	15
2116	3c. Charles Lindbergh (vert)	15	15
2117	4c. "Spirit of St. Louis" crossing Atlantic	15	15
2118	5c. Charles Lindbergh standing by "Spirit of St. Louis"	15	15
2119	20c. Lindbergh, route and "Spirit of St. Louis"	15	15
2120	55c. Lindbergh landing in Nicaragua (1928) (air)	20	20
2121	80c. "Spirit of St. Louis" and route map	30	20
2122	2cor. "Spirit of St. Louis" flying along Nicaraguan coast	50	30
2123	10cor. Passing Momotombo (Nicaragua)	2·50	2·00
MS2124	124×80 mm. 20cor. "Spirit of St. Louis" in flight	6·25	5·00

303 Christmas Festival

1977. Christmas. Scenes from Tchaikovsky's "Nutcracker" Suite. Multicoloured.

2125	1c. Type **303**	15	15
2126	2c. Doll's dance	15	15
2127	3c. Clara and snowflakes	15	15
2128	4c. Snow fairy and prince	15	15
2129	5c. Snow fairies	15	15
2130	15c. Sugar fairy and prince	15	15
2131	40c. Waltz of the Flowers	15	15
2132	90c. Chinese dance	30	30
2133	1cor. Senora Bonbonierre	40	30
2134	10cor. Arabian dance	2·50	2·20
MS2135	130×109 mm. 20cor. Finale (air)	5·25	5·00

304 "Mr. and Mrs. Andrews". (Gainsborough)

1978. Paintings. Multicoloured.

2136	1c. Type **304** (postage)	10	10
2137	2c. "Giovanna Bacelli" (Gainsborough)	10	10
2138	3c. "Blue Boy" (Gainsborough)	10	10
2139	4c. "Francis I" (Titian)	10	10
2140	5c. "Charles V at Battle of Muhlberg" (Titian)	10	10
2141	25c. "Sacred Love" (Titian)	20	10
2142	5cor. "Hippopotamus and Crocodile Hunt" (Rubens) (air)	1·20	1·00
2143	10cor. "Duke of Lerma on Horseback" (Rubens)	2·50	2·00
MS2144	130×105 mm. 20cor. Rubens (from painting of Rubens and Isabella Brandt)	5·25	4·50

305 Gothic Portal with Rose Window, Small Basilica of St. Francis

1978. 750th Anniv of Canonisation of St. Francis of Assisi. Multicoloured.

2145	1c. Type **305** (postage)	10	10
2146	2c. St. Francis preaching to birds	10	10
2147	3c. Painting of St. Francis	10	10
2148	4c. Franciscan genealogical tree	10	10
2149	5c. Portiuncola	10	10
2150	15c. Autographed blessing	10	10
2151	25c. Windows of Large Basilica	10	10
2152	80c. St. Francis and wolf (air)	20	15
2153	10cor. St. Francis	2·10	1·80
MS2154	121×105 mm. 20cor. Our Lady of Conception (patron saint of Nicaragua)	4·25	3·50

306 Locomotive No. 6, 1921

1978. Centenary of Railway. Multicoloured.

2155	1c. Type **306** (postage)	25	20
2156	2c. Lightweight cargo locomotive	25	20
2157	3c. Steam locomotive No. 10, 1909	25	20
2158	4c. Baldwin steam locomotive No. 31, 1906	25	20
2159	5c. Baldwin steam locomotive No. 21, 1911	25	20
2160	15c. Presidential Pullman coach	30	20
2161	35c. Steam locomotive No. 33, 1907 (air)	40	20
2162	4cor. Baldwin steam locomotive No. 36, 1907	1·70	1·20
2163	10cor. Juniata steam locomotive, 1914, U.S.A.	2·75	2·00
MS2164	140×107 mm. 20cor. Map of Nicaraguan railway system	7·25	5·00

307 Mongol Warriors ("Michael Strogoff")

1978. 150th Birth Anniv of Jules Verne. Multicoloured.

2165	1c. Type **307** (postage)	10	10
2166	2c. Sea scene ("The Mysterious Island")	10	10
2167	3c. Sea monsters ("Journey to the Centre of the Earth")	10	10
2168	4c. Balloon and African elephant ("Five Weeks in a Balloon")	10	10
2169	90c. Submarine ("Twenty Thousand Leagues Under the Sea") (air)	30	20
2170	10cor. Balloon, Indian, steam locomotive and elephant ("Around the World in Eighty Days")	2·10	1·80
MS2171	113×87 mm. 20cor. Space ship ("From Earth to Moon")	6·25	5·00

308 Icarus

1978. 75th Anniv of History of Aviation. First Powered Flight. Multicoloured.

2172	1c. Type **308** (postage)	10	10
2173	2c. Montgolfier balloon (vert)	10	10
2174	3c. Wright Flyer I	10	10
2175	4c. Orville Wright in Wright Type A (vert)	10	10
2176	55c. Vought-Sikorsky VS-300 helicopter prototype (air)	30	20
2177	10cor. Space Shuttle	1·60	1·20
MS2178	143×114 mm. 20cor. "Flyer" III	6·25	5·00

309 Ernst Ocwirk and Alfredo di Stefano

1978. World Cup Football Championship, Argentina. Multicoloured.

2179	20c. Type **309** (postage)	15	15
2180	25c. Ralk Edstrom and Oswaldo Piazza	15	15
2181	50c. Franz Beckenbauer and Dennis Law (air)	20	20
2182	5cor. Dino Zoff and Pele	1·60	1·00
MS2183	102×77 mm. 20cor. Dominique Rocheteau and Johan Neeskens	6·25	5·00

310 "St. Peter" (Goya)

1978. Christmas. Multicoloured.

2184	10c. Type **310** (postage)	10	10
2185	15c. "St. Gregory" (Goya)	15	10
2186	3cor. "The Apostles John and Peter" (Durer) (air)	50	40
2187	10cor. "The Apostles Paul and Mark" (Durer)	1·70	1·20
MS2188	143×104 mm. 20cor. "The Child with Garland" (Durer)	4·25	3·50

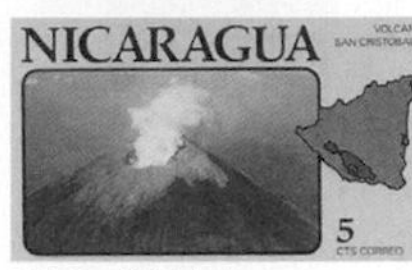

311 San Cristobal

1978. Volcanoes and Lakes. Multicoloured.

2189	5c. Type **311** (postage)	10	10
2190	5c. Lake de Cosiguina	10	10
2191	20c. Telica	15	10
2192	20c. Lake Jiloa	15	10
2193	35c. Cerro Negro (air)	20	20
2194	35c. Lake Masaya	20	20
2195	90c. Momotombo	30	20
2196	90c. Lake Asososca	30	20
2197	1cor. Mombacho	30	20
2198	1cor. Lake Apoyo	30	20
2199	10cor. Concepcion	2·30	1·50
2200	10cor. Lake Tiscapa	2·30	1·50

312 General O'Higgins

1979. Air. Birth Bicentenary of Bernardo O'Higgins (liberation hero).

2201	**312** 20cor. multicoloured	5·25	4·00

313 Ginger Plant and Broad-tailed Hummingbird

1979. Air. Flowers. Multicoloured.

2202	50c. Type **313**	30	20
2203	55c. Orchids	30	20
2204	70c. Poinsettia	30	20
2205	80c. "Poro poro"	30	20
2206	2cor. "Morpho cypris" (butterfly) and Guayacan flowers	40	30
2207	4cor. Iris	85	60

314 Children with football

315 Indian Postal Runner

316 Einstein and Albert Schweitzer

317 Loggerhead Turtle

1980. Year of Liberation (1979) and Nicaragua's Participation in Olympic Games. Unissued stamps overprinted. (a) International Year of the Child. Multicoloured.

2208 20c. Children on roundabout (postage) 30 20
2209 90c. Type **314** (air) 1·00 1·00
2210 2cor. Children with stamp albums 2·10 2·00
2211 2cor.20 Children playing with toy steam train and aircraft 12·50 12·00
2212 10cor. Baseball 4·25 4·00
MS2213 130×105 mm. 5cor. As No. 2211 (30×47 mm); 15cor. Dr. Hermann Gmeiner (30×47 mm) 50·00 50·00

(b) Death Centenary of Sir Rowland Hill. Multicoloured.

2214 20c. Type **315** (postage) 1·10 1·10
2215 35c. Pony express 2·30 2·20
2216 1cor. Pre-stamp letter (horiz) 4·75 4·50
2217 1cor.80 Sir Rowland Hill examining sheet of Penny Black stamps (air) 8·25 8·00
2218 2cor.20 Penny Blacks (horiz) 10·50 10·00
2219 5cor. Nicaraguan Zeppelin flight cover (horiz) 23·00 22·00
MS2220 130×105 mm. 20cor. Sir Rowland Hill and Indian postal runner (36×47 mm) 50·00 50·00

(c) Birth Centenary of Albert Einstein (physicist). Multicoloured.

2221 5c. Type **316** (postage) 70 70
2222 10c. Einstein and equation 2·00 90
2223 15c. Einstein and 1939 World Fair pavilion 1·60 1·50
2224 20c. Einstein and Robert Oppenheimer 1·90 1·80
2225 25c. Einstein in Jerusalem 2·50 2·50
2226 1cor. Einstein and Nobel Prize medal (air) 7·75 7·50
2227 2cor.75 Einstein and space exploration 17·00 16·00
2228 10cor. Einstein and Mahatma Gandhi 50·00 50·00
MS2229 130×105 mm. 5cor. Einstein at work (53×36 mm); 15cor. As No. 2228 (53×36 mm) 41·00 40·00

(d) Endangered Turtles. Multicoloured.

2230 90c. Type **317** 6·25 6·00
2231 2cor. Leatherback turtle 10·50 10·00
2232 2cor.20 Ridley turtle 11·50 11·00
2233 10cor. Hawksbill turtle 36·00 35·00
MS2234 150×105 mm. 5cor. As No. 2231 (51×32 mm); 15cor. Green turtles (51×32 mm) 41·00 40·00

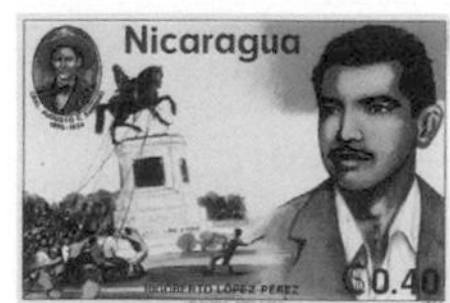

318 Rigoberto Lopez Perez and Crowds pulling down Statue

1980. First Anniv of the Revolution. Multicoloured.

2235 40c. Type **318** 10 10
2236 75c. Street barricade 10 10
2237 1cor. "Learn to Read" emblem (vert) 20 10
2238 1cor.25 German Pomares Ordonez and jungle fighters 30 20
2239 1cor.85 Victory celebrations (vert) 40 20
2240 2cor.50 Carlos Fonesca and camp-fire 50 40
2241 5cor. Gen. Augusto Sandino and flag (vert) 1·20 1·00
MS2242 118×90 mm. 10cor. Nicaraguan landscape 6·25 5·00

1980. Literacy Year. Unissued stamps optd **1980 ANO DE LA ALFABETIZACION**. (a) International Year of the Child. As Nos. 2208/12.

2243 - 20c. Children on roundabout (postage) 1·80 1·70
2244 **314** 90c. Children with football (air) 1·80 1·70
2245 - 2cor. Children with stamp albums 1·80 1·70
2246 - 2cor.20 Children playing with toy steam train and airplane 23·00 22·00
2247 - 10cor. Baseball 8·25 8·00
MS2248 105×90 mm. 10cor. Dr. Hermann Gmeiner 41·00 40·00

(b) Death Centenary of Sir Rowland Hill. Nos. 2214/16.

2249 **315** 20c. Indian postal runner 1·20 1·20
2250 - 35c. Pony express 1·20 1·20
2251 - 1cor. Pre-stamp letter (horiz) 1·20 1·20
MS2252 83×100 mm. 10cor. Penny Black and Nicaraguan 2c. stamp 12·50 12·00

(c) Birth Centenary of Albert Einstein (physicist). As Nos. 2221/8.

2253 5c. Optd **"YURI GAGARIN/12/IV/1961/LER HOMBRE EN EL ESPACIO"** (postage) 6·25 6·00
2254 10c. Optd **"LURABA 1981"** and space shuttle 6·25 6·00
2255 15c. Optd **"SPACE SHUTTLE"** and craft 6·25 6·00
2256 20c. Optd **ANO DE LA ALFABETIZACION** 6·25 6·00
2257 25c. Optd **"16/VII/1969/LER HOMBRE A LA LUNA"** and **"APOLLO XI"** 6·25 6·00
2258 1cor. Optd As No. 2256 (air) 6·25 6·00
2259 2cor.75 Optd As No. 2256 6·25 6·00
2260 10cor. Optd **"LUNOJOD 1"** and vehicle 6·25 6·00
MS2261 111×85 mm. 10cor. Einstein at work £100 £100

(d) Air. Endangered Species. Turtles. As Nos. 2230/3. Multicoloured.

2262 **317** 90c. Loggerhead turtle 4·25 4·00
2263 - 2cor. Leatherback turtle 4·25 4·00
2264 - 2cor.20 Ridley turtle 4·25 4·00
2265 - 10cor. Hawksbill turtle 4·25 4·00
MS2266 140×105 mm. 5cor. Green turtles £100 £100

320 Resplendent Quetzal

1981. "WIPA" 1981 International Stamp Exhibition, Vienna. Sheet 93×55 mm.

MS2267 **320** 10cor. multicoloured 3·00 2·20

321 Footballer and El Molinon Stadium

1981. World Cup Football Championship, Spain. (1st issue). Venues. Multicoloured.

2268 5c. Type **321** 10 10
2269 20c. Sanchez Pizjuan, Seville 10 10
2270 25c. San Mames, Bilbao 10 10
2271 30c. Vincent Calderon, Madrid 15 10
2272 50c. R.C.D. Espanol, Barcelona 15 10
2273 4cor. New Stadium, Valladolid 50 30
2274 5cor. Balaidos, Vigo 65 35
2275 10cor. Santiago Bernabeu, Madrid 1·40 80
MS2276 65×79 mm. 10cor. Nou Camp, Barcelona (36×28 mm) 2·10 1·50

See also Nos. 2325/**MS**2332.

322 Adult Education

1981. Second Anniv of Revolution. Multicoloured.

2277 50c. Type **322** (postage) 15 10
2278 2cor.10 Workers marching (air) 30 30
2279 3cor. Roadbuilding and container ship 45 30
2280 6cor. Medical services 85 50

323 Allegory of Revolution

1981. 20th Anniv of Sandinista National Liberation Front. Multicoloured.

2281 50c. Type **323** (postage) 15 10
2282 4cor. Sandinista guerrilla (air) 60 40

324 Postman

1981. 12th Postal Union of the Americas and Spain Congress, Managua. Multicoloured.

2283 50c. Type **324** (postage) 10 10
2284 2cor.10 Pony Express (air) 30 20
2285 3cor. Postal Headquarters, Managua 50 20
2286 6cor. Government building, globe and flags of member countries 1·00 50

325 Reliefs depicting Bulgarian History (image scaled to 51% of original size)

1981. Air. 1300th Anniv of Bulgarian State. Sheet 96×70 mm. Imperf.

MS2287 **325** 10cor. multicoloured 3·00 2·00

326 "Nymphaea capensis"

1981. Water Lilies. Multicoloured.

2288 50c. Type **326** (postage) 15 10
2289 1cor. "Nymphaea daubenyana" 20 15
2290 1cor.20 "Nymphaea Marliacea Chromat" 30 20
2291 1cor.80 "Nymphaea Dir. Geo. T. Moore" 40 20
2292 2cor. "Nymphaea lotus" 50 30
2293 2cor.50 "Nymphaea B.G. Berry" 60 40
2294 10cor. "Nymphaea Gladstoniana" (air) 2·10 1·00

327 Giant Panda

1981. Air. "Philatokyo 81 International Stamp Exhibition". Sheet 100×61 mm.

MS2295 **327** 10cor. multicoloured 2·10 1·80

328 Cardinal Tetra

1981. Tropical Fish. Multicoloured.

2296 50c. Type **328** (postage) 15 10
2297 1cor. Guppy 20 15
2298 1cor.85 Striped headstander 30 20
2299 2cor.10 Skunk corydoras 40 20
2300 2cor.50 Black-finned pearlfish 50 30
2301 3cor.50 Long-finned killie (air) 60 40
2302 4cor. Red swordtail 85 50

329 Frigate

1981. Air. "Espamer 81 Stamp Exhibition, Buenos Aires". Sheet 98×59 mm.

MS2303 **329** 10cor. multicoloured 2·10 1·80

330 Lineated Woodpecker

1981. Birds. Multicoloured.

2304 50c. Type **330** (postage) 30 20
2305 1cor.20 Keel-billed toucan (horiz) 40 20
2306 1cor.80 Finsch's conure (horiz) 50 30
2307 2cor. Scarlet macaw 50 30
2308 3cor. Slaty-tailed trogon (air) 60 30
2309 4cor. Violet sabrewing (horiz) 75 40
2310 6cor. Blue-crowned motmot 1·10 70

331 Satellite in Orbit

1981. Satellite Communications. Multicoloured.

2311 50c. Type **331** (postage) 15 10
2312 1cor. "Intelsat IVA" 20 15
2313 1cor.50 "Intelsat V" moving into orbit 30 20
2314 2cor. Rocket releasing "Intelsat V" 30 30
2315 3cor. Satellite and Space Shuttle (air) 60 40
2316 4cor. "Intelsat V" and world maps 1·00 50
2317 5cor. Tracking stations 1·30 60

332 Steam Locomotive at Lake Granada

1981. Locomotives. Multicoloured.

2318 50c. Type **332** (postage) 15 10
2319 1cor. Vulcan Iron Works steam locomotive No. 35, 1946 30 15
2320 1cor.20 Baldwin steam locomotive No. 21, 1911 (inscribed "Philadelphia Iron Works") 35 20
2321 1cor.80 Steam crane, 1909 50 30
2322 2cor. General Electric Model "U10B" diesel locomotive, 1960s 60 30
2323 2cor.50 German diesel railbus, 1954 (dated "1956") 70 40
2324 6cor. Japanese-built diesel railbus, 1967 (air) 1·90 70

333 Heading Ball

1982. World Cup Football Championship, Spain (2nd issue). Multicoloured.

2325 5c. Type **333** (postage) 15 10
2326 20c. Running with ball 15 10
2327 25c. Running with ball (different) 15 10
2328 2cor.50 Saving goal 40 35
2329 3cor.50 Goalkeeper diving for ball (horiz) 60 40
2330 4cor. Kicking ball (air) 70 40
2331 10cor. Tackle (horiz) 1·40 80
MS2332 98×61 mm. 10cor. Goalkeeper attempting save (39×31 mm) 3·00 2·00

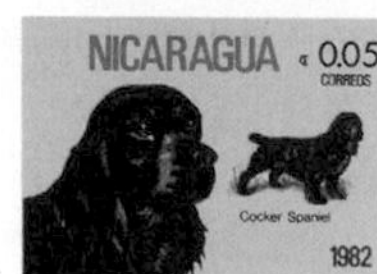

334 Cocker Spaniel

1982. Pedigree Dogs. Multicoloured.

2333	5c. Type **334** (postage)	10	10
2334	20c. Alsatian	15	10
2335	25c. English setter	15	10
2336	2cor.50 Brittany spaniel	50	30
2337	3cor. Boxer (air)	60	35
2338	3cor.50 Pointer	60	40
2339	6cor. Collie	90	60

335 Satellite Communications

1982. Air. I.T.U. Congress.

2340	**335** 25cor. multicoloured	4·25	3·00

336 *Dynamine myrrhina*

1982. Butterflies. Multicoloured.

2341	50c. Type **336** (postage)	15	10
2342	1cor.20 *Eunica alcmena*	30	20
2343	1cor.50 *Callizona acesta*	30	20
2344	2cor. *Adelpha leuceria*	40	30
2345	3cor. *Parides iphidamas* (air)	75	30
2346	3cor.50 *Consul hippona*	90	40
2347	4cor. *Morpho peleides*	1·10	40

337 Laika and Rocket

1982. Space Exploration. Multicoloured.

2348	5c. Type **337** (postage)	10	10
2349	15c. Satellite (vert)	10	10
2350	50c. "Apollo–Soyuz" link	15	10
2351	1cor.50 Satellite	30	20
2352	2cor.50 Docking in space	50	30
2353	5cor. Russian space station (air)	85	40
2354	6cor. Space shuttle "Columbia" (vert)	1·00	50

338 Mailcoach

1982. Centenary of U.P.U. Membership. Multicoloured.

2355	50c. Type **338** (postage)	15	10
2356	1cor.20 "Victoria" (packet steamer)	25	15
2357	3cor.50 Steam locomotive, 1953 (air)	50	30
2358	10cor. Boeing 727-100 airliner	1·50	90

339 Cyclists

1982. 14th Central American and Caribbean Games. Multicoloured.

2359	10c. Type **339** (postage)	10	10
2360	15c. Swimming (horiz)	10	10
2361	25c. Basketball	10	10
2362	50c. Weightlifting	15	10
2363	2cor.50 Handball (air)	50	30
2364	3cor. Boxing (horiz)	60	40
2365	9cor. Football (horiz)	2·10	1·00
MS2366	65×90 mm. 10cor. Baseball (30×39 mm)	2·50	1·50

340 Balloon

1982. Air. "Philexfrance 82 International Stamp Exhibition, Paris". Sheet 79×91 mm.

MS2367	**340** 15cor. multicoloured	3·00	2·00

341 Washington passing through Trenton

1982. 250th Birth Anniv of George Washington. Multicoloured.

2368	50c. Mount Vernon, Washington's house (39×49 mm) (postage)	15	10
2369	1cor. Washington signing the Constitution (horiz)	25	20
2370	2cor. Type **341**	40	25
2371	2cor.50 Washington crossing the Delaware (horiz) (air)	50	30
2372	3cor.50 Washington at Valley Forge (horiz)	65	40
2373	4cor. Washington at the Battle of Trenton	85	40
2374	6cor. Washington at Princeton	1·20	60

342 Carlos Fonseca, Dove and Flags

1982. Third Anniv of Revolution. Multicoloured.

2375	50c. Type **342** (postage)	15	10
2376	2cor.50 Ribbons forming dove (vert) (air)	50	30
2377	1cor. Augusto Sandino and dove (vert)	70	40
2378	6cor. Dove	1·20	60

343 "Vase of Flowers" (R. Penalba)

1982. Paintings. Multicoloured.

2379	25c. Type **343** (postage)	10	10
2380	50c. "El Gueguense" (M. Garcia) (horiz)	10	10
2381	1cor. "The Couple" (R. Perez)	20	10
2382	1cor.20 "Canales Valley" (A. Mejias) (horiz)	20	10
2383	1cor.85 "Portrait of Senora Castellon" (T. Jerez)	40	20
2384	2cor. "The Vendors" (L. Cerrato)	40	25
2385	9cor. "Sitting Woman" (A. Morales) (horiz) (air)	2·30	1·10
MS2386	86×64 mm. 10cor. "Roosters" (P. Ortiz) (horiz)	2·50	1·50

344 Lenin and Dimitrov, Moscow, 1921

1982. Birth Centenary of Georgi Dimitrov (Bulgarian statesman). Multicoloured.

2387	50c. Type **344** (postage)	10	10
2388	2cor.50 Dimitrov & Todor Yikov, Sofia, 1946 (air)	45	30
2389	4cor. Dimitrov and flag	75	50

345 Ausberto Narvaez

1982. 26th Anniv of State of Resistance Movement. Multicoloured.

2390	50c. Type **345** (postage)	10	10
2391	2cor.50 Cornelio Silva	50	30
2392	4cor. Rigoberto Lopez Perez (air)	60	45
2393	6cor. Edwin Castro	1·00	65

346 Old Ruins at Leon

1982. Tourism. Multicoloured.

2394	50c. Type **346** (postage)	10	10
2395	1cor. Ruben Dario Theatre and Park, Managua	20	10
2396	1cor.20 Independence Square, Granada	35	20
2397	1cor.80 Corn Island	35	20
2398	2cor. Carter Santiago Volcano, Masaya	45	30
2399	2cor.50 El Coyotepe Fortress, Masaya (air)	45	30
2400	3cor.50 Luis A. Velazquez Park, Managua	55	45

347 Karl Marx and View of Trier

1982. Death Centenary of Karl Marx. Multicoloured.

2401	1cor. Type **347** (postage)	20	10
2402	4cor. Marx and grave in Highgate Cemetery (air)	75	45

348 Stacking Cane and Fruit

1982. World Food Day. Multicoloured.

2403	50c. Picking Fruit (horiz)	20	20
2404	1cor. Type **348**	20	20
2405	2cor. Cutting sugar cane (horiz)	35	25
2406	10cor. F.A.O. and P.A.N. emblems (horiz)	1·50	1·30

349 "Santa Maria"

1982. 490th Anniv of Discovery of America. Multicoloured.

2407	50c. Type **349** (postage)	20	10
2408	1cor. "Nina"	25	20
2409	1cor.50 "Pinta"	35	20
2410	2cor. Columbus and fleet	45	30
2411	2cor.50 Fleet and map of route (air)	50	30
2412	4cor. Arrival in America	75	40
2413	7cor. Death of Columbus	1·30	85
MS2414	71×56 mm. 10cor. "Santa Maria" (vert)	2·75	1·60

350 *Lobelia laxiflora*

1982. Woodland Flowers. Multicoloured.

2415	50c. Type **350** (postage)	10	10
2416	1cor.20 *Bombacopsis quinata*	25	20
2417	1cor.80 *Mimosa albida*	40	25
2418	2cor. *Epidendrum alatum*	40	25
2419	2cor.50 Passion flower *Passiflora foetida* wrongly inscr *Pasiflora* (air)	40	25
2420	3cor.50 *Clitoria* sp.	60	40
2421	5cor. *Russelia sarmentosa*	85	50

351 "Micrurus lemniscatus"

1982. Reptiles. Multicoloured.

2422	10c. Type **351** (postage)	10	10
2423	50c. Common iguana "Iguana iguana" (horiz)	20	10
2424	2cor. "Lachesis muta" (snake) (horiz)	45	30
2425	2cor.50 Hawksbill turtle "Eretmochelys imbricata" (horiz) (air)	90	30
2426	3cor. Boa constrictor "Constrictor constrictor"	1·10	35
2427	3cor.50 American crocodile "Crocodilus acutus" (horiz)	1·20	40
2428	5cor. Diamond-back rattlesnake "Sistrurus catenatus" (horiz)	1·90	65

352 Tele-cor Building, Managua

1982. Telecommunications Day. Multicoloured.

2429	1cor. Type **352** (postage)	20	10
2430	50c. Interior of radio transmission room (air)	10	10

353 Girl with Dove

1983. Air. Non-Aligned States Conference.

2431	**353** 4cor. multicoloured	85	45

354 Jose Marti and Birthplace

1983. 130th Birth Anniv of Jose Marti (Cuban revolutionary).

2432	**354** 1cor. multicoloured	30	15

355 Boxing

1983. Olympic Games, Los Angeles (1st issue). Multicoloured.

2433	50c. Type **355** (postage)	25	10
2434	1cor. Gymnastics	25	15
2435	1cor.50 Running	30	20
2436	2cor. Weightlifting	40	20
2437	4cor. Discus (air)	75	40
2438	5cor. Basketball	95	45
2439	6cor. Cycling	1·20	65
MS2440	60×88 mm. 15cor. Sailing (31×39 mm)	3·00	1·60

See also Nos. 2609/**MS**2616.

356 *Neomarica coerulea*

1983. Flowers.

2441	**356**	1cor. blue	20	10
2442	-	1cor. violet	20	10
2443	-	1cor. mauve	20	10
2444	-	1cor. brown	20	10
2445	-	1cor. green	20	10
2446	-	1cor. blue	20	10
2447	-	1cor. green	20	10
2448	-	1cor. green	20	10
2449	-	1cor. mauve	20	10
2450	-	1cor. red	20	10
2451	-	1cor. grey	20	10
2452	-	1cor. yellow	20	10
2453	-	1cor. brown	20	10
2454	-	1cor. purple	20	10
2455	-	1cor. green	20	10
2456	-	1cor. black	20	10

DESIGNS: No. 2442, "Tabebula ochraceae"; 2443, "Laella sp"; 2444, "Plumeria rubra"; 2445, "Brassavola nodosa"; 2446, "Stachytarpheta indica"; 2447, "Cochiospermum sp"; 2448, "Malvaviscus arboreus"; 2449, "Telecoma stans"; 2450, "Hibiscus rosa-sinensis"; 2451, "Cattleya lueddemanniana"; 2452, "Tagetes erecta"; 2453, "Senecio sp"; 2454, "Sobralia macrantha"; 2455, "Thumbergia alata"; 2456, "Bixa orellana".

See also Nos. 2739/54, 2838/53 and 3087/3102.

357 Momotombo Geothermal Electrical Plant

1983. Air. Energy.

2457	**357**	2cor.50 multicoloured	50	35

358 Map of Nicaragua and Girl picking Coffee

1983. Papal Visit.

2458	-	50c. red, black and blue (postage)	20	10
2459	**358**	1cor. multicoloured	30	20
2460	-	4cor. multicoloured (air)	1·00	60
2461	-	7cor. multicoloured	1·50	85
MS2462		80×66 mm. 15cor. multicoloured (31×39 mm)	3·25	1·90

DESIGNS: 50c. Demonstrating crowd; 4cor. Pres. Cordova Rivas and Pope John Paul II; 7cor. Pope outside Managua Cathedral; Pope John Paul II.

359 "Xilophanes chiron"

1983. Moths. Multicoloured.

2463	15c. Type **359** (postage)	25	10
2464	50c. "Protoparce ochus"	25	10
2465	65c. "Pholus lasbruscae"	25	10
2466	1cor. "Amphypterus gannascus"	25	15
2467	1cor.50 "Pholus licaon"	30	20
2468	2cor. "Agrius cingulata"	40	25
2469	10cor. "Rothschildia jurulla" (vert) (air)	2·00	1·10

360 La Recoleccion Church, Leon

1983. Monuments. Multicoloured.

2470	50c. Subtiava Church, Leon (horiz) (postage)	10	10
2471	1cor. La Inmaculada Castle, Rio San Juan (horiz)	25	10
2472	2cor. Type **360**	40	20
2473	4cor. Ruben Dario Monument, Managua (air)	80	45

361 Passenger Carriage

1983. Railway Wagons. Multicoloured.

2474	15c. Type **361** (postage)	10	10
2475	65c. Goods wagon No. 1034	25	10
2476	1cor. Tanker wagon No. 931	30	15
2477	1cor.50 Xolotlan hopper wagon	35	15
2478	4cor. Railcar (air)	75	40
2479	5cor. Tipper truck	85	50
2480	7cor. Railbus	1·50	70

362 Helping Earthquake Victim

1983. Red Cross. Multicoloured.

2481	50c. Aiding flood victims (horiz) (postage)	10	10
2482	1cor. Placing stretcher patient into ambulance (horiz)	20	10
2483	4cor. Type **362** (air)	75	40
2484	5cor. Doctor examining wounded soldier (horiz)	85	65

363 Raising Telephone Pole

1983. World Communications Year.

2485	**363**	1cor. multicoloured	25	15

364 Ibex

1983. Air. "Tembal 83 International Stamp Exhibition, Basel". Sheet 79×64 mm.

MS2486	**364** 15cor. multicoloured	2·50	1·50

365 Basketball

1983. Ninth Pan-American Games. Multicoloured.

2487	15c. Basketball (horiz) (postage)	15	10
2488	50c. Water polo (horiz)	15	10
2489	65c. Running (horiz)	20	10
2490	1cor. Type **365**	20	10
2491	2cor. Weightlifting	45	25
2492	7cor. Fencing (horiz) (air)	1·20	70
2493	8cor. Gymnastics (horiz)	1·30	75

MS2494	75×85 mm. 15cor. Boxing (39×31 mm)	2·50	1·30

366 Boeing 727-100

1983. Air. "Expo Filnic National Stamp Exhibition". Sheet 79×60 mm.

MS2495	**366** 10cor. multicoloured	2·50	1·30

367 Container Ship being Unloaded

1983. Fourth Anniv of Revolution. Multicoloured.

2496	1cor. Type **367**	20	10
2497	2cor. Telcor building, Leon	45	25

368 Carlos Fonseca

1983. Founders of Sandinista National Liberation Front. Multicoloured.

2498	50c. Escobar, Navarro, Ubeda, Pomares and Ruiz (postage)	10	10
2499	1cor. Santos Lopez, Borge, Buitrago and Mayorga	20	10
2500	4cor. Type **368** (air)	85	50

369 Simon Bolivar on Horseback

1983. Birth Bicentenary of Simon Bolivar. Multicoloured.

2501	50c. Bolivar and Sandinista guerrilla	10	10
2502	1cor. Type **369**	20	10

370 Jaguar

1983. Air. "Brasiliana 83 International Stamp Exhibition, Rio de Janeiro. Sheet 95×65 mm.

MS2503	**370** 15cor. multicoloured	5·50	2·50

371 Movements of a Pawn

1983. Chess. Multicoloured.

2504	15c. Type **371** (postage)	15	10
2505	65c. Knight's movements	20	10
2506	1cor. Bishop's movements	20	10
2507	2cor. Rook's movements	35	25
2508	4cor. Queen's movements (air)	65	45
2509	5cor. King's movements	85	50
2510	7cor. Game in progress	1·20	70

372 Speed Skating

1983. Winter Olympic Games, Sarajevo (1984) (1st issue). Multicoloured.

2511	50c. Type **372** (postage)	10	10
2512	1cor. Slalom	20	10
2513	1cor.50 Luge	25	20
2514	2cor. Ski jumping	35	25
2515	4cor. Figure skating (air)	65	40
2516	5cor. Downhill skiing	85	50
2517	6cor. Biathlon	1·10	60
MS2518	51×80 mm. 15cor. Ice hockey (31×39 mm)	2·75	1·70

373 Soldiers with German Shepherd Dog

1983. Armed Forces.

2519	**373**	4cor. multicoloured	65	45

374 "Madonna of the Chair"

1983. 500th Birth Anniv of Raphael. Multicoloured.

2520	50c. Type **374** (postage)	10	10
2521	1cor. "Esterhazy Madonna"	20	10
2522	1cor.50 "Sistine Madonna"	30	15
2523	2cor. "Madonna of the Linnet"	35	20
2524	4cor. "Madonna of the Meadow" (air)	75	45
2525	5cor. "Madonna of the Garden"	95	50
2526	6cor. "Adoration of the Kings"	1·10	70
MS2527	86×123 mm. 15cor. "Foligno Madonna"	2·75	1·30

375 Pottery Idol

1983. Archaeological Finds. Multicoloured.

2528	50c. Type **375** (postage)	10	10
2529	1cor. Pottery dish with ornamental lid	20	10
2530	2cor. Vase with snake design	35	25
2531	4cor. Pottery dish (air)	85	45

376 Metal being poured into Moulds

1983. Nationalization of Mines. Multicoloured.

2532	1cor. Type **376** (postage)	20	10
2533	4cor. Workers and mine (air)	85	60

377 Radio Operator and Sinking Liner

1983. "Fracap '83" Congress of Radio Amateurs of Central America and Panama. Multicoloured.

2534	1cor. Type **377**	30	15
2535	4cor. Congress emblem and town destroyed by earthquake	75	45

378 Tobacco

1983. Agrarian Reform.

No.	Type	Description	Unused	Used
2536	378	1cor. green	20	15
2537	-	2cor. orange	35	25
2538	-	4cor. brown	75	40
2539	-	5cor. blue	85	50
2540	-	6cor. lavender	1·10	60
2541	-	7cor. purple	1·30	70
2542	-	8cor. purple	1·30	80
2543	-	10cor. brown	1·70	95

DESIGNS: 2cor. Cotton; 4cor. Maize; 5cor. Sugar; 6cor. Cattle; 7cor. Rice; 8cor. Coffee; 10cor. Bananas.

See also Nos. 2755/62 and 2854/61.

379 Fire Engine with Ladder

1983. Fire Engines. Multicoloured.

No.	Description	Unused	Used
2544	50c. Type **379** (postage)	15	10
2545	1cor. Water tanker	20	15
2546	6cor. Crew vehicle, 1930	1·10	60
2547	1cor.50 Pump with extension fire hoses (air)	35	20
2548	2cor. Pump with high-pressure tank	45	25
2548a	4cor. Water tanker	60	40
2549	5cor. Fire engine, 1910	95	50

380 Jose Marti and General Sandino

1983. Nicaragua–Cuba Solidarity. Multicoloured.

No.	Description	Unused	Used
2550	1cor. Type **380** (postage)	20	10
2551	4cor. Teacher, doctor and welder (air)	75	45

381 "Adoration of the Shepherds" (Hugo van der Gaes)

1983. Christmas. Multicoloured.

No.	Description	Unused	Used
2552	50c. Type **381** (postage)	10	10
2553	1cor. "Adoration of the Kings" (Domenico Ghirlandaio)	20	10
2554	2cor. "Adoration of the Shepherds" (El Greco)	35	25
2555	7cor. "Adoration of the Kings" (Konrad von Soest) (air)	1·10	50

382 Anniversary Emblem

1984. Air. 25th Anniv of Cuban Revolution.

No.	Type	Description	Unused	Used
2557	382	4cor. red, blue and black	75	50
2558	-	6cor. multicoloured	1·10	70

DESIGN: 6cor. Fidel Castro and Che Guevara.

383 Bobsleigh

1984. Winter Olympic Games, Sarajevo.(2nd issue) Multicoloured.

No.	Description	Unused	Used
2559	50c. Type **383** (postage)	10	10
2560	50c. Biathlon	10	10
2561	1cor. Slalom	20	10
2562	1cor. Speed skating	20	10
2563	4cor. Skiing (air)	75	45
2564	5cor. Ice-dancing	95	60
2565	10cor. Ski-jumping	1·60	85
MS2566	64×73 mm. 15cor. Ice hockey (31×35 mm)	3·75	1·90

384 Chinchilla

1984. Cats. Multicoloured.

No.	Description	Unused	Used
2567	50c. Type **384** (postage)	30	15
2568	50c. Longhaired white	30	15
2569	1cor. Red tabby	35	15
2570	2cor. Tortoiseshell	45	25
2571	4cor. Burmese	95	45
2572	3cor. Siamese (air)	75	45
2573	7cor. Longhaired silver	1·40	80

385 National Arms

1984. 50th Death Anniv of Augusto Sandino. Multicoloured.

No.	Description	Unused	Used
2574	1cor. Type **385** (postage)	30	15
2575	4cor. Augusto Sandino (air)	95	45

386 Blanca Arauz

1984. International Women's Day.

No.	Type	Description	Unused	Used
2576	386	1cor. multicoloured	20	15

387 Sunflower

1984. Agricultural Flowers. Multicoloured.

No.	Description	Unused	Used
2577	50c. Type **387** (postage)	30	15
2578	50c. "Poinsettia pulcherrima"	30	15
2579	1cor. "Cassia alata"	35	15
2580	1cor. "Antigonon leptopus"	35	15
2581	3cor. "Bidens pilosa" (air)	55	35
2582	4cor. "Althaea rosea"	75	45
2583	5cor. "Rivea corymbosa"	95	60

388 "Soyuz"

1984. Space Anniversaries. Multicoloured.

No.	Description	Unused	Used
2584	50c. Type **388** (15th anniv of "Soyuz 6", "7" and "8" flights) (postage)	10	10
2585	50c. "Soyuz" (different) (15th anniv of "Soyuz 6", "7" and "8" flights)	10	10
2586	1cor. "Apollo 11" approaching Moon (15th anniv of 1st manned landing)	20	15
2587	2cor. "Luna I" (25th anniv of 1st Moon satellite)	45	25
2588	3cor. "Luna II" (25th anniv of 1st Moon landing) (air)	65	45
2589	4cor. "Luna III" (25th anniv of 1st photographs of far side of Moon)	85	60
2590	9cor. Rocket (50th anniv of Korolev's book on space flight)	1·80	85

389 "Noli me Tangere" (detail)

1984. 450th Death Anniv of Correggio (artist). Multicoloured.

No.	Description	Unused	Used
2591	50c. Type **389** (postage)	10	10
2592	50c. "Madonna of St. Jerome" (detail)	10	10
2593	1cor. "Allegory of Virtue"	20	15
2594	2cor. "Allegory of Pleasure"	35	25
2595	3cor. "Ganymedes" (detail) (air)	55	35
2596	5cor. "The Danae" (detail)	85	50
2597	8cor. "Leda and the Swan" (detail)	1·30	85
MS2598	116×81 mm. 15cor. "St. John the Evangelist"	3·25	1·50

390 Daimler, 1886

1984. 150th Birth Anniv of Gottlieb Daimler (automobile designer). Multicoloured.

No.	Description	Unused	Used
2599	1cor. Type **390** (postage)	20	10
2600	1cor. Abadal, 1914 (horiz)	20	10
2601	2cor. Ford, 1903	45	25
2602	2cor. Renault, 1899	45	25
2603	3cor. Rolls Royce, 1910 (horiz) (air)	55	45
2604	4cor. Metallurgique, 1907 (horiz)	75	50
2605	7cor. Bugatti "Mod 40" (horiz)	1·30	60

391 "Cardinal Infante Dom Fernando"

1984. Air. "Espana 84 International Stamp Exhibition, Madrid". Sheet 76×98 mm.

No.	Type	Description	Unused	Used
MS2606	391	15cor. multicoloured	3·75	1·70

392 Mail Transport

1984. Air. 19th Universal Postal Union Congress Philatelic Salon, Hamburg.

No.	Description	Unused	Used
2607	15cor. Type **392**	3·25	1·70
MS2608	101×60 mm. 5cor. Zeppelin "Bodensee"	4·00	2·20

393 Basketball

1984. Olympic Games, Los Angeles (2nd issue). Multicoloured.

No.	Description	Unused	Used
2609	50c. Type **393** (postage)	20	10
2610	50c. Volleyball	20	10
2611	1cor. Hockey	30	15
2612	2cor. Tennis (air)	35	25
2613	3cor. Football (horiz)	55	45
2614	4cor. Water polo (horiz)	75	50
2615	9cor. Soccer (horiz)	1·90	85
MS2616	105×67 mm. 15cor. Baseball (horiz)	2·75	1·70

394 Horses and Carriage

1984. Air. "Expofilnic 84 National Stamp Exhibition". Sheet 86×66 mm.

No.	Type	Description	Unused	Used
MS2617	394	15cor. multicoloured	2·30	1·70

395 Rural Construction Site

1984. Fifth Anniv of Revolution. Multicoloured.

No.	Description	Unused	Used
2618	5c. Type **395** (postage)	20	10
2619	1cor. Diesel locomotive, Pacific–Atlantic line	45	25
2620	4cor. Ploughing with oxen and tractor (Agrarian reform) (air)	65	35
2621	7cor. State Council building	1·30	60

396 "Children defending Nature" (Pablo Herrera Berrios)

1984. UNESCO Environmental Protection Campaign. Multicoloured.

No.	Description	Unused	Used
2622	50c. Type **396** (postage)	20	10
2623	1cor. Living and dead forests	30	15
2624	2cor. Fisherman and dried river bed	45	25
2625	10cor. Hands holding plants (vert) (air)	1·90	1·00

397 Red Cross Airplane and Ambulance

1984. 50th Anniv of Nicaraguan Red Cross. Multicoloured.

No.	Description	Unused	Used
2626	1cor. Type **397** (postage)	30	15
2627	7cor. Battle of Solferino (125th anniv) (air)	1·20	60

398 "Discovery"

1984. Air. "Ausipex 84 International Stamp Exhibition, Melbourne". Sheet 74×94 mm.

No.	Type	Description	Unused	Used
MS2628	398	15cor. multicoloured	2·10	1·25

399 Ventura Escalante and Dominican Republic Flag

1984. Baseball. Multicoloured.

No.	Description	Unused	Used
2629	50c. Type **399** (postage)	20	15
2630	50c. Danial Herrera and Mexican flag	20	15
2631	1cor. Adalberto Herrera and Venezuelan flag	30	20
2632	1cor. Roberto Clemente and Nicaraguan flag	30	20
2633	3cor. Carlos Colas and Cuban flag (air)	55	45
2634	4cor. Stanley Cayasso and Argentinian flag	80	50
2635	5cor. Babe Ruth and U.S.A. flag	1·00	60

400 Central American Tapir

1984. Wildlife Protection. Multicoloured.

No.	Description	Mint	Used
2636	25c. Type **400** (postage)	30	15
2637	25c. Young tapir	30	15
2638	3cor. Close-up of tapir (air)	95	45
2639	4cor. Mother and young	1·30	50

401 Football in 1314

1985. World Cup Football Championship, Mexico (1986) (1st issue). Multicoloured.

No.	Description	Mint	Used
2640	50c. Type **401** (postage)	20	10
2641	50c. Football in 1500	20	10
2642	1cor. Football in 1872	30	15
2643	1cor. Football in 1846	30	15
2644	2cor. Football in 1883 (air)	35	25
2645	4cor. Football in 1890	55	35
2646	6cor. Football in 1953	95	50
MS2647	92×81 mm. 10cor. Footballers	2·30	1·30

See also Nos. 2731/**MS**2738 and 2812/**MS**2819.

402 *Strobilomyces retisporus*

1985. Fungi. Multicoloured.

No.	Description	Mint	Used
2648	50c. Type **402** (postage)	20	10
2649	50c. *Boletus calopus*	20	10
2650	1cor. *Boletus luridus*	30	15
2651	1cor. *Xerocomus illudens* (air)	30	15
2652	4cor. *Gyrodon merulioides*	75	35
2653	5cor. *Tylopilus plumbeoviolaceus*	95	45
2654	8cor. *Gyroporus castaneus*	1·40	70

403 Postal Runner and Map

1985. 13th Postal Union of the Americas and Spain Congress. Multicoloured.

No.	Description	Mint	Used
2655	1cor. Type **403** (postage)	50	15
2656	7cor. Casa Aviocar mail plane over map (air)	2·50	50

404 Cyclist

1985. Air. "Olymphilex 85 International Stamp Exhibition, Lausanne". Sheet 53×82 mm.

No.	Description	Mint	Used
MS2657	**404** 15cor. multicoloured	2·00	1·00

405 Cuban Crocodile

1985. Air. "Espamer 85 International Stamp Exhibition, Havana". Sheet 94×60 mm.

No.	Description	Mint	Used
MS2658	**405** 10cor. multicoloured	1·40	85

406 Steam Locomotive, Oldenburg

1985. 150th Anniv of German Railway. Multicoloured.

No.	Description	Mint	Used
2659	1cor. Type **406** (postage)	30	15
2660	1cor. Electric locomotive, Prussia	30	15
2661	9cor. Steam locomotive No. 88, Prussia (air)	1·00	45
2662	9cor. Double-deck tram	1·00	45
2663	15cor. Steam locomotive, Wurttemberg	1·70	70
2664	21cor. Steam locomotive, Germany	2·30	1·00
MS2665	80×60 mm. 42cor. Steam engine with tender (35×26 mm)	6·50	4·00

The miniature sheets also commemorates centenary of Nicaraguan railways.

407 Douglas, 1928

1985. Centenary of Motor Cycle. Multicoloured.

No.	Description	Mint	Used
2666	50c. Type **407** (postage)	35	15
2667	50c. FN, 1928	35	15
2668	1cor. Puch, 1938	45	25
2669	2cor. Wanderer, 1939 (air)	55	35
2670	4cor. Honda, 1949	1·20	45
2671	5cor. BMW, 1984	1·50	60
2672	7cor. Honda, 1984	2·00	85

408 "Matelea quirosii"

1985. Flowers. Multicoloured.

No.	Description	Mint	Used
2673	50c. Type **408** (postage)	35	15
2674	50c. "Ipomea nil"	35	15
2675	1cor. "Lysichitum americanum"	45	25
2676	2cor. "Clusia sp." (air)	85	35
2677	4cor. "Vanilla planifolia"	1·70	50
2678	7cor. "Stemmadenia obovata"	2·75	85

409 "Capitulation of German Troops" (P. Krivonogov)

1985. 40th Anniv of End of World War II. Multicoloured.

No.	Description	Mint	Used
2679	9cor.50 Type **409** (postage)	1·00	50
2680	28cor. Woman behind barbed wire and Nuremberg trial (air)	3·25	1·60

411 Bassett Hound

1985. "Argentina 85 International Stamp Exhibition, Buenos Aires. Sheet 76×96 mm.

No.	Description	Mint	Used
MS2683	**411** 75cor. multicoloured (4.47)	4·75	2·50

412 Victoria de Julio Sugar Factory

1985. Air. Sixth Anniv of Revolution. Multicoloured.

No.	Description	Mint	Used
2684	9cor. Type **412**	1·10	70
2685	9cor. Soldier and flag	1·10	70

413 Common Pheasant

1985. Domestic Birds. Multicoloured.

No.	Description	Mint	Used
2686	50c. Type **413**	30	15
2687	50c. Hen	30	15
2688	1cor. Helmeted guineafowl	35	20
2689	2cor. Swan goose	75	25
2690	6cor. Ocellated turkey	2·00	85
2691	8cor. Duck	2·75	1·30

414 Luis A. Delgadillo

1985. International Music Year. Multicoloured.

No.	Description	Mint	Used
2692	1cor. Type **414** (postage)	30	15
2693	1cor. Masked dancer with floral headdress	30	15
2694	9cor. Masked procession (air)	1·10	45
2695	9cor. Crowd outside church	1·10	45
2696	15cor. Masked dancer in brimmed hat	1·50	70
2697	21cor. Procession resting	2·20	1·20

415 Zeledon

1985. Air. Birth Centenary of Benjamin Zeledon.

No.	Description	Mint	Used
2698	**415** 15cor. multicoloured	1·40	70

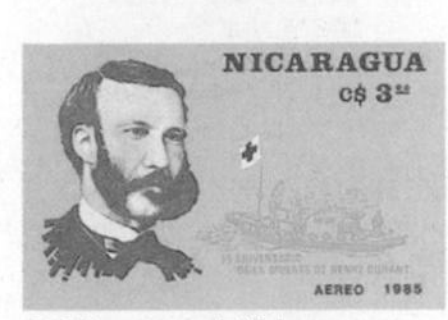

416 Dunant and Lifeboat

1985. 75th Death Anniv of Henri Dunant (founder of Red Cross). Multicoloured.

No.	Description	Mint	Used
2699	3cor. Type **416**	30	15
2700	15cor. Dunant and Ilyushin Il-86 and Tupolev Tu-154 aircraft	1·10	60

417 Fire Engine

1985. Sixth Anniv of SINACOI Fire Service. Multicoloured.

No.	Description	Mint	Used
2701	1cor. Type **417** (postage)	30	15
2702	1cor. Fire station	30	15
2703	1cor. Engine with water jet	30	15
2704	3cor. Foam tender (air)	55	25
2705	9cor. Airport fire engine	95	35
2706	15cor. Engine at fire	1·40	60
2707	21cor. Fireman in protective clothing	1·90	85

418 Halley, Masaya Volcano and Comet

1985. Appearance of Halley's Comet. Multicoloured.

No.	Description	Mint	Used
2708	1cor. Type **418** (postage)	30	15
2709	3cor. Armillary sphere and 1910 trajectory	35	20
2710	3cor. "Venus" space probe and Tycho Brahe underground observatory	35	20
2711	9cor. Habermel's astrolabe and comet's path through solar system (air)	1·10	25
2712	15cor. Hale Telescope, Mt. Palomar, and Herschel's telescope	1·90	50
2713	21cor. Galileo's telescope and sections through telescopes of Newton, Cassegrain and Ritchey	2·50	85

419 Tapir eating

1985. Protected Animals. Baird's Tapir. Multicoloured.

No.	Description	Mint	Used
2714	1cor. Type **419** (postage)	30	15
2715	3cor. Tapir in water (air)	65	20
2716	5cor. Tapir in undergrowth	1·10	45
2717	9cor. Mother and calf	1·90	60

420 "Rosa spinosissima"

1986. Wild Roses. Multicoloured.

No.	Description	Mint	Used
2718	1cor. Type **420**	20	15
2719	1cor. Dog rose ("R. canina")	20	15
2720	3cor. "R. eglanteria"	30	20
2721	5cor. "R. rubrifolia"	35	25
2722	9cor. "R. foetida"	55	35
2723	100cor. "R. rugosa"	4·25	1·60

421 Crimson Topaz

1986. Birds. Multicoloured.

No.	Description	Mint	Used
2724	1cor. Type **421**	20	15
2725	3cor. Orange-billed nightingale thrush	30	20
2726	3cor. Troupial	30	20
2727	5cor. Painted bunting	35	25
2728	10cor. Frantzius's nightingale thrush	55	35

2729	21cor. Great horned owl	1·10	60
2730	75cor. Great kiskadee	3·00	1·70

422 Footballer and Statue

1986. World Cup Football Championship, Mexico (2nd issue). Multicoloured.

2731	1cor. Type **422** (postage)	10	10
2732	1cor. Footballer and sculptured head	10	10
2733	3cor. Footballer and water holder with man as stem (air)	20	15
2734	3cor. Footballer and sculpture	20	15
2735	5cor. Footballer and sculptured head (different)	30	20
2736	9cor. Footballer and sculpture (different)	35	25
2737	100cor. Footballer and sculptured snake's head	3·00	1·40
MS2738	83×93 mm. 100cor. Footballer's leg and ball	3·25	1·70

1986. (a) Flowers. As Nos. 2441/56 but values changed.

2739	5cor. blue	35	15
2740	5cor. violet	35	15
2741	5cor. purple	35	15
2742	5cor. orange	35	15
2743	5cor. green	35	15
2744	5cor. blue	35	15
2745	5cor. green	35	15
2746	5cor. green	35	15
2747	5cor. mauve	35	15
2748	5cor. red	35	15
2749	5cor. grey	35	15
2750	5cor. orange	35	15
2751	5cor. brown	35	15
2752	5cor. brown	35	15
2753	5cor. green	35	15
2754	5cor. black	35	15

DESIGNS: No. 2739, Type **356**; 2740, "Tabebula ochraceae"; 2741, "Laella sp"; 2742, Frangipani ("Plumeria rubra"); 2743, "Brassavola nodosa"; 2744, "Strachytarpheta indica"; 2745, "Cochlospermum sp"; 2746, "Malvaviscus arboreus"; 2747, "Tecoma stans"; 2748, Chinese hibiscus ("Hibiscus rosa-sinensis"); 2749, "Cattleya lueddemanniana"; 2750, African marigold ("Tagetes erecta"); 2751, "Senecio sp"; 2752, "Sobralia macrantha"; 2753, "Thumbergia alata"; 2754, "Bixa orellana".

(b) Agrarian Reform. As T **378**.

2755	1cor. brown	20	10
2756	9cor. violet	30	15
2757	15cor. purple	45	20
2758	21cor. red	55	30
2759	33cor. orange	80	45
2760	42cor. green	1·00	60
2761	50cor. brown	1·30	70
2762	100cor. blue	2·20	1·70

DESIGNS: 1cor. Type **378**; 9cor. Cotton; 15cor. Maize; 21cor. Sugar; 33cor. Cattle; 42cor. Rice; 50cor. Coffee; 100cor. Bananas.

423 Alfonso Cortes

1986. National Libraries. Latin American Writers. Multicoloured.

2763	1cor. Type **423** (postage)	10	10
2764	3cor. Azarias H. Pallais	20	15
2765	3cor. Salomon de la Selva	20	15
2766	5cor. Ruben Dario	30	20
2767	9cor. Pablo Neruda	35	25
2768	15cor. Alfonso Reyes (air)	45	35
2769	100cor. Pedro Henriquez Urena	3·25	1·50

424 Great Britain Penny Black and Nicaragua 1929 25c. Stamp

1986. Air. 125th Anniv of Nicaraguan Stamps. Designs showing G.B. Penny Black and Nicaragua stamps.

2770	**424** 30cor. multicoloured	95	25
2771	- 40cor. brown, black and grey	1·10	45
2772	- 50cor. red, black and grey	1·30	60
2773	- 100cor. blue, black and grey	2·75	1·10

DESIGNS: 40c. 1903 1p. stamp; 50c. 1892 5p. stamp; 1p. 1862 2c. stamp.

425 Sapodilla

1986. 40th Anniv of F.A.O. Multicoloured.

2774	1cor. Type **425** (postage)	20	10
2775	1cor. Maranon	20	10
2776	3cor. Tree-cactus	30	15
2777	3cor. Granadilla	30	15
2778	5cor. Custard-apple (air)	35	20
2779	21cor. Melocoton	95	35
2780	100cor. Mamey	3·50	1·50

426 Rainbow and Globe

1986. Air. International Peace Year. Multicoloured.

2781	5cor. Type **426**	20	10
2782	10cor. Dove and globe	35	15

427 Lockheed L-1011 TriStar 500

1986. "Stockholmia 86" International Stamp Exhibition. Multicoloured.

2783	1cor. Type **427** (postage)	20	10
2784	1cor. Yakovlev Yak-40	20	10
2785	3cor. B.A.C. One Eleven	30	15
2786	3cor. Boeing 747-100	30	15
2787	9cor. Airbus Industrie A300 (air)	45	25
2788	15cor. Tupolev Tu-154	65	35
2789	100cor. Concorde (vert)	3·25	1·50
MS2790	60×73 mm. 100cor. SAAb "FAirchild 340" (39×31 mm)	3·75	1·70

428 "Pinta" and 16th-century Map

1986. 500th Anniv (1992) of Discovery of America by Columbus (1st issue). Multicoloured.

2791	1cor. Type **428** (postage)	30	15
2792	1cor. "Santa Maria" and "Nina"	30	15
2793	9cor. Juan de la Cosa (air)	35	20
2794	9cor. Christopher Columbus	35	20
2795	21cor. King and Queen of Spain	1·00	45
2796	100cor. Courtiers behind Columbus and Indians	4·25	1·50
MS2797	Two sheets each 155×80 mm. (a) Nos. 2971/2; (b) Nos. 2793/6	10·50	9·75

The designs of the same value and Nos. 2795/6 were printed together in *se-tenant* pairs within their sheets, Nos. 2791/2 and 2795/6 forming composite designs.

See also Nos. 2911/16.

429 Fonseca and Flags

1986. Air. 25th Anniv of Sandinista Front and 10th Death Anniv of Carlos Fonseca (co-founder).

2798	**429** 15cor. multicoloured	35	15

430 Rhinoceros

1986. Air. Endangered Animals. Multicoloured.

2799	15cor. Type **430**	45	15
2800	15cor. Zebra	45	15
2801	25cor. Elephant	75	35
2802	25cor. Giraffe	75	35
2803	50cor. Tiger	1·60	80
2804	50cor. Mandrill	1·60	80

431 *Theritas coronata*

1986. Butterflies. Multicoloured.

2805	10cor. Type **431** (postage)	45	15
2806	15cor. *Salamis cacta* (air)	75	25
2807	15cor. *Charayes nitebis*	75	25
2808	15cor. *Papilio maacki*	75	25
2809	25cor. *Palaeochrysophonus hippothoe*	1·20	50
2810	25cor. *Euphaedro cyparissa*	1·20	50
2811	30cor. *Ritra aurea*	1·40	60

432 Player and French Flag

1986. Air. World Cup Football Championship, Mexico (3rd issue). Finalists. Multicoloured. Designs showing footballers and national flags.

2812	10cor. Type **432**	45	15
2813	10cor. Argentina	45	15
2814	10cor. West Germany	45	15
2815	15cor. England	75	25
2816	15cor. Brazil	75	25
2817	25cor. Spain	95	35
2818	50cor. Belgium (horiz)	1·90	80
MS2819	95×65 mm. 100cor. Players	4·25	1·70

433 Ernesto Mejia Sanchez

1987. Ruben Dario Cultural Order of Independence. Multicoloured.

2820	10cor. Type **433** (postage)	25	15
2821	10cor. Fernando Gordillo	25	15
2822	10cor. Francisco Perez Estrada	25	15
2823	15cor. Order medal (air)	35	20
2824	30cor. Julio Cortazar	75	45
2825	60cor. Enrique Fernandez Morales	1·50	85

434 Ice Hockey

1987. Winter Olympic Games, Calgary (1988). Multicoloured.

2826	10cor. Type **434** (postage)	35	15
2827	10cor. Speed skating	35	15
2828	15cor. Downhill skiing (air)	55	15
2829	15cor. Figure skating	55	15
2830	20cor. Shooting	75	25
2831	30cor. Slalom	1·30	45
2832	40cor. Ski jumping	1·70	70
MS2833	75×66 mm. 110cor. Ice hockey (different) (39×31 mm)	3·75	3·00

435 Development

1987. UNICEF Child Survival Campaign. Multicoloured.

2834	10cor. Type **435** (postage)	45	15
2835	25cor. Vaccination (air)	85	45
2836	30cor. Oral rehydration therapy	1·20	50
2837	50cor. Breast-feeding	1·70	85

1987. (a) Flowers. As Nos. 2441/56 and 2739/54 but values changed.

2838	10cor. blue	35	15
2839	10cor. violet	35	15
2840	10cor. purple	35	15
2841	10cor. red	35	15
2842	10cor. green	35	15
2843	10cor. blue	35	15
2844	10cor. green	35	15
2845	10cor. green	35	15
2846	10cor. mauve	35	15
2847	10cor. red	35	15
2848	10cor. green	35	15
2849	10cor. orange	35	15
2850	10cor. brown	35	15
2851	10cor. purple	35	15
2852	10cor. turquoise	35	15
2853	10cor. black	35	15

DESIGNS: No. 2838, Type **356**; 2839, "Tabebula ochraceae"; 2840, "Laella sp"; 2841, Frangipani; 2842, "Brassavola nodosa"; 2843, "Stachytarpheta indica"; 2844, "Cochlospermum sp"; 2845, "Malvaviscus arboreus"; 2846, "Tecoma stans"; 2847, Chinese hibiscus; 2848, "Cattleya lueddermanniana"; 2849, African marigold; 2850, "Senecio sp"; 2851, "Sobralla macrantha"; 2852, "Thumbergia alata"; 2853, "Bixa orellana".

(b) Agrarian Reform. As T **378**. Dated "1987".

2854	10cor. brown	30	15
2855	10cor. violet	30	15
2856	15cor. purple	45	25
2857	25cor. red	65	45
2858	30cor. orange	85	60
2859	50cor. brown	1·30	95
2860	60cor. green	1·60	1·30
2861	100cor. blue	2·50	1·90

DESIGNS: No. 2854, Type **378**; 2855, Cotton; 2856, Maize; 2857, Sugar; 2858, Cattle; 2859, Coffee; 2860, Rice; 2861, Bananas.

436 Flags and Buildings

1987. 77th Interparliamentary Conf, Managua.

2862	**436** 10cor. multicoloured	20	10

437 *Mammuthus columbi*

1987. Prehistoric Animals. Multicoloured.

2863	10cor. Type **437** (postage)	80	15

2864 10cor. Triceratops 35 15
2865 10cor. Dimetrodon 35 15
2866 15cor. Uintaterium (air) 65 25
2867 15cor. Dinichthys 65 25
2868 30cor. Pteranodon 1·40 45
2869 40cor. Tilosaurus 1·90 50

438 Tennis Player

1987. "Capex 87" International Stamp Exhibition, Toronto.
2870 10cor. multicoloured (Type **438**) (postage) 45 15
2871 10cor. mult 45 15
2872 15cor. mult (male player) (air) 65 20
2873 15cor. mult (female player) 65 20
2874 20cor. multicoloured 75 25
2875 30cor. multicoloured 1·40 45
2876 40cor. multicoloured 1·90 50
MS2877 49×60 mm. 110cor. multicoloured (31×39 mm) 3·75 3·25
DESIGNS: Nos. 2871/**MS**2877, Various tennis players.

439 Dobermann Pinscher

1987. Dogs. Multicoloured.
2878 10cor. Type **439** (postage) 30 15
2879 10cor. Bull mastiff 30 15
2880 15cor. Japanese spaniel (air) 55 20
2881 15cor. Keeshond 55 20
2882 20cor. Chihuahua 95 25
2883 30cor. St. Bernard 1·40 45
2884 40cor. West Gotha spitz 1·90 70

440 Modern Wooden Houses

1987. Air. International Year of Shelter for the Homeless. Multicoloured.
2885 20cor. Type **440** 55 25
2886 30cor. Modern brick-built houses 95 45

441 Levski

1987. Air. 150th Birth Anniv of Vasil Levski (revolutionary).
2887 **441** 30cor. multicoloured 85 35

442 *Opuntia acanthocarpa major*

1987. Cacti. Multicoloured.
2888 10cor. Type **442** (postage) 35 15
2889 10cor. *Lophocereus schottii* 35 15
2890 10cor. *Echinocereus engelmanii* 35 15
2891 20cor. Saguaros (air) 85 35
2892 20cor. *Lemaireocereus thurberi* 85 35
2893 30cor. *Opuntia fulgida* 1·30 50
2894 50cor. *Opuntia ficus indica* 1·90 80

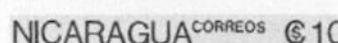

443 High Jumping

1987. Tenth Pan-American Games, Indiana. Multicoloured.
2895 10cor. Type **443** (postage) 30 15
2896 10cor. Handball 30 15
2897 15cor. Running (air) 45 20
2898 15cor. Gymnastics 45 20
2899 20cor. Baseball 75 25
2900 30cor. Synchronized swimming (vert) 1·10 45
2901 40cor. Weightlifting (vert) 1·40 60
MS2902 57×67 mm 110cor. Gymnastics (different) (31×39 mm) 3·25 2·50

444 Television Tower, East Berlin

1987. Air. 750th Anniv of Berlin. Sheet 69×96 mm.
MS2903 **443** 130cor. multicoloured 3·75 1·70

445 "Cosmos"

1987. Cosmonautics Day. Multicoloured.
2904 10cor. Type **445** (postage) 35 15
2905 10cor. "Sputnik" 35 15
2906 15cor. "Proton" (air) 65 20
2907 25cor. "Luna" 1·00 25
2908 25cor. "Meteor" 1·00 25
2909 30cor. "Electron" 1·10 45
2910 50cor. "Mars-1" 1·60 75

446 Native Huts and Terraced Hillside

1987. Air. 500th Anniv (1992) of Discovery of America by Columbus (2nd issue). Multicoloured.
2911 15cor. Type **446** 65 15
2912 15cor. Columbus's fleet 65 15
2913 20cor. Spanish soldiers in native village 75 25
2914 30cor. Mounted soldiers killing natives 1·10 45
2915 40cor. Spanish people and houses 1·50 60
2916 50cor. Church and houses 1·70 75

447 Tropical Gar

1987. World Food Day. Fish. Multicoloured.
2917 10cor. Type **447** (postage) 45 15
2918 10cor. Atlantic tarpon ("Tarpon atlanticus") 45 15
2919 10cor. Jaguar guapote ("Cichlasoma managuense") 45 15
2920 15cor. Banded astyanax ("Astyana fasciatus") (air) 75 35
2921 15cor. Midas cichlid ("Cichlasoma citrimellum") 75 35
2922 20cor. Wolf cichlid 1·20 45
2923 50cor. Lake Nicaragua shark 2·40 85

448 Lenin

1987. 70th Anniv of Russian Revolution. Multicoloured.
2924 10cor. Type **448** (postage) 35 15
2925 30cor. "Aurora" (cruiser) (horiz) (air) 95 35
2926 50cor. Russian arms 1·40 60

449 "Nativity"

1987. Christmas. Details of Painting by L. Saenz. Multicoloured.
2927 10cor. Type **449** 30 15
2928 20cor. "Adoration of the Magi" 55 20
2929 25cor. "Adoration of the Magi" (close-up detail) 65 25
2930 50cor. "Nativity" (close-up detail) 1·40 50

1987. Surch.
2931 **435** 400cor. on 10cor. mult (postage) 1·40 50
2932 - 600cor. on 50cor. mult (No. 2837) 1·60 60
2933 - 1000cor. on 25cor. mult (No. 2835) 2·20 90
2934 - 5000cor. on 30cor. mult (No. 2836) 2·75 1·10
2935 **440** 200cor. on 20cor. multicoloured (air) 2·50 1·10
2936 - 3000cor. on 30cor. mult (No. 2886) 80 30

451 Cross-country Skiing

1988. Winter Olympic Games, Calgary. Multicoloured.
2937 10cor. Type **451** 30 15
2938 10cor. Rifle-shooting (horiz) 30 15
2939 15cor. Ice hockey 55 20
2940 20cor. Ice skating 85 35
2941 25cor. Downhill skiing 1·10 45
2942 30cor. Ski jumping (horiz) 2·10 50
2943 40cor. Slalom 1·60 70
MS2944 66×74 mm. 100cor. Ice skating (pairs) (39×27 mm) 4·25 3·25

452 Flag around Globe

1988. Tenth Anniv of Nicaragua Journalists' Association. Multicoloured.
2945 1cor. Type **452** (postage) 35 15
2946 5cor. Churches of St. Francis Xavier, Sandino and Fatima, Managua, and speaker addressing journalists (42×27 mm) (air) 95 45

453 Basketball

1988. Olympic Games, Seoul. Multicoloured.
2947 10cor. Type **453** 30 15
2948 10cor. Gymnastics 30 15
2949 15cor. Volleyball 55 20
2950 20cor. Long jumping 85 35
2951 25cor. Football 1·10 45
2952 30cor. Water polo 1·20 50
2953 40cor. Boxing 1·80 70
MS2954 70×60 mm. 100cor. Baseball (39×31 mm) 4·25 3·25

454 Brown Bear

1988. Mammals and their Young. Multicoloured.
2955 10c. Type **454** (postage) 10 10
2956 15c. Lion 20 15
2957 25c. Cocker spaniel 25 20
2958 50c. Wild boar 30 25
2959 4cor. Cheetah (air) 1·30 35
2960 7cor. Spotted hyena 1·80 80
2961 8cor. Red fox 2·10 85
MS2962 61×71 mm. 15cor. Kittens (31×39 mm) 4·25 3·25

455 Slide Tackle

1988. "Essen '88" International Stamp Fair and European Football Championship, Germany. Multicoloured.
2963 50c. Type **455** (postage) 20 10
2964 1cor. Footballers 30 15
2965 2cor. Lining up shot (vert) (air) 45 20
2966 3cor. Challenging for ball (vert) 75 25
2967 4cor. Heading ball (vert) 1·10 35
2968 5cor. Tackling (vert) 1·40 45
2969 6cor. Opponent winning possession 1·60 50
MS2970 58×71 mm. 15cor. Players challenging goalkeeper (31×39 mm) 4·25 3·25

456 Bell JetRanger III

1988. "Finlandia 88" International Stamp Exhibition, Helsinki. Helicopters. Multicoloured.
2971 4cor. Type **456** (postage) 35 10
2972 12cor. MBB-Kawasaki BK-117A-3 (air) 35 15
2973 16cor. Boeing-Vertol B-360 55 20
2974 20cor. Agusta A.109 MR11 70 25
2975 24cor. Sikorsky S-61N 85 30
2976 28cor. Aerospatiale SA.365 Dauphin 2 95 35
2977 56cor. Sikorsky S-76 Spirit 2·00 70
MS2978 97×52 mm. 120cor. "NH-90" (39×31 mm) 4·25 3·25

457 Flags and Map

1988. Ninth Anniv of Revolution. Multicoloured.
2979 1cor. Type **457** (postage) 30 15
2980 5cor. Landscape and hands releasing dove (air) 95 35

458 Casimiro Sotelo Montenegro

1988. Revolutionaries.
2981 **458** 4cor. blue (postage) 20 10
2982 - 12cor. mauve (air) 30 10
2983 - 16cor. green 35 15
2984 - 20cor. red 45 20
2985 - 24cor. brown 55 25
2986 - 28cor. violet 65 35
2987 - 50cor. red 1·10 55
2988 - 100cor. purple 2·20 1·10
DESIGNS: 12cor. Ricardo Morales Aviles; 16cor. Silvio Mayorga Delgado; 20cor. Pedro Arauz Palacios; 24cor. Oscar A. Turcios Chavarrias; 28cor. Julio C. Buitrago Urroz; 50cor. Jose B. Escobar Perez; 100cor. Eduardo E. Contreras Escobar.

459 *Acacia baileyana*

1988. Flowers. Multicoloured.

2989	4cor. Type **459** (postage)	20	10
2990	12cor. *Anigozanthos manglesii* (air)	35	15
2991	16cor. *Telopia speciosissima*	45	20
2992	20cor. *Eucalyptus ficifolia*	60	25
2993	24cor. *Boronia heterophylla*	70	30
2994	28cor. *Callistemon speciosus*	80	40
2995	30cor. *Nymphaea caerulea* (horiz)	90	45
2996	50cor. *Clianthus formosus*	1·30	60

460 West Indian Fighting Conch

1988. Molluscs. Multicoloured.

2997	4cor. Type **460** (postage)	30	10
2998	12cor. Painted polymita (air)	35	15
2999	16cor. Giant sundial	55	20
3000	20cor. Japanese baking oyster	75	25
3001	24cor. Yoka star shell	1·00	35
3002	28cor. Gawdy frog shell	1·10	40
3003	50cor. Mantled top	1·90	60

461 Zapotecan Funeral Urn

1988. 500th Anniv (1992) of Discovery of America by Columbus (3rd issue). Multicoloured.

3004	4cor. Type **461** (postage)	25	10
3005	12cor. Mochican ceramic seated figure (air)	45	15
3006	16cor. Mochican ceramic head	60	20
3007	20cor. Tainan ceramic vessel	75	25
3008	28cor. Nazcan vessel (horiz)	95	35
3009	100cor. Incan ritual pipe (horiz)	2·75	1·10
MS3010	100×65 mm. 120cor. Aztec ceramic head (39×31 mm)	4·25	3·25

462 *Chrysina macropus*

1988. Beetles. Multicoloured.

3011	4cor. Type **462** (postage)	30	10
3012	12cor. *Plusiotis victoriana* (air)	35	15
3013	16cor. *Ceratotrupes bolivari*	60	20
3014	20cor. *Gymnetosoma stellata*	80	25
3015	24cor. *Euphoria lineoligera*	1·00	35
3016	28cor. *Euphoria candezei*	1·10	45
3017	50cor. *Sulcophanaeus chrysеicollis*	1·90	55

463 Dario

1988. Air. Centenary of Publication of "Blue" by Ruben Dario.

3018	**463**	25cor. multicoloured	1·20	25

464 Simon Bolivar, Jose Marti, Gen. Sandino and Fidel Castro

1989. Air. 30th Anniv of Cuban Revolution.

3019	**464**	20cor. multicoloured	1·10	25

465 Pochomil Tourist Centre

1989. Tourism. Multicoloured.

3020	4cor. Type **465** (postage)	20	10
3021	12cor. Granada Tourist Centre (air)	45	15
3022	20cor. Olof Palme Convention Centre	65	20
3023	24cor. Masaya Volcano National Park	70	25
3024	28cor. La Boquita Tourist Centre	90	30
3025	30cor. Xiloa Tourist Centre	1·00	35
3026	50cor. Managua Hotel	1·50	60
MS3027	101×50 mm. 160cor. Beach, Montelimar International Tourist Centre (39×31 mm)	4·25	3·25

466 Footballers

1989. Air. World Cup Football Championship, Italy (1990).

3028	**466**	100cor. multicoloured	20	15
3029	-	200cor. multicoloured	25	20
3030	-	600cor. multicoloured	30	25
3031	-	1000cor. multicoloured	45	30
3032	-	2000cor. multicoloured	95	45
3033	-	3000cor. multicoloured	1·40	50
3034	-	5000cor. multicoloured	2·10	70
MS3035		90×70 mm. 9000cor. multicoloured (31×39 mm)	4·25	3·00

DESIGNS: 200cor. to 9000cor. Different footballers.

467 Downhill Skiing

1989. Air. Winter Olympic Games, Albertville (1992) (1st issue). Multicoloured.

3036	50cor. Type **467**	45	10
3037	300cor. Ice hockey	50	15
3038	600cor. Ski jumping	55	20
3039	1000cor. Ice skating	65	25
3040	2000cor. Biathlon	90	35
3041	3000cor. Slalom	1·20	45
3042	5000cor. Skiing	1·60	60
MS3043	86×65 mm. 9000cor. Two-man bobsleighing (31×39 mm)	3·50	2·50

See also Nos. 3184/**MS**3191.

468 Water Polo

1989. Air. Olympic Games, Barcelona (1992). Multicoloured.

3044	100cor. Type **468**	45	10
3045	200cor. Running	50	15
3046	600cor. Diving	55	20
3047	1000cor. Gymnastics	65	25
3048	2000cor. Weightlifting	90	35
3049	3000cor. Volleyball	1·20	45
3050	5000cor. Wrestling	1·60	60
MS3051	80×60 mm. 9000cor. Hockey (31×39 mm)	3·50	2·50

See also Nos. 3192/**MS**3199.

469 Procession of States General at Versailles

1989. "Philexfrance 89" International Stamp Exhibition, Paris, and Bicentenary of French Revolution. Multicoloured.

3052	50cor. Type **469** (postage)	20	10
MS3053	66×96 mm. 9000cor. Words and score of "The Marseille" (28×36 mm)	4·75	4·00
3054	300cor. Oath of the Tennis Court (36×28 mm) (air)	30	15
3055	600cor. "The 14th of July" (29×40 mm)	35	20
3056	1000cor. Tree of Liberty (36×28 mm)	50	25
3057	2000cor. "Liberty guiding the People" (Eugene Delacroix) (29×40 mm)	95	35
3058	3000cor. Storming the Bastille (36×28 mm)	1·50	50
3059	5000cor. Lafayette taking oath (28×36 mm)	2·40	80

471 Anniversary Emblem

1989. Air. Tenth Anniv of Revolution. Multicoloured.

3068	300r. Type **471**	20	15
MS3069	97×77 mm. 9000cor. Concepcion volcano (36×28 mm)	3·25	2·20

472 Animal-shaped Vessel

1989. Air. America. Pre-Columbian Artefacts.

3070	**472**	2000cor. multicoloured	85	25

Currency Reform. 150000 (old) cordoba = 1 (new) cordoba

The following issues, denominated in the old currency, were distributed by agents but were not issued (each set consists of seven values and is dated "1990"):
"London 90" International Stamp Exn. Ships
World Cup Football Championship, Italy
Olympic Games, Barcelona (1992)
Fungi
Winter Olympic Games, Albertville (1992)

473 Little Spotted Kiwi

1991. "New Zealand 1990" International Stamp Exhibition, Auckland. Birds. Multicoloured.

3071	5c. Type **473**	20	10
3072	5c. Takahe	20	10
3073	10c. Red-fronted parakeet	30	15
3074	20c. Weka rail	45	25
3075	30c. Kagu (vert)	85	45
3076	60c. Kea	1·60	85
3077	70c. Kakapo	1·90	1·10
MS3078	90×68 mm. 1cor.51 Black swan (40×31 mm)	4·75	3·25

474 Jaguar

1991. 45th Anniv of Food and Agriculture Organization. Animals. Multicoloured.

3079	5c. Type **474**	20	10
3080	5c. Ocelot (vert)	20	10
3081	10c. Black-handed spider monkey (vert)	30	15
3082	20c. Baird's tapir	50	20
3083	30c. Nine-banded armadillo	90	35
3084	60c. Coyote	1·80	80
3085	70c. Two-toed sloth	2·00	90

475 Dr. Chamorro

1991. Dr. Pedro Joaquin Chamorro (campaigner for an independent Press).

3086	**475**	2cor.25 multicoloured	1·10	45

1991. Flowers. As T **356** but with currency inscribed in "oro".

3087	-	1cor. blue	40	15
3088	-	2cor. green	85	15
3089	-	3cor. brown	1·30	15
3090	-	4cor. purple	1·70	15
3091	-	5cor. red	2·10	20
3092	-	6cor. green	2·30	20
3093	**356**	7cor. blue	3·00	20
3094	-	8cor. green	3·25	20
3095	-	9cor. green	3·75	25
3096	-	10cor. violet	4·25	25
3097	-	11cor. mauve	4·75	25
3098	-	12cor. yellow	5·00	30
3099	-	13cor. red	5·50	30
3100	-	14cor. green	5·75	30
3101	-	15cor. mauve	6·25	35
3102	-	16cor. black	6·75	35

DESIGNS: 1cor. "Stachytarpheta indica"; 2cor. "Cochlospermum sp."; 3cor. "Senecio sp."; 4cor. "Sobralia macrantha"; 5cor. Frangipani; 6cor. "Brassavola nodosa"; 8cor. "Malvaviscus arboreus"; 9cor. "Cattleya lueddemanniana"; 10cor. "Tabebula ochraceae"; 11cor. "Laelia sp."; 12cor. African marigold; 13cor. Chinese hibiscus; 14cor. "Thumbergia alata"; 15cor. "Tecoma stans"; 16cor. "Bixa orellana".

476 Steam Locomotive, 1920s, Peru

1991. Steam Locomotives of South and Central America. Multicoloured.

3103	25c. Type **476**	20	15
3104	25c. Locomotive No. 508, 1917, Bolivia	20	15
3105	50c. Class N/O locomotive, 1910s, Argentina	35	20
3106	1cor.50 Locomotive, 1952, Chile	60	35
3107	2cor. Locomotive No. 61, 1944, Colombia	80	45
3108	3cor. Locomotive No. 311, 1947, Brazil	1·20	50
3109	3cor.50 Locomotive No. 60, 1910, Paraguay	1·40	80
MS3110	Two sheets each 100×70 mm. (a) 7cor.50 Guatemala; (b) 7cor.50 Nicaragua	7·00	5·25

477 Match Scene (West Germany versus Netherlands)

1991. West Germany, Winners of World Cup Football Championship (1990). Multicoloured.

3111	25c. Type **477**	10	10
3112	25c. Match scene (West Germany versus Colombia) (vert)	10	10
3113	50c. West German players and referee	20	15
3114	1cor. West German players forming wall (vert)	45	20
3115	1cor.50 Diego Maradona (Argentina) (vert)	70	35
3116	3cor. Argentinian players and Italian goalkeeper (vert)	1·50	65
3117	3cor.50 Italian players	1·80	80
MS3118	100×70 mm. 7cor.50 West German team celebrating with World Cup trophy	3·50	1·90

478 *Prepona praeneste*

1991. Butterflies. Multicoloured.
3119 25c. Type **478** 10 10
3120 25c. "Anartia fatima" 10 10
3121 50c. "Eryphanis aesacus" 25 15
3122 1cor. "Heliconius melpomene" 45 20
3123 1cor.50 "Chlosyne janais" 70 25
3124 3cor. "Marpesia iole" 1·40 65
3125 3cor.50 Rusty-tipped page 1·80 85
MS3126 100×70 mm. 7cor.50 Emperor 3·50 1·90

479 Dove and Cross

1991. 700th Anniv of Swiss Confederation.
3127 **479** 2cor.25 red, black and yellow 1·10 80

480 Yellow-headed Amazon

1991. "Rainforest is Life". Fauna. Multicoloured.
3128 2cor.25 Type **480** 95 45
3129 2cor.25 Keel-billed toucan 95 45
3130 2cor.25 Scarlet macaw 95 45
3131 2cor.25 Resplendent quetzal 95 45
3132 2cor.25 Black-handed spider monkey 95 45
3133 2cor.25 White-throated capuchin 95 45
3134 2cor.25 Three-toed sloth 95 45
3135 2cor.25 Chestnut-headed oropendola 95 45
3136 2cor.25 Violet sabrewing 95 45
3137 2cor.25 Tamandua 95 45
3138 2cor.25 Jaguarundi 95 45
3139 2cor.25 Boa constrictor 95 45
3140 2cor.25 Common iguana 95 45
3141 2cor.25 Jaguar 95 45
3142 2cor.25 White-necked jacobin 95 45
3143 2cor.25 "Doxocopa clothilda" (butterfly) 95 45
3144 2cor.25 "Dismorphia deione" (butterfly) 95 45
3145 2cor.25 Golden arrow-poison frog 95 45
3146 2cor.25 "Callithomia hezia" (butterfly) 95 45
3147 2cor.25 Chameleon 95 45

Nos. 3128/47 were issued together, *se-tenant*, forming a composite design.

481 "Isochilus major"

1991. Orchids. Multicoloured.
3148 25c. Type **481** 10 10
3149 25c. "Cycnoches ventricosum" 10 10
3150 50c. "Vanilla odorata" 25 15
3151 1cor. "Helleriella nicaraguensis" 45 25
3152 1cor.50 "Barkeria spectabilis" 65 35
3153 3cor. "Maxillaria hedwigae" 1·30 60
3154 3cor.50 "Cattleya aurantiaca" 1·50 1·20
MS3155 100×70 mm. 7cor.50 *Psygmorchis pusilla* (27×41 mm) 3·25 1·90

482 Concepcion Volcano

1991. America (1990).
3156 **482** 2cor.25 multicoloured 1·10 50

483 Warehouse and Flags

1991. 30th Anniv of Central American Bank of Economic Integration.
3157 **483** 1cor.50 multicoloured 75 50

484 "The One-eyed Man"

1991. Death Centenary (1990) of Vincent van Gogh (painter). Multicoloured.
3158 25c. Type **484** 10 10
3159 25c. "Head of Countrywoman with Bonnet" 10 10
3160 50c. "Self-portrait" 30 15
3161 1cor. "Vase with Carnations and other Flowers" 45 20
3162 1cor.50 "Vase with Zinnias and Geraniums" 70 25
3163 3cor. "Portrait of Tanguy Father" 1·40 55
3164 3cor.50 "Portrait of a Man" (horiz) 1·60 70
MS3165 127×102 mm. 7cor.50 "Footpath with Poplars". Imperf 3·00 1·80

485 Painting by Rafaela Herrera (1st-prize winner)

1991. National Children's Painting Competition.
3166 **485** 2cor.25 multicoloured 1·10 45

486 Golden Pavilion

1991. "Phila Nippon '91" International Stamp Exhibition, Tokyo. Multicoloured.
3167 25c. Type **486** 10 10
3168 50c. Himaji Castle 25 15
3169 1cor. Head of Bunraku doll 35 20
3170 1cor.50 Japanese cranes 65 25
3171 2cor.50 Phoenix pavilion 1·00 45
3172 3cor. "The Guardian" (statue) 1·30 50
3173 3cor.50 Kabuki actor 1·50 70
MS3174 100×71 mm. 7cor.50 Mizusahi vase 3·00 2·40

487 Turquoise-browed Motmot

1992. Birds. Multicoloured.
3175 50c. Type **487** 20 15
3176 75c. Collared trogon 30 15
3177 1cor. Broad-billed motmot 35 20
3178 1cor.50 Wire-tailed manakin 55 25
3179 1cor.75 Paradise tanager (horiz) 75 35
3180 2cor.25 Resplendent quetzal 1·40 65
3181 2cor.25 Black-spotted bare-eye 1·40 65
MS3182 Two sheets each 100×70 mm. (a) 7cor.50 Crimson-rumped toucanet; (b) 7cor.50 Spotted antbird 7·00 5·25

488 Columbus's Fleet

1992. America (1991). Voyages of Discovery.
3183 **488** 2cor.25 multicoloured 1·10 65

489 Ice Hockey

1992. Winter Olympic Games, Albertville (2nd issue). Multicoloured.
3184 25c. Type **489** 20 10
3185 25c. Four-man bobsleighing 20 10
3186 50c. Skiing (vert) 30 15
3187 1cor. Speed skating 45 25
3188 1cor.50 Cross-country skiing 70 35
3189 3cor. Double luge 1·40 65
3190 3cor.50 Ski jumping (vert) 1·50 80
MS3191 100×70 mm. 7cor.50 Skiing. Imperf 3·00 1·70

490 Fencing

1992. Olympic Games, Barcelona (2nd issue) Multicoloured.
3192 25c. Type **490** 20 15
3193 25c. Throwing the javelin (horiz) 20 15
3194 50c. Basketball 30 20
3195 1cor.50 Running 70 35
3196 2cor. Long jumping 90 45
3197 3cor. Running 1·30 50
3198 3cor.50 Show jumping 1·40 80
MS3199 100×70 mm. 7cor.50 Canoeing. Imperf 3·00 1·70

491 Ceramic Vase with Face (Lorenza Pineda Co-operative)

1992. Contemporary Arts and Crafts. Multicoloured.
3200 25c. Type **491** 20 15
3201 25c. Ceramic spouted vessel (Jose Ortiz) (horiz) 20 15
3202 50c. Blue-patterned ceramic vase (Elio Gutierrez) 30 20
3203 1cor. "Christ" (Jose de los Santos) 45 25
3204 1cor.50 "Family" (sculpture, Erasmo Moya) 70 35
3205 3cor. "Bird-fish" (Silvio Chavarria Co-operative) (horiz) 1·40 75
3206 3cor.50 Filigree ceramic vessel (Maria de los Angeles Bermudez) 1·50 80
MS3207 100×70 mm., 7cor.50 Masks (Jose Flores). Imperf 3·00 1·70

492 "Picnic Table with Three Objects" (Alejandro Arostegui)

1992. Contemporary Paintings. Multicoloured.
3208 25c. Type **492** 20 15
3209 25c. "Prophetess of the New World" (Alberto Ycaza) 20 15
3210 50c. "Flames of Unknown Origin" (Bernard Dreyfus) (horiz) 30 20
3211 1cor.50 "Owl" (Orlando Sobalvarro) (horiz) 70 35
3212 2cor. "Pegasus at Liberty" (Hugo Palma) (horiz) 90 45
3213 3cor. "Avocados" (Omar d'Leon) (horiz) 1·30 65
3214 3cor.50 "Gueguense" (Carlos Montenegro) 1·40 80
MS3215 100×71 mm. 7cor.50 "Shipment" (Federico Nordalm). Imperf 3·00 1·70

493 Rivoli's Hummingbird

1992. Second U.N. Conference on Environment and Development, Rio de Janeiro. Tropical Forest Wildlife. Multicoloured.
3216 1cor.50 Type **493** 60 35
3217 1cor.50 Harpy eagle ("Aguila arpia") 60 35
3218 1cor.50 Orchid 60 35
3219 1cor.50 Keel-billed toucan and morpho butterfly 60 35
3220 1cor.50 Resplendent quetzal 60 35
3221 1cor.50 Guardabarranco 60 35
3222 1cor.50 Howler monkey ("Mono aullador") 60 35
3223 1cor.50 Sloth ("Perezoso") 60 35
3224 1cor.50 Squirrel monkey ("Mono ardilla") 60 35
3225 1cor.50 Blue and yellow macaw ("Guacamaya") 60 35
3226 1cor.50 Emerald boa and scarlet tanager 60 35
3227 1cor.50 Poison-arrow frog 60 35
3228 1cor.50 Jaguar 60 35
3229 1cor.50 Anteater 60 35
3230 1cor.50 Ocelot 60 35
3231 1cor.50 Coati 60 35

Nos. 3216/31 were issued together, *se-tenant*, forming a composite design of a forest.

494 Fabretto with Children

1992. Father Fabretto, "Benefactor of Nicaraguan Children".
3232 **494** 2cor.25 multicoloured 1·00 45

495 "Nicaraguan Identity" (Claudia Gordillo)

1992. Winning Entry in Photography Competition.
3233 **495** 2cor.25 multicoloured 1·00 45

496 "The Indians of Nicaragua" (Milton Jose Cruz)

1992. Winning Entry in Children's Painting Competition.
3234 **496** 2cor.25 multicoloured 1·00 45

497 Eucharistical Banner

1993. 460th Anniv of Catholic Church in Nicaragua. Multicoloured.
3235 25c. Type **497** 20 15

3236 50c. "Shrine of the Immaculate Conception" 30 20
3237 1cor. 18th-century document 45 25
3238 1cor.50 16th-century baptismal font 70 40
3239 2cor. "The Immaculate Conception" 90 45
3240 2cor.25 Monsignor Diego Alvarez Osorio (1st Bishop of Leon) 1·00 55
3241 3cor. "Christ on the Cross" 1·30 70

498 Rivas Cross, 1523

1993. America (1992). 500th Anniv of Discovery of America by Columbus.
3242 **498** 2cor.25 multicoloured 1·00 45

499 Cathedral

1993. Inauguration of Cathedral of the Immaculate Conception of Mary, Managua. Multicoloured.
3243 3cor. Type **499** 1·10 50
3244 4cor. Cross, Virgin Mary and map of Nicaragua (2nd Provincial Council) 1·50 70

Nos. 3243/4 were issued together, *se-tenant*, forming a composite design.

500 Emblem and Voters queueing outside Poll Station

1993. 23rd General Assembly of Organization of American States.
3245 **500** 3cor. multicoloured 1·40 80

501 Anniversary Emblem

1993. 90th Anniv of Pan-American Health Organization.
3246 **501** 3cor. multicoloured 1·40 80

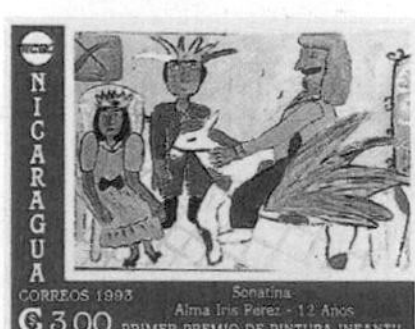

502 "Sonatina" (Alma Iris Perez)

1993. Winning Entry in Children's Painting Competition.
3247 **502** 3cor. multicoloured 1·20 85

503 Racoon Buttterflyfish

1993. Butterflyfish. Multicoloured.
3248 1cor.50 Type **503** 55 30
3249 1cor.50 Rainford's butterflyfish ("Chaetodon rainfordi") 55 30
3250 1cor.50 Mailed butterflyfish ("Chaetodon reticulatus") 55 30
3251 1cor.50 Thread-finned butterfly-fish ("Chaetodon auriga") 55 30
3252 1cor.50 Pennant coralfish ("Heniochus acuminatus") 55 30
3253 1cor.50 Dark-banded butterfly-fish ("Coradion fulvocinctus") 55 30
3254 1cor.50 Mirror butterflyfish ("Chaetodon speculum") 55 30
3255 1cor.50 Lined butterflyfish ("Chaetodon lineolatus") 55 30
3256 1cor.50 Bennett's butterflyfish ("Chaetodon bennetti") 55 30
3257 1cor.50 Black-backed butterfly-fish ("Chaetodon melanotus") 55 30
3258 1cor.50 Golden butterflyfish ("Chaetodon aureus") 55 30
3259 1cor.50 Saddle butterflyfish ("Chaetodon ephippium") 55 30
3260 1cor.50 Pyramid butterflyfish ("Hemitaurichthys polylepis") 55 30
3261 1cor.50 Dotted butterflyfish ("Chaetodon semeion") 55 30
3262 1cor.50 Klein's butterflyfish ("Chaetodon kleinii") 55 30
3263 1cor.50 Copper-banded butter-flyfish ("Chelmon rostratus") 55 30

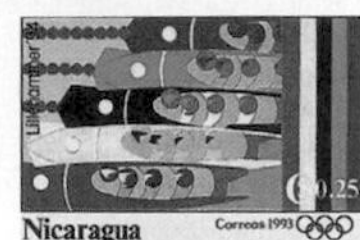

504 Four-man Bobsleigh

1993. Multicoloured. (a) Winter Olympic Games, Lillehammer, Norway (1994).
3264 25c. Type **504** 20 10
3265 25c. Skiing 20 10
3266 50c. Speed skating 30 15
3267 1cor.50 Ski jumping 70 40
3268 2cor. Women's figure skating 90 45
3269 3cor. Pairs' figure skating 1·30 70
3270 3cor.50 Shooting (biathlon) 1·40 90

470 American Darter

1989. Air. "Brasiliana 89" International Stamp Exhibition, Rio de Janeiro. Birds. Multicoloured.
3060 100cor. Type **470** 20 15
3061 200cor. Swallow-tailed kite 25 15
3062 600cor. Turquoise-browed motmot 30 20
3063 1000cor. Painted redstart 45 25
3064 2000cor. Great antshrike (horiz) 95 35
3065 3000cor. Northern royal flycatcher 1·40 50
3066 5000cor. White-flanked antwren (horiz) 2·30 85
MS3067 61×91 mm. 9000cor. Yellow-crowned amazon (31×39 mm) 3·75 2·20

(b) Olympic Games, Atlanta (1996).
3271 25c. Swimming 20 10
3272 25c. Diving 20 10
3273 50c. Long distance running 30 15
3274 1cor. Hurdling 70 40
3275 1cor.50 Gymnastics 90 45
3276 3cor. Throwing the javelin 1·30 70
3277 3cor.50 Sprinting 1·40 90
MS3278 Two sheets each 100×70 mm. (a) 7cor.50 Flags; (b) 7cor.50 Olympic torch and hands 6·75 4·25

505 "Bromeliaceae sp."

1994. Tropical Forest Flora and Fauna. Multicoloured.
3279 2cor. Type **505** 75 45
3280 2cor. Sparkling-tailed humming-bird ("Tilmatura dupontii") 75 45
3281 2cor. "Anolis biporcatus" (lizard) 75 45
3282 2cor. Lantern fly ("Fulgara laternaria") 75 45
3283 2cor. Sloth ("Bradypus sp.") 75 45
3284 2cor. Ornate hawk eagle ("Spizaetus ornatus") 75 45
3285 2cor. Lovely cotinga ("Cotinga amabilis") 75 45
3286 2cor. Schegel's lance-head snake ("Bothrops schlegelii") 75 45
3287 2cor. "Odontoglossum sp." (orchid) and bee 75 45
3288 2cor. Red-eyed tree frog ("Agalychnis callidryas") 75 45
3289 2cor. "Heliconius sapho" (butterfly) 75 45
3290 2cor. Passion flower ("Passiflora vitifolia") 75 45
MS3291 Two sheets each 105×77 mm. (a) 10cor. Agouti; (b) 10cor. "Melinaea lilies" (butterfly) 8·50 5·25

Nos. 3279/90 were issued together, *se-tenant*, forming a composite design.

506 Tomas Brolin (Sweden)

1994. World Cup Football Championship, U.S.A. Players.
3292 50c. Type **506** 30 15
3293 1cor. Jan Karas (Poland) and Antonio Luiz Costa (Brazil) 45 30
3294 1cor. Maxime Bossis and Michel Platini (France) 45 30
3295 1cor.50 Harold Schumacher (Germany) 75 40
3296 2cor. Andoni Zubizarreta (Spain) 95 50
3297 2cor.50 Lothar Matthaeus (Germany) and Diego Maradona (Argentine Republic) 1·20 70
3298 3cor.50 Bryan Robson (England) and Carlos Santos (Portugal) 1·60 85
MS3299 71×100 mm. 10cor. Carlos Valderrama (Colombia) 5·00 3·50

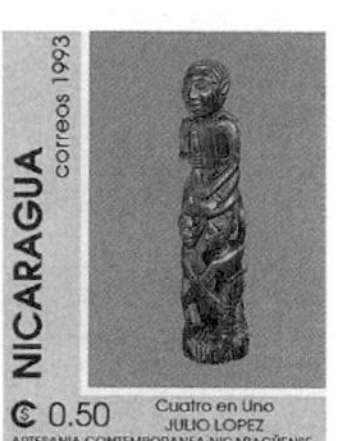

507 "Four in One" (Julio Lopez)

1994. Contemporary Arts. Multicoloured.
3300 50c. Rush mat (Rosalia Sevilla) (horiz) 15 10
3301 50c. Type **507** 15 10
3302 1cor. Ceramic church (Auxiliadora Bush) 35 25
3303 1cor. Statuette of old woman (Indiana Robleto) 35 25
3304 2cor.50 "Santiago" (Jose de los Santos) 85 45
3305 3cor. "Gueguense" (Ines Gutierrez de Chong) 1·00 60
3306 4cor. Ceramic hornet's nest (Elio Gutierrez) 1·30 75
MS3307 100×70 mm. 10cor. "Metate" (grinding stone) (Saul Carballo). Imperf 3·75 2·30

508 *Callicore patelina*

1994. "Hong Kong '94" International Stamp Exhibition. Butterflies. Multicoloured.
3308 1cor.50 Type **508** 50 30
3309 1cor.50 "Chlosyne narva" 50 30
3310 1cor.50 Giant brimstone ("Anteos maerula") 50 30
3311 1cor.50 Diadem ("Marpesia petreus") 50 30
3312 1cor.50 "Pierella helvetia" 50 30
3313 1cor.50 "Eurytides epidaus" 50 30
3314 1cor.50 Doris ("Heliconius doris") 50 30
3315 1cor.50 "Smyrna blomfildia" 50 30
3316 1cor.50 "Eueides lybia olympia" 50 30
3317 1cor.50 "Adelpha heraclea" 50 30
3318 1cor.50 "Heliconius hecale zuleika" 50 30
3319 1cor.50 "Parides montezuma" 50 30
3320 1cor.50 "Morpho polyphemus" 50 30
3321 1cor.50 "Eresia alsina" 50 30
3322 1cor.50 "Prepona omphale octavia" 50 30
3323 1cor.50 "Morpho grenadensis" 50 30

509 "The Holy Family" (anonymous)

1994. Christmas (1993). Paintings. Multicoloured.
3324 1cor. Type **509** 25 15
3325 4cor. "Nativity" (Lezamon) 1·10 50

510 Sculpture

1994. Chontal Culture Statuary. Multicoloured, colour of frame given.
3326 **510** 50c. yellow 15 10
3327 - 50c. yellow 15 10
3328 - 1cor. emerald 35 25
3329 - 1cor. green 35 25
3330 - 2cor.50 blue 85 45
3331 - 3cor. blue 1·00 60
3332 - 4cor. green 1·50 75
MS3333 100×70 mm. 10cor. Twin totems. Imperf 3·00 1·40

DESIGNS: 50c. (3327) to 10cor. Different sculptures.

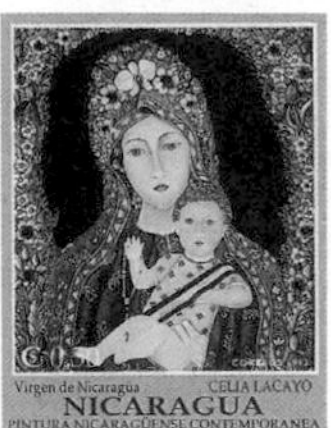

511 "Virgin of Nicaragua" (Celia Lacayo)

1994. Contemporary Paintings. Multicoloured.
3334 50c. Type **511** 15 10
3335 50c. "Woman embroidering" (Guillermo Rivas Navas) 15 10
3336 1cor. "Couple dancing" (June Beer) 35 25
3337 1cor. "Song of Peace" (Alejandro Canales) 35 25
3338 2cor.50 "Sapodilla Plums" (Genaro Lugo) (horiz) 85 45
3339 3cor. "Figure and Fragments" (Leonel Vanegas) 1·00 60
3340 4cor. "Eruption of Agua Volcano" (Asilia Guillen) (horiz) 1·30 75
MS3341 100×70 mm. 10cor. "Still-life" (Alejandro Alonso Rochi). Imperf 3·00 1·40

512 Nicolas Copernicus and Satellite

1994. Astronomers. Multicoloured.
3342 1cor.50 Type **512** 45 25
3343 1cor.50 Tycho Brahe and astronomers 45 25
3344 1cor.50 Galileo Galilei and "Galileo" space probe 45 25
3345 1cor.50 Sir Isaac Newton and telescope 45 25
3346 1cor.50 Edmond Halley, space probe and Halley's Comet 45 25
3347 1cor.50 James Bradley and Greenwich Observatory 45 25
3348 1cor.50 William Herschel and telescope 45 25
3349 1cor.50 John Goodricke and Algol (star) 45 25
3350 1cor.50 Karl Friedrich Gauss and Gottingen Observatory 45 25
3351 1cor.50 Friedrich Bessel and 1838 star telescope 45 25
3352 1cor.50 William Cranch Bond (wrongly inscr "Granch") and Harvard College Observatory 45 25
3353 1cor.50 Sir George Airy and stellar disk 45 25

3354	1cor.50 Percival Lowell and Flagstaff Observatory, Arizona, U.S.A.	45	25
3355	1cor.50 George Hale (wrongly inscr "Halle") and solar spectroscope	45	25
3356	1cor.50 Edwin Hubble and Hubble telescope	45	25
3357	1cor.50 Gerard Kuiper and Miranda (Uranus moon)	45	25
MS3358	144×84 mm. 10cor. Nicolas Copernicus and interstellar probe	3·25	2·50

Nos. 3342/57 were issued together, *se-tenant*, forming a composite design.

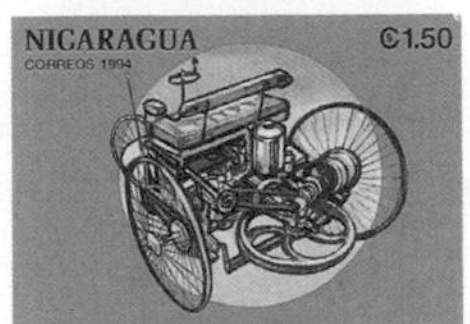

513 1886 Benz Tricycle

1994. Automobiles. Multicoloured.

3359	1cor.50 Type **513**	45	25
3360	1cor.50 1909 Benz Blitzen	45	25
3361	1cor.50 1923 Mercedes Benz 24/100/140	45	25
3362	1cor.50 1928 Mercedes Benz SSK	45	25
3363	1cor.50 1934 Mercedes Benz 500K Cabriolet	45	25
3364	1cor.50 1949 Mercedes Benz 170S	45	25
3365	1cor.50 1954 Mercedes Benz W196	45	25
3366	1cor.50 1954 Mercedes Benz 300SL	45	25
3367	1cor.50 1896 Ford Quadricycle	45	25
3368	1cor.50 1920 Ford taxi cab	45	25
3369	1cor.50 1928 Ford Roadster	45	25
3370	1cor.50 1932 Ford V-8	45	25
3371	1cor.50 1937 Ford V-8 78	45	25
3372	1cor.50 1939 Ford 91 Deluxe Tudor Sedan	45	25
3373	1cor.50 1946 Ford V-8 Sedan Coupe	45	25
3374	1cor.50 1958 Ford Custom 300	45	25
MS3375	120×84 mm. 10cor. Henry Ford, 1903 Ford Model A, Karl Benz and 1897 5CH	3·75	2·20

514 Hugo Eckener and Count Ferdinand von Zeppelin

1994. Zeppelin Airships. Multicoloured.

3376	1cor.50 Type **514**	45	25
3377	1cor.50 "Graf Zeppelin" over New York, 1928	45	25
3378	1cor.50 "Graf Zeppelin" over Tokyo, 1929	45	25
3379	1cor.50 "Graf Zeppelin" over Randolph Hearst's villa, 1929	45	25
3380	1cor.50 Charles Lindbergh, Hugo Eckener and "Graf Zeppelin" at Lakehurst, 1929	45	25
3381	1cor.50 "Graf Zeppelin" over St. Basil's Cathedral, Moscow (wrongly inscr "Santra Sofia")	45	25
3382	1cor.50 "Graf Zeppelin" over Paris, 1930	45	25
3383	1cor.50 "Graf Zeppelin" over Cairo, Egypt, 1931	45	25
3384	1cor.50 "Graf Zeppelin" over Arctic Sea	45	25
3385	1cor.50 "Graf Zeppelin" over Rio de Janeiro, 1932	45	25
3386	1cor.50 "Graf Zeppelin" over St. Paul's Cathedral, London, 1935	45	25
3387	1cor.50 "Graf Zeppelin" over St. Peter's Cathedral, Rome	45	25
3388	1cor.50 "Graf Zeppelin" over Swiss Alps	45	25
3389	1cor.50 "Graf Zeppelin over Brandenburg Gate, Berlin	45	25
3390	1cor.50 Hugo Eckener piloting "Graf Zeppelin"	45	25
3391	1cor.50 Captain Ernest Lehman, "Graf Zeppelin" and Dornier Do-X flying boat	45	25
MS3392	Two sheets each 96×69 mm. (a) 10cor. Hugo Eckener and *Graf Zeppelin*; (b) 10cor. Count Ferdinand von Zeppelin and Airship	6·50	4·25

515 Gabriel Horvilleur

1994. Nicaraguan Philatelists. Multicoloured.

3393	1cor. Type **515**	35	25
3394	3cor. Jose Cauadra	1·00	60
3395	4cor. Alfredo Pertz	1·30	75

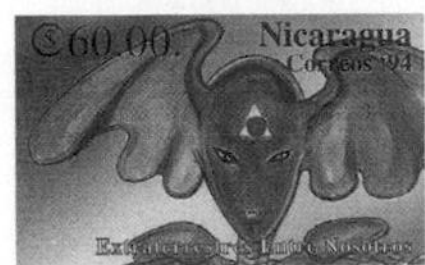

516 August 21 1955 Sighting at Kentucky

1994. Alien Sightings. Eight sheets each 105×75 mm containing horiz designs as T **516**.

MS3396	Eight sheets. (a) 60cor. Type **516**; (b) 60cor. September 19 1961 sighting, New Hampshire, USA; (c) 60cor. 28 July 1965 sighting, Argentina; (d) 60cor. May 8 1973 sighting, Texas, USA; (e) 60cor. September 22 1976 sighting, Canary Islands; (f) 60cor. October 26 1978 sighting, Pennsylvania, USA; (g) 60cor. November 7 1989 sighting, Kansas, USA; (h) 61cor. July 21 1991 sighting, Missouri, USA	£140	£140

517 "Poponjoche" (Thelma Gomez)

1994. First Nicaraguan Tree Conference.

3397	**517**	4cor. multicoloured	1·20	75

518 Conference Emblem

1994. Second International Conference on New and Restored Democracies, Managua.

3398	**518**	3cor. multicoloured	1·00	60

518a Chocolate Point Himalayan

1994. Cats. Two sheets containing T **518a** and similar vert designs. Multicoloured.

MS3399	(a) 146×203 mm. 1cor.50×12, Type **518a**; Somali; American shorthair; Russian blue; Scottish fold; Persian; Egyptian mau; Blue cream Manx; Blue Birman; Seal point Balinese; Blue oriental shorthair; Persian; Angora; Siamese; Two seal point Birman kittens; Devon rex. (b) 136×100 mm. 15cor. Golden Persian (38×50 mm). Set of 2 sheets	13·00	13·00

The stamps of **MS**3399a form a composite design.

519 Pulpit, Leon Cathedral

1994. Religious Art. Multicoloured.

3400	50c. Type **519**	15	10
3401	50c. "St. Anna" (porcelain figure), Chinandega Church	15	10
3402	1cor. "St. Joseph and Child" (porcelain figure), St. Peter's Church, Rivas	35	25
3403	1cor. "St. James", Jinotepe Church	35	25
3404	2cor.50 Gold chalice, Subtiava Temple, Leon	85	45
3405	3cor. Processional cross, Niquinohomo Church, Masaya	1·00	60
3406	4cor. "Lord of Miracles" (crucifix), Lord of Miracles Temple, Managua	1·30	75
MS3407	100×70 mm. 10cor. Silver altar hanging, St. Peter's Church, Rivas. Imperf	3·25	2·30

520 Mascot and Emblem

1994. 32nd World Amateur Baseball Championship.

3408	**520**	4cor. multicoloured	1·40	1·30

520a "Verdad" (Aparicio Arthola)

1994. Sculpture. Multicoloured.

3409	50c. Type **520a**	20	10
3410	1cor. "Buho" (Oelando Sobalvarro)	35	25
3411	1cor.50 "Pequeno Lustrador" (Noel Flores Castro)	55	40
3412	2cor. "Exodo II" (Miguel Angel Abarca)	85	60
3413	2cor.50 "Raza" (Fernando Saravia)	1·00	75
3414	3cor. "Dolor Incognito" (Edith Gron)	1·20	90
3415	4cor. "Garza" (Ernesto Cardenal)	1·60	1·10
MS3416	Two sheets, each 70×100 mm. (a) 15cor. "Atlante" (Jorge Navas Cordonero). Imperf. (b) 15cor. "Maternidad" (Rodrigo Penalba). Imperf. Set of 2 sheets	6·00	6·00

521 Mt. Sorak

1994. "Philakorea 1994" International Stamp Exhibition, Seoul. Views of South Korea. Mult.

3417	1cor.50 Type **521**	45	25
3418	1cor.50 Bronze Statue of Kim Yu-Shin	45	25
3419	1cor.50 Woedolgae (solitary rock)	45	25
3420	1cor.50 Stream, Mt. Hallasan, Cheju Island	45	25
3421	1cor.50 Mirukpong and Pisondae	45	25
3422	1cor.50 Ch'onbuldong Valley	45	25
3423	1cor.50 Bridge of the Seven Nymphs	45	25
3425	1cor.50 Piryong Waterfall	25	10
MS3425	106×76 mm. 10cor. Child surrounded by food on first birthday	2·75	2·50

522 Piano on Stage

1994. 25th Anniv of Ruben Dario National Theatre, Managua.

3426	**522**	3cor. multicoloured	1·10	85

523 Tyrannosaurus Rex

1994. Prehistoric Animals. Multicoloured.

3427	1cor.50 Type **523**	45	25
3428	1cor.50 Plateosaurus	45	25
3429	1cor.50 Pteranodon	45	25
3430	1cor.50 Camarasaurus	45	25
3431	1cor.50 Euplocephalus	45	25
3432	1cor.50 Sacuanjoche	45	25
3433	1cor.50 Deinonychus	45	25
3434	1cor.50 Chasmosaurus	45	25
3435	1cor.50 Dimorphodon	45	25
3436	1cor.50 Ametriorhynchids	45	25
3437	1cor.50 Ichthyosaurus	45	25
3438	1cor.50 Pterapsis and compsognathus	45	25
3439	1cor.50 Cephalopod	45	25
3440	1cor.50 Archelon	45	25
3441	1cor.50 Griphognatus and gyroptychius	45	25
3442	1cor.50 Plesiosaur and nautiloid	45	25

Nos. 3427/42 were issued together, *se-tenant*, forming a composite design.

523a Chapel, Granada

1994. Cultural Heritage. Multicoloured.

3443	50c. Type **523a**	20	10
3444	1cor. San Francisco Convent, Granada (horiz)	35	25
3445	1cor.50 Santiago tower, Leon	55	40
3446	2cor. Santa Ana parish church, Nindiri (horiz)	85	60
3447	2cor.50 Santa Ana parish church, Nandaime	1·00	75
3448	3cor. Arched doorway, Los Leones, Granada (horiz)	1·20	90
3449	4cor. La Inmaculada Concepcion castle, Rio San Juan (horiz)	1·60	1·10
MS3450	100×70 mm. 15cor. San Jacinto hacienda, Managua. Imperf	6·00	6·00

523b Rai (Brazil)

1994. World Cup Football Championship, USA. Three sheets containing T **523** and similar multicoloured designs showing players.

MS3451	(a) 149×120 mm. 3cor.×8, Type **523b**; Freddy Rincon (Colombia); Luis Garcia (Mexico); Thomas Dooley (USA); Franco Barest (Italy); Tony Meola (USA); Enzo Francescoli (Uruguay); Roy Wegerle (USA). (b) 70×100 mm. 10cor. Faustino Asprilla (Colombia). (c) 106×76 mm. 10cor. Aldolfo Valencia (Colombia) (horiz). Set of 3 sheets	15·00	15·00

524 Hawker Typhoon 1B

1994. 50th Anniv of D-Day. Multicoloured.

3452 3cor. Type **524** 1·10 70
3453 3cor. Douglas C-47 Skytrain transport dropping paratroops 1·10 70
3454 3cor. H.M.S. "Mauritius" (cruiser) bombarding Houlgate, Normandy 1·10 70
3455 3cor. Formation of Mulberry Harbours to transport supplies to beach 1·10 70
3456 3cor. British AVRE Churchill tank 1·10 70
3457 3cor. Tank landing craft 1·10 70

525 Renate Stecher (women's 200 m, 1972)

1994. Centenary of International Olympic Committee. Gold Medal Winners. Multicoloured.

3458 3cor.50 Type **525** 1·70 1·00
3459 3cor.50 Cassius Clay (Muhammad Ali) (boxing, 1960) 1·70 1·00
MS3460 106×76 mm. 10cor. Claudia Pechstein (5000 metres speed skating, 1994) 3·75 3·75

526 Detachment of Command module "Eagle"

1994. 25th Anniv of First Manned Moon Landing. Multicoloured.

3461 3cor. Type **526** 95 50
3462 3cor. Launch of "Saturn V", Cape Canaveral, Florida 95 50
3463 3cor. Command module orbiting Moon 95 50
3464 3cor. Footprint on Moon 95 50
3465 3cor. Primary space capsule separating 95 50
3466 3cor. Command module 95 50
3467 3cor. Lunar module landing on Moon 95 50
3468 3cor. Astronaut on Moon 95 50
MS3469 Two sheets each 81×116 mm. (a) 10cor. Buzz Aldrin, Neil Armstrong and Michael Collins (crew) (46×28 mm); (b) 10cor. Astronaut on Moon saluting American flag (28×46 mm) 7·50 7·50

527 "The Death Cart" (Erick Joanello Montoya)

1994. First Prize in Children's Painting Competition.

3470 **527** 4cor. multicoloured 1·40 85

528 Black-crowned Night Heron

1994. Woodland Animals. Multicoloured.

3471 2cor. Type **528** 65 35
3472 2cor. Scarlet macaw ("Ara macao") 65 35
3473 2cor. Cattle egrets ("Bubulcus ibis") (wrongly inscr "Bulbulcus") 65 35
3474 2cor. American black vultures ("Coragyps atratus") 65 35
3475 2cor. Brazilian rainbow boa ("Epicrates cenchria") 65 35
3476 2cor. Red-legged honeycreepers ("Cyanerpes cyaneus") 65 35
3477 2cor. Plain chachalaca ("Ortalis vetula") 65 35
3478 2cor. Sloth ("Bradypus griseus") 65 35
3479 2cor. Jaguar ("Felis onca") 65 35
3480 2cor. American darter ("Anhinga anhinga") 65 35
3481 2cor. Baird's tapir ("Tapirus bairdi") 65 35
3482 2cor. Anteater ("Myrmecophaga jubata") 65 35
3483 2cor. Iguana ("Iguana iguaana") 65 35
3484 2cor. Snapping turtle ("Chelydra serpentina") 65 35
3485 2cor. Red-billed whistling ducks ("Dendrocygna autumnalis") 65 35
3486 2cor. Ocelot ("Felis pardalis") 65 35
MS3487 100×70 mm. 15cor. American anhingas (as central motif of No. 3462) 4·25 4·25

Nos. 3471/86 were issued together, *se-tenant*, forming a composite design.

529 "The Kid" (dir. Charlie Chaplin)

1994. Centenary of Motion Pictures. Multicoloured.

3488 2cor. Type **529** 65 35
3489 2cor. "Citizen Kane" (dir. Orson Welles) 65 35
3490 2cor. "Lawrence of Arabia" (dir. David Lean) 65 35
3491 2cor. "Ivan the Terrible" (dir. Sergio Eisenstein) 65 35
3492 2cor. "Metropolis" (dir. Fritz Lang) 65 35
3493 2cor. "The Ten Commandments" (dir. Cecil B. De Mille) 65 35
3494 2cor. "Gandhi" (dir. Richard Attenborough) 65 35
3495 2cor. "Casablanca" (dir. Michael Curtiz) 65 35
3496 2cor. "Platoon" (dir. Oliver Stone) 65 35
3497 2cor. "The Godfather" (dir. Francis Ford Coppola) 65 35
3498 2cor. "2001: A Space Odyssey" (dir. Stanley Kubrick) 65 35
3499 2cor. "The Ocean Depths" (dir. Jean Renoir) 65 35
MS3500 80×109 mm. 15cor. "Gone with the Wind" (dir. Victor Fleming) 4·75 4·75

530 "Discovery of America"

1994. 15th Death Anniv of Rodrigo Penalba (artist). Multicoloured.

3501 50c. Type **530** 20 10
3502 1cor. "Portrait of Mauricio" 35 15
3503 1cor.50 "Portrait of Franco" 55 25
3504 2cor. "Portrait of Mimi Hammer" 75 35
3505 2cor.50 "Seated Woman" 95 45
3506 3cor. "Still-life" (horiz) 1·10 50
3507 4cor. "Portrait of Maria Augusta" 1·50 70
MS3508 70×100 mm. 15cor. "Entrance to Anticoli" (66×96 mm). Imperf 3·75 3·75

531 Hen and Cock

1994. Endangered Species. The Highland Guan. Multicoloured.

3509 50c. Type **531** 20 10
3510 1cor. Cock 35 15
3511 2cor.50 Hen 1·00 50
3512 3cor. Cock and hen (different) 1·20 60
MS3513 100×70 mm. 15cor. Heads of cock and hen 5·75 5·75

532 M.W. Jung

1995. Korea Baseball Championship. Eight sheets, each 147×200 mm containing T **532** and similar vert designs showing players and team emblems. Multicoloured.

MS3514 (a) 3cor.50×9, Type **532**; K.K. Kim; H.J. Kim; M.T. Chung; Pacific Dolphins emblem; B.W. An; D.G. Yoon; S.D. Choi; D.K. Kim. (b) 3cor.50×9, J.H. Jang; Y.D. Han; K.D. Lee; J.S. Park; Hanwha Eagles emblem; M.C. Jeong; J.W. Song; J.G. Kang; D.S. Koo. (c) 3cor.50×9, R.J. Park; K.J. Cho; K.T. Kim; W.H. Kim; Raiders emblem; I.H. Baik; S.K. Park; K.L. Kim; J.S. Park. (d) 3cor.50×9, J.I. Ryu; S.Y. Kim; S.R. Kim; B.C. Dong; Samsung Lions emblem; K.W. Kang; C.S. Park; J.H. Yang; T.H. Kim.(e) 3cor.50×9, D.H. Han; Y.S. Kim; J.H. Yoo; Y.B. Seo; LG Twins emblem; J.H. Park; S.H. Lee; D.S. Kim; J.H. Kim. (f) 3cor.50×9, H.K. Yoon; D.H. Park; H.K. Joo; E.G. Kim; Lotte Giants emblem; J.T. Park; P.S. Kong; J.S. Yeom; M.H. Kim. (g) 3.50×9, D.Y Sun; J.B. Lee; J.S. Kim; S.H. Kim; Haitai Tigers emblem; G.C. Lee; G.H. Cho; S.H. Kim (different); S.C. Lee. (h) 3cor.50×9, M.S. Lee; C.S. Park; H.S. Lim; K.W. Kim; OB Bears emblem; J.S. Kim; T.H. Kim; H.S. Kim; S.J. Kim. Set of 8 sheets 95·00 95·00

533 "Avanzamos Hacia El Siglo 21" (Maria Jose Zamora)

1995. FUNCOD (environmental organization) Art Prize. Multicoloured.

3515 1cor. Type**533** 35 15
3516 2cor. "Naturaleza Muerta" (Rafael Castellon) 65 35
3517 4cor. "Aguas Cautivas" (Alvaro Gutierrez) 1·40 70

534 Greater Bird of Paradise (*Paradisaea apoda*)

1995. Birds. Two sheets containing T **534** and similar vert designs. Multicoloured.

MS3518 (a) 120×164 mm. 2cor.×12, Type **534**; *Dryocopus galeatus*; Montezuma oropendola (*Psarocolius Montezuma*); Black-capped kingfisher (*Halcyon pileata*); White-throated magpie jay (*Calocitta Formosa*); Green-winged macaw (*Ara chloroptera*); Eastern rosella (*Platycercus eximius*); Palawan peacock pheasant (*Polyplectron emphanum*); Red-legged seriema (*Cariama cristata*); Hoatzin (*Opisthocomus hoatzin*); Blue-bellied roller (*Coracias cyanogaster*). (b) 75×102 mm. 10cor. *Dryocopus galeatus* (different). Set of 2 sheets 10·00 10·00

The stamps of **MS**3518a form a composite design.

535 Hovercraft

1995. British–Nicaraguan San Juan River Expedition.

3519 **535** 4cor. multicoloured 1·40 85

536 "Fiesta de Boaco" (Ernesto Brown)

1995. Centenary of Boaco City.

3520 **536** 4cor. multicoloured 1·40 85

537 Villa Rivas and Cannon

1995. 275th Anniv of Villa Rivas. 160th Anniv of Rivas City.

3521 **537** 3cor. multicoloured 1·10 70

538 Louis Pasteur

1995. Death Centenary of Louis Pasteur (research scientist).

3522 **538** 4cor. multicoloured 1·40 85

539 Crocodile

1995. Fauna. Three sheets containing T **541** and similar multicoloured designs.

MS3523 (a) 140×100 mm. 2cor.50×9, Type **539**; Opossum; Peccary; Paca; Tree frog; Iguana; Scarlet macaw; Capybara; Vampire bat. (b) 110×80 mm. 15cor. Jaguar (vert). (c) 110×80 mm. 15cor. Ornate hawk eagle (vert). Set of 3 sheets 10·50 10·50

540 "Children love Nature" (Brenda Gutierrez)

1995. Winning Design in Children's Drawing Competition.

3524 **540** 3cor. multicoloured 1·10 70

541 Carlos Drummond De Andrade

1995. Twentieth Century Writers. Sheet 112×210 mm containing T **541** and similar vert designs showing writers and their country flags. Multicoloured.

MS3525 3cor.×12, Type **541**; Cesar Vallejo; Jorge Luis Borges; James Joyce; Marcel Proust; William Faulkner; Vladimir Maiakovski; Ezra Pound; Franz Kafka; T.S. Eliot; Rainer Maria Rilke; Federico Garcia Lorca 11·00 11·00

542 Child and Maize

1995. 50th Anniv of United Nations Food and Agriculture Organization (FAO).

3526 **542** 4cor. multicoloured 1·40 85

543 "Ferry Boat"

1995. Paintings by Armando Morales. Multicoloured.

3527 50c. Type **543** 20 10
3528 1cor. "Oliverio Castaneda" (vert) 35 15
3529 1cor. 50 "Desnudo Sentado" (vert) 55 25
3530 2cor. "Las Senoritas de Puerto Cabezas" 75 35
3531 2cor. 50 "El Automovil de la Compania" (vert) 95 45
3532 3cor. "Paisaje Taurino" (vert) 1·10 50
3533 4cor. "Anonas" 1·50 70
MS3534 100×70 mm. 15cor. "Mujer Dormida". Imperf 4·25 4·25

544 Doves and UN Flag

1995. 50th Anniv of United Nations. Multicoloured.

3535 3cor. Type **544** 95 45
3536 4cor. Lion and lamb 1·10 50
3537 5cor. Dove sitting on UN helmet 1·40 70
MS3538 70×100 mm. 10cor. Dove and children 3·50 3·50

Nos. 3535/7 were issued together, *se-tenant*, forming a composite design.

545 African Map Butterfly (*Cyrestis Camillus*)

1995. Butterflies. Two sheets containing T **545** and similar multicoloured designs.

MS3539 (a) 138×125 mm. 2cor.50×12, Type **545**; Lilac beauty (*Salamis cacta*); Giant charaxes (*Charaxes castor*); Beautiful monarch (*Danaus Formosa*); Red swallowtail (*Graphium ridleyanus*); Hewitson's forest blue (*Hewitsonia boisduvali*); Club-tailed charaxes (*Charaxes zoolina*); *Kalima cymodoce*; Blue spot commodore (*Precis westermanni*); African giant swallowtail (*Papilio antimachus*); Red glider (*Cymothoe sangaris*); Giant blue swallowtail (*Papilio zalmoxis*). (b) 106×76 mm. *Danaus Formosa* (vert). Set of 2 sheets 13·50 13·50

The stamps of **MS**3539a form a composite design.

546 Paul Harris (founder) and Emblem

1995. 90th Anniv of Rotary International (charitable organization). Multicoloured.

3540 15cor. Type **546** 6·00 4·00
MS3541 106×76 mm. 25cor. Emblems from 1905 and 1995 8·50 8·50

547 Michael Jordan (basketball)

1995. Olympic Games, Atlanta. Three sheets containing T **547** and similar vert designs. Multicoloured.

MS3542 (a) 110×100 mm. 5cor.×6, Type **547**; Heike Henkel (high jump); Linford Christie (running); Vitaly Chterchbo (gymnastic); Heike Drechsler (long jump); Mark Tewksbury (swimming). (b) 112×78 mm. 20cor. Pierre de Coubertin (founder) and Runner. (c) 112×78 mm. 20cor. Javelin throw and Pierre de Coubertin (horiz). Set of 3 sheets 19·00 19·00

548 John Lennon

1995. 15th Death Anniv of John Lennon (musician).

3543 **548** 2cor. multicoloured 75 50

549 Stylized Nativity

1995. Christmas.

3544 **549** 4cor. multicoloured 1·40 85

550 Otto Meyerhof (medicine, 1922)

1995. Centenary of the Nobel Prize. Five sheets containing T **550** and similar vert designs showing prize winners. Multicoloured.

MS3545 (a) 102×180 mm. 2cor.50×9, Type **550**; Leon Bourgeois (peace, 1920); James Frank (physics, 1925); Leo Esaki (physics, 1973); Miguel Angel Asturias (literature, 1967); Henri Bergson (literature, 1927); Friedrich Bergius (chemistry, 1931); Klaus von Klitzing (physics, 1985); Eisaku Sato (peace, 1974). (b) 130×179 mm. 2cor.50×2, Wilhelm Rontgen (physics, 1901); Theodor Mommsen (literature, 1902); Philipp von Lenard (physics, 1905); Walther Nernst (chemistry, 1920); Hans Spemann (medicine,1935); Jean-Paul Sartre (literature, 1964); T.S. Eliot (literature, 1948); Albert Camus (literature, 1957); Ludwig Quidde (peace, 1927); Werner Heisenberg (physics, 1932); Joseph Brodsky (literature, 1987); Carl von Ossietzky (peace, 1935). (c) 107×76 mm.15cor. Johannes Stark (physics, 1919). (d) 107×76 mm. 15cor. Sin-itiro Tomonaga (physics, 1965). (e) 107×76 mm. 15cor. Oscar Arias Sanchez (peace, 1987) 30·00 30·00

The stamps of **MS**3545a/b, respectively, each form a composite design.

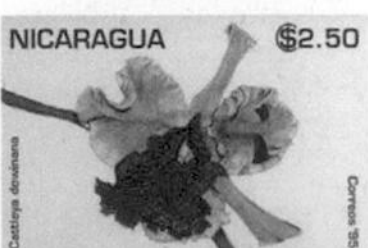

551 *Cattleya downiana*

1995. Orchids. Three sheets containing T **551** and similar horiz designs. Multicoloured.

MS3546 (a) 139×95 mm. 2cor.50×9, Type **551**; *Odontoglossum maculatum*; *Barkeria Lindleyana*; *Rossioglossum grande*; *Brassavola digbyana* (inscr "Brassavp"); *Miltonia Schroederiana*; *Oncidium ornithorhynchum*; *Odontoglossum cervantesii*; *Chysis Tricostata*. (b) 139×95 mm. 3cor.×9, *Lycaste Auburn*; *Lemboglossum cordatum*; *Cyrtochilum macranthum*; *Miltassia Aztec*; *Masdevallia ignea*; *Oncidium Sniffen*; *Brassolaeliocattleya*; *Ascocenda*; *Phalaenopsis*. (c) 106×76 mm. 15cor. *Odontoglossum uro-skinneri*. Set of 3 sheets 20·00 20·00

The stamps of **MS**3546b form a composite design.

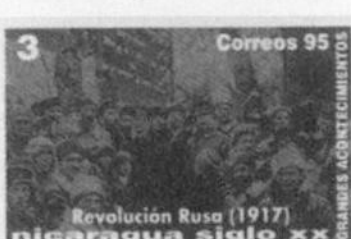

552 Russian Revolution (1917)

1995. 20th-century Events. Multicoloured.

3547 30cor. Type **552** 85 50
3548 30cor. Chinese revolution (1945) 85 50
3549 30cor. Creation of United Nations (1945) 85 50
3550 30cor. Destruction of Berlin wall (1989) 85 50
3551 30cor. World War I (inscr "1914—17") (vert) 85 50
3552 30cor. Creation of Israel (1948) (vert) 85 50
3553 30cor. World War II (vert) 85 50
3554 30cor. Vatican Council (1962—5) (vert) 85 50
3555 30cor. Hiroshima atomic bomb (1945) 85 50
3556 30cor. Vietnam war (1962—73) 85 50
3557 30cor. Gulf war (1991); End of apartheid (1991) 85 50
3558 3 cor. End of apartheid (1991) 9·25 5·50

553 Beyer-Garrat Locomotive, South Africa

1996. Trains. Multicoloured.

3559 2cor. Type **553** 75 45
3560 2cor. Beyer-Garrat locomotive, Rhodesia 75 45
3561 2cor. Mombasa mail train, Uganda 75 45
3562 2cor. Class 31 steam locomotive, East Africa 75 45
3563 2cor. Red steam locomotive, East Africa 75 45
3564 2cor. Electric locomotive, South Africa 75 45
3565 4cor. Plusmarquista 440 No. 999, USA 1·10 70
3566 4cor. Class 638 4.6.2. Pacific, Australia 1·10 70
3567 4cor. 2 .10.2 locomotive *Baldwin*, Bolivia 1·10 70
3568 4cor. Vulcan 4.8.4. locomotive, China 1·10 70
3569 4cor. Paris—Orleans 4.6.2. Pacific, France 1·10 70
3570 4cor. Class 062-4.6.4., Japan 1·10 70
MS3571 Three sheets, each 104×74 mm. Size 85×28 mm. (a) 15cor. Trans Siberian cargo train. (b) 15cor. Midland 4.4.0. compound steam locomotive, UK. (c) 15cor. Steam locomotive, Russia 15·00 15·00

554 Allied Troops crossing Rhine

1996. 50th Anniv (1995) of End of World War II. Multicoloured.

3572 3cor. Type **554** 85 50
3573 3cor. Winston Churchill, Franklin Roosevelt and Joseph Stalin 85 50
3574 3cor. American soldiers raising flag 85 50
3575 3cor. Marine infantry entering Okinawa 85 50
3576 3cor. American and Russian troops 85 50
3577 3cor. Freeing prisoners 85 50
3578 3cor. United Nations treaty 85 50
3579 3cor. American fleet entering Tokyo port 85 50
MS3580 110×80 mm. 10cor. German fighter aircraft 3·75 3·75

555 Pope John Paul II

1996. Visit of Pope John Paul II to Nicaragua.

3581 **555** 5cor. multicoloured 1·90 1·30

556 *Mayflower*

1996. Ships. Multicoloured.

3582 2cor. Type **556** 75 50
3583 2cor. *Young America* 75 50
3584 2cor. *Preussen* 75 50
3585 2cor. Pirate ship 75 50
3586 2cor. *Cutty Sark* 75 50
3587 2cor. Pirate barque 75 50
3588 2cor. Galleon 75 50
3589 2cor. Inscr "El Sol Real" 75 50
3590 2cor. *Santa Maria* 75 50
3591 2cor. HMS *Bountyt* 75 50
3592 2cor. *El Presidente* 75 50
3593 2cor. Inscr "El Principe Guillermo" 75 50
3594 2cor. *Vuelo Nublado* 75 50
3595 2cor. Nile sail boat 75 50
3596 2cor. *Europa* 75 50
3597 2cor. *Vasa* 75 50
3598 2cor. Junk 75 50
3599 2cor. *San Gabriel* 75 50
MS3600 Two sheets, each 100×70 mm. (a) 15cor. Junk (vert). (b) 15cor. *Passat* (vert) 9·75 9·75

557 Collie carrying Lead

1996. Dogs. Multicoloured.

3601 1cor. Type **557** 35 25
3602 1cor. Cairn terrier wearing neckerchief 35 25
3603 2cor. Otter hound holding biscuit 75 50
3604 2cor. Puppy with ball 75 50
3605 3cor. Bulldog 1·10 80
3606 3cor. Siberian husky 1·10 80
3607 4cor. Beagle carrying newspaper 1·40 1·00
3608 4cor. Dalmatian puppy and kitten 1·40 1·00
MS3609 Two sheets. (a) 104×73 mm. 16cor. Chihuahua (b) 73×104 mm. 16cor. Poodle 10·00 10·00

558 Indira Gandhi

1996. United Nations' Fourth Women's Conference. Famous Women. Multicoloured.

3610 2cor. Type **558** 75 50
3611 2cor. Madame Chaing Kai-Shek 75 50
3612 2cor. Mother Teresa 75 50
3613 2cor. Marie Curie 75 50
3614 2cor. Margaret Thatcher 75 50
3615 2cor. Eleanor Roosevelt 75 50
3616 2cor. Eva Peron 75 50
3617 2cor. Golda Meir 75 50
3618 2cor. Violetta Barrios de Chamorro 75 50
MS3619 Three sheets, each 127×102 mm. (a) 15cor. Valentina Tereshkova (vert). (b) 15cor. Aung San Suu Kyi (vert). (c) 15cor. Jacqueline Kennedy Onassis (vert) 15·00 15·00

559 Lou Gehrig

1996. Baseball. Multicoloured.

3620 4cor. Type **559** 1·10 80
3621 4cor. Rogers Hornby 1·10 80

3622	4cor. Mike Schmidt	1·10	80
3623	4cor. Honus Wagner	1·10	80
3624	4cor. Ty Cobb	1·10	80
3625	4cor. Roberto Clemente	1·10	80
3626	4cor. Babe Ruth	1·10	80
3627	4cor. Johnny Bench	1·10	80
3628	4cor. Tom Seaver	1·10	80
MS3629	130×97 mm. 10cor. Reggie Jackson	9·25	9·25

560 Takehide Nakatani (judo gold medallist—1964)

1996. Olympic Games, Atlanta. Multicoloured.

3630	1cor. Type **560**	30	15
3631	2cor. Olympic stadium, Japan 1964	55	35
3632	2cor.50 Basketball	75	45
3633	2cor.50 Baseball	75	45
3634	2cor.50 Boxing	75	45
3635	2cor.50 Hurdling	75	45
3636	2cor.50 Judo	75	45
3637	2cor.50 Handball	75	45
3638	2cor.50 Volleyball	75	45
3639	2cor.50 Water polo	75	45
3640	2cor.50 Tennis	75	45
3641	3cor. Al Oerter (discus gold medallist—1956, 1960, 1964 and 1968) (vert)	85	50
3642	10cor. Olympic rings and early athlete	2·75	2·90

561 Andrew Maynard

1996. Boxing Gold Medallists. Multicoloured.

3643	2cor.50 Type **561**	75	50
3644	2cor.50 Rudi Fink	75	50
3645	2cor.50 Peter Lessov	75	50
3646	2cor.50 Angel Herrera	75	50
3647	2cor.50 Patrizio Oliva	75	50
3648	2cor.50 Armando Martinez	75	50
3649	2cor.50 Slobodan Kacar	75	50
3650	2cor.50 Teofilo Stevenson	75	50
3651	2cor.50 George Foreman	75	50
MS3652	107×76 mm. 25cor. Cassius Clay (horiz)	8·50	8·50

Nos. 3643/51 were issued together, *se-tenant*, with the background forming a composite design.

562 Bay

1996. Horses. Multicoloured.

3653	1cor. Type **562**	35	25
3654	2cor. Liver chestnut	75	50
3655	2cor.18 th-century Persian light cavalry harness	75	50
3656	2cor.15 th-century Italian harness	75	50
3657	2cor.15 th-century German horse armour	75	50
3658	2cor.17 th-century Turkish light cavalry harness	75	50
3659	2cor.50 Bright bay with black and white socks	95	65
3660	3cor. Dark bay	1·10	70
3661	3cor. Chestnut with pale mane and tail and white socks (vert)	1·10	70
3662	4cor. Yellow dun	1·60	1·10
3663	4cor. Black with white socks and snip	1·60	1·10
MS3664	105×75 mm. 16cor. Dappled grey	5·50	5·50
MS3665	101×71 mm. 25cor. 16th-century German horse armour	8·50	8·50

563 Shark

1996. Marine Life. Multicoloured.

MS3666 (a) Two sheets, each 151×111 mm. (i) 2cor.50×9, Type **563**; Diver and hammer-head shark; Moray eel; Mackerel; Mackerel and hammer-head shark; Butterfly fish; Spotted grouper; Squid; Manta ray. (ii) 2cor.50×9, Butterfly fish; Barracuda; Manatee; Medusa; Octopus; Yellow comber; Lemon shark; Squirrel fish; Red snapper. (b) Two sheets, each 106×76 mm. (i) 20cor. Angelfish. (ii) 20cor. Striped butterfly fish Set of 4 sheets 28·00 28·00

The stamps and margins of **MS**3665a form composite designs.

564 Flags and Emblem

1996. Central American Integration System.

3667	**564**	5cor. multicoloured	2·00	1·40

565 Rat

1996. New Year. Year of the Ox. China 96 International Stamp Exhibition (**MS**3680). Multicoloured.

3668	2cor. Type **565**	55	35
3669	2cor. Ox	55	35
3670	2cor. Tiger	55	35
3671	2cor. Rabbit	55	35
3672	2cor. Dragon	55	35
3673	2cor. Snake	55	35
3674	2cor. Horse	55	35
3675	2cor. Goat	55	35
3676	2cor. Monkey	55	35
3677	2cor. Rooster	55	35
3678	2cor. Dog	55	35
3679	2cor. Pig	55	35
MS3680	100×141 mm. 4cor. Pagoda	1·70	1·70
MS3681	188×128 mm. 10cor. Ox (81×48 mm)	4·00	4·00

567 "Paisaje con Bolsa" (Frederico Nordalm)

1996

3682	**566**	4cor. multicoloured	1·40	1·10

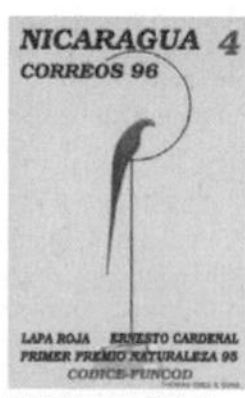

566 "Lapa Roja" (Ernesto Cardenal)

1996. Nicaragua—Taiwan Diplomatic Relations. Multicoloured.

3683	10cor. Type **567**	1·90	1·50
3684	20cor. President Lee Tang (Taiwan) and President Violetta Barrios de Chamorro (Nicaragua) (horiz)	3·75	3·00

568 Violeta Chamorro

1997. Violeta Barrios de Chamorro (president 1990–1996). Self-adhesive.

3685	**568**	3cor. multicoloured	1·10	80

569 House and Garden

1997. 60th Anniv of Plan Internacional. Self-adhesive.

3686	**569**	7cor.50 multicoloured	3·00	1·90

570 "Noctorno con dos Figuras" (Alejandro Arostegui)

1998. Art.

3687	**570**	7cor.50 multicoloured	2·40	1·70

571 Map of India and Flag

1998. 50th Anniv (1997) of Indian Independence.

3688	**571**	3cor. multicoloured	65	45
3689	**571**	9cor. multicoloured	1·90	1·30

572 Mombacho Volcano

1998. National Parks. Multicoloured.

3690	1cor.50 Type **572**	30	20
3691	2cor.50 La Flor	55	40
3692	3cor. Zapatera archipelago	65	45
3693	3cor.50 Miraflor	75	50
3694	5cor. Cosiguina volcano	1·00	75
3695	6cor.50 Masaya volcano	1·40	95
3696	7cor.50 Juan Venado Island	1·50	1·10
3697	8cor. Rio Escalante Chacocente	1·70	1·20
3698	10cor. Mountains (national system of protected areas)	1·90	1·50
MS3699	65×95 mm. 12cor. Bosawas. Imperf	2·75	2·75

573 Footprints

1998. Centenary Huellas de Acahualinca (Footprints of Acahualinca) Museum.

3700	**573**	3cor.50 multicoloured	75	50

574 "Descendimiento"

1998. 90th Birth Anniv of Rodrigo Penalba (artist). Multicoloured.

3701	2cor.50 Type **574**	55	40
3702	3cor.50 "Victoria y Piere"	75	50
3703	5cor. "Maternidad"	1·00	75
MS3704	95×65 mm. 10cor. "El gueguense" Imperf	2·00	2·00

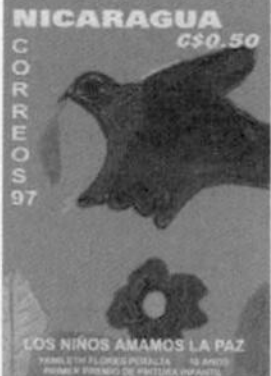

575 Dove (Yamileth Flores Peralta)

1998. Winning Design in Children's Painting Competition.

3705	**575**	50c. multicoloured	20	10

576 Frontispiece

1998. Centenary of Publication of "Prosas Profanos". Ruben Garcia Sarmiento Felix (Ruben Dario) (poet) Commemoration. Multicoloured.

3706	3cor.50 Type **576**	75	40
3707	5cor. Ruben Dario	1·10	75

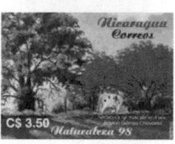

577 "Vaca y Malinche" (Bayron Gomez Chavarria)

1998. Naturaleza 98 (art and culture).

3708	**577**	3cor.50 multicoloured	75	50

578 Post Box

1998. Stamp Day.

3709	**578**	6cor.50 multicoloured	1·40	95

579 "Dialogo de Nicaragua" (painting)

1998. Meeting between Nicarao Chief and Gil Gonzalez Davila (Spanish explorer).

3710	**579**	5cor. multicoloured	1·00	75

580 Lolita Soriano de Guerrero (founder of (Leoncio Saenz) Lola Soriano Grammar school)

1998. America. Famous Women. Multicoloured.

3711	3cor.50 Type **580**	75	90
3712	7cor.50 Violeta Barrios de Chamorro (president 1990—1996)	1·60	1·10

581 "50", Emblem and Faces

1998. 50th Anniv of Universal Declaration of Human Rights.

3713	**581**	12cor. multicoloured	2·30	1·80

582 The Nativity (clay)

1998. Christmas. Multicoloured.

3714 50c. Type **582** 10 10
3715 1cor. Jesus (carved gourd) 20 15
3716 2cor. The Nativity (statues) (horiz) 35 30
3717 3cor. Modern Nativity (painting) (horiz) 65 45
MS3718 95×65 mm. 7cor.50 Hark the Herald Angels. Imperf 1·70 1·70

583 Managua before the Earthquake

1998. 25th (1997) Anniv of Managua Earthquake. Multicoloured.

3719 3cor. Type **583** 65 45
3720 7cor.50 After the earthquake (horiz) 1·70 1·10
MS3721 65×95 mm.10cor.50 Clock and stylized buildings 2·30 2·30

584 Diana, Princess of Wales

1999. Diana, Princess of Wales Commemoration. Multicoloured.

3722 5cor. Type **584** 1·10 70
3723 7cor.50 Wearing tiara 1·70 1·20
3724 10cor. Wearing drop earrings 2·30 1·60

585 *Metamorpha stelenes*

1999. Butterflies. Multicoloured.

3725 2cor. Type **585**; 55 35
3726 2cor. *Erateina staudinger* 55 35
3727 2cor. *Premolis semirufa* 55 35
3728 2cor. Inscr "Heliconius eisini" 55 35
3729 2cor. Inscr "Phoebis phlea" 55 35
3730 2cor. *Dione juno* 55 35
3731 2cor. *Helicopis cupido* 55 35
3732 2cor. Inscr "Catonephele numili" 55 35
3733 2cor. *Anteos clorinde* 55 35
3734 3cor.50 Inscr "Papilionidae ornithoptera alexandrae" 75 50
3735 8cor. Inscr "Nymphalidae cepheutychia cephus" 1·80 1·30
3736 9cor. Inscr "Nymphalidae eryphanis polyxena" 1·90 1·30
3737 9cor. Inscr "Nymphalidae callicore maimuna" 1·90 1·30
3738 9cor. Inscr "Nymphalidae hypolimmas salmacis" 1·90 1·30
3739 9cor. Inscr "Nymphalidae precis octavia" 1·90 1·30
3740 9cor. Inscr "Papilionidae troides-brookiana" 1·90 1·30
3741 9cor. Inscr "Nymphalidae cithaerias esmeralda" 1·90 1·30
3742 9cor. Inscr "Papilionidae parides coon" 1·90 1·30
3743 9cor. Inscr "Nymphalidae heliconius" 1·90 1·30
3744 9cor. Inscr "Nymphalidae morpho rhetenor" 1·90 1·30
3745 12cor.50 Inscr "Pieridae phoebis philea" 2·75 1·90
MS3746 110×85 mm. 15cor. Inscr "Papiliomidae papilio glaucus" 2·75 2·75
MS3747 110×80 mm. 25cor. Inscr "Thecla coronata" 4·50 4·50
MS3748 105×72 mm. Inscr "Ufefheisa bela" 4·50 4·50

Nos. 3736/44 were issued together, *se-tenant*, forming a composite design.

586 *Eudyptes chrysocome*

1999. Sea Birds. Multicoloured.

3749 5cor. Type **586** 1·00 70
3749a 5cor.50 Inscr "Speniscus magellanious" 1·00 70
3756 6cor. Inscr "Speniscus magellanious" 1·10 80
3756a 6cor. Pygoscelis Antarctica 1·10 80
3757 6cor. Inscr "Phalacrocorax punctatus featherstoni" (horiz) 1·20 85
3758 2cor. *Phalacrocorax bougainvillii* (horiz) 1·20 85
3759 6cor. *Anhinga anhinga* (horiz) 1·20 85
3760 6cor. *Phalacrocorax punctatus punctatus* (horiz) 1·20 80
3761 6cor. *Phalacrocorax sulcirostris* (horiz) 1·20 85
3762 6cor. *Pelicanus occidentalis* (horiz) 1·20 85
3763 7cor.50 Inscr "Magadyptes antipodes" 1·50 1·00
MS3764 Two sheets, each 85×110 mm (a) 12cor. Inscr "Pygos papua". (b) 12cor. *Aptenodytes forsteri* 4·75 4·75

587 *Eagle* (1851)

1999. Ships. Multicoloured.

3765 2cor. Type **587** 35 25
3766 3cor. HMS *Rodney* (1830) (31×40 mm) 55 35
3767 3cor. *Boyne* (1700) (31×40 mm)
3768 3cor. *Castor* (1800) (31×40 mm) 55 35
3769 3cor. *Mutin* (1800) (31×40 mm) 55 35
3770 3cor. *Britannia* (1820) (31×40 mm) 55 35
3771 3cor. *Goulden Leeuw* (1600) (31×40 mm) 55 35
3772 3cor. *Hercules* (1600) (31×40 mm) 55 35
3773 3cor. *Resolotion* (1667) (31×40 mm) 55 35
3774 3cor. *Royal George* (1756) (31×40 mm) 55 35
3775 3cor. HMS *Vanguard* (Inscr "Vaguard") (1700) (31×40 mm) 55 35
3776 3cor. *Prince Royal* (1600) (31×40 mm) 55 35
3777 3cor. *Zeven Provincien* (1600) (31×40 mm) 55 35
3778 4cor. *Contest* (1800) 75 50
3779 5cor. *Architect* (1847—8) 1·00 65
3780 10cor. *Edward O'Brien* (1863) 2·00 1·60
MS3781 Two sheets, each 115×84 mm (a) 15cor. *Pamir* (1905). (b) 15cor. *Great Expedition* (1700) 6·00 6·00

588 Sordes

1999. Pre-Historic Animals. Multicoloured.

3782 5cor. Type **588** 1·00 65
3783 5cor. Dimorphodon 1·00 65
3784 5cor. Anurognathus 1·00 65
3785 5cor. Rhamphorynchus 1·00 65
3786 5cor. Pterodaustro 1·00 65
3787 5cor. Pteranodon 1·00 65
3788 6cor. Macroplata 1·20 85
3789 6cor. Coelurus 1·20 85
3790 6cor. Inscr "Stegosaurus" 1·20 85
3791 6cor. Corythosaurus 1·20 85
3792 6cor. Inscr "Thadeosaurus" 1·20 85
3793 6cor. Inscr "Brachsaurus" 1·20 85
MS3794 Two sheets, each 115×84 mm (a) 12cor. Platecarpus. (b) 12cor. Pterodactylus 4·75 4·75

Nos. 3782/7 and 3788/93 were issued together, *se-tenant*, with enlarged illustrated margins, the whole, in each case, forming a composite design.

589 *Anteos clorinde*

1999. Fauna and Flora. Multicoloured.

3795 5cor. Type **589** 95 65
3796 5cor. Palm tree (vert) 95 65
3797 5cor. *Phaethon lepturus* (vert) 95 65
3798 5cor. *Cinlocerthia ruficauda* (vert) 95 65
3799 5cor. *Myadestes genbarbis* (vert) 95 65
3800 5cor. *Rosa sinesis* (vert) 95 65
3801 5cor. *Cyanophaia bicolor* (vert) 95 65
3802 5cor. *Delphinus delphinus* (vert) 95 65
3803 5cor. *Anolis carolinensis* (vert) 95 65
3804 5cor. *Dynastes titvus* (vert) 95 65
3805 5cor. *Iguana iguana* (vert) 95 65
3806 5cor. *Prepona meander* (vert) 95 65
3809 6cor. *Coereba flaveola* 1·20 80
3810 7cor.50 *Rynchops niger* 1·50 1·00
3811 7cor.50 *Chaetodon striatus* 1·50 1·00
MS3812 100×70 mm. 10cor. *Anisotremus virginicus* 1·90 1·90
MS3813 70×100 mm. 10cor. *Ceryle torquata* (vert) 1·90 1·90

Nos. 3796/808 were issued together, *se-tenant*, with enlarged illustrated margins, the whole forming a composite design.

590 U25B Rock Island No. 213 General Electric Locomotive (1960)

1999. Railways. Multicoloured.

3814 1cor. Type **590** 20 15
3815 5cor. C-630 Century Santa Fe Railroad Alco (1965) 1·00 75
3816 5cor. CR Alco RS11 No. 7610 (1956) 1·00 75
3817 5cor. Metra No. 167 GE EMD F40 (1983) 1·00 75
3818 5cor. British Columbia Railways GF6C 1·00 75
3819 5cor. Amtrak GE EMD AEM7 No. 908 (1981) 1·00 75
3820 5cor. C-40-9 Norfolk Southern No. 8845 GE EMD (1986) 1·00 75
3821 5cor. C-630 No. 5308 "Big Alco" Reading RR (1967) 1·00 75
3823 6cor. British Columbia Railways General Motors GF6C (1983) 1·20 80
3824 6cor. Alco Indian Railways WDM C-C (1962) 1·20 80
3825 6cor. Clyde Engineering GM Powerhouse Class 421 No. 42106 Australia (1982) 1·20 80
3826 6cor. Clyde Engineering GM Powerhouse Class M821 No. 8136 Australia (1986) 1·20 80
3827 6cor. Via Canada LRC BB Alco No. 6903 (1982) 1·20 80
3828 6cor. Clyde Engineering Victorian Railways GM class X No. X49 (1966) 1·20 80
3830 6cor.50 General Motors Class DD 41 AX Centennial DD Union Pacific (1969) 1·30 90
3831 7cor.50 F Series BB EMD Maryland DOT No. 7185 1·50 1·00
MS3832 Two sheets, each 116×76 mm (a) 15cor. Queen Victoria. (b) 15cor. Donald A. Smith drives the "Last Spike", Canadian and Pacific Railway (vert) 6·00 6·00

591 *Tricholoma ustaloides*

1999. Fungi. Multicoloured.

3833 5cor. Type **591** 1·10 70
3834 5cor. *Tricholoma pardinum* 1·10 70
3835 5cor. *Amanita echinocephala* 1·10 70
3836 5cor. *Tricholoma saponaceum* 1·10 70
3837 5cor. *Amanita inaurata* 1·10 70
3838 5cor. *Amanita rubescens* 1·10 70
3839 7cor.50 *Amanita*; 1·50 1·00
3840 7cor.50 Inscr "Cryptotrama asprata" 1·50 1·00
3841 7cor.50 *Amanita gemmata* 1·50 1·00
3842 7cor.50 *Catathelasma imperiale* 1·50 1·00
3843 7cor.50 *Collybia fusipes* 1·50 1·00
3844 7cor.50 *Collybia butyracea* 1·50 1·00
MS3845 Two sheets, each 100×70 mm. (a) 12cor.50 *Tricholomopsis rutilans*. (b) 12cor.50 *Tricholoma virgatum* 4·75 4·75

592 *Cattleya skinneri*

1999. Orchids. Multicoloured.

3846 2cor. Type **592** 35 25
3847 3cor. *Odontoglossum rossii* 55 35
3848 3cor. *Cattleya aurantiaca* 55 35
3849 3cor. *Encyclia cordigera* 55 35
3850 3cor. *Phragmipedium besseae* 55 35
3851 3cor. *Brassavola nodosa* 55 35
3852 3cor. *Cattleya forbesii* 55 35
3853 3cor. *Barkeria spectabilis* 55 35
3854 3cor. *Dracula erythrochaete* 55 35
3855 3cor. *Cochleanthes discolor* 55 35
3856 3cor. *Encyclia cochleata* 55 35
3857 3cor. *Lycaste aromatica* 55 35
3858 3cor. *Brassia maculate* 55 35
3859 4cor. *Lycaste aromatica* (different) 85 50
3860 5cor. *Odontoglossum cervantesii* 1·00 65
3861 10cor. *Brassia verrucosa* 2·00 1·60
MS3862 Two sheets, each 85×110 mm. (a) 25cor. *Odontoglossum rossii* (different). (b) 25cor. *Phragmipedium longifolium* 10·00 10·00

593 Fishing Boats, Puerto Cabezas

1999. Nicaragua—Japan Friendship. Multicoloured.

MS3863 150×120 mm. 3cor.50 Type **593**; 5cor. Grain production; 6cor. Japanese school; 7cor.50 Pan American Highway bridge; 8cor. Japanese aqueduct, Managua; 9cor. Japan—Nicaragua Friendship Hospital 9·25 9·25

594 Tiberius Cavallo (early researcher into gases)

1999. Ballooning. Multicoloured.

3864 12cor. Type **594** 2·50 1·80
3865 12cor. *Breitling Orbiter 3* (1990) 2·50 1·80
3866 12cor. Bertrand Piccard and Brian Jones (balloonists) 2·50 1·80
3867 12cor. Brian Jones (captain) 2·50 1·80
3868 12cor. *Breitling Orbiter 3* (first non-stop circumnavigation of the world, 1999) 2·50 1·80
3869 12cor. Bertrand Picard (co-pilot) 2·50 1·80
3870 12cor. *Breitling Orbiter 3* over Alps 2·50 1·80
3871 12cor. Leonardo da Vinci (experiments with heavier than air) 2·50 1·80
3872 12cor. Bertrand Piccard and Brian Jones (different) 2·50 1·50
3873 12cor. *Solo Spirit 3* (first crossing of South Atlantic, 1998) 2·50 1·80
3874 12cor. *BreitlingOrbiter 3* emblem 2·50 1·80
3875 12cor. ICO Global (1998) 2·50 1·80
MS3876 Three sheets, each 70×100 mm. (a) 25cor. Pilatre de Rozier (first manned flight). (b) 25cor. Madame Thible (first woman solo balloon flight). (c) 25cor. J. A. C. Charles (early balloon producer) 17·00 17·00
MS3877 100×70 mm. 25cor. Jean Pierre Blanchard (balloon pioneer) 5·50 5·50

595 Bank Building, Washington

1999. 40th Anniv of Inter-American Development Bank.
3878 **595** 7cor.50 multicoloured 1·60 1·10

596 Dove carrying Olive Branch

1999. America. New Millennium without Arms.
3879 **596** 7cor.50 multicoloured 1·70 1·20

597 Theatre at Night

1999. 30th Anniv of Ruben Dario Theatre.
3880 **597** 7cor.50 multicoloured 1·90 1·30

598 Municipal Building, Grenada

1999. 475th Anniv of Grenada (3872/7) and Leon (3878/83). Multicoloured.

3881	3cor.50 Type **598**	75	50
3882	3cor.50 Guadalupe Church, Central Plaza	75	50
3883	3cor.50 Houses with verandas, Gral	75	50
3884	3cor.50 Ponciano Corral	75	50
3885	3cor.50 Casa de los Leones	75	50
3886	3cor.50 Colonial and neo-classical buildings, El Consulado	75	50
3887	7cor.50 Leon Cathedral	1·70	1·20
3888	7cor.50 Municipal theatre	1·70	1·20
3889	7cor.50 La Recoleccion Church	1·70	1·20
3890	7cor. Ruben Dario Archive Musuem	1·70	1·20
3891	7cor.50 TELCOR building	1·70	1·20
3892	7cor.50 Cural de Subtiava	1·70	1·20

599 Building

1999. 125th Anniv of Universal Postal Union.
3893 **599** 7cor.50 multicoloured 1·90 1·30

600 Azawakh Dog

2000. Dogs and Cats. Multicoloured.

3894	1cor. Type **600**	30	15
3895	2cor. Chihuahua dog	55	35
3896	2cor.50 Chocolate colour point Birman cat (horiz)	65	45
3897	3cor. Norwegian forest cat (horiz)	75	50
3898	6cor. Clumber spaniel	1·60	1·10
3899	6cor. Australian sheepdog	1·60	1·10
3900	6cor. German wire-haired pointer	1·60	1·10
3901	6cor. Dog with long ears and rough coat	1·60	1·10
3902	6cor. Ibizan hound	1·60	1·10
3903	6cor. Norwegian elkhound	1·60	1·10
3904	6cor. Italian blue colour point	1·60	1·10
3905	6cor. Turkish longhair	1·60	1·10
3906	6cor. Incr "Tiffany Rojo"	1·60	1·10
3907	6cor. Longhair	1·60	1·10
3908	6cor. Inscr "Calico Pelocorto sin Pedigree"	1·60	1·10
3909	6cor. Oriental blue	1·60	1·10

MS3910 110×86 mm. 12cor. Burmese cat (57×42 mm) 3·25 3·25
MS3911 86×110 mm. 12cor. Braque de Bourbonnais (42×57 mm) 3·25 3·25

601 Queen Elizabeth

2000. Birth Centenary of Queen Elizabeth, Queen Mother. Two sheets, each 151×155 mm containing T **601** and similar vert designs. Multicoloured.
MS3912 (a) 10cor.×4, Type **601**; Seated facing right; With King George VI ; Wearing blue hat. (b) Wearing tiara, facing left (38×51 mm) 17·00 17·00

602 Bristol F2B

2000. Aviation. Multicoloured.

3913	7cor.50 Montgolfier balloon (41×60 mm)	1·90	1·30
3914	7cor.50 Type **602**	1·90	1·30
3915	7cor.50 Inscr "Provost Jet"	1·90	1·30
3916	7cor.50 Inscr "Hunter"	1·90	1·30
3917	7cor.50 Wessex helicopter	1·90	1·30
3918	7cor.50 Inscr "Redwing II Trainer" (41×60 mm)	1·90	1·30
3919	7cor.50 Montgolfier balloon (41×60 mm) (different)	1·90	1·30
3920	7cor.50 Hawker Hart	1·90	1·30
3921	7cor.50 Westland Lysander		
3922	7cor.50 ; British Aerospace Harrier	1·90	1·30
3923	7cor.50 VC10	1·90	1·30
3924	7cor.50 Bleriot and De Havilland Fox Moth (41×60 mm)	1·90	1·30

MS3925 Two sheets, each 86×110 mm. (a) 25cor. Spartan Arrow and De Havilland Tiger Moth. (b) 25cor. Tiger Moth and Spartan Arrow (different) 13·00 13·00

603 British Rail Class 470 APT-P

2000. Railways. Showing locomotives. Multicoloured.

3926	3cor. Type **603**	75	50
3927	3cor. Swedish State Railways Class DM3	75	50
3928	3cor. New Zealand Railways Class EW 165	75	50
3929	3cor. British Rail Class 87	75	50
3930	3cor. British Rail Class 40	75	50
3931	3cor. Swiss Class GE6/6 Crocodile	75	50
3932	3cor. Spanish Railways Class 277 No. 1737	75	50
3933	3cor. B-23-7 Metro North Commuter	75	50
3934	3cor. Long Island EMD DE30	75	50
3935	3cor. General Motors EMD F40 PHM-2C	75	50
3936	3cor. Pennsylvania Railroad GG1	75	50
3937	3cor. New Jersey Transit MK GP40 FH-2	75	50
3938	3cor. Amtrak EMD F59 PHI	75	20
3939	4cor. Swedish State Railways X-2000 Tilting Express	1·00	70
3940	5cor. New South Wales XPT	1·30	75
3941	10cor. British Rail IIST 125	2·75	1·90

MS3942 110×86 mm. 25cor. British Rail Class 44 6·50 6·50
MS3943 86×110 mm. 25cor. Metra EMD P69PN-AC 6·50 6·50

604 Great White Shark

2000. Marine Life. Multicoloured.

3944	3cor.50 Type **604**	95	65
3945	5cor. Humpback whale	1·30	95
3946	6cor. Sea turtle	1·60	1·10
3947	9cor. Sperm whale	2·40	1·60

MS3948 Two sheets, each 163×89 mm. (a) 7cor.50×6, Bridled burrfish; Manta ray; Black grouper; Tiger grouper; Moray eel; Atlantic squid. (b) 7cor.50×6, Hawksbill turtle; Jellyfish; Reef shark; Reef turtle; Dolphin; Stingray 24·00 24·00
MS3949 Two sheets, each 85×110 mm. (a) 25cor. Tiger shark. (b) 25cor. Dolphins 13·00 13·00

The stamps and margins of **MS**3948a/b form composite designs.

605 *Cotinga amabilis*

2000. Birds. Multicoloured.

3950	5cor. Type **605**	1·30	95
3951	7cor.50 *Galbula ruficauda*	1·90	1·30
3952	10cor. *Guiraca caerulea*	2·50	1·80
3953	12cor.50 *Momotus momoto*	3·50	2·50

MS3954 157×108 mm. 3cor.×10, *Ara macao; Amazona ochrocephala; Chloroceryleamericana; Archilocus colubris; Pharamachrus mocinno; Ramphastossalfuratus; Coereba flaveola; Piculus rubiginosus; Passerina ciris; Busarella nigricollis* 8·00 8·00
MS3955 Two sheets, each 85×110 mm. (a) 25cor. *Aulacorhynchus prasinus.* (b) 25cor. *Megaceryle alcyon* 13·00 13·00

The stamps and margins of **MS**3954 form a composite design.

606 Recovery of Spacecraft

2000. Space Exploration. Multicoloured.

3956	5cor. Type **6061**	30	95
3957	5cor. Earth from space	1·30	95
3958	5cor. Malcolm Scott Carpenter in dinghy	1·30	95
3959	5cor. Helicopter rescue of Alan Shepherd	1·30	95
3960	5cor. USS *Intrepid* (rescue craft)	1·30	95
3961	5cor. Launch of *Friendship 7*	1·30	95
3962	5cor. *Mercury 9* splash down	1·30	95
3963	5cor. *Mercury 6* suspended from helicopter	1·30	95

MS3964 123×187 mm. All vert. 5cor.×8, Donald Kent Slayton; Malcolm Scott Carpenter; Walter Marty Schirra; John Herschel Glenn; Leroy Gordon Cooper; Virgil Ivan Grissom; Mercury Redstone-3 spacecraft; Alan Shepherd 10·00 10·00
MS3965 85×115 mm. 25cor. John Glenn (different) (vert) 6·50 6·50
MS3966 115×85 mm. 25cor. Alan Shepherd (different) 6·50 6·50

The stamps and margins of **MS**3964 form a composite design.

607 Pope Leo XIII

2000. 20th Century Popes. Multicoloured.

3967	3cor. Type **607**	75	50
3968	3cor. Worker with raised arm (Leo XIII's proclamation of worker's rights)	75	50
3969	3cor. Pius X	75	50
3970	3cor. Monk holding harp (Pius X's revision of ecclesiastical music)	75	50
3971	3cor. Benedict XV	75	50
3972	3cor. Joan of Arc (Benedict XV's campaign for the canonization of Joan of Arc)	75	50
3973	3cor. Pius XI	75	50
3974	3cor. Radio and globe (establishment of Radio Vatican)	75	50
3975	3cor. John XXIII	75	50
3976	3cor. Peace symbol	75	50
3977	3cor. Paul VI	75	50
3978	3cor. Paul VI's flag	75	50
3979	3cor. John Paul I	75	50
3980	3cor. Lamb and cross (symbol of Papal humility)	75	50
3981	3cor. John Paul II	75	50
3982	3cor. Globe and hands holding dove (symbol of John Paul II's ministry)	75	50

MS3983 Two sheets, each 108×115 mm. (a) 25cor. Pope John XXIII (38×51 mm). (b) 25cor. Pope John Paul II (38×51 mm) 13·00 13·00

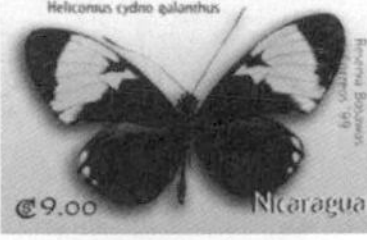
608 *Heliconius cydno galanthus*

2000. Butterflies. Multicoloured.

3984	9cor. *Catonephele numilla esite*	2·00	1·40
3985	9cor. *Marpesia marcella*	2·00	1·40
3986	9cor. *Heliconius hecalesia*	2·00	1·40
3987	9cor. *Acinote thalia anteas*	2·00	1·40
3988	9cor. *Boxocopa larentia cherubina*	2·00	1·40
3989	9cor. *Napeogenes tolosa mombachoensis*	2·00	1·40
3990	9cor. Type **608**	2·00	1·40
3991	9cor. *Nessaea aglaura*	2·00	1·40
3992	9cor. *Godyris zavaleta sosunga*	2·00	1·40
3993	9cor. *Caligo atreusdionysos*	2·00	1·40
3994	9cor. *Morpho amonte*	2·00	1·40
3995	9cor. *Eryphanis polyxena lycomedon*	2·00	1·40

MS3996 Two sheets, each 106×75 mm. (a) 25cor. *Papillo garamas.* (b) 25cor. *Cithaerias menader* 13·00 13·00

609 Indira Ghandhi

2000. Twentieth Century Leaders. Multicoloured.

3997	5cor. Type **609**	1·30	95
3998	5cor. Indira Ghandhi, soldier and elephant (57×43 mm)	1·30	95
3999	5cor. Ronald Reagan (57×43 mm)	1·30	95
4000	5cor. Ronald Reagan and flags	1·30	95
4001	5cor. Vladimir Lenin	1·30	95
4002	5cor. Vladimir Lenin and national symbols (57×43 mm)	1·30	95
4003	5cor. Charles de Gaulle (57×43 mm)	1·30	95
4004	5cor. Charles de Gaulle wearing uniform	1·30	95
4005	5cor. Kemal Ataturk	1·30	95
4006	5cor. Kemal Ataturk and national flag (57×43 mm)	1·30	95
4007	5cor. John F. Kennedy (57×43 mm)	1·30	95
4008	5cor. John F. Kennedy and space craft	1·30	95
4009	5cor. Winston Churchill	1·30	95
4010	5cor. Winston Churchill wearing uniform (57×43 mm)	1·30	95
4011	5cor. Jomo Kenyatta (57×43 mm)	1·30	95
4012	5cor. Jomo Kenyatta and mountains	1·30	95

MS4013 76×105 mm. 25cor. Chiang Kai-Shek 6·50 6·50
MS4014 105×76 mm. 25cor. Theodore Roosevelt 6·50 6·50

610 Founder Members

2000. Charitable Organizations. Lions Club International (4015/20) or Rotary International (4021/6). Multicoloured.
4015 5cor. Type **610** 1·30 95

4016 5cor. Headquarters building, Chicago 1·30 95
4017 5cor. Helen Keller 1·30 95
4018 5cor. Koffi Annan (United Nations Secretary General) and Kajit Haadananananda (Lions Club president) 1·30 95
4019 5cor. Melvin Jones (founder) 1·30 95
4020 5cor. Andre de Villiers (design a "Peace Poster" winner) 1·30 95
4021 7cor. Clowns and children (vert) 1·90 1·30
4022 7cor. Nurse giving Polio vaccine drops (vert) 1·90 1·30
4023 7cor. Women using water pump, Burkina Faso (vert) 1·90 1·30
4024 7cor. Women attending literacy class, Nepal (vert) 1·90 1·30
4025 7cor. Transport for people with physical disabilities (vert) 1·90 1·30
4026 7cor. Campaign to reduce urban violence, Northern Ireland 1·90 1·30
MS4027 Two sheets, each 114×101 mm. (a) 25cor. Melvin Jones (vert). (b) 25cor. Rotary International emblem (vert) 13·00 13·00

611 Puente El Tamarindo

2001. Nicaragua—Japan Friendship. Bridges. Sheet 150×141 mm containing T **611** and similar horiz designs. Multicoloured.
MS4028 6cor.50 Type **611**; 7cor.50 Puente Ochomogo; 9cor. Puente Gil Gonzalez; 10cor. Puente Las Lajas; 12cor. Puente Rio Negro 12·00 12·00

612 Globe

2001. Stamp Day.
4029 **612** 6cor.50 multicoloured 1·60 1·10

613 Ruins, Leon Viejo

2001. America. World Heritage.
4030 **613** 10cor. multicoloured 2·00 1·40

615 *Ramphastos swaisonii* (inscr "Rtamphastos")

2001. Fauna. Sheet 111×110 mm containing T **615** and similar vert designs. Multicoloured.
MS4032 5cor. Type **615**; 6cor.50 *Amazona auropalliata*; 8cor.*Buteo magnirostris*; 9cor. *Ateles geoffroy* (Inscr "Atteles");10cor. *Leopardus wiedii*; 12cor. *Puma concolor* 6·50 6·50
The stamps and margins of **MS**4032 form a composite design.

616 Children

2001. 50th Anniv of SOS Children's Villages.
4033 **616** 5cor.50 multicoloured 1·00 85

617 Cardinal Obando Bravo

2002. Cardinal Miguel Obando Bravo (archbishop of Managua).
4034 **617** 6cor.50 multicoloured 1·10 95

621 Early Village and Ships

2002. 500th Anniv of Discovery of Nicaragua. Multicoloured.
4038 7cor.50 Type **621** 1·40 1·30

622 Josemaria Escriva

2002. Birth Centenary of Josemaria Escriva de la Balaguer (founder of Opus Dei (religious organization)).
4040 **622** 2cor.50 multicoloured 45 45

623 Children enclosing Book

2002. America. Literacy Campaign.
4041 **623** 7cor.50 multicoloured 1·40 1·30

624 Puertos de Nicaragua-Corinto

2002. Ports.
4042 **624** 5cor. multicoloured 95 85

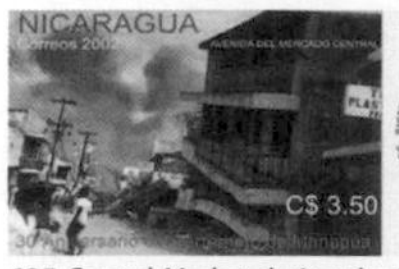

625 Central Market during the Earthquake and SNPMAD (disaster organization) Emblem

2002. 30th Anniv of Managua Earthquake. Multicoloured.
4043 3cor.50 Type **625** 65 60
4044 7cor.50 Managua Cathedral (vert) 1·40 1·30

626 Duke and Duchess of Luxembourg

2003. First Visit of Duke and Duchess of Luxembourg.
4045 **626** 12cor. multicoloured 2·30 2·20

627 "En Diriamba de Nicaragua, capturaronme amigo" (Roger Perez De la Rocha)

2003. Art. Multicoloured.
4046 3cor. Type **627** 45 45
4047 5cor. "San Gabriel Arcangel" (Orlando Sobalvarro) 75 70
4048 6cor.50 "Ave Fenex" (Alejandro Arostegul) 1·00 95
4049 7cor.50 "Abstraccion de frutas" (Leonel Vanegas) 1·10 1·00
4050 8cor. "Suite en Turquesa y azules" (Bernard Dreyfus) (horiz) 1·20 1·10
4051 9cor. "Ana III" (Armando Morales) (horiz) 1·40 1·30
4052 10cor. "Coloso IV" (Arnoldo Guillen) (horiz) 1·50 1·40

628 Pope John Paul II

2003. 25th Anniv of Pontificate of Pope John Paul II. Sheet 85×110 mm containing T **628** and similar vert design. Multicoloured.
MS4053 3cor. Type **628**; 10cor. Wearing mitre 2·00 2·00

629 Hospicio San Juan de Dios Leon

2003. Centenary of La Salle Christian Education. Multicoloured.
4055 3cor. Type **629** 45 45
4056 5cor. Octavio de Jesus (vert) 75 70
4057 6cor.50 Bodran Marie (vert) 1·00 95
4058 7cor.50 Agustin Herve (vert) 1·10 1·00
4059 9cor. Vauthier de Jesus (vert) 1·40 1·30
4060 10cor. Father Mariano Dubón (vert) 1·50 1·40
MS4060a 97×66 mm. 12cor. John Baptist de la Salle (founder) (vert) 1·90 1·70

630 *Fulgora laternaria*

2003. Insects. Two sheets, each 111×110 mm containing T **630** and similar horiz designs. Multicoloured.
MS4061 (a) 6cor.50×6 Type **630**; *Acraephia perspicillata; Copidocephala guttata;. Pterodictya reticularis; Phrictus quinquepartitus; Odontoptera carrenoi* (b) 8cor.x6 *Golofa pizarro; Phanaeus pyrois* (Inscr "Phaneus"); *Plusiotis aurigans; Polyphylla concurrens; Dynastes hercules septentrionalis; Phanaeus demon excelsus* (Inscr "Phaneus") 5·00 5·00
The stamps of **MS**4061a/b respectively form composite background design.

632 *Victoria*

2003. River Boat Mail Transportation. Steam Boats. Multicoloured.
4080 3cor. Type **632** 45 45
4081 5cor. *Irma* 75 70
4082 6cor.50 *Hollenbeck* 1·00 95
4083 7cor.50 *Managua* 1·10 1·00

633 *Corytophanes cristatus*

2003. America. Fauna and Flora. Multicoloured.
4084 10cor. Type **633** 1·50 1·40
4085 12cor. *Guaiacum sanctum* 1·80 1·60

634 Beachfront

2003. 150th Anniv of San Juan del Sur Port.
4086 **634** 10cor. multicoloured 1·50 1·40

635 Model AA (1936)

2003. Toyota Cars. Multicoloured.
4087 7cor.50 Type **635** 1·10 1·00
4088 7cor.50 AB Phaeton (1936) 1·10 1·00
4089 7cor.50 Model SA (1947) 1·10 1·00
4090 7cor.50 Model BJ (1951) 1·10 1·00
4091 7cor.50 Crown RSD (1955) 1·10 1·00
4092 7cor.50 Model FJ28VA 1·10 1·00

636 Ruben Dario and Book Cover

2004. Centenary of "Tierras Solares" by Ruben Dario.
4093 **636** 10cor. multicoloured 1·50 1·40

637 *Tabebuia rosea*

2004. Flowering Trees. Multicoloured.
4094 3cor. Type **637** 45 45
4095 5cor. *Cassia fistula* 75 70
4096 6cor.50 *Delonix regia* 1·00 95

638 Cerro Kilambe Nature Reserve

2004. America. Environmental Protection. Multicoloured.
4097 7cor.50 Type **638** 1·10 1·00
4098 7cor.50 Bosawas Rio Bocay reserve 1·10 1·00

639 Hurdling

2004. Olympic Games, Athens. Multicoloured.
4099 7cor.50 Type **639** 1·10 1·00
4100 10cor. Swimming 1·50 1·40
4101 12cor. Shooting 1·90 1·70

640 Judo and Kickboxing

2004. Central American Student Games, Managua. Multicoloured.
4102 3cor. Type **640** 45 45
4103 5cor. Football and baseball 75 70
4104 6cor.50 High jump and swimming 95 85

641 *Selenidera spectabilis*

2004. Birds. Multicoloured.

4105	5cor. Type **641**	75	70
4106	6cor.50 *Nycticorax nycticorax*	1·00	95
4107	7cor.50 *Caracara plancus*	1·10	1·00
4108	10cor. *Myiozetetes similes*	1·50	1·40

642 Station Building

2004. Granada Railway Station.

4109	**642**	3cor. multicoloured	45	45

643 Mambacho Volcano Reserve

2004. Tourism. Multicoloured.

4110	7cor.50 Type **643**	1·10	1·00
4111	7cor.50 Tapou river, San Juan river wildlife reserve	1·10	1·00

644 "Frutas Ocultas" (Federico Nordalm)

2004. Contemporary Art. Multicoloured.

4112	3cor. Type **644**	45	45
4113	7cor.50 "Nicaraguapa" (Efren Medina) (vert)	1·10	1·00
4114	10cor. "Bambues" (Genaro Lugo)	1·50	1·40

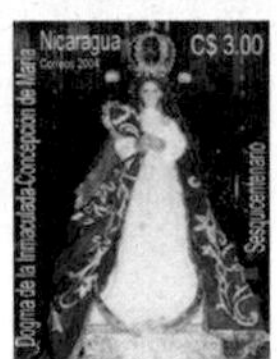

645 Mary (statue)

2004. 150th Anniv of Dogma of Immaculate Conception of Virgin Mary.

4115	**645**	3cor. multicoloured	45	45

646 Pablo Neruda

2004. Birth Centenary of Neftalí Ricardo Reyes Basoalto (Pablo Neruda) (winner of Nobel Prize for Literature, 1971).

4116	**646**	7cor.50 multicoloured	1·10	1·00

No. 4117 and Type **647** are left for Birth Centenary of Ruben Dario issued on 7 February 2005, not yet received.

No. 4118/21 and Type **648** are left for Centenary of Festival issued on 4 May 2007, not yet received.

649 Village

2007. Towards a Mine-free Nicaragua. 15th Anniv of Assistance Program for Demining in Central America (PADCA).

4122	**649**	19cor. multicoloured	2·75	2·50

No. 4123/6 and Type **650** are left for Augusto Sandino Commemoration issued on 18 May 2007, not yet received.

651 *Casmerodius albus* (great egret)

2007. Environmental Protection. Multicoloured.

4127	4cor.50 Type **651**	75	70
4128	11cor.50 *Amazilia tzacatl* (rufous-tailed hummingbird)	1·70	1·50
4129	13cor.50 *Jacana spinosa* (northern jacana)	2·10	1·90
4130	14cor.50 Rio Mico	2·30	2·00

No. 4131/4 and Type **652** are left for Alphabet issued on 9 October 2007, not yet received.

653 Puerto Corinto

2009. Ports. Multicoloured.

4135	1cor. Type **653**	15	10
4136	2cor. Puerto El Rama	25	20
4137	5cor. Puerto de Granada	85	75
4138	10cor. Puerto San Juan del Sur	1·60	1·50
4139	15cor. Puerto Sandino	2·20	2·00
4140	25cor. Puerto Salvador Allende	3·75	3·50

654 Sandino Monument

2009. Augusto Nicolas Calderon Sandino (revolutionary leader) Commemoration. Multicoloured.

4141	10cor. Type **654**	1·60	1·50
4142	10cor. With his wife Blanca Arauz	1·60	1·50

655 Victor Raul Haya de la Torre

2009. 30th Death Anniv of Victor Raul Haya de la Torre (Peruvian political leader).

4143	**655**	12cor. multicoloured	1·80	1·60

656 Augusto Sandino

2009. 30th Anniv of Revolution. Multicoloured

4144	4cor. Type **656**	55	50
4145	5cor. Day of Triumph–19th July 1979	75	70
4146	60cor. Insurrection	8·00	7·00

657 Nurse examing Child

2009. 50th Anniv of National Institute of Social Security. Multicoloured.

4147	4cor. Type **657** (protection of children)	55	50
4148	14cor. Hands, flag and anniversary emblem (solidarity)	2·00	1·80
4149	16cor. Elderly woman and carer (protection of the elderly)	2·40	2·20
4150	25cor. Man wearing mask (risk assessment)	3·50	3·00

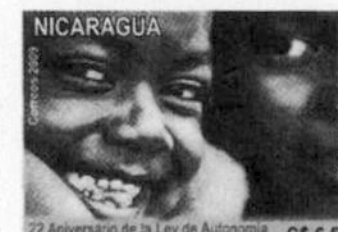

599 Creole Children

2009. 22th Anniv of Caribbean Coast of Nicaragua Autonomy. Multicoloured.

4151	6cor.50 Type **658**	60	65
4152	10cor. Mayagnas and map	1·40	1·30
4153	14cor. Garifuna people (vert)	2·00	1·80
4154	60cor. Dancers	8·00	7·00

599 Assembly Building

2010. 25th Anniv of National Assembly

4155	**659**	60cor. multicoloured	8·00	7·00

599 First Polymer Banknotes (2007)

2010. 50th Anniv of Central Bank. Multicoloured.

4156	15cor. Type **606**	2·10	1·90
4157	15cor. Bank emblem and '50'	2·10	1·90

SILVER CURRENCY

The following were for use in all places on the Atlantic coast of Nicaragua where the silver currency was in use. This currency was worth about 50c. to the peso.

Earlier issues (overprints on Nicaraguan stamps) were also issued for Zelaya. These are listed in the Stanley Gibbons Part 15 (Central America) Catalogue.

Z1 Steam Locomotive

1912

Z1	**Z1**	1c. green	1·20	75
Z2	**Z1**	2c. red	80	55
Z3	**Z1**	3c. brown	1·20	75
Z4	**Z1**	4c. lake	1·20	55
Z5	**Z1**	5c. blue	1·20	55
Z6	**Z1**	6c. red	4·75	2·75
Z7	**Z1**	10c. grey	1·20	1·10
Z8	**Z1**	15c. lilac	1·20	1·10
Z9	**Z1**	20c. blue	1·20	1·10
Z10	**Z1**	25c. black and green	1·80	1·70
Z11	**Z1**	35c. black and brown	2·30	1·70
Z12	**Z1**	50c. green	2·30	1·70
Z13	**Z1**	1p. orange	3·50	2·00
Z14	**Z1**	2p. brown	4·75	3·25
Z15	**Z1**	5p. green	20·00	7·25

OFFICIAL STAMPS

Overprinted FRANQUEO OFICIAL.

1890. Stamps of 1890.

O37	**6**	1c. blue	35	40
O38	**6**	2c. blue	35	40
O39	**6**	5c. blue	35	40
O40	**6**	10c. blue	35	50
O41	**6**	20c. blue	35	85
O42	**6**	50c. blue	35	1·00
O43	**6**	1p. blue	35	1·60
O44	**6**	2p. blue	35	2·10
O45	**6**	5p. blue	35	3·00
O46	**6**	10p. blue	35	5·25

7

1891. Stamps of 1891.

O47	**7**	1c. green	35	45
O48	**7**	2c. green	35	45
O49	**7**	5c. green	35	45
O50	**7**	10c. green	35	45
O51	**7**	20c. green	35	70
O52	**7**	50c. green	35	1·30
O53	**7**	1p. green	35	1·60
O54	**7**	2p. green	35	1·70
O55	**7**	5p. green	35	3·00
O56	**7**	10p. green	35	5·25

8 First Sight of the New World

1892. Stamps of 1892.

O57	**8**	1c. brown	35	40
O58	**8**	2c. brown	35	40
O59	**8**	5c. brown	35	40
O60	**8**	10c. brown	35	40
O61	**8**	20c. brown	35	85
O62	**8**	50c. brown	35	1·10
O63	**8**	1p. brown	35	1·60
O64	**8**	2p. brown	35	3·00
O65	**8**	5p. brown	35	3·50
O66	**8**	10p. brown	35	5·75

1893. Stamps of 1893.

O67	**9**	1c. black	35	40
O68	**9**	2c. black	35	40
O69	**9**	5c. black	35	40
O70	**9**	10c. black	35	40
O71	**9**	20c. black	35	60
O72	**9**	25c. black	35	80
O73	**9**	50c. black	35	1·00
O74	**9**	1p. black	35	1·70
O75	**9**	2p. black	35	2·50
O76	**9**	5p. black	35	3·50
O77	**9**	10p. black	35	5·75

1894. Stamps of 1894.

O78	**10**	1c. orange	45	40
O79	**10**	2c. orange	45	40
O80	**10**	5c. orange	45	40
O81	**10**	10c. orange	45	40
O82	**10**	20c. orange	45	65
O83	**10**	50c. orange	45	1·20
O84	**10**	1p. orange	45	1·70
O85	**10**	2p. orange	45	2·75
O86	**10**	5p. orange	2·75	4·00
O87	**10**	10p. orange	2·75	5·25

1895. Stamps of 1895.

O88A	**11**	1c. green	25	40
O89A	**11**	2c. green	25	40
O90A	**11**	5c. green	25	40
O91A	**11**	10c. green	25	40
O92A	**11**	20c. green	25	60
O93A	**11**	50c. green	25	1·20
O94A	**11**	1p. green	25	1·70
O95A	**11**	2p. green	25	2·10
O96A	**11**	5p. green	25	3·00
O97A	**11**	10p. green	25	5·25

1896. Stamps of 1896, dated "1896", optd **FRANQUEO OFICIAL** in oval frame.

O99A	**12**	1c. red	2·50	3·00
O100A	**12**	2c. red	2·50	3·00
O101A	**12**	5c. red	2·50	3·00
O102A	**12**	10c. red	2·50	3·00
O103A	**12**	20c. red	3·25	3·00
O104A	**12**	50c. red	5·25	5·25
O105A	**12**	1p. red	12·50	12·50
O106A	**12**	2p. red	12·50	12·50
O107A	**12**	5p. red	17·00	17·00

1896. Nos. D99/103 handstamped Franqueo Oficial.

O108A	**D13**	1c. orange		7·25
O109A	**D13**	2c. orange		7·25
O110A	**D13**	5c. orange		5·25
O111A	**D13**	10c. orange		5·25
O112A	**D13**	20c. orange		5·25

1897. Stamps of 1897, dated "1897", optd **FRANQUEO OFICIAL** in oval frame.

O113A	**12**	1c. red	3·25	3·25
O114A	**12**	2c. red	3·25	3·25
O115A	**12**	5c. red	3·25	3·25
O116A	**12**	10c. red	3·25	3·25
O117A	**12**	20c. red	3·25	3·25
O118A	**12**	50c. red	5·25	5·25
O119A	**12**	1p. red	12·50	12·50
O120A	**12**	2p. red	12·50	12·50
O121A	**12**	5p. red	17·00	17·00

1898. Stamps of 1898 optd **FRANQUEO OFICIAL** in oval frame.

O124	**13**	1c. red	3·50	3·50
O125	**13**	2c. red	3·50	3·50
O126	**13**	4c. red	3·50	3·50
O127	**13**	5c. red	2·50	2·50
O128	**13**	10c. red	4·00	4·00
O129	**13**	15c. red	6·00	6·00
O130	**13**	20c. red	6·00	6·00

O131	**13**	50c. red	8·50	8·50
O132	**13**	1p. red	11·00	11·00
O133	**13**	2p. red	11·00	11·00
O134	**13**	5p. red	11·00	11·00

1899. Stamps of 1899 optd **FRANQUEO OFICIAL** in scroll.

O137	**14**	1c. green	30	1·00
O138	**14**	2c. brown	30	1·00
O139	**14**	4c. red	30	1·00
O140	**14**	5c. blue	30	55
O141	**14**	10c. orange	20	1·00
O142	**14**	15c. brown	30	2·00
O143	**14**	20c. green	30	3·00
O144	**14**	50c. red	30	3·00
O145	**14**	1p. orange	30	10·00
O146	**14**	2p. violet	30	10·00
O147	**14**	5p. blue	30	16·00

O16

1900

O148	**O16**	1c. purple	60	60
O149	**O16**	2c. orange	50	50
O150	**O16**	4c. olive	60	60
O151	**O16**	5c. blue	1·30	50
O152	**O16**	10c. violet	1·30	40
O153	**O16**	20c. brown	1·00	40
O154	**O16**	50c. lake	1·30	50
O155	**O16**	1p. blue	3·50	2·50
O156	**O16**	2p. orange	4·25	4·00
O157	**O16**	5p. black	5·25	5·00

1903. Stamps of 1900 surch **OFICIAL** and value, with or without ornaments.

O197	**15**	1c. on 10c. mauve	40	40
O198	**15**	2c. on 3c. green	40	50
O199	**15**	4c. on 3c. green	1·60	1·50
O200	**15**	4c. on 10c. mauve	1·60	1·50
O201	**15**	5c. on 3c. green	25	25

1903. Surch.

O202	**O16**	10c. on 20c. brown	30	30
O203	**O16**	30c. on 20c. brown	30	30
O204	**O16**	50c. on 20c. brown	60	40

O38

1905

O219	**O38**	1c. green	30	30
O220	**O38**	2c. red	30	30
O221	**O38**	5c. blue	30	30
O222	**O38**	10c. brown	30	30
O223	**O38**	20c. orange	30	30
O224	**O38**	50c. olive	30	30
O225	**O38**	1p. lake	30	30
O226	**O38**	2p. violet	30	30
O227	**O38**	5p. black	30	30

1907. Surch **Vale 10 c.**

O239	10c. on 1c. green	1·00	1·00
O241	10c. on 2c. red	26·00	25·00
O243	20c. on 2c. red	26·00	20·00
O245	50c. on 1c. green	2·10	2·00
O247	50c. on 2c. red	16·00	15·00

1907. Surch **Vale 20 cts or Vale $1.00.**

O249	20c. on 1c. green	1·60	1·50
O250	$1 on 2c. red	2·10	2·00
O251	$2 on 2c. red	2·10	2·50
O252	$3 on 2c. red	2·50	2·00
O253	$4 on 5c. blue	2·50	2·50

1907. No. 206 surch **OFICIAL** and value.

O256	**49**	10c. on 1c. green	16·00	13·00
O257	**49**	15c. on 1c. green	16·00	13·00
O258	**49**	20c. on 1c. green	16·00	13·00
O259	**49**	50c. on 1c. green	16·00	13·00
O260	**49**	1p. on 1c. green	16·00	13·00
O261	**49**	2p. on 1c. green	16·00	13·00

1907. Fiscal stamps as T **50** surch **10 cts. CORREOS 1907 OFICIAL 10 CTS.**

O262	**50**	10c. on 2c. orange	20	20
O263	**50**	35c. on 1c. blue	20	20
O264	**50**	70c. on 1c. blue	20	20
O266	**50**	1p. on 2c. orange	20	20
O267	**50**	2p. on 2c. orange	20	20
O268	**50**	3p. on 5c. brown	20	20
O269	**50**	4p. on 5c. brown	20	20
O270	**50**	5p. on 5c. brown	30	30

1908. Stamp of 1905 surch **OFICIAL VALE** and value.

O271	**37**	10c. on 3c. violet	16·00	15·00
O272	**37**	15c. on 3c. violet	16·00	15·00
O273	**37**	20c. on 3c. violet	16·00	15·00
O274	**37**	35c. on 3c. violet	16·00	15·00
O275	**37**	50c. on 3c. violet	16·00	15·00

1908. Fiscal stamps as T **50** surch as last but dated 1908.

O276	**50**	10c. on 1c. blue	85	60
O277	**50**	10c. on 2c. orange	1·20	70
O278	**50**	35c. on 1c. blue	85	60
O279	**50**	35c. on 2c. orange	1·20	70
O280	**50**	50c. on 1c. blue	85	60
O281	**50**	50c. on 2c. orange	1·20	70
O282	**50**	70c. on 2c. orange	1·20	70
O283	**50**	1p. on 1c. blue	41·00	40·00
O284	**50**	1p. on 2c. orange	1·20	70
O285	**50**	2p. on 1c. blue	1·00	80
O286	**50**	2p. on 2c. orange	1·20	70

1909. Stamps of 1905 optd **OFICIAL.**

O290	**37**	10c. lake	30	20
O291	**37**	15c. black	85	60
O292	**37**	20c. olive	1·20	80
O293	**37**	50c. green	1·70	1·10
O294	**37**	1p. yellow	1·90	1·30
O295	**37**	2p. red	3·00	2·20

1911. Stamps of 1905 optd **OFICIAL** and surch **Vale** and value.

O296	5c. on 3c. orange	7·25	7·00
O297	10c. on 4c. violet	6·25	6·00

1911. Railway tickets, surch **Timbre Fiscal Vale 10 ctvs.** further surch **for official postal use.** Printed in red.

(a) Surch **Correo oficial Vale** and value on front.

O334	**64**	10c. on 10c. on 1st class	3·00	3·00
O335	**64**	15c. on 10c. on 1st class	3·00	3·00
O336	**64**	20c. on 10c. on 1st class	3·00	3·00
O337	**64**	50c. on 10c. on 1st class	4·25	4·00
O338	**64**	$1 on 10c. on 1st class	5·25	7·00
O339	**64**	$2 on 10c. on 1st class	6·25	12·00

(b) Surch **CORREO OFICIAL** and new value on front.

O340	10c. on 10c. on 1st class	26·00	25·00
O341	15c. on 10c. on 1st class	26·00	25·00
O342	20c. on 10c. on 1st class	26·00	25·00
O343	50c. on 10c. on 1st class	19·00	18·00

(c) No. 322 surch on front **Correo Oficial Vale 1911** and new value and with 15 cts. on back obliterated by heavy bar.

O344	5c. on 10c. on 1st class	5·25	7·00
O345	10c. on 10c. on 1st class	6·25	8·00
O346	15c. on 10c. on 1st class	7·25	9·00
O347	20c. on 10c. on 1st class	7·25	10·00
O348	50c. on 10c. on 1st class	9·25	11·00

(d) No. 322 surch on front **Correo Oficial 1912** and new value and with the whole surch on back obliterated.

O349	5c. on 10c. on 1st class	10·50	10·00
O350	10c. on 10c. on 1st class	10·50	10·00
O351	15c. on 10c. on 1st class	10·50	10·00
O352	20c. on 10c. on 1st class	10·50	10·00
O353	25c. on 10c. on 1st class	10·50	10·00
O354	50c. on 10c. on 1st class	10·50	10·00
O355	$1 on 10c. on 1st class	10·50	10·00

1913. Stamps of 1912 optd **OFICIAL.**

O356	**70**	1c. blue	20	20
O357	**70**	2c. blue	20	20
O358	**70**	3c. blue	20	20
O359	**70**	4c. blue	20	20
O360	**70**	5c. blue	20	20
O361	**70**	6c. blue	20	20
O362	**70**	10c. blue	20	20
O363	**70**	15c. blue	20	20
O364	**70**	20c. blue	20	20
O365	**70**	25c. blue	30	30
O366	**71**	35c. blue	40	40
O367	**70**	50c. blue	1·90	1·80
O368	**70**	1p. blue	50	50
O369	**70**	2p. blue	60	60
O370	**70**	5p. blue	70	70

1915. Optd **OFICIAL.**

O406	**79**	1c. blue	20	20
O407	**80**	2c. blue	20	20
O408	**79**	3c. blue	30	20
O409	**80**	4c. blue	20	20
O410	**79**	5c. blue	20	20
O411	**80**	6c. blue	20	20
O412	**80**	10c. blue	30	30
O413	**79**	15c. blue	30	30
O414	**80**	20c. blue	30	30
O415	**79**	25c. blue	50	50
O416	**80**	50c. blue	85	80

1925. Optd **Oficial** or **OFICIAL.**

O513	**79**	½c. green	20	20
O514	**79**	1c. violet	20	20
O515	**80**	2c. red	20	20
O516	**79**	3c. olive	20	20
O517	**80**	4c. red	20	20
O518	**79**	5c. black	20	20
O519	**80**	6c. brown	20	20
O520	**80**	10c. yellow	20	20
O521	**79**	15c. brown	20	20
O522	**80**	20c. brown	20	20
O523	**79**	25c. orange	30	30
O524	**80**	50c. blue	40	40

1929. Air. Official stamps of 1925 additionally optd **Correo Aereo.**

O618	**79**	25c. orange	65	65
O619	**80**	50c. blue	85	80

1931. Stamp of 1924 surch **OFICIAL C$ 0.05 Correos 1928.**

O651	**99**	5c. on 10c. brown	30	20

1931. No. 648 additionally surch **OFICIAL** and value.

O652	5c. on 10c. brown	30	20

1931. Stamps of 1914 optd **1931** (except 6c., 10c.), and also optd **OFICIAL.**

O670	**79**	1c. olive (No. 762)	20	20
O707	**80**	2c. red	7·00	6·75
O671	**79**	3c. blue	20	20
O672	**79**	5c. sepia	20	20
O673	**80**	6c. brown	30	25
O674	**80**	10c. blue (No. 697)	1·50	1·40
O675	**80**	10c. brown	30	25
O710	**79**	15c. orange	95	90
O711	**79**	25c. sepia	95	90
O712	**79**	25c. violet	2·00	2·00

1932. Air. Optd **Correo Aereo OFICIAL** only.

O688		15c. orange	55	55
O689	**80**	20c. orange	65	65
O690	**79**	25c. violet	65	65
O691	**80**	50c. green	75	70
O692	**80**	1cor. yellow	1·10	1·10

1932. Air. Optd **1931 Correo Aereo OFICIAL.**

O693	**79**	25c. sepia	47·00	45·00

1932. Optd **OFICIAL.**

O694		1c. olive	20	20
O695	**80**	2c. red	20	20
O696	**79**	3c. blue	20	20
O697	**80**	4c. blue	20	20
O698	**79**	5c. sepia	30	25
O699	**80**	6c. brown	30	20
O700	**80**	10c. brown	30	20
O701	**79**	15c. orange	50	25
O702	**80**	20c. orange	80	35
O703	**79**	25c. violet	2·30	70
O704	**80**	50c. green	30	20
O705	**80**	1cor. yellow	35	25

1933. 441st Anniv of Columbus's Departure from Palos. As T **133**, but inscr **"CORREO OFICIAL"**. Roul.

O777	1c. yellow	1·80	1·70
O778	2c. yellow	1·80	1·70
O779	3c. brown	1·80	1·70
O780	4c. brown	1·80	1·70
O781	5c. brown	1·80	1·70
O782	6c. blue	2·30	2·20
O783	10c. violet	2·30	2·20
O784	15c. purple	2·30	2·20
O785	20c. green	2·30	2·20
O786	25c. green	3·00	3·00
O787	50c. red	3·75	3·50
O788	1cor. red	5·25	5·00

1933. Optd with T **134** and **OFICIAL.**

O814	**79**	1c. green	20	20
O815	**80**	2c. red	20	20
O816	**79**	3c. blue	20	20
O817	**80**	4c. blue	20	20
O818	**79**	5c. brown	20	20
O819	**80**	6c. grey	20	20
O820	**80**	10c. brown	20	20
O821	**79**	15c. red	20	20
O822	**80**	20c. orange	20	20
O823	**79**	25c. violet	20	20
O824	**80**	50c. green	20	20
O825	**80**	1cor. yellow	45	25

1933. Air. Optd with T **134** and **CORREO Aereo OFICIAL.**

O826	**79**	15c. violet	30	25
O827	**80**	20c. green	30	25
O828	**79**	25c. olive	30	25
O829	**80**	50c. green	35	35
O830	**80**	1cor. red	60	50

1935. Nos. O814/25 optd **RESELLO – 1935** in a box.

O864A	**79**	1c. green	30	25
O865A	**80**	2c. red	30	25
O866A	**79**	3c. blue	30	25
O867A	**80**	4c. blue	30	25
O868A	**79**	5c. brown	30	25
O869A	**80**	6c. grey	30	25
O870A	**80**	10c. brown	30	25
O871A	**79**	15c. red	30	25
O872A	**80**	20c. orange	30	25
O873A	**79**	25c. violet	30	25
O874A	**80**	50c. green	30	25
O875A	**80**	1cor. yellow	35	35

1935. Air. Nos. O826/30 optd **RESELLO – 1935** in a box.

O877	**79**	15c. violet	30	25
O878	**80**	20c. green	30	25
O879	**79**	25c. olive	30	30
O880	**80**	50c. green	90	90
O881	**80**	1cor. red	90	90

(O141)

1937. Nos. 913, etc, optd with Type **O141.**

O935	**79**	1c. red	20	20
O936	**80**	2c. blue	20	20
O937	**79**	3c. brown	30	25
O938	**79**	5c. red	35	25
O939	**80**	10c. green	65	35
O940	**79**	15c. green	95	55
O941	**79**	25c. orange	1·10	70
O942	**80**	50c. brown	1·40	90
O943	**80**	1cor. blue	2·75	1·30

1937. Air. Nos. 926/30 optd with Type **O141.**

O944	**112**	15c. orange	1·10	55
O945	**112**	20c. red	1·10	55
O946	**112**	25c. black	1·10	70
O947	**112**	50c. violet	1·10	70
O948	**112**	1cor. orange	1·10	70

O151 Islets in the Great Lake

1939

O1020	**O151**	2c. red	35	35
O1021	**O151**	3c. blue	35	35
O1022	**O151**	6c. brown	35	35
O1023	**O151**	7½c. green	35	35
O1024	**O151**	10c. brown	35	35
O1025	**O151**	15c. orange	35	35
O1026	**O151**	25c. violet	45	45
O1027	**O151**	50c. green	60	60

O152 Pres. Somoza

1939. Air.

O1028	**O152**	10c. brown	35	35
O1029	**O152**	15c. blue	35	35
O1030	**O152**	20c. yellow	35	35
O1031	**O152**	25c. violet	35	35
O1032	**O152**	30c. red	45	45
O1033	**O152**	50c. orange	80	80
O1034	**O152**	1cor. olive	1·50	1·50

O175 Managua Airport

1947. Air.

O1120	**O175**	5c. brown and black	30	30
O1121	-	10c. blue and black	30	30
O1122	-	15c. violet and black	30	30
O1123	-	20c. orange & black	30	30
O1124	-	25c. blue and black	30	30
O1125	-	50c. red and black	30	30
O1126	-	1cor. grey and black	50	50
O1127	-	2cor.50 brown and black	1·60	1·50

DESIGNS: 10c. Sulphur lagoon, Nejapa; 15c. Ruben Dario Monument, Managua; 20c. Baird's tapir; 25c. Genizaro Dam; 50c. Thermal baths, Tipitapa; 1cor. Highway and Lake Managua; 2cor.50, Franklin D. Roosevelt Monument, Managua.

O181 U.P.U. Offices, Berne

1950. Air. 75th Anniv of U.P.U. Inscr as in Type **O181**. Frames in black.

O1159		5c. purple	20	20
O1160		10c. green	20	20
O1161		25c. purple	30	30
O1162	**O181**	50c. orange	30	30
O1163	-	1cor. blue	30	30
O1164	-	2cor.60 black	2·50	2·50

MSO1165 Six sheets each 121×96 mm. Nos. O1159/64 in blocks of four 25·00 25·00

DESIGNS—HORIZ: 5c. Rowland Hill; 10c. Heinrich von Stephan; 25c. Standehaus, Berne; 1cor. Monument, Berne; 2cor.60, Congress Medal.

1961. Air. Consular Fiscal stamps as T **203/4** with serial Nos. in red, surch **Oficial Aereo** and value.

O1448	10c. on 1cor. olive	20	20
O1449	15c. on 20cor. brown	20	20
O1450	20c. on 100cor. lake	20	20
O1451	25c. on 50c. blue	20	20
O1452	35c. on 50cor. brown	20	20
O1453	50c. on 3cor. red	20	20
O1454	1cor. on 2cor. green	30	30
O1455	2cor. on 5cor. red	50	50
O1456	5cor. on 10cor. violet	1·20	1·20

POSTAGE DUE STAMPS

D13

1896

D99A	**D13**	1c. orange	65	1·60
D100A	**D13**	2c. orange	65	1·60
D101A	**D13**	5c. orange	65	1·60
D102A	**D13**	10c. orange	65	1·60
D103A	**D13**	20c. orange	65	1·60
D104A	**D13**	30c. orange	65	1·60
D105A	**D13**	50c. orange	65	1·60

1897

D108A	1c. violet	65	1·50
D109A	2c. violet	65	1·50
D110A	5c. violet	65	1·50
D111A	10c. violet	65	1·50
D112A	20c. violet	1·50	1·90
D113A	30c. violet	65	1·50
D114A	50c. violet	65	1·50

1898

D124	1c. green	30	2·00
D125	2c. green	30	2·00
D126	5c. green	30	2·00
D127	10c. green	30	2·00
D128	20c. green	30	2·00
D129	30c. green	30	2·00
D130	50c. green	30	2·00

1899

D137	1c. red	30	2·00
D138	2c. red	30	2·00
D139	5c. red	30	2·00
D140	10c. red	30	2·00
D141	20c. red	30	2·00
D142	50c. red	30	2·00

D16

1900

D146	**D16**	1c. red	1·20
D147	**D16**	2c. orange	1·20
D148	**D16**	5c. blue	1·20
D149	**D16**	10c. violet	1·20
D150	**D16**	20c. brown	1·20
D151	**D16**	30c. green	2·30
D152	**D16**	50c. lake	2·30

APPENDIX

The following stamps have either been issued in excess of postal needs, or have not been available to the public in reasonable quantities at face value. Such stamps may later be given full listings if there is evidence of regular postal use. Miniature sheets and imperforate stamps are excluded from this listing.

1996

Fauna. 2cor.×12. 2cor×12.
Animals. 2cor.50×12.; 2cor.50×9; 2cor.50×6.

Pt. 6, Pt. 14

NIGER

Area south of the Sahara. In 1920 was separated from Upper Senegal and Niger to form a separate colony. From 1944 to 1959 used the stamps of French West Africa.

In 1958 Niger became an autonomous republic within the French Community and on 3 August 1960 an independent republic.

100 centimes = 1 franc.

1921. Stamps of Upper Senegal and Niger optd **TERRITOIRE DU NIGER**.

1	7	1c. violet and purple	35	3·75
2	7	2c. purple and grey	45	3·50
3	7	4c. blue and black	1·10	5·75
4	7	5c. chocolate and brown	75	2·50
5	7	10c. green and light green	2·30	4·25
25	7	10c. pink on blue	1·40	6·00
6	7	15c. yellow and brown	80	3·50
7	7	20c. black and purple	1·50	4·00
8	7	25c. green and black	1·30	3·25
9	7	30c. carmine and red	3·00	6·00
26	7	30c. red and green	1·10	4·75
10	7	35c. violet and red	1·90	4·75
11	7	40c. red and grey	1·60	5·00
12	7	45c. brown and blue	1·20	7·25
13	7	50c. blue and ultramarine	2·00	5·50
27	7	50c. blue and grey	1·20	5·25
28	7	60c. red	1·50	4·00
14	7	75c. brown and yellow	1·60	8·25
15	7	1f. purple and brown	1·50	5·50
16	7	2f. blue and green	1·90	8·75
17	7	5f. black and violet	2·30	8·50

1922. Stamps of 1921 surch.

18	25c. on 15c. yellow & brown	1·10	7·25
19	25c. on 2f. blue and green	2·30	6·25
20	25c. on 5f. black and violet	1·70	5·75
21	60 on 75c. violet on pink	85	4·50
22	65 on 45c. brown and blue	2·50	8·50
23	85c. on 75c. brown & yellow	2·50	9·50
24	1f.25 on 1f. light blue & blue	1·40	8·50

3 Wells

4 Canoe on River Niger

5 Zinder Fort

1926

29	3	1c. green and purple	35	2·50
30	3	2c. red and grey	10	3·50
31	3	3c. brown and mauve	10	4·25
32	3	4c. black and brown	35	5·00
33	3	5c. green and red	55	3·00
34	3	10c. green and blue	10	80
35	3	15c. light green and green	1·00	3·50
36	3	15c. red and lilac	35	4·25
37	4	20c. brown and blue	40	5·50
38	4	25c. pink and black	90	2·50
39	4	30c. light green and green	2·30	4·75
40	4	30c. mauve and yellow	1·40	5·00
41	4	35c. blue and red on blue	1·00	4·00
42	4	35c. green and deep green	2·00	7·25
43	4	40c. grey and purple	10	2·30
44	4	45c. mauve and yellow	1·40	5·00
45	4	45c. green and turquoise	1·30	8·00
46	4	50c. green and red on green	35	30
47	4	55c. brown and red	2·30	8·25
48	4	60c. brown and red	65	7·75
49	4	65c. red and green	1·50	4·75
50	4	70c. red and green	2·30	8·25
51	4	75c. mauve and green on pink	1·80	5·00
52	4	80c. green and purple	2·30	8·00
53	4	90c. red and carmine	1·90	8·25
54	4	90c. green and red	2·00	6·25
55	5	1f. green and red	7·00	13·00
56	5	1f. orange and red	2·30	3·00
57	5	1f. red and green	1·70	7·00
58	5	1f.10 green and brown	6·00	12·00
59	5	1f.25 red and green	2·50	3·00
60	5	1f.25 orange and red	3·25	8·00
61	5	1f.40 brown and mauve	2·50	8·50
62	5	1f.50 light blue and blue	1·40	2·00
63	5	1f.60 green and brown	2·50	8·75
64	5	1f.75 brown and mauve	2·75	3·75
65	5	1f.75 ultramarine and blue	1·80	8·75
66	5	2f. brown and orange	1·80	2·00
67	5	2f.25 ultramarine and blue	2·50	6·75
68	5	2f.50 brown	3·50	6·50
69	5	3f. grey and mauve	2·00	1·60
70	5	5f. black and purple on pink	1·30	2·50
71	5	10f. mauve and lilac	1·80	4·25
72	5	20f. orange and green	2·75	6·25

1931. "Colonial Exhibition" key types inscr "NIGER".

73	**E**	40c. green	7·00	10·00
74	**F**	50c. mauve	5·50	8·50
75	**G**	90c. red	5·00	14·00
76	**H**	1f.50 blue	9·25	14·00

4a

1937. International Exhibition, Paris.

77	**4a**	20c. violet	1·20	5·75
78	**4a**	30c. green	1·30	6·25
79	**4a**	40c. red	90	4·75
80	**4a**	50c. brown and agate	1·00	4·00
81	**4a**	90c. red	1·10	3·50
82	**4a**	1f.50 blue	90	4·25

MS82a 120×100 mm. 3f. mauve Imperf 12·00 24·00

1938. Int Anti-cancer Fund. As T **17a** of Oceanic Settlements.

83	1f.75+50c. blue	14·00	50·00

4b

1939. Caille.

84	**4b**	90c. orange	80	3·75
85	**4b**	2f. violet	75	1·60
86	**4b**	2f.25 blue	65	4·25

1939. New York World's Fair. As T **17b** of Oceanic Settlements.

87	1f.25 red	2·00	5·75
88	2f.25 blue	80	7·00

1939. 150th Anniv of French Revolution. As T **17c** of Oceanic Settlements.

89	45c.+25c. green and black	10·00	23·00
90	70c.+30c. brown and black	10·00	23·00
91	90c.+35c. orange and black	10·00	23·00
92	1f.25+1f. red and black	10·00	23·00
93	2f.25+2f. blue and black	10·00	23·00

4c

1940. Air.

94	**4c**	1f.90 blue	2·30	4·25
95	**4c**	2f.90 red	1·40	4·75
96	**4c**	4f.50 green	2·30	5·00
97	**4c**	4f.90 olive	1·60	6·50
98	**4c**	6f.90 orange	1·90	4·00

1941. National Defence Fund. Surch **SECOURS NATIONAL** and additional value.

98a	4	+1f. on 50c. green and red on green	6·00	9·50
98b	4	+2f. on 80c. green & pur	8·75	19·00
98c	5	+2f. on 1f.50 lt blue & bl	17·00	27·00
98d	5	+3f. on 2f. brown & orge	12·00	27·00

5a Zinder Fort

1942. Marshal Petain issue.

98e	**5a**	1f. green	65	5·50
98f	**5a**	2f.50 blue	75	5·50

5b Weighing Baby

1942. Air. Colonial Child Welfare Fund.

98g	-	1f.50+3f.50 green	80	6·00
98h	-	2f.+6f. brown	90	6·00
98i	**5b**	3f.+9f. red	1·00	5·50

DESIGNS: 49×28 mm: 1f.50, Maternity Hospital, Dakar; 2f. Dispensary, Mopti.

5c "Vocation"

1942. Air. Imperial Fortnight.

98j	**5c**	1f.20+1f.80 blue and red	1·40	7·25

5e

1942. Air. As T **5e** but inscr "NIGER" at foot.

98k	**5e**	50f. red and yellow	3·00	7·00

7 Giraffes

8 Carmine Bee Eater

1959. Wild Animals and Birds. Inscr "PROTECTION DE LA FAUNE".

99	-	50c. turquoise, green and black (postage)	1·80	5·25
100	-	1f. multicoloured	1·80	5·25
101	-	2f. multicoloured	1·80	5·25
102	-	5f. mauve, black and brown	2·75	2·30
103	-	7f. red, black and green	5·25	5·00
104	-	10f. multicoloured	3·00	3·00
105	-	15f. sepia and turquoise	3·00	3·00
106	-	20f. black and violet	2·75	2·30
107	7	25f. multicoloured	3·00	2·30
108	7	30f. brown, bistre and green	2·50	2·75
109	-	50f. blue and brown	16·00	4·00
110	-	60f. sepia and green	20·00	7·50
111	-	85f. brown and bistre	7·50	4·75
112	-	100f. bistre and green	13·00	4·50
113	8	200f. multicoloured (air)	55·00	25·00
114	-	500f. green, brown and blue	23·00	23·00

DESIGNS—As Type **7**: HORIZ: 50c., 10f. African manatee. VERT: 1, 2f. Crowned cranes; 5, 7f. Saddle-bill stork; 15, 20f. Barbary sheep; 50, 60f. Ostriches; 85, 100f. Lion. As Type **8**: VERT: 500f. Game animals.

8a

1960. Tenth Anniv of African Technical Co-operation Commission.

115	**8a**	25f. brown and ochre	1·80	4·50

9 Conseil de l'Entente Emblem

1960. First Anniv of Conseil de l'Entente.

116	**9**	25f. multicoloured	1·80	4·50

1960. Independence. No. 112 surch **200 F Independance 3-8-60**.

117	200f. on 100f. bistre and green	13·50	13·50

11 Pres. Diori Hamani

1960

118	**11**	25f. black and bistre	60	45

12 U.N. Emblem and Niger Flag

1961. Air. First Anniv of Admission into U.N.

119	**12**	25f. red, green and orange	65	35
120	**12**	100f. green, red and emerald	2·40	1·20

12a

1962. Air. "Air Afrique" Airline.

121	**12a**	100f. violet, black and brown	1·90	95

12b

1962. Malaria Eradication.

122	**12b**	25f.+5f. brown	75	75

13 Athletics

1962. Abidjan Games, 1961. Multicoloured.

123	15f. Boxing and cycling (vert)	45	25
124	25f. Basketball and football (vert)	60	30
125	85f. Type **13**	1·80	80

13a

1962. First Anniv of Union of African and Malagasy States.

126	**13a**	30f. mauve	95	60

14 Pres. Hamani and Map

1962. Fourth Anniv of Republic.

127	**14**	25f. multicoloured	60	35

14a

1963. Freedom from Hunger.

128	**14a**	25f.+5f. purple, brn & olive	75	75

15 Running

1963. Dakar Games.

129	-	15f. brown and blue	45	25
130	**15**	25f. red and brown	60	25
131	-	45f. black and green	1·10	55

DESIGNS—HORIZ: 15f. Swimming. VERT: 45f. Volleyball.

16 Agadez Mosque

1963. Air. Second Anniv of Admission to U.P.U. Multicoloured.

132	50f. Type **16**	1·20	45
133	85f. Gaya Bridge	1·90	80
134	100f. Presidential Palace, Niamey	2·00	1·00

17 Wood-carving

1963. Traditional Crafts. Multicoloured.

135	5f. Type **17** (postage)	30	20
136	10f. Skin-tanning (horiz)	35	20
137	25f. Goldsmith	60	30
138	30f. Mat-making (horiz)	1·00	45
139	85f. Potter	2·40	1·20
140	100f. Canoe building (horiz) (47×27 mm) (air)	3·00	1·60

17a

1963. Air. African and Malagasy Posts and Telecommunications Union.

141	**17a**	85f. multicoloured	1·50	80

1963. Air. Red Cross Centenary. Optd with cross and Centenaire de la Croix-Rouge in red.

142	**12**	25f. red, green and orange	90	60
143	**12**	100f. green, red and emerald	2·20	1·10

19 Costume Museum

1963. Opening of Costume Museum, Niamey. Vert costume designs. Multicoloured.

144	15f. Berber woman	35	25
145	20f. Haussa woman	55	25
146	25f. Tuareg woman	75	30
147	30f. Tuareg man	85	30
148	60f. Djerma woman	2·00	80
149	85f. Type **19**	2·20	1·00

20 "Europafrique"

1963. Air. European–African Economic Convention.

150	**20**	50f. multicoloured	4·25	3·00

21 Groundnut Cultivation

1963. Air. Groundnut Cultivation Campaign.

151	**21**	20f. blue, brown and green	55	30
152	-	45f. brown, blue and green	1·10	50
153	-	85f. multicoloured	2·00	1·00
154	-	100f. olive, brown and blue	2·50	1·30
MS154a		130×100 mm. Nos. 151/4	7·75	7·75

DESIGNS: 45f. Camel transport; 85f. Fastening sacks; 100f. Dispatch of groundnuts by lorry.

21a

1963. Air. First Anniv of "Air Afrique" and DC-8 Service Inauguration.

155	**21a**	50f. multicoloured	1·00	65

22 Man and Globe

1963. 15th Anniv of Declaration of Human Rights.

156	**22**	25f. blue, brown and green	75	40

23 "Telstar"

1964. Air. Space Telecommunications.

157	**23**	25f. olive and violet	50	25
158	-	100f. green and purple	1·60	1·10

DESIGN: 100f. "Relay".

24 "Parkinsonia aculeata"

1964. Flowers. Multicoloured.

159	5f. Type **24**	80	45
160	10f. "Russelia equisetiformis"	75	45
161	15f. "Lantana camara"	1·20	60
162	20f. "Agryeia nervosa"	1·20	60
163	25f. "Luffa cylindrica"	1·30	60
164	30f. "Hibiscus rosa-sinensis"	1·80	70
165	45f. "Plumierai rubra"	2·75	1·30
166	50f. "Catharanthus roseus"	3·00	1·40
167	60f. "Caesalpinia pulcherrima"	4·50	1·70

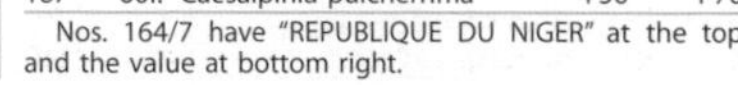
Nos. 164/7 have "REPUBLIQUE DU NIGER" at the top and the value at bottom right.

25 Statue, Abu Simbel

1964. Air. Nubian Monuments Preservation.

168	**25**	25f. green and brown	95	65
169	**25**	30f. brown and blue	1·50	90
170	**25**	50f. blue and purple	2·75	1·70

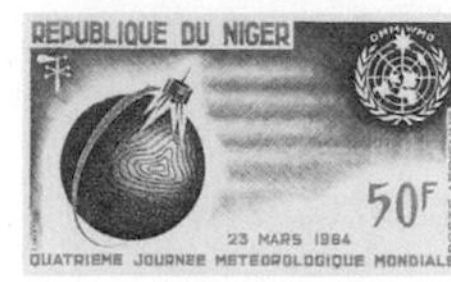

26 Globe and "Tiros" Satellite

1964. Air. World Meteorological Day.

171	**26**	50f. brown, blue and green	1·30	85

27 Sun Emblem and Solar Flares

1964. International Quiet Sun Years.

172	**27**	30f. red, violet and sepia	75	50

28 Convoy of Lorries

1964. O.M.N.E.S. (Nigerian Mobile Medical and Sanitary Organization) Commemoration.

173	**28**	25f. orange, olive and blue	55	15
174	-	30f. multicoloured	70	25
175	-	50f. multicoloured	95	45
176	-	60f. purple, orange & turq	1·20	1·40

DESIGNS: 30f. Tending children; 50f. Tending women; 60f. Open-air laboratory.

29 Rocket, Stars and Stamp Outline

1964. Air. "PHILATEC 1964" Int Stamp Exn, Paris.

177	**29**	50f. mauve and blue	1·30	80

30 European, African and Symbols of Agriculture and Industry

1964. Air. First Anniv of European-African Economic Convention.

178	**30**	50f. multicoloured	1·00	65

31 Pres. Kennedy

1964. Air. Pres. Kennedy Commemoration.

179	**31**	100f. multicoloured	2·30	1·70
MS179a		90×129 mm. No. 179 in block of four	6·75	6·50

32 Water-polo

1964. Air. Olympic Games, Tokyo.

180	**32**	60f. brown, deep green and purple	1·00	80
181	-	85f. brown, blue and red	2·00	95
182	-	100f. blue, red and green	2·20	1·10
183	-	250f. blue, brown and green	5·00	2·75
MS183a		191×100 mm. Nos. 180/3	13·00	13·00

DESIGNS—HORIZ: 85f. Relay-racing. VERT: 100f. Throwing the discus; 250f. Athlete holding Olympic Torch.

32a

1964. French, African and Malagasy Co-operation.

184	**32a**	50f. brown, orange and violet	1·00	60

33 Azawak Tuareg Encampment

1964. Native Villages. Multicoloured.

185	15f. Type **33**	30	25
186	20f. Songhai hut	45	25
187	25f. Wogo and Kourtey tents	45	25
188	30f. Djerma hut	50	25
189	60f. Sorkawa fishermen's encampment	1·20	40
190	85f. Hausa urban house	1·80	60

34 Doctors and Patient and Microscope Slide

1964. Anti-leprosy Campaign.

191	**34**	50f. multicoloured	95	60

35 Abraham Lincoln

1965. Death Centenary of Abraham Lincoln.

192	**35**	50f. multicoloured	95	70

36 Instruction by "Radio-Vision"

1965. "Human Progress". Inscr as in T **36**.

193	**36**	20f. brown, yellow and blue	45	25
194	-	25f. sepia, brown and green	55	25
195	-	30f. purple, red and green	80	40
196	-	50f. purple, blue and brown	1·10	50

DESIGNS: 25f. Student; 30f. Adult class; 50f. Five tribesmen ("Alphabetization").

37 Ader's Telephone

1965. I.T.U. Centenary.

197	**37**	25f. black, lake and green	75	25
198	-	30f. green, purple and red	95	40
199	-	50f. green, purple and red	1·30	70

DESIGNS: 30f. Wheatstone's telegraph; 50f. "Telautographe".

38 Pope John XXIII

1965. Air. Pope John Commemoration.

200	**38**	100f. multicoloured	1·80	1·00

39 Hurdling

1965. First African Games, Brazzaville.

201	**39**	10f. purple, green and brown	30	15
202	-	15f. red, brown and grey	50	25
203	-	20f. purple, blue and green	60	25
204	-	30f. purple, green and lake	95	25

DESIGNS—VERT: 15f. Running; 30f. Long-jumping. HORIZ: 20f. Pole-vaulting.

40 "Capture of Cancer" (the Crab)

1965. Air. Campaign against Cancer.

205	**40**	100f. brown, black and green	1·80	1·10

41 Sir Winston Churchill

1965. Air. Churchill Commemoration.

206	**41**	100f. multicoloured	1·80	1·10

42 Interviewing

1965. Radio Club Promotion.

207	**42**	30f. brown, violet and green	45	25
208	-	45f. red, black and buff	75	25
209	-	50f. multicoloured	95	40
210	-	60f. purple, blue and ochre	90	45

DESIGNS—VERT: 45f. Recording; 50f. Listening to broadcast. HORIZ: 60f. Listeners' debate.

43 "Agricultural and Industrial Workers"

1965. Air. International Co-operation Year.

211	**43**	50f. brown, black and bistre	1·00	55

44 Fair Scene and Flags

1965. Air. International Fair, Niamey.

212	**44**	100f. multicoloured	1·50	95

45 Dr. Schweitzer and Diseased Hands

1966. Air. Schweitzer Commemoration.

213	**45**	50f. multicoloured	1·30	70

46 "Water Distribution and Control"

1966. Int Hydrological Decade Inauguration.

214	**46**	50f. blue, orange and violet	1·00	45

47 Weather Ship "France I"

1966. Air. Sixth World Meteorological Day.

215	**47**	50f. green, purple and blue	1·50	70

48 White and "Gemini" Capsule

1966. Air. Cosmonauts.

216	**48**	50f. black, brown and green	1·20	60
217	-	50f. blue, violet and orange	1·20	60

DESIGN: No. 217, Leonov and "Voskhod" capsule.

49 Head-dress and Carvings

1966. World Festival of Negro Arts, Dakar.

218	**49**	30f. black, brown and green	60	35
219	-	50f. violet, brown and blue	95	50
220	-	60f. lake, violet and brown	1·00	60
221	-	100f. black, red and blue	1·90	95

DESIGNS: 50f. Carved figures and mosaics; 60f. Statuettes, drums and arch; 100f. Handicrafts and church.

50 "Diamant" Rocket and Gantry

1966. Air. French Space Vehicles. Multicoloured designs each showing different satellites.

222	45f. Type **50**	90	55
223	60f. "A 1" (horiz)	1·20	65
224	90f. "FR 1" (horiz)	1·50	85
225	100f. "D 1" (horiz)	2·00	1·20

51 Goalkeeper saving Ball

1966. World Cup Football Championship.

226	-	30f. red, brown and blue	80	25
227	**51**	50f. brown, blue and green	1·10	40
228	-	60f. blue, purple and bistre	1·40	70

DESIGNS—VERT: 30f. Player dribbling ball; 60f. Player kicking ball.

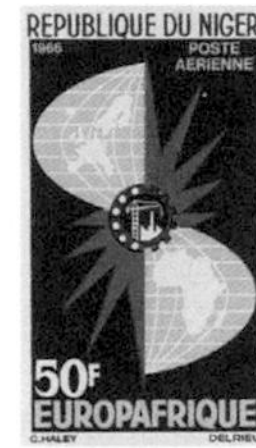

52 Cogwheel Emblem and Hemispheres

1966. Air. Europafrique.

229	**52**	50f. multicoloured	1·00	60

53 Parachutist

1966. Fifth Anniv of National Armed Forces. Multicoloured.

230	20f. Type **53**	45	25
231	30f. Soldiers with standard (vert)	55	25
232	45f. Armoured patrol vehicle (horiz)	80	45

53a

1966. Air. Inauguration of DC-8F Air Services.

233	**53a**	30f. olive, black and grey	75	40

54 Inoculating cattle

1966. Campaign for Prevention of Cattle Plague.
234 **54** 45f. black, brown and blue 1·50 70

55 "Voskhod 1"

1966. Air. Astronautics.
235 **55** 50f. blue, indigo and lake 95 55
236 - 100f. violet, blue and lake 2·00 1·10
DESIGN—HORIZ: 100f. "Gemini 6" and "7".

56 UNESCO "Tree"

1966. 20th Anniv of UNESCO.
237 **56** 50f. multicoloured 95 45

57 Japanese Gate, Atomic Symbol and Cancer ("The Crab")

1966. Air. International Cancer Congress, Tokyo.
238 **57** 100f. multicoloured 1·70 1·00

58 Furnace

1966. Malbaza Cement Works.
239 **58** 10f. blue, orange and brown 30 10
240 - 20f. blue and green 50 20
241 - 30f. brown, grey and blue 65 25
242 - 50f. indigo, brown and blue 95 40
DESIGNS—HORIZ: 20f. Electrical power-house; 30f. Works and cement silos; 50f. Installation for handling raw materials.

59 Niamey Mosque

1967. Air.
243 **59** 100f. blue, green and grey 2·00 1·10

60 Durer (self-portrait)

1967. Air. Paintings. Multicoloured.
244 50f. Type **60** 1·30 90
245 100f. David (self-portrait) 2·30 1·30
246 250f. Delacroix (self-portrait) 5·50 3·00
See also Nos. 271/2 and 277/9.

61 Red-billed Hornbill

1967. Birds.
247 **61** 1f. bistre, red and green (postage) 25 15
248 - 2f. black, brown and green 25 15
249 - 30f. multicoloured 75 40
249a - 40f. purple, orange and green 3·50 1·10
250 - 45f. brown, green and blue 1·40 45
250a - 65f. yellow, brown & pur 3·75 90
251 - 70f. multicoloured 2·40 80
251a - 250f. blue, purple and green (48×27 mm) (air) 3·75 2·10
BIRDS: 2f. Lesser pied kingfishers; 30f. Common gonolek; 40f. Red bishop; 45f., 65f. Little masked weaver; 70f. Chestnut-bellied sandgrouse; 250f. Splendid glossy starlings.

62 Bobsleigh Course, Villard-de-Lans

1967. Grenoble—Winter Olympics Town (1968).
252 **62** 30f. brown, blue and green 55 30
253 - 45f. brown, blue and green 95 45
254 - 60f. brown, blue and green 1·00 65
255 - 90f. brown, blue and green 1·70 90
DESIGNS: 45f. Ski-jump, Autrans; 60f. Ski-jump, St. Nizier du Moucherotte; 90f. Slalom course, Chamrousse.

63 Family and Lions Emblem

1967. 50th Anniv of Lions International.
256 **63** 50f. blue, red and green 95 55

64 Weather Ship

1967. Air. World Meteorological Day.
257 **64** 50f. red, black and blue 1·80 95

65 View of World Fair

1967. Air. World Fair, Montreal.
258 **65** 100f. black, blue and purple 1·70 70

66 I.T.Y. Emblem and Jet Airliner

1967. International Tourist Year.
259 **66** 45f. violet, green and purple 75 45

67 Scouts around Campfire

1967. World Scout Jamboree, Idaho, U.S.A.
260 **67** 30f. brown, lake and blue 55 25
261 - 45f. blue, brown and orange 95 30
262 - 80f. lake, slate and bistre 1·50 55
DESIGNS—HORIZ: 45f. Jamboree emblem and scouts. VERT: 80f. Scout cooking meal.

68 Audio-Visual Centre

1967. Air. National Audio-Visual Centre, Niamey.
263 **68** 100f. violet, blue and green 1·50 75

69 Carrying Patient

1967. Nigerian Red Cross.
264 **69** 45f. black, red and green 95 30
265 - 50f. black, red and green 1·00 45
266 - 60f. black, red and green 1·40 50
DESIGNS: 50f. Nurse with mother and child; 60f. Doctor giving injection.

70 "Europafrique"

1967. Europafrique.
267 **70** 50f. multicoloured 95 45

71 Dr. Konrad Adenauer

1967. Air. Adenauer Commemoration.
268 **71** 100f. brown and blue 2·20 1·00
MS269 120×161 mm. No. 268 in block of four 10·00 10·00

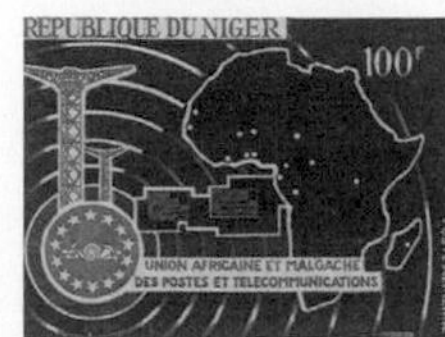

71a

1967. Air. Fifth Anniv of African and Malagasy Post and Telecommunications Union (U.A.M.P.T.).
270 **71a** 100f. violet, green and red 1·70 75

1967. Air. Death Centenary of Jean Ingres (painter). Paintings by Ingres. As T 60. Multicoloured.
271 100f. "Jesus among the Doctors" (horiz) 3·00 1·50
272 150f. "Jesus restoring the Keys to St. Peter" (vert) 4·50 2·20

72 African Women

1967. U.N. Women's Rights Commission.
273 **72** 50f. brown, yellow and blue 95 45

72a

1967. Fifth Anniv of West African Monetary Union.
274 **72a** 30f. green and purple 55 25

73 Nigerian Children

1967. Air. 21st Anniv of UNICEF.
275 **73** 100f. brown, blue and green 2·00 1·30

74 O.C.A.M. Emblem

1968. Air. O.C.A.M. Conference, Niamey.
276 **74** 100f. orange, green and blue 1·50 70

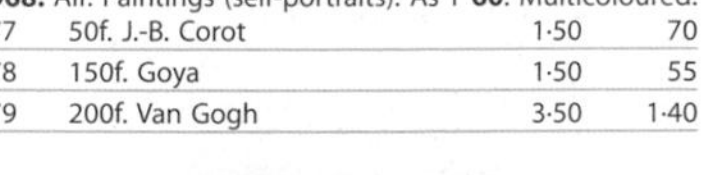

1968. Air. Paintings (self-portraits). As T **60**. Multicoloured.
277 50f. J.-B. Corot 1·50 70
278 150f. Goya 1·50 55
279 200f. Van Gogh 3·50 1·40

75 Allegory of Human Rights

1968. Human Rights Year.
280 **75** 50f. indigo, brown and blue 1·20 55

76 Breguet 27 Biplane over Lake

1968. Air. 35th Anniv of First France–Niger Airmail Service.
281 **76** 45f. blue, green and mauve 1·20 45
282 - 80f. slate, brown and blue 1·80 70
283 - 100f. black, green and blue 2·75 95
DESIGNS—Potez 25TOE biplane: 80f. On ground; 100f. In flight.

77 "Joyous Health"

1968. 20th Anniv of W.H.O.
284 **77** 50f. indigo, blue and brown 75 35

78 Cyclists of 1818 and 1968

1968. Air. 150th Anniv of Bicycle.
285 **78** 100f. green and red 2·30 90

79 Beribboned Rope

1968. Air. Fifth Anniv of Europafrique.
286 **79** 50f. multicoloured 95 55

80 Fencing

1968. Air. Olympic Games, Mexico.
287 **80** 50f. purple, violet and green 80 50
288 - 100f. black, purple and blue 1·50 70
289 - 150f. purple and orange 2·20 95
290 - 200f. blue, brown and green 3·00 1·70
MS291 240×104 mm. Nos. 287/90 10·00 10·00
DESIGNS—VERT: 100f. High-diving; 150f. Weight-lifting. HORIZ: 200f. Horse-jumping.

81 Woodland Kingfisher

1969. Birds. Dated "1968". Multicoloured.
292 5f. African grey hornbill (postage) 45 35
293 10f. Type **81** 55 35
294 15f. Senegal coucal 1·10 40
295 20f. Rose-ringed parakeets 1·20 55
296 25f. Abyssinian roller 1·90 50
297 50f. Cattle egret 2·75 1·00
298 100f. Violet starling (27×49 mm) (air) 5·25 1·90
See also Nos. 372/7, 567/8 and 714/15.

82 Mahatma Gandhi

1968. Air. "Apostles of Non-Violence".
299 **82** 100f. black and yellow 1·50 80
300 - 100f. black and turquoise 1·50 80
301 - 100f. black and grey 1·60 80
302 - 100f. black and orange 1·50 80
MS303 120×160 mm. Nos. 299/302 8·75 8·75
PORTRAITS: No. 300, President Kennedy; No. 301, Martin Luther King; No. 302, Robert F. Kennedy.

82a "Pare, Minister of the Interior" (J. L. La Neuville)

1968. Air. "Philexafrique" Stamp Exhibition, Abidjan (Ivory Coast, 1969) (1st issue).
304 **82a** 100f. multicoloured 3·75 3·75

83 Arms of the Republic

1968. Air. Tenth Anniv of Republic.
305 **83** 100f. multicoloured 1·80 75

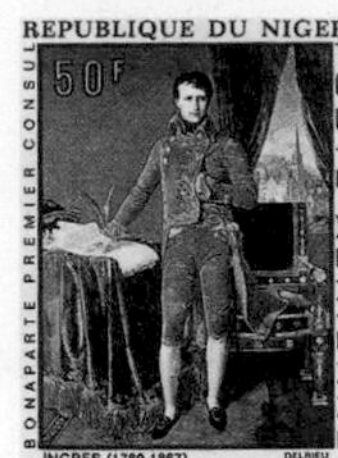

83a "Napoleon as First Consul" (Ingres)

1969. Air. Napoleon Bonaparte. Birth Bicentenary. Multicoloured.
306 50f. Type **83a** 2·50 1·40
307 100f. "Napoleon visiting the plague victims of Jaffa" (Gros) 3·75 2·10
308 150f. "Napoleon Enthroned" (Ingres) 6·00 2·20
309 200f. "The French Campaign" (Meissonier) 8·00 4·00

83b Giraffes and stamp of 1926

1969. Air. "Philexafrique" Stamp Exhibition, Abidjan, Ivory Coast (2nd issue).
310 **83b** 50f. brown, blue and orange 3·50 2·10

84 Boeing 707 over Rain-cloud and Anemometer

1969. Air. World Meteorological Day.
311 **84** 50f. black, blue and green 95 55

85 Workers supporting Globe

1969. 50th Anniv of I.L.O.
312 **85** 30f. red and green 60 30
313 **85** 50f. green and red 95 50

86 Panhard and Levassor (1909)

1969. Air. Veteran Motor Cars.
314 **86** 25f. green 75 40
315 - 45f. violet, blue and grey 95 40
316 - 50f. brown, ochre and grey 1·70 55
317 - 70f. purple, red and grey 2·50 90
318 - 100f. green, brown and grey 3·00 1·10
DESIGNS: 45f. De Dion Bouton 8 (1904); 50f. Opel "Doktor-wagen" (1909); 70f. Daimler (1910); 100f. Vermorel 12/16 (1912).

87 Mother and Child

1969. 50th Anniv of League of Red Cross Societies.
319 **87** 45f. red, brown and blue 95 30
320 - 50f. red, grey and green 1·00 45
321 - 70f. red, brown and ochre 1·50 65
DESIGNS—VERT: 70f. Man with Red Cross parcel. HORIZ: 50f. Symbolic Figures, Globe and Red Crosses.

88 Mouth and Ear

1969. First French Language Cultural Conf, Niamey.
322 **88** 100f. multicoloured 1·50 70

89 School Building

1969. National School of Administration.
323 **89** 30f. black, green and orange 55 30

1969. Air. First Man on the Moon. No. 114 optd **L'HOMME SUR LA LUNE JUILLET 1969 APOLLO 11** and moon module.
324 500f. green, brown and blue 10·00 10·00

91 "Apollo 8" and Rocket

1969. Air. Moon Flight of "Apollo 8". Embossed on gold foil.
325 **91** 1000f. gold 25·00 25·00

91a

1969. Fifth Anniv of African Development Bank.
326 **91a** 30f. brown, green and violet 75 30

92 Child and Toys

1969. Air. International Toy Fair, Nuremburg.
327 **92** 100f. blue, brown and green 1·70 75

93 Linked Squares

1969. Air. "Europafrique".
328 **93** 50f. yellow, black and violet 95 45

94 Trucks crossing Sahara

1969. Air. 45th Anniv of "Croisiere Noire" Trans-Africa Expedition.
329 **94** 50f. brown, violet & mauve 1·40 55
330 - 100f. violet, red and blue 2·50 80
331 - 150f. multicoloured 3·50 1·40
332 - 200f. green, indigo and blue 5·25 1·80
DESIGNS: 100f. Crossing the mountains; 150f. African children and expedition at Lake Victoria; 200f. Route Map, European greeting African and Citroen truck.

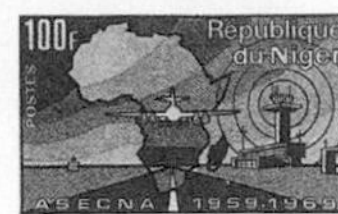

94a Aircraft, Map and Airport

1969. Tenth Anniv of Aerial Navigation Security Agency for Africa and Madagascar (A.S.E.C.N.A.).
333 **94a** 100f. red 1·60 85

95 Classical Pavilion

1970. National Museum.
334 **95** 30f. blue, green and brown 45 25
335 - 45f. blue, green and brown 75 25
336 - 50f. blue, brown and green 80 35
337 - 70f. brown, blue and green 95 55
338 - 100f. brown, blue and green 1·50 80
DESIGNS: 45f. Temporary exhibition pavilion; 50f. Audio-visual pavilion; 70f. Local musical instruments gallery; 100f. Handicrafts pavilion.

96 Niger Village and Japanese Pagodas

1970. Air. "EXPO 70" World Fair, Osaka, Japan (1st issue).
339 **96** 100f. multicoloured 1·50 70

97 Hypodermic "Gun" and Map

1970. One Hundred Million Smallpox Vaccinations in West Africa.
340 **97** 50f. blue, purple and green 95 45

98 Education Symbols

1970. Air. International Education Year.
341 **98** 100f. slate, red and purple 1·50 70

99 Footballer

1970. World Cup Football Championship, Mexico.

342	**99**	40f. green, brown and purple	95	35
343	-	70f. purple, brown and blue	1·30	55
344	-	90f. red and black	1·80	70

DESIGNS: 70f. Football and Globe; 90f. Two footballers.

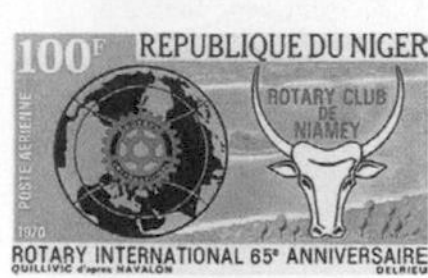

100 Rotary Emblems

1970. Air. 65th Anniv of Rotary International.

345	**100**	100f. multicoloured	1·80	80

101 Bay of Naples and Niger Stamp

1970. Air. Tenth "Europafrique" Stamp Exn, Naples.

346	**101**	100f. multicoloured	1·50	65

102 Clement Ader's "Avion III" and Modern Airplane

1970. Air. Aviation Pioneers.

347	**102**	50f. grey, blue and red	1·00	45
348	-	100f. red, grey and blue	2·10	70
349	-	150f. lt brown, brn & grn	2·50	1·10
350	-	200f. red, bistre and violet	3·25	1·60
351	-	250f. violet, grey and red	4·50	1·90

DESIGNS: 100f. Joseph and Etienne Montgolfier balloon and rocket; 150f. Isaac Newton and gravity diagram; 200f. Galileo and rocket in planetary system; 250f. Leonardo da Vinci's drawing of a "flying machine" and Chanute's glider.

103 Cathode Ray Tube illuminating Books, Microscope and Globe

1970. Air. World Telecommunications Day.

352	**103**	100f. brown, green and red	1·70	75

1970. Inauguration of New U.P.U. Headquarters Building, Berne. As T **81** of New Caledonia.

353	30f. red, slate and brown	55	25
354	60f. violet, red and blue	95	45

1970. Air. Safe Return of "Apollo 13". Nos. 348 and 350 optd **Solidarite Spatiale Apollo XIII 11-17 Avril 1970.**

355	100f. red, slate and blue	1·50	70
356	200f. red, bistre and violet	2·75	1·10

105 U.N. Emblem, Man, Woman and Doves

1970. Air. 25th Anniv of U.N.O.

357	**105**	100f. multicoloured	1·50	70
358	**105**	150f. multicoloured	2·20	1·10

106 Globe and Heads

1970. Air. International French Language Conference, Niamey. Die-stamped on gold foil.

359	**106**	250f. gold and blue	5·25	5·25

107 European and African Women

1970. Air. "Europafrique".

360	**107**	50f. red and green	95	45

108 Japanese Girls and "EXPO 70" Skyline

1970. Air. "EXPO 70" World Fair, Osaka, Japan. (2nd issue).

361	**108**	100f. purple, orange and green	1·30	65
362	-	150f. blue, brown and green	2·20	95

DESIGN: 150f. "No" actor and "EXPO 70" by night.

109 Gymnast on Parallel Bars

1970. Air. World Gymnastic Championships, Ljubljana.

363	**109**	50f. blue	75	45
364	-	100f. green	1·70	75
365	-	150f. purple	2·50	1·10
366	-	200f. red	3·00	1·50

GYMNASTS—HORIZ: 100f. Gymnast on vaulting-horse; 150f. Gymnast in mid-air. VERT: 200f. Gymnast on rings.

1970. Air. Moon Landing of "Luna 16". Nos. 349 and 351 surch **LUNA 16 – Sept. 1970 PREMIERS PRELEVEMENTS AUTOMATIQUES SUR LA LUNE** and value.

367	100f. on 150f. light brown, brown and green	2·00	80
368	200f. on 250f. violet, grey and red	4·00	1·60

111 Beethoven, Keyboard and Manuscripts

1970. Air. Birth Bicentenary of Beethoven. Multicoloured.

369	100f. Type **111**	2·00	70
370	150f. Beethoven and allegory, "Hymn of Joy"	2·75	1·00

112 John F. Kennedy Bridge, Niamey

1970. Air. 12th Anniv of Republic.

371	**112**	100f. multicoloured	1·80	75

1971. Birds. Designs similar to T **81**. Variously dated between 1970 and 1972. Multicoloured.

372	5f. African grey hornbill	30	25
373	10f. Woodland kingfisher	30	25
374	15f. Senegal coucal	65	40
375	20f. Rose-ringed parakeet	1·30	40
376	35f. Broad-tailed paradise whydah	2·50	70
377	50f. Cattle egret	6·50	1·80

The Latin inscription on No. 377 is incorrect, reading "Bulbucus ibis" instead of "Bubulcus ibis".

See also Nos. 714/15.

114 Pres. Nasser

1971. Air. Death of Pres. Gamal Nasser (Egyptian statesman). Multicoloured.

378	100f. Type **114**	1·20	50
379	200f. Nasser waving	2·30	1·10

115 Pres. De Gaulle

1971. Air. De Gaulle Commemoration. Embossed on gold foil.

380	**115**	1000f. gold	90·00	90·00

116 "MUNICH" and Olympic Rings

1971. Air. Publicity for 1972 Olympic Games, Munich.

381	**116**	150f. purple, blue & green	2·20	95

117 "Apollo 14" leaving Moon

1971. Air. Moon Mission of "Apollo 14".

382	**117**	250f. green, orange & blue	3·75	2·00

118 Symbolic Masks

1971. Air. Racial Equality Year.

383	**118**	100f. red, green and blue	1·30	70
384	-	200f. brown, green & blue	3·00	1·10

DESIGN: 200f. "Peoples" and clover-leaf emblem.

119 Niamey on World Map

1971. First Anniv of French-speaking Countries Co-operative Agency.

385	**119**	40f. multicoloured	80	55

120 African Telecommunications Map

1971. Air. Pan-African Telecommunications Network.

386	**120**	100f. multicoloured	1·00	50

121 African Mask and Japanese Stamp

1971. Air. "PHILATOKYO 71" International Stamp Exhibition, Japan.

387	**121**	50f. olive, purple and green	1·00	50
388	-	100f. violet, red and green	1·80	75

DESIGN: 100f. Japanese scroll painting and Niger stamp.

122 "Longwood House, St. Helena" (C. Vernet)

1971. Air. 150th Anniv of Napoleon's Death. Paintings. Multicoloured.

389	150f. Type **122**	2·75	95
390	200f. "Napoleon's Body on his Camp-bed" (Marryat)	4·25	1·40

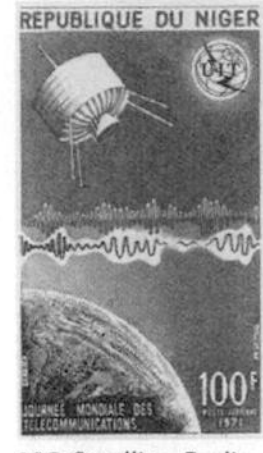

123 Satellite, Radio Waves, and Globe

1971. Air. World Telecommunications Day.

391	**123**	100f. multicoloured	1·80	75

124 Pierre de Coubertin and Discus-throwers

1971. Air. 75th Anniv of Modern Olympic Games.

392	**124**	50f. red and blue	95	35
393	-	100f. multicoloured	1·60	65
394	-	150f. blue and purple	2·50	1·20

DESIGNS—VERT: 100f. Male and female athletes holding torch. HORIZ: 150f. Start of race.

125 Scout Badges and Mount Fuji

1971. 13th World Scout Jamboree, Asagiri, Japan.

395	**125**	35f. red, purple and orange	55	25
396	-	40f. brown, plum and green	55	25
397	-	45f. green, red and blue	95	40
398	-	50f. green, violet and red	90	40

DESIGNS—VERT: 40f. Scouts and badge; 45f. Scouts converging on Japan. HORIZ: 50f. "Jamboree" in rope, and marquee.

126 "Apollo 15" on Moon

1971. Air. Moon Mission of "Apollo 15".

399	**126**	150f. blue, violet & brown	2·20	1·10

127 Linked Maps

1971. Second Anniv of Renewed "Europafrique" Convention, Niamey.

400	**127**	50f. multicoloured	1·00	50

128 Gouroumi (Hausa)

1971. Musical Instruments.

401	**128**	25f. brown, green and red	40	10
402	-	30f. brown, violet and green	55	25
403	-	35f. blue, green and purple	65	45
404	-	40f. brown, orange & grn	95	40
405	-	45f. ochre, brown and blue	1·30	60
406	-	50f. brown, red and black	1·70	70

DESIGNS: 30f. Molo (Djerma); 35f. Garaya (Hausa); 40f. Godjie (Djerma-Sonrai); 45f. Inzad (Tuareg); 50f. Kountigui (Sonrai).

129 De Gaulle in Uniform

1971. Air. First Death Anniv of Gen. Charles De Gaulle (French statesman).

407	**129**	250f. multicoloured	11·50	6·75

129a U.A.M.P.T. H.Q. and Rural Scene

1971. Air. Tenth Anniv of African and Malagasy Posts and Telecommunications Union.

408	**129a**	100f. multicoloured	1·50	70

130 "Audience with Al Hariri" (Baghdad, 1237)

1971. Air. Moslem Miniatures. Multicoloured.

409	100f. Type **130**	1·50	70
410	150f. "Archangel Israfil" (Iraq, 14th-cent) (vert)	2·50	95
411	200f. "Horsemen" (Iraq, 1210)	3·50	1·80

131 Louis Armstrong

1971. Air. Death of Louis Armstrong (American jazz musician). Multicoloured.

412	100f. Type **131**	2·20	70
413	150f. Armstrong playing trumpet	3·25	1·10

132 "Children of All Races"

1971. 25th Anniv of UNICEF.

414	**132**	50f. multicoloured	75	50

133 "Adoration of the Magi" (Di Bartolo)

1971. Air. Christmas. Paintings. Multicoloured.

415	100f. Type **133**	1·50	60
416	150f. "The Nativity" (D. Ghirlandaio) (vert)	2·20	95
417	200f. "Adoration of the Shepherds" (Perugino)	3·00	1·30

134 Presidents Pompidou and Hamani

1972. Air. Visit of Pres. Pompidou of France.

418	**134**	250f. multicoloured	8·25	5·00

135 Ski "Gate" and Cherry Blossom

1972. Air. Winter Olympic Games, Sapporo, Japan.

419	**135**	100f. violet, red and green	1·50	70
420	-	150f. red, purple and violet	2·30	1·00
MS421		130×100 mm. Nos. 419/20	4·00	4·00

DESIGN—HORIZ: 150f. Snow crystals and Olympic flame.

135a "The Masked Ball"

1972. Air. UNESCO "Save Venice" Campaign.

422	**135a**	50f. multicoloured (vert)	1·40	55
423	-	100f. multicoloured (vert)	2·50	90
424	-	150f. multicoloured (vert)	3·75	1·30
425	-	200f. multicoloured	4·50	1·70

DESIGNS: Nos. 422/5 depict various details of Guardi's painting, "The Masked Ball".

136 Johannes Brahms and Music

1972. Air. 75th Death Anniv of Johannes Brahms (composer).

426	**136**	100f. green, myrtle and red	2·10	70

137 Saluting Hand

1972. Air. Int Scout Seminar, Cotonou, Dahomey.

427	**137**	150f. violet, blue & orange	2·00	70

138 Star Symbol and Open Book

1972. International Book Year.

428	**138**	35f. purple and green	55	25
429	-	40f. blue and lake	80	30

DESIGN: 40f. Boy reading, 16th-century galleon and early aircraft.

139 Heart Operation

1972. Air. World Heart Month.

430	**139**	100f. brown and red	1·80	70

140 Bleriot XI crossing the Channel, 1909

1972. Air. Milestones in Aviation History.

431	**140**	50f. brown, blue and lake	1·20	45
432	-	75f. grey, brown and blue	1·80	70
433	-	100f. ultramarine, blue and purple	3·50	1·60

DESIGNS: 75f. Lindbergh crossing the Atlantic in "Spirit of St. Louis"; 100f. First flight of Concorde, 1969.

141 Satellite and Universe

1972. Air. World Telecommunications Day.

434	**141**	100f. brown, purple & red	1·70	65

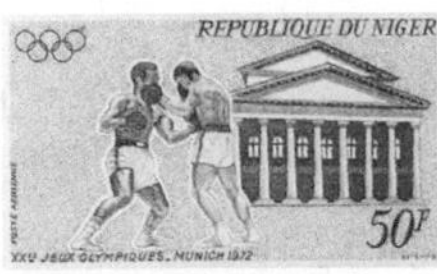

142 Boxing

1972. Air. Olympic Games, Munich. Sports and Munich Buildings.

435	**142**	50f. brown and blue	80	30
436	-	100f. brown and green	1·30	60
437	-	150f. brown and red	2·00	95
438	-	200f. brown and mauve	3·00	1·20
MS439		200×100 mm. Nos. 435/438	7·75	7·75

DESIGNS—VERT: 100f. Long-jumping; 150f. Football. HORIZ: 200f. Running.

143 A. G. Bell and Telephone

1972. Air. 50th Death Anniv of Alexander Graham Bell (inventor of telephone).

440	**143**	100f. blue, purple and red	1·50	50

144 "Europe on Africa" Map

1972. Air. "Europafrique" Co-operation.

441	**144**	50f. red, green and blue	75	30

145 Herdsman and Cattle

1972. Medicinal Salt-ponds at In-Gall. Multicoloured.

442	35f. Type **145**	1·00	35
443	40f. Cattle in salt-pond	1·80	40

146 Lottery Wheel

1972. Sixth Anniv of National Lottery.

444	**146**	35f. multicoloured	75	45

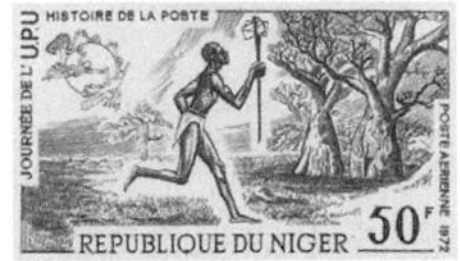

147 Postal Runner

1972. Air. U.P.U. Day. Postal Transport.

445	**147**	50f. brown, green and lake	1·00	45
446	-	100f. green, blue and lake	1·50	70
447	-	150f. green, violet and lake	2·50	90

DESIGNS: 100f. Rural mail van; 150f. Loading Fokker Friendship mail plane.

147a

1972. Tenth Anniv of West African Monetary Union.

448	**147a**	40f. grey, violet and brown	75	40

1972. Air. Gold Medal Winners. Munich Olympic Games. Nos. 435/8 optd with events and names, etc.

449	**142**	50f. brown and blue	80	35
450	-	100f. brown and green	1·30	60
451	-	150f. brown and red	2·10	80
452	-	200f. brown and mauve	2·75	1·20

OVERPRINTS: 50f. **WELTER CORREA MEDAILLE D'OR**; 100f. **TRIPLE SAUT SANEIEV MEDAILLE D'OR**; 150f. **FOOTBALL POLOGNE MEDAILLE D'OR**; 200f. **MARATHON SHORTER MEDAILLE D'OR.**

148 "The Raven and the Fox"

1972. Air. Fables of Jean de la Fontaine.

453	**148**	25f. black, brown and green	1·30	45
454	-	50f. brown, green and purple	2·50	70
455	-	75f. brown, green and brown	3·75	1·40

DESIGNS: 50f. "The Lion and the Rat"; 75f. "The Monkey and the Leopard".

149 Astronauts on Moon

1972. Air. Moon Flight of "Apollo 17".

456	**149**	250f. multicoloured	4·50	1·80

150 Dromedary Race

1972. Niger Sports.

457	**150**	35f. purple, red and blue	1·20	60
458	-	40f. lake, brown and green	1·50	85

DESIGN: 40f. Horse race.

151 Pole Vaulting

1973. Second African Games, Lagos, Nigeria. Multicoloured.

459	35f. Type **151**	45	40
460	40f. Basketball	50	40
461	45f. Boxing	75	40
462	75f. Football	1·00	50

152 "Young Athlete"

1973. Air. Antique Art Treasures.

463	**152**	50f. red	75	35
464	-	100f. violet	1·50	55

DESIGN: 100f. "Head of Hermes".

153 Knight and Pawn

1973. World Chess Championships, Reykjavik, Iceland.

465	**153**	100f. green, blue and red	3·50	1·40

154 "Abutilon pannosum"

1973. Rare African Flowers. Multicoloured.

466	30f. Type **154**	1·00	45
467	45f. "Crotalaria barkae"	1·20	45
468	60f. "Dichrostachys cinerea"	1·60	55
469	80f. "Caralluma decaisneana"	2·20	70

155 Interpol Badge

1973. 50th Anniv of International Criminal Police Organization (Interpol).

470	**155**	50f. multicoloured	75	30

156 Scout with Radio

1973. Air. Scouting in Niger.

471	**156**	25f. brown, green and red	45	25
472	-	50f. brown, green and red	95	25
473	-	100f. brown, green and red	1·50	70
474	-	150f. brown, green and red	2·10	85

DESIGNS: 50f. First aid; 100f. Care of animals; 150f. Care of the environment.

157 Hansen and Microscope

1973. Centenary of Dr. Hansen's Discovery of Leprosy Bacillus.

475	**157**	50f. brown, green and blue	1·30	50

158 Nurse tending Child

1973. 25th Anniv of W.H.O.

476	**158**	50f. brown, red and blue	75	30

159 "The Crucifixion" (Hugo van der Goes)

1973. Air. Easter. Paintings. Multicoloured.

477	50f. Type **159**	95	25
478	100f. "The Deposition" (Cima de Conegliano) (horiz)	1·70	75
479	150f. "Pieta" (Bellini) (horiz)	2·40	85

160 Douglas DC-8 and Mail Van

1973. Air. Stamp Day.

480	**160**	100f. brown, red and green	2·00	75

161 W.M.O. Emblem and "Weather Conditions"

1973. Air. Centenary of W.M.O.

481	**161**	100f. brown, red and green	1·50	70

162 "Crouching Lioness" (Delacroix)

1973. Air. Paintings by Delacroix. Multicoloured.

482	150f. Type **162**	3·25	1·60
483	200f. "Tigress and Cub"	5·25	2·75

163 Crocodile

1973. Wild Animals from "Park W".

484	**163**	25f. multicoloured	70	25
485	-	35f. grey, gold and black	90	40
486	-	40f. multicoloured	1·20	40
487	-	80f. multicoloured	2·20	60

DESIGNS: 35f. African elephant; 40f. Hippopotamus; 80f. Warthog.

164 Eclipse over Mountain

1973. Total Eclipse of the Sun.

488	**164**	40f. violet	75	45

1973. Air. 24th International Scouting Congress, Nairobi, Kenya. Nos. 473/4 optd **24 Conference Mondiale du Scoutisme NAIROBI 1973**.

489	100f. brown, green and red	1·50	60
490	150f. brown, green and red	2·20	85

166 Palomino

1973. Horse-breeding. Multicoloured.

491	50f. Type **166**	1·20	55
492	75f. French trotter	1·60	80
493	80f. English thoroughbred	2·00	90
494	100f. Arab thoroughbred	2·50	1·10

1973. Pan-African Drought Relief. African Solidarity. No. 436 surch **SECHERESSE SOLIDARITE AFRICAINE** and value.

495	**145**	100f. on 35f. multicoloured	2·00	1·40

168 Rudolf Diesel and Oil Engine

1973. 60th Death Anniv of Rudolf Diesel (engineer).

496	**168**	25f. blue, purple and grey	80	35
497	-	50f. grey, green and blue	1·50	55
498	-	75f. blue, black and mauve	2·20	90
499	-	125f. blue, red and green	3·25	1·40

DESIGNS: 50f. Series "BB 100" diesel locomotive; 75f. Type "060-DB1" diesel locomotive, France; 125f. Diesel locomotive No. 72004, France.

168a

1973. African and Malagasy Posts and Telecommunications Union.

500	**168a**	100f. red, green and brown	1·20	75

168b African Mask and Old Town Hall, Brussels

1973. Air. African Fortnight, Brussels.

501	**168b**	100f. purple, blue and red	1·50	70

169 T.V. Set and Class

1973. Schools Television Service.

502	**169**	50f. black, red and blue	95	40

1973. Third International French Language and Culture Conf, Liege. No. 385 optd **3e CONFERENCE DE LA FRANCOPHONIE LIEGE OCTOBRE 1973**.

503	**110**	40f. multicoloured	95	40

171 "Apollo"

1973. Classical Sculptures.

504	**171**	50f. green and brown	1·70	55
505	-	50f. black and brown	1·70	55
506	-	50f. brown and red	1·70	55
507	-	50f. purple and red	1·70	55

DESIGNS: No. 505, "Atlas"; No. 506, "Hercules"; No. 507, "Venus".

172 Bees and Honeycomb

1973. World Savings Day.

508	**172**	40f. brown, red and blue	95	40

173 "Food for the World"

1973. Air. Tenth Anniv of World Food Programme.

509	**173**	50f. violet, red and blue	95	45

174 Copernicus and "Sputnik 1"

1973. Air. 500th Birth Anniv of Copernicus (astonomer).

510	**174**	150f. brown, blue and red	2·20	95

175 Pres. John Kennedy

1973. Air. Tenth Death Anniv of U.S. President Kennedy.

511	**175**	100f. multicoloured	1·50	70

MS512 80×100 mm. 200f. multicoloured 3·00 3·00

176 Kounta Songhai Blanket

1973. Niger Textiles. Multicoloured.

513 35f. Type **176** 80 40
514 40f. Tcherka Snghai blanket (horiz) 1·20 55

177 Barges on River Niger

1974. Air. First Anniv of Ascent of Niger by "Fleet of Hope".

515 **177** 50f. blue, green and red 1·20 70
516 - 75f. purple, blue and green 1·80 70

DESIGN: 75f. "Barban Maza" (tug) and barge.

178 Lenin

1974. Air. 50th Death Anniv of Lenin.

517 **178** 50c. brown 2·20 80

179 Slalom Skiing

1974. Air. 50th Anniv of Winter Olympic Games.

518 **179** 200f. red, brown and blue 3·75 1·40

180 Newly-born Baby

1974. World Population Year.

519 **180** 50f. multicoloured 75 40

181 Footballers and "Global" Ball

1974. Air. World Cup Football Championship, West Germany.

520 **181** 75f. violet, black & brown 70 45
521 - 150f. brown, green & turq 1·50 85
522 - 200f. blue, orange & green 2·10 1·50

MS523 130×100 mm. 250f. green, bistre and brown 3·75 3·75

DESIGNS: 150f. to 250f. Football scenes similar to Type **181**.

182 "The Crucifixion" (Grunewald)

1974. Air. Easter. Paintings. Multicoloured.

524 50f. Type **182** 80 40
525 75f. "Avignon Pieta" (attributed to E. Quarton) 1·20 55
526 125f. "The Entombment" (G. Isenmann) 1·90 75

183 Class 230K Locomotive, 1948, France and Locomotive No. 5511, 1938, U.S.A.

1974. Famous Railway Locomotives of the Steam Era.

527 **183** 50f. green, black and violet 1·30 55
528 - 75f. green, black & brown 2·00 75
529 - 100f. multicoloured 2·75 1·30
530 - 150f. brown, black and red 4·00 1·40

DESIGNS: 75f. Class 21 locomotive, 1893, France; 100f. Locomotive, 1866, U.S.A. and "Mallard", Great Britain; 150f. Marc Seguin locomotive, 1829, France and Stephenson's "Rocket", 1829.

184 Map of Member Countries

1974. 15th Anniv of Conseil de l'Entente.

531 **184** 40f. multicoloured 90 45

185 Knights

1974. Air. 21st Chess Olympiad, Nice.

532 **185** 50f. brown, blue & indigo 2·10 90
533 - 75f. purple, brown & green 2·50 1·10

DESIGN: 75f. Kings.

186 Marconi and "Elettra" (steam yacht)

1974. Birth Centenary of Guglielmo Marconi (radio pioneer).

534 **186** 50f. blue, brown & mauve 95 45

187 Astronaut on Palm of Hand

1974. Air. Fifth Anniv of 1st Landing on Moon.

535 **187** 150f. brown, blue & indigo 2·00 90

188 Tree on Palm of Hand

1974. National Tree Week.

536 **188** 35f. turquoise, grn & brn 95 50

189 "The Rhinoceros" (Longhi)

1974. Air. Europafrique.

537 **189** 250f. multicoloured 8·50 4·25

190 Camel Saddle

1974. Handicrafts.

538 **190** 40f. red, blue and brown 75 30
539 - 50f. blue, red and brown 95 45

DESIGN: 50f. Statuettes of horses.

1974. Air. West Germany's Victory in World Cup Football Championships. No. **MS**523 optd **R.F.A. HOLLANDE 1**.

MS540 130×100 mm. **181** 250f. green, bistre and brown 3·75 3·75

192 Frederic Chopin

1974. 125th Death Anniv of Frederic Chopin.

541 **192** 100f. black, red and blue 2·10 80

1974. Beethoven's Ninth Symphony Commemoration. As T **192**.

542 100f. lilac, blue and indigo 2·10 80

DESIGN: 100f. Beethoven.

193 European Woman and Douglas DC-8 Airliners

1974. Air. Centenary of U.P.U.

543 **193** 50f. turquoise, grn & pur 95 40
544 - 100f. blue, mauve & ultram 2·00 70
545 - 150f. brown, blue & indigo 2·20 1·10
546 - 200f. brown, orange & red 3·00 1·30

DESIGNS: 100f. Japanese woman and electric locomotives; 150f. American Indian woman and liner; 200f. African woman and road vehicles.

194 "Skylab" over Africa

1974. Air. "Skylab" Space Laboratory.

547 **194** 100f. violet, brown & blue 1·50 60

195 Don-don Drum

1974

548 **195** 60f. purple, green and red 1·40 70

196 Tree and Compass Rose

1974. First Death Anniv of Tenere Tree (desert landmark).

549 **196** 50f. brown, blue and ochre 3·00 1·40

197 "Virgin and Child" (Correggio)

1974. Air. Christmas. Multicoloured.

550 100f. Type **197** 1·50 55
551 150f. "Virgin and Child, and St. Hilary" (F. Lippi) 2·30 80
552 200f. "Virgin and Child" (Murillo) 3·00 1·40

198 "Apollo" Spacecraft

1975. Air. "Apollo–Soyuz" Space Test Project.

553 **198** 50f. green, red and blue 80 45
554 - 100f. grey, red and blue 1·20 60
555 - 150f. purple, plum & blue 2·00 85

DESIGNS: 100f. "Apollo" and "Soyuz" docked; 150f. "Soyuz" spacecraft.

199 European and African Women

1975. Air. Europafrique.

556 **199** 250f. brown, purple & red 3·75 1·90

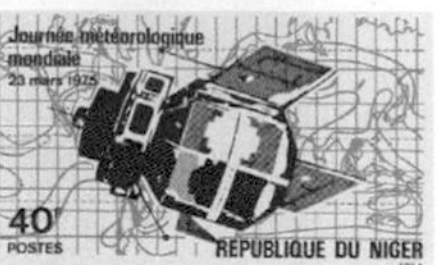

200 Communications Satellite and Weather Map

1975. World Meteorological Day.

557 **200** 40f. red, black and blue 75 40

201 "Christ in the Garden of Olives" (Delacroix)

1975. Air. Easter. Multicoloured.

558	75f. Type **201**	1·00	45
559	125f. "The Crucifixion" (El Greco) (vert)	1·80	75
560	150f. "The Resurrection" (Limousin) (vert)	2·30	95

202 Lt-Col. S. Kountche, Head of State

1975. Air. First Anniv of Military Coup.

561	**202**	100f. multicoloured	1·50	75

203 "City of Truro", 1903, Great Britain

1975. Famous Locomotives. Multicoloured.

562	50f. Type **203**	1·40	45
563	75f. Class 05 steam locomotive No. 003, 1937, Germany	2·00	50
564	100f. "General", 1855, U.S.A. (dated "1863")	2·75	90
565	125f. Series BB 15000 electric locomotive, 1971, France	4·00	1·40

1975. Birds. As Nos. 296 and 298, but dated "1975". Multicoloured.

567	25f. Abyssinian roller (postage)	1·80	55
568	100f. Violet starlings (air)	3·25	1·10

205 "Zabira" Leather Bag

1975. Niger Handicrafts. Multicoloured.

569	35f. Type **205**	45	25
570	40f. Chequered rug	55	40
571	45f. Flower pot	75	45
572	60f. Gourd	1·20	55

206 African Woman and Child

1975. International Women's Year.

573	**206**	50f. blue, brown and red	95	45

207 Dr. Schweitzer and Lambarene Hospital

1975. Birth Centenary of Dr. Albert Schweitzer.

574	**207**	100f. brown, green & black	1·70	85

208 Peugeot, 1892

1975. Early Motor-cars.

575	**208**	50f. blue and mauve	1·20	55
576	-	75f. purple and blue	1·70	70
577	-	100f. mauve and green	2·50	90
578	-	125f. green and red	3·00	1·30

DESIGNS: 75f. Daimler, 1895; 100f. Fiat, 1899; 125f. Cadillac, 1903.

209 Tree and Sun

1975. National Tree Week.

579	**209**	40f. green, orange and red	95	45

210 Boxing

1975. Traditional Sports.

580	**210**	35f. brown, orange and black	55	25
581	-	40f. brown, green and black	75	30
582	-	45f. brown, blue and black	75	45
583	-	50f. brown, red and black	85	50

DESIGNS—VERT: 40f. Boxing; 50f. Wrestling. HORIZ: 45f. Wrestling.

211 Leontini Tetradrachme

1975. Ancient Coins.

584	**211**	50f. grey, blue and red	80	25
585	-	75f. grey, blue and mauve	1·10	45
586	-	100f. grey, orange and blue	1·60	55
587	-	125f. grey, purple and green	2·20	85

COINS: 75f. Athens tetradrachme; 100f. Himer diadrachme; 125f. Gela tetradrachme.

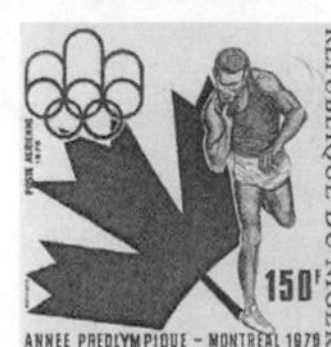

212 Putting the Shot

1975. Air. "Pre-Olympic Year". Olympic Games, Montreal (1976).

588	**212**	150f. brown and red	2·00	80
589	-	200f. red, chestnut and brown	2·50	1·10

DESIGN: 200f. Gymnastics.

213 Starving Family

1975. Pan-African Drought Relief.

590	**213**	40f. blue, brown & orange	90	50
591	-	45f. brown and blue	2·20	1·10
592	-	60f. blue, green and orange	1·30	65

DESIGNS: 45f. Animal skeletons; 60f. Truck bringing supplies.

214 Trading Canoe crossing R. Niger

1975. Tourism. Multicoloured.

593	40f. Type **214**	80	45
594	45f. Boubon Camp entrance	95	45
595	50f. Boubon Camp view	1·00	55

215 U.N. Emblem and Peace Dove

1975. Air. 30th Anniv of U.N.O.

596	**215**	100f. light blue and blue	1·30	55

216 "Virgin of Seville" (Murillo)

1975. Air. Christmas. Multicoloured.

597	50f. Type **216**	75	40
598	75f. "Adoration of the Shepherds" (Tintoretto) (horiz)	1·20	55
599	125f. "Virgin with Angels" (Master of Burgo d'Osma)	1·80	1·10

1975. Air. "Apollo–Soyuz" Space Link. Nos. 533/5 optd **JONCTION 17 Juillet 1975**.

600	**198**	50f. green, red and blue	80	35
601	-	100f. grey, red and blue	1·20	60
602	-	150f. purple, plum & blue	1·80	60

218 "Ashak"

1976. Literacy Campaign. Multicoloured.

603	25f. Type **218**	30	10
604	30f. "Kaska"	30	25
605	40f. "Iccee"	35	25
606	50f. "Tuuri-nya"	45	25
607	60f. "Lekki"	65	25

219 Ice Hockey

1976. Winter Olympic Games, Innsbruck, Austria. Multicoloured.

608	40f. Type **219** (postage)	45	25
609	50f. Tobogganing	60	30
610	150f. Ski-jumping	1·80	65
611	200f. Figure-skating (air)	1·80	80
612	300f. Cross-country skiing	2·75	1·20
MS613	117×78 mm. 500f. Speed Ice-skating	5·25	2·20

220 Early Telephone and Satellite

1976. Telephone Centenary.

614	**220**	100f. orange, blue & green	1·50	70

221 Baby and Ambulance

1976. World Health Day.

615	**221**	50f. red, brown and purple	95	30

222 Washington crossing the Delaware (after Leutze)

1976. Bicentenary of American Revolution. Multicoloured.

616	40f. Type **222** (postage)	40	10
617	50f. First soldiers of the Revolution	55	25
618	150f. Joseph Warren – martyr of Bunker Hill (air)	1·20	40
619	200f. John Paul Jones aboard the "Bonhomme Richard"	2·00	80
620	300f. Molly Pitcher – heroine of Monmouth	2·75	1·20
MS621	128×97 mm. 500f. "Soldiers' farewell; the beginning of the revolution" (after F. Darley)	5·25	2·10

223 Distribution of Provisions

1976. Second Anniv of Military Coup. Multicoloured.

622	50f. Type **223**	55	25
623	100f. Soldiers with bulldozer (horiz)	1·20	55

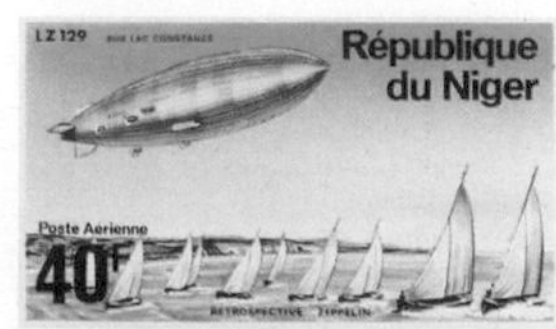

224 "Hindenburg" crossing Lake Constance

1976. Air. 75th Anniv of Zeppelin Airships. Multicoloured.

624	40f. Type **224**	55	20
625	50f. LZ-3 over Wurzberg	75	25
626	150f. L-9 over Friedrichshafen	2·20	60
627	200f. LZ-2 over Rothenburg (vert)	2·75	80
628	300f. "Graf Zeppelin II" over Essen	3·75	95
MS629	129×103 mm. 500f. "LZ-127" crossing Alps	6·00	2·00

225 "Europafrique" Symbols

1976. "Europafrique".
630 **225** 100f. multicoloured 1·50 70

226 Plant Cultivation

1976. Communal Works. Multicoloured.
631 25f. Type **226** 30 25
632 30f. Harvesting rice 40 25

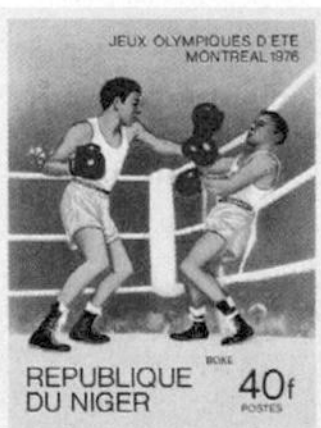

227 Boxing

1976. Olympic Games, Montreal. Multicoloured.
633 40f. Type **227** 35 15
634 50f. Basketball 50 15
635 60f. Football 60 15
636 80f. Cycling (horiz) 95 25
637 100f. Judo (horiz) 1·20 45
MS638 194×79 mm. 150f. Athletics (horiz) 2·00 90

228 Motobecane "125"

1976. Motorcycles.
639 **228** 50f. violet, brown & turq 85 30
640 - 75f. green, red & turquoise 1·20 50
641 - 100f. brown, orange & pur 1·90 70
642 - 125f. slate, olive and black 2·20 1·10
DESIGNS: 75f. Norton "Challenge"; 100f. B.M.W. "903"; 125f. Kawasaki "1000".

229 Cultivation Map

1976. Operation "Sahel Vert". Multicoloured.
643 40f. Type **229** 45 25
644 45f. Tending plants (vert) 60 25
645 60f. Planting sapling (vert) 1·00 35

1976. International Literacy Day. Nos. 603/7 optd **JOURNEE INTERNATIONALE DE L'ALPHABETISATION.**
646 **218** 25f. multicoloured 30 15
647 - 30f. multicoloured 30 15
648 - 40f. multicoloured 40 25
649 - 50f. multicoloured 45 25
650 - 60f. multicoloured 55 25

231 Basket Making

1976. Niger Women's Association. Multicoloured.
651 40f. Type **231** 55 25
652 45f. Hairdressing (horiz) 60 40
653 50f. Making pottery 85 40

232 Wall Paintings

1976. "Archaeology". Multicoloured.
654 40f. Type **232** 2·20 55
655 50f. Neolithic statuettes 2·50 55
656 60f. Dinosaur skeleton 4·50 80

233 "The Nativity" (Rubens)

1976. Air. Christmas. Multicoloured.
657 50f. Type **233** 80 25
658 100f. "Holy Night" (Correggio) 1·50 65
659 150f. "Adoration of the Magi" (David) (horiz) 2·30 1·10

234 Benin Ivory Mask

1977. Second World Festival of Negro-African Arts, Lagos.
660 **234** 40f. brown 55 25
661 - 50f. blue 95 45
DESIGNS—HORIZ: 50f. Nigerian stick dance.

235 Students in Class

1977. Alphabetization Campaign.
662 **235** 40f. multicoloured 45 25
663 **235** 50f. multicoloured 55 30
664 **235** 60f. multicoloured 95 35

236 Examining Patient

1977. Village Health. Multicoloured.
665 40f. Type **236** 60 25
666 50f. Examining baby 95 45

237 Rocket Launch

1977. "Viking" Space Mission. Multicoloured.
667 50f. Type **237** (postage) 55 25
668 80f. "Viking" approaching Mars (horiz) 95 30
669 100f. "Viking" on Mars (horiz) (air) 95 25
670 150f. Parachute descent 1·30 50
671 200f. Rocket in flight 1·90 95
MS672 104×77 mm. 400f. "Viking" landing on Mars (horiz) 3·75 1·50

238 Marabou Stork

1977. Fauna Protection.
673 **238** 80f. sepia, bistre and red 2·30 1·00
674 - 90f. brown and turquoise 2·50 1·00
DESIGN: 90f. Bushbuck.

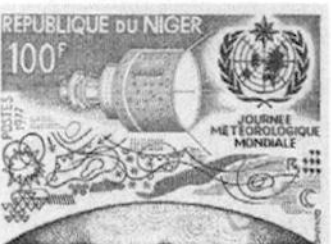

239 Satellite and Weather Symbols

1977. World Meteorological Day.
675 **239** 100f. blue, black & turq 1·50 70

240 Gymnastic Exercise

1977. Second Youth Festival, Tahoua. Multicoloured.
676 40f. Type **240** 50 30
677 50f. High jumping 75 45
678 80f. Choral ensemble 1·10 55

241 Red Cross and Children playing

1977. World Health Day. Child Immunization Campaign.
679 **241** 80f. red, mauve and orange 95 40

242 Fly, Dagger, and W.H.O. Emblem in Eye

1977. Fight against Onchocerciasis (blindness caused by worm infestation).
680 **242** 100f. blue, grey and red 1·30 70

243 Guirka Tahoua Dance

1977. "Popular Arts and Traditions". Multicoloured.
681 40f. Type **243** 65 40
682 50f. Maifilafili Gaya 95 45
683 80f. Naguihinayan Loga 4·25 60

244 Four Cavalrymen

1977. Chiefs' Traditional Cavalry. Multicoloured.
684 40f. Type **244** 80 30
685 50f. Chieftain at head of cavalry 95 45
686 60f. Chieftain and cavalry 1·30 70

245 Planting Crops

1977. "Operation Green Sahel" (recovery of desert).
687 **245** 40f. multicoloured 75 40

246 Albert John Luthuli (Peace, 1960)

1977. Nobel Prize Winners. Multicoloured.
688 50f. Type **246** 45 25
689 80f. Maurice Maeterlinck (Literature, 1911) 95 25
690 100f. Allan L. Hodgkin (Medicine, 1963) 1·00 30
691 150f. Albert Camus (Literature, 1957) 1·60 45
692 200f. Paul Ehrlich (Medicine, 1908) 2·00 60
MS693 117×80 mm. 500f. Theodore Roosevelt (Peace, 1906) 5·50 1·60

247 Mao Tse-tung

1977. First Death Anniv of Mao Tse-tung (Chinese leader).
694 **247** 100f. black and red 3·50 1·80

248 Vittorio Pozzo (Italy)

1977. World Football Cup Elimination Rounds. Multicoloured.
695 40f. Type **248** 45 10
696 50f. Vincente Feola, Spain 50 25
697 80f. Aymore Moreira, Portugal 75 25
698 100f. Sir Alf Ramsey, England 1·30 45
699 200f. Helmut Schoen, West Germany 2·10 65
MS700 117×78 mm. 500f. Sepp Herberger (Germany) 5·50 2·10

249 Horse's Head and Parthenon

1977. UNESCO Commemoration.
701 **249** 100f. blue, red and pale blue 2·00 90

250 Carrying Water

1977. Women's Work. Multicoloured.
702 40f. Type **250** 55 25
703 50f. Pounding maize 65 40

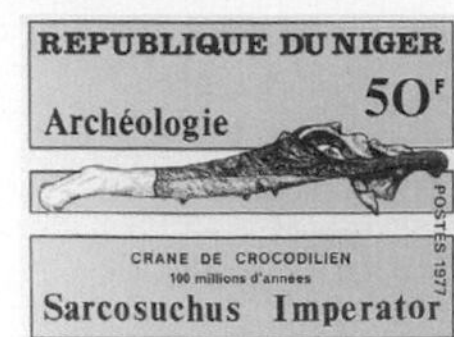

251 Crocodile Skull

1977. Archaeology. Multicoloured.

704	50f. Type **251**	1·30	70
705	80f. Neolithic tools	1·80	1·10

252 Paul Follereau and Leper

1978. 25th Anniv of World Leprosy Day.

706	**252**	40f. red, blue and orange	55	25
707	-	50f. black, red and orange	70	35

DESIGN—HORIZ: 50f. Follereau and two lepers.

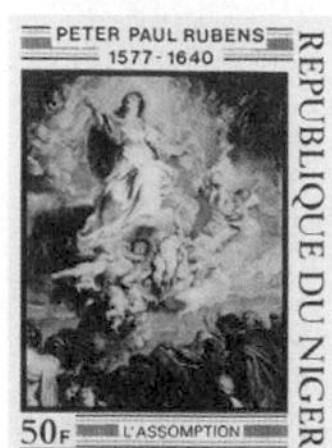

253 "The Assumption"

1978. 400th Birth Anniv of Peter Paul Rubens. Paintings. Multicoloured.

708	50f. Type **253**	45	15
709	70f. "The Artist and his Friends" (horiz)	55	25
710	100f. "History of Maria de Medici"	1·00	40
711	150f. "Alathea Talbot"	1·70	55
712	200f. "Portrait of the Marquise de Spinola"	2·30	70
MS713	85×111 mm. 500f. "St. Ildofonse and the Virgin"	6·00	1·70

1978. As Nos. 376/7 but redrawn and background colour of 35f. changed to blue, 35f. undated, 50f. dated "1978".

714	35f. Broad-tailed paradise whydah	2·20	70
715	50f. Cattle egret	1·80	60

The 50f. is still wrongly inscribed "Balbucus".

254 Putting the Shot

1978. National Schools and University Sports Championships. Multicoloured.

716	40f. Type **254**	35	15
717	50f. Volleyball	45	25
718	60f. Long-jumping	55	25
719	100f. Throwing the javelin	95	40

255 Nurse assisting Patient

1978. Niger Red Cross.

720	**255**	40f. multicoloured	45	25

256 Station and Dish Aerial

1978. Goudel Earth Receiving Station.

721	**256**	100f. multicoloured	1·00	65

257 Football and Flags of Competing Nations

1978. World Cup Football Championship, Argentina. Multicoloured.

722	40f. Type **257**	35	10
723	50f. Football in net	70	25
724	100f. Globe and goal	1·00	30
725	200f. Tackling (horiz)	1·80	75
MS726	102×78 mm. 300f. Footballer and globe	3·00	1·60

258 "Fireworks"

1978. Air. Third African Games, Algiers. Multicoloured.

727	40f. Type **258**	45	25
728	150f. Olympic rings emblem	1·60	80

259 Niamey Post Office

1978. Niamey Post Office. Multicoloured.

729	40f. Type **259**	40	25
730	60f. Niamey Post Office (different)	55	40

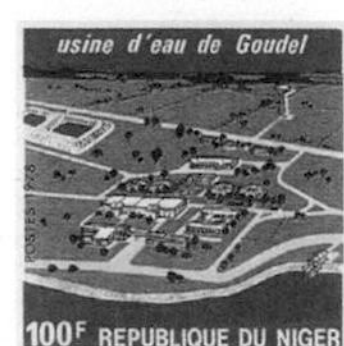

260 Aerial View of Water-works

1978. Goudel Water-works.

731	**260**	100f. multicoloured	1·00	60

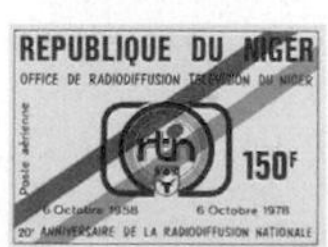

261 R.T.N. Emblem

1978. Air. 20th Anniv of Niger Broadcasting.

732	**261**	150f. multicoloured	1·50	85

262 Golden Eagle and Oldenburg 2g. Stamp of 1859

1978. Air. "Philexafrique" Stamp Exhibition, Libreville, Gabon (1st issue) and Int Stamp Fair, Essen, West Germany. Multicoloured.

733	100f. Type **262**	2·75	2·10
734	100f. Giraffes and Niger 1959 2f. stamp	2·75	2·10

See also Nos. 769/70.

263 Giraffe

1978. Endangered Animals. Multicoloured.

735	40f. Type **263**	1·00	35
736	50f. Ostrich	1·60	45
737	70f. Cheetah	2·30	60
738	150f. Scimitar oryx (horiz)	4·75	1·10
739	200f. Addax (horiz)	7·00	1·60
740	300f. Hartebeest (horiz)	9·25	2·20

1978. World Cup Football Championship Finalists. Nos. 695/9 optd.

741	**248**	40f. multicoloured	45	25
742	-	50f. multicoloured	60	25
743	-	80f. multicoloured	1·00	40
744	-	100f. multicoloured	1·20	70
745	-	200f. multicoloured	2·30	1·10
MS746		117×78 mm. 500f. Optd as No. 745	5·50	5·25

OVERPRINTS: 40f. **EQUIPE QUATRIEME: ITALIE**; 50f. **EQUIPE TROISIEME: BRESIL**; 80f. **EQUIPE SECONDE: PAYS BAS**; 100f. **EQUIPE VAINQUEUR: ARGENTINE**. 200 f; **ARGENTINE - PAYS BAS 3 - 1**.

265 Dome of the Rock, Jerusalem

1978. Palestinian Welfare.

747	**265**	40f.+5f. multicoloured	55	40

266 Laying Foundation Stone, and View of University

1978. Air. Islamic University of Niger.

748	**266**	100f. multicoloured	95	55

267 Tinguizi

1978. Musicians. Multicoloured.

749	100f. Type **267**	1·20	65
750	100f. Chetima Ganga (horiz)	1·20	65
751	100f. Dan Gourmou	1·20	65

268 "The Homecoming" (Daumier)

1979. Paintings. Multicoloured.

752	50f. Type **268**	95	25
753	100f. "Virgin in Prayer" (Durer)	95	25
754	150f. "Virgin and Child" (Durer)	1·50	45
755	200f. "Virgin and Child" (Durer) (different)	2·00	65
MS756	103×78 mm. 500f. "Virgin and Child with Garland"	6·00	1·80

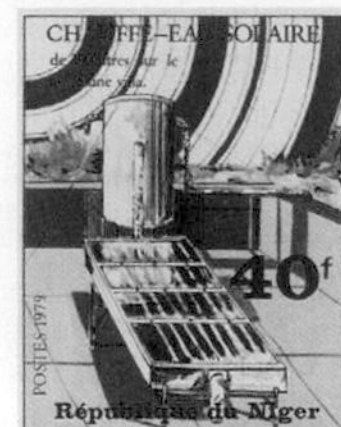

269 Feeder Tanks

1979. Solar Energy. Multicoloured.

757	40f. Type **269**	45	25
758	50f. Solar panels on house roofs (horiz)	55	40

270 Langha Contestants

1979. Traditional Sports. Multicoloured.

759	40f. Type **270**	45	25
760	50f. Langha contestants clasping hands	55	30

271 Children with Building Bricks

1979. International Year of the Child. Multicoloured.

761	40f. Type **271**	45	20
762	100f. Children with book	1·00	30
763	150f. Children with model airplane	1·80	60

272 Rowland Hill, Peugeot Mail Van and French "Ceres" Stamp of 1849

1979. Death Centenary of Sir Rowland Hill. Mult.

764	40f. Type **272**	50	20
765	100f. Canoes and Austrian newspaper stamp, 1851	1·20	30
766	150f. "DC-3" aircraft & U.S. "Lincoln" stamp, 1869	1·80	45
767	200f. Advanced Passenger Train (APT), Great Britain and Canada 7½d. stamp, 1857	2·20	65
MS768	119×81 mm. 400f. French electric train and Niger 75c. stamp, 1926	4·50	1·70

273 Zabira Decorated Bag and Niger 45f. Stamp, 1965

1979. "Philexafrique 2" Exhibition, Gabon (2nd issue).

769	**273**	50f. multicoloured	1·50	1·10
770	-	150f. blue, red and carmine	3·75	2·10

DESIGN: 150f. Talking Heads, world map, satellite and U.P.U. emblem.

274 Alcock and Brown Statue and Vickers Vimy Aircraft

1979. 60th Anniv of First Transatlantic Flight.

771	**274**	100f. multicoloured	1·30	45

275 Djermakoye Palace

1979. Historic Monuments.

772	**275**	100f. multicoloured	1·00	60

276 Bororos in Festive Headdress

1979. Annual Bororo Festival. Multicoloured.

773	45f. Type **276**	50	45
774	60f. Bororo women in traditional costume (vert)	70	45

277 Boxing

1979. Pre-Olympic Year.

775	**277**	45f. multicoloured	20	10
776	-	100f. multicoloured	1·00	30
777	-	150f. multicoloured	1·50	45
778	-	250f. multicoloured	2·50	65
MS779 117×79 mm. 500f. multicoloured			4·50	1·60

DESIGNS: 100f. to 500f. Various boxing sheets.

278 Class of Learner-drivers

1979. Driving School.

780	**278**	45f. multicoloured	55	40

279 Douglas DC-10 over Map of Niger

1979. Air. 20th Anniv of ASECNA (African Air Safety Organization).

781	**279**	150f. multicoloured	1·20	40

1979. "Apollo 11" Moon Landing. Nos. 667/8, 670/1 optd **alunissage apollo XI juillet 1969** and lunar module.

782	50f. Type **237** (postage)	45	25
783	80f. "Viking" approaching Mars (horiz)	80	45
784	150f. Parachute descent (air)	1·50	80
785	200f. Rocket in flight	2·00	1·10
MS786 104×77 mm. 400f. "Viking" landing on Mars (horiz)		4·00	4·00

281 Four-man Bobsleigh

1979. Winter Olympic Games, Lake Placid (1980). Multicoloured.

787	40f. Type **281**	45	15
788	60f. Downhill skiing	55	25
789	100f. Speed skating	95	40
790	150f. Two-man bobsleigh	1·50	55
791	200f. Figure skating	2·00	70
MS792 116×78 mm. 300f. Cross-country skiing		3·25	1·40

282 Le Gaweye Hotel

1980. Air.

793	**282**	100f. multicoloured	95	55

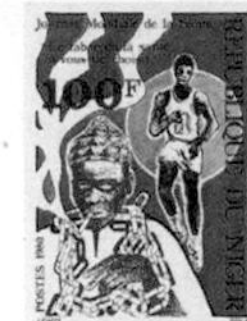

283 Sultan and Court

1980. Sultan of Zinder's Court. Multicoloured.

794	45f. Type **283**	45	25
795	60f. Sultan and court (different)	55	25

284 Chain Smoker and Athlete

1980. World Health Day. Anti-smoking Campaign.

796	**284**	100f. multicoloured	95	60

285 Walking

1980. Olympic Games, Moscow. Multicoloured.

797	60f. Throwing the javelin	60	20
798	90f. Type **285**	1·00	25
799	100f. High jump (horiz)	1·20	45
800	300f. Running (horiz)	2·75	90
MS801 105×79 mm. 500f. High jump-ing (different)		4·50	1·60

1980. Winter Olympic Games Medal Winners. Nos. 787/**MS**792 optd.

802	**281**	40f. **VAINQUEUR R.D.A.**	45	25
803	-	60f. **VAINQUEUR STENMARK SUEDE**	55	25
804	-	100f. **VAINQUEUR HEIDEN Etats-Unis**	95	55
805	-	150f. **VAINQUEURS SCHERER-BENZ Suisse**	1·40	75
806	-	200f. **VAINQUEUR COUSINS Grande Bretagne**	2·10	95
MS807 116×78 mm. 300f. **VAINQUEUR ZIMIATOV/U.R.S.S**			3·25	3·00

287 Village Scene

1980. Health Year.

808	**287**	150f. multicoloured	1·40	75

288 Class 150 (first locomotive in Japan, 1871)

1980. Steam Locomotives. Multicoloured.

809	45f. Type **288**	55	30
810	60f. "Fred Merril", 1848, U.S.A.	75	35
811	90f. Series 61, 1934, Germany	1·10	40
812	100f. Type P2, 1900, Prussia	1·40	70
813	130f. "Aigle", 1846, France	2·10	85
MS814 105×92 mm. 425f. "Rocket"		5·75	5·75

289 Steve Biko and Map of Africa

1980. Fourth Death Anniv of Steve Biko (South African Anti-apartheid Worker).

815	**289**	150f. multicoloured	1·20	85

1980. Olympic Medal Winners. Nos. 787/**MS**801 optd.

816	**285**	60f. **KULA (URSS)**	55	25
817	-	90f. **DAMILANO (IT)**	95	35
818	-	100f. **WZSOLA (POL)**	1·20	40
819	-	300f. **YIFTER (ETH)**	2·75	1·20
MS820 105×79 mm. 500f. *WESSIG (RDA)*			4·00	3·50

291 Footballer

1980. World Cup Football Championship, Spain (1982). Various designs showing Football.

821	**291**	45f. multicoloured	35	15
822	-	60f. multicoloured	45	15
823	-	90f. multicoloured	95	25
824	-	100f. multicoloured	95	40
825	-	130f. multicoloured	1·10	40
MS826 113×91 mm. 425f. multicoloured			4·50	1·50

292 U.A.P.T. Emblem

1980. Fifth Anniv of African Posts and Telecommunications Union.

827	**292**	100f. multicoloured	95	60

293 Earthenware Statuettes

1981. Kareygorou Culture Terracotta Statuettes. Multicoloured.

828	45f. Type **293**	35	25
829	60f. Head (vert)	55	25
830	90f. Head (different) (vert)	80	40
831	150f. Three heads	1·50	70

294 "Self-portrait"

1981. Paintings by Rembrandt. Multicoloured.

832	60f. Type **294**	70	25
833	90f. "Portrait of Hendrickje at the Window"	90	25
834	100f. "Portrait of an Old Man"	1·00	40
835	130f. "Maria Trip"	1·50	40
836	200f. "Self-portrait" (different)	2·00	70
837	400f. "Portrait of Saskia"	4·00	1·40

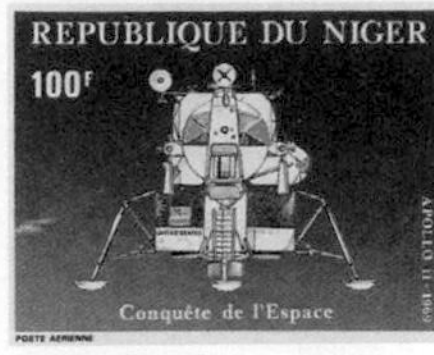

295 Ostrich

1981. Animals. Multicoloured.

839	10f. Type **295**	80	30
840	20f. Scimitar oryx	40	30
841	25f. Addra gazelle	45	30
842	30f. Arabian bustard	1·30	55
843	60f. Giraffe	85	35
844	150f. Addax	2·00	75

296 "Apollo 11"

1981. Air. Conquest of Space. Multicoloured.

845	100f. Type **296**	95	45
846	150f. Boeing 747 SCA carrying space shuttle	1·40	45
847	200f. Rocket carrying space shuttle	1·80	70
848	300f. Space shuttle flying over planet	2·75	95
MS848a 101×78 mm. 500f. Space shuttle returning to Earth		4·50	1·70

297 Tanks

1981. Seventh Anniv of Military Coup.

849	**297**	100f. multicoloured	95	60

298 Disabled Archer

1981. International Year of Disabled People.

850	**298**	50f. dp brown, red & brown	95	35
851	-	100f. brown, red and green	1·30	65

DESIGN: 100f. Disabled draughtsman.

299 Ballet Mahalba

1981. Ballet Mahalba. Multicoloured.

852	100f. Type **299**	95	55
853	100f. Ballet Mahalba (different)	95	55

300 "Portrait of Olga in an Armchair"

1981. Air. Birth Centenary of Pablo Picasso (artist). Multicoloured.

854	60f. Type **300**	75	25
855	90f. "The Family of Acrobats"	1·00	40
856	120f. "The Three Musicians"	1·50	55
857	200f. "Paul on a Donkey"	2·50	80
858	400f. "Young Girl drawing in an Interior" (horiz)	4·25	1·40

301 Mosque and Ka'aba

1981. 15th Centenary of Hejira.
859 **301** 100f. multicoloured 95 55

302 Carriage

1981. British Royal Wedding.
860 **302** 150f. multicoloured 1·30 45
861 - 200f. multicoloured 2·00 60
862 - 300f. multicoloured 2·75 85
MS863 117×78 mm. 400f. multicoloured 3·75 1·50
DESIGNS: 200f. to 400f. Similar designs showing carriages.

303 Sir Alexander Fleming

1981. Birth Centenary of Sir Alexander Fleming (discoverer of Penicillin).
864 **303** 150f. blue, brown and green 2·50 1·10

304 Pen-nibs, Envelope, Flower and U.P.U. Emblem

1981. International Letter Writing Week.
865 **304** 65f. on 45f. blue and red 60 30
866 - 85f. on 60f. blue, orange and black 95 50
DESIGN: 85f. Quill, hand holding pen and U.P.U. emblem.

305 Crops, Cattle and Fish

1981. World Food Day.
867 **305** 100f. multicoloured 95 55

306 Tackling

1981. World Cup Football Championship, Spain (1982). Multicoloured.
868 40f. Type **306** 40 15
869 65f. Goalkeeper fighting for ball 55 15
870 85f. Passing ball 80 30
871 150f. Running with ball 1·50 55
872 300f. Jumping for ball 2·75 95
MS873 103×78 mm. 500f. Running for ball 4·50 1·70

307 Peugeot, 1912

1981. 75th Anniv of French Grand Prix Motor Race. Multicoloured.
874 20f. Type **307** 45 25
875 40f. Bugatti, 1924 60 25
876 65f. Lotus-Climax, 1962 95 30
877 85f. Georges Boillot 1·20 55
878 150f. Phil Hill 2·30 70
MS879 119×96 mm. 450f. United States Grand Prix, 1967 6·50 2·30

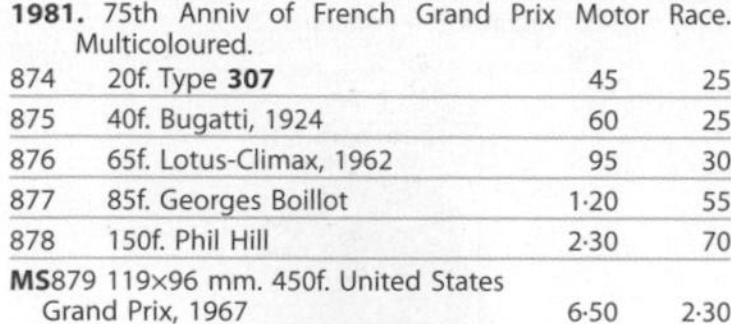

308 "Madonna and Child" (Botticelli)

1981. Christmas. Various Madonna and Child Paintings by named artists. Multicoloured.
880 100f. Type **308** 95 45
881 200f. Botticini 1·80 70
882 300f. Botticini (different) 2·75 1·00

309 Children watering Plants

1982. School Gardens. Multicoloured.
883 65f. Type **309** 60 30
884 85f. Tending plants and examining produce 90 50

310 Arturo Toscanini (conductor, 25th death anniv)

1982. Celebrities' Anniversaries. Multicoloured.
885 120f. Type **310** 1·70 55
886 140f. "Fruits on a Table" (Manet, 150th birth anniv) (horiz) 1·70 80
887 200f. "L'Estaque" (Braque, birth centenary) (horiz) 2·75 1·00
888 300f. George Washington (250th birth anniv) 3·75 1·30
889 400f. Goethe (poet, 150th death anniv) 5·00 1·70
890 500f. Princess of Wales (21st birthday) 5·50 2·00
MS891 80×104 mm. 500f. Princess of Wales (different) 4·50 1·70

311 Palace of Congresses

1982. Palace of Congresses.
892 **311** 150f. multicoloured 1·50 85

312 Martial Arts

1982. Seventh Youth Festival, Agadez. Multicoloured.
893 65f. Type **312** 55 25
894 100f. Traditional wrestling 95 60

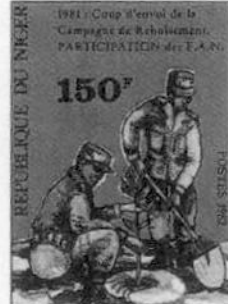

313 Planting a Tree

1982. National Re-afforestation Campaign. Multicoloured.
895 150f. Type **313** 1·50 55
896 200f. Forest and desert 1·80 85

314 Scouts in Pirogue

1982. 75th Anniv of Boy Scout Movement. Multicoloured.
897 65f. Type **314** 75 25
898 85f. Scouts in inflatable dinghy 1·00 25
899 130f. Scouts in canoe 1·30 55
900 200f. Scouts on raft 1·90 75
MS901 80×104 mm. 400f. Scouts on beach 4·00 2·00

315 Map of Africa showing Member States

1982. Economic Community of West African States.
902 **315** 200f. yellow, black and blue 1·80 90

316 Casting Net

1982. Niger Fishermen. Multicoloured.
903 65f. Type **316** 75 40
904 85f. Net fishing 95 55

1982. Birth of Prince William of Wales. Nos. 860/MS863 optd **NAISSANCE ROYALE 1982**.
905 **302** 150f. multicoloured 1·30 60
906 - 200f. multicoloured 2·00 85
907 - 300f. multicoloured 2·75 1·10
MS908 117×78 mm. 400f. multicoloured 3·75 3·50

318 Hands reaching towards Mosque

1982. 13th Islamic Foreign Ministers Meeting, Niamey.
909 **318** 100f. multicoloured 95 55

319 "Flautist"

1982. Norman Rockwell Paintings. Multicoloured.
910 65f. Type **319** 60 30
911 85f. "Clerk" 95 30
912 110f. "Teacher and Pupil" 1·20 35
913 150f. "Girl Shopper" 1·50 60

320 World Map and Satellite

1982. I.T.U. Delegates' Conference, Nairobi.
914 **320** 130f. blue, light blue and black 1·20 70

1982. World Cup Football Championship Winners. Nos. 868/MS873 optd.
915 40f. Type **306** 40 15
916 65f. Goalkeeper fighting for ball 55 25
917 85f. Passing ball 75 40
918 150f. Running with ball 1·50 60
919 300f. Jumping for ball 2·75 1·40
MS920 103×78 mm. 500f. Running for ball 4·50 4·50
OVERPRINTS: 40f. **1966 VAINQUEUR GRANDE - BRETAGNE**; 65f. **1970 VAINQUEUR BRESIL**; 85f. **1974 VAINQUEUR ALLEMAGNE (RFA)**; 150f. **1978 VAINQUEUR ARGENTINE**; 300f. **1982 VAINQUEUR ITALIE**. 500f. **ITALIE-ALLEMAGNE (RFA) 3I**.

322 Laboratory Workers with Microscopes

1982. Laboratory Work. Multicoloured.
921 65f. Type **322** 75 60
922 115f. Laboratory workers 1·20 80

323 "Adoration of the Kings"

1982. Air. Christmas. Paintings by Rubens. Multicoloured.
923 200f. Type **323** 1·80 45
924 300f. "Mystic Marriage of St. Catherine" 2·75 1·30
925 400f. "Virgin and Child" 4·00 1·10

324 Montgolfier Balloon

1983. Air. Bicent of Manned Flight. Multicoloured.
926 65f. Type **324** 55 25
927 85f. Charles's hydrogen balloon 55 25
928 200f. Goodyear Aerospace airship (horiz) 95 25
929 250f. Farman H.F.III biplane (horiz) 1·50 40
930 300f. Concorde 1·80 70
931 500f. "Apollo 11" spacecraft 2·75 80
No. 928 is wrongly inscribed "Zeppelin".

325 Harvesting Rice

1983. Self-sufficiency in Food. Multicoloured.
932 65f. Type **325** 3·75 90
933 85f. Planting rice 5·50 1·10

326 E.C.A. Anniversary Emblem

1983. 25th Anniv of Economic Commission for Africa.

934	**326**	120f. multicoloured	1·20	65
935	**326**	200f. multicoloured	1·80	90

327 "The Miraculous Draught of Fishes"

1983. 500th Birth Anniv of Raphael. Multicoloured.

936	65f. Type **327**	55	20
937	85f. "Grand Ducal Madonna" (vert)	75	20
938	100f. "The Deliverance of St. Peter"	95	35
939	150f. "Sistine Madonna" (vert)	1·40	55
940	200f. "The Fall on the Way to Calvary" (vert)	1·70	65
941	300f. "The Entombment"	2·50	90
942	400f. "The Transfiguration" (vert)	3·50	1·10
943	500f. "St. Michael fighting the Dragon" (vert)	4·75	1·40

328 Surveying

1983. The Army in the Service of Development. Multicoloured.

944	85f. Type **328**	75	45
945	150f. Road building	1·50	70

329 Palace of Justice

1983. Palace of Justice, Agadez.

946	**329**	65f. multicoloured	55	25

330 Javelin

1983. Air. Olympic Games, Los Angeles. Multicoloured.

947	85f. Type **330**	75	25
948	200f. Shotput	1·80	60
949	250f. Throwing the hammer (vert)	2·30	80
950	300f. Discus	2·75	90
MS951	104×80 mm. 500f. Shotput (different)	4·50	1·70

331 Rural Post Vehicle

1983. Rural Post Service. Multicoloured.

952	65f. Type **331**	55	25
953	100f. Post vehicle and map	95	45

332 Dome of the Rock

1983. Palestine.

954	**332**	65f. multicoloured	75	30

333 Class watching Television

1983. International Literacy Day. Multicoloured.

955	40f. Type **333**	45	10
956	65f. Teacher at blackboard (vert)	55	25
957	85f. Learning weights (vert)	95	45
958	100f. Outdoor class	95	55
959	150f. Woman reading magazine (vert)	1·50	70

334 Three Dancers

1983. 7Sevenh Dosso Dance Festival. Multicoloured.

960	65f. Type **334**	60	35
961	85f. Four dancers	95	55
962	120f. Two dancers	1·30	70

335 Post Van

1983. World Communications Year. Multicoloured.

963	80f. Type **335**	75	60
964	120f. Sorting letters	1·00	60
965	150f. W.C.Y. emblem (vert)	1·50	75

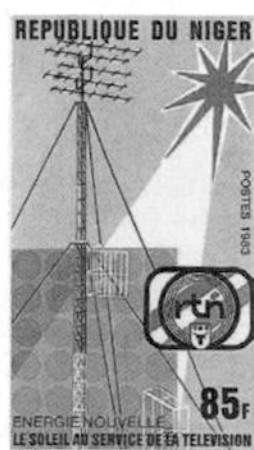

336 Television Antenna and Solar Panel

1983. Solar Energy in the Service of Television. Multicoloured.

966	85f. Type **336**	75	40
967	130f. Land-rover and solar panel	1·20	55

337 "Hypolimnas misippus"

1983. Butterflies. Multicoloured.

968	75f. Type **337**	1·00	45
969	120f. "Papilio demodocus"	1·50	70
970	250f. "Vanessa antiopa"	2·75	90
971	350f. "Charexes jasius"	3·75	1·40
972	500f. "Danaus chrisippus"	6·25	2·10

338 "Virgin and Child with Angels"

1983. Air. Christmas. Paintings by Botticelli. Multicoloured.

973	120f. Type **338**	1·20	50
974	350f. "Adoration of the Magi" (horiz)	3·75	1·00
975	500f. "Virgin of the Pomegranate"	4·50	1·80

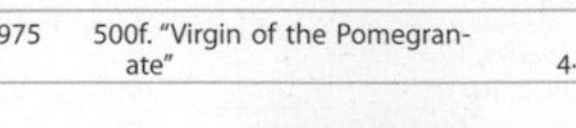

339 Samariya Emblem

1984. Samariya.

976	**339**	80f. black, orange & green	75	45

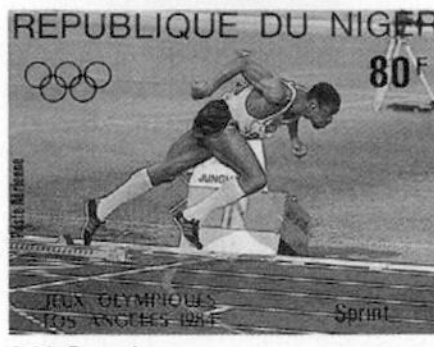

340 Running

1984. Air. Olympic Games, Los Angeles. Multicoloured.

977	80f. Type **340**	75	25
978	120f. Pole vault	1·00	25
979	140f. High jump	1·50	40
980	200f. Triple jump (vert)	1·70	55
981	350f. Long jump (vert)	3·50	1·30
MS982	104×79 mm. 500f. Hurdles	4·50	1·50

341 Boubon's Tetra

1984. Fish.

983	**341**	120f. multicoloured	2·75	80

342 Obstacle Course

1984. Military Pentathlon. Multicoloured.

984	120f. Type **342**	1·20	60
985	140f. Shooting	1·40	90

343 Radio Station

1984. New Radio Station.

986	**343**	120f. multicoloured	1·20	55

344 Flags, Agriculture and Symbols of Unity and Growth

1984. 25th Anniv of Council of Unity.

987	**344**	65f. multicoloured	60	35
988	**344**	85f. multicoloured	95	55

345 "Paris" (early steamer)

1984. Ships. Multicoloured.

989	80f. Type **345**	75	25
990	120f. "Jacques Coeur" (full-rigged ship)	95	40
991	150f. "Bosphorus" (full-rigged ship)	1·50	55
992	300f. "Comet" (full-rigged ship)	2·75	85

346 Daimler

1984. Motor Cars. Multicoloured.

993	100f. Type **346**	1·20	25
994	140f. Renault	1·40	45
995	250f. Delage "D 8"	2·40	80
996	400f. Maybach "Zeppelin"	3·75	1·40

347 "Rickmer Rickmers" (full-rigged ship)

1984. Universal Postal Union Congress, Hamburg.

997	**347**	300f. blue, brown and green	4·00	2·30

348 Cattle

1984. Ayerou Market. Multicoloured.

998	80f. Type **348**	95	60
999	120f. View of market	1·40	85

349 Viper

1984

1000	**349**	80f. multicoloured	1·20	70

350 Carl Lewis (100 and 200 m)

1984. Air. Olympic Games Medal Winners. Multicoloured.

1001	80f. Type **350**	70	35
1002	120f. J. Cruz (800 m)	1·20	50
1003	140f. A. Cova (10,000 m)	1·40	65
1004	300f. Al Joyner (Triple jump)	2·75	1·20
MS1005	101×78 mm. 500f. D. Mogenburg (high jump) (horiz)	4·50	2·75

351 Emblem

1984. Tenth Anniv of Economic Community of West Africa.

1006	**351**	80f. multicoloured	75	45

352 Emblem and Extract from General Kountche's Speech

1984. United Nations Disarmament Decennials.

1007	**352**	400f. black and green	3·75	1·70
1008	**352**	500f. black and blue	4·25	2·50

353 Football

1984. Air. Preliminary Rounds of World Cup Football Championship, Mexico.

1009	**353**	150f. multicoloured	1·50	60
1010	-	250f. multicoloured	2·50	1·00
1011	-	450f. multicoloured	4·00	1·70
1012	-	500f. multicoloured	4·50	2·00

DESIGNS: 250 to 500f. Footballing scenes.

354 "The Visitation" (Ghirlandaio)

1984. Air. Christmas. Multicoloured.

1013	100f. Type **354**	95	40
1014	200f. "Virgin and Child" (Master of Saint Verdiana)	2·00	85
1015	400f. "Virgin and Child" (J. Koning)	3·75	1·80

1984. Drought Relief. Nos. 895/6 optd **Aide au Sahel 84**.

1016	150f. multicoloured	1·70	1·10
1017	200f. multicoloured	2·20	1·50

356 Organization Emblem

1985. Tenth Anniv of World Tourism Organization.

1018	**356**	100f. black, orange and green	1·00	55

357 Breast-feeding Baby

1985. Infant Survival Campaign. Multicoloured.

1019	85f. Type **357**	85	40
1020	110f. Feeding baby and changing nappy	1·20	60

358 Black-necked Stilt

1985. Air. Birth Centenary of John J. Audubon (ornithologist). Multicoloured.

1021	110f. Type **358**	1·20	50
1022	140f. Greater flamingo (vert)	1·50	65
1023	200f. Atlantic puffin	2·00	90
1024	350f. Arctic tern (vert)	3·75	1·60

1985. International Exhibitions. Nos. **MS**814, **MS**848, **MS**879, **MS**901 and **MS**951 variously optd.

MS1025 Five sheets. (a) 400f. **MOPHILA'85 HAMBOURG**; (b) 425f. **TSUKUBA EXPO '85**. (c) 450f. **Italia '85 ROME** and emblem; (d) 500f. **ARGENTINA '85 BUENOS AIRES** and emblem; (e) 500f. **OLYMPHILEX '85 LAUSANNE** and emblem 26·00 26·00

360 Profile and Emblem

1985. 15th Anniv of Technical and Cultural Co-operation Agency.

1026	**360**	110f. brown, red & violet	95	55

361 Dancers

1985. Eighth Niamey Festival. Multicoloured.

1027	85f. Type **361**	75	55
1028	110f. Four dancers (vert)	95	70
1029	150f. Dancers (different)	1·50	85

362 Wolf ("White Fang") and Jack London

1985. International Youth Year. Multicoloured.

1030	85f. Type **362**	95	35
1031	105f. Woman with lion and Joseph Kessel	95	50
1032	250f. Capt. Ahab harpooning white whale ("Moby Dick")	2·75	1·10
1033	450f. Mowgli on elephant ("Jungle Book")	4·25	1·80

363 Two Children on Leaf

1985. "Philexafrique" Stamp Exhibition, Lome, Togo (1st issue). Multicoloured.

1034	200f. Type **363**	2·00	1·40
1035	200f. Mining	2·00	1·40

See also Nos. 1064/5.

364 "Hugo with his Son Francois" (A. de Chatillon)

1985. Death Centenary of Victor Hugo (writer).

1036	**364**	500f. multicoloured	5·75	2·20

365 French Turbotrain TGV 001, Satellite and Boeing 737 on Map

1985. Europafrique.

1037	**365**	110f. multicoloured	1·20	60

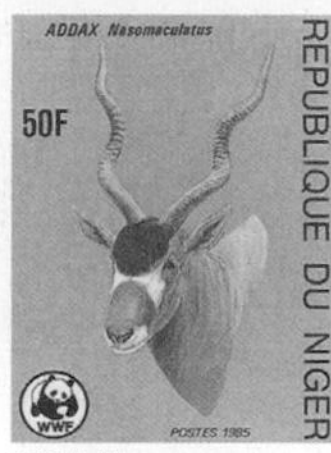

366 Addax

1985. Endangered Animals. Multicoloured.

1038	50f. Type **366**	2·75	40
1039	60f. Addax (different) (horiz)	3·25	55
1040	85f. Two scimitar oryxes (horiz)	4·75	70
1041	110f. Oryx	7·50	95

367 "Oedaleus sp" on Millet

1985. Vegetation Protection. Multicoloured.

1042	85f. Type **367**	1·00	40
1043	110f. "Dysdercus volkeri" (beetle)	1·40	70
1044	150f. Fungi attacking sorghum and millet (horiz)	1·80	80
1045	210f. Sudan golden sparrows in tree	2·50	1·10
1046	390f. Red-billed queleas in tree	4·50	2·50

368 Cross of Agadez

1985

1047	**368**	85f. green	75	25
1048	-	110f. brown	1·00	30

DESIGN: 110f. Girl carrying water jar on head.

369 Arms, Flags and Agriculture

1985. 25th Anniv of Independence.

1049	**369**	110f. multicoloured	1·20	60

370 Baobab

1985. Protected Trees. Multicoloured.

1050	110f. Type **370**	1·20	70
1051	210f. "Acacia albida"	2·00	1·40
1052	390f. Baobab (different)	4·25	2·20

371 Man watching Race

1985. Niamey–Bamako Powerboat Race. Multicoloured.

1053	110f. Type **371**	1·00	50
1054	150f. Helicopter and powerboat	1·50	75
1055	250f. Powerboat and map	2·50	1·40

1985. "Trees for Niger". As Nos. 1050/2 but new values and optd **DES ARBRES POUR LE NIGER**.

1056	**370**	30f. multicoloured	55	45
1057	-	85f. multicoloured	1·00	70
1058	-	110f. multicoloured	1·60	90

373 "Boletus"

1985. Fungi. Multicoloured.

1059	85f. Type **373**	1·00	45
1060	110f. "Hypholoma fasciculare"	1·50	55
1061	200f. "Coprinus comatus"	2·20	95
1062	300f. "Agaricus arvensis" (horiz)	3·75	1·60
1063	400f. "Geastrum fimbriatum" (horiz)	4·50	2·20

374 First Village Water Pump

1985. "Philexafrique" Stamp Exhibition, Lome, Togo (2nd issue). Multicoloured.

1064	250f. Type **374**	2·50	1·60
1065	250f. Handicapped youths playing dili (traditional game)	2·50	1·60

375 "Saving Ant" and Savings Bank Emblem

1985. World Savings Day.

1066	**375**	210f. multicoloured	2·00	1·10

376 Gouroumi

1985. Musical Instruments. Multicoloured.

1067	150f. Type **376**	1·50	90
1068	210f. Gassou (drums) (horiz)	2·20	1·30
1069	390f. Algaita (flute)	3·75	2·20
MS1070	114×79 mm. 500f. Biti (drums) (horiz)	5·00	4·25

377 "The Immaculate Conception"

1985. Air. Christmas. Paintings by Murillo. Multicoloured.

1071	110f. "Madonna of the Rosary"	95	40
1072	250f. Type **377**	2·30	1·00
1073	390f. "Virgin of Seville"	3·75	1·60

378 Comet over Paris, 1910

1985. Air. Appearance of Halley's Comet. Multicoloured.

1074	110f. Type **378**	1·00	45
1075	130f. Comet over New York	1·20	50
1076	200f. "Giotto" satellite	2·00	80
1077	300f. "Vega" satellite	3·00	1·20
1078	390f. "Planet A" space probe	4·00	1·60

379 National Identity Card

1986. Civil Statutes Reform. Each black, green and orange.

1079	85f. Type **379**	85	40
1080	110f. Civil registration emblem	1·20	55

380 Road Signs

1986. Road Safety Campaign.

1081	**380**	85f. black, yellow and red	80	40
1082	-	110f. black, red and green	1·20	55

DESIGN: 110f. Speed limit sign, road and speedometer ("Watch your speed").

381 Oumarou Ganda (film producer)

1986. Honoured Artists. Multicoloured.

1083	60f. Type **381**	55	25
1084	85f. Idi na Dadaou	75	45
1085	100f. Dan Gourmou	95	55
1086	130f. Koungoui (comedian)	1·40	80

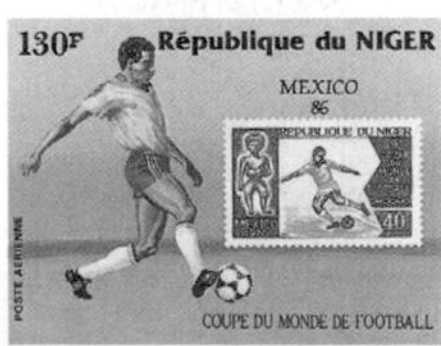
382 Martin Luther King

1986. Air. 18th Death Anniv of Martin Luther King (human rights activist).

1087	**382**	500f. multicoloured	4·50	2·20

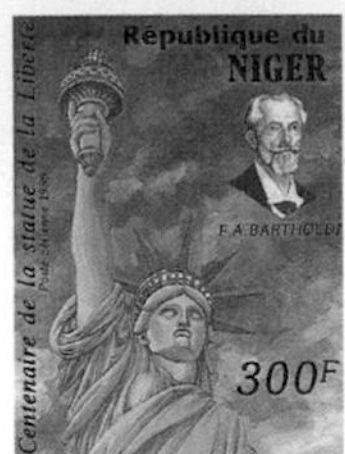
383 Footballer and 1970 40f. Stamp

1986. Air. World Cup Football Championship, Mexico. Multicoloured.

1088	130f. Type **383**	1·20	45
1089	210f. Footballer and 1970 70f. stamp	1·80	85
1090	390f. Footballer and 1970 90f. stamp	4·00	1·50
1091	400f. Footballer and Mexican figure on "stamp"	4·00	1·50
MS1092	102×78 mm. 500f. Footballer and trophy on "stamp"	4·50	3·00

384 Statue and F. A. Bartholdi

1986. Air. Centenary of Statue of Liberty.

1093	**384**	300f. multicoloured	3·00	1·50

385 Truck

1986. "Trucks of Hope". Multicoloured.

1094	85f. Type **385**	1·00	45
1095	110f. Mother and baby (vert)	1·30	60

386 Nelson Mandela and Walter Sisulu

1986. International Solidarity with S. African and Namibian Political Prisoners Day. Multicoloured.

1096	200f. Type **386**	2·20	1·00
1097	300f. Nelson Mandela	3·75	1·40

387 Food Co-operatives

1986. 40th Anniv of F.A.O. Multicoloured.

1098	50f. Type **387**	45	25
1099	60f. Anti-desertification campaign	55	40
1100	85f. Irrigation	95	55
1101	100f. Rebuilding herds of livestock	95	55
1102	110f. Reafforestation	1·20	70

388 Trees and Woman with Cooking Pots

1987. "For a Green Niger". Multicoloured.

1103	85f. Type **388**	1·00	45
1104	110f. Trees, woman and cooking pots (different)	1·30	65

389 *Sphodromantis* sp.

1987. Protection of Vegetation. Useful Insects. Multicoloured.

1105	85f. Type **389**	1·10	70
1106	110f. *Delta* sp.	1·50	90
1107	120f. *Cicindela* sp.	2·00	1·10

390 Transmitter, Map and Woman using Telephone

1987. Liptako–Gourma Telecommunications Network.

1108	**390**	110f. multicoloured	1·00	70

391 Morse Key and Operator, 19th-century

1987. 150th Anniv of Morse Telegraph. Multicoloured.

1109	120f. Type **391**	1·00	55
1110	200f. Samuel Morse (inventor) (vert)	1·80	80
1111	350f. Morse transmitter and receiver	3·25	1·60

392 Tennis Player

1987. Olympic Games, Seoul (1988). Multicoloured.

1112	85f. Type **392**	75	60
1113	110f. Pole vaulter	1·00	60
1114	250f. Footballer	2·50	1·20
MS1115	120×90 mm. 500f. Runner	4·50	4·00

393 Ice Hockey

1987. Winter Olympic Games, Calgary (1988) (1st issue). Multicoloured.

1116	85f. Type **393**	75	55
1117	110f. Speed skating	1·20	55
1118	250f. Figure skating (pairs)	2·30	1·20
MS1119	120×87 mm. 500f. Downhill skiing (51×30 mm)	4·50	4·00

See also Nos. 1146/**MS**1150.

394 Long-distance Running

1987. African Games, Nairobi. Multicoloured.

1120	85f. Type **394**	75	55
1121	110f. High jumping	95	55
1122	200f. Hurdling	2·00	95
1123	400f. Javelin throwing	3·75	1·90

395 Chief's Stool, Sceptre and Crown

1987. Tenth Anniv of National Tourism Office. Multicoloured.

1124	85f. Type **395**	75	45
1125	110f. Nomad, caravan and sceptre handle	95	55
1126	120f. Houses	1·20	60
1127	200f. Bridge over River Niger	2·00	1·00

396 Yaama Mosque at Dawn

1987. Aga Khan Prize.

1128	**396**	85f. multicoloured	75	55
1129	-	110f. multicoloured	95	55
1130	-	250f. multicoloured	2·75	1·20

DESIGNS: 110, 250f. Yaama mosque at various times of the day.

397 Court Building

1987. Appeal Court, Niamey. Multicoloured.

1131	85f. Type **397**	75	45
1132	110f. Front entrance	95	55
1133	140f. Side view	1·50	80

398 "Holy Family of the Sheep" (Raphael)

1997. Christmas. Multicoloured.

1134	110f. Type **398** (postage)	1·30	65
MS1135	1235×92 mm. 500f. "Adoration of the Magi" (detail) (Hans Memling) (30×51 mm) (air)	4·75	4·75

399 Water Drainage

1988. Health Care. Multicoloured.

1136	85f. Type **399**	1·20	80
1137	110f. Modern sanitation	1·50	85
1138	165f. Refuse collection	2·50	1·10

400 Singer and Band

1988. Award of Dan-Gourmou Music Prize.

1139	**400**	85f. multicoloured	1·50	90

1988. Winter Olympic Games Winners. Nos. 1116/18 optd.

1140	85f. **Medaille d'or URSS**	75	55
1141	110f. **Medaille d'or 5.000-10.000 m GUSTAFSON (Suede)**	95	70
1142	250f. **Medaille d'or E. GORDEEVA - S. GRINKOV URSS**	2·75	1·50

402 New Great Market, Niamey

1988

1143	**402**	85f. multicoloured	95	55

403 Mother and Child

1988. UNICEF Child Vaccination Campaign and 40th Anniv of W.H.O. Multicoloured.

1144	85f. Type **403**	80	55
1145	110f. Doctor and villagers	1·20	80

404 Kayak

1988. Air. Olympic Games, Seoul (2nd issue) and 125th Birth Anniv of Pierre de Coubertin (founder of modern Olympic Games). Multicoloured.

1146	85f. Type **404**	95	30
1147	165f. Rowing (horiz)	1·50	55
1148	200f. Two-man kayak (horiz)	2·00	70
1149	600f. One-man kayak	5·50	2·20
MS1150	105×80 mm. 750f. One-man kayak (different)	7·25	4·00

405 Emblem

1988. 25th Anniv of Organization of African Unity.

1151	**405**	85f. multicoloured	95	45

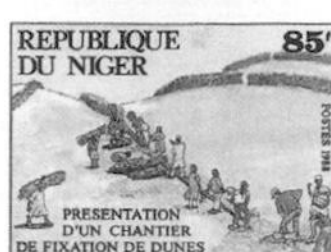

406 Team working

1988. Dune Stabilization.

1152	**406**	85f. multicoloured	1·20	70

407 Anniversary Emblem

1988. 125th Anniv of International Red Cross.

1153	**407**	85f. multicoloured	80	40
1154	**407**	110f. multicoloured	1·20	60

409 Emblem

1989. Niger Press Agency.

1159	**409**	85f. black, orange & grn	95	40

410 Couple, Globe and Laboratory Worker

1989. Campaign against AIDS.

1160	**410**	85f. multicoloured	85	35
1161	**410**	110f. multicoloured	1·30	55

411 Radar, Tanker and Signals

1989. 30th Anniv of International Maritime Organization.

1162	**411**	100f. multicoloured	95	45
1163	**411**	120f. multicoloured	1·30	65

412 General Ali Seybou (Pres.)

1989. 15th Anniv of Military Coup. Multicoloured.

1164		85f. Type **412**	75	35
1165		110f. Soldiers erecting flag	1·00	55

413 Eiffel Tower

1989. "Philexfrance 89" International Stamp Exhibition, Paris. Multicoloured.

1166		100f. Type **413**	95	60
1167		200f. Flags on stamps	2·00	85

414 "Planting a Tree of Liberty"

1989. Bicentenary of French Revolution.

1168	**414**	250f. multicoloured	3·00	1·60

415 Telephone Dial, Radio Mast, Map and Stamp

1989. 30th Anniv of West African Posts and Telecommunications Association.

1169	**415**	85f. multicoloured	95	45

416 "Apollo 11" Launch

1989. Air. 20th Anniv of First Manned Landing on Moon. Multicoloured.

1170		200f. Type **416**	1·80	75
1171		300f. Crew	2·75	1·00
1172		350f. Astronaut and module on lunar surface	3·25	1·20
1173		400f. Astronaut and U.S. flag on lunar surface	3·75	1·40

417 Emblem

1989. 25th Anniv of African Development Bank.

1174	**417**	100f. multicoloured	1·10	50

418 Before and After Attack, and "Schistocerca gregaria"

1989. Locusts.

1175	**418**	85f. multicoloured	1·20	70

419 Auguste Lumiere and 1st Cine Performance, 1895

1989. 35th Death Anniv of Auguste Lumiere and 125th Birth Anniv of Louis Lumiere (photo-graphy pioneers). Multicoloured.

1176		150f. Type **419**	1·70	80
1177		250f. Louis Lumiere and first cine-camera, 1894	2·75	1·40
1178		400f. Lumiere brothers and first colour cine-camera, 1920	4·75	2·00

420 Tractor, Map and Pump

1989. 30th Anniv of Agriculture Development Council.

1179	**420**	75f. multicoloured		23·00

421 Zinder Regional Museum

1989. Multicoloured.. Multicoloured..

1180		85f. Type **421**		23·00
1181		145f. Carawan	80·00	
1182		165f. Temet dunes	80·00	

422 "Russelia equisetiformis"

1989. Flowers. Multicoloured.

1183		10f. Type **422**	15	10
1184		20f. "Argyreia nervosa"	30	10
1185		30f. "Hibiscus rosa-sinensis"	30	25
1186		50f. "Catharanthus roseus"	50	25
1187		100f. "Cymothoe sangaris" (horiz)	1·30	55

423 Emblem

1990. Tenth Anniv of Pan-African Postal Union.

1188	**423**	120f. multicoloured	1·20	60

424 Adults learning Alphabet

1990. International Literacy Year. Multicoloured.

1189		85f. Type **424**	80	35
1190		110f. Adults learning arithmetic	1·20	50

425 Emblem

1990. 20th Anniv of Islamic Conference Organization.

1191	**425**	85f. multicoloured	95	45

426 Footballers and Florence

1990. Air. World Cup Football Championship, Italy. Multicoloured.

1192		130f. Type **426**	1·20	55
1193		210f. Footballers and Verona	2·00	70
1194		500f. Footballers and Bari	4·75	80
1195		600f. Footballers and Rome	5·25	1·40

427 Leland and Child

1990. Mickey Leland (American Congressman) Commemoration.

1196	**427**	300f. multicoloured	2·75	1·40
1197	**427**	500f. multicoloured	4·75	2·20

428 Emblem

1990. First Anniv of National Movement for the Development Society.

1198	**428**	85f. multicoloured	95	45

429 Flags and Envelopes on Map

1990. 20th Anniv of Multinational Postal Training School, Abidjan.

1199	**429**	85f. multicoloured	95	50

430 Gymnastics

1990. Olympic Games, Barcelona (1992). Multicoloured.

1200		85f. Type **430**	75	30
1201		110f. Hurdling	1·20	35
1202		250f. Running	2·30	1·00
1203		400f. Show jumping	3·75	1·40
1204		500f. Long jumping	4·75	1·70
MS1205		92×70 mm. 600f. Cycling	5·75	4·25

431 Arms, Map and Flag

1990. 30th Anniv of Independence.

1206	**431**	85f. multicoloured	80	40
1207	**431**	110f. multicoloured	1·20	60

432 Emblem

1990. 40th Anniv of United Nations Development Programme.

1208	**432**	100f. multicoloured	95	45

433 The Blusher

1991. Butterflies and Fungi. Multicoloured.

1209		85f. Type **433** (postage)	1·00	25
1210		110f. "Graphium pylades" (female)	1·10	25
1211		200f. "Pseudacraea hostilia"	2·30	65
1212		250f. Cracked green russula	2·50	80
1213		400f. "Boletus impolitus" (air)	3·75	1·30
1214		500f. "Precis octavia"	4·50	1·20
MS1215		98×85 mm. 600f. "Pseudacraea boisduvali" (female) and "Chanterelle" ("Cantharellus cibarius") (29×37 mm)	6·00	3·75

434 Christopher Columbus and "Santa Maria"

1991. 540th Birth of Christopher Columbus. Multicoloured.

1216	85f. Type **434** (postage)	80	25
1217	110f. 15th-century Portuguese caravel	1·00	25
1218	200f. 16th-century four-masted caravel	1·80	60
1219	250f. "Estremadura" (Spanish caravel), 1511	2·50	75
1220	400f. "Vija" (Portuguese caravel), 1600 (air)	3·75	90
1221	500f. "Pinta"	4·50	1·30
MS1222	108×68 mm. 600f. "Nina"	6·50	4·00

435 Speed Skating

1991. Winter Olympic Games, Albertville (1992). Multicoloured.

1223	110f. Type **435**	1·10	45
1224	300f. Ice-hockey	2·75	1·30
1225	500f. Women's downhill skiing	4·50	1·80
1226	600f. Two-man luge	5·25	1·80

436 Flag and Boy holding Stone

1991. Palestinian "Intifada" Movement.

1227	**436**	110f. multicoloured	1·20	55

437 Hairstyle

1991. Traditional Hairstyles. Multicoloured.

1228	85f. Type **437**	2·00	55
1229	110f. Netted hairstyle	1·50	45
1230	165f. Braided hairstyle	2·20	75
1231	200f. Plaited hairstyle	2·50	1·00

438 Boubon Market

1991. African Tourism Year. Multicoloured.

1232	85f. Type **438**	85	35
1233	110f. Timia waterfalls (vert)	1·20	55
1234	130f. Ruins at Assode	1·50	70
1235	200f. Tourism Year emblem (vert)	2·50	1·10

439 Anatoly Karpov and Gary Kasparov

1991. Anniversaries and Events. Multicoloured.

1236	85f. Type **439** (World Chess Championship) (postage)	75	25
1237	110f. Ayrton Senna and Alain Prost (World Formula 1 motor racing championship)	1·20	40
1238	200f. Reading of Declaration of Human Rights and Comte de Mirabeau (bicentenary of French Revolution)	1·80	40
1239	250f. Dwight D. Eisenhower, Winston Churchill and Field-Marshal Montgomery (50th anniv of America's entry into Second World War)	5·00	1·10
1240	400f. Charles de Gaulle and Konrad Adenauer (28th anniv of Franco-German Co-operation Agreement) (air)	5·50	90
1241	500f. Helmut Kohl and Brandenburg Gate (2nd anniv of German reunification)	6·00	1·10
MS1242	119×56 mm. 600f. Pope John Paul II (visit to Africa)	6·25	6·25

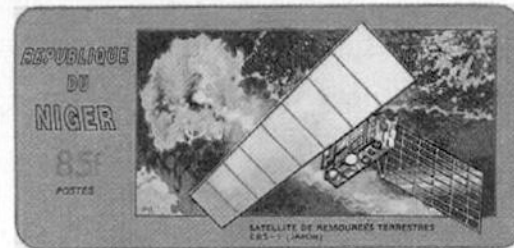

440 Japanese "ERS-1" Satellite

1991. Satellites and Transport. Multicoloured.

1243	85f. Type **440** (postage)	75	25
1244	110f. Japanese satellite observing Aurora Borealis	95	25
1245	200f. Louis Favre and "BB 415" diesel locomotive	2·20	45
1246	250f. "BB-BB 301" diesel locomotive	2·75	70
1247	400f. "BB 302" diesel locomotive (air)	4·25	90
1248	500f. Lockheed Stealth fighter-bomber and Concorde	4·50	1·10
MS1249	120×86 mm. 600f. George Nagelmacker and "Orient Express"	6·00	3·75

441 Crowd and Emblem on Map

1991. National Conference (to determine new constitution).

1250	**441**	85f. multicoloured	95	45

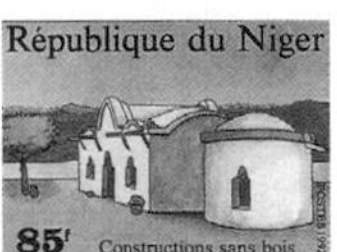

442 Timberless House

1992

1251	**442**	85f. multicoloured	95	45

443 Couple adding Final Piece to Globe Jigsaw

1992. World Population Day. Multicoloured.

1252	85f. Type **443**	85	45
1253	110f. Children flying globe kite (after Robert Parker)	1·20	50

444 Columbus and Fleet

1992. 500th Anniv of Discovery of America by Columbus.

1254	**444**	250f. multicoloured	2·75	1·20

445 Zaleye

1992. Second Death Anniv of Hadjia Haqua Issa (Zaleye) (singer).

1255	**445**	150f. multicoloured	1·50	70

446 Conference Emblem

1992. International Nutrition Conference, Rome.

1256	**446**	145f. multicoloured	1·50	70
1257	**446**	350f. multicoloured	3·50	1·50

447 College Emblem

1993. 30th Anniv of African Meteorology and Civil Aviation College.

1258	**447**	110f. blue, black & green	95	55

448 Girl planting Sapling

1993. Anti-desertification Campaign.

1259	**448**	85f. multicoloured	75	55
1260	**448**	165f. multicoloured	1·70	80

449 Aerosol spraying Globe (Patricia Charets)

1993. World Population Day. Children's Drawings. Multicoloured.

1261	85f. Type **449**	85	45
1262	110f. Tree and person with globe as head looking at high-rise tower blocks (Mathieu Chevrault)	1·20	70

450 Jerusalem

1993. "Jerusalem, Holy City".

1268	**450**	110f. multicoloured	1·20	70

451 People of Different Races

1994. Award of Nobel Peace Prize to Nelson Mandela and F. W. de Klerk (South African statesmen).

1269	**451**	270f. multicoloured	1·50	80

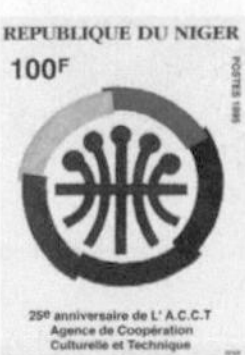

452 Emblem

1995. 25th Anniv of ACCT (cooperation and cultural agency).

1270	**452**	100f. multicoloured

453 Map enclosing Figures

1995. 20th Anniv ECOWAS Commission.

1271	**453**	125f. multicoloured

454 Replenishment of Stock

1995. Agriculture. Multicoloured.

1272	125f. Type **454**
1273	300f. Irrigation

455 Emblem

1995. 30th Anniv of African Development Bank.

1274	**455**	300f. emerald and scarlet

456 Donkey Cart

1995. Children's Drawings. Multicoloured.

1275	500f. Type **456**
1276	1000f. Courtesan's Mount

457 Race Car

1997. Agades–Dakar Rally. Multicoloured.

1277	125f. Type **457**
1278	175f. Quad bike
1279	300f. Lorry
1280	500f. Motor cycle
MS1281	113×117 mm. Nos. 1277/80

458 *Tockus nastus* (grey hornbill)

1997. Birds. Multicoloured.

1282	5f. Type **458**
1283	15f. *Psittacula krameri* (ring-necked parakeet)
1284	25f. *Coracias abyssinica* (Abyssinian roller)
1285	35f. *Bubulcus ibis* (inscr 'Bubulcus ibis') (cattle egret)

459 Abdou Moumouni Dioffo

1998. Abdou Moumouni Dioffo (university president) Commemoration.

1286	**459**	125f. multicoloured

461 Ibrahim Bare Mainassara

1998. Ibrahim Bare Mainassara (president 1996–1999).

1290	**461**	500f. multicoloured

Nos. 1287/9 and Type **460** have been left for 'Flowers', issued on 17 June 1998, not yet received

462 Woman and Cloth

1998. FIMA NIGER 98–International African Fashion Festival, Tiguidit and Agades. Multicoloured.

1291	175f. Type **462**
1292	225f. Woman and desert

463 1849 20c. Stamp of France (As No. 6)

1999. 150th Anniv of First French Stamp.

1293	**463**	200f. multicoloured

464 Couple and Farmer

1999. 40th Anniv of Council for Rural Development.

1294	**464**	150f. multicoloured
1295	**464**	175f. multicoloured

465 Tracks in Sand

2000. International Day against Deserts and Desertification. Multicoloured.

1296	150f. Type **465**
1297	200f. Figures and scrub
1298	225f. Open landscape

466 Air Mountains, Chiriet

2001

1299	**466**	150f. multicoloured

467 Emblem

2001. International Year of Volunteers.

1300	**467**	150f. multicoloured

468 Cow's Head

2002

1301	**468**	50f. multicoloured

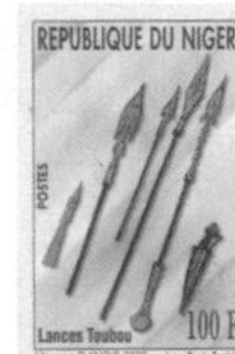

469 Tobou Spears

2002

1302	**469**	100f. multicoloured

470 Birds

2002

1303	**470**	225f. multicoloured

471 Hippopotamus

2000. Hippopotamas in Captivity

1304	**471**	100f. multicoloured

472 Cow

2001. Boudouma Cattle. Multicoloured.

1305	150f. Type **472**
1306	225f. Calf (35××35 mm)

479 Messenger from Madaoua

2006. Messenger from Madaoua

1316	**479**	25f. multicoloured

480 Decorated Pots

2006. Pottery

1317	**480**	150f. multicoloured

481 Camel Driver of Tahoua

2006. Camel Driver of Tahoua

1318	**481**	1000f. multicoloured

482 Emblem

2007. 24th UPU Congress, Nairobi

1319	**482**	500f. multicoloured

483 Giraffes

2007. African Fauna. Multicoloured.

1320	200f. Type **483**
1321	400f. Addax
1322	600f. Ostriches

484 Women pounding Meal, Bathing Child and Cow grazing

2008. Village Life

1323	**484**	100f. multicoloured

485 Dancers

2008. Bororo Dance

1324	**485**	350f. multicoloured

486 Mounted Warriors

2008. Bodyguard to Traditional Leaders

1325	**486**	1000f. multicoloured

487 Young Bororos drawing Water

2009. Young Bororos at the Well

1326	**487**	300f. multicoloured

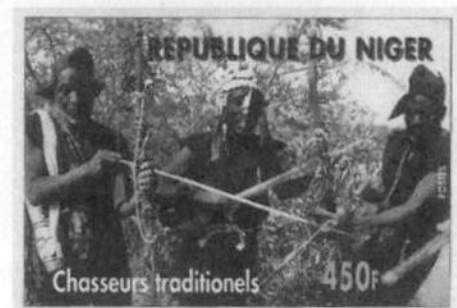

488 Traditional Hunters

2009. Traditional Hunters

1327	**488**	450f. multicoloured

489 Baobab Tree of the Sahel

2010. Baobab Tree of the Sahel

1328	**489**	500f. multicoloured

490 Téra-téra Blanket

2010. Cultural Heritage

1329	**490**	700f. multicoloured

491 Two Women

2010. Cultural Heritage. Traditional Hairstyles

1330	**491**	1500f. multicoloured

492 Anniversary Emblem

2010. 50th Anniv of Independence

1331	**492**	1000f. multicoloured

OFFICIAL STAMPS

O13 Djerma Women

1962. Figures of value in black.

O121	**O13**	1f. violet	10	10
O122	**O13**	2f. green	10	10
O123	**O13**	5f. blue	10	10
O124	**O13**	10f. red	30	10
O125	**O13**	20f. blue	30	25
O126	**O13**	25f. orange	30	25
O127	**O13**	30f. blue	45	25
O128	**O13**	35f. green	55	40
O129	**O13**	40f. brown	55	40
O130	**O13**	50f. slate	55	40
O131	**O13**	60f. turquoise	75	45
O132	**O13**	85f. turquoise	1·00	45
O133	**O13**	100f. purple	1·20	45
O134	**O13**	200f. blue	2·50	95

1988. As Type **O13**, but figures of value in same colour as remainder of design.

O1155	5f. blue	10	10
O1156	10f. red	20	15
O1157	15f. yellow	15	15
O1158	20f. blue	30	15
O1159	45f. orange	45	25
O1160	50f. green	60	25

POSTAGE DUE STAMPS

1921. Postage Due stamps of Upper Senegal and Niger "Figure" key-type optd **TERRITOIRE DU NIGER.**

D18	**M**	5c. green	45	6·25
D19	**M**	10c. red	65	6·25
D20	**M**	15c. grey	60	6·00
D21	**M**	20c. brown	35	4·00
D22	**M**	30c. blue	90	4·75
D23	**M**	50c. black	1·30	5·75
D24	**M**	60c. orange	1·30	9·00
D25	**M**	1f. violet	1·40	6·00

D6 Zinder Fort

1927

D73	**D6**	2c. red and blue	20	4·25
D74	**D6**	4c. black and orange	20	3·25
D75	**D6**	5c. violet and yellow	35	4·25
D76	**D6**	10c. violet and red	20	3·25
D77	**D6**	15c. orange and green	35	5·75
D78	**D6**	20c. sepia and red	35	3·50
D79	**D6**	25c. sepia and black	35	3·75
D80	**D6**	30c. grey and violet	65	6·50
D81	**D6**	50c. red on green	55	8·00
D82	**D6**	60c. orange & lilac on bl	45	7·25
D83	**D6**	1f. violet & blue on blue	1·10	4·25
D84	**D6**	2f. mauve and red	1·70	8·50
D85	**D6**	3f. blue and brown	2·00	9·25

D13 Cross of Agadez

1962

D123	**D13**	50c. green	15	15
D124	**D13**	1f. violet	15	15
D125	**D13**	2f. myrtle	15	15
D126	**A**	3f. mauve	15	15
D127	**A**	5f. green	30	25
D128	**A**	10f. orange	30	25
D129	**B**	15f. blue	30	25
D130	**B**	20f. red	30	25
D131	**B**	50f. brown	50	50

DESIGNS: A, Cross of Iferouane; B, Cross of Tahoua.

D450 Cross of Iferouane

1993

D1263	**D450**	5f. multicoloured	10	10
D1264	**D450**	10f. orange and black	10	10
D1265	-	15f. multicoloured	10	10
D1266	-	20f. mve, yell & blk	15	15
D1267	-	50f. multicoloured	45	40

DESIGN: 15 to 50f. Cross of Tahoua.

APPENDIX

The following stamps have either been issued in excess of postal needs, or have not been available to the public in reasonable quantities at face value. Such stamps may later be given full listings if there is evidence of regular postal use. Miniature sheets and imperforate stamps are excluded from this listing.

1994

Entertainers. 175, 300, 400, 600, 700f.×2; 750f.; 800f.×2

1996

World Scout Jamboree, Netherlands. 350, 500f.
90th Anniv of Rotary International.150, 200f.×2; 700, 900, 1000f.
80th Anniv of Lions International. 300, 600f.
50th Anniv of United Nations and UNICEF. 150, 22, 475, 550f.
Red Cross. 250, 400f.
Winter Olympic Games, Nagano (1st issue). Overprinted in red or blue. 85, 200, 400, 500f.
Sport. 300, 450, 500, 700f.
Olympic Games, Atlanta. 250, 350, 400, 600f.
Football World Cup, France. 125f.; 175f.; 750f.; 1000f.
Winter Olympic Games, Nagano (2nd issue). 125, 175, 700, 800f.
Traditional Musical Instruments. 125, 175f.
Butterflies. 150f, 200, 750, 800f.

1997

Chinese New Year. Year of the Ox. 500f.×2

1998

Diana, Princess of Wales. 180f.×4
Gazelles. 250f.×4
Birds. 5, 15, 25, 35f.

Pt. 1

NIGER COAST PROTECTORATE

A district on the west coast of Africa. In 1900 became part of Southern Nigeria.

12 pence = 1 shilling; 20 pence = 1 pound.

1892. Stamps of Gt. Britain (Queen Victoria) optd **BRITISH PROTECTORATE OIL RIVERS.**

1	**71**	½d. red	21·00	13·00
2	**57**	1d. lilac	13·00	11·00
3	**73**	2d. green and red	35·00	9·00
4	**74**	2½d. purple and blue	9·50	2·50
5	**78**	5d. purple and blue	19·00	6·50
6	**82**	1s. green	70·00	90·00

1893. Half of No. 2 surch **½d.**

7	**57**	½d. on half of 1d. lilac	£160	£140

1893. Nos. 1 to 6 surch in words (½d., 1s.) or figures (others).

20	**73**	½d. on 2d. green and red	£475	£250
21	**74**	½d. on 2½d. purple on blue	£375	£180
37	**73**	1s. on 2d. green and red	£450	£375
40	**73**	5s. on 2d. green and red	£9000	£11000
41	**78**	10s. on 5d. purple and blue	£6500	£10000
42	**82**	20s. on 1s. green	£140000	

13

1893. Various frames with "OIL RIVERS" barred out and "NIGER COAST" above.

45a	**13**	½d. red	7·00	12·00
46c	**13**	1d. blue	4·00	4·75
47d	**13**	2d. green	19·00	17·00
48	**13**	2½d. red	17·00	4·25
49b	**13**	5d. lilac	22·00	13·00
50	**13**	1s. black	14·00	15·00

14

1894. Various frames.

66	**14**	½d. green	7·50	1·50
67d	**14**	1d. red	2·50	2·75
68	**14**	2d. red	4·00	2·00
69	**14**	2½d. blue	7·50	2·50
55a	**14**	5d. purple	9·00	5·50
71	**14**	6d. brown	7·00	8·00
72	**14**	1s. black	15·00	29·00
73b	**14**	2s.6d. brown	22·00	90·00
74ba	**14**	10s. violet	£120	£200

1894. Surch with large figures.

58	½ on half 1d. (No. 46)	£1200	£375
59	1 on half 2d. (No. 2)	£1700	£375

1894. No. 67 bisected and surch.

64	½d. on half of 1d. red	£3500	£500

1894. Surch **ONE HALF PENNY** and bars.

65	½d. on 2½d. blue	£425	£250

Pt. 1

NIGERIA

A former British colony on the west coast of Africa, comprising the territories of Northern and Southern Nigeria and Lagos. Attained full independence within the British Commonwealth in 1960 and became a Federal Republic in 1963.

The Eastern Region (known as Biafra (q.v.)) seceded in 1967, remaining independent until overrun by Federal Nigerian troops during January 1970.

1914. 12 pence = 1 shilling; 20 shillings = 1 pound.
1973. 100 kobo = 1 naira.

1

1914

15	**1**	½d. green	1·25	40
16b	**1**	1d. red	1·75	35
17	**1**	1½d. orange	7·50	15
18	**1**	2d. grey	1·50	8·00
20	**1**	2d. brown	3·00	15
21	**1**	2½d. blue	1·25	11·00
5a	**1**	3d. purple on yellow	1·50	2·75
22	**1**	3d. violet	6·00	3·50
23	**1**	3d. blue	10·00	1·00
24	**1**	4d. black and red on yellow	65	55
25a	**1**	6d. purple	7·00	8·00
26	**1**	1s. black on green	4·75	2·00
9	**1**	2s.6d. black and red on blue	16·00	6·50
10	**1**	5s. green and red on yellow	22·00	60·00
11d	**1**	10s. green and red on green	35·00	£120
12a	**1**	£1 purple and black on red	£225	£250

1935. Silver Jubilee. As T **143a** of Newfoundland.

30	1½d. blue and grey	1·00	1·50
31	2d. green and blue	2·00	2·00
32	3d. brown and blue	3·25	19·00
33	1s. grey and purple	9·25	42·00

3 Apapa Wharf **11** Victoria–Buea Road

1936

34	**3**	½d. green	1·50	1·40
35	-	1d. red	50	40
36	-	1½d. brown	2·00	40
37	-	2d. black	50	80
38	-	3d. blue	2·00	1·50
39	-	4d. brown	2·25	2·00
40	-	6d. violet	50	60
41	-	1s. green	1·75	4·75
42	**11**	2s.6d. black and blue	7·00	38·00
43	-	5s. black and green	19·00	55·00
44	-	10s. black and grey	85·00	£130
45	-	£1 black and orange	£120	£190

DESIGNS—VERT: 1d. Cocoa; 1½d. Tin dredger; 2d. Timber industry; 3d. Fishing village; 4d. Cotton ginnery; 6d. Habe minaret; 1s. Fulani cattle. HORIZ: 5s. Oil palms; 10s. River Niger at Jebba; £1 Canoe pulling.

1937. Coronation. As T **143b** of Newfoundland.

46	1d. red	1·00	2·50
47	1½d. brown	3·00	3·00
48	3d. blue	3·00	5·50

15 King George VI

1938

49	**15**	½d. green	10	10
50a	**15**	1d. red	75	30
50b	**15**	1d. lilac	10	20
51a	**15**	1½d. brown	20	10
52	**15**	2d. black	10	3·25
52ab	**15**	2d. red	50	70
52b	**15**	2½d. orange	10	3·00
53	**15**	3d. blue	10	10
53b	**15**	3d. black	15	3·25
54	**15**	4d. orange	50·00	3·75
54a	**15**	4d. blue	15	4·50
55	**15**	6d. purple	40	10
56	**15**	1s. olive	60	10
57	**15**	1s.3d. blue	1·00	30
58b	-	2s.6d. black and blue	3·25	3·50
59a	-	5s. black and orange	7·50	4·50

DESIGNS: 2s.6d., 5s. As Nos. 42 and 44 but with portrait of King George VI.

1946. Victory. As T **4a** of Pitcairn Islands.

60	1½d. brown	50	10
61	4d. blue	50	2·50

1948. Royal Silver Wedding. As T **4b/4c** of Pitcairn Islands.

62	1d. mauve	35	40
63	5s. orange	17·00	24·00

1949. U.P.U. As T **4d/4g** of Pitcairn Islands.

64	1d. purple	15	30
65	3d. blue	1·25	3·75
66	6d. purple	30	3·75
67	1s. olive	50	2·00

1953. Coronation. As T **4h** of Pitcairn Islands.

68	1½d. black and green	50	10

18 Old Manilla Currency

26 Victoria Harbour

29 New and Old Lagos

1953

69	**18**	½d. black and orange	15	30
70	-	1d. black and bronze	20	10
71	-	1½d. turquoise	50	40
72	-	2d. black and ochre	4·00	30
72c	-	2d. slate	3·00	2·00
73	-	3d. black and purple	55	10
74	-	4d. black and blue	2·50	20
75	-	6d. brown and black	30	10
76	-	1s. black and purple	50	10
77	**26**	2s.6d. black and green	16·00	1·25
78	-	5s. black and orange	5·50	1·40
79	-	10s. black and brown	24·00	3·25
80	**29**	£1 black and violet	35·00	16·00

DESIGNS—HORIZ (As Type **18**): 1d. Bornu horsemen; 1½d. "Groundnuts"; 2d. "Tin"; 3d. Jebba Bridge and R. Niger; 4d. "Cocoa"; 1s. "Timber". (As Type **26**): 5s. "Palm oil"; 10s. "Hides and skins". VERT (As Type **18**): 6d. Ife bronze.

1956. Royal Visit. No. 72 optd **ROYAL VISIT 1956.**

81	2d. black and ochre	40	30

31 Victoria Harbour

1958. Centenary of Victoria, S. Cameroons.

82	**31**	3d. black and purple	40	30

32 Lugard Hall

1959. Attainment of Self-government. Northern Region of Nigeria.

83	**32**	3d. black and purple	30	10
84	-	1s. black and green	95	60

DESIGN: 1s. Kano Mosque.

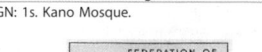

35 Legislative Building

1960. Independence Commemoration.

85	**35**	1d. black and red	10	10
86	-	3d. black and blue	15	10
87	-	6d. green and brown	20	20
88	-	1s.3d. blue and yellow	40	20

DESIGNS—As Type **35**: 3d. African paddling canoe; 6d. Federal Supreme Court. LARGER (40×24 mm): 1s.3d. Dove, torch and map.

39 Groundnuts **48** Central Bank

1961

89	**39**	½d. green	10	60
90	-	1d. violet	80	10
91	-	1½d. red	80	2·25
92	-	2d. blue	30	10
93	-	3d. green	40	10
94	-	4d. blue	40	2·00
95	-	6d. yellow and black	80	10
96	-	1s. green	4·50	10

97	-	1s.3d. orange	1·50	10
98	**48**	2s.6d. black and yellow	2·75	15
99	-	5s. black and green	65	1·25
100	-	10s. black and blue	3·75	4·25
101	-	£1 black and red	14·00	18·00

DESIGNS—VERT (as Type **39**): 1d. Coal mining; 1½d. Adult education; 2d, Pottery; 3d. Oyo carver; 4d. Weaving; 6d. Benin mask; 1s. Yellow casqued hornbill; 1s.3d. Camel train. HORIZ (as Type **48**: 5s. Nigeria Museum; 10s. Kano airport; £1 Lagos railway station.

52 Globe and Diesel-electric Locomotive

1961. Admission into U.P.U. Inscr as in T **52**.

102	**52**	1d. orange and blue	30	10
103	-	3d. olive and black	30	10
104	-	1s.3d. blue and red	80	20
105	-	2s.6d. green and blue	85	2·00

DESIGNS: 3d. Globe and mail van; 1s.3d. Globe and Bristol 175 Britannia aircraft; 2s.6d. Globe and liner.

56 Coat of Arms

1961. First Anniv of Independence.

106	**56**	3d. multicoloured	10	10
107	-	4d. green and orange	30	50
108	-	6d. green	40	10
109	-	1s.3d. grey and blue	45	10
110	-	2s.6d. green and blue	55	1·75

DESIGNS—HORIZ: 4d. Natural resources map; 6d. Nigerian eagle; 1s 3d. Eagles in flight; 2s.6d. Nigerians and flag.

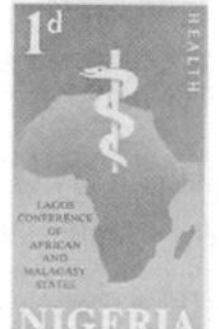

61 "Health"

1962. Lagos Conf of African and Malagasy States.

111	**61**	1d. bistre	10	10
112	-	3d. purple	10	10
113	-	6d. green	15	10
114	-	1s. brown	20	10
115	-	1s.3d. blue	25	20

DESIGNS: Map and emblems symbolising Culture (3d.); Commerce (6d.); Communications (1s.); Co-operation (1s.3d.).

66 Malaria Eradication Emblem and Parasites

1962. Malaria Eradication.

116	**66**	3d. green and red	15	10
117	-	6d. blue and purple	20	10
118	-	1s.3d. mauve and blue	30	10
119	-	2s.6d. blue and brown	45	90

DESIGNS (embodying emblem): 6d. Insecticide-spraying; 1s.3d. Aerial spraying; 2s.6d. Mother, child and microscope.

70 National Monument

1962. Second Anniv of Independence.

120	**70**	3d. green and blue	10	10
121	-	5s. red, green and violet	1·00	1·00

DESIGN—VERT: 5s. Benin bronze.

72 Fair Emblem

1962. International Trade Fair, Lagos.

122	**72**	1d. red and olive	10	10
123	-	6d. black and red	15	10
124	-	1s. black and brown	15	10
125	-	2s.6d. yellow and blue	60	20

DESIGNS—HORIZ: 6d. "Cogwheels of Industry"; 1s. "Cornucopia of Industry"; 2s.6d. Oilwells and tanker.

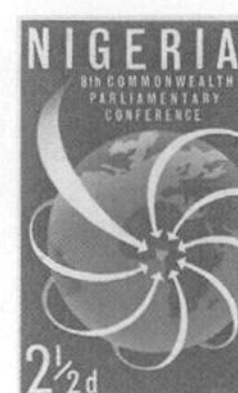

76 "Arrival of Delegates"

1962. Eighth Commonwealth Parliamentary Conference, Lagos.

126	**76**	2½d. blue	15	1·10
127	-	4d. blue and rose	15	30
128	-	1s.3d. sepia and yellow	20	20

DESIGNS—HORIZ: 4d. National Hall. VERT: 1s.3d. Mace as Palm Tree.

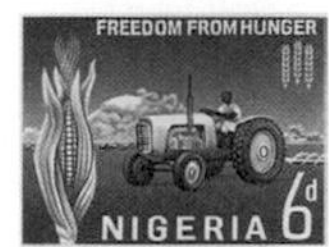

80 Tractor and Maize

1963. Freedom from Hunger.

129		3d. olive	2·00	20
130	**80**	6d. mauve	2·25	20

DESIGN—VERT: 3d. Herdsman.

81 Mercury Capsule and Kano Tracking Station

1963. "Peaceful Use of Outer Space".

131	**81**	6d. blue and green	25	10
132	-	1s.3d. black and turquoise	35	20

DESIGN: 1s.3d. Satellite and Lagos Harbour.

83 Scouts shaking Hands

1963. 11th World Scout Jamboree. Marathon.

133	**83**	3d. red and bronze	30	20
134	-	1s. black and red	95	80
MS134a		93×95 mm. Nos. 133/4	1·75	1·75

DESIGN: 1s. Campfire.

85 Emblem and First Aid Team

1963. Centenary of Red Cross.

135	**85**	3d. red and blue	60	10
136	-	6d. red and green	80	10
137	-	1s.3d. red and sepia	1·00	70
MS137a		102×102 mm. No. 137 (block of four)	8·50	11·00

DESIGNS: 6d. Emblem and "Hospital Services"; 1s.3d. Patient and emblem.

88 President Azikiwe and State House

1963. Republic Day.

138	**88**	3d. olive and green	10	10
139	-	1s.3d. brown and sepia	10	10
140	-	2s.6d. turquoise and blue	15	15

The buildings on the 1s.3d. and the 2s.6d. are the Federal Supreme Court and the Parliament Building respectively.

90 "Freedom of worship"

1963. 15th Anniv of Declaration of Human Rights.

141		3d. red	10	10
142	**90**	6d. green	15	10
143	-	1s.3d. blue	30	10
144	-	2s.6d. purple	45	30

DESIGNS—HORIZ: 3d. (Inscr "1948–1963"), Charter and broken whip. VERT: 1s.3d. "Freedom from Want"; 2s.6d. "Freedom of Speech".

93 Queen Nefertari

1964. Nubian Monuments Preservation.

145	**93**	6d. olive and green	50	10
146	-	2s.6d. brown, olive & green	1·75	2·25

DESIGN: 2s.6d. Rameses II.

95 President Kennedy

1964. Pres. Kennedy Memorial Issue.

147	**95**	1s.3d. lilac and black	30	15
148	-	2s.6d. multicoloured	40	65
149	-	5s. multicoloured	70	1·75
MS149a		154×135 mm. No. 149 (block of four). Imperf	7·00	12·00

DESIGNS: 2s.6d. Kennedy and flags; 5s. Kennedy (U.S. coin head) and flags.

98 President Azikiwe

1964. First Anniv of Republic.

150	**98**	3d. brown	10	10
151	-	1s.3d. green	35	10
152	-	2s.6d. green	70	90

DESIGNS—25×42 mm: 1s.3d. Herbert Macaulay; 2s.6d. King Jaja of Opobo.

101 Boxing Gloves

1964. Olympic Games, Tokyo.

153	**101**	3d. sepia and green	45	10
154	-	6d. green and blue	60	10
155	-	1s.3d. sepia and olive	1·00	15
156	-	2s.6d. sepia and brown	1·75	3·75

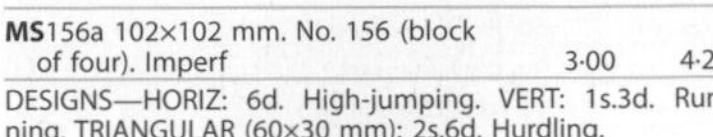

MS156a	102×102 mm. No. 156 (block of four). Imperf	3·00	4·25

DESIGNS—HORIZ: 6d. High-jumping. VERT: 1s.3d. Running. TRIANGULAR (60×30 mm): 2s.6d. Hurdling.

105 Scouts on Hill-top

1965. 50th Anniv of Nigerian Scout Movement.

157	**105**	1d. brown	10	40
158	-	3d. red, black and green	15	10
159	-	6d. red, sepia and green	25	20
160	-	1s.3d. brown, yellow and deep green	40	55
MS160a		76×104 mm. No. 160 (block of four). Imperf	5·00	8·50

DESIGNS: 3d. Scout badge on shield; 6d. Scout badges; 1s.3d. Chief Scout and Nigerian scout.

109 "Telstar"

1965. International Quiet Sun Years.

161	**109**	6d. violet and turquoise	15	15
162	-	1s.3d. green and lilac	15	15

DESIGN: 1s.3d. Solar satellite.

111 Native Tom-tom and Modern Telephone

1965. Centenary of I.T.U.

163	**111**	3d. black, red and brown	30	10
164	-	1s.3d. black, green & blue	2·75	1·00
165	-	5s. multicoloured	7·00	7·00

DESIGNS—VERT: 1s.3d. Microwave aerial. HORIZ: 5s. Telecommunications satellite and part of globe.

114 I.C.Y. Emblem and Diesel-hydraulic Locomotive

1965. International Co-operation Year.

166	**114**	3d. green, red and orange	3·50	20
167	-	1s. black, blue and lemon	3·00	40
168	-	2s.6d. green, blue & yellow	9·00	7·00

DESIGNS: 1s. Students and Lagos Teaching Hospital; 2s.6d. Kainji (Niger) Dam.

117 Carved Frieze

1965. Second Anniv of Republic.

169	**117**	3d. black, red and yellow	10	10
170	-	1s.3d. brown, green & blue	25	10
171	-	5s. brown, sepia and green	60	1·25

DESIGNS—VERT: 1s.3d. Stone Images at Ikom; 5s. Tada bronze.

121 African Elephants

1965

172		½d. multicoloured	1·00	2·75
173	**121**	1d. multicoloured	50	15
174	-	1½d. multicoloured	8·00	10·00
222a	-	2d. multicoloured	1·00	1·75
176	-	3d. multicoloured	1·25	30
177a	-	4d. multicoloured	30	10

178	-	6d. multicoloured	2·00	40
179	-	9d. blue and red	3·00	60
227	-	1s. multicoloured	2·50	20
181	-	1s.3d. multicoloured	8·50	2·00
182	**227**	2s.6d. light brown, buff and brown	75	2·50
183	-	5s. chestnut, yellow and brown	2·00	3·50
184	-	10s. multicoloured	6·50	3·25
185	-	£1 multicoloured	20·00	9·00

DESIGNS—VERT (as T **121**): ½d. Lion and cubs; 6d. Saddle-bill stork. (26½×46 mm): 10s. Hippopotamus. HORIZ (as T **121**): 1½d. Splendid sunbird; 2d. Village weaver and red-headed malimbe; 3d. Cheetah; 4d. Leopards; 9d. Grey parrots. (46×26½ mm): 1s. Blue-breasted kingfishers; 1s.3d. Crowned cranes; 2s.6d. Kobs; 5s. Giraffes; £1 African buffalo.

The 1d., 3d., 4d., 1s., 1s.3d., 2s.6d., 5s. and £1 exist optd **F.G.N.** (Federal Government of Nigeria) twice in black. They were prepared in November 1968 as official stamps, but the scheme was abandoned. Some stamps held at a Head Post Office were sold in error and passed through the post. The Director of Posts then decided to put limited supplies on sale, but they had no postal validity.

1966. Commonwealth Prime Ministers' Meeting, Lagos. Optd **COMMONWEALTH P. M. MEETING 11. JAN. 1966.**

186	**48**	2s.6d. black and yellow	30	30

135 Y.W.C.A. Emblem and H.Q., Lagos

1966. Diamond Jubilee of Nigerian Y.W.C.A.

187	**135**	4d. multicoloured	15	10
188	**135**	9d. multicoloured	15	60

137 Telephone Handset and Linesman

1966. Third Anniv of Republic.

189	-	4d. green	10	10
190	**137**	1s.6d. black, brown & violet	30	50
191	-	2s.6d. multicoloured	1·00	2·25

DESIGNS—VERT: 4d. Dove and flag. HORIZ: 2s.6d. North Channel Bridge over River Niger, Jebba.

139 "Education, Science and Culture"

1966. 20th Anniv of UNESCO.

192	**139**	4d. black, lake and orange	65	20
193	**139**	1s.6d. black, lake & turq	3·00	3·50
194	**139**	2s.6d. black, lake and pink	4·00	9·50

140 Children drinking

1966. Nigerian Red Cross.

195	**140**	4d.+1d. black, vio & red	30	30
196	-	1s.6d.+3d. multicoloured	55	3·75
197	-	2s.6d.+3d. multicoloured	65	4·25

DESIGNS—VERT: 1s.6d. Tending patient. HORIZ: 2s.6d. Tending casualties and badge.

143 Surveying

1967. Int Hydrological Decade. Multicoloured.

198	4d. Type **143**	10	10
199	2s.6d. Water gauge on dam (vert)	40	2·00

145 Globe and Weather Satellite

1967. World Meteorological Day.

200	**145**	4d. mauve and blue	15	10
201	-	1s.6d. black, yellow & blue	65	90

DESIGN: 1s.6d. Passing storm and sun.

147 Eyo Masqueraders

1967. Fourth Anniv of Republic. Multicoloured.

202	4d. Type **147**	15	10
203	1s.6d. Crowds watching acrobat	50	1·50
204	2s.6d. Stilt dancer (vert)	75	3·50

150 Tending Sick Animal

1967. Rinderpest Eradication Campaign.

205	**150**	4d. multicoloured	15	10
206	**150**	1s.6d. multicoloured	55	1·50

151 Smallpox Vaccination

1968. 20th Anniv of W.H.O.

207	**151**	4d. mauve and black	15	10
208	-	1s.6d. orange, lemon & blk	55	1·00

DESIGN: 1s.6d. African and mosquito.

153 Chained Hands and Outline of Nigeria

1968. Human Rights Year.

209	**153**	4d. blue, black and yellow	15	10
210	-	1s.6d. green, red and black	40	1·00

DESIGN—VERT: 1s.6d. Nigerian flag and Human Rights emblem.

155 Hand grasping at Doves of Freedom

1968. Fifth Anniv of Federal Republic.

211	**155**	4d. multicoloured	10	10
212	**155**	1s.6d. multicoloured	20	20

156 Map of Nigeria and Olympic Rings

1968. Olympic Games, Mexico.

213	**156**	4d. black, green and red	20	10
214	-	1s.6d. multicoloured	80	30

DESIGN: 1s.6d. Nigerian athletes, flag and Olympic rings.

158 G.P.O., Lagos

1969. Inauguration of Philatelic Service.

215	**158**	4d. black and green	10	10
216	**158**	1s.6d. black and blue	20	50

159 Yakubu Gowon and Victoria Zakari

1969. Wedding of General Gowon.

217	**159**	4d. brown and green	10	10
218	**159**	1s.6d. black and green	90	30

160 Bank Emblem and "5th Anniversary"

1969. Fifth Anniv of African Development Bank.

233	**160**	4d. orange, black and blue	10	10
234	-	1s.6d. yellow, black and purple	20	1·25

DESIGN: 1s.6d. Bank emblem and rays.

162 I.L.O. Emblem

1969. 50th Anniv of I.L.O.

235	**162**	4d. black and violet	10	10
236	-	1s.6d. green and black	75	1·50

DESIGN: 1s.6d. World map and I.L.O. emblem.

164 Olumo Rock

1969. International Year of African Tourism.

237	**164**	4d. multicoloured	15	10
238	-	1s. black and green	20	10
239	-	1s.6d. multicoloured	1·25	95

DESIGNS—VERT: 1s. Traditional musicians; 1s.6d. Assob Falls.

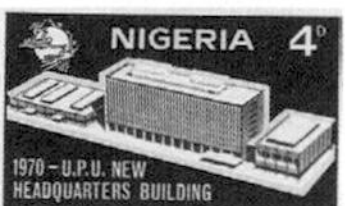

167 Symbolic Tree

1970. "Stamp of Destiny". End of Civil War.

240	**167**	4d. gold, blue and black	10	10
241	-	1s. multicoloured	10	10
242	-	1s.6d. green and black	15	10
243	-	2s. multicoloured	20	20

DESIGNS—VERT: 1s. Symbolic wheel; 1s.6d. United Nigerians supporting map. HORIZ: 2s. Symbolic torch.

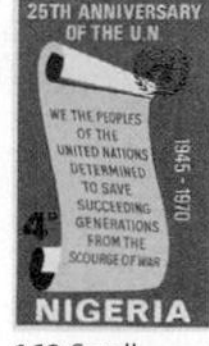

168 U.P.U. Headquarters Building

1970. New U.P.U. Headquarters Building.

244	**168**	4d. violet and yellow	10	10
245	**168**	1s.6d. blue and indigo	40	20

169 Scroll

1970. 25th Anniv of United Nations.

246	**169**	4d. brown, buff and black	10	10
247	-	1s.6d. blue, brown & gold	30	20

DESIGN: 1s.6d. U.N. Building.

170 Oil Rig

1970. Tenth Anniv of Independence.

248	2d. Type **170**	25	25
249	4d. University graduate	15	10
250	6d. Durbar horsemen	30	10
251	9d. Servicemen raising flag	40	10
252	1s. Footballer	40	10
253	1s.6d. Parliament building	40	40
254	2s. Kainji Dam	70	90
255	2s.6d. Agricultural produce	70	1·40

171 Children and Globe

1971. Racial Equality Year. Multicoloured.

256	4d. Type **171**	10	10
257	1s. Black and white men uprooting "Racism" (vert)	15	10
258	1s.6d. "The World in Black and White" (vert)	20	75
259	2s. Black and white men united	20	1·75

172 Ibibio Face Mask

1971. Antiquities of Nigeria.

260	**172**	4d. black and blue	10	10
261	-	1s.3d. brown and ochre	15	30
262	-	1s.9d. green, brown & yell	20	1·25

DESIGNS: 1s.3d. Benin bronze; 1s.9d. Ife bronze.

173 Children and Symbol

1971. 25th Anniv of UNICEF.

263	**173**	4d. multicoloured	10	10
264	-	1s.3d. orange, red & brn	15	40
265	-	1s.9d. turquoise and deep turquoise	15	1·00

DESIGNS: Each with UNICEF symbol: 1s.3d. Mother and child; 1s.9d. Mother carrying child.

174 Mast and Dish Aerial

1971. Opening of Nigerian Earth Satellite Station.

266	**174**	4d. multicoloured	15	10
267	-	1s.3d. green, blue & black	25	50
268	-	1s.9d. brown, orange & blk	25	1·00
269	-	3s. mauve, black and purple	45	2·00

DESIGNS: Nos. 267/9 as Type **174**, but showing different views of the Satellite Station.

175 Trade Fair Emblem

1972. All-Africa Trade Fair.

270	**175**	4d. multicoloured	10	10
271	-	1s.3d. lilac, yellow & gold	15	35
272	-	1s.9d. yellow, orange & blk	15	1·60

DESIGNS—HORIZ: 1s.3d. Map of Africa with pointers to Nairobi. VERT: 1s.9d. Africa on globe.

176 Traffic

1972. Change to Driving on the Right.

273	**176**	4d. orange, brown & black	50	10
274	-	1s.3d. multicoloured	1·25	70
275	-	1s.9d. multicoloured	1·25	1·25
276	-	3s. multicoloured	1·75	3·00

DESIGNS: 1s.3d. Roundabout; 1s.9d. Highway; 3s. Road junction.

177 Nok Style Terracotta Head

1972. All-Nigeria Arts Festival. Multicoloured.

277	4d. Type **177**	10	10
278	1s.3d. Bronze pot from Igbo-Ukwu	25	60
279	1s.9d. Bone harpoon (horiz)	30	1·75

178 Hides and Skins

1973

290	**178**	1k. multicoloured	10	20
281	-	2k. multicoloured	35	10
292	-	3k. multicoloured	15	10
282a	-	5k. multicoloured	50	10
294	-	7k. multicoloured	30	1·25
295	-	8k. multicoloured	40	10
344	-	10k. multicoloured	2·00	20
297	-	12k. black, green and blue	30	3·25
298	-	15k. multicoloured	30	60
299	-	18k. multicoloured	50	30
300	-	20k. multicoloured	65	30
301	-	25k. multicoloured	85	45
302	-	30k. black, yellow & blue	40	1·50
303	-	35k. multicoloured	6·00	4·25
288a	-	50k. multicoloured	50	90
305	-	1n. multicoloured	50	75
306	-	2n. multicoloured	75	2·00

DESIGNS—HORIZ: 2k. Natural gas tanks; 3k. Cement works; 5k. Cattle-ranching; 7k. Timber mill; 8k. Oil refinery; 10k. Cheetahs, Yankari Game Reserve; 12k. New Civic Building; 15k. Sugar-cane harvesting; 20k. Vaccine production; 25k. Modern wharf; 35k. Textile machinery; 1n. Eko Bridge; 2n. Teaching Hospital, Lagos. VERT: 18k. Palm oil production; 30k. Argungu Fishing Festival; 50k. Pottery.

179 Athlete

1973. Second All-African Games, Lagos.

307	**179**	5k. lilac, blue and black	15	10
308	-	12k. multicoloured	25	50
309	-	18k. multicoloured	45	1·00
310	-	25k. multicoloured	50	1·50

DESIGNS—HORIZ: 12k. Football; 18k. Table tennis. VERT: 25k. National stadium.

180 All-Africa House, Addis Ababa

1973. Tenth Anniv of O.A.U. Multicoloured.

311	5k. Type **180**	10	10
312	18k. O.A.U. flag (vert)	30	40
313	30k. O.A.U. emblem and symbolic flight of ten stairs (vert)	50	80

181 Dr. Hansen

1973. Centenary of Discovery of Leprosy Bacillus.

314	**181**	5k.+2k. brown, pink and black	30	1·00

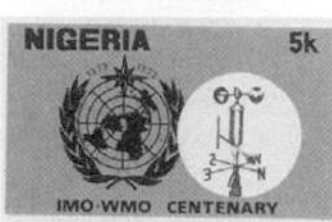

182 W.M.O. Emblem and Weather-vane

1973. Centenary of I.M.O./W.M.O.

315	**182**	5k. multicoloured	30	10
316	**182**	30k. multicoloured	1·50	2·25

183 University Complex

1973. 25th Anniv of Ibadan University. Multicoloured.

317	5k. Type **183**	10	10
318	12k. Students' population growth (vert)	15	20
319	18k. Tower and students	25	35
320	30k. Teaching Hospital	35	65

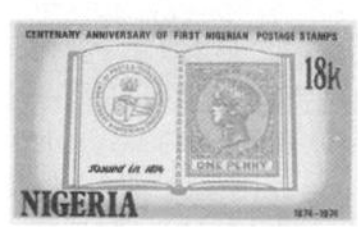

184 Lagos 1d. Stamp of 1874

1974. Stamp Centenary.

321	-	5k. green, orange & black	15	10
322	-	12k. multicoloured	30	40
323	**184**	18k. green, mauve & black	40	70
324	-	30k. multicoloured	1·25	2·00

DESIGNS: 5k. Graph of mail traffic growth; 12k. Northern Nigeria £25 stamp of 1904; 30k. Forms of mail transport.

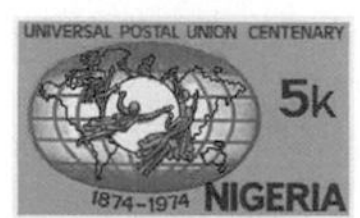

185 U.P.U. Emblem on Globe

1974. Centenary of U.P.U.

325	**185**	5k. blue, orange and black	15	10
326	-	18k. multicoloured	2·00	60
327	-	30k. brown, green & black	1·75	1·75

DESIGNS: 18k. World transport map; 30k. U.P.U. emblem and letters.

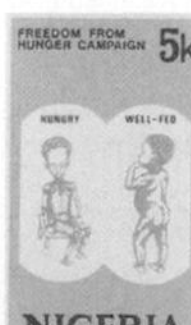

186 Starving and Well-fed Children

1974. Freedom from Hunger Campaign.

328	**186**	5k. green, buff and black	10	10
329	-	12k. multicoloured	30	50
330	-	30k. multicoloured	80	1·75

DESIGNS—HORIZ: 12k. Poultry battery. VERT: 30k. Water-hoist.

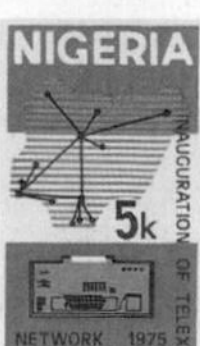

187 Telex Network and Teleprinter

1975. Inauguration of Telex Network.

331	**187**	5k. black, orange & green	10	10
332	-	12k. black, yellow & brn	20	20
333	-	18k. multicoloured	30	30
334	-	30k. multicoloured	50	50

DESIGNS: 12, 18, 30k. are as Type **187** but with the motifs arranged differently.

188 Queen Amina of Zaria

1975. International Women's Year.

335	**188**	5k. green, yellow and blue	35	10
336	**188**	18k. purple, blue & mauve	1·00	80
337	**188**	30k. multicoloured	1·25	1·60

190 Alexander Graham Bell

1976. Centenary of Telephone.

355	**190**	5k. multicoloured	10	10
356	-	18k. multicoloured	40	55
357	-	25k. blue, light blue and brown	70	1·00

DESIGNS—HORIZ: 18k. Gong and modern telephone system. VERT: 25k. Telephones, 1876 and 1976.

191 Child writing

1976. Launching of Universal Primary Education.

358	**191**	5k. yellow, violet & mauve	10	10
359	-	18k. multicoloured	45	85
360	-	25k. multicoloured	70	1·25

DESIGNS—VERT: 18k. Children entering school; 25k. Children in class.

192 Festival Emblem

1976. Second World Black and African Festival of Arts and Culture, Nigeria.

361	**192**	5k. gold and brown	35	10
362	-	10k. brown, yellow & blk	35	55
363	-	12k. multicoloured	80	90
364	-	18k. yellow, brown & blk	90	90
365	-	30k. red and black	1·00	1·50

DESIGNS: 10k. National Arts Theatre; 12k. African hairstyles; 18k. Musical instruments; 30k. "Nigerian arts and crafts".

193 General Murtala Muhammed and Map of Nigeria

1977. First Death Anniv of General Muhammed (Head of State). Multicoloured.

366	5k. Type **193**	10	10
367	18k. General in dress uniform (vert)	20	35
368	30k. General in battle dress (vert)	30	70

194 Scouts saluting

1977. First All-African Scout Jamboree, Jos, Nigeria. Multicoloured.

369	5k. Type **194**	15	10
370	18k. Scouts cleaning street (horiz)	50	70
371	25k. Scouts working on farm (horiz)	60	1·25
372	30k. Jamboree emblem and map of Africa (horiz)	70	2·00

195 Trade Fair Complex

1977. First Lagos Int Trade Fair.

373	**195**	5k. black, blue and green	10	10
374	-	18k. black, blue and purple	20	25
375	-	30k. multicoloured	30	45

DESIGNS: 18k. Globe and Trade Fair emblem; 30k. Weaving and basketry.

196 Map showing Nigerian Universities

1978. Global Conference on Technical Co-operation between Developing Countries, Buenos Aires.

376	**196**	5k. multicoloured	10	10
377	-	12k. multicoloured	15	15
378	-	18k. multicoloured	25	25
379	-	30k. yellow, violet & black	45	60

DESIGNS: 12k. Map of West African highways and telecommunications; 18k. Technologists undergoing training; 30k. World map.

197 Microwave Antenna

1978. Tenth World Telecommunications Day.

380	**197**	30k. multicoloured	50	60

198 Students on "Operation Feed the Nation"

1978. "Operation Feed the Nation" Campaign. Multicoloured.

381	5k. Type **198**	10	10
382	18k. Family backyard farm	20	20
383	30k. Plantain farm (vert)	35	60

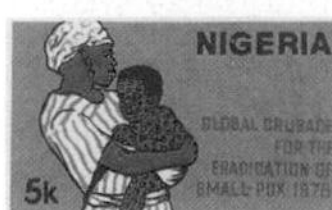

199 Mother with Infected Child

1978. Global Eradication of Smallpox.

384	**199**	5k. black, brown and lilac	15	10
385	-	12k. multicoloured	25	40
386	-	18k. black, brown & yell	40	45
387	-	30k. black, silver and pink	55	1·40

DESIGNS—HORIZ: 12k. Doctor and infected child; 18k. Group of children being vaccinated. VERT: 30k. Syringe.

200 Nok Terracotta Human Figure, Bwari (900 B.C.–100 A.D.)

1978. Antiquities.

388	**200**	5k. black, blue and red	10	10
389	-	12k. multicoloured	15	10
390	-	18k. black, blue and red	20	15
391	-	30k. multicoloured	25	20

DESIGNS—HORIZ: 12k. Igbo-Ukwu bronze snail shell, Igbo Isaiah (9th-century A.D.). VERT: 18k. Ife bronze statue of a king (12th–15th century A.D.); 30k. Benin bronze equestrian figure (about 1700 A.D.).

201 Anti-Apartheid Emblem

1978. International Anti-Apartheid Year.
392 **201** 18k. black, yellow and red 15 15

202 Wright Brothers and Wright Type A

1978. 75th Anniv of Powered Flight.
393 **202** 5k. multicoloured 20 10
394 - 18k. black, blue and light blue 60 20
DESIGN: 18k. Nigerian Air Force formation.

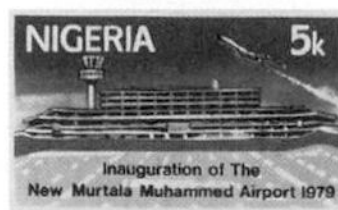

203 Murtala Muhammed Airport

1979. Opening of Murtala Muhammed Airport.
395 **203** 5k. black, grey and blue 40 30

204 Child with Stamp Album

1979. Tenth Anniv of National Philatelic Service.
396 **204** 5k. multicoloured 10 20

205 Mother and Child

1979. International Year of the Child. Multicoloured.
397 5k. Type **205** 10 10
398 18k. Children studying 35 30
399 25k. Children playing (vert) 40 50

206 Trainee Teacher making Audio Visual Aid Materials

1979. 50th Anniv of International Bureau of Education. Multicoloured.
400 10k. Type **206** 10 10
401 30k. Adult education class 25 30

207 Necom House

1979. 50th Anniv of Consultative Committee of International Radio.
402 **207** 10k. multicoloured 15 30

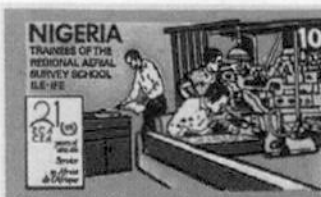

208 Trainees of the Regional Air Survey School, Ile-Ife

1979. 21st Anniv of Economic Commission for Africa.
403 **208** 10k. multicoloured 20 30

209 Football Cup and Map of Nigeria

1980. African Cup of Nations Football Competition, Nigeria. Multicoloured.
404 10k. Type **209** 20 10
405 30k. Footballer (vert) 60 50

210 Wrestling

1980. Olympic Games, Moscow.
406 **210** 10k. multicoloured 10 10
407 - 20k. black and green 10 10
408 - 30k. black, orange & blue 15 15
409 - 45k. multicoloured 20 20
DESIGNS—VERT: 20k. Long jump; 45k. Netball. HORIZ: 30k. Swimming.

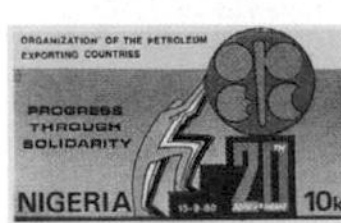

211 Figures supporting O.P.E.C. Emblem

1980. 20th Anniv of O.P.E.C. (Organization of Petroleum Exporting Countries).
410 **211** 10k. black, blue and yellow 15 10
411 - 45k. black, blue and mauve 70 60
DESIGN—VERT: 45k. O.P.E.C. emblem and globe.

212 Tank Locomotive No. 2, Wushishi Tramway

1980. 25th Anniv of Nigerian Railway Corporation. Multicoloured.
412 10k. Type **212** 75 10
413 20k. Loading goods train 1·00 1·25
414 30k. Freight train 1·40 1·50

213 Metric Scales

1980. World Standards Day.
415 **213** 10k. red and black 10 10
416 - 30k. multicoloured 35 90
DESIGN—HORIZ: 30k. Quality control.

214 "Communication" Symbols and Map of West Africa

1980. Fifth Anniv of Economic Community of West African States.
417 **214** 10k. black, orange & olive 10 10
418 - 25k. black, green and red 30 10
419 - 30k. black, yellow & brn 20 15
420 - 45k. black, turquoise & bl 25 25
DESIGNS: 25k. "Transport"; 30k. "Agriculture"; 45k. "Industry".

215 Disabled Woman sweeping

1981. International Year for Disabled Persons.
421 **215** 10k. multicoloured 20 10
422 - 30k. black, brown and blue 65 65
DESIGN: 30k. Disabled man filming.

216 President launching "Green Revolution" (food production campaign)

1981. World Food Day.
423 **216** 10k. multicoloured 10 10
424 - 25k. black, yellow & green 20 50
425 - 30k. multicoloured 25 55
426 - 45k. black, brown & yell 45 85
DESIGNS—VERT: 25k. Food crops; 30k. Harvesting tomatoes. HORIZ: 45k. Pig farming.

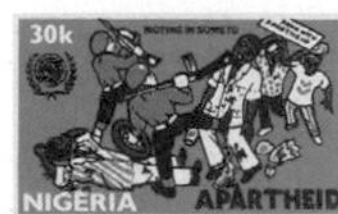

217 Rioting in Soweto

1981. Anti-Apartheid Movement.
427 **217** 30k. multicoloured 40 55
428 - 45k. black, red and green 60 1·50
DESIGN—VERT: 45k. "Police brutality".

218 "Preservation of Wildlife"

1982. 75th Anniv of Boy Scout Movement. Multicoloured.
429 30k. Type **218** 50 55
430 45k. Lord Baden-Powell taking salute 75 1·25

219 Early Inoculation

1982. Centenary of Robert Koch's Discovery of Tubercle Bacillus.
431 **219** 10k. multicoloured 20 15
432 - 30k. black, brown and green 50 65
433 - 45k. black, brown and green 80 1·75
DESIGNS—HORIZ: 30k. Technician and microscope. VERT: 45k. Patient being X-rayed.

220 "Keep Your Environment Clean"

1982. Tenth Anniv of U.N. Conference on Human Environment.
434 **220** 10k. multicoloured 10 10
435 - 20k. orange, grey and black 20 40
436 - 30k. multicoloured 35 60
437 - 45k. multicoloured 55 85
DESIGNS: 20k. "Check air pollution"; 30k. "Preserve natural environment"; 45k. "Reafforestation concerns all".

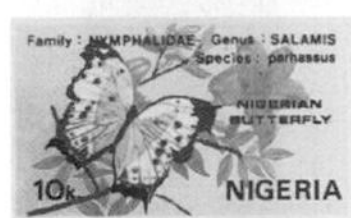

221 "Salamis parhassus"

1982. Nigerian Butterflies. Multicoloured.
438 10k. Type **221** 15 10
439 20k. "Iterus zalmoxis" 30 30
440 30k. "Cymothoe beckeri" 40 40
441 45k. "Papilio hesperus" 70 1·25

222 Carving of "Male and Female Twins"

1982. 25th Anniv of National Museum. Multicoloured.
442 10k. Type **222** 10 10
443 20k. Royal bronze leopard (horiz) 20 35
444 30k. Soapstone seated figure 35 90
445 45k. Wooden helmet mask 50 1·75

223 Three Generations

1983. Family Day. Multicoloured.
446 10k. Type **223** 15 10
447 30k. Parents with three children (vert) 50 65

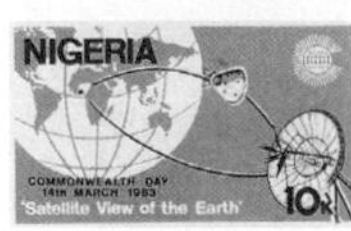

224 Satellite View of Globe

1983. Commonwealth Day.
448 **224** 10k. brown and black 10 10
449 - 25k. multicoloured 20 30
450 - 30k. black, purple and grey 75 35
451 - 45k. multicoloured 35 45
DESIGNS—HORIZ: 25k. National Assembly Buildings. VERT: 30k. Drilling for oil; 45k. Athletics.

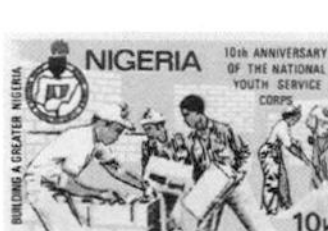

225 Corps Members on Building Project

1983. Tenth Anniv of National Youth Service Corps. Multicoloured.
452 10k. Type **225** 15 10
453 25k. On the assault-course (vert) 30 30
454 30k. Corps members on parade 40 40

226 Postman on Bicycle

1983. World Communications Year. Multicoloured.
455 10k. Type **226** 15 10
456 25k. Newspaper kiosk (horiz) 30 55
457 30k. Town crier blowing elephant tusk (horiz) 35 90
458 45k. T.V. newsreader (horiz) 45 1·25

227 Pink Shrimp

1983. World Fishery Resources.
459 **227** 10k. red, blue and black 15 10
460 - 25k. multicoloured 30 40
461 - 30k. multicoloured 30 45
462 - 45k. multicoloured 40 70
DESIGNS: 25k. Long-necked croaker; 30k. Barracuda; 45k. Fishing techniques.

228 On Parade

1983. Centenary of Boys' Brigade and 75th Anniv of Founding in Nigeria. Multicoloured.

463	10k. Type **228**	40	10
464	30k. Members working on cassava plantation (horiz)	1·50	1·50
465	45k. Skill training (horiz)	2·25	2·75

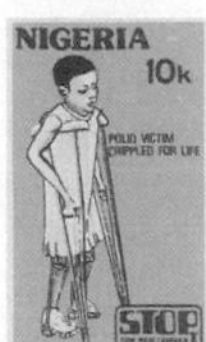

229 Crippled Child

1984. Stop Polio Campaign.

466	**229**	10k. blue, black and brown	20	15
467	-	25k. orange, black & yell	40	75
468	-	30k. red, black and brown	60	1·10

DESIGNS—HORIZ: 25k. Child receiving vaccine. VERT: 30k. Healthy child.

230 Waterbuck

1984. Nigerian Wildlife.

469	**230**	10k. green, brown & black	15	10
470	-	25k. multicoloured	30	50
471	-	30k. brown, black & green	40	90
472	-	45k. blue, orange & black	45	1·50

DESIGNS—HORIZ: 25k. Hartebeest; 30k. African buffalo. VERT: 45k. Diademed monkey.

231 Obverse and Reverse of 1969 £1 Note

1984. 25th Anniv of Nigerian Central Bank.

473	**231**	10k. multicoloured	20	10
474	-	25k. brown, black & green	45	80
475	-	30k. red, black and green	55	1·10

DESIGNS: 25k. Central Bank; 30k. Obverse and reverse of 1959 £5 note.

232 Boxing

1984. Olympic Games, Los Angeles. Multicoloured.

476	10k. Type **232**	15	10
477	25k. Discus-throwing	35	50
478	30k. Weightlifting	40	60
479	45k. Cycling	60	90

233 Irrigation Project, Lesotho

1984. 20th Anniv of African Development Bank.

480	**233**	10k. multicoloured	15	10
481	-	25k. multicoloured	30	50
482	-	30k. black, yellow and blue	35	60
483	-	45k. black, brown and blue	1·75	90

DESIGNS—HORIZ: 25k. Bomi Hills Road, Liberia; 30k. School building project, Seychelles; 45k. Coal mining, Niger.

234 Pin-tailed Whydah

1984. Rare Birds. Multicoloured.

484	10k. Type **234**	75	20
485	25k. Spur-winged plover	1·50	70
486	30k. Red bishop	1·50	1·75
487	45k. Double-spurred francolin	1·75	2·50

235 Boeing 747 Airliner taking-off

1984. 40th Anniv of International Civil Aviation Organization. Multicoloured.

488	10k. Type **235**	40	10
489	45k. Boeing 707 airliner circling globe	1·50	2·25

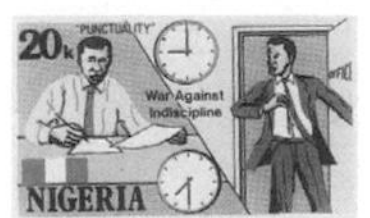

236 Office Workers and Clocks ("Punctuality")

1985. "War against Indiscipline". Multicoloured.

490	20k. Type **236**	30	35
491	50k. Cross over hands passing banknotes ("Discourage Bribery")	55	75

237 Footballers receiving Flag from Major-General Buhari

1985. International Youth Year. Multicoloured.

492	20k. Type **237**	30	20
493	50k. Girls of different tribes with flag (vert)	55	70
494	55k. Members of youth organizations with flags (vert)	55	80

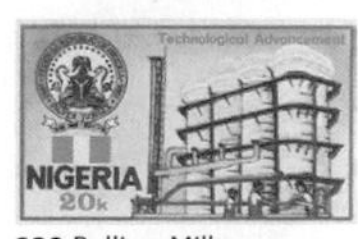

238 Rolling Mill

1985. 25th Anniv of Independence. Multicoloured.

495	20k. Type **238**	25	10
496	50k. Map of Nigeria	40	40
497	55k. Remembrance Arcade	40	60
498	60k. Eleme, first Nigerian oil refinery	1·00	1·75
MS499	101×101 mm. Nos. 495/8	5·00	6·50

239 Globe and O.P.E.C. Emblem

1985. 25th Anniv of Organization of Petroleum Exporting Countries.

500	**239**	20k. blue and red	75	35
501	-	50k. black and blue	1·50	75

DESIGN—HORIZ: 50k. World map and O.P.E.C. emblem.

240 Waterfall

1985. World Tourism Day. Multicoloured.

502	20k. Type **240**	35	10
503	50k. Pottery, carved heads and map of Nigeria (horiz)	45	50
504	55k. Calabash carvings and Nigerian flag	45	50
505	60k. Leather work	45	55

241 Map of Nigeria and National Flag

1985. 40th Anniv of United Nations Organization and 25th Anniv of Nigerian Membership.

506	**241**	20k. black, green and blue	20	10
507	-	50k. black, blue and red	35	85
508	-	55k. black, blue and red	35	95

DESIGNS—HORIZ: 50k. United Nations Building, New York; 55k. United Nations logo.

242 Rock Python

1986. African Reptiles.

509	**242**	10k. multicoloured	30	10
510	-	20k. black, brown and blue	50	90
511	-	25k multicoloured	50	1·00
512	-	30k. multicoloured	50	1·00

DESIGNS: 20k. Long snouted crocodile; 25k. Gopher tortoise; 30k. Chameleon.

243 Social Worker with Children

1986. Nigerian Life. Multicoloured.

513	1k. Type **243**	40	1·00
514	2k. Volkswagen motor assembly line (horiz)	40	1·00
515	5k. Modern housing estate (horiz)	15	50
516	10k. Harvesting oil palm fruit	20	10
517	15k. Unloading freighter (horiz)	1·25	10
518	20k. "Tecoma stans" (flower)	25	10
519	25k. Hospital ward (horiz)	30	60
519a	30k. Birom dancers (horiz)	30	10
520	35k. Telephonists operating switchboard (horiz)	30	10
521	40k. Nkpokiti dancers	30	75
522	45k. Hibiscus (horiz)	30	75
523a	50k. Post Office counter (horiz)	1·00	75
524	1n. Stone quarry (horiz)	30	15
525a	2n. Students in laboratory (horiz)	40	10
525be	10n. Lekki Beach (horiz)	1·00	50
525c	20n. Ancient wall, Kano (horiz)	7·50	2·00
525d	50n. Rock bridge (horiz)	5·00	4·00
525e	100n. Ekpe masquerader	3·00	3·75
525f	500n. National Theatre (horiz)	20·00	12·00

244 Emblem and Globe

1986. International Peace Year. Multicoloured.

526	10k. Type **244**	20	10
527	20k. Hands of five races holding globe	60	1·50

245 "Goliathus goliathus" (beetle)

1986. Nigerian Insects. Multicoloured.

528	10k. Type **245**	30	10
529	20k. "Vespa vulgaris" (wasp)	40	40
530	25k. "Acheta domestica" (cricket)	45	90
531	30k. "Anthrenus verbasci" (beetle)	55	1·50
MS532	119×101 mm. Nos. 528/31	3·00	5·50

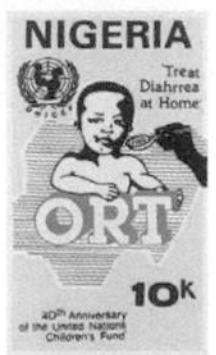

246 Oral Rehydration Therapy

1986. 40th Anniv of UNICEF.

533	**246**	10k. multicoloured	30	10
534	-	20k. black, brown & yell	40	40
535	-	25k. multicoloured	45	70
536	-	30k. multicoloured	55	1·00

DESIGNS: 20k. Immunization; 25k. Breast-feeding; 30k. Mother and child.

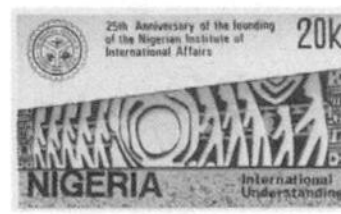

247 Stylized Figures on Wall ("International Understanding")

1986. 25th Anniv of Nigerian Institute of International Affairs.

537	**247**	20k. black, blue and green	50	50
538	-	30k. multicoloured	75	1·25

DESIGN—VERT: 30k. "Knowledge" (bronze sculpture).

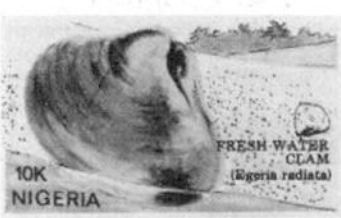

248 Freshwater Clam

1987. Shells.

539	**248**	10k. multicoloured	55	10
540	-	20k. black, brown and pink	80	1·75
541	-	25k. multicoloured	80	2·00
542	-	30k. multicoloured	1·00	2·50

DESIGNS: 20k. Periwinkle; 25k. Bloody cockle (inscr "BLOODY COCKLE"); 30k. Mangrove oyster.

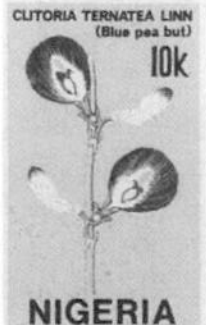

249 "Clitoria ternatea"

1987. Nigerian Flowers.

543	**249**	10k. multicoloured	10	10
544	-	20k. brown, yellow and green	15	25
545	-	25k. multicoloured	15	45
546	-	30k. multicoloured	20	1·00

DESIGNS: 20k. "Hibiscus tiliaceus"; 25k. "Acanthus montanus"; 30k. "Combretum racemosum".

250 Doka Hairstyle

1987. Women's Hairstyles.

547	**250**	10k. black, brown and grey	10	10
548	-	20k. multicoloured	30	30
549	-	25k. black, brown and red	30	55
550	-	30k. multicoloured	30	1·00

DESIGNS: 20k. Eting; 25k. Agogo; 30k. Goto.

251 Family sheltering under Tree

1987. International Year of Shelter for the Homeless. Multicoloured.

551	20k. Type **251**	15	15
552	30k. Family and modern house	15	90

252 Red Cross Worker distributing Food

1988. 125th Anniv of International Red Cross. Multicoloured.

553	20k. Type **252**	65	30
554	30k. Carrying patient to ambulance	65	1·75

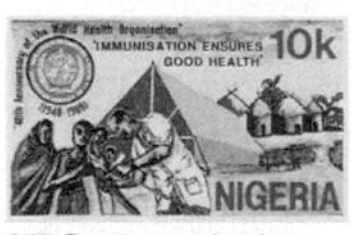
253 Doctor vaccinating Baby

1988. 40th Anniv of W.H.O. Multicoloured.

555	10k. Type **253**	25	10
556	20k. W.H.O. logo and outline map of Nigeria	60	70
557	30k. Doctor and patients at mobile clinic	60	70

254 O.A.U. Logo

1988. 25th Anniv of Organization of African Unity.

558	**254**	10k. brown, green & orge	15	15
559	-	20k. multicoloured	15	15

DESIGN: 20k. Four Africans supporting map of Africa.

255 Pink Shrimp

1988. Shrimps.

560	**255**	10k. multicoloured	20	10
561	-	20k. black and green	30	15
562	-	25k. black, red and brown	30	25
563	-	30k. orange, brown & blk	30	60
MS564		120×101 mm. Nos. 560/3	1·50	2·00

DESIGNS: 20k. Tiger shrimp; 25k. Deepwater roseshrimp; 30k. Estuarine prawn.

256 Weightlifting

1988. Olympic Games, Seoul. Multicoloured.

565	10k. Type **256**	25	10
566	20k. Boxing	35	35
567	30k. Athletics (vert)	50	65

257 Banknote Production Line

1988. 25th Anniv of Nigerian Security Printing and Minting Co. Ltd.

568	**257**	10k. multicoloured	10	10
569	-	20k. black, silver and green	20	20
570	-	25k. multicoloured	30	30
571	-	30k. multicoloured	50	50

DESIGNS—HORIZ (As T **257**): 20k. Coin production line. VERT (37×44 mm): 25k. Montage of products; 30k. Anniversary logos.

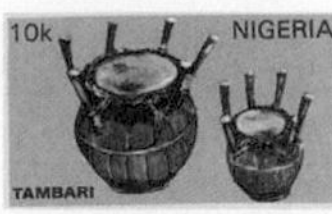
258 Tambari

1989. Nigerian Musical Instruments.

572	**258**	10k. multicoloured	15	10
573	-	20k. multicoloured	25	20
574	-	25k. brown, green & black	35	30
575	-	30k. brown and black	60	50

DESIGNS: 20k. Kundung; 25k. Ibid; 30k. Dundun.

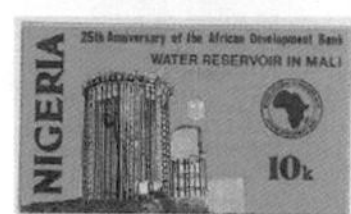
259 Construction of Water Towers, Mali

1989. 25th Anniv of African Development Bank. Multicoloured.

576	10k. Type **259**	10	10
577	20k. Paddy field, Gambia	15	15
578	25k. Bank Headquarters, Abidjan, Ivory Coast	25	25
579	30k. Anniversary logo (vert)	35	35

260 Lighting Campfire

1989. 70th Anniv of Nigerian Girl Guides Association. Multicoloured.

580	10k. Type **260**	30	10
581	20k. Guide on rope bridge (vert)	70	60

261 Etubom Costume

1989. Traditional Costumes. Multicoloured.

582	10k. Type **261**	45	10
583	20k. Fulfulde	50	25
584	25k. Aso-Ofi	60	85
585	30k. Fuska Kura	65	1·75

262 Dove with Letter and Map of Africa

1990. Tenth Anniv of Pan African Postal Union. Multicoloured.

586	10k. Type **262**	25	10
587	20k. Parcel and map of Africa	50	50

263 Oil Lamps

1990. Nigerian Pottery.

588	**263**	10k. black, brown & violet	15	10
589	-	20k. black, brown & violet	25	25
590	-	25k. brown and violet	35	35
591	-	30k. multicoloured	40	45
MS592		120×100 mm. Nos. 588/91	1·40	1·50

DESIGNS: 20k. Water pots; 25k. Musical pots; 50k. Water jugs.

264 Teacher and Class

1990. International Literacy Year.

593	**264**	20k. multicoloured	20	10
594	-	30k. brown, blue & yellow	30	40

DESIGN: 30k. Globe and book.

265 Globe and OPEC Logo

1990. 30th Anniv of the Organization of Petroleum Exporting Countries. Multicoloured.

595	10k. Type **265**	10	10
596	20k. Logo and flags of member countries (vert)	20	25
597	25k. World map and logo	25	30
598	30k. Logo within inscription "Co-operation for Global Energy Security" (vert)	35	45

266 Grey Parrot

1990. Wildlife. Multicoloured.

599	20k. Type **266**	20	20
600	30k. Roan antelope	20	10
601	1n.50 Grey-necked bald crow ("Rockfowl")	60	1·00
602	2n.50 Mountain gorilla	85	1·50
MS603	118×119 mm. Nos. 599/602	1·75	2·50

267 Eradication Treatment

1991. National Guineaworm Eradication Day. Multicoloured.

604	10k. Type **267**	15	10
605	20k. Women collecting water from river (horiz)	25	30
606	30k. Boiling pot of water	25	40

268 Hand holding Torch (Progress)

1991. Organization of African Unity Heads of State and Governments Meeting, Abuja. Each showing outline map of Africa. Multicoloured.

607	20k. Type **268**	15	10
608	30k. Cogwheel (Unity)	20	25
609	50k. O.A.U. flag (Freedom)	20	45

269 National Flags

1991. Economic Community of West African States Summit Meeting, Abuja. Multicoloured.

610	20k. Type **269**	15	10
611	50k. Map showing member states	30	45

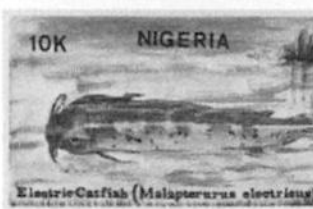
270 Electric Catfish

1991. Nigerian Fish. Multicoloured.

612	10k. Type **270**	15	10
613	20k. Nile perch	25	25
614	30k. Nile mouthbrooder ("Talapia")	35	35
615	50k. Sharp-toothed catfish	50	85
MS616	121×104 mm. Nos. 612/15	2·00	2·50

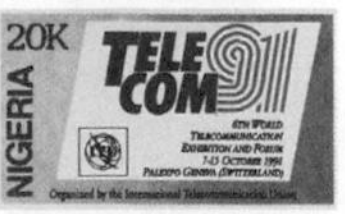
271 Telecom '91 Emblem

1991. "Telecom '91" 6th World Telecommunication Exhibition, Geneva.

617	**271**	20k. black, green and violet	30	10
618	-	50k. multicoloured	40	50

DESIGN—VERT: 50k. Emblem and patchwork.

272 Boxing

1992. Olympic Games, Barcelona (1st issue). Multicoloured.

619	50k. Type **272**	20	15
620	1n. Nigerian athlete winning race	30	25
621	1n.50 Table tennis	40	50
622	2n. Taekwondo	55	70
MS623	120×117 mm. Nos. 619/22	2·00	2·25

See also No. 624.

273 Football

1992. Olympic Games, Barcelona (2nd issue).

624	**273**	1n.50 multicoloured	65	65

274 Blood Pressure Gauge

1992. World Health Day. Multicoloured.

625	50k. Type **274**	15	15
626	1n. World Health Day '92 emblem	20	20
627	1n.50 Heart and lungs	30	45
628	2n. Interior of heart	45	60
MS629	123×111 mm. Nos. 625/8	1·10	1·25

275 Map of World and Stamp on Globe

1992. "Olymphilex '92" Olympic Stamp Exhibition, Barcelona. Multicoloured.

630	50k. Type **275**	20	10
631	1n.50 Examining stamps	40	55
MS632	120×109 mm. Nos. 630/1	1·60	1·75

276 Gathering Plantain Fruit

1992. 25th Anniv of International Institute of Tropical Agriculture.

633	**276**	50k. multicoloured	1·60	1·75
634	-	1n. multicoloured	15	15
635	-	1n.50 black, brown & grn	20	20
636	-	2n. multicoloured	25	25
MS637		121×118 mm. Nos. 633/6	1·25	1·50

DESIGNS—VERT: 1n.50, Harvesting cassava tubers; 2n. Stacking yams. HORIZ: 1n. Tropical foods.

277 Centre Emblem

1992. Commissioning of Maryam Babangida National Centre for Women's Development.

638	**277**	50k. gold, emerald and green	10	10
639	-	1n. multicoloured	15	15
640	-	1n.50 multicoloured	20	20
641	-	2n. multicoloured	30	30

DESIGNS—VERT: 1n. Women working in fields; 2n. Woman at loom. HORIZ: 1n.50, Maryam Babangida National Centre.

All examples of No. 641 are without a "NIGERIA" inscription.

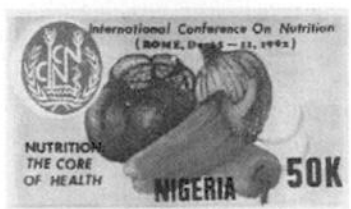

278 Healthy Food and Emblem

1992. International Conference on Nutrition, Rome. Multicoloured.

642	50k. Type **278**	10	10
643	1n. Child eating	15	15
644	1n.50 Fruit (vert)	20	20
645	2n. Vegetables	25	25
MS646	120×100 mm. Nos. 642/5	2·00	2·50

279 Sabada Dance

1992. Traditional Dances. Multicoloured.

647	50k. Type **279**	10	10
648	1n. Sato	15	15
649	1n.50 Asian Ubo Ikpa	20	20
650	2n. Dundun	25	25
MS651	126×107 mm. Nos. 647/50	1·50	1·75

280 African Elephant

1993. Wildlife. Multicoloured.

652	1n.50 Type **280**	1·75	50
653	5n. Stanley crane (vert)	3·00	1·00
654	20n. Roan antelope	8·00	4·00
655	30n. Lion	6·00	6·00

281 Suburban Garden

1993. World Environment Day. Multicoloured.

656	1n. Type **281**	10	10
657	1n.50 Water pollution	15	10
658	5n. Forest road	50	60
659	10n. Rural house	90	1·50

282 Oni Figure

1993. 50th Anniv of National Museums and Monuments Commission. Multicoloured.

660	1n. Type **282**	10	10
661	1n.50 Bronze head of Queen Mother	10	10
662	5n. Bronze pendant (horiz)	30	50
663	10n. Nok head	70	1·00

283 "Bulbophyllum distans"

1993. Orchids. Multicoloured.

664	1n. Type **283**	10	25
665	1n.50 "Eulophia cristata"	15	25
666	5n. "Eulophia horsfalli"	45	55
667	10n. "Eulophia quartiniana"	1·00	1·25
MS668	103×121 mm. Nos. 664/7	1·75	2·25

284 Children in Classroom and Adults carrying Food

1994. International Year of the Family. Multicoloured.

669	1n.50 Type **284**	10	10
670	10n. Market	1·00	1·50

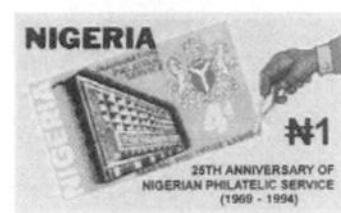

285 Hand with Tweezers holding 1969 4d. Philatelic Service Stamp

1994. 25th Anniv of Nat Philatelic Service. Multicoloured.

671	1n. Type **285**	10	10
672	1n.50 Philatelic Bureau	15	10
673	5n. Stamps forming map of Nigeria	45	60
674	10n. Philatelic counter	1·00	1·40

286 "I Love Stamps"

1994. 120th Anniv of First Postage Stamps in Nigeria. Multicoloured.

675	1n. Type **286**	10	10
676	1n.50 "I Collect Stamps"	15	10
677	5n. 19th-century means of communication	45	60
678	10n. Lagos stamp of 1874	1·00	1·40

287 Magnifying Glass over Globe

1994. "Philakorea '94" International Stamp Exhibition, Seoul.

679	**287**	30n. multicoloured	1·75	2·50
MS680		127×115 mm. **287** 30n. multicoloured	2·25	4·00

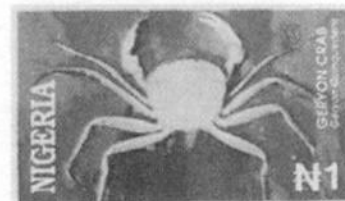

288 Geryon Crab

1994. Crabs. Multicoloured.

681	1n. Type **288**	10	10
682	1n.50 Spider crab	10	10
683	5n. Red spider crab	45	45
684	10n. Geryon maritae crab	90	1·25

289 Sewage Works

1994. 30th Anniv of African Development Bank. Multicoloured.

685	1n.50 Type **289**	15	10
686	30n. Development Bank emblem and flowers	1·75	2·40

290 Letterbox

1995. Tenth Anniv of Nigerian Post and Telecommunication Corporations. Multicoloured.

687	1n. Type **290**	10	10
688	1n.50 Letter showing "1 JAN 1985" postmark (horiz)	10	10
689	5n. Nipost and Nitel emblems (horiz)	30	45
690	10n. Mobile telephones	60	1·00

291 Woman preparing Food

1995. Family Support Programme. Multicoloured.

691	1n. Type **291**	10	10
692	1n.50 Mother teaching children	10	10
693	5n. Family meal	30	45
694	10n. Agricultural workers and tractor	60	1·00

292 "Candlestick" Telephone

1995. Cent of First Telephone in Nigeria. Multicoloured.

695	1n.50 Type **292**	10	10
696	10n. Early equipment	60	1·00

293 F.A.O. Emblem

1995. 50th Anniv of F.A.O. Multicoloured.

697	1n.50 Type **293**	10	10
698	30n. Fishing canoes	1·90	2·75

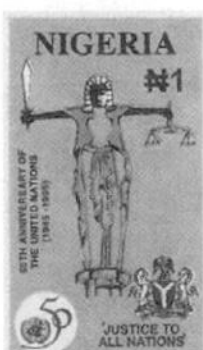

294 "Justice" and 50th Anniversary Emblem

1995. 50th Anniv of United Nations. Multicoloured.

699	1n. Type **294**	10	10
700	1n.50 Toxic waste (horiz)	10	10
701	5n. Tourist hut (horiz)	30	40
702	10n. Nigerian armoured car on U.N. duty (horiz)	1·25	1·40

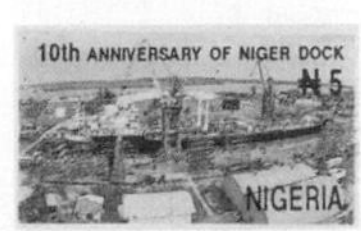

295 Container Ship in Dock

1996. Tenth Anniv of Niger Dock. Multicoloured.

703	5n. Type **295**	35	30
704	10n. "Badagri" (tourist launch) on crane	65	60
705	20n. Shipping at dock	1·00	1·50
706	30n. "Odoragushin" (ferry)	1·50	2·50

296 Scientist and Crops

1996. 21st Anniv of E.C.O.W.A.S. (Economic Community of West African States). Multicoloured.

707	5n. Type **296**	30	30
708	30n. Queue at border crossing	2·00	2·50

297 Judo

1996. Olympic Games, Atlanta. Multicoloured.

709	5n. Type **297**	35	30
710	10n. Tennis	80	60
711	20n. Relay race	1·00	1·50
712	30n. Football	1·50	2·25

298 Nigerian Flag and Exhibition Emblem

1996. "ISTANBUL '96" International Stamp Exhibition.

713	**298**	30n. mauve, green and black	1·50	2·25

299 "Volvariella esculenta"

1996. Fungi. Multicoloured.

714	5n. Type **299**	40	30
715	10n. "Lentinus subnudus"	70	60
716	20n. "Tricholoma lobayensis"	80	1·50
717	30n. "Pleurotus tuber-regium"	1·00	2·25

300 Boy with Toys

1996. 50th Anniv of UNICEF. Multicoloured.

718	5n. Type **300**	30	30
719	30n. Girl reading book (horiz)	1·50	2·50

301 Literacy Logo

1996. Fifth Anniv of Mass Literacy Commission.

720	**301**	5n. emerald, green and black	30	30
721	-	30n. emerald, green and black	1·50	2·50

DESIGN: 30n. Hands holding book and literacy logo.

302 Three Footballers

1998. World Cup Football Championship, France. Multicoloured.

722	5n. Type **302**	25	30
723	10n. Player with ball (vert)	55	60
724	20n. Player receiving ball (vert)	1·10	1·25
725	30n. Two opposing players	1·60	2·50

303 University Tower and Complex

1998. 50th Anniv of Ibadan University. Multicoloured.

726	5n. Type **303**	25	30
727	30n. Anniversary logo and University crest	1·60	2·50

304 Ship and Logo

1998. Eighth Anniv of Economic Community of West African States Military Arm (ECOMOG). Multicoloured.

728	5n. Type **304**	25	30
729	30n. Logo and original member states	1·25	1·75
730	50n. Current member states	2·25	3·50

305 Caged Steam Locomotive

1999. Centenary of Nigerian Railway Corporation. Multicoloured.

731	5n. Type **305**	25	30
732	10n. Iddo Terminus	55	60
733	20n. Diesel locomotive No. 2131	1·10	1·25
734	30n. Passenger train pulling into station	1·60	2·50

306 Football and Globe

1999. 11th World Youth Football Championship, Nigeria. Multicoloured.

735	5n.+5n. Type **306**	15	20
736	10n.+5n. Player throwing ball	20	25
737	20n.+5n. Player scoring goal	30	50
738	30n.+5n. Map of Nigeria showing venues	40	70
739	40n.+5n. World Youth Football Championship logo	50	80
740	50n.+5n. Player being tackled	65	90
MS741	120×115 mm. Nos. 735/40	2·00	3·00

307 Sea Life and F.E.P.A. Emblem

1999. Tenth Anniv of Federal Environmental Protection Agency. Multicoloured.

742	5n. Type **307**	30	30
743	10n. Forest	65	60
744	20n. Monkeys	1·40	1·10
745	30n. Villagers and wildlife	2·75	2·75

308 Nicon Emblem

1999. 30th Anniv of Nicon Insurance Corporation. Multicoloured.

746	5n. Type **308**	25	30
747	30n. Emblem and Nicon Building (horiz)	1·00	1·75

309 Map of Nigeria in 1900

2000. New Millennium (1st Issue). Multicoloured.

748	10n. Type **309**	50	15
749	20n. Map of Nigeria in 1914	70	40
750	30n. Coat of arms	75	80
751	40n. Map of Nigeria in 1996	1·10	1·60

See also Nos. 786/9.

310 Sunshine Hour Recorder

2000. 50th Anniv of World Meteorological Organization.

752	**310**	10n. multicoloured	25	15
753	-	30n. brown and blue	75	1·00

DESIGN—HORIZ: 30n. Meteorological station.

311 "Freedom of the Press"

2000. Return to Democracy. Multicoloured.

754	10n. Type **311**	20	15
755	20n. "Justice for All" (horiz)	35	30
756	30n. Parliamentary Mace	55	55
757	40n. President Olusegun Obasanjo	75	1·40
MS758	99×109 mm. Nos. 754/7	1·75	2·25

312 Boxing

2000. Olympic Games, Sydney. Multicoloured.

759	10n. Type **312**	1·00	15
760	20n. Weightlifting	35	30
761	30n. Women's football	1·00	55
762	40n. Men's football	75	1·40
MS763	136×118 mm. Nos. 759/62	2·25	2·50

313 Obafemi Awolowo

2000. 40th Anniv of Nigeria's Independence.

764	**313**	10n. black, emerald and green	1·00	15
765	-	20n. black, emerald and green	35	30
766	-	30n. black, emerald and green	55	45
767	-	40n. multicoloured	80	80
768	-	50n. multicoloured	95	1·25

DESIGNS—VERT: 20n. Abubakar Tafawa Balewa; 30n. Nnamdi Azikiwe. HORIZ: 40n. Liquified gas station; 50n. Container ships.

314 Hug Plum

2001. Fruit. Multicoloured.

769	20n. Type **314**	55	30
770	30n. White star apple	65	40
771	40n. African breadfruit	85	85
772	50n. Akee apple	95	1·40

315 *Daily Times* Headquarters, Lagos

2001. 75th Anniv of The Daily Times of Nigeria. Multicoloured.

773	20n. Type **315**	40	30
774	30n. First issue of *Nigerian Daily Times*, 1926	55	45
775	40n. *Daily Times* printing works, Lagos	75	85
776	50n. *Daily Times* masthead, 1947	90	1·40

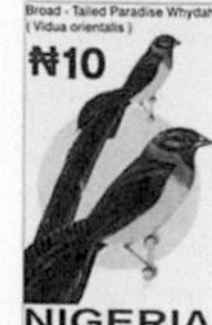

316 Broad-tailed Paradise Whydah

2001. Wildlife. Multicoloured.

777	10n. Type **316**	50	15
778	15n. Fire-bellied woodpecker	60	20
779	20n. Grant's zebra (horiz)	60	20
780	25n. Aardvark (horiz)	60	25
781	30n. Preuss's guenon (monkey)	60	30
782	40n. Great ground pangolin (horiz)	70	40
783	50n. Pygmy chimpanzee (*Pan paniscus*) (horiz)	90	70
784	100n. Red-eared guenon (monkey)	1·50	1·25

317 "Children encircling Globe" (Urska Golob)

2001. U.N. Year of Dialogue among Civilisations.

785	**317**	20n. multicoloured	50	50

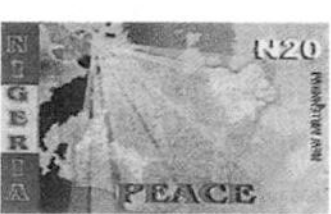

318 Map of Nigeria and Dove

2002. New Millennium (2nd issue). Multicoloured.

786	20n. Type **318**	40	30
787	30n. Globe and satellite dish	55	40
788	40n. Handshake across flag in shape of Nigeria	95	95
789	50n. Two overlapping hearts	85	1·40

319 Kola Nuts

2002. Cash Crops. Multicoloured.

790	20n. Type **319**	30	25
791	30n. Oil palm	40	35
792	40n. Cassava	50	60
793	50n. Maize (vert)	60	80

320 Nigerian Player dribbling Ball

2002. World Cup Football Championship, Japan and Korea. Multicoloured.

794	20n. Type **320**	30	25
795	30n. Footballs around Globe	40	35
796	40n. Footballer's legs and World Cup Trophy (horiz)	50	60
797	50n. World Cup Trophy	60	80

321 Nurse caring for Patient

2003. World AIDS Day. Multicoloured.

798	20n. Type **321**	40	20
799	50n. Counselling on AIDS	85	1·10

322 Girl and Boy in Class

2003. Universal Basic Education. Multicoloured.

800	20n. Type **322**	40	20
801	50n. Boy writing in book (horiz)	1·00	1·50

2003. Eighth All Africa Games, Abuja. Multicoloured.

802	20n. Type **323**	40	20
803	30n. High jump (horiz)	50	35
804	40n. Taekwondo (horiz)	70	80
805	50n. Long jump	80	1·00
MS806	172×98 mm. Nos. 802/5	2·25	2·50

324 Logo and Map of Nigeria

2003. Commonwealth Heads of Government Meeting, Abuja. Multicoloured.

807	20n. Type **324**	40	20
808	50n. Logo (vert)	1·00	1·25

325 Female with Cubs

2003. Endangered Species. Side-Striped Jackal. Multicoloured.

809	20n. Type **325**	35	20
810	40n. Adult jackal	65	40
811	80n. Two jackals	1·25	1·40
812	100n. Adult jackal (with head lowered, looking through grass)	1·50	2·00

326 Athletes

2004. Olympic Games, Athens. Multicoloured.

813	50n. Type **326**	80	90
814	120n. Basketball	2·00	2·50
MS814a	168×107 mm. Nos. 813/14		

327 Children carrying Water and Food (Zainab Jalloh)

2004. Children's Day. Multicoloured.

815	50n. Type **327**	70	45
816	90n. Book with lightening bolt and hand-cuffed hands (Jessica Umaru) (horiz)	1·25	1·40
817	120n. Skulls, outline of Nigeria and forbidden weapons (Chinonso Chukwougor)(horiz)	1·50	2·25
818	150n. Skull smoking, drugs and alcohol (Sanusi Omolola)	1·75	2·50
MS819	170×104 mm. Nos. 815/18	4·75	6·00

328 Emblems in "100"

2005. Centenary of Rotary International. Multicoloured.

820	50n. Type **328**	70	50
821	120n. Map of world and Rotary and centenary emblems	1·50	2·25

329 Outline of Stamp

2005. 131st Year of Commemorative Postage Stamps. Multicoloured.

823	50n. Type **329**	70	50
824	90n. Outlines of Nigeria and postage stamp	1·25	1·00
825	120n. "1874 2005" and Nigerian flag in outline map	1·50	2·00
826	150n. 1961 3d. 1st anniv of independence and 2002 50n. maize stamps	1·75	2·25

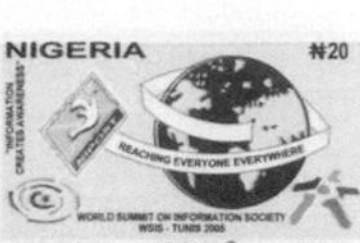

330 Nipost Emblem and Globe

2005. World Summit on the Information Society, Tunis. Multicoloured.

827	20n. Type **330**	30	20
828	50n. Motorcycle courier, satellite dish and globe (vert)	70	85
829	120n. Type **330**	1·75	2·25

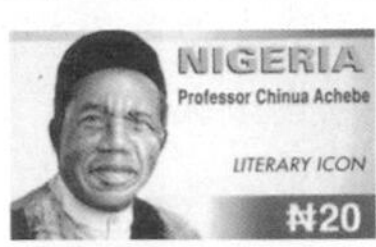

331 Prof. Chinua Achebe (novelist)

2006. Nigerian Personalities. Multicoloured.

830	20n. Type **331**	30	20
831	40n. Alhaji Abubakar Imam (journalist and writer)	50	55
832	50n. Prof. Wole Soyinka (dramatist and writer)	60	70
833	50n. Prof. Ayodele Awojobi (engineer and educationist) (vert)	60	70
834	50n. Prof. Gabriel Oyibo (mathematician and physicist) (vert)	60	70
835	50n. As No. 833 (vert)	60	70
836	100n. As No. 833 (vert)	1·50	1·75
837	120n. As No. 834 (vert)	1·75	1·90
838	150n. As No. 835 (vert)	2·75	3·00

332 International Conference Centre, Abuja

2006. 52nd Commonwealth Parliamentary Conference, Abuja. Sheet 159×97 mm containing T **332** and similar horiz design. Multicoloured. Imperf.

839	20n. Type **332**	30	20
840	50n. National Assembly Building, Abuja	70	80
MS841	159×97 mm. 20n. As Type **332**; 50n. As No. 840. Imperf	1·25	1·50

Stamps from **MS**841 differ slightly from the sheet stamps in design. The 20n. from **MS**841 has a smaller face value in white and the inscription "NIGERIA International Conference Centre" in a grey panel. The 50n. from **MS**841 has the face value in green (red on No. 840) and the inscription "NIGERIA National Assembly" on a white background (green panel on No. 840).

333 Queen Elizabeth II on Visit to Nigeria, 2003

2006. 80th Birthday of Queen Elizabeth II. Multicoloured.

842	20n. Type **333**	50	25
843	50n. Queen Elizabeth II (vert)	90	1·25

334 Agbani Darego

2006. Crowning of Miss Nigeria Agbani Darego as Miss World 2001. Multicoloured.

844	20n. Type **334**	35	25
845	50n. Agbani Darego and world map (horiz)	65	1·00

335 Entrance to Abuja and Fireworks

2006. Tenth Anniv of Abuja. Multicoloured.

846	20n. Type **335**	35	25
847	50n. Emblem inside outline map (vert)	65	1·00

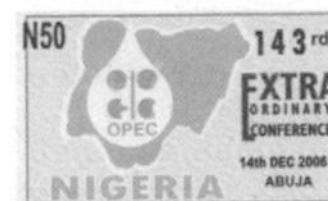

336 Emblem and Outline Map

2006. 143rd Extraordinary OPEC Conference, Abuja.

848	**336**	50n. multicoloured	65	85

337 Mungo Park and Memorial to Park

2007. Death Bicentenary (2006) of Mungo Park (explorer). Multicoloured.

849	20n. Type **337**	25	25
850	50n. Mungo Park and river Niger (horiz)	75	85

338 CBAAC and FESTAC '77 Emblems and Richard Lander, Jebba

2007. 30th Anniv of FESTAC '77 Second World Black and African Festival of Arts and Culture, Lagos.

851	**338**	50n. multicoloured	1·00	1·00

338a Fulani Man, north-west Nigeria

2007. 24th UPU Congress, Nairobi. Ceremonial Costumes

851a	20n. Type **338a**	35	35
851b	20n. Igbo couple, south-east Nigeria	35	35
851c	30n. South Zone costume	35	35
851d	30n. Tiv couple, north-central Nigeria (horiz)	35	35
851e	50n. North East Zone costume	35	35
851f	50n. Yoruba couple, south-west Nigeria	35	35
MS851g	100×164 mm. Nos. 851*a/f*. Imperf	3·50	3·50

The horiz stamp No. 851*d* is laid vertically within **MS**851*g*

339 Silverback (adult male) Gorilla

2008. Endangered Species. Cross River Gorilla (*Gorilla gorilla diehli*). Multicoloured.

852	20n. Type **339**	45	30
853	50n. Silverback with female and baby (horiz)	90	75
854	100n. Baby riding on female's back (horiz)	1·60	1·75
855	150n. Head of gorilla	2·25	2·50

340 Hands and Money ('Treasury Looting kills the Economy')

2008. EFCC (Economic and Financial Crimes Commission) Anti-Corruption Campaign. Multicoloured.

856	20n. Type **340**	40	35
857	50n. Stop sign and 'LET'S FIX NIGERIA'	1·25	85
858	100n. Clasped hands and 'UNITED WE WIN'	1·50	1·75

341 Athletes breaking Finish Tape

2008. Olympic Games, Beijing. Multicoloured.

859	20n. Type **341**	30	30
860	50n. Footballer scoring goal	75	75
861	100n. Wrestling (vert)	1·50	1·75

342 Overloaded Vehicle

2008. 20th Anniv of the Federal Road Safety Commission Nigeria

862	**342**	50n. multicoloured	1·00	75

343 Emblem

2009. 30th Anniv of the Nigerian Institute of Advanced Legal Studies

863	**343**	50n. multicoloured	75	75

344 Emblem

2010. 30th Anniv of Pan African Postal Union

864	**344**	50n. multicoloured	75	75

345 Pres. Umaru Musa Yar'Adua and Nigerian Flag

2010. Tenth Anniv of Return to Democracy. Multicoloured.

865	50n. Type **345**	70	80
866	50n. Scales, mace and lawyer's wig ('The Rule of Law') (vert)	70	80

346 Footballers heading Ball

2010. World Cup Football Championship, South Africa

867	20n. Type **346**	35	25
868	30n. Trophy, football and globe (vert)	50	45
869	50n. Footballers and stadium	75	90

347 Woman, Globe and GT Bank Emblem

2010. 20th Anniv of Guaranty Trust Bank

870	**347**	20n. multicoloured	50	25
871	**347**	50n. multicoloured	1·00	50
872	**347**	100n. multicoloured	2·00	2·00
873	**347**	120n. multicoloured	2·25	2·50

348 Emblem

2010. 50th Anniv of OPEC (Organization of Petroleum Exporting Countries). Multicoloured.

874	50n. Type **348**	1·00	55
875	120n. '50' emblem	2·25	2·50

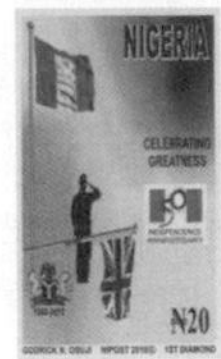

349 Lowered Union Jack and Raised Nigerian Flag

2010. 50th Anniv of Independence

876	20n. Type **349**	35	20
877	30n. Arms in '50th'	55	50
878	50n. 'Founding Fathers' and Nigerian flag (80×25 mm)	1·00	1·10
879	50n. Montage of photographs showing equestrian statue, refinery and workers (56×40 mm)	1·00	1·10

350 Terracotta Head, Ile-Ife

2010. 2000 Years of Nigerian Arts and Wildlife

(a) Litho Kalamazoo Security Print Ltd. Incorporating round hologram. "NIGERIA" and face value in fluorescent ink

880	20n. Type **350** (Type I)	45	45
881	30n. Bronze bowl, Awka	65	65
882	50n. Lander Brothers Anchorage, Asaba (Type I)	1·10	1·10
883	50n. Slave chain, Badagry	1·10	1·10
884	90n. Elephants at Yankari Game reserve (*horiz*)	1·40	1·40
885	120n. Seated human figure, Tada-Niger State	2·50	2·50

(b) Litho Superflex Int Ltd, Lagos ("SIL")". Incorporating square hologram and overall multiple "NIPOST" and dove diagonal fluorescent overprint

888	20n. Ife Terracotta (Type II) (2011)	—	—
889	30n. Igbo-ukwu bronze (*horiz*) (2011)	—	—
890	50n. Nok terracotta head, Kaduna	1·10	1·10
891	50n. Monkey Colony, Lagwa-Mbaise	1·10	1·10
892	50n. Lander Brothers Anchorage, Asaba (Type III) (2011)	—	—
893	100n. Argungu fishing festival (*horiz*)	2·25	2·25

(c) Litho Nigerian Security Printing and Minting Co

897	50n. Lander Brothers Anchorage, Asaba (Type II)	14·00	14·00

351 Gugur Waterfall on Katsina Ala River

2011. Benue State. Multicoloured.

901	20n. Type **351**	30	30
902	30n. Basket of produce ('Benue State - Food basket of the Nation')	45	45
903	50n. Senator Joseph Sarwuan Tarka (1932-1980)	75	75
904	100n. Benue Bridge, opened May 24, 1932	1·50	1·50

MS905 160×100 mm. Nos. 901/4. Imperf 3·50 3·50

352 Heart and Arteries ('Tax Sustains a Nation' 'Pay your Taxes for National Development')

2011. 'Pay your Taxes'. Multicoloured.

906 20n. Type **352** 30 30
907 50n. Light bulb and tap ('For Infrastructural Facilities and Social Amenities Pay your Taxes!') 75 75
908 100n. Taxcard ('Be Patriotic Pay your Tax') 1·50 1·50

353 Anniversary Emblem

2011. 50th Anniv of the Nigerian Institute of Management

909 **353** 50n. multicoloured 75 75
MS909*a* As No. 909. Imperf 1·00 1·00

354 Emblem

2012. Phila Africa African Exhibition of Postage Stamps and Philatelic Products, Abuja

910 **354** 50n. multicoloured 75 75
MS911 147×100 mm. As No. 910. Imperf 2·50 2·50

POSTAGE DUE STAMPS

D1

1959

D1 **D1** 1d. orange 15 1·00
D2 **D1** 2d. orange 20 1·00
D3 **D1** 3d. orange 25 1·50
D4 **D1** 6d. orange 25 5·00
D5 **D1** 1s. black 50 6·50

1961

D6 1d. red 15 40
D7 2d. blue 20 45
D8 3d. green 25 60
D9 6d. yellow 30 1·40
D10 1s. blue 50 2·25

1973. As Type **D1**.

D11 2k. red 10 30
D12 3k. blue 10 30
D13 5k. yellow 15 30
D14 10k. green 20 30

Pt. 1

NIUAFO'OU

A remote island, part of the Kingdom of Tonga, with local autonomy.

100 seniti = 1 pa'anga.

1 Map of Niuafo'ou

1983

1 **1** 1s. stone, black and red 40 90
2 **1** 2s. stone, black and green 40 90
3 **1** 3s. stone, black and blue 40 90
4 **1** 3s. stone, black and brown 40 90
5 **1** 5s. stone, black and purple 50 90
6 **1** 6s. stone, black and blue 50 90
7 **1** 9s. stone, black and green 50 90
8 **1** 10s. stone, black and blue 50 90
9 **1** 13s. stone, black and green 75 90
10 **1** 15s. stone, black and brown 80 1·25
11 **1** 20s. stone, black and blue 85 1·25
12 **1** 29s. stone, black and purple 1·10 80
13 **1** 32s. stone, black and green 1·10 90
14 **1** 47s. stone, black and red 1·40 1·40

1983. No. 820 of Tonga optd **NIUAFO'OU KINGDOM OF TONGA** or surch also.

15 1p. on 2p. green and black 2·50 3·50
16 2p. green 3·50 5·00

2a SPIA de Havilland DHC-6 Twin Otter 300

1983. Inauguration of Niuafo'ou Airport.

17 **2a** 29s. multicoloured 1·50 1·00
18 **2a** 1p. multicoloured 3·00 3·25

1983. As T **1**, but without value, surch.

19 3s. stone, black and blue 30 50
20 5s. stone, black and blue 30 50
21 32s. stone, black and blue 1·75 1·25
22 2p. stone, black and blue 8·50 10·00

4 Eruption of Niuafo'ou

1983. 25th Anniv of Re-settlement. Multicoloured.

23 5s. Type **4** 60 55
24 29s. Lava flow 1·25 1·00
25 32s. Islanders fleeing to safety 1·40 1·00
26 1p.50 Evacuation by canoe 4·00 6·00

5 Purple Swamphen

1983. Birds of Niuafo'ou.

27 **5** 1s. black and mauve 1·50 1·25
28 - 2s. black and blue 1·50 1·25
29 - 3s. black and green 1·50 1·25
30 - 5s. black and yellow 1·75 1·25
31 - 6s. black and orange 2·00 1·60
32 - 9s. multicoloured 2·25 1·25
33 - 10s. multicoloured 2·25 2·00
34 - 13s. multicoloured 2·75 1·60
35 - 15s. multicoloured 2·75 2·50
36 - 20s. multicoloured 3·00 2·75
37 - 29s. multicoloured 3·00 1·50
38 - 32s. multicoloured 3·00 1·60
39 - 47s. multicoloured 3·50 2·25
40 - 1p. multicoloured 6·00 8·50
41 - 2p. multicoloured 8·00 12·00

DESIGNS—VERT (22×29 mm): 2s. White collared kingfisher; 3s. Red-headed parrot finch; 5s. Buff-banded rail ("Banded Rail"); 6s. Polynesian scrub hen ("Niuafo'ou megapode"); 9s. Green honeyeater; 10s. Purple swamphen (different). (22×36 mm): 29s. Red-headed parrot finch (different); 32s. White-collared kingfisher (different). (29×42 mm): 1p. As 10s. HORIZ (29×22 mm): 13s. Buff-banded rail ("Banded Rail") (different); 15s. Polynesian scrub hen (different). (36×22 mm): 20s. As 13s.; 47s. As 15s. (42×29 mm): 2p. As 15s.

6 Green Turtle

1984. Wildlife and Nature Reserve. Multicoloured.

42 29s. Type **6** 70 70
43 32s. Insular flying fox (vert) 70 70
44 47s. Humpback whale 3·50 1·75
45 1p.50 Polynesian scrub hen ("Niuafo'ou megapode") (vert) 5·50 7·50

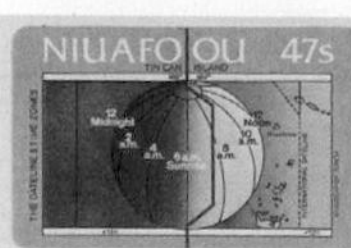

7 Diagram of Time Zones

1984. Cent of International Dateline. Multicoloured.

46 47s. Type **7** 75 50
47 2p. Location map showing Niuafo'ou 2·75 3·50

8 Australia 1913 £2 Kangaroo Definitive

1984. "Ausipex" International Stamp Exhibition, Melbourne. Multicoloured.

48 32s. Type **8** 75 60
49 1p.50 Niuafo'ou 1983 10s. map definitive 2·25 3·00
MS50 90×100 mm. As Nos. 48/9, but without exhibition logo and with face value at foot 1·75 2·50

9 Dutch Brass Band entertaining Tongans

1985. 400th Birth Anniv of Jacob Le Maire (discoverer of Niuafo'ou).

51 **9** 13s. brown, yellow & orange 25 40
52 - 32s. brown, yellow and blue 55 60
53 - 47s. brown, yellow and green 75 80
54 - 1p.50 brown, cinnamon and yellow 2·25 3·00
MS55 90×90 mm. 1p.50 brown, light brown and blue. Imperf 1·50 2·00

DESIGNS: 32s. Tongans preparing kava; 47s. Tongan canoes and outriggers; 1p.50, "Eendracht" at anchor off Tafahi Island.

10 "Ysabel", 1902

1985. Mail Ships. Multicoloured.

56B 9s. Type **10** 35 55
57A 13s. "Tofua I", 1908 70 55
58B 47s. "Mariposa", 1934 1·10 1·60
59B 1p.50 "Matua", 1936 2·50 4·00

11 Preparing to fire Rocket

1985. Niuafo'ou Rocket Mails. Multicoloured.

60 32s. Type **11** 1·25 80
61 42s. Rocket in flight 1·50 1·00
62 57s. Ship's crew watching rocket's descent 1·60 1·40
63 1p.50 Islanders reading mail 3·50 5·00

12 Halley's Comet, 684 A.D.

1986. Appearance of Halley's Comet. Multicoloured.

64 42s. Type **12** 5·50 3·50
65 42s. Halley's Comet, 1066, from Bayeux Tapestry 5·50 3·50
66 42s. Edmond Halley 5·50 3·50
67 42s. Halley's Comet, 1910 5·50 3·50
68 42s. Halley's Comet, 1986 5·50 3·50
69 57s. Type **12** 5·50 3·50
70 57s. As No. 65 5·50 3·50
71 57s. As No. 66 5·50 3·50
72 57s. As No. 67 5·50 3·50
73 57s. As No. 68 5·50 3·50

Nos. 64/8 and 69/73 were printed together, *se-tenant*, forming composite designs.

1986. Nos. 32/9 surch.

74 4s. on 9s. Green honeyeater 1·00 2·75
75 4s. on 10s. Purple swamphen 1·00 2·75
76 42s. on 13s. Buff-banded rail ("Banded Rail") 3·25 2·25
77 42s. on 15s. Polynesian scrub hen 3·25 2·25
78 57s. on 29s. Red-headed parrot finch 3·75 2·50
79 57s. on 32s. White-collared kingfisher 3·75 2·50
80 2p.50 on 20s. Buff-banded rail ("Banded Rail") 12·00 14·00
81 2p.50 on 47s. Polynesian scrub hen 12·00 14·00

13a Peace Corps Surveyor and Pipeline

1986. "Ameripex '86" International Stamp Exhibition, Chicago. 25th Anniv of United States Peace Corps. Multicoloured.

82 57s. Type **13a** 1·25 1·25
83 1p.50 Inspecting crops 2·25 3·00
MS84 90×90 mm. Nos. 82/3, magnifying glass and tweezers. Imperf 3·75 5·00

14 Swimmers with Mail

1986. Centenary of First Tonga Stamps. Designs showing Niuafo'ou mail transport. Multicoloured.

85 42s. Type **14** 90 90
86 57s. Collecting tin can mail 1·10 1·10
87 1p. Ship firing mail rocket 2·00 2·50
88 2p.50 "Collecting the Mails" (detail) (C. Mayger) 3·50 4·75
MS89 135×80 mm. No. 88 5·00 7·00

15 Woman with Nourishing Foods ("Eat a balanced diet")

1987. Red Cross. Preventive Medicine. Multicoloured.

90 15s. Type **15** 60 60
91 42s. Nurse with baby ("Give them post-natal care") 1·60 1·60
92 1p. Man with insecticide ("Insects spread disease") 2·50 3·25
93 2p.50 Boxer ("Say no to alcohol, drugs, tobacco") 4·00 5·50

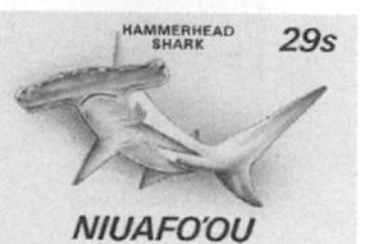

16 Hammerhead

1987. Sharks. Multicoloured.

94 29s. Type **16** 2·00 1·75
95 32s. Tiger shark 2·00 1·75
96 47s. Grey nurse shark 2·50 2·25

97 1p. Great white shark 4·00 6·00
MS98 90×90 mm. 2p. Shark and fishes 11·00 12·00

17 Capt. E. C. Musick and Sikorsky S.42A Flying Boat "Samoan Clipper"

1987. Air Pioneers of the South Pacific. Multicoloured.
99 42s. Type **17** 2·50 1·60
100 57s. Capt. J. W. Burgess and Short S. 30 modified "G" Class flying boat "Aotearoa" 2·75 1·75
101 1p.50 Sir Charles Kingsford Smith and Fokker F.VIIa/3m "Southern Cross" 5·00 4·50
102 2p. Amelia Earhart and Lockheed 10E Electra 5·50 6·00

18 Polynesian Scrub Hen and 1983 1s. Map Definitive

1988. Fifth Annivs of First Niuafo'ou Postage Stamp (42, 57s.) and Niuafo'ou Airport Inauguration (1, 2p.). Multicoloured.
103 42s. Type **18** 1·00 75
104 57s. As Type **18**, but with stamp at left 1·00 95
105 1p. Concorde and 1983 Airport Inauguration 29s. stamp 5·50 3·25
106 2p. As 1p. but with stamp at left 6·00 4·00

19 Sailing Ship and Ship's Boat

1988. Bicentenary of Australian Settlement. Sheet 115×110 mm containing T **19** and similar vert designs. Multicoloured.
MS107 42s. Type **19**; 42s. Aborigines; 42s. Early settlement; 42s. Marine and convicts; 42s. Sheep station; 42s. Mounted stockman; 42s. Kangaroos and early Trans Continental locomotive; 42s. Kangaroos and train carriages; 42s. Flying Doctor aircraft; 42s. Cricket match; 42s. Wicket and Sydney skyline; 42s. Fielders and Sydney Harbour Bridge 38·00 35·00

Each horizontal strip of 4 within No. **MS**107 shows a composite design.

20 Audubon's Shearwaters and Blowholes, Houma, Tonga

1988. Islands of Polynesia. Multicoloured.
108 42s. Type **20** 1·50 95
109 57s. Brown kiwi at Akaroa Harbour, New Zealand 2·25 1·40
110 90s. Red-tailed tropic birds at Rainmaker Mountain, Samoa 2·50 2·50
111 2p.50 Laysan albatross at Kapoho Volcano, Hawaii 4·75 6·00

21 Sextant

1989. Bicentenary of Mutiny on the Bounty. Sheet 115×110 mm containing T **21** and similar vert designs. Multicoloured.
MS112 42s. Type **21**; 42s. Capt. Bligh; 42s. Lieutenant, 1787; 42s. Midshipman, 1787; 42s. Tahitian woman and contemporary newspaper; 42s. Breadfruit plant; 42s. Pistol and extract from "Mutiny on the Bounty"; 42s. Book illustration of Bligh cast adrift; 42s. Profile of Tahitian woman and extract from contemporary newspaper; 42s. Signatures of "Bounty officers"; 42s. Fletcher Christian; 42s. Tombstone of John Adams, Pitcairn Island 17·00 16·00

22 Spiny Hatchetfish

1989. Fish of the Deep. Multicoloured.
113 32s. Type **22** 85 1·00
114 42s. Snipe eel 1·00 1·00
115 57s. Viperfish 1·25 1·50
116 1p.50 Football anglerfish 3·00 4·00

23 Formation of Earth's Surface

1989. The Evolution of the Earth. Multicoloured. (a) Size 27×35½ mm.
117 1s. Type **23** 60 1·00
118 2s. Cross-section of Earth's crust 60 1·00
119 5s. Volcano 70 1·00
120 10s. Cross-section of Earth during cooling 70 1·00
120a 13s. Gem stones 1·75 90
121 15s. Sea 70 1·00
122 20s. Mountains 70 1·00
123 32s. River gorge 85 50
124 42s. Early plant life, Silurian era 1·00 65
124a 45s. Early marine life 1·50 90
125 50s. Fossils and Cambrian lifeforms 1·25 80
126 57s. Carboniferous forest and coal seams 1·50 80
126a 60s. Dinosaurs feeding 2·25 1·25
126b 80s. Tyrannosaurus and triceratops fighting 2·75 2·00

(b) Size 25½×40 mm.
127 1p. Dragonfly and amphibians, Carboniferous era 2·25 2·00
128 1p.50 Dinosaurs, Jurassic era 3·25 3·50
129 2p. Archaeopteryx and mammals, Jurassic era 3·75 4·00
130 5p. Human family and domesticated dog, Pleistocene era 6·00 7·00
130a 10p. Mammoth and sabre-tooth tiger 10·00 12·00

24 Astronaut on Moon and Newspaper Headline

1989. "World Stamp Expo '89" International Stamp Exhibition, Washington.
131 **24** 57s. multicoloured 2·00 1·50

1989. 20th Universal Postal Union Congress, Washington. Miniature sheet, 185×150 mm, containing designs as Nos. 117/20, 121/4, 125/6 and 127/30, but wuth U.P.U. emblem at top right and some new values.
MS132 32s.×5 (as Nos. 117/20, 121); 42s.×5 (as Nos. 122/4, 125/6); 57s.×5 (as Nos. 127/30, 131) 23·00 24·00

25 Lake Vai Lahi

1990. Niuafo'ou Crater Lake. Multicoloured.
133 42s. Type **25** 70 1·00
134 42s. Islands in centre of lake 70 1·00
135 42s. South-west end of lake and islet 70 1·00
136 1p. Type **25** 1·40 1·60
137 1p. As No. 134 1·40 1·60
138 1p. As No. 135 1·40 1·60

Nos. 133/8 were printed together in *se-tenant* strips of each value, forming a composite design.

26 Penny Black and Tin Can Mail Service

1990. 150th Anniv of the Penny Black. Multicoloured.
139 42s. Type **26** 1·25 1·00
140 57s. U.S.A. 1847 10c. stamp 1·40 1·25
141 75s. Western Australia 1854 1d. stamp 1·60 2·00
142 2p.50 Mafeking Siege 1900 1d. stamp 5·00 6·00

27 Humpback Whale surfacing

1990. Polynesian Whaling. Multicoloured.
143 15s. Type **27** 2·25 1·75
144 42s. Whale diving under canoe 2·75 1·90
145 57s. Tail of Blue whale 3·00 1·90
146 2p. Old man and pair of whales 8·00 9·00
MS147 120×93 mm. 1p. Pair of whales (38×30 mm) 10·00 11·00

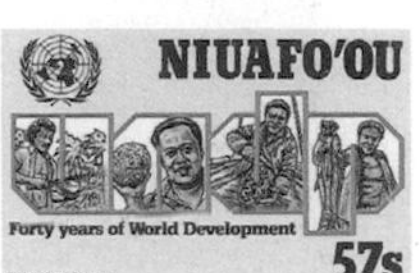

27a Agriculture and Fisheries

1990. 40th Anniv of U.N. Development Programme. Multicoloured.
148 57s. Type **27a** 90 1·40
149 57s. Education 90 1·40
150 2p.50 Healthcare 3·25 4·00
151 2p.50 Communications 3·25 4·00

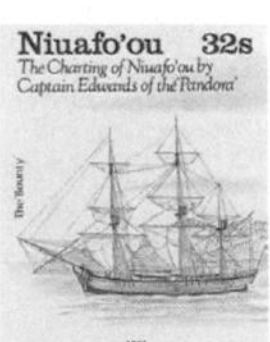

28 H.M.S. "Bounty"

1991. Bicentenary of Charting of Niuafo'ou. Multicoloured.
152 32s. Type **28** 1·25 1·75
153 42s. Chart of "Pandora's" course 1·40 1·75
154 57s. H.M.S. "Pandora" (frigate) 1·75 1·75
MS155 120×93 mm. 2p. Capt. Edwards of the "Pandora"; 3p. Capt. Bligh of the "Bounty" 14·00 14·00

1991. Ornithological and Scientific Expedition to Niuafo'ou. No. **MS**147 surch **1991 ORNITHOLOGICAL AND SCIENTIFIC EXPEDITION T $1**.
MS156 120×93 mm. 1p. on 1p. multicoloured 3·25 4·00

30 Longhorned Beetle Grub

1991. Longhorned Beetle. Multicoloured.
157 42s. Type **30** 80 1·00
158 57s. Adult beetle 90 1·00
159 1p.50 Grub burrowing 2·75 3·25
160 2p.50 Adult on tree trunk 4·00 4·50

31 Heina meeting the Eel

1991. Christmas. The Legend of the Coconut Tree. Multicoloured.
161 15s. Type **31** 65 75
162 42s. Heina crying over the eel's grave 1·25 1·25
MS163 96×113 mm. 15s. Type **31**; 42s. No. 162; 1p.50, Heina's son collecting coconuts; 3p. Milk flowing from coconut 9·00 10·00

31a Columbus

1992. 500th Anniv of Discovery of America by Columbus. Sheet 119×109 mm. containing vert designs as T **31a**. Multicoloured.
MS164 57s. Columbus; 57s. Queen Isabella and King Ferdinand; 57s. Columbus being blessed by Abbot of Palos; 57s. 15th-century compass; 57s. Wooden traverse, windrose and the "Nina"; 57s. Bow of "Santa Maria"; 57s. Stern of "Santa Maria"; 57s. The "Pinta"; 57s. Crew erecting cross; 57s. Sailors and Indians; 57s. Columbus reporting to King and Queen; 57s. Coat of Arms 22·00 24·00

31b American Battleship Ablaze, Pearl Harbor

1992. 50th Anniv of War in the Pacific. Multicoloured.
165 42s. Type **31b** 1·75 1·75
166 42s. Destroyed American Douglas B-18 Bolo aircraft, Hawaii 1·75 1·75
167 42s. Newspaper and Japanese Mitsubishi A6M Zero-Sen fighter 1·75 1·75
168 42s. Pres. Roosevelt signing Declaration of War 1·75 1·75
169 42s. Japanese T95 light tank and Gen. MacArthur 1·75 1·75
170 42s. Douglas SBD Dauntless dive bomber and Admiral Nimitz 1·75 1·75
171 42s. Bren gun and Gen. Sir Thomas Blamey 1·75 1·75
172 42s. Australian mortar crew, Kokoda 1·75 1·75
173 42s. U.S.S. *Mississippi* in action and Maj. Gen. Julian C. Smith 1·75 1·75
174 42s. U.S.S. *Enterprise* (aircraft carrier) 1·75 1·75
175 42s. American marine and Maj. Gen. Curtis Lemay 1·75 1·75
176 42s. Boeing B-29 Superfortress bomber and Japanese surrender, Tokyo Bay 1·75 1·75

Nos. 165/76 were printed together, *se-tenant*, forming a composite design.

31c King Taufa'ahau Tupou IV and Queen Halaevalu During Coronation

1992. 25th Anniv of the Coronation of King Tupou IV.
177 **31c** 45s. multicoloured 75 75
178 - 80s. multicoloured 1·50 1·75
179 - 80s. black and brown 1·50 1·75
180 - 80s. multicoloured 1·50 1·75
181 - 2p. multicoloured 2·50 3·00

DESIGNS—(34×23 mm): No. 177, Type **31c**. (48×35 mm): No. 178, King Tupou IV and Tongan national anthem; 179, Extract from Investiture ceremony; 180, Tongan choir; 181, As 45s.

Nos. 177/81 show the King's first name incorrectly spelt as "Tauf'ahau".

32 Male and Female Scrub Hens searching for Food

1992. Endangered Species. Polynesian Scrub Hen. Multicoloured.

182	45s. Type **32**	1·00	1·25
183	60s. Female guarding egg	1·25	1·40
184	80s. Chick	1·60	1·75
185	1p.50 Head of male	2·75	3·50

33 1983 2s. Map Definitive and 1993 60s. Dinosaur Definitive

1993. Tenth Anniv of First Niuafo'ou Stamp. Multicoloured.

186	60s. Type **33**	1·25	1·40
187	80s. 1983 5s. definitive and 1993 80s. dinosaurs definitive	1·50	1·75

34 de Havilland Twin Otter 200/300 of South Pacific Island Airways

1993. Tenth Anniv of First Flight to Niuafo'ou. Multicoloured.

188	1p. Type **34**	1·50	2·00
189	2p.50 de Havilland Twin Otter 200/300 of Friendly Islands Airways	3·50	4·50

34a King Tupou IV and "Pangai" (patrol boat)

1993. 75th Birthday of King Taufa'ahau Tupou IV. Multicoloured.

190	45s. Type **34a**	90	65
191	80s. King Tupou IV and musical instruments (38½×51 mm)	1·40	1·75
192	80s. King Tupou IV and sporting events (38½×51 mm)	1·40	1·75
193	80s. King Tupou IV with De Havilland Twin Otter 200/300 airplane and telecommunications	1·40	1·75
194	2p. As 45s. but larger (38½×51 mm)	3·00	3·25

35 Blue-crowned Lorikeets

1993. Natural History of Lake Vai Lahi. Multicoloured.

195	60s. Type **35**	1·00	1·25
196	60s. White-tailed tropic bird and reef heron	1·00	1·25
197	60s. Black admiral (butterfly) and Niuafo'ou coconut beetle	1·00	1·25
198	60s. Niuafo'ou dragonfly, pacific black ducks and Niuafo'ou moths	1·00	1·25
199	60s. Niuafo'ou megapode	1·00	1·25

Nos. 195/9 were printed together, *se-tenant*, forming a composite design.

35a "Crater Lake Megapode and Volcano" (Paea Puletau)

1993. Children's Painting Competition Winners.

200	**35a**	10s. multicoloured	50	1·00
201	-	10s. black and grey	50	1·00
202	-	1p. multicoloured	3·50	3·75
203	-	1p. multicoloured	3·50	3·75

DESIGNS: Nos. 200 and 202, Type **35a**; Nos. 201 and 203, "Ofato Beetle Grubs of Niuafo'ou" (Peni Finau).

36 "Scarabaeidea"

1994. Beetles. Multicoloured.

204	60s. Type **36**	85	1·00
205	80s. "Coccinellidea"	1·10	1·40
206	1p.50 "Cerambycidea"	2·00	2·50
207	2p.50 "Pentatomidae"	3·75	4·25

37 Stern of H.M.S. "Bounty"

1994. Sailing Ships. Multicoloured.

208	80s. Type **37**	1·75	2·25
209	80s. Bow of H.M.S. "Bounty"	1·75	2·25
210	80s. H.M.S. "Pandora" (frigate)	1·75	2·25
211	80s. Whaling ship	1·75	2·25
212	80s. Trading schooner	1·75	2·25

38 Blue-crowned Lory and Lava Flows

1994. Volcanic Eruptions on Niuafo'ou. Multicoloured.

213	80s. Type **38**	1·25	1·75
214	80s. Pacific ducks over lava flows	1·25	1·75
215	80s. Megapodes and palm trees	1·25	1·75
216	80s. White-tailed tropic birds and inhabitants	1·25	1·75
217	80s. Reef heron and evacuation, 1946	1·25	1·75

Nos. 213/17 were printed together, se-tenant, forming a composite design.

1995. Visit South Pacific Year '95. Save the Whales. Nos. 143/6 surch **SAVE THE WHALES VISIT SOUTH PACIFIC YEAR '95**, emblem and value.

218	60s. on 42s. Whale diving under canoe	2·00	1·75
219	80s. on 15s. Type **27**	2·25	2·25
220	80s. on 57s. Tail of blue whale	2·25	2·25
221	2p. on 2p. Old man and pair of whales	4·25	4·50
MS222	120×93 mm. 1p.50 on 1p. Pair of whales (38×30 mm)	3·50	4·25

39a American Marine

1995. 50th Anniv of End of World War II in the Pacific.

223	**39a**	60s. yellow, black and blue	1·40	1·60
224	-	60s. yellow, black and blue	1·40	1·60
225	-	60s. yellow, black and blue	1·40	1·60
226	-	60s. yellow, black and blue	1·40	1·60
227	-	60s. yellow, black and blue	1·40	1·60
228	**39a**	80s. yellow, black and red	1·40	1·60
229	-	80s. yellow, black and red	1·40	1·60
230	-	80s. yellow, black and red	1·40	1·60
231	-	80s. yellow, black and red	1·40	1·60
232	-	80s. yellow, black and red	1·40	1·60

DESIGNS: Nos. 224 and 229, Marine firing and side of tank; 225 and 230, Tank; 226 and 231, Marines leaving landing craft; 227 and 232, Beach assault and palm trees.

Nos. 223/32 were printed together, *se-tenant*, forming two composite designs.

39b Dinosaurs Feeding

1995. "Singapore '95" International Stamp Exhibitions. Designs showing exhibition emblem. Multicoloured.

233	45s. Type **39b** (as No. 126a)	1·00	1·50
234	60s. Tyrannosaurus fighting Triceratops (as No. 126b)	1·00	1·50
MS235	110×70 mm. 2p. Plesiosaurus	2·50	3·50

39c Great Wall of China (image scaled to 57% of original size)

1995. Beijing International Coin and Stamp Show '95. Sheet 143×87 mm.

MS236	**39c** 1p.40 multicoloured	2·25	3·00

39d St. Paul's Cathedral and Searchlights

1995. 50th Anniv of United Nations and End of Second World War.

237	**39d**	60s. multicoloured	1·75	1·75
238	-	60s. black and blue	1·75	1·75
239	-	60s. multicoloured	1·75	1·75
240	-	80s. multicoloured	1·75	1·75
241	-	80s. blue and black	1·75	1·75
242	-	80s. multicoloured	1·75	1·75

DESIGNS—HORIZ: No. 239, Concorde; 240, Allied prisoners of war and Burma Railway; 242, Mt. Fuji and express train. VERT—25×35 mm: Nos. 238 and 241, U.N. anniversary emblem.

40 Charles Ramsay and Swimmers with Poles

1996. Tin Can Mail Pioneers. Multicoloured.

243	45s. Type **40**	90	90
244	60s. Charles Ramsay and encounter with shark	1·25	1·25
245	1p. Walter Quensell and transferring mail from canoes to ship	2·00	2·00
246	3p. Walter Quensell and Tin Can Mail cancellations	6·50	6·00

40a Cave Painting, Lake Village and Hunter

1996. 13th Congress of International Union of Prehistoric and Protohistoric Sciences, Forli, Italy. Multicoloured.

247	1p. Type **40a**	2·25	2·25
248	1p. Egyptians with Pyramid, Greek temple, and Romans with Colosseum	2·25	2·25

40b Dolls, Model Truck and Counting Balls

1996. 50th Anniv of UNICEF. Children's Toys. Multicoloured.

249	80s. Type **40b**	1·75	2·00
250	80s. Teddy bear, tricycle and model car	1·75	2·00
251	80s. Book, model helicopter, pedal car and roller skates	1·75	2·00

Nos. 249/51 were printed together, *se-tenant*, forming a composite design.

41 Island and Two Canoes

1996. 50th Anniv of Evacuation of Niuafo'ou. Multicoloured.

252	45s. Type **41**	1·00	1·10
253	45s. Erupting volcano and canoes	1·00	1·10
254	45s. End of island, volcanic cloud and canoe	1·00	1·10
255	45s. Family and livestock in outrigger canoe	1·00	1·10
256	45s. Islanders reaching "Matua" (inter-island freighter)	1·00	1·10
257	60s. Type **41**	1·00	1·10
258	60s. As No. 253	1·00	1·10
259	60s. As No. 254	1·00	1·10
260	60s. As No. 255	1·00	1·10
261	60s. As No. 256	1·00	1·10

Nos. 252/6 and 257/61 respectively were printed together, *se-tenant*, forming the same composite design.

42 Plankton

1997. The Ocean Environment.

262	**42**	60s. multicoloured	1·00	1·00
263	-	80s. multicoloured	1·25	1·25
264	-	1p.50 multicoloured	2·25	2·50
265	-	2p.50 multicoloured	3·00	3·50

DESIGNS: 80s. to 2p.50, Different plankton.

42a Black-naped Tern

1997. "Pacific '97" International Stamp Exhibition, San Francisco. Sheet 85×110 mm.

MS266	**42a** 2p. multicoloured	3·00	3·75

42b King and Queen on Wedding Day

1997. King and Queen of Tonga's Golden Wedding and 30th Anniv of Coronation. Multicoloured.

267	80s. Type **42b**	1·75	1·75
268	80s. King Tupou in Coronation robes	1·75	1·75
MS269	82×70 mm. 5p. King Tupou with pages (horiz)	6·00	7·50

43 Blue-crowned Lory Nestlings

1998. Endangered Species. Blue-crowned Lory. Multicoloured.

270	10s. Type **43**	1·50	1·50
271	55s. Feeding on flowers	3·00	1·25
272	80s. Perched on branch	4·00	2·00
273	3p. Pair on branch	8·00	9·00
MS274	160×112 mm. Nos. 270/3×2	30·00	30·00

1998. Diana, Princess of Wales Commemoration. Sheet, 145×70 mm, containing vert designs as T **91** of Kiribati. Multicoloured.

MS275	10s. Princess Diana in tartan jacket, 1987; 80s. Wearing white dress, 1992; 1p. Wearing check jacket, 1993; 2p.50, Wearing black jacket (sold at 4p.40+50s. charity premium)	3·00	5·00

43a King Taufa'ahau Tupou IV

1998. 80th Birthday of King Taufa'ahau Tupou IV.

276	**43a**	2p.70 multicoloured	2·50	3·25

43b Tiger and Top Left Quarter of Clock Face

1998. Chinese New Year ("Year of the Tiger"). Sheet, 126×85 mm, containing horiz designs as T **43b**, each showing tiger and quarter segment of clock face. Multicoloured.

MS277	55s. Type **43b**; 80s. Top right quarter; 1p. Bottom left quarter; 1p. Bottom right quarter	4·75	5·00

No. **MS**277 also includes "SINGPEX '98" Stamp Exhibition, Singapore emblem on the sheet margin.

43c "Amphiprion melanopus"

1998. International Year of the Ocean. Multicoloured.

278	10s. Type **43c**	40	50
279	55s. "Amphiprion perideraion"	80	90
280	80s. "Amphiprion chrysopterus"	1·00	1·10

43d Angel playing lute (inscr in Tongan)

1998. Christmas. Multicoloured.

281	20s. Type **43d**	80	55
282	55s. Angel playing violin (inscr in English)	1·25	60
283	1p. Children and bells (inscr in Tongan)	1·75	1·90
284	1p.60 Children and candles (inscr in English)	2·50	4·00

43e Rabbit on Hind Legs

1999. Chinese New Year ("Year of the Rabbit"). Sheet 126×85 mm, containing horiz designs as T **43e**, showing rabbits and segments of flower (each red, yellow and grey).

MS285	10s. Type **43e**; 55s. Rabbit facing left; 80s. Rabbit facing right; 1p. Two rabbits	3·25	3·75

44 "Eendracht" (Le Maire)

1999. Early Explorers. Multicoloured.

286	80s. Type **44**	2·50	1·25
287	2p.70 Tongiaki (outrigger canoe)	3·75	4·50
MS288	120×72 mm. Nos. 286/7	6·00	7·00

No. **MS**288 also includes the "Australia '99" emblem on the sheet margin.

44a "Cananga odorata"

1999. Fragrant Flowers. Multicoloured.

289	55s. Type **44a**	75	60
290	80s. "Gardenia tannaensis" (vert)	1·00	80
291	1p. "Coleus amboinicus" (vert)	1·40	1·50
292	2p.50 "Hernandia moerenhoutiana"	2·75	3·75

45 Dove over Tafahi Island

2000. New Millennium. Sheet, 120×80 mm, containing T **45** and similar vert design. Multicoloured.

MS293	1p. Type **45**; 2p.50, Kalia (traditional canoe) passing island	3·50	4·00

45a Dragon in the Sky

2000. Chinese New Year ("Year of the Dragon"). Sheet, 126×85 mm, containing horiz designs as T **45a**. Multicoloured.

MS294	10s. Type **45a**; 55s. Dragon in the sky (facing left); 80s. Sea dragon (facing right); 1p. Sea dragon (facing left)	2·25	2·75

45b Queen Elizabeth the Queen Mother

2000. "The Stamp Show 2000" International Stamp Exhibition, London. Queen Elizabeth the Queen Mother's 100th Birthday. Sheet, 105×71 mm, containing designs as T **45b**.

MS295	1p.50, Type **45b**; 2p.50, Queen Salote Tupou III of Tonga	3·50	4·00

46 Tongan Couple

2000. "EXPO 2000" World Stamp Exhibition, Anaheim, U.S.A. Space Communications. Sheet, 120×90 mm, containing T **46** and similar vert designs. Multicoloured.

MS296	10s. Type **46**; 2p.50, Telecom dish aerial; 2p.70, "Intelsat" satelite	4·50	5·50

47 *Jamides bochus* (butterfly)

2000. Butterflies. Multicoloured.

297	55s. Type **47**	95	80
298	80s. *Hypolimnas bolina*	1·40	1·25
299	1p. *Eurema hecabe aprica*	1·60	1·60
300	2p.70 *Danaus plexippus*	3·25	4·00

48 Snake

2001. Chinese New Year ("Year of the Snake") and "Hong Kong 2001" Stamp Exhibition. Sheet, 125×87 mm, containing horiz designs as T **48** showing decorative snakes.

MS301	10s. multicoloured; 55s. multicoloured; 80s. multicoloured; 1p. multicoloured	3·50	4·00

49 Seale's Flying Fish

2001. Fish. Multicoloured.

302	80s. Type **49**	1·75	1·25
303	1p. Swordfish	1·90	1·75
304	2p.50 Skipjack tuna	3·75	4·50
MS305	121×92 mm. Nos. 302/4	7·00	7·50

50 Pawpaw

2001. Tropical Fruit. Sheet, 120×67 mm, containing T **50** and similar vert designs. Multicoloured.

MS306	55s. Type **50**; 80s. Limes; 1p. Mango; 2p.50, Bananas	4·25	5·50

51 Barn Owl in Flight

2001. Barn Owls. Multicoloured.

307	10s. Type **51**	50	60
308	55s. Adult feeding young in nest	1·25	55
309	2p.50 Adult and fledglings in nest	2·50	2·75
310	2p.70 Barn owl in palm tree	2·50	2·75
MS311	170×75 mm. Nos. 307/10	6·00	6·50

51a Queen Elizabeth with Princess Elizabeth, Coronation, 1937

2002. Golden Jubilee. Sheet 162×95 mm, containing designs as T **51a**.

MS312	15s. brown, violet and gold; 90s. multicoloured; 1p.20, multicoloured; 1p.40, multicoloured; 2p.25, multicoloured	8·50	9·00

DESIGNS—HORIZ (as Type **51a**): 15s. Type **51a**; 90s. Queen Elizabeth in lilac outfit; 1p.20, Princess Elizabeth in garden; 1p.40, Queen Elizabeth in red hat and coat. VERT (38×51 mm): 2p.25, Queen Elizabeth after Annigoni.

51b Two Horses with Foal

2002. Chinese New Year ("Year of the Horse"). Sheet, 126×89 mm, containing vert designs as T **51b**. Multicoloured.

MS313	65s. Two horses with foal; 80s. Horse drinking from river; 1p. Horse standing in river; 2p.50 Horse and foal on river bank	6·00	6·50

52 Polynesian Scrub Fowl with Eggs

2002. Polynesian Scrub Fowl. Multicoloured.

314	15s. Type **52**	30	50
315	70s. Two birds on rocks	90	90
316	90s. Polynesian scrub fowl by tree (vert)	1·10	1·10
317	2p.50 Two birds in undergrowth (vert)	2·25	2·75
MS318	72×95 mm. Nos. 316/17	4·50	5·00

53 Octopus (*Octopus vulgaris*)

2002. Cephalopods. Multicoloured.

319	80s. Type **53**	1·40	1·00
320	1p. Squid (*Sepioteuthls lessoniana*)	1·50	1·40
321	2p.50 Nautilus (*Nautilus belauensis*)	3·75	4·50
MS322	120×83 mm. Nos. 319/21	7·00	8·00

54 CASA C-212 Aviocar

2002. Mail Planes. Sheet, 140×80 mm, containing T **54** and similar horiz designs. Multicoloured.

MS323	80s. Type **54**; 1p.40 Britten-Norman Islander; 2p.50 DHC 6-300 Twin Otter	9·00	9·00

54a Ram

2003. Chinese New Year ("Year of the Sheep"). Sheet 128×88 mm, containing horiz designs as T **54a**.

MS324	65s. Type **54a**, 80s. Three ewes; 1p. Three black-faced ewes; 2p.50 Two ewes	6·00	6·50

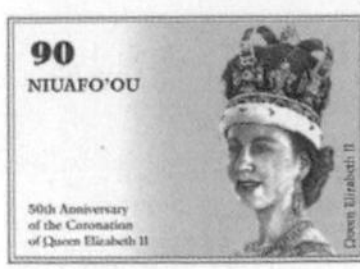

54b Queen Elizabeth II

2004. 50th Anniv of Coronation.

325	**54b**	90s. purple, blue and bistre	90	80
326	-	1p.20 green, blue and bistre	1·40	1·25
327	-	1p.40 blue, purple and bistre	1·60	1·50
328	-	2p.50 multicoloured	3·25	4·00

DESIGNS: 1p.20 Queen Elizabeth II on throne; 1p.40 Queen Salote in open-top car; 2p.50 Queen Salote.

54c Spider Monkey

2004. Chinese New Year ("Year of the Monkey"). Sheet 95×85 mm containing horiz designs as T **54c**. Each azure, black and scarlet.

MS329	60s. Spider monkey; 80s; Ring-tailed Lemur; 1p. Cotton-top tamarin; 2p.50 White-cheeked gibbon	5·50	6·50

55 King George Tupou II (1893–1918)

2004. Royal Succession. Multicoloured.

330	30s. King George Tupou I (1875–93)	40	40
331	65s. Type **55**	70	70
332	80s. Queen Salote Tupou III (1918–65)	80	80
333	$3.05 King Taufa'ahau Tupou IV (1965–)	3·00	4·25
MS334	160×65 mm. Nos. 330/3	5·50	6·00

Stamps in the same designs were also issued by Tonga.

56 Pawpaw Tree

2004. Fruit Trees. Multicoloured.

335	45s. Type **56**	90	60
336	60s. Banana tree	1·25	85
337	80s. Coconut tree	1·50	1·25
338	1p.80 Lime tree	2·75	4·00

57 Mary and Baby Jesus

2004. Christmas. Multicoloured.

339	15s. Type **57**	35	40
340	90s. Mary and Joseph on the way to Bethlehem	1·00	80
341	1p.20 The Shepherds	1·40	1·50
342	2p.60 The Three Wise Men	2·75	4·00

58 Rooster and Hen

2005. Chinese New Year ("Year of the Rooster"). Sheet 95×85 mm, containing T **58** and similar horiz designs. Multicoloured.

MS343	65s. Type **58**; 80s. Rooster, hen and three chicks; 1p. Rooster, hen and chick; 2p.50 Rooster and hen on nest	5·50	6·00

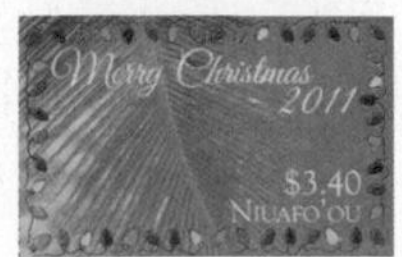

59 Palm Frond and Christmas Lights

2011. Christmas. Multicoloured.

344	3p.40 Type **59**	3·50	4·00
345	5p. Light and snowflakes	5·00	5·50

60 Humpback Whale

2012. Humpback Whale (*Megaptera novaeangliae*). Multicoloured.

MS346	1p. Type **60**; 1p.40 Humpback Whale leaping above water; 1p.60 Tail fin of Humpback Whale	4·00	4·00
MS347	2p. Head of Humpback Whale; 2p.25 Humpback Whale underwater; 2p.40 Three Humpback Whales	6·75	6·75

61 Zebra Shark

2012. Endangered Species. Zebra Shark (*Stegostoma fasciatum*). Multicoloured.

348	45s. Type **61**	50	30
349	2p. Zebra Shark (dark background)	2·00	2·25
350	2p.40 Zebra Shark on coral reef	2·50	2·75
351	3p.40 Juvenile Zebra Shark	3·50	4·00

62 Australian Meadow-argus (*Junonia villida*)

2012. Butterflies. Multicoloured.

352	45s. Type **62**	45	30
353	1p.95 Crow Butterfly (*Euploea core*) on pink flower	2·00	2·25
354	2p. Monarch Butterfly (*Danaus plexippus*) on orange flower	2·00	2·25
355	2p.40 Monarch Butterfly (*Danaus plexippus*) on purple flower	2·40	2·75
356	2p.50 Blue Moon Butterfly (*Hypolimnas bolina*)	2·50	2·75
357	3p. Australian Meadow-argus (*Junonia villida*) on white flower	3·00	3·50
358	3p.40 Crow Butterfly (*Euploea core*) on twig	3·50	4·00
359	4p. Blue Moon Butterfly (*Hypolimnas bolina*) (different)	4·00	4·50
360	5p. Monarch Butterfly on blue daisy	5·00	5·50
361	6p. Blue Moon Butterfly (*Hypolimnas bolina*) on pink flower	6·00	6·50
362	7p.30 Crow Butterfly (*Euploea core*) on white flower	7·50	8·00
363	8p. Australian Meadow-argus (*Junonia villida*) (wings half closed)	8·00	8·50
MS364	180×181 mm. Nos. 352/63	45·00	45·00

Stamps from **MS**364 have pale blue frames.

63 *Titanic*

2012. Centenary of the Sinking of the *Titanic*. Multicoloured.

MS365	119×88 mm. 45c. Type **63**; $3.40 *Titanic* (ship pale grey)	3·75	4·00
MS366	216×153 mm. $3.40×4 *Titanic* (ship in grey); *Titanic* (pale lavender-grey background); *Titanic* at sea (brownish grey sea background); *Titanic* (funnels smoking)	13·50	13·50

64 Books

2012. Education

367	**64**	$3 multicoloured	3·00	3·50

In Loving Memory of Diana, Princess of Wales
31 August 1997
Her Legacy will live on forever
William snd Kate, Duke and Duchess of Cambridge
1st Anniversary of their Royal Wedding 2011

65 (image scaled to 49% of original size)

2012. 15th Death Anniv of Princess Diana

MS368	4p. on 10s. Princess Diana in tartan jacket, 1987; 4p. on 80s. Wearing white dress, 1992; 4p. on 1p. Wearing check jacket, 1993; 4p. on 2p.50, Wearing black jacket	16·00	16·00

No. **MS**368 was optd across all four stamps with each stamp surch $4.

E1 Three Barn Owls

2012. Barn Owl (*Tyto alba*). Multicoloured.

E1	25p. Type E **1**	20·00	20·00
E2	25p. Barn Owl (looking towards left)	20·00	20·00
E3	25p. Barn Owl (facing right)	20·00	20·00
E4	25p. Barn Owl (wings half open)	20·00	20·00
MSE5	161×135 mm. As Nos. E1/4	80·00	80·00

66 Angels

2012. Christmas. *Nativity* (Giotto di Bondone, c. 1311-20). Multicoloured.

MS369	1p.×12 Type **66**; Three angels above roof; Six angels above roof; Four angels looking at Infant Jesus; Six angels looking at Infant Jesus; Angel, walls and tree; Virgin Mary holding Infant Jesus, ox and ass in background; Shepherds; Joseph; Joseph holding Infant Jesus; Virgin Mary, sheep right foreground; Sheep	12·00	12·50

The stamps, two stamp-size labels and margins of **MS**369 form a composite design showing the complete painting.

NIUAFO'OU $3

67

2012. Personalized Stamp

370	**67**	3p. black, grey and bright scarlet	3·00	3·50

68 Snake

2013. Chinese New Year. Year of the Snake. Multicoloured.

MS371	2p.45×4 Type **68**; As Type **68** but green snake on orange background; Purple snake on pink background; Yellow snake on blue background	10·00	10·00

Pt. 1

NIUE

One of the Cook Is. group in the S. Pacific. A dependency of New Zealand, the island achieved local self-government in 1974.

1902. 12 pence = 1 shilling; 20 shillings = 1 pound.
1967. 100 cents = 1 dollar.

1902. T **42** of New Zealand optd **NIUE** only

1	**42**	1d. red	£300	£300

1902. Pictorials of 1898 etc.

8	**23**	½d. green	1·00	1·00
9	**42**	1d. red	60	1·00
2	**26**	2½d. blue (B)	1·50	4·00
13	**28**	3d. brown	9·50	5·00
14	**31**	6d. red	14·00	11·00
16	**34**	1s. orange	40·00	48·00

1911. King Edward VII stamps.

17	**51**	½d. green	50	50
18	**51**	6d. red	2·00	7·00
19	**51**	1s. orange	6·50	48·00

1917. Dominion and King George V stamps.

21	**53**	1d. red	23·00	5·50
22	**62**	3d. brown	50·00	95·00

1917. Stamps of New Zealand (King George V, etc) optd **NIUE.** only.

23		½d. green	70	2·50
24	**53**	1d. red	10·00	13·00
25	**62**	1½d. grey	1·00	2·25
26	**62**	1½d. brown	70	8·00
28a	**62**	2½d. blue	1·25	14·00
29a	**62**	3d. brown	1·25	1·50
30a	**62**	6d. red	4·75	24·00
31a	**62**	1s. orange	5·50	27·00

1918. Stamps of New Zealand optd **NIUE**.

33	**F4**	2s. blue	16·00	32·00
34	**F4**	2s.6d. brown	23·00	48·00
35	**F4**	5s. green	25·00	55·00
37b	**F4**	10s. red	95·00	£160
37	**F4**	£1 red	£180	£275

1920. Pictorial types as Cook Islands (1920), but inscr "NIUE".

38	**9**	½d. black and green	3·75	3·75
45	-	1d. black and red	1·75	1·00
40	-	1½d. black and red	2·75	17·00
46	-	2½d. black and blue	4·25	11·00
41	-	3d. black and blue	1·75	15·00
47	**7**	4d. black and violet	7·00	20·00
42	-	6d. brown and green	4·25	18·00
43	-	1s. black and brown	4·25	18·00

1927. Admiral type of New Zealand optd as **NIUE**

49	**71**	2s. blue	18·00	32·00

1931. No. 40 surch **TWO PENCE**.

50	2d. on 1½d. black and red	4·75	1·00

1931. Stamps of New Zealand (Arms types) optd **NIUE**.

83	**F6**	2s.6d. brown	4·00	10·00
84	**F6**	5s. green	14·00	13·00
53	**F6**	10s. red	35·00	£110
86	**F6**	£1 pink	65·00	75·00

1932. Pictorial stamps as Cook Islands (1932) but inscr additionally "NIUE".

89	**20**	½d. black and green	50	4·75
56	-	1d. black and red	1·00	50
64	**22**	2d. black and brown	50	1·75
92	-	2½d. black and blue	60	2·50
93	-	4d. black and blue	4·25	1·00
67	-	6d. black and orange	70	75
61	-	1s. black and violet	2·75	5·00

1935. Silver Jubilee. As Nos. 63, 92 and 67, with colours changed, optd **SILVER JUBILEE OF KING GEORGE V. 1910-1935.**

69	1d. red	60	3·50
70	2½d. blue	4·25	13·00
71	6d. green and orange	4·75	9·00

1937. Coronation. New Zealand stamps optd **NIUE**.

72	**106**	1d. red	30	10
73	**106**	2½d. blue	40	1·50
74	**106**	6d. orange	40	20

1938. As 1938 issue of Cook Islands, but inscr "NIUE COOK ISLANDS".

95	**29**	1s. black and violet	1·50	85
96	**30**	2s. black and brown	8·50	3·50
97	-	3s. blue and green	15·00	8·50

1940. As No. 132 of Cook Islands but inscr "NIUE COOK ISLANDS".

78	**32**	3d. on 1½d. black and purple	75	20

1946. Peace. New Zealand stamps optd **NIUE** (twice on 2d.).

98	**132**	1d. green	40	10
99	-	2d. purple (No. 670)	40	10
100	-	6d. brown & red (No. 674)	40	80
101	**139**	8d. black and red	50	80

18 Map of Niue

19 H.M.S. *Resolution*

1950

113	**18**	½d. orange and blue	20	1·75
114	**19**	1d. brown and green	2·25	3·00
115	-	2d. black and red	1·25	3·00
116	-	3d. blue and violet	10	20
117	-	4d. olive and purple	10	20
118	-	6d. green and orange	1·00	1·25
119	-	9d. orange and brown	15	1·40
120	-	1s. purple and black	15	20
121	-	2s. brown and green	6·00	6·00
122	-	3s. blue and black	5·50	5·50

DESIGNS—HORIZ: 2d. Alofi landing; 3d. Native hut; 4d. Arch at Hikutavake; 6d. Alofi bay; 1s. Cave, Makefu. VERT: 9d. Spearing fish; 2s. Bananas; 3s. Matapa Chasm.

1953. Coronation. As Types of New Zealand but inscr "NIUE".

123	**164**	3d. brown	65	40
124	**168**	6d. grey	95	40

26

1967. Decimal Currency

(a) Nos. 113/22 surch.

125	**17**	½c. on ½d.	10	10
126	**19**	1c. on 1d.	1·10	15
127	-	2c. on 2d.	10	10
128	-	2½c. on 3d.	10	10
129	-	3c. on 4d.	10	10
130	-	5c. on 6d.	10	10
131	-	8c. on 9d.	10	10
132	-	10c. on 1s.	10	10
133	-	20c. on 2s.	35	2·00
134	-	30c. on 3s.	65	1·50

(b) Arms type of New Zealand without value, surch as in T **26**.

135	**26**	25c. brown	30	55
136	**26**	50c. green	70	80
137	**26**	$1 mauve	45	1·25
138	**26**	$2 pink	50	2·00

1967. Christmas. As T **278** of New Zealand but inscr "NIUE".

139	2½c. multicoloured	10	10

1969. Christmas. As No. 905 of New Zealand but inscr "NIUE".

140	2½c. multicoloured	10	10

27 "Pua"

1969. Flowers. Multicoloured; frame colours given.

141	**27**	½c. green	10	10
142	-	1c. red	10	10
143	-	2c. olive	10	10
144	-	2½c. brown	10	10
145	-	3c. blue	10	10
146	-	5c. red	10	10
147	-	8c. violet	10	10
148	-	10c. yellow	10	10
149	-	20c. blue	35	1·50
150	-	30c. green	1·10	2·00

DESIGNS: 1c. "Golden Shower"; 2c. Flamboyant; 2½c. Frangipani; 3c. Niue crocus; 5c. Hibiscus; 8c. "Passion Fruit"; 10c. "Kampui"; 20c. Queen Elizabeth II (after Anthony Buckley); 30c. Tapeu orchid.

For 20c. design as 5c. see No. 801.

37 Kalahimu

1970. Indigenous Edible Crabs. Multicoloured.

151	3c. Type **37**	10	10
152	5c. Kalavi	10	10
153	30c. Unga	30	25

1970. Christmas. As T **314** of New Zealand, but inscr "NIUE".

154	2½c. multicoloured	10	10

38 Outrigger Canoe, and Fokker F.27 Friendship over Jungle

1970. Opening of Niue Airport. Multicoloured.

155	3c. Type **38**	10	20
156	5c. "Tofua II" (cargo liner) and Fokker F.27 Friendship over harbour	15	20
157	8c. Fokker F.27 Friendship over airport	15	30

39 Spotted Triller

1971. Birds. Multicoloured.

158	5c. Type **39**	15	35
159	10c. Purple-capped fruit dove	40	20
160	20c. Blue-crowned lory	60	20

1971. Christmas. As T **325** of New Zealand, but inscr "Niue".

161	3c. multicoloured	10	10

40 Niuean Boy

1971. Niuean Portraits. Multicoloured.

162	4c. Type **40**	10	10
163	6c. Girl with garland	10	20
164	9c. Man	10	40
165	14c. Woman with garland	15	80

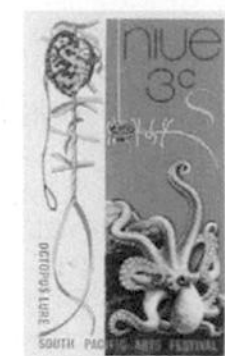

41 Octopus Lure

1972. South Pacific Arts Festival, Fiji. Multicoloured.

166	3c. Type **41**	10	10
167	5c. War weapons	15	15
168	10c. Sika throwing (horiz)	20	15
169	25c. Vivi dance (horiz)	30	25

42 Alofi Wharf

1972. 25th Anniv of South Pacific Commission. Multicoloured.

170	4c. Type **42**	10	10
171	5c. Medical services	15	10
172	6c. Schoolchildren	15	10
173	18c. Dairy cattle	25	20

1972. Christmas. As T **332** of New Zealand, but inscr "NIUE".

174	3c. multicoloured	10	10

43 Silver Sweeper

1973. Fish. Multicoloured.

175	8c. Type **43**	25	25
176	10c. Peacock hind ("Loi")	25	30
177	15c. Yellow-edged lyretail ("Malau")	30	40
178	20c. Ruby snapper ("Palu")	30	45

44 "Large Flower Piece" (Jan Brueghel)

1973. Christmas. Flower studies by the artists listed. Multicoloured.

179	4c. Type **44**	10	10
180	5c. Bollongier	10	10
181	10c. Ruysch	20	20

45 Capt. Cook and Bowsprit

1974. Bicent of Capt. Cook's Visit. Multicoloured.

182	2c. Type **45**	20	20
183	3c. Niue landing place	20	20
184	8c. Map of Niue	20	30
185	20c. Ensign of 1774 and Administration Building	30	65

46 King Fataaiki

1974. Self-government. Multicoloured.

186	4c. Type **46**	10	15
187	8c. Annexation Ceremony, 1900	10	15
188	10c. Legislative Assembly Chambers (horiz)	15	10
189	20c. Village meeting (horiz)	25	15

47 Decorated Bicycles

1974. Christmas. Multicoloured.

190	3c. Type **47**	10	10
191	10c. Decorated motorcycle	10	10
192	20c. Motor transport to church	20	30

48 Children going to Church

1975. Christmas. Multicoloured.

193	4c. Type **48**	10	10
194	5c. Child with balloons on bicycle	10	10
195	10c. Balloons and gifts on tree	20	20

49 Hotel Buildings

1975. Opening of Tourist Hotel. Multicoloured.

196	8c. Type **49**	10	10
197	20c. Ground-plan and buildings	20	20

50 Preparing Ground for Taro

1976. Food Gathering. Multicoloured.

198	1c. Type **50**	10	10
199	2c. Planting taro	10	10
200	3c. Banana gathering	10	10
201	4c. Harvesting taro	10	10
202	5c. Gathering shellfish	30	10
203	10c. Reef fishing	10	10
204	20c. Luku gathering	15	15
205	50c. Canoe fishing	20	60
206	$1 Coconut husking	25	80
207	$2 Uga gathering	45	1·40

See also Nos. 249/58 and 264/73.

51 Water

1976. Utilities. Multicoloured.

208	10c. Type **51**	10	10
209	15c. Telecommunications	15	15
210	20c. Power	15	15

52 Christmas Tree, Alofi

1976. Christmas. Multicoloured.

211	9c. Type **52**	15	15
212	15c. Church service, Avatele	15	15

53 Queen Elizabeth II and Westminster Abbey

1977. Silver Jubilee. Multicoloured.

213	$1 Type **53**	60	50
214	$2 Coronation regalia	80	75
MS215	72×104 mm. Nos. 213/14	1·10	1·60

Stamps from the miniature sheet have a blue border.

54 Child Care

1977. Personal Services. Multicoloured.

216	10c. Type **54**	15	10
217	15c. School dental clinic	20	20
218	20c. Care of the aged	20	20

55 "The Annunciation"

1977. Christmas. Paintings by Rubens. Multicoloured.

219	10c. Type **55**	20	10
220	12c. "Adoration of the Magi"	20	15
221	20c. "Virgin in a Garland"	35	40
222	35c. "The Holy Family"	55	90
MS223	82×129 mm. Nos. 219/22	1·10	2·25

1977. Nos. 198/207, 214, 216 and 218 surch.

224	12c. on 1c. Type **50**	25	25
225	16c. on 2c. Planting taro	30	30
226	30c. on 3c. Banana gathering	30	40
227	35c. on 4c. Harvesting taro	30	45
228	40c. on 5c. Gathering shellfish	30	50
229	60c. on 20c. Luku gathering	30	55
230	70c. on $1 Coconut husking	30	55
231	85c. on $2 Uga gathering	30	60
232	$1.10 on 10c. Type **22**	30	60
233	$2.60 on 20c. Care of the aged	50	70
234	$3.20 on $2 Coronation regalia	60	80

57 "An Island View in Atooi"

1978. Bicent of Discovery of Hawaii. Paintings by John Webber. Multicoloured.

235	12c. Type **57**	85	40
236	16c. "A View of Karakaooa, in Owhyhee"	95	50
237	20c. "An Offering before Capt. Cook in the Sandwich Islands"	1·00	60
238	30c. "Tereoboo, King of Owhyhee bringing presents to Capt. Cook"	1·10	70
239	35c. "A Canoe in the Sandwich Islands, the rowers masked"	1·25	80
MS240	121×121 mm. Nos. 235/9	4·75	2·75

58 "The Deposition of Christ" (Caravaggio)

1978. Easter. Paintings from the Vatican Galleries. Multicoloured.

241	10c. Type **58**	20	10
242	20c. "The Burial of Christ" (Bellini)	40	25
MS243	102×68 mm. Nos. 241/2	1·00	1·00

1978. Easter. Children's Charity. Designs as Nos. 241/2 in separate miniature sheets 64×78 mm, each with a face value of 70c.+5c.

MS244	As Nos. 241/2 Set of 2 sheets	1·00	2·00

59 Flags of Niue and U.K.

1978. 25th Anniv of Coronation. Multicoloured.

245	$1.10 Type **59**	60	90
246	$1.10 Coronation portrait by Cecil Beaton	60	90
247	$1.10 Queen's personal flag for New Zealand	60	90
MS248	87×98 mm. Nos. 245/7 with white borders	2·00	1·50

1978. Designs as Nos. 198/207 but margin colours changed and silver frame.

249	12c. Type **50**	20	20
250	16c. Planting taro	20	20
251	30c. Banana gathering	30	25
252	35c. Harvesting taro	30	30
253	40c. Gathering shellfish	30	40
254	60c. Reef fishing	30	35
255	75c. Luku gathering	30	40
256	$1.10 Canoe fishing	35	80
257	$3.20 Coconut husking	50	90
258	$4.20 Uga gathering	55	95

60 "Festival of the Rosary"

1978. Christmas. 450th Death Anniv of Durer. Multicoloured.

259	20c. Type **60**	40	20
260	30c. "The Nativity"	50	30
261	35c. "Adoration of the Magi"	60	35
MS262	143×82 mm. Nos. 259/61	1·50	2·00

1978. Christmas. Children's Charity. Designs as Nos. 259/61 in separate miniature sheets 74×66 mm., each with a face value of 60c.+5c.

MS263	As Nos. 259/61 Set of 3 sheets	1·00	2·00

1979. Air. Designs as Nos. 249/58 but gold frames and additionally inscr "AIRMAIL".

264	15c. Planting taro	20	15
265	20c. Banana gathering	20	15
266	23c. Harvesting taro	25	15
267	50c. Canoe fishing	80	20
268	90c. Reef fishing	80	35
269	$1.35 Type **50**	80	1·50
270	$2.10 Gathering shellfish	80	1·75
271	$2.60 Luku gathering	80	1·75
272	$5.10 Coconut husking	80	1·75
273	$6.35 Uga gathering	80	1·75

61 "Pieta" (Gregorio Fernandez)

1979. Easter. Paintings. Multicoloured.

274	30c. Type **61**	30	25
275	35c. "Burial of Christ" (Pedro Roldan)	35	25
MS276	82×82 mm. Nos. 274/5	1·00	1·00

1979. Easter. Children's Charity. Designs as Nos. 274/5 in separate miniature sheets 86×69 mm., each with a face value of 70c.+5c.

MS277	As Nos. 274/5 Set of 2 sheets	1·10	1·75

62 "The Nurse and Child" (Franz Hals)

1979. International Year of the Child. Details of Paintings. Multicoloured.

278	16c. Type **62**	20	15
279	20c. "Child of the Duke of Osuna" (Goya)	20	20
280	30c. "Daughter of Robert Strozzi" (Titian)	35	35
281	35c. "Children eating Fruit" (Murillo)	45	40
MS282	80×115 mm. Nos. 278/81	1·25	2·25

1979. International Year of the Child. Children's Charity. Designs as Nos. 278/81 in separate miniature sheets 99×119 mm, each with a face value of 70c.+5c.

MS283	As Nos. 278/81 Set of 4 sheets	1·00	1·50

63 Penny Black Stamp

1979. Death Cent of Sir Rowland Hill. Multicoloured.

284	20c. Type **63**	15	15
285	20c. Sir Rowland Hill and original Bath mail coach	15	15
286	30c. Basel 1845 2½r. stamp	15	20
287	30c. Sir Rowland Hill and Alpine village coach	15	20
288	35c. U.S.A. 1847 5c. stamp	20	20
289	35c. Sir Rowland Hill and *Washington* (first transatlantic U.S.A. mail vessel)	20	20
290	50c. France 1849 20c. stamp	25	20
291	50c. Sir Rowland Hill and French Post Office railway van, 1849	25	20
292	60c. Bavaria 1849 1k. stamp	25	20
293	60c. Sir Rowland Hill and Bavarian coach with mail	25	20
MS294	143×149 mm. Nos. 284/93	2·50	3·00

The two versions of each value were issued *se-tenant* within the sheet, forming composite designs.

64 Cook's Landing at Botany Bay

1979. Death Bicentenary of Captain Cook. Multicoloured.

295	20c. Type **64**	55	30
296	30c. Cook's men during a landing on Erromanga	75	40
297	35c. H.M.S. "Resolution" and H.M.S. "Discovery" in Queen Charlotte's Sound	85	45
298	75c. Death of Captain Cook, Hawaii	1·25	70
MS299	104×80 mm. Nos. 295/8	3·25	2·50

65 Launch of "Apollo 11"

1979. Tenth Anniv of First Manned Moon Landing. Multicoloured.

300	30c. Type **65**	35	20
301	35c. Lunar module on Moon	45	25
302	60c. Sikorsky Sea King helicopter, recovery ship and command module after splashdown	90	40
MS303	120×82 mm. Nos. 300/2	1·50	1·60

Stamps from No. **MS**303 have the inscription in gold on a blue panel.

66 "Virgin of Tortosa" (P. Serra)

1979. Christmas. Paintings. Multicoloured.

304	20c. Type **66**	10	10
305	25c. "Virgin with Milk" (R. di Mur)	15	15
306	30c. "Virgin and Child" (S. di G. Sassetta)	20	20
307	50c. "Virgin and Child" (J. Huguet)	25	25
MS308	95×113 mm. Nos. 304/7	75	1·25

1979. Christmas Children's Charity. Designs as Nos. 304/7 in separate miniature sheets, 49×84 mm, each with a face value of 85c.+5c.

MS309	As Nos. 304/7 Set of 4 sheets	1·00	2·00

1980. Hurricane Relief. Surch **HURRICANE RELIEF** Plus **2c**.

(a) On Nos. 284/93 **HURRICANE RELIEF** spread over each *se-tenant* pair

310	**63**	20c. +2c. multicoloured	20	40
311	-	20c. +2c. multicoloured (No. 285)	20	40
312	-	30c. +2c. multicoloured (No. 286)	25	45
313	-	30c. +2c. multicoloured (No. 287)	25	45
314	-	35c. +2c. multicoloured (No. 288)	30	50
315	-	35c. +2c. multicoloured (No. 289)	30	50
316	-	50c. +2c. multicoloured (No. 290)	35	65
317	-	50c. +2c. multicoloured (No. 291)	35	65
318	-	60c. +2c. multicoloured (No. 292)	35	70
319	-	60c. +2c. multicoloured (No. 293)	35	70

(b) On Nos. 295/8.

320	**64**	20c. +2c. multicoloured	60	50
321	-	30c. +2c. multicoloured	60	60
322	-	35c. +2c. multicoloured	65	65
323	-	75c. +2c. multicoloured	1·00	1·10

(c) On Nos. 300/2.

324	**65**	30c. +2c. multicoloured	35	40
325	-	35c. +2c. multicoloured	35	45
326	-	60c. +2c. multicoloured	70	75

(d) On Nos. 304/7.

327	**66**	20c. +2c. multicoloured	20	35
328	-	25c. +2c. multicoloured	20	40
329	-	30c. +2c. multicoloured	20	45
330	-	50c. +2c. multicoloured	30	70

68 "Pieta" (Bellini)

1980. Easter. "Pieta". Paintings. Multicoloured.

331	25c. Type **68**	20	15
332	30c. Botticelli	25	20
333	35c. A. van Dyck	25	20
MS334	75×104 mm. As Nos. 331/3, but each with additional premium of **+ 2c.**	55	90

The premiums on No. **MS**334 were used to support Hurricane Relief.

1980. Easter. Hurricane Relief. Designs as Nos. 331/3 in separate miniature sheets, 75×52 mm, each with a face value of 85c.+5c.

MS335	As Nos. 331/3 Set of 3 sheets	1·00	1·50

69 Ceremonial Stool, New Guinea

1980. South Pacific Festival of Arts, New Guinea. Multicoloured.

336	20c. Type **69**	10	10
337	20c. Ku-Tagwa plaque, New Guinea	10	10
338	20c. Suspension hook, New Guinea	10	10
339	20c. Ancestral board, New Guinea	10	10
340	25c. Platform post, New Hebrides	10	10
341	25c. Canoe ornament, New Ireland	10	10
342	25c. Carved figure, Admiralty Islands	10	10
343	25c. Female with child, Admiralty Islands	10	10
344	30c. The God A'a, Rurutu (Austral Islands)	15	15
345	30c. Statue of Tangaroa, Cook Islands	15	15
346	30c. Ivory pendant, Tonga	15	15
347	30c. Tapa (Hiapo) cloth, Niue	15	15
348	35c. Feather box (Waka), New Zealand	15	15
349	35c. Hei-Tiki amulet, New Zealand	15	15
350	35c. House post, New Zealand	15	15
351	35c. Feather image of god Ku, Hawaii	15	15
MS352	Four sheets, each 86×124 mm. (a) Nos. 336, 340, 344, 348; (b) Nos. 337, 341, 345, 349; (c) Nos. 338, 342, 346, 350; (d) Nos. 339, 343, 347, 351. Each stamp with an additional premium of 2c. Set of 4 sheets	1·50	2·00

1980. "Zeapex '80" International Stamp Exhibition, Auckland. Nos. 284/93 optd (A) **ZEAPEX'80 AUCKLAND** or (B) **NEW ZEALAND STAMP EXHIBITION** and emblem.

353	**63**	20c. multicoloured (A)	20	15
354	-	20c. multicoloured (B)	20	15
355	-	30c. multicoloured (A)	20	15
356	-	30c. multicoloured (B)	20	15
357	-	35c. multicoloured (A)	20	15
358	-	35c. multicoloured (B)	20	15
359	-	50c. multicoloured (A)	25	20
360	-	50c. multicoloured (B)	25	20
361	-	60c. multicoloured (A)	25	20
362	-	60c. multicoloured (B)	25	20
MS363		143×149 mm. Nos. 353/62, each additionally surcharged **+ 2c.**	3·00	2·75

72 Queen Elizabeth the Queen Mother

1980. 80th Birthday of The Queen Mother.

364	**72**	$1.10 multicoloured	80	1·50
MS365		55×80 mm. **72** $3 multicoloured	1·00	1·75

73 100 m Dash

1980. Olympic Games, Moscow.

366	**73**	20c. multicoloured	20	15
367	-	20c. multicoloured	20	15
368	-	25c. multicoloured	20	20
369	-	25c. multicoloured	20	20
370	-	30c. multicoloured	25	20
371	-	30c. multicoloured	25	20
372	-	35c. multicoloured	25	25
373	-	35c. multicoloured	25	25
MS374		119×128 mm. Nos. 366/73, each stamp including premium of 2c.	1·00	1·00

DESIGNS: No. 367, Allen Wells, Great Britain (winner 100 m dash); 368, 400 m freestyle 369, Ines Diers (winner, D.D.R.); 370, Soling Class; 371, Winner, Denmark; 372, Football; 373, Winner, Czechoslovakia.

Nos. 366/7, 368/9, 370/1 and 372/3 were printed se-tenant in pairs each pair forming a composite design. On the 25c. and 35c. stamps the face value is at right on the first design and at left on the second in each pair. For the 30c. No. 370 has a yacht with a green sail at left and No. 371 a yacht with a red sail.

74 "The Virgin and Child"

1980. Christmas.

375	**74**	20c. multicoloured	15	15
376	-	25c. multicoloured	15	15
377	-	30c. multicoloured	20	20
378	-	35c. multicoloured	20	20
MS379		87×112 mm. Nos. 375/8	85	1·25

DESIGNS: 25c. to 35c. Various Virgin and Child paintings by Andrea del Sarto.

1980. Christmas. Children's Charity. Designs as Nos. 375/8 in separate miniature sheets 62×84 mm, each with a face value of 80c.+5c.

MS380	As Nos. 375/8 Set of 4 sheets	1·25	1·75

75 "Phalaenopsis sp."

1981. Flowers (1st series). Multicoloured.

381	2c. Type **75**	10	10
382	2c. Moth orchid	10	10
383	5c. "Euphorbia pulcherrima"	10	10
384	5c. Poinsettia	10	10
385	10c. "Thunbergia alata"	10	10
386	10c. Black-eyed Susan	10	10
387	15c. "Cochlospermum hibiscoides"	15	15
388	15c. Buttercup tree	15	15
389	20c. "Begonia sp."	20	20
390	20c. Begonia	20	20
391	25c. "Plumeria sp."	25	25
392	25c. Frangipani	25	25
393	30c. "Strelitzia reginae"	30	30
394	30c. Bird of Paradise	30	30
395	35c. "Hibiscus syriacus"	30	30
396	35c. Rose of Sharon	30	30
397	40c. "Nymphaea sp."	35	35
398	40c. Water lily	35	35
399	50c. "Tibouchina sp."	45	45
400	50c. Princess flower	45	45
401	60c. "Nelumbo sp."	55	55
402	60c. Lotus	55	55
403	80c. "Hybrid hibiscus"	60	75
404	80c. Yellow hibiscus	60	75
405	$1 Golden shower tree ("cassia fistula")	75	75
406	$2 "Orchid var"	3·00	1·75
407	$3 "Orchid sp."	3·25	2·50
408	$4 "Euphorbia pulcherrima poinsettia"	2·00	4·00
409	$6 "Hybrid hibiscus"	2·25	6·00
410	$10 Scarlet hibiscus ("hibiscus rosa-sinensis")	3·50	9·00

Nos. 405/10 are larger, 47×35 mm.
See also Nos. 527/36.

76 "Jesus Defiled" (El Greco)

1981. Easter. Details of Paintings. Multicoloured.

425	35c. Type **76**	40	30
426	50c. "Pieta" (Fernando Gallego)	60	50
427	60c. "The Supper of Emmaus" (Jacopo de Pontormo)	65	55
MS428	69×111 mm. As Nos. 425/7, but each with charity premium of 2c.	1·00	1·75

1981. Easter. Children's Charity. Designs as Nos. 425/7 in separate miniature sheets 78×86 mm, each with a face value of 80c.+5c.

MS429	As Nos. 425/7 Set of 3 sheets	1·00	2·00

77 Prince Charles

1981. Royal Wedding. Multicoloured.

430	75c. Type **77**	25	60
431	95c. Lady Diana Spencer	30	70
432	$1.20 Prince Charles and Lady Diana Spencer	30	80
MS433	78×85 mm. Nos. 430/2	1·50	2·25

78 Footballer Silhouettes

1981. World Cup Football Championship, Spain (1982).

434	**78**	30c. green, gold and blue	20	20
435	-	30c. green, gold and blue	20	20
436	-	30c. green, gold and blue	20	20
437	-	35c. blue, gold and orange	20	20
438	-	35c. blue, gold and orange	20	20
439	-	35c. blue, gold and orange	20	20
440	-	40c. orange, gold and green	20	20
441	-	40c. orange, gold and green	20	20
442	-	40c. orange, gold and green	20	20
MS443		162×122 mm. 30c.+3c., 35c.+3c., 40c.+3c. (each×3). As Nos. 434/42	1·60	2·00

DESIGNS—Various footballer silhouettes: 435, gold figure 3rd from left; 436, gold figure 4th from left; 437, gold figure 3rd from left; 438, gold figure 4th from left; 439, gold figure 2nd from left; 440, gold figure 3rd from left displaying close control; 441, gold figure 2nd from left; 442, gold figure 3rd from left, heading.

1982. International Year for Disabled Persons. Nos. 430/2 surch **+5c.**

444	75c. +5c. Type **77**	50	85
445	95c. +5c. Lady Diana Spencer	60	1·00
446	$1.20 +5c. Prince Charles and Lady Diana	60	1·25
MS447	78×85 mm. As Nos. 444/6, with each surcharged **+ 10c.**	1·75	4·50

80 "The Holy Family with Angels" (detail)

1981. Christmas. 375th Birth Anniv of Rembrandt. Multicoloured.

448	20c. Type **80**	65	45
449	35c. "Presentation in the Temple"	85	55
450	50c. "Virgin and Child in Temple"	95	1·10
451	60c. "The Holy Family"	1·25	1·50
MS452	79×112 mm. Nos. 448/51	3·25	3·75

1982. Christmas. Children's Charity. Designs as Nos. 448/51 in separate miniature sheets 66×80 mm, each with a face value of 80c.+5c.

MS453	As Nos. 448/51 Set of 4 sheets	2·00	2·50

1982. 21st Birthday of Princess of Wales. Multicoloured.

454	50c. Type **81**	40	55
455	$1.25 Prince and Princess of Wales	60	90
456	$2.50 Princess of Wales	1·50	1·40
MS457	81×101 mm. Nos. 454/6	5·00	3·50

The stamps from No. **MS**457 are without white borders.

1982. Birth of Prince William of Wales (1st issue). Nos. 430/3 optd.

458	75c. Type **77**	1·50	2·00
459	75c. Type **77**	1·50	2·00
460	95c. Lady Diana Spencer	2·50	2·50
461	95c. Lady Diana Spencer	2·50	2·50
462	$1.20 Prince Charles and Lady Diana Spencer	2·50	2·75
463	$1.20 Prince Charles and Lady Diana Spencer	2·50	2·75
MS464	78×85 mm. Nos. 430/2	6·00	6·00

OVERPRINTS: Nos. 458, 460 and 462 **COMMEMORATING THE ROYAL BIRTH 21 JUNE 1982**; 459, 461 and 463 **BIRTH OF PRINCE WILLIAM OF WALES 21 JUNE 1982**; **MS**464 **PRINCE WILLIAM OF WALES 21 JUNE 1982.**

81 Prince of Wales

1982. Birth of Prince William of Wales (2nd issue). As Nos. 454/6, but with changed inscriptions. Multicoloured.

465	50c. Type **81**	50	65
466	$1.25 Prince and Princess of Wales	1·00	1·25
467	$2.50 Princess of Wales	4·00	3·25
MS468	81×101 mm. As Nos. 465/7	7·00	5·50

83 Infant

1982. Christmas. Paintings of Infants by Bronzion, Murillo and Boucher.

469	**83**	40c. multicoloured	1·50	80
470	-	52c. multicoloured	1·60	95
471	-	83c. multicoloured	2·50	2·50
472	-	$1.05 multicoloured	2·75	2·75
MS473		110×76 mm. Designs as Nos. 469/72 (each 31×27 mm), but without portrait of Princess and Prince William	6·00	4·50

84 Prince and Princess of Wales with Prince William

1982. Christmas. Children's Charity. Sheet 72×58 mm.

MS474	**84**	80c.+5c. multicoloured	1·50	1·50

85 Prime Minister Robert Rex

1983. Commonwealth Day. Multicoloured.

475	70c. Type **85**	50	55
476	70c. H.M.S. "Resolution" and H.M.S. "Adventure" off Niue, 1774	50	55
477	70c. Passion flower	50	55
478	70c. Limes	50	55

86 Scouts signalling

1983. 75th Anniv of Boy Scout Movement and 125th Birth Anniv of Lord Baden-Powell. Multicoloured.

479	40c. Type **86**	35	40
480	50c. Planting sapling	45	50
481	83c. Map-reading	85	90
MS482	137×90 mm. As Nos. 479/81, but each with premium of 3c.	1·25	1·75

1983. 15th World Scout Jamboree, Alberta, Canada. Nos. 479/81 optd **XV WORLD JAMBOREE CANADA.**

483	40c. Type **86**	35	40
484	50c. Planting sapling	45	50
485	83c. Map-reading	85	90
MS486	137×90 mm. As Nos. 483/5, but each with premium of 3c.	1·60	1·75

88 Black Right Whale

1983. Protect the Whales. Multicoloured.

487	12c. Type **88**	75	65
488	25c. Fin whale	95	80
489	35c. Sei whale	1·50	1·25
490	40c. Blue whale	1·75	1·50
491	58c. Bowhead whale	1·90	1·60
492	70c. Sperm whale	2·25	1·75
493	83c. Humpback whale	2·50	2·25
494	$1.05 Minke whale	3·00	2·50
495	$2.50 Grey whale	4·25	4·00

89 Montgolfier Balloon, 1783

1983. Bicentenary of Manned Flight. Multicoloured.

496	25c. Type **89** (postage)	55	25
497	40c. Wright Brothers Flyer I, 1903	1·40	45
498	58c. Airship "Graf Zeppelin", 1928	1·50	60
499	70c. Boeing 247, 1933	1·75	85
500	83c. "Apollo 8", 1968	1·75	1·00
501	$1.05 Space shuttle "Columbia", 1982	2·00	1·40
MS502	118×130 mm. Nos. 496/501 (air)	3·00	3·25

90 "The Garvagh Madonna"

1983. Christmas. 500th Birth Anniv of Raphael. Multicoloured.

503	30c. Type **90**	90	40
504	40c. "Madonna of the Granduca"	95	45
505	58c. "Madonna of the Goldfish"	1·40	60
506	70c. "The Holy Family of Francis I"	1·50	70
507	83c. "The Holy Family with Saints"	1·60	80
MS508	120×114 mm. As Nos. 503/7 but each with a premium of 3c.	3·25	2·75

1983. Various stamps surch

(a) Nos. 393/4, 399/404 and 407

509	52c. on 30c. "Strelitzia reginae"	70	45
510	52c. on 30c. Bird of paradise	70	45
511	58c. on 50c. "Tibouchina sp."	70	55
512	58c. on 50c. Princess flower	70	55
513	70c. on 60c. "Nelumbo sp."	85	60
514	70c. on 60c. Lotus	85	60
515	83c. on 80c. "Hybrid hibiscus"	1·00	75
516	83c. on 80c. Yellow hibiscus	1·00	75
517	$3.70 on $3 "Orchid sp."	6·00	3·25

(b) Nos. 431/2 and 455/6.

518	$1.10 on 95c. Lady Diana Spencer	2·50	2·25
519	$1.10 on $1.25 Prince and Princess of Wales	1·50	2·00
520	$2.60 on $1.20 Prince Charles and Lady Diana	3·00	3·50
521	$2.60 on $2.50 Princess of Wales	2·75	3·25

1983. Christmas. 500th Birth Anniv of Raphael. Children's Charity. Designs as Nos. 503/7 in separate miniature sheets, 65×80 mm, each with face value of 85c.+5c.

MS522	As Nos. 503/7 Set of 5 sheets	3·50	2·75

91 Morse Key Transmitter

1984. World Communications Year. Multicoloured.

523	40c. Type **91**	30	35
524	52c. Wall-mounted phone	40	45
525	83c. Communications satellite	60	65
MS526	114×90 mm. Nos. 523/5	1·10	1·50

92 "Phalaenopsis sp."

1984. Flowers (2nd series). Multicoloured.

527	12c. Type **92**	25	15
528	25c. "Euphorbia pulcherrima"	35	20
529	30c. "Cochlospermum hibiscoides"	40	25

530	35c. "Begonia sp."	40	25
531	40c. "Plumeria sp."	50	30
532	52c. "Strelitzia reginae"	65	40
533	58c. "Hibiscus syriacus"	70	45
534	70c. "Tibouchina sp."	1·00	60
535	83c. "Nelumbo sp."	1·10	70
536	$1.05 "Hybrid hibiscus"	1·25	85
537	$1.75 "Cassia fistula"	2·00	1·50
538	$2.30 "Orchid var"	4·50	2·00
539	$3.90 "Orchid sp."	6·00	4·00
540	$5 "Euphorbia pulcherrima poinsettia"	4·00	4·50
541	$6.60 "Hybrid hibiscus"	4·50	6·00
542	$8.30 "Hibiscus rosa-sinensis"	6·00	7·00

Nos. 537/42 are larger, 39×31 mm.

93 Discus throwing

1984. Olympic Games, Los Angeles. Multicoloured.

547	30c. Type **93**	25	30
548	35c. Sprinting (horiz)	30	35
549	40c. Horse racing (horiz)	35	40
550	58c. Boxing (horiz)	50	55
551	70c. Javelin-throwing	60	65

94 Koala

1984. "Ausipex" International Stamp Exhibition, Melbourne

(a) Designs showing Koala Bears

552	94	25c. multicoloured (postage)	70	50
553	-	35c. multicoloured	80	55
554	-	40c. multicoloured	90	60
555	-	58c. multicoloured	1·00	85
556	-	70c. multicoloured	1·25	1·00

(b) Vert designs showing Kangaroos

557	83c. multicoloured (air)	1·50	1·25
558	$1.05 multicoloured	1·75	1·60
559	$2.50 multicoloured	3·00	4·00
MS560	110×64 mm. $1.75 Wallaby; $1.75 Koala bear	4·50	4·00

See also Nos. **MS**566/7.

1984. Olympic Gold Medal Winners, Los Angeles. Nos. 547/51 optd.

561	30c. Type **93**	65	30
562	35c. Sprinting	70	35
563	40c. Horse racing	75	35
564	58c. Boxing	80	50
565	70c. Javelin-throwing	85	60

OPTS: 30c. **Discus Throw Rolf Danneberg Germany**; 35c. **1,500 Metres Sebastian Coe Great Britain**; 40c. **Equestrian Mark Todd New Zealand**; 58c. **Boxing Tyrell Biggs United States**; 70c. **Javelin Throw Arto Haerkoenen Finland**.

1984. "Ausipex" International Stamp Exhibition, Melbourne (2nd issue). Designs as Nos. 552/60 in miniature sheets of six or four. Multicoloured.

MS566	109×105 mm. Nos. 552/6 and $1.75 Koala bear (as No. **MS**560)	6·00	4·75
MS567	80×105 mm. Nos. 557/9 and $1.75 Wallaby (as No. **MS**560)	6·00	4·75

96 Niue National Flag and Premier Sir Robert Rex

1984. Tenth Anniv of Self-government. Multicoloured.

568	40c. Type **96**	1·10	50
569	58c. Map of Niue and Premier Rex	1·10	50
570	70c. Premier Rex receiving proclamation of self-government	1·10	70
MS571	110×83 mm. Nos. 568/70	2·00	2·00
MS572	100×74 mm. $2.50 As 70c. (50×30 mm)	2·00	2·00

1984. Birth of Prince Henry. Nos. 430 and 454 surch $2 Prince Henry 15. 9. 84.

573	$2 on 50c. on 50c. Type **81**	2·50	2·75
574	$2 on 75c. on 75c. Type **77**	2·50	2·75

98 "The Nativity" (A. Vaccaro)

1984. Christmas. Multicoloured.

575	40c. Type **98**	70	35
576	58c. "Virgin with Fly" (anon, 16th-century)	85	50
577	70c. "The Adoration of the Shepherds" (B. Murillo)	95	60
578	80c. "Flight into Egypt" (B. Murillo)	1·10	70
MS579	115×111 mm. As Nos. 575/8 but each stamp with a 5c. premium	2·50	2·25
MS580	Four sheets, each 66×98 mm. As Nos. 575/8, but each stamp 30×42 mm. with a face value of 95c.+10c. Set of 4 sheets	4·00	3·00

99 House Wren

1985. Birth Bicentenary of John J. Audubon (ornithologist). Multicoloured.

581	40c. Type **99**	2·75	1·00
582	70c. Veery	3·00	1·60
583	83c. Grasshopper sparrow	3·25	2·00
584	$1.50 Henslow's sparrow	3·50	2·25
585	$2.50 Vesper sparrow	5·00	4·25
MS586	Five sheets, each 54×60 mm. As Nos. 581/5 but each stamp 34×26 mm with a face value of $1.75 and without the commemorative inscription Set of 5 sheets	13·00	8·50

100 The Queen Mother in Garter Robes

1985. Life and Times of Queen Elizabeth the Queen Mother. Multicoloured.

587	70c. Type **100**	1·50	1·50
588	$1.15 In open carriage with the Queen	1·60	1·60
589	$1.50 With Prince Charles during 80th birthday celebrations	1·75	1·75
MS590	70×70 mm. $3 At her desk in Clarence House (38×35 mm)	6·50	2·75

See also No. **MS**627.

1985. South Pacific Mini Games, Rarotonga. Nos. 547/8 and 550/1 surch **MINI SOUTH PACIFIC GAMES, RAROTONGA** and emblem.

591	52c. on 70c. Javelin throwing	40	55
592	83c. on 58c. Boxing	65	80
593	95c. on 35c. Sprinting	75	90
594	$2 on 30c. Type **93**	1·50	2·00

1985. Pacific Islands Conference, Rarotonga. Nos. 475/8 optd **PACIFIC ISLANDS CONFERENCE, RAROTONGA** and emblem.

595	70c. Type **85**	55	75
596	70c. "Resolution" and "Adventure" off Niue, 1774	55	75
597	70c. Passion flower	55	75
598	70c. Limes	55	75

Nos. 595 also shows an overprinted amendment to the caption which now reads **Premier Sir Robert Rex K.B.E.**.

103 "R. Strozzi's Daughter" (Titian)

1985. International Youth Year. Multicoloured.

599	58c. Type **103**	2·25	90
600	70c. "The Fifer" (E. Manet)	2·50	1·00
601	$1.15 "Portrait of a Young Girl" (Renoir)	3·25	1·90
602	$1.50 "Portrait of M. Berard" (Renoir)	3·50	2·50
MS603	Four sheets, each 63×79 mm. As Nos. 599/602 but each with a face value of $1.75+10c. Set of 4 sheets	16·00	11·00

104 "Virgin and Child"

1985. Christmas. Details of Paintings by Correggio. Multicoloured.

604	58c. Type **104**	1·50	85
605	85c. "Adoration of the Magi"	1·75	1·40
606	$1.05 "Virgin with Child and St. John"	2·25	2·50
607	$1.45 "Virgin and Child with St. Catherine"	2·75	3·50
MS608	83×123 mm. As Nos. 604/7 but each stamp with a face value of 60c.+10c.	3·00	2·75
MS609	Four sheets, each 80×90 mm. 65c. Type **104**; 95c. As No. 605; $1.20, As No. 606; $1.75, As No. 607 (each stamp 49×59 mm). Imperf Set of 4 sheets	4·00	4·00

105 "The Constellations" (detail)

1986. Appearance of Halley's Comet. Designs showing details from ceiling painting "The Constellations" by Giovanni de Vecchi. Nos. 611/13 show different spacecraft at top left. Multicoloured.

610	60c. Type **105**	50	50
611	75c. "Vega" spacecraft	65	65
612	$1.10 "Planet A" spacecraft	90	90
613	$1.50 "Giotto" spacecraft	1·25	1·25
MS614	125×91 mm. As Nos. 610/13 but each stamp with a face value of 95c.	4·75	4·25

Stamps from No. **MS**614 are without borders.

106 Queen Elizabeth II and Prince Philip

1986. 60th Birthday of Queen Elizabeth II. Multicoloured.

615	$1.10 Type **106**	80	1·00
616	$1.50 Queen and Prince Philip at Balmoral	1·00	1·25
617	$2 Queen at Buckingham Palace	1·50	1·75
MS618	110×70 mm. As Nos. 615/17, but each stamp with a face value of 75c.	2·75	3·25
MS619	58×89 mm. $3 Queen and Prince Philip at Windsor Castle	3·50	4·25

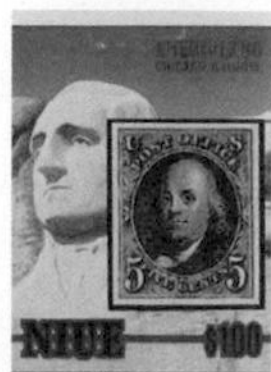

107 U.S.A. 1847 Franklin 5c. Stamp and Washington Sculpture, Mt. Rushmore, U.S.A.

1986. "Ameripex '86" International Stamp Exhibition, Chicago. Multicoloured.

620	$1 Type **107**	3·50	3·50
621	$1 Flags of Niue and U.S.A. and Mt. Rushmore sculptures	3·50	3·50

Nos. 620/1 were printed together, *se-tenant*, forming a composite design.

108 "Statue under Construction, Paris, 1883" (Victor Dargaud)

1986. Centenary of Statue of Liberty. Multicoloured.

622	$1 Type **108**	2·00	2·00
623	$2.50 "Unveiling of Statue of Liberty" (Edmund Morand)	2·75	2·75
MS624	107×73 mm. As Nos. 622/3, but each stamp with a face value of $1.25	2·50	3·00

See also No. **MS**648.

109 Prince Andrew, Miss Sarah Ferguson and Westminster Abbey

1986. Royal Wedding.

625	**109**	$2.50 multicoloured	3·25	3·25
MS626		106×68 mm. $5 Prince Andrew and Miss sarah Ferguson (43×30 mm)	7·50	8·00

1986. 86th Birthday of Queen Elizabeth the Queen Mother. Nos. 587/9 in miniature sheet, 109×83 mm.

MS627	Nos. 587/9	13·00	13·00

110 Great Egret

1986. "Stampex '86" Stamp Exhibition, Adelaide. Australian Birds. Multicoloured.

628	40c. Type **110**	3·00	1·75
629	60c. Painted finch (horiz)	3·25	2·00
630	75c. Australian king parrot	3·50	2·25
631	80c. Variegated wren (horiz)	3·75	2·50
632	$1 Peregrine falcon	4·25	2·75
633	$1.65 Azure kingfisher (horiz)	6·00	4·00
634	$2.20 Budgerigars	6·50	6·00
635	$4.25 Emu (horiz)	8·00	7·50

111 "Virgin and Child" (Perugino)

1986. Christmas. Paintings from Vatican Museum. Multicoloured.

636	80c. Type **111**	2·25	1·75
637	$1.15 "Virgin of St. N. dei Frari" (Titian)	2·50	2·00
638	$1.80 "Virgin with Milk" (Lorenzo di Credi)	3·50	3·75
639	$2.60 "Madonna of Foligno" (Raphael)	4·50	5·50
MS640	87×110 mm. As Nos. 636/9, but each stamp with a face value of $1.50	10·00	6·00
MS641	70×100 mm. $7.50 As No. 639, but 27×43 mm	8·00	9·00

1986. Visit of Pope John Paul II to South Pacific. Nos. 636/9 surch **CHRISTMAS VISIT TO SOUTH PACIFIC OF POPE JOHN PAUL II NOVEMBER 21 24 1986.**

642	80c. +10c. Type **111**	3·50	2·50
643	$1.10 +10c. "Virgin of St. N. dei Frari" (Titian)	4·00	3·00
644	$1.80 +10c. "Virgin with Milk" (Lorenzo di Credi)	5·50	4·00
645	$2.60 +10c. "Madonna of Foligno" (Raphael)	6·50	5·00
MS646	87×110 mm. As Nos. 642/5, but each stamp with a face value of $1.50+10c.	18·00	12·00
MS647	70×100 mm. $7.50+50c. As No. 645, but 27×43 mm	18·00	12·00

112a Sailing Ship under Brooklyn Bridge

1987. Centenary of Statue of Liberty (1986) (2nd issue). Two sheets, each 122×122 mm, containing T **112a** and similar multicoloured designs.

MS648 Two sheets. (a) 75c. Type **112a**; 75c. Restoring Statue's flame; 75c. Steam-cleaning Statue's torch; 75c. "Esmerelda" (children cadet barquentine) off Manhattan; 75c. Cadet barque at dusk. (b) 75c. Statue of Liberty at night (vert); 75c. Statue at night (side view) (vert); 75c. Cleaning Statue's crown (vert); 75c. Statue at night (rear view) (vert); 75c. Cleaning a finial (vert) Set of 2 sheets 8·00 9·00

113 Boris Becker, Olympic Rings and Commemorative Coin

1987. Olympic Games, Seoul (1988). Tennis (1st issue). Designs showing Boris Becker in play.

649	**113**	80c. multicoloured	2·75	2·00
650	-	$1.15 multicoloured	3·00	2·25
651	-	$1.40 multicoloured	3·25	2·50
652	-	$1.80 multicoloured	4·00	3·25

1987. Olympic Games, Seoul (1988). Tennis (2nd issue). As T **113** but showing Steffi Graf.

653	85c. multicoloured	2·75	1·75
654	$1.05 multicoloured	3·00	2·00
655	$1.30 multicoloured	3·25	2·25
656	$1.75 multicoloured	3·50	2·75

1987. Royal Ruby Wedding. Nos. 616/17 surch **40TH WEDDING ANNIV. 4.85**.

657	$4.85 on $1.50 Queen and Prince Philip at Balmoral	5·00	4·50
658	$4.85 on $2 Queen at Buckingham Palace	5·00	4·50

115 "The Nativity"

1987. Christmas. Religious Paintings by Durer. Multicoloured.

659	80c. Type **115**	1·50	1·25
660	$1.05 "Adoration of the Magi"	1·75	1·75
661	$2.80 "Celebration of the Rosary"	3·75	3·75
MS662	100×140 mm. As Nos. 659/61, but each size 48×37 mm with a face value of $1.30	8·00	6·00
MS663	90×80 mm. $7.50 As No. 661, but size 51×33 mm	8·50	7·00

Nos. 659/61 each include detail of an angel with lute as in T **115**.

Stamps from the miniature sheets are without this feature.

116 Franz Beckenbauer in Action

1988. West German Football Victories. Multicoloured.

664	20c. Type **116**	80	70
665	40c. German "All Star" team in action	1·00	90
666	60c. Bayern Munich team with European Cup, 1974	1·25	1·10
667	80c. World Cup match, England, 1966	1·60	1·40
668	$1.05 World Cup match, Mexico, 1970	1·75	1·60
669	$1.30 Beckenbauer with pennant, 1974	2·25	2·00
670	$1.80 Beckenbauer and European Cup, 1974	2·50	2·25

1988. Steffi Graf's Tennis Victories. Nos. 653/6 optd.

671	85c. mult (optd **Australia 24 Jan 88 French Open 4 June 88**)	2·25	1·50
672	$1.05 multicoloured (optd **Wimbledon 2 July 88 U S Open 10 Sept. 88**)	2·75	1·75
673	$1.30 multicoloured (optd **Women's Tennis Grand Slam: 10 September 88**)	2·75	1·90
674	$1.75 mult (optd **Seoul Olympic Games Gold Medal Winner**)	2·75	2·10

118 Angels

1988. Christmas. Details from "The Adoration of the Shepherds" by Rubens. Multicoloured.

675	60c. Type **118**	1·75	1·50
676	80c. Shepherds	2·00	1·75
677	$1.05 Virgin Mary	2·75	2·50
678	$1.30 Holy Child	3·50	3·00
MS679	83×103 mm. $7.20 The Nativity (38×49 mm)	6·00	7·50

119 Astronaut and "Apollo 11" Emblem

1989. 20th Anniv of First Manned Landing on Moon. Multicoloured.

680	$1.50 Type **119**	4·75	4·50
681	$1.50 Earth and Moon	4·75	4·50
682	$1.50 Astronaut and "Apollo 11" emblem	4·75	4·50
MS683	160×64 mm. As Nos. 680/2, but each stamp with a face value of $1.15	5·00	5·00

120 Priests

1989. Christmas. Details from "Presentation in the Temple" by Rembrandt. Multicoloured.

684	70c. Type **120**	3·00	2·75
685	80c. Virgin and Christ Child in Simeon's arms	3·00	2·75
686	$1.05 Joseph	3·50	3·25
687	$1.30 Simeon and Christ Child	4·00	3·75
MS688	84×110 mm. $7.20 "Presentation in the Temple" (39×49 mm)	12·00	11·00

121 Fritz Walter

1990. World Cup Football Championship, Italy. German Footballers. Multicoloured.

689	80c. Type **121**	2·50	2·50
690	$1.15 Franz Beckenbauer	2·75	2·75
691	$1.40 Uwe Seeler	3·00	3·00
692	$1.80 German team emblem and signatures of former captains	4·00	4·00

122 "Merchant Maarten Looten" (Rembrandt)

1990. 150th Anniv of the Penny Black. Rembrandt Paintings. Multicoloured.

693	80c. Type **122**	2·50	2·50
694	$1.05 "Rembrandt's Son Titus with Pen in Hand"	3·75	3·00
695	$1.30 "The Shipbuilder and his Wife"	4·00	3·25
696	$1.80 "Bathsheba with King David's Letter"	5·00	3·50
MS697	82×143 mm. As Nos. 693/6, but each with a face value of $1.50	7·50	8·50

123 Queen Elizabeth the Queen Mother

1990. 90th Birthday of Queen Elizabeth the Queen Mother.

698	**123**	$1.25 multicoloured	4·75	4·00
MS699		84×64 mm. **123** $7 multicoloured	15·00	13·00

124 "Adoration of the Magi" (Dirk Bouts)

1990. Christmas. Religious Paintings. Multicoloured.

700	70c. Type **124**	3·00	2·75
701	80c. "Holy Family" (Fra Bartolommeo)	3·25	3·00
702	$1.05 "Nativity" (Memling)	3·50	3·50
703	$1.30 "Adoration of the Kings" (Bruegel the Elder)	4·50	4·50
MS704	100×135 mm. $7.20 "Virgin and Child Enthroned" (detail, Cosimo Tura)	11·00	13·00

1990. "Birdpex '90" Stamp Exhibition, Christchurch, New Zealand. No. 410 optd **Birdpex '90** and logo.

705	$10 Scarlet hibiscus	11·00	12·00

1991. 65th Birthday of Queen Elizabeth II. No. 409 optd **SIXTY FIFTH BIRTHDAY QUEEN ELIZABETH II**.

706	$6 "Hybrid hibiscus"	12·00	13·00

1991. Tenth Wedding Anniv of Prince and Princess of Wales. Nos. 430/2 optd **TENTH ANNIVERSARY**.

707A	75c. Type **77**	2·25	1·75
708A	95c. Lady Diana Spencer	3·25	2·75
709A	$1.20 Prince Charles and Lady Diana	3·75	2·75

129 "The Virgin and Child with Sts. Jerome and Dominic" (Lippi)

1991. Christmas. Religious Paintings. Multicoloured.

710	20c. Type **129**	1·50	1·00
711	50c. "The Isenheim Altarpiece" (M. Grunewald)	2·50	1·75
712	$1 "The Nativity" (G. Pittoni)	3·75	3·50
713	$2 "Adoration of the Kings" (J. Brueghel the Elder)	5·00	5·50
MS714	79×104 mm. $7 "Adoration of the Sheperds" (G. Reni)	12·00	14·00

130 Buff-banded Rail

1992. Birds. Multicoloured.

718	20c. Type **130**	2·00	1·00
719	50c. Red-tailed tropic bird	2·00	1·10
720	70c. Purple swamphen	3·00	1·25
721	$1 Pacific pigeon	3·50	1·75
722	$1.50 White-collared kingfisher	2·50	2·25
723	$2 Blue-crowned lory	2·50	2·50
724	$3 Purple-capped fruit dove	2·75	3·00
726	$5 Barn owl	6·50	5·50
727	$7 Longtailed koel ("Cockoo") (48½×35 mm)	5·50	7·50
728	$10 Reef heron (48½×35 mm)	7·50	9·50
729	$15 Spotted triller ("Polynesian Triller") (48½×35 mm)	11·00	14·00

131 Columbus before King Ferdinand and Queen Isabella

1992. 500th Anniv of Discovery of America by Columbus. Multicoloured.

731	$2 Type **131**	3·50	3·00
732	$3 Fleet of Columbus	6·00	5·50
733	$5 Claiming the New World for Spain	7·00	6·50

132 Tennis and $10 Commemorative Coin

1992. Olympic Games, Barcelona. Multicoloured.

734	$2.50 Type **132**	6·50	5·00
735	$2.50 Olympic flame and national flags	6·50	5·00
736	$2.50 Gymnastics and different $10 coin	6·50	5·00
MS737	152×87 mm. $5 Water polo	13·00	14·00

1992. Sixth Festival of Pacific Arts, Rarotonga. Nos. 336/51 surch **$1**.

738	$1 on 20c. Type **69**	1·10	1·10
739	$1 on 20c. Ku-Tagwa plaque, New Guinea	1·10	1·10
740	$1 on 20c. Suspension hook, New Guinea	1·10	1·10
741	$1 on 20c. Ancestral board, New Guinea	1·10	1·10
742	$1 on 25c. Platform post, New Hebrides	1·10	1·10
743	$1 on 25c. Canoe ornament, New Ireland	1·10	1·10
744	$1 on 25c. Carved figure, Admiralty Islands	1·10	1·10
745	$1 on 25c. Female with child, Admiralty Islands	1·10	1·10
746	$1 on 30c. The God A'a, Rurutu, Austral Islands	1·10	1·10
747	$1 on 30c. Statue of Tangaroa, Cook Islands	1·10	1·10
748	$1 on 30c. Ivory pendant, Tonga	1·10	1·10
749	$1 on 30c. Tapa (Hiapo) cloth, Niue	1·10	1·10
750	$1 on 35c. Feather box (Waka), New Zealand	1·10	1·10
751	$1 on 35c. Hei-Tiki amulet, New Zealand	1·10	1·10
752	$1 on 35c. House post, New Zealand	1·10	1·10
753	$1 on 35c. Feather image of god Ku, Hawaii	1·10	1·10

134 "St. Catherine's Mystic Marriage" (detail) (Memling)

1992. Christmas.

754	**134**	20c. multicoloured	1·50	75
755	-	50c. multicoloured	2·25	1·50
756	-	$1 multicoloured	3·25	3·00
757	-	$2 multicoloured	4·75	5·50
MS758		87×101 mm. $7 multicoloured (as 50c., but larger (36×47 mm)	13·00	14·00

DESIGNS: 50c., $1, $2 Different details from "St. Catherine's Mystic Marriage" by Hans Memling.

135 Queen on Official Visit

1992. 40th Anniv of Queen Elizabeth II's Accession. Multicoloured.

759	70c. Type **135**	2·50	1·75
760	$1 Queen in green evening dress	3·00	2·25
761	$1.50 Queen in white embroidered evening dress	3·50	2·75
762	$2 Queen with bouquet	4·25	3·25

136 Rough-toothed Dolphin

1993. Endangered Species. South Pacific Dolphins. Multicoloured.

763	20c. Type **136**	1·25	90
764	50c. Fraser's dolphin	2·00	1·60
765	75c. Pantropical spotted dolphin	2·50	2·75
766	$1 Risso's dolphin	3·00	3·50

1993. Premier Sir Robert Rex Commemoration. Nos. 568/70 optd **1909 IN MEMORIAM 1992 SIR ROBERT R REX K.B.E.** or surch also.

767	40c. Type **96**	2·50	2·50
768	58c. Map of Niue and Premier Rex	2·50	2·50
769	70c. Premier Rex receiving proclamation of self-government	2·50	2·50
770	$1 on 40c. Type **96**	2·75	2·75
771	$1 on 58c. Map of Niue and Premier Rex	2·75	2·75
772	$1 on 70c. Premier Rex receiving proclamation of self-government	2·75	2·75

138 Queen Elizabeth II in Coronation Robes and St. Edward's Crown

1993. 40th Anniv of Coronation.

773	**138**	$5 multicoloured	12·00	12·00

139 "Virgin of the Rosary" (detail) (Guido Reni)

1993. Christmas.

774	**139**	20c. multicoloured	85	75
775	-	70c. multicoloured	2·00	1·25
776	-	$1 multicoloured	2·25	1·50
777	-	$1. 50 multicoloured	3·00	3·50
778	-	$3 multicoloured (32×47 mm)	4·75	6·50

DESIGNS: 70c. to $3 Different details of "Virgin of the Rosary" (Reni).

140 World Cup and Globe with Flags of U.S.A. and Previous Winners

1994. World Cup Football Championship, U.S.A.

779	**140**	$4 multicoloured	6·50	7·50

141 "Apollo 11" and Astronaut on Moon

1994. 25th Anniv of First Manned Moon Landing. Multicoloured.

780	$2.50 Type **141**	6·00	6·00
781	$2.50 Astronaut and flag	6·00	6·00
782	$2.50 Astronaut and equipment	6·00	6·00

142 "The Adoration of the Kings" (Jan Gossaert)

1994. Christmas. Religious Paintings. Multicoloured.

783	70c. Type **142**	1·00	1·25
784	70c. "Madonna and Child with Sts. John and Catherine" (Titian)	1·00	1·25
785	70c. "The Holy Family and Shepherd" (Titian)	1·00	1·25
786	70c. "The Virgin and Child with Saints" (Gerard David)	1·00	1·25
787	$1 "The Adoration of the Shepherds" (cherubs detail) (Poussin)	1·25	1·50
788	$1 "The Adoration of the Shepherds" (Holy Family detail) (Poussin)	1·25	1·50
789	$1 "Madonna and Child with Sts. Joseph and John" (Sebastiano)	1·25	1·50
790	$1 "The Adoration of the Kings" (Veronese)	1·25	1·50

143 Long John Silver and Jim Hawkins ("Treasure Island")

1994. Death Centenary of Robert Louis Stevenson (author). Multicoloured.

791	$1.75 Type **143**	4·00	3·25
792	$1.75 Transformation of Dr. Jekyll ("Dr. Jekyll and Mr. Hyde")	4·00	3·25
793	$1.75 Attack on David Balfour ("Kidnapped")	4·00	3·25
794	$1.75 Robert Louis Stevenson, tomb and inscription	4·00	3·25

1996. Nos. 720 and 722 surch.

795	50c. on 70c. Purple swamphen	7·00	4·00
796	$1 on $1.50 White-collared kingfisher	8·50	6·50

145 Tapeu Orchid

1996. Flowers. Multicoloured.

797	70c. Type **145**	80	80
798	$1 Frangipani	1·00	1·00
799	$1.20 "Golden Shower"	1·40	1·75
800	$1.50 "Pua"	1·90	2·50

1996. Redrawn design as No. 146.

801	20c. red and green	50	1·00

146 "Jackfish" (yacht)

1996. Sailing Ships. Multicoloured.

802	70c. Type **146**	1·10	1·10
803	$1 "Jennifer" (yacht)	1·60	1·60
804	$1.20 "Mikeva" (yacht)	1·90	2·00
805	$2 "Eye of the Wind" (cadet brig)	2·50	3·00

147 "Desert Star" (ketch)

1996. "Taipei '96" International Philatelic Exhibition, Taiwan. Sheet 90×80 mm.

MS806	**147** $1.50 multicoloured	2·00	2·50

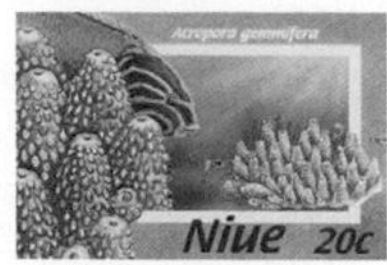

148 "Acropora gemmifera"

1996. Corals. Multicoloured.

807	20c. Type **148**	70	70
808	50c. "Acropora nobilis"	1·00	75
809	70c. "Goniopora lobata"	1·25	85
810	$1 "Sylaster sp."	1·50	1·25
811	$1.20 "Alveopora catalai"	1·75	1·75
812	$1.50 "Fungia scutaria"	2·00	2·00
813	$2 "Porites solida"	2·50	2·75
814	$3 "Millepora sp."	3·25	3·75
815	$4 "Pocillopora eydouxi"	3·75	4·50
816	$5 "Platygyra pini"	4·00	4·75

149 Ox

1997. "HONG KONG '97" International Stamp Exhibition. Chinese New Year ("Year of the Ox"). Sheet 120×90 mm.

MS817	**149** $1.50 multicoloured	1·50	2·25

150 Steps to Lagoon

1997. Island Scenes. Multicoloured.

818	$1 Type **150**	1·25	1·50
819	$1 Islands in lagoon	1·25	1·50
820	$1 Beach with rocks in foreground	1·25	1·50
821	$1 Over-hanging rock on beach	1·25	1·50

Nos. 818/21 were printed together, *se-tenant*, forming a composite design.

151 Humpback Whale

1997. Whales (1st series). Multicoloured.

822	20c. Type **151**	50	45
823	$1 Humpback whale and calf (vert)	1·25	1·25
824	$1.50 Humpback whale surfacing (vert)	1·75	2·00
MS825	120×90 mm. Nos. 822/4	3·25	3·75

No. **MS**825 shows the "Pacific '97" International Stamp Exhibition, San Francisco, emblem on the margin.

See also Nos. 827/9.

152 Niue 1902 Ovpt on New Zealand 1d.

1997. "Aupex '97" Stamp Exhibition, Auckland (1st issue). Sheet 136×90 mm.

MS826	**152** $2+20c. multicoloured	2·10	2·50

1997. Whales (2nd series). As T **151**. Multicoloured.

827	50c. Killer whale (vert)	85	85
828	70c. Minke whale (vert)	1·00	1·00
829	$1.20 Sperm whale (vert)	1·25	1·25

153 Niue 1918–29 Overprint on New Zealand £1

1997. "Aupex '97" Stamp Exhibition, Auckland (2nd issue). Sheet 90×135 mm.

MS830	**153** $2+20c. multicoloured	1·90	2·50

154 Floral Display in Woven Basket

1997. Christmas. Floral Displays. Multicoloured.

831	20c. Type **154**	45	40
832	50c. Display in white pot	70	60
833	70c. Display in white basket	90	90
834	$1 Display in purple vase	1·25	1·50

1998. Diana, Princess of Wales Commemoration. Sheet 145×70 mm, containing vert designs as T **91** of Kiribati. Multicoloured.

MS835	20c. Wearing white jacket, 1992; 50c. Wearing pearl-drop earrings, 1988; $1 In raincoat, 1990; $2 With Mother Theresa, 1992 (sold at $3.70+50c. charity premium)	2·50	3·50

155 Divers and Turtle

1998. Diving. Multicoloured.

836	20c. Type **155**	45	45
837	70c. Diver exploring coral reef	75	75
838	$1 Exploring underwater chasm (vert)	90	90
839	$1.20 Divers and coral fronds	1·10	1·25
840	$1.50 Divers in cave	1·40	1·75

157 Pacific Black Duck

1998. Coastal Birds (1st series). Multicoloured.

841	20c. Type **157**	70	60
842	70c. White tern ("Fairy Tern")	1·25	80
843	$1 Great frigate bird (vert)	1·25	1·10
844	$1.20 Pacific golden plover ("Lesser Golden Plover")	1·40	1·50
845	$2 Common noddy ("Brown Noddy")	2·00	2·50

See also Nos. 875/8.

158 Golden Cowrie

1998. Shells. Multicoloured.

846	20c. Type **158**	40	30
847	70c. Cowrie shell	75	65
848	$1 Spider conch	1·00	1·00
849	$5 Helmet shell	5·00	7·00

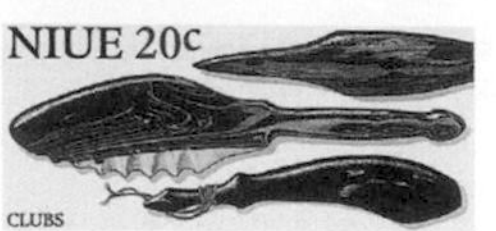

159 Clubs

1998. Ancient Weapons. Multicoloured.

850	20c. Type **159**	60	50
851	$1.20 Three spears (59×24 mm)	1·25	1·25
852	$1.50 Five spears (59×24 mm)	1·50	2·25
853	$2 Throwing stones	1·75	2·25

160 Outrigger Canoe (first migration of Niue Fekai)

1999. "Australia '99" World Stamp Exhibition, Melbourne. Maritime History. Each blue.

854	70c. Type **160**	70	60
855	$1 H.M.S. "Resolution" (Cook)	1·25	1·00
856	$1.20 "John Williams" (missionary sailing ship)	1·40	1·60
857	$1.50 Captain James Cook	1·60	2·00

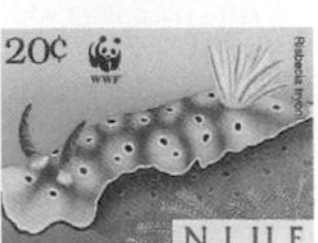

161 "Risbecia tryoni"

1999. Endangered Species. Nudibranchs. Multicoloured.

858	20c. Type **161**	45	40
859	$1 "Chromodoris lochi"	1·10	1·00
860	$1.20 "Chromodoris elizabethina"	1·25	1·40
861	$1.50 "Chromodoris bullocki"	1·50	2·00
MS862	190×105 mm. Nos. 858/61×2	6·50	8·00

162 Togo Chasm

1999. Scenic Views. Multicoloured.

863	$1 Type **162**	1·10	1·00
864	$1.20 Matapa Chasm	1·25	1·25
865	$1.50 Tufukia (horiz)	1·50	2·00
866	$2 Talava Arches (horiz)	1·75	2·50

163 Shallow Baskets

1999. Woven Baskets. Multicoloured.

867	20c. Type **163**	70	90
868	70c. Tray and bowl	80	1·10
869	$1 Tall basket and deep bowls (44×34 mm)	1·00	1·40
870	$3 Tall basket and shallow bowls (44×34 mm)	2·10	2·50

164 Children, Yachts and Forest

1999. 25th Anniv of Self-Government. Sheet, 120×74 mm, containing T **164** and similar horiz design. Multicoloured.

MS871	20c. Type **164**; $5 Scuba diver, young child and sunset	5·00	6·00

165 Family and Man in Canoe

1999. New Millennium. Multicoloured.

872	20c. Type **165**	1·25	1·50
873	70c. People pointing up	1·75	2·25
874	$4 Diver and man in traditional dress	2·75	3·25

Nos. 872/4 were printed together, se-tenant, with the backgrounds forming a composite design.

166 Purple-capped Fruit Dove

2000. Coastal Birds (2nd series). Multicoloured.

875	20c. Type **166**	45	40
876	$1 Purple swamphen	1·00	90
877	$1.20 Barn owl	1·40	1·40
878	$2 Blue-crowned lory	1·75	2·25

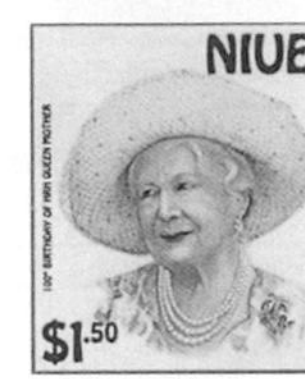

167 Queen Elizabeth the Queen Mother

2000. 100th Birthday of Queen Elizabeth the Queen Mother and 18th Birthday of Prince William. Multicoloured.

879	$1.50 Type **167**	1·75	1·75
880	$3 Queen Elizabeth the Queen Mother and Prince William (horiz)	2·50	3·25

168 Pole Vault

2000. Olympic Games, Sydney. Multicoloured.

881	50c. Type **168**	60	45
882	70c. Diving	75	65
883	$1 Hurdling	1·10	1·10
884	$3 Gymnastics	2·25	3·25

169 Couple in Traditional Costumes

2000. Island Dances. Multicoloured.

885	20c. Type **169**	70	90
886	70c. Woman in red costume	1·25	1·50
887	$1.50 Woman in white costume	1·50	1·75
888	$3 Child in costume made of leaves	1·90	2·75

Nos. 885/8 were printed together, *se-tenant*, with the backgrounds forming a composite design of flowers.

170 New Zealand Overprinted 1d. of 1902

2001. Centenary of First Niue Stamps. Multicoloured.

889	70c. Type **170**	75	75
890	$3 New Zealand overprinted £1 stamp of 1918–29	2·00	2·75

171 Large Green-banded Blue

2001. Butterflies. Multicoloured.

891	20c. Type **171**	40	35
892	70c. Leafwing	80	70
893	$1.50 Cairns birdwing	1·25	1·40
894	$2 Meadow argus	1·50	2·00

172 Green Turtle

2001. Turtles. Multicoloured.

895	50c. Type **172**	60	60
896	$1 Hawksbill turtle	1·00	1·00
897	$3 Green turtle on beach	2·50	3·50

173 Coconut Crab emerging from Sea

2001. Coconut Crabs. Multicoloured.

898	20c. Type **173**	40	30
899	70c. Crab on beach with coconut palms	80	70
900	$1.50 Crab climbing coconut palm	1·25	1·50
901	$3 Crab with coconut	2·50	3·00

174 Government Offices

2001. Centenary of Annexation to New Zealand. Multicoloured.

902	$1.50 Type **174**	1·25	1·50
903	$2 New Zealand Commissioner and Niue Chief	1·50	1·75

175 Three Wise Men

2001. Christmas. Multicoloured.

904	20c. Type **175**	35	60
905	70c. Dove	80	1·10
906	$1 Angel	1·10	1·40
907	$2 Star	2·00	2·50

2002. World Wildlife Fund. No. 858 surch **$10.00**.

908	$10 on 20c. *Risbecia tryoni*	50·00	55·00

177 Great Clam

2002. Great Clam. Multicoloured.

909	50c. Type **177**	70	70
910	70c. Clam with black spots around opening	90	90
911	$1 Clam with barnacles attached	1·25	1·40
912	$1.50 Clam with white coral attached	1·75	2·00
MS913	163×101 mm. Nos. 909/12, each×2	7·00	9·00

178 Cadillac Eldorado (1953)

2003. Centenary of the Cadillac. Multicoloured.

MS916	115×155 mm. $1.50 Type **178**; $1.50 Cadillac Eldorado (2002); $1.50 Cadillac Eldorado (1967); $1.50 Cadillac Sedan DeVille (1961)	6·00	6·25
MS917	108×82 mm. $4 Cadillac Seville (1978)	3·00	3·25

179 Corvette Convertible (1954)

2003. 50th Anniv of the Corvette. Multicoloured.

MS918	117×156 mm. $1.50 Type **179**; $1.50 Corvette (1979); $1.50 Corvette Convertible (1956); $1.50 Corvette Stingray (1964)	6·00	6·25
MS919	109×82 mm. $4 Corvette (1979)	4·00	4·25

180 Queen Elizabeth II

2003. Golden Jubilee. Multicoloured.

MS920	147×78 mm. $1.50 Type **180**; $1.50 Wearing tiara; $1.50 Wearing Imperial State Crown	4·00	4·50
MS921	97×68 mm. $4 Holding bouquet	4·00	4·25

181 Nicholas Frantz (1927)

2003. Centenary of Tour de France Cycle Race. Multicoloured.

MS922	156×96 mm. $1.50 Type **181**; $1.50 Nicholas Frantz (1928); $1.50 Maurice De Waele (1929); $1.50 Andre Leducq wearing round neck t-shirt (1930)	6·00	7·00
MS923	106×76 mm. $4 Andre Leducq wearing collared shirt (1930)	5·00	6·00

182 Prince William

2003. 21st Birthday of Prince William. Two sheets containing T **182** and similar vert designs. Multicoloured.

MS924	147×78 mm. $1.50 Wearing suit and white spotted tie; $1.50 Type **182**; $1.50 Wearing suit and square patterned tie	9·00	9·50
MS925	68×98 mm. $4 Wearing blue patterned shirt	5·00	5·50

183 Boeing 737-200

2003. Centenary of Powered Flight. Two sheets containing T **183** and similar horiz designs. Multicoloured.

MS926	107×176 mm. 80c. Type **183**; 80c. Boeing Stratocruiser; 80c. Boeing Model SA-307B; 80c. Douglas DC-2; 80c. Wright Flyer 1; 80c. DeHavilland D.H.4A	8·50	9·00
MS927	106×76 mm. $4 Boeing 767	5·00	5·50

184 Wrinkled Hornbill

2004. Birds. Two sheets containing T **184** and similar multicoloured designs.

MS928	79×104 mm. $1.50 Type **184**; $1.50 Toco toucan; $1.50 Roseate spoonbill; $1.50 Blue and yellow ("Gold") macaw	9·00	9·50
MS929	52×76 mm. $3 Green-winged Macaw (horiz)	5·50	6·00

185 Garibaldi Fish

2004. Fish. Two sheets containing T **185** and similar horiz designs. Multicoloured.

MS930	104×79 mm. $1.50 Type **185**; $1.50 Golden dddamselfish; $1.50 Squarespot anthias; $1.50 Orange-fin anemonefish	6·00	6·50
MS931	76×52 mm. $3 Maculosus angel	6·00	6·50

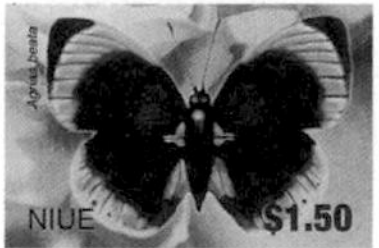

186 *Agrias beata*

2004. Butterflies. Two sheets containing T **186** and similar horiz designs. Multicoloured.

MS932	104×79 mm. $1.50 Type **186**; $1.50 *Papilio blume*; $1.50 *Cethosia bibbis*; $1.50 *Cressida Cressida*	10·00	11·00
MS933	52×76 mm. $3 *Morpho rhetenor rhetenor*	7·00	7·50

187 Allied Air Forces

2004. 60th Anniv of D-Day Landings. Two sheets containing T **187** and similar horiz designs. Multicoloured.

MS934	140×100 mm. $1.50 Type **187**; $1.50 Allied naval guns; $1.50 Paratroopers; $1.50 Advance of Allies	8·50	9·00
MS935	98×68 mm. $3 Landing on Normandy	4·50	4·75

188 520 Class 4-8-4, Australia

2004. Bicentenary of Steam Locomotives. Two sheets containing T **188** and similar horiz designs. Multicoloured.

MS936	200×103 mm. $1.50 Type **188**; $1.50 FEF-2 Class 4-8-4, U.S.A; $1.50 Royal Scot Class 4-6-0, Great Britain; $1.50A4 Class 4-6-2, Great Britain	8·50	9·00
MS937	100×70 mm. $3 Class GS-4 4-8-4, U.S.A	4·50	4·75

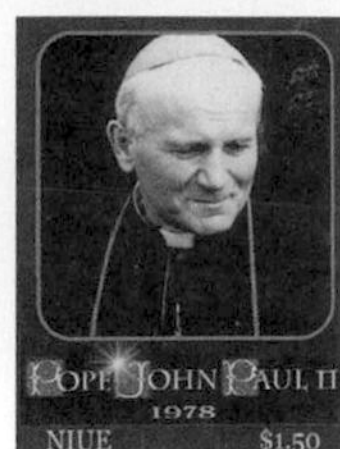

189 Pope John Paul II

2004. 25th Anniv of the Pontificate of Pope John Paul II. Sheet 126×198 mm containing T **189** and similar vert designs.. Multicoloured.

MS938	$1.50 Type **189**; $1.50 Waving; $1.50 At the Wailing Wall; $1.50 Holding Crucifix	9·00	9·00

190 Lily

2004. United Nations International Year of Peace. Flowers. Sheet 139×177 mm containing T **190** and similar vert designs. Multicoloured.

MS939	75c. Type **190**; 75c. Thistle; 75c. Lily of the Valley; 75c. Rose; 75c. Garland flower; 75c. Crocus; 75c. Lotus; 75c. Iris	5·50	6·50

191 Pope John Paul II

2005. Pope John Paul II Commemoration.

940	**191**	$2 multicoloured	4·00	4·00

192 Children

2005. Centenary of Rotary International. Multicoloured.

MS941	132×95 mm. (a) $1.50 Type **192**; $1.50 Paul Harris (founder); $1.50 Carlo Ravizza (President 1999–2000). (b) $3 Jonas Salk (polio vaccine)	10·00	11·00

The two left-hand stamps within **MS**941 form a composite background design showing children.

193 D-Day Invasion, Normandy

2005. 60th Anniv of VE Day. Multicoloured.

942	$1.25 Type **193**	2·50	2·50
943	$1.25 "Monty's Double", Lt. Meyrick Clifton-James, R.A.P. Corps	2·50	2·50
944	$1.25 RAF Hawker Typhoon over French coast	2·50	2·50
945	$1.25 Allied war cemetery, St. Laurent-sur-Mer	2·50	2·50
MS946	70×99 mm. $3 Sir Winston Churchill	7·50	7·50

194 Entertaining the Troops in the Pacific

2005. 60th Anniv of VJ Day. Multicoloured.

947	75c. Type **194**	1·50	1·50
948	75c. Reading letters from home, USS *Argonaut*, August 1942	1·50	1·50
949	75c. Japan surrenders, USS *Missouri*, 1945	1·50	1·50
950	75c. A toast to peace, Naval Air Station, South Carolina	1·50	1·50
951	75c. Entertainment at sea	1·50	1·50
952	75c. Headline "Japs Sign, 6-Yr. War Ends"	1·50	1·50
MS953	99×70 mm. $3 Franklin Delano Roosevelt (US President 1932–45) (vert)	5·50	6·00

195 Frank Bauman, 2002

2005. 75th Anniv of the First World Cup Football Championship, Uruguay. Designs showing players from German World Cup teams. Multicoloured.

954	$1.50 Type **195**	2·75	2·75
955	$1.50 Marcus Babbel, 1998	2·75	2·75
956	$1.50 Dietmar Hamann, 2002	2·75	2·75
MS957	123×105 mm. $3 Christian Worns, 2004	5·50	6·50

196 Hans Christian Andersen

2005. Birth Bicentenary of Hans Christian Andersen (writer). Multicoloured.

958	$1.50 Type **196**	2·50	2·50
959	$1.50 In profile, facing right	2·50	2·50
960	$1.50 Holding book	2·50	2·50
MS961	70×100 mm. $3 In profile, facing left	5·00	6·00

197 Pope Benedict XVI

2005. Inauguration of Pope Benedict XVI.

962	**197**	$1.50 multicoloured	4·00	4·00

198 *Life Study of a Young Man pulling a Rope* (detail)

2007. 400th Birth Anniv (2006) of Rembrandt Harmenszoon van Rijn. Multicoloured.

963	75c. Type **198**	1·25	1·25
964	$1.25 *Self-Portrait*	2·25	2·25
965	$1.50 *Joseph Telling His Dreams*	3·00	3·00
966	$2 *The Blindness of Tobit*	3·50	3·50
MS967	70×99 mm. $3 *Christ in the Storm on the Lake of Galilee*. Imperf	6·25	6·25

199 Young Queen Elizabeth II

2007. 80th Birthday (2006) of Queen Elizabeth II. Multicoloured.

968	$1.50 Type **199**	3·00	3·00
969	$1.50 Wearing pale pink jacket	3·00	3·00
970	$1.50 Speaking, wearing orange-brown dress	3·00	3·00
971	$1.50 In recent years, wearing white	3·00	3·00
MS972	120×120 mm. $3 In recent years, wearing violet dress	6·25	6·25

200 Elvis Presley

2007. 50th Anniv of Purchase of Gracelands by Elvis Presley. Multicoloured.

973	$1.50 Type **200**	3·00	3·00
974	$1.50 Seated, playing guitar	3·00	3·00
975	$1.50 Standing, playing guitar and singing	3·00	3·00
976	$1.50 Standing, holding guitar	3·00	3·00

201 *Stardust* at Kennedy Space Center

2007. Space Anniversaries. Multicoloured

(a) Stardust Spacecraft's encounter with Comet Wild 2, (2004)

977	$1 Type **201**	2·00	2·00
978	$1 *Stardust* Dust Collector with Aerogel	2·00	2·00
979	$1 *Stardust* Navigation Camera	2·00	2·00
980	$1 *Stardust* Whipple Shield	2·00	2·00
981	$1 Cometary and Interstellar Dust Analyzer	2·00	2·00
982	$1 *Stardust* and Comet Wild 2	2·00	2·00

(b) NASA Future Projects (artists renditions).

983	$1.50 Astrobiology Field Laboratory	3·00	3·00
984	$1.50 Deep-Drill Lander	3·00	3·00
985	$1.50 Mars Science Laboratory	3·00	3·00
986	$1.50 The Phoenix Lander	3·00	3·00

202 Palaha Cave

2007. Island Scenes. Multicoloured.

987	20c. Type **202**	40	40
988	70c. White pua flowers	1·10	1·10
989	$1 Talava Natural Arch	2·00	2·00
990	$1.20 Avaiki Pool	2·25	2·25
991	$1.50 Coral rock spears	3·00	3·00
992	$2 Humpback whale	3·50	3·50
993	$3 Spinner dolphins	6·25	6·25

203 Diana, Princess of Wales

2007. Tenth Death Anniv of Diana, Princess of Wales. Multicoloured.

994	$1 Type **203**	2·00	2·00
995	$1 Wearing tiara and black evening dress	2·00	2·00
996	$1 Wearing green, with chin cupped in hand	2·00	2·00
997	$1 As Type **203** but in close-up	2·00	2·00
998	$1 As No. 995 but in close-up	2·00	2·00
999	$1 As No. 996 but head and shoulders photograph	2·00	2·00
MS1000	70×100 mm. $3 Wearing black dress, with hand resting on chin	6·25	6·25

204 Queen Elizabeth II and Duke of Edinburgh

2007. Diamond Wedding of Queen Elizabeth II and Duke of Edinburgh. Multicoloured.

1001	$1 Type **204**	2·00	2·00
1002	$1 Queen Elizabeth wearing green dress and hat	2·00	2·00
MS1003	100×70 mm. $3 Queen Elizabeth and Duke of Edinburgh waving (horiz)	6·25	6·25

205 Final Landing of Concorde F-BVFC at Toulouse

2007. Concorde. Multicoloured.

1004	$1 Type **205** (bistre frame)	2·00	2·00
1005	$1 Crew waving to crowd from cockpit (grey frame)	2·00	2·00
1006	$1 As Type **205** but olive frame	2·00	2·00
1007	$1 As No. 1005 but brown frame	2·00	2·00
1008	$1 As Type **205** (grey frame)	2·00	2·00
1009	$1 As No. 1005 but blue frame	2·00	2·00
1010	$1 Concorde G-BOAD on ground (grey background, blue tint to aircraft)	2·00	2·00
1011	$1 Concorde G-BOAD in flight (natural colours)	2·00	2·00
1012	$1 As No. 1010 but brown background	2·00	2·00
1013	$1 As No. 1011 but lilac tint	2·00	2·00
1014	$1 As No. 1010 but drab background	2·00	2·00
1015	$1 As No. 1011 but blue tint	2·00	2·00

Nos. 1004/9 show the last flight of Concorde F-BVFC from Paris to Toulouse on 27 June 2003.

Nos. 1010/15 show the final flight of Concorde G-BOAD from London Heathrow Airport to New York on 10 November 2003.

206 Marilyn Monroe

2007. 80th Birth Anniv of Marilyn Monroe (actress). Multicoloured.

1016	$1.50 Type **206**	3·00	3·00
1017	$1.50 Smiling, looking over shoulder	3·00	3·00
1018	$1.50 Wearing halter-neck dress	3·00	3·00
1019	$1.50 Speaking, wearing black	3·00	3·00
1020	$1.50 Half-profile, looking to her left	3·00	3·00
1021	$1.50 Close-up of face	3·00	3·00
1022	$1.50 Wearing pale blouse with stand-up collar	3·00	3·00
1023	$1.50 Head and neck portrait	3·00	3·00

207 Marriage of John Rolfe to Pocahontas

2007. 400th Anniv of Jamestown, Virginia, USA. Multicoloured.

1024	$1 Type **207**	2·00	2·00
1025	$1 First settlers reach James-town (on board ship)	2·00	2·00
1026	$1 Tobacco plant imported by John Rolfe	2·00	2·00
1027	$1 Captain John Smith	2·00	2·00
1028	$1 Jamestown Tercentenary Monument	2·00	2·00
1029	$1 Map of Jamestown	2·00	2·00
MS1030	100×70 mm. $3 Queen Elizabeth II and Prince Philip at Jamestown Settlement	6·25	6·25

208 Pope Benedict XVI

2007. 80th Birthday of Pope Benedict XVI.

1031	**208**	70c. multicoloured	1·75	1·75

209 Ferrari 166FL, 1949

2007. 60th Anniv of Ferrari Motor Company. Multicoloured.

1032	$1 Type **209**	2·00	2·00
1033	$1 512 TR, 1991	2·00	2·00
1034	$1 Challenge Stradale, 2003	2·00	2·00
1035	$1 F1 87/88C, 1988	2·00	2·00
1036	$1 F2007, 2007	2·00	2·00
1037	$1 Ferrari Headquarters, Italy	2·00	2·00

210 Coconut Palm

2009. Niue Scenes. Multicoloured.

1038	10c. Type **210**	30	30
1039	20c. Sunset over the sea	60	60
1040	30c. Humpback whale	75	75
1041	50c. Rainbow over dead tree and rainforest	90	90
1042	$1 Hio Beach	1·75	1·75
1043	$1.20 Talava Arches	2·50	2·50
1044	$1.40 Limu Pools	2·75	2·75
1045	$1.70 Limestone caves	3·00	3·00
1046	$2 Snorkelling in Limu Pools	3·25	3·25
1047	$3 Coastline	3·75	3·75
1048	$5 Liku Cave	6·00	6·00
MS1049	150×80 mm. Nos. 1038/43	6·00	6·00
MS1050	150×80 mm. Nos. 1044/8	14·00	14·00

211 'Devotion to the Lord', Ekalesia Millennium Hall

2009. Christmas. Stained Glass Windows. Multicoloured.

1051	30c. Type **211**	75	75
1052	80c. Dove, Lakepa Ekalesia Church	1·50	1·50
1053	$1.20 Chalice and bread, Lakepa Ekalesia Church	2·50	2·50
1054	$1.40 'Steward of the Lord', Ekalesia Millennium Hall	2·75	2·75
MS1055	148×80 mm. Nos. 1051/4. Phosphorised paper	6·75	6·75

OFFICIAL STAMPS

1985. Nos. 409/10 and 527/42 optd **O.H.M.S.**

O1	12c. Type **92**	35	30
O2	25c. "Euphorbia pulcherrima"	40	35
O3	30c. "Cochlospermum hibis-coides"	45	35
O4	35c. "Begonia sp."	50	40
O5	40c. "Plumeria sp."	50	45
O6	52c. "Strelitzia reginae"	60	50
O7	58c. "Hibiscus syriacus"	60	55
O8	70c. "Tibouchina sp."	75	70
O9	83c. "Nelumbo sp."	90	80
O10	$1.05 "Hybrid hibiscus"	1·25	1·00
O11	$1.75 "Cassia fistula"	1·75	1·75
O12	$2.30 Orchid var.	5·50	2·75
O13	$3.90 Orchid sp.	6·00	4·25
O14	$4 "Euphorbia pulcherrima poinsettia"	5·50	6·00
O15	$5 "Euphorbia pulcherrima poinsettia"	5·50	6·00
O16	$6 "Hybrid hibiscus"	8·00	9·00
O17	$6.60 "Hybrid hibiscus"	8·00	9·00
O18	$8.30 "Hibiscus rosa-sinensis"	9·00	10·00
O19	$10 Scarlet hibiscus	10·00	11·00

1993. Nos. 718/29 optd **O.H.M.S.**

O20	20c. Type **130**	2·50	1·50
O21	50c. Red-tailed tropic bird	3·00	1·75
O22	70c. Purple swamphen	4·00	2·00
O23	$1 Pacific pigeon	3·25	2·00
O24	$1.50 White-collared kingfisher	4·00	3·00
O25	$2 Blue-crowned lory	4·00	3·25
O26	$3 Crimson-crowned fruit dove	2·75	3·50
O27	$5 Barn owl	9·50	6·50
O28	$7 Longtailed cuckoo (48½×35 mm)	6·50	8·50
O29	$10 Eastern reef heron (48½×35 mm)	7·50	10·00
O30	$15 Spotted triller ("Polynesian Triller") (48½×35 mm)	16·00	18·00

Pt. 1

NORFOLK ISLAND

A small island East of New South Wales, administered by Australia until 1960 when local government was established.

1947. 12 pence = 1 shilling; 20 shillings = 1 pound.
1966. 100 cents = $1 Australian.

1 Ball Bay

1947

1	1	½d. orange	85	60
2	1	1d. violet	50	60
3	1	1½d. green	50	70
4	1	2d. mauve	55	40
5	1	2½d. red	80	30
6	1	3d. brown	70	70
6a	1	3d. green	12·00	11·00
7	1	4d. red	1·75	40
8	1	5½d. blue	70	30
9	1	6d. brown	70	30
10	1	9d. pink	1·25	40
11	1	1s. green	70	40
12	1	2s. brown	1·00	1·25
12a	1	2s. blue	15·00	11·00

2 Warder's Tower

12 "Hibiscus insularis"

22 Red-tailed Tropic Bird

17 Queen Elizabeth II (after Annigoni) and Cereus

4 Old Stores (Crankmill)

1953

24	**12**	1d. green	15	10
25	-	2d. red and green	20	10
26	-	3d. green	70	15
13	**2**	3½d. red	1·00	90
27	-	5d. purple	55	20
14	-	6½d. green	2·25	3·75
15	**4**	7½d. blue	1·50	3·00
28	-	8d. red	80	50
16	-	8½d. brown	1·75	4·75
29	**17**	9d. blue	80	45
17	-	10d. violet	1·00	75
30	-	10d. brown and violet	1·25	1·00
31	-	1s. on 1d. red	80	35
32	-	2s. brown	4·00	1·00
33	-	2s. on 5d. violet	1·00	40
34	-	2s. on 8d. brown and green	2·25	55
18	-	5s. brown	35·00	8·50
35	-	5s. brown and green	2·75	75
36	**22**	10s. green	26·00	38·00

DESIGNS—VERT: 2d. "Lagunaria patersonii"; 5d. Lantana; 8d. Red hibiscus; 8½d. Barracks entrance; 10d. Salt house; 1s.1d. Fringed hibiscus; 2s. Solander's petrel; 2s.5d. Passion-flower; 2s.8d. Rose apple. HORIZ: 3d. White tern; 6½d. Airfield; 5s. Bloody Bridge.

For Nos. 25 and 28 with face values in decimal currency see Nos. 600/1.

8 Norfolk Is. Seal and Pitcairners Landing

1956. Cent of Landing of Pitcairners on Norfolk Is.

19	**8**	3d. green	75	40
20	**8**	2s. violet	1·25	1·00

1958. Surch.

21	**4**	7d. on 7½d. blue	1·25	1·00
22	-	8d. on 8½d. brown (No. 16)	1·25	1·00

1959. 150th Anniv of Australian P.O. No. 331 of Australia surch **NORFOLK ISLAND 5D.**

23	**143**	5d. on 4d. slate	35	30

1960. As Nos. 13 and 14/15 but colours changed and surch.

37	**2**	1s.1d. on 3½d. blue	2·00	1·00
38	**2**	2s.5d. on 6½d. turquoise	3·00	1·75
39	**4**	2s.8d. on 7½d. sepia	7·00	7·50

26 Queen Elizabeth II and Map

1960. Introduction of Local Government.

40	**26**	2s.8d. purple	4·00	6·50

27 Open Bible and Candle

1960. Christmas.

41	**27**	5d. mauve	40	50

28 Open Prayer Book and Text

1961. Christmas.

42	**28**	5d. blue	30	70

29 Stripey

1962. Fish.

43	**29**	6d. sepia, yellow and green	60	25
44	-	11d. orange, brown and blue	1·00	80
45	-	1s. blue, pink and olive	60	25
46	-	1s.3d. blue, brown and green	1·00	2·00
47	-	1s.6d. sepia, violet and blue	1·25	80
48	-	2s.3d. multicoloured	2·50	80

DESIGNS: 11d. Gold-mouthed emperor; 1s. Surge wrasse ("Po'ov"); 1s.3d. Seachub ("Dreamfish"); 1s.6d. Giant grouper; 2s.3d. White trevally.

30 "Madonna and Child"

1962. Christmas.

49	**30**	5d. blue	45	80

31 "Peace on Earth ..."

1963. Christmas.

50	**31**	5d. red	40	70

32 Overlooking Kingston

1964. Overlooking Kingston. Multicoloured..

51	5d. Type **32**	60	1·00
52	8d. Kingston	1·00	1·50
53	9d. The Arches (Bumboras)	1·00	30
54	10d. Slaughter Bay	1·00	30

33 Norfolk Pine

1964. 50th Anniv of Norfolk Island as Australian Territory.

55	33	5d. black, red and orange	40	15
56	33	8d. black, red and green	40	1·10

34 Child looking at Nativity Scene

1964. Christmas.

57	34	5d. multicoloured	30	40

1965. 50th Anniv of Gallipoli Landing. As T 22 of Nauru, but slightly larger (22×34½ mm).

58	5d. brown, black and green	15	10

35 Nativity Scene

1965. Christmas.

59	35	5d. multicoloured	15	10

38 "Hibiscus insularis"

38 "Hibiscus insularis"

1966. Decimal Currency. As earlier issue but with values in cents and dollars. Surch in black on silver tablets obliterating old value as in T 38.

60	38	1c. on 1d.	20	10
61	-	2c. on 2d. (No. 25)	20	10
62	-	3c. on 3d. (No. 26)	1·50	1·00
63	-	4c. on 5d. (No. 27)	25	10
64	-	5c. on 8d. (No. 28)	30	10
65	-	10c. on 10d. (No. 30)	1·00	15
66	-	15c. on 1s.1d. (No. 31)	50	1·25
67	-	20c. on 2s. (No. 32)	2·75	3·00
68	-	25c. on 2s.5d. (No. 33)	1·00	40
69	-	30c. on 2s.8d. (No. 34)	1·00	50
70	-	50c. on 5s. (No. 35)	1·75	75
71	22	$1 on 10s.	2·50	2·50

39 Headstone Bridge

1966. Headstone Bridge. Multicoloured..

72	7c. Type **39**	40	15
73	9c. Cemetery Road	40	15

41 St. Barnabas' Chapel (interior)

1966. Centenary of Melanesian Mission. Multicoloured.

74	4c. Type **41**	10	10
75	25c. St. Barnabas' Chapel (exterior)	20	20

43 Star over Philip Island

1966. Christmas.

76	43	4c. multicoloured	10	10

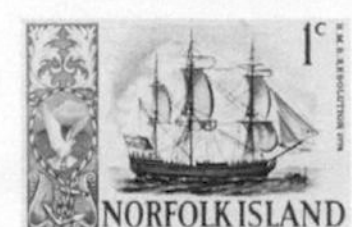

44 H.M.S. "Resolution", 1774

1967. H.M.S. "Resolution" 1774. Multicoloured..

77	1c. Type **44**	10	10
78	2c. "La Boussole" and "L'Astrolabe", 1788	15	10
79	3c. H.M.S. "Supply" (brig), 1788	15	10
80	4c. H.M.S. "Sirius" (frigate), 1790	75	10
81	5c. "Norfolk" (sloop), 1798	20	10
82	7c. H.M.S. "Mermaid" (survey cutter), 1825	20	10
83	9c. "Lady Franklin" (full-rigged ship), 1853	20	10
84	10c. "Morayshire" (full-rigged transport), 1856	20	50
85	15c. "Southern Cross" (missionary ship), 1866	50	30
86	20c. "Pitcairn" (missionary schooner), 1891	60	40
87	25c. "Black Billy" (Norfolk Island whaleboat), 1895	1·50	75
88	30c. "Iris" (cable ship), 1907	1·50	2·00
89	50c. "Resolution" (schooner), 1926	2·50	2·75
90	$1 "Morinda" (freighter), 1931	3·00	2·75

45 Lions Badge and 50 Stars

1967. 50th Anniv of Lions International.

91	45	4c. black, green and yellow	10	10

46 Prayer of John Adams and Candle

1967. Christmas.

92	46	5c. black, olive and red	10	10

47 Queen Elizabeth II

1968

93	47	3c. black, brown and red	10	10
94	47	4c. black, brown and green	10	10
95	47	5c. black, brown and violet	10	10
95a	47	6c. black, brown and lake	30	60

59 Avro Type 691 Lancastrian and Douglas DC-4 Aircraft

1968. 21st Anniv of QANTAS Air Service, Sydney–Norfolk Island.

96	59	5c. black, red and blue	15	10
97	59	7c. brown, red and turquoise	15	10

60 Bethlehem Star and Flowers

1968. Christmas.

98	60	5c. multicoloured	10	10

61 Captain Cook, Quadrant and Chart of Pacific Ocean

1969. Captain Cook Bicentenary (1st issue). Observation of the transit of Venus across the Sun from Tahiti.

99	61	10c. multicoloured	10	10

See also Nos. 118/19, 129, 152/5, 200/2 and 213/14.

62 Van Diemen's Land, Norfolk Island and Sailing Cutter

1969. 125th Anniv of Annexation of Norfolk Island to Van Diemen's Land.

100		5c. multicoloured	10	10
101	62	30c. multicoloured	50	1·00

63 "The Nativity" (carved mother-of- pearl plaque)

1969. Christmas.

102	63	5c. multicoloured	10	10

64 New Zealand Grey Flyeater

1970. Birds. Multicoloured.

103	1c. Scarlet robin (vert)	30	10
104	2c. Golden whistler (vert)	30	40
105	3c. Type **64**	30	10
106	4c. Long-tailed koels	60	10
107	5c. Red-fronted parakeet (vert)	1·50	60
108	7c. Long-tailed triller (vert)	45	10
109	9c. Island thrush	70	10
110	10c. Boobook owl (vert)	1·75	3·00
111	15c. Norfolk Island pigeon (vert)	1·25	65
112	20c. White-chested white-eye	6·00	3·50
113	25c. Norfolk Island parrots (vert)	1·25	40
114	30c. Collared grey fantail	6·00	2·00
115	45c. Norfolk Island starlings	1·00	80
116	50c. Crimson rosella (vert)	1·25	2·00
117	$1 Sacred kingfisher	7·00	10·00

65 Cook and Map of Australia

1970. Captain Cook Bicentenary (2nd issue). Discovery of Australia's East Coast. Mult.

118	5c. Type **65**	15	10
119	20c. H.M.S. "Endeavour" and aborigine	40	10

66 First Christmas Service, 1788

1970. Christmas.

120	66	5c. multicoloured	10	10

67 Bishop Patteson, and Martyrdom of St. Stephen

1971. Death Cent of Bishop Patteson. Multicoloured.

121	6c. Type **67**	10	35
122	6c. Bible, Martyrdom of St. Stephen and knotted palm-frond	10	35
123	10c. Bishop Patteson and stained glass	10	35
124	10c. Cross and Bishop's Arms	10	35

68 Rose Window, St. Barnabas Chapel, Kingston

1971. Christmas.

125	68	6c. multicoloured	10	10

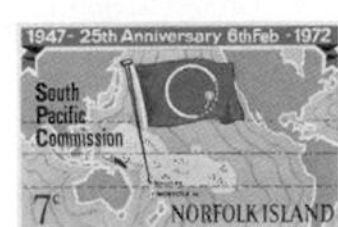

69 Map and Flag

1972. 25th Anniv of South Pacific Commission.

126	69	7c. multicoloured	15	20

70 "St. Mark" (stained glass window) (All Saints, Norfolk Is.)

1972. Christmas.

127	70	7c. multicoloured	10	10

71 Cross and Pines (stained-glass window, All Saints Church)

1972. Cent of First Pitcairner-built Church.

128	71	12c. multicoloured	10	10

72 H.M.S. "Resolution" in the Antarctic

1973. Capt. Cook Bicentenary (3rd issue). Crossing of the Antarctic Circle.

129	72	35c. multicoloured	1·75	1·75

73 Child and Christmas Tree

1973. Christmas. Multicoloured.

130	7c. Type **73**	20	10
131	12c. Type **73**	25	10
132	35c. Fir trees and star	70	90

74 Protestant Clergyman's Quarters

1973. Historic Buildings. Multicoloured.

133	1c. Type **74**	10	10
134	2c. Royal Engineers' Office	10	10
135	3c. Double Quarters for Free Overseers	20	1·00
136	4c. Guard House	15	20
137	5c. Entrance to Pentagonal Gaol	20	15
138	7c. Pentagonal Gaol	25	25
139	8c. Prisoners' Barracks	1·00	2·25
140	10c. Officers' Quarters, New Military Barracks	35	45
141	12c. New Military Barracks	35	30
142	14c. Beach Stores	35	50
143	15c. The Magazine	1·00	35
144	20c. Entrance, Old Military Barracks	40	1·00
145	25c. Old Military Barracks	1·00	1·50
146	30c. Old Stores (Crankmill)	40	40
147	50c. Commissariat Stores	40	1·50
148	$1 Government House	1·00	2·75

75 Royal Couple and Map

1974. Royal Visit.

149	**75**	7c. multicoloured	40	20
150	**75**	25c. multicoloured	70	80

76 Chichester's De Havilland Gipsy Moth Seaplane "Madame Elijah"

1974. First Aircraft Landing on Norfolk Island.

151	**76**	14c. multicoloured	75	70

77 "Captain Cook" (engraving by J. Basire)

1974. Capt. Cook Bicentenary (4th issue). Discovery of Norfolk Is. Multicoloured.

152	7c. Type **77**	45	50
153	10c. H.M.S. "Resolution" (H. Roberts)	80	90
154	14c. Norfolk Island pine	50	90
155	25c. "Norfolk Island flax" (G. Raper)	50	1·25

78 Nativity Scene (pearl-shell pew carving)

1974. Christmas.

156	**78**	7c. multicoloured	15	10
157	**78**	30c. multicoloured	60	75

79 Norfolk Pine

1974. Centenary of Universal Postal Union. Multicoloured. Imperf. Self-adhesive.

158	10c. Type **79**	35	50
159	15c. Offshore islands	45	50
160	35c. Crimson rosella and sacred kingfisher	1·00	85
161	40c. Pacific map	1·00	95
MS162	106×101 mm. Map of Norfolk Is. cut-to-shape with reduced size replicas of Nos. 158/61	20·00	24·00

80 H.M.S. "Mermaid" (survey cutter)

1975. 150th Anniv of Second Settlement. Multicoloured.

163	10c. Type **80**	40	1·10
164	35c. Kingston, 1835 (from painting by T. Seller)	60	1·25

81 Star on Norfolk Island Pine

1975. Christmas.

165	**81**	10c. multicoloured	15	10
166	**81**	15c. multicoloured	20	10
167	**81**	35c. multicoloured	30	35

82 Memorial Cross

1975. Cent of St. Barnabas Chapel. Multicoloured.

168	30c. Type **82**	20	15
169	60c. Laying foundation stone, and Chapel in 1975	40	40

83 Launching of "Resolution"

1975. 50th Anniv of Launching of "Resolution" (schooner). Multicoloured.

170	25c. Type **83**	25	40
171	45c. "Resolution" at sea	40	70

84 Whaleship "Charles W. Morgan"

1976. Bicent of American Revolution. Multicoloured.

172	18c. Type **84**	20	35
173	25c. Thanksgiving Service	20	35
174	40c. Boeing B-17 Flying Fortress over Norfolk Island	30	85
175	45c. California quail	45	85

85 Antarctic Tern and Sun

1976. Christmas.

176	**85**	18c. multicoloured	25	15
177	**85**	25c. multicoloured	35	20
178	**85**	45c. multicoloured	50	50

86 "Vanessa ita"

1977. Butterflies and Moths. Multicoloured.

179	1c. Type **86**	10	40
180	2c. "Utetheisa pulchelloides"	10	40
181	3c. "Agathia asterias"	10	20
182	4c. "Cynthia kershawi"	10	60
183	5c. "Leucania loreyimima"	15	1·10
184	10c. "Hypolimnas bolina"	30	1·10
185	15c. "Pyrrhorachis pyrrhogona"	30	30
186	16c. "Austrocarea iocephala"	30	30
187	17c. "Pseudocoremia christiani"	35	30
188	18c. "Cleora idiocrossa"	35	30
189	19c. "Simplicia caeneusalis"	35	30
190	20c. "Austrocidaria ralstonae"	40	30
191	30c. "Hippotion scrofa"	50	75
192	40c. "Papilio amynthor (ilioneus)"	50	40
193	50c. "Tiracola plagiata"	50	1·00
194	$1 "Precis villida"	60	75
195	$2 "Cepora perimale"	75	1·40

87 Queen's View, Kingston

1977. Silver Jubilee.

196	**87**	25c. multicoloured	35	30

88 Hibiscus Flowers and Oil Lamp

1977. Christmas.

197	**88**	18c. multicoloured	15	10
198	**88**	25c. multicoloured	15	10
199	**88**	45c. multicoloured	30	35

89 Captain Cook (from a portrait by Nathaniel Dance)

1978. Capt. Cook Bicentenary (5th issue). Discovery of Hawaii. Multicoloured.

200	18c. Type **89**	30	20
201	25c. Discovery of northern Hawaiian islands	30	30
202	80c. British flag against island background	60	70

90 Guide Flag and Globe

1978. 50th Anniv of Girl Guides. Multicoloured. Imperf. Self-adhesive.

203	18c. Type **90**	25	50
204	25c. Trefoil and scarf badge	30	60
205	35c. Trefoil and Queen Elizabeth	45	85
206	45c. Trefoil and Lady Baden-Powell	55	85

91 St. Edward's Crown

1978. 25th Anniv of Coronation. Multicoloured.

207	25c. Type **91**	15	15
208	70c. Coronation regalia	40	45

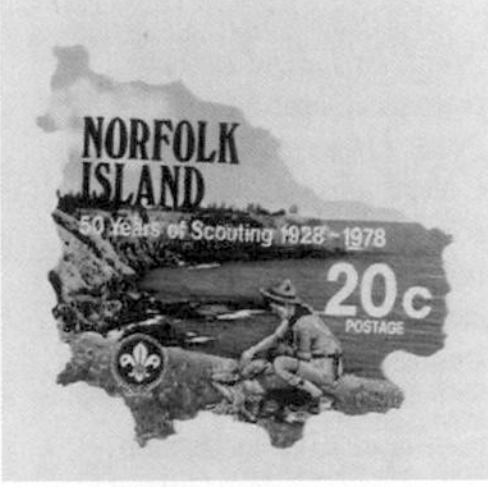

92 View of Duncombe Bay with Scout at Camp Fire

1978. 50th Anniv of Boy Scout Movement. Multicoloured. Imperf. Self-adhesive.

209	20c. Type **92**	30	45
210	25c. View from Kingston and emblem	35	55
211	35c. View of Anson Bay and Link Badge	50	90
212	45c. Sunset scene and Lord Baden-Powell	55	95

93 Chart showing Route of Arctic Voyage

1978. Captain Cook Bicentenary (6th issue). Northernmost Voyages. Multicoloured.

213	25c. Type **93**	30	30
214	90c. "H.M.S. "Resolution" and H.M.S. "Discovery" in Pack Ice" (Webber)	80	80

94 Poinsettia and Bible

1978. Christmas. Multicoloured.

215	20c. Type **94**	15	10
216	30c. Native oak and bible	20	15
217	55c. Hibiscus and bible	30	30

95 Cook and Village of Staithes near Marton

1978. 250th Birth Anniv of Captain Cook. Multicoloured.

218	20c. Type **95**	30	25
219	80c. Cook and Whitby Harbour	70	1·25

96 H.M.S. "Resolution"

1979. Death Bicent of Captain Cook. Multicoloured.

220	20c. Type **96**	25	30
221	20c. Cook (statue)	25	30
222	40c. Cook's death	30	50
223	40c. Cook's death (different)	30	50

Nos. 220/1 were issued se-tenant, in horizontal pairs throughout the sheet, forming a composite design. A chart of Cook's last voyage is shown in the background. Nos. 222/3 were also issued se-tenant, the horizontal pair forming a composite design taken from an aquatint by John Cleveley.

97 Assembly Building

1979. First Norfolk Island Legislative Assembly.

224	**97**	$1 multicoloured	50	50

98 Tasmania 1853 1d. Stamp and Sir Rowland Hill

1979. Death Centenary of Sir Rowland Hill.

225	**98**	20c. blue and brown	20	10
226	-	30c. red and grey	20	15
227	-	55c. violet and indigo	30	30
MS228		142×91 mm. No. 227	55	1·25

DESIGNS: 30c. Great Britain 1841 1d. red; 55c. 1947 "Ball Bay" 1d. stamp.

99 I.Y.C. Emblem and Map of Pacific showing Norfolk Island as Pine Tree

1979. International Year of the Child.

229	**99**	80c. multicoloured	40	45

100 Emily Bay

1979. Christmas.

230	**100**	15c. multicoloured	15	15
231	-	20c. multicoloured	15	15
232	-	30c. multicoloured	15	15
MS233		152×83 mm. Nos. 230/2	1·00	1·40

DESIGNS: 20, 30c. Different scenes.

Nos. 230/2 were printed together, *se-tenant*, forming a composite design.

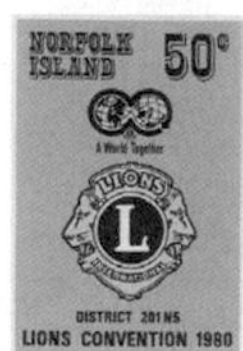

101 Lions International Emblem

1980. Lions Convention.

234	**101**	50c. multicoloured	35	30

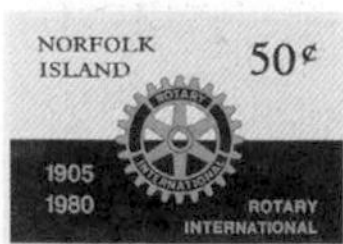

102 Rotary International Emblem

1980. 75th Anniv of Rotary International.

235	**102**	50c. multicoloured	35	30

103 de Havilland Gipsy Moth Seaplane "Madame Elijah"

1980. Airplanes. Multicoloured.

236	1c. Hawker Siddeley H.S.748	15	20
237	2c. Type **103**	15	20
238	3c. Curtis P-40E Kittyhawk I	15	20
239	4c. Chance Vought F4U-1 Corsair	15	30
240	5c. Grumman TBF Avenger	15	30
241	15c. Douglas SBD-5 Dauntless	30	30
242	20c. Cessna 172D Skyhawk	30	30
243	25c. Lockheed 414 Hudson	30	35
244	30c. Lockheed PV-1 Ventura	40	2·00
245	40c. Avro Type 685 York	50	55
246	50c. Douglas DC-3	65	65
247	60c. Avro Type 691 Lancastrian	75	75
248	80c. Douglas DC-4	1·00	1·00
249	$1 Beech 200 Super King Air	1·00	1·00
250	$2 Fokker F.27 Friendship	2·00	3·00
251	$5 Lockheed C-130 Hercules	2·25	2·00

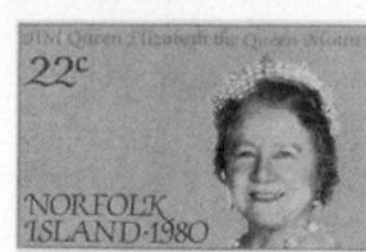

104 Queen Elizabeth the Queen Mother

1980. 80th Birthday of The Queen Mother.

252	**104**	22c. multicoloured	20	20
253	**104**	60c. multicoloured	35	40

105 Red-tailed Tropic Birds

1980. Christmas. Birds. Multicoloured.

254	15c. Type **105**	30	25
255	22c. White terns	30	25
256	35c. White-capped noddys	30	25
257	60c. White terns (different)	40	45

106 "Morayshire" and View of Norfolk Island

1981. 125th Anniv of Pitcairn Islanders' Migration to Norfolk Island. Multicoloured.

258	5c. Type **106**	15	15
259	35c. Islanders arriving ashore	40	30
260	60c. View of new settlement	60	45
MS261	183×127 mm. Nos. 258/60	1·00	1·25

107 Wedding Bouquet from Norfolk Island

1981. Royal Wedding. Multicoloured.

262	35c. Type **107**	15	15
263	55c. Prince Charles at horse trials	25	25
264	60c. Prince Charles and Lady Diana Spencer	25	35

108 Uniting Church in Australia

1981. Christmas. Churches. Multicoloured.

265	18c. Type **108**	10	10
266	24c. Seventh Day Adventist Church	15	15
267	30c. Church of the Sacred Heart	15	20
268	$1 St. Barnabas Chapel	35	70

109 Pair of White-chested White-Eyes

1981. White-chested White-Eye ("Silvereye"). Multicoloured.

269	35c. Type **109**	25	35
270	35c. Bird on nest	25	35
271	35c. Bird with egg	25	35
272	35c. Parents with chicks	25	35
273	35c. Fledgelings	25	35

110 Aerial view of Philip Island

1982. Philip and Nepean Islands. Multicoloured.

274	24c. Type **110**	20	20
275	24c. Close-up view of Philip Island landscape	20	20
276	24c. Gecko ("Phyllodactylus guentheri"), Philip Island	20	20
277	24c. Sooty tern, Philip Island	20	20
278	24c. Philip Island hibiscus ("hibiscus insularis")	20	20
279	35c. Aerial view of Nepean Island	20	25
280	35c. Close-up view of Nepean Island landscape	20	25
281	35c. Gecko ("phyllodactylus guentheri"), Nepean Island	20	25
282	35c. Blue-faced boobies, Nepean Island	20	25
283	35c. "Carpobrotus glaucescens" (flower), Nepean Island	20	25

111 Sperm Whale

1982. Whales.

284	**111**	24c. multicoloured	50	35
285	-	55c. multicoloured	70	95
286	-	80c. black, mauve & stone	80	2·25

DESIGNS: 55c. Black right whale; 80c. Humpback whale.

112 "Diocet", Wrecked 20 April 1873

1982. Shipwrecks. Multicoloured.

287	24c. H.M.S. "Sirius", wrecked 19 March 1790	50	50
288	27c. Type **112**	50	50
289	35c. "Friendship", wrecked 17 May 1835	90	1·25
290	40c. "Mary Hamilton", wrecked 6 May 1873	90	1·25
291	55c. "Fairlie", wrecked 14 February 1840	1·25	1·50
292	65c. "Warrigal", wrecked 18 March 1918	1·25	2·25

113 R.N.Z.A.F. Lockheed 414 Hudson dropping Christmas Supplies, 1942

1982. Christmas. 40th Anniv of First Supply-plane Landings on Norfolk Island (Christmas Day 1942). Multicoloured.

293	27c. Type **113**	80	35
294	40c. R.N.Z.A.F. Lockheed 414 Hudson landing Christmas supplies 1942	1·00	70
295	75c. Christmas, 1942	1·25	2·25

114 50th (Queen's Own) Regiment

1982. Military Uniforms. Multicoloured.

296	27c. Type **114**	25	35
297	40c. 58th (Rutlandshire) Regiment	30	75
298	55c. 80th (Staffordshire Volunteers) Battalion Company	35	95
299	65c. 11th (North Devonshire) Regiment	40	1·25

115 "Panaeolus papilionaceus"

1983. Fungi. Multicoloured.

300	27c. Type **115**	25	35
301	40c. "Coprinus domesticus"	30	50
302	55c. "Marasmius niveus"	40	70
303	65c. "Cymatoderma elegans var lamellatum"	45	85

116 Beechcraft 18

1983. Bicentenary of Manned Flight. Multicoloured.

304	10c. Type **116**	15	15
305	27c. Fokker F.28 Fellowship	25	35
306	45c. French military Douglas C-54	40	60
307	75c. Sikorsky S-61N helicopter	60	95
MS308	105×100 mm. Nos. 304/7	1·40	2·50

117 St. Matthew

1983. Christmas. 150th Birth Anniv of Sir Edward Burne-Jones.

309	5c. Type **117**	10	10
310	24c. St. Mark	15	30
311	30c. Jesus Christ	20	40
312	45c. St. Luke	30	55
313	85c. St. John	40	1·10

DESIGNS: showing stained glass windows from St. Barnabas Chapel, Norfolk Island.

118 Cable Ship "Chantik"

1983. World Communications Year. ANZCAN Cable. Multicoloured.

314	30c. Type **118**	25	40
315	45c. "Chantik" during in-shore operations	30	55
316	75c. Cable ship "Mercury"	40	95
317	85c. Diagram of cable route	40	1·10

119 Popwood

1984. Flowers. Multicoloured.

318	1c. Type **119**	30	70
319	2c. Strand morning glory	40	70
320	3c. Native phreatia	45	70
321	4c. Philip Island wisteria	45	70
322	5c. Norfolk Island palm	50	70
323	10c. Evergreen	50	70
324	15c. Bastard oak	50	70
325	20c. Devil's guts	50	70
326	25c. White oak	50	80
327	30c. Ti	50	1·00
328	35c. Philip Island hibiscus	50	1·00
329	40c. Native wisteria	50	1·25
330	50c. Native jasmine	55	1·25
331	$1 Norfolk Island hibiscus	60	1·75
332	$3 Native oberonia	70	3·00
333	$5 Norfolk Island pine	1·00	3·50

120 Morwong

1984. Reef Fish. Multicoloured.

334	30c. Type **120**	20	45
335	45c. Black-spotted goatfish	25	65
336	75c. Surgeonfish	30	1·10
337	85c. Three-striped butterflyfish	35	1·40

121 Owl with Eggs

1984. Boobook Owl. Multicoloured.

338	30c. Type **121**	55	85
339	30c. Fledgeling	55	85
340	30c. Young owl on stump	55	85
341	30c. Adult on branch	55	85
342	30c. Owl in flight	55	85

122 1953 7½d. and 1974 Cook Bicent 10c. Stamps

1984. "Ausipex" International Stamp Exhibition, Melbourne. Multicoloured.

343	30c. Type **122**	25	35
344	45c. John Buffett commemorative postal stationery envelope	35	75
345	75c. Design from Presentation Pack for 1982 Military Uniforms issue	50	1·75
MS346	151×93 mm. Nos. 343/5	3·25	5·00

123 Font, Kingston Methodist Church

1984. Christmas. Centenary of Methodist Church on Norfolk Island. Multicoloured.

347	5c. Type **123**	10	30
348	24c. Church service in Old Barracks, Kingston, late 1800s	20	40
349	30c. The Revd. & Mrs. A. H. Phelps and sailing ship	20	45
350	45c. The Revd. A. H. Phelps and First Congregational Church, Chester, U.S.A.	25	65
351	85c. Interior of Kingston Methodist Church	40	1·40

124 The Revd. Nobbs teaching Pitcairn Islanders

1984. Death Centenary of Revd. George Hunn Nobbs (leader of Pitcairn community). Multicoloured.

352	30c. Type **124**	20	45
353	45c. The Revd. Nobbs with sick islander	25	65
354	75c. Baptising baby	35	1·10
355	85c. Presented to Queen Victoria, 1852	45	1·40

125 "Fanny Fisher"

1985. 19th-Century Whaling Ships (1st series). Multicoloured.

356	5c. Type **125**	30	1·25
357	33c. "Costa Rica Packet"	60	55
358	50c. "Splendid"	1·00	1·50
359	90c. "Onward"	1·25	3·25

See also Nos. 360/3.

1985. 19th-Century Whaling Ships (2nd series). As T **125**. Multicoloured.

360	15c. "Waterwitch"	50	1·10
361	20c. "Canton"	55	1·10
362	60c. "Aladdin"	1·00	2·00
363	80c. "California"	1·00	2·50

126 The Queen Mother (from photo by Norman Parkinson)

1985. Life and Times of Queen Elizabeth the Queen Mother. Multicoloured.

364	5c. The Queen Mother (from photo by Dorothy Wilding)	10	40
365	33c. With Princess Anne at Trooping the Colour	25	25
366	50c. Type **126**	40	55
367	90c. With Prince Henry at his christening (from photo by Lord Snowdon)	60	1·00
MS368	91×73 mm. $1 With Princess Anne at Ascot Races	2·75	2·25

127 "Swimming"

1985. International Youth Year. Children's Paintings. Multicoloured.

369	33c. Type **127**	40	40
370	50c. "A Walk in the Country"	70	85

128 Prize-winning Cow and Owner

1985. 125th Anniv of Royal Norfolk Island Agricultural and Horticultural Show. Multicoloured.

371	80c. Type **128**	60	80
372	90c. Show exhibits	65	90
MS373	132×85 mm. Nos. 371/2	2·50	3·25

129 Shepherds with Flock

1985. Christmas. Multicoloured.

374	27c. Type **129**	30	30
375	33c. Mary and Joseph with donkey	35	40
376	50c. The Three Wise Men	60	65
377	90c. The Nativity	1·00	1·25

130 Long-spined Sea Urchin

1986. Marine Life. Multicoloured.

378	5c. Type **130**	10	10
379	33c. Blue starfish	25	35
380	55c. Southern eagle ray	40	85
381	75c. Snowflake moray	55	1·50
MS382	100×95 mm. Nos. 378/81	2·50	4·00

131 "Giotto" Spacecraft

1986. Appearance of Halley's Comet. Multicoloured.

383	$1 Type **131**	50	1·50
384	$1 Halley's Comet	50	1·50

Nos. 383/4 were printed together, *se-tenant*, forming a composite design.

132 Isaac Robinson (U.S. Consul 1887–1908)

1986. "Ameripex '86" International Stamp Exhibition, Chicago. Multicoloured.

385	33c. Type **132**	30	35
386	50c. Ford "Model T" (first vehicle on island) (horiz)	40	50
387	80c. Statue of Liberty	40	1·10
MS388	125×100 mm. Nos. 385/7	1·00	2·25

No. 387 also commemorates the Centenary of the Statue of Liberty.

133 Princess Elizabeth and Dog

1986. 60th Birthday of Queen Elizabeth II. Multicoloured.

389	5c. Type **133**	20	40
390	33c. Queen Elizabeth II	40	35
391	80c. Opening Norfolk Island Golf Club	2·25	1·60
392	90c. With Duke of Edinburgh in carriage	1·25	1·60

134 Stylized Dove and Norfolk Island

1986. Christmas.

393	**134**	30c. multicoloured	25	30
394	**134**	40c. multicoloured	30	45
395	**134**	$1 multicoloured	70	1·50

135 British Convicts, 1787

1986. Bicentenary (1988) of Norfolk Island Settlement (1st issue). Governor Phillip's Commission. Multicoloured.

396	36c. Type **135**	50	35
397	55c. Judge passing sentence of transportation	1·00	85
398	90c. Governor Phillip meeting Home Secretary (inscr "Home Society")	2·00	3·75
399	90c. As No. 398, but correctly inscr "Home Secretary"	2·00	3·75
400	$1 Captain Arthur Phillip	2·00	2·75

See also Nos. 401/4, 421/4, 433/5, 436/7 and 438/43.

136 Stone Tools

1986. Bicentenary (1988) of Norfolk Island Settlement (2nd issue). Pre-European Occupation. Multicoloured.

401	36c. Type **136**	35	85
402	36c. Bananas and taro	35	85
403	36c. Polynesian outrigger canoe	35	85
404	36c. Maori chief	35	85

137 Philip Island from Point Ross

1987. Norfolk Island Scenes. Multicoloured.

405	1c. Cockpit Creek Bridge	50	1·50
406	2c. Cemetery Bay Beach	50	1·50
407	3c. Island guesthouse	50	1·50
408	5c. Type **137**	30	1·00
409	15c. Cattle in pasture	80	2·00
410	30c. Rock fishing	30	1·25
411	37c. Old Pitcairner-style house	1·40	2·00
412	40c. Shopping centre	35	1·25
413	50c. Emily Bay	45	1·25
414	60c. Bloody Bridge	2·00	3·00
415	80c. Pitcairner-style shop	1·75	2·75
416	90c. Government House	1·25	2·25
417	$1 Melanesian Memorial Chapel	1·00	1·75
418	$2 Convict Settlement, Kingston	1·25	3·50
419	$3 Ball Bay	2·00	5·00
420	$5 Northern cliffs	2·50	7·00

1987. Bicentenary of Norfolk Island Settlement (1988) (3rd issue). The First Fleet. As T **135**. Multicoloured.

421	5c. Loading supplies, Deptford	50	1·50
422	55c. Fleet leaving Spithead	2·00	2·50
423	55c. H.M.S. "Sirius" leaving Spithead	2·00	2·50
424	$1 Female convicts below decks	2·25	3·00

Nos. 422/3 were printed together, *se-tenant*, forming a composite design.

138 Male Red-fronted Parakeet

1987. Red-fronted Parakeet ("Green Parrot"). Multicoloured.

425	5c. Type **138**	2·00	2·00
426	15c. Adult with fledgeling and egg	2·50	2·50
427	36c. Young parakeets	2·75	2·75
428	55c. Female parakeet	3·75	3·75

139 Christmas Tree and Restored Garrison Barracks

1987. Christmas. Multicoloured.

429	30c. Type **139**	30	30
430	42c. Children opening presents	45	55
431	58c. Father Christmas with children	60	1·00
432	63c. Children's party	70	1·25

1987. Bicentenary of Norfolk Island Settlement (1988) (4th issue). Visit of La Perouse (navigator). As T **135**. Multicoloured.

433	37c. La Perouse with King Louis XVI	95	55
434	90c. "L'Astrolabe" and "La Boussole" off Norfolk Island	2·75	3·00
435	$1 "L'Astrolabe" wrecked in Solomon Islands	2·75	3·00

1988. Bicentenary of Norfolk Island Settlement (5th issue). Arrival of First Fleet at Sydney. As T **135**. Multicoloured.

436	37c. Ship's cutter approaching Port Jackson	1·75	75
437	$1 Landing at Sydney Cove	3·25	3·75

1988. Bicentenary of Norfolk Island Settlement (6th issue). Foundation of First Settlement. As T **135**. Multicoloured.

438	5c. Lt. Philip Gidley King	20	50
439	37c. Raising the flag, March 1788	85	75
440	55c. King exploring	1·75	1·50
441	70c. Landing at Sydney Bay, Norfolk Island	2·00	2·50
442	90c. H.M.S. "Supply" (brig)	2·25	2·75
443	$1 Sydney Bay settlement, 1788	2·25	2·75

140 Airliner, Container Ship and Sydney Harbour Bridge

1988. "Sydpex '88" National Stamp Exhibition, Sydney. Multicoloured.

444	37c. Type **140**	55	1·25
445	37c. Exhibition label under magnifying glass (horiz)	55	1·25
446	37c. Telephone and dish aerial	55	1·25
MS447	118×84 mm. Nos. 444/6	6·00	7·00

141 Flowers and Decorations

1988. Christmas. Multicoloured.

448	30c. Type **141**	30	40
449	42c. Flowers	40	70
450	58c. Fishes and beach	50	85
451	63c. Norfolk Island	55	1·00

142 Pier Store and Boat Shed

1988. Restored Buildings from the Convict Era. Multicoloured.

452	39c. Type **142**	30	35
453	55c. Royal Engineers Building	40	50
454	90c. Old Military Barracks	60	1·40
455	$1 Commissariat Store and New Military Barracks	65	1·40

143 "Lamprima aenea"

1989. Endemic Insects. Multicoloured.

456	39c. Type **143**	50	40
457	55c. "Insulascirtus nythos"	75	75
458	90c. "Caedicia araucariae"	1·10	2·25
459	$1 "Thrincophora aridela"	1·25	2·25

144 H.M.S. "Bounty" off Tasmania

1989. Bicentenary of the Mutiny on the "Bounty". Multicoloured.

460	5c. Type **144**	60	60
461	39c. Mutineers and Polynesian women, Pitcairn Island	1·75	1·25
462	55c. Lake Windermere, Cumbria (Christian's home county)	2·25	2·25
463	$1.10 "Mutineers casting Bligh adrift" (Robert Dodd)	3·50	4·50
MS464	110×85 mm. 39c. No. 461; 90c. Isle of Man 1989 Mutiny 35p., No. 414; $1 Pitcairn Islands 1989 Settlement Bicent 90c., No. 345	7·50	8·50

145 Norfolk Island Flag

1989. Tenth Anniv of Internal Self-government. Multicoloured.

465	41c. Type **145**	90	55
466	55c. Old ballot box	95	65
467	$1 Norfolk Island Act, 1979	1·40	2·25
468	$1.10 Island crest	1·40	3·25

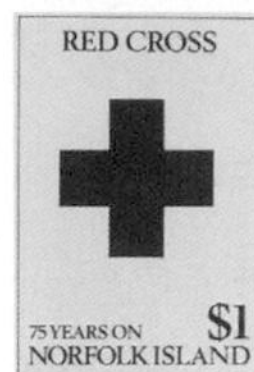

146 Red Cross

1989. 75th Anniv of Red Cross on Norfolk Island.

469	**146**	$1 red and blue	3·00	3·25

147 "Gethsemane"

1989. Christmas. Designs showing opening lines of hymns and local scenes. Multicoloured.

470	36c. Type **147**	80	40
471	60c. "In the Sweet Bye and Bye"	1·50	2·00
472	75c. "Let the Lower Lights be Burning"	1·75	3·25
473	80c. "The Beautiful Stream"	1·75	3·25

148 John Royle (first announcer)

1989. 50th Anniv of Radio Australia. Designs each showing Kingston buildings. Multicoloured.

474	41c. Type **148**	95	70
475	65c. Radio waves linking Australia and Norfolk Island	1·75	2·50
476	$1.10 Anniversary kookaburra logo	2·75	4·50

149 H.M.S. "Bounty" on fire, Pitcairn Island, 1790

1990. History of the Norfolk Islanders (1st series). Settlement on Pitcairn Island. Multicoloured.

477	70c. Type **149**	2·50	3·00
478	$1.10 Arms of Norfolk Island	2·75	3·50

See also Nos. 503/4 and 516/17.

150 H.M.S. "Sirius" striking Reef

1990. Bicentenary of Wreck of H.M.S. "Sirius". Multicoloured.

479	41c. Type **150**	1·50	2·00
480	41c. H.M.S. "Sirius" failing to clear bay	1·50	2·00
481	65c. Divers at work on wreck	2·00	3·00
482	$1 Recovered artifacts and chart of site	2·25	3·25

Nos. 479/80 were printed together, *se-tenant*, forming a composite design.

151 Unloading Lighter, Kingston

152 "Ile de Lumiere" (freighter)

1990. Ships.

483	**151**	5c. brown	20	50
484	**151**	10c. brown	20	50
485	-	45c. multicoloured	1·00	60
486	-	50c. multicoloured	1·00	1·00
487	-	65c. multicoloured	1·00	1·25
488	**152**	70c. multicoloured	1·00	1·25
489	-	75c. multicoloured	1·50	2·00
490	-	80c. multicoloured	1·50	2·25
491	-	90c. multicoloured	1·50	2·25
492	-	$1 multicoloured	1·50	2·00
493	-	$2 multicoloured	1·50	3·50
494	-	$5 multicoloured	2·50	7·00

DESIGNS—As T **152**: 45c. "La Dunkerquoise" (French patrol vessel); 50c. "Dmitri Mendeleev" (Russian research vessel); 65c. "Pacific Rover" (tanker); 75c. "Norfolk Trader" (freighter); 80c. "Roseville" (transport); 90c. "Kalia" (container ship); $1 "Bounty" (replica); $2 H.M.A.S. "Success" (supply ship); $5 H.M.A.S. "Whyalla" (patrol vessel).

153 Santa on House Roof

1990. Christmas. Multicoloured.

499	38c. Type **153**	60	35
500	43c. Santa at Kingston Post Office	65	40
501	65c. Santa over Sydney Bay, Kingston (horiz)	1·25	2·00
502	85c. Santa on Officers' Quarters (horiz)	1·50	2·50

154 William Charles Wentworth

1990. History of the Norfolk Islanders (2nd series). The First Generation.

503	**154**	70c. brown and cinnamon	1·25	1·50
504	-	$1.20 brown and cinnamon	2·00	2·50

DESIGN: $1.20, Thursday October Christian.

155 Adult Robin and Chicks in Nest

1990. "Birdpex '90" Stamp Exhibition, Christchurch, New Zealand. Scarlet Robin. Multicoloured.

505	65c. Type **155**	1·25	1·50
506	$1 Hen on branch	1·75	2·00
507	$1.20 Cock on branch	1·75	2·25
MS508	70×90 mm. $1 Hen; $1 Cock and hen	4·50	4·75

Each inscribed "Norfolk Island Robin".

156 Map of Norfolk Island

1991. Ham Radio Network. Multicoloured.

509	43c. Type **156**	1·25	70
510	$1 Globe showing Norfolk Island	2·75	3·00
511	$1.20 Map of south-west Pacific	2·75	4·00

157 Display in "Sirius" Museum

1991. Norfolk Island Museums. Multicoloured.

512	43c. Type **157**	60	50
513	70c. 19th-century sitting room, House Museum (horiz)	1·00	2·25
514	$1 Carronade, "Sirius" Museum (horiz)	1·25	2·50
515	$1.20 Reconstructed jug and beaker, Archaeological Museum	1·25	3·50

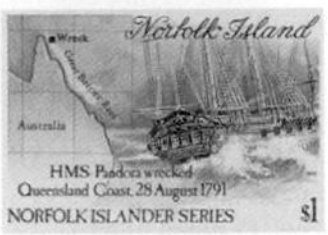

158 H.M.S. "Pandora" wrecked on Great Barrier Reef (1791)

1991. History of the Norfolk Islanders (3rd series). Search for the "Bounty". Multicoloured.

516	$1 Type **158**	2·75	2·50
517	$1.20 H.M.S. "Pandora" leaving bay	2·75	3·00

159 Hibiscus and Island Scene

1991. Christmas.

518	**159**	38c. multicoloured	70	45
519	**159**	43c. multicoloured	80	55
520	**159**	65c. multicoloured	1·25	2·00
521	**159**	85c. multicoloured	1·50	2·50

160 Tank and Soldier in Jungle

1991. 50th Anniv of Outbreak of Pacific War. Multicoloured.

522	43c. Type **160**	1·25	65
523	70c. Boeing B-17 Flying Fortress on jungle airstrip	2·25	2·75
524	$1 Warships	2·75	3·50

161 Coat of Arms

1992. 500th Anniv of Discovery of America by Columbus. Multicoloured.

525	45c. Type **161**	85	55
526	$1.05 "Santa Maria"	2·00	2·75
527	$1.20 Columbus and globe	2·50	3·25

162 Deployment Map

1992. 50th Anniv of Battle of the Coral Sea. Multicoloured.

528	45c. Type **162**	1·25	60
529	70c. H.M.A.S. "Australia" (cruiser)	2·00	2·50
530	$1.05 U.S.S. "Yorktown" (aircraft carrier)	2·75	3·50

1992. 50th Anniv of Battle of Midway. As T **162**. Multicoloured.

531	45c. Battle area	1·25	60
532	70c. Consolidated PBY-5 Catalina flying boat over task force	2·00	2·50

533	$1.05 Douglas SBD Dauntless dive bomber and "Akagi" (Japanese aircraft carrier) burning	2·75	3·50

1992. 50th Anniv of Battle of Guadalcanal. As T **162**. Multicoloured.

534	45c. American troops landing (horiz)	1·25	60
535	70c. Machine-gun crew (horiz)	2·00	2·50
536	$1.05 Map of Pacific with Japanese and American flags (horiz)	4·50	4·25

163 Norfolk Pines above Ball Bay

1992. Christmas. Multicoloured.

537	40c. Type **163**	70	40
538	45c. Headstone Creek	75	45
539	75c. South side of Ball Bay	1·50	2·25
540	$1.20 Rocky Point Reserve	2·00	3·00

164 Boat Shed and Flaghouses, Kingston

1993. Tourism. Historic Kingston. Multicoloured.

541	45c. Type **164**	70	1·00
542	45c. Old Military Barracks	70	1·00
543	45c. All Saints Church	70	1·00
544	45c. Officers' Quarters	70	1·00
545	45c. Quality Row	70	1·00

Nos. 541/5 were printed together, *se-tenant*, forming a composite design.

165 Fire Engine

1993. Emergency Services. Multicoloured.

546	45c. Type **165**	1·00	60
547	70c. Cliff rescue squad	1·10	1·75
548	75c. Ambulance	1·40	1·90
549	$1.20 Police car	2·50	3·00

166 Blue Sea Lizard ("Glaucus atlanticus")

1993. Nudibranchs. Multicoloured.

550	45c. Type **166**	60	55
551	45c. Ocellate nudibranch ("Phyllidia ocellata")	60	55
552	75c. "Bornella sp."	1·00	1·25
553	85c. "Glossodoris rubroannolata"	1·00	2·00
554	95c. "Halgerda willeyi"	1·25	2·50
555	$1.05 "Ceratosoma amoena"	1·25	2·50

167 Christmas Wreath

1993. Christmas.

556	**167**	40c. multicoloured	50	40
557	**167**	45c. multicoloured	50	40
558	**167**	75c. multicoloured	75	1·25
559	**167**	$1.20 multicoloured	1·25	2·75

168 Maori Stone Clubs

1993. Bicentenary of Contact with New Zealand. Multicoloured.

560	70c. Type **168**	75	1·25
561	$1.20 First Maori map of New Zealand, 1793	1·25	2·25

169 Alvaro de Saavedra, Route Map and "Florida"

1994. Pacific Explorers. Multicoloured.

562	5c. Vasco Nunez de Balboa, map and "Barbara"	1·00	1·50
563	10c. Ferdinand Magellan, map and "Vitoria"	1·25	1·75
564	20c. Juan Sebastian del Cano, map and "Vitoria"	1·75	1·50
565	50c. Type **169**	1·75	1·25
566	70c. Ruy Lopez de Villalobos, map and "San Juan"	2·25	1·50
567	75c. Miguel Lopez de Legaspi, map and "San Lesmes"	2·25	2·00
568	80c. Sir Francis Drake, map and "Golden Hind"	2·50	2·00
569	85c. Alvaro de Mendana, map and "Santiago"	2·25	2·00
570	90c. Pedro Fernandes de Quiros, map and "San Pedro y Pablo"	2·25	2·00
571	$1 Luis Baez de Torres, map and "San Pedrico"	2·25	2·00
572	$2 Abel Tasman, map and "Heemskerk"	3·00	4·50
573	$5 William Dampier, map and "Cygnet"	5·00	8·00
MS574	100×80 mm. $1.20 "Golden Hind" (Drake) (32×52 mm)	5·00	5·50

170 Sooty Tern

1994. Sea Birds. Multicoloured.

575	45c. Type **170**	95	1·25
576	45c. Red-tailed tropic bird	95	1·25
577	45c. Australian gannet	95	1·25
578	45c. Wedge-tailed shearwater	95	1·25
579	45c. Masked booby	95	1·25

Nos. 575/9 were printed together, *se-tenant*, forming a composite design.

171 House and Star

1994. Christmas. Multicoloured. Self-adhesive.

580	45c. Type **171**	80	55
581	75c. Figures from stained-glass windows	1·50	2·00
582	$1.20 Rainbow and "The Church of God" (missionary sailing ship)	2·50	3·50

172 Chevrolet, 1926

1995. Vintage Motor Vehicles. Multicoloured.

583	45c. Type **172**	60	55
584	75c. Ford Model "A", 1928	80	1·25
585	$1.05 Ford Model "A A/C", 1929	1·00	1·60
586	$1.20 Ford Model "A", 1930	1·25	2·00

173 Tail Flukes of Humpback Whale

1995. Humpback Whale Conservation. Multicoloured.

587	45c. Type **173**	1·00	55
588	75c. Mother and calf	1·50	2·00
589	$1.05 Whale breaching (vert)	1·75	2·50
MS590	107×84 mm. $1.20 Humpback whale (29×49 mm)	3·25	4·00

174 Dot-and-Dash Butterflyfish

1995. Butterflyfish. Multicoloured.

591	5c. Type **174**	30	75
592	45c. Blue-spotted butterflyfish	85	50
593	$1.20 Three-belted butterflyfish	2·25	2·75
594	$1.50 Three-finned butterflyfish	2·50	3·25

1995. "JAKARTA '95" Stamp Exhibition, Indonesia. No. **MS**590 optd **"Selamat Hari Merdeka"** and emblem on sheet margin in gold.

MS595	107×84 mm. $1.20 Humpback whale	1·75	2·75

175 International 4×4 Refueller, 1942

1995. Second World War Vehicles. Multicoloured.

596	5c. Type **175**	30	75
597	45c. Ford Sedan, 1942	75	45
598	$1.20 Ford 3 ton tipper, 1942	2·00	2·50
599	$2 D8 caterpillar with scraper	3·00	4·00

1995. Flower designs as 1960 issues, but with face values in decimal currency.

600	5c. pink and green (as No. 25)	20	50
601	5c. red (as No. 28)	20	50

176 Servicing Fighter

1995. 50th Anniv of End of Second World War in the Pacific. Multicoloured.

602	5c. Type **176**	55	1·00
603	45c. Sgt. Tom Derrick, VC (vert)	85	45
604	75c. Gen. Douglas MacArthur (vert)	1·50	1·50
605	$1.05 Girls celebrating victory	2·25	2·25
606	$10 Pacific War medals (50×30 mm)	20·00	24·00

The $10 also includes the "Singapore '95" International stamp exhibition logo.

177 Peace Dove and Anniversary Emblem

1995. Christmas. 50th Anniv of United Nations. Each including U.N. anniversary emblem.

607	**177**	45c. gold and blue	45	45
608	-	75c. gold and violet	65	70
609	-	$1.05 gold and red	80	2·00
610	-	$1.20 gold and green	90	2·00

DESIGNS: 75c. Star of Bethlehem; $1.05, Symbolic candles on cake; $1.20, Olive branch.

178 Skink on Bank

1996. Endangered Species. Skinks and Geckos. Multicoloured.

611	5c. Type **178**	60	85
612	5c. Gecko on branch	60	85
613	45c. Skink facing right	80	85
614	45c. Gecko on flower	80	85

179 Sopwith Pup Biplane and Emblem

1996. 75th Anniv of Royal Australian Air Force. Aircraft. Multicoloured.

615	45c. Type **179**	60	60
616	45c. Wirraway fighter	60	60
617	75c. F-111C jet fighter	1·00	1·50
618	85c. F/A-18 Hornet jet fighter	1·10	1·60

180 Rat

1996. Chinese New Year ("Year of the Rat"). Sheet 100×75 mm.

MS619	**180** $1 black, red and brown	1·50	2·25

181 "Naticarlus oncus"

1996. Shells. Multicoloured.

620	45c. Type **181**	70	85
621	45c. "Janthina janthina"	70	85
622	45c. "Cypraea caputserpentis"	70	85
623	45c. "Argonauta nodosa"	70	85

182 Shopping

1996. Tourism. Multicoloured.

624	45c. Type **182**	50	50
625	75c. Celebrating Bounty Day	1·00	1·00
626	$2.50 Horse riding	3·75	4·50
627	$3.70 Unloading lighter	4·50	5·75

183 The Nativity

1996. Christmas. Multicoloured.

628	45c. Type **183**	50	50
629	45c. Star and boat sheds	50	50
630	75c. Star, bungalow and ox	90	1·50
631	85c. Star, fruit, flowers and ox	1·10	1·75

184 Coat of Arms

1997

632	**184**	5c. blue and yellow	25	50
633	-	5c. brown	25	50

DESIGN: No. 633, Great Seal of Norfolk Island.

185 Calf

1997. Beef Cattle. Sheet 67×67 mm.

MS634	**185** $1.20 multicoloured	2·00	2·75

1997. "HONG KONG '97" International Stamp Exhibition. As No. **MS**634, but with exhibition emblem on sheet margin.

MS635	67×67 mm. **185** $1.20 multi-coloured	3·25	4·00

186 "Cepora perimale"

1997. Butterflies. Multicoloured.

636	75c. Type **186**	1·10	1·00
637	90c. "Danaus chrysippus"	1·40	1·60
638	$1 "Danaus hamata"	1·40	1·60
639	$1.20 "Danaus plexippus"	1·50	2·25

187 Dusky Dolphins

1997. Dolphins. Multicoloured.

640	45c. Type **187**	75	60
641	75c. Common dolphin and calf	1·25	1·40
MS642	106×80 mm. $1.05 Dolphin	2·75	3·25

1997. "Pacific '97" International Stamp Exhibition, San Francisco. As No. **MS**642, but with exhibition emblem on sheet margin.

MS643	106×80 mm. $1.05 Dolphin	4·75	5·50

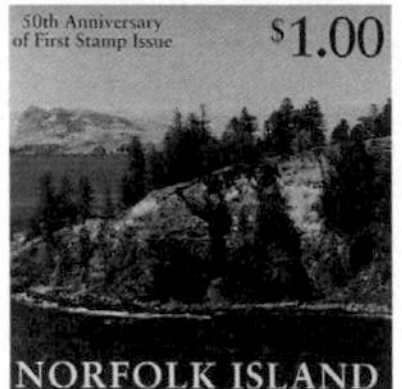

188 Ball Bay, Norfolk Island

1997. 50th Anniv of Norfolk Island Stamps. Multicoloured.

644	$1 Type **188**	1·25	2·25
645	$1.50 1947 2d. stamp	1·25	2·25
646	$8 Ball Bay and 1947 2s. bistre stamp (90×45 mm)	7·50	12·00

188a Queen Elizabeth II

1997. Golden Wedding of Queen Elizabeth and Prince Philip. Multicoloured.

647	20c. Type **188a**	50	60
648	25c. Prince Philip in carriage-driving trials	50	60
649	25c. Prince Philip	55	65
650	50c. Queen in phaeton at Trooping the Colour	70	80
MS651	110×70 mm. $1.50 Queen Elizabeth and Prince Philip in landau (horiz)	2·25	2·75

Nos. 647/8 and 649/50 were each printed together, *se-tenant*, with the backgrounds forming composite designs.

189 Royal Yacht "Britannia" leaving Hong Kong

1997. Return of Hong Kong to China. Sheet 126×91 mm.

MS652	**189** 45c. multicoloured	1·00	1·50

No. **MS**652 is inscribed "Brittania" in error.

190 Christmas Tree

1997. Annual Festivals. Multicoloured.

653	45c. Type **190**	60	45
654	75c. Fireworks (New Year's Eve)	90	1·25
655	$1.20 Rose (Valentine's Day)	1·40	2·00

191 Oriental Pearl T.V. Tower, Shanghai

1997. "Shanghai '97" International Stamp and Coin Exhibition, shanghai. Sheet 103×138 mm.

MS656	**191** 45c. multicoloured	1·00	1·50

192 Tiger Mask

1998. Chinese New Year ("Year of the Tiger"). Sheet 75×95 mm.

MS657	**192** 45c. multicoloured	1·00	1·50

193 "Pepper"

1998. Cats. Multicoloured.

658	45c. Type **193**	65	65
659	45c. "Tabitha" at window	65	65
660	75c. "Midnight"	85	1·25
661	$1.20 "Rainbow" with flower pot	1·25	1·75

194 Entrance to Pentagonal Gaol

1998

662	**194**	5c. black and blue	25	50
663	-	5c. black and green	25	50

DESIGN: No. 663, Ruined First Settlement cottage.

194a Princess Diana with Bouquet, 1991

1998. Diana, Princess of Wales Commemoration. Multicoloured.

664	45c. Type **194a**	60	60
MS665	145×70 mm. 45c. Wearing blue and white dress, 1989; 45c. Wearing pearl earrings, 1990; 45c. No. 664; 45c. Wearing striped dress (sold at $1.80+45c. charity premium)	1·25	2·00

195 Tweed Trousers

1998. Reef Fish. Multicoloured.

666	10c. Type **195**	30	40
667	20c. Conspicuous angelfish	55	50
668	30c. Moon wrasse	65	50
669	45c. Wide-striped clownfish	75	50
670	50c. Racoon butterflyfish	80	80
671	70c. Artooti (juvenile)	1·00	1·00
672	75c. Splendid hawkfish	1·00	1·00
673	85c. Scorpion fish	1·25	1·25
674	90c. Orange fairy basslet	1·25	1·25
675	$1 Sweetlips	1·25	1·25
676	$3 Moorish idol	2·75	3·50
677	$4 Gold-ribbon soapfish	3·25	4·25
MS678	110×85 mm. $1.20 Shark (29×39 mm)	1·50	2·00

Nos. 672 and 675 are incorrectly inscribed "Splendid Hawkefish" and "Sweetlip".

196 Hammer Throwing

1998. 16th Commonwealth Games, Kuala Lumpur.

679	**196**	75c. red and black	60	75
680	-	95c. violet and black	70	1·25
681	-	$1.05 mauve and black	80	1·40
MS682		80×100 mm. 85c. green and black	1·00	1·75

DESIGNS—HORIZ: 95c. Trap shooting. VERT: 85c. Flag bearer; $1.05, Lawn bowls.

197 "Norfolk" (sloop)

1998. Bicentenary of the Circumnavigation of Tasmania by George Bass and Matthew Flinders.

683	**197**	45c. multicoloured	1·90	1·25
MS684		101×69 mm. **197** $1.20 multicoloured	4·25	4·75

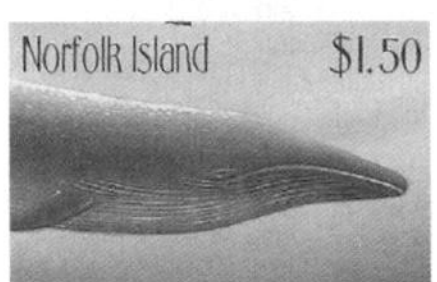

198 Blue whale

1998. Whales of the Southern Oceans (joint issue with Namibia and South Africa). Sheet 103×70 mm.

MS685	**198** $1.50 multicoloured	1·90	2·75

199 "Peace on Earth"

1998. Christmas. Multicoloured.

686	45c. Type **199**	55	50
687	75c. "Joy to the World"	85	80
688	$1.05 "A Season of Love"	1·25	1·75
689	$1.20 "Light of the World"	1·25	1·75

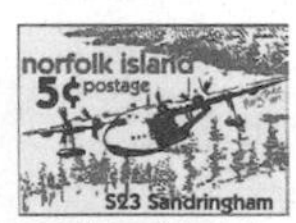

200 Short S.23 Sandringham (flying boat)

1999. Aircraft. Each red and green.

690	5c. Type **200**	30	60
691	5c. DC-4 "Norfolk Trader"	30	60

201 Soft Toy Rabbit

1999. Chinese New Year ("Year of the Rabbit"). Sheet 80×100 mm.

MS692	**201** 95c. multicoloured	1·00	1·75

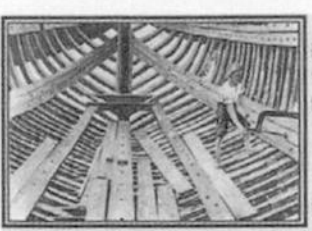

202 Hull of "Resolution" under Construction

1999. "Australia '99" International Stamp Exhibition, Melbourne. Schooner "Resolution". Multicoloured.

693	45c. Type **202**	1·60	2·00
694	45c. After being launched	1·60	2·00
695	45c. In Emily Bay	1·60	2·00
696	45c. Off Cascade	1·60	2·00
697	45c. Alongside at Auckland	1·60	2·00

203 Pacific Black Duck

1999. "iBRA '99" International Stamp Exhibition, Nuremburg. Sheet 80×100 mm.

MS698	**203** $2.50 multicoloured	5·50	6·50

204 Solander's Petrel in Flight

1999. Endangered Species. Solander's Petrel ("Providence Petrel"). Multicoloured.

699	75c. Type **204**	2·50	1·75
700	$1.05 Head of Solander's petrel (horiz)	3·00	2·50
701	$1.20 Adult and fledgling (horiz)	3·25	3·50
MS702	130×90 mm. $4.50 Solander's petrel in flight (35×51 mm)	10·00	12·00

See also No. **MS**738.

205 "Cecile Brunner" Rose

1999. Roses. Multicoloured.

703	45c. Type **205**	60	40
704	75c. Green rose	85	90
705	$1.05 "David Buffett" rose	1·25	1·75
MS706	60×81 mm. $1.20 "A Country Woman" Rose	1·40	2·00

No. **MS**706 also commemorates the 50th anniversary of the Country Women's Association on Norfolk Island.

1999. "China '99" International Stamp Exhibition, Beijing. No. **MS**692 with "China '99" logo optd on the margin in red.

MS707	80×100 mm. 95c. Type **201**	2·00	2·50

206 Pottery

1999. Handicrafts of Norfolk Island. Multicoloured.

708	45c. Type **206**	70	70
709	45c. Woodcarving	70	70
710	75c. Quilting	1·25	1·25
711	$1.05 Basket-weaving	1·50	2·25

206a Inspecting Bomb Damage, Buckingham Palace, 1940

1999. "Queen Elizabeth the Queen Mother's Century". Multicoloured (except $1.20).

712	45c. Type **206a**	70	70

713	45c. At Abergeldy Castle sale of work, 1955	70	70
714	75c. Queen Mother, Queen Elizabeth and Prince William, 1994	95	95
715	$1.20 Inspecting the King's Regiment (black)	1·50	1·75
MS716	145×70 mm. $3 Queen Elizabeth, 1937, and Amy Johnson's flight to Australia, 1930	3·50	4·00

207 Bishop George Augustus Selwyn

1999. Christmas. 150th Anniv of Melanesian Mission. Multicoloured (except 75c.).

717	45c. Type **207**	1·50	1·75
718	45c. Bishop John Coleridge Patteson	1·50	1·75
719	75c. "150 YEARS MELANESIAN MISSION" (black)	1·75	1·90
720	$1.05 Stained-glass windows	2·00	2·25
721	$1.20 "Southern Cross" (missionary ship) and religious symbols	2·25	2·50

Nos. 717/21 were printed together, *se-tenant*, with the backgrounds forming a composite design.

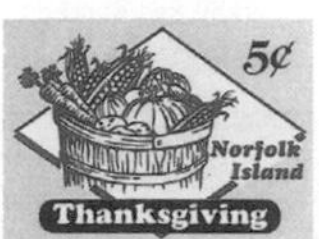
208 Basket of Food (Thanksgiving)

2000. Festivals.

722	**208**	5c. black and blue	40	65
723	-	5c. black and blue	40	65

DESIGN: No. 723, Musician playing guitar (Country Music Festival).

209 Dragon

2000. Chinese New Year ("Year of the Dragon"). Sheet 106×86 mm.

MS724	**209** $2 multicoloured	3·00	3·50

210 Domestic Goose

2000. Ducks and Geese. Multicoloured.

725	45c. Type **210**	1·25	70
726	75c. Pacific black duck	2·00	1·25
727	$1.05 Mallard drake	2·25	2·50
728	$1.20 Aylesbury duck	2·25	2·50

211 Honour Roll for First World War

2000. Anzac Day. Multicoloured.

729	45c. Type **211**	1·50	1·00
730	75c. Honour rolls for Second World War and Korea	2·00	1·75

212 Young Boy, Shipwright and Whaleboat

2000. "Whaler Project 2000". Two sheets, each 96×76 mm, containing T **212**. Multicoloured.

MS731	**212** $4 multicoloured	8·00	9·00
MS732	$4 mult ("THE STAMP SHOW 2000" and Crown Agents logos added in gold) Imperf	8·00	9·00

213 Captain William Bligh and Bounty

2000. "Bounty" Day. Multicoloured.

733	45c. Type **213**	2·00	1·50
734	75c. Fletcher Christian and Tahiti	2·25	2·00

214 Turtle

2000. Eighth Festival of Pacific Arts, New Caledonia. Multicoloured. (a) Size 24×29 mm. Self-adhesive.

735	45c. Urn and swat	1·50	1·50

(b) Sheet 130×70 mm.

MS736	75c. Type **214**; $1.05 Traditional mosaic; $1.20 Mask and spearhead; $2 Decorated utensils	7·50	8·50

215 Malcolm Champion (Olympic Gold Medal Winner, Stockholm, 1912)

2000. "Olymphilex 2000" International Stamp Exhibition, Sydney. Sheet 120×70 mm.

MS737	**215** $3 multicoloured	7·00	8·00

2000. "Canpex 2000" National Stamp Exhibition, Christchurch, New Zealand. Sheet 120×90 mm.

MS738	$2.40 No. 701×2	8·50	9·00

216 Sun over Pines

2000. Christmas. Multicoloured.

739	45c. Type **216**	1·50	55
740	75c. Candle over pines	2·00	85
741	$1.05 Moon over pines	2·50	3·00
742	$1.20 Star over pines	2·75	3·00

217 "Norfolk Island in 1825 and 2001" (Jessica Wong and Mardi Pye)

2000. New Millennium. Children's drawings. Multicoloured.

743	45c. Type **217**	2·00	2·00
744	45c. "Seabirds over Norfolk Island" (Roxanne Spreag)	2·00	2·00
745	75c. "Trees and Clothes" (Tara Grube)	3·25	3·25
746	75c. "Underwater Scene" (Thomas Greenwood)	3·25	3·25

218 Red-fronted Parakeet ("Green Parrot")

2001. Green Parrot.

747	**218**	5c. red and green	30	70

219 Purple Swamphen

2001. Chinese New Year "Year of the Snake" and International Stamp Exhibition, Hong Kong.

748	**219**	45c. multicoloured	2·00	2·25
MS749		110×70 mm. $2.30 Norfolk Island eel and purple swamphen (as Type **219**, but without country inscr and face value). Imperf	3·25	4·00

220 "Old Clothes"

2001. Centenary of Australian Federation. Cartoons from The Bulletin Magazine. Multicoloured.

750	45c. Type **220**	70	80
751	45c. "Tower of Babel"	70	80
752	45c. "The Political Garotters"	70	80
753	45c. "Promises, Promises!"	70	80
754	45c. "The Gout of Federation"	70	80
755	45c. "The Federal Spirit"	70	80
756	75c. "Australia Faces the Dawn"	1·00	1·00
757	$1.05 "The Federal Capital Question"	1·25	1·60
758	$1.20 "The Imperial Fowl-Yard"	1·40	1·75

221 Satellite over China

2001. Invercargill "Stamp Odyssey 2001" National Stamp Exhibition, New Zealand. Sheet, 136×105 mm, containing T **221** and similar vert designs. Multicoloured.

MS759	75c. Type **221**; 75c. Satellite over Pacific; 75c. Satellite over Australia	4·00	5·00

222 Woman and Child in Victorian Dress

2001. Bounty Day.

760	**222**	5c. black and green	30	60

223 *Jasminium simplicifolium*

2001. Perfume from Norfolk Island. Multicoloured.

761	45c. Type **223**	50	35
762	75c. Girl's face in perfume bottle	70	70
763	$1.05 Girl and roses	90	1·25
764	$1.20 Taylor's Road, Norfolk Island	90	1·50

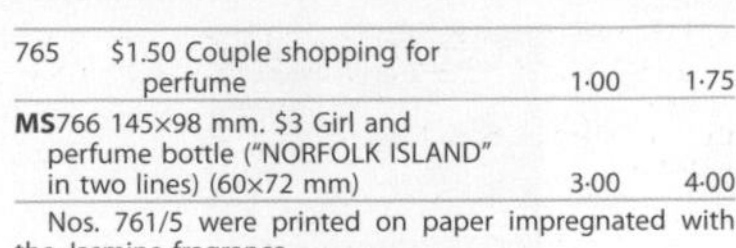

765	$1.50 Couple shopping for perfume	1·00	1·75
MS766	145×98 mm. $3 Girl and perfume bottle ("NORFOLK ISLAND" in two lines) (60×72 mm)	3·00	4·00

Nos. 761/5 were printed on paper impregnated with the Jasmine fragrance.

224 Whaleboat

2001. Local Boats. Multicoloured.

768	45c. Type **224**	1·50	50
769	$1 Motor launch	2·50	2·75
770	$1 Family rowing boat (horiz)	2·50	2·75
771	$1.50 Sailing cutter (horiz)	3·00	3·25

No. 768 also comes self-adhesive.

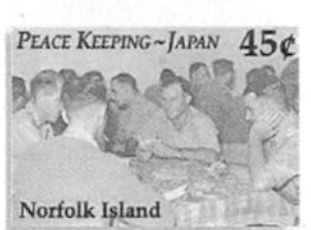
225 Australian Soldiers playing Cards

2001. Centenary of Australian Army. B.C.O.F. Japan.

773	**225**	45c. brown and blue	1·50	1·50
774	-	45c. brown and blue	1·50	1·50
775	-	$1 brown and green	3·25	3·25
776	-	$1 brown and green	3·25	3·25

DESIGNS: No. 774, Christmas float; 775, Birthday cake; 776, Australian military policeman directing traffic.

226 Miamiti (cartoon owl) holding Island Flag

2001. Sixth South Pacific Mini Games (1st issue).

777	**226**	10c. brown and green	40	60

See also Nos. 794/5.

227 Strawberry Guava

2001. Christmas. Island Plants. Each incorporating carol music. Multicoloured.

778	45c. Type **227**	1·25	1·25
779	45c. Poinsettia	1·25	1·25
780	$1 Christmas croton	2·00	2·00
781	$1 Hibiscus	2·00	2·00
782	$1.50 Indian shot	2·50	2·50

No. 779 is inscribed "Pointsettia" in error.

228 Sacred Kingfisher

2002. "Nuffka" (Sacred Kingfisher).

783	**228**	10c. deep blue and blue	65	80

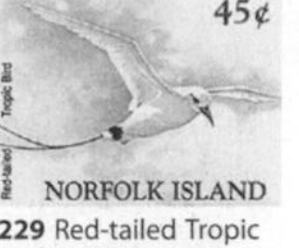
229 Red-tailed Tropic Bird

2002. Cliff Ecology. Multicoloured.

784	45c. Type **229**	2·00	1·00
785	$1 White oak blossom	2·75	2·75
786	$1 White oak tree	2·75	2·75
787	$1.50 Eagle ray	3·00	3·25

229a Elizabeth Duchess of York with Princesses Elizabeth and Margaret, 1930

2002. Golden Jubilee.

788	**229a**	45c. black, red and gold	1·25	55
789	-	75c. multicoloured	1·40	1·00
790	-	$1 black, red and gold	1·75	1·25
791	-	$1.50 multicoloured	2·25	2·75
MS792		162×95 mm. Nos. 788/91 and $3 multicoloured	6·50	7·50

DESIGNS:—HORIZ: 75c. Queen Elizabeth in multicoloured hat, 1977; $1 Queen Elizabeth wearing Imperial State Crown, Coronation 1953; $1.50, Queen Elizabeth at Windsor Horse Show, 2000. VERT (38×51 mm)— $3 Queen Elizabeth after Annigoni.

Designs as Nos. 788/91 in No. **MS**792 omit the gold frame around each stamp and the "Golden Jubilee 1952-2002" inscription.

230 Derelict Steam Engine

2002. Restoration of Yeaman's Mill Steam Engine.

793	**230**	$4.50 multicoloured	8·50	10·00

231 Miamiti (cartoon owl) running

2002. Sixth South Pacific Mini Games (2nd issue). Multicoloured.

794	50c. Type **231**	1·50	1·00
795	$1.50 Miamiti playing tennis	2·75	3·25

232 Lawn Bowls Player

2002. Bounty Bowls Tournament.

796	**232**	10c. black and green	30	60

233 *Streblorrhiza speciosa*

2002. Phillip Island Flowers. Multicoloured.

797	10c. Type **233**	75	1·00
798	20c. *Plumbago zeylanica*	55	45
799	30c. *Canavalia rosea*	1·25	65
800	40c. *Ipomea pes-caprae*	60	60
801	45c. *Hibiscus insularis*	60	45
802	50c. *Solanum laciniatum*	1·75	55
803	95c. *Phormium tenax*	1·00	1·25
804	$1 *Lobelia anceps*	2·50	1·50
805	$1.50 *Carpobrotus glaucescens*	4·25	4·00
806	$2 *Abutilon julianae*	2·50	4·00
807	$3 *Wollastonia biflora*	5·50	6·00
808	$5 *Oxalis corniculata*	6·00	7·50

No. 797 is inscribed "specioca" in error.

234 Running

2002. 17th Commonwealth Games, Manchester. Multicoloured.

809	10c. Type **234**	55	75
810	45c. Cycling (horiz)	3·50	1·25
811	$1 Lawn bowls	2·00	2·00
812	$1.50 Shooting (horiz)	3·00	3·50

235 Adult Sperm Whale and Calf

2002. Norfolk Island—New Caledonia Joint Issue. Operation Cetaces (marine mammal study). Multicoloured.

813	$1 Type **235**	3·00	3·00
814	$1 Sperm whale attacked by giant squid	3·00	3·00

A similar set was issued by New Caledonia.

236 White Tern incubating Egg

2002. Christmas. White Tern. Multicoloured.

815	45c. Type **236**	1·50	1·25
816	45c. White tern chick	1·50	1·25
817	$1 Two White terns in flight	2·50	1·75
818	$1.50 White tern landing	3·50	5·00

237 Horses in Riding School

2003. Horses on Norfolk Island. Multicoloured.

819	45c. Type **237**	1·40	1·50
820	45c. Mares and foals in paddock	1·40	1·50
821	45c. Showjumpers	1·40	1·50
822	75c. Racehorses	1·60	1·75
823	75c. Draught horses	1·60	1·75

238 Old Warehouse Buildings at Seashore

2003. Photographic Scenes of Norfolk Island (1st series). Multicoloured.

824	50c. Type **238**	1·50	75
825	95c. Beached boat (with rainbow markings) and sandy shore	2·50	2·25
826	$1.10 Grazing cattle and pine trees	2·75	2·25
827	$1.65 Sandy shore and head-land with single pine tree	3·75	5·50

See also Nos. 859/62.

239 "Southern Prize"

2003. Day Lilies. Multicoloured.

828	50c. Type **239**	65	75
829	50c. "Becky Stone"	65	75
830	50c. "Cameroons"	65	75
831	50c. "Chinese Autumn"	65	75
832	50c. "Scarlet Orbit"	65	75
833	50c. "Ocean Rain"	65	75
834	50c. "Gingerbread Man"	65	75
835	50c. "Pink Corduroy"	65	75
836	50c. "Elizabeth Hinrichsen"	65	75
837	50c. "Simply Pretty"	65	75

240 Maeve and Gil Hitch

2003. First Norfolk Island Writer's Festival. Black, violet and lilac (Nos. 838/9 and 844/5) or multicoloured (Nos. 840/3).

838	10c. Type **240**	60	75
839	10c. Alice Buffett	60	75
840	10c. Nan Smith	60	75
841	10c. Archie Bigg	60	75
842	50c. Colleen McCullough	60	75
843	50c. Peter Clarke	60	75
844	50c. Bob Tofts	60	75
845	50c. Merval Hoare	60	75

241 Seashore with Trees and Stream

2004. Island Landscapes. Multicoloured.

846	50c. Type **241**	1·75	1·90
847	50c. Sandy shore with wooden post and small boat	1·75	1·90
848	50c. Rocky bay with pine trees on headland	1·75	1·90
849	50c. Grazing cattle, pine trees and ruined building	1·75	1·90

242 Queen Elizabeth II wearing Imperial State Crown

2003. 50th Anniv of Coronation.

MS850	115×85 mm. 10c. Type **242** (black, deep violet and violet); $3 Queen wearing flowered hat and dress (multicoloured)	4·50	5·50

243 Globe ("Peace on Earth")

2003. Christmas. Multicoloured.

851	50c. Type **243**	1·25	1·00
852	50c. Bird and rainbow ("Joy to the World")	1·25	1·00
853	$1.10 Heart-shaped Christmas present ("Give the gift of Love")	2·25	1·75
854	$1.65 Candle ("Trust in Faith")	3·00	4·00

244 de Havilland DH.60G Gipsy Moth Floatplane (first aircraft at Norfolk Island, 1931)

2003. Centenary of Powered Flight. Multicoloured (except Type **244**).

855	50c. Type **244** (black, brown and violet)	1·75	85
856	$1.10 Boeing 737 (Norfolk Island–Australia service)	2·75	1·90
857	$1.65 Douglas DC-4 (passenger service 1949–977)	4·25	6·00
MS858	110×83 mm. $1.65 Wright *Flyer I*, 1903 (47×29 mm)	6·00	6·50

245 Timbers from Prow of Boat and Houses

2004. Photographic Scenes of Norfolk Island (2nd series). Multicoloured.

859	50c. Type **245**	1·50	1·00
860	95c. Waterfall	2·75	2·50
861	$1.10 Cattle and pine trees	2·75	2·50
862	$1.65 Beach and headland at sunset	4·00	5·00

246 Whale Shark

2004. Sharks. Multicoloured.

863	10c. Type **246**	65	1·00
864	50c. Hammerhead shark	1·75	70
865	$1.10 Tiger shark	3·25	2·75
866	$1.65 Bronze whaler shark	4·50	5·50

247 Golden Orb Spider

2004. Spiders. Multicoloured.

867	50c. Type **247**	1·00	1·00
868	50c. Community spider	1·00	1·00
869	$1 St. Andrews Cross	1·60	1·60
870	$1.65 Red-horned spider	2·50	3·75
MS871	120×80 mm. $1.50 Red-horned spider (48×40 mm)	2·50	3·50

248 Loading Cargo into Light Craft

2004. Werken Dar Shep. Multicoloured.

872	50c. Type **248**	1·25	70
873	$1.10 Transporting cargo	2·00	2·00
874	$1.65 Two light craft	2·25	3·50
MS875	130×85 mm. $1.65 Craft moored alongside dock	3·25	4·00

249 Apple Blossom

2004. Hippeastrums. Multicoloured.

876	50c. Type **249**	80	95
877	50c. Carnival	80	95
878	50c. Cherry blossom	80	95
879	50c. Lilac wonder	80	95
880	50c. Millennium star	80	95
881	50c. Cocktail	80	95
882	50c. Milady	80	95
883	50c. Pacific sunset	80	95
884	50c. Geisha girl	80	95
885	50c. Lady Jane	80	95

250 Three Children

2004. 25th Anniv of Quota International (humanitarian organisation). Sheet 135×73 mm containing T **250** and similar horiz designs. Multicoloured.

MS886	50c. Type **250**; $1.10 Feet painted with "WE CARE"; $1.65 Boy drawing "Quota" in sand	5·00	6·50

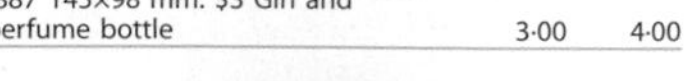

2004. Perfume from Norfolk Island. Special Edition. No. **MS**766 optd with **SPECIAL EDITION**.

MS887	145×98 mm. $3 Girl and perfume bottle	3·00	4·00

252 Tree and "Twas the Night Before Christmas"

2004. Christmas. Designs showing Christmas tree and excerpt of carol.

No.	Type	Description	Unused	Used
890	**252**	50c. green and silver	75	70
891	-	50c. lilac and silver	75	70
892	-	$1.10 carmine and silver	1·50	1·40
893	-	$1.65 orange and silver	2·25	3·75

DESIGNS: No. 890, Type **252**; 891, "Silent Night"; 892, "Twelve Days of Christmas"; 893, "Oh Holy Night".

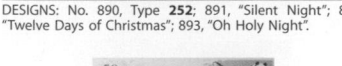

253 Sacred Kingfisher

2004. Sacred Kingfisher. Multicoloured.

No.	Type	Description	Unused	Used
894		50c. Type **253**	1·40	1·25
895		50c. Two sacred kingfishers	1·40	1·25
896		$1 Sacred kingfisher perched	2·50	2·00
897		$2 Sacred kingfisher from back	4·00	5·00
MS898		130×158 mm. Nos. 894/7, each ×2	13·00	16·00

251 Tree Fern

2004. Norfolk Island Palm and Fern.

No.	Type	Description	Unused	Used
888	**251**	10c. green and black	25	60
889	-	10c. yellow and black	25	60

DESIGNS: No. 888, Type **251**; 889, Palm.

254 Coat of Arms and Flag

2004. 25th Anniv of Self-Government.

No.	Type	Description	Unused	Used
899	**254**	$5 multicoloured	7·50	9·00

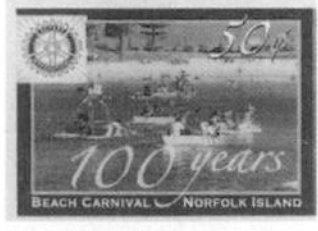

255 Boat Race

2005. Centenary of Rotary International (humanitarian organisation). Multicoloured.

No.	Type	Description	Unused	Used
900		50c. Type **255**	75	75
901		50c. Tree planting (vert)	75	75
902		$1.20 Paul Harris (founder)	1·50	1·40
903		$1.80 Rotary Youth Leadership Awards (vert)	2·25	3·75
MS904		110×80 mm. $2 District 9910 (Rotary community)	3·00	4·25

256 Tea Cup, 1856

2005. Norfolk Island Museum, Kingston. Multicoloured.

No.	Type	Description	Unused	Used
905		50c. Type **256**	1·25	1·00
906		50c. Salt cellar from HMS *Bounty*, 1856	1·25	1·00
907		$1.10 Medicine cups, 1825–55	2·00	1·75
908		$1.65 Stoneware jar, 1825–55	2·75	3·75

257 Polynesian Explorer and Voyaging Canoe

2005. Pacific Explorers. Multicoloured.

No.	Type	Description	Unused	Used
909		50c. Type **257**	70	50
910		$1.20 *Vitoria* (Magellan)	1·75	1·60
911		$1.80 Captain Cook ashore at Norfolk Island and HMS *Resolution*	2·50	3·25
MS912		140×85 mm. $2 Early map of Pacific (45×31 mm)	2·75	3·50

No. **MS**912 also commemorates Pacific Explorer 2005 World Stamp Expo, Sydney.

258 Branka House

2005. Old Island Houses. Multicoloured.

No.	Type	Description	Unused	Used
913		50c. Type **258**	60	55
914		50c. Greenacres	60	55
915		$1.20 Ma Annas	1·40	1·40
916		$1.80 Naumai	2·00	3·50

259 Red-tailed Tropic Bird

2005. Seabirds of Norfolk Island. Multicoloured.

No.	Type	Description	Unused	Used
917		10c. Type **259**	15	20
918		25c. White tern	30	35
919		40c. Sooty tern	50	40
920		50c. Australasian gannet	60	40
921		70c. Black-winged petrel	75	65
922		$1 Black noddy	1·10	1·10
923		$1.50 Grey ternlet	1·50	1·25
924		$2 Masked booby	2·00	2·25
925		$3 Wedge-tailed shearwater	3·00	3·25
926		$5 White-necked petrel	5·50	5·75
MS927		(a) 65×90 mm. $2.50 Sooty tern in flight. (b) 100×70 mm. $4 Red-tailed tropic bird (horiz). Set of 2 sheets	9·00	10·00

260 "Marjory Brown"

2005. Hibiscus Varieties. Multicoloured.

No.	Type	Description	Unused	Used
928		50c. Type **260**	60	75
929		50c. "Aloha"	60	75
930		50c. "Pulau Tree"	60	75
931		50c. "Ann Miller"	60	75
932		50c. "Surfrider"	60	75
933		50c. "Philip Island"	60	75
934		50c. "Rose of Sharon"	60	75
935		50c. "D. J. O'Brien"	60	75
936		50c. "Elaine's Pride"	60	75
937		50c. "Castle White"	60	75
938		50c. Skeleton Hibiscus	60	75
939		50c. "Pink Sunset"	60	75

261 Anson Bay

2005. Christmas. Multicoloured.

No.	Type	Description	Unused	Used
940		50c. Type **261**	75	40
941		$1.20 Cascade Bay	1·60	1·40
942		$1.80 Ball Bay	2·25	3·75

262 Drummer

2005. Norfolk Island Jazz Festival. Multicoloured.

No.	Type	Description	Unused	Used
943		50c. Type **262**	75	50
944		$1.20 Saxophone player	1·60	1·40
945		$1.80 Guitarist and pine tree	2·25	3·75

263 Baton and Norfolk Island Pines

2006. Commonwealth Games Queen's Baton Relay on Norfolk Island. Multicoloured.

No.	Type	Description	Unused	Used
946		$1.50 Type **263**	2·75	2·75
947		$1.50 Prow of ship and girl carrying baton	2·75	2·75

264 Shooting

2006. Commonwealth Games. Multicoloured.

No.	Type	Description	Unused	Used
948		50c. Type **264**	70	50
949		$1.50 Lawn bowls	1·50	1·50
950		$2 Squash	2·00	3·50

265 HMS *Bounty* at Portsmouth, 1789

2006. 150th Anniv of Migration of Pitcairn Islanders to Norfolk Island (1st issue). Departure from Pitcairn Island. Designs showing scenes from cyclorama on Norfolk Island depicting the "Bounty" story. Multicoloured.

No.	Type	Description	Unused	Used
951		50c. Type **265**	1·75	1·75
952		50c. Collecting breadfruit at Tahiti	1·75	1·75
953		$1.20 Capt. Bligh cast adrift in Bounty's launch	3·25	2·50
954		$1.50 Burning of HMS *Bounty* at Pitcairn Island	3·75	4·00
955		$1.80 Pitcairn Islanders arriving at Norfolk Island, 1856	4·00	4·50

266 Re-enactment Procession

2006. 150th Anniv of Migration of Pitcairn Islanders to Norfolk Island (2nd issue). Arrival on Norfolk Island. Designs showing Bounty Day re-enactment and celebrations. Multicoloured.

No.	Type	Description	Unused	Used
956		10c. Type **266**	75	1·00
957		30c. Laying wreath at war memorial	1·25	1·00
958		50c. Honouring ancestors	1·50	1·50
959		50c. Community picnic	1·50	1·50
960		$4 Bounty ball	9·00	11·00

267 Hat with Decorated Brim

2006. Traditional Hats. Multicoloured.

No.	Type	Description	Unused	Used
961		50c. Type **267** (blue)	1·50	1·75
962		50c. Hat with pale woven band (blue)	1·50	1·75
963		50c. Hat with flowers on brim (green)	1·50	1·75
964		50c. Plain hat (green)	1·50	1·75
965		50c. Hat with white decoration around brim (violet)	1·50	1·75
966		50c. Plain hat (different) (violet)	1·50	1·75

268 "Wal"

2006. Dogs of Norfolk Island ("Year of the Dog"). Multicoloured.

No.	Type	Description	Unused	Used
967		10c. Type **268**	90	1·00
968		50c. "Axel"	2·00	75
969		$1 "Wag"	3·00	2·00
970		$2.65 "Gemma"	8·00	10·00

269 Norfolk Island Central School, Middlegate, c. 1906

2006. Centenary of Norfolk Island Central School, Middlegate. Multicoloured.

No.	Type	Description	Unused	Used
971		$2 Type **269**	7·00	8·00
972		$2 Norfolk Island Central School, Middlegate, 2006	7·00	8·00

270 Adult and Juvenile Boobies enclosed in Bauble

2006. Christmas. Multicoloured.

No.	Type	Description	Unused	Used
973		50c. Type **270**	1·50	1·00
974		50c. Prow of boat and houses in bauble and fish decoration	1·50	1·00
975		$1.20 Old Military Barracks, Kingston, in bauble and star decoration	3·00	2·00
976		$1.80 Hibiscus flower in bauble and bird decoration	4·50	6·00

271 *Lantana camara*

2007. Flowers. Multicoloured.

No.	Type	Description	Unused	Used
977		50c. Type **271**	1·75	1·50
978		50c. *Ageratina riparia* (Crofton weed)	1·75	1·50
979		$1.20 *Ipomoea cairica* (morning glory)	3·25	2·25
980		$1.80 *Solanum mauritianum* (wild tobacco)	4·50	6·50

272 Sea Kayaking

2007. Adventure Sports. Multicoloured.

No.	Type	Description	Unused	Used
981		50c. Type **272**	1·50	1·25
982		50c. Wind surfing	1·50	1·25
983		$1.20 Mountain biking	3·00	2·25
984		$1.80 Surfing	4·50	6·00

273 Kentia Palms

2007. Kentia Palm Seed Harvest. Sheet 82×82 mm containing T **273** and similar multicoloured designs and one label.

No.	Type	Description	Unused	Used
MS985		50c. Type **273**; 50c. Dog guarding buckets of palm seeds (horiz); 50c. Emptying bucket into wooden crates (horiz); 50c. Kentia palm tree laden with seeds	4·25	4·75

274 The Violin Teacher and Government House

2007. Ghosts of Norfolk Island. Multicoloured.

No.	Description	Mint	Used
986	10c. Type **274**	50	85
987	50c. Ghosts in graveyard	1·50	75
988	$1 Emily (lady in white) at Kingston Pier	3·00	2·25
989	$1.80 Officer on guard at entrance to Barracks	5·00	6·00

275 Queen Victoria

2007. 120th Anniv of Queen Victoria Scholarship at Norfolk Island Central School. Self-adhesive.

No.	Type	Description	Mint	Used
990	**275**	10c. multicoloured	30	60
		(b) Sheet stamp		
991	**275**	$5 multicoloured (25×32 mm)	14·00	16·00

276 Squash player

2007. South Pacific Games, Samoa. Multicoloured.

No.	Description	Mint	Used
992	50c. Type **276**	1·25	75
993	$1 Golf	2·50	1·75
994	$1.20 Netball player	2·00	2·00
995	$1.80 Athlete running	3·50	5·00
MS996	115×90 mm. $2 Emblem	3·00	4·00

277 HMS *Sirius* and *Supply* off Kingston

2007. Bicentenary of Transfer of First Convict Settlement to Tasmania. Multicoloured.

No.	Description	Mint	Used
997	10c. Type **277**	75	1·00
998	50c. Shipping Signal, Kingston	2·00	75
999	$1.20 First Settlement, Kingston	3·75	2·75
1000	$1.80 *Lady Nelson* leaving for Tasmania, 1807	5·00	6·50

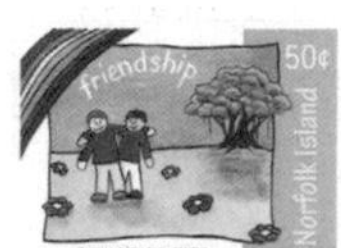

278 Two Children ('friendship')

2007. 30th Anniv of Banyan Park Play Centre. Multicoloured.

No.	Description	Mint	Used
1001	50c. Type **278**	1·75	1·00
1002	$1 Four children ('Community')	2·50	2·00
1003	$1.20 Three children playing ('Play grow learn together')	2·75	2·75
1004	$1.80 Two children reading book ('read books')	4·50	6·00

279 Young Norfolk Island Pine

2007. Christmas. 'Fairy Lights'. Multicoloured.

No.	Description	Mint	Used
1005	50c. Type **279**	1·75	75
1006	$1.20 Back of Melanesian Chapel	3·25	2·25
1007	$1.80 Old lighter on Kingston foreshore	4·75	6·00

280 Ford Falcon XP, 1965

2008. Classic Cars. Each showing car and photograph of Norfolk Island scene. Multicoloured.

No.	Description	Mint	Used
1008	50c. Type **280**	1·75	1·00
1009	$1 Chevrolet Styleline, 1952	2·75	2·00
1010	$1.20 Pontiac Silver Arrow, 1953	2·75	2·75
1011	$1.80 Rolls Royce Silver Shadow, 1971	4·50	6·00

281 Andre Nobbs

2008. Faces of Norfolk Island. Portraits by Adam Jauczius. Multicoloured.

No.	Description	Mint	Used
1012	50c. Type **281**	1·25	1·00
1013	$1 Darlene Buffett	2·00	2·00
1014	$1.20 Colin Lindsay Buffett ('Boonie')	2·50	2·50
1015	$1.80 Tania Grube and her baby son	3·50	4·00

282 Limousin Cross Calf

2008. Calves. Multicoloured.

No.	Description	Mint	Used
1016	50c. Type **282**	1·25	1·00
1017	$1 Murray Grey	2·25	2·00
1018	$1.20 Poll Hereford	2·50	2·50
1019	$1.80 Brahman cross	3·50	4·00

283 Gravestone

2008. A Jewish Resting Place

No.	Type	Description	Mint	Used
1020	**283**	50c. multicoloured	2·00	1·00
1021	–	$1.20 multicoloured	3·25	2·50
1022	–	$1.80 multicoloured	4·75	6·00

2008. Israel 2008 World Stamp Championship, Tel-Aviv. Sheet 103×80 mm containing stamp as T **283** but 30×40 mm, optd **World Championship Israel 2008 Tel-Aviv 14–21 May** and emblem on right-hand sheet margin.

No.	Description	Mint	Used
MS1023	Jewish gravestone	11·00	10·00

284 Past and Present Members

2008. 25th Anniv of St. John's Ambulance in Norfolk Island. Multicoloured.

No.	Description	Mint	Used
1024	30c. Type **284**	1·25	75
1025	40c. Re-enactment: putting casualty in recovery position	1·40	1·00
1026	95c. Re-enactment: loading casualty into ambulance	3·00	2·00
1027	$4 Re-enactment: taking casualty into hospital	11·00	13·00

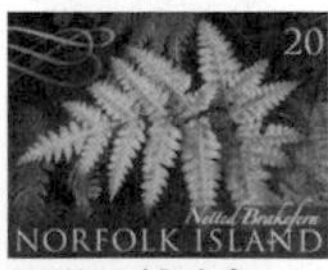

285 Netted Brakefern

2008. Rare Ferns. Multicoloured.

No.	Description	Mint	Used
1028	20c. Type **285**	90	1·25
1029	20c. *Pteris zahlbruckneriana*	90	1·25
1030	50c. Robinsonia	1·75	2·00
1031	50c. *Asplenium australasicum f. robinsonii*	1·75	2·00
1032	80c. Hanging fork fern	2·25	2·50
1033	80c. *Tmesipteris norfolkensis*	2·25	2·50
1034	$2 King fern	4·25	4·50
1035	$2 *Marattia salicina*	4·25	4·50

286 *Norfolk* (sloop), 1798

2008. Ships built on Norfolk Island. Multicoloured.

No.	Description	Mint	Used
1036	50c. Type **286**	2·25	1·00
1037	$1.20 *Resolution* (schooner), 1925	3·75	2·75
1038	$1.80 *Endeavour* (schooner), 1808	5·50	7·25

287 Royal Engineers Cottage, Store and Guard Houses from Second Settlement

2008. 'Isles of Exile'. Multicoloured.

No.	Description	Mint	Used
1039	25c. Type **287**	1·00	1·00
1040	55c. Commissariat Stores	1·75	80
1041	$1.75 Cemetery	4·00	4·00
1042	$2.50 Aerial view of Pentagonal Gaol from the Second Settlement	6·00	8·00

288 Child at Prayer

2008. Christmas. Multicoloured.

No.	Description	Mint	Used
1043	55c. Type **288**	1·25	80
1044	$1.40 Virgin Mary and baby Jesus	2·75	2·25
1045	$2.05 Three Magi carrying gifts	4·25	5·50

289 Fish Mosaic

2009. Norfolk Island Mosaics. Multicoloured

No.	Description	Mint	Used
	(a) Ordinary gum		
1046	5c. Type **289**	15	40
1047	15c. Lily	35	60
1048	55c. Red-tailed tropic bird	1·00	85
1049	$1.40 Tree	2·10	2·50
	(b) Self-adhesive.		
1050	15c. Sea turtle (Jasmine Kiernan)	40	65
1051	15c. Starfish on urn (Jeannie Sheridan)	50	65

2009. Norfolk Island Cattle (2nd series). Cattle Breeds. As T **282**. Multicoloured.

No.	Description	Mint	Used
1052	15c. Shorthorn	25	50
1053	55c. South Devon	1·00	85
1054	$1.40 Norfolk Blue	2·50	2·50
1055	$2.05 Lincoln Red	3·50	5·00
MS1056	110×84 mm. $5 Young cattle in pasture	8·50	10·00

290 *Gyrodon* sp.

2009. Fungi of Norfolk Island. Multicoloured.

No.	Description	Mint	Used
1057	15c. Type **290**	25	50
1058	55c. *Stereum ostrea*	1·00	85
1059	$1.40 *Cymatoderma elegans var lamellatum*	2·50	2·50
1060	$2.05 *Chlorophyllum molybdites*	3·50	5·00
MS1061	130×71 mm. Nos. 1057/60	6·50	8·50

291 Bridled Nailtail Wallaby

2009. Species at Risk. Multicoloured.

No.	Description	Mint	Used
1062	55c. Type **291**	2·50	2·50
1063	55c. Norfolk Island green parrot	2·50	2·50
1064	55c. Subantarctic fur seal	2·50	2·50
1065	55c. Christmas Island blue-tailed skink	2·50	2·50
1066	55c. Green turtle	2·50	2·50
MS1067	150×85 mm. Nos. 3247 and 3249/51 of Australia and No. 1063	9·00	9·50

Similar designs were issued by Australia.

No. **MS**1067 is identical to No. **MS**3252 of Australia. Nos. 1062/**MS**1067 of Norfolk Island and Nos. 3247/**MS**3252 of Australia were all issued on August 2010.

292 Grey Fantail

2009. Bush Birds. Multicoloured.

No.	Description	Mint	Used
1068	15c. Type **292**	50	70
1069	55c. Pacific robin	1·40	90
1070	$1.40 Golden whistler	3·25	3·25
1071	$2.05 Sacred kingfisher	4·00	5·00

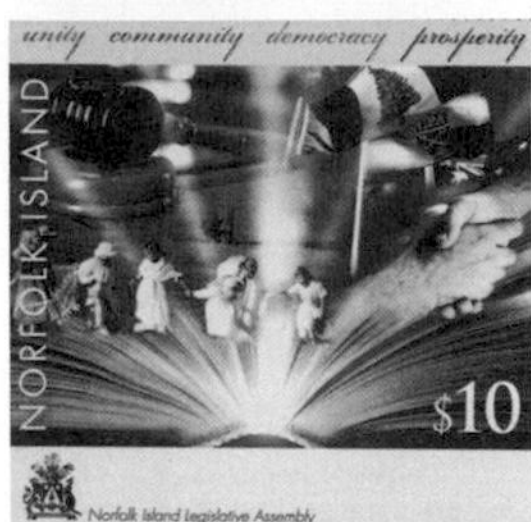

293 Children in Bounty Day Dress, Gavel, Handshake and Flags of Norfolk Island, Commonwealth Parliamentary Association and Australia

2009. 30th Anniv of Self-Government (Norfolk Island Legislative Assembly).

No.	Type	Description	Mint	Used
1072	**293**	$10 multicoloured	20·00	23·00

294 St. Mathew, St. Barnabas Chapel

2009. Christmas. Stained Glass Windows from St. Barnabas Chapel and All Saints Church. Multicoloured.

No.	Description	Mint	Used
1073	15c. Type **294**	45	45
1074	50c. Rose window, St. Barnabas Chapel	1·25	85
1075	$1.45 Christ in Glory, All Saints Church, Kingston	3·00	2·75
1076	$2.10 Memorial window to missionaries at St. Barnabas Chapel	4·25	5·50

295 Pottery from Second Convict Settlement

2010. Artefacts from Norfolk Island's Museums (1st series). Multicoloured.

No.	Description	Mint	Used
1077	5c. Type **295**	20	40
1078	55c. Polynesian ivory fish hook, c.1450	1·50	1·00
1079	$1.10 Regimental badge	2·50	1·50
1080	$1.45 Brass wall fitting from wreck of HMS *Sirius*	3·00	2·50
1081	$1.65 Bottles from Convict Settlement's hospital	3·50	3·50
1082	$2.10 The Bounty Ring	4·25	5·00

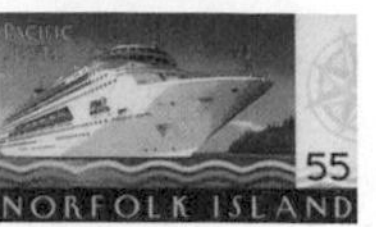

296 *Pacific Jewel*

2010. Cruise Ships to Norfolk Island. Multicoloured.

No.	Description	Mint	Used
1083	55c. Type **296**	1·75	1·00
1084	$1.45 *Pacific Sun*	2·25	1·60
1085	$1.65 *Pacific Pearl*	3·50	3·50
1086	$1.75 *Pacific Dawn*	3·75	3·75
1087	$2.10 RMS *Strathaird*	4·25	4·75

297 Pitcairn Island Girls on Norfolk Island, 1857

2010. 'They came aboard the *Morayshire*'. Multicoloured.

1088	55c. Type **297**	1·60	1·00
1089	$1.10 Pitcairn Islanders aboard the *Morayshire*, 1856	2·00	1·40
1090	$1.45 Pitcairn Island men on Norfolk Island, 1861	3·00	2·75
1091	$2.75 Naomi and Jane Nobbs	5·50	7·00

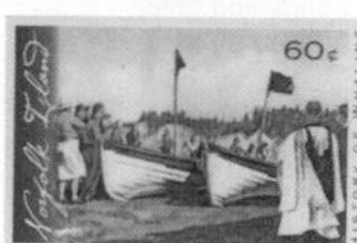

298 Blessing of the Boats

2010. History of Whaling in Norfolk Island. Multicoloured.

1092	60c. Type **298**	1·25	90
1093	60c. Launching boat from shore	1·25	90
1094	$1.20 Women on cliff tops burning fires to guide boats back to shore	2·50	1·75
1095	$3 Whale products	6·00	7·00

299 Crimson Rosella

2010. Christmas. Parrots. Multicoloured.

1096	15c. Type **299**	60	45
1097	55c. Crimson rosella and Norfolk Island green parrot	1·75	1·00
1098	60c. Norfolk Island green parrot and wrapped present	1·90	1·10
1099	$1.30 Crimson rosella with ribbon and bauble in beak	4·25	4·50

2010. 'Beijing 2010' International Stamp and Coin Expo, Beijing, China. No. **MS**1061 inscr 'INTERNATIONAL STAMP & COIN EXPO BEIJING 7th-10th NOVEMBER 2010' and BEIJING 2010 emblem on sheet margins

MS1099a	130×71 mm. Nos. 1057/60	6·50	8·50

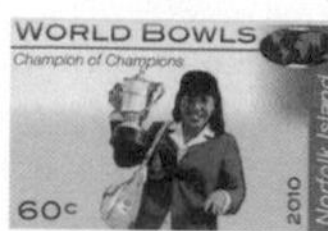

300 Bowler holding Trophy

2010. World Bowls Champion of Champions. Multicoloured.

1100	60c. Type **300**	1·75	1·00
1101	$1.50 Bowler	3·25	2·50
1102	$2.20 Bowls and jack	5·00	6·00

301 Construction of St. Barnabas Chapel, 1880

2010. 130th Anniv of St. Barnabas Chapel. Multicoloured.

MS1103	60c.×3 Type **301**; St. Barnabas Chapel and congregation; Chapel wall and builders	6·00	6·00

2011. Artefacts from Norfolk Island's Museums (2nd series). Multicoloured.

1104	15c. Iron from No. 10 Quality Row	60	45
1105	60c. Mug with personal scratch mark of Thursday October Christian	1·60	1·00
1106	$1.20 Bone dominoes from Convict Settlement	3·00	2·00
1107	$1.50 Clay pipes and ceramics from the civil Hospital	3·50	3·00
1108	$1.80 Doll fragments from privies, Quality Row	4·25	4·25
1109	$3 Wooden and shell hair items from the Melanesian Mission	7·00	9·50

302 *Cirsotrema zelebori* (zelebor wentletrap) and *Canarium labiatum* (plicate conch)

2011. Shells of Norfolk Island. Multicoloured.

1110	15c. Type **302**	60	45
1111	60c. *Janthina janthina* (violet snail) and *Spirula spirula* (ram's horn)	1·75	1·50
1112	$1.50 *Conus capitaneus* (captain cone) and *Conus ebraeus* (Hebrew cone)	3·50	3·75
1113	$1.80 *Cypraea vitellus* (Pacific dear cowrie) and *Cypraea caputserpentis* (serpent's head cowrie)	4·25	4·25
1114	$3 *Nerita atramentosa* (black nerite) and *Nerita turrita* (turreted nerite)	6·75	7·50

303 Norfolk Island Abutilon (*Abutilon julianae*)

2011. 25th Anniv of Norfolk Island National Park. Multicoloured.

1115	25c. Type **303**	70	65
1116	60c. Phillip Island hibiscus (*Hibiscus insularis*)	1·75	1·60
1117	$1.55 Popwood (*Myoporum obscurum*)	3·50	3·50
1118	$2.25 Broad-leaved meryta (*Meryta latifolia*)	5·50	6·50

304 Guard House, 1796-1826

2011. World Heritage. Kingston and Arthur's Vale Historic Area. Multicoloured.

1119	60c. Type **304**	1·40	1·50
1120	60c. The Graveyard, 1790s/1825	1·40	1·50
1121	60c. Government House, 1804/28	1·40	1·50
1122	60c. Pier Store, 1825	1·40	1·50
1123	60c. The Crank Mill, 1827	1·40	1·50
1124	60c. Bloody Bridge, 1835	1·40	1·50
1125	60c. Commissariat Store, 1835	1·40	1·50
1126	60c. Kingston Pier, 1839	1·40	1·50
1127	60c. No. 9 Quality Row, 1839	1·40	1·50
1128	60c. Flaghouses, 1840s	1·40	1·50
1129	60c. New Gaol, 1847	1·40	1·50
1130	60c. Royal Engineers Office, 1851	1·40	1·50

Nos. 1119/30 commemorate the first anniversary of the declaration of Kingston and Arthur's Vale Historical Area as a world heritage site.

305 Bounty Day, c. 1933

2011. 80th Anniv of the Norfolk Island Police Force (NIPF). Multicoloured.

1131	60c. Type **305**	2·00	1·50
1132	$1.55 Police car, 1970s	4·00	3·50
1133	$2.25 Modern policeman watching ship ('Watching the seas')	6·00	6·50

306 Protea

2011. Christmas. Flowers. Multicoloured.

1134	15c. Type **306**	55	50
1135	55c. Frangipani	1·60	1·40
1136	60c. Cordyline	1·75	1·50
1137	$1.35 Orchid	3·50	4·00

(307)

2012. No. 917 surch with T **307**

1138	$4 on 10c. Type **259**		

308 Collecting Hi Hi (Periwinkle) Shells

2012. Iconic Activities. Multicoloured.

1139	60c. Type **308**	1·40	1·40
1140	75c. Collecting whale bird eggs	1·75	1·75
1141	$1.55 Fishing off the rocks	3·50	3·50
1142	$2.75 Clifftop barbecue	6·50	6·50

309 Commemorative Plaque at Queen Elizabeth Avenue, Norfolk Island

2012. Diamond Jubilee. Multicoloured.

MS1143	$1.60×3 Type **309**; Beacon at Queen Elizabeth Lookout; Illuminated pine tree at Government House	11·00	11·00

310 Dishes from *Norfolk Island Cookery Book*

2012. 51st Anniv of the Sunshine Club (assists senior citizens and people needing offshore medical treatment). Multicoloured.

1144	60c. Type **310**	1·40	1·40
1145	$1.60 Wicker basket lined with patchwork containing fruit, sugar and flour	3·75	3·75
1146	$1.65 Ingredients, flan case and *Norfolk Island Cookery Book*	3·75	3·75
1147	$2.35 Cupped hands and sunset	5·50	5·50

311 Pearl Inlay and Lyrics from Carol 'Silent Night'

2012. Christmas. Pearl Inlays from Pews at St. Barnabas Chapel and Lyrics from Carols and Hymns. Multicoloured.

1148	15c. Type **311**	35	35
1149	55c. Three pearl inlays and lyrics from 'O Come All Ye Faithful'	1·25	1·25
1150	$1.55 Pearl inlay with square surrounded by four triangles design and hymn lyrics	3·50	3·50
1151	$2.35 Pearl inlay with geometric flower design and hymn lyrics	5·50	5·50

312 RNZAF Hudson Bomber

2012. 70th Anniv of First Aircraft Landing on Norfolk Island. Multicoloured.

1152	60c. Type **312**	1·40	1·40
1153	60c. DC-3	1·40	1·40
1154	60c. Lancastrian	1·40	1·40
1155	60c. DC-4 Skymaster	1·40	1·40
1156	60c. Fokker F27 Friendship	1·40	1·40
1157	60c. Beechcraft Super King Air 200	1·40	1·40
1158	60c. Fokker F28 Fellowship	1·40	1·40
1159	60c. C-130 Hercules	1·40	1·40
1160	60c. BAe 146	1·40	1·40
1161	60c. Boeing 737-300	1·40	1·40
1162	60c. F/A 18 Hornet	1·40	1·40
1163	60c. Airbus A320	1·40	1·40

313 Bell, All Saints Church, Kingston

2013. Church Bell, Norfolk Island

1164	**313**	$5 multicoloured	10·00	11·00

314 Boots on Sands of Emily Bay

2013. 20th Anniv (2014) of Norfolk Island Country Music Festival. Multicoloured.

1165	15c. Type **314**	35	35
1166	60c. Adam Harvey	1·40	1·40
1167	$1.60 Guitar	3·75	3·75
1168	$1.65 Dennis Marsh	3·75	3·75
1169	$2.35 Guitar player on main street of Burnt Pine	5·50	5·50

315 Ball Bay

2013. Shorelines of Norfolk Island. Multicoloured.

1170	15c. Type **315**	35	35
1171	60c. Second Sands	1·40	1·40
1172	95c. Anson Bay	2·00	2·00
1173	$1.20 Slaughter Bay	2·75	2·75
1174	$1.70 Bumboras	3·75	3·75
1175	$1.85 Emily Bay	4·00	4·00

Nos. 1176/81 are left for Part 2 of this definitive stamp issue.

316 Driftwood Wreath

2013. Christmas. Items made from Driftwood. Multicoloured.

1182	15c. Type **316**	35	35
1183	55c. Driftwood pine tree and beach	1·25	1·25
1184	$1.10 Seabird driftwood sculpture and sea	2·50	2·50
1185	$1.65 Three driftwood stars and beach	3·75	3·75

317 Joe McNaughton

2013. Trans Tasman FMX (Freestyle Motor Cross) Challenge. Multicoloured.

1186	50c. Type **317**	1·10	1·10
1187	$1 Joe McNaughton (holding back of bike)	2·25	2·25
1188	$1.50 Joe McNaughton (in air above bike)	3·50	3·50
1189	$1.60 Callum Shaw	3·75	3·75

Pt. 1

NORTH BORNEO

A territory in the north of the Island of Borneo in the China Sea, formerly under the administration of the British North Borneo Company. A Crown Colony since 1946. Joined Malaysia in 1963 and renamed Sabah in 1964.

100 cents = 1 dollar (Malayan).

1

1883. "POSTAGE NORTH BORNEO" at top.

8	1	½c. mauve	£120	£200
9	1	1c. orange	£180	£325
10	1	2c. brown	45·00	40·00

11	1	4c. pink	18·00	50·00
12	1	8c. green	21·00	50·00
13	1	10c. blue	55·00	65·00

1883. Surch **EIGHT CENTS**.

2	8c. on 2c. brown	£1300	£800
3	8c. on 2c. brown	£500	£190

Where there are three price columns, prices in the second column are for postally used stamps and those in the third column are for stamps cancelled with black bars.

4

5

1883. Inscr "NORTH BORNEO".

4	**4**	50c. violet	£200	£275
5	**5**	$1 red	£170	£250

For these designs with "BRITISH" in place of value in words at top, see Nos. 46/7.

1886. Optd **and Revenue**.

14	**1**	½c. mauve	£225	£325
15	**1**	10c. blue	£275	£350

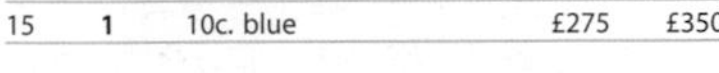

1886. Surch in words and figures

18	3c. on 4c. pink	£130	£150
19	5c. on 8c. green	£140	£150

9

10

13

19

1886. Inscr "BRITISH NORTH BORNEO"

22	**9**	½c. red	4·00	19·00
24	**9**	1c. orange	2·00	16·00
25	**9**	2c. brown	2·00	14·00
26	**9**	4c. pink	5·00	19·00
27	**9**	8c. green	28·00	28·00
28	**9**	10c. blue	14·00	45·00
45	**10**	25c. blue	£100	£100
46	-	50c. violet	£120	£140
47	-	$1 red	60·00	£110
48	**13**	$2 green	£225	£225
49	**19**	$5 purple	£350	£375
50	-	$10 brown	£350	£400

DESIGNS: 50c. As Type **4**; $1, As Type **5**. $10 As Type **19** but with different frame.

14

1888. Inscr "POSTAGE & REVENUE".

36*b*	**14**	½c. red	1·50	8·50
37	**14**	1c. orange	6·50	7·00
38*b*	**14**	2c. brown	7·50	25·00
39	**14**	3c. violet	2·50	13·00
40	**14**	4c. pink	13·00	50·00
41	**14**	5c. grey	2·75	30·00
42	**14**	6c. red	18·00	32·00
43*a*	**14**	8c. green	28·00	38·00
44*b*	**14**	10c. blue	6·50	22·00

1890. Surch in words.

51	**10**	2c. on 25c. blue	80·00	90·00
52	**10**	8c. on 25c. blue	£120	£130

1891. Surch in figures and words.

63	**14**	1c. on 4c. pink	27·00	14·00
64	**14**	1c. on 5c. grey	7·00	6·00
54	**9**	6c. on 8c. green	£9000	£5000
55	**14**	6c. on 8c. green	29·00	10·00
56	**9**	6c. on 10c. blue	60·00	22·00
57	**14**	6c. on 10c. blue	£200	26·00
65	**10**	8c. on 25c. blue	£180	£190

24 Dyak Chief

25 Sambar Stag ("Cervus unicolor")

26 Sago Palm

27 Great Argus Pheasant

28 Arms of the Company

29 Malay Prau

30 Estuarine Crocodile

31 Mt. Kinabalu

32 Arms of the Company with Supporters

1894

66	**24**	1c. black and bistre	1·25	9·50
69	**25**	2c. black and red	5·50	3·50
70	**26**	3c. green and mauve	2·75	8·50
72	**27**	5c. black and red	14·00	11·00
73a	**28**	6c. black and brown	4·50	18·00
74	**29**	8c. black and lilac	6·50	11·00
75a	**30**	12c. black and blue	29·00	80·00
78	**31**	18c. black and green	28·00	50·00
79c	**32**	24c. blue and red	23·00	70·00

1894. As Nos. 47, etc, but inscr "THE STATE OF NORTH BORNEO".

81	25c. blue	9·50	30·00
82	50c. violet	50·00	65·00
83	$1 red	12·00	30·00
84	$2 green	26·00	75·00
85	$5 purple	£275	£325
86	$10 brown	£325	£375

1895. No. 83 surch in figures and words.

87	4c. on $1 red	7·00	1·50
88	10c. on $1 red	27·00	1·75
89	20c. on $1 red	50·00	17·00
90	30c. on $1 red	45·00	38·00
91	40c. on $1 red	60·00	65·00

37 Orang-utan

41 Sun Bear

43 Borneo Steam Train

1897. As 1894 issue with insertion of native inscriptions.

92a	**24**	1c. black and bistre	11·00	2·75
94a	**25**	2c. black and red	25·00	1·50
95	**25**	2c. black and green	70·00	2·00
97	**26**	3c. green and mauve	32·00	3·00
98	**37**	4c. black and green	13·00	—
99	**37**	4c. black and red	40·00	12·00
100a	**27**	5c. black & orange	£120	2·00
101a	**28**	6c. black and brown	55·00	4·25
103	**29**	8c. black and brown	16·00	45·00
104	**41**	10c. brown and grey	£150	55·00
106b	**30**	12c. black and blue	£150	35·00
107	**43**	16c. green & brown	£140	90·00
108	**31**	18c. black and green	35·00	75·00
110b	**31**	18c. black & green*	£130	12·00
109	**32**	24c. blue and red*	35·00	90·00
111b	**32**	24c. blue and red*	55·00	55·00

*No. 110b is inscribed "POSTAGE & REVENUE" at the sides instead of "POSTAL REVENUE" as in No. 108. No. 111b has the words "POSTAGE & REVENUE" at the sides below the Arms; these words were omitted in No. 109.

1899. Stamps of 1897 and Nos. 81/6 surch **4 CENTS**.

112a	4c. on 5c. black and orange	48·00	10·00
113	4c. on 6c. black and brown	19·00	24·00
114	4c. on 8c. black and lilac	17·00	10·00
115	4c. on 12c. black and blue	40·00	13·00
116	4c. on 18c. black and green (110)	20·00	14·00
117	4c. on 24c. blue and red (111)	42·00	21·00
118	4c. on 25c. blue	5·50	8·50
119	4c. on 50c. violet	25·00	16·00
121	4c. on $1 red	5·50	12·00
122	4c. on $2 green	5·50	13·00
125	4c. on $5 on $5 purple	7·50	16·00
126	4c. on $10 on $10 brown	7·50	16·00

1901. Stamps of 1897 and Nos. 81/6 optd **BRITISH PROTECTORATE**.

127a	1c. black and bistre	2·50	1·75
128	2c. black and green	8·00	1·00
129	3c. green and mauve	1·75	5·50
130	4c. black and red	9·00	1·00
131a	5c. black and orange	14·00	3·25
132b	6c. black and brown	4·00	15·00
133	8c. black and lilac	4·50	3·75
134	10c. brown and grey	95·00	5·00
135	12c. black and blue	65·00	12·00
136	16c. green and brown	£200	38·00
137	18c. black & green (110b)	17·00	26·00
138	24c. blue and red (111b)	16·00	40·00
139	25c. blue	2·00	10·00
140	50c. violet	2·75	11·00
142	$1 red	6·50	38·00
143	$2 green	45·00	£100
144	$5 purple (with full point)	£425	£550
184	$5 purple (without full point)	£1800	£2000
145	$10 brown (with full point)	£700	£1000
185	$10 brown (without full point)	£2000	—

1904. Stamps of 1897 and Nos. 81/6 surch **4 cents**.

146	4c. on 5c. blk & orge	50·00	55·00
147	4c. on 6c. black & brn	7·00	21·00
148	4c. on 8c. blk & lilac	19·00	26·00
149	4c. on 12c. black & bl	50·00	40·00
150	4c. on 18c. black and green (110b)	14·00	38·00
151a	4c. on 24c. blue and red (111b)	23·00	50·00
152	4c. on 25c. blue	5·50	25·00
153	4c. on 50c. violet	6·00	38·00
154	4c. on $1 red	6·00	48·00
155	4c. on $2 green	6·00	48·00
156	4c. on $5 purple	13·00	48·00
157	4c. on $10 brown	12·00	48·00

1909. No. 177 is surch **20 CENTS**

277	**51**	1c. black and brown	1·00	70
160	**52**	2c. black and green	1·00	70
278	**52**	2c. black and red	85	60
162	-	3c. black and red	4·00	2·75
279	-	3c. black and green	3·00	75
280	-	4c. black and red	50	10
281	-	5c. black and brown	6·50	2·75
282	-	6c. black and green	15·00	90
283	-	8c. black and red	7·50	50
284	-	10c. black and blue	4·25	90
285	-	12c. black and blue	30·00	80
174	-	16c. black and brown	26·00	5·50
175	-	18c. black and green	£160	32·00
177	-	20c. on 18c. blk & grn	7·00	1·00
176	-	24c. black and mauve	28·00	3·00
289	**64**	25c. black and green	22·00	4·25
179	-	50c. black and blue	22·00	6·00
180	-	$1 black and brown	20·00	4·00
181	-	$2 black and lilac	85·00	17·00
182	-	$5 black and red	£190	£140
183	-	$10 black and orange	£700	£750

DESIGNS—As T **51**: 3c. Jesselton railway station; 4c. Sultan of Sulu, his staff and W. C. Cowie, first Chairman of the Company; 5c. Asiatic elephant; 8c. Ploughing with buffalo; 24c. Dwarf cassowary. As T **52**: 6c. Sumatran rhinoceros; 10c. Wild boar; 12c. Palm cockatoo; 16 c Rhinoceros hornbill; 18 c Banteng. As T **64** but Arms with supporters: $5, $10.

1916. Stamps of 1909 surch.

186	2c. on 3c. black and red	30·00	15·00
187	4c. on 6c. black and olive	32·00	24·00
188	10c. on 12c. black and blue	60·00	70·00

(68)

1916. Nos. 277 etc, optd with T **68**.

189	1c. black and brown	8·50	35·00
203	2c. black and green	28·00	50·00
191	3c. black and red	27·00	50·00
192	4c. black and red	5·50	32·00
193	5c. black and brown	55·00	55·00
206	6c. black and green	65·00	80·00
207	8c. black and red	29·00	55·00
196	10c. black and blue	60·00	70·00
197	12c. black and blue	£110	£110
198	16c. black and brown	£120	£120
199	20c. on 18c. black and green	65·00	£110
200	24c. black and mauve	£140	£140
201	25c. black and green	£375	£475

1918. Nos. 159, etc, surch **RED CROSS TWO CENTS**.

214	1c. +2c. black and brown	3·50	16·00
215	2c. +2c. black and green	1·00	8·50
216	3c. +2c. black and red	14·00	19·00
218	4c. +2c. black and red	70	5·00
219	5c. +2c. black and brown	8·00	35·00
221	6c. +2c. black and olive	5·00	35·00
222	8c. +2c. black and red	5·50	11·00
223	10c. +2c. black and blue	8·00	30·00
224	12c. +2c. black and blue	21·00	55·00
225	16c. +2c. black and brown	22·00	45·00
226	24c. +2c. black and mauve	22·00	45·00
229	25c. +2c. black and green	10·00	45·00
230	50c. +2c. black and blue	12·00	45·00
231	$1 +2c. black and brown	50·00	55·00
232	$2 +2c. black and lilac	75·00	95·00
233	$5 +2c. black and red	£500	£800
234	$10 +2c. black and orange	£600	£850

The premium of 2c. on each value was for Red Cross Funds.

1918. Nos. 159, etc. surch **FOUR CENTS** and a red cross.

235	1c. +4c. black and brown	60	5·00
236	2c. +4c. black and green	65	8·00
237	3c. +4c. black and red	1·00	3·75
238	4c. +4c. black and red	40	4·75
239	5c. +4c. black and brown	2·00	25·00
240	6c. +4c. black and olive	1·90	12·00
241	8c. +4c. black and red	1·25	9·50
242	10c. +4c. black and blue	3·75	12·00
243	12c. +4c. black and blue	14·00	14·00
244	16c. +4c. black and brown	8·00	16·00
245	24c. +4c. black and mauve	11·00	20·00
246	25c. +4c. black and green	12·00	50·00
248	50c. +4c. black and blue	15·00	45·00
249	$1 +4c. black and brown	26·00	60·00
250	$2 +4c. black and lilac	55·00	80·00
251	$5 +4c. black and red	£300	£400
252	$10 +4c. black and orange	£400	£475

The premium of 4c. on each value was for Red Cross Funds.

1922. Nos. 159, etc, optd **MALAYA-BORNEO EXHIBITION 1922**.

253	1c. black and brown	24·00	90·00
255	2c. black and green	3·75	29·00
256	3c. black and red	16·00	65·00
257	4c. black and red	3·75	50·00
258	5c. black and brown	10·00	70·00
260	6c. black and green	10·00	70·00
261	8c. black and red	9·50	50·00
263	10c. black and blue	21·00	70·00
265	12c. black and blue	13·00	21·00
267	16c. black and brown	29·00	75·00
268	20c. on 18c. black and green	29·00	95·00
270	24c. black and mauve	55·00	80·00
274	25c. black and green	14·00	75·00
275	50c. black and blue	19·00	75·00

1923. No. 280 surch **THREE CENTS** and bars.

276	3c. on 4c. black and red	4·50	6·00

73 Head of a Murut

76 Mount Kinabalu

1931. 50th Anniv of North Borneo Company.

295	**73**	3c. black and green	1·50	80
296	-	6c. black and orange	20·00	3·50
297	-	10c. black and red	5·50	13·00
298	**76**	12c. black and blue	5·50	8·00
299	-	25c. black and violet	48·00	35·00
300	-	$1 black and green	27·00	£110
301	-	$2 black and brown	48·00	£110
302	-	$5 black and purple	£180	£700

DESIGNS—VERT: 6c. Orang-utan; 10c. Dyak warrior; $1, $2, $5 Arms. HORIZ: 25c. Clouded leopard.

81 Buffalo Transport

82 Palm Cockatoo

1939

303	**81**	1c. green and brown	4·75	2·50
304	**82**	2c. purple and blue	5·00	3·25
305	-	3c. blue and green	6·00	3·50

306	-	4c. green and violet	17·00	1·00
307	-	6c. blue and red	13·00	17·00
308	-	8c. red	23·00	2·25
309	-	10c. violet and green	42·00	9·00
310	-	12c. green and blue	50·00	9·50
311	-	15c. green and brown	35·00	16·00
312	-	20c. violet and blue	27·00	9·00
313	-	25c. green and brown	42·00	18·00
314	-	50c. brown and violet	45·00	17·00
315	-	$1 brown and red	£140	23·00
316	-	$2 violet and olive	£275	£180
317	-	$5 indigo and blue	£800	£425

DESIGNS—VERT: 3c. Native; 4c. Proboscis monkey; 6c. Mounted Bajaus; 10c. Orang-utan; 15c. Dyak; $1, $2 Arms. HORIZ: 8c. Map of Eastern Archipelago; 12c. Murut with blow-pipe; 20c. River scene; 25c. Native boat; 50c. Mt. Kinabalu; $5 Arms with supporters.

1941. Optd **WAR TAX**.

318	**81**	1c. green and brown	2·75	5·50
319	**82**	2c. purple and blue	11·00	6·00

1945. British Military Administration. Stamps of 1939 optd **BMA**.

320	**81**	1c. green and brown	22·00	3·00
321	**82**	2c. purple and blue	14·00	2·00
322	-	3c. blue and green	1·25	1·25
323	-	4c. green and violet	25·00	16·00
324	-	6c. blue and red	1·25	1·25
325	-	8c. red	3·00	75
326	-	10c. violet and green	3·00	40
327	-	12c. green and blue	6·00	5·00
328	-	15c. green and brown	3·50	1·00
329	-	20c. violet and blue	8·50	3·25
330	-	25c. green and brown	7·50	2·00
331	-	50c. brown and violet	7·50	3·25
332	-	$1 brown and red	65·00	40·00
333	-	$2 violet and olive	70·00	50·00
334	-	$5 indigo and blue	38·00	21·00

1947. Stamps of 1939 optd with Crown over GR monogram and bars obliterating "THE STATE OF" and "BRITISH PROTECTORATE".

335	**81**	1c. green and brown	30	1·00
336	**82**	2c. purple and blue	2·25	1·00
337	-	3c. blue and green	30	1·00
338	-	4c. green and violet	1·00	1·00
339	-	6c. blue and red	40	20
340	-	8c. red	1·00	20
341	-	10c. violet and green	1·50	40
342	-	12c. green and blue	5·50	2·75
343	-	15c. green and brown	2·25	30
344	-	20c. violet and blue	4·75	85
345	-	25c. green and brown	3·00	50
346	-	50c. brown and violet	4·25	85
347	-	$1 brown and red	17·00	1·75
348	-	$2 violet and olive	22·00	18·00
349	-	$5 indigo and blue	38·00	32·00

1948. Silver Wedding. As T **4b/4c** of Pitcairn Islands.

350	8c. red	30	80
351	$10 mauve	32·00	38·00

1949. U.P.U. As T **4d/4g** of Pitcairn Islands.

352	8c. red	60	30
353	10c. brown	3·25	1·75
354	30c. brown	1·25	1·75
355	55c. blue	1·25	2·75

100 Mt. Kinabalu

102 Coconut Grove

1950

356	**100**	1c. brown	15	1·25
357	-	2c. blue	15	50
358	**102**	3c. green	30	15
359	-	4c. purple	1·00	10
360	-	5c. violet	1·00	10
361	-	8c. red	2·75	85
362	-	10c. purple	2·25	15
363	-	15c. blue	2·25	65
364	-	20c. brown	3·25	10
365	-	30c. buff	5·50	30
366	-	50c. red ("JESSLETON")	2·75	6·00
366a	-	50c. red ("JESSELTON")	17·00	3·25
367	-	$1 orange	8·00	1·75
368	-	$2 green	16·00	23·00
369	-	$5 green	27·00	35·00
370	-	$10 blue	70·00	95·00

DESIGNS—VERT: 4c. Hemp drying; 5c. Cattle at Kota Belud; 30c. Suluk river canoe; 50c. Clock tower, Jesselton; $1 Bajau horsemen. HORIZ: 2c. Musician; 8c. Map; 10c. Log pond; 15c. Malay prau, Sandakan; 20c. Bajau chief; $2 Murut with blowpipe; $5 Net fishing; $10, King George VI and arms.

1953. Coronation. As T **4h** of Pitcairn Islands.

371	10c. black and red	2·50	1·00

1954. As 1950 but with portrait of Queen Elizabeth II.

372	1c. brown	10	30
373	2c. blue	1·25	15
374	3c. green	4·00	2·00
375	4c. purple	1·75	20
376	5c. violet	1·00	10
377	8c. red	1·25	30
378	10c. purple	30	10
379	15c. blue	1·00	10
380	20c. brown	50	15
381	30c. buff	3·25	20
382	50c. red (No. 366a)	6·00	20
383	$1 orange	6·50	20
384	$2 green	17·00	1·25
385	$5 green	12·00	35·00
386	$10 blue	30·00	40·00

117 Malay Prau

1956. 75th Anniv of Foundation of British North Borneo Co. Inscr "CHARTER 1ST NOVEMBER 1881".

387	-	10c. black and red	1·25	40
388	**117**	15c. black and brown	1·00	30
389	-	35c. black and green	1·00	1·50
390	-	$1 black and slate	1·00	2·50

DESIGNS—HORIZ: 10c. Borneo Railway, 1902; 35c. Mt. Kinabalu. VERT: $1 Arms of Chartered Company.

120 Sambar Stag

1961

391	**120**	1c. green and red	20	10
392	-	4c. olive and orange	1·00	90
393	-	5c. sepia and violet	30	10
394	-	6c. black and turquoise	75	40
395	-	10c. green and red	1·25	10
396	-	12c. brown and myrtle	50	10
397	-	20c. turquoise and blue	4·00	10
398	-	25c. black and red	1·50	1·50
399	-	30c. sepia and olive	1·75	20
400	-	35c. slate and brown	2·75	2·50
401	-	50c. green and bistre	2·25	20
402	-	75c. blue and purple	18·00	90
403	-	$1 brown and green	18·00	1·75
404	-	$2 brown and slate	35·00	4·00
405	-	$5 green and purple	38·00	23·00
406	-	$10 red and blue	55·00	50·00

DESIGNS—HORIZ: 4c. Sun bear; 5c. Clouded leopard; 6c. Dusun woman with gong; 10c. Map of Borneo; 12c. Banteng; 20c. Butterfly orchid; 25c. Sumatran rhinoceros; 30c. Murut with blow-pipe; 35c. Mt. Kinabalu; 50c. Dusun and buffalo transport; 75c. Bajau horseman. VERT: $1 Orang-utan; $2 Rhinoceros hornbill; $5 Crested wood partridge; $10 Arms of N. Borneo.

1963. Freedom from Hunger. As T **20a** of Pitcairn Islands.

407	12c. blue	1·75	75

POSTAGE DUE STAMPS

Overprinted POSTAGE DUE.

1895. Issue of 1894.

D2	**25**	2c. black and red	27·00	24·00
D3	**26**	3c. green & mve	6·00	16·00
D5	**27**	5c. black and red	70·00	32·00
D6a	**28**	6c. black & brn	25·00	50·00
D7	**29**	8c. black and lilac	60·00	50·00
D8b	**30**	12c. black & blue	70·00	50·00
D10	**31**	18c. black & grn	70·00	60·00
D11b	**32**	24c. blue and red	32·00	55·00

1897. Issue of 1897.

D12	**25**	2c. black and red	11·00	9·00
D13	**25**	2c. black & green	£100	†
D14	**26**	3c. green & mve	42·00	†
D16a	**26**	4c. black and red	90·00	†
D17a	**27**	5c. black & orge	27·00	55·00
D18	**28**	6c. black & brn	9·00	45·00
D20	**29**	8c. black & lilac	12·00	†
D21a	**30**	12c. black & blue	£170	†
D22	**31**	18c. black and green (No. 108)	†	†
D23	**31**	18c. black and green (No. 110b)	£100	†
D24	**32**	24c. blue and red (No. 109)		†
D25	**32**	24c. blue and red (No. 111b)	70·00	†

1902. Issue of 1901.

D37	1c. black and bistre		†
D38	2c. black and green	35·00	4·50
D39	3c. green and mauve	9·00	4·25
D40	4c. black and red	28·00	7·00
D41	5c. black and orange	55·00	5·50
D42	6c. black and brown	26·00	11·00
D43	8c. black and lilac	32·00	5·00
D45	10c. brown and grey	£140	25·00
D46	12c. black and blue	50·00	24·00
D47	16c. green & brown	£100	32·00
D48	18c. black and green	21·00	24·00
D49	24c. blue and red	22·00	40·00

1919. Issue of 1909.

D52	2c. black and green	12·00	75·00
D66	2c. black and red	1·50	2·00
D77	3c. black and green	14·00	42·00
D55	4c. black and red	1·00	1·25
D57	5c. black and brown	10·00	35·00
D80	6c. black and olive	8·50	2·50
D62	8c. black and red	1·50	1·50
D63	10c. black and blue	19·00	19·00
D64	12c. black and blue	80·00	55·00
D65a	16c. black and brown	29·00	55·00

POSTAGE DUE

D2 Crest of the Company

1939

D85	**D2**	2c. brown	7·00	80·00
D86	**D2**	4c. red	9·50	£110
D87	**D2**	6c. violet	35·00	£160
D88	**D2**	8c. green	42·00	£300
D89	**D2**	10c. blue	80·00	£475

For later issues see **SABAH**.

JAPANESE OCCUPATION

1942. Stamps of North Borneo optd as T **1** of Japanese Occupation of Brunei

(a) Issue of 1939

J1	**81**	1c. green and brown	£180	£250
J2	**82**	2c. purple and blue	£200	£275
J3	-	3c. blue and green	£170	£300
J4a	-	4c. green and violet	65·00	£140
J5	-	6c. blue and red	£190	£350
J6	-	8c. red	£250	£190
J7	-	10c. violet and green	£225	£350
J8	-	12c. green and blue	£250	£500
J9	-	15c. green and brown	£225	£500
J10	-	20c. violet and blue	£300	£650
J11	-	25c. green and brown	£275	£650
J12	-	50c. brown and violet	£350	£700
J13	-	$1 brown and red	£425	£900
J14	-	$2 violet and olive	£600	£1100
J15	-	$5 blue	£700	£1200

(b) War Tax Issue of 1941.

J16	**81**	1c. green and brown	£700	£325
J17	**82**	2c. purple and blue	£2000	£650

2 Mt. Kinabalu

3 Borneo Scene

1943

J18	**2**	4c. red	32·00	60·00
J19	**3**	8c. blue	28·00	55·00

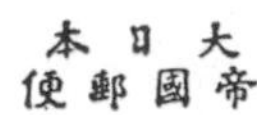

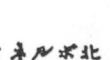

(4) ("Imperial Japanese Postal Service, North Borneo")

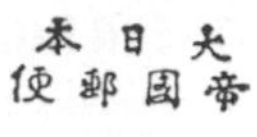

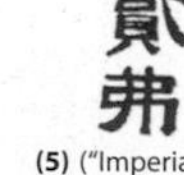

(5) ("Imperial Japanese Postal Service, North Borneo")

1944. Optd with T **4**

(a) On stamps of North Borneo

J20	**81**	1c. green and brown	8·00	12·00
J21	**82**	2c. purple and blue	8·00	9·00
J22	-	3c. blue and green	8·00	10·00
J23	-	4c. green and violet	16·00	25·00
J24	-	6c. blue and red	11·00	6·50
J25	-	8c. red	10·00	17·00
J26	-	10c. violet and green	8·50	13·00
J27	-	12c. green and blue	17·00	13·00
J28	-	15c. green and brown	17·00	16·00
J29	-	20c. violet and blue	38·00	50·00
J30	-	25c. green and brown	38·00	50·00
J31	-	50c. brown and violet	80·00	£120
J32	-	$1 brown and red	95·00	£150

(b) On stamps of Japanese Occupation of North Borneo.

J21a	2c. purple and blue (J2)	£450	
J22a	3c. blue and green (J3)	£450	
J25a	8c. red (J6)	£450	
J26b	10c. violet and green (J7)	£250	£475
J27a	12c. green and blue (J8)	£450	
J28a	15c. green and brown (J9)	£450	

1944. No. J1 surch with T **5**.

J33	**81**	$2 on 1c. green and brown	£6000	£4750

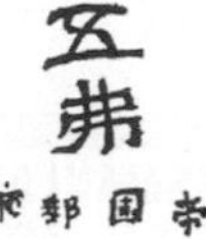

(6)

1944. No. 315 of North Borneo surch with T **6**.

J34	$5 on $1 brown and red	£5000	£3750

1944. Stamps of Japan optd as bottom line in T **4**.

J35	**126**	1s. brown	9·00	38·00
J36	**84**	2s. red	7·50	29·00
J37	-	3s. green (No. 319)	9·00	38·00
J38	**129**	4s. green	18·00	27·00
J39	-	5s. red (No. 396)	15·00	32·00
J40	-	6s. orange (No. 322)	24·00	35·00
J41	-	8s. violet (No. 324)	6·50	35·00
J42	-	10s. red (No. 399)	15·00	35·00
J43	-	15s. blue (No. 401)	14·00	35·00
J44	-	20s. blue (No. 328)	85·00	90·00
J45	-	25s. brown (No. 329)	65·00	90·00
J46	-	30s. blue (No. 330)	£180	95·00
J47	-	50s. olive and brown (No. 331)	80·00	85·00
J48	-	1y. brown (No. 332)	85·00	£110

POSTAGE DUE

便郵國帝本日大

(1)

1942. Nos. D85/6 and D88 of North Borneo handstamped with **T1** in black

JD1	2c. brown	—	£5000
JD2	4c. scarlet	—	£5000
JD3	8c. green	—	£5000

Pt. 7

NORTH GERMAN CONFEDERATION

The North German Confederation was set up on 1 January 1868, and comprised the postal services of Bremen, Brunswick, Hamburg Lubeck, Mecklenburg (both), Oldenburg, Prussia (including Hanover, Schleswig-Holstein with Bergedorf and Thurn and Taxis) and Saxony.

The North German Confederation joined the German Reichspost on 4 May 1871, and the stamps of Germany were brought into use on 1 January 1872.

Northern District: 30 groschen = 1 thaler.
Southern District: 60 kreuzer = 1 gulden.

1

1868. Roul or perf. (a) Northern District.

19	1	¼g. mauve	20·00	23·00
22	1	⅓g. green	7·25	4·00
23	1	½g. orange	7·25	5·25
25	1	1g. red	5·50	2·30
27	1	2g. blue	10·00	3·00
29	1	5g. bistre	12·50	15·00

(b) Southern District.

30	1k. green	18·00	15·00
13	2k. orange	80·00	80·00
33	3k. red	10·00	4·75
36	7k. blue	16·00	18·00
18	18k. bistre	50·00	95·00

The 1k. to 18k. have the figures in an oval.

3

1869. Perf.

38	3	10g. grey	£450	95·00
39	-	30g. blue	£325	£200

The frame of the 30g. is rectangular.

OFFICIAL STAMPS

O5

1870. (a) Northern District.

O40	**O 5**	¼g. black and brown	39·00	65·00
O41	**O 5**	⅓g. black and brown	13·50	29·00
O42	**O 5**	½g. black and brown	4·00	5·75
O43	**O 5**	1g. black and brown	4·00	3·00
O44	**O 5**	2g. black and brown	10·00	7·00

(b) Southern District.

O45	1k. black and grey	45·00	£375
O46	2k. black and grey	£110	£1300
O47	3k. black and grey	33·00	70·00
O48	7k. black and grey	60·00	£400

Pt. 10

NORTH INGERMANLAND

Stamps issued during temporary independence of this Russian territory, which adjoins Finland.

100 pennia = 1 mark.

1 18th-century Arms of Ingermanland

1920

1	**1**	5p. green	3·75	6·25
2	**1**	10p. red	3·75	6·25
3	**1**	25p. brown	3·75	6·25
4	**1**	50p. blue	3·75	6·25
5	**1**	1m. black and red	55·00	90·00
6	**1**	5m. black and purple	£225	£250
7	**1**	10m. black and brown	£500	£450

4 Gathering Crops

1920. Inscr as in T **4**.

8	-	10p. blue and green	6·25	15·00
9	-	30p. green and brown	6·25	15·00
10	-	50p. brown and blue	6·25	15·00
11	-	80p. grey and red	6·25	15·00
12	**4**	1m. grey and red	38·00	65·00
13	-	5m. red and violet	15·00	31·00
14	-	10m. violet and brown	15·00	31·00

DESIGNS—VERT: 10p. Arms; 30p. Reaper; 50p. Ploughing; 80p. Milking. HORIZ: 5m. Burning church; 10m. Zither players.

Pt. 10

NORTH WEST RUSSIA

Issues made for use by the various Anti-Bolshevist Armies during the Russian Civil War, 1918-20.

100 kopeks = 1 rouble.

NORTHERN ARMY

1 "OKCA" = Osobiy Korpus Severnoy Armiy—(trans "Special Corps, Northern Army")

1919. As T **1** inscr "OKCA".

1	**1**	5k. purple	25	50
2	**1**	10k. blue	25	50
3	**1**	15k. yellow	25	50
4	**1**	20k. red	25	50
5	**1**	50k. green	25	50

NORTH-WESTERN ARMY

Сѣв. Зап.
Армія

(2)

1919. Arms types of Russia optd as T **2**. Imperf or perf.

6	**22**	2k. green	6·50	13·00
16	**22**	3k. red	6·50	13·00
7	**22**	5k. lilac	6·50	13·00
8	**23**	10k. blue	13·00	20·00
9	**10**	15k. blue and brown	9·75	13·00
10	**14**	20k. red and blue	13·00	20·00
11	**10**	20k. on 14k. red and blue	£450	
12	**10**	25k. violet and green	9·75	13·00
13	**14**	50k. green and purple	16·00	23·00
14	**15**	1r. orange & brown on brn	33·00	46·00
17	**11**	3r.50 green and red	65·00	80·00
18	**22**	5r. blue on green	55·00	65·00
19	**11**	7r. pink and green	£200	£250
15	**20**	10r. grey and red on yellow	£130	£160

1919. No. 7 surch.

20	**22**	10k. on 5k. lilac	9·75	13·00

WESTERN ARMY

1919. Stamps of Latvia optd with Cross of Lorraine in circle with plain background. Imperf. (a) Postage stamps.

21	**1**	3k. lilac	65·00	85·00
22	**1**	5k. red	65·00	85·00
23	**1**	10k. blue	£225	£400
24	**1**	20k. orange	65·00	85·00
25	**1**	25k. grey	65·00	85·00
26	**1**	35k. brown	65·00	85·00
27	**1**	50k. violet	65·00	85·00
28	**1**	75k. green	65·00	£130

(b) Liberation of Riga issue.

29	**4**	5k. red	65·00	85·00
30	**4**	15k. green	33·00	65·00
31	**4**	35k. brown	33·00	70·00

1919. Stamps of Latvia optd with Cross of Lorraine in circle with burele background and characters 3. A (= "Z. A."). Imperf. (a) Postage stamps.

32	**1**	3k. lilac	9·75	16·00
33	**1**	5k. red	9·75	16·00
34	**1**	10k. blue	£200	£325
35	**1**	20k. orange	20·00	33·00
36	**1**	25k. grey	46·00	£100
37	**1**	35k. brown	33·00	46·00
38	**1**	50k. violet	33·00	46·00
39	**1**	75k. green	33·00	46·00

(b) Liberation of Riga issue.

40	**4**	5k. red	6·50	13·00
41	**4**	15k. green	6·50	13·00
42	**4**	35k. brown	6·50	13·00

1919. Arms type of Russia surch with Cross of Lorraine in ornamental frame and LP with value in curved frame. Imperf or perf.

43	**22**	10k. on 2k. green	9·75	13·00
44	**23**	30k. on 4k. red	13·00	16·00
45	**22**	40k. on 5k. lilac	9·75	13·00
46	**23**	50k. on 10k. blue	9·75	13·00
47	**10**	70k. on 15k. blue and brown	9·75	13·00
48	**14**	90k. on 20k. red and blue	20·00	26·00
49	**10**	1r. on 25k. violet and green	9·75	13·00
50	**10**	1r.50 on 35k. green & brown	85·00	£100
51	**14**	2r. on 50k. green and purple	20·00	26·00
52	**10**	4r. on 70k. red and brown	33·00	46·00
53	**15**	6r. on 1r. orange, brown on brown	46·00	65·00
54	**22**	20k. on 3k. red	13·00	13·00
56	**11**	10r. on 3r.50 green & pur	£130	£130

Pt. 1

NORTHERN NIGERIA

A British protectorate on the west coast of Africa. In 1914 incorporated into Nigeria.

12 pence = 1 shilling; 20 shillings = 1 pound.

1

1900

1	**1**	½d. mauve and green	7·50	20·00
2	**1**	1d. mauve and red	4·50	5·00
3	**1**	2d. mauve and yellow	16·00	60·00
4	**1**	2½d. mauve and blue	13·00	42·00
5	**1**	5d. mauve and brown	29·00	70·00
6	**1**	6d. mauve and violet	29·00	50·00
7	**1**	1s. green and black	29·00	85·00
8	**1**	2s.6d. green and blue	£180	£550
9	**1**	10s. green and brown	£325	£900

1902. As T **1**, but portrait of King Edward VII.

10	½d. purple and green	2·00	1·00
11	1d. purple and red	4·25	75
12	2d. purple and yellow	2·00	3·00
13	2½d. purple and blue	1·75	10·00
14	5d. purple and brown	7·00	7·00
15	6d. purple and violet	17·00	6·50
16	1s. green and black	7·00	7·00
17	2s.6d. green and blue	17·00	75·00
18	10s. green and brown	50·00	55·00

1910. As last. New colours etc.

28	½d. green	2·00	1·25
29	1d. red	4·50	1·25
30	2d. grey	8·50	4·00
31	2½d. blue	2·75	8·00
32	3d. purple on yellow	3·75	75
34	5d. purple and green	6·00	15·00
35a	6d. purple	5·00	6·00
36	1s. black and green	3·50	75
37	2s.6d. black and red on blue	16·00	42·00
38	5s. green and red on yellow	28·00	75·00
39	10s. green and red on green	55·00	48·00

5

1912

40	**5**	½d. green	4·00	60
41	**5**	1d. red	4·00	60
42	**5**	2d. grey	6·00	14·00
43	**5**	3d. purple on yellow	2·25	1·25
44	**5**	4d. black and red on yellow	1·25	2·25
45	**5**	5d. purple and olive	4·00	17·00
46	**5**	6d. purple and violet	4·00	4·25
47	**5**	9d. purple and red	2·00	12·00
48	**5**	1s. black on green	4·50	2·25
49	**5**	2s.6d. black and red on blue	8·00	55·00
50	**5**	5s. green and red on yellow	24·00	85·00
51	**5**	10s. green and red on green	42·00	48·00
52	**5**	£1 purple and black on red	£180	£110

Pt. 1

NORTHERN RHODESIA

A British territory in central Africa, north of the Zambesi. From 1954 to 1963 part of the central African Federation and using the stamps of Rhodesia and Nyasaland (q.v.). A new constitution was introduced on 3 January 1964, with internal self-government and independence came on 24 October 1964 when the country was renamed Zambia (q.v.).

12 pence = 1 shilling; 20 shillings = 1 pound.

1

1925. The shilling values are larger and the view is in first colour.

1	**1**	½d. green	1·75	80
2	**1**	1d. brown	1·75	10
3	**1**	1½d. red	4·25	30
4	**1**	2d. orange	4·50	10
5	**1**	3d. blue	4·50	1·25
6	**1**	4d. violet	7·50	50
7	**1**	6d. grey	8·00	40
8	**1**	8d. purple	8·00	55·00
9	**1**	10d. olive	8·00	50·00
10	**1**	1s. orange and black	4·25	1·75
11	**1**	2s. brown and blue	27·00	40·00
12	**1**	2s.6d. black and green	24·00	15·00
13	**1**	3s. violet and blue	40·00	25·00
14	**1**	5s. grey and violet	50·00	19·00
15	**1**	7s.6d. purple and black	£160	£275
16	**1**	10s. green and black	£100	95·00
17	**1**	20s. red and purple	£275	£325

1935. Silver Jubilee. As T **143a** of Newfoundland.

18	1d. blue and olive	1·50	1·50
19	2d. green and blue	3·00	2·75
20	3d. brown and blue	4·00	11·00
21	6d. grey and purple	10·00	1·75

1937. Coronation. As T **143b** of Newfoundland.

22	1½d. red	30	50
23	2d. brown	40	1·00
24	3d. blue	60	1·25

1938. As 1925, but with portrait of King George VI facing right and "POSTAGE & REVENUE" omitted.

25	½d. green	10	10
26	½d. brown	2·25	1·50
27	1d. brown	20	20
28	1d. green	1·50	2·25
29	1½d. red	50·00	75
30	1½d. orange	75	10
31	2d. orange	50·00	1·75
32	2d. red	1·75	50
33	2d. purple	60	1·50
34	3d. blue	70	30
35	3d. red	60	3·00
36	4d. violet	40	40
37	4½d. blue	3·25	12·00
38	6d. grey	40	10
39	9d. violet	3·25	12·00
40	1s. orange and black	4·00	60
41	2s.6d. black and green	13·00	7·00
42	3s. violet and blue	26·00	18·00
43	5s. grey and violet	26·00	18·00
44	10s. green and black	30·00	32·00
45	20s. red and purple	70·00	80·00

1946. Victory. As T **8a** of Pitcairn Islands.

46	1½d. orange	1·00	1·75
47	2d. red	10	50

1948. Silver Wedding. As T **8b/c** of Pitcairn Islands.

48	1½d. orange	30	10
49	20s. red	90·00	85·00

1949. U.P.U. As T **8d/g** of Pitcairn Islands.

50	2d. red	20	1·00
51	3d. blue	2·00	3·00
52	6d. grey	1·25	3·00
53	1s. orange	75	2·25

5 Cecil Rhodes and Victoria Falls

1953. Birth Centenary of Cecil Rhodes.

54	**5**	½d. brown	55	2·00
55	**5**	1d. green	45	2·25
56	**5**	2d. mauve	75	30
57	**5**	4½d. blue	45	4·50
58	**5**	1s. orange and black	1·25	4·75

6 Arms of the Rhodesias and Nyasaland

1953. Rhodes Centenary Exhibition.

59	**6**	6d. violet	70	1·50

1953. Coronation. As T **8h** of Pitcairn Islands.

60	1½d. black and orange	1·00	20

1953. As 1938 but with portrait of Queen Elizabeth II facing left.

61	½d. brown	65	10
62	1d. green	65	10
63	1½d. orange	1·25	10
64	2d. purple	1·25	10
65	3d. red	80	10
66	4d. violet	1·25	2·00
67	4½d. blue	1·50	4·50
68	6d. grey	1·25	10
69	9d. violet	1·25	4·25
70	1s. orange and black	70	10
71	2s.6d. black and green	15·00	8·00
72	5s. grey and purple	17·00	15·00
73	10s. green and black	13·00	38·00
74	20s. red and purple	30·00	40·00

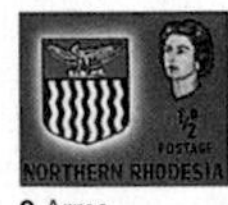

9 Arms

1963. Arms black, gold and blue; portrait and inscriptions black; background colours given.

75	**9**	½d. violet	70	1·25
76	**9**	1d. blue	1·50	10
77	**9**	2d. brown	70	10
78	**9**	3d. yellow	1·25	10
79	**9**	4d. green	70	30
80	**9**	6d. green	1·00	10
81	**9**	9d. bistre	70	1·60
82	**9**	1s. purple	50	10
83	**9**	1s.3d. purple	2·25	10
84	**9**	2s. orange	2·50	6·50
85	**9**	2s.6d. lake	2·75	2·50
86	**9**	5s. mauve	12·00	9·00
87	**9**	10s. mauve	20·00	23·00
88	**9**	20s. blue	22·00	42·00

Nos. 84/88 are larger (27×23 mm).

POSTAGE DUE STAMPS

D1

1929

D1	**D1**	1d. black	3·00	2·50
D2	**D1**	2d. black	8·00	3·00
D3	**D1**	3d. black	3·00	26·00
D4	**D1**	4d. black	12·00	42·00

D2

1963

D5	**D2**	1d. orange	3·00	6·50
D6	**D2**	2d. blue	3·00	5·00
D7	**D2**	3d. lake	3·00	8·50
D8	**D2**	4d. blue	3·00	15·00
D9	**D2**	6d. purple	9·50	11·00
D10	**D2**	1s. green	11·00	35·00

For later issues see **ZAMBIA**.

Pt. 11

NORWAY

In 1814 Denmark ceded Norway to Sweden, from 1814 to 1905 the King of Sweden was also King of Norway after which Norway was an independent Kingdom.

1855. 120 skilling = 1 speciedaler.
1877. 100 ore = 1 krone.

1

1855. Imperf.

1	**1**	4s. blue	£6500	£180

3 King Oscar I

1856. Perf.

4	**3**	2s. yellow	£750	£150
6	**3**	3s. lilac	£450	95·00
7	**3**	4s. blue	£325	18·00
11	**3**	8s. red	£1500	50·00

4

1863

12	**4**	2s. yellow	£750	£225
13	**4**	3s. lilac	£650	£500
21	**4**	4s. blue	£130	90·00
17	**4**	8s. pink	£1100	65·00
18	**4**	24s. brown	48·00	£140

5

1867

22	**5**	1s. black	90·00	55·00
23	**5**	2s. buff	25·00	55·00
26	**5**	3s. lilac	£450	£150
27	**5**	4s. blue	£180	14·00
29	**5**	8s. red	£750	65·00

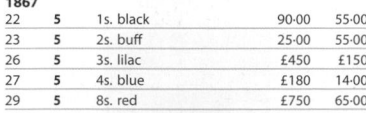

6

1872. Value in "Skilling".

33	**6**	1s. green	16·00	50·00
36	**6**	2s. blue	16·00	80·00
39	**6**	3s. red	£110	38·00
42	**6**	4s. mauve	16·00	75·00
44	**6**	6s. brown	£500	75·00
45	**6**	7s. brown	80·00	75·00

10 With background shading

A

1877. Letters without serifs as Type **A**. Value in "ore".

47	**10**	1ore brown	8·75	7·50
83	**10**	2ore brown	4·50	8·75
84c	**10**	3ore orange	90·00	12·50
52	**10**	5ore blue	£325	48·00
85d	**10**	5ore green	65·00	2·50
86a	**10**	10ore red	70·00	2·50
55	**10**	12ore green	£130	25·00
75b	**10**	12ore brown	31·00	29·00
76	**10**	20ore brown	£190	19·00
87	**10**	20ore blue	£130	7·50
88	**10**	25ore mauve	19·00	18·00
61	**10**	35ore green	25·00	16·00
62	**10**	50ore purple	65·00	12·50
63	**10**	60ore blue	65·00	11·50

9 King Oscar II

1878

68	**9**	1k. green and light green	31·00	14·00
69	**9**	1k.50 blue and ultramarine	65·00	50·00
70	**9**	2k. brown and pink	48·00	29·00

1888. Surch **2 ore**.

89a	**6**	2ore on 12ore brown	3·25	3·25

D

1893. Letters with serifs as Type **D**.

133	**10**	1ore drab	50	75
134	**10**	2ore brown	50	45
135	**10**	3ore orange	40	30
136	**10**	5ore green	5·00	40
529	**10**	5ore purple	70	35
138	**10**	7ore green	75	40
139	**10**	10ore red	6·25	40
140	**10**	10ore green	7·50	65
529a	**10**	10ore grey	70	35
141	**10**	12ore violet	1·00	1·90
143	**10**	15ore blue	5·75	40
530	**10**	15ore brown	70	70
144	**10**	20ore blue	7·50	40
530a	**10**	20ore green	4·75	60
146	**10**	25ore mauve	50·00	40
147	**10**	25ore red	6·25	1·00
531	**10**	25ore blue	35	35
148	**10**	30ore grey	10·00	50
149	**10**	30ore blue	8·75	7·50
119	**10**	35ore green	12·50	8·75
150	**10**	35ore brown	10·00	40
151	**10**	40ore green	7·50	75
152	**10**	40ore blue	31·00	40
531b	**10**	50ore purple	35	35
154	**10**	60ore blue	25·00	65
531c	**10**	60ore orange	35	45
531d	**10**	70ore orange	50	60
531e	**10**	80ore brown	50	45
531f	**10**	90ore brown	50	60

See also Nos. 279 etc and 1100/3.

1905. Surch.

122	**5**	1k. on 2s. buff	44·00	48·00
123	**5**	1k.50 on 2s. buff	75·00	£100
124	**5**	2k. on 2s. buff	90·00	95·00

1906. Surch.

162	**10**	5ore on 25ore mauve	50	75
125	**6**	15ore on 4s. mauve	5·00	6·25
126	**6**	30ore on 7s. brown	8·25	11·50

15 King Haakon VII

1907

127	**15**	1k. green	44·00	38·00
128	**15**	1½k. blue	95·00	95·00
129	**15**	2k. red	£150	£150

16 King Haakon VII

1910

155a	**16**	1k. green	75	40
156	**16**	1½k. blue	3·25	1·50
157	**16**	2k. red	3·75	1·50
158	**16**	5k. violet	6·25	7·50

17 Constitutional Assembly (after O. Wergeland)

1914. Centenary of Independence.

159	**17**	5ore green	90	75
160	**17**	10ore red	2·50	1·00
161	**17**	20ore blue	10·00	11·50

19

1922

163	**19**	10ore green	9·50	8·75
164	**19**	20ore purple	16·00	40
165	**19**	25ore red	29·00	75
166	**19**	45ore blue	1·30	1·80

20

1925. Air. Amundsen's Polar Flight.

167	**20**	2ore brown	2·50	3·75
168	**20**	3ore orange	5·00	5·75
169	**20**	5ore mauve	11·50	19·00
170	**20**	10ore green	16·00	31·00
171	**20**	15ore blue	16·00	31·00
172	**20**	20ore mauve	25·00	38·00
173	**20**	25ore red	6·25	8·25

21

1925. Annexation of Spitzbergen.

183	**21**	10ore green	7·50	12·50
184	**21**	15ore blue	6·25	6·25
185	**21**	20ore purple	6·25	2·50
186	**21**	45ore blue	6·25	8·25

22

1926. Size 16×19½ mm.

187	**22**	10ore green	70	40
187a	**22**	14ore orange	2·75	3·75
188	**22**	15ore brown	85	40
189	**22**	20ore purple	28·00	50
189a	**22**	20ore red	85	40
190	**22**	25ore red	14·00	3·25
190a	**22**	25ore brown	1·40	40
190b	**22**	30ore blue	1·40	40
191	**22**	35ore brown	85·00	40
191a	**22**	35ore violet	2·75	40
192	**22**	40ore blue	5·00	1·80
193	**22**	40ore grey	2·10	40
194	**22**	50ore pink	2·10	40
195	**22**	60ore blue	2·10	40

For stamps as Type **22** but size 17×21 mm, see Nos. 284, etc.

1927. Surcharged with new value and bar.

196		20ore on 25ore red	2·75	3·25
197	**19**	30ore on 45ore blue	14·00	3·25
198	**21**	30ore on 45ore blue	5·00	8·75

24 Akershus Castle

1927. Air.

199a	**24**	45ore blue (with frame-lines)	5·50	5·00
323	**24**	45ore blue (without frame-lines)	75	35

25 Ibsen

1928. Ibsen Centenary.

200	**25**	10ore green	7·00	3·75
201	**25**	15ore brown	4·25	4·50
202	**25**	20ore red	3·50	75
203	**25**	30ore blue	5·00	4·50

1929. Postage Due stamps optd **Post Frimerke** (204/6 and 211) or **POST** and thick bar (others).

204	**D12**	1ore brown	40	1·30
205	**D12**	4ore mauve (No. D96a)	40	75
206	**D12**	10ore green	2·75	5·00
207	**D12**	15ore brown	3·50	7·50
208	**D12**	20ore purple	1·40	75
209	**D12**	40ore blue	2·75	1·10
210	**D12**	50ore purple	11·00	10·00
211	**D12**	100ore yellow	5·00	3·75
212	**D12**	200ore violet	6·25	3·75

28 Abel

1929. Death Cent of N. H. Abel (mathematician).

213	**28**	10ore green	2·75	1·00
214	**28**	15ore brown	2·75	2·30
215	**28**	20ore red	1·40	50
216	**28**	30ore blue	3·50	3·25

1929. Surch **14 ORE 14**.

217	**5**	14ore on 2s. buff	4·25	6·25

30 St. Olaf (sculpture, Brunlanes Church)

31 Nidaros Trondhjem Cathedral

32 Death of St. Olaf (after P. N. Arbo)

1930. Ninth Death Centenary of St. Olaf.

219	**30**	10ore green	10·50	75
220	**31**	15ore sepia and brown	1·40	90
221	**30**	20ore red	1·40	65
222	**32**	30ore blue	5·50	4·50

33 North Cape and "Bergensfjord" (liner)

1930. Norwegian Tourist Association Fund. Size 35½×21½ mm.

223	**33**	15ore+25ore brown	3·50	5·00
224	**33**	20ore+25ore red	49·00	55·00
225	**33**	30ore+25ore blue	£110	£110

For smaller stamps in this design see Nos. 349/51, 442/66 and 464/6.

34 Radium Hospital

1931. Radium Hospital Fund.

226	**34**	20ore+10ore red	10·50	7·50

35 Bjornson

1932. Birth Cent of Bjornstjerne Bjornson (writer).

227	**35**	10ore green	10·50	1·00
228	**35**	15ore brown	2·10	1·90
229	**35**	20ore red	1·40	65
230	**35**	30ore blue	4·25	3·75

36 L. Holberg

1934. 250th Birth Anniv of Holberg (writer).

231	**36**	10ore green	2·10	65
232	**36**	15ore brown	85	1·00

233	**36**	20ore red	14·00	50
234	**36**	30ore blue	4·25	3·75

37 Dr. Nansen

1935. Nansen Refugee Fund.

235	**37**	10ore+10ore green	4·25	5·75
236	**37**	15ore+10ore brown	12·50	16·00
237	**37**	20ore+10ore red	3·50	3·25
238	**37**	30ore+10ore blue	10·50	16·00

See also Nos. 275/8.

38 No background shading

1937

279	**38**	1ore green	40	25
280	**38**	2ore brown	40	25
281	**38**	3ore orange	40	25
282	**38**	5ore mauve	40	25
283	**38**	7ore green	40	25
413	**38**	10ore grey	95	35
285	**38**	12ore violet	75	2·50
414	**38**	15ore green	2·40	70
415	**38**	15ore brown	70	35
416	**38**	20ore brown	4·75	3·00
417	**38**	20ore green	60	35
531a	**38**	40ore brown	35	35

1937. As T **22**, but size 17×21 mm.

284	**22**	10ore green	50	25
286	**22**	14ore orange	1·40	4·50
287	**22**	15ore green	55	50
288a	**22**	20ore red	40	50
289	**22**	25ore brown	1·40	25
289a	**22**	25ore red	40	25
290	**22**	30ore blue	2·10	50
290a	**22**	30ore grey	5·00	40
291	**22**	35ore violet	2·10	40
292	**22**	40ore grey	1·40	40
292a	**22**	40ore blue	3·50	50
293	**22**	50ore purple	1·40	40
293a	**22**	55ore orange	12·50	50
294	**22**	60ore blue	1·40	40
294a	**22**	80ore brown	12·50	50

38b King Haakon VII

1937

255	**38b**	1k. green	40	40
256	**38b**	1k.50 blue	1·10	4·50
257	**38b**	2k. red	85	12·50
258	**38b**	5k. purple	7·00	65·00

39 Reindeer

41 Joelster in Sunnfjord

1938. Tourist Propaganda.

262	**39**	15ore brown	2·75	3·75
263	-	20ore red	12·50	50
264	**41**	30ore blue	1·10	75

DESIGN—As T **39** but VERT: 20ore, Stave Church, Borgund.

42 Queen Maud

1939. Queen Maud Children's Fund.

267	**42**	10ore+5ore green	55	14·00
268	**42**	15ore+5ore brown	55	14·00
269	**42**	20ore+5ore red	55	11·50
270	**42**	30ore+5ore blue	55	16·00

43 Lion Rampant

1940

271	**43**	1k. green	1·40	40
272	**43**	1½k. blue	2·75	45
273	**43**	2k. red	3·75	1·90
274	**43**	5k. purple	5·50	6·25

See also Nos. 318/21.

44 Dr. Nansen

1940. National Relief Fund.

275	**44**	10ore+10ore green	2·50	5·00
276	**44**	15ore+10ore brown	3·50	6·25
277	**44**	20ore+10ore red	75	1·90
278	**44**	30ore+10ore blue	1·80	3·75

46 Femboring (fishing boat) and Iceberg

1941. Haalogaland Exhibition and Fishermen's Families Relief Fund.

295	**46**	15ore+10ore blue	1·70	7·50

47 Colin Archer (founder) and Lifeboat "Colin Archer"

1941. 50th Anniv of National Lifeboat Institution.

296	**47**	10ore+10ore green	1·10	3·25
297	**47**	15ore+10ore brown	1·40	3·75
298	-	20ore+10ore red	40	1·00
299	-	30ore+10ore blue	2·75	8·75

DESIGN—VERT: 20ore, 30ore, "Osloskoyta" (lifeboat).

48 Soldier and Flags

1941. Norwegian Legion Support Fund.

300	**48**	20ore+80ore red	35·00	£110

1941. Stamps of 1937 optd **V** (= Victory).

301B	**38**	1ore green	45	6·25
302B	**38**	2ore brown	45	11·00
303B	**38**	3ore orange	75	6·25
304B	**38**	5ore mauve	45	45
305A	**38**	7ore green	60	5·75
306B	**22**	10ore green	45	25
307B	**38**	12ore violet	90	20·00
308A	**22**	14ore orange	1·50	23·00
309A	**22**	15ore green	60	1·20
310B	**22**	20ore red	45	25
311B	**22**	25ore brown	60	70
312B	**22**	30ore blue	90	4·00
313A	**22**	35ore violet	1·20	1·20
314B	**22**	40ore grey	90	90
315B	**22**	50ore purple	1·20	4·00
316A	**22**	60ore blue	1·10	2·30
317B	**43**	1k. green	90	90
318B	**43**	1½k. blue	3·75	18·00
319B	**43**	2k. red	11·50	60·00
320B	**43**	5k. purple	23·00	£140

1941. As No. T **43**, but with "V" incorporated in the design.

321	10ore green	1·20	14·00

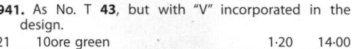

51 Oslo University

1941. Centenary of Foundation of Oslo University Building.

322	**51**	1k. green	23·00	65·00

52 Queen Ragnhild's Dream

53 Stiklestad Battlefield

1941. 700th Death Anniv of Snorre Sturlason (historian).

324	**52**	10ore green	45	25
325	-	15ore brown	45	70
326	-	20ore red	60	35
327	-	30ore blue	1·10	2·30
328	-	50ore violet	90	1·70
329	**53**	60ore blue	1·40	2·30

DESIGNS (illustrations from "Sagas of Kings")—As T **53**: 15ore Einar Tambarskjelve at Battle of Svolder; 30ore King Olav II sails to his wedding; 50ore Svipdag's men enter Hall of the Seven Kings. As T **52**: 20ore Snorre Sturlason.

55 Vidkun Quisling

1942. (a) Without opt.

330	**55**	20ore+30ore red	3·75	29·00

(b) Optd **1-2-1942**.

331	20ore+30ore red	3·75	29·00

See also No. 336.

56 Rikard Nordraak

57 Embarkation of the Viking Fleet

1942. Birth Centenary of Rikard Nordraak (composer).

332	**56**	10ore green	1·50	3·00
333	**57**	15ore brown	1·50	3·00
334	**56**	20ore red	1·50	3·00
335	-	30ore blue	1·50	3·00

DESIGN—As Type **57**: 30ore Mountains across sea and two lines of the National Anthem.

1942. War Orphans' Relief Fund. As T **55** but inscr "RIKSTINGET 1942".

336	20ore+30ore red	45	7·00

58 J. H. Wessel

1942. Birth Bicentenary of Wessel (poet).

337	**58**	15ore brown	45	45
338	**58**	20ore red	45	45

59 Reproduction of Types **55** and **1**

1942. Inaug of European Postal Union, Vienna.

339	**59**	20ore red	45	1·70
340	**59**	30ore blue	45	3·00

60 "Sleipner" (Destroyer)

1943

341	**60**	5ore purple	45	35
342	-	7ore green	45	45
343	**60**	10ore green	45	35
344	-	15ore green	60	1·70
345	-	20ore red	45	35
346	-	30ore blue	75	1·80
347	-	40ore green	75	1·80
348	-	60ore blue	75	1·80

DESIGNS: 7ore, 30ore Merchant ships in convoy; 15ore Airman; 20ore "Vi Vil Vinne" (We will win) written on the highway; 40ore Soldiers on skis; 60ore King Haakon VII.

For use on correspondence posted at sea on Norwegian merchant ships and (in certain circumstances) from Norwegian camps in Gt. Britain during the German Occupation of Norway. After liberation all values were put on sale in Norway.

1943. Norwegian Tourist Association Fund. As T **33**, but reduced to 27×21 mm.

349	**33**	15ore+25ore brown	1·20	2·30
350	**33**	20ore+25ore red	2·30	3·50
351	**33**	30ore+25ore blue	2·30	3·50

61 Edvard Grieg

1943. Birth Centenary of Grieg (composer).

352	**61**	10ore green	45	35
353	**61**	20ore red	45	35
354	**61**	40ore green	45	45
355	**61**	60ore blue	45	45

62 Soldier's Emblem

1943. Soldiers' Relief Fund.

356	**62**	20ore+30ore red	45	7·50

63 Fishing Station

1943. Winter Relief Fund.

357	**63**	10ore+10ore green	90	8·00
358	-	20ore+10ore red	90	8·00
359	-	40ore+10ore grey	90	8·00

DESIGNS: 20ore Mountain scenery; 40ore Winter landscape.

64 Sinking of "Baroy" (freighter)

1944. Shipwrecked Mariners' Relief Fund.

360	**64**	10ore+10ore green	75	8·00
361	-	15ore+10ore brown	75	8·00
362	-	20ore+10ore red	75	8·00

DESIGNS—HORIZ: 15ore "Sanct Svithun" (cargo liner) attacked by Bristol Type 142 Blenheim Mk IV airplane. VERT: 20ore Sinking of "Irma" (freighter).

65 Gran's Bleriot XI "Nordsjoen"

1944. 30th Anniv of First North Sea Flight, by Tryggve Gran.

363	**65**	40ore blue	45	4·50

66 Girl Spinning

1944. Winter Relief Fund. Inscr as in T **66**.

364	**66**	5ore+10ore mauve	60	8·00
365	-	10ore+10ore green	60	8·00
366	-	15ore+10ore purple	60	8·00
367	-	20ore+10ore red	60	8·00

DESIGNS: 10ore Ploughing; 15ore Tree felling; 20ore Mother and children.

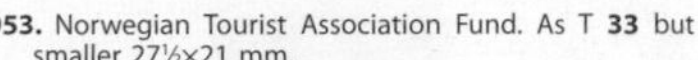

67 Arms

1945

368	**67**	1½k. blue	90	70

68 Henrik Wergeland

1945. Death Centenary of Wergeland (poet).

369	**68**	10ore green	45	35
370	**68**	15ore brown	60	1·40
371	**68**	20ore red	45	35

69 Red Cross Sister

1945. Red Cross Relief Fund and Norwegian Red Cross Jubilee.

372	**69**	20ore+10ore red	60	1·20

70 Folklore Museum Emblem

1945. 50th Anniv of National Folklore Museum.

373	**70**	10ore green	60	70
374	**70**	20ore red	60	60

71 Crown Prince Olav

1946. National Relief Fund.

375	**71**	10ore+10ore green	95	70
376	**71**	15ore+10ore brown	95	70
377	**71**	20ore+10ore red	1·10	70
378	**71**	30ore+10ore blue	3·00	2·30

72 "R.N.A.F."

1946. Honouring Norwegian Air Force trained in Canada.

379	**72**	15ore red	85	1·40

73 King Haakon VII

1946

380	**73**	1k. green	3·00	35
381	**73**	1½k. blue	7·25	35
382	**73**	2k. brown	55·00	35
383	**73**	5k. violet	39·00	90

74 Fridtjof Nansen, Roald Amundsen and "Fram"

1947. Tercentenary of Norwegian Post Office.

384	-	5ore mauve	70	35
385	-	10ore green	70	35
386	-	15ore brown	1·40	35
387	-	25ore red	1·20	35
388	-	30ore grey	2·75	35
389	-	40ore blue	5·50	35
390	-	45ore violet	3·50	90
391	-	50ore brown	6·00	45
392	**74**	55ore orange	7·75	35
393	-	60ore grey	7·25	2·10
394	-	80ore brown	7·75	70

DESIGNS: 5ore Hannibal Sehested (founder of postal service) and Akershus Castle; 10ore "Postal-peasant"; 15ore Admiral Tordenskiold and 18th-century warship; 25ore Christian M. Falsen; 30ore Cleng Peerson and "Restaurationen" (emigrant sloop), 1825; 40ore "Constitutionen" (paddle-steamer), 1827; 45ore First Norwegian locomotive "Caroline"; 50ore Svend Foyn and "Spes et Fides" (whale catcher); 60ore Coronation of King Haakon and Queen Maud in Nidaros Cathedral; 80ore King Haakon and Oslo Town Hall.

75 Petter Dass

1947. Birth Tercentenary of Petter Dass (poet).

395	**75**	25ore red	1·40	1·20

76 King Haakon VII

1947. 75th Birthday of King Haakon VII.

396	**76**	25ore orange	85	80

77 Axel Heiberg

1948. 50th Anniv of Norwegian Forestry Society and Birth Centenary of Axel Heiberg (founder).

397	**77**	25ore red	1·20	80
398	**77**	80ore brown	3·25	45

1948. Red Cross. Surch **25+5** and bars.

399	**69**	25+5 ore on 20+10 ore red	70	1·20

1949. Nos. 288a and 292a surch.

400	**22**	25ore on 20ore red	50	35
401	**22**	45ore on 40ore blue	4·25	80

80 A. L. Kielland

1949. Birth Centenary of Alexander L. Kielland (author).

402	**80**	25ore red	2·20	45
403	**80**	40ore blue	2·40	80
404	**80**	80ore brown	3·00	1·20

81 Symbolising Universe

82 Pigeons and Globe

1949. 75th Anniv of U.P.U.

405	**81**	10ore green and purple	50	70
406	**82**	25ore red	70	45
407	-	40ore blue	70	70

DESIGN—37×21 mm: 40ore Dove, globe and signpost.

84 King Harald Haardraade and Oslo Town Hall

1950. 900th Anniv of Founding of Oslo.

408	**84**	15ore green	95	90
409	**84**	25ore red	95	45
410	**84**	45ore blue	95	90

85 Child with Flowers

1950. Infantile Paralysis Fund.

411	**85**	25ore+5ore red	2·40	1·70
412	**85**	45ore+5ore blue	9·00	8·75

87 King Haakon VII

1950

418	**87**	25ore red	95	35
419	**87**	25ore grey	27·00	45
419a	**87**	25ore green	1·80	35
420	**87**	30ore grey	10·00	1·20
421	**87**	30ore red	95	35
422a	**87**	35ore red	6·00	35
422b	**87**	40ore purple	2·40	35
423	**87**	45ore blue	2·75	3·50
424	**87**	50ore brown	6·00	35
425	**87**	55ore orange	2·40	1·70
426	**87**	55ore blue	3·00	80
427	**87**	60ore blue	19·00	35
427a	**87**	65ore blue	1·80	45
427b	**87**	70ore brown	22·00	35
428	**87**	75ore purple	3·50	35
429	**87**	80ore brown	4·25	45
430	**87**	90ore orange	2·20	35

"NOREG" on the stamps was the spelling advocated by Arne Garborg.

88 Arne Garborg (after O. Rusti)

1951. Birth Centenary of Garborg (author).

431	**88**	25ore red	95	45
432	**88**	45ore blue	3·50	3·50
433	**88**	80ore brown	3·50	2·30

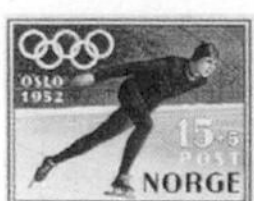
89 Ice Skater

1951. Sixth Winter Olympic Games. Inscr "OSLO 1952".

434	**89**	15ore+5ore green	3·50	3·50
435	-	30ore+10ore red	3·50	3·50
436	-	55ore+20ore blue	15·00	14·50

DESIGNS—As T **89**: 30ore Ski jumping. 38×21 mm: 55ore Winter landscape.

1951. Surch in figures.

437	**87**	30ore on 25ore red	95	45
440	**38**	20ore on 15ore green	60	35

92 King Haakon VII

1952. 80th Birthday of King Haakon.

438	**92**	30ore scarlet and red	50	45
439	**92**	55ore blue and grey	1·40	1·40

94 "Supplication"

1953. Anti-cancer Fund.

441	**94**	30ore+10ore red and cream	3·00	3·00

1953. Norwegian Tourist Association Fund. As T **33** but smaller 27½×21 mm.

442	**33**	20ore+10ore green	15·00	14·50
464	**33**	25ore+10ore green	7·75	7·50
443	**33**	30ore+15ore red	18·00	17·00
465	**33**	35ore+15ore red	9·50	9·25
444	**33**	55ore+25ore blue	21·00	20·00
466	**33**	65ore+25ore blue	6·00	5·75

95 Medieval Sculpture

1953. Eighth Cent of Archbishopric of Nidaros.

445	**95**	30ore red	1·40	80

96 Stephenson Locomotive on Hoved Railway, 1854, and Horse-drawn Sledge

1954. Centenary of Norwegian Railways.

446	**96**	20ore green	1·30	70
447	-	30ore red	1·40	45
448	-	55ore blue	2·20	1·70

DESIGNS: 30ore Diesel-hydraulic express train; 55ore Alfred Andersen (engine driver) in locomotive cab.

97 C. T. Nielsen (first Director)

1954. Centenary of Telegraph Service.

449	**97**	20ore black and green	70	60
450	-	30ore red	70	45
451	-	55ore blue	1·40	1·30

DESIGNS: 30ore Radio masts at Tryvannshogda; 55ore Telegraph lineman on skis.

98 "Posthorn" Type Stamp

1955. Norwegian Stamp Centenary.

452		20ore blue and green	50	45
453	**98**	30ore deep red and red	50	35
454	-	55ore blue and grey	80	70

DESIGNS: 20ore Norway's first stamp; 55ore "Lion" type stamp.

1955. Stamp Cent and Int Stamp Exn, Oslo. Nos. 452/4 with circular opt **OSLO NORWEX**.

455		20ore blue and green	17·00	16·00
456	**98**	30ore deep red and red	17·00	16·00
457	-	55ore blue and grey	17·00	16·00

Nos. 455/7 were only on sale at the Exhibition P.O. at face plus 1k. entrance fee.

100 King Haakon and Queen Maud

1955. Golden Jubilee of King Haakon.

458	**100**	30ore red	50	45
459	**100**	55ore blue	70	70

101 Crown Princess Martha

1956. Crown Princess Martha Memorial Fund.

460	**101**	35ore+10ore red	1·80	1·70
461	**101**	65ore+10ore blue	4·75	4·50

101a Whooper Swans

1956. Northern Countries' Day.

462	**101a**	35ore red	70	70
463	**101a**	65ore blue	70	70

102 Jan Mayen Island (after aquarell, H. Mohn)
103 Map of Spitzbergen

1957. Int Geophysical Year. Inscr "INTERN. GEOFYSISK AR 1957–1958".

467	**102**	25ore green	70	60
468	**103**	35ore red and grey	70	45
469	-	65ore green and blue	70	65

DESIGN—VERT: 65ore Map of Antarctica showing Queen Maud Land.

104 King Haakon VII

1957. 85th Birthday of King Haakon.

470	**104**	35ore red	60	45
471	**104**	65ore blue	1·20	1·20

105 King Olav V
106 King Olav V

1958

472	**105**	25ore green	1·80	35
473	**105**	30ore violet	2·40	35
474	**105**	35ore red	1·10	35
474a	**105**	35ore green	7·25	35
475	**105**	40ore red	1·10	35
475a	**105**	40ore grey	4·75	2·75
476	**105**	45ore red	1·40	35
477	**105**	50ore brown	7·75	35
478	**105**	50ore red	11·00	35
479	**105**	55ore grey	2·40	2·30
480	**105**	60ore violet	6·50	1·20
481	**105**	65ore blue	3·00	60
482	**105**	80ore brown	15·00	1·20
483	**105**	85ore brown	2·40	35
484	**105**	90ore orange	1·70	35
485	**106**	1k. green	2·20	35
486	**106**	1k.50 blue	4·25	35
487	**106**	2k. red	15·00	35
488	**106**	5k. purple	60·00	35
489	**106**	10k. orange	9·00	35

107 Asbjorn Kloster (founder)

1959. Cent of Norwegian Temperance Movement.

490	**107**	45ore brown	70	35

108 Society's Centenary Medal

1959. 150th Anniv of Royal Norwegian Agricultural Society.

491	**108**	45ore brown and red	70	65
492	**108**	90ore grey and blue	2·40	2·30

109 Sower

1959. Centenary of Norwegian Royal College of Agriculture.

493	**109**	45ore black and brown	95	70
494	-	90ore black and blue	1·80	1·70

DESIGN—VERT: 90ore Ears of corn.

110 White Anemone

1960. Tuberculosis Relief Funds.

495	**110**	45ore+10ore yellow, green and red	4·25	4·00
496	-	90ore+10ore mult	9·50	9·25

DESIGN: 90ore Blue anemone.

111 Society's Original Seal

1960. Bicentenary of Royal Norwegian Society of Scientists.

497	**111**	45ore red on grey	70	60
498	**111**	90ore blue on grey	2·20	2·10

112 Refugee Mother and Child

1960. World Refugee Year.

499	**112**	45ore+25ore black and pink	7·75	7·50
500	**112**	90ore+25ore blk & bl	16·00	15·00

113 Viking Longship

1960. Norwegian Ships.

501	**113**	20ore black and grey	2·20	1·70
502	-	25ore black and green	1·30	1·30
503	-	45ore black and red	1·30	60
504	-	55ore black and brown	3·50	3·50
505	-	90ore black and blue	4·75	3·00

SHIPS: 25ore Hanse kogge; 45ore "Skomvaer" (barque); 55ore "Dalfon" (tanker); 90ore "Bergensfjord" (liner).

113a Conference Emblem

1960. Europa.

506	**113a**	90ore blue	70	65

113b Douglas DC-8

1961. Tenth Anniv of Scandinavian Airlines System (SAS).

507	**113b**	90ore blue	1·10	1·00

114 Throwing the Javelin

1961. Centenary of Norwegian Sport.

508	**114**	20ore brown	1·20	1·20
509	-	25ore green	95	90
510	-	45ore red	85	45
511	-	90ore mauve	1·40	1·30

DESIGNS: 25ore Ice skating; 45ore Ski jumping; 90ore Yachting.

115 Haakonshallen Barracks and Rosencrantz Tower

1961. 700th Anniv of Haakonshallen, Bergen.

512	**115**	45ore black and red	85	70
513	**115**	1k. black and green	1·20	45

116 Oslo University

1961. 150th Anniv of Oslo University.

514	**116**	45ore red	70	60
515	**116**	1k.50 blue	1·30	45

117 Nansen

1961. Birth Centenary of Fridtjof Nansen (polar explorer).

516	**117**	45ore black and red	95	45
517	**117**	90ore black and blue	1·80	1·70

118 Amundsen, "Fram" and Dog-team

1961. 50th Anniv of Amundsen's Arrival at South Pole.

518	**118**	45ore red and grey	1·20	70
519	-	90ore deep blue and blue	2·20	2·10

DESIGN: 90ore Amundsen's party and tent at South Pole.

119 Frederic Passy and Henri Dunant (winners in 1901)

1961. Nobel Peace Prize.

520	**119**	45ore red	60	45
521	**119**	1k. green	1·80	60

120 Prof. V. Bjerknes

1962. Birth Centenary of Prof. Vilhelm Bjerknes (physicist).

522	**120**	45ore black and red	60	45
523	**120**	1k.50 black and blue	1·40	60

121 Etrich/Rumpler Taube Monoplane "Start"

1962. 50th Anniv of Norwegian Aviation.

524	**121**	1k.50 brown and blue	4·25	80

122 Branch of Fir, and Cone

1962. Cent of State Forestry Administration.

525	**122**	45ore grey, black and red	70	65
526	**122**	1k. grey, black and green	7·75	45

123 Europa "Tree"

1962. Europa.

527	**123**	50ore red	70	65
528	**123**	90ore blue	1·80	1·70

125 Reef Knot

1962

531g	-	25ore green	1·40	35
532	-	30ore drab	4·75	4·50
532a	-	30ore green	50	35
533	**125**	35ore green	50	35
533a	-	40ore red	4·75	35
534	-	40ore green	35	35
534a	-	45ore green	70	70
535	**125**	50ore red	4·75	35
535a	**125**	50ore grey	35	35
536	-	55ore brown	70	70
536a	**125**	60ore green	14·50	35
537a	**125**	60ore red	2·40	90
537b	-	65ore violet	3·50	45
538	**125**	65ore red	60	35
538a	**125**	70ore brown	35	35
539	-	75ore green	50	35
539a	-	80ore purple	12·00	4·50
539b	-	80ore brown	50	45
540	-	85ore brown	60	35
540a	-	85ore buff	50	45
540b	-	90ore blue	60	35
541	-	100ore violet	70	35
541a	-	100ore red	95	35
542	-	110ore red	60	35
542a	-	115ore brown	1·20	60
543	-	120ore blue	70	70
543a	-	125ore red	85	35
544	-	140ore blue	70	70
544a	-	750ore brown	3·75	35

DESIGNS: 25, 40, 90, 100 (2), 110, 120, 125ore, Runic drawings; 30, 45, 55, 75, 85ore, Ear of wheat and Atlantic cod; 65 (537b), 80, 140ore, "Stave" (wooden) church and "Aurora Borealis"; 115ore Fragment of Urnes stave-church; 750ore Sigurd Farnesbane (the Dragon killer) and Regin (the blacksmith), portal from Hylestad stave-church.

126 Camilla Collett

1963. 150th Birth Anniv of Camilla Collett (author).

545	**126**	50ore red	70	45
546	**126**	90ore blue	1·70	1·60

127 Boatload of Wheat

1963. Freedom from Hunger.

547	**127**	25ore bistre	60	45
548	**127**	35ore green	95	90
549	-	50ore red	95	90
550	-	90ore blue	1·70	1·60

DESIGN—37½×21 mm: 50, 90ore Birds carrying food on cloth.

128 River Mail Boat

1963. Tercentenary of Southern-Northern Norwegian Postal Services.

551	**128**	50ore red	1·20	1·20
552	-	90ore blue	3·50	3·50

DESIGN: 90ore Femboring (Northern sailing vessel).

129 Ivar Aasen

1963. 150th Birth Anniv of Ivar Aasen (philologist).

553	**129**	50ore red and grey	70	45
554	**129**	90ore blue and grey	2·20	2·10

The note after No. 433 re "NOREG" also applies here.

130 "Co-operation"

1963. Europa.

555	**130**	50ore orange and purple	95	80
556	**130**	90ore green and blue	2·40	2·30

131 "Herringbone" Pattern

1963. 150th Anniv of Norwegian Textile Industry.

557	**131**	25ore green and bistre	95	90
558	**131**	35ore ultramarine and blue	1·70	1·60
559	**131**	50ore purple and red	70	70

132 Edvard Munch (self-portrait)

1963. Birth Centenary of Edvard Munch (painter and engraver).

560	**132**	25ore black	50	45
561	-	35ore green	50	45
562	-	50ore brown	70	45
563	-	90ore blue and indigo	1·20	1·20

DESIGNS (woodcuts)—HORIZ: 35ore "Fecundity"; 50ore "The Solitaries". VERT: 90ore "The Girls on the Bridge".

133 Eilert Sundt (founder)

1964. Centenary of Oslo Workers' Society.

564	**133**	25ore green	70	70
565	-	50ore purple	70	35

DESIGN: 50ore Beehive emblem of O.W.S.

134 C. M. Guldberg and P. Waage (chemists)

1964. Centenary of Law of Mass Action.

566	**134**	35ore green	85	80
567	**134**	55ore stone	1·80	1·70

135 Eidsvoll Manor

1964. 150th Anniv of Norwegian Constitution.

568	**135**	50ore grey and red	1·10	70
569	-	90ore black and blue	2·40	2·30

DESIGN: 90ore Storting (Parliament House), Oslo.

On 1 June 1964 a stamp depicting the U.N. refugee emblem and inscr "PORTO BETALT ... LYKKEBREVET 1964" was put on sale. It had a franking value of 50ore but was sold for 2k.50, the balance being for the Refugee Fund. In addition, each stamp bore a serial number representing participation in a lottery which took place in September. The stamp was on sale until 15 July and had validity until 10 August.

136 Harbour Scene

1964. Cent of Norwegian Seamen's Mission.

570	**136**	25ore green and yellow	70	70
571	**136**	90ore blue and cream	2·40	2·30

137 Europa "Flower"

1964. Europa.

572	**137**	90ore deep blue and blue	4·25	4·00

138 H. Anker and O. Arvesen (founders)

1964. Cent of Norwegian Folk High Schools.

573	**138**	50ore pink	95	60
574	**138**	90ore blue	3·00	3·00

The note after No. 433 re "NOREG" also applies here.

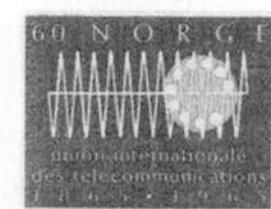

139 "Radio-telephone"

1965. Centenary of I.T.U.

575	**139**	60ore purple	70	45
576	-	90ore grey	1·70	1·60

DESIGN: 90ore "T.V. transmission".

140 Dove of Peace and Broken Chain

1965. 20th Anniv of Liberation.

577	**140**	30ore+10ore brown, green and sepia	50	45
578	-	60ore+10ore blue and red	85	60

DESIGN: 60ore Norwegian flags.

141 Mountain Landscapes

1965. Centenary of Norwegian Red Cross.

579	**141**	60ore brown and red	95	70
580	-	90ore blue and red	4·75	4·50

DESIGN: 90ore Coastal view.

142 Europa "Sprig"

1965. Europa.

581	**142**	60ore red	95	45
582	**142**	90ore blue	2·20	2·10

143 St. Sunniva and Bergen Buildings

1965. Bicentenary of Harmonien Philharmonic Society.

583	-	30ore black and green	60	45
584	**143**	90ore black and blue	2·00	2·00

DESIGN—VERT: 30ore St. Sunniva.

144 Rondane Mountains (after H. Sohlberg)

1965. Rondane National Park.

585	**144**	1k.50 blue	3·00	45

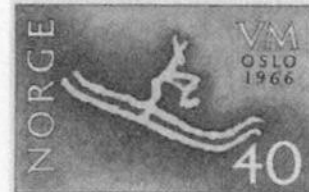

145 "Rodoy Skier" (rock carving)

1966. World Skiing Championships, Oslo. Inscr "VM OSLO 1966".

586	**145**	40ore brown	1·70	1·40
587	-	55ore green	1·90	1·80
588	-	60ore brown	95	45
589	-	90ore blue	1·80	1·70

DESIGNS—HORIZ: 55ore Ski jumper; 60ore Cross-country skier. VERT: 90ore Holmenkollen ski jumping tower, Oslo.

146 "The Bible"

1966. 150th Anniv of Norwegian Bible Society.

590	**146**	60ore red	70	45
591	**146**	90ore blue	1·70	1·60

147 Guilloche Pattern

1966. 150th Anniv of Bank of Norway.

592	**147**	30ore green	75	70
593	-	60ore red (Bank building)	65	45

No. 593 is size 27½×21 mm.

148 J. Sverdrup (after C. Krohg)

1966. 150th Birth Anniv of Johan Sverdrup (statesman).

594	**148**	30ore green	75	70
595	**148**	60ore purple	65	45

149 Europa "Ship"

1966. Europa.

596	**149**	60ore red	75	45
597	**149**	90ore blue	2·30	2·10

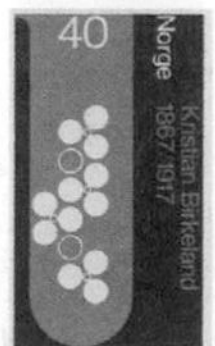

150 Molecules in Test-tube

1966. Birth Centenaries of S. Eyde (industrialist) (1966) and K. Birkeland (scientist) (1967), founders of Norwegian Nitrogen Industry.

598	**150**	40ore blue and light blue	1·90	1·70
599	-	55ore mauve and red	2·50	2·30

DESIGN: 55ore Ear of wheat and conical flask.

151 E.F.T.A. Emblem

1967. European Free Trade Association.

600	**151**	60ore red	65	45
601	**151**	90ore blue	2·50	2·30

152 "Owl" and Three Swords

1967. 150th Anniv of Higher Military Training.

602	**152**	60ore brown	1·00	90
603	**152**	90ore green	3·75	3·50

153 Cogwheels

1967. Europa.

604	**153**	60ore deep plum, plum and purple	75	45
605	**153**	90ore deep violet, violet and blue	1·80	1·60

154 Johanne Dybwad

1967. Birth Centenary of J. Dybwad (actress).

606	**154**	40ore blue	65	60
607	**154**	60ore red	65	60

155 I. Skrefsrud (missionary and founder)

1967. Centenary of Norwegian Santal Mission.

608	**155**	60ore brown	75	45
609	-	90ore blue	1·80	1·60

DESIGN—HORIZ: 90ore Ebenezer Church, Benagaria, Santal, India.

156 Climbers on Mountain-top

1968. Centenary of Norwegian Mountain Touring Association.

610	**156**	40ore brown	1·50	1·40
611	-	60ore red	1·00	45
612	-	90ore blue	1·50	1·40

DESIGNS: 60ore Mountain cairn and scenery; 90ore Glitretind peak.

157 "The Blacksmiths"

1968. Norwegian Handicrafts.

613	**157**	65ore brown, black & red	65	45
614	**157**	90ore brown, black & blue	1·60	1·50

158 Vinje

1968. 150th Birth Anniv of Aasmund Vinje (poet).

615	**158**	50ore brown	75	70
616	**158**	65ore red	65	45

See note below No. 433.

159 Cross and Heart

1968. Centenary of Norwegian Lutheran Home Mission Society.

617	**159**	40ore red and green	3·25	3·00
618	**159**	65ore red and violet	65	45

160 Cathinka Guldberg (first deaconess)

1968. Centenary of Deaconess House, Oslo.
619 **160** 50ore blue 65 60
620 **160** 65ore red 65 45

161 K. P. Arnoldson and F. Bajer

1968. Nobel Peace Prize Winners of 1908.
621 **161** 65ore brown 75 70
622 **161** 90ore blue 2·50 2·30

161a Viking Ships (from old Swedish coin)

1969. 50th Anniv of Northern Countries' Union.
623 **161a** 65ore red 65 45
624 **161a** 90ore blue 1·80 1·60

162 Transport

1969. Centenary of "Rutebok for Norge" ("Communications of Norway") and Road Safety Campaign.
625 **162** 50ore green 1·30 1·20
626 - 65ore red and green 65 45
DESIGN: 65ore Pedestrian-crossing.

163 Colonnade

1969. Europa.
627 **163** 65ore black and red 75 45
628 **163** 90ore black and blue 2·00 1·80

164 J. Hjort and Atlantic Cod Eggs

1969. Birth Centenary of Professor Johan Hjort (fisheries pioneer).
629 **164** 40ore brown and blue 1·30 1·20
630 - 90ore blue and green 2·50 2·30
DESIGN: 90ore Hjort and polyp.

165 Traena Islands

1969
631 **165** 3k.50 black 2·30 35

166 King Olav V

1969
632 **166** 1k. green 65 35
633 **166** 1k.50 blue 90 35
634 **166** 2k. red 1·00 35
635 **166** 5k. blue 2·50 35
636 **166** 10k. brown 7·00 35
637 **166** 20k. brown 12·50 35
637a **166** 50k. green 20·00 2·30

167 "Mother and Child"

1969. Birth Centenary of Gustav Vigeland (sculptor).
638 **167** 65ore black and red 65 45
639 - 90ore black and blue 1·50 1·40
DESIGN: 90ore "Family" (sculpture).

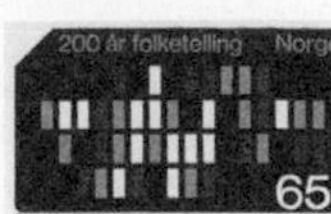

168 Punched Cards

1969. Bicentenary of First National Census. Multicoloured.
640 65ore Type **168** 65 45
641 90ore "People" (diagram) 1·50 1·40

169 Queen Maud

1969. Birth Centenary of Queen Maud.
642 **169** 65ore purple 65 45
643 **169** 90ore blue 1·80 1·60

170 Wolf ("Canis lupus")

1970. Nature Conservation Year.
644 **170** 40ore brown and blue 1·50 1·40
645 - 60ore grey and brown 3·25 3·00
646 - 70ore brown and blue 1·50 70
647 - 100ore brown and blue 2·30 2·10
DESIGNS—VERT: 60ore Pale pasque flower ("Pulsatilla vernalis"); 70ore Voringsfossen Falls. HORIZ: 100ore White-tailed sea eagle ("Haliaeetus albicilla").

171 "V" Symbol

1970. 25th Anniv of Liberation.
648 **171** 70ore red and violet 2·50 70
649 - 100ore blue and green 2·50 2·00
DESIGN—HORIZ: 100ore Merchant ships in convoy.

172 "Citizens"

1970. 900th Anniv of Bergen.
650 **172** 40ore green 2·30 1·40
651 - 70ore purple 3·25 60
652 - 1k. blue 2·50 2·30
DESIGNS: 70ore "City between the Mountains"; 1k. "Ships".

173 Hands reaching for Globe

1970. 25th Anniv of United Nations.
653 **173** 70ore red 3·25 70
654 **173** 100ore green 1·90 1·70

174 G. O. Sars

1970. Norwegian Zoologists.
655 **174** 40ore brown 1·50 1·40
656 - 50ore lilac 1·50 1·00
657 - 70ore brown 1·50 60
658 - 100ore blue 1·50 1·40
ZOOLOGISTS: 50ore Hans Strom; 70ore J. E. Gunnerus; 100ore Michael Sars.

175 Ball-game

1970. Centenary of Central School of Gymnastics, Oslo.
659 **175** 50ore brown and blue 1·00 60
660 - 70ore brown and red 1·30 45
DESIGN—HORIZ: 70ore "Leapfrog" exercise.

176 Tonsberg's Seal c. 1340

1971. 1100th Anniv of Tonsberg.
661 **176** 70ore red 1·00 45
662 **176** 100ore blue 1·50 1·40

177 Parliament House, Oslo

1971. Centenary of Introduction of Annual Parliamentary Sessions.
663 **177** 70ore lilac and red 75 45
664 **177** 100ore green and blue 1·50 1·40

178 "Helping Hand"

1971. "Help for Refugees".
665 **178** 50ore green and black 65 60
666 **178** 70ore red and black 65 45

179 "Hauge addressing Followers" (A. Tidemand)

1971. Birth Centenary of Hans Nielson Hauge (church reformer).
667 **179** 60ore black 75 70
668 **179** 70ore brown 65 45

180 Bishop welcoming Worshippers

1971. 900th Anniv of Oslo Bishopric.
669 - 70ore black and red 50 45
670 **180** 1k. black and blue 2·00 1·80
DESIGN—VERT: 70ore Masons building first church.

181 Roald Amundsen and Treaty Emblem

1971. Tenth Anniv of Antarctic Treaty.
671 **181** 100ore red and blue 4·50 3·00

182 "The Preacher and the King"

1971. Norwegian Folk Tales. Drawings by Erik Werenskiold.
672 - 40ore black and green 1·00 60
673 **182** 50ore black and blue 1·00 45
674 - 70ore black and purple 65 45
DESIGNS—VERT: 40ore "The Farmer and the Woman"; 70ore "The Troll and the Girl".

183 Anniversary Symbol

1972. 150th Anniv of Norwegian Savings Banks.
675 **183** 80ore gold and red 75 45
676 **183** 1k.20 gold and blue 1·60 1·50

184 3s. "Posthorn" Stamp

1972. Centenary of Norwegian "Posthorn" Stamps.
677 **184** 80ore red and brown 75 45
678 **184** 1k. blue and violet 75 60
MS679 120×71 mm. Nos. 677/8 (sold at 2k.50) 7·50 8·75

185 Alstad "Picture" Stone (detail)

1972. 1100th Anniv of Norway's Unification. Relics.
680 **185** 50ore green 75 70
681 - 60ore brown 1·80 1·60
682 - 80ore red 1·80 60
683 - 1k.20 blue 2·00 1·80
DESIGNS: 60ore Portal, Hemsedal Church (detail); 80ore Figurehead of Oseberg Viking ship; 1k.20, Sword-hilt (Lodingen).

186 King Haakon VII

1972. Birth Centenary of King Haakon VII.
684 **186** 80ore red 3·50 60
685 **186** 1k.20 blue 2·10 1·80

187 "Joy" (Ingrid Ekrem)

1972. "Youth and Leisure".
686 **187** 80ore mauve 90 45
687 - 1k.20 blue 1·60 1·50
DESIGN: 1k.20, "Solidarity" (Ole Instefjord).

1972. "Interjunex 1972" Stamp Exhibition, Oslo. Nos. 686/7 optd **INTERJUNEX 72**.
688 **187** 80ore mauve 3·25 3·00
689 - 1k.20 blue 3·25 3·00

189 "Maud"

1972. Norwegian Polar Ships.
690 **189** 60ore olive and green 1·80 1·40
691 - 80ore red and black 3·25 60
692 - 1k.20 blue and red 2·30 1·80
DESIGNS: 80ore "Fram" (Amundsen and Nansen's ship); 1k.20, "Gjoa".

190 "Little Man"

1972. Norwegian Folk Tales. Drawings of Trolls by Th. Kittelsen.

693	**190**	50ore black and green	1·00	45
694	-	60ore black and blue	1·30	90
695	-	80ore black and pink	1·00	45

TROLLS: 60ore "The troll who wonders how old he is"; 80ore "Princess riding on a bear".

191 Dr. Hansen and Bacillus Diagram

1973. Centenary of Hansen's Identification of Leprosy Bacillus.

696	**191**	1k. red and blue	65	45
697	-	1k.40 blue and red	1·60	1·50

DESIGN: 1k.40, As Type **191** but bacillus as seen in modern microscope.

192 Europa "Posthorn"

1973. Europa.

698	**192**	1k. red, scarlet and carmine	3·25	45
699	**192**	1k.40 emerald, green and blue	1·90	1·70

192a "The Nordic House", Reykjavik

1973. Nordic Countries' Postal Co-operation.

700	**192a**	1k. multicoloured	1·30	60
701	**192a**	1k.40 multicoloured	1·50	1·40

193 King Olav V

1973. King Olav's 70th Birthday.

702	**193**	1k. brown and purple	1·50	45
703	**193**	1k.40 brown and blue	1·50	1·40

194 J. Aall

1973. Birth Centenary of Jacob Aall (industrialist).

704	**194**	1k. purple	75	45
705	**194**	1k.40 blue	1·50	1·40

195 Bone Carving

1973. Lapp Handicrafts.

706	**195**	75ore brown and cream	75	60
707	-	1k. red and cream	1·10	45
708	-	1k.40 black and blue	1·50	1·40

DESIGNS: 1k. Detail of weaving; 1k.40, Detail of tin-ware.

196 Yellow Wood Violet

1973. Mountain Flowers. Multicoloured.

709	65ore Type **196**	65	60
710	70ore Rock speedwell	75	70
711	1k. Mountain heath	75	45

197 Land Surveying

1973. Bicent of Norwegian Geographical Society.

712	**197**	1k. red	75	45
713	-	1k.40 blue	1·50	1·40

DESIGN: 1k.40, Old map of Hestbraepiggene (mountain range).

198 Lindesnes

1974. Norwegian Capes.

714	**198**	1k. green	1·30	70
715	-	1k.40 blue	3·25	3·00

DESIGN: 1k.40, North Cape.

199 "Bridal Procession on Hardanger Fjord" (A. Tidemand and H. Gude)

1974. Norwegian Paintings. Multicoloured.

716	1k. Type **199**	75	45
717	1k.40 "Stugunoset from Filefjell" (J. Dahl)	1·40	1·30

200 Gulating Law Manuscript, 1325

1974. 700th Anniv of King Magnus Lagaboter National Legislation.

718	**200**	1k. red and brown	75	45
719	-	1k.40 blue and brown	1·50	1·40

DESIGN: 1k.40, King Magnus Lagaboter (sculpture in Stavanger Cathedral).

201 Trees and Saw Blade

1974. Industrial Accident Prevention.

720	**201**	85ore green, deep green and emerald	2·50	2·30
721	-	1k. carmine, red and orange	1·50	60

DESIGN: 1k. Flower and cogwheel.

202 J. H. L. Vogt

1974. Norwegian Geologists.

722	**202**	65ore brown and green	50	45
723	-	85ore brown and purple	2·50	2·30
724	-	1k. brown and orange	75	35
725	-	1k.40 brown and blue	1·50	1·40

DESIGNS: 85ore V. M. Goldschmidt; 1k. Th. Kjerulf; 1k.40, W. C. Brogger.

203 Buildings of the World

1974. Centenary of Universal Postal Union.

726	**203**	1k. brown and green	75	45
727	-	1k.40 blue and brown	1·50	1·40

DESIGN: 1k.40, People of the World.

204 Detail of Chest of Drawers

1974. Norwegian Folk Art. Rose Painting. Multicoloured.

728	85ore Type **204**	65	60
729	1k. Detail of cupboard	65	45

205 Woman Skier, 1900

1975. Norwegian Skiing.

730	**205**	1k. red and green	1·00	45
731	-	1k.40 blue and brown	1·30	1·20

DESIGN: 1k.40, Skier making telemark turn.

206 "Three Women with Ivies" Gate, Vigeland Park, Oslo

1975. International Women's Year.

732	**206**	1k.25 violet and purple	75	35
733	**206**	1k.40 ultramarine and blue	1·30	1·20

207 Nusfjord Fishing Harbour, Lofoten Islands

1975. European Architectural Heritage Year.

734	**207**	1k. green	1·00	70
735	-	1k.25 red	75	35
736	-	1k.40 blue	1·30	1·20

DESIGNS: 1k.25, Old Stavanger; 1k.40, Roros.

208 Norwegian 1k. Coin, 1875 (Monetary Convention)

1975. Cent of Monetary and Metre Conventions.

737	**208**	1k.25 red	1·00	35
738	-	1k.40 blue	1·10	90

DESIGN: 1k.40, O. J. Broch (original Director of the International Bureau of Weights and Measures) (Metre Convention).

209 Camping and Emblem

1975. World Scout Jamboree, Lillehammer. Multicoloured.

739	1k.25 Type **209**	1·10	45
740	1k.40 Skiing and emblem	1·50	1·40

210 Colonist's Peat House

1975. 150th Anniv of First Emigrations to America.

741	**210**	1k.25 brown	1·00	35
742	-	1k.40 blue	1·30	1·20

DESIGNS: 1k.40, C. Peerson and extract from letter to America, 1874.

211 "Templet" (Temple Mountain), Tempelfjord, Spitzbergen

1975. 50th Anniv of Norwegian Administration of Spitzbergen.

743	**211**	1k. grey	1·00	70
744	-	1k.25 purple	1·00	35
745	-	1k.40 blue	2·30	2·10

DESIGNS: 1k.25, Miners leaving pit; 1k.40, Polar bear.

212 "Television Screen" (T. E. Johnsen)

1975. 50th Anniv of Norwegian Broadcasting System. Multicoloured.

746	1k.25 Type **212**	75	35
747	1k.40 Telecommunications antenna (N. Davidsen) (vert)	1·00	90

213 "The Annunciation"

1975. Paintings from "Altaket" (wooden vault) of "Al" Stave Church, Hallingdal.

748	80ore Type **213**	50	45
749	1k. "The Visitation"	65	60
750	1k.25 "The Nativity" (30×38 mm)	75	35
751	1k.40 "The Adoration" (30×38 mm)	1·00	90

214 "Halling" (folk dance)

1976. Norwegian Folk Dances. Multicoloured.

752	80ore Type **214**	1·00	70
753	1k. "Springar"	1·00	45
754	1k.25 "Gangar"	75	35

215 Silver Sugar Caster, Stavanger, 1770

1976. Centenary of Oslo Museum of Applied Art.

755	**215**	1k.25 brown, red and pink	75	45
756	-	1k.40 lilac, blue and azure	1·00	90

DESIGN: 1k.40, Goblet, Nostetangen Glass-works, 1770.

216 Bishop's "Mitre" Bowl, 1760

1976. Europa. Early Products of Herrebo Potteries, Halden.

757	**216**	1k.25 red and mauve	75	60
758	-	1k.40 ultramarine & blue	1·00	90

DESIGN: 1k.40, Decorative plate, 1760.

217 "The Pulpit", Lyse Fjord

1976. Norwegian Scenery. Multicoloured.

759	1k. Type **217**	75	35
760	1k.25 Peak of Gulleplet ("The Golden Apple"), Balestrand, Sognefjord	1·30	35

218 Social Development Graph

1976. Cent of Norwegian Central Bureau of Statistics.

761	**218**	1k.25 red	65	35
762	-	2k. blue	1·10	45

DESIGN: 2k. National productivity graph.

219 Olav Duun and Cairn, Dun Mountain, Joa Island, Namsen Fjord

1976. Birth Centenary of Olav Duun (novelist).

763	**219**	1k.25 multicoloured	65	35
764	**219**	1k.40 multicoloured	1·00	90

220 "Slindebirkin" (T. Fearnley)

1976. Norwegian Paintings. Multicoloured.

765	1k.25 Type **220**	65	45
766	1k.40 "Gamle Furutraer" (L. Hertervig)	1·10	1·00

221 Details of "April"

1976. Tapestry from Baldishol Stave Church. Multicoloured.

767	80ore Type **221**	50	45
768	1k. Detail of "May"	65	45
769	1k.25 "April" and "May" section of tapestry (48×30 mm)	75	35

222 Five Water-lilies

1977. Nordic Countries Co-operation in Nature Conservation and Environment Protection.

770	**222**	1k.25 multicoloured	90	45
771	**222**	1k.40 multicoloured	1·00	90

223 Akershus Castle, Oslo

1977

772	-	1k. green	50	35
773	-	1k.10 purple	65	35
774	**223**	1k.25 red	65	35
775	-	1k.30 brown	65	35
776	-	1k.40 lilac	75	35
777	-	1k.50 red	75	35
778	-	1k.70 green	1·00	70
779	-	1k.75 green	75	35
780	-	1k.80 blue	90	45
781	-	2k. red	75	35
782	-	2k.20 blue	1·10	70
783	-	2k.25 violet	1·00	45
784	-	2k.50 red	1·00	35
785	-	2k.75 red	1·50	1·20
786	-	3k. blue	1·00	35
787	-	3k.50 violet	1·50	45

DESIGNS—HORIZ: 1k. Austraat Manor; 1k.10, Trondenes Church, Harstad; 1k.30, Steinviksholm Fortress, Asen Fjord; 1k.40, Ruins of Hamar Cathedral; 2k.20, Tromsdalen Church; 2k.50, Loghouse, Breiland; 2k.75, Damsgard Palace, Laksevag, near Bergen; 3k. Ruins of Selje Monastery; 3k.50, Lindesnes lighthouse. VERT: 1k.50, Stavanger Cathedral; 1k.70, Rosenkrantz Tower, Bergen; 1k.75, Seamen's commemoration hall, Stavern; 1k.80, Torungen lighthouses, Arendal; 2k. Tofte royal estate, Dovre; 2k.25, Oscarshall (royal residence), Oslofjord.

224 Hamnoy, Lofoten Islands

1977. Europa. Multicoloured.

795	1k.25 Type **224**	90	35
796	1k.80 Huldrefossen, Nordfjord (vert)	1·30	80

225 Spruce

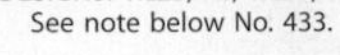

1977. Norwegian Trees.

797	**225**	1k. green	65	45
798	-	1k.25 brown	90	45
799	-	1k.80 black	1·10	1·00

DESIGNS: 1k.25, Fir; 1k.80, Birch.
See note below No. 433.

226 "Constitutionen" (paddle-steamer) at Arendal

1977. Norwegian Coastal Routes.

800	**226**	1k. brown	65	35
801	-	1k.25 red	1·00	35
802	-	1k.30 green	1·90	1·70
803	-	1k.80 blue	1·30	1·00

DESIGNS: 1k.25, "Vesteraalen" (coaster) off Bodo; 1k.30, "Kong Haakon" and "Dronningen" at Stavanger, 1893 (ferries); 1k.80, "Nordstjernen" and "Harald Jarl" (ferries).

227 "From the Herring Fishery" (after photo by S. A. Borretzen)

1977. Fishing Industry.

804	**227**	1k.25 brown on orange	1·00	35
805	-	1k.80 blue on blue	1·10	1·00

DESIGN: 1k.80, Saithe and fish hooks.
See note below No. 433.

228 "Saturday Evening" (H. Egedius)

1977. Norwegian Paintings. Multicoloured.

806	1k.25 Type **228**	50	45
807	1k.80 "Forest Lake in Lower Telemark" (A. Cappelen)	1·10	1·00

229 "David with the Bells"

1977. Miniatures from the Bible of Aslak Bolt. Multicoloured.

808	80ore Type **229**	50	45
809	1k. "Singing Friars"	65	35
810	1k.25 "The Holy Virgin with the Child" (34×27 mm)	65	35

230 "Peer and the Buck Reindeer" (after drawing by P. Krohg for "Peer Gynt")

1978. 150th Birth Anniv of Henrik Ibsen (dramatist).

811	**230**	1k.25 black and stone	65	35
812	-	1k.80 multicoloured	1·10	1·00

DESIGN: 1k.80, Ibsen (after E. Werenskiold).

231 Heddal Stave Church, Telemark

1978. Europa.

813	**231**	1k.25 brown and orange	1·10	35
814	-	1k.80 green and blue	1·50	1·40

DESIGN: 1k.80, Borgund stave church, Sogn.

232 Lenangstindene and Jaegervasstindene, Troms

1978. Norwegian Scenery. Multicoloured.

815	1k. Type **232**	75	35
816	1k.25 Gaustatoppen, Telemark	1·10	35

233 King Olav in Sailing-boat

1978. 75th Birthday of King Olav V.

817	**233**	1k.25 brown	1·00	35
818	-	1k.80 violet	1·10	80

DESIGN—VERT: 1k.80, King Olav delivering royal speech at opening of Parliament.

234 Amundsen's Polar Flight Stamp of 1925

1978. "Norwex 80" International Stamp Exhibition (1st issue).

819	**234**	1k.25 green and grey	1·00	90
820	**234**	1k.25 blue and grey	1·00	90
821	-	1k.25 green and grey	1·00	90
822	-	1k.25 blue and grey	1·00	90
823	**234**	1k.25 purple and grey	1·00	90
824	**234**	1k.25 red and grey	1·00	90
825	-	1k.25 purple and grey	1·00	90
826	-	1k.25 blue and grey	1·00	90

DESIGNS: Nos. 821/2, 825/6, Annexation of Spitzbergen stamp of 1925.

On Nos. 819/26 each design incorporates a different value of the 1925 issues.

See also Nos. **MS**847 and **MS**862.

235 Willow Pipe Player

1978. Musical Instruments.

827	**235**	1k. green	65	35
828	-	1k.25 red	75	35
829	-	1k.80 blue	1·30	90
830	-	7k.50 grey	5·00	35
831	-	15k. brown	6·25	45

DESIGNS: 1k.25, Norwegian violin; 1k.80, Norwegian zither; 7k.50, Ram's horn; 15k. Jew's harp.
See note below No. 433.

236 Wooden Doll, c. 1830

1978. Christmas. Antique Toys from Norwegian Folk Museum. Multicoloured.

835	80ore Type **236**	50	35
836	1k. Toy town, 1896/7	65	45
837	1k.25 Wooden horse from Torpo, Hallingdal	65	35

237 Ski Jumping at Huseby, 1879

1979. Centenary of Skiing Competitions at Huseby and Holmenkollen.

838	**237**	1k. green	75	45
839	-	1k.25 red	75	35
840	-	1k.80 blue	1·10	1·00

DESIGNS: 1k.25, Crown Prince Olav ski jumping at Holmenkollen, 1922; 1k.80, Cross-country skiing at Holmenkollen, 1976.

238 "Portrait of Girl" (M. Stoltenberg)

1979. International Year of the Child. Multicoloured.

841	1k.25 Type **238**	65	35
842	1k.80 "Portrait of Boy" (H. C. F. Hosenfelder)	1·00	90

239 Road to Briksdal Glacier

1979. Norwegian Scenery. Multicoloured.

843	1k. Type **239**	75	35
844	1k.25 Skjernoysund, near Mandal	1·00	35

240 Falkberget (after Harald Dal)

1979. Birth Centenary of Johan Falkberget (novelist).

845	**240**	1k.25 brown	65	35
846	-	1k.80 blue	1·00	90

DESIGN: 1k.80, "Ann-Magritt and the Hovi Bullock" (statue by Kristofer Leirdal).

241 Dornier Do-J Wal Flying Boat N-25

1979. "Norwex 80" International Stamp Exhibition, Oslo (2nd issue). Arctic Aviation. Sheet 113×91 mm containing T **241** and similar horiz designs, each black, yellow and ultramarine.

MS847 1k.25 Type **241** (Amundsen and Ellsworth, 1925); 2k. Airship N.1 *Norge* (Amundsen, Ellsworth and Nobile, 1926); 2k.80, Loening OA-2 amphibian *Live Eriksson* (Thor Solberg, 1935); 4k. Douglas DC-7C *Reider Viking* (first scheduled flight over North Pole, 1957) (sold at 15k.)	7·50	7·25

242 Steam Train on Kylling Bridge, Verma, Romsdal

1979. Norwegian Engineering.

848	**242**	1k.25 black and brown	70	35
849	-	2k. black and blue	1·10	35
850	-	10k. brown and bistre	5·50	60

DESIGNS: 2k. Vessingsjo Dam, Nea, Sor- Trondelag; 10k. Statfjord A offshore oil drilling and production platform.

243 Glacier Buttercup ("Ranunculus glacialis")

1979. Flowers. Multicoloured.

851	80ore Type **243**	55	35
852	1k. Alpine cinquefoil ("Potentilla crantzii")	55	35
853	1k.25 Purple saxifrage ("Saxifraga oppositifolia")	70	35

See also Nos. 867/8.

244 Leaf and Emblems

1980. Centenary of Norwegian Christian Youth Association. Multicoloured.

854	1k. Type **244**	70	35
855	1k.80 Plant and emblems	1·10	95

245 Oystercatcher Chick ("Haematopus ostralegus")

1980. Birds (1st series). Multicoloured.

856	1k. Type **245**	55	35
857	1k. Mallard chick ("Anas platyrhynchos")	55	35
858	1k.25 White-throated dipper ("Cinclus cinclus")	70	35
859	1k.25 Great tit ("Parus major")	70	35

See also Nos. 869/72, 894/5 and 914/15.

246 Telephone and Dish Aerial

1980. Centenary of Norwegian Telephone Service.

860	**246**	1k.25 brown, purple & bl	70	35
861	-	1k.80 multicoloured	1·10	95

DESIGN: 1k.80, Erecting a telephone pole.

247 *Bergen* (paddle-steamer)

1980. "Norwex 80" International Stamp Exhibition, Oslo (3rd issue). Sheet 113×90 mm containing T **247** and similar horiz designs.

MS862	1k.25, red and black; 2k. yellow and black; 2k.80, yellow, green and black; 4k. dull blue and black (sold at 15k.)	6·00	5·75

DESIGNS: 2k. Steam locomotive and carriages, 1900; 2k.80, Motor coach, 1940; 4k. Boeing 737 and Douglas DC-9 aircraft.

248 "Vulcan as an Armourer" (Hassel Jerverk after Bech)

1980. Nordic Countries' Postal Co-operation. Cast-iron Stove Ornaments.

863	**248**	1k.25 brown	70	35
864	-	1k.80 violet	1·10	95

DESIGN: 1k.80, "Hercules at a burning Altar" (Moss Jerverk after Henrich Bech).

249 "Jonsokbal" (Nikolai Astrup)

1980. Norwegian Paintings. Multicoloured.

865	1k.25 Type **249**	70	35
866	1k.80 "Seljefloyten" (Christian Skredsvig)	1·10	95

1980. Flowers. As T **243**. Multicoloured.

867	80ore Rowan berries ("Sorbus aucparia")	40	35
868	1k. Dog rose hips ("Rosa canina")	45	40

1981. Birds (2nd series). As T **245**. Multicoloured.

869	1k.30 Lesser white-fronted goose ("Anser erythropus")	70	60
870	1k.30 Peregrine falcon ("Falco peregrinus")	70	60
871	1k.50 Atlantic puffin ("Fratercula arctica")	80	35
872	1k.50 Black guillemot ("Cepphus grylle")	80	35

250 Cow

1981. Centenary of Norwegian Milk Producers' National Association. Multicoloured.

873	1k.10 Type **250**	70	35
874	1k.50 Goat	80	50

See note below No. 433.

251 "The Mermaid" (painting by Kristen Aanstad on wooden dish from Hol)

1981. Europa. Multicoloured.

875	1k.50 Type **251**	1·10	35
876	2k.20 "The Proposal" (painting by Ola Hansson on box from Nes)	1·40	1·20

See note below No. 433.

252 Weighing Anchor

1981. Sailing Ship Era.

877	**252**	1k.30 green	80	50
878	-	1k.50 red	80	35
879	-	2k.20 blue	1·20	1·10

DESIGNS—VERT: 1k.50, Climbing the rigging. HORIZ: 2k.20, "Christian Radich" (cadet ship).

253 "Skibladner" (paddle-steamer)

1981. Norwegian Lake Shipping.

880	**253**	1k.10 brown	70	35
881	-	1k.30 green	80	60
882	-	1k.50 red	80	35
883	-	2k.30 blue	1·20	60

DESIGNS: 1k.30, "Victoria" (ferry); 1k.50, "Faemund II" (ferry); 2k.30, "Storegut" (train ferry).

254 Handicapped People as Part of Community

1981. International Year of Disabled Persons.

884	**254**	1k.50 pink, red and blue	80	35
885	-	2k.20 blue, deep blue and red	1·20	1·10

DESIGN: 2k.20, Handicapped and non-handicapped people walking together.

255 "Interior in Blue" (Harriet Backer)

1981. Norwegian Paintings. Multicoloured.

886	1k.50 Type **255**	80	35
887	1k.70 "Peat Moor on Jaeren" (Kitty Lange Kielland)	1·10	95

256 Hajalmar Branting and Christian Lange

1981. Nobel Peace Prize Winners of 1921.

888	**256**	5k. black	2·75	35

257 "One of the Magi" (detail from Skjak tapestry, 1625)

1981. Tapestries. Multicoloured.

889	1k.10 Type **257**	55	40
890	1k.30 "Adoration of Christ" (detail, Skjak tapestry, 1625)	70	50
891	1k.50 "Marriage in Cana" (pillow slip from Storen, 18th century) (29×36 mm)	80	35

258 Ski Sticks

1982. World Ski Championships, Oslo.

892	**258**	2k. red and blue	80	35
893	-	3k. blue and red	1·10	60

DESIGN: 3k. Skis.

1982. Birds (3rd series). As T **245**. Multicoloured.

894	2k. Bluethroat ("Luscinia svecica")	80	35
895	2k. European robin ("Erithacus rubecula")	80	35

259 Nurse

1982. Anti-tuberculosis Campaign. Multicoloured.

896	2k. Type **259**	80	35
897	3k. Microscope	1·20	1·10

See note below No. 433.

260 King Haakon VII disembarking from "Heimdal" after Election, 1905

1982. Europa.

898	**260**	2k. brown	2·00	35
899	-	3k. blue	2·40	70

DESIGN: 3k. Crown Prince Olav greeting King Haakon VII after liberation, 1945.

261 "Girls from Telemark" (Erik Werenskiold)

1982. Norwegian Paintings. Multicoloured.

900	1k.75 Type **261**	80	60

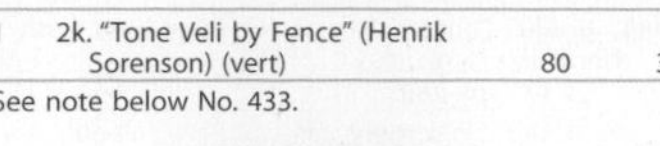

901	2k. "Tone Veli by Fence" (Henrik Sorenson) (vert)	80	35

See note below No. 433.

262 Consecration Ceremony, Nidaros Cathedral, Trondheim

1982. 25th Anniv of King Olav V's Reign.

902	**262**	3k. violet	1·60	1·20

263 "Bjornstjerne Bjornson on Balcony at Aulestad" (Erik Werenskiold)

1982. Writers' Birth Anniversaries. Multicoloured.

903	1k.75 Type **263** (150th anniv)	1·10	50
904	2k. "Sigrid Undset" (after A. C. Svarstad) (birth centenary)	1·10	35

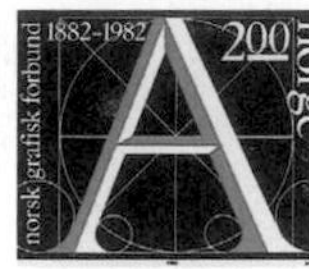

264 Construction of Letter "A"

1982. Centenary of Graphical Union of Norway.

905	**264**	2k. yellow, green and black	80	50
906	-	3k. multicoloured	1·40	70

DESIGN: 3k. Offset litho printing rollers.

265 Fridtjof Nansen

1982. 1922 Nobel Peace Prize Winner.

907	**265**	3k. blue	1·60	70

See note below No. 433.

266 "Christmas Tradition" (Adolf Tidemand)

1982. Christmas.

908	**266**	1k.75 multicoloured	70	35

267 Buhund (farm dog)

1983. Norwegian Dogs. Multicoloured.

909	2k. Type **267**	1·10	60
910	2k.50 Elkhound	1·40	35
911	3k.50 Lundehund (puffin hunter)	2·00	95

See note below No. 433.

268 Mountain Scenery

1983. Nordic Countries' Postal Co-operation. "Visit the North". Multicoloured.

912	2k.50 Type **268**	1·20	35
913	3k.50 Fjord scenery	1·60	95

1983. Birds (4th series). As T **245**. Multicoloured.

914	2k.50 Barnacle goose ("Branta leucopsis")	1·50	35
915	2k.50 Little auk ("Alle alle")	1·50	3·50

269 Edvard Grieg with Concerto in A minor

1983. Europa.

916	**269**	2k.50 red	2·00	35
917	-	3k.50 blue and green	2·40	95

DESIGN—VERT: 3k.50, Statue of Niels Henrik Abel (mathematician) by Gustav Vigeland.

270 Arrows forming Posthorn

1983. World Communications Year. Multicoloured.

918	2k.50 Type **270**	1·20	35
919	3k.50 Arrows circling globe	1·60	95

271 King Olav V and Royal Birch, Molde

1983. 80th Birthday of King Olav V.

920	**271**	5k. green	2·75	50

272 Lie

1983. 150th Birth Anniv of Jonas Lie (author).

921	**272**	2k.50 red	1·20	35

273 Northern Femboring

1983. North Norwegian Ships.

922	**273**	2k. blue and brown	1·20	60
923	-	3k. brown and blue	1·60	95

DESIGNS: 3k. Northern jekt.
See note below No. 433.

274 "The Sleigh Ride" (Axel Ender)

1983. Christmas. Multicoloured.

924	2k. Type **274**	1·20	50
925	2k.50 "The Guests are arriving" (Gustav Wendel)	1·40	50

275 Post Office Counter

1984. Postal Work. Multicoloured.

926	2k. Type **275**	1·40	50
927	2k.50 Postal sorting	1·40	35
928	3k.50 Postal delivery	2·00	70

276 Freshwater Fishing

1984. Sport Fishing.

929	**276**	2k.50 red	95	35
930	-	3k. green	1·40	60
931	-	3k.50 blue	1·60	60

DESIGNS: 3k. Atlantic salmon fishing; 3k.50, Sea fishing.

277 Magnetic Meridians and Parallels

1984. Birth Bicentenary of Christopher Hansteen (astronomer and geophysicist).

932	**277**	3k.50 blue	1·90	60
933	-	5k. red	2·75	50

DESIGN—VERT: 5k. Portrait of Hansteen by Johan Gorbitz.

278 Bridge

1984. Europa. 25th Anniv of European Post and Telecommunications Conference.

934	**278**	2k.50 multicoloured	1·90	35
935	**278**	3k.50 multicoloured	2·20	95

279 Vegetables, Fruit and Herbs

1984. Centenary of Norwegian Horticultural Society. Multicoloured.

936	2k. Type **279**	1·10	50
937	2k.50 Rose and garland of flowers	1·20	35

280 Honey Bees

1984. Centenaries of Norwegian Beekeeping Society and Norwegian Poultry-breeding Society. Multicoloured.

938	2k.50 Type **280**	1·20	35
939	2k.50 Leghorn cock	1·20	35

See note below No. 433.

281 Holberg (after J. M. Bernigeroth)

1984. 300th Birth Anniv of Ludvig Holberg (writer).

940	**281**	2k.50 red	1·40	35

282 Children reading

1984. 150th Anniv of "Norsk Penning-Magazin" (1st weekly magazine in Norway).

941	**282**	2k.50 purple, blue and red	1·10	35
942	-	3k.50 orange and violet	1·40	60

DESIGN: 3k.50, 1st edition of "Norsk Penning-Magazin".

283 Entering Parliamentary Chamber, 2 July 1884

1984. Cent of Norwegian Parliament.

943	**283**	7k.50 brown	5·50	1·20

284 Karius and Baktus (tooth decay bacteria)

1984. Characters from Stories by Thorbjorn Egner. Multicoloured.

944	2k. Type **284**	2·00	35
945	2k. The tree shrew playing guitar	2·00	35
946	2k.50 Kasper, Jesper and Jonatan (Rovers) in Kardemomme Town	2·75	50
947	2k.50 Chief Constable Bastian	2·75	50

285 Mount Sagbladet (Saw Blade)

1985. Antarctic Mountains. Multicoloured.

948	2k.50 Type **285**	2·00	35
949	3k.50 Mount Hoggestabben (Chopping Block)	2·75	95

286 Return of Crown Prince Olav, 1945

1985. 40th Anniv of Liberation.

950	**286**	3k.50 red and blue	2·20	70

287 Kongsten Fort

1985. 300th Anniv of Kongsten Fort.

951	**287**	2k.50 multicoloured	2·00	35

288 Bronze Cannon, 1596

1985. Artillery Anniversaries. Multicoloured.

952	3k. Type **288** (300th anniv of Artillery)	2·00	95
953	4k. Cannon on sledge carriage, 1758 (bicentenary of Artillery Officers Training School)	2·75	70

289 "Boy and Girl" (detail)

1985. International Youth Year. Sculptures in Vigeland Park, Oslo. Multicoloured.

954	2k. Type **289**	1·20	50
955	3k.50 Bronze fountain (detail)	2·00	1·10

See note below No. 433.

290 Torgeir Augundsson (fiddler)

1985. Europa. Music Year.

956	**290**	2k.50 red	2·00	35
957	-	3k.50 blue	2·75	70

DESIGN: 3k.50, Ole Bull (composer and violinist).

291 Workers at Glomfjord

1985. Centenary of Electricity in Norway.

958	**291**	2k.50 red and scarlet	1·40	35
959	-	4k. blue and green	2·20	50

DESIGN: 4k. Men working on overhead cable.

292 Ekofisk Centre

1985. Stamp Day. Norwegian Working Life (1st series). Offshore Oil Industry. Sheet 112×91 mm containing T **292** and similar horiz designs. Multicoloured.

MS960	2k.+1k. Type **292**; 2k.+1k. Drilling rig *Treasure Scout* and supply ship *Odin Viking*; 2k.+1k. Towing *Statfjord C* platform to oil field, 1984; 2k.+1k. Drilling team on rig *Neptuno Nordraug*	8·75	9·50

See also Nos. **MS**989 and **MS**1012.

293 Carl Deichman on Book Cover

1985. Bicentenary of Public Libraries.

961	**293**	2k.50 sepia and brown	1·60	35
962	-	10k. green	6·75	70

DESIGN—HORIZ: 10k. Library interior.

294 Wreath

1985. Christmas. Multicoloured.

963	2k. Type **294**	2·00	35
964	2k.50 Northern bullfinches	2·75	50

295 "Berghavn" (dredger)

1985. 250th Anniv of Port Authorities and Bicentenary of Hydrography in Norway.

965	**295**	2k.50 purple, orange & bl	1·40	35
966	-	5k. blue, green and brown	3·50	60

DESIGN: 5k. Sextant and detail of chart No. 1 of Lt. F.C. Grove showing Trondheim sealane, 1791.

296 Sun

1986

967	**296**	2k.10 orange and brown	1·40	35
968	-	2k.30 green and blue	1·50	35
969	-	2k.70 pink and red	1·60	40
970	-	4k. blue and green	2·00	50

DESIGNS: 2k.30, Atlantic cod and herring; 2k.70, Flowers; 4k. Star ornaments.

297 Marksman in Prone Position

1986. World Biathlon Championships. Multicoloured.

977	2k.50 Type **297**	1·40	35
978	3k.50 Marksman standing to take aim	2·00	1·20

298 Industry and Countryside

1986. Europa. Multicoloured.

979	2k.50 Type **298**	1·60	35
980	3k.50 Dead and living forest, mountains and butterflies	2·40	1·40

299 Stone Cutter

1986. Centenary of Norwegian Craftsmen's Federation.

981	**299**	2k.50 lake and red	1·40	35
982	-	7k. blue and red	4·75	95

DESIGN: 7k. Carpenter.

300 Moss

1986. Nordic Countries' Postal Co-operation. Twinned Towns. Multicoloured.

983	2k.50 Type **300**	1·40	35
984	4k. Alesund	2·00	60

See note below No. 433.

301 Hans Polson Egede (missionary) and Map

1986. Birth Anniversaries.

985	**301**	2k.10 brown and red	1·10	95
986	-	2k.50 red, green and blue	1·20	35
987	-	3k. brown and red	1·60	50
988	-	4k. purple and lilac	2·00	60

DESIGNS: 2k.10, Type **301** (300th anniv); 2k.50, Herman Wildenvey (poet) and poem carved in wall at Stavern (centenary); 3k. Tore Ojasaeter (poet) and old cupboard from Skjak (centenary); 4k. Engebret Soot (engineer) and lock gates, Orje (centenary).

See note below No. 433.

302 Timber being debarked and cut

1986. Stamp Day. Norwegian Working Life (2nd series). Paper Industry. Sheet 113×91 mm containing T **302** and similar horiz designs. Multicoloured.

MS989 2k.50+1k. Type **302**; 2k.50+1k. Boiling plant; 2k.50+1k. Paper factory; 2k.50+1k. Paper being dried and rolled into bales — 13·50 — 13·00

303 "Olav Kyrre founds Diocese in Nidaros"

1986. Christmas. Stained Glass Windows by Gabriel Kielland in Nidaros Cathedral, Trondheim. Multicoloured.

990	2k.10 Type **303**	2·00	30
991	2k.50 "The King and the Peasant at Sul"	2·20	35

304 Doves

1986. International Peace Year.

992	**304**	15k. red, blue and green	11·00	85

305 Numeral

1987

993	**305**	3k.50 yellow, red and blue	2·00	95
994	**305**	4k.50 blue, yellow & green	2·75	70

306 Wooden Building

1987. Europa. Multicoloured.

1000	2k.70 Type **306**	1·40	35
1001	4k.50 Building of glass and stone	2·75	85

307 The Final Vote

1987. 150th Anniv of Laws on Local Councils (granting local autonomy).

1002	**307**	12k. green	8·00	70

308 Rehabilitation Centre, Mogadishu

1987. Norwegian Red Cross in Somalia. Sheet 113×92 mm.

MS1003 **308** 4k.50 multicoloured — 3·50 — 3·25

309 Funnel-shaped Chanterelle ("Cantharellus tubaeformis")

1987. Fungi (1st series). Multicoloured.

1004	2k.70 Type **309**	1·60	35
1005	2k.70 The gypsy ("Rozites caperata")	1·60	35

See also Nos. 1040/1 and 1052/3.

310 Bjornstad Farm from Vaga

1987. Centenary of Sandvig Collections, Maihaugen.

1006	**310**	2k.70 sepia and brown	1·20	35
1007	-	3k.50 purple and blue	2·20	95

DESIGN: 3k.50, "Horse and Rider" (wooden carving, Christen Erlandsen Listad).

311 Valevag Churchyard

1987. Birth Centenary of Fartein Valen (composer).

1008	**311**	2k.30 blue and green	1·20	1·10
1009	-	4k.50 brown	2·40	50

DESIGN—VERT: 4k.50, Fartein Valen.

See note below No. 433.

312 "Storm at Sea" (Christian Krohg)

1987. Paintings. Multicoloured.

1010	2k.70 Type **312**	1·60	35
1011	5k. "The Farm" (Gerhard Munthe)	3·50	60

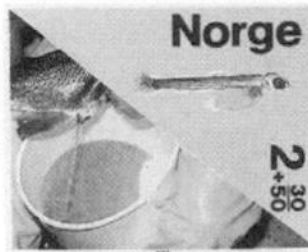

313 Eggs and Alevin

1987. Stamp Day. Norwegian Working Life (3rd series). Atlantic Salmon Farming. Sheet 113×91 mm containing T **313** and similar horiz designs. Multicoloured.

MS1012 2k.30+50ore Type **313**; 2k.70+50ore Hatching tanks and parr; 3k.50+50ore Marine stage; 4k.50+50ore Harvested salmon — 15·00 — 16·00

314 Cat with Children making Decorations

1987. Christmas. Multicoloured.

1013	2k.30 Type **314**	1·40	70
1014	2k.70 Dog with children making gingersnaps	1·90	50

315 Dales Pony

1987. Native Ponies.

1015	**315**	2k.30 deep brown, green and brown	1·10	95
1016	-	2k.70 buff, brown & blue	1·40	35
1017	-	4k.50 brown, red and blue	2·40	70

DESIGNS: 2k.70, Fjord pony; 4k.50, Nordland pony.

See note below No. 433.

316 Western Capercaillie

1988. Wildlife.

1018		2k.60 deep brown, brown and green	1·50	25
1019	**316**	2k.90 black, brn & grn	2·00	25
1020	-	3k. brown, grey and green	2·20	30
1021	-	3k.20 ultramarine, green and blue	2·30	35
1022	-	3k.80 brown, blue & blk	2·40	35
1023	-	4k. brown, red and green	2·50	40
1024	-	4k.50 brown, green & bl	2·75	50
1025	-	5k.50 brown, grey & grn	3·00	60
1026	-	6k.40 brown, blk & grn	3·50	85

DESIGNS: 2k.60, Fox; 3k. Stoat; 3k.20, Mute swan; 3k.80, Reindeer; 4k. Eurasian red squirrel; 4k.50, Beaver; 5k.50, Lynx; 6k.40, Tengmalm's owl.

317 Band

1988. Centenary of Salvation Army in Norway. Multicoloured.

1035	2k.90 Type **317**	1·60	35
1036	4k.80 Othilie Tonning (early social worker) and Army nurse	3·50	1·10

318 Building Fortress

1988. Military Anniversaries.

1037	**318**	2k.50 green	1·40	50
1038	-	2k.90 brown	1·60	50
1039	-	4k.60 blue	2·75	85

DESIGNS: 2k.50, Type **318** (300th anniv of Defence Construction Service); 2k.90, Corps members in action (centenary of Army Signals corps); 4k.60, Making pontoon bridge (centenary of Engineer Corps).

1988. Fungi (2nd series). As T **309**. Multicoloured.

1040	2k.90 Wood blewits ("Lepista nuda")	1·60	35
1041	2k.90 "Lactarius deterrimus"	1·60	35

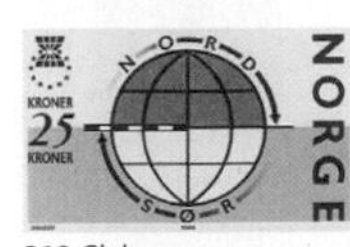

319 Globe

1988. European Campaign for Interdependence and Solidarity of North and South.

1042	**319**	25k. multicoloured	13·50	1·80

320 King Olav V

1988. 85th Birthday of King Olav V. Multicoloured.

1043	2k.90 Type **320**	1·60	35

MS1044 121×91 mm. 2k.90 King Olav arriving as baby; 2k.90 Type **320**; 2k.90 King Olav at Holmenkollen — 6·75 — 6·50

321 "Prinds Gustav" (paddle-steamer)

1988. Europa. Transport and Communications.

1045	**321**	2k.90 black, red and blue	2·00	60
1046	-	3k.80 blue, red & yellow	2·75	1·80

DESIGN: 3k.80, Heroybrua Bridge.

322 King Christian IV

1988. 400th Anniv of Christian IV's Accession to Danish and Norwegian Thrones.

1047	**322**	2k.50 black, stone & vio	2·00	35
1048	-	10k. multicoloured	6·75	60

DESIGN: 10k. 1628 silver coin and extract from decree on mining in Norway.

323 Handball

1988. Stamp Day. Sport. Sheet 113×91 mm containing T **323** and similar horiz designs. Multicoloured.

MS1049 2k.90 Type **323**; 2k.90 Football; 2k.90 Basketball; 2k.90 Volleyball (sold at 15k.) — 13·50 — 13·00

324 Ludvig with Ski Stick

1988. Christmas. Multicoloured.

1050	2k.90 Type **324**	2·00	35
1051	2k.90 Ludvig reading letter	2·00	35

1989. Fungi (3rd series). As T **309**. Multicoloured.

1052	3k. Chanterelle ("Cantharellus cibarius")	1·60	35
1053	3k. Butter mushroom ("Suillus luteus")	1·60	35

325 Start and Finish of Race

1989. World Cross-country Championship, Stavanger.
1054 **325** 5k. multicoloured 2·75 50

326 Vardo

1989. Town Bicentenaries.
1055 **326** 3k. blue, red & light blue 1·60 35
1056 - 4k. purple, blue & orange 2·75 95
DESIGN: 4k. Hammerfest.

327 Setesdal Woman

1989. Nordic Countries' Postal Co-operation. Traditional Costumes. Multicoloured.
1057 3k. Type **327** 1·60 35
1058 4k. Kautokeino man 2·75 95

328 Children making Snowman

1989. Europa. Children's Games. Multicoloured.
1059 3k.70 Type **328** 2·40 1·10
1060 5k. Cat's cradle 3·50 1·20
See note below No. 433.

329 Rooster and Cover of 1804 First Reader

1989. 250th Anniv of Primary Schools.
1061 **329** 2k.60 multicoloured 1·60 70
1062 - 3k. brown 1·60 35
DESIGN: 3k. Pocket calculator and child writing.

330 "Impressions of the Countryside" (detail)

1989. Stamp Day. Sheet 107×85 mm. containing T **330** and similar horiz designs, forming a composite design of the painting by Jakob Weidemann.
MS1063 3k.×4 multicoloured (sold at 15k.) 11·50 11·00

331 Bjorg Eva Jensen (300m. speed skating 1980)

1989. Winter Olympic Games, Lillehammer (1994) (1st issue). Norwegian Gold Medallists. Sheet 113×91 mm containing T **331** and similar horiz designs. Multicoloured.
MS1064 4k. Type **331**; 4k. Eirik Kvalfoss (biathlon, 1984); 4k. Tom Sandberg (combined cross-country and ski-jumping, 1984); 4k. Women's team (10km cross-country relay, 1984) (sold at 20k.) 11·00 10·00

See also Nos. **MS**1083, **MS**1097, **MS**1143, 1150/1, **MS**1157, 1169/70 and 1175/80.

332 Arnulf Overland (poet, centenary)

1989. Writers' Birth Anniversaries.
1065 **332** 3k. red and blue 1·60 35
1066 - 25k. blue, orange & green 12·00 1·80
DESIGN: 25k. Hanna Winsnes (pseudonym Hugo Schwartz) (bicentenary).

333 Star Decoration

1989. Christmas. Tree Decorations. Multicoloured.
1067 3k. Type **333** 1·60 35
1068 3k. Bauble 1·60 35

334 Larvik Manor

1989. Manor Houses.
1069 **334** 3k. brown 1·60 35
1070 - 3k. green 1·60 35
DESIGN: No. 1070, Rosendal Barony.

335 Emblem

1990. Winter Cities Events, Tromso.
1071 **335** 5k. multicoloured 2·75 60

336 Common Spotted Orchid ("Dactylorhiza fuchsii")

1990. Orchids (1st series). Multicoloured.
1072 3k.20 Type **336** 1·20 35
1073 3k.20 Dark red helleborine ("Epipactis atrorubens") 1·20 35
See also Nos. 1141/2.

337 Merchant Navy, Airforce, Home Guard, "Moses" (coastal gun) and Haakon VII's Monogram

1990. 50th Anniv of Norway's Entry into Second World War. Multicoloured.
1074 3k.20 Type **337** 2·40 35
1075 4k. Second Battle of Narvik, 1940 2·75 1·10

338 Penny Black

1990. 150th Anniv of the Penny Black. Sheet 113×91 mm containing T **338** and similar vert design.
MS1076 5k. Type **338**; 5k. First Norwegian stamp (sold at 15k.) 10·00 9·50

339 Trondheim Post Office

1990. Europa. Post Office Buildings. Multicoloured.
1077 3k.20 Type **339** 2·00 60
1078 4k. Longyearbyen Post Office 2·75 1·20

340 "Tordenskiold" (from print by J. W. Tegner after Balthazar Denner)

1990. 300th Birth Anniv of Admiral Tordenskiold (Peter Wessel). Multicoloured.
1079 3k.20 Type **340** 2·00 35
1080 5k. Tordenskiold's coat-of-arms 2·75 85

341 Svendsen

1990. 150th Birth Anniv of Johan Svendsen (composer and conductor).
1081 **341** 2k.70 black and red 1·60 70
1082 - 15k. brown and yellow 8·75 1·40
DESIGN: 15k. Svendsen Monument (Stinius Fredriksen), Oslo.

342 Thoreleif Haug (cross-country skiing, 1924)

1990. Winter Olympic Games, Lillehammer (1994) (2nd issue). Norwegian Gold Medallists. Sheet 113×91 mm containing T **342** and similar horiz designs. Multicoloured.
MS1083 4k. Type **342**; 4k. Sonja Henie (figure skating, 1928, 1932, 1936); 4k. Ivar Ballangrud (speed skating, 1928, 1936); 4k. Hjalmar Andersen (speed skating, 1952) (sold at 20k.) 11·00 10·50

343 "Children and Snowman" (Ragni Engstrom Nilsen)

1990. Christmas. Children's Prize-winning Drawings. Multicoloured.
1084 3k.20 Type **343** 1·40 50
1085 3k.20 "Christmas Church" (Jorgen Ingier) 1·40 50

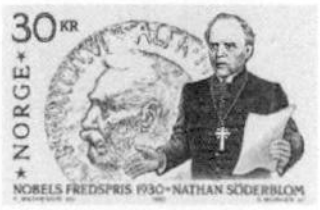

344 Nobel Medal and Soderblom

1990. 60th Anniv of Award of Nobel Peace Prize to Nathan Soderblom, Archbishop of Uppsala.
1086 **344** 30k. brown, blue and red 16·00 1·80

345 Plan and Elevation of Container Ship and Propeller

1991. Centenaries of Federation of Engineering Industries (1989) and Union of Iron and Metal Workers.
1087 **345** 5k. multicoloured 2·75 95

346 Satellite transmitting to Tromso

1991. Europa. Europe in Space. Multicoloured.
1088 3k.20 Type **346** 2·20 60
1089 4k. Rocket leaving Andoya rocket range 4·75 1·20
See note below No. 433.

347 Christiansholm Fortress (late 17th-century)

1991. 350th Anniv of Kristiansand. Each black, blue and red.
1090 3k.20 Type **347** 1·90 35
1091 5k.50 Present day view of Christiansholm Fortress 2·75 50

348 Fountain, Vigeland Park, Oslo

1991. Nordic Countries' Postal Co-operation. Tourism. Multicoloured.
1092 3k.20 Type **348** 1·90 35
1093 4k. Globe, North Cape Plateau 3·50 1·70

349 "Skomvaer III" (lifeboat)

1991. Centenary of Norwegian Society for Sea Rescue.
1094 **349** 3k.20 brown, black & grn 1·90 60
1095 - 27k. brown, grey & purple 13·50 2·40
DESIGN—VERT: 27k. "Colin Archer" (first lifeboat).

350 Engraving on Steel

1991. Stamp Day. Stamp Engraving. Sheet 113×91 mm containing T **350** and similar horiz designs.
MS1096 2k.70 Type **350**; 3k.20 Engraver using magnifying glass; 4k. Engraver's hands seen through magnifying glass; 5k. Positive impression of engraving and burin (sold at 20k.) 10·00 9·50

351 Birger Ruud (ski jumping, 1932, 1936; downhill, 1936)

1991. Winter Olympic Games, Lillehammer (1994) (3rd issue). Norwegian Gold Medallists. Sheet 113×91 mm containing T **351** and similar horiz designs. Multicoloured.
MS1097 4k. Type **351**; 4k. Johann Grottumsbraten (cross-country skiing, 1928, 1932); 4k. Knut Johannesen (speed skaing, 1960, 1964); 4k. Magnar Solberg (biathlon, 1960, 1968, 1972) (sold at 20k.) 11·00 10·50

352 Posthorn

1991
1098 **352** 1k. black and orange 55 25
1099 **352** 2k. red and green 70 30

1100	**352**	3k. green and blue	1·10	35
1101	**352**	4k. red and orange	1·40	40
1102	**352**	5k. blue and green	1·60	50
1103	**352**	6k. red and green	2·00	95
1104	**352**	7k. blue and brown	2·40	95
1105	**352**	8k. green and purple	2·75	50
1106	**352**	9k. brown and blue	3·25	60

353 Guisers with Goat Head

1991. Christmas. Guising. Multicoloured.

1120	3k.20 Type **353**	1·40	35
1121	3k.20 Guisers with lantern	1·40	35

354 Queen Sonja

355 King Harald

356 King Harald

1992

1122	**354**	2k.80 lake, purple & red	1·60	35
1123	**354**	3k. green, deep green and turquoise	1·40	50
1124	**355**	3k.30 blue, ultramarine and light blue	1·90	35
1125	**355**	3k.50 black and grey	1·60	50
1126	**355**	4k.50 deep red and red	1·90	50
1127	**355**	5k.50 brown, sepia & blk	2·20	50
1128	**355**	5k.60 orange, red and vermilion	2·75	35
1129	**355**	6k.50 emerald, green and turquoise	2·00	85
1130	**355**	6k.60 maroon, purple and brown	3·50	50
1131	**355**	7k.50 violet, lilac and purple	3·00	2·20
1132	**355**	8k.50 chestnut, deep brown and brown	3·50	2·20
1133	**356**	10k. green	3·50	35
1438	**356**	20k. violet	7·25	1·70
1138	**356**	30k. blue	10·00	60
1139	**356**	50k. green	16·00	2·20

1992. Orchids (2nd series). As T **336**. Multicoloured.

1141	3k.30 Lady's slipper orchid ("Cypripedium calceolus")	1·40	35
1142	3k.30 Fly orchid ("Ophrys insectifera")	1·40	35

357 Hallgeir Brenden (cross-country skiing, 1952, 1956)

1992. Winter Olympic Games, Lillehammer (4th issue). Norwegian Gold Medallists. Sheet 113×91 mm containing T **357** and similar horiz designs. Multicoloured.

MS1143 4k. Type **357**; 4k. Arnfinn Bergmann (ski jumping, 1952); 4k. Stein Eriksen (super slalom, 1952); 4k. Simon Slattvik (combined, 1952) (sold at 20k.) 11·00 10·00

358 "Restaurationen" (emigrant sloop)

1992. Europa. 500th Anniv of Discovery of America by Columbus. Transatlantic Ships. Multicoloured.

1144	3k.30 Type **358**	2·20	60
1145	4k.20 "Stavangerfjord" (liner) and American skyline	2·75	1·20

See note below No. 433.

359 Norwegian Pavilion, Rainbow and Ship

1992. "Expo '92" World's Fair, Seville. Multicoloured.

1146	3k.30 Type **359**	1·60	60
1147	5k.20 Mountains, rainbow, fish and oil rig	2·75	85

360 Molde

1992. 250th Anniversaries of Molde and Kristiansund.

1148	**360**	3k.30 blue, green & brn	1·90	35
1149	-	3k.30 blue, brown & lt bl	1·90	35

DESIGN: No. 1149, Kristiansund.

361 Banners and Lillehammer Buildings

1992. Winter Olympic Games, Lillehammer (1994) (5th issue). Multicoloured.

1150	3k.30 Type **361**	1·60	35
1151	4k.20 Flags	2·20	95

362 Flask with Etched Figures (Serre Petersen)

1992. Stamp Day. Sheet 113×91 mm containing T **362** and similar horiz designs. Multicoloured.

MS1152 2k.80 Type **362**; 3k.30 Monogrammed carafe; 4k.20 Cut-glass salad bowl; 5k.20 Engraved goblet (Heinrich Gottlieb Kohler) (sold at 20k.) 10·00 9·50

363 Gnomes below Pillar Box

1992. Christmas. Christmas card designs by Otto Moe. Multicoloured.

1153	3k.30 Type **363**	1·20	35
1154	3k.30 Gnome posting letter	1·20	35

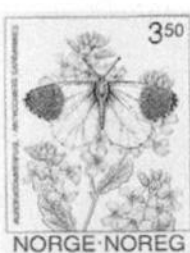

364 Orange-tip ("Anthocaris cardamines")

1993. Butterflies (1st series). Multicoloured.

1155	3k.50 Type **364**	1·40	35
1156	3k.50 Small tortoiseshell ("Aglais urticae")	1·40	35

See also Nos. 1173/4.

365 Finn Chr. Jagge (slalom)

1993. Winter Olympic Games, Lillehammer (1994) (6th issue). Norwegian Gold Medallists at 1992 Games. Sheet 113×91 mm containing T **365** and similar horiz designs. Multicoloured.

MS1157 4k.50 Type **365**; 4k.50 Bjorn Daehlie (cross-country skiing); 4k.50 Geir Karlstad (speed skating); 4k.50 Vegard Ulvang (cross-country skiing) 9·50 9·00

366 Grieg

1993. 150th Birth Anniv of Edvard Grieg (composer). Multicoloured.

1158	3k.50 Type **366**	2·00	35
1159	5k.50 "Spring"	3·00	60

367 Two-man Kayak on Lake

1993. Nordic Countries' Postal Co-operation. Tourist Activities. Multicoloured.

1160	4k. Type **367**	2·40	50
1161	4k.50 White-water rafting	2·75	60

368 Richard With (founder) and "Vesteraalen"

1993. Centenary of Express Coaster Service.

1162	**368**	3k.50 blue, violet and red	2·00	35
1163	-	4k.50 multicoloured	2·75	85

DESIGN: 4k.50, "Kong Harald".

369 Handball

1993. Sports Events. Multicoloured.

1164	3k.50 Type **369** (Women's World Championship, Norway)	2·00	60
1165	5k.50 Cycling (World Championships, Oslo and Hamar)	3·00	95

370 Johann Castberg (politician)

1993. Centenary of Workforce Protection Legislation.

1166	**370**	3k.50 brown and blue	2·00	60
1167	-	12k. blue and brown	6·00	1·20

DESIGN: 12k. Betzy Kjelsberg (first woman factory inspector).

371 Deail of Altarpiece (Jakob Klukstad), Lesja Church

1993. Stamp Day. Wood Carvings of Acanthus Leaves. Sheet 113×91 mm containing T **371** and similar horiz designs. Multicoloured.

MS1168 3k. Type **371**; 3k.50 Detail of dresser (Ola Teigeroen); 4k.50 Detail of Fliksaker chest (Jens Strammerud); 5k.50 Detail of pulpit, Our Saviour's Church, Oslo (sold at 21k.) 10·00 9·50

372 Torch Bearer on Skis

1993. Winter Olympic Games, Lillehammer (1994) (7th issue). Morgedal–Lillehammer Torch Relay. Multicoloured.

1169	3k.50 Type **372**	1·20	35
1170	3k.50 Lillehammer	1·20	35

Nos. 1169/70 were issued together, *se-tenant*, forming a composite design.

373 Store Mangen Chapel

1993. Christmas. Multicoloured.

1171	3k.50 Type **373**	1·20	35
1172	3k.50 Stamnes church, Sandnessjoen	1·20	35

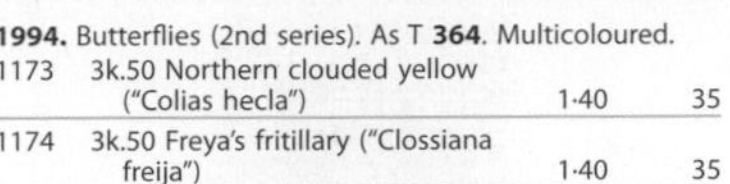
1994. Butterflies (2nd series). As T **364**. Multicoloured.

1173	3k.50 Northern clouded yellow ("Colias hecla")	1·40	35
1174	3k.50 Freya's fritillary ("Clossiana freija")	1·40	35

374 Flags

1994. Winter Olympic Games, Lillehammer (8th issue). Multicoloured.

1175	3k.50 Type **374**	1·20	35
1176	3k.50 Flags (different)	1·20	35
1177	3k.50 Lillehammer (church) and rings	1·20	35
1178	3k.50 Lillehammer (ski jump) and rings	1·20	35
1179	4k.50 Flags of European countries	1·90	50
1180	5k.50 Flags of non-European countries	2·40	60

Nos. 1175/8 were issued together, *se-tenant*, forming a composite design.

375 Cross-country Skiing

1994. Paralympic Games, Lillehammer. Multicoloured.

1181	4k.50 Type **375**	1·80	60
1182	5k.50 Downhill skiing	1·80	60

376 King Christian VII's Signature and Seal

1994. Bicentenary of Tromso.

1183	**376**	3k.50 red, bistre & brn	2·00	35
1184	-	4k.50 blue, yellow and light blue	2·75	70

DESIGN: 4k.50, Tromsdalen church.

377 Mount Floy Incline Railway Cars, Bergen

1994. Tourism. Multicoloured.

1185	4k. Type **377**	2·00	50
1186	4k.50 "Svolvaer Goat" (rock formation), Lofoten	2·40	60
1187	5k.50 Beacon, World's End, Tjome	2·75	85

378 Osterdal Farm Buildings

1994. Cent of Norwegian Folk Museum, Bygdoy.

1188	**378**	3k. multicoloured	1·60	50
1189	-	3k.50 blue, yellow and purple	2·00	60

DESIGN: 3k.50, Horse-drawn sleigh, 1750 (Torsten Hoff).

379 Technological Symbols and Formula ("Glass Flasks")

1994. EUREKA (European technology co-operation organization) Conference of Ministers, Lillehammer. Multicoloured.

1190	4k. Type **379**	2·00	60
1191	4k.50 Technological symbols ("Electronic Chips")	2·75	95

380 Electric Tram and Street Plan of Oslo, 1894

1994. Centenary of Electric Trams. Multicoloured.

1192	3k.50 Type **380**	2·00	60
1193	12k. Articulated tram and Oslo route map	6·75	1·20

381 Engraved Brooch

1994. Stamp Day. Jewellery. Sheet 113×91 mm containing T **381** and similar horiz designs. Multicoloured.

MS1194	3k. Type **381**; 3k.50 Silver and gem studded brooch; 4k.50 "Rings" brooch; 5k.50 Brooch with medallions and central stone (sold at 21k.)	11·00	10·00

382 Sledge

1994. Christmas.

1195	**382**	3k.50 red and black	1·20	35
1196	-	3k.50 ultramarine, blue and black	1·20	35

DESIGN: No. 1196, Kick-sledge.

383 Cowberry ("Vaccinium vitis-idaea")

1995. Wild Berries (1st Series). Multicoloured.

1197	3k.50 Type **383**	1·40	35
1198	3k.50 Bilberry ("Vaccinium myrtillus")	1·40	35

See also Nos. 1224/5.

384 Swan Pharmacy, Bergen

1995. 400th Anniv of Norwegian Pharmacies. Multicoloured.

1199	3k.50 Type **384**	2·00	60
1200	25k. Scales, pestle and mortar and ingredients	12·00	3·00

385 German Commander saluting Terje Rollem (Home Guard commander)

1995. 50th Anniv of Liberation of Norway.

1201	**385**	3k.50 silver, green and black	2·00	60
1202	-	4k.50 silver, blue and black	2·40	95
1203	-	5k.50 silver, red and black	2·75	1·20

DESIGNS: 4k.50, King Haakon VII and family returning to Norway; 5k.50, Children waving Norwegian flags.

386 Old Moster Church

1995. Millenary of Christianity in Norway. Multicoloured.

1204	3k.50 Type **386**	2·00	60
1205	15k. Slettebakken Church, Bergen	6·75	2·40

387 Skudeneshavn

1995. Nordic Countries' Postal Co-operation. Tourism. Multicoloured.

1206	4k. Type **387**	1·40	60
1207	4k.50 Hole in the Hat (coastal rock formation)	1·60	95

388 Flagstad as Isolde

1995. Birth Centenary of Kirsten Flagstad (opera singer). Multicoloured.

1208	3k.50 Type **388**	2·00	60
1209	5k.50 Flagstad in scene from "Lohengrin" (Wagner)	2·75	85

389 Disputants in Conflict

1995. Bicentenary of Conciliation Boards. Multicoloured.

1210	7k. Type **389**	3·50	1·20
1211	12k. Disputants in conciliation with mediator	5·50	1·80

390 Letter and Vice-regent Hannibal Sehested (founder)

1995. 350th Anniv (1997) of Norwegian Postal Service (1st issue). Multicoloured.

1212	3k.50 Type **390** (letter post, 1647)	1·40	70
1213	3k.50 Wax seal (registered post, 1745)	1·40	70
1214	3k.50 Postmarks (1845)	1·40	70
1215	3k.50 Banknotes, coins and money orders (transfer of funds, 1883)	1·40	70
1216	3k.50 Editions of "Norska Intelligenz-Sedler" and "Arkiv" (newspapers and magazines, 1660)	1·40	70
1217	3k.50 Address label, cancellations and "Constitutionen" (paddle-steamer) (parcel post, 1827)	1·40	70
1218	3k.50 Stamps (1855)	1·40	70
1219	3k.50 Savings book (Post Office Savings Bank, 1950)	1·40	70

The dates are those of the introduction of the various services.

See also Nos. 1237/44 and 1283/90.

391 Trygve Lie (first Secretary-General) and Emblem

1995. 50th Anniv of U.N.O. Multicoloured.

1220	3k.50 Type **391**	2·00	50
1221	5k.50 Relief worker, water pump and emblem	2·75	85

392 Woolly Hat

1995. Christmas. Multicoloured.

1222	3k.50 Type **392**	1·20	35
1223	3k.50 Mitten	1·20	35

1996. Wild Berries (2nd series). As T **383**. Multicoloured.

1224	3k.50 Wild strawberries ("Fragaria vesca")	1·20	35
1225	3k.50 Cloudberries ("Rubus chamaemorus")	1·20	35

393 Advent Bay

1996. Svalbard Islands. Multicoloured.

1226	10k. Type **393**	4·75	1·20
1227	20k. Polar bear	8·75	3·50

394 Cross-country Skier (Hakon Paulsen)

1996. Centenary of Modern Olympic Games. Children's Drawings. Multicoloured.

1228	3k.50 Type **394**	2·00	60
1229	5k.50 Athlete (Emil Tanem)	2·75	1·20

395 Besseggen

1996. Tourism. UNESCO World Heritage Sites. Multicoloured.

1230	4k. Type **395**	1·40	85
1231	4k.50 Stave church, Urnes	1·60	95
1232	5k.50 Rock carvings, Alta	2·00	1·20

See also Nos. 1291/3.

396 Steam Train, Urskog-Holand Line

1996. Railway Centenaries. Multicoloured.

1233	3k. Type **396**	1·60	60
1234	4k.50 Steam train, Setesdal line	2·00	1·20

397 Location Map and Height Indicator

1996. Natural Gas Production at Troll, near Bergen. Multicoloured.

1235	3k.50 Type **397**	1·60	60
1236	25k. Planned route map of pipelines to Europe for next 200 years	10·00	4·75

398 Postal Courier crossing Mountains

1996. 350th Anniv (1997) of Postal Service (2nd issue). Multicoloured.

1237	3k.50 Type **398**	1·40	70
1238	3k.50 "Framnaes" (fjord steamer)	1·40	70
1239	3k.50 Postal truck in Oslo	1·40	70
1240	3k.50 Taking mail on board Junkers W-34 "Ternen" (seaplane) on Jonsvatn Lake, Trondheim	1·40	70
1241	3k.50 Loading mail train at East Station, Oslo	1·40	70
1242	3k.50 Rural postman at Mago farm, Nittedal	1·40	70
1243	3k.50 Serving customer, Elverum post office	1·40	70
1244	3k.50 Computer, letters and globe	1·40	70

399 Leif Juster, Sean Connery, Liv Ullmann and Olsen Gang

1996. Centenary of Motion Pictures. Multicoloured.

1245	3k.50 Type **399**	1·60	70
1246	5k.50 Wenche Foss, Jack Fjeldstad, Marilyn Monroe, blood and gun	2·00	95
1247	7k. Charlie Chaplin in "Modern Times", Ottar Gladvedt, Laurel and Hardy and Marlene Dietrich	3·00	1·30

400 Left Detail of Embroidery

1996. Christmas. Embroidery Details from Telemark Folk Costume. Multicoloured.

1248	3k.50 Type **400**	1·20	50
1249	3k.50 Right detail	1·20	50

Nos. 1248/9 were issued together, *se-tenant*, forming a composite design.

401 Skram

1996. 150th Birth Anniv of Amalie Skram (writer).

1250	**401**	3k.50 red	1·60	60
1251	-	15k. violet and red	6·75	3·00

DESIGN: 15k. Scene from dramatisation of "People of Hellemyr".

402 Posthorn

1997. Multicoloured, colour of oval given.

1252	**402**	10ore red	40	25
1253	**402**	20ore blue	40	25
1254	**402**	30ore orange	40	25
1255	**402**	40ore black	40	25
1256	**402**	50ore green	40	25

403 Coltsfoot

1997. Flowers. Multicoloured.

1259	3k.20 Red clover	1·10	35
1260	3k.40 Marsh marigold	1·20	35
1261	3k.60 Red campion	1·40	60
1262	3k.70 Type **403**	1·50	35
1263	3k.80 Wild pansy	1·60	40
1264	4k. Wood anemone	1·80	50
1265	4k.30 Lily of the valley	2·00	50
1266	4k.50 White clover	2·20	70
1267	5k. Harebell	2·30	60
1268	5k.40 Oeder's lousewort	2·40	85
1269	5k.50 Hepatica	2·50	70
1270	6k. Ox-eye daisy	2·75	70
1271	7k. Yellow wood violet	2·75	1·20
1272	7k.50 Pale pasque flower	3·00	1·30
1273	8k. White water-lily	3·00	1·60
1274	13k. Purple saxifrage	4·75	2·40
1275	14k. Globe flower	5·50	3·50
1276	25k. Melancholy thistle	9·50	4·75

404 Bumble Bee

1997. Insects (1st series). Multicoloured.

1277	3k.70 Type **404**	1·20	35
1278	3k.70 Ladybird	1·20	35

See also Nos. 1306/7.

405 Ski Jumping

1997. World Nordic Skiing Championships, Trondheim. Multicoloured.
1279 3k.70 Type **405** 1·60 60
1280 5k. Speed skiing 2·20 1·20

406 King Harald (photo by Erik Johansen)

1997. 60th Birthdays of King Harald and Queen Sonja. Multicoloured.
1281 3k.70 Type **406** 1·80 60
1282 3k.70 Queen Sonja and King Harald (photo by Knut Falch) (horiz) 1·80 60

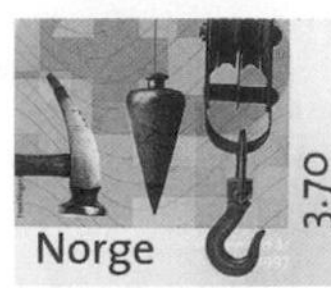

407 Hammer, Plumb Line and Hook (post-war reconstruction)

1997. 350th Anniv of Postal Service (3rd issue). Post-war History. Multicoloured.
1283 3k.70 Type **407** 1·40 85
1284 3k.70 "Kon Tiki" (replica of balsa raft) (Thor Heyerdahl's expedition from Peru to Polynesia, 1947) 1·40 85
1285 3k.70 Grouse feather (official bird of Rondane National Park (first National Park, 1962)) 1·40 85
1286 3k.70 Hands of man and woman (Welfare State (introduction of National Insurance, 1967)) 1·40 85
1287 3k.70 Drilling platform, Ekofisk oil field (discovery of oil in Norwegian sector of North Sea, 1969) 1·40 85
1288 3k.70 Grete Waitz (first women's world Marathon champion, 1983) 1·40 85
1289 3k.70 Askoy Bridge, 1992 (communications) 1·40 85
1290 3k.70 Crown Prince Haakon Magnus lighting Olympic flame (Winter Olympic Games, Lillehammer, 1994) 1·40 85

1997. Tourism. As T **395**. Multicoloured.
1291 4k.30 Roros 1·60 85
1292 5k. Faerder Lighthouse 1·90 1·20
1293 6k. Nusfjord 2·20 1·30

408 University, Cathedral, Statue of King Olav, City Gate and Broadcasting Tower

1997. Millenary of Trondheim. Multicoloured.
1294 3k.70 Type **408** 1·60 60
1295 12k. Trees, mine, King Olav, pilgrims, burning buildings and harbour 5·50 1·80

409 Gerhardsen and Storting (Parliament House)

1997. Birth Centenary of Einar Gerhardsen (Prime Minister 1945–51, 1955–63 and 1963–65).
1296 **409** 3k.70 black, stone and red 1·60 60
1297 - 25k. black, flesh and green 10·00 4·75
DESIGN: 25k. Gerhardsen, mountain, factory and electricity pylon.

410 Thematic Subjects

1997. Inauguration of National Junior Stamp Club. Multicoloured.
1298 3k.70 Type **410** 1·60 60
1299 3k.70 Thematic subjects including fish and tiger 1·60 60

411 Harald Saeverud (composer)

1997. Birth Centenaries.
1300 **411** 10k. blue 4·75 1·20
1301 - 15k. green 6·75 3·00
DESIGN: 15k. Tarjei Vesaas (writer).

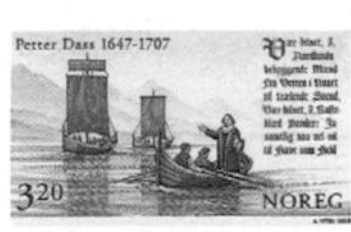

412 Dass in Rowing Boat

1997. 350th Birth Anniv of Petter Dass (priest and poet). Multicoloured.
1302 **412** 3k.20 blue and brown 1·40 95
1303 - 3k.70 green, blue and brown 1·60 1·10
DESIGN: 3k.70, Dass and Alstahaug Church.

413 Golden Calendar Stick Symbols against Candle Flames

1997. Christmas. Multicoloured. Self-adhesive.
1304 3k.70 Type **413** 1·20 60
1305 3k.70 Silver calendar stick symbols against night sky 1·20 60

1998. Insects (2nd series). As T **404**. Multicoloured.
1306 3k.80 Dragonfly 1·40 70
1307 3k.80 Grasshopper 1·40 70

414 Roses

1998. St. Valentine's Day. Self-adhesive.
MS1308 multicoloured 5·50 5·50

415 "Hornelen" (passenger and mail steamer)

1998. Nordic Countries' Postal Co-operation. Ships.
1309 **415** 3k.80 blue and green 1·40 60
1310 - 4k.50 green and blue 2·40 1·80
DESIGN: No. 1310, "Kommandoren" (passenger catamaran).

416 Holmenkollen Ski Jump, Oslo

1998. Tourist Sights. Multicoloured.
1311 3k.80 Type **416** 1·40 95
1312 4k.50 Fisherman, Alesund Harbour 1·60 1·20
1313 5k.50 Mt Hamaroyskaftet 2·00 1·40

417 Egersund Harbour

1998. Bicentenary of Egersund.
1314 **417** 3k.80 blue and pink 1·40 95
1315 - 6k. blue and mauve 2·20 1·40
DESIGN: No. 1315, Egersund ceramics.

418 Silver

1998. Minerals. Multicoloured.
1316 3k.40 Type **418** 1·40 60
1317 5k.20 Cobalt 2·00 1·20

419 "Water Rider" (Frans Widerberg)

1998. Contemporary Art. Multicoloured.
1318 6k. Type **419** 2·20 1·20
1319 7k.50 "Red Moon" (carpet, Synnove Anker Aurdal) 3·50 1·80
1320 13k. "King Haakon VII" (sculpture, Nils Aas) 5·50 3·00

420 Hopscotch

1998. Children's Games (1st series). Multicoloured.
1321 3k.80 Type **420** 1·40 95
1322 5k.50 Throwing coins at a stick 2·00 1·40
See also Nos 1355/6.

421 Boeing 747, Douglas DC-3 and Junkers Ju 52/3m Airliners

1998. Inauguration of Oslo Airport, Gardermoen. Multicoloured.
1323 3k.80 Type **421** 1·40 95
1324 6k. Boeing 737 airliner and map of former approaches to Gardermoen Airport 2·75 1·40
1325 24k. Terminal building, control tower and wings drawn by Leonardo da Vinci 9·50 4·75

422 Main Entrance and Guard

1998. 150th Anniv of Royal Palace, Oslo.
1326 **422** 3k.40 purple 1·20 85
1327 - 3k.80 blue, pink and yellow 1·40 95
DESIGN: 3k.80, Main front of palace.

423 Music Score

1998. Christmas. Multicoloured. Self-adhesive.
1328 3k.80 Type **423** (red background) 1·40 60
1329 3k.80 Music score (blue background) 1·40 60

424 Cheese Slicer (Thor Bjorklund)

1999. Norwegian Inventions. Self-adhesive.
1330 **424** 3k.60 black and blue 1·20 60
1331 - 4k. black and red 1·40 70
1332 - 4k.20 black and green 1·80 1·20
DESIGNS: 4k. Paper clip (Johan Vaaler); 4k.20 Aerosol can (Erik Rotheim).

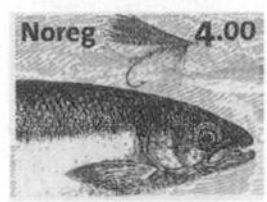

425 Salmon and Fly

1999. Fish and Fishing Flies. Multicoloured. Self-adhesive.
1333 4k. Type **425** 1·40 85
1334 4k. Cod and fly 1·40 85

426 Heart blowing Flowers out of Posthorn

1999. St. Valentine's Day.
1335 **426** 4k. multicoloured 1·40 85

427 "The Pioneer" (statue, Per Palle Storm)

1999. Centenary of Norwegian Confederation of Trade Unions.
1336 **427** 4k. multicoloured 1·40 85

428 Poland v Norway, Class B Championship, 1998

1999. World Ice Hockey Championships, Norway. Multicoloured.
1337 4k. Type **428** 1·40 85
1338 7k. Switzerland v Sweden, Class A Championship, 1998 2·75 1·20

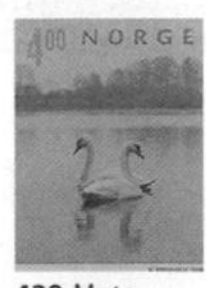

429 Mute Swans

1999. Tourism. Multicoloured.
1339 4k. Type **429** 1·40 95
1340 5k. Hamar Cathedral 1·60 1·20
1341 6k. Sami man from Troms 2·00 1·60

430 Emigration

1999. "Norway 2000" (1st issue). Norwegian History. Multicoloured.
1342 4k. Type **430** 1·40 95
1343 6k. King Olav and Bible (conversion to Christianity, 11th century) 2·20 1·20
1344 14k. Medal of King Christian IV and quarry workers (union of Norway and Denmark) 5·50 3·00
1345 26k. Oslo at Beier Bridge, 1850s (industrialization) 9·50 4·75

431 Horse Ferry, Amli, East Agder, 1900

1999. "Norway 2000" (2nd issue). Photographs of Everyday Life. Multicoloured.

1346	4k. Type **431**	1·60	85
1347	4k. Men hewing rock during construction of Valdres railway line, 1900	1·60	85
1348	4k. Taxi driver Aarseth Odd filling up car with petrol, Kleive, 1930	1·60	85
1349	4k. Dairymaid Mathea Isaksen milking cow, Karmoy, 1930	1·60	85
1350	4k. Haymakers, Hemsedal, 1943	1·60	85
1351	4k. Cross-country skier Dagfinn Knutsen, 1932	1·60	85
1352	4k. "Bolgen" (coastal fishing boat), Varanger Fjord, 1977	1·60	85
1353	4k. Boy Jon Andre Koch holding football, 1981	1·60	85
MS1354	136×148 mm. Nos. 1346/53	13·50	13·00

432 Skateboarding

1999. Children's Games (2nd series). Multicoloured.

1355	4k. Type **432**	1·40	85
1356	6k. Inline skating	2·75	1·20

433 Wenche Foss and Per Haugen in "An Ideal Husband" (Oscar Wilde)

1999. Centenary of National Theatre.

1357	**433**	3k.60 purple and orange	1·20	85
1358	-	4k. ultramarine and blue	1·40	95

DESIGN: 4k. Toralv Maurstad and Tore Segelcke in "Per Gynt" (Henrik Ibsen).

434 Family bringing in Logs

1999. Christmas. Multicoloured. Self-adhesive.

1359	4k. Type **434**	1·40	60
1360	4k. Family sitting by window	1·40	60

435 "Sunset" (Sverre Simonsen)

1999. Year 2000. Winning entries in photographic competition. Multicoloured. Self-adhesive.

1361	4k. Type **435**	1·60	70
1362	4k. "Winter Nights" (Poul Christensen)	1·60	70

436 Eye within Heart

2000. St. Valentine's Day.

1363	**436**	4k. multicoloured	1·80	95

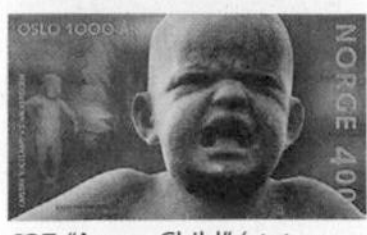

437 "Angry Child" (statue, Gustav Vigeland)

2000. Millenary of Oslo City. Multicoloured.

1364	4k. Type **437**	1·40	85
1365	6k. Christian IV statue	2·20	1·20
1366	8k. City Hall and clock face	3·00	1·80
1367	27k. Oslo Stock Exchange and Mercury (statue)	9·50	5·50

438 Golden Eagle

2000. Endangered Species. Multicoloured.

1368	5k. Type **438**	1·60	85
1369	6k. European moose	2·00	1·20
1370	7k. Sperm whale	2·40	1·60

439 "Power and Energy"

2000. "EXPO 2000" World's Fair, Hanover, Germany. Paintings by Marianne Heske. Multicoloured.

1371	4k.20 "The Quiet Room"	2·00	1·10
1372	6k.30 Type **439**	2·50	1·70

440 Cadets, 1750

2000. 250th Anniv of Royal Norwegian Military Academy.

1373	**440**	3k.60 multicoloured	1·30	90
1374	-	8k. blue, yellow and red	3·25	2·20

DESIGN: 8k. Cadets, 2000.

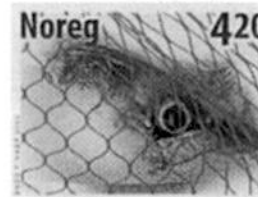

441 Mackerel

2000. Fish. Multicoloured. Self-adhesive.

1375	4k.20 Type **441**	1·30	55
1376	4k.20 Herring	1·30	55

442 Spaceman (May-Therese Vorland)

2000. "Stampin the Future". Winning Entries in Children's International Painting Competition. Multicoloured.

1377	4k.20 Type **442**	2·00	1·10
1378	6k.30 Rocket and Earth (Jann Fredrik Ronning)	2·50	1·70

443 "Monument to Log Drivers" (sculpture, Trygve M. Barstad)

2000. Millennium of Skien City. Multicoloured.

1379	4k.20 Type **443**	2·00	55
1380	15k. Skien Church	5·75	3·25

444 Laestadius, Lifelong Saxifrage and Laestadius Poppy

2000. Birth Bicentenary of Lars Levi Laestadius (clergyman and botanist).

1381	**444**	5k. multicoloured	2·20	1·30

445 Nils og Blamann with Goat and Cart

2000. Cartoon Characters. Multicoloured. Self-adhesive.

1382	4k.20 Type **445**	1·30	90
1383	4k.20 Soldier No. 91 Stomperud and birds	1·30	90

446 Woven Altar Piece, Hamaroy Church

2000. Altar Pieces. Multicoloured.

1384	3k.60 Type **446**	1·30	1·00
1385	4k.20 Ski Church	1·60	1·10

2000

1388	**352**	1k. multicoloured	50	35
1389	**352**	2k. multicoloured	65	45
1390	**352**	3k. multicoloured	1·00	85
1391	**352**	5k. multicoloured	1·70	90
1392	**352**	6k. multicoloured	1·80	1·10
1393	**352**	7k. multicoloured	2·30	1·30
1394	**352**	9k. multicoloured	2·75	1·70

447 Sekel Rose

2001. Roses (1st series). Multicoloured. Self-adhesive.

1395	4k.50 Type **447**	1·40	90
1396	4k.50 Namdal rose	1·40	90

See also Nos 1418/19 and 1491/2.

448 Place Mat

2001. Crafts (1st series). Multicoloured. Self-adhesive.

1397	4k. Type **448**	1·30	75
1398	4k.50 Pot with lid	1·40	90
1399	7k. Bunad (woven cloth)	2·50	1·70

See also Nos. 1415/17.

449 Aase Bye

2001. Thespians (1st series).

1400	**449**	4k. black and brown	1·60	75
1401	-	4k.50 black and blue	1·80	90
1402	-	5k.50 black and brown	2·30	1·10
1403	-	7k. black and purple	2·75	1·40
1404	-	8k. black and grey	3·00	1·70

DESIGNS: 4k.50, Per Aabel; 5k.50, Alfred Maurstad; 7k. Lillebil Ibsen; 8k. Tore Segelcke.

See also Nos 1410/14 and 1450/4.

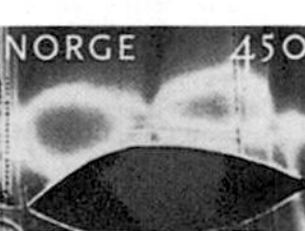

450 "Ties that Bind" (Magne Furuholmen)

2001. St. Valentine's Day.

1405	**450**	4k.50 multicoloured	1·80	1·20

451 Whitewater Kayaking

2001. Sports. Multicoloured. Self-adhesive.

1406	4k.50 Type **451**	1·90	75
1407	7k. Rock climbing	2·75	1·10

452 Tuba Player

2001. Centenary of School Bands. Multicoloured.

1408	4k.50 Type **452**	1·60	1·10
1409	9k. Majorette	3·50	2·20

453 Lalla Carlsen

2001. Thespians (2nd series). Multicoloured.

1410	5k. Type **453**	1·90	1·10
1411	5k.50 Leif Juster	2·00	1·20
1412	7k. Kari Diesen	2·75	1·70
1413	9k. Arvid Nilssen	3·25	1·90
1414	10k. Einar Rose	3·75	2·20

2001. Crafts (2nd series). As T **448**. Multicoloured.

1415	5k. Wooden drinking vessel	1·90	90
1416	5k.50 Crocheted doll's clothing	2·00	1·10
1417	8k.50 Knitted woollen hat	3·50	2·20

454 Rose "Heidekonigin"

2001. Roses (2nd series). Multicoloured. Self-adhesive.

1418	5k.50 Type **454**	2·00	1·10
1419	5k.50 Rose "Old Master"	2·00	1·10

Nos. 1418/19 are impregnated with the scent of roses.

455 Old Bank of Norway

2001. Norwegian Architecture. Multicoloured.

1420	5k.50 Type **455**	2·00	1·10
1421	8k.50 Ivar Aasen Centre	3·50	2·20

456 Kittens

2001. Pets. Multicoloured.

1422	5k.50 Type **456**	2·00	1·10
1423	7k.50 Goat	2·75	1·70

457 Aung San Suu Kyi (Burmese opposition leader), 1991

2001. Centenary of Nobel Prizes. Peace Prize Winners (Nos. 1424/5 and 1427). Multicoloured.

1424	5k.50 Type **457**	1·90	90
1425	5k.50 Nelson Mandela (South African President), 1993	1·90	90
1426	7k. Alfred Nobel (Prize Fund founder)	2·40	1·40
1427	7k. Henry Dunant (founder of Red Cross), 1901	2·40	1·40
1428	9k. Fridtjof Nansen (Norwegian organizer for League of Nations refugee relief), 1922	3·00	1·80
1429	9k. Mikhail Gorbachev (Soviet President), 1990	3·00	1·80
1430	10k. Martin Luther King (Civil Rights leader), 1964	3·50	2·20
1431	10k. Rigoberta Menchu Tum (Guatemalan Civil Rights leader), 1992	3·50	2·20
MS1432	170×64 mm. No. 1426	3·50	3·25

Dates are those on which the Prize was awarded.

458 Snow-covered Trees and Lights

2001. Northern Lights. Multicoloured.

1433	5k. Type **458**	1·80	1·10
1434	5k.50 Lights and reindeer	2·10	1·30

459 Gingerbread Man

2001. Christmas. Multicoloured. Self-adhesive.

1435	5k.50 Type **459**	2·00	1·20
1436	5k.50 Gingerbread house	2·00	1·20

460 Tordis Maurstad

2002. Thespians (3rd series). Showing caricatures by Arne Roar Lund.

1450 **460** 5k. black and lilac 1·80 1·10
1451 - 5k.50 black and grey 2·00 1·20
1452 - 7k. black and green 2·50 1·50
1453 - 9k. black and green 3·00 1·90
1454 - 10k. black and brown 3·50 2·10

DESIGNS: 5k.50 Rolf Just Nilsen; 7k. Lars Tvinde; 9k. Henry Gleditsch; 10k. Norma Balean.

461 Boys tackling

2002. Centenary of Norwegian Football Association (1st issue). Multicoloured. Self-adhesive.

1455 5k.50 Type **461** 2·50 1·50
1456 5k.50 German referee Peter Hertel and player 2·50 1·50
1457 5k.50 Girls tackling 2·50 1·50
1458 5k.50 Boy kicking ball 2·50 1·50

See also Nos. 1469/**MS**1475.

462 Scene from "Askeladden and the Good Helpers" (animated film by Ivo Caprino)

2002. Fairytale Characters. Multicoloured. Self-adhesive.

1459 5k.50 Type **462** 2·10 1·30
1460 9k. Giant troll (drawing by Theodor Kittelsen) 3·50 2·10

463 "Monument to Whaling" (Sivert Donali)

2002. Nordic Countries' Postal Co-operation. Modern Art. Sculptures. Multicoloured.

1461 7k.50 Type **463** 2·75 1·60
1462 8k.50 "Throw" (Kåre Groven) 3·00 1·80

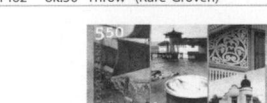

464 Holmestrand

2002. City Charter Anniversaries. Multicoloured.

1463 5k.50 Type **464** (300th anniv) 2·10 1·30
1464 5k.50 Kongsberg (200th anniv) 2·10 1·30

465 Abel

2002. Birth Bicentenary of Niels Henrik Abel (mathematician). Multicoloured.

1465 5k.50 Type **465** 2·10 1·30
1466 22k. Mathematical rosette 8·50 5·00

466 Johan Borgen

2002. Writers' Birth Centenaries. Portraits by Nils Aas.

1467 **466** 11k. yellow and green 4·00 2·50
1468 - 20k. green and blue 7·25 4·50

DESIGN: 20k. Nordahl Grieg.

467 Norwegian Team (Olympic Games, Berlin, 1936)

2002. Centenary of Norwegian Football Association (2nd issue). Multicoloured.

1469 5k. Type **467** (2-0 victory over Germany, 1936 Olympics) 1·80 1·10
1470 5k.50 No. 9 player and Brazil No. 4 player (2-1 victory over Brazil, World Cup, France, 1998) 2·10 1·30
1471 5k.50 Norway and U.S.A. women players (3-2 victory over USA, Olympic Games, Sydney, 2000) 2·10 1·30
1472 7k. Player capturing ball from Sweden No. 11 player (3-1 victory over Sweden, 1960) 2·50 1·50
1473 9k. Player with chevron sleeves (2-1 victory over England, 1981) 3·25 2·00
1474 10k. Team members of Rosenborg F.C. celebrrating (2-1 victory over Milan, Champions League, 1996) 3·75 2·20
MS1475 140×127 mm. Nos. 1469/74 17·00 16·00

468 Clown on Tightrope

2002. Europa. Circus. Multicoloured.

1476 5k.50 Type **468** 2·10 1·30
1477 8k.50 Elephant, horse and chimpanzee 3·50 2·10

2002. "Nordia 2002" Nordic Stamp Exhibition, Kristiansand. Nos. 1465/6 surch **NORDIC 2002**.

1478 5k.50 multicoloured 4·25 3·50
1479 22k. multicoloured 14·00 13·00

470 Landstad on Horseback and Frontispiece of "Norske Folkeviser"

2002. Birth Bicentenary of Magnus Brostrup Landstad (folk-song collector and hymn writer). Multicoloured.

1480 5k. Type **470** 2·00 1·20
1481 5k.50 Landstad and frontispiece of Kirkefalmebog 2·20 1·40

471 Straw Heart-shaped Decoration

2002. Christmas. Multicoloured. Self-adhesive.

1482 5k.50 Type **471** 2·10 1·30
1483 5k.50 Paper star-shaped decoration 2·10 1·30

472 "Nordmandens Krone" (Kare Espolin Johnson)

2003. Graphic Art (1st series). Multicoloured.

1484 5k. Type **472** 2·00 1·20
1485 8k.50 "Bla Hester" (Else Hagen) 3·25 2·00
1486 9k. "Dirigent og Solist" (Niclas Gulbrandsen) 3·50 2·10
1487 11k. "Olympia" (Svein Strand) 4·25 2·50
1488 22k. "Still Life XVII" (Rigmor Hansen) 9·75 6·00

See also Nos. 1515/16.

473 Heart

2003. St. Valentine.

1489 **473** 5k.50 multicoloured 2·10 1·30

474 Doudji Knife Handle (Havard Larsen)

2003. Crafts. Coil stamp. Self-adhesive.

1490 **474** 5k.50 multicoloured 2·10 1·30

475 Rose "Grand Prix"

2003. Roses (3rd series). Multicoloured. Self-adhesive.

1491 5k.50 Type **475** 2·10 1·30
1492 5k.50 Rose "Champagne" 2·10 1·30

476 Operating Theatre

2003. 400th Anniv of Public Health Service. Multicoloured.

1493 5k.50 Type **476** 2·10 1·30
1494 7k. Doctor examining baby 2·75 1·70

477 Forest Troll

2003. Fairytale Characters (2nd series). Showing drawings by Theodor Kittelsen. Self-adhesive. Multicoloured.

1495 5k.50 Type **477** 2·10 1·30
1496 9k. Water sprite (horiz) 3·50 2·10

478 Hand and Violin

2003. Bergen International Festival. Multicoloured.

1497 5k.50 Type **478** 2·10 1·30
1498 10k. Children's faces 4·25 2·50

479 Child holding Bread

2003. World Refugee Day. Multicoloured.

1499 5k.50 Type **479** 2·10 1·30
1500 10k. Refugees 3·50 2·10

480 Crown Prince Olav as a Child

2003. Birth Centenary of King Olav V (1903–1991). Multicoloured.

1501 5k.50 Type **480** 2·10 1·30
1502 8k.50 Crown Prince Olav and Crown Princess Martha 3·50 2·10
1503 11k. King Olav V 4·25 2·50
MS1504 170×101 mm. Nos. 1501/3 11·00 10·00

481 Baby

2003. Greetings Stamps. Multicoloured. Self-adhesive.

1505 5k.50 Type **481** 2·30 1·50
1506 5k.50 Hand wearing ring 2·30 1·50
1507 5k.50 Lily 2·30 1·50
1508 5k.50 Couple 2·30 1·50
1509 5k.50 Children and cake 2·30 1·50

482 Dagbladet (Per Krohg)

2003. Europa. Poster Art. Multicoloured.

1510 8k.50 Type **482** 3·25 2·20
1511 9k. Winter Olympics, Oslo (Knut Yran) 3·50 2·30
1512 10k. Music festival (Willibald Storn) 3·75 2·50

483 Bjornstjerne Bjornson (literature, 1903)

2003. Norwegian Nobel Prize Winners (1st series). Multicoloured.

1513 11k. Type **483** 4·50 3·00
1514 22k. Lars Onsager (chemistry, 1968) 9·75 6·50

See also Nos. 1549/50.

484 "Goatherd and Goats" (Rolf Nesch)

2003. Graphic Art (2nd series). Multicoloured.

1515 5k. Type **484** 2·30 1·50
1516 5k.50 "Winter Landscape 1980" (Terje Grostad) 2·40 1·60

485 Santa Claus

2003. Christmas. Self-adhesive gum. Multicoloured.

1517 5k.50 Type **485** 2·10 1·40
1518 5k.50 Present 2·10 1·40

486 Coronet Medusa (*Periphylla periphylla*)

2004. Marine Life (1st series). Multicoloured. Self-adhesive.

1519 5k.50 Type **486** 2·30 1·50
1520 6k. Catfish (*Anarhichas lupus*) 2·50 1·70
1521 9k. Little cuttlefish (*Sepiola atlantica*) 3·75 2·50

See also Nos. 1576/7, 1608, 1621/2, 1649 and 1658/61.

487 Couple

2004. Greetings Stamps. Self-adhesive gum. Each green and grey.

1522 6k. Type **487** 2·75 1·80
1523 6k. Globe 2·75 1·80

488 "Idyll" (Christian Skredsbvig)

2004. Painters' Birth Anniversaries. Multicoloured.

1524	6k. Type **488** (150th anniv)	2·75	1·80
1525	9k.50 "Stetind in Fog" (Peder Balke) (bicentenary)	3·50	2·40
1526	10k.50 "Workers' Protest" (Reidar Aulie) (centenary)	4·00	2·50

489 Heart

2004. St. Valentine's Day.

1527	**489** 6k. multicoloured	3·00	2·00

490 Cyclist

2004. Europa. Holidays. Multicoloured.

1528	6k. Type **490**	2·40	1·80
1529	7k.50 Canoeist	3·00	2·20
1530	9k.50 Skiers	3·75	2·75

491 Otto Sverdrup

2004. 150th Birth Anniv of Otto Sverdrup (polar explorer). Each purple and buff.

1531	6k. Type **491**	2·40	1·80
1532	9k.50 *Fram* (polar research ship)	4·00	3·00
MS1533	166×60 mm. Nos. 1541/2 plus 1 label	7·25	7·00

No. **MS**1533 was issued with a stamp-sized label showing design of Greenland stamp.

Stamps of similar designs were issued by Greenland and Canada.

492 Sea God Njord

2004. Nordic Mythology. Multicoloured.

1534	7k.50 Type **492**	3·25	2·40
1535	10k.50 Balder's funeral	4·75	3·50
MS1536	106×70 mm. Nos. 1544/5	9·50	9·25

Stamps of a similar theme were issued by Aland Islands, Denmark, Faeroe Islands, Finland, Greenland, Iceland and Sweden.

493 Princess Ingrid Alexandra

2004. Birth of Princess Ingrid Alexandra of Norway. Sheet 94×61 mm.

MS1537	6k. multicoloured	4·00	3·75

494 Steam Locomotive, Koppang Station

2004. 150th Anniv of Norwegian Railways. Multicoloured.

1538	6k. Type **494**	2·40	2·00
1539	7k.50 Passengers and staff, Dovre station	3·25	2·50
1540	9k.50 Early diesel locomotive, Flatmark halt	4·00	3·25
1541	10k.50 Airport Express locomotive	7·25	5·75

495 Hakon Hakonsson

2004. 800th Birth Anniv of Hakon Hakonsson (Viking leader). Multicoloured.

1542	12k. Type **495**	4·75	4·00
1543	22k. Outline of Hakon's hall and sword	8·75	7·25

496 Smiley (emblem)

2004. Youth Stamps. Multicoloured.

1544	6k. Type **496**	2·40	2·00
1545	9k. Badges	4·00	3·25

497 Ship's Prow and Barrels

2004. Centenary of Archaeological Discovery, Oseberg. Multicoloured.

1546	7k.50 Type **497**	3·00	2·30
1547	9k.50 Sled	3·75	3·00
1548	12k. Bed	4·75	3·75

2004. Norwegian Nobel Prize Winners (2nd series). As T **483**. Multicoloured.

1549	5k.50 Odd Hassel (chemistry, 1969)	2·40	2·00
1550	6k. Christian Lous Lange (peace, 1921)	3·25	2·50

498 "Friends" (Hanne Soteland)

2004. Christmas. Winning Designs in UNICEF Painting Competition. Multicoloured. Self-adhesive.

1551	6k. Type **498**	2·40	2·00
1552	6k. "Caring" (Synne Amalie Lund Kallak)	2·40	2·00

499 Princesses and Guard

2005. 150th Birth Anniv of Erik Werenskiold (artist). Illustrations from "The Three Princesses in the Blue Hill" fairytale by Peter Christen Asbjornsen and Jorgen Moe. Multicoloured.

1553	7k.50 Type **499**	3·00	2·30
1554	9k.50 Royal cradle	3·75	3·00

500 Soup Kitchen, Møllergata (1953)

2005. 150th Anniv of Church City Missions (humanitarian organization). Multicoloured.

1555	5k.50 Type **500**	2·20	1·80
1556	6k. Ministers giving communion at street service, Oslo	2·40	2·00

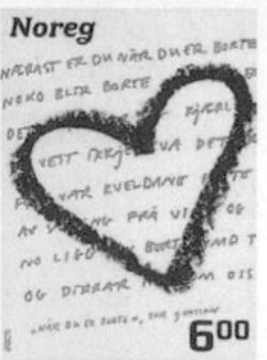

501 Heart and "Nar du er Borte" (poem by Tor Jonsson)

2005. St. Valentine's Day.

1557	**501** 6k. carmine and silver	2·40	2·00

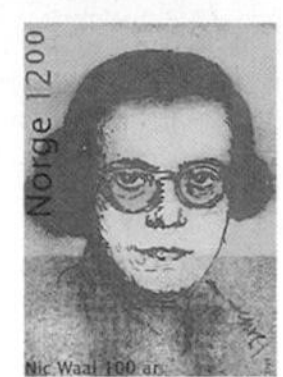

502 Caroline (Nic) Waal

2005. Birth Centenaries. Multicoloured.

1558	12k. Type **502** (first child psychiatrist)	4·75	4·00
1559	22k. Aase Gruda Skard (first child psychologist)	8·50	7·00

503 "City of the Future" (Maja Anna Marszalek)

2005. Winning Entries in Children's Drawing Competition. Multicoloured.

1560	6k. Type **503**	2·40	2·00
1561	7k.50 "The Modern Classroom" (Tobias Abrahamsen)	3·00	2·30

504 Fjord, Geiranger

2005. Tourism. Self-adhesive. Multicoloured.

1562	6k. Type **504**	2·40	2·00
1563	9k.50 Kjosfossen, Flam	3·75	3·00
1564	10k.50 Polar bear, Svalbard	4·25	3·50

505 Prime Minister Christian Michelsen (Norway)

2005. Centenary of Dissolution of Union with Sweden. Multicoloured.

1565	6k. Type **505**	2·40	2·00
1566	7k.50 King Haakon VII (Sweden)	3·00	2·30
MS1567	162×94 mm. Nos. 1565/56	5·50	5·25

506 King Haakon VII taking Oath (1905)

2005. 20th-century Events. Multicoloured.

1568	6k. Type **506**	2·50	2·10
1569	6k. Crown Prince Olav riding through Oslo (1945)	2·50	2·10
1570	6k. King Olav V appearing on first Norwegian television broadcast (1960)	2·50	2·10
1571	6k. Prime Minster Trygve Bratteli opening Ekofisk oilfield (1971)	2·50	2·10
1572	9k. Kjetil Rekdal scoring winning goal in World Cup match against Brazil (1998)	2·50	2·10

507 *Christian Radich*

2005. Ships. Multicoloured.

1573	6k. Type **507**	2·50	2·10
1574	9k.50 *Sorlandet*	3·75	3·00
1575	10k.50 *Statsraad Lehmkuhl*	4·25	3·50

508 Killer Whale (*Orcinus orca*)

2005. Marine Life (2nd series). Multicoloured. Self-adhesive.

1576	B (5k.50) Type **508**	2·40	2·10
1577	A (6k.) Sea anemone (*Urticina eques*)	2·75	2·40

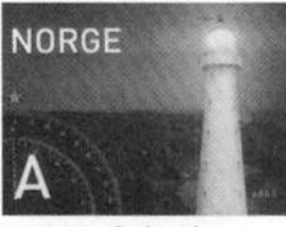

509 Jomfruland Lighthouse

2005. Lighthouses. Self-adhesive. Multicoloured.

1578	(6k.) Type **509**	2·75	2·40
1579	(6k.) Tranoy	2·75	2·40

510 Thortveitite (rare mineral)

2005. Centenary of Geological Society. Multicoloured.

1580	5k.50 Type **510**	2·40	2·10
1581	6k. Drilling rig, ship, continental shelf, stylized rock section and *Lamprocyclas maritalis*	2·75	2·40

511 Transmitting Apparatus

2005. 150th Anniv of Telegraph in Norway. Multicoloured.

1582	6k. Type **511**	2·75	2·40
1583	10k.50 Girl using mobile phone	4·50	4·00

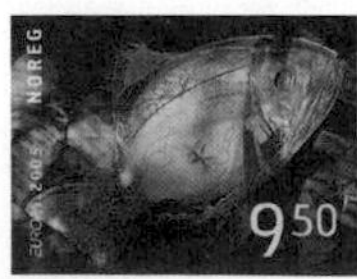

512 Fish

2005. Europa. Gastronomy. Multicoloured.

1584	9k.50 Type **512**	4·25	3·75
1585	10k.50 Decorated table	4·50	4·00

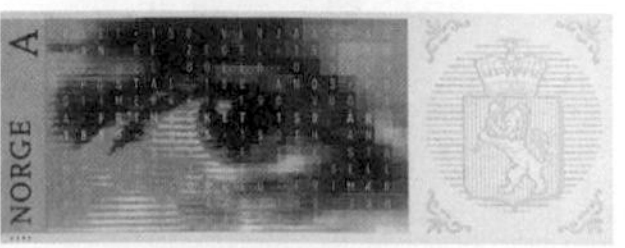

513 Eye and "150th Anniversary"

2005. 150th Anniv of Norwegian Stamps. Multicoloured.

1586	(6k.) Type **513**	2·75	2·40
MS1587	170×60 mm. (6k.) Type **513**; 12k. First stamp and woman writing letter	8·25	8·00

514 King Haakon holding Crown Prince Olav and Prime Minister Christian Michelsen

2005. Centenary of Norwegian Royal House. Multicoloured.

1588	6k. Type **514**	2·75	2·40
1589	6k. King Harald VII and Crown Prince Haakon holding Princess Ingrid Alexandra	2·75	2·40

515 Gingerbread Christmas Tree

2005. Christmas. Multicoloured. Self-adhesive.

1590	(6k.) Type **515**	2·50	2·30
1591	(6k.) Spiced oranges	2·50	2·30

516 Comet and "Tanke og draum er himmelske køyrety" (Olav Hauge)

2006. Centenary of Language Society.

1592	**516**	6k. multicoloured	2·75	2·40

517 Kari Traa performing Iron Cross

2006. Winter Olympic Games, Turin. Multicoloured.

1593	6k. Type **517**	2·75	2·40
1594	22k. Elinar Bjørndalen (biathlete)	9·50	8·50

518 Heart and Blossom

2006. St. Valentine's Day.

1595	**518**	A (6k.) multicoloured	2·75	2·40

519 Flower

2006. Greetings Stamps. Multicoloured. Self-adhesive.

1596	A (6k.) Type **519**	2·50	2·30
1597	A (6k.) Baby	2·50	2·30
1598	A (6k.) Heart and rings	2·50	2·30
1599	A (6k.) Cake	2·50	2·30

520 Lifeguard carrying Victim

2006. Centenary of Lifesaving Society. Multicoloured.

1600	10k. Type **520**	4·25	3·75
1601	10k.50 Baby swimming	4·50	4·00

521 Shaman's Drum (detail)

2006. Nordic Mythology. Sheet 105×70 mm containing T **521** and similar horiz design. Multicoloured.

MS1602	A (6k.) Type **521**; 10k.50 Fafnir (dragon) (carved door panel)	7·25	7·00

Stamps of a similar theme were issued by Aland Islands, Denmark, Faroe Islands, Finland, Greenland, Iceland and Sweden.

522 Lynx

2006. Wildlife. Multicoloured.

1603	6k.50 Type **522**	2·75	2·40
1604	8k.50 Capercaillie	3·50	3·00
1605	10k. Golden eagle	4·25	3·75
1606	10k.50 Artic fox	4·50	4·00
1607	13k. Mountain hare	5·50	5·00

523 *Polycera quadrilineata*

2006. Marine Life. (3rd series). Self-adhesive.

1608	**523**	10k. multicoloured	4·25	3·75

524 Shopper c. 1947

2006. Centenary of Cooperative Movement.

1609	**524**	6k.50 multicoloured	2·75	2·40

525 *Skibladner*

2006. Tourism. Multicoloured. Self-adhesive.

1610	6k.50 Type **525**	2·75	2·40
1611	6k.50 Maihaugen, Lillehammer	2·75	2·40
1612	8k.50 Kirkenporten, Nordkapp	3·50	3·00
1613	8k.50 Nordkapp	3·50	3·00
1614	10k.50 Bryggen, Bergen	4·50	4·00
1615	10k.50 Atlanterhavsveien	4·50	4·00

526 Surveying c. 1906

2006. Centenary of Prince Albert I of Monaco's Expedition to Svalbard, Arctic Circle and Establishment of Longyearbyen and Stoke Norske Coal Mining Company. Multicoloured.

1616	6k.50 Type **526**	2·50	2·30
1617	8k.50 Coal transport terminal	6·00	5·25
1618	22k. Longyearbyen today	9·25	8·25
MS1619	171×100 mm. Nos. 1616/18	19·00	18·00

527 Dove

2006. Personalised Stamp. Self-adhesive.

1620	**527**	A (6k.50) multicoloured	3·00	2·50

528 Sea urchin (*Strongylocentrotus droebachiensis*)

2006. Marine Life. (4th series). Multicoloured. Self-adhesive.

1621	B (6k.) Type **528**	2·75	2·40
1622	A (6k.50) Cuckoo wrasse (*Labrus bimaculatus*)	3·00	2·50

529 On Parade

2006. 150th Anniv of King's Guard. Multicoloured.

1623	6k.50 Type **529**	3·00	2·50
1624	13k. Field training	5·50	5·00
MS1625	178×65 mm. Nos. 1623/4	8·75	8·50

530 Lantern

2006. Personalised Stamp. Self-adhesive.

1626	**530**	A (6k.50) multicoloured	3·00	2·50

531 Children and Tree

2006. Christmas. Multicoloured. Self-adhesive.

1627	A (6k.50) Type **531**	3·00	2·50
1628	A (6k.50) Snowman	3·00	2·50

532 Circle of Children

2006. Europa. Integration. Multicoloured.

1629	8k.50 Type **532**	3·75	3·25
1630	13k. Children and ball	5·50	5·00

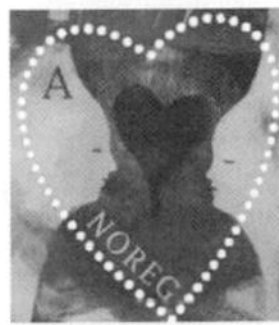

533 Heart

2007. St. Valentine's Day.

1631	**533**	A (6k.50) multicoloured	2·75	2·40

534 Petter Solberg driving Subaru Impreza

2007. Motor Sport. Norway Winter Rally. Multicoloured.

1632	A (6k.50) "Innland" Type **534**	2·75	2·40
1633	A (8k.50) "Europa" Henning Solberg driving Peugeot 307	3·50	3·25
1634	A (10k.50) "Verden" Thomas Schie driving Ford Focus	4·50	4·00
MS1635	170×100 mm. Nos. 1632/4	10·50	10·00

No. 1632 was for use on priority domestic mail, 1633 was for use on priority mail within Europe and 1634 was for use on worldwide priority mail.

535 King Harald V

2007. 70th Birthday of King Harald V.

1636	**535**	6k.50 multicoloured	2·75	2·40

536 Water Samples and CTD Machine

2007. International Polar Year. Sheet 170×100 mm containing T **536** and similar horiz design. Multicoloured.

MS1637	170×100 mm. 10k.50 Type **536**; 13k. *Svalbard* (research ship) and antenna	9·75	9·50

537 Hedgehog

2007. Wildlife. Multicoloured.

1638	12k. Type **537**	5·00	4·50
1639	22k. Red squirrel	9·25	8·00

538 Arms, *Dionne* (barque), Customs House and Perfume Bottle

2007. Bicentenary of Porgrunn. Value expressed by letter.

1640	**538**	A "Innland" (7k.) mult	3·00	2·75

No. 1640 was for use on Priority mail within Norway.

539 Free Fall over Voss

2007. Tourism. Multicoloured. Self-adhesive.

1641	A "Innland" (7k.) Type **539**	3·00	2·75
1642	A "Innland" (7k.) Cyclists on Old Navvy Road, Finse	3·00	2·75
1643	A "Europa" (9k.) Houses, Roros	4·00	3·50
1644	A "Europa" (9k.) River, Fredrikstad	4·00	3·50
1645	A "Verden" (11k.) House and bay, Portor	4·50	4·00
1646	A "Verden" (11k.) View from sea, Reine	4·50	4·00

Nos. 1641/2 was for use on priority domestic mail, 1643/4 was for use on priority mail within Europe and 1645/6 was for use on priority mail worldwide.

540 "Et Overfall" (An Attack)

2007. 150th Birth Anniv of Theodor Kittelsen (artist). Multicoloured.

1647	A "Europa" (9k.) Type **540**	4·00	3·50
1648	A "Verden" (11k.) "For tidlig Nedkomst" (Premature Delivery)	4·50	4·00

Nos. 1647 was for use on priority mail within Europe and 1648 was for use on priority mail worldwide.

541 Mackerel (*Scomber scombrus*)

2007. Marine Life (5th series). Multicoloured. Self-adhesive.

1649	**541**	11k. multicoloured	4·50	4·00

542 Scouts and Knots

2007. Europa. Centenary of Scouting. Multicoloured.

1650	9k. Type **542**	4·00	3·50
1651	11k. Camp	4·50	4·00

543 Church of Our Lady, Trondheim

2007. Architectural Anniversaries. Multicoloured.

1652	14k. Type **543** (800th anniv)	6·00	5·25
1653	23k. Vardohus Fortress (700th anniv)	9·25	8·25

544 Ona Lighthouse

2007. Lighthouses. Multicoloured. Self-adhesive.
1654 (7k.) Type **544** 3·00 2·75
1655 (7k.) Tungeneset 3·00 2·75
See also Nos. 1578/9.

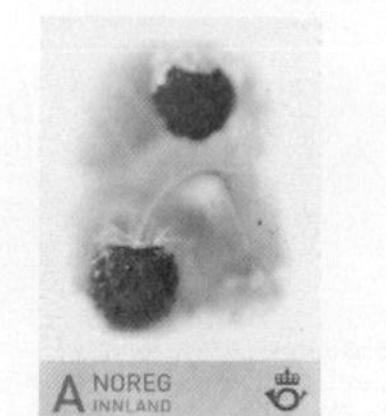

545 Strawberries

2007. Personalised Stamp. Self-adhesive.
1656 **545** (7k.) multicoloured 3·00 2·75

546 'Ingen tanke er tenkt fo den er stot i ord' (Inge Loning)

2007. Centenary of Riksmaal (language) Society.
1657 **546** 7k. multicoloured 3·00 2·75

547 *Pandalus montagui*

2007. Marine Life (6th series). Mlticoloured. Self-adhesive.
1658 (7k.) Type **547** 3·00 2·75
1659 (7k.) *Homarus gammarus* 3·00 2·75
1660 (7k.) *Cancer pagurus* 3·00 2·75
1661 (7k.) *Galathea strigosa* 3·00 2·75

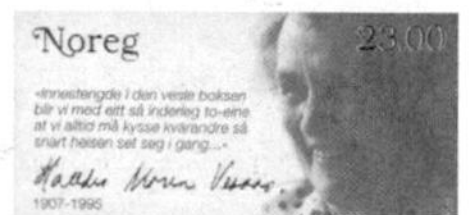

548 Halldis Moren

2007. Birth Centenary of Halldis Moren Vesaas (poet and translator).
1662 **548** 23k. bronze, black and gold 9·50 8·50

549 Reindeer

2007. Personal Stamp. Self-adhesive A-Priority Domestic Stamp.
1663 **549** (7k.) blue and vermilion 3·00 2·75
No. 1663 was inscr 'A INNLAND'.

550 Star

2007. Christmas. A-Priority Domestic Stamps. Multicoloured. Self-adhesive.
1664 (7k.) Type **550** 3·00 2·75
1665 (7k.) Three Wise Men 3·00 2·75
Nos. 1664/5 were inscr 'A INNLAND'.

551 Academy Building and Machinery

2007. Scientific Anniversaries. Multicoloured.
1666 14k. Type **551** (250th anniv of Kongsberg Mining Academy) 6·00 5·50
1667 14k. Molecule and microscope (150th anniv of Academy of Science and Letters) 6·00 5·50

552 'Love'

2008. St Valentine's Day. Multicoloured. (a) Inscr 'INNLAND A'.
1668 (7k.) Type **552** 3·00 2·75

(b) Inscr 'EUROPA A'.
1669 (9k.) Letter, roses and doves 4·00 3·50
No. 1668 was for use on domestic mail and No. 1669 for use on mail within Europe.

553 Elk

2008. Wildlife. Multicoloured.
1670 11k. Type **553** 4·75 4·25
1671 14k. Brown bear 6·00 5·50
1672 23k. Wolf 9·75 8·75

554 Thorleif Haug

2008. Centenary of Norwegian Ski Federation. Multicoloured. Self adhesive.
1673 A (7k.) Type **554** (Olympic cross country and Nordic gold medallist–1924) 3·00 2·75
1674 A (7k.) Espen Bredesen (Olympic hill gold medallist–1994) 3·00 2·75
1675 A (7k.) Children skiing 3·00 2·75
1676 A (7k.) Kjetil Andre Aamodt (four times Olympic alpine gold medallist) 3·00 2·75

555 Harald Fairhair and Snofrid

2008. Norse Mythology. Mythological Places. Sheet 105×70 mm containing T **555** and similar horiz design. Multicoloured.
MS1677 A (70k.)×2, Type **555**; Snøhetta (home of giants) in Dovre mountains 7·25 7·00
The stamps and margins of **MS**1677 form a composite design.

556 Building Facade

2008. Inauguration of New Opera House, Oslo.
1678 **556** A (7k.) multicoloured 3·00 2·75

557 Frederick Stang

2008. Birth Bicentenaries. Multicoloured.
1679 A (7k.) Type **557** (politician) 3·00 2·75
1680 A (7k.) Henrick Wergland (lyricist) 3·00 2·75

558 Oslo Harbour

2008. Tourism. Multicoloured. Self-adhesive. (a) Inscr 'INNLAND A'.
1681 A (7k.) Type **558** 3·00 2·75
1682 A (7k.) *Divers* (sculpture) (Ola Enstad) 3·00 2·75

(b) Inscr 'EUROPA A'.
1683 A (9k.) The Blade, Molladalen (Sunnmore alps) 4·00 3·50
1684 A (9k.) Wedged boulder, Kjerag plateau, Lyse Fjord 4·00 3·50

(c) Inscr 'VERDEN A'.
1685 A (11k.) Yacht and Lyngør lighthouse 4·75 4·25
1686 A (11k.) Houses, Lyngor 4·75 4·25
Nos. 1681/2 was for use on priority domestic mail, 1683/4 was for use on priority mail within Europe and 1685/6 was for use on priority mail worldwide.

559 *Boroysund*

2008. Transportation Centenaries.
1687 7k. olive and brown 3·00 2·75
1688 9k. indigo and crimson 4·00 3·50
1689 25k. brown and blue 10·50 9·50
1690 30k. lilac and green 13·00 11·50
DESIGNS: 7k. Type **559**; 9k. *Oster* (ice breaker and transport ship); 25k. French Unic 1907 bus and driver; 30k. Thamshavn electric railway locomotive and train.

560 *Dancer in a Cultural Landscape* (composed photograph by Marcel Lelienhof)

2008. Stavanger–European Capital of Culture, 2008 (1st issue). Multicoloured.
1691 7k. Type **560** 3·00 2·75
1692 14k. *Swords in Rock* (sculpture by Fritz Roed) 6·00 5·25
1693 23k. 'Eye' (character from *The Thousandth Heart* (musical)) (vert) 9·75 8·75

561 Andreas Thorkildsen (javelin)

2008. Olympic Games, Beijing. Multicoloured.
1694 9k. Type **561** 4·00 3·50
1695 23k. Gro Hammerseng (handball) 9·75 8·75

562 New Post Logo

2008. Personalised Stamp.
1696 **562** A (7k.) multicoloured 3·00 2·75
No. 1696 was for use on priority domestic mail, and originally sold for 7k.

2008. Stavanger–European Capital of Culture, 2008 (2nd issue). As T **560**. Multicoloured.
MS1697 170×65 mm. Nos. 1691/3 19·00 18·00

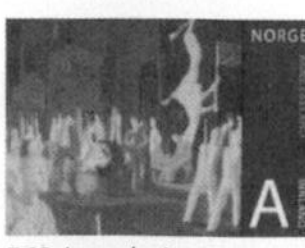

563 *I revolusjonens forgard* (Arne Ekeland)

2008. Norwegian Art. Multicoloured. Self-adhesive.
1698 A (7k.) Type **563** 3·00 2·75
1699 A (7k.) *Svalbardmotiv* (Kare Tveter) 3·00 2·75
1700 A (7k.) *Komposisjon i rodt* (Inge Sitter) 3·00 2·75
1701 A (7k.) *Fra Sagorsk ca 1985* (Terje Bergstad) 3·00 2·75
No. 1698/701 were for use on priority domestic mail, and originally sold for 7k.

564 Gnomes and Amperhaugen Farm

2008. Christmas. Multicoloured. Self-adhesive.
1702 A (7k.) Type **564** 3·00 2·75
1703 A (7k.) Gnome looking down on Nordre Lien farm 3·00 2·75
Nos. 1702/3 were for use on priority domestic mail, and originally sold for 7k.

2009. Norwegian Art (2nd series). Self-adhesive Coil Stamps. As T **563**. Multicoloured.
1704 B (7k.50) *Sommernatt til E.M.* (Kjell Nupen) 3·25 2·75
1705 12k. *Lyset ved pinsetider* (Irmo Salo Jæger) 5·25 4·75
No. 1704 was for use on economy domestic mail, and originally sold for 7k.50.

565 Roe Deer

2009. Wildlife. Multicoloured.
1706 11k.50 Type **565** 5·00 4·25
1707 15k.50 Reindeer 6·75 5·75
1708 25k. Willow grouse 10·50 9·50

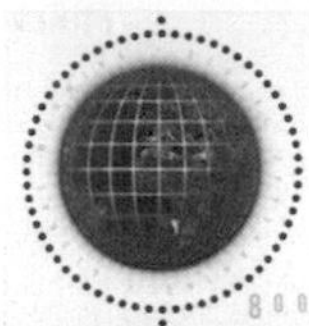

566 Over-heated Globe

2009. Preserve Polar Regions and Glaciers. Sheet 120×80 mm containing T **566** and similar circular design. Multicoloured.
MS1709 8k.×2, Type **566**; Polar ice 8·50 8·25

567 Hepatica

2009. Personal Stamp. Self-adhesive.
1710 **567** A (8k.) multicoloured 3·25 2·75
No. 1710 was for use on priority domestic mail, and originally sold for 8k.

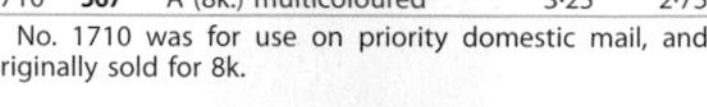

568 Bergen Railway Line

2009. Tourism. Self-adhesive Booklet Stamps. Multicoloured.
1711 A (8k.) Type **568** 3·25 2·75
1712 A (8k.) Locomotive in snow 3·25 2·75
1713 A (10k.) Stottafjorden, Meloy, Nordland 4·00 3·50
1714 A (10k.) Revtangen, Kiepp, Rogaland 4·00 3·50
1715 A (12k.) Bleik, Andoya, Nordland 4·75 4·25
1716 A (12k.) Kennesteinen, Vagsoy, Sogh og Fjordane 4·75 4·25
Nos. 1711/12 were for use on priority domestic mail, and originally sold for 8k. Nos. 1713/14 were for use on priority mail within Europe, and originally sold for 10k. Nos. 1715/16 were for use on priority worldwided mail, and originally sold for 12k.

569 Procession

2009. 150th Anniv of National Anthem.
1717 **569** 12k. multicoloured 5·00 4·50

570 Telephone Kiosk (designed by Georg Fasting, 1932)

2009. Norwegian Year of Cultural Heritage. Coil stamps. Multicoloured. Self-adhesive.
1718 (8k.) Type **570** 3·25 2·75
1719 (8k.) Kurer radio (1950) 3·25 2·75

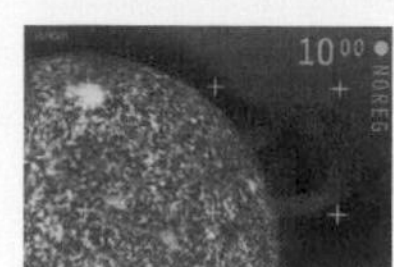

571 Explosion on Sun's Surface

2009. Europa. Astronomy. Multicoloured.
1720 10k. Type **571** 4·00 3·50
1721 12k. Moon 4·75 4·25
MS1722 156×108 mm. Nos. 1720/1 8·75 8·50

572 Symbols of Development

2009. Bicentenary of Royal Norwegian Society for Development.
1723 **572** 12k. multicoloured 4·75 4·25

573 *Kobben* (1909)

2009. Centenary of Naval Submarines. Multicoloured.
1724 14k.50 Type **573** 5·75 5·00
1725 15k.50 Modern Ula class submarine 6·00 5·50

574 Knut Hamsun

2009. 150th Birth Anniv of Knut Hamsun (writer and winner of 1920 Nobel Prize for Literature).
1726 **574** 25k. deep claret, silver and gold 9·75 8·75

575 Roald Stensby

2009. Norwegian Rock Pioneers. Multicoloured. Self-adhesive.
1727 A (8k.) Type **575** 3·25 2·75
1728 A (8k.) Rocke-Pelle (Per Hartvig) 3·25 2·75
1729 A (8k.) Jan Rhode 3·25 2·75
1730 A (8k.) Per 'Elvis' Granberg 3·25 2·75

576 Cruise Ship

2009. Centenary of Shipowners' Association.
1731 **576** 15k.50 multicoloured 6·00 5·50

577 Man with Guide Dog and White Stick

2009. Centenary of Norwegian Association of the Blind and Partially Sighted.
1732 **577** 8k. vermilion 3·50 3·25

No. 1732 is embossed with Braille letters.

578 Apple

2009. Christmas. Booklet Stamps. Multicoloured. Self-adhesive.
1733 A (8k.) Type **578** 3·50 3·25
1734 A (8k.) Star 3·50 3·25

Nos. 1733/4 were for use on priority domestic mail, and originally sold for 8k.

579 *Woman on a Man's Lap* (Gustav Vigeland)

2009. Modern Art. Multicoloured. Self-adhesive.
1735 A (8k.) Type **579** 3·50 3·25
1736 A (8k.) *Crow* (Nils Aas) 3·50 3·25
1737 A (8k.) *Birds in Flight* (Arnold Haukeland) 3·50 3·25
1738 A (8k.) *Granite Head on Side* (Kristian Blystad) 3·50 3·25

No. 1735/8 were for use on priority domestic mail, and originally sold for 8k.

580 *Mann som drikker* (Per Salle Storm)

2010. Modern Art. Self-adhesive.
1739 **580** 13k. multicoloured 5·50 5·00

581 Otter

2010. Fauna. Multicoloured.
1740 15k. Type **581** 6·25 5·75
1741 16k. Lemming 6·75 6·00
1742 26k. Wolverine 11·00 10·00

582 Ole Bull (violinist)

2010. Birth Bicentenaries. Multicoloured. Self-adhesive.
1743 A (8k.) Type **582** 3·50 3·25
1744 A (8k.) Peter Andreas Munch (historian) 3·50 3·25

No. 1743/4 were for use on priority domestic mail, and originally sold for 8k.

583 Fish on Drying Rack, Lofoten

2010. Norden. Life at the Coast
MS1745 **583** A (11k.) multicoloured 4·75 4·50

Stamps of a similar theme were issued by Denmark, Greenland, Faröe Islands, Finland, Iceland, Aland Islands and Sweden.

584 Valdresflya

2010. Tourism. Multicoloured.
1746 A INNLAND (8k.50) Type **584** 3·50 3·25
1747 A INNLAND (8k.50) Gamle Strynefjellsveien 3·50 3·25
1748 A EUROPA (11k.) Sognfjellet 4·75 4·25
1749 A EUROPA (11k.) Trollstigen 4·75 4·25
1750 A VERDA (13k.) Helgelandskysten Nord 5·50 5·00
1751 A VERDA (13k.) Lofoten 5·50 5·00

Nos. 1746/7 were for use on priority domestic mail, and originally sold for 8k.50

Nos. 1748/9 were for use on priority mail within Europe, and originally sold for 11k

Nos. 1750/1 were for use on priority worldwide mail, and originally sold for 13k.

585 Heather

2010. Personal Stamp
1752 **585** A INNLAND (8k.50) multicoloured 4·75 4·25

586 Jahn Teigen

2010. Eurovision Song Contest Performers.. Multicoloured.
1753 A INNLAND (8k.50) Type **586** 3·50 3·25
1754 A INNLAND (8k.50) Alexander Rybak 3·50 3·25
1755 A INNLAND (8k.50) Secret Garden 3·50 3·25
1756 A INNLAND (8k.50) Bobbysocks 3·50 3·25

587 Nils Petter Molvær (trumpeter)

2010. 50th (2011) Anniv of Molde Jazz Festival
1757 **587** 13k. black and turquoise-blue 5·50 5·00

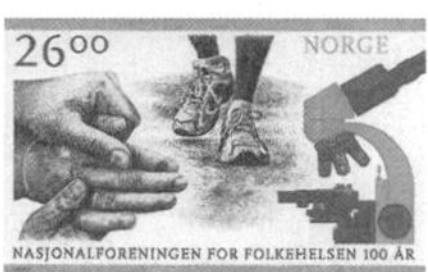

588 Hands, Feet and Microscope

2010. Centenary of Norwegian National Health Association
1758 **588** 26k. multicoloured 11·00 10·00

589 Bjørnen Teodor, Komekameratene,Pompel & Piltand Titten Tei (children's television)

2010. 50th Anniv of Norwegian Television. Multicoloured.

(a) Coil stamps. Self-adhesive
1759 A INNLAND (8k.50) Type **589** 4·00 3·75
1760 A INNLAND (8k.50) Trond Kirkvåg as *Skremmer'n*, Robert Stolenberg as *Narvestad*, Rolv Wesenlund as *Fleksnes* and Trond-Viggo Torgesen as *Vaktmester'n* (comedy) 4·00 3·75
1761 A INNLAND (8k.50) Erik Diesen, Dan Børge Åkerø, Ivar Dyrhaug and Anne Grosvald (entertainment) 4·00 3·75
1762 A INNLAND (8k.50) Arne Scheie, Ingrid Espelid Høvig, Erik Bye and Ragnhild Sælthun Fjørtoft (personalities) 4·00 3·75

(b) Miniature sheet. Ordinary gum
MS1763 120×80 mm. A INNLAND (8k.50)×2, As Type **589** and As No. 1762 8·25 8·00

590 Norwegian University of Technology and Science, Gloshaugen (centenary)

2010. Anniversaries. Multicoloured.
1764 8k.50 Type **590** 4·00 3·75
1765 13k. Society seal and building, Klalvskinnet, Trondheim (Royal Norwegian Society of Science and Letters (250th anniv)) 6·00 5·50

591 'YTRINGSFRIHET' (freedom of speech)

2010. Centenary of Norwegian Press Association and Norwegian Media Businesses' Association
1766 **591** 11k. multicoloured 5·00 4·50

592 Boatswain Mikel Våge aboard Stavanger (1973)

2010. Centenary of Norwegian Seafarers' Union
1767 **592** 16k. multicoloured 7·25 6·50

Nos. 1768/9 and Type **593** are left for DKNVS and NTNU Anniversaries issude on 15 September 2010, not yet received.

2010. Posthorn. Multicoloured, colour of oval given.
1770 4k. royal blue 2·00 1·80
1771 8k. deep carmine-red 3·75 3·50
1772 30k. reddish lilac 14·00 13·00

594 Christmas Goat

2010. Christmas. Multicoloured.
1773 A (8k.50) Type **594** 4·00 3·75
1774 A (8k.50) Candlestick with candles 4·00 3·75

Nos. 1773/4 were both inscribed 'INNLAND' and were for use on priority domestic mail, and originally sold for 8k.60.

595 In the Sledge

2010. Europa. Multicoloured.
1775 A (8k.50) Type **595** 4·00 3·75
1776 A (11k.) Father, Mother, Grandmother and children approaching cottage 5·00 4·50

Nos. 1775 was inscribed 'INNLAND' and was for use on priority domestic mail, and originally sold for 8k.60. No. 1776 was inscribed 'EUROPA' and were for use on priority European mail, and originally sold for 11k.

596 Athletes

2011. 150th Anniv of Norwegian Confederation of Sports
1777 **596** 14k. multicoloured 6·50 6·00

597 Polar Bear

2011. Fauna. Multicoloured.
1778 17k. Type **597** 8·00 7·50
1779 27k. Musk ox 12·50 11·50

597a New Holmenkollen Ski Jump

2011. Nordic World Ski Championships, Oslo, 2011. Multicoloured.

1779a 9k. Type **597a** 4·25 3·75
1779b 12k. Marit Bjørgen and Kristin Størmer Steira, 2010 World Cup in Holmenkollen 5·75 5·25
MS1779c 156×108 mm. Nos. 1779a/b 10·50 10·00

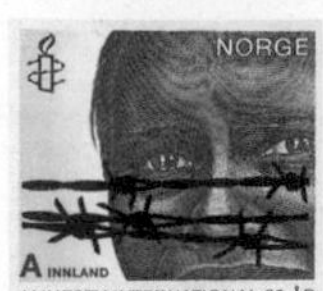

598 Barbed Wire and Face

2011. 50th Anniv of Amnesty International

1780 **598** A (9k.) multicoloured 4·25 3·75

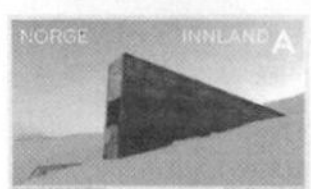

599 Svalbard Global Seed Vault

2011. Tourism. Modern Architecture. Multicoloured.

1781 A INNLAND (9k.) Type **599** 4·25 3·75
1782 A EUROPA (12k.) Borgund Visitor Centre 5·50 5·00
1783 A VERDEN (14k.) Preikestolen Mountain Lodge 6·50 6·00

No. 1781 as for use on priority domestic mail, and originally sold for 9k.

No. 1782 was for use on priority mail within Europe, and originally sold for 12k.

No. 1783 was for use on priority worldwide mail, and originally sold for 13k.

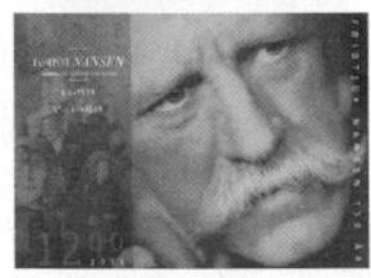

600 Fridtjof Nansen

2011. 150th Birth Anniv of Fridtjof Nansen (first High Commissioner for Refugees at League of Nation and winner of 1922 Nobel Peace Prize)

1784 **600** 12k. multicoloured 5·50 5·00

601 Roald Amudsen (expedition leader), Olav Bjaaland, Helmer Hanssen, Sverre Hassel and Oscar Wisting

2011. Centenary of First Men at South Pole. Multicoloured.

1785 14k. Type **601** 6·50 6·00
1786 17k. Sled dogs and *Fram* (expedition ship) 8·00 7·25

602 Waterfront

2011. Bicentenary of Drammen

1787 **602** 9k. multicoloured 4·25 3·75

603 Fire and Rescue Team from the Sagene Fire Station, Oslo

2011. 150th Anniv of Fire and Rescue Services. Multicoloured.

1788 9k. Type **603** 4·25 3·75
1789 27k. Training in rescue from burning building 12·50 11·50

604 Modern Harvester at Work in Bjønnsåsen Forest

2011. Europa. Forests. Multicoloured.

1790 12k. Type **604** 5·50 5·00
1791 14k. Conifers and dead tree, Farris, Siljan, Telemark 6·50 6·00

605 Ionic Columns, Domus Media

2011. Bicentenary of University of Oslo

1792 **605** 9k. agate and vermilion 4·25 3·75

606 Sissel Kyrkjebø

2011. Norwegian Female Singers. Multicoloured.

1793 A Type **606** 4·25 3·75
1794 A Mari Boine 4·25 3·75
1795 A Inger Lise Rypdal 4·25 3·75
1796 A Wenche Myhre 4·25 3·75

607 Bird in the Nest (created by John Arne Sæterøy (Jason), from *Mjau mjau*)

2011. Centenary of First Norwegian Comic Strip. Multicoloured.

1797 9k. Type **607** 4·25 4·00
1798 14k. Hold Brillan (created by Christopher Nielsen, from *Bygdegutar*) 6·50 6·00
1799 17k. Nemi (created by Lise Myhre) 8·00 7·25
1800 20k. Pondus (drawn and written by Frode Øverli) 9·25 8·50

2011. Posthorn. Multicoloured, colour of oval given.

1801 50k. greenish slate 27·00 26·50

608 Boy holding Envelope

2011. Christmas. Multicoloured.

1802 (9k.50) Type **608** 4·50 4·25
1803 (9k.50) Girl holding parcel 4·50 4·25

Nos. 1803/3 were both inscribed 'INNLAND' and were for use on priority domestic mail, and originally sold for 9k.50.

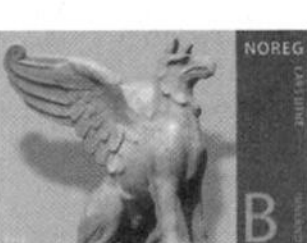

609 Griffin (Lars Utne)

2012. Modern Art. Multicoloured.

1804 (9k.) Type **609** 4·25 4·00
1805 14k. *Branntomt* (Fire site), (Håkon Stenstadvold) 6·50 6·00

No. 1804 was both inscribed 'B"INNLAND' and was for use on economy domestic mail, and originally sold for 9k.

610 Blossom

2012. Personal Stamp

1806 **610** (9k.50) multicoloured 4·50 4·25

611 Sea King Rescue Helicopter

2012. Norden. Life at the Coast. Sheet 105×70 mm

MS1807 **611** A (13k.) multicoloured 6·75 6·00

Stamps of a similar theme were issued by Denmark, Greenland, Faröe Islands, Finland, Iceland, Aland Islands and Sweden.

612 Queen Sonja

2012. 75th Birthdays of King Harald V and Queen Sonja

1808 9k.50 purple and sage-green 4·50 4·25
1809 13k. deep ultramarine and sage-green 6·25 5·75

DESIGNS: 9k.50, Type **612**; 13k. King Harald V

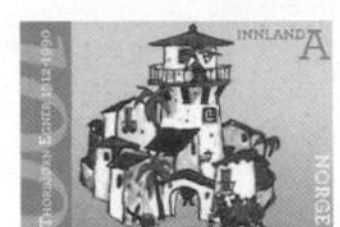

613 Cardamom Town (When the Robbers Came to Cardamom Town)

2012. Birth Centenaries. Multicoloured.

1810 (9k.50) Type **613** (Thorbjørn Egner) 4·50 4·25
1811 (9k.50) Sonja Henie (ice skater) 4·50 4·25
1812 (9k.50) Thorbjørn Egner (children's writer and illustrator) 4·50 4·25
1813 (9k.50) Sonja Henie skating 4·50 4·25

614 Nidaros Cathedral

2011. Tourism. Walking on Historic Ground. Multicoloured.

1814 (9k.) Type **614** 4·50 4·25
1815 (12k.) Monastery ruins on Selja Island, Nordfjord 6·25 5·75
1816 (14k.) Walkers on the way over Dovre Mountains 7·25 6·50

No. 1814 as for use on priority domestic mail, and originally sold for 9k.

No. 1815 was for use on priority mail within Europe, and originally sold for 12k.

No. 1816 was for use on priority worldwide mail, and originally sold for 14k.

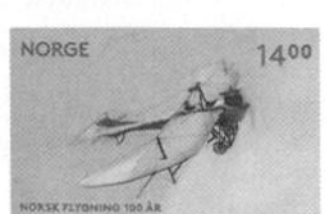

615 Start (Rumpler Taube) (Norway's first aeroplane)

2012. Centenary of Norwegian Aviation. Multicoloured.

1817 14k. Type **615** 6·75 6·00
1818 15k. Douglas DC-3 (Dakota) 7·25 6·50
1819 27k. Glider 13·50 12·00
MS1820 115×80 mm. Nos. 1817/19 27·00 26·00

616 Kavringen Lighthouse

2012. Lighthouses. Multicoloured.

1821 (9k.50) Type **616** 4·50 4·25
1822 (9k.50) Medfjordbåen 4·50 4·25

Nos. 1821/2 were both inscribed 'A' 'INNLAND' and were for use on priority domestic mail, and originally sold for 9k.50.

617 Decanter, Glasses and Glassblower

2012. 250th Anniv of Hadeland Glassverk

1823 **617** 13k. multicoloured 6·25 5·75

618 Sondre Lerche

2012. Norwegian Male Singers. Multicoloured.

1824 A Type **618** 4·50 4·25
1825 A Ole Paus 4·50 4·25
1826 A Åge Aleksandersen 4·50 4·25
1827 A Morten Abel 4·50 4·25

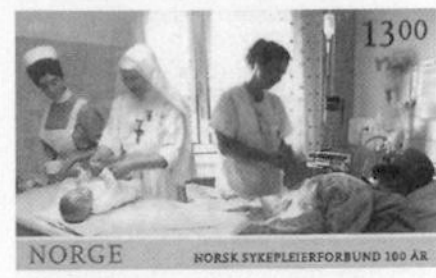

619 Nurses

2012. Centenary of Norwegian Nurses Organization (Norsk Sykepleierskeforbund)

1828 **619** 13k. multicoloured 6·25 5·75

620 Knud Knudsen (contributor to Norwegian language reform)

2012. Birth Bicentenaries. Multicoloured.

1829 14k. Type **620** 6·75 6·00
1830 15k. Peter Christen Asbjørnsen and Jørgen Moe (writers of Norwegian folktales) 7·25 6·50

621 Carpenter Andersen and Santa Claus

2012. Christmas. *Carpenter Andersen and Santa Claus* (by Alf Prøysen). Multicoloured.

1831 (9k.50) Type **621** 4·50 4·25
1832 (9k.50) Mrs Claus and children 4·50 4·25

622 Hamar Cathedral Ruins

2012. Centenary of the Directorate for Cultural Heritage

1833 **622** 15k. multicoloured 7·25 6·50

2012. Posthorn. Multicoloured, colour of oval given.

1834 40k. dark grey 10·00 9·50

623 Woman's Outfit, Nina Skarra's Autumn/ Winter 2012 Collection

2013. Norwegian Fashion. Fashion Designs by Nina Skarra and Camilla Bruerberg. Multicoloured.

1835 15k. Type **623** 7·25 6·50
1836 15k. Men's clothes by Camilla Bruerburg 7·25 6·50

624 *Self-Portrait in Front of the House Wall*

2013. 150th Birth Anniv of Edvard Munch (artist). Multicoloured.

1837 13k. Type **624** 6·50 5·75
1838 15k. *The Sick Child* 7·25 6·50
1839 17k. *Madonna* 7·75 7·00
1840 20k. *The Scream* 8·25 7·50
MS1841 100×70 mm. 20k. *The Sun* 10·00 10·00

625 Ice Climbing, Jostedal Glacier

2013. Tourism. Active Leisure Pursuits. Booklet Stamps. Multicoloured.

1842	A INNLAND (9k.50) Type **625**	4·50	4·25
1843	A INNLAND (9k.50) Bøya Glacier (arm of Jostedal Glacier	4·50	4·25
1844	A EUROPA (13k.) Hiking, Gaustatoppen	6·50	5·75
1845	A EUROPA (13k.) Hiking, Gaustatoppen (different)	6·50	5·75
1846	A VERDA (15k.) Rafting in Sjoa river	7·25	6·50
1847	A VERDA (15k.) Riverboarding in Sjoa river	7·25	6·50

626 Karl Johan Monument, The Royal Palace

2013. 250th Birth Anniv of King Karl Johan

1848	**626**	30k. multicoloured	9·00	8·25

627 Harley-Davidson Motorcycle

2013. Europa. Postal Transport. Multicoloured.

1849	13k. Type **627**	6·50	5·75
1850	15k. Ford El-Connect post van	7·25	6·50

628 Student Cap and Profiles

2013. Bicentenary of Norwegian Student Society

1851	**628**	17k. multicoloured	7·75	7·00

629 Crown Prince Haakon

2013. 40th Birthdays of Crown Prince Haakon and Crown Princess Mette-Marit. Multicoloured.

1852	A INNLAND (9k.50) Type **629**	4·50	4·25
1853	A INNLAND (9k.50) Crown Princess Mette-Marit	4·50	4·25
1854	A INNLAND (9k.50) Crown Prince and family	4·50	4·25
1855	A INNLAND (9k.50) King Harald and the current heirs to the throne	4·50	4·25

630 Camilla Collett and Cover of *Amtmandens Døttre*

2013. Centenary of Norwegian Women's Suffrage. Multicoloured.

1856	17k. Type **630**	7·75	7·00
1857	30k. Anna Rogstad and Parliament building	9·00	8·25

631 Lasse Kolstad in Scene from *Fiddler on the Roof* at Det Norske Teatret

2013. National Year of Languages. Multicoloured.

1858	A INNLAND (9k.50) Type **631** (centenary of Det Norske Teatret)	4·50	4·25
1859	A INNLAND (9k.50) Ivar Aasen and text from *Mellom bakkar og berg* (birth bicentenary)	4·50	4·25

632 Pussycats

2013. Norwegian Bands. Multicoloured.

1860	A INNLAND (9k.50) Type **632**	4·50	4·25
1861	A INNLAND (9k.50) DumDum Boys	4·50	4·25
1862	A INNLAND (9k.50) Turbonegro	4·50	4·25
1863	A INNLAND (9k.50) deLillos	4·50	4·25

OFFICIAL STAMPS

O22

1925

O187	**O22**	5ore mauve	1·10	1·90
O188	**O22**	10ore green	55	40
O189	**O22**	15ore blue	2·75	4·50
O190	**O22**	20ore purple	55	50
O191	**O22**	30ore grey	3·50	8·25
O192	**O22**	40ore blue	1·70	2·50
O193	**O22**	60ore blue	3·75	9·50

1929. Surch **2 2**.

O219	2ore on 5ore mauve	1·70	1·90

O36

1933

O231	**O36**	2ore brown	55	2·50
O243	**O36**	5ore purple	1·70	5·00
O233	**O36**	7ore orange	5·50	10·00
O245	**O36**	10ore green	70	75
O235	**O36**	15ore green	85	1·30
O247	**O36**	20ore red	1·70	65
O237	**O36**	25ore brown	85	1·30
O238	**O36**	30ore blue	85	1·50
O248	**O36**	35ore violet	85	75
O249	**O36**	40ore grey	1·70	90
O250	**O36**	60ore blue	1·70	1·50
O241	**O36**	70ore brown	1·40	5·00
O242	**O36**	100ore blue	2·50	3·75

O39

1937

O267	**O39**	5ore mauve	40	40
O268	**O39**	7ore orange	40	1·30
O269	**O39**	10ore green	40	40
O270	**O39**	15ore brown	40	50
O271	**O39**	20ore red	40	40
O260	**O39**	25ore brown	85	1·30
O273	**O39**	25ore red	40	40
O261	**O39**	30ore blue	85	1·30
O275	**O39**	30ore grey	70	65
O276	**O39**	35ore purple	85	65
O277	**O39**	40ore grey	55	50
O278	**O39**	40ore blue	2·75	50
O279	**O39**	50ore lilac	55	50
O280	**O39**	60ore blue	55	50
O281	**O39**	100ore blue	1·10	50
O282	**O39**	200ore orange	2·10	50

O58 Quisling Emblem

1942

O336	**O58**	5ore mauve	45	3·00
O337	**O58**	7ore orange	45	3·00
O338	**O58**	10ore green	45	45
O339	**O58**	15ore brown	1·80	23·00
O340	**O58**	20ore red	45	45
O341	**O58**	25ore brown	3·75	35·00
O342	**O58**	30ore blue	3·00	35·00
O343	**O58**	35ore purple	3·00	14·50
O344	**O58**	40ore grey	45	45
O345	**O58**	60ore blue	2·30	17·00
O346	**O58**	1k. blue	2·30	23·00

1949. Surch **25** and bar.

O402	**O39**	25ore on 20ore red	50	45

O89

1951

O434	**O89**	5ore mauve	1·40	45
O435	**O89**	10ore grey	1·40	35
O436	**O89**	15ore brown	1·80	1·20
O437	**O89**	30ore red	95	35
O438	**O89**	35ore brown	1·40	90
O439	**O89**	60ore blue	1·80	35
O440	**O89**	100ore violet	2·40	70

O99

1955

O458	**O99**	5ore purple	70	35
O459	**O99**	10ore grey	35	35
O460	**O99**	15ore brown	5·50	4·50
O461	**O99**	20ore green	95	35
O736	**O99**	25ore green	40	45
O463	**O99**	30ore red	4·25	1·00
O464	**O99**	30ore green	3·00	45
O465	**O99**	35ore red	60	35
O466	**O99**	40ore lilac	1·60	45
O467	**O99**	40ore green	6·00	2·30
O468	**O99**	45ore red	2·20	35
O469	**O99**	50ore brown	3·50	45
O470	**O99**	50ore red	3·00	35
O471	**O99**	50ore blue	70	45
O738	**O99**	50ore grey	40	35
O473	**O99**	60ore red	95	35
O739	**O99**	60ore blue	2·50	7·00
O475	**O99**	65ore red	1·80	35
O476	**O99**	70ore brown	6·50	1·20
O477	**O99**	70ore red	50	45
O478	**O99**	75ore purple	19·00	17·00
O479	**O99**	75ore green	95	1·20
O481	**O99**	80ore brown	70	45
O741	**O99**	80ore red	65	35
O482	**O99**	85ore brown	1·20	3·00
O483	**O99**	90ore orange	1·80	35
O484	**O99**	1k. violet	2·20	35
O485	**O99**	1k. red	50	45
O486	**O99**	1k.10 red	95	1·20
O744	**O99**	1k.25 red	2·50	35
O745	**O99**	1k.30 purple	2·30	3·00
O746	**O99**	1k.50 red	75	45
O747	**O99**	1k.75 green	2·30	2·30
O748	**O99**	2k. green	1·00	35
O749	**O99**	2k. red	1·50	45
O750	**O99**	3k. violet	2·30	80
O488	**O99**	5k. violet	7·75	1·20
O752	**O99**	5k. blue	1·90	35

POSTAGE DUE STAMPS

D12

1889. Inscr "at betale" and "PORTOMAERKE".

D95	**D12**	1ore green	1·00	1·90
D96a	**D12**	4ore mauve	1·50	1·00
D97	**D12**	10ore red	3·75	75
D98	**D12**	15ore brown	2·50	1·30
D99	**D12**	20ore blue	3·25	65
D94	**D12**	50ore purple	5·00	2·75

1922. Inscr "a betale" and "PORTOMERKE".

D162		4ore purple	7·50	19·00
D163		10ore green	3·75	2·50
D164		20ore purple	5·00	4·50
D165		40ore blue	7·50	1·50
D166		100ore yellow	25·00	14·00
D167		200ore violet	65·00	31·00

Pt. 6

NOSSI-BE

An island north-west of Madagascar, declared a French protectorate in 1840. In 1901 it became part of Madagascar and Dependencies.

100 centimes = 1 franc.

1889. Stamp of French Colonies, "Peace and Commerce" type, surch.

8	**H**	25c. on 40c. red on yellow	£2250	£800

1889. Stamps of French Colonies, "Commerce" type, surch.

4	**J**	5c. on 10c. black on lilac	£2750	£800
2	**J**	5c. on 20c. red on green	£3000	£850
6	**J**	15 on 20c. red on green	£2750	£800
7	**J**	25 on 30c. brown on drab	£2750	£650
9	**J**	25 on 40c. red on yellow	£2250	£650

1890. Stamps of French Colonies, "Commerce" type, surch. (a) **N S B 0 25**.

10	0 25 on 20c. red on green	£325	£225
11	0 25 on 75c. red on pink	£275	£225
12	0 25 on 1f. green	£325	£225

(b) **N S B 25 c**.

13	25c. on 20c. red on green	£325	£225
14	25c. on 75c. red on pink	£325	£225
15	25c. on 1f. green	£325	£225

(c) **N S B 25** in frame.

16	25 on 20c. red on green	£750	£550
17	25 on 75c. red on pink	£750	£550
18	25 on 1f. green	£750	£550

1893. Stamps of French Colonies, "Commerce" type, surch **NOSSI-BE** and bar over value in figures.

36	25 on 20c. red on green	60·00	60·00
37	50 on 10c. black on lilac	65·00	60·00
38	75 on 15c. blue	£225	£170
39	1f. on 5c. green	£120	£100

1893. Stamps of French Colonies, "Commerce" type, optd **Nossi Be**.

40a	10c. black on lilac	40·00	9·25
41	15c. blue	40·00	12·00
42	20c. red on green	£425	28·00

1894. "Tablet" key-type inscr "NOSSI-BE" in red (1, 5, 15, 25, 75c., 1f.) or blue (others).

44	**D**	1c. black on blue	1·90	1·70
45	**D**	2c. brown on buff	2·50	3·50
46	**D**	4c. brown on grey	3·00	3·50
47	**D**	5c. green on green	3·25	3·00
48	**D**	10c. black on lilac	3·25	5·25
49	**D**	15c. blue	14·00	4·50
50	**D**	20c. red on green	11·00	10·50
51	**D**	25c. black on pink	14·00	12·50
52	**D**	30c. brown on drab	11·00	20·00
53	**D**	40c. red on yellow	17·00	23·00
54	**D**	50c. red on pink	6·00	7·75
55	**D**	75c. brown on orange	34·00	27·00
56	**D**	1f. green	11·00	46·00

POSTAGE DUE STAMPS

1891. Stamps of French Colonies, "Commerce" type, surch **NOSSI-BE chiffre-taxe A PERCEVOIR** and value.

D19	**J**	0.20 on 1c. black on blue	£275	£200
D20	**J**	0.30 on 2c. brown on buff	£275	£200
D21	**J**	0.35 on 4c. brown on grey	£300	£225
D22	**J**	0.35 on 20c. red on green	£325	£225
D23	**J**	0.50 on 30c. brn on drab	£110	85·00
D24	**J**	1f. on 35c. black on orge	£180	£140

1891. Stamps of French Colonies, "Commerce" type, surch **Nossi-Be A PERCEVOIR** and value.

D25	5c. on 20c. red on green	£140	£140
D33	0.10 on 5c. green	33·00	19·00
D26	10c. on 15c. blue on blue	£150	£150
D27	15c. on 10c. black on lilac	£140	£140
D34	0.15 on 20c. red on green	40·00	42·00
D28	25c. on 5c. green on green	£140	£140
D35	0.25 on 75c. red on pink	£425	£425

Pt. 1

NOVA SCOTIA

An eastern province of the Dominion of Canada, whose stamps it now uses.

Currency: As Canada.

1

2 Emblem of the United Kingdom

1851. Imperf.

1	1	1d. brown	£3000	£475
4	2	3d. blue	£1000	£150
5	2	6d. green	£4750	£550
8	2	1s. purple	£18000	£3500

3

4

1863. Perf.

10	3	1c. black	4·25	18·00
23	3	2c. purple	4·75	13·00
13	3	5c. blue	£475	25·00
14	4	8½c. green	4·75	65·00
28	4	10c. red	5·00	42·00
17	4	12½c. black	38·00	30·00

Pt. 1

NYASALAND PROTECTORATE

A British Protectorate in central Africa. Formerly known as British Central Africa. From 1954 to 1963 part of the Central African Federation using the stamps of Rhodesia and Nyasaland (q.v.). From July 1964 independent within the Commonwealth under its new name of Malawi.

12 pence = 1 shilling; 20 shillings = 1 pound.

1891. Stamps of Rhodesia optd **B.C.A.**

1	1	1d. black	12·00	10·00
2	1	2d. green and red	13·00	4·50
3	1	4d. brown and black	13·00	7·00
5	1	6d. blue	18·00	9·50
6	1	8d. red and blue	19·00	30·00
7	1	1s. brown	27·00	19·00
8	1	2s. red	48·00	60·00
9	1	2s.6d. purple	85·00	£100
10	1	3s. brown and green	85·00	85·00
11	1	4s. black and red	95·00	£110
12	1	5s. yellow	£100	£110
13	1	10s. green	£190	£225
14	-	£1 blue	£1200	£700
15	-	£2 red	£1300	£1600
16	-	£5 olive	£1900	
17	-	£10 brown	£4250	£5000

1892. Stamps of Rhodesia surch **B.C.A.** and value in words.

18	1	3s. on 4s. black and red	£375	£375
19	1	4s. on 5s. yellow	£100	£100

1895. No. 2 surch **ONE PENNY.** and bar.

20	1d. on 2d. green and red	35·00	60·00

5 Arms of the Protectorate

1895. The 2s.6d. and higher values are larger.

32	5	1d. black	3·25	9·50
33	5	2d. black and green	21·00	5·50
34	5	4d. black and orange	35·00	17·00
35	5	6d. black and blue	50·00	16·00
36	5	1s. black and red	50·00	25·00
37	5	2s.6d. black and mauve	£200	£150
38	5	3s. black and yellow	£180	75·00
39	5	5s. black and olive	£275	£275
29	5	£1 black and orange	£1200	£600
40	5	£1 black and blue	£1200	£650
30	5	£10 black and orange	£8000	£5500
31	5	£25 black and green	£15000	£15000

7 Arms of the Protectorate

1897. The 2s.6d. and higher values are larger.

43	7	1d. black and blue	3·25	1·25
57d	7	1d. purple and red	2·75	50
44	7	2d. black and yellow	3·25	2·00
45	7	4d. black and red	6·50	1·50
57e	7	4d. purple and olive	12·00	11·00
46	7	6d. black and green	60·00	4·25
58	7	6d. purple and brown	9·50	4·00
47	7	1s. black and purple	11·00	7·00
48	7	2s.6d. black and blue	95·00	50·00
49	7	3s. black and green	£350	£375
50	7	4s. black and red	£120	£100
50a	7	10s. black and olive	£300	£325
51	7	£1 black and purple	£475	£250
52	7	£10 black and yellow	£8000	£2750

1897. No. 49 surch **ONE PENNY.**

53	1d. on 3s. black and green	10·00	19·00

10

1898

56a	10	1d. red and blue (imperf)	£6500	£190
57	10	1d. red and blue (perf)	£6000	35·00

11

1903. The 2s.6d. and higher values are larger.

68	11	1d. grey and red	8·50	2·75
60	11	2d. purple	3·50	1·00
61	11	4d. green and black	2·50	9·00
62	11	6d. grey and brown	3·75	2·00
62b	11	1s. grey and blue	4·75	16·00
63	11	2s.6d. green	65·00	£100
64	11	4s. purple	90·00	90·00
65	11	10s. green and black	£200	£300
66	11	£1 grey and red	£325	£225
67	11	£10 grey and blue	£8000	£4750

13

14

1908

73	13	½d. green	1·75	2·25
74	13	1d. red	8·00	1·00
75	13	3d. purple on yellow	1·75	4·25
76	13	4d. black and red on yellow	1·75	1·50
77	13	6d. purple	4·75	11·00
72	13	1s. black on green	5·00	16·00
78	14	2s.6d. black and red on blue	75·00	£110
79	14	4s. red and black	£110	£180
80	14	10s. green and red on green	£200	£325
81	14	£1 purple and black on red	£650	£750
82	14	£10 purple and blue	£12000	£8000

1913. As 1908, but portrait of King George V.

100	½d. green	3·00	50
101	1d. red	2·75	50
102	1½d. orange	3·25	17·00
103	2d. grey	3·00	50
89	2½d. blue	2·50	7·00
90	3d. purple on yellow	7·50	4·50
91	4d. black and red on yellow	2·00	2·50
107	6d. purple	5·00	3·25
93a	1s. black on green	5·50	1·50
109	2s. purple and blue on blue	20·00	12·00
94	2s.6d. black and red on blue	11·00	24·00
111	4s. red and black	23·00	42·00
112	5s. green and red on yellow	55·00	85·00
113	10s. green and red on green	£120	£120
98	£1 purple and black on red	£200	£170
99e	£10 purple and blue	£4000	£2000

17 King George V and Symbol of the Protectorate

1934

114	17	½d. green	75	1·25
115	17	1d. brown	75	75
116	17	1½d. red	75	3·00
117	17	2d. grey	1·00	1·25
118	17	3d. blue	3·00	1·75
119	17	4d. mauve	5·50	3·50
120	17	6d. violet	2·75	50
121	17	9d. olive	8·50	13·00
122	17	1s. black and orange	23·00	14·00

1935. Silver Jubilee. As T **143a** of Newfoundland.

123	1d. blue and grey	1·00	2·00
124	2d. green and blue	1·00	1·50
125	3d. brown and blue	10·00	22·00
126	1s. grey and purple	28·00	55·00

1937. Coronation. As T **143b** of Newfoundland.

127	½d. green	30	2·25
128	1d. brown	50	1·50
129	2d. grey	50	3·25

1938. As T **17** but with head of King George VI and "POSTAGE REVENUE" omitted.

130	½d. green	30	2·50
130a	½d. brown	10	2·50
131	1d. brown	4·00	30
131b	1d. green	30	2·25
132	1½d. red	9·00	8·50
132a	1½d. grey	30	8·50
133	2d. grey	8·00	1·25
133a	2d. red	30	1·75
134	3d. blue	1·00	1·50
135	4d. mauve	3·00	2·00
136	6d. violet	2·75	2·00
137	9d. olive	3·00	5·00
138	1s. black and orange	3·50	3·25

1938. As T **14** but with head of King George VI facing right.

139	2s. purple and blue on blue	10·00	17·00
140	2s.6d. black and red on blue	15·00	22·00
141	5s. green and red on yellow	55·00	35·00
142	10s. green and red on green	55·00	80·00
143	£1 purple and black on red	50·00	50·00

20 Lake Nyasa

21 King's African Rifles

1945

144	20	½d. black and brown	50	10
145	21	1d. black and green	20	70
160	-	1d. brown and green	50	30
146	-	1½d. black and grey	30	50
147	-	2d. black and red	1·50	85
148	-	3d. black and blue	30	30
149	-	4d. black and red	2·00	80
150	-	6d. black and violet	3·00	90
151	20	9d. black and olive	4·25	3·00
152	-	1s. blue and green	3·75	20
153	-	2s. green and purple	9·50	6·00
154	-	2s.6d. green and blue	9·50	7·50
155	-	5s. purple and blue	7·00	6·50
156	-	10s. red and green	22·00	19·00
157	-	20s. red and black	29·00	42·00

DESIGNS—HORIZ: 1½d., 6d. Tea estate; 2d., 1s., 10s. Map of Nyasaland; 4d., 2s.6d. Tobacco; 5s., 20s. Badge of Nyasaland. VERT: 1d. (No. 160), Leopard and sunrise; 3d., 2s. Fishing village.

1946. Victory. As T **8a** of Pitcairn Islands.

158	1d. green	20	30
159	2d. red	30	30

1948. Silver Wedding. As T **8b/8c** of Pitcairn Islands.

161	1d. green	15	10
162	10s. mauve	18·00	30·00

1949. U.P.U. As T **8d/8g** of Pitcairn Islands.

163	1d. green	30	20
164	3d. blue	2·25	4·25
165	6d. purple	50	70
166	1s. blue	30	50

27 Arms in 1891 and 1951

1951. Diamond Jubilee of Protectorate.

167	27	2d. black and red	1·25	1·50
168	27	3d. black and blue	1·25	1·50
169	27	6d. black and violet	1·50	2·00
170	27	5s. black and blue	6·00	8·00

1953. Rhodes Centenary Exhibition. As T **6** of Northern Rhodesia.

171	6d. violet	50	30

1953. Coronation. As T **8h** of Pitcairn Islands.

172	2d. black and orange	70	80

29 Grading Cotton

1953. As 1945 but with portrait of Queen Elizabeth II as in T **29**. Designs as for corresponding values except where stated.

173	20	½d. black and brown	10	1·75
174	-	1d. brn & grn (as No. 160)	65	65
175	-	1½d. black and grey	30	1·90
176a	-	2d. black and orange	55	30
177	29	2½d. green and black	30	50
178	-	3d. black and red (as 4d.)	30	20
179	-	4½d. black and blue (as 3d.)	1·00	40
180	-	6d. black and violet	1·00	1·50
181	20	9d. black and olive	1·25	2·75
182	-	1s. blue and green	3·75	50
183	-	2s. green and red	3·50	3·75
184	-	2s.6d. green and blue	4·25	7·50
185	-	5s. purple and blue	12·00	7·50
186	-	10s. red and green	14·00	23·00
187	-	20s. red and black	27·00	40·00

30

1963. Revenue stamps optd **POSTAGE** as in T **30** or surch also.

188	30	½d. on 1d. blue	30	30
189	30	1d. green	30	10
190	30	2d. red	30	30
191	30	3d. blue	30	10
192	30	6d. purple	30	10
193	30	9d. on 1s. red	40	25
194	30	1s. purple	45	10
195	30	2s.6d. black	1·25	2·75
196	30	5s. brown	3·25	3·00
197	30	10s. olive	5·50	8·50
198	30	£1 violet	5·50	9·00

32 Mother and Child

34 Tea Industry

1964

199	32	½d. violet	10	30
200	-	1d. black and green	10	10
201	-	2d. brown	10	10
202	-	3d. brown, green and bistre	10	10
203	-	4d. blue and yellow	20	30
204	34	6d. purple, green and blue	85	70
205	-	1s. brown, blue and yellow	15	10
206	-	1s.3d. bronze and brown	3·75	10
207	-	2s.6d. brown and blue	3·25	50
208	-	5s. blue, green, yellow & blk	1·50	1·75
209	-	10s. green, salmon and black	2·50	3·25
210	-	£1 brown and yellow	8·50	14·00

DESIGNS—HORIZ (as Type **32**): 1d. Chambo (fish); 2d. Zebu bull; 3d. Groundnuts; 4d. Fishing. (As Type **34**): 1s. Timber; 1s.3d. Turkish tobacco industry; 2s.6d. Cotton industry; 5s. Monkey Bay, Lake Nyasa; 10s. Forestry, Afzelia. VERT (as Type **34**): £1 Nyala.

POSTAGE DUE STAMPS

D1

1950. As Type D **1.**

D1		1d. red	4·25	32·00
D2		2d. blue	20·00	32·00
D3		3d. green	17·00	6·00
D4		4d. purple	30·00	60·00
D5		6d. orange	42·00	£160

For later issues see **MALAWI**.

Pt. 9

NYASSA COMPANY

In 1894 Portugal granted a charter to the Nyassa Company to administer an area in the Northern part of Mozambique, including the right to issue its own stamps. The lease was terminated in 1929 and the administration was transferred to Mozambique whose stamps were used there.

1898. 1000 reis = 1 milreis.
1913. 100 centavos = 1 escudo.

1898. "Figures" and "Newspaper" key-types inscr "MOCAMBIQUE" optd **NYASSA**.

1	V	2½r. brown	3·75	3·50
2	R	5r. orange	3·75	3·50
3	R	10r. mauve	3·75	3·50
4	R	15r. brown	3·75	3·50
5	R	20r. lilac	3·75	3·50
6	R	25r. green	3·75	3·50
7	R	50r. blue	3·75	3·50
8	R	75r. pink	4·50	4·25
9	R	80r. green	4·50	4·25
10	R	100r. brown on buff	4·50	4·25
11	R	150r. red on pink	14·00	13·00
12	R	200r. blue on blue	8·25	7·50
13	R	300r. blue on brown	8·25	7·50

1898. "King Carlos" key-type inscr "MOCAMBIQUE" optd **NYASSA**.

14	S	2½r. grey	2·50	2·50
15	S	5r. red	2·50	2·50
16	S	10r. green	2·50	2·50
17	S	15r. brown	3·50	2·75
18	S	20r. lilac	3·50	2·75
19	S	25r. green	3·50	2·75
20	S	50r. blue	3·50	2·75
21	S	75r. pink	3·75	3·50
22	S	80r. mauve	4·50	2·50
23	S	100r. blue on blue	4·50	2·50
24	S	150r. brown on yellow	4·50	2·50
25	S	200r. purple on pink	4·75	2·75
26	S	300r. blue on pink	6·25	2·75

2 Giraffe 3 Dromedaries

1901

27	2	2½r. brown and black	2·30	1·20
28	2	5r. violet and black	2·30	1·20
29	2	10r. green and black	2·30	1·20
30	2	15r. brown and black	2·30	1·20
31	2	20r. red and black	2·30	1·50
32	2	25r. orange and black	2·30	1·50
33	2	50r. blue and black	2·30	1·50
34	3	75r. red and black	2·75	1·90
35	3	80r. bistre and black	2·75	1·90
36	3	100r. brown and black	2·75	1·90
37	3	150r. brown and black	3·25	2·20
38	3	200r. green and black	3·25	2·20
39	3	300r. green and black	3·25	2·20

1903. (a) Surch in figures and words.

40		65r. on 80r. mauve and black	2·10	1·60
41		115r. on 150r. brown & black	2·10	1·60
42		130r. on 300r. green & black	2·10	1·60

(b) Optd **PROVISORIO**.

43	2	15r. brown and black	2·10	1·60
44	2	25r. orange and black	2·10	1·60

1910. Optd **PROVISORIO** and surch in figures and words.

50		5r. on 2½r. brown and black	2·20	1·80
51	3	50r. on 100r. bistre and black	2·20	1·80

9 Dromedaries

12 Vasco de Gama's Flagship "Sao Gabriel"

1911. Optd **REPUBLICA**.

53	9	2½r. violet and black	2·10	1·30
54	9	5r. black	2·10	1·30
55	9	10r. green and black	2·10	1·30
56	-	20r. red and black	2·10	1·30
57	-	25r. brown and black	2·10	1·30
58	-	50r. blue and black	2·10	1·30
59	-	75r. brown and black	2·10	1·30
60	-	100r. brown & black on green	2·10	1·30
61	-	200r. green & black on orge	2·30	2·10
62	12	300r. black on blue	5·00	3·50
63	12	400r. brown and black	5·75	4·00
64	12	500r. violet and green	7·50	6·25

DESIGNS—HORIZ: 20, 25, 50r. Common zebra. VERT: 75, 100, 200r. Giraffe.

1918. Surch **REPUBLICA** and value in figures. (a) Stamps of 1901.

65	2	¼c. on 2½c. brown and black	£275	£200
66	2	½c. on 5r. violet and black	£275	£200
67	2	1c. on 10r. green and black	£275	£200
68	2	1½c. on 15r. brown and black	4·50	2·30
69	2	2c. on 20r. red and black	2·75	2·10
70	2	3½c. on 25r. orange and black	2·75	2·10
71	2	5c. on 50r. blue and black	2·75	2·10
72	3	7½c. on 75r. red and black	2·75	2·10
73	3	8c. on 80r. mauve and black	2·75	2·10
74	3	10c. on 100r. bistre and black	2·75	2·10
75	3	15c. on 150r. brown & black	4·50	4·25
76	3	20c. on 200r. green and black	4·25	4·25
77	3	30c. on 300r. green and black	6·75	5·00

(b) Nos. 43/4 and 40/2.

78	2	1½c. on 15r. brown and black	8·50	6·50
79	2	3½c. on 25r. orange and black	3·25	2·10
80	3	40c. on 65r. on 80r.	38·00	35·00
81	3	50c. on 115r. on 150r.	5·50	4·25
82	3	1E. on 130r. on 300r.	5·50	4·25

1921. Stamps of 1911 surch in figures and words.

83A	9	¼c. on 2½r. violet and black	3·25	3·25
85A	9	½c. on 5r. black	3·25	3·25
86A	9	1c. on 10r. green and black	3·25	3·25
87A	12	1½c. on 300r. black on blue	3·25	3·25
88A	-	2c. on 20r. red and black	3·25	3·25
89A	-	2½c. on 25r. brown and black	3·25	3·25
90A	12	3c. on 400r. brown & black	3·25	3·25
91A	-	5c. on 50r. blue and black	3·25	3·25
92A	-	7½c. on 75r. brown & black	3·25	3·25
93A	-	10c. on 100r. brown and black on green	3·25	3·25
94A	12	12c. on 500r. violet & green	3·25	3·25
95A	-	20c. on 200r. green and black on orange	3·25	3·25

16 Giraffe

19 Common Zebra

1921

96	16	¼c. purple	1·90	1·40
97	16	½c. blue	1·90	1·40
98	16	1c. black and green	1·90	1·40
99	16	1½c. orange and black	1·90	1·40
100	-	2c. black and red	1·90	1·40
101	-	2½c. green and black	1·90	1·40
102	-	4c. red and black	1·90	1·40
103	-	5c. black and blue	1·90	1·40
104	-	6c. violet and black	1·90	1·40
123	-	7½c. brown and black	1·50	1·20
124	-	8c. green and black	1·50	1·20
125	-	10c. brown and black	1·50	1·20
126	-	15c. red and black	1·50	1·20
127	-	20c. blue and black	1·50	1·20
110	19	30c. brown and black	1·90	1·40
111	19	40c. blue and black	1·90	1·40
112	19	50c. green and black	1·90	1·40
113	19	1e. brown and black	1·90	1·40
114	-	2e. black and brown	6·25	5·00
115	-	5e. brown and blue	5·75	4·50

DESIGNS—As Type **16**: 2c. to 6c. Vasco da Gama; 7½c. to 20c. Vasco da Gama's flagship "Sao Gabriel". As Type **19**: 2, 5e. Native dhow.

CHARITY TAX STAMPS

The notes under this heading in Portugal also apply here.

1925. Marquis de Pombal Commem. Nos. C327/9 of Mozambique optd **NYASSA**.

C141	C22	15c. brown	12·50	10·00
C142	-	15c. brown	12·50	10·00
C143	C 25	15c. brown	12·50	10·00

POSTAGE DUE STAMPS

D21 "Sao Gabriel"

1924

D132	-	½c. green	4·50	3·50
D133	-	1c. blue	4·50	3·50
D134	-	2c. red	4·50	3·50
D135	-	3c. red	4·50	3·50
D136	D21	5c. brown	4·50	3·50
D137	D21	6c. brown	4·50	3·50
D138	D21	10c. purple	4·50	3·50
D139	-	20c. red	4·50	3·50
D140	-	50c. purple	4·50	3·50

DESIGNS: ½c., 1c. Giraffe; 2c., 3c. Common zebra; 20c., 50c. Vasco da Gama.

1925. De Pombal stamps of Mozambique, Nos. D327/9, optd **NYASSA**.

D144	C22	30c. brown	15·00	15·00
D145	-	30c. brown	15·00	15·00
D146	C25	30c. brown	15·00	15·00

Pt. 6

OBOCK

A port and district on the Somali Coast. During 1894 the administration was moved to Djibouti, the capital of French Somali Coast, and the Obock post office was closed.

1892. Stamps of French Colonies, "Commerce" type, optd **OBOCK**.

1	J	1c. black on blue	55·00	60·00
2	J	2c. brown on buff	60·00	65·00
12	J	4c. brown on grey	14·00	22·00
13	J	5c. green on green	20·00	20·00
14	J	10c. black on lilac	25·00	42·00
15	J	15c. blue	14·00	32·00
16	J	20c. red on green	65·00	60·00
17	J	25c. black on pink	21·00	30·00
8	J	35c. black on orange	£325	£325
18	J	40c. red on buff	60·00	65·00
19	J	75c. red on pink	£250	£225
20	J	1f. green	70·00	70·00

1892. Nos. 14, 15, 17 and 20 surch.

39		1 on 25c. black on red	11·00	13·00
40		2 on 10c. black on lilac	80·00	65·00
41		2 on 15c. blue	8·25	30·00
42		4 on 15c. blue	12·00	42·00
43		4 on 25c. black on red	12·00	10·00
44		5 on 25c. black on red	30·00	40·00
45		20 on 10c. black on lilac	95·00	95·00
46		30 on 10c. black on lilac	£100	£100
47		35 on 25c. black on red	£100	80·00
48		75 on 1f. olive	£100	£110
49		5f. on 1f. olive	£700	£600

1892. "Tablet" key-type inscr "OBOCK" in red (1, 5, 15, 25, 75c., 1f.) or blue (others).

50	D	1c. black on blue	4·75	5·25
51	D	2c. brown on buff	2·75	3·75
52	D	4c. brown on grey	2·50	1·80
53	D	5c. green on green	7·00	9·00
54	D	10c. black on lilac	9·00	12·00
55	D	15c. blue	25·00	17·00
56	D	20c. red on green	40·00	48·00
57	D	25c. black on pink	36·00	42·00
58	D	30c. brown on drab	29·00	26·00
59	D	40c. red on yellow	21·00	18·00
60	D	50c. red on pink	16·00	16·00
61	D	75c. brown on orange	50·00	22·00
62	D	1f. green	40·00	60·00

5

1893

63	5	2f. grey	70·00	70·00
64	5	5f. red	£130	£130

The 5f. stamp is larger than the 2f.

6

7

1894

65	6	1c. black and red	75	90
66	6	2c. red and green	2·30	1·70
67	6	4c. red and orange	1·40	1·20
68	6	5c. green and brown	2·10	1·40
69	6	10c. black and green	5·50	3·75
70	6	15c. blue and red	2·30	1·20
71	6	20c. orange and purple	7·75	1·40
72	6	25c. black and blue	9·00	2·75
73	6	30c. yellow and green	20·00	9·25
74	6	40c. orange and green	10·00	7·25
75	6	50c. red and blue	8·25	4·50
76	6	75c. lilac and orange	11·00	6·50
77	6	1f. olive and purple	9·25	8·25
78	7	2f. orange and lilac	£130	£130
79	7	5f. red and blue	£120	£120
80	7	10f. lake and red	£150	£150
81	7	25f. blue and brown	£750	£750
82	7	50f. green and lake	£800	£800

Length of sides of Type **7**: 2f. 37 mm; 5f. 42 mm; 10f. 46 mm; 25, 50f. 49 mm.

POSTAGE DUE STAMPS

1892. Postage Due stamps of French Colonies optd **OBOCK**.

D25	U	1c. black	65·00	70·00
D26	U	2c. black	55·00	65·00
D27	U	3c. black	55·00	70·00
D28	U	4c. black	48·00	60·00
D29	U	5c. black	18·00	13·00
D30	U	10c. black	60·00	60·00
D31	U	15c. black	30·00	44·00
D32	U	20c. black	36·00	55·00
D33	U	30c. black	55·00	60·00
D34	U	40c. black	75·00	75·00
D35	U	60c. black	95·00	95·00
D36	U	1f. brown	£170	£170
D37	U	2f. brown	£180	£180
D38	U	5f. brown	£350	£350

For later issues see **DJIBOUTI**.

Pt. 6

OCEANIC SETTLEMENTS

Scattered French islands in the E. Pacific Ocean, including Tahiti and the Marquesas.

In 1957 the Oceanic Settlements were renamed French Polynesia.

1892. "Tablet" key-type.

1	D	1c. black and red on blue	80	1·00
2	D	2c. brown and blue on buff	1·50	1·70
3	D	4c. brown and blue on grey	2·75	2·75
14	D	5c. green and red	2·75	1·60
5	D	10c. black and blue on lilac	22·00	12·50
15	D	10c. red and blue	3·25	1·40
6	D	15c. blue and red	20·00	11·50
16	D	15c. grey and red	5·75	4·75
7	D	20c. red and blue on green	16·00	14·00
8	D	25c. black and red on pink	42·00	28·00
17	D	25c. blue and red	23·00	13·00
9	D	30c. brown and blue on drab	16·00	16·00
18	D	35c. black and red on yellow	7·75	8·25
10	D	40c. red and blue on yellow	£110	£100
19	D	45c. black and red on green	6·00	7·00
11	D	50c. red and blue on pink	8·00	10·50
20	D	50c. brown and red on blue	£200	£225
12	D	75c. brown and red on orange	12·50	15·00
13	D	1f. green and red	16·00	18·00

2 Tahitian Woman **3** Kanakas

4 Valley of Fautaua

1913

21	**2**	1c. brown and violet	30	45
22	**2**	2c. grey and brown	55	1·10
23	**2**	4c. blue and orange	90	1·50
24	**2**	5c. light green and green	1·70	1·70
46	**2**	5c. black and blue	1·30	2·50
25	**2**	10c. orange and red	3·00	1·90
47	**2**	10c. light green and green	2·75	4·25
48	**2**	10c. purple and red on blue	2·75	3·50
25a	**2**	15c. black and orange	2·50	2·75
26	**2**	20c. violet and black	85	3·75
49	**2**	20c. green	2·30	6·00
50	**2**	20c. brown and red	3·25	4·00
27	**3**	25c. blue and ultramarine	4·00	3·00
51	**3**	25c. red and violet	2·10	2·30
28	**3**	30c. brown and grey	6·75	8·25
52	**3**	30c. red and carmine	2·75	9·00
53	**3**	30c. red and black	2·50	2·75
54	**3**	30c. green and blue	3·50	6·00
29	**3**	35c. red and green	2·30	3·50
30	**3**	40c. green and black	2·40	2·50
31	**3**	45c. red and orange	2·50	4·75
32	**3**	50c. black and brown	13·00	15·00
55	**3**	50c. blue and ultramarine	2·30	3·00
56	**3**	50c. blue and grey	2·20	2·10
57	**3**	60c. black and green	1·90	6·25
58	**3**	65c. mauve and brown	5·00	4·50
33	**3**	75c. violet and purple	3·00	3·50
59	**3**	90c. mauve and red	15·00	29·00
34	**4**	1f. black and red	4·00	2·75
60	**4**	1f.10 brown and mauve	4·25	6·25
61	**4**	1f.40 violet and brown	7·50	8·00
62	**4**	1f.50 light blue and blue	17·00	11·50
35	**4**	2f. green and brown	7·25	7·00
36	**4**	5f. blue and violet	11·50	25·00

1915. "Tablet" key-type optd **E F O 1915** and bar.

37	**D**	10c. red	2·10	4·50

1915. Red Cross. No. 37 surch **5c** and red cross.

38	10c.+5c. red	15·00	34·00

1915. Red Cross. Surch **5c** and red cross.

41	**2**	10c.+5c. orange and red	3·75	6·25

1916. Surch.

42		10c. on 15c. black and orange	2·75	3·00
71	**4**	20f. on 5f. mauve and red	26·00	25·00
67	**4**	25c. on 2f. green and brown	1·00	8·00
68	**4**	25c. on 5f. blue and violet	1·00	8·00
63	**3**	60 on 75c. brown and blue	55	2·75
64	**4**	65 on 1f. brown and blue	1·90	4·50
65	**4**	85 on 1f. brown and blue	1·60	3·50
66	**3**	90 on 75c. mauve and red	3·25	5·50
69	**4**	1f.25 on 1f. ultramarine & bl	85	3·50
70	**4**	1f.50 on 1f. light blue & blue	3·25	3·25

1921. Surch 1921 and new value.

43	**2**	05 on 2c. grey and brown	40·00	40·00
44	**3**	10 on 45c. red and orange	50·00	50·00
45	**2**	25 on 15c. black and orange	6·25	12·00

1924. Surch **45c**. 1924.

72	45c. on 10c. orange and red	5·25	8·25

1926. Surch in words.

73	**4**	3f. on 5f. blue and grey	2·75	4·00
74	**4**	10f. on 5f. black and green	5·50	6·25

13 Papetoia Bay

1929

75	**13**	3f. sepia and green	7·50	8·00
76	**13**	5f. sepia and blue	10·50	18·00
77	**13**	10f. sepia and red	32·00	50·00
78	**13**	20f. sepia and mauve	43·00	55·00

1931. "International Colonial Exhibition", Paris, key-types.

79	**E**	40c. black and green	7·50	11·50
80	**F**	50c. black and mauve	8·00	14·00
81	**G**	90c. black and red	8·00	16·00
82	**H**	1f.50 black and blue	8·00	11·50

14 Spearing Fish **15** Tahitian Girl

16 Native Gods

1934

83	**14**	1c. black	20	2·10
84	**14**	2c. red	20	2·75
85	**14**	3c. blue	30	6·25
86	**14**	4c. orange	20	5·75
87	**14**	5c. mauve	35	3·00
88	**14**	10c. brown	25	3·75
89	**14**	15c. green	25	4·50
90	**14**	20c. red	35	4·00
91	**15**	25c. blue	1·60	2·75
92	**15**	30c. green	2·20	6·75
93	**15**	30c. orange	65	4·50
94	**16**	35c. green	3·25	11·00
95	**15**	40c. mauve	55	5·75
96	**15**	45c. red	12·00	18·00
97	**15**	45c. green	2·20	7·50
98	**15**	50c. violet	75	1·40
99	**15**	55c. blue	6·50	16·00
100	**15**	60c. black	1·00	4·00
101	**15**	65c. brown	5·75	5·50
102	**15**	70c. pink	3·25	7·00
103	**15**	75c. olive	8·75	12·50
104	**15**	80c. purple	2·50	7·75
105	**15**	90c. red	1·40	3·25
106	**16**	1f. brown	1·50	2·75
107	**16**	1f.25 purple	12·00	11·50
108	**16**	1f.25 red	2·20	7·25
109	**16**	1f.40 orange	1·80	7·00
110	**16**	1f.50 blue	1·70	2·10
111	**16**	1f.60 violet	1·90	7·50
112	**16**	1f.75 green	10·00	9·00
113	**16**	2f. red	95	3·25
114	**16**	2f.25 blue	2·20	7·50
115	**16**	2f.50 black	2·30	7·00
116	**16**	3f. orange	1·30	8·00
117	**16**	5f. mauve	2·00	8·00
118	**16**	10f. green	1·90	10·50
119	**16**	20f. brown	2·00	11·00

MS126a 120×100 mm. 3f. emerald-green, Imperf 32·00 65·00

17 Flying Boat

1934. Air.

120	**17**	5f. green	2·00	5·50

1937. International Exhibition, Paris. As Nos. 168/73 of St.-Pierre et Miquelon.

121	20c. violet	2·50	4·00
122	30c. green	2·50	4·00
123	40c. red	2·10	3·50
124	50c. brown	3·25	3·50
125	90c. red	3·50	4·50
126	1f.50 blue	4·00	6·25

17a Pierre and Marie Curie

1938. International Anti-cancer Fund.

127	**17a**	1f.75+50c. blue	12·50	23·00

17b

1939. New York World's Fair.

128	**17b**	1f.25 red	2·00	4·00
129	**17b**	2f.25 blue	2·00	4·00

17c Storming the Bastille

1939. 150th Anniv of French Revolution.

130	**17c**	45c.+25c. green and black (postage)	17·00	29·00
131	**17c**	70c.+30c. brown & black	17·00	29·00
132	**17c**	90c.+35c. orange & black	17·00	29·00
133	**17c**	1f.25+1f. red and black	17·00	29·00
134	**17c**	2f.25+2f. blue and black	17·00	29·00
135	**17c**	5f.+4f. black & orge (air)	42·00	50·00

1941. Adherence to General de Gaulle. Optd **FRANCE LIBRE**. (a) Nos. 75/8.

136	**13**	3f. brown and green	5·25	9·75
137	**13**	5f. brown and blue	5·25	15·00
138	**13**	10f. brown and red	16·00	28·00
139	**13**	20f. brown and mauve	80·00	£130

(b) Nos. 106 and 115/19.

140	**16**	1f. brown	4·00	16·00
141	**16**	2f.50 black	4·00	21·00
142	**16**	3f. red	4·50	21·00
143	**16**	5f. mauve	5·25	20·00
144	**16**	10f. green	42·00	90·00
145	**16**	20f. brown	40·00	90·00

(c) Air stamp of 1934.

146	**17**	5f. green	3·75	6·50

19 Polynesian Travelling Canoe

19a Airplane

1942. Free French Issue. (a) Postage.

147	**19**	5c. brown	20	6·75
148	**19**	10c. blue	20	4·25
149	**19**	25c. green	55	6·75
150	**19**	30c. red	35	5·75
151	**19**	40c. green	35	6·75
152	**19**	80c. purple	75	6·75
153	**19**	1f. mauve	80	1·40
154	**19**	1f.50 red	1·30	4·75
155	**19**	2f. black	1·30	2·30
156	**19**	2f.50 blue	1·60	7·25
157	**19**	4f. violet	1·20	5·00
158	**19**	5f. yellow	1·10	4·00
159	**19**	10f. brown	2·30	4·75
160	**19**	20f. green	2·10	7·00

(b) Air. As T **19a**.

161	1f. orange	1·80	5·75
162	1f.50 red	1·80	6·50
163	5f. purple	2·00	7·75
164	10f. black	2·50	8·50
165	25f. blue	3·25	10·00
166	50f. green	4·00	10·00
167	100f. red	3·75	10·00

19b

1944. Mutual Aid and Red Cross Funds.

168	**19b**	5f.+20f. blue	1·10	9·00

1945. Surch in figures.

169	**19**	50c. on 5c. brown	55	7·00
170	**19**	60c. on 5c. brown	70	7·00
171	**19**	70c. on 5c. brown	60	7·50
172	**19**	1f.20 on 5c. brown	85	7·00
173	**19**	2f.40 on 25c. green	1·10	7·25
174	**19**	3f. on 25c. green	1·00	4·00
175	**19**	4f.50 on 25c. green	1·60	8·00
176	**19**	15f. on 2f.50 blue	1·40	6·25

20a Felix Eboue

1945. Eboue.

177	**20a**	2f. black	30	7·25
178	**20a**	25f. green	1·60	9·50

20b "Victory"

1946. Air. Victory.

179	**20b**	8f. green	1·10	9·25

20c Legionaries by Lake Chad

1946. Air. From Chad to the Rhine.

180	**20c**	5f. red	1·60	8·25
181	-	10f. brown	1·30	10·00
182	-	15f. green	1·60	9·50
183	-	20f. red	2·00	9·00
184	-	25f. purple	2·10	9·25
185	-	50f. black	2·20	13·00

DESIGNS: 10f. Battle of Koufa; 15f. Tank Battle, Mareth; 20f. Normandy Landings; 25f. Liberation of Paris; 50f. Liberation of Strasbourg.

21 Mooréa Coastline **22** Tahitian Girl

23 Wandering Albatross over Mooréa

1948. (a) Postage as T **21/22**.

186	**21**	10c. brown	35	55
187	**21**	30c. green	45	60
188	**21**	40c. blue	60	4·25
189	-	50c. lake	60	3·50
190	-	60c. olive	55	5·25
191	-	80c. blue	65	6·50
192	-	1f. lake	2·75	1·10
193	-	1f.20 blue	2·75	7·25
194	-	1f.50 blue	1·10	3·00
195	**22**	2f. brown	2·75	90
196	**22**	2f.40 lake	3·25	8·00
197	**22**	3f. violet	8·50	80
198	**22**	4f. blue	2·50	70
199	-	5f. brown	3·75	1·80
200	-	6f. blue	3·75	90
201	-	9f. brown, black and red	4·25	7·00
202	-	10f. olive	4·00	55
203	-	15f. red	5·75	1·40
204	-	20f. blue	5·75	80
205	-	25f. brown	5·50	1·70

(b) Air. As T **23**.

206		13f. light blue and deep blue	7·50	5·75
207	**23**	50f. lake	28·00	18·00
208	-	100f. violet	17·00	12·50
209	-	200f. blue	44·00	25·00

DESIGNS: As T **22**: 50c. to 80c. Kanaka fisherman; 9f. Bora-Bora girl; 1f. to 1f.50, Faa village; 5, 6, 10f. Bora-Bora and Pandanus pine; 15f. to 25f. Polynesian girls. As T **23**: 13f. Pahia Peak and palms; 100f. Airplane over Mooréa; 200f. Wandering albatross over Maupiti Island.

POSTAGE DUE STAMPS

1926. Postage Due stamps of France surch **Etabts Francais de l'Oceanie 2 francs a percevoir** (No. D80) or optd **Etablissements Francais de l'Oceanie** (others).

D73	**D11**	5c. blue	65	3·25
D74	**D11**	10c. brown	65	2·75

24a People of Five Races, Aircraft and Globe

1949. Air. 75th Anniv of U.P.U.

210	**24a**	10f. blue	12·50	21·00

24b Doctor and Patient

1950. Colonial Welfare.

211	**24b**	10f.+2f. green and blue	7·50	9·25

24c

1952. Centenary of Military Medals.

212	**24c**	3f. violet, yellow and green	10·50	10·50

25 "Nafea" (after Gauguin)

1953. Air. 50th Death Anniv of Gauguin (painter).

213	**25**	14f. sepia, red and turquoise	50·00	70·00

25a Normandy Landings, 1944

1954. Air. Tenth Anniv of Liberation.

214	**25a**	3f. green and turquoise	11·50	11·50

26 Schooner in Dry Dock, Papeete

1956. Economic and Social Development Fund.

215	**26**	3f. turquoise	2·30	2·30

D75	**D11**	20c. olive	1·20	3·25
D76	**D11**	30c. red	1·50	3·50
D77	**D11**	40c. red	2·75	5·25
D78	**D11**	60c. green	2·75	4·75
D79	**D11**	1f. red on yellow	2·75	5·25
D80	**D11**	2f. on 1f. red	3·00	5·75
D81	**D11**	3f. mauve	10·50	17·00

D14 Fautaua Falls

1929

D82	**D14**	5c. brown and blue	65	2·50
D83	**D14**	10c. green and orange	65	3·00
D84	**D14**	30c. red and brown	1·60	3·50
D85	**D14**	50c. brown and green	1·50	3·00
D86	**D14**	60c. green and violet	3·25	5·75
D87	-	1f. mauve and blue	3·00	4·50
D88	-	2f. brown and red	2·10	4·00
D89	-	3f. green and blue	2·30	4·75

DESIGN: 1 to 3f. Polynesian man.

D24

1948

D210	**D24**	10c. green	20	1·90
D211	**D24**	30c. brown	20	2·75
D212	**D24**	50c. red	35	2·75
D213	**D24**	1f. blue	95	2·75
D214	**D24**	2f. green	95	3·50
D215	**D24**	3f. red	1·90	4·00
D216	**D24**	4f. violet	2·00	4·50
D217	**D24**	5f. mauve	2·75	5·00
D218	**D24**	10f. blue	3·75	6·25
D219	**D24**	20f. lake	5·25	7·50

For later issues see **FRENCH POLYNESIA**.

Pt. 7

OLDENBURG

A former Grand Duchy in North Germany. In 1867 it joined the North German Federation.

72 grote = 1 thaler

1

1852. Imperf.

2	**1**	1/30th. black on blue	£500	41·00
5	**1**	1/15th. black on red	£1100	£120
8	**1**	1/10th. black on yellow	£1100	£140
1	**1**	⅓sgr. black on green	£1800	£1600

2

1859. Imperf.

17	**2**	¼g. yellow	£425	£6000
10	**2**	⅓g. black on green	£3750	£4250
19	**2**	⅓g. green	£650	£1300
21	**2**	½g. brown	£600	£750
11	**2**	1g. black on blue	£1000	70·00
23	**2**	1g. blue	£325	£225
15	**2**	2g. black on red	£1400	£900
26	**2**	2g. red	£600	£600
16	**2**	3g. black on yellow	£1400	£900
28	**2**	3g. yellow	£600	£600

3

1862. Roul.

30	**3**	⅓g. green	£275	£275
32	**3**	½g. orange	£275	£160
42	**3**	1g. red	28·00	80·00
36	**3**	2g. blue	£275	70·00
39	**3**	3g. bistre	£300	75·00

Pt. 19

OMAN (SULTANATE)

In January 1971, the independent Sultanate of Muscat and Oman was renamed Sultanate of Oman.

NOTE. Labels inscribed "State of Oman" or "Oman Imamate State" are said to have been issued by a rebel administration under the Imam of Oman. There is no convincing evidence that these labels had any postal use within Oman and they are therefore omitted. They can be found, however, used on covers which appear to emanate from Amman and Baghdad.

1971. 1000 baizas = 1 rial saidi.
1972. 1000 baizas = 1 rial omani.

1971. Nos. 110/21 of Muscat and Oman optd **SULTANATE of OMAN** in English and Arabic.

122	**12**	5b. purple	12·00	55
142	**12**	10b. brown	40·00	23·00
124	**12**	20b. brown	16·00	85
125	**A**	25b. black and violet	2·10	55
126	**A**	30b. black and blue	3·25	95
127	**A**	40b. black and orange	4·00	1·10
128	**14**	50b. mauve and blue	5·25	1·50
129	**B**	75b. green and brown	8·00	2·00
130	**C**	100b. blue and orange	10·50	3·50
131	**C**	¼r. brown and green	27·00	8·50
132	**E**	½r. violet and red	55·00	15·00
133	**F**	1r. red and violet	£120	30·00

19 Sultan Qabus and Buildings ("Land Development")

1971. National Day. Multicoloured.

134	**F**	10b. Type **19**	2·75	45
135	**F**	40b. Sultan in military uniform and Omanis ("Freedom")	10·50	95
136	**F**	50b. Doctors and patients ("Health Services")	14·00	1·60
137	**F**	100b. Children at school ("Education")	27·00	5·25

1971. No. 94 of Muscat and Oman surch **SULTANATE of OMAN 5** in English and Arabic.

138	5b. on 3b. purple	£140	21·00

21 Child in Class

1971. 25th Anniv of UNICEF.

139	**21**	50b.+25b. multicoloured	32·00	7·00

22 Book Year Emblem

1972. International Book Year.

140	**22**	25b. multicoloured	25·00	3·25

سلطنة عمان

25 B ٢٥ ب

(24)

1972. Nos. 102 of Muscat and Oman and 127 of Oman optd with T **24**.

145	25b. on 40b. black and orange	£160	£160
144	25b. on 1r. blue and orange	£160	£160

26 Matrah, 1809

1972

158	**26**	5b. multicoloured	40	10
147	**26**	10b. multicoloured	1·50	30
148	**26**	20b. multicoloured	1·80	30
149	**26**	25b. multicoloured	2·40	30
150	-	30b. multicoloured	3·00	30
151	-	40b. multicoloured	3·00	30
152	-	50b. multicoloured	4·00	50
153	-	75b. multicoloured	9·25	1·00
154	-	100b. multicoloured	12·50	1·60
155	-	¼r. multicoloured	29·00	3·25
156	-	½r. multicoloured	55·00	9·75
157	-	1r. multicoloured	85·00	20·00

DESIGNS—26×21 mm: 30b. to 75b. Shinas, 1809. 42×25 mm: 100b. to 1r. Muscat, 1809.

29 Government Buildings

1973. Opening of Ministerial Complex.

170	**29**	25b. multicoloured	3·50	1·30
171	**29**	100b. multicoloured	12·50	3·25

30 Oman Crafts (dhow building)

1973. National Day. Multicoloured.

172	15b. Type **30**	2·00	60
173	50b. Seeb International Airport	9·75	2·50
174	65b. Dhow and tanker	10·50	2·50
175	100b. "Ship of the Desert" (camel)	14·50	4·00

31 Aerial View of Port

1974. Inauguration of Port Qabus.

176	**31**	100b. multicoloured	15·00	5·25

32 Map on Open Book

1974. Illiteracy Eradication Campaign. Multicoloured.

177	25b. Type **32**	3·50	60
178	100b. Hands reaching for open book (vert)	11·50	3·50

33 Sultan Qabus bin Said and Emblems

1974. Centenary of U.P.U.

179	**33**	100b. multicoloured	3·50	2·10

34 Arab Scribe

1975. "Eradicate Illiteracy".

180	**34**	25b. multicoloured	9·25	3·00

35 New Harbour, Mina Raysoot

1975. National Day. Multicoloured.

181	30b. Type **35**	1·30	70
182	50b. Stadium and map	2·75	80
183	75b. Water desalination plant	3·50	1·50
184	100b. Television station	5·00	2·40
185	150b. Satellite Earth station and map	7·25	3·50
186	250b. Telecommunications symbols and map	13·50	7·25

36 Arab Woman and Child with Nurse

1975. International Women's Year. Multicoloured.

187	75b. Type **36**	3·00	1·20
188	150b. Mother and children (vert)	5·25	2·40

37 Presenting Colours and Opening of Seeb–Nizwa Highway

1976. National Day. Multicoloured.

201	25b. Type **37**	1·10	35
202	40b. Parachutists and harvesting	3·25	75
203	75b. Agusta-Bell AB-212 helicopters and Victory Day procession	6·25	1·60
204	150b. Road construction and Salalah T.V. Station	7·75	2·75

38 Great Bath, Moenjodaro

1977. "Save Moenjodaro" Campaign.

205	**38**	125b. multicoloured	7·25	3·25

39 A.P.U. Emblem

1977. 25th Anniv of Arab Postal Union.

206	**39**	30b. multicoloured	3·75	1·00
207	**39**	75b. multicoloured	7·25	3·00

40 Coffee Pots

1977. National Day. Multicoloured.

208	40b. Type **40**	1·50	55
209	75b. Earthenware pots	3·25	1·00
210	100b. Khor Rori inscriptions	5·50	1·50
211	150b. Silver jewellery	8·50	2·00

1978. Surch in English and Arabic.

212	40b. on 150b. mult (No. 185)	£400	£325
213	50b. on 150b. mult (No. 188)	£450	£450
214	75b. on 250b. mult (No. 186)	£2000	£450

42 Mount Arafat, Pilgrims and Kaaba

1978. Pilgrimage to Mecca.

215	**42**	40b. multicoloured	6·00	2·50

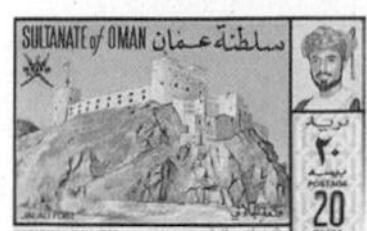
43 Jalali Fort

1978. National Day. Forts. Multicoloured.

216	20b. Type **43**	1·10	35
217	25b. Nizwa Fort	1·20	45
218	40b. Rostaq Fort	3·00	80
219	50b. Sohar Fort	3·25	90
220	75b. Bahla Fort	4·00	1·50
221	100b. Jibrin Fort	6·00	2·00

44 World Map, Koran and Symbols of Arab Achievements

1979. The Arabs.

222	**44**	40b. multicoloured	2·50	65
223	**44**	100b. multicoloured	5·00	1·50

45 Child on Swing

1979. International Year of the Child.

224	**45**	40b. multicoloured	3·75	2·50

46 Gas Plant

1979. National Day. Multicoloured.

225	25b. Type **46**	2·75	90
226	75b. Dhow and modern trawler	8·25	2·75

47 Sultan Qabus on Horseback

1979. Armed Forces Day. Multicoloured.

227	40b. Type **47**	6·00	1·80
228	100b. Soldier	12·50	4·00

48 Mosque, Mecca

1980. 1400th Anniv of Hegira. Multicoloured.

229	50b. Type **48**	5·00	1·20
230	150b. Mosque and Kaaba	8·50	3·75

49 Bab Alkabir

1980. National Day. Multicoloured.

231	75b. Type **49**	2·30	1·20
232	100b. Corniche	3·00	2·00
233	250b. Polo match	6·25	5·00
234	500b. Omani women	12·00	9·00

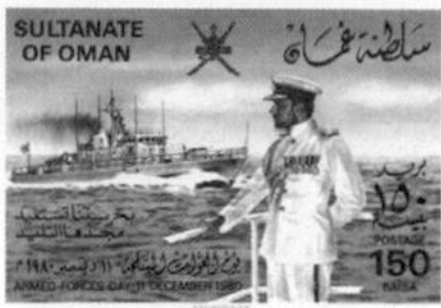

50 Sultan and Naval Patrol Boat

1980. Armed Forces Day. Multicoloured.

235	150b. Type **50**	6·25	3·25
236	750b. Sultan and mounted soldiers	32·00	15·00

51 Policewoman helping Children across Road

1981. National Police Day. Multicoloured.

237	50b. Type **51**	3·75	1·10
238	100b. Police bandsmen	4·25	2·20
239	150b. Mounted police	5·00	3·25
240	½r. Police headquarters	14·50	10·00

1981. Nos. 231, 234 and 235/6 surch **POSTAGE** and new value in English and Arabic.

241	**50**	20b. on 150b. multicoloured	4·25	90
242	-	30b. on 750b. multicoloured	5·50	1·30
243	**49**	50b. on 75b. multicoloured	6·75	2·20
244	-	100b. on 500b. multicoloured	11·00	3·75

53 Sultan's Crest

1981. Welfare of Blind.

245	**53**	10b. black, blue and red	26·00	3·00

54 Palm Tree, Fishes and Wheat

1981. World Food Day.

246	**54**	50b. multicoloured	6·75	2·75

55 Pilgrims at Prayer

1981. Pilgrimage to Mecca.

247	**55**	50b. multicoloured	8·25	3·50

56 Al Razha

1981. National Day. Multicoloured.

248	160b. Type **56**	5·75	3·25
249	300b. Sultan Qabus bin Said	9·75	5·00

57 Muscat Port, 1981

1981. Retracing the Voyage of Sinbad. Multicoloured.

250	50b. Type **57**	2·50	1·20
251	100b. The "Sohar" (replica of medieval dhow)	5·25	3·00
252	130b. Map showing route of voyage	6·25	4·00
253	200b. Muscat Harbour, 1650	8·75	5·75
MS254	172×130 mm. Nos. 250/3	41·00	21·00

58 Parachute-drop

1981. Armed Forces Day. Multicoloured.

255	100b. Type **58**	7·25	3·50
256	400b. Missile-armed corvettes	18·00	8·75

59 Police Launch

1982. National Police Day. Multicoloured.

257	50b. Type **59**	3·00	1·50
258	100b. Royal Oman Police Band at Cardiff	6·25	3·00

60 "Nerium mascatense"

1982. Flora and Fauna. Multicoloured.

259	5b. Type **60**	30	20
260	10b. "Dionysia mira"	30	20
261	20b. "Teucrium mascatense"	60	25
262	25b. "Geranium mascatense"	60	30
263	30b. "Cymatium boschi" (horiz)	90	40
264	40b. Eloise's acteon (horiz)	90	40
265	50b. Teulere's cowrie (horiz)	1·00	60
266	75b. Lovely cowrie (horiz)	1·30	90
267	100b. Arabian chukar (25×33 mm)	4·50	1·50
268	¼r. Hoopoe (25×33 mm)	11·50	6·25
269	½r. Arabian tahr (25×39 mm)	13·50	8·75
270	1r. Arabian oryx (25×39 mm)	23·00	16·00

Nos. 259/62 show flowers, Nos. 263/6 shells, Nos. 267/8 birds and Nos. 269/70 animals.

61 Palm Tree

1982. Arab Palm Tree Day. Multicoloured.

271	40b. Type **61**	4·75	2·30
272	100b. Palm tree and nuts	9·75	3·50

62 I.T.U. Emblem

1982. I.T.U. Delegates Conference, Nairobi.

273	**62**	100b. multicoloured	10·50	4·00

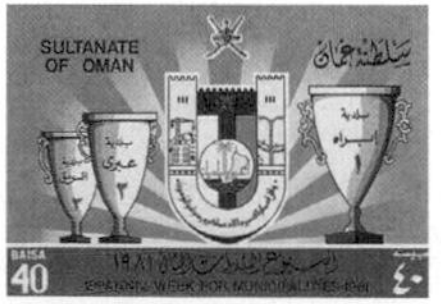

63 Emblem and Cups

1982. Municipalities Week.

274	**63**	40b. multicoloured	7·25	3·00

64 State Consultative Council Inaugural Session

1982. National Day. Multicoloured.

275	40b. Type **64**	4·00	2·10
276	100b. Petroleum refinery	8·25	3·50

65 Sultan meeting Troops

1982. Armed Forces Day. Multicoloured.
277 50b. Type **65** 4·00 2·10
278 100b. Mounted army band 8·25 4·00

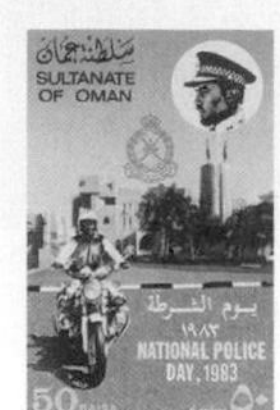

66 Police Motorcyclist and Headquarters

1983. National Police Day.
279 **66** 50b. multicoloured 7·25 2·50

67 Satellite, W.C.Y. Emblem and Dish Aerial

1983. World Communications Year.
280 **67** 50b. multicoloured 6·25 3·00

68 Bee Hives

1983. Bee-keeping. Multicoloured.
281 50b. Type **68** 4·50 3·50
282 50b. Bee collecting nectar 4·50 3·50

Nos. 281/2 were issued together, *se-tenant*, each pair forming a composite design.

69 Pilgrims at Mudhalfa

1983. Pilgrimage to Mecca.
283 **69** 40b. multicoloured 10·50 3·50

70 Emblem, Map and Sultan

1983. Omani Youth Year.
284 **70** 50b. multicoloured 7·25 3·00

71 Sohar Copper Mine

1983. National Day. Multicoloured.
285 50b. Type **71** 4·50 2·30
286 100b. Sultan Qabus University and foundation stone 8·75 4·50

72 Machine Gun Post

1983. Armed Forces Day.
287 **72** 100b. multicoloured 8·25 3·00

73 Police Cadets Parade

1984. National Police Day.
288 **73** 100b. multicoloured 9·25 3·50

74 Footballers and Cup

1984. Seventh Arabian Gulf Cup Football Tournament. Multicoloured.
289 40b. Type **74** 3·50 1·70
290 50b. Emblem and pictograms of footballers 5·75 2·40

75 Stoning the Devil

1984. Pilgrimage to Mecca.
291 **75** 50b. multicoloured 6·25 2·75

76 New Central Post Office and Automatic Sorting Machine

1984. National Day. Multicoloured.
292 130b. Type **76** 6·75 3·25
293 160b. Map of Oman with telecommunications symbols 8·75 4·00

77 Scouts reading Map

1984. 16th Arab Scouts Conference, Muscat. Multicoloured.
294 50b. Scouts pegging tent 2·10 70
295 50b. Type **77** 2·10 70
296 130b. Scouts assembled round flag 6·25 2·20
297 130b. Scout, cub, guide, brownie and scout leaders 6·25 2·20

78 Sultan, Jet Fighters and "Al Munassir" (landing craft)

1984. Armed Forces Day.
298 **78** 100b. multicoloured 10·50 4·50

79 Bell 214ST Helicopter lifting Man from "Al-Ward" (tanker)

1985. National Police Day.
299 **79** 100b. multicoloured 9·25 4·00

80 Al-Khaif Mosque and Tent, Mina

1985. Pilgrimage to Mecca.
300 **80** 50b. multicoloured 5·25 1·80

81 I.Y.Y. Emblem and Youth holding Olive Branches

1985. International Youth Year. Multicoloured.
301 50b. Type **81** 3·00 1·10
302 100b. Emblem and young people at various activities 5·25 2·40

82 Palace before and after Restoration

1985. Restoration of Jabrin Palace. Multicoloured.
303 100b. Type **82** 3·50 2·10
304 250b. Restored ceiling 8·75 5·75

83 Drummers

1985. International Omani Traditional Music Symposium.
305 **83** 50b. multicoloured 5·75 2·10

84 Scenes of Child Care and Emblem

1985. UNICEF Child Health Campaign.
306 **84** 50b. multicoloured 4·50 1·70

85 Flags around Map of Gulf

1985. Sixth Supreme Council Session of Gulf Co-operation Council, Muscat. Multicoloured.
307 40b. Type **85** 3·00 1·30
308 50b. Portraits of rulers of Council member countries 3·75 1·50

86 Sultan Qabus University and Students

1985. National Day. Multicoloured.
309 20b. Type **86** 1·50 1·00
310 50b. Tractor and oxen ploughing field 3·00 2·10
311 100b. Port Qabus cement factory and Oman Chamber of Commerce 5·25 3·00
312 200b. Road bridge, Douglas DC-10 airliner and communications centre 8·75 5·75
313 250b. Portrait of Sultan Qabus (vert) 10·50 6·75

87 Military Exercise at Sea

1985. Armed Forces Day.
314 **87** 100b. multicoloured 9·25 2·40

88 Red-tailed Butterflyfish

1985. Marine Life. Multicoloured.
315 20b. Type **88** 60 20
316 50b. Black-finned melon butterflyfish 1·20 50
317 100b. Gardiner's butterflyfish 1·80 1·20
318 150b. Narrow-barred Spanish mackerel 2·75 2·10
319 200b. Lobster (horiz) 4·00 2·75

89 Frankincense Tree

1985. Frankincense Production.
320 **89** 100b. multicoloured 1·30 1·30
321 **89** 3r. multicoloured 38·00 33·00

90 Camel Corps Member

1986. National Police Day.
322 **90** 50b. multicoloured 5·75 1·80

91 Cadet Barquentine "Shabab Oman", 1986

1986. Participation of "Shabab Oman" in Statue of Liberty Centenary Celebrations. Multicoloured.
323 50b. "Sultana" (full-rigged sailing ship), 1840 4·50 1·70
324 100b. Type **91** 6·75 3·00
MS325 162×128 mm. Nos. 323/4 (sold at 250b.) 26·00 14·50

92 Crowd around Holy Kaaba

1986. Pilgrimage to Mecca.
326 **92** 50b. multicoloured 4·00 1·60

93 Scouts erecting Tent

1986. 17th Arab Scout Camp, Salalah. Multicoloured.
327 50b. Type **93** 3·00 1·20
328 100b. Scouts making survey 5·25 2·40

94 Sports Complex

1986. Inauguration of Sultan Qabus Sports Complex.
329 **94** 100b. multicoloured 4·00 2·10

95 Mother and Baby, Emblem and Tank on Globe

1986. International Peace Year.

330	**95**	130b. multicoloured	3·50	1·80

96 Al-Sahwa Tower

1986. National Day. Multicoloured.

331	50b. Type **96**	1·80	1·00
332	100b. Sultan Qabus University (inauguration)	4·25	2·10
333	130b. 1966 stamps and F.D.C. cancellation (20th anniv of first Oman stamp issue) (57×27 mm)	5·25	2·50

97 Camel Corps

1987. National Police Day.

334	**97**	50b. multicoloured	4·00	1·80

98 Family

1987. Arabian Gulf Social Work Week.

335	**98**	50b. multicoloured	3·00	1·20

99 Aqueduct

1987. International Environment Day. Multicoloured.

336	50b. Greater flamingoes	3·00	1·00
337	130b. Type **99**	5·25	1·50

100 Crowd around Holy Kaaba

1987. Pilgrimage to Mecca. Multicoloured.

338	50b. Type **100**	1·70	1·10
339	50b. Al-Khaif Mosque and tents, Mina	1·70	1·10
340	50b. Stoning the Devil	1·70	1·10
341	50b. Pilgrims at Mudhalfa	1·70	1·10
342	50b. Pilgrims at prayer	1·70	1·10
343	50b. Mount Arafat, pilgrims and Kaaba	1·70	1·10

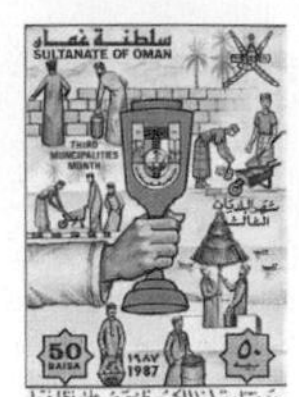

101 Examples of Work and Hand holding Cup

1987. Third Municipalities Month.

344	**101**	50b. multicoloured	2·50	1·10

102 Marine Science and Fisheries Centre

1987. National Day. Multicoloured.

345	50b. Type **102**	1·20	80
346	130b. Royal Hospital	3·50	2·00

103 Radio Operators

1987. 15th Anniv of Royal Omani Amateur Radio Society.

347	**103**	130b. multicoloured	3·50	1·80

104 Weaver

1988. Traditional Crafts. Multicoloured.

348	50b. Type **104**	1·30	80
349	100b. Potter	2·00	1·10
350	150b. Halwa maker	2·75	1·80
351	200b. Silversmith	3·25	2·10
MS352	165×135 mm. Nos. 348/51 (sold at 600b.)	18·00	12·50

105 Show Jumping

1988. Olympic Games, Seoul. Multicoloured.

353	100b. Type **105**	1·70	1·10
354	100b. Hockey	1·70	1·10
355	100b. Football	1·70	1·10
356	100b. Running	1·70	1·10
357	100b. Swimming	1·70	1·10
358	100b. Shooting	1·70	1·10
MS359	160×160 mm. Nos. 353/8 (sold at 700b.)	23·00	17·00

106 Emblem

1988. 40th Anniv of W.H.O. "Health for All".

360	**106**	100b. multicoloured	2·50	1·50

107 Tending Land and Crops

1988. National Day. Agriculture Year. Multicoloured.

361	100b. Type **107**	1·80	1·30
362	100b. Livestock	1·80	1·30

108 Dhahira Region (woman's)

1989. Costumes. Multicoloured.

363	30b. Type **108**	1·00	50
364	40b. Eastern region (woman's)	1·30	80
365	50b. Batinah region (woman's)	1·50	1·00
366	100b. Interior region (woman's)	3·00	2·10
367	130b. Southern region (woman's)	4·00	3·00
368	150b. Muscat region (woman's)	4·50	3·25
369	200b. Dhahira region (man's)	2·30	1·80
370	¼r. Eastern region (man's)	3·00	2·50
371	½r. Southern region (man's)	5·25	5·00
372	1r. Muscat region (man's)	10·50	9·25
MS373	210×145 mm. Nos. 363/8 (sold at 700b.)	18·00	15·00
MS374	210×145 mm. Nos. 369/72 (sold at 2r.)	31·00	24·00

109 Fishing

1989. National Day. Agriculture Year. Multicoloured.

375	100b. Type **109**	1·50	1·00
376	100b. Agriculture	1·50	1·00

110 Flags and Omani State Arms

1989. Tenth Supreme Council Session of Arab Co-operation Council, Muscat. Multicoloured.

377	50b. Type **110**	90	70
378	50b. Council emblem and Sultan Qabus	90	70

111 Emblem and Map

1990. Fifth Anniv (1989) of Gulf Investment Corporation.

379	**111**	50b. multicoloured	2·50	1·20
380	**111**	130b. multicoloured	3·50	1·80

112 Emblem and Douglas DC-10 Airliner

1990. 40th Anniv of Gulf Air.

381	**112**	80b. multicoloured	5·25	2·10

113 Map

1990. Omani Ophiolite Symposium, Muscat.

382	**113**	80b. multicoloured	1·30	90
383	**113**	150b. multicoloured	2·75	2·00

114 Ahmed bin Na'aman al-Ka'aby (envoy), "Sultana" and Said bin Sultan al-Busaidi

1990. 150th Anniv of First Omani Envoy's Journey to U.S.A.

384	**114**	200b. multicoloured	3·00	2·00

115 Sultan Qabus Rose

1990. 20th Anniv of Sultan Qabus's Accession.

385	**115**	200b. multicoloured	3·00	2·00

116 National Day Emblem

1990. National Day.

386	**116**	100b. red and green on gold foil	1·80	1·00
387	-	200b. green and red on gold foil	3·75	2·10
MS388		160×114 mm. Nos. 386/7 (sold at 500b.)	7·75	7·75

DESIGN: 200b. Sultan Qabus.

117 Donor and Recipient

1991. Blood Donation.

389	**117**	50b. multicoloured	80	60
390	**117**	200b. multicoloured	3·50	2·00

118 Industrial Emblems

1991. National Day and Industry Year. Multicoloured.

391	100b. Type **118**	3·50	1·20
392	200b. Sultan Qabus	5·75	2·40
MS393	172×123 mm. Nos. 391/2 (sold at 400b.)	9·25	5·75

119 Weapons, Military Transport and Sultan Qabus

1991. Armed Forces Day.

394	**119**	100b. multicoloured	2·50	1·30

120 Interior of Museum and National Flags

1992. Inaug of Omani-French Museum, Muscat.

395	**120**	100b. multicoloured	2·10	1·30
MS396		141×100 mm. No. 395 (sold at 300b.)	13·50	6·75

121 Satellite Picture of Asia

1992. World Meteorological Day.

397	**121**	220b. multicoloured	3·50	2·40

122 Emblem and Hands

1992. World Environment Day.

398	**122**	100b. multicoloured	2·30	1·30

123 Emblem and Hands protecting Handicapped Child

1992. Welfare of Handicapped Children.

399	**123**	70b. multicoloured	1·80	90

124 Sultan Qabus and Books

1992. Publication of Sultan Qabus "Encyclopedia of Arab Names".

400	**124**	100b. multicoloured	2·50	1·40

125 Sultan Qabus, Factories and Industry Year Emblem

1992. National Day. Multicoloured.

401	100b. Type **125**	2·75	1·80
402	200b. Sultan Qabus and Majlis As'shura (Consultative Council) emblem	4·50	2·75

126 Mounted Policemen and Sultan Qabus

1993. National Police Day.

403	**126**	80b. multicoloured	2·10	1·10

127 Census Emblem

1993. Population, Housing and Establishments Census.

404	**127**	100b. multicoloured	2·10	1·30

128 Frigate and Sultan Qabus presenting Colours

1993. Navy Day.

405	**128**	100b. multicoloured	3·00	1·50

129 Youth Year Emblem

1993. National Day and Youth Year. Multicoloured.

406	100b. Type **129**	2·10	1·50
407	200b. Sultan Qabus	3·50	2·10

130 Scout Headquarters and Emblem

1993. 61st Anniv of Scouting in Oman (408) and Tenth Anniv of Sultan Qabus as Chief Scout (409). Multicoloured.

408	100b. Type **130**	1·50	1·30
409	100b. Scout camp and Sultan Qabus	1·30	1·30

Nos. 408/9 were issued together, *se-tenant*, forming a composite design.

131 Sei Whale and School of Dolphins

1993. Whales and Dolphins in Omani Waters. Multicoloured.

410	100b. Type **131**	3·00	1·80
411	100b. Sperm whale and dolphins	3·00	1·80
MS412	160×120 mm. Nos. 410/11 (sold at 400b.)	39·00	28·00

Nos. 410/11 were issued together, se-tenant, forming a composite design.

132 Water Drops and Falaj (ancient water system)

1994. World Water Day.

413	**132**	50b. multicoloured	1·50	80

133 Municipality Building

1994. 70th Anniv of Muscat Municipality.

414	**133**	50b. multicoloured	2·10	1·00

134 Centenary Emblem and Sports Pictograms

1994. Centenary of International Olympic Committee.

415	**134**	100b. multicoloured	16·00	8·25

135 Emblem

1994. National Day. Multicoloured.

416	50b. Type **135**	1·00	70
417	50b. Sultan Qabus	1·00	70

136 Airplane and Emblem

1994. 50th Anniv of I.C.A.O.

418	**136**	100b. multicoloured	6·25	3·00

137 Arms

1994. 250th Anniv of Al-Busaid Dynasty. Multicoloured.

419	50b. Type **137** dated "1744–1775"	1·60	60
420	50b. Type **137** dated "1775–1779"	1·60	60
421	50b. Type **137** dated "1779–1792"	1·60	60
422	50b. Type **137** dated "1792–1804"	1·60	60
423	50b. Type **137** dated "1804–1807"	1·60	60
424	50b. Said bin Sultan (1807–1856)	1·60	60
425	50b. Type **137** dated "1856–1866"	1·60	60
426	50b. Type **137** dated "1866–1868"	1·60	60
427	50b. Type **137** dated "1868–1871"	1·60	60
428	50b. Turki bin Said (1871–1888)	1·60	60
429	50b. Feisal bin Turki (1888–1913)	1·60	60
430	50b. Taimur bin Feisal (1913–1932)	1·60	60
431	50b. Arms, Sultan Qabus and family tree	1·60	60
432	50b. Said bin Taimur (1932–1970)	1·60	60
433	50b. Sultan Qabus (1970–)	1·60	60
MS434	140×110 mm. 200d. As No. 431. Imperf	5·25	3·50

138 Meeting

1995. Open Parliament.

435	**138**	50b. multicoloured	1·80	1·00

139 Emblem and National Colours

1995. 50th Anniv of Arab League.

436	**139**	100b. multicoloured	2·10	1·00

140 Anniversary Emblem

1995. 50th Anniv of U.N.O.

437	**140**	100b. multicoloured	3·50	1·50

141 Sultan Qabus in Robes

1995. National Day. Multicoloured.

438	50b. Type **141**	1·40	80
439	100b. Sultan Qabus in military uniform	2·20	1·00
MS440	150×110 mm. Nos. 438/9 (sold at 300b.)	5·25	4·00

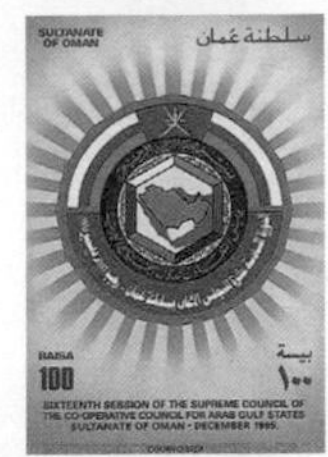
142 Council Emblem

1995. 16th Supreme Council Session of Gulf Co-operation Council, Oman. Multicoloured.

441	100b. Type **142**	2·75	1·30
442	200b. Sultan Qabus, members' flags and map	4·00	2·00

143 Ash'shashah

1996. Omani Sailing Vessels. Multicoloured.

443	50b. Type **143**	30	20
444	100b. Al-Battil	70	60
445	200b. Al-Boum	1·30	1·20
446	250b. Al-Badan	1·70	1·40
447	350b. As'sanbuq	2·50	2·10
448	450b. Al-Galbout	3·00	2·50
449	650b. Al-Baghlah	4·00	3·75
450	1r. Al-Ghanjah	7·00	5·75

144 Emblem, Poppy Head, Skull-like Face smoking Cigarette and Syringe

1996. United Nations Decade against Drug Abuse.

451	**144**	100b. multicoloured	21·00	15·00

145 Shooting

1996. Olympic Games, Atlanta. Multicoloured.

452	100b. Type **145**	5·75	3·00
453	100b. Swimming	5·75	3·00
454	100b. Cycling	5·75	3·00
455	100b. Running	5·75	3·00

Nos. 452/5 were issued together, se-tenant, forming a composite design.

146 Tournament Emblem and Flags of Participating Countries

1996. 13th Arabian Gulf Cup Football Championship.

456	**146**	100b. multicoloured	2·10	1·20

147 Sultan Qabus and Sur (left detail)

1996. National Day. Multicoloured.

457	50b. Type **147**	1·10	90
458	50b. Sultan Qabus and Sur (right detail)	1·10	90

Nos. 457/8 were issued together, *se-tenant*, forming a composite design.

148 Mother with Children

1996. 50th Anniv of UNICEF.

459	**148**	100b. multicoloured	1·70	1·10

149 Nakl Fort

1997. Tourism. Multicoloured.

460	100b. Type **149**	2·00	1·50
461	100b. Wadi Tanuf (waterfall in centre of stamp)	2·00	1·50
462	100b. Fort on Muthrah Corniche	2·00	1·50
463	100b. Wadi Dayqah Dam	2·00	1·50
464	100b. Bahla fort (overlooking tree-covered plain)	2·00	1·50
465	100b. Wadi Darbut waterfall (near top of stamp)	2·00	1·50

150 Sultan Qabus and Dhofar Waterfalls

1997. National Day. Multicoloured.

466	100b. Type **150**	2·00	1·50
467	100b. Sultan Qabus seated by waterfalls	2·00	1·50

151 Guide Activities

1997. 25th Anniv of Oman Girl Guides.

468	**151**	100b. multicoloured	2·20	1·50

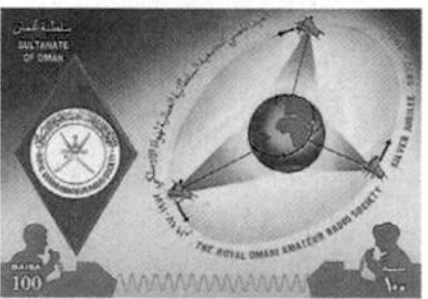
152 Society and Anniversary Emblems

1997. 25th Anniv of Royal Omani Amateur Radio Society.

469	**152**	100b. multicoloured	3·25	2·00

153 Dagger and Sheath

1998. Al-Khanjar Assaidi. Multicoloured, background colours given.

470	**153**	50b. green	80	65
471	**153**	50b. red	80	65
471a	**153**	80b. yellow	1·60	1·20
472	**153**	100b. violet	2·00	1·50
473	**153**	200b. brown	3·25	2·50

154 Car, Traffic Lights, Hand and Police Motor Cycle

1998. Gulf Co-operation Council Traffic Week.

474	**154**	100b. multicoloured	7·75	4·00

155 Sohar Fort

1998. Tourism. Multicoloured.

475	100b. Type **155**	2·20	1·60
476	100b. Wadi Shab	2·20	1·60
477	100b. Nizwa town	2·20	1·60
478	100b. Eid celebration (religious holiday)	2·20	1·60
479	100b. View of river	2·20	1·60
480	100b. Three young girls by an aqueduct	2·20	1·60

156 Exhibition Emblem

1998. Fourth Arab Gulf Countries Stamp Exhibition, Muscat.

481	**156**	50b. multicoloured	1·10	80

157 U.P.U. Emblem and Doves

1998. World Stamp Day.

482	**157**	100b. multicoloured	1·70	1·50

158 Year Emblem

1998. National Day. Year of the Private Sector. Multicoloured.

483	100b. Sultan Qabus	4·25	2·75
484	100b. Type **158**	4·25	2·75
MS485	160×80 mm. Nos. 483/4	30·00	30·00

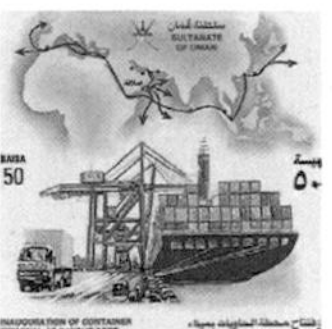
159 Map and Container Ship at Quayside

1998. Inauguration of Salalah Port Container Terminal.

486	**159**	50b. multicoloured	4·50	2·20

160 Sultan Qabus, Dove and Olive Branch

1998. International Peace Award.

487	**160**	500b. multicoloured	17·00	12·50

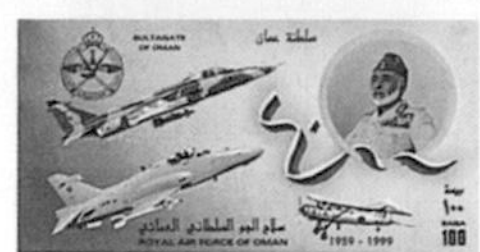
161 Military Aircraft and Sultan Qabus

1999. 40th Anniv of Royal Air Force of Oman.

488	**161**	100b. multicoloured	2·75	1·70

162 African Monarch

1999. Butterflies. Multicoloured.

489	100b. Type **162**	2·75	2·00
490	100b. Chequered swallowtail (*Papilio demoleus*)	2·75	2·00
491	100b. Blue pansy (*Precis orithya*)	2·75	2·00
492	100b. Yellow pansy (*Precis hierta*)	2·75	2·00
MS493	110×110 mm. Nos. 489/92	28·00	17·00

163 Longbarbel Goatfish

1999. Marine Life. Multicoloured.

494	100b. Type **163**	1·50	1·10
495	100b. Red-eyed round herring (*Etrumeus teres*)	1·50	1·10
496	100b. Brown-spotted grouper (*Epinephelus chlorostigma*)	1·50	1·10
497	100b. Blue-spotted emperor (*Lethrinus lentjan*)	1·50	1·10
498	100b. Blood snapper (*Lutjanus erythropterus*)	1·50	1·10
499	100b. Wahoo (*Acanthocybium solandri*)	1·50	1·10
500	100b. Long-tailed tuna (*Thunnus tonggol*)	1·50	1·10
501	100b. Crimson jobfish (*Pristipomoides filamentosus*)	1·50	1·10
502	100b. Yellow-finned tuna (*Thunnus albacares*)	1·50	1·10
503	100b. Cultured shrimp (*Penaeus indicus*)	1·50	1·10
504	100b. Pharaoh cuttlefish (*Sepia pharaonis*)	1·50	1·10
505	100b. Tropical rock lobster (*Panulirus homarus*)	1·50	1·10

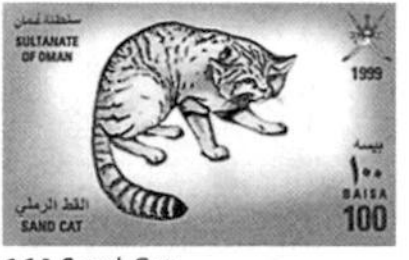
164 Sand Cat

1999. Wildlife. Multicoloured.

506	100b. Type **164**	1·50	1·10
507	100b. Genet	1·50	1·10
508	100b. Leopard	1·50	1·10
509	100b. Sand fox	1·50	1·10
510	100b. Caracal lynx	1·50	1·10
511	100b. Hyena	1·50	1·10
MS512	175×96 mm. Nos. 506/11	33·00	22·00

165 Globe and Emblem

1999. 125th Anniv of Universal Postal Union.

513	**165**	200b. multicoloured	2·20	2·20

166 Sultan Qabus and Musicians

1999. National Day. Multicoloured.

514	100b. Type **166**	2·20	1·50
515	100b. Sultan Qabus and horsemen	2·20	1·50

Nos. 514/15 were issued together, *se-tenant*, forming a composite design.

167 Sultan Qabus, Globe and "2000"

2000. New Year. Sheet 80×95 mm.

MS516	500b. multicoloured	14·50	11·00

168 Water Droplet and Dried Earth

2000. World Water Week.

517	**168**	100b. multicoloured	1·70	1·10

169 Emblem, Airplane and Silhouette of Bird

2000. 50th Anniv of Gulf Air.

518	**169**	100b. multicoloured	2·00	1·10

170 Crimson-tip Butterfly (*Colotis danae*)

2000. Butterflies. Multicoloured.

519	100b. Type **170**	2·00	1·10
520	100b. *Anaphaeis aurota*	2·00	1·10
521	100b. *Tarucus rosaceus*	2·00	1·10
522	100b. Long-tailed blue (*Lampides boeticus*)	2·00	1·10
MS523	110×110 mm. Nos. 519/22	25·00	13·50

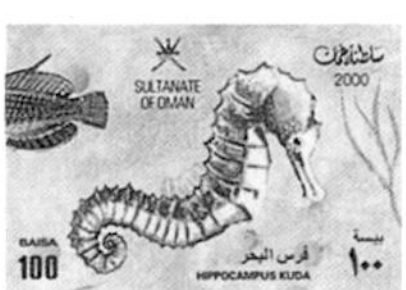
171 Yellow Seahorse (*Hippocampus kuda*)

2000. Marine Life. Multicoloured.

524	100b. Type **171**	2·75	1·30
525	100b. Yellow boxfish (*Ostracion cubicus*)	2·75	1·30
526	100b. Japanese pineconefish (*Monocentris japonica*)	2·75	1·30
527	100b. Broad-barred lionfish (*Pterois antennata*)	2·75	1·30
528	100b. *Rhinecanthus assasi*	2·75	1·30
529	100b. Blue-spotted stingray (*Taeniura lymma*)	2·75	1·30
MS530	130×125 mm. Nos. 524/9	22·00	11·00

172 Arabian Tahr

2000. Mammals. Multicoloured.

531	100b. Type **172**	2·00	1·20
532	100b. Nubian ibex	2·00	1·20
533	100b. Arabian oryx	2·00	1·20
534	100b. Arabian gazelle	2·00	1·20
MS535	130×96 mm. Nos. 531/4	19·00	11·00

173 Emblem

2000. Olympic Games, Sydney. Multicoloured.

536	100b. Type **173**	2·10	1·70
537	100b. Running	2·10	1·70
538	100b. Swimming	2·10	1·70
539	100b. Rifle-shooting	2·10	1·70
MS540	121×100 mm. Nos. 536/9	28·00	17·00

174 Sultan Qabus

2000. National Day. Multicoloured.

541	100b. Type **174**	1·90	1·10
542	100b. Sitting	1·90	1·10
543	100b. Wearing uniform including red beret	1·90	1·10
544	100b. Wearing (white) naval uniform	1·90	1·10
545	100b. Anniversary emblem	1·90	1·10
546	100b. Wearing (beige) police uniform	1·90	1·10
MS547	175×120 mm. Nos. 541/6	13·50	7·75

175 Egret and Sea Birds

2001. Environment Day. Sheet 83×46 mm.

MS548	**175** 200b. multicoloured	13·50	11·00

176 Dagger and Sheath

2001. Al-Khanjar A'suri. Multicoloured, background colours given. (a) Size 24×27 mm.

549	**176**	50b. red	65	55
550	**176**	80b. yellow	1·10	1·00

(b) Size 26×34 mm.

551	100b. blue	1·30	1·20
552	200b. white	2·50	2·20
MS553	80×100 mm. Nos. 549/552	7·75	5·00

177 Child and Tank

2001. Al Aqsa Uprising. Sheet 105×100 mm.

MS554	**177** 100b. multicoloured	6·75	2·20

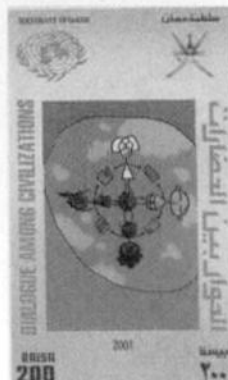
178 Children encircling Globe

2001. United Nations Year of Dialogue among Civilizations.

555	**178**	200b. multicoloured	5·50	3·25

179 Globe, Tree, Map and Sunrise

2001. National Day. Year of the Environment. Multicoloured.

556	100b. Type **179**	1·70	1·10
557	100b. Sunrise and Sultan Qabas	1·70	1·10

Nos. 556/7 were issued together, *se-tenant*, forming a composite design.

180 *Cerithium caeruleum*

2001. Shells. Multicoloured.

558	100b. Type **180**	1·30	1·10
559	100b. *Nassarius coronatus*	1·30	1·10
560	100b. *Cerithdea cingulata*	1·30	1·10
561	100b. *Epitoneum pallash*	1·30	1·10

181 Necklace

2001. Traditional Jewellery. Four sheets, each 71×71 mm containing T **181** and similar multicoloured designs.

MS562 (a) 100b. Type **181**; (b) 100b. Necklace with barred pendant (horiz) (63×28 mm); (c) 100b. "Mazrad" necklace (circular) (38×38 mm); (d) 100b. Hair decoration (triangular) (64×32 mm) 17·00 11·00

182 Map enclosed in Circle

2001. 22nd Supreme Session of Gulf Co-operation Council, Oman. Multicoloured.

563	50b. Type **182**	90	55
564	100b. Sultan Qabas	1·90	1·10

183 Interior of Dome

2002. Inauguration of Sultan Qabus Grand Mosque, Baushar. Multicoloured.

565	50b. Type **183**	1·00	55
566	50b. Dome	1·00	55
567	50b. Entrance	1·00	55
568	50b. Decorated roof	1·00	55
MS569	120×90 mm. 100b. Aerial view of mosque. Imperf	5·50	2·20

184 Olive Ridley Turtle

2002. Turtles. Multicoloured.

570	100b. Type **184**	1·70	1·10
571	100b. Atlantic green turtle	1·70	1·10
572	100b. Hawksbill	1·70	1·10
573	100b. Loggerhead	1·70	1·10
MS574	130×98 mm. Nos. 570/3. Imperf	11·00	7·75

185 Adult and Child's Hands

2002. Early Intervention for Children with Special Needs. Ordinary or self-adhesive gum.

575	**185**	100b. multicoloured	3·25	1·70

186 Sultan Qabus and Cheetah

2002. National Day. Year of the Environment. Sheet 100×80 mm.

MS577	**186** 100b. multicoloured	5·50	3·25

187 Collared Dove (*Streptopelia decaocto*)

2002. Birds. Multicoloured.

578	50b. Type **187**	1·10	55
579	50b. Black-headed tchagra (*Tchagra senegala*)	1·10	55
580	50b. Ruppell's weaver (*Ploceus galbula*)	1·10	55
581	50b. Bonelli's eagle (*Hieraetus fasciatus*)	1·10	55
582	50b. White-eyed bulbul (*Pycnontus xanthopygos*)	1·10	55
583	50b. Northern eagle owl (*Bubo bubo*)	1·10	55
584	50b. Dunn's lark (*Eremalauda dunni*)	1·10	55
585	50b. Cape dikkop (*Burhinus capensis*)	1·10	55
586	50b. Graceful prinia (*Prinia gracilis*)	1·10	55
587	50b. Indian grey francolin (*Francolinus pondicerianus*)	1·10	55
588	50b. Tristram's grackle (*Onychognathus tristramii*)	1·10	55
589	50b. Red-wattled plover (*Vanellus indicus* (inscr "Hoplopterus indicus"))	1·10	55
590	50b. House crow (*Corvus splendens*)	1·10	55
591	50b. Houbara bustard (*Chlamydotis undulate*)	1·10	55
592	50b. White-collared kingfisher (*Halcyon chloris*)	1·10	55
593	50b. Crowned sand grouse (*Pterocles coronatus*)	1·10	55

188 Muscat Gate and Festival Emblem

2003. Muskat Festival.

594	**188**	100b. multicoloured	1·70	1·10

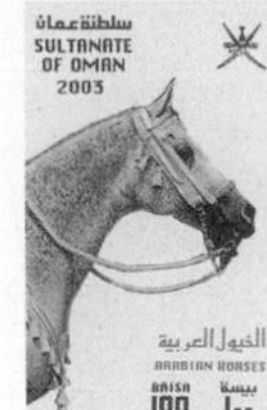

189 Horse's Head

2003. Arabian Horses. Four sheets, each 95×80 mm containing T **189** and similar vert designs. Multicoloured.

MS595 (a) 100b. Type **189**; (b) 100b. Chestnut; (c) 100b. Grey; (d) 100b. Wearing tasselled breast harness 9·00 5·50

190 Chinese and Omani Buildings

2003. 25th Anniv of Oman—China Diplomatic Relations.

596	**190**	70b. multicoloured	1·70	1·10

191 Census Emblem

2003. National Census. Multicoloured.

597	50b. Type **191**	90	55
598	50b. Emblem and numbers	90	55

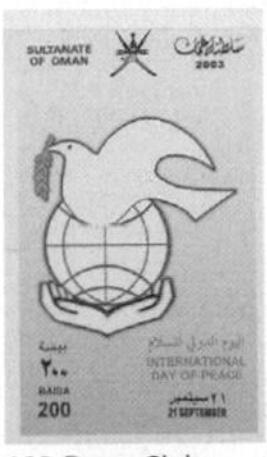
192 Dove, Globe and Hands

2003. International Day of Peace.

599	**192**	200b. multicoloured	2·20	2·00

193 Emblem

2003. Organization of Islamic Conference.

600	**193**	100b. multicoloured	1·10	1·00

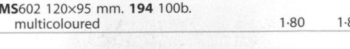

194 Emblem

2003. SANAD (Self-employment and national autonomous development) Project. (a) Self-adhesive gum.

601	**194**	100b. multicoloured	1·20	1·10

(b) Miniature sheet. Ordinary gum.

MS602	120×95 mm. **194** 100b. multicoloured	1·80	1·80

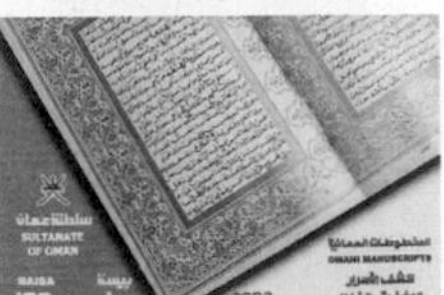
195 Illuminated Manuscript

2003. Manuscripts. Multicoloured.

603	100b. Type **195**	1·20	1·20
604	100b. Mathematical drawing	1·20	1·20
605	100b. Compass	1·20	1·20
606	100b. Diagram	1·20	1·20
MS607	151×122 mm. 50b. ×4, Showing ships; As No. 606; As No. 603; Script enclosed in circle	2·40	2·40

Nos. 603/6 were issued together, *se-tenant* forming a composite design.

196 Sultan Qabus

2003. National Day. Multicoloured.

608	50b. Type **196**	60	55
609	50b. Wearing dark robe facing left	60	55
610	50b. Wearing white robe and multicoloured turban	60	55
611	50b. Wearing white turban facing right	60	55

197 *Anogeissus* (inscr "dhoafrica")

2004. Flowers. Multicoloured.

612	50b. Type **197**	60	55
613	50b. *Tecomella undulate*	60	55
614	50b. *Euyrops pinifolius*	60	55
615	50b. *Aloe dhofarensis*	60	55
616	50b. *Cleome glaucescens*	60	55
617	50b. *Cassia italica*	60	55
618	50b. *Cibirhiza dhofarensis*	60	55
619	50b. *Ipomoea nil*	60	55
620	50b. *Viola cinera*	60	55
621	50b. *Dyschoriste dalyi*	60	55
622	50b. *Calotropis procera*	60	55
623	50b. *Lavandula dhofarensis*	60	55
624	50b. *Teucrium mascatense*	60	55
625	50b. *Capparis mucronifolia*	60	55
626	50b. *Geranium mascatense*	60	55
627	50b. *Convolvulus arvensis*	60	55

198 Emblem

2004. Centenary of FIFA (Federation Internationale de Football Association).

628	**198**	250b. multicoloured	3·00	2·75

199 Leopard

2004. Arabian Leopard. Multicoloured.

629	50b. Type **199**	65	65
630	50b. Two leopards	65	65
631	50b. Leopard facing left	65	65
632	50b. Leopard with raised paw	65	65

Nos. 629/32 were issued together, *se-tenant*, forming a composite design.

200 *Montipora*

2004. Corals. Multicoloured.

633	100b. Type **200**	1·30	1·30
634	100b. *Porites*	1·30	1·30
635	100b. *Acropora*	1·30	1·30
636	100b. *Cycloeris*	1·30	1·30

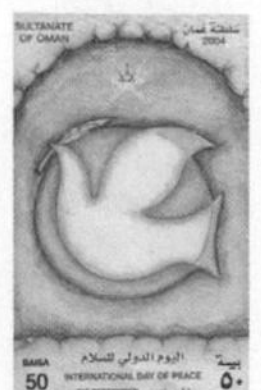

201 Dove holding Olive Branch

2004. International Day of Peace. Multicoloured.

637	50b. Type **201**	40	40
638	100b. Doves becoming olive branch and globe	80	80

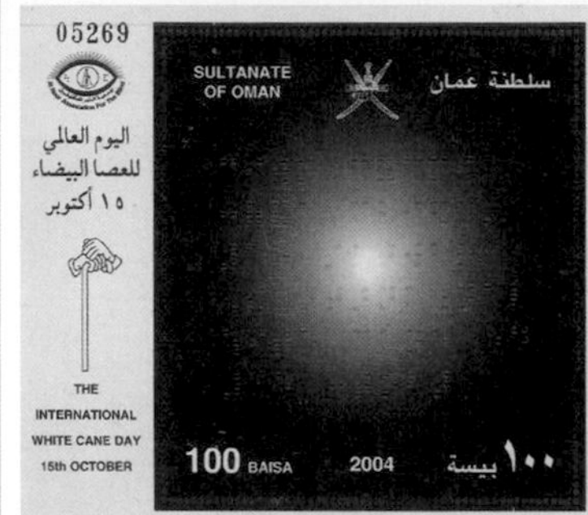

202 Sun in Black Sky (image scaled to 42% of original size)

2004. International White Cane Day. Sheet 118×105 mm.

MS639	**202**	100b. black	3·25	3·25

No. **MS**639 was embossed with Braille letters.

203 Emblem

2004. Tenth Gulf Cooperation Council Stamp Exhibition, Muscat. Ordinary or self-adhesive gum.

640	**203**	50c. multicoloured	1·00	1·00

204 Sultan Qabus

2004. National Day. Multicoloured.

642	100b. Type **204**	1·30	1·30
643	100b. Facing left	1·30	1·30
644	100b. Wearing blue turban facing right	1·30	1·30
645	100b. Wearing pink turban facing right	1·30	1·30

205 Oasis (Al Masarrat Water Supply Scheme)

2004. Al Masarrat and Ash'Sharqiyah Water Supply Schemes. Multicoloured.

646	50b. Type **205**	65	65
647	50b. Oasis (Ash'Sharqiyah Water Supply Scheme)	65	65

Nos. 646/7 were issued together, *se-tenant*, forming a composite design.

206 Children and Rescue Workers

2005. Civil Defence. Multicoloured.

648	50b. Type **206**	65	65
649	100b. Fire fighters and rescue team	1·30	1·30

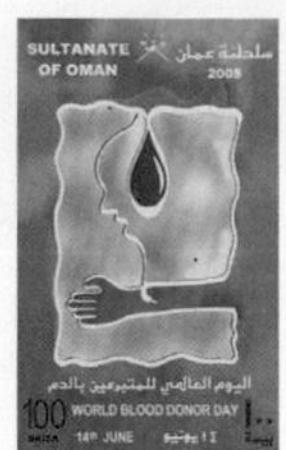

207 Blood Droplet and Arm

2005. International Blood Donor Day.

650	**207**	100b. multicoloured	1·30	1·30

208 Animals and Census Recorders

2005. Agricultural Census. Multicoloured.

651	100b. Type **208**	1·30	1·30
652	100b. Recorder, farmer, palm and shrub	1·30	1·30

Nos. 651/2 were issued together, *se-tenant*, forming a composite design.

209 Emblem and Faces

2005. World Information Society Summit, Tunis.

653	**209**	100b. multicoloured	1·30	1·30

210 Aircraft and Satellite Dishes

2005. National Day. Multicoloured.

654	100b. Type **210**	1·30	1·30
655	100b. Helicopter and cavalry	1·30	1·30
656	100b. Sultan Qabus	1·30	1·30
657	100b. Musicians and dancers	1·30	1·30
658	100b. Aircraft, ship and tanks	1·30	1·30
659	100b. Castle and inlet	1·30	1·30
660	100b. Clock tower and computers	1·30	1·30
661	100b. Emblem	1·30	1·30
662	100b. Woodlands	1·30	1·30
663	100b. Oil refinery	1·30	1·30

2005. Al-Khanjar A'suri. Multicoloured, background colours given. Size 27×35 mm.

664	**176**	250b. green	3·25	3·25
665	**176**	300b. mauve	4·00	4·00
666	**176**	400b. ochre	5·25	5·25

211 Flag

2006. 25th Anniv of Gulf Co-operation Council. Multicoloured.

667	100b. Type **211**	5·25	5·25
MS668	165×105 mm. 500b. Flags of member states. Imperf	21·00	21·00

Stamps of similar designs were issued by Kuwait, Bahrain, Qatar, Saudi Arabia and United Arab Emirates.

212 Emblem

2006. Muscat–Arab Capital of Culture, 2006. Sheet 100×60 mm.

MS669	100b. multicoloured	2·50	2·50

213 Boy and Flowers

2006. International Day of Tourism. Multicoloured.

670	100b. Type **213**	1·20	1·20
671	100b. Musicians	1·20	1·20
672	100b. Beach	1·20	1·20
673	100b. Nomads and textiles	1·20	1·20

214 Emblem

2006. Postal Service.

674	**214**	100b. ultramarine and silver	1·30	1·30
675	**214**	250b. ultramarine and silver	3·25	3·25

The No. 675 is as No. 674 but with the colours reversed.

215 Sultan Qaboos

2006. National Day.

676	**215**	100b. multicoloured	1·30	1·30

216 Cultural Symbols

2006. Sultan Qaboos Prize for Cultural Innovation.

677	**216**	250b. multicoloured	3·25	3·25

217 Refinery and Tanker

2007. 40th Anniv of Oil Exports. Multicoloured.

678	100b. Type **217**	1·30	1·30
679	100b. Refinery, well head and pipeline	1·30	1·30

Nos. 678/9 were issued together, *se-tenant*, forming a composite design.

218 Emblem

2007. Symposium on Sustainable Agriculture.

680	**218**	100b. multicoloured	1·30	1·30

219 Sultan Qaboos

2007. National Day.

681	**219**	100b. multicoloured	1·30	1·30

220 Khasab Castle

2007. Tourism. Multicoloured.

682	100b. Type **220**	1·30	1·30
683	100b. Shop keeper	1·30	1·30
684	100b. Children reading	1·30	1·30
685	100b. Entrance and cannon	1·30	1·30

221 Modern and Early Scouts

2007. Centenary of World Scouting. 75th Anniv of Scouting in Oman.

686	**221**	250b. multicoloured	3·25	3·25

223 Flags of Council Members, Muscat

2008. GCC Supreme Council Session, Muscat. Multicoloured.

688	100b. Type **223**	1·30	1·30
MS689	161×81 mm. 300b. Sultan Qaboos and council members. Imperf	4·00	4·00

224 Carrier Pigeon

2008. Arab Post Day. Multicoloured.

MS690	200b.×2, Type **224**; Camels	5·25	5·25

226 Dome of the Rock

2009. Al-Quds - Capital of Arab Culture

692	**226**	250b. multicoloured	3·25	3·25

227 Exhibition Emblem

2009. 15th Gulf Cooperation Council Stamp Exhibition, Muscat. Multicoloured.

(a) Booklet stamp. Self-adhesive

693	50b. Type **227**	70	70

(b) Ordinary gum

MS694	231×153 mm. 200b.×9 As Type **227**×9	13·00	13·00

228 Sultan Qaboos

2009. National Day

695	**228**	200b. multicoloured	2·75	2·75

229 Trophy

2009. Arabian Gulf Cup

696	**229**	200b. multicoloured	2·75	2·75

230 Oman Census Emblem

2010. GCC Census. Multicoloured.

698	50b. Type **230**	70	70
699	50b. GCC Census emblem	70	70

231 Wadi Dayqah Dam

2010. Arab Water Day

701	**231**	100b. multicoloured	1·30	1·30

232 Oman Pavilion, Expo 2010

2010. Expo, 2010, Shanghai

(a) Self-adhesive

702	50b. Type **232**	70	70

(b) Ordinary gum

MS703	146×86 mm. 100b. Oman Pavilion (side view to represent Sinbad's ship) (50×30 mm)	1·30	1·30

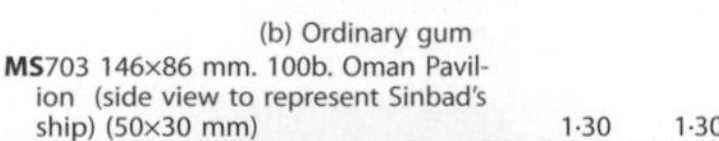

233 Jewel of Muscat

2010. Voyage of *Jewel of Muscat* (copy Arabian dhow found off Belitung Island, Indonesia) from Muscat to Singapore. Sheet 90×90 mm

MS704	**233** 100b. multicoloured	1·30	1·30

234 Sultan Qaboos

2010. Blessed Renaissance Day - Glorious 23rd of July. Multicoloured.

MS705	50b.×5, Type **234**; Army; Navy; Summer; Army (with no crossbelt)	3·50	3·50

235 Emblem

2010. Traffic Safety Day. Multicoloured.

(a) Self-adhesive

706	50b. Type **235**	70	70

(b) Ordinary gum

MS707	120×90 mm 100b. As Type **235** (beige background)	1·30	1·30

236 Anniversary Emblem

2010. National Day. Multicoloured.

MS708	100b. Type **236**; 150b. Sultan Qaboos	3·25	3·25

Pt. 1

ORANGE FREE STATE (ORANGE RIVER COLONY)

British possession 1848–54. Independent 1854–99. Annexed by Great Britain, 1900. Later a province of the Union of South Africa.

12 pence = 1 shilling; 20 shillings = 1 pound.

1

1869

48	1	½d. brown	7·00	50
84	1	½d. yellow	2·75	35
2	1	1d. brown	20·00	45
68	1	1d. purple	4·75	30
50	1	2d. mauve	21·00	30
51	1	3d. blue	7·50	2·00
19	1	4d. blue	5·00	4·25
7	1	6d. red	17·00	2·00
87	1	1s. brown	30·00	1·50
9	1	1s. orange	60·00	1·50
20	1	5s. green	12·00	18·00

1877. Surch in figures.

75	½d. on 3d. blue	8·00	5·00
36	½d. on 5s. green	24·00	5·50
54	1d. on 3d. blue	8·50	1·00
57	1d. on 4d. blue	42·00	12·00
22	1d. on 5s. green	60·00	28·00
53	2d. on 3d. blue	55·00	2·00
67	2½d. on 3d. blue	20·00	70
83	2½d. on 3d. blue	9·50	80
40	3d. on 4d. blue	48·00	22·00
12	4d. on 6d. red	£200	38·00

1896. Surch **Halve Penny.**

77	½d. on 3d. blue	1·00	50

1900. Surch **V.R.I.** and value in figures.

112	½d. on ½d. orange	30	20
113	1d. on 1d. purple	30	20
114	2d. on 2d. mauve	3·25	30
104	2½d. on 3d. blue (No. 83)	21·00	21·00
117	3d. on 3d. blue	2·00	30
118	4d. on 4d. blue	3·00	4·50
108	6d. on 6d. red	45·00	40·00
120	6d. on 6d. blue	1·00	40
121	1s. on 1s. brown	10·00	45
122	5s. on 5s. green	9·50	15·00

1900. Stamps of Cape of Good Hope optd **ORANGE RIVER COLONY.**

133	**17**	½d. green	65	10
134	**17**	1d. red	2·00	10
135	**6**	2½d. blue	3·50	1·00

1902. No. 120 surch **4d** and bar.

136	**1**	4d. on 6d. blue	1·50	2·25

1902. Surch **E. R. I. 6d.**

137	6d. on 6d. blue	6·00	18·00

1902. No. 20 surch **One Shilling** and star.

138	1s. on 5s. green	9·50	23·00

38 King Edward VII, Springbok and Gnu

1903

148	**38**	½d. green	16·00	1·00
140	**38**	1d. red	8·50	10
141	**38**	2d. brown	9·50	1·00
142	**38**	2½d. blue	6·00	1·25
143	**38**	3d. mauve	9·50	1·25
150	**38**	4d. red and green	4·50	5·00
145	**38**	6d. red and mauve	8·50	1·25
146	**38**	1s. red and brown	48·00	3·00
147	**38**	5s. blue and brown	£150	29·00

MILITARY FRANK STAMP

M1

1899

M1	**M1**	(-) black on yellow	28·00	60·00

POLICE FRANK STAMPS

PF1

1896

PF2	**PF1**	(-) black	£170	£225

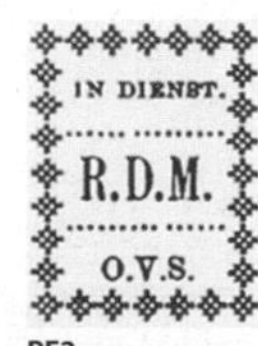

PF2

1899

PF3	**PF2**	(-) black on yellow	£140	£160

Pt. 1

ORCHHA

A state of Central India. Now uses Indian stamps.

12 pies = 1 anna; 16 annas = 1 rupee.

A set of four stamps ½a. red, 1a. violet, 2a. yellow and 4a. deep blue-green, in a design similar to T **2**, was prepared in 1897 with State authority but not put into use. These exist both imperforate and pin-perforated *(Price for set of 4, £18 unused or c.t.o.)*

1

1913. Imperf.

1	**1**	½a. green	48·00	£150
2	**1**	1a. red	22·00	£250

2

1914. Imperf.

3*a*	2	¼a. blue	40	5·50
4	2	½a. green	55	7·50
5	2	1a. red	2·50	9·50
6	2	2a. brown	4·50	24·00
7*a*	2	4a. yellow	11·00	55·00

3 Maharaja Vir Singh II

1935

8b	3	¼a. purple and grey	60	6·00
9	3	½a. grey and mauve	1·00	4·50
10	3	¾a. mauve and green	50	4·25
11	-	1a. green and brown	50	5·00
12	3	1¼a. grey and mauve	50	5·00
13	3	1½a. brown and red	75	4·50
14	3	2a. blue and orange	50	5·00
15	3	2½a. brown and orange	65	5·00
16	3	3a. blue and mauve	75	4·50
17	3	4a. purple and green	65	6·50
18	3	6a. black and buff	1·75	8·00
19	3	8a. brown and purple	2·50	11·00
20	3	12a. green and purple	1·00	11·00
21	3	12a. blue and purple	50·00	£170
22	3	1r. brown and green	1·25	12·00
24	3	2r. brown and yellow	3·25	38·00
25	3	3r. black and blue	3·00	42·00
26	3	4r. black and brown	6·00	45·00
27	3	5r. blue and purple	4·50	50·00
28	-	10r. green and red	7·00	55·00
29	-	15r. black and green	12·00	£130
30	-	25r. orange and blue	18·00	£140

DESIGN: 1a., 10r. to 25r. As Type **3**, but inscr "POSTAGE & REVENUE". There are two different versions of the portrait for the 1r. value.

5 Maharaja Vir Singh II

1939

31	5	¼a. brown	8·00	£130
32	5	½a. green	7·50	90·00
33	5	¾a. blue	8·50	£150
34	5	1a. red	7·50	32·00
35	5	1¼a. blue	9·00	£150
36	5	1½a. mauve	8·00	£180
37	5	2a. red	7·50	£110
38	5	2½a. green	9·50	£350
39	5	3a. violet	9·00	£170
40	5	4a. slate	11·00	42·00
41	5	8a. mauve	14·00	£350
42	-	1r. green	32·00	£850
43	-	2r. violet	90·00	£1200
44	-	5r. orange	£275	£4000
45	-	10r. green	£1100	£6500
46	-	15r. lilac	£25000	
47	-	25r. purple	£18000	

The rupee values are larger (25×30 mm) and have different frame.

Pt. 1

PAHANG

A state of the Federation of Malaya, incorporated in Malaysia in 1963.

100 cents = 1 dollar (Straits or Malayan).

1889. Nos. 52/3 and 63 of Straits Settlements optd **PAHANG**.

4*a*	2c. red	14·00	14·00
2	8c. orange	£1800	£1800
3	10c. grey	£225	£275

1891. No. 68 of Straits Settlements surch **PAHANG Two CENTS**.

7	2c. on 24c. green	£275	£300

9 Tiger

1891

11	9	1c. green	4·25	3·25
12	9	2c. red	4·50	3·75
13	9	5c. blue	11·00	48·00

10 Tiger

1895

14	10	3c. purple and red	10·00	3·50
15	10	4c. purple and red	17·00	19·00
16	10	5c. purple and yellow	55·00	24·00

1897. No. 13 divided, and each half surch.

18	9	2c. on half of 5c. blue	£1500	£400
18d	9	3c. on half of 5c. blue	£1500	£400

1898. Stamps of Perak optd **Pahang**.

(a) Nos. 72/5 of Perak optd with **Pahang**

19	44	10c. purple and orange	27·00	30·00
20	44	25c. green and red	85·00	£170
21	44	50c. purple and black	£475	£550
22	44	50c. green and black	£300	£425

(b) Nos. 76 and 79 of Perak optd **Pahang**

23	45	$1 green	£400	£650
24	45	$5 green and blue	£1600	£3000

1898. Stamp of Perak surch **Pahang Four cents**.

25	44	4c. on 8c. purple and blue	11·00	11·00

1899. No. 16 surch **Four cents**.

28	10	4c. on 5c. purple and yellow	24·00	75·00

15 Sultan Sir Abu Bakar

1935

29	15	1c. black	30	40
30	15	2c. green	3·50	50
31a	15	3c. green	27·00	27·00
32	15	4c. orange	70	50
33	15	5c. brown	70	10
34	15	6c. red	30·00	1·75
35	15	8c. grey	60	10
36	15	8c. red	11·00	80·00
37	15	10c. purple	2·50	10
38	15	12c. blue	6·00	1·25
39	15	15c. blue	42·00	70·00
40	15	25c. purple and red	3·00	1·50
41	15	30c. purple and orange	1·25	1·10
42	15	40c. red and purple	1·00	2·00
43	15	50c. black on green	6·50	1·50
44	15	$1 black and red on blue	6·50	8·00
45	15	$2 green and red	42·00	50·00
46	15	$5 green and red on green	15·00	90·00

1948. Silver Wedding. As T **8b/8c** of Pitcairn Islands.

47	10c. violet	15	60
48	$5 green	25·00	50·00

1949. U.P.U. As T **8d/8g** of Pitcairn Islands.

49	10c. purple	30	25
50	15c. blue	1·10	1·50
51	25c. orange	35	2·50
52	50c. black	70	4·00

16 Sultan Sir Abu Bakar

1950

53	16	1c. black	20	10
54	16	2c. orange	30	10
55	16	3c. green	55	80
56	16	4c. brown	2·50	10
57*a*	16	5c. purple	70	15
58	16	6c. grey	1·25	30
59	16	8c. red	65	1·50
60	16	8c. green	1·50	75
61	16	10c. mauve	35	10
62	16	12c. red	3·00	1·25
63	16	15c. blue	1·00	10
64	16	20c. black and green	1·50	2·75
65	16	20c. blue	4·00	10
66	16	25c. purple and orange	1·00	10
67	16	30c. red and purple	4·25	35
68	16	35c. red and purple	1·50	25
69	16	40c. red and purple	4·75	9·00
70	16	50c. black and blue	1·75	10
71	16	$1 blue and purple	4·00	3·50
72	16	$2 green and red	16·00	29·00
73	16	$5 green and brown	80·00	£100

1953. Coronation. As T **8h** of Pitcairn Islands.

74	10c. black and purple	2·75	10

1957. As Nos. 92/102 of Kedah but inset portrait of Sultan Sir Abu Bakar.

75	1c. black	10	10
76	2c. red	15	10
77	4c. sepia	15	10
78	5c. lake	15	10
79	8c. green	4·25	2·25
80	10c. sepia	1·25	10
81	10c. purple	4·25	30
82	20c. blue	2·25	20
83	50c. black and blue	45	75
84	$1 blue and purple	14·00	2·25
85	$2 green and red	12·00	9·00
86	$5 brown and green	12·00	15·00

17 "Vanda hookeriana"

1965. Flowers as in T **17**.

87	17	1c. multicoloured	10	1·25
88	-	2c. multicoloured	10	1·25
89	-	5c. multicoloured	15	10
90	-	6c. multicoloured	30	1·25
91	-	10c. multicoloured	20	10
92	-	15c. multicoloured	1·00	10
93	-	20c. multicoloured	1·60	40

The higher values used in Pahang were Nos. 20/7 of Malaysia (National Issue).

18 "Precis orithya"

1971. Butterflies. as T **18**.

96		1c. multicoloured	20	2·00
97		2c. multicoloured	50	2·25
98		5c. multicoloured	1·00	50
99		6c. multicoloured	1·50	2·25
100		10c. multicoloured	1·00	30
101	18	15c. multicoloured	1·75	10
102	-	20c. multicoloured	2·00	1·00

The higher values in use with this issue were Nos. 64/71 of Malaysia (National Issues).

19 Sultan Haji Ahmad Shah

1975. Installation of the Sultan.

103	19	10c. green, lilac and gold	50	1·25
104	19	15c. black, yellow and green	60	10
105	19	50c. black, blue and green	1·75	4·25

1977. As Nos. 97/8, 100/102 but with portrait of Sultan Haji Ahmad Shah.

106	-	2c. multicoloured	85·00	75·00
107	-	5c. multicoloured	70	1·25
108	-	10c. multicoloured	1·00	75
109	18	15c. multicoloured	1·00	30
110	-	20c. multicoloured	3·25	2·25

20 "Rhododendron scortechinii"

1979. Flowers. as T **20**.

111	1c. "Rafflesia hasseltii"	10	1·00
112	2c. "Pterocarpus indicus"	10	1·00
113	5c. "Lagerstroemia speciosa"	10	30
114	10c. "Durio zibethinus"	15	10
115	15c. "Hibiscus rosa-sinensis"	15	10
116	20c. Type **20**	20	10
117	25c. "Etlingera elatior" (inscr "Phaeomeria speciosa")	40	40

21 Rice

1986. National Products as T **21**.

125	1c. Coffee	10	50
126	2c. Coconuts	15	35
127	5c. Cocoa	15	15
128	10c. Black pepper	25	10
129	15c. Rubber	40	10
130	20c. Oil palm	40	15
131	30c. Type **21**	40	15

2002. As T **21** but redenominated in 'sen'. Multicoloured.

132	30s. Rice	2·00	10

22 *Nelumbium nelumbo* (sacred lotus)

2007. Garden Flowers. As T 22. Multicoloured.

133	5s. Type **22**	10	10
134	10s. *Hydrangea macrophylla*	15	10
135	20s. *Hippeastrum reticulatum*	25	15
136	30s. *Bougainvillea*	40	20
137	40s. *Ipomoea indica*	50	30
138	50s. *Hibiscus rosa-sinensis*	65	35
MS139	100×85 mm. Nos. 133/8	2·00	2·00
MS139	100×85 mm. Nos. 133/8	2·00	1·25

Pt. 17

PAKHOI

An Indo-Chinese Post Office in China, closed in 1922.

1903. Stamps of Indo-China, "Tablet" key-type, surch **PACKHOI** and value in Chinese.

1	D	1c. black and red on blue	25·00	28·00
2	D	2c. brown and blue on buff	11·00	14·00
3	D	4c. brown and blue on grey	8·50	16·00
4	D	5c. green and red	4·25	5·00
5	D	10c. red and blue	3·50	5·75
6	D	15c. grey and red	4·50	7·50
7	D	20c. red and blue on green	14·50	14·00
8	D	25c. blue and red	9·50	21·00
9	D	25c. black and red on pink	7·75	13·00
10	D	30c. brown and blue on drab	24·00	37·00
11	D	40c. red and blue on yellow	95·00	£100
12	D	50c. red and blue on pink	£450	£425
13	D	50c. brown and red on blue	£110	£140
14	D	75c. brown and red on orange	£110	£140
15	D	1f. green and red	£120	£140
16	D	5f. mauve and blue on lilac	£170	£160

1906. Stamps of Indo-China surch **PAK-HOI** and value in Chinese.

17	8	1c. green	4·50	3·50
18	8	2c. red on yellow	2·75	2·30
19	8	4c. mauve on blue	3·25	2·75
20	8	5c. green	7·50	2·10
21	8	10c. red	4·00	2·75
22	8	15c. brown on blue	12·00	12·00
23	8	20c. red on green	6·00	4·50
24	8	25c. blue	5·50	6·50
25	8	30c. brown on cream	11·00	5·75
26	8	35c. black on yellow	6·25	5·50
27	8	40c. black on grey	6·25	8·00
28	8	50c. olive on green	20·00	11·50
29	D	75c. brown on orange	£110	£110
30	8	1f. green	60·00	50·00
31	8	2f. brown on yellow	80·00	80·00
32	D	5f. mauve on lilac	£160	£150
33	8	10f. red on green	£170	£160

1908. Stamps of Indo-China (Native types) surch **PAKHOI** and value in Chinese.

34	10	1c. black and brown	1·70	1·00
35	10	2c. black and brown	1·20	1·40
36	10	4c. black and blue	1·80	2·00
37	10	5c. black and green	2·20	2·30
38	10	10c. black and red	2·20	6·50
39	10	15c. black and violet	3·50	7·00

40	**11**	20c. black and violet	3·50	8·00
41	**11**	25c. black and blue	4·25	9·75
42	**11**	30c. black and brown	4·25	13·00
43	**11**	35c. black and green	4·50	13·00
44	**11**	40c. black and brown	4·25	13·00
45	**11**	50c. black and red	4·50	13·00
46	**12**	75c. black and orange	13·00	20·00
47	-	1f. black and red	20·00	26·00
48	-	2f. black and green	34·00	60·00
49	-	5f. black and blue	£130	£150
50	-	10f. black and violet	£170	£160

1919. As last, surch in addition in figures and words.

51	**10**	⅖c. on 1c. black and green	70	7·25
52	**10**	⅘c. on 2c. black and brown	1·60	9·00
53	**10**	1⅗c. on 4c. black and blue	1·30	7·75
54	**10**	2c. on 5c. black and green	3·25	8·25
55	**10**	4c. on 10c. black and red	6·00	6·25
56	**10**	6c. on 15c. black and violet	4·00	9·00
57	**11**	8c. on 20c. black and violet	8·50	8·00
58	**11**	10c. on 25c. black and blue	8·00	10·50
59	**11**	12c. on 30c. black & brown	4·00	5·00
60	**11**	14c. on 35c. black and green	4·75	4·25
61	**11**	16c. on 40c. black & brown	4·50	5·25
62	**11**	20c. on 50c. black and red	7·00	6·25
63	**12**	30c. on 75c. black & orange	5·50	11·00
64	-	40c. on 1f. black and red	25·00	37·00
65	-	80c. on 2f. black and green	11·00	16·00
66	-	2pi. on 5f. black and blue	17·00	23·00
67	-	4pi. on 10f. black and violet	60·00	70·00

Pt. 1

PAKISTAN

A Dominion created in 1947 from territory with predominantly Moslem population in Eastern and Western India. Became an independent Islamic Republic within the British Commonweath in 1956. The eastern provinces declared their independence in 1971 and are now known as Bangladesh.

On 30 January 1972 Pakistan left the Commonweath but rejoined on 1 October 1989.

1947. 12 pies = 1 anna; 16 annas = 1 rupee.
1961. 100 paisa = 1 rupee.

1947. King George VI stamps of India optd **PAKISTAN**.

1	**100a**	3p. grey	30	10
2	**100a**	½a. purple	30	10
3	**100a**	9p. green	30	10
4	**100a**	1a. red	30	10
5	**101**	1½a. violet	1·75	10
6	**101**	2a. red	30	20
7	**101**	3a. violet	35	20
8	**101**	3½a. blue	1·00	2·25
9	**102**	4a. brown	35	20
10	**102**	6a. green	1·00	1·25
11	**102**	8a. violet	45	60
12	**102**	12a. red	1·00	20
13	-	14a. purple (No. 277)	3·25	3·75
14	**93**	1r. grey and brown	6·00	1·25
15	**93**	2r. purple and brown	3·50	4·50
16	**93**	5r. green and blue	9·00	7·00
17	**93**	10r. purple and claret	9·00	11·00
18	**93**	15r. brown and green	85·00	£140
19	**93**	25r. violet and purple	90·00	90·00

3 Constituent Assembly Building, Karachi

1948. Independence.

20	**3**	1½a. blue	1·25	2·00
21	-	2½a. green	1·25	20
22	-	3a. brown	1·25	35
23	-	1r. red	1·25	70

DESIGNS—HORIZ: 2½a. Entrance to Karachi Airport; 3a. Gateway to Lahore Fort. VERT: 1r. Crescent and Stars in foliated frame.

7 Scales of Justice

9 Lloyds Barrage

12 Salimullah Hostel, Dacca University

13 Khyber Pass

1948. Designs with crescent moon pointing to right.

24	**7**	3p. red	10	10
25	**7**	6p. violet	1·25	10
26	**7**	9p. green	50	10
27	-	1a. blue	20	50
28	-	1½a. green	20	10
29	-	2a. red	5·00	70
30	**9**	2½a. green	7·00	11·00
31	-	3a. green	7·50	1·00
32	**9**	3½a. blue	7·00	5·50
33	**9**	4a. brown	1·25	10
34	-	6a. blue	2·00	50
35	-	8a. black	1·50	1·50
36	-	10a. red	6·50	12·00
37	-	12a. red	8·50	1·00
38	**12**	1r. blue	20·00	10
39	**12**	2r. brown	20·00	75
40a	**12**	5r. red	14·00	25
41b	**13**	10r. mauve	19·00	3·25
42	**13**	15r. green	18·00	28·00
210b	**13**	25r. violet	7·50	10·00

DESIGNS—VERT (as Type **7**): 1a., 1½a., 2a. Star and Crescent; 6a., 8a., 12a. Karachi Port Trust. HORIZ (as Type **12**): 3a., 10a. Karachi Airport.

1949. As 1948 but with crescent moon pointing to left.

44	1a. blue	4·00	85
45a	1½a. green	3·50	10
46	2a. red	4·50	10
47	3a. green	16·00	1·00
48	6a. blue	22·00	2·50
49	8a. black	22·00	2·50
50	10a. red	26·00	3·75
51	12a. red	28·00	60

16

1949. First Death Anniv of Mohammed Ali Jinnah.

52	**16**	1½a. brown	3·00	2·00
53	**16**	3a. green	3·00	1·50
54	-	10a. black	8·50	8·00

DESIGN: 10a. inscription reads "QUAID-I-AZAM MOHAMMAD ALI JINNAH" etc.

17 Pottery

1951. Fourth Anniv of Independence.

55	**17**	2½a. red	1·75	1·25
56	-	3a. purple	1·00	10
57	**17**	3½a. blue (A)	1·25	8·50
57a	-	3½a. blue (B)	4·50	6·00
58	-	4a. green	1·50	10
59	-	6a. orange	1·50	10
60	-	8a. sepia	4·50	25
61	-	10a. violet	2·00	2·25
62	-	12a. slate	2·00	10

DESIGNS—VERT: 3, 12a. Airplane and hour-glass; 4, 6a. Saracenic leaf pattern. HORIZ: 8, 10a. Archway and lamp.

(A) has Arabic fraction on left as in Type **17**, (B) has it on right.

For similar 3½a. see No. 88.

21 "Scinde Dawk" Stamp and Ancient and Modern Transport

1952. Cent of "Scinde Dawk" Issue of India.

63	**21**	3a. green on olive	1·00	85
64	**21**	12a. brown on salmon	1·25	15

22 Kaghan Valley

24 Tea Plantation, East Pakistan

1954. Seventh Anniv of Independence.

65	**22**	6p. violet	25	10
66	-	9p. blue	3·75	3·00
67	-	1a. red	30	10
68	-	1½a. red	30	10
69	**24**	14a. myrtle	6·00	10
70	-	1r. green	11·00	10
71	-	2r. orange	3·00	10

DESIGNS—HORIZ (as Type **22**): 9p. Mountains, Gilgit; 1a. Badshahi Mosque, Lahore. (As Type **24**): 1r. Cotton plants, West Pakistan; 2r. Jute fields and river, East Pakistan. VERT (as Type **22**): 1½a. Mausoleum of Emperor Jehangir, Lahore.

29 View of K2

1954. Conquest of K2 (Mount Godwin-Austen).

72	**29**	2a. violet	40	40

30 Karnaphuli Paper Mill, East Bengal

1955. Eighth Anniv of Independence.

73	**30**	2½a. red (A)	50	1·40
73a	-	2½a. red (B)	1·50	1·40
74	-	6a. blue	1·50	10
75	-	8a. violet	3·75	10
76	-	12a. red and orange	4·00	10

DESIGNS: 6a. Textile mill, W. Pakistan; 8a. Jute mill, E. Pakistan; 12a. Main Sui gas plant.

(A) has Arabic fraction on left as in Type **30**, (B) has it on right.

For similar 2½a. see No. 87.

1955. Tenth Anniv of U.N. Nos. 68 and 76 optd **TENTH ANNIVERSARY UNITED NATIONS 24.10.55.**

77	1½a. red	1·50	5·00
78	12a. red and orange	50	3·50

35 Map of West Pakistan

1955. West Pakistan Unity.

79	**35**	1½a. green	1·25	1·75
80	**35**	2a. brown	1·00	10
81	**35**	12a. red	1·50	50

36 Constituent Assembly Building, Karachi

1956. Republic Day.

82	**36**	2a. green	80	10

37

1956. Ninth Anniv of Independence.

83	**37**	2a. red	65	10

38 Map of East Pakistan

1956. First Session of National Assembly of Pakistan at Dacca.

84	**38**	1½a. green	40	1·50
85	**38**	2a. brown	40	10
86	**38**	12a. red	40	1·25

41 Orange Tree

1957. First Anniv of Republic.

87	-	2½a. red	25	10
88	-	3½a. blue	30	10
89	**41**	10r. green and orange	1·00	25

DESIGNS: 2½a. as Type **30** without value in Arabic at right; 3½a. as Type **17** without value in Arabic at right.

42 Pakistani Flag

1957. Centenary of Struggle for Independence (Indian Mutiny).

90	**42**	1½a. green	50	10
91	**42**	12a. blue	1·25	10

43 Pakistani Industries

1957. Tenth Anniv of Independence.

92	**43**	1½a. blue	20	30
93	**43**	4a. salmon	45	1·50
94	**43**	12a. mauve	45	50

44 Coconut tree

1958. Second Anniv of Republic.

95	**44**	15r. red and purple	2·50	1·50

45

1958. 20th Death Anniv of Mohammed Iqbal (poet).

96	**45**	1½a. olive and black	55	1·00
97	**45**	2a. brown and black	55	10
98	**45**	14a. turquoise and black	90	10

46 U.N. Charter and Globe

1958. Tenth Anniv of Declaration of Human Rights.

99	**46**	1½a. turquoise	10	10
100	**46**	14a. sepia	45	10

1958. Scout Jamboree. Optd **PAKISTAN BOY SCOUT 2nd NATIONAL JAMBOREE CHITTAGONG Dec. 58-Jan. 59.**

101	**22**	6p. violet	20	10
102	-	8a. violet (No. 75)	40	10

1959. Revolution Day. No. 74 optd **REVOLUTION DAY Oct. 27, 1959.**

103		6a. blue	80	10

49 "Centenary of An Idea"

1959. Red Cross Commemoration.

104	**49**	2a. red and green	30	10
105	**49**	10a. red and blue	55	10

50 Armed Forces Badge

1960. Armed Forces Day.

106	**50**	2a. red, blue and green	50	10
107	**50**	14a. red and blue	1·00	10

51 Map of Pakistan

1960

108	**51**	6p. purple	40	10
109	**51**	2a. red	60	10
110	**51**	8a. green	1·25	10
111	**51**	1r. blue	2·00	10

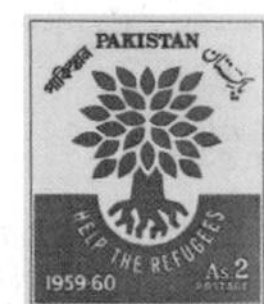

52 "Uprooted Tree"

1960. World Refugee Year.

112	**52**	2a. red	20	10
113	**52**	10a. green	30	10

53 Punjab Agricultural College

1960. Golden Jubilee of Punjab Agricultural College, Lyallpur.

114	**53**	2a. blue and red	15	10
115	-	8a. green and violet	40	10

DESIGN: 8a. College arms.

55 "Land Reforms, Rehabilitation and Reconstruction"

1960. Revolution Day.

116	**55**	2a. green, pink and brown	10	10
117	**55**	14a. green, yellow and blue	50	75

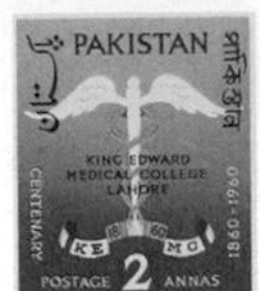

56 Caduceus

1960. Centenary of King Edward Medical College, Lahore.

118	**56**	2a. yellow, black and blue	50	10
119	**56**	14a. green, black and red	1·75	1·00

57 "Economic Co-operation"

1960. Int Chamber of Commerce C.A.F.E.A. Meeting, Karachi.

120	**57**	14a. brown	75	20

58 Zam-Zama Gun, Lahore ("Kim's Gun" after Rudyard Kipling)

1960. Third Pakistan Boy Scouts' National Jamboree, Lahore.

121	**58**	2a. red, yellow and green	80	30

1961. Surch in "PAISA".

122	-	1p. on 1½a. red (No. 68)	40	10
123	**7**	2p. on 3p. red	10	10
124	**51**	3p. on 6p. purple	15	10
125	-	7p. on 1a. red (No. 67)	40	10
126	**51**	13p. on 2a. red	40	10
127	**37**	13p. on 2a. red	30	10

See also Nos. 262/4.

60 Khyber Pass

61 Shalimar Gardens, Lahore

62 Chota Sona Masjid (gateway)

1961

170	**60**	1p. violet	10	10
132	**60**	2p. red	1·00	10
133	**60**	3p. purple	75	10
173	**60**	5p. blue	10	10
135	**60**	7p. green	2·00	10
175	**61**	10p. brown	10	10
176	**61**	13p. violet	10	10
176a	**61**	15p. purple	20	10
176b	**61**	20p. green	30	10
138	**61**	25p. blue	5·50	10
178	**61**	40p. purple	15	30
179	**61**	50p. green	15	10
141	**61**	75p. red	40	70
142	**61**	90p. green	70	70
204	**62**	1r. red	1·00	10
144	**62**	1r.25 violet	1·00	1·25
206	**62**	2r. orange	1·00	15
207	**62**	5r. green	5·50	1·00

1961. Lahore Stamp Exn. No. 110 optd **LAHORE STAMP EXHIBITION 1961** and emblem.

145	**51**	8a. green	1·00	1·75

64 Warsak Dam and Power Station

1961. Completion of Warsak Hydro-electric Project.

146	**64**	40p. black and blue	60	10

65 Narcissus

1961. Child Welfare Week.

147	**65**	13p. turquoise	50	10
148	**65**	90p. mauve	1·25	20

66 Ten Roses

1961. Co-operative Day.

149	**66**	13p. red and green	40	10
150	**66**	90p. red and blue	85	90

67 Police Crest and "Traffic Control"

1961. Police Centenary.

151	**67**	13p. silver, black and blue	50	10
152	**67**	40p. silver, black and red	1·00	20

68 Locomotive "Eagle", 1861

1961. Railway Centenary.

153	**68**	13p. green, black and yellow	75	80
154	-	50p. yellow, black and green	1·00	1·50

DESIGN: 50p. Diesel locomotive No. 20 and tracks forming "1961".

1962. First Karachi–Dacca Jet Flight. No. 87 surch with Boeing 720B airliner and **FIRST JET FLIGHT KARACHI–DACCA 13 Paisa.**

155		13p. on 2½a. red	1·75	1·25

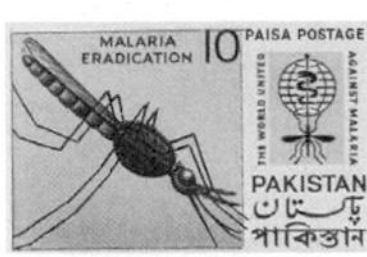

71 "Anopheles sp." (mosquito)

1962. Malaria Eradication.

156	**71**	10p. black, yellow and red	35	10
157	-	13p. black, lemon and red	35	10

DESIGN: 13p. Mosquito pierced by blade.

73 Pakistan Map and Jasmine

1962. New Constitution.

158	**73**	40p. green, turquoise & grey	85	10

74 Football

1962. Sports.

159	**74**	7p. black and blue	10	10
160	-	13p. black and green	60	2·25
161	-	25p. black and purple	20	10
162	-	40p. black and brown	2·00	2·25

DESIGNS: 13p. Hockey; 25p. Squash; 40p. Cricket.

78 Marble Fruit Dish and Bahawalpuri Clay Flask

1962. Small Industries.

163	**78**	7p. lake	10	10
164	-	13p. green	2·50	2·50
165	-	25p. violet	10	10
166	-	40p. green	10	10
167	-	50p. red	10	10

DESIGNS: 13p. Sports equipment; 25p. Camelskin lamp and brassware; 40p. Wooden powder-bowl and basket-work; 50p. Inlaid cigarette-box and brassware.

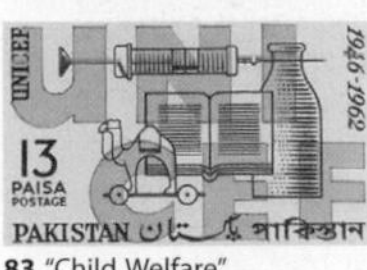

83 "Child Welfare"

1962. 16th Anniv of UNICEF.

168	**83**	13p. black, blue and purple	35	10
169	**83**	40p. black, yellow and blue	35	10

1963. Pakistan U.N. Force in West Irian. Optd **U.N. FORCE W. IRIAN.**

182	**61**	13p. violet	10	1·50

85 "Dancing" Horse, Camel and Bull

1963. National Horse and Cattle Show.

183	**85**	13p. blue, sepia and pink	10	10

86 Wheat and Tractor

1963. Freedom from Hunger.

184	**86**	13p. brown	3·00	10
185	-	50p. bistre	4·50	55

DESIGN: 50p. Lifting rice.

1963. Second International Stamp Exhibition, Dacca. Surch **13 PAISA INTERNATIONAL DACCA STAMP EXHIBITION 1963.**

186	**51**	13p. on 2a. red	50	50

89 Centenary Emblem

1963. Centenary of Red Cross.

187	**89**	40p. red and olive	2·25	15

90 Paharpur

1963. Archaeological Series.

188	**90**	7p. blue	55	10
189	-	13p. sepia	55	10
190	-	40p. red	90	10
191	-	50p. violet	95	10

DESIGNS—VERT: 13p. Moenjodaro. HORIZ: 40p. Taxila; 50p. Mainamati.

1963. Centenary of Pakistan Public Works Department. Surch **100 YEARS OF P.W.D. OCTOBER, 1963 13.**

192	**60**	13p. on 3p. purple	10	10

95 Ataturk's Mausoleum

1963. 25th Death Anniv of Kemal Ataturk.

193	**95**	50p. red	50	10

96 Globe and UNESCO Emblem

1963. 15th Anniv of Declaration of Human Rights.

194	**96**	50p. brown, red and blue	40	10

97 Thermal Power Installations

1963. Completion of Multan Thermal Power Station.
195 **97** 13p. blue 10 10

99 Temple of Thot, Queen Nefertari and Maids

1964. Nubian Monuments Preservation.
211 **99** 13p. blue and red 30 10
212 - 50p. purple and black 70 10
DESIGN: 50p. Temple of Abu Simbel.

101 "Unisphere" and Pakistan Pavilion

1964. New York World's Fair.
213 **101** 13p. blue 10 10
214 - 1r.25 blue and orange 40 20
DESIGN—VERT: 1r.25, Pakistan Pavilion on "Unisphere".

103 Shah Abdul Latif's Mausoleum

1964. Death Bicentenary of Shah Abdul Latif of Bhit.
215 **103** 50p. blue and red 1·00 10

104 Mausoleum of Quaid-i-Azam

1964. 16th Death Anniv of Mohammed Ali Jinnah (Quaid-i-Azam).
216 **104** 15p. green 1·00 10
217 - 50p. green 2·25 10
DESIGN: 50p. As Type **104**, but 26½×31½ mm.

106 Bengali and Urdu Alphabets

1964. Universal Children's Day.
218 **106** 15p. brown 10 10

107 University Building

1964. First Convocation of the West Pakistan University of Engineering and Technology, Lahore.
219 **107** 15p. brown 10 10

108 "Help the Blind"

1965. Blind Welfare.
220 **108** 15p. blue and yellow 20 10

109 I.T.U. Emblem and Symbols

1965. Centenary of I.T.U.
221 **109** 15p. purple 1·50 30

110 I.C.Y. Emblem

1965. International Co-operation Year.
222 **110** 15p. black and blue 50 15
223 **110** 50p. green and yellow 1·50 40

111 "Co-operation"

1965. First Anniv of Regional Development Co-operation Pact. Multicoloured.
224 15p. Type **111** 20 10
225 50p. Globe and flags of Turkey, Iran and Pakistan (54¾×30¾ mm) 1·10 10

113 Soldier and Tanks

1965. Pakistan Armed Forces. Multicoloured.
226 7p. Type **113** 75 30
227 15p. Naval Officer and "Tughril" (destroyer) 1·50 10
228 50p. Pilot and Lockheed F-104C Starfighters 2·50 30

116 Army, Navy and Air Force Crests

1966. Armed Forces Day.
229 **116** 15p. blue, green and buff 1·00 10

117 Atomic Reactor, Islamabad

1966. Inauguration of Pakistan's First Atomic Reactor.
230 **117** 15p. black 10 10

118 Bank Crest

1966. Silver Jubilee of Habib Bank.
231 **118** 15p. green, orange & sepia 10 10

119 Children

1966. Universal Children's Day.
232 **119** 15p. black, red and yellow 10 10

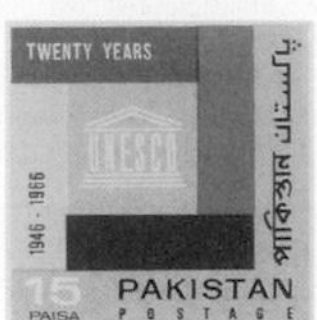

120 UNESCO Emblem

1966. 20th Anniversary of UNESCO.
233 **120** 15p. multicoloured 3·75 30

121 Flag, Secretariat Building and President Ayub

1966. Islamabad (new capital).
234 **121** 15p. multicoloured 35 10
235 **121** 50p. multicoloured 65 10

122 Avicenna

1966. Foundation of Health and Tibbi Research Institute.
236 **122** 15p. green and salmon 40 10

123 Mohammed Ali Jinnah

1966. 90th Birth Anniv of Mohammed Ali Jinnah.
237 **123** 15p. black, orange & blue 15 10
238 - 50p. black, purple and blue 35 10
DESIGN: 50p. Same portrait as 15p. but different frame.

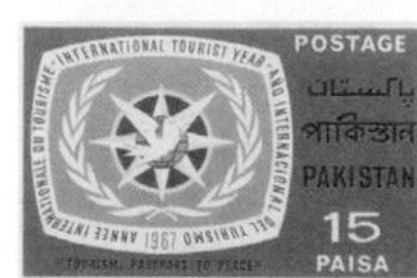

124 Tourist Year Emblem

1967. International Tourist Year.
239 **124** 15p. black, blue and brown 10 10

125 Emblem of Pakistan T.B. Association

1967. Tuberculosis Eradication Campaign.
240 **125** 15p. red, sepia and brown 10 10

126 Scout Salute and Badge

1967. Fourth National Scout Jamboree.
241 **126** 15p. brown and purple 15 10

127 "Justice"

1967. Cent of West Pakistan High Court.
242 **127** 15p. multicoloured 10 10

128 Dr. Mohammed Iqbal (philosopher)

1967. Iqbal Commemoration.
243 **128** 15p. sepia and red 15 10
244 **128** 1r. sepia and green 35 10

129 Hilal-i-Isteqlal Flag

1967. Award of Hilal-i-Isteqlal (for Valour) to Lahore, Sialkot and Sargodha.
245 **129** 15p. multicoloured 10 10

130 "20th Anniversary"

1967. 20th Anniv of Independence.
246 **130** 15p. red and green 10 10

131 "Rice Exports"

1967. Pakistan Exports. Multicoloured.
247 10p. Type **131** 10 15
248 15p. Cotton plant, yarn and textiles (vert) (27×45 mm) 10 10
249 50p. Raw jute, bale and bags (vert) (27×45 mm) 20 15

134 Clay Toys

1967. Universal Children's Day.
250 **134** 15p. multicoloured 10 10

135 Shah and Empress of Iran and Gulistan Palace, Teheran

1967. Coronation of Shah Mohammed Riza Pahlavi and Empress Farah of Iran.
251 **135** 50p. purple, blue and ochre 1·25 10

136 "Each For All–All for Each"

1967. Co-operative Day.
252 **136** 15p. multicoloured 10 10

137 Mangla Dam

1967. Indus Basin Project.

253	**137**	15p. multicoloured	10	10

138 Crab pierced by Sword

1967. The Fight Against Cancer.

254	**138**	15p. red and black	70	10

139 Human Rights Emblem

1968. Human Rights Year.

255	**139**	15p. red and blue	10	15
256	**139**	50p. red, yellow and grey	10	15

140 Agricultural University, Mymensingh

1968. First Convocation of East Pakistan Agricultural University.

257	**140**	15p. multicoloured	10	10

141 W.H.O. Emblem

1968. 20th Anniv of W.H.O.

258	**141**	15p. orange and green	10	15
259	**141**	50p. orange and blue	10	15

142 Kazi Nazrul Islam (poet, composer and patriot)

1968. Nazrul Islam Commemoration.

260	**142**	15p. sepia and yellow	35	15
261	**142**	50p. sepia and red	65	15

1968. Nos. 56, 74 and 61 surch.

262	4p. on 3a. purple	1·00	1·75
263	4p. on 6a. blue	1·25	1·75
264	60p. on 10a. violet	1·00	35

144 Children running with Hoops

1968. Universal Children's Day.

265	**144**	15p. multicoloured	10	10

145 National Assembly

1968. "A Decade of Development".

266	**145**	10p. multicoloured	10	10
267	-	15p. multicoloured	10	10
268	-	50p. multicoloured	2·00	20
269	-	60p. blue, purple and red	50	35

DESIGNS: 15p. Industry and Agriculture; 50p. Army, Navy and Air Force; 60p. Minaret and atomic reactor plant.

149 Chittagong Steel Mill

1969. Pakistan's First Steel Mill, Chittagong.

270	**149**	15p. grey, blue and olive	10	10

150 "Family"

1969. Family Planning.

271	**150**	15p. purple and blue	10	10

151 Olympic Gold Medal and Hockey Player

1969. Olympic Hockey Champions.

272	**151**	15p. multicoloured	75	50
273	**151**	1r. multicoloured	2·25	1·00

152 Mirza Ghalib and Lines of Verse

1969. Death Centenary of Mirza Ghalib (poet).

274	**152**	15p. multicoloured	20	15
275	**152**	50p. multicoloured	50	15

The lines of verse on No. 275 are different from those in Type **152**.

153 Dacca Railway Station

1969. First Anniv of New Dacca Railway Station.

276	**153**	15p. multicoloured	50	10

154 I.L.O. Emblem and "1919–1969"

1969. 50th Anniv of I.L.O.

277	**154**	15p. buff and green	10	10
278	**154**	50p. brown and red	40	10

155 "Lady on Balcony" (18th-cent Mogul)

1969. Fifth Anniv of Regional Co-operation for Development. Miniatures. Multicoloured.

279	20p. Type **155**	15	10
280	50p. "Kneeling Servant" (17th-cent Persian)	15	10
281	1r. "Suleiman the Magnificent holding Audience" (16th-cent Turkish)	20	10

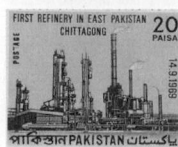

158 Eastern Refinery, Chittagong

1969. First East Pakistan Oil Refinery.

282	**158**	20p. multicoloured	10	10

159 Children playing outside "School"

1969. Universal Children's Day.

283	**159**	20p. multicoloured	10	10

160 Japanese Doll and P.I.A. Air Routes

1969. Inauguration of P.I.A. Pearl Route, Dacca–Tokyo.

284	**160**	20p. multicoloured	40	10
285	**160**	50p. multicoloured	60	40

161 "Reflection of Light" Diagram

1969. Millenary Commemorative of Ibn-al-Haitham (physicist).

286	**161**	20p. black, yellow and blue	10	10

162 Vickers Vimy and Karachi Airport

1969. 50th Anniv of First England–Australia Flight.

287	**162**	50p. multicoloured	1·25	35

163 Flags, Sun Tower and Expo Site Plan

1970. "Expo-70" World Fair, Osaka.

288	**163**	50p. multicoloured	20	30

164 New U.P.U. H.Q. Building

1970. New U.P.U. Headquarters Building.

289	**164**	20p. multicoloured	15	10
290	**164**	50p. multicoloured	25	25

165 U.N. H.Q. Building

1970. 25th Anniv of United Nations. Multicoloured.

291	20p. Type **165**	10	10
292	50p. U.N. emblem	15	20

167 I.E.Y. Emblem, Book and Pen

1970. International Education Year.

293	**167**	20p. multicoloured	10	10
294	**167**	50p. multicoloured	20	20

168 Saiful Malook Lake (Pakistan)

1970. Sixth Anniv of Regional Co-operation for Development. Multicoloured.

295	20p. Type **168**	15	10
296	50p. Seeyo-Se-Pol Bridge, Esfahan (Iran)	20	10
297	1r. View from Fethiye (Turkey)	20	15

171 Asian Productivity Symbol

1970. Asian Productivity Year.

298	**171**	50p. multicoloured	20	20

172 Dr. Maria Montessori

1970. Birth Centenary of Dr. Maria Montessori (educationist).

299	**172**	20p. multicoloured	15	10
300	**172**	50p. multicoloured	15	30

173 Tractor and Fertilizer Factory

1970. Tenth Near East F.A.O. Regional Conference, Islamabad.

301	**173**	20p. green and brown	15	50

174 Children and Open Book

1970. Universal Children's Day.

302	**174**	20p. multicoloured	15	10

175 Pakistan Flag and Text

1970. Elections for National Assembly.

303	**175**	20p. green and violet	15	10

1970. Elections for Provincial Assemblies. As No. 303 but inscr "PROVINCIAL ASSEMBLIES".

304	20p. green and red	15	10

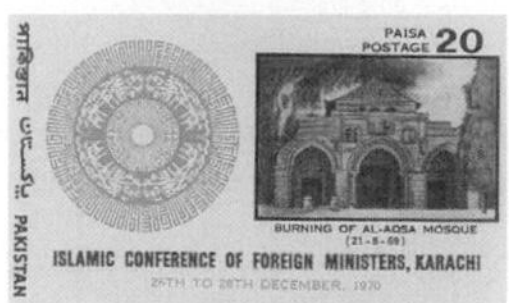

176 Conference Crest and burning Al-Aqsa Mosque

1970. Conference of Islamic Foreign Ministers, Karachi.

305	**176**	20p. multicoloured	15	15

177 Coastal Embankments

1971. East Pakistan Coastal Embankments Project.

306	**177**	20p. multicoloured	15	15

178 Emblem and United Peoples of the World

1971. Racial Equality Year.

307	**178**	20p. multicoloured	10	15
308	**178**	50p. multicoloured	20	45

179 Maple Leaf Cement Factory, Daudkhel

1971. 20th Anniv of Colombo Plan.

309	**179**	20p. brown, black & violet	10	10

180 Chaharbagh School (Iran)

1971. Seventh Anniv of Regional Co-operation for Development. Multicoloured.

310	10p. Selimiye Mosque (Turkey) (horiz)	10	15
311	20p. Badshahi Mosque, Lahore (horiz)	20	25
312	50p. Type **180**	30	35

181 Electric Train and Boy with Toy Train

1971. Universal Children's Day.

313	**181**	20p. multicoloured	1·75	50

182 Horseman and Symbols

1971. 2500th Anniv of Persian Monarchy.

314	**182**	10p. multicoloured	25	30
315	**182**	20p. multicoloured	35	40
316	**182**	50p. multicoloured	50	75

183 Hockey-player and Trophy

1971. World Cup Hockey Tournament, Barcelona.

317	**183**	20p. multicoloured	1·75	1·00

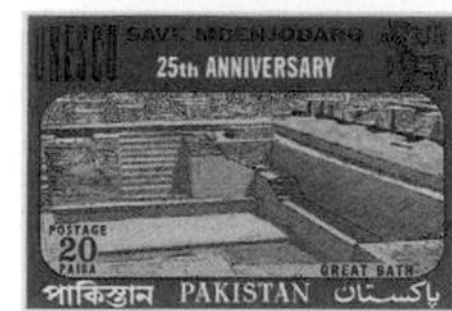

184 Great Bath, Moenjodaro

1971. 25th Anniv of UNESCO and Campaign to save the Moenjodaro Excavations.

318	**184**	20p. multicoloured	20	30

185 UNICEF Symbol

1971. 25th Anniv of UNICEF.

319	**185**	50p. multicoloured	30	60

186 King Hussein and Jordanian Flag

1971. 50th Anniv of Hashemite Kingdom of Jordan.

320	**186**	20p. multicoloured	15	20

187 Badge of Hockey Federation and Trophy

1971. Hockey Championships Victory.

321	**187**	20p. multicoloured	2·50	1·00

188 Reading Class

1972. International Book Year.

322	**188**	20p. multicoloured	20	40

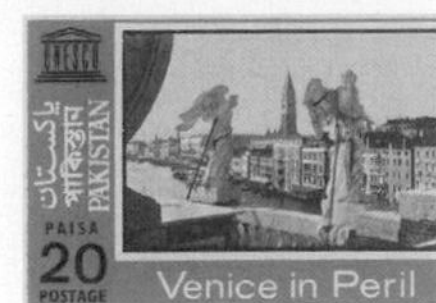

189 View of Venice

1972. UNESCO Campaign to Save Venice.

323	**189**	20p. multicoloured	30	40

190 E.C.A.F.E. Emblem and Discs

1972. 25th Anniv of E.C.A.F.E.

324	**190**	20p. multicoloured	15	30

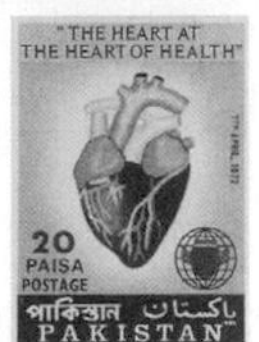

191 Human Heart

1972. World Health Day.

325	**191**	20p. multicoloured	20	30

192 "Only One Earth"

1972. U.N. Conference on the Human Environment, Stockholm.

326	**192**	20p. multicoloured	20	30

193 "Fisherman" (Cevat Dereli)

1972. Eighth Anniv of Regional Co-operation for Development. Multicoloured.

327	10p. Type **193**	20	20
328	20p. "Iranian Woman" (Behzad)	35	25
329	50p. "Will and Power" (A. R. Chughtai)	55	70

194 Mohammed Ali Jinnah and Tower

1972. 25th Anniv of Independence. Multicoloured.

330	10p. Type **194**	10	10
331	20p. "Land Reform" (74×23½)	20	30
332	20p. "Labour Reform" (74×23½)	20	30
333	20p. "Education Policy" (74×23½)	20	30
334	20p. "Health Policy" (74×23½)	20	30
335	60p. National Assembly Building (46×28 mm)	25	40

195 Donating Blood

1972. National Blood Transfusion Service.

336	**195**	20p. multicoloured	20	30

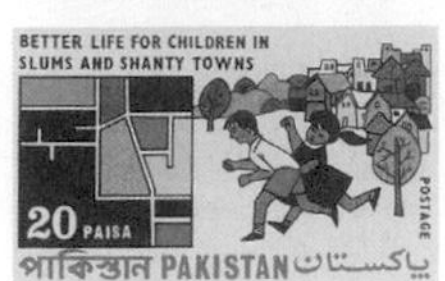

196 People and Squares

1972. Centenary of Population Census.

337	**196**	20p. multicoloured	20	20

197 Children from Slums

1972. Universal Children's Day.

338	**197**	20p. multicoloured	20	30

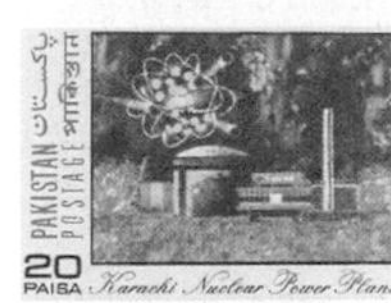

198 People and Open Book

1972. Education Week.

339	**198**	20p. multicoloured	20	30

199 Nuclear Power Plant

1972. Inauguration of Karachi Nuclear Power Plant.

340	**199**	20p. multicoloured	20	40

200 Copernicus in Observatory

1973. 500th Birth Anniv of Nicholas Copernicus (astronomer).

341	**200**	20p. multicoloured	20	30

201 Moenjodaro Excavations

1973. 50th Anniv of Moenjodaro Excavations.

342	**201**	20p. multicoloured	20	30

202 Elements of Meteorology

1973. Centenary of I.M.O./W.M.O.

343	**202**	20p. multicoloured	30	40

203 Prisoners-of-war

1973. Prisoners-of-war in India.

344	**203**	1r.25 multicoloured	1·75	2·50

204 National Assembly Building and Constitution Book

1973. Constitution Week.

345	**204**	20p. multicoloured	70	65

205 Badge and State Bank Building

1973. 25th Anniv of Pakistan State Bank.

346	**205**	20p. multicoloured	15	30
347	**205**	1r. multicoloured	30	50

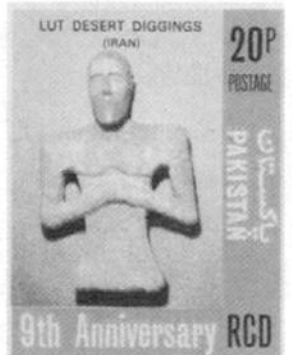

206 Lut Desert Excavations (Iran)

1973. Ninth Anniv of Regional Co-operation for Development. Multicoloured.

348	20p. Type **206**	30	20
349	60p. Main Street, Moenjodaro (Pakistan)	55	50
350	1r.25 Mausoleum of Antiochus I (Turkey)	75	1·25

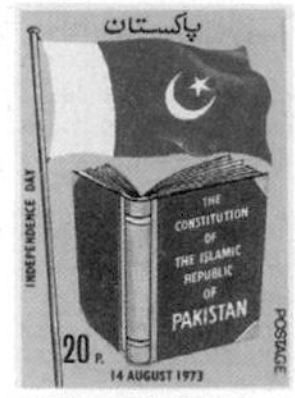

207 Constitution Book and Flag

1973. Independence Day and Enforcement of the Constitution.

351	**207**	20p. multicoloured	15	30

208 Mohammed Ali Jinnah (Quaid-i-Azam)

1973. 25th Death Anniv of Mohammed Ali Jinnah.

352	**208**	20p. green, yellow & black	15	30

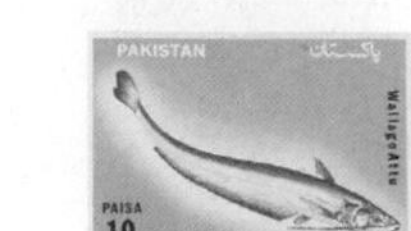

209 Wallago

1973. Fish. Multicoloured.

353	10p. Type **209**	1·10	1·10
354	20p. Rohu	1·25	1·25
355	60p. Mozambique mouth-brooder	1·40	1·40
356	1r. Catla	1·40	1·40

210 Children's Education

1973. Universal Children's Day.

357	**210**	20p. multicoloured	15	40

211 Harvesting

1973. Tenth Anniv of World Food Programme.

358	**211**	20p. multicoloured	60	40

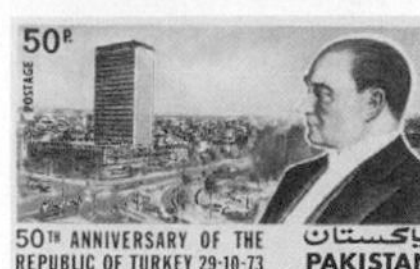

212 Ankara and Kemal Ataturk

1973. 50th Anniv of Turkish Republic.

359	**212**	50p. multicoloured	45	35

213 Boy Scout

1973. National Silver Jubilee Jamboree.

360	**213**	20p. multicoloured	1·75	50

214 "Basic Necessities"

1973. 25th Anniv of Declaration of Human Rights.

361	**214**	20p. multicoloured	30	40

215 Al-Biruni and Nandana Hill

1973. Al-Biruni Millennium Congress.

362	**215**	20p. multicoloured	50	20
363	**215**	1r.25 multicoloured	1·25	90

216 Dr. Hansen, Microscope and Bacillus

1973. Centenary of Hansen's Discovery of Leprosy Bacillus.

364	**216**	20p. multicoloured	1·00	80

217 Family and Emblem

1974. World Population Year.

365	**217**	20p. multicoloured	10	10
366	**217**	1r.25 multicoloured	30	40

218 Conference Emblem

1974. Islamic Summit Conference, Lahore. Multicoloured.

367	20p. Type **218**	10	10
368	65p. Emblem on "Sun" (42×30 mm)	25	60

MS369 102×102 mm. Nos. 367/8. Imperf	1·50	4·75

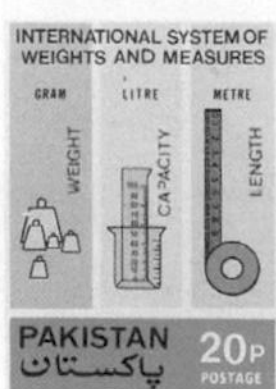

219 Units of Weight and Measurement

1974. Adoption of Int Weights and Measures System.

370	**219**	20p. multicoloured	15	25

220 "Chand Chauthai" Carpet, Pakistan

1974. Tenth Anniversary of Regional Co-operation for Development. Multicoloured.

371	20p. Type **220**	20	15
372	60p. Persian carpet, 16th-century	40	55
373	1r.25 Anatolian carpet, 15th-century	65	1·25

221 Hands protecting Sapling

1974. Tree Planting Day.

374	**221**	20p. multicoloured	50	60

222 Torch and Map

1974. Namibia Day.

375	**222**	60p. multicoloured	50	80

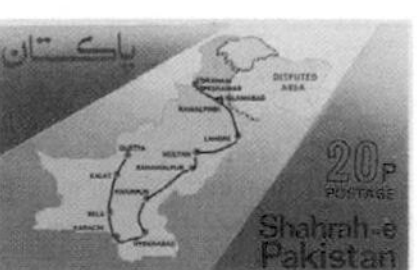

223 Highway Map

1974. Shahrah-e-Pakistan (Pakistan Highway).

376	**223**	20p. multicoloured	1·25	1·00

224 Boy at Desk

1974. Universal Children's Day.

377	**224**	20p. multicoloured	30	40

225 U.P.U. Emblem

1974. Centenary of U.P.U. Multicoloured.

378	20p. Type **225**	20	20
379	2r.25 U.P.U. emblem, Boeing 707 and mail-wagon (30×41 mm)	55	1·40

MS380 100×101 mm. Nos. 378/9. Imperf	1·25	5·00

226 Liaquat Ali Khan

1974. Liaquat Ali Khan (First Prime Minister of Pakistan).

381	**226**	20p. black and red	30	40

227 Dr. Mohammed Iqbal (poet and philosopher)

1974. Birth Centenary of Dr. Iqbal (1977) (1st issue).

382	**227**	20p. multicoloured	30	40

See also Nos. 399, 433 and 445/9.

228 Dr. Schweitzer and River Scene

1975. Birth Centenary of Dr. Albert Schweitzer.

383	**228**	2r.25 multicoloured	4·50	3·25

229 Tourism Year Symbol

1975. South East Asia Tourism Year.

384	**229**	2r.25 multicoloured	60	1·00

230 Assembly Hall, Flags and Prime Minister Bhutto

1975. First Anniv of Islamic Summit Conference, Lahore.

385	**230**	20p. multicoloured	35	35
386	**230**	1r. multicoloured	75	1·40

231 "Scientific Research"

1975. International Women's Year. Multicoloured.

387	20p. Type **231**	25	25
388	2r.25 Girl teaching woman ("Adult Education")	1·25	2·00

232 "Globe" and Algebraic Symbol

1975. International Congress of Mathematical Sciences, Karachi.

389	**232**	20p. multicoloured	50	60

233 Pakistani Camel-skin Vase

1975. 11th Anniv of Regional Co-operation for Development. Multicoloured.

390	20p. Type **233**	30	30
391	60p. Iranian tile (horiz)	60	1·00
392	1r.25 Turkish porcelain vase	90	1·50

234 Sapling and Dead Trees

1975. Tree Planting Year.

393	**234**	20p. multicoloured	35	70

235 Black Partridge

1975. Wildlife Protection (1st series).

394	**235**	20p. multicoloured	1·25	35
395	**235**	2r.25 multicoloured	4·00	4·75

See also Nos. 400/1, 411/12, 417/18, 493/6, 560, 572/3, 581/2, 599, 600, 605, 621/2, 691, 702, 752, 780/3, 853 and 1027.

236 "Today's Girls"

1975. Universal Children's Day.

396	**236**	20p. multicoloured	30	50

237 Hazrat Amir Khusrau, Sitar and Tabla

1975. 700th Birth Anniv of Hazrat Amir Khusrau (poet and musician).

397	**237**	20p. multicoloured	20	50
398	**237**	2r.25 multicoloured	80	2·00

238 Dr. Mohammed Iqbal

1975. Birth Cent (1977) of Dr. Iqbal (2nd issue).

399	**238**	20p. multicoloured	30	50

239 Urial (wild sheep)

1975. Wildlife Protection (2nd series).

400	**239**	20p. multicoloured	30	30
401	**239**	3r. multicoloured	1·75	3·25

240 Moenjodaro Remains

1976. "Save Moenjodaro" (1st issue). Multicoloured.

402	10p. Type **240**	65	80
403	20p. Remains of houses	75	90
404	65p. The Citadel	75	90
405	3r. Well inside a house	75	90
406	4r. The "Great Bath"	85	1·00

See also Nos. 414 and 430.

241 Dome and Minaret of the Rauza-e-Mubarak

1976. International Congress on Seerat.

407	**241**	20p. multicoloured	15	20
408	**241**	3r. multicoloured	55	90

242 Alexander Graham Bell and Dial

1976. Telephone Centenary.

409	**242**	3r. multicoloured	1·25	2·00

243 College Arms within "Sun"

1976. Cent of National College of Arts, Lahore.

410	**243**	20p. multicoloured	30	50

244 Common Peafowl

1976. Wildlife Protection (3rd series).

411	**244**	20p. multicoloured	1·00	35
412	**244**	3r. multicoloured	3·50	4·50

245 Human Eye

1976. Prevention of Blindness.

413	**245**	20p. multicoloured	1·00	70

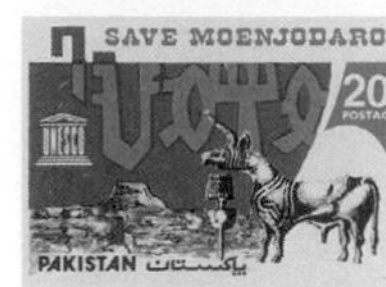

246 Unicorn and Ruins

1976. "Save Moenjodaro" (2nd series).

414	**246**	20p. multicoloured	30	40

247 Jefferson Memorial

1976. Bicent of American Revolution. Multicoloured.

415	90p. Type **247**	75	60
416	4r. "Declaration of Independence" (47×36 mm)	3·00	5·00

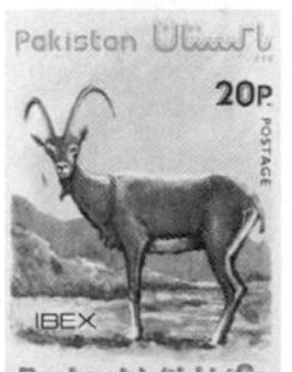

248 Ibex

1976. Wildlife Protection (4th series).

417	**248**	20p. multicoloured	30	35
418	**248**	3r. multicoloured	1·25	2·50

249 Mohammed Ali Jinnah

1976. 12th Anniv of Regional Co-operation for Development. Multicoloured.

419	20p. Type **249**	65	90
420	65p. Reza Shah the Great (Iran)	65	90
421	90p. Kemal Ataturk (Turkey)	65	90

250 Urdu Text

1976. Birth Cent of Mohammed Ali Jinnah (1st issue). (a) Type **250**.

(a) Type **250**

422	**250**	5p. black, blue and yellow	20	25
423	**250**	10p. black, yellow & pur	20	25
424	**250**	15p. black and blue	20	25
425	**250**	1r. black, yellow and blue	30	30

251 Mohammed Ali Jinnah and Wazir Mansion

(b) Type **251**. Background Buildings given. Multicoloured.

426	20p. Type **251**	20	25
427	40p. Sind Madressah	20	25
428	50p. Minar Qarardad-e-Pakistan	20	25
429	3r. Mausoleum	45	50

See also No. 436.

252 Dancing-girl, Ruins and King Priest

1976. "Save Moenjodaro" (3rd series).

430	**252**	65p. multicoloured	35	80

253 U.N. Racial Discrimination Emblem

1976. U.N. Decade to Combat Racial Discrimination.

431	**253**	65p. multicoloured	30	60

254 Child in Maze and Basic Services

1976. Universal Children's Day.

432	**254**	20p. multicoloured	60	60

255 Verse from "Allama Iqbal"

1976. Birth Centenary (1977) of Dr. Iqbal (3rd issue).

433	**255**	20p. multicoloured	15	30

256 Mohammed Ali Jinnah giving Scout Salute

1976. Quaid-i-Azam Centenary Jamboree.

434	**256**	20p. multicoloured	1·00	60

257 Children Reading

1976. Children's Literature.

435	**257**	20p. multicoloured	65	65

258 Mohammed Ali Jinnah

1976. Birth Centenary of Mohammed Ali Jinnah (2nd issue).

436	**258**	10r. green and gold	2·75	3·50

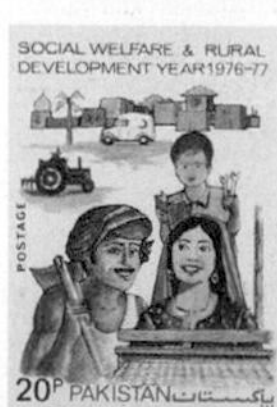

259 Rural Family

1977. Social Welfare and Rural Development Year.

437	**259**	20p. multicoloured	40	20

260 Turkish Vase, 1800 B.C.

1977. 13th Anniv of Regional Co-operation for Development.

438	**260**	20p. orange, blue & black	45	10
439	-	65p. multicoloured	65	40
440	-	90p. multicoloured	90	1·50

DESIGNS: 60p. Pakistani toy bullock cart from Moenjodaro; 90p. Pitcher with spout from Sialk Hill, Iran.

261 Forest

1977. National Tree Plantation Campaign.

441	**261**	20p. multicoloured	20	30

262 Desert Scene

1977. U.N. Conference on Desertification, Nairobi.

442	**262**	65p. multicoloured	1·25	45

263 "Water for Children of the World"

1977. Universal Children's Day.

443	**263**	50p. multicoloured	40	30

264 Aga Khan III

1977. Birth Centenary of Aga Khan III.

444	**264**	2r. multicoloured	55	1·00

265 Iqbal and Spirit of the Poet Roomi (from painting by Behzad)

1977. Birth Centenary of Dr. Mohammed Iqbal (4th issue). Multicoloured.

445	20p. Type **265**	60	70
446	65p. Iqbal looking at Jamalud-din Afghani and Saeed Haleem Pasha at prayer (Behzad)	60	70
447	1r.25 Urdu verse	65	75
448	2r.25 Persian verse	70	85
449	3r. Iqbal	75	95

266 The Holy "Khana-Kaaba" (House of God, Mecca)

1977. Haj (pilgrimage to Mecca).

450	**266**	65p. multicoloured	30	30

267 Rheumatic Patient and Healthy Man

1977. World Rheumatism Year.

451	**267**	65p. blue, black and yellow	30	20

268 Woman in Costume of Rawalpindi-Islamabad

1978. Indonesia–Pakistan Economic and Cultural Co-operation Organization.

452	**268**	75p. multicoloured	30	20

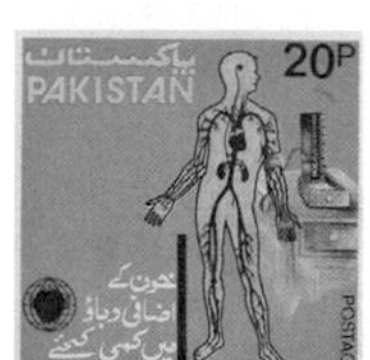

269 Human Body and Sphygmomanometer

1978. World Hypertension Month.

453	**269**	20p. multicoloured	25	10
454	-	2r. multicoloured	75	90

The 2r. value is as Type **269** but has the words "Down with high blood pressure" instead of the Urdu inscription at bottom left.

270 Henri Dunant

1978. 150th Birth Anniv of Henri Dunant (founder of the Red Cross).

455	**270**	1r. multicoloured	1·00	20

271 Red Roses (Pakistan)

1978. 14th Anniv of Regional Co-operation for Development. Roses. Multicoloured.

456	20p. Type **271**	35	25
457	90p. Pink roses (Iran)	50	35
458	2r. Yellow rose (Turkey)	75	50

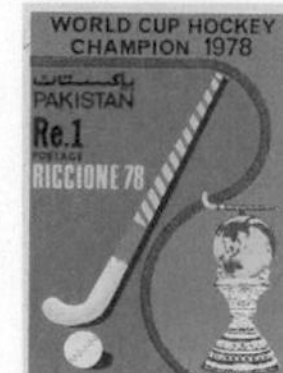

272 "Pakistan, World Cup Hockey Champions"

1978. "Riccione '78" International Stamp Fair. Multicoloured.

459	1r. Type **272**	1·25	25
460	2r. Fountain at Piazza Turismo	50	35

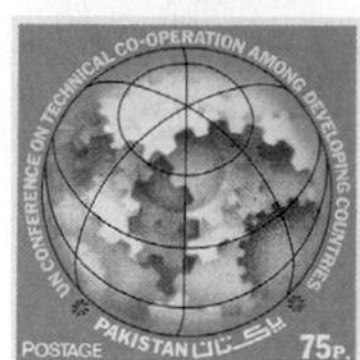

273 Cogwheels within Globe Symbol

1978. U.N. Technical Co-operation amongst Developing Countries Conference.

461	**273**	75p. multicoloured	25	20

274 St. Patrick's Cathedral, Karachi

1978. Centenary of St. Patrick's Cathedral, Karachi. Multicoloured.

462	1r. Type **274**	15	10
463	2r. Stained glass window	30	30

275 Minar-i-Qarardad-e-Pakistan

1978

464	**275**	2p. green	10	10
465	**275**	3p. black	10	10
466	**275**	5p. blue	10	10
467	-	10p. blue and turquoise	10	10
468	-	20p. green	60	10
469	-	25p. green and mauve	1·25	10
470	-	40p. blue and mauve	10	10
471	-	50p. lilac and green	30	10
472	-	60p. black	10	10
473b	-	75p. red	1·75	10
474	-	90p. mauve and blue	30	10
475	-	1r. green	60	10
476	-	1r.50 orange	20	10
477	-	2r. red	20	10
478	-	3r. blue	20	10
479	-	4r. black	20	10
480	-	5r. brown	20	10

DESIGNS—HORIZ (25×20 mm): 10p. to 90p. Tractor. VERT (21×25 mm): 1r. to 5r. Mausoleum of Ibrahim Khan Makli, Thatta.

277 Emblem and "United Races" Symbol

1978. International Anti-Apartheid Year.

481	**277**	1r. multicoloured	15	15

278 Maulana Mohammad Ali Jauhar

1978. Birth Centenary of Maulana Mohammad Ali Jauhar (patriot).

482	**278**	50p. multicoloured	50	20

279 Panavia MRCA Tornado, De Havilland Dragon Rapide and Wright Flyer I

1978. 75th Anniv of Powered Flight. Multicoloured.

483	65p. Type **279**	1·00	1·75
484	1r. McDonnell Douglas Phantom II, Lockheed Tristar 500 and Wright Flyer I	1·10	1·75
485	2r. North American X-15, Tupolev Tu-104 and Wright Flyer I	1·25	2·00
486	2r.25 Mikoyan Gurevich MiG-15, Concorde and Wright Flyer I	1·25	2·25

280 "Holy Koran illuminating Globe" and Raudha-e-Mubarak (mausoleum)

1979. "12th Rabi-ul-Awwal" (Prophet Mohammed's birthday).

487	**280**	20p. multicoloured	40	15

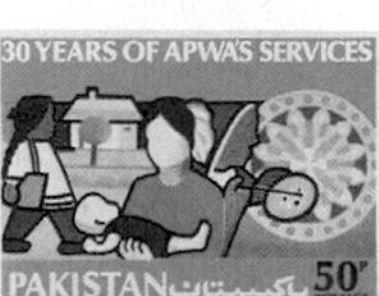

281 "Aspects of A.P.W.A."

1979. 30th Anniv of A.P.W.A. (All Pakistan Women's Association).

488	**281**	50p. multicoloured	75	15

282 Tippu Sultan Shaheed of Mysore

1979. Pioneers of Freedom (1st series). Multicoloured.

490	10r. Type **282**	75	1·60
491	15r. Sir Syed Ahmad Khan	1·00	2·25
492	25r. Altaf Hussain Hali	1·50	2·25

See also Nos. 757, 801/27, 838/46, 870/2, 904/6, 921/8, 961/2, 1007, 1019/20 and 1075/7.

283 Himalayan Monal Pheasant

1979. Wildlife Protection (5th series). Pheasants. Multicoloured.

493		20p. Type **283**	1·25	60
494		25p. Kalij pheasant	1·25	80
495		40p. Koklass pheasant	1·60	1·75
496		1r. Cheer pheasant	3·00	2·00

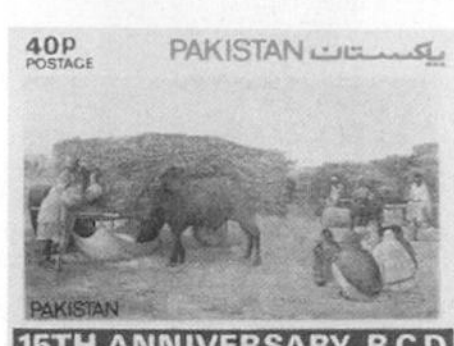

284 "Pakistan Village Scene" (Ustad Bakhsh)

1979. 15th Anniv of Regional Co-operation for Development. Multicoloured.

497		40p. Type **284**	20	25
498		75p. "Iranian Goldsmith" (Kamal al Molk)	20	25
499		1r.60 "Turkish Harvest" (Namik Ismail)	25	30

285 Guj Embroidered Shirt (detail)

1979. Handicrafts (1st series). Multicoloured.

500		40p. Type **285**	20	20
501		1r. Enamel inlaid brass plate	25	25
502		1r.50 Baskets	30	30
503		2r. Chain-stitch embroidered rug (detail)	40	40

See also Nos. 578/9, 595/6 and 625/8.

286 Children playing on Climbing-frame

1979. S.O.S. Children's Village, Lahore.

504	**286**	50p. multicoloured	40	40

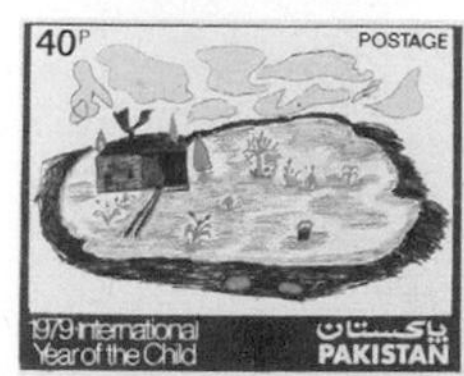

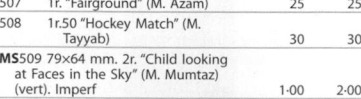

287 "Island" (Z. Maloof)

1979. International Year of the Child. Children's Paintings. Multicoloured.

505		40p. Type **287**	15	15
506		75p. "Playground" (R. Akbar)	25	25
507		1r. "Fairground" (M. Azam)	25	25
508		1r.50 "Hockey Match" (M. Tayyab)	30	30
MS509		79×64 mm. 2r. "Child looking at Faces in the Sky" (M. Mumtaz) (vert). Imperf	1·00	2·00

288 Warrior attacking Crab

1979. "Fight Against Cancer".

510	**288**	40p. black, yellow and purple	70	70

289 Pakistan Customs Emblem

1979. Centenary of Pakistan Customs Service.

511	**289**	1r. multicoloured	30	30

290 Boeing 747-200 and Douglas DC-3 Airliners

1980. 25th Anniv of Pakistan International Air Lines.

512	**290**	1r. multicoloured	1·75	90

291 Islamic Pattern

1980

513	**291**	10p. green and yellow	10	10
514	**291**	15p. deep green and green	20	10
515	**291**	25p. violet and red	30	50
516	**291**	35p. red and green	40	1·00
517	-	40p. red and brown	40	10
518	-	50p. violet and green	40	50
519	-	80p. green and black	60	50

The 40 to 80p. values also show different Islamic patterns, the 40p. being horizontal and the remainder vertical.

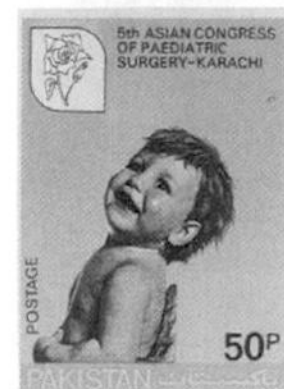

292 Young Child

1980. Fifth Asian Congress of Paediatric Surgery, Karachi.

530	**292**	50p. multicoloured	75	1·50

293 Conference Emblem

1980. 11th Islamic Conference of Foreign Ministers, Islamabad.

531	**293**	1r. multicoloured	1·25	75

294 Karachi Port

1980. Centenary of Karachi Port Authority.

532	**294**	1r. multicoloured	1·75	2·00

1980. "Riccione 80" International Stamp Exhibition. Nos. 505/8 optd **RICCIONE 80**.

533	**287**	40p. multicoloured	30	80
534	-	75p. multicoloured	40	90
535	-	1r. multicoloured	45	90
536	-	1r.50 multicoloured	60	1·10

296 College Emblem with Old and New Buildings

1980. 75th Anniv of Command and Staff College, Quetta.

537	**296**	1r. multicoloured	20	15

1980. World Tourism Conference, Manila. No. 496 optd **WORLD TOURISM CONFERENCE MANILA 80**.

538		1r. Cheer pheasant	1·25	40

298 Birth Centenary Emblem

1980. Birth Cent of Hafiz Mahmood Shairani.

539	**298**	40p. multicoloured	30	1·00

299 Shalimar Gardens, Lahore

1980. Aga Khan Award for Architecture.

540	**299**	2r. multicoloured	40	1·75

300 Rising Sun

1980. 1400th Anniv of Hegira (1st issue). Multicoloured.

541		40p. Type **300**	15	10
542		2r. Ka'aba and symbols of Moslem achievement (33×33 mm)	40	45
543		3r. Holy Koran illuminating the World (30×54 mm)	55	80
MS544		106×84 mm. 4r. Candles. Imperf	60	1·00

See also No. 549.

301 Money Order Form

1980. Centenary of Money Order Service.

545	**301**	40p. multicoloured	20	60

302 Postcards encircling Globe

1980. Centenary of Postcard Service.

546	**302**	40p. multicoloured	20	60

303 Heinrich von Stephan and U.P.U. Emblem

1981. 150th Birth Anniv of Heinrich von Stephan (U.P.U. founder).

547	**303**	1r. multicoloured	30	20

304 Aircraft and Airmail Letters

1981. 50th Anniv of Airmail Service.

548	**304**	1r. multicoloured	75	20

305 Mecca

1981. 1400th Anniv of Hegira (2nd issue).

549	**305**	40p. multicoloured	20	60

306 Conference Emblem and Afghan Refugees

1981. Islamic Summit Conference (1st issue). Multicoloured.

550		40p. Type **306**	30	15
551		40p. Conference emblem encircled by flags and Afghan refugees (28×58 mm)	30	15
552		1r. Type **306**	50	15
553		1r. As No. 551	50	15
554		2r. Conference emblem and map showing Afghanistan (48×32 mm)	65	50

307 Conference Emblem

1981. Islamic Summit Conference (2nd issue). Multicoloured.

555		40p. Type **307**	15	15
556		40p. Conference emblem and flags (28×46 mm)	15	15
557		85p. Type **307**	20	40
558		85p. As No. 556	20	40

308 Kemal Ataturk

1981. Birth Centenary of Kemal Ataturk (Turkish statesman).

559	**308**	1r. multicoloured	50	15

309 Green Turtle

1981. Wildlife Protection (6th series).

560	**309**	40p. multicoloured	1·25	40

310 Dome of the Rock

1981. Palestinian Welfare.

561	**310**	2r. multicoloured	1·25	60

311 Malubiting West

1981. Mountain Peaks (1st series). Karakoram Range. Multicoloured.

562	40p. Type **311**	40	40
563	40p. Malubiting West (24×31 mm)	40	40
564	1r. Haramosh	55	75
565	1r. Haramosh (24×31 mm)	55	75
566	1r.50 K6	70	1·00
567	1r.50 K6 (24×31 mm)	70	1·00
568	2r. K2, Broad Peak, Gasherbrum 4 and Gasherbrum 2	70	1·40
569	2r. K2 (24×31 mm)	70	1·40

See also Nos. 674/5.

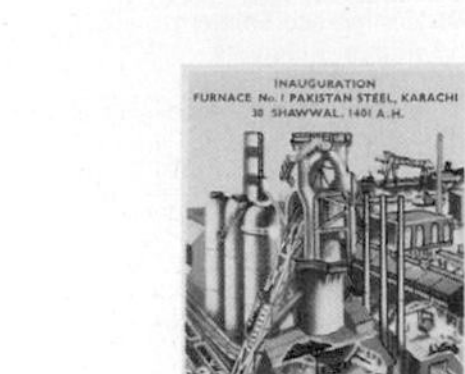

312 Pakistan Steel "Furnace No. 1"

1981. First Firing of Pakistan Steel "Furnace No. 1", Karachi.

570	**312**	40p. multicoloured	20	10
571	**312**	2r. multicoloured	60	1·75

313 Western Tragopan

1981. Wildlife Protection (7th series).

572	**313**	40p. multicoloured	2·25	75
573	-	2r. multicoloured	4·25	4·25

DESIGN: 2r. As Type **313** but with background showing a winter view.

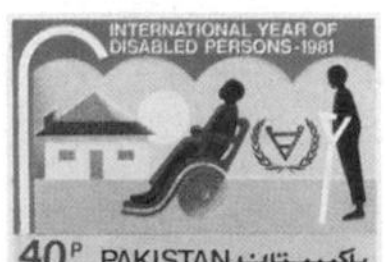

314 Disabled People and I.Y.D.P. Emblem

1981. International Year for Disabled Persons.

574	**314**	40p. multicoloured	30	50
575	**314**	2r. multicoloured	1·10	1·75

315 World Hockey Cup below Flags of participating Countries

1982. Pakistan—World Cup Hockey Champions. Multicoloured.

576	1r. Type **315**	2·00	1·50
577	1r. World Hockey Cup above flags of participating countries	2·00	1·50

316 Camel Skin Lamp

1982. Handicrafts (2nd series). Multicoloured.

578	1r. Type **316**	70	80
579	1r. Hala pottery	70	80

See also Nos. 595/6.

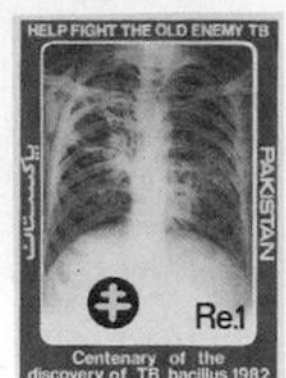

317 Chest X-Ray of Infected Person

1982. Centenary of Robert Koch's Discovery of Tubercle Bacillus.

580	**317**	1r. multicoloured	1·25	1·50

318 Indus Dolphin

1982. Wildlife Protection (8th series).

581	**318**	40p. multicoloured	1·50	1·50
582	-	1r. multicoloured	3·00	2·50

DESIGN: 1r. As Type **318** but with design reversed.

319 "Apollo–Soyuz" Link-up, 1975

1982. Peaceful Use of Outer Space.

583	**319**	1r. multicoloured	2·00	1·25

320 Sukkur Barrage

1982. 50th Anniv of Sukkur Barrage.

584	**320**	1r. multicoloured	30	30

321 Pakistan National Flag and Stylized Sun

1982. Independence Day. Multicoloured.

585	40p. Type **321**	20	30
586	85p. Map of Pakistan and stylized torch	45	1·25

1982. "Riccione '82" Stamp Exhibition. No. 584 optd **RICCIONE-82.**

587	1r. multicoloured	20	20

323 Arabic Inscription and University Emblem

1982. Centenary of the Punjab University.

588	**323**	40p. multicoloured	1·25	1·00

324 Scout Emblem and Tents

1983. 75th Anniv of Boy Scout Movement.

589	**324**	2r. multicoloured	50	50

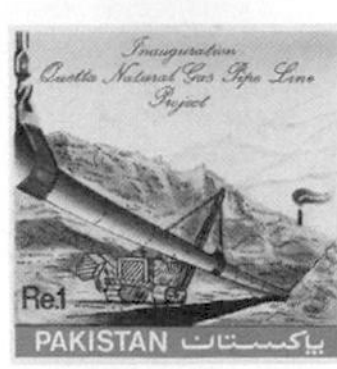

325 Laying Pipeline

1983. Inaug of Quetta Natural Gas Pipeline Project.

590	**325**	1r. multicoloured	30	30

326 "Papilio polyctor"

1983. Butterflies. Multicoloured.

591	40p. Type **326**	1·25	20
592	50p. "Atrophaneura aristolochiae"	1·50	20
593	60p. "Danaus chrysippus"	1·75	60
594	1r.50 "Papilio demoleus"	2·50	2·25

1983. Handicrafts (3rd series). As T **316**. Multicoloured.

595	1r. Five flower motif needlework, Sind	15	15
596	1r. Straw mats	15	15

327 School of Nursing and University Emblem

1983. Presentation of Charter to Aga Khan University, Karachi.

597	**327**	2r. multicoloured	1·75	2·00

328 Yak Caravan crossing Zindiharam-Darkot Pass, Hindu Kush

1983. Trekking in Pakistan.

598	**328**	1r. multicoloured	1·50	1·50

329 Marsh Crocodile

1983. Wildlife Protection (9th series).

599	**329**	3r. multicoloured	3·50	2·00

330 Goitred Gazelle

1983. Wildlife Protection (10th series).

600	**330**	1r. multicoloured	2·50	2·00

331 Floral Design

1983. 36th Anniv of Independence. Multicoloured.

601	60p. Type **331**	10	10
602	4r. Hand holding flaming torch	40	45

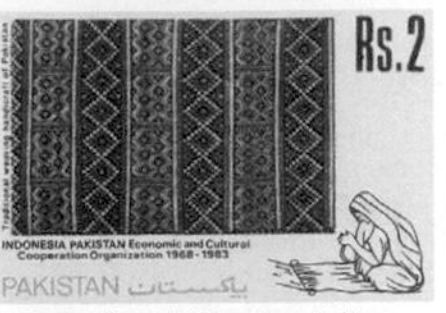

332 Traditional Weaving, Pakistan

1983. Indonesian–Pakistan Economic and Cultural Co-operation Organization, 1969–1983. Mult.

603	2r. Type **332**	20	25
604	2r. Traditional weaving, Indonesia	20	25

333 "Siberian Cranes" (Great White Cranes) (Sir Peter Scott)

1983. Wildlife Protection (11th series).

605	**333**	3r. multicoloured	3·75	3·25

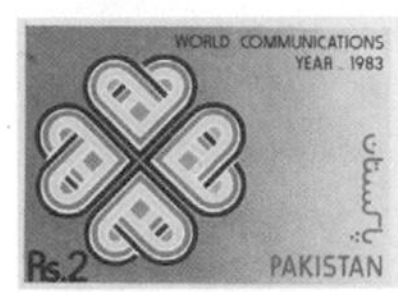

334 W.C.Y. Emblem

1983. World Communications Year. Multicoloured.

606	2r. Type **334**	20	25
607	3r. W.C.Y. emblem (different) (33×33 mm)	30	35

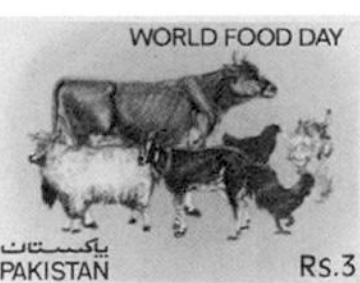

335 Farm Animals

1983. World Food Day. Multicoloured.

608	3r. Type **335**	1·50	1·75
609	3r. Fruit	1·50	1·75
610	3r. Crops	1·50	1·75
611	3r. Sea food	1·50	1·75

336 Agriculture Produce and Fertilizer Factory

1983. National Fertilizer Corporation.

612	**336**	60p. multicoloured	20	30

337 Lahore, 1852

1983. National Stamp Exn, Lahore. Multicoloured.

613	60p. Musti Durwaza Dharmsala	60	75
614	60p. Khabgha	60	75
615	60p. Type **337**	60	75
616	60p. Summan Burj Hazuri	60	75

617 60p. Flower Garden, Samadhi Northern Gate 60 75
618 60p. Budda Darya, Badshahi Masjid 60 75

338 Winner of "Enterprise" Event

1983. Yachting Champions, Asian Games, Delhi. Multicoloured.
619 60p. Type **338** 1·75 1·75
620 60p. Winner of "OK" Dinghy event 1·75 1·75

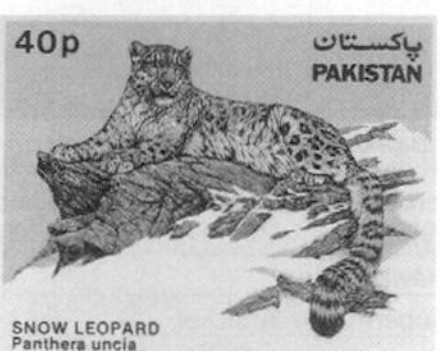

339 Snow Leopard

1984. Wildlife Protection (12th series).
621 **339** 40p. multicoloured 1·75 90
622 **339** 1r.60 multicoloured 4·75 6·00

340 Jahangir Khan (World Squash Champion)

1984. Squash.
623 **340** 3r. multicoloured 2·25 1·75

341 P.I.A. Boeing 707 Airliner

1984. 20th Anniv of Pakistan International Airways Service to China.
624 **341** 3r. multicoloured 5·00 5·50

342 Glass-work

1984. Handicrafts (4th series). Multicoloured, frame colours given.
625 **342** 1r. blue 30 20
626 - 1r. red 30 20
627 - 1r. green 30 20
628 - 1r. violet 30 20

DESIGNS: showing glass-work in Sheesh Mahal, Lahore Fort. Nos. 627/8 are horizontal designs.

343 Attock Fort

1984. Forts.
629 5p. black and purple 40 60
630 10p. black and red 40 10
631 15p. violet and brown 75 10
632 **343** 20p. black and violet 1·50 10
633 - 50p. brown and red 1·50 10
634 - 60p. light brown & brown 1·25 10
635 - 70p. blue 1·50 10
636 - 80p. brown and red 1·50 10

DESIGNS: 5p. Kot Diji Fort; 10p. Rohtas Fort; 15p. Bala Hissar Fort; 50p. Hyderabad Fort; 60p. Lahore Fort; 70p. Sibi Fort; 80p. Ranikot Fort.

344 Shah Rukn i Alam's Tomb, Multan

1984. Aga Khan Award for Architecture.
647 **344** 60p. multicoloured 2·50 2·75

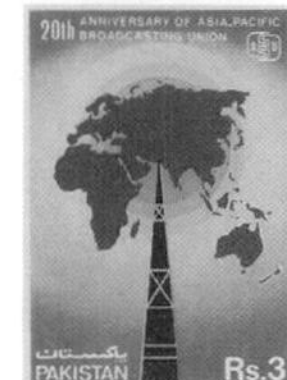

345 Radio Mast and Map of World

1984. 20th Anniv of Asia–Pacific Broadcasting Union.
648 **345** 3r. multicoloured 1·00 60

346 Wrestling

1984. Olympic Games, Los Angeles. Multicoloured.
649 3r. Type **346** 1·25 1·50
650 3r. Boxing 1·25 1·50
651 3r. Athletics 1·25 1·50
652 3r. Hockey 1·25 1·50
653 3r. Yachting 1·25 1·50

347 Jasmine (National flower) and Inscription

1984. Independence Day. Multicoloured.
654 60p. Type **347** 10 10
655 4r. Symbolic torch 45 50

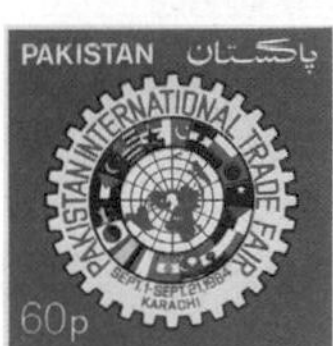

348 Gearwheel Emblem and Flags of Participating Nations

1984. Pakistan International Trade Fair.
656 **348** 60p. multicoloured 1·00 30

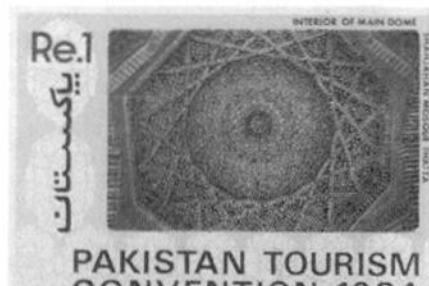

349 Interior of Main Dome

1984. Tourism Convention, Shahjahan Mosque, Thatta. Multicoloured.
657 1r. Type **349** 50 60
658 1r. Brick and glazed tile work 50 60
659 1r. Gateway 50 60
660 1r. Symmetrical archways 50 60
661 1r. Interior of a dome 50 60

350 Bank Emblem in Floral Pattern

1984. 25th Anniv of United Bank Ltd.
662 **350** 60p. multicoloured 1·00 1·00

351 Conference Emblem

1984. 20th United Nations Conference of Trade and Development.
663 **351** 60p. multicoloured 80 40

352 Postal Life Insurance Emblem within Hands

1984. Centenary of Postal Life Insurance. Multicoloured.
664 60p. Type **352** 70 15
665 1r. "100" and Postal Life Insurance emblem 90 15

353 Bull (wall painting)

1984. UNESCO Save Moenjadoro Campaign. Multicoloured.
666 2r. Type **353** 1·40 1·00
667 2r. Bull (seal) 1·40 1·00

354 International Youth Year Emblem and "75"

1985. 75th Anniv of Girl Guide Movement.
668 **354** 60p. multicoloured 3·25 1·50

355 Smelting Ore

1985. Inauguration of Pakistan Steel Corporation. Multicoloured.
669 60p. Type **355** 65 25
670 1r. Pouring molten steel from ladle (28×46 mm) 1·10 25

356 Map of Pakistan and Rays of Sun

1985. Presidential Referendum of 19 December 1984.
671 **356** 60p. multicoloured 1·75 55

357 Ballot Box and Voting Paper

1985. March Elections. Multicoloured.
672 1r. Type **357** 65 15
673 1r. Minar-e-Qarardad-e-Pakistan Tower, and word "Democracy" (31×43 mm) 65 15

1985. Mountain Peaks (2nd series). As T **311**. Multicoloured.
674 40p. Rakaposhi (Karakoram Range) 1·75 75
675 2r. Nangaparbat (Western Himalayas) 3·75 6·00

358 Trophy and Medals from Olympic Games 1984, Asia Cup 1985 and World Cup 1982

1985. Pakistan Hockey Team "Grand Slam" Success.
676 **358** 1r. multicoloured 2·50 2·25

359 King Edward Medical College

1985. 125th Anniv of King Edward Medical College, Lahore.
677 **359** 3r. multicoloured 1·75 1·00

360 Illuminated Inscription in Urdu

1985. Independence Day. Multicoloured.
678 60p. Type **360** 65 1·00
679 60p. Illuminated "XXXVIII" (inscr in English) 65 1·00

361 Sind Madressah-tul-Islam, Karachi

1985. Centenary of Sind Madressah-tul-Islam (theological college), Karachi.
680 **361** 2r. multicoloured 1·75 1·00

362 Jamia Masjid Mosque by Day

1985. Inauguration of New Jamia Masjid Mosque, Karachi. Multicoloured.
681 1r. Type **362** 90 50
682 1r. Jamia Masjid illuminated at night 90 50

363 Lawrence College, Murree

1985. 125th Anniv of Lawrence College, Murree.
683 **363** 3r. multicoloured 2·50 2·25

1989. 25th Anniv of Television Broadcasting in Pakistan.
787 **417** 3r. multicoloured 50 50

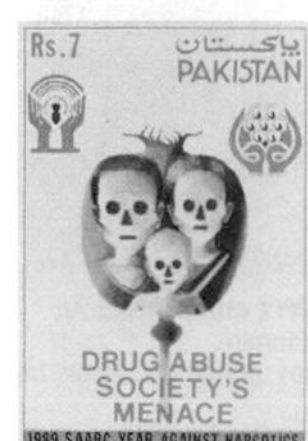
418 Family of Drug Addicts in Poppy Bud

1989. South Asian Association for Regional Co-operation Anti-Drugs Campaign.
788 **418** 7r. multicoloured 2·25 1·40

419 Murray College, Sialkot

1989. Centenary of Murray College, Sialkot.
789 **419** 6r. multicoloured 1·50 1·25

420 Government College, Lahore

1989. 125th Anniv of Government College, Lahore.
790 **420** 6r. multicoloured 1·00 1·25

421 Fields, Electricity Pylons and Rural Buildings

1989. Tenth Anniv of Centre for Asia and Pacific Integrated Rural Development.
791 **421** 3r. multicoloured 1·00 75

422 Emblem and Islamic Patterns

1990. 20th Anniv of Organization of the Islamic Conference.
792 **422** 1r. multicoloured 1·75 40

423 Hockey Match

1990. Seventh World Hockey Cup, Lahore.
793 **423** 2r. multicoloured 4·50 4·25

424 Mohammed Iqbal addressing Crowd and Liaquat Ali Khan taking Oath

1990. 50th Anniv of Passing of Pakistan Resolution. Multicoloured.

794	1r. Type **424**	1·00	1·25
795	1r. Maulana Mohammad Ali Jauhar and Mohammed Ali Jinnah with banner	1·00	1·25
796	1r. Women with Pakistan flag, and Mohammed Ali Jinnah taking Governor-General's oath, 1947	1·00	1·25
797	7r. Minar-i-Qarardad-e-Pakistan Monument and Resolution in Urdu and English (86×42 mm)	2·50	3·00

Nos. 794/6 were printed together, *se-tenant*, forming a composite design.

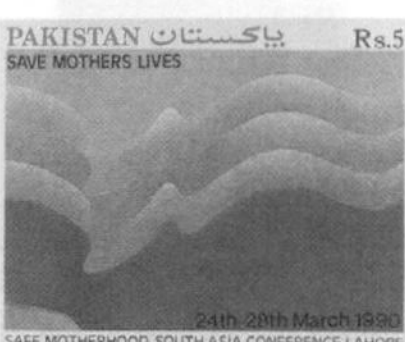
425 Pregnant Woman resting

1990. "Safe Motherhood" South Asia Conference, Lahore.
798 **425** 5r. multicoloured 1·00 1·25

426 "Decorated Verse by Ghalib" (Shakir Ali)

1990. Painters of Pakistan (1st series). Shakir Ali.
799 **426** 1r. multicoloured 2·25 1·25
See also Nos. 856/7.

427 Satellite in Night Sky

1990. Launch of "Badr I" Satellite.
800 **427** 3r. multicoloured 3·50 3·50

428 Allama Mohammed Iqbal

1990. Pioneers of Freedom (3rd series). Each brown and green.

801	1r. Type **428**	40	45
802	1r. Mohammed Ali Jinnah	40	45
803	1r. Sir Syed Ahmad Khan	40	45
804	1r. Nawab Salimullah	40	45
805	1r. Mohtarma Fatima Jinnah	40	45
806	1r. Aga Khan III	40	45
807	1r. Nawab Mohammad Ismail Khan	40	45
808	1r. Hussain Shaheed Suhrawardy	40	45
809	1r. Syed Ameer Ali	40	45
810	1r. Nawab Bahadur Yar Jung	40	45
811	1r. Khawaja Nazimuddin	40	45
812	1r. Maulana Obaidullah Sindhi	40	45
813	1r. Sahibzada Abdul Qaiyum Khan	40	45
814	1r. Begum Jahanara Shah Nawaz	40	45
815	1r. Sir Ghulam Hussain Hiday-atullah	40	45
816	1r. Qazi Mohammad Isa	40	45
817	1r. Sir M. Shahnawaz Khan Mamdot	40	45
818	1r. Pir Sahib of Manki Sharif	40	45
819	1r. Liaquat Ali Khan	40	45
820	1r. Maulvi A. K. Fazl-ul-Haq	40	45
821	1r. Allama Shabbir Ahmad Usmani	40	45
822	1r. Sadar Abdur Rab Nishtar	40	45
823	1r. Bi Amma	40	45
824	1r. Sir Abdullah Haroon	40	45
825	1r. Chaudhry Rahmat Ali	40	45
826	1r. Raja Sahib of Mahmudabad	40	45
827	1r. Hassanally Effendi	40	45

See also Nos. 838/46, 870/2, 904/6, 921/8, 961/2, 1007, 1019/20 and 1075/7.

429 Cultural Aspects of Indonesia and Pakistan

1990. Indonesia–Pakistan Economic and Cultural Co-operation Organization.
828 **429** 7r. multicoloured 3·50 3·50

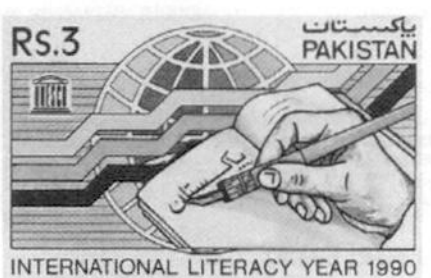
430 Globe, Open Book and Pen

1990. International Literacy Year.
829 **430** 3r. multicoloured 1·00 1·50

431 College Crests

1990. Joint Meeting between Royal College of Physicians, Edinburgh, and College of Physicians and Surgeons, Pakistan.
830 **431** 2r. multicoloured 60 75

432 Children and Globe

1990. U.N. World Summit for Children, New York.
831 **432** 7r. multicoloured 75 1·25

433 Girl within Members' Flags

1990. South Asian Association for Regional Co-operation Year of Girl Child.
832 **433** 2r. multicoloured 70 75

434 Paper passing over Rollers

1990. 25th Anniv of Security Papers Limited.
833 **434** 3r. multicoloured 4·50 2·50

435 Civil Defence Worker protecting Islamabad

1991. International Civil Defence Day.
834 **435** 7r. multicoloured 1·75 1·75

436 Logo and Flags of Member Countries

1991. South and West Asia Postal Union Commemoration.
835 **436** 5r. multicoloured 1·60 1·90

437 Globe and Figures

1991. World Population Day.
836 **437** 10r. multicoloured 1·90 2·50

438 Mentally Handicapped Athlete

1991. Pakistan Participation in Special Olympic Games.
837 **438** 7r. multicoloured 1·75 2·50

1991. Pioneers of Freedom (4th series). As T **428**. Each brown and green.

838	1r. Maulana Zafar Ali Khan	70	80
839	1r. Maulana Mohamed Ali Jauhar	70	80
840	1r. Chaudhry Khaliquzzaman	70	80
841	1r. Hameed Nizami	70	80
842	1r. Begum Ra'ana Liaquat Ali Khan	70	80
843	1r. Mirza Abol Hassan Ispahani	70	80
844	1r. Raja Ghazanfar Ali Khan	70	80
845	1r. Malik Barkat Ali	70	80
846	1r. Mir Jaffer Khan Jamali	70	80

439 Habib Bank Headquarters and Emblem

1991. 50th Anniv of Habib Bank.
847 **439** 1r. multicoloured 1·25 25
848 **439** 5r. multicoloured 3·75 4·00

440 St. Joesph's Convent School

1991. 130th Anniv (1992) of St. Joesph's Convent School, Karachi.
849 **440** 5r. multicoloured 4·00 4·00

441 Emperor Sher Shah Suri

1991. Emperor Sher Shah Suri (founder of road network) Commemoration.
850 **441** 5r. multicoloured 2·25 2·50

MS851 92×80 mm. 7r. Emperor on horseback and portrait as Type **441**. Imperf 1·75 2·75

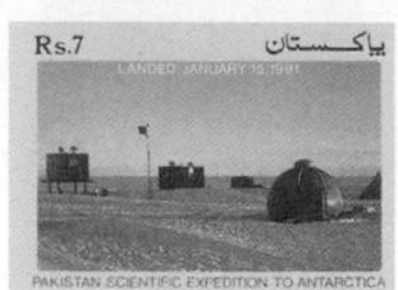

442 Jinnah Antarctic Research Station

1991. Pakistan Scientific Expedition to Antarctica.

852	**442**	7r. multicoloured	3·00	2·75

443 Houbara Bustard

1991. Wildlife Protection (17th series).

853	**443**	7r. multicoloured	2·50	2·75

444 Mosque

1991. 300th Death Anniv of Hazrat Sultan Bahoo.

854	**444**	7r. multicoloured	2·25	3·00

445 Development Symbols and Map of Asia

1991. 25th Anniv of Asian Development Bank.

855	**445**	7r. multicoloured	3·25	3·25

1991. Painters of Pakistan (2nd series). As T **426**. Multicoloured.

856	1r. "Procession" (Haji Muhammad Sharif)	2·50	1·75
857	1r. "Women harvesting" (Ustad Allah Bux)	2·50	1·75

446x 446 American Express Travellers Cheques of 1891 and 1991

1991. Centenary of American Express Travellers Cheques.

858	**446**	7r. multicoloured	1·75	2·50

447 Flag, Banknote and Banking Equipment

1992. First Anniv of Muslim Commercial Bank Privatization. Multicoloured.

859	1r. Type **447**	20	10
860	7r. Flag with industrial and commercial scenes	1·25	1·40

448 Imran Khan (team captain) and Trophy

1992. Pakistan's Victory in World Cricket Championship. Multicoloured.

861	2r. Type **448**	70	70
862	5r. Trophy and national flags (horiz)	1·50	1·50
863	7r. Pakistani flag, trophy and symbolic cricket ball	1·75	2·00

449 "Rehber-1" Rocket and Satellite View of Earth

1992. International Space Year. Multicoloured.

864	1r. Type **449**	40	10
865	2r. Satellite orbiting Earth and logo	60	60

450 Surgical Instruments

1992. Industries. Multicoloured.

866	10r. Type **450**	1·25	1·60
867	15r. Leather goods	1·75	2·50
868	25r. Sports equipment	2·75	3·50

451 Globe and Symbolic Family

1992. Population Day.

869	**451**	6r. multicoloured	1·00	1·25

1992. Pioneers of Freedom (5th series). As T **428**. Each brown and green.

870	1r. Syed Suleman Nadvi	1·40	1·60
871	1r. Nawab Iftikhar Hussain Khan Mamdot	1·40	1·60
872	1r. Maulana Muhammad Shibli Naumani	1·40	1·60

452 Scout Badge and Salute

1992. Sixth Islamic Scout Jamboree and 4th Islamic Scouts Conference. Multicoloured.

873	6r. Type **452**	50	75
874	6r. Conference centre and scout salute	50	75

453 College Building

1992. Centenary of Islamia College, Lahore.

875	**453**	3r. multicoloured	70	75

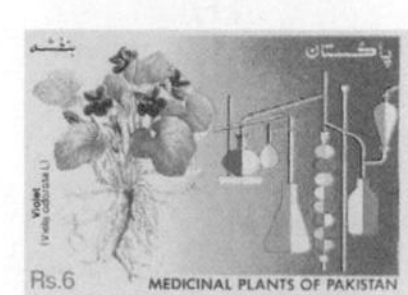

454 "Viola odorata" (flower) and Symbolic Drug Manufacture

1992. Medicinal Plants (1st series).

876	**454**	6r. multicoloured	3·25	2·25

See also Nos. 903, 946, 1010, 1026, 1037, 1099, 1123, 1142, 1159, 1185 and 1333/4.

455 Emblem

1992. Extraordinary Ministerial Council Session of Economic Co-operation Organization, Islamabad.

877	**455**	7r. multicoloured	1·00	1·75

456 Emblems and Field

1992. International Conference on Nutrition, Rome.

878	**456**	7r. multicoloured	70	1·25

457 Alhambra Palace, Granada, Spain

1992. Cultural Heritage of Muslim Granada.

879	**457**	7r. multicoloured	1·00	1·50

458 Mallard

1992. Water Birds. Multicoloured.

880	5r. Type **458** (A)	60	70
881	5r. Type **458** (B)	60	70
882	5r. Type **458** (C)	60	70
883	5r. Type **458** (D)	60	70
884	5r. Greylag goose (A)	60	70
885	5r. As No. 884 (B)	60	70
886	5r. As No. 884 (C)	60	70
887	5r. As No. 884 (D)	60	70
888	5r. Gadwall (A)	60	70
889	5r. As No. 888 (B)	60	70
890	5r. As No. 888 (C)	60	70
891	5r. As No. 888 (D)	60	70
892	5r. Common shelduck (A)	60	70
893	5r. As No. 892 (B)	60	70
894	5r. As No. 892 (C)	60	70
895	5r. As No. 892 (D)	60	70

Four different versions of designs as T **458**:

Type A. "Rs.5" at right with rainbow 8 mm beneath "P" of "PAKISTAN"

Type B. "Rs.5" at right with rainbow 2 mm beneath "P"

Type C. "Rs.5" at left with rainbow 2 mm beneath "N" of "PAKISTAN"

Type D. "Rs.5" at left with rainbow 8 mm beneath "N"

Nos. 880/95 were printed together, *se-tenant*, each horizontal row having a composite design of a rainbow.

459 Baluchistan Costume

1993. Women's Traditional Costumes. Multicoloured.

896	6r. Type **459**	1·25	1·50
897	6r. Punjab	1·25	1·50
898	6r. Sindh	1·25	1·50
899	6r. North-west Frontier Province	1·25	1·50

460 Clasped Hands and Islamic Symbols

1993. 21st Conference of Islamic Foreign Ministers, Karachi.

900	**460**	1r. multicoloured	75	10
901	**460**	6r. multicoloured	2·25	2·75

461 I.T.U. Emblem

1993. 25th Anniv of World Telecommunication Day.

902	**461**	1r. multicoloured	1·50	30

1993. Medicinal Plants (2nd issue). As T **454**. Multicoloured.

903	6r. Fennel and symbolic drug manufacture	3·50	2·75

1993. Pioneers of Freedom (6th series). As T **428**. Each brown and red.

904	1r. Ghulam Mohammad Bhurgri	1·40	1·40
905	1r. Ahmed Yar Khan	1·40	1·40
906	1r. Mohammad Pir Sahib Zakori Sharif	1·40	1·40

462 College Building and Arms

1993. Centenary of Gordon College, Rawalpindi.

907	**462**	2r. multicoloured	2·25	2·00

463 Juniper Forest

1993. Campaign to Save the Juniper Forest, Ziarat.

907a	**463**	1r. multicoloured	2·00	35
908	**463**	7r. multicoloured	4·00	3·50

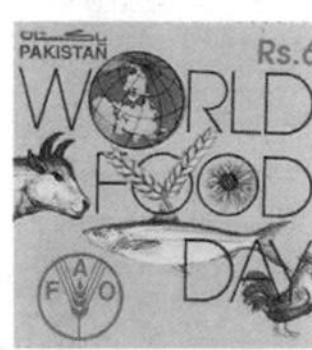

464 Globe, Produce and Emblem

1993. World Food Day.

909	**464**	6r. multicoloured	1·50	1·60

465 Burn Hall Institution, Abbottabad

1993. 50th Anniv of Burn Hall Institutions.

910	**465**	7r. multicoloured	3·00	3·25

466 Peace Dove carrying Letter and National Flags

1993. South and West Asia Postal Union Commemoration.

911	**466**	7r. multicoloured	3·00	3·25

467 Congress Emblem

1993. Pakistan College of Physicians and Surgeons International Medical Congress.
912 **467** 1r. multicoloured 2·50 40

468 Wazir Mansion (birthplace)

1993. 45th Death Anniv of Mohammed Ali Jinnah.
913 **468** 1r. multicoloured 2·00 30

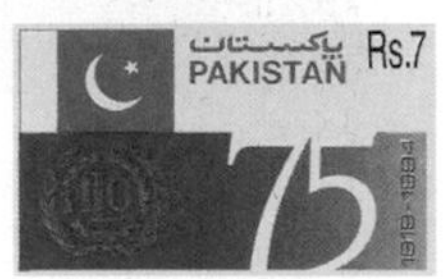

469 Emblem and National Flag

1994. 75th Anniv of I.L.O.
914 **469** 7r. multicoloured 1·75 2·75

470 Ratan Jot (flower)

1994. Ratification of International Biological Diversity Convention. Multicoloured.
915 6r. Type **470** 50 65
916 6r. Wetlands habitat 50 65
917 6r. Golden mahseer ("Tor puttitora") (fish) 50 65
918 6r. Brown bear 50 65

471 Silhouette of Family and Emblem

1994. International Year of the Family.
919 **471** 7r. multicoloured 80 1·00

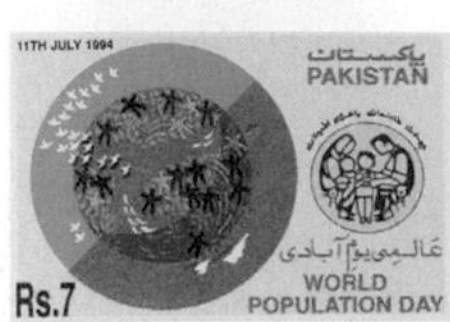

472 Symbolic Globe and Logo

1994. World Population Day.
920 **472** 7r. multicoloured 1·00 1·00

1994. Pioneers of Freedom (7th series). As T **428**. Each brown and green.
921 1r. Nawab Mohsin-Ul-Mulk 35 45
922 1r. Sir Shahnawaz Bhutto 35 45
923 1r. Nawab Viqar-Ul-Mulk 35 45
924 1r. Pir Ilahi Bux 35 45
925 1r. Sheikh Abdul Qadir 35 45
926 1r. Dr. Sir Ziauddin Ahmed 35 45
927 1r. Jam Mir Ghulam Qadir Khan 35 45
928 1r. Sardar Aurangzeb Khan 35 45

473 Hala Pottery, Pakistan

1994. Indonesia–Pakistan Economic and Cultural Co-operation Organization. Multicoloured.
929 10r. Type **473** 2·00 2·50
930 10r. Lombok pottery, Indonesia 2·00 2·50

474 Boy writing and Globe

1994. International Literacy Day.
931 **474** 7r. multicoloured 1·00 1·25

475 Mohammed Ali Jinnah and Floral Pattern

1994
932 **475** 1r. multicoloured 35 10
933 **475** 2r. multicoloured 50 10
934 **475** 3r. multicoloured 65 10
935 **475** 4r. multicoloured 70 10
936 **475** 5r. multicoloured 75 15
937 **475** 7r. multicoloured 1·00 20
938 **475** 10r. multicoloured 80 30
939 **475** 12r. multicoloured 90 60
940 **475** 15r. multicoloured 1·00 80
941 **475** 20r. multicoloured 1·10 1·00
942 **475** 25r. multicoloured 1·25 1·25
942z **475** 28r. multicoloured 1·25 1·25
943 **475** 30r. multicoloured 1·40 1·40

476 Gateway and Emblem

1994. Second South Asian Association for Regional Co-operation and 12th National Scout Jamborees, Quetta.
944 **476** 7r. multicoloured 1·00 1·10

477 Engraver

1994. First Int Festival of Islamic Artisans at Work.
945 **477** 2r. multicoloured 1·50 60

478 Henbane

1994. Medicinal Plants (3rd issue).
946 **478** 6r. multicoloured 1·00 1·00

479 Abu-l Kasim Firdausi (poet)

1994. Millenary of "Shah Namah" (poem).
947 **479** 1r. multicoloured 35 15

480 Museum Building

1994. Centenary of Lahore Museum.
948 **480** 4r. multicoloured 60 80

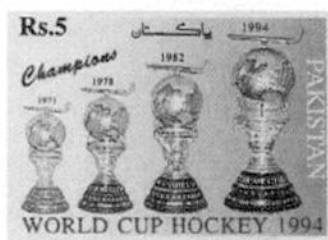

481 World Cup Trophies for 1971, 1978, 1982 and 1994

1994. Victory of Pakistan in World Cup Hockey Championship.
949 **481** 5r. multicoloured 1·00 1·00

482 Tourist Attractions

1995. 20th Anniv of World Tourism Organization.
950 **482** 4r. multicoloured 1·25 1·40

483 Khan Khushal of Khattak and Army

1995. Khan Khushal of Khattak (poet) Commemoration.
951 **483** 7r. multicoloured 2·25 2·25

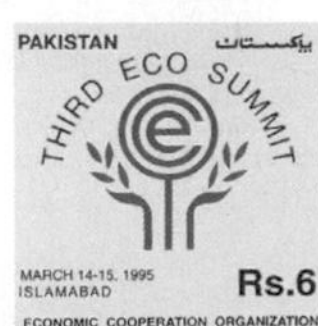

484 E.C.O. Emblem

1995. Third Economic Co-operation Organization Summit, Islamabad.
952 **484** 6r. multicoloured 1·50 1·50

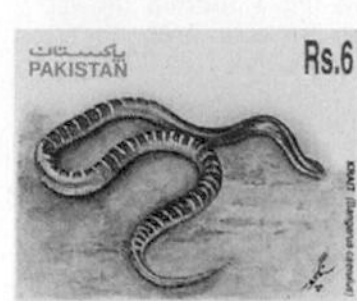

485 Common Indian Krait

1995. Snakes. Multicoloured.
953 6r. Type **485** 70 90
954 6r. Indian cobra 70 90
955 6r. Indian python 70 90
956 6r. Russell's viper 70 90

486 Globe and Environments

1995. Earth Day.
957 **486** 6r. multicoloured 70 80

487 Victoria Carriage, Karachi

1995. Traditional Transport.
958 **487** 5r. multicoloured 1·00 1·00

488 Prime Minister Tansu Ciller of Turkey and Rose

1995. First Muslim Women Parliamentarians' Conference, Islamabad. Multicoloured.
959 5r. Type **488** 1·00 1·50
960 5r. Prime Minister Benazir Bhutto and jasmine 1·00 1·50

1995. Pioneers of Freedom (8th series). As T **428**. Each brown and green.
961 1r. Maulana Shaukat Ali 80 70
962 1r. Chaudhry Ghulam Abbas 80 70

489 Oil Sardine

1995. Fish. Multicoloured.
963 6r. Type **489** 70 85
964 6r. Mozambique mouthbrooder ("Tilapia") 70 85
965 6r. Brown trout 70 85
966 6r. Rohu 70 85

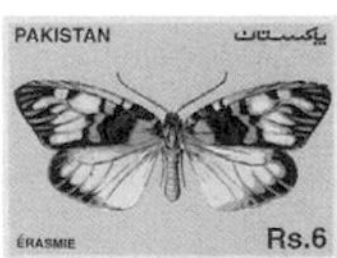

490 "Erasmia pulchella"

1995. Butterflies. Multicoloured.
967 6r. Type **490** 70 90
968 6r. "Callicore astarte" (inscr "Catogramme") 70 90
969 6r. "Ixias pyrene" 70 90
970 6r. "Heliconius" 70 90

491 Major Raja Aziz Bhatti Shaheed and Medal

1995. Defence Day.
971 **491** 1r.25 multicoloured 2·00 1·50

492 Presentation Convent School, Rawalpindi

1995. Centenary of Presentation Convent School, Rawalpindi.
972 **492** 1r.25 multicoloured 1·50 1·00

493 Women Soldiers, Golfer and Scientist

1995. Fourth World Conference on Women, Peking. Multicoloured.

973	1r.25 Type **493**	30	45
974	1r.25 Women graduates, journalist, computer operator and technicians	30	45
975	1r.25 Sewing machinist and women at traditional crafts	30	45
976	1r.25 Army officer and women at traditional tasks	30	45

494 "Louis Pasteur in Laboratory" (Edelfelt)

1995. Death Centenary of Louis Pasteur (chemist).

977	**494**	5r. multicoloured	1·00	1·00

495

1995

978	**495**	5p. blue, orange and brown	15	20
979	**495**	15p. orange, violet and brown	40	20
980	**495**	25p. blue, mauve and purple	50	10
981	**495**	75p. green, brown and deep brown	1·25	10

496 Liaquat Ali Khan

1995. Birth Centenary (1995) of Liaquat Ali Khan (statesman).

987	**496**	1r.25 multicoloured	1·00	40

497 Village and Irrigated Fields

1995. 50th Anniv of F.A.O.

988	**497**	1r.25 multicoloured	1·00	40

498 Pakistani Soldier treating Somali Refugees

1995. 50th Anniv of United Nations.

989	**498**	7r. multicoloured	1·25	1·60

499 Education Emblem

1995. 80th Anniv (1993) of Kinnaird College for Women, Lahore.

990	**499**	1r.25 multicoloured	1·00	40

500 Hand holding Book, Eye and Pen Nib

1995. International Conference of Writers and Intellectuals, Islamabad.

991	**500**	1r.25 multicoloured	1·00	40

501 Children holding Hands and S.A.A.R.C. Logo

1995. Tenth Anniv of South Asian Association for Regional Co-operation.

992	**501**	1r.25 multicoloured	60	30

502 Jet Skier

1995. National Water Sports Gala, Karachi. Multicoloured.

993	1r.25 Type **502**	35	45
994	1r.25 Local punts	35	45
995	1r.25 Sailboard	35	45
996	1r.25 Water skier	35	45

503 Mortar Board and Books

1995. 20th Anniv of Allama Iqbal Open University.

997	**503**	1r.25 multicoloured	60	30

504 Balochistan Quetta University Building

1995. 25th Anniv of Balochistan Quetta University.

998	**504**	1r.25 multicoloured	60	30

505 Zulfikar Ali Bhutto,Flag and Crowd

1996. 17th Death Anniv of Zulfikar Ali Bhutto (former Prime Minister). Multicoloured.

999	1r.25 Type **505**	1·25	20
1000	4r. Zulfikar Ali Bhutto and flag (53×31 mm)	2·75	2·25
MS1001	118×74 mm. 8r. Zulfikar Ali Bhutto and crowd. Imperf	2·25	2·50

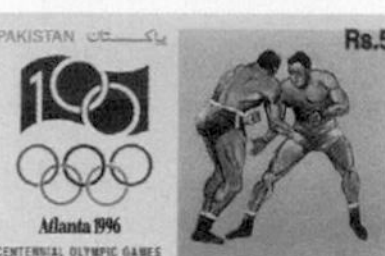
506 Wrestling

1996. Olympic Games, Atlanta. Multicoloured.

1002	5r. Type **506**	65	80
1003	5r. Boxing	65	80
1004	5r. Pierre de Coubertin	65	80
1005	5r. Hockey	65	80
MS1006	112×100 mm. 25r. Designs as Nos. 1002/5, but without face values. Imperf	3·00	3·75

1996. Pioneers of Freedom (9th series). Allama Abdullah Yousuf Ali. As T **428**.

1007	1r. brown and green	40	20

507 G.P.O. Building, Lahore

1996. Restoration of G.P.O. Building, Lahore.

1008	**507**	5r. multicoloured	50	60

508 Symbolic Open Book and Text

1996. International Literacy Day.

1009	**508**	2r. multicoloured	40	30

509 Yarrow

1996. Medicinal Plants (4th series).

1010	**509**	3r. multicoloured	1·75	1·00

510 Faiz Ahmed Faiz

1997. 86th Birth Anniv of Faiz Ahmed Faiz (poet).

1011	**510**	3r. multicoloured	60	60

511 Golden Jubilee and O.I.C. Emblems

1997. Special Summit Conference of Organization of Islamic Countries commemorating 50th anniv of Pakistan.

1012	**511**	2r. multicoloured	35	35

512 Amir Timur

1997. 660th Birth Anniv of Timur (founder of Timurid Empire).

1013	**512**	3r. multicoloured	60	60

513 Jalal-al-din Moulana Rumi

1997. Pakistan–Iran Joint Issue.

1014	3r. Type **513**	50	65
1015	3r. Allama Mohammad Iqbal (poet)	50	65

514 Apple

1997. Fruit.

1016	**514**	2r. multicoloured	35	35

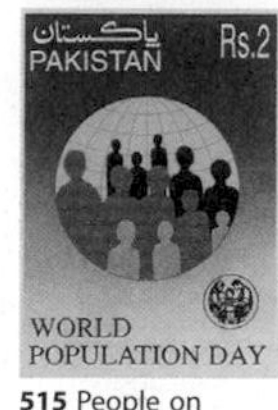
515 People on Globe

1997. World Population Day.

1017	**515**	2r. multicoloured	35	35

516 Stylized Dove of Peace

1997. 40th Anniv of Co-operation between International Atomic Energy Agency and Pakistan Atomic Energy Corporation.

1018	**516**	2r. multicoloured	70	35

1997. Pioneers of Freedom (10th series). As T **428**. Each brown and green.

1019	1r. Mohammad Ayub Khuhro	75	75
1020	1r. Begum Salma Tassaduq Hussain	75	75

517 Mohammed Ali Jinnah

1997. 50th Anniv of Independence. Multicoloured.

1021	3r. Type **517**	60	70
1022	3r. Allama Mohammad Iqbal	60	70
1023	3r. Mohtarma Fatima Jinnah	60	70
1024	3r. Liaquat Ali Khan	60	70

518 College Building

1997. 75th Anniv of Lahore College for Women.

1025	**518**	3r. multicoloured	1·50	1·00

519 Garlic

1997. Medicinal Plants (5th series).

1026	**519**	2r. multicoloured	1·50	65

520 Himalayan Monal Pheasant

1997. Wildlife Protection (18th series).

1027	**520**	2r. multicoloured	2·25	1·25

521 Globe and Cracked Ozone Layer

1997. Save Ozone Layer Campaign.

1028	**521**	3r. multicoloured	1·60	1·25

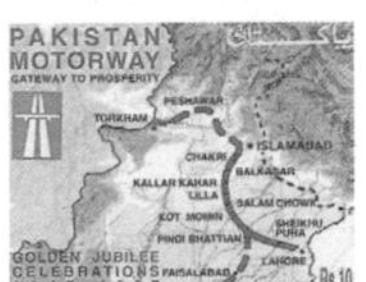

522 Map of Pakistan Motorway Project

1997. Pakistan Motorway Project.

1029	**522**	10r. multicoloured	2·25	2·50
MS1030 117×97 mm. No. 1029 (sold at 15r.)			2·75	3·00

523 Emblem and Disabled People

1997. International Day for the Disabled.

1031	**523**	4r. multicoloured	1·50	1·00

524 Karachi Grammar School

1997. 150th Anniv of Karachi Grammar School.

1032	**524**	2r. multicoloured	1·50	70

525 Mirza Ghalib

1998. Birth Bicentenary (1997) of Mirza Ghalib (poet).

1033	**525**	2r. multicoloured	60	30

No. 1033 is inscr "DEATH ANNIVERSARY".

526 Servicemen, Pakistan Flag and "50"

1998. 50th Anniv (1997) of Armed Forces.

1034	**526**	7r. multicoloured	1·00	1·00

527 Sir Syed Ahmed Khan

1998. Death Centenary of Sir Syed Ahmed Khan (social reformer).

1035	**527**	7r. brown, green & stone	1·00	1·25

528 Olympic Torch and Sports

1998. 27th National Games, Peshawar.

1036	**528**	7r. multicoloured	1·00	1·10

529 Thornapple

1998. Medicinal Plants (6th series).

1037	**529**	2r. multicoloured	1·50	55

530 Silver Jubilee Emblem

1998. 25th Anniv of Senate.

1038	**530**	2r. multicoloured	30	15
1039	**530**	5r. multicoloured	70	85

531 Mohammed Ali Jinnah

1998

1039a	**531**	1r. red and black	15	10
1040	**531**	2r. blue and red	25	10
1041	**531**	3r. green and brown	30	10
1042	**531**	4r. purple and orange	40	10
1043	**531**	5r. brown and green	40	10
1044	**531**	6r. green and blue	50	20
1045	**531**	7r. red and violet	60	25
1045z		8r. black, emerald and dull orange (1.10.10)		

532 College Building

1998. Cent of Government College, Faisalabad.

1046	**532**	5r. multicoloured	70	70

533 "Mohammed Ali Jinnah" (S. Akhtar)

1998. 50th Death Anniv of Mohammed Ali Jinnah.

1047	**533**	15r. multicoloured	2·25	2·50
MS1048 72×100 mm. **533** 15r. multi-coloured (sold at 20r.)			2·50	3·00

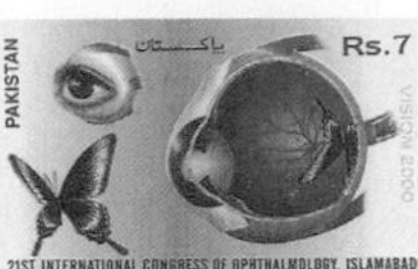

534 Cross-section of Eye

1998. 21st International Ophthalmology Congress, Islamabad.

1049	**534**	7r. multicoloured	1·50	1·50

535 United Nations Emblems and Bukhari

1998. Birth Centenary of Syed Ahmed Shah Patrus Bukhari.

1050	**535**	5r. multicoloured	1·25	1·00

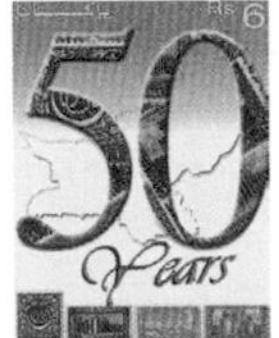

536 Map, "50 years" and Stamps

1998. 50th Anniv of Philately in Pakistan.

1051	**536**	6r. multicoloured	65	65

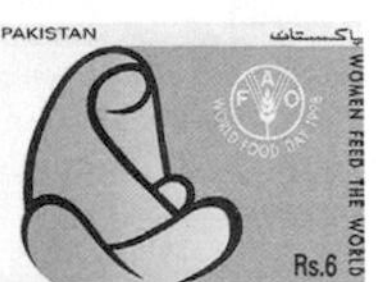

537 Mother and Child

1998. World Food Day.

1052	**537**	6r. multicoloured	75	75

538 Dr. Abdus Salam

1998. Scientists of Pakistan (1st series). Dr. Abdus Salam.

1053	**538**	2r. multicoloured	50	25

See also No. 1068.

539 Satellite Dish Aerial

1998. "Better Pakistan" Development Plan. Multicoloured.

1054	2r. Type **539**	45	55
1055	2r. Combine harvester	45	55
1056	2r. Airliner	45	55
1057	2r. Children and doctor	45	55

540 Globe and Human Rights Emblem

1998. 50th Anniv of Universal Declaration of Human Rights.

1058	**540**	6r. multicoloured	1·25	1·25

541 Pakistani Woman carrying Water Pot

1998. 50th Anniv of UNICEF in Pakistan. Multicoloured.

1059	2r. Type **541**	30	40
1060	2r. Woman reading	30	40
1061	2r. Woman with goitre	30	40
1062	2r. Young boy receiving oral vaccine	30	40

542 Earth seen from Space

1998. International Year of the Ocean.

1063	**542**	5r. multicoloured	1·25	1·00

543 Marchers and Route Map

1998. Qaumi Parcham March, Khyber to Chaghi.

1064	**543**	2r. multicoloured	40	25

544 Centenary Logo

1999. Centenary of Saudi Dynasty of Saudi Arabia. Multicoloured.

1065	2r. Type **544**	30	10
1066	15r. As Type **544**, but with mosaic pattern in corners	1·75	2·00
MS1067 73×100 mm. 15r. No. 1066 (sold at 20r.)		2·50	3·00

545 Dr. Salimuz Zaman Siddiqui

1999. Scientists of Pakistan (2nd series). Dr. Salimuz Zaman Siddiqui.

1068	**545**	5r. multicoloured	60	60

546 Mountains and Pakistan Flag

1999. "Atoms for Peace".

1069	**546**	5r. multicoloured	60	60

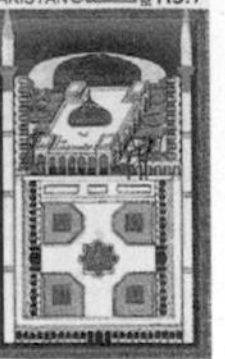

547 Plan and View of Mosque

1999. Completion of Data Darbar Mosque Complex, Lahore.
1070 **547** 7r. multicoloured 75 1·00

548 Fasting Buddha Statue (drapery on left knee)

1999. Archaeological Heritage. Multicoloured.
1071 7r. Type **548** 70 85
1072 7r. Fasting Buddha (drapery on right knee) 70 85
MS1073 107×90 mm. Nos. 1071/2 (sold at 25r.) 2·25 3·00

No. **MS**1073 includes the "China '99" International Stamp Exhibition, Beijing, logo on the margin.

549 Red Cross International Committee Emblem and "50"

1999. 50th Anniv of Geneva Conventions.
1074 **549** 5r. red and black 60 50

1999. Pioneers of Freedom (11th series). As T **428**. Each brown and green.
1075 2r. Maulana Abdul Hamid Badayuni 45 50
1076 2r. Chaudhry Muhammad Ali 45 50
1077 2r. Sir Adamjee Haji Dawood 45 50

550 Ustad Nusrat Fateh Ali Khan

1999. Ustad Nusrat Fateh Ali Khan (musician) Commemoration.
1078 **550** 2r. multicoloured 1·25 60

551 Islamic Development Bank Building

1999. 25th Anniv of Islamic Development Bank.
1079 **551** 5r. multicoloured 1·00 1·00

552 Crowd celebrating

1999. 50th Anniv of People's Republic of China. Multicoloured.
1080 2r. Type **552** 20 20
1081 15r. Bust of Mao Tse-tung (Chinese leader) and emblem (horiz) 1·25 1·75

553 "Enterprise" Sailing Dinghy

1999. Ninth Asian Sailing Championship. Sailing Craft. Multicoloured.
1082 2r. Type **553** 50 50
1083 2r. "470" dinghy 50 50
1084 2r. "Optimist" dinghy 50 50
1085 2r. "Laser" dinghy 50 50
1086 2r. "Mistral" sailboard 50 50

554 "Optimist" Sailing Dinghies

1999. Tenth Asian "Optimist" Sailing Championship.
1087 **554** 2r. multicoloured 60 40

555 U.P.U. Emblem

1999. 125th Anniv of Universal Postal Union.
1088 **555** 10r. multicoloured 1·00 1·25

556 Hakim Mohammed Said

1999. First Death Anniv of Hakim Mohammed Said.
1089 **556** 5r. multicoloured 60 60

557 National Bank of Pakistan Building

1999. 50th Anniv of National Bank of Pakistan.
1090 **557** 5r. multicoloured 1·25 70

558 Evolution of the "Shell" Emblem

1999. Centenary of Shell in Pakistan.
1091 **558** 4r. multicoloured 1·25 75

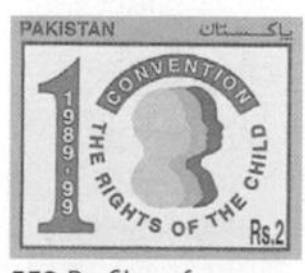

559 Profiles of Children in "10"

1999. Tenth Anniv of United Nations Rights of the Child Convention.
1092 **559** 2r. emerald, green and red 30 30

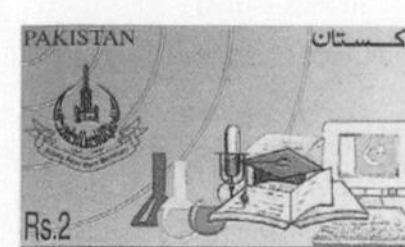

560 Science Equipment, Books and Computer

1999. 25th Anniv of Allama Iqbal Open University. Multicoloured.
1093 2r. Type **560** 20 15
1094 3r. Scholastic symbols as Type **560** 30 30
1095 5r. Map of Pakistan 1·25 90

561 Josh Malihabadi

1999. Birth Centenary of Josh Malihabadi (poet).
1096 **561** 5r. multicoloured 60 60

562 Dr. Afzal Qadri and Locusts

1999. 25th Death Anniv of Dr. Afzal Qadri (scientist).
1097 **562** 3r. multicoloured 60 40

563 Ghulam Bari Aleeg

1999. 50th Death Anniv of Ghulam Bari Aleeg (writer).
1098 **563** 5r. multicoloured 1·00 65

564 Plantain

1999. Medicinal Plants (7th series).
1099 **564** 5r. multicoloured 1·75 1·00

565 Mosque

1999. Eid-ul-Fitr Greetings.
1100 **565** 2r. multicoloured 40 25
1101 **565** 15r. multicoloured 2·50 3·00

566 Woman and Young Boy

2000. 25th Anniv of S.O.S. Children's Villages in Pakistan.
1102 **566** 2r. multicoloured 65 30

567 Racing Cyclists

2000. Centenary of International Cycling Union.
1103 **567** 2r. multicoloured 1·75 80

568 Doves

2000. Pakistan Convention on Human Rights and Human Dignity.
1104 **568** 2r. multicoloured 60 30

569 College Building

2000. Centenary of Edwardes College, Peshawar.
1105 **569** 2r. multicoloured 60 30

570 Mahomed Ali Habib

2000. Mahomed Ali Habib (founder of Habib Bank Ltd) Commemoration.
1106 **570** 2r. multicoloured 60 30

571 Emblems and Symbols

2000. 50th Anniv of Institute of Cost and Management Accountants. Multicoloured.
1107 2r. Type **571** 30 20
1108 15r. Emblems, graph, keyboard and globe 2·00 2·50

572 Ahmed Jaffer

2000. Tenth Death Anniv of Ahmed Jaffer (prominent businessman).
1109 **572** 10r. multicoloured 1·25 1·25

573 "Sarfaroshaane Tehreeke Pakistan" (detail)

2000. "Sarfaroshaane Tehreeke Pakistan" (painting). Showing different details. Multicoloured.
1110 5r. Type **573** 50 55
1111 5r. Bullock carts with tree in foreground 50 55
1112 5r. Bullock carts and crowd carrying Pakistan flag 50 55
1113 5r. Unloading bullock cart 50 55

574 Captain Muhammad Sarwar

2000. Defence Day. Showing winners of Nishan-e-Haider medal. Multicoloured.
1114 5r. Type **574** 1·00 1·00
1115 5r. Major Tufail Muhammad 1·00 1·00

See also No. 1173/4.

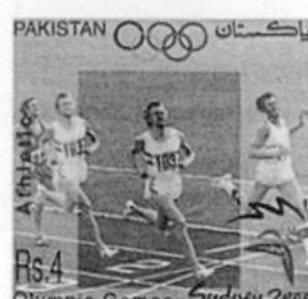

575 Athletics

2000. Olympic Games, Sydney. Multicoloured.
1116 4r. Type **575** 70 70
1117 4r. Hockey 70 70
1118 4r. Weightlifting 70 70
1119 4r. Cycling 70 70

576 Emblem and Building

2000. 125th Anniv of National College of Arts, Lahore.
1120 **576** 5r. multicoloured 55 65

577 Conference Emblem

2000. "Creating the Future" Business Conference.
1121 **577** 5r. multicoloured 1·00 75

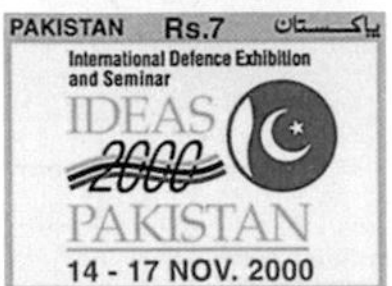

578 Exhibition Emblem

2000. "Ideas 2000" International Defence Exhibition and Seminar.
1122 **578** 7r. multicoloured 1·25 1·25

579 Liquorice

2000. Medicinal Plants (8th series).
1123 **579** 2r. multicoloured 1·50 45

580 Crippled Child and Rotary Emblem

2000. "A World Without Polio" Campaign.
1124 **580** 2r. multicoloured 60 25

581 Refugee Family and Emblems

2000. 50th Anniv of United Nations High Commissioner for Refugees.
1125 **581** 2r. multicoloured 35 25

582 Hafeez Jalandhri

2001. Birth Centenary of Hafeez Jalandhri (poet).
1126 **582** 2r. multicoloured 1·00 40

583 Habib Bank AG Zurich Head Office

2001. Habib Bank AG Zurich Commemoration.
1127 **583** 5r. multicoloured 1·50 1·25

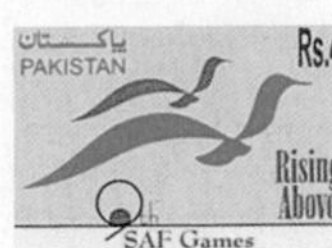

584 Chashma Nuclear Power Station

2001. Opening of Chashma Nuclear Power Station.
1128 **584** 4r. multicoloured 1·25 1·00

585 S.A.F. Games Emblem

2001. Ninth S.A.F. Games, Islamabad.
1129 **585** 4r. multicoloured (blue background) 75 80
1130 **585** 4r. multicoloured (pink background) 75 80

586 "Ma Gu's Birthday Offering"

2001. 50th Anniv of Pakistan–China Friendship. Multicoloured.
1131 4r. Type **586** 70 80
1132 4r. "Two Pakistani Women drawing Water" 70 80
1133 4r. Girls in traditional Yugur and Hunza costumes 70 80
No. 1131 is inscribed "BIRTTHDAY" in error.

587 Mohammad Ali Jinnah

2001. 125th Birth Anniv of Mohammad Ali Jinnah ("Quaid-e-Azam") (1st issue).
1134 **587** 4r. multicoloured 60 80
See also Nos. 1152/6.

2001. Defence Day. As T **574** showing winners of Nishan-e-Haider medal. Multicoloured.
1135 4r. Major Shabbir Sharif Shaheed 75 75
1136 4r. Major Mohammad Akram Shaheed 75 75

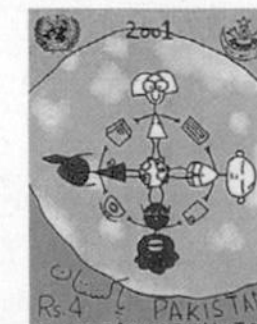

588 Goat Emblem and Traditional Architecture

2001. Sindh Festival, Karachi.
1137 **588** 4r. yellow, black and green 60 60

589 Khawaja Ghulam Farid

2001. Death Centenary of Khawaja Ghulam Farid (poet).
1138 **589** 5r. multicoloured 60 60

590 "Children encircling Globe" (Urska Golob)

2001. U.N. Year of Dialogue among Civilizations.
1139 **590** 4r. multicoloured 50 50

591 Syed Imitaz Ali Taj

2001. Syed Imitaz Ali Taj (writer) Commemoration.
1140 **591** 5r. multicoloured 60 60

592 Pres. Saparmurat Niyazov of Turkmenistan

2001. Tenth Anniv of Turkmenistan Independence.
1141 **592** 5r. multicoloured 60 60

593 Peppermint

2001. Medicinal Plants (9th series).
1142 **593** 4r. multicoloured 2·00 1·25

594 Convent of Jesus and Mary, Lahore

2001. 125th Anniv of Convent of Jesus and Mary, Lahore.
1143 **594** 4r. multicoloured 1·00 75

595 Dr. Ishtiaq Husain Qureshi

2001. 20th Death Anniv of Dr. Ishtiaq Husain Qureshi (historian).
1144 **595** 4r. multicoloured 50 50

596 Blue Throat

2001. Birds. Multicoloured.
1145 4r. Type **596** 1·25 1·25
1146 4r. Hoopoe 1·25 1·25
1147 4r. Pin-tailed sandgrouse 1·25 1·25
1148 4r. Magpie robin 1·25 1·25

597 Handshake beneath Flags of U.A.E. and Pakistan

2001. 30th Anniv of Diplomatic Relations between Pakistan and United Arab Emirates. Multicoloured.
1149 5r. Type **597** 50 25
1150 30r. Pres. Sheikh Zayed bin Sultan Al Nahyan of U.A.E. and Mohammed Ali Jinnah (horiz) 3·25 4·00

598 Nishtar Medical College, Multan

2001. 50th Anniv of Nishtar Medical College, Multan.
1151 **598** 5r. multicoloured 70 55

599 Mohammad Ali Jinnah taking Oath as Governor General, 1947

2001. 125th Birth Anniv of Mohammad Ali Jinnah ("Quaid-e-Azam") (2nd issue). Multicoloured.
1152 4r. Type **599** 30 35
1153 4r. Opening State Bank, Karachi, 1948 30 35
1154 4r. Taking salute, Peshawar, 1948 30 35
1155 4r. Inspecting guard of honour, 1948 (55×27 mm) 30 35
1156 4r. With anti-aircraft gun crew, 1948 (55×27 mm) 30 35

600 Troops and Ordnance

2001. 50th Anniv of Pakistan Ordnance Factories.
1157 **600** 4r. multicoloured 1·00 60

601 Samandar Khan Samandar

2002. Samandar Khan Samandar (poet) Commemoration.
1158 **601** 5r. multicoloured 60 60

602 Hyssop

2002. Medicinal Plants (10th series).
1159 **602** 5r. multicoloured 1·75 1·25

603 Statues of Buddha

2002. 50th Anniv of Diplomatic Relations between Pakistan and Japan.
1160 **603** 5r. multicoloured 50 50

604 Pakistan and Kyrgyzstan Flags

2002. Tenth Anniv of Diplomatic Relations between Pakistan and Kyrgyzstan.
1161 **604** 5r. multicoloured 50 50

605 Anwar Ratol Mangoes

2002. Fruit of Pakistan. Mangoes. Multicoloured.
1162 4r. Type **605** 65 75
1163 4r. Dusehri mangoes 65 75
1164 4r. Chaunsa mangoes 65 75
1165 4r. Sindhri mango 65 75

606 Begum Noor us Sabah

2002. 55th Independence Day Celebrations. Political Figures. Multicoloured.
1166 4r. Type **606** 60 75
1167 4r. I. Chundrigar 60 75
1168 4r. Habib Ibrahim Rahimtoola 60 75
1169 4r. Qazi Mureed Ahmed 60 75

607 Children with Animals and Pakistan Flag

2002. World Summit on Sustainable Development, Johannesburg. Multicoloured.
1170 4r. Type **607** 50 50
1171 4r. Mountain and cartoon character (37×37 mm) 50 50

608 Mohammad Aly Rangoonwala (politician/ philanthropist)

2002. Mohammad Aly Rangoonwala Commem.
1172 **608** 4r. multicoloured 60 50

2002. Defence Day. As T **574** showing winners of Nishan-e-Haider medal. Multicoloured.
1173 4r. Lance Naik Muhammad Mahfuz Shaheed 70 70
1173b 4r. Sawar Muhammad Hussain Shaheed 70 70

609 Muhammad Iqbal in Academic Gown

2002. 125th Birth Anniv of Muhammad Iqbal (writer). Multicoloured.
1174 4r. Type **609** 50 50
1175 4r. Muhammad Iqbal in library 50 50

610 "Eid Mubarak"

2002. Eid-ul-Fitr Festival.
1176 **610** 4r. multicoloured 50 50

611 Hakim Muhammad Hassan Qarshi and Plants

2002. Hakim Muhammad Hassan Qarshi (pioneer of Tibb homeopathic medicine) Commemoration.
1177 **611** 4r. multicoloured 1·00 55

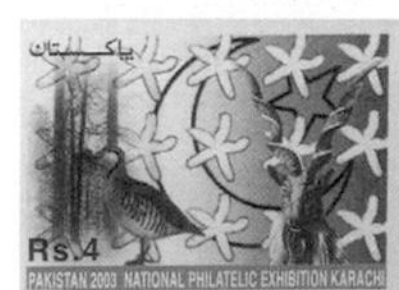
612 Red-legged Partridge, Markhor and White Flowers

2003. National Philatelic Exhibition, Karachi.
1178 **612** 4r. multicoloured 1·50 1·10

613 Anniversary Emblem

2003. 50th Anniv of Pakistan Academy of Sciences.
1179 **613** 4r. multicoloured 70 70

614 Minaret Emblem

2003. Centenary Celebrations of North West Frontier Province.
1180 **614** 4r. multicoloured 60 60

615 Golden Jubilee Emblem

2003. 50th Anniv of Pakistan Council of Scientific and Industrial Research, Islamabad.
1181 **615** 4r. brown, green and yellow 60 60

616 Prof. A. B. A. Haleem

2003. Prof. A. B. A. Haleem (1st Vice Chancellor of Karachi University) Commemoration.
1182 **616** 2r. multicoloured 55 35

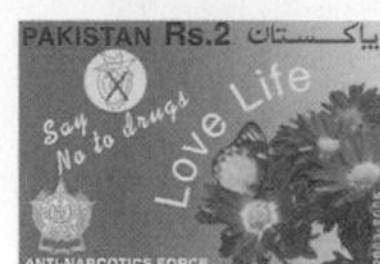
617 Flowers and Anti Narcotics Force Badge

2003. "Say No to Drugs".
1183 **617** 2r. multicoloured 1·00 55

618 Sir Syed Memorial, Islamabad

2003. Sir Syed Memorial, Islamabad.
1184 **618** 2r. multicoloured 45 30

619 *Rosa damascene*

2003. Medicinal Plants (11th series).
1185 **619** 2r. multicoloured 1·50 65

620 Fatima Jinnah

2003. 110th Birth Anniv of Fatima Jinnah (politician and campaigner for women's rights).
1186 **620** 4r. multicoloured 55 45

621 Abdul Rahman (PO employee killed in raid, 2002)

2003. Commemorations. Multicoloured.
1187 2r. Type **621** 35 35
1188 2r. M. A. Rahim (trade union leader and philanthropist) 35 35

622 Moulana Abdul Sattar Khan Niazi (politician, 88th)

2003. Birth Anniversaries. Multicoloured.
1189 2r. Type **622** 40 50
1190 2r. Muhammad Yousaf Khattak (politician, 86th) 40 50
1191 2r. Moulana Muhammad Ismail Zabeeh (politician, centenary) 40 50

623 Emblem

2003. United Nations Literacy Decade.
1192 **623** 1r. multicoloured 20 20

624 Pilot Officer Rashid Minhas Shaheed and Nishan-e-Haider Medal

2003. 32nd Death Anniv of Pilot Officer Rashid Minhas.
1193 **624** 2r. multicoloured 1·25 55

625 Pakistan Academy of Letters, Islamabad

2003. 25th Anniv of Pakistan Academy of Letters (2001).
1194 **625** 2r. multicoloured 40 25

626 Karakoram Highway

2003. 25th Anniv of Karakoram Highway.
1195 **626** 2r. multicoloured 1·00 50

627 Nanga Parbat

2003. 50th Anniv of First Ascent of Nanga Parbat Mountain.
1196 **627** 2r. multicoloured 1·00 50

628 PAF Public School, Sargodha

2003. 50th Anniv of PAF Public School, Sargodha.
1197 **628** 4r. multicoloured 1·25 1·00

629 Leather Coats

2003. Achievement of Ten Billion US Dollar Exports Target, 2002–3. Multicoloured.
1198 1r. Type **629** 35 40
1199 1r. Towels 35 40
1200 1r. Readymade garments 35 40
1201 1r. Cargo ship being loaded by crane, Port Qasim 35 40
1202 1r. Fisheries 35 40
1203 1r. Yarn 35 40
1204 1r. Sports equipment 35 40
1205 1r. Fabrics 35 40
1206 1r. Furniture 35 40
1207 1r. Surgical instruments 35 40
1208 1r. Gems and jewellery 35 40
1209 1r. Leather goods 35 40
1210 1r. Information technology 35 40
1211 1r. Rice 35 40
1212 1r. Auto parts 35 40
1213 1r. Carpets 35 40
1214 1r. Marble and granite 35 40
1215 1r. Fruits 35 40
1216 1r. Cutlery 35 40
1217 1r. Engineering goods 35 40

630 Boy in Wheelchair with Boy and Girl

2003. International Day for Disabled.

1218	**630**	2r. multicoloured	1·00	50

631 Globe

2003. World Summit on the Information Society, Geneva (Switzerland) and Tunis (Tunisia).

1219	**631**	2r. multicoloured	75	40

632 Khalid Class Submarine (Agosta 90B)

2003. Submarine Construction in Pakistan. Multicoloured.

1220	1r. Type **632**	75	25
1221	2r. Khalid Class submarine (Agosta 90B) and Pakistan flag (horiz)	1·50	85

633 Pakistan Air Force Plane, Siachen, 1988–90

2003. Centenary of Powered Flight. Pakistan Air Force. Multicoloured.

1222	2r. Type **633**	80	80
1223	2r. Old and modern Pakistan Air Force planes	80	80

634 Emblem

2004. 12th Summit Meeting of South Asian Association for Regional Co-operation, Islamabad.

1224	**634**	4r. multicoloured	50	50

635 Sadiq Public School, Bahawalpur

2004. 50th Anniv of Sadiq Public School, Bahawalpur.

1225	**635**	4r. multicoloured	60	50

636 South Asian Federation Games Medal

2004. Ninth South Asian Federation (S.A.F.) Games, Islamabad. Multicoloured.

1226	2r. Type **636**	35	40
1227	2r. Sprinting	35	40
1228	2r. Squash	35	40
1229	2r. Boxing	35	40
1230	2r. Wrestling	35	40
1231	2r. Judo	35	40
1232	2r. Javelin throwing	35	40
1233	2r. Football	35	40
1234	2r. Rowing	35	40
1235	2r. Shooting	35	40
1236	2r. Shot-putting	35	40
1237	2r. Badminton	35	40
1238	2r. Weight lifting	35	40
1239	2r. Volleyball	35	40
1240	2r. Table tennis	35	40
1241	2r. Swimming	35	40

637 Justice Pir Muhammad Karam Shah Al-Azhari

2004. Justice Pir Muhammad Karam Shah Al-Azhari Commemoration.

1242	**637**	2r. multicoloured	50	25

638 Cadet College, Hasanabdal

2004. 50th Anniv of Cadet College, Hasanabdal.

1243	**638**	4r. multicoloured	50	50

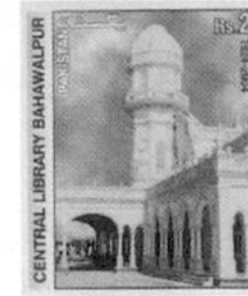
639 Central Library, Bahawalpur

2004. 80th Anniv of Central Library, Bahawalpur.

1244	**639**	2r. multicoloured	40	25

640 Bhong Mosque, Rahim Yar Khan

2004. Bhong Mosque.

1245	**640**	4r. multicoloured	70	60

641 Footballer and FIFA Emblem

2004. Centenary of FIFA (Federation Internationale de Football Association). Multicoloured.

1246	5r. Type **641**	75	75
1247	5r. FIFA emblem	75	75
1248	5r. As No. 1246 with stadium background extended behind FIFA emblem	75	75

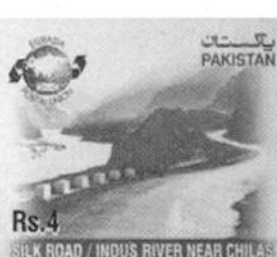
642 Silk Road alongside Indus River

2004. Silk Road. Multicoloured.

1249	4r. Type **642**	50	50
1250	4r. Silk Road and Haramosh Peak (vert)	50	50

643 Juniper Forest and Emblems

2004. 50th Anniv of Sui Southern Gas Company. Protecting National Heritage.

1251	**643**	4r. multicoloured	60	55

644 K2

2004. 50th Anniv of First Ascent of K2. Multicoloured.

1252	5r. Type **644**	60	60
MS1253	**1253** 96×64 mm. 30r. Views of K2. Imperf	2·75	3·50

645 Running

2004. Olympic Games, Athens. Multicoloured.

1254	5r. Type **645**	55	55
1255	5r. Boxing	55	55
1256	5r. Hockey	55	55
1257	5r. Wrestling	55	55

646 Muhammad Ali Jinnah

647

648 Muhammad Ali Jinnah

649

2004. 57th Anniv of Independence.

1258	**646**	5r. multicoloured	45	45
1259	**647**	5r. multicoloured	45	45
1260	**648**	5r. multicoloured	45	45
1261	**649**	5r. multicoloured	45	45

Nos. 1258/61 each show Muhammad Ali Jinnah beside Urdu text, which differs on each stamp.

650 Maulvi Abdul Haq

2004. Maulvi Abdul Haq (scholar) Commemoration.

1262	**650**	4r. multicoloured	40	40

651 Calligraphic Dove with Olive Branch and Emblem

2004. Fourth International Calligraphy and Calligraph-Art Exhibition and Competition.

1263	**651**	5r. multicoloured	40	40

652 Striped Gourami

2004. Fish. Multicoloured.

1264	2r. Type **652**	55	55
1265	2r. Black widow	55	55
1266	2r. Yellow dwarf cichlid	55	55
1267	2r. Tiger barb	55	55
1268	2r. Neon tetra	55	55

653 Training for Handicapped

2004. 50th Anniv of Japan's International Co-Operation and Assistance. Multicoloured.

1269	5r. Type **653**	75	75
1270	5r. Polio eradication	75	75
1271	5r. Ghazi Barotha hydropower	75	75
1272	5r. Friendship tunnel (Kohat)	75	75
MS1273	128×68 mm. 30r. Looking down Friendship Tunnel and designs as Nos. 269/72	2·75	3·50

654 Children and Daffodils

2004. Year of Child Welfare and Rights.

1274	**654**	4r. multicoloured	45	45

655 Open University Emblems

2004. 30th Anniv of Allama Iqbal Open University, Islamabad.

1275	**655**	20r. multicoloured	1·50	2·00

656 Khyber Medical College

2004. Centenary of Khyber Medical College.

1276	**656**	5r. multicoloured	60	50

657 Prof. Ahmed Ali

2005. 95th Birth Anniv of Prof. Ahmed Ali.

1277	**657**	5r. multicoloured	50	50

658 Allama Iqbal (Pakistani), Mihai Emineseu (Romanian) and Monument

2005. Pakistani and Romanian Poets. Multicoloured.

1278	5r. Type **658**	70	70
1279	5r. Allama Iqbal, Mihai Emineseu and book title	70	70

659 Saadat Hasan Manto

2005. 50th Death Anniv of Saadat Hasan Manto (short story writer).

1280	**659**	5r. multicoloured	45	45

660 Muhammad Ali Jinnah and Tempest II Airplane

2005. Air Force. Multicoloured.

1281	5r. Type **660**	1·00	1·00
1282	5r. Visit of Muhammad Ali Jinnah to the Air Force academy (vert)	1·00	1·00
1283	5r. Fighter plane and air force base facilities	1·00	1·00
1284	5r. Roundel and fighter plane	1·00	1·00

661 Command and Staff College

2005. Centenary of Command and Staff College, Quetta.
1285 **661** 5r. multicoloured 50 50

662 Muhammad Ali Jinnah and Mustafa Kemal Atatürk

2005. 85th Anniversary of Turkish Grand National Assembly. Multicoloured.
1286 10r. Type **662** 1·00 1·40
1287 10r. Mustafa Kemal Atatürk 1·00 1·40

663 Institute of Business Administration, Karachi

2005. 50th Anniv of Institute of Business Administration, Karachi. Multicoloured.
1288 3r. Type **663** 50 50
1289 3r. Entrance to Institute 50 50

664 Entrance

2005. 95th Anniv of Islamia High School, Quetta. Paper with fluorescent fibres.
1290 **664** 5r. multicoloured 50 50

665 Akhtar Shairani

2005. Birth Centenary of Akhtar Shairani (poet).
1291 **665** 5r. multicoloured 50 50

666 Emblem

2005. World Summit on the Information Society, Tunis.
1292 **666** 5r. multicoloured 50 50

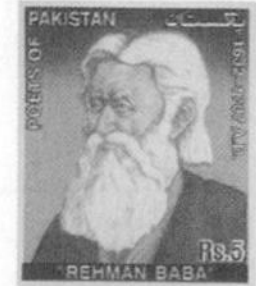

667 Abdul Rehman Baba

2005. Abdul Rehman Baba (poet) Commemoration.
1293 **667** 5r. multicoloured 50 50

668 Marathon Runners

2005. Lahore Marathon.
1294 **668** 5r. multicoloured 50 50

669 *Lepiota procera*

2005. Mushrooms. Multicoloured.
1295 5r. Type **669** 75 75
1296 5r. *Tricholoma gambosum* 75 75
1297 5r. *Amanita caesarea* 75 75
1298 5r. *Cantharellus cibarius* 75 75
1299 5r. *Boletus luridus* 75 75
1300 5r. *Morchella vulgaris* 75 75
1301 5r. *Amanita vaginata* 75 75
1302 5r. *Agaricus arvensis* 75 75
1303 5r. *Coprinus comatus* 75 75
1304 5r. *Clitocybe geotropa* 75 75

669a 'HELP EARTHQUAKE VICTIMS'

2005. President's Relief Fund for Earthquake Victims. Sheet 174×147 mm. Multicoloured.
MS1304a Type **669a** and 17 stamp size labels (sold for 100r.) 4·50 5·50

No. **MS**1304a the sheet was sold at 100r., a premium of 60r. for the President's Relief Fund for Earthquake Victims.

670 Silhouettes and Sports Equipment

2005. International Year of Sports and Physical Education.
1305 **670** 5r. multicoloured 50 50

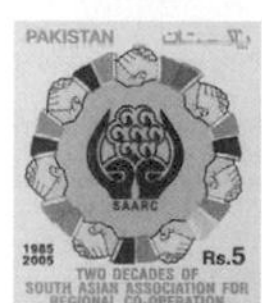

671 Emblem and Clasped Hands

2005. 20th Anniv of South Asian Association for Regional Co-operation.
1306 **671** 5r. multicoloured 50 50

672 Khwaja Sarwar Hasan

2005. Khwaja Sarwar Hasan (founder of Pakistan Institute of International Affairs) Commemoration.
1307 **672** 5r. multicoloured 50 50

673 Emblem and Silhouettes of Children

2005. 30th Anniv of SOS Children's Villages of Pakistan.
1308 **673** 5r. multicoloured 50 50

674 Emblem and Players

2005. 20th World Men's Team Squash Championship, Islamabad.
1309 **674** 5r. multicoloured 1·00 60

675 Supreme Court Building

2006. 50th Anniv of Supreme Court of Pakistan. Multicoloured.
1310 4r. Type **675** 60 30
1311 15r. Supreme Court at night 2·25 2·75

676 Muhammed Ali Jinnah inspecting Troops and Tanks

2006. Muhammad Ali Jinnah's visit to Armoured Corps Centre, Nowshera, 1948. Multicoloured.
1312 5r. Type **676** 50 50
1313 5r. Col. Stroud (Commandant), Muhammad Ali Jinnah and Begum Ra'na Liaquat Ali Khan 50 50

677 Begum Ra'na Liaquat Ali Khan

2006. Birth Centenary (2005) of Begum Ra'na Liaquat Ali Khan.
1314 **677** 4r. multicoloured 60 50

678 Gurdwara Dera Sahib, Lahore

2006. 400th Death Anniv of Arjun Dev Ji (Sikh Guru).
1315 **678** 5r. multicoloured 65 60

679 Polo at Shandur Pass

2006. Shandur Polo Festival, Chitral.
1316 **679** 5r. multicoloured 1·00 75

680 Hanna Lake, Quetta

2006. "Visit Pakistan 2006". Lakes. Multicoloured.
1317 5r. Type **680** 70 70
1318 5r. Lake Payee, Kaghan 70 70
1319 5r. Lake Saiful Maluk, Kaghan 70 70
1320 5r. Lake Dudi Pat Sar, Kaghan 70 70

681 Prof. Shakir Ali

2006. Painters of Pakistan. Each showing the artist and one of their paintings. Multicoloured.
1321 4r. Type **681** 55 55
1322 4r. Anna Molka Ahmed 55 55
1323 4r. Sadequain 55 55
1324 4r. Ali Imam 55 55
1325 4r. Zubeida Agha 55 55
1326 4r. Laila Shahzada 55 55
1327 4r. Ahmed Parvez 55 55
1328 4r. Bashir Mirza 55 55
1329 4r. Zahooral Akhlaque 55 55
1330 4r. Askari Mian Irani 55 55

682 Centenary Emblem

2006. Centenary of Hamdard Services.
1331 **682** 5r. multicoloured 60 50

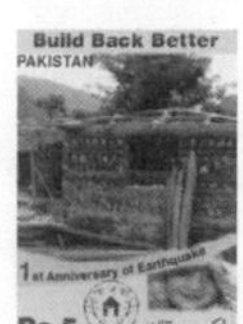

683 New Houses under Construction

2006. First Anniv of Earthquake.
1332 **683** 5r. multicoloured 60 50

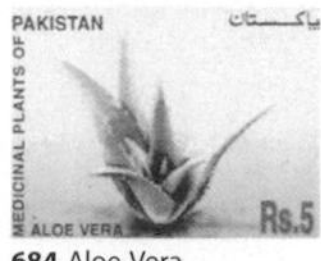

684 Aloe Vera

2006. Medicinal Plants (12th series). Multicoloured.
1333 5r. Type **684** 90 90
1334 5r. Chamomilla (vert) 90 90

685 UN Emblem

2006. United Nations International Anti-Corruption Day.
1335 **685** 5r. multicoloured 60 60

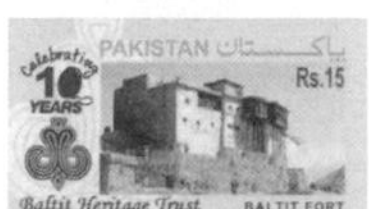

686 Baltit Fort, Karimabad

2006. Tenth Anniv of Baltit Heritage Trust.
1336 **686** 15r. multicoloured 2·25 2·75

687 Muhammed Ali Jinnah joins Muslim League, 1913

2006. Centenary of the Muslim League. Multicoloured.
1337 4r. Type **687** 50 50
1338 4r. Muhammed Ali Jinnah ("Quaid") in 1937 50 50
1339 4r. Addressing Lucknow Session, 1937 50 50
1340 4r. With Fatima Jinnah and youth and women of Muslim League, 1938 50 50
1341 4r. Hoisting Muslim League flag, Manto Park, Lahore, 1940 50 50
1342 4r. Addressing Lahore session, 1940 50 50
1343 4r. Ballot box and crowd (elections victory, 1945–6) 50 50
1344 4r. Addressing first Constituent Assembly, 1947 50 50

688 Old KMC Building, Karachi

2007. 75th Anniv of Inauguration of KMC (Karachi Municipal Corporation) Building.

1345	**688**	10r. multicoloured	1·50	1·50

689 Cadet College, Petaro and Arms

2007. 50th Anniv of Cadet College, Petaro.

1346	**689**	10r. multicoloured	1·00	1·00

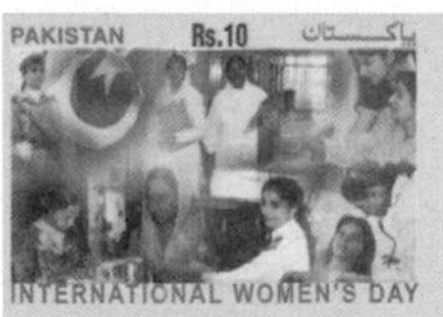
690 Women at Work

2007. International Women's Day.

1347	**690**	10r. multicoloured	1·00	1·00

691 Hugh Catchpole

2007. Birth Centenary of Hugh Catchpole (educationist).

1348	**691**	10r. multicoloured	1·00	1·00

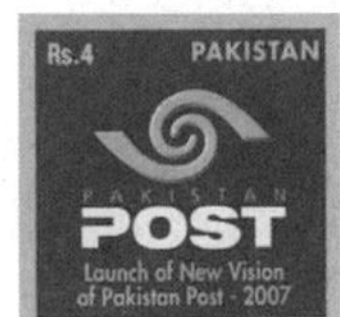
692 Emblem

2007. 'Launch of New Vision of Pakistan Post'.

1349	**692**	4r. vermilion and yellow	1·00	1·00

693 JF-17 Thunder

2007. Pakistan Air Force Defence Day.

1350	**693**	5r. multicoloured	1·50	1·00

694 Members Flags and Map

2007. ECO (Economic Co-operation Organization) Postal Authorities Conference, Ankara (2006).

1351	**694**	10r. multicoloured	1·75	1·50

No. 1351 is inscr '650 Rials I.R. Iran' at top left and the country name 'PAKISTAN' is missing from the stamp.

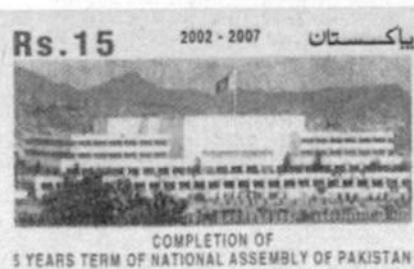
695 National Assembly Building

2007. Completion of Five Years Term of National Assembly of Pakistan.

1352	**695**	15r. multicoloured	1·50	1·75

696 Church Building, Medallion and Nave

2007. Centenary of Catholic Cathedral Church, Lahore.

1353	**696**	5r. multicoloured	1·00	1·00

697 Zulfikar Ali Bhutto, Benazir Bhutto and Crowd

2008. 29th Death Anniv of Zulfikar Ali Bhutto.

1354	**697**	4r. multicoloured	1·25	1·00
MS1355	106×70 mm. **696** 20r. multicoloured. Imperf		2·00	2·50

698 Benazir Bhutto

2008. 55th Birth Anniv of Benazir Bhutto (Prime Minister of Pakistan 1988–90, 1993–6). Multicoloured.

1356		4r. Type **698**	1·25	1·00
1357		5r. Benazir Bhutto waving (34×56 mm)	1·25	1·00
MS1358	67×98 mm. 20r. As No. 1357. Imperf		2·00	2·50

699 Girls in Class and Rebuilt School

2008. Third Anniv of Earthquake.

1359	**699**	4r. multicoloured	1·25	1·00

700 Benazir Bhutto

2008. United Nations Human Rights Award for Benazir Bhutto.

1360	**700**	4r. multicoloured	1·25	1·00

701 Benazir Bhutto and Pakistan Flag

2008. First Death Anniv of Benazir Bhutto.

1361	**701**	4r. multicoloured	1·25	1·00
MS1362	99×67 mm. **701** 20r. multicoloured. Imperf		2·00	2·50

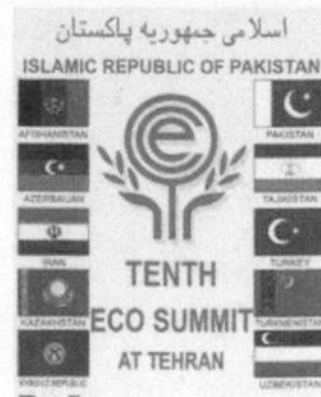
702 Members Flags

2009. Tenth ECO Summit, Tehran, Iran.

1363	**702**	5r. multicoloured	75	75

703 Deodar

2009. National Year of the Environment. Multicoloured.

1364		5r. Type **703**	70	70
1365		5r. Chukar	70	70
1366		5r. Markhor	70	70
1367		5r. Jasmine	70	70

704 Entrance to 'Habib Education Centre'

2009. 50th Anniv of Habib Public School, Karachi.

1368	**704**	5r. multicoloured	50	50

705 High School Building, Karachi

2009. 150th Anniv of Bai Virbaiji Soparivala Parsi High School, Karachi.

1369	**705**	5r. multicoloured	50	50

706 KCCI Building, Karachi

2009. 75th Anniv of Karachi Chamber of Commerce and Industry Building.

1370	**706**	4r. multicoloured	45	45

707 Ahmad Nadeem Qasmi

2009. Ahmad Nadeem Qasmi (Urdu poet and writer) Commemoration.

1371	**707**	5r. multicoloured	50	50

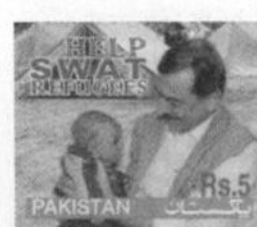
708 Prime Minister holding Refugee Baby

2009. Prime Minister's Relief Fund for Swat Refugees. Sheet 174×153 mm. Multicoloured.

MS1372	5r.×8 Type **708** and 17 stamp size labels (sold for 100r.)		4·50	5·50

No. **MS**1372 was sold for 100r., a premium of 60r. for the Prime Minister's Relief Fund for Swat Refugees.

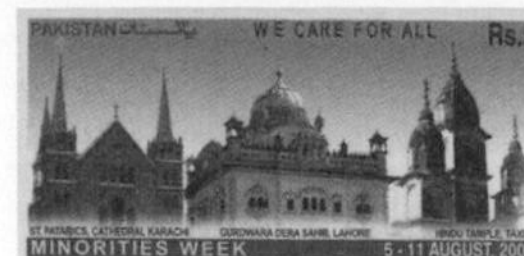
709 St. Patrick's Cathedral, Karachi, Gurdwara Dera Sahib, Lahore and Hindu Temple, Taxila

2010. Minorities Week

1373	**709**	5r. multicoloured	50	50

No. 1373 is incorrectly inscr 'ST. PATARICS'.

710 Teacher, Students and National Flag

2009. Independence Day.

1374	**710**	5r. multicoloured	50	50

711 Mausoleum of Hazrat Musa Pak Shaheed

2009. Mausoleum of Hazrat Musa Pak Shaheed.

1375	**711**	5r. multicoloured	50	50

712 Peace Dove

2009. 'United for Peace'.

1376	**712**	5r. dull violet, azure and black	50	50

713 National Flags of Pakistan and Philippines

2009. 60th Anniv of Diplomatic Relations between Pakistan and the Philippines.

1377	**713**	5r. multicoloured	50	50

714 Sun, Chinese Flag and Outline Map of China

2009. 60th Anniv of the People's Republic of China.

1378	**714**	5r. multicoloured	50	50

715 Aseefa Bhutto Zardari and Benazir Bhutto

2009. 'Polio Free Pakistan Mother's Vision Daughter's Mission'. Multicoloured.

1379	5r. Type **715**	50	50

716 Mr. Yousaf Raza Gillani, Chief Ministers, Cabinet Members and Portrait of Benazir Bhutto

2010. Seventh National Finance Commission Award

1380	**716**	8r. multicoloured	1·00	1·00

717 Gwadar Port

2010. Aghaz-e-Haqooq-e-Balochistan (government development package for Balochistan)

1381	**717**	8r. multicoloured	1·00	1·00

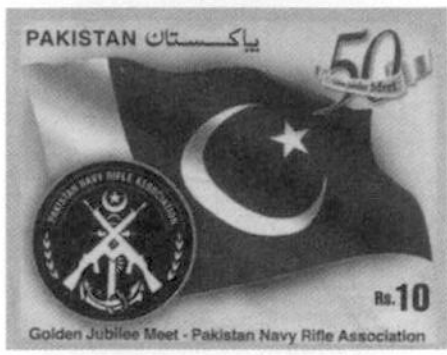

718 Pakistan Flag and Navy Rifle Insignia

2010. 50th Anniv of the Pakistan Navy Rifle Association

1382	**718**	10r. multicoloured	1·00	1·00

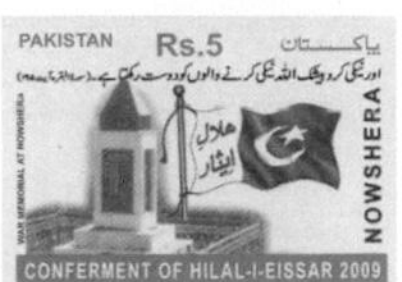

719 War Memorial, Nowshera

2010. Conferment of Hilal-i-Eissar on Cities of Nowshera, Peshawar, Swabi, Mardan and Charsadda. Multicoloured.

1383	5r. Type **719**	50	50
1384	5r. Islamia College, Peshawar	50	50
1385	5r. Judicial Complex, Swabi	50	50
1386	5r. Takht-e-Barhi, Mardan	50	50
1387	5r. Sugar mills, Charsadda	50	50

Nos. 1383/7 were printed together, *se-tenant*, as horizontal strips of five stamps in sheets of 40 (4×10).

720 OICCI Building

2010. 150th Anniv of the Overseas Investors Chamber of Commerce and Industry

1388	**720**	8r. multicoloured	1·00	1·00

721 Athletes and Olympic Rings

2010. Youth Olympic Games, Singapore

1389	**721**	8r. multicoloured	1·00	1·00

722 Junior School Building

2010. 150th Anniv of Lawrence College, Ghora Gali, Murree Hills. Multicoloured.

1390	8r. Type **722**	40	40
1391	8r. Lawrence Asylum, 1860	40	40
1392	8r. Aerial view of Senior School bulding	40	40
1393	8r. Prep School building	40	40

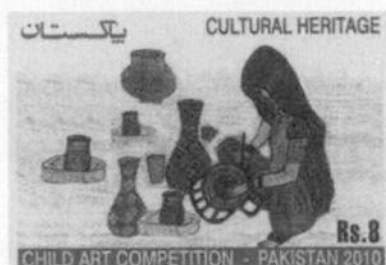

723 Craftswoman (Ilma Tariq)

2010. 'Pakistan 2010' National Stamp Exhibition, Karachi

1394	**723**	8r. multicoloured	1·00	1·00

724 International Islamic University, Islamabad

2010. 25th Anniv of International Islamic University, Islamabad

1395	**724**	8r. multicoloured	1·00	1·00

725 Islamabad

2010. 50th Anniv of Islamabad

1396	**725**	5r. multicoloured	1·00	1·00

726 Cellular Phone

2011. PTA (Pakistan Telecommunication Authority) '100 Million Cellular Subscribers'

1397	**726**	8r. multicoloured	1·00	1·00

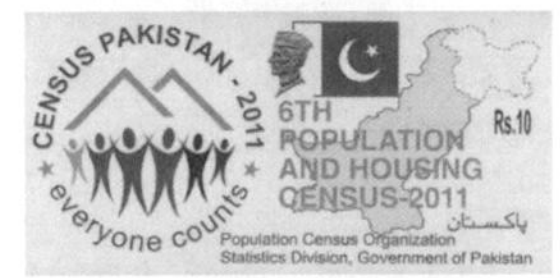

727 Census Emblem and Map of Pakistan

2011. Sixth Population and Housing Census

1398	**727**	10r. multicoloured	1·00	1·00

728 Train

2011. 150th Anniv of Pakistan Railways

1399	**728**	8r. multicoloured	1·00	1·00

729 Asif Ali Zardari (Pakistan President) and Hu Jintao (Chinese President)

2011. 60th Anniv of Diplomatic Relations between Pakistan and China (People's Republic). Multicoloured.

1400	8r. Type **729**	50	50
1401	8r. Yousuf Raza Gilani (Pakistan Prime Minister) and Wen Jiabao (Chinese Prime Minister)	50	50

730 Hands supporting Globe and AIDS Ribbon

2011. 'Uniting for HIV Prevention'

1402	**730**	8r. multicoloured	1·00	1·00

731 Faisal Mosque, Islamabad and St. Basil's Cathedral, Moscow

2011. Pakistan Russia Friendship

1403	**731**	8r. multicoloured	1·00	1·00

732 Interior of a House in Swat (Mahnoor Rafi)

2011. Child Art Competition at 'Kurrachee 2011' National Stamp Exhibition, Karachi. Multicoloured.

1404	8r. Type **732**	50	50
1405	8r. Independence Day Celebrations, with traditional dress of the Provinces (Khurram Jahangir Khan)	50	50
1406	8r. Historical Monuments of Pakistan (Almen Khan)	50	50
1407	8r. Campaign against Pollution in Karachi (Laiba Jawaid)	50	50
1408	8r. Bread making in Village in Sindh (Vania Rizvi)	50	50
1409	8r. Girls performing Traditional Dance, Kalash Valley (Naveera Jabeen)	50	50
1410	8r. Sunrise over Beach, Karachi (Mehnur Zahid)	50	50
1411	8r. Pollution Free Pakistan (Ali Nazim)	50	50

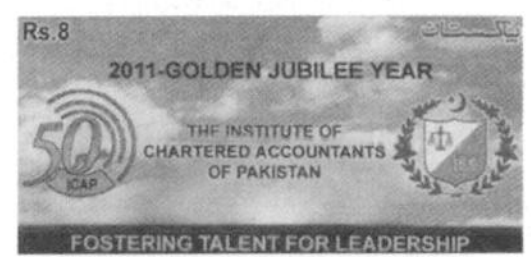

733 Anniversary and ICAP Emblems

2011. 50th Anniv of the Institute of Chartered Accountants of Pakistan

1412	**733**	8r. multicoloured	1·00	1·00

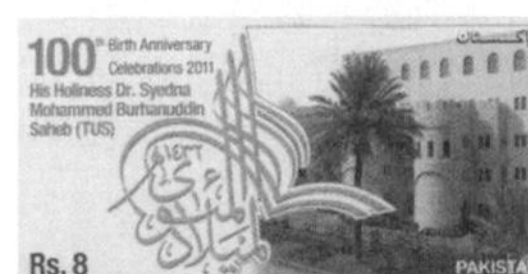

734 Al Jama-tus-Saifiyah Building (Dawoodi Bohra university for Islamic Studies)

2011. Birth Centenary Celebrations of Dr. Syedna Mohammed Burhanuddin Saheb (spiritual leader of Dawoodi Bohra community)

1413	**734**	8r. multicoloured	1·00	1·00

735 Zarai Taraqiati Bank

2011. 50th Anniv of Zarai Taraqiati Bank Ltd

1414	**735**	8r. multicoloured	1·00	1·00

736 Satellite, Radio, Telephones, Television and Satellite Dish

2011. 60th Anniv of Managing Radio Frequency Spectrum by Frequency Allocation Board

1415	**736**	8r. multicoloured	1·00	1·00

737 Milad Tower, Tehran

2011. Pakistan-Iran Joint Issue. Multicoloured.

1416	8r. Type **737**	50	50
1417	8r. Minar-e-Pakistan, Lahore	50	50

Stamps in similar designs were issued by Iran.

738 Satellite and SUPARCO Emblem

2011. 50th Anniv of Pakistan Space and Upper Atmosphere Research Commission

1418	**738**	8r. multicoloured	1·00	1·00

739 Karachi Gymkhana

2011. 125th Anniv of Karachi Gymkhana (club). Multicoloured.

1419	8r. Type **739**	50	50
1420	8r. Karachi Gymkhana buildings (post at right)	50	50
1421	8r. Entrance	50	50
1422	8r. Cricket ground	50	50

740 Emblem, Figures and Rainbow

2011. Breast Cancer Awareness Campaign in Pakistan

1423	**740**	8r. multicoloured	1·25	1·25

741 Victory Monument, Bangkok and Minar-e-Pakistan, Lahore

2011. 60th Anniv of Diplomatic Relations between Pakistan and Thailand

1424	**741**	8r. multicoloured	1·25	1·25

742 School Buildings

2011. 150th Anniv of St. Patrick's High School, Karachi

1425	**742**	8r. multicoloured	1·25	1·25

743 Cabinet Meeting, 25 December 2011

2012. 100th Meeting of the Federal Cabinet of Pakistan
1426 **743** 8r. multicoloured 1·25 1·25

744 Arfa Karim Randhawa

2012. Arfa Karim Randhawa (computer genius and World's youngest Microsoft Certified Professional) Commemoration
1427 **744** 8r. multicoloured 1·25 1·25

745 Air Marshal Nur Khan and North American F-86 Sabre Plane

2012. Air Marshal Nur Khan Commemoration
1428 **745** 8r. multicoloured 1·25 1·25

746 Emerald

2012. Gems and Minerals of Pakistan. Multicoloured.
1429 8r. Type **746** 1·25 1·25
1430 8r. Ruby 1·25 1·25
1431 8r. Sapphire 1·25 1·25
1432 8r. Peridot 1·25 1·25

747 Aitchison College, Lahore

2012. 125th Anniv of Aitchison College, Lahore
1433 **747** 8r. multicoloured 1·25 1·25

748 St. Joseph's Convent School, Karachi

2012. 150th Anniv of St. Joseph's Convent School, Karachi
1434 **748** 8r. multicoloured 1·25 1·25

749 Emblem

2012. 50th Anniv of Asian-Pacific Postal Union (APPU)
1435 **749** 8r. multicoloured 1·25 1·25

750 Government High School No. 1

2012. Centenary of Government High School No. 1, Thana, Malakand Division
1436 **750** 8r. multicoloured 1·25 1·25

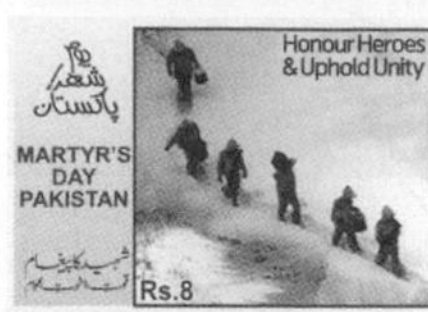

751 Mountain Troops ('Honour Heroes & Uphold Unity')

2012. Martyrs Day
1437 **751** 8r. multicoloured 1·25 1·25

752 King Bhumibol Adulyadej and Queen Sirikit

2012. 50th Anniv of State Visit of King Bhumibol Adulyadej and Queen Sirikit of Thailand to Pakistan
1438 **752** 8r. multicoloured 1·25 1·25

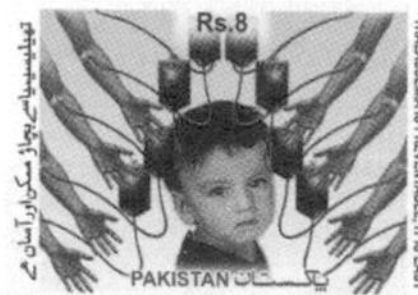

753 Young Boy and Blood Donors

2012. Prevention of Thalassemia Major in Pakistan
1439 **753** 8r. multicoloured 1·25 1·25

754 Lake Saiful Malook

2012. 40th Anniv of United Nations Environment Programme (UNEP). World Environment Day. Multicoloured.
1440 8r. Type **754** 1·25 1·25
1441 8r. Polo at Shandur Pass 1·25 1·25
1442 8r. Shalimar Garden, Lahore 1·25 1·25
1443 8r. Khyber Gateway 1·25 1·25

755 Ayub Bridge

2012. 50th Anniv of Ayub Bridge
1444 **755** 8r. multicoloured 1·25 1·25

756 Oven (Priya Parkash Mansha)

2012. Child Art Competition at 'Kurrachee 2012' National Stamp Exhibition, Karachi. Multicoloured.
1445 8r. Type **756** 1·25 1·25
1446 8r. Tower, Faisal Mosque, Islamabad and gateway (Ali Muhammad Nizar) 1·25 1·25
1447 8r. Narwhal (Samayan Hasan Khan) 1·25 1·25
1448 8r. River and wildlife (Sheza Ashraf) 1·25 1·25
1449 8r. Independence Monument, dove, crescent and star (Yamna Naveed) 1·25 1·25
1450 8r. Monument and child flying kite (Ayesha Qureshi) 1·25 1·25
1451 8r. Toucan and parrot (Vania Rizvi) 1·25 1·25
1452 8r. Quetzals (Marium Shahzad) 1·25 1·25

757 Pale Yellow Roses

2012. Eid Greetings. Roses. Multicoloured.
1453 8r. Type **757** 1·25 1·25
1454 8r. Pink roses 1·25 1·25
1455 8r. White roses 1·25 1·25
1456 8r. Deep yellow roses 1·25 1·25

758 King Edward Medical University, Lahore

2012. 150th Anniv of King Edward Medical University, Lahore
1457 **758** 8r. multicoloured 1·25 1·25

759 Abdur Rahman Chughtai (1897-1975, artist) and 1948 1r. Scarlet Independence Stamp

2012. 65th Anniv of Independence
1458 **759** 10r. multicoloured 1·50 1·50

760 Sialkot Chamber of Commerce and Industry

2012. 30th Anniv of Sialkot Chamber of Commerce and Industry
1459 **760** 8r. multicoloured 1·25 1·25

761 White Storks

2012. Migratory Birds in Pakistan. Multicoloured.
1460 8r. Type **761** 1·25 1·25
1461 8r. Shoveler Ducks 1·25 1·25
1462 8r. Snow Geese 1·25 1·25
1463 8r. Siberian Cranes 1·25 1·25

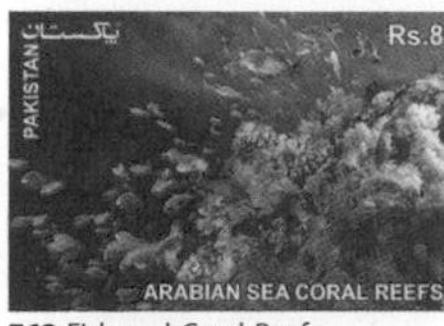

762 Fish and Coral Reef

2012. Arabian Sea Coral Reefs. Multicoloured.
1464 8r. Type **762** 1·25 1·25
1465 8r. Yellow and orange fish and coral reef (face value at top left) 1·25 1·25
1466 8r. Orange fish and green coral reef (face value at top right) 1·25 1·25
1467 8r. School of silver fish and blue and red corals (face value at top left) 1·25 1·25

763 Hameed Naseem

2012. Hameed Naseem (1920-98, poet, writer and broadcaster) Commemoration
1468 **763** 8r. multicoloured 1·25 1·25

764 Department Building

2012. 60th Anniv of Department of Geography, University of Karachi
1469 **764** 15r. multicoloured 2·40 2·40

765 Certificate

2012. 50th Anniv of National Investment Trust Ltd
1470 **765** 15r. multicoloured 2·40 2·40

766 *Muhammad Luthfullah Khan* (Prof. Saeed Akhtar)

2012. Muhammad Luthfullah Khan (1916-2012, archivist) Commemoration
1471 **766** 15r. multicoloured 2·40 2·40

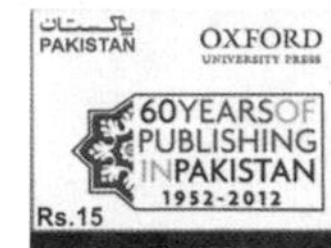

767 Emblem

2012. 60th Anniv of Oxford University Press Publishing in Pakistan
1472 **767** 15r. multicoloured 2·40 2·40

768 Wind Farm

2012. Commercial Operation of First Wind Farm Project in Pakistan
1473 **768** 15r. multicoloured 2·40 2·40

769 Syed Nasir Raza Kazmi

2013. Syed Nasir Raza Kazmi (1925-72, poet) Commemoration
1474 **769** 15r. multicoloured 2·40 2·40

770 Qudrat Ullah Shabab

2013. Qudrat Ullah Shabab (1917-86, writer) Commemoration
1475 **770** 15r. multicoloured 2·40 2·40

771 Allama Muhammad Asad

2013. Allama Muhammad Asad (1900-92, writer) Commemoration

1476	**771**	15r. multicoloured	2·40	2·40

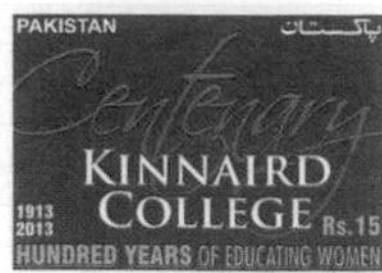

772 'Centenary KINNAIRD COLLEGE'

2013. Centenary of Kinnaird College for Women

1477	**772**	15r. multicoloured	2·40	2·40

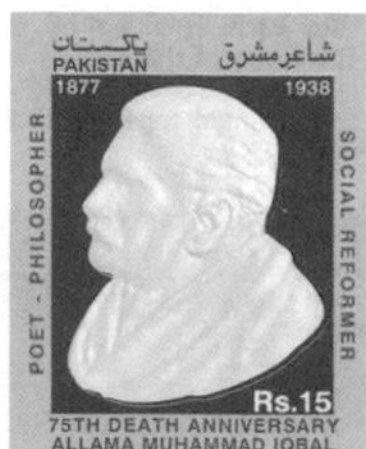

773 Allama Muhammad Iqbal

2013. 75th Death Anniv of Allama Muhammad Iqbal (1877-1938, poet, philosopher and social reformer)

1478	**773**	15r. multicoloured	2·40	2·40

774 Sufi Barkat Ali

2013. Sufi Barkat Ali (1911-97, Muslim Sufi saint) Commemoration

1479	**774**	8r. multicoloured	1·25	1·25

775 Statue of Subedar Khuda Dad Khan and Pak Army Museum

2013. Inauguration of Pak Army Museum, Rawalpindi

1480	**775**	15r. multicoloured	2·40	2·40

776 Havildar Lalak Jan Shaheed (1967-99) and Nishan-e-Haider Medal

2013. Recipients of Nishan-e-Haider and Hilal-e-Kashmir Medals. Multicoloured.

1481	8r. Type **776**	1·25	1·25
1482	8r. Captain Karnal Sher Khan Shaheed (1970-99) and Nishan-e-Haider medal	1·25	1·25
1483	8r. Naik Saif Ali Janjua Shaheed (1922-48) and Hilal-i-Kashmir medal	1·25	1·25

777 Casting Vote

2013. Election 2013

1484	**777**	8r. multicoloured	1·25	1·25

778 Nawab Sadiq Muhammad Khan Abbasi V

2013. Nawab Sadiq Muhammad Khan Abbasi V (1904-66, Nawab of Bahawalpur) Commemoration

1485	**778**	8r. multicoloured	1·25	1·25

779 Syed Zamir Jafri

2013. Syed Zamir Jafri (1916-99, poet) Commemoration

1486	**779**	8r. multicoloured	1·25	1·25

780 Islamia College, Peshawar

2013. Centenary of Islamia College, Peshawar

1487	**780**	8r. multicoloured	1·25	1·25

OFFICIAL STAMPS

1947. King George VI Official stamps of India optd **PAKISTAN**.

O1	**O20**	3p. slate	3·50	2·75
O2	**O20**	½a. purple	60	10
O3	**O20**	9p. green	5·50	4·50
O4	**O20**	1a. red	60	10
O5	**O20**	1½a. violet	60	10
O6	**O20**	2a. orange	60	60
O7	**O20**	2½a. violet	7·50	15·00
O8	**O20**	4a. brown	1·50	1·75
O9	**O20**	8a. violet	2·25	3·25
O10	**93**	1r. slate and brown (No. O138)	1·25	4·00
O11	**93**	2r. purple and brown (No. O139)	11·00	10·00
O12	**93**	5r. green and blue (No. O140)	32·00	60·00
O13	**93**	10r. purple and red (No. O141)	85·00	£170

1948. Optd **SERVICE**. Crescent moon pointing to right.

O14	**7**	3p. red	10	10
O15	**7**	6p. violet	10	10
O37	**7**	9p. green	10	10
O17	-	1a. blue	3·75	10
O18	-	1½a. green	3·50	10
O19	-	2a. red	1·50	10
O20	-	3a. green	26·00	18·00
O21	**9**	4a. brown	2·50	10
O22	-	8a. black	2·75	10·00
O23	**12**	1r. blue	1·50	10
O42	**12**	2r. brown	7·50	30
O61	**12**	5r. red	7·50	15
O26	**13**	10r. mauve	24·00	80·00

1949. Optd **SERVICE**. Crescent moon pointing to left.

O38	1a. blue	10	10
O39	1½a. green	10	10
O40	2a. red	20	10
O30	3a. green	42·00	7·50
O31	8a. black	65·00	25·00

1951. Fourth Anniv of Independence. As Nos. 56, 58 and 60 but inscr "SERVICE" instead of "PAKISTAN POSTAGE".

O32	3a. purple	10·00	10·00
O33	4a. green	2·50	20
O34	8a. sepia	11·00	8·50

1954. Seventh Anniv of Independence. Nos. 65/71 optd **SERVICE**.

O53	6p. violet	10	10
O54	9p. blue	15	10
O55	1a. red	15	10
O56	1½a. red	15	10
O57	14a. myrtle	75	5·00
O58	1r. green	75	10
O51	2r. orange	6·00	15

1955. Eighth Anniv of Independence. Nos. 74/5 optd **SERVICE**.

O63	6a. blue	20	10
O64	8a. violet	45	10

1959. Ninth Anniv of Independence. Optd **SERVICE**.

O65	**37**	2a. red	10	10

1961. First Anniv of Republic. Optd **SERVICE**.

O62	**41**	10r. green and orange	7·00	11·00

1961. Optd **SERVICE**.

O66	**51**	8a. green	25	10
O67	**51**	1r. blue	25	10

1961. New currency. Provisional stamps. Nos. 122 etc. optd **SERVICE**.

O68	-	1p. on 1½a. red	10	10
O69	**7**	2p. on 3p. red	10	10
O70	**51**	3p. on 6p. purple	10	10
O71	-	7p. on 1a. red	10	10
O72	**51**	13p. on 2a. red	10	10
O73	**37**	13p. on 2a. red	10	10

1961. Definitive issue optd **SERVICE**.

O74	**60**	1p. violet	10	10
O75	**60**	2p. red	10	10
O79	**60**	3p. purple	10	10
O94	**60**	5p. blue	10	10
O81	**60**	7p. green	10	10
O82	**61**	10p. brown	10	10
O83	**61**	13p. violet	10	10
O98	**61**	15p. purple	10	2·25
O99	**61**	20p. green	10	40
O100	**61**	25p. blue	22·00	5·50
O85	**61**	40p. purple	10	10
O102	**61**	50p. turquoise	15	15
O87	**61**	75p. red	20	10
O104	**61**	90p. green	15·00	10·00
O88	**62**	1r. red	35	10
O89	**62**	2r. orange	1·50	20
O90	**62**	5r. green	4·25	8·50

1979. Optd **SERVICE**.

O109	**275**	2p. green	10	30
O110	-	3p. black	10	30
O111	-	5p. blue	10	30
O112	**275**	10p. blue and turquoise	10	30
O113	-	20p. green (No. 468)	10	10
O114	-	25p. green and mauve (No. 489)	10	10
O115	-	40p. blue and mauve (No. 470)	30	10
O116	-	50p. lilac and green (No. 471)	10	10
O117	-	60p. black (No. 472)	1·00	10
O118	-	75p. red (No. 473)	1·00	10
O119	-	1r. green (No. 475)	2·25	10
O120	-	1r.50 orange (No. 476)	20	30
O121	-	2r. red (No. 477)	20	10
O122	-	3r. blue (No. 478)	30	30
O123	-	4r. black (No. 479)	3·50	50
O124	-	5r. brown (No. 480)	3·50	50

1980. As Nos. 513/19 but inscr "SERVICE".

O125	**291**	10p. green and yellow	1·00	10
O126	**291**	15p. deep green & green	1·00	10
O127	**291**	25p. violet and red	15	1·00
O128	**291**	35p. red and green	20	1·50
O129	-	40p. red and brown	1·00	10
O130	-	50p. red and green	20	60
O131	-	80p. green and black	30	1·50

1984. Nos. 629/30 and 632/6 optd **SERVICE**.

O132		5p. black and purple	10	60
O133		10p. black and red	15	40
O135	**343**	20p. black and violet	30	40
O136	-	50p. brown and red	40	40
O137	-	60p. lt brown & brown	45	50
O138	-	70p. blue	50	70
O139	-	80p. brown and red	55	70

1989. No. 773 optd **SERVICE**.

O140	**411**	1r. multicoloured	5·00	85

O7 State Bank of Pakistan Building, Islamabad

1990

O141	**O7**	1r. red and green	15	10
O142	**O7**	2r. red and pink	25	15
O143	**O7**	3r. red and blue	35	15
O144	**O7**	4r. red and brown	45	15
O145	**O7**	5r. red and purple	50	15
O146	**O7**	10r. red and brown	1·25	40

Pt. 22

PALAU

Formerly part of the United States Trust Territory of the Pacific Islands, Palau became an autonomous republic on 1 January 1981. Until 1983 it continued to use United States stamps.

Palau became an independent republic on 1 October 1994.

100 cents = 1 dollar.

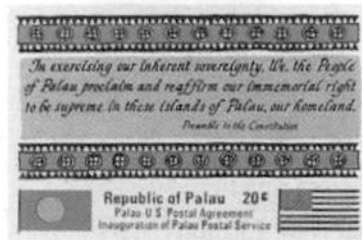

1 Preamble to Constitution

1983. Inaug of Postal Independence. Multicoloured.

1	20c. Type **1**	80	70
2	20c. Natives hunting (design from Koror meeting house)	80	70
3	20c. Preamble to Constitution (different)	80	70
4	20c. Three fishes (design from Koror meeting house)	80	70

2 Palau Fruit Dove

1983. Birds. Multicoloured.

5	20c. Type **2**	65	55
6	20c. Morning bird	65	55
7	20c. Palau white-eye (inscr "Giant White-eye")	65	55
8	20c. Palau fantail	65	55

3 Map Cowrie

1983. Marine Life. Multicoloured.

9	1c. Sea fan	30	20
10	3c. Type **3**	30	20
11	5c. Jellyfish	30	20
12	10c. Hawksbill turtle	30	20
13	13c. Giant clam	30	20
14	14c. Trumpet triton	45	40
15	20c. Parrotfish	50	45
16	22c. Indo-Pacific hump-headed ("Bumphead") parrotfish	80	70
17	25c. Soft coral and damselfish	85	75
17a	28c. Chambered nautilus	75	65
18	30c. Dappled sea cucumber	75	65
18a	33c. Sea anemone and anemonefish ("Clownfish")	1·20	1·00
19	37c. Sea urchin	85	75
19a	39c. Green sea turtle	1·30	1·10
19b	44c. Sailfish	1·50	1·30
20	50c. Starfish	1·20	1·00
21	$1 Common squid	2·30	2·00
22	$2 Dugong	6·25	5·25
23	$5 Pink sponge	14·50	12·50
24	$10 Spinner dolphin	28·00	24·00

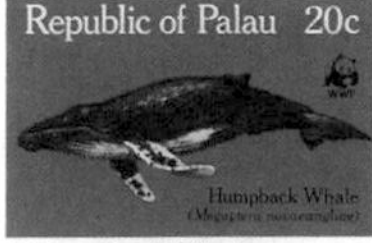

4 Humpback Whale

1983. World Wildlife Fund. Whales. Multicoloured.

25	20c. Type **4**	1·50	1·30
26	20c. Blue whale	1·50	1·30
27	20c. Fin whale	1·50	1·30
28	20c. Sperm whale	1·50	1·30

5 "Spear fishing at New Moon"

1983. Christmas. Paintings by Charlie Gibbons. Multicoloured.

29	20c. Type **5**	75	65
30	20c. "Taro Gardening"	75	65
31	20c. "First Child Ceremony"	75	65

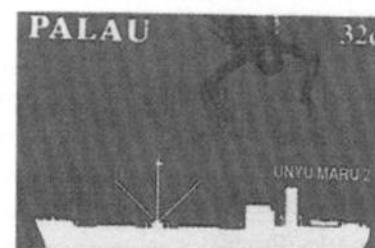

103 "Unyu Maru 2" (tanker)

1995. Japanese Fleet Sunk off Rock Islands (1944). Multicoloured.

851	32c. Type **103**	85	80
852	32c. "Wakatake" (destroyer)	85	80
853	32c. "Teshio Maru" (freighter)	85	80
854	32c. "Raizan Maru" (freighter)	85	80
855	32c. "Chuyo Maru" (freighter)	85	80
856	32c. "Shinsei Maru" (No. 18 freighter)	85	80
857	32c. "Urakami Maru" (freighter)	85	80
858	32c. "Ose Maru" (tanker)	85	80
859	32c. "Iro" (tanker)	85	80
860	32c. "Shosei Maru" (freighter)	85	80
861	32c. Patrol Boat 31	85	80
862	32c. "Kibi Maru" (freighter)	85	80
863	32c. "Amatsu Maru" (tanker)	85	80
864	32c. "Gozan Maru" (freighter)	85	80
865	32c. "Matuei Maru" (freighter)	85	80
866	32c. "Nagisan Maru" (freighter)	85	80
867	32c. "Akashi" (repair ship)	85	80
868	32c. "Kamikazi Maru" (freighter)	85	80

Nos. 851/68 were issued together, *se-tenant*, forming a composite design.

104 "Pteranodon sternbergi"

1995. 25th Anniv of Earth Day. Prehistoric Winged Animals. Multicoloured.

869	32c. Type **104**	85	80
870	32c. "Pteranodon ingens"	85	80
871	32c. Pterodactyls	85	80
872	32c. Dorygnathus	85	80
873	32c. Dimorphodon	85	80
874	32c. Nyctosaurus	85	80
875	32c. "Pterodactylus kochi"	85	80
876	32c. Ornithodesmus	85	80
877	32c. "Diatryma" sp.	85	80
878	32c. Archaeopteryx	85	80
879	32c. Campylognathoides	85	80
880	32c. Gallodactylus	85	80
881	32c. Batrachognathus	85	80
882	32c. Scaphognathus	85	80
883	32c. Peteinosaurus	85	80
884	32c. "Ichthyornis" sp.	85	80
885	32c. Ctenochasma	85	80
886	32c. Rhamphorhynchus	85	80

Nos. 869/86 were issued together, *se-tenant*, forming a composite design.

105 Fairey Delta 2

1995. Research and Experimental Jet-propelled Aircraft. Multicoloured.

887	50c. Type **105**	1·30	1·20
888	50c. B-70 Valkyrie	1·30	1·20
889	50c. Douglas X-3 Stiletto	1·30	1·20
890	50c. Northrop/Nasa HL-10	1·30	1·20
891	50c. Bell XS-1	1·30	1·20
892	50c. Tupolev Tu-144	1·30	1·20
893	50c. Bell X-1	1·30	1·20
894	50c. Boulton Paul P.111	1·30	1·20
895	50c. EWR VJ 101C	1·30	1·20
896	50c. Handley Page HP-115	1·30	1·20
897	50c. Rolls Royce TMR "Flying Bedstead"	1·30	1·20
898	50c. North American X-15	1·30	1·20
MS899	$2 Concorde (84×28 mm) (postage)	5·00	4·75

106 Scuba Gear

1995. Submersibles. Multicoloured.

900	32c. Type **106**	85	80
901	32c. Cousteau midget submarine "Denise"	85	80
902	32c. Jim suit	85	80
903	32c. Beaver IV	85	80
904	32c. "Ben Franklin"	85	80
905	32c. U.S.S. "Nautilus" (submarine)	85	80
906	32c. Deep Rover	85	80
907	32c. Beebe bathysphere	85	80
908	32c. "Deep Star IV"	85	80
909	32c. U.S. Navy Deep Submergence Rescue Vehicle	85	80
910	32c. "Aluminaut" (aluminium submarine)	85	80
911	32c. "Nautile"	85	80
912	32c. "Cyana"	85	80
913	32c. French Navy (F.N.R.S.) bathyscaphe	85	80
914	32c. Woods Hole Oceanographic Institute's "Alvin"	85	80
915	32c. "Mir I" (research submarine)	85	80
916	32c. "Archimede" (bathyscaphe)	85	80
917	32c. "Trieste" (bathyscaphe)	85	80

Nos. 900/917 were issued together, *se-tenant*, forming a composite design.

107 Dolphins, Diver and Pufferfish

1995. "Singapore'95" International Stamp Exhibition. Marine Life. Multicoloured.

918	32c. Type **107**	80	75
919	32c. Turtle and diver	80	75
920	32c. Grouper, anemonefish and crab on sea-bed (emblem on right)	80	75
921	32c. Parrotfish, lionfish and angelfish (emblem on left)	80	75

108 Dove in Helmet (Peace)

1995. 50th Annivs of U.N.O. and F.A.O. Multicoloured.

922	60c. Type **108**	1·50	1·40
923	60c. Ibedul Gibbons (Palau chief) in flame (human rights)	1·50	1·40
924	60c. Palau atlas in open book (education)	1·50	1·40
925	60c. Bananas in tractor (agriculture)	1·50	1·40
MS926	Two sheets each 116×83 mm. (a) $2 National flag and Palau fruit dove; (b) $2 Irrigation of crops and anniversary emblem (FAO) (vert)	9·75	9·00

Nos. 922/5 were issued together, *se-tenant*, the centre of each block forming a composite design of the U.N. emblem.

109 Palau Fruit Doves

1995. First Anniv of Independence. Each showing Palau national flag. Multicoloured.

927	20c. Type **109**	50	45
928	20c. Rock Islands	50	45
929	20c. Map of Palau islands	50	45
930	20c. Orchid and hibiscus	50	45
931	32c. Raccoon butterflyfish, soldierfish and conch shell	80	75

110 "Preparing Tin-Fish" (William Draper)

1995. 50th Anniv of the End of Second World War. Multicoloured.

932	32c. Type **110**	80	75
933	32c. "Hellcat's Take-off into Palau's Rising Sun" (Draper)	80	75
934	32c. "Dauntless Dive Bombers over Malakal Harbor" (Draper)	80	75
935	32c. "Planes Return from Palau" (Draper)	80	75
936	32c. "Communion Before Battle" (Draper)	80	75
937	32c. "The Landing" (Draper)	80	75
938	32c. "First Task Ashore" (Draper)	80	75
939	32c. "Fire Fighters save Flak-torn Pilot" (Draper)	80	75
940	32c. "Young Marine Headed for Peleliu" (Tom Lea)	80	75
941	32c. "Peleliu" (Lea)	80	75
942	32c. "Last Rites" (Lea)	80	75
943	32c. "The Thousand Yard Stare" (Lea)	80	75
944	60c. "Admiral Chester W. Nimitz" (Albert Murray) (vert)	1·80	1·70
945	60c. "Admiral William F. Halsey" (Murray) (vert)	1·80	1·70
946	60c. "Admiral Raymond A. Spruance" (Murray) (vert)	1·80	1·70
947	60c. "Vice-Admiral Marc A. Mitscher" (Murray) (vert)	1·80	1·70
948	60c. "General Holland M. Smith" (Murray) (vert)	1·80	1·70
MS949	129×90 mm. $3 Nose art on B-29 bomber Bock's Car (38×24½ mm)	7·25	6·75

111 Angel with Animals

1995. Christmas. "We Three Kings of Orient Are" (carol). Multicoloured.

950	32c. Type **111**	80	75
951	32c. Two wise men	80	75
952	32c. Shepherd at crib	80	75
953	32c. Wise man and shepherd	80	75
954	32c. Children with goat	80	75

Nos. 950/4 were issued together, *se-tenant*, forming a composite design.

112 Mother and Young in Feeding Area

1995. Year of the Sea Turtle. Multicoloured.

955	32c. Type **112**	85	80
956	32c. Young adult females meeting males	85	80
957	32c. Sun, cockerel in tree and mating area	85	80
958	32c. Woman and hatchlings	85	80
959	32c. Couple and nesting area	85	80
960	32c. House and female swimming to lay eggs	85	80

Nos. 955/60 were issued together, *se-tenant*, forming a composite design of the turtle's life cycle.

113 Lennon

1995. 15th Death Anniv of John Lennon (entertainer).

961	113	32c. multicoloured	1·20	1·10

114 Rats leading Procession

1996. Chinese New Year. Year of the Rat. Multicoloured.

962	10c. Type **114**	55	50
963	10c. Three rats playing instruments	55	50
964	10c. Rats playing tuba and banging drum	55	50
965	10c. Family of rats outside house	55	50
MS966	131×63 mm. 60c. Family of rats outside house and rats playing tuba and banging drum (56×42 mm); (b) 60c. Rats playing instruments and leading procession (56×42 mm) (air)	2·75	2·50

Nos. 962/5 were issued together, *se-tenant*, forming a composite design of a procession.

115 Girls

1996. 50th Anniv of UNICEF. Each showing three children. Multicoloured.

967	32c. Type **115**	75	70
968	32c. Girl in centre wearing lei around neck	75	70
969	32c. Girl in centre wearing headscarf	75	70
970	32c. Boy in centre and girls holding bunches of grass	75	70

Nos. 967/70 were issued together, *se-tenant*, forming a composite design of the children around a globe and the UNICEF emblem.

116 Basslet and Vermiculate Parrotfish ("P")

1996. Underwater Wonders. Illuminated letters spelling out PALAU. Multicoloured.

971	32c. Type **116**	75	70
972	32c. Yellow-striped cardinalfish ("A")	75	70
973	32c. Pair of atoll butterflyfish ("L")	75	70
974	32c. Starry moray and slate-pencil sea urchin ("A")	75	70
975	32c. Blue-streaked cleaner wrasse and coral hind ("Grouper") ("U")	75	70

117 Ferdinand Magellan and "Vitoria"

1996. "CAPEX'96" International Stamp Exhibition, Toronto, Canada. Circumnavigators. Multicoloured. (a) POSTAGE

976	32c. Type **117** (postage)	75	70
977	32c. Charles Wilkes and U.S.S. "Vincennes" (sail frigate)	75	70
978	32c. Joshua Slocum and "Spray" (yacht)	75	70
979	32c. Ben Carlin and "Half-Safe" (amphibian)	75	70
980	32c. Edward Beach and U.S.S. "Triton" (submarine)	75	70
981	32c. Naomi James and "Express Crusader" (yacht)	75	70
982	32c. Sir Ranulf Fiennes and snow vehicle	75	70
983	32c. Rick Hansen and wheelchair	75	70
984	32c. Robin Knox-Johnson and "Enza New Zealand" (catamaran)	75	70
MS985	Two sheets each 110×80 mm. (a) $3 Sir Francis Chichester and "Gypsy Moth IV" (yacht); (b) $3 Bob Martin, Mark Sullivan and Troy Bradley and "Odyssey" (helium balloon)	14·50	13·50

(b) AIR

986	60c. Lowell Smith and Douglas world cruiser seaplanes (air)	1·50	1·40
987	60c. Ernst Lehmann and "Graf Zeppelin" (dirigible airship)	1·50	1·40
988	60c. Wiley Post and Lockheed Vega "Winnie Mae"	1·50	1·40
989	60c. Yuri Gagarin and "Vostok I" (spaceship)	1·50	1·40
990	60c. Jerrie Mock and Cessna 180 "Spirit of Columbus"	1·50	1·40
991	60c. H. Ross Perot jnr. and Bell LongRanger III helicopter "Spirit of Texas"	1·50	1·40
992	60c. Brooke Knapp and Gulfstream III "The American Dream"	1·50	1·40
993	60c. Jeana Yeager and Dick Rutan and "Voyager"	1·50	1·40
994	60c. Fred Lasby and Piper Commanche	1·50	1·40

118 Simba, Nala and Timon ("The Lion King")

1996. Disney Sweethearts. Multicoloured.

995 1c. Type **118** 25 10
996 2c. Georgette, Tito and Oliver ("Oliver & Company") 25 10
997 3c. Duchess, O'Malley and Marie ("The Aristocats") 25 10
998 4c. Bianca, Jake and Polly ("The Rescuers Down Under") 25 10
999 5c. Tod, Vixey and Copper ("The Fox and the Hound") 25 10
1000 6c. Thumper, Flower and their Sweethearts ("Bambi") 25 10
1001 60c. As No. 995 1·80 1·70
1002 60c. Bernard, Bianca and Mr. Chairman ("The Rescuers") 1·80 1·70
1003 60c. As No. 996 1·80 1·70
1004 60c. As No. 997 1·80 1·70
1005 60c. As No. 998 1·80 1·70
1006 60c. As No. 999 1·80 1·70
1007 60c. Robin Hood, Maid Marian and Alan-a-Dale ("Robin Hood") 1·80 1·70
1008 60c. As No. 1000 1·80 1·70
1009 60c. Pongo, Perdita and the Puppies ("101 Dalmatians") 1·80 1·70
MS1010 Two sheets each 110×131 mm. (a) $2 Bambi and Faline; (b) $2 Lady ("Lady and the Tramp") (vert) 11·50 10·50

119 Hakeem Olajuwan (basketball)

1996. Centenary of Modern Olympic Games and Olympic Games, Atlanta. Multicoloured.

1011 32c. Type **119** 80 75
1012 32c. Pat McCormick (gymnastics) 80 75
1013 32c. Jim Thorpe (pentathlon and decathlon) 80 75
1014 32c. Jesse Owens (athletics) 80 75
1015 32c. Tatyana Gutsu (gymnastics) 80 75
1016 32c. Michael Jordan (basketball) 80 75
1017 32c. Fu Mingxia (diving) 80 75
1018 32c. Robert Zmelik (decathlon) 80 75
1019 32c. Ivan Pedroso (long jumping) 80 75
1020 32c. Nadia Comaneci (gymnastics) 80 75
1021 32c. Jackie Joyner-Kersee (long jumping) 80 75
1022 32c. Michael Johnson (running) 80 75
1023 32c. Kristin Otto (swimming) 80 75
1024 32c. Vitai Scherbo (gymnastics) 80 75
1025 32c. Johnny Weissmuller (swimming) 80 75
1026 32c. Babe Didrikson (track and field athlete) 80 75
1027 32c. Eddie Tolan (track athlete) 80 75
1028 32c. Krisztina Egerszegi (swimming) 80 75
1029 32c. Sawao Kato (gymnastics) 80 75
1030 32c. Aleksandr Popov (swimming) 80 75
1031 40c. Fanny Blankers-Koen (track and field athlete) (vert) 90 85
1032 40c. Bob Mathias (decathlon) (vert) 90 85
1033 60c. Torchbearer entering Wembley Stadium, 1948 1·50 1·40
1034 60c. Entrance to Olympia Stadium, Athens, and flags 1·50 1·40

Nos. 1011/30 were issued together, *se-tenant*, forming a composite design of the athletes and Olympic rings.

120 The Creation

1996. 3000th Anniv of Jerusalem. Illustrations by Guy Rowe from "In Our Image: Character Studies from the Old Testament". Multicoloured.

1035 20c. Type **120** 45 40
1036 20c. Adam and Eve 45 40
1037 20c. Noah and his Wife 45 40
1038 20c. Abraham 45 40
1039 20c. Jacob's Blessing 45 40
1040 20c. Jacob becomes Israel 45 40
1041 20c. Joseph and his Brethren 45 40
1042 20c. Moses and Burning Bush 45 40
1043 20c. Moses and the Tablets 45 40
1044 20c. Balaam 45 40
1045 20c. Joshua 45 40
1046 20c. Gideon 45 40
1047 20c. Jephthah 45 40
1048 20c. Samson 45 40
1049 20c. Ruth and Naomi 45 40
1050 20c. Saul anointed 45 40
1051 20c. Saul denounced 45 40
1052 20c. David and Jonathan 45 40
1053 20c. David and Nathan 45 40
1054 20c. David mourns 45 40
1055 20c. Solomon praying 45 40
1056 20c. Solomon judging 45 40
1057 20c. Elijah 45 40
1058 20c. Elisha 45 40
1059 20c. Job 45 40
1060 20c. Isaiah 45 40
1061 20c. Jeremiah 45 40
1062 20c. Ezekiel 45 40
1063 20c. Nebuchadnezzar's Dream 45 40
1064 20c. Amos 45 40

121 Nankeen Night Heron

1996. Birds over Palau Lagoon. Multicoloured.

1065 50c. Eclectus parrot (female) ("Iakkotsiang") 1·20 1·10
1066 50c. Type **121** 1·20 1·10
1067 50c. Micronesian pigeon ("Belochel") 1·20 1·10
1068 50c. Eclectus parrot (male) ("Iakkotsiang") 1·20 1·10
1069 50c. White tern ("Sechosech") 1·20 1·10
1070 50c. Common noddy ("Mechadelbedaoch") 1·20 1·10
1071 50c. Nicobar pigeon ("Laib") 1·20 1·10
1072 50c. Chinese little bittern ("Cheloteachel") 1·20 1·10
1073 50c. Little pied cormorant ("Deroech") 1·20 1·10
1074 50c. Black-naped tern ("Kerkirs") 1·20 1·10
1075 50c. White-tailed tropic bird ("Dudek") 1·20 1·10
1076 50c. Sulphur-crested cockatoo ("Iakkotsiang") (white bird) 1·20 1·10
1077 50c. White-capped noddy ("Bedaoch") 1·20 1·10
1078 50c. Bridled tern ("Bedebedchakl") 1·20 1·10
1079 50c. Reef heron (grey) ("Sechou") 1·20 1·10
1080 50c. Grey-tailed tattler ("Kekereielderariik") 1·20 1·10
1081 50c. Reef heron (white) ("Sechou") 1·20 1·10
1082 50c. Audubon's shearwater ("Ochaieu") 1·20 1·10
1083 50c. Black-headed gull ("Oltirakladial") 1·20 1·10
1084 50c. Ruddy turnstone ("Omechederiibabad") 1·20 1·10

Nos. 1065/84 were issued together, se-tenant, forming a composite design.

122 Lockheed U-2

1996. Spy Planes. Multicoloured.

1085 40c. Type **122** 1·00 95
1086 40c. General Dynamics EF-111A 1·00 95
1087 40c. Lockheed YF-12A 1·00 95
1088 40c. Lockheed SR-71 1·00 95
1089 40c. Teledyne Ryan Tier II Plus 1·00 95
1090 40c. Lockheed XST 1·00 95
1091 40c. Lockheed ER-2 1·00 95
1092 40c. Lockheed F-117A Nighthawk 1·00 95
1093 40c. Lockheed EC-130E 1·00 95
1094 40c. Ryan Firebee 1·00 95
1095 40c. Lockheed Martin/Boeing Darkstar 1·00 95
1096 40c. Boeing E-3A Sentry 1·00 95
MS1097 120×90 mm. $3 Northrop B-2A Stealth Bomber (41×56 mm) 7·75 7·25

123 "The Birth of a New Nation"

1996. Second Anniv of Independence. Illustrations from "Kirie" by Koh Sekiguchi. Multicoloured.

1098 20c. Type **123** 50 45
1099 20c. "In the Blue Shade of Trees" 50 45

124 Pandanus

1996. Christmas. "O Tannenbaum" (carol). Decorated Trees. Multicoloured.

1100 32c. Type **124** 80 75
1101 32c. Mangrove 80 75
1102 32c. Norfolk Island pine 80 75
1103 32c. Papaya 80 75
1104 32c. Casuarina 80 75

Nos. 1100/4 were issued together, se-tenant, forming a composite design.

125 "Viking I" in Orbit (½-size illustration)

1996. Space Missions to Mars. Multicoloured.

1105 32c. Type **125** 80 75
1106 32c. "Viking I" emblem (top half) 80 75
1107 32c. "Mars Lander" firing de-orbit engines 80 75
1108 32c. "Viking I" emblem (bottom half) 80 75
1109 32c. Phobos (Martian moon) 80 75
1110 32c. "Mars Lander" entering Martian atmosphere 80 75
1111 32c. "Mariner 9" (first mission, 1971) 80 75
1112 32c. Parachute opens for landing and heat shield jettisons 80 75
1113 32c. Projected U.S./Russian manned spacecraft, 21st century (top half) 80 75
1114 32c. "Lander" descent engines firing 80 75
1115 32c. Projected U.S./Russian spacecraft (bottom half) 80 75
1116 32c. "Viking I Lander" on Martian surface, 1976 80 75
MS1117 Two sheets each 98×78 mm. (a) $3 Mars Rover (projected 1997 mission) (37×30 mm); (b) $3 Water probe (projected 1999 mission) 14·50 13·50

Nos. 1105/16 were issued together, se-tenant, forming several composite designs.

126 Northrop XB-35 Bomber

1996. Oddities of the Air. Aircraft Designs. Multicoloured.

1118 60c. Type **126** 1·50 1·40
1119 60c. Leduc O.21 1·50 1·40
1120 60c. Convair Model 118 flying car 1·50 1·40
1121 60c. Blohm und Voss BV 141 1·50 1·40
1122 60c. Vought V-173 1·50 1·40
1123 60c. McDonnell XF-85 Goblin 1·50 1·40
1124 60c. North American F-82B Twin Mustang fighter 1·50 1·40
1125 60c. Lockheed XFV-1 vertical take-off fighter 1·50 1·40
1126 60c. Northrop XP-79B 1·50 1·40
1127 60c. Saunders Roe SR/A1 flying boat fighter 1·50 1·40
1128 60c. "Caspian Sea Monster" hovercraft 1·50 1·40
1129 60c. Grumman X-29 demonstrator 1·50 1·40
MS1130 $3 Martin Marieeta X-24B (84×28 mm) 7·75 7·25

127 Ox Cart

1997. Chinese New Year. Year of the Ox. Sheet 76×106 mm.

MS1131 **127** $2 multicoloured 5·25 4·75

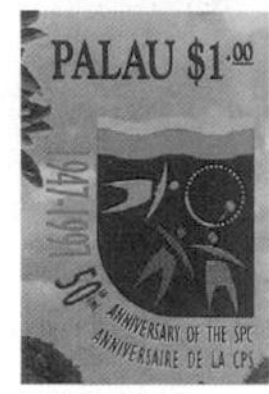

128 Emblem

1997. 50th Anniv of South Pacific Commission. Sheet 103×70 mm.

MS1132 **128** $1 multicoloured 2·40 2·30

129 Pemphis

1997. "Hong Kong '97" Stamp Exhibition. Flowers. Multicoloured.

1133 1c. Type **129** 25 15
1134 2c. Sea lettuce 25 15
1135 3c. Tropical almond 25 15
1136 4c. Guettarda 25 15
1137 5c. Pacific coral bean 25 15
1138 32c. Black mangrove 80 75
1139 32c. Cordia 80 75
1140 32c. Lantern tree 80 75
1141 32c. Palau rock-island flower 80 75
1142 50c. Fish-poison tree 1·20 1·10
1143 50c. Indian mulberry 1·20 1·10
1144 50c. Pacific poison-apple 1·20 1·10
1145 50c. "Ailanthus" sp. 1·20 1·10
1146 $3 Sea hibiscus (73×48 mm) 7·25 6·75

130 "Apollo 15" Command Module splashing-down

1997. Bicentenary of the Parachute. Multicoloured. (a) POSTAGE

1147 32c. Type **130** (postage) 80 75
1148 32c. Skydiving team in formation (40×23 mm) 80 75
1149 32c. Cargo drop from airplane 80 75
1150 32c. Parasailing (40×23 mm) 80 75
1151 32c. Parachutist falling to earth 80 75
1152 32c. Parachute demonstration team (40×23 mm) 80 75
1153 32c. Parachutist falling into sea 80 75
1154 32c. Drag-racing car (40×23 mm) 80 75
MS1155 Two sheets. (a) 72×102 mm. $2 Training tower, Fort Benning, Georgia (27×84 mm); (b) 102×72 mm. $2 "Funny Car" safety parachute (56×42 mm) 12·00 11·50

(b) AIR

1156 60c. Parachuting demonstration (air) 1·50 1·40
1157 60c. "The Blue Flame" (world land-speed record attempt) (40× 23 mm) 1·50 1·40
1158 60c. Atmospheric Re-entry Demonstrator (capsule with three canopies) 1·50 1·40
1159 60c. Spies parachuting behind enemy lines during Second World War (40×23 mm) 1·50 1·40
1160 60c. Andre Jacques Garnerin's first successful parachute descent (from balloon), 1797 1·50 1·40

2007. Tenth Death Anniv of Princess Diana. Two sheets containing T **296** and similar vert designs. Multicoloured.

MS2296	150×101 mm. 90c.×4, Type **296**;Wearing pearl necklace; Facing left, longer hair; Facing right, large pearl earring	11·00	10·50
MS2297	100×70 mm. $2 Wearing hat with veil	6·25	5·75

297 *Troides amphrysus*

2007. Butterflies. Multicoloured.

2298	2c. Type **297**	15	15
2299	3c. Inscr 'Paraeronia boebera'	15	15
2300	4c. *Delias catisa*	15	15
2301	5c. *Chilasa clytia*	25	20
2302	11c. *Ornithoptera goliath*	40	35
2303	15c. Insc 'Graphium delesseru'	45	45
2304	20c. *Euploea*	60	60
2305	23c. *Papilio euchenor*	70	65
2306	26c. *Ornithoptera tithonus*	85	80
2307	41c. *Hypolimnas misippus*	1·30	1·20
2308	45c. *Delias meeki*	1·40	1·30
2309	50c. *Papilio ulysses*	1·50	1·50
2310	75c. *Ornithoptera croseus*	2·30	2·20
2311	90c. *Trogonoptera brookiana*	3·00	2·75
2312	$1 *Idea lynceus*	3·00	3·00
2313	$2 *Parantica weiskei*	6·25	5·75
2314	$3 *Graphium weiskei*	9·25	8·75
2315	$4 *Ornithoptera goliath* (different)	12·50	11·50
2316	$5 *Attacus lorquini*	15·00	14·50
2317	$10 *Delias henningia*	31·00	29·00

298 Elvis Presley

2007. 30th Death Anniv of Elvis Presley. Two sheets containing T **298** and similar vert designs. Multicoloured.

MS2318	195×132 mm. 75c.×6, Type **298**; Holding guitar, mauve overlay; As Type **298**, greenish silver suit, olive-brown country and value imprint; Holding guitar, claret overlay; As Type **298**, silver suit, new blue country and value imprint; Holding guitar, orange-yellow/yellow-orange overlay	14·00	13·00
MS2319	100×70 mm. 75c.×6, Wearing dark grey shirt; Wearing green shirt; Wearing reddish shirt, eyes closed; As Type **298**, gold suit, white background; Standing wearing white shirt; Standing wearing blackish lilac suit	14·00	13·00

299 Eduardo Sevilla, Nicaragua

2007. United Nations General Assembly adoption of Holocaust Remembrance Resolution No. 60/7 (1 November 2005). Sheet 198×158 mm containing T **299** and similar vert designs. Multicoloured.

MS2320	50c.×8, Type **299**; Aminu Bashir Wali, Nigeria; Stuart Beck, Palau; Ricardo Alberto Arias, Panama; Robert Aisi, Papua New Guinea; Eladio Loizaga, Paraguay; Jorge Voto-Bernales, Peru; Ban-Ki Moon, Secretary General	12·50	11·50

300 Baubles

2007. Christmas. T **300** and similar vert designs. Multicoloured.

2321	22c. Type **301**	70	65
2322	26c. Green bauble	85	80
2323	41c. Blue baubles	1·30	1·20
2324	90c. Orange bauble with red bow	3·00	2·75

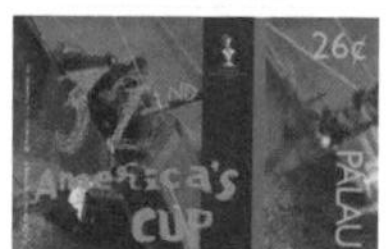

301 '32nd America's cup' and Yachts

2007. 32nd America's Cup. Designs showing emblem and yachts. Multicoloured.

2325	26c. Type **300**	85	80
2326	80c. Yacht with black and red keel, yellow-orange emblem	2·50	2·30
2327	$1.14 Yacht with inscribed dark blue keel, turquoise-green emblem	3·75	3·50
2328	$2 Yacht crowded with rescued crew, scarlet-vermilion emblem	6·25	5·75

Nos. 2325/8 were printed, *se-tenant*, in horizontal or vertical strips of four stamps within sheets of 16.

302 Rat

2008. Chinese New Year. Year of the Rat.

2329	**302**	50c. multicoloured	1·50	1·50

303 Crowd and 'Kennedy for President' Poster

2008. 45th Death Anniv of John F. Kennedy. Sheet 132×110 mm containing T **303** and similar vert designs. Multicoloured.

MS2330	90c.×4, Type **303**; John F. Kennedy reaching down into crowd; Speaking from podium; Speaking into microphones	11·00	10·50

304 1908 Fencing Poster

2008. History of the Olympic Games. London–1908. Sheet 178×102 mm containing T **304** and similar vert designs. Multicoloured.

MS2331	50c.×4, Type **304**; 1908 Olympic Games poster; Wyndham Halswelle–track gold medalist; Dorando Pietri–marathon runner	6·25	5·75

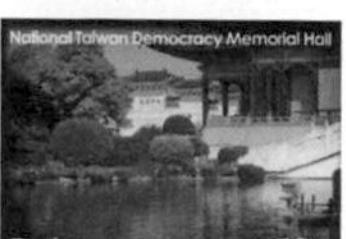

305 National Democracy Memorial Hall

2008. Sites and Scenes of Taiwan. Two sheets containing T **305** and similar horiz designs. Multicoloured.

MS2332	100×108 mm. 50c.×4, Type **305**; Chinese ornamental garden, Taipei; Taipei 101 tower and city-scape; Eastern coast	6·25	5·75
MS2333	100×70 mm. $2 Illuminated temple in southern Taiwan (51×47 mm)	6·25	5·75

306 Entrance to the City of David (image scaled to 49% of original size)

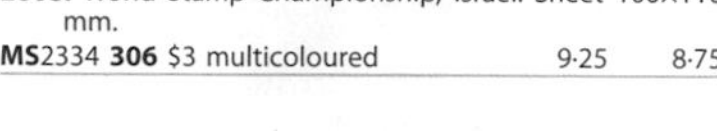

2008. World Stamp Championship, Israel. Sheet 100×110 mm.

MS2334 **306**	$3 multicoloured	9·25	8·75

307 Edmund Hillary and Prince Charles

2008. Sir Edmund Percival Hillary (first man to reach the summit of Mount Everest) Commemoration. Sheet 131×118 mm containing T **307** and similar horiz designs. Multicoloured.

MS2335	90c.×4, Type **307**; Facing left; With Lokendra Bahdur Chand (prime minister of Nepal); With cockatoo on shoulder	11·00	10·50

308 Pope Benedict XVI

2008. Visit of Pope Benedict XVI to the USA. Sheet 127×177 mm containing T **308** and similar horiz designs showing Pope Benedict XVI. Multicoloured

MS2336	90c.×4, Type **308**; As Type **308**, red smudge, central left shoulder; As Type **308**, two red smudges, front and rear of left shoulder; As Type **308**, heavier red strip, leaching into margin	11·00	10·50

Nos. 2337/40 and Type **309** are vacant.

310 Barack Obama

2009. Inauguration of President Barack Obama. Multicoloured.

MS2341	133×100 mm. 94c.×4, Type **310**; Facing left; Facing right; With hand raised	11·00	11·00
MS2342	111×80 mm. $2 Facing left with presidential seal in background (38×51 mm)	6·25	6·25

311 Ox

2009. Chinese New Year. Year of the Ox. Multicoloured.

MS2343	94c.×4, Type **311**×2; As Type **311** but with white central inscriptions×2	11·00	11·00

Pt. 1

PALESTINE

A territory at the extreme east of the Mediterranean Sea, captured from the Turks by Great Britain in 1917 and under Military Occupation until 1920. It was a British Mandate of the League of Nations from 1923 to May 1948 when the State of Israel was proclaimed.

1918. 10 milliemes = 1 piastre.
1927. 1,000 mills = £P1.

1

1918

3	**1**	1p. blue	2·00	2·00

(2)

1918. Surch with T **2**.

4	5m. on 1p. blue	8·00	2·75

3 "E.E.F." = Egyptian Expeditionary Force

1918

5	**3**	1m. brown	30	40
6	**3**	2m. green	30	45
7	**3**	3m. brown	50	35
8	**3**	4m. red	35	40
9a	**3**	5m. orange	65	30
10	**3**	1p. blue	50	25
11	**3**	2p. olive	3·50	60
12	**3**	5p. purple	3·75	2·50
13	**3**	9p. ochre	12·00	7·50
14	**3**	10p. blue	12·00	4·50
15	**3**	20p. grey	18·00	20·00

Nos. 1/15 were also valid in Transjordan, Cilicia, Lebanon and Syria.

فلسطين

PALESTINE

פלשתינה א״י

(4)

1920. Optd with T **4**.

71	1m. brown	2·25	30
61	2m. green	3·00	30
72	2m. yellow	3·00	30
62	3m. brown	3·25	30
73	3m. blue	3·25	15
74	4m. red	3·25	20
64	5m. orange	3·50	20
76	6m. green	2·75	30
77	7m. brown	2·75	30
78	8m. red	2·75	30
65	1p. blue	2·75	35
79	1p. grey	3·25	30
80	13m. blue	4·00	15
66	2p. olive	4·75	60
82	5p. purple	6·00	1·25
87	9p. ochre	9·50	9·00
88	10p. blue	8·50	4·00
26	20p. grey	35·00	50·00
89	20p. violet	11·00	5·50

9 Rachel's Tomb

10 Dome of the Rock

11 Citadel, Jerusalem

12 Sea of Galilee

1927

90	**9**	2m. blue	2·75	10

91	9	3m. green	1·75	10
92	10	4m. red	9·00	1·25
104	10	4m. purple	3·00	10
93	11	5m. orange	4·25	10
94a	10	6m. green	1·50	20
95	11	7m. red	11·00	60
105	11	7m. violet	1·00	10
96	10	8m. brown	18·00	6·50
106	10	8m. red	1·25	20
97	9	10m. grey	2·00	10
98	10	13m. blue	17·00	30
107	10	13m. brown	3·50	10
108a	10	15m. blue	5·50	40
99a	11	20m. olive	2·25	15
100	12	50m. purple	3·25	30
101	12	90m. bistre	85·00	60·00
102	12	100m. blue	2·25	70
103	12	200m. violet	8·00	5·00
109	12	250m. brown	7·50	3·50
110	12	500m. red	8·50	3·50
111	12	£P1 black	12·00	3·50

POSTAGE DUE STAMPS

D1

1920

D1	D1	1m. brown	26·00	38·00
D2	D1	2m. green	21·00	10·00
D3	D1	4m. red	10·00	13·00
D4	D1	8m. mauve	7·50	7·00
D5	D1	13m. blue	7·50	8·00

D2

1924

D6	D2	1m. brown	1·00	2·00
D7	D2	2m. yellow	4·00	1·75
D8	D2	4m. green	2·00	1·25
D9	D2	8m. red	3·00	90
D10	D2	13m. blue	3·25	2·50
D11	D2	5p. violet	14·00	1·75

1928. As Type **D2**, but inscr "MIL" instead of "MILLIEME".

D12	1m. brown	2·50	85
D13	2m. yellow	3·50	60
D14	4m. green	4·00	1·60
D15	6m. brown	18·00	5·00
D16	8m. red	2·75	1·75
D17	10m. grey	1·75	60
D18	13m. blue	4·50	2·75
D19	20m. olive	4·50	1·25
D20	50m. violet	4·75	2·25

Pt. 19

PALESTINIAN AUTHORITY

Following negotiations in Oslo, during which the Israeli government recognized the Palestine Liberation Organization as representing the Arab inhabitants of those areas occupied by Israel since 1967 and the P.L.O. accepted Israel's right to exist within secure borders, an agreement was signed in Washington on 13 September 1993 under which there was to be limited Palestinian self-rule in the Gaza Strip and in an enclave around Jericho on the West Bank. Further talks followed, leading to the Cairo Agreement of 4 May 1994, which inaugurated Palestinian Authority rule in Gaza and Jericho.

Under the Taba Accord of 28 September 1995 the Israeli army progressively withdrew from much of the remainder of the West Bank, which was then placed under Palestinian Authority administration.

1000 fils = 1 dinar

CURRENCY Israeli currency continued to be used in the Palestinian Authority areas. The first stamp issues had face values in mils, the currency of the Palestine Mandate period, but the Israeli authorities objected to this notional currency with the result that the face values were subsequently shown in the Jordanian currency of 1000 fils = 1 dinar.

PA1 Monument from Hisham Palace, Jericho

1994. Multicoloured.

PA1	5m. Type PA **1**	10	10
PA2	10m. Type PA **1**	10	10
PA3	20m. Type PA **1**	10	10
PA4	30m. Church of the Holy Sepulchre, Jerusalem	15	15
PA5	40m. As No. PA4	20	20
PA6	50m. As No. PA4	25	25
PA7	75m. As No. PA4	35	35
PA8	125m. Flags of Palestinian Authority	45	45
PA9	150m. As No. PA8	60	60
PA10	250m. As No. PA8	1·20	1·20
PA11	300m. As No. PA8	1·50	1·50
PA12	500m. Flags of Palestinian Authority (51×29 mm)	2·10	2·10
PA13	1000m. Dome of the Rock, Jerusalem (51×29 mm)	4·75	4·75

PA2 Arms of Palestinian Authority

1994

PA14	**PA2**	50m. yellow	25	25
PA15	**PA2**	100m. green	35	35
PA16	**PA2**	125m. blue	45	45
PA17	**PA2**	200m. orange	95	95
PA18	**PA2**	250m. yellow	1·20	1·20
PA19	**PA2**	400m. purple	1·70	1·70

PA3 Prime Minister Rabin of Israel and Chairman Arafat of P.L.O. with Pres. Clinton

1994. Gaza and Jericho Peace Agreement. Sheet 105×70 mm.

MSPA20 PA **3** 750m.+250m. multicoloured 4·75 4·75

PA4 "Land of My Dreams" (Ibrahim Hazimeh)

1995. 50th Anniv of Arab League. Sheet 105×70 mm.

MSPA21 PA **4** 750f.+250f. multicoloured 4·75 4·75

1995. Award of Nobel Peace Prize to Yasser Arafat, Yitzhak Rabin and Shimon Peres. No. MSPA20 surch FILS English and Arabic.

MSPA22 PA **3** 740f.+250f. multicoloured 5·75 5·75

NEW CURRENCY. From No. PA23 the face values are expressed as 1000 fils = 1 Jordanian dinar.

PA6 Palestine Mandate 1927 2m. Stamp

1995. Palestine Postal History.

PA23	**PA6**	150f. green and black	70	70
PA24	-	350f. orange and black	1·60	1·60
PA25	-	500f. red and black	2·10	2·10

DESIGNS: 350f. Palestine Mandate 1927; 5m. stamp; 500f. Palestine Mandate 1932; 8m. stamp.

PA7 Woman in Embroidered Costume

1995. Traditional Palestinian Women's Costumes. Multicoloured.

PA26	250f. Type PA **7**	1·20	1·20
PA27	300f. Woman carrying basket	1·40	1·40
PA28	550f. Woman in cloak	2·75	2·75
PA29	900f. Woman in veiled head-dress	4·00	4·00

1995. Nos. PA1/13 surch **FILS** in English and Arabic.

PA30	**PA1**	5f. on 5m. mult	10	10
PA31	**PA1**	10f. on 10m. mult	10	10
PA32	**PA1**	20f. on 20m. mult	10	10
PA33	-	30f. on 30m. mult	15	15
PA34	-	40f. on 40m. mult	20	20
PA35	-	50f. on 50m. mult	25	25
PA36	-	75f. on 75m. mult	35	35
PA37	-	125f. on 125m. mult	45	45
PA38	-	150f. on 150m. mult	60	60
PA39	-	250f. on 250m. mult	1·20	1·20
PA40	-	300f. on 300m. mult	1·50	1·50
PA41	-	500f. on 500m. mult	2·10	2·10
PA42	-	1000f. on 1000m. mult	4·75	4·75

PA9

1995. Handstamped Fils within circle in English and Arabic, twice on each stamp. As Type **PA9**. (a) On Nos. PA1/13.

PA43	**PA1**	5f. on 5m. mult	10	10
PA44	**PA1**	10f. on 10m. mult	10	10
PA45	**PA1**	20f. on 20m. mult	10	10
PA46	-	30f. on 30m. mult	15	15
PA47	-	40f. on 40m. mult	20	20
PA48	-	50f. on 50m. mult	25	25
PA49	-	75f. on 75m. mult	35	35
PA50	-	125f. on 125m. mult	45	45
PA51	-	150f. on 150m. mult	60	60
PA52	-	250f. on 250m. mult	1·20	1·20
PA53	-	300f. on 300m. mult	1·50	1·50
PA54	-	500f. on 500m. mult	2·10	2·10
PA55	-	1000f. on 1000m. mult	4·75	4·75

(b) On Nos. **PA14/19**.

PA56	**PA2**	50f. on 50m. yellow	25	25
PA57	**PA2**	100f. on 100m. green	35	35
PA58	**PA2**	125f. on 125m. blue	45	45
PA59	**PA2**	200f. on 200m. orange	95	95
PA60	**PA2**	250f. on 250m. yellow	1·20	1·20
PA61	**PA2**	400f. on 400m. purple	1·70	1·70

MSPA62 PA **3** 750f.+250f. on 750m.+250m. multicoloured 5·75 5·75

PA10 Bethlehem (old print)

1995. Christmas. Multicoloured.

PA63	10f. Type PA**10**	15	15
PA64	20f. Manger Square, Bethlehem	20	20
PA65	50f. Entrance to Church of the Nativity (vert)	25	25
PA66	100f. Pope John Paul II with Yasser Arafat	70	70
PA67	1000f. Site of the Nativity	6·50	6·50

PA11 Yasser Arafat

1996

PA68	**PA11**	10f. black and lilac	10	10
PA69	**PA11**	20f. black and yellow	20	20
PA70	**PA11**	50f. black and blue	25	25
PA71	**PA11**	100f. black and green	60	60
PA72	**PA11**	1000f. black & brown	5·25	5·25

PA12 Summer Palace, Peking

1996. Int Stamp Exhibitions and Fairs. Multicoloured.

PA73	20f. Type PA **12** ("China '96")	25	25
PA74	50f. Hagia Sofia Mosque, Istanbul ("Istanbul '96")	35	35
PA75	100f. Villa Hugel, Essen (Essen stamp fair)	60	60
PA76	1000f. Modern skyline, Toronto ("Capex '96")	5·75	5·75

PA13 Crowd of Palestinians

1996. First Presidential Legislative and Presidential Elections. Sheet 105×70 mm.

MSPA77 PA **13** 1250f. multicoloured 7·00 7·00

PA14 Boxing

1996. Olympic Games, Atlanta. Multicoloured.

PA78	30f. Type PA **14**	15	15
PA79	40f. Olympic medal of 1896	25	25
PA80	50f. Running	35	35
PA81	150f. Olympic flame and flag	80	80
PA82	1000f. Palestinian Olympic Committee emblem	6·00	6·00
PAPA83	140×105 mm. Nos. PA78 and PA80/1	4·75	4·75

PA15 Poppy

1996. Flowers and Fruit. Multicoloured.

PA84	10f. Type **PA15**	10	10
PA85	25f. Hibiscus	15	15
PA86	100f. Thyme	60	60
PA87	150f. Lemon	95	95
PA88	750f. Orange	4·75	4·75
MSPA89	105×70 mm. 1000f. Olive	5·75	5·75

PA 16 Three Wise Men

1996. Christmas. Sheet 165×105 mm containing Type **PA16** and similar square designs. Multicoloured.

MSPA90 150f. Type PA **16**; 350f. Bethlehem; 500f. Shepherds; 750f. The Nativity 9·25 9·25

No. **MS**PA90 form a composite design.

PA17 Great Tits

1997. Birds. Multicoloured.

PA91	25f. Type PA **17**	35	35
PA92	75f. Blue rock thrushes	45	45
PA93	150f. Golden orioles	1·00	1·00
PA94	350f. Hoopoes	2·20	2·20
PA95	600f. Peregrine falcons	3·00	3·00

PA18 Gaza

1997. Palestinian Towns in 1839. Each brown and black.

PA96	350f. Type PA **18**	1·50	1·50
PA97	600f. Hebron	2·50	2·50

PA19 Chinese Junk

1997. Return of Hong Kong to China. Sheet 140X90 mm.

MSPA98 PA **19** 225f. multicoloured	1·20	1·20

PA20 Yasser Arafat and Wischnewski

1997. Friends of Palestine (1st series). Hans-Jurgen Wischnewski (German politician). Multicoloured.

PA99 600f. Type PA **20**	2·10	2·10
PA100 600f. Wischnewski congratulating Yasser Arafat	2·10	2·10

See also Nos. PA103/4.

PA21 "The Young Jesus in the Temple" (Anton Wollenek)

1997. Christmas.

PA101 **PA21** 350f. multicoloured	1·30	1·30
PA102 **PA21** 700f. multicoloured	2·50	2·50

PA22 Mother Teresa and Street Scene

1997. Friends of Palestine (2nd series). Mother Teresa (founder of Missionaries of Charity). Multicoloured.

PA103 600f. Type PA **22**	2·10	2·10
PA104 600f. Mother Teresa with Yasser Arafat	2·10	2·10

PA23 Baal, Tyre and Bull

1998. Baal (Canaanite god). Sheet 72×109 mm.

MSPA105 PA **23** 600f. multicoloured	3·00	3·00

PA24 Hare and Palm Tree

1998. Mosaics from Jabalia. Multicoloured.

PA106 50f. Type PA **24**	35	35
PA107 125f. Goat, hare and hound	80	80
PA108 200f. Lemon tree and baskets	1·30	1·30
PA109 400f. Lion	2·30	2·30

PA25 Sea Onion

1998. Medicinal Plants. Multicoloured.

PA110 40f. Type PA **25**	15	15
PA111 80f. "Silybum marianum"	35	35
PA112 500f. "Foeniculum vulgare"	2·10	2·10
PA113 800f. "Inula viscosa"	3·50	3·50

PA 26 Emblem

1998. Admission of Palestinian Authority as Non-voting Member to United Nations Organization. Sheet 82×65 mm.

MSPA114 PA**26** 700f. multicoloured	3·25	3·25

PA27 Bonelli's Eagle

1998. Birds of Prey. Multicoloured.

PA115 20f. Type PA **27**	15	15
PA116 60f. Northern hobby ("Hobby")	25	25
PA117 340f. Verreaux's eagle	1·40	1·40
PA118 600f. Bateleur	2·50	2·50
PA119 900f. Common buzzard ("Buzzard")	3·75	3·75

PA 28 Southern Swallowetail (Papilio alexanor)

1998. Butterflies. Sheet 106×84 mm containing Type **PA28** and similar horiz designs. Multicoloured.

MSPA120 100f. Type PA **28**; 200f. African monarch; 300f. *Gonepteryx cleopatra*; 400f. *Melanargia titea*	5·50	5·50

PA 29 Ornamental Star

1998. Christmas. Sheet 90×140 mm.

MSPA121 PA **29** 1000f. multicoloured	5·00	5·00

PA 30 Yasser Arafat and U.S. Pres Clinton signing Agreement

1999. Wye River Middle East Peace Agreement. Sheet 83×65 mm.

MSPA122 PA **30** 900f. multicoloured	4·00	4·00

PA31 Control Tower

1999. Inauguration of Gaza International Airport. Multicoloured.

PA123 80f. Type PA **31**	25	25
PA124 300f. Fokkar F.27 Friendship airliner (horiz)	1·00	1·00
PA125 700f. Terminal building (horiz)	2·75	2·75

PA32 Peking ("China'99")

1999. International Stamp Exhibitions and Anniversary. Multicoloured.

PA126 20f. Type PA **32**	25	25
PA127 80f. Melbourne ("Australia 99")	35	35
PA128 260f. Nuremberg ("iBRA'99")	1·30	1·30
PA129 340f. Paris ("Philexfrance 99")	1·60	1·60
PA130 400f. Emblem and landscape (face value at right) (125th anniv of U.P.U.)	1·70	1·70
PA131 400f. As No. PA130 but face value at left	1·70	1·70

PA33 Relief by Anton Wollenek

1999. Hebron.

PA132 **PA33** 400f. multicoloured	1·90	1·90
PA133 **PA33** 500f. multicoloured	2·50	2·50

PA34 Horse and Foal

1999. Arabian Horses. Multicoloured.

PA134 25f. Type PA **34**	25	25
PA135 75f. Black horse	35	35
PA136 150f. Horse rearing	70	70
PA137 350f. Horse trotting	1·60	1·60
PA138 800f. Brown horse	4·25	4·25

PA35 Madonna and Child

1999. Christmas (1st series).

PA139 **PA35** 60f. blue, black and ochre	20	20
PA140 **PA35** 80f. multicoloured	25	25
PA141 **PA35** 100f. multicoloured	35	35
PA142 **PA35** 280f. multicoloured	95	95
PA143 **PA35** 300f. multicoloured	1·00	1·00
PA144 **PA35** 400f. multicoloured	1·40	1·40
PA145 **PA35** 500f. multicoloured	1·90	1·90
PA146 **PA35** 560f. multicoloured	2·10	2·10

See also Nos. PA147/57.

PA36 Nativity

1999. Christmas (2nd series). Designs with frames and face values in colours indicated.

PA147 **PA36** 200f. multicoloured (black)	35	35
PA148 **PA36** 200f. multicoloured (silver)	1·00	1·00
PA149 **PA36** 280f. multicoloured (white)	45	45
PA150 **PA36** 280f. multicoloured (silver)	1·40	1·40
PA151 - 380f. multicoloured (black)	60	60
PA152 - 380f. multicoloured (silver)	1·70	1·70
PA153 - 460f. multicoloured (white)	75	75
PA154 - 460f. multicoloured (silver)	2·20	2·20
PA155 - 560f. multicoloured (lemon)	95	95
PA156 - 560f. multicoloured (silver)	3·50	3·50
PA157 **PA 36** 2000f. multicoloured	8·25	8·25

DESIGNS: 380, 460f. Adoration of the Magi; 560f. Flight into Egypt.

PA 37 Palestine Sunbird

1999. Sheet 105×70 mm.

MSPA158 PA **37** 750f. multicoloured	3·50	3·50

PA 38 *The Last Supper*

2000. Easter. Paintings by Giotto di Bondone. Multicoloured.

PA159 150f. Type PA **38**	45	45
PA160 200f. As Type PA **38**	70	70
PA161 750f. *Lamentation*	95	95
PA162 800f. As No. PA161	1·40	1·40
PA163 1000r. *Crucificion*	2·30	2·30
MSPA164 155×98 mm. 2000f. As No. PA163.	8·25	8·25

No. **MS**PA164 has the outline of the cross embossed in gold foil.

PA 39 Landscape

2000. Children's Drawings. Multicoloured.

PA165 50f. Type PA **39**	35	35
PA166 100f. Two boys	45	45
PA167 350f. Buildings	1·50	1·50
PA168 400f. Woman crying	2·00	2·00

PA 40 Pope John Paul II and Yassar Arafat

2000. Papal Visit. Multicoloured.

PA169 500f. Type PA **40**	1·70	1·70
PA170 600f. Pope John Paul II	2·10	2·10
PA171 750f. With hand on Yassar Arafat	2·50	2·50
PA172 800f. Looking at crib	3·00	3·00
PA173 1000r. Talking to Yassar Arafat	3·50	3·50

2000. Bethlehem 2000.As Type **PA36.** Multicoloured.

PA174 2000f. As No. PA157 but face value at top left	7·00	7·00
PA175 2000f. As **MS**PA164 but inscription in white (horiz)	7·00	7·00
PA176 2000f. *Madonna and Child* (Fra Angelico)	7·00	7·00

PA 41 Yasser Arafat and Gerhard Schroder (German Chancellor)

2000. Yasser Arafat's Visit to Germany. Multicoloured.

PA177 200f. Type PA **41**	80	80
PA178 300f. With President Johannes Rau	1·30	1·30

PA 42 Parrotfish

2000. Marine Fauna. Sheet 175×105 mm containing Type **PA42** and similar square designs. Multicoloured.

MSPA179 700f.×8, Type PA **42**; Mauve stinger; Ornate wrasse; Rainbow wrasse; Redstarfish; Common octopus; Purple sea urchin; Striated hermit crab	19·00	19·00

The stamps and margins of **MS**PA179 form a composite design of the seabed.

PA 43 *Blue Madonna*

2000. Sheet 70×110 mm.

MSPA180	multicoloured	3·50	3·50

PA 44 *Nativity* (Gentile da Fabriano)

2000. Christmas. Multicoloured.

PA181	100f. Type PA 44	25	25
PA182	150f. *Adoration of the Magi* (Gentile da Fabriano)	60	60
PA183	250f. *Annunciation* (Fra Angelico)	95	95
PA184	350f. *Madonna and Child* (Fra Angelico) (As No. PA176) (vert)	1·40	1·40
PA185	500f. As Type PA **44**	1·70	1·70
PA186	1000f. As No. PA184 (vert)	3·25	3·25
MSPA187	56×71 mm. As No. PA184	7·25	7·25

No. **MS**PA187 has halos and dress decoration embossed in gold foil.

PA 45 *Christ carrying the Cross* (Fra Angelico)

2000. Easter. Multicoloured.

PA188	150f. Type PA **45**	60	60
PA189	200f. As Type PA **45**	70	70
PA190	300f. *Removing Christ from the Cross* (Fra Angelico)	1·30	1·30
PA191	350f. As No. PA190	1·60	1·60
MSPA192	155×98 mm. 2000f. *Crucificion* (Giotto di Bondone) (vert).	7·25	7·25

No. **MS**PA192 has the figure of Christ embossed in gold foil.

PA 46 Palestine Authority and Organization for African Unity

2001. International Co-operation. Designs showing Palestine flag conjoined with other organizations. Multicoloured.

PA193	50f. Type PA **46**	25	25
PA194	100f. Organisation of the Islamic Conference	45	45
PA195	200f. European Union	70	70
PA196	500f. Arab League	1·70	1·70

PA 47 *Jerusalem after Rain*

2001. Art for Peace. Sheet 127×138 mm containing Type **PA47** and similar vert designs showing paintings by Ibrahim Hazimeh. Multicoloured.

MSPA197	350f. Type PA **47**; 550f. *Mysticism*; 850f. *Ramallah*; 900f. *Remembrance*	9·25	9·25

PA 48 Scene from *Aladdin and the Wonderful Lamp*

2001. Tales from the Arabian Nights. Designs showing scenes from the stories. Multicoloured.

PA198	300f. Type PA **48**	95	95
PA199	450f. *Adventures of Sinbad*	1·50	1·50
PA200	650f. *The Enchanted Horse'*	2·30	2·30
PA201	800f. *Ali Baba and the Forty Thieves*	2·75	2·75

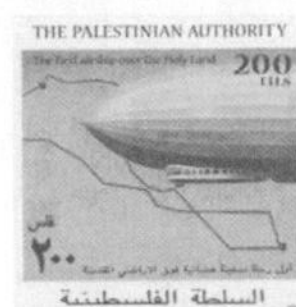

PA 49 Airship and Map of Route

2001. 70th Anniv of Flight of Graf Zeppelin (LZ-127) over Palestine. Multicoloured.

PA202	200f. Type PA **49**	95	95
PA203	600f. Airship over Palestine	2·50	2·50

PA 50 Male Displaying

2001. Houbara Bustard (Chlamydotis undulata). Multicoloured.

PA204	350f. Type PA **50**	1·70	1·70
PA205	350f. Chick	1·70	1·70
PA206	750f. Female	3·50	3·50
PA207	750f. Male	3·50	3·50

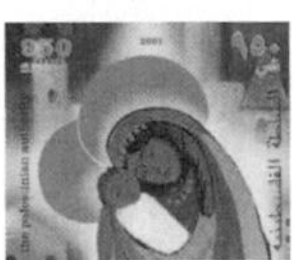

PA 51 Madonna and Child

2001. Peace for Bethlehem. Sheet 90×90 mm.

MSPA208	multicoloured	3·50	3·50

PA 52 Woman

2002. Traditional Costumes. Designs showing women wearing traditional dress. Multicoloured.

PA209	50f. Type PA **52**	25	25
PA210	100f. Wearing tall headdress and yellow skirt	45	45
PA211	500f. White head veil and panelled skirt	2·10	2·10

PA 53 Jerusalem

2002. Historic City Views. Multicoloured.

PA212	450f. Type PA **53**	1·70	1·70
PA213	650f. El-Eizariya	2·30	2·30
PA214	850f. Nablus	3·00	3·00

PA 54 Madonna and Child

2002. Christmas. Sheet 98×85 mm.

MSPA215	multicoloured	3·75	3·75

PA 55 Prickly Pear

2003. Flora. Multicoloured.

PA216	550f. Type PA **55**	2·00	2·00
PA217	600f. Euphorbia	2·20	2·20
PA218	750f. Agave (century plant)	2·75	2·75
MSPA219	110×66 mm. Nos. PA216/18	7·25	7·25

PA 56 Olive Tree

2003. Trees. Multicoloured.

PA220	300f. Type PA **56**	1·40	1·40
PA221	700f. Blessing tree	2·75	2·75

PA 57 Al-Azhar University, Gaza

2003. Universities. Multicoloured.

PA222	250f. Type PA **57**	95	95
PA223	650f. Hebron University	2·30	2·30
PA224	800f. Arab American University, Jenin	3·00	3·00

PA 58 Glass Necklace

2003. Handicrafts. Multicoloured.

PA225	150f. Type PA **58**	70	70
PA226	200f. Headdress	80	80
PA227	450f. Embroidery	2·00	2·00
PA228	500f. Embroidery on costume	2·30	2·30
PA229	950f. Head veil	4·25	4·25

PA 59 Madonna and Child

2004. Christmas. Sheet 100×75 mm.

MSPA230	**PA59** 1000f. multicoloured	5·00	5·00

PA 60 Yasser Arafat and Jaques Chirac (French president 1995–2007)

2004. Friends of Peace. Sheet 100×100 mm containing Type **PA60** and similar horiz design. Multicoloured.

MSPA231	200f.×2, Type PA **60**×2; 450f.×2, Jaques Chirac×2	6·50	6·50

PA 61 Town

2005. 60th Anniv of Arab League. Sheet 105×70 mm.

MSPA232	**PA 61** 750f. multicoloured	3·75	3·75

PA 62 Mahmud Darwish

2008. Visit (2007) of Mahmud Darwish (Palestinian writer).

PA233	**PA 62** 350f. multicoloured	1·70	1·70

Nos. PA234/6 are left for additions to Visit (2007) of Mahmud Darwish (Palestinian writer).

PA 63 Emblem and Skyline

2009. Al Quds–Arab Capital of Culture. Multicoloured.

PA237	100f. Type PA **63**		
PA238	150f. As Type PA **63**		
PA239	500f. Type PA **63**		
PA240	1000f. Emblem (central, large)		

Pt. 15

PANAMA

Country situated on the C. American isthmus. Formerly a State or Department of Colombia, Panama was proclaimed an independent republic in 1903.

1878. 100 centavos = 1 peso.
1906. 100 centesimos = 1 balboa.

1 Coat of Arms

1878. Imperf. The 50c. is larger.

1A	1	5c. green	31·00	37·00
2A	1	10c. blue	80·00	80·00
3A	1	20c. red	44·00	35·00
4B	1	50c. yellow	17·00	

3 Map

1887. Perf.

5	3	1c. black on green	1·20	95
6	3	2c. black on pink	1·80	1·40
7	3	5c. black on blue	1·20	35
7a	3	5c. black on grey	1·40	45
8	3	10c. black on yellow	1·40	45
9	3	20c. black on lilac	1·70	55
10	3	50c. brown	2·50	1·20

5 Map of Panama

1892

12a	5	1c. green	30	30
12b	5	2c. red	50	30
12c	5	5c. blue	2·10	65
12d	5	10c. orange	40	30
12e	5	20c. violet	65	45
12f	5	50c. brown	70	45
12g	5	1p. lake	7·25	4·25

1894. Surch **HABILITADO 1894** and value.

13		1c. on 2c. red	70	45
15	3	5c. on 20c. black on lilac	3·50	1·90
18	3	10c. on 50c. brown	3·75	3·75

1903. Optd **REPUBLICA DE PANAMA**.

70B	5	1c. green	95	95
36B	5	2c. red	1·30	1·20
72B	5	5c. blue	1·30	1·00
38A	5	10c. orange	2·75	2·50
39A	5	20c. violet	5·25	4·50
40B	5	50c. brown	12·50	9·25
75B	3	50c. brown	31·00	26·00
41B	5	1p. lake	65·00	50·00

1903. Optd **PANAMA** twice.

53	5	1c. green	30	30
54	5	2c. red	30	30
55	5	5c. blue	40	30
56	5	10c. orange	40	30
64	5	20c. violet	6·25	6·00
65	5	50c. brown	12·50	12·00
66	5	1p. lake	15·00	15·00

1904. Optd **Republica de Panama**.

94		1c. green	50	45
97		2c. red	60	55
98		5c. blue	60	55
99		10c. orange	60	55
100		20c. violet	60	55
103	3	50c. brown	3·75	3·75
104	5	1p. lake	18·00	16·00

38 Map of Panama

1905

151	38	½c. orange	1·20	55
136	38	1c. green	75	55
137	38	2c. red	1·20	65

1906. Surch **PANAMA** twice and new value and thick bar.

138	5	1c. on 20c. violet	30	30
139	5	2c. on 50c. brown	30	30
140	5	5c. on 1p. lake	70	45

41 Panamanian Flag
42 Vasco Nunez de Balboa
43 F. de Cordoba

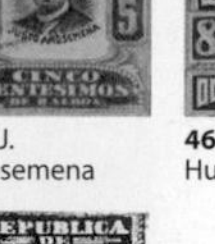
44 Arms of Panama
45 J. Arosemena
46 M. J. Hurtado
47 J. de Obaldia

1906

142	41	½c. multicoloured	75	65
143	42	1c. black and green	75	65
144	43	2c. black and red	1·10	65
145	44	2½c. red	1·10	65
146	45	5c. black and blue	1·30	65
147	46	8c. black and purple	1·60	1·20
148	47	10c. black and violet	1·60	65
149	-	25c. black and brown	3·75	2·00
150	-	50c. black	9·75	6·50

DESIGNS: 25c. Tomas Herrera; 50c. Jose de Fabrega.

48 Balboa
49 De Cordoba
50 Arms

51 Arosemena
52 Hurtado
53 Obaldia

1909

152	48	1c. black and green	1·20	95
153	49	2c. black and red	1·20	55
154	50	2½c. red	1·60	55
155	51	5c. black and blue	2·10	55
156	52	8c. black and purple	9·75	5·50
157	53	10c. black and purple	4·00	2·00

56 Balboa viewing Pacific Ocean

1913. 400th Anniv of Discovery of Pacific Ocean.

160	56	2½c. yellow and green	1·90	75

57 Balboa reaches the Pacific

1915. Panama Exhibition and Opening of Canal.

161	-	½c. black and olive	50	35
162	-	1c. black and green	1·10	35
163	57	2c. black and red	85	35
164	-	2½c. black and red	1·20	45
165	-	3c. black and violet	1·70	65
166	-	5c. black and blue	2·40	45
167	-	10c. black and orange	2·30	85
168	-	20c. black and brown	11·50	3·50

DESIGNS: ½c. Chorrera Falls; 1c. Relief Map of Panama Canal; 2½c. Cathedral ruins, Old Panama; 3c. Palace of Arts, National Exhibition; 5c. Gatun Locks; 10c. Culebra Cut; 20c. Archway, S. Domingo Monastery.

62 Balboa Docks

1918. Views of Panama Canal.

178		12c. black and violet	17·00	6·50
179		15c. black and blue	11·50	4·00
180		24c. black and brown	17·00	4·00
181	62	50c. black and orange	34·00	24·00
182	-	1b. black and violet	42·00	28·00

DESIGNS: 12c. "Panama" (cargo liner) in Gaillard Cut, north; 15c. "Panama" in Gaillard Cut, south; 24c. "Cristobal" (cargo liner) in Gatun Locks; 1b. "Nereus" (U.S. Navy collier) in Pedro Miguel Locks.

1919. 400th Anniv of Founding of City of Panama. No. 164 surch **1519 1919 2 CENTESIMOS 2**.

183		2c. on 2½c. black and red	50	50

64 Arms of Panama

65 Vallarino

68 Bolivar's Speech

1921. Independence Centenary. Dated "1821 1921".

184	64	½c. orange	85	30
185	65	1c. green	1·20	30
186	-	2c. red ("Land Gate", Panama City)	1·40	30
187	65	2½c. red (Bolivar)	3·00	1·50
188	-	3c. violet (Cervantes statue)	3·00	1·50
189	68	5c. blue	3·00	55
190	65	8c. olive (Carlos Ycaza)	10·50	4·00
191	-	10c. violet (Government House 1821–1921)	7·25	1·90
192	-	15c. blue (Balboa statue)	8·75	2·40
193	-	20c. brown (Los Santos Church)	15·00	4·00
194	65	24c. sepia (Herrera)	15·00	4·75
195	-	50c. black (Fabrega)	27·00	9·25

70 Hurtado

1921. Birth Centenary of Manuel Jose Hurtado (writer).

196	70	2c. green	70	65

1923. No. 164 surch **1923 2 CENTESIMOS 2**.

197		2c. on 2½c. black and red	50	45

72

1924

198	72	½c. orange	30	20
199	72	1c. green	30	20
200	72	2c. red	30	20
201	72	5c. blue	60	25
202	72	10c. violet	70	30
203	72	12c. olive	85	45
204	72	15c. blue	1·10	45
205	72	24c. brown	2·10	65
206	72	50c. orange	5·25	1·20
207	72	1b. black	7·75	2·75

73 Simon Bolivar

74 Statue of Bolivar

75 Congress Hall, Panama

1926. Bolivar Congress.

208	73	½c. orange	60	30
209	73	1c. green	60	30
210	73	2c. red	75	35
211	73	4c. grey	95	45
212	73	5c. blue	1·50	65
213	74	8c. purple	2·40	1·00
214	74	10c. violet	1·70	95
215	74	12c. olive	2·75	1·40
216	74	15c. blue	3·50	1·70
217	74	20c. brown	7·25	2·40
218	75	24c. slate	8·75	2·40
219	75	50c. black	14·50	6·50

78 "Spirit of St. Louis" over Map

1928. Lindbergh's Flying Tour.

222	-	2c. red on rose	40	30
223	78	5c. blue on green	60	45

DESIGN—VERT: 2c. "Spirit of St. Louis" over Old Panama with opt **HOMENAJE A LINDBERGH**.

1928. 25th Anniv of Independence. Optd **1903 NOV 3 BRE 1928**.

224	70	2c. green	30	30

1929. Air. No. E226 surch with Fokker Universal airplane and **CORREO AEREO 25 25 VEINTICINCO CENTESIMOS**.

225	E81	25c. on 10c. orange	1·20	95

1929. Air. Nos. E226/7 optd **CORREO AEREO** or additionally surch with new value in CENTESIMOS.

238		5c. on 10c. orange	60	55
228		10c. orange	60	55
268		10c. on 20c. brown	95	65
229		15c. on 10c. orange	60	55
269		20c. brown	1·20	65
230		25c. on 20c. brown	1·30	1·10

83

1930. Air.

231	83	5c. blue	25	20
232	83	5c. orange	30	30
233	83	7c. red	30	30
234	83	8c. black	30	30
235	83	15c. green	40	30
236	83	20c. red	60	30
237	83	25c. blue	75	75

1930. No. 182 optd with airplane and **CORREO AEREO**.

239		1b. black and violet	21·00	16·00

87

1930. Air.

244	87	5c. blue	30	30
245	87	10c. orange	40	30
246	87	30c. violet	6·25	4·25
247	87	50c. red	1·70	55
248	87	1b. black	6·25	4·25

1930. Bolivar's Death Centenary. Surch **1830 - 1930 17 DE DICIEMBRE UN CENTESIMO**.

249	73	1c. on 4c. grey	30	25

89 Seaplane over Old Panama

1931. Air. Opening of service between Panama City and western provinces.

250	89	5c. blue	95	1·10

1932. Optd **HABILITADA** or surch also.

251	64	½c. orange (postage)	50	25
252	73	½c. orange	30	25
253	73	1c. green	50	25
270	68	1c. on 5c. blue	50	45
254	73	2c. red	50	25
255	73	5c. blue	95	50
256	-	10c. violet (No. 191)	1·40	85
258	74	10c. on 12c. olive	1·40	85
259	74	10c. on 15c. blue	1·20	65
257	74	20c. brown	2·50	2·00
260	83	20c. on 25c. blue (air)	6·75	80

92 Manuel Amador Guerrero

1932. Birth Centenary of Dr. Guerrero (first president of republic).

261	92	2c. red	50	30

95 National Institute

1934. 25th Anniv of National Institute.

262	-	1c. green	1·20	65
263	-	2c. red	1·20	60
264	-	5c. blue	1·50	1·10
265	**95**	10c. brown	3·50	2·00
266	-	12c. green	5·75	2·20
267	-	15c. blue	7·75	2·75

DESIGNS—VERT: 1c. J. D. de Obaldia; 2c. E. A. Morales; 5c. Sphinx and Quotation from Emerson. HORIZ: 12c. J. A. Facio; 15c. P. Arosemena.

(98)

1936. Birth Centenary of Pablo Arosemena. (a) Postage. Surch as T **98**, but without CORREO AEREO.

271	**72**	2c. on 24c. brown	75	75

(b) Air. Surch with T **98**.

272		5c. on 50c. orange	1·40	1·10

100 Urraca Monument

99 Custom House Ruins, Portobelo

1936. Fourth Spanish–American Postal Congress (1st issue). Inscr "IV CONGRESO POSTAL AMERICO–ESPANOL".

273	**99**	½c. orange (postage)	60	40
274	-	1c. green	60	30
275	-	2c. red	60	30
276	-	5c. blue	85	55
277	-	10c. violet	1·90	95
278	-	15c. blue	1·90	1·00
279	-	20c. red	2·10	1·90
280	-	25c. brown	3·75	2·40
281	-	50c. orange	8·25	6·00
282	-	1b. black	19·00	17·00

DESIGNS: 1c. "Panama" (Old tree); 2c. "La Pollera" (woman in costume); 5c. Bolivar; 10c. Ruins of Old Panama Cathedral; 15c. Garcia y Santos; 20c. Madden Dam; 25c. Columbus; 50c. "Resolute" (liner) in Gaillard Cut; 1b. Panama Cathedral.

283	**100**	5c. blue (air)	75	55
284	-	10c. orange	85	75
285	-	20c. red	2·10	1·90
286	-	30c. violet	3·75	3·00
287	-	50c. red	8·75	7·00
288	-	1b. black	10·50	7·50

DESIGNS—HORIZ: 10c. "Man's Genius Uniting the Oceans"; 20c. Panama; 50c. San Pedro Miguel Locks; 1b. Courts of Justice. VERT: 30c. Balboa Monument.

1937. Fourth Spanish–American Postal Congress (2nd issue). Nos. 273/88 optd **UPU**.

289	**99**	½c. orange (postage)	40	35
290	-	1c. green	50	30
291	-	2c. red	50	30
292	-	5c. blue	75	35
293	-	10c. violet	1·30	45
294	-	15c. blue	5·75	4·00
295	-	20c. red	2·10	1·90
296	-	25c. brown	3·00	1·90
297	-	50c. orange	9·75	8·00
298	-	1b. black	18·00	12·00
299	**99**	5c. blue (air)	50	45
300	-	10c. orange	75	60
301	-	20c. red	1·90	1·30
302	-	30c. violet	5·00	4·00
303	-	50c. red	20·00	19·00
304	-	1b. black	24·00	19·00

1937. Optd **1937-38**.

305	**73**	½c. orange	1·30	1·20
306	**65**	1c. green	40	35
307	**73**	1c. green	40	35
308	**70**	2c. green	50	45
309	**73**	2c. red	60	55

1937. Surch **1937-38** and value.

310		2c. on 4c. grey	75	55
311	**78**	2c. on 8c. olive	75	75
312	**74**	2c. on 8c. purple	75	55
313	**74**	2c. on 10c. violet	75	65
314	**74**	2c. on 12c. olive	75	55
315	-	2c. on 15c. blue (No. 192)	75	75
316	**65**	2c. on 24c. sepia	75	1·00
317	**65**	2c. on 50c. black	75	55

1937. Air. Optd **CORREO AEREO** or surch also.

318	**73**	5c. blue	95	95
319	**74**	5c. on 15c. blue	95	95
320	**74**	5c. on 20c. brown	95	95
321	**75**	5c. on 24c. slate	95	95
322	**62**	5c. on 1b. black and violet	95	55
323	-	10c. on 10c. violet (No. 191)	2·10	1·80
324	**75**	10c. on 50c. black	3·00	2·40

105 Fire-Engine

106 Firemen's Monument

107 Fire-Brigade Badge

1937. 50th Anniv of Fire Brigade.

325	-	½c. orange (postage)	2·30	45
326	-	1c. green	2·30	45
327	-	2c. red	2·30	55
328	**105**	5c. blue	4·25	65
329	**106**	10c. violet	7·75	1·60
330	-	12c. green	12·50	2·40
331	**107**	5c. blue (air)	3·75	75
332	-	10c. orange	5·25	1·40
333	-	20c. red	7·75	1·00

DESIGNS—VERT: ½c. R. Arango; 1c. J. A. Guizado; 10c. (No. 332), F. Arosemena; 12c. D. H. Brandon; 20c. J. G. Duque. HORIZ: 2c. House on fire.

108 Basketball Player

1938. Air. Central American and Caribbean Olympic Games.

334	**108**	1c. red	2·40	45
335	-	2c. green (Baseball player) (horiz)	2·40	30
336	-	7c. grey (Swimmer) (horiz)	3·50	50
337	-	8c. brown (Boxers) (horiz)	3·50	50
338	-	15c. blue (Footballer)	5·25	2·50

MS339 140×140 mm. Nos. 334/8 (sold at 35c.) 21·00 20·00

1938. Opening of Aguadulce Normal School, Santiago. Optd **NORMAL DE SANTIAGO JUNIO 5 1938** or surch also.

340	**72**	2c. red (postage)	50	40
341	**87**	7c. on 30c. violet (air)	60	55
342	**83**	8c. on 15c. green	60	55

111 Old Panama Cathedral and Statue of Liberty

1938. 150th Anniv of U.S. Constitution. Flags in red, white and blue.

343	**111**	1c. black and green (postage)	40	35
344	**111**	2c. black and red	60	30
345	**111**	5c. black and blue	85	35
346	**111**	12c. black and olive	1·50	1·10
347	**111**	15c. black and blue	1·90	1·70
348	**111**	7c. black and grey (air)	40	35
349	**111**	8c. black and blue	60	55
350	**111**	15c. black and brown	75	55
351	**111**	50c. black and orange	8·75	7·00
352	**111**	1b. black	8·75	7·00

Nos. 343/7 are without the Douglas DC-3 airliner.

112 Pierre and Marie Curie

1939. Obligatory Tax. Cancer Research Fund. Dated "1939".

353	**112**	1c. red	70	25
354	**112**	1c. green	70	25
355	**112**	1c. orange	70	25
356	**112**	1c. blue	70	25

113 Gatun Locks

1939. 25th Anniv of Opening of Panama Canal.

357	**113**	½c. yellow (postage)	40	25
358	-	1c. green	60	25
359	-	2c. red	70	25
360	-	5c. blue	1·10	30
361	-	10c. violet	1·30	45
362	-	12c. olive	1·30	60
363	-	15c. blue	1·30	1·00
364	-	50c. orange	3·00	1·80
365	-	1b. brown	6·25	3·75

DESIGNS: 1c. "Santa Elena" (liner) in Pedro Miguel Locks; 2c. Allegory of canal construction; 5c. "Rangitata" (liner) in Culebra Cut; 10c. Panama canal ferry; 12c. Aerial view; 15c. Gen. Gorgas; 50c. M. A. Guerrero; 1b. Woodrow Wilson.

366		1c. red (air)	50	25
367		2c. green	50	25
368		5c. blue	70	25
369		10c. violet	75	30
370		15c. blue	1·70	40
371		20c. red	4·25	1·90
372		50c. brown	5·25	95
373		1b. black	7·75	5·00

PORTRAITS: 1c. B. Porras; 2c. Wm. H. Taft; 5c. P. J. Sosa; 10c. L. B. Wise; 15c. A. Reclus; 20c. Gen. Goethals; 50c. F. de Lesseps; 1b. Theodore Roosevelt.

115 Flags of American Republics

1940. Air. 50th Anniv of Pan-American Union.

374	**115**	15c. blue	50	35

1940. Air. No. 370 surch **55**.

375		5c. on 15c. blue	30	30

No. 363 surch **AEREO SIETE**.

376		7c. on 15c. blue	50	30

No. 371 surch **SIETE**.

377		7c. on 20c. red	50	30

No. 374 surch **8-8**.

378		8c. on 15c. blue	50	30

1941. Obligatory Tax. Cancer Research Fund. Optd **LUCHA CONTRA EL CANCER**.

379	**72**	1c. green	1·70	1·00

1941. Enactment of New Constitution. (a) Postage. Optd **CONSTITUCION 1941**.

380		½c. orange	40	30
381		1c. green	40	30
382		2c. red	40	30
383		5c. blue	60	30
384		10c. violet	85	55
385		15c. blue	1·80	75
386		50c. orange	6·75	3·75
387		1b. black	15·00	6·50

(b) Air. Surch **CONSTITUCION 1941 AEREO** and value in figures.

388	**E81**	7c. on 10c. orange	1·10	1·00
389	**72**	15c. on 24c. brown	2·50	2·40

(c) Air. Optd **CONSTITUCION 1941**.

390	**83**	20c. red	2·10	2·00
391	**87**	50c. red	6·25	4·00
392	**87**	1b. black	14·50	10·00

1941. Obligatory Tax. Cancer Research Fund. Dated "1940".

393	**112**	1c. red	70	30
394	**112**	1c. green	70	30
395	**112**	1c. orange	70	30
396	**112**	1c. blue	70	30

120a "Liberty"

1942. Telegraph stamps as T **120a** optd or surch. (a) Optd **CORREOS 1942** and (No. 397) surch **2c**.

397		2c. on 5c. blue	1·80	65
398		10c. violet	1·50	1·20

(b) Air. Optd **CORREO AEREO 1942**.

399		20c. brown	4·25	3·25

123 Flags of Panama and Costa Rica

1942. First Anniv of Revised Frontier Agreement between Panama and Costa Rica.

400	**123**	2c. red (postage)	40	35
401	**123**	15c. green (air)	75	30

1942. Obligatory Tax. Cancer Research Fund. Dated "1942".

402	**112**	1c. violet	60	30

127 Balboa reaches Pacific

129 J. D. Arosemena Normal School

1942. (a) Postage stamps.

403	-	½c. red, blue and violet	30	30
404	-	½c. blue, orange and red	30	30
405	-	1c. green	30	30
406	-	1c. red	30	30
407	-	2c. red ("ACARRERO")	30	30
408	-	2c. red ("ACARREO")	1·00	30
409	-	2c. black and red	30	30
410	**127**	5c. black and blue	30	30
411	-	5c. blue	50	30
412	-	10c. orange and red	70	30
413	-	10c. orange and purple	1·10	30
414	-	15c. black and blue	1·30	65
415	-	15c. black	95	35
416	-	50c. black and red	2·75	1·20
417	-	1b. black	3·75	1·20

DESIGNS—VERT: ½c. National flag; 1c. Farm girl; 10c. Golden Altar, Church of St. Jose; 50c. San Blas Indian woman and child. HORIZ: 2c. Oxen drawing sugar cart; 15c. St. Thomas's Hospital; 1b. National highway.

(b) Air.

418		2c. red	95	30
419		7c. red	95	30
420		8c. black and brown	30	30
421		10c. black and blue	30	30
422		15c. violet	50	30
423		15c. grey	50	30
424	**129**	20c. brown	70	30
425	**129**	20c. green	50	30
426	-	50c. green	1·30	45
427	-	50c. red	7·75	3·75
428	-	50c. blue	3·75	1·20
429	-	1b. orange, yellow and black	3·00	95

DESIGNS—HORIZ: 2c., 7c. Black marlin; 8c., 10c. Gate of Glory, Portobelo; 15c. Taboga Is; 50c. Fire Brigade H.Q., Panama City; 1b. Idol (Golden Beast).

1943. Obligatory Tax. Cancer Research Fund. Dated "1943".

433	**112**	1c. green	60	30
434	**112**	1c. red	60	30
435	**112**	1c. orange	60	30
436	**112**	1c. blue	60	30

131 A. G. Melendez

1943. Air.

437	**131**	3b. grey	5·75	5·50
438	-	5b. blue (T. Lefevre)	8·75	8·50

1945. Obligatory Tax. Cancer Research Fund. Dated "1945".

439	**112**	1c. red	1·60	35
440	**112**	1c. green	1·60	35
441	**112**	1c. orange	1·60	35
442	**112**	1c. blue	1·60	35

1946. Obligatory Tax. Cancer Research Fund. Surch **CANCER B/. 0.01 1947.**

443	**72**	1c. on ½c. orange	1·20	30
444	**72**	1c. on 1c. green	1·20	30
445	-	1c. on ½c. red, blue and violet (No. 403)	1·10	30
446	**72**	1c. on 12c. olive	1·10	35
447	**72**	1c. on 24c. brown	1·10	35

1947. Air. Surch **AEREO 1947** and value.

448	-	5c. on 7c. red (No. 419)	30	30
449	**83**	5c. on 8c. black	30	30
450	-	5c. on 8c. black and brown (No. 420)	30	30
451	**83**	10c. on 15c. green	60	55
452	-	10c. on 15c. violet (422)	30	30

134 Flag of Panama

135 National Theatre

1947. Second Anniv of National Constitutional Assembly.

453	**134**	2c. red, deep red and blue (postage)	25	20
454	-	5c. blue	25	25
455	**135**	8c. violet (air)	50	30

DESIGN—As Type **134**: 5c. Arms of Panama.

1947. Cancer Research Fund. Dated "1947".

456	**112**	1c. red	1·40	25
457	**112**	1c. green	1·40	25
458	**112**	1c. orange	1·40	25
459	**112**	1c. blue	1·40	25

1947. Surch **HABILITADA CORREOS** and value.

460	**83**	½c. on 8c. black	10	10
461	-	½c. on 8c. black and brown (No. 420)	20	20
462	-	1c. on 7c. red (No. 419)	20	20
463	**135**	2c. on 8c. violet	40	20

1947. Surch **Habilitada CORREOS B/. 0.50.**

464	**72**	50c. on 24c. brown	2·10	1·80

138 J. A. Arango

1948. Air. Honouring members of the Revolutionary Junta of 1903.

465	-	3c. black and blue	50	30
466	**138**	5c. black and brown	50	30
467	-	10c. black and orange	50	30
468	-	15c. black and red	50	30
469	-	20c. black and red	85	65
470	-	50c. black	1·50	95
471	-	1b. black and green	4·75	3·25
472	-	2b. black and yellow	10·50	7·50

PORTRAITS—HORIZ: 3c. M. A. Guerrero; 10c. F. Boyd; 15c. R. Arias. VERT: 20c. M. Espinosa; 50c. Carlos Arosemena (engineer); 1b. N. de Obarrio; 2b. T. Arias.

140 Firemen's Monument

1948. 50th Anniv of Colon Fire Brigade.

473	**140**	5c. black and red	70	25
474	-	10c. black and orange	95	35
475	-	20c. black and blue	1·90	65
476	-	25c. black and brown	1·90	1·00
477	-	50c. black and violet	3·75	1·00
478	-	1b. black and green	5·25	2·00

DESIGNS—HORIZ: 10c. Fire engine; 20c. Fire hose; 25c. Fire Brigade Headquarters. VERT: 50c. Commander Walker; 1b. First Fire Brigade Commander.

142 F. D. Roosevelt and J. D. Arosemena

144 Roosevelt Monument, Panama

1948. Air. Homage to F. D. Roosevelt.

479	**142**	5c. black and red	30	20
480	-	10c. orange	40	35
481	**144**	20c. green	50	45
482	-	50c. black and blue	75	75
483	-	1b. black	1·90	1·50

DESIGNS—HORIZ: 10c. Woman with palm symbolizing "Four Freedoms"; 50c. Map of Panama Canal. VERT: 1b. Portrait of Roosevelt.

147 Cervantes

148 Monument to Cervantes

1948. 400th Birth Anniv of Cervantes.

484	**147**	2c. black and red (postage)	85	30
485	**148**	5c. black and blue (air)	60	30
486	-	10c. black and mauve	95	35

DESIGN—HORIZ: 10c. Don Quixote and Sancho Panza (inscr as Type **148**).

1949. Air. Jose Gabriel Duque (philanthropist). Birth Centenary. No. 486 optd **"CENTENARIO DE JOSE GABRIEL DUQUE" "18 de Enero de 1949".**

487	10c. black and mauve	75	65

1949. Obligatory Tax. Cancer Research Fund. Surch **LUCHA CONTRA EL CANCER** and value.

488	**142**	1c. on 5c. black and red	70	30
489	-	1c. on 10c. orange (No. 480)	70	30

1949. Incorporation of Chiriqui Province Cent. Stamps of 1930 and 1942 optd **1849 1949 CHIRIQUI CENTENARIO.** (a) On postage stamps as No. 407. (i) Without surcharge.

491	2c. red	30	30

(ii) Surch **1 UN CENTESIMO 1** also.

490	1c. on 2c. red	30	30

(b) Air.

492	-	2c. red (No. 418)	30	30
493	**83**	5c. blue	30	30
494	-	15c. grey (No. 423)	75	75
495	-	50c. red (No. 427)	3·00	2·75

1949. 75th Anniv of U.P.U. Stamps of 1930 and 1942/3 optd **1874 1949 U.P.U.** No. 625 is also surch **B/0.25.**

496		1c. green (No. 405) (postage)	30	20
497		2c. red (No. 407)	50	30
498	**127**	5c. blue	75	45
499	-	2c. red (No. 418) (air)	30	30
500	**83**	5c. orange	95	65
501	-	10c. black and blue (No. 421)	95	75
502	**131**	25c. on 3b. grey	1·40	1·30
503	-	50c. red (No. 427)	4·25	4·00

1949. Cancer Research Fund. Dated "1949".

504	**112**	1c. brown	2·10	30

153 Father Xavier

154 St. Xavier University

1949. Bicentenary of Founding of St. Xavier University.

505	**153**	2c. black and red (postage)	30	30
506	**154**	5c. black and blue (air)	50	30

155 Dr. Carlos J. Finlay

156 "Aedes aegypti"

1950. Dr. Finlay (medical research worker).

507	**155**	2c. black and red (postage)	50	30
508	**156**	5c. black and blue (air)	1·70	75

1950. Death Centenary of San Martin. Optd **CENTENARIO del General** (or **Gral.**) **Jose de San Martin 17 de Agosto de 1950** or surch also. The 50c. is optd **AEREO** as well.

509	-	1c. green (No. 405) (postage)	30	30
510	-	2c. on ½c. blue, orange and red (No. 404)	30	30
511	**127**	5c. black and blue	40	30
512	-	2c. red (No. 418) (air)	60	35
513	**83**	5c. orange	70	45
514	-	10c. black & blue (No. 421)	70	55
515	**83**	25c. blue	1·10	95
516	-	50c. black & violet (No. 477)	2·10	1·60

158 Badge

159 Stadium

1950. Obligatory Tax. Physical Culture Fund. Dated "1950".

517		1c. black and red	1·70	45
518	**158**	1c. black and blue	1·70	45
519	**159**	1c. black and green	1·70	45
520	-	1c. black and orange	1·70	45
521	-	1c. black and violet	1·70	45

DESIGNS—VERT: No. 520, as Type **159** but medallion changed and incorporating four "F"s; 521, Discus thrower. HORIZ: No. 517, as Type **159** but front of stadium.

1951. Birth Tercentenary of Jean-Baptiste de La Salle (educational reformer). Optd **Tercer Centenario del Natalicio de San Juan Baptista de La Salle. 1651-1951.**

522	2c. black and red (No. 409)	30	30
523	5c. blue (No. 411)	50	30

1952. Air. Surch **AEREO 1952** and value.

524	2c. on 10c. black and blue (No. 421)	30	30
525	5c. on 10c. black and blue (No. 421)	40	35
526	1b. on 5b. blue (No. 438)	31·00	30·00

1952. Surch **1952** and figure of value.

527	1c. on ½c. (No. 404)	30	30

Air. Optd **AEREO** also.

528	5c. on 2c. (No. 408)	30	30
529	25c. on 10c. (No. 413)	1·40	1·40

164 Isabella the Catholic

1952. 500th Birth Anniv of Isabella the Catholic.

530	**164**	1c. black & grn (postage)	50	30
531	**164**	2c. black and red	50	30
532	**164**	5c. black and blue	50	30
533	**164**	10c. black and violet	75	35
534	**164**	4c. black and orange (air)	50	30
535	**164**	5c. black and olive	50	30
536	**164**	10c. black and buff	70	35
537	**164**	25c. black and slate	1·80	35
538	**164**	50c. black and brown	2·75	85
539	**164**	1b. black	8·00	3·75

1953. Surch **B/.0.01 1953.**

540	1c. on 10c. (No. 413)	30	30
541	1c. on 15c. black (No. 415)	30	30

1953. Air. No. 421 surch **5 1953.**

542	5c. on 10c. black and blue	50	30

167 Masthead of "La Estrella"

1953. Air. Centenary of "La Estrella de Panama", Newspaper.

543	**167**	5c. red	30	30
544	**167**	10c. blue	50	35

168 Pres. and Senora Amador Guerrero

1953. 50th Anniv of Panama Republic.

545	-	2c. violet (postage)	50	25
546	**168**	5c. orange	60	25
547	-	12c. purple	1·40	25
548	-	20c. indigo	2·40	40
549	-	50c. yellow	3·75	95
550	-	1b. blue	5·50	2·10

DESIGNS—VERT: 2c. Blessing the flat; 50c. Old Town Hall. HORIZ: 12c. J. A. Santos and J. De La Ossa; 20c. Revolutionary council; 1b. Obverse and reverse of coin.

551	2c. blue (air)	50	25
552	5c. green	50	25
553	7c. grey	60	25
554	25c. black	3·75	1·00
555	50c. brown	2·40	1·20
556	1b. orange	5·50	2·40

DESIGNS—VERT: 2c. Act of Independence. HORIZ: 5c. Pres. and Senora Remon Cantera; 7c. Girl in national costume; 25c. National flower; 50c. Salazar, Huertas and Domingo; 1b. National dance.

1954. Surch in figures.

557	-	3c. on 1c. red (No. 406) (postage)	25	25
558	**167**	1c. on 5c. red (air)	25	25
559	**167**	1c. on 10c. blue	25	25

170 Gen. Herrera at Conference Table

1954. Death Centenary of Gen. Herrera.

560	-	3c. violet (postage)	25	20
561	**170**	6c. green (air)	25	20
562	-	1b. black and red	3·75	2·75

DESIGNS—VERT: 3c. Equestrian statue. HORIZ: 1b. Cavalry charge.

171 Rotary Emblem and Map

1955. Air. 50th Anniv of Rotary International.

563	**171**	6c. violet	25	20
564	**171**	21c. red	70	40
565	**171**	1b. black	5·50	3·50

172 Tocumen Airport

1955

566	**172**	½c. brown	50	20

173 President Remon Cantera

1955. National Mourning for Pres. Remon Cantera.

567	**173**	3c. black & pur (postage)	25	20
568	**173**	6c. black and violet (air)	25	20

174 V. de la Guardia y Azala and M. Chiaria

1955. Centenary of Cocle Province.

569	**174**	5c. violet	40	20

175 F. de Lesseps

1955. 150th Birth Anniv of De Lesseps (engineer).

570	**175**	3c. lake on pink (postage)	60	20
571	-	25c. blue on blue	2·40	1·60
572	-	50c. violet on lilac	3·00	1·80
573	-	5c. myrtle on green (air)	40	20
574	-	1b. black and mauve	5·25	2·75

DESIGNS—VERT: 5c. P. J. Sosa; 50c. T. Roosevelt. HORIZ: 25c. First excavations for Panama Canal; 1b. "Ancon I" (first ship to pass through canal) and De Lesseps.

1955. Air. No. 564 surch.

575	**171**	15c. on 21c. red	60	45

177 Pres. Eisenhower (United States)

178 Bolivar Statue

1956. Air. Pan-American Congress, Panama and 30th Anniv of First Congress.

576	-	6c. black and blue	50	30
577	-	6c. black and bistre	50	30
578	-	6c. black and green	50	30
579	-	6c. sepia and green	50	30
580	-	6c. green and yellow	50	30
581	-	6c. green and violet	50	30
582	-	6c. blue and lilac	50	30
583	-	6c. green and purple	50	30
584	-	6c. blue and olive	50	30
585	-	6c. sepia and yellow	50	30
586	-	6c. blue and sepia	50	30
587	-	6c. green and mauve	50	30
588	-	6c. sepia and red	50	30
589	-	6c. green and blue	50	30
590	-	6c. sepia and blue	50	30
591	-	6c. black and orange	50	30
592	-	6c. sepia and grey	50	30
593	-	6c. black and pink	50	30
594	**177**	6c. blue and red	50	30
595	-	6c. blue and grey	50	30
596	-	6c. green and brown	50	30
597	**178**	20c. grey	1·30	90
598	-	50c. green	1·90	1·60
599	-	1b. sepia	4·50	2·75

PRESIDENTIAL PORTRAITS as Type **177**: No. 576, Argentina; 577, Bolivia; 578, Brazil; 579, Chile; 580, Colombia; 581, Costa Rica; 582, Cuba; 583, Dominican Republic; 584, Ecuador; 585, Guatemala; 586, Haiti; 587, Honduras; 588, Mexico; 589, Nicaragua; 590, Panama; 591, Paraguay; 592, Peru; 593, Salvador; 595, Uruguay; 596, Venezuela. As Type **178**—HORIZ: No. 598, Bolivar Hall. VERT: No. 599, Bolivar Medallion.

179 Arms of Panama City

1956. Sixth Inter-American Congress of Municipalities, Panama City.

600	**179**	3c. green (postage)	25	20
601	-	25c. red (air)	70	45
602	-	50c. black	1·40	1·10
MS603 125×76 mm. Nos. 600/2. Imperf (sold at 85c.)			3·25	3·25

DESIGNS: 25c. Stone bridge, Old Panama; 50c. Town Hall, Panama.

180 Pres. Carlos A. Mendoza

1956. Birth Centenary of Pres. Carlos A. Mendoza.

604	**180**	10c. green and red	40	25

182 Dr. Belisario Porras

1956. Birth Centenary of Dr. Porras.

605	-	15c. grey (postage)	75	30
606	**182**	25c. blue and red	1·20	65
607	-	5c. green (air)	30	25
608	-	15c. red	50	30

DESIGNS—HORIZ: 15c. (No. 605), National Archives; 15c. (No. 608), St. Thomas's Hospital. VERT: 5c. Porras Monument.

183 Isthmus Highway

1957. Seventh Pan-American Highway Congress.

609	**183**	3c. green (postage)	30	20
610	-	10c. black (air)	30	20
611	-	20c. black and blue	70	55
612	-	1b. green	3·00	2·75
MS613 85c. No. **MS**603 optd **VII CONGRESO INTERAMERICANO DE CARRETERAS 1957**			17·00	17·00

DESIGNS—VERT: 10c. Highway under construction; 20c. Darien Forest; 1b. Map of Pan-American Highway.

1957. Air. Surch **1957 x 10c x**.

614	**173**	10c. on 6c. black & violet	30	25

185 Manuel E. Batista

1957. Birth Centenary of Manuel Espinosa Batista (independence leader).

615	**185**	5c. blue and green	25	20

186 Portobelo Castle

1957. Air. Buildings. Centres in black.

616	**186**	10c. grey	30	25
617	-	10c. purple	30	25
618	-	10c. violet	30	25
619	-	10c. grey and green	30	25
620	-	10c. blue	30	25
621	-	10c. brown	30	25
622	-	10c. orange	30	25
623	-	10c. light blue	30	25
624	-	1b. red	3·00	1·90

DESIGNS—HORIZ: No. 617, San Jeronimo Castle; 618, Portobelo Customs-house; 619, Panama Hotel; 620, Pres. Remon Cantera Stadium; 621, Palace of Justice; 622, Treasury; 623, San Lorenzo Castle. VERT: No. 624, Jose Remon Clinics.

1957. Surch **1957** and value.

625	**172**	1c. on ½c. brown	20	20
626	**172**	3c. on ½c. brown	25	20

1958. Air. Surch **1958** and value.

627	**170**	5c. on 6c. green	35	20

189 U.N. Emblem

1958. Air. Tenth Anniv of U.N.O.

628	**189**	10c. green	25	20
629	**189**	21c. blue	50	30
630	**189**	50c. orange	1·30	1·00
631	-	1b. red, blue and grey	2·50	1·90
MS632 127×102 mm. Nos. 628/31. Imperf (sold at 2b.)			6·75	6·50

DESIGN: 1b. Flags of Panama and United Nations.

1958. No. 547 surch **3c 1958**.

633		3c. on 12c. purple	25	20

191 Flags Emblem

1958. Tenth Anniv of Organization of American States. Emblem (T **191**) multicoloured within yellow and black circular band; background colours given below.

634	**191**	1c. grey (postage)	25	20
635	**191**	2c. green	25	20
636	**191**	3c. red	30	20
637	**191**	7c. blue	30	25
638	**191**	5c. blue (air)	25	20
639	**191**	10c. red	30	25
640	-	50c. black, yellow and grey	75	75
641	**191**	1b. black	2·40	1·90

DESIGN—VERT: 50c. Headquarters building.

192 Brazilian Pavilion

1958. Brussels International Exhbition.

642	**192**	1c. green & yellow (postage)	20	20
643	-	3c. green and blue	25	20
644	-	5c. slate and brown	25	25
645	-	10c. brown and blue	30	25
646	-	15c. violet and grey (air)	30	30
647	-	50c. brown and slate	75	75
648	-	1b. turquoise and lilac	1·70	1·70
MS649 130×105 mm. Nos. 642/8 (sold at 2b.)			5·75	5·50

DESIGNS—PAVILIONS: As Type **192**: 3c. Argentina; 5c. Venezuela; 10c. Great Britain; 15c. Vatican City; 50c. United States; 1b. Belgium.

193 Pope Pius XII

1959. Pope Pius XII Commemoration.

650	**193**	3c. brown (postage)	25	20
651	-	5c. violet (air)	25	25
652	-	30c. mauve	70	45
653	-	50c. grey	95	75
MS654 127×86 mm. Nos. 650/3. Imperf (sold at 1b.)			2·40	2·30

PORTRAITS (Pope Pius XII): 5c. when Cardinal; 30c. wearing Papal tiara; 50c. enthroned.

194 Children on Farm

1959. Obligatory Tax. Youth Rehabilitation Institute. Size 35×24 mm.

655	**194**	1c. grey and red	25	20

195 U.N. Headquarters, New York

1959. Tenth Anniv of Declaration of Human Rights.

656	**195**	3c. olive & brown (postage)	25	20
657	-	15c. green and orange	45	30
658	-	5c. blue and green (air)	25	20
659	-	10c. brown and grey	30	25
660	-	20c. slate and brown	30	30
661	-	50c. blue and green	85	75
662	**195**	1b. blue and red	1·70	1·70

DESIGNS: 5c., 15c. Family looking towards light; 10c., 20c. U.N. emblem and torch; 50c. U.N. flag.

1959. Eighth Latin-American Economic Commission Congress. Nos. 656/61 optd **8A REUNION C.E.P.A.L. MAYO 1959** or surch also.

663		3c. olive and brown (postage)	20	20
664	-	15c. green and orange	45	25
665	-	5c. blue and green (air)	25	25
666	-	10c. brown and grey	30	25
667	-	20c. slate and brown	50	30
668	-	1b. on 50c. blue and green	2·40	2·30
MS669 No. **MS**654, but larger in two lines (sold at 1b.)			6·75	6·50

197 J. A. Facio

1959. 50th Anniv of National Institute.

670		3c. red (postage)	20	20
671		13c. green	50	25
672		21c. blue	75	40
673	**197**	5c. black (air)	20	20
674	-	10c. black	25	20

DESIGNS—VERT: 3c. E. A. Morales (founder); 10c. Ernesto de la Guardia, Nr; 13c. A. Bravo. HORIZ: 21c. National Institute building.

1959. Obligatory Tax. Youth Rehabilitation Institute. As No. 655, but colours changed and inscr "1959".

675	**194**	1c. green and black	25	20
676	**194**	1c. blue and black	25	20

See also No. 690.

198 Football

1959. Third Pan-American Games, Chicago. Inscr "III JUEGOS DEPORTIVOS PANAMERICANOS".

677	**198**	1c. green & grey (postage)	20	20
678	-	3c. brown and blue	40	20
679	-	20c. brown and green	1·80	1·10
680	-	5c. brown and black (air)	40	30
681	-	10c. brown and grey	75	40
682	-	50c. brown and blue	3·00	1·70

DESIGNS: 3c. Swimming; 5c. Boxing; 10c. Baseball; 20c. Hurdling; 50c. Basketball.

1960. Air. World Refugee Year. Nos. 554/6 optd **NACIONES UNIDAS ANO MUNDIAL. REFUGIADOS. 1959–1960.**

683		25c. black	95	30
684		50c. brown	1·40	45
685		1b. orange	2·10	1·50

200 Administration Building

1960. Air. 25th Anniv of National University.

686	**200**	10c. green	25	20
687	-	21c. blue	60	25
688	-	25c. blue	85	45
689	-	30c. black	1·10	50

DESIGNS: 21c. Faculty of Science; 25c. Faculty of Medicine; 30c. Statue of Dr. Octavio Mendez Pereira (first rector) and Faculty of Law.

1960. Obligatory Tax. Youth Rehabilitation Institute. As No. 655 but smaller (32×22 mm) and inscr "1960".

690	**194**	1c. grey and red	20	20

202 Fencing

1960. Olympic Games.

No.	Type	Description	Mint	Used
691	**202**	3c. purple & violet (postage)	25	20
692	-	5c. green and turquoise	50	20
693	-	5c. red and orange (air)	25	20
694	-	10c. black and bistre	60	30
695	-	25c. deep blue and blue	1·30	70
696	-	50c. black and brown	2·50	1·30
MS697		127×76 mm. Nos. 695/6. Imperf (sold at 80c.)	4·75	4·75

DESIGNS—VERT: 5c. (No. 692), Football; (No. 693), Basketball; 25c. Javelin-throwing; 50c. Runner with Olympic Flame. HORIZ: 10c. Cycling.

204 "Population"

1960. Air. Sixth National Census (5c.) and Central American Census.

No.	Type	Description	Mint	Used
698	**204**	5c. black	20	20
699	-	10c. brown	25	25

DESIGN: 10c. Two heads and map.

205 Boeing 707 Airliner

1960. Air.

No.	Type	Description	Mint	Used
700	**205**	5c. blue	25	20
701	**205**	10c. green	30	20
702	**205**	20c. brown	50	30

206 Pastoral Scene

1961. Agricultural Census (16th April).

No.	Type	Description	Mint	Used
703	**206**	3c. turquoise	25	20

206a U.N. Emblem

1961. Air. 15th Anniv of United Nations (1960). Sheet 65×77 mm. Imperf.

No.	Description	Mint	Used
MS704	80c. cerise and black	2·50	2·40

207 Helen Keller School

1961. 25th Anniv of Lions Club.

No.	Type	Description	Mint	Used
705	-	3c. blue (postage)	25	20
706	**207**	5c. black (air)	25	25
707	-	10c. green	35	25
708	-	21c. blue, red and yellow	40	30

DESIGNS: 3c. Nino Hospital; 10c. Children's Colony, Verano; 21c. Lions emblem, arms and slogan.

1961. Air. Obligatory Tax. Youth Rehabilitation Fund. Surch **1 c "Rehabilitacion de Menores"**.

No.	Type	Description	Mint	Used
709		1c. on 10c. black and bistre (No. 694)	25	20
710	**205**	1c. on 10c. green	25	20

1961. Air. World Refugee Year (1959–60). Sheet No. **MS**704 optd with uprooted oak emblem and **ANO DE LOS REFUGIADOS**.

No.	Description	Mint	Used
MS711	80c. cerise and black	4·50	4·50

1961. Air. Surch **HABILITAD. en** and value.

No.	Type	Description	Mint	Used
712	**200**	1c. on 10c. green	25	20
713	-	1b. on 25c. blue and blue (No. 695)	2·50	2·40

210 Flags of Costa Rica and Panama

1961. Meeting of Presidents of Costa Rica and Panama.

No.	Type	Description	Mint	Used
715	**210**	3c. red and blue (postage)	25	20
716	-	1b. black and gold (air)	3·00	2·50

DESIGN: 1b. Pres. Chiari of Panama and Pres. Echandi of Costa Rica.

211 Girl using Sewing-machine

1961. Obligatory Tax. Youth Rehabilitation Fund.

No.	Type	Description	Mint	Used
717	**211**	1c. violet	25	20
718	**211**	1c. yellow	25	20
719	**211**	1c. green	25	20
720	**211**	1c. blue	25	20
721	**211**	1c. purple	25	20
722	-	1c. mauve	25	20
723	-	1c. grey	25	20
724	-	1c. blue	25	20
725	-	1c. orange	25	20
726	-	1c. red	25	20

DESIGN: Nos. 722/6, Boy sawing wood.

212 Campaign Emblem

1961. Air. Malaria Eradication.

No.	Type	Description	Mint	Used
727	**212**	5c.+5c. red	1·40	95
728	**212**	10c.+10c. blue	1·40	95
729	**212**	15c.+15c. green	1·40	95

213 Dag Hammarskjold

1961. Air. Death of Dag Hammarskjold.

No.	Type	Description	Mint	Used
730	**213**	10c. black and grey	35	20

1962. Air. (a) Surch **Vale B/.0.15**.

No.	Type	Description	Mint	Used
731	**200**	15c. on 10c. green	40	30

(b) No. 810 surch **XX** over old value and **VALE B/.1.00**.

No.	Description	Mint	Used
732	1b. on 25c. deep blue and blue	3·00	1·50

214 Arms of Panama

1962. Third Central American Inter-Municipal Cooperation Assembly.

No.	Type	Description	Mint	Used
733	**214**	3c. red, yellow and blue (postage)	30	30
734	-	5c. black and blue (air)	30	25

DESIGN—HORIZ: 5c. City Hall, Colon.

215 Mercury on Cogwheel

1962. First Industrial Census.

No.	Type	Description	Mint	Used
735	**215**	3c. red	20	20

1962. Surch **VALE** and value with old value obliterated.

No.	Type	Description	Mint	Used
736	**212**	10c. on 5c.+5c. red	1·50	1·10
737	**212**	20c. on 10c.+10c. blue	2·30	2·20

217 Social Security Hospital

1962. Opening of Social Security Hospital, Panama City.

No.	Type	Description	Mint	Used
738	**217**	3c. black and red	25	20

218 Colon Cathedral

1962. "Freedom of Worship". Inscr "LIBERTAD DE CULTOS". Centres in black.

No.	Type	Description	Mint	Used
739	-	1c. red and blue (postage)	20	20
740	-	2c. red and cream	20	20
741	-	3c. blue and cream	25	20
742	-	5c. red and green	25	25
743	-	10c. green and cream	30	25
744	-	10c. mauve and blue	30	25
745	-	15c. blue and green	35	30
746	**218**	20c. red and pink	60	35
747	-	25c. green and pink	70	50
748	-	50c. blue and pink	1·30	65
749	-	1b. violet and cream	2·75	2·00

DESIGNS—HORIZ: 1c. San Francisco de Veraguas Church; 3c. David Cathedral; 25c. Orthodox Greek Temple; 1b. Colon Protestant Church. VERT: 2c. Panama Old Cathedral; 5c. Nata Church; 10c. Don Bosco Temple; 15c. Virgin of Carmen Church; 50c. Panama Cathedral.

No.	Description	Mint	Used
750	5c. violet and flesh (air)	20	20
751	7c. light mauve and mauve	25	20
752	8c. violet and blue	25	20
753	10c. violet and salmon	25	20
754	10c. green and purple	25	25
755	15c. red and orange	35	25
756	21c. sepia and blue	60	50
757	25c. blue and pink	70	45
758	30c. mauve and blue	75	55
759	50c. purple and green	1·10	75
760	1b. blue and salmon	2·20	1·50
MS761	132×107 mm. Nos. 747/8, 757 and 759. Imperf	6·25	6·00

DESIGNS—HORIZ: 5c. Cristo Rey Church; 7c. San Miguel Church; 21c. Canal Zone Synagogue; 25c. Panama Synagogue; 50c. Canal Zone Protestant Church. VERT: 8c. Santuario Church; 10c. Los Santos Church; 15c. Santa Ana Church; 30c. San Francisco Church; 1b. Canal Zone Catholic Church.

1962. Air. Ninth Central American and Caribbean Games, Jamaica. Nos. 693 and 695 optd **"IX JUEGOS C.A. Y DEL CARIBE KINGSTON - 1962"** or surch also.

No.	Description	Mint	Used
762	5c. red and orange	20	20
764	10c. on 25c. deep blue & blue	70	45
765	15c. on 25c. deep blue & blue	85	60
766	20c. on 25c. deep blue & blue	95	65
763	25c. deep blue and blue	1·10	90

220 Thatcher Ferry Bridge nearing Completion

1962. Opening of Thatcher Ferry Bridge, Canal Zone.

No.	Type	Description	Mint	Used
767	**220**	3c. black and red (postage)	25	20
768	-	10c. black and blue (air)	25	20

DESIGN: 10c. Completed bridge.

221 Col. Glenn and Capsule "Friendship 7"

1962. Air. Col. Glenn's Space Flight.

No.	Type	Description	Mint	Used
769	**221**	5c. red	20	20
770	-	10c. yellow	40	30
771	-	31c. blue	1·60	95
772	-	50c. green	1·90	1·40
MS773		77×110 mm. Nos. 769/72. Imperf (sold at 1b.)	4·25	4·25

DESIGNS—HORIZ: "Friendship": 10c. Over Earth; 31c. In space. VERT: 50c. Col. Glenn.

222 U.P.A.E. Emblem

1963. Air. 50th Anniv of Postal Union of Americas and Spain.

No.	Type	Description	Mint	Used
774	**222**	10c. multicoloured	40	20

223 Water Exercise

1963. 75th Anniv of Panama Fire Brigade.

No.	Type	Description	Mint	Used
775	**223**	1c. black & green (postage)	20	20
776	-	3c. black and blue	25	20
777	-	5c. black and red	30	20
778	-	10c. black and orange (air)	40	25
779	-	15c. black and purple	50	30
780	-	21c. blue, gold and red	95	75

DESIGNS: 3c. Brigade officers; 5c. Brigade president and advisory council; 10c. "China" pump in action, 1887; 15c. "Cable 14" station and fire-engine; 21c. Fire Brigade badge.

1963. Air. Red Cross Cent (1st issue). Nos. 769/71 surch with red cross **1863 1963** and premium.

No.	Type	Description	Mint	Used
781	**215**	5c.+5c. red	1·60	1·50
782	-	10c.+10c. yellow	3·50	3·00
783	-	31c.+15c. blue	3·50	3·00

See also No. 797.

225 F.A.O. Emblem

1963. Air. Freedom from Hunger.

No.	Type	Description	Mint	Used
784	**225**	10c. red and green	40	30
785	**225**	15c. red and blue	50	40

1963. Air. 22nd Central American Lions Convention. Optd **"XXII Convencion Leonistica Centroamericana Panama, 18-21 Abril 1963"**.

No.	Type	Description	Mint	Used
786	**207**	5c. black	75	20

1963. Air. Surch **HABILITADO Vale B./0.04**.

No.	Type	Description	Mint	Used
789	**200**	4c. in 10c. green	30	20

1963. Air. Nos. 743 and 769 optd **AEREO** vert.

No.	Description	Mint	Used
790	10c. green and cream	30	20
791	20c. brown and green	70	40

1963. Air. Freedom of the Press. No. 693 optd **LIBERTAD DE PRENSA 20-VIII-63**.

No.	Description	Mint	Used
792	5c. red and orange	30	20

1963. Air. Visit of U.S. Astronauts to Panama. Optd **"Visita Astronautas Glenn-Schirra Sheppard Cooper a Panama"** or surch also.

No.	Type	Description	Mint	Used
793	**221**	5c. red	3·50	3·25
794	**221**	10c. on 5c. red	4·75	4·75
MS795		77×100 mm. No. **MS**773 (sold at 1b.)	55·00	50·00

1963. Air. Surch **HABILITADO 10c**.

No.	Description	Mint	Used
796	10c. on 5c. red	9·75	9·25

1963. Air. Red Cross Centenary (2nd issue). No. 781 surch **"Centenario Cruz Roja Internacional 10c"** with premium obliterated.

No.	Description	Mint	Used
797	10c. on 5c.+5c. red	7·75	6·00

1963. Surch **VALE** and value.

No.	Type	Description	Mint	Used
798	**217**	4c. on 3c. black and red (postage)	25	20
799	-	4c. on 3c. black, blue and cream (No. 741)	25	20
800	**220**	4c. on 3c. black and red	25	20
801	-	4c. on 3c. black and blue (No. 776)	25	20
802	**182**	10c. on 25c. blue and red	45	25
803	-	10c. on 25c. blue (No. 688) (air)	35	20

234 Pres. Orlich (Costa Rica) and Flags

1963. Presidential Reunion, San Jose (Costa Rica). Multicoloured. Presidents and flags of their countries.

No.	Description	Mint	Used
804	1c. Type **234** (postage)	20	20
805	2c. Somoza (Nicaragua)	20	20
806	3c. Villeda (Honduras)	25	20
807	4c. Chiari (Panama)	30	25
808	5c. Rivera (El Salvador) (air)	30	30
809	10c. Ydigoras (Guatemala)	60	35
810	21c. Kennedy (U.S.A.)	1·60	1·20

235 Innsbruck

1963. Winter Olympic Games, Innsbruck.

No.	Description	Mint	Used
811	½c. red and blue (postage)	20	10
812	1c. red, brown and turquoise	20	10
813	3c. red and blue	60	25
814	4c. red, brown and green	70	30
815	5c. red, brown and mauve (air)	85	35
816	15c. red, brown and blue	1·60	95
817	21c. red, brown and myrtle	2·75	1·40
818	31c. red, brown and blue	3·75	2·40
MS819	100×65 mm. Nos. 817/18 but colours changed. Imperf	21·00	20·00

DESIGNS: ½c. (expressed "B/0.005"), 3c. Type **235**; 1, 4c. Speed-skating; 5c. to 31c. Skiing (slalom).

236 Vasco Nunez de Balboa

1964. 450th Anniv of Discovery of Pacific Ocean.

No.	Type	Description	Mint	Used
820	**236**	4c. green on flesh (postage)	25	20
821	**236**	10c. violet on pink (air)	30	30

237 Boy Scout

1964. Obligatory Tax for Youth Rehabilitation Institute.

No.	Type	Description	Mint	Used
822	**237**	1c. red	25	20
823	**237**	1c. grey	25	20
824	**237**	1c. light blue	25	20
825	**237**	1c. olive	25	20
826	**237**	1c. violet	25	20
827	-	1c. brown	25	20
828	-	1c. orange	25	20
829	-	1c. turquoise	25	20
830	-	1c. violet	25	20
831	-	1c. yellow	25	20

DESIGN: Nos. 827/31, Girl guide.

238 St. Paul's Cathedral, London

1964. Air. Ecumenical Council, Vatican City (1st issue). Cathedrals. Centres in black.

No.	Description	Mint	Used
832	21c. red (Type **238**)	1·50	1·10
833	21c. blue (Kassa, Hungary)	1·50	1·10
834	21c. green (Milan)	1·50	1·10
835	21c. black (St. John's, Poland)	1·50	1·10
836	21c. brown (St. Stephen's, Vienna)	1·50	1·10
837	21c. brown (Notre Dame, Paris)	1·50	1·10
838	21c. violet (Moscow)	1·50	1·10
839	21c. violet (Lima)	1·50	1·10
840	21c. red (Stockholm)	1·50	1·10
841	21c. mauve (Cologne)	1·50	1·10
842	21c. bistre (New Delhi)	1·50	1·10
843	21c. deep turquoise (Basel)	1·50	1·10
844	21c. green (Toledo)	1·50	1·10
845	21c. red (Metropolitan, Athens)	1·50	1·10
846	21c. olive (St. Patrick's, New York)	1·50	1·10
847	21c. green (Lisbon)	1·50	1·10
848	21c. turquoise (Sofia)	1·50	1·10
849	21c. deep brown (New Church, Delft, Netherlands)	1·50	1·10
850	21c. deep sepia (St. George's Patriarchal Church, Istanbul)	1·50	1·10
851	21c. blue (Basilica, Guadalupe, Mexico)	1·50	1·10
852	1b. blue (Panama)	8·25	7·00
853	2b. green (St. Peter's, Rome)	15·00	13·00
MS854	198×138 mm. Nos. 832, 837/8, 846 and 852/3. Imperf (sold at 3b.85)	16·00	16·00

See also Nos. 822/**MS**888.

1964. As Nos. 749 and 760 but colours changed and optd **HABILITADA**.

No.	Description	Mint	Used
855	1b. black, red & blue (postage)	3·00	2·30
856	1b. black, green & yellow (air)	3·25	2·75

1964. Air. No. 756 surch **VALE B/. 0.50**.

No.	Description	Mint	Used
857	50c. on 21c. black, sepia and blue	1·90	1·20

241 Discus-thrower

1964. Olympic Games, Tokyo.

No.	Description	Mint	Used
858	½c. ("B/0.005") purple, red, brown and green (postage)	15	15
859	1c. multicoloured	20	15
860	5c. black, red and olive (air)	40	30
861	10c. black, red and yellow	70	35
862	21c. multicoloured	1·40	75
863	50c. multicoloured	2·50	1·50
MS864	66×95 mm. No. 863	21·00	20·00

DESIGNS: ½c. Type **241**; 1c. Runner with Olympic Flame; 5c. to 50c. Olympic Stadium, Tokyo, and Mt. Fuji.

1964. Air. Nos. 692 and 742 surch **Aereo B/.0.10**.

No.	Description	Mint	Used
865	10c. on 5c. green and turquoise	35	20
866	10c. on 5c. black, red and green	35	20

243 Space Vehicles (Project "Apollo")

1964. Space Exploration. Multicoloured.

No.	Description	Mint	Used
867	½c. ("B/0.005") Type **243** (postage)	15	10
868	1c. Rocket and capsule (Project "Gemini")	15	10
869	5c. W. M. Schirra (air)	35	35
870	10c. L. G. Cooper	60	45
871	21c. Schirra's capsule	1·30	1·10
872	50c. Cooper's capsule	6·25	4·50
MS873	60×95 mm. No. 872	21·00	19·00

1964. No. 687 surch Correos **B/. 0.10**.

No.	Description	Mint	Used
874	10c. on 21c. blue	35	25

245 Water-skiing

1964. Aquatic Sports. Multicoloured.

No.	Description	Mint	Used
875	½c. ("B/0.005") Type **245** (postage)	25	20
876	1c. Underwater swimming	25	20
877	5c. Fishing (air)	35	25
878	10c. Sailing (vert)	1·90	65
879	21c. Speedboat racing	3·50	1·20
880	31c. Water polo at Olympic Games, 1964	4·50	1·50
MS881	95×65 mm. No. 880	21·00	19·00

1964. Air. Ecumenical Council, Vatican City (2nd issue). Stamps of 1st issue optd **1964**. Centres in black.

No.	Description	Mint	Used
882	21c. red (No. 832)	1·20	75
883	21c. green (No. 834)	1·20	75
884	21c. olive (No. 836)	1·20	75
885	21c. deep sepia (No. 850)	1·20	75
886	1b. blue (No. 852)	4·50	3·25
887	2b. green (No. 853)	9·25	7·50
MS888	No. **MS**854 optd **1964** and coat-of-arms (sold at 3b.65)	80·00	80·00

247 General View

1964. Air. New York's World Fair.

No.	Type	Description	Mint	Used
889	**247**	5c. black and yellow	60	45
890	-	10c. black and red	1·40	1·10
891	-	15c. black and green	2·40	1·50
892	-	21c. black and blue	3·50	2·75
MS893		127×76 mm. No. 892	5·75	5·50

DESIGNS: 10c., 15c. Fair pavilions (different); 21c. Unisphere.

248 Eleanor Roosevelt

1964. Mrs. Eleanor Roosevelt Commemoration.

No.	Type	Description	Mint	Used
894	**248**	4c. black and red on yellow (postage)	30	20
895	**248**	20c. black and green on buff (air)	50	35
MS896		87×76 mm. Nos. 894/5Imperf (sold at 25c.)	2·00	1·90

249 Dag Hammarskjold

1964. Air. U.N. Day.

No.	Type	Description	Mint	Used
897	**249**	21c. black and blue	1·20	75
898	-	21c. blue and black	1·20	75
MS899		98×80 mm. No. 897/8. Imperf	6·25	6·00

DESIGN: No. 898, U.N. Emblem.

250 Pope John XXIII

1964. Air. Pope John Commemoration.

No.	Type	Description	Mint	Used
900	**250**	21c. black and bistre	95	65
901	-	21c. mult (Papal Arms)	95	65
MS902		97×80 mm. Nos. 900/1	9·25	8·75

251 Slalom Skiing Medals

1964. Winter Olympic Winners' Medals. Medals in gold, silver and bronze.

No.	Type	Description	Mint	Used
903	**251**	½c. ("B/0.005") turquoise (postage)	20	10
904	-	1c. deep blue	20	10
905	-	2c. brown	25	15
906	-	3c. mauve	50	20
907	-	4c. lake	75	40
908	-	5c. violet (air)	60	50
909	-	6c. blue	75	65
910	-	7c. violet	1·30	1·00
911	-	10c. green	1·90	1·60
912	-	21c. red	2·10	1·80
913	-	31c. blue	3·75	3·25
MS914		142×103 mm. Nos. 911/13	21·00	20·00

DESIGNS—Medals for: 1c., 7c. Speed-skating; 2c., 21c. Bobsleighing; 3c., 10c. Figure-skating; 4c. Ski-jumping; 5c., 6c., 31c. Cross-country skiing. Values in the same design show different medal-winners and country names.

252 Red-billed Toucan

1965. Birds. Multicoloured.

No.	Description	Mint	Used
915	1c. Type **252** (postage)	70	20
916	2c. Scarlet macaw	70	20
917	3c. Woodpecker sp.	1·10	20
918	4c. Blue-grey tanager (horiz)	1·10	20
919	5c. Troupial (horiz) (air)	1·50	45
920	10c. Crimson-backed tanager (horiz)	2·75	45

253 Red Snapper

1965. Marine Life. Multicoloured.

No.	Description	Mint	Used
921	1c. Type **253** (postage)	40	20
922	2c. Dolphin (fish)	40	20
923	8c. Shrimp (air)	50	20
924	12c. Smooth hammerhead	65	35
925	13c. Sailfish	75	45
926	25c. Lined seahorse (vert)	1·50	75

254 Double Daisy and Emblem

1966. Air. 50th Anniv of Junior Chamber of Commerce. Flowers. Multicoloured: background colour given.

No.	Type	Description	Mint	Used
927	**254**	30c. mauve	95	45
928	-	30c. flesh (Hibiscus)	95	45
929	-	30c. olive (Mauve orchid)	95	45
930	-	40c. green (Water lily)	1·40	45
931	-	40c. blue (Gladiolus)	1·40	45
932	-	40c. pink (White orchid)	1·40	45

Each design incorporates the Junior Chamber of Commerce Emblem.

1966. Surch. (a) Postage.

No.	Description	Mint	Used
933	13c. on 25c. (No. 747)	50	30

(b) Air.

No.	Description	Mint	Used
934	3c. on 5c. (No. 680)	30	30
935	13c. on 25c. (No. 695)	50	35

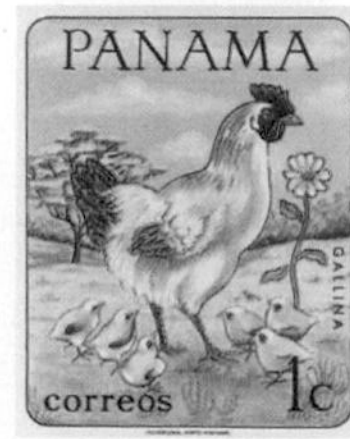

256 Chicken

1967. Domestic Animals. Multicoloured.

No.	Description	Mint	Used
936	1c. Type **256** (postage)	10	10
937	3c. Cockerel	10	10
938	5c. Pig (horiz)	20	10
939	8c. Cow (horiz)	30	20
940	10c. Pekingese dog (air)	50	35
941	13c. Zebu (horiz)	60	35
942	30c. Cat	1·20	80
943	40c. Horse (horiz)	1·40	95

257 American Darter

1967. Wild Birds. Multicoloured.

944		½c. Type **257**	1·10	20
945		1c. Resplendent quetzal	1·10	20
946		3c. Turquoise-browed motmot	1·30	30
947		4c. Red-necked aracari (horiz)	1·50	30
948		5c. Chestnut-fronted macaw	1·90	30
949		13c. Belted kingfisher	7·25	1·20

258 "Deer" (F. Marc)

1967. Wild Animals. Paintings. Multicoloured.

950		1c. Type **258** (postage)	10	10
951		3c. "Cougar" (F. Marc) (vert)	10	10
952		5c. "Monkeys" (F. Marc)	20	10
953		8c. "Fox" (F. Marc)	40	10
954		10c. "St. Jerome and the Lion" (Durer) (vert) (air)	40	30
955		13c. "The Hare" (Durer) (vert)	60	35
956		20c. "Lady with the Ermine" (Da Vinci) (vert)	85	45
957		30c. "The Hunt" (Delacroix)	1·30	75

259 Map of Panama and People

1969. National Population Census.

958	**259**	5c. blue	30	30
959	-	10c. purple	45	20

DESIGN—VERT: 10c. People and map of the Americas.

260 Cogwheel

1969. 50th Anniv of Rotary Int in Panama.

960	**260**	13c. black, yellow and blue	45	20

261 Cornucopia and Map

1969. First Anniv of 11 October Revolution.

961	**261**	10c. multicoloured	40	20

262 Tower and Map

1969

962	**262**	3c. black and orange	15	10
963	-	5c. green	20	10
964	-	8c. brown	25	20
965	-	13c. black and green	35	20
966	-	20c. brown	50	30
967	-	21c. yellow	50	35
968	-	25c. green	70	35
969	-	30c. black	85	55
970	-	34c. brown	1·10	55
971	-	38c. blue	1·20	55
972	-	40c. yellow	1·40	75
973	-	50c. black and purple	1·50	90
974	-	59c. purple	2·10	95

DESIGNS—HORIZ: 5c. Peasants; 13c. Hotel Continental; 25c. Del Rey Bridge; 34c. Panama Cathedral; 38c. Municipal Palace; 40c. French Plaza; 50c. Thatcher Ferry Bridge; 59c. National Theatre. VERT: 8c. Nata Church; 20c. Virgin of Carmen Church; 21c. Altar, San Jose Church; 30c. Dr. Arosemena statue.

263 Discus-thrower and Stadium

1970. 11th Central American and Caribbean Games, Panama (1st series).

975	**263**	1c. multicoloured (postage)	15	10
976	**263**	2c. multicoloured	15	10
977	**263**	3c. multicoloured	15	10
978	**263**	5c. multicoloured	15	10
979	**263**	10c. multicoloured	20	20
980	**263**	13c. multicoloured	30	20
981	-	13c. multicoloured	35	20
982	**263**	25c. multicoloured	1·00	75
983	**263**	30c. multicoloured	1·20	80
984	-	13c. multicoloured (air)	1·00	40
985	-	30c. multicoloured	1·20	80

DESIGNS—VERT: No. 981, "Flor del Espirited Santo" (flowers); 985, Indian girl. HORIZ: No. 984, Thatcher Ferry Bridge and palm.

See also Nos. 986/94.

264 J. D. Arosemena and Stadium

1970. Air. 11th Central American and Caribbean Games, Panama (2nd series). Multicoloured.

986		1c. Type **264**	15	15
987		2c. Type **264**	15	15
988		3c. Type **264**	15	15
989		5c. Type **264**	20	15
990		13c. Basketball	45	20
991		13c. New Gymnasium	45	20
992		13c. Revolution Stadium	45	20
993		13c. Panamanian couple in festive costume	45	20
994		30c. Eternal Flame and stadium	1·20	65
MS995		85×75 mm. No. 994. Imperf	2·10	2·00

265 A. Tapia and M. Sosa (first comptrollers)

1971. 40th Anniv of Panamanian Comptroller-General's Office. Multicoloured.

996		3c. Comptroller-General's Building (1970) (vert)	15	10
997		5c. Type **265**	15	10
998		8c. Comptroller-General's emblem (vert)	20	15
999		13c. Comptroller-General's Building (1955–70)	25	15

266 "Man and Alligator"

1971. Indian Handicrafts.

1000	**266**	8c. multicoloured	80	25

267 Map of Panama on I.E.Y. Emblem

1971. International Education Year.

1001	**267**	1b. multicoloured	3·50	3·00

268 Astronaut on Moon

1971. Air. "Apollo 11" and "Apollo 12" Moon Missions. Multicoloured.

1002		13c. Type **268**	60	40
1003		13c. "Apollo 12" astronauts	60	40

269 Panama Pavilion

1971. Air. "EXPO 70" World Fair, Osaka, Japan.

1004	**269**	10c. multicoloured	25	25

270 Conference Text and Emblem

1971. Ninth Inter-American Loan and Savings Association Conference, Panama City.

1005	**270**	25c. multicoloured	95	75

271 Panama Flag

1971. Air. American Tourist Year. Multicoloured.

1006		5c. Type **271**	15	10
1007		13c. Map of Panama and Western Hemisphere	45	25

272 New U.P.U. H.Q. Building

1971. Inauguration of New U.P.U. Headquarters Building, Berne. Multicoloured.

1008		8c. Type **272**	25	10
1009		30c. U.P.U. Monument, Berne (vert)	1·00	75

273 Cow and Pig

1971. Third Agricultural Census.

1010	**273**	3c. multicoloured	25	20

274 Map and "4S" Emblem

1971. "4S" Programme for Rural Youth.

1011	**274**	2c. multicoloured	20	20

275 Gandhi

1971. Air. Birth Centenary (1969) of Mahatma Gandhi.

1012	**275**	10c. multicoloured	70	40

276 Central American Flags

1971. Air. 150th Anniv of Central American States' Independence from Spain.

1013	**276**	13c. multicoloured	35	25

277 Early Panama Stamp

1971. Air. Second National, Philatelic and Numismatic Exhibition, Panama.

1014	**277**	8c. blue, black and red	25	20

278 Altar, Nata Church

1972. Air. 450th Anniv of Nata Church.

1015	**278**	40c. multicoloured	85	75

279 Telecommunications Emblem

1972. Air. World Telecommunications Day.

1016	**279**	13c. black, blue & lt blue	50	40

280 "Apollo 14" Badge

1972. Air. Moon Flight of "Apollo 14".

1017	**280**	13c. multicoloured	85	60

281 Children on See-saw

1972. 25th Anniv (1971) of UNICEF. Multicoloured.

1018		1c. Type **281** (postage)	10	10
1019		5c. Boy sitting by kerb (vert) (air)	15	10
1020		8c. Indian mother and child (vert)	25	25
1021		50c. UNICEF emblem (vert)	1·30	65
MS1022		86×75 mm. No. 1021. Imperf	1·70	1·70

282 Tropical Fruits

1972. Tourist Publicity. Multicoloured.

1023		1c. Type **282** (postage)	10	10
1024		2c. "Isle of Night"	10	10
1025		3c. Carnival float (vert)	15	10

329 Pele (Brazilian footballer)

1982. World Cup Football Championship, S
Multicoloured.
1314 50c. Italian team (horiz) (postage) 1·40
1315 23c. Football emblem and map of Panama (air) 70
1316 35c. Type **329** 95
1317 41c. World Cup Trophy 1·30
MS1318 85×75 mm. No. 1316. Imperf (sold at 1b.) 13·00

330 Chamber of Trade Emblem

1983. "Expo Comer" Chamber of Trade Exhibition.
1319 **330** 17c. lt blue, blue, & gold 50

331 Dr. Nicolas Solano

1983. Air. Birth Centenary (1982) of Dr. Nicola
(anti-tuberculosis pioneer).
1320 **331** 23c. brown 50

332 Pope John Paul II giving Blessing

1983. Papal Visit. Multicoloured.
1321 6c. Type **332** (postage) 4
1322 17c. Pope John Paul II 8
1323 35c. Pope and map of Panama (air) 1·

333 Map of Americas and Sunburst

1983. 24th Assembly of Inter-American I
Bank Governors.
1324 **333** 50c. light blue, blue and gold

334 Simon Bolivar

1983. Birth Bicentenary of Simon Bolivar.
1325 **334** 50c. multicoloured
MS1326 85×75 mm. **334** 1b. multicoloured. Impref

1026 5c. San Blas textile (air) 15 15
1027 8c. Chaquira (beaded collar) 25 15
1028 25c. Ruined fort, Portobelo 80 60
MS1029 96×120 mm. Nos. 1026 and 1028. Imperf 3·50 2·50

283 Map and Flags

1973. Obligatory Tax. Panama City Post Office Building Fund. Seventh Bolivar Games.
1030 **283** 1c. black 20 15

284 Baseball Players

1973. Air. Seventh Bolivar Games.
1031 **284** 8c. red and yellow 25 15
1032 - 10c. black and blue 25 20
1033 - 13c. multicoloured 35 25
1034 - 25c. black, red and green 70 35
1035 - 50c. multicoloured 1·50 80
1036 - 1b. multicoloured 3·00 1·50
DESIGNS—VERT: 10c. Basketball; 13c. Flaming torch. HORIZ: 25c. Boxing; 50c. Panama map and flag, Games emblem and Bolivar; 1b. Games' medals.

1973. U.N. Security Council Meeting, Panama City. Various stamps surch **O.N.U.** in laurel leaf, **CONSEJO DE SEGURIDAD 15 - 21 Marzo 1973** and value.
1037 8c. on 59c. (No. 974) (postage) 15 15
1038 10c. on 1b. (No. 1001) 20 15
1039 13c. on 30c. (No. 969) 35 20
1040 13c. on 40c. (No. 1015) (air) 45 25

286 Farming Co-operative

1973. Obligatory Tax. Post Office Building Fund.
1041 **286** 1c. green and red 45 25
1042 - 1c. grey and red 45 25
1043 - 1c. yellow and red 45 25
1044 - 1c. orange and red 45 25
1045 - 1c. blue and red 45 25
DESIGNS: No. 1042, Silver coins; 1043, V. Lorenzo; 1044, Cacique Urraca; 1045, Post Office building.
See also Nos. 1061/2.

287 J. D. Crespo (educator)

1973. Famous Panamanians. Multicoloured.
1046 3c. Type **287** (postage) 15 10
1047 5c. Isabel Obaldia (educator) (air) 15 10
1048 8c. N. V. Jaen (educator) 25 20
1049 10c. "Forest Scene" (Roberto Lewis, painter) 35 25
1050 13c. R. Miro (poet) 50 25
1051 13c. "Portrait of a Lady" (M. E. Amador, painter) 50 25
1052 20c. "Self-Portrait" (Isaac Benitez, painter) 70 40
1053 21c. M. A. Guerrero (statesman) 80 50
1054 25c. Dr. B. Porras (statesman) 85 50
1055 30c. J. D. Arosemena (statesman) 1·00 60
1056 34c. Dr. O. M. Pereira (writer) 1·10 70
1057 38c. Dr. R. J. Alfaro (writer) 1·30 80

1973. Air. 50th Anniv of Isabel Obaldia Professional School. Nos. 1047, 1054 and 1056 optd **1923 1973 Godas de Oro Escuela Profesional Isabel Herrera Obaldia** and EP emblem.
1058 5c. multicoloured 15 10
1059 25c. multicoloured 85 50
1060 34c. multicoloured 1·10 85

1974. Obligatory Tax. Post Office Building Fund. As Nos. 1044/5.
1061 1c. orange 45 25
1062 2c. blue 45 25

1974. Surch **VALE** and value.
1063 5c. on 30c. black (No. 969) (postage) 15 15
1064 10c. on 34c. brown (No. 970) 25 15
1065 13c. on 21c. yellow (No. 967) 25 20
1066 1c. on 25c. multicoloured (No. 1028) (air) 10 10
1067 3c. on 20c. mult (No. 1052) 10 10
1068 8c. on 38c. mult (No. 1057) 20 15
1069 10c. on 34c. mult (No. 1056) 25 20
1070 13c. on 21c. mult (No. 1053) 25 20

290 Women's upraised Hands

1975. Air. International Women's Year.
1071 **290** 17c. multicoloured 70 40

291 Bayano Dam

1975. Air. Seventh Anniv of October 1968 Revolution.
1073 **291** 17c. black, brown & blue 70 40
1074 - 27c. blue and green 95 65
1075 - 33c. multicoloured 1·10 75
DESIGNS—VERT: 27c. Victoria sugar plant, Veraguas, and sugar cane. HORIZ: 33c. Tocumen International Airport.

1975. Obligatory Tax. Various stamps surch **VALE PRO EDIFICIO** and value.
1076 1c. on 30c. black (No. 969) (postage) 25 20
1077 1c. on 40c. yellow (No. 972) 25 20
1078 1c. on 50c. black and purple (No. 973) 25 20
1079 1c. on 30c. mult (No. 1009) 25 20
1080 **282** 1c. on 1c. multicoloured 25 20
1081 - 1c. on 2c. multicoloured (No. 1024) 25 20
1082 **278** 1c. on 40c. mult (air) 25 20
1083 - 1c. on 25c. mult (No. 1028) 25 20
1084 - 1c. on 25c. mult (No. 1052) 25 20
1085 - 1c. on 20c. mult (No. 1054) 25 20
1086 - 1c. on 30c. mult (No. 1055) 25 20

1975. Obligatory Tax. Post Office Building Fund. As No. 1045.
1087 1c. red 45 25

294 Bolivar and Thatcher Ferry Bridge

1976. 150th Anniv of Panama Congress (1st issue). Multicoloured.
1088 6c. Type **294** (postage) 15 10
1089 23c. Bolivar Statue (air) 60 25
1090 35c. Bolivar Hall, Panama City (horiz) 95 40
1091 41c. Bolivar and flag 1·00 75

295 "Evibacus princeps"

1976. Marine Fauna. Multicoloured.
1092 2c. Type **295** (postage) 45 20
1093 3c. "Ptitosarcus sinuosus" (vert) 45 20
1094 4c. "Acanthaster planci" 45 20
1095 7c. "Oreaster reticulatus" 45 25
1096 17c. Porcupinefish (vert) (air) 85 35
1097 27c. "Pocillopora damicornis" 1·30 50
MS1098 100×100 mm. 1b. *Mithrax spinossimus*. Imperf 5·25 5·00

296 "Simon Bolivar"

1976. 150th Anniv of Panama Congress (2nd issue). Designs showing details of Bolivar Monument or flags of Latin-American countries. Multicoloured.
1099 20c. Type **296** 60 60
1100 20c. Argentina 60 60
1101 20c. Bolivia 60 60
1102 20c. Brazil 60 60
1103 20c. Chile 60 60
1104 20c. "Battle scene" 60 60
1105 20c. Colombia 60 60
1106 20c. Costa Rica 60 60
1107 20c. Cuba 60 60
1108 20c. Ecuador 60 60
1109 20c. El Salvador 60 60
1110 20c. Guatemala 60 60
1111 20c. Guyana 60 60
1112 20c. Haiti 60 60
1113 20c. "Congress assembly" 60 60
1114 20c. "Liberated people" 60 60
1115 20c. Honduras 60 60
1116 20c. Jamaica 60 60
1117 20c. Mexico 60 60
1118 20c. Nicaragua 60 60
1119 20c. Panama 60 60
1120 20c. Paraguay 60 60
1121 20c. Peru 60 60
1122 20c. Dominican Republic 60 60
1123 20c. "Bolivar and standard-bearer" 60 60
1124 20c. Surinam 60 60
1125 20c. Trinidad and Tobago 60 60
1126 20c. Uruguay 60 60
1127 20c. Venezuela 60 60
1128 20c. "Indian Delegation" 60 60
MS1129 81×122 mm. 30c. Bolivar and flag-bearer; 30c. Top of Monument; 40c. Inscribed tablet. Perf or Imperf 3·50 3·25

297 Nicanor Villalaz (designer of Panama Arms)

1976. Villalaz Commemoration.
1130 **297** 5c. blue 25 20

298 National Lottery Building, Panama City

1976. "Progressive Panama".
1131 **298** 6c. multicoloured 25 20

299 Cerro Colorado, Copper Mine

1976. Air.
1132 **299** 23c. multicoloured 50 25

300 Contadora Island

1977. Tourism.
1133 **300** 3c. multicoloured 25 20

301 Secretary-General of Pan-American Union, A. Orfila

1978. Signing of Panama–U.S.A. Treaty. Multicoloured.
1134 3c. Type **301** 15 15
1135 23c. Treaty signing scene (horiz) 60 25
1136 40c. President Carter 1·00 60
1137 50c. Gen. O. Torrijos of Panama 1·30 90
Nos. 1134 and 1136/7 were issued together se-tenant in horizontal stamps of three showing Treaty signing as No. 1135.

302 Signing Ratification of Panama Canal Treaty

1978. Ratification of Panama Canal Treaty.
1138 **302** 3c. multicoloured 15 10
1139 - 5c. multicoloured 20 10
1140 - 35c. multicoloured 95 40
1141 - 41c. multicoloured 1·00 50
DESIGNS: 5, 35, 41c. As Type **302**, but with the design of the Ratification Ceremony spread over the three stamps, issued as a se-tenant strip in the order 5c. (29×39 mm), 41c. (44×39 mm), 35c. (29×39 mm).

303 Colon Harbour and Warehouses

1978. 30th Anniv of Colon Free Zone.
1142 **303** 6c. multicoloured 25 20

304 Children's Home and Melvin Jones

1978. Birth Centenary of Melvin Jones (founder of Lions International).
1143 **304** 50c. multicoloured 1·30 85

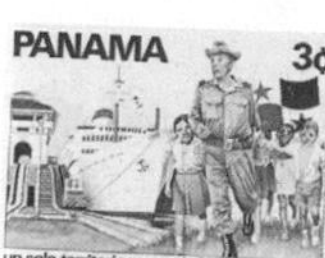

305 Pres. Torrijos, "Flavia" (liner) and Children

1979. Return of Canal Zone. Multicoloured.
1144 3c. Type **305** 25 15
1145 23c. Presidents Torrijos and Carter, liner and flags of Panama and U.S.A. 60 35

306 "75" and Bank Emblem

1979. 75th Anniv of National Bank.
1146 **306** 6c. black, red and blue 25 20

307 Rotary Emblem

1979. 75th Anniv of Rotary International.
1147 **307** 17c. blue and yellow 45 35

308 Children inside Heart

1979. International Year of the Child.
1148 **308** 50c. multicoloured 1·3

309 U.P.U. Emblem and Globe

1979. 18th Universal Postal Union Congr Janeiro.
1149 **309** 35c. multicoloured

310 Colon Station

1980. Centenary of Trans-Panamanian Railwa
1150 **310** 1c. purple and lilac

311 Postal Headquarters, Balboa (inauguration)

1980. Anniversaries and Events.
1151 **311** 3c. multicoloured
1152 - 6c. multicoloured
1153 - 17c. multicoloured
1154 - 23c. multicoloured
1155 - 35c. blue, black and red
1156 - 41c. pink and black
1157 - 50c. multicoloured
DESIGNS—HORIZ: 17c. Map of Central An (census of the Americas); 23c. Tourism a Centre (opening); 35c. Bank emblem (Inte velopment Bank, 25th anniv); 41c. F. de L Canal cent); 50c. Olympic Stadium, Mo Games). VERT: 6c. National flag (return of

1980. Olympic Games, Lake Placid and M **1980 LAKE PLACID MOSCU** and ver
1158 20c. (No. 1099)
1160 20c. (1101)
1162 20c. (1103)
1164 20c. (1105)
1166 20c. (1107)
1168 20c. (1109)
1170 20c. (1111)
1172 20c. (1113)
1174 20c. (1115)
1176 20c. (1117)
1178 20c. (1119)
1180 20c. (1121)
1182 20c. (1123)
1184 20c. (1125)
1186 20c. (1127)

(b) Optd with Lake Placid Olympic emb total of country indicat
1159 20c. "**ALEMANIA D.**" (1100)
1161 20c. "**AUSTRIA**" (1102)
1163 20c. "**SUECIA**" (1104)
1165 20c. "**U.R.S.S.**" (1106)
1167 20c. "**ALEMANIA F.**" (1108)
1169 20c. "**ITALIA**" (1110)
1171 20c. "**U.S.A.**" (1112)
1173 20c. "**SUIZA**" (1114)
1175 20c. "**CANADA/GRAN BRETANA**" (1116)
1177 20c. "**NORUEGA**" (1118)
1179 20c. "**LICHTENSTEIN**" (1120)
1181 20c. "**HUNGRIA/BULGARIA**" (1122)
1183 20c. "**FINLANDIA**" (1124)
1185 20c. "**HOLANDA**" (1126)
1187 20c. "**CHECOS-LOVAQUIA/FRANCIA**" (1128)

Nos. 1158, etc, occur on 1st, 3rd Nos. 1159, etc, occur on the others.

406 Columbus's Fleet

1992. America. 500th Anniv of Discovery of America by Columbus. Multicoloured.
1539 20c. Type **406** 60 50
1540 35c. Columbus planting flag 1·10 90

407 Flag and Map of Europe

1992. European Single Market.
1541 **407** 10c. multicoloured 35 25

408 Mascot

1992. "Expo '92" World's Fair, Seville.
1542 **408** 10c. multicoloured 25 25

409 Occupations

1992. American Workers' Health Year.
1543 **409** 15c. multicoloured 45 40

410 Angel and Shepherds

1992. Christmas. Multicoloured.
1544 20c. Type **410** 60 50
1545 35c. Mary and Joseph arriving at Bethlehem 1·10 90

411 Jesus lighting up the Americas

1993. 500th Anniv (1992) of Evangelization of the American Continent.
1546 **411** 10c. multicoloured 25 25

412 Woman on Crutches and Wheelchair-bound Man

1993. National Day of Disabled Persons.
1547 **412** 5c. multicoloured 25 15

413 Herrera (bust)

1993. 32nd Death Anniv of Dr. Jose de la Cruz Herrera (essayist).
1548 **413** 5c. multicoloured 25 15

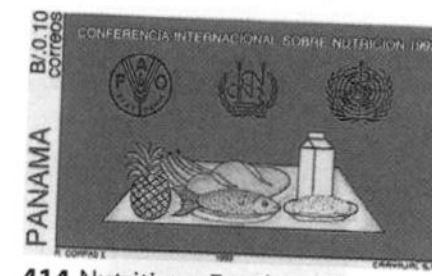

414 Nutritious Foods and Emblems

1993. International Nutrition Conference, Rome.
1549 **414** 10c. multicoloured 25 25

415 Caravel and Columbus in Portobelo Harbour

1994. 490th Anniv (1992) of Columbus's Fourth Voyage and Exploration of the Panama Isthmus.
1550 **415** 50c. multicoloured 1·50 1·30

416 Panama Flag and Greek Motifs

1995. 50th Anniv of Greek Community in Panama. Multicoloured.
1551 20c. Type **416** 50 50
MS1552 100×50 mm. 75c. Acropolis, Athens; 75c. Greek Orthodox Church, Panama (horiz) 4·25 4·25

1995. Various stamps surch.
1553 - 20c. on 23c. multicoloured (1459) 50 40
1554 **373** 25c. on 45c. multicoloured 70 50
1555 - 30c. on 45c. multicoloured (1510) 85 55
1556 **375** 35c. on 45c. brown and bistre 95 65
1557 - 35c. on 45c. multicoloured (1477) 1·00 70
1558 - 40c. on 41c. multicoloured (1461) 1·10 80
1559 - 50c. on 60c. multicoloured (1511) 1·70 1·00
1560 - 1b. on 50c. multicoloured (1480) 3·00 1·90

418 Chinese Family and House

1996. Chinese Presence in Panama. 142nd Anniv of Arrival of First Chinese Immigrants. Multicoloured.
1561 60c. Type **418** 2·20 1·50
MS1562 90×78 mm. 1b.50 Motifs for winter, spring, summer and autumn. Imperf 4·75 4·50

419 The King's Bridge from the North (16th century)

1996. 475th Anniv (1994) of Founding by the Spanish of Panama City. Multicoloured.
1563 15c. Type **419** 45 40
1564 20c. City arms, 1521 (vert) 60 50
1565 25c. Plan of first cathedral 80 65

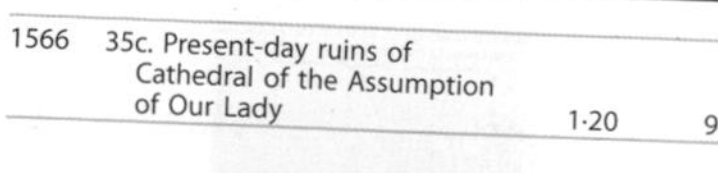
1566 35c. Present-day ruins of Cathedral of the Assumption of Our Lady 1·20 90

420 "60", Campus and Emblem

1996. 60th Anniv of Panama University.
1567 **420** 40c. multicoloured 1·20 1·10

421 Anniversary Emblem

1996. 75th Anniv of Panama Chapter of Rotary International.
1568 **421** 5b. multicoloured 14·50 13·00

422 Great Tinamou

1996. America (1993). Endangered Species.
1569 **422** 20c. multicoloured 1·00 50

423 Northern Coati

1996. Mammals. Multicoloured.
1570 25c. Type **423** 70 65
1571 25c. Collared anteater ("Tamandua mexicana") 70 65
1572 25c. Two-toed anteater ("Cyclopes didactylus") 70 65
1573 25c. Puma 70 65

424 De Lesseps

1996. Death Centenary of Ferdinand, Vicomte de Lesseps (builder of Suez Canal).
1574 **424** 35c. multicoloured 1·10 90

425 "50" and Emblem

1996. 50th Anniv of U.N.O.
1575 **425** 45c. multicoloured 1·40 1·20

426 Emblem and Motto

1996. 25th Anniv (1993) of Panama Chapter of Kiwanis International.
1576 **426** 40c. multicoloured 1·20 1·10

427 Bello

1996. 25th Anniv (1995) of Andres Bello Covenant for Education, Science, Technology and Culture.
1577 **427** 35c. multicoloured 1·10 90

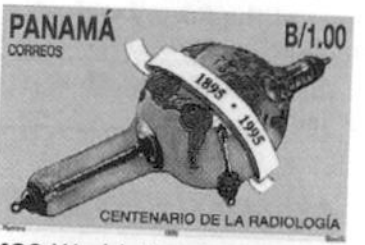

428 World Map on X-ray Equipment

1996. Centenary of Discovery of X-rays by Wilhelm Rontgen.
1578 **428** 1b. multicoloured 3·00 2·75

429 Madonna and Child

1996. Christmas.
1579 **429** 35c. multicoloured 1·10 90

430 Diesel Train and Panama Canal

1996. America (1994). Postal Transport.
1580 **430** 30c. multicoloured 85 85

431 "Panama, More than a Canal" (C. Gonzalez)

1997. 20th Anniv of Torrijos–Carter Treaty (transferring Control of Canal Zone to Panama in Year 2000). Multicoloured.
1581 20c. Type **431** 60 60
1582 30c. "A Curtain of Our Flag" (A. Siever) (vert) 95 90
1583 45c. "Perpetual Steps" (R. Martinez) 1·40 1·30
1584 50c. Kurt Waldheim (U.N. Secretary-General), President Carter of U.S.A. and President Torrijos of Panama at signing ceremony 1·60 1·50
MS1585 127×102 mm. 3, 40, 50c. Composite design as No. 1584 (sold at 1b.50) 1·75 1·40

432 Pedro Miguel Locks

1997. World Congress on Panama Canal. Multicoloured.
1586 45c. Type **432** 1·40 1·30
1587 45c. Miraflores Locks 1·40 1·30
MS1588 100×75 mm. 1b.50 Gatun Locks (75×30 mm) 4·75 4·50

433 "Gandhi Spinning" (P. Biswas)

1997. 50th Anniv of Independence of India.
1589 **433** 50c. multicoloured 1·60 1·40

434 Crocodile on Rock

1997. The American Crocodile. Multicoloured.

1590	25c. Type **434**	70	50
1591	25c. Looking across water	70	50
1592	25c. Two crocodiles	70	50
1593	25c. Head with mouth open	70	50

435 Mary and Joseph searching for Lodgings

1997. Christmas.

1594	**435**	35c. multicoloured	1·10	85

436 Fire Engines from 1941 and 1948

1997. Centenary of Colon City Fire Brigade.

1595	**436**	20c. multicoloured	60	45

437 "Eleutherodactylus biporcatus" (robber frog)

1997. Frogs. Multicoloured.

1596	25c. Type **437**	80	50
1597	25c. "Hyla colymba" (tree frog)	80	50
1598	25c. "Hyla rufitela" (tree frog)	80	50
1599	25c. "Nelsonephryne aterrima"	80	50

438 Women wearing Polleras

1997. America (1996). Traditional Costumes.

1600	**438**	20c. multicoloured	60	40

439 Arosemena

1997. Death Centenary of Justo Arosemena (President, 1855–56).

1601	**439**	40c. multicoloured	1·30	1·10

440 Emblem

1997. 85th Anniv of Colon Chamber of Commerce, Agriculture and Industry.

1602	**440**	1b. multicoloured	3·00	2·75

441 Douglas DC-3

1997. 50th Anniv of Panamanian Aviation Company. Multicoloured.

1603	35c. Type **441**	1·00	85
1604	35c. Martin 4-0-4	1·00	85
1605	35c. Avro HS-748	1·00	85
1606	35c. Lockheed L-188 Electra	1·00	85
1607	35c. Boeing 727-100	1·00	85
1608	35c. Boeing 737-200 Advanced	1·00	85

442 Wailing Wall

1997. 3000th Anniv of Jerusalem. Multicoloured.

1609	20c. Type **442**	60	40
1610	25c. Service in the Basilica of the Holy Sepulchre	80	60
1611	60c. Dome of the Rock	1·70	1·50
MS1612	100×75 mm. 2b.50 Motifs of Nos. 1609/11	4·75	4·50

443 Building Facade and Emblem

1998. 50th Anniv of Organization of American States.

1613	**443**	40c. multicoloured	1·30	1·10

444 Central Avenue, San Felipe

1998. Tourism. Multicoloured.

1614	10c. Type **444**	25	10
1615	20c. Tourists in rainforest	60	40
1616	25c. Gatun Locks, Panama Canal (horiz)	80	60
1617	35c. Panama City (horiz)	1·10	90
1618	40c. San Jeronimo Fort, San Felipe de Portobelo (horiz)	1·30	1·10
1619	45c. Rubber raft, River Chagres (horiz)	1·50	1·20
1620	60c. Beach, Dog's Island, Kuna Yala (horiz)	1·90	1·70

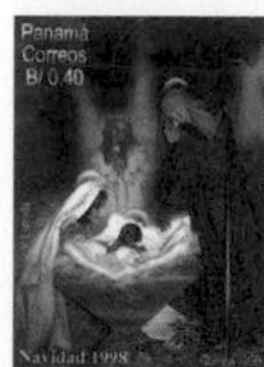
445 Nativity

2000. Christmas.

1621	**445**	40c. multicoloured	1·40	1·20

446 Pavilion

2000. "World Expo'98" World's Fair, Lisbon, Portugal.

1622	**446**	45c. multicoloured	1·60	1·30

447 Harpy Eagle (L. Melillo)

2000. The Harpy Eagle. Entries in painting competition by named artist.

1623	**447**	20c. black and green	70	50
1624	-	20c. multicoloured	70	50
1625	-	20c. multicoloured	70	50
1626	-	20c. multicoloured	70	50

DESIGNS: No. 1624, J. JimEnez; 1625, S. Castro; 1626, J. Ramos.

448 Emblem

2000. 40th Anniv of Business Executives' Association.

1627	**448**	50c. multicoloured	2·20	1·70

449 Emblem

2000. 50th Anniv of Colon Free Trade Zone.

1628	**449**	15c. multicoloured	70	50

450 Emblem

2000. 50th Anniv of Universal Declaration of Human Rights.

1629	**450**	15c. multicoloured	70	50

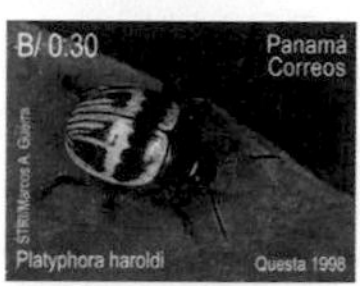
451 *Platyphora haroldi*

2000. Beetles. Multicoloured.

1630	30c. Type **451**	1·10	90
1631	30c. *Stilodes leopardа*	1·10	90
1632	30c. *Stilodes fuscolineata*	1·10	90
1633	30c. *Platyphora boucardi*	1·10	90

452 Cruise Ship

2000. Return of Control of Panama Canal to Panama (1999). Multicoloured.

1634	20c. Type **452**	95	75
1635	35c. Cruise ship at lock gate	1·60	1·40
1636	40c. View down canal	1·70	1·50
1637	45c. Cruise ship passing through lock	2·10	1·80

453 Constructing Canal

2000. 85th Anniv of Panama Canal. Multicoloured.

1638	40c. Type **453**	1·90	1·70
1639	40c. Construction of canal (different)	1·90	3·75
MS1640	106×56 mm. 1b.50 View of canal at early stage of construction	7·25	7·25

454 Crowd and Madrid wearing surgical mask

2001. Birth Centenary of Dr. Arnulfo Arias Madrid.

1641	**454**	20c. black and brown	70	50
1642	-	20c. black and sepia	70	50
1643	-	30c. multicoloured	95	75
1644	-	30c. multicoloured	95	75

DESIGNS: No. 1642, Crowd and Madrid holding glasses; 1643, Flag, building façade and Madrid; 1644, Crowd and Madrid.

Nos. 1641/25 and 1643/4 respectively were each issued together, se-tenant, forming a composite design.

455 Baby Jesus

2001. Year 2000.

1645	**455**	20c. multicoloured	85	65

456 Crowned Globe, Rainbow and Birds (D. Ortega)

2001. "Dreaming of the Future". Winning Entries in Stamp Design Competition. Multicoloured.

1646	20c. Type **456**	85	65
1647	20c. Globe in flower (L. Guerra)	85	65
MS1648	105×54 mm. 75c. Tree, birds, globe and children (J. Aguilar) (horiz); 75c. Blue birds holding ribbons, globe and children holding hands (S. Sitton) (horiz)	6·50	6·50

457 Angel and Baby Jesus

2001. Christmas.

1649	**457**	35c. multicoloured	80	60

458 Banco General Tower (Carlos Medina)

2001. Architecture of 1990s. Multicoloured.

1650	35c. Type **458**	1·60	1·30
1651	35c. Los Delfines condominium (Edwin Brown)	1·60	1·30
MS1652	104×54 mm. 75c. Circular building (Ricardo Moreno and Jesus Santamaria) (horiz); 75c. Building with three gables (Ricardo Moreno and Jesus Santamaria) (horiz)	6·50	6·50

459 *Psychopsis krameriana*

2001. Orchids. Multicoloured.

1653	35c. Type **459**	1·60	1·30
1654	35c. *Cattleya dowiana*	1·60	1·30
MS1655	104×54 mm. 75c. *Peristeria elata*; 75c. *Miltoniopsis roezlii*	6·50	6·50

460 1878 50c. Sovereign State and 1904 1c. Republic of Panama Stamps

2001. 18th U. P. A. E. P. Congress, Panama.

1656	**460**	5b. multicoloured	22·00	21·00

461 Hospital Buildings and Dr Jaime de la Guardia (founder)

2001. 50th Anniv of San Fernando Clinical Hospital.

1657	**461**	20c. multicoloured	85	65

462 Pres. Moscoso and Cornucopia

2002. Mireya Moscoso, First Woman President of Panama. (1st issue).

1658	**462**	35c. multicoloured	1·60	1·30

See also No. 1720.

463 Couple and Drums

2002. Christmas, 2001. Multicoloured.

1659	60c. Type **463**	2·20	2·00
1660	1b. Hat, instruments and candles	4·00	3·50
1661	2b. Vase, gourds and holly	7·75	5·75

464 Helmeted Warrior (allegorical painting)

2002. 180th Anniv of Independence. Multicoloured.

1662	15c. Type **464**	60	40
1663	15c. Woman charioteer (allegorical painting)	60	40

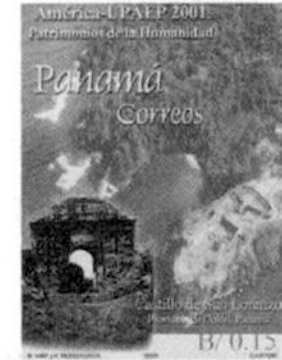

465 San Lorenzo Castle

2002. America. Cultural Heritage. Multicoloured.

1664	15c. Type **465**	70	50
1665	15c. Panama city	70	50
1666	1b. 50 Metropolitan Cathedral church (horiz)	6·25	4·25
1667	1b. 50 Portobelo fortifications (horiz)	6·25	4·25

466 Natives and Ship

2002. 500th Anniv of Discovery of Panama Isthmus. Multicoloured.

1668	50c. Type **466**	1·90	1·70
1669	5b. Native woman and Spanish conquistador	19·00	17·00

467 Spaniard and Natives (allegorical painting)

2002. Artistic Treasures of Las Garzas Palace. Painting by Robert Lewis. Multicoloured.

1670	5c. Type **467**	25	15
1671	5c. Battle scene	25	15
1672	5c. Mythical figures	25	15
1673	5c. Spanish women	25	15

468 *Montastraea annualaris*

2002. Corals. Multicoloured.

1674	10c. Type **468**	35	25
1675	10c. *Pavona chiriquiensis*	35	25
1676	1b. *Siderastrea glynni*	3·75	3·25
1677	2b. *Pocillopora*	7·50	6·50

469 *Ophioderes maternal*

2002. Butterflies and Moths. Multicoloured.

1678	10c. Type **469**	45	25
1679	10c. *Rhuda focula*	45	25
1680	1b. *Morpho peleides*	4·25	3·25
1681	2b. *Tarchon felderi*	8·50	6·50

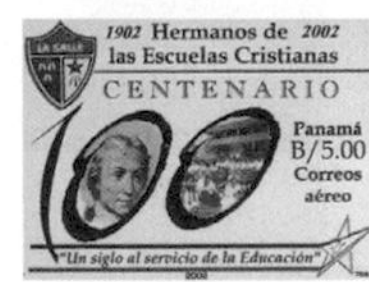

470 "100" enclosing Jean Baptiste de La Salle (founder) and Children

2003. Air. Centenary of La Salle Christian Schools.

1682	**470**	5b. multicoloured	16·00	13·00

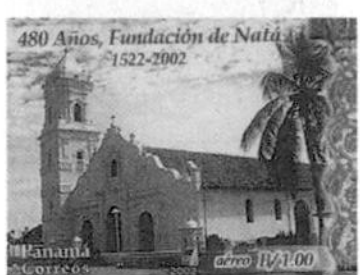

471 Nata Church

2003. Air. 480th Anniv of Nata.

1683	**471**	1b. multicoloured	3·00	2·50

472 Girl and Nativity Figures

2003. Christmas (2002).

1684	**472**	15c. multicoloured	50	35

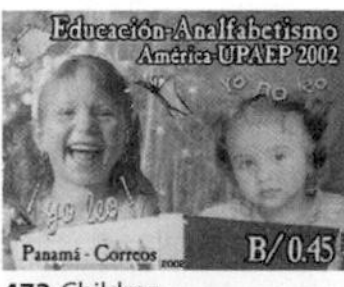

473 Children

2003. America. Literacy Campaign.

1685	**473**	45c. multicoloured	1·40	1·20

474 Clara Gonzalez de Behringer

2003. Famous Women. Clara Gonzalez de Behringer (first woman lawyer).

1686	**474**	30c. multicoloured	1·00	85

475 "Colon" (steam locomotive)

2003. Air. First Transcontinental Railway. Multicoloured.

1687	40c. Type **475**	1·30	1·10
1688	50c. Locomotive in station (vert)	1·60	1·40

476 Columbus Monument

2003. 150th Anniv of Colon City (2002).

1689	**476**	15c. multicoloured	50	35

477 Spanish Soldiers and Native Americans

2003. Air. 500th Anniv of Santa Maria de Belen.

1690	**477**	1b.50 multicoloured	4·75	4·25

478 Christopher Columbus and his Ships

2003. Air. 500th Anniv of Fourth Voyage of Christopher Columbus (2002).

1691	**478**	2b. multicoloured	6·50	5·00

479 Luis Russell

2003. Birth Centenary of Luis Russell (musician).

1692	**479**	10c. multicoloured	35	15

480 Muse of Music (statue)

2003. Artistic Treasures of National Theatre. Multicoloured.

1693	5c. Type **480** (postage)	15	10
1694	5c. Muse of theatre (statue)	15	10

(b) Size 40×30 mm.

1695	50c. Decorated balcony (air)	1·60	1·40
1696	60c. Portico and decorated ceiling	1·80	1·60

481 Village and Woman's Face

2003. Kuna Indians of San Blas Archipelago. Multicoloured.

1697	50c. Type **481**	1·60	1·40
1698	50c. Couple wearing traditional costume (vert)	1·60	1·40
1699	60c. Traditional dance	1·90	1·60
1700	60c. Woman's hands sewing mola (traditional cloth)	1·90	1·60
MS1701	100×50 mm. 1b.50 Fish (mola design) (50×46 mm)	5·50	5·50

482 Josemaria Escriva de Balaguer

2003. Birth Centenary (2002)of Josemaria Escriva de Balaguer (founder of Opus Dei (religious organization).

1702	**482**	10c. multicoloured	35	15

483 Hospital Building and St. Tomas de Villanueva (founder)

2003. Air. Panamanian Medicine Multicoloured.

1703	50c. Type **483** (300th anniv of St. Tomas Hospital)	1·60	1·40
1704	50c. Building facade and William Crawford Gorgas (founder) (75th anniv of Gorgas Medical Institute)	1·60	1·40

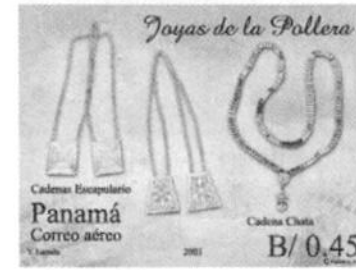

484 Necklaces

2003. Air. Pollera (Latin American folk costume) Jewellery. Multicoloured.

1705	45c. Type **484**	1·40	1·20
1706	60c. Broaches	1·80	1·60

485 National Arms

2003. Centenary of Panama Republic (1st issue). Multicoloured.

1707	5c. Type **485**	15	10
1708	10c. National flag	35	15
1709	15c. Manuel Amador Guerrero (president, 1903)	50	35
1710	15c. Mireya Mascoso (president, 2003)	50	35
1711	25c. Act of Independence	80	60
1712	30c. Sterculia apetala	1·00	85
1713	30c. Peristeria elata	1·00	85
1714	35c. Revolutionary junta	1·20	95
1715	45c. Constitutional conference members	1·40	1·20

See also No. 1717.

486 Harpy Eagle (*Harpia harpia*) and Harlequin Frog (*Atelopus varius*)

2003. America. Endangered Species.

1716	**486**	2b. multicoloured	6·50	5·00

487 Panama City and Nativity

2003. Centenary of Panama Republic (2nd issue). Christmas.

1717	**487**	10c. multicoloured	35	15

488 Building Facade

2003. 150th Anniv of *La Estrella* Newspaper.
1718 **488** 40c. multicoloured 1·30 1·10

489 Panama City and Emblems

2003. Panama City, Ibero-American Cultural Capital, 2003.
1719 **489** 5c. multicoloured 15 10

490 Pres. Moscoso and Cornucopia

2004. Mireya Moscoso, First Woman President of Panama (2nd issue).
1720 **490** 35c. multicoloured 1·10 90

491 Don Quixote and Sanco Panza (based on drawing by Salvador Dali)

2007. 400th (2005) Anniv of Publication of *El Ingenioso Hidalgo Don Quixote de la Mancha* (novel) by Miguel de Cervantes.
1721 **491** 45c. multicoloured 1·50 1·50

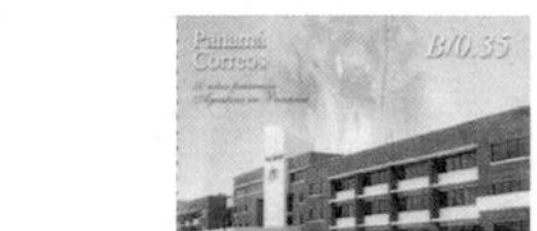
492 Building Facade

2007. 50th Anniv of Augustinians in Panama.
1722 **492** 35c. multicoloured 1·30 1·30

493 Red-backed Squirrel Monkey

2007. Red-backed Squirrel Monkey (*Saimiri oerstedi*). Multicoloured.
1723 20c. Type **493** 75 75
1724 20c. Mother and baby 75 75
1725 20c. Two monkeys 75 75
1726 20c. Monkey chewing stick and mother with baby 75 75

Nos. 1723/6 were issued together, *se-tenant*, forming a composite design.

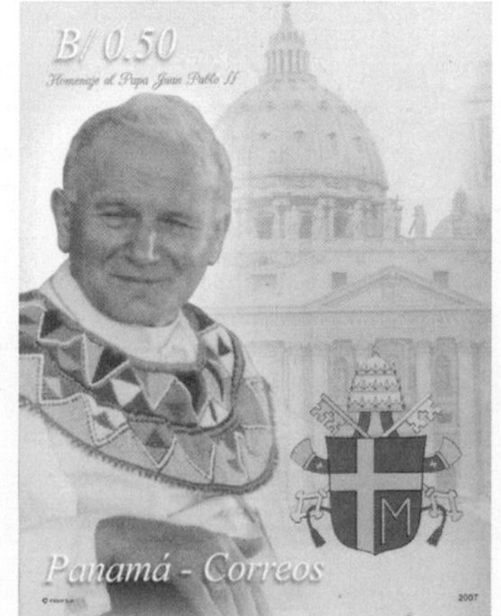
494 Pope John Paul II

2007. Pope John Paul II and Pope Benedict XVI. Sheet 150×100 mm containing Type **494** and similar vert design. Multicoloured.
MS1727 50c.×2, Type **494**; Pope Benedict XVI 3·25 3·25

495 Children looking at Atlas

2007. Tourism includes People. National Secretariat for Social Integration of Disabled Persons of Panama (SENADIS).
1728 **495** 5c. multicoloured 15 15

496 'Crossing the Isthmus'

2007. 150th (2005) Anniv of Panama Canal Railway. Multicoloured.
1729 20c. Type **496** 75 75
1730 30c. Locomotive 1·20 1·20

497 Diablico Sucio

2008. Tourism. Multicoloured.
1731 15c. Type **497** 60 60
1732 20c. Salto de la Chorrera (vert) 75 75
1733 25c. Sarigua Park 90 90
1734 35c. Ancient pots 1·30 1·30
1735 45c. Casa Fuerte de San Fernando 1·50 1·50
1736 60c. Colonial buildings (vert) 3·50 3·50

498 Boeing 737 – 700, Boeing 737 – 800 and Embraer 190

2010. 60th Anniv of Copa Airlines. Sheet 100×150 mm
MS1737 **498** 1b. multicoloured 2·75 2·75

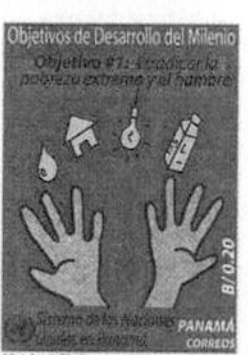
499 Hands and Symbols of Health (Eradicate extreme poverty and hunger)

2010. United Nations Systems in Pananma. Millennium Development Goals. Multicoloured.
1738 20c. Type **499** 75 75
1739 20c. Hand holding pencil (Universal primary education) 75 75
1740 20c. Two hands and equal sign (Equality between the sexes and autonomy for women) 75 75
1741 20c. Breast feeding (Reduce infant mortality) 75 75

Nos. 1738/41 were printed, *se-tenant*, in sheets of four stamps with an enlarged inscribed right margin.

500 St. John Bosco (founder)

2010. Centenary of Salesians in Panama
1742 **500** 20c. multicoloured 75 75

501 Scout Jamboree

2010. Centenary of Scouting
1743 **501** 20c. multicoloured 75 75

502 General Torrijo and Pres. Jimmy Carter

2010. 30th Anniv of Torrijos - Carter Treaties (returning control of Panama canal)
1744 **502** 35c. multicoloured 1·30 1·30

ACKNOWLEDGEMENT OF RECEIPT STAMPS

1898. Handstamped A. R. COLON COLOMBIA.
AR24 **5** 5c. blue 6·75 5·75
AR27 **5** 10c. orange 12·00 11·50

1902. Handstamped AR in circle.
AR32 5c. blue 5·75 5·50
AR33 10c. orange 11·50 11·00

1903. No. AR169 of Colombia handstamped AR in circle.
AR34 **AR 60** 5c. red 23·00 22·00

AR37

1904
AR135 **AR 37** 5c. blue 1·20 95

1916. Optd **A.R.**
AR177 **50** 2½c. red 1·20 95

EXPRESS LETTER STAMPS

1926. Optd **EXPRESO.**
E220 **57** 10c. black and orange 9·75 3·75
E221 **57** 20c. black and brown 11·50 3·75

E81 Cyclist Messenger

1929
E226 **E 81** 10c. orange 1·40 1·10
E227 **E 81** 20c. brown 5·25 3·25

INSURANCE STAMPS

1942. Surch **SEGURO POSTAL HABILITADO** and value.
IN430 5c. on 1b. black (No. 373) 60 55
IN431 10c. on 1b. brown (No. 365) 95 95
IN432 25c. on 50c. brown (No. 372) 2·50 2·40

POSTAGE DUE STAMPS

D58 San Geronimo Castle Gate, Portobelo

1915
D169 **D58** 1c. brown 3·75 95
D170 - 2c. brown 5·75 75
D171 - 4c. brown 7·75 1·50
D172 - 10c. brown 5·75 2·00

DESIGNS—VERT: 2c. Statue of Columbus. HORIZ: 4c. House of Deputies. VERT: 10c. Pedro J. Sosa.

No. D169 is wrongly inscr "CASTILLO DE SAN LORENZO CHAGRES".

D86

1930
D240 **D86** 1c. green 1·20 75
D241 **D86** 2c. red 1·20 75
D242 **D86** 4c. blue 1·70 95
D243 **D86** 10c. violet 1·70 95

REGISTRATION STAMPS

R4

1888
R12 **R4** 10c. black on grey 9·25 7·50

1897. Handstamped R COLON in circle.
R22 **5** 10c. orange 6·75 6·25

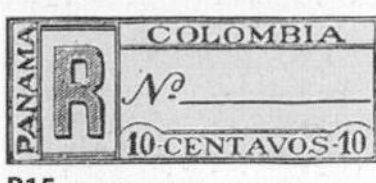
R15

1900
R29 **R15** 10c. black on blue 5·75 4·75
R30 **R15** 10c. red 39·00 22·00

1902. No. R30 surch by hand.
R31 20c. on 10c. red 23·00 18·00

1903. Type **R85** of Colombia optd **REPUBLICA DE PANAMA.**
R42A 20c. red on blue 60·00 50·00
R43A 20c. blue on blue 60·00 50·00

1903. Nos. R42/3 surch.
R46 10c. on 20c. red on blue 75·00 70·00
R47 10c. on 20c. blue on blue 75·00 70·00

1904. Optd **PANAMA.**
R60 **5** 10c. orange 3·75 3·00

1904. Type **R6** of Colombia surch **Panama 10** and bar.
R67 10c. on 20c. red on blue 90·00 85·00
R68 10c. on 20c. blue on blue 70·00 60·00

1904. Type **R85** of Colombia optd **Republica de Panama.**
R106 20c. red on blue 6·75 6·50

R35

1904
R133 **R35** 10c. green 1·20 55

1916. Stamps of Panama surch **R 5 cts.**
R175 **46** 5c. on 8c. black & purple 4·00 3·50
R176 **52** 5c. on 8c. black & purple 4·75 2·40

TOO LATE STAMPS

1903. Too Late stamp of Colombia optd **REPUBLICA DE PANAMA.**
L44A **L86** 5c. violet on red 14·50 10·00

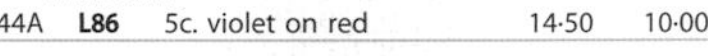

L36

1904
L134 **L36** 2½c. red 1·20 75

1910. Typewritten optd **Retardo.**
L158 **50** 2½c. red £140 £110

1910. Optd **RETARDO.**
L159 2½c. red 70·00 55·00

1916. Surch **RETARDO UN CENTESIMO.**
L173 **38** 1c. on ½c. orange 1·20 1·10

APPENDIX

The following stamps have either been issued in excess of postal needs or have not been available to the public in reasonable quantites at face value. Such stamps may later be given full listing if there is evidence of regular postal use.

1964

Satellites. Postage ½, 1c.; Air 5, 10, 21, 50c.

1965

Tokyo Olympic Games Medal Winners. Postage ½, 1, 2, 3, 4c.; Air 5, 6, 7, 10, 21, 31c.
Space Research. Postage ½, 1, 2, 3c.; Air 5, 10, 11, 31c.
400th Birth Anniv of Galileo. Air 10, 21c.
Peaceful Uses of Atomic Energy. Postage ½, 1, 4c.; Air 6, 10, 21c.
Nobel Prize Medals. Air 10, 21c.
Pres. John Kennedy. Postage ½, 1c.; Air 10+5c., 21+10c., 31+15c.

1966

Pope Paul's Visit to U.N. in New York. Postage ½, 1c.; Air 5, 10, 21, 31c.
Famous Men. Postage ½c.; Air 10, 31c.
Famous Paintings. Postage ½c.; Air 10, 31c.
World Cup Football Championship. Postage ½, ½c.; Air 10, 10, 21, 21c.
Italian Space Research. Postage ½, 1c.; Air 5, 10, 21c.
Centenary of I.T.U. Air 31c.
World Cup Winners. Optd on 1966 World Cup Issue. Postage ½, ½c.; Air 10, 10, 21, 21c.
Religious Paintings. Postage ½, 1, 2, 3c.; Air 21, 21c.
Churchill and Space Research. Postage ½c.; Air 10, 31c.
3rd Death Anniv of Pres. John Kennedy. Postage ½, 1c.; Air 10, 31c.
Jules Verne and Space Research. Postage ½, 1c.; Air 5, 10, 21, 31c.

1967

Religious Paintings. Postage ½, 1c.; Air 5, 10, 21, 31c.
Mexico Olympics. Postage ½, 1c.; Air 5, 10, 21, 31c.
Famous Paintings. Postage 5c.×3; Air 21c.×3.
Goya's Paintings. Postage 2, 3, 4c.; Air 5, 8, 10, 13, 21c.

1968

Religious Paintings. Postage 1, 1, 3c.; Air 4, 21, 21c.
Mexican President's Visit. Air 50c., 1b.
Winter Olympic Games, Grenoble. Postage ½, 1c.; Air 5, 10, 21, 31c.
Butterflies. Postage ½, 1, 3, 4c.; Air 5, 13c.
Ship Paintings. Postage ½, 1, 3, 4c.; Air 5, 13c.
Fishes. Postage ½, 1, 3, 4c.; Air 5, 13c.
Winter Olympic Medal Winners. Postage 1, 2, 3, 4, 5, 6, 8c.; Air 13, 30c.
Paintings of Musicians. Postage 5, 10, 15, 20, 25, 30c.
Satellite Transmissions from Panama T.V. (a) Olympic Games, Mexico. Optd on 1964 Satellites issue. Postage ½c.; Air 50c. (b) Pope Paul's Visit to Latin America. Postage ½c.; Air 21c. (c) Panama Satellite Transmissions. Inauguration. (i) optd on Space Research issue of 1965. Postage 5c.; Air 31c. (ii) optd on Churchill and Space Research issue of 1966. Postage ½c.; Air 10c.
Hunting Paintings. Postage 1, 3, 5, 10c.; Air 13, 30c.
Horses and Jockeys. Postage 5, 10, 15, 20, 25, 30c.
Mexico Olympics. Postage 1, 2, 3, 4, 5, 6, 8c.; Air 13, 30c.

1969

1st International Philatelic and Numismatic Exhibition. Optd on 1968 Issue of Mexican President's Visit. Air 50c., 1b.
Telecommunications Satellites. Air 5, 10, 15, 20, 25, 30c.
Provisionals. Surch "Decreto No. 112 (de 6 de marzo de 1969)" and new values on No. 781 and 10c.+5c. and 21c.+10c. of 1965 Issue of 3rd Death Anniv of Pres. John Kennedy. Air 5c. on 5c.+5c., 5c. on 10c.+5c., 10c. on 21c.+10c.
Pope Paul VI Visit to Latin America. Religious Paintings. Postage 1, 2, 3, 4, 5c.; Air 6, 7, 8, 10c.

Pt. 8

PAPAL STATES

Parts of Italy under Papal rule till 1870 when they became part of the Kingdom of Italy.

1852. 100 bajoochi = 1 scudo.
1866. 100 centesimi = 1 lira.

1

2

1852. Papal insignia as in T **1** and **2** in various shapes and frames. Imperf.

2	½b. black on grey	£800	75·00
5	½b. black on lilac	95·00	£170
10	1b. black on green	£150	£120
11	2b. black on green	£275	21·00
14	2b. black on white	27·00	£120
15	3b. black on brown	£275	90·00
16	3b. black on yellow	32·00	£160
17	4b. black on brown	£8500	£110
19	4b. black on yellow	£325	£110
20	5b. black on pink	£300	21·00
22	6b. black on lilac	£1700	£300
23	6b. black on grey	£1300	£110
25	7b. black on blue	£2000	£110
26	8b. black on white	£750	65·00
27	50b. blue	£19000	£2000
29	1s. pink	£4750	£4000

1867. Same types. Imperf.

30	2c. black on green	£140	£350
32	3c. black on grey	£3250	£3000
33	5c. black on blue	£250	£325
34	10c. black on red	£2250	£130
35	20c. black on red	£250	£150
36	40c. black on yellow	£250	£225
37	80c. black on pink	£250	£600

1868. Same types. Perf.

42	2c. black on green	16·00	£100
43	3c. black on grey	75·00	£4250
45	5c. black on blue	48·00	90·00
46	10c. black on orange	5·25	21·00
49	20c. black on mauve	7·50	48·00
50	20c. black on red	4·25	20·00
52	40c. black on yellow	16·00	£120
55	80c. black on pink	75·00	£475

Pt. 1

PAPUA

The eastern portion of the island of New Guinea, to the North of Australia, a territory of the Commonwealth of Australia, now combined with New Guinea. Australian stamps were used after the Japanese defeat in 1945 until the combined issue appeared in 1952.

12 pence = 1 shilling; 20 shilling = 1 pound.

(Formerly BRITISH NEW GUINEA)

1 Lakatoi (native canoe) with Hanuabada Village in Background

1901

9	1	½d. black and green	22·00	3·75
10	1	1d. black and red	10·00	2·00
11	1	2d. black and violet	12·00	4·25
12	1	2½d. black and blue	30·00	12·00
13	1	4d. black and brown	38·00	55·00
6	1	6d. black and green	65·00	35·00
7	1	1s. black and orange	75·00	70·00
8	1	2s.6d. black and brown	£650	£550

1906. Optd **Papua**.

38	½d. black and green	20·00	25·00
39	1d. black and red	9·00	5·00
40	2d. black and violet	6·00	2·25
42	4d. black and brown	50·00	70·00
43	6d. black and green	50·00	45·00
19	1s. black and orange	24·00	42·00
24	2½d. black and blue	9·00	15·00
37	2s.6d. black and brown	50·00	75·00

6

1907

66	6	½d. black and green	3·00	4·00
94	6	1d. black and red	1·75	1·25
68	6	2d. black and purple	8·50	11·00
51*a*	6	2½d. black and blue	13·00	6·50
63	6	4d. black and brown	4·75	9·00
80	6	6d. black and green	8·50	10·00
81	6	1s. black and orange	10·00	20·00
82	6	2s.6d. black and brown	55·00	55·00

1911

84*a*	½d. green	70	2·25
85	1d. red	2·00	75
86	2d. mauve	3·50	75
87	2½d. blue	6·50	8·50
88	4d. olive	2·25	11·00
89	6d. brown	3·75	5·00
90	1s. yellow	9·50	15·00
91	2s.6d. red	42·00	50·00

1916

93	½d. green and olive	80	1·00
95	1½d. blue and brown	1·50	80
96	2d. purple and red	1·75	75
97	2½d. green and blue	4·75	12·00
98	3d. black and turquoise	4·00	1·75
99	4d. brown and orange	2·50	5·00
100	5d. grey and brown	4·25	16·00
101	6d. purple	4·00	9·50
127	9d. lilac and violet	6·00	38·00
102	1s. brown and olive	4·75	7·00
128	1s.3d. lilac and blue	8·50	38·00
103	2s.6d. red and pink	23·00	40·00
104	5s. black and green	55·00	48·00
105	10s. green and blue	£170	£180

1917. Surch **ONE PENNY**.

106a	1d. on ½d. green	1·00	1·25
107	1d. on 2d. mauve	12·00	15·00
108	1d. on 2½d. blue	1·25	3·75
109	1d. on 4d. green	1·75	4·50
110	1d. on 6d. brown	8·50	21·00
111	1d. on 2s.6d. red	2·00	6·00

1929. Air. Optd **AIR MAIL**.

114	3d. black and turquoise	1·75	9·00

(11)

1930. Air. Optd with T **11**.

118	3d. black and turquoise	1·50	6·00
119	6d. purple	5·50	17·00
120	1s. brown and olive	4·25	13·00

1931. Surch in words or figures and words.

122	2d. on 1½d. blue and brown	1·00	2·00
125	5d. on 1s. brown and olive	1·00	2·00
126	9d. on 2s.6d. red and pink	5·50	9·00
123	1s.3d. on 5s. black and green	5·00	11·00

15 Motuan Girl

18 Raggiana Bird of Paradise

20 Native Mother and Child

1932

130	15	½d. black and orange	3·50	3·50
131	-	1d. black and green	3·00	60
132	-	1½d. black and red	3·50	8·00
133	18	2d. red	12·00	30
134	-	3d. black and blue	3·50	6·50
135	20	4d. olive	12·00	9·50
136	-	5d. black and green	6·00	3·00
137	-	6d. brown	7·50	5·50
138	-	9d. black and violet	11·00	21·00
139	-	1s. green	8·00	8·50
140	-	1s.3d. black and purple	16·00	28·00
141	-	2s. black and green	15·00	24·00
142	-	2s.6d. black and mauve	25·00	38·00
143	-	5s. black and brown	70·00	55·00
144	-	10s. violet	£150	£120
145	-	£1 black and grey	£275	£180

DESIGNS—VERT (as T **15**): 1d. Chieftain's son; 1½d. Tree houses; 3d. Papuan dandy; 5d. Masked dancer; 9d. Shooting fish; 1s. Ceremonial platform; 1s.3d. Lakatoi; 2s. Papuan art; 2s.6d. Pottery-making; 5s. Native policeman; £1 Delta house. VERT (as T **18**): 6d. Papuan mother. HORIZ: (as T **20**): 10s. Lighting fire.

31 Hoisting the Union Jack

1934. 50th Anniv of Declaration of British Protectorate. Inscr "1884 1934".

146	31	1d. green	2·25	3·50
147	-	2d. red	2·00	3·00
148	31	3d. blue	2·25	3·00
149	-	5d. purple	11·00	20·00

DESIGN: 2d., 5d. Scene on H.M.S. "Nelson".

1935. Silver Jubilee. Optd **HIS MAJESTY'S JUBILEE 1910 1935** (**1910 – 1935** on 2d.).

150		1d. black & green (No. 131)	1·50	3·25
151	18	2d. red	7·00	6·50
152	-	3d. black and blue (No. 134)	4·25	3·25
153	-	5d. black & green (No. 136)	3·75	3·25

35 King George VI

1937. Coronation.

154	35	1d. green	45	20
155	35	2d. red	45	1·25
156	35	3d. blue	45	1·25
157	35	5d. purple	45	1·75

36 Port Moresby

1938. Air. 50th Anniv of Declaration of British Possession.

158	36	2d. red	3·00	3·50
159	36	3d. blue	3·00	2·50
160	36	5d. green	3·00	3·75
161	36	8d. red	6·00	24·00
162	36	1s. mauve	25·00	27·00

37 Natives poling Rafts

1939. Air.

163	37	2d. red	3·50	8·50
164	37	3d. blue	3·50	14·00
165	37	5d. green	3·50	2·50
166	37	8d. red	8·00	6·00
167	37	1s. mauve	13·00	10·00

OFFICIAL STAMPS

1931. Optd **O S**.

O55	6	½d. green and olive	2·75	4·75
O56	6	1d. black and red	7·50	17·00
O56*a*	6	1d. black and red	6·50	16·00
O57	6	1½d. blue and brown	1·60	12·00
O58	6	2d. brown and purple	7·50	18·00
O59	6	3d. black and turquoise	2·50	22·00
O60	6	4d. brown and orange	2·50	18·00
O61	6	5d. grey and brown	6·00	38·00
O62	6	6d. purple and red	4·00	8·50
O63	6	9d. lilac and violet	30·00	48·00
O64	6	1s. brown and olive	9·00	30·00
O65	6	1s.3d. lilac and blue	30·00	48·00
O66	6	2s.6d. red and pink	48·00	95·00

Pt. 1

PAPUA NEW GUINEA

Combined territory on the island of New Guinea administered by Australia under trusteeship. Self-government was established during 1973.

1952. 12 pence = 1 shilling; 20 shillings = 1 pound.
1966. 100 cents = $1 Australian.
1975. 100 toea = 1 kina.

1 Matschie's Tree Kangaroo

7 Kiriwina Chief House

1952

1	1	½d. green	30	10
2	-	1d. brown	20	10
3	-	2d. blue	35	10
4	-	2½d. orange	3·00	50
5	-	3d. myrtle	50	10
6	-	3½d. red	50	10
6a	-	3½d. black	6·00	1·00
18	-	4d. red	60	10
19	-	5d. green	60	10
7	7	6½d. purple	1·25	10
20	-	7d. green	2·25	10
8	-	7½d. blue	2·50	1·00
21	-	8d. blue	60	1·00
9	-	9d. brown	2·50	40
10	-	1s. green	1·50	10
11	-	1s.6d. myrtle	2·75	60
22	-	1s.7d. brown	5·50	3·00
12	-	2s. blue	2·50	10
23	-	2s.5d. red	1·50	1·00
13	-	2s.6d. purple	2·50	40
24	-	5s. red and olive	3·00	1·00
14	-	10s. slate	32·00	13·00
15	-	£1 brown	38·00	15·00

DESIGNS—VERT (as T **1**): 1d. Buka head-dresses; 2d. Native youth; 2½d. Greater bird of paradise; 3d. Native policeman; 3½d. Papuan head-dress; 4d., 5d. Cacao plant. (As T **7**): 7½d. Kiriwina Yam house; 1s.6d. Rubber tapping; 2s. Sepik dancing masks; 5s. Coffee beans; £1 Papuan shooting fish. HORIZ (as T **7**): 7, 8d. Klinki plymill; 9d. Copra making; 1s. Lakatoi; 1s.7d., 2s.5d. Cattle; 2s.6d. Native shepherd and flock; 10s. Map of Papua and New Guinea.

1957. Nos. 4, 1 and 10 surch.

16		4d. on 2½d. orange	1·25	10
25	1	5d. on ½d. green	75	10
17		7d. on 1s. green	40	10

23 Council Chamber, Port Moresby

1961. Reconstitution of Legislative Council.

26	23	5d. green and yellow	75	25
27	23	2s.3d. green and salmon	2·00	1·75

24 Female, Goroka, New Guinea

26 Female Dancer

39 Waterfront, Port Moresby

28 Traffic Policeman

1961

28	**24**	1d. lake	70	10
29	-	3d. blue	30	10
47	**39**	8d. green	30	15
30	**26**	1s. green	1·00	15
31	-	2s. purple	45	15
48	-	2s.3d. blue	30	30
32	**28**	3s. green	1·00	2·00

DESIGNS—As Type **24**: 3d. Tribal elder, Tari, Papua. As Type **39**: 2s.3d. Piaggio P-166B Portofino aircraft landing at Tapini. As Type **26**: 2s. Male dancer.

29 Campaign Emblem

1962. Malaria Eradication.

33	**29**	5d. lake and blue	30	15
34	**29**	1s. red and brown	50	25
35	**29**	2s. black and green	60	70

30 Map of South Pacific

1962. Fifth South Pacific Conference, Pago Pago.

36	**30**	5d. red and green	50	15
37	**30**	1s.6d. violet and yellow	75	1·00
38	**30**	2s.6d. green and blue	75	1·40

31 Throwing the Javelin

1962. Seventh British Empire and Commonwealth Games, Perth.

39	**31**	5d. brown and blue	20	10
40	-	5d. brown and orange	20	10
41	-	2s.3d. brown and green	70	75

SPORTS—As T **31**: No. 40, High jump. 32×23 mm: No. 41, Runners.

34 Raggiana Bird of Paradise

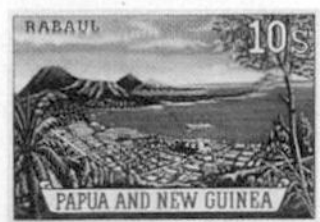

36 Rabaul

37 Queen Elizabeth II

1963

42	**34**	5d. yellow, brown and sepia	70	10
43	-	6d. red, brown and grey	50	1·00
44	**36**	10s. multicoloured	9·50	4·50
45	**37**	£1 brown, gold and green	1·25	1·75

DESIGN—As Type **34**: 6d. Common phalanger.

38 Centenary Emblem

1963. Centenary of Red Cross.

46	**38**	5d. red, grey and green	75	10

40 Games Emblem

1963. First South Pacific Games, Suva.

49	**40**	5d. brown	10	10
50	**40**	1s. green	30	60

41 Watam Head

1964. Native Artefacts. Multicoloured.

51		11d. Type **41**	25	10
52		2s.5d. Watam head (different)	30	1·75
53		2s.6d. Bosmun head	30	10
54		5s. Medina head	35	20

45 Casting Vote

1964. Common Roll Elections.

55	**45**	5d. brown and drab	10	10
56	**45**	2s.3d. brown and blue	20	25

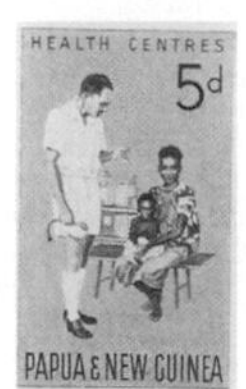

46 "Health Centres"

1964. Health Services.

57	**46**	5d. violet	10	10
58	-	8d. green	10	10
59	-	1s. blue	15	10
60	-	1s.2d. red	20	35

DESIGNS: 8d. "School health"; 1s. "Infant child and maternal health"; 1s.2d. "Medical training".

50 Striped Gardener Bowerbird

1964. Birds. Multicoloured.

61		1d. Type **50**	50	10
62		3d. Adelbert bowerbird	50	30
63		5d. Blue bird of paradise	55	10
64		6d. Lawes's parotia	60	10
65		8d. Black-billed sicklebill	1·00	20
66		1s. Emperor of Germany bird of paradise	1·50	10
67		2s. Brown sicklebill	60	30
68		2s.3d. Lesser bird of paradise	60	85
69		3s. Magnificent bird of paradise	60	1·25
70		5s. Twelve-wired bird of paradise	6·00	1·00
71		10s. Magnificent riflebird	1·75	6·50

Nos. 66/71 are larger, 25½×36½ mm.

61 Canoe Prow

1965. Sepik Canoe Prows in Port Moresby Museum.

72	**61**	4d. multicoloured	30	10
73	-	1s.2d. multicoloured	1·00	1·75
74	-	1s.6d. multicoloured	30	10
75	-	4s. multicoloured	40	50

Each show different carved prows as Type **61**.

61a "Simpson and his Donkey"

1965. 50th Anniv of Gallipoli Landing.

76	**61a**	2s.3d. brown, black & green	20	10

65 Urban Plan and Native House

1965. Sixth South Pacific Conference, Lae.

77	**65**	6d. multicoloured	10	10
78	-	1s. multicoloured	10	10

No. 78 is similar to Type **65** but with the plan on the right and the house on the left. Also "URBANISATION" reads downwards.

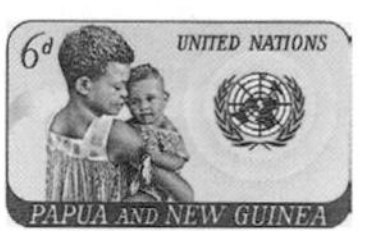

66 Mother and Child

1965. 20th Anniv of U.N.O.

79	**66**	6d. sepia, blue and turquoise	10	10
80	-	1s. brown, blue and violet	10	10
81	-	2s. blue, green and olive	10	10

DESIGNS—VERT: 1s. Globe and U.N. emblem; 2s. U.N. emblem and globes.

69 "Papilio ulysses"

1966. Decimal Currency. Butterflies. Multicoloured.

82		1c. Type **69**	40	1·00
83		3c. "Cyrestis acilia"	40	1·00
84		4c. "Graphium weiskei"	40	1·00
85		5c. "Terinos alurgis"	40	10
86		10c. "Ornithoptera priamus" (horiz)	50	30
86a		12c. "Euploea callithoe" (horiz)	4·00	2·25
87		15c. "Papilio euchenor" (horiz)	1·00	80
88		20c. "Parthenos sylvia" (horiz)	50	25
89		25c. "Delias aruna" (horiz)	70	1·25
90		50c. "Apaturina erminea" (horiz)	10·00	1·25
91		$1 "Doleschallia dascylus" (horiz)	2·75	2·50
92		$2 "Ornithoptera paradisea" (horiz)	5·00	9·00

80 "Molala Harai"

1966. Folklore. Elema Art (1st series).

93	**80**	2c. black and red	10	10
94	-	7c. black, yellow and blue	10	65
95	-	30c. black, red and green	15	15
96	-	60c. black, red and yellow	40	65

DESIGNS: 7c. "Marai"; 30c. "Meavea Kivovia"; 60c. "Toivita Tapaivita".

84 Throwing the Discus

1966. South Pacific Games, Noumea. Multicoloured.

97		5c. Type **84**	10	10
98		10c. Football	15	10
99		20c. Tennis	20	40

87 "Mucuna novoguineensis"

1966. Flowers. Multicoloured.

100		5c. Type **87**	15	10
101		10c. "Tecomanthe dendrophila"	15	10
102		20c. "Rhododendron macgregoriae"	20	10
103		60c. "Rhododendron konori"	50	1·40

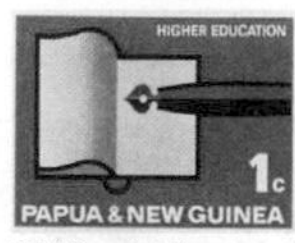

91 "Fine Arts"

1967. Higher Education. Multicoloured.

104		1c. Type **91**	10	10
105		3c. "Surveying"	10	15
106		4c. "Civil Engineering"	10	15
107		5c. "Science"	10	10
108		20c. "Law"	15	10

96 "Sagra speciosa"

1967. Fauna Conservation (Beetles). Multicoloured.

109		5c. Type **96**	15	10
110		10c. "Eupholus schoenherri"	15	10
111		20c. "Sphingnotus albertisi"	25	10
112		25c. "Cyphogastra albertisi"	25	10

100 Laloki River

1967. Laloki River Hydro-electric Scheme, and "New Industries". Multicoloured.

113		5c. Type **100**	10	10
114		10c. Pyrethrum	10	10
115		20c. Tea plant	15	10
116		25c. Type **100**	15	10

103 Air Attack at Milne Bay

1967. 25th Anniv of Pacific War. Multicoloured.

117		2c. Type **103**	10	50
118		5c. Kokoda Trail (vert)	10	10
119		20c. The Coast watchers	25	10
120		50c. Battle of the Coral Sea	80	70

107 Papuan Lory

1967. Christmas. Territory Parrots. Multicoloured.

No.	Description	Mint	Used
121	5c. Type **107**	20	10
122	7c. Pesquet's parrot	25	90
123	20c. Dusky lory	30	10
124	25c. Edward's fig parrot	35	10

111 Chimbu Head-dress

1968. "National Heritage". Designs showing different Head-dresses. Multicoloured.

No.	Description	Mint	Used
125	5c. Type **111**	10	10
126	10c. Southern Highlands (horiz)	15	10
127	20c. Western Highlands (horiz)	15	10
128	60c. Chimbu (different)	40	45

115 "Hyla thesaurensis"

1968. Fauna Conservation (Frogs). Multicoloured.

No.	Description	Mint	Used
129	5c. Type **115**	15	10
130	10c. "Hyla iris"	15	20
131	15c. "Ceratobatrachus guentheri"	15	30
132	20c. "Nyctimystes narinosa"	20	60

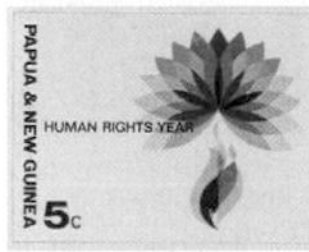

119 Human Rights Emblem and Papuan Head-dress (abstract)

1968. Human Rights Year. Multicoloured.

No.	Description	Mint	Used
133	5c. Type **119**	10	10
134	10c. Human Rights in the World (abstract)	10	10

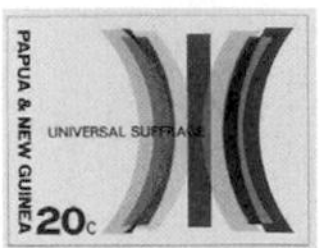

121 Leadership (abstract)

1968. Universal Suffrage. Multicoloured.

No.	Description	Mint	Used
135	20c. Type **121**	15	20
136	25c. Leadership of the Community (abstract)	15	30

123 Common Egg Cowrie

1968. Sea Shells. Multicoloured.

No.	Description	Mint	Used
137	1c. Type **123**	10	10
138	3c. Laciniate conch	30	1·25
139	4c. Lithograph cone	20	1·25
140	5c. Marbled cone (*Conus marmoreus marmoreus*)	25	10
141	7c. Episcopal mitre	35	10
142	10c. "Cymbiola rutila ruckeri"	45	10
143	12c. Checkerboard bonnet	1·25	2·00
144	15c. Scorpion conch	60	1·00
145	20c. Fluted giant clam or scale tridacna	70	10
146	25c. Camp pitar venus	70	1·75
147	30c. Ramose murex	70	1·00
148	40c. Chambered or pearly nautilus	75	1·25
149	60c. Trumpet triton	70	50
150	$1 Manus green papuina	1·00	60
151	$2 Glory of the sea cone (*Conus gloriamaris*)	10·00	1·50

138 Tito Myth

1969. Folklore. Elema Art (2nd series).

No.	Type	Description	Mint	Used
152	**138**	5c. black, yellow and red	10	60
153	-	5c. black, yellow and red	10	60
154	-	10c. black, grey and red	15	60
155	-	10c. black, grey and red	15	60

DESIGNS: No. 153, Iko Myth; 154, Luvuapo Myth; 155, Miro Myth.

142 "Fireball" Class Dinghy

1969. Third South Pacific Games, Port Moresby.

No.	Type	Description	Mint	Used
156	**142**	5c. black	10	10
157	-	10c. violet	10	20
158	-	20c. green	15	30

DESIGNS—HORIZ: 10c. Swimming pool, Boroko; 20c. Games arena, Konedobu.

145 "Dendrobium ostrinoglossum"

1969. Flora Conservation (Orchids). Multicoloured.

No.	Description	Mint	Used
159	5c. Type **145**	25	10
160	10c. "Dendrobium lawesii"	25	70
161	20c. "Dendrobium pseudofrigidum"	30	90
162	30c. "Dendrobium conanthum"	30	70

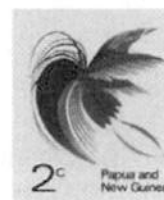

149 Bird of Paradise

1969

No.	Type	Description	Mint	Used
162a	**149**	2c. blue, black and red	10	65
163	**149**	5c. green, brown & orge	10	10

150 Native Potter

1969. 50th Anniv of I.L.O.

No.	Type	Description	Mint	Used
164	**150**	5c. multicoloured	10	10

151 Tareko

1969. Musical Instruments.

No.	Type	Description	Mint	Used
165	**151**	5c. multicoloured	10	10
166	-	10c. black, green & yellow	10	10
167	-	25c. black, yellow & brown	15	15
168	-	30c. multicoloured	25	15

DESIGNS: 10c. Garamut; 25c. Iviliko; 30c. Kundu.

155 Prehistoric Ambun Stone

1970. "National Heritage". Multicoloured.

No.	Description	Mint	Used
169	5c. Type **155**	10	10
170	10c. Masawa canoe of Kula Circuit	10	10
171	25c. Torres' map, 1606	40	15
172	30c. H.M.S. "Basilisk" (paddle-sloop), 1873	65	25

159 King of Saxony Bird of Paradise

1970. Fauna Conservation. Birds of Paradise. Multicoloured.

No.	Description	Mint	Used
173	5c. Type **159**	40	15
174	10c. King bird of paradise	40	45
175	15c. Raggiana bird of paradise	55	80
176	25c. Sickle-crested bird of paradise	65	50

163 Douglas DC-6B and Mt. Wilhelm

1970. Australian and New Guinea Air Services. Multicoloured.

No.	Description	Mint	Used
177	5c. Type **163**	25	30
178	5c. Lockheed Electra and Mt. Yule	25	30
179	5c. Boeing 727-100 and Mt. Giluwe	25	30
180	5c. Fokker Friendship and Manam Island	25	30
181	25c. Douglas DC-3 and Matupi Volcano	35	40
182	30c. Boeing 707 and Hombrom's Bluff	35	60

169 N. Miklouho-Maclay (scientist) and Effigy

1970. 42nd A.N.Z.A.A.S. Congress, Port Moresby. Multicoloured.

No.	Description	Mint	Used
183	5c. Type **169**	10	10
184	10c. B. Malinowski (anthropologist) and native hut	20	10
185	15c. T. Salvadori (ornithologist) and double-wattled cassowary	70	25
186	20c. F. R. R. Schlechter (botanist) and flower	40	25

A.N.Z.A.A.S. = Australian–New Zealand Association for the Advancement of Science.

170 Wogeo Island Food Bowl

1970. Native Artefacts. Multicoloured.

No.	Description	Mint	Used
187	5c. Type **170**	10	10
188	10c. Lime pot	20	10
189	15c. Albom sago storage pot	20	10
190	30c. Manus island bowl (horiz)	25	30

171 Eastern Highlands Dwelling

1971. Native Dwellings. Multicoloured.

No.	Description	Mint	Used
191	5c. Type **171**	10	10
192	7c. Milne Bay stilt dwelling	15	90
193	10c. Purari Delta dwelling	15	10
194	40c. Sepik dwelling	25	90

172 Spotted Phalanger

1971. Fauna Conservation. Multicoloured.

No.	Description	Mint	Used
195	5c. Type **172**	30	10
196	10c. Long-fingered possum	35	10
197	15c. Feather-tailed possum	50	80
198	25c. Long-tailed echidna	70	80
199	30c. Ornate tree kangaroo (horiz)	70	50

173 "Basketball"

1971. Fourth South Pacific Games, Papeete. Multicoloured.

No.	Description	Mint	Used
200	7c. Type **173**	10	10
201	14c. "Sailing"	15	20
202	21c. "Boxing"	15	30
203	28c. "Athletics"	15	40

174 Bartering Fish for Vegetables

1971. Primary Industries. Multicoloured.

No.	Description	Mint	Used
204	7c. Type **174**	10	10
205	9c. Man stacking yams	15	30
206	14c. Vegetable market	25	10
207	30c. Highlanders cultivating garden	45	65

175 Sia Dancer

1971. Native Dancers. Multicoloured.

No.	Description	Mint	Used
208	7c. Type **175**	20	10
209	9c. Urasena dancer	20	20
210	20c. Siassi Tubuan dancers (horiz)	50	75
211	28c. Sia dancers (horiz)	65	90

176 Papuan Flag over Australian Flag

1971. Constitutional Development.

No.	Type	Description	Mint	Used
212	**176**	7c. multicoloured	30	10
213	-	7c. multicoloured	30	10

DESIGN: No. 213, Crest of Papua New Guinea and Australian coat of arms.

177 Map of Papua New Guinea and Flag of South Pacific Commission

1972. 25th Anniv of South Pacific Commission.

No.	Type	Description	Mint	Used
214	**177**	15c. multicoloured	45	55
215	-	15c. multicoloured	45	55

DESIGN: No. 215, Man's face and flag of the Commission.

178 Turtle

1972. Fauna Conservation (Reptiles). Multicoloured.

No.	Description	Mint	Used
216	7c. Type **178**	35	10

217	14c. Rainforest dragon	50	1·25
218	21c. Green python	55	1·50
219	30c. Salvador's monitor	60	1·25

179 Curtiss MF-6 Seagull and "Eureka" (schooner)

1972. 50th Anniv of Aviation. Multicoloured.

220	7c. Type **179**	40	10
221	14c. De Havilland D.H.37 and native porters	60	1·25
222	20c. Junkers G.31 and gold dredger	70	1·25
223	25c. Junkers F-13 and mission church	70	1·25

180 New National Flag

1972. National Day. Multicoloured.

224	7c. Type **180**	20	10
225	10c. Native drum	25	25
226	30c. Trumpet triton	45	50

181 Rev. Copland King

1972. Christmas. Missionaries. Multicoloured.

227	7c. Type **181**	25	40
228	7c. Rev. Dr. Flierl	25	40
229	7c. Bishop Verjus	25	40
230	7c. Pastor Ruatoka	25	40

182 Mt. Tomavatur Station

1973. Completion of Telecommunications Project, 1968–72. Multicoloured.

231	7c. Type **182**	15	20
232	7c. Mt. Kerigomma Station	15	20
233	7c. Sattelburg Station	15	20
234	7c. Wideru Station	15	20
235	9c. Teleprinter	15	20
236	30c. Network map	35	50

Nos. 235/6 are larger, 36×26 mm.

183 Queen Carola's Parotia

1973. Birds of Paradise. Multicoloured.

237	7c. Type **183**	80	35
238	14c. Goldie's bird of paradise	1·75	1·00
239	21c. Ribbon-tailed bird of paradise	2·00	1·50
240	28c. Princess Stephanie's bird of paradise	2·00	2·00

Nos. 239/40 are size 18×49 mm.

184 Wood Carver

1973. Multicoloured.. Multicoloured..

241	1c. Type **184**	10	10
242	3c. Wig-makers	15	10
243	5c. Mt. Bagana	55	10
244	6c. Pig exchange	80	1·50
245	7c. Coastal village	15	10
246	8c. Arawe mother	20	30
247	9c. Fire dancers	15	20
248	10c. Tifalmin hunter	20	10
249	14c. Crocodile hunters	35	70
250	15c. Mt. Elimbari	30	30
251	20c. Canoe-racing, Manus	60	40
252	21c. Making sago	30	1·00
253	25c. Council House	30	45
254	28c. Menyamya bowmen	30	1·00
255	30c. Shark-snaring	1·00	50
256	40c. Fishing canoes, Madang	30	40
257	60c. Tapa cloth-making	40	50
258	$1 Asaro Mudmen	45	1·10
259	$2 Enga "Sing Sing"	1·75	6·00

185 Stamps of German New Guinea, 1897

1973. 75th Anniv of Papua New Guinea Stamps.

260	**185**	1c. multicoloured	10	15
261	-	6c. indigo, blue and silver	15	30
262	-	7c. multicoloured	15	30
263	-	9c. multicoloured	15	30
264	-	25c. orange and gold	30	80
265	-	30c. plum and silver	30	90

DESIGNS—As Type **185**: 6c. 2 mark stamp of German New Guinea, 1900; 7c. Surcharged registration label of New Guinea, 1914. 46×35 mm: 9c. Papuan 1s. stamp, 1901. 45×38 mm: 25c. ½d. stamp of New Guinea, 1925; 30c. Papuan 10s. stamp, 1932.

186 Native Carved Heads

1973. Self-government.

266	**186**	7c. multicoloured	30	15
267	**186**	10c. multicoloured	50	65

187 Queen Elizabeth II (from photo by Karsh)

1974. Royal Visit.

268	**187**	7c. multicoloured	25	15
269	**187**	30c. multicoloured	75	1·50

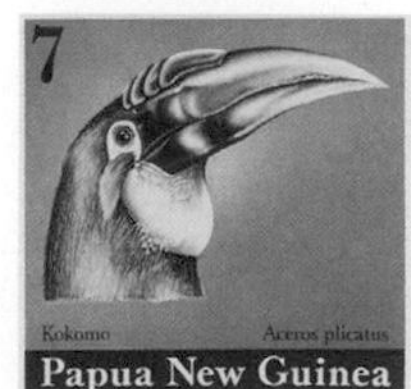

188 Blyth's Hornbill

1974. Birds' Heads. Multicoloured.

270	7c. Type **188**	1·00	70
271	10c. Double-wattled cassowary (33×49 mm)	1·75	3·00
272	30c. New Guinea harpy eagle	3·25	7·50

189 "Dendrobium bracteosum"

1974. Flora Conservation. Multicoloured.

273	7c. Type **189**	30	10
274	10c. "D. anosmum"	40	70
275	20c. "D. smillieae"	50	1·50
276	30c. "D. insigne"	60	1·90

190 Motu Lakatoi

1974. National Heritage. Canoes. Multicoloured.

277	7c. Type **190**	30	10
278	10c. Tami two-master morobe	30	55
279	25c. Aramia racing canoe	60	3·25
280	30c. Buka Island canoe	60	1·00

191 1-toea Coin

1975. New Coinage. Multicoloured.

281	1t. Type **191**	10	30
282	7t. New 2t. and 5t. coins	20	10
283	10t. New 10t. coin	20	30
284	20t. New 20t. coin	30	70
285	1k. New 1k. coin	90	4·00

SIZES: 10, 20t. As Type **191**; 7t., 1k. 45×26 mm.

192 "Ornithoptera alexandrae"

1975. Fauna Conservation (Birdwing Butterflies). Multicoloured.

286	7t. Type **192**	25	10
287	10t. "O. victoriae"	30	65
288	30t. "O. allottei"	60	2·00
289	40t. "O. chimaera"	75	3·50

193 Boxing

1975. Fifth South Pacific Games, Guam. Multicoloured.

290	7t. Type **193**	10	10
291	20t. Running	15	30
292	25t. Basketball	30	45
293	30t. Swimming	30	50

194 Map and National Flag

1975. Independence. Multicoloured.

294	7t. Type **194**	20	10
295	30t. Map and National emblem	40	65
MS296	116×58 mm. Nos. 294/5	1·10	1·75

195 M.V. "Bulolo"

1976. Ships of the 1930s. Multicoloured.

297	7t. Type **195**	20	10
298	15t. M.V. "Macdhui"	30	30
299	25t. M.V. "Malaita"	35	65
300	60t. S.S. "Montoro"	50	2·50

196 Rorovana Carvings

1976. Bougainville Art. Multicoloured.

301	7t. Type **196**	10	10
302	20t. Upe hats	20	35
303	25t. Kapkaps	25	1·50
304	30t. Canoe paddles	30	80

197 Rabaul House

1976. Native Dwellings. Multicoloured.

305	7t. Type **197**	10	10
306	15t. Aramia house	15	20
307	30t. Telefomin house	25	60
308	40t. Tapini house	25	1·75

198 Landscouts

1976. 50th Annivs of Survey Flight and Scouting in Papua New Guinea. Multicoloured.

309	7t. Type **198**	15	10
310	10t. De Havilland D.H.50A seaplane	15	20
311	15t. Seascouts	20	40
312	60t. De Havilland D.H.50A seaplane on water	60	3·00

199 Father Ross and New Guinea Highlands

1976. William Ross Commemoration.

313	**199**	7t. multicoloured	40	15

200 Picture Wrasse

1976. Fauna Conservation (Tropical Fish). Multicoloured.

314	5t. Type **200**	15	10
315	15t. Emperor angelfish	25	45
316	30t. Six-blotched hind	40	80
317	40t. Thread-finned butterflyfish	45	1·10

201 Man from Kundiawa

202 Headdress, Wasara Tribe

1977. Headdresses. Multicoloured.

318	1t. Type **201**	10	10
319	5t. Masked dancer, Abelam area of Maprik	10	10
320	10t. Headdress from Koiari	20	15
321	15t. Woman with face paint, Hanuabada	20	20
322	20t. Orokaiva dancer	30	30
323	25t. Haus Tambaran dancer, Abelam area of Maprik	25	30
324	30t. Asaro Valley headdress	25	35
325	35t. Singsing costume, Garaina	25	45
326	40t. Waghi Valley headdress	25	35
327	50t. Trobriand Island dancer	30	60
328	1k. Type **202**	40	1·50
329	2k. Headdress, Meko tribe	75	3·00

SIZES: 1, 5, 20t. 25×31 mm; 35, 40t. 23×38 mm; 1k. 28×35 mm; 2k. 33×23 mm; others 26×26 mm.

203 National Flag and Queen Elizabeth II

1977. Silver Jubilee. Multicoloured.

330	7t. Type **203**	20	10
331	15t. The Queen and national emblem	25	35
332	35t. The Queen and map of P.N.G.	40	70

204 White-breasted Ground Pigeon

1977. Fauna Conservation (Birds). Multicoloured.

333	5t. Type **204**	25	10
334	7t. Victoria crowned pigeon	25	10
335	15t. Pheasant pigeon	40	50
336	30t. Orange-fronted fruit dove	60	85
337	50t. Banded imperial pigeon	75	3·00

205 Guides and Gold Badge

1977. 50th Anniv of Guiding in Papua New Guinea. Multicoloured.

338	7t. Type **205**	20	10
339	15t. Guides mapping	25	20
340	30t. Guides washing	40	50
341	35t. Guides cooking	40	60

206 Kari Marupi Myth

1977. Folklore. Elema Art (3rd series).

342	**206**	7t. multicoloured	15	10
343	-	20t. multicoloured	35	35
344	-	30t. red, blue and black	40	75
345	-	35t. red, yellow and black	40	75

DESIGNS: 20t. Savoripi clan myth; 30t. Oa-Laea myth; 35t. Oa-Iriarapo myth.

207 Blue-tailed Skink

1978. Fauna Conservation (Skinks). Multicoloured.

346	10t. Type **207**	20	10
347	15t. Green tree skink	25	25
348	35t. Crocodile skink	30	70
349	40t. New Guinea blue-tongued skink	45	85

208 "Roboastra arika"

1978. Sea Slugs. Multicoloured.

350	10t. Type **208**	20	10
351	15t. "Chromodoris fidelis"	25	30
352	35t. "Flabellina macassarana"	45	85
353	40t. "Chromodoris marginata"	50	1·00

209 Present Day Royal Papua New Guinea Constabulary

1978. History of Royal Papua New Guinea Constabulary. Uniformed Police and Constabulary Badges. Multicoloured.

354	10t. Type **209**	20	10
355	15t. Mandated New Guinea Constabulary, 1921–41	25	15
356	20t. British New Guinea Armed Constabulary, 1890–1906	25	40
357	25t. German New Guinea Police, 1899–1914	30	45
358	30t. Royal Papua and New Guinea Constabulary, 1906–64	30	60

210 Ocarina

1979. Musical Instruments. Multicoloured.

359	7t. Type **210**	10	10
360	20t. Musical bow (horiz)	20	20
361	28t. Launut	25	30
362	35t. Nose flute (horiz)	30	45

211 East New Britain Canoe Prow

1979. Traditional Canoe Prows and Paddles. Multicoloured.

363	14t. Type **211**	20	15
364	21t. Sepik war canoe	30	25
365	25t. Trobriand Island canoe	30	30
366	40t. Milne Bay canoe	40	60

212 Katudababila (waist belt)

1979. Traditional Currency. Multicoloured.

367	7t. Type **212**	10	10
368	15t. Doga (chest ornament)	20	30
369	25t. Mwali (armshell)	35	55
370	35t. Soulava (necklace)	45	75

213 "Aenetus cyanochlora"

1979. Fauna Conservation. Moths. Multicoloured.

371	7t. Type **213**	20	10
372	15t. "Celerina vulgaris"	30	35
373	20t. "Alcidis aurora" (vert)	30	75
374	25t. "Phyllodes conspicillator"	35	1·00
375	30t. "Lyssa patroclus" (vert)	40	1·00

214 "The Right to Affection and Love"

1979. International Year of the Child. Multicoloured.

376	7t. Type **214**	10	10
377	15t. "The right to adequate nutrition and medical care"	15	15
378	30t. "The right to play"	20	20
379	60t. "The right to a free education"	45	60

215 "Post Office Service"

1980. Admission to U.P.U. (1979). Multicoloured.

380	7t. Type **215**	10	10
381	25t. "Wartime mail"	25	25
382	35t. "U.P.U. emblem	35	40
383	40t. "Early postal services"	40	50

216 Detail from Betrothal Ceremony Mural, Minj District, Western Highlands Province

1980. South Pacific Festival of Arts.

384	**216**	20t. yellow, orange & blk	15	45
385	-	20t. mult (two figures, left-hand in black and yellow; right-hand in black, yellow and red)	15	45
386	-	20t. mult (two figures, left-hand in black and orange; right-hand in black)	15	45
387	-	20t. mult (two figures, one behind the other)	15	45
388	-	20t. mult (one figure)	15	45

DESIGNS: Nos. 385/8, further details of Betrothal Ceremony.

Nos. 384/8 were issued together in horizontal se-tenant strips of five within the sheet, forming a composite design.

217 Family being Interviewed

1980. National Census. Multicoloured.

389	7t. Type **217**	10	10
390	15t. Population symbol	15	15
391	40t. Papua New Guinea map	30	40
392	50t. Heads symbolizing population growth	35	50

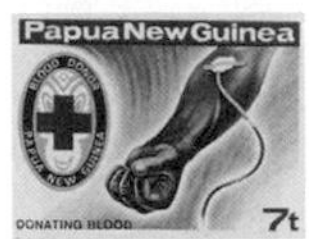
218 Donating Blood

1980. Red Cross Blood Bank. Multicoloured.

393	7t. Type **218**	15	10
394	15t. Receiving transfusion	20	20
395	30t. Map of Papua New Guinea showing blood transfusion centres	25	25
396	60t. Blood and its components	40	60

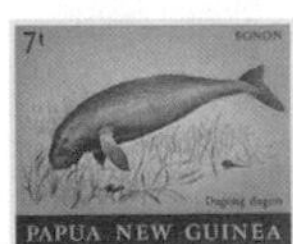
219 Dugong

1980. Mammals. Multicoloured.

397	7t. Type **219**	10	10
398	30t. New Guinea marsupial cat (vert)	30	45
399	35t. Tube-nosed bat (vert)	30	45
400	45t. Rufescent bandicoot	40	55

220 White-headed Kingfisher

1981. Kingfishers. Multicoloured.

401	3t. Type **220**	25	80
402	7t. Forest kingfisher	25	10
403	20t. Sacred kingfisher	30	50
404	25t. White-tailed kingfisher (26×46 mm)	30	85
405	60t. Blue-winged kookaburra	60	3·50

221 Native Mask

1981

406	**221**	2t. violet and orange	10	20
407	-	5t. red and green	10	20

DESIGN: 5t. Hibiscus flower.

222 Mortar Team

1981. Defence Force. Multicoloured.

408	7t. Type **222**	15	10
409	15t. Douglas DC-3 and aircrew	25	25
410	40t. "Aitape" (patrol boat) and seamen	35	65
411	50t. Medical team examining children	35	75

223 M.A.F. (Missionary Aviation Fellowship) Cessna Super Skywagon

1981. "Mission Aviation". Multicoloured.

412	10t. Type **223**	20	10
413	15t. Catholic mission British Aircraft Swallow "St. Paulus"	25	15
414	20t. S.I.L. (Summer Institute of Linguistics) Hiller 12E helicopter	25	25
415	30t. Lutheran mission Junkers F-13	35	40
416	35t. S.D.A. (Seventh Day Adventist Church) Piper PA-23 Aztec	35	55

224 Scoop Net Fishing

1981. Fishing. Multicoloured.

417	10t. Type **224**	15	10
418	15t. Kite fishing	20	30
419	30t. Rod fishing	30	50
420	60t. Scissor net fishing	55	85

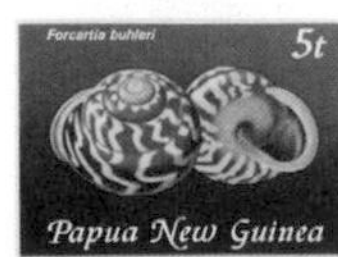
225 Buhler's Papuina

1981. Land Snail Shells. Multicoloured.

421	5t. Type **225**	10	10
422	15t. Yellow naninia	20	25
423	20t. Adonis papuina and Hermoine papuina	20	35
424	30t. Hinde's papuina and New Pommeranian papuina	30	50
425	40t. "Papuina strabo"	40	80

226 Lord Baden-Powell and Flag-raising Ceremony

1981. 75th Anniv of Boy Scout Movement. Multicoloured.

426	15t. Type **226**	25	15
427	25t. Scout leader and camp	25	30
428	35t. Scout and hut building	25	45
429	50t. Percy Chaterton and Scouts administering first aid	35	75

227 Yangoru and Boiken Bowls, East Sepik

1981. Native Pottery. Multicoloured.

430	10t. Type **227**	10	10
431	20t. Utu cooking pot and small Gumalu pot, Madang	20	30
432	40t. Wanigela pots, Northern (37×23 mm)	40	55
433	50t. Ramu Valley pots, Madang (37×23 mm)	45	80

228 "Eat Healthy Foods"

1982. Food and Nutrition. Multicoloured.

434	10t. Type **228**	10	10
435	15t. Protein foods	20	30
436	30t. Protective foods	40	55
437	40t. Energy foods	45	70

229 "Stylophora sp."

1982. Multicoloured.

438	1t. Type **229**	10	20
439	3t. "Dendrophyllia sp." (vert)	60	1·75
440	5t. "Acropora humilis"	15	10
441	10t. "Dendronephthya sp." (vert)	80	1·00
442	12t. As 10t.	3·50	6·00
443	15t. "Distichopora sp."	20	20
444	20t. "Isis sp" (vert)	90	25
445	25t. "Acropora sp." (vert)	50	50
446	30t. "Dendronephthya sp." (different) (vert)	1·25	90
447	35t. "Stylaster elegans" (vert)	1·25	50
448	40t. "Antipathes sp." (vert)	1·25	1·75
449	45t. "Turbinarea sp." (vert)	2·00	1·00
450	1k. "Xenia sp."	1·00	85
451	3k. "Distichopora sp." (vert)	2·25	3·50
452	5k. Raggiana bird of paradise (33×33 mm)	7·00	10·00

230 Missionaries landing on Beach

1982. Centenary of Catholic Church in Papua New Guinea. Mural on Wall of Nordup Catholic Church, East New Britain. Multicoloured.

457	10t. Type **230**	20	75
458	10t. Missionaries talking to natives	20	75
459	10t. Natives with slings and spears ready to attack	20	75

Nos. 457/9 were issued together, se-tenant, forming a composite design.

231 Athletics

1982. Commonwealth Games and "Anpex 82" Stamp Exhibition, Brisbane. Multicoloured.

460	10t. Type **231**	15	10
461	15t. Boxing	20	25
462	45t. Rifle-shooting	40	70
463	50t. Bowls	45	75

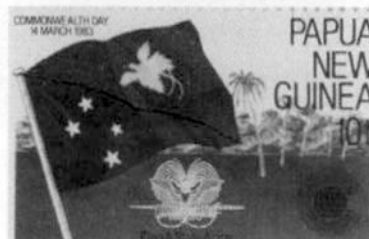

232 National Flag

1983. Commonwealth Day. Multicoloured.

464	10t. Type **232**	15	10
465	15t. Basket-weaving and cabbage-picking	20	30
466	20t. Crane hoisting roll of material	25	35
467	50t. Lorries and ships	60	75

233 Transport Communications

1983. World Communications Year. Multicoloured.

468	10t. Type **233**	30	10
469	25t. "Postal service"	50	25
470	30t. "Telephone service"	55	30
471	60t. "Transport service"	1·10	90

234 "Chelonia depressa"

1984. Turtles. Multicoloured.

472	5t. Type **234**	20	10
473	10t. "Chelonia mydas"	25	10
474	15t. "Eretmochelys imbricata"	30	30
475	20t. "Lepidochelys olivacea"	40	35
476	25t. " Caretta caretta"	45	50
477	40t. "Dermochelys coriacea"	60	75

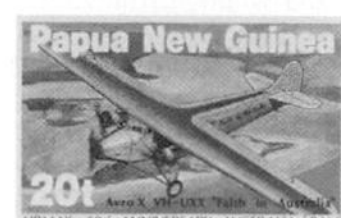

235 Avro Type 618 Ten "Faith in Australia"

1984. 50th Anniv of First Airmail Australia–Papua New Guinea. Multicoloured.

478	20t. Type **235**	40	30
479	25t. De Havilland Dragon Express "Carmania"	40	45
480	40t. Westland Widgeon	50	80
481	60t. Consolidated PBY-5 Catalina flying boat	70	1·25

236 Parliament House

1984. Opening of New Parliament House.

482	**236**	10t. multicoloured	30	30

237 Ceremonial Shield and Club, Central Province

1984. Ceremonial Shields. Multicoloured.

483	10t. Type **237**	20	10
484	20t. Ceremonial shield, West New Britain	30	35
485	30t. Ceremonial shield, Madang Province	45	75
486	50t. Ceremonial shield, East Sepik	75	3·00

See also Nos. 558/61.

238 H.M.S. "Nelson" at Port Moresby, 1884

1984. Centenary of Protectorate Proclamations for British New Guinea and German New Guinea. Multicoloured.

487	10t. Type **238**	35	55
488	10t. Papua New Guinea flag and Port Moresby, 1984	35	55
489	45t. Papua New Guinea flag and Rabaul, 1984	50	1·90
490	45t. German warship "Elizabeth" at Rabaul, 1884	50	1·90

Nos. 487/8 and 489/90 were issued in *se-tenant* pairs, each pair forming a composite picture.

239 Fergusson Island

1985. Tourist Scenes. Multicoloured.

491	10t. Type **239**	25	10
492	25t. Sepik River	50	60
493	40t. Chimbu Gorge (horiz)	75	1·50
494	60t. Dali Beach, Vanimo (horiz)	1·25	2·00

1985. No. 408 surch **12t.**

495	**222**	12t. on 7t. multicoloured	60	75

241 Dubu Platform, Central Province

1985. Ceremonial Structures. Multicoloured.

496	15t. Type **241**	35	15
497	20t. Tamuniai house, West New Britain	50	50
498	30t. Traditional yam tower, Trobriand Island	65	80
499	60t. Huli grave, Tari	1·00	1·75

242 Head of New Britain Collared Sparrow Hawk

1985. Birds of Prey. Multicoloured.

500	12t. Type **242**	50	1·25
501	12t. New Britain collared sparrow hawk in flight	50	1·25
502	30t. Doria's goshawk	60	1·40
503	30t. Doria's goshawk in flight	60	1·40
504	60t. Long-tailed honey buzzard	70	1·50
505	60t. Long-tailed honey buzzard in flight	70	1·50

244 Early Postcard, Aerogramme, Inkwell and Spectacles

1985. Tenth Anniv of Independence.

506	**243**	12t. multicoloured	60	1·00

243 National Flag and Parliament House

1985. Centenary of Papua New Guinea Post Office. Multicoloured.

507	12t. Type **244**	45	10
508	30t. Queensland 1897 1d. die with proof and modern press printing stamps	1·10	1·00
509	40t. Newspaper of 1885 announcing shipping service and loading mail into aircraft	1·75	2·25
510	60t. Friedrich-Wilhelmshafen postmark of 1892 and Port Moresby F.D.C. postmark of 9 October 1985	2·00	3·75

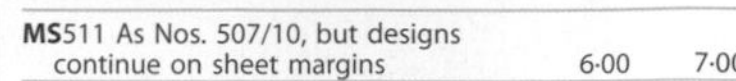

MS511	As Nos. 507/10, but designs continue on sheet margins	6·00	7·00

245 Figure with Eagle

1985. Nombowai Wood Carvings. Multicoloured.

512	12t. Type **245**	50	10
513	30t. Figure with clam shell	1·00	60
514	60t. Figure with dolphin	1·75	2·75
515	80t. Figure of woman with cockerel	2·00	4·50

246 Valentine or Prince Cowrie

1986. Sea Shells. Multicoloured.

516	15t. Type **246**	60	15
517	35t. Bulow's olive	1·25	1·40
518	45t. Parkinson's olive	1·50	2·25
519	70t. Golden cowrie	2·00	5·75

246a Princess Elizabeth in A.T.S. Uniform, 1945

1986. 60th Birthday of Queen Elizabeth II. Multicoloured.

520	15t. Type **246a**	15	15
521	35t. Silver Wedding Anniversary photograph (by Patrick Lichfield), Balmoral, 1972	20	40
522	50t. Queen inspecting guard of honour, Port Moresby, 1982	40	85
523	60t. On board Royal Yacht "Britannia", Papua New Guinea, 1982	65	1·00
524	70t. At Crown Agents' Head Office, London, 1983	40	1·25

247 Rufous Fantail

1986. "Ameripex '86" International Stamp Exhibition, Chicago. Small Birds (1st series). Multicoloured.

525	15t. Type **247**	70	30
526	35t. Streaked berry pecker	1·25	1·00
527	45t. Red-breasted pitta	1·40	1·00
528	70t. Olive-yellow robin (vert)	2·00	5·50

See also Nos. 597/601.

248 Martin Luther nailing Theses to Cathedral Door, Wittenberg and Modern Lutheran Pastor

1986. Centenary of Lutheran Church in Papua New Guinea. Multicoloured.

529	15t. Type **248**	60	15
530	70t. Early church, Finschhafen, and modern Martin Luther Chapel, Lae Seminary	1·90	3·75

249 "Dendrobium vexillarius"

1986. Orchids. Multicoloured.
531 15t. Type **249** 95 20
532 35t. "Dendrobium lineale" 2·00 75
533 45t. "Dendrobium johnsoniae" 2·00 1·10
534 70t. "Dendrobium cuthbertsonii" 2·75 6·00

250 Maprik Dancer

1986. Papua New Guinea Dancers. Multicoloured.
535 15t. Type **250** 65 15
536 35t. Kiriwina 1·25 80
537 45t. Kundiawa 1·40 1·10
538 70t. Fasu 2·25 5·50

251 White-bonnet Anemonefish

1987. Anemonefish. Multicoloured.
539 17t. Type **251** 55 25
540 30t. Orange-finned anemonefish 75 85
541 35t. Fire anemonefish ("Tomato clownfish") 85 1·00
542 70t. Spine-cheeked anemonefish 1·25 5·50

252 "Roebuck" (Dampier), 1700

1987. Ships. Multicoloured.
543 1t. "La Boudeuse" (De Bougainville, 1768) 50 1·50
544 5t. Type **252** 1·00 2·00
545 10t. H.M.S. "Swallow" (Philip Carteret), 1767 1·25 2·00
546 15t. H.M.S. "Fly" (Blackwood), 1845 1·75 1·00
547 17t. As 15t. 1·75 75
548 20t. H.M.S. "Rattlesnake" (Owen Stanley), 1849 1·75 1·00
549 30t. "Vitiaz" (Maclay), 1871 1·75 2·50
550 35t. "San Pedrico" (Torres) and zabra, 1606 70 1·00
551 40t. "L'Astrolabe" (D'Urville), 1827 2·00 3·00
552 45t. "Neva" (D. Albertis), 1876 75 1·50
553 60t. Spanish galleon (Jorge de Meneses), 1526 2·25 4·00
554 70t. "Eendracht" (Schouten and Le Maire), 1616 1·75 2·75
555 1k. H.M.S. "Blanche" (Simpson), 1872 2·25 3·00
556 2k. "Merrie England" (steamer), 1889 2·50 3·00
557 3k. "Samoa" (German colonial steamer), 1884 2·75 6·00

For some of these designs redrawn for "Australia '99" World Stamp Exhibition see Nos. 857/60.

1987. War Shields. As T **237**. Multicoloured.
558 15t. Gulf Province 20 25
559 35t. East Sepik 45 50
560 45t. Madang Province 55 60
561 70t. Telefomin 85 90

1987. No. 442 surch **15t.**
562 15t. on 12t. "Dendronephthya sp." (vert) 65 65

254 "Protoreaster nodosus"

1987. Starfish. Multicoloured.
563 17t. Type **254** 45 25
564 35t. "Gomophia egeriae" 75 60
565 45t. "Choriaster granulatus" 80 70
566 70t. "Neoferdina ocellata" 1·40 3·50

255 Cessna Stationair 6 taking off, Rabaraba

1987. Aircraft in Papua New Guinea. Multicoloured.
567 15t. Type **255** 1·25 25
568 35t. Britten Norman Islander over Hombrum Bluff 2·00 90
569 45t. De Havilland Twin Otter 100 over Highlands 2·00 1·00
570 70t. Fokker F.28 Fellowship over Madang 3·00 7·00

256 Pre-Independence Policeman on Traffic Duty and Present-day Motorcycle Patrol

1988. Centenary of Royal Papua New Guinea Constabulary. Multicoloured.
571 17t. Type **256** 45 25
572 35t. British New Guinea Armed Constabulary, 1890, and Governor W. MacGregor 80 50
573 45t. Police badges 90 65
574 70t. German New Guinea Police, 1888, and Dr. A Hahl (founder) 1·50 1·75

257 Lakatoi (canoe) and Sydney Opera House

1988. "Sydpex '88" Nat Stamp Exn, Sydney.
575 **257** 35t. multicoloured 80 1·25

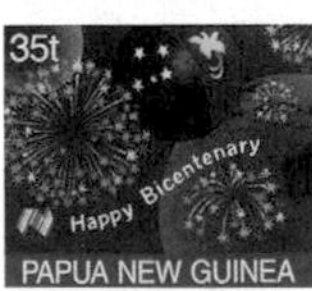

258 Papua New Guinea Flag on Globe and Fireworks

1988. Bicent of Australian Settlement. Multicoloured.
576 35t. Type **258** 75 1·25
577 35t. Australian flag on globe and fireworks 75 1·25
MS578 90×50 mm. Nos. 576/7 1·50 2·25

Nos. 576/7 were printed together, *se-tenant*, forming a composite design.

259 Male and Female Butterflies in Courtship

1988. Endangered Species. "Ornithoptera alexandrae" (butterfly). Multicoloured.
579 5t. Type **259** 1·00 2·00
580 17t. Female laying eggs and mature larva (vert) 2·00 40
581 25t. Male emerging from pupa (vert) 2·75 4·00
582 35t. Male feeding 3·25 3·50

260 Athletics

1988. Olympic Games, Seoul. Multicoloured.
583 17t. Type **260** 30 30
584 45t. Weightlifting 70 70

261 "Rhododendron zoelleri"

1989. Rhododendrons. Multicoloured.
585 3t. Type **261** 10 10
586 20t. "Rhododendron cruttwellii" 50 30
587 60t. "Rhododendron superbum" 1·25 1·50
588 70t. "Rhododendron christianae" 1·50 2·00

263 Writing Letter

1989. Int Letter Writing Week. Multicoloured.
589 20t. Type **263** 30 30
590 35t. Stamping letter 55 50
591 60t. Posting letter 90 1·10
592 70t. Reading letter 1·10 1·60

264 Village House, Buka Island, North Solomons

1989. Traditional Dwellings. Multicoloured.
593 20t. Type **264** 40 35
594 35t. Tree house, Koiari, Central Province 70 60
595 60t. Longhouse, Lauan, New Ireland 1·25 1·50
596 70t. Decorated house, Basilaki, Milne Bay 1·50 1·75

265 Tit Berrypecker (female)

1989. Small Birds (2nd issue). Multicoloured.
597 20t. Type **265** 1·00 1·25
598 20t. Tit berrypecker (male) 1·00 1·25
599 35t. Blue-capped babbler 1·50 80
600 45t. Black-throated robin 1·50 1·00
601 70t. Large mountain sericornis 2·25 3·00

1989. No. 539 surch **20t.**
602 20t. on 17t. Type **251** 60 70

266 Motu Motu Dancer, Gulf Province

1989. Traditional Dancers. Multicoloured.
603 20t. Type **266** 55 35
604 35t. Baining, East New Britain 80 90
605 60t. Vailala River, Gulf Province 1·75 2·50
606 70t. Timbunke, East Sepik Province 1·75 3·00

267 Hibiscus, People going to Church and Gope Board

1989. Christmas. Designs showing flowers and carved panels. Multicoloured.
607 20t. Type **267** 40 20
608 35t. Rhododendron, Virgin and Child and mask 60 40
609 60t. D'Albertis creeper, Christmas candle and war shield 1·25 1·75
610 70t. Pacific frangipani, peace dove and flute mask 1·40 2·25

268 Guni Falls

1990. Waterfalls. Multicoloured.
611 20t. Type **268** 60 35
612 35t. Rouna Falls 85 75
613 60t. Ambua Falls 1·40 1·50
614 70t. Wawoi Falls 1·60 2·00

269 Boys and Census Form

1990. National Census. Multicoloured.
615 20t. Type **269** 40 30
616 70t. Family and census form 1·50 2·50

270 Gwa Pupi Dance Mask

1990. Gogodala Dance Masks. Multicoloured.
617 20t. Type **270** 65 30
618 35t. Tauga paiyale 1·00 55
619 60t. A: ga 1·75 3·00
620 70t. Owala 1·75 3·50

271 Sepik and Maori Kororu Masks

1990. "New Zealand 1990" International Stamp Exhibition, Auckland.
621 **271** 35t. multicoloured 75 1·00

272 Dwarf Cassowary and Great Spotted Kiwi

1990. 150th Anniv of Treaty of Waitangi. Multicoloured.
622 20t. Type **272** 1·25 50
623 35t. Double-wattled cassowary and brown kiwi 1·50 1·50

273 Whimbrel

1990. Migratory Birds. Multicoloured.

624	20t. Type **273**	85	40
625	35t. Sharp-tailed sandpiper	1·25	80
626	60t. Ruddy turnstone	2·25	3·25
627	70t. Terek sandpiper	2·50	3·25

274 Jew's Harp

1990. Musical Instruments. Multicoloured.

628	20t. Type **274**	60	30
629	35t. Musical bow	90	50
630	60t. Wantoat drum	1·75	2·25
631	70t. Gogodala rattle	1·75	2·50

275 Weigman's Papuina

1991. Land Shells. Multicoloured.

632	21t. Type **275**	65	30
633	40t. "Papuina globula" and "Papuina azonata"	1·00	85
634	50t. "Planispira deaniana"	1·40	1·60
635	80t. Chance's papuina and golden-mouth papuina	2·00	2·75

276 Magnificent Riflebird

1991. Birds of Paradise. Multicoloured. (a) Face values shown as "t" or "K".

636	1t. Type **276**	15	40
637	5t. Loria's bird of paradise	20	40
638	10t. Sickle-crested bird of paradise	20	40
639	20t. Wahnes' parotia	50	30
640	21t. Crinkle-collared manucode	1·75	30
641	30t. Goldie's bird of paradise	30	40
642	40t. Wattle-billed bird of paradise	50	50
643	45t. King bird of paradise	5·50	80
644	50t. Short-tailed paradigalla bird of paradise	50	55
645	60t. Queen Carola's parotia	8·50	2·75
646	90t. Emperor of Germany bird of paradise	9·00	4·00
647	1k. Magnificent bird of paradise	1·75	1·75
648	2k. Superb bird of paradise	1·90	2·00
649	5k. Trumpet Manucode	2·25	6·50
650	10k. Lesser bird of paradise (32×32 mm)	6·00	11·00

(b) Face values shown as "T".

650a	21t. Crinkle-collared manucode	1·00	40
650b	45t. King bird of paradise	2·00	1·00
650c	60t. Queen Carola's parotia	2·25	2·25
650d	90t. Emperor of Germany bird of paradise	2·75	3·50

For designs as Nos. 642, 644 and 647/8 but without "1992 BIRD OF PARADISE" at foot, see Nos. 704/7.

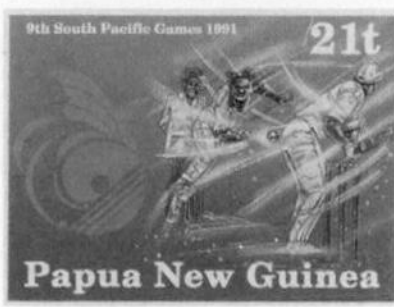

277 Cricket

1991. Ninth South Pacific Games. Multicoloured.

651	21t. Type **277**	1·50	40
652	40t. Athletics	1·00	1·00
653	50t. Baseball	1·25	2·25
654	80t. Rugby Union	2·25	4·00

278 Cathedral of St. Peter and St. Paul, Dogura

1991. Cent of Anglican Church in Papua New Guinea. Multicoloured.

655	21t. Type **278**	60	20
656	40t. Missionaries landing, 1891, and Kaieta shrine	1·10	1·10
657	80t. First church and Modawa tree	1·75	3·50

279 Rambusto Headdress, Manus Province

1991. Tribal Headdresses. Multicoloured.

658	21t. Type **279**	50	20
659	40t. Marawaka, Eastern Highlands	80	1·10
660	50t. Tufi, Oro Province	85	1·50
661	80t. Sina Sina, Simbu Province	1·40	4·00

280 "Nina"

1992. 500th Anniv of Discovery of America by Columbus and "EXPO '92" World's Fair, Seville. Multicoloured.

662	21t. Type **280**	60	30
663	45t. "Pinta"	1·25	1·00
664	60t. "Santa Maria"	1·75	2·00
665	90t. Christopher Columbus and ships	2·25	3·50

1992. "World Columbian Stamp Expo '92", Chicago. Sheet, 110×80 mm, containing Nos. 664/5.

MS666	60t. "Santa Maria"; 90t. Christopher Columbus and ships (sold at 1k. 70)	4·25	5·50

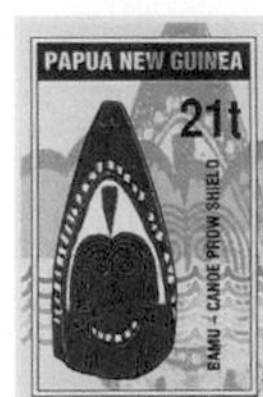

281 Canoe Prow Shield, Bamu

1992. Papuan Gulf Artefacts. Multicoloured.

667	21t. Type **281**	40	30
668	45t. Skull rack, Kerewa	85	75
669	60t. Ancestral figure, Era River	1·25	1·50
670	90t. Gope (spirit) board, Urama	1·60	2·75

282 Papuan Infantryman

1992. 50th Anniv of Second World War Campaigns in Papua New Guinea. Multicoloured.

671	21t. Type **282**	60	30
672	45t. Australian militiaman	1·25	90
673	60t. Japanese infantryman	1·75	2·25
674	90t. American infantryman	2·50	3·75

283 "Hibiscus tiliaceus"

1992. Flowering Trees. Multicoloured.

675	21t. Type **283**	50	20
676	45t. "Castanospermum australe"	1·10	70
677	60t. "Cordia subcordata"	1·75	2·50
678	90t. "Acacia auriculiformis"	2·25	3·75

284 Three-striped Dasyure

1993. Mammals. Multicoloured.

679	21t. Type **284**	35	20
680	45t. Striped bandicoot	65	55
681	60t. Dusky black-eared giant rat	85	1·10
682	90t. Painted ringtail possum	1·40	2·75

285 Rufous Wren Warbler

1993. Small Birds. Multicoloured.

683	21t. Type **285**	45	30
684	45t. Superb pitta	90	80
685	60t. Mottled whistler	1·25	1·50
686	90t. Slaty-chinned longbill	1·60	2·75

1993. "Taipei '93" Asian Int Stamp Exn, Taiwan. Nos. 683/6 optd **TAIPEI'93** and emblem.

687	21t. Type **285**	75	30
688	45t. Superb pitta	1·40	80
689	60t. Mottled whistler	1·60	2·75
690	90t. Slaty-chinned longbill	2·00	4·50

287 Thread-finned Rainbowfish

1993. Freshwater Fish. Multicoloured.

691	21t. Type **287**	60	30
692	45t. Peacock gudgeon	1·00	55
693	60t. Northern rainbowfish	1·40	1·75
694	90t. Popondetta blue-eye	1·75	4·00

288 Blue Bird of Paradise

1993. "Bangkok '93" Asian International Stamp Exhibition, Thailand. Sheet 100×65 mm.

MS695	**288** 2k. multicoloured	6·00	8·00

289 Douglas DC-3

1993. 20th Anniv of Air Niugini. Multicoloured.

696	21t. Type **289**	75	25
697	45t. Fokker F.27 Friendship	1·75	70
698	60t. De Havilland D.H.C.7 Dash Seven	2·00	2·25
699	90t. Airbus Industrie A310	2·75	4·50

290 Girl holding Matschie's Tree Kangaroo

1994. Matschie's (Huon Gulf) Tree Kangaroo. Multicoloured.

700	21t. Type **290**	35	25
701	45t. Adult male	90	60
702	60t. Female with young in pouch	1·25	1·75
703	90t. Adolescent on ground	1·90	3·50

1994. "Hong Kong '94 International Stamp Exhibition. Designs as Nos. 642, 644 and 647/8, but without "1992 BIRD OF PARADISE" at foot. Multicoloured.

704	40t. Yellow-breasted bird of paradise	85	1·25
705	50t. Short-tailed paradigalla bird of paradise	1·25	1·50
706	1k. Magnificent bird of paradise	2·00	2·75
707	2k. Superb bird of paradise	3·00	4·00

1994. Nos. 541 and 551 surch.

708	21t. on 35t. Fire anemonefish	7·00	50
709	1k.20 on 40t. "L'Astrolabe" (D'Urville)	1·50	1·50

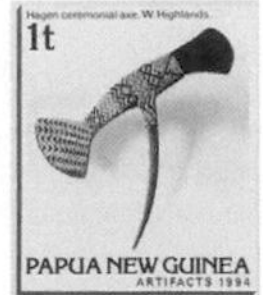

292 Hagen Axe, Western Highlands

1994. Artefacts. Multicoloured.

710	1t. Type **292**	10	1·00
711	2t. Telefomin shield, West Sepik	10	1·00
712	20t. Head mask, Gulf Province	80	75
713	21t. Kanganaman stool, East Sepik	1·00	10
714	45t. Trobriand lime gourd, Milne Bay	50	25
715	60t. Yuat River flute stopper, East Sepik	1·00	30
716	90t. Tami Island dish, Morobe	60	40
717	1k. Kundu (drum), Ramu River estuary	4·25	2·50
723	5k. Gogodala dance mask, Western Province	1·75	2·00
724	10k. Malanggan mask, New Ireland	4·50	4·75

293 Ford Model "T", 1920

1994. Historical Cars. Multicoloured.

725	21t. Type **293**	35	25
726	45t. Chevrolet "490", 1915	90	60
727	60t. Austin "7", 1931	1·25	1·75
728	90t. Willys jeep, 1942	1·90	3·50

294 Grizzled Tree Kangaroo

1994. "Phila Korea '94" International Stamp Exhibition, Seoul. Tree Kangaroos. Sheet 106×70 mm, containing T **294** and similar vert design. Multicoloured.

MS729	90t. Type **294**; 1k.20, Doria's tree kangaroo	3·00	3·50

1994. Surch.

730	-	5t. on 35t. mult (No. 604)	1·00	75
731	-	5t. on 35t. mult (No. 629)	14·00	10·00
732	271	10t. on 35t. mult	24·00	5·50
733	-	10t. on 35t. mult (No. 623)	10·00	3·50
734	-	21t. on 80t. mult (No. 635)	45·00	75
735	-	50t. on 35t. mult (No. 612)	29·00	13·00
736	-	50t. on 35t. mult (No. 618)	90·00	18·00
737	-	65t. on 70t. mult (No. 542)	2·00	1·40
738	-	65t. on 70t. mult (No. 616)	2·00	1·40
739	-	1k. on 70t. mult (No. 614)	17·00	5·00
740	-	1k. on 70t. mult (No. 620)	2·00	3·00

297 "Daphnis hypothous pallescens"

1994. Moths. Multicoloured.

741	21t. Type **297**	35	25

742	45t. "Tanaorhinus unipuncta"	80	65
743	60t. "Neodiphthera sciron"	1·10	1·50
744	90t. "Parotis marginata"	1·60	2·50

298 Peter To Rot

1995. Beatification of Peter To Rot (catechist) and Visit of Pope John Paul II. Multicoloured.

745	21t. Type **298**	1·00	1·00
746	1k. on 90t. Pope John Paul II	2·50	2·50

No. 746 was not issued without surcharge.

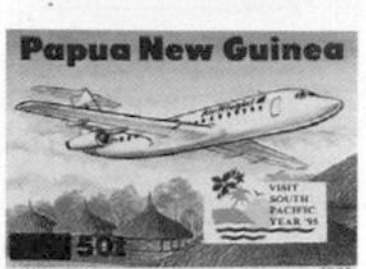

299 Airliner over Holiday Village

1995. Tourism. Multicoloured.

747	21t. "Melanesian Discoverer" (cruise ship) and launch	90	1·25
748	21t. Tourist taking photo of traditional mask	90	1·25
749	50t. on 45t. Type **299**	1·50	2·75
750	50t. on 45t. Holiday homes	1·50	1·75
751	65t. on 60t. Tourists and guide crossing river	1·75	2·00
752	65t. on 60t. White water rafting	1·75	2·00
753	1k. on 90t. Scuba diver and "Chertan" (launch)	2·00	2·50
754	1k. on 90t. Divers and wreck of aircraft	2·00	2·50

Nos. 749/54 were not issued without surcharge.

1995. Nos. 643, 646, 650b, 650d and 692/4 surch **21t**.

755	21t. on 45t. King bird of paradise (643)	1·50	1·00
756	21t. on 90t. Emperor of Germany bird of paradise (646)	1·50	1·00
757	21t. on 45t. King bird of paradise (650b)	5·00	3·00
758	21t. on 90t. Emperor of Germany bird of paradise (650d)	6·50	1·00
759	21t. on 45t. Peacock gudgeon	55	40
760	21t. on 60t. Northern rainbowfish	1·50	2·00
761	21t. on 90t. Popondetta blue-eye	55	60

302 "Lentinus umbrinus"

302a "Lentinus umbrinus"

1995. Fungi. Multicoloured.

762	25t. Type **302**	45	30
763	50t. "Amanita hemibapha"	80	80
764	65t. "Boletellus emodensis"	95	1·25
765	1k. "Ramaria zippellii"	1·60	2·25
765a	25t. Type **302a**	1·00	60

On Type **302a** the fungi illustration is larger, 26×32 mm instead of 27×30½ mm, face value and inscriptions are in a different type and there is no imprint date at foot.

303 Anniversary Emblem and Map of Papua New Guinea

1995. 20th Anniv of Independence. Multicoloured.

766	21t. Type **303**	30	25
767	50t. Emblem and lines on graph	70	80
768	1k. As 50t.	1·40	2·25

304 "Dendrobium rigidifolium"

1995. "Singapore '95" International Stamp Exhibition. Orchids. Sheet 150×95 mm, containing T 304 and similar horiz designs. Multicoloured.

MS769	21t. Type **304**; 45t. "Dendrobium convolutum"; 60t. "Dendrobium spectabile"; 90t. "Dendrobium tapiniense" (sold at 3k.)	1·25	1·50

305 Pig

1995. Chinese New Year ("Year of the Pig"). Sheet 150×95 mm.

MS770	**305** 3k. multicoloured	3·50	3·75

No. **MS**770 is inscribed "BEIJING '95" on the sheet margin.

306 Volcanic Eruption, Tavarvur

1995. First Anniv of Volcanic Eruption, Rabaul.

771	**306** 2k. multicoloured	1·25	1·60

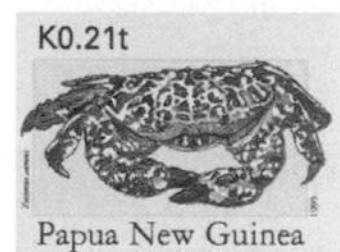

307 "Zosimus aeneus"

1995. Crabs. Multicoloured.

772	21t. Type **307**	40	25
773	50t. "Cardisoma carnifex"	75	60
774	65t. "Uca tetragonon"	90	1·25
775	1k. "Eriphia sebana"	1·25	2·00

308 Pesquet's Parrot

1996. Parrots. Multicoloured.

776	25t. Type **308**	1·75	30
777	50t. Rainbow lory	2·25	75
778	65t. Green-winged king parrot	2·50	2·00
779	1k. Red-winged parrot	3·00	4·00

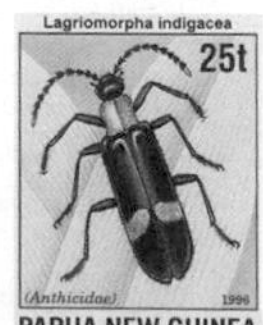

309 "Lagriomorpha indigacea"

1996. Beetles. Multicoloured.

780	25t. Type **309**	15	15
781	50t. "Eupholus geoffroyi"	20	25
782	65t. "Promechus pulcher"	30	40
783	1k. "Callistola pulchra"	45	70

310 Guang Zhou Zhong Shang Memorial Hall

1996. "China '96" 9th Asian International Stamp Exhibition, Peking. Sheet 105×70 mm.

MS784	**310** 70t. multicoloured	75	1·00

311 Rifle-shooting

1996. Olympic Games, Atlanta. Multicoloured.

785	25t. Type **311**	15	15
786	50t. Athletics	25	20
787	65t. Weightlifting	30	35
788	1k. Boxing	45	70

312 Air Traffic Controller

1996. Centenary of Radio. Multicoloured.

789	25t. Type **312**	15	15
790	50t. Radio disc-jockey	25	20
791	65t. Dish aerials	30	35
792	1k. Early radio transmitter	45	70

313 Dr. Sun Yat-sen

1996. "TAIPEI '96" Tenth Asian International Stamp Exhibition, Taiwan. Sheet 105×70 mm, containing T **313** and similar vert design. Multicoloured.

MS793	65t. Type **313**; 65t. Dr. John Guise (former speaker of Papua New Guinea House of Assembly)	1·75	2·00

314 "Hibiscus rosa-sinensis"

1996. Flowers. Multicoloured.

794	1t. Type **314**	10	50
795	5t. "Bougainvillea spectabilis"	10	50
796	10t. "Thunbergia fragrans" (vert)	20	50
797	20t. "Caesalpinia pulcherrima" (vert)	30	20
798	25t. "Hoya sp." (vert)	30	15
799	30t. "Heliconia spp." (vert)	30	15
800	50t. "Amomum goliathensis" (vert)	50	20
801	65t. "Plumeria rubra"	50	25
802	1k. "Mucuna novoguineensis"	60	60

315 Ox and National Flag

1997. "HONG KONG '97" International Stamp Exhibition. Sheet 130×90 mm.

MS808	**315** 1k.50 multicoloured	1·00	1·25

316 Gogodala Canoe Prow

1997. Canoe Prows. Multicoloured.

809	25t. Type **316**	15	15
810	50t. East New Britain	25	20
811	65t. Trobriand Island	35	35
812	1k. Walomo	50	70

1997. Golden Wedding of Queen Elizabeth and Prince Philip. As T **87** of Kiribati. Multicoloured.

813	25t. Prince Philip on polo pony, 1972	25	35
814	25t. Queen Elizabeth at Windsor Polo Club	25	35
815	50t. Prince Philip carriage-driving, 1995	40	55
816	50t. Queen Elizabeth and Prince Edward on horseback	40	55
817	1k. Prince Philip waving and Peter and Zara Phillips on horseback	75	1·00
818	1k. Queen Elizabeth waving and Prince Harry on horseback	75	1·00
MS819	105×71 mm. 2k. Queen Elizabeth and Prince Philip in landau (horiz)	2·50	3·50

Nos. 813/14, 815/16 and 818/19 respectively were printed together, se-tenant, with the backgrounds forming composite designs.

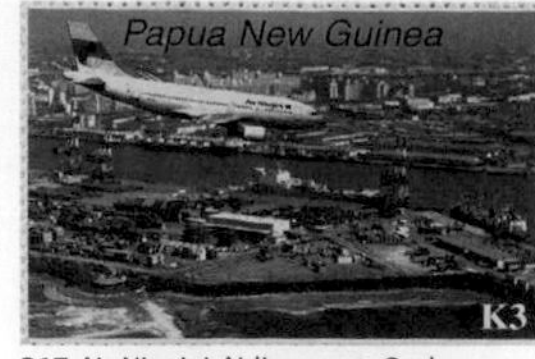

317 Air Niugini Airliner over Osaka

1997. Inaugural Air Niugini Port moresby to Osaka Flight. Sheet 110×80 mm.

MS820	**317** 3k. multicoloured	1·50	1·75

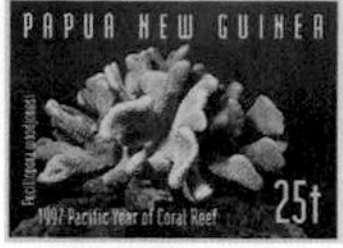

318 "Pocillopora woodjonesi"

1997. Pacific Year of the Coral Reef. Corals. Multicoloured.

821	25t. Type **318**	15	15
822	50t. "Subergorgia mollis"	25	20
823	65t. "Oxypora glabra"	35	35
824	1k. "Turbinaria reinformis"	60	70

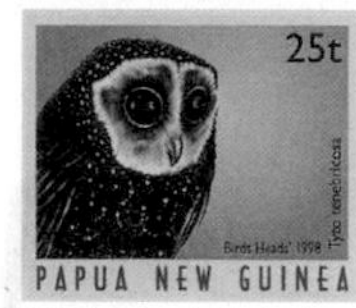

319 Greater Sooty Owl

1998. Birds. Multicoloured.

825	25t. Type **319**	50	20
826	50t. Wattled brush turkey	70	45
827	65t. New Guinea grey-headed goshawk	80	1·00
828	1k. Forest bittern	1·25	2·25

1998. Diana, Princess of Wales Commemoration. Sheet, 145×70 mm, containing vert designs as T **91** or Kiribati. Multicoloured.

MS829	1k., Wearing pink jacket, 1992; 1k. Wearing purple dress; 1988; 1k. wearing tartan jacket, 1990; 1k. Carrying bouquets, 1990 (sold at 4k.+50t. charity premium)	1·25	1·60

320 Mother Teresa and Child

1998. Mother Teresa Commemoration. Multicoloured.

830	65t. Type **320**	80	80
831	1k. Mother Teresa	80	80

1998. No. 774 surch **25t.**

832	25t. on 65t. "Uca tetragonon"	60	25

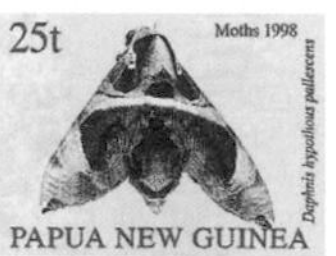

322 "Daphnis hypothous pallescens"

1998. Moths. Multicoloured.

833	25t. Type **322**	20	15
834	50t. "Theretra polistratus"	40	25
835	65t. "Psilogramma casurina"	55	50
836	1k. "Meganoton hyloicoides"	1·00	1·50

323 "Coelogyne fragrans"

1998. Orchids. Multicoloured.

837	25t. Type **323**	20	15
838	50t. "Den cuthbertsonii"	30	20
839	65t. "Den vexillarius "var" retroflexum"	40	40
840	1k. "Den finisterrae"	65	75

324 Weightlifting

1998. 16th Commonwealth Games, Kuala Lumpur, Malaysia. Multicoloured.

841	25t. Type **324**	20	15
842	50t. Lawn bowls	25	20
843	65t. Rugby Union	35	35
844	1k. Squash	60	75

325 Double Kayak

1998. Sea Kayaking World Cup, Manus Island. Multicoloured.

845	25t. Type **325**	20	15
846	50t. Running	30	20
847	65t. Traditional canoe and modern kayak	40	40
848	1k. Single kayak and stylized bird of paradise	65	75

326 The Holy Child

1998. Christmas. Multicoloured.

849	25t. Type **326**	20	15
850	50t. Mother breast-feeding baby	30	20
851	65t. Holy Child and tribal elders	40	40
852	1k. Map of Papua New Guinea and festive bell	65	75

1999. "Australia '99" World Stamp Exhibition, Melbourne. Designs as Nos. 543, 552 and 556/7, showing ships, redrawn to include exhibition emblem at top right and with some face values changed. Multicoloured.

853	25t. "La Boudeuse" (De Bougainville) (as No. 543)	20	15
854	50t. "Neva" (D'Albertis) (as No. 552)	30	20
855	65t. "Merrie England" (steamer) (as No. 556)	40	40
856	1k. "Samoa" (German colonial steamer) (as No. 557)	60	75
MS857	165×110 mm. 5t. H.M.S. "Rattlesnake" (Owen Stanley) (as No. 548); 10t. H.M.S. "Swallow" (Philip Carterat) (as No. 545); 15t. "Roebuck" (Dampier) (as No. 544); 20t. H.M.S. "Blanche" (Simpson) (as No. 55); 30t. "Vitaz" (Maclay) (as No. 549); 40t. "San Pedrico" (Torres) and zabra (as No. 550); 60t. Spanish galleon (Jorge de Meneses) (as No. 553); 1k.20, "L' Astrolabe" (D' Urville) (as No. 551)	1·40	1·40

No. 855 is inscribed "Merrir England" in error. Of the designs in No. **MS**857 the 5t. is inscribed "Simpson Blanche 1872", 10t. "Carterel", 15t. "Dampien", 40t. "eabra" and 60t. "Menesis", all in error.

327 German New Guinea 1900 Yacht Type 2m. Stamp

1999. "iBRA '99" International Stamp Exhibition, Nuremberg. Multicoloured.

858	1k. Type **327**	55	65
859	1k. German New Guinea 1897 3pf. and 5pf. optd on Germany	55	65

328 Father Jules Chevalier

1999. "PhilexFrance '99" International Stamp Exhibition, Paris. Famous Frenchmen. Mult.

860	25t. Type **328**	20	15
861	50t. Bishop Alain-Marie	30	20
862	65t. Joseph-Antoine d'Entrecasteaux (explorer)	40	40
863	1k. Louis de Bougainville (explorer)	65	75

329 Hiri Claypot and Traditional Dancer

1999. Hiri Moale Festival. Multicoloured (except No. **MS**686).

864	25t. Type **329**	20	15
865	50t. Three dancers	30	20
866	65t. Hiri Lakatoi (trading canoe) and dancer	40	40
867	1k. Hiri Sorcerer and dancer	65	75
MS868	140×64 mm. 1k. Hiri Sorcerer (deep blue and blue); 1k. Hiri Claypot (deep purple and blue); 1k. Hiri Lakatoi (green and blue)	1·50	1·75

330 Lap-top Computer, Globe and Watch

1999. New Millennium. Modern Technology. Each showing Globe. Multicoloured.

869	25t. Type **330**	20	15
870	50t. Globe within concentric circles	35	25
871	65t. Compact disc, web site and man using computer	50	45
872	1k. Keyboard, dish aerial and solar eclipse	70	90

331 *Turbo petholatus*

2000. Sea Shells. Multicoloured.

873	25t. Type **331**	25	15
874	50t. *Charonia tritonis*	40	20
875	65t. *Cassis cornuta*	60	50
876	1k. *Ovula ovum*	85	1·25

332 Rabbit

2000. Chinese New Year ("Year of the Rabbit") (1999). Sheet, 145×70 mm, containing T **332** and similar vert designs. Multicoloured.

MS877	65t. Type **332**; 65t. Light brown rabbit running; 65t. White rabbit grinning; 65t. Pink rabbit hiding behind grass knoll	1·75	2·00

333 Shell

2000. 25th Anniv of Independence. Multicoloured.

878	25t. Type **333**	30	15
879	50t. Raggiana bird of Paradise	50	30
880	65t. Ornament	70	50
881	1k. Red bird of Paradise perched on spear and drums	1·10	1·25
MS882	145×75 mm. Nos. 878/81	2·40	2·50

334 Athletics

2000. Olympic Games, Sydney. Multicoloured.

883	25t. Type **334**	25	15
884	50t. Swimming	40	30
885	65t. Boxing	50	50
886	1k. Weightlifting	80	95
MS887	80×90 mm. 3k. Runner with Olympic Torch (34×45 mm) (sold at 3k.50)	2·75	3·25

No. **MS**887 includes the "Olymphilex 2000" stamp exhibition logo on the sheet margin.

335 Queen Mother in Yellow Coat and Hat

2000. Queen Elizabeth the Queen Mother's 100th Birthday. Multicoloured.

888	25t. Type **335**	25	15
889	50t. Queen Mother with bouquet of roses	45	30
890	65t. Queen Mother in green coat	55	50
891	1k. Lady Elizabeth Bowes-Lyon	80	1·00

336 Comb-crested Jacana

2001. Water Birds. Multicoloured.

892	35t. Type **336**	35	20
893	70t. Masked lapwing	60	40
894	90t. Australian white ibis	80	65
895	1k.40 Black-tailed godwit	1·40	1·75

337 Cessna 170 Aircraft

2001. 50th Anniv of Mission Aviation Fellowship. Multicoloured.

896	35t. Type **337**	35	15
897	70t. Auster Autocar	65	45
898	90t. Cessna 260	85	80
899	1k.40 Twin Otter	1·40	1·75

338 Flags of China and Papua New Guinea

2001. 25th Anniv of Diplomatic Relations between Papua New Guinea and China. Multicoloured.

900	10t. Type **338**	10	10
901	50t. Dragon and bird of paradise	30	20
902	2k. Tian An Men (Gate of Heavenly Peace), Beijing, and Parliament House, Port Moresby	1·10	1·40

2001. Nos. 745, 862, 866, 871 and 883 surch.

903	50t. on 21t. Type **248**	2·00	65
904	50t. on 25t. Type **334**	40	30
905	50t. on 65t. Compact disc, web site and man using computer	40	30
906	2k.65 on 65t. Joseph-Antoine d'Entrecasteaux	2·25	2·50
907	2k.65 on 65t. Hiri Lakatoi (trading canoe) and dancer	2·25	2·50

341 Flag of Enga Province

2001. Provincial Flags. Multicoloured.

908	10t. Type **341**	20	20
909	15t. Simbu Province	20	20
910	20t. Manus Province	20	20
911	50t. Central Province	50	20
912	2k. New Ireland Province	1·75	1·75
913	5k. Sandaun Province	3·00	4·00

2002. Golden Jubilee. As T **211** of St. Helena.

914	1k.25 multicoloured	50	50
915	1k.45 multicoloured	60	65
916	2k. black, brown and gold	90	1·00
917	2k.65 multicoloured	1·10	1·40
MS918	162×95 mm. Nos. 914/17 and 5k. multicoloured	4·25	4·75

DESIGNS—HORIZ:1k.25, Queen Elizabeth with Princesses Elizabeth and Margaret, 1941; 1k.45, Queen Elizabeth in evening dress, 1975; 2k. Princess Elizabeth, Duke of Edinburgh and children, 1951; 2k.65, Queen Elizabeth at Henley-on-Thames. VERT (38×51 mm)—5k. Queen Elizabeth after Annigoni.

Designs as Nos. 914/17 in No. **MS**918 omit the gold frame around each stamp and the "Golden Jubilee 1952–2002" inscription.

342 Lakatoi (trading canoe) and Hanuabada Village

2002. Centenary of First Papuan Stamps (2001).

919	**342**	5t. black and mauve	10	20
920	**342**	15t. black and brown	25	20
921	**342**	20t. black and blue	30	20
922	**342**	1k.25 black and brown	75	70
923	**342**	1k.45 black and green	75	70
924	**342**	10k. black and orange	5·00	6·50
MS925		127×99 mm. Nos. 919/24	7·50	8·50

The design of Type **342** is adapted from that of the first Papua issue of 1901.

343 Queen Elizabeth with Princess Elizabeth in South Africa

2002. Queen Elizabeth the Queen Mother Commemoration. Multicoloured (No. 929) or black and blue (others).

926	2k. Type **343**	1·10	1·10
927	2k. Queen Elizabeth with Princess Elizabeth at Balmoral, 1951	1·10	1·10
928	2k. Queen Mother at Sandown races, 2001 (26×30 mm)	1·10	1·10
929	2k. Queen Mother with Irish Guards, 1988 (41×30 mm)	1·10	1·10
930	2k. Queen Mother at the Derby, 1988 (26×30 mm)	1·10	1·10
931	2k. Queen Mother at Ascot races, 1966	1·10	1·10
932	2k. King George VI with Queen Elizabeth at Balmoral, 1951	1·10	1·10
MS933	Two sheets, each 65×101 mm. (a) 3k. Queen Mother at Lord Linley's wedding, 1993; 3k. At Aintree racecourse, 1991 (wearing brooch). (b) 3k. Lady Elizabeth Bowes-Lyon as a young girl; 3k. Queen Mother on Remembrance Day, 1988 (each 26×40 mm)	7·00	7·50

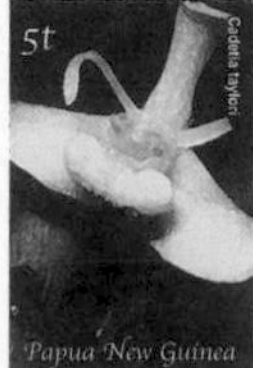

344 *Cadetia taylori*

2002. Orchids. Multicoloured.

934	5t. Type **344**	15	50
935	30t. *Dendrobium anosmum*	45	20
936	45t. *Dendrobium bigibbum*	60	25
937	1k.25 *Dendrobium cuthbertsonii*	1·25	90
938	1k.45 *Spiranthes sinensis*	1·40	1·25
939	2k.65 *Thelymitra carnea*	2·00	2·50
MS940	135×135 mm. 2k. *Dendrobium bracteosum*; 2k. *Calochilus campestris*; 2k. *Anastomus oscitans*; 2k. *Thelymitra carnea*; 2k. *Dendrobium macrophyllum*; 2k. *Dendrobium johnsoniae* (all horiz)	8·50	9·00
MS940a	110×74 mm. 7k. *Bulbophyllum graveolens* (horiz)	8·00	8·00

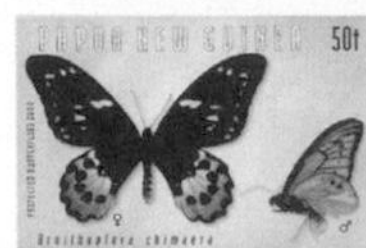
345 *Ornithoptera chimaera*

2002. Birdwing Butterflies. Multicoloured.

941 50t. Type **345** 70 55
942 50t. *Ornithoptera goliath* 70 55
943 1k.25 *Ornithoptera meridionalis* 1·40 1·00
944 1k.45 *Ornithoptera paradisea* 1·60 1·25
945 2k.65 *Ornithoptera victoriae* 2·50 2·75
946 5k. *Ornithoptera alexandrae* 4·25 5·50

346 Globe covered in National Flags and New York Skyline

2002. "United We Stand". Support for Victims of 11 September 2001 Terrorist Attacks. Sheet 174×123 mm.

MS947 **346** 50t.×4 multicoloured 2·25 2·50

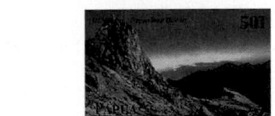

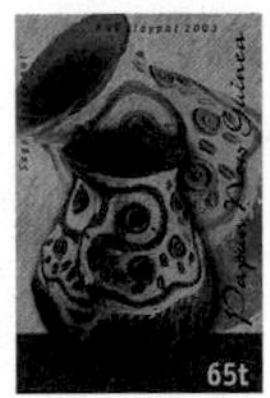
347 Mt. Wilhelm, Papua New Guinea

2002. International Year of Mountains. Multicoloured

948 50t. Type **347** 45 20
949 1k.25 Matterhorn, Switzerland 90 75
950 1k.45 Mount Fuji, Japan 1·10 1·00
951 2k.65 Massif des Aravis, France 1·75 2·50

348 Sago Storage Pot

2003. Clay Pots. Multicoloured.

952 65t. Type **348** 55 25
953 1k. Smoking pot 75 40
954 1k.50 Water jar 1·10 90
955 2k.50 Water jar on stand 1·75 2·00
956 4k. Ridge pot 2·50 4·00

349 Papuan Scout Troop

2003. 20th World Scout Jamboree, Thailand. Multicoloured.

957 50t. Type **349** 35 20
958 1k.25 Scouts in workshop 75 65
959 1k.45 Scouts on wooden platform with banner 85 85
960 2k.65 Scouts 1·50 2·50

350 Princess Elizabeth

2003. 50th Anniv of Coronation.

961 **350** 65t. brown, bistre and black 50 40
962 - 65t. deep lilac, lilac and black 50 40
963 - 1k.50 deep blue, blue and black 90 65
964 - 2k. deep purple, purple and black 1·10 1·25
965 - 2k.50 black and grey 1·60 2·00
966 - 4k. brown, cinnamon and black 2·50 3·50

MS967 146×116 mm. 2k. multicoloured; 2k. multicoloured; 2k. multicoloured; 2k. multicoloured; 2k. multicoloured 6·00 7·00
MS968 97×67 mm. 8k. multicoloured 5·50 6·50

DESIGNS: No. 962, Queen Elizabeth II in Coronation robes and crown; 963, Queen wearing white evening dress, sash and tiara; 964, Queen seated, wearing tiara; 965, Queen in Coronation robes, with Imperial State Crown and sceptre; 966, Princess Elizabeth as teenager; **MS**967, Princess Elizabeth aged 21; Queen wearing diadem, 1952; Wearing hat with blue flowers, c. 1958; Wearing tiara, c. 1970; Wearing red hat with black bow, c. 1985; Wearing black robes and hat with white cockade, c. 1992; **MS**968, Wearing garter robes (from painting by Annigoni).

351 Prince William

2003. 21st Birthday of Prince William of Wales. Multicoloured.

969 65t. Type **351** 65 55
970 65t. Wearing red and blue t-shirt 65 55
971 1k.50 As toddler 1·50 1·10
972 2k. Wearing grey jacket and blue tie 1·75 1·25
973 2k.50 Prince William 2·25 2·50
974 4k. Playing polo 3·75 4·50

MS975 146×116 mm. 2k. As toddler; 2k. Wearing sunglasses; 2k. Wearing blue jacket and tie (facing forwards); 2k. Wearing blue jacket and tie (facing right); 2k. Wearing blue shirt; 2k. Wearing black and yellow t-shirt 6·00 7·00
MS976 95×66 mm. 8k. Prince William 5·50 6·50

352 Gabagaba Village

2003. Coastal Villages. Multicoloured.

977 65t. Type **352** 50 45
978 65t. Wanigela (Koki) 50 45
979 1k.50 Tubuserea 1·10 80
980 2k. Hanuabada 1·25 1·25
981 2k.50 Barakau 1·50 2·00
982 4k. Porebada 2·50 3·50

353 Orville Wright circling Fort Myer, Virginia, 1908

2003. Centenary of Powered Flight. Multicoloured (except No. **MS**987).

983 65t. Type **353** 60 40
984 1k.50 Orville Wright piloting "Baby Grand" biplane, Belmont New York, 1910 1·25 80
985 2k.50 Wilbur Wright holding anemometer, Pau, France, 1909 2·25 2·50
986 4k. Wilbur Wright piloting Wright Model A, Pau, France, 1909 3·75 4·50

MS987 176×96 mm. 2k.50 Wright *Flyer I* outside hangar, Kitty Hawk, North Carolina, 1903 (multicoloured); 2k.50 Wright *Flyer I* rolled out from hangar (black, grey and brown); 2k.50 Wright *Flyer I* being prepared for takeoff (black, green and brown); 2k.50 Wright *Flyer I* taking off, 1903 (multicoloured) 5·50 6·50
MS988 105×76 mm. 10k. Wright *Flyer I*, 1903 5·50 6·50

354 Matschie's Tree Kangaroo

2003. Endangered Species. Tree Kangaroos. Multicoloured.

989 65t. Grizzled tree kangaroo 1·40 1·60
990 1k.50 Type **354** 1·75 2·25
991 2k.50 Doria's tree kangaroo 2·00 2·50
992 4k. Goodfellow's tree kangaroo 2·50 2·75

MS993 168×127 mm. As Nos. 989/92, each ×2, but without white margins 10·00 12·00

355 Indo-Pacific Hump-backed Dolphin

2003. Protected Species. Dolphins. Multicoloured.

994 65t. Type **355** 60 50
995 65t. Two Indo-Pacific bottlenose dolphins 60 50
996 1k.50 Indo-Pacific bottlenose dolphin leaping 1·25 85
997 2k. Irrawaddy dolphin 1·50 1·50
998 2k.50 Indo-Pacific hump-backed dolphin leaping 1·75 2·00
999 4k. Irrawaddy dolphin with diver 2·75 3·50

MS1000 147×112 mm. 1k.50 Indo-Pacific hump-backed dolphin; 1k.50 Indo-Pacific bottlenose dolphin; 1k.50 Two Indo-Pacific bottlenose dolphins; 1k.50 Irrawaddy dolphin with diver; 1k.50 Irrawaddy dolphin; 1k.50 Indo-Pacific hump-backed dolphin 5·50 6·50

2004. Nos. 977/8 surch.

1001 70t. on 65t. Type **352** 1·00 65
1002 70t. on 65t.Wanigela (Koki) 1·00 65

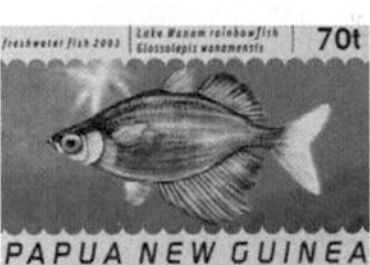

357 Lake Wanam Rainbowfish

2004. Freshwater Fish. Multicoloured.

1003 70t. Type **357** 55 65
1004 70t. Kokoda mogurnda 55 65
1005 1k. Sepik grunter 70 50
1006 2k.70 Papuan black bass 1·75 1·50
1007 4k.60 Lake Tebera rainbowfish 2·50 2·75
1008 20k. Wichmann's mouth almighty 10·00 12·00

358 Ankylosaurus

2004. Prehistoric Animals. Multicoloured.

1009 70t. Type **358** 75 40
1010 1k. Oviraptor 1·00 50
1011 2k. Tyranosaurus 1·50 1·25
1012 2k.65 Gigantosaurus 1·75 1·75
1013 2k.70 Centrosaurus 1·75 1·75
1014 4k.60 Carcharodontsaurus 3·00 4·00

MS1015 146×106 mm. 1k.50 Edmontonia; 1k.50 Struthiomimus; 1k.50 Psittacosaurus; 1k.50 Gastonia; 1k.50 Shunosaurus; 1k.50 Iguanadon 8·00 8·50
MS1016 116×86 mm. 7k. Afrovenator 6·50 7·00

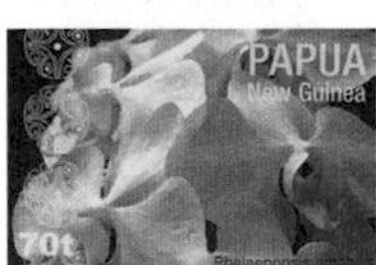

359 *Phalaenopsis amabilis*

2004. Orchids. Multicoloured.

1017 70k. Type **359** 75 40
1018 1k. *Phaius tankervilleae* 1·00 50
1019 2k. *Bulbophyllum macranthum* 1·50 1·25
1020 2k.65 *Dendrobium rhodostictum* 1·75 1·75
1021 2k.70 *Diplocaulobium ridleyanum* 1·75 1·75
1022 4k.60 *Spathoglottis papuana* 3·00 4·00

MS1023 146×106 mm. 2k. *Dendrobium cruttwellii*; 2k. *Dendrobium coeloglossum*; 2k. *Dendrobium alaticaulinum*; 2k. *Dendrobium Obtusisepalum*; 2k. *Dendrobium johnsoniae*; 2k. *Dendrobium insigne* 7·50 8·50
MS1024 116×86 mm. 7k. *Dendrobium biggibum* 6·00 7·00

360 Headdress from East Sepik Province

2004. Local Headdresses. Multicoloured.

1025 70t. Type **360** 55 65
1026 70t. Simbu Province 55 65
1027 2k.65 Southern Highlands Province 1·50 1·50
1028 2k.70 Western Highlands Province 1·50 1·50
1029 4k.60 Eastern Highlands Province 2·50 3·25
1030 5k. Central Province 2·50 3·25

2004. No. 910 and Nos. 994/5 surch.

1031 5t. on 20t. Manus Province (910) 40 65
1032 70t. on 65t. Type **355** (994) 1·25 75
1033 70t. on 65t. Two Indo-Pacific bottlenose dolphins (995) 1·25 75

363 Swimming

2004. Olympic Games, Athens. Multicoloured.

1034 70t. Type **363** 50 30
1035 2k.65 Weight lifting (vert) 1·25 1·50
1036 2k.70 "The Torch Race" (Greek art) (vert) 1·25 1·50
1037 4k.60 Olympic poster, Helsinki 1952 (vert) 2·25 2·75

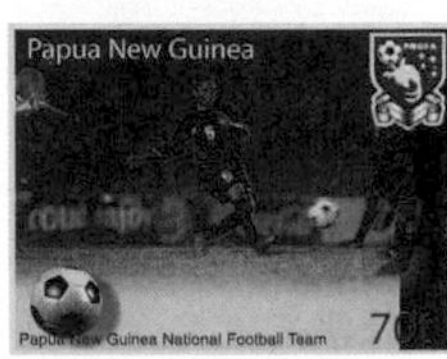

364 Papua New Guinea Football Player

2004. Centenary of FIFA (Federation Internationale de Football Association). Multicoloured.

1038 70t. Type **364** 50 30
1039 2k.65 Shooting at goal 1·25 1·50
1040 2k.70 Two players 1·25 1·50
1041 4k.60 Players and referee 2·25 2·75

MS1042 165×85 mm. 2k.50 Bruno Conti, Italy; 2k.50 Oliver Kahn, Germany; 2k.50 Mario Kempes, Argentina; 2k.50 Bobby Moore, England (51×20 mm) 5·50 6·50
MS1043 93×76 mm. 10k. Bobby Robson, England (51×20 mm) 5·50 6·50

365 Flag of East New Britain Province

2004. Provincial Flags. Multicoloured.

1044 70t. Type **365** 60 50
1045 70t. Madang Province 60 50
1046 2k.65 Eastern Highlands Province 1·75 1·75
1047 2k.70 Morobe Province 1·75 1·75
1048 4k.60 Milne Bay Province 2·75 3·00
1049 10k. East Sepik Province 5·50 6·50

366 *Phalium areola*

2004. Sea Shells. Multicoloured.

1050 70t. Type **366** 55 50
1051 70t. *Conus auratus* 55 50
1052 2k.65 *Oliva miniacea* 1·60 1·60
1053 2k.70 *Lambis chiragra* 1·60 1·60
1054 4k.60 *Conus suratensis* 2·50 2·75
1055 10k. *Architectonica perspective* 5·50 6·50

2005. Nos. 1003/4 and 1025/6 surch **75t**.

1056 75t. on 70t. Type **357** 1·00 80
1057 75t. on 70t. Kokoda mogurnda 1·00 80
1058 75t. on 70t. Type **360** 1·00 80
1059 75t. on 70t. Simbu Province 1·00 80

369 Little Egret

2005. Coastal Birds. Multicoloured.

1060 5t. Type **369** 40 60
1061 75t. White-faced heron 1·25 75
1062 75t. Nankeen night heron 1·25 75
1063 3k. Crested tern 2·25 2·75
1064 3k.10 Bar-tailed godwit 2·25 2·75
1065 5k.20 Little pied heron 3·75 4·50

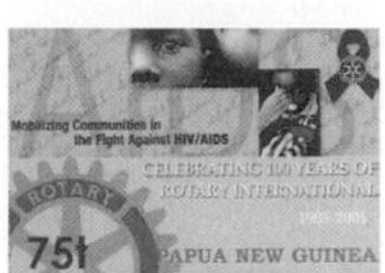

370 Children, Handwriting and Rotary Emblem

2005. Centenary of Rotary International (Humanitarian organisation). Multicoloured.

1066 75t. Type **370** 90 35
1067 3k. Child and PolioPlus emblem 2·00 2·25
1068 3k.10 Co-Founders of the first Rotary club 2·00 2·25
1069 4k. Silvester Schiele (1st Rotary Pres.) (vert) 2·50 2·75
1070 4k. Paul Harris (Founder of Rotary International) (vert) 2·50 2·75
1071 4k. Three children (vert) 2·50 2·75
1072 5k.20 Chicago skyline 2·75 3·25
MS1073 107×74 mm. 10k. Globe and "Mankind is our Business" (vert) 5·50 6·50

371 Lady in Pink

2005. Frangipani Flowers. Multicoloured.

1074 75t. Type **371** 1·00 65
1075 75t. Evergreen 1·00 65
1076 1k. Carmine flush 1·40 65
1077 3k. *Cultivar acutifolia* 2·50 2·75
1078 3k.10 American beauty 2·50 2·75
1079 5k.20 Golden kiss 3·25 3·75

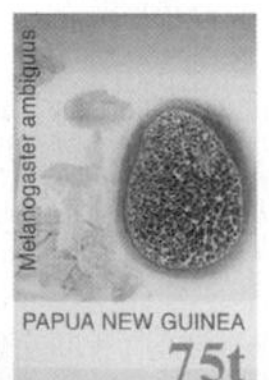

372 *Melanogaster ambiguus*

2005. Mushrooms. Multicoloured.

1080 75t. Type **372** 75 45
1081 75t. *Gymnopilus spectabilis* 75 45
1082 2k. *Amanita muscaria* 1·50 1·50
1083 2k. *Amanita rubescens* 1·50 1·50
1084 2k. *Suillus luteus* 1·50 1·50
1085 2k. *Stropharia cubensis* 1·50 1·50
1086 2k. *Aseroe rubra* 1·50 1·50
1087 2k. *Psilocybe aucklandii* 1·50 1·50
1088 3k.10 *Microporus xanthopus* 2·25 2·50
1089 5k.20 *Psilocybe subcubensis* 3·25 3·75
MS1090 100×70 mm. 10k. *Mycena pura* 5·50 6·50

373 *Promechus pulcher*

2005. Beetles. Multicoloured.

1091 75t. Type **373** 1·00 1·00
1092 75t. *Callistola pulchra* 1·00 1·00
1093 1k. *Lagriomorpha indigacea* 1·25 1·00
1094 3k. *Hellerhinus papuanus* 3·00 3·25
1095 3k.10 *Aphorina australis* 3·00 3·25
1096 5k.20 *Bothricara pulchella* 4·50 5·50

374 Pope John Paul II on Visit to Papua New Guinea

2005. Pope John Paul II Commemoration. Multicoloured. Country name and value colour given.

1097 **374** 2k. blue 2·25 2·25
1098 **374** 2k. green 2·25 2·25
1099 **374** 2k. orange 2·25 2·25
1100 **374** 2k. mauve 2·25 2·25

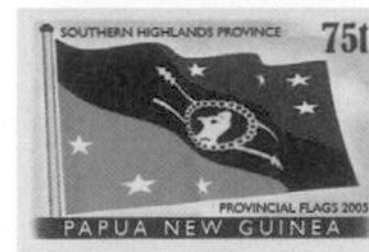

375 Flag of Southern Highlands Province

2005. Provincial Flags. Multicoloured.

1101 75t. Type **375** 1·00 65
1102 75t. Gulf Province 1·00 65
1103 1k. North Solomons Province 1·40 65
1104 3k. Oro Province 3·00 3·25
1105 3k.10 Western Highlands Province 3·00 3·25
1106 5k.20 Western Province 4·75 6·50

376 Ruddy Somali (inscr "Rudy")

2005. Cats and Dogs. Multicoloured.

1107 75t. Type **376** 1·25 75
1108 75t. Balinese seal lynx point 1·25 75
1109 3k. Sphynx brown mackerel tabby and white 3·25 3·50
1110 3k.10 Korat blue 3·25 3·50
1111 5k.20 Bengal brown spotted tabby 5·50 6·50
MS1112 232×100 mm. 2k.50 Yorkshire terrier; 2k.50 Basenji; 2k.50 Neapolitan mastiff (wrongly inscr "Msastiff"); 2k.50 Poodle 9·00 9·50
MS1113 100×70 mm. 10k. Boston terrier (horiz) 9·00 9·50

The stamps and margins of No. **MS**1112 form a composite background design spelling "DOGS".

377 Adult Literacy Class

2006. 50th Anniv of SIL (Summer Institute of Linguistics). Multicoloured.

1114 80t. Type **377** 1·25 75
1115 80t. Postmarking letters (Postal Services) 1·25 75
1116 1k. Dr. Jim Dean (first director of SIL Papua New Guinea Branch, 1956–64) 1·40 75
1117 3k.20 Learning to read in mother tongue (Tokples Preschools) 3·00 3·25
1118 3k.25 Rural people and aircraft (SIL Aviation) 3·00 3·25
1119 5k.35 SIL worker teaching woman to use sewing machine (Community Development) 5·00 6·00

378 Queen with President Bill Clinton

2006. 80th Birthday of Queen Elizabeth II. Two sheets each 162×152 mm containing T **378** and similar vert designs. Multicoloured.

MS1120 (a) 80t. Type **378**; 3k.20 Dancing with Pres. Gerald Ford; 3k.25 At banquet with Pres. Ronald Reagan; 5k.35 With Pres. George Bush. (b) 2k.50 Wearing polka dot dress; 2k.50 Line engraving of Queen; 2k.50 Line engraving of Queen (facing left); 2k.50 With Queen Mother 18·00 20·00

379 "Spirit House" (interior of Sepik Haus Tambaran)

2006. Contemporary Art in Papua New Guinea (1st series). Multicoloured.

1121 5t. Type **379** 25 50
1122 80t. "Rhythm and Harmony" (two heads) 1·25 65
1123 80t. "The Chief" (man with nose ring) 1·25 65
1124 3k.20 "Reaching out to the People" 3·00 3·25
1125 3k.25 "Protecting our Women" 3·00 3·25
1126 5k.35 "Man as Art" 4·50 5·50

See also Nos. 1214/**MS**1220.

380 Stylised England Player

2006. World Cup Football Championship, Germany. Sheet 127×102 mm containing T **380** and similar horiz designs showing cartoon players and team colours. Multicoloured.

MS1127 80t. Type **380**; 3k.20 Germany; 3k.25 Argentina; 5k.35 Australia 9·75 11·00

381 "50th Anniversary" Emblem

2006. 50th Anniv of the Salvation Army in Papua New Guinea. Multicoloured.

1128 5t. Type **381** 25 50
1129 80t. Papua New Guinea and Salvation Army flags 1·40 60
1130 1k. Lt. Ian Cutmore and Major Keith Baker (pioneer officers, 1956) 1·40 60
1131 3k.20 Colonels Andrew and Julie Kalai (first Papua New Guinean commanders) 3·25 3·50
1132 3k.25 Kei Geno (first Papua New Guinean convert) 3·25 3·50
1133 5k.35 Lt. Dorothy Elphick (pioneer officer in Highlands) holding baby 4·50 5·50

2006. Nos. 1050/1 surch **80t.**

1134 80t. on 70t. Type **366** 80 70
1135 80t. on 70t. *Conus auratus* 80 70

383 *Delias iltis*

2006. Butterflies. Multicoloured.

1136 80t. Type **383** 1·40 50
1137 3k.20 *Ornithoptera paradisea* 3·50 3·50
1138 3k.25 *Taenaris catops* 3·50 3·50
1139 5k.35 *Papilio ulysses autolycus* 5·00 6·50

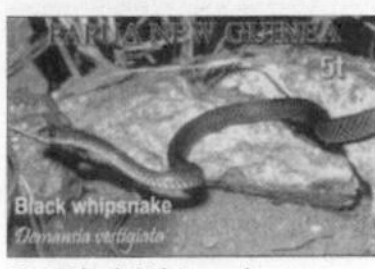

384 Black Whipsnake

2006. Snakes of Papua New Guinea. Multicoloured.

1140 5t. Type **384** 25 70
1141 80t. Papuan taipan 1·25 50
1142 2k. Smooth-scaled death adder 1·90 1·75
1143 3k.20 Papuan blacksnake 3·00 3·25
1144 3k.25 New Guinea small-eyed snake 3·00 3·25
1145 5k.35 Eastern brownsnake 4·00 5·00

385 Elvis Presley

2006. Elvis Presley Commemoration. Multicoloured.

1146 80t. Type **385** 1·25 50
1147 3k.20 Holding microphone, wearing red shirt 3·00 3·00
1148 3k.25 Wearing white jacket and bow tie 3·00 3·00
1149 5k.35 Playing guitar 4·75 5·50
MS1150 127×190 mm. 80t. Wearing gold suit, "Elvis Gold Records–Volume 2"; 3k.20 Aged 2, "Elvis Country"; 3k.25 Playing piano, "His Hand in Mine"; 5k.35 "King Creole" (all 50×37 mm) 11·00 12·00
MS1151 100×70 mm. 10k. Holding three teddy bears 8·50 8·50

The stamps within No. **MS**1150 all show album covers.

386 Mango

2007. Tropical Fruit. Multicoloured.

1152 5t. Type **386** 25 70
1153 85t. Pineapple 1·25 65
1154 85t. Watermelon 1·25 65
1155 3k.35 Guava 3·00 3·25
1156 3k.35 Pawpaw 3·00 3·25
1157 5k.35 Lemon 4·50 6·00

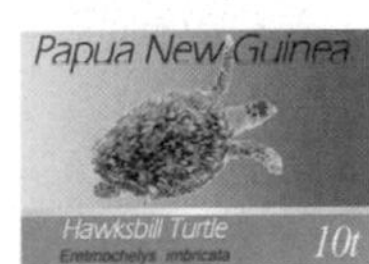

387 Hawksbill Turtle

2007. Endangered Marine Turtles. Multicoloured.

1158 10t. Type **387** 40 70
1159 35t. Flatback turtle (adult) 1·00 60
1160 85t. Loggerhead turtle 1·50 1·10
1161 3k. Leatherback turtle (adult) 3·75 4·00
1162 3k.35 Green turtle (adult) 3·75 4·00
1163 5k.35 Olive Ridley turtle (adult on beach) 5·50 6·50
MS1164 176×96 mm. 85t. Flatback turtle hatchling; 3k. Leatherback turtle hatchling reaching sea; 3k.35 Young green turtle emerging from egg; 5k.35 Young Olive Ridley turtle swimming 12·00 13·00

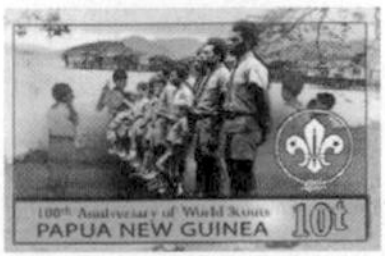

388 Scouts on Parade

2007. Centenary of Scouting. Multicoloured.

1165 10t. Type **388** 35 60
1166 85t. Papua New Guinea scouts in procession 1·25 75
1167 3k.35 Papua New Guinea scouts seated on ground 3·25 3·50
1168 5k.35 Papua New Guinea scout leaders 4·75 6·00
MS1169 177×98 mm. Nos. 1165/8 8·50 9·00
MS1170 116×86 mm. 10k. Lord Baden-Powell (founder) (vert) 8·50 9·00

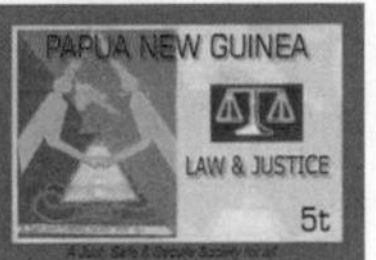

389 Handshake and Scales of Justice (Joshua Weka)

2007. National Stamp Design Competition. Designs showing winning entries. Multicoloured.

1171 5t. Type **389** ('A Just, Safe & Secure Society for all') 20 70

1172	30t. Open book between totem poles (David Moripi) ('Prosperity through self reliance')	45	30
1173	85t. AIDS ribbon and outline map (Kokenu Makita) ('STOP Aids Now')	1·50	75
1174	3k. Saluting policemen, arms and scales of justice (Tenison Paki) ('Crime Reduction')	3·25	3·25
1175	3k.35 Nurse and mother breast feeding baby (Kopoi Boi) ('Infant Care & Child Immunization')	3·25	3·25
1176	5k.35 Teacher and tribesmen in classroom (Paul Gemis) ('Minimizing illiteracy')	4·75	6·00

No. 1176 is incorrectly spelled 'literacy'.

390 *Den. conanthum* and *Den. lasianthera*

391 Pale Yellow Orchid with Mauve Lip

2007. Personalised Stamps. Orchids of Papua New Guinea. Multicoloured. (a) As T **390**.

1177	85t. Type **390**	1·75	75
1178	3k. *Dendrobium conanthum* Schltr	3·75	3·75
1179	3k.35 *Dendrobium lasianthera* var May River Red	3·75	3·75
1180	5k.35 *Dendrobium wulaiense* Howcroft	6·00	7·00

(b) As T **391**.

1181	1k. Type **391**	1·40	1·40
1182	1k. Cream orchid with twisted petals and mauve lip	1·40	1·40
1183	1k. White orchids	1·40	1·40
1184	1k. Orchid with mauve lip and white and pink petals	1·40	1·40
1185	1k. White orchid with deep red markings on petals	1·40	1·40
1186	1k. Yellow orchid with brownish shading	1·40	1·40
1187	1k. Pale mauve orchid with deep mauve lip	1·40	1·40
1188	1k. White Stanhopea orchid with yellow blotch in throat and reddish veining	1·40	1·40
1189	1k. Pale pink orchid with mauve veining on lip	1·40	1·40
1190	1k. Many bloomed red-brown orchid	1·40	1·40
1191	1k. Yellow orchid with greenish column	1·40	1·40
1192	1k. Greenish orchid with dark shading	1·40	1·40

392 Separated Siamese Twins Eustina and Eustocia Bosin, 1996

2007. 50th Anniv of First Rotary Club in Papua New Guinea. Multicoloured.

1193	85t. Type **392** (ROMAC medical aid for children)	1·00	60
1194	3k.35 Distribution of insecticide treated mosquito nets	3·25	3·25
1195	5k. List of Papua New Guinea Rotary Clubs	3·75	4·50
1196	5k.35 Rotary members and container of donated goods	4·25	5·00
MS1197	146×106 mm. Nos. 1193/6	12·00	13·00

393 Lady Diana Spencer, 1965

2007. Tenth Death Anniv of Diana, Princess of Wales. Multicoloured.

MS1198	130×100 mm. 85t. Type **393**; 2k.45 Lady Diana Spencer, 1971; 3k.35 Lady Diana Spencer, 1981; 5k.35 Princess Diana, 1983	10·50	10·50
MS1199	70×100 mm. 10k. Princess Diana	9·75	9·75

394 Queen Elizabeth II and Prince Philip

2007. Diamond Wedding of Queen Elizabeth II and Prince Philip. Multicoloured.

1200	2t. Type **394** (mauve border)	2·50	2·50
1201	2k. Queen Elizabeth II (mauve border)	2·50	2·50
1202	2k. As No. 1201 (lavender border)	2·50	2·50
1203	2k. As Type **394** (lavender border)	2·50	2·50
1204	2k. As Type **394** (stone border)	2·50	2·50
1205	2k. As No. 1201 (stone border)	2·50	2·50
MS1206	70×100 mm. 10k. Princess Elizabeth and Philip Mountbatten, c. 1949	13·00	13·00

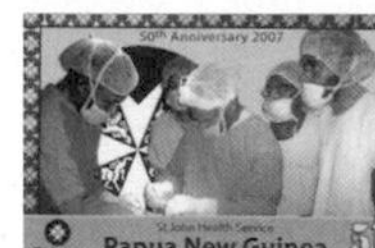

395 St. John Health Service

2007. 50th Anniv of St. John Ambulance in Papua New Guinea. Multicoloured.

1207	5t. Type **395**	35	70
1208	20t. St. John Blood Service	75	40
1209	85t. St. John Blind Service	1·75	75
1210	1k. St. John Ambulance Service	1·90	1·10
1211	3k.35 St. John Volunteer Service	4·50	4·50
1212	5k.35 The Order of St. John	6·00	7·50
MS1213	186×114 mm. Nos. 1207/12	14·00	14·00

396 'Blended Culture' (Oro Gagara)

2007. Contemporary Art in Papua New Guinea (2nd series). Multicoloured.

1214	5t. Type **396**	25	70
1215	30t. Tribesman – Western Province	50	35
1216	85t. 'The Sorcerer – Cultural Initiation' (Begesin/Madang)	1·10	60
1217	3k. 'Blended Culture' (Hewa Wigman)	3·25	3·50
1218	3k.35 'Pigs into Python – Legend' (Bukawa, Morobe Province)	3·25	3·50
1219	5k.35 Tolai masks – East New Britain Province	5·50	7·00
MS1220	186×114 mm. Nos. 1214/19 (sold at 12k.55)	12·50	12·50

No. **MS**1220 was sold at 12k.55, a discount of 35t. over the face value.

397 Papuan Hornbill

2008. Protected Birds. Multicoloured.

1221	10t. Type **397**	70	90
1222	50t. Osprey	2·00	1·00
1223	85t. New Guinea harpy eagle	2·75	1·25
1224	3k. Victoria crowned pigeon	7·00	7·00
MS1225	145×101 mm. Nos. 1221/3; 1k. Palm cockatoo; No. 1224; 5k.35 Great white egret	12·00	12·00
MS1226	115×86 mm. 10k. Palm cockatoo	16·00	16·00

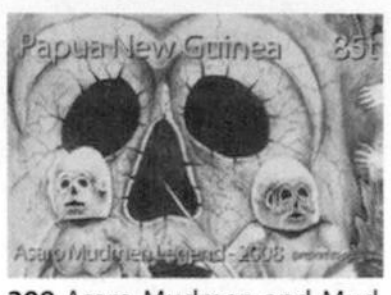

398 Asaro Mudmen and Mud Mask

2008. Asaro Mudmen Legend. Multicoloured.

1227	85t. Type **398**	1·25	65
1228	3k. Mudmen hiding in bushes	3·25	3·25
1229	3k.35 Firing arrows at enemy	3·25	3·25
1230	5k.35 Enemy tribe fleeing believing mudmen are ghosts	5·50	6·00
MS1231	176×80 mm. Nos. 1227/30	12·00	12·00
MS1232	115×86 mm. 10k. As Type **398**	10·00	10·00

399 *Sarcophyton* sp. (leather coral)

2008. Marine Biodiversity. Multicoloured.

1233	85t. Type **399**	1·75	65
1234	3k. *Chromodoris kunei*	3·75	3·75
1235	3k.35 *Lambis scorpius* (scorpion spider snail)	3·75	3·75
1236	5k.35 *Clatheia mima* (veined sponge)	6·50	7·50
MS1237	85t. *Astropyga radiata* (radiant sea urchin); 3k. *Phyllidia varicosa*; 3k.35 *Nephtheis fascicularis* (sea squirt); 5k.35 *Celerina heffernani* (Heffernan's sea star)	12·00	12·00
MS1238	116×85 mm. 10k. *Euphyllia cristata* (white grape coral)	10·00	10·00

400 Weightlifting

2008. Olympic Games, Beijing. Multicoloured.

1239	1k.40 Type **400**	1·90	1·90
1240	1k.40 Diving	1·90	1·90
1241	1k.40 Hurdling	1·90	1·90
1242	1k.40 Boxing	1·90	1·90

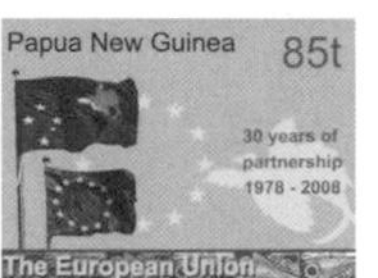

401 Papua New Guinea and EU Flags

2008. 30 Years of Papua New Guinea – European Union Partnership. Multicoloured; background colours given.

1243	**401**	85t. grey	1·25	75
1244	**401**	3k. yellow	3·25	3·25
1245	**401**	3k.35 rose	3·25	3·25
1246	**401**	5k.35 blue	5·00	6·00
MS1247		100×120 mm. As Nos. 1243/6	11·50	12·00
MS1248		85×85 mm. 10k. blue	10·00	10·00

Stamps from **MS**1247 have dark blue borders at foot. Nos. 1243/6 have dark blue borders at foot with white patterns.

402 *Long Hair*

2008. Pioneer Art by Akis (Timothy Akis). Multicoloured.

1249	85t. Type **402**	1·25	60
1250	3k. *Alone*	3·50	3·50
1251	3k.35 *Woman with Cassowary and Child*	3·50	3·50
1252	5k.35 *Man shooting Cassowary*	6·50	7·50
MS1253	128×155 mm. 85t. *Five Men in their Gardens* (top portion); 3k. Crocodile woman; 3k.35 *Five Men in their Gardens* (bottom portion); 5k.35 Two-headed man	12·50	12·50
MS1254	80×90 mm. 10k. *Flying Fox*	10·00	10·00

The 3k. and 5k.35 values from **MS**1253 form a complete drawing: *The Crocodile Woman and Two-headed Man.*

403 Headdress

2008. Traditional Headdress. Multicoloured.

1255	85t. Type **403**	1·40	90
1256	3k. Headdress with red feathers and white plume	3·75	3·75
1257	3k.35 Headdress with white feathers and brown plume	4·00	4·00
1258	5k.35 Man wearing headdress of white feathers with brown markings	6·50	7·50
MS1259	145×105 mm. 85t. Man wearing headdress with light brown plumes; 3k. Headdress with shells and dark red feathers; 3k. 35 Man with white painted face wearing black and white headdress; 5k.35 Red headdress	13·50	13·50
MS1260	86×115 mm. 10k. Red and yellow headdress with white feathers	10·50	10·50

404 Marilyn Monroe

2008. Marilyn Monroe Commemoration. Multicoloured.

MS1261	100×140 mm. 85c. Type **404**; 3k. Looking over shoulder; 3k.35 Smiling at camera; 5k.35 With hand raised to face	13·50	13·50
MS1262	100×70 mm. 10k. Leaning on car door	10·50	10·50

405 *Paradisaea guilielmi*

2008. Birds of Paradise. Previously issued designs as Nos. 64, 66/7, 69, 173/4, 176 and 239/40 redrawn with new values and inscriptions as T **405**. Multicoloured.

1263	85t. Type **405** (66)	1·75	1·10
1264	3k. *Parotia lawesi* (64)	4·50	4·50
1265	3k.35 *Epimachus meyeri* (67)	4·50	4·50
1266	5k.35 *Diphyllodes magnificus* (69)	6·50	7·50
MS1267	146×106 mm. 85t. *Astrapia stephaniae* (240); 3k. *Cnemophilus macgregorii* (176); 3k.35 *Pteridophora albertii* (173); 5k.35 *Astrapia mayeri* (239)	16·00	16·00
MS1268	116×86 mm. 10k. *Cicinnurus regius* (174)	12·00	12·00

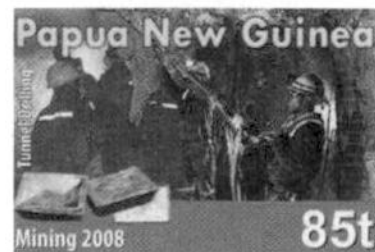

406 Tunnel drilling

2008. Mining. Multicoloured.

1269	85t. Type **406**	2·00	1·10
1270	3k. Mine truck (Logistics)	5·50	4·50
1271	3k.35 Refinery	5·50	4·50
1272	5k.35 Gold bars	8·00	8·50
MS1273	145×105 mm. 85t. Open pit mining; 3k. Conveyor belt; 3k.35 Plant site; No. 1272	14·00	14·00
MS1274	116×86 mm. 10k. Close up of gold bar	15·00	15·00

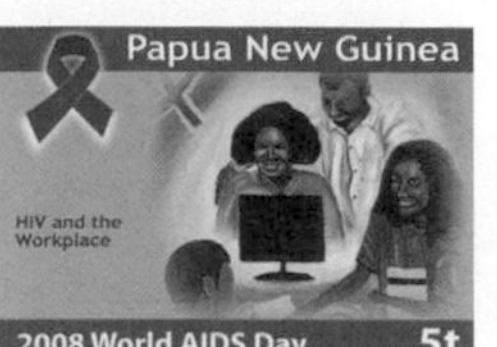

407 'HIV and the Workplace'

2008. World AIDS Day. Multicoloured.

1275	5t. Type **407**	30	70
1276	10t. 'Voluntary Counselling and Testing'	40	70
1277	50t. Condom ('Role of Men and Women')	1·25	50

1278 85t. Teaching children about HIV/AIDS ('Education') 1·60 75
1279 1k. 'Eradicating Stigma and Discrimination' 1·75 1·00
1280 2k. 'Living with the Virus' 3·00 2·50
1281 3k. Couple ('Care, Support and the Role of Family') 4·00 3·75
1282 3k.70 AIDS ribbons in pattern ('Building Leadership') 5·00 5·00
1283 6k. Anti-AIDS drugs and fruit ('Health and Nutrition') 9·50 11·00
MS1284 146×106 mm. As Nos. 1278 and 1281/3 but 42×28 mm 17·00 17·00
MS1285 115×86 mm. 10k. As No. 1279 but 42×28 mm 14·50 14·50

No. MS1284 was sold at 13k., a discount of 55t. over the face value.

408 The Nativity ('Joy to the World')

2008. Christmas. Multicoloured.
1286 85t. Type **408** 2·00 50
1287 3k. Santa riding reindeer ('Ho ho ho... Merry Christmas') 4·50 3·50
1288 3k.35 Book and candle ('Amazing Grace') 5·00 3·75
1289 5k.35 Book and bell ('Jingle Bells') 7·00 8·00
MS1290 146×106 mm. 85t. 'The Journey to Bethlehem'; 3k. Native huts and Christmas star ('Silent Night'); 3k.35 Shepherds following Star ('Behold that Star'); 5k.35 Three Papuan men carrying gifts ('The 3 Wise Men') 17·00 17·00
MS1291 116×86 mm. 10k. Wrapped Christmas gift 13·50 13·50

409 *Bixa orellana*

2009. Plants. Multicoloured.
1292 85t. Type **409** 1·50 50
1293 3k. Perfume tree (*Cananga odorata*) 5·00 3·50
1294 3k.70 Beach kalofilum (*Calophyllum inophyllum*) 6·00 3·50
1295 6k. *Macaranga tenarius* 10·00 11·00
MS1296 146×106 mm. 85t. Native frangipani (*Hymenosporum flavum*); 3k. Ten cent flower (*Fagraea berteriana*); 3k.70 Beach terminali (*Terminalia catappa*); 6k. Red beech (*Dillenia alata*) 20·00 20·00
MS1297 111×66 mm. 10k. Beach convolvulus or morning glory (*Ipomoea pes-caprae*) 15·00 15·00

410 *Albericus siegfriedi*

2009. Frogs. Multicoloured.
1298 85t. Type **410** 1·75 50
1299 3k. *Cophixalus nubicola* 5·50 3·50
1300 3k.70 *Nyctimystes pulcher* 6·50 3·50
1301 6k. *Sphenophryne cornuta* 11·00 12·00
MS1302 146×113 mm. 85t. *Litoria sauroni*; 3k. *Litoria prora*; 3k.70 *Litoria multiplica*; 6k. *Litoria pronimia* 20·00 20·00
MS1303 117×93 mm. 10k. *Oreophyrne* sp. 15·00 15·00

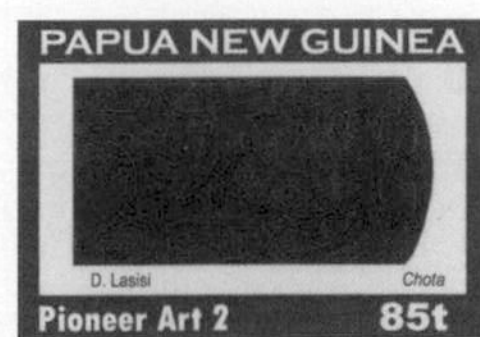

411 *Chota*

2009. 'Pioneer Art' (2nd series) by David Lasisi. Multicoloured.
1304 85t. Type **411** 1·50 50
1305 3k. *Stability* 5·00 3·50
1306 3k.70 *Taumirmir* 6·00 3·50
1307 6k. *The Moieties* 10·00 11·00
MS1308 146×107 mm. 85t. *Like a Log being Adrifted*; 3k. *Lasisi*; 3k.70 *Lupa*; 6k. *InMemory of Marker Craftsman* 20·00 20·00
MS1309 116×86 mm. 10k. *Trapped by Cobweb of Stinging Pain* 15·00 15·00

412 Vessel (lian or Zun) with Design of Deities, Animals and Masks (265–316)

2009. China 2009 World Stamp Exhibition, Luoyang. Multicoloured.
1310 5t. Type **412** 30 70
1311 10t. *Evening in the Peach and Plum Garden* (Li Bai) (1644–1911) 40 70
1312 85t. Reliquary with Buddhist figures (960–1127) 1·60 75
1313 1k. Pink peony 1·75 1·00
1314 3k. Brick relief figure (1279–1368) 4·00 3·75
1315 3k.70 Round tray with scroll designs (206BCE–8CE) 5·00 5·00
1316 6k. Plate in shape of two peach halves with design of two foxes (618–907) 9·50 11·00
MS1317 108×154 mm. As Nos. 1310/15 but with different background design. P 14½×14 19·00 19·00
MS1318 70×101mm. 6k. Two pink peonies (44×44 mm) 8·50 9·00

Nos. 1310/15 all show the right hand part of a plate at left of the stamp. The stamps within **MS**1317 each have a background showing part of the plate design.

413 Fish ('Sustainable Income & Food Security')

2009. Coral Triangle Programme (Marine Conservation). Multicoloured.
1319 85t. Type **413** 1·75 75
1320 3k. Green turtle 6·00 4·00
1321 3k.70 Mangroves 6·00 4·00
1322 6k. Coral reefs 11·00 12·00
MS1323 146×106 mm. 85t. Dolphin; 3k. Green turtle; 3k.70 Reef fish; 6k. Killer whale 22·00 20·00
MS1324 116×87 mm. 10k. Grouper 15·00 15·00

No. **MS**1323 contains four triangular stamps laid tête-beche, the stamps and margins forming a composite background design showing a coral reef and fish.

414 Guides helping Trekker down Steep Slope

2009. Kokoda Trail. Multicoloured.
1325 85t. Type **414** 1·50 50
1326 3k. Crossing Vabuyavi River 4·25 3·00
1327 3k.70 Waterfall near Abuari 4·50 3·00
1328 6k. Trekkers crossing Lake Myola 1 7·50 8·00
MS1329 146×106 mm. 85t. Crossing Emune River; 3k. Entering Imita Ridge; Crossing Alo Creek; 6k. Camping at Templeton's Crossing No. 2 16·00 16·00
MS1330 86×116 mm. 10k. 'Golden Staircase', Imita Ridge 12·00 12·00

415 Black-bellied Bat (*Melanycteris melanops*)

2009. Bats of Papua New Guinea. Multicoloured.
1331 85t. Type **415** 1·50 50
1332 3k. Least blossom bat (*Macroglossus minimus*) 5·00 3·50
1333 3k.70 Sanborn's broad-nosed bat (*Scotorepens sanborni*) 6·00 3·50
1334 6k. Mantled mastiff bat (*Otomops secundus*) 10·00 11·00
MS1335 146×106 mm. 85t. Trident leaf-nosed bat (*Aselliscus tricuspidatus*); 3k. Flower-faced bat (*Anthops ornatus*); 3k.70 Eastern horseshoe bat (*Phinolophus megaphyllus*); 6k. Greater tubed-nose bat (*Nyctimene aello*) 20·00 20·00
MS1336 116×86 mm. 10k. Bougainville's fruit bat (*Pteralopex anceps*) 12·00 12·00

416 Abraham Lincoln

2009. International Day of Non-Violence. Multicoloured.
1337 85t. Type **416** 1·50 50
1338 3k. Princess Diana 4·25 3·00
1339 3k.70 Nelson Mandela 4·50 3·00
1340 6k. Pres. Barack Obama (facing left) 7·50 8·00
MS1341 106×146 mm. 85t. As No. 1340; 3k. Martin Luther King; 3k.70 Mahatma Gandhi; 6k. As No. 1338 16·00 16·00
MS1342 86×116 mm. 10k. Pres Barack Obama (facing right) (37×51 mm) 12·00 12·00

417 Mt. Vulcan, Rabaul

2009. Volcanoes. Multicoloured.
1343 85t. Type **417** 2·00 50
1344 3k. Foreshore with buildings and Mt. Tavurvur, Rabaul 5·50 3·50
1345 3k.70 Mt. Bagana, Bougainville 5·50 3·50
1346 6k. Forest and volcano, Manam Island, Madang 9·50 10·00
MS1347 146×106 mm. 85t. Mt. Tavurvur, Rabaul, emitting black smoke; 3k. Volcano, Manam Island, Madang; 3k.70 Mt. Tavurvur, Rabaul, emitting black cloud; 6k. Mt. Ulawun, Rabaul 20·00 18·00
MS1348 116×86 mm. 10k. Mt. Tavurvur, Rabaul, erupting red lava at sunset 14·00 14·00

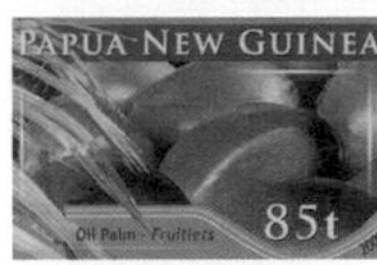

418 Oil Palm Fruitlets

2009. Oil Palm Farming. Multicoloured.
1349 85t. Type **418** 1·25 50
1350 3k. Oil palm nursery 3·75 3·00
1351 3k.70 Bunches of oil palm fruit 4·00 3·00
1352 6k. Collection of fruit by lorry 7·00 8·00
MS1353 146×106 mm. 85t. Irrigation of oil palm seedlings; 3k. As No. 1351; 3k.70 Loose fruits; 6k. Oil palm mill 16·00 16·00
MS1354 116×86 mm. 10k. Hand holding fruitlets 12·00 12·00

419 Canoe, Mortlock Island, North Solomon Province

2009. Traditional Canoes. Multicoloured.
1355 85t. Type **419** 1·50 50
1356 3k. Manus Province 4·00 3·00
1357 3k.70 Bilbil, Madang Province 4·25 3·00
1358 6k. Central Province 7·00 8·00
MS1359 146×106 mm. 85t. Kimbe, West New Britain Province; 3k. Vuvulu Island, East Sepik Province; 3k.70 Suau Island, Milne Bay Province; 6k. Mailu, Central Province 16·00 16·00
MS1360 116×86 mm. 10k. Gogodala, Western Province 12·00 12·00

420 Engagement Dance, Western Highlands Province

2009. Traditional Dance (Romance). Multicoloured.
1361 1k. Type **420** 1·50 50
1362 3k. Bride Price Dance, Central Province 4·00 3·00
1363 4k.65 Engagement Dance, Manus Province 4·25 3·00
1364 6k.30 Tobriand Love Dance, Milne Bay Province 7·00 8·00
MS1365 146×107 mm. 1k. Courtship Dance, Chimbu Province; 3k. Engagement Dance, Enga Province; 4k.65 Engagement Dance, Central Province; 6k.30 Womanhood, Central Province 17·00 17·00
MS1366 116×86 mm. 10k. Tobriand Love Dance, Milne Bay Province 12·00 12·00

421 *Fish Man*

2010. Pioneer Art (3rd series) by Jakupa Ako. Multicoloured.
1367 1k. Type **421** 1·75 50
1368 3k. *Story Board* (vert) 4·50 3·00
1369 4k.65 *Hunting Trip* (vert) 4·75 3·00
1370 6k.30 *Warrior* (vert) 8·00 9·00
MS1371 106×146 mm. 1k. *Bird Art*; 3k. *Bird Eating*; 4k.65 *Bird Nest*; 6k.30 *Marsupial* (all vert) 17·00 17·00
MS1372 116×86 mm. 10k. *Spirit Mask* (vert) 12·00 12·00

422 *Bohadschia similis* ('Chalkfish')

2010. Sea Cucumbers (Beche-de-Mer). Multicoloured.
1373 1k. Type **422** 1·75 50
1374 3k. *Holothuria (Microthele) fuscopunctata* ('Elephant trunk fish') 4·50 3·00
1375 4k.65 *Stichopus hermanni* ('Curryfish') 4·75 3·00
1376 6k.30 *Bohadschia argus* ('Tigerfish') 8·00 9·00
MS1377 146×106 mm. 1k. *Actinopyga mauritiana* ('Surf redfish'); 3k. *Holothuria (Halodeima) atra* ('Lollyfish'); 4k.65 *Bohadschia vitiensis* ('Brown sandfish'); 6k.30 *Holothuria scabra* ('Sandfish') 17·00 16·00
MS1378 86×116 mm. 10k. *Holothuria (Halodeima) edulis* ('Pinkfish') 11·00 11·00

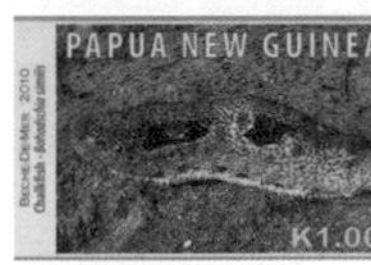

423 Huene Island

2010. Climate Change. Sinking Islands (Carterets). Multicoloured.
1379 1k. Type **423** 1·50 50
1380 3k. Upsurge of sea through man made barriers 4·00 3·00
1381 4k.65 Flooded forest ('Saltwater Intrusion') 5·50 3·50
1382 6k.30 Uprooted tree and branches at forest edge ('Saltwater Claims') 8·00 9·00
MS1383 146×106 mm. 1k. Dwindling Island; 3k. Uprooted tree on beach ('Saltwater Claims'); 4k.65 Storm surge and erosion; 6k.30 Man made barriers 16·00 15·00
MS1384 116×86 mm. 10k. Divided atolls 10·00 10·00

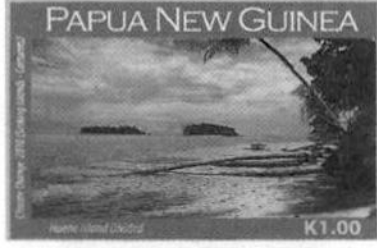

424 *Nelumbium nelumbo* (sacred lotus)

2010. Centenary of Girl Guiding.. Multicoloured.
1385 1k. Type **424** 1·00 50
1386 3k. Creating wash bowl stand for badge work 2·75 2·00
1387 4k.65 Trainer teaching knots at Guide Leaders training 4·00 3·50
1388 6k.30 Brownies displaying their badge work 6·25 7·50

MS1389 146×107 mm. 1k. Lady Kala Olewale, Second PNG Chief Commissioner, 1980s–90s; 3k. Lady Christian Chartterton, founder of Guiding in PNG, 1927; 4k.65 Princess Anne's visit to PNG, 1970; 6k.30 Enny Moaitz, first PNG Chief Commissioner, 1970s–80s 12·50 12·50

MS1390 117×86 mm. 10k. Lady Olave Baden-Powell, World Chief Guide, 1930–77 8·50 8·50

425 Australian Soldiers on Kokoda Trail, 1942

2010. Kokoda Trail Campaign, World War II. Multicoloured.

1391	1k. Type **425**	1·40	1·40
1392	1k. Papua New Guineans helping wounded soldiers along trail, 1942	1·40	1·40
1393	1k. Trekker, guide and memorial	1·40	1·40
1394	4k.65 Veterans at Kokoda Isurava Memorial	4·25	4·25
1395	4k.65 Kokoda veterans	4·25	4·25
MS1396	160×90 mm. Nos. 1391/5	13·50	13·50

Stamps in the same designs were issued by Australia on the same date. .

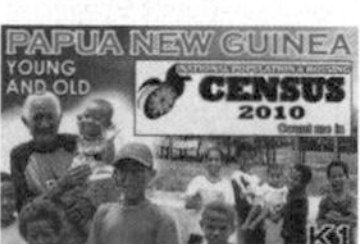

426 Elderly Man holding Infant and Children ('Young and Old')

2010. National Census 2010. Multicoloured.

1397	1k. Type **426**	1·25	1·25
1398	1k. 'Youths'	1·25	1·25
1399	3k. Village women with produce ('Villagers')	3·00	3·00
1400	3k. Working mother with baby from town and village houses ('Infants')	3·00	3·00
MS1401	145×106 mm. 1k. Davau Pre-School class and teacher, Ugabega, National Capital District ('School Kids'); 1k. 'Elderly men'; 3k. Women from Deacon Mothers of Mahuru United Church, National Capital District ('Elderly women'); 3k. People outside Post PNG, Boroko ('All walks of life')	8·25	8·25

427 Summer Palace, Wenchang Tower

2010. Expo 2010, Shanghai, China. Multicoloured.

1402	1k. Type **427**	90	50
1403	3k. Ballet dancer, Shanghai International Culture and Art Festival	2·50	1·75
1404	4k.65 Oriental Pearl Tower, Pudong, Shanghai	3·25	3·00
1405	6k.30 Chinese acrobatic performers (two men)	5·00	6·00
MS1406	131×181 mm. 5t. As Type **427**; 10t. As No. 1403; 85t. As No. 1404; 3k. Chinese acrobatic performers (three women); 3k.70 As No. 1405; 6k. Ancient Chinese building	11·00	11·00
MS1407	100×70 mm. 10k. Tower, Suzhou	8·00	8·00

428 Female Angler

2010. Game Fishing. Multicoloured.

1408	1k. Type **428**	1·00	50
1409	3k. Anglers with sailfish	2·75	1·75
1410	4k.65 Anglers with 25kg sailfish	3·25	3·00
1411	6k.30 Angler with 10kg barramundi	5·00	6·00
MS1412	146×106 mm. 1k. Game fishing boat; 3k. Angler; 4k.65 Angler with 14kg wahoo; 6k.30 Angler with 11kg barramundi	12·00	12·00
MS1413	86×116 mm. 10k. Irene Robinson with world record catch (2.6kg blue fin trevally on 4kg line)	8·00	8·00

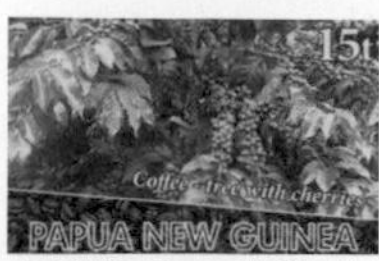

429 Coffee Tree with Cherries

2010. Coffee. Multicoloured.

1414	15t. Type **429**	40	60
1415	1k. Coffee nursery (budding)	80	50
1416	4k.65 Coffee green cherries	3·25	3·00
1417	6k.30 Coffee red cherries	5·00	6·00
MS1418	146×107 mm. 1k. Harvesting coffee; 3k. Coffee fermentation; 4k.65 Coffee drying parchment; 6k.30 Coffee green beans	11·50	11·50
MS1419	116×86 mm. 10k. Coffee cherries	8·00	8·00

430 Macgregor's Gardener Bowerbird (*Amblyornis macgregoriae*)

2010. Bowerbirds. Multicoloured.

1420	5t. Type **430**	30	1·00
1421	1k. Flame bowerbird (*Sericulus aureus*) (male with bower)	1·75	60
1422	4k.65 Archbold's bowerbird (*Archboldia papuensis*)	6·00	4·00
1423	6k.30 Adelbert regent bowerbird (*Sericulus bakeri*)	9·00	8·00
MS1424	106×146 mm. 1k. Flame bowerbird (*Sericulus aureus*) (pair); 3k. Yellow-fronted gardener bowerbird (*Amblyornis flavifrons*); 4k.65 Vogelkop gardener bowerbird (*Amblyornis inornatus*); 6k.30 Lauterbach's bowerbird (*Chlamydera lautabachi*)	17·00	15·00
MS1425	86×116 mm. 10k. Flame bowerbird (*Sericulus aureus*) (close-up of male)	10·00	10·00

431 Rugby Sevens

2010. 19th Commonwealth Games, Delhi. Multicoloured.

1426	1k. Type **431**	1·00	50
1427	3k. Boxing	2·75	1·75
1428	4k.65 Netball	3·25	3·00
1429	6k.30 Hurdling	5·00	6·00
MS1430	146×106 mm. 1k. Power lifting; 3k. Swimming; 4k.65 Bowling; 6k.30 Sprinting	12·00	12·00
MS1431	87×116 mm. 10k. Tennis	8·00	8·00

432 *Dendrobium lasianthera* 'May River Red'

2010. Orchids. Multicoloured.

1432	1k. Type **432**	1·00	50
1433	3k. *Dendrobium violaceoflavens* J. J. Smith	2·75	1·75
1434	4k.65 *Dendrobium mirbelianum* var. Vanimo	3·25	3·00
1435	6k.30 *Dendrobium helix*	5·00	6·00
MS1436	146×106 mm. 1k. *Dendrobium nindii* W. Hill; 3k. *Dendrobium* sp. *aff. D. gouldii Reichb.f.*; 4k.65 *Dendrobium gouldii Reichb.f.* var. Bougainville White; 6k.30 *Dendrobium discolor* var. pink Bensbach	12·00	12·00
MS1437	116×87 mm. 10k. *Dendrobium lasianthera* var. Sepik Blue	8·00	8·00

433 Mother Teresa, New Delhi, 1997

2010. Birth Centenary of Mother Teresa (founder of Missionaries of Charity). Multicoloured.

1438	1k. Type **433**	1·00	50
1439	3k. On visit to Rome, Italy, 1971	2·75	1·75
1440	4k.65 Mother Teresa in 1988	3·25	3·00
1441	6k.30 Arriving in Bhopal, India, 1984	5·00	6·00

434 Pope John Paul II meeting Pilgrims, Czestochowa

2010. Fifth Death Anniv of Pope John Paul II. Multicoloured.

MS1442	112×152 mm. 5t. Type **434**; 10t. In Nigeria; 1k. In Poland (giving blessing); 3k. In Poland (wearing mitre); 4k.65 Greeting Easter crowds, St. Peter's Square, Rome; 6k.30 In England	12·00	12·00

435 Pope Benedict XVI

2010. Fifth Anniv of Pontificate of Pope Benedict XVI

MS1443	**435** 10k. multicoloured	10·00	10·00

436 *Nephila pilipes*

2010. Spiders. Multicoloured.

1444	1k. Type **436**	1·40	80
1445	3k. *Argiope aemula*	3·50	2·75
1446	4k.65 *Gasteracantha* (black and yellow spider)	5·00	4·00
1447	6k.30 *Cyrtophora moluccensis*	7·00	8·00
MS1448	106×146 mm. 1k. *Leucauge celebesiana*; 3k. *Holconia*; 4k.65 *Gasterocantha* (black and white spider); 6k.30 *Ocrisiona*	14·00	14·00
MS1449	86×116 mm. 10k. *Nephila pilipes* (different)	12·00	12·00

437 Warrior with Bow and Arrow, Western Highlands Province

2010. Traditional Dance (2nd series). War. Multicoloured.

1450	50t. Type **437**	40	40
1451	1k.05 Simbu warrior with spear, Chimbu Province	85	60
1452	5k. Warrior with spear and shield, Western Highlands Province	4·00	4·25
1453	7k. Mudman with bow and arrow, Eastern Highlands Province	6·00	7·00
MS1454	86×116 mm. 10k. Tasman Island knife dancer, North Solomons Province	8·25	8·50

438 Emerald Tree Monitor (Varanus prasinus)

2011. Monitor Lizards. Multicoloured.

1455	1k.05 Type **438**	1·00	50
1456	5k. Papuan argus monitor (*Varanus panoptes horni*)	4·00	3·25
1457	5k. Papuan Monitor (*Varanus salvadori*)	4·00	3·25
1458	7k. Blue-tailed monitor (*Varanus doreanus*) (head and front foot)	5·50	6·50
MS1459	146×107 mm. 1k.05 Blue-tailed monitor (*Varanus doreanus*); 2k. Spotted tree monitor (*Varanus similis*); 5k. Mangrove monitor (*Varanus indicus*); 5k. Peach-throat monitor (*Varanus jobiensis*)	14·00	14·00
MS1460	116×86 mm. 5k. Papuan argus monitor (*Varanus panoptes horni*) (head)	5·00	5·00

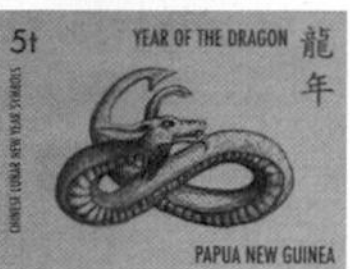

439 Year of the Dragon

2011. Chinese Lunar New Year Symbols. Multicoloured.

1461	5t. Type **439**	15	50
1462	50t. Year of the Tiger	75	70
1463	1k.05 Year of the Horse	1·25	75
1464	2k. Year of the Monkey	1·50	1·50
1465	5k. Year of the Snake	4·50	5·00
1466	5k. Year of the Dog	4·50	5·00
MS1467	150×101 mm. 5t. Cow and calf ('Year of the Ox'); 50t. Year of the Rooster; 55t. Year of the Sheep; 1k.05 Year of the Rat; 5k. Year of the Boar; 7k. Year of the Rabbit	11·50	11·50

440 *Pailet draivim balus* (Pilot flying an aeroplane) (Mathias Kauage)

2011. Pioneer Arts (4th issue) by Mathias Kauage. Multicoloured.

1468	1k.05 Type **440**	1·00	50
1469	5k. *Fes Misineri* (First Missionary)	4·00	3·25
1470	5k. *Pailet i trein long draivim balus* (Trainee pilot at training)	4·00	3·25
1471	7k. *Eia bas* (Air Niugini's Airbus)	5·50	6·50
MS1472	146×106 mm. Design as No. 1471: 1k.05 Top left portion; 5k. Top right portion; 5k. Bottom left portion; 7k. Bottom right portion	16·00	16·00
MS1473	86×116 mm. 10k. *Barasut man* (Parachute man)	9·00	9·00

441 *Cephalopholis miniata* (coral hind)

2011. Reef Fish (Grouper). Multicoloured.

1474	1k.05 Type **441**	1·50	1·25
1475	1k.05 *Cromileptes altivelis* (mouse grouper)	1·50	1·25
1476	5k. *Plectropomus areolatus* (Square tail coral grouper)	5·50	5·00
1477	7k. *Epinephelus lanceolatus* (giant grouper)	7·50	8·00
MS1478	116×86 mm. 10k. *Epinephelus polyphekadion* (camouflage grouper)	13·00	13·00

442 Abraham Lincoln

2011. Abraham Lincoln (US President 1861-5) Commemoration and 150th Anniv of the American Civil War. Multicoloured.

1479	1k. Type **442**	1·00	70
1480	1k.05 Abraham Lincoln and 'Of the people by the people for the people'	1·00	70
1481	5k. Shackled slave	5·00	4·50

1482	7k. Abraham Lincoln, Jefferson Davis and Union and Confederate flags	7·00	8·00
MS1483	146×106 mm. 5t. Sherman, Grant, Lincoln and Porter ('The Peacemakers'); 50t. Fort Sumter burning; 55t. Pres. Lincoln with cabinet ('Emancipation Proclamation'); 1k.05 Pres. Lincoln, General Grant and General Lee; 5k. Pres. Lincoln, negro and 'If Slavery is not wrong, nothing is wrong'; 7k. Battle of Gettysburg	12·50	12·50
MS1484	87×117 mm. 10k. Pres. Lincoln ('A house divided cannot stand')	8·75	8·75

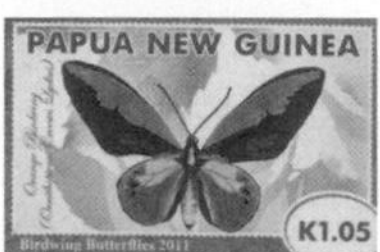

443 Orange Birdwing (*Ornithoptera croesus lydias*)

2011. Birdwing Butterflies. Multicoloured.

1485	1k.05 Type **443**	1·75	1·25
1486	1k.05 Green birdwing (*Ornithoptera priamus*)	1·75	1·25
1487	5k. Blue birdwing (*Ornithoptera urvillianus*)	6·50	4·75
1488	7k. Goliath birdwing (*Ornithoptera goliathus*)	8·50	8·50
MS1489	87×116 mm. 10k. Pair of Queen Alexandra's birdwing (*Ornithoptera alexandrae*)	14·00	13·00

444 African Queen Pineapple Variety sliced

2011. Pineapple Fragrance. Multicoloured.

1490	1k.05 Type **444**	1·25	1·00
1491	1k.05 African Queen and Hawaiian pineapple species sliced	1·25	1·00
1492	5k. Two African Queen in basket and Hawaiian pineapple species	5·00	4·50
1493	7k. Two African and one Hawaiian species pineapples in two baskets	7·00	8·00
MS1494	146×107 mm. 10t. Tops of two pineapples and growing pineapples; 2k. Pineapple and top of pineapple; 5k. Two pineapples in dish and growing pineapples (at left); 7k. Two pineapples in dish and growing pineapples (at right)	13·00	13·00
MS1495	117×86 mm. 10k. African pineapple species sliced into three portions	9·50	9·50

445 Yumi Lukautim Mosbi Logo

2011. Urban Safety and Crime Prevention (Yumi Lukautim Mosbi) ("Law and Justice"). Multicoloured.

1496	5t. Type **445**	15	50
1497	1k.05 Gun free zone emblem ('Krismas SEIF Kempan')	1·50	75
1498	5k. Meri Seif Ples logo	5·00	4·50
1499	7k. Certificate of Recognition by UN-Habitat	7·00	8·00
MS1500	146×107 mm. 1k.05 Women's Resource Centre, Kaugere; 1k.05 Krismas SEIF Kempan members; 5k. Stop and shop supermarkets ('Meri SEIF Ples'); 7k. Port Moresby Chamber of Commerce and Industry emblem ('Innovative Job Creation')	13·50	13·50
MS1501	116×86 mm. 10k. Yumi Lukautim Mosbi logo ('Linking Government, Private Sector and Community')	9·50	9·50

446 Harvesting Cocoa Pods

2011. Cocoa in Papua New Guinea. Multicoloured.

1502	5t. Type **446**	15	50
1503	1k.05 Breaking cocoa pod	1·50	75
1504	5k. Drying cocoa	5·00	4·50
1505	7k. Exporting cocoa bags	7·00	8·00
MS1506	145×107 mm. 1k.05 Cocoa seedling; 1k.05 Cocoa flower; 5k. Pruning cocoa trees; 7k. Cocoa pods	13·50	13·50
MS1507	117×86 mm. 10k. Exporting cocoa bags, Rabaul Harbour	9·50	9·50

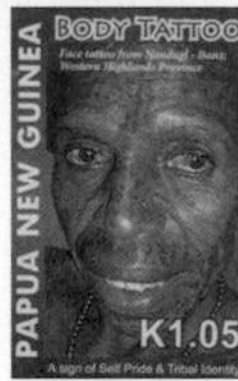

447 Face Tattoo from Nondugl-Banz, Western Highlands Province

2011. Body Tattoos. Multicoloured.

1508	1k.05 Type **447**	80	70
1509	1k.05 Face tattoo from Tufi, Popondetta, Oro Province	80	70
1510	5k. Face tattoo from Asaro, Eastern Highlands Province	3·50	3·00
1511	7k. Face tattoo from Kudjip, Western Highlands Province	5·50	6·50
MS1512	147×106 mm. 1k.05 Arm tattoo from Kairuku, Central Province; 1k.05 Chest tattoo from Gumine, Simbu Province; 5k. Leg tattoo from South Whagi, Western Highlands Province; 7k. Eagle arm tattoo from Minei tribe, Manus, Manus Province	13·50	13·50
MS1513	117×87 mm. 10k.Face tattoo from Tufi, Popondetta, Oro Province	9·50	9·50

448 Weaned Chick feeding

2011. Southern Cassowary (*Casuarius casuarius*). Multicoloured.

1514	1k.05 Type **448**	1·60	1·25
1515	1k.05 Two newly weaned chicks feeding	1·60	1·25
1516	5k. Adult feeding	6·00	4·50
1517	7k. Two adults, showing detail of head	8·00	7·50
MS1518	146×107 mm. 1k05 Head and shoulder of adult; 1k.05 Back hump of adult; 5k. Chick; 7k. Legs of adult	14·00	14·00
MS1519	116×87 mm. 10k. Adult in forest, waterfall in background	13·00	13·00

449 Kesesoru Falls, Eastern Highlands Province

2011. Waterfalls. Multicoloured.

1520	1k.05 Type **449**	1·40	1·25
1521	1k.05 Aerial view of Mageni Falls, East New Britain Province	1·40	1·25
1522	5k. Outlet of Mageni Falls, East New Britain Province	5·00	4·00
1523	7k. Waghi Falls, Western Highland Province	7·00	8·00
MS1524	146×106 mm. 1k.05 Sogeri Falls, Central Province; 1k.05 Beaver Falls, Southern Highlands Province; 5k. Wawoi Falls, Western Province; 7k. Remote Island Falls, East New Britain Province	14·00	14·00
MS1525	115×87 mm. 10k. Ambua Falls, Southern Highlands Province	10·00	10·00

450 Catherine, Duchess of Cambridge

2011. Royal Wedding. Multicoloured.

1526	1k.05 Type **450**	1·40	1·25
1527	1k.05 Miss Catherine Middleton and bridesmaid Pippa Middleton	1·40	1·25
1528	5k. Prince William	5·00	4·00
1529	7k. Duke and Duchess of Cambridge	7·00	8·00
MS1530	106×146 mm. 1k.05 Catherine, Duchess of Cambridge (in profile); 1k.05 Duke and Duchess of Cambridge waving; 5k. Duke and Duchess of Cambridge; 7k. Prince William (in profile)	14·50	14·50
MS1531	117×86 mm. 10k. Profiles of Duke and Duchess of Cambridge	10·50	10·50

451 American B-17E Plane 41-2446 ("The Swamp Ghost")

2011. War Relics. Multicoloured.

1532	1k.05 Type **451**	1·50	1·25
1533	1k.05 Japanese Ki-21 Sally plane at former Lakunai Airport, Rabaul	1·50	1·25
1534	5k. Wreckage of American P-38F-42-12647 S plane on salt flats near Lea Lea	5·50	4·00
1535	7k. Wreckage of American B-17E plane 41-9234 at Black Cap Pass	7·50	8·00
MS1536	116×86 mm. 1k.05 Japanese 95 Ha Go tanker; 1k.05 Wreckage of Australian RAAF Hudson A16-91 plane; 5k. New Zealand RNZAF PV-1 Ventura NZ4613 Tail 13; 7k. Japanese 120mm dual purpose gun, Kokopo War Museum	16·00	16·00
MS1537	116×86 mm. 10k. Underwater wreckage of American B-17F "Black Jack" plane, Milne Bay Province	12·00	12·00

452 Kiriwina, Milne Bay Province

2011. Traditional Dance (3rd series). Victory. Multicoloured.

1538	1k.05 Type **452**	1·40	1·25
1539	1k.05 Oro, Northern Province	1·40	1·25
1540	5k. Kandep, Enga Province	5·00	4·00
1541	7k. Siasi, Morobe Province	7·00	8·00
MS1542	146×106 mm. 1k.05 Kerowagi, Simbu Province; 1k.05 Tolai, East New Britain Province; 5k. Rigo, Central Province; 7k. Huli, Southern Highlands Province	15·00	15·00
MS1543	116×86 mm. 10k. Baining fire dancer, East New Britain Province	10·50	10·50

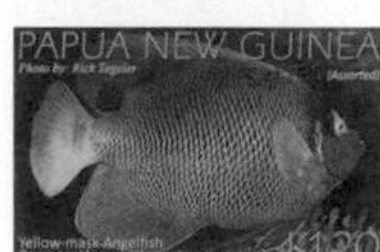

453 Yellow-mask Angelfish (*Pomacanthus xanthometopon*)

2012. Reef Fish. Multicoloured.

1544	1k.20 Type **453**	1·75	1·50
1545	1k.20 Emperor angelfish (*Pomacanthus imperator*)	1·75	1·50
1546	6k. Meyer's butterflyfish (*Chaetodon meyeri*)	6·50	5·50
1547	8k. Barrier reef anemonefish (*Amphiprion akindynos*)	8·50	9·50
MS1548	146×106 mm. 1k.20 Clown anemonefish (*Amphiprion percula*); 1k.20 Clown triggerfish (*Balistoides conspicullum*); 6k. Clark's anemonefish (*Amphiprion clarkii*); 8k. Spotfin lionfish (*Pterois antennata*)	17·00	17·00
MS1549	117×86 mm. 10k. Bearded scorpionfish (*Scorpaenopsis cirrhosa*)	10·50	10·50

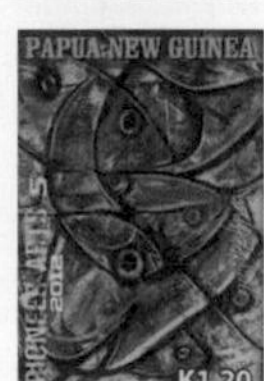

454 *Fish Berserk*

2012. Pioneer Art (5th series) by Philip Yobale. Multicoloured.

1550	1k.20 Type **454**	1·50	1·25
1551	1k.20 *Facing Faces*	1·50	1·25
1552	6k. *Face without Eye*	6·00	4·75
1553	8k. *Regiana Bird of Paradise*	8·00	9·00
MS1554	119×86 mm. 1k20 Montage of three faces; 1k.20 Face; 6k. Eye and profiles; 8k. Montage of faces (all untitled)	15·00	15·00
MS1555	120×86 mm. 10k. *On-looking Eyes*	10·50	10·50

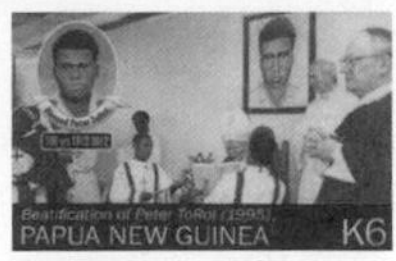

455 Beatification of Peter To Rot, 1995

2012. Birth Centenary of Peter To Rot (Catholic martyr). Multicoloured.

1556	1k.20 Type **455**	1·50	1·25
1557	1k.20 Peter ToRot baptising child	1·50	1·25
1558	6k. Beatification of Peter To Rot, 1995 (different)	6·00	4·75
1559	8k. Peter To Rot giving Holy Communion	8·00	9·00
MS1560	117×86 mm. 1k.20 Peter To Rot in Taliligap Catechist School; 1k.20 Peter To Rot conducting Matrimony; 6k. Peter To Rot leading Worship and Devotion; 8k. Peter To Rot murdered in prison cell by Japanese, 1945	15·00	15·00
MS1561	117×86 mm. 10k. Statue of Peter To Rot	10·50	10·50

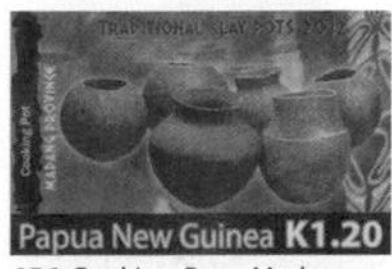

456 Cooking Pots, Madang Province

2012. Traditional Clay Cooking Pots. Multicoloured.

1562	1k.20 Type **456**	1·50	1·25
1563	1k.20 Cooking pot, Central Province	1·50	1·25
1564	6k. Cooking pot, Bougainville	6·00	4·75
1565	8k. Cooking pot, East Sepik Province	8·00	9·00
MS1566	116×86 mm. 1k.20 Cooking pot, Milne Bay Province (terracotta); 1k.20 Cooking pot, Milne Bay Province (dark grey); 6k. Cooking pot, East Sepik Province; 8k. Cooking pot, Manus Bay Province	15·00	15·00
MS1567	116×86 mm. 10k. Cooking pot, West Sepik Province	10·50	10·50

457 Common Grey Cuscus (*Phalanger orientalis*)

2012. Cuscus and Possums. Multicoloured.

1568	1k.20 Type **457**	1·50	1·25
1569	1k.20 Common Spotted Cuscus (*Spilocuscus maculatus*) (male)	1·50	1·25
1570	6k. Black Spotted Cuscus (*Spilocuscus rufoniger*)	6·00	4·75
1571	8k. Woodlark Cuscus (*Phalanger lullulae*)	8·00	9·00
MS1572	126×86 mm. 1k.20 Sugar Glider (*Petaurus breviceps*); 1k.20 Feather-tail Possum (*Distoechurus pennatus*); 6k. Striped Possum (*Dactylopsila trivirgata*); 8k. Northern Glider (*Petaurus abidi*)	15·00	15·00
MS1573	115×85 mm. 10k. Common Spotted Cuscus (*Spilocuscus maculatus*) (different)	10·50	10·50

458 Iamo Launa (athletics)

2012. Sports Legends. Multicoloured.

1574	1k.20 Type **458**	1·50	1·25
1575	1k.20 Martin Beni (boxing)	1·50	1·25
1576	6k. Stanley Nandex (kick boxing)	6·00	4·75
1577	8k. Will Genia (rugby union)	8·00	9·00
MS1578	116×86 mm. 1k.20 Tau John (marathon running); 1k.20 Iwila Jacobs (weight lifting); 6k. Takale Tuna (athletics); 8k. John Aba (boxing)	15·00	15·00
MS1579	10k. Will Genia (rugby union) (different)	10·50	10·50

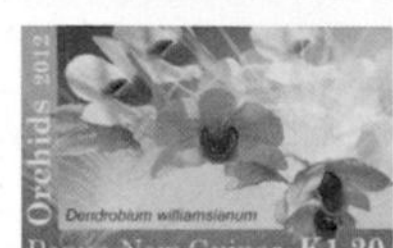

459 *Dendrobium williamsianum*

2012. Orchids. Multicoloured.

1580 1k.20 Type **459** 1·75 1·25
1581 1k.20 *Dendrobium macrophyllum* 1·75 1·25
1582 6k. *Dendrobium bracteosum* (pink) 6·50 4·75
1583 8k. *Philaenopsis amabilis* 8·50 9·00
MS1584 116×86 mm. 1k.20 *Dendrobium bracteosum* (white); 1k.20 *Dendrobium bifalce*; 6k. *Dendrobium strepsiceros*; 8k. *Vanda hindsii* 17·00 16·00
MS1585 117×86 mm. 10k. *Dendrobium spectabile* 12·00 12·00

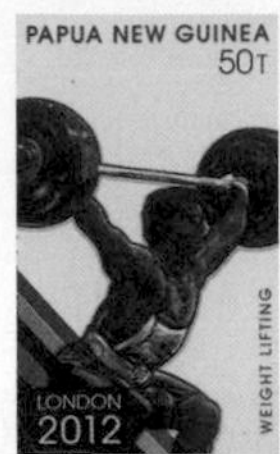

460 Weightlifting

2012. Olympic Games, London. Multicoloured.

MS1586 146×106 mm. 50t. Type **460**; 55t. Swimming; 1k. Relay race 2·50 2·75
MS1587 116×86 mm. 5k. Boxing 4·75 5·00

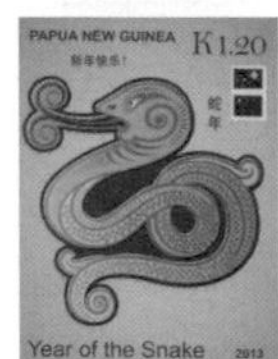

461 Snake

2012. Chinese New Year. Year of the Snake. Multicoloured: background colours given.

1588 **461** 1k.20 pale new blue 1·50 1·25
1589 **461** 1k.20 mauve 1·50 1·25
1590 6k. orange-yellow 6·00 4·75
1591 8k. bright green 8·00 9·00
MS1592 86×117 mm. **461** 1k.20 pale apple-green; 1k.20 orange-yellow; 6k. bright purple; 8k. pale blue 15·00 15·00
MS1593 86×116 mm. **461** 10k. greenish yellow 10·50 10·50

462 Man wearing Penis Gourd, Telefomin, Sandaun Province

2012. Traditional Cloths. Multicoloured.

1594 1k.20 Type **462** 1·50 1·25
1595 1k.20 Woman wearing traditional grass skirt, Pomio, East New Britain 1·50 1·25
1596 6k. Women wearing traditional grass skirts, Central Province 6·00 4·75
1597 8k. Duna woman wearing grass skirt made from reeds and traditional rain covering made from pandanus leaves, and carrying child 8·00 9·00
MS1598 86×116 mm. 1k.20 Mendi bride painted black and dressed in tree bark fibres, Southern Highlands Province; 1k.20 Tari woman wearing grass skirt and tree bark rain covering over her head and back, Southern Highlands Province; 6k. Woman wearing grass skirt and carrying child, and man wearing pandanus pants, Tobriand Islands; 8k. Mukawa women wearing grass skirts made from pandanus and banana leaves, Milne Bay Province 15·00 15·00
MS1599 86×116 mm. 10k. Popondetta widows wearing tapa cloth (from tree bark) during mourning 10·50 10·50

463 Prince of Wales and Duchess of Cornwall (visit to Papua New Guinea)

2012. Diamond Jubilee. Multicoloured.

1600 25t. Type **463** 45 45
1601 50t. Prince of Wales, Commander and Chief of Papua New Guinea Defence Force 75 60
1602 1k. Prince of Wales and Duchess of Cornwall on their wedding day and Queen Elizabeth II and Prince Philip 1·25 75
1603 1k.20 Prince of Wales in Papua New Guinea, 1975 1·50 1·25
1604 6k. Queen Elizabeth II and Prince of Wales 6·00 4·75
1605 8k. Queen Elizabeth II and Prince Philip 8·00 9·00
MS1606 211×148 mm. 10k. Queen Elizabeth II (vert) 11·00 11·00

464 PMV (Passenger Motor Vehicle) Truck – Rural Routes

2013. Public Transport. Multicoloured.

1607 1k.30 Type **464** 1·75 1·25
1608 1k.30 Banana boat - coastline service 1·75 1·25
1609 6k. Airline - Remote Service 6·00 4·75
1610 8k.70 Trading canoe - open sea 8·00 9·00
MS1611 117×86 mm. 1k.30 Taxi - Urban Routes; 1k30 PMV (Passenger Motor Vehicle) Bus - Urban/Highway Routes; 6k. Airline - Domestic/International; 8k.70 Marine Vessel - Coastal Islands 16·00 16·00
MS1612 117×86 mm. 10k. Dugout Canoe - Rivers/Lakes 10·50 10·50

465 *Kundu* Slit Gong

2013. Pioneer Art (6th series). Metal Sculptures by Gickmai Kundun. Multicoloured.

1613 1k.30 Type **465** 1·50 1·25
1614 1k.30 *Hiri Trade Canoe* (Lakatoi) 1·50 1·25
1615 6k. *Hiri Moale Queen* 6·00 4·75
1616 8k.70 *Bird of Paradise* 8·00 9·00
MS1617 87×117 mm. 1k.30 *Follow the Leader*; 1k.30 *Walking Together*; 6k. *Relieving Education Burden*; 8k.70 *Inherited Believe System* 15·00 15·00
MS1618 88×116 mm. 10k. *Indo-Pacific Lionfish* (*Pterois*) 10·50 10·50

466 Pres. John F. Kennedy

2013. 50th Death Anniv of Pres. John F. Kennedy (1917-63, US President 1961-3)

1619 1k.30 Type **466** 1·50 1·25
1620 1k.30 Pres. Kennedy, Mrs. Kennedy and Vice President Lyndon Johnson 1·50 1·25
1621 6k. Pres. Kennedy riding in open car in motorcade 6·00 4·75
1622 8k.70 US servicemen carrying US flag 8·00 9·00
MS1623 115×86 mm. 1k.30 Pres. Kennedy and US flag; 1k.30 Pres. and Mrs. Kennedy; 6k. Pres. Kennedy's coffin lying in state; 8k.70 Vice President Lyndon Johnson taking the oath 15·00 15·00
MS1624 116×86 mm. 10k. Pres. John F. Kennedy (vert) 10·50 10·50

467 Cassava (*Manihot esculerta Crantz*)

2013. Root Crops. Multicoloured.

1625 1k.30 Type **467** 1·50 1·25
1626 1k.30 Chinese Taro (*Xanthosoma sagittifolium*) 1·50 1·25
1627 6k. Sweet Potato (*Ipomoea batatas*) 6·00 4·75
1628 8k.70 Taro (*Colocasia esculenta*) 8·00 9·00
MS1629 116×87 mm. 1k.30 Five Leaflet Yam (*Dioscorea pentaphylla L.*); 1k.30 Lesser Yam (*Dioscorea esculenta* (*Loureiro*) *Burkil*); 6k. Greater Yam (*Dioscorea alata L*); 8k.70 Nummularia Yam (*Dioscorea mummularia Lamarck.*) 15·00 15·00
MS1630 116×87 mm. 10k. Queensland Arrowroot (*Canna edulis*) 10·50 10·50

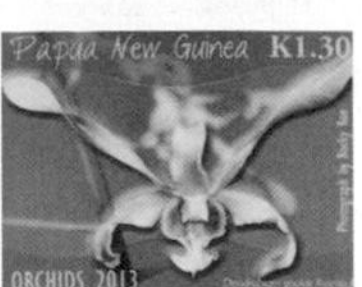

468 *Dendrobium gouldii Reichb. f.*

2013. Orchids. Multicoloured.

1631 1k.30 Type **468** 1·75 1·25
1632 1k.30 *Dendrobium lineale* var. Kui Island Blue 1·75 1·25
1633 6k. *Dendrobium mirbelianum* Gaudich 6·50 4·75
1634 8k.70 *Dendrobium* sp. *aff. D. cochilioides* Schltr. 8·50 9·00
MS1635 116×86 mm. 1k.30 *Dendrobium* sp. *aff. D. gouldii* Reichb. f.; 1k.30 *Dendrobium* sp. *aff. D. conanthum* Schltr.; 6k. *Dendrobium lineale*; 8k.70 *Den. carronii* Lavarack & P. J. Cribb 17·00 14·50
MS1636 116×87 mm. 10k. *Dendrobium mussauense* P. Ormd. 12·00 12·00

469 Salyut 6 Space Station

2013. 15th Anniv of Launch of International Space Station. Multicoloured.

1637 1k.30 Type **469** 1·50 1·25
1638 1k.30 Skylab Space Station 1·50 1·25
1639 6k. Spacehab 6·00 4·75
1640 8k.70 Mir Space Station 8·00 9·00
MS1641 116×86 mm. 1k.30 Skylab Space Station; 1k.30 Salyut Space Station; 6k. Shuttle's atmospheric re-entry; 8k.70 Mir Space Station 15·00 15·00
MS1642 116×86 mm. 10k. Shuttle as seen from Space Station window 10·50 10·50

470 Common 'Tolai' Carry Basket, East New Britain Province

2013. Woven Baskets. Multicoloured.

1643 1k.30 Type **470** 1·50 1·25
1644 1k.30 Pepeni (yam basket), Kitava Island, Milne Bay Province 1·50 1·25
1645 6k. Multicoloured carry basket with handle, Milne Bay Province 6·00 4·75
1646 8k.70 Carry baskets, lalibu, Southern Highlands Province 8·00 9·00
MS1647 116×86 mm. 1k.30 Common Sepik basket, East Sepik Province; 1k.30 Check pattern carry basket with popper fastening, Milne Bay Province; 6k. Carry basket, Gulf Province; 8k.70 Manus carry basket, Manus Province 15·00 15·00
MS1648 116×86 mm. 10k. Temporary palm leaf baskets (bombom), Coastal and Island Provinces 10·50 10·50

471 Green Coconuts

2013. Coconuts (*Cocos nucifera*). Multicoloured.

1649 4k. Type **471** 3·00 3·00
1650 6k. Coconut husking (exocarp) 4·25 4·25
1651 8k.70 Coconut juice (liquid endosperm) 6·25 6·25
1652 12k. Coconut meat (endosperm) 8·75 8·75
MS1653 116×86 mm. 1k. Dry coconut; 1k.30 Three coconuts, one with new shoot (inner shell (endocarp)); 6k. One halved coconut (Meat (endosperm)); 8k.70 Apple (cotyledon) 11·50 11·50
MS1654 116×86 mm. 10k. Coconuts with new leaves (inner shell (endocarp)) 7·25 7·25

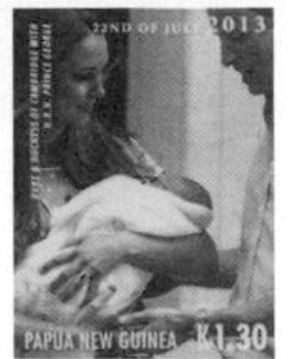

472 Duke and Duchess of Cambridge with Prince George

2013. Birth of Prince George of Cambridge. Multicoloured.

1655 1k.30 Type **472** 1·50 1·25
1656 1k.30 Prince William Duke of Cambridge holding Prince George 1·50 1·25
1657 6k. Catherine, Duchess of Cambridge holding Prince George 6·00 4·75
1658 8k.70 Catherine, Duchess of Cambridge handing Prince George to Duke of Cambridge 8·00 9·00
MS1659 116×86 mm. Nos. 1655/8 15·00 15·00
MS1660 116×86 mm. 10k. Prince George 10·50 10·50

473 Fish Drying on Platform

2013. Cooking Methods. Multicoloured.

1661 1k.30 Type **473** 95 95
1662 1k.30 Food boiling in clay pot 95 95
1663 6k. Fish drying in clay jar 4·25 4·25
1664 8k.70 Corn roasting in open fire 6·25 6·25
MS1665 116×86 mm. 1k.30 Mumu pit; 1k.30 Heating stones in pit; 6k. Food placed in mumu pit with fire on top 11·50 11·50
MS1666 117×86 mm. 10k. Cooking aigir (chicken, greens, banana and coconut cream heated in pot with hot stones) 7·25 7·25

POSTAGE DUE STAMPS

1960. Stamps of 1952 surch **POSTAL CHARGES** and value.

In (A) value and "POSTAGE" is obliterated by a solid circle and a series of "IX's" but these are omitted in (B).

D1 6d. on 7½d. blue (A) £850 £450

D2 1d. on 6½d. purple 2·50 4·00
D3 3d. on ½d. green 4·25 1·25
D4 6d. on 7½d. blue (B) 40·00 5·50
D5 1s.3d. on 3½d. black 2·50 1·25
D6 3s. on 2½d. orange 10·00 2·25

D3

1960

D7 **D3** 1d. orange 55 75
D8 **D3** 3d. brown 60 60
D9 **D3** 6d. blue 65 30
D10 **D3** 9d. red 65 1·50
D11 **D3** 1s. green 65 35
D12 **D3** 1s.3d. violet 1·00 1·00
D13 **D3** 1s.6d. blue 2·75 4·50
D14 **D3** 3s. yellow 1·00 35

Pt. 20

PARAGUAY

A republic in the centre of S. America, independent since 1811.

1870. 8 reales = 1 peso.
1878. 100 centavos = 1 peso.
1944. 100 centimos = 1 guarani.

1

1870. Various frames. Values in "reales". Imperf.

1	**1**	1r. red	4·50	8·25
3	**1**	2r. blue	90·00	£100
4	**1**	3r. black	£160	£180

1878. Handstamped with large 5. Imperf.

5	**1**	5c. on 1r. red	£100	£130
9	**1**	5c. on 2r. blue	£500	£425
13	**1**	5c. on 3r. black	£600	£600

7

1879. Prepared for use but not issued (wrong currency). Values in "reales". Perf.

14	**7**	5r. orange	80	
15	**7**	10r. brown	95	

1879. Values in "centavos". Perf.

16	**7**	5c. brown	1·20	1·10
17	**7**	10c. green	3·75	3·75

1881. Handstamped with large figures.

18	**7**	1 on 10c. green	17·00	16·00
19	**7**	2 on 10c. green	17·00	16·00

1881. As T **1** (various frames), but value in "centavos". Perf.

20	**1**	1c. blue	90	85
21a	**1**	2c. red	65	95
22	**1**	4c. brown	65	65

1884. No. 1 handstamped with large 1. Imperf.

23	**1**	1c. on 1r. red	7·25	7·00

13

1884. Perf.

24	**13**	1c. green	65	85
25	**13**	2c. red	50	55
26	**13**	5c. blue	75	70

24

1887

32	**24**	1c. green	20	15
33a	**24**	2c. red	25	15
34	**24**	5c. blue	25	15
35	**24**	7c. brown	65	50
36	**24**	10c. mauve	55	35
37	**24**	15c. orange	55	35
38	**24**	20c. pink	55	35
50	**24**	40c. blue	2·40	1·20
51	**24**	60c. orange	1·00	55
52	**24**	80c. blue	90	55
53	**24**	1p. green	90	55

25

1889. Imperf or perf.

40	**25**	15c. purple	1·80	1·50

27 C. Rivarola

1892

42	**27**	1 CENTAVOS grey	20	10
54	**27**	1 CENTAVO grey	20	10
43	-	2c. green	20	10
44	-	4c. red	20	10
57	-	5c. purple	20	20
46	-	10c. violet	20	20
47	-	14c. brown	55	55
48	-	20c. red	90	55
49	-	30c. green	1·30	85
84	-	1p. blue	45	20

PORTRAITS: 2c. S. Jovellano; 4c. J. Bautista Gil; 5c. H. Uriarte; 10c. C. Barreiro; 14c. Gen. B. Caballero; 20c. Gen. P. Escobar; 30c. J. Gonzales; 1p. J. B. Egusquisa.

1892. 400th Anniv of Discovery of America. No. 46 optd **1492 12 DE OCTUBRE 1892** in oval.

41	10c. violet	6·00	2·75

1895. Surch **PROVISORIO 5**.

59	**24**	5c. on 7c. brown	55	55

30

1896. Telegraph stamps as T **30** surch **CORREOS 5 CENTAVOS** in oval.

60	**30**	5c. on 2c. brown, blk & grey	55	30
61	**30**	5c. on 4c. orange, blk & grey	55	30

1898. Surch **Provisorio 10 Centavos**.

63	**24**	10c. on 15c. orange	55	45
62	**24**	10c. on 40c. blue	20	20

1900. Telegraph stamps as T **30** surch with figures of value twice and bar.

64	**30**	5c. on 30c. green, blk & grey	1·80	1·20
65	**30**	10c. on 50c. lilac, blk & grey	4·00	2·75

39

1900

76	**39**	1c. green	20	20
67	**39**	2c. grey	20	20
73	**39**	2c. pink	45	20
68	**39**	3c. brown	20	20
78	**39**	4c. blue	20	20
69	**39**	5c. green	20	20
74	**39**	5c. brown	45	20
79	**39**	5c. lilac	20	20
80	**39**	8c. brown	35	30
71	**39**	10c. red	35	20
72	**39**	24c. blue	55	55
82	**39**	28c. orange	75	65
83	**39**	40c. blue	65	55

1902. Surch **Habilitado en** and new values.

88	-	1c. on 14c. brown (No. 47)	30	20
91	-	1c. on 1p. blue (No. 84)	30	25
86	**39**	5c. on 8c. brown (No. 80)	35	25
87	**39**	5c. on 28c. orange (No. 82)	35	25
89	**24**	5c. on 60c. orange (No. 51)	35	25
90	**24**	5c. on 80c. blue (No. 52)	30	25
85	**39**	20c. on 24c. blue (No. 72)	35	20

46

1903

92	**46**	1c. grey	30	25
93	**46**	2c. green	30	25
94a	**46**	5c. blue	45	25
95	**46**	10c. brown	45	25
96	**46**	20c. red	45	25
97	**46**	30c. blue	55	25
98	**46**	60c. violet	1·30	85

47

1903

99	**47**	1c. green	30	25
100	**47**	2c. orange	30	25
101	**47**	5c. blue	30	25
102	**47**	10c. violet	30	25
103	**47**	20c. green	90	45
104	**47**	30c. blue	1·00	25
105	**47**	60c. brown	1·10	65

48

1904

106	**48**	10c. blue	35	20

1904. End of successful Revolt against Govt. (begun in August). Surch **PAZ 12 Dic. 1904. 30 centavos.**

107	**48**	30c. on 10c. blue	55	30

50

51 National Palace, Asuncion

1905

108	**50**	1c. orange	35	25
109	**50**	1c. red	35	25
110	**50**	1c. blue	35	25
112	**50**	2c. green	41·00	
113	**50**	2c. red	35	25
114	**50**	5c. blue	35	25
116	**50**	5c. yellow	35	25
117	**50**	10c. brown	35	25
118	**50**	10c. green	35	25
119	**50**	10c. blue	35	25
120	**50**	20c. lilac	45	25
121	**50**	20c. brown	45	25
122	**50**	20c. green	35	25
123	**50**	30c. blue	45	25
124	**50**	30c. grey	45	25
125	**50**	30c. lilac	55	25
126	**50**	60c. brown	35	25
128	**50**	60c. pink	5·00	2·75
129	**51**	1p. black and red	1·80	95
130	**51**	1p. black and brown	65	30
131	**51**	1p. black and green	65	30
132	**51**	2p. black and blue	35	25
133	**51**	2p. black and red	45	25
134	**51**	2p. black and brown	35	25
135	**51**	5p. black and red	1·10	65
136	**51**	5p. black and blue	1·10	65
137	**51**	5p. black and green	1·10	65
138	**51**	10p. black and brown	1·10	65
139	**51**	10p. black and blue	1·00	65
141	**51**	20p. black and green	2·40	2·20
142	**51**	20p. black and yellow	2·40	2·20
143	**51**	20p. black and purple	2·40	2·20

1907. Surch **Habilitado en** and value and bars.

159	**50**	5c. on 1c. blue	30	25
145	**50**	5c. on 2c. green	35	25
160	**50**	5c. on 2c. red	30	25
172	**39**	5c. on 28c. orange	1·80	1·50
173	**39**	5c. on 40c. blue	55	45
162	**50**	5c. on 60c. pink	30	25
163	**50**	5c. on 60c. brown	30	25
175	**50**	20c. on 1c. blue	30	25
177	**50**	20c. on 2c. red	5·00	3·75
180	**24**	20c. on 2c. red	3·50	2·75
178	**50**	20c. on 30c. blue	2·10	2·00
179	**50**	20c. on 30c. lilac	30	25

1907. Official stamps surch **Habilitado en**, value and bars. Where not otherwise stated, the design is as T **50** but with "OFICIAL" below the lion.

149	-	5c. on 10c. brown	30	25
150	-	5c. on 10c. lilac	30	25
164	-	5c. on 10c. green	30	25
181	**24**	5c. on 15c. orange (No. O63)	3·75	2·30
151	-	5c. on 20c. green	55	45
152	-	5c. on 20c. lilac	55	45
166	-	5c. on 20c. brown	55	45
167	-	5c. on 20c. pink	55	45
182	**24**	5c. on 20c. pink (No. O64)	55·00	45·00
154	-	5c. on 30c. blue	30	25
157	**46**	5c. on 30c. blue (No. O104)	1·80	1·50
168	-	5c. on 30c. grey	30	25
169	-	5c. on 30c. yellow	30	25
183	**24**	5c. on 50c. grey (No. O65)	24·00	17·00
155	-	5c. on 60c. brown	30	25
158	**46**	5c. on 60c. violet (No. O105)	65	45
171	-	5c. on 60c. blue	30	25
174	**46**	20c. on 5c. blue (No. O101)	2·10	1·70
184	**24**	20c. on 5c. blue (No. O60)	2·10	1·70

1907. Official stamps, as T **50** and **51** with "OFICIAL" added, optd **Habilitado** and one bar.

146	5c. grey	55	25
148	5c. blue	55	25
185	1p. black and orange	55	55
186	1p. black and red	45	30

1907. Official stamps, as T **51** with "OFICIAL" added, surch **Habilitado 1908 UN CENTAVO** and bar.

188	1c. on 1p. black and red	30	25
189	1c. on 1p. black and brown	6·50	3·25

1908. Optd **1908**.

190	**50**	1c. green	15	15
191	**50**	5c. yellow	15	15
192	**50**	10c. brown	20	20
193	**50**	20c. orange	15	15
194	**50**	30c. red	30	25
195	**50**	60c. mauve	25	25
196	**51**	1p. blue	25	25

1909. Optd **1909**.

197	**50**	1c. blue	35	35
198	**50**	1c. red	30	25
199	**50**	5c. green	30	25
200	**50**	5c. orange	30	25
201	**50**	10c. red	30	25
202	**50**	10c. brown	30	25
203	**50**	20c. lilac	30	25
204	**50**	20c. yellow	35	30
205	**50**	30c. brown	75	65
206	**50**	30c. blue	65	55

62

1910

207	**62**	1c. brown	30	25
208	**62**	5c. lilac	30	25
209	**62**	5c. green	30	25
210	**62**	5c. blue	30	25
211	**62**	10c. green	30	25
212	**62**	10c. violet	30	25
213	**62**	10c. red	30	25
214	**62**	20c. red	30	25
215	**62**	50c. red	45	25
216	**62**	75c. blue	30	25

1911. No. 216 perf diagonally and each half used as 20c.

217	**62**	20c. (½ of 75c.) blue	30	20

63

1911. Independence Centenary.

218	**63**	1c. black and olive	20	10
219	**63**	2c. black and blue	20	20
220	**63**	5c. black and red	35	20
221	**63**	10c. brown and blue	35	20
222	**63**	20c. blue and olive	35	20
223	**63**	50c. blue and lilac	65	30
224	**63**	75c. purple and olive	65	30

1912. Surch **Habilitada en VEINTE** and thin bar.

225	**62**	20c. on 50c. red	30	20

65

1913

226	**65**	1c. black	30	10
227	**65**	2c. orange	30	10
228	**65**	5c. mauve	30	10
229	**65**	10c. green	30	10
230	**65**	20c. red	30	10
231	**65**	40c. red	30	10
232	**65**	75c. blue	30	10
233	**65**	80c. yellow	30	10
234	**65**	1p. blue	30	10
235	**65**	1p.25 blue	30	20
236	**65**	3p. green	30	20

1918. No. D242 surch **HABILITADO EN 0.05 1918** and bar.

237		5c. on 40c. brown	30	25

1918. Nos. D239/42 optd **HABILITADO 1918**.

238		5c. brown	20	20
239		10c. brown	20	20
240		20c. brown	30	20
241		40c. brown	30	20

1918. Surch **HABILITADO EN 0.30 1918** and bar.

242	**65**	30c. on 40c. red	10	10

1920. Surch **HABILITADO en**, value and **1920**.

243	**65**	50c. on 80c. yellow	20	20
244	**65**	1p.75 on 3p. green	1·10	95

1920. Nos. D243/4 optd **HABILITADO 1920** or surch also.

245		1p. brown	35	25
246		1p. on 1p.50 brown	35	25

72 Parliament House, Asuncion

1920. Jubilee of Constitution.

247	**72**	50c. black and red	35	25
248	**72**	1p. black and blue	1·00	45
249	**72**	1p.75 black and blue	20	25
250	**72**	3p. black and yellow	1·50	25

1920. Surch **50**.

251	**65**	50 on 75c. blue	45	25

1921. Surch **50** and two bars.

252	**62**	50 on 75c. blue	30	25
253	**65**	50 on 75c. blue	30	25

75

1922

254	**75**	50c. blue and red	30	20
255	**75**	1p. brown and blue	30	20

77 Starting-point of Conspirators

1922. Independence.

256	**77**	1p. blue	35	10
258	**77**	1p. blue and red	35	25
259	**77**	1p. grey and purple	35	25
260	**77**	1p. grey and orange	35	25
257	**77**	5p. purple	55	30
261	**77**	5p. brown and blue	55	30
262	**77**	5p. black and green	55	30
263	**77**	5p. blue and red	55	30

Between 1922 and 1936 many regular postage stamps were overprinted **C** (= Campana—country), these being used at post offices outside Asuncion but not for mail sent abroad. The prices quoted are for whichever is the cheapest.

1924. Surch **Habilitado en**, value and **1924**.

265	**65**	50c. on 75c. blue	30	25
266	**65**	$1 on 1p.25 blue	30	25
267	-	$1 on 1p.50 brown (No. D244)	30	25

80 Map

1924

268	**80**	1p. blue	20	10
269	**80**	2p. red	35	10
270	**80**	4p. blue	45	30

81 Gen. Jose E. Diaz

1925

271	**81**	50c. red	10	10
272	**81**	1p. blue	10	10
273	**81**	1p. green	20	10

82 Columbus

1925

274	**82**	1p. blue	20	10

1926. Surch **Habilitado en** and new value.

275	**62**	1c. on 5c. blue	10	10
276	**62**	$0.02 on 5c. blue	10	10
277	**65**	7c. on 40c. red	30	15
278	**65**	15c. on 75c. blue	10	10
279	**50**	$0.50 on 60c. purple (No. 195)	30	25
280	-	$0.50 on 75c. blue (No. O243)	20	10
281	-	$1.50 on 1p.50 brown (No. D244)	30	20
282	**80**	$1.50 on 4p. blue	20	10

86

87 P. J. Caballero

88 Paraguay

89 Cassel Tower, Asuncion

90 Columbus

1927

283	**86**	1c. red	10	10
284	**86**	2c. orange	10	10
285	**86**	7c. lilac	10	10
286	**86**	7c. green	10	10
287	**86**	10c. green	10	10
288	**86**	10c. red	10	10
290	**86**	10c. blue	10	10
291	**86**	20c. blue	10	10
292	**86**	20c. purple	10	10
293	**86**	20c. violet	10	10
294	**86**	20c. pink	10	10
295	**86**	50c. blue	10	10
296	**86**	50c. red	20	20
299	**86**	50c. mauve	10	10
300	**86**	50c. pink	10	10
323	**86**	50c. orange	10	10
326	**86**	50c. green	10	10
301	**86**	70c. blue	20	20
304	**87**	1p. orange	10	10
328	**87**	1p. green	10	10
329	**87**	1p. red	10	10
330	**87**	1p. purple	10	10
331	**87**	1p. blue	10	10
332	**87**	1p. violet	10	10
307	**88**	1p.50 pink	20	10
333	**88**	1p.50 brown	10	10
334	**88**	1p.50 lilac	10	10
335	**88**	1p.50 blue	10	10
308	-	2p.50 bistre	10	10
337	-	2p.50 violet	10	10
310	-	3p. red	20	45
311	-	3p. violet	10	10
338	-	3p. grey	20	10
312	**89**	5p. brown	55	45
314	**89**	5p. orange	20	10
340	**89**	5p. violet	15	10
315	**90**	10p. red	1·70	75
317	**90**	10p. blue	1·70	75
318	**88**	20p. red	3·75	3·00
319	**88**	20p. green	3·75	3·00
320	**88**	20p. purple	3·75	3·00

DESIGNS—As Type **87**: 2p.50, Fulgencio Yegros; 3p. V. Ignacio Yturbe.

92 Arms of De Salazarde Espinosa, founder of Asuncion

1928. Foundation of Asuncion, 1537.

342	**92**	10p. purple	1·90	1·30

93 Pres. Hayes of U.S.A. and Villa Hayes

1928. 50th Anniv of Hayes's Decision to award Northern Chaco to Paraguay.

343	**93**	10p. brown	9·25	4·25
344	**93**	10p. grey	9·25	4·25

1929. Air. Surch **Correo Aereo Habilitado en** and value.

357	**86**	$0.95 on 7c. lilac	30	25
358	**86**	$1.90 on 20c. blue	30	25
345	-	$2.85 on 5c. purple (No. O239)	1·10	95
348	-	$3.40 on 3p. grey (No. 338)	2·75	1·60
359	**80**	$3.40 on 4p. blue	35	25
360	**80**	$4.75 on 4p. blue	65	65
346	-	$5.65 on 10c. green (No. O240)	75	55
361	-	$6.80 on 3p. grey (No. 338)	75	75
349	**80**	$6.80 on 4p. blue	2·75	1·60
347	-	$11.30 on 50c. red (No. O242)	1·10	75
350	**89**	$17 on 5p. brown (A)	2·75	1·60
362	**89**	$17 on 5p. brown (B)	2·20	2·10

On No. 350 (A) the surcharge is in four lines, and on No. 362 (B) it is in three lines.

95

1929. Air.

352	**95**	2.85p. green	35	20
353	-	5.65p. brown	1·10	55
354	-	5.65p. red	55	30
355	-	11.30p. purple	75	55
356	-	11.30p. blue	35	30

DESIGNS: 5.65p. Carrier pigeon; 11.30p. Stylized airplane.

1930. Air. Optd **CORREO AEREO** or surch also in words.

363	**86**	5c. on 10c. green	30	25
364	**86**	5c. on 70c. blue	30	25
365	**86**	10c. green	35	20
366	**86**	20c. blue	35	20
367	**87**	20c. on 1p. red	35	25
368	**86**	40c. on 50c. orange	35	25
369	**87**	1p. green	75	75
370	-	3p. grey (No. 338)	75	75
371	**90**	6p. on 10p. red	1·30	1·10
372	**88**	10p. on 20p. red	5·50	5·25
373	**88**	10p. on 20p. purple	5·50	5·25

101

103

1930. Air.

374	**101**	95c. blue on blue	55	30
375	**101**	95c. red on pink	55	30
376	-	1p.90 purple on blue	55	30
377	-	1p.90 red on pink	55	30
378	**103**	6p.80 black on blue	55	30
379	**103**	6p.80 green on pink	55	30

DESIGN: 1p.90, Asuncion Cathedral.

104 Declaration of Independence

1930. Air. Independence Day.

380	**104**	2p.85 blue	55	30
381	**104**	3p.40 green	55	25
382	**104**	4p.75 purple	55	25

105

1930. Red Cross Fund.

383	**105**	1p.50+50c. blue	2·20	1·30
384	**105**	1p.50+50c. red	2·20	1·30
385	**105**	1p.50+50c. lilac	2·20	1·30

106 Portraits of Archbishop Bogarin

1930. Consecration of Archbishop Bogarin.

386	**106**	1p.50 blue	2·20	1·60
387	**106**	1p.50 red	2·20	1·60
388	**106**	1p.50 violet	2·20	1·60

1930. Surch **Habilitado en CINCO**.

389	**86**	5c. on 7c. green	10	10

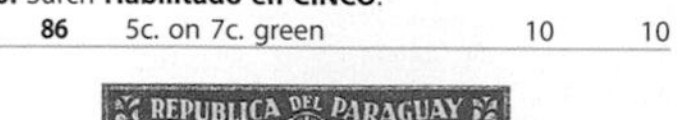

108 Planned Agricultural College at Ypacarai

1931. Agricultural College Fund.

390	**108**	1p.50+50c. blue on red	65	65

109 Arms of Paraguay

1931. 60th Anniv of First Paraguay Postage Stamps.

391	**109**	10p. brown	1·20	55
392	**109**	10p. red on blue	1·20	55
393	**109**	10p. blue on red	1·20	55
395	**109**	10p. grey	1·00	45
396	**109**	10p. blue	35	30

110 Gunboat "Paraguay"

1931. Air. 60th Anniv of Constitution and Arrival of new Gunboats.

397	**110**	1p. red	20	20
398	**110**	1p. blue	20	20
399	**110**	2p. orange	35	30
400	**110**	2p. brown	35	30
401	**110**	3p. green	75	75
402	**110**	3p. blue	75	75
403	**110**	3p. red	65	65
404	**110**	6p. green	1·10	1·10
405	**110**	6p. mauve	1·10	1·10
406	**110**	6p. blue	1·10	1·10
407	**110**	10p. red	1·10	3·75
408	**110**	10p. green	2·40	2·10
409	**110**	10p. blue	1·90	1·80
410	**110**	10p. brown	2·75	2·75
411	**110**	10p. pink	2·75	2·75

1931. As T **110**.

412		1p.50 violet	55	30
413		1p.50 blue	35	30

DESIGN: Gunboat "Humaita".
No. 413 is optd with large **C**.

112 War Memorial

113 Orange Tree and Yerba Mate

114 Yerba Mate

115 Palms

116 Yellow-headed Caracara

1931. Air.

414	112	5c. blue	20	10
415	112	5c. green	15	20
416	112	5c. red	35	20
417	112	5c. purple	10	10
418	113	10c. violet	20	20
419	113	10c. red	20	20
420	113	10c. brown	20	10
421	113	10c. blue	10	10
422	114	20c. red	20	10
423	114	20c. blue	35	30
424	114	20c. green	30	10
425	114	20c. brown	10	10
426	115	40c. green	30	20
426a	115	40c. blue	20	10
426b	115	40c. red	35	25
427	116	80c. blue	55	30
428	116	80c. green	35	25
428a	116	80c. red	30	25

1931. Air. Optd with airship "Graf Zeppelin" and **Correo Aereo "Graf Zeppelin"** or surch also.

429	80	3p. on 4p. blue	17·00	16·00
430	80	4p. blue	17·00	16·00

118 Farm Colony

1931. 50th Anniv of Foundation of San Bernardino.

431	118	1p. green	35	25
432	118	1p. red	35	25

1931. New Year. Optd **FELIZ ANO NUEVO 1932**.

433	106	1p.50 blue	2·00	2·00
434	106	1p.50 red	2·00	2·00

120 "Graf Zeppelin"

1932. Air.

435	120	4p. blue	3·25	3·25
436	120	8p. red	3·75	3·75
437	120	12p. green	5·00	5·00
438	120	16p. purple	6·50	6·50
439	120	20p. brown	6·50	6·50

121 Red Cross H.Q.

1932. Red Cross Fund.

440	121	50c.+50c. pink	65	55

122 (Trans: "Has been, is and will be")

1932. Chaco Boundary Dispute.

441	122	1p. purple	30	20
442	122	1p.50 pink	30	20
443	122	1p.50 brown	30	20
444	122	1p.50 green	30	20
445	122	1p.50 blue	30	20

Nos. 443/5 are optd with a large **C**.

1932. New Year. Surch **CORREOS FELIZ ANO NUEVO 1933** and value.

446	120	50c. on 4p. blue	35	25
447	120	1p. on 8p. red	75	65
448	120	1p.50 on 12p. green	75	65
449	120	2p. on 16p. purple	75	65
450	120	5p. on 20p. brown	1·90	1·50

124 "Graf Zeppelin" over Paraguay

125 "Graf Zeppelin" over Atlantic

1933. Air. "Graf Zeppelin" issue.

451	124	4p.50 blue	2·20	1·50
452	124	9p. red	3·75	2·75
453	124	13p.50 green	3·75	2·75
454	125	22p.50 brown	10·00	7·50
455	125	45p. violet	13·00	13·00

126 Columbus's Fleet

1933. 441st Anniv of Departure of Columbus from Palos. Maltese Crosses in violet.

456	126	10c. olive and red	35	30
457	126	20c. blue and lake	35	30
458	126	50c. red and green	35	30
459	126	1p. brown and blue	45	45
460	126	1p.50 green and blue	55	55
461	126	2p. green and sepia	75	75
462	126	5p. lake and olive	1·70	1·60
463	126	10p. sepia and blue	1·70	1·60

127 G.P.O., Asuncion

1934. Air.

464	127	33p.75 blue	2·20	1·90
466	127	33p.75 green	2·75	2·10
467	127	33p.75 brown	75	75
468	127	33p.75 red	2·00	1·90

1934. Air. Optd **1934**.

469	124	4p.50 blue	2·20	1·90
470	124	9p. red	2·75	2·10
471	124	13p.50 green	7·75	7·00
472	125	22p.50 brown	6·00	5·25
473	125	45p. violet	11·00	9·00

1935. Air. Optd **1935**.

474	124	4p.50 red	2·75	1·90
475	124	9p. green	3·75	2·10
476	124	13p.50 brown	7·75	7·00
477	125	22p.50 purple	6·00	5·25
478	125	45p. blue	11·00	9·00

131 Tobacco Plant

1935. Air.

479	131	17p. brown	11·00	3·25
480	131	17p. red	21·00	5·75
481	131	17p. blue	14·50	3·75
482	131	17p. green	8·75	2·10

132 Church of the Incarnation

1935. Air.

483	132	102p. red	6·00	3·50
485	132	102p. blue	3·75	2·75
486	132	102p. brown	3·75	2·75
487	132	102p. violet	2·00	1·50
487a	132	102p. orange	1·80	1·30

1937. Air. Surch **Habilitado en** and value in figures.

488	127	$24 on 33p.75 blue	75	55
489	132	$65 on 102p. grey	2·00	1·40
490	132	$84 on 102p. green	2·00	1·20

134 Arms of Asuncion

1937. Fourth Centenary of Asuncion (1st issue).

491	134	50c. purple and violet	35	25
492	134	1p. green and bistre	35	25
493	134	3p. blue and red	35	25
494	134	10p. yellow and red	35	25
495	134	20p. grey and blue	35	25

135 Monstrance

1937. First National Eucharistic Congress.

496	135	1p. red, yellow and blue	35	25
497	135	3p. red, yellow and blue	35	25
498	135	10p. red, yellow and blue	35	25

136 Oratory of the Virgin of Asuncion

1938. Fourth Centenary of Asuncion (2nd issue).

499	136	5p. olive	35	30
500	136	5p. red	55	30
501	136	11p. brown	55	45

137 Asuncion

1939. Air.

502	137	3p.40 blue	75	75
503	137	3p.40 green	45	30
504	137	3p.40 brown	45	30

138 J. E. Diaz

1939. Reburial in National Pantheon of Ashes of C. A. Lopez and J. E. Diaz.

505	138	2p. brown and blue	45	30
506	-	2p. brown and blue	45	30

DESIGN—VERT: No. 506, C. A. Lopez.

139 Pres. Caballero and Senator Decoud

1939. 50th Anniv of Asuncion University.

507	-	50c. blk & orge (postage)	20	10
508	-	1p. black and blue	45	20
509	-	2p. black and red	65	30
510	139	5p. black and blue	90	55
511	139	28p. black and red (air)	10·00	9·50
512	139	90p. black and green	12·00	11·50

DESIGN: Nos. 507/9, Pres. Escobar and Dr. Zubizarreta.

140 Coats of Arms

141 Pres. Baldomir and Flags of Paraguay and Uruguay

1939. Chaco Boundary Peace Conference, Buenos Aires (1st issue).

513	140	50c. blue (postage)	45	30
514	141	1p. olive	35	20
515	A	2p. green	45	30
516	B	3p. brown	90	65
517	C	5p. orange	65	45
518	D	6p. violet	1·80	1·40
519	E	10p. brown	1·30	85
520	F	1p. brown (air)	20	20
521	140	3p. blue	35	20
522	E	5p. olive	35	30
523	D	10p. violet	45	30
524	C	30p. orange	65	45
525	B	50p. brown	1·10	65
526	A	100p. green	1·50	1·40
527	141	200p. green	8·75	5·75
528	-	500p. black	22·00	21·00

DESIGNS (flag on right is that of country named): A, Benavides (Peru); B, Eagle (USA); C, Alessandri (Chile); D, Vargas (Brazil); E, Ortiz (Argentina); F, Figure of "Peace" (Bolivia); 500p. (30×40 mm), Map of Chaco frontiers.

See also Nos. 536/43.

143 Arms of New York

144 Asuncion–New York Air Route

1939. New York World's Fair.

529	143	5p. red (postage)	45	30
530	143	10p. blue	90	65
531	143	11p. green	1·30	1·10
532	143	22p. grey	1·80	1·40
533	144	30p. brown (air)	8·25	5·25
534	144	80p. orange	10·00	9·50
535	144	90p. violet	13·00	13·00

145 Soldier

147 Waterfall

1940. Chaco Boundary Peace Conference, Buenos Aires (2nd issue). Inscr "PAZ DEL CHACO".

536	145	50c. orange	35	20
537	-	1p. purple	35	20
538	-	3p. green	35	20
539	-	5p. brown	35	20
540	-	10p. mauve	35	20
541	-	20p. blue	65	45
542	-	50p. green	1·50	65
543	147	100p. black	3·25	2·10

DESIGNS: As Type **145**: VERT: 1p. Water-carrier; 5p. Ploughing with oxen. HORIZ: 3p. Cattle Farming. As Type **147**: VERT: 10p. Fishing in the Paraguay River. HORIZ: 20p. Bullock-cart, 50p. Cattle-grazing.

148 Western Hemisphere

1940. 50th Anniv of Pan-American Union.

544	148	50c. orange (postage)	10	10
545	148	1p. green	20	20
546	148	5p. blue	35	30
547	148	10p. brown	1·20	1·20
548	148	20p. red (air)	55	45
549	148	70p. blue	1·40	55
550	148	100p. green	1·70	1·60
551	148	500p. violet	7·25	5·75

149 Reproduction of Paraguay No. 1

1940. Cent of First Adhesive Postage Stamps. Inscr "CENTENARIO DEL SELLO POSTAL 1940".

552	**149**	1p. purple and green	75	30
553	-	5p. brown and green	1·00	45
554	-	6p. blue and brown	2·20	95
555	-	10p. black and red	2·20	1·50

DESIGNS: 5p. Sir Rowland Hill; 6p., 10p. Early Paraguayan stamps.

1940. National Mourning for Pres. Estigarribia. Surch **7-IX-40/DUELO NACIONAL/5 PESOS** in black border.

556	**145**	5p. on 50c. orange	55	55

152 Dr. Francia

1940. Death Centenary of Dr. Francia (dictator).

557	**152**	50c. red	40	25
558	-	50c. purple	40	25
559	**152**	1p. green	40	25
560	-	5p. blue	40	25

PORTRAIT: Nos. 558 and 560, Dr. Francia seated in library.

1941. Visit of President Vargas of Brazil. Optd **Visita al Paraguay Agosto de 1941**.

560a	6p. violet (No. 518)	55	55

154 Our Lady of Asuncion

1941. Mothers' Fund.

561	**154**	7p.+3p. brown	45	35
562	**154**	7p.+3p. violet	45	35
563	**154**	7p.+3p. red	45	35
564	**154**	7p.+3p. blue	45	35

1942. Nos. 520/2 optd **Habilitado** and bar(s).

565	-	1p. brown	45	30
566	**140**	3p. blue	45	30
567	-	5p. olive	45	30

156 Arms of Paraguay

1942

568	**156**	1p. green	35	25
569	**156**	1p. orange	35	20
570	**156**	7p. blue	35	20
571	**156**	7p. brown	35	20

For other values as Type **156** see Nos. 631, etc.

158 Irala's Vision

1942. Fourth Centenary of Asuncion.

572	-	2p. green (postage)	1·20	55
573	**158**	5p. red	1·20	55
574	-	7p. blue	1·20	55
575	-	20p. purple (air)	1·00	55
576	**158**	70p. brown	2·75	1·70
577	-	500p. olive	7·75	5·25

DESIGNS—VERT: 2p., 20p. Indian hailing ships; 7p., 500p. Irala's Arms.

160 Columbus sighting America

161 Pres. Morinigo and Symbols of Progress

1943. 450th Anniv of Discovery of America by Columbus.

578	**160**	50c. violet	35	25
579	**160**	1p. brown	35	25
580	**160**	5p. green	65	30
581	**160**	7p. blue	35	25

1943. Three Year Plan.

582	**161**	7p. blue	20	20

NOTE: From No. 583 onwards, the currency having been changed, the letter "c" in the value description indicates "centimos" instead of "centavos".

1944. St. Juan Earthquake Fund. Surch **U.P.A.E. Adhesion victimas San Juan y Pueblo Argentino centimos** and bar.

583	**E**	10c. on 10p. brown (No. 519)	75	55

1944. No. 311 surch **Habilitado en un centimo**.

584	1c. on 3p. violet	35	25

1944. Surch **1944/5 Centimos 5**.

585	**160**	5c. on 7p. blue	30	15
586	**161**	5c. on 7p. blue	30	15

164 Primitive Indian Postmen

181 Jesuit Relics of Colonial Paraguay

1944

587	**164**	1c. black (postage)	10	15
588	-	2c. brown	20	15
589	-	5c. olive	2·20	30
590	-	7c. blue	65	45
591	-	10c. green	90	55
592	-	15c. blue	90	55
593	-	50c. black	1·20	85
594	-	1g. red	3·75	2·10

DESIGNS—HORIZ: 2c. Ruins of Humaita Church; 7c. Marshal Francisco S. Lopez; 1g. Ytororo Heroes' Monument. VERT: 5c. First Paraguayan railway locomotive; 10c. "Tacuary" (paddle-steamer); 15c. Port of Asuncion; 50c. Meeting place of Independence conspirators.

595	-	1c. blue (air)	10	10
596	-	2c. green	20	20
597	-	3c. purple	45	30
598	-	5c. green	35	30
599	-	10c. violet	55	45
600	-	20c. brown	1·70	1·30
601	-	30c. blue	75	65
602	-	40c. olive	1·30	1·20
603	-	70c. red	1·80	1·60
604	**181**	1g. orange	2·75	2·75
605	-	2g. brown	4·50	3·75
606	-	5g. brown	11·00	10·50
607	-	10g. blue	28·00	27·00

DESIGNS—HORIZ: 1c. Port of Asuncion; 2c. First telegraphic apparatus in S. America; 3c. Paddle-steamer "Tacuary"; 5c. Meeting place of Independence Conspirators; 10c. Antequera Monument; 20c. First Paraguayan railway locomotive; 40c. Government House. VERT: 30c. Ytororo Heroes' Monument; 70c. As Type **164** but vert: 2g. Ruins of Humaita Church; 5g. Oratory of the Virgin; 10g. Marshal Francisco S. Lopez.

See also Nos. 640/51.

1945. No. 590 surch with figure **5** over ornaments deleting old value.

608	5c. on 7c. blue	35	20

186 Clasped Hands and Flags

1945. President Morinigo's Goodwill Visits. Designs of different sizes inscr "CONFRATERNIDAD" between crossed flags of Paraguay and another American country, mentioned in brackets. (a) Postage.

609	**186**	1c. green (Panama)	10	10
610	**186**	3c. red (Venezuela)	20	20
611	**186**	5c. grey (Ecuador)	20	20
612	**186**	2g. brown (Peru)	2·75	2·75

(b) Air.

613	20c. orange (Colombia)	55	55
614	40c. olive (Bolivia)	55	55
615	70c. red (Mexico)	55	55
616	1g. blue (Chile)	1·10	1·10
617	2g. violet (Brazil)	1·70	1·60
618	5g. green (Argentina)	3·25	3·25
619	10g. brown (U.S.A.)	22·00	21·00

The 5 and 10g. are larger, 32×28 and 33½×30 mm respectively.

1945. Surch **1945 5 Centimos 5**.

620	**160**	5c. on 7p. blue	55	45
621	**161**	5c. on 7p. blue	45	45
622	-	5c. on 7p. blue (No. 590)	90	45

1945. Surch **1945** and value.

623	**154**	2c. on 7p.+3p. brown	35	20
624	**154**	2c. on 7p.+3p. violet	35	20
625	**154**	2c. on 7p.+3p. red	35	20
626	**154**	2c. on 7p.+3p. blue	35	20
627	**154**	5c. on 7p.+3p. brown	40	20
628	**154**	5c. on 7p.+3p. violet	40	20
629	**154**	5c. on 7p.+3p. red	40	20
630	**154**	5c. on 7p.+3p. blue	40	20

1946. As T **156** but inscr "U.P.U." at foot.

631	**156**	5c. grey	35	20
631a	**156**	5c. pink	35	20
631b	**156**	5c. brown	35	20
686	**156**	10c. blue	35	20
687	**156**	10c. pink	35	20
631c	**156**	30c. green	35	20
631d	**156**	30c. brown	35	20
775	**156**	45c. green	35	25
631e	**156**	50c. mauve	35	20
776	**156**	50c. purple	35	25
858	**156**	70c. brown	35	25
777	**156**	90c. blue	35	25
778	**156**	1g. violet	35	25
860	**156**	1g.50 mauve	35	25
814	**156**	2g. ochre	35	25
780	**156**	2g.20 mauve	35	25
781	**156**	3g. brown	35	25
782	**156**	4g.20 green	35	25
862	**156**	4g.50 blue	35	25
816	**156**	5g. red	35	25
689	**156**	10g. orange	1·10	75
784	**156**	10g. green	35	25
818	**156**	12g.45 green	35	25
819	**156**	15g. orange	35	25
786	**156**	20g. blue	55	30
820	**156**	30g. bistre	55	30
812	**156**	50g. brown	35	20
821	**156**	100g. blue	1·50	1·20

See also Nos. 1037/49.

1946. Surch **1946 5 Centimos 5**.

632	**154**	5c. on 7p.+3p. brown	1·20	95
633	**154**	5c. on 7p.+3p. violet	1·20	95
634	**154**	5c. on 7p.+3p. red	1·20	95
635	**154**	5c. on 7p.+3p. blue	1·20	95

1946. Air. Surch **1946 5 Centimos 5**.

636	5c. on 20c. brown (No. 600)	1·80	1·70
637	5c. on 30c. blue (No. 601)	1·80	1·70
638	5c. on 40c. olive (No. 602)	1·80	1·70
639	5c. on 70c. red (No. 603)	1·80	1·70

1946. As Nos. 587/607 but colours changed and some designs smaller.

640	-	1c. red (postage)	15	10
641	-	2c. violet	20	15
642	**164**	5c. blue	30	15
643	-	10c. orange	45	25
644	-	15c. olive	55	35
645	**181**	50c. green	1·10	55
646	-	1g. blue	1·70	1·10

DESIGNS—VERT: 1c. Paddle-steamer "Tacuary"; 1g. Meeting place of Independence Conspirators. HORIZ: 2c. First telegraphic apparatus in S. America; 10c. Antequera Monument; 15c. Ytororo Heroes' Monument.

647	10c. red (air)	20	20
648	20c. green	35	30
649	1g. brown	1·10	1·10
650	5g. purple	3·25	3·25
651	10g. red	17·00	16·00

DESIGNS—VERT: 10c. Ruins of Humaita Church. HORIZ: 20c. Port of Asuncion; 1g. Govt. House; 5g. Marshal Francisco S. Lopez; 10g. Oratory of the Virgin.

189 Marshal Francisco Lopez

1947. Various frames.

652	**189**	1c. violet (postage)	15	15
653	**189**	2c. red	15	15
654	**189**	5c. green	20	20
655	**189**	15c. blue	20	20
656	**189**	50c. green	1·20	1·20
657	**189**	32c. red (air)	20	20
658	**189**	64c. brown	55	55
659	**189**	1g. blue	1·10	1·10
660	**189**	5g. purple and blue	2·75	2·75
661	**189**	10g. green and red	5·50	5·25

190 Archbishop of Paraguay

1947. 50th Anniv of Archbishopric of Paraguay.

662	**190**	2c. grey (postage)	10	10
663	-	5c. red	20	20
664	-	10c. black	35	20
665	-	15c. green	65	55
666	-	20c. black (air)	20	20
667	-	30c. grey	35	30
668	-	40c. mauve	55	55
669	**190**	70c. red	55	55
670	-	1g. lake	75	75
671	-	2g. red	2·20	2·10
672	**190**	5g. slate and red	3·75	3·75
673	-	10g. brown and green	6·50	6·50

DESIGNS: 5, 20c., 10g. Episcopal Arms; 10, 30c, 1g. Sacred Heart Monument; 15, 40c., 2g. Vision of projected monument.

194 Torchbearer

1948. Honouring the "Barefeet" (political party). Badge in red and blue.

674	**194**	5c. red (postage)	20	20
675	**194**	15c. orange	35	30
676	**194**	69c. green (air)	1·20	1·40
677	**194**	5g. blue	8·75	5·25

195 C. A. Lopez, J. N. Gonzalez and "Paraguari" (freighter)

1948. Centenary of Paraguay's Merchant Fleet. Centres in black, red and blue.

678	**195**	2c. orange	10	10
679	**195**	5c. blue	20	10
680	**195**	10c. black	30	10
681	**195**	15c. violet	45	15
682	**195**	50c. green	55	20
683	**195**	1g. red	65	45

1949. Air. National Mourning for Archbishop of Paraguay. Surch **DUELO NACIONAL 5 CENTIMOS 5**.

684	**190**	5c. on 70c. red	35	30

1949. Air. Aid to Victims of Ecuadorean Earthquake. No. 667 surch **AYUDA AL ECUADOR 5 + 5** and two crosses.

685	5c.+5c. on 30c. slate	35	30

198 "Postal Communications"

1950. Air. 75th Anniv of U.P.U.

691	**198**	20c. violet and green	75	45
692	**198**	30c. brown and purple	1·10	65
693	**198**	50c. green and grey	1·70	85
694	**198**	1g. brown and blue	2·20	1·10
695	**198**	5g. black and red	5·50	2·75

199 President Roosevelt

1950. Air. Honouring F. D. Roosevelt. Flags in red and blue.

696	**199**	20c. orange	35	30
697	**199**	30c. black	35	30
698	**199**	50c. purple	35	30
699	**199**	1g. green	35	30
700	**199**	5g. blue	65	65

1951. First Economic Congress of Paraguay. Surch **PRIMER CONGRESO DE ENTIDADES ECONOMICAS DEL PARAGUAY 18–IV–1951** and shield over a block of four stamps.

700a	**156**	5c. pink	35	20
700b	**156**	10c. blue	55	30
700c	**156**	30c. green	90	65

Prices are for single stamps. Prices for blocks of four, four times single prices.

200 Columbus Lighthouse **201** Urn

1952. Columbus Memorial Lighthouse.

701	**200**	2c. brown (postage)	40	35
702	**200**	5c. blue	40	35
703	**200**	10c. pink	40	35
704	**200**	15c. blue	40	35
705	**200**	20c. purple	40	35
706	**200**	50c. orange	40	35
707	**200**	1g. green	40	35
708	**201**	10c. blue (air)	40	35
709	**201**	20c. green	40	35
710	**201**	30c. purple	40	35
711	**201**	40c. pink	40	35
712	**201**	50c. bistre	40	35
713	**201**	1g. blue	40	35
714	**201**	2g. orange	40	35
715	**201**	5g. lake	55	55

202 Isabella the Catholic

1952. Air. 500th Birth Anniv of Isabella the Catholic.

716	**202**	1g. blue	35	30
717	**202**	2g. brown	45	45
718	**202**	5g. green	90	85
719	**202**	10g. purple	2·20	2·10

203 S. Pettirossi (aviator)

1954. Pettirossi Commemoration.

720	**203**	5c. blue (postage)	55	30
721	**203**	20c. red	55	30
722	**203**	50c. purple	55	30
723	**203**	60c. violet	55	30
724	**203**	40c. brown (air)	55	30
725	**203**	55c. green	55	30
726	**203**	80c. blue	55	30
727	**203**	1g.30 grey	55	30

204 San Roque Church, Asuncion

1954. Air. San Roque Church Centenary.

728	**204**	20c. red	20	15
729	**204**	30c. purple	20	15
730	**204**	50c. blue	20	15
731	**204**	1g. purple and brown	35	25
732	**204**	1g. black and brown	35	25
733	**204**	1g. green and brown	35	25
734	**204**	1g. orange and brown	35	25
735	**204**	5g. yellow and brown	55	45
736	**204**	5g. olive and brown	55	45
737	**204**	5g. violet and brown	55	45
738	**204**	5g. buff and brown	55	45
MS738a		Two sheets each 124×108 mm. Nos. 731/4 and 735/8. No gum	9·00	9·00

205 Marshal Lopez, C. A. Lopez and Gen. Caballero

1954. National Heroes.

739	**205**	5c. violet (postage)	10	10
740	**205**	20c. blue	10	10
741	**205**	50c. mauve	10	10
742	**205**	1g. brown	15	10
743	**205**	2g. green	35	30
744	**205**	5g. violet (air)	45	30
745	**205**	10g. olive	90	75
746	**205**	20g. grey	1·40	1·20
747	**205**	50g. pink	3·00	3·00
748	**205**	100g. blue	10·00	9·50

206 Presidents Stroessner and Peron

1955. Visit of President Peron. Flags in red and blue.

749	**206**	5c. brown & buff (postage)	10	10
750	**206**	10c. lake and buff	10	10
751	**206**	50c. grey	20	10
752	**206**	1g.30 lilac and buff	35	30
753	**206**	2g.20 blue and buff	65	65
754	**206**	60c. olive and buff (air)	10	10
755	**206**	2g. green	45	30
756	**206**	3g. red	45	30
757	**206**	4g.10 mauve and buff	65	55

207 Trinidad Campanile

1955. Sacerdotal Silver Jubilee of Mgr. Rodriguez.

758	**207**	5c. brown (postage)	40	35
759	-	20c. brown	40	35
760	-	50c. brown	40	35
761	-	2g.50 green	40	35
762	-	5g. brown	40	35
763	-	15g. green	40	35
764	-	25g. green	75	45
765	**207**	2g. blue (air)	40	35
766	-	3g. green	40	35
767	-	4g. green	40	35
768	-	6g. brown	40	35
769	-	10g. red	40	35
770	-	20g. brown	40	35
771	-	30g. green	55	45
772	-	50g. blue	65	55

DESIGNS—HORIZ: 20c., 3g. Cloisters in Trinidad; 5, 10g. San Cosme Portico; 15, 20g. Church of Jesus. VERT: 50c., 4g. Cornice in Santa Maria; 2g.50, 6g. Santa Rosa Tower; 25, 30g. Niche in Trinidad; 50g. Trinidad Sacristy.

208 Angel and Marching Soldiers **209** Soldier and Flags

1957. Chaco Heroes. Inscr "HOMENAJE A LOS HEROES DEL CHACO". Flags in red, white and blue.

787	**208**	5c. green (postage)	35	30
788	**208**	10c. red	35	30
789	**208**	15c. blue	35	30
790	**208**	20c. purple	35	30
791	**208**	25c. black	35	30
792	-	30c. blue	35	30
793	-	40c. black	35	30
794	-	50c. lake	35	30
795	-	1g. turquoise	35	30
796	-	1g.30 blue	35	30
797	-	1g.50 purple	35	30
798	-	2g. green	35	30
799	**209**	10c. blue (air)	35	30
800	**209**	15c. purple	35	30
801	**209**	20c. red	35	30
802	**209**	25c. blue	35	30
803	**209**	50c. turquoise	35	30
804	**209**	1g. red	35	30
805	-	1g.30 purple	35	30
806	-	1g.50 blue	35	30
807	-	2g. green	35	30
808	-	4g.10 vermilion and red	35	30
809	-	5g. black	35	30
810	-	10g. turquoise	35	30
811	-	25g. blue	45	30

DESIGNS—HORIZ: Nos. 792/8, Man, woman and flags; 805/11, "Paraguay" and kneeling soldier.

212 R. Gonzalez and St. Ignatius

1958. Fourth Centenary of St. Ignatius of Loyola.

822	**212**	50c. green	35	30
823	-	50c. brown	35	30
824	-	1g.50 violet	35	30
825	-	3g. blue	35	30
826	**212**	6g.25 red	35	30

DESIGNS—VERT: 50c. brown; 3g. Statue of St. Ignatius. HORIZ: 1g.50, Jesuit Fathers' house, Antigua.

See also Nos. 1074/81.

213 President Stroessner

1958. Re-election of Pres. Stroessner. Portrait in black.

827	**213**	10c. red (postage)	10	10
828	**213**	15c. violet	10	10
829	**213**	25c. green	10	10
830	**213**	30c. lake	10	10
831	**213**	50c. mauve	10	10
832	**213**	75c. blue	10	10
833	**213**	5g. turquoise	20	15
834	**213**	10g. brown	65	55
835	**213**	12g. mauve (air)	75	65
836	**213**	18g. orange	90	75
837	**213**	23g. brown	1·20	1·10
838	**213**	36g. green	1·90	1·60
839	**213**	50g. olive	2·20	2·10
840	**213**	65g. grey	3·75	3·25

1959. Nos. 758/72 surch with star enclosed by palm leaves and value.

841	1g.50 on 5c. ochre (postage)	10	10
842	1g.50 on 20c. brown	10	10
843	1g.50 on 50c. purple	10	10
844	3g. on 2g.50 olive	10	10
845	6g.25 on 5g. brown	15	15
846	20g. on 15g. turquoise	65	65
847	30g. on 25g. green	1·00	95
848	4g. on 2g. blue (air)	20	10
849	12g.45 on 3g. olive	45	30
850	18g.15 on 6g. brown	65	55
851	23g.40 on 10g. red	90	65
852	34g.80 on 20g. bistre	1·20	95
853	36g. on 4g. green	1·40	95
854	43g.95 on 30g. green	1·70	1·10
855	100g. on 50g. blue	3·75	2·30

215 U.N. Emblem

1959. Air. Visit of U.N. Secretary-General.

856	**215**	5g. blue and orange	90	65

216 U.N. Emblem and Map of Paraguay

1959. Air. U.N. Day.

857	**216**	12g.45 orange and blue	45	30

217 Football

1960. Olympic Games, Rome. Inscr "1960".

863	**217**	30c. red & green (postage)	40	35
864	**217**	50c. purple and blue	40	35
865	**217**	75c. green and orange	40	35
866	**217**	1g.50 violet and green	40	35
867	-	12g.45 blue and red (air)	40	35
868	-	18g.15 green and purple	40	35
869	-	36g. red and green	65	65

DESIGN—AIR: Basketball.

218 "Uprooted Tree"

1960. World Refugee Year (1st issue).

870	**218**	25c. pink and green (postage)	45	35
871	**218**	50c. green and red	45	35
872	**218**	70c. brown and mauve	55	35
873	**218**	1g.50 blue and deep blue	55	35
874	**218**	3g. grey and brown	1·10	85
875	-	4g. pink and green (air)	90	75
876	-	12g.45 green and blue	1·80	1·30
877	-	18g.15 orange and red	2·40	1·40
878	-	23g.40 blue and red	2·75	2·75

DESIGN—AIR. As Type **218** but with "ANO MUNDIAL" inscr below tree.

See also Nos. 971/7.

219 U.N. Emblem

1960. "Human Rights". Inscr "DERECHOS HUMANOS".

879	**219**	1g. red and blue (postage)	40	35
880	-	3g. orange and blue	40	35
881	-	6g. orange and green	40	35
882	-	20g. yellow and red	40	35
MS882a		140×95 mm. Nos. 879/82	6·00	6·00
883	**219**	40g. blue and red (air)	45	45
884	-	60g. red and green	55	55
885	-	100g. red and blue	1·30	1·30
MS885a		140×95 mm. Nos. 883/5	22·00	22·00

DESIGNS: 3g., 60g. Hand holding scales; 6g. Hands breaking chain; 20g., 100g. "Freedom flame".

220 U.N. Emblem and Flags

1960. U.N. Day. Flags and inscr in blue and red.

886	**220**	30c. blue (postage)	40	35
887	**220**	75c. yellow	40	35
888	**220**	90c. mauve	40	35
889	**220**	3g. orange (air)	40	35
890	**220**	4g. green	40	35

221 Bridge with Arms of Brazil and Paraguay

1961. Inauguration of International Bridge between Brazil and Paraguay.

891	**221**	15c. green (postage)	10	10
892	**221**	30c. blue	10	10
893	**221**	50c. orange	10	10
894	**221**	75c. blue	10	10
895	**221**	1g. violet	10	10
896	-	3g. red (air)	35	20
897	-	12g.45 lake	65	55
898	-	18g.15 green	75	65
899	-	36g. blue	1·50	1·30
MS899a		125×181 mm. Nos. 896/9. Imperf	3·25	3·25

DESIGN—HORIZ: Nos. 896/9, Aerial view of bridge.

222 Timber Truck

1961. Paraguayan Progress. Inscr "PARAGUAY EN MARCHA".

900	**222**	25c. red & green (postage)	10	10
901	-	90c. yellow and blue	10	10
902	-	1g. red and orange	10	10
903	-	2g. green and pink	10	10
904	-	5g. violet and green	35	20
905	**222**	12g.45 blue and buff (air)	65	55
906	-	18g.15 violet and buff	90	75
907	-	22g. blue and orange	1·00	85
908	-	36g. yellow, green and blue	1·70	1·50

DESIGNS: 90c., 2g., 18g.15, Motorized timber barge; 1, 5, 22g. Radio mast; 36g. Boeing 707 jetliner.

223 P. J. Caballero, J. G. R. de Francia and F. Yegros

1961. 150th Anniv of Independence. (a) 1st issue.

909	**223**	30c. green (postage)	10	10
910	**223**	50c. mauve	10	10
911	**223**	90c. violet	10	10
912	**223**	1g.50 blue	10	10
913	**223**	3g. bistre	10	10
914	**223**	4g. blue	20	10
915	**223**	5g. brown	20	20
916	-	12g.45 red (air)	55	30
917	-	18g.15 blue	65	55
918	-	23g.40 green	90	75
919	-	30g. violet	1·10	85
920	-	36g. red	1·40	1·30
921	-	44g. brown	1·80	1·40

DESIGN: Nos. 916/21, Declaration of Independence.

224 "Chaco Peace"

(b) 2nd issue. Inscr "PAZ DEL CHACO".

922	**224**	25c. red (postage)	10	10
923	**224**	30c. green	10	10
924	**224**	50c. brown	10	10
925	**224**	1g. violet	10	10
926	**224**	2g. blue	10	10
927	-	3g. blue (air)	55	45
928	-	4g. purple	65	55
929	-	100g. green	3·75	3·25

DESIGN: Nos. 927/9, Clasped hands.

225 Puma

(c) 3rd issue.

930	**225**	75c. violet (postage)	90	30
931	**225**	1g.50 brown	90	30
932	**225**	4g.50 green	90	30
933	**225**	10g. blue	90	30
934	-	12g.45 purple (air)	2·75	1·70
935	-	18g.15 blue	2·75	2·10
936	-	34g.80 brown	5·00	3·75

DESIGN: Nos. 934/6, Brazilian tapir.

226 Arms of Paraguay

(d) 4th issue.

937	**226**	15c. blue (postage)	35	30
938	**226**	25c. red	35	30
939	**226**	75c. green	35	30
940	**226**	1g. red	35	30
941	**226**	3g. brown (air)	35	30
942	**226**	12g.45 mauve	35	30
943	**226**	36g. turquoise	75	75

The air stamps have a background pattern of horiz lines.

227 Grand Hotel, Guarani

(e) 5th issue.

944	**227**	50c. grey (postage)	35	30
945	**227**	1g. green	35	30
946	**227**	4g.50 violet	35	30
947	-	3g. brown (air)	35	30
948	-	4g. blue	35	30
949	-	18g.15 orange	45	45
950	-	36g. red	75	75

The air stamps are similar to Type **227** but inscr "HOTEL GUARANI" in upper left corner. See also Nos. 978/85 and 997/1011.

228 Racquet, Net and Balls

1961. 28th South American Tennis Championships, Asuncion (1st issue). Centres multicoloured; border colours given.

951	**228**	35c. pink (postage)	10	10
952	**228**	75c. yellow	10	10
953	**228**	1g.50 blue	10	10
954	**228**	2g.25 turquoise	15	15
955	**228**	4g. grey	30	25
MS955a 105×160 mm. Nos. 951/5 in block of 4 with colours changed. Imperf			29·00	28·00
956	**228**	12g.45 orange (air)	1·00	95
957	**228**	20g. orange	1·90	1·80
958	**228**	50g. orange	4·75	4·50

See also Nos. 978/85.

229

1961. "Europa".

959	**229**	50c. red, blue and mauve	55	20
960	**229**	75c. red, blue and green	55	20
961	**229**	1g. red, blue and brown	55	20
962	**229**	1g.50 red, blue & lt blue	55	20
963	**229**	4g.50 red, blue and yellow	1·30	55
MS963a 180×139 mm. Nos. 959/63. Imperf			29·00	29·00

230 Comm. Alan Shepard and Solar System

1961. Commander Shepard's Space Flight.

964	-	10c. brown and blue (postage)	35	10
965	-	25c. mauve and blue	35	10
966	-	50c. orange and blue	35	10
967	-	75c. green and blue	35	10
968	**230**	18g.15 blue and green (air)	13·00	6·50
969	**230**	36g. blue and orange	13·00	6·50
970	**230**	50g. blue and mauve	18·00	7·50
MS970a 124×94 mm. No. 970			33·00	33·00

DESIGN—HORIZ: Nos. 964/7, Comm. Shepard.

231

1961. World Refugee Year (2nd issue).

971	**231**	10c. deep blue and blue (postage)	10	10
972	**231**	25c. purple and orange	10	10
973	**231**	50c. mauve and pink	10	10
974	**231**	75c. blue and green	10	10
975	-	18g.15 red and brown (air)	75	75
976	-	36g. green and red	1·90	1·80
977	-	50g. orange and green	2·40	2·30
MS977a 119×80 mm. No. 977			19·00	19·00

Nos. 975/7 have a different background and frame.

232 Tennis-player

1962. 150th Anniv of Independence (6th issue) and 28th South American Tennis Championships, Asuncion (2nd issue).

978	**232**	35c. blue (postage)	1·00	30
979	**232**	75c. violet	1·00	30
980	**232**	1g.50 brown	1·00	30
981	**232**	2g.25 green	1·00	30
982	-	4g. red (air)	1·00	30
983	-	12g.45 purple	1·00	30
984	-	20g. turquoise	1·90	65
985	-	50g. brown	2·75	1·10

Nos. 982/5 show tennis-player using backhand stroke.

233 Scout Bugler

1962. Boy Scouts Commemoration.

986	**233**	10c. green & pur (postage)	10	10
987	**233**	20c. green and red	10	10
988	**233**	25c. green and brown	10	10
989	**233**	30c. green and emerald	10	10
990	**233**	50c. green and blue	10	10
991	-	12g.45 mauve & blue (air)	1·20	1·20
992	-	36g. mauve and green	3·50	3·50
993	-	50g. mauve and yellow	5·00	4·75
MS993a 128×101 mm. No. 993			19·00	19·00

DESIGN: Nos. 991/3, Lord Baden-Powell.

234 Pres. Stroessner and the Duke of Edinburgh

1962. Air. Visit of Duke of Edinburgh.

994	**234**	12g.45 blue, buff & green	35	30
995	**234**	18g.15 blue, pink and red	35	30
996	**234**	36g. blue, yellow & brown	65	65
MS996a 130×80 mm. No. 995			10·00	10·00

235 Map of the Americas

1962. 150th Anniv of Independence (7th issue) and Day of the Americas.

997	**235**	50c. orange (postage)	35	30
998	**235**	75c. blue	35	30
999	**235**	1g. violet	35	30
1000	**235**	1g.50 green	35	30
1001	**235**	4g.50 red	35	30
1002	-	20g. mauve (air)	35	30
1003	-	50g. orange	75	75

DESIGN: 20g., 50g. Hands supporting Globe.

236 U.N. Emblem

1962. 150th Anniv of Independence (8th issue).

1004	**236**	50c. brown (postage)	10	10
1005	**236**	75c. purple	10	10
1006	**236**	1g. blue	10	10
1007	**236**	2g. brown	10	10
1008	-	12g.45 violet (air)	65	65
1009	-	18g.15 green	1·10	1·10
1010	-	23g.40 red	1·50	1·50
1011	-	30g. red	1·80	1·70

DESIGN: Nos. 1008/11, U.N. Headquarters, New York.

237 Mosquito and W.H.O. Emblem

1962. Malaria Eradication.

1012	**237**	30c. black, blue and pink (postage)	10	10
1013	**237**	50c. black, green & bistre	10	10
1014	-	75c. black, bistre and red	10	10
1015	-	1g. black, bistre and green	10	10
1016	-	1g.50 black, bistre & brown	10	10
1017	**237**	3g. black, red & blue (air)	10	10
1018	**237**	4g. black, red and green	10	10
1019	-	12g.45 black, grn & brn	55	45
1020	-	18g.15 black, red and purple	1·30	75
1021	-	36g. black, blue and red	3·25	2·10
MS1021a 105×70 mm. No. 1021			22·00	22·00

DESIGN: Nos. 1014/16, 1019/21, Mosquito on U.N. emblem, and microscope.

238 Football Stadium

1962. World Cup Football Championship, Chile.

1022	**238**	15c. brown & yell (postage)	10	10
1023	**238**	25c. brown and green	10	10
1024	**238**	30c. brown and violet	10	10
1025	**238**	40c. brown and orange	10	10
1026	**238**	50c. brown and green	10	10
1027	-	12g.45 black, red and violet (air)	1·20	55
1028	-	18g.15 black, brn & vio	1·90	75
1029	-	36g. black, grey & brown	3·50	1·40
MS1029a 105×70 mm. No. 1029			33·00	32·00

DESIGN—HORIZ: Nos. 1027/9, Footballers and Globe.

239 "Lago Ypoa" (freighter)

1962. Paraguayan Merchant Marine Commem.

1030	**239**	30c. brown (postage)	45	45
1031	-	90c. blue	45	45
1032	-	1g.50 purple	45	45
1033	-	2g. green	45	45
1034	-	4g.20 blue	45	45
1035	-	12g.45 red (air)	45	45
1036	-	44g. blue	75	65

DESIGNS—HORIZ: 90c. Freighter; 1g.50, "Olympo" (freighter); 2g. Freighter (diff); 4g.20, "Rio Apa" (freighter). VERT: 12g.45, 44g. Ship's wheel.

1962. As Nos. 631, etc, but with taller figures of value.

1037	**156**	50c. blue	45	30
1038	**156**	70c. lilac	45	30
1039	**156**	1g.50 violet	45	30
1040	**156**	3g. blue	45	30
1041	**156**	4g.50 brown	45	30
1042	**156**	5g. mauve	45	30

1043	**156**	10g. mauve	45	30
1044	**156**	12g.45 blue	45	30
1045	**156**	15g.45 red	45	30
1046	**156**	18g.15 purple	45	30
1047	**156**	20g. brown	45	30
1048	**156**	50g. brown	65	30
1049	**156**	100g. grey	1·40	75

241 Gen. A. Stroessner

1963. Re-election of Pres. Stroessner to Third Term of Office.

1050	**241**	50c. brown and drab (postage)	45	45
1051	**241**	75c. brown and pink	45	45
1052	**241**	1g.50 brown and mauve	45	45
1053	**241**	3g. brown and green	45	45
1054	**241**	12g.45 red and pink (air)	45	45
1055	**241**	18g.15 green and pink	45	45
1056	**241**	36g. violet and pink	1·50	95

242 Popes Paul VI, John XXIII and St. Peter's

1964. Popes Paul VI and John XXIII.

1057	**242**	1g.50 yellow and red (postage)	10	10
1058	**242**	3g. green and red	10	10
1059	**242**	4g. brown and red	10	10
1060	-	12g.45 olive & grn (air)	55	45
1061	-	18g.15 green and violet	75	55
1062	-	36g. green and blue	2·75	1·90

DESIGNS: Nos. 1060/2, Cathedral, Asuncion.

243 Arms of Paraguay and France

1964. Visit of French President.

1063	**243**	1g.50 brown (postage)	10	10
1064	-	3g. blue	10	10
1065	**243**	4g. grey	15	10
1066	-	12g.45 violet (air)	45	45
1067	**243**	18g.15 green	65	65
1068	-	36g. red	2·75	1·90

DESIGNS: 3, 12g.45, 36g. Presidents Stroessner and De Gaulle.

245 Map of the Americas

1965. Sixth Reunion of the Board of Governors of the Inter-American Development Bank. Optd **Centenario de la Epopeya Nacional 1,864–1,870** as in T **245**.

1069	**245**	1g.50 green (postage)	35	30
1070	**245**	3g. pink	35	30
1071	**245**	4g. blue	35	30
1072	**245**	12g.45 brown (air)	35	30
1073	**245**	36g. violet	1·00	65

The overprint refers to the National Epic of 1864–70, the war with Argentina, Brazil and Uruguay and this inscription occurs on many other issues from 1965 onwards.

Nos. 1069/73 without the overprint were not authorized.

246 R. Gonzalez and St. Ignatius

1966. 350th Anniv of Founding of San Ignacio Guazu Monastery.

1074	**246**	15c. blue (postage)	35	30
1075	**246**	25c. blue	35	30
1076	**246**	75c. blue	35	30
1077	**246**	90c. blue	35	30
1078	-	3g. brown (air)	35	30
1079	-	12g.45 brown	35	30
1080	-	18g.15 brown	45	45
1081	-	23g.40 brown	45	45

DESIGNS: Nos. 1078/81, Jesuit Fathers' house, Antigua.

For similar stamps with different inscriptions, see Nos. 822, 824 and 826.

247 Ruben Dario

1966. 50th Death Anniv of Ruben Dario (poet).

1082	**247**	50c. blue	10	10
1083	**247**	70c. brown	10	10
1084	**247**	1g.50 lake	10	10
1085	**247**	3g. violet	10	10
1086	**247**	4g. turquoise	10	10
1087	**247**	5g. black	10	10
1088	-	12g.45 blue (air)	35	20
1089	-	18g.15 violet	55	45
1090	-	23g.40 brown	65	55
1091	-	36g. green	1·00	75
1092	-	50g. red	1·70	1·20

DESIGNS: Nos. 1088/92, Open book inscr "Paraguay de Fuego ..." by Dario.

248 Lions' Emblem on Globe

1967. 50th Anniv of Lions International.

1093	**248**	50c. violet (postage)	35	30
1094	**248**	70c. blue	35	30
1095	-	1g.50 blue	35	30
1096	-	3g. brown	35	30
1097	-	4g. blue	35	30
1098	-	5g. brown	35	30
1099	-	12g.45 brown (air)	35	30
1100	-	18g.15 violet	35	30
1101	-	23g.40 purple	35	30
1102	-	36g. blue	45	30
1103	-	50g. red	55	30

DESIGNS—VERT: 1g.50, 3g. M. Jones; 4, 5g. Lions headquarters, Chicago. HORIZ: 12g.45, 18g.15, Library–"Education"; 23g.40, 36g., 50g. Medical laboratory–"Health".

249 W.H.O. Emblem

1968. 20th Anniv of W.H.O.

1104	**249**	3g. turquoise (postage)	10	10
1105	**249**	4g. purple	10	10
1106	**249**	5g. brown	10	10
1107	**249**	10g. violet	10	10
1108	-	36g. brown (air)	90	45
1109	-	50g. red	1·00	65
1110	-	100g. blue	2·20	1·30

DESIGN—VERT: Nos. 1108/10, W.H.O. emblem on scroll.

250

1969. World Friendship Week.

1111	**250**	50c. red	10	10
1112	**250**	70c. blue	10	10
1113	**250**	1g.50 brown	10	10
1114	**250**	3g. mauve	10	10
1115	**250**	4g. green	10	10
1116	**250**	5g. violet	10	10
1117	**250**	10g. purple	35	10

251

1969. Air. Campaign for Houses for Teachers.

1118	**251**	36g. blue	1·10	55
1119	**251**	50g. brown	1·30	1·10
1120	**251**	100g. red	5·00	4·00

252 Pres. Lopez

1970. Death Centenary of Pres. F. Solano Lopez.

1121	**252**	1g. brown (postage)	35	30
1122	**252**	2g. violet	35	30
1123	**252**	3g. pink	35	30
1124	**252**	4g. red	35	30
1125	**252**	5g. blue	35	30
1126	**252**	10g. green	35	30
1127	**252**	15g. blue (air)	35	30
1128	**252**	20g. brown	35	30
1129	**252**	30g. green	35	30
1130	**252**	40g. purple	45	30

253 Paraguay 2r. Stamp of 1870

1970. Centenary of First Paraguayan Stamps.

1131	**253**	1g. red (postage)	10	10
1132	**A**	2g. blue	10	10
1133	**B**	3g. brown	10	10
1134	**253**	5g. violet	10	10
1135	**A**	10g. lilac	35	20
1136	**B**	15g. purple (air)	55	45
1137	**253**	30g. green	1·20	85
1138	**A**	36g. red	1·30	1·10

DESIGNS: First Paraguay stamps. A, 1r.; B, 3r.

254 Teacher and Pupil

1971. International Education Year–UNESCO.

1139	**254**	3g. blue (postage)	10	10
1140	**254**	5g. lilac	10	10
1141	**254**	10g. green	10	10
1142	**254**	20g. red (air)	45	30
1143	**254**	25g. mauve	55	45
1144	**254**	30g. brown	65	55
1145	**254**	50g. green	1·20	75

255 UNICEF Emblem

1972. 25th Anniv of UNICEF.

1146	**255**	1g. brown (postage)	35	30
1147	**255**	2g. blue	35	30
1148	**255**	3g. red	35	30
1149	**255**	4g. purple	35	30
1150	**255**	5g. green	35	30
1151	**255**	10g. purple	35	30
1152	**255**	20g. blue (air)	35	30
1153	**255**	25g. green	35	30
1154	**255**	30g. brown	35	30

256 Acaray Dam

1972. Tourist Year of the Americans.

1155	**256**	1g. brown (postage)	10	10
1156	-	2g. brown	10	10
1157	-	3g. blue	10	10
1158	-	5g. red	10	10
1159	-	10g. green	30	10
1160	-	20g. red (air)	45	30
1161	-	25g. grey	65	45
1162	-	50g. lilac	1·30	85
1163	-	100g. mauve	2·40	1·70

DESIGNS: 2g. Statue of Lopez; 3g. Friendship Bridge; 5g. Rio Tebicuary Bridge; 10g. Grand Hotel, Guarani; 20g. Motor coach; 25g. Social Service Institute Hospital; 50g. Liner "Presidente Stroessner"; 100g. Lockheed Electra airliner.

257 O.E.A. Emblem

1973. 25th Anniv of Organization of American States (O.E.A.).

1164	**257**	1g. mult (postage)	10	10
1165	**257**	2g. multicoloured	10	10
1166	**257**	3g. multicoloured	10	10
1167	**257**	4g. multicoloured	10	10
1168	**257**	5g. multicoloured	10	10
1169	**257**	10g. multicoloured	20	10
1170	**257**	20g. multicoloured (air)	35	10
1171	**257**	25g. multicoloured	55	10
1172	**257**	50g. multicoloured	1·30	10
1173	**257**	100g. multicoloured	2·20	10

258 Exhibition Emblem

1973. International Industrial Exhibition, Paraguay.

1174	**258**	1g. brown (postage)	35	30
1175	**258**	2g. red	35	30
1176	**258**	3g. blue	35	30
1177	**258**	4g. green	35	30
1178	**258**	5g. lilac	35	30
1179	**258**	20g. mauve (air)	35	30
1180	**258**	25g. red	35	30

259 Carrier Pigeon with Letter

1975. Centenary of U.P.U.

1181	**259**	1g. violet & blk (postage)	10	10
1182	**259**	2g. red and black	10	10
1183	**259**	3g. blue and black	10	10
1184	**259**	5g. blue and black	10	10
1185	**259**	10g. purple and black	35	10
1186	**259**	20g. brown & black (air)	65	30
1187	**259**	25g. green and black	75	30

260 Institute Buildings

1976. Inauguration (1974) of Institute of Higher Education.

1188	**260**	5g. violet, red and black (postage)	10	10
1189	**260**	10g. blue, red and black	20	10
1190	**260**	30g. brn, red & blk (air)	65	55

261 Rotary Emblem

1976. 70th Anniv of Rotary International.

1191	**261**	3g. blue, bistre and black (postage)	10	10
1192	**261**	4g. blue, bistre and mauve	10	10
1193	**261**	25g. blue, bistre and green (air)	75	45

262 Woman and I.W.Y. Emblem

1976. International Women's Year.

1194	**262**	1g. brown & blue (postage)	35	30
1195	**262**	2g. brown and red	35	30
1196	**262**	20g. brown & green (air)	35	30

263 Black Palms

1977. Flowering Plants and Trees. Multicoloured.

1197	2g. Type **263** (postage)	35	25
1198	3g. Mburucuya flowers	35	25
1199	20g. Marsh rose (tree) (air)	1·00	55

264 Nanduti Lace

1977. Multicoloured.. Multicoloured..

1200	1g. Type **264** (postage)	30	25
1201	5g. Nanduti weaver	30	25
1202	25g. Lady holding jar (air)	45	45

265 F. S. Lopez

1977. 150th Birth Anniv of Marshal Francisco Solano Lopez.

1203	**265**	10g. brown (postage)	35	60
1204	**265**	50g. blue (air)	75	55
1205	**265**	100g. green	1·50	1·10

266 General Bernardino Caballero National College

1978. Cent of National College of Asuncion.

1206	**266**	3g. red (postage)	10	10
1207	**266**	4g. blue	10	10
1208	**266**	5g. violet	10	10
1209	**266**	20g. brown (air)	45	20
1210	**266**	25g. purple	55	30
1211	**266**	30g. green	65	45

267 Marshal Jose F. Estigarribia, Trumpeter and Flag

1978. "Salon de Bronce" Commemoration.

1212	**267**	3g. purple, blue and red (postage)	10	10
1213	**267**	5g. violet, blue and red	10	10
1214	**267**	10g. grey, blue and red	20	10
1215	**267**	20g. green, bl & red (air)	35	20
1216	**267**	25g. violet, blue and red	45	30
1217	**267**	30g. purple, blue and red	55	30

268 Congress Emblem

1979. 22nd Latin American Tourism Congress, Asuncion.

1218	**268**	10g. black, blue and red (postage)	35	30
1219	**268**	50g. black, blue and red (air)	55	45

269 Spanish Colonial House, Pilar

1980. Bicentenary of Pilar City.

1220	**269**	5g. mult (postage)	10	10
1221	**269**	25g. multicoloured (air)	55	10

270 Boeing 707

1980. Inauguration of Paraguayan Airlines Boeing 707 Service.

1222	**270**	20g. mult (postage)	55	10
1223	**270**	100g. multicoloured (air)	2·40	1·30

271 Seminary, Communion Cup and Bible

1981. Air. Centenary of Metropolitan Seminary, Asuncion.

1224	**271**	5g. blue	10	10
1225	**271**	10g. brown	20	10
1226	**271**	25g. green	55	30
1227	**271**	50g. black	1·10	75

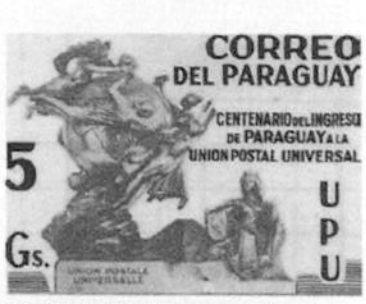

272 U.P.U. Monument, Berne

1981. Centenary of Admission to U.P.U.

1228	**272**	5g. red and black (postage)	10	10
1229	**272**	10g. mauve and black	20	10
1230	**272**	20g. green and black (air)	45	20
1231	**272**	25g. red and black	55	30
1232	**272**	50g. blue and black	1·10	65

273 St. Maria Mazzarello

1981. Air. Death Centenary of Mother Maria Mazzarello (founder of Daughters of Mary).

1233	**273**	20g. green and black	35	30
1234	**273**	25g. red and black	35	30
1235	**273**	50g. violet and black	55	45

274 Stroessner and Bridge over River Itaipua

1983. 25th Anniv of President Stroessner City.

1236	**274**	3g. green, blue & blk (postage)	10	10
1237	**274**	5g. red, blue and black	10	10
1238	**274**	10g. violet, blue and black	10	10
1239	**274**	20g. grey, blue & blk (air)	35	20
1240	**274**	25g. purple, blue & black	55	30
1241	**274**	50g. blue, grey and black	90	65

275 Sun and Map of Americas

1985. Air. 25th Anniv of Inter-American Development Bank.

1242	**275**	3g. orange, yellow & pink	30	25
1243	**275**	5g. orange, yellow & mauve	30	25
1244	**275**	10g. orange, yellow & mauve	30	25
1245	**275**	50g. orange, yellow & brown	30	25
1246	**275**	65g. orange, yellow & bl	30	25
1247	**275**	95g. orange, yellow & green	30	25

276 U.N. Emblem

1986. Air. 40th Anniv of U.N.O.

1248	**276**	5g. blue and brown	30	25
1249	**276**	10g. blue and grey	30	25
1250	**276**	50g. blue and black	30	25

277 1886 1c. Stamp

1986. Centenary of First Official Stamp.

1251	**277**	5g. deep blue, brown and blue (postage)	20	20
1252	**277**	15g. deep blue, brown and blue	20	20
1253	**277**	40g. deep blue, brown and blue	45	20
1254	-	65g. blue, green and red (air)	65	20
1255	-	100g. blue, green and red	1·10	30
1256	-	150g. blue, green and red	1·90	65

DESIGNS: 65, 100, 150g. 1886 7c. stamp.

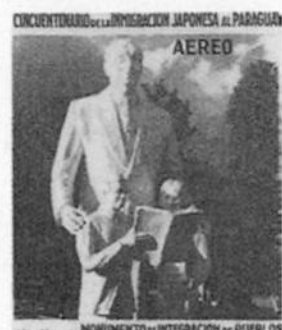

278 Integration of the Nations Monument, Colmena

1986. Air. 50th Anniv of Japanese Immigration. Multicoloured.

1257	5g. La Colmena vineyards (horiz)	20	10
1258	10g. Flowers of cherry tree and lapacho (horiz)	20	10
1259	20g. Type **278**	20	10

279 Caballero, Stroessner and Road

1987. Centenary of National Republican Association (Colorado Party).

1260	**279**	5g. multicoloured (postage)	10	10
1261	**279**	10g. multicoloured	10	10
1262	**279**	25g. multicoloured	10	10
1263	-	150g. multicoloured (air)	75	65
1264	-	170g. multicoloured	90	75
1265	-	200g. multicoloured	1·10	85

DESIGN: 150 to 200g. Gen. Bernardino Caballero (President 1881–86 and founder of party), Pres. Alfredo Stroessner and electrification of countryside.

280 Emblem of Visit

1988. Visit of Pope John Paul II.

1266	**280**	10g. blue and black (postage)	20	20
1267	**280**	20g. blue and black	20	20
1268	**280**	50g. blue and black	20	20
1269	-	100g. multicoloured (air)	65	45
1270	-	120g. multicoloured	75	55
1271	-	150g. multicoloured	90	75

DESIGN—HORIZ: 100 to 150g. Pope and Caacupe Basilica.

281 Silver Mate

1988. Air. Centenary of New Germany Colony. Multicoloured.

1272	90g. Type **281**	65	45
1273	105g. Mate ("Ilex paraguayensis") plantation	65	55
1274	120g. As No. 1273	75	65

1988. Air. 75th Anniv of Paraguay Philatelic Centre. No. 1249 optd * **75o ANIVERSARIO DE FUNDACION CENTRO FILATELICO DEL PARAGUAY 15 JUNIO-1913 - 1988.**

1275	**276**	10g. blue and grey	20	20

283 Pres. Stroessner and Government Palace

1988. Air. Re-election of President Stroessner.

1276	**283**	200g. multicoloured	55	45
1277	**283**	500g. multicoloured	1·50	1·50
1278	**283**	1000g. multicoloured	2·75	2·75

1989. "Parafil 89" Stamp Exhibition. Nos. 1268 and 1270 optd **PARAFIL 89.**

1279	**280**	50g. blue and black (postage)	4·00	3·75
1280	-	120g. multicoloured (air)	9·25	9·00

285 Green-winged Macaw

1989. Birds. Multicoloured.

1281	50g. Type **285** (postage)	20	10
1282	100g. Brazilian merganser (horiz) (air)	35	20
1283	300g. Greater rhea (horiz)	75	55
1284	500g. Toco toucan (horiz)	1·30	1·10
1285	1000g. Bare-faced curassow (horiz)	2·40	2·10
1286	2000g. Wagler's macaw and blue and yellow macaw	4·75	4·25

286 Anniversary Emblem

1990. Centenary of Organization of American States. Multicoloured.

1287	50g. Type **286**	20	10
1288	100g. Organization and anniversary emblems (vert)	45	30
1289	200g. Map of Paraguay	90	65

287 Basket

1990. America. Pre-Columbian Life. Multicoloured.

1290	150g. Type **287** (postage)	75	55
1291	500g. Guarani post (air)	2·50	1·70

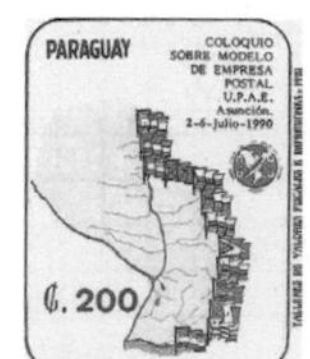

288 Flags on Map

1990. Postal Union of the Americas and Spain Colloquium. Multicoloured.

1292	200g. Type **288**	90	45
1293	250g. First Paraguay stamp	1·00	55
1294	350g. Paraguay 1990 America first day cover (horiz)	1·50	65

289 Planned Building

1990. Centenary of National University. Multicoloured.

1295	300g. Type **289**	1·30	95
1296	400g. Present building	1·80	1·40
1297	600g. Old building	2·75	2·10

290 Guarambare Church

1990. Franciscan Churches. Multicoloured.

1298	50g. Type **290**	20	10
1299	100g. Yaguaron Church	45	30
1300	200g. Ita Church	90	65

1991. Visit of King and Queen of Spain. Nos. 1290/1 optd **Vista de sus Majestades Los Reyes de Espana 22-24 Octubre 1990.**

1301	287	150g. mult (postage)	65	55
1302	-	500g. multicoloured (air)	2·20	1·70

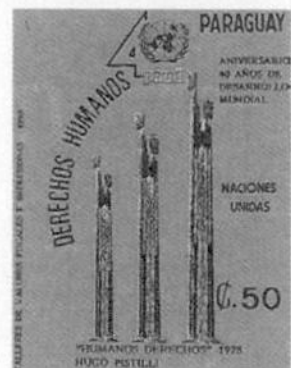

292 "Human Rights" (Hugo Pistilli)

1991. 40th Anniv of United Nations Development Programme. Multicoloured.

1303	50g. Type **292**	20	10
1304	100g. "United Nations" (sculpture, Hermann Guggiari)	45	30
1305	150f. First Miguel de Cervantes prize, awarded to Augusto Roa Bastos, 1989	65	55

294 Hands and Ballot Box (free elections)

1991. Democracy. Multicoloured.

1308	50g. Type **294** (postage)	25	10
1309	100g. Sun (State and Catholic Church) (vert)	30	15
1310	200g. Arrows and male and female symbols (human rights) (vert)	60	40
1311	300g. Dove and flag (freedom of the press) (vert) (air)	95	75
1312	500g. Woman and child welcoming man (return of exiles)	2·40	1·30
1313	3000g. Crowd with banners (democracy)	9·50	8·25

295 Julio Manuel Morales (gynaecologist)

1991. Medical Professors.

1314	**295**	50g. mult (postage)	25	10
1315	-	100g. multicoloured	30	15
1316	-	200g. multicoloured	60	45
1317	-	300g. brown, black & green	95	75
1318	-	350g. brown, black and green (air)	1·10	90
1319	-	500g. multicoloured	1·70	1·30

DESIGNS: 100g. Carlos Gatti (surgeon); 200g. Gustavo Gonzalez (symptomatologist); 300g. Juan Max Boettner (physician and musician); 350g. Juan Boggino (pathologist); 500g. Andres Barbero (founder of Paraguayan Red Cross).

1991. "Espamer '91" Spain–Latin America Stamp Exhibition, Buenos Aires. Nos. 1298/1300 optd **ESPAMER 91 BUENOS AIRES 5 14 Jul** and **Conquistador** in oval.

1323	50g. multicoloured	35	20
1324	100g. multicoloured	40	30
1325	200g. multicoloured	70	55

298 Ruy Diaz de Guzman (historian)

1991. Writers and Musicians. Multicoloured.

1326	50g. Type **298** (postage)	25	15
1327	100g. Maria Talavera (war chronicler) (vert)	35	20
1328	150g. Augusto Roa Bastos (writer and 1989 winner of Miguel de Cervantes Prize) (vert)	60	45
1329	200g. Jose Asuncion Flores (composer of "La Guarania") (vert) (air)	85	65
1330	250g. Felix Perez Cardozo (harpist and composer)	1·10	90
1331	300g. Juan Carlos Moreno Gonzalez (composer)	1·30	1·00

299 Battle of Tavare

1991. America. Voyages of Discovery. Multicoloured.

1332	100g. Type **299** (postage)	45	35
1333	300g. Arrival of Domingo Martinez de Irala in Paraguay (air)	1·40	1·00

300 "Compass of Life" (Alfredo Moraes)

1991. Paintings. Multicoloured.

1334	50g. Type **300** (postage)	25	15
1335	100g. "Callejon Illuminated" (Michael Burt)	35	20
1336	150g. "Arete" (Lucy Yegros)	60	45
1337	200g. "Itinerants" (Hugo Bogado Barrios) (air)	85	65
1338	250g. "Travellers without a Ship" (Bernardo Ismachoviez)	1·10	90
1339	300g. "Guarani" (Lotte Schulz)	1·30	1·00

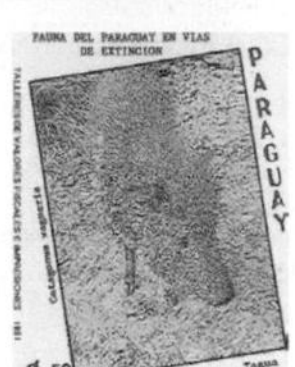

301 Chaco Peccary

1992. Endangered Mammals. Multicoloured.

1340	50g. Type **301**	25	15
1341	100g. Ocelot (horiz)	35	20
1342	150g. Brazilian tapir	60	45
1343	200g. Maned wolf	85	65

302 Geometric Design, Franciscan Church, Caazapa

1992. 500th Anniv of Discovery of America by Columbus (1st series). Church Roof Tiles. Mult.

1344	50g. Type **302**	25	15
1345	100g. Church, Jesuit church, Trinidad	35	20
1346	150g. Missionary ship, Jesuit church, Trinidad	60	45
1347	200g. Plant, Franciscan church, Caazapa	85	65

See also Nos. 1367/71.

1992. "Granada '92" International Thematic Stamp Exhibition. Nos. 1344/7 optd **GRANADA '92** and emblem.

1348	50g. multicoloured	25	10
1349	100g. multicoloured	35	20
1350	150g. multicoloured	85	35
1351	200g. multicoloured	95	45

304 Malcolm L. Norment (founder) and Emblem

1992. 68th Anniv of Paraguay Leprosy Foundation. Multicoloured.

1352	50g. Type **304**	35	20
1353	250g. Gerhard Hansen (discoverer of leprosy bacillus)	1·10	90

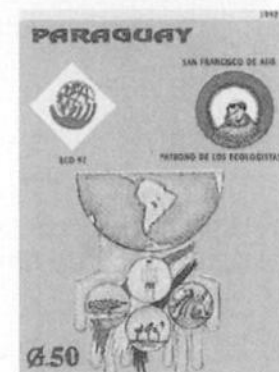

305 Southern Hemisphere and Ecology Symbols on Hands

1992. Second United Nations Conference on Environment and Development, Rio de Janeiro. Multicoloured.

1354	50g. Type **305**	30	20
1355	100g. Butterfly and chimneys emitting smoke	35	30
1356	250g. Tree and map of South America on globe	1·10	90

306 Factories and Cotton (economy)

1992. National Population and Housing Census. Multicoloured.

1357	50g. Type **306**	30	20
1358	200g. Houses (vert)	85	65
1359	250g. Numbers and stylized people (population) (vert)	1·10	90
1360	300g. Abacus (education)	1·30	1·00

307 Football

1992. Olympic Games, Barcelona. Multicoloured.

1361	50g. Type **307**	25	15
1362	100g. Tennis	35	20
1363	150g. Running	60	45
1364	200g. Swimming (horiz)	85	65
1365	250g. Judo	1·10	90
1366	350g. Fencing (horiz)	1·40	1·20

308 Brother Luis Bolanos

1992. 500th Anniv of Discovery of America by Columbus (2nd series). Evangelists. Multicoloured.

1367	50g. Type **308** (translator of Catechism into Guarani and founder of Guarani Christian settlements)	30	20
1368	100g. Brother Juan de San Bernardo (Franciscan and first Paraguayan martyr)	35	30
1369	150g. St. Roque Gonzalez de Santa Cruz (Jesuit missionary and first Paraguayan saint)	60	45
1370	200g. Fr. Amancio Gonzalez (founder of Melodia settlement)	85	65
1371	250g. Mgr. Juan Sinforiano Bogarin (first Archbishop of Asuncion) (vert)	1·10	90

309 Fleet approaching Shore

1992. America. 500th Anniv of Discovery of America by Columbus. Multicoloured.

1372	150g. Type **309** (postage)	70	55
1373	350g. Christopher Columbus (vert) (air)	1·50	1·20

1992. 30th Anniv of United Nations Information Centre in Paraguay. Nos. 1354/6 optd **NACIONES UNIDAS 1992 - 30 ANOS CENTRO INFORMACION OUN EN PARAGUAY.**

1374	50g. multicoloured	30	20
1375	100g. multicoloured	35	30
1376	250g. multicoloured	1·10	90

1992. Christmas. Nos. 1367/9 optd **Navidad 92**.

1377	50g. multicoloured	30	20
1378	100g. multicoloured	35	30
1379	150g. multicoloured	60	45

1992. "Parafil 92" Paraguay–Argentina Stamp Exhibition, Buenos Aires. Nos. 1372/3 optd **PARAFIL 92**.

1380	150g. multicoloured (postage)	35	20
1381	350g. multicoloured (air)	95	55

313 Planting and Hoeing

1992. 50th Anniv of Pan-American Agricultural Institute. Multicoloured.

1382	50g. Type **313**	30	20
1383	100g. Test tubes	35	30
1384	200g. Cotton plant in cupped hands	85	65
1385	250g. Cattle and maize plant	1·10	90

314 Yolanda Bado de Artecona

1992. Centenary of Paraguayan Writers' College. Multicoloured.

1386	50g. Type **314**	30	20
1387	100g. Jose Ramon Silva	35	30
1388	150g. Abelardo Brugada Valpy	60	45
1389	200g. Tomas Varela	85	65
1390	250g. Jose Livio Lezcano	1·10	90
1391	300g. Francisco I. Fernandez	1·20	1·00

315 Members' Flags and Map of South America

1993. First Anniv (1992) of Treaty of Asuncion forming Mercosur (common market of Argentina, Brazil, Paraguay and Uruguay). Multicoloured.

1392	50g. Type **315**	30	20
1393	350g. Flags encircling globe showing map of South America	1·40	1·20

316 Orange Flowers (Gilda Hellmers)

1993. 50th Anniv of St. Isabel Leprosy Association. Flower paintings by artists named. Multicoloured.

1394	50g. Type **316**	30	20
1395	200g. Luis Alberto Balmelli	85	65
1396	250g. Lili del Monico	1·10	90
1397	350g. Brunilde Guggiari	1·40	1·20

317 Goethe (after J. Lips) and Manuscript of Poem

1993. Centenary of Goethe College.

1398	**317**	50g. brown, black & blue	30	20
1399	-	200g. multicoloured	85	65

DESIGN: 200g. Goethe (after J. Tischbein).

1993. "Brasiliana 93" International Stamp Exhibition, Rio de Janeiro. Nos. 1398/9 optd **BRASILIANA 93**.

1400	50g. brown, black and blue	30	20
1401	200g. multicoloured	85	65

319 Palace (Michael Burt)

1993. Centenary (1992) of Los Lopez (Government) Palace, Asuncion. Paintings of palace by artists named. Multicolured.

1402	50g. Type **319**	30	20
1403	100g. Esperanza Gill	35	30
1404	200g. Emili Aparici	85	65
1405	250g. Hugo Bogado Barrios (vert)	1·10	90

320 Couple sitting on Globe and Emblem

1993. 35th Anniv of World Friendship Crusade.

1406	**320**	50g. black, blue and mauve	30	20
1407	-	100g. multicoloured	35	30
1408	-	200g. multicoloured	85	65
1409	-	250g. multicoloured	1·10	90

DESIGNS: 100g. Dr. Ramon Artemio Bracho (founder), map of Americas and emblem; 200g. Children and sun emerging from cloud; 250g. Couple hugging and emblem.

1993. Inauguration of President Juan Carlos Wasmosy. Nos. 1402/5 optd **TRANSMISION DEL MANDO PRESIDENCIAL GRAL. ANDRES RODRIGUEZ ING. JUAN C. WASMOSY 15 DE AGOSTO 1993**.

1410	50g. multicoloured	30	20
1411	100g. multicoloured	35	30
1412	200g. multicoloured	85	65
1413	250g. multicoloured	1·10	90

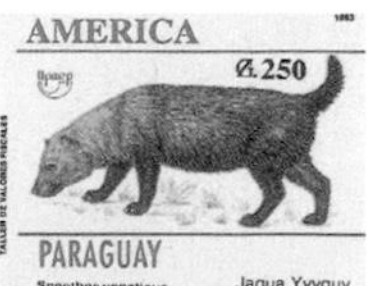

322 "Church of the Incarnation" (Juan Guerra Gaja)

1993. Centenary of Church of the Incarnation. Paintings. Multicoloured.

1414	50g. Type **322**	25	10
1415	350g. "Church of the Incarnation" (Hector Blas Ruiz) (horiz)	1·20	55

323 Bush Dog

1993. America. Endangered Animals. Multicoloured.

1416	250g. Type **323** (postage)	1·70	55
1417	50g. Great anteater (air)	1·10	45

1993. 80th Anniv of World Food Programme. Nos. 1383/4 optd **'30 ANOS DEL PROGRAMA MUNDIAL DE ALIMENTOS'** and emblem.

1418	100g. multicoloured	30	10
1419	200g. multicoloured	60	35

325 Children Carol-singing

1993. Christmas. Multicoloured.

1420	50g. Type **325**	25	10
1421	250g. Wise men following star	70	45

326 Boy and Girl Scouts

1993. 80th Anniv of Paraguay Scouts Association. Multicoloured.

1422	50g. Type **326**	25	10
1423	100g. Boy scouts in camp	30	15
1424	200g. Lord Robert Baden-Powell (founder of Scouting movement)	60	35
1425	250g. Girl scout with flag	70	45

327 Cecilio Baez

1994. Centenary of First Graduation of Lawyers from National University, Asuncion.

1426	**327**	50g. red and crimson	30	20
1427	-	100g. yellow and orange	35	30
1428	-	250g. yellow and green	45	35
1429	-	500g. blue and deep blue	95	75

DESIGNS—VERT: 100g. Benigno Riquelme. HORIZ: 250g. Emeterio Gonzalez; 500g. J. Gaspar Villamayor.

328 Basketball

1994. 50th Anniv of Phoenix Sports Association. Multicoloured.

1430	50g. Type **328**	30	20
1431	200g. Football	35	30
1432	250g. Pedro Andres Garcia Arias (founder) and tennis (horiz)	60	35

329 Penalty Kick

1994. World Cup Football Championship, U.S.A. Multicoloured.

1433	250g. Type **329**	45	20
1434	500g. Tackle	1·10	45
1435	1000g. Dribbling ball past opponent	2·00	1·00

330 Runner

1994. Centenary of International Olympic Committee. Multicoloured.

1436	350g. Type **330**	70	55
1437	400g. Athlete lighting Olympic Flame	85	65

331 World Map and Emblem

1994. World Congress of International Federation for Physical Education, Asuncion. Multicoloured.

1438	200g. Type **331**	60	45
1439	1000g. Family exercising and flag (vert)	3·00	2·40

1994. Brazil, Winners of World Cup Football Championship. Nos. 1433/5 optd **BRASIL Campeon Mundial de Futbol Estados Unidos '94.**

1440	250g. multicoloured	70	55
1441	500g. multicoloured	1·50	1·20
1442	1000g. multicoloured	3·00	2·40

1994. 25th Anniv of First Manned Moon Landing. No. 1407 optd **25 Anos, Conquista de la Luna por el hombre 1969 - 1994.**

1443	100g. multicoloured	35	20

334 Barrios

1994. 50th Death Anniv of Agustin Pio Barrios Mangore (guitarist). Multicoloured.

1444	250g. Type **334**	70	55
1445	500g. Barrios wearing casual clothes and a hat	1·50	1·20

335 Police Commandant, 1913

1994. 151st Anniv of Police Force. Multicoloured.

1446	50g. Type **335**	35	20
1447	250g. Carlos Bernardino Cacabelos (first Commissioner) and Pedro Nolasco Fernandez (first Chief of Asuncion Police Dept)	70	55

336 Maguari Stork

1994. "Parafil 94" Stamp Exhibition. Birds. Multicoloured.

1448	100g. Type **336**	60	35
1449	150g. Yellow-billed cardinal	95	45
1450	400g. Green kingfisher (vert)	2·40	1·00
1451	500g. Jabiru (vert)	3·00	1·20

337 Nicolas Copernicus and Eclipse

1994. Total Eclipse of the Sun, November 1994. Astronomers. Multicoloured.

1452	50g. Type **337**	35	20
1453	200g. Johannes Kepler and sun dial, St. Cosmas and Damian Jesuit settlement	70	55

338 Steam Locomotive

1994. America. Postal Transport. Multicoloured.

1454	100g. Type **338**	40	30
1455	1000g. Express mail motor cycle	3·50	2·75

339 Mother and Child

1994. International Year of the Family. Details of paintings by Olga Blinder. Multicoloured.

1456	50g. Type **339**	35	20
1457	250g. Mother and children	85	65

340 Holy Family and Angels

1994. Christmas. Ceramic Figures. Multicoloured.

1458	150g. Type **340**	45	35
1459	700g. Holy Family (vert)	2·40	1·80

341 Red Cross Workers and Dr. Andres Barbero (founder)

1994. 75th Anniv of Paraguay Red Cross. Multicoloured.

1460	150g. Scouts, anniversary emblem and Henri Dunant (founder of International Red Cross)	45	35
1461	700g. Type **341**	2·40	1·80

342 Sculpture by Herman Guggiari and Pope John Paul II

1994. 90th Anniv of San Jose College. Multicoloured.

1462	200g. Type **342**	60	45
1463	250g. College entrance and Pope John Paul II	85	55

343 Pasteur and Hospital Facade

1995. Paraguayan Red Cross. Death Centenary of Louis Pasteur (chemist) and Centenary of Clinical Hospital.

1464	**343** 1000g. multicoloured	2·40	1·50

344 Couple

1995. Anti-AIDS Campaign. Multicoloured.

1465	500g. Type **344**	1·30	75
1466	1000g. Sad and happy blood droplets	2·40	1·50

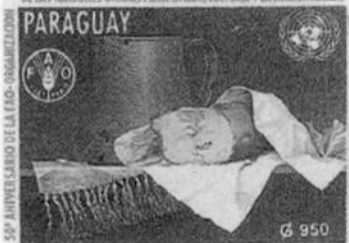

345 Jug and Loaf

1995. 50th Anniv of F.A.O. Paintings by Hernan Miranda. Multicoloured.

1467	950g. Type **345**	2·20	1·40
1468	2000g. Melon and leaf	5·00	2·75

346 Olive-backed Warbler

1995. Fifth Neo-tropical Ornithological Congress, Asuncion. Multicoloured.

1469	100g. Type **346**	45	35
1470	200g. Swallow-tailed manakin	60	35
1471	600g. Troupial	2·00	90
1472	1000g. Hooded siskin	3·00	1·50

347 River Monday Rapids

1995. Fifth International Town, Ecology and Tourism Symposium. Multicoloured.

1473	1150g. Type **347**	1·90	1·20
1474	1300g. Aregua railway station	2·10	1·30

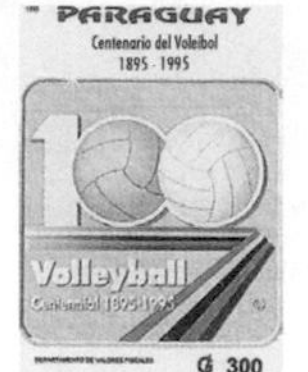

348 "100"

1995. Centenary of Volleyball.

1475	**348**	300g. multicoloured	50	25
1476	-	600g. blue and black	1·00	60
1477	-	1000g. multicoloured	1·70	1·10

DESIGNS: 600g. Ball hitting net; 1000g. Hands, ball and net.

349 Macizo, Acahay

1995. America. Environmental Protection. Multicoloured.

1478	950g. Type **349**	3·00	1·10
1479	2000g. Tinfunque Reserve, Chaco (vert)	5·50	2·40

350 Anniversary Emblem

1995. 50th Anniv of U.N.O. Multicoloured.

1480	200g. Type **350**	35	25
1481	3000g. Stylized figures supporting emblem	5·25	3·25

351 Couple holding Star

1995. Christmas. Multicoloured.

1482	200g. Type **351**	35	25
1483	1000g. Crib	2·00	1·30

352 Marti and "Hedychium coronarium"

1995. Birth Cent of Jose Marti (revolutionary). Multicoloured.

1484	200g. Type **352**	35	25
1485	1000g. Marti, Cuban national flag and "Hedychium coronarium" (horiz)	2·00	1·30

353 "Railway Station" (Asuncion)

1996. 25th Latin American and Caribbean Forum of Lions International. Paintings by Esperanza Gill. Multicoloured.

1486	200g. Type **353**	35	25
1487	1000g. "Viola House"	2·00	1·30

354 "Cattleya nobilior"

1996. Orchids. Multicoloured.

1488	100g. Type **354**	30	10
1489	200g. "Oncidium varicosum"	35	25
1490	1000g. "Oncidium jonesianum" (vert)	1·70	95
1491	1150g. "Sophronitis cernua"	2·00	1·10

355 Emblems and Gymnast on "Stamp"

1996. Centenary of Modern Olympic Games and Olympic Games, Atlanta. Multicoloured.

1492	500g. Type **355**	85	45
1493	1000g. Emblems and runner on "stamp"	1·70	95

356 Bosco, Monks and Boys

1996. Centenary of Salesian Brothers in Paraguay. Multicoloured.

1494	200g. Type **356**	35	25
1495	300g. Madonna and Child, Pope John Paul II and St. John Bosco (vert)	50	35
1496	1000g. St. John Bosco (founder) and map	1·70	1·40

357 Family Outing (Silvia Cacares Baez)

1996. 50th Anniv of UNICEF. Multicoloured.

1497	1000g. Type **357**	1·70	1·40
1498	1300g. Families (Cinthia Perez Alderete)	2·20	1·90

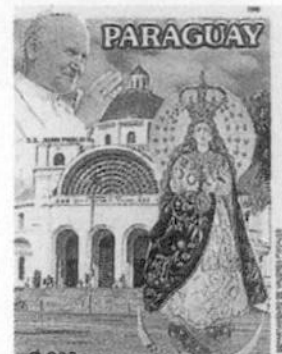

358 Pope John Paul II, Caacupe Cathedral and Virgin

1996. Our Lady of Caacupe. Multicoloured.

1499	200g. Type **358**	35	30
1500	1300g. Pope John Paul II, floodlit cathedral and Virgin (horiz)	2·20	1·90

359 Woman

1996. America. Traditional Costumes. Multicoloured.

1501	500g. Type **359**	85	70
1502	1000g. Couple	1·80	1·40

360 Boxes and Food

1996. International Year for Eradication of Poverty. Multicoloured.

1503	1000g. Type **360**	1·70	1·40
1504	1150g. Boy with boxes and food (vert)	2·00	1·70

361 Mother and Baby

1996. Christmas. Multicoloured.

1505	200g. Type **361**	35	30
1506	1000g. Mother with smiling child	1·70	95

362 "Eryphanis automedon"

1997. Butterflies. Multicoloured.

1507	200g. Type **362**	60	35
1508	500g. "Dryadula phaetusa"	1·80	45
1509	1000g. "Vanessa myrinna"	3·00	95
1510	1150g. Rare tiger	3·75	1·10

363 First Government Palace (legislative building)

1997. Buildings. Multicoloured.

1511	200g. Type **363**	35	30
1512	1000g. Patri Palace (postal headquarters)	2·00	1·10

364 Crucifix, Piribebuy

1997. Year of Jesus Christ.

1513	**364**	1000g. multicoloured	1·70	95

365 Summit Emblem

1997. 11th Group of Rio Summit Meeting, Asuncion.

1514	**365**	1000g. multicoloured	1·80	1·20

366 Cactus

1997. "The Changing Climate—Everyone's Concern". Plants. Multicoloured.

1515	300g. Type **366**	60	35
1516	500g. "Bromelia balansae" (vert)	85	60
1517	1000g. "Monvillea kroenlaini"	1·80	1·20

367 Tiger Cat

1997. First Mercosur (South American Common Market), Chile and Bolivia Stamp Exhibition, Asuncion. Mammals. Multicoloured.

1518	200g. Type **367**	25	10
1519	1000g. Black howler monkey (vert)	1·80	1·20
1520	1150g. Paca	2·10	1·30

368 Members' Flags and Southern Cross

1997. Sixth Anniv of Mercosur (South American Common Market).

1521	**368**	1000g. multicoloured	1·80	1·20

369 Postman and Letters circling Globe

1997. America. The Postman. Multicoloured.

1522	1000g. Type **369**	2·75	1·20
1523	1150g. Weather and terrain aspects of postal delivery and postman (horiz)	3·00	1·40

370 Neri Kennedy (javelin)

1997. 50th Anniv of National Sports Council. Multicoloured.

1524	200g. Type **370**	35	30
1525	1000g. Ramon Milciades Gimenez Gaona (discus)	2·20	1·30

1997. "Mevifil '97" First International Exhibition of Philatelic Audio-visual and Computer Systems, Buenos Aires, Argentina. Nos. 1446/7 optd **MEVIFIL '97**.

1526	50g. multicoloured	85	60
1527	250g. multicoloured	4·25	2·40

372 Mother and Child (Olga Blinder)

1997. Christmas. Multicoloured.

1528	200g. Type **372**	25	10
1529	1000g. Mother and child (Hernan Miranda)	1·80	1·20

373 Boy

1997. "Children of the World with AIDS". Children's Paintings. Multicoloured.

1530	500g. Type **373**	85	60
1531	1000g. Girl	1·80	1·20

374 Drinking Vessel and Emblem forming "70"

1997. 70th Anniv of Asuncion Rotary Club.

1532	**374**	1150g. multicoloured	2·10	1·30

375 Julio Cesar Romero (1986 World Cup team member)

1998. World Cup Football Championship, France. Multicoloured.

1533	200g. Type **375**	25	10
1534	500g. Carlos Gamarra (World Cup team member) tackling opponent	85	60
1535	1000g. World Cup team (horiz)	1·80	1·20

376 Silver Tetra

1998. Fish. Multicoloured.

1536	200g. Type **376**	60	35
1537	300g. Spotted sorubim	85	35
1538	500g. Dorado	1·30	60
1539	1000g. Pira jagua	2·75	1·20

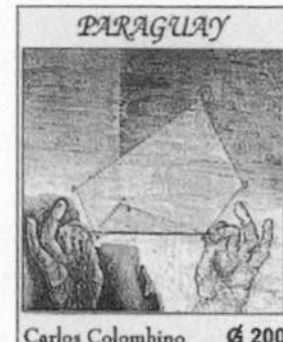
377 Painting by Carlos Colombino

1998. Paintings by artists named. Multicoloured.

1540	200g. Type **377**	25	10
1541	300g. Felix Toranzos	60	35
1542	400g. Edith Gimenez	75	45
1543	1000g. Ricardo Migliorisi (horiz)	1·80	1·20

378 Cep

1998. Fungi. Multicoloured.

1544	400g. Type **378**	80	50
1545	600g. Parasol mushroom	1·00	60
1546	1000g. Collared earthstar	1·90	1·20

379 Carlos Lopez's House, Botanical and Zoological Gardens, Asuncion

1998. 50th Anniv of Organization of American States. Multicoloured.

1547	500g. Type **379**	90	60
1548	1000g. Villa Palmerola, Aregua	1·90	1·20

380 Door of Sanctuary, Caazapa Church

1998. 400th Anniv of Ordination of First Paraguayan Priests by Brother Hernando de Trejo y Sanabria. Multicoloured.

1549	400g. Type **380**	80	50
1550	1700g. Statue of St. Francis of Assisi, Atyra Church (horiz)	3·50	2·20

381 "Acacia caven"

1998. Flowers. Multicoloured.

1551	100g. Type **381**	25	10
1552	600g. "Cordia trichotoma"	1·30	75
1553	1900g. "Glandularia" sp.	4·00	2·40

382 Ruins of the Mission of Jesus, Itapua

1998. Mercosur (South American Common Market) Heritage Sites.

1554	**382**	5000g. multicoloured	10·50	6·75

383 Serafina Davalos (first female lawyer in Paraguay) and National College

1998. America. Famous Women. Multicoloured.

1555	1600g. Type **383**	3·50	2·10
1556	1700g. Adela Speratti (first director) and Teachers' Training College	3·75	2·20

384 Abstract (Carlos Colombino)

1998. 50th Anniv of Universal Declaration of Human Rights. Multicoloured.

1557	500g. Type **384**	90	60
1558	1000g. Man on crutches (after Joel Filartiga)	1·90	1·20

385 Crib

1998. Christmas. Multicoloured.

1559	300g. Type **385**	65	35
1560	1600g. Crib (different) (vert)	3·50	2·10

386 Coral Cobra

1999. Reptiles. Multicoloured.

1561	100g. Type **386**	25	10
1562	300g. Ground lizard	65	35
1563	1600g. Red-footed tortoise	3·50	2·10
1564	1700g. Paraguay caiman	3·75	2·20

1999. "Chaco Peace 99" Stamp Exhibition, Paraguay and Bolivia. No. 1542 optd **1era. Exposicion Filatellca Paraguayo-Boliviana PAZ DEL CHACO 99**.

1565	400g. multicoloured	90	50

388 Painting by Ignacio Nunes Soler

1999. Paintings. Showing paintings by named artists.

1566	500g. Type **388**	90	60
1567	1600g. Modesto Delgado Rodas	2·75	1·80
1568	1700g. Jaime Bestard	3·00	2·00

389 Carlos Humberto Parades being tackled

1999. American Cup Football Championship, Paraguay. Multicoloured.

1569	300g. Type **389**	50	25
1570	500g. South American Football Federation Building, Luque, Paraguay (horiz)	90	50
1571	1900g. Feliciano Caceres Stadium, Luque (horiz)	3·50	2·10

390 Toucan

1999. 50th Anniv of S.O.S. Children's Villages. Multicoloured.

1572	1700g. Type **390**	2·75	1·60
1573	1900g. Toucan (different) (vert)	3·00	1·90

391 Government Palace

1999. Assassination of Dr. Luis Marua Argana (Vice-president, 1998–99). Multicoloured.

1574	100g. Type **391**	25	10
1575	500g. Dr. Argana (vert)	65	40
1576	1500g. Crowd before National Congress building	2·30	1·40

392 *Cochlospermum regium*

1999. Medicinal Plants. Multicoloured.

1577	600g. Type **392**	95	50
1578	700g. *Borago officinalis*	1·00	65
1579	1700g. *Passiflora cincinnata*	2·50	1·50

393 "The Man who carries the Storm"

1999. America. A New Millennium without Arms. Showing paintings by Ricardo Migliorisi. Mult.

1580	1500g. Type **393**	2·10	1·40
1581	3000g. "The Man who dominates the Storm" (vert)	4·75	3·25

394 "Couple" (Olga Blinder)

1999. International Year of the Elderly. Multicoloured.

1582	1000g. Type **394**	1·50	1·00
1583	1900g. "Old Woman" (Marma de los Reyes Omella Herrero) (vert)	3·00	1·90

395 "Mother and Child" (Manuel Viedma)

1999. Christmas. Multicoloured.

1584	300g. Type **395**	55	25
1585	1600g. "Nativity" (Federico Ordinana)	2·40	1·50

396 *Tabebuia impetiginosa*

1999. Centenary of Pedro Juan Caballero City. Multicoloured.

1586	1000g. Type **396**	1·50	1·00
1587	1600g. *Tabebuia pulcherrima* (vert)	2·40	1·50

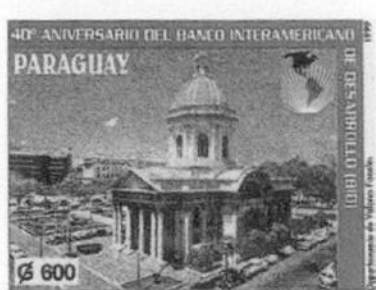

397 Oratory of the Virgin Our Lady of the Assumption and National Mausoleum

1999. 40th Anniv of Inter-American Development Bank. Multicoloured.

1588	600g. Type **397**	95	65
1589	700g. Government Palace	1·10	75

398 Carmen Casco de Lara Castro and "Conjunction" (bronze sculpture, Domingo Rivarola)

2000. International Women's Day. Carmen Casco de Lara Castro (founder of National Commission for Human Rights). Multicoloured.

1590	400g. Type **398**	65	40
1591	2000g. Carmen Casco de Lara Castro and "Violation" (bronze sculpture, Gustavo Beckelman)	3·25	2·20

399 Hydroelectric Dam, Yacyreta, and Marsh Deer

2000. "EXPO 2000" World's Fair, Hanover, Germany. Showing bi-lateral development projects. Multicoloured.

1592	500g. Type **399** (Paraguay–Argentine Republic)	80	50
1593	2500g. Hydroelectric dam, Itaipu and Brazilian tapir (Paraguay–Brazil)	4·00	2·75

400 Students and Pope John Paul II

2000. Centenary of the Daughters of Maria Auxiliadora College. Multicoloured.

1594	600g. Type **400**	95	65
1595	2000g. College building	3·25	2·20

401 Footballers chasing Ball

2000. Olympic Games, Sydney. Multicoloured.

1596	2500g. Type **401**	4·00	2·75
1597	3000g. Francisco Rojas Soto (athlete), Munich Olympics, 1972 (horiz)	4·75	3·25

402 Adult Hands protecting Child (Nahuel Moreno Lezcano)

2000. Tenth Anniv of United Nations Convention on the Rights of the Child. Multicoloured.

1598	1500g. Type **402**	2·10	1·40
1599	1700g. Hand prints (Claudia Alessandro Irala Chavez) (horiz)	2·75	1·60

403 Firemen attending to Fire

2000. 95th Anniv of Fire Service. Multicoloured.

1600	100g. Type **403**	25	15
1601	200g. Badge and fireman wearing 1905 dress uniform	40	20
1602	1500g. Firemen attending fire (horiz)	2·10	1·40
1603	1600g. Firemen using hose (horiz)	2·40	1·50

404 Stretch of Road from San Bernardino to Altos

2000. Road Development Scheme. Multicoloured.

1604	500g. Type **404**	80	50
1605	3000g. Gaspar Rodriguez de Francia motorway	4·75	3·25

405 Signpost and Emblem

2000. America. AIDS Awareness Campaign. Multicoloured.

1606	1500g. Type **405**	2·10	1·40
1607	2500g. Ribbon emblem on noughts and crosses grid	4·00	2·75

406 "Love and Peace" (metal sculpture, Hugo Pistilli)

2000. International Year of Culture and Peace. Multicoloured.

1608	500g. Type **406**	80	50
1609	2000g. "For Peace" (metal sculpture, Herman Guggiari)	3·25	2·20

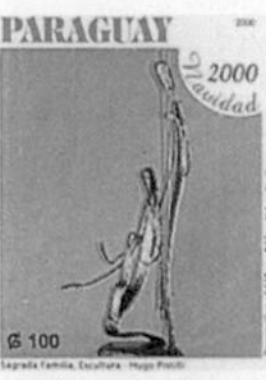

407 "Holy Family" (metal sculpture, Hugo Pistilli)

2000. Christmas. Multicoloured.

1610	100g. Type **407**	25	15
1611	500g. Poem, pen and Jose Luis Appleyard (poet and writer)	80	50
1612	2000g. Nativity (crib firgures) (horiz)	3·25	2·20

408 Country Woman (sculpture, Behage)

2000. Art. Multicoloured.

1613	200g. Type **408**	40	20
1614	1500g. Drinking vessels (Quintin Velazquez) (horiz)	2·10	1·40
1615	2000g. Silver orchid brooch (Quirino Torres)	3·25	2·20

409 Flores

2000. 30th Birth Anniv (2002) of Jose Asuncion Flores (musician). Multicoloured.

1616	100g. Type **409**	25	15
1617	1500g. Violin	2·10	1·40
1618	2500g. Trombone	4·00	2·75

410 Presidents of Argentina, Brazil, Paraguay and Uruguay signing Treaty

2001. Tenth Anniv of Asuncion Treaty (cooperation treaty). Multicoloured.

1619	500g. Type **410**	80	50
1620	2500g. Map of South America (vert)	4·00	2·75

411 *Opuntia*

2001. Cacti. Multicoloured.

1621	2000g. Type **411**	3·25	2·20
1622	2500g. *Cerus stenogonus*	4·00	2·75

412 Three Players

2001. Under 20's Football Championship, Argentina. Multicoloured.

1623	2000g. Type **412**	3·25	2·20
1624	2500g. Two players (vert)	4·00	2·75

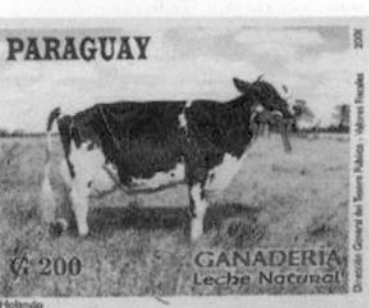

413 Holando Cow (Friesian)

2001. Cattle. Multicoloured.

1625	200g. Type **413**	40	20
1626	500g. Nelore bull (Brahmin)	80	50
1627	1500g. Pampa Chaqueno bull	2·10	1·40

414 Donkey Riders (Josefina Pla)

2001. Xylographs (wood engravings).

1628 **414** 500g. multicoloured 85 55
1629 - 500g. multicoloured (vert) 85 55
1630 - 1500g. black, green and lemon 2·20 1·50
1631 - 2000g. multicoloured 3·50 2·40

DESIGNS: 500g. Type **414**; 500g. Women (Leonor Cecotto); 1500g. Frog (Jacinta Rivero); 2000g. (Livio Abramo).

415 Eichu (Pleiades)

2001. Guarani (Native Americans) Mythology. Multicoloured.

1632 100g. Type **415** 30 15
1633 600g. Mborevi Rape (Milky Way) 95 70
1634 1600g. Jagua Ho'u Jasy (Eclipse of the moon) 2·50 1·70

416 Inocencio Lezcano

2001. Teachers' Day. Multicoloured.

1635 200g. Type **416** 40 20
1636 1600g. Ramon Cardozo 2·50 1·70

417 Jesuit Mission Ruins, Trinidad and St. Ignacio de Loyola (statue)

2001. America. Cultural Heritage. Multicoloured.

1637 500g. Type **417** 85 55
1638 2000g. Ruins (different) 3·50 2·40

Nos. 1637/8 were issued together, *se-tenant*, in strips of two stamps and two labels, the whole forming a composite design.

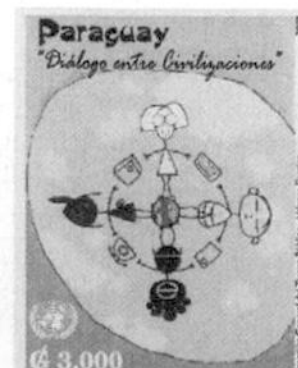

418 Children encircling Globe

2001. United Nations Year of Dialogue among Civilization.

1639 **418** 3000g. multicoloured 4·75 3·50

419 Dough Nativity (Gladys Feliciangeli)

2001. Christmas. Multicoloured.

1640 700g. Type **419** 1·10 85
1641 4000g. Clay and banana leaf Nativity (Mercedes Servin) 6·25 4·25

420 World Trade Buildings, New York

2001. "No to Terrorism". Multicoloured.

1642 700g. Type **420** 1·10 85
1643 5000g. Chain links changing to doves and flags (horiz) 7·50 5·50

421 *Passiflora carulea*

2001. Tenth Anniv of Mercosur (South American Common Market).

1644 **421** 4000g. multicoloured 6·25 4·25

422 Tree Frog (*Phyllomedusa sauvagei*)

2002. Scout Jamboree, Loma Plata.

1645 **422** 6000g. multicoloured 9·00 7·00

423 Rowers, Club Building and Cormorant

2002. Centenary of "El Mbigua" (cormorant) Social Club.

1646 **423** 700g. multicoloured 1·10 85

424 "The Pieta" (statue)

2002. 25th Anniv of Juan de Salzar Cultural Centre, Asuncion. Multicoloured.

1647 2500g. Type **424** 4·25 3·00
1648 5000g. St. Michael (statue) 7·50 5·50

425 Team Members

2002. Football World Cup Championships, Japan and South Korea. Multicoloured.

1649 3000g. Type **425** 4·75 3·50
1649a 3000g. As Type **425** but with no inscription 4·75 3·50
1649b 5000g. Players celebrating 7·50 5·50

426 Mennonite Church, Filadelfia

2002. 75th Anniv of Arrival of Mennonite Christians. Multicoloured.

1650 2000g. Type **426** 3·50 2·40
1651 4000g. Church, Loma Plata 6·25 4·25

427 Criollo Mare and Foal

2002. Horses. Multicoloured.

1652 700g. Type **427** 1·10 85
1653 1000g. Quarto de Milla 1·50 1·10
1654 6000g. Arabian 9·00 7·00

428 Players holding Cup

2002. Centenary of Olimpia Football Club.

1655 **428** 700g. multicoloured 1·10 85

429 *Stevia rebaudiana*

2002. Centenary of Pan American Health Organization. Multicoloured.

1656 4000g. Type **429** 6·25 4·25
1657 5000g. *Ilex paraguayensis* 7·50 5·50

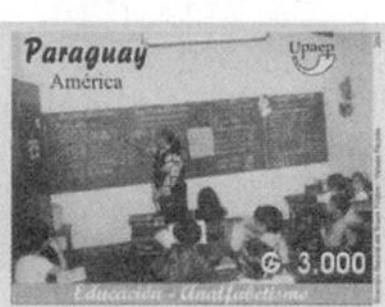

432 Teacher and Class

2002. America. Literacy Campaign. Multicoloured.

1661 3000g. Type **432** 4·75 3·50
1662 6000g. Children playing 9·00 7·00

435 San Antonio Church and Saint Anthony (statue)

2003. Centenary of San Antonio District.

1667 **435** 700g. multicoloured 1·10 85

436 Decorated Plate and Josefina Pla

2003. Birth Centenary of Josefina Pla (ceramist and writer). Multicoloured.

1668 700g. Type **436** 1·10 85
1669 6000g. Josefina Pla and engraving 9·00 7·00

437 Blue-fronted Amazon (*Amazona aestiva*)

2003. Parrots. Multicoloured.

1670 1000g. Type **437** 1·50 1·10
1671 2000g. Monk parrot (*Myiopsitta monachus*) 3·50 2·40
1672 4000g. White-eyed conure (*Aratinga leucophtalmus*) 6·25 4·25

438 Legislative Palace

2003. Inauguration of New Legislative Palace.

1674 **438** 4000g. multicoloured 6·25 4·25

No. 1673 is vacant.

439 Pope John Paul II and Our Lady of Asuncion Church

2003. 25th Anniv of Pontificate of Pope John Paul II.

1675 **439** 6000g. multicoloured 9·00 7·00

440 Pig

2003. Domestic Animals. Multicoloured.

1676 1000g. Type **440** 1·40 1·00
1677 3000g. Sheep 4·50 3·25
1678 8000g. Goat 9·75 7·75

441 Sweets

2003. Gastronomy. Multicoloured.

1679 700g. Type **441** 1·00 80
1680 2000g. Sopa Paraguaya (cake) 3·25 2·30
1681 3000g. Chipa (bread) 4·50 3·25

442 Julio Correa

2003. Folklorists. Multicoloured.

1682 700g. Type **442** 1·00 80
1683 1000g. Emilano Rivarola Fernadez 1·40 1·00
1684 2000g. Manuel Ortiz Guerrero 3·25 2·30

443 La Golondriana

2003. National Dances. Multicoloured.

1685 700g. Type **443** 1·00 80
1686 3000g. Polca 4·50 3·25
1687 4000g. Galopera 5·75 4·00

444 Footballers

2003. Centenary of Guarani Football Club.

1688 **444** 700g. multicoloured 1·00 80

445 Poncho Para i (60 stripe poncho)

2003. Mercosur. Crafts. Multicoloured.

1689 4000g. Type **445** 5·75 4·00

1690 5000g. Shirt made from Ao Poi fabric 7·25 5·25

446 Flight into Egypt

2003. Christmas. Patchwork designs made by Santa Maria de Fe Mission. Multicoloured.

1691 700g. Type **446** 1·00 80

1692 1000g. Shepherd and star 1·40 1·00

1693 4000g. Holy Family 5·75 4·00

447 Footballers

2003. Futsal (Indoor Football) Championship, Sol de America Stadium, Asuncion, Paraguay. Multicoloured.

1694 4000g. Type **447** 5·75 4·00

1695 5000g. Two players 7·25 5·25

2003. Paraguay's Qualification for Futsal World Cup Championship, Taiwan . Nos. 1694/5 optd **PARAGUAY CAMPEON MUNDIAL**. Multicoloured.

1696 4000g. As Type **447** 5·75 4·00

1697 5000g. As No. 1695 7·25 5·25

449 *Cordia bordasii*

2003. America. Endangered Species. Multicoloured.

1698 1000g. Type **449** 1·40 1·00

1699 5000g. *Chorisia insignis* 7·25 5·25

1700 5000g. *Bulnesia sarmientoi* 7·25 5·25

450 Anahi (C. Gomez)

2004. Comics written by Robin Wood. Multicoloured.

1701 1000g. Type **450** 1·40 1·00

1702 3000g. Nippur de Lagash (L. Olivera) 4·50 3·25

1703 5000g. Dago (A. Salinas) 7·25 5·25

451 Footballer

2004. Centenary of National Football Team.

1704 **451** 700g. multicoloured 1·00 80

452 Statues, Alter Piece, San Jose Church

2004. Centenary of San Jose College, Asuncion.

1705 **452** 700g. multicoloured 1·00 80

453 Pablo Neruda (statue) (Hugo Pistilli)

2004. Birth Centenary of Ricardo Eliecer Neftali Reyes Basoalto. (Pablo Neruda) (writer).

1706 **453** 5000g. multicoloured 7·25 5·25

454 Monday Waterfall

2004. Tourism. Multicoloured.

1707 700g. Type **454** 1·00 80

1708 6000g. Tobati 8·50 6·50

455 Asuncion (fresco) (Jose Laterza Parodi)

2004. Museum of Independence. Multicoloured.

1709 700g. Type **455** 1·00 80

1710 5000g. Museum building 7·25 5·25

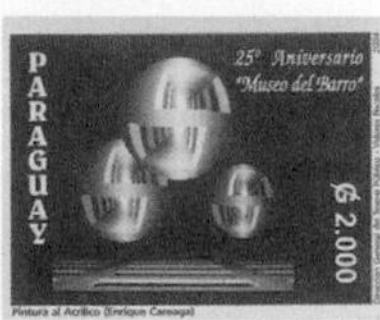

456 Abstract (Enrique Careaga)

2004. Centenary of Museo del Barro (art museum). Multicoloured.

1711 2000g. Type **456** 3·25 2·30

1712 3000g. Female figure (Mercedes Noguera) (vert) 4·50 3·25

1713 4000g. Crucified Christ (Jesuit Mission) (vert) 5·75 4·00

457 Jose Flores and Musical Score

2004. Birth Centenary of Jose Asuncion Flores (composer).

1714 **457** 5000g. multicoloured 7·25 5·25

458 Camello Locomotive (1911)

2004. 150th Anniv of Railways. Multicoloured.

1715 2000g. Type **458** 3·25 2·30

1716 3000g. El Coqueto locomotive (1911) (horiz) 4·50 3·25

MS1717 117×82 mm. 6000g. Sapucai locomotive (1886) (50×40 mm) 8·50 8·50

459 *Procias nudicollis*

2004. America. Environmental Protection. Multicoloured.

1718 6000g. Type **459** 8·50 6·50

MS1719 117×82 mm. 6000g. *Ceratophys cranwelli* (50×40 mm) 8·50 8·50

460 Ocelot (*Felis pardalis*)

2004. Mercosur. Aquifer Conservation. Multicoloured.

1720 2000g. Type **460** 3·25 2·30

1721 4000g. Giant anteater (*Myrmecophaga tridactyla*), Hippopotamus (*Hydrochoerus hydrochaeris*) and crested screamer (*Chauna torquata*) 5 75 4·00

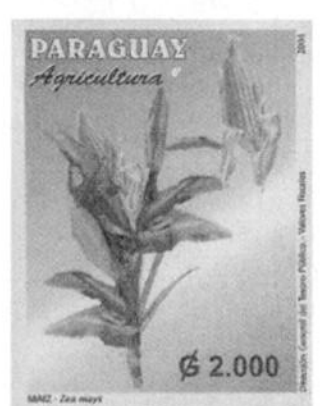

461 Maize (Zea mays)

2004. Agricultural Crops. Multicoloured.

1722 2000g. Type **461** 3·25 2·30

1723 4000g. Cotton (*Gossypium hirsutum*) 5·75 4·00

1724 6000g. Soya bean (*Glicine max*) 8·50 6·50

462 Mary and Jesus

2004. Christmas. Paintings by Ricardo Migliorisi. Multicoloured.

1725 3000g. Type **462** 4·50 3·25

1726 5000g. Angel (vert) 7·25 5·25

463 1870 3r. Stamp and Emblem

2004. 40th Anniv of Latin American Parliament.

1727 **463** 4000g. multicoloured 5·75 4·00

464 Turbines

2004. 30th Anniv of Paraguay—Brazil Hydro-Electric Generation (ITAIPU). Multicoloured.

1728 4000g. Type **464** 5·75 4·00

1729 5000g. Dam (vert) 7·25 5·25

2005. Pope John Paul II Commemoration (1st issue). No. 1713 optd **S.S. JUNA PABLO II EN LA GLORIA DE DIOS 2 ABRIL 2005**. Multicoloured.

1730 4000g. Crucified Christ (Jesuit Mission) 5·75 4·00

See also No. 1742.

466 La Santisima Trinidad de Paraná Ruins

2005. Centenary of Rotary International. Multicoloured.

1731 3000g. Type **466** 4·50 3·25

1732 4000g. Statue (vert) 5·75 4·00

467 Building and Jose Gaspar Rodríguez de Francia (1st post-independence leader)

2005. Bicentenary of Casa Castelvi.

1733 **467** 5000g. multicoloured 7·25 5·25

468 Orchestra and Herminio Gimenez

2005. Birth Centenary of Herminio Gimenez (composer).

1734 **468** 700g. multicoloured 1·00 80

469 Building Facade

2005. First Anniv of El Cabildo National Cultural Centre.

1735 **469** 1000g. multicoloured 1·40 1·00

470 Monument to the Pioneers

2005. 75th Anniv of Fernheim Mennonite Colony. Multicoloured.

1736 5000g. Type **470** 7·25 5·25

MS1737 116×82 mm. 6000g. Ox cart (50×40 mm) 8·50 8·50

471 Team Members (1955)

2005. Centenary of Club Libertad Football Club.

1738 **471** 700g. multicoloured 1·00 80

472 Don Quixote and Sancho Panza

2005. 400th Anniv of Don Quixote De La Mancha novel by Miguel de Cervantes Saavedra.

1739	**472**	8000g. multicoloured	9·75	7·75

473 Herib Campos Cervera

2005. Mercosur. Writers. Multicoloured.

1740	3000g. Type **473**	4·50	3·25
1741	5000g. Gabriel Casaccia	7·25	5·25

474 Pope John Paul II

2005. Pope John Paul II Commemoration (2nd issue).

1742	**474**	2000g. multicoloured	3·25	2·30

475 Chains, Bird and Justice (statue)

2005. Truth and Justice.

1743	**475**	8000g. multicoloured	9·75	7·75

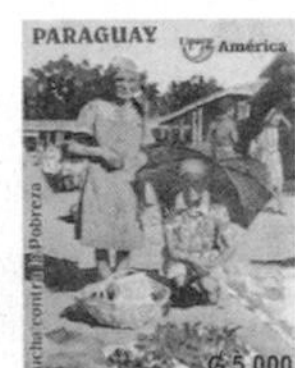

476 Elderly Women

2005. America. Struggle against Poverty. Multicoloured.

1744	5000g. Type **476**	7·25	5·25
1745	6000g. Man mending shoes	8·50	6·50

477 Cats

2005. Cats and Dogs. Multicoloured.

1746	2000g. Type **477**	3·25	2·30
1747	2000g. Samoyed dog	3·25	2·30
1748	3000g. White shorthair cat	4·50	3·25
1749	3000g. Inscr "German dog"	4·50	3·25

478 Branislava Susnik and Chamacoco Bracelet

2005. Anthropologists. Multicoloured.

1750	1000g. Type **478**	1·40	1·00
1751	2000g. Miguel Chase-Sardi and Nivacle poncho	3·25	2·30
1752	8000g. Leon Cadogan and Mbya basket	9·75	7·75

479 Lucy Aguero (athlete)

2005. International Year of Sports Education. Multicoloured.

1753	5000g. Type **479**	7·25	5·25
MS1754	116×81 mm. 6000g. Carlos Franco (golfer) (50×40 mm)	8·50	8·50

480 Angels

2005. Christmas. Multicoloured.

1755	700g. Type **480**	1·00	80
1756	5000g. The Nativity	7·25	5·25

481 Dam and Plant

2005. Yacyreta Hydroelectric Plant. Multicoloured.

1757	3000g. Type **481**	4·50	3·25
1758	5000g. Aerial view of plant	7·25	5·25

482 Monumento a Las Residentas (statue) (Francisco Javier Baez Rolon)

2005. 150th Anniv of Ministry of Defence. Multicoloured.

1759	700g. Type **482**	1·00	80
1760	1000g. Ministry of Defence building	1·40	1·00

483 Karl Benz Vehicle, 1886

2006. 50th Anniv of Paraguay—Germany Chamber of Commerce.

1761	**483**	8000g. multicoloured	9·75	7·75

484 Paraguay Team

2006. World Cup Football Championship, Germany. Multicoloured.

1762	3000g. Type **484**	4·50	3·25
1763	5000g. Emblem and trophy	7·25	5·25

485 Eiffel Tower and Pot

2006. 50th Anniv of Asuncion French Alliance.

1764	**485**	8000g. multicoloured	9·75	7·75

486 Miguel de Cervantes Saavedra and Letter, 1616

2006. 50th Anniv of Cervantes Grammar School.

1765	**486**	700g. multicoloured	1·00	80

488 *Cattleya* (orchid)

2006. Centenary of Commercial School.

1767	**488**	700g. multicoloured	1·00	80

489 *Junonia evarete*

2005. 70th Anniv of Japanese Immigration. Butterflies. Multicoloured.

1768	1000g. Type **489**	1·40	1·00
1769	2000g. *Anartia jatrophae*	3·25	2·30
1770	3000g. *Agraulis vanillae*	4·50	3·25
MS1771	116×83 mm. 6000g. *Danaus plexippus* (50×40 mm)	8·50	8·50

490 Surfacing Route 10

2006. 30th Anniv of OPEC International Development Fund.

1772	**490**	8000g. multicoloured	9·75	7·75

491 Virgin of Schoenstatt (inscr "Schoenstant")

2006. 25th Anniv of Tuparenda Sanctuary.

1773	**491**	700g. multicoloured	1·00	80

492 Windmills

2006. America. Energy Conservation. Multicoloured.

1774	5000g. Type **492**	7·25	5·25
1775	6000g. Solar panels	8·50	6·50

493 Livestock

2006. 30th Anniv of Veterinary and Agricultural School. Multicoloured.

1776	4000g. Type **493** (veterinary faculty)	5·75	4·00
1777	4000g. Symbols of agriculture (agricultural faculty)	5·75	4·00

494 Building and Monument

2006. 90th Anniv of Confederacion Sudamericana de Futbol (CONMEBOL).

1778	**494**	8000g. multicoloured	9·75	7·75

495 Harp

2006. Mercosur. Musical Instruments. Multicoloured.

1779	5000g. Type **495**	7·25	5·25
1780	6000g. Guitar	8·50	6·50

496 Nuestra Senora de la Asuncion Cathedral

2006. Christmas. Multicoloured.

1781	4000g. Type **496**	5·75	4·00
1782	6000g. Santisima Trinidad Church (horiz)	8·50	6·50

497 Battle Area

2007. 80th Death Anniv of Adolfo Rojas Silva (casualty during 'Chaco War'). Multicoloured.

1783	4000g. Type **497**	5·75	4·00
1784	6000g. Adolfo Rojas Silva (vert)	8·50	6·50

498 Flower

2007. 50th Anniv of B'nai B'rith Organization (Jewish service organization) in Paraguay.

1785	**498**	8000g. multicoloured	9·75	7·75

499 Parrot

2007. Asuncion 2007–Americas Conference.

1786	**499**	8000g. multicoloured	9·75	7·75

500 Smoky Atmosphere

2007. Freedom from Tobacco Day. Multicoloured.

1787	5000g. Type **500**	7·25	5·25
1788	6000g. Clean atmosphere (vert)	8·50	6·50

501 Masks

2007. 25th Anniv of Arlequin Theatre.

1789	**501**	700g. multicoloured	1·00	80

502 *Felis pardalis* (ocelot)

2007. Inter-American Philatelic Association. Chaco National Park. Multicoloured.

1790	700g. Type **502**	1·00	80
1791	8000g. Postman riding ox	9·75	7·75

503 Horse-drawn Cart (inscr 'Sulki')

2007. 45th Anniv of Paraguay–Korea Diplomatic Relations. Multicoloured.

1792	1000g. Type **503**	1·40	1·00
1793	2000g. Covered horse-drawn cart (inscr 'Carumbe')	3·25	2·30
1794	3000g. Ox cart (vert)	4·50	3·25
MS1795	116×81 mm. 6000g. Mugungfa (Korean national flower) (50×40 mm)	8·50	8·50

504 Taipei 101 Tower

2007. 50th Anniv of Paraguay–Republic of China (Taiwan) Friendship.

1796	**504**	7000g. multicoloured	9·00	7·25

505 Tree and Building

2007. 25th Anniv of Paraguay–Indonesia Diplomatic Relations.

1797	**505**	11000g. multicoloured	13·00	10·50

506 Bull

2007. 40th Anniv of SENASCA (veterinary services). Multicoloured.

1798	5000g. Type **506**	7·25	5·25
1799	7000g. Vet, cattle and prize bull (horiz)	9·00	7·25

507a Celebration

2007. America. Education for All

1800	**507a**	5000g. Type **507a**	1·50	1·10
1800a		6000g. Teacher and pupils		

508a Nautilus Building

2007. Mercosur. Architecture. Multicoloured.

1801	6000g. Type **508a**	6·00	6·50
1802	7000g. Barro Museum (horiz)	8·50	6·50

509 martin McMahon

2007. General Martin McMahon Commemoration.

1803	700g. **509** multicoloured	1·00	80

510 Anniversary Emblem

2007. 40th Anniv of Peace Corps.

1804	7000g. **510** multicoloured	9·00	7·25

511 Scouts and Campfire

2007. Centenary of Scouting. Multicoloured.

1805	700g. Type **511**	1·00	80
1806	6000g. Girl scout	8·50	6·50

512 Stadium Façade

2007. Inauguration of New Stadium.

1807	700g. **512** multicoloured	1·00	80

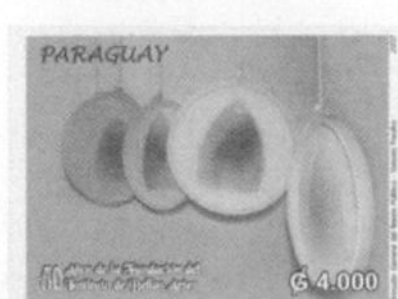

513 Pendants (Engelberto Gimenez Legal)

2007. 50th Anniv of Institute of Fine Arts. Multicoloured.

1808	4000g. Type **513**	5·75	4·00
1809	8000g. Hands releasing bird (sculpture) (Hugo Pistilli) (vert)	9·75	7·75

No. 1803 and Type **509** have been left for 'General McMahon', issued on 19 Sept 2007, not yet received.

No. 1804 and Type **510** have been left for '40th Anniv of Peace Corps', issued on19 Sept 2007, not yet received.

Nos. 1805/6 and Type **511** have been left for 'Boy Scouts', issued on 11 Oct 2007, not yet received.

No. 1807 and Type **512** have been left for 'Stadium', issued on 22 October 2007, not yet received.

514 Gabriel Casaccia

2007. Birth Centenary of Gabriel Casaccia Bibolini (writer).

1810	**514**	8000g. multicoloured	9·75	7·75

515 Fronds

2007. Christmas. Multicoloured.

1811	700g. Type **515**	1·00	80
1812	8000g. The Nativity	9·75	7·75

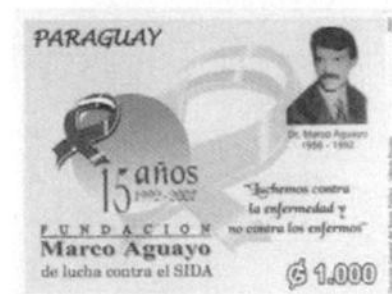

516 Emblem and Marco Aguayo

2007. 15th Anniv of Marco Aguayo AIDS Foundation. Multicoloured.

1813	1000g. Type **516**	9·75	7·75
1814	8000g. Emblem (different)	1·40	1·10

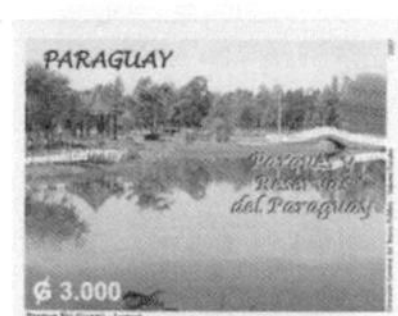

517 Nu Guarza Parks

2007. National Parks. Multicoloured.

1815	3000g. Type **517**	4·50	3·25
MS1816	117×82 mm. 6000g. *Alouatta caraya* (50×40 mm) (rouletted)	8·50	6·50

518 Tree in Desert

2007. International Year of Deserts and Desertification.

1817	**518**	7000g. multicoloured	9·00	7·25

519 Flower

40th Anniv of Nasta Advertising.

1818	700g. Type **519**	1·00	80
1819	5000g. Stylized tulip (vert)	7·25	5·25

520 Emblem

2008. 80th Anniv of Asunción Rotary Club. Multicoloured.

1820	2000g. Type **520**	3·25	2·30
1821	8000g. Parkland (Martin Luis Vallejos Cuevas) (horiz)	9·75	7·75

522 *Coryphospingus cucullatus* (red crested finch)

2008. Mercosur. Birds. Multicoloured.

1822	5000g. Type **522**	6·25	5·25
1823	6000g. *Pitangus sulpphuratus* (great kiskadee)	8·25	6·25

523 Building Facade

2008. 125th Anniv of Fundacion del Anteo Paraguayo.

1824	**523**	700g. multicoloured	1·00	80

524 Celebration

2008. America. Festivals.

1825	**524**	11000g. multicoloured	12·00	10·50

525 Signing

2008. 30th Anniv (2007) of Torrijos-Carter Treaties (two treaties signed by the United States and Panama guaranteeing Panama control of Panama Canal after 1999). Multicoloured.

1826	700g. Type **525**	1·00	80
1827	7000g. Pres. Omar Torrijos, Pres. Jimmy Carter and Panama Canal	9·00	7·25

526 Scouts and Tent

2008. 70th Anniv of Scouting in Paraguay. Multicoloured.

1828	3000g. Type **526**	4·25	3·25
1829	4000g. Capitan Figan troop	4·50	3·25

527 Virgin and Child

2008. Christmas. Multicoloured.

1830	700g. Type **527**	1·00	80
1831	5000g. Holy Family	7·25	5·25

528 Cathedral and Cotton

2008. 250th Anniv of Corniel Oviedo City. Multicoloured.

1832	3000g. Type **528**	4·25	3·25
1833	7000g. Approach to city	9·00	7·25

529 Pres. Hayes

2008. 130th Anniv of Pres. Hayes' Arbitration.

1834	**529**	1000g. multicoloured	1·40	1·00

530 Children and Flower

2008. 25th Anniv of SOS Children's Village, Zeballos Cue. Multicoloured.

1835	2000g. Type **530**	3·25	2·30
1836	7000g. Emblem	9·00	7·25

531 Harpist

2008. Year of the Harp.

1837	**531**	5000g. multicoloured	7·25	5·25

532 Father Joseph Kentenich (founder) and Virgin and child (statue)

2009. 50th Anniv of Schoenstatt Movement in Paraguay

1838	**533**	3000g. multicoloured	4·50	3·25

533 'Virgen Nuestra Senora de Caacupe'

2009. Christmas. Multicoloured.

1839	800g. Type **533**	95	75
1840	5000g. 'Virgen Nuestra Senora de la Asunción'	7·25	5·25

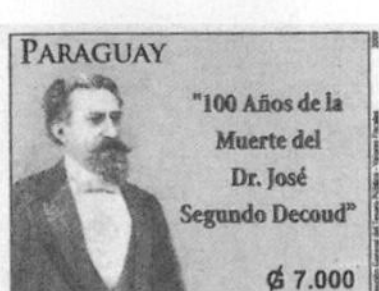
534 J. S. Decoud

2009. Death Centenary of José Segundo Decoud

1841	**534**	7000g. multicoloured	9·00	7·25

535 Nelore Bull

2009. Mercosur. Exports. Multicoloured.

1842	2000g. Type **535**	3·25	2·30
1843	5000g. *Steevia rebaudiana*	7·25	5·25

536 'EL MALABARISTA'

2009. Arsenio Erico (footballer) Commemoration. Multicoloured.

1844	700g. Type **536**	1·00	80
1845	1000g. Holding footballs (vert)	1·40	1·00

537 Trompo

2010. America. Children's Games. Multicoloured.

1846	4000g. Type **537**	5·75	4·00
1847	7000g. Tikichuela (horiz)	9·00	7·25

538 Government House

2010. Bicentenary of Independence (1st issue). Multicoloured.

1848	700g. Type **538**	1·00	80
1849	2000g. *Request for Surrender, May* 1811 (Jaime Bestard)	3·25	2·30

539 Galileo and Telescope

2010. 400th Anniv of Publication of *Sidereus Nuncius* by Galileo Galilei

1850	**539**	2500g. multicoloured	3·50	2·50

540 Roses

2010. Centenary of Paraguay - Russia Diplomatic Relations

1851	**540**	7000g. multicoloured	9·00	7·25

Nos. 1852/3 and Type **541** are left for Darwin, issued on 26 May 2010, not yet received.

542 Paraguayan Team

2010. World Cup Football Championships, South Africa. Multicoloured.

1854	700g. Type **542**	1·00	80
1855	6000g. Team (different)	8·50	6·50

543 National Hymn (fragment)

2010. America. Patriotic Symbols. Multicoloured.

1856	5000g. Type **543**	7·00	5·00
1857	6000g. Flag and arms (horiz)	8·50	6·50

544 Three Magi

2010. Christmas. Multicoloured.

1857a	700g. Type **544**	1·00	80
1858	6000g. The Holy Family (vert)	8·50	6·50
1859	11000g. Joseph leading Mary seated on donkey	12·50	10·50

545 Venancio López Palace

2010. Bicentenary of Independence (2nd issue). Multicoloured.

1860	700g. Type **545**	1·00	80
1861	2000g. Heritage residence	3·25	2·30

546 Campaign Mascot

2010. Road Safety Day in Paraguay

1862	**546**	700g. multicoloured	1·00	80

547 Hand receiving Yellow Rose

2010. Tenth Anniv of Mercosur. A Culture of Peace. Multicoloured.

1863	2000g. Type **547**	3·25	2·30
1864	6000g. Hand holding yellow rose	8·50	6·50

548 Diego Galeano Harrison

2010. Youth Games, Singapore. Multicoloured.

1865	2000g. Type **548**	3·25	2·30
1866	5000g. Parguayan athletes	7·00	5·00

549 Flags of Members on Map of Americas

2011. Centenary of UPAEP. Centenary of Uniting Cultures. Multicoloured.

1867	6000g. Type **549**	8·50	6·50
1868	11000g. Members flags and building (horiz)	12·50	10·50

550 Bank Building

2011. 50th Anniv of National Development Bank

1869	**550**	700g. multicoloured	1·00	80

551 National Pantheon of Heroes

2011. Bicentenary of Independence (3rd issue). Multicoloured.

1870	6000g. Type **551**	8·50	6·50
1871	6000g. National Pantheon of Martyrs of Revolution	8·50	6·50

552 Woman

2011. Stop Violence against Women at Home and at Work

1872	**552**	700g. multicoloured	1·00	80

553 Marie Curie

2011. International Year of Chemistry

1873	**553**	2000g. multicoloured	3·25	2·30

No. 1874 is vacant.

554 Pope John Paul II

2011. Beatification of Pope John Paul II. Sheet 115×80 mm

MS1875	**554**	10000g. multicoloured	14·00	14·00

555 Asunción Cathedral

2011. Bicentenary of Independence (4th issue). Multicoloured.

1876	1000g. Type **555**	1·70	1·20
1877	1000g. Railway Station	1·70	1·20
1878	1000g. Government Palace	1·70	1·20
1879	1000g. Municipal Theatre	1·70	1·20
1880	1000g. Pink lit building (Cabildo)	1·70	1·20
MS1881	115×82 mm. 11000g. House of Independence. Imperf	12·50	10·50

556 Temple

2011. 140th Anniv of Freemasonary in Paraguay

1882	**556**	11000g. multicoloured	12·50	10·50

556a *Trichocentrum jonesianum* (Orchid)

2011. International Day of Friendship

1882a	**556a**	700g. multicoloured	1·00	80

557 *Buteogallus meridionalis* (Savanna Hawk)

2011. 75th Anniv of 'Caritas 680' Radio Station Universidad Católica

1883	**557**	700g. multicoloured	1·00	80

558 Tower

2011. Centenary of San Jose School

1884	**558**	700g. multicoloured	1·00	80

559 Three Wise Men

2011. Christmas. Multicoloured.

1885	700g. Type **559**	1·00	80
1886	5000g. Star above Mary and Infant Jesus	7·25	5·25
1887	11000g. Shepherd, lambs, Mary and Infant Jesus	12·00	10·50

560 AIDS Ribbon

2011. 30th Anniv of AIDS Prevention Campaign

1888	**560**	1000g. multicoloured	1·40	1·00

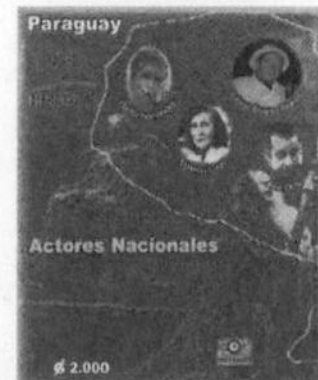

561 Actors

2011. Mercosur. National Actors. Multicoloured.

1889	2000g. Type **561**	3·25	2·30
MS1890	111×82 mm. 6000g. Edda de los Rios. Rouletted	9·00	7·25

562 Post Box

2011. America. Mail Boxes. Multicoloured.

1891	5000g. Type **562**	7·25	75·25
1892	6000g. Green full size postbox	8·25	6·25

OFFICIAL STAMPS

O14 **O19** **O20**

1886. Various types as O14, O19 and O20 optd **OFICIAL**.

(a) Imperf.

O32	1c. orange	3·50	3·50
O33	2c. violet	3·50	3·50
O34	5c. orange	3·50	3·50
O35	7c. green	3·50	3·50
O36	10c. brown	3·50	3·50
O37	15c. blue	3·50	3·50
O38	20c. lake	3·50	3·50

(b) New colours. Perf.

O39	1c. green	55	55
O40	2c. red	55	55
O41	5c. blue	55	55
O42	7c. orange	55	55
O43	10c. lake	55	55
O44	15c. brown	55	55
O45	20c. blue	55	55

1889. Stamp of 1889 surch **OFICIAL** and value. Perf.

O47	**25**	1 on 15c. purple	2·50	2·40
O48	**25**	2 on 10c. purple	2·50	2·40

1889. Stamp of 1889 surch **OFICIAL** and value. Imperf.

O49	**25**	3 on 15c. purple	2·50	2·40
O50	**25**	5 on 15c. brown	2·50	2·40

1890. Stamps of 1887 optd **OFICIAL** or **Oficial**.

O58	**24**	1c. green	20	20
O59	**24**	2c. red	20	20
O60	**24**	5c. blue	20	20
O61	**24**	7c. brown	4·00	1·80
O55	**24**	10c. mauve	35	30
O63	**24**	15c. orange	35	20
O64	**24**	20c. pink	75	30
O65	**24**	50c. grey	65	30
O86	**24**	1p. green	35	30

O37

1901

O73	**O37**	1c. blue	65	60
O74	**O37**	2c. red	10	10
O75	**O37**	4c. brown	10	10
O76	**O37**	5c. green	10	10
O77	**O37**	8c. brown	20	20
O78	**O37**	10c. red	35	20
O79	**O37**	20c. blue	45	30

1903. Stamps of 1903, optd **OFICIAL**.

O99	**46**	1c. grey	35	30
O100	**46**	2c. green	35	30
O101	**46**	5c. blue	35	30
O102	**46**	10c. brown	35	30
O103	**46**	20c. red	35	30
O104	**46**	30c. blue	35	30
O105	**46**	60c. violet	35	30

1904. As T **50**, but inscr "OFICIAL".

O106	1c. green	20	10
O107	1c. olive	90	15
O108	1c. orange	35	15
O109	1c. red	45	20
O110	2c. orange	20	15
O111	2c. green	20	15
O112	2c. red	1·40	45
O113	2c. grey	75	30
O114	5c. blue	35	20
O116	5c. grey	1·40	1·20
O117	10c. lilac	20	10
O118	20c. lilac	1·20	75

1913. As T **65**, but inscr "OFICIAL".

O237	1c. grey	35	30
O238	2c. orange	35	30
O239	5c. purple	35	30
O240	10c. green	35	30
O241	20c. red	35	30
O242	50c. red	35	30
O243	75c. blue	35	30
O244	1p. blue	35	30
O245	2p. yellow	35	30

1935. Optd **OFICIAL**.

O474	**86**	10c. blue	35	30
O475	**86**	50c. mauve	35	30
O476	**87**	1p. orange	35	30
O477	**122**	1p.50 green	35	30
O478	-	2p.50 violet (No. 337)	35	30

1940. 50th Anniv of Asuncion University. As T **139**, inscr "SERVICIO OFICIAL", but portraits of Pres. Escobar and Dr. Zubizarreta.

O513	50c. black and red	35	30
O514	1p. black and red	35	30
O515	2p. black and blue	35	30
O516	5p. black and blue	35	30
O517	10p. black and blue	35	30
O518	50p. black and orange	55	55

POSTAGE DUE STAMPS

D48

1904

D106	**D48**	2c. green	55	55
D107	**D48**	4c. green	55	55
D108	**D48**	10c. green	55	55
D109	**D48**	20c. green	55	55

1913. As T **65**, but inscr "DEFICIENTE".

D237	1c. brown	45	45
D238	2c. brown	45	45
D239	5c. brown	45	45
D240	10c. brown	45	45
D241	20c. brown	45	45
D242	40c. brown	45	45
D243	1p. brown	45	45
D244	1p.50 brown	45	45

APPENDIX

The following stamps have either been issued in excess of postal needs or have not been available to the public in reasonable quantities at face value. Such stamps may later be given full listing if there is evidence of regular postal use.

1962

Manned Spacecraft. Postage 15, 25, 30, 40, 50c.; Air 12g.45, 18g.15, 36g.
Previous Olympic Games (1st series). Vert designs. Postage 15, 25, 30, 40, 50c.; Air 12g.45, 18g.15, 36g.
Vatican Council. Postage 50, 70c., 1g.50, 2, 3g.; Air 5, 10g., 12g.45, 18g.15, 23g.40, 36g.
Europa. Postage 4g.; Air 36g.
Solar System. Postage 10, 20, 25, 30, 50c.; Air 12g.45, 36g., 50g.

1963

Previous Olympic Games (2nd series). Horiz designs. Postage 15, 25, 30, 40, 50c.; Air 12g.45, 18g.15, 36g.
Satellites and Space Flights. Vert designs. Postage 10, 20, 25, 30, 50c.; Air 12g.45, 36, 50g.
Previous Winter Olympic Games. Postage 10, 20, 25, 30, 50c.; Air 12g.45, 36, 50g.
Freedom from Hunger. Postage 10, 25, 50, 75c.; Air 18g.15, 36, 50g.
"Mercury" Space Flights. Postage 15, 25, 30, 40, 50c.; Air 12g.45, 18g.15, 50g.
Winter Olympic Games. Postage 15, 25, 30, 40, 50c.; Air 12g.45, 18g.15, 50g.

1964

Tokyo Olympic Games. Postage 15, 25, 30, 40, 50c.; Air 12g.45, 18g.15, 50g.
Red Cross Centenary. Postage 10, 25, 30, 50c.; Air 18g.15, 36, 50g.
"Gemini", "Telstar" and "Apollo" Projects. Postage 15, 25, 30, 40, 50c.; Air 12g.45, 18g.15, 50g.
Spacecraft Developments. Postage 15, 25, 30, 40, 50c.; Air 12g.45, 18g.15, 50g.
United Nations. Postage 15, 25, 30, 40, 50c.; Air 12g.45, 18g.15, 50g.
American Space Research. Postage 10, 15, 20, 30, 40c.; Air 12g.45+6g., 18g.15+9g., 20g.+20g.
Eucharistic Conference. Postage 20g.+10g., 30g.+15g., 50g.+25g., 100g.+50g.
Pope John Memorial Issue. Postage 20g.+10g., 30g.+15g., 50g.+25g., 100g.+50g.

1965

Scouts. Postage 10, 15, 20, 30, 50c.; Air 12g.45, 18g.15, 36g.
Tokyo Olympic Games Medals. Postage 15, 25, 30, 40, 50c.; Air 12g.45, 18g.15, 50g.
Famous Scientists. Postage 10, 15, 20, 30, 40c.; Air 12g.45+6g., 18g.15+9g., 20g.+20g.
Orchids and Trees. Postage 20, 30, 90c., 1g.50, 4g.50.; Air 3, 4, 66g.
Kennedy and Churchill. Postage 15, 25, 30, 40, 50c.; Air 12g.45, 18g.15, 50g.
I.T.U. Centenary. Postage 10, 15, 20, 30, 40c.; Air 12g.45+6g., 18g.15+9g., 20g.+10g.
Pope Paul VI. Visit to United Nations. Postage 10, 15, 20, 30, 50c.; Air 12g.45, 18g.15, 36g.

1966

"Gemini" Space Project. Postage 15, 25, 30, 40, 50c.; Air 12g.45, 18g.15, 50g.
Events of 1965. Postage 10, 15, 20, 30, 50c.; Air 12g.45, 18g.15, 36g.
Mexico Olympic Games. Postage 10, 15, 20, 30, 50c.; Air 12g.45, 18g.15, 36g.
German Space Research. Postage 10, 15, 20, 30, 50c.; Air 12g.45, 18g.15, 36g.
Famous Writers. Postage 10, 15, 20, 30, 50c.; Air 12g.45, 18g.15, 36g.
Italian Space Research. Postage 10, 15, 20, 30, 50c.; Air 12g.45, 18g.15, 36g.
Moon Missions. Postage 10, 15, 20, 30, 50c.; Air 12g.45, 18g.15, 36g.
Sports Commemorative Issue. Postage 10, 15, 20, 30, 50c.; Air 12g.45, 18g.15, 36g.
3rd Death Anniv of Pres. John Kennedy. Postage 10, 15, 20, 30, 50c.; Air 12g.45, 18g.15, 36g.
Famous Paintings. Postage 10, 15, 20, 30, 50c.; Air 12g.45, 18g.15, 36g.

1967

Religious Paintings. Postage 10, 15, 20, 30, 50c.; Air 12g.45, 18g.15, 36g.
16th-century. Religious Paintings. Postage 10, 15, 20, 30, 50c.; Air 12g.45, 18g.15, 36g.
Impressionist Paintings. Postage 10, 15, 20, 30, 50c.; Air 12g.45, 18g.15, 36g.
European Paintings of 17th and 18th Cent. Postage 10, 15, 20, 25, 30, 50c.; Air 12g.45, 18g.15, 36g.
Birth Anniv of Pres. John Kennedy. Postage 10, 15, 20, 25, 30, 50c.; Air 12g.45, 18g.15, 36g.
Sculpture. Postage 10, 15, 20, 25, 30, 50c.; Air 12g.45, 18g.15, 50g.
Mexico Olympic Games. Archaeological Relics. Postage 10, 15, 20, 25, 30, 50c.; Air 12g.45, 18g.15, 36g.

1968

Religious Paintings. Postage 10, 15, 20, 25, 30, 50c.; Air 12g.45, 18g.15, 36g.
Winter Olympic Games, Grenoble. Paintings. Postage 10, 15, 20, 25, 30, 50c.; Air 12g.45, 18g.15, 36g.
Paraguayan Stamps from 1870–1970. Postage 10, 15, 20, 25, 30, 50c.; Air 12g.45, 18g.15, 36g.
Mexico Olympic Games, Paintings of Children. Postage 10, 15, 20, 25, 30, 50c.; Air 12g.45, 18g.15, 36g. (Sailing ship and Olympic Rings).
Visit of Pope Paul VI to Eucharistic Congress. Religious Paintings. Postage 10, 15, 20, 25, 30, 50c.; Air 12g.45, 18g.15, 36g.
Important Events of 1968. Postage 10, 15, 20, 25, 30, 50c.; Air 12g.45, 18g.15, 50g.

1969

Gold Medal Winners of 1968 Mexico Olympic Games. Postage 10, 15, 20, 25, 30, 50c.; Air 12g.45, 18g.15, 50g.
Int. Projects in Outer Space. Postage 10, 15, 20, 25, 30, 50c.; Air 12g.45, 18g.15, 50g.
Latin American Wildlife. Postage 10, 10, 15, 15, 20, 20, 25, 25, 30, 30, 50, 50, 75, 75 c; Air 12g.45×2, 18g.15×2.
Gold Medal Winners in Olympic Football, 1900–1968. Postage 10, 15, 20, 25, 30, 50, 75c.; Air 12g.45, 18g.15.
Paraguayan Football Champions, 1930–1966. Postage 10, 15, 20, 25, 30, 50, 75c.; Air 12g.45, 18g.15.
Paintings by Goya. Postage 10, 15, 20, 25, 30, 50, 75c.; Air 12g.45, 18g.15.
Christmas. Religious Paintings. Postage 10, 15, 20, 25, 30, 50, 75c.; Air 12g.45, 18g.15.

1970

Moon Walk. Postage 10, 15, 20, 25, 30, 50, 75c.; Air 12g.45, 18g.15.
Easter. Paintings. Postage 10, 15, 20, 25, 30, 50, 75c.; Air 12g.45, 18g.15.
Munich Olympic Games. Postage 10, 15, 20, 25, 30, 50, 75c.; Air 12g.45, 18g.15.
Paintings from the Pinakothek Museum in Munich. Postage 10, 15, 20, 25, 30, 50, 75c.; Air 12g.45, 18g.15.
"Apollo" Space Programme. Postage 10, 15, 20, 25, 30, 50, 75c.; Air 12g.45, 18g.15.
Space Projects in the Future. Postage 10, 15, 20, 25, 30, 50, 75c.; Air 12g.45, 18g.15.
"Expo 70" World Fair, Osaka, Japan. Japanese Paintings. Postage 10, 15, 20, 25, 30, 50, 75c.; Air 12g.45, 18g.15, 50g.
Flower Paintings. Postage 10, 15, 20, 25, 30, 50, 75c.; Air 12g.45, 18g.15, 50g.
Paintings from Prado Museum, Madrid. Postage 10, 15, 20, 25, 30, 50, 75c.; Air 12g.45, 18g.15, 50g.
Paintings by Durer. Postage 10, 15, 20, 25, 30, 50, 75c.; Air 12g.45, 18g.15, 50g.

1971

Christmas 1970/71. Religious Paintings. Postage 10, 15, 20, 25, 30, 50, 75c.; Air 12g.45, 18g.15, 50g.
Munich Olympic Games, 1972. Postage 10, 15, 20, 25, 30, 50, 75c.; Air 12g.45, 18g.15, 50g.
Paintings of Horses and Horsemen. Postage 10, 15, 20, 25, 30, 50, 75c.; Air 12g.45, 18g.15, 50g.
Famous Paintings from the Louvre, Paris. Postage 10, 15, 20, 25, 30, 50, 75c.; Air 12g.45, 18g.15, 50g.
Paintings in the National Museum, Asuncion. Postage 10, 15, 20, 25, 30, 50, 75c.; Air 12g.45, 18g.15, 50g.
Hunting Paintings. Postage 10, 15, 20, 25, 30, 50, 75c.; Air 12g.45, 18g.15, 50g.
Philatokyo '71, Stamp Exhibition, Tokyo. Japanese Paintings. Postage 10, 15, 20, 25, 30, 50, 75c.; Air 12g.45, 18g.15, 50g.
Winter Olympic Games, Sapporo, 1972. Japanese Paintings. Postage 10, 15, 20, 25, 30, 50, 75c.; Air 12g.45, 18g.15, 50g.
150th Death Anniv of Napoleon. Paintings. Postage 10, 15, 20, 25, 30, 50, 75c.; Air 12g.45, 18g.15, 50g.
Famous Paintings from the Dahlem Museum, Berlin. Postage 10, 15, 20, 25, 30, 50, 75c.; Air 12g.45, 18g.15, 50g.

1972

Locomotives (1st series). Postage 10, 15, 20, 25, 30, 50, 75c.; Air 12g.45, 18g.15, 50g.
Winter Olympic Games, Sapporo. Postage 10, 15, 20, 25, 30, 50, 75c.; Air 12g.45, 18g.15, 50g.

Racing Cars. Postage 10, 15, 20, 25, 30, 50, 75c.; Air 12g.45, 18g.15, 50g.
Famous Sailing Ships. Postage 10, 15, 20, 25, 30, 50, 75c.; Air 12g.45, 18g.15, 50g.
Famous Paintings from the Vienna Museum. Postage 10, 15, 20, 25, 30, 50, 75c.; Air 12g.45, 18g.15, 50g.
Famous Paintings from the Asuncion Museum. Postage 10, 15, 20, 25, 30, 50, 75c.; Air 12g.45, 18g.15, 50g.
Visit of the Argentine President to Paraguay. Postage 10, 15, 20, 25, 30, 50, 75c.; Air 12g.45, 18g.15.
Visit of President of Paraguay to Japan. Postage 10, 15, 20, 25, 30, 50, 75c.; Air 12g.45, 18g.15.
Paintings of Animals and Birds. Postage 10, 15, 20, 25, 30, 50, 75c.; Air 12g.45, 18g.15.
Locomotives (2nd series). Postage 10, 15, 20, 25, 30, 50, 75c.; Air 12g.45, 18g.15.
South American Fauna. Postage 10, 15, 20, 25, 30, 50, 75c.; Air 12g.45, 18g.15.

1973

Famous Paintings from the Florence Museum. Postage 10, 15, 20, 25, 30, 50, 75c.; Air 5, 10, 20g.
South American Butterflies. Postage 10, 15, 20, 25, 30, 50, 75c.; Air 5, 10, 20g.
Cats. Postage 10, 15, 20, 25, 30, 50, 75c.; Air 5, 10, 20g.
Portraits of Women. Postage 10, 15, 20, 25, 30, 50, 75c.; Air 5, 10, 20g.
World Cup Football Championship, West Germany (1974) (1st issue). Postage 10, 15, 20, 25, 30, 50, 75c.; Air 5, 10, 20g.
Paintings of Women. Postage 10, 15, 20, 25, 30, 50, 75c.; Air 5, 10, 20g.
Birds. Postage 10, 15, 20, 25, 30, 50, 75c.; Air 5, 10, 20g.
"Apollo" Moon Missions and Future Space Projects. Postage 10, 15, 20, 25, 30, 50, 75c.; Air 5, 10, 20g.
Visit of Pres. Stroessner to Europe and Morocco. Air 5, 10, 25, 50, 150g.
Folk Costume. Postage 25, 50, 75c., 1g., 1g.50, 1g.75, 2g.25.
Flowers. Postage 10, 20, 25, 30, 40, 50, 75c.

1974

World Cup Football Championship, West Germany (2nd issue). Air 5, 10, 20g.
Roses. Postage 10, 15, 20, 25, 30, 50, 75c.
Famous Paintings from the Gulbenkian Museum, New York. Postage 10, 15, 20, 25, 30, 50, 75 c; Air 5, 10, 20g.
U.P.U. Centenary. Postage 10, 15, 20, 25, 30, 50, 75c.; Air 5, 10, 20g.
Famous Masterpieces. Postage 10, 15, 20, 25, 30, 50, 75c.; Air 5, 10, 20g.
Visit of Pres. Stroessner to France. Air 100g.
World Cup Football Championship, West Germany (3rd issue). Air 4, 5, 10g.
Ships. Postage 5, 10, 15, 20, 25, 35, 40, 50c.
Events of 1974. Air 4g. (U.P.U.), 5g. (President of Chile's visit), 10g. (President Stroessner's visit to South Africa).
Centenary of U.P.U. Air 4, 5, 10, 20g.

1975

Paintings. Postage 5, 10, 15, 20, 25, 35, 40, 50c.
Christmas (1974). Postage 5, 10, 15, 20, 25, 35, 40, 50c.
"Expo '75" Okinawa, Japan. Air 4, 5, 10g.
Paintings from National Gallery, London. Postage 5, 10, 15, 20, 25, 35, 40, 50c.
Dogs. Postage 5, 10, 15, 20, 25, 35, 40, 50c.
South American Fauna. Postage 5, 10, 15, 20, 25, 35, 40, 50c.
"Espana '75". Air 4, 5, 10g.
500th Birth Anniv of Michelangelo. Postage 5, 10, 15, 20, 25, 35, 40, 50c.; Air 4, 5, 10g.
Winter Olympic Games, Innsbruck (1976). Postage 1, 2, 3, 4, 5g.; Air 10, 15, 20g.
Olympic Games, Montreal (1976). Gold borders. Postage 1, 2, 3, 4, 5g.; Air 10, 15, 20g.
Various Commemorations. Air 4g. (Zeppelin), 5g. (1978 World Cup), 10g. (Nordposta Exhibition).
Bicent (1976) of American Revolution (1st issue). Paintings of Sailing Ships. Postage 5, 10, 15, 20, 25, 35, 40, 50c.
Bicent (1976) of American Revolution (2nd issue). Paintings. Postage 5, 10, 15, 20, 25, 35, 40, 50c.
Bicent (1976) of American Revolution (3rd issue). Lunar Rover and American Cars. Air 4, 5, 10g.
Various Commemorations. Air 4g. (Concorde), 5g. (Lufthansa), 10g. ("Exfilmo" and "Espamer" Stamp Exhibitions).
Paintings by Spanish Artists. Postage 1, 2, 3, 4, 5g.; Air 10, 15, 20g.

1976

Holy Year. Air 4, 5, 10g.
Cats. Postage 5, 10, 15, 20, 25, 35, 40, 50c.
Railway Locomotives (3rd series). Postage 1, 2, 3, 4, 5g.; Air 10, 15, 20g.
Butterflies. Postage 5, 10, 15, 20, 25, 35, 40, 50c.
Domestic Animals. Postage 1, 2, 3, 4, 5g.; Air 10, 15, 20g.
Bicent of American Revolution (4th issue) and U.S. Postal Service. Postage 1, 2, 3, 4, 5g.; Air 10, 15, 20g.
"Paintings and Planets". Postage 1, 2, 3, 4, 5g.; Air 10, 15, 20g.
Ship Paintings. Postage 1, 2, 3, 4, 5g.; Air 10, 15, 20g.
German Ship Paintings (1st issue). Postage 1, 2, 3, 4, 5g.; Air 10, 15, 20g.
Bicentenary of American Revolution (5th issue). Paintings of Cowboys and Indians. Postage 1, 2, 3, 4, 5g.; Air 10, 15, 20g.
Gold Medal Winners. Olympic Games, Montreal. Postage 1, 2, 3, 4, 5g.; Air 10, 15, 20g.
Paintings by Titian. Postage 1, 2, 3, 4, 5g.; Air 10, 15, 20g.
History of the Olympics. Postage 1, 2, 3, 4, 5g.; Air 10, 15, 20g.

1977

Paintings by Rubens (1st issue). Postage 1, 2, 3, 4, 5g.; Air 10, 15, 20g.
Bicent of American Revolution (6th issue). Astronautics. Postage 1, 2, 3, 4, 5g.; Air 10, 15, 20g.
"Luposta 77" Stamp Exn. Zeppelin and National Costumes. Postage 1, 2, 3, 4, 5g.; Air 10, 15, 20g.
History of Aviation. Postage 1, 2, 3, 4, 5g.; Air 10, 15, 20g.
Paintings. Postage 1, 2, 3, 4, 5g.; Air 10, 15, 20g.
German Ship Paintings (2nd issue). Postage 1, 2, 3, 4, 5g.; Air 10, 15, 20g.
Nobel Prize-winners for Literature. Postage 1, 2, 3, 4, 5g.; Air 10, 15, 20g.
History of World Cup (1st issue). Postage 1, 2, 3, 4, 5g.; Air 10, 15, 20g.
History of World Cup (2nd issue). Postage 1, 2, 3, 4, 5g.; Air 10, 15, 20g.

1978

Paintings by Rubens (2nd issue). Postage 1, 2, 3, 4, 5g.; Air 10, 15, 20g.
Chess Olympiad, Buenos Aires. Paintings of Chess Games. Postage 1, 2, 3, 4, 5g.; Air 10, 15, 20g.
Paintings by Jordaens. Postage 3, 4, 5, 6, 7, 8, 20g.; Air 10, 25g.
450th Death Anniv of Durer (1st issue). Postage 3, 4, 5, 6, 7, 8, 20g.; Air 10, 25g.
Paintings by Goya. Postage 3, 4, 5, 6, 7, 8, 20g.; Air 10, 25g.
Astronautics of the Future. Postage 3, 4, 5, 6, 7, 8, 20g.; Air 10, 25g.
Racing Cars. Postage 3, 4, 5, 6, 7, 8, 20g.; Air 10, 25g.
Paintings by Rubens (3rd issue). Postage 3, 4, 5, 6, 7, 8, 20g.; Air 10, 25g.
25th Anniv of Queen Elizabeth's Coronation (reproduction of stamps). Postage 3, 4, 5, 6, 7, 8, 20g.; Air 10, 25g.
Paintings and Stamp Exhibition Emblems. Postage 3, 4, 5, 6, 7, 8, 20g.; Air 10, 25g.
Various Commemorations. Air 75g. (Satellite Earth Station), 500g. (Coat of Arms), 1000g. (Pres. Stroessner).
International Year of the Child (1st issue). Snow White and the Seven Dwarfs. Postage 3, 4, 5, 6, 7, 8, 20g.; Air 10, 25g.
Military Uniforms. Postage 3, 4, 5, 6, 7, 8, 20g.; Air 10, 25g.

1979

World Cup Football Championship, Argentina. Postage 3, 4, 5, 6, 7, 8, 20g.; Air 10, 25g.
Christmas (1978). Paintings of Madonnas. Postage 3, 4, 5, 6, 7, 8, 20g.; Air 10, 25g.
History of Aviation. Postage 3, 4, 5, 6, 7, 8, 20g.; Air 10, 25g.
450th Death Anniv of Durer (2nd issue). Postage 3, 4, 5, 6, 7, 8, 20g.; Air 10, 25g.
Death Centenary of Sir Rowland Hill (1st issue). Reproduction of Stamps. Postage 3, 4, 5, 6, 7, 8, 20g.; Air 10, 25g.
International Year of the Child (2nd issue). Cinderella. Postage 3, 4, 5, 6, 7, 8, 20g.; Air 10, 25g.
Winter Olympic Games, Lake Placid (1980). Postage 3, 4, 5, 6, 7, 8, 20g.; Air 10, 25g.
Sailing Ships. Postage 3, 4, 5, 6, 7, 8, 20g.; Air 10, 25g.
International Year of the Child (3rd issue). Cats. Postage 3, 4, 5, 6, 7, 8, 20g.; Air 10, 25g.
International Year of the Child (4th issue). Little Red Riding Hood. Postage 3, 4, 5, 6, 7, 8, 20g.; Air 10, 25g.
Olympic Games, Moscow (1980). Greek Athletes. Postage 3, 4, 5, 6, 7, 8, 20g.; Air 10, 25g.
Centenary of Electric Locomotives. Postage 3, 4, 5, 6, 7, 8, 20g.; Air 10, 25g.

1980

Death Centenary of Sir Rowland Hill (2nd issue). Military Aircraft. Postage 3, 4, 5, 6, 7, 8, 20 g; Air 10, 25g.
Death Centenary of Sir Rowland Hill (3rd issue). Stamps. Postage 3, 4, 5, 6, 7, 8, 20g.; Air 10, 25g.
Winter Olympic Games Medal Winners (1st issue). Postage 3, 4, 5, 6, 7, 8, 20g.; Air 10, 25g.
Composers. Scenes from Ballets. Postage 3, 4, 5, 6, 7, 8, 20g.; Air 20, 25g.
International Year of the Child (1979) (5th issue). Christmas. Postage 3, 4, 5, 6, 7, 8, 20g.; Air 10, 25g.
Exhibitions. Paintings of Ships. Postage 3, 4, 5, 6, 7, 8, 20g.; Air 10, 25g.
World Cup Football Championship, Spain (1982) (1st issue). Postage 3, 4, 5, 6, 7, 8, 20g.; Air 10, 25g.
World Chess Championship, Merano. Postage 3, 4, 5, 6, 7, 8, 20g.; Air 10, 25g.

1981

Winter Olympic Games Medal Winners (2nd issue). Postage 25, 50c., 1, 2, 3, 4, 5g.; Air 5, 10, 30g.
International Year of the Child (1979) (6th issue). Children and Flowers. Postage 10, 25, 50, 100, 200, 300, 400g.; Air 75, 500, 1000g.
"WIPA 1981" International Stamp Exhibition, Vienna. 1980 Composers stamp optd. Postage 4g.; Air 10g.
Wedding of Prince of Wales (1st issue). Postage 25, 50c., 1, 2, 3, 4, 5g.; Air 5, 10, 30g.
Costumes and Treaty of Itaipu. Postage 10, 25, 50, 100, 200, 300, 400g.
Paintings by Rubens. Postage 25, 50c., 1, 2, 3, 4, 5g.
Anniversaries and Events. Air 5g. (250th birth anniv of George Washington), 10g. (80th birthday of Queen Mother), 30g. ("Philatokyo '81").
Flight of Space Shuttle. Air 5, 10, 30g.
Birth Bicentenary of Ingres. Postage 25, 50c., 1, 2, 3, 4, 5g.
World Cup Football Championship, Spain (1982) (2nd issue). Air 5, 10, 30g.
Birth Centenary of Picasso. Postage 25, 50c., 1, 2, 3, 4, 5g.
"Philatelia '81" International Stamp Exhibition, Frankfurt. Picasso stamps optd. Postage 25, 50c., 1, 2, 3, 4g.
"Espamer '81" International Stamp Exhibition. Picasso stamps optd. Postage 25, 50c., 1, 2, 3, 4g.
Wedding of Prince of Wales (2nd issue). Postage 25, 50c., 1, 2, 3, 4, 5g.; Air 5, 10, 30g.
International Year of the Child (1979) (7th issue). Christmas. Postage 25, 50c., 1, 2, 3, 4, 5g.
Christmas. Paintings. Air 5, 10, 30g.

1982

International Year of the Child (1979) (8th issue). Puss in Boots. Postage 25, 50c., 1, 2, 3, 4, 5g.
World Cup Football Championship, Spain (3rd issue). Air 5, 10, 30g.
75th Anniv of Boy Scout Movement and 125th Birth Anniv of Lord-Baden Powell (founder). Postage 25, 50c., 1, 2, 3, 4, 5g.; Air 5, 10, 30g.
"Essen 82" International Stamp Exhibition, 1981 International Year of the Child (7th issue) Christmas stamps optd. Postage 25, 50c., 1, 2, 3, 4g.
Cats. Postage 25, 50c., 1, 2, 3, 4, 5g.
Chess paintings. Air 5, 10, 30g.
"Philexfrance 82" International Stamp Exhibition. 1981 Ingres stamps optd. Postage 25, 50c., 1, 2, 3g.
World Cup Football Championship, Spain (4th issue). Postage 25, 50c., 1, 2, 3, 4, 5g.; Air 5, 10, 30g.
"Philatelia 82" International Stamp Exhibition, Hanover. 1982 Cats issue optd. Postage 25, 50c., 1, 2, 3, 4, 5g.
500th Birth Anniv of Raphael (1st issue). Postage 25, 50c., 1, 2, 3, 4, 5g.
500th Birth Anniv of Raphael (2nd issue) and Christmas (1st issue). Postage 25, 50c., 1, 2, 3, 4, 5g.
World Cup Football Championship Results. Air 5, 10, 30g.
Christmas (2nd issue). Paintings by Rubens. Air 5, 10, 30g.
Paintings by Durer. Life of Christ. Postage 25, 50c., 1, 2, 3, 4, 5g.
500th Birth Anniv of Raphael (3rd issue) and Christmas (3rd issue). Air 5, 10, 30g.

1983

Third International Railways Congress, Malaga (1982). Postage 25, 50c., 1, 2, 3, 4, 5g.
Racing Cars. Postage 25, 50c., 1, 2, 3, 4, 5g.
Paintings by Rembrandt. Air 5, 10, 30g.
German Astronautics. Air 5, 10, 30g.
Winter Olympic Games, Sarajevo (1984). Postage 25, 50c., 1, 2, 3, 4, 5g.
Bicentenary of Manned Flight. Air 5, 10, 30g.
Pope John Paul II. Postage 25, 50c., 1, 2, 3, 4, 5g.
Olympic Games, Los Angeles (1984). Air 5, 10, 30g.
Veteran Cars. Postage 25, 50c., 1, 2, 3, 4, 5g.; Air 5, 10, 30g.
"Brasiliana '83" International Stamp Exhibition and 52nd F.I.P. Congress (1st issue). 1982 World Cup (4th issue) stamps optd. Postage 25, 50c., 1, 2, 3, 4g.
"Brasiliana '83" International Stamp Exhibition and 52nd F.I.P. Congress (2nd issue). 1982 Raphael/Christmas stamps optd. Postage 25, 50c., 1, 2, 3, 4g.
Aircraft Carriers. Postage 25, 50c., 1, 2, 3, 4, 5g.
South American Flowers. Air 5, 10, 30g.
South American Birds. Postage 25, 50c., 1, 2, 3, 4, 5g.
25th Anniv of International Maritime Organization. Air 5, 10, 30g.
"Philatelia '83" International Stamp Exhibition, Dusseldorf. 1983 International Railway Congress stamps optd. Postage 25, 50c., 1, 2, 3, 4g.
"Exfivia - 83" International Stamp Exn, Bolivia. 1982 Durer paintings optd. Postage 25, 50c., 1, 2, 3, 4g.
Flowers, Postage 10, 25g.; Chaco soldier, Postage 50g.; Dams, Postage 75g; Air 100g.; President, Air 200g.

1984

Bicent of Manned Flight. Postage 25, 50c., 1, 2, 3, 4, 5g.
World Communications Year. Air 5, 10, 30g.
Dogs. Postage 25, 50c., 1, 2, 3, 4, 5g.
Olympic Games, Los Angeles. Air 5, 10, 30g.
Animals. Postage 10, 25, 50, 75g.
1983 Anniversaries. Air 100g. (birth bicentenary of Bolivar), 200g. (76th anniv of boy scout movement).
Christmas (1983) and New Year. Postage 25, 50c., 1, 2, 3, 4, 5g.
Winter Olympic Games, Sarajevo. Air 5, 10, 30g.
Troubador Knights. Postage 25, 50c., 1, 2, 3, 4, 5g.
World Cup Football Championship, Spain (1982) and Mexico (1986). Air 5, 10, 30g.
International Stamp Fair, Essen. 1983 Racing Cars stamps optd. Postage 25, 50c., 1, 2, 3, 4g.
Extinct Animals. Postage 25, 50c., 1, 2, 3, 4, 5g.
60th Anniv of International Chess Federation. Air 5, 10, 30g.
19th Universal Postal Union Congress Stamp Exhibition, Hamburg (1st issue). Sailing Ships. Postage 25, 50c., 1, 2, 3, 4, 5g.
19th Universal Postal Union Congress Stamp Exhibition, Hamburg (2nd issue). Troubadour Knights stamp optd. Postage 5g.
Leaders of the World. British Railway Locomotives. Postage 25, 50c., 1, 2, 3, 4, 5g.
50th Anniv of First Lufthansa Europe–South America Direct Mail Flight. Air 5, 10, 30g.
30th Anniv of Presidency of Alfredo Stroessner. Dam stamp optd. Air 100g.
"Ausipex 84" International Stamp Exhibition, Melbourne. 1974 U.P.U. Centenary stamps optd. Postage 10, 15, 20, 25, 30, 50, 75c.
"Phila Korea 1984" International Stamp Exhibition, Seoul. Olympic Games, Los Angeles, and Extinct Animals stamps optd. Postage 5g.; Air 30g.
German National Football Championship and Sindelfingen Stamp Bourse. 1974 World Cup stamps (1st issue) optd. Postage 10, 15, 20, 25, 30, 50, 75c.
Cats. Postage 25, 50c., 1, 2, 3, 4, 5g.
Winter Olympic Games Medal Winners. Air 5, 10, 30g.
Centenary of Motor Cycle. Air 5, 10, 30g.

1985

Olympic Games Medal Winners. Postage 25, 50c., 1, 2, 3, 4, 5g.
Christmas (1984). Costumes. Air 5, 10, 30g.
Fungi. Postage 25, 50c., 1, 2, 3, 4, 5g.
Participation of Paraguay in Preliminary Rounds of World Cup Football Championship. Air 5, 10, 30g.
"Interpex 1985" and "Stampex 1985" Stamp Exhibitions. 1981 Queen Mother's Birthday stamp optd. Postage 10g.×2.
International Federation of Aero-Philatelic Societies Congress, Stuttgart. 1984 Lufthansa Europe–South America Mail Flight stamp optd. Air 10g.
Paraguayan Animals and Extinct Animals. Postage 25, 50c., 1, 2, 3, 4, 5g.
"Olymphilex 85" Olympic Stamps Exhibition, Lausanne. 1984 Winter Olympics Games Medal Winners stamp optd. Postage 10g.
"Israphil 85" International Stamp Exhibition, Tel Aviv. 1982 Boy Scout Movement stamp optd. Postage 5g.
Music Year. Air 5, 10, 30g.
Birth Bicentenary of John J. Audubon (ornithologist). Birds. Postage 25, 50c., 1, 2, 3, 4, 5g.
Railway Locomotives. Air 5, 10, 30g.
"Italia '85" International Stamp Exhibition, Rome (1st issue). 1983 Pope John Paul II stamp optd. Postage 5g.
50th Anniv of Chaco Peace (1st issue). 1972 Visit of Argentine President stamp optd. Postage 30c.
"Mophila 85" Stamp Exhibition, Hamburg. 1984 U.P.U. Congress Stamp Exhibition (1st issue) stamp optd. Postage 5g.
"Lupo 85" Stamp Exhibition, Lucerne. 1984 Bicentenary of Manned Flight stamp optd. Postage 5g.
"Expo 85" World's Fair, Tsukuba. 1981 "Philatokyo '81" stamp optd. Air 30g.
International Youth Year. Mark Twain. Postage 25, 50c., 1, 2, 3, 4, 5g.
75th Death Anniv of Henri Dunant (founder of Red Cross). Air 5, 10, 30g.
150th Anniv of German Railways (1st issue). Postage 25, 50c., 1, 2, 3, 4, 5g.
International Chess Federation Congress, Graz. Air 5, 10, 30g.
50th Anniv of Chaco Peace (2nd issue) and Government Achievements. Postage 10, 25, 50, 75g.; Air 100, 200g.
Paintings by Rubens. Postage 25, 50c., 1, 2, 3, 4, 5g.
Explorers and their Ships. Air 5, 10, 30g.
"Italia '85" International Stamp Exhibition, Rome (2nd issue). Paintings. Air 5, 10, 30g.

1986

Paintings by Titian. Postage 25, 50c., 1, 2, 3, 4, 5g.
International Stamp Fair, Essen. 1985 German Railways stamps optd. Postage 25, 50c., 1, 2, 3, 4g.
Fungi. Postage 25, 50c., 1, 2, 3, 4, 5g.
"Ameripex '86" International Stamp Exhibition, Chicago. Air 5, 10, 30g.
Lawn Tennis (1st issue). Inscriptions in black or red. Air 5, 10, 30g.
Centenary of Motor Car. Postage 25, 50c., 1, 2, 3, 4, 5g.
Appearance of Halley's Comet. Air 5, 10, 30g.
Qualification of Paraguay for World Cup Football Championship Final Rounds, Mexico (1st issue). Postage 25, 50c., 1, 2, 3, 4, 5g.
Tenth Pan-American Games, Indianapolis (1987). 1985 Olympic Games Medal Winners stamp optd. Postage 5g.
Maybach Cars. Postage 25, 50c., 1, 2, 3, 4, 5g.
Freight Trains. Air 5, 10, 30g.
Qualification of Paraguay for World Cup Football Championship Final Rounds (2nd issue). Air 5, 10, 30g.
Winter Olympic Games, Calgary (1988) (1st issue). 1983 Winter Olympic Games stamp optd. Postage 5g.
Centenary of Statue of Liberty. Postage 25, 50c., 1, 2, 3, 4, 5g.
Dogs. Postage 25, 50c., 1, 2, 3, 4, 5g.
150th Anniv of German Railways (2nd issue). Air 5, 10, 30g.
Lawn Tennis (2nd issue). Postage 25, 50c., 1, 2, 3, 4, 5g.
Visit of Prince Hitachi of Japan. 1972 Visit of President of Paraguay to Japan stamps optd. Postage 10, 15, 20, 25, 30, 50, 75c.
International Peace Year. Paintings by Rubens. Air 5, 10, 30g.
Olympic Games, Seoul (1988) (1st issue). Postage 25, 50c., 1, 2, 3, 4, 5g.
27th Chess Olympiad, Dubai. 1982 Chess Paintings stamp optd. Air 10g.

1987

World Cup Football Championship, Mexico (1986) and Italy (1990). Air 5, 10, 20, 25, 30g.
12th Spanish American Stamp and Coin Exhibition, Madrid, and 500th Anniv of Discovery of America by Columbus. 1975 South American Fauna and 1983 25th Anniv of I.M.O. stamps optd. Postage 15, 20, 25, 35, 40g.; Air 10g.
Tennis as Olympic Sport. 1986 Lawn Tennis (1st issue) stamps optd. Air 10, 30g.
Olympic Games, Barcelona (1992). 1985 Olympic Games Medal Winners stamps optd. Postage 25, 50c., 1, 2, 3, 4g.
"Olymphilex '87" Olympic Stamps Exhibition, Rome. 1985 Olympic Games Medal Winners stamp optd. Postage 5g.
Cats. Postage 1, 2, 3, 5, 60g.
Paintings by Rubens (1st issue). Postage 1, 2, 3, 5, 60g.
Saloon Cars. Air 5, 10, 20, 25, 30g.
National Topics. Postage 10g. (steel plant), 25g. (Franciscan monk), 50g. (400th anniv of Ita and Yaguaron), 75g. (450th Anniv of Asuncion); Air 100g. (airliner), 200g. (Pres. Stroessner).
"Capex 87" International Stamp Exhibition, Toronto. Cats stamps optd. Postage 1, 2, 3, 5g.
500th Anniv of Discovery of America by Columbus. Postage 1, 2, 3, 5, 60g.
Winter Olympic Games, Calgary (1988) (2nd issue). Air 5, 10, 20, 25, 30g.
Centenary of Colorado Party. National Topics and 1978 Pres. Stroessner stamps optd. Air 200, 1000g.
750th Anniv of Berlin (1st issue) and "Luposta '87" Air Stamps Exhibition, Berlin. Postage 1, 2, 3, 5, 60g.
Olympic Games, Seoul (1988) (2nd issue). Air 5, 10, 20, 25, 30g.
Rally Cars. Postage 1, 2, 3, 5, 60g.
"Exfivia 87" Stamp Exhibition, Bolivia. National Topics stamps optd. Postage 75g.; Air 100g.
"Olymphilex '88" Olympic Stamps Exhibition, Seoul. 1986 Olympic Games, Seoul (1st issue) stamps optd. Postage 2, 3, 4, 5g.
"Philatelia '87" International Stamp Exhibition, Cologne. 1986 Lawn Tennis (2nd issue) stamps optd. Postage 25, 50c., 1, 2, 3, 4g.
Italy–Argentina Match at Zurich to Launch 1990 World Cup Football Championship, Italy. 1986 Paraguay Qualification (2nd issue) stamps optd. Air 10, 30g.
"Exfilna '87" Stamp Exhibition, Gerona. 1986 Olympic Games, Seoul (1st issue) stamps optd. Postage 25, 50c.
Spanish Ships. Postage 1, 2, 3, 5, 60g.
Paintings by Rubens (2nd issue). Air 5, 10, 20, 25, 30g.
Christmas. Air 5, 10, 20, 25, 30g.
Winter Olympic Games, Calgary (1988) (3rd issue). Postage 1, 2, 3, 5, 60g.

1988

150th Anniv of Austrian Railways. Air 5, 10, 20, 25, 30g.
"Aeropex 88" Air Stamps Exhibition, Adelaide, 1987. 750th Anniv of Berlin and "Luposta '87" stamps optd. Postage 1, 2, 3, 5g.
"Olympex" Stamp Exhibition, Calgary. 1987 Winter Olympic Games (3rd issue) stamps optd. Postage 1, 2, 3g.
Olympic Games, Seoul (3rd issue). Equestrian Events. Postage 1, 2, 3, 5, 60g.
Space Projects. Air 5, 10, 20, 25, 30g.
750th Anniv of Berlin (2nd issue). Paintings. Postage 1, 2, 3, 5, 60g.
Visit of Pope John Paul II. Postage 1, 2, 3, 5, 60g.
"Lupo Wien 88" Stamp Exhibition, Vienna. 1987 National Topics stamp optd. Air 100g.
World Wildlife Fund. Extinct Animals. Postage 1, 2, 3, 5g.
Paintings in West Berlin State Museum. Air 5, 10, 20, 25, 30g.
Bicentenary of Australian Settlement. 1981 Wedding of Prince of Wales (1st issue) optd. Postage 25, 50c., 1, 2g.

History of World Cup Football Championship (1st issue). Air 5, 10, 20, 25, 30g.
New Presidential Period, 1988–1993. 1985 Chaco Peace and Government Achievements issue optd. Postage 10, 25, 50, 75g.; Air 100, 200g.
Olympic Games, Seoul (4th issue). Lawn Tennis and Medal. Postage 1, 2, 3, 5, 60g.
Calgary Winter Olympics Gold Medal Winners. Air 5, 10, 20, 25, 30g.
History of World Cup Football Championship (2nd issue). Air 5, 10, 20, 25, 30g.
"Prenfil '88" International Philatelic Press Exhibition, Buenos Aires. "Ameripex '86" stamp optd. Air 30g.
"Philexfrance 89" International Stamp Exhibition, Paris. 1985 Explorers stamp optd. Air 30g.

Pt. 8

PARMA

A former Grand Duchy of N. Italy, united with Sardinia in 1860 and now part of Italy.

100 centesimi = 1 lira.

1 Bourbon "fleur-de-lis"

1852. Imperf.

2	**1**	5c. black on yellow	£160	£180
11	**1**	5c. yellow	£9000	£850
4	**1**	10c. black	£160	£180
5	**1**	15c. black on pink	£4750	£110
13	**1**	15c. red	£12000	£250
7	**1**	25c. black on purple	£19000	£325
14	**1**	25c. brown	£12000	£475
9	**1**	40c. black on blue	£3000	£475

2

1857. Imperf.

17	**2**	15c. red	£475	£425
19	**2**	25c. purple	£750	£250
20	**2**	40c. blue	£130	£650

3

1859. Imperf.

28	**3**	5c. green	£3250	£5000
29	**3**	10c. brown	£1400	£850
32	**3**	20c. blue	£800	£10000
33	**3**	40c. red	£800	£9500
35	**3**	80c. yellow	£8500	

NEWSPAPER STAMPS

1853. As T **3**. Imperf.

N1	6c. black on pink	£2500	£500
N3	9c. black on blue	£1400	£28000

Pt. 1

PATIALA

A "convention" state in the Punjab, India.

12 pies = 1 anna; 16 annas = 1 rupee.

1884. Stamps of India (Queen Victoria) with curved opt **PUTTIALLA STATE** vert.

1	**23**	½a. turquoise	6·50	4·75
2	-	1a. purple	80·00	£110
3	-	2a. blue	20·00	16·00
4	-	4a. green (No. 96)	£140	£160
5	-	8a. mauve	£550	£1600
6	-	1r. grey (No. 101)	£190	£900

1885. Stamps of India (Queen Victoria) optd **PUTTIALLA STATE** horiz.

7	**23**	½a. turquoise	3·75	30
11	-	1a. purple	1·00	40
8	-	2a. blue	20·00	1·75
9	-	4a. green (No. 96)	8·00	4·25
12	-	8a. mauve	48·00	£100
10	-	1r. grey (No. 101)	45·00	£130

Stamps of India optd PATIALA STATE.

1891. Queen Victoria.

32	**40**	3p. red	30	15
13	**23**	½a. turquoise (No. 84)	1·50	10
33	-	½a. green (No. 114)	1·10	1·25
14	-	9p. red	1·25	2·50
15	-	1a. purple	1·75	30
34	-	1a. red	2·50	3·00
17	-	1a.6p. brown	3·00	3·00
18	-	2a. blue	3·25	40
20	-	3a. orange	3·75	1·00
21	-	4a. green (No. 95)	5·50	1·50
23	-	6a. brown (No. 80)	4·75	17·00
26	-	8a. mauve	7·50	17·00
27	-	12a. purple on red	5·50	18·00
28	**37**	1r. green and red	10·00	65·00
29	**38**	2r. red and orange	£250	£1400
30	**38**	3r. brown and green	£300	£1500
31	**38**	5r. blue and violet	£350	£1500

1903. King Edward VII.

35	3p. grey	40	10
37	½a. green (No. 122)	1·50	15
38	1a. red (No. 123)	3·25	10
39	2a. lilac	3·50	65
40	3a. orange	2·75	35
41	4a. olive	5·50	1·50
42	6a. bistre	6·00	16·00
43	8a. mauve	5·50	4·00
44	12a. purple on red	13·00	40·00
45	1r. green and red	8·00	9·00

1912. King Edward VII. Inscr "INDIA POSTAGE & REVENUE".

46	½a. green (No. 149)	40	25
47	1a. red (No. 150)	1·75	1·25

1912. King George V. Optd in two lines.

48	**55**	3p. grey	75	10
49	**56**	½a. green	1·50	60
50	**57**	1a. red	2·00	20
61	**57**	1a. brown	3·00	50
51	**58**	1½a. brown (A)	50	55
52	**59**	2a. purple	2·75	1·75
53	**62**	3a. orange	4·00	2·25
62	**62**	3a. blue	5·00	14·00
54	**63**	4a. olive	6·00	3·75
55	**64**	6a. ochre	4·25	4·75
56	**65**	8a. mauve	6·50	4·75
57	**66**	12a. red	7·50	11·00
58	**67**	1r. brown and green	16·00	21·00
59	**67**	2r. red and brown	20·00	£160
60	**67**	5r. blue and violet	55·00	£350

1928. King George V. Optd in one line.

63	**55**	3p. grey	2·00	10
64	**56**	½a. green	50	10
75	**79**	½a. green	1·50	30
65*a*	**80**	9p. green	3·00	35
66	**57**	1a. brown	1·25	25
76	**81**	1a. brown	1·10	20
67	**82**	1a.3p. mauve	3·75	15
68	**70**	2a. lilac	1·75	40
77	**59**	2a. red	40	1·50
69	**61**	2a.6p. orange	7·50	4·25
70	**62**	3a. blue	4·25	3·00
78w	**62**	3a. red	6·00	14·00
71	**71**	4a. green	8·25	2·25
79	**63**	4a. olive	2·50	4·25
72	**65**	8a. mauve	11·00	5·50
73	**66**	1r. brown and green	10·00	16·00
74w	**66**	2r. red and orange	14·00	80·00

1937. King George VI. Optd in one line.

80	**91**	3p. grey	15·00	35
81	**91**	½a. brown	8·00	50
82	**91**	9p. green	5·00	1·00
83	**91**	1a. red	3·00	20
84	**92**	2a. red	2·50	14·00
85	-	2a.6p. violet	9·50	38·00
86	-	3a. green	14·00	15·00
87	-	3a.6p. blue	12·00	40·00
88	-	4a. brown	28·00	24·00
89	-	6a. green	40·00	90·00
90	-	8a. violet	45·00	70·00
91	-	12a. red	32·00	95·00
92	**93**	1r. grey and brown	38·00	60·00
93	**93**	2r. purple and brown	35·00	£160
94	**93**	5r. green and blue	45·00	£375
95	**93**	10r. purple and red	70·00	£600
96	**93**	15r. brown and green	£150	£950
97	**93**	25r. grey and purple	£225	£950

1943. King George VI. Optd **PATIALA** only

(a) Issue of 1938

98	**94**	3p. grey	21·00	3·75
99	**94**	½a. brown	6·50	3·25
100	**94**	9p. green	£550	16·00
101	**94**	1a. red	40·00	3·50
102	**93**	1r. grey and brown	15·00	85·00

(b) Issue of 1940.

103	**92**	3p. grey	3·00	15
104	**92**	½a. mauve	1·00	15
105	**92**	9p. green	1·75	15
106	**92**	1a. red	3·00	10
107	**101**	1a.3p. bistre	1·75	4·00
108*a*	**102**	1½a. violet	14·00	6·00
109	**101**	2a. red	2·00	50
110	**101**	3a. violet	2·00	3·75
111	**101**	3½a. blue	19·00	48·00
112	**102**	4a. brown	3·00	4·75
113	**102**	6a. green	2·00	40·00
114	**102**	8a. violet	2·00	15·00
115	**102**	12a. purple	40·00	£120

OFFICIAL STAMPS
Overprinted SERVICE.

1884. Nos. 1 to 3 (Queen Victoria).

O1	**23**	½a. turquoise	28·00	50
O2	-	1a. purple	1·00	10
O3	-	2a. blue	£8500	£140

1885. Nos. 7, 11 and 8 (Queen Victoria).

O5	-	1a. purple	2·50	10
O6	**23**	½a. turquoise	2·75	10
O7	-	2a. blue	1·00	40

1891. Nos. 13 to 28 and No. 10 (Queen Victoria).

O8	**23**	½a. turquoise (No. 13)	1·25	10
O9	-	1a. purple	8·50	10
O20	-	1a. red	2·25	10
O10*a*		2a. blue	5·00	4·00
O12	-	3a. orange	4·75	4·50
O13*a*		4a. green	4·50	30
O15	-	6a. brown	3·75	45
O16	-	8a. mauve	5·50	1·75
O18	-	12a. purple on red	3·75	65
O19	-	1r. grey	4·25	70
O21	**37**	1r. green and red	7·50	10·00

1903. Nos. 36 to 45 (King Edward VII).

O22	3p. grey	50	10
O24	½a. green	1·50	10
O25	1a. red	60	10
O28	3a. brown	6·00	3·75
O29	4a. olive	4·25	20
O30	8a. mauve	2·75	75
O32	1r. green and red	3·00	80

1907. Nos. 46/7 (King Edward VII). Inscr "INDIA POSTAGE & REVENUE".

O33	½a. green	50	20
O34	1a. red	1·25	10

1913. Official stamps of India (King George V). Optd **PATIALA STATE** in two lines.

O35	**55**	3p. grey	10	20
O36	**56**	½a. green	10	20
O37	**57**	1a. red	10	10
O38	**57**	1a. brown	8·50	1·00
O39	**59**	2a. mauve	1·25	1·25
O40	**63**	4a. olive	50	35
O41	**64**	6a. bistre	3·00	2·50
O42	**65**	8a. mauve	70	70
O43	**67**	1r. brown and green	2·25	1·40
O44	**67**	2r. red and brown	22·00	55·00
O45	**67**	5r. blue and violet	22·00	35·00

1927. Postage stamps of India (King George V) optd **PATIALA STATE SERVICE** in two lines.

O47	**55**	3p. grey	10	10
O48	**56**	½a. green	1·00	55
O58	**79**	½a. green	50	10
O49	**57**	1a. brown	15	10
O59	**81**	1a. brown	35	30
O50	**82**	1a.3p. mauve	40	10
O51	**70**	2a. purple	30	30
O52	**70**	2a. red	50	35
O60	**59**	2a. red	15	30
O53w	**61**	2a.6p. orange	2·00	80
O54	**71**	4a. green	50	30
O62	**63**	4a. olive	5·00	1·75
O55	**65**	8a. purple	2·75	65
O55w	**65**	8a. purple	1·60	80
O56w	**67**	1r.	3·00	4·00
O57	**66**	2r. red and orange	18·00	60·00

1938. Postage stamps of India (King George VI) optd **PATIALA STATE SERVICE.**

O63	**91**	½a. brown	1·00	20
O64	**91**	9p. green	14·00	85·00
O65	**91**	1a. red	1·00	40
O66	**93**	1r. grey and brown	1·00	9·50
O67	**93**	2r. purple and green	9·00	5·00
O68	**93**	5r. green and blue	19·00	80·00

1939. Surch **1A SERVICE 1A.**

O69w	**82**	1a. on 1a.3p. mauve	11·00	3·25

1940

Official stamps of India optd **PATIALA**

O71	**O20**	3p. grey	1·00	10
O72	**O20**	½a. brown	1·50	10
O73	**O20**	½a. purple	1·25	10
O74	**O20**	9p. green	1·60	50
O75	**O20**	1a. red	1·50	10
O76	**O20**	1a.3p. bistre	1·40	25
O77	**O20**	1½a. violet	8·00	1·50
O78	**O20**	2a. orange	10·00	35
O79	**O20**	2½a. violet	4·00	1·00
O80	**O20**	4a. brown	2·00	2·50
O81	**O20**	8a. violet	7·50	6·00

(b) Postage stamps of India (King George VI) optd **PATIALA SERVICE**

O82	**93**	1r. slate and brown	5·00	11·00
O83	**93**	2r. purple and brown	16·00	85·00
O84	**93**	5r. green and blue	27·00	£100

Pt. 1

PENANG

A British Settlement which became a state of the Federation of Malaya, incorporated in Malaysia in 1963.

100 cents = 1 dollar (Straits or Malayan).

1948. Silver Wedding. As T **8b/8c** of Pitcairn Islands.

1	10c. violet	30	20
2	$5 brown	38·00	38·00

1949. As Nos. 278/92 of Straits Settlement.

3	1c. black	1·75	20
4	2c. orange	1·75	20
5	3c. green	60	1·00
6	4c. brown	50	10
7	5c. purple	7·00	4·00
8	6c. grey	2·00	20
9	8c. red	1·25	6·50
10	8c. green	7·00	4·00
11	10c. mauve	50	10
12	12c. red	7·00	13·00
13	15c. blue	2·00	30
14	20c. black and green	3·25	1·50
15	20c. blue	7·50	1·25
16	25c. purple and orange	3·75	1·50
17	35c. red and purple	7·00	1·25
18	40c. red and purple	7·50	16·00
19	50c. black and blue	7·50	20
20	$1 blue and purple	20·00	3·50
21	$2 green and red	23·00	2·00
22	$3 green and brown	48·00	3·00

1949. U.P.U. As T **8d/8g** of of Pitcairn Islands.

23	10c. purple	20	10
24	15c. blue	2·50	3·75
25	25c. orange	45	3·75
26	30c. black	1·50	3·50

1953. Coronation. As T **8h** of Pitcairn Islands.

27	10c. black and purple	2·75	10

1954. As T **1** of Malacca, but inscr "PENANG".

28	1c. black	10	70
29	2c. orange	50	30
30	4c. brown	2·00	10
31	5c. mauve	2·00	4·75
32	6c. grey	20	80
33	8c. green	40	3·50
34	10c. purple	20	10
35	12c. red	40	3·50
36	20c. blue	50	10
37	25c. purple and orange	40	10
38	30c. red and purple	40	10
39	35c. red and purple	70	60
40	50c. black and blue	75	10
41	$1 blue and purple	3·00	30
42	$2 green and red	21·00	3·75
43	$5 green and brown	48·00	3·75

1957. As Nos. 92/102 of Kedah, but inset portrait of Queen Elizabeth II.

44	1c. black	10	1·50
45	2c. red	10	1·00
46	4c. sepia	10	10
47	5c. lake	10	30
48	8c. green	3·00	2·25
49	10c. brown	30	10
50	20c. blue	1·00	40
51	50c. black and blue	2·00	70
52	$1 blue and purple	14·00	1·00
53	$2 green and red	23·00	20·00
54	$5 brown and green	27·00	14·00

1 Copra

1960. As Nos. 44/54, but with inset Arms of Penang as in T **1**.

55	1c. black	10	1·60
56	2c. red	10	1·60
57	4c. brown	10	10
58	5c. lake	10	10
59	8c. green	2·75	4·50
60	10c. purple	30	10
61	20c. blue	55	10
62	50c. black and blue	30	30
63	$1 blue and purple	7·50	1·75
64	$2 green and red	13·00	9·00
65	$5 brown and green	15·00	9·00

2 "Vanda hookeriana"

1965. Flowers as T **2**.

66	**2**	1c. multicoloured	10	1·25
67	-	2c. multicoloured	10	1·50
68	-	5c. multicoloured	1·25	10
69	-	6c. multicoloured	30	1·25
70	-	10c. multicoloured	20	10
71	-	15c. multicoloured	1·00	10
72	-	20c. multicoloured	1·60	30

The higher values used in Penang were Nos. 20/7 of Malaysia (National Issues).

3 "Valeria valeria"

1971. Butterflies as T **3**.

75		1c. multicoloured	40	2·25
76		2c. multicoloured	70	2·25
77		5c. multicoloured	1·50	40
78		6c. multicoloured	1·50	2·00
79		10c. multicoloured	1·50	15
80		15c. multicoloured	1·50	10
81	**3**	20c. multicoloured	1·75	60

The higher values in use with this issue were Nos. 64/71 of Malaysia (National Issues).

4 "Etlingera elatior" (inscr "Phaeomeria speciosa")

1979. Flowers as T **4**.

86	1c. "Rafflesia hasseltii"	10	1·00
87	2c. "Pterocarpus indicus"	10	1·00
88	5c. "Lagerstroemia speciosa"	10	35
89	10c. "Durio zibethinus"	15	10
90	15c. "Hibiscus rosa-sinensis"	15	10
91	20c. "Rhododendron scorte-chinii"	20	10
92	25c. Type **4**	40	30

1986. As Nos. 152/8 of Kedah but with Arms of Penang and inscr "PULAU PINANG".

100	1c. Coffee	10	50
101	2c. Coconuts	10	50
102	5c. Type **5**	15	15
103	10c. Black pepper	20	10
104	15c. Rubber	40	10
105	20c. Oil palm	40	15
106	30c. Rice	40	15

2003. As 106 but redenominated in 'sen'. Multicoloured.

107	30s. Rice	1·75	10

6 *Nelumbium nelumbo* (sacred lotus)

2007. Garden Flowers. As Nos. 210/15 of Johore, but with Arms of Penang as in T **6**. Multicoloured.

108	5s. Type **6**	10	10
109	10s. *Hydrangea macrophylla*	15	10
110	20s. *Hippeastrum reticulatum*	25	15
111	30s. *Bougainvillea*	40	20
112	40s. *Ipomoea indica*	50	30
113	50s. *Hibiscus rosa-sinensis*	65	35
MS114	100×85 mm.Nos. 108/13	2·00	2·00

Pt. 1

PENRHYN ISLAND

One of the Cook Islands in the South Pacific. A dependency of New Zealand. Used Cook Islands stamps until 1973 when further issues for use in the Northern group of the Cook Islands issues appeared.

A. NEW ZEALAND DEPENDENCY

1902. Stamps of New Zealand (Pictorials) surch **PENRHYN ISLAND.** and value in native language.

4	**23**	½d. green	1·00	14·00
10	**42**	1d. red	1·25	9·00
1	**26**	2½d. blue (No. 249)	12·00	12·00
14	**28**	3d. brown	10·00	40·00
15	**31**	6d. red	15·00	50·00
16*a*	**34**	1s. orange	42·00	42·00

1914. Stamps of New Zealand (King Edward VII) surch **PENRHYN ISLAND.** and value in native language.

19	**51**	½d. green	80	12·00
22	**51**	6d. red	23·00	75·00
23	**51**	1s. orange	48·00	£100

1917. Stamps of New Zealand (King George V) optd **PENRHYN ISLAND.**

28	**62**	½d. green	1·00	2·00
29	**62**	1½d. grey	6·50	27·00
30	**62**	1½d. brown	60	27·00
24a	**62**	2½d. blue	2·00	10·00
31	**62**	3d. brown	4·00	42·00
26a	**62**	6d. red	5·00	21·00
27a	**62**	1s. orange	12·00	35·00

1920. Pictorial types as Cook Islands (1920), but inscr "PENRHYN".

32	**9**	½d. black and green	1·00	23·00
33	-	1d. black and red	1·50	15·00
34	-	1½d. black and violet	6·50	19·00
40	-	2½d. brown and black	14·00	42·00
35	-	3d. black and red	2·50	15·00
36	-	6d. brown and red	3·25	20·00
37	-	1s. black and blue	10·00	26·00

B. PART OF COOK ISLANDS

1973. Nos. 228/9, 231, 233/6, 239/40 and 243/5 of Cook Islands optd **PENRHYN NORTHERN** or **PENRHYN** ($1 ,2)

41B	1c. multicoloured	10	10
42B	2c. multicoloured	10	10
43B	3c. multicoloured	20	10
44B	4c. multicoloured	10	10
45B	5c. multicoloured	10	10
46B	6c. multicoloured	15	30
47B	8c. multicoloured	20	40
48B	15c. multicoloured	30	50
49B	20c. multicoloured	1·50	80
50B	50c. multicoloured	50	1·75
51B	$1 multicoloured	50	2·00
52B	$2 multicoloured	50	2·25

1973. Nos. 450/2 of Cook Is. optd **PENRHYN NORTHERN**.

53	**138**	25c. multicoloured	30	20
54	-	30c. multicoloured	30	20
55	-	50c. multicoloured	30	20

10 "Ostracion sp."

1974. Fish. Multicoloured.

(a) T **10** and similar horiz designs showing fishes

56	½c. Type **10**	50	75
57	1c. "Monodactylus argenteus"	70	75
58	2c. "Pomacanthus imperator"	80	75
59	3c. "Chelmon rostratus"	80	50
60	4c. "Chaetodon ornatissimus"	80	50
61	5c. "Chaetodon melanotus"	80	50
62	8c. "Chaetodon raffessi"	80	50
63	10c. "Chaetodon ephippium"	85	50
64	20c. "Pygoplites diacanthus"	1·75	50
65	25c. "Heniochus acuminatus"	1·75	50
66	60c. "Plectorhynchus chaeto-donoides"	2·50	90
67	$1 "Balistipus undulatus"	3·25	1·25

(b) Larger designs

68	$2 Bird's-eye view of Penrhyn	3·00	12·00
69	$5 Satellite view of Australasia	3·00	5·00

11 Penrhyn Stamps of 1902

1974. Cent of Universal Postal Union. Multicoloured.

70	25c. Type **11**	20	45
71	50c. Stamps of 1920	35	55

12 "Adoration of the Kings" (Memling)

1974. Christmas. Multicoloured.

72	5c. Type **12**	20	30
73	10c. "Adoration of the Shepherds" (Hugo van der Goes)	25	30
74	25c. "Adoration of the Magi" (Rubens)	40	45
75	30c. "The Holy Family" (Borgianni)	45	65

13 Churchill giving "V" sign

1974. Birth Cent of Sir Winston Churchill.

76	**13**	30c. brown and gold	35	85
77	-	50c. green and gold	45	90

DESIGN: 50c. Full-face portrait.

1975. "Apollo–Soyuz" Space Project. Optd **KIA ORANA ASTRONAUTS** and emblem.

78	$5 Satellite view of Australasia	1·50	2·50

15 "Virgin and Child" (Bouts)

1975. Christmas. Paintings of the "Virgin and Child" by artists given below. Multicoloured.

79	7c. Type **15**	40	10
80	15c. Leonardo da Vinci	70	20
81	35c. Raphael	1·10	35

16 "Pieta"

1976. Easter. 500th Birth Anniv of Michelangelo.

82	**16**	15c. brown and gold	25	15
83	-	20c. lilac and gold	30	15
84	-	35c. green and gold	40	20
MS85		112×72 mm. Nos. 82/4	85	1·25

DESIGNS: Nos. 83/4 show different views of the "Pieta".

17 "Washington crossing the Delaware" (E. Leutze)

1976. Bicentenary of American Revolution.

86	**17**	30c. multicoloured	25	15
87	-	30c. multicoloured	25	15
88	-	30c. multicoloured	25	15
89	-	50c. multicoloured	30	20
90	-	50c. multicoloured	30	20
91	-	50c. multicoloured	30	20
MS92		103×103 mm. Nos. 86/91	1·25	1·25

DESIGNS: Nos. 86/88, "Washington crossing the Delaware" (E. Leutze); Nos. 89/91, "The Spirit of "76" (A. M. Willard).

Nos. 86/88 and 89/91 were each printed together, se-tenant, forming a composite design of the complete painting. Type **17** shows the left-hand stamp of the 30c. design.

18 Running

1976. Olympic Games, Montreal. Multicoloured.

93	25c. Type **18**	25	15
94	30c. Long jumping	30	15
95	75c. Throwing the javelin	55	25
MS96	86×128 mm. Nos. 93/5	1·10	2·00

19 "The Flight into Egypt"

1976. Christmas. Durer Engravings.

97	**19**	7c. black and silver	15	10
98	-	15c. blue and silver	25	15
99	-	35c. violet and silver	35	25

DESIGNS: 15c. "Adoration of the Magi"; 35c. "The Nativity".

20 The Queen in Coronation Robes

1977. Silver Jubilee. Multicoloured.

100	50c. Type **20**	25	60
101	$1 The Queen and Prince Philip	35	65
102	$2 Queen Elizabeth II	50	80
MS103	128×87 mm. Nos. 100/2	1·00	1·50

Stamps from the miniature sheet have silver borders.

21 "The Annunciation"

1977. Christmas. Illustrations by J. S. von Carolsfeld.

104	**21**	7c. brown, purple and gold	40	15
105	-	15c. red, purple and gold	60	15
106	-	35c. deep green, green and gold	1·00	30

DESIGNS: 15c. "The Announcement to the Shepherds"; 35c. "The Nativity".

22 Iiwi

1978. Bicentenary of Discovery of Hawaii. Birds and Artefacts. Multicoloured.

107	20c. Type **22**	80	30
108	20c. Elgin cloak	80	30
109	30c. Apapane	90	40
110	30c. Feather image of a god	90	40
111	35c. Moorhen	90	45
112	35c. Feather cape, helmet and staff	90	45
113	75c. Hawaii O-o	1·50	80
114	75c. Feather image and cloak	1·50	80
MS115	Two sheets, each 78×119 mm. containing. (a) Nos. 107, 109, 111, 113. (b) Nos. 108, 110, 112, 114	5·00	7·00

23 "The Road to Calvary"

1978. Easter. 400th Birth Anniv of Rubens. Multicoloured.

116	10c. Type **23**	20	10
117	15c. "Christ on the Cross"	25	15
118	35c. "Christ with Straw"	45	25
MS119	87×138 mm. Nos. 116/18	1·00	1·60

Stamps from No. **MS**119 are slightly larger (28×36 mm).

1978. Easter. Children's Charity. Designs as Nos. 116/18 in separate miniature sheets, 49×68 mm, each with a face value of 60c.+5c.

MS120	As Nos. 116/18. Set of 3 sheets	1·00	1·50

24 Royal Coat of Arms

1978. 25th Anniv of Coronation.

121 **24** 90c. black, gold and mauve 30 60
122 - 90c. multicoloured 30 60
123 - 90c. black, gold and green 30 60
MS124 75×122 mm. Nos. 121/3 1·10 2·00

DESIGNS: No. 122, Queen Elizabeth II; No. 123, New Zealand coat of arms.

25 "Madonna of the Pear"

1978. Christmas. 450th Death Anniv of Albrecht Durer. Multicoloured.

125 30c. Type **25** 65 30
126 35c. "The Virgin and Child with St. Anne" (Durer) 65 30
MS127 101×60 mm. Nos. 125/6 1·00 1·25

26 Sir Rowland Hill and G.B. Penny Black Stamp

1979. Death Centenary of Sir Rowland Hill. Multicoloured.

128 75c. Type **26** 40 55
129 75c. 1974 U.P.U. Centenary 25c. and 50c. commemoratives 40 55
130 90c. Sir Rowland Hill 45 70
131 90c. 1978 Coronation Anniversary 90c. commemorative 45 70
MS132 116×58 mm. Nos. 128/31 1·25 1·50

Stamps from No. **MS**132 have cream backgrounds.

27 Max and Moritz

1979. International Year of the Child. Illustrations from "Max and Moritz" stories by Wilhelm Busch. Multicoloured.

133 12c. Type **27** 15 15
134 12c. Max and Moritz looking down chimney 15 15
135 12c. Max and Moritz making off with food 15 15
136 12c. Cook about to beat dog 15 15
137 15c. Max sawing through bridge 20 15
138 15c. Pursuer approaching bridge 20 15
139 15c. Collapse of bridge 20 15
140 15c. Pursuer in river 20 15
141 20c. Baker locking shop 20 20
142 20c. Max and Moritz emerge from hiding 20 20
143 20c. Max and Moritz falling in dough 20 20
144 20c. Max and Moritz made into buns 20 20

28 "Christ carrying Cross" (Book of Ferdinand II)

1980. Easter. Scenes from 15th-cent Prayer Books. Multicoloured.

145 12c. Type **28** 15 20
146 20c. "The Crucifixion" (William Vrelant, Book of Duke of Burgundy) 20 25
147 35c. "Descent from the Cross" (Book of Ferdinand II) 30 45
MS148 111×65 mm. Nos. 145/7 55 1·00

Stamps from No. **MS**148 have cream borders.

1980. Easter. Children's Charity. Designs as Nos. 145/7 in separate miniature sheets 54×85 mm, each with a face value of 70c.+5c.

MS149 As Nos. 145/7. Set of 3 sheets 75 1·00

29 "Queen Elizabeth, 1937" (Sir Gerald Kelly)

1980. 80th Birthday of The Queen Mother.

150 **29** $1 multicoloured 1·00 1·25
MS151 55×84 mm. **29** $2.50 multicoloured 1·60 1·60

30 Falk Hoffman, East Germany (platform diving) (gold)

1980. Olympic Medal Winners. Multicoloured.

152 10c. Type **30** 30 10
153 10c. Martina Jaschke, East Germany (platform diving) 30 10
154 20c. Tomi Polkolainen, Finland (archery) 35 15
155 20c. Kete Losaberidse, U.S.S.R. (archery) 35 15
156 30c. Czechoslovakia (football) 35 20
157 30c. East Germany (football) 40 20
158 50c. Barbel Wockel, East Germany (200 m) 50 30
159 50c. Pietro Mennea, Italy (200 m) 50 30
MS160 150×106 mm. Nos. 152/9 1·40 1·75

Stamps from No. **MS**160 have gold borders.

31 "The Virgin of Counsellors" (Luis Dalmau)

1980. Christmas. Multicoloured.

161 20c. Type **31** 15 15
162 35c. "Virgin and Child" (Serra brothers) 20 20
163 50c. "The Virgin of Albocacer" (Master of the Porciuncula) 30 30
MS164 135×75 mm. Nos. 161/3 1·50 1·50

1980. Christmas. Children's Charity. Design as Nos. 161/3 in separate miniature sheets, 54×77 mm, each with a face value of 70c.+5c.

MS165 As Nos. 161/3. Set of 3 sheets 1·00 1·50

32 Amatasi

1981. Sailing Craft and Ships (1st series). Multicoloured.

166 1c. Type **32** 20 15
167 1c. Ndrua (canoe) 20 15
168 1c. Waka (canoe) 20 15
169 1c. Tongiaki (canoe) 20 15
170 3c. Va'a Teu'ua (canoe) 50 15
171 3c. "Vitoria" (Del Cano's ship) 50 15
172 3c. "Golden Hind" (Drake's ship) 50 15
173 3c. "La Boudeuse" (Bougainville's ship) 50 15
174 4c. H.M.S. "Bounty" 50 15
175 4c. "L'Astrolabe" (Dumont d'Urville's ship) 50 15
176 4c. "Star of India" (full-rigged ship) 50 15
177 4c. "Great Republic" (clipper) 50 15
178 6c. "Balcutha" (clipper) 50 20
179 6c. "Coonatto" (clipper) 50 20
180 6c. "Antiope" (clipper) 50 20
181 6c. "Taeping" (clipper) 50 20
182 10c. "Preussen" (full-rigged ship) 50 75
183 10c. "Pamir" (barque) 50 75
184 10c. "Cap Hornier" (full-rigged ship) 50 75
185 10c. "Patriarch" (clipper) 50 75
186 15c. Type **32** 50 85
187 15c. As No. 167 50 85
188 15c. As No. 168 50 85
189 15c. As No. 169 50 85
190 20c. As No. 170 50 85
191 20c. As No. 171 50 85
192 20c. As No. 172 50 85
193 20c. As No. 173 50 85
194 30c. As No. 174 50 95
195 30c. As No. 175 50 95
196 30c. As No. 176 50 95
197 30c. As No. 177 50 95
198 50c. As No. 178 1·00 1·75
199 50c. As No. 179 1·00 1·75
200 50c. As No. 180 1·00 1·75
201 50c. As No. 181 1·00 1·75
202 $1 As No. 182 2·50 1·50
203 $1 As No. 183 2·50 1·50
204 $1 As No. 184 2·50 1·50
205 $1 As No. 185 2·50 1·50
206 $2 "Cutty Sark" (clipper) 4·50 3·25
207 $4 "Mermerus" (clipper) 9·00 5·00
208 $6 H.M.S. "Resolution" and H.M.S. "Discovery" (Cook's ships) 15·00 12·00

Nos. 186/201 are 41×35 mm, Nos. 202/5 41×25 mm and Nos. 206/8 47×33 mm in size.

Nos. 181 and 201 are wrongly inscribed "TEAPING".

See also Nos. 337/55.

33 "Jesus at the Grove" (Veronese)

1981. Easter. Paintings. Multicoloured.

218 30c. Type **33** 40 20
219 40c. "Christ with Crown of Thorns" (Titian) 55 25
220 50c. "Pieta" (Van Dyck) 60 30
MS221 110×68 mm. Nos. 218/20 2·75 2·00

1981. Easter. Children's Charity. Designs as Nos. 218/20 in separate miniature sheets 70×86 mm, each with a face value of 70c.+5c.

MS222 As Nos. 218/20. Set of 3 sheets 1·00 1·50

34 Prince Charles as Young Child

1981. Royal Wedding. Multicoloured.

223 40c. Type **34** 15 35
224 50c. Prince Charles as schoolboy 15 40
225 60c. Prince Charles as young man 20 40
226 70c. Prince Charles in ceremonial Naval uniform 20 45
227 80c. Prince Charles as Colonel-in-Chief, Royal Regiment of Wales 20 45
MS228 99×89 mm. Nos. 223/7 1·00 2·00

1981. International Year for Disabled Persons. Nos. 223/7 surch **+5c**.

229 **34** 40c.+5c. +5c. multicoloured 15 50
230 - 50c.+5c. +5c. multicoloured 15 55
231 - 60c.+5c. +5c. multicoloured 20 55
232 - 70c.+5c. +5c. multicoloured 20 60
233 - 80c.+5c. +5c. multicoloured 20 65
MS234 99×89 mm. As Nos. 229/33, but 10c. premium on each stamp 80 2·50

35 Footballers

1981. World Cup Football Championship, Spain (1982). Multicoloured.

235 15c. Type **35** 20 15
236 15c. Footballer wearing orange jersey with black and mauve stripes 20 15
237 15c. Player in blue jersey 20 15
238 35c. Player in blue jersey 30 25
239 35c. Player in red jersey 30 25
240 35c. Player in yellow jersey with green stripes 30 25
241 50c. Player in orange jersey 40 35
242 50c. Player in mauve jersey 40 35
243 50c. Player in black jersey 40 35
MS244 113×151 mm. As Nos. 235/43, but each stamp with a premium of 3c. 4·75 2·50

36 "The Virgin on a Crescent"

1981. Christmas. Engravings by Durer.

245 **36** 30c. violet, purple and stone 90 1·00
246 - 40c. violet, purple and stone 1·25 1·40
247 - 50c. violet, purple and stone 1·50 1·75
MS248 134×75 mm. As Nos. 245/7, but each stamp with a premium of 2c. 2·00 2·25
MS249 Designs as Nos. 245/7 in separate miniature sheets, 58×85 mm, each with a face value of 70c.+5c. Set of 3 sheets 1·50 1·75

DESIGNS: 40c. "The Virgin at the Fence"; 50c. "The Holy Virgin and Child".

37 Lady Diana Spencer as Baby

1982. 21st Birthday of Princess of Wales. Multicoloured.

250 30c. Type **37** 30 30
251 50c. As young child 40 45
252 70c. As schoolgirl 60 60
253 80c. As teenager 70 80
254 $1.40 As a young lady 1·10 1·25
MS255 87×110 mm. Nos. 250/4 6·50 3·50

1982. Birth of Prince William of Wales (1st issue). Nos. 223/7 optd **BIRTH OF PRINCE WILLIAM OF WALES 21 JUNE 1982**.

256 40c. Type **34** 30 35
257 50c. Prince Charles as schoolboy 40 45
258 60c. Prince Charles as young man 45 55
259 70c. Prince Charles in ceremonial Naval uniform 50 60
260 80c. Prince Charles as Colonel-in-Chief, Royal Regiment of Wales 50 65
MS261 99×89 mm. Nos. 256/60 5·00 7·00

1982. Birth of Prince William of Wales (2nd issue). As Nos. 250/5 but with changed inscriptions. Multicoloured.

262 30c. As Type **37** (A) 30 30
263 30c. As Type **37** (B) 60 55
264 50c. As No. 251 (A) 60 55
265 50c. As No. 251 (B) 70 65
266 70c. As No. 252 (A) 90 80
267 70c. As No. 252 (B) 90 80
268 80c. As No. 253 (A) 95 85
269 80c. As No. 253 (B) 95 85
270 $1.40 As No. 254 (A) 1·40 1·25
271 $1.40 As No. 254 (B) 1·40 1·25
MS272 88×109 mm. As No. **MS**255 (C) 4·75 3·25

INSCR: A. "21 JUNE 1982. BIRTH OF PRINCE WILLIAM OF WALES"; B. "COMMEMORATING THE BIRTH OF PRINCE WILLIAM OF WALES"; C. "21 JUNE 1982. ROYAL BIRTH PRINCE WILLIAM OF WALES".

39 "Virgin and Child" (detail, Joos Van Cleve)

1982. Christmas. Details from Renaissance Paintings of "Virgin and Child". Multicoloured.

273 25c. Type **39** 30 40
274 48c. "Virgin and Child" (Filippino Lippi) 45 55
275 60c. "Virgin and Child" (Cima da Conegliano) 60 70
MS276 134×73 mm. As Nos. 273/5 but each with 2c. charity premium 1·00 2·00

1982. Christmas. Children's Charity. Designs as Nos. 273/5, but without frames, in separate miniature sheets, 60×85 mm, each with a face value of 70c.+5c.

MS277 As Nos. 273/5. Set of 3 sheets 1·25 1·60

40 Red Coral

1983. Commonwealth Day. Multicoloured.

278 60c. Type **40** 40 45
279 60c. Aerial view of Penrhyn atoll 40 45
280 60c. Eleanor Roosevelt on Penrhyn during Second World War 40 45
281 60c. Map of South Pacific 40 45

41 Scout Emblem and Blue Tropical Flower

1983. 75th Anniv of Boy Scout Movement. Multicoloured.

282 36c. Type **41** 1·50 60
283 48c. Emblem and pink flower 1·75 90
284 60c. Emblem and orange flower 1·75 1·00
MS285 86×46 mm. $2 As 48c., but with elements of design reversed 1·50 3·00

1983. 15th World Scout Jamboree, Alberta, Canada. Nos. 282/4 optd **XV WORLD JAMBOREE CANADA 1983**.

286 36c. Type **41** 1·25 45
287 48c. Emblem and pink flower 1·50 60
288 60c. Emblem and orange flower 1·60 75
MS289 86×46 mm. $2 As 48c., but with elements of design reversed 1·50 3·50

43 School of Sperm Whales

1983. Whale Conservation. Multicoloured.

290 8c. Type **43** 1·00 70
291 15c. Harpooner preparing to strike 1·40 95
292 35c. Whale attacking boat 2·00 1·40
293 60c. Dead whales marked with flags 3·00 2·00
294 $1 Dead whales on slipway 3·75 3·00

44 "Mercury" (cable ship)

1983. World Communications Year. Multicoloured.

295 36c. Type **44** 80 35
296 48c. Men watching cable being laid 85 45
297 60c. "Mercury" (different) 1·10 60
MS298 115×90 mm. As Nos. 295/7 but each with charity premium of 3c. 1·25 1·60

On No. **MS**298 the values are printed in black and have been transposed with the World Communications Year logo.

1983. Various stamps surch

(a) Nos. 182/5, 190/7 and 206

299 18c. on 10c. on 10c. "Preussen" 1·25 50
300 18c. on 10c. on 10c. "Pamir" 1·25 50
301 18c. on 10c. on 10c. "Cap Hornier" 1·25 50
302 18c. on 10c. on 10c. "Patriarch" 1·25 50
303 36c. on 20c. on 20c. Va'a Teu'ua 1·50 70
304 36c. on 20c. on 20c. "Vitoria" 1·50 70
305 36c. on 20c. on 20c. "Golden Hind" 1·50 70
306 36c. on 20c. on 20c. "La Boudeuse" 1·50 70
307 36c. on 30c. on 30c. H.M.S. "Bounty" 1·50 70
308 36c. on 30c. on 30c. "L'Astrolabe" 1·50 70
309 36c. on 30c. on 30c. "Star of India" 1·50 70
310 36c. on 30c. on 30c. "Great Republic" 1·50 70
311 $1.20 on $2 on $2 "Cutty Sark" 5·00 2·00

(b) Nos. 252/3

312 72c. on 70c. on 70c. Princess Diana as schoolgirl 4·00 1·50
313 96c. on 80c. on 80c. Princess Diana as teenager 4·00 1·75

1983. Nos. 225/6, 268/9, 253 and 208 surch.

314 48c. on 60c. on 60c. Prince Charles as young man 3·75 1·75
315 72c. on 70c. on 70c. Prince Charles in ceremonial Naval uniform 4·25 1·90
316 96c. on 80c. on 80c. As No. 253 (inscr "21 JUNE 1982 ...") 3·00 1·10
317 96c. on 80c. on 80c. As No. 253 (inscr "COMMEMORATING ...") 2·00 1·10
318 $1.20 on $4.40 on $1.40 As young lady 3·50 1·60
319 $5.60 on $6 on $6 H.M.S. "Resolution" and "Discovery" 18·00 10·00

45 George Cayley's Airship Design, 1837

1983. Bicentenary of Manned Flight. Multicoloured

A. Inscr "NORTHERN COOK ISLANDS"

320A 36c. Type **45** 1·50 80
321A 48c. Dupuy de Lome's man-powered airship, 1872 1·75 90
322A 60c. Santos Dumont's airship "Ballon No. 6", 1901 2·00 1·25
323A 96c. Lebaudy-Juillot's airship, No. 1 "La Jaune", 1902 2·75 1·75
324A $1.32 Airship LZ-127 "Graf Zeppelin", 1929 3·25 2·50
MS325A 113×138 mm. Nos. 320A/4A 6·50 11·00

B. Corrected spelling optd in black on silver over original inscription

320B 36c. Type **45** 40 35
321B 48c. Dupuy de Lome's man-powered airship, 1872 50 45
322B 60c. Santos Dumont's airship "Ballon No. 6", 1901 55 50
323B 96c. Lebaudy-Juillot's airship No. 1 "La Jaune", 1902 80 80
324B $1.32 Airship LZ-127 "Graf Zeppelin", 1929 1·10 1·10
MS325B 113×138 mm. Nos. 320B/4B 2·25 4·25

46 "Madonna in the Meadow"

1983. Christmas. 500th Birth Anniv of Raphael. Multicoloured.

326 36c. Type **46** 60 40
327 42c. "Tempi Madonna" 60 40
328 48c. "The Smaller Cowper Madonna" 80 50
329 60c. "Madonna della Tenda" 95 60
MS330 87×115 mm. As Nos. 326/9 but each with a charity premium of 3c. 2·00 2·50

1983. Nos. 266/7, 227 and 270 surch.

331 72c. on 70c. As No. 252 (inscr "21 JUNE 1982 ...") 2·00 80
332 72c. on 70c. As No. 252 (inscr "COMMEMORATING ...") 1·25 60
333 96c. on 80c. Prince Charles as Colonel-in-Chief, Royal Regiment of Wales 2·00 65
334 $1.20 on $1.40 As No. 254 (inscr "21 JUNE 1982 ...") 2·25 70
335 $1.20 on $1.40 As No. 254 (inscr "COMMEMORATING ...") 1·75 65

1983. Christmas. 500th Birth Anniv of Raphael. Children's Charity. Designs as Nos. 326/9 in separate miniature sheets, 65×84 mm, each with a face value of 75c.+5c.

MS336 As Nos. 326/9. Set of 4 sheets 1·75 3·00

47 Waka

1984. Sailing Craft and Ships (2nd series). Multicoloured.

337 2c. Type **47** 70 70
338 4c. Amatasi 70 70
339 5c. Ndrua 70 70
340 8c. Tongiaki 70 70
341 10c. "Vitoria" 70 70
342 18c. "Golden Hind" 1·25 70
343 20c. "La Boudeuse" 80 70
344 30c. H.M.S. "Bounty" 1·25 70
345 36c. "L'Astrolabe" 1·00 70
346 48c. "Great Republic" 1·00 70
347 50c. "Star of India" 1·00 70
348 60c. "Coonatto" 1·00 70
349 72c. "Antiope" 1·00 70
350 80c. "Balcutha" 1·00 70
351 96c. "Cap Hornier" 1·00 85
352 $1.20 "Pamir" 2·50 1·40
353 $3 "Mermerus" (41×31 mm) 5·00 3·00
354 $5 "Cutty Sark" (41×31 mm) 5·50 5·00
355 $9.60 H.M.S. "Resolution" and H.M.S. "Discovery" (41×31 mm) 22·00 23·00

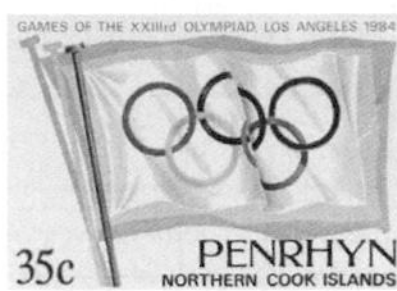

48 Olympic Flag

1984. Olympic Games, Los Angeles. Multicoloured.

356 35c. Type **48** 30 35
357 60c. Olympic torch and flags 50 55
358 $1.80 Ancient athletes and Coliseum 1·00 1·60
MS359 103×86 mm. As Nos. 356/8 but each with a charity premium of 5c. 1·90 2·50

49 Penrhyn Stamps of 1978, 1979 and 1981

1984. "Ausipex" International Stamp Exhibition, Melbourne. Multicoloured.

360 60c. Type **49** 50 75
361 $1.20 Location map of Penrhyn 1·00 1·25
MS362 90×90 mm. As Nos. 360/1, but each with a face value of 96c. 1·75 2·00

1984. Birth of Prince Harry. Nos. 223/4 and 250/1 surch **$2 Birth of Prince Harry 15 Sept. 1984**.

363 $2 on 30c. on 30c. Type **37** 1·40 1·50
364 $2 on 40c. on 40c. Type **34** 1·40 1·50
365 $2 on 50c. on 50c. Prince Charles as schoolboy 1·40 1·50
366 $2 on 50c. on 50c. Lady Diana as young child 1·40 1·50

51 "Virgin and Child" (Giovanni Bellini)

1984. Christmas. Paintings of the Virgin and Child by different artists. Multicoloured.

367 36c. Type **51** 60 35
368 48c. Lorenzo di Credi 75 45
369 60c. Palma the Older 80 50
370 96c. Raphael 1·00 80
MS371 93×118 mm. As Nos. 367/70, but each with a charity premium of 5c. 2·00 3·00

1984. Christmas. Children's Charity. Designs as Nos. 367/70, but without frames, in separate miniature sheets 67×81 mm, each with a face value of 96c.+10c.

MS372 As Nos. 367/70. Set of 4 sheets 2·50 3·50

52 Harlequin Duck

1985. Birth Bicentenary of John J. Audubon (ornithologist). Multicoloured.

373 20c. Type **52** 2·00 1·75
374 55c. Sage grouse 2·75 2·75
375 65c. Solitary sandpiper 3·00 3·00
376 75c. Dunlin 3·25 3·50
MS377 Four sheets, each 70×53 mm. As Nos. 373/6, but each with a face value of 95c. 9·00 6·50

Nos. 373/6 show original paintings.

53 Lady Elizabeth Bowes-Lyon, 1921

1985. Life and Times of Queen Elizabeth the Queen Mother. Each violet, silver and yellow.

378 75c. Type **53** 40 65
379 95c. With baby Princess Elizabeth, 1926 50 80
380 $1.20 Coronation Day, 1937 65 1·00
381 $2.80 On her 70th birthday 1·25 2·00
MS382 66×90 mm. $5 The Queen Mother 2·40 3·25

See also No. **MS**403.

54 "The House in the Wood"

1985. International Youth Year. Birth Centenary of Jacob Grimm (folklorist). Multicoloured.

383 75c. Type **54** 2·75 2·50
384 95c. "Snow-White and Rose-Red" 3·00 2·75
385 $1.15 "The Goose Girl" 3·25 3·00

55 "The Annunciation"

1985. Christmas. Paintings by Murillo. Multicoloured.

386 75c. Type **55** 1·25 1·25
387 $1.15 "Adoration of the Shepherds" 1·75 1·75
388 $1.80 "The Holy Family" 2·50 2·50
MS389 66×131 mm. As Nos. 386/8, but each with a face value of 95c. 2·75 3·00
MS390 Three sheets, each 66×72 mm. As Nos. 386/8, but with face values of $1.20, $1.45 and $2.75. Set of 3 sheets 4·50 4·75

56 Halley's Comet

1986. Appearance of Halley's Comet. Design showing details of the painting "Fire and Ice" by Camille Rendal. Multicoloured.

391 $1.50 Type **56** 2·25 1·50
392 $1.50 Stylized "Giotto" spacecraft 2·25 1·50

MS393 108×43 mm. $3 As Nos. 391/2 (104×39 mm). Imperf 2·25 2·50

Nos. 391/2 were printed together, forming a composite design of the complete painting.

57 Princess Elizabeth aged Three, 1929, and Bouquet

1986. 60th Birthday of Queen Elizabeth II. Multicoloured.

394 95c. Type **57** 1·50 80

395 $1.45 Profile of Queen Elizabeth and St. Edward's Crown 2·00 1·25

396 $2.50 Queen Elizabeth aged three and in profile with Imperial State Crown (56×30 mm) 2·50 2·00

58 Statue of Liberty under Construction, Paris

1986. Centenary of Statue of Liberty. Each black, gold and green.

397 95c. Type **58** 65 70

398 $1.75 Erection of Statue, New York 1·10 1·25

399 $3 Artist's impression of Statue, 1876 2·10 2·25

See also No. **MS**412.

59 Prince Andrew and Miss Sarah Ferguson

1986. Royal Wedding. Multicoloured.

400 $2.50 Type **59** 3·50 3·50

401 $3.50 Profiles of Prince Andrew and Miss Sarah Ferguson 4·00 4·00

1986. "Stampex '86" Stamp Exhibition, Adelaide. No. **MS**362 surch **$2** in black on gold.

MS402 $2 on 96c. × 2 6·00 7·00

The "Stampex '86" exhibition emblem is overprinted on the sheet margin.

1986. 86th Birthday of Queen Elizabeth the Queen Mother. Nos. 378/81 in miniature sheet, 90×120 mm.

MS403 Nos. 378/81 12·00 11·00

61 "Adoration of the Shepherds"

1986. Christmas. Engravings by Rembrandt. Each brown, ochre and gold.

404 65c. Type **61** 1·75 1·75

405 $1.75 "Virgin and Child" 3·00 3·00

406 $2.50 "The Holy Family" 4·25 4·25

MS407 120×87 mm. As Nos. 404/6, but each size 31×39 mm with a face value of $1.50 13·00 10·00

1986. Visit of Pope John Paul II to South Pacific. Nos. 404/6 surch **SOUTH PACIFIC VISIT 21 TO 24 NOVEMBER 1986 +10c**.

408 65c. +10c. Type **61** 4·50 2·75

409 $1.75 +10c. "Virgin and Child" 6·00 4·00

410 $2.50 +10c. "The Holy Family" 7·00 4·25

MS411 120×87 mm. As Nos. 408/10, but each size 31×39 mm with a face value of $1.50+10c. 20·00 12·00

1987. Centenary of Statue of Liberty (1986) (2nd issue). Two sheets, each 122×122 mm, containing multicoloured designs as T **112a** of Niue.

MS412 Two sheets. (a) 65c. Head and torch of Statue; 65c. Torch at sunset; 65c. Restoration workers with flag; 65c. Statue and Manhattan skyline; 65c. Workers and scaffolding. (b) 65c. Workers on Statue crown (horiz); 65c. Aerial view of Ellis Island (horiz); 65c. Ellis Island Immigration Centre (horiz); 65c. View from Statue to Ellis Island and Manhattan (horiz); 65c. Restoration workers (horiz). Set of 2 sheets 7·50 11·00

1987. Royal Ruby Wedding. Nos. 68/9 optd **Fortieth Royal Wedding Anniversary 1947–87**.

413 $2 Birds-eye view of Penrhyn 2·00 2·25

414 $5 Satellite view of Australasia 3·50 4·25

65 "The Garvagh Madonna"

1987. Christmas. Religious Paintings by Raphael. Multicoloured.

415 95c. Type **65** 1·50 1·50

416 $1.60 "The Alba Madonna" 2·00 2·00

417 $2.25 "The Madonna of the Fish" 3·00 3·00

MS418 91×126 mm. As Nos. 415/17, but each with a face value of $1.15 15·00 15·00

MS419 70×86 mm. $4.80 As No. 417, but size 36×39 mm. 15·00 15·00

1988. Olympic Games, Seoul. Multicoloured.

420 55c. Type **66** 75 65

421 95c. Pole vaulting (vert) 1·25 1·00

422 $1.25 Shot putting 1·50 1·40

423 $1.50 Lawn tennis (vert) 2·50 1·75

MS424 110×70 mm. As Nos. 421 and 423, but each with a face value of $2.50 4·00 5·00

66 Athletics

1988. Olympic Gold Medal Winners, Seoul. Nos. 420/3 optd.

425 55c. Type **66** (optd **CARL LEWIS UNITED STATES 100 METERS**) 80 60

426 95c. Pole vaulting (optd **LOUISE RITTER UNITED STATES HIGH JUMP**) 1·25 90

427 $1.25 Shot putting (optd **ULF TIMMERMANN EAST GERMANY SHOT-PUT**) 1·50 1·25

428 $1.50 Lawn tennis (optd **STEFFI GRAF WEST GERMANY WOMEN'S TENNIS**) 5·00 1·75

MS429 110×70 mm. $2.50 As No. 421 (optd **JACKIE JOYNER-KERSEE United States Heptathlon**); $2.50 As No. 423 (optd **STEFFI GRAF West Germany Women's Tennis MILOSLAV MECIR Czechoslovakia Men's Tennis**) 5·50 5·50

67 "Virgin and Child"

1988. Christmas. Designs showing different "Virgin and Child" paintings by Titian.

430 **67** 70c. multicoloured 90 90

431 - 85c. multicoloured 1·00 1·00

432 - 95c. multicoloured 1·25 1·25

433 - $1.25 multicoloured 1·50 1·50

MS434 100×80 mm. $6.40 As type **67**, but diamond-shaped (57×57 mm) 6·00 7·00

68 Neil Armstrong stepping onto Moon

1989. 20th Anniv of First Manned Moon Landing. Multicoloured.

435 55c. Type **68** 1·60 70

436 75c. Astronaut on Moon carrying equipment 1·75 85

437 95c. Conducting experiment on Moon 2·25 1·10

438 $1.25 Crew of "Apollo 11" 2·50 1·40

439 $1.75 Crew inside "Apollo 11" 2·75 1·90

69 Virgin Mary

1989. Christmas. Details from "The Nativity" by Durer. Multicoloured.

440 55c. Type **69** 80 80

441 70c. Christ Child and cherubs 90 90

442 85c. Joseph 1·25 1·25

443 $1.25 Three women 1·60 1·60

MS444 88×95 mm. $6.40 "The Nativity" (31×50 mm) 6·50 7·50

70 Queen Elizabeth the Queen Mother

1990. 90th Birthday of Queen Elizabeth the Queen Mother.

445 **70** $2.25 multicoloured 2·50 2·50

MS446 85×73 mm. **70** $7.50 multicoloured 14·00 14·00

71 "Adoration of the Magi" (Veronese)

1990. Christmas. Religious Paintings. Multicoloured.

447 55c. Type **71** 1·00 1·00

448 70c. "Virgin and Child" (Quentin Metsys) 1·40 1·40

449 85c. "Virgin and Child Jesus" (Hugo van der Goes) 1·60 1·60

450 $1.50 "Adoration of the Kings" (Jan Gossaert) 2·50 2·50

MS451 108×132 mm. $6.40 "Virgin and Child with Saints, Francis, John the Baptist, Zenobius and Lucy" (Domenico Veneziano) 8·00 9·00

1990. "Birdpex '90" Stamp Exhibition, Christchurch, New Zealand. Nos. 373/6 surch **Birdpex '90** and emblem.

452 $1.50 on 20c. on 20c. Type **52** 1·90 2·25

453 $1.50 on 55c. on 55c. Sage grouse 1·90 2·25

454 $1.50 on 65c. on 65c. Solitary sandpiper 1·90 2·25

455 $1.50 on 75c. on 75c. Dunlin 1·90 2·25

1991. 65th Birthday of Queen Elizabeth II. No. 208 optd **COMMEMORATING 65th BIRTHDAY OF H.M. QUEEN ELIZABETH II**.

456 $6 H.M.S. "Resolution" and "Discovery", 1776–80 12·00 13·00

74 "The Virgin and Child with Saints" (G. David)

1991. Christmas. Religious Paintings. Multicoloured.

457 55c. Type **74** 1·00 1·00

458 85c. "Nativity" (Tintoretto) 1·50 1·50

459 $1.15 "Mystic Nativity" (Botticelli) 1·75 1·75

460 $1.85 "Adoration of the Shepherds" (B. Murillo) 2·75 3·25

MS461 79×103 mm. $6.40 "The Madonna of the Chair" (Raphael) (vert) 12·00 13·00

74a Running

1992. Olympic Games, Barcelona. Multicoloured.

462 75c. Type **74a** 1·60 1·60

463 95c. Boxing 1·75 1·75

464 $1.15 Swimming 2·00 2·00

465 $1.50 Wrestling 2·25 2·25

75 Marquesan Canoe

1992. Sixth Festival of Pacific Arts, Rarotonga. Multicoloured.

466 $1.15 Type **75** 1·60 1·60

467 $1.75 Tangaroa statue from Rarotonga 2·00 2·00

468 $1.95 Manihiki canoe 2·25 2·25

1992. Royal Visit by Prince Edward. Nos. 466/8 optd **ROYAL VISIT**.

469 $1.15 Type **75** 3·00 2·50

470 $1.75 Tangaroa statue from Rarotonga 4·00 3·50

471 $1.95 Manihiki canoe 4·25 4·00

76 "Virgin with Child and Saints" (Borgognone)

1992. Christmas. Religious Paintings by Ambrogio Borgognone. Multicoloured.

472 55c. Type **76** 75 75

473 85c. "Virgin on Throne" 1·10 1·10

474 $1.05 "Virgin on Carpet" 1·40 1·40

475 $1.85 "Virgin of the Milk" 2·25 2·25

MS476 101×86 mm. $6.40 As 55c., but larger (36×46 mm) 8·00 9·00

77 Vincente Pinzon and "Nina"

1992. 500th Anniv of Discovery of America by Columbus. Multicoloured.

477 $1.15 Type **77** 2·50 2·50

478 $1.35 Martin Pinzon and "Pinta" 2·75 2·75

479 $1.75 Christopher Columbus and "Santa Maria" 3·50 3·50

78 Queen Elizabeth II in 1953

1993. 40th Anniv of Coronation.

480 **78** $6 multicoloured 6·50 8·50

79 Bull-mouth Helmet

1993. Marine Life. Multicoloured.

No.	Description		
481	5c. Type **79**	30	50
482	10c. Daisy coral	35	50
483	15c. Hydroid coral	45	50
484	20c. Feather-star	50	50
485	25c. Sea star	50	50
486	30c. Varicose nudibranch	50	50
487	50c. Smooth sea star	70	70
488	70c. Black-lip pearl oyster	1·00	1·00
489	80c. Four-coloured nudibranch	1·00	1·00
490	85c. Prickly sea cucumber	1·00	1·00
491	90c. Organ pipe coral	1·00	1·00
492	$1 Blue sea lizard	1·00	2·00
493	$2 Textile cone shell	1·50	2·75
494	$3 Starfish	2·25	2·75
495	$5 As $3	3·75	4·50
496	$8 As $3	5·00	6·50
497	$10 As $3	10·00	11·00

Nos. 494/7 are larger, 47×34 mm, and include a portrait of Queen Elizabeth II at top right.

80 "Virgin on Throne with Child" (detail) (Tura)

1993. Christmas.

No.	Type	Description		
499	**80**	55c. multicoloured	1·00	1·00
500	-	85c. multicoloured	1·50	1·50
501	-	$1.05 multicoloured	1·75	1·75
502	-	$1.95 multicoloured	2·75	3·00
503	-	$4.50 mult (32×47 mm)	6·00	7·00

DESIGNS: 80c. to $4.50, Different details from "Virgin on Throne with Child" (Cosme Tura).

81 Neil Armstrong stepping onto Moon

1994. 25th Anniv of First Manned Moon Landing.

No.	Type	Description		
504	**81**	$3.25 multicoloured	7·50	8·00

82 "The Virgin and Child with Sts. Paul and Jerome" (Vivarini)

1994. Christmas. Religious Paintings. Multicoloured.

No.	Description		
505	90c. Type **82**	1·10	1·25
506	90c. "The Virgin and Child with St. John" (Luini)	1·10	1·25
507	90c. "The Virgin and Child with Sts. Jerome and Dominic" (Lippi)	1·10	1·25
508	90c. "Adoration of the Shepherds" (Murillo)	1·10	1·25
509	$1 "Adoration of the Kings" (detail of angels) (Reni)	1·10	1·25
510	$1 "Madonna and Child with the Infant Baptist" (Raphael)	1·10	1·25
511	$1 "Adoration of the Kings" (detail of manger) (Reni)	1·10	1·25
512	$1 "Virgin and Child" (Borgognone)	1·10	1·25

83 Battleship Row burning, Pearl Harbor

1995. 50th Anniv of End of Second World War. Multicoloured.

No.	Description		
513	$3.75 Type **83**	9·00	8·00
514	$3.75 Boeing B-25 Superfortress "Enola Gay" over Hiroshima	9·00	8·00

84 Queen Elizabeth the Queen Mother at Remembrance Day Ceremony

1995. 95th Birthday of Queen Elizabeth the Queen Mother.

No.	Type	Description		
515	**84**	$4.50 multicoloured	10·00	9·50

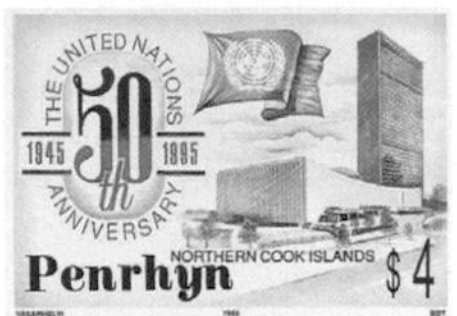

85 Anniversary Emblem, United Nations Flag and Headquarters

1995. 50th Anniv of United Nations.

No.	Type	Description		
516	**85**	$4 multicoloured	4·50	6·00

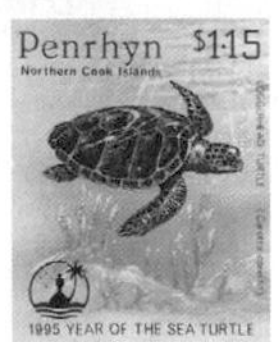

86 Loggerhead Turtle

1995. Year of the Sea Turtle. Multicoloured.

No.	Description		
517	$1.15 Type **86**	1·75	2·00
518	$1.15 Hawksbill turtle	1·75	2·00
519	$1.65 Olive ridley turtle	2·25	2·50
520	$1.65 Green turtle	2·25	2·50

87 Queen Elizabeth II and Rose

1996. 70th Birthday of Queen Elizabeth.

No.	Type	Description		
521	**87**	$4.25 multicoloured	5·00	6·50

88 Olympic Flame, National Flags and Sports

1996. Centenary of Modern Olympic Games.

No.	Type	Description		
522	**88**	$5 multicoloured	6·50	8·00

89 Royal Wedding, 1947

1997. Golden Wedding of Queen Elizabeth and Prince Philip.

No.	Type	Description		
523	**89**	$3 multicoloured	4·25	3·75
MS524		42×28 mm. **89** $4 multicoloured	4·25	5·00

90 Diana, Princess of Wales with Sons

1998. Diana, Princess of Wales Commemoration.

No.	Type	Description		
525	**90**	$1.50 multicoloured	1·10	1·75
MS526		70×100 mm. **90** $3.75 multicoloured	2·50	4·00

1998. Children's Charities. No. **MS**526 surch **+$1 CHILDREN'S CHARITIES**.

No.	Description		
MS527	70×100 mm. **90** $3.75+$1 multicoloured	4·50	5·50

1999. New Millennium. Nos. 466/8 optd **KIA ORANA THIRD MILLENNIUM**.

No.	Description		
528	$1.15 Type **75**	1·25	1·25
529	$1.75 Tangaroa statue from Rarotonga	1·60	1·60
530	$1.95 Manihiki canoe	1·75	1·75

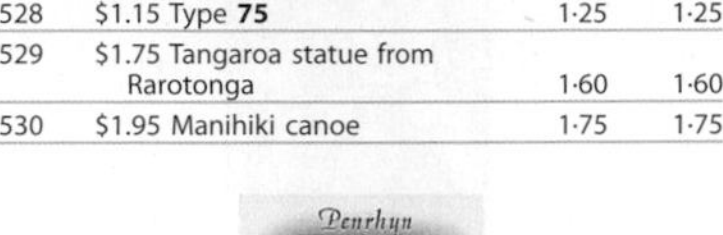

90a King George VI and Queen Elizabeth on Wedding Day

2000. Queen Elizabeth the Queen Mother's 100th Birthday.

No.	Type	Description		
531	**90a**	$2.50 purple and brown	2·75	2·75
532	-	$2.50 brown	2·75	2·75
533	-	$2.50 green and brown	2·75	2·75
534	-	$2.50 blue and brown	2·75	2·75
MS535		72×100 mm. $10 multicoloured	9·50	10·00

DESIGNS: No. 532, Queen Elizabeth with young Princess Elizabeth; 533, Royal Family in 1930; 534, Queen Elizabeth with Princesses Elizabeth and Margaret; **MS**535, Queen Elizabeth wearing blue gown.

90b Ancient Greek Javelin-throwers

2000. Olympic Games, Sydney. Multicoloured.

No.	Description		
536	$2.75 Type **90b**	2·40	2·50
537	$2.75 Modern javelin-thrower	2·40	2·50
538	$2.75 Ancient Greek discus-thrower	2·40	2·50
539	$2.75 Modern discus-thrower	2·40	2·50
MS540	90×99 mm. $3.50 Cook Islands Olympic Torch Relay runner in traditional costume (vert)	3·25	4·00

91 Ocean Sunfish

2003. Endangered Species. Ocean Sunfish.

No.	Type	Description		
541	**91**	80c. multicoloured	1·40	1·60
542	-	90c. multicoloured	1·40	1·60
543	-	$1.15 multicoloured	1·60	1·90
544	-	$1.95 multicoloured	2·00	2·75

DESIGNS: 90c. to $1.95, Ocean sunfish.

91a Statue of Liberty

2003. "United We Stand". Support for Victims of 11 September 2001 Terrorist Attacks. Multicoloured.

No.	Description		
MS545	75×109 mm. **91a** $1.50×4 Statue of Liberty, Twin Towers and flags of USA and Cook Islands	5·50	6·50

92 Pope John Paul II

2005. Pope John Paul II Commemoration.

No.	Type	Description		
546	**92**	$1.45 multicoloured	2·50	2·50

93 Pacific Reef Egrets (white and dark grey morphs)

2008. WWF Pacific Reef-egret (*Egretta sacra*). Multicoloured.

No.	Description		
547	80c. Type **93**	1·75	1·90
548	90c. Egret (dark grey morph) on shore	1·75	1·90
549	$1.15 Egret (white morph) in flight	1·90	2·00
550	$1.95 Egret (dark grey morph) at nest with chicks	2·25	2·50

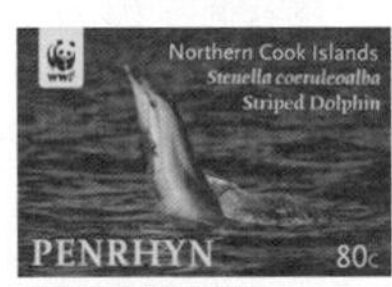

94 Striped Dolphin

2010. Endangered Species. Striped Dolphin (*Stenella coeruleoalba*). Multicoloured.

No.	Description		
551	80c. Type **94**	1·50	1·60
552	90c. Two striped dolphins	1·50	1·60
553	$1.10 Striped dolphin (swimming to right)	1·75	1·90
554	$1.20 School of dolphins	1·75	1·90

2011. Royal Engagement. Multicoloured designs as T **299** of Cook Islands. Multicoloured.

No.	Description		
555	55c. Prince William laying wreath at the Cenotaph, London, 2009	85	85
556	50c. Prince William competing in Chakravarty Cup, Beaufort Polo Club	85	85
557	50c. Kate Middleton, Prince William in background	85	85
558	50c. Prince William	85	85
559	50c. Kate Middleton	85	85
560	50c. Prince William and Kate Middleton	85	85
561	50c. Kate Middleton wearing black hat	85	85
562	50c. Prince William (head and shoulders)	85	85
563	50c. Prince William and Kate Middleton (facing each other)	85	85
564	50c. Engagement ring on Kate Middleton's hand	85	85
565	$2 Prince William arriving at Imperial War Museum for 'Night of Heroes' event, 15 December 2009	16·00	16·00
566	$2 Kate Middleton (wearing white jacket) at wedding of Rose Astor and Hugh van Cutsem, Burford	16·00	16·00
MS567	108×70 mm. Nos. 565/6	35·00	35·00
MS568	144×93 mm. $8.10 Prince William and Kate Middleton (38×50 mm)	6·75	6·72
MS569	58×95 mm. $11 As No. 565 (38×50 mm)	13·50	13·50
MS570	58×95 mm. $11 As No. 566 (38×50 mm)	13·50	13·50

95 Shark

2011. Pearl Industry. Multicoloured.

No.	Description		
MS571	128×222 mm. 20c. Type **95**; 30c. Diver; 50c. Pearls; $1 Pearl held iin tweezers; $2 Oysters	6·75	6·75
MS572	108×135 mm. 80c. Atoll; 90c. Twelve pearls; $1.10 Diver holding up rope of oysters; $1.20 Diver and oysters (*Pinctada margaritifera*) growing on ropes	6·75	6·75

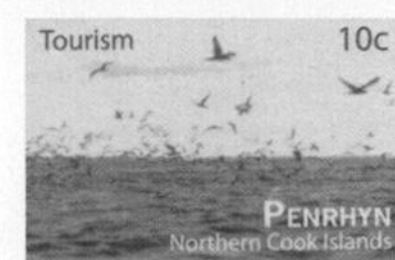

96 Seabirds over Ocean

2011. Tourism. Island Views. Multicoloured.

573	10c. Type **96**	35	40
574	20c. Stingray	45	50
575	30c. Village, shore and palm trees	55	60
576	40c. Shore with rock pools in coral	70	75
577	50c. Road lined with palm trees	85	90
578	60c. Waves breaking on rocky shore	95	1·00
579	70c. Aerial view of atolls and beaches	1·10	1·25
580	80c. Moonlight over ocean	1·25	1·40
581	90c. Palm tree lined shore at sunset	1·50	1·60
582	$1 Shark	1·50	1·60
583	$1.10 Atoll and Saab 340 aircraft	1·75	1·90
584	$1.20 Pearls	1·90	2·00
585	$1.50 Green turtle	2·25	2·40
586	$2 Aerial view of atoll and beach	3·25	3·50
587	$3 Sunset over island with palm trees	4·50	4·75
MS588	240×180 mm. Nos. 573/87	26·00	26·00

97 Duke and Duchess of Cambridge walking down the Aisle

2011. Royal Wedding. Sheet 108×73 mm containing T **97** and similar vert design. Multicoloured.

MS589	$1 Duke and Duchess of Cambridge; $1.20 Type **97**	4·00	4·00

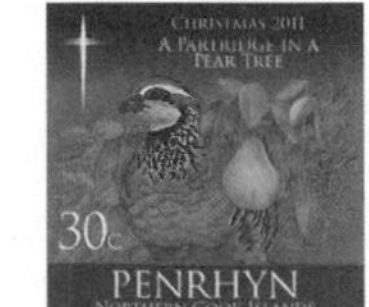

98 A Partridge in a Pear Tree

2011. Christmas. The Twelve Days of Christmas (carol). Multicoloured.

590	30c. Type **98**	55	60
591	50c. Two Turtle Doves	85	90
592	90c. Three French Hens	1·50	1·60
593	$2 Four Calling Birds	3·25	3·50
MS594	203×137 mm. Nos. 590/3 and eight imperforate labels	6·00	6·50

99 Pope Benedict XVI

2012. Beatification of Pope John Paul II. Multicoloured.

595	$1.20 Type **99**	1·90	2·00
596	$5 Pope John Paul II	7·50	7·50

100 *Christ taking Leave of his Mother* (c. 1512)

2012. Christmas. Paintings by Antonio Allegri da Correggio. Multicoloured.

597	80c. Type **100**	1·25	1·40
598	80c. *Deposition* (c. 1525)	1·25	1·40
599	90c. *The Martyrdom of Four Saints* (c. 1523)	1·50	1·60
600	90c. *Mystic Marriage of St. Catherine with St. Sebastian* (c. 1526-7)	1·50	1·60
601	$3 *Nativity* (c. 1510s)	5·00	5·25
602	$3 *The Nativity of Christ* (c. 1529-30)	5·00	5·25
MS603	149×140 mm. As Nos. 597/602 but with gold frames	15·00	15·00

Nos. 597/602 have white borders, but stamps from **MS**603 have gold frames.

OFFICIAL STAMPS

1978. Optd or surch **O.H.M.S.**

O1	1c. multicoloured (No. 57)	15	10
O2	2c. multicoloured (No. 58)	15	10
O3	3c. multicoloured (No. 59)	25	10
O4	4c. multicoloured (No. 60)	25	10
O5	5c. multicoloured (No. 61)	30	10
O6	8c. multicoloured (No. 62)	35	15
O7	10c. multicoloured (No. 63)	40	15
O8	15c. on 60c. on 60c. mult (No. 66)	45	25
O9	18c. on 60c. on 60c. mult (No. 66)	50	25
O10	20c. multicoloured (No. 64)	50	25
O11	25c. multicoloured (No. 65)	55	30
O12	30c. on 60c. on 60c. mult (No. 66)	55	35
O13	50c. multicoloured (No. 89)	90	55
O14	50c. multicoloured (No. 90)	90	55
O15	50c. multicoloured (No. 91)	90	55
O16	$1 multicoloured (No. 101)	2·25	45
O17	$2 multicoloured (No. 102)	4·00	50

1985. Nos. 206/8, 278/81, 337/47 and 349/55 optd **O.H.M.S.** or surch also.

O18	2c. Type **47**	70	80
O19	4c. Amatasi	70	80
O20	5c. Ndrua	70	80
O21	8c. Tongiaki	70	80
O22	10c. "Vitoria"	70	80
O23	18c. "Golden Hind"	2·00	90
O24	20c. "La Boudeuse"	1·75	90
O25	30c. H.M.S. "Bounty"	2·75	1·00
O26	40c. on 36c. "L'Astrolabe"	1·75	90
O27	50c. "Star of India"	1·75	90
O28	55c. on 48c. "Great Republic"	1·75	90
O39	65c. on 60c. Type **40**	80	1·00
O40	65c. on 60c. Aerial view of Penrhyn atoll	80	1·00
O41	65c. on 60c. Eleanor Roosevelt on Penrhyn during Second World War	80	1·00
O42	65c. on 60c. Map of South Pacific	80	1·00
O29	75c. on 72c. "Antiope"	2·50	1·60
O30	75c. on 96c. "Cap Hornier"	2·50	1·60
O31	80c. "Balcutha"	2·50	1·60
O32	$1.20 "Pamir"	2·75	1·60
O33	$2 "Cutty Sark"	5·00	3·25
O34	$3 "Mermerus"	4·25	3·50
O35	$4 "Mermerus"	5·50	5·00
O36	$5 "Cutty Sark"	8·00	6·50
O37	$6 H.M.S. "Resolution" and H.M.S. "Discovery"	11·00	9·50
O38	$9.60 H.M.S. "Resolution" and H.M.S. "Discovery"	14·00	13·00

1998. Nos. 481/93 optd **O.H.M.S.**

O43	5c. Type **79**	35	50
O44	10c. Daisy coral	35	50
O45	15c. Hydroid coral	50	50
O46	20c. Feather-star	50	50
O47	25c. Sea star	50	50
O48	30c. Varicose nudibranch	50	50
O49	50c. Smooth sea star	70	70
O50	70c. Black-lip pearl oyster	1·00	1·00
O51	80c. Four-coloured nudibranch	1·00	1·00
O52	85c. Prickly sea cucumber	1·00	1·00
O53	90c. Organ pipe coral	1·00	1·00
O54	$1 Blue sea lizard	1·00	1·00
O55	$2 Textile cone shell	1·75	2·00

Pt. 1

PERAK

A state of the Federation of Malaya, incorporated in Malaysia in 1963.

100 cents = 1 dollar (Straits or Malayan).

Stamps of Straits Settlement optd or surch.

1878. No. 11 optd with crescent and star and P in oval.

1	2c. brown	£2000	£2250

1880. Optd **PERAK**.

10	**9**	2c. brown	24·00	85·00
17	**9**	2c. red	8·00	3·75

1883

16	2c. on 4c. red	£750	£300

1886. No. 63a surch **ONE CENT PERAK**, without full point

29	1c. on 2c. red	4·00	18·00

1886. No. 63a surch **ONE CENT PERAK**, with final full point

26	1c. on 2c. red	75·00	90·00

1886. No. 63a surch **1 CENT PERAK**.

28	1c. on 2c. red	£200	£200

No. 63a surch **One CENT PERAK**

33*b*	1c. on 2c. red	2·75	3·50

1889. No. 17 surch **ONE CENT** (with full point).

41	1c. on 2c. red	£350	£130

1891. Surch **PERAK One CENT.**

57	1c. on 2c. red	2·25	13·00
43	1c. on 6c. lilac	60·00	35·00

1891. Surch **PERAK TWO Cents**

48	2c. on 24c. green	28·00	16·00

42 Tiger

1892

61	**42**	1c. green	2·25	15
62	**42**	2c. red	1·75	30
63	**42**	2c. orange	1·00	8·00
64	**42**	5c. blue	3·25	7·50

1895. Surch **3 CENTS.**

65	3c. on 5c. red	3·75	5·00

44 Tiger

45 Elephants

1895

66	**44**	1c. purple and green	2·75	50
67	**44**	2c. purple and brown	3·25	50
68	**44**	3c. purple and red	3·75	50
69	**44**	4c. purple and red	18·00	6·50
70	**44**	5c. purple and yellow	10·00	75
71	**44**	8c. purple and blue	45·00	65
72	**44**	10c. purple and orange	16·00	50
73	**44**	25c. green and red	£225	12·00
74	**44**	50c. purple and black	48·00	48·00
75	**44**	50c. green and black	£225	£170
76	**45**	$1 green	£300	£225
77	**45**	$2 green and red	£450	£350
78	**45**	$3 green and yellow	£600	£550
79	**45**	$5 green and blue	£650	£600
80	**45**	$25 green and orange	£9500	£4000

1900. Surch in words.

81	**44**	1c. on 2c. purple and brown	60	2·25
82	**44**	1c. on 4c. purple and red	1·00	17·00
83	**44**	1c. on 5c. purple and yellow	2·75	21·00
84	**44**	3c. on 8c. purple and blue	12·00	17·00
85	**44**	3c. on 50c. green and black	5·00	11·00
86	**45**	3c. on $1 green	55·00	£150
87	**45**	3c. on $2 green and red	50·00	85·00

50 Sultan Iskandar

1935

88	**50**	1c. black	3·00	10
89	**50**	2c. green	3·00	10
90	**50**	4c. orange	3·25	10
91	**50**	5c. brown	75	10
92	**50**	6c. red	12·00	6·00
93	**50**	8c. grey	1·00	10
94	**50**	10c. purple	80	15
95	**50**	12c. blue	4·50	1·00
96	**50**	25c. purple and red	3·25	1·00
97	**50**	30c. purple and orange	4·50	1·50
98	**50**	40c. red and purple	7·50	6·50
99	**50**	50c. black on green	9·50	1·25
100	**50**	$1 black and red on blue	2·75	1·25
101	**50**	$2 green and red	42·00	7·00
102	**50**	$5 green and red on green	£150	35·00

51 Sultan Iskandar

1938

103	**51**	1c. black	18·00	10
104	**51**	2c. green	13·00	10
105	**51**	2c. orange	3·50	22·00
106a	**51**	3c. green	2·75	13·00
107	**51**	4c. orange	42·00	10
108	**51**	5c. brown	6·50	10
109	**51**	6c. red	27·00	10
110	**51**	8c. grey	38·00	10
111	**51**	8c. red	1·00	90·00
112	**51**	10c. purple	40·00	10
113	**51**	12c. blue	29·00	1·00
114	**51**	15c. blue	4·25	13·00
115	**51**	25c. purple and red	50·00	3·50
116	**51**	30c. purple and orange	11·00	2·25
117	**51**	40c. red and purple	50·00	2·25
118	**51**	50c. black on green	32·00	75
119	**51**	$1 black and red on blue	£140	30·00
120	**51**	$2 green and red	£225	75·00
121	**51**	$5 green and red on green	£425	£475

1948. Silver Wedding. As T **8b/c** of Pitcairn Islands.

122	10c. violet	15	10
123	$5 green	23·00	48·00

1949. U.P.U. As T **8d/g** of Pitcairn Islands.

124	10c. purple	15	10
125	15c. blue	1·50	2·00
126	25c. orange	30	5·50
127	50c. black	1·25	3·50

52 Sultan Yussuf 'Izzuddin Shah

1950

128	**52**	1c. black	10	10
129	**52**	2c. orange	20	10
130	**52**	3c. green	6·00	10
131	**52**	4c. brown	80	10
132	**52**	5c. purple	75	2·75
133	**52**	6c. grey	50	10
134	**52**	8c. red	3·00	3·00
135	**52**	8c. green	1·50	1·00
136	**52**	10c. purple	30	10
137	**52**	12c. red	1·50	7·50
138	**52**	15c. blue	1·25	10
139	**52**	20c. black and green	1·75	65
140	**52**	20c. blue	1·50	10
141	**52**	25c. purple and orange	1·00	10
142	**52**	30c. red and purple	3·00	20
143	**52**	35c. red and purple	1·75	25
144	**52**	40c. red and purple	9·00	6·00
145	**52**	50c. black and blue	9·00	10
146	**52**	$1 blue and purple	9·00	1·00
147	**52**	$2 green and red	24·00	7·00
148	**52**	$5 green and brown	45·00	30·00

1953. Coronation. As T **8h** of Pitcairn Islands.

149	10c. black and purple	2·50	10

1957. As Nos. 92/102 of Kedah, but portrait of Sultan Yussuf Izzuddin Shah.

150	1c. black	10	20
151	2c. orange	30	1·00
152	4c. brown	20	10
153	5c. lake	20	10
154	8c. green	2·00	3·50
155	10c. sepia	2·75	10
156	10c. purple	11·00	10
157	20c. blue	2·25	10
158a	50c. black and blue	40	10
159	$1 blue and purple	6·50	40
160	$2 green and red	4·00	7·50
161a	$5 brown and green	18·00	8·50

53 Sultan Idris Shah

1963. Installation of Sultan of Perak.

162	**53**	10c. multicoloured	15	10

54 "Vanda hookeriana"

1965. As Nos. 115/21 of Kedah, but with inset portrait of Sultan Idris as in T **54**.

No.	Type	Description	Mint	Used
163	**54**	1c. multicoloured	10	50
164	-	2c. multicoloured	10	70
165	-	5c. multicoloured	10	10
166	-	6c. multicoloured	15	40
167	-	10c. multicoloured	15	10
168	-	15c. multicoloured	80	10
169	-	20c. multicoloured	1·25	10

The higher values used in Perak were Nos. 20/7 of Malaysia (National Issues).

55 "Delias ninus"

1971. Butterflies. As Nos. 124/30 of Kedah, but with portrait of Sultan Idris as In T **55**.

No.	Type	Description	Mint	Used
172	**55**	1c. multicoloured	40	2·00
173	-	2c. multicoloured	1·00	2·50
174	-	5c. multicoloured	1·25	10
175	-	6c. multicoloured	1·25	2·00
176	-	10c. multicoloured	1·25	10
177	-	15c. multicoloured	1·00	10
178	-	20c. multicoloured	1·75	30

The higher values in use with this issue were Nos. 64/71 of Malaysia (National Issues).

56 "Rafflesia hasseltii"

1979. Flowers. As Nos. 135/41 of Kedah but with portrait of Sultan Idris as in T **56**.

No.	Description	Mint	Used
184	1c. Type **56**	10	85
185	2c. "Pterocarpus indicus"	10	85
186	5c. "Lagerstroemia speciosa"	10	20
187	10c. "Durio zibethinus"	15	10
188	15c. "Hibiscus rosa-sinensis"	15	10
189	20c. "Rhododendron scorte-chinii"	20	10
190	25c. "Etlingera elatior" (inscr"Phaeomeria speciosa")	40	20

57 Coffee

1986. As Nos. 152/8 of Kedah but with portrait of Sultan Azlan Shah as in T **57**.

No.	Description	Mint	Used
198	1c. Type **57**	10	40
199	2c. Coconuts	10	40
200	5c. Cocoa	15	10
201	10c. Black pepper	20	10
202	15c. Rubber	40	10
203	20c. Oil palm	40	15
204	30c. Rice	40	15

58 *Nelumbium nelumbo* (sacred lotus)

2007. Garden Flowers. As Nos. 210/15 of Johore, but with portrait of Sultan Azlan Shah and Arms of Penang as in T **58**. Multicoloured.

No.	Description	Mint	Used
205	5s. Type **58**	10	10
206	10s. *Hydrangea macrophylla*	15	10
207	20s. *Hippeastrum reticulatum*	25	15
208	30s. *Bougainvillea*	40	20
209	40s. *Ipomoea indica*	50	30
210	50s. *Hibiscus rosa-sinensis*	65	35
MS211	100×85 mm. Nos. 205/10	2·00	2·00

OFFICIAL STAMPS

1889. Stamps of Straits Settlements optd **P.G.S.**

No.	Type	Description	Mint	Used
O1	**30**	2c. red	7·50	9·50
O2	**30**	4c. brown	32·00	35·00
O3	**30**	6c. lilac	40·00	55·00
O4	**30**	8c. orange	50·00	65·00
O5	**38**	10c. grey	75·00	75·00
O6	**30**	12c. blue	£325	£325
O7	**30**	12c. purple	£250	£325
O9	**30**	24c. green	£200	£225

1894. No. 64 optd **Service.**

No.	Description	Mint	Used
O10	5c. blue	£130	1·00

1895. No. 70 optd **Service.**

No.	Type	Description	Mint	Used
O11	**31**	5c. purple and yellow	3·00	50

Pt. 1

PERLIS

A state of the Federation of Malaya, incorporated in Malaysia in 1963.

100 cents = 1 dollar (Straits or Malayan).

1948. Silver Wedding. As T **8b/c** of Pitcairn Islands.

No.	Description	Mint	Used
1	10c. violet	30	2·75
2	$5 brown	32·00	55·00

1949. U.P.U. As T **8d/g** of Pitcairn Islands.

No.	Description	Mint	Used
3	10c. purple	30	2·25
4	15c. blue	1·25	4·75
5	25c. orange	45	4·50
6	50c. black	1·00	3·75

1 Raja Syed Putra

1951

No.	Type	Description	Mint	Used
7	**1**	1c. black	20	1·00
8	**1**	2c. orange	75	1·00
9	**1**	3c. green	2·00	5·50
10	**1**	4c. brown	2·00	1·75
11	**1**	5c. purple	1·00	4·75
12	**1**	6c. grey	1·50	2·75
13	**1**	8c. red	6·00	10·00
14	**1**	8c. green	2·75	3·50
15	**1**	10c. purple	1·75	50
16	**1**	12c. red	3·75	8·00
17	**1**	15c. blue	7·00	10·00
18	**1**	20c. black and green	7·00	15·00
19	**1**	20c. blue	1·75	1·50
20	**1**	25c. purple and orange	3·00	5·00
21	**1**	30c. red and purple	2·50	18·00
22	**1**	35c. red and purple	4·25	9·50
23	**1**	40c. red and purple	7·00	40·00
24	**1**	50c. black and blue	5·50	8·00
25	**1**	$1 blue and purple	9·00	32·00
26	**1**	$2 green and red	26·00	70·00
27	**1**	$5 green and brown	80·00	£140

1953. Coronation. As T **8h** of Pitcairn Islands.

No.	Description	Mint	Used
28	10c. black and purple	2·25	3·25

1957. As Nos. 92/102 of Kedah, but inset portrait of Raja Syed Putra.

No.	Description	Mint	Used
29	1c. black	10	50
30	2c. red	15	50
31	4c. brown	15	40
32	5c. lake	15	15
33	8c. green	2·00	1·75
34	10c. brown	1·50	2·25
35	10c. purple	16·00	4·75
36	20c. blue	4·00	5·50
37	50c. black and blue	1·50	4·00
38	$1 blue and purple	14·00	19·00
39	$2 green and red	14·00	11·00
40	$5 brown and green	15·00	15·00

2 "Vanda hookeriana"

1965. As Nos. 115/21 of Kedah, but with inset portrait of Tunku Bendahara Abu Bakar as in T **2**.

No.	Type	Description	Mint	Used
41	**2**	1c. multicoloured	10	1·00
42	-	2c. multicoloured	10	1·50
43	-	5c. multicoloured	15	40
44	-	6c. multicoloured	65	1·50
45	-	10c. multicoloured	65	40
46	-	15c. multicoloured	1·00	40
47	-	20c. multicoloured	1·00	1·75

The higher values used in Perlis were Nos. 20/7 of Malaysia (National Issues).

3 "Danaus melanippus"

1971. Butterflies. As Nos. 124/30 of Kedah, but with portrait of Raja Syed Putra as in T **3**.

No.	Type	Description	Mint	Used
48		1c. multicoloured	20	1·25
49	**3**	2c. multicoloured	40	2·25
50	-	5c. multicoloured	1·25	1·25
51	-	6c. multicoloured	1·50	3·25
52	-	10c. multicoloured	1·50	1·25
53	-	15c. multicoloured	1·50	50
54	-	20c. multicoloured	1·50	2·50

The higher values in use with this issue were Nos. 64/71 of Malaysia (National Issues).

4 Raja Syed Putra

1971. 25th Anniv of Installation of Raja Syed Putra.

No.	Type	Description	Mint	Used
56	**4**	10c. multicoloured	30	2·25
57	**4**	15c. multicoloured	30	75
58	**4**	50c. multicoloured	80	4·25

5 "Pterocarpus indicus"

1979. Flowers. As Nos. 135/41 of Kedah, but with portrait of Raja Syed Putra as in T **5**.

No.	Description	Mint	Used
59	1c. "Rafflesia hasseltii"	10	1·00
60	2c. Type **5**	10	1·00
61	5c. "Lagerstroemia speciosa"	10	1·00
62	10c. "Durio zibethinus"	15	30
63	15c. "Hibiscus rosa-sinensis"	15	10
64	20c. "Rhododendron scorte-chinii"	20	10
65	25c. "Etlingera elatior" (inscr "Phaeomeria speciosa")	40	85

6 Coconuts

1986. As Nos. 152/8 of Kedah, but with portrait of Raja Syed Putra as in T **6**.

No.	Description	Mint	Used
73	1c. Coffee	10	65
74	2c. Type **6**	15	65
75	5c. Cocoa	20	50
76	10c. Black pepper	25	15
77	15c. Rubber	50	10
78	20c. Oil palm	40	15
79	30c. Rice	45	15

7 Raja Syed Putra and Aspects of Perlis

1995. 50th Anniv of Raja Syed Putra's Accession. Multicoloured.

No.	Description	Mint	Used
80	30c. Type **7**	75	50
81	$1 Raja Syed Putra and Palace	2·25	3·50

8 *Nelumbium nelumbo* (sacred lotus)

2007. Garden Flowers. As Nos. 210/15 of Johore, but with portrait of Raja Tuanku Syed Sirajuddin and Arms of Perlis as in T **8**. Multicoloured.

No.	Description	Mint	Used
82	5s. Type 8	10	10
83	10s. *Hydrangea macrophylla*	15	10
84	20s. *Hippeastrum reticulatum*	25	15
85	30s. *Bougainvillea*	40	20
86	40s. *Ipomoea indica*	50	30
87	50s. *Hibiscus rosa-sinensis*	65	35
MS88	100×85. Nos. 82/7	2·00	2·00

Pt. 20

PERU

A republic on the N.W. coast of S. America independent since 1821.

1857. 8 reales = 1 peso.
1858. 100 centavos = 10 dineros = 5 pesetas = 1 peso.
1874. 100 centavos = 1 sol.
1985. 100 centimos = 1 inti.
1991. 100 centimos = 1 sol.

7

1858. T **7** and similar designs with flags below arms. Imperf.

No.	Type	Description	Mint	Used
5	**7**	½ peso yellow	£2750	£375
8	**7**	1d. blue	£180	10·50
13	**7**	1 peseta red	£250	27·00

8

1862. Various frames. Imperf.

No.	Type	Description	Mint	Used
14	**8**	1d. red	14·50	4·50
20	**8**	1d. green	19·00	3·75
16	**8**	1 peseta, brown	£120	37·00
22	**8**	1 peseta, yellow	£150	55·00

10 Vicuna 13 14

1866. Various frames. Perf.

No.	Type	Description	Mint	Used
17	**10**	5c. green	10·50	95
18	-	10c. red	10·50	2·30
19	-	20c. brown	35·00	7·00

See also No. 316.

1871. 20th Anniv of First Railway in Peru (Callao–Lima–Chorillos). Imperf.

No.	Type	Description	Mint	Used
21a	**13**	5c. red	£130	43·00

1873. Roul by imperf.

No.	Type	Description	Mint	Used
23	**14**	2c. blue	50·00	£325

15 Sun-god 16 20

21

1874. Various frames. Perf.

No.	Type	Description	Mint	Used
24	**15**	1c. orange	90	65
25a	**16**	2c. violet	1·10	85
26	**16**	5c. blue	1·40	45
27	**16**	10c. green	45	30
28	**16**	20c. red	3·50	1·10
29	**20**	50c. green	15·00	4·25
30	**21**	1s. pink	2·40	2·30

For further stamps in these types, see Nos. 278, 279/84 and 314/5.

(24)

1880. Optd with T **24**.

No.	Type	Description	Mint	Used
36	**15**	1c. green	90	65
37	**16**	2c. red	1·80	1·10
39	**16**	5c. blue	3·50	1·70
40	**20**	50c. green	46·00	28·00
41	**21**	1s. red	70·00	50·00

1881. Optd as T **24**, but inscr "LIMA" at foot instead of "PERU".

42	**15**	1c. green	1·30	95
43	**16**	2c. red	24·00	15·00
44	**16**	5c. blue	2·75	1·30
286	**16**	10c. green	2·00	1·90
45	**20**	50c. green	£750	£425
46	**21**	1s. red	£140	90·00

(27) Arms of Chile

1881. Optd with T **27**.

57	**15**	1c. orange	45	85
58	**16**	2c. violet	45	3·50
59	**16**	2c. red	1·40	15·00
60	**16**	5c. blue	50·00	55·00
61	**16**	10c. green	45	1·40
62	**16**	20c. red	70·00	£110

(28)

1882. Optd with T **27** and T **28**.

63	**15**	1c. green	45	70
64	**16**	5c. blue	70	70
66	**20**	50c. red	1·40	1·70
67	**21**	1s. blue	3·00	3·75

1883. Optd with T **28** only.

200	**15**	1c. green	2·20	2·10
201	**16**	2c. red	2·20	6·50
202	**16**	5c. blue	3·50	3·50
203	**20**	50c. pink	55·00	
204	**21**	1s. blue	55·00	

(28a)

1883. Handstamped with T **28a** only.

206	**15**	1c. orange	1·30	1·10
210	**16**	5c. blue	13·00	7·00
211	**16**	10c. green	1·30	1·10
216	**20**	50c. green	6·00	4·25
220	**21**	1s. red	9·25	8·00

1883. Optd with T **24** and **28a**, the inscription in oval reading "PERU".

223	**20**	50c. green	2·10	£110
225	**21**	1s. red	£250	£160

1883. Optd with T **24** and **28a**, the inscription in oval reading "LIMA".

227	**15**	1c. green	7·25	7·00
228	**16**	2c. red	7·75	7·50
232	**16**	5c. blue	11·00	10·00
234	**20**	50c. green	£250	£150
236	**21**	1s. red	£275	£275

1883. Optd with T **28** and **28a**.

238	**15**	1c. green	90	85
241	**16**	2c. red	1·70	1·30
246	**16**	5c. blue	2·20	1·60

1884. Optd **CORREOS LIMA** and sun.

277		5c. blue	45	25

1886. Re-issue of 1866 and 1874 types.

278	**15**	1c. violet	90	30
314	**15**	1c. red	65	30
279	**16**	2c. green	1·30	30
315	**16**	2c. blue	55	30
280	**16**	5c. orange	1·00	45
316	**10**	5c. lake	2·20	85
281	**16**	10c. black	65	30
317	-	10c. orange (Llamas)	1·00	55
282	**16**	20c. blue	8·75	1·10
318	-	20c. blue (Llamas)	10·50	2·30
283	**20**	50c. red	2·75	1·10
284	**21**	1s. brown	2·20	85

71 Pres. R. M. Bermudez

1894. Optd with T **71**.

294	**15**	1c. orange	1·00	65
295	**15**	1c. green	65	55
296c	**16**	2c. violet	40	35
297	**16**	2c. red	65	55
298	**16**	5c. blue	4·50	2·75
299	**16**	10c. green	65	55
300	**20**	50c. green	2·40	2·00

1894. Optd with T **28** and **71**.

301	**16**	2c. red	55	45
302	**16**	5c. blue	1·80	85
303	**20**	50c. red	70·00	43·00
304	**21**	1s. blue	£170	£150

73

1895. Installation of Pres. Nicolas de Pierola.

328	**73**	1c. violet	1·90	1·10
329	**73**	2c. green	1·90	1·10
330	**73**	5c. yellow	1·90	1·10
331	**73**	10c. blue	1·90	1·10
332	-	20c. orange	1·90	1·30
333	-	50c. blue	10·00	7·00
334	-	1s. lake	55·00	36·00

Nos. 332/4 are larger (30×36 mm) and the central device is in a frame of laurel.

See also Nos. 352/4.

75 Atahualpa **76** Pizarro **77** General de la Mar

1896

335	**75**	1c. blue	90	30
336	**75**	1c. green	90	30
337	**75**	2c. blue	90	30
338	**75**	2c. red	90	30
340	**76**	5c. green	1·30	30
341	**76**	5c. blue	90	55
342	**76**	10c. yellow	1·70	45
343	**76**	10c. black	1·70	30
344	**76**	20c. orange	3·50	45
345	**77**	50c. red	8·75	1·60
346	**77**	1s. red	13·00	1·60
347	**77**	2s. lake	3·50	1·20

1897. No. D31 optd **FRANQUEO**.

348	**D 22**	1c. brown	90	75

82 Suspension Bridge at Paucartambo **83** Pres. D. Nicolas de Pierola

1897. Opening of New Postal Building. Dated "1897".

349	**82**	1c. blue	1·20	55
350	-	2c. brown	1·20	30
351	**83**	5c. red	1·70	55

DESIGN: 2c. G.P.O. Lima.

1899. As Nos. 328/34, but vert inscr replaced by pearl ornaments.

352	**73**	22c. green	55	30
353	-	5s. red	2·75	2·75
354	-	10s. green	£850	£600

84 President Eduardo Lopez de Romana

1900

357	**84**	22c. black and green	13·00	1·30

85 Admiral Grau

1901. Advent of the Twentieth Century.

358	**85**	1c. black and green	1·70	45
359	-	2c. black and red	1·70	45
360	-	5c. black and lilac	1·70	45

PORTRAITS: 2c. Col. Bolognesi; 5c. Pres. Romana.

90 Municipal Board of Health Building

1905

361	**90**	12c. black and blue	1·70	45

1907. Surch.

362		1c. on 12c. black and blue	35	30
363		2c. on 12c. black and blue	65	45

97 Bolognesi Monument **98** Admiral Grau **99** Llama

101 Exhibition Buildings **103** G.P.O., Lima

1907

364	**97**	1c. black and green	55	30
365	**98**	2c. purple and red	55	30
366	**99**	4c. olive	9·25	1·30
367	-	5c. black and blue	1·00	30
368	**101**	10c. black and brown	1·70	45
369	-	20c. black and green	39·00	75
370	**103**	50c. black	39·00	1·60
371	-	1s. green and violet	£200	3·75
372	-	2s. black and blue	£200	£160

DESIGNS—VERT: As Type **98**: 5c. Statue of Bolivar. (24×33 mm): 2c. Columbus Monument. HORIZ: As Type **101**: 20c. Medical School, Lima. (33×24 mm): 1s. Grandstand, Santa Beatrice Race-course, Lima.

107 Columbus

1909. Portraits.

373		1c. grey (Manco Capac)	35	15
374	**107**	2c. green	35	15
375	-	4c. red (Pizarro)	45	30
376	-	5c. purple (San Martin)	35	15
377	-	10c. blue (Bolivar)	75	30
378	-	12c. blue (de la Mar)	1·70	30
379	-	20c. brown (Castilla)	1·90	45
380	-	50c. orange (Grau)	8·25	55
381	-	1s. black and lake (Bolognesi)	17·00	65

See also Nos. 406/13, 431/5, 439/40 and 484/9.

1913. Surch **UNION POSTAL 8 Cts. Sud Americana** in oval.

382	**90**	8c. on 12c. black and blue	90	30

1915. As 1896, 1905 and 1907, surch **1915** and value.

383	**75**	1c. on 1c. green	28·00	23·00
384	**97**	1c. on 1c. black and green	1·10	1·10
385	**98**	1c. on 2c. purple and red	1·70	1·60
387	**99**	1c. on 4c. green	3·25	2·75
386	**76**	1c. on 10c. black	1·70	1·30
388	**101**	1c. on 10c. black & brown	1·70	1·30
389	**101**	2c. on 10c. black & brown	£170	£130
390	**90**	2c. on 12c. black and blue	45	30
391	-	2c. on 20c. black and green (No. 369)	22·00	21·00
392	**103**	2c. on 50c. black	3·25	3·25

1916. Surch **VALE**, value and **1916**.

393		1c. on 12c. blue (378)	35	15
394		1c. on 20c. brown (379)	35	15
395		1c. on 50c. orange (380)	35	15
396		2c. on 4c. red (375)	35	15
397		10c. on 1s. black & lake (381)	75	55

1916. Official stamps of 1909 optd **FRANQUEO 1916** or surch **VALE 2 Cts** also.

398	**O108**	1c. red	20	15
399	**O108**	2c. on 50c. olive	35	15
400	**O108**	10c. brown	35	15

1916. Postage Due stamps of 1909 surch **FRANQUEO VALE 2 Cts. 1916.**

401	**D109**	2c. on 1c. brown	65	65
402	**D109**	2c. on 5c. brown	20	15
403	**D109**	2c. on 10c. brown	20	15
404	**D109**	2c. on 50c. brown	20	15

1917. Surch **Un Centavo**.

405		1c. on 4c. (No. 375)	55	55

1918. Portraits as T **107**.

406		1c. black & orge (San Martin)	35	10
407		2c. black and green (Bolivar)	35	10
408		4c. black and red (Galvez)	45	30
409		5c. black and blue (Pardo)	45	30
410		8c. black and brown (Grau)	1·30	45
411		10c. black and blue (Bolognesi)	55	30
412		12c. black and lilac (Castilla)	1·70	30
413		20c. black and green (Caceres)	2·10	30

126 Columbus at Salamanca University

1918

414	**126**	50c. black and brown	8·25	55
415a	-	1s. black and green	21·00	75
416	-	2s. black and blue	35·00	1·10

DESIGNS: 1s. Funeral of Atahualpa; 2s. Battle of Arica.

129 A. B. Leguia

1920. New Constitution.

417	**129**	5c. black and blue	35	30
418	**129**	5c. black and brown	35	30

130 San Martin **131** Oath of Independence

132 Admiral Cochrane **137** J. Olaya

1921. Centenary of Independence.

419	**130**	1c. brown (San Martin)	35	15
420	**130**	2c. green (Arenales)	55	30
421	**130**	4c. red (Las Heras)	1·90	65
422	**131**	5c. brown	45	15
423	**132**	7c. violet	1·90	65
424	**130**	10c. blue (Guisse)	1·90	65
425	**130**	12c. black (Vidal)	4·50	75
426	**130**	20c. black and red (Leguia)	4·50	75
427	**130**	50c. violet and purple (S. Martin Monument)	13·00	3·75
428	**131**	1s. green and red (San Martin and Leguia)	19·00	8·00

1923. Surch **CINCO Centavos 1923**.

429		5c. on 8c. black & brn (No. 410)	75	55

1924. Surch **CUATRO Centavos 1924**.

430		4c. on 5c. (No. 409)	55	15

1924. Portraits as T **107**. Size 18½×23 mm.

431		2c. olive (Rivadeneyra)	35	10
432		4c. green (Melgar)	35	10
433		8c. black (Iturregui)	3·25	3·25
434		10c. red (A. B. Leguia)	35	10
435		15c. blue (De la Mar)	1·00	30
439		1s. brown (De Saco)	15·00	1·60
440		2s. blue (J. Leguia)	39·00	8·00

1924. Monuments.

436	**137**	20c. blue	1·70	30
437	**137**	20c. yellow	2·75	30
438	-	50c. purple (Bellido)	8·25	45

See also Nos. 484/9.

139 Simon Bolivar

140

1924. Cent of Battle of Ayacucho. Portraits of Bolivar.

441		2c. olive	35	10
442	**139**	4c. green	45	20
443	**139**	5c. black	2·20	20
444	**140**	10c. red	35	10
445	-	20c. blue	2·20	30
446	-	50c. lilac	5·50	1·10
447	-	1s. brown	13·00	4·25
448	-	2s. blue	35·00	18·00

1925. Surch **DOS Centavos 1925.**

449	**137**	2c. on 20c. blue	1·70	1·10

1925. Optd **Plebiscito.**

450	10c. red (No. 434)	1·70	1·70

143 The Rock of Arica

1925. Obligatory Tax. Tacna–Arica Plebiscite.

451	**143**	2c. orange	1·10	30
452	**143**	5c. blue	2·75	75
453	**143**	5c. red	1·40	55
454	**143**	5c. green	1·30	55
455	-	10c. brown	5·50	23·00
456	-	50c. green	35·00	17·00

DESIGNS—HORIZ: 39×30 mm: 10c. Soldiers with colours. VERT: 27×33 mm: 50c. Bolognesi Statue.

146 The Rock of Arica

1927. Obligatory Tax. Figures of value not encircled.

457	**146**	2c. orange	1·10	30
458	**146**	2c. brown	1·10	30
459	**146**	2c. blue	1·10	30
460	**146**	2c. violet	1·10	30
461	**146**	2c. green	1·10	30
462	**146**	20c. red	5·50	1·80

1927. Air. Optd **Servicio Aereo.**

463	**9**	50c. purple (No. 438)	50·00	26·00

148 Pres. A. B. Leguia

1927. Air.

464	**148**	50c. green	1·10	55

149 The Rock of Arica

1928. Obligatory Tax. Plebiscite Fund.

465	**149**	2c. mauve	55	20

1929. Surch Habilitada **2 Cts. 1929.**

466	-	2c. on 8c. (No. 410)	1·30	1·30
468	**137**	15c. on 20c. (No. 437)	1·30	1·30

1929. Surch Habilitada **2 centavos 1929.**

467	2c. on 8c. (No. 410)	1·30	1·30

1930. Optd **Habilitada Franqueo.**

469	**149**	2c. mauve	55	55

1930. Surch **Habilitada 2 Cts. 1930.**

470	**137**	2c. on 20c. yellow	55	55

1930. Surch **Habilitada Franqueo 2 Cts. 1930.**

471	**148**	2c. on 50c. green	55	55

156 Arms of Peru

157 Lima Cathedral

1930. Sixth (inscribed "seventh") Pan-American Child Congress.

472	**156**	2c. green	1·70	75
473	**157**	5c. red	3·75	2·10
474	-	10c. blue	2·20	1·60
475	-	50c. brown	31·00	19·00

DESIGNS—HORIZ: 10c. G.P.O., Lima. VERT: 50c. Madonna and Child.

1930. Fall of Leguia Govt. No. 434 optd with Arms of Peru or surch with new value in four corners also.

477	2c. on 10c. red	35	20
478	4c. on 10c. red	35	20
479	10c. red	35	20
476	15c. on 10c. red	35	20

159 Simon Bolivar

1930. Death Centenary of Bolivar.

480	**159**	2c. brown	55	55
481	**159**	4c. red	90	65
482	**159**	10c. green	45	30
483	**159**	15c. grey	90	85

1930. As T **107** and **137** but smaller, 18×22 mm.

484	-	2c. olive (Rivadeneyra)	45	30
485	-	4c. green (Melgar)	45	30
486	-	15c. blue (De la Mar)	1·30	30
487	**137**	20c. yellow (Olaya)	2·10	30
488	-	50c. purple (Bellido)	2·10	45
489	-	1s. brown (De Saco)	3·25	55

1931. Obligatory Tax. Unemployment Fund. Surch **Habilitada Pro Desocupados 2 Cts.**

490	**159**	2c. on 4c. red	1·80	75
491	**159**	2c. on 10c. green	75	75
492	**159**	2c. on 15c. grey	75	75

161 Pizarro

162 The Old Stone Bridge, Lima

1931. First Peruvian Philatelic Exhibition.

493	**161**	2c. slate	2·10	1·80
494	**161**	4c. brown	2·10	1·80
495	**162**	10c. red	2·10	1·80
496	**162**	10c. green and mauve	2·10	1·80
497	**161**	15c. green	2·10	1·80
498	**162**	15c. red and grey	2·10	1·80
499	**162**	15c. blue and orange	2·10	1·80

163 Manco Capac

164 Oil Well

1931

500	**163**	2c. olive	35	10
501	**164**	4c. green	65	30
502	-	10c. orange	1·70	10
503	-	15c. blue	2·00	30
504	-	20c. yellow	8·25	30
505	-	50c. lilac	8·25	30
506	-	1s. brown	20·00	1·40

DESIGNS—VERT: 10c. Sugar Plantation; 15c. Cotton Plantation; 50c. Copper Mines. 1s. Llamas. HORIZ: 20c. Guano Islands.

170

1931. Obligatory Tax. Unemployment Fund.

507	**170**	2c. green	10	10
508	**170**	2c. red	10	10

171 Arms of Piura

1932. Fourth Centenary of Piura.

509	**171**	10c. blue (postage)	8·25	8·00
510	**171**	15c. violet	8·25	8·00
511	**171**	50c. red (air)	26·00	23·00

172 Parakas

1932. 400th Anniv of Spanish Conquest of Peru. Native designs.

512	**172**	10c. purple (22×19½ mm)	35	10
513	-	15c. lake (25×19½ mm)	65	30
514	-	50c. brown (19½×22 mm)	1·50	30

DESIGNS: 15c. Chimu; 50c. Inca.

175 Arequipa and El Misti

176 Pres. Sanchez Cerro

1932. First Anniv of Constitutional Government.

515	**175**	2c. blue	20	55
527	**175**	2c. black	20	10
528	**175**	2c. green	20	10
516	**175**	4c. brown	20	10
529	**175**	4c. orange	20	10
517	**176**	10c. red	28·00	16·00
530	-	10c. red	75	10
518	-	15c. blue	55	10
531	-	15c. mauve	55	10
519	-	20c. lake	75	10
532	-	20c. violet	75	20
520	-	50c. green	1·10	20
521	-	1s. orange	11·00	1·60
533	-	1s. brown	11·00	1·10

DESIGNS—VERT: 10c. (No. 530), Statue of Liberty; 15c. to 1s. Bolivar Monument, Lima.

178 Blacksmith

1932. Obligatory Tax. Unemployment Fund.

522	**178**	2c. grey	20	10
523	**178**	2c. violet	35	10

179 Monument of 2nd May to Battle of Callao

1933. Obligatory Tax. Unemployment Fund.

524	**179**	2c. violet	20	10
525	**179**	2c. orange	20	10
526	**179**	2c. purple	20	10

181 Hawker Hart Bomber

1934. Air.

534	**181**	2s. blue	6·50	65
535	**181**	5s. brown	15·00	1·20

1934. Obligatory Tax. Unemployment Fund. Optd Pro-Desocupados. (a) In one line.

536	**176**	2c. green	20	10
585	-	2c. purple (No. 537)	10	10

(b) In two lines.

566	2c. purple (No. 537)	20	10

184 F. Pizarro

185 Coronation of Huascar

186 The Inca

1934

537	-	2c. purple	20	10
538	-	4c. green	20	10
539	**184**	10c. red	20	10
540	**184**	15c. blue	55	20
541	**185**	20c. blue	75	20
542	**185**	50c. brown	1·10	20
543	**186**	1s. violet	11·00	1·10

DESIGNS: 2, 4c. show the scene depicted in Type **189**.

187 Lake of the Marvellous Cure

188 Grapes

1935. Tercentenary of Founding of Ica.

544	-	4c. black	35	1·40
545	**187**	5c. red	45	1·40
546	**188**	10c. mauve	6·50	3·25
547	**187**	20c. green	2·20	2·10
548	-	35c. red	11·00	8·00
549	-	50c. brown and orange	7·75	7·00
550	-	1s. red and violet	22·00	17·00

DESIGNS—HORIZ: 4c. City of Ica; 50c. Don Diego Lopez and King Philip IV of Spain. VERT: 35c. Cotton blossom; 1s. Supreme God of the Nazcas.

189 Pizarro and "The Thirteen"

192 Funeral of Atahualpa

1935. Fourth Centenary of Founding of Lima.

551	**189**	2c. brown (postage)	55	30
552	-	4c. violet	55	65
553	-	10c. red	55	30
554	-	15c. blue	1·10	75
555	**189**	20c. grey	2·20	95
556	-	50c. green	3·25	1·90
557	-	1s. blue	6·00	3·75
558	-	2s. brown	14·50	10·00

DESIGNS—HORIZ: 4c. Lima Cathedral. VERT: 10c., 50c. Miss L. S. de Canevaro; 15c., 2s. Pizarro; 1s. The "Tapada" (a veiled woman).

559	**192**	5c. green (air)	35	20
560	-	35c. brown	45	45
561	-	50c. yellow	90	75
562	-	1s. purple	1·70	1·20
563	-	2s. orange	2·75	2·30
564	**192**	5s. purple	11·00	7·00
565	**189**	10s. blue	44·00	30·00

DESIGNS—HORIZ: 35c. Airplane near San Cristobal Hill; 50c., 1s. Airplane over Avenue of Barefoot Friars. VERT: 2s. Palace of Torre Tagle.

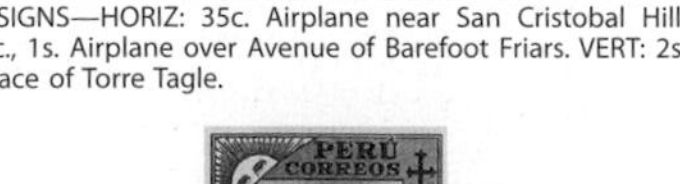

207 "San Cristobal" (caravel)

1936. Callao Centenary.

567	**207**	2c. black (postage)	75	30
568	-	4c. green	75	30
569	-	5c. brown	75	30
570	-	10c. blue	75	30
571	-	15c. green	75	30
572	-	20c. brown	1·00	30

573	-	50c. lilac	1·90	55
574	-	1s. olive	12·00	1·80
575	-	2s. purple	20·00	9·00
576	-	5s. red	28·00	19·00
577	-	10s. brown and red	65·00	55·00
578	-	35c. slate (air)	3·25	1·80

DESIGNS—HORIZ: 4c. La Punta Naval College; 5c. Independence Square, Callao; 10c. Aerial view of Callao; 15c. "Reina del Pacifico" (liner) in Callao Docks and Custom House; 20c. Plan of Callao, 1746; 35c. "La Callao" (locomotive); 1s. Gunboat "Sacramento"; 10s. Real Felipe Fortifications. VERT: 50c. D. Jose de la Mar; 2s. Don Jose de Velasco; 5s. Fort Maipo and miniature portraits of Galvez and Nunez.

1936. Obligatory Tax. St. Rosa de Lima Cathedral Construction Fund. Optd **"Ley 8310"**.

579	**179**	2c. purple	10	10

1936. Surch **Habilitado** and value in figures and words.

580	-	2c. on 4c. green (No. 538) (postage)	35	20
581	**185**	10c. on 20c. blue	35	20
582	**186**	10c. on 1s. violet	55	55
583	**181**	5c. on 2s. blue (air)	55	30
584	**181**	25c. on 5s. brown	1·10	55

211 Guanay Cormorants

217 Mail Steamer "Inca" on Lake Titicaca

1936

586	**211**	2c. brown (postage)	75	30
616	**211**	2c. green	1·00	30
587	-	4c. brown	75	30
617	-	4c. black	45	30
618	-	10c. red	35	30
619	-	15c. blue	45	30
590	-	20c. black	90	30
620	-	20c. brown	35	30
591	-	50c. yellow	3·25	85
621	-	50c. grey	1·00	30
592	-	1s. purple	6·50	1·10
622	-	1s. blue	1·90	30
593	-	2s. blue	13·00	2·75
623	-	2s. violet	4·50	85
594	-	5s. blue	13·00	2·75
595	-	10s. brown and violet	75·00	37·00

DESIGNS—VERT: 4c. Oil well; 10c. Inca postal runner; 1s. G.P.O., Lima; 2s. M. de Amat y Junyent; 5s. J. A. de Pando y Riva; 10s. J. D. Condemarin. HORIZ: 15c. Paseo de la Republica, Lima; 20c. Municipal Palace and Natural History Museum; 50c. University of San Marcos, Lima.

596		5c. green (air)	35	20
625	**217**	15c. blue	35	20
598		20c. grey	1·50	20
626	-	20c. green	1·00	30
627	-	25c. red	45	10
628	-	30c. brown	1·50	10
600		35c. brown	2·75	2·30
601		50c. yellow	45	30
629	-	50c. red	65	10
630	-	70c. green	1·00	85
603		80c. black	6·50	5·00
631	-	80c. green	1·30	55
604		1s. blue	4·75	45
632	-	1s. brown	2·40	30
605		1s.50 brown	7·75	5·25
633	-	1s.50 orange	4·75	45
606		2s. blue	13·00	7·50
634	-	2s. green	9·25	75
607		5s. green	17·00	3·50
608		10s. brown and red	£130	£110

DESIGNS—HORIZ: 5c. La Mar Park; 20c. Native recorder player and llama; 30c. Chuquibambilla ram; 25, 35c. J. Chavez; 50c. Mining Area; 70c. Ford "Tin Goose" airplane over La Punta; 1s. Steam train at La Cima; 1s.50, Aerodrome at Las Palmas, Lima. 2s. Douglas DC-2 mail plane; 5s. Valley of R. Inambari. VERT: 80c. Infiernillo Canyon, Andes; 10s. St. Rosa de Lima.

223 St. Rosa de Lima

1937. Obligatory Tax. St. Rosa de Lima Construction Fund.

609	**223**	2c. red	15	10

1937. Surch **Habilit.** and value in figures and words. (a) Postage.

610		1s. on 2s. blue (593)	3·25	3·25

(b) Air.

611		15c. on 30c. brown (599)	65	45
612		15c. on 35c. brown (600)	65	45
613		15c. on 70c. green (630)	4·50	3·50
614		25c. on 80c. black (603)	4·50	3·50
615		1s. on 2s. blue (606)	7·75	6·50

225 Bielovucic over Lima

226 Jorge Chavez

1937. Air. Pan-American Aviation Conference.

635	**225**	10c. violet	65	20
636	**226**	15c. green	90	20
637	-	25c. brown	65	20
638	-	1s. black	3·00	2·10

DESIGNS—As T **225**: 25c. Limatambo Airport; 1s. Peruvian air routes.

229 "Protection" (by John Q. A. Ward)

1938. Obligatory Tax. Unemployment Fund.

757c	**229**	2c. brown	10	10

230 Children's Holiday Camp

1938. Designs as T **230**.

693	**230**	2c. green	55	30
694	-	4c. brown	55	30
642	-	10c. red	35	10
696	-	15c. blue	55	30
727	-	15c. turquoise	35	10
644	-	20c. purple	20	10
740	-	20c. violet	35	10
698	-	50c. blue	55	30
741	-	50c. brown	35	10
699	-	1s. purple	65	30
742	-	1s. brown	65	10
700	-	2s. green	1·70	30
731	-	2s. blue	1·90	30
701	-	5s. brown and violet	10·50	95
732	-	5s. purple and blue	1·90	65
702	-	10s. blue and black	13·00	1·30
733	-	10s. black and green	5·50	1·30

DESIGNS—VERT: 4c. Chavin pottery; 10c. Automobile roads in Andes; 20c. (2) Industrial Bank of Peru; 1s. (2) Portrait of Toribio de Luzuriaga; 5s. (2) Chavin Idol. HORIZ: 15c. (2) Archaeological Museum, Lima; 50c. (2) Labourers' homes at Lima; 2s. (2) Fig Tree; 10s. (2) Mt. Huascaran.

240 Monument on Junin Plains

1938. Air. As T **240**.

650		5c. brown	20	10
743	-	5c. green	20	10
651	**240**	15c. brown	20	10
652	-	20c. red	55	30
653	-	25c. green	20	10
654	-	30c. orange	20	10
735	-	30c. red	20	10
655	-	50c. green	45	30
656	-	70c. grey	65	30
736	-	70c. blue	35	10
657	-	80c. green	1·20	30
737	-	80c. red	1·30	45
658	-	1s. green	10·00	4·25
705	-	1s.50 violet	75	30
738	-	1s.50 purple	90	55
660	-	2s. red and blue	3·75	95
661	-	5s. purple	18·00	1·70
662	-	10s. blue and green	70·00	38·00

DESIGNS—VERT: 20c. Rear-Admiral M. Villar; 70c. (No. 656, 736), Infiernillo Canyon; 2s. Stele from Chavin Temple. HORIZ: 5c. People's restaurant, Callao; 25c. View of Tarma; 30c. Ica River irrigation system; 50c. Port of Iquitos; 80c. Mountain roadway; 1s. Plaza San Martin, Lima; 1s.50, Nat. Radio Station, San Miguel; 5s. Ministry of Public Works; 10s. Heroe's Crypt, Lima.

248 Seal of City of Lima

1938. Eighth Pan-American Congress, Lima.

663		10c. grey (postage)	65	45
664	**248**	15c. gold, blue, red & blk	1·10	55
665	-	1s. brown	2·75	1·60

DESIGNS (39×32½ mm): 10c. Palace and Square, 1864; 1s. Palace, 1938.

666		25c. blue (air)	90	65
667		1s.50 lake	2·40	1·90
668		2s. black	1·50	75

DESIGNS—VERT: 26×37 mm: 25c. Torre Tagle Palace. HORIZ: 39×32½ mm: 1s.50, National Congress Building, Lima; 2s. Congress Presidents, Ferreyros, Paz Soldan and Arenas.

1940. No. 642 surch **Habilitada 5 cts.**

669		5c. on 10c. red	20	10

251 National Broadcasting Station

1941. Optd **FRANQUEO POSTAL**.

670	**251**	50c. yellow	3·25	15
671	**251**	1s. violet	3·25	30
672	**251**	2s. green	5·25	85
673	**251**	5s. brown	31·00	8·50
674	**251**	10s. mauve	46·00	7·00

1942. Air. No. 653 surch **Habilit 0.15**.

675		15c. on 25c. green	1·70	20

253 Map of S. America showing R. Amazon

254 Francisco de Orellana

255 Francisco Pizarro

1943. 400th Anniv of Discovery of R. Amazon.

676	-	2c. red	35	10
677	**254**	4c. grey	35	10
678	**255**	10c. brown	35	10
679	**253**	15c. blue	65	30
680	-	20c. olive	35	30
681	-	25c. orange	2·20	55
682	**254**	30c. red	55	30
683	**253**	50c. green	55	45
685	-	70c. violet	2·75	1·30
686	-	80c. blue	2·75	1·30
687	-	1s. brown	5·50	75
688	**255**	5s. black	11·00	5·00

DESIGNS—As Type **254**: 2, 70c. Portraits of G. Pizarro and Orellana in medallion; 20, 80c. G. Pizarro. As Type **253**: 25c., 1s. Orellana's Discovery of the R. Amazon.

1943. Surch with Arms of Peru (as Nos. 483, etc) above **10 CTVS.**

689		10c. on 10c. red (No. 642)	20	10

257 Samuel Morse

1944. Centenary of Invention of Telegraphy.

691	**257**	15c. blue	35	30
692	**257**	30c. brown	1·00	30

1946. Surch **Habilitada S/o 0.20.**

706		20c. on 1s. purple (No. 699)	75	30

259

261

1947. First National Tourist Congress, Lima. Unissued designs inscr "V Congreso Pan Americano de Carreteras 1944" optd Habilitada I Congreso Nac. de Turismo Lima–1947.

707	**259**	15c. black and red	65	30
708	-	1s. brown	1·10	45
709	-	1s.35 green	1·10	45
710	**261**	3s. blue	2·00	75
711	-	5s. green	4·50	1·60

DESIGNS—VERT: 1s. Mountain road; 1s.35, Forest road. HORIZ: 5s. Road and house.

1947. Air. First Peruvian Int Airways Lima–New York Flight. Optd with PIA badge and **PRIMER VUELO LIMA - NUEVA YORK.**

712		5c. brown (No. 650)	55	20
713		50c. green (No. 655)	55	30

263 Basketball Players

1948. Air. Olympic Games.

714	-	1s. blue	4·00	2·75
715	**263**	2s. brown	5·50	3·50
716	-	5s. green	9·25	5·75
717	-	10s. yellow	11·00	7·00
MS717a		116×151 mm. Nos. 714/17	50·00	50·00

DESIGNS: 1s. Map showing air route from Peru to Great Britain; 5s. Discus thrower; 10s. Rifleman.

No. 714 is inscr "AEREO" and Nos. 715/17 are optd **AEREO**.

The above stamps exist overprinted **MELBOURNE 1956** but were only valid for postage on one day.

1948. Air. Nos. 653, 736 and 657 surch **Habilitada S/o.** and value.

722		5c. on 25c. green	20	10
723		10c. on 25c. green	20	10
718		10c. on 70c. blue	35	10
719		15c. on 70c. blue	35	10
720		20c. on 70c. blue	35	10
724		30c. on 80c. green	1·10	65
721		55c. on 70c. blue	35	10

263a

263b

1949. Anti-tuberculosis Fund. Surch **Decreto Ley No. 18** and value.

724a	**263a**	3c. on 4c. blue	1·10	10
724b	**263b**	3c. in 10c. blue	1·10	10

264 Statue of Admiral Grau

1949

726	**264**	10c. blue and green	35	10

264a "Education"

1950. Obligatory Tax. National Education Fund.

851	**264a**	3c. lake (16½×21 mm)	10	10
897	**264a**	3c. lake (18×21½ mm)	20	10

265 Park, Lima

1951. Air. 75th Anniv of U.P.U. Unissued stamps inscr "VI CONGRESO DE LA UNION POSTAL DE LAS AMREICAS Y ESPANA-1949" optd **U.P.U. 1874–1949**.

745	**265**	5c. green	10	10
746	-	30c. red and black	20	10
747	-	55c. green	20	10
748	-	95c. turquoise	20	15
749	-	1s.50 red	35	30
750	-	2s. blue	35	30
751	-	5s. red	4·00	3·25
752	-	10s. violet	5·25	4·50
753	-	20s. blue and brown	8·75	7·00

DESIGNS: 30c. Peruvian flag; 55c. Huancayo Hotel; 95c. Ancash Mtns; 1s.50, Arequipa Hotel; 2s. Coaling Jetty; 5s. Town Hall, Miraflores; 10s. Congressional Palace; 20s. Pan-American flags.

1951. Air Surch **HABILITADA S/o. 0.25**.

754	25c. on 30c. red (No. 735)	20	10

1951. Surch **HABILITADA S/.** and figures.

755	1c. on 2c. (No. 693)	20	10
756	5c. on 15c. (No. 727)	20	10
757	10c. on 15c. (No. 727)	20	10

268 Obrero Hospital, Lima

1951. Fifth Pan-American Highways Congress. Unissued "VI CONGRESO DE LA UNION POSTAL" stamps, optd **V Congreso Panamericano de Carreteras 1951.**

758	-	2c. green	35	10
759	**268**	4c. red	35	10
760	-	15c. grey	35	10
761	-	20c. brown	35	10
762	-	50c. purple	35	10
763	-	1s. blue	55	30
764	-	2s. blue	90	30
765	-	5s. red	2·20	2·10
766	-	10s. brown	4·00	2·10

DESIGNS—HORIZ: 2c. Aguas Promenade; 50c. Archiepiscopal Palace, Lima; 1s. National Judicial Palace; 2s. Municipal Palace; 5s. Lake Llanganuco, Ancash. VERT: 15c. Inca postal runner; 20c. Old P.O., Lima; 10s. Machu-Picchu ruins.

269 Father Tomas de San Martin and Capt. J. de Aliaga

1951. Air. Fourth Cent of S. Marcos University.

767	**269**	30c. black	35	30
768	-	40c. blue	35	30
769	-	50c. mauve	35	30
770	-	1s.20 green	35	30
771	-	2s. grey	1·40	30
772	-	5s. multicoloured	3·00	30

DESIGNS: 40c. San Marcos University; 50c. Santo Domingo Convent; 1s.20, P. de Peralto Barnuevo, Father Tomas de San Martin and Jose Baquijano; 2s. Toribio Rodriguez, Jose Hipolito Unanue and Jose Cayetano Heredia; 5s. University Arms in 1571 and 1735.

270 Engineer's School

1952. (a) Postage.

774		2c. purple	10	10
775		5c. green	10	10
776		10c. green	20	10
777		15c. grey	10	10
777a		15c. brown	65	10
829	-	20c. brown	20	10
779	**270**	25c. red	20	10
779a	**270**	25c. green	65	10
780	-	30c. blue	20	10
780a	-	30c. red	35	10
830	-	30c. mauve	20	10
831	-	50c. purple	20	10
924	-	50c. green	35	10
782	-	1s. brown	55	10
782a	-	1s. blue	55	10
783	-	2s. turquoise	1·10	10
783a	-	2s. grey	1·10	10

DESIGNS—As Type **270**: HORIZ: 2c. Hotel, Tacna; 5c. Tuna fishing boat and indigenous fish; 10c. View of Matarani; 15c. Steam train; 30c. Public Health and Social Assistance. VERT: 20c. Vicuna. Larger (35×25 mm): HORIZ: 50c. Inca maize terraces; 1s. Inca ruins, Paramonga Fort; 2s. Agriculture Monument, Lima.

(b) Air.

784	40c. green	10	10
785	75c. brown	1·50	30
834	80c. red	35	10
786	1s.25 blue	35	10
787	1s.50 red	45	30
788	2s.20 blue	2·20	45
789	3s. brown	1·90	65
835	3s. green	1·10	45
836	3s.80 orange	2·20	55
790	5s. brown	1·50	30
791	10s. brown	3·75	85
838	10s. red	2·20	65

DESIGNS—As Type **270**. HORIZ: 40c. Gunboat "Maranon"; 1s.50, Housing Complex. VERT: 75c., 80c. Colony of Guanay cormorants. Larger (25×25 mm.): HORIZ: 1s.25, Corpac-Limatambo Airport; 2s.20, 3s.80, Inca Observatory, Cuzco; 5s. Garcilaso (portrait). VERT: 3s. Tobacco plant, leaves and cigarettes; 10s. Manco Capac Monument (25×37 mm).

See also Nos. 867, etc.

271 Isabella the Catholic

272 "Santa Maria", "Pinta" and "Nina"

1953. Air. 500th Birth Anniv of Isabella the Catholic.

792	**271**	40c. red	20	10
793	**272**	1s.25 green	65	15
794	**271**	2s.15 purple	1·10	55
795	**272**	2s.20 black	1·30	65

273

1954. Obligatory Tax. National Marian Eucharistic Congress Fund. Roul.

796	**273**	5c. blue and red	35	10

274 Gen. M. Perez Jimenez

1956. Visit of President of Venezuela.

797	**274**	25c. brown	10	10

275 Arms of Lima and Bordeaux

1957. Air. Exhibition of French Products, Lima.

798	**275**	40c. lake, blue and green	20	10
799	-	50c. black, brown & green	20	10
800	-	1s.25 deep blue, green and blue	55	45
801	-	2s.20 brown and blue	90	65

DESIGNS—HORIZ: 50c. Eiffel Tower and Lima Cathedral; 1s.25, Admiral Dupetit-Thouars and frigate "La Victorieuse"; 2s.20, Exhibition building, Pres. Prado and Pres. Coty.

276 1857 Stamp

1957. Air. Centenary of First Peruvian Postage Stamp.

802		5c. black and grey	10	10
803	**276**	10c. turquoise and mauve	10	10
804	-	15c. brown and green	10	10
805	-	25c. blue and yellow	10	10
806	-	30c. brown and chocolate	10	10
807	-	40c. ochre and black	20	10
808	-	1s.25 brown and blue	75	55
809	-	2s.20 red and blue	1·10	75
810	-	5s. red and mauve	2·40	75
811	-	10s. violet and green	4·50	85

DESIGNS: 5c. Pre-stamp Postmarks; 15c. 1857 2r. stamp; 25c. 1d. 1858; 30c. 1p. 1858 stamp; 40c. ½ peso 1858 stamp; 1s.25, J. Davila Condemarin, Director of Posts, 1857; 2s.20, Pres. Ramon Castilla; 5s. Pres. D. M. Prado; 10s. Various Peruvian stamps in shield.

277 Carlos Paz Soldan (founder)

1958. Air. Centenary of Lima–Callao Telegraph Service.

812	**277**	40c. brown and red	20	10
813	-	1s. green	35	20
814	-	1s.25 blue and purple	55	30

DESIGNS—VERT: 1s. Marshal Ramon Castilla. HORIZ: 1s.25, Pres. D. M. Prado and view of Callao.

No. 814 also commemorates the political centenary of the Province of Callao.

278 Flags of France and Peru

1958. Air. "Treasures of Peru" Exhibition, Paris.

815	**278**	50c. red, blue & deep blue	10	10
816	-	65c. multicoloured	15	15
817	-	1s.50 brown, purple & bl	35	20
818	-	2s.50 purple, turq & grn	65	30

DESIGNS—HORIZ: 65c. Lima Cathedral and girl in national costume; 1s.50, Caballero and ancient palace. VERT: 2s.50, Natural resources map of Peru.

279 Father Martin de Porras Velasquez

1958. Air. Birth Centenary of D. A. Carrion Garcia (patriot).

819	**279**	60c. multicoloured	10	10
820	-	1s.20 multicoloured	15	10
821	-	1s.50 multicoloured	20	10
822	-	2s.20 black	65	65

DESIGNS—VERT: 1s.20, D. A. Carrion Garcia. 1s.50, J. H. Unanue Pavon. HORIZ: 2s.20, First Royal School of Medicine (now Ministry of Government Police, Posts and Telecommunications).

280 Gen. Alvarez Thomas

1958. Air. Death Centenary of Gen. Thomas.

823	**280**	1s.10 purple, red & bistre	20	15
824	**280**	1s.20 black, red and bistre	55	55

281 Association Emblems

1958. Air. 150th Anniv of Advocates' College, Lima. Emblems in bistre and blue.

825	**281**	80c. green	20	10
826	**281**	1s.10 red	20	10
827	**281**	1s.20 blue	35	10
828	**281**	1s.50 purple	35	10

292 Symbol of Eucharist

1960. Obligatory Tax. 6th National Eucharistic Congress Fund.

839	**282**	10c. multicoloured	20	10
839a	**282**	10c. blue and red	35	10

283

1960. Air. World Refugee Year.

840	**283**	80c. multicoloured	55	55
841	**283**	4s.30 multicoloured	1·00	95
MS841a		150×100 mm. Nos. 840/1. Imperf (sold at 15s.)	17·00	17·00

284 Sea Bird bearing Map

1960. Air. International Pacific Fair, Lima.

842	**284**	1s. multicoloured	3·75	45

285 Congress Emblem

1960. Sixth National Eucharistic Congress, Piura.

843	**285**	50c. red, black and blue	20	20
844	-	1s. multicoloured (Eucharistic symbols)	55	30

286 1659 Coin

1961. Air. First National Numismatic Exhibition, Lima.

845		1s. grey and brown	55	30
846	**286**	2s. grey and blue	55	30

DESIGNS: 1s. 1659 coin.

287 "Amazonas"

1961. Air. Centenary of World Tour of Cadet Sailing Ship "Amazonas".

847	**287**	50c. green and brown	20	10
848	**287**	80c. red and purple	35	10
849	**287**	1s. black and green	55	15

288 Globe, Moon and Stars

1961. Air. I.G.Y.

850	**288**	1s. multicoloured	1·40	65

289 Olympic Torch

1961. Air. Olympic Games, 1960.

852	**289**	5c. blue and black	90	55
853	**289**	10s. red and black	2·00	1·30
MS853a		100×80 mm. Nos. 852/3. Imerf	28·00	28·00

290 "Balloon"

1961. Christmas and New Year.

854	**290**	20c. blue	55	30

291 Fair Emblem

1961. Air. Second International Pacific Fair, Lima.

855	**291**	1s. multicoloured	35	30

292 Symbol of Eucharist

1962. Obligatory Tax. Seventh National Eucharistic Congress Fund. Roul.

857	**292**	10c. blue and yellow	10	10

293 Sculptures "Cahuide" and "Cuauhtemoc"

1962. Air. Peruvian Art Treasures Exhibition, Mexico 1960. Flags red and green.

859	**293**	1s. red	20	10
860	-	2s. turquoise	45	30
861	-	3s. brown	65	55

DESIGNS: 2s. Tupac-Amaru and Hidalgo; 3s. Presidents Prado and Lopez.

294 Frontier Maps

1962. Air. 20th Anniv of Ecuador–Peru Border Agreement.

862	**294**	1s.30 black & red on grey	35	30
863	**294**	1s.50 multicoloured	35	30
864	**294**	2s.50 multicoloured	65	65

295 The Cedar, Pomabamba

1962. Centenary of Pomabamba and Pallasca Ancash.

865	**295**	1s. green and red (postage)	55	30
866	-	1s. black and grey (air)	35	10

DESIGN: No. 866, Agriculture, mining, etc, Pallasca Ancash (31½×22 mm.).

1962. As Nos. 774/91 but colours and some designs changed and new values. (a) Postage.

867	20c. purple	20	10
921	20c. red	35	10
922	30c. blue (as No. 776)	35	10
923	40c. orange (as No. 784)	35	10
871	60c. black (as No. 774)	55	10
925	1s. red	35	10

(b) Air.

873	1s.30 ochre (as No. 785)	75	20
874	1s.50 purple	55	10
875	1s.80 blue (as No. 777)	55	20
876	2s. green	55	10
926	2s.60 green (as No. 783)	1·00	30
877	3s. purple	55	10
927	3s.60 purple (as No. 789)	1·40	45
878	4s.30 orange	1·30	30
928	4s.60 orange (as No. 788)	1·50	55
879	5s. green	1·30	35
880	10s. blue	2·75	75

296 "Man"

1963. Air. Chavin Excavations Fund. Pottery.

881	-	1s.+50c. grey and pink	35	30
882	-	1s.50+1s. grey and blue	55	55
883	-	3s.+2s.50 grey & green	65	95
884	**296**	4s.30+3s. grey and green	1·70	1·60
885	-	6s.+4s. grey and olive	2·00	1·90

FIGURES—HORIZ: 1s. "Griffin"; 1s.50, "Eagle"; 3s. "Cat". VERT: 6s. "Deity".

297 Campaign and Industrial Emblems

1963. Freedom from Hunger.

886	**297**	1s. bistre and red (postage)	20	10
887	**297**	4s.30 bistre and green (air)	1·40	75

298 Henri Dunant and Centenary Emblem

1964. Air. Red Cross Centenary.

888	**298**	1s.30+70c. multicoloured	55	55
889	**298**	4s.30+1s.70 multicoloured	1·10	1·10

299 Chavez and Wing

1964. Air. 50th Anniv of Jorge Chavez's Trans-Alpine Flight.

890	**299**	5s. blue, purple and brn	90	45

300 Alliance Emblem

1964. "Alliance for Progress". Emblem black, green and blue.

891	**300**	40c. black & yell (postage)	10	10
892	-	1s.30 black & mauve (air)	20	10
893	**300**	3s. black and blue	75	55

DESIGN—HORIZ: 1s.30, As Type **300**, but with inscription at right.

301 Fair Poster

1965. Air. Third International Pacific Fair, Lima.

894	**301**	1s. multicoloured	10	10

302 Net, Flag and Globe

1965. Air. Women's World Basketball Championships, Lima.

895	**302**	1s.30 violet and red	75	30
896	**302**	4s.30 bistre and red	1·70	75

303 St. Martin de Porras (anonymous)

1965. Air. Canonization of St. Martin de Porras (1962). Paintings. Multicoloured.

898	1s.30 Type **303**	35	10
899	1s.80 "St. Martin and the Miracle of the Animals" (after painting by Camino Brent)	45	20
900	4s.30 "St. Martin and the Angels" (after painting by Fausto Conti)	90	85

Porras is wrongly spelt "Porres" on the stamps.

304 Fair Emblem

1965. Fourth International Pacific Fair, Lima.

901	**304**	1s.50 multicoloured	35	15
902	**304**	2s.50 multicoloured	35	20
903	**304**	3s.50 multicoloured	45	30

305 Father Christmas and Postmarked Envelope

1965. Christmas.

904	**305**	20c. black and red	20	10
905	**305**	50c. black and green	45	30
906	**305**	1s. black and blue	75	55

The above stamps were valid for postage only on November 2nd. They were subsequently used as postal employees' charity labels.

1966. Obligatory Tax. Journalists' Fund. (a) Surch **HABILITADO "Fondo del Periodista Peruano" Ley 16078 S/o. 0.10.**

907	**264a**	10c. on 3c. (No. 897)	35	20

(b) Surch **Habilitado "Fondo del Periodista Peruano" Ley 16078 S/. 0.10.**

909	10c. on 3c. (No. 897)	35	20

1966. Obligatory Tax. Journalists' Fund. No. 857 optd **Periodista Peruano LEY 16078.**

910	**292**	10c. blue and yellow	10	10

1966. Nos. 757c, 851 and 897 surch **XX Habilitado S/. 0.10.**

911	**229**	10c. on 2c. brown	10	10
912	**264a**	10c. on 3c. lake (No. 897)	10	10
912b	**264a**	10c. on 3c. lake (No. 851)	1·30	20

312 2nd May Monument and Battle Scene

1966. Air. Centenary of Battle of Callao. Multicoloured.

913	1s.90 Type **312**	65	30
914	3s.60 Monument and sculpture	75	45
915	4s.60 Monument and Jose Galvez	1·30	55

313 Funerary Mask

1966. Gold Objects of Chimu Culture. Multicoloured.

916	1s.90+90c. Type **313**	1·20	1·20
917	2s.60+1s.30 Ceremonial knife (vert)	1·50	1·50
918	3s.60+1s.80 Ceremonial urn	2·20	2·10
919	4s.60+2s.30 Goblet (vert)	3·00	2·75
920	20s.+10s. Ear-ring	12·00	11·50

314 Civil Guard Emblem

1966. Air. Civil Guard Centenary Multicoloured.

929	90c. Type **314**	10	10
930	1s.90 Emblem and activities of Civil Guard	55	20

315 Map and Mountains

1966. Opening of Huinco Hydro-electric Scheme.

931	**315**	70c. black, deep blue and blue (postage)	35	20
932	**315**	1s.90 black, blue and violet (air)	35	20

316 Globe

1967. Air. Peruvian Photographic Exhibition, Lima.

933	-	2s.60 red and black	35	20
934	-	3s.60 black and blue	45	55
935	**316**	4s.60 multicoloured	55	55

DESIGNS: 2s.60, "Sun" carving; 3s.60, Map of Peru within spiral.

317 Symbol of Construction

1967. Six-year Construction Plan.

936	**317**	90c. black, gold and mauve (postage)	35	15
937	**317**	1s.90 black, gold and ochre (air)	45	30

318 "St. Rosa" (from painting by A. Medoro)

1967. Air. 350th Death Anniv of St. Rosa of Lima. Designs showing portraits of St. Rosa by artists given below. Multicoloured.

938		1s.90 Type **318**	65	15
939		2s.60 C. Maratta	1·10	30
940		3s.60 Anon., Cusquena School	1·20	55

319 Vicuna within Figure "5"

1967. Fifth International Pacific Fair, Lima.

941	**319**	1s. black, green and gold (postage)	20	10
942	**319**	1s. purple, black and gold (air)	35	20

320 Pen-nib made of Newspaper

1967. Obligatory Tax. Journalists' Fund.

943	**320**	10c. black and red	10	10

321 Wall Reliefs (fishes)

1967. Obligatory Tax. Chan-Chan Excavation Fund.

944	**321**	20c. black and blue	10	10
945	-	20c. black and mauve	10	10
946	-	20c. black and brown	10	10
947	-	20c. multicoloured	10	10
948	-	20c. multicoloured	10	10
949	-	20c. black and green	10	10

DESIGNS: No. 945, Ornamental pattern; No. 946, Carved "bird"; No. 947, Temple on hillside; No. 948, Corner of Temple; No. 949, Ornamental pattern (birds).

322 Lions' Emblem

1967. Air. 50th Anniv of Lions International.

950	**322**	1s.60 violet, blue and grey	45	30

323 Nazca Jug

1968. Air. Ceramic Treasures of Nazca Culture. Designs showing painted pottery jugs. Multicoloured.

951		1s.90 Type **323**	65	30
952		2s.60 Falcon	75	55
953		3s.60 Round jug decorated with bird	75	55
954		4s.60 Two-headed snake	1·10	75
955		5s.60 Sea Bird	2·20	1·10

324 Alligator

1968. Gold Sculptures of Mochica Culture. Multicoloured.

956		1s.90 Type **324**	2·20	45
957		2s.60 Bird (vert)	3·25	55
958		3s.60 Lizard	4·00	65
959		4s.60 Bird (vert)	4·75	65
960		5s.60 Jaguar	4·75	95

325 "Antarqui" (Airline Symbol)

1968. Air. 12th Anniv of APSA (Peruvian Airlines).

961	**325**	3s.60 multicoloured	55	30
962	-	5s.60 brown, black & red	75	55

DESIGN: 5s.60, Alpaca and stylized Boeing 747.

326 Human Rights Emblem

1968. Air. Human Rights Year.

963	**326**	6s.50 red, green & brown	55	55

327 "The Discus-thrower"

1968. Air. Olympic Games, Mexico.

964	**327**	2s.30 brown, blue & yell	35	10
965	**327**	3s.50 blue, red and green	35	20
966	**327**	5s. black, blue and pink	35	30
967	**327**	6s.50 purple, brown & bl	55	45
968	**327**	8s. blue, mauve and lilac	55	55
969	**327**	9s. violet, green and orange	55	65

328

1968. Obligatory Tax. Unissued stamps surch as in T **328**.

970	**328**	20c. on 50c. violet, orange and black	90	85
971	**328**	20c. on 1s. blue, orange and black	90	85

1968. Obligatory Tax. Journalists' Fund. No. 897 surch **Habilitado Fondo Periodista Peruano Ley 17050 S/.** and value.

972	**264a**	20c. on 3c. lake	10	10

1968. Christmas. No. 900 surch **PRO NAVIDAD Veinte Centavos R.S. 5-11-68.**

973		20c. on 4s.30 multicoloured	65	55

331 Indian's Head and Wheat

1969. Unissued Agrarian Reform stamps, surch as in T **331**. Multicoloured.

974		2s.50 on 90c. Type **331** (postage)	20	10
975		3s. on 90c. Man digging	35	20
976		4s. on 90c. As No. 975	45	30
977		5s.50 on 1s.90 Corn-cob and hand scattering cobs (air)	55	30
978		6s.50 on 1s.90 As No. 977	75	45

333 First Peruvian Coin (obverse and reverse)

1969. Air. 400th Anniv of 1st Peruvian Coinage.

979	**333**	5s. black, grey and yellow	55	20
980	**333**	5s. black, grey and green	55	20

334 Worker holding Flag and Oil Derrick

1969. Nationalization of International Petroleum Company's Oilfields and Refinery (9 October 1968).

981	**334**	2s.50 multicoloured	35	15
982	**334**	3s. multicoloured	35	20
983	**334**	4s. multicoloured	65	30
984	**334**	5s.50 multicoloured	65	30

335 Castilla Monument

1969. Air. Death Centenary of President Ramon Castilla.

985	**335**	5s. blue and green	55	30
986	-	10s. brown and purple	1·30	65

DESIGN—(21×37 mm): 10s. President Castilla.

336 Boeing 707, Globe and "Kon Tiki" (replica of balsa raft)

1969. First A.P.S.A. (Peruvian Airlines) Flight to Europe.

987	**336**	2s.50 mult (postage)	55	10
988	**336**	3s. multicoloured (air)	35	10
989	**336**	4s. multicoloured	55	15
990	**336**	5s.50 multicoloured	65	30
991	**336**	6s.50 multicoloured	65	55

337 Dish Aerial, Satellite and Globe

1969. Air. Inauguration of Lurin Satellite Telecommunications Station, Lima.

992	**337**	20s. multicoloured	2·20	1·10
MS993		110×81 mm. No. 992. Imperf	4·00	4·00

338 Captain Jose A. Quinones Gonzales (military aviator)

1969. Quinones Gonzales Commemoration.

994	**338**	20s. mult (postage)	2·75	1·30
995	**338**	20s. multicoloured (air)	2·75	1·30

339 W.H.O. Emblem

1969. Air. 20th Anniv (1968) of W.H.O.

996	**339**	5s. multicoloured	35	30
997	**339**	6s.50 multicoloured	45	30

340 Peasant breaking Chains

1969. Agrarian Reform Decree.

998	**340**	2s.50 deep blue, blue and red (postage)	10	10
999	**340**	3s. purple, lilac and black (air)	35	15
1000	**340**	4s. brown and light brown	55	30

341 Arms of the Inca Garcilaso de la Vega (historian)

1969. Air. Garcilaso de la Vega Commemoration.

1001	**341**	2s.40 black, silver & grn	20	10
1002	-	3s.50 black, buff and blue	35	15
1003	-	5s. multicoloured	55	20
MS1004		127×88 mm. Nos. 1001/1003. Imperf	1·90	1·90

DESIGNS: 3s.50, Title page, "Commentarios Reales", Lisbon, 1609; 5s. Inca Garcilaso de la Vega.

342 Admiral Grau and Ironclad Warship "Huascar"

1969. Navy Day.

1005	**342**	50s. multicoloured	5·50	3·25

343 "6" and Fair Flags

1969. Sixth International Pacific Fair, Lima.

1006	**343**	2s.50 mult (postage)	55	10
1007	**343**	3s. multicoloured (air)	55	10
1008	**343**	4s. multicoloured	55	15

344 Father Christmas and Greetings Card

1969. Christmas.

1009	**344**	20c. black and red	35	20
1010	**344**	20c. black and orange	35	20
1011	**344**	20c. black and brown	35	20

345 Col. F. Bolognesi and Soldier

1969. Army Day.

1012	**345**	1s.20 black, gold and blue (postage)	35	10
1013	**345**	50s. black, gold and brown (air)	4·50	1·90

346 Arms of Amazonas

1970. Air. 150th Anniv (1971) of Republic (1st issue).

1014	**346**	10s. multicoloured	1·20	75

See also Nos. 1066/70, 1076/80 and 1081/90.

347 I.L.O. Emblem on Map

1970. Air. 50th Anniv of I.L.O.

1015	**347**	3s. deep blue and blue	35	10

348 "Motherhood"

1970. Air. 24th Anniv of UNICEF.

1016	**348**	5s. black and yellow	45	30
1017	**348**	6s.50 black and pink	65	45

349 "Puma" Jug

1970. Vicus Culture. Ceramic Art. Multicoloured.

1018	2s.50 Type **349** (postage)	75	10
1019	3s. Squatting warrior (statuette) (air)	1·10	30
1020	4s. Animal jug	1·10	30
1021	5s.50 Twin jugs	2·20	85
1022	6s.50 Woman with jug (statuette)	3·25	1·10

350 Ministry Building

1970. Ministry of Transport and Communications.

1023	**350**	40c. black and purple	35	10
1024	**350**	40c. black and yellow	35	10
1025	**350**	40c. black and grey	35	10
1026	**350**	40c. black and red	35	10
1027	**350**	40c. black and brown	35	10

351 Peruvian Anchovy

1970. Fish. Multicoloured.

1028	2s.50 Type **351** (postage)	2·00	30
1029	2s.50 Chilean hake	2·00	30
1030	3s. Swordfish (air)	2·00	30
1031	3s. Yellow-finned tuna	2·00	30
1032	5s.50 Atlantic wolffish	2·00	30

352 Telephone and Skyline

1970. Air. Nationalization of Lima Telephone Service.

1033	**352**	5s. multicoloured	55	20
1034	**352**	10s. multicoloured	1·10	55

353 "Soldier and Farmer"

1970. Unity of Armed Forces and People.

1035	**353**	2s.50 mult (postage)	55	10
1036	**353**	3s. multicoloured (air)	55	20
1037	**353**	5s.50 multicoloured	1·10	20

354 U.N. Headquarters and Dove

1970. Air. 25th Anniv of U.N.O.

1038	**354**	3s. blue and light blue	35	30

355 Rotary Emblem

1970. Air. 50th Anniv of Lima Rotary Club.

1039	**355**	10s. gold, red and black	1·30	75

356 Military Parade (Army Staff College, Chorrillos)

1970. Military, Naval and Air Force Academies. Multicoloured.

1040	2s.50 Type **356**	90	30
1041	2s.50 Parade, Naval Academy, La Punta	90	30
1042	2s.50 Parade, Air Force Officer Training School, Las Palmas	90	30

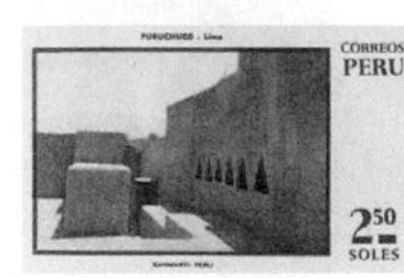

357 Puruchuco, Lima

1970. Tourism. Multicoloured.

1043	2s.50 Type **357** (postage)	1·10	30
1044	3s. Chan-Chan-Trujillo, La Libertad (air)	1·10	30
1045	4s. Sacsayhuaman, Cuzco (vert)	1·30	30
1046	5s.50 Lake Titicaca, Pomata, Puno (vert)	1·90	45
1047	10s. Machu-Picchu, Cuzco (vert)	2·75	95
MS1048	127×95 mm. Nos. 1043/7. Imperf	5·50	5·50

358 Festival Procession

1970. Air. October Festival, Lima. Multicoloured.

1049	3s. Type **358**	20	10
1050	4s. "The Cock-fight" (T. Nunez Ureta)	35	20
1051	5s.50 Altar, Nazarenas Shrine (vert)	65	45
1052	6s.50 "The Procession" (J. Vinatea Reinoso)	75	55
1053	8s. "The Procession" (Jose Sabogal) (vert)	1·10	65

359 "The Nativity" (Cuzco School)

1970. Christmas. Paintings by Unknown Artists. Multicoloured.

1054	1s.20 Type **359**	35	20
1055	1s.50 "The Adoration of the Magi" (Cuzquena School)	35	20
1056	1s.80 "The Adoration of the Shepherds" (Peruvian School)	35	20

360 "Close Embrace" (petroglyph)

1971. Air. "Gratitude for World Help in Earthquake of May 1970".

1057	**360**	4s. olive, black and red	55	30
1058	**360**	5s.50 blue, flesh and red	55	30
1059	**360**	6s.50 grey, blue and red	55	30

361 "St. Rosa de Lima" (F. Laso)

1971. 300th Anniv of Canonization of St. Rosa de Lima.

1060	**361**	2s.50 multicoloured	35	10

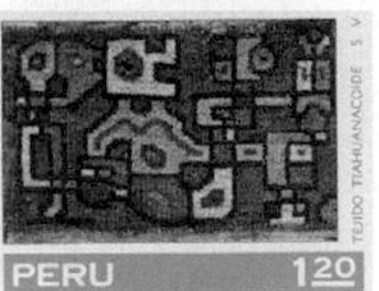

362 Tiahuanaco Fabric

1971. Ancient Peruvian Textiles.

1061	**362**	1s.20 mult (postage)	20	10
1062	-	2s.50 multicoloured	55	10
1063	-	3s. multicoloured (air)	1·10	20
1064	-	4s. pink, green & dp grn	1·10	30
1065	-	5s.50 multicoloured	1·70	55

DESIGNS—HORIZ: 2s.50, Chancay fabric; 4s. Chancay lace. VERT: 3s. Chancay tapestry; 5s.50, Paracas fabric.

363 M. Garcia Pumacahua

1971. 150th Anniv of Independence (2nd issue). National Heroes.

1066	**363**	1s.20 blk & red (postage)	10	10
1067	-	2s.50 black and blue	35	15
1068	-	3s. black and mauve (air)	15	15
1069	-	4s. black and green	35	20
1070	-	5s.50 black and brown	55	20

DESIGNS: 2s.50, F. Antonio de Zela; 3s. T. Rodriguez de Mendoza; 4s. J. P. Viscardo y Guzman; 5s.50, J. G. Condorcanqui, Tupac Amani.

See also Nos. 1076/80 and Nos. 1081/90.

364 Violet Amberjack (Nazca Culture)

1971. "Traditional Fisheries of Peru". Piscatorial Ceramics. Multicoloured.

1071	1s.50 Type **364** (postage)	35	10
1072	3s.50 Pacific bonito (Chimu Inca) (air)	65	20
1073	4s. Peruvian anchovy (Mochica)	75	20
1074	5s.50 Chilian hake (Chimu)	1·20	55
1075	8s.50 Peruvian menhaden (Nazca)	1·80	1·10

1971. 150th Anniv of Independence. National Heroes (3rd issue). As T **363**. Multicoloured.

1076	1s.20 M. Melgar (postage)	10	10
1077	2s.50 J. Baquijano y Carrillo	35	20
1078	3s. J. de la Riva Aguero (air)	20	15
1079	4s. H. Unanue	35	15
1080	5s.50 F. J. de Luna Pizarro	55	20

366 Liberation Expedition Monument

1971. 150th Anniv of Independence (4th issue). As T **366**. Multicoloured.

1081	1s.50 M. Bastidas (postage)	20	10
1082	2s. J. F. Sanchez Carrion	20	10
1083	2s.50 M. J. Guise	35	20
1084	3s. F. Vidal (air)	20	20
1085	3s.50 J. de San Martin	35	20
1086	4s.50 Type **366**	35	20
1087	6s. "Surrender of the 'Numancia Battalion'" (horiz) (42×35 mm)	65	30
1088	7s.50 Alvarez de Arenales Monument (horiz) (42×39 mm)	75	55
1089	9s. Monument to Founders of the Republic, Lima (horiz) (42×39 mm)	75	55
1090	10s. "Proclamation of Independence" (horiz) (46×35 mm)	55	65

367 R. Palma (author and poet)

1971. Air. 150th Anniv of National Library.

1091	**367**	7s.50 black and brown	1·10	55

368 Weightlifting

1971. Air. 25th World Weightlifting Championships, Huampani, Lima.

1092	**368**	7s.50 black and blue	1·10	55

369 "Gongora portentosa"

1971. Peruvian Flora (1st series). Orchids. Multicoloured.

1093	1s.50 Type **369**	90	10
1094	2s. "Odontoglossum cristatum"	1·10	20
1095	2s.50 "Mormolyca peruviana"	1·10	10
1096	3s. "Trichocentrum pulchrum"	1·30	20
1097	3s.50 "Oncidium sanderae"	2·20	20

See also Nos. 1170/4 and 1206/10.

370 Family and Flag

1971. Air. Third Anniv of October 3rd Revolution.

1098	**370**	7s.50 black, red and blue	90	30
MS1099		110×82 mm. No. 1089. Imperf	2·75	2·75

371 Schooner "Sacramento" of 1821

1971. Air. 150th Anniv of Peruvian Navy and "Order of the Peruvian Sun".

1100 **371** 7s.50 blue and light blue 1·00 55

1101 - 7s.50 multicoloured 55 30

DESIGN: No. 1101, Order of the Peruvian Sun.

372 "Development and Liberation" (detail)

1971. Second Ministerial Meeting of "The 77" Group.

1102 **372** 1s.20 multicoloured (postage) 10 10

1103 - 3s.50 multicoloured 45 20

1104 - 50s. multicoloured (air) 6·50 2·30

DESIGNS—As Type **372**: 3s.50, 50s. Detail from the painting "Development and Liberation".

373 "Plaza de Armas, 1843" (J. Rugendas)

1971. "Exfilima" Stamp Exhibition, Lima.

1105 **373** 3s. black and green 65 30

1106 - 3s.50 black and pink 65 30

DESIGN: 3s.50, "Plaza de Armas, 1971" (C. Zeiter).

374 Fair Emblem

1971. Air. Seventh International Pacific Fair, Lima.

1107 **374** 4s.50 multicoloured 55 20

375 Army Crest

1971. 150th Anniv of Peruvian Army.

1108 **375** 8s.50 multicoloured 1·30 55

376 "The Flight into Egypt"

1971. Christmas. Multicoloured.

1109 1s.80 Type **376** 35 30

1110 2s.50 "The Magi" 55 30

1111 3s. "The Nativity" 65 30

377 "Fishermen" (J. Ugarte Elespuru)

1971. Social Reforms. Paintings. Multicoloured.

1112 3s.50 Type **377** 1·10 20

1113 4s. "Threshing Grain in Cajamarca" (Camilo Blas) 1·10 20

1114 6s. "Hand-spinning Huanca Native Women" (J. Sabogal) 1·70 20

378 Chimu Idol

1972. Peruvian Antiquities. Multicoloured.

1115 3s.90 Type **378** 1·10 20

1116 4s. Chimu statuette 1·10 20

1117 4s.50 Lambayeque idol 1·30 30

1118 5s.40 Mochica collar 1·30 30

1119 6s. Lambayeque "spider" pendant 1·80 55

379 Peruvian Bigeye

1972. Peruvian Fish. Multicoloured.

1120 1s.20 Type **379** (postage) 55 20

1121 1s.50 Common guadana 55 20

1122 2s.50 Jack mackerel 1·20 20

1123 3s. Diabolico (air) 1·30 30

1124 5s.50 Galapagos hogfish 2·40 65

380 "Peruvian Family" (T. Nunez Ureta)

1972. Air. Education Reforms.

1125 **380** 6s.50 multicoloured 75 45

381 Mochica Warrior

1972. Peruvian Art (1st series). Mochica Ceramics. Multicoloured.

1126 1s.20 Type **381** 55 20

1127 1s.50 Warrior's head 55 20

1128 2s. Kneeling deer 1·20 20

1129 2s.50 Warrior's head (different) 1·30 20

1130 3s. Kneeling warrior 1·90 20

See also Nos. 1180/4.

382 White-tailed Trogon

1972. Air. Peruvian Birds. Multicoloured.

1131 2s. Type **382** 2·40 30

1132 2s.50 Amazonian umbrellabird 2·40 30

1133 3s. Andean cock of the rock 2·75 30

1134 6s.50 Red-billed toucan 5·00 55

1135 8s.50 Blue-crowned motmot 7·75 65

383 "The Harvest" (July)

1972. 400th Anniv of G. Poma de Ayala's "Inca Chronicles". Woodcuts.

1136 **383** 2s.50 black and red 1·90 30

1138 - 2s.50 black and pink 1·90 30

1140 - 2s.50 black and orange 1·90 30

1142 - 2s.50 black and brown 1·90 30

1144 - 2s.50 black and blue 1·90 30

1146 - 2s.50 black and mauve 1·90 30

1137 - 3s. black and green 1·90 30

1139 - 3s. black and blue 1·90 30

1141 - 3s. black and lilac 1·90 30

1143 - 3s. black and green 1·90 30

1145 - 3s. black and orange 1·90 30

1147 - 3s. black and yellow 1·90 30

DESIGNS: No. 1137, "Land Purification" (August); No. 1138, "Sowing" (September); No. 1139, "Invocation of the Rains" (October); No. 1140, "Irrigation" (November); No. 1141, "Rite of the Nobility" (December); No. 1142, "Maize Cultivation Rights" (January); No. 1143, "Ripening of the Maize" (February); No. 1144, "Birds in the Maize" (March); No. 1145, "Children as camp-guards" (April); No. 1146, "Gathering the harvest" (May); No. 1147, "Removing the harvest" (June).

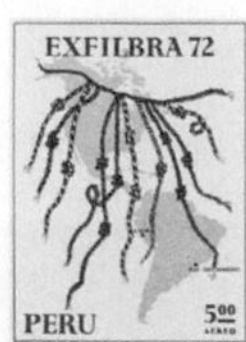

384 "Quipu" on Map

1972. Air. "Exfibra 72" Stamp Exn, Rio de Janeiro.

1148 **384** 5s. multicoloured 1·00 30

385 "The Messenger"

1972. Air. Olympic Games, Munich.

1149 **385** 8s. multicoloured 1·10 55

386 Catacaos Woman

1972. Air. Provincial Costumes (1st series). Multicoloured.

1150 2s. Tupe girl 35 20

1151 3s.50 Type **386** 1·30 55

1152 4s. Conibo Indian 1·50 65

1153 4s.50 Agricultural worker playing "quena" and drum 90 30

1154 5s. "Moche" (Trujillo) girl 75 30

1155 6s.50 Ocongate (Cuzco) man and woman 2·20 85

1156 8s. "Chucupana" (Ayacucho) girl 1·70 65

1157 8s.50 "Cotuncha" (Junin) girl 1·70 65

1158 10s. "Pandilla" dancer 1·70 75

See also Nos. 1248/9.

387 Ruins of Chavin (Ancash)

1972. Air. 25th Death Anniv Julio C. Tello (archaeologist). Multicoloured.

1159 1s.50 "Stone of the 12 Angles", Cuzco (vert) 55 10

1160 3s.50 Type **387** 75 20

1161 4s. Burial-tower, Sillustani (Puno) (vert) 75 20

1162 5s. Gateway, Chavin (Ancash) 1·10 30

1163 8s. "Wall of the 3 Windows", Machu Picchu (Cuzco) 1·80 55

388 "Territorial Waters"

1972. Fourth Anniv of Armed Forces Revolution. Multicoloured.

1164 2s. Agricultural Workers ("Agrarian Reform") (vert) 35 30

1165 2s.50 Type **388** 35 30

1166 3s. Oil rigs ("Nationalization of Petroleum Industry") (vert) 35 30

389 "The Holy Family" (wood-carving)

1972. Christmas. Multicoloured.

1167 1s.50 Type **389** 35 10

1168 2s. "The Holy Family" (carved Huamanga stone) (horiz) 35 20

1169 2s.50 "The Holy Family" (carved Huamanga stone) 35 20

390 "Ipomoea purpurea"

1972. Peruvian Flora (2nd series). Multicoloured.

1170 1s.50 Type **390** 55 20

1171 2s.50 "Amaryllis ferreyrae" 65 20

1172 3s. "Liabum excelsum" 90 20

1173 3s.50 "Bletia catenulata" 1·10 20

1174 5s. "Cantua buxifolia cantuta" 1·80 55

391 Inca Poncho

1973. Air. Ancient Inca Textiles.

1175 **391** 2s. multicoloured 55 20

1176 - 3s.50 multicoloured 75 30

1177 - 4s. multicoloured 75 30

1178 - 5s. multicoloured 75 55

1179 - 8s. multicoloured 1·90 55

DESIGNS: Nos. 1176/9, similar to T **391**.

392 Mochica Cameo and Cups

1973. Air. Peruvian Art (2nd series). Jewelled Antiquities. Multicoloured.

1180 1s.50 Type **392** 1·20 30

1181 2s.50 Gold-plated arms and hands (Lambayeque) 1·20 30

1182 4s. Bronze effigy (Mochica) 1·20 30

1183 5s. Gold pendants (Nazca) 1·50 65

1184 8s. Gold cat (Mochica) 2·75 75

393 Andean Condor

1973. Air. Fauna Protection (1st series). Multicoloured.

1185 2s.50 Lesser rhea 1·90 30

1186 3s.50 Giant otter 2·75 55

1187 4s. Type **393** 55 20

1188 5s. Vicuna 75 45

1189 6s. Chilian flamingo 3·75 55

1190 8s. Spectacled bear 1·70 75

1191 8s.50 Bush dog (horiz) 3·75 75

1192 10s. Short-tailed chinchilla (horiz) 4·75 1·30

See also Nos. 1245/6.

394 "The Macebearer" (J. Sabogal)

1973. Air. Peruvian Paintings. Multicoloured.

1193		1s.50 Type **394**	35	20
1194		8s. "Yananacu Bridge" (E. C. Brent) (horiz)	1·10	30
1195		8s.50 "Portrait of a Lady" (D. Hernandez)	40	15
1196		10s. "Peruvian Birds" (T. N. Ureta)	1·80	55
1197		20s. "The Potter" (F. Laso)	2·75	1·10
1198		50s. "Reed Boats" (J. V. Reinoso) (horiz)	7·75	2·10

395 Basketball Net and Map

1973. Air. First World Basketball Festival.

1199	**395**	5s. green	65	30
1200	**395**	20s. purple	2·75	85

396 "Spanish Mayor on Horseback"

1973. 170th Birth Anniv of Pancho Fierro (painter). Multicoloured.

1201		1s.50 Type **396**	35	10
1202		2s. "Peasants"	35	10
1203		2s.50 "Father Abregu"	55	20
1204		3s.50 "Dancers"	55	20
1205		4s.50 "Esteban Arredondo on horseback"	1·30	65

1973. Air. Peruvian Flora (3rd series). Orchids. As T **390**. Multicoloured.

1206		1s.50 "Lycaste reichenbachii"	1·50	30
1207		2s.50 "Masdevallia amabilis"	2·00	30
1208		3s. "Sigmatostalix peruviana"	2·10	30
1209		3s.50 "Porrogossum peruvianum"	2·75	30
1210		8s. "Oncidium incarum"	5·50	1·10

398 Fair Emblem (poster)

1973. Air. Eighth International Pacific Fair, Lima.

1211	**398**	8s. red, black and grey	1·10	30

399 Symbol of Flight

1973. Air. 50th Anniv of Air Force Officers' School.

1212	**399**	8s.50 multicoloured	1·10	30

400 "The Presentation of the Child"

1973. Christmas. Paintings of the Cuzco School. Multicoloured.

1213		1s.50 Type **400**	20	10
1214		2s. "The Holy Family" (vert)	35	20
1215		2s.50 "The Adoration of the Kings"	35	30

401 Freighter "Ilo"

1973. Air. National Development. Multicoloured.

1216		1s.50 Type **401**	20	20
1217		2s.50 Trawlers	35	30
1218		8s. B.A.C. One Eleven 200 airliner and seagull	1·50	30

402 House of the Mulberry Tree, Arequipa

1974. Air. "Landscapes and Cities". Multicoloured.

1219		1s.50 Type **402**	20	10
1220		2s.50 El Misti (peak), Arequipa	55	10
1221		5s. Giant puya, Cordillera Blanca, Ancash (vert)	75	20
1222		6s. Huascaran (peak), Cordillera Blanca, Ancash	1·10	20
1223		8s. Lake Querococha, Cordillera Blanca, Ancash	1·80	65

403 Peruvian 2c. Stamp of 1873

1974. Stamp Day and 25th Anniv of Peruvian Philatelic Association.

1224	**403**	6s. blue and grey	90	30

404 Room of the Three Windows, Machu Picchu

1974. Air. Archaeological Discoveries. Multicoloured. (a) Cuzco Relics.

1225		3s. Type **404**	75	20
1226		5s. Baths of Tampumacchay	75	20
1227		10s. "Kencco"	1·10	20

(b) Dr. Tello's Discoveries at Chavin de Huantar. Stone carvings.

1228		3s. Mythological jaguar (vert)	1·10	20
1229		5s. Rodent ("Vizcacha") (vert)	2·20	65
1230		10s. Chavin warrior (vert)	2·20	65

405 Church of San Jeronimo, Cuzco

1974. Air. Architectural Treasures. Multicoloured.

1231		1s.50 Type **405**	90	30
1232		3s.50 Cathedral of Santa Catalina, Cajamarca	90	30
1233		5s. Church of San Pedro, Zepita, Puno (horiz)	1·30	30
1234		6s. Cuzco Cathedral	1·30	45
1235		8s.50 Wall of the Coricancha, Cuzco	2·20	55

406 "Colombia" Bridge, Tarapoto–Juanjui Highway

1974. "Structural Changes". Multicoloured.

1236		2s. Type **406**	20	10
1237		8s. Tayacaja hydro-electric scheme	1·10	55
1238		10s. Tablachaca dam	1·10	55

407 "Battle of Junin" (F. Yanez)

1974. 150th Anniv of Battle of Junin.

1239	**407**	1s.50 mult (postage)	20	20
1240	**407**	2s.50 multicoloured	35	30
1241	**407**	6s. multicoloured (air)	90	30

408 "Battle of Ayacucho" (F. Yanez)

1974. 150th Anniv of Battle of Ayacucho.

1242	**408**	2s. mult (postage)	20	20
1243	**408**	3s. multicoloured	35	30
1244	**408**	7s.50 multicoloured (air)	90	30

1974. Air. Fauna Protection (2nd series). As T **393**. Multicoloured.

1245		8s. Red uakari	1·10	20
1246		20s. As 8s.	2·75	1·10

409 Chimu Gold Mask

1974. Air. Eighth World Mining Congress, Lima.

1247	**409**	8s. multicoloured	1·90	30

1974. Air. Provincial Costumes (2nd series). As T **386**. Multicoloured.

1248		5s. Horseman in "chalan" (Cajamarca)	55	20
1249		8s.50 As 5s.	1·10	55

410 Pedro Paulet and Spacecraft

1974. Air. Centenary of U.P.U. and Birth Centenary of Pedro E. Paulet (aviation scientist).

1250	**410**	8s. violet and blue	75	30

411 Copper Smelter, La Oroya

1974. Expropriation of Cerro de Pasco Mining Complex.

1251	**411**	1s.50 blue and deep blue	20	10
1252	**411**	3s. red and brown	55	20
1253	**411**	4s.50 green and grey	90	45

412 "Capitulation of Ayacucho" (D. Hernandez)

1974. Air. 150th Anniv of Spanish Forces' Capitulation at Ayacucho.

1254	**412**	3s.50 multicoloured	55	20
1255	**412**	8s.50 multicoloured	1·10	30
1256	**412**	10s. multicoloured	1·30	65

413 "Madonna and Child"

1974. Christmas. Paintings of the Cuzco Shool. Multicoloured.

1257		1s.50 Type **413** (postage)	20	20
1258		6s.50 "Holy Family" (air)	55	30

414 "Andean Landscape" (T. Nunez Ureta)

1974. Air. Andean Pact Communications Ministers' Meeting, Cali, Colombia.

1259	**414**	6s.50 multicoloured	65	45

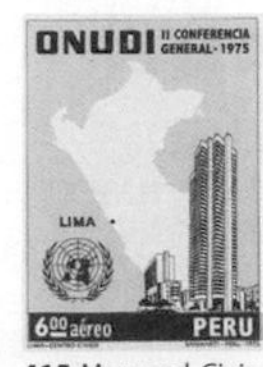

415 Map and Civic Centre, Lima

1975. Air. Second General Conference of U.N. Organization for Industrial Development.

1260	**415**	6s. black, red and grey	55	20

1975. Air. Various stamps surch.

1261	-	1s.50 on 3s.60 purple (No. 927)	35	20
1262	-	2s. on 2s.60 green (No. 926)	35	20
1263	-	2s. on 3s.60 purple (No. 927)	35	20
1263a	-	2s. on 3s.60 black and blue (No. 934)	35	20
1264	-	2s. on 4s.30 orange (No. 878)	45	20
1265	-	2s. on 4s.30 multicoloured (No. 900)	35	20
1266	-	2s. on 4s.60 orange (No. 928)	35	20
1267	-	2s.50 on 4s.60 orange (No. 928)	55	20
1268	-	3s. on 2s.60 green (No. 926)	45	20
1294	-	3s.50 on 4s.60 orange (No. 928)	20	20
1269	-	4s. on 2s.60 green (No. 926)	45	30
1270	-	4s. on 3s.60 purple (No. 927)	45	30
1271	-	4s. on 4s.60 orange (No. 928)	45	20
1295	-	4s.50 on 3s.80 orange (No. 836)	20	20
1272	-	5s. on 3s.60 purple (No. 927)	35	20
1273	-	5s. on 3s.80 orange (No. 836)	55	45
1296	-	5s. on 4s.30 orange (No. 878)	35	20
1277	**316**	6s. on 4s.60 multicoloured (No. 935)	65	30
1297	-	6c. on 4s.60 orange (No. 928)	55	20
1278	-	7s. on 4s.30 orange (No. 878)	45	30
1279	-	7s.50 on 3s.60 purple (No. 927)	75	45
1280	-	8s. on 3s.60 purple (No. 927)	1·00	30
1281	**271**	10s. on 2s.15 purple (No. 794)	75	30
1298	-	10s. on 2s.60 green (No. 926)	65	65
1282	-	10s. on 3s.60 purple (No. 927)	1·20	45
1283	-	10s. on 3s.60 multicoloured (No. 940)	1·10	45
1284	-	10s. on 4s.30 orange (No. 878)	55	30
1285	-	10s. on 4s.60 orange (No. 928)	1·10	30
1286	-	20s. on 3s.60 purple (No. 927)	1·10	65
1287	-	24s. on 3s.60 multicoloured (No. 953)	1·10	65
1288	-	28s. on 4s.60 multicoloured (No. 954)	2·20	1·10
1289	-	32s. on 5s.60 multicoloured (No. 955)	2·20	1·10
1290	-	50s. on 2s.60 green (No. 926)	5·50	1·80
1299	-	50s. on 3s.60 purple (No. 927)	1·30	2·10
1292	-	100s. on 3s.80 orange (No. 836)	5·50	3·75

417 Lima on World Map

1975. Air. Conference of Non-aligned Countries' Foreign Ministers, Lima.

1311	**417**	6s.50 multicoloured	1·10	30

418 Maria Parado de Bellido

1975. "Year of Peruvian Women" and International Women's Year. Multicoloured.

1312	1s.50 Type **418**	20	10
1313	2s. Micaela Bastidas (vert)	35	10
1314	2s.50 Juana Alarco de Dammert	35	10
1315	3s. I.W.Y. emblem (vert)	65	10

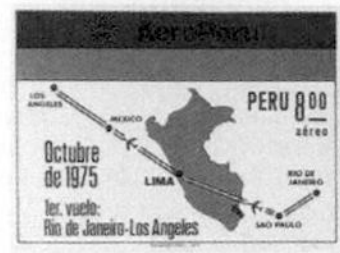

419 Route Map of Flight

1975. Air. First "Aero Peru" Flight, Rio de Janeiro–Lima–Los Angeles.

1316	**419**	8s. multicoloured	1·00	30

420 San Juan Macias

1975. Canonization of St. Juan Macias.

1317	**420**	5s. multicoloured	55	20

421 Fair Poster

1975. Air. Ninth International Pacific Fair, Lima.

1318	**421**	6s. red, brown and black	75	30

422 Col. F. Bolognesi

1975. Air. 159th Birth Anniv of Colonel Francisco Bolognesi.

1319	**422**	20s. multicoloured	2·75	85

423 "Nativity"

1976. Air. Christmas (1975).

1320	**423**	6s. multicoloured	75	30

424 Louis Braille

1976. 150th Anniv of Braille System for Blind.

1321	**424**	4s.50 red, black and grey	55	20

426 Inca Postal Runner

1976. Air. 11th UPAE Congress, Lima.

1322	**426**	5s. black, brown and red	75	20

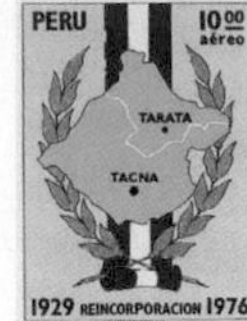

427 Map on Riband

1976. Air. Reincorporation of Tacna.

1323	**427**	10s. multicoloured	75	30

428 Peruvian Flag

1976. First Anniv of Second Phase of Revolution.

1324	**428**	5s. red, black and grey	35	20

429 Police Badge

1976. Air. 54th Anniv of Peruvian Special Police.

1325	**429**	20s. multicoloured	1·30	75

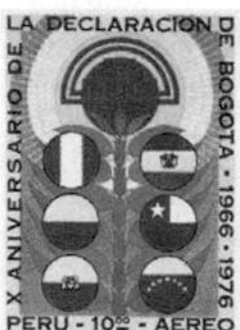

430 "Tree of Badges"

1976. Air. Tenth Anniv of Bogota Declaration.

1326	**430**	10s. multicoloured	75	20

431 Chairman Pal Losonczi

1976. Air. Visit of Hungarian Head of State.

1327	**431**	7s. black and blue	75	30

432 "St. Francis of Assisi" (El Greco)

1976. 750th Death Anniv of St. Francis of Assisi.

1328	**432**	5s. brown and gold	75	20

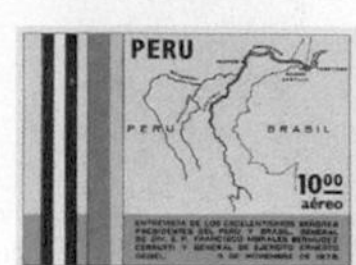

433 Map and National Colours

1976. Air. Meeting of Presidents of Peru and Brazil.

1329	**433**	10s. multicoloured	75	30

434 "Nativity"

1976. Christmas.

1330	**434**	4s. multicoloured	65	20

435 Military Monument and Symbols

1977. Air. Army Day.

1331	**435**	20s. black, buff and red	1·70	75

436 Map and Scroll

1977. Air. Visit of Peruvian President to Venezuela.

1332	**436**	12s. multicoloured	1·10	55

437 Printed Circuit

1977. Air. World Telecommunications Day.

1333	**437**	20s. red, black and silver	2·20	75

438 Inca Postal Runner

1977

1334	**438**	6s. black and turquoise (postage)	55	20
1335	**438**	8s. black and red	55	20
1336	**438**	10s. black and blue	55	55
1337	**438**	12s. black and green	55	55
1338	**438**	24s. black and red (air)	1·70	75
1339	**438**	28s. black and blue	2·75	75
1340	**438**	32s. black and brown	1·70	1·10

439 Petrochemical Plant, Map and Tanker

1977. Air. Bayovar Petrochemical Complex.

1341	**439**	14s. multicoloured	75	55

440 Arms of Arequipa

1977. Air. "Gold of Peru" Exhibition, Arequipa.

1342	**440**	10s. multicoloured	35	20

441 President Videla

1977. Air. Visit of President Videla of Argentina.

1343	**441**	36s. multicoloured	1·10	30

1977. Various stamps surch **FRANQUEO** and new value.

1344	**325**	6s. on 3s.60 multicoloured	75	55
1345	**325**	8s. on 3s.60 multicoloured	90	65
1347	**305**	10s. on 50c. black & grn	45	30
1346	-	10s. on 5s.60 brown, black and red (No. 962)	1·10	75
1348	**305**	20s. on 20c. black and red	90	55
1349	**305**	30s. on 1s. black and blue	1·20	75

444 Fair Emblem and Flags

1977. Tenth International Pacific Fair.

1350	**444**	10s. multicoloured	35	20

445 Republican Guard Badge

1977. 58th Anniv of Republican Guard.

1351	**445**	12s. multicoloured	55	30

446 Admiral Miguel Grau

1977. Air. Navy Day.

1352	**446**	28s. multicoloured	75	45

447 "The Holy Family"

1977. Christmas. Multicoloured.

1353	8s. Type **447** (postage)	45	20
1354	20s. "The Adoration of the Shepherds" (air)	75	55

448 Open Book of Flags

1978. Air. Eighth Meeting of Education Ministers.

1355	**448**	30s. multicoloured	10	10

449 Inca Head

1978

1356	**449**	6s. green (postage)	10	10
1357	**449**	10s. red	20	20
1358	**449**	16s. brown	45	45
1359	**449**	24s. mauve (air)	65	20
1360	**449**	30s. pink	75	20
1361	**449**	65s. blue	1·80	1·10
1362	**449**	95s. blue	2·75	1·10

450 Emblem and Flags of West Germany, Argentina, Austria and Brazil

1978. World Cup Football Championship, Argentina (1st issue). Multicoloured.

1367		10s. Type **450**	65	30
1368		10s. Emblem and flags of Hungary, Iran, Italy and Mexico	65	30
1369		10s. Emblem and flags of Scotland, Spain, France and Netherlands	65	30
1370		10s. Emblem and flags of Peru, Poland, Sweden and Tunisia	65	30

See also Nos. 1412/15.

451 Microwave Antenna

1978. Air. Tenth World Telecommunications Day.

1371	**451**	50s. grey, deep blue and blue	1·20	1·20

1978. Various stamps surch **Habilitado Dif.-Porte** and value (Nos. 1372/4), **Habilitado R.D. No. 0118** and value (Nos. 1377/8, 1381, 1384, 1390) or with value only (others).

1372	**229**	2s. on 2c. brown (postage)	20	20
1373	**229**	4s. on 2c. brown	20	20
1374	**229**	5s. on 2c. brown	20	20
1375	**313**	20s. on 1s.90+90c. multicoloured	1·10	1·10
1376	-	30s. on 2s.60+1s.30 multicoloured (No. 917)	1·10	1·10
1377	**229**	35s. on 2c. brown	1·70	1·60
1378	**229**	50s. on 2c. brown	5·50	5·25
1379	-	55s. on 3s.60+1s.80 multicoloured (No. 918)	1·70	1·60
1380	-	65s. on 4s.60+2s.30 multicoloured (No. 919)	1·70	1·60
1381	-	80s. on 5s.60 mult (No. 960)	1·40	1·40
1382	-	85s. on 20s.+10s. multicoloured (No. 920)	2·75	2·75
1383	-	25s. on 4s.60 mult (No. 954) (air)	55	45
1384	**316**	34s. on 4s.60 mult	55	45
1385	**302**	40s. on 4s.30 bistre and red	65	55
1386	**449**	45s. on 28s. green	1·10	55
1387	-	70s. on 2s.60 green (No. 926)	1·10	85
1388	**449**	75s. on 28s. green	1·70	1·10
1389	-	105s. on 5s.60 mult (No. 955)	2·40	1·60
1390	-	110s. on 3s.60 purple (No. 927)	2·75	65
1391	-	265s. on 4s.30 mult (No. 900)	4·00	3·75

The 28s. value as Type **449** was not issued without a surcharge.

1978. Surch **SOBRE TASA OFICIAL** and value.

1400	**229**	3s. on 2s. brown	20	20
1401	**229**	6s. on 2c. brown	20	20

456 San Martin

1978. Air. Birth Bicentenary of General Jose de San Martin.

1410	**456**	30s. multicoloured	75	75

457 Elmer Faucett and Stinson-Faucett F-19 and Boeing 727-200 Aircraft

1978. 50th Anniv of Faucett Aviation.

1411	**457**	40s. multicoloured	1·00	45

1978. World Cup Football Championship, Argentina (2nd issue). Multicoloured.

1412		16s. As Type **450**	65	45
1413		16s. As No. 1368	65	45
1414		16s. As No. 1369	65	45
1415		16s. As No. 1370	65	45

458 Nazca Bowl

1978

1416	**458**	16s. blue	55	20
1417	**458**	20s. green	55	20
1418	**458**	25s. green	65	20
1419	**458**	35s. red	1·10	30
1420	**458**	45s. brown	1·30	55
1421	**458**	50s. black	1·50	65
1422	**458**	55s. mauve	1·50	65
1423	**458**	70s. mauve	1·90	95
1424	**458**	75s. blue	2·10	75
1425	**458**	80s. brown	2·10	95
1426	**458**	200s. violet	5·25	3·25

459 Peruvian Nativity

1978. Christmas.

1436	**459**	16s. multicoloured	65	45

460 Ministry of Education, Lima

1979. National Education.

1437	**460**	16s. multicoloured	45	45

461 Queen Sophia and King Juan Carlos

1979. Air. Visit of King and Queen of Spain.

1438	**461**	75s. multicoloured	1·10	30

462 Red Cross Emblem

1979. Centenary of Peruvian Red Cross Society.

1439	**462**	16s. multicoloured	45	45

463 "Naval Battle of Iquique" (E. Velarde)

1979. Pacific War Centenary. Multicoloured.

1440		14s. Type **463**	45	45
1441		25s. "Col. Jose Joaquin Inclan" (vert)	65	30
1442		25s. "Arica Blockade-runner, the Corvette "Union"	1·00	45
1443		25s. "Heroes of Angamos"	1·00	45
1444		25s. "Lt. Col. Pedro Ruiz Gallo" (vert)	55	10
1445		85s. "Marshal Andres H. Caceres" (vert)	1·10	75
1446		100s. "Battle of Angamos" (T. Castillo)	1·20	75
1447		100s. "Battle of Tarapaca"	1·30	75
1448		115s. "Admiral Miguel Grau" (vert)	2·40	1·40
1449		200s. "Bolognesi's Reply" (Leppiani)	2·40	1·90
1450		200s. "Col. Francisco Bolognesi" (vert)	2·40	1·90
1451		200s. "Col. Alfonso Ugarte" (Morizani)	3·50	1·90

A similar 200s. value, showing the Crypt of the Fallen was on sale for a very limited period only.

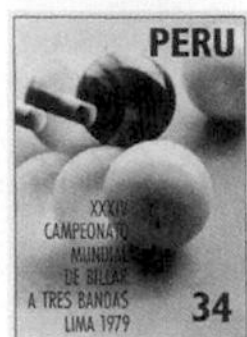

464 Billiard Balls and Cue

1979. 34th World Billiards Championship, Lima.

1456	**464**	34s. multicoloured	65	45

465 Arms of Cuzco

1979. Inca Sun Festival, Cuzco.

1457	**465**	50s. multicoloured	1·40	45

466 Flag and Arch

1979. 50th Anniv of Reincorporation of Tacna into Peru.

1458	**466**	16s. multicoloured	65	45

1979. Surch in figures only.

1459	**229**	7s. on 2c. brown	45	45
1460	**229**	9s. on 2c. brown	45	45
1461	**229**	15s. on 2c. brown	45	45

468 Exposition Emblem

1979. Third World Telecommunications Exhibition, Geneva.

1467	**468**	15s. orange, blue and grey	45	45

469 Caduceus

1979. Int Stomatology Congress, Lima, and 50th Anniv of Peruvian Academy of Stomatology.

1468	**469**	25s. gold, black & turq	45	45

470 Fair Emblem on World Map

1979. 11th International Pacific Fair.

1469	**470**	55s. multicoloured	75	55

471 Regalia of Chimu Chief (Imperial period)

1979. Rafael Larco Herrera Museum of Archaeology.

1470	**471**	85s. multicoloured	2·00	65

472 Angel with Lute

1980. Christmas.

1471	**472**	25s. multicoloured	65	45

1980. Various stamps surch.

1472	**466**	20s. on 16s. multicoloured (postage)	45	45
1473	**463**	25s. on 14s. multicoloured	55	45
1474	**464**	65s. on 34s. multicoloured	1·00	75
1475	**458**	80s. on 70s. mauve	1·40	55
1476	**449**	35s. on 24s. mauve (air)	55	45
1477	**438**	45s. on 32s. black and brown	5·50	45

474 "Respect and Comply with the Constitution"

1980. Citizens' Duties.

1478	**474**	15s. turquoise	40	55
1479	-	20s. red	45	45
1480	-	25s. blue	45	45
1481	-	30s. mauve	45	45
1482	-	35s. black	45	45
1483	-	45s. green	55	45
1484	-	50s. brown	1·00	45

INSCRIPTIONS: 20s. "Honour your country and protect your interests"; 25s. "Comply with the elective process"; 30s. "Comply with your military service"; 35s. "Pay your taxes"; 45s. "Work and contribute to national progress"; 50s. "Respect the rights of others".

475 Ceramic Vase (Chimu Culture)

1980. Rafael Larco Herrera Archaeological Museum.

1485	**475**	35s. multicoloured	1·20	45

476 "Liberty" and Map of Peru

1980. Return to Democracy.

1486	**476**	25s. black, buff and red	65	45
1487	-	35s. black and red	90	45

DESIGN: 35s. Handshake.

477 Machu Picchu

1980. World Tourism Conference, Manila.

1488	**477**	25s. multicoloured	2·40	45

478 Rebellion Memorial, Cuzco (Joaquin Ugarte)

1980. Bicentenary of Tupac Amaru Rebellion.

1489	**478**	25s. multicoloured	45	30

See also No. 1503.

479 Nativity

1980. Christmas.

1490	**479**	15s. multicoloured	65	45

480 Bolivar and Flags

1981. 150th Death Anniv of Simon Bolivar.

1491	**480**	40s. multicoloured	55	30

1981. Various stamps surch.

1492	-	25s. on 35s. black and red (No. 1487)	35	20
1493	**482**	40s. on 25s. multicoloured	1·00	55
1494	**458**	85s. on 200s. violet	1·20	85
1495	-	100s. on 115s. mult (No. 1448)	1·30	95
1496	**482**	130s. on 25s. mult	1·00	55
1497	**482**	140s. on 25s. mult	1·00	55

482 Presidential Badge of Office, Laurel Leaves and Open Book

1981. Re-establishment of Constitutional Government.

1498	25s. multicoloured	65	45

483 Stone Head, Pallasca

1981

1499	**483**	30s. violet	75	45
1500	-	40s. blue	90	45
1501	-	100s. mauve	2·20	85
1502	-	140s. green	3·00	1·30

DESIGNS—VERT: 40s. Stone head, Huamachuco; 100s. Stone head (Chavin culture). HORIZ: 140s. Stone puma head (Chavin culture).

484 Tupac Amaru and Micaela Bastidas (sculptures by Miguel Boca Rossi)

1981. Bicentenary of Revolution of Tupac Amaru and Micaela Bastidas.

1503	**484**	60s. multicoloured	90	65

485 Post Box, 1859

1981. 50th Anniv of Postal and Philatelic Museum, Lima.

1504	**485**	130s. multicoloured	1·10	1·10

486 Map of Peru and I.Y.D.P. Emblem

1981. International Year of Disabled Persons.

1505	**486**	100s. violet, mauve and gold	1·50	75

487 Victor Raul Haya de la Torre (President of Constitutional Assembly)

1981. Constitution.

1506	**487**	30s. violet and grey	45	45

1981. No. 801 surch.

1507	30s. on 2s.20 brown & blue	55	55
1508	40s. on 2s.20 brown & blue	55	30

1981. 12th International Pacific Fair. No. 801 surch with **12 Feria Internacional del Pacifico 1981 140**.

1509	140s. on 2s.20 brown & blue	2·00	1·30

490 Inca Messenger (drawing by Guaman Ponce de Ayala)

1981. Christmas.

1510	**490**	30s. black and mauve	1·70	30
1511	**490**	40s. black and red	1·30	65
1512	**490**	130s. black and green	3·25	75
1513	**490**	140s. black and blue	3·25	95
1514	**490**	200s. black and brown	5·00	1·30

1982. Various stamps surch **Habilitado Franq**. Postal and value (Nos. 1520/1) or with value only (others).

1515	**229**	10s. on 2c. brown (postage)	45	45
1516	-	10s. on 10c. red (No. 642)	35	20
1517	**292**	40s. on 10c. blue and yellow	35	20
1518	**273**	70s. on 5c. blue and red	45	30
1519	**264a**	80s. on 3c. lake	35	20
1520	**D 109**	80s. on 10c. green	35	20
1521	**O 108**	80s. on 10c. brown	35	20
1522	**292**	100s. on 10c. blue and yellow	45	45
1523	-	140s. on 50c. brown, yellow and red	55	45
1524	-	140s. on 1s. mult	55	45
1525	**264a**	150s. on 3c. lake	65	65
1526	**264a**	180s. on 3c. lake	65	65
1527	**264a**	200s. on 3c. lake	75	75
1528	**273**	280s. on 5c. blue and red	1·20	1·20
1529	-	40s. on 1s.25 blue and purple (No. 814) (air)	35	20
1530	-	100s. on 2s.20 brown and blue (No. 801)	55	55
1531	-	240s. on 1s.25 blue and purple (No. 814)	1·30	1·30

Nos. 1523/4 are surcharged on labels for the Seventh Eucharistic Congress which previously had no postal validity.

493 Inca Pot

1982. Indian Ceramics.

1532	**493**	40s. orange	90	30
1533	**493**	80s. lilac	2·20	85
1534	-	80s. red	2·20	65
1535	**493**	180s. green	5·25	95
1536	-	240s. blue	3·00	1·20
1537	-	280s. violet	4·25	1·60

DESIGNS: 80s., (No. 1534), 240, 280s. Nazca fish ceramic.

494 Jorge Basadre (after Oscar Lopez Aliaga)

1982. Jorge Basadre (historian) Commemoration.

1538	**494**	100s. black and green	45	30

495 Julio C. Tello (bust, Victoria Macho)

1982. Birth Centenary of Julio C. Tello (archaeologist).

1539	**495**	200s. green and blue	90	55

496 Championship Emblem

1982. Ninth World Women's Volleyball Championship, Peru.

1540	**496**	80s. red and black	35	30

497 Disabled Person in Wheelchair

1982. Rights for the Disabled Year.

1541	**497**	200s. blue and red	1·10	30

498 Andres A. Caceres Medallion

1982. Centenary of Brena Campaign.

1542	**498**	70s. brown and grey	35	30

499 Footballers

1982. World Cup Football Championship, Spain.

1543	**499**	80s. multicoloured	1·00	30

500 Congress Emblem

1982. 16th Int Latin Notaries Congress, Lima.

1544	**500**	500s. black, gold and red	1·70	1·10

501 Bull (clay jar)

1982. Handicrafts Year.

1545	**501**	200s. red, brown and black	65	30

502 Pedro Vilcapaza

1982. Death Bicentenary of Pedro Vilcapaza (Indian leader).

1546	**502**	240s. brown and black	75	55

503 Jose Davila Condemarin (after J. Y. Pastor)

1982. Death Centenary of Jose Davila Condemarin (Director General of Posts).

1547	**503**	150s. black and blue	45	45

504 "Nativity" (Hilario Mendivil)

1982. Christmas.

1548	**504**	280s. multicoloured	90	85

505 Centre Emblem and Hand holding Potatoes

1982. Tenth Anniv of International Potato Centre.

1549	**505**	240s. brown and grey	75	55

506 Arms of Piura

1982. 450th Anniv of San Miguel de Piura.

1550	**506**	280s. multicoloured	1·10	75

507 Microscope

1982. Centenary of Discovery of Tubercule Bacillus.

1551	**507**	240s. green	75	75

508 "St. Theresa of Avila" (Jose Espinoza de los Monteros)

1983. 400th Death Anniv of St. Theresa of Avila.

1552	**508**	100s. multicoloured	35	30

509 Civil Defence Badge and Interlocked Hands

1983. Tenth Anniv of Civil Defence System.

1553	**509**	100s. blue, orange & blk	35	30

510 Silver Shoe

1983. "Peru, Land of Silver".

1554	**510**	250s. silver, black & blue	75	55

511 Map of Signatories and 200 Mile Zone

1983. 30th Anniv of Santiago Declaration.

1555	**511**	280s. brown, blue & black	1·10	75

512 Boeing 747-200

1983. 25th Anniv of Lima–Bogota Airmail Service.

1556	**512**	150s. multicoloured	75	20

513 "75"

1983. 75th Anniv of Lima and Callao State Lotteries.

1557	**513**	100s. blue and purple	35	20

514 Cruiser "Almirante Grau"

1983. Peruvian Navy. Multicoloured.

1558	150s. Type **514**	1·00	30
1559	350s. Submarine "Ferre"	2·75	65

1983. Various stamps surch.

1560	**493**	100s. on 40s. orange	1·40	20
1561	**498**	100s. on 70s. brown and grey	1·40	20
1562	**496**	100s. on 80s. red and black	1·40	20
1563	**502**	100s. on 240s. brown and black	1·40	20
1564	**505**	100s. on 240s. ochre, deep brown and brown	1·40	20
1565	**507**	100s. on 240s. green	1·40	20
1566	**506**	150s. on 280s. mult	1·80	65
1567	**511**	150s. on 280s. brown, blue and black	1·80	65
1568	**504**	200s. on 280s. mult	2·75	75
1569	**493**	300s. on 180s. green	4·25	1·30
1570	**493**	400s. on 180s. green	5·00	1·60
1571	**499**	500s. on 80s. mult	6·50	1·80

516 Simon Bolivar

1983. Birth Bicentenary of Simon Bolivar.

1572	**516**	100s. blue and black	90	30

517 "Virgin and Child" (Cuzquena School)

1983. Christmas.

1573	**517**	100s. multicoloured	1·20	30

518 Fair Emblem

1983. 14th International Pacific Fair.

1574	**518**	350s. multicoloured	1·20	65

519 W.C.Y. Emblem

1984. World Communications Year.

1575	**519**	700s. multicoloured	2·75	1·30

520 Leoncio Prado

1984. Death Centenary (1983) of Colonel Leoncio Prado.

1576	**520**	150s. bistre and brown	75	20

521 Container Ship "Presidente Jose Pardo" at Wharf

1984. Peruvian Industry.

1577	**521**	250s. purple	75	30
1578	-	300s. blue	90	30

DESIGN: 300s. "Presidente Jose Pardo" (container ship).

522 Ricardo Palma

1984. 150th Birth Anniv (1983) of Ricardo Palma (writer).

1579	**522**	200s. violet	55	20

523 Pistol Shooting

1984. Olympic Games, Los Angeles.

1580	**523**	500s. mauve and black	1·10	55
1581	-	750s. red and black	1·70	75

DESIGN: 750s. Hurdling.

524 Arms of Callao

1984. Town Arms.

1582	**524**	350s. grey	65	20
1583	-	400s. brown	1·50	30
1584	-	500s. brown	2·00	30

DESIGNS: 400s. Cajamarca; 500s. Ayacucho.

525 Water Jar

1984. Wari Ceramics (1st series).

1585	**525**	100s. brown	90	30
1586	-	150s. brown	90	30
1587	-	200s. brown	90	30

DESIGNS: 150s. Llama; 200s. Vase.
See also Nos. 1616/18.

526 Hendee's Woolly Monkeys

1984. Fauna.

1588	**526**	1000s. multicoloured	2·75	75

527 Signing Declaration of Independence

1984. Declaration of Independence.

1589	**527**	350s. black, brown & red	75	30

528 General Post Office, Lima

1984. Postal Services.

1590	**528**	50s. olive	35	30

529 "Canna edulis"

1984. Flora.

1591	**529**	700s. multicoloured	1·30	55

530 Grau (after Pablo Muniz)

1984. 150th Anniv of Admiral Miguel Grau. Multicoloured.

1592	600s. Type	1·30	30
1593	600s. Battle of Angamos (45×35 mm)	1·30	30
1594	600s. Grau's seat, National Congress	1·30	30
1595	600s. "Battle of Iquique" (Guillermo Spier) (45×35 mm)	1·30	30

531 Hipolito Unanue

1984. 150th Death Anniv (1983) of Hipolito Unanue (founder of School of Medicine).

1596	**531**	50s. green	55	10

532 Destroyer "Almirante Guise"

1984. Peruvian Navy.

1597	**532**	250s. blue	1·00	30
1598	-	400s. turquoise and blue	1·00	30

DESIGN: 400s. River gunboat "America".

533 "The Adoration of the Shepherds"

1984. Christmas.

1599	**533**	1000s. multicoloured	75	55

534 Belaunde

1984. Birth Centenary (1983) of Victor Andres Belaunde (diplomat).

1600	**534**	100s. purple	55	10

535 Street in Cuzco

1984. 450th Anniv of Founding of Cuzco by the Spanish.

1601	**535**	1000s. multicoloured	1·20	55

536 Fair Emblem

1984. 15th International Pacific Fair, Lima.

1602	**536**	1000s. blue and red	1·20	55

537 "Foundation of Lima" (Francisco Gonzalez Gamarra)

1985. 450th Anniv of Lima.
1603 **537** 1500s. multicoloured 2·75 65

538 Pope John Paul II

1985. Papal Visit.
1604 **538** 2000s. multicoloured 3·00 55

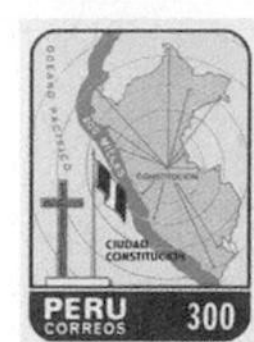

539 Dish Aerial, Huancayo

1985. 15th Anniv (1984) of Entel Peru (National Telecommunications Enterprise).
1605 **539** 1100s. multicoloured 1·30 45

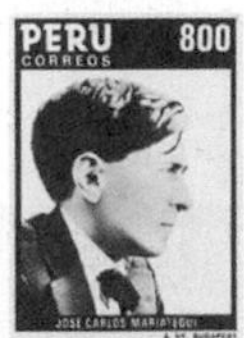

540 Jose Carlos Mariategui

1985. 60th Death Anniv (1984) of Jose Carlos Mariategui (writer).
1606 **540** 800s. red 65 30

541 Emblem

1985. 25th Meeting of American Airforces Co-operation System.
1607 **541** 400s. multicoloured 65 20

542 Captain Quinones

1985. 44th Death Anniv of Jose Abelardo Quinones Gonzales (airforce captain).
1608 **542** 1000s. multicoloured 1·20 45

543 Arms of Huancavelica

1985
1609 **543** 700s. orange 1·00 45
See also Nos. 1628/9.

544 Globe and Emblem

1985. 14th Latin-American Air and Space Regulations Days, Lima.
1610 **544** 900s. blue 75 30

545 Francisco Garcia Calderon (head of 1881 Provisional Government)

1985. Personalities.
1611 **545** 500s. green 55 20
1612 - 800s. green 65 30
DESIGN: 800s. Oscar Miro Quesada (philosopher and jurist).

546 Cross, Flag and Map

1985. First Anniv of Constitucion City.
1613 **546** 300s. multicoloured 75 45

547 General Post Office, Lima

1985. Postal Services.
1614 **547** 200s. grey 75 45

548 Society Emblem, Satellite and Radio Equipment

1985. 55th Anniv of Peruvian Radio Club.
1615 **548** 1300s. blue and orange 1·20 45

549 Robles Moqo Style Cat Vase

1985. Wari Ceramics (2nd series).
1616 **549** 500s. brown 45 45
1617 - 500s. brown 45 45
1618 - 500s. brown 45 45
DESIGNS: No. 1617, Cat, Huaura style; No. 1618, Llama's head, Robles Moqo Style.

550 St. Francis's Monastery, Lima

1985. Tourism Day.
1619 **550** 1300s. multicoloured 75 20

551 Title Page of "Doctrina Christiana"

1985. 400th Anniv of First Book printed in South America.
1620 **551** 300s. black and stone 90 30

552 Emblem and Curtiss "Jenny" Airplane

1985. 40th Anniv of I.C.A.O.
1621 **552** 1100s. black, blue and red 1·00 45

553 Humboldt Penguin

1985. Fauna.
1622 **553** 1500s. multicoloured 1·30 20

554 "Virgin and Child" (Cuzquena School)

1985. Christmas.
1623 **554** 2i.50 multicoloured 1·10 30

555 Postman lifting Child

1985. Postal Workers' Christmas and Children's Restaurant Funds.
1624 **555** 2i.50 multicoloured 75 45

556 Cesar Vallejo

1986. Poets.
1625 **556** 800s. blue 65 30
1626 - 800s. brown 65 30
DESIGN: No. 1626, Jose Santos Chocano.

557 Arms

1986. 450th Anniv of Trujillo.
1627 **557** 3i. multicoloured 1·20 45

1986. Town Arms. As T **543**.
1628 700s. blue 1·00 45
1629 900s. brown 1·40 45
DESIGNS: 700s. Huanuco; 900s. Puno.

558 Stone Carving of Fish

1986. Restoration of Chan-Chan.
1630 **558** 50c. multicoloured 1·10 30

559 "Hymenocallis amancaes"

1986. Flora.
1631 **559** 1100s. multicoloured 1·00 45

560 Alpaca and Textiles

1986. Peruvian Industry.
1632 **560** 1100s. multicoloured 1·00 45

561 St. Rosa de Lima (Daniel Hernandez)

1986. 400th Birth Anniv of St. Rosa de Lima.
1633 **561** 7i. multicoloured 2·75 1·60

562 Daniel Alcides Carrion

1986. Death Centenary (1985) of Daniel Alcides Carrion.
1634 **562** 50c. brown 45 45

563 Emblems and "16"

1986. 16th International Pacific Fair, Lima.
1635 **563** 1i. multicoloured 75 45

564 Woman Handspinning and Boy in Reed Canoe

1986. International Youth Year.
1636 **564** 3i.50 multicoloured 75 55

565 Pedro Vilcapaza

1986. 205th Anniv of Vilcapaza Rebellion.
1637 **565** 50c. brown 55 10

566 U.N. Building, New York

1986. 40th Anniv (1985) of U.N.O.
1638 **566** 3i.50 multicoloured 1·30 55

567 Fernando and Justo Albujar Fayaque and Manuel Guarniz

1986. National Heroes.
1639 **567** 50c. brown 55 10

568 Nasturtium

1986. Flora.
1640 **568** 80c. multicoloured 55 10

569 Submarine "Casma (R-1)", 1926

1986. Peruvian Navy. Each blue.
1641 1i.50 Type **569** 1·10 45
1642 2i.50 Submarine "Abtao", 1954 1·50 45

570 Tinta Costumes, Canchis Province

1986. Costumes.
1643 **570** 3i. multicoloured 1·40 45

571 Sacsayhuaman Fort, Cuzco

1986. Tourism Day (1st issue).
1644 **571** 4i. multicoloured 2·00 75
See also No. 1654.

572 La Tomilla Water Treatment Plant

1986. 25th Anniv of Inter-American Development Bank.
1645 **572** 1i. multicoloured 45 45

573 "Datura candida"

1986. Flora.
1646 **573** 80c. multicoloured 55 20

574 Pope John Paul and Sister Ana

1986. Beatification of Sister Ana of the Angels Monteagudo.
1647 **574** 6i. multicoloured 2·40 85

575 Chavez, Bleriot XI and Simplon Range

1986. 75th Anniv of Trans-Alpine Flight by Jorge Chavez Dartnell.
1648 **575** 5i. multicoloured 1·70 85

576 Emblem

1986. National Vaccination Days.
1649 **576** 50c. blue 45 45

577 "Martyrs of Uchuraccay"

1986. Peruvian Journalists' Fund.
1650 **577** 1i.50 black and blue 55 20

578 "Canis nudus"

1986. Fauna.
1651 **578** 2i. multicoloured 1·30 55

579 Brigantine "Gamarra"

1986. Navy Day.
1652 **579** 1i. blue and light blue 1·00 45
1653 - 1i. blue and red 1·00 45
DESIGN: No. 1653, Battleship "Manco Capac".

580 Intihuatana Cuzco

1986. Tourism Day (2nd issue).
1654 **580** 4i. multicoloured 2·75 65

581 Institute Building

1986. 35th Anniv (1985) of Institute of Higher Military Studies.
1655 **581** 1i. multicoloured 45 20

582 Children

1986. Postal Workers' Christmas and Children's Restaurant Funds.
1656 **582** 2i.50 black and brown 75 55

583 White-winged Guan

1986. Fauna.
1657 **583** 2i. multicoloured 1·70 55

584 Galvez

1986. Birth Centenary (1985) of Jose Galvez Barrenechea (poet).
1658 **584** 50c. brown 45 45

585 "St. Joseph and Child" (Cuzquena School)

1986. Christmas.
1659 **585** 5i. multicoloured 2·10 1·20

586 Flags, and Hands holding Cogwheel

1986. 25th Anniv of "Senati" (National Industrial Training Organization).
1660 **586** 4i. multicoloured 1·30 85

587 Shipibo Costumes

1987. Christmas.
1661 **587** 3i. multicoloured 1·50 85

588 Harvesting Mashua

1987. World Food Day.
1662 **588** 50c. multicoloured 65 20

589 Dr. Reiche and Diagram of Nazca Lines

1987. Dr. Maria Reiche (Nazca Lines researcher).
1663 **589** 8i. multicoloured 3·50 1·70

590 Santos

1987. Mariano Santos (Hero of War of the Pacific).
1664 **590** 50c. violet 55 20

591 Show Jumping

1987. 50th Anniv of Peruvian Horse Club.
1665 **591** 3i. multicoloured 90 65

592 Salaverry

1987. 150th Death Anniv (1986) of General Felipe Santiago Salaverry (President, 1835–36).
1666 **592** 2i. multicoloured 90 45

593 Colca Canyon

1987. "Arequipa 87" National Stamp Exhibition.
1667 **593** 6i. multicoloured 1·00 75

594 1857 1 & 2r. Stamps

1987. "Amifil 87" National Stamp Exhibition, Lima.
1668 **594** 1i. brown, blue and grey 45 45

595 Arguedas

1987. 75th Birth Anniv (1986) of Jose Maria Arguedas (writer).
1669 **595** 50c. brown 45 45

596 Carving, Emblem and Nasturtium

1987. Centenary of Arequipa Chamber of Commerce and Industry.
1670 **596** 2i. multicoloured 45 20

597 Vaccinating Child

1987. Child Vaccination Campaign.
1671 **597** 50c. red 45 45

598 De la Riva Aguero

1987. Birth Centenary (1985) of Jose de la Riva Aguero (historian).
1672 **598** 80c. brown 55 20

599 Porras Barrenechea

1987. 90th Birth Anniv of Raul Porras Barrenechea (historian).
1673 **599** 80c. brown 55 20

600 Footballers

1987. World Cup Football Championship, Mexico (1986).
1674 **600** 4i. multicoloured 1·00 55

601 Stone Carving of Man

1987. Restoration of Chan-Chan.
1675 **601** 50c. multicoloured 1·20 45

602 Comet and "Giotto" Space Probe

1987. Appearance of Halley's Comet (1986).
1676 **602** 4i. multicoloured 1·90 55

603 Chavez

1987. Birth Centenary of Jorge Chavez Dartnell (aviator).
1677 **603** 2i. brown, ochre and gold 65 20

604 Osambela Palace

1987. 450th Birth Anniv of Lima.
1678 **604** 2i.50 multicoloured 65 20

605 Machu Picchu

1987. 75th Anniv (1986) of Discovery of Machu Picchu.
1679 **605** 9i. multicoloured 3·50 95

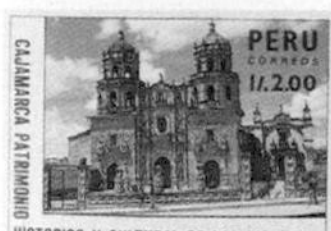

606 St. Francis's Church

1987. Cajamarca, American Historical and Cultural Site.
1680 **606** 2i. multicoloured 55 20

607 National Team, Emblem and Olympic Rings

1988. 50th Anniv (1986) of First Peruvian Participation in Olympic Games (at Berlin).
1681 **607** 1i.50 multicoloured 75 20

608 Children

1988. 150th Anniv of Ministry of Education.
1682 **608** 1i. multicoloured 1·00 55

609 Statue and Pope

1988. Coronation of Virgin of Evangelization, Lima.
1683 **609** 10i. multicoloured 1·00 55

610 Emblems

1988. Rotary International Anti-Polio Campaign.
1684 **610** 2i. blue, gold and red 55 20

611 Postman and Lima Cathedral

1988. Postal Workers' Christmas and Children's Restaurant Funds.
1685 **611** 9i. blue 1·10 30

612 Flags

1988. First Meeting of Eight Latin American Presidents of Contadora and Lima Groups, Acapulco, Mexico.
1686 **612** 9i. multicoloured 1·50 45

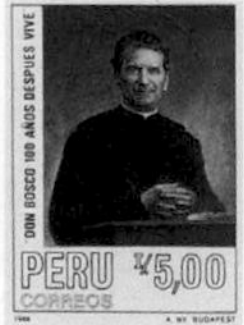

613 St. John Bosco

1988. Death Centenary of St. John Bosco (founder of Salesian Brothers).
1687 **613** 5i. multicoloured 45 45

614 Supply Ship "Humboldt" and Globe

1988. First Peruvian Scientific Expedition to Antarctica.
1688 **614** 7i. multicoloured 65 20

615 Clay Wall

1988. Restoration of Chan-Chan.
1689 **615** 4i. brown and black 55 20

616 Vallejo (after Picasso)

1988. 50th Death Anniv of Cesar Vallejo (poet).
1690 **616** 25i. black, yellow & brn 1·20 55

617 Journalists at Work

1988. Peruvian Journalists' Fund.
1691 **617** 4i. blue and brown 45 45

618 1908 2s. Columbus Monument Stamp

1988. "Exfilima 88" Stamp Exhibition, Lima, and 500th Anniv of Discovery of America by Christopher Columbus.
1692 **618** 20i. blue, pink and black 55 20

619 "17" and Guanaco

1988. 17th International Pacific Fair, Lima.
1693 **619** 4i. multicoloured 1·20 45

620 "Village Band"

1988. Birth Centenary of Jose Sabogal (painter).
1694 **620** 12i. multicoloured 45 45

621 Dogs

1988. "Canino '88" International Dog Show, Lima.
1695 **621** 20i. multicoloured 2·00 55

622 Silva and Score of "Splendour of Flowers"

1988. 50th Death Anniv (1987) of Alfonso de Silva (composer).
1696 **622** 20i. grey, deep brown and brown 75 30

623 Pope

1988. Second Visit of Pope John Paul II.
1697 **623** 50i. multicoloured 75 30

624 Volleyball

1988. Olympic Games, Seoul.
1698 **624** 25i. multicoloured 75 45

625 Volleyball

1988. Postal Workers' Christmas and Children's Restaurant Funds. Unissued stamp surch as in T **625**.
1699 **625** 95i. on 300s. black and red 1·80 75

626 Ceramic Vase

1988. Chavin Culture. Unissued stamps surch as in T **626**.
1700 **626** 40i. on 100s. red 1·50 65
1701 **626** 80i. on 10s. black 2·20 70

627 Map

1989. Forest Boundary Road. Unissued stamp surch as in T **627**.

1702	**627**	70i. on 80s. green, black and blue	60	30

628 Arm

1989. Laws of the Indies. Unissued stamp surch as in T **628**.

1703	**628**	230i. on 300s. brown	1·10	60

629 Huari Weaving

1989. Centenary of Credit Bank of Peru.

1704	**629**	500i. multicoloured	1·70	90

630 Special Postal Services Emblem

1989. Postal Services.

1705	**630**	50i. blue and green	45	35
1706	-	100i. red and pink	55	40

DESIGN: 100i. National Express Post emblem.

631 Newspaper Offices

1989. 150th Anniv of "El Comercio" (newspaper).

1707	**631**	600i. multicoloured	1·20	60

632 Garcilaso de la Vega

1989. 450th Birth Anniv of Garcilaso de la Vega (writer).

1708	**632**	300i. multicoloured	60	25

633 Emblem

1989. Express Mail Service.

1709	**633**	100i. red, blue and orange	45	35

634 Dr. Luis Loli Roca (founder of Journalists' Federation)

1989. Peruvian Journalists' Fund.

1710	**634**	100i. blue, deep blue and black	45	35

635 Relief of Birds

1989. Restoration of Chan-Chan.

1711	**635**	400i. multicoloured	2·40	1·10

636 Old Map of South America

1989. Centenary of Lima Geographical Society.

1712	**636**	600i. multicoloured	2·50	1·30

637 Painting

1989. 132nd Anniv of Society of Founders of Independence.

1713	**637**	300i. multicoloured	60	35

638 Lake Huacachina

1989. Third Meeting of Latin American Presidents of Contadora and Lima Groups, Ica.

1714	**638**	1300i. multicoloured	3·00	1·50

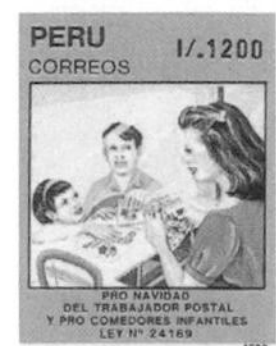

639 Children buying Stamps for Commemorative Envelopes

1989. Postal Workers' Christmas and Children's Restaurant Funds.

1715	**639**	1200i. multicoloured	60	25

640 "Corryocactus huincoensis"

1989. Cacti. Multicoloured.

1716	500i. Type **640**	60	45
1717	500i. "Haagocereus clavispinus" (vert)	60	45
1718	500i. "Loxanthocereus acanthurus"	60	45
1719	500i. "Matucana cereoides" (vert)	60	45
1720	500i. "Trichocereus peruvianus" (vert)	60	45

641 Vessel with Figure of Doctor examining Patient

1989. America. Pre-Columbian Ceramics. Multicoloured.

1721	5000i. Type **641**	8·25	3·50
1722	5000i. Vessel with figure of surgeon performing cranial operation	8·25	3·50

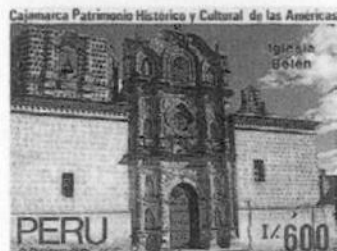

642 Bethlehem Church

1990. Cajamarca, American Historical and Cultural Site.

1723	**642**	600i. multicoloured	1·80	1·20

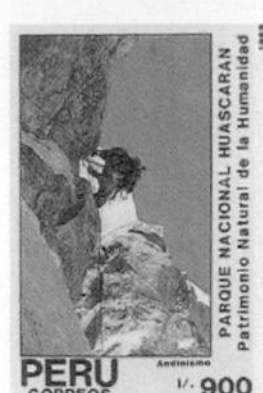

643 Climber in Andes

1990. Huascaran National Park. Multicoloured.

1724	900i. Type **643**	70	45
1725	900i. Llanganuco Lake (horiz)	70	45
1726	1000i. "Puya raimondi" (plant)	85	60
1727	1000i. Snow-covered mountain peak (horiz)	85	60
1728	1100i. Huascaran Mountain (horiz)	95	70
1729	1100i. Andean condor over mountain slopes (horiz)	95	70

644 Pope and Virgin of Evangelization

1990. Second Visit of Pope John Paul II.

1730	**644**	1250i. multicoloured	1·10	45

645 "Agrias beata" (female)

1990. Butterflies. Multicoloured.

1731	1000i. Type **645**	2·40	95
1732	1000i. "Agrias beata" (male)	2·40	95
1733	1000i. "Agrias amydon" (female)	2·40	95
1734	1000i. "Agrias sardanapalus" (female)	2·40	95
1735	1000i. "Agrias sardanapalus" (male)	2·40	95

646 Victor Raul Haya de la Torre (President of Constituent Assembly)

1990. Tenth Anniv of Political Constitution.

1736	**646**	2100i. multicoloured	1·20	60

647 Emblem

1990. 40th Anniv of Peruvian Philatelic Association.

1737	**647**	300i. brown, blk & cream	60	35

648 Globe and Exhibition Emblem

1990. "Prenfil '88" International Philatelic Literature Exhibition, Buenos Aires.

1738	**648**	300i. multicoloured	35	25

649 "Republic" (Antoine-Jean Gros)

1990. Bicentenary of French Revolution. Paintings. Multicoloured.

1739	2000i. Type **649**	95	60
1740	2000i. "Storming the Bastille" (Hubert Robert)	95	60
1741	2000i. "Lafayette at the Festival of the Republic" (anon)	95	60
1742	2000i. "Jean Jacques Rousseau and Symbols of the Revolution" (E. Jeaurat)	95	60

650 "Founding Arequipa" (Teodoro Nunez Ureta)

1990. 450th Anniv of Arequipa.

1743	**650**	50000i. multicoloured	1·20	60

651 Pelado Island Lighthouse

1990. Peruvian Navy. Unissued stamps, each light blue and blue, surch as in T 651.

1744	110000i. on 200i. Type **651**	1·70	75
1745	230000i. on 400i. "Morona" (hospital ship)	3·50	1·50

652 Games Mascot

1990. Fourth South American Games (1st issue). Multicoloured.

1746	110000i. Type **652**	1·20	60
1747	280000i. Shooting	2·75	1·80
1748	290000i. Athletics (horiz)	3·00	1·90
1749	300000i. Football	3·00	1·90

See also Nos. 1753/6.

653 1857 1r. Stamp and Container Ship

1990. 150th Anniv of Pacific Steam Navigation Company. Multicoloured. Self-adhesive.

1750	250000i. Type **653**	3·00	1·80
1751	350000i. 1857 2r. stamp and container ship	4·25	2·50

654 Postal Van

1990. Postal Workers' Christmas and Children's Restaurant Funds.

1752	**654**	310000i. multicoloured	3·50	1·80

1991. Fourth South American Games (2nd issue). As T 652. Multicoloured.

1753	560000i. Swimming	4·25	2·50
1754	580000i. Show jumping (vert)	4·50	3·00

1755		600000i. Yachting (vert)	4·75	3·00
1756		620000i. Tennis (vert)	5·25	3·50

655 Maria Jesus Castaneda de Pardo

1991. Red Cross. Unissued stamp surch.

1757	**655**	0.15i/m. on 2500i. red	1·20	60

Note. "i/m" on No. 1757 onwards indicates face value in million intis.

656 Adelie Penguins, Scientist and Station

1991. Second Peruvian Scientific Expedition to Antarctica. Unissued stamps surch. Multicoloured.

1758		0.40i/m. on 50000i. Type **656**	4·25	1·90
1759		0.45i/m. on 80000i. Station and Pomarine skua	5·00	2·10
1760		0.50i/m. on 100000i. Whale, map and station	5·50	2·50

657 "Siphoonandra elliptica" (plant No. 1 in University herbarium)

1991. 300th Anniv of National University of St. Anthony Abad del Cusco. Multicoloured.

1761		10c. Type **657**	40	25
1762		20c. Bishop Manuel de Mollinedo y Angulo (first Chancellor)	95	60
1763		1s. University arms	4·75	3·00

658 "Virgin of the Milk"

1991. Postal Workers' Christmas and Children's Restaurant Funds. Paintings by unknown artists. Multicoloured.

1764		70c. Type **658**	4·25	3·00
1765		70c. "Divine Shepherdess"	4·25	3·00

659 Lake

1991. America (1990). The Natural World. Multicoloured.

1766		0.50i/m. Type **659**	3·00	1·80
1767		0.50i/m. Waterfall (vert)	3·00	1·80

660 Sir Rowland Hill and Penny Black

1992. 150th Anniv (1990) of the Penny Black.

1768	**660**	0.40i/m. black, grey & bl	1·80	85

661 Arms and College

1992. 150th Anniv (1990) of Our Lady of Guadalupe College.

1769	**661**	0.30i/m. multicoloured	1·40	70

662 Arms

1992. 80th Anniv (1991) of Entre Nous Society, Lima (literature society for women).

1770	**662**	10c. multicoloured	35	25

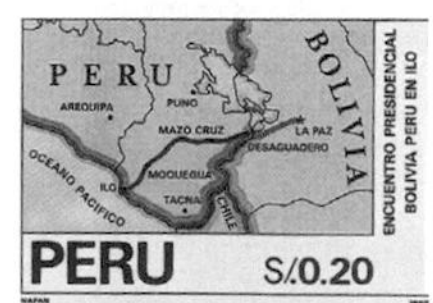

663 Map

1992. Bolivia–Peru Presidential Meeting, Ilo.

1771	**663**	20c. multicoloured	95	60

664 Tacaynamo Idol

1992. Restoration of Chan-Chan.

1772	**664**	0.15i/m. multicoloured	1·30	70

See note below No. 1757.

665 Raimondi

1992. Death Centenary of Jose Antonio Raimondi (naturalist).

1773	**665**	0.30i/m. multicoloured	1·40	85

See note below No. 1757.

666 First Issue

1992. Bicentenary (1990) of "Diario de Lima" (newspaper).

1774	**666**	35c. black and yellow	1·40	85

667 Melgar

1992. Birth Bicentenary (1990) of Mariano Melgar (poet).

1775	**667**	60c. multicoloured	2·50	1·20

668 1568 Eight Silver Reales Coin

1992. First Peruvian Coinage.

1776	**668**	70c. multicoloured	2·50	1·20

669 Emblem

1992. 75th Anniv of Catholic University of Peru.

1777	**669**	90c. black and stone	3·50	1·80

670 Emblem

1992. 90th Anniv of Pan-American Health Organization. Self-adhesive. Imperf.

1778	**670**	3s. multicoloured	7·00	6·00

1992. Various stamps surch.

1779	-	40c. on 500i. multicoloured (1717)	10·50	4·75
1780	-	40c. on 500i. multicoloured (1718)	10·50	4·75
1781	-	40c. on 500i. multicoloured (1719)	10·50	4·75
1782	-	40c. on 500i. multicoloured (1720)	10·50	4·75
1783	**493**	50c. on 180s. green	1·30	85
1784	**648**	50c. on 300i. mult	12·00	5·25
1785	**645**	50c. on 1000i. mult	12·00	5·25
1786	-	50c. on 1000i. mult (1732)	12·00	5·25
1787	-	50c. on 1000i. mult (1733)	12·00	5·25
1788	-	50c. on 1000i. mult (1734)	12·00	5·25
1789	-	50c. on 1000i. mult (1735)	12·00	5·25
1790	**647**	1s. on 300i. brown, black and cream	22·00	6·00
1791	**644**	1s. on 1250i. mult	22·00	6·00
1792	**638**	1s. on 1300i. mult	3·00	1·80

672 "Virgin of the Spindle" (painting, Santa Clara Monastery, Cuzco)

1993. Self-adhesive. Imperf.

1793	**672**	80c. multicoloured	3·00	1·30

673 Gold Figures

1993. Sican Culture (1st series). Multicoloured. Self-adhesive. Imperf.

1794		2s. Type **673**	5·00	3·00
1795		5s. Gold foil figure (vert)	13·00	6·00

See also Nos. 1814/15.

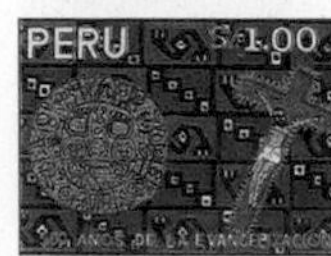

674 Incan Gold Decoration and Crucifix on Chancay Robe

1993. 500th Anniv of Evangelization of Peru.

1796	**674**	1s. multicoloured	3·50	1·50

675 "The Marinera" (Monica Rojas)

1993. Paintings of Traditional Scenes. Multicoloured. Self-adhesive. Imperf.

1797		1s.50 Type **675**	5·25	2·40
1798		1s.50 "Fruit Sellers" (Angel Chavez)	5·25	2·40

676 "Madonna and Child" (statue)

1993. Centenary (1991) of Salesian Brothers in Peru. Self-adhesive. Imperf.

1799	**676**	70c. multicoloured	2·10	95

677 Francisco Pizarro and Spanish Galleon

1993. America (1991). Voyages of Discovery. Multicoloured.

1800		90c. Type **677**	2·00	1·20
1801		1s. Spanish galleon and route map of Pizarros' second voyage	2·40	1·40

Nos. 1800/1 were issued together, se-tenant, forming a composite design.

678 Gold Mask

1993. Jewels from Funerary Chamber of "Senor of Sipan" (1st series).

1802	**678**	50c. multicoloured	12·00	10·50

See also Nos. 1830/1.

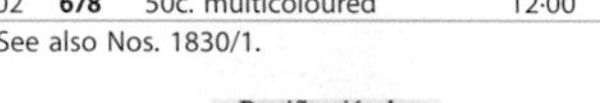

679 Escriva

1993. First Anniv of Beatification of Josemaria Escriva (founder of Opus Dei). Self-adhesive. Imperf.

1803	**679**	30c. multicoloured	95	40

680 Cherry Blossom and Nazca Lines Hummingbird

1993. 120th Anniv of Diplomatic Relations and Peace, Friendship, Commerce and Navigation Treaty with Japan. Multicoloured.

1804		1s.50 Type **680**	4·25	1·80
1805		1s.70 Peruvian and Japanese children and Mts. Huascaran (Peru) and Fuji (Japan)	4·25	2·00

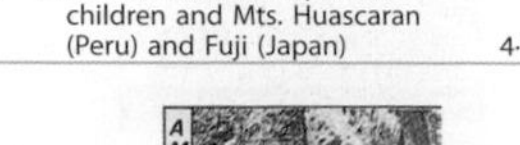

681 Sea Lions

1993. Stamp Exhibitions. Multicoloured.

1806 90c. Type **681** ("Amifil '93" National Stamp Exhibition, Lima) 2·40 95

1807 1s. Blue and yellow macaw ("Brasiliana '93" International Stamp Exhibition, Rio de Janeiro) (vert) 2·50 1·20

682 Delgado

1993. Birth Centenary of Dr. Honorio Delgado (psychiatrist and neurologist). Self-adhesive. Imperf.

1808 **682** 50c. brown 1·70 70

683 Morales Macedo

1993. Birth Centenary of Rosalia de Lavalle de Morales Macedo (founder of Society for Protection of Children and of Christian Co-operation Bank). Self-adhesive. Imperf.

1809 **683** 80c. orange 3·00 1·30

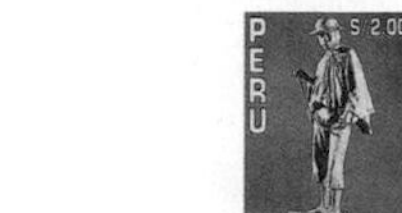

684 "The Sling" (Quechua Indians)

1993. Ethnic Groups (1st series). Statuettes by Felipe Lettersten. Multicoloured. Self-adhesive. Imperf.

1810 2s. Type **684** 13·00 4·75

1811 3s.50 "Fire" (Orejon Indians) 15·00 7·75

See also Nos. 1850/1.

685 "20" on Stamp

1993. 20th International Pacific Fair.

1812 **685** 1s.50 multicoloured 6·50 3·50

686 "Virgin of Loreta"

1993. Christmas.

1813 **686** 1s. multicoloured 3·00 1·50

687 Artefacts from Tomb, Poma

1993. Sican Culture (2nd series). Multicoloured. Self-adhesive. Imperf.

1814 2s.50 Type **687** 12·00 7·00

1815 4s. Gold mask 19·00 10·50

688 Ceramic Figure

1993. Chancay Culture. Multicoloured. Self-adhesive. Imperf.

1816 10s. Type **688** 47·00 24·00

1817 20s. Textile pattern (horiz) 95·00 47·00

689 "With AIDS There is No Tomorrow"

1993. International AIDS Day.

1818 **689** 1s.50 multicoloured 4·75 2·40

690 Computer Graphics

1994. 25th Anniv of National Council for Science and Technology. Self-adhesive. Imperf.

1819 **690** 1s. multicoloured 3·00 1·30

691 "The Bridge" (woodcut from "New Chronicle and Good Government" by Poma de Ayala)

1994. Self-adhesive. Imperf.

1820 **691** 20c. blue 1·20 45

1821 **691** 40c. orange 2·20 95

1822 **691** 50c. violet 3·00 1·20

For similar design see Nos. 1827/9.

1994. Multicoloured. Self-adhesive. Imperf.

1823 1s.50 Type **692** 4·25 2·10

1824 1s.50 Engraved silver and mate vessel (vert) 4·25 2·10

1825 3s. Figure of bull from Pucara 8·75 3·50

1826 3s. Glazed plate decorated with fishes 8·75 3·50

693 "The Bridge" (Poma de Ayala)

1994

1827 **693** 30c. brown 1·30 45

1828 **693** 40c. black 2·10 85

1829 **693** 50c. red 2·50 1·10

694 Gold Trinkets

1994. Jewels from Funerary Chamber of Senor de Sipan (2nd series). Multicoloured.

1830 3s. Type **694** 11·00 4·75

1831 5s. Gold mask (vert) 19·00 8·25

695 El Brujo

1994. Archaeology. El Brujo Complex, Trujillo.

1832 **695** 70c. multicoloured 2·00 95

696 "Baby Emmanuel" (Cuzco sculpture)

1995. Christmas (1994). Multicoloured.

1833 1s.80 Type **696** 4·75 2·40

1834 2s. "Nativity" (Huamanga ceramic) 5·25 2·75

697 Brazilian Player

1995. World Cup Football Championship, U.S.A. (1994). Multicoloured.

1835 60c. Type **697** 1·20 70

1836 4s.80 Mascot, pitch and flags 9·50 6·00

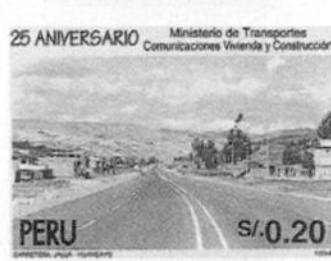

698 Jauja–Huancayo Road

1995. 25th Anniv (1994) of Ministry of Transport, Communications, Housing and Construction.

1837 **698** 20c. multicoloured 35 30

699 Mochican Pot (Rafael Larco Herrera Museum of Archaeology)

1995. Museum Exhibits. Multicoloured.

1838 40c. Type **699** 1·30 60

1839 80c. Mochican gold and gemstone ornament of man with slingshot (Rafael Larco Herrera Museum of Archaeology, Lima) 2·50 95

1840 90c. Vessel in shape of beheaded man (National Museum) 3·00 1·20

700 Juan Parra del Reigo (poet) (after David Alfaro)

1995. Writers' Birth Centenaries (1994). Mult.

1841 90c. Type **700** 3·25 1·80

1842 90c. Jose Carlos Mariategui 3·25 1·80

701 Church

1995. 350th Anniv (1993) of Carmelite Monastery, Lima.

1843 **701** 70c. multicoloured 2·40 1·20

702 Violoncello and Music Stand

1995. Musical Instruments. Multicoloured.

1844 20c. Type **702** 60 35

1845 40c. Andean drum 1·30 85

703 Steam-powered Fire Engine

1995. Volunteer Firemen. Multicoloured.

1846 50c. Type **703** 1·80 1·40

1847 90c. Modern fire engine 3·00 2·40

704 Union Club and Plaza de Armas

1995. World Heritage Site. Lima. Multicoloured.

1848 90c. Type **704** 5·00 2·20

1849 1s. Cloisters of Dominican Monastery 5·75 2·50

705 "Bora Child"

1995. Ethnic Groups (2nd series). Statuettes by Felipe Lettersten. Multicoloured.

1850 1s. Type **705** 3·25 2·00

1851 1s.80 "Aguaruna Man" 6·00 3·50

706 Woman fishing

1995. 30th Anniv (1993) of World Food Programme.

1852 **706** 1s.80 multicoloured 5·50 3·50

707 Potato Plant

1995. The Potato. Multicoloured.

1853 1s.80 Type **707** 5·50 3·50

1854 2s. Mochican ceramic of potato tubers 6·50 4·25

708 Reed Sailing Canoe

1995. Tourism and Ecology. Lake Titicaca.

1855 **708** 2s. multicoloured 6·50 4·75

709 Great Horned Owl

1995. Endangered Animals. Multicoloured.

1856 1s. Type **709** 4·25 3·00

1857 1s.80 Jaguar on branch (horiz) 5·50 4·25

710 Anniversary Emblem

1995. 25th Anniv of Andean Development Corporation.

1858 **710** 5s. multicoloured 15·00 10·50

711 Ollantaytambo

1995. World Tourism Day.

1859	**711**	5s.40 multicoloured	21·00	12·00

712 Ancient Letterbox, Head Post Office

1995. World Post Day.

1860	**712**	1s.80 multicoloured	5·25	3·50

713 Columbus landing on Beach

1995. America (1992 and 1993). Multicoloured.

1861	1s.50 Type **713** (500th anniv of discovery of America)	4·75	3·00
1862	1s.70 Guanaco (vert)	5·25	3·50

714 Cart

1995. America (1994). Postal Transport. Multicoloured.

1863	1s.80 Type **714**	5·25	3·50
1864	2s. Post vans	6·00	3·75

715 Lima Cathedral (rear entrance)

1995. Doorways. Multicoloured.

1865	30c. Type **715**	1·10	70
1866	70c. St. Francis's Church (side entrance)	2·40	1·50

716 Peruvian Delegation, San Francisco Conference, 1945

1995. 50th Anniv of U.N.O.

1867	**716**	90c. multicoloured	3·00	1·80

717 Ceramic Church (National Culture Museum)

1995. Museum Exhibits. Multicoloured.

1868	20c. Type **717**	95	45
1869	20c. "St. John the Apostle" (figurine) (Riva Aguero Institute Museum of Popular Art)	95	45
1870	40c. "Allegory of Asia" (alabaster figurine) (National Culture Museum)	1·80	85
1871	50c. "Archangel Moro" (figurine) (Riva Aguero Institute Museum of Popular Art)	2·20	95

718 Lady Olave Baden-Powell (Girl Guides)

1995. Scouting. Multicoloured.

1872	80c. Type **718**	2·00	1·20
1873	1s. Lord Robert Baden Powell (founder of Boy Scouts)	2·50	1·80

Nos. 1872/3 were issued together, *se-tenant*, forming a composite design.

719 "Festejo"

1995. Folk Dances. Multicoloured.

1874	1s.80 Type **719**	5·25	3·50
1875	2s. "Marinera Limena" (horiz)	5·50	3·75

720 Stream in Sub- tropical Forest

1995. Manu National Park, Madre de Dios. Multicoloured.

1876	50c. Type **720**	7·00	4·75
1877	90c. American chamaeleon (horiz)	8·25	3·50

721 Toma de Huinco

1995. Electricity and Development. Multicoloured.

1878	20c. Type **721**	60	35
1879	40c. Antacoto Lake	1·20	85

722 St. Toribio de Mogrovejo (Archbishop of Lima)

1995. Saints. Multicoloured.

1880	90c. Type **722**	2·50	1·80
1881	1s. St. Francisco Solano (missionary)	2·75	1·90

723 Cultivating Crops

1996. 50th Anniv (1995) of F.A.O.

1882	**723**	60c. multicoloured	1·80	95

724 Crib

1996. Christmas (1995). Porcelain Figures. Multicoloured.

1883	30c. Type **724**	85	60
1884	70c. Three Wise Men (horiz)	1·90	1·30

725 Lachay National Park

1996. America (1995). Environmental Protection. Multicoloured.

1885	30c. Type **725**	1·20	60
1886	70c. Black caiman	2·40	1·30

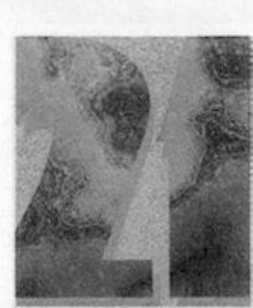

726 "21"

1996. 21st International Pacific Fair, Lima.

1887	**726**	60c. multicoloured	1·70	95

727 Rifle Shooting

1996. Olympic Games, Barcelona (1992). Multicoloured.

1888	40c. Type **727**	95	60
1889	40c. Tennis	95	60
1890	60c. Swimming	1·40	95
1891	60c. Weightlifting	1·40	95

Nos. 1888/91 were issued together, *se-tenant*, forming a composite design of the sports around the games emblem.

728 Archaeological Find from Sipan

1996. "Expo'92" World's Fair, Seville.

1892	**728**	1s.50 multicoloured	7·75	3·50

729 Vallejo (after Gaston Garreu)

1996. Birth Centenary of Cesar Vallejo (writer).

1893	**729**	50c. black	2·10	1·10

730 Avenue of the Descalzos

1996. UNESCO World Heritage Site. Lima.

1894	**730**	30c. brown and stone	85	45

731 "Kon Tiki" (replica of balsa raft)

1997. 50th Anniv of Thor Heyerdahl's "Kon Tiki" Expedition (voyage from Peru to Tuamoto Island, South Pacific).

1895	**731**	3s.30 multicoloured	7·00	4·75

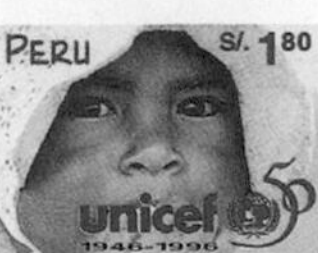

732 Child

1997. 50th Anniv (1996) of UNICEF.

1896	**732**	1s.80 multicoloured	4·75	2·50

733 Owl

1997. Mochica Culture.

1897	**733**	20c. green	85	35
1898	-	30c. violet	1·30	55
1899	-	50c. black	2·20	85
1900	-	1s. orange	4·25	1·90
1901	-	1s.30 red	6·00	2·40
1902	-	1s.50 brown	6·50	3·00

DESIGNS—Vessels in shape of: 30c. Crayfish; 50c. Cormorant; 1s. Monkeys; 1s.30, Duck; 1s.50, Jaguar.

See also Nos. 1942/6.

734 Shooting

1997. Olympic Games, Atlanta, U.S.A. (1996). Multicoloured.

1903	2s.70 Type **734**	4·75	3·00
1904	2s.70 Volleyball	4·75	3·00
1905	2s.70 Boxing	4·75	3·00
1906	2s.70 Football	4·75	3·00

735 White-bellied Caique

1997. 25th Anniv of Peru Biology College.

1907	**735**	5s. multicoloured	8·75	6·25

736 Scout Badge and Tents

1997. 90th Anniv of Boy Scout Movement.

1908	**736**	6s.80 multicoloured	12·00	8·25

737 Man on Reed Raft

1997. Eighth International Anti-corruption Conference, Lima.

1909	**737**	2s.70 multicoloured	4·75	3·00

738 Emblem

1997. Tenth Anniv of Montreal Protocol (on reduction of use of chlorofluorocarbons).

1910	**738**	6s.80 multicoloured	18·00	9·50

739 Pectoral

1997. Funerary Chamber of "Senor of Sipan". Multicoloured.

1911	2s.70 Type **739**	7·00	3·50
1912	3s.30 Ear-cap (vert)	8·25	4·50
MS1913	80×59 mm. 10s. Open tomb	24·00	24·00

740 Von Stephan

1997. Death Centenary of Heinrich von Stephan (founder of U.P.U.).

1914	**740**	10s. multicoloured	24·00	24·00

741 Shipibo Woman

1997. America (1996). Traditional Costumes. Multicoloured.

1915	2s.70 Type **741**	6·50	3·50
1916	2s.70 Shipibo man	6·50	3·50

742 Inca Messenger

1997. America. The Postman. Multicoloured.

1917	2s.70 Type **742**	6·50	3·50
1918	2s.70 Modern postman	6·50	3·50

743 Castilla

1997. Birth Bicentenary of Ramon Castilla (President, 1845–51 and 1855–62).

1919	**743**	1s.80 multicoloured	5·00	2·75

744 Tennis

1997. 13th Bolivarian Games, Arequipa. Multicoloured.

1920	2s.70 Type **744**	5·25	3·50
1921	2s.70 Football	5·25	3·50
1922	2s.70 Basketball	5·25	3·50
1923	2s.70 Volleyball	5·25	3·50

Nos. 1920/3 were issued together, *se-tenant*, containing a composite design of a ball in the centre.

745 River Kingfisher

1997. Manu National Park. Birds. Multicoloured.

1924	3s.30 Type **745**	6·00	4·25
1925	3s.30 Green woodpecker	6·00	4·25
1926	3s.30 Red crossbill	6·00	4·25
1927	3s.30 Eagle	6·00	4·25
1928	3s.30 Jabiru	6·00	4·25
1929	3s.30 Cuban screech owl	6·00	4·25

746 Concentric Circles over Map

1997. 30th Anniv of Treaty of Tlatelolco (banning nuclear weapons in Latin America and the Caribbean).

1930	**746**	20s. multicoloured	47·00	30·00

747 Map and Krill

1997. Eighth Peruvian Scientific Expedition to Antarctica.

1931	**747**	6s. multicoloured	14·00	8·25

748 Holy Family

1997. Christmas.

1932	**748**	2s.70 multicoloured	6·50	3·75

749 Map, Emblem and Unanue

1997. 25th Anniv (1996) of Hipolito Unanue Agreement (health co-operation in Andes region).

1933	**749**	1s. multicoloured	2·40	1·30

750 Obverse and Reverse of 1897 1 Libra Coin

1997. Centenary of Gold Libra in Peru. Sheet 80×59 mm.

MS1934	**750**	10s. multicoloured	33·00	33·00

751 Facade

1997. Cent of Posts and Telegraph Headquarters.

1935	**751**	1s. multicoloured	2·40	1·30

752 School and Cadets

1998. Centenary of Chorrillos Military School.

1936	**752**	2s.70 multicoloured	6·50	3·50

753 Map and Emblem

1998. 50th Anniv of Organization of American States.

1937	**753**	2s.70 multicoloured	6·50	3·50

754 Cuzco Cathedral

1998. 25th Anniv of Aeroperu. Multicoloured.

1938	1s.50 Type **754**	3·75	2·10
1939	2s.70 Airbus Industrie A320 jetliner	7·00	4·00

755 "Paso Horse" (Enrique Arambur Ferreyros)

1998. 50th Anniv of National Association of Breeders and Owners of Paso Horses.

1940	**755**	2s.70 violet	7·75	4·25

756 Lima Cathedral

1998. Centenary of Restoration of Lima Cathedral.

1941	**756**	2s.70 red, yellow and black	6·00	3·50

1998. Mochica Culture. As Nos. 1897 and 1899/1902 but values and/or colours changed.

1942	1s. blue	4·25	1·50
1943	1s.30 purple	5·25	1·90
1944	1s.50 blue	6·50	2·30
1945	2s.70 bistre	11·00	4·50
1946	3s.30 black	13·00	4·75

DESIGNS: 1s.30, Type **733**; 1s.50, Jaguar; 2s.70, Cormorant; 3s.30, Duck.

758 Goalkeeper

1998. "Inti-Raymi" Inca Festival.

1947	**757**	5s. multicoloured	11·00	6·75

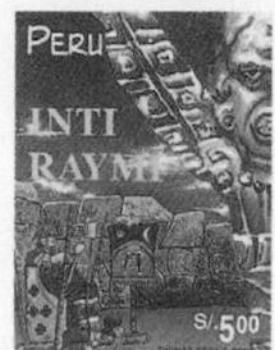

757 Ceremony, Sacsayhuaman, Cuzco

1998. World Cup Football Championship, France. Multicoloured.

1948	2s.70 Type **758**	6·00	3·50
1949	3s.30 Two players	6·50	4·25
MS1950	100×79 mm. 10s. Player kicking ball (horiz)	24·00	24·00

Nos. 1948/9 were issued together, se-tenant, forming a composite design.

759 Lloque Yupanqui

1998. Inca Chiefs (1st issue). Multicoloured.

1951	2s.70 Type **759**	8·75	6·75
1952	2s.70 Sinchi Roca	8·75	6·75
1953	9s.70 Mancoc Capau	31·00	27·00

See also Nos. 2008/11.

760 Soldiers

1998. Heroes of (River) Cenepa (Peru-Ecuador border dispute). Sheet 110×80 mm.

MS1954	**760**	10s. multicoloured	24·00	24·00

761 Fishermen (Moche sculpture) and Emblem

1998. International Year of the Ocean.

1955	**761**	6s.80 multicoloured	15·00	15·00

762 Bars of Music and Conductor's Hands

1998. 60th Anniv of National Symphony Orchestra.

1956	**762**	2s.70 multicoloured	6·00	4·75

763 Mother Teresa and Baby

1998. First Death Anniv of Mother Teresa (founder of Missionaries of Charity).

1957	**763**	2s.70 multicoloured	6·00	4·75

764 Children with Toys

1998. Peruvian Children's Foundation.

1958	**764**	8s.80 multicoloured	21·00	17·00

765 Princess of Ampato (Inca mummy)

1998. Third Anniv of Discovery by Johann Reinhard of Best Preserved Pre-Hispanic Corpse. Sheet 100×80 mm.

MS1959	**765**	10s. multicoloured	24·00	24·00

766 Tropical Forest

1998. Manu National Park.

1960	**766**	1s.50 multicoloured	3·50	2·75

767 1858 1 Dinero Stamp

1998. World Stamp Day.

1961	**767**	6s.80 multicoloured	14·00	12·00

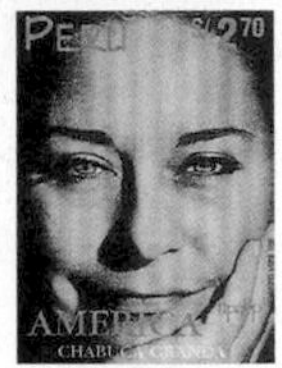
768 Chabuca Granda (singer)

1998. America. Famous Women.

1962	**768**	2s.70 multicoloured	6·00	4·75

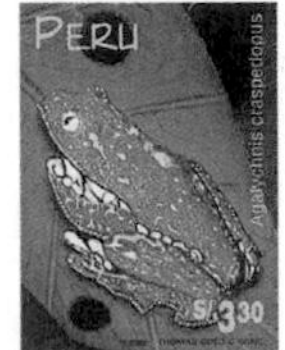

769 "Agalychnis craspedopus"

1998. Frogs. Multicoloured.

1963	3s.30 Type **769**	5·00	3·75
1964	3s.30 Amazonian horned frog ("Ceratophrys cornuta")	5·00	3·75
1965	3s.30 "Epipedobates macero"	5·00	3·75
1966	3s.30 "Phyllomedusa vaillanti" (leaf frog)	5·00	3·75
1967	3s.30 "Dendrobates biolat" (poison arrow frog)	5·00	3·75
1968	3s.30 "Hemiphractus probosci-deus" (horned frog)	5·00	3·75

Nos. 1963/8 were issued together, *se-tenant*, forming a composite design.

770 "Chulucanas Nativity" (Lizzy Lopez)

1998. Christmas.

1969	**770**	3s.30 multicoloured	5·00	3·75

771 Dove and Flags of Peru, Ecuador and Guarantor Countries

1998. Signing of Peru–Ecuador Peace Agreement, Brasilia.

1970	**771**	2s.70 multicoloured	4·75	3·75

772 Children on Hillside

1998. 50th Anniv of Universal Declaration of Human Rights.

1971	**772**	5s. multicoloured	6·50	5·25

773 Scout Badge and Tents

1999. 19th World Scout Jamboree, Chile. Multicoloured.

1972	5s. Type **773**	6·50	5·25
1973	5s. Emblem and tents	6·50	5·25

774 Emblem

1999. 50th Anniv of Peruvian Philatelic Association.

1974	**774**	2s.70 multicoloured	3·50	2·75

775 "Evening Walk"

1999. 120th Death Anniv of Pancho Fierro (artist). Multicoloured.

1975	2s.70 Type **775**	3·50	2·75
1976	3s.30 "The Sound of the Devil"	4·25	3·25

776 Dancer and Detail from Costume

1999. "Puno" (traditional dance).

1977	**776**	3s.30 multicoloured	4·25	3·25

1999. Mochica Culture. As Nos. 1943/46 but values and or colours changed.

1978	1s. red	1·40	1·10
1979	1s.50 blue	1·90	1·50
1980	1s.80 brown	2·40	1·90
1981	2s. orange	2·50	2·10

DESIGNS: Vessels in shape of—1s. Jaguar; 1s.50, Duck; 1s.80, Type **733**; 2s. Cormorant.

777 Inca blowing Conch Shell

1999. 25th Anniv of Peruvian Folklore Centre (CENDAF).

1982	**777**	1s.80 multicoloured	2·40	1·90

778 Malinowski and Train crossing Bridge

1999. Death Centenary of Ernest Malinowski (designer of iron bridge between Lima and La Oroya).

1983	**778**	5s. multicoloured	6·50	5·25

779 Sick and Healthy Hearts with Smiling Face

1999. Child Heart Care.

1984	**779**	2s.70 multicoloured	3·50	2·75

780 Origami Birds

1999. Centenary of Japanese Immigration.

1985	**780**	6s.80 multicoloured	8·75	7·00

781 Miner and Crowbars

1999. 50th Anniv of Milpo S.A. Mining Company.

1986	**781**	1s.50 multicoloured	1·90	1·50

782 Wildlife

1999. Flora and Fauna.

1987 **782**	5s. multicoloured	6·50	5·25
MS1988	79×98 mm. 10s. Jaguar, Manu National Park (horiz)	17·00	17·00

1999. Nos. 1888/91 surch.

1989	1s. on 40c. Rifle shooting	1·30	1·00
1990	1s. on 40c. Tennis	1·30	1·00
1991	1s. on 60c. Swimming	1·30	1·00
1992	1s. on 60c. Weightlifting	1·30	1·00
1993	1s.50 on 40c. Rifle shooting	1·90	1·50
1994	1s.50 on 40c. Tennis	1·90	1·50
1995	1s.50 on 60c. Swimming	1·90	1·50
1996	1s.50 on 60c. Weightlifting	1·90	1·50
1997	2s.70 on 40c. Rifle shooting	3·50	2·75
1998	2s.70 on 40c. Tennis	3·50	2·75
1999	2s.70 on 60c. Swimming	3·50	2·75
2000	2s.70 on 60c. Weightlifting	3·50	2·75
2001	3s.30 on 40c. Rifle shooting	4·25	3·25
2002	3s.30 on 40c. Tennis	4·25	3·25
2003	3s.30 on 60c. Swimming	4·25	3·25
2004	3s.30 on 60c. Weightlifting	4·25	3·25

1999. No. 1894 surch.

2005	2s.40 on 30c. brown and ochre	3·00	2·40

785 Penguin and Antarctic Vessel

1999. 40th Anniv of Antarctic Treaty.

2006	**785**	6s.80 multicoloured	10·00	8·00

786 Bird

1999. Nazca Lines. Sheet 98×79 mm.

MS2007	**786**	10s. multicoloured	13·00	13·00

1999. Inca Chiefs (2nd issue). As T **759**. Multicoloured.

2008	3s.30 Maita Capac	4·25	3·25
2009	3s.30 Inca Roca	4·25	3·25
2010	3s.30 Capac Yupanqui	4·25	3·25
2011	3s.30 Yahuar Huaca	4·25	3·25

787 Galena

1999. Minerals. Multicoloured.

2012	2s.70 Type **787**	3·50	2·75
2013	3s.30 Scheelita	4·25	3·25
2014	5s. Virgotrigonia peterseni	6·50	5·25

788 Virgin of Carmen

1999

2015	**788**	3s.30 multicoloured	6·00	4·75

789 Building

1999. St. Catalina Monastery, Arequipa.

2016	**789**	2s.70 multicoloured	3·50	2·75

790 Emblem and Dragon

1999. 150th Anniv of Chinese Immigration to Peru.

2017	**790**	1s.50 red and black	3·25	2·50

791 Taking Pulse

1999. 25th Anniv of Peruvian Medical Society.

2018	**791**	1s.50 multicoloured	1·90	1·50

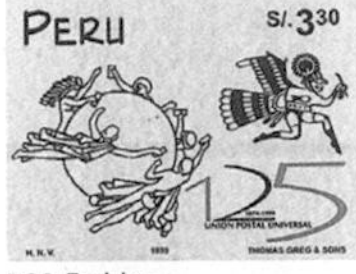

792 Emblem

1999. 125th Anniv of Universal Postal Union.

2019	**792**	3s.30 multicoloured	4·50	3·50

793 Sunflower growing out of Gun

1999. America. A New Millennium without Arms. Multicoloured.

2020	2s.70 Type **793**	3·50	2·75
2021	3s.30 Man emerging from Globe (horiz)	4·50	3·50

794 Woman with Fumigator

1999. Señor de los Milagros Festival, Lima. Multicoloured.

2022	1s. Type **794**	1·40	1·10
2023	1s.50 Procession	1·90	1·50

795 Young Child and Emblem

1999. 40th Anniv of Inter-American Development Bank.

2024	**795**	1s.50 multicoloured	1·90	1·50

796 *Pterourus zagreus chrysomelus*

1999. Butterflies. Multicoloured.

2025	3s.30 Type **796**	4·50	3·50
2026	3s.30 *Asterope buckleyi*	4·50	3·50
2027	3s.30 *Parides chabrias*	4·50	3·50
2028	3s.30 *Mimoides pausanias*	4·50	3·50
2029	3s.30 *Nessaea obrina*	4·50	3·50
2030	3s.30 *Pterourus zagreus zagreus*	4·50	3·50

797 Map of Cunhuime Sur Sub-sector

1999. First Anniv of Peru–Ecuador Border Peace Agreement. Multicoloured.

2031	1s. Type **797**	1·40	1·10
2032	1s. Map of Lagartococha-Gueppi sector	1·40	1·10
2033	1s. Map of Cusumasa Bumbuiza-Yaupi Santiago sub-sector (horiz)	1·40	1·10

798 Globe

1999. Fifth Anniv of Serpost S.A. (Peruvian postal services).

2034	**798**	2s.70 multicoloured	3·50	2·75

799 Virgin of Belen

1999. Christmas.

2035	**799**	2s.70 multicoloured	4·50	3·50

800 Mujica and Factory

1999. Birth Centenary of Ricardo Bentin Mujica (industrialist).

2036	**800**	2s.70 multicoloured	3·50	2·75

801 Flags encircling Globe

2000. New Millennium. Sheet 79×99 mm.

MS2037	**801**	10s. multicoloured	13·00	13·00

802 Oberti and Foundry

2000. Ricardo Cilloniz Oberti (founder of Peruvian steel industry).

2038	**802**	1s.50 multicoloured	1·90	1·50

803 Llamas

2000. Michell Group (Peruvian alpaca exporters). Multicoloured.

2039	1s.50 Type **803**	1·90	1·50
2040	1s.50 Llamas (different)	1·90	1·50

Nos. 2039/40 were issued together, *se-tenant*, forming a composite design.

804 Power Station

2000. 25th Anniv of Peruvian Institute of Nuclear Energy (I.P.E.N.).

2041	**804**	4s. multicoloured	5·25	4·25

805 Miner

2000. Mining Industry. Multicoloured.

2042	1s. Type **805**	1·30	1·00
2043	1s. View of mine	1·30	1·00

Nos. 2042/3 were issued together, se-tenant, forming a composite design.

806 Stylized Outline of Peru

2000. 70th Anniv of Comptroller General of Republic.

2044	**806**	3s.30 multicoloured	4·50	3·50

807 Field and Emilio Guimoye Hernandez

2000. Poblete Agriculture Group.

2045	**807**	1s.50 multicoloured	1·90	1·50

808 Pupils carrying Flags

2000. National School Sports Games.

2046	**808**	1s.80 multicoloured	2·50	2·10

809 Machu Picchu

2000. World Heritage Sites.

2047	**809**	1s.30 multicoloured	1·90	1·60

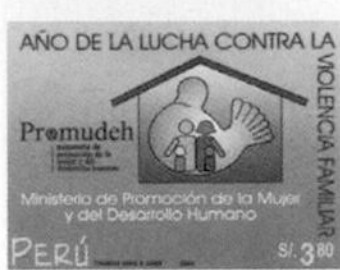
810 Emblem

2000. Campaign Against Domestic Violence.

2048	**810**	3s.80 multicoloured	5·25	4·50

811 Emblem

2000. Year.

2049	**811**	3s.20 multicoloured	4·75	4·00

812 "Cataratas de Ahuashiyacu" (Susan Hidalgo Bacalla)

2000. Winning Entries in Students' Painting Competition. Multicoloured.

2050	3s.20 Type **812**	4·75	4·00
2051	3s.20 "Laguna Yarinacocha" (Mari Trini Ramos Vargas) (horiz)	4·75	4·00
2052	3s.80 "La Campina Arequipena" (Anibal Lajo Yanez) (horiz)	5·25	4·50

813 Member Flags and Emblem

2000. United Nations Millennium Summit, New York, U.S.A.

2053	**813**	3s.20 multicoloured	4·75	4·00

814 San Martín

2000. 150th Death Anniv of General Jose de San Martin.

2054	**814**	3s.80 multicoloured	5·25	4·50

815 Bus, Map of South America and Road

2000. 30th Anniv of Peru—North America Bus Route. Multicoloured.

2055	1s. Type **815**	1·50	1·30
2056	2s.70 Bus, map of North America and road	3·75	3·25

Nos. 2055/6 were issued together, *se-tenant*, forming a composite design.

816 Cyclist

2000. Centenary of International Cycling Union.

2057	**816**	3s.20 multicoloured	4·75	4·00

817 Sun Dial

2000. 50th Anniv of World Meteorological Organization.

2058	**817**	1s.50 multicoloured	2·00	1·70

818 Western Leaf Lizard (*Tropidurus plica*)

2000. Lizards. Multicoloured.

2059	3s.80 Type **818**	5·25	4·50
2060	3s.80 Haitian ameiva (*Ameiva ameiva*)	5·25	4·50
2061	3s.80 Two-lined skink (*Mabouya bistriata*)	5·25	4·50
2062	3s.80 *Neusticurus ecpleopus*	5·25	4·50
2063	3s.80 Blue-lipped forest anole (*Anolis fuscoauratus*)	5·25	4·50
2064	3s.80 Horned wood lizard (*Enyalioides palpebralis*)	5·25	4·50

Nos. 2059/64 were issued together, *se-tenant*, forming a composite design.

819 *Matucana madisoniorum*

2000. Cacti.

2065	**819**	3s.80 multicoloured	5·25	4·50

820 Noriega and Space Shuttle

2000. Carlos Noriega (first Peruvian astronaut).

2066	**820**	3s.80 multicoloured	5·25	4·50

821 De Mendoza and Library

2000. 250th Birth Anniv Toribio Rodríguez de Mendoza.

2067	**821**	3s.20 multicoloured	4·75	4·00

822 Symbols of Ucayali

2000. Centenary of Ucayali Province.

2068	**822**	3s.20 multicoloured	4·75	4·00

823 Grape Vine and Flag

2000. Wines of Peru.
2069 **823** 3s.80 multicoloured 5·25 4·50

824 Flags on Watch Parts

2000. 20th Anniv of ALADI (Latin-American integration association).
2070 **824** 10s.20 multicoloured 18·00 18·00

825 Emblem

2000. 50th Anniv of Federation of Journalists.
2071 **825** 1s.50 multicoloured 2·10 1·70

826 Petrified Forest, Santa Cruz

2000
2072 **826** 1s.50 multicoloured 2·30 1·90

827 Male and Female Symbols

2000. America. Anti-AIDS Campaign.
2073 **827** 3s.80 multicoloured 5·50 4·50

828 Justice Palace, Trujillo

2000. New Judicial Powers.
2074 **828** 1s.50 multicoloured 2·10 1·70

829 Child at Table

2000. 90th Anniv of Peruvian Salvation Army.
2075 **829** 1s.50 multicoloured 2·10 1·70

830 Ribbon and Medal

2000. 50th Anniv of League against Cancer.
2076 **830** 1s.50 multicoloured 2·10 1·70

831 Steam Locomotive

2000. 150th Anniv of Peruvian Railways.
2077 **831** 1s.50 multicoloured 2·10 1·70

832 Monument, Parliament Building

2000. National Congress.
2078 **832** 3s.80 multicoloured 5·50 4·50

833 Doris Gibson (first editor)

2000. 50th Anniv of "Caretas" Magazine.
2079 **833** 3s.20 multicoloured 4·75 4·00

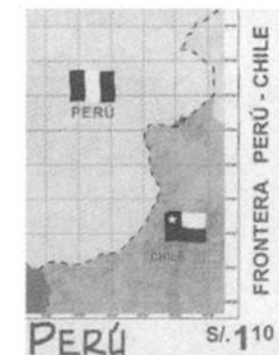

834 Map showing Peru—Chile Border

2000. National Borders. Multicoloured. Designs showing maps of borders.
2080 1s.10 Type **834** 1·70 1·40
2081 1s.50 Peru—Brazil 2·10 1·70
2082 2s.10 Peru—Colombia (horiz) 3·00 2·40
2083 3s.20 Peru—Ecuador (horiz) 4·75 4·00
2084 3s.80 Peru—Bolivia 5·50 4·50

835 Luis Alberto Sanchez

2000. Birth Centenary of Luis Alberto Sanchez (writer).
2085 **835** 3s.20 multicoloured 4·75 4·00

836 *Haageocereus acranthus*

2000. Cacti. Multicoloured.
2086 1s.10 Type **836** 1·70 1·40
2087 1s.50 *Cleistocactus xylorhizus* 2·10 1·70
2088 2s.10 *Mila caespitose* 3·00 2·40
2089 2s.10 *Haageocereus setosus* (horiz) 3·00 2·40
2090 3s.20 *Opuntia pachypus* (horiz) 4·75 4·00
2091 3s.80 *Haageocereus tenuis* 5·50 4·50

837 University Arms

2001. 450th Anniv of San Marco University.
2092 **837** 1s.50 multicoloured 2·10 1·70

838 Footballers

2001. Centenary of Club Alianza Lima (Lima football club). Multicoloured.
2093 3s.20 Type **838** 4·75 4·00
2094 3s.20 Two players and ball 4·75 4·00
Nos. 2093/4 were issued together, *se-tenant*, forming a composite design.

839 Symbols of Abuse and Family

2001. International Day against Drug Abuse.
2095 **839** 1s.10 multicoloured 1·70 1·40

840 Roque Saenz Pena

2001. 150th Birth Anniv of Roque Saenz Pena (Argentinean general).
2096 **840** 3s.80 multicoloured 5·50 4·50

841 Walls, Sun, Tree and Horseman

2001. Rio Lurin Valley.
2097 **841** 1s.10 multicoloured 1·70 1·40

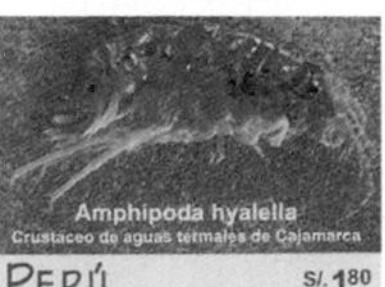

842 *Hyalella* (amphipod crustacean)

2001
2098 **842** 1s.80 multicoloured 2·50 2·10

843 Early Post Cart

2001. 70th Anniv of Post and Philately Museum.
2099 **843** 3s.20 multicoloured 4·75 4·00

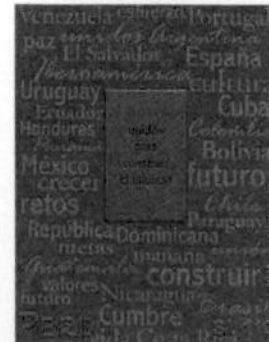
844 Names of Participating Countries

2002. Ibero-American Conference, Lima.
2100 **844** 1s.10 black and scarlet 1·70 1·40
2101 - 2s.70 scarlet and orange 4·00 3·25
DESIGN: 2s.70, Triangle.

845 Ruins and Hand

2002. 150th Anniv of Peru—Costa Rica Diplomatic Relations. Multicoloured.
2102 1s.10 Type **845** 1·70 1·40
2103 2s.70 Hand and grassland 4·00 3·25
Nos. 2102/3 were issued, together, *se-tenant*, forming a composite design.

846 People from Many Races

2002. International Conference to Combat Racism.
2104 **846** 3s.80 multicoloured 5·50 4·50

847 Multicultural Symbols

2002. International Day of Indigenous Peoples.
2105 **847** 5s.80 multicoloured 8·00 6·75

848 Airplane and Passengers

2002. 50th Anniv of International Organization for Migration.
2106 **848** 3s.80 multicoloured 5·50 4·50

849 "100" enclosing Map of Americas

2002. Centenary of Pan American Health Organization.
2107 **849** 3s.20 multicoloured 4·75 4·00

850 Early University Building

2002. Centenary of La Molina Agricultural University. Multicoloured.
2108 1s.10 Type **850** 1·70 1·40
2109 2s.70 Modern building 4·00 3·25

851 Distillation Equipment

2002. Pisco (brandy) Distilling. Multicoloured.
2110 3s.20 Type **851** 4·75 4·00
2111 3s.80 Amphora 5·50 4·50
MS2112 100×80 mm. 10s. "Pisco Festival" (Jose Sabogal) 18·00 18·00

852 *Stanhopea*

2002. Orchids. Multicoloured.

2113	1s.50 Type **852**	2·10	1·70
2114	3s.20 *Chloraea pavoni*	4·75	4·00
2115	3s.80 *Psychopsis*	5·50	4·50

853 *Solanum stenotomum*

2002. Native Tuberous Plants. Multicoloured.

2116	1s.10 Type **853**	1·70	1·40
2117	1s.50 *Ipomea batatas*	2·10	1·70
2118	2s.10 *Ipomea purpurea*	3·00	2·40

854 Balcony, Osambela Palace

2002. America. Cultural Heritage. Multicoloured.

2119	2s.70 Type **854**	4·00	3·25
2120	5s.80 Balcony, Torre Tagle Palace	8·00	6·75

855 Flower enclosing Globe

2002. United Nations Year (2001) of Dialogue among Civilizations. Multicoloured.

2121	1s.50 Type **855**	2·10	1·70
2122	1s.80 Children encircling globe	2·50	2·10

856 Blue-faced Booby (*Sula dactiilatra*)

2002. Paracus National Reserve. Multicoloured.

2123	1s.10 Type **856**	1·70	1·40
2124	1s.50 Peruvian booby (*Sula variegate*) (horiz)	2·10	1·70
2125	3s.20 American oystercatcher (*Haematopus palliates*) (horiz)	4·75	4·00
2126	3s.80 *Grapus grapus* (crab) (horiz)	5·50	4·50

857 Giant Otter (*Pteronura brasiliensis*)

2002. Endangered Species. Sheet 80×100 mm.

MS2127	**857** 8s. multicoloured	14·50	14·50

858 Figure with Crab's Claws, Sipan

2002. Tourism. Archaeological Sites. Multicoloured.

2128	1s.50 Type **858**	2·10	1·70
2129	3s.20 Warrior (metal decoration), Sican	4·75	4·00
2130	3s.80 Gold pectoral decoration, Kuntur Wasi (horiz)	5·50	4·50
MS2131	80×100 mm. 10s.20 Los Pinchudos, Gran Pajaten (horiz)	18·00	18·00

859 La Zamacueca

2002. Peruvian Dances. Multicoloured.

2132	2s.10 Type **859**	3·00	2·50
2133	2s.70 El Alcatraz	4·00	3·25

860 Robert Baden Powell (founder of Scout movement)

2002. 90th Anniv of Peruvian Scouts. Multicoloured.

2134	3s.20 Type **860**	5·00	4·25
2135	3s.20 Juan Luis Rospigliosi (co-founder of Peruvian Scouts)	5·00	4·25
MS2136	100×80 mm. 10s.20 First Peruvian Scout group	19·00	19·00

Nos. 2134/5 were issued together, *se-tenant*, forming a composite design.

861 Globe and Postal Emblems

2002. Postal Services.

2137	**861** 20s. multicoloured	35·00	35·00

862 Viracocha

2002. Ancient Rulers (1st series). Multicoloured.

2138	1s.50 Type **862**	2·10	1·80
2139	2s.70 Pachacutec	4·00	3·25
2140	3s.20 Inca Yupanqui	5·00	4·25
2141	3s.80 Tupac Inca Yupanqui	5·75	4·75

See also Nos. 2191/3.

863 Peruvian Red-necked Owl Monkey (*Aotus nancymai* (inscr "nancymaea"))

2002. Primates. Multicoloured.

2142	3s.80 Type **863**	5·75	4·75
2143	3s.80 Grey monk saki (*Pithecia irrorata*)	5·75	4·75
2144	3s.80 Equatorial saki (*Pithecia aequatorialis*)	5·75	4·75
2145	3s.80 White-fronted capuchin (*Cebus albifrons*)	5·75	4·75
2146	3s.80 Bolivian squirrel monkey (*Saimiri boliviensis*)	5·75	4·75
2147	3s.80 Owl monkey (*Aotus vociferans*)	5·75	4·75

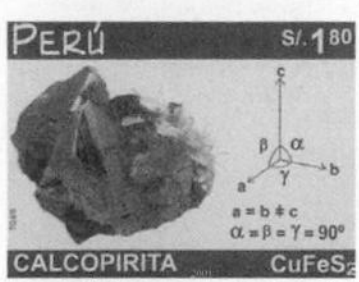

864 Chalcopyrite (CuFeS2)

2002. Minerals (1st series). Multicoloured.

2148	1s.80 Type **864**	2·75	2·20
2149	3s.20 Zinc sulphide (Zns)	5·00	4·25
2150	3s.20 Pyrargyrite (inscr "AgSbS3")	5·00	4·25

See also Nos. 2187/8.

865 Miguel Grau

2002. Miguel Grau (naval hero) Commemoration.

2151	**865** 3s.80 multicoloured	5·75	4·75

866 Spanish and Peruvian Flags and Coins

2002. Peru—Spain Business Conference.

2152	**866** 3s.80 multicoloured	5·75	4·75

867 Flags, Bridge and Map

2002. Peru—Bolivia Integrated Development Plan.

2153	**867** 3s.20 multicoloured	5·00	4·25

868 Andean and Amazonian People

2002. National Commission for Andean and Amazonian Peoples.

2154	**868** 1s.50 multicoloured	2·10	1·80

869 Fishermen

2002. 50th Anniv of National Fishing Society.

2155	**869** 3s.20 multicoloured	5·00	4·25

870 Alexander von Humboldt

2002. Bicentenary of Visit by Alexander von Humboldt (geologist).

2156	**870** 3s.20 multicoloured	5·00	4·25

871 Surveyor

2003. Centenary of Hydro-graphic Mapping.

2157	**871** 1s.10 multicoloured	1·70	1·40

872 Emblem

2003. 25th Anniv of Movimiento Manuela Ramos (organization for sexual equality).

2158	**872** 3s.80 scarlet and black	5·75	4·75

873 Transmitter

2003. 40th Anniv of RPP Radio.

2159	**873** 4s. multicoloured	6·00	5·00

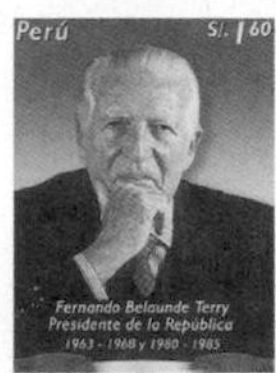

874 Fernando Terry

2003. First Death Anniv of Fernando Belaunde Terry (president 1963—68 and 1980—1985).

2160	**874** 1s.60 multicoloured	2·30	1·90

875 Jose Maria Escriva de Balaguer

2003. Canonization of Jose Maria Escriva de Balaguer (founder of Opus Dei (religious organization)).

2161	**875** 1s.20 multicoloured	1·70	1·40

876 Teresa de la Cruz

2003. 50th Death Anniv of Teresa de la Cruz Candamo.

2162	**876** 4s. brown and yellow	6·00	5·00

877 Map of the Americas

2003. 150th Anniv of Peru—Italy Treaty of Friendship and Trade. Multicoloured.

2163	2s. Type **877**	3·00	2·40
2164	2s. Map of Europe, Africa and Asia	3·00	2·40

Nos. 2163/4 were issued together, *se-tenant*, forming a composite design.

878 Emblems

879 Emblem and Children

2003. Serpente de Agua Exhibition (cultural project). Multicoloured.
2165 2s. Type **878** 3·00 2·40
2166 2s. Early and modern children 3·00 2·40

2003. 50th Anniv of UNESCO Associated Schools.
2167 **879** 1s.20 multicoloured 1·90 1·50

880 Four Birds

2003. Endangered Species. Andean Cock of the Rock (Rupicola peruviana). Multicoloured.
2168 2s. Type **880** 3·00 2·40
2169 2s. Single bird 3·00 2·40
Nos. 2168/9 were issued together, *se-tenant*, forming a composite design.

881 1570 Map (Diego Mendez)

2003. 150th Anniv of Peru—Panama Diplomatic Relations.
2170 **881** 4s. multicoloured 6·00 5·00

882 *Wright Flyer*, Orville and Wilbur Wright

2003. Centenary of Powered Flight. Multicoloured.
2171 4s.80 Type **882** 7·00 5·75
2172 4s.80 "Arriba siempre arriba hasta alcanzar la gloria" 1·60 95
Nos. 2171/2 were issued together, *se-tenant*, forming a composite design.

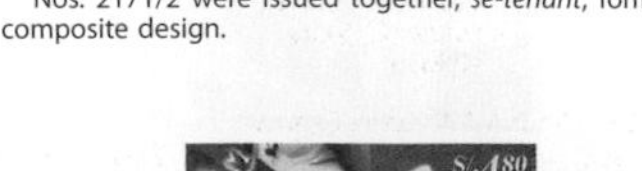

883 Musician and Notes

2003. Cajon (wooden box played as musical instrument).
2173 **883** 4s.80 multicoloured 7·00 5·75

884 Chess Board and Globe

2004. Chess.
2174 **884** 1s.20 multicoloured 1·90 1·50

885 Free-style Crawl

2004. Swimming.
2175 **885** 1s.20 multicoloured 1·90 1·50

886 Wheelchair User, Amputee and Boy using Crutches

2004. National Institute of Rehabilitation. Year of the Rights for the Disabled.
2176 **886** 1s.20 multicoloured 1·90 1·50

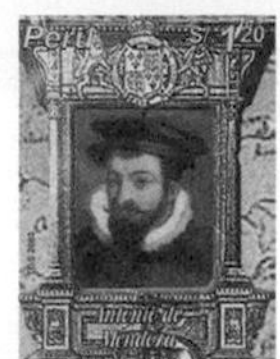

887 Antonio de Mendoza

2004. Viceroys. Multicoloured.
2177 1s.20 Type **887** 1·90 1·50
2178 1s.20 Andreas Hurtado de Mendoza 1·90 1·50
2179 1s.20 Diego Lopez de Zuniga y Velasco 1·90 1·50
2180 4s.80 Blasco Nunez de Vela 7·00 5·75

888 The Nativity

2004. Christmas (2003).
2181 **888** 4s.80 multicoloured 6·75 5·50

889 Emblem

2004. 30th Anniv of Civil Defence Organization.
2182 **889** 4s.80 multicoloured 7·00 5·75

890 Cebiche (fish)

2004. Traditional Dishes.
2183 **890** 4s.80 multicoloured 7·00 5·75

891 *Chaubardia heteroclite*

2004. Orchids. Multicoloured.
2184 1s.20 Type **891** 1·90 1·50
2185 2s.20 *Cochleanthes amazonica* (incr "Cochleanther") 3·00 2·50
2186 4s.80 *Sobralia* (horiz) 7·00 5·75

892 Orpiment

2004. Minerals (2nd series). Multicoloured.
2187 1s.20 Type **892** 1·90 1·50
2188 4s.80 Rodocrosita 7·00 5·75

893 St. Martin de Porres

2004. Peruvian Saints. Multicoloured.
2189 4s.80 Type **893** 7·00 5·75
2190 4s.80 St. Rosa de Lima (horiz) 7·00 5·75

2004. Ancient Rulers (2nd series). As T **862**. Multicoloured.
2191 1s.20 Huascar 1·90 1·50
2192 1s.20 Atahualpa 1·90 1·50
2193 3s.20 Huayna Capac 7·00 5·75

894 Locomotive

2004. Railways. Multicoloured.
2194 1s.20 Type **894** 1·90 1·50
2195 4s.80 "Puente Galeros" viaduct 7·00 5·75

895 Marine Otter (*Lontra feline*) (inscr "Londra")

2004. Endangered Species. Multicoloured.
2196 1s.80 Type **895** 2·75 2·20
2197 1s.80 Ara couloni (vert) 2·75 2·20

896 Fire Fighters

2004. Fire Service. Multicoloured.
2198 2s.20 Type **896** 3·00 2·50
2199 2s.20 Fire appliance 3·00 2·50

897 Jorge Basadre

2004. Birth Centenary of Jorge Basadre Grohmann (writer) (2003).
2200 **897** 4s.80 indigo 7·00 5·75

898 *Matucana haynei*

2004. Cacti (2nd series). Multicoloured.
2201 1s.20 Type **898** 1·90 1·50
2202 1s.20 *Eriosyce islayensis* 1·90 1·50
2203 4s.80 *Pymaeocereus bylesianus* (inscr "Pigmaeocereus") 7·00 5·75

899 Gentoo Penguin (*Pygoscelis papua*) (inscr "Pygosceles")

2004. Antarctic Fauna. Multicoloured.
2204 1s.80 Type **899** 2·75 2·20
2205 1s.80 *Asteroidea* 2·75 2·20
2206 1s.80 *Leucocarbo atriceps* (horiz) 2·75 2·20

900 Tree and Children

2004. Environmental Awareness. Multicoloured.
2207 4s.80 Type **900** (Population Control Day) 7·00 5·75
2208 4s.80 Plants and animals (National Biological Diversity Day) 7·00 5·75

901 Stadium

2004. Football. Multicoloured.
2209 4s.80 Type **901** (50th anniv of National Stadium, Lima) 7·00 5·75
2210 4s.80 Players, emblem and trophy (World Cup Football Championships, Japan and South Korea (2002)) 7·00 5·75

902 Ruben Vargas Ugarte (historian)

2004. Personalities. Multicoloured.
2211 4s.80 Type **902** 7·00 5·75
2212 4s.80 Jose Jimenez Borja (writer) (vert) 7·00 5·75

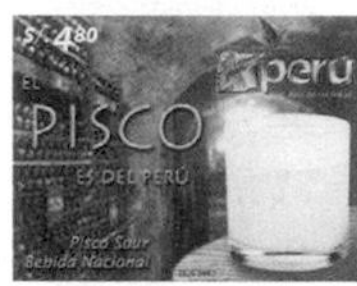

903 Glass

2004. Pisco Sour National Drink.
2213 **903** 4s.80 multicoloured 7·00 5·75

904 Daniel Carrion

2004. Daniel Alcides Carrion (medical student who died after inoculation experiment) Commemoration.
2214 **904** 4s.80 multicoloured 7·00 5·75

905 "Founding of Juaja" (Wenceslao Hinostroza)

2004. 470th Anniv of Founding of Juaja. Sheet 100×80 mm.
MS2215 **905** 7s. multicoloured 11·50 11·50

906 Alpaca

2004. Llamas. Multicoloured.

2216	20c. Type **906**	40	35
2217	30c. Vicuna	55	45
2218	40c. Guanaco	65	55
2219	50c. Llama	80	65

907 *Bothros roedingeri*

2004. Snakes. Multicoloured.

2220	1s.80 Type **907**	2·75	2·20
2221	1s.80 *Micrurus lemniscalus*	2·75	2·20
2222	1s.80 *Bothrops atrox*	2·75	2·20
2223	1s.80 *Bothrops microphtlalmus*	2·75	2·20
2224	1s.80 *Micrurus surinamensis*	2·75	2·20
2225	1s.80 *Bothrops barnetti*	2·75	2·20

Nos. 2220/5 were issued together, *se-tenant*, forming a composite design.

908 Mount Huascaran

2004. International Year of Mountains (2002). Sheet 100×80 mm.

MS2226 **908** 7s. multicoloured 11·50 11·50

909 Artefacts and Building

2004. Royal Tombs of Sipan Museum, Lambayeque.

2227	**909**	4s.80 multicoloured	7·00	5·75

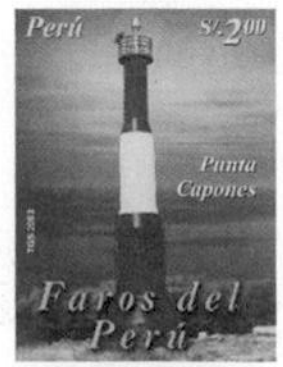
910 Punta Capones Lighthouse

2004. Lighthouses (1st issue). Multicoloured.

2228	2s. Type **910**	3·00	2·40
2229	2s. Islas Chincha	3·00	2·40

See also Nos. 2286/7 and **MS**2404.

911 Fire Fighter

2004. 130th Anniv of Volunteer Fire Brigades.

2230	**911**	4s.80 multicoloured	7·00	5·75

912 *Trachurus murphyi*

2004. Fish. Sheet 140×112 mm containing T **912** and similar horiz designs. Multicoloured.

MS2231 1s.60×5, Type **912**; *Mugil cephalus; Engraulis ringens; Odontesthes regia; Merluccius peruanus* 15·00 15·00

The stamps and margin of **MS**2231 form a composite design.

913 Cathedral Tower, Arequipa

2004. Tourism. Sheet 100×80 mm containing T **913** and similar multicoloured design.

MS2232 4s.×2, Type **913**; El Misti volcano 14·50 14·50

The stamps and margin of **MS**2232 form a composite design.

914 Solar Clock, Intihuatana

2004. World Heritage Site. Machu Picchu. Multicoloured.

2233	1s.20 Type **914**	1·90	1·50
2234	1s.20 Temple	1·90	1·50
2235	1s.20 Waterfall, Huayna Picchu	1·90	1·50
2236	4s.80 Ciudadela	7·00	5·75

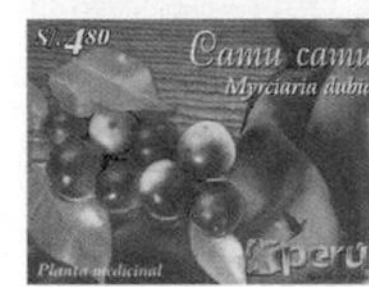
915 *Myrciaria dubia*

2004. Medicinal Plants. Multicoloured.

2237	4s.80 Type **915**	7·00	5·75
2238	4s.80 *Lepidium meyenii*	7·00	5·75
2239	4s.80 *Uncaria tomentosa*	7·00	5·75

916 Map and Emblem

2004. Inter-American Development Bank Governors' Assembly Annual Reunion.

2240	**916**	4s.80 multicoloured	7·00	5·75

917 Italian Volpino Spitz

2004. Dogs. Multicoloured.

2241	4s.80 Type **917**	7·00	5·75
2242	4s.80 Peruvian Inca Orchid	7·00	5·75
2243	4s.80 Beauceron (Pastor de Beauce)	7·00	5·75
2244	4s.80 Italian Spinone	7·00	5·75

918 Huaylash

2004. Traditional Dances. Multicoloured.

2245	1s.20 Type **918**	1·90	1·50
2246	1s.20 Huayno	1·90	1·50

919 Scientists and Weather Map

2004. Preparation for "El Nino".

2247	**919**	4s.80 multicoloured	7·00	5·75

920 Paca Lake, Jauja

2004. Tourism. Multicoloured.

2248	4s.80 Type **920**	7·00	5·75
2249	4s.80 Banos del Inca (thermal springs), Cajamarca (vert)	7·00	5·75
2250	4s.80 Ballestas island, Paracas, Ica (vert)	7·00	5·75
2251	4s.80 Caballitos (handmade totora reed boats) (vert)	7·00	5·75

921 Santiago Apostol Church, Pomata

2004. Cultural Heritage.

2252	**921**	1s.80 multicoloured	2·75	2·20

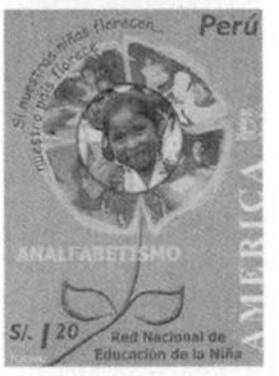
922 Flower containing Children

2004. America. Literacy Campaign. Multicoloured.

2253	1s.20 Type **922**	1·90	1·50
2254	1s.20 Child and computer (horiz)	1·90	1·50

923 Aboriginal Footballer

2004. Americas' Cup Football Championship, Peru. Sheet 74×74 mm.

MS2255 **923** 5s. multicoloured 8·00 8·00

No. **MS**2255 was cut round in the shape of a football.

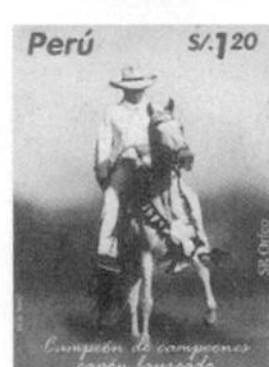
924 SR Orfeo

2004. Peruvian Gaited Horses. Multicoloured.

2256	1s.20 Type **924**	1·90	1·50
2257	1s.20 JyEP Pretencioso	1·90	1·50
2258	1s.20 MSP Morenita	1·90	1·50
2259	4s.80 Horse's head	7·00	5·75

925 Otter

2004. Endangered Species. Giant Otter (Pteronura brasiliensis). Sheet 90×115 mm containing T **925** and similar vert designs. Multicoloured.

MS2260 30c. Type **925**; 50c. Snarling; 1s.50 Eating fish; 1s.50 Mother and cubs 6·25 6·25

926 Living and Dead Trees

2004. America. Environmental Protection.

2261	**926**	4s.50 multicoloured	6·75	5·50

927 Central Railway (1870)

2004. National Railways. Multicoloured.

2262	5s. Type **927**	7·25	6·00

MS2263 80×60 mm. 10s. Train on Puente Infiernillo bridge (horiz) 19·00 19·00

928 Musical Instruments

2004. 60th Anniv of Cancion Criolla Day.

2264	**928**	5s. multicoloured	7·25	6·00

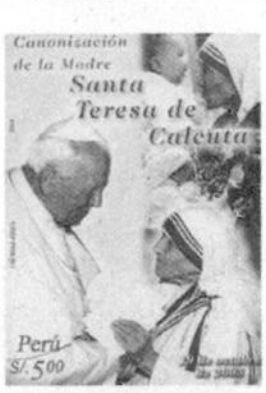
929 Pope John Paul II and Mother Teresa

2004. Canonization of Mother Teresa.

2265	**929**	5s. multicoloured	7·25	6·00

930 Anniversary Emblem

2004. Centenary of FIFA (Federation Internationale de Football Association).

2266	**930**	5s. multicoloured	7·25	6·00

931 Pope John Paul II

2004. 25th Anniv of Pope John Paul II's Pontificate.

2267	**931**	5s. multicoloured	7·25	6·00

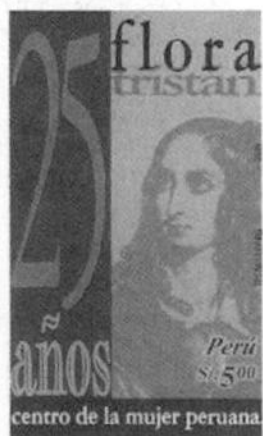
932 Flora Tristan (women's rights activist)

2004. 25th Anniv of Women's Centre.

2268	**932**	5s. multicoloured	7·25	6·00

933 World Map and Exports

2004. Exporters Day.

2269	**933**	5s. multicoloured	7·25	6·00

934 Piranha (*Serrasalmus*)

2004. Fish. Multicoloured.

2270	2s. Type **934**	3·00	2·40

2271	4s.50 La Plata river dolphin (*Pontoporia blainvillei*)	6·75	5·50
2272	5s. Pirarucu (*Arapaima gigas*) (vert)	7·25	6·00

935 "40"

2004. 40th Anniv of Latin American Parliament. Multicoloured.

2273	2s.50 Type **935**	3·75	3·00
2274	2s.50 Andres Townsend Escurra (first president) and flags	3·75	3·00

936 Couple

2004. Mochica Ceramics. Designs showing jugs. Multicoloured.

2275	4s.50 Type **936**	6·75	5·50
2276	4s.50 Couple (different)	6·75	5·50
2277	5s. Two animals (horiz)	7·25	6·00

937 Gavel and Regalia

2004. Bicentenary of Law College.

2278	**937**	5s. multicoloured	7·25	6·00

938 Envelope

2004. Tenth Anniv of Serpost.

2279	**938**	5s. multicoloured	7·25	6·00

939 Juan Diego Florez

2004. Musicians. Sheet 121×95 mm containing T **939** and similar multicoloured designs.

MS2280 2s.×5, Type **939**; Susana Baca; Gian Marco; Eva Ayllon (horiz); Libido (horiz) 19·00 19·00

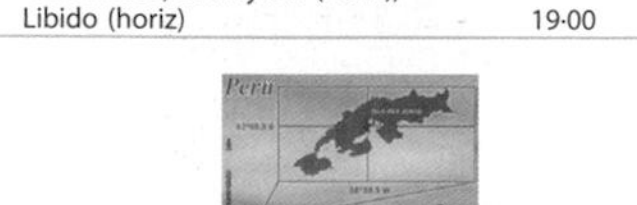

940 Machu Picchu Base

2004. Antarctic. Multicoloured.

2281	1s.50 Type **940**	2·10	1·80
2282	2s. *Megaptera novaeagliae* (horiz)	3·00	2·40
2283	4s.50 *Orcinus orca* (horiz)	6·75	5·50

941 Smilodon neogaeus

2004. Pre historic Animals. Multicoloured.

2284	1s.80 Type **941**	2·75	2·20
2285	3s.20 Toxodon platensis	5·00	4·25

Nos. 2284/5 were issued together, *se-tenant*, forming a composite design.

2004. Lighthouses (2nd issue). As T **910**. Multicoloured.

2286	4s.50 Pijuayal	6·75	5·50
2287	4s.50 Suana	6·75	5·50

942 The Nativity

2004. Christmas.

2288	**942**	5s. multicoloured	7·25	6·00

943 Flags

2004. Latin-American Presidential Summit.

2289	**943**	5s. multicoloured	7·25	6·00

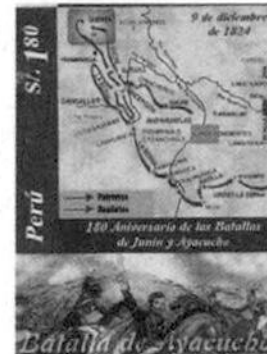

944 Map and Battle of Ayacucho

2004. 180th Anniv of Battles. Multicoloured.

2290	1s.80 Type **944**	2·75	2·20
2291	3s.20 Battle of Junin	5·00	4·25

945 Emblem

2004. 50th Anniv of Art Museum, Lima.

2292	**945**	5s. multicoloured	7·25	6·00

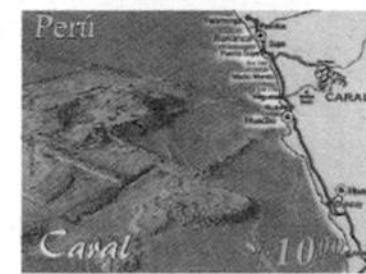

946 Ruins

2004. Caral Archaeological Site. Sheet 80×60 mm.

MS2293 **946** 10s. multicoloured 19·00 19·00

947 *Cantua buxifolia*

2005. 40th Anniv of Las Leyendas Park. Multicoloured.

2294	5s. Type **947**	7·25	6·00
2295	5s. Puma (*Puma concolor*)	7·25	6·00

Nos. 2294/5 were issued together, se-tenant, forming a composite design.

948 Trophies and Emblem

2005. Cienciano Football Club—South American Cup Champions, 2003 and South American Recopa Champions, (2004).

2296	**948**	5s. multicoloured	7·25	6·00

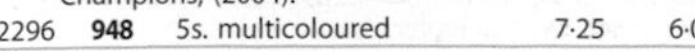

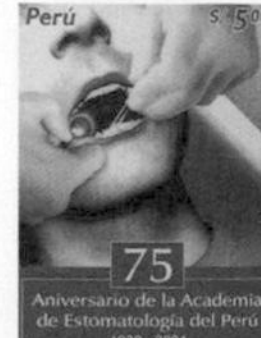

949 Dental Examination

2005. 75th Anniv (2004) of Stomatology Academy.

2297	**949**	5s. multicoloured	7·25	6·00

950 Children and Teacher

2005. Campaign for Rights and Responsibilities for Health.

2298	**950**	2s. multicoloured	3·00	2·40

951 San Cristobal Church, Huamanga

2005. Churches. Multicoloured.

2299	4s.50 Type **951**	6·75	5·50
2300	5s. Huancayo Cathedral	7·25	6·00

952 Don Ramon Castilla (president 1845—51 and 1855—62) and Slaves

2005. 150th Anniv of Abolition of Slavery.

2301	**952**	5s. crimson	7·25	6·00

953 Tank

2005. Armed Forces. Multicoloured.

2302	1s.80 Type **953**	2·75	2·20
2303	3s.20 Sukoi aircraft	5·00	4·25
2304	3s.20 Soldiers	5·00	4·25
2305	1s.80 Submarine	2·75	2·20
2306	1s.80 Mirage fighters and ship	2·75	2·20
2307	3s.20 Missile frigate	5·00	4·25

Nos. 2302/4 and 2305/7, respectively were issued together, *se-tenant*, forming a composite design.

954 *Eugenia stipitata*

2005. Fruit. Multicoloured.

2308	4s.50 Type **954**	6·75	5·50
2309	4s.50 *Maurita flexuosa*	6·75	5·50
2310	5s. *Solanum sessiliflorum* (vert)	7·25	6·00

955 Luis Alva Talledo

2005. Luis Alva Talledo (singer and founder of Prolirica (music association)).

2311	**955**	1s.50 multicoloured	2·10	1·80

956 Northern Chestnut-tailed Ant Bird

2005. Allpahuayo-Mishana Reserve. Multicoloured.

2312	4s.50 Type **956**	6·75	5·50
2313	4s.50 *Mishana tyrannulet*	6·75	5·50
2314	4s.50 Tree frog	6·75	5·50
2315	4s.50 Iguana	6·75	5·50

Nos. 2312/15 were issued together, *se-tenant*, forming a composite design.

957 Soldier and Woman (Pancho Fierro)

2005. Art. Multicoloured.

2316	2s. Type **957**	3·00	2·40
2317	2s. Old woman, child, old man and woman wearing fur trimmed robe (Ignacio Merino)	3·00	2·40
2318	2s. Portrait of man (Daniel Hernandes)	3·00	2·40
2319	2s. Mountains and church (Camilo Blas)	3·00	2·40
2320	2s. Portrait of woman (Ricardo Grau)	3·00	2·40
2321	2s. Abstract (Fernando de Szyszlo)	3·00	2·40

958 Stone Carvings, Chavin de Huantar

2005. 180th Birth Anniv (2004) of Antonio Raimondi (scientist). Multicoloured.

2322	1s.80 Type **958**	2·75	2·20
2323	3s.20 Inca tern and bat	5·00	4·25
2324	4s.50 *Stanhophea*	6·75	5·50
2325	5s. Huallanca periwinkle fossil (*Roemoceras subplanum*)	7·25	6·00

959 White-winged Guan (*Penelope albipennis*)

2005. Rediscovery of White-winged Guan (presumed extinct) in Laquipampa Reserve. Sheet 81×60 mm.

MS2326 **959** 10s. multicoloured 19·00 19·00

960 Government Palace

2005. Architecture. Multicoloured.

2327	4s.50 Type **960**	6·75	5·50
2328	4s.50 Museum of Italian Art	6·75	5·50
2329	5s. Tourist and Entertainment Centre, Larco Mer	7·25	6·00
2330	5s. Mega Plaza	7·25	6·00

961 Paper Plane

2005. Postal Giros.

2331	**961**	5s. multicoloured	7·25	6·00

962 Pope John Paul II

2005. Pope John Paul II Commemoration.

2332	**962**	1s.80 multicoloured	2·75	2·20

963 Spain 1968 3p.50 Stamp (As T **393**) and Machica Medallion

2005. 50th Anniv of Europa Stamps. Showing stamps of Spain and Pre-historic gold ornaments. Multicoloured.

2333	2s. Type **963**	3·00	2·40
2334	2s. 1960 1p. (As No. 1355) and Chimu ceremonial accoutrements	3·00	2·40
2335	2s. 1969 3p.50 (As T **400**) and Mochica turquoise and Lapis Lazuli roundels	3·00	2·40
2336	2s. 1970 3p.50 (T **410**) and Mochica frontal decoration	3·00	2·40

964 Punta Malpelo, 1828

2005. Naval Victories. Designs showing naval battles. Multicoloured.

2337	2s. Type **964**	3·00	2·40
2338	2s. Callao, May, 1880	3·00	2·40
2339	2s. Collapse of *Covadonga*, December, 1880	3·00	2·40
2340	2s. Abtao, 1866	3·00	2·40
2341	2s. Iquique, 1879	3·00	2·40
2342	2s. Pedrera, 1911	3·00	2·40

Nos. 2337/42 were issued together, *se-tenant*, with the background forming a composite design of the battle.

965 Skull

2005. 35th Anniv of Medical College.

2343	**965**	5s.50 multicoloured	8·00	6·50

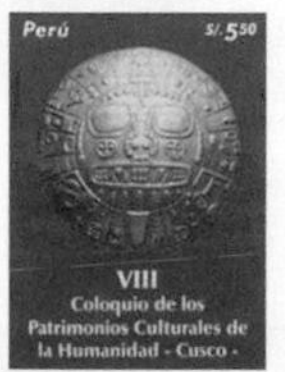

966 Gold Medallion

2006. Cultural Heritage. Cusco.

2344	**966**	5s.50 multicoloured	8·00	6·50

967 The Nativity

2006. Christmas (2005).

2345	**967**	5s.50 multicoloured	8·00	6·50

968 Sister Ana de los Angeles

2006. 400th Birth Anniv of Sister Ana de los Angeles Monteagudo.

2346	**968**	5s.50 multicoloured	8·00	6·50

969 Pope Benedict XVI

2006. Enthronement (2005) of Pope Benedict XVI. Multicoloured.

2347	2s.50 Type **969**	3·75	3·00
2348	2s.50 Giving blessing	3·75	3·00

970 Reading

2006. 400th (2005) Anniv of "Don Quixote de la Mancha" (novel by Miguel de Cervantes).

2349	**970**	5s. multicoloured	7·25	6·00

971 Children

2006. Centenary (2005) of Rotary International.

2350	**971**	5s.50 multicoloured	8·00	6·50

972 Child with Outstretched Hand

2006. America (2005). Struggle against Poverty.

2351	**972**	5s.50 multicoloured	8·00	6·50

973 Pichpichu

2006. Volcanoes. Multicoloured.

2352	2s.50 Type **973**	3·75	3·00
2353	2s.50 Chachani	3·75	3·00
2354	2s.50 Misti	3·75	3·00

974 Church Facade

2006. San Pedro Church, Lima. Multicoloured.

2355	2s.50 Type **974**	3·75	3·00
2356	2s.50 Interior	3·75	3·00

975 Academy Medallion

2006. Centenary (2005) of National History Academy.

2357	**975**	5s.50 multicoloured	8·00	6·50

976 Emblems

2006. 85th (2005) Anniv of YMCA.

2358	**976**	5s.50 multicoloured	8·00	6·50

977 Julio Tello

2006. 125th Birth Anniv (2005) of Julio Tello (anthropologist).

2359	**977**	5s. multicoloured	7·25	6·00

978 Emblems

2006. 75th (2005) Anniv of Contraloria General de la Republica.

2360	**978**	5s.50 multicoloured	8·00	6·50

979 Building Facade

2006. 150th Anniv of Cajamarca City.

2361	**979**	6s. multicoloured	8·75	7·25

980 Chupe de Camarones

2006. Food. Multicoloured.

2362	2s. Type **980**	3·00	2·40
2363	2s. Juane	3·00	2·40
2364	2s. Arroz con Pato	3·00	2·40
2365	2s. Rocoto Relleno	3·00	2·40

981 *Heliconius sara*

2006. Butterflies. Multicoloured.

2366	2s. Type **981**	3·00	2·40
2367	2s. *Morpho Achilles*	3·00	2·40
2368	2s. *Dryas iulia*	3·00	2·40
2369	2s. *Caligo eurilochus*	3·00	2·40

Nos. 2366/9 were issued together, *se-tenant*, forming a composite design.

982 Scouts

2006. XII Pan American Scout Jamboree. Multicoloured.

2370	2s. Type **982**	3·00	2·40
2371	2s. Scouts carrying flags	3·00	2·40

Nos. 2370/1 were issued together, *se-tenant*, forming a composite design.

983 Ceramics, Chavin, 1200 BC

2006. Cultural Heritage. Multicoloured.

2372	6s. Type **983**	8·75	7·25
2373	6s. Mummy and textiles, Paracas, 500 BC	8·75	7·25

984 Los Hermanos Ayar

2006. Myths and Legends.

2374	**984**	6s. multicoloured	8·75	7·25

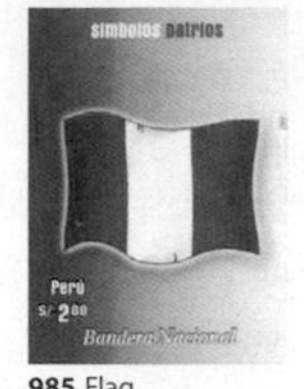

985 Flag

2006. National Symbols. Multicoloured.

2375	2s. Type **985**	3·00	2·40
2376	2s. Emblem	3·00	2·40
2377	2s. Hymn, Jose Bernado Alcedo (composer) and Jose de la Torre Ugarte (writer)	3·00	2·40

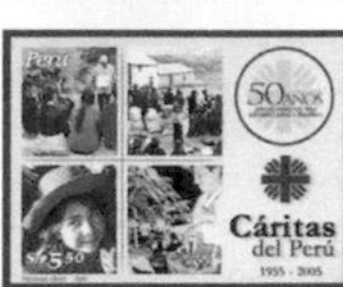

986 Discussion, Market, Child and Grower

2006. 50th (2005) Anniv of Caritas.

2378	**986**	5s.50 multicoloured	8·00	6·50

987 Lucuma

2006. Fruit. Multicoloured.

2379	6s. Type **987**	8·75	7·25
2380	6s. Chirimoya	8·75	7·25

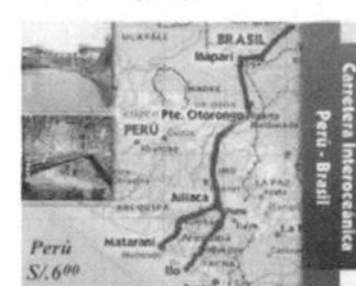

988 Map of Highway

2006. Peru—Brazil Interoceanica Highway.

2381	**988**	6s. multicoloured	8·75	7·25

989 Alfredo Bryce Echenique

2006. Writers. Each brown.

2382	6s. Type **989**	8·75	7·25
2383	6s. Mario Vargas Llosa	8·75	7·25

990 Emblem

2006. 70th (2005) Anniv of Ministry of Health.

2384	**990**	6s. multicoloured	8·75	7·25

991 Emblem

2006. 25th (2005) Anniv of ALADI (Latin American integration association).

2385	**991**	6s. multicoloured	8·75	7·25

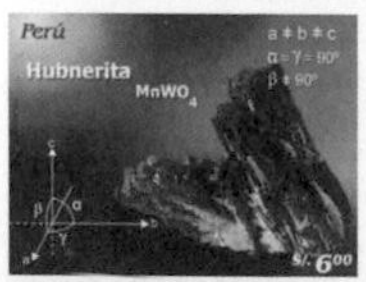
992 Hubnerite

2006. Minerals.

2386	**992**	6s. multicoloured	8·75	7·25

993 Chicha de Maiz Morado

2006. National Drink.

2387	**993**	6s. multicoloured	8·75	7·25

994 *Orestias*

2006. Fauna of Lake Titicaca. Multicoloured.

2388	5s.50 Type **994**	8·00	6·50
2389	5s.50 *Plegadis ridgwayi*	8·00	6·50
2390	5s.50 *Phoenicoparrus andinus*	8·00	6·50
2391	5s.50 *Telmatobius coleus*	8·00	6·50

Nos. 2388/91 were issued together, *se-tenant*, block forming a composite design.

995 Micaela Bastidas (freedom fighter)

2006. Precursor of Independence. Multicoloured.

2392	2s. Type **995**	3·00	2·40
2393	2s. Cusco Plaza	3·00	2·40

Nos. 2392/3 were issued together, *se-tenant*, forming a composite design.

996 *Pionopsitta barrabandi*

2006. Parrots. Multicoloured.

2394	5s.50 Type **996**	8·00	6·50
2395	5s.50 *Touit huetii* (Inscr "Tovit")	8·00	6·50
2396	5s.50 *Pionites melanocephala*	8·00	6·50
2397	5s.50 *Ara severa*	8·00	6·50
2398	5s.50 *Amazona festiva*	8·00	6·50
2399	5s.50 *Ara ararauna*	8·00	6·50

2006. Viceroys. As T **887**. Multicoloured.

2400	5s.50 Francisco de Toledo	8·00	6·50
2401	5s.50 Martin Enriquez de Almansa	8·00	6·50
2402	5s.50 Fernando Torres y Portugal	8·00	6·50
2403	5s.50 Garcia Hurtado de Mendoza	8·00	6·50

2006. Lighthouses (3rd issue). Sheet 102×82 mm containing vert designs as T **910**. Multicoloured.

MS2404 6s.×2, Isla Lobos de Tierra; Isla Blanca	20·00	20·00

997 Simon Bolivar

2006. 180th Anniv of El Peruano Newspaper.

2405	**997**	6s. multicoloured	8·75	7·25

998 Inscr "Tortolita moteada" (*Metriopelia ceciliae*)

2006. Birds. Multicoloured.

2406	6s. Type **998**	8·75	7·25
2407	6s. Inscr "Perlita de Iquitos" (*Polioptila clementsi*)	8·75	7·25
2408	6s. Inscr "Ganso Andino" (*Chloephaga melanoptera*)	8·75	7·25

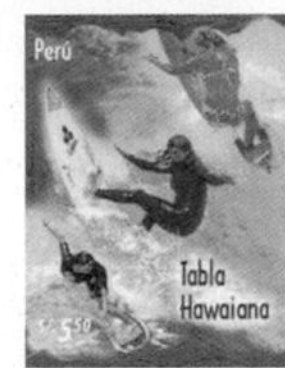
999 Surfing

2006. Sofia Mulanovich World Champion Surfer—2004.

2409	5s.50 Type **999**	8·00	6·50
2410	5s.50 Holding trophy	8·00	6·50

1000 Early Steam Locomotive

2006. 150th (2005) Anniv of Lima—Callao Railway. Sheet 81×60 mm.

MS2411 **1000** 6s. multicoloured	9·00	9·00

1001 Chan Chan, Trujillo

2006. Tourism. Multicoloured.

2412	5s.50 Type **1001**	8·00	6·50
2413	5s.50 Sipan man, Lambayeque	8·00	6·50
2414	5s.50 Ventanas de Otuzco, Cajamarca	8·00	6·50
2415	5s.50 Kuelap fort, Amazonas	8·00	6·50
2416	5s.50 Rio Abiseo National Park, San Martin	8·00	6·50
2417	5s.50 Pacaya Samiria, Loreto	8·00	6·50

1002 Pope John Paul II

2006. Pope John Paul II's Visit to Peru. Designs showing Pope John Paul II. Multicoloured.

2418	2s. Type **1002**	3·00	2·40
2419	2s. With two nuns	3·00	2·40
2420	2s. With dignitaries	3·00	2·40
2421	2s. Wearing native poncho	3·00	2·40
2422	2s. Accepting straw hat	3·00	2·40
2423	2s. With statue of the Virgin	3·00	2·40
2424	2s. Wearing native hat	3·00	2·40
2425	2s. Waving to crowd	3·00	2·40

1003 Couple, Arequipa

2006. Carnival Costumes. Multicoloured.

2426	6s. Type **1003**	8·75	7·25
2427	6s. Devil masked dancer, Puno	8·75	7·25
2428	6s. Guitarist, Cajamarca	8·75	7·25

1004 Emblem

2006. National Air Force. Multicoloured.

2429	6s. Type **1004**	8·75	7·25
2430	6s. Pilot	8·75	7·25

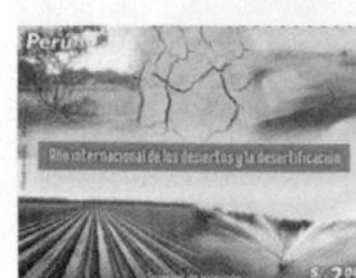
1005 Arid and Irrigated Land

2006. International Year of Deserts and Desertification.

2431	**1005**	2s. multicoloured	3·00	2·40

1006 The Nativity and Cathedral Museum

2006. Christmas.

2432	**1006**	2s. multicoloured	3·00	2·40

1007 Mozart and Score

2006. 250th Birth Anniv of Wolfgang Amadeus Mozart.

2433	**1007**	5s.50 multicoloured	8·00	6·50

1008 Flags and Ball

2006. World Cup Football Championship, Germany.

2434	**1008**	8s.50 multicoloured	14·50	14·50

1009 Christopher Columbus

2006. 500th Death Anniv of Christopher Columbus.

2435	**1009**	6s. multicoloured	8·75	7·25

1010 Solar Energy Collection Panels

2006. America. Energy Conservation. Multicoloured.

2436	3s. Type **1010**	4·25	3·50
2437	5s.50 Gas	8·00	6·50

Nos. 2436/7 were issued together, se-tenant, forming a composite design.

1011 Giant Panda

2006. 35th Anniv of Peru–China Diplomatic Relations. Multicoloured.

2438	2s. Type **1011**	3·00	2·40
2439	2s. Guanaco	3·00	2·40
2440	2s. Machu Pichu mountain	3·00	2·40
2441	2s. Great Wall of China	3·00	2·40

Nos. 2438/41 were issued together, se-tenant, forming a composite design.

1012 As Type **162**

2006. 75th Anniv of First Stamp Exhibition in Peru.

2442	**1012**	8s.50 multicoloured	14·50	14·50

1013 Pirates

2007. Movies (1st issue). Piratas en el Callao (first 3D animated film in Peru). Multicoloured.

2443	2s. Type **1013**	3·00	2·40
2444	2s. Children	3·00	2·40

See also Nos. 2453/4.

1014 Abstract (painting) (Fernando de Szyszlo)

2007. Peruvian Artists. Multicoloured.

2445	2s.20 Type **1014**	3·00	2·50
2446	2s.20 Horse (sculpture) (Victor Delfin)	3·00	2·50

1015 Purussaurus Skull

2007. Fossils. Sheet 101×81 mm.

MS2447 8s.50 multicoloured	15·00	15·00

1016 Quena

2007. Musical Instruments of the Andes. Multicoloured.

2448	5s.50 Type **1016**	8·00	6·50
2449	5s.50 Zampona	8·00	6·50
2450	5s.50 Antara	8·00	6·50

1017 Toribio de Mogrovejo

2007. 400th Death Anniv of Toribio de Mogrovejo (Archbishop of Lima).

2451	**1017**	2s. purple	3·00	2·40

1018 Senor de los Milagros

2007. Religious Festivals. Sheet 90×110 mm containing T **1018** and similar vert designs. Multicoloured.

MS2452 5s.50×4 Type **1018**; Virgen de las Mercedes; Virgen de la Candelaria; Senor de Muruhuay 32·00 32·00

The stamps and margins of No. **MS**2452 share a composite background design.

1019 Flying Dragons

2007. Movies (2nd issue). Dragones. Destino de Fuego (animation based on book by Hernan Garrido Lecca). Multicoloured.

2453	2s. Type **1019**	3·00	2·40
2454	2s. Head of large dragon	3·00	2·40

1020 Clasped Hands

2007. 75th Anniv of National Jury of Elections.

2455	**1020** 2s.20 sepia	3·00	2·50

1021 Suspiro de Limena

2007. Gastronomy. Desserts. Multicoloured.

2456	2s.50 Type **1021**	3·75	3·00
2457	2s.50 Picarones	3·75	3·00
2458	2s.50 Mazamorra morada	3·75	3·00

1022 Perro Sin Pelo (Peruvian hairless dog)

2007. Dogs. Multicoloured.

2459	6s. Type **1022**	8·75	7·25
2460	6s. Dachshund	8·75	7·25
2461	6s. Samoyed	8·75	7·25
2462	6s. Siberian husky	8·75	7·25

Nos. 2459/62 were issued together, *se-tenant*, forming a composite design.

1023 San Augustin Church

2007. Cultural Heritage. Lima. Multicoloured.

2463	5s.50 Type **1023**	8·00	6·50
2464	5s.50 San Francisco Sacristy	8·00	6·50
2465	5s.50 Santa Apolonia	8·00	6·50
2466	5s.50 Metropolitan Cathedral	8·00	6·50

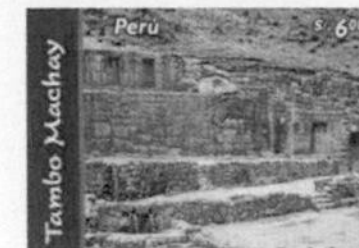

1024 Tambo Machay, Cusco

2007. Archaeology (1st issue). Inca Temples. Multicoloured.

2467	6s. Type **1024**	8·75	7·25
2468	6s. Pachacamac, Lima	8·75	7·25
2469	6s. Tambo Colorado, Ica	8·75	7·25

See also Nos. 2472/3.

1025 Felipe Pinglo Alva

2007. 70th (2006) Death Anniv of Felipe Pinglo Alva (singer and musician). Multicoloured.

2470	3s. Type **1025**	4·25	3·50
2471	3s. Photograph and guitar	4·25	3·50

Nos. 2470/1 were issued together, se-tenant, forming a composite design.

1026 Cat-shaped Pot and Gold Mask (Vicus c. 500BC)

2007. Archaeology (2nd issue). Multicoloured.

2472	6s. Type **1026**	8·75	7·25
2473	6s. Two anthropomorphic pots, decorated pot and jug (Salinar c. 200BC)	8·75	7·25

1027 Danza de los Negritos

2007. Traditional Costumes and Dances. Multicoloured.

2474	2s.50 Type **1027**	3·75	3·00
2475	2s.50 Danza de las Tijeras	3·75	3·00
2476	2s.50 Danza Capac Colla	3·75	3·00
2477	2s.50 Danza Diablada	3·75	3·00

Nos. 2474/7 were issued together, *se-tenant*, forming a composite design.

1028 Asparagus

2007. Exports. Multicoloured.

2478	6s. Type **1028**	8·75	7·25
2479	6s. Mangoes	8·75	7·25
2480	6s. Alpaca wool	8·75	7·25

1029 White Water Rafting (canoeing)

2007. Adventurous Sports. Multicoloured.

2481	6s. Type **1029**	8·75	7·25
2482	6s. Off road cycling (cycling)	8·75	7·25
2483	6s. Rock climbing (climbing)	8·75	7·25

1030 Provisional Headquarters of Chamber of Deputies

2007. 185th Anniv of First Constitutional Congress. Sheet 176×146 mm containing T **1030** and similar vert designs. Multicoloured.

MS2484 2s.50×8, Type **1030**; First constitutional congress; Former local court of the Inquisition, headquarters of the chamber of senators; Simon Bolivar (statue); Legislative Palace at night; Pasos Perdidos hall; Window showing 'Mother Peru'; Portico, Legislative Palace 29·00 29·00

2007. Viceroys. As T **887**. Multicoloured.

2485	6s. Luis de Velasco	8·75	7·25
2486	6s. Gaspar de Zuniga y Acevedo	8·75	7·25
2487	6s. Juan de Mendoza y Luna	8·75	7·25
2488	6s. Francisco de Borja y Aragon	8·75	7·25

1031 Giuseppe Garibaldi

2007. Birth Bicentenary of Giuseppe Garibaldi (soldier and nationalist).

2489	**1031** 6s. multicoloured	8·75	7·25

1032 *Oncifelis colocolo* (pampas cat)

2007. Endangered Species. Multicoloured.

2490	3s. Type **1032**	4·25	3·50
2491	3s. *Lontra felina* (marine otter)	4·25	3·50
2492	6s. *Harpia harpyja* (harpy eagle)	8·75	7·25
2493	6s. *Odocoileus virginianus* (white-tailed deer)	8·75	7·25

Nos. 2490/3 were issued together, se-tenant, forming a composite design.

1033 Emblem

2007. Centenary of Scouting. Multicoloured.

2494	3s. Type **1033**	4·25	3·50
2495	3s. Robert Baden-Powell and world flags	4·25	3·50

1034 *Bixa orellana*

2007. Medicinal Plants. Multicoloured.

2496	2s.50 Type **1034**	3·75	3·00
2497	2s.50 *Cestrum auriculatum*	3·75	3·00
2498	2s.50 *Brugmansia suaveolens*	3·75	3·00
2499	2s.50 *Anacardium occidentale*	3·75	3·00
2500	2s.50 *Caesalpinia spinosa*	3·75	3·00
2501	2s.50 *Croton lechleri*	3·75	3·00

1035 Raul Maria Pereira and Postal Building

2007. 130th Birth Anniv of Raul Maria Pereira (artist and architect).

2502	**1035** 2s. multicoloured	3·00	2·40

A stamp of a similar design was issued by Portugal.

No. 2503 has been left for 'Victor de la Torre' Commemoration, issued on 16 August 2007, not yet received.

1036 Institute Building

2007. 60th Anniv of Riva–Aguero Institute. Sheet 100×81 mm.

MS2504 10s.50 multicoloured 19·00 19·00

1037 *Pyrocephalus rubinus* (vermilion flycatcher)

2007. Birds. Multicoloured.

2505	5s.50 Type **1037**	8·00	6·50
2506	5s.50 *Mimus longicaudatus* (long-tailed mockingbird)	8·00	6·50
2507	5s.50 *Coereba flaveola* (bananaquit)	8·00	6·50
2508	5s.50 *Sarcoramphus papa* (king vulture)	8·00	6·50

1038 Band Members

2007. Centenary of National Band. Multicoloured.

2509	2s. Type **1037**	3·00	2·40
2510	8s.50 Band marching	14·50	12·00

1039 Symbols of Masons

2007. 125th Anniv of Grand Masonic Lodge.

2511	**1039** 6s.50 multicoloured	9·25	7·75

1040 Auburn Speedster 851 SC

2007. Classic Cars. Sheet 141×100 mm containing T **1040** and similar horiz designs. Multicoloured.

MS2512 3s.×5, Type **1040**; Inscr 'Clement Brass Phaeton 9 CV'; Dodge Brothers Special Pickup; Inscr 'Stutz BB Sedan Convertible Victoria'; Inscr 'Pierce Arrow 1603 Touring D 700' 21·00 21·00

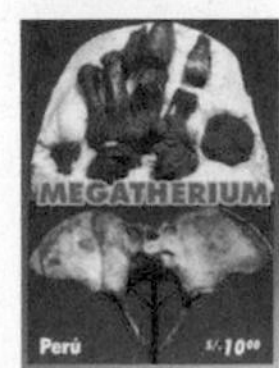

1041 Fossilized Bones

2007. Megatherium. Sheet 101×81 mm.

MS2513 multicoloured 17·00 17·00

1042 Map Outline and Service Personnel

2007. 50th Anniv of Joint Command of Armed Forces. Sheet 101×81 mm.

MS2514 multicoloured 21·00 21·00

1043 Courtyard

2007. 450th Anniv (2008) of Santa Clara Monastery, Cusco.
2515 **1043** 5s.50 multicoloured 8·00 6·50

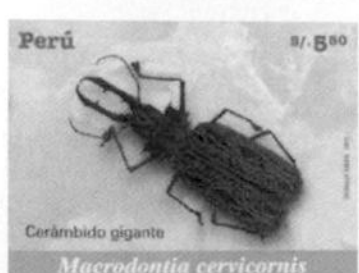

1044 *Macrodontia cervicornis*

2007. Terrestrial Invertebrates. Sheet 110×91 mm containing T **1044** and similar horiz designs. Multicoloured.
MS2516 5s.50×4, Type **1044**; *Dynastes hercules*; *Titanus giganteus*; *Megasoma* 24·00 24·00

1045 Angora

2007. Cats. Multicoloured.
2517 6s. Type **1045** 8·75 7·25
2518 6s. Persian 8·75 7·25
2519 6s. Bengal 8·75 7·25
2520 6s. Siamese 8·75 7·25

1046 Daniel Alcides Carrion

2007. 150th Birth Anniv of Daniel Alcides Carrion (medical student after whom Carrion's disease is named (died after self testing of theory)).
2521 **1046** 3s. brown 4·25 3·50

1047 Francisco Ruiz Lozano (first professor of mathematics)

2007. 350th Anniv of First Nautical Skills Academy.
2522 **1047** 5s.50 multicoloured 8·00 6·50

1048 Woman and Child reading

2007. America. Education for All. Multicoloured.
2523 5s.50 Type **1048** 8·00 6·50
2524 5s.50 Two children reading 8·00 6·50

1049 *Dictyophora indusiata* (inscr 'Dyctiophora indusiata')

2007. Fungi. Sheet 115×127 mm containing T **1049** and similar vert designs. Multicoloured.
MS2525 2s.50×4, Type **1049**; *Sepultaria arenicola*; *Marasmius haematocephalus*; *Marasmiellus volvatus* 15·00 15·00

1050 Bush Dog

2007. Endangered Species. Bush Dog (Speothos venaticus). Sheet 115×127 mm containing T **1050** and similar horiz designs. Multicoloured.
MS2526 2s.×2, Type **1050**; Two bush dogs; 5s.50×2, Preparing to pounce; Facing left 22·00 22·00

1051 Soldiers on Parade

2007. Architecture. Fortaleza del Real Felipe. Sheet 80×100 mm.
MS2527 multicoloured 8·75 7·25

1052 Merryweather Fire Appliance, 1908

2007. Centenary of Volunteer Firefighters. Multicoloured.
2528 3s. Type **1052** 4·25 3·50
2529 3s. Mack fire appliance, 1969 4·25 3·50

Nos. 2528/9 were issued together, *se-tenant*, forming a composite design.

1053 *Familia serrana* (Camilo Blas)

2007. Art.
2530 **1053** 6s. multicoloured 8·75 7·25

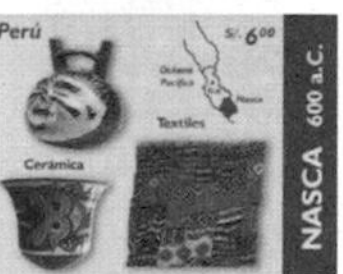

1054 Nasca Artefacts

2007. Cultural Heritage. Multicoloured.
2531 6s. Type **1054** 8·75 7·25
2532 7s. Mohica artefacts 11·00 9·00

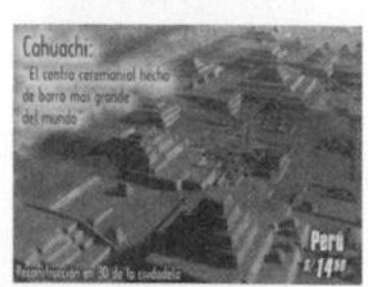

1055 Cahuachi

2007. Archaeology. Sheet 100×80 mm.
MS2533 multicoloured 23·00 23·00

1056 Emblem

2007. Asia—Pacific Economic Cooperation Forum, 2008.
2534 **1056** 6s. multicoloured 8·75 7·25

1057 House on Stilts (Juan Chuquipiondo Mesia) (1st place)

2007. Winning Designs in Children's Painting Competition 'Flora and Fauna of My Region'. Multicoloured.
2535 2s. Type **1057** 3·00 2·40
2536 2s. Egret in swamp (Ruben Saavedra Cobenas) (2nd place) (vert) 3·00 2·40

1058 1857 1r. stamp (Type **1**)

2007. 150th Anniv of First Peruvian Stamps (1st series). Multicoloured.
2537 2s.50 Type **1058** 3·75 3·00
2538 2s.50 1857 2r. stamp (As Type **1**) 3·75 3·00

1059 Bronze Cross of Society of the Founders of Independence and Woman holding Arms of Peru

2007. 150th Anniv of Society of the Founders of Independence.
2539 **1059** 6s. multicoloured 8·75 7·25

1060 Iglesia de las Carmelitas (Church of the Carmelites)

2007. Chuirch Altars. Multicoloured.
2540 6s. Type **1060** 8·75 7·25
2541 8s.50 Catedral de Lima (Lima Cathedral) 14·50 12·00

1061 Litany of the Blessed Virgin

2007. Christmas.
2542 **1061** 6s.50 multicoloured 8·75 7·25

1062 Yuca (*Manihot esculenta*) (Cassava)

2007. Root Vegetables. Multicoloured.
2543 6s. Type **1062** 8·75 7·25
2544 6s. Yacon (*Manihot esculenta*) 8·75 7·25

1063 Pedro Paulet Mostajo (astrononautical pioneer)

2007. First Anniv of Launch of Paulet I Space Probe. Multicoloured.
2545 3s. Type **1063** 4·25 3·50
2546 3s. Paulet I on launch pad 4·25 3·00

Nos. 2545/6 were issued together, se-tenant, forming a composite design.

1064 Victor Raul Haya de la Torre

2008. Victor Raul Haya de la Torre Commemoration (American Popular Revolutionary Alliance founder).
2547 **1064** 3s. brown 4·25 3·00

1065 1858 1dinero Stamp (As Type **3**)

2008. 150th Anniv of First Peruvian Stamps (2nd series). Multicoloured.
2548 5s.50 Type **1065** 8·00 6·50
2549 5s.50 1858 1/2 peso stamp 8·00 6·50
2550 5s.50 1858 1dinero stamp 8·00 6·50

1066a Nun and Interior

2008. 300th Anniv of Santa Rosa de Santa Maria Convent.
2551 **1066a** 5s.50 **1066a** multicoloured 8·00 6·50

1067 Research Ship

2008. 20th Anniv of First Antarctic Expedition. Sheet 100×80 mm containing T **1067** and similar multicoloured design.
MS2552 10s.×2, Type **1067**; Scientists and crew (horiz) 33·00 33·00

1068 '100 Anos' and Violin

2008. Centenary of Philharmonic Orchestra. Multicoloured.
2553 3s. Type **1068** 4·25 3·50
2554 3s. Photograph of members 4·25 3·50

1069 Statue

2008. Bicentenary of Matias Maestro Cemetery. Multicoloured.
2555 6s.50 Type **1069** 9·25 7·75
2556 6s.50 Memorial (horiz) 9·25 7·75

No. 2553/4 and Type **1068** have been left for 'Centenary of Philharmonic Society' issued on 8 June 2008, not yet received.

2008. Viceroys. As T **887**. Multicoloured.

2557	6s. Luis Enriquez de Guzman	8·75	7·25
2558	6s. Diego de Benavides y de la Cueva	8·75	7·25
2559	6s. Pedro Antonio Fernandez de Castro	8·75	7·25
2560	6s. Baltasar de la Cueva Enriquez	8·75	7·25

1070 Aboriginal (Inti Raymi (Festival of the Sun))

2008. America. Festivals. Multicoloured.

2561	6s.50 Type **1070**	9·25	7·75
2562	6s.50 Grapes and dancer (Festival de la Vendima)	9·25	7·75

1071 Postman and Customers

2008. Serpost–Ease of Exports.

2563	**1071**	10s. multicoloured	17·00	13·00

1072 Beibel

2008. Olympic Games, Beijing. Multicoloured.

2564	1s.40 Type **1072**	2·00	1·60
2565	1s.40 Jingjing	2·00	1·60
2566	1s.40 Yingying	2·00	1·60
2567	1s.40 Nini	2·00	1·60

1073 Ruins

2008. ALC–UE (Latin American and Caribbean—European Union Cooperation) Summit.

2568	**1073**	6s.50 vermilion and black	9·25	7·75

1074 Flags and Arms

2008. Euro-Latin American Parliamentary Assembly, Lima.

2569	**1074**	6s.50 multicoloured	9·25	7·75

1075 Aurelio Sosa

2008. Birth Centenary of Aurelio Miro Queseda Sosa (journalist and writer).

2570	2s.50 **1075** multic coloured	3·75	3·00

1076 Woman writing on Blackboard

2008. National Literacy Campaign.

2571	**1076**	2s.50 multicoloured	3·75	3·00

1077 Petra, Jordan

2008. New Seven Wonders of the World. Sheet 150×130 mm containing T **1077** and similar horiz designs.. Multicoloured.

MS2572	2s.50 Type **1077**; 2s.50 Machu Pichu, Peru; 2s.50 Great Wall, China; 2s.50 Christo Redentor, Brazil; 7s.50 Chichen Itza, Mexico; 10s. Colosseum, Rome; 10s.50 Taj Mahal, India	32·00	32·00

1078 Avocados

2008. Exports. Multicoloured.

2573	5s.50 Type **1078**	8·00	6·50
2574	5s.50 Olives	8·00	6·50
2575	5s.50 Cotton flowers	8·00	6·50

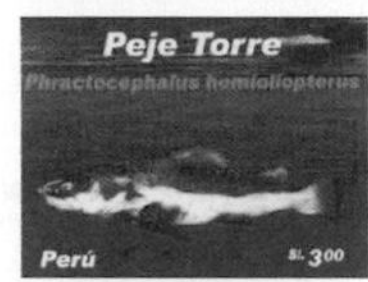

1079 *Phractocephalus hemioliopterus*

2008. Fish. Sheet 135×96 mm containing T **1079** and similar horiz designs. Multicoloured.

MS2576	3s.×5, Type **1079**; *Mylossoma duriventre; Piaractus brachypomus* (inscr 'braphypomus'); *Ageneiosus ucayalensis; Brycon melanopterus*	21·00	21·00

The stamps and margins of **MS**2576 form a composite design.

1080 Christ sat in Judgement

2008. The Last Judgement, Cathedral, Lima. Multicoloured.

2577	6s.50 Type **1080**	9·25	7·75
2578	6s.50 Angels and the damned	9·25	7·75
2579	6s.50 Christ holding sword and the damned	9·25	7·75
2580	6s.50 Christ, Saints and the saved	9·25	7·75

1081 Edwin Vasquez Cam

2008. 60th Anniv of Edwin Vasquez Cam's Olympic Gold Medal for Pistol Shooting.

2581	**1081**	6s. multicoloured	8·75	7·25

1082 *Espostoa mirabilis*

2008. Peruvian Cacti. Multicoloured.

2582	7s.50 Type **1082**	11·00	9·00
2583	7s.50 *Matucana oreodoxa*	11·00	9·00
2584	7s.50 *Melocactus onychacanthus*	11·00	9·00

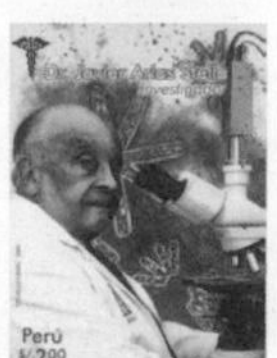
1083 Javier Arias Stella

2008. Javier Arias Stella (scientist, politician, Minister of Health and Foreign Minister).

2585	**1083**	2s. multicoloured	3·00	2·40

1084 Girl and Potatoes

2008. International Year of Potato.

2586	**1084**	5s.50 multicoloured	8·00	6·50

1085 *Cattleya rex*

2008. Orchids. Multicoloured.

2587	7s. Type **1085**	10·50	8·50
2588	7s. *Cattleya maxima*	10·50	8·50

1086 Facade

2008. Centenary of Crypt of Heroes. Sheet 100×80 mm.

MS2589	multicoloured	17·00	17·00

1087 Architecture, Ceramics and Silver, Tiahuanaco

2008. Cultural Heritage. Multicoloured.

2590	2s. Type **1087**	3·00	2·40
2591a	6s. Ceramics and metallurgy, Recuay	8·75	7·25

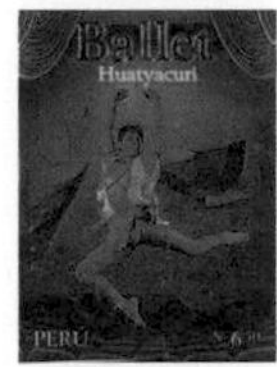
1088 *Huatyacuri* (ballet)

2008. Ballet and Theatre. Multicoloured.

2592	6s.50 Type **1088**	9·25	7·75
2593	6s.50 *Na Catita* (theatre)	9·25	7·75

1089 Mochica Ceramic

2008. 50th Anniv of Faculty of Medicine, National University of Trujillo.

2594	**1089**	6s. multicoloured	8·75	7·25

1090 *Araneidae micrathena*

2008. Spiders. Sheet 80×100 mm containing T **1090** and similar horiz designs.. Multicoloured.

MS2595	2s.×4 Type **1088**; *Lycosidae lyscosinae; Salticidae; Lycosidae aglaoctenus*	12·00	9·50

1091 1822 2r. Note

2008. First Currency of Independence. Sheet 80×100 mm containing T **1091** and similar horiz designs. Multicoloured.

MS2596	8s.50×2, Type **1091**; 1822 8r. peso	7·25	7·25

1092 Choquequirao

2008. Cultural Heritage. Choquequirao. Sheet 100×80 mm.

MS2597	multicoloured	17·00	17·00

1093 Portico

2008. 40th Anniv of Inquisition Museum. Multicoloured.

2598	6s. Type **1093**	8·75	7·25
2599	6s. Seated inquisitors	8·75	7·25

1094 Traffic Policeman

2008. Traffic Control Campaign.

2600	**1094**	6s.50 multicoloured	9·25	7·75

1095 Emblem

2008. 50th Anniv of Edgardo Rebagliati Martins National Hospital.

2601	**1095**	2s. multicoloured	3·00	2·40

1096 Textile

2008. Textiles. Manto Paracas. Multicoloured.

2602	6s. Type **1096**	8·75	7·25
2603	6s. Geometric shapes, red-brown background	8·75	7·25
2604	6s. Squares on black background, stylized figures in border	8·75	7·25
2605	6s. Ochre and brown background, stylized figures	8·75	7·25

1097 *Xenoglaux loweryi* (long-whiskered owlet)

2008. Endangered Species.

2606	**1097**	7s.50 multicoloured	11·00	9·00

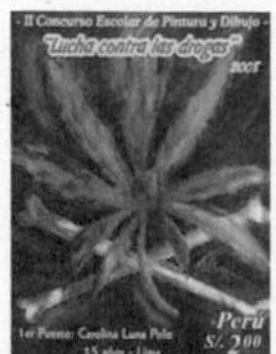

1098 Cannabis Leaves and Crossed Bones (Carolina Luna Polo) (1st)

2008. Fight against Drug Abuse. Winning Designs in Children's Painting Competition. Multicoloured.

2607 2s. Type **1098** 3·00 2·40

2608 2s. Sad and happy children (Diego Gutierrez) (2nd) (horiz) 3·00 2·40

1099 The Nativity

2008. Christmas.

2609 **1099** 8s.50 multicoloured 13·00 11·00

1100 Presidents Alan Garcia Perez (Peru) and George W. Bush (USA)

2008. First Anniv of Peru–USA Trade Promotion Agreement.

2610 **1100** 6s. multicoloured 8·75 7·25

1101 Jeronimo de Loayza Gonzalez

2008. Jeronimo de Loayza Gonzalez (first archbishop of Lima) Commemoration.

2611 **1101** 2s. multicoloured 3·00 2·40

1102 Wiracocha

2008. Myths and Legends. Wiracocha (creator god). Sheet 152×76 mm containing T **1102** and similar horiz designs. multicoloured.

MS2612 2s.50×3, Type **1102**; Creating flowers; Walking through landscape 11·25 11·25

1103 Ice Cliffs, South Pole

2009. Preserve Polar Regions and Glaciers. Sheet 120×80 mm containing T **1103** and similar horiz designs. Multicoloured.

MS2613 2s.20×4, Type **1103**; Raising flag; Emblem of International Polar Year; Quelcayya glacier, Cusco 12·00 12·00

1104 Emblem

2009. 30th Anniv of Business Administration College

2614 **1104** 6s.50 multicoloured 9·00 7·25

1105 Sun and Planets

2009. International Heliophysical Year.

2615 **1105** 5s.50 multicoloured 9·00 6·50

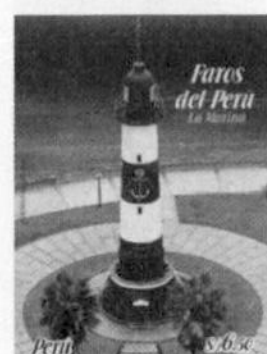

1106 La Marina

2008. Lighthouses. Multicoloured.

2617 6s.50 Type **1106** 9·25 7·75

2618 6s.50 Muelle Darsena 9·25 7·75

1107 Sunflower

2009. Sunflowers. Multicoloured.

2619 2s.50 Type **1107** 3·75 3·00

2620 2s.50 Sunflower in frame 3·75 3·00

1108 Faces of Different Ethnicity and 'HONRADEZ'

2009. Honesty and Punctuality. Multicoloured.

2621 6s.50 Type **1108** 9·00 6·50

2622 6s.50 Torso with clock for face and 'PUNTUALIDAD' (vert) 9·00 6·50

1109 Symbols of Weather

2009. International Meteorological Day.

2623 **1109** 2s. multicoloured 3·00 2·40

1110 Canon del Colca

2009. Canyons. Multicoloured.

2624 2s. Type **1110** 3·00 2·40

2625 2s. Canon de Cotahuasi 3·00 2·40

2626 2s. Canon del Pato 3·00 2·40

Nos. 2624/6 were printed, *se-tenant*, forming a composite design.

1111 Parachutist

2009. Adventurous Sports. Parachuting. Multicoloured.

2627 7s. Type **1111** 12·00 10·00

2628 7s. Parachutist in close up 12·00 10·00

Nos. 2627/8 were printed, *se-tenant* forming a composite design.

1112 Boy riding Ox

2009. Chinese New Year. Year of the Ox. Multicoloured.

2629 2s.50 Type **1112** 3·75 3·00

2630 2s.50 Symbol and ox's head 3·75 3·00

1113 Hand holding Globe

2009. Earth Day.

2631 **1113** 5s.50 multicoloured 8·00 6·50

2009. Viceroys. As T **887**. Multicoloured.

2632 6s. Melchor de Linan y Cisneros 8·75 7·25

2633 6s. Melchor de Navarra y Rocafull 8·75 7·25

2634 6s. Melchor Portocarrero Lasso de la Vega 8·75 7·25

2635 6s. Manuel de Oms y de Santa Pau 8·75 7·25

No. 2636 and Type **1114** are left for 50th Anniv of Central University, issued on 30 April 2009, not yet received.

No. 2639/42 and Type **1116** are left for Endangered Species, issued on 4 May 2009, not yet received.

1115 Frontispiece

2009. 400th Anniv of Royal Commentaries of the Incas

2637 2s. Type **1115** 1·10 90

2638 2s. GarciLaso De la Vega (author) 1·10 90

2009. First Currency of Independence. One sheet 80×100 mm containing multicoloured designs as T **1091**.

MS2643 3s.×2, 1826 'Libertad Parada' (vert); Obverse 8·75 7·25

1117 Horse Riders (Munequeria Cusquena)

2009. Peruvian Crafts. Multicoloured.

2644 6s.50 Type **1117** 8·00 7·50

2645 6s.50 Retalbo (Retalbo Ayacuchano) 8·00 7·50

2646 6s.50 Bull (Torito de Pucara) 8·00 7·50

No. 2647 and Type **1118** are left for Dog, issued on 15 May 2009, not yet received.

1119 *Farfantepenaeus califoniensis*

2009. Crustaceans. Multicoloured.

2648 10s. Type **1119** 15·00 15·00

2649 10s. *Sicyonia aliaffinis* 15·00 15·00

2650 10s. *Ucides occidentalis* 15·00 15·00

2651 10s. *Palinurus elephas* 15·00 15·00

Nos. 2648/51 were printed, *se-tenant* forming a composite design.

1120 Gateway and Bell Tower

2008. 80th Anniv of Santiago de Surco Municipality.

2652 **1120** 5s.50 multicoloured 8·00 6·50

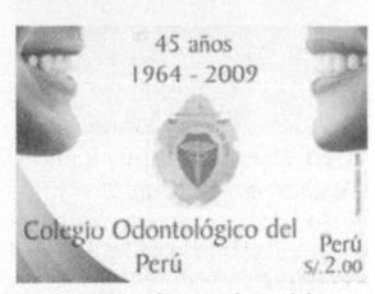

1121 *Pisagua*

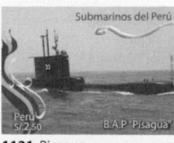

2009. Submarines. Multicoloured.

2653 2s.50 Type **1121** 3·75 3·00

2654 2s.50 *Arica* 3·75 3·00

1122 Mouths and Emblem

2009. 45th Anniv of School of Dentistry.

2655 **1122** 2s. multicoloured 3·00 2·40

1123 Building

2009. 25th Anniv of Cusco as UNESCO World Heritage Site.

2656 **1123** 2s.50 multicoloured 3·75 3·00

1124 Emblem and Dog

2009. Rabies Awareness Day.

2657 **1124** 5s.50 multicoloured 8·00 6·50

1125 Louis Braille

2009. Birth Bicentenary of Louis Braille (inventor of Braille writing for the blind). Multicoloured.

2658 2s.50 Type **1125** 3·75 3·00

2659 2s.50 Braille letters 3·75 3·00

1126 Ceramics and Textiles

2009. Cultural Heritage. Multicoloured.

2660 2s. Type **1126** 3·00 2·40

2661 2s. Metals and textile 3·00 2·40

1127 Ciro Alegria

2009. Birth Centenary of Ciro Alegria (journalist, politician, and novelist).

2662 **1127** 2s.50 multicoloured 3·75 3·00

1128 Rock Formation

2009. Cumbemayo Archaeological Complex, Cajamarca.

2663 **1128** 7s.50 multicoloured 13·00 12·00

1129 Loreto River

2009. Rivers and Lakes. Multicoloured.
2664 2s.50 Type **1129** 3·75 3·00
2665 2s.50 Lake Titicaca 3·75 3·00

1130 Anniversary Emblem

2009. 60th Anniv of Philatelic Association.
2666 **1130** 2s. multicoloured 3·00 2·40

1131 Victor Raul Haya de la Torre

2009. 30th Death Anniv of Victor Raul Haya de la Torre (political leader).
2667 **1131** 2s. multicoloured 3·00 2·40
Type **1132** is vacant

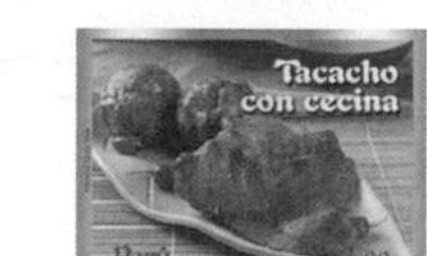

1133 Tacacho con cecina

2009. Peruvian Gastronomy. Sheet 95×135 mm containing T **1133** and similar horiz designs. Multicoloured.
MS2667a 3s.×5, Type **1133**; Ocupa; Cebiche de conchas negras; Picante de papa con cuy frito; Frejoles con cabrito 21·00 21·00

1134 Puente Inca de Qeswachaka

2009. Inca Path. Sheet 91×117 mm containing T **1134** and similar horiz designs. Multicoloured.
MS2668 6s. Type **1134**; 6s. Camino Inca Wanacaure; 6s. Escalerayoe, Lima; 7s.50 Quebrada Huarautambo, Pasco 35·00 35·00

1135 Presidents Alan Garcia of Peru and Hu Jintao of China

2009. Peru–China Commercial Agreement.
2669 **1135** 7s.50 multicoloured 11·00 9·00

1136 Guinea Pig

2009. Exports. Multicoloured.
2670 2s.50 Type **1136** 3·75 3·00
2671 2s.50 Coffee beans 3·75 3·00

1137 Baguatherium (Pyrotheria)

2009. Prehistoric Animals. Sheet 100×80 mm.
MS2672 **1137** 7s. multicoloured 12·00 10·00

1138 *Megalobulimus popuilirianus*

2009. Molluscs. Sheet 110×90 mm containing T **1138** and similar horiz designs. Multicoloured.
MS2673 6s.50×4, Type **1138**; *Megalobulimus capillaccus; Scutalus versicolor; Scutalus proteus* 35·00 35·00

1139 Symbols of China

2009. 160th Anniv of Chinese Immigration to Peru.
2674 **1139** 8s.50 multicoloured 11·00 9·25

1140 Building Façade

2009. National Museum of Archaeology, Anthropology and History.
2675 **1140** 5s.50 multicoloured 8·00 6·50

1141 *Actitis macularia* (spotted sandpiper)

2009. Birds. Sheet 110×91 mm containing T **1141** and similar horiz designs. Multicoloured.
MS2676 6s.×4, Type **1141**; *Glaucidium brasilianum* (ferruginous pygmy owl); *Numenius phaeopus* (whimbrel); *Egretta caerula* (little blue heron) 34·00 34·00

1142 Luciano Pavarotti

2009. Luciano Pavarotti (tenor) Commemoration.
2677 **1142** 10s.50 multicoloured 16·00 13·00

1143 Orchid and Parrot (Ahmed Lonia Heredia Perez)

2009. Protection of Environment. Winning Designs in Children's Painting Competition. Multicoloured.
2678 2s. Type **1143** 3·00 2·40
2679 2s. Hill as woman feeding hummingbird (Scarle Estefany Rojas Reategui) 3·00 2·40

1144 Virgen de Chapi

2009. Christmas.
2680 **1144** 2s.20 multicoloured 3·25 2·50

1145 Decorated Wall

2010. Chachapoya Culture. Multicoloured.
MS2681 3s.×3, Type **1145**; Main entrance; Corner made of large flat stones 5·75 5·75

1146 Roadway, Barrier and Transit Route

2010. Transport. Multicoloured.
2682 2s. Type **1146** 1·10 90
2683 2s. Buses using transit route 1·10 90
Nos. 2682/3 were printed, *se-tenant*, forming a composite design

1147 Musical Instruments

2010. Day of Afro-Peruvian Culture. Multicoloured.
2684 10c. Type **1146** 30 25
2685 10c. Afro-Peruvian museum, Lima 30 25
Nos. 2684/5 were printed, *se-tenant*, forming a composite design

1148 Rebeca Carrión Cachot

2010. 50th Death Anniv of Rebeca Carrión Cachot (historian and archaeologist)
2686 **1148** 40c. multicoloured 30 25

1149 Virgen de Chapi

2010. 400th Anniv of Arequipa Diocese
2687 **1149** 2s. multicoloured 1·10 90

1150 Zakumi (championship mascot)

2010. World Cup Football Championships, South Africa.. Multicoloured.
MS2688 10s.×4, Type **1150**; Championship emblem; Trophy; Player heading ball 19·00 19·00

1151 San Francisco Solano

2010. 400th Death Anniv of Francisco Sánchez-Solano Jiménez (San Francisco Solano) (Franciscan friar)
2689 **1151** 40c. multicoloured 30 25

1153 Gustavo Pons Muzzo

2010. Gustavo Pons Muzzo (historian) Commemoration
2692 **1153** 50c. multicoloured 30 25

1154 Javier Pérez de Cuéllar

2010. 90th Birth Anniv of Javier Pérez de Cuéllar y de la Guerra (diplomat and Secretary-General of the United Nations, 1982-1991)
2693 **1154** 50c. black and brown-red 30 25

1157 Jorge Chávez, Blériot XI Aircraft and Alps

2010. Centenary of Jorge Chávez's Flight (first person to fly across the Alps)
2700 **1157** 2s. multicoloured 1·10 90

1158 Club Emblem

2010. Colegio Nacional de Iquitos Football Club
2701 **1158** 3s. multicoloured 1·60 1·30

1159 Windsurfing (inscr 'VELA' (sailing))

2010. Adventurous Sports
2702 **1159** 3s. multicoloured 1·60 1·30

1160 Club Emblem

2010. Melgar Football Club
2703 **1160** 3s. multicoloured 1·60 1·30

1161 *Anguloa virginalis*

2010. Orchids. Multicoloured.
MS2704 3s.×4, Type **1161**; *Masdevallia pernix; Stanhopea marizaiana; Telipogon campoverdi* 6·00 6·00

1162 *Thalassocnus littoralis*

2010. Pre-historic Animal Fossils

MS2705	**1162**	10s. multicoloured	4·75	4·75

1163 Child enclosed in Water Droplet (second place)

2010. Winning Designs in Painting Competition 'Cuidemos el Agua'. Multicoloured.

2707	2s. Type **1163**	1·10	90
2708	2s. Figure sweeping rubbish under water, watched by eyes in the sky (first place)	1·10	90

1164 Club Emblem

2010. Alianza Lima Football Club

2709	**1164**	3s. multicoloured	1·60	1·30

1165 Retablo (cajones sanmarcos) (Jesús Urbano Rojas), Ayacucho

2010. Peruvian Craftmanships. Multicoloured.

2710	2s. Type **1165**	1·10	90
2711	2s. Polychrome stone carving (Fidel Barrientos Bustos), La Procession San Pedro, Apurimac	1·10	90
2712	2s. La Virgen del Pino (statue) (Antonio Olave Palomino), Cusco	1·10	90

1166 Frédéric Chopin

2010. Birth Bicentenary of Frédéric François Chopin

2713	**1166**	3s. multicoloured	1·60	1·30

1167 Reverse of Seated Liberty

2010. Seated Liberty 1 sol Coin (1863)

MS2713a	**1167**	3s. multicoloured	1·60	1·30

1168 Tiger

2010. Chinese New Year. Year of the Tiger. Multicoloured.

2714	20c. Type **1168**	30	25
2715	20c. Emblem and tiger looking over left shoulder	30	25

Nos. 2714/15 were printed, *se-tenant*, forming a composite design

1169 *Suillus luteos*

2010. Fungi. Multicoloured.

2716	6s. Type **1169**	2·75	2·20
2717	6s. *Pleurotus cornucopiae*	2·75	2·20

Nos. 2716/17 were printed, *se-tenant* forming a composite design

1170 Cabezas Clavas de Chavin

2010. Archaeology

MS2718	**1170**	10s. multicoloured	4·75	4·75

1171 Circuito Magico del Agua, Lima

2010. Tourism. Multicoloured.

2719	3s. Type **1171**	1·60	1·30
2720	3s. Laguna del Parque, Huascar (Huascar Park Lagoon)	1·60	1·30

1172 Christmas Tree

2010. Christmas

2721	**1172**	10s. multicoloured	4·75	3·75

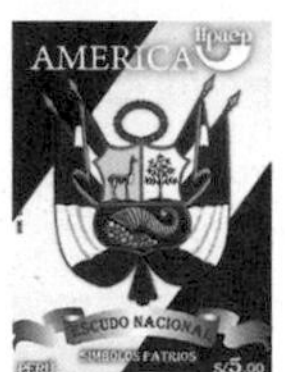

1173 Arms

2010. America. Multicoloured.

2722	5s. Type **1173**	2·75	2·20
2723	5s. Flag	2·75	2·20

1174 Merry Weather Steam Pump (1860)

2010. 150th anniv of Volunteer Firefighters Corps of Peru. Multicoloured.

2724	6s. Type **1174**	3·25	3·00
2725	6s. Modern Pierce Contender firefighting appliance	3·25	3·00

Nos. 2724/5 were printed, *se-tenant*, forming a composite design

1174a Cathedral and Plaza Mayor

2011. 40th Lions Forum Latin America and Caribbean - 2011 (XL FOLAC), Lima, Peru

2726	**1174a**	7s.80 multicoloured	4·25	3·25

1175 Jose Maria Arguedas

2011. Birth Centenary of Jose Maria Arguedas (writer and anthropologist)

2727	**1175**	6s.60 multicoloured	3·25	2·40

No. 2728 and Type **1176** are left for Centenary of UPAEP.

1177 South Quay, Callao Port

2011. Infrastructure. Multicoloured.

2729	5s. Type **1177**	2·75	2·10
2730	5s.20 South Inter-Oceanic Highway	3·00	2·30

1178 Girl Scout

2011. Centenary of Scouting in Peru. Multicoloured.

2731	6s.40 Type **1178**	3·00	2·30
2732	6s.40 Boy scout	3·00	2·30

1179 Anniversary Emblem and Array

2011. 50th Anniv of Radio Telescope, Jicamarca

2733	**1179**	6s.60 multicoloured	3·25	2·40

1180 Mario Vargas Llosa receiving Award from King Carl XVI Gustaf of Sweden

2011. Mario Vargas Llosa's Nobel Prize for Literature, 2010

2734	**1180**	7s.80 multicoloured	4·25	3·25

1181 Submarine

2011. Centenary of Submarine Forces in Peru. Multicoloured.

2735	7s.20 Type **1181**	3·50	2·60
2736	7s.20 Submarines, large conning tower in foreground	3·50	2·60

Nos. 2745/6 were printed, *se-tenant*, forming a composite design.

1182 Javier Pulgar Vidal

2011. Birth Centenary of Javier Pulgar Vidal (geographer)

2737	**1182**	2s.40 multicoloured	1·30	1·00

1183 Male Figure and AIDS Ribbon (left)

2011. AIDS Prevention Day. Each scarlet-vermilion and black.

2738	5s.50 Type **1183**	2·75	2·10
2739	5s.50 AIDS ribbon (right) and female figure	2·75	2·10

Nos. 2748/9 were printed, *se-tenant*, forming a composite design.

1184 Francisco Antonio de Zela

2011. Birth Bicentenary of Francisco Antonio de Zela y Arizaga. Multicoloured.

2740	7s.20 Type **1184**	3·50	2·60
2741	7s.20 Francisco Antonio de Zela (statue)	3·50	2·60

1185 Anniversary Emblem and Campus

2011. 50th Anniv of National University of Peruvian Amazon (UNAP)

2742	**1185**	2s.70 multicoloured	1·40	1·10

1186 Theatre Façade

2011. National Theatre of Peru

2743	**1186**	5s. multicoloured	2·75	2·10

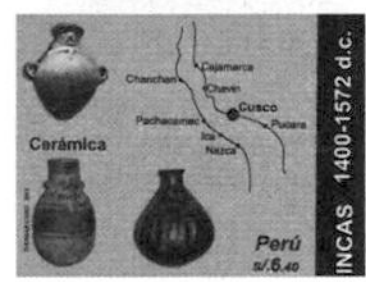

1187 Inca Ceramics and Map of Cusco Area

2011. Cutural Heritage. Ceramics. Multicoloured.

2744	6s.40 Type **1187**	3·00	2·30
2745	6s.40 Chachapoyas ceramics and map	3·00	2·30

2011. Viceroys. Multicoloured.

2746	7s.80 Jose Antonio de Mendoza	4·25	3·25
2747	7s.80 Jose Antonio Manso de Velasco	4·25	3·25
2748	7s.80 Manuel de Amat y Junyent	4·25	3·25
2749	7s.80 Manuel Guirior	4·25	3·25

1188 Rabbit

2011. Chinese New Year. Year of the Rabbit

2750	5s.50 Type **1188**	2·75	2·10
2751	5s.50 Chinese character	2·75	2·10

Nos. 2750/1 were printed, *se-tenant*, forming a composite design.

1189 Motocross

2011. Adventurous Sports

2752	**1189**	7s.80 multicoloured	4·25	3·25

No. 2753 and Type **1190** are left for Centenary of Machu Pichu, issued on 5 July 2011, not yet received.

1191 Huaconada

2011. Cultural Heritage. Dances. Multicoloured.

2754	9s. Type **1191**	4·50	3·50
2755	9s. Danza de las Tijeras	4·50	3·50

1192 Engine

2011. Electric Train Transportation. Lima Subway. Multicoloured.

2756	5s.50 Type **1192**	2·75	2·10
2757	5s.50 Train in station	2·75	2·10

1193 *Maxillaria pyhalae*

2011. Endangered Species. Orchid. *Maxillaria pyhalae*

2758	**1193**	10s.50 multicoloured	5·25	4·00

Nos. 2759/808 and Type **1194** are left for Presidents, issued on 25 July 2011, not yet received.

1195 Arms, 'Au' (gold) and Symbols of Chemistry

2011. International Year of Chemistry

2809	**1195**	7s.20 multicoloured	3·50	2·60

1196 Sherley Breshley Suchupe Calderon (1st place)

2011. School Children's Painting Competition. Prevention of Natural Disasters. Prize Winners. Multicoloured.

2810	20c. Carlos Renato Huaynasi Calcina (2nd Place)	15	10
2811	2s.40 Type **1196**	1·30	1·10

1197 Manuscripts

2011. 150th Anniv of National Archives

2812	**1197**	5s.80 multicoloured	2·75	2·30

1198 'Lomo Saltado'

2011. Gastronomy. Multicoloured.

MS2813 7s.80×4, Type **1198**; 'Aji de Gllina'; 'Tiradito de Pescado'; 'Chicharrón'	17·00	17·00

1199 Clorinda Matto de Turner

2011. Clorinda Matto de Turner (writer) Commemoration

2814	**1199**	3s.60 multicoloured	1·90	1·30

1200 Reverse of 1838 South Peruvian 8 Escudos Coin

2011. Peruvian Coins. Multicoloured.

2815	5s.80 Type **1200**	3·00	2·50
2816	5s.80 Obverse	3·00	2·50

Nos. 2825/6 were printed, *se-tenant*, forming a composite design.

1201 University Campus

2011. 50th Anniv of Cayetano Heredia University

2817	**1201**	3s.60 multicoloured	1·90	1·50

1202 Juan Bielovucic Cavalie

2011. Centenary of First Flight in Peru

2818	**1202**	7s.20 multicoloured	3·50	2·60

1203 *Lagothrix flavicauda*

2011. Primates. Multicoloured.

MS2819 7s.80×4, Type **1203**; *Callicebus oenanthe*; *Aotus miconax*; *Cacajao calvus*	17·00	17·00

1204 Bud

2011. Native Flora. *Gossypium barbadense*. Multicoloured.

2820	8s.50 Type **1204**	4·00	3·00
2821	8s.50 Cotton boll	4·00	3·00

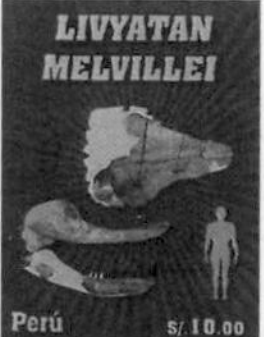

1205 Livyatan melvillei

2011. Pre-historic Animal Fossils. Sheet 80×100 mm

MS2822 **1205** 10s. multicoloured	4·75	4·75

No. 2823 and Type **1206** are left for Birth Bicentenary of Liszt, issued on 22 October 2011, not yet received.

No. 2824/5 and Type **1207** are left for Birds, issued on 28 October 2011, not yet received.

1208 Inscr 'PINTURA CUSQUEÑA'

2011. Christmas

2826	**1208**	5s.50 multicoloured	2·75	2·30

1209 Lion-shaped Box

2011. America. Mailboxes. Multicoloured.

2827	10s. Type **1209**	5·00	3·75
2828	10s. Red Post Office box	5·00	3·75

1210 Martin Chambi

2011. Photography. Martin Chambi (first major indigenous Latin American photographer) Commemoration

2829	**1210**	5s.20 multicoloured	2·50	1·90

No. 2830 and Type **1211** are left for South America-Arabic Countries Summit, issued on 10 November 2011, not yet received.

1212 Coffee Cups

2011. Peruvian Coffee. Organic Champion

2831	**1212**	6s.60 multicoloured	3·00	2·20

1213 San Sebastian

2011. San Sebastian, Patron of Province of Chepen

2832	**1213**	2s. multicoloured	1·10	85

EXPRESS LETTER STAMPS

1908. Optd **EXPRESO**.

E373	**76**	10c. black	26·00	19·00
E382	-	10c. blue (No. 377)	24·00	20·00
E383	**101**	10c. black and brown	40·00	23·00

OFFICIAL STAMPS

1890. Stamps of 1866 optd **GOBIERNO** in frame.

O287	**15**	1c. violet	2·40	2·30
O324	**15**	1c. red	13·00	13·00
O288	**16**	2c. green	2·40	2·30
O325	**16**	2c. blue	13·00	13·00
O289	**16**	5c. orange	3·50	2·75
O326	**10**	5c. lake	11·00	11·00
O290	**16**	10c. black	1·90	1·20
O291	**16**	20c. blue	5·50	3·50

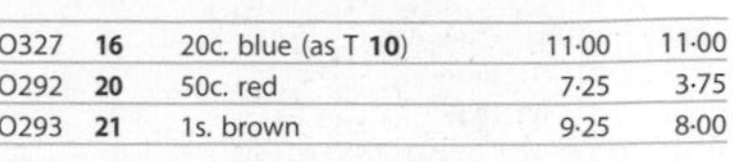

O327	**16**	20c. blue (as T **10**)	11·00	11·00
O292	**20**	50c. red	7·25	3·75
O293	**21**	1s. brown	9·25	8·00

1894. Stamps of 1894 (with "Head" optd) optd **GOBIERNO** in frame.

O305	**15**	1c. orange (No. 294)	40·00	34·00
O306	**15**	1c. green (No. 295)	2·40	2·30
O307	**16**	2c. violet (No. 296)	2·40	2·30
O308	**16**	2c. red (No. 297)	2·40	2·30
O309	**16**	5c. blue (No. 298)	19·00	16·00
O310	**16**	10c. green (No. 299)	6·00	5·75
O311	**20**	50c. green (No. 300)	9·25	9·00

1894. Stamps of 1894 (with "Head" and "Horseshoe" optd) optd **GOBIERNO** in frame.

O312	**16**	2c. red (No. 301)	3·50	3·50
O313	**16**	5c. blue (No. 302)	3·50	3·50

1896. Stamps of 1896 optd **GOBIERNO**.

O348	**75**	1c. blue	35	30
O349	**76**	10c. yellow	2·00	85
O350	**76**	10c. black	35	30
O351	**77**	50c. red	5·00	5·00

O108

1909

O382	**108**	1c. red	55	30
O385	**108**	10c. purple	90	45
O572	**108**	10c. brown	20	10
O573	**108**	50c. green	65	65

1935. Optd **Servicio Oficial.**

O567	**184**	10c. red	35	20

PARCEL POST STAMPS

P79

1895. Different frames.

P348	**79**	1c. purple	4·00	3·50
P349	**79**	2c. brown	5·50	3·75
P350	**79**	5c. blue	19·00	10·50
P351	**79**	10c. brown	24·00	18·00
P352	**79**	20c. pink	29·00	23·00
P353	**79**	50c. green	85·00	75·00

1903. Surch in words.

P361	1c. on 20c. pink	11·00	6·75
P362	1c. on 50c. green	11·00	10·00
P363	5c. on 10c. brown	70·00	55·00

POSTAGE DUE STAMPS

D22 D23

1874

D31	**D 22**	1c. brown	45	30
D32	**D 23**	5c. red	55	30
D33	**D 23**	10c. orange	65	30
D34	**D 23**	20c. blue	1·10	55
D35	**D 23**	50c. brown	17·00	6·50

1881. Optd with T **24** ("LIMA" at foot instead of "PERU").

D47	**D 22**	1c. brown	6·00	5·75
D48	**D 23**	5c. red	12·00	11·50
D49	**D 23**	10c. orange	12·00	11·50
D50	**D 23**	20c. blue	46·00	34·00
D51	**D 23**	50c. brown	£100	95·00

1881. Optd **LIMA CORREOS** in double-lined circle.

D52	**D 22**	1c. brown	9·25	9·25
D53	**D 23**	5c. red	11·00	10·50
D54	**D 23**	10c. orange	13·00	13·00
D55	**D 23**	20c. blue	55·00	38·00
D56	**D 23**	50c. brown	£130	£130

1883. Optd with T **24** (inscr "LIMA" instead of "PERU") and also with T **28a**.

D247	**D 22**	1c. brown	9·25	6·50
D250	**D 23**	5c. red	17·00	16·00
D253	**D 23**	10c. orange	13·00	13·00
D256	**D 23**	20c. blue	£850	£850
D258	**D 23**	50c. brown	60·00	60·00

1884. Optd with T **28a** only.

D259	**D 22**	1c. brown	90	85
D262	**D 23**	5c. red	90	85
D267	**D 23**	10c. orange	90	85
D269	**D 23**	20c. blue	1·90	85
D271	**D 23**	50c. brown	5·50	1·70

1894. Optd **LIMA CORREOS** in double-lined circle and with T **28a**.

D275	**D 22**	1c. brown	31·00	31·00

1896. Optd **DEFICIT**.

D348		1c. brown (D31)	65	55
D349	**D 23**	5c. red (D32)	75	45
D350	**D 23**	10c. orange (D33)	1·00	65
D351	**D 23**	20c. blue (D34)	1·20	85
D352	**20**	50c. red (283)	1·30	85
D353	**21**	1s. brown (284)	1·90	1·20

1899. As T **73**, but inscr "DEFICIT" instead of "FRANQUEO".

D355	5s. green	1·90	10·50
D356	10s. brown	£1700	£1700

1902. Surch **DEFICIT** and value in words.

D361	1c. on 10s. (D356)	75	75
D362	5c. on 10s. (354)	1·90	1·60

1902. Surch **DEFICIT** and value in words.

D363	**23**	1c. on 20c. (D34)	1·10	75
D364	**23**	5c. on 20c. (D34)	2·75	1·80

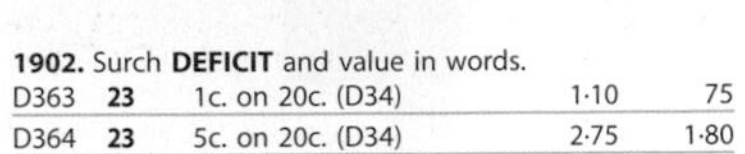

D109

1909

D382	**109**	1c. brown	90	30
D419	**109**	1c. purple	45	30
D420	**109**	2c. purple	45	30
D570	**109**	2c. brown	45	45
D383	**109**	5c. brown	90	30
D421	**109**	5c. purple	65	30
D384	**109**	10c. brown	1·10	45
D422	**109**	10c. purple	90	45
D571	**109**	10c. green	90	85
D385	**109**	50c. brown	1·70	45
D423	**109**	50c. purple	2·75	1·30
D424	**109**	1s. purple	13·00	5·25
D425	**109**	2s. purple	22·00	6·50

1935. Optd **Deficit**.

D568	-	2c. purple (No. 537)	1·30	45
D569	**184**	10c. red	1·30	45

Pt. 9, Pt. 22, Pt. 21

PHILIPPINES

A group of islands in the China Sea, E. of Asia, ceded by Spain to the United States after the war of 1898. Under Japanese Occupation from 1941 until 1945. An independent Republic since 1946.

1854. 20 cuartos = 1 real; 8 reales = 1 peso plata fuerte.
1864. 100 centimos = 1 peso plata fuerte.
1871. 100 centimos = 1 escudo (= ½ peso).
1872. 100 centimos = 1 peseta (=⅕peso).
1876. 1000 milesimas = 100 centavos or centimos = 1 peso.
1899. 100 cents = 1 dollar.
1906. 100 centavos = 1 peso.
1962. 100 sentimos = 1 piso.

SPANISH ADMINISTRATION

1 Queen Isabella II

1854. Imperf.

1	**1**	5c. red	£2500	£425
3	**1**	10c. red	£850	£300
5	**1**	1r. blue	£950	£325
7	**1**	2r. green	£1300	£225

On the 1r. the inscriptions are reversed.

4 Queen Isabella II

1859. Imperf.

13	**4**	5c. red	24·00	7·75
14	**4**	10c. pink	24·00	23·00

5 Queen Isabella II

1861. Larger lettering. Imperf.

17	**5**	5c. red	65·00	16·00

7

1863. Imperf.

19	**7**	5c. red	21·00	7·50
20	**7**	10c. red	65·00	65·00
21	**7**	1r. mauve	£1100	£650
22	**7**	2r. blue	£800	£550

8

1863. Imperf.

25	**8**	1r. green	£170	55·00

1864. As T **14** of Spain, but value in "centimos de peso". Imperf.

26	3⅛c. black on buff	5·25	2·75
27	6 2/8c. green on pink	5·25	1·60
28	12 4/8c. blue on pink	10·50	1·30
29	25c. red on pink	21·00	7·50
30	25c. red on white	16·00	4·75

1868. Optd **HABILITADO POR LA NACION.** (a) On 1854 to 1863 issues of Philippines.

41	**7**	5c. red	£100	55·00
53	**4**	10c. pink	£140	80·00
36		1r. green	70·00	29·00
42	**7**	1r. mauve	£950	£550
52	**1**	1r. blue	£3250	£1600
43	**7**	2r. blue	£800	£375

(b) On 1864 issues of Philippines.

31	**7**	3⅛c. black on buff	27·00	6·50
32	**7**	6 2/8c. green on pink	27·00	6·50
33	**7**	12 4/8c. blue on pink	70·00	37·00
34	**7**	25c. red	32·00	21·00

(c) On Nos. 10/11a of Cuba (as T **8** of Philippines).

44	1r. green	£275	£150
45	2r. red	£375	£150

12

1871

37	**12**	5c. blue	85·00	9·00
38	**12**	10c. green	11·50	7·75
39	**12**	20c. brown	£100	55·00
40	**12**	40c. red	£130	27·00

13 King Amadeo

1872

46	**13**	12c. pink	20·00	7·50
47	**13**	16c. blue	£190	49·00
48a	**13**	25c. grey	15·00	7·00
49	**13**	62c. mauve	46·00	13·00
50	**13**	1p.25 brown	85·00	41·00

14

1874

54	**14**	12c. grey	21·00	6·50
55	**14**	25c. blue	8·25	2·75
56	**14**	62c. pink	65·00	6·50
57	**14**	1p.25 brown	£350	95·00

15

1875. With rosettes each side of "FILIPINAS".

58	**15**	2c. pink	3·00	1·10
59	**15**	2c. blue	£325	£130
60	**15**	6c. orange	15·00	3·50
61	**15**	10c. blue	4·00	1·10
62	**15**	12c. mauve	4·25	1·10
63	**15**	20c. brown	27·00	4·50
64	**15**	25c. green	32·00	1·10

16

1878. Without rosettes.

65	**16**	25m. black	4·25	65
66	**16**	25m. green	95·00	41·00
67	**16**	50m. purple	48·00	17·00
68a	**16**	(62½m.) 0.0625 lilac	85·00	27·00
69	**16**	100m. red	£160	65·00
70	**16**	100m. green	15·00	3·75
71	**16**	125m. blue	7·00	65
72	**16**	200m. pink	49·00	9·25
74	**16**	250m. brown	19·00	3·75

1877. Surch **HABILITADO 12 CS. PTA.** in frame.

75	**15**	12c. on 2c. pink	£160	40·00
76	**16**	12c. on 25m. black	£160	40·00

1879. Surch **CONVENIO UNIVERSAL DE CORREOS HABILITADO** and value in figures and words.

78	2c. on 25m. green	80·00	15·00
79	8c. on 100m. red	55·00	10·00

1880. "Alfonso XII" key-type inscr "FILIPINAS".

97	**X**	1c. green	45	20
82a	**X**	2c. red	1·20	2·30
83	**X**	2½c. brown	11·50	2·30
95	**X**	2 4/8c. blue	85	30
99	**X**	50m. bistre	70	20
85	**X**	5c. grey	1·20	2·30
100	**X**	6c. brown	18·00	2·50
87	**X**	6 2/8c. green	8·50	13·00
88	**X**	8c. brown	60·00	30·00
89	**X**	10c. brown	4·75	2·30
90	**X**	10c. purple	9·50	19·00
91	**X**	10c. green	£600	£350
92	**X**	12 4/8c. pink	2·75	2·30
93	**X**	20c. brown	4·75	2·30
94	**X**	25c. brown	6·25	2·30

1881. "Alfonso XII" key-type inscr "FILIPINAS" with various circular surcharges. (a) **HABILITADO U. POSTAL** and value.

111		1c. on 2 4/8c. blue	1·20	75
102	**X**	10c. on 2 4/8c. blue	11·50	2·30

(b) **HABILITADO CORREOS 2 CENTS. DE PESO.**

101	**X**	2c. on 2½c. brown	5·75	2·30

(c) **HABILITADO PA. U. POSTAL 8 CMOS.**

106	**X**	8c. on 2c. red	11·50	2·75

(d) **HABILITADO PA. CORREOS DE** and value.

107	**X**	10c. cuartos on 2c. red	7·00	2·10
112	**X**	16 cuartos on 2 4/8c. blue	18·00	4·50
103	**X**	20c. on 8c. brown	15·00	5·25
113	**X**	1r. on 2c. red	11·50	4·50
109	**X**	1r. on 5c. lilac	9·50	4·00
110	**X**	1r. on 8c. brown	18·00	7·00
105	**X**	2r. on 2 4/8c. blue	9·50	2·75

25

29

30

31

1881. Fiscal and telegraph stamps. (a) with circular surch **HABILITADO CORREOS, HABILITADO PARA CORREOS, HABILITADO PA. U. POSTAL** or **HABILITADO PA. CORREOS** and value in figures and words.

115	**25**	2c. on 10 cuartos bistre	41·00	26·00
129	**29**	2c. on 200m. green	9·00	4·50
116	**25**	2 4/8c. on 10 cuartos bistre	5·75	1·30
117	**25**	2 4/8c. on 2r. blue	£300	£130
124	**25**	6 2/8c. on 12 4/8c. lilac	9·00	5·25
119	**25**	8c. on 10c. brown	£325	£250
118	**25**	8c. on 2r. blue	16·00	4·25
123	**25**	16 cmos. on 2r. blue	10·50	4·50
137	**31**	20c. on 150m. blue	†	†
134	**31**	20c. on 250m. blue	£550	£325
127	**25**	1r. on 10 cuartos bistre	21·00	7·50
121	**25**	1r. on 12 4/8c. lilac	15·00	7·00
130	**29**	1r. on 200m. green	£110	70·00
131	**29**	1r. on 1 peso green	55·00	27·00
132	**30**	1r. on 10 pesetas bistre	80·00	41·00
133	**31**	2r. on 250m. blue	18·00	5·75

(b) With two circular surcharges as above, showing two different values.

128	**25**	8c. on 2r. on 2r. blue	†	†
136	**31**	1r. on 20c. on 250m. blue	19·00	8·00

(c) Optd **HABILITADO PARA CORREOS** in straight lines.

122	**25**	10 cuartos bistre	£300	£130
126	**25**	1r. green	£160	£120

1887. Various stamps with oval surch **UNION GRAL. POSTAL HABILITADO** (No. 142) or **HABILITADO PARA COMMUNICACIONES** and new value. (a) "Alfonso XII" key-type inscr "FILIPINAS".

138	**X**	2 4/8c. on 1c. green	3·75	2·10
139	**X**	2 4/8c. on 5c. lilac	2·50	1·20
140	**X**	2 4/8c. on 50m. bistre	3·50	2·30
141	**X**	2 4/8c. on 10c. green	2·50	1·30
142	**X**	8c. on 2 4/8c. blue	1·50	85

34

(b) "Alfonso XII" key-type inscr "FILIPAS-IMPRESOS".

143	2 4/8c. on⅛c. green	85	30

(c) Fiscal and telegraph stamps.

144	**29**	2 4/8c. on 200m. green	7·50	3·25
146	**34**	2 4/8c. on 1c. bistre	1·50	1·10
145	**29**	2 4/8c. on 20c. brown	20·00	9·00

1889. Various stamps with oval surch **RECARGO DE CONSUMOS HABILITADO** and new value. (a) "Alfonso XII" key-type inscr "FILIPINAS".

147	**X**	2 4/8c. on 1c. green	†	†
148	**X**	2 4/8c. on 2c. red	†	†
149	**X**	2 4/8c. on 2 4/8c. blue	†	†
150	**X**	2 4/8c. on 5c. lilac	†	†
151	**X**	2 4/8c. on 50m. bistre	†	†
152	**X**	2 4/8c. on 12 4/8c. pink	†	†

(c) Fiscal and telegraph stamps.

153	**34**	2 4/8c. on 1c. bistre	†	†
154	**34**	2 4/8c. on 2c. red	†	†
155	**34**	2 4/8c. on 2 4/8c. brown	†	†
156	**34**	2 4/8c. on 5c. blue	†	†
157	**34**	2 4/8c. on 10c. green	†	†
158	**34**	2 4/8c. on 10c. mauve	†	†
159	**34**	2 4/8c.on 20c. mauve	†	†
161	-	17 4/8c. on 5p. green	†	†

No. 161 is a fiscal stamp inscribed "DERECHO JUDICIAL" with a central motif as T **43** of Spain.

(b) "Alfonso XII" key-type inscr "FILIPAS-IMPRESOS".

160	2 4/8c. on⅛c. green	†	†

1890. "Baby" key-type inscr "FILIPINAS".

176	**Y**	1c. violet	1·40	45
188	**Y**	1c. red	27·00	11·50
197	**Y**	1c. green	3·75	1·10
162	**Y**	2c. red	20	20
177	**Y**	2c. violet	65	20
190	**Y**	2c. brown	30	20
198	**Y**	2c. blue	45	25
163	**Y**	2 4/8c. blue	75	20
178	**Y**	2 4/8c. grey	45	20
164	**Y**	5c. green	75	20
165	**Y**	5c. blue	75	20
199	**Y**	5c. brown	15·00	5·50
181	**Y**	6c. purple	45	20
192	**Y**	6c. red	2·75	1·30
166	**Y**	8c. green	45	20
182	**Y**	8c. blue	1·10	45
193	**Y**	8c. red	1·30	45
167	**Y**	10c. green	2·75	45
172	**Y**	10c. pink	1·20	35
202	**Y**	10c. brown	95	45
173	**Y**	12 4/8c. green	30	20
184	**Y**	12 4/8c. orange	1·20	20
185	**Y**	15c. brown	1·40	45
195	**Y**	15c. red	3·00	1·30
203	**Y**	15c. green	3·50	2·50
169	**Y**	20c. red	£140	70·00
186	**Y**	20c. brown	3·50	55
196	**Y**	20c. purple	32·00	11·50
204	**Y**	20c. orange	7·50	2·75
170	**Y**	25c. brown	10·50	2·10
175	**Y**	25c. blue	2·20	85

205	Y	40c. purple	32·00	9·25
206	Y	80c. red	43·00	30·00

1897. Surch **HABILITADO CORREOS PARA 1897** and value in frame. (a) "Baby" key-type inscr "FILIPINAS".

212		5c. on 5c. green	7·50	4·25
208	Y	15c. on 15c. red	4·25	2·30
213		15c. on 15c. brown	6·50	3·75
209		20c. on 20c. purple	30·00	17·00
214		20c. on 20c. brown	10·50	6·50
210		20c. on 25c. brown	21·00	14·00

(b) "Alfonso XII" key-type inscr "FILIPINAS".

215	X	5c. on 5c. lilac	8·50	4·00

1898. "Curly Head" key-type inscr "FILIPNAS 1898 y 99".

217	Z	1m. brown	20	20
218	Z	2m. brown	20	20
219	Z	3m. brown	20	20
220	Z	4m. brown	13·00	2·50
221	Z	5m. brown	20	20
222	Z	1c. purple	20	20
223	Z	2c. green	20	20
224	Z	3c. brown	20	20
225	Z	4c. orange	21·00	15·00
226	Z	5c. red	45	20
227	Z	6c. blue	1·50	80
228	Z	8c. brown	70	20
229	Z	10c. red	2·75	1·50
230	Z	15c. grey	2·50	1·20
231	Z	20c. purple	2·50	1·80
232	Z	40c. lilac	1·50	1·20
233	Z	60c. black	6·50	4·00
234	Z	80c. brown	8·50	4·00
235	Z	1p. green	30·00	19·00
236	Z	2p. blue	43·00	23·00

STAMPS FOR PRINTED MATTER

1886. "Alfonso XII" key-type inscr "FILIPAS-IMPRESOS".

P138	X	1m. red	30	20
P139	X	⅛c. green	30	20
P140	X	2m. blue	30	20
P141	X	5m. brown	30	20

1890. "Baby" key-type inscr "FILIPAS-IMPRESOS".

P171	Y	1m. purple	20	20
P172	Y	⅛c. purple	20	20
P173	Y	2m. purple	20	20
P174	Y	5m. purple	20	20

1892. "Baby" key-type inscr "FILIPAS-IMPRESOS".

P192		1m. green	3·75	95
P193		⅛c. green	1·70	20
P194		2m. green	4·50	95
P191	Y	5m. green	£400	85·00

1894. "Baby" key-type inscr "FILIPAS-IMPRESOS".

P197	1m. grey	35	35
P198	⅛c. brown	35	35
P199	2m. grey	35	35
P200	5m. grey	35	35

1896. "Baby" key-type inscr "FILIPAS-IMPRESOS".

P205	1m. blue	45	20
P206	⅛c. blue	1·50	1·10
P207	2m. brown	55	20
P208	5m. blue	4·25	2·50

UNITED STATES ADMINISTRATION

1899. United States stamps of 1894 (No. 267 etc) optd **PHILIPPINES**.

252	-	1c. green	3·50	70
253	-	2c. red	2·30	1·00
255	-	3c. violet	9·00	1·40
256	-	4c. brown	34·00	6·25
257	-	5c. blue	9·00	1·10
258	-	6c. purple	45·00	8·50
259	-	8c. brown	45·00	9·00
260	-	10c. brown	34·00	5·00
262	-	15c. green	50·00	9·00
263	83	50c. orange	£160	45·00
264	-	$1 black	£550	£350
266	-	$2 blue	£550	£425
267	-	$5 green	£1000	£950

1903. United States stamps of 1902 optd **PHILIPPINES**.

268	103	1c. green	6·25	45
269	104	2c. red	9·00	1·40
270	105	3c. violet	85·00	16·00
271a	106	4c. brown	90·00	25·00
272	107	5c. blue	17·00	1·10
273	108	6c. lake	£100	28·00
274	109	8c. violet	55·00	18·00
275	110	10c. brown	32·00	2·75
276	111	13c. purple	45·00	20·00
277	112	15c. olive	75·00	18·00
278	113	50c. orange	£150	45·00
279	114	$1 black	£650	£350
280	115	$2 blue	£950	£950
281	116	$5 green	£1300	£5500

1904. United States stamp of 1903 optd **PHILIPPINES**.

282a	117	2c. red	8·00	2·75

45 Rizal

46 Arms of Manila

1906. Various portraits as T **45** and T **46**.

337	45	2c. green	25	25
338	-	4c. red (McKinley)	25	25
339	-	6c. violet (Magellan)	35	25
340	-	8c. brown (Legaspi)	45	25
341	-	10c. blue (Lawton)	35	25
288	-	12c. red (Lincoln)	6·75	2·30
342	-	12c. orange (Lincoln)	35	35
289	-	16c. black (Sampson)	5·75	35
298	-	16c. green (Sampson)	4·00	1·40
344	-	16c. olive (Dewey)	1·10	25
290	-	20c. brown (Washington)	5·75	35
345	-	20c. yellow (Washington)	45	25
291	-	26c. brown (Carriedo)	8·00	2·75
346	-	26c. green (Carriedo)	55	55
292	-	30c. green (Franklin)	6·25	1·80
313	-	30c. blue (Franklin)	4·25	55
347	-	30c. grey (Franklin)	70	35
293	46	1p. orange	36·00	8·50
363a	46	1p. violet	5·75	5·00
294	46	2p. black	50·00	1·70
364	46	2p. brown	£400	£160
350	46	4p. blue	32·00	55
351	46	10p. green	65·00	6·25

Nos. 288, 289, 298, 290, 291, 292, 313, 293 and 294 exist perf only, the other values perf or imperf.

1926. Air. Madrid–Manila Flight. Stamps as last, optd **AIR MAIL 1926 MADRID-MANILA** and aeroplane propeller.

368	45	2c. green	18·00	18·00
369	45	4c. red	23·00	23·00
370	-	6c. violet	70·00	55·00
371	-	8c. brown	70·00	55·00
372	-	10c. blue	70·00	55·00
373	-	12c. orange	70·00	55·00
374	-	16c. green (Sampson)	£3750	£1800
375	-	16c. olive (Dewey)	90·00	90·00
376	-	20c. yellow	85·00	85·00
377	-	26c. green	85·00	85·00
378	-	30c. grey	85·00	85·00
383	46	1p. violet	£250	£225
379	46	2p. brown	£700	£375
380	46	4p. blue	£900	£650
381	46	10p. green	£1700	£850

49 Legislative Palace

1926. Inauguration of Legislative Palace.

384	49	2c. black and green	55	35
385	49	4c. black and red	55	35
386	49	16c. black and olive	1·10	90
387	49	18c. black and brown	1·10	90
388	49	20c. black and orange	1·70	1·40
389	49	24c. black and grey	2·30	90
390	49	1p. black and mauve	55·00	36·00

1928. Air. London–Orient Flight by British Squadron of Seaplanes. Stamps of 1906 optd **L.O.F.** (= London Orient Flight), 1928 and Fairey IIID seaplane.

402	45	2c. green	80	45
403	-	4c. red	90	70
404	-	6c. violet	2·75	2·30
405	-	8c. brown	3·25	2·50
406	-	10c. blue	3·25	2·50
407	-	12c. orange	4·50	3·50
408	-	16c. olive (Dewey)	4·00	2·30
409	-	20c. yellow	4·50	3·50
410	-	26c. green	13·50	8·00
411	-	30c. grey	13·50	8·00
412	46	1p. violet	65·00	34·00

54 Mayon Volcano

57 Vernal Falls, Yosemite National Park, California, wrongly inscr "PAGSANJAN FALLS"

1932

424	54	2c. green	70	80
425	-	4c. red	55	45
426	-	12c. orange	80	70
427	57	18c. red	32·00	11·50
428	-	20c. yellow	1·00	90
429	-	24c. violet	1·70	1·00
430	-	32c. brown	1·70	1·10

DESIGNS—HORIZ: 4c. Post Office, Manila; 12c. Freighters at Pier No. 7, Manila Bay; 20c. Rice plantation; 24c. Rice terraces; 32c. Baguio Zigzag.

1932. No. 350 surch in words in double circle.

431	46	1p. on 4p. blue	4·25	70
432	46	2p. on 4p. blue	7·50	90

1932. Air. Nos. 424/30 optd with Dornier Do-J flying boat "Gronland Wal" and **ROUND-THE-WORLD FLIGHT VON GRONAU 1932**.

433	2c. green	90	45
434	4c. red	90	45
435	12c. orange	1·40	70
436	18c. red	6·25	4·00
437	20c. yellow	3·75	2·00
438	24c. violet	3·75	2·00
439	32c. brown	2·75	2·00

1933. Air. Stamps of 1906 optd **F. REIN MADRID-MANILA FLIGHT-1933** under propeller.

440	45	2c. green	55	45
441	-	4c. red	70	45
442	-	6c. violet	1·10	90
443	-	8c. brown	3·50	1·80
444	-	10c. blue	3·50	1·40
445	-	12c. orange	3·25	1·40
446	-	16c. olive (Dewey)	3·25	1·40
447	-	20c. orange	3·25	1·40
448	-	26c. green	3·50	1·80
449	-	30c. grey	3·50	2·30

1933. Air. Nos. 337 and 425/30 optd with **AIR MAIL** on wings of airplane.

450	2c. green	70	55
451	4c. red	35	25
452	12c. orange	55	25
453	20c. yellow	55	25
454	24c. violet	70	35
455	32c. brown	90	45

66 Baseball

1934. Tenth Far Eastern Championship Games.

456	66	2c. brown	1·80	1·00
457	-	6c. blue	35	25
458	-	16c. purple	70	70

DESIGNS—VERT: 6c. Tennis; 16c. Basketball.

69 Dr. J. Rizal

72 Pearl Fishing

1935. Designs as T **69/70** in various sizes (sizes in millimetres).

459	2c. red (19×22)	25	25
460	4c. green (34×22)	25	25
461	6c. brown (22½×28)	25	25
462	8c. violet (34×22)	25	25
463	10c. red (34×22)	35	25
464	12c. black (34×22)	35	25
465	16c. blue (34×22)	35	25
466	20c. bistre (19×22)	35	25
467	26c. blue (34×22)	45	35
468	30c. red (34×22)	45	35
469	1p. black and orange (37×27)	2·75	2·00
470	2p. black and brown (37×27)	6·75	2·00
471	4p. black and blue (37×27)	6·75	4·00
472	5p. black and green (27×37)	17·00	4·00

DESIGNS: 4c. Woman, Carabao and Rice-stalks; 6c. Filipino girl; 10c. Fort Santiago; 12c. Salt springs; 16c. Magellan's landing; 20c. "Juan de la Cruz"; 26c. Rice terraces; 30c. Blood Compact; 1p. Barasoain Church; 2p. Battle of Manila Bay; 4p. Montalban Gorge; 5p. George Washington (after painting by John Faed).

COMMONWEALTH OF THE PHILIPPINES

83 "Temples of Human Progress"

1935. Inauguration of Commonwealth of the Philippines.

483	83	2c. red	25	25
484	83	6c. violet	25	25
485	83	16c. blue	35	35
486	83	36c. green	45	45
487	83	50c. brown	70	70

1935. Air. "China Clipper" Trans-Pacific Air Mail Flight. Optd **P.I. U.S. INITIAL FLIGHT December-1935** and Martin M-130 flying boat.

488	10c. red (No. 463)	45	35
489	30c. red (No. 468)	70	70

85 J. Rizal y Mercado

1936. 75th Birth Anniv of Rizal.

490	85	2c. yellow	25	25
491	85	6c. blue	25	25
492	85	36c. brown	70	70

1936. Air. Manila–Madrid Flight by Arnaiz and Calvo. Stamps of 1906 surch **MANILA-MADRID ARNACAL FLIGHT-1936** and value.

493	45	2c. on 4c. red	25	25
494	45	6c. on 12c. orange	25	25
495	45	16c. on 26c. green	35	35

1936. Stamps of 1935 (Nos. 459/72) optd **COMMON-WEALTH** (2c., 6c., 20c.) or **COMMONWEALTH** (others).

496	2c. red	25	25
497	4c. green	70	5·75
526	6c. brown	25	25
527	8c. violet	25	25
528	10c. red	25	25
529	12c. black	25	25
530	16c. blue	25	25
531	20c. bistre	25	25
532	26c. blue	35	35
505	30c. red	55	25
534	1p. black and orange	70	25
535	2p. black and brown	5·75	90
508	4p. black and blue	34·00	6·75
509	5p. black and green	8·00	2·30

89 Manuel L. Quezon

1936. First Anniv of Autonomous Government.

510	89	2c. brown	25	25
511	89	6c. green	25	25
512	89	12c. blue	35	35

90 Philippine Is

1937. 33rd International Eucharistic Congress.

513	90	2c. green	25	25
514	90	6c. brown	25	25
515	90	12c. blue	25	25
516	90	20c. orange	35	25
517	90	36c. violet	55	55
518	90	50c. red	80	45

1937

522	92	10p. grey	6·00	2·50
523	92	20p. brown	4·00	2·00

92 Arms of Manila

1939. Air. First Manila Air Mail Exhibition. Surch **FIRST AIR MAIL EXHIBITION Feb 17 to 19, 1939** and value.

548a	-	8c. on 26c. green (346)	90	55
549	92	1p. on 10p. grey	3·75	2·75

1939. First National Foreign Trade Week. Surch **FIRST FOREIGN TRADE WEEK MAY 21-27, 1939** and value.

551	-	2c. on 4c. green (460)	25	25
552a	45	6c. on 26c. green (346)	1·10	35
553	92	50c. on 20p. brown	1·40	1·40

101 Triumphal Arch

102 Malacanan Palace

103 Pres. Quezon taking Oath of Office

1939. 4th Anniv of National Independence.

554	**101**	2c. green	25	25
555	**101**	6c. red	25	25
556	**101**	12c. blue	35	25
557	**102**	2c. green	25	25
558	**102**	6c. orange	25	25
559	**102**	12c. red	35	25
560	**103**	2c. orange	25	25
561	**103**	6c. green	25	25
562	**103**	12c. violet	35	25

104 Jose Rizal

1941

563	**104**	2c. green	25	55
623	-	2c. brown	35	25

In No. 623 the head faces to the right.

105 Filipino Vinta and Boeing 314 Flying Boat

1941. Air.

566	**105**	8c. red	25	70
567	**105**	20c. blue	3·25	55
568	**105**	60c. green	2·75	1·10
569	**105**	1p. sepia	1·10	55

For Japanese Occupation issues of 1941–45 see **JAPANESE OCCUPATION OF PHILIPPINE ISLANDS**.

1945. Victory issue. Nos. 496, 525/31, 505, 534 and 522/3 optd **VICTORY**.

610	2c. red	25	25
611	4c. green	25	25
612	6c. brown	35	25
613	8c. violet	35	25
614	10c. red	35	25
615	12c. black	25	25
616	16c. blue	45	25
617	20c. bistre	55	25
618	30c. red	70	55
619	1p. black and orange	2·00	45
620	10p. grey	70·00	17·00
621	20p. brown	65·00	18·00

INDEPENDENT REPUBLIC

111 "Independence"

1946. Proclamation of Independence.

625	**111**	2c. red	60	55
626	**111**	6c. green	1·20	60
627	**111**	12c. blue	1·80	75

1946. Optd **PHILIPPINES 50TH ANNIVERSARY MARTYRDOM OF RIZAL 1896–1946**.

628	**104**	2c. brown (No. 623)	60	35

113 Bonifacio Monument

1947

629	-	4c. brown	25	20
630	**113**	10c. red	30	20
631	-	12c. blue	35	20
632	-	16c. grey	3·50	2·20
633	-	20c. brown	80	20
634	-	50c. green	2·30	55
635	-	1p. violet	4·75	1·10

DESIGNS—VERT: 4c. Rizal Monument; 50c., 1p. Avenue of Palm Trees. HORIZ: 12c. Jones Bridge; 16c. Santa Lucia Gate; 20c. Mayon Volcano.

115 Manuel L. Quezon

1947

636	**115**	1c. green	45	20
MS637		64×85 mm. No. 636 in block of four. Imperf	3·25	2·50

116 Pres. Roxas taking Oath of Office

1947. First Anniv of Independence.

638	**116**	4c. red	35	20
639	**116**	6c. green	95	75
640	**116**	16c. purple	2·20	1·40

117 Presidents Quezon and Roosevelt

1947. Air.

641	**117**	6c. green	1·20	1·00
642	**117**	40c. orange	2·50	2·30
643	**117**	80c. blue	6·50	5·75

119 United Nations Emblem

1947. Conference of Economic Commission for Asia and Far East, Baguio. Imperf or perf.

648	**119**	4c. red and pink	3·50	3·25
649	**119**	6c. violet and light violet	4·75	4·25
650	**119**	12c. blue and light blue	5·25	5·00

121 General MacArthur

1948. Third Anniv of Liberation.

652	**121**	4c. violet	1·20	35
653	**121**	6c. red	2·10	1·30
654	**121**	16c. blue	3·00	1·60

122 Threshing Rice

1948. United Nations Food and Agriculture Organization Conference, Baguio.

655	**122**	2c. green & yell (postage)	1·80	1·10
656	**122**	6c. brown and stone	2·10	1·40
657	**122**	18c. blue and light blue	5·50	4·00
658	**122**	40c. red and pink (air)	28·00	14·00

125 Dr. Jose Rizal

1948

662	**125**	2c. green	35	20

126 Pres. Manuel Roxas

1948. President Roxas Mourning Issue.

663	**126**	2c. black	35	20
664	**126**	4c. black	70	35

127 Scout and Badge

1948. 25th Anniv of Philippine Boy Scouts. Perf or imperf.

665	**127**	2c. green and brown	3·00	1·10
666	**127**	4c. pink and brown	3·50	1·60

128 Sampaguita, National Flower

1948. Flower Day.

667	**128**	3c. green and black	70	55

130 Santos, Tavera and Kalaw

131 "Doctrina Christiana" (first book published in Philippines)

1949. Library Rebuilding Fund.

671	**130**	4c.+2c. brown	2·10	1·40
672	**131**	6c.+4c. violet	6·50	4·00
673	-	18c.+7c. blue	8·75	6·50

DESIGN—VERT: 18c. Title page of Rizal's "Noli Me Tangere".

132 U.P.U. Monument, Berne

1949. 75th Anniv of U.P.U.

674	**132**	4c. green	30	15
675	**132**	6c. violet	35	20
676	**132**	18c. blue	1·50	55
MS677		106×92 mm. Nos. 674/6. Imperf	3·25	3·00

133 General del Pilar at Tirad Pass

1949. 50th Death Anniv of Gen. Gregorio del Pilar.

678	**133**	2c. brown	25	20
679	**133**	4c. green	70	55

134 Globe

1950. Fifth International Congress of Junior Chamber of Commerce.

680	**134**	2c. violet (postage)	35	15
681	**134**	6c. green	45	20
682	**134**	18c. blue	1·10	35
683	**134**	30c. orange (air)	80	25
684	**134**	50c. red	1·40	40

135 Red Lauan Trees

1950. 15th Anniv of Forestry Service.

685	**135**	2c. green	70	35
686	**135**	4c. violet	1·40	55

136 Franklin D. Roosevelt

1950. 25th Anniv of Philatelic Association.

687	**136**	4c. brown	60	35
688	**136**	6c. pink	1·20	65
689	**136**	18c. blue	2·50	1·60
MS690		61×51 mm. **136** 80c. green. Imperf	4·75	4·25

137 Lions Emblem

1950. "Lions" International Convention, Manila.

691	**137**	2c. orange (postage)	1·30	1·20
692	**137**	4c. lilac	1·90	1·70
693	**137**	30c. green (air)	1·90	1·30
694	**137**	50c. blue	2·10	1·70
MS695		91×88 mm. Nos. 693/4	4·75	4·25

138 President Quirino taking Oath of Office

1950. Pres. Quirino's Inauguration.

696	**138**	2c. red	30	10
697	**138**	4c. purple	35	15
698	**138**	6c. green	45	20

1950. Surch **ONE CENTAVO**.

699	**125**	1c. on 2c. green	25	10

140 Dove and Map

1950. Baguio Conference.

701	**140**	5c. green	55	25
702	**140**	6c. red	60	35
703	**140**	18c. blue	1·40	85

141 War Widow and Children

1950. Aid to War Victims.

704	**141**	2c.+2c. red	25	10
705	-	4c.+4c. violet	80	75

DESIGN: 4c. Disabled veteran.

142 Arms of Manila

1950. As T **142**. Various arms and frames. (a) Arms inscr "MANILA".

706	5c. violet	1·20	85
707	6c. grey	95	65
708	18c. blue	1·20	85

(b) Arms inscr "CEBU".

709	5c. red	1·20	85

710		6c. brown	95	65
711		18c. violet	1·20	85

(c) Arms inscr "ZAMBOANGA".

712		5c. green	1·20	85
713		6c. brown	95	65
714		18c. blue	1·20	85

(d) Arms inscr "ILOILO".

715		5c. green	1·20	85
716		6c. violet	95	65
717		18c. blue	1·20	85

143 Soldier and Peasants

1951. Guarding Peaceful Labour. Perf or imperf.

718	**143**	5c. green	35	25
719	**143**	6c. purple	60	55
720	**143**	18c. blue	1·60	1·50

144 Philippines Flag and U.N. Emblem

1951. U.N. Day.

721	**144**	5c. red	1·80	65
722	**144**	6c. green	1·20	55
723	**144**	18c. blue	3·00	2·00

145 Statue of Liberty

1951. Human Rights Day.

724	**145**	5c. green	95	55
725	**145**	6c. orange	1·40	85
726	**145**	18c. blue	2·50	1·40

146 Schoolchildren

1952. 50th Anniv of Philippine Educational System.

727	**146**	5c. orange	1·20	85

147 M. L. Quezon

1952. Portraits.

728	**147**	1c. brown	25	20
729	-	2c. black (J. Abad Santos)	25	20
730	-	3c. red (A. Mabini)	25	20
731	-	5c. red (M. H. del Pilar)	25	20
732	-	10c. blue (Father J. Burgos)	25	20
733	-	20c. red (Lapu-Lapu)	60	25
734	-	25c. green (Gen. A. Luna)	80	35
735	-	50c. red (C. Arellano)	1·80	55
736	-	60c. red (A. Bonifacio)	1·90	75
737	-	2p. violet (G. L. Jaena)	6·50	2·00

149 Aurora A. Quezon

1952. Fruit Tree Memorial Fund.

742	**149**	5c.+1c. blue	25	20
743	**149**	6c.+2c. pink	80	75

See also No. 925.

150 Milkfish and Map of Oceania

1952. Indo-Pacific Fisheries Council.

744	**150**	5c. brown	2·30	1·30
745	**150**	6c. blue	1·40	1·10

151 "A Letter from Rizal"

1952. Pan-Asiatic Philatelic Exhibition, Manila.

746	**151**	5c. blue (postage)	1·20	20
747	**151**	6c. brown	1·30	35
748	**151**	30c. red (air)	2·50	2·00

152 Wright Park, Baguio City

1952. Third Lions District Convention.

749	**152**	5c. red	1·80	1·60
750	**152**	6c. green	2·50	2·00

153 F. Baltazar (poet)

1953. National Language Week.

751	**153**	5c. bistre	95	65

154 "Gateway to the East"

1953. International Fair, Manila.

752	**154**	5c. turquoise	65	20
753	**154**	6c. red	70	25

155 Pres. Quirino and Pres. Sukarno

1953. Visit of President to Indonesia. Flags in yellow, blue and red.

754	**155**	5c. blue, yellow and black	35	20
755	**155**	6c. green, yellow and black	60	55

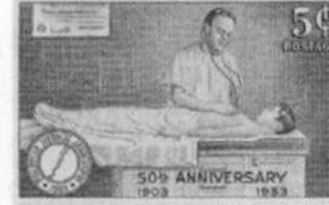
156 Doctor examining patient

1953. 50th Anniv of Philippines Medical Association.

756	**156**	5c. mauve	60	55
757	**156**	6c. blue	80	65

1954. Optd **FIRST NATIONAL BOY SCOUTS JAMBOREE APRIL 23-30, 1954** or surch also.

758		5c. red (No. 731)	2·50	2·00
759		18c. on 50c. green (No. 634)	4·25	2·75

158 Stamp of 1854, Magellan and Manila P.O.

1954. Stamp Centenary. Central stamp in orange.

760	**158**	5c. violet (postage)	1·50	1·10
761	**158**	18c. blue	3·00	2·40
762	**158**	30c. green	7·00	4·00
763	**158**	10c. brown (air)	3·00	2·40
764	**158**	20c. green	5·25	4·00
765	**158**	50c. red	10·50	8·25

159 Diving

1954. Second Asian Games, Manila.

766	-	5c. blue on blue (Discus)	1·80	1·20
767	**159**	18c. green on green	2·75	2·00
768	-	30c. red on pink (Boxing)	4·25	3·25

1954. Surch **MANILA CONFERENCE OF 1954** and value.

769	**113**	5c. on 10c. red	35	20
770	-	18c. on 20c. brown (No. 633)	1·50	1·30

161 "Independence"

1954. Independence Commemoration.

771	**161**	5c. red	60	35
772	**161**	18c. blue	1·80	1·00

162 "The Immaculate Conception" (Murillo)

1954. Marian Year.

773	**162**	5c. blue	1·10	65

163 Mayon Volcano and Filipino Vinta

1955. 50th Anniv of Rotary International.

774	**163**	5c. blue (postage)	70	35
775	**163**	18c. red	2·30	1·10
776	**163**	50c. green (air)	4·75	1·80

164 "Labour"

1955. Labour-Management Congress, Manila.

777	**164**	5c. brown	3·00	1·00

165 Pres. Magsaysay

1955. Ninth Anniv of Republic.

778	**165**	5c. blue	40	35
779	**165**	20c. red	1·50	1·40
780	**165**	30c. green	2·50	2·30

166 Lt. J. Gozar

1955. Air. Air Force Heroes.

781	**166**	20c. violet	1·60	25
782	-	30c. red (Lt. C. F. Basa)	2·10	45
783	**166**	50c. green	2·50	55
784	-	70c. blue (Lt. C. F. Basa)	3·75	2·30

167 Liberty Well

1956. Artesian Wells for Rural Areas.

785	**167**	5c. violet	75	70
786	**167**	20c. green	1·60	1·40

1956. Fifth Conference of World Confederation of Organizations of the Teaching Profession. No. **731** optd **WCOTP CONFERENCE MANILA**.

787		5c. red	75	70

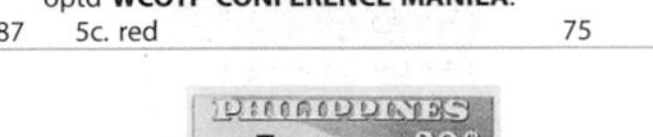

169 Nurse and War Victims

1956. 50th Anniv of Philippines Red Cross.

788	**169**	5c. violet and red	1·00	90
789	**169**	20c. brown and red	1·50	1·00

170 Monument (landing marker) in Leyte

1956. Liberation Commem. Perf or imperf.

790	**170**	5c. red	25	20

171 St. Thomas's University

1956. University of St. Thomas.

791	**171**	5c. brown and red	75	45
792	**171**	60c. brown and mauve	4·25	2·30

172 Statue of the Sacred Heart

1956. Second National Eucharistic Congress and Centenary of the Feast of the Sacred Heart.

793	**172**	5c. green	75	55
794	**172**	20c. pink	1·60	1·50

1956. Surch **5 5**.

795		5c. on 6c. brown (No. 710)	25	20
796		5c. on 6c. brown (No. 713)	25	20
797		5c. on 6c. violet (No. 716)	25	20

174 Girl Guide, Badge and Camp

1957. Girl Guides' Pacific World Camp, Quezon City, and Birth Centenary of Lord Baden-Powell. Perf or imperf.

798 **174** 5c. blue 1·40 1·20

175 Pres. Ramon Magsaysay

1957. Death of Pres. Magsaysay.

799 **175** 5c. black 65 25

176 Sergio Osmena (Speaker) and First Philippine Assembly

1957. 50th Anniv of First Philippine Assembly.

800 **176** 5c. green 65 25

177 "The Spoliarium" after Juan Luna

1957. Birth Centenary of Juan Luna (painter).

801 **177** 5c. red 65 25

1957. Inauguration of President C. P. Garcia and Vice-President D. Macapagal. Nos. 732/3 surch **GARCIA-MACAPAGAL INAUGURATION DEC. 30, 1957** and value.

802 5c. on 10c. blue 40 35
803 10c. on 20c. red 65 55

179 University of the Philippines

1958. Golden Jubilee of University of the Philippines.

804 **179** 5c. red 75 35

180 Pres. Garcia

1958. 12th Anniv of Republic.

805 **180** 5c. multicoloured 25 15
806 **180** 20c. multicoloured 1·10 80

181 Main Hospital Building, Quezon Institute

1958. Obligatory Tax. T.B. Relief Fund.

807 **181** 5c.+5c. green and red 40 35
808 **181** 10c.+5c. violet and red 90 80

182 The Immaculate Conception and Manila Cathedral

1958. Inauguration of Manila Cathedral.

809 **182** 5c. multicoloured 65 25

1959. Surch **One Centavo.**

810 1c. on 5c. red (No. 731) 65 15

1959. 14th Anniv of Liberation. Nos. 704/5 surch.

812 **141** 1c. on 2c.+2c. red 30 15
813 - 6c. on 4c.+4c. violet 40 25

186 Philippines Flag

1959. Adoption of Philippine Constitution.

814 **186** 6c. red, blue and yellow 25 10
815 **186** 20c. red, blue and yellow 40 35

187 Bulacan Seal

1959. Provincial Seals. (a) Bulacan Seal and 60th Anniv of Malolos Constitution.

816 **187** 6c. green 40 10
817 **187** 20c. red 50 35

(b) Capiz Seal and 11th Death Anniv of Pres. Roxas.

818 6c. brown 40 10
819 25c. violet 50 45

The shield within the Capiz seal bears the inset portrait of Pres. Roxas.

(c) Bacolod Seal.

820 6c. green 40 10
821 10c. purple 40 25

188 Scout at Campfire

1959. Tenth World Scout Jamboree, Manila.

822 **188** 6c.+4c. red on yellow (postage) 25 15
823 **188** 6c.+4c. red 75 70
824 - 25c.+5c. blue on yellow 1·10 1·00
825 - 25c.+5c. blue 1·50 1·40
826 - 30c.+10c. green (air) 1·30 1·10
827 - 70c.+20c. brown 2·50 2·30
828 - 80c.+20c. violet 3·75 3·50

MS829 171×90 mm. Nos. 823, 825/8 (sold at 4p.) 25·00 24·00

DESIGNS: 25c. Scout with bow and arrow; 30c. Scout cycling; 70c. Scout with model airplane; 80c. Pres. Garcia with scout.

190 Bohol Sanatorium

1959. Obligatory Tax. T.B. Relief Fund. Nos. 807/8 surch **HELP FIGHT T B** with Cross of Lorraine and value and new design (T 190).

830 **181** 3c.+5c. on 5c.+5c. 40 35
831 **181** 6c.+5c. on 10c.+5c. 40 35
832 **190** 6c.+5c. green and red 40 35
833 **190** 25c.+5c. blue and red 90 70

191 Pagoda and Gardens at Camp John Hay

1959. 50th Anniv of Baguio.

834 **191** 6c. green 25 10
835 **191** 25c. red 75 35

1959. U.N. Day. Surch **6c UNITED NATIONS DAY.**

836 **132** 6c. on 18c. blue 65 15

193 Maria Cristina Falls

1959. World Tourist Conference, Manila.

837 **193** 6c. green and violet 25 15
838 **193** 30c. green and brown 1·10 80

1959. No. 629 surch **One** and bars.

839 1c. on 4c. brown 65 15

195

1959. Centenary of Manila Athenaeum (school).

840 **195** 6c. blue 25 10
841 **195** 30c. red 1·00 70

196 Dr. Jose Rizal

1959

842 **196** 6c. blue 65 15

197 Book of the Constitution

1960. 25th Anniv of Philippines Constitution.

844 **197** 6c. brn & gold (postage) 40 25
845 **197** 30c. blue and silver (air) 1·00 55

198 Congress Building

1960. Fifth Anniv of Manila Pact.

846 **198** 6c. green 25 10
847 **198** 25c. orange 90 70

199 Sunset, Manila Bay

1960. World Refugee Year.

848 **199** 6c. multicoloured 40 25
849 **199** 25c. multicoloured 1·00 55

200 North American F-86 Sabre and Boeing P-12 Fighters

1960. Air. 25th Anniv of Philippine Air Force.

850 **200** 10c. red 40 25
851 **200** 20c. blue 90 55

1960. Surch.

852 **134** 1c. on 18c. blue 40 25
853 **161** 5c. on 18c. blue 40 25
854 **163** 5c. on 18c. red 65 30
855 **158** 10c. on 18c. orange & blue 40 25
856 **140** 10c. on 18c. blue 65 25

202 Lorraine Cross

1960. 50th Anniv of Philippine Tuberculosis Society. Lorraine Cross and wreath in red and gold.

857 **202** 5c. green 40 10
858 **202** 6c. blue 40 10

1960. Obligatory Tax. T.B. Relief Fund. Surch **6+5 HELP PREVENT TB.**

859 **181** 6c.+5c. on 5c.+5c. green and red 75 25

204 Pres. Quezon

1960

860 **204** 1c. green 65 15

205 Basketball

1960. Olympic Games.

861 **205** 6c. brown & grn (postage) 25 10
862 - 10c. brown and purple 40 25
863 - 30c. brown and orange (air) 1·00 80
864 - 70c. purple and blue 2·10 1·70

DESIGNS: 10c. Running; 30c. Rifle-shooting; 70c. Swimming.

206 Presidents Eisenhower and Garcia

1960. Visit of President Eisenhower.

865 **206** 6c. multicoloured 40 25
866 **206** 20c. multicoloured 1·00 55

207 "Mercury" and Globe

1961. Manila Postal Conference.

867 **207** 6c. multicoloured (postage) 25 10
868 **207** 30c. multicoloured (air) 75 55

1961. Surch **20 20.**

869 20c. on 25c. green (No. 734) 65 25

1961. Second National Scout Jamboree, Zamboanga. Nos. 822/5 surch **2nd National Boy Scout Jamboree Pasonanca Park** and value.

870 10c. on 6c.+4c. red on yellow 25 15
871 10c. on 6c.+4c. red 1·00 90
872 30c. on 25c.+5c. blue on yellow 75 70
873 30c. on 25c.+5c. blue 1·10 1·00

210 La Salle College

1961. 50th Anniv of La Salle College.

874 **210** 6c. multicoloured 25 10
875 **210** 10c. multicoloured 40 25

211 Rizal when Student, School and University Buildings

1961. Birth Centenary of Dr. Jose Rizal.

876	**211**	5c. multicoloured	15	10
877	-	6c. multicoloured	20	10
878	-	10c. brown and green	40	35
879	-	20c. turquoise and brown	50	45
880	-	30c. multicoloured	90	55

DESIGNS: 6c. Rizal and birthplace at Calamba, Laguna; 10c. Rizal, mother and father; 20c. Rizal extolling Luna and Hidalgo at Madrid; 30c. Rizal's execution.

1961. 15th Anniv of Republic. Optd **IKA 15 KAARAWAN Republika ng Pilipinas Hulyo 4, 1961**.

881	**198**	6c. green	40	35
882	**198**	25c. orange	90	80

213 Roxas Memorial T.B. Pavilion

1961. Obligatory Tax. T.B. Relief Fund.

883	**213**	6c.+5c. brown and red	75	25

214 Globe, Plan Emblem and Supporting Hand

1961. Seventh Anniv of Admission of Philippines to Colombo Plan.

884	**214**	5c. multicoloured	25	15
885	**214**	6c. multicoloured	40	35

1961. Philippine Amateur Athletic Federation's Golden Jubilee. Surch with P.A.A.F. monogram and **6c PAAF GOLDEN JUBILEE 1911 1961**.

886	**200**	6c. on 10c. red	65	35

216 Typist

1961. Government Employees' Association.

887	**216**	6c. violet and brown	40	15
888	**216**	10c. blue and brown	65	35

1961. Inauguration of Pres. Macapagal and Vice-Pres. Pelaez. Surch **MACAPAGAL-PELAEZ DEC. 30, 1961 INAUGURATION 6c**.

889		6c. on 25c. violet (No. 819)	65	15

1962. Cross obliterated by Arms and surch **6s**.

890	**181**	6c. on 5c.+5c. green and red	65	25

220 Waling-Waling

1962. Orchids. Multicoloured.

892	5c. Type **220**	45	25
893	6c. White Mariposa	50	25
894	10c. "Dendrobium sanderii"	65	35
895	20c. Sanggumay	90	55

221 A. Mabini (statesman)

1962. New Currency.

896	-	1s. brown	15	10
897	**221**	3s. red	15	10
898	-	5s. red	20	10
899	-	6s. brown	25	10
900	-	6s. blue	25	10
901	-	10s. purple	40	10
902	-	20s. blue	50	15
903	-	30s. red	90	25
904	-	50s. violet	1·50	35
905	-	70s. blue	1·90	80
906	-	1p. green	3·75	70
907	-	1p. orange	1·50	55

PORTRAITS: 1s. M. L. Quezon; 5s. M. H. del Pilar; 6s. (2) J. Rizal (different); 10s. Father J. Burgos; 20s. Lapu-Lapu; 30s. Rajah Soliman; 50s. C. Arellano; 70s. S. Osmena; 1p. (No. 906) E. Jacinto; 1p. (No. 907) J. M. Panganiban.

225 Pres. Macapagal taking Oath

1962. Independence Day.

915	**225**	6s. multicoloured	25	10
916	**225**	10s. multicoloured	40	25
917	**225**	30s. multicoloured	65	35

226 Valdes Memorial T.B. Pavilion

1962. Obligatory Tax Stamps. T.B. Relief Fund. Cross in red.

918	**226**	6s.+5s. purple	25	15
919	**226**	30s.+5s. blue	90	55
920	**226**	70s.+5s. blue	2·10	1·70

1962. Malaria Eradication.

921	**227**	6s. multicoloured	25	15
922	**227**	10s. multicoloured	40	25
923	**227**	70s. multicoloured	3·00	1·90

227 Lake Taal

1962. Bicentenary of Diego Silang Revolt. No. 734 surch **1762 1962 BICENTENNIAL Diego Silang Revolt 20**.

924		20s. on 25c. green	65	35

1962. No. 742 with premium obliterated.

925	**149**	5c. blue	65	25

230 Dr. Rizal playing Chess

1962. Rizal Foundation Fund.

926	**230**	6s.+4s. green and mauve	40	35
927	-	30s.+5s. blue and purple	90	80

DESIGN: 30s. Dr. Rizal fencing.

1963. Surch.

928	**221**	1s. on 3s. red	25	10
929	-	5s. on 6s. brown (No. 899)	40	25

1963. Diego Silang Bicentenary Art and Philatelic Exhibition, G.P.O., Manila. No. 737 surch **1763 1963 DIEGO SILANG BICENTENNIAL ARPHEX** and value.

930	6c. on 2p. violet	25	15
931	20c. on 2p. violet	65	55
932	70c. on 2p. violet	1·80	1·40

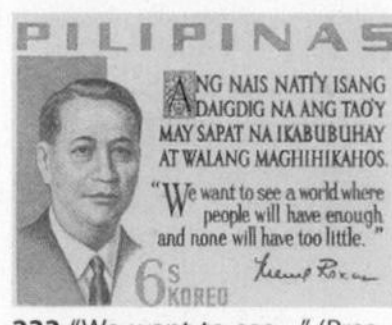

233 "We want to see ..." (Pres. Roxas)

1963. Presidential Sayings (1st issue).

933	**233**	6s. blue and black	25	10
934	**233**	30s. brown and black	90	25

See also Nos. 959/60, 981/2, 1015/16, 1034/5, 1055/6, 1148/9 and 1292/3.

234 Lorraine Cross on Map

1963. Obligatory Tax. T.B. Relief Fund. Cross in red.

935	**234**	6s.+5s. pink and violet	20	10
936	**234**	10s.+5s. pink and green	25	20
937	**234**	50s.+5s. pink & brown	1·60	95

235 Globe and Flags

1963. First Anniv of Asian-Oceanic Postal Union.

938	**235**	6s. multicoloured	25	20
939	**235**	20s. multicoloured	40	25

236 Centenary Emblem

1963. Red Cross Centenary. Cross in red.

940	**236**	5s. grey and violet	20	10
941	**236**	6s. grey and blue	25	20
942	**236**	20s. grey and green	90	35

237 Tinikling (dance)

1963. Folk Dances. Multicoloured.

943	5s. Type **237**	40	25
944	6s. Pandanggo sa Ilaw	40	25
945	10s. Itik-Itik	50	35
946	20s. Singkil	65	45

238 Pres. Macapagal and Philippine Family

1963. President's Social-Economic Programme.

947	**238**	5s. multicoloured	25	20
948	**238**	6s. multicoloured	25	20
949	**238**	20s. multicoloured	65	35

239 Presidents' Meeting

1963. Visit of President Mateos of Mexico.

950	**239**	6s. multicoloured	25	15
951	**239**	30s. multicoloured	90	25

240 Bonifacio and Flag

1963. Birth Cent of Andres Bonifacio (patriot).

952	**240**	5s. multicoloured	30	20
953	**240**	6s. multicoloured	40	25
954	**240**	25s. multicoloured	80	45

1963. 15th Anniv of Declaration of Human Rights. Sheet No. **MS**677 optd with **UN ADOPTION OF HUMAN RIGHTS 15TH ANNIVERSARY DEC. 10, 1963,** by Philippine Bureau of Printing.

MS955 106×92 mm	4·50	3·75

241 Harvester

1963. Freedom from Hunger.

956	**241**	6s. multicoloured (postage)	25	20
957	**241**	30s. multicoloured (air)	1·20	80
958	**241**	50s. multicoloured	1·90	1·40

1963. Presidential Sayings (2nd issue). As T **233** but with portrait and saying changed.

959	6s. black and violet	25	10
960	30s. black and green	65	25

PORTRAIT AND SAYING: Pres. Magsaysay, "I believe ...".

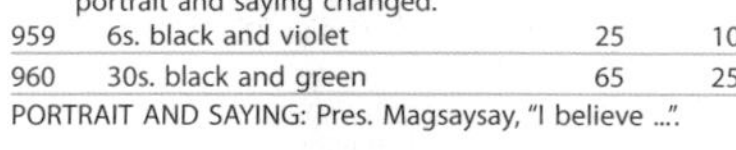

242 Bamboo Organ, Catholic Church, Las Pinas

1964. Las Pinas Organ Commemoration.

961	**242**	5s. multicoloured	25	15
962	**242**	6s. multicoloured	25	20
963	**242**	20s. multicoloured	90	35

243 A. Mabini (patriot)

1964. Birth Centenary of A. Mabini.

964	**243**	6s. gold and violet	20	10
965	**243**	10s. gold and brown	25	20
966	**243**	30s. gold and green	65	25

244 Negros Oriental T.B. Pavilion

1964. Obligatory Tax. T.B. Relief Fund. Cross in red.

967	**244**	5s.+5s. purple	25	20
968	**244**	6s.+5s. blue	25	20
969	**244**	30s.+5s. brown	90	60
970	**244**	70s.+5s. green	1·90	1·50

245 S.E.A.T.O. Emblems and Flags

1964. Tenth Anniv of S.E.A.T.O.

971	245	6s. multicoloured	25	15
972	245	10s. multicoloured	40	20
973	245	25s. multicoloured	50	25

246 President signing the Land Reform Code

1964. Agricultural Land Reform Code. President and inscr at foot in brown, red and sepia.

974	246	3s. green (postage)	40	20
975	246	6s. blue	50	25
976	246	30s. brown (air)	1·00	35

247 Basketball

1964. Olympic Games, Tokyo. Sport in brown. Perf or imperf.

977	247	6s. blue and gold	25	20
978	-	10s. pink and gold	40	25
979	-	20s. yellow and gold	90	35
980	-	30s. green and gold	1·20	80

SPORTS: 10s. Relay-racing; 20s. Hurdling; 30s. Football.

1965. Presidential Sayings (3rd issue). As T **233** but with portrait and saying changed.

981	6s. black and green	25	15
982	30s. black and purple	65	25

PORTRAIT AND SAYING: Pres. Quirino, "So live ...".

248 Presidents Luebke and Macapagal

1965. Visit of President of German Federal Republic.

983	248	6s. multicoloured	25	10
984	248	10s. multicoloured	40	20
985	248	25s. multicoloured	65	45

249 Meteorological Emblems

1965. Cent of Philippines Meteorological Services.

986	249	6s. multicoloured	20	15
987	249	20s. multicoloured	25	20
988	249	50s. multicoloured	1·20	60

250 Pres. Kennedy

1965. John F. Kennedy (U.S. President) Commemoration.

989	250	6s. multicoloured	25	20
990	250	10s. multicoloured	40	25
991	250	30s. multicoloured	90	35

251 King Bhumibol and Queen Sirikit, Pres. Macapagal and Wife

1965. Visit of King and Queen of Thailand.

992	251	2s. multicoloured	20	10
993	251	6s. multicoloured	25	20
994	251	30s. multicoloured	1·00	35

252 Princess Beatrix and Mrs. Macapagal

1965. Visit of Princess Beatrix of the Netherlands.

995	252	2s. multicoloured	15	10
996	252	6s. multicoloured	25	20
997	252	10s. multicoloured	40	25

1965. Obligatory Tax. T.B. Relief Fund. Surch.

998	244	1s.+5s. on 6s.+5s.	25	10
999	244	3s.+5s. on 6s.+5s.	40	25

254 Hand holding Cross and Rosary

1965. 400th Anniv of Philippines Christianisation. Multicoloured.

1000	3s. Type **254** (postage)	25	10
1001	6s. Legaspi-Urdaneta, monument	40	20
1002	30s. Baptism of Filipinos by Father Urdaneta, Cebu (horiz) (48×27 mm) (air)	90	45
1003	70s. "Way of the Cross"–ocean map of Christian voyagers' route, Spain to the Philippines (horiz) (48×27 mm)	2·20	1·20
MS1004	170×105 mm. Nos. 1000/3. Imperf	6·00	5·75

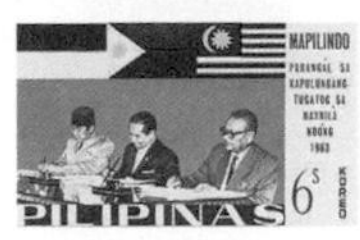

256 Signing Agreement

1965. "MAPILINDO" Conference, Manila.

1005	256	6s. blue, red and yellow	25	20
1006	256	10s. multicoloured	30	20
1007	256	25s. multicoloured	90	35

The above stamps depict Pres. Sukarno of Indonesia, former Pres. Macapagal of the Philippines and Prime Minister Tunku Abdul Rahman of Malaysia.

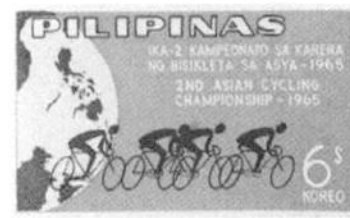

257 Cyclists and Globe

1965. Second Asian Cycling Championships, Philippines.

1008	257	6s. multicoloured	25	20
1009	257	10s. multicoloured	40	25
1010	257	25s. multicoloured	90	60

1965. Inauguration of Pres. Marcos and Vice-Pres. Lopez. Nos. 926/7 surch **MARCOS-LOPEZ INAUGURATION DEC. 30, 1965** and value.

1011	230	10s. on 6s.+4s.	40	35
1012	-	30s. on 30s.+5s.	90	80

259 Dr. A. Regidor

1966. Regidor (patriot) Commemoration.

1013	259	6s. blue	25	20
1014	259	30s. brown	65	35

1966. Presidential Sayings (4th issue). As T **233** but with portrait and saying changed.

1015	6s. black and red	25	10
1016	30s. black and blue	65	35

PORTRAIT AND SAYING: Pres. Aguinaldo, "Have faith ...".

1966. Campaign Against Smuggling. No. 900 optd **HELP ME STOP SMUGGLING Pres. MARCOS**.

1017	6s. blue	65	25

261 Girl Scout

1966. Silver Jubilee of Philippines Girl Scouts.

1018	261	3s. multicoloured	20	10
1019	261	6s. multicoloured	25	20
1020	261	20s. multicoloured	90	35

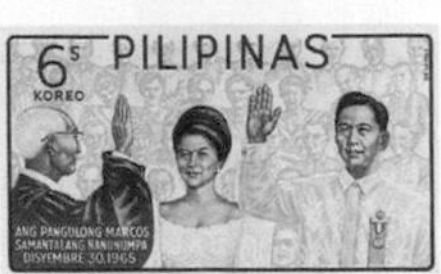

262 Pres. Marcos taking Oath

1966. Inauguration (1965) of Pres. Marcos.

1021	262	6s. multicoloured	20	15
1022	262	20s. multicoloured	25	20
1023	262	30s. multicoloured	65	35

263 Manila Seal and Historical Scenes

1966. Introduction of New Seal for Manila.

1024	263	6s. multicoloured	25	20
1025	263	30s. multicoloured	65	25

264 Bank Facade and 1 peso Coin

265 "Progress"

1966. 50th Anniv of Philippines National Bank. Multicoloured.

1026	6s. Type **264**	25	10
1027	10s. Old and new bank buildings	40	25
MS1028	157×70 mm. **265** 70s. multicoloured	4·00	3·75

266 Bank Building

1966. 60th Anniv of Postal Savings Bank.

1029	266	6s. violet, yellow & green	25	20
1030	266	10s. red, yellow and green	40	25
1031	266	20s. blue, yellow & green	90	35

1966. Manila Summit Conference. Nos. 1021 and 1023 optd **MANILA SUMMIT CONFERENCE 1966 7 NATIONS** and emblem.

1032	262	6s. multicoloured	40	25
1033	262	30s. multicoloured	65	60

1966. Presidential Sayings (5th issue). As T **233** but with portrait and saying changed.

1034	6s. black and brown	25	10
1035	30s. black and blue	65	25

PORTRAIT AND SAYING: Pres. Laurel; "No one can love the Filipinos better ...".

1967. 50th Anniv of Lions International. Nos. 977/80 optd with Lions emblem and **50th ANNIVERSARY LIONS INTERNATIONAL 1967**. Imperf.

1036	247	6c. blue and gold	25	15
1037	-	10c. pink and gold	40	25
1038	-	20c. yellow and gold	90	35
1039	-	30c. green and gold	1·30	1·20

269 "Succour" (after painting by F. Amorsolo)

1967. 25th Anniv of Battle of Bataan.

1040	269	5s. multicoloured	25	10
1041	269	20s. multicoloured	40	25
1042	269	2p. multicoloured	4·75	2·30

1967. Nos. 900 and 975 surch.

1043	-	4s. on 6s. blue	50	10
1044	246	5s. on 6s. blue	65	15

271 Stork-billed Kingfisher

1967. Obligatory Tax. T.B. Relief Fund. Birds. Multicoloured.

1045	1s.+5s. Type **271**	40	20
1046	5s.+5s. Rufous hornbill	50	30
1047	10s.+5s. Philippine eagle	80	35
1048	30s.+5s. Great-billed parrot	1·60	80

See also Nos. 1113/16.

272 Gen. MacArthur and Paratroopers landing on Corregidor

1967. 25th Anniv of Battle of Corregidor.

1049	272	6s. multicoloured	25	10
1050	272	5p. multicoloured	9·00	7·00

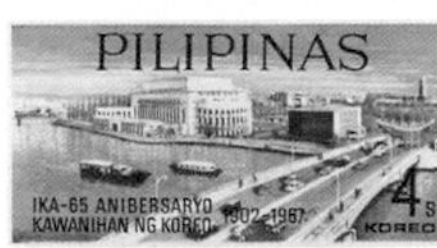

273 Bureau of Posts Building, Manila

1967. 65th Anniv of Philippines Bureau of Posts.

1051	273	4s. multicoloured	25	20
1052	273	20s. multicoloured	40	25
1053	273	50s. multicoloured	1·20	80

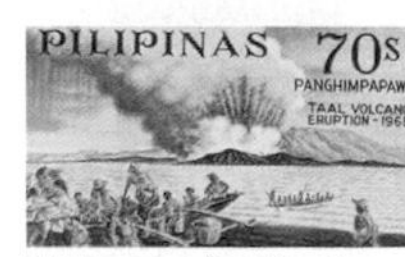

274 Escaping from Eruption

1967. Obligatory Tax. Taal Volcano Eruption (1965) (1st issue).

1054	274	70s. multicoloured	1·90	1·40

For compulsory use on foreign air mail where the rate exceeds 70s. in aid of Taal Volcano Rehabilitation Committee.

See also No. 1071.

1967. Presidential Sayings (6th issue). As T **233** but with portrait and saying changed.

1055	10s. black and blue	25	10
1056	30s. black and violet	65	25

PORTRAIT AND SAYING: Pres. Quezon. "Social justice is far more beneficial ...".

275 "The Holy Family" (Filipino version)

1967. Christmas.

1057	275	10s. multicoloured	40	25
1058	275	40s. multicoloured	90	70

276 Pagoda, Pres. Marcos and Chiang Kai-shek

1967. China–Philippines Friendship.

1059	276	5s. multicoloured	20	10
1060	-	10s. multicoloured	25	20
1061	-	20s. multicoloured	40	25

DESIGNS (with portraits of Pres. Marcos and Chiang Kai-shek): 10s. Gateway, Chinese Garden, Rizal Park, Luneta; 20s. Chinese Garden, Rizal Park, Luneta.

277 Ayala Avenue, Manila, Inaugural Ceremony and Rotary Badge

1968. First Anniv of Makati Centre Post Office, Manila.

1062	**277**	10s. multicoloured	25	20
1063	**277**	20s. multicoloured	40	35
1064	**277**	40s. multicoloured	1·20	1·10

1968. Surch.

1065	-	5s. on 6s. (No. 981)	25	10
1066	-	5s. on 6s. (No. 1034)	25	10
1067	**244**	10s. on 6s.+5s.	30	20

280 Calderon, Barasoain Church and Constitution

1968. Birth Centenary of Felipe G. Calderon (lawyer and author of Malolos Constitution).

1068	**280**	10s. multicoloured	25	20
1069	**280**	40s. multicoloured	1·20	80
1070	**280**	75s. multicoloured	2·30	2·00

281 Eruption

1968. Taal Volcano Eruption (1965) (2nd issue).

1071	**281**	70s. multicoloured	1·90	1·80

Two issues were prepared by an American Agency under a contract signed with the Philippine postal authority but at the last moment this contract was cancelled by the Philippine Government. In the meanwhile the stamps had been on sale in the U.S.A. but they were never issued in the Philippines and they had no postal validity.

They comprise a set for the Mexican Olympic Games in the values 1, 2, 3 and 15s. postage and 50, 75s., 1, 2p. airmail and a set in memory of J. F. Kennedy and Robert Kennedy in the values 1, 2, 3s. postage and 5, 10p. airmail.

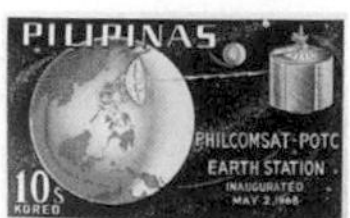

282 "Philcomsat", Earth Station and Globe

1968. Inauguration of "Philcomsat"–POTC Earth Station, Tanay, Rizal, Luzon.

1072	**282**	10s. multicoloured	40	25
1073	**282**	40s. multicoloured	1·20	80
1074	**282**	75s. multicoloured	1·90	1·60

283 "Tobacco Production" (mural)

1968. Philippines Tobacco Industry.

1075	**283**	10s. multicoloured	25	20
1076	**283**	40s. multicoloured	1·20	95
1077	**283**	70s. multicoloured	2·20	1·60

284 "Kudyapi"

1968. St. Cecilia's Day. Musical Instruments. Multicoloured.

1078	10s. Type **284**	20	10
1079	20s. "Ludag"	25	20
1080	30s. "Kulintangan"	65	45
1081	50s. "Subing"	1·00	80

285 Concordia College

1968. Centenary of Concordia Women's College.

1082	**285**	10s. multicoloured	25	10
1083	**285**	20s. multicoloured	40	20
1084	**285**	70s. multicoloured	1·30	95

286 Children singing Carols

1968. Christmas.

1085	**286**	10s. multicoloured	25	20
1086	**286**	40s. multicoloured	1·00	80
1087	**286**	75s. multicoloured	1·90	1·40

287 Philippine Tarsier

1969. Philippines Fauna. Multicoloured.

1088	2s. Type **287**	25	20
1089	10s. Tamarau	40	25
1090	20s. Water buffalo	50	35
1091	75s. Greater Malay chevrotain	3·50	1·90

288 President Aguinaldo and Cavite Building

1969. Birth Centenary of President Amilio Aguinaldo.

1092	**288**	10s. multicoloured	40	25
1093	**288**	40s. multicoloured	1·20	60
1094	**288**	70s. multicoloured	1·90	1·40

289 Rotary Emblem and "Bastion of San Andres"

1969. 50th Anniv of Manila Rotary Club.

1095	**289**	10s. mult (postage)	25	20
1096	**289**	40s. multicoloured (air)	90	60
1097	**289**	75s. multicoloured	1·90	1·40

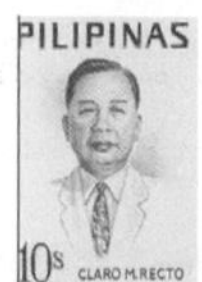

290 Senator C. M. Recto

1969. Recto Commemoration.

1098	**290**	10s. purple	25	10

1969. Philatelic Week. No. 1051 optd **PHILATELIC WEEK NOV. 24-30, 1968.**

1099	**273**	4s. multicoloured	65	20

292 Jose Rizal College

1969. 50th Anniv of Jose Rizal College, Mandaluyong, Rizal.

1100	**292**	10s. multicoloured	25	20
1101	**292**	40s. multicoloured	1·00	70
1102	**292**	50s. multicoloured	1·60	1·10

1969. Fourth National Boy Scout Jamboree, Palayan City. No. 1019 surch **4th NATIONAL BOY SCOUT JAMBOREE PALAYAN CITY–MAY, 1969 5s.**

1103	5s. on 6s. multicoloured	65	25

294 Red Cross Emblems and Map

1969. 50th Anniv of League of Red Cross Societies.

1104	**294**	10s. red, blue and grey	25	20
1105	**294**	40s. red, blue and cobalt	90	45
1106	**294**	75s. red, brown and buff	1·40	1·20

295 Pres. and Mrs. Marcos harvesting Rice

1969. "Rice for Progress".

1107	**295**	10s. multicoloured	25	20
1108	**295**	40s. multicoloured	90	60
1109	**295**	75s. multicoloured	1·40	1·20

296 "The Holy Child of Leyte" (statue)

1969. 80th Anniv of Return of the "Holy Child of Leyte" to Tacloban.

1110	**296**	5s. mult (postage)	20	10
1111	**296**	10s. multicoloured	25	20
1112	**296**	40s. multicoloured (air)	90	60

1969. Obligatory Tax. T.B. Relief Fund. Birds as T **271**.

1113	1s.+5s. Common gold-backed woodpecker	50	20
1114	5s.+5s. Philippine trogon	65	25
1115	10s.+5s. Johnstone's (inscr "Mt. Apo") lorikeet	90	35
1116	40s.+5s. Scarlet (inscr "John-stone's") minivet	1·20	60

297 Bank Building

1969. Inauguration of Philippines Development Bank, Makati, Rizal.

1117	**297**	10s. black, blue and green	25	15
1118	**297**	40s. black, purple and green	1·60	70
1119	**297**	75s. black, brown & grn	2·30	1·50

298 "Philippine Birdwing"

1969. Philippine Butterflies. Multicoloured.

1120	10s. Type **298**	90	35
1121	20s. Tailed jay	1·40	45
1122	30s. Red Helen	2·30	60
1123	40s. Birdwing	3·50	95

299 Children of the World

1969. 15th Anniv of Universal Children's Day.

1124	**299**	10s. multicoloured	25	10
1125	**299**	20s. multicoloured	30	25
1126	**299**	30s. multicoloured	40	30

300 Memorial and Outline of Landing

1969. 25th Anniv of U.S. Forces' Landing on Leyte.

1127	**300**	5s. multicoloured	25	10
1128	**300**	10s. multicoloured	40	25
1129	**300**	40s. multicoloured	90	45

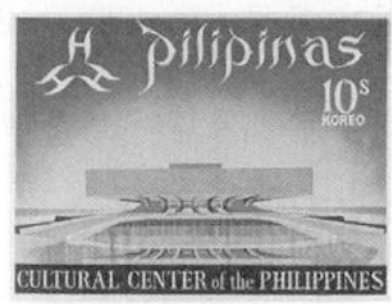

301 Cultural Centre

1969. Cultural Centre, Manila.

1130	**301**	10s. blue	40	25
1131	**301**	30s. purple	90	35

1969. Philatelic Week. Nos. 943/6 (Folk Dances) optd **1969 PHILATELIC WEEK** or surch also.

1132	5s. multicoloured	20	15
1133	5s. on 6s. multicoloured	25	20
1134	10s. multicoloured	35	30
1135	10s. on 20s. multicoloured	40	35

303 Melchora Aquino

1969. 50th Death Anniv of Melchora Aquino, "Tandang Sora" (Grand Old Woman of the Revolution).

1136	**303**	10s. multicoloured	25	20
1137	**303**	20s. multicoloured	40	25
1138	**303**	30s. multicoloured	90	35

1969. Second-term Inaug of President Marcos. Surch **PASINAYA, IKA-2 PANUNUNGKULAN PANGULONG FERDINAND E. MARCOS DISYEMBRE 30, 1969.**

1139	**262**	5s. on 6s. multicoloured	40	25

305 Ladle and Steel Mills

1970. Iligan Integrated Steel Mills.

1140	**305**	10s. multicoloured	25	20
1141	**305**	20s. multicoloured	65	35
1142	**305**	30s. multicoloured	1·20	45

1970. Nos. 900, 962 and 964 surch.

1143	-	4s. on 6s. blue	25	15
1144	**242**	5s. on 6s. multicoloured	40	20
1145	**243**	5s. on 6s. multicoloured	40	20

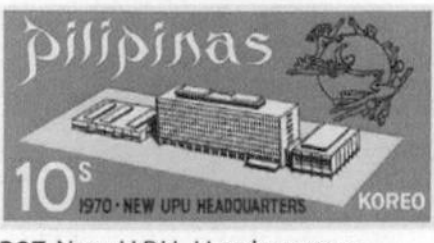

307 New U.P.U. Headquarters Building

1970. New U.P.U. Headquarters Building, Berne.

1146	**307**	10s. ultramarine, yellow and blue	25	20
1147	**307**	30s. blue, yellow and green	1·00	45

1970. Presidential Sayings (7th issue). As T **233** but with portrait and saying changed.

1148	10s. black and purple	25	15
1149	40s. black and green	65	25

PORTRAIT AND SAYING: Pres. Osmena, "Ante todo el bien de nuestro pueblo" ("The well-being of our nation comes above all").

308 Dona Julia V. de Ortigas and T.B. Society Headquarters

1970. Obligatory Tax. T.B. Relief Fund.
1150 **308** 1s.+5s. multicoloured 25 15
1151 **308** 5s.+5s. multicoloured 40 35
1152 **308** 30s.+5s. multicoloured 1·30 80
1153 **308** 70s.+5s. multicoloured 1·70 1·10

309 I.C.S.W. Emblem

1970. 15th Int Conference on Social Welfare.
1154 **309** 10s. multicoloured 25 20
1155 **309** 20s. multicoloured 50 30
1156 **309** 30s. multicoloured 1·00 35

310 "Crab" (after sculpture by A. Calder)

1970. "Fight Cancer" Campaign.
1157 **310** 10s. multicoloured 40 25
1158 **310** 40s. multicoloured 80 35
1159 **310** 50s. multicoloured 1·20 60

311 Scaled Tridacna

1970. Sea Shells. Multicoloured.
1160 5s. Type **311** 65 20
1161 10s. Royal spiny oyster 80 25
1162 20s. Venus comb murex 1·00 35
1163 40s. Glory-of-the-sea cone 3·25 70

1970. Nos. 986, 1024 and 1026 surch with new values in figures and words.
1164 **249** 4s. on 6s. 25 15
1165 **263** 4s. on 6s. 25 15
1166 **264** 4s. on 6s. 25 15

313 The "Hundred Islands" and Ox-cart

1970. Tourism (1st series). Multicoloured.
1167 10s. Type **313** 25 20
1168 20s. Tree-house, Pasonanca Park, Zamboanga City 40 25
1169 30s. "Filipino" (statue) and sugar plantation, Negros Island 50 45
1170 2p. Calesa (horse-carriage) and Miagao Church, Iloilo 3·25 1·90
See also Nos. 1186/9, 1192/5 and 1196/9.

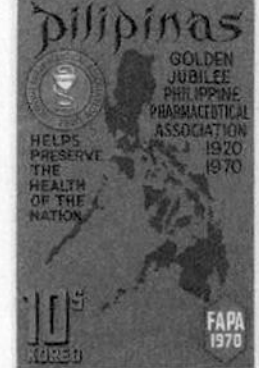

314 Map of the Philippines

1970. Golden Jubilee of Philippine Pharmaceutical Association.
1171 **314** 10s. multicoloured 25 20
1172 **314** 50s. multicoloured 1·30 60

1970. U.P.U./A.O.P.U. Regional Seminar, Manila. No. 938 surch **UPU-AOPU REGIONAL SEMINAR NOV. 23 - DEC. 5, 1970 TEN 10s**.
1173 **235** 10s. on 6s. multicoloured 65 25

1970. Philatelic Week. No. 977 surch **1970 PHILATELIC WEEK 10s TEN**.
1174 **247** 10s. on 6s. brown, blue and gold 80 20

317 Pope Paul VI and Map

1970. Pope Paul's Visit to the Philippines.
1175 **317** 10s. mult (postage) 25 20
1176 **317** 30s. multicoloured 50 30
1177 **317** 40s. multicoloured (air) 80 35

318 Mariano Ponce

1970
1178 **318** 10s. red 45 15
1179 - 15s. brown 50 20
1180 - 40s. red 65 25
1181 - 1p. blue 1·70 60
DESIGNS: 15s. Josefa Llanes Escoda; 40s. Gen. Miguel Malvar; 1p. Julian Felipe.

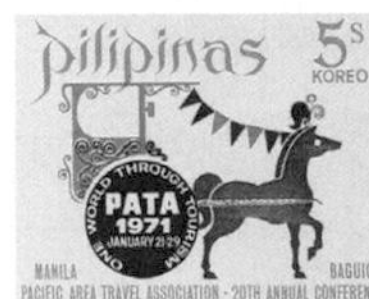

320 "PATA" Horse and Carriage

1971. 20th PATA Conference and Workshop, Manila.
1183 **320** 5s. multicoloured 40 20
1184 **320** 10s. multicoloured 50 25
1185 **320** 70s. multicoloured 1·00 60

1971. Tourism (2nd series). Views as T **313**. Multicoloured.
1186 10s. Nayong Pilipino resort 15 10
1187 20s. Fish farm, Iloilo 25 15
1188 30s. Pagsanjan Falls 40 25
1189 5p. Watch-tower, Punta Cruz 3·00 2·50

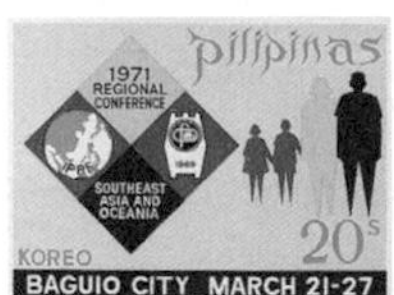

321 Emblem and Family

1971. Regional Conference of International Planned Parenthood Federation for South-East Asia and Oceania.
1190 **321** 20s. multicoloured 25 15
1191 **321** 40s. multicoloured 40 25

1971. Tourism (3rd series). As T **313**. Multicoloured.
1192 10s. Aguinaldo pearl farm 30 20
1193 20s. Coral-diving, Davao 40 25
1194 40s. Taluksengay Mosque 50 35
1195 1p. Ifugao woman and Banaue rice-terraces 3·25 1·10

1971. Tourism (4th series). As T **313**. Multicoloured.
1196 10s. Cannon and Filipino vintas, Fort del Pilar 20 15
1197 30s. Magellan's Cross, Cebu City 25 20
1198 50s. "Big Jar", Calamba, Laguna (Rizal's birthplace) 50 35
1199 70s. Mayon Volcano and diesel train 2·75 70

1971. Surch **FIVE 5s**.
1200 **264** 5s. on 6s. multicoloured 80 20

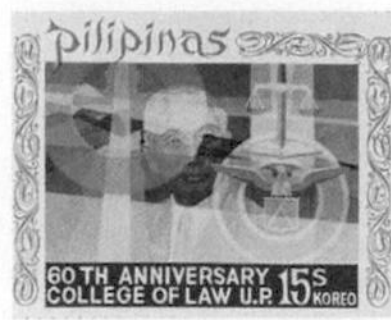

323 G. A. Malcolm (founder) and Law Symbols

1971. 60th Anniv of Philippines College of Law.
1201 **323** 15s. mult (postage) 50 25
1202 **323** 1p. multicoloured (air) 2·50 1·20

324 Commemorative Seal

1971. 400th Anniv of Manila.
1203 **324** 10s. multicoloured (postage) 40 25
1204 **324** 1p. multicoloured (air) 2·20 1·30

325 Arms of Faculties

1971. Centenaries of Faculties of Medicine and Surgery, and of Pharmacy, Santo Tomas University.
1205 **325** 5s. mult (postage) 25 15
1206 **325** 2p. multicoloured (air) 2·75 2·30

1971. University Presidents' World Congress, Manila. Surch **MANILA MCMLXX1 CONGRESS OF UNIVERSITY PRESIDENTS 5s FIVE** and emblem.
1207 **266** 5s. on 6s. violet, yellow and green 80 20

327 "Our Lady of Guia"

1971. 400th Anniv of "Our Lady of Guia", Ermita, Manila.
1208 **327** 10s. multicoloured 25 20
1209 **327** 75s. multicoloured 1·00 80

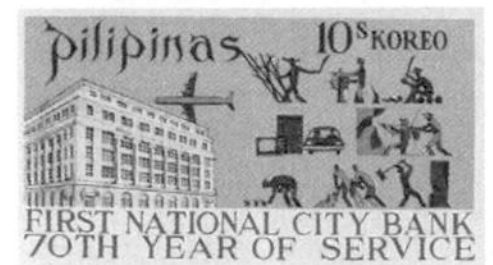

328 Bank and "Customers"

1971. 70th Anniv of First National City Bank.
1210 **328** 10s. multicoloured 25 20
1211 **328** 30s. multicoloured 50 35
1212 **328** 1p. multicoloured 1·30 95

1971. Surch in figure and word.
1213 **259** 4s. on 6s. blue 50 15
1214 **259** 5s. on 6s. blue 65 20

1971. Philatelic Week. Surch **1971 - PHILATELIC WEEK 5s FIVE**.
1215 **266** 5s. on 6s. violet, yellow and green 65 20

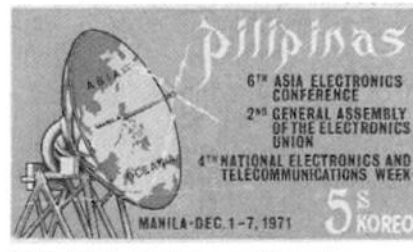

331 Dish Aerial and Events

1972. Sixth Asian Electronics Conference, Manila (1971) and Related Events.
1216 **331** 5s. multicoloured 25 10
1217 **331** 40s. multicoloured 1·00 60

332 Fathers Burgos, Gomez and Zamora

1972. Centenary of Martyrdom of Fathers Burgos, Gomez and Zamora.
1218 **332** 5s. multicoloured 25 15
1219 **332** 60s. multicoloured 80 70

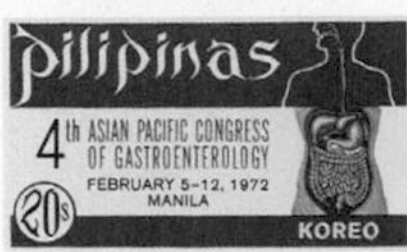

333 Human Organs

1972. Fourth Asian–Pacific Gastro-enterological Congress, Manila.
1220 **333** 20s. mult (postage) 40 25
1221 **333** 40s. multicoloured (air) 80 60

1972. Surch **5s FIVE**.
1222 **263** 5s. on 6s. multicoloured 65 20

1972. No. O914 with optd **G.O.** obliterated by bars.
1223 50s. violet 80 35

1972. Surch.
1224 **245** 10s. on 6s. multicoloured 25 10
1225 **251** 10s. on 6s. multicoloured 25 10
1226 - 10s. on 6s. black and red (No. 1015) 25 10

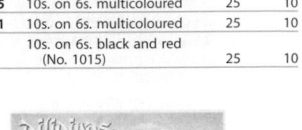

336 Memorial Gardens, Manila

1972. Tourism. "Visit Asean Lands" Campaign.
1227 **336** 5s. multicoloured 25 10
1228 **336** 50s. multicoloured 1·60 35
1229 **336** 60s. multicoloured 2·10 60

337 "KKK" Flag

1972. Evolution of Philippines' Flag.
1230 **337** 30s. red and blue 2·50 45
1231 - 30s. red and blue 2·50 45
1232 - 30s. red and blue 2·50 45
1233 - 30s. black and blue 2·50 45
1234 - 30s. red and blue 2·50 45
1235 - 30s. red and blue 2·50 45
1236 - 30s. red and blue 2·50 45
1237 - 30s. red and blue 2·50 45
1238 - 30s. black, red and blue 2·50 45
1239 - 30s. yellow, red and blue 2·50 45
FLAGS: No. 1231, Three "K"s in pyramid; No. 1232, Single "K"; No. 1233, "K", skull and crossbones; No. 1234, Three "K"s and sun in triangle; No. 1235, Sun and three "K"s; No. 1236, Ancient Tagalog "K" within sun; No. 1237, Face in sun; No. 1238, Tricolor; No. 1239, Present national flag—sun and stars within triangle, two stripes.

338 Mabol, Santol and Papaya

1972. Obligatory Tax. T.B. Relief Fund. Fruit. Multicoloured.
1240 1s.+5s. Type **338** 40 20
1241 10s.+5s. Bananas, balimbang and mangosteen 50 25
1242 40s.+5s. Guava, mango, duhat and susongkalabac 80 60
1243 1p.+5s. Orange, pineapple, lanzones and sirhuelas 1·60 1·30

339 Bridled Parrotfish

1972. Fish. Multicoloured.
1244 5s. Type **339** (postage) 80 20
1245 10s. Klein's butterflyfish 1·00 25
1246 20s. Moorish idol 1·30 35
1247 50s. Two-spined angelfish (air) 5·25 70

340 Bank Headquarters

1972. 25th Anniv of Philippines Development Bank.

1248	**340**	10s. multicoloured	20	10
1249	**340**	20s. multicoloured	25	20
1250	**340**	60s. multicoloured	1·00	60

341 Pope Paul VI

1972. First Anniv of Pope Paul's Visit to Philippines.

1251	**341**	10s. mult (postage)	40	25
1252	**341**	50s. multicoloured	90	60
1253	**341**	60s. multicoloured (air)	1·90	1·10

1972. Various stamps surch.

1254	**240**	10s. on 6s. (No. 953)	50	15
1255	-	10s. on 6s. (No. 959)	50	15
1256	**250**	10s. on 6s. (No. 989)	50	15

343 "La Barca de Aqueronte" (Hidalgo)

1972. 25th Anniv of Stamps and Philatelic Division, Philippines Bureau of Posts. Filipino Paintings. Multicoloured.

1257	5s. Type **343**	25	20
1258	10s. "Afternoon Meal of the Rice Workers" (Amorsolo)	55	25
1259	30s. "Espana y Filipinas" (Luna) (27×60 mm)	65	40
1260	70s. "The Song of Maria Clara" (Amorsolo)	2·40	1·00

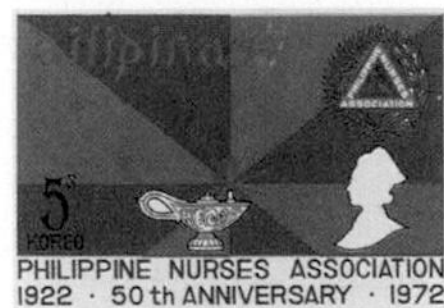

344 Lamp, Emblem and Nurse

1972. 50th Anniv of Philippine Nurses Assn.

1261	**344**	5s. multicoloured	20	15
1262	**344**	10s. multicoloured	25	20
1263	**344**	70s. multicoloured	80	65

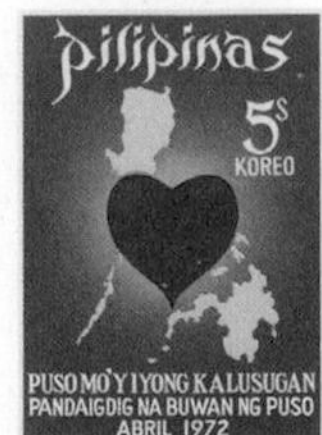

345 Heart on Map

1972. World Heart Month.

1264	**345**	5s. red, green and violet	25	15
1265	**345**	10s. red, green and blue	40	20
1266	**345**	30s. red, blue and green	55	40

346 "The First Mass" (C. V. Francisco)

1972. 450th Anniv of First Mass in Limasawa (1971).

1267	**346**	10s. mult (postage)	55	25
1268	**346**	60s. multicoloured (air)	1·20	75

1972. Asia-Pacific Scout Conference, Manila. Various stamps surch **ASIA PACIFIC SCOUT CONFERENCE NOV, 1972** and value.

1269	**233**	10s. on 6s. (No. 933)	1·60	40
1270	**240**	10s. on 6s. (No. 953)	1·60	40
1271	-	10s. on 6s. (No. 981)	1·60	40

348 Olympic Emblems and Torch

1972. Olympic Games, Munich.

1272	**348**	5s. multicoloured	25	20
1273	**348**	10s. multicoloured	40	25
1274	**348**	70s. multicoloured	1·30	75

1972. Philatelic Week. Nos. 950 and 983 surch **1972 PHILATELIC WEEK TEN 10s**.

1275	**239**	10s. on 6s. multicoloured	55	25
1276	**248**	10s. on 6s. multicoloured	55	25

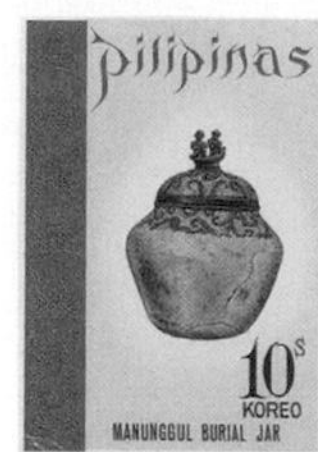

350 Manunggul Burial Jar

1972. Philippine Archaeological Discoveries. Multicoloured.

1277	10s. Type **350**	55	15
1278	10s. Ritual earthenware vessel	55	15
1279	10s. Metal pot	55	15
1280	10s. Earthenware vessel	55	15

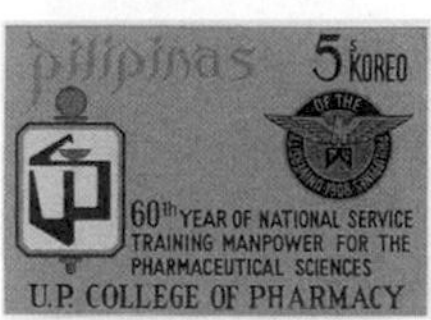

351 Emblems of Pharmacy and University of the Philippines

1972. 60th Anniv of National Training for Pharmaceutical Sciences, University of the Philippines.

1281	**351**	5s. multicoloured	25	15
1282	**351**	10s. multicoloured	40	20
1283	**351**	30s. multicoloured	55	25

352 "The Lantern-makers" (J. Pineda)

1972. Christmas.

1284	**352**	10s. multicoloured	40	20
1285	**352**	30s. multicoloured	55	25
1286	**352**	50s. multicoloured	95	65

353 President Roxas and Wife

1972. 25th Anniv of Philippines Red Cross.

1287	**353**	5s. multicoloured	25	15
1288	**353**	20s. multicoloured	40	25
1289	**353**	30s. multicoloured	55	40

1973. Nos. 948 and 1005 surch **10s**.

1290	**238**	10s. on 6s. multicoloured	35	15
1291	**256**	10s. on 6s. blue. red and yellow	35	15

1973. Presidential Sayings (8th issue). As T **233** but with portrait and saying changed.

1292	10s. black and bistre	25	15
1293	30s. black and mauve	65	25

PORTRAIT AND SAYING: 10s., 30s. Pres. Garcia, "I would rather be right than successful".

355 University Building

1973. 60th Anniv of St. Louis University, Baguio City.

1294	**355**	5s. multicoloured	20	15
1295	**355**	10s. multicoloured	25	20
1296	**355**	75s. multicoloured	1·10	90

356 Col. J. Villamor and Air Battle

1973. Villamor Commemoration.

1297	**356**	10s. multicoloured	25	15
1298	**356**	2p. multicoloured	2·40	2·30

1973. Various stamps surch.

1299	**252**	5s. on 6s. multicoloured	25	15
1300	**266**	5s. on 6s. violet, yellow and green	25	15
1301	**318**	15s. on 10s. red (No. O1182)	40	25

359 Actor and Stage Performance

1973. First "Third-World" Theatre Festival, Manila.

1302	**359**	5s. multicoloured	15	15
1303	**359**	10s. multicoloured	20	15
1304	**359**	50s. multicoloured	65	40
1305	**359**	70s. multicoloured	1·10	65

1973. President Marcos's Anti-smuggling Campaign. No. 1017 surch **5s**.

1306	5s. on 6s. blue	65	15

1973. Tenth Death Anniv of John F. Kennedy. No. 989 surch **5s**.

1307	5s. on 6s. multicoloured	65	15

1973. Compulsory Tax Stamps. T.B. Relief Fund. Nos. 1241/2 surch.

1308	15s.+5s. on 10s.+5s. mult	40	25
1309	60s.+5s. on 40s.+5s. mult	1·20	90

363 Proclamation Scenes

1973. 75th Anniv of Philippine Independence.

1310	**363**	15s. multicoloured	40	25
1311	**363**	45s. multicoloured	55	40
1312	**363**	90s. multicoloured	1·20	1·10

364 M. Agoncillo (maker of first national flag)

1973. Perf or imperf.

1313	-	15s. violet	65	25
1314	**364**	60s. brown	80	65
1315	-	90s. blue	1·10	50
1316	-	1p.10 blue	1·90	65
1317	-	1p.50 red	2·00	1·40
1318	-	1p.50 brown	2·00	65
1319	-	1p.80 green	3·00	1·80
1320	-	5p. blue	8·00	5·75

DESIGNS: 15s. Gabriela Silang (revolutionary); 90s. Teodoro Yangco (businessman); 1p.10, Pio Valenzuela (physician); 1p.50 (No. 1317), Pedro Paterno (revolutionary); 1p.50 (No. 1318), Teodora Alonso (mother of Jose Rizal); 1p.80, E. Evangelista (revolutionary); 5p. F. M. Guerrero (writer).

For similar designs see Nos. 1455/8.

365 Imelda Marcos

1973. Projects Inaugurated by Sra Imelda Marcos.

1321	**365**	15s. multicoloured	25	20
1322	**365**	50s. multicoloured	55	50
1323	**365**	60s. multicoloured	65	60

366 Malakanyang Palace

1973. Presidential Palace, Manila.

1324	**366**	15s. mult (postage)	40	25
1325	**366**	50s. multicoloured	65	40
1326	**366**	60s. multicoloured (air)	95	65

367 Interpol Emblem

1973. 50th Anniv of International Criminal Police Organization (Interpol).

1327	**367**	15s. multicoloured	25	15
1328	**367**	65s. multicoloured	80	40

368 Scouting Activities

1973. Golden Jubilee of Philippine Boy Scouts. Perf or imperf.

1329	**368**	15s. bistre and green	65	40
1330	-	65s. blue and yellow	1·20	50

DESIGN: 65s. Scouts reading brochure.

369 Bank Emblem, Urban and Agricultural Landscapes

1974. 25th Anniv of Central Bank of the Philippines. Multicoloured.

1331	15s. Type **369**	40	15
1332	60s. Bank building, 1949	80	40
1333	1p.50 Bank complex, 1974	1·90	1·00

370 "Maria Clara" Costume

1974. Centenary of U.P.U. Philippine Costumes. Multicoloured.

1334		15s. Type **370**	40	25
1335		60s. "Balintawak"	80	40
1336		80s. "Malong"	1·20	50

1974. Philatelic Week (1973). No. 1303 surch **1973 PHILATELIC WEEK 15s.**

1337	**359**	15s. on 10s. multicoloured	55	15

1974. 25th Anniv of Philippine "Lionism". Nos. 1297 and 1180 surch **PHILIPPINE LIONISM 1949-1974 15s** and Lions emblem.

1338	**356**	15s. on 10s. multicoloured	40	15
1339	-	45s. on 40s. red	55	40

373 Map of South-East Asia

1974. Asian Paediatrics Congress, Manila. Perf or imperf.

1340	**373**	30s. red and blue	80	25
1341	**373**	1p. red and green	1·50	65

374 Gen. Valdes and Hospital

1974. Obligatory Tax. T.B. Relief Fund. Perf or imperf.

1342	**374**	15s.+5s. green and red	25	15
1343	**374**	1p.10+5s. blue and red	80	65

1974. Nos. 974, 1024 and 1026 surch.

1344	**246**	5s. on 3s. green	40	15
1345	**263**	5s. on 6s. multicoloured	40	15
1346	**264**	5s. on 6s. multicoloured	40	15

378 W.P.Y. Emblem

1974. World Population Year. Perf or imperf.

1347	**378**	5s. black and orange	1·10	25
1348	**378**	2p. blue and green	2·75	1·00

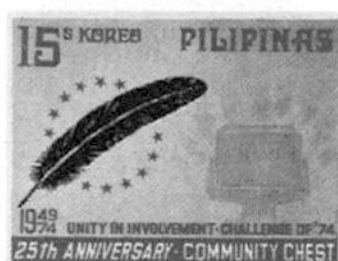

379 Red Feather Emblem

1974. 25th Anniv of Community Chest Movement in the Philippines. Perf or imperf.

1349	**379**	15s. red and blue	40	20
1350	**379**	40s. red and green	65	25
1351	**379**	45s. red and brown	95	30

381 Sultan Mohammad Kudarat, Map, Malayan Prau and Order

1975. Sultan Kudarat of Mindanao Commem.

1352	**381**	15s. multicoloured	65	15

382 Association Emblem

1975. 25th Anniv of Philippine Mental Health Association. Perf or imperf.

1353	**382**	45s. green and orange	55	25
1354	**382**	1p. green and purple	1·20	50

383 Rafael Palma

1975. Birth Centenary of Rafael Palma (educationalist and statesman). Perf or imperf (15s.), perf (30s.).

1355	**383**	15s. green	65	25
1436	**383**	30s. brown	95	20

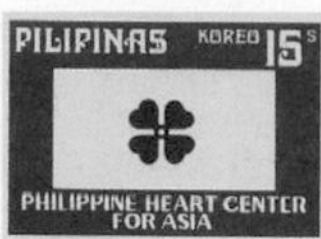

384 Heart Centre Emblem

1975. Inauguration of Philippine Heart Centre for Asia, Quezon City. Perf or imperf.

1356	**384**	15s. red and blue	55	25
1357	**384**	50s. red and green	1·20	50

385 Cadet in Full Dress, and Academy Building

1975. 70th Anniv of Philippine Military Academy.

1358	**385**	15s. multicoloured	40	25
1359	**385**	45s. multicoloured	95	40

387/9, 392/4 "Helping the Disabled"

1975. 25th Anniv (1974) of Philippines Orthopaedic Association. Perf or imperf.

1360	-	45s. green (inscr at left and top)	80	50
1361	**387**	45s. green	80	50
1362	**388**	45s. green	80	50
1363	**389**	45s. green	80	50
1364	-	45s. green (inscr at top and right)	80	50
1365	-	45s. green (inscr at left and bottom)	80	50
1366	**392**	45s. green	80	50
1367	**393**	45s. green	80	50
1368	**394**	45s. green	80	50
1369	-	45s. green (inscr at bottom and right)	80	50

DESIGNS—23×30 mm: Nos. 1360, 1364/5, 1369, Details of corners of the mural.

Nos. 1360/9 were issued together, se-tenant, forming a composite design.

1975. Nos. 1153 and 1342/3 surch.

1370	**374**	5s. on 15s.+5s. green and red	25	20
1371	**308**	60s. on 70s.+5s. multicoloured	80	40
1372	**374**	1p. on 1p.10+5s. blue and red	95	50

397 Planting Sapling

1975. Forest Conservation. Multicoloured.

1373		45s. Type **397**	55	25
1374		45s. Sapling and tree-trunks	55	25

398 Jade Vine

1975

1375	**398**	15s. multicoloured	55	15

399 Imelda Marcos and I.W.Y. Emblem

1975. International Women's Year. Perf or imperf.

1376	**399**	15s. black, blue & dp blue	55	25
1377	**399**	80s. black, blue and pink	80	65

400 Commission Badge

1975. 75th Anniv of Civil Service Commission. Perf or imperf.

1378	**400**	15s. multicoloured	55	25
1379	**400**	50s. multicoloured	80	40

401 Angat River Barrage

1975. 25th Anniv of International Irrigation and Drainage Commission. Perf or imperf.

1380	**401**	40s. blue and orange	40	25
1381	**401**	1p.50 blue and mauve	1·30	75

402 "Welcome to Manila"

1975. Centenary of Hong Kong and Shanghai Banking Corporation's Service in the Philippines.

1382	**402**	1p.50 multicoloured	2·75	65

403 N. Romualdez (legislator and writer)

1975. Birth Centenaries. Perf or imperf.

1383	**403**	60s. lilac	1·50	25
1384	-	90s. mauve	1·90	25

DESIGN: 90s. General G. del Pilar.

405 Boeing 747-100 Airliner and Martin M-130 Flying Boat

1975. 40th Anniv of First Trans-Pacific China Clipper Airmail Flight. San Francisco–Manila.

1385	**405**	60s. multicoloured	95	40
1386	**405**	1p.50 multicoloured	2·40	1·10

1975. Airmail Exn. Nos. 1314 and 1318 optd **AIRMAIL EXHIBITION NOV 22-DEC 9.**

1387	**364**	60s. brown	65	40
1388	-	1p.50 brown	1·60	1·10

407 APO Emblem

1975. 25th Anniv of APO Philatelic Society. Perf or imperf.

1389	**407**	5s. multicoloured	40	25
1390	**407**	1p. multicoloured	95	65

408 E. Jacinto

1975. Birth Centenary of Emilio Jacinto (military leader). Perf or imperf.

1391	**408**	65s. mauve	1·10	25

409 San Agustin Church

1975. Holy Year. Churches. Perf or imperf.

1392	**409**	20s. blue	55	20
1393	-	30s. black and yellow	65	25
1394	-	45s. red, pink and black	1·10	40
1395	-	60s. bistre, yellow & black	1·70	50

DESIGNS—HORIZ: 30s. Morong Church; 45s. Taal Basilica. VERT: 60s. San Sebastian Church.

410 "Conducting" Hands

1976. 50th Anniv of Manila Symphony Orchestra.

1396	**410**	5s. multicoloured	25	20
1397	**410**	50s. multicoloured	65	50

411 Douglas DC-3 and DC-10

1976. 30th Anniv of Philippines Airlines (PAL).

1398	**411**	60s. multicoloured	80	25
1399	**411**	1p.50 multicoloured	2·50	1·10

412 Felipe Agoncillo (statesman)

1976. Felipe Agoncillo Commemoration.

1400	**412**	1p.60 black	3·00	40

413 University Building

1976. 75th Anniv of National University.

1401	**413**	45s. multicoloured	65	25
1402	**413**	60s. multicoloured	95	40

414 "Foresight Prevents Blindness"

1976. World Health Day.
1403 **414** 15s. multicoloured 95 40

415 Emblem on Book

1976. 75th Anniv of National Archives.
1404 **415** 1p.50 multicoloured 1·60 1·30

416 College Emblem and University Tower

1976. 50th Anniv of Colleges of Education and Science, Saint Thomas's University.
1405 **416** 15s. multicoloured 40 15
1406 **416** 50s. multicoloured 65 40

417 College Building

1976. 50th Anniv of Maryknoll College.
1407 **417** 15s. multicoloured 25 15
1408 **417** 1p.50 multicoloured 1·50 1·00

1976. Olympic Games, Montreal. Surch **15s Montreal 1976 21st OLYMPICS, CANADA** and emblem.
1409 **348** 15s. on 10s. mult 1·10 40

419 Constabulary Headquarters, Manila

1976. 75th Anniv of Philippine Constabulary. Perf or imperf.
1410 **419** 15s. multicoloured 40 25
1411 **419** 60s. multicoloured 95 40

420 Land and Aerial Surveying

1976. 75th Anniv of Lands Bureau.
1412 **420** 80s. multicoloured 1·90 65

1976. Air. Bicentenary of American Revolution. No. MS1004 optd **U.S.A. BICENTENNIAL 1776—1976** and individual stamps surch.
MS1413 170×105 mm. 5s. on 3s., 5s. on 6s., 15s. on 30s., 50s. on 70s. Imperf 7·25 7·00

422 Badges of Banking Organizations

1976. International Monetary Fund and World Bank Joint Board of Governors Annual Meeting, Manila.
1414 **422** 60s. multicoloured 55 40
1415 **422** 1p.50 multicoloured 1·60 1·00

423 Virgin of Antipolo

1976. 350th Anniv of "Virgin of Antipolo".
1416 **423** 30s. multicoloured 55 25
1417 **423** 90s. multicoloured 1·30 40

1976. Philatelic Week. Surch **1976 PHILATELIC WEEK 30s.**
1418 **355** 30s. on 10s. mult 80 25

425 "Going to Church"

1976. Christmas.
1419 **425** 15s. multicoloured 65 15
1420 **425** 30s. multicoloured 1·30 25

426 Facets of Education

1976. 75th Anniv of Philippine Educational System.
1421 **426** 30s. multicoloured 25 20
1422 **426** 75s. multicoloured 95 40

1977. Surch.
1423 1p.20 on 1p.10 blue (No. 1316) 1·30 65
1424 3p. on 5p. blue (No. 1320) 3·25 2·10

428 Jose Rizal

1977. Famous Filipinos. Multicoloured.
1425 30s. Type **428** 65 15
1426 2p.30 Dr. Galicano Apacible 1·70 1·10

429 Flags, Map and Emblem

1977. 15th Anniv of Asian–Oceanic Postal Union.
1427 **429** 50s. multicoloured 65 15
1428 **429** 1p.50 multicoloured 1·30 75

430 Worker and Cogwheels

1977. Tenth Anniv of Asian Development Bank.
1429 **430** 90s. multicoloured 80 65
1430 **430** 2p.30 multicoloured 1·70 1·40

431 Commission Emblem

1977. National Rural Credit Commission.
1431 **431** 30s. multicoloured 65 15

432 Dutch Windmill and First Stamps of The Netherlands and the Philippines

1977. Air. "Amphilex77" International Stamp Exhibition, Amsterdam. Sheet 73×90 mm.
MS1432 7p.50 ×3, multicoloured 20·00 19·00

433 Solicitor-General's Emblem

1977. 75th Anniv of Office of Solicitor-General.
1433 **433** 1p.65 multicoloured 1·30 40

434 Conference Emblem

1977. World Law Conference, Manila.
1434 **434** 2p.20 multicoloured 1·60 50

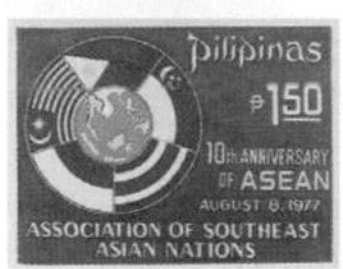

435 A.S.E.A.N. Emblem

1977. Tenth Anniv of Association of South East Asian Nationals (A.S.E.A.N.).
1435 **435** 1p.50 multicoloured 1·50 65

436 Cable Ship "Mercury" and Map

1977. Inauguration of OLUHO Cable (Okinawa–Luzon–Hong Kong).
1437 **436** 1p.30 multicoloured 1·10 65

437 President Marcos

1977. 60th Birthday of President Marcos.
1438 **437** 30s. multicoloured 25 15
1439 **437** 2p.30 multicoloured 1·90 1·10

438 People raising Flag

1977. Fifth Anniv of "New Society".
1440 **438** 30s. multicoloured 25 15
1441 **438** 2p.30 multicoloured 1·90 1·10

439 Bishop Gregorio Aglipay (founder)

1977. 75th Anniv of Aglipayan Church.
1442 **439** 30s. multicoloured 65 20
1443 **439** 90s. multicoloured 1·60 40

440 Bull and early Spanish Stamps

1977. Air. "Espamer 77" International Stamp Exhibition, Barcelona. Sheet 75×90 mm.
MS1444 7p.50 ×3, multicoloured 27·00 25·00

441 Fokker F.7 Trimotor "General New" and World Map

1977. 50th Anniv of First Pan-Am International Air Service.
1445 **441** 2p.30 multicoloured 2·75 1·00

442 Eight-pointed Star and Children

1977. Christmas.
1446 **442** 30s. multicoloured 40 15
1447 **442** 45s. multicoloured 55 25

1977. Philatelic Week. Surch **90s 1977 PHILATELIC WEEK.**
1448 **407** 90s. on 1p. multicoloured 1·20 40

444 Scouts and Map of Philippines

1977. National Scout Jamboree.
1449 **444** 30s. multicoloured 95 25

445 University Badge

1978. 50th Anniv of Far Eastern University.
1450 **445** 30s. multicoloured 80 20

446 Sipa Player

1978. "Sipa" (Filipino ball game).
1451 **446** 5s. multicoloured 25 15
1452 - 10s. multicoloured 40 20
1453 - 40s. multicoloured 55 25
1454 - 75s. multicoloured 1·10 40

DESIGNS: Nos. 1452/4, Different players.

Nos. 1451/4 were issued together, se-tenant, forming a composite design.

447 Jose Rizal

1978

1455	**447**	30s. blue	65	15
1456	-	30s. mauve	65	15
1457	-	90s. green	80	20
1458	-	1p.20 red	95	25

DESIGNS: No. 1456, Rajah Kalantiaw (Panay chief); 1457, Lope K. Santos ("Father of Filipino grammar"); 1458, Gregoria de Jesus (patriot).

448 Arms of Meycauayan

1978. 400th Anniv of Meycauayan.

1459	**448**	1p.05 multicoloured	1·10	40

449 Horse-drawn Mail Cart

1978. "CAPEX 78" International Stamp Exhibition, Toronto. Multicoloured.

1460	2p.50 Type **449**	2·00	1·30
1461	5p. Filipino vinta (sailing canoe)	5·25	3·25
MS1462	Two sheets, each 90×73 mm, each containing 4 ×7p.50. (a) With blue backgrounds; (b) With green backgrounds	65·00	65·00

DESIGNS—36×22 mm : 7p.50 (i) As No. 1461; (ii) As No. 1460; (iii) Early staem locomotive; (iv) Schooner.

450 Andres Bonifacio Monument (Guillermo Tolentino)

1978. Andres Bonifacio Monument.

1463	**450**	30s. multicoloured	65	20

451 Knight, Rook and Globe

1978. World Chess Championship, Baguio City.

1464	**451**	30s. red and violet	65	25
1465	**451**	2p. red and violet	2·30	65

452 Miner

1978. 75th Anniv of Benguet Consolidated Mining Company.

1466	**452**	2p.30 multicoloured	2·40	75

453 Pres. Quezon

1978. Birth Centenary of Manuel L. Quezon (former President).

1467	**453**	30s. multicoloured	75	20
1468	**453**	1p. multicoloured	1·50	25

454 Law Association and Conference Emblems

1978. 58th Int Law Association Conf, Manila.

1469	**454**	2p.30 multicoloured	1·60	1·10

455 Pres. Osmena

1978. Birth Centenary of Sergio Osmena (former President).

1470	**455**	30s. multicoloured	60	15
1471	**455**	1p. multicoloured	1·00	40

456 Map of Cable Route and Cable Ship "Mercury"

1978. Inauguration of Philippines–Singapore Submarine Cable.

1472	**456**	1p.40 multicoloured	2·00	40

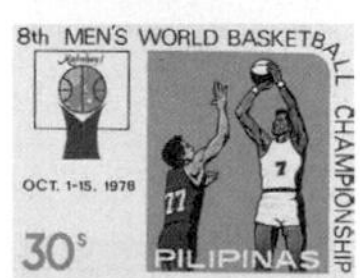

457 Basketball

1978. Eighth Men's World Basketball Championship, Manila.

1473	**457**	30s. multicoloured	75	25
1474	**457**	2p.30 multicoloured	2·50	1·10

458 Dr. Catalino Gavino and Hospital

1978. 400th Anniv of San Lazaro Hospital.

1475	**458**	50s. multicoloured	75	20
1476	**458**	90s. multicoloured	1·50	40

459 Nurse vaccinating Child

1978. Global Eradication of Smallpox.

1477	**459**	30s. multicoloured	60	25
1478	**459**	1p.50 multicoloured	2·50	65

1978. Philatelic Week. No. 1391 surch **1978 PHILATELIC WEEK 60s**.

1479	**408**	60s. on 65s. mauve	1·00	20

461 Man on Telephone, Map and Satellite

1978. 50th Anniv of Philippine Long Distance Telephone Company. Multicoloured.

1480	30s. Type **461**	45	25
1481	2p. Woman on telephone and globe	1·80	95

Nos. 1480/1 were issued together, se-tenant, forming a composite design.

462 Family travelling in Ox-drawn Cart

1978. Decade of the Filipino Child.

1482	**462**	30s. multicoloured	75	20
1483	**462**	1p.35 multicoloured	1·50	40

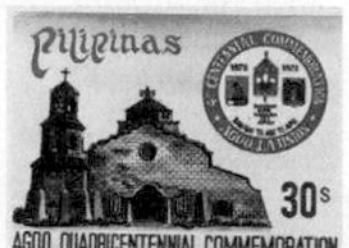

463 Spanish Colonial Church and Arms

1978. 400th Anniv of Agoo Town.

1484	**463**	30s. multicoloured	60	15
1485	**463**	45s. multicoloured	90	25

464 Church and Arms

1978. 400th Anniv of Balayan Town.

1486	**464**	30s. multicoloured	60	15
1487	**464**	90s. multicoloured	1·20	25

465 Dr. Sison

1978. Dr. Honoria Acosta Sison (first Filipino woman physician) Commemoration.

1488	**465**	30s. multicoloured	90	25

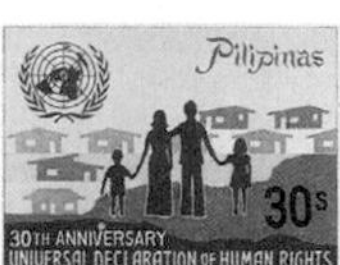

466 Family and Houses

1978. 30th Anniv of Declaration of Human Rights.

1489	**466**	30s. multicoloured	45	25
1490	**466**	3p. multicoloured	3·00	1·50

467 Melon butterflyfish

1978. Fish. Multicoloured.

1491	30s. Type **467**	45	15
1492	1p.20 Black triggerfish	1·30	25
1493	2p.20 Picasso triggerfish	2·20	65
1494	2p.30 Copper-banded butterflyfish	2·30	80
1495	5p. Atoll butterflyfish ("Chaetodon mertensi")	5·00	1·90
1496	5p. Yellow-faced butterflyfish ("Euxiphipops xanthometapon")	5·00	1·90

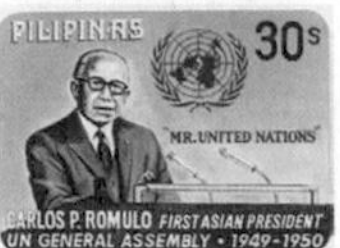

468 Carlos P. Romulo

1979. 80th Anniv of Carlos P. Romulo (1st Asian President of U.N. General Assembly).

1497	**468**	30s. multicoloured	60	25
1498	**468**	2p. multicoloured	2·20	80

469 Cogwheel (Rotary Emblem)

1979. 60th Anniv of Manila Rotary Club.

1499	**469**	30s. multicoloured	45	15
1500	**469**	2p.30 multicoloured	2·00	65

470 Rosa Sevilla de Alvero

1979. Birth Centenary of Rosa Sevilla de Alvero (writer and educator).

1501	**470**	30s. mauve	75	20

471 Burning-off Gas and Map

1979. First Oil Production. Nido Complex, Palawan.

1502	**471**	30s. multicoloured	45	15
1503	**471**	45s. multicoloured	75	25

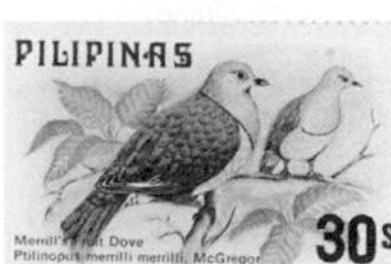

472 Merrill's Fruit Dove

1979. Birds. Multicoloured.

1504	30s. Type **472**	1·50	25
1505	1p.20 Brown tit-babbler	3·00	80
1506	2p.20 Mindoro zone-tailed (inscr "Imperial") pigeon	4·50	1·10
1507	2p.30 Steere's pitta	5·75	1·30
1508	5p. Koch's pitta and red-breasted pitta	14·50	3·25
1509	5p. Great eared nightjar	14·50	3·25

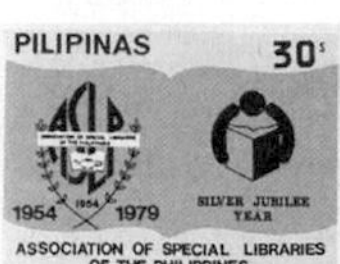

473 Association Emblem

1979. 25th Anniv of Association of Special Libraries of the Philippines.

1510	**473**	30s. green, black & yell	60	25
1511	**473**	75s. green, black & yell	90	40
1512	**473**	1p. green, black & orange	1·50	55

474 Conference Emblem

1979. Fifth U.N. Conference on Trade and Development, Manila.

1513	**474**	1p.20 multicoloured	90	25
1514	**474**	2p.30 multicoloured	2·30	65

475 Malay Civet

1979. Animals. Multicoloured.

1515	30s. Type **475**	45	25
1516	1p.20 Crab-eating macaque	1·00	40
1517	2p.20 Javan pig	1·80	80
1518	2p.30 Leopard cat	1·90	95
1519	5p. Oriental small-clawed otter	4·50	2·40
1520	5p. Malayan pangolin	4·50	2·40

476 Dish Aerial

1979. World Telecommunications Day. Multicoloured.

1521	90s. Type **476**	90	25
1522	1p.30 Hemispheres	1·20	40

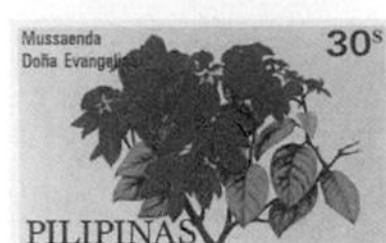

477 Mussaenda "Dona Evangelina"

1979. Cultivated Mussaendas. Multicoloured.

1523	30s. Type **477**	60	15
1524	1p.20 "Dona Esperanza"	1·20	25
1525	2p.20 "Dona Hilaria"	2·00	65
1526	2p.30 "Dona Aurora"	2·20	80
1527	5p. "Gining Imelda"	4·50	1·90
1528	5p. "Dona Trining"	4·50	1·90

478 Manila Cathedral

1979. 400th Anniv of Archdiocese of Manila.

1529	**478**	30s. multicoloured	45	15
1530	**478**	75s. multicoloured	60	20
1531	**478**	90s. multicoloured	90	40

479 "Bagong Lakas" (patrol boat)

1979. Philippine Navy Foundation Day.

1532	**479**	30s. multicoloured	75	15
1533	**479**	45s. multicoloured	1·00	25

1979. Air. First Scout Philatelic Exhibition and 25th Anniv of First National Jamboree. Surch **1ST SCOUT PHILATELIC EXHIBITION JULY 4.14, 1979 QUEZON CITY AIRMAIL 90s.**

1534	**188**	90s. on 6c.+4c. red on yellow	75	65
MS1535		171×90 mm. Nos. 823, 825/8 each surch **50s.**	6·25	6·00

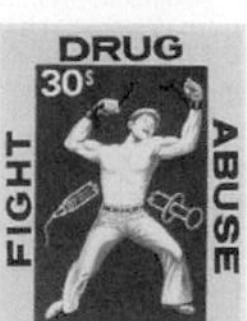

481 Drug Addict breaking Manacles

1979. "Fight Drug Abuse" Campaign.

1536	**481**	30s. multicoloured	45	15
1537	**481**	90s. multicoloured	1·00	25
1538	**481**	1p.05 multicoloured	1·30	40

482 Afghan Hound

1979. Cats and Dogs. Multicoloured.

1539	30s. Type **482**	45	15
1540	90s. Tabby cats	1·30	25
1541	1p.20 Dobermann pinscher	1·60	40
1542	2p.20 Siamese cats	3·00	55
1543	2p.30 German shepherd dog	3·50	1·60
1544	5p. Chinchilla cats	6·50	2·00

483 Children flying Kites

1979. International Year of the Child. Paintings by Rod Dayao. Multicoloured.

1545	15s. Type **483**	60	15
1546	20s. Boys fighting with catapults	75	20
1547	25s. Girls dressing-up	90	25
1548	1p.20 Boy playing policeman	1·50	40

484 Hands holding Emblems

1979. 80th Anniv of Methodism in the Philippines.

1549	**484**	30s. multicoloured	45	15
1550	**484**	1p.35 multicoloured	1·30	25

485 Anniversary Medal and 1868 Coin

1979. 50th Anniv of Philippine Numismatic and Antiquarian Society.

1551	**485**	30s. multicoloured	60	15

486 Concorde over Manila and Paris

1979. 25th Anniv of Air France Service to the Philippines. Multicoloured.

1552	1p.05 Type **486**	1·50	65
1553	2p.20 Concorde over monument	3·75	1·20

1979. Philatelic Week. Surch **1979 PHILATELIC WEEK 90s.**

1554	**412**	90s. on 1p.60 black	1·50	25

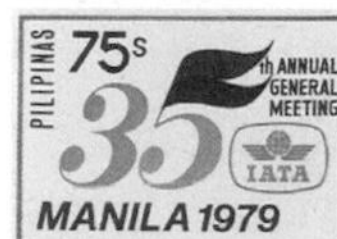

488 "35" and I.A.T.A. Emblem

1979. 35th Annual General Meeting of International Air Transport Association, Manila.

1555	**488**	75s. multicoloured	1·00	25
1556	**488**	2p.30 multicoloured	2·75	1·30

489 Bureau of Local Government Emblem

1979. Local Government Year.

1557	**489**	30s. multicoloured	45	15
1558	**489**	45s. multicoloured	60	25

490 Christmas Greetings

1979. Christmas. Multicoloured.

1559	30s. Type **490**	75	25
1560	90s. Stars	1·50	65

491 Rheumatism Victim

1980. Fourth Congress of Southeast Asia and Pacific Area League Against Rheumatism, Manila.

1561	**491**	30s. multicoloured	1·20	20
1562	**491**	90s. multicoloured	3·25	40

492 Birthplace and MacArthur Memorial Foundation

1980. Birth Centenary of General Douglas MacArthur (U.S. Army Chief of Staff). Multicoloured.

1563	30s. Type **492**	45	20
1564	75s. General MacArthur	1·00	25
1565	2p.30 Hat, pipe and glasses	3·50	1·50
MS1566	76×76 mm. 5p. Landing in the Philippines (horiz). Imperf	7·25	6·00

493 Columbus and Emblem

1980. 75th Anniv of Knights of Columbus Organization in Philippines.

1567	**493**	30s. multicoloured	45	25
1568	**493**	1p.35 multicoloured	2·00	95

494 Soldiers and Academy Emblem

1980. 75th Anniv of Philippine Military Academy.

1569	**494**	30s. multicoloured	45	25
1570	**494**	1p.20 multicoloured	1·90	65

495 Tirona, Benitez and University

1980. 60th Anniv of Philippine Women's University.

1571	**495**	30s. multicoloured	30	15
1572	**495**	1p.05 multicoloured	1·50	65

496 Boats and Burning City

1980. 75th Anniv of Rotary International. Details of painting by Carlos Francisco. Multicoloured.

1573	30s. Type **496**	45	25
1574	30s. Priest with cross, swords-men and soldier	45	25
1575	30s. "K K K" flag and group around table	45	25
1576	30s. Man in midst of spearmen and civilian scenes	45	25
1577	30s. Reading the Constitution, soliders and U.S. and Philippine flags	45	25
1578	2p.30 Type **496**	3·25	1·20
1579	2p.30 As No. 1574	3·25	1·20
1580	2p.30 As No. 1575	3·25	1·20
1581	2p.30 As No. 1576	3·25	1·20
1582	2p.30 As No. 1577	3·25	1·20

Nos. 1573/7 and 1578/82 were issued together in se-tenant strips of five, each strip forming a composite design.

497 Mosque and Koran

1980. 600th Anniv of Islam in the Philippines.

1583	**497**	30s. multicoloured	75	25
1584	**497**	1p.30 multicoloured	3·75	65

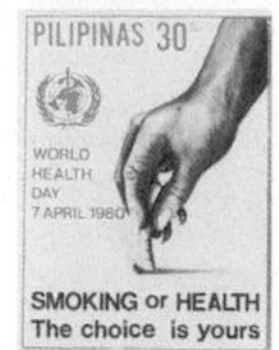

498 Hand stubbing out Cigarette

1980. World Health Day. Anti-smoking Campaign.

1585	**498**	30s. multicoloured	75	25
1586	**498**	75s. multicoloured	1·50	40

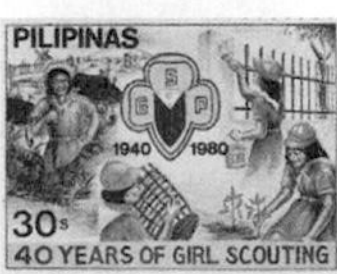

499 Scouting Activities and Badge

1980. 40th Anniv of Girl Scouting in the Philippines.

1587	**499**	30s. multicoloured	75	25
1588	**499**	2p. multicoloured	2·20	65

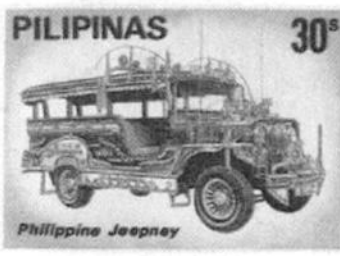

500 Jeepney

1980. Philippine Jeepneys (decorated jeeps). Multicoloured.

1589	30s. Type **500**	60	25
1590	1p.20 Side view of Jeepney	1·80	65

1980. 82nd Anniv of Independence. Surch **PHILIPPINE INDEPENDENCE 82ND ANNIVERSARY 1898 1980.**

1591	**412**	1p.35 on 1p.60 black	1·80	80
1592	**412**	1p.50 on 1p.80 green (No. 1319)	2·30	95

502 Association Emblem

1980. Seventh General Conference of International Association of Universities, Manila.

1593	**502**	30s. multicoloured	30	15
1594	**502**	2p.30 multicoloured	3·00	2·75

503 Map and Emblems

1980. 46th Congress of International Federation of Library Associations and Institutions, Manila.

1595	**503**	30s. green and black	45	25
1596	**503**	75s. blue and black	1·00	40
1597	**503**	2p.30 red and black	3·25	1·70

504 Filipinos and Emblem

1980. Fifth Anniv of Kabataang Barangay (national council charged with building the "New Society").

1598	**504**	30s. multicoloured	45	15
1599	**504**	40s. multicoloured	60	25
1600	**504**	1p. multicoloured	1·30	55

1980. Nos. 1433, 1501, 1536, 1557 and 1559 surch.

1601	**470**	40s. on 30s. mauve	45	15

1602	**481**	40s. on 30s. multicoloured	45	15
1603	**489**	40s. on 30s. multicoloured	45	15
1604	**490**	40s. on 30s. multicoloured	45	15
1605	**433**	2p. on 1p.65 mult	3·00	1·30

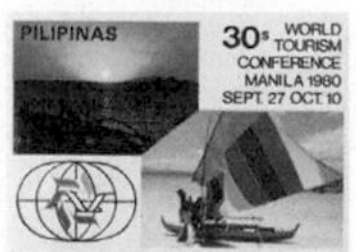

506 Sunset, Filipino Vinta and Conference Emblem

1980. World Tourism Conference, Manila.

1606	**506**	30s. multicoloured	45	25
1607	**506**	2p.30 multicoloured	3·25	1·60

507 Magnifying Glass and Stamps

1980. Postage Stamp Day.

1608	**507**	40s. multicoloured	45	25
1609	**507**	1p. multicoloured	1·30	55
1610	**507**	2p. multicoloured	2·75	1·20

508 U.N. Headquarters and Philippines Flag

1980. 35th Anniv of U.N.O.

1611	40s. Type **508**	75	25
1612	3p.20 U.N. Headquarters and U.N. and Philippines flags	4·50	2·75

509 Alabaster Murex

1980. Shells. Multicoloured.

1613	40s. Type **509**	90	25
1614	60s. Giant frog shell	1·50	40
1615	1p.20 Zambo's murex	2·75	65
1616	2p. Pallid carrier shell	5·25	1·20

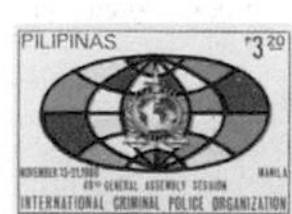

510 Interpol Emblem on Globe

1980. 49th General Assembly of Interpol, Manila.

1617	**510**	40s. multicoloured	45	25
1618	**510**	1p. multicoloured	1·50	65
1619	**510**	3p.20 multicoloured	4·75	2·75

511 University and Faculty Emblems

1980. 75th Anniv of Central Philippine University. Multicoloured, background colour given.

1620	**511**	40s. blue	60	15
1621	**511**	3p.20 green	3·75	2·40

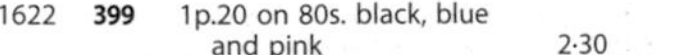

1980. Philatelic Week. No. 1377 surch **1980 PHILATELIC WEEK P1.20.**

1622	**399**	1p.20 on 80s. black, blue and pink	2·30	55

513 Christmas Tree and Presents

1980. Christmas.

1623	**513**	40s. multicoloured	90	20

1981. Various stamps surch.

1624	**244**	10s. on 6s.+5s. blue	1·20	20
1625	**462**	10s. on 30s. mult	30	10
1626	**408**	40s. on 65s. mauve	75	25
1627	**458**	40s. on 90s. mult	90	25
1628	**481**	40s. on 90s. mult	45	15
1629	-	40s. on 90s. mult (No. 1560)	90	25
1630	**448**	40s. on 1p.05 mult	90	25
1631	**462**	40s. on 1p.35 mult	90	25
1632	**399**	85s. on 80s. black, blue and pink	1·00	55
1633	**408**	1p. on 65s. mauve	3·00	55
1634	**401**	1p. on 1p.50 blue and mauve	3·00	55
1635	**422**	1p. on 1p.50 mult	1·60	55
1636	-	1p.20 on 1p.50 brown (No. 1318)	1·90	65
1637	**433**	1p.20 on 1p.65 mult	3·50	65
1638	-	1p.20 on 1p.80 green (No. 1319)	3·50	65
1639	**401**	2p. on 1p.50 blue and mauve	2·75	1·20
1640	**434**	3p.20 on 2p.20 mult	8·75	1·90

1981. 30th Anniv of APO Philatelic Society. Surch **NOV. 30, 1980 APO PHILATELIC SOCIETY PEARL JUBILEE 40s.**

1641	**455**	40s. on 30s. mult	90	20

516 Von Stephan and U.P.U. Emblem

1981. 150th Birth Anniv of Heinrich von Stephan (founder of U.P.U.).

1642	**516**	3p.20 multicoloured	3·75	1·70

1981. Girl Scouts Camp. No. 1589 surch **GSP RJASIA-PACIFIC REGIONAL CAMP PHILIPPINES DECEMBER 23, 1980 40s.**

1643	**500**	40s. on 30s. mult	3·00	25

518 Pope John Paul II

1981. Papal Visit. Multicoloured.

1644	90s. Type **518**	1·00	40
1645	1p.20 Pope and cardinals	1·30	55
1646	2p.30 Pope blessing crowd (horiz)	2·75	1·20
1647	3p. Pope and Manila Cathedral (horiz)	3·25	1·50
MS1648	75×91 mm. 7p.50 Pope and map of Philippines	11·50	8·00

519 Parliamentary Debate

1981. Interparliamentary Union Meeting, Manila.

1649	**519**	2p. multicoloured	2·75	1·10
1650	**519**	3p.20 multicoloured	3·75	1·90

520 Monument

1981. Jose Rizal Monument, Luneta Park.

1651	**520**	40s. black, yellow & brn	75	20

521 President Aguinaldo's Car

1981. 50th Anniv of Philippine Motor Association. Multicoloured.

1652	40s. Type **521**	1·20	25
1653	40s. 1930 model car	1·20	25
1654	40s. 1937 model car	1·20	25
1655	40s. 1937 model car (different)	1·20	25

522 Bubble Coral

1981. Corals. Multicoloured.

1656	40s. Type **522**	1·20	25
1657	40s. Branching corals	1·20	25
1658	40s. Brain coral	1·20	25
1659	40s. Table coral	1·20	25

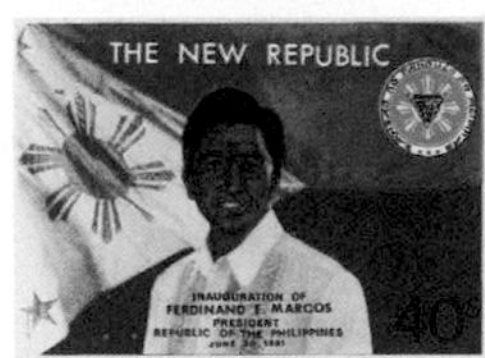

523 President Marcos and Flag

1981. Inauguration of President Marcos. Perf or imperf.

1660	**523**	40s. multicoloured	75	20
MS1661		78×78 mm. 5p. As No. 1660 but design smaller with inscriptions below. Imperf	7·25	3·25

524 St. Ignatius de Loyola (founder)

1981. 400th Anniv of Jesuits in the Philippines. Multicoloured.

1662	40s. Type **524**	90	25
1663	40s. Dr. Jose P. Rizal and Intramuros Ateneo	90	25
1664	40s. Father Frederico Faura (director) and Manila Observatory	90	25
1665	40s. Father Saturnino Urios (missionary) and map of Mindanao	90	25
MS1666	89×89 mm. As Nos. 1662/5 but smaller. Imperf (sold at 2p.)	6·50	4·00

525 F. R. Castro

1981. Chief Justice Fred Ruiz Castro.

1667	**525**	40s. multicoloured	60	15

526 Pres. Ramon Magsaysay

1981. Portraits. As T **526**

1668	-	1p. brown and black	1·30	55
1669	**526**	1p.20 brown and black	1·60	65
1670	-	2p. purple and black	2·75	1·20

DESIGNS: 1p. General Gregorio del Pilar; 2p. Ambrosio R. Bautista.

See also Nos. 1699/1704, 1807 etc. and 2031/3.

527 Man in Wheelchair

1981. International Year of Disabled Persons.

1671	**527**	40s. multicoloured	60	25
1672	**527**	3p.20 multicoloured	3·75	1·90

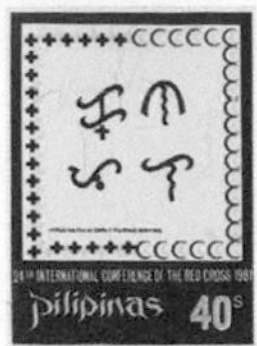

528 Early Filipino Writing

1981. 24th International Red Cross Conference.

1673	**528**	40s. black, red and bistre	30	20
1674	**528**	2p. black and red	2·75	95
1675	**528**	3p.20 black, red and mauve	4·00	1·70

529 Isabel II Gate, Manila

1981

1676	**529**	40s. black	75	15

530 Concert in Park

1981. Opening of Concert at Park 200.

1677	**530**	40s. multicoloured	1·00	15

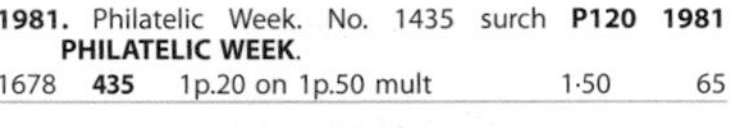

1981. Philatelic Week. No. 1435 surch **P120 1981 PHILATELIC WEEK**.

1678	**435**	1p.20 on 1p.50 mult	1·50	65

532 Running

1981. 11th South-east Asian Games, Manila.

1679	**532**	40s. yellow, green & brn	60	15
1680	-	1p. multicoloured	1·60	55
1681	-	2p. multicoloured	3·00	1·10
1682	-	2p.30 multicoloured	3·25	1·20
1683	-	2p.80 multicoloured	3·75	1·50
1684	-	3p.20 violet and blue	4·00	1·90

DESIGNS: 1p. Cycling; 2p. President Marcos and Juan Antonio Samaranch (president of International Olympic Committee); 2p.30, Football; 2p.80, Shooting; 3p.20, Bowling.

533 Manila Film Centre

1982. Manila International Film Festival. Multicoloured.

1685	40s. Type **533**	75	25
1686	2p. Front view of trophy	3·25	1·20
1687	3p.20 Side view of trophy	4·00	2·00

534 Carriedo Fountain

1982. Centenary of Manila Metropolitan Waterworks and Sewerage System.

1688	**534**	40s. blue	75	15
1689	**534**	1p.20 brown	1·80	65

535 Lord Baden-Powell (founder)

1982. 75th Anniv of Boy Scout Movement. Multicoloured.

1690	40s. Type **535**	45	25
1691	2p. Scout	3·25	1·20

536 Embroidered Banner

1982. 25th Anniv of Children's Museum and Library Inc. Multicoloured.

1692	40s. Type **536**	60	25
1693	1p.20 Children playing	1·50	55

537 President Marcos presenting Sword of Honour

1982. Military Academy.

1694	**537**	40s. multicoloured	60	25
1695	**537**	1p. multicoloured	1·60	55

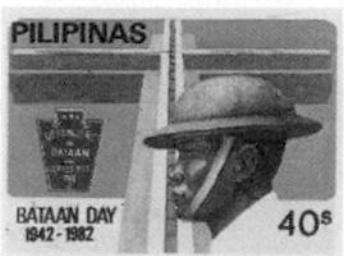

538 Soldier and Memorial

1982. Bataan Day.

1696	**538**	40s. multicoloured	45	25
1697	-	2p. multicoloured	3·25	1·20

MS1698 76×76 mm. 3p.20 purple and black. Imperf 5·00 3·00

DESIGNS: 2p. Doves and rifles; 3p.20, Field gun and flag.

1982. Portraits. As T **526**.

1699	40s. blue	45	25
1700	1p. red	1·50	55
1701	1p.20 brown	1·60	65
1702	2p. mauve	2·75	1·20
1703	2p.30 purple	3·25	1·30
1704	3p.20 blue	4·00	1·90

DESIGNS: 40s. Isabelo de los Reyes (founder of first workers' union); 1p. Aurora Aragon Quezon (social worker and former First Lady); 1p.20, Francisco Dagohoy; 2p. Juan Sumulong (politician); 2p.30, Professor Nicanor Abelardo (composer); 3p.20, General Vicente Lim.

For these designs in other values, see Nos. 1811/15.

539 Worker with Tower Award

1982. Tower Awards (for best "Blue Collar" Workers). Multicoloured.

1705	40s. Type **539** (inscr "MANG-GAGAWA")	90	15
1705d	40s. Type **539** (inscr "MANGA-GAWA")	90	15
1706	1p.20 Cogwheel and tower award (inscr "MANGGA-GAWA")	2·00	65
1706b	1p.20 As No. 1706 but inscr "Mangagawa"	2·00	65

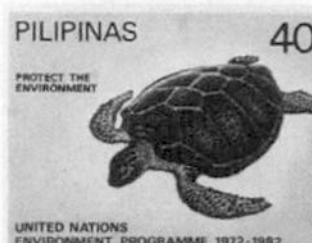

541 Green Turtle

1982. Tenth Anniv of United Nations Environment Programme. Multicoloured.

1707	40s. Type **541**	1·50	25
1708	3p.20 Philippine eagle	5·75	1·70

542 K.K.K. Emblem

1982. Inauguration of Kilusang Kabuhayan at Kaunlaran (national livelihood movement).

1709	**542**	40s. green, light green and black	75	15
1816	**542**	60s. green, light green and black	75	25
1817	**542**	60s. green, red and black	75	25

543 Chemistry Apparatus and Emblem

1982. 50th Anniv of Adamson University.

1710	**543**	40s. multicoloured	75	15
1711	**543**	1p.20 multicoloured	1·50	65

544 Dr. Fernando G. Calderon and Emblems

1982. 75th Anniv of College of Medicine, University of the Philippines.

1712	**544**	40s. multicoloured	60	25
1713	**544**	3p.20 multicoloured	3·75	1·90

545 President Marcos

1982. 65th Birthday of President Ferdinand Marcos.

1714	**545**	40s. multicoloured	45	20
1715	**545**	3p.20 multicoloured	3·75	1·90

MS1716 76×76 mm. Nos. 1714/15. Imperf 5·75 3·00

546 Hands supporting Family

1982. 25th Anniv of Social Security System.

1717	**546**	40s. black, orange & blue	45	25
1718	**546**	1p.20 black, orange and green	1·50	65

547 Emblem and Flags forming Ear of Wheat

1982. 15th Anniv of Association of South East Asian Nations.

1719	**547**	40s. multicoloured	75	25

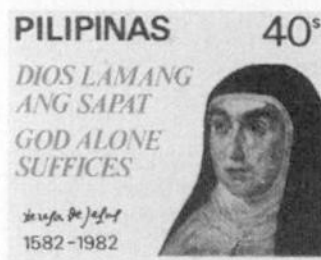

548 St. Theresa of Avila

1982. 400th Death Anniv of St. Theresa of Avila. Multicoloured.

1720	40s. Type **548**	45	25
1721	1p.20 St. Theresa and map of Europe, Africa and Asia	1·60	65
1722	2p. As 1p.20	3·25	1·20

549 St. Isabel College

1982. 350th Anniv of St. Isabel College.

1723	**549**	40s. multicoloured	60	25
1724	**549**	1p. multicoloured	1·80	55

550 President Marcos signing Decree and Tenant Family

1982. Tenth Anniv of Tenant Emancipation Decree.

1725a	**550**	40s. green, brown and black (37×27 mm)	1·50	20
1726	**550**	40s. green, brown and black (32×22½ mm)	2·20	25

551 "Reading Tree"

1982. Literacy Campaign.

1727	**551**	40s. multicoloured	45	25
1728	**551**	2p.30 multicoloured	3·25	1·20

552 Helmeted Heads

1982. 43rd World Congress of Skal Clubs, Manila.

1729	40s. Type **552**	45	25
1730	2p. Head in feathered head-dress	3·25	1·20

553 Dancers with Parasols

1982. 25th Anniv of Bayanihan Folk Arts Centre. Multicoloured.

1731	40s. Type **553**	75	15
1732	2p.80 Dancers (different)	4·00	1·50

554 Dr. Robert Koch and Bacillus

1982. Cent of Discovery of Tubercule Bacillus.

1733	**554**	40s. red, blue and black	45	15
1734	**554**	2p.80 multicoloured	3·75	1·50

555 Father Christmas in Sleigh

1982. Christmas.

1735	**555**	40s. multicoloured	1·20	25
1736	**555**	1p. multicoloured	3·00	55

556 Presidential Couples and Flags

1982. State Visit of Pres. Marcos to United States.

1737	**556**	40s. multicoloured	60	25
1738	**556**	3p.20 multicoloured	3·00	1·60

MS1739 76×75 mm. Nos. 1737/8. Imperf 6·25 2·75

557 Woman with Sewing Machine

1982. U.N. World Assembly on Ageing.

1740a	**557**	1p.20 green and orange	1·50	65
1741a	-	2p. pink and blue	3·00	1·10

DESIGN: 2p. Man with carpentry tools.

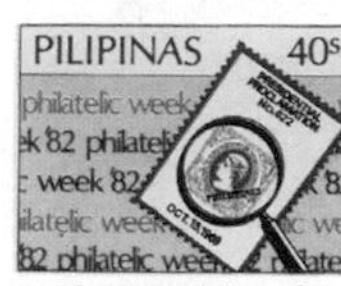

558 Stamp and Magnifying Glass

1983. Philatelic Week.

1742	**558**	40s. multicoloured	45	25
1743	**558**	1p. multicoloured	1·50	55

559 Eulogio Rodriguez

1983. Birth Centenary of Eulogio Rodriguez (former President of Senate).

1744a	**559**	40s. multicoloured	45	15
1745	**559**	1p.20 multicoloured	1·50	65

560 Symbolic Figure and Film Frame

1983. Manila International Film Festival.

1746a	**560**	40s. multicoloured	75	25
1747a	**560**	3p.20 multicoloured	3·75	1·70

561 Monument

1983. Second Anniv of Beatification of Lorenzo Ruiz.

1748	**561**	40s. yellow, red and black	60	15
1749	**561**	1p.20 multicoloured	1·60	65

562 Early Printing Press

1983. 390th Anniv of First Local Printing Press.

1750	**562**	40s. green and black	75	15

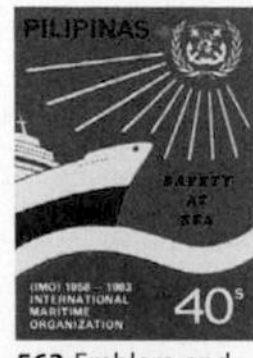

563 Emblem and Ship

1983. 25th Anniv of International Maritime Organization.

1751	**563**	40s. red, black and blue	75	15

1983. Seventh National Scout Jamboree. No. 1709 optd **7TH BSP NATIONAL JAMBOREE 1983**.

1752	**542**	40s. green, light green and black	75	15

1983. Nos. 1360/9 surch **40s**.

1753	-	40s. on 45c. green	90	25
1754	**387**	40s. on 45c. green	90	25
1755	**388**	40s. on 45c. green	90	25
1756	**389**	40s. on 45c. green	90	25
1757	-	40s. on 45c. green	90	25
1758	-	40s. on 45c. green	90	25
1759	**392**	40s. on 45c. green	90	25
1760	**393**	40s. on 45c. green	90	25
1761	**394**	40s. on 45c. green	90	25
1762	-	40s. on 45c. green	90	25

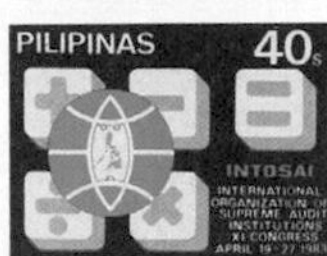

566 Calculator Keys

1983. 11th International Organization of Supreme Audit Institutions Congress.

1763	**566**	40s. blue, light blue and silver	45	15
1764	-	2p.80 multicoloured	3·75	1·50
MS1765 77×76 mm. Nos. 1763/4. Imperf			6·50	4·00

DESIGN: 2p.80, Congress emblem.

567 Smiling Children

1983. 75th Anniv of Philippine Dental Association.

1766	**567**	40s. green, mauve & brn	75	25

568 Detail of Statue

1983. 75th Anniv of University of the Philippines.

1767	**568**	40s. brown and green	60	25
1768	-	1p.20 multicoloured	1·60	55

DESIGN: 1p.20, Statue and diamond.

569 Yasuhiro Nakasone and Pres. Marcos

1983. Visit of Japanese Prime Minister.

1769	**569**	40s. multicoloured	75	25

570 Agriculture and Natural Resources

1983. 25th Anniv of National Science and Technology Authority. Multicoloured.

1770	40s. Type **570**		75	25
1771	40s. Heart, medical products and food (Health and nutrition)		75	25
1772	40s. Industrial complex and air (Industry and energy)		75	25
1773	40s. House, scientific equipment and book (Sciences and social science)		75	25

571 Globes and W.C.Y. Emblem

1983. World Communication Year.

1774	**571**	3p.20 multicoloured	3·75	1·60

572 Postman

1983. Bicent of Philippine Postal System.

1775	**572**	40s. multicoloured	75	25

573 Woman with Tambourine

1983. Christmas. Multicoloured.

1776	40s. Type **573**	60	25
1777	40s. Man turning spit (left side)	60	25
1778	40s. Pig on spit	60	25
1779	40s. Man turning spit (right side)	60	25
1780	40s. Man with guitar	60	25
MS1781 153×77 mm. Nos. 1776/80. Imperf		5·75	4·00

Nos. 1776/80 were issued together, se-tenant, forming a composite design.

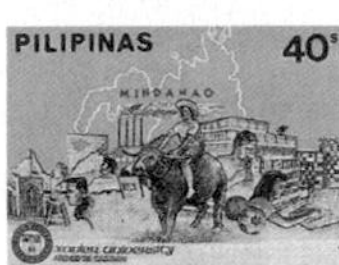

574 University Activities

1983. 50th Anniv of Xavier University.

1782	**574**	40s. multicoloured	75	25
1783	**574**	60s. multicoloured	1·20	35

575 Woman casting Vote

1983. 50th Anniv of Female Suffrage.

1784	**575**	40s. multicoloured	75	25
1785	**575**	60s. multicoloured	1·20	35

576 Workers

1983. 50th Anniv of Ministry of Labour and Employment.

1786	**576**	40s. multicoloured	75	25
1787	**576**	60s. multicoloured	1·20	35

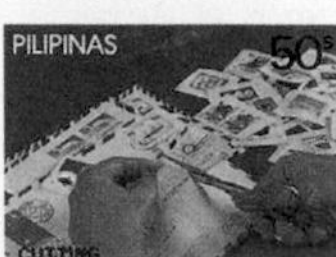

577 Cutting Stamp from Envelope

1983. Philatelic Week. Multicoloured.

1788	50s. Type **577**	1·00	25
1789	50s. Sorting stamps	1·00	25
1790	50s. Soaking stamps	1·00	25
1791	50s. Hinging stamp	1·00	25
1792	50s. Mounting stamp in album	1·00	25

578 Red-vented Cockatoo

1984. Parrots. Multicoloured.

1793	40s. Type **578**	2·30	55
1794	2p.30 Guaiabero	3·25	60
1795	2p.80 Mountain racket-tailed parrot	3·75	65
1796	3p.20 Great-billed parrot	4·75	80
1797	3p.60 Muller's parrot	5·00	1·20
1798	5p. Philippine hanging parrot	5·75	1·50

579 Princess Tarhata Kiram

1984. Fifth Death Anniv of Princess Tarhata Kiram.

1799	**579**	3p. deep green, green and red	3·00	55

580 Nun and Congregation

1984. 300th Anniv of Religious Congregation of the Virgin Mary.

1800	**580**	40s. multicoloured	45	25
1801	**580**	60s. multicoloured	90	25

581 Dona Concha Felix de Calderon

1984. Birth Centenary of Dona Concha Felix de Calderon.

1802	**581**	60s. green and black	75	25
1803	**581**	3p.60 green and red	2·20	40

1984. Various stamps surch.

1804	**545**	60s. on 40s. multicoloured	75	25
1805	**558**	60s. on 40s. multicoloured	75	25
1806	-	3p.60 on 3p.20 blue (No. 1704)	4·50	55

1984. Portraits. as T **526**.

1807	60s. brown and black	75	25
1808	60s. violet and black	75	25
1809	60s. black	75	25
1889	60s. brown	75	15
1913	60s. blue	75	25
1914	60s. red	75	25
1811	1p.80 blue	1·50	35
1812	2p.40 purple	1·80	40
1813	3p. brown	1·80	45
1814	3p.60 red	2·75	55
1815	4p.20 purple	3·00	65

DESIGNS: No. 1807, General Artemio Ricarte; 1808, Teodoro M. Kalaw (politician); 1809, Carlos P. Garcia (4th President); 1913, Quintin Paredes (senator); 1889, Dr. Deogracias V. Villadolid; 1914, Santiago Fonacier (former Senator and army chaplain); 1811, General Vicente Lim; 1812, Professor Nicanor Abelardo; 1813, Francisco Dagohoy; 1814, Aurora Aragon Quezon; 1815, Juan Sumulong.

583 Manila

1984. 150th Anniv of Ayala Corporation.

1818	**583**	70s. multicoloured	45	15
1819	**583**	3p.60 multicoloured	3·00	40

584 "Lady of the Most Holy Rosary with St. Dominic" (C. Francisco)

1984. "Espana 84" International Stamp Exhibition, Madrid. Multicoloured.

1820	2p.50 Type **584**	1·50	25
1821	5p. "Spoliarum" (Juan Luna)	3·00	65
MS1822 99×73 mm. 7p.50, As No. 1821; 7p.50, Virgin of Manila and Spanish galleon; 7p.50, Illustrations from Rizal's "The Monkey and the Turtle"; 7p.50, As No. 1820. Perf or imperf		26·00	20·00

585 Maria Paz Mendoza Guazon

1984. Birth Centenary of Dr. Maria Paz Mendoza Guazon.

1823	**585**	60s. red and blue	1·50	15
1824	**585**	65s. red, black and blue	1·60	20

586 "Adolias amlana"

1984. Butterflies. Multicoloured.

1825	60s. Type **586**	60	25
1826	2p.40 "Papilio daedalus"	1·50	40
1827	3p. "Prothoe franckii semperi"	1·80	55
1828	3p.60 Philippine birdwing	2·30	55
1829	4p.20 Lurcher	2·75	95
1830	5p. "Chilasa idaeoides"	3·75	1·10

1984. National Children's Book Day. Stamp from miniature sheet ("The Monkey and the Turtle") surch **7-17-84 NATIONAL CHILDREN'S BOOK DAY 20.** Perf or imperf.

1831	7p.20 on 7p.50 multicoloured	44·00	24·00

1984. 420th Anniv of Philippine–Mexican Friendship. Stamp from miniature sheet (Virgin of Manila) surch **420TH PHIL-MEXICAN FRIENDSHIP 8-3-84 20.** Perf or imperf.

1832	7p.20 on 7p.50 multicoloured	44·00	24·00

589 Running

1984. Olympic Games, Los Angeles. Multicoloured.

1833	60s. Type **589**	75	40
1834	2p.40 Boxing	2·20	65
1835	6p. Swimming	4·50	1·10
1836	7p.20 Windsurfing	5·00	1·50
1837	8p.40 Cycling	5·75	1·60
1838	20p. Running (woman athlete)	11·50	4·00
MS1839 87×129 mm. 6p. ×4, As Nos. 1834 and 1836/8		26·00	20·00

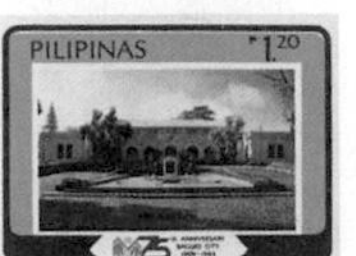

590 The Mansion

1984. 75th Anniv of Baguio City.

1840	**590**	1p.20 multicoloured	90	25

1984. 300th Anniv of Our Lady of Holy Rosary Parish. Stamp from miniature sheet ("Lady of the Most Holy Rosary") surch **9-1-84 300TH YR O.L. HOLY ROSARY PARISH 20.** Perf or imperf.

1841	7p.20 on 7p.50 multicoloured	60·00	55·00

592 Electric Train on Viaduct

1984. Light Railway Transit.

1842	**592**	1p.20 multicoloured	1·90	25

593 Australian and Philippine Stamps and Koalas

1984. "Ausipex 84" International Stamp Exhibition, Melbourne.

1843	**593**	3p. multicoloured	4·00	65
1844	**593**	3p.60 multicoloured	4·50	80
MS1845 75×90 mm. **593** 20p. ×3, multicoloured			50·00	47·00

1984. National Museum Week. Stamp from miniature sheet (as No. 1821) surch **NATIONAL MUSEUM WEEK 10-5-84 20.** Perf or imperf.

1846	7p.20 on 7p.50 multicoloured	35·00	27·00

1984. Asia Regional Conference of Rotary International. No. 1728 surch **14-17 NOV. 84 R.I. ASIA REGIONAL CONFERENCE P1.20.**

1847	**551**	1p.20 on 2p.30 mult	2·20	25

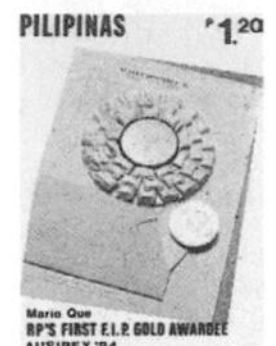

596 Gold Award

1984. Philatelic Week. Gold Award at "Ausipex 84" to Mario Que. Multicoloured.

1848	1p.20 Type **596**	1·20	25
1849	3p. Page of Que's exhibit	2·50	40

597 Caracao

1984. Water Transport. Multicoloured.

1850	60s. Type **597**	30	20
1851	1p.20 Chinese junk	45	25
1852	6p. Spanish galleon	2·50	1·10
1853	7p.20 Casco (Filipino cargo prau)	3·00	1·30
1854	8p.40 Early paddle-steamer	3·25	1·60
1855	20p. Modern liner	8·00	3·50

1984. No. **MS**1666 surch **3 00** with T **598**.

MS1856 89×89 mm. 3p. on 2p. multicoloured	7·25	3·25

599 Anniversary Emblem

1984. 125th Anniv of Ateneo de Manila University.

1857	**599**	60s. blue and gold	1·00	25
1858	**599**	1p.20 blue and silver	1·50	40

600 Virgin and Child

1984. Christmas. Multicoloured.

1859	60s. Type **600**	75	25
1860	1p.20 Holy Family	2·20	40

601 Manila–Dagupan Steam Locomotive, 1892

1984. Rail Transport. Multicoloured.

1861	60s. Type **601**	75	25
1862	1p.20 Light Rail Transit eletric train, 1984	90	35
1863	6p. Bicol express, 1955	3·75	1·10
1864	7p.20 Electric tram, 1905	4·50	1·30
1865	8p.40 Diesel commuter railcar, 1972	5·75	1·60
1866	20p. Horse tram, 1898	11·00	3·50

602 Abstract

1984. Tenth Anniv of Philippine Jaycees' Ten Outstanding Young Men Awards. Abstracts by Raul Isidro. Multicoloured.

1867	60s. brown background in circle	60	25
1868	60s. Type **602**	60	25
1869	60s. red background	60	25
1870	60s. blue and purple background	60	25
1871	60s. orange and brown background	60	25
1872	3p. As No. 1867	1·30	65
1873	3p. Type **602**	1·30	65
1874	3p. As No. 1869	1·30	65
1875	3p. As No. 1870	1·30	65
1876	3p. As No. 1871	1·30	65

603 Tobacco Plant and Dried Leaf

1985. 25th Anniv of Philippine Virginia Tobacco Administration.

1877	**603**	60s. multicoloured	90	25
1878	**603**	3p. multicoloured	2·75	65

1985. Philatelic Week, 1984. Nos. 1848/9 optd **Philatelic Week 1984**.

1879	**596**	1p.20 multicoloured	75	25
1880	-	3p. multicoloured	2·20	80

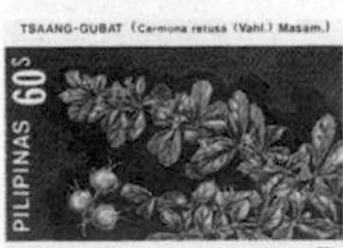

605 National Research Council Emblem

1985. Fifth Pacific Science Association Congress.

1881	**605**	60s. black, blue and light blue	60	25
1882	**605**	1p.20 black, blue and orange	1·30	40

606 "Carmona retusa"

1985. Medicinal Plants. Multicoloured.

1883a	60s. Type **606**	90	40
1884	1p.20 "Orthosiphon aristatus"	1·30	55
1885	2p.40 "Vitex negundo"	3·75	65
1886	3p. "Aloe barbadensis"	5·75	95
1887	3p.60 "Quisqualis indica"	5·75	95
1888	4p.20 "Blumea balsamifera"	11·50	1·30

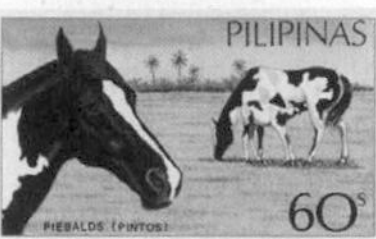

607 "Early Bird" Satellite

1985. 20th Anniv of International Telecommunications Satellite Organization.

1896	**607**	60s. multicoloured	60	25
1897	**607**	3p. multicoloured	1·80	65

608 Piebalds

1985. Horses. Multicoloured.

1898	60s. Type **608**	60	20
1899	1p.20 Palominos	75	25
1900	6p. Bays	3·00	1·20
1901	7p.20 Browns	3·75	1·60
1902	8p.40 Greys	4·00	1·90
1903	20p. Chestnuts	10·00	4·00
MS1904 123×84 mm. 8p.40 ×4, As Nos. 1899/1901 and 1903		22·00	20·00

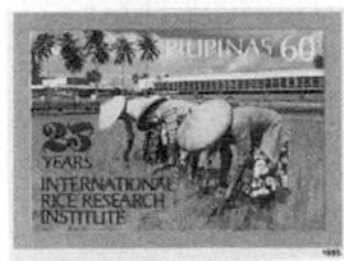

609 Emblem

1985. 25th Anniv of National Tax Research Centre.

1905	**609**	60s. multicoloured	90	20

610 Transplanting Rice

1985. 25th Anniv of International Rice Research Institute, Los Banos. Multicoloured.

1906	60s. Type **610**	60	25
1907	3p. Paddy fields	1·30	40

611 Image of Holy Child of Cebu

1985. 420th Anniv of Filipino–Spanish Treaty. Multicoloured.

1908	1p.20 Type **611**	1·50	25
1909	3p.60 Rajah Tupas and Miguel Lopez de Lagazpi signing treaty	5·00	55

1985. Tenth Anniv of Diplomatic Relations with Chinese People's Republic. No. **MS**1661 optd **10th ANNIVERSARY PHILIPPINES AND PEOPLE'S REPUBLIC OF CHINA DIPLOMATIC RELATIONS 1975–1985.**

MS1910a 78×78 m. 5p. multicoloured	8·75	5·25

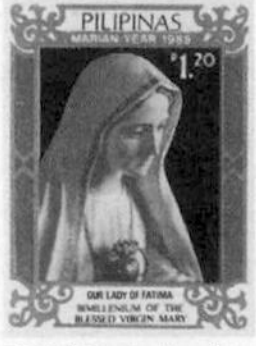

613 Early Anti-TB Label

1985. 75th Anniv of Philippine Tuberculosis Society. Multicoloured.

1911	60s. Screening for TB, laboratory work, health education and inoculation	75	25
1912	1p.20 Type **613**	2·20	40

1985. 45th Anniv of Girl Scout Charter. No. 1409 surch **45th ANNIVERSARY GIRL SCOUT CHARTER**, emblem and new value.

1917	**348**	2p.40 on 15s. on 10s. multicoloured	2·20	55
1918	**348**	4p.20 on 15s. on 10s. multicoloured	4·50	65
1919	**348**	7p.20 on 15s. on 10s. multicoloured	5·00	1·10

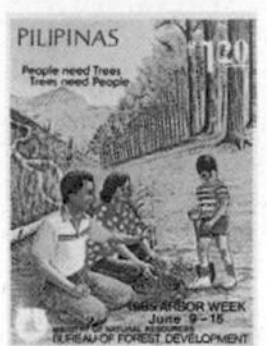

616 "Our Lady of Fatima"

1985. Marian Year. 2000th Birth Anniversary of Virgin Mary. Multicoloured.

1920	1p.20 Type **616**	1·80	40
1921	2p.40 "Our Lady of Beaterio" (Juan Bueno Silva)	2·20	45
1922	3p. "Our Lady of Penafrancia"	2·75	55
1923	3p.60 "Our Lady of Guadalupe"	4·50	65

617 Family planting Tree

1985. Tree Week. International Year of the Forest.

1924	**617**	1p.20 multicoloured	1·20	25

618 Battle of Bessang Pass

1985. 40th Anniv of Bessang Pass Campaign.

1925	**618**	1p.20 multicoloured	1·20	25

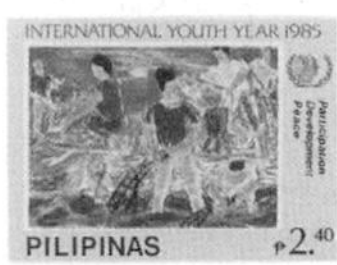

619 Vicente Orestes Romualdez

1985. Birth Centenary of Vicente Orestes Romualdez (lawyer).

1926a	**619**	60s. blue	90	20
1927a	**619**	2p. mauve	1·30	25

620 Fishing

1985. International Youth Year. Children's Paintings. Multicoloured.

1928	2p.40 Type **620**	1·50	25
1929	3p.60 Picnic	3·00	40

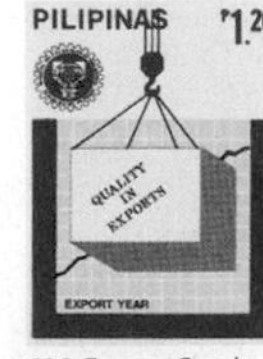

621 Banawe Rice Terraces

1985. World Tourism Organization Congress, Sofia, Bulgaria.

1930	**621**	2p.40 multicoloured	3·00	40

622 Export Graph and Crane lifting Crate

1985. Export Promotion Year.

1931	**622**	1p.20 multicoloured	2·00	40

1985. No. 1815 surch **P360.**

1932	3p.60 on 4p.20 purple	3·00	80

624 Emblem and Dove with Olive Branch

1985. 40th Anniv of U.N.O.

1933	**624**	3p.60 multicoloured	1·20	55

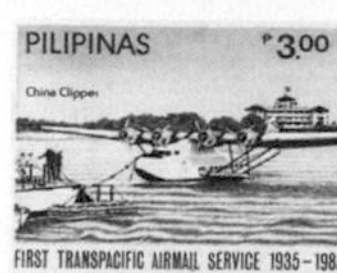

625 Martin M-130 Flying Boat "China Clipper"

1985. 50th Anniv of First Trans-Pacific Commercial Flight (San Francisco–Manila). Multicoloured.

1934		3p. Type **625**	1·30	40
1935		3p.60 Route map, "China Clipper" and anniversary emblem	1·80	55

1985. Philatelic Week. Nos. 1863/4 surch **PHILATELIC WEEK 1985**, No. 1937 further optd **AIRMAIL**.

1936		60s. on 6p. mult (postage)	1·50	25
1937		3p. on 7p.20 mult (air)	4·50	65

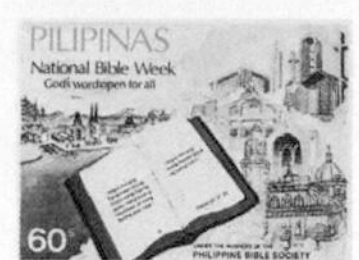

627 Bible and Churches

1985. National Bible Week.

1938	**627**	60s. multicoloured	90	25
1939	**627**	3p. multicoloured	3·25	65

628 Panuluyan (enactment of search for an inn)

1985. Christmas. Multicoloured.

1940		60s. Type **628**	90	25
1941		3p. Pagdalaw (nativity)	3·25	65

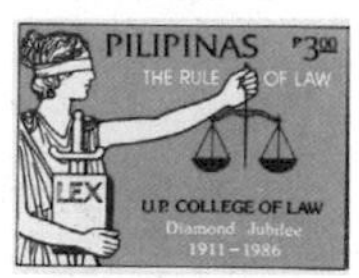

629 Justice holding Scales

1986. 75th Anniv of College of Law.

1942	**629**	60s. mauve and black	75	25
1943	**629**	3p. green, purple & black	3·00	65

See also No. 2009.

630 Rizal and "Noli Me Tangere"

1986. Centenary of Publication of "Noli Me Tangere" (Jose Rizal's first book).

1944	**630**	60s. violet	75	25
1945	-	1p.20 green	1·50	55
1946	-	3p.60 brown	1·80	65

DESIGNS: 1p.20, 3p.60, Rizal, "To the Flowers of Heidelberg" (poem) and Heidelberg University.

631 Douglas DC-3, 1946

1986. 45th Anniv of Philippine Airlines. Each red, black and blue.

1947		60s. Type **631**	90	40
1948		60s. Douglas DC-4 Skymaster, 1946	90	40
1949		60s. Douglas DC-6, 1948	90	40
1950		60s. Vickers Viscount 784, 1957	90	40
1951		2p.40 Fokker F.27 Friendship, 1960	1·50	55
1952		2p.40 Douglas DC-8-50, 1962	1·50	55
1953		2p.40 B.A.C. One Eleven 500, 1964	1·50	55
1954		2p.40 Douglas DC-10-30, 1974	1·50	55
1955		3p.60 Beech 18, 1941	2·75	80
1956		3p.60 Boeing 747-200, 1980	2·75	80

See also No. 2013.

632 Oil Refinery, Manila Bay

1986. 25th Anniv of Bataan Refinery Corporation.

1957	**632**	60s. silver and green	90	25
1958	-	3p. silver and blue	2·75	55

DESIGN—HORIZ: 3p. Refinery (different).

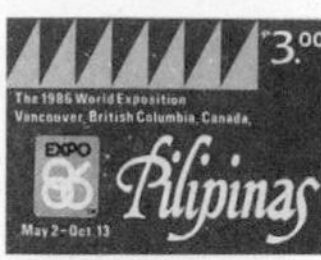

633 Emblem

1986. "Expo 86" World's Fair, Vancouver.

1959	**633**	60s. multicoloured	1·20	25
1960	**633**	3p. multicoloured	2·30	65

634 Emblem and Industrial and Agricultural Symbols

1986. 25th Anniv of Asian Productivity Organization.

1961	**634**	60s. black, green & orge	1·20	25
1962	**634**	3p. black, green & orange	2·00	65
1963	**634**	3p. brown (30×22 mm)	2·00	65

635 1906 2c. Stamp

1986. "Ameripex 86" Int Stamp Exhibition, Chicago.

1964	**635**	60s. green, black & yellow	1·20	25
1965	-	3p. bistre, black and green	2·30	65

DESIGN: 3p. 1935 20c. stamp.

See also No. 2006.

637 Corazon Aquino, Salvador Laurel and Hands

1986. "People Power". Multicoloured.

1966		60s. Type **637**	75	25
1967		1p.20 Radio antennae, helicopter and people	90	40
1968		2p.40 Religious procession	1·50	55
1969		3p. Crowds around soldiers in tanks	1·60	65
MS1970		76×76 mm. 7p.20, Crowd, Pres. Aquino and Vice-Pres. Laurel (42×32 mm). Imperf	6·50	6·00

638 Monument and Paco and Taft Schools

1986. 75th Anniv of First La Salle School in Philippines.

1971	**638**	60s. black, lilac and green	75	40
1972	-	2p.40 black, blue & grn	2·20	55
1973	-	3p. black, yellow & green	3·00	65
MS1974		75×75 mm. 7p.20, black and emerald. Imperf	13·00	12·00

DESIGNS: 2p.40, St. Miguel Febres Cordero and Paco school; 3p. St. Benilde and Taft school; 7p.20, Founding brothers of Paco school.

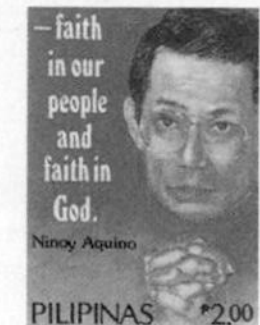

639 Aquino praying

1986. Third Death Anniv of Benigno S. Aquino, jun.

1975		60s. green	75	40
1976	**639**	2p. multicoloured	1·20	55
1977	-	3p.60 multicoloured	2·75	65
MS1978		75×75 mm. 10p. multicoloured. Imperf	7·25	6·75

DESIGNS: 27×36 mm (as T **526**—60s. Aquino. HORIZ (as T **639**)—3p.60 Aquino (different); 10p. Crowd and Aquino.

See also No. 2007.

640 "Vanda sanderiana"

1986. Orchids. Multicoloured.

1979		60s. Type **640**	75	25
1980		1p.20 "Epigeneium lyonii"	1·60	40
1981		2p.40 "Paphiopedilum philippinense"	2·75	55
1982		3p. "Amesiella philippinense"	3·25	65

641 "Christ carrying the Cross"

1986. 400th Anniv of Quiapo District.

1983	**641**	60s. red, black and mauve	75	25
1984	-	3p.60 blue, black & grn	2·20	65

DESIGN—HORIZ: 3p.60, Quiapo Church.

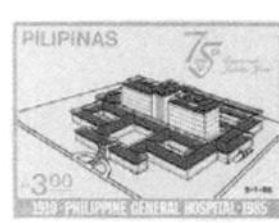

642 Hospital

1986. 75th Anniv of Philippine General Hospital.

1985	**642**	60s. multicoloured	75	25
1986	**642**	3p. multicoloured	2·20	65
2012	**642**	5p. brown	3·50	65

643 Comet and Earth

1986. Appearance of Halley's Comet. Multicoloured.

1987		60s. Type **643**	1·00	25
1988		2p.40 Comet, Moon and Earth	2·75	65

644 Handshake

1986. 74th International Dental Federation Congress, Manila. Multicoloured.

1989		60s. Type **644**	2·20	25
1990		3p. Jeepney, Manila	5·00	80

See also Nos. 2008 and 2011.

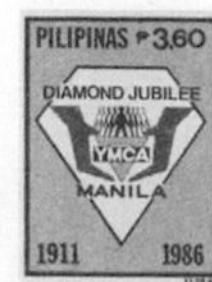

645 Emblem

1986. 75th Anniv of Manila Young Men's Christian Association.

1991	**645**	2p. blue	1·50	40
1992	**645**	3p.60 red	2·20	80
2058	**645**	4p. blue	3·25	1·10

646 Old and New Buildings

1986. 85th Anniv of Philippine Normal College.

1993	-	60s. multicoloured	75	25
1994	**646**	3p.60 yellow, brown & bl	4·50	1·10

DESIGN: 60s. Old and new buildings (different).

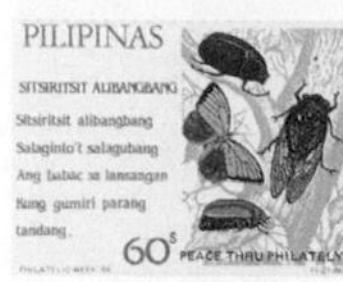

647 Butterfly and Beetles

1986. Philatelic Week and International Peace Year.

1995	**647**	60s. multicoloured	60	25
1996	-	1p. blue and black	1·20	40
1997	-	3p. multicoloured	3·75	80

DESIGNS—VERT: 1p. Peace Year emblem. HORIZ: 3p. Dragonflies.

648 Mother and Child

1986. Christmas. Multicoloured.

1998		60s. Type **648**	75	25
1999		60s. Couple with child and cow	75	25
2000		60s. Mother and child with doves	75	25
2001		1p. Mother and child receiving gifts (horiz)	1·30	40
2002		1p. Mother and child beneath arch (horiz)	1·30	40
2003		1p. Madonna and shepherd adoring child (horiz)	1·30	40
2004		1p. Shepherds and animals around child in manger (horiz)	1·30	40

1987. No. 1944 surch **P100**.

2005	**630**	1p. on 60s. violet	1·50	25

1987. As previous issues but smaller, 22×30 mm, 30×22 mm or 32×22 mm (5p.50), and values and colours changed.

2006	-	75s. green (As No. 1965)	75	25
2007	-	1p. blue (As No. 1975)	90	35
2008	**644**	3p.25 green	2·20	40
2009	**629**	3p.50 brown	2·30	45
2011	-	4p.75 green (As No. 1990)	3·25	60
2013	-	5p.50 blue (As No. 1956)	3·75	80

650 Manila Hotel, 1912

1987. 75th Anniv of Manila Hotel.

2014	**650**	1p. bistre and black	75	40
2015	-	4p. multicoloured	3·75	80
2016	-	4p.75 multicoloured	4·50	1·10
2017	-	5p.50 multicoloured	5·00	1·20

DESIGNS: 4p. Hotel; 4p.75, Lobby; 5p.50, Staff in ante-lobby.

651 Emblem

1987. 50th Anniv of International Eucharistic Congress, Manila. Multicoloured.

2018		75s. Type **651**	75	25
2019		1p. Emblem (different) (horiz)	1·30	40

652 Pres. Cory Aquino taking Oath

1987. Ratification of New Constitution.

2020	**652**	1p. multicoloured	75	40
2021	-	5p.50 blue and brown	3·25	1·50
2060	-	5p.50 green and brown (22×31 mm)	2·50	45

DESIGN: 5p.50, Constitution on open book and dove.

653 Dr. Jose P. Laurel (founder) and Tower

1987. 35th Anniv of Lyceum.

2022	**653**	1p. multicoloured	75	25
2023	**653**	2p. multicoloured	2·20	40

654 City Seal, Man with Philippine Eagle and Woman with Fruit

1987. 50th Anniv of Davao City.

2024	**654**	1p. multicoloured	90	25

655 Salary and Policy Loans

1987. 50th Anniv of Government Service Insurance System. Multicoloured.

2025	1p. Type **655**	90	40
2026	1p.25 Disability and medicare	1·00	45
2027	2p. Retirement benefits	1·30	55
2028	3p.50 Survivorship benefits	2·20	80

656 Emblem and People in Hand

1987. 50th Anniv of Salvation Army in Philippines.

2029	**656**	1p. multicoloured	1·20	25

657 Woman, Ballot Box and Map

1987. 50th Anniv of League of Women Voters.

2030	**657**	1p. blue and mauve	1·80	40

1987. Portraits As T **526**.

2031	1p. green	1·00	25
2032	1p. blue	1·00	25
2033	1p. red	1·00	25
2034	1p. purple and red	1·00	25

DESIGNS: No. 2031, Gen. Vicente Lukban; 2032, Wenceslao Q. Vinzons; 2033, Brigadier-General Mateo M. Capinpin; 2034, Jesus Balmori.

658 Map and Flags as Leaves

1987. 20th Anniv of Association of South-East Asian Nations.

2035	**658**	1p. multicoloured	1·30	25

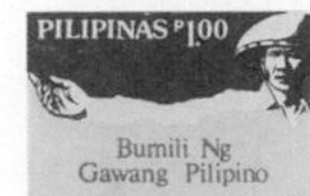

659 Man with Outstretched Arm

1987. Exports.

2036	**659**	1p. multicoloured	75	25
2037	-	2p. green, yellow & brn	1·00	40
2059	-	4p.75 blue and black	2·20	40

DESIGN: 2p., 4p.75, Man, cogwheel and factory.

660 Nuns, People and Crucifix within Flaming Heart

1967. 125th Anniv of Daughters of Charity in the Philippines.

2038	**660**	1p. blue, red and black	1·50	35

661 Statue and Stained Glass Window

1987. Canonization of Blessed Lorenzo Ruiz de Manila (first Filipino saint). Multicoloured.

2039	1p. Type **661**	1·00	40
2040	5p.50 Lorenzo Ruiz praying before execution	4·50	80
MS2041	56×56 mm. 8p. As No. 2040. Imperf	7·25	6·75

1987. No. 2012 surch **P4.75**.

2042	**642**	4p.75 on 5p. brown	3·00	40

663 Nun and Emblem

1987. 75th Anniv of Good Shepherd Sisters in Philippines.

2043	**663**	1p. multicoloured	2·20	25

664 Founders

1987. 50th Anniv of Philippines Boy Scouts.

2044	**664**	1p. multicoloured	1·80	25

665 Family with Stamp Album

1987. 50th Anniv of Philippine Philatelic Club.

2045	**665**	1p. multicoloured	1·80	25

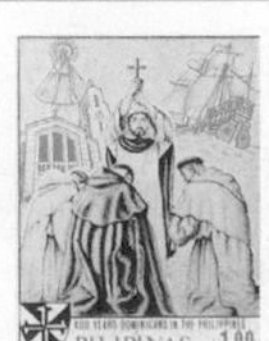

666 Monks, Church and Wrecked Galleon

1987. 400th Anniv of Dominican Order in Philippines.

2046	**666**	1p. black, blue and orange	75	40
2047	-	4p.75 multicoloured	2·20	65
2048	-	5p.50 multicoloured	3·75	1·10

DESIGNS: 4p.75, J. A. Jeronimo Guerrero, Diego de Sta. Maria and Letran Dominican college; 5p.50, Pope and monks.

667 Flags

1987. Third Association of South-east Asian Nations Summit Meeting.

2049	**667**	4p. multicoloured	3·75	55

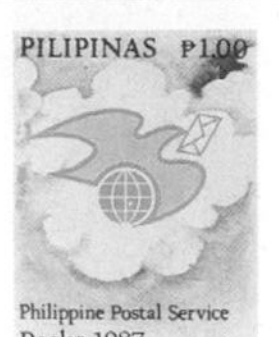

668 Dove with Letter

1987. Christmas. Multicoloured.

2050	1p. Type **668**	75	40
2051	1p. People and star decoration	75	40
2052	4p. Crowd going to church	3·00	55
2053	4p.75 Mother and children exchanging gifts	3·75	65
2054	5p.50 Children and bamboo cannons	5·00	80
2055	8p. Children at table bearing festive fare	5·75	1·20
2056	9p.50 Woman at table	6·50	1·60
2057	11p. Woman having Christmas meal	7·25	2·00

669 Emblem, Headquarters and Dr. Rizal

1987. 75th Anniv of Grand Lodge of Philippine Masons.

2061	**669**	1p. multicoloured	1·20	25

670 Foodstuffs in Split Globe

1987. 40th Anniv of U.N.O. Multicoloured.

2062	1p. Type **670** (International Fund for Agricultural Development)	1·20	40
2063	1p. Means of transport and communications (Asian and Pacific Transport and Communications Decade)	1·20	40
2064	1p. People and hands holding houses (International Year of Shelter for the Homeless)	1·20	40
2065	1p. Happy children playing musical instruments (World Health Day: UNICEF child vaccination campaign)	1·20	40

671 Official Seals and Gavel

1988. Opening Session of 1987 Congress. Multicoloured.

2066	1p. Type **671**	1·00	25
2067	5p.50 Congress in session and gavel (horiz)	4·75	1·10

672 Children and Bosco

1988. Death Centenary of St. John Bosco (founder of Salesian Brothers).

2068	**672**	1p. multicoloured	75	25
2069	**672**	5p.50 multicoloured	3·00	1·10

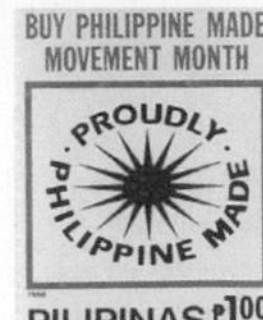

673 Emblem

1988. Buy Philippine-Made Movement Month.

2070	**673**	1p. multicoloured	90	35

1988. Various stamps surch **P 3.00**.

2071	-	3p. on 3p.60 brown (No. 1946)	3·75	55
2072	**645**	3p. on 3p.60 red	5·75	95
2073	-	3p. on 3p.60 mult (No. 1977)	4·50	60
2074	-	3p. on 3p.60 blue, black and green (No. 1984)	4·75	65
2075	**646**	3p. on 3p.60 yellow, brown and blue	5·25	80

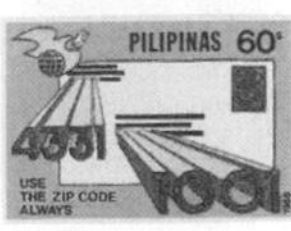

675 Envelope with Coded Addresses

1988. Postal Codes.

2076	**675**	60s. multicoloured	75	25
2077	**675**	1p. multicoloured	1·50	40

676 "Vesbius purpureus" (soldier bug)

1988. Insect Predators. Multicoloured.

2078	1p. Type **676**	75	25
2079	5p.50 "Campsomeris aurulenta" (dagger wasp)	3·25	1·10

677 Solar Eclipse

1988

2080	**677**	1p. multicoloured	75	25
2081	**677**	5p.50 multicoloured	6·50	1·10

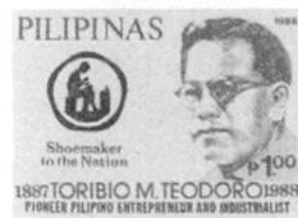

678 Teodoro

1988. 101st Birth Anniv of Toribio Teodoro (industrialist).

2082	**678**	1p. cinnamon, brn & red	90	25
2083	**678**	1p.20 blue, brown & red	1·30	40

679 Emblem

1988. 75th Anniv of College of Holy Spirit.

2084	**679**	1p. brown, gold & black	75	25
2085	-	4p. brown, green & black	3·00	65

DESIGN: 4p. Arnold Janssen (founder) and Sister Edelwina (director, 1920–47).

680 Emblem

1988. Newly Restored Democracies International Conference.

2086	**680**	4p. blue, ultram & blk	3·25	65

681 Luna and Hidalgo

1988. National Juan Luna and Felix Resurreccion Hidalgo Memorial Exhibition.

2087 **681** 1p. black, yellow & brn 75 25

2088 **681** 5p.50 black, cinnamon and brown 3·00 80

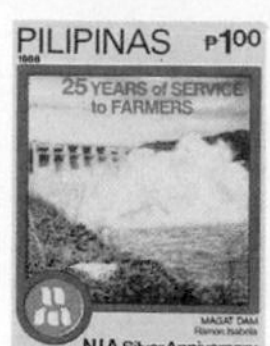

682 Magat Dam, Ramon, Isabela

1988. 25th Anniv of National Irrigation Administration.

2089 **682** 1p. multicoloured 3·00 1·30

2090 **682** 5p.50 multicoloured 3·75 2·00

683 Scuba Diving, Siquijor

1988. Olympic Games, Seoul (1st issue). Multicoloured. Perf or imperf.

2091 1p. Type **683** 45 35

2092 1p.20 Big game fishing, Aparri, Cagayan 60 40

2093 4p. Yachting, Manila Central 1·90 1·10

2094 5p.50 Mountain climbing, Mt. Apo, Davao 2·75 1·60

2095 8p. Golfing, Cebu City 3·75 2·30

2096 11p. Cycling (Tour of Mindanao), Marawi City 5·50 3·25

See also Nos. 2113/18.

684 Headquarters, Plaza Santa Cruz, Manila

1988. Banking Anniversaries. Multicoloured.

2097 1p. Type **684** (50th anniv of Philippine International Commercial Bank) 75 40

2098 1p. Family looking at factory and countryside (25th anniv of Land Bank) 75 40

2099 5p.50 Type **684** 3·75 1·20

2100 5p.50 As No. 2098 3·75 1·20

1988. Various stamps surch.

2101 1p.90 on 2p.40 mult (No. 1968) 1·90 40

2102 1p.90 on 2p.40 black, blue and green (No. 1972) 1·90 40

2103 1p.90 on 2p.40 mult (No. 1981) 1·90 40

2104 1p.90 on 2p.40 mult (No. 1988) 1·90 40

686 Balagtas

1988. Birth Bicentenary of Francisco Balagtas Baltasco (writer). Each green, brown and yellow.

2105 1p. Type **686** 90 25

2106 1p. As Type **686** but details reversed 90 25

687 Hospital

1988. 50th Anniv of Quezon Institute (tuberculosis hospital).

2107 **687** 1p. multicoloured 75 40

2108 **687** 5p.50 multicoloured 2·75 1·30

688 Brown Mushroom

1988. Fungi. Multicoloured.

2109 60s. Type **688** 75 25

2110 1p. Rat's ear fungus 90 40

2111 2p. Abalone mushroom 1·80 55

2112 4p. Straw mushroom 3·50 1·10

689 Archery

1988. Olympic Games, Seoul (2nd issue). Multicoloured. Perf or imperf.

2113 1p. Type **689** 90 25

2114 1p.20 Tennis 1·00 40

2115 4p. Boxing 3·50 65

2116 5p.50 Athletics 4·50 80

2117 8p. Swimming 6·50 1·30

2118 11p. Cycling 7·25 2·30

MS2119 101×76 mm. 5p.50, Weightlifting; 5p.50, Basketball; 5p.50, Judo; 5p.50, Shooting. Imperf 18·00 16·00

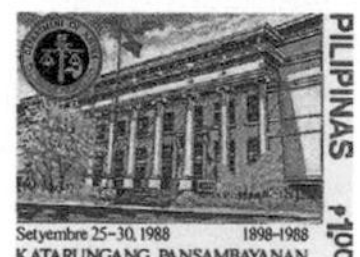

690 Department of Justice

1988. Law and Justice Week.

2120 **690** 1p. multicoloured 90 25

691 Red Cross Work

1988. 125th Anniv of Red Cross.

2121 **691** 1p. multicoloured 75 40

2122 **691** 5p.50 multicoloured 3·75 1·30

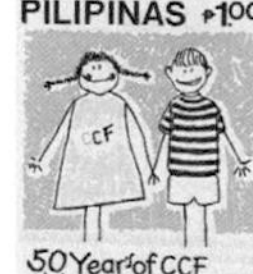

692 Girl and Boy

1988. 50th Anniv of Christian Children's Fund.

2123 **692** 1p. multicoloured 1·00 25

693 Map and Shrimps

1988. 50th Anniv of Bacolod City Charter.

2124 **693** 1p. multicoloured 1·00 25

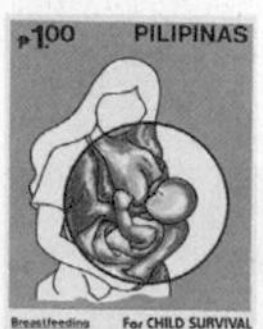

694 Breastfeeding

1988. Child Survival Campaign. Multicoloured.

2125 1p. Type **694** 1·00 25

2126 1p. Growth monitoring 1·00 25

2127 1p. Immunization 1·00 25

2128 1p. Oral rehydration 1·00 25

2129 1p. Access for the disabled (U.N. Decade of Disabled Persons) 1·00 25

695 A. Aragon Quezon

1988. Birth Centenary of Aurora Aragon Quezon.

2130 **695** 1p. multicoloured 45 25

2131 **695** 5p.50 multicoloured 2·30 1·30

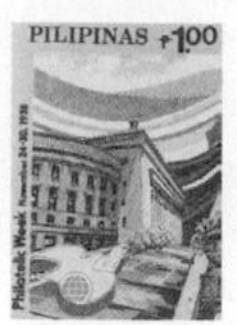

696 Post Office

1988. Philatelic Week. Multicoloured.

2132 1p. Type **696** (inscr "1938") 60 25

2132b 1p. Type **696** (inscr "1988") 2·20 65

2133 1p. Stamp counter 60 25

2134 1p. Fern and stamp displays 60 25

2135 1p. People looking at stamp displays 60 25

697 Sampaloc Branch Transmitter

1988. Ten Years of Technological Improvements by Philippine Long Distance Telephone Company.

2136 **697** 1p. multicoloured 90 25

698 Clasped Hands and Dove

1988. Christmas. Multicoloured.

2137 75s. Type **698** 75 25

2138 1p. Children making decorations (horiz) 90 35

2139 2p. Man carrying decorations on yoke (horiz) 1·30 40

2140 3p.50 Christmas tree 2·20 65

2141 4p.75 Candle and stars 3·00 80

2142 5p.50 Reflection of star forming heart (horiz) 3·75 1·10

699 Crowd with Banners

1988. Commission on Human Rights (2143) and 40th Anniv of Universal Declaration of Human Rights (2144). Multicoloured.

2143 1p. Type **699** 75 25

2144 1p. Doves escaping from cage 75 25

700 Church, 1776

1988. 400th Anniv of Malate. Multicoloured.

2145 1p. Type **700** 75 25

2146 1p. Our Lady of Remedies Church anniversary emblem and statue of Virgin (Eduardo Castrillo) 75 25

2147 1p. Church, 1880 75 25

2148 1p. Church, 1988 75 25

701 Statue and School

1988. 50th Anniv of University of Santo Tomas Graduate School.

2149 **701** 1p. multicoloured 1·00 25

702 Order's Activities

1989. 50th Anniv of Oblates of Mary Immaculate.

2150 **702** 1p. multicoloured 1·00 25

703 Miguel Ver (first leader)

1989. 47th Anniv of Recognition of Hunters ROTC Guerrilla Unit (formed by Military Academy and University students). Multicoloured.

2151 1p. Type **703** 1·00 25

2152 1p. Eleuterio Adevoso (leader after Ver's death) 1·00 25

704 Foodstuffs and Paulino Santos

1989. 50th Anniv of General Santos City.

2153 **704** 1p. multicoloured 1·00 25

705 Sinulog

1989. "Fiesta Islands '89" (1st series). Multicoloured.

2154 4p.75 Type **705** 1·90 95

2155 5p.50 Cenaculo (Lenten festival) 2·20 1·10

2156 6p.25 Iloilo Paraw Regatta 2·50 1·50

See also Nos. 2169/71, 2177/9, 2194/6 and 2210.

706 Tomas Mapua

1989. Birth Centenaries. Multicoloured.

2157 1p. Type **706** 75 25

2158 1p. Camilo Osias 75 25

2159 1p. Dr. Olivia Salamanca 75 25

2160 1p. Dr. Francisco Santiago 75 25

2161 1p. Leandro Fernandez 75 25

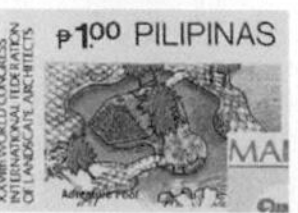

707 Adventure Pool

1989. 26th International Federation of Landscape Architects World Congress, Manila. Multicoloured.

2162 1p. Type **707** 75 25

2163 1p. Paco Park 75 25

2164 1p. Street improvements in Malacanang area 75 25

2165 1p. Erosion control on upland farm 75 25

708 Palawan Peacock-Pheasant

1989. Environment Month. Multicoloured.

2166	1p. Type **708**	1·50	40
2167	1p. Palawan bear cat	1·50	40

709 Entrance and Statue of Justice

1989. Supreme Court.

2168	**709**	1p. multicoloured	1·00	40

1989. "Fiesta Islands '89" (2nd series). As T **705**. Multicoloured.

2169	60s. Turumba	45	20
2170	75s. Pahiyas	60	40
2171	3p.50 Independence Day	1·30	65

710 Birds, Quill, "Noli Me Tangere" and Flags

1989. Bicentenary of French Revolution and Decade of Philippine Nationalism.

2172	**710**	1p. multicoloured	75	40
2173	**710**	5p.50 multicoloured	3·00	1·30

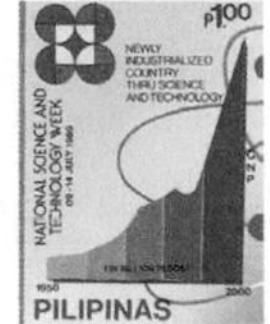

711 Graph

1989. National Science and Technology Week. Multicoloured.

2174	1p. Type **711**	1·50	25
2175	1p. "Man" (Leonardo da Vinci) and emblem of Philippine Science High School)	1·50	25

1989. New Constitution stamp of 1987 surch **P4 75**.

2176	4p.75 on 5p.50 green and brown (2060)	2·50	1·20

1989. "Fiesta Island 89" (3rd series). As T **705**.

2177	1p. Pagoda Sa Wawa (carnival float)	60	40
2178	4p.75 Cagayan de Oro Fiesta	2·20	80
2179	5p.50 Penafrancia Festival	2·75	1·10

713 Monument, Flag, Civilian and Soldier

1989. 50th Anniv of National Defence Department.

2180	**713**	1p. multicoloured	1·00	40

714 Map and Satellite

1989. Tenth Anniv of Asia–Pacific Telecommunity.

2181	**714**	1p. multicoloured	1·00	40

715 Annunciation

1989. Christmas. Multicoloured.

2182	60s. Type **715**	45	20
2183	75s. Mary and Elizabeth	60	25
2184	1p. Mary and Joseph travelling to Bethlehem	75	35
2185	2p. Search for an inn	90	40
2186	4p. Magi and star	1·80	1·10
2187	4p.75 Adoration of shepherds	2·00	1·20

716 Lighthouse, Liner and Lifebelt

1989. International Maritime Organization.

2188	**716**	1p. multicoloured	1·00	40

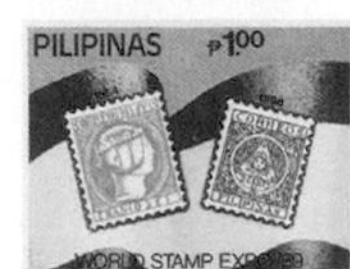

717 Spanish Philippines 1854 5c. and Revolutionary Govt 1898 2c. Stamps

1989. "World Stamp Expo '89" International Stamp Exhibition, Washington D.C. Multicoloured.

2189	1p. Type **717**	75	25
2190	4p. U.S. Administration 1899 50c. and Commonwealth 1935 6c. stamps	3·75	1·20
2191	5p.50 Japanese Occupation 1942 2c. and Republic 1946 6c. stamps	4·50	1·30

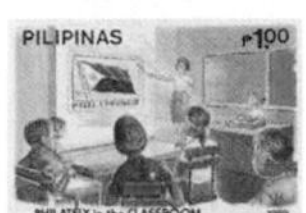

718 Teacher using Stamp as Teaching Aid

1989. Philatelic Week. Philately in the Classroom. Multicoloured.

2192	1p. Type **718**	90	25
2193	1p. Children working with stamps	90	25

1989. "Fiesta Islands '89" (4th series). As T **705**.

2194	1p. Masked festival, Negros	60	40
2195	4p.75 Grand Canao, Baguio	2·20	80
2196	5p.50 Fireworks	2·50	1·10

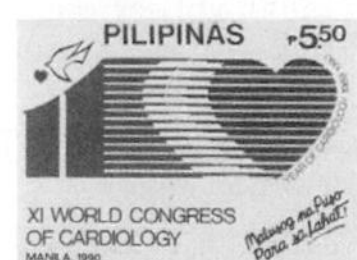

719 Heart

1990. 11th World Cardiology Congress, Manila.

2197	**719**	5p.50 red, blue and black	2·50	1·10

720 Glasses of Beer

1990. Centenary of San Miguel Brewery.

2198	**720**	1p. multicoloured	75	40
2199	**720**	5p.50 multicoloured	3·00	1·10

721 Houses and Family

1990. Population and Housing Census. Multicoloured, colours of houses given.

2200	**721**	1p. blue	75	25
2201	**721**	1p. pink	75	25

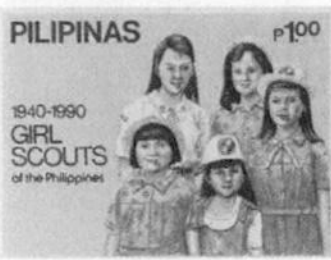

722 Scouts

1990. 50th Anniv of Philippine Girl Scouts.

2202	**722**	1p. multicoloured	90	25
2203	**722**	1p.20 multicoloured	1·00	40

723 Claro Recto (politician)

1990. Birth Centenaries. Multicoloured.

2204	1p. Type **723**	75	25
2205	1p. Manuel Bernabe (poet)	75	25
2206	1p. Guillermo Tolentino (sculptor)	75	25
2207	1p. Elpidio Quirino (President 1948–53)	75	25
2208	1p. Dr. Bienvenido Gonzalez (University President, 1937–51)	75	25

724 Badge and Globe

1990. 50th Anniv of Legion of Mary.

2209	**724**	1p. multicoloured	90	25

1990. "Fiesta Islands '89" (5th series). As No. 2179 but new value.

2210	4p. multicoloured	2·50	80

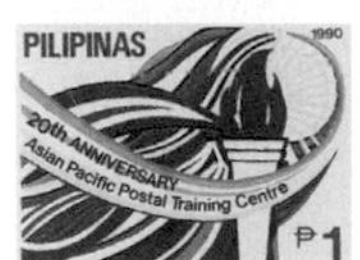

725 Torch

1990. 20th Anniv of Asian–Pacific Postal Training Centre.

2211	**725**	1p. multicoloured	60	40
2212	**725**	4p. multicoloured	1·80	80

726 Catechism Class

1990. National Catechetical Year.

2213	**726**	1p. multicoloured	45	25
2214	**726**	3p.50 multicoloured	1·50	80

727 Waling Waling Flowers

1990. 29th Orient and South-East Asian Lions Forum, Manila. Multicoloured.

2215	1p. Type **727**	75	40
2216	4p. Sampaguita flowers	2·00	65

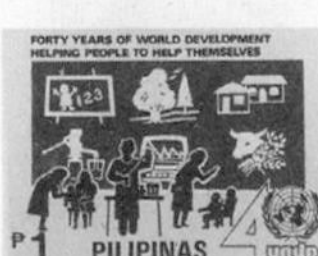

728 Areas for Improvement

1990. 40th Anniv of United Nations Development Programme.

2217	**728**	1p. multicoloured	60	25
2218	**728**	5p.50 multicoloured	2·30	1·30

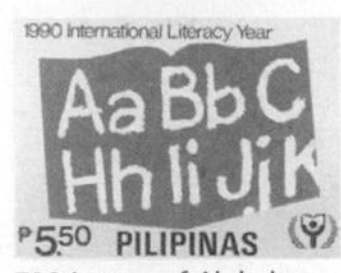

729 Letters of Alphabet

1990. International Literacy Year.

2219	**729**	1p. green, orange & black	60	25
2220	**729**	5p.50 green, yellow & blk	2·30	1·30

730 "Laughter" (A. Magsaysay-Ho)

1990. Philatelic Week. Multicoloured.

2221	1p. "Family" (F. Amorsolo) (horiz)	45	25
2222	4p.75 "The Builders" (V. Edades)	3·00	1·30
2223	5p.50 Type **730**	3·50	1·70

731 Star

1990. Christmas. Multicoloured.

2224	1p. Type **731**	45	25
2225	1p. Stars within stars (blue background)	45	25
2226	1p. Red and white star	45	25
2227	1p. Gold and red star (green background)	45	25
2228	5p.50 Geometric star (Paskuhan Village, San Fernando)	2·75	1·10

732 Figures

1990. International White Cane Safety Day.

2229	**732**	1p. black, yellow and blue	90	25

733 La Solidaridad in 1990 and 1890 and Statue of Rizal

1990. Centenary of Publication of "Filipinas Dentro de Cien Anos" by Jose Rizal.

2230	**733**	1p. multicoloured	90	25

734 Crowd before Figure of Christ

1991. Second Plenary Council of the Philippines.

2231	**734**	1p. multicoloured	90	25

735 Tailplane and Stewardess

1991. 50th Anniv of Philippine Airlines.

2232	**735**	1p. mult (postage)	45	20
2233	**735**	5p.50 multicoloured (air)	2·20	1·30

736 Gardenia

1991. Flowers. Multicoloured.

2234	60s. Type **736**	45	15
2235	75s. Yellow bell	45	15
2236	1p. Yellow plumeria	60	20
2237	1p. Red plumeria	60	20
2238	1p. Pink plumeria	60	20
2239	1p. White plumeria	60	20
2475	1p. Yellow bell	90	25
2240	1p.20 Nerium	90	25
2241	3p.25 Ylang-ylang	2·75	80
2242	4p. Pink ixora	3·00	95
2243	4p. White ixora	3·00	95
2244	4p. Yellow ixora	3·00	95
2245	4p. Red ixora	3·00	95
2246	4p.75 Orange bougainvillea	3·25	1·10
2247	4p.75 Purple bougainvillea	3·25	1·10
2248	4p.75 White bougainvillea	3·25	1·10
2249	4p.75 Red bougainvillea	3·25	1·10
2250	5p. Canna	3·50	1·30
2251	5p.50 Red hibiscus	3·75	1·50
2252	5p.50 Yellow hibiscus	3·75	1·50
2253	5p.50 White hibiscus	3·75	1·50
2254	5p.50 Pink hibiscus	3·75	1·50

See also Nos. 2322/41.

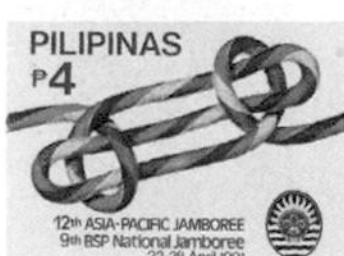

737 Sheepshank

1991. 12th Asia–Pacific and 9th National Boy Scouts Jamboree. Multicoloured.

2255	1p. Reef knot	45	20
2256	4p. Type **737**	1·50	55
2257	4p.75 Granny knot	1·60	65
MS2258	88×82 mm. Nos. 2255/7. Imperf (sold at 16p.50)	7·25	6·75

738 Jorge Vargas

1991. Birth Centenaries. Multicoloured.

2259	1p. Type **738**	75	25
2260	1p. Ricardo Paras	75	25
2261	1p. Jose Laurel	75	25
2262	1p. Vicente Fabella	75	25
2263	1p. Maximo Kalaw	75	25

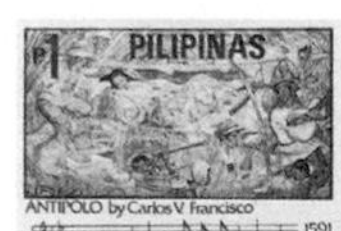

739 "Antipolo" (Carlos Francisco) and Score

1991. 400th Anniv of Antipolo.

2264	**739**	1p. multicoloured	75	25

740 Philippine Eagle

1991. Endangered Species. The Philippine Eagle. Multicoloured.

2265	1p. Type **740**	1·50	65
2266	4p.75 Eagle on branch	5·00	3·00
2267	5p.50 Eagle in flight	5·75	3·50
2268	8p. Eagle feeding chick	8·00	5·00

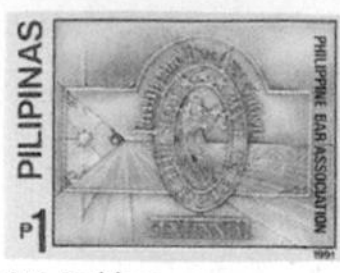

741 Emblem

1991. Centenary of Founding of Society of Lawyers (from 1904 Philippine Bar Association).

2269	**741**	1p. multicoloured	90	25

742 Flags and Induction Ceremony

1991. 50th Anniv of Induction of Philippine Reservists into United States Army Forces in the Far East. Background colours given where necessary in brackets. (a) T **742**.

2270	**742**	1p. multicoloured	1·00	25
MS2271		82×88 mm. **742** 16p. multicoloured. Imperf	7·25	6·75

743 First Regular Division Emblem

(b) Showing Division emblems.

2272	**743**	2p. red, black and yellow	75	25
2273	-	2p. multicoloured (yellow) (2nd Regular)	75	25
2274	-	2p. multicoloured (yellow) (11th)	75	25
2275	-	2p. blue, yellow and black (yellow) (21st)	75	25
2276	**743**	2p. red and black	75	25
2277	-	2p. black, blue and red (2nd Regular)	75	25
2278	-	2p. multicoloured (white) (11th)	75	25
2279	-	2p. blue, yellow and black (white) (21st)	75	25
2280	-	2p. multicoloured (yellow) (31st)	75	25
2281	-	2p. multicoloured (yellow) (41st)	75	25
2282	-	2p. multicoloured (yellow) (51st)	75	25
2283	-	2p. multicoloured (yellow) (61st)	75	25
2284	-	2p. red, blue and black (31st)	75	25
2285	-	2p. multicoloured (white) (41st)	75	25
2286	-	2p. blue, black and red (51st)	75	25
2287	-	2p. multicoloured (white) (61st)	75	25
2288	-	2p. multicoloured (yellow) (71st)	75	25
2289	-	2p. multicoloured (yellow) (81st)	75	25
2290	-	2p. multicoloured (yellow) (91st)	75	25
2291	-	2p. multicoloured (yellow) (101st)	75	25
2292	-	2p. multicoloured (white) (71st)	75	25
2293	-	2p. multicoloured (white) (81st)	75	25
2294	-	2p. multicoloured (white) (91st)	75	25
2295	-	2p. multicoloured (white) (101st)	75	25
2296	-	2p. blue, black and yellow (Bataan Force)	75	25
2297	-	2p. yellow, red and black (yellow) (Philippine)	75	25
2298	-	2p. multicoloured (yellow) (Air Corps)	75	25
2299	-	2p. black, blue and yellow (Offshore Patrol)	75	25
2300	-	2p. blue and black (Bataan Force)	75	25
2301	-	2p. yellow, red and black (white) (Philippine)	75	25
2302	-	2p. multicoloured (white) (Air Corps)	75	25
2303	-	2p. black and blue (Offshore Patrol)	75	25

Nos. 2272/2303 (all as T **743**) show divisional emblems.

744 Basilio

1991. Centenary of Publication of "El Filibusterismo" by Jose Rizal. Characters from the novel. Each red, blue and black.

2304	1p. Type **744**	75	40
2305	1p. Simoun	75	40
2306	1p. Father Florentino	75	40
2307	1p. Juli	75	40

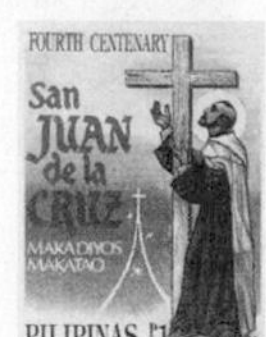

745 St. John of the Cross

1991. 400th Death of St. John of the Cross. Multicoloured.

2308	Type **745**	75	25
MS2309	59×59 mm. 16p. St. John praying, signature and Type **745**. Imperf	11·00	10·00

746 Faces (Children's Fund)

1991. United Nations Agencies.

2310	**746**	1p. multicoloured	45	25
2311	-	4p. multicoloured	1·50	40
2312	-	5p.50 black, red and blue	2·00	80

DESIGNS: 4p. Hands supporting boatload of people (High Commissioner for Refugees); 5p.50, 1951 15c. and 1954 3c. U.N. stamps (40th anniv of Postal Administration).

747 "Bayanihan" (Carlos "Botong" Francisco)

1991. Philatelic Week. Multicoloured.

2313	2p. Type **747**	75	35
2314	7p. "Sari-Sari Vendor" (Mauro Malang Santos)	2·50	1·10
2315	8p. "Give Us This Day" (Vicente Manansala)	3·00	1·30

748 Gymnastics

1991. 16th South-East Asian Games, Manila. Multicoloured.

2316	2p. Type **748**	90	40
2317	2p. Gymnastics (emblem at bottom)	90	40
2318	6p. Arnis (martial arts) (emblem at left) (vert)	2·20	80
2319	6p. Arnis (emblem at right) (vert)	2·20	80
MS2320	Two sheets. (a) 90×60 mm. Nos. 2318/19. Imperf; (b) 65×98 mm. Nos. 2316/19	17·00	15·00

Designs of the same value were issued together, se-tenant, each pair forming a composite design.

1991. Fitst Philippine Philatelic Convention, Manila. No. **MS**1698 surch **p4**.

MS2321	4p. on 3p.20 purple and black	4·50	4·00

1991. Flowers. As T **736**. Multicoloured.

2322	1p.50 Type **736**	1·80	35
2323	2p. Yellow plumeria	1·90	40
2324	2p. Red plumeria	1·90	40
2325	2p. Pink plumeria	1·90	40
2326	2p. White plumeria	1·90	40
2327	3p. Nerium	2·30	65
2328	5p. Ylang-ylang	3·00	1·20
2329	6p. Pink ixora	3·75	1·30
2330	6p. White ixora	3·75	1·30
2331	6p. Yellow ixora	3·75	1·30
2332	6p. Red ixora	3·75	1·30
2333	7p. Orange bougainvillea	4·50	1·70
2334	7p. Purple bougainvillea	4·50	1·70
2335	7p. White bougainvillea	4·50	1·70
2336	7p. Red bougainvillea	4·50	1·70
2337	8p. Red hibiscus	5·00	1·90
2338	8p. Yellow hibiscus	5·00	1·90
2339	8p. White hibiscus	5·00	1·90
2340	8p. Pink hibiscus	5·00	1·90
2341	10p. Canna	5·75	2·30

750 Church

1991. Christmas. Children's Paintings. Multicoloured.

2342	2p. Type **750**	75	25
2343	6p. Christmas present	2·00	80
2344	7p. Santa Claus and tree	2·20	95
2345	8p. Christmas tree and star	3·00	1·10

751 Player

1991. Centenary of Basketball. Multicoloured.

2346	2p. Type **751**	1·20	40
2347	6p. Basketball player and map (issue of first basketball stamp, 1934) (horiz)	2·75	65
2348	7p. Girls playing basketball (introduction of basketball in Philippines, 1904) (horiz)	3·00	80
2349	8p. Players	3·75	1·20
MS2350	Two sheets (a) 60×60 mm. Match scene. Imperf; (b) 73×101 mm. Nos. 2346/9	20·00	18·00

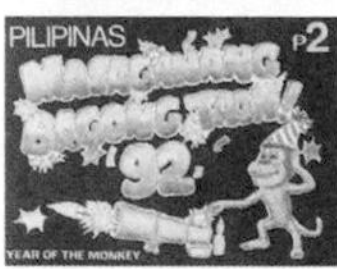

752 Monkey firing Cannon

1991. New Year. Year of the Monkey.

2351	**752**	2p. multicoloured	1·80	40
2352	**752**	6p. multicoloured	4·75	65

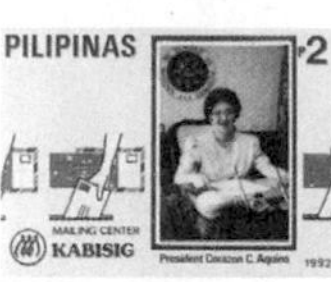

753 Pres. Aquino and Mailing Centre Emblem

1992. Kabisig Community Projects Organization. Multicoloured.

2353	2p. Type **753**	75	40
2354	6p. Housing	1·80	55
2355	7p. Livestock	2·00	65
2356	8p. Handicrafts	2·30	80

754 "Curcuma longa"

1992. Asian Medicinal Plants Symposium, Los Banos, Laguna. Multicoloured.

2357	2p. Type **754**	1·20	55
2358	6p. "Centella asiatica"	2·30	65
2359	7p. "Cassia alata"	3·00	80
2360	8p. "Ervatamia pandacaqui"	3·25	1·10

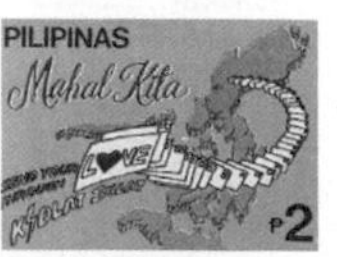

755 "Mahal Kita", Envelopes and Map

1992. Greetings Stamps. Multicoloured.

2361	2p. Type **755**	75	40
2362	2p. As No. 2361 but inscr "I Love You"	75	40
2363	6p. Heart and doves ("Mahal Kita")	2·20	80
2364	6p. As No. 2363 but inscr "I Love You"	2·20	80
2365	7p. Basket of flowers ("Mahal Kita")	2·30	95

2366	7p. As No. 2365 but inscr "I Love You"	2·30	95
2367	8p. Cupid ("Mahal Kita")	4·50	1·10
2368	8p. As No. 2367 but inscr "I Love You"	4·50	1·10

756 Philippine Pavilion and Couple Dancing

1992. "Expo '92" World's Fair, Seville. Multicoloured.

2369	2p. Type **756**	75	40
2370	8p. Pavilion, preacher and conquistador holding globe	2·75	1·10
MS2371	63×76 mm. 16p. Pavilion (horiz). Imperf	11·00	10·00

757 "Our Lady of the Sun" (icon)

1992. 300th Anniv of Apparition of Our Lady of the Sun at Gate, Vaga Cavite.

2372	**757**	2p. multicoloured	75	40
2373	**757**	8p. multicoloured	2·75	1·10

758 Fish Farming

1992. 75th Anniv of Department of Agriculture. Multicoloured.

2374	2p. Type **758**	90	40
2375	2p. Pig farming	90	40
2376	2p. Sowing seeds	90	40

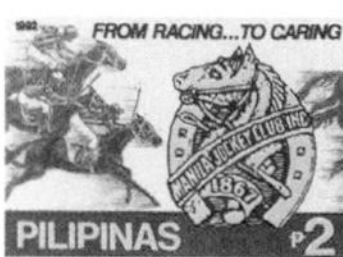

759 Race Horses and Emblem

1992. 125th Anniv of Manila Jockey Club.

2377	**759**	2p. multicoloured	1·50	40
MS2378		74×63 mm. **759** 8p. multicoloured. Imperf	6·50	6·00

760 Manuel Roxas (President, 1946–48)

1992. Birth Centenaries. Multicoloured.

2379	2p. Type **760**	75	40
2380	2p. Natividad Almeda-Lopez (judge)	75	40
2381	2p. Roman Ozaeta (judge)	75	40
2382	2p. Engracia Cruz-Reyes (women's rights campaigner and environmentalist)	75	40
2383	2p. Fernando Amorsolo (artist)	75	40

761 Queen, Bishop and 1978 30s. Stamp

1992. 30th Chess Olympiad, Manila. Multicoloured.

2384	2p. Type **761**	90	40
2385	6p. King, queen and 1962 6s.+4s. stamp	2·30	1·10
MS2386	89×63 mm. 8p. Type **761**; 8p. As No. 2385. Imperf	6·50	6·00

762 Bataan Cross

1992. 50th Anniv of Pacific Theatre in Second World War. Multicoloured.

2387	2p. Type **762**	90	40
2388	6p. Map inside "W"	1·90	1·10
2389	8p. Corregidor eternal flame	3·00	1·50
MS2390	Two sheets. (a) 63×75 mm. 16p. Map of Bataan and cross; (b) 76×63 mm. 16p. Map of Corregidor and Eternal flame	22·00	20·00

763 President Aquino and President-elect Ramos

1992. Election of Fidel Ramos to Presidency.

2391	**763**	2p. multicoloured	1·00	40

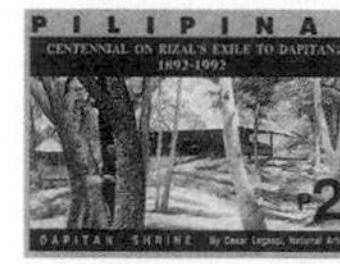

764 "Dapitan Shrine" (Cesar Legaspi)

1992. Centenary of Dr. Jose Rizal's Exile to Dapitan. Multicoloured.

2392	2p. Type **764**	1·50	45
2393	2p. Portrait (after Juan Luna) (vert)	1·50	45

765 "Spirit of ASEAN" (Visit Asean Year)

1992. 25th Anniv of Association of South-East Asian Nations. Multicoloured.

2394	2p. Type **765**	75	40
2395	2p. "ASEAN Sea" (25th Ministerial Meeting and Postal Ministers' Conf)	75	40
2396	6p. Type **765**	1·80	1·10
2397	6p. As No. 2395	1·80	1·10

766 Member of the Katipunan

1992. Centenary of Katipunan ("KKK") (revolutionary organization). Multicoloured.

2398	2p. Type **766**	1·00	35
2399	2p. Revolutionaries	1·00	35
2400	2p. Plotting (horiz)	1·00	35
2401	2p. Attacking (horiz)	1·00	35

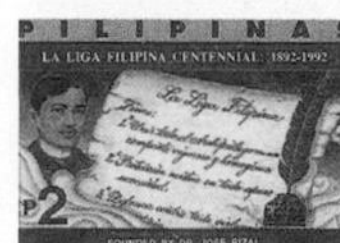

767 Dr. Jose Rizal, Text and Quill

1992. Centenary of La Liga Filipina.

2402	**767**	2p. multicoloured	1·20	40

768 Swimming

1992. Olympic Games, Barcelona. Multicoloured.

2403	2p. Type **768**	75	40
2404	7p. Boxing	2·00	1·20
2405	8p. Hurdling	2·75	1·50
MS2406	87×85 mm. 1p. Type **768**; 7p. No. 2404; 8p. No. 2405. Imperf	13·00	12·00

769 School, Emblem and Students

1992. Centenaries. Multicoloured.

2407	2p. Type **769** (Sisters of the Assumption in the Philippines)	1·20	40
2408	2p. San Sebastian's Basilica, Manila (centenary (1991) of blessing of fifth construction) (vert)	1·20	40

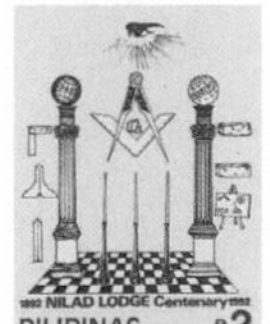

770 Masonic Symbols

1992. Centenary of Nilad Lodge (first Filipino Masonic Lodge).

2409	**770**	2p. black and green	90	40
2410	-	6p. multicoloured	1·90	1·10
2411	-	8p. multicoloured	2·75	1·50

DESIGNS: 6p. Antonio Luna and symbols; 8p. Marcelo del Pilar ("Father of Philippine Masonry") and symbols.

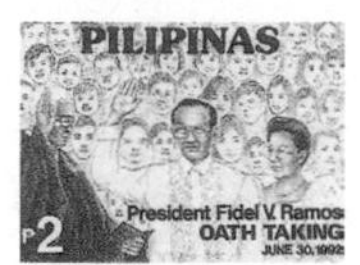

771 Ramos taking Oath

1992. Swearing in of President Fidel Ramos. Multicoloured.

2412	2p. Type **771**	60	25
2413	8p. President taking oath in front of flag	2·50	1·10

772 Flamingo Guppy

1992. Freshwater Aquarium Fish (1st series). Multicoloured.

2414	1p.50 Type **772**	75	25
2415	1p.50 Neon tuxedo guppy	75	25
2416	1p.50 King cobra guppy	75	25
2417	1p.50 Red-tailed guppy	75	25
2418	1p.50 Tiger lace-tailed guppy	75	25
2419	2p. Pearl-scaled goldfish	1·00	40
2420	2p. Red-capped goldfish	1·00	40
2421	2p. Lion-headed goldfish	1·00	40
2422	2p. Black moor goldfish	1·00	40
2423	2p. Bubble-eyed goldfish	1·00	40
2424	4p. Delta topsail platy ("Variatus")	2·20	1·50
2425	4p. Orange-spotted hi-fin platy	2·20	1·50
2426	4p. Red lyre-tailed swordtail	2·20	1·50
2427	4p. Bleeding heart hi-fin platy	2·20	1·50
MS2428	Two sheets. (a) 132×78 mm. 6p. Green discus; 6p. Brown discus; 7p. Red discus; 7p. Harald's blue discus; (b) 88×61 mm. 8p. Golden arowana. Imperf	20·00	19·00

See also Nos. 2543/**MS**2557.

1992. Philippines Stamp Exhibition, Taipeh, Taiwan. No. **MS**2428 optd **PHILIPPINE STAMP EXHIBITION 1992 – TAIPEI.**

MS2429	Two sheets. (a) 132×79 mm. 6p. ×2, 7p. ×2, multicoloured; (b) 88×61 mm. 8p. multicoloured	60·00	55·00

774 Couple

1992. Greetings Stamps. "Happy Birthday". Multicoloured.

2430	2p. Type **774**	60	35
2431	6p. Type **774**	1·60	1·10
2432	7p. Balloons and candles on birthday cake	1·90	1·20
2433	8p. As No. 2432	2·50	1·50

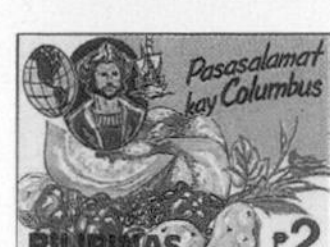

775 Melon, Beans, Tomatoes and Potatoes

1992. 500th Anniv of Discovery of America by Columbus. Multicoloured.

2434	2p. Type **775**	75	40
2435	6p. Maize and sweet potatoes	2·20	1·10
2436	8p. Pineapple, cashews, avocado and water melon	2·75	1·50

1992. Second National Philatelic Convention. No. **MS**2271 optd **Second National Philatelic Convention Cebu, Philippines, Oct 22—24, 1992.**

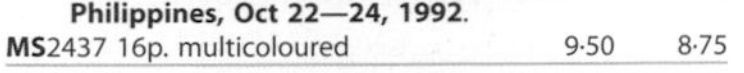

MS2437	16p. multicoloured	9·50	8·75

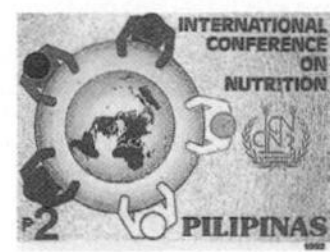

777 Figures around World Map

1992. International Nutrition Conference, Rome.

2438	**777**	2p. multicoloured	1·00	40

778 Mother and Child

1992. Christmas.

2439	**778**	2p. multicoloured	60	35
2440	-	6p. multicoloured	1·60	1·10
2441	-	7p. multicoloured	1·90	1·20
2442	-	8p. multicoloured	2·50	1·50

DESIGNS: 6p. to 8p. Various designs showing mothers and children.

1992. Inauguration of Postal Museum and Philatelic Library. No. **MS**1566 optd **INAUGURATION OF THE PHILIPPINE POSTAL MUSEUM AND PHILTATELIC LIBRARY NOVEMBER 10 1992.**

MS2443	76×76 mm. 5p. multicoloured	5·50	5·00

780 Family and Canoe

1992. Anti-drugs Campaign. Multicoloured.

2444	2p. Type **780**	75	40
2445	8p. Man carrying paddle, children and canoe	2·50	1·50

781 Damaged Trees

1992. Mt. Pinatubo Fund (for victims of volcanic eruption). Multicoloured.

2446	25s. Type **781**	45	15
2447	1p. Mt. Pinatubo erupting	75	25
2448	1p. Cattle in ash-covered field	75	25
2449	1p. Refugee settlement	75	25
2450	1p. People shovelling ash	75	25

782 Red Junglefowl

1992. New Year. Year of the Cock. Multicoloured.

2451	2p. Type **782**	90	40
2452	6p. Maranao Sarimanok (mythical bird)	2·75	1·10
MS2453	98×87 mm. Nos. 2451/2 plus two labels. Perf or Imperf	4·50	4·00

1992. Philippine Stamp Exhibition, Taipeh. No. **MS**2453 optd **PHILIPPPINE STAMP EHXIBIT TAIPEI DECEMBER 1—3 1992.**

MS2454	98×87 mm. 2, 6p. multicoloured	10·00	9·25

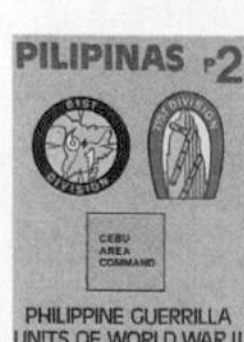

784 Badges of 61st and 71st Divisions, Cebu Area Command

1992. Philippine Guerrilla Units of Second World War (1st series). Multicoloured.

2455	2p. Type **784**	90	40
2456	2p. Vinzon's Guerrillas and badges of 48th Chinese Guerrilla Squadron and 101st Division	90	40
2457	2p. Anderson's Command, Luzon Guerrilla Army Forces and badge of Bulacan Military Area	90	40
2458	2p. President Quezon's Own Guerrillas and badges of Marking's Fil-American Troops and Hunters ROTC Guerrillas	90	40

See also Nos. 2594/7, 2712/15 and 2809/12.

785 "Family" (Cesar Legaspi) (family ties)

1992. Philatelic Week. Multicoloured.

2459	2p. Type **785**	75	40
2460	6p. "Pounding Rice" (Nena Saguil) (hard work and industry)	1·90	1·10
2461	7p. "Fish Vendors" (Romeo Tabuena) (flexibility and adaptability)	2·20	1·20

786 Black Shama

1992. Endangered Birds. Multicoloured. (a) As T **786**.

2462	2p. Type **786**	90	40
2463	2p. Blue-headed fantail	90	40
2464	2p. Mindoro zone-tailed (inscr "Imperial") pigeon	90	40
2465	2p. Sulu hornbill	90	40
2466	2p. Red-vented (inscr "Philippine") cockatoo	90	40

(b) Size 29×39 mm.

2467	2p. Philippine trogon	90	40
2468	2p. Rufous hornbill	90	40
2469	2p. White-bellied black woodpecker	90	40
2470	2p. Spotted wood kingfisher	90	40

(c) Size 36×26½ mm.

2471	2p. Brahminy kite	90	40
2472	2p. Philippine falconet	90	40
2473	2p. Reef heron	90	40
2474	2p. Philippine duck (inscr "Mallard")	90	40

787 Flower (Jasmine)

1993. National Symbols. Multicoloured. (a) As T **787**. "Pilipinas" in brown at top.

2476	1p. Type **787**	45	20
2571	2p. Flag	75	35
2478	6p. Leaf (palm)	1·80	1·10
2479	7p. Costume	2·00	1·20
2480	8p. Fruit (mango)	2·50	1·50

788 Flower (Jasmine)

(b) As T **788**. "Pilipinas" in red at foot.

2481	60s. Tree	50	15
2512	1p. Flag	60	25
2513	1p. House	60	25
2514	1p. Costume	60	25
2515	1p. As No. 2481	60	25
2516	1p. Type **788**	60	25
2517	1p. Fruit	60	25
2518	1p. Leaf	60	25
2519	1p. Fish (milkfish)	60	25
2520	1p. Animal (water buffalo)	60	25
2521	1p. Bird (Philippine trogons)	60	25
2482	1p.50 As No. 2519	60	25
2565	2p. Hero (Dr. Jose Rizal)	75	35
2566	2p. As No. 2513	75	35
2567	2p. As No. 2514	75	35
2568	2p. Dance ("Tinikling")	75	35
2569	2p. Sport (Sipa)	75	35
2570	2p. As No. 2521	75	35
2572	2p. As No. 2520	75	35
2573	2p. Type **788**	75	35
2574	2p. As No. 2481	75	35
2575	2p. As No. 2517	75	35
2576	2p. As No. 2518	75	35
2577	2p. As No. 2519	75	35
2578	2p. As No. 2512	75	35
2644	3p. As No. 2520	75	40
2645	5p. As No. 2521	1·90	80
2646	6p. As No. 2518	2·00	1·10
2647	7p. As No. 2514	2·20	1·20
2486	8p. As No. 2517	2·75	1·50
2649	10p. As No. 2513	3·25	1·70

See also Nos. **MS**2663, 2717/19, **MS**2753, 2818/20, **MS**2906, 2973/5, **MS**3010, 3017/19, 3089/3092, 3093/7, 3103/5, **MS**3106, 3107/21, **MS**3178 and 3200/9.

789 "Euploea mulciber dufresne"

1993. Butterflies. Multicoloured. (a) As T **789**.

2488	2p. Type **789**	1·50	40
2489	2p. "Cheritra orpheus"	1·50	40
2490	2p. "Delias henningia"	1·50	40
2491	2p. "Mycalesis ita"	1·50	40
2492	2p. "Delias diaphana"	1·50	40

(b) Size 28×35 mm.

2493	2p. "Papilio rumanzobia"	1·50	40
2494	2p. "Papilio palinurus"	1·50	40
2495	2p. "Trogonoptera trojana"	1·50	40
2496	2p. Tailed jay ("Graphium agamemnon")	1·50	40
MS2497	10p. "Papilio iowi", "Valeria boebera" and "Delias themis"	18·00	16·00

1993. Indopex 93 International Stamp Exhibition, Surabaya. No. **MS**2497 optd **INDOPEX 93 INDONESIA PHILATELIC EXHIBITION 1993, 6th ASIAN INTERNATIONAL PHILATELIC EXHIBITION 29th MAY – 4th JUNE 1993 SURABAYA – INDONESIA.**

MS2498	140×70 mm. 10p. multicoloured	19·00	17·00

791 Nicanor Abelardo

1993. Birth Centenaries. Multicoloured.

2499	2p. Type **791**	75	40
2500	2p. Pilar Hidalgo-Lim	75	40
2501	2p. Manuel Viola Gallego	75	40
2502	2p. Maria Ylagan-Orosa	75	40
2503	2p. Eulogio B. Rodriguez	75	40

792 Boxing and Judo

1993. 17th South-East Asian Games, Singapore. Multicoloured.

2504	2p. Weightlifting, archery, fencing and shooting (79×29 mm)	1·00	40
2505	2p. Type **792**	1·00	40
2506	2p. Athletics, cycling, gymnastics and golf (79×29 mm)	1·00	40
2507	6p. Table tennis, football, volleyball and badminton (79×29 mm)	3·00	1·10
2508	6p. Billiards and bowling	3·00	1·10
2509	6p. Swimming, water polo, yachting and diving (79×29 mm)	3·00	1·10
MS2510	84×96 mm. 10p. Basketball (vert)	8·00	7·25

1993. 46th Anniv of Philippine Air Force. No. MS2497 optd Towards the Year 2000, 46th PAF Anniversary 1 July 1993.

MS2511	140×70 mm. 10p. multicoloured	25·00	23·00

794 "Spathoglottis chrysantha"

1993. Orchids. Multicoloured.

2522	2p. Type **794**	75	40
2523	2p. "Arachnis longicaulis"	75	40
2524	2p. "Phalaenopsis mariae"	75	40
2525	2p. "Coelogyne marmorata"	75	40
2526	2p. "Dendrobium sanderae"	75	40
2527	3p. "Dendrobium serratilabium"	1·20	55
2528	3p. "Phalaenopsis equestris"	1·20	55
2529	3p. "Vanda merrillii"	1·20	55
2530	3p. "Vanda luzonica"	1·20	55
2531	3p. "Grammatophyllum martae"	1·20	55
MS2532	Two sheets, each 58×99 mm. (a) 8p. "Aerides quinquevulnera" (27×77 mm); (b) 8p. "Vanda lamellate" (27×77 mm). Imperf	7·25	6·75

1993. "Taipei '93" Asian Stamp Exhibition. No. **MS**2532 optd **ASIAN INTERNATIONAL INVITATION STAMP EXHIBITION TAIPEI '93.**

MS2533	Two sheets, each 58×99 mm. Perf. (a) 8p. multicoloured; (b) 8p. multicoloured. Imperf	14·50	13·50

796 Dog in Window ("Thinking of You")

1993. Greetings Stamps. Multicoloured.

2534	2p. Type **796**	90	40
2535	2p. As No. 2534 but inscr "Naaalala Kita"	90	40
2536	6p. Dog looking at clock ("Thinking of You")	2·75	1·10
2537	6p. As No. 2536 but inscr "Naaalala Kita"	2·75	1·10
2538	7p. Dog looking at calendar ("Thinking of You")	3·00	1·20
2539	7p. As No. 2538 but inscr "Naaalala Kita"	3·00	1·20
2540	8p. Dog with pair of slippers ("Thinking of You")	3·25	1·50
2541	8p. As No. 2540 but inscr "Naaalala Kita"	3·25	1·50

797 Palms and Coconuts

1993. "Tree of Life".

2542	**797** 2p. multicoloured	1·00	40

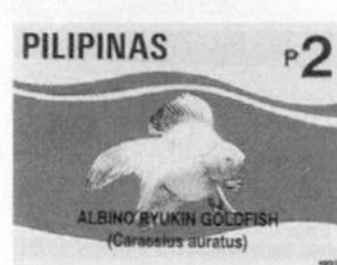

798 Albino Ryukin Goldfish

1993. Freshwater Aquarium Fish (2nd series). Multicoloured. (a) As T **798**.

2543	2p. Type **798**	90	35
2544	2p. Black oranda goldfish	90	35
2545	2p. Lion-headed goldfish	90	35
2546	2p. Celestial goldfish	90	35
2547	2p. Pompon goldfish	90	35
2548	2p. Paradise fish	90	35
2549	2p. Pearl gourami	90	35
2550	2p. Red-tailed black shark (carp)	90	35
2551	2p. Tiger barb	90	35
2552	2p. Cardinal tetra	90	35

(b) Size 29×39 mm.

2553	2p. Pearl-scaled freshwater angelfish	2·20	55
2554	2p. Zebra freshwater angelfish	2·20	55
2555	2p. Marble freshwater angelfish	2·20	55
2556	2p. Black freshwater angelfish	2·20	55
MS2557	Two sheets. (a) 138×78 mm. 3p. Neon Siamese fighting fish; 3p. Libby Siamese fighting fish; 3p. Split-tailed Siamese fighting fish; 3p. Butterfly Siamese fighting fish. Perf. (b) 87×60 mm. 6p. Albino oscar. Imperf	25·00	23·00

799 Map and Emblem

1993. Basic Petroleum and Minerals Inc. "Towards Self-sufficiency in Energy".

2558	**799** 2p. multicoloured	90	40

1993. "Bangkok '93" International Stamp Exhibition, Thailand. No. **MS**2557 optd **QUEEN SIRIKIT NATIONAL CONVENTION CENTRE 1-10 OCTOBER 1993, BANGKOK WORLD PHILATELIC EXHIBITION 1993.**

MS2559	Two sheets. (a) 3p. ×4, multicoloured; (b) 6p. multicoloured	29·00	27·00

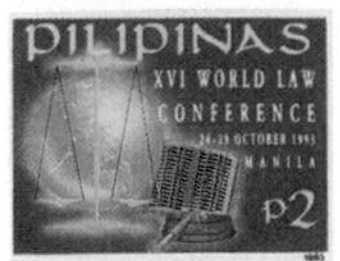

801 Globe, Scales, Book and Gavel

1993. 16th Int Law Conference, Manila. Multicoloured.

2560	2p. Type **801**	90	40
2561	6p. Globe, scales, gavel and conference emblem on flag of Philippines (vert)	2·20	1·10
2562	7p. Woman holding scales, conference building and globe	2·75	1·20
2563	8p. Fisherman pulling in nets and emblem (vert)	3·00	1·60

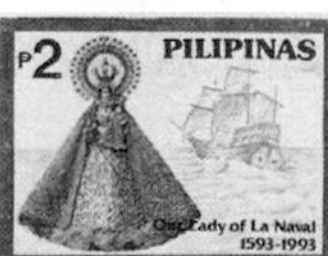

802 Our Lady of La Naval (statue) and Galleon

1993. 400th Anniv of Our Lady of La Naval.

2564	**802** 2p. multicoloured	1·20	40

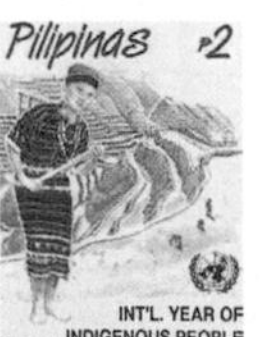

803 Woman and Terraced Hillside

1993. International Year of Indigenous Peoples. Women in traditional costumes. Multicoloured.

2579	2p. Type **803**	75	40
2580	6p. Woman, plantation and mountain	2·20	1·10
2581	7p. Woman and mosque	2·50	1·20
2582	8p. Woman and Filipino vintas (sail canoes)	2·75	1·60

804 Trees

1993. Philatelic Week. "Save the Earth". Multicoloured.

2583	2p. Type **804**	75	40
2584	6p. Marine flora and fauna	2·20	1·10
2585	7p. Dove and irrigation system	2·50	1·20
2586	8p. Effects of industrial pollution	2·75	1·60

805 1949 6c.+4c. Stamp and Symbols

1993. 400th Anniv of Publication of "Doctrina Christiana" (first book published in Philippines).

2587	**805**	2p. multicoloured	90	40

806 Moon-buggy and Society Emblem

1993. 50th Anniv of Filipino Inventors Society. Multicoloured.

2588	2p. Type **806**	90	40
2589	2p. Rice-harvesting machine	90	40

Nos. 2588/9 were issued together, se-tenant, forming a composite design.

807 Holy Family

1993. Christmas. Multicoloured.

2590	2p. Type **807**	75	40
2591	6p. Church goers	2·20	1·10
2592	7p. Cattle and baskets of food	2·50	1·20
2593	8p. Carol-singers	2·75	1·60

808 Northern Luzon

1993. Philippine Guerrilla Units of Second World War (2nd series). Multicoloured.

2594	2p. Type **808**	1·30	45
2595	2p. Bohol Area Command	1·30	45
2596	2p. Leyte Area Command	1·30	45
2597	2p. Palawan Special Battalion and Sulu Area Command	1·30	45

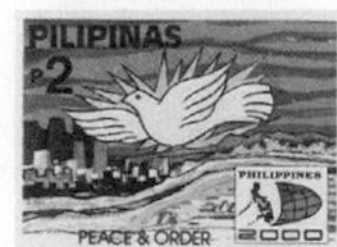

809 Dove over City (peace and order)

1993. "Philippines 2000" (development plan). Multicoloured.

2598	2p. Type **809**	75	40
2599	6p. Means of transport and communications	2·20	1·10
2600	7p. Offices, roads and factories (infrastructure and industry)	2·50	1·20
2601	8p. People from different walks of life (people empowerment)	2·75	1·60
MS2602	110×85 mm. 8p. Various motifs on themes of peace, transport and communication, infrastructure and industry and people power. Imperf	5·75	5·25

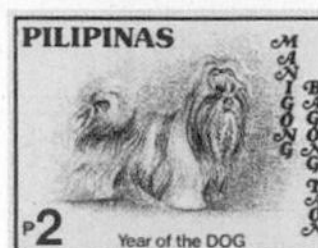

810 Shih Tzu

1993. New Year. Year of the Dog. Multicoloured.

2603	2p. Type **810**	60	35
2604	6p. Chow	1·80	1·10
MS2605	98×88 mm. Nos. 2603/4 plus two labels. Perf or imperf	8·75	8·00

811 Jamboree Emblem and Flags

1993. First Association of South-East Asian Nations Scout Jamboree, Makiling. Multicoloured.

2606	2p. Type **811**	60	35
2607	6p. Scout at camp-site, flags and emblem	1·80	1·10
MS2608	86×86 mm. Nos. 2606/7	5·50	5·00

812 Club Emblem on Diamond

1994. 75th Anniv of Manila Rotary Club.

2609	**812**	2p. multicoloured	90	40

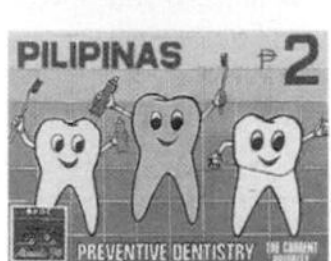

813 Teeth and Dental Hygiene Products

1994. 17th Asian–Pacific Dental Congress, Manila. Multicoloured.

2610	2p. Type **813**	90	40
2611	6p. Teeth, flags of participating countries and teeth over globe with Philippines circled (vert)	2·20	1·10

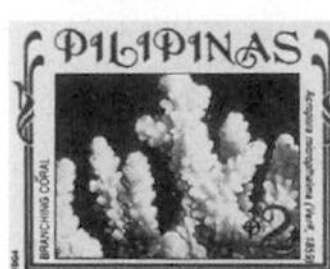

814 "Acropora micropthalma"

1994. Corals. Multicoloured.

2612	2p. Type **814**	90	40
2613	2p. "Seriatopora hystrix"	90	40
2614	2p. "Acropora latistella"	90	40
2615	2p. "Millepora tenella"	90	40
2616	2p. "Millepora tenella" (different)	90	40
2617	2p. "Pachyseris valenciennesi"	90	40
2618	2p. "Pavona decussata"	90	40
2619	2p. "Galaxea fascicularis"	90	40
2620	2p. "Acropora formosa"	90	40
2621	2p. "Acropora humilis"	90	40
2622	2p. "Isis sp." (vert)	2·20	55
2623	2p. "Plexaura sp." (vert)	2·20	55
2624	2p. "Dendronepthya sp." (vert)	2·20	55
2625	2p. "Heteroxenia sp." (vert)	2·20	55
MS2626	135×78 mm. 3p. "Xenia puertogalerae"; 3p. "Plexaura" sp. (different); 3p. "Dendrophyllia gracilis"; 3p. "Plerogyra sinuosa"	14·50	13·50

815 New Year Stamps of 1991 and 1992 bearing Exhibition Emblem

1994. "Hong Kong '94" Stamp Exhibition. Multicoloured.

2627	2p. Type **815**	60	35
2628	6p. 1993 New Year stamps	1·60	1·10
MS2629	Two sheets, each 98×72 mm. (a) Nos. 2627/8 (blue margin); (b) Nos. 2627/8 (green margin)	5·75	5·25

816 Class of 1944 Emblem

1994. 50th Anniv of Philippine Military Academy Class of 1944.

2630	**816**	2p. multicoloured	90	40

1994. Naphilcon 94 First National Philatelic Congress. As No. **MS**2626 but with additional inscription in the central gutter.

MS2631	135×78 mm. 3p. ×4 multicoloured	23·00	21·00

817 Airplane over Harbour, Man and Cogwheel and Emblem

1994. Federation of Filipino–Chinese Chambers of Commerce and Industry.

2632	**817**	2p. multicoloured	90	40

818 Stork carrying Baby ("Binabati Kita")

1994. Greetings Stamps. Multicoloured.

2633	2p. Type **818**	60	35
2634	2p. As No. 2633 but inscr "Congratulations"	60	35
2635	2p. Bouquet ("Binabati Kita")	60	35
2636	2p. As No. 2635 but inscr "Congratulations"	60	35
2637	2p. Mortar board, scroll and books ("Binabati Kita")	60	35
2638	2p. As No. 2637 but inscr "Congratulations"	60	35
2639	2p. Bouquet, doves and heads inside heart ("Binabati Kita")	60	35
2640	2p. As No. 2639 but inscr "Congratulations"	60	35

819 Gloria Diaz (Miss Universe 1969)

1994. Miss Universe Beauty Contest. Multicoloured.

2653	2p. Type **819**	60	25
2654	2p. Margie Moran (Miss Universe 1973)	60	25
2655	6p. Crown	1·80	80
2656	7p. Contestant	2·20	1·10
MS2657	90×80 mm. 8p. As No. 2653; 8p. As No. 2654	5·00	4·75

820 Antonio Molina (composer)

1994. Birth Centenaries. Multicoloured.

2658	2p. Type **820**	60	35
2659	2p. Jose Yulo (Secretary of Justice)	60	35
2660	2p. Josefa Jara-Martinez (social worker)	60	35
2661	2p. Nicanor Reyes (accountant)	60	35
2662	2p. Sabino Padilla (judge)	60	35

1994. Centenary of Declaration of Philippine Independence (2nd issue). National Landmarks. Sheet 100×80 mm containing vert designs as T **788**. Multicoloured.

MS2663	2p. Aguinaldo Shrine; 2p. Barasoain Shrine; 3p. Rizal Shrine; 3p. Mabini Shrine	3·75	3·25

821 Map, Forest and Emblem (Baguio City)

1994. Export Processing Zones. Multicoloured.

2664	2p. Type **821**	75	40
2665	2p. Cross on hilltop (Bataan)	75	40
2666	2p. Octagonal building (Mactan)	75	40
2667	2p. Aguinaldo Shrine (Cavite)	75	40
2668	7p. Map and products	2·75	1·20
2669	8p. Globe and products	3·00	1·50

Nos. 2264/7 and 2668/9 respectively were issued together, se-tenant, forming composite designs.

822 Cross through "ILLEGAL RECRUITMENT"

1994. Anti-illegal Recruitment Campaign.

2670	**822**	2p. multicoloured	90	40

823 Palawan Bearcat

1994. Mammals. Multicoloured.

2671	6p. Type **823**	2·20	1·10
2672	6p. Philippine tarsier	2·20	1·10
2673	6p. Malayan pangolin (inscr "Scaly Anteater")	2·20	1·10
2674	6p. Indonesian ("Palawan") porcupine	2·20	1·10
MS2675	96×67 mm. 12p. Visayan spotted deer (79×29 mm)	13·00	12·00

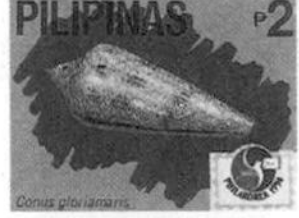

824 Glory of the Sea Cone ("Conus gloriamaris")

1994. "Philakorea 1994" International Stamp Exhibition, Seoul. Shells. Multicoloured.

2676	2p. Type **824**	1·50	45
2677	2p. Striate cone ("Conus striatus")	1·50	45
2678	2p. Geography cone ("Conus geographus")	1·50	45
2679	2p. Textile cone ("Conus textile")	1·50	45
MS2680	Two sheets, each 88×78 mm. (a) 6p. Striate cone; 6p. "Conus marmoreus" (Marble cone); (b) 6p. Marble cone; 6p. Geography cone	18·00	16·00

1994. "Singpex '94" National Stamp Exhibition, Singapore. As No. **MS**2675 but additionally inscribed "Singpex '94 31 August–3 September 1994" and emblem.

MS2681	96×67 mm. 12p. multicoloured	20·00	19·00

825 Sergio Osmena, Snr.

1994. 50th Anniv of Leyte Gulf Landings. Multicoloured.

2682	2p. Type **825**	1·00	35
2683	2p. Soldiers landing at Palo	1·00	35
2684	2p. "Peace – A Better World" emblem	1·00	35
2685	2p. Carlos Romulo	1·00	35

Nos. 2682/5 were issued together, se-tenant, forming a composite design.

826 Family (International Year of the Family)

1994. Anniversaries and Event. Multicoloured.
2686 2p. Type **826** 60 25
2687 6p. Workers (75th anniv of I.L.O.) 1·90 1·10
2688 7p. Aircraft and symbols of flight (50th anniv of I.C.A.O.) 2·30 1·50

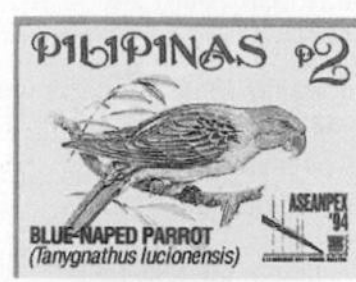

827 Blue-naped Parrot

1994. "Aseanpex '94" Stamp Exhibition, Penang, Malaysia. Birds. Muilticoloured.
2689 2p. Type **827** 2·20 55
2690 2p. Luzon bleeding heart ("Bleeding Heart Pigeon") 2·20 55
2691 2p. Palawan peacock-pheasant 2·20 55
2692 2p. Koch's pitta 2·20 55
MS2693 69×55 mm. 12p. Philippine eagle (vert) 14·50 13·50

828 Presidents Fidel Ramos and W. Clinton

1994. Visit of United States President William Clinton to Philippines.
2694 **828** 2p. multicoloured 75 40
2695 **828** 8p. multicoloured 3·00 1·50

829 Convention Emblem

1994. Association of South-East Asian Nations Eastern Business Convention, Davao City.
2696 **829** 2p. multicoloured 60 25
2697 **829** 6p. multicoloured 1·90 1·20

830 "Soteranna Puson y Quintos de Ventenilla" (Dionisio de Castro)

1994. Philatelic Week. Portraits. Multicoloured.
2698 2p. Type **830** 75 40
2699 6p. "Quintina Castor de Sadie" (Simon Flores y de la Rosa) 1·90 1·20
2700 7p. "Portrait of the Artist's Mother" (Felix Hidalgo y Padilla) 2·30 1·50
2701 8p. "Una Bulaquena" (Juan Luna y Novicio) 2·75 1·60
MS2702 60×100 mm. 12p. "Cirilo and Severina Quaison Family" (Simon Flores y de la Rosa) (28½×79 mm) 5·00 4·75

831 Wreath

1994. Christmas. Multicoloured.
2703 2p. Type **831** 75 40
2704 6p. Angels 1·90 1·20
2705 7p. Bells 2·30 1·50
2706 8p. Christmas basket 2·75 1·60

832 Piggy Bank

1994. New Year. Year of the Pig. Multicoloured.
2707 2p. Type **832** 90 40
2708 6p. Pig couple 2·20 1·20
MS2709 98×88 mm. Nos. 2707/8 plus two labels. Perf or imperf 4·75 4·25

833 Raid on Prison

1994. 50th Anniversaries of Raid by Hunters ROTC Guerrillas on Psew Bilibi Prison and of Mass Escape by Inmates. Multicoloured.
2710 2p. Type **833** 75 40
2711 2p. Inmates fleeing 75 40
Nos. 2710/11 were issued together, se-tenant, forming a composite design.

834 East Central Luzon Guerrilla Area

1994. Philippine Guerrilla Units of Second World War (3rd series). Multicoloured.
2712 2p. Type **834** 60 25
2713 2p. Mindoro Provincial Battalion and Marinduque Guerrilla Force 60 25
2714 2p. Zambales Military District and Masbate Guerrilla Regiment 60 25
2715 2p. Samar Area Command 60 25

835 Ribbon on Globe

1994. National AIDS Awareness Campaign.
2716 **835** 2p. multicoloured 90 40

836 Flag

1994. Centenary of Declaration of Philippine Independence. Multicoloured.
2717 2p. Type **836** 75 40
2718 2p. Present state flag 75 40
2719 2p. Anniversary emblem 75 40
Nos. 2717/19 were issued together, se-tenant, forming a composite design.

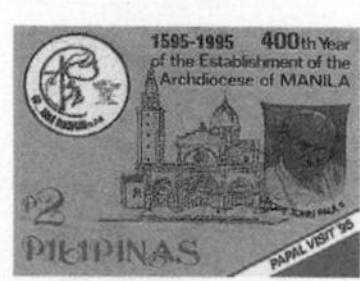

837 Pope John Paul II and Manila Cathedral

1995. Papal Visit. Multicoloured.
2720 2p. Type **837** (400th anniv of Manila Archdiocese) 75 40
2721 2p. Pope and Cebu Cathedral (400th anniv of Diocese) 75 40
2722 2p. Pope and Caceres Cathedral (400th anniv of Diocese) 75 40
2723 2p. Pope and Nueva Segovia Cathedral (400th anniv of Diocese) 75 40
2724 2p. Pope, globe and Pope's arms 75 40
2725 6p. Pope and Federation of Asian Bishops emblem (6th Conference, Manila) 1·50 95
2726 8p. Pope, youths and emblem (10th World Youth Day) 2·20 1·20
MS2727 81×60 mm. 8p. Pope and President Fidel Ramos 4·75 4·25

1995. "Christypex '95" Philatelic Exhibition, Manila. No. **MS**2727 optd **CHRISTYPEX '95 JANUARY 4-16, 1995 University of Santo Tomas, Manila PHILIPPINE PHILATELIC FEDERATION**.
MS2728 81×60 mm. 8p. multicoloured 5·00 4·75

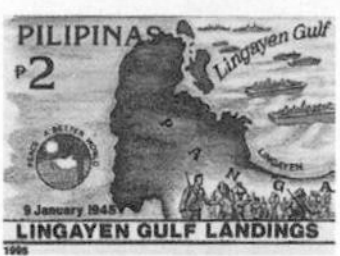

839 Landing Craft and Map

1995. 50th Anniv of Lingayen Gulf Landings. Multicoloured.
2729 2p. Type **839** 90 40
2730 2p. Map and emblems of 6th, 37th, 40th and 43rd army divisions 90 40
Nos. 2729/30 were issued together, se-tenant, forming a composite design.

840 Monument (Peter de Guzman) and Ruins of Intramuros

1995. 50th Anniv of Battle for the Liberation of Manila. Multicoloured.
2731 2p. Type **840** 90 40
2732 8p. Monument and ruins of Legislative Building and Department of Agriculture 2·75 1·20

841 Diokno

1995. Eighth Death Anniv of Jose Diokno (politician).
2733 **841** 2p. multicoloured 90 40

842 Anniversary Emblem and Ethnic Groups

1995. 75th Anniv of International School, Manila. Multicoloured.
2734 2p. Type **842** 60 35
2735 8p. Globe and cut-outs of children 2·75 1·50

843 Greater Malay Mouse Deer

1995. Mammals. Multicoloured.
2736 2p. Type **843** 75 35
2737 2p. Tamarau 75 35
2738 2p. Visayan warty pig 75 35
2739 2p. Palm civet 75 35
MS2740 89×80 mm. 8p. Flying lemur; 8p. Philippine deer 5·25 4·75

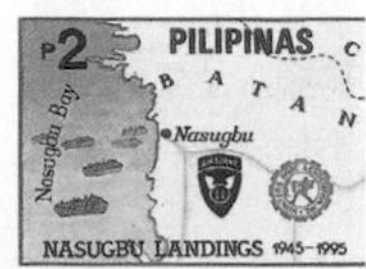

844 Nasugbu Landings

1995. 50th Anniversaries. Multicoloured.
2741 2p. Type **844** 75 35
2742 2p. Tagaytay Landings 75 35
2743 2p. Battle of Nichols Airbase and Fort McKinley 75 35
Nos. 2741/2 were issued together, se-tenant, forming a composite design.

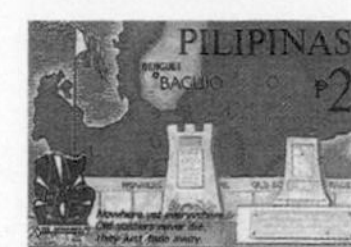

845 Memorial

1995. 50th Anniv of Liberation of Baguio.
2744 **845** 2p. multicoloured 75 35

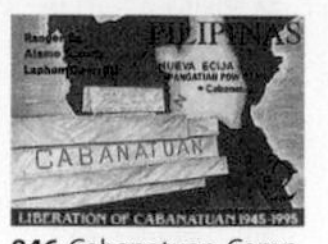

846 Cabanatuan Camp

1995. 50th Anniv of Liberation of Internment and Prisoner of War Camps. Multicoloured.
2745 2p. Type **846** 75 35
2746 2p. Entrance to U.S.T. camp 75 35
2747 2p. Los Banos camp 75 35
Nos. 2746/7 are wrongly inscribed "Interment".

847 Victorio Edades (artist)

1995. Birth Centenaries. Multicoloured.
2748 2p. Type **847** 60 25
2749 2p. Jovita Fuentes (opera singer) 60 25
2750 2p. Candido Africa (medical researcher) 60 25
2751 2p. Asuncion Arriola-Perez (politician) 60 25
2752 2p. Eduardo Quisumbing (botanist) 60 25

1995. Centenary of Declaration of Philippine Independence (3rd issue). 123rd Anniv of Cavite Mutiny. Sheet 100×80 mm. containing vert designs as T **788**.
MS2753 2p. Cavite shipyard; 2p. Centenary memorial; 3p. San Filipe fortress; 3p. Crisanto de los Reyes y Mendoza (death centenary) 11·50 10·50

848 Emblems and Bible

1995. 50th Anniv of Philippine Catholic Bishops' Conference, Manila.
2754 **848** 2p. multicoloured 90 40

849 Ferrer

1995. Eighth Death Anniv of Jaime Ferrer (administrator).
2755 **849** 2p. multicoloured 90 40

850 Neolithic Burial Jar, Manunggul

1995. Archaeology. Multicoloured.
2756 2p. Type **850** 90 40
2757 2p. Iron age secondary burial jar, Ayub Cave, Mindanao 90 40
2758 2p. Iron age secondary burial jar (different), Ayub Cave 90 40
2759 2p. Neolithic ritual drinking vessel, Leta-Leta Cave, Palawan 90 40
MS2760 100×70 mm. 12p. 14th–15th century double-spouted vessel and presentation tray, Laurel, Batangas (80×30 mm) 5·00 4·75
See also No.**MS**2767.

851 Philippine Eagle

1995. Adoption of the Philippine Eagle as National Bird. Sheet 69×55 mm.
MS2761 16p. multicoloured 13·00 12·00

852 Right Hand supporting Wildlife

1995. Association of South-East Asian Nations Environment Year. Multicoloured.
2762 2p. Type **852** 1·20 55
2763 2p. Left hand supporting wildlife 1·20 55
MS2764 89×78 mm. 6p. Type **852**; 6p. As No. 2766 8·75 8·00
Nos. 2762/3 were issued together, se-tenant, forming a composite design.

853 Anniversary Emblem, Buildings and Trolley

1995. 50th Anniv of Mercury Drug Corporation.
2765 **853** 2p. multicoloured 90 40

854 Parish Church

1995. 400th Anniv of Parish of Saint Louis Bishop, Lucban.
2766 **854** 2p. multicoloured 90 40

1995. "Jakarta 95" Asian Stamp Exhibition. As No. **MS**2760 but with additional inscription at foot.
MS2767 100×70 mm. 12p. multicoloured 5·25 5·00

855 Instructor and Pupils

1995. 25th Anniv of Asian-Pacific Postal Training Centre, Bangkok.
2768 **855** 6p. multicoloured 2·00 1·20

856 Crops and Child drinking from Well

1995. 50th Anniv of F.A.O.
2769 **856** 8p. multicoloured 3·00 1·70

857 Carlos Romulo

1995. 50th Anniv of U.N.O. Multicoloured.
2770 2p. Jose Bengzon (inscr "Cesar Bengzon") £250 £225
2771 2p. Rafael Salas (Assistant Secretary General) 1·50 1·30
2772 2p. Salvador Lopez (Secretary) 1·50 1·30
2773 2p. Jose Ingles (Under-secretary) 1·50 1·30
MS2774 71×57 mm. 16p. Carlos Romulo (President of General Assembly) 5·75 5·25
2775 2p. Type **857** 75 40
No. 2770 depicts Jose Bengzon in error for his brother Cesar.

858 Anniversary Emblem

1995. 50th Anniv of Manila Overseas Press Club.
2779 **858** 2p. multicoloured 90 40

859 Eclipse

1995. Total Solar Eclipse.
2780 **859** 2p. multicoloured 90 40

860 Flag

1995. National Symbols. With blue barcode at top. "Pilipinas" in red. Variously dated. Multicoloured.
2781 2p. Flag ("Pilipinas" at top) 60 25
2782 2p. Hero (Jose Rizal) 60 25
2783 2p. House 60 25
2784 2p. Costume 60 25
2785 2p. Dance 60 25
2786 2p. Sport 60 25
2787 2p. Bird (Philippine eagle) 60 25
2788 2p. Type **860** 60 25
2789 2p. Animal (water buffalo) 60 25
2790 2p. Flower (jasmine) 60 25
2791 2p. Tree 60 25
2792 2p. Fruit (mango) 60 25
2793 2p. Leaf (palm) 60 25
2794 2p. Fish (milkfish) 60 25
For designs with barcode but "Pilipinas" in blue, see Nos. 2822/44.

861 "Two Igorot Women" (Victorio Edades)

1995. National Stamp Collecting Month (1st issue). Paintings by Filipino artists. Multicoloured.
2795 2p. Type **861** 75 40
2796 6p. "Serenade" (Carlos Francisco) 2·30 1·20
2797 7p. "Tuba Drinkers" (Vicente Manansala) 2·50 1·60
2798 8p. "Genesis" (Hernando Ocampo) 2·75 1·90
MS2799 99×70 mm. "The Builders" (Victorio Edades) (79×29 mm) 7·25 6·75
See also No. **MS**2805.

862 Tambourine

1995. Christmas. Musical instruments and Lines from Carols. Multicoloured.
2800 2p. Type **862** 75 40
2801 6p. Maracas 2·30 1·20
2802 7p. Guitar 2·50 1·60
2803 8p. Drum 2·75 1·90

863 Abacus and Anniversary Emblem

1995. 50th Anniv of Sycip Gorres Velayo & Co. (accountants).
2804 **863** 2p. multicoloured 75 40

864 Pres. Ramos signing Stamp Month Proclamation

1995. National Stamp Collecting Month (2nd issue). Sheet 80×60 mm.
MS2805 8p. multicoloured 4·75 4·25

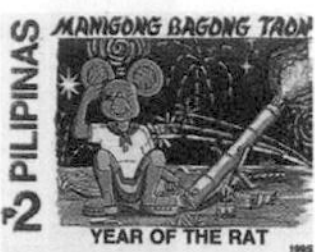

865 Rat and Fireworks

1995. New Year. Year of the Rat. Multicoloured.
2806 2p. Type **865** 75 40
2807 6p. Model of rat 2·00 1·20
MS2808 98×88 mm. Nos. 2806/7 plus two greetings labels. Perf or imperf 7·25 6·75

866 Badge of Fil-American Irregular Troops Veterans Legion

1995. Philippine Guerrilla Units of Second World War (4th series). Multicoloured.
2809 2p. Type **866** 75 40
2810 2p. Badge of Bicol Brigade Veterans 75 40
2811 2p. Map of Fil-American Guerrilla forces (Cavite) and Hukbalahap unit (Pampanga) 75 40
2812 2p. Map of South Tarlac military district and Northwest Pampanga 75 40

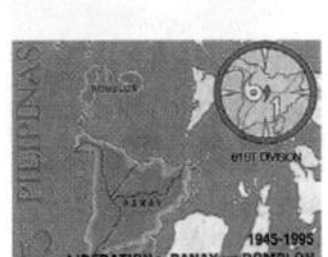

867 Liberation of Panay and Romblon

1995. 50th Anniversaries. Multicoloured.
2813 2p. Type **867** 60 25
2814 2p. Liberation of Cebu 60 25
2815 2p. Battle of Ipo Dam 60 25
2816 2p. Battle of Bessang Pass 60 25
2817 2p. Surrender of General Yamashita 60 25

868 Jose Rizal

1995. Centenary of Declaration of Philippine Independence Revolutionaries. Multicoloured.
2818 2p. Type **868** 75 40
2819 2p. Andres Bonifacio 75 40
2820 2p. Apolinario Mabini 75 40

869 Top detail of Map of Islands

1995. 50th Anniv of End of Second World War. Dated "1995". Two sheets containing new designs as T **869** and previous designs. Multicoloured.
MS2821 Two sheets. (a) 177×139 mm. 2p. ×8, Nos. 2682/5, 2729/30 and 2741/2; 2p. ×4, As T **869** forming composite design of map of Philippine Islands (blue background). (b) 179×199 mm. 2p. ×13, Nos. 2710/11, 2731, 2743/7 and 2813/17; 2p. ×4 As T **869** forming composite design of map of Philippine Islands (green background); 2p. As No. 2732 23·00 21·00

1996. National Symbols. As T **860**, with blue barcode at top. "Pilipinas" in blue. Variously dated. Multicoloured.
2822 1p. Flower (jasmine) 45 25
2823 1p.50 Fish (milkfish) 60 40
2823a 2p. Flower (jasmine) 80 55
2824 3p. Animal (water buffalo) 90 65
2825 4p. Flag ("Pilipinas" at top) 1·50 80
2826 4p. Hero (Jose Rizal) 1·50 80
2827 4p. House 1·50 80
2828 4p. Costume 1·50 80
2829 4p. Dance 1·50 80
2830 4p. Sport 1·50 80
2831 4p. Bird (Philippine eagle) 1·50 80
2832 4p. Type **860** 1·50 80
2833 4p. Animal (head of water buffalo) (dated "1995") 1·50 80
2834 4p. Flower (jasmine) 1·50 80
2835 4p. Tree 1·50 80
2836 4p. Fruit (mango) 1·50 80
2837 4p. Leaf (palm) 1·50 80
2838 4p. Fish (milkfish) 1·50 80
2839 4p. Animal (water buffalo) (dated "1996") 1·50 80
2840 5p. Bird (Philippine eagle) 2·00 1·90
2841 6p. Leaf (palm) 2·20 1·30
2842 7p. Costume 2·30 1·50
2843 8p. Fruit (mango) 3·00 1·90
2844 10p. House 3·75 2·10

870 "Treating Patient" (Manuel Baldemor)

1996. 23rd International Congress of Internal Medicine, Manila.
2856 **870** 2p. multicoloured 1·20 40

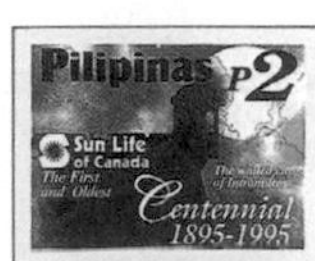

871 Walled City of Intramuros

1996. Centenary of Sun Life of Canada (insurance company). Multicoloured.
2857 2p. Type **871** 60 35
2858 8p. Manila Bay sunset 3·00 1·70

872 Pair of Eastern Rosella (birds) on Branch ("I Love You")

1996. Greetings Stamps. Multicoloured.
2859 2p. Type **872** 60 35
2860 2p. Eastern rosella (birds) ("Happy Valentine") 60 35
2861 6p. Cupid holding banner ("I Love You") 1·90 1·20
2862 6p. Cupid holding banner ("Happy Valentine") 1·90 1·20
2863 7p. Box of chocolates ("I Love You") 2·50 1·60
2864 7p. Box of chocolates ("Happy Valentine") 2·50 1·60
2865 8p. Butterfly and roses ("I Love You") 3·25 1·90
2866 8p. Butterfly and roses ("Happy Valentine") 3·25 1·90
Nos. 2861/2 were issued together, se-tenant, forming a composite design.

873 University Building and Map of Islands on Grid

1996. 50th Anniv of Gregorio Araneta University Foundation.
2867 **873** 2p. multicoloured 1·20 40

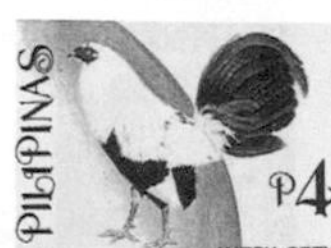

921 Hatch Grey

1997. Gamecocks. Multicoloured.

3035	4p. Type **921**	1·00	60
3036	4p. Spangled roundhead	1·00	60
3037	4p. Racey mug	1·00	60
3038	4p. Silver grey	1·00	60
3039	4p. Grey (vert)	1·00	60
3040	4p. Kelso (vert)	1·00	60
3041	4p. Bruner roundhead (vert)	1·00	60
3042	4p. Democrat (vert)	1·00	60
MS3043	Two sheets. (a) 55×69 mm. 12p. Cocks fighting (vert); (b) 99×59 mm. 16p. Cocks preparing to fight (79×29 mm)	9·50	8·25

922 Philippine Eagle

1997. National Symbols. Multicoloured.

3044	20p. Type **922**	3·50	3·00
3045	30p. Philippine eagle (different)	5·25	4·50
3046	50p. Philippine eagle (different)	9·00	7·50

923 Flag and Stars

1998. 50th Anniv of Art Association of the Philippines. Multicoloured.

3047	4p. Type **923**	1·10	95
3048	4p. Hand clasping paintbrushes	1·10	95

924 Mother Philippines, Club Building and Emblem

1998. Centenary of Club Filipino (social club).

3049	**924**	4p. multicoloured	1·10	95

925 Marie Eugenie

1998. Death Centenary of Blessed Marie Eugenie (founder of the Sisters of the Assumption).

3050	**925**	4p. multicoloured	1·10	95

926 Philippine and United States Flags

1998. 50th Anniv of Fulbright (student exchange) Program.

3051	**926**	4p. multicoloured	1·10	95

927 Emilio Jacinto

1998. Heroes of the Revolution. Multicoloured. White backgrounds. Blue barcode at foot.

3052	2p. Type **927**	40	25
3054	4p. Melchora Aquino	1·10	70
3055	4p. Jose Rizal	1·10	70
3056	5p. Antonio Luna	1·10	70
3057	8p. Marcelo del Pilar	1·40	1·10
3058	10p. Gregorio del Pilar	1·80	1·30
3059	11p. Andres Bonifacio	1·90	1·40
3060	13p. Apolinario Mabini	2·20	1·50
3061	15p. Emilio Aguinaldo	2·50	2·00
3062	18p. Juan Luna	3·00	2·30

See also Nos. 3179/88 and 3189/98.

928 Mt. Apo, Bagobo Woman, Orchids and Fruit

1998. 50th Anniv of Apo View Hotel, Davao City.

3070	**928**	4p. multicoloured	1·10	95

929 School and Emblem

1998. 75th Anniv of Philippine Cultural High School.

3071	**929**	4p. multicoloured	1·10	95

930 Old and Present School Buildings

1998. 75th Anniv of Victorino Mapa High School, San Rafael.

3072	**930**	4p. multicoloured	1·10	95

931 Lighthouse, Warship and Past and Present Uniforms

1998. Centenary of Philippine Navy.

3073	**931**	4p. multicoloured	1·10	95

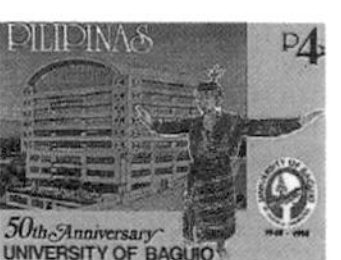

932 University and Igorot Dancer

1998. 50th Anniv of University of Baguio.

3074	**932**	4p. multicoloured	1·10	95

933 Training Ship and Emblem

1998. 50th Anniv of Philippine Maritime Institute.

3075	**933**	4p. multicoloured	1·10	95

934 Forest, Palawan

1998. "EXPO '98" World's Fair, Lisbon. Multicoloured.

3076	4p. Type **934**	1·10	95
3077	15p. Filipino vinta (sail canoe), Zamboanga (horiz)	2·75	2·30
MS3078	102×81 mm. 15p. Main Lobby of Philippine Pavilion (79×29 mm)	4·75	4·00

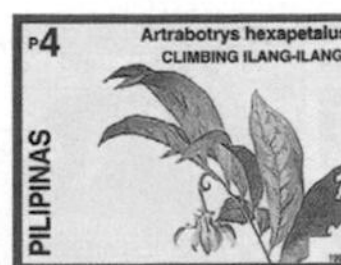

935 Climbing Ilang-ilang

1998. "Florikultura'98" International Garden Festival, San Fernando, Pampanga. Illustrations from "Flowers of the Philippines" by Manuel Blanco. Multicoloured.

3079	4p. Type **935**	1·10	95
3080	4p. "Hibiscus rosa-sinensis"	1·10	95
3081	4p. "Nerium oleander"	1·10	95
3082	4p. Arabian jasmine ("Jasminum sambac")	1·10	95
3083	4p. "Gardenia jasminoides" (vert)	1·10	95
3084	4p. Flame-of-the-forest ("Ixora coccinea") (vert)	1·10	95
3085	4p. Indian coral bean ("Erythrina indica") (vert)	1·10	95
3086	4p. "Abelmoschus moschatus" (vert)	1·10	95
MS3087	61×70 mm. 15p. "Medinilla magnifica" (vert)	7·00	6·50

936 City and Clark International Airport

1998. Clark Special Economic Zone.

3088	**936**	15p. multicoloured	2·75	2·30

937 Manila Galleon

1998. Centenary of Declaration of Philippine Independence. Philippines–Mexico–Spain Friendship. Multicoloured.

3089	15p. Type **937**	2·75	2·30
3090	15p. Philippine woman with flag, Legaspi-Urdaneta Monument and galleon	2·75	2·30
3091	15p. Spanish and Philippine flags, Cebu Basilica (after M. Miguel) and "Holy Child" (statuette)	2·75	2·30
MS3092	145×90 mm. Nos. 3089/91 plus three labels	7·00	6·50

938 "Spoliarium" (Juan Luna)

1998. Centenary of Declaration of Philippine Independence. Multicoloured.

3093	4p. Type **938**	55	45
3094	8p. General Emilio Aguinaldo introducing Philippine national flag at Cavite	85	70
3095	16p. Execution of Jose Rizal, 1896	6·25	5·25
3096	16p. Andres Bonifacio and Katipunan monument	6·25	5·25
3097	20p. Barasoain Church (venue of first Philippine Congress, 1898)	7·00	5·75

939 Andres Soriano (accountant)

1998. Birth Centenaries. Multicoloured.

3098	4p. Type **939**	85	70
3099	4p. Tomas Fonacier (Univeristy dean and historian)	85	70
3100	4p. Josefa Escoda (founder of Filipino Girl Scouts and social reformer)	85	70
3101	4p. Lorenzo Tanada (politician)	85	70
3102	4p. Lazaro Francisco (writer)	85	70

940 Melchora Aquino

1998. Centenary of Declaration of Philippine Independence Women Revolutionaries. Multicoloured.

3103	4p. Type **940**	85	70
3104	4p. Nazaria Lagos	85	70
3105	4p. Agueda Kahabagan	85	70

1998. Centenary of Philippine Independence (13th issue). Events of 1898. Sheet 100×80 mm containing vert designs as T **860** but with barcode sideways at right.

MS3106	4p. Cebu uprising; 4p. Negros uprising; 4p. Iligan uprising; 4p. Centenary emblem	8·25	7·50

1998. Centenary of Declaration of Philippine Independence (14th issue). Nos. 2644 (1993), 2825/32 and 2834/9 optd **1898 1998 KALAYAAN** and emblem.

3107	3p. Animal (head of water buffalo)	55	45
3108	4p. Flag ("Pilipinas" at top)	70	60
3109	4p. Hero (Jose Rizal)	70	60
3110	4p. House	70	60
3111	4p. Costume	70	60
3112	4p. Dance	70	60
3113	4p. Sport	70	60
3114	4p. Bird (Philippine eagle)	70	60
3115	4p. Type **860**	70	60
3116	4p. Flower (jasmine)	70	60
3117	4p. Tree	70	60
3118	4p. Fruit (mango)	70	60
3119	4p. Leaf (palm)	70	60
3120	4p. Fish	70	60
3121	4p. Animal (water buffalo)	70	60

942 River Pasig

1998. River Pasig Environmental Campaign.

3122	**942**	4p. multicoloured	95	80

943 Bottle-nosed ("Bottlenose") Dolphin

1998. Marine Mammals. Multicoloured.

3123	4p. Type **943**	85	70
3124	4p. Humpback whale	85	70
3125	4p. Fraser's dolphin	85	70
3126	4p. Melon-headed whale	85	70
3127	4p. Minke whale	85	70
3128	4p. Striped dolphin	85	70
3129	4p. Sperm whale	85	70
3130	4p. Pygmy killer whale	85	70
3131	4p. Cuvier's beaked whale	85	70
3132	4p. Killer whale	85	70
3133	4p. Bottle-nosed ("Bottlenose") dolphin (different)	85	70
3134	4p. Spinner dolphin ("Long-snouted spinner dolphin")	85	70
3135	4p. Risso's dolphin	85	70
3136	4p. Finless porpoise	85	70
3137	4p. Pygmy sperm whale	85	70
3138	4p. Pantropical spotted dolphin	85	70
3139	4p. False killer whale	85	70
3140	4p. Blainville's beaked whale	85	70
3141	4p. Rough-toothed dolphin	85	70
3142	4p. Bryde's whale	85	70
MS3143	83×60 mm. 15p. Dugong	5·50	5·25

944 Coconuts and Products

1998. Centenary of Philippine Coconut Industry.

3144	**944**	4p. multicoloured	95	80

945 Grapes, Emblem and Nun

1998. 75th Anniv of Holy Spirit Adoration Sisters in the Philippines.
3145 **945** 4p. multicoloured 95 80

946 Child posting Letter

1998. Centenary of Postal Service. Multicoloured.
3146 6p. Type **946** 1·10 95
3147 6p. Globe and handshake 1·10 95
3148 6p. Philippine stamps, globe, airplane, galleon and building 1·10 95
3149 6p. Flags, dove and letters floating down to girl 1·10 95
MS3150 102×60 mm. 15p. Boy holding letter and letters encircling globe 5·50 5·25

947 Holly Wreath

1998. Christmas. Multicoloured.
3151 6p. Type **947** 1·10 95
3152 11p. Star wreath 1·80 1·50
3153 13p. Flower wreath 2·20 1·90
3154 15p. Bell wreath 2·50 2·10

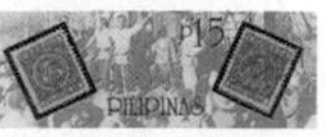

948 2c. Postage Stamps

1998. "Philipinas 98" International Stamp Exhibition, Mandaluyong City. Six sheets each 121×60 mm containing horiz designs as T **948** showing 1898 Filipino Revolutionary Government Stamps. Multicoloured.
MS3155 Six sheets (a) 15p. Type **948** (blue background); (b) 15p. 2c. Postage and 1m. imperforate and perforate Printed Matter ("IMPRESOS") stamps; (c) 15p. 2 and 5c. Telegraph stamps; (d) 15p. 8c. Registered Letter ("CERTIFICADO") and 10c. Revenue ("RECIBOS") stamps; (e) 15p. Local issue and 5p. "LIBERTAD" stamp; (f) 15p. As No. **MS**3154a but imperforate and with green background 41·00 39·00

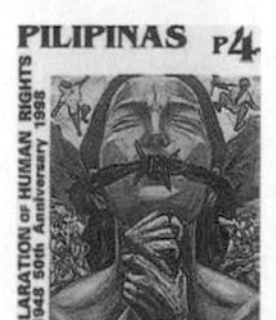

949 Person gagged with Barbed Wire

1998. 50th Anniv of Universal Declaration of Human Rights.
3156 **949** 4p. multicoloured 1·10 95

950 Papal Mitre

1998. Shells. Multicoloured.
3157 4p. Type **950** 1·10 95
3158 4p. "Vexillum citrinum" 1·10 95
3159 4p. "Rugose mitre" ("Vexillum rugosum") 1·10 95
3160 4p. "Volema carinifera" 1·10 95
3161 4p. "Teramachia dalli" 1·10 95
3162 4p. "Nassarius vitiensis" 1·10 95
3163 4p. "Cymbiola imperialis" 1·10 95
3164 4p. "Cymbiola aulica" 1·10 95
MS3165 97×70 mm. 8p. "Nassarius papillosus"; 8p. Trapezium horse conch ("Fasciolaria trapezium") 8·25 7·50

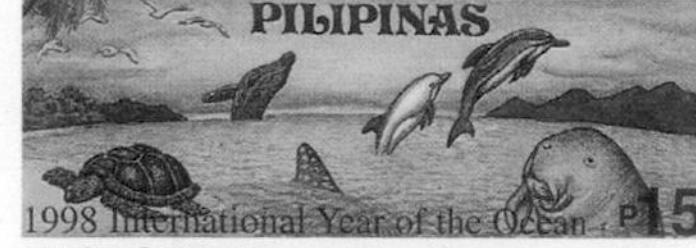

951 Sea Creatures

1998. International Year of the Ocean.
3166 **951** 15p. multicoloured 2·50 2·10
MS3167 101×71 mm. No. 3166 7·00 6·50

952 Taking Oath

1998. Inauguration of President Joseph Ejercito Estrada. Multicoloured.
3168 6p. Type **952** 1·10 95
3169 15p. Inaugural speech 2·50 2·10

953 Rabbit

1998. New Year. Year of the Rabbit. Multicoloured.
3170 4p. Type **953** 85 70
3171 11p. Two rabbits 2·10 1·80
MS3172 97×89 mm. Nos. 3170/1 plus two labels. Perf or Imperf 4·75 4·00

954 "Dyesebel"

1998. National Stamp Collecting Month. Film Posters.
3173 **954** 6p. blue and black 1·10 95
3174 - 11p. brown and black 1·80 1·50
3175 - 13p. mauve and black 2·20 1·90
3176 - 15p. green and black 2·50 2·10
MS3177 58×101 mm. 15p. black 4·50 3·75
DESIGNS—As T **954** 11p. "Ang Sawa sa Lumang Simboryo"; 13p. "Prinsipe Amante"; 10p. (3176) "Anak Dalita". 26×76 mm—15p. (**MS**3177) "Siete Infantes de Lara".

955 "Noli Me Tangere" (Jose Rizal) (Pride in the Citizenry)

1998. Centenary of Declaration of Independence of Philippine Independence (15th issue). The Six Prides. Six sheets, each 84×90 mm containing vert designs as T **955**. Multicoloured.
MS3178 Six sheets. (a) 15p. Type **955**; (b) 15p. Banaue Rice Terraces (engineering); (c) 15p. Monument and woman holding national flag (Filipino people); (d) 15p. Malay woman in traditional costume (heritage); (e) 15p. Woman decorating pot and scripts (literature); (f) 15p. Woman with eagle on arm (resources) 28·00 26·00

1998. Heroes of the Revolution. As Nos. 3052/62. Multicoloured. Blue barcode at foot. (a) Yellow backgrounds.
3179 6p. Type **927** 1·20 1·10
3180 6p. Melchora Aquino 1·20 1·10
3181 6p. Jose Rizal 1·20 1·10
3182 6p. Antonio Luna 1·20 1·10
3183 6p. Marcelo del Pilar 1·20 1·10
3184 6p. Gregorio del Pilar 1·20 1·10
3185 6p. Andres Bonifacio 1·20 1·10
3186 6p. Apolinario Mabini 1·20 1·10
3187 6p. Emilio Aguinaldo 1·20 1·10
3188 6p. Juan Luna 1·20 1·10

(c) Pink background.
3229 5p. Jose Rizal 95 80

(b) Green backgrounds.
3189 15p. Type **927** 2·50 2·20
3190 15p. Melchora Aquino 2·50 2·20
3191 15p. Jose Rizal 2·50 2·20
3192 15p. Antonio Luna 2·50 2·20
3193 15p. Marcelo del Pilar 2·50 2·20
3194 15p. Gregorio del Pilar 2·50 2·20
3195 15p. Andres Bonifacio 2·50 2·20
3196 15p. Apolinario Mabini 2·50 2·20
3197 15p. Emilio Aguinaldo 2·50 2·20
3198 15p. Juan Luna 2·50 2·20

956 Old and New Bank Emblems

1999. 50th Anniv of Central Bank of the Philippines.
3199 **956** 6p. multicoloured 1·20 1·10

957 Anniversary Emblem

1999. Centenary of Declaration of Philippine Independence. Multicoloured.
3200 6p. Type **957** 1·20 1·10
3201 6p. General Emilio Aguinaldo's house (site of declaration, June 1898) 1·20 1·10
3202 6p. Malolos Congress, Barasoain Church, Bulacan (ratification by regions of declaration, September 1898) 1·20 1·10
3203 6p. House in Western Negros (uprising of 5 November 1898) 1·20 1·10
3204 6p. Cry of Santa Barbara, Iloilo (inauguration of government, 17 November 1898) 1·20 1·10
3205 6p. Cebu City (Victory over Colonial Forces of Spain, December 1898) 1·20 1·10
3206 6p. Philippine flag and emblem (declaration in Butaan City of sovereignty over Mindanao, 17 January 1899) 1·20 1·10
3207 6p. Facade of Church (Ratification of Constitution, 22 January 1899) 1·20 1·10
3208 6p. Carnival procession, Malolos (Inauguration of Republic, 23 January 1899) 1·20 1·10
3209 6p. Barosoain Church and anniversary emblem 1·20 1·10

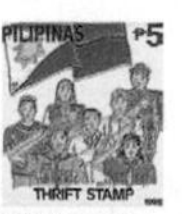

958 Scouts and Guides

1999
3210 5p. Type **958** 2·75 2·30
3211 5p. Children gardening 2·75 2·30
Nos. 3210/11 were originally issued as Savings Bank stamps in 1995, but were authorized for postal use from 16 January 1999.

959 Cruise Liner

1999. Centenary of Department of Transportation and Communication. Multicoloured.
3212 6p. Type **959** 95 80
3213 6p. Airplane 95 80
3214 6p. Air traffic control tower 95 80
3215 6p. Satellite dish aerial and bus 95 80
MS3216 114×70 mm. 15p. Globe, stamps, Philpost headquarters and letters (79×27 mm) 4·25 3·75
Nos. 3212/15 were issued together, se-tenant, forming a composite design.

960 San Juan del Monte Bridge

1999. Centenary of American–Filipino War.
3217 **960** 5p. multicoloured 95 80

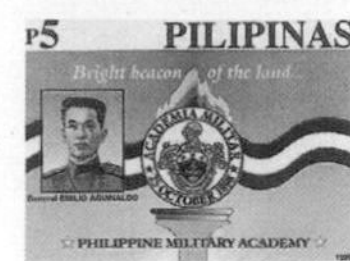

961 General Emilio Aguinaldo and Academy Arms

1999. Centenary (1998) of Philippine Military Academy.
3218 **961** 5p. multicoloured 95 80

962 Green-backed Heron

1999. Birds. Multicoloured.
3219 5p. Type **962** 1·10 95
3220 5p. Common tern 1·10 95
3221 5p. Greater crested tern 1·10 95
3222 5p. Ruddy Turnstone 1·10 95
3223 5p. Black-winged stilt 1·10 95
3224 5p. Asiatic Dowitcher 1·10 95
3225 5p. Whimbrel 1·10 95
3226 5p. Reef heron 1·10 95
MS3227 84×71 mm. 8p, Spotted greenshank; 8p. Tufted duck 9·75 8·75
MS3228 84×71 mm. As No. **MS**3227 but with different margin and emblem and inscription for "Australia 99" World Stamp Exhibition, Melbourne 10·50 8·75

963 Man holding Crutches

1999. 50th Anniv of Philippine Orthopaedic Association.
3230 **963** 5p. multicoloured 95 80

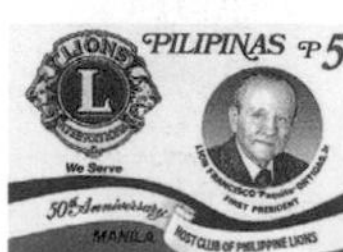

964 Francisco Ortigas and Emblem

1999. 50th Anniv of Manila Lions Club.
3231 **964** 5p. multicoloured 95 80

965 Entrance to Garden

1999. La Union Botanical Garden, San Fernando.
3232 5p. Type **965** 95 80
3233 5p. Kiosk 95 80
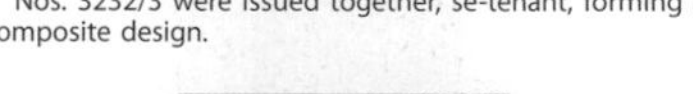
Nos. 3232/3 were issued together, se-tenant, forming a composite design.

966 Gliding Tree Frog

1999. Frogs. Multicoloured.
3234 5p. Type **966** 95 80
3235 5p. Common forest frog 95 80
3236 5p. Woodworth's frog 95 80
3237 5p. Giant Philippine frog 95 80
MS3238 108×86 mm. 5p. Spiny tree frog; 5p. Truncate-toed chorus frog; 5p. Variable-backed frog 7·00 6·50

967 Manta Ray

1999. Marine Life. Multicoloured.
3239 5p. Type **967** 95 80
3240 5p. Painted rock lobster 95 80
3241 5p. Sea squirt 95 80
3242 5p. Banded sea snake 95 80
MS3243 111×88 mm. 5p. Sea grapes; 5p. Branching coral; 5p. Sea urchin 8·25 7·50

968 Nakpil

1999. Birth Centenary of Juan Nakpil (architect).
3244 **968** 5p. multicoloured 1·10 95

969 Child writing Letter and Globe

1999. 125th Anniv of Universal Postal Union. Multicoloured.
3245 5p. Type **969** 1·10 95
3246 15p. Girl with stamp album 3·00 2·30

970 Waling-Waling and Cattleya "Queen Sirikit"

1999. 50 Years of Philippines–Thailand Diplomatic Relations. Multicoloured.
3247 5p. Type **970** 1·10 95
3248 11p. As Type **970** but with flowers transposed 2·50 2·20

971 Child writing

1999. 150th Anniv of Mongol Pencils.
3249 **971** 5p. multicoloured 1·10 95

972 Emblem and Handicapped Children

1999. 75th Anniv of Masonic Charities for Handicapped Children.
3250 **972** 5p. multicoloured 1·10 95

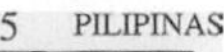

973 Sampaguita and Rose of Sharon

1999. 50 Years of Philippines–South Korea Diplomatic Relations. Multicoloured.
3251 5p. Type **973** 1·10 95
3252 11p. As Type **973** but with flowers transposed 2·50 2·20

974 Teachers, Nurses and Machinists

1999. 50th Anniv of Community Chest Foundation.
3253 **974** 5p. multicoloured 1·10 95

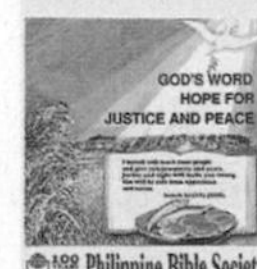

975 Dove, Fishes, Bread and Quotation from Isaiah

1999. Centenary of Philippine Bible Society.
3254 **975** 5p. multicoloured 1·10 95

976 Score, Jose Palma (lyricist) and Julian Felipe (composer)

1999. Centenary of National Anthem.
3255 **976** 5p. multicoloured 1·10 95

977 St. Francis of Assisi and Parish Church

1999. 400th Anniv of St. Francis of Assisi Parish, Sariaya, Quezon.
3256 **977** 5p. multicoloured 1·10 95

1999. 25th Anniv of International Philippine Philatelic Society. No. **MS**3092 optd **25th ANNIVERSARY IPPS** on each stamp and in the margins with anniversary inscr and emblems in silver.
MS3257 145×90 mm. Nos. 3089/91 plus three labels 8·25 7·50

979 Flags and Official Seal

1999. The Senate.
3258 **979** 5p. multicoloured 1·10 95

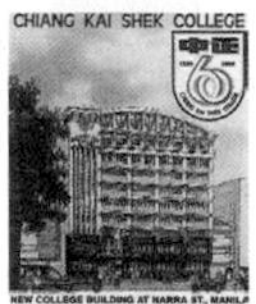

980 New Business, Arts and Sciences Faculty Building

1999. 60th Anniv of Chiang Kai Shek College, Manila.
3259 **980** 5p. multicoloured 1·10 95

981 School Building

1999. 50th Anniv of Tanza National High School.
3260 **981** 5p. multicoloured 1·10 95

982 St. Agustin Church, Paoay (World Heritage Day)

1999. United Nations Day. Multicoloured.
3261 5p. Type **982** 1·10 95
3262 11p. Elderly couple (International Year of the Older Person) 2·40 2·00
3263 15p. "Rizal Learns the Alphabet and Prayers from his Mother" (Miguel Galvez) (World Teachers' Day) 3·50 3·00

983 Angel

1999. Christmas. Multicoloured.
3264 5p. Type **983** 1·00 85
3265 11p. Angel holding star 2·00 1·70
3266 13p. Angel holding ribbon 2·50 2·10
3267 15p. Angel holding flowers 3·00 2·50
MS3268 141×95 mm. Nos. 3264/7 8·75 8·00

984 Tamaraw and Polar Bear

1999. 50 Years of Philippines–Canada Diplomatic Relations. Multicoloured.
3269 5p. Type **984** 1·00 85
3270 15p. As Type **984** but with animals transposed 3·00 2·50

985 Coliseum

1999. Renovation of Araneta Coliseum.
3271 **985** 5p. multicoloured 1·00 85

986 Sunrise

1999. Third Informal Summit of Association of South-east Asian Nations, Manila.
3272 **986** 5p. multicoloured 1·00 85
3273 **986** 11p. multicoloured 2·10 1·80

987 "Kristo" (Arturo Luz)

1999. National Stamp Collecting Month. Modern Sculptures. Multicoloured.
3274 5p. Type **987** 1·00 85
3275 11p. "Homage to Dodgie Laurel" (J. Elizalde Navarro) 2·00 1·70
3276 13p. "Hilojan" (Napoleon Abueva) 2·50 2·10
3277 15p. "Mother and Child" (Napoleon Abueva) 3·00 2·50
MS3278 100×90 mm. 5p. "Mother's Revenge" (Jose Rival); 15p. "El Ermitano" (Jose Rival) (horiz) 5·00 4·75

988 Dragon

1999. New Year. Year of the Dragon. Multicoloured.
3279 5p. Type **988** 1·10 95
3280 15p. Dragon amongst clouds 2·50 2·10
MS3281 98×88 mm. Nos. 3279/80 plus two labels. Perf or imperf 4·75 4·00

989 Gen. Gregorio H. del Pilar

1999. Centenary of the Battle of Tirad Pass.
3282 **989** 5p. multicoloured 1·10 95

990 *Paphiopedilum urbanianum*

1999. Orchids. Multicoloured.
3283 5p. Type **990** 1·10 95
3284 5p. *Phalaenopsis schilleriana* 1·10 95
3285 5p. *Dendrobium amethystoglossum* 1·10 95
3286 5p. *Paphiopedilum barbatum* 1·10 95
MS3287 132×83 mm. 5p. "Paphiopedilum haynaldianum" (horiz); 5p. "Phalaenopsis stuartiana" (horiz); 5p. "Trichoglottis brachiata" (horiz); 5p. "Ceratostylis rubra" (horiz) 5·00 4·75

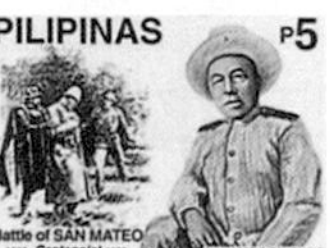

991 General Licerio Geronimo

1999. Centenary of Battle of San Mateo.
3288 **991** 5p. multicoloured 1·10 95

992 Crowds around Soldiers in Tanks

1999. New Millennium (1st series). "People Power". Multicoloured.
3289 5p. Type **992** 1·10 95
3290 5p. Radio antennae, helicopters and people 1·10 95
3291 5p. Religious procession 1·10 95
Nos. 3289/91 were issued together, se-tenant, forming a composite design.
See also Nos. 3311/13, 3357/9 and 3394/6.

993 Woman holding Gender Signs

2000. 25th Anniv of National Commission on Role of Filipino Women.
3292 **993** 5p. multicoloured 1·00 85

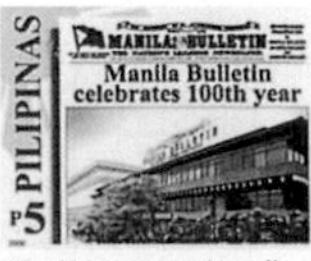

994 Newspaper Headline and Headquarters

2000. Centenary of the Manila Bulletin (newspaper).
3293 **994** 5p. multicoloured 1·00 85

995 Manuel Roxas (1946–48)

2000. Presidential Office. Multicoloured.
3294 5p. Type **995** 1·00 85
3295 5p. Elpidio Quirino (1948–53) 1·00 85

996 Golfer, Sailing Boat and Swimmers

2000. 150th Anniv of La Union Province. Multicoloured.

3296	5p. Type **996**	1·00	85
3297	5p. Tractor, building and worker	1·00	85
3298	5p. Government building	1·00	85
3299	5p. Airplane, bus, satellite dish, workers and bus	1·00	85

997 Joseph Ejercito Estrada (1998–2000)

2000. Presidential Office. Multicoloured.

3300	5p. Presidential seal (face value at top left)	90	75
3301	5p. Type **997**	90	75
3302	5p. Fidel V. Ramos (1992–98)	90	75
3303	5p. Corazon C. Aquino (1986–92)	90	75
3304	5p. Ferdinand E. Marcos (1965–86)	90	75
3305	5p. Diosdado Macapagal (1961–65)	90	75
3306	5p. Carlos P. Garcia (1957–61)	90	75
3307	5p. Ramon Magsaysay (1953–57)	90	75
3308	5p. Elpidio Quirino (1948–53)	90	75
3309	5p. Manuel Roxas (1946–48)	90	75

998 Workers and Emblem

2000. Centenary of the Civil Service Commission.

3310	**998**	5p. multicoloured	1·00	85

999 Golden Garuda, Palawan

2000. New Millennium (2nd series). Artefacts. Multicoloured.

3311	5p. Type **999**	1·30	1·10
3312	5p. Sunrise at Pusan Point, Davao Oriental	1·30	1·10
3313	5p. Golden Tara, Agusan	1·30	1·10

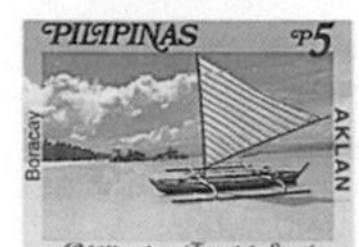

1000 Outrigger Canoe, Boracay Island

2000. Tourist Sites. Multicoloured.

3314	5p. Type **1000**	1·00	85
3315	5p. Chocolate Hills, Bohol	1·00	85
3316	5p. El Nido Forest, Palawan	1·00	85
3317	5p. Vigan House, Ilocos Sur	1·00	85
MS3318	99×59 mm. 15p. Bananue rice terraces, Ifugao (79×29 mm)	5·00	4·50

1001 Great Wall of China and Chinese Phoenix

2000. 25th Anniv of Diplomatic Relations with Republic of China. Multicoloured.

3319	5p. Type **1001**	1·30	1·10
3320	11p. Banaue rice terraces and Philippine Sarimanok	2·50	2·10
MS3321	98×60 mm. 5p. Great Wall of China (39×29 mm); 11p. Banaue rice terraces (39×29 mm)	3·75	3·50

1002 Television and Emblem

2000. 50th Anniv of GMA Television and Radio Network.

3322	**1002**	5p. multicoloured	1·00	85

1003 Church Building

2000. 400th Anniv of St. Thomas de Aquinas Parish, Mangaldan.

3323	**1003**	5p. multicoloured	1·00	85

1004 Carlos P. Garcia

2000. Presidential Office. Multicoloured.

3324	10p. Type **1004**	2·30	1·90
3325	10p. Ramon Magsaysay	2·30	1·90
3326	11p. Ferdinand E. Marcos	2·40	2·00
3327	11p. Diosdado Macapagal	2·40	2·00
3328	13p. Corazon C. Aquino	2·50	2·10
3329	13p. Fidel V. Ramos	2·50	2·10
3330	15p. Joseph Ejercito Estrada	3·00	2·50
3331	15p. Presidential seal (face value at top right)	3·00	2·50

See also Nos. 3489/98.

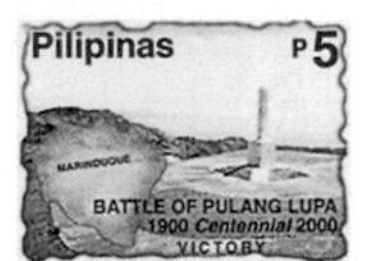

1005 Memorial and Map

2000. Battle Centenaries. Multicoloured.

3332	5p. Type **1005** (Battle of Pulang Lupa)	1·10	95
3333	5p. Memorial and soldiers (Battle of Mabitac)	1·10	95
3334	5p. Sun and soldiers (Battles of Cagayan, Agusan Hill and Makahambus Hill) (vert)	1·10	95
3335	5p. Map, memorial and bamboo signalling device (Battle of Paye) (vert)	1·10	95

1006 Joseph Ejercito Estrada

2000. Presidential Office. Multicoloured.

3336	5p. Presidential seal	1·10	95
3337	5p. Type **1006**	1·10	95
3338	5p. Fidel V. Ramos	1·10	95
3339	5p. Corazon C. Aquino	1·10	95
3340	5p. Ferdinand E. Marcos	1·10	95
3341	5p. Diosdado Macapagal	1·10	95
3342	5p. Carlos P. Garcia	1·10	95
3343	5p. Ramon Magsaysay	1·10	95
3344	5p. Elpidio Quirino	1·10	95
3345	5p. Manuel Roxas	1·10	95

1007 Ornate Chequered Beetle

2000. Insects. Multicoloured.

3346	5p. Type **1007**	1·10	95
3347	5p. Sharpshooter bug	1·10	95
3348	5p. Milkweed bug	1·10	95
3349	5p. Spotted cucumber beetle	1·10	95
3350	5p. Green June beetle	1·10	95
3351	5p. Convergent ladybird beetle	1·10	95
3352	5p. Eastern hercules beetle	1·10	95
3353	5p. Harlequin cabbage bug	1·10	95
MS3354	Two sheets, each 99×19 mm. (a) Nos. 3346/9; (b) Nos. 3350/3	16·00	14·00

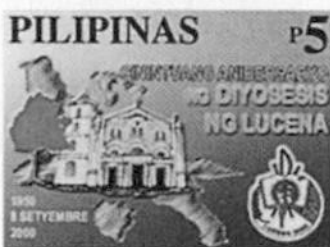

1008 St. Ferdinand Cathedral, Map and Emblem

2000. 50th Anniv of Lucena Diocese.

3355	**1008**	5p. multicoloured	1·30	1·10

1009 Nurses and Patients

2000. 50th Anniv of Occupational Health Nurses' Association.

3356	**1009**	5p. multicoloured	1·30	1·10

1010 Balanghai

2000. New Millennium (3rd series). Traditional Sea Craft. Multicoloured.

3357	5p. Type **1010**	1·30	1·10
3358	5p. Vinta	1·30	1·10
3359	5p. Caracoa	1·30	1·10

1011 Jars, Bank Note, Circuit Board, Computer Mouse and Emblem

2000. 50th Anniv of Equitable PCI Bank.

3360	**1011**	5p. multicoloured	1·30	1·10

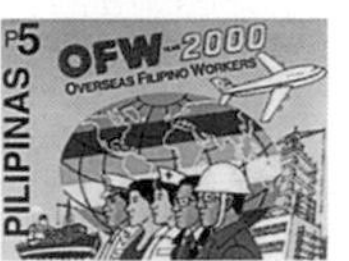

1012 Ship, Globe, Airplane and Workers

2000. Year of Overseas Filipino Workers.

3361	**1012**	5p. multicoloured	1·30	1·10

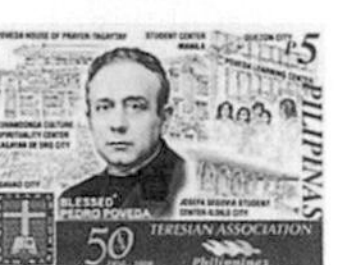

1013 Pedro Poveda (founder), Buildings and Emblem

2000. 50th Anniv of the Teresian Association (international lay preacher association) in the Philippines.

3362	**1013**	5p. multicoloured	1·30	1·10

1014 Congress in Session

2000. House of Representatives.

3363	**1014**	5p. multicoloured	1·30	1·10

1015 Soldiers, Tank and Emblem

2000. 50th Anniv of Philippine Marine Corps.

3364	**1015**	5p. multicoloured	1·30	1·10

1016 Running

2000. Olympic Games, Sydney. Multicoloured.

3365	5p. Type **1016**	1·30	1·10
3366	5p. Archery	1·30	1·10
3367	5p. Rifle shooting	1·30	1·10
3368	5p. Diving	1·30	1·10
MS3369	100×85 mm. 5p. Boxing (horiz); 5p. Show jumping (horiz); 5p. Rowing (horiz); 5p. Taekwondo (horiz)	7·00	6·50

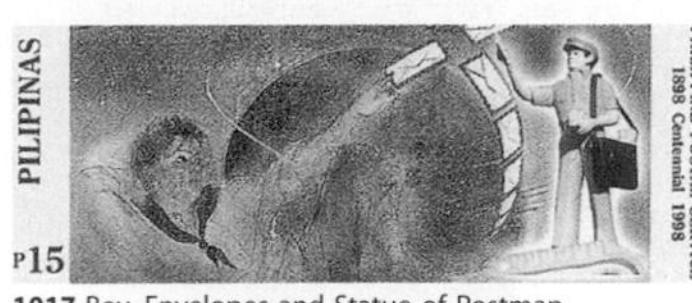

1017 Boy, Envelopes and Statue of Postman

2000. Postal Service. Sheet 100×60 mm.

MS3370	**1017**	15p. multicoloured	4·50	3·75

1018 B'laan Woman's Blouse, Davao del Sur

2000. "Sheer Realities: Clothing and Power in 19th-century Philippines" Exhibition, Manila. Multicoloured.

3371	5p. Type **1018**	1·30	1·10
3372	5p. T'boli T'nalak abaca cloth, South Cotabato	1·30	1·10
3373	5p. Kalinga/Gaddang cotton loincloth, Cordilleras (vert)	1·30	1·10
3374	5p. Portrait of Leticia Jimenez (anon) (vert)	1·30	1·10
MS3375	101×70 mm. 5p. Portrait of Teodora Devera Ygnacio (Justiniano Asuncion); 15p. Tawsug silk sash, Sulu Archipelago	5·75	5·25

1019 Angel cradling Sunflowers

2000. Christmas. Multicoloured.

3376	5p. Type **1019**	1·20	1·00
3377	5p. As No. 3376 but inscribed "CHRISTMAS JUBILEUM"	1·20	1·00
3378	11p. Angel with basket of fruit and swag of leaves	2·10	1·80
3379	13p. Angel with basket of fruit on shoulder	2·40	2·00
3380	15p. Angel with garland of flowers	2·75	2·30

1020 1955 5c. Labour Management Congress Stamp

2000. 50th Anniv of Amateur Philatelists Organization Philatelic Society. Multicoloured.

3381	5p. Type **1020**	1·20	1·00
3382	5p. 1957 5c. Juan Luna birth centenary stamp (horiz)	1·20	1·00
3383	5p. 1962 5c. orchid stamp	1·20	1·00
3384	5p. 1962 6 + 4c. Rizal Foundation Fund stamp (horiz)	1·20	1·00

2000. No. 1977 surch **P5.00.**

3385	5p on 3p.60 multicoloured	8·25	7·50

1022 "Portrait of an Unknown Lady" (Juan Novicio Luna)

2000. Modern Art. Multicoloured.

3386	5p. Type **1022**	1·20	1·00
3387	11p. "Nude" (Jose Joya) (horiz)	2·10	1·80
3388	13p. "Lotus Odalisque" (Rodolfo Paras-Perez) (horiz)	2·40	2·00
3389	15p. "Untitled (Nude)" (Fernando Amorsolo) (horiz)	2·75	2·30
MS3390	100×80 mm. 15p. "The Memorial" (Cesar Legaspi) (79×29 mm)	6·75	6·25

1023 Snake

2000. New Year. Year of the Snake. Multicoloured.

3391	5p. Type **1023**	1·50	1·30
3392	11p. Snake	3·00	2·50
MS3393	98×88 mm. Nos. 3391/2. Perf or imperf	9·00	8·25

1024 Ships in Port (Trade and Industry)

2000. New Millennium (4th series). Multicoloured.

3394	5p. Type **1024**	1·40	1·10
3395	5p. Pupils and teacher (Education and Knowledge)	1·40	1·10
3396	5p. Globe, satellite, family using computer and woman using telephone (Communications and Technology)	1·40	1·10

1025 Pesos Fuertes (1st Philippines Banknote)

2001. 150th Anniv of Philippines Bank.

3397	**1025**	5p. multicoloured	1·20	1·00

1026 Eagle

2001. "Hong Kong 2001" International Stamp Exhibition. Flora and Fauna. Multicoloured.

3398	5p. Type **1026**	1·20	1·00
3399	5p. Philippine tarsier	1·20	1·00
3400	5p. "Talisman Cove" (flower)	1·20	1·00
3401	5p. Turtle	1·20	1·00
3402	5p. Tamaraw	1·20	1·00
MS3403	Five sheets, each 80×71 mm. (a) 11p. As Type **1026**. (b) 11p. As No. 3399. (c) 11p. As No. 3400. (d) 11p. As No. 3401. (e) 11p. As No. 3402	20·00	19·00

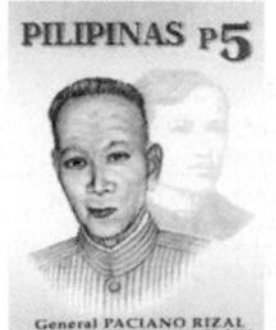

1027 Rizal

2001. 150th Birth Anniv of General Paciano Rizal.

3404	**1027**	5p. multicoloured	1·10	90

1028 Facade

2001. Centenary of San Beda College.

3405	**1028**	5p. multicoloured	1·10	90

1029 High Altar, St. Peter's Basilica, Rome

2001. 50th Anniv of Diplomatic Relations with Vatican City. Multicoloured.

3406	5p. Type **1029**	1·10	90
3407	15p. High altar, San Agustin Church, Manila	3·00	2·50
MS3408	90×71 mm. 15p. Adam; 15p. God	7·50	7·00

The two stamps in No. **MS**3408 form the composite design of "Creation of Adam" (Michaelangelo).

1030 Presidential Seal

2001. Multicoloured, background colour given.

3409	**1030**	5p. yellow	90	75
3410	**1030**	10p. green	2·10	1·80
3411	**1030**	11p. red	2·30	1·90
3412	**1030**	13p. black	2·75	2·40
3413	**1030**	15p. blue	3·25	2·75

1031 Our Lady of Manaoag

2001. 75th Anniv of Canonical Coronation of Our Lady of the Rosary of Manaoag.

3414	**1031**	5p. multicoloured	1·10	90

1032 Pres. Macapagal-Arroyo taking Presidential Oath

2001. President Gloria Macapagal-Arroyo. Multicoloured.

3415	5p. Type **1032**	1·10	90
3416	5p. Pres. Macapagal-Arroyo waving	1·10	90

1033 Sydney Opera House and Philippines Cultural Centre

2001. Philippine-Australia Diplomatic Relations. Multicoloured.

3417	5p. Type **1033**	1·10	90
3418	13p. As Type **1033** but with subjects transposed	2·75	2·40
MS3419	96×60 mm. 13p. Philippines Cultural Centre and Sydney Opera House (79×29 mm)	5·50	5·00

1034 Philippine Normal University

2001. University Centenaries. Multicoloured.

3420	5p. Type **1034**	1·10	90
3421	5p. Facade of Silliman University	1·10	90

1035 Scales of Justice and Court Building

2001. Centenary of Supreme Court.

3422	**1035**	5p. multicoloured	1·10	90

1036 Joaquin J. Ortega

2001. Anniversaries. Multicoloured.

3423	5p. Type **1036** (centenary of appointment as first Civil Governor of the Province of La Union)	1·10	90
3424	5p. Eugenio H. Lopez (businessman, birth centenary)	1·10	90

1037 Visayan Couple

2001. "PHILANIPPON '01" International Stamp Exhibition, Japan. Boxer Codex (manuscript depicting Philippine lifestyle during first century of Spanish contact). Multicoloured.

3425	5p. Type **1037**	1·20	1·00
3426	5p. Tagalog couple	1·20	1·00
3427	5p. Moros of Luzon (man wearing red tunic)	1·20	1·00
3428	5p. Moros of Luzon (woman wearing blue dress)	1·20	1·00
MS3429	82×107 mm. 5p. Tattooed Pintados; 5p. Pintados wearing costumes; 5p. Cagayan woman; 5p. Zambal	4·75	4·50

1038 Teachers and Thomas (transport)

2001. Centenary of Arrival of American Teachers. Multicoloured.

3430	5p. Type **1038**	1·20	1·00
3431	15p. Pupils and school building	3·25	2·75

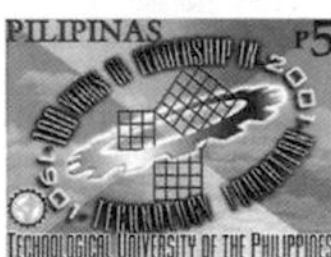

1039 Emblem

2001. Centenary of Technology University, Manila.

3432	**1039**	5p. multicoloured	1·20	1·00

1040 Museum Artefacts

2001. Centenary of National Museum.

3433	**1040**	5p. multicoloured	1·20	1·00

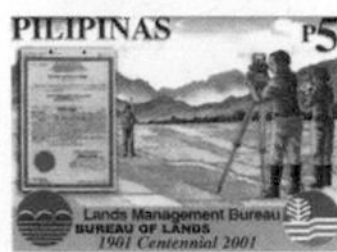

1041 1901 Lands Management Charter, Modern Surveyors and Emblems

2001. Centenary of Lands Management Bureau.

3434	**1041**	5p. multicoloured	1·20	1·00

1042 Statue of St. Joseph and Seminary Building

2001. 400th Anniv of San Jose Seminary.

3435	**1042**	5p. multicoloured	1·20	1·00

1043 Makati City Financial District

2001

3436	**1043**	5p. multicoloured	1·20	1·00

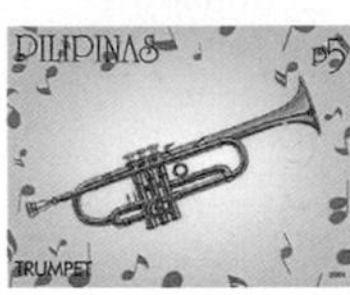

1044 Trumpet

2001. Musical Instruments. Multicoloured.

3437	5p. Type **1044**	1·20	1·00
3438	5p. Tuba	1·20	1·00
3439	5p. French horn	1·20	1·00
3440	5p. Trombone	1·20	1·00
MS3441	81×106 mm. VERT:—5p. ×4 Bass drum; Clarinet and oboe; Xylophone; Sousaphone	5·50	5·00

1045 Off Shore Production Platform

2001. Malampaya Deep Water Gas to Power Project. Multicoloured.

3442	5p. Type **1045**	1·20	1·00
3443	15p. As No. 3442 but with gold border	3·25	2·75

1046 Two Stylized Figures

2001. International Year of Volunteers.

3444	**1046**	5p. multicoloured	1·20	1·00

1047 Children surrounding globe

2001. United Nations Year of Dialogue among Civilizations.

3445	**1047**	15p. multicoloured	3·75	3·25

1048 Girls and Singers ("Herald Angels")

2001. Christmas. Multicoloured.

3446	5p. Type **1048**	1·20	1·00
3447	11p. Boy and Christmas baubles ("Kumukutikutitap")	2·30	1·90
3448	13p. Children and lanterns ("Pasko ni Bitoy")	2·50	2·10
3449	15p. Children blowing trumpets ("Pasko na naman")	3·25	2·75

1049 William Tell Monument

2001. 150th Anniv of Philippines–Switzerland Diplomatic Relations. Multicoloured.

3450	5p. Type **1049**	1·20	1·00
3451	15p. Jose P. Rizal Monument	3·25	2·75
MS3452	98×62 mm. 15p. Mayon volcano and Matterhorn (horiz) (80×30 mm)	4·75	4·50

1050 St. George and Dragon

2001. Centenary of Solicitor General's Office.

3453	**1050** 5p. multicoloured	1·20	1·00

1051 "Puj" (Antonio Austria)

2001. National Stamp Collecting Month. Art. Multicoloured.

3454	5p. Type **1051**	1·20	1·00
3455	17p. "Hesus Nazereno" (Angelito Antonio)	3·50	3·00
3456	21p. "Three Women with Basket" (Anita Magsaysay-Ho) (vert)	4·25	3·50
3457	22p. "Church with Yellow background" (Mauro Santos)	4·50	3·75
MS3458	102×74 mm. 22p. "Komedya ng Pakil" (Danilo Dalena) (80×30 mm)	4·75	4·50

1052 Couple (woman wearing brown apron)

2001. Inhabitants of Manila drawn by Jean Mallet. Multicoloured.

3462	5p. Couple in riding dress	1·20	1·00
3468	17p. Type **1052**	3·50	3·00
3469	21p. Couple (woman wearing blue apron)	4·25	3·50
3470	22p. Couple using pestles and mortar	4·50	3·75

1053 Red Horse

2001. New Year. Year of the Horse. Multicoloured.

3471	5p. Type **1053**	1·20	1·00
3472	17p. White horse	3·50	3·00
MS3473	100×89 mm. As Nos. 3471/2 plus 2 labels	7·50	7·00

No. **MS**3473 also exists imperforate.

1054 "Sanctification in Ordinary Life" (Godofredo F. Zapanta)

2002. Birth Centenary of Josemaria Escriva de Balaguer (founder of Opus Dei religious order).

3474	**1054** 5p. multicoloured	1·20	1·00

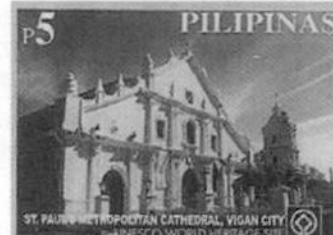

1055 St. Paul's Metropolitan Cathedral

2002. UNESCO World Heritage Sites, Vigan City, Ilocos Sur Province. Multicoloured.

3475	5p. Type **1055**	1·20	1·00
3476	22p. Calee Crisologo	4·50	4·00

1056 Salvador Araneta

2002. Birth Centenary of Salvador Araneta (nationalist politician and philanthropist).

3477	**1056** 5p. multicoloured	1·20	1·00

1057 "Manila Customs" (painting, Auguste Nicolas Vaillant)

2002. Centenary of Customs Bureau.

3478	**1057** 5p. multicoloured	1·20	1·00

1058 Envelope and "I Love You"

2002. St. Valentine's Day. Multicoloured.

3479	5p. Type **1058**	1·20	1·00
3480	5p. Couple enclosed in heart	1·20	1·00
3481	5p. Cat and dog	1·20	1·00
3482	5p. Air balloon	1·20	1·00

1059 "Image of the Resurrection" (detail, Fernando Amorsolo) and Hospital Façade

2002. Centenary of Baguio General Hospital and Medical Centre.

3483	**1059** 5p. multicoloured	1·20	1·00

1060 Pedro Calungsod

2002. 330th Death Anniv of Pedro Calungsod. Multicoloured.

3484	5p. Type **1060**	1·20	1·00
MS3485	102×72 mm. 22p. Pedro Calungsod holding crucifix. Imperf	4·50	3·75

1061 Virgin and Child (painting) and School Façade

2002. Centenary of Negros Occidental High School.

3486	**1061** 5p. multicoloured	1·20	1·00

1062 College Facade

2002. Centenary of La Consolacion College, Manila.

3487	**1062** 5p. multicoloured	1·20	1·00

1063 Stupa, Buddha and Lotus Blossom

2002. Vesak Day.

3488	**1063** 5p. multicoloured	1·20	1·00

1064 Gloria Macapagal-Arroyo (2001–)

2002. Presidential Office (2nd series). With blue barcode at foot. Multicoloured.

3489	5p. Type **1064**	1·20	1·00
3490	5p. Joseph Ejercito Estrada (1998–2000)	1·20	1·00
3491	5p. Fidel V. Ramos (1992–98)	1·20	1·00
3492	5p. Corazon C. Aquino (1986–92)	1·20	1·00
3493	5p. Ferdinand E. Marcos (1965–86)	1·20	1·00
3494	5p. Diosdado Macapagal (1961–65)	1·20	1·00
3495	5p. Carlos P. Garcia (1957–61)	1·20	1·00
3496	5p. Ramon Magsaysay (1953–57)	1·20	1·00
3497	5p. Elpidio Quirino (1948–1953)	1·20	1·00
3498	5p. Manuel Roxas (1946–1948)	1·20	1·00

1065 National Flag and School Façade

2002. Centenary of Cavite National High School.

3499	**1065** 5p. multicoloured	1·20	1·00

1066 Emblem and Cathedral Façade

2002. Centenary Iglesia Filipina Independiente (religious movement).

3500	**1066** 5p. multicoloured	1·20	1·00

1067 Fish

2002. Marine Conservation. Multicoloured.

3501	5p. Type **1067**	1·20	1·00
3502	5p. Fish laid head to head	1·20	1·00
3503	5p. Edge of mangrove swamp	1·20	1·00
3504	5p. Hands holding minnows	1·20	1·00
MS3505	90×77 mm. 5p. ×4, Man using binoculars from catamaran (no fishing); Mangrove swamp (reforestation of mangroves); Divers (reef monitoring); Rows of seaweed (seaweed farming)	4·75	4·50

No. **MS**3505 has a brief description of each stamp in the lower margin.

1068 Edge of Mangrove Swamp

2002. Philakorea 2002 International Stamp Exhibition, Seoul. Two sheets, each 97×86 mm containing T **1068** and similar vert design. Multicoloured.

MS3506	(a) 5p. Type **1068**; 17p. As No. 3488 (b) As No. **MS**3506a but with gold horizontal band	5·50	5·00

2002. No. 2476 optd **3p.**

3507	3p. on 60s. multicoloured	1·10	90

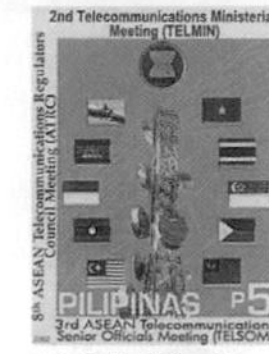

1070 Participating Countries' Flags surrounding Communication Mast

2002. TELMIN, TELSOM and ATRC Telecommunications Meetings held in Manila.

3508	**1070** 5p. multicoloured	1·20	1·00

1071 Kapitan Moy Building and Giant Shoe

2002. Shoe Manufacture in Marikina City.

3509	**1071** 5p. multicoloured	1·20	1·00

1072 Gerardo de Leon

2002. National Stamp Collecting Month. Multicoloured.

3510	5p. Type **1072** (filmmaker)	1·20	1·00
3511	17p. Francisca Reyes Aquino (folk dance researcher)	3·50	3·00
3512	21p. Pablo Antonio (architect)	4·00	3·25
3513	22p. Jose Garcia Villa (writer)	4·50	3·75
MS3514	100×74 mm. 22p. Honorata de la Rama (singer and actress) Imperf	4·75	4·50

1073 Kutsinta (rice cakes)

2002. Christmas. Multicoloured.

3515	5p. Type **1073**	1·20	1·00
3516	17p. Sapin-sapin (multilayered cake)	3·50	3·00
3517	21p. Bibingka (rice and coconut cake)	4·00	3·25
3518	22p. Puto bumbong (cylindrical rice cakes)	4·50	3·75

1074 Dove, Family and Crucifix

2002. Fourth World Meeting of Families (papal initiative), Manila (1st issue).

3519	**1074** 11p. multicoloured	2·50	2·10

See also No. 3528.

3674	6p. Logwood (vert)	1·20	1·00
3675	6p. Kamuning Binangonan octagonal pot Bantolinao (vert)	1·20	1·00
MS3676	146×95 mm. 6p.×4, Lemonsito; Bougainvillea on stand; Bougainvillea in flower; Kalyos	6·25	5·75

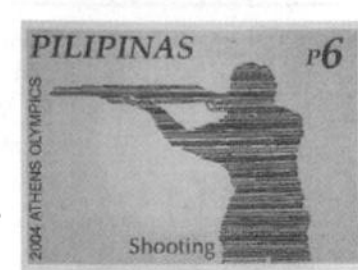

1129 Rifle Shooting

2004. Olympic Games, Athens. Multicoloured.

3677	6p. Type **1129**	1·20	1·00
3678	17p. Taekwondo	3·25	2·75
3679	21p. Swimming	4·00	3·50
3680	22p. Archery	4·25	3·75
MS3681	60×61 mm. 22p. Boxing	5·00	4·50

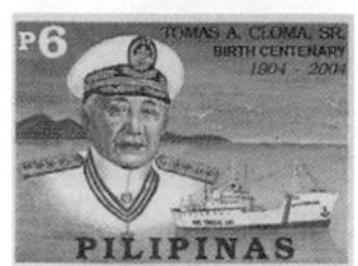

1130 Tomas Cloma

2004. Birth Centenary of Tomas Cloma (maritime educationalist).

3682	**1130**	6p. multicoloured	1·20	1·00

1131 "Sandugo" (Carlos Francisco)

2004. 600th Birth Anniv of Miguel Lopez De Legazpi (first Governor General of Philippines).

3683	**1131**	6p. multicoloured	1·20	1·00

1132 Rat

2004. Lunar New Year. Multicoloured.

3684	6p. Type **1132**	1·20	1·00
3685	6p. Ox	1·20	1·00
3686	6p. Tiger	1·20	1·00
3687	6p. Pig	1·20	1·00
3688	6p. Rabbit	1·20	1·00
3689	6p. Dog	1·20	1·00
3690	6p. Dragon	1·20	1·00
3691	6p. Rooster	1·20	1·00
3692	6p. Snake	1·20	1·00
3693	6p. Monkey	1·20	1·00
3694	6p. Goat	1·20	1·00
3695	6p. Horse	1·20	1·00

1133 Building Facade

2004. Centenary of Manila University.

3696	**1133**	6p. multicoloured	1·20	1·00

1134 Decorated Tree

2004. Christmas. Decorated trees. Multicoloured.

3697	6p. Type **1134**	1·20	1·00
3698	17p. With red ribbons and bells	3·25	2·75
3699	21p. With poinsettia flowers	4·00	3·50
3700	22p. With white stems	4·25	3·75

1135 Intamuros, Manila

2004. Centenary of Filipino—Chinese Chamber of Commerce. Multicoloured.

3701	6p. Type **1135**	1·20	1·00
3702	6p. Great Wall, China	1·20	1·00

Nos. 3701/2 were issued together, se-tenant, forming a composite design.

1136 People enclosed in Rice Grain (Maria Enna T. Alegre)

2004. International Year of Rice. Winning Entries in Design a Stamp Competition. Multicoloured.

3703	6p. Type **1136**	1·20	1·00
3704	6p. Woman, rice and family (Lady Fatima Velasco)	1·20	1·00
3705	6p. Boy amongst plants (Gary Manalo)	1·20	1·00
3706	6p. Dove, rice stalk and family (Michael Villadolid)	1·20	1·00
3707	6p. Rice grains (Ljian Delgado)	1·20	1·00
3708	6p. Doves and man cradling rice plant (Sean Pajaron)	1·20	1·00

1137 19th-century Facade

2004. 400th Anniv of San Augustin Church. Multicoloured.

3709	6p. Type **1137**	1·20	1·00
3710	6p. Modern facade	1·20	1·00

1138 Lapu-Lapu (Francisco Coching)

2004. Stamp Collecting Month. Comics. Multicoloured.

3711	6p. Type **1138**	1·20	1·00
3712	6p. El Vibora (Frederico Javinal)	1·20	1·00
3713	6p. Kulafu (Francisco Reyes) (horiz)	1·20	1·00
3714	6p. Darna (Nestor Redondo) (horiz)	1·20	1·00
MS3715	68×95 mm. 22p. Darna (Mats Revelo) (30×80 mm)	5·75	5·25

1139 Rooster

2004. New Year. Year of the Rooster. Multicoloured.

3716	6p. Type **1139**	1·20	1·00
3717	17p. Rooster (different)	3·25	2·75
MS3718	138×80 mm. Nos. 3416/17 each×2	8·25	7·75

1140 *Otus megalottis nigrorum*

2004. Owls. Multicoloured.

3719	6p. Type **1140**	1·70	1·40
3720	6p. *Ninox philippensis centralis*	1·70	1·40
3721	6p. *Mimizuku gurneyi*	1·70	1·40
3722	6p. *Bubo philippensis*	1·70	1·40

1141 Chapel and North Academy Cluster Building

2005. 50th Anniv of Liceo de Cagayan University.

3723	**1141**	6p. multicoloured	1·20	1·00

1142 Baguio Country Club, 1930

2005. Centenary of Baguio Country Club. Multicoloured.

3724	6p. Type **1142**	1·20	1·00
3725	6p. Modern building facade	1·20	1·00

1143 Christ, Manila Skyline and Emblem

2005. Centenary of the Seventh Day Adventists' Church in the Philippines.

3726	**1143**	6p. multicoloured	1·20	1·00

1144 *Arisbe decolour stratos*

2005. Butterflies. Multicoloured.

3727	1p. Type **1144**	25	15
3728c	2p. *Arthopala anthelus impar* (with all over pale pink ground)	25	15
3729	3p. *Zophoessa dataensis nihirai*	50	30
3730	4p. *Liphyra brassolis justini*	65	45
3731	5p. *Parantica danatti*	35	20
3732	6p. *Hebomoia* (inscr "Hebe-moia") *glaucippe philippensis*	50	30
3733	6p. *Moduza urdaneta*	65	45
3734	6p. *Lexias satrapes hiwaga*	75	65
3735	6p. *Cherita orpheus*	85	70
3736	6p. *Achillides chikae*	85	70
3737	6p. *Arisbe ideaoides* (inscr "ideaoiedes")	85	70
3738	6p. *Delias schoenigi hermeli*	85	70
3739	6p. *Achillides palinurus daedalus*	85	70
3740	6p. *Delias levicki justini*	85	70
3741	6p. *Troides magellanus*	85	70
3742	7p. *Hebomoia* (inscr "Hebe-moia") *glaucippe philippensis*	85	70
3743	7p. *Moduza urdaneta*	85	70
3744	7p. *Lexias satrapes hiwaga*	85	70
3745	7p. *Cherita orpheus*	90	80
3746	7p. *Achillides chikae*	90	80
3747	7p. *Arisbe ideaoides* (inscr "ideaoiedes")	90	80
3748	7p. *Delias schoenigi hermeli*	90	80
3749	7p. *Achillides palinurus daedalus*	90	80
3750	7p. *Delias levicki justini*	90	80
3751	7p. *Troides magellanus*	90	80
3755	7p. *Cherita orpheus* (with all over white ground)	90	80
3756	7p. *Achillides chikae* (with all over white ground)	90	80
3757	7p. *Arisbe ideaoides* (inscr "ideaoiedes") (with all over white ground)	90	80
3759	7p. *Achillides palinurus daedalus* (with all over white ground and microprint)	90	80
3762	9p. *Lexias satrapes amiana*	1·20	1·00
3763	10p. *Tanaecia aruna pallida*	1·30	1·10
3764	17p. *Idea electra*	90	80
3765	17p. *Charaxes bajula adoracion*	90	80
3766	17p. *Tanaecia calliphorus*	90	80
3767	17p. *Trogonoptera trojana*	90	80
3768	20p. *Idea electra electra*	2·30	2·00
3769	20p. *Charaxes bajula adoracion*	2·30	2·00
3770	20p. *Tanaecia calliphorus calliphorus*	2·30	2·00
3771	20p. *Trogonoptera trojana*	2·30	2·00
3772	21p. *Cethosia biblis barangingi*	90	80
3772b	21p. *Menelaides* (inscr "Me-nalaides") *polytes ledebouria*	90	80
3772c	21p. *Appias nero palawanica*	90	80
3772d	21p. *Udara tyotaroi*	90	80
3773	22p. *Parantica noeli*	90	80
3773b	22p. *Chilasa osmana osmana*	90	80
3773c	22p. *Graphium sandawanum joreli*	90	80
3773d	22p. *Papilio xuthus benguetanus*	90	80
3774	24p. *Cethosia biblis baranginigi*	90	80
3774b	24p. *Menalaides polytes ledebouria*	1·20	1·00
3774c	24p. *Appias nero palawanica*	1·30	1·10
3774d	24p. *Trogonoptera trojana*	2·20	1·80
3775	26p. *Udara tyotaroi*	2·20	1·80
3775b	26p. *Chilasa osmana osmana*	2·20	1·80
3775c	26p. *Graphium sandawanum joreli*	2·20	1·80
3775d	26p. *Papilio xuthus benguetanus*	2·30	2·00
3776	30p. *Appias nero domitia*	2·30	2·00
3778	100p. *Cepora Aspasia olga*	2·30	2·00

1145 *Chlamys senatoria*

2005. Shells (1st issue). Multicoloured.

3780	6p. Type **1145**	1·20	1·00
3781	6p. *Siphonofusus vicdani*	1·20	1·00
3782	6p. *Epitonium scalare*	1·20	1·00
3783	6p. *Harpa harpa*	1·20	1·00
3784	6p. *Chicoreus saulii*	1·20	1·00
3785	6p. *Spondylus varians*	1·20	1·00
3786	6p. *Spondylus linquaefelis*	1·20	1·00
3787	6p. *Melo broderipii*	1·20	1·00
MS3788	131×86 mm. 6p.×4, *Siliquaria armata*; *Argonauta argo*; *Perotrochus vicdani*; *Corculum cardissa*	5·00	4·25

See also Nos. 3803/**MS**3811.

1146 Presidents Gloria Macapagal-Arroyo and Hu Jintao

2005. 30th Anniv of Philippines—China Diplomatic Relations. State Visit of President Hu Jintao of People's Republic of China. Multicoloured.

3789	6p. Type **1146**	1·00	85
3790	17p. As No. 3789 but design reversed	2·75	2·00
MS3791	79×108 mm. Nos. 3789/90	4·75	4·00

1147 Ernesto dela Cruz Ancestral House

2005. Historic Houses. Multicoloured.

3792	6p. Type **1147**	1·00	85
3793	6p. Limjoco residence	1·00	85
3794	6p. Pelaez ancestral house	1·00	85
3795	6p. Vergara house	1·00	85
MS3796	94×102 mm. 6p.×4, Gliceria Marella Villavicencio; Lasala-Guarin house; Claparols house; Ilagan ancestral house	4·25	3·50

1148 University Church, Iloilo

2005. Centenary of Central Philippine University.

3797	**1148**	6p. multicoloured	1·20	1·00

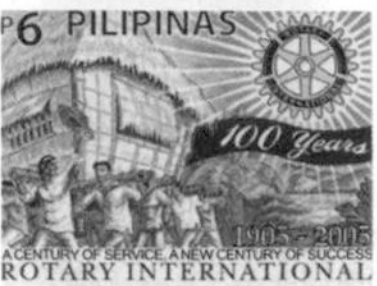

1149 Men carrying House (Bayanihan)

2005. Centenary of Rotary International. Multicoloured.

3798	6p. Type **1149**	85	70
3799	22p. As No. 3798 but design reversed	3·25	2·75
MS3800	100×144 mm. No. 3798×6 and 3799×2	11·50	10·00

1150 Pope John Paul II

2005. Pope John Paul II Commemoration.

3801	6p. Type **1150**	85	70
3802	22p. Leaning on staff	3·25	2·75

2005. Shells (2nd issue). As T **1145**. Multicoloured.

3803	6p. *Cochlostyla imperator* (vert)	1·00	85
3804	6p. *Helicostyla turbinoides* (vert)	1·00	85
3805	6p. *Helicostyla lignaria* (vert)	1·00	85
3806	6p. *Amphidromus dubius* (vert)	1·00	85
3807	6p. *Chrysallis fischeri* (vert)	1·00	85
3808	6p. *Helicostyla bicolorata* (vert)	1·00	85
3809	6p. *Helicostyla dobiosa* (vert)	1·00	85
3810	6p. *Helicostyla portei* (vert)	1·00	85
MS3811	131×86 mm. 6p.×4, *Cochlostyla depressa; Cochlostyla sarcinosa; Calocochliaschadenbergi; Helicostyla pulcherrina*	6·75	5·75

1151 Blas Ople

2005. Second Death Anniv of Blas Ople (journalist and politician).

3812	**1151** 6p. multicoloured	1·00	85

1152 San Bartolome Parish Church

2005. 400th Anniv of San Bartolome Parish, Magalang.

3813	**1152** 6p. multicoloured	1·00	85

1153 "Celebrating the Eucharist with Mary" (Carlos Vincent H. Ruiz)

2005. International Year of the Eucharist. Winning Designs in Painting Competition. Designs on the theme "Celebrating the Eucharist with Mary", artist names given. Multicoloured.

3814	6p. Type **1153**	1·00	85
3815	6p. Rommer A. Fajardo	1·00	85
3816	6p. Telly Farolan-Somara	1·00	85
3817	6p. Allen A. Moran	1·00	85
3819	6p. Elouiza Athena Tentativa	1·00	85
3820	6p. Jianina Marishka C. Montealto	1·00	85
MS3821	114×190 mm. Nos. 3814/20	7·50	6·50

2005. Tenth Anniv of Filipinas Stamp Collectors Club. No. **MS**2041 surch **15p FILIPINAS STAMP COLLECTORS CLUB 10TH YEAR 1995–2006**. Imperf.

MS3822	15p. on 8p. multicoloured	4·75	4·00

1155 Children, Flame and Dove (Rojohn Daniel R. Olivar)

2005. 60th Anniv of United Nations. International Year of Sports' Education. Winning Designs in Children's Painting Competition (3823/5) or Millennium Development Goals (3826). Multicoloured.

3823	6p. Type **1155**	1·00	85
3824	6p. As No. 3823 but with dove and emblem at left	1·00	85
3825	6p. Dove and open book (Sarahbeth B. Almeiro)	1·00	85
3826	10p. Emblem	1·00	85
MS3827	Two sheets, each 110×78 mm. (a) Nos. 3823, 3825/6. (b) Nos. 3824/6	5·00	4·25

1156 Building Facade

2005. Centenary of Bureau of Correction.

3828	**1156** 6p. multicoloured	1·00	85

1157 Pres. Macapagal-Arroyo taking Oath

2005. Inauguration of President Gloria Macapagal-Arroyo. Multicoloured.

3829	6p. Type **1157**	85	70
3830	22p. Giving inaugural speech	3·25	2·75

1158 Church, Pony and Trap

2005. Christmas. Multicoloured.

3831	6p. Type **1158**	85	70
3832	6p. The Nativity enclosed in rock	2·30	2·00
3833	6p. Joseph leading donkey carrying Mary	3·00	2·50
3834	6p. Thatched buildings and Three Kings	3·25	2·75

1159 Boxing

2005. 23rd South East Asian Games. Designs showing Gilas (games mascot) as athlete. Multicoloured.

3835	6p. Type **1159**	1·00	85
3836	6p. Cycling	1·00	85
3837	6p. Wushu (martial art)	1·00	85
3838	6p. Bowling	1·00	85
3839	6p. Badminton	1·00	85
3840	6p. Billiards	1·00	85
MS3841	102×111 mm. 5p. Arnis (hand, foot and stick fighting) (horiz); 6p. Chess (horiz); 6p. Dragonboat (horiz)	3·25	2·75
MS3842	111×102 mm. 5p. Shooting; 6p. Archery; 6p. Equestrian sports	3·25	2·75

1160 "The Fourth Horseman" (Tequi)

2005. Stamp Collecting Month. Print Makers. Multicoloured.

3843	6p. Type **1160**	1·00	85
3844	6p. "Bulbs" (M. Parial)	1·00	85
3845	6p. "Breaking Ground" (R. Olazo)	1·00	85
3846	6p. "Pinoy Worker Abr'd" (Ben Cab)	1·00	85
MS3847	99×68 mm. 22p. "Form XV" (Brenda Fajardo) (80×30 mm)	4·25	4·00

1161 Shih Tzu

2005. New Year. Year of the Dog. Multicoloured.

3848	6p. Type **1161**	85	70
3849	17p. German shepherd	2·50	2·10
MS3850	138×81 mm. Nos. 3848/9, each×2	6·75	6·50

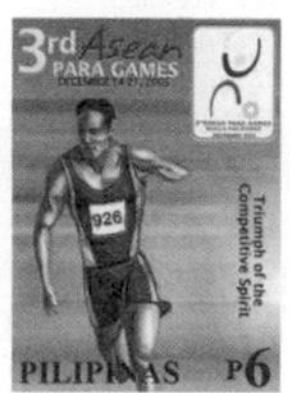

1162 Amputee Runner

2005. Third ASEAN Para Games. Multicoloured.

3851	6p. Type **1162**	1·00	85
3852	17p. Wheelchair racer	3·00	2·50

1163 Cape Santiago Lighthouse, Calatagan

2005. Lighthouses. Multicoloured.

3853	6p. Type **1163**	1·00	85
3854	6p. Bagacay, Liloan	1·00	85
3855	6p. Malabrigo, Lobo	1·00	85
3856	6p. Capones, San Antonio	1·00	85
MS3857	141×85 mm. 6p.×4, Tubbataha, Cagayancillo; Cape Bojeador, Burgos; Cape Bolinao, Bolinao; San Fernando Point, San Fernando	5·00	4·50

See also Nos. 3875/**MS**3879.

1164 College Building

2006. Centenary of St. Scholastica's College.

3858	**1164** 6p. multicoloured	1·00	85

1165 Working in Fields (Allen A. Moran)

2006. Centenary of Filipinos in Hawaii. Winning Designs in Painting Competition. Multicoloured.

3859	6p. Type **1165**	85	70
3860	22p. Skyline, people, globe and flags (Cristanto S. Umali)	3·25	2·75
MS3861	90×85 mm. Nos. 3859/60	3·75	3·25

1166 Original Building and Rebecca Parish (founder)

2006. Centenary of Mary Johnston Hospital. Multicoloured.

3862	6p. Type **1166**	1·00	85
3863	6p. Surgery and modern building	1·00	85

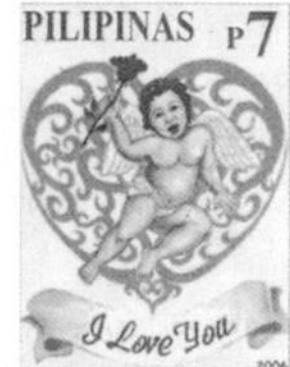

1167 Cupid

2006. St. Valentine's Day. Multicoloured.

3864	7p. Type **1167**	1·00	85
3865	7p. Cupid holding envelope	1·00	85

1168 Archbishop Sin

2006. Cardinal Jaime Lachica Sin (Archbishop of Manila) Commemoration. Multicoloured.

3866	22p. Type **1168**	1·00	85
3867	22p. Seated	3·00	2·50
MS3868	142×86 mm. Nos. 3866/7	8·25	7·75

2006. First Death Anniv of Pope John Paul II. Sheet 75×91 mm. No. **MS**1648 surch **26p.**

MS3869	26p. on 7p.50 multicoloured	5·25	5·00

No. **MS**3869 was additionally inscribed for the anniversary in the margins.

1170 *Lepidochelys olivacea*

2006. Turtles. Multicoloured.

3870	7p. Type **1170**	1·20	1·00
3871	7p. *Eretmochelys imbricate*	1·20	1·00
3872	7p. *Caretta caretta*	1·20	1·00
3873	7p. *Dermochelys coriacea*	1·20	1·00
MS3874	100×70 mm. 26p *Chelonia mydas* (80×30 mm)	4·75	4·25

Nos. 3870/3 were issued together, *se-tenant*, forming a composite design.

2006. Lighthouses. As T **1163**. Multicoloured.

3875	7p. Bugui Point Lighthouse, Aroroy, Masbate	1·20	1·00
3876	7p. Capul Island, Samar del Norte	1·20	1·00
3877	7p. Corregidor Island, Cavite	1·20	1·00
3878	7p. Rio Del Pasig, Manila	1·20	1·00
MS3879	141×85 mm. 7p.×4, Engano Cape, Cagayan Province; Cabra Point, Lubang; Melville Cape, Balabac Island; Gintotolo Island, Balud	5·00	5·00

1171 Badges

2006. 50th Anniv of Xavier School. Multicoloured.

3880	7p. Type **1171**	1·20	1·00
3881	7p. School façade	1·20	1·00
3882	7p. Paul Hsu Kuangchi (first Christian convert)	1·20	1·00
3883	7p. St. Francis Xavier (500th birth anniv)	1·20	1·00

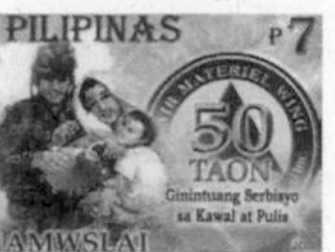

1172 Soldier, Wife, Child and Piggy Bank

2006. 50th Anniv of Air Material Wing Savings and Loan Association (AMWSLAI) (Military and Police Association). Multicoloured.

3884	7p. Type **1172**	1·00	85
3885	7p. Headquarters	1·00	85

2006. 60th Anniv of Philippines—United Kingdom Diplomatic Relations. No. 1853 surch **60 Years of RP–UK Relations 1946–2006 20p**.

3886	26p. on 7p.20 multicoloured	3·75	3·50

1174 Family and George Willmann (first Philippine director)

2006. Centenary (2005) of Knights Of Columbus (charitable organization).

3887	**1174**	7p. multicoloured	1·00	85

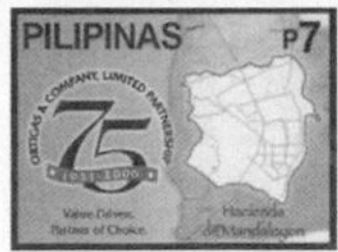

1175 Anniversary Emblem and Map

2006. 75th Anniv of Ortigas & Company. Multicoloured.

3888	7p. Type **1175**	1·00	85
3889	26p. Headquarters and emblem	3·25	2·75
MS3890	180×80 mm. Nos. 3888/9, each×2	8·25	7·75

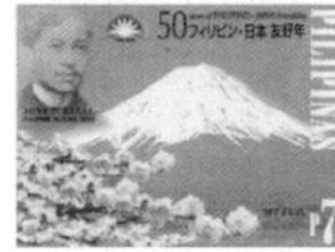

1176 Jose Rizal, Snow-covered Mount Fuji and Blossom

2006. 50th Anniv of Philippines—Japan Diplomatic Relations. Multicoloured.

3891	7p. Type **1176**	1·00	85
3892	20p. J. Rizal, smoking Mount Fuji and blossom	2·75	2·40
MS3893	178×80 mm. Nos. 3891/2, each×2	7·75	7·00

1177 Roque Ablan, Flag and Coastline

2006. Birth Centenary of Roque B. Ablan (guerrilla leader and war hero).

3894	**1177**	7p. multicoloured	1·00	85

2006. Tenth Anniv of Quezon Philatelic Society. No. 1980 surch and optd **7p.00 Anniversary Quezon Philatelic Society 1996–2006**.

3895	7p. on 1p.20 multicoloured	1·00	85

1179 Emblem

2006. Centenary of Chan-Chu Association. Multicoloured.

3896	7p. Type **1179**	1·00	85
3897	7p. Seated figure	1·00	85

1180 Inscr "Himalayan Cat"

2006. Cats. Multicoloured. Phosphorescent markings.

3898	7p. Type **1180**	1·00	85
3899	7p. Maine Coon	1·00	85
3900	7p. Red point Siamese	1·00	85
3901	7p. Persian	1·00	85
3902	7p. Japanese bobtail	1·00	85
3903	7p. Ragdoll	1·00	85
3904	7p. Egyptian mau	1·00	85
3905	7p. Abyssinian	1·00	85

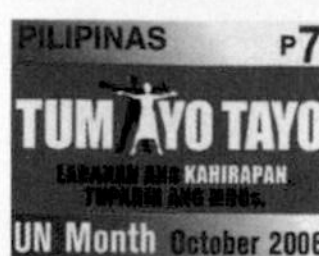

1181 "TUMAYO TAYO"

2006. United Nations Month. Multicoloured.

3906	7p. Type **1181**	85	70
3907	26p. "STAND UP"	3·25	2·75

1182 Manila Post Office in Ruins

2006. 110th (2008) Anniv of Philippine Post. Multicoloured.

3908	7p. Type **1182**	1·00	85
3909	7p. Modern Central Post Office	1·00	85

Nos. 3908/9 were issued in horizontal *se-tenant* pairs with the sheet.

1183 Lower Slopes

2006. First Philippine Ascent of Mount Everest. Multicoloured.

3910	7p. Type **1183**	85	70
3911	20p. Team members	2·50	2·10
3912	26p. Summit	3·25	2·75
MS3913	130×90 mm. 7p. As No. 3912; 7p. As No. 3910; 10p. As No. 3911	3·75	3·50

1184 Manila Cathedral

2006. Christmas. Multicoloured.

3914	7p. Type **1184**	1·00	85
3915	20p. St. Augustine Church, Paoay	2·75	2·40
3916	24p. Church of Santo Tomas de Villanueva, Miagao	3·25	2·75
3917	26p. Barasoain Church	3·75	3·00

1185 Pig

2006. New Year. Year of the Pig. Multicoloured.

3918	7p. Type **1185**	85	70
3919	20p. Pig facing left	2·50	2·10

1186 Jackfruit

2006. Fruit. Multicoloured.

3920	7p. Type **1186**	85	70
3921	7p. Lanzones	85	70
3922	7p. Coconut	85	70
3923	7p. Bananas	85	70

1187 Graciano Lopez Jaena

2006. Birth Centenary of Graciano Lopez Jaena (journalist and reformer).

3924	**1187**	7p. multicoloured	1·00	85

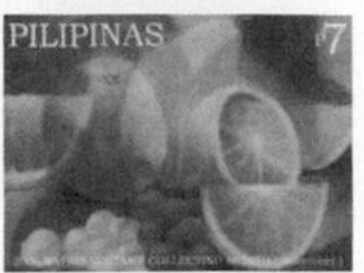

1188 Oranges and Grapes

2006. Stamp Collecting Month (November). Pastel Paintings. Multicoloured.

3925	7p. Type **1188**	1·00	85
3926	7p. Coconut and melon	1·00	85
3927	7p. Fish and vegetables	1·00	85
3928	7p. Mother and child (vert)	1·00	85
MS3929	50×100 mm. 26p. Roses (50×80 mm)	3·75	3·50

1189 Fort

2007. 250th Anniv of Ozamiz Cotta.

3930	**1189**	7p. multicoloured	1·00	85

1190 University Facade

2007. Centenary of Centro Escolar University.

3931	**1190**	7p. multicoloured	1·00	85

1191 Flag Pole and School Building

2007. Centenary of National School for the Deaf.

3932	**1191**	7p. multicoloured	1·00	85

1192 Emblem

2007. Centenary of Manulife.

3933	**1192**	7p. multicoloured	1·00	85

1193 Puente de Isabel II, Cavite

2007. Bridges. Multicoloured.

3934	7p. Type **1193**	1·00	85
3935	7p. Puente Dampol Dupax, Nueva Viscaya	1·00	85
3936	7p. Puente de Barit Laoag, Ilocos Norte	1·00	85
3937	7p. Puente de Blanco Bimondo, Manila	1·00	85

1194 *Medinilla magnifica*

2007. Flowers. Multicoloured.

3938	7p. Type **1194**	85	70
3939	7p. *Strongylodon elmeri*	85	70
3940	7p. *Amyema imcarnatiflora*	85	70
3941	7p. *Dillenia monatha*	85	70
3942	7p. *Xanthostemon fruticosus*	85	70
3943	7p. *Plumiera acuminate*	85	70
3944	7p. *Paphiopedilum adductum*	85	70
3945	7p. *Rafflesia manillana*	85	70
MS3946	134×60 mm. 26p. *Rafflesia manillana* (120×30 mm)	3·75	3·50

1195 Symbols of France

2007. 60th Anniv of Philippines–France Diplomatic Relations. Multicoloured.

3947	7p. Type **1195**	85	70
3948	26p. Symbols of Philippines	3·25	2·75
MS3949	52×92 mm. 26p. Symbols of France and Philippines (30×80 mm)	3·75	3·50

1196 Inscr 'Diana'

2007. Fish. Multicoloured.

3950	7p. Type **1196**	85	70
3951	7p. Giant trevally	85	70
3952	7p. Skipjack tuna	85	70
3953	7p. Yellowfin tuna	85	70
MS3954	134×56 mm. 7p. Cuttlefish 20p. Bigfin reef squid (80×30 mm)	3·75	3·50

Nos. 3950/3 were issued together, se-tenant, forming a composite background design.

1197 Emblems

2007. Centenary of Scouting. Multicoloured.

3955	7p. Type **1197**	85	70
3956	7p. Hand and flag	85	70

1198 Tufted Duck

2007. Ducks. Multicoloured.

3957	7p. Type **1198**	1·00	85
3958	7p. Cotton pygmy goose	1·00	85
3959	7p. Mallard	1·00	85
3960	7p. Green-winged teal	1·00	85
3961	7p. Northern pintail	1·00	85
3962	7p. Common shelduck	1·00	85
3963	7p. Northern shoveler	1·00	85
3964	7p. Greater scaup	1·00	85

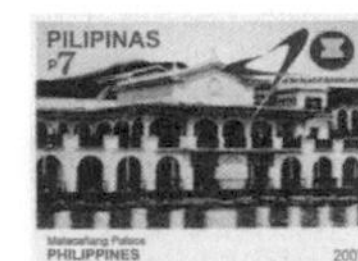

1199 Malacanang Palace, Manila

2007. Architecture. 40th Anniv of ASEAN (Association of South-east Asian Nations). Multicoloured.

3965	7p. Type **1199**	1·00	85
3966	20p. Secretariat Building, Bandar Seri Begawan, Brunei Darusslam	2·75	2·30
3967	20p. National Museum, Cambodia	2·75	2·30
3968	20p. Fatahillah Museum, Jakarta	2·75	2·30
3969	20p. Traditional house, Laos	2·75	2·30
3970	20p. Railway Headquarters Building, Malaysia	2·75	2·30
3971	20p. Yangon Post Office, Union of Myanmar	2·75	2·30
3972	20p. As Type **1199**	2·75	2·30
3973	20p. National Museum, Singapore	2·75	2·30
3974	20p. Vimanmek Mansion, Bangkok, Thailand	2·75	2·30
3975	20p. Presidential Palace, Hanoi, Vietnam	2·75	2·30
MS3976	102×59 mm 20p. Malacanang Palace, Manila (80×30 mm)	4·00	3·75

Stamps of a similar design were issued by all member countries.

1200 Ramon Magsaysay

2007. Birth Centenary of Ramon del Fierro Magsaysay (president from 1953–7).

3977	**1200**	7p. multicoloured	85	70

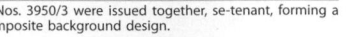

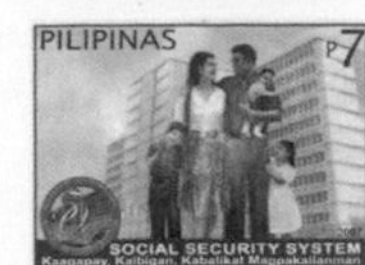

1201 Family

2007. 50th Anniv of Social Security. Multicoloured.

3978	7p. Type **1201**	85	70
3979	7p. President Magsaysay	85	70
3980	7p. President signing Social Security Act	85	70
3981	7p. Social Security building	85	70

No. 3982/3 and Type **1202** have been left for 'Centenary of First Assembly', issued on 16 October 2007, not yet received.

1203 *La Bulakena*

2007. 150th Birth Anniv of Juna Luna (artist). Multicoloured.

3984	7p. Type **1203**	1·00	85

Nos. 3985/7 have been left for stamps not yet received. See also Nos. **MS**4058 and **MS**4703.

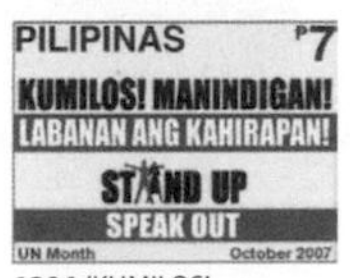

1204 'KUMILOS! MANINDIGAN'

2007. United Nations Month. Multicoloured.

3988	7p. Type **1204**	1·00	85
3989	26p. STAND UP	3·25	2·75

1205 Asian Fairy Bluebird

2007. Birds. Multicoloured.

3990	1p. Black-naped oriole	35	30
3991	2p. Type **1205**	35	30
3992	3p. Writhed hornbill	50	45
3993	4p. Crimson sunbird	60	50
3994	5p. Brown shrike (P 13½×14) (11.1.2010) (inscr '2009C')	65	55
3995	7p. Mindanao bleeding heart pigeon	85	70
3995b	7p. Nicobar pigeon	1·00	85
3995c	7p. Black chinned fruit dove	1·20	1·00
3995d	7p. Metallic pigeon	1·30	1·10
3995e	7p. Pink necked green pigeon	2·30	2·00
3995f	7p. Amethyst brown dove	2·75	2·40
3995g	7p. Grey Imperial pigeon	3·00	2·50
3995h	7p. Red turtle dove	5·75	5·00
3995i	7p. Pied Imperial pigeon	11·50	10·00
3995j	7p. Spotted Imperial pigeon	35	30
3996	8p. Hoopoe	1·20	1·00
3997	9p. Short eared owl	35	30
4017	9p. Crested serpent eagle	1·20	1·00
3998	10p. Blue winged pitta	35	30
3999	20p. Dwarf kingfisher	1·20	1·00
3999b	20p. Blue capped wood kingfisher	35	30
3999c	20p. White throated kingfisher	15	10
3999d	20p. White collared kingfisher	35	30
4000	24p. Inscr 'Green faced parrot finch'	40	35
4019	24p. Philippine Eagle Owl	3·25	2·75
4019b	24p. Luzon Scops Owl	3·25	2·75
4019c	24p. Philippine Scops Owl	3·25	2·75
4019d	24p. Spotted Wood Owl	3·25	2·75
4000b	24p. Java sparrow	50	45
4000c	24p. Yellow breasted bunting	65	55
4000d	24p. White cheeked bullfinch	85	70
4001	26p. Great billed parrot	1·00	85
4001b	26p. Philippine cockatoo	1·20	1·00
4001c	26p. Blue naped parrot	1·30	1·10
4001d	26p. Blue backed parrot	3·25	2·75
4037	26p. Philippine tailorbird	3·50	3·00
4037b	26p. Mountain tailorbird	3·50	3·00
4037c	26p. Black-headed tailorbird	3·50	3·00
4037d	26p. Ashy tailorbird (2009) (inscr '2009B')	3·50	3·00
4002	50p. Philippine eagle (29×39 mm)	6·75	5·75
4050a	50p. Grey-headed fish eagle	6·75	5·75
4021	100p. Philippine hawk eagle	13·50	11·50

Nos. 4022/50 have been left for possible additions to this series.

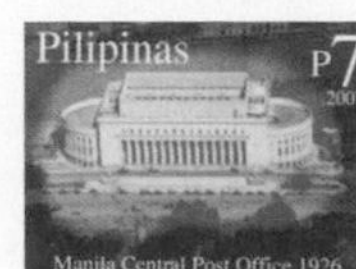

1206 Manila Central Post Office (1926)

2007. 110th (2008) Anniv of National Postal Service. Multicoloured.

4051	7p. Type **1206**	85	70
4052	20p. Manila Post Office and Juan Marcos de Guzman Arellano (architect) (80×30 mm)	85	70

1207 San Diego de Alcala Cathedral

2007. 425th Anniv of San Diego de Alcala Parish.

4053	**1207** 7p. multicoloured	85	70

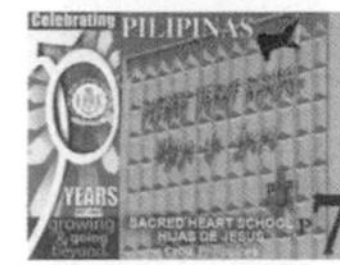

1208 Emblem and School Building Façade

2007. 50th Anniv of Sacred Heart School—Hijas de Jesus. Multicoloured.

4054	7p. Type **1208**	85	70
4055	7p. Statue and building	85	70
4056	7p. Mother Superior Eloisa Alonso and arms	85	70
4057	7p. Building and entrance	85	70

2007. National Stamp Collecting Month. 150th Birth Anniv of Juan Luna (2nd issue). Sheet 100×100 mm containing multicoloured designs as T **1203**.

MS4058	7p.×4, *Picnic in Normandy* (59×39 mm) (imperf); *El Violinista*; *Indio Bravo*; *Old Man with Pipe*	3·25	2·75

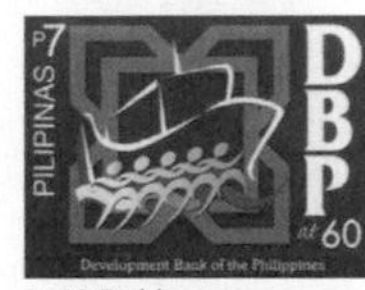

1209 Emblem

2007. 60th Anniv of Development Bank of the Philippines. Multicoloured.

4059	7p. Type **1209**	85	70
4060	7p. Street corner building facade	85	70
4061	7p. Multi-storey building and trees	85	70
4062	7p. Six storey building	85	70

1210 Rat

2007. New Year. Year of the Rat. Multicoloured.

4063	7p. Type **1210**	85	70
4064	20p. Rat seated	2·30	2·00
MS4065	139×80 mm. Nos. 4063/4, each×2	7·00	6·75

1211 Pres. Ramon Magsaysay and Rev. Bob Pierce (World Vision founder)

2007. 50th Anniv of World Vision. Multicoloured.

4066	7p. Type **1211**	85	70
4067	20p. 50	2·30	2·00

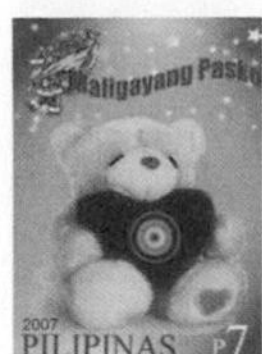

1212 Teddy

2007. Christmas. Toys. Multicoloured.

4068	7p. Type **1212**	85	70
4069	20p. Train	2·30	2·00
4070	24p. Quad bike	3·00	2·50
4071	26p. Angel doll	3·25	2·75

2007. 25th Anniv of Cebu Philatelic Society. No. 1981 surch **p7.00**and optd **Cebu Philatelic Society 25th Anniversary 1982–2007**.

4072	7p. on 2p.40 multicoloured	1·00	85

(1213)

2007. 150th Birth Anniv of Juan Luna (3rd issue). Sheet 125×100 mm containing horiz designs as T **1203**. Multicoloured, background colour given.

MS4073	7p.×4, *Parisian Life* (73×48 mm) (imperf); *Parisian Life* (green); *Parisian Life* (red); *Parisian Life* (cerise)	3·25	2·75

1214 St. Dominic de Guzman

2008. 50th Anniv of Dominican School, Manila. Multicoloured.

4074	7p. Type **1214**	85	70
4075	7p. School campus	85	70
4076	7p. School and anniversary emblems	85	70
4077	7p. School building	85	70

1215 Heart filled with Roses

2008. St. Valentine's Day. Multicoloured.

4078	7p. Type **1215**	85	70
4079	7p. Cupid and hearts	85	70

1216 St. Therese, Alfredo Maria Obviar and Anniversary Emblem

2008. 50th Anniv of Missionary Catechists of St. Therese of the Infant Jesus. Multicoloured.

4080	7p. Type **1216**	85	70
4081	7p. MCST emblem	85	70

1217 *Batomys granti* (Luzon furry-tailed rat)

2008. Rats and Mice of Luzon Island. Multicoloured.

4082	7p. Type **1217**	85	70
4083	7p. *Chrotomys whiteheadi* (Luzon striped earth rat)	85	70
4084	7p. *Apomys datae* (Cordillera forest mouse)	85	70
4085	7p. *Archboldomys* (Cordillera shrew mouse)	85	70
MS4086	115×85 mm. 7p. *Phloeomys pallidus* (northern giant cloud rat); 7p. *Carpomys phaeurus* (lesser dwarf cloud rat); 20p. *Crateromys schadenbergi* (bushy-tailed cloud rat) (40×70 mm). Imperf)	4·25	4·00

2008. Taipei 2008–International Stamp Exhibition. Sheet 130×155 mm containing vert stamps as Type **1205**. Multicoloured.

MS4087	7p.×10, As Nos. 3995a/4004a but without microprinting; 7p. Philippine eagle perched; 7p. As No. 4017a but without microprinting; 7p. Java sparrow; 7p. Blue-capped wood kingfisher	13·50	13·00

No. **MS**4087 was on sale for 125p.

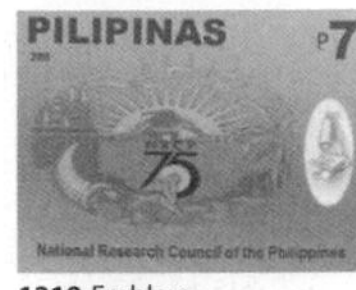

1218 Emblem

2008. 75th Anniv of National Research Council.

4088	**1218** 7p. multicoloured	85	70

1219 Tents

2008. Centenary of Teachers' Camp, Baguio. Multicoloured.

4089	7p. Type **1219**	85	70
4090	7p. Teachers	85	70

1220 Gasan Bridge, Marinduque

2008. American Colonial Bridges. Multicoloured.

4091	7p. Type **1220**	85	70
4092	7p. Hinigaran Bridge, Negros Occidental	85	70
4093	7p. Wahig Bridge, Dagohoy, Bohol	85	70
4094	7p. Pan-ay Bridge, Capiz	85	70
MS4095	170×60 mm. 7p.×4, Quezon Bridge, Quiapo, Manila; Governor Reynolds Bridge, Guinobatan, Albay; Mauca Railway Bridge, Ragay, Camarines Sur; Balucuan Bridge, Dao, Capiz	4·00	3·50

1221 Manny Pacquiao

2008. Emmanuel 'Pacman' Pacquiao (champion boxer). Sheet 100×100 mm containing T **1221** and similar vert designs showing Manny Pacquiao. Multicoloured.

MS4096	7p.×4, Type **1221**; Wearing robe; Wearing champion's belt; Looking right	3·25	3·00

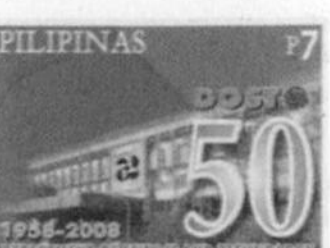

1222 Building Facade

2008. 50th Anniv Department of Science and Technology (4097) or 50th Anniv of Nuclear Research Institute (4098). Multicoloured.

4097	7p. Type **1222**	85	70
4098	7p. Institute building	85	70

1224 Tai Bei Kong (Most Honored Ancestor)

2008. Centenary of Liong Tek Go Family Association. Multicoloured.

4099	7p. Type **1224**	85	70
4100	7p. Anniversary emblem	85	70

Type **1223** is vacant.

1225 University Seal

2008. Centenary of University of the Philippines. Multicoloured. (a) Size 21×25 mm.

4101	7p. Type **1225**	85	70
4102	7p. *Carillion* (Juan Nakpil)	85	70
4103	7p. *Oblation* (statue) (Guillermo Tolentino)	85	70
4104	7p. Centenary emblem	85	70

(b) Size 40×30 mm.

4105	7p. As No. 4102	85	70
4106	7p. As No. 4104	85	70
4107	7p. As Type **1225**	85	70
4108	7p. As No. 4103	85	70
MS4109	181×75 mm. 7p.×4, As Nos. 4105/8	3·25	2·75

1226 Fr. Andres de Urdaneta and Monument

2008. 500th Birth Anniv of Fr. Andres (Fray) de Urdaneta. Spanish-Philippine Friendship Day.

4110	**1226** 7p. multicoloured	85	70

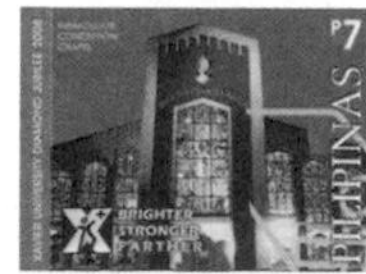

1227 Immaculate Conception Chapel

2008. 75th Anniv of Xavier University, Ateneo de Cagayan. Multicoloured.

4111	7p. Type **1227**	85	70
4112	7p. St. Francis Xavier (statue)	85	70
4113	7p. Archbishop T. G. Hayes	85	70
4114	7p. Science centre	85	70

1228 College Building

2008. 60th Anniv of Ateneo de Davao University. Multicoloured

4115	7p. Type **1228**	85	70
4116	7p. High School Building	85	70
4117	7p. Preschool and Grade School Building	85	70
4118	7p. *Assumption* (stained glass)	85	70
MS4119	181×75 mm. 7p.×4, As Nos. 4115/18	3·25	2·75

Nos. 4115/18 were printed, *se-tenant*, in blocks of four stamps within the sheet.

The stamps of No. **MS**4119 are arranged in two vertical pairs separated by a large central gutter.

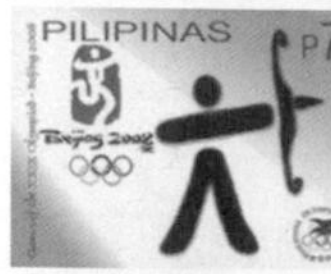

1229 Archery

2008. Olympic Games, Beijing. Designs showing stylized athletes. Multicoloured.

4120	7p. Type **1229**	85	70
4121	20p. Taekwondo	2·50	2·10
4122	24p. Equestrian	3·00	2·50
4123	26p. Weight lifting	3·25	2·75

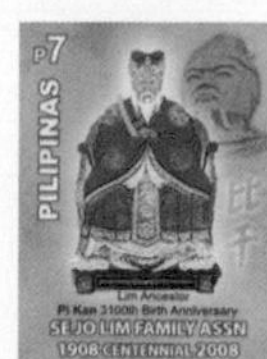

1230 Pi Kan (Great Ancestor)

2008. Centenary of Se Jo Tong Lim Family Association. T **1230** and similar horiz designs. Multicoloured

4124	7p. Type **1230**	85	70
4125	7p. Gen. Vicente Lim (WW II Hero) and Senator Roseller Lim	85	70
4126	7p. Binondo Church and Chinese Gate	85	70
4127	7p. Se Jo Tong emblem over symbolic Philippine flag	85	70
MS4128	181×75 mm. 7p.×4, As Nos. 4124/7. Imperf between vertical pairs	3·25	2·75

1231 *Pemphis acidula*

2008. 35th Anniv of Philippine Bonsai Association. Multicoloured.

4129	7p. Type **1231**	85	70
4130	7p. *Ficus microcarpa*	85	70
4131	7p. *Serissa foetida*	85	70
4132	7p. *Pemphis acidula* with wide shallow pot	85	70
4133	7p. *Pemphis acidula* leaning to lower left with deep pot	85	70
4134	7p. *Triphasia trifolia*	85	70
4135	7p. *Pemphis acidula* leaning left with wide pot	85	70
4136	7p. *Bougainville*	85	70
4137	7p. *Murraya* (vert)	85	70
4138	7p. *Pemphis acidula* short upright growth, one large and one smaller branches (vert)	85	70
4139	7p. *Pemphis acidula* single branch on thick bare stem (vert)	85	70
4140	7p. *Pemphis acidula* short twisted growth, single stem with wide base (vert)	85	70
4141	7p. *Pemphis acidula*, two branches, wide base in shallow tray (vert)	85	70
4142	7p. *Antidesma bunius* (vert)	85	70
4143	7p. *Maba buxifolia* (vert)	85	70
4144	7p. *Ficus concina* (vert)	85	70
MS4145	181×75 mm. 7p.×4, *Lagerstroemia indica*; *Pemphis acidula* hexagonal pot and stand; *Vitex*; *Ixora chinensis*	3·25	2·75

2008. Jakarta 2008–International Stamp Exhibition. Sheet 140×175 mm containing vert stamps as Type **1205**. Multicoloured.

MS4146	7p. Brahminy kite; 7p. Olive-backed sunbird; 7p. Purple-throated sunbird; 7p. Metallic-winged sunbird; 7p. Grey-headed fish eagle; 7p. Plain-throated sunbird; 7p. Lina's sunbird; 7p. Apo sunbird; 7p. Copper-throated sunbird; 7p. Flaming sunbird; 7p. Grey-hooded sunbird; 7p. Lovely sunbird; 7p. Crested serpent eagle; 7p. Philippine hawk eagle; 7p. Blue-crowned racquet tail; 7p. Philippine eagle owl; 7p. Common flameback	17·00	16·00

No. **MS**4087 was on sale for 150p.

1232 Ban Ki-moon

2008. Visit of United Nations Secretary General Ban Ki-moon. Multicoloured.

4147	7p. Type **1232**	85	70
4148	26p. Ban Ki-moon with President Gloria Macapagal	3·25	2·75

1233 Boracay Beach, Aklan

2008. 110th Anniv of Postal Service. Tourism. Multicoloured.

4149	7p. Type **1233**	85	70
4150	7p. Intramuros, Manila	85	70
4151	7p. Banaue Rice Terraces, Mountain Province	85	70
4152	7p. Mayon Volcano, Bicol	85	70
4153	20p. Puerto Princesa Underground River, Palawan	2·50	2·10
4154	24p. Chocolate Hills, Bohol	3·00	2·50
4155	26p. Tuddataila Reef, Palawan	3·25	2·75

1234 Mother and Child

2008. Christmas–Mother and Child. Multicoloured.

4156	7p. Type **1234**	85	70
4157	20p. Mother and child (facing left)	2·50	2·10
4158	24p. Mother and child holding dove	3·00	2·50
4159	26p. Mother carrying child in sling	3·25	2·75
MS4160	118×95 mm 7p. Virgin and Child; 26p. Mother and child	4·00	3·50

1235 Joaquin Bordado

2008. National Stamp collecting Month. Comics. T **1235** and similar vert designs showing comic book heroes created by Carlo J. Caparas (Magno Jose J. Caparas). Multicoloured.

4161	7p. Type **1235**	85	70
4162	20p. Totoy Bato	85	70
4163	24p. Gagambino	85	70
4164	26p. Pieta	85	70
MS4165	89×79 mm 7p. Ang Panday; 20p. Panday	3·25	2·75

1236 Benigno Aquino Jr.

2008. 25th Death Anniv of Benigno S. Aquino Jr. (senator, governor of Tarlac and opposition leader to Pres. Ferdinand Marcos. He was assassinated at Manila International Airport). Multicoloured.

4166	7p. Type **1236**	85	70
4167	26p. Pen and ink portrait	2·50	2·10

1237 Fernando Bautista

2008. Birth Centenary of Fernando Bautista (founder of University of Baguio).

4168	**1237** 7p. multicoloured	85	70

1238 Ox

2008. Chinese New Year. Year of the Ox. Multicoloured.

4169	7p. Type **1238**	85	70
4170	80p. Ox facing left	2·50	2·10
MS4171	139×80 mm. Nos. 4169/70, each×2	8·25	7·75

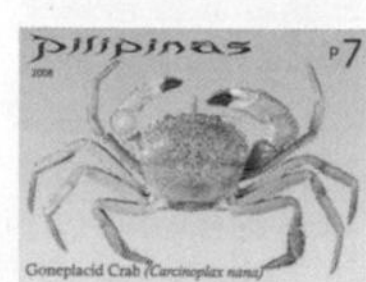

1239 *Carinoplax nana*

2008. Crabs. Multicoloured.

4172	7p. Type **1239**	85	70
4173	7p. *Cyrtomaia largoi*	85	70
4174	7p. *Hirsutodynomene vespertilio*	85	70
4175	7p. *Dicranodromia danielae*	85	70
MS4176	170×110 mm 20p. *Oxypleurodon stimpson*; 20p. *Cyrtomaia ericina*	6·75	6·50

1240 Manuel S. Enverga

2009. Birth Centenary Manuel Sarmiento Enverga (founder Manuel S. Enverga University Foundation, Lucena City).

4177	**1240** 7p. multicoloured	85	70

1241 Envelope of Hearts

2009. St. Valentine's Day. Multicoloured.

4178	7p. Type **1241**	85	70
4179	7p. Heart and roses	85	70

1242 'SINING BISWAL' (Visual Arts)

2009. International Arts Festival. Multicoloured.

4180	7p. Type **1242**	85	70
4181	7p. Masks (drama and poetry)	85	70
4182	7p. Dancer (music and dance)	85	70
4183	7p. Building and film credits (architecture and cinema)	85	70

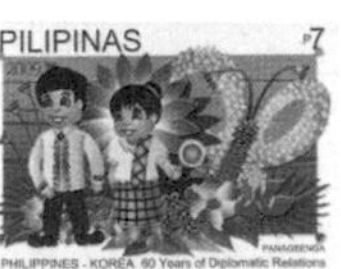

1243 Panagbenga Flower Festival, Philippines

2009. 60th Anniv of Philippines–South Korea Diplomatic Relations. Multicoloured.

4184	7p. Type **1243**	85	70
4185	7p. Hangawi Sonori (cow play), Korea	85	70

1244 Quartz

2009. Minerals. Multicoloured.

4186	7p. Type **1244**	85	70
4187	7p. Rhodochrisite	85	70
4188	7p. Malachite	85	70
4189	7p. Nickel	85	70
MS4190	136×80 mm 7p.×4, Cinnabar; Gold; Copper; Magnetite	4·25	4·00

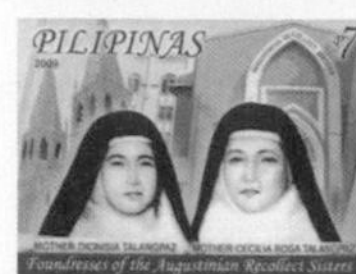

1245 Mother Dionisia Talangpaz and Mother Cecilia Rosa Talangpaz

2009. Augustinian Recollect Sisters.

4191	**1245**	7p. multicoloured	85	70

1246 King's Theatre

2009. Architectural Heritage. Art Deco Theatres and Cinemas. Sheet 100×102 mm containing T **1246** and similar horiz designs. Multicoloured.

4192	7p. Type **1246**	85	70
4193	7p. Capitol Theatre	85	70
4194	7p. Joy Theatre	85	70
4195	7p Scala Theatre	85	70
MS4196	7p.×4, Life Theatre; Times Theatre; Bellevue Theatre; Pines Theatre	3·25	2·75

1247 Rodolfo Cornejo

2009. Birth Centenary of Rodolfo S. Cornejo (musician and composer).

4197	**1247**	7p. multicoloured	85	70

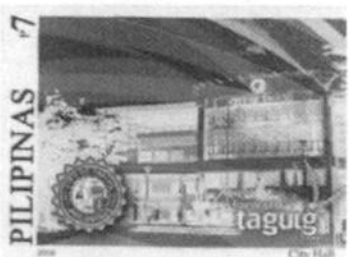

1248 City Hall

2009. Taguig–Global City. Multicoloured.

4198	7p. Type **1248**	85	70
4199	7p. Global City	85	70
4200	7p. St. Ana Church	85	70
4201	7p. Blue Mosque	85	70

1249 Tinikling, Philippine Folk Dance

2009. 60th Anniv of Philippines–Thailand Diplomatic Relations. Multicoloured.

4202	7p. Type **1249**	85	70
4203	7p. Ten Krathop Sark, Thailand Folk Dance	85	70

1250 Anniversary Emblem

2009. 150th Anniv of Ateneo de Manila University. Multicoloured

4204	7p. Type **1250**	85	70
4205	7p. Blue Eagle	85	70
4206	7p. Ignatius de Loyola	85	70
4207	7p. Dr. Jose Rizal	85	70
MS4208	192×101 mm. 7p.×4, As Nos. 4204/7	†	†

1251 Early Church

2009. 400th Anniv of Baler. Multicoloured.

4209	7p. Type **1251**	85	70
4210	7p. New Church	85	70

1252 Chua Tiong (Ancestor)

2009. Centenary of Che Yong Cua and Chua Family Association (1st issue). Multicoloured.

4211	7p. Type **1252**	85	70
4212	7p. Chua Siok To (Grand Ancestor)	85	70
MS4213	167×89 mm. 7p.×4, As Nos. 4124/7,each ×2. Imperf between horizontal pair	3·25	2·75

1253 Pheepoy

2009. Postal Corporation Mascot.

4214	**1253**	7p. multicoloured	85	70

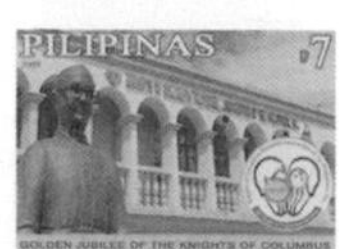

1254 George J. Willmann (founder)

2009. 50th Anniv of Knights of Columbus Fraternal Association of the Philippines.

4215	**1254**	7p. multicoloured	85	70
4216	**1254**	9p. multicoloured	1·20	1·00

1255 President Gloria Macapagal-Arroyo and Sultan Haji Hassanal Bolkiah of Brunei

2009. Philippines–Brunei Agricultural Cooperation.

4217	**1255**	7p. multicoloured	85	70

1256 Bamban Bridge, Philippines

1257 Marcelo B. Fernan Bridge, Cebu, Philippines

1258 Cavenagh Bridge, Singapore

1259 Henderson Waves and Alexandra Arch, Singapore

2009. 40th Anniv of Diplomatic Relations between Singapore and the Philippines. Bridges.

4218	**1256**	7p. multicoloured	85	70
4219	**1257**	7p. multicoloured	85	70
4220	**1258**	7p. multicoloured	85	70
4221	**1259**	7p. multicoloured	85	70

Stamps of a similar designs were issued by Singapore.

1260 Hand, Emblem and Mansion House

2009. Centenary of Baguio City. Multicoloured.

4222	7p. Type **1260**	85	70
4223	7p. Emblem and Mines View Park	85	70
4224	7p. Emblem, photographs and Baguio Cathedral	85	70
4225	7p. Emblem and Kennon Road	85	70
MS4226	100×100 mm. As Nos. 4222/5	3·25	2·75

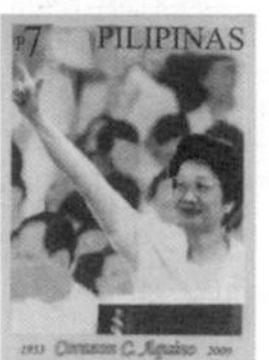

1261 Cory Aquino

2009. María Corazón (Cory) Sumúlong Cojuangco Aquino (president 1986–1992) Commemoration. Multicoloured.

4227	7p. Type **1261**	85	70
4228	7p. Facing right	85	70

1262 Pina Barong and Dress

2008. International Year of Natural Fibres. Multicoloured.

4229	7p. Type **1262**	85	70
4230	7p. Abaca bag and hats	85	70
4231	7p. Bank notes made from Abaca	85	70
4232	7p. Abaca rope	85	70

2009. María Corazón (Cory) Sumúlong Cojuangco Aquino (president 1986–1992) Commemoration. As T **1261**. Multicoloured.

4233	7p. As Type **1261**	85	70
4234	7p. Facing right	85	70

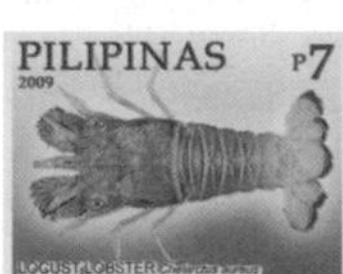

1263 *Chelarctus aureus*

2009. Lobsters. Multicoloured.

4235	7p. Type **1263**	85	70
4236	7p. *Polycheles coccifer*	85	70
4237	7p. *Metanephrops australiensis*	85	70
4238	7p. *Remiarctus bertholdii*	85	70
MS4239	136×80 mm. 7p.×4, *Metanephrops neptunus; Ibacus ciliatus; Petrarchus brevicomis; Puerulus angulatus*	3·25	2·75

1264 President Manuel L. Quezon and Philippine Flag

2009. 70th Anniv of Quezon City. Multicoloured.

4240	7p. Type **1264**	85	70
4241	7p. Quezon City Hall	85	70
4242	7p. Araneta Center	85	70
4243	7p. Eastwood City	85	70
MS4244	136×80 mm. 7p.×4, Nos. 4240/3	3·25	2·75

2009. Centenary of Che Yong Cua and Chua Family Association (2nd issue). As T **1252**.

4245	7p. As Type **1252**	85	70
4246	7p. Cua Lo (Ancestor)	85	70
MS4247	167×89 mm. 7p.×4, As Nos. 4245/6,each ×2. Imperf between horizontal pair	3·25	2·75

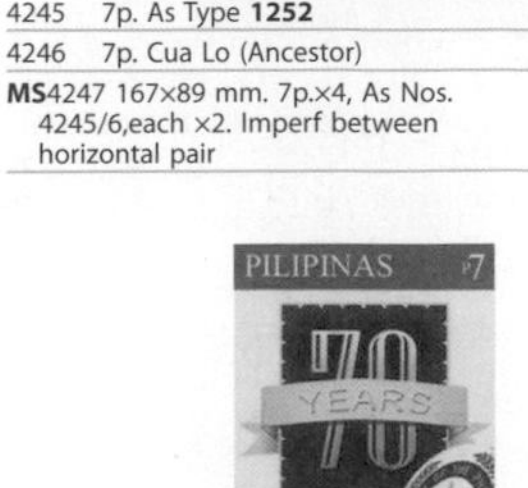

1265 70th Anniversary Emblem

2009. 70th Anniv of University of the Philippines Alpha Phi Beta. Multicoloured.

4248	7p. Type **1265**	85	70
4249	7p. Quezon Hall	85	70
4250	7p. Malcolm Hall (UP College of Law)	85	70
4251	7p. Founder members	85	70

1266 Tumbang Preso

2009. Stamp Colllecting Month. Children's Games. Multicoloured.

4252	7p. Type **1266**	85	70
4253	7p. Luksong Tinik	85	70
4254	7p. Holen	85	70
4255	7p. Sungka	85	70
MS4256	128×102 mm. 7p.×6, Taguan (30×40 mm); Sipa (30×40 mm); Saranggola (30×40 mm); Bangkang papel (30×40 mm); Paluan ng palayok (48×38 mm); Luksong lubid (48×38 mm)	5·00	4·75

1267 Children Caroling

2009. Christmas. Multicoloured.

4257	7p. Type **1267**	85	70
4258	7p. The Nativity	85	70
4259	7p. Three Kings	85	70
4260	7p. Angels	85	70
4261	7p. Christmas decorations	85	70

1268 Cecilia Munoz Palma

2009. Cecilia Munoz Palma (first woman Supreme Court Associate Justice) Commemoration.

4262	**1268**	7p. multicoloured	85	70

1269 Whale Shark (*Rhincodon typus*)

2009. 60th Anniv of Philippines–India Diplomatic Relations. Endangered Marine Life. Multicoloured.

4263	7p. Type **1269**	85	70
4264	7p. Gangetic dolphin (*Platanista gangetica*)	85	70
MS4265	100×80 mm. 7p. As No. 4264; 20p. As Type **1269**	3·25	2·75

1270 Tiger

2009. Chinese New Year. Year of the Tiger. Multicoloured.

4266	7p. Type **1270**	30	30
4267	20p. Tiger facing left	30	30
MS4268	138×81 mm. 7p. As Type **1270**×2; 20p. As No. 4267×2	6·75	6·50

1271 *Hypselodoris apolegma*

2009. Marine Biodiversity. Nudibranchs. Multicoloured.

4269	7p. Type **1271**	85	70
4270	7p. *Glossodoris colemani*	85	70
4271	7p. *Chromodoris sp.*	85	70
4272	7p. *Chromodoris elisabethina*	85	70
MS4273	168×87 mm. 7p.×6, *Jorunna funebris; Chromodoris lochi; Noumea alboannulata ; Chromodoris hintuanesis; Risbechi tryoni; Chromodoris leopardus*	5·00	4·75

1272 Greek Goddess of Flight

2009. 65th Anniv of International Civil Aviation Organization (ICAO). Multicoloured.

4274	7p. Type **1272**	85	70
MS4275	82×106 mm. 7p.×4, As Type **1272**, top left; As Type **1272**, top right; As Type **1272**, bottom left; As Type **1272**, bottom right;	3·25	2·75

1273 Return Ceremony and Seals of Philippines and USA

2009. 50th Anniv of Return of Olongapo to the Philippines. Multicoloured.

4276	7p. Type **1273**	85	70
4277	7p. Parade of Philippine and USA Flags and seals	85	70

2009. Postal Corporation Mascot (Pheepoy).

4278	7p. As Type **1253**	85	70

1274 PCSO Building and Presidents Manuel L. Quezon and Gloria Macapagal Arroyo

2008. 75th Anniv of Charity Sweepstakes Office. Multicoloured.

4279	7p. Type **1274**	85	70
4280	7p. PCSO Building	85	70
4281	7p. PCSO Building and Filipino family	85	70
4282	7p. Building and PCSO employees	85	70
MS4283	135×96 mm. 7p.×4, As Nos. 4279/82	3·25	2·75

1275 Damili (Pottery)

2009. Centenary of San Nicolas, Ilocos Norte.

4284	**1275** 7p. multicoloured	85	70

1276 'Shower the world with LOVE'

2010. St Valentine's Day. Multicoloured.

4285	7p. Type **1276**	85	70
4286	7p. Cupid	85	70

2010. Postal Corporation Mascot (Pheepoy)

4287	7p. As Type **1253**	85	70

1277 Dove

2010. 90th Anniv of Philippine Rotary Club. Multicoloured.

4288	7p. Type **1277**	85	70
4289	7p. Housing project	85	70
4290	7p. Care workers giving child polio vaccine	85	70
4291	7p. Rizal monument and globe	85	70
MS4292	100×86 mm. As Nos. 4288/91. Imperf	3·25	2·75

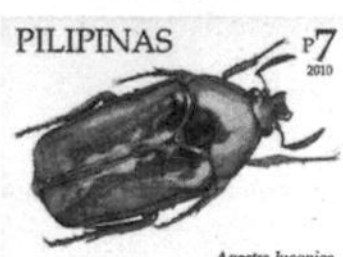

1278 *Agestra Luconia*

2010. Beetles. Multicoloured.

4293	7p. Type **1278**	85	70
4294	7p. *Glycyphana*	85	70
4295	7p. *Paraplectrone Crassa*	85	70
4296	7p. *Astrea*	85	70
MS4296a	135×80 mm. 7p.×4, *Agestra Semperi Heterorhina Clerota rodriguerzi Agestra antoinei*	3·25	2·75

1279 *Spirobranchus giganteus*

2010. Marine Biodiversity. Multicoloured.

4297	1p. Type **1279**	15	10
4298	1p. *Hippocampus kuda*	15	10
4299	1p. *Manta birostris*	15	10
4300	1p. *Dendronephthya*	15	10
4301	1p. *Rhinecanthus aculeatus*	15	10
4302	2p. *Glossodoris cruentus*	15	10
4303	2p. *Heterocentrotus mammillatus*	15	10
4304	2p. *Lutjanus kasmira*	25	15
4305	2p. *Conus marmorues*	25	15
4306	3p. *Siphonogorgia godeffroyi*	25	15
4307	3p. *Heteractis magnifica*	25	15
4308	3p. *Acanthus lineatus*	35	20
4309	4p. *Architectonica perspectiva*	25	15
4310	4p. *Linckia laevigata*	25	15
4311	4p. *Vexillum taeniatum*	50	30
4312	5p. *Cyerce nigrans* (incorrectly inscr 'Sea Hare')	35	20
4313	5p. *Tridacna crocea* (15.6.10)	35	20
4314	5p. *Chelonia mydas*	35	20
4315	5p. *Cyerce nigrans*	50	30
4316	5p. *Pseudocolochirus violaceus*	65	55
4317	5p. *Chelmon rostratus*	65	55
4318	7p. *Pterois volitans*	50	30
4319	7p. *Amphiprion percula*	50	30
4320	7p. *Ostracion meleagris*	85	70
4321	8p. *Hymenocera*	65	55
4322	9p. *Centropyge bispinosus*	65	55
4323	9p. *Pomacanthus annularis*	65	55
4324	9p. *Sepia latimanus*	1·20	1·00
4325	10p. *Synchiropus splendidsus*	65	55
4326	10p. *Rhinomuraena quaesita*	65	55
4327	10p. *Fungia scutaria*	1·30	1·10
4328	10p. *Charonia tritonis*	1·30	1·10
4329	15p. *Rhina ancylostoma*	65	55
4330	17p. *Sepioteuthis lessoniana*	85	70
4331	17p. *Taeniura lymma*	85	70
4332	17p. *Lactoria cornuta*	2·20	1·80
4333	20p. *Rhopalaea crassa*	85	70
4334	20p. *Pseudoceros ferrugineus*	1·00	85
4335	20p. *Amphiprion clarkii*	2·75	2·30
4336	20p. *Oxycomanthus bennettii*	2·75	2·30
4337	24p. *Actiniaria* (inscr 'Actineria')	1·20	1·00
4338	25p. *Lybia tesselata* (inscr 'Lybia tessellata')	1·20	1·00
4339	26p. *Neopetrolisthes maculata*	1·20	1·00
4340	30p. *Nautilus pompilius*	1·30	1·10
4341	30p. *Naso lituratus*	4·00	3·50
4342	30p. *Centropyge eibli*	4·00	3·50
4343	35p. *Cephalopholis miniata* (Cephalopholis miniatus)	1·30	1·10
4344	35p. *Gymnothorax Javanicus*	1·30	1·10
4345	40p. *Conus textile*	1·30	1·10
4346	40p. *Paraglyphidodon melanopus*	5·00	4·25
4347	50p. *Fromia monilis*	2·00	1·70
4348	50p. *Cassiopea*	2·20	1·80
4349	100p. *Tursiops aduncus*	2·20	1·80
4350	100p. *Hapalochlaena maculosa*	2·20	1·80
4350a	100p. *Cribrochalina olemda* (40×30 mm)	2·75	2·30

1280 Anniversary Emblem

2010. 50th Anniv of International Rice Research Institute. Multicoloured.

4351	7p. Type **1280**	95	80
4352	7p. Institute campus	95	80
4353	7p. Rice field and irrigation canal	95	80
4354	7p. Rice	95	80
MS4355	81×100 mm. Nos. 4351/4	3·75	3·25

1281 Eraño de Guzman Manalo

1282 Eraño de Guzman Manalo

1283 Eraño de Guzman Manalo

1284 Eraño de Guzman Manalo

2010. Eraño de Guzman Manalo (Executive Minister of the Iglesia ni Cristo (Church of Christ), 1963–2009) Commemoration

4356	**1281** 7p. multicoloured	95	80
4357	**1282** 7p. multicoloured	95	80
4358	**1283** 7p. multicoloured	95	80
4359	**1284** 7p. multicoloured	95	80

1285 *Sabungero* (1982)

2010. Birth Centenary of Vicente Manansala (artist). Multicoloured.

4360	7p. Type **1285**	95	80
4361	7p. *Bayanishan* (1982) (horiz)	95	80
4362	7p. *Nipa Hut* (1984) (horiz)	95	80
4363	7p. *Fish Vendor* (1982) (horiz)	95	80
4364	7p. *Planting of the First Cross* (1965) (80×30 mm)	3·00	2·40
MS4365	132×84 mm. 7p.×4, *Rooster* (1957); *Mamimintakasi* (1954); *I Believe in God* (1948); *Three Carabaos* (1958)	3·75	3·25

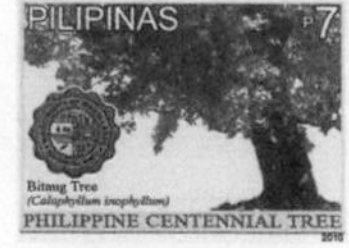

1286 Tree and Emblem

2010. Bitaug Tree (*Calophyllum inophyllum*) (oldest tree in Philippines). Multicoloured.

4366	7p. Type **1286**	95	80
4367	9p. As Type **1286** but with design reversed	1·30	1·10

1287 University Entrance

2010. 86th Anniv of Bukidnon State University. Multicoloured.

4368	7p. Type **1287**	95	80
4369	7p. Building and lawn	95	80

1288 Emblem and Battle Scene

2010. 50th Anniv of Veterans Federation of the Philippines. Multicoloured.

4370	7p. Type **1288**	95	80
4371	7p. Taking prisoners	95	80

1289 Train on Viaduct

2010. 30th Anniv of Light Rail Transit Authority (LRTA). Multicoloured.

4372	7p. Type **1289**	95	80
4373	7p. Electric locomotive	95	80
4374	7p. Electric locomotive, side view and skyline	95	80
4375	7p. LRT Megatren locomotive on viaduct and roadway	95	80
MS4376	170×80 mm. 10p.×4, as Nos 4372/5. Imperf	6·25	5·75

1290 Oath Taking

2010. President Benigno Simeon Cojuangco Aquino III's Inauguration. Multicoloured.

4377	7p. Type **1290**	95	80
4378	40p. Inaugural speech (vert)	5·75	5·00

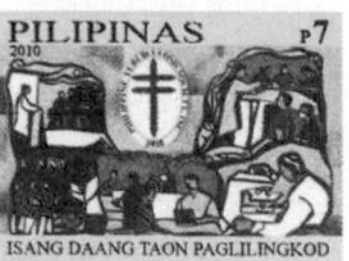

1291 Emblem and Symbols of TB Control and Treatment

2010. Centenary of Philippine Tuberculosis Society. Multicoloured.

4379	7p. Type **1291**	95	80
4380	9p. As Type **1291** but inscription in English	1·30	1·10
MS4381	165×86 mm. 26p. Manuel Quezon birthday seal (1935) (120×30 mm)	3·75	3·25

1292 Our Lady of Peñafrancia (photograph, 1924)

2010. 300 Years of Devotion to Our Lady of Peñafrancia. Multicoloured.

4382	7p. Type **1292**	95	80
4383	7p. Our Lady of Peñafrancia (2009)	95	80
4384	7p. Our Lady of Peñafrancia shrine (early photograph)	95	80
4385	7p. Basilica Minore of Our Lady of Peñafrancia, Naga City	95	80
MS4386	100×51 mm. 28p. Our Lady of Peñafrancia shrine, Naga City (early photograph) (80×30 mm)	3·75	3·25

1293 Chow Chow

2010. Dogs. Multicoloured.

4387	7p. Type **1293**	95	80
4388	7p. Bull terrier	95	80
4389	7p. Labrador retriever	95	80
4390	7p. Beagle	95	80
MS4391	135×80 mm. 7p.×4, Inscr 'Amerikan Eskimo Dog'; Black and tan coonhound; Afghan hound; Mastiff	3·75	3·25

1294 Hand above Globe above Sea

2010. Protect the Ozone Layer Campaign. Multicoloured.

4392	7p. Type **1294**	95	80
4393	7p. Hands enclosing globe with ozone layer	95	80

1295 CMU Administration Building and Mt. Musuan

2010. Centenary of Central Mindanao University (CMU). Multicoloured.

4394	7p. Type **1295**	95	80
4395	7p. CMU Main Building	95	80

1296 President Macapagal

2010. Birth Centenary of President Diosdado Macapagal

4396	**1296** 7p. multicoloured	95	80

1297 Galleon

1298 Galleon

2010. Dia del Galeon Festival, 2010. Multicoloured.

4397	7p. Type **1297**	95	80
4398	7p. Type **1298**	95	80
MS4399	175×80 mm. As Types **1297** and **1298**	1·90	1·60
MS4400	175×80 mm. 7p. As Type **1297**; 40p. As Type **1298**	5·75	5·25

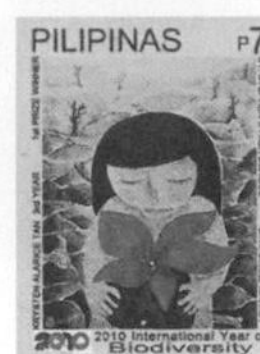

1298a Girl holding Plant (Krysten Alarice Tan)

2010. United Nations International Year of Biodiversity. Multicoloured.

4400a	7p. Type **1298a**	95	80
4400b	7p. Girl holding globe and symbols of diversity (Justen Paul Tolentino)	95	80

1298b PhilRice Administrative Building

2010. 25th Anniv of Philippine Rice Institute (PhilRice). Multicoloured.

4401	7p. Type **1298b**	95	80
4402	7p. Test tube	95	80
4403	7p. Field of rice	95	80
4404	7p. Mechanical harvesting	95	80

1299 Pheepoy driving Mail Van

2010. Postal Corporation Mascot (Pheepoy). Multicoloured.

4405	7p. Type **1299**	95	80
MS4406	80×100mm. 7p.×4, As Type **1253**; No. 4278; No. 4287; Type **1299**	3·75	3·25
MS4407	110×70 mm. 7p.×4, As Type **1253**; No. 4278; No. 4287; Type **1299**. Imperf	3·75	3·25

1300 Levi Celerio (Music)

2010. Stamp Collecting Month. Multicoloured.

4408	7p. Type **1300**	95	80
4409	7p. Leonor Orosa Goquingco (Dance)	95	80
4410	7p. Carlos L. Quirino (Historical Literature)	95	80
4411	7p. Nick Joaquin (Literature)	95	80
MS4412	137×80 mm. Vert. 7p.×3, *Ang Panday Ikatlong Yugto*; *Umpishan Mo Tatapustin Ko*; *Pipeng Kaliwete* (Fernando Poe, Jr. (Film))	3·00	2·75

1301 Oath Taking

2010. Vice President Jejomar Binay's Inauguration

4413	**1301** 7p. multicoloured	95	80

1302 Mary and Joseph in Philippino Costume and Vatican

2010. Christmas. Multicoloured.

4414	7p. Type **1302**	95	80
4415	7p. Holy family	95	80
4416	7p. Holy family in jar	95	80
4417	7p. Holy family and shepherds	95	80

1303 Fernando Poe Jr.

2010. National Stamp Collecting Month (2nd issue). Fernando Poe Jr. (film actor) Commemoration. Multicoloured.

4418	7p. Type **1303**	1·00	90
4419	7p. *Ang Panday Ikatlong Yugto*	1·00	90
4420	7p. *Umpishan Mo Tatapustin Ko*	1·00	90
4421	7p. *Pipeng Kaliwete*	1·00	90

Nos. 4419/21 are as the stamps of **MS**4412.

1304 'Fabilioh!' (official emblem)

2010. Ateneo de Manila Class '60 Re-union. Multicoloured.

4422	7p. Type **1304**	1·00	90
4423	7p. 'We stand on a hill, between the earth and sky'	1·00	90
4424	7p. 'Mary for you, for your white and blue'	1·00	90
4425	7p. 'The Bell Ringers of GESU'	1·00	90

1305 Rabbit and 'Manigong Bagong Taon'

2010. Chinese New Year. Year of the Rabbit. Multicoloured.

4426	7p. Type **1305**	1·00	90
4427	30p. Rabbit and 'Happy New Year'	4·50	4·00
MS4428	140×80 mm. 7p.×2, Type **1305**×2; 30p.×2, Rabbit and 'Happy New Year'×2	8·00	7·25

1306 Portrait and As Politician

2010. Birth Centenary of Senator Ambrosio Padilla. Multicoloured.

4429	7p. Type **1306**	1·00	90
4430	7p. Portrait and as basketball player	1·00	90

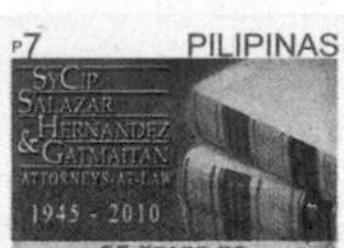

1307 Law Books

2010. 65th Anniv SyCip, Salazar, Hernandez & Gatmaitan Law Firm

4430a	**1307** 7p. multicoloured	1·00	90

1308 New Building

2010. 60th Anniv of Grace Christian College (GCC). Multicoloured.

4431	7p. Type **1308**	1·00	90
4432	7p. Anniversary emblem	1·00	90
4433	7p. Building, 1966	1·00	90
4434	7p. Founders, Ms. Julia L. Tan, Dr. and Mrs. Edward Spahr	1·00	90
MS4435	170×80 mm. 7p.×4, Nos. 4431/4	4·00	3·50

1309 Pheepoy (Philpost Mascot) Delivering Chocolates

2011. St Valentine's Day. Multicoloured.

4436	7p. Type **1309**	1·00	90
4437	7p. Pheepoy delivering flowers	1·00	90

1310 Philippine National Flag, Emblem of Kiwanis Club of Manila and Child

2011. Kiwanis Club of Manila

4438	**1310** 7p. multicoloured	1·00	90

1311 Main Building

2011. University of Santo Tomas. Multicoloured.

4439	7p. Type **1311**	1·00	90
4440	7p. Central Seminary	1·00	90
4441	7p. Arch of Centules	1·00	90
4442	7p. *Foundation of the University of Santo Tomas*	1·00	90
MS4443	110×76 mm. Vert. 7p. Benavides Monument by Tony Noel; 30p. Quattro Mondial Monument by Ramon Orlina	5·50	5·00

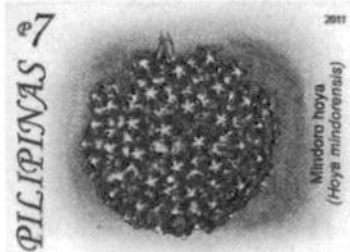

1312 Mindoro Hoya (*Mindora mindorensis*)

2011. Philippine Hoyas. Multicoloured.

4444	7p. Type **1312**	1·00	90
4445	7p. Grandmother's Wax Plant (*Hoya camosa*)	1·00	90
4446	7p. Summer Hoya (*Hoya obscura*)	1·00	90
4447	7p. Benito Tan's Hoya (*Hoya benitotanii*)	1·00	90
MS4448	130×75 mm. 7p.×4, Siar's Hoya (*Hoya siariae*); Shooting Star Hoya (*Hoya multiflora*); Imperial Hoya (*Hoya imperialis*); Buot's Hoya (*Hoya buotii*)	4·00	3·50

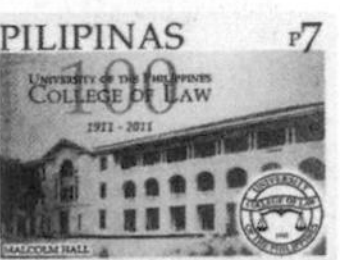

1313 Malcolm Hall and UP College of Law Emblem

2011. Centenary of University of Philippines College of Law. Multicoloured.

4449	7p. Type **1313**	1·00	90
4450	7p. As Type **1313** , but with centenary emblem	1·00	90

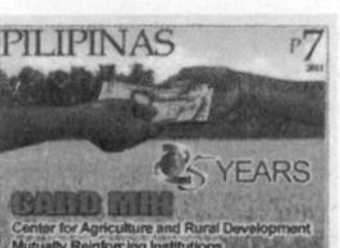

1314 Exchange of Money and CARD MRI Anniversary Emblem

2011. 25th Anniv of CARD MRI (Center for Agriculture and Rural Development Mutually Reinforcing Institutions)

4451	**1314** 7p. multicoloured	1·00	90

1315 DBM Complex, DBM Emblem and DBM Anniversary Emblem

2011. 75th Anniv of Department of Budget and Management (DBM)

4452 **1315** 7p. multicoloured 1·00 90

1316 Wenceslao Vinzons

2011. Birth Centenary of Wenceslao Quinito Vinzons (politician and leader of armed resistance)

4452a **1316** 7p. multicoloured 1·00 90

2011. 60th Anniv of Grace Christian College (GCC) (2nd issue). Multicoloured.

4453 7p. As Type **1308** 1·00 90
4454 7p. Anniversary emblem 1·00 90
4455 7p. Building, 1966 1·00 90
4456 7p. Founders, Ms. Julia L. Tan, Dr. and Mrs. Edward Spahr 1·00 90
MS4457 170×80 mm. 7p.×4, Nos. 4453/6 4·00 3·50

1317

2011. 50th Anniv of WWF. Philippine Crocdiles (*Crocodylus mindorensis*). Multicoloured.

4458 7p. Type **1317** 1·00 90
4459 7p. Young adult, speckled, facing left 1·00 90
4460 7p. Hatchling and eggs 1·00 90
4461 7p. Head of adult with open mouth 1·00 90

1318 Combatants wearing Body Armour

2011. Arnis, National Sport. Multicoloured.

4462 7p. Type **1318** 1·00 90
4463 7p. Combatants wearing white costumes 1·00 90

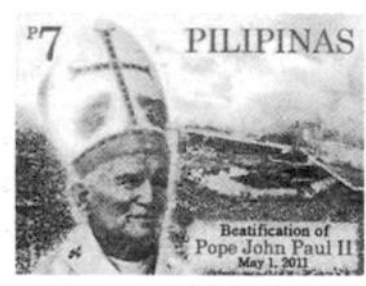

1319 Pope John Paul II at Grandstand, Rizal Park

2011. Beatification of Pope John Paul II. Multicoloured.

4464 7p. Type **1319** 1·00 90
4465 7p. At University of Santo Tomas 1·00 90
4466 7p. At Philippine International Convention Center 1·00 90
4467 7p. Pope John Paul II and Popemobile along Roxas Boulevard 1·00 90
MS4468 110×76 mm. 40p. With arm raised in blessing (vert) 6·00 5·25

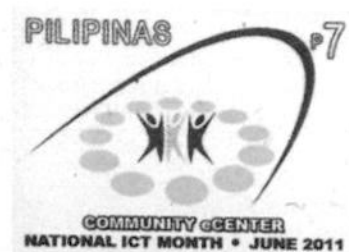

1320 Emblem (Community eCenter)

2011. National Information and Communications Technology Month. Multicoloured.

4469 7p. Type **1320** 1·00 90
4470 7p. Flying vehicle (Creative Content Industries) 1·00 90
4471 7p. Nationwide automated elections 1·00 90
4472 7p. Keyboard and headset (Business Process Outsourcing) 1·00 90

1321 Plaza Goiti, Manila (1951) and Ayala, Makati (2011) Corporate Headquarters

2011. 60th Anniv of Security Bank Corporation. Multicoloured.

4473 10p. Type **1321** 1·00 90
4474 10p. Corporate emblems 1·00 90

1322 Rizal Statue, Wilhelmsfeld, Germany

2011. 50th Anniv of Goethe Institute in the Philippines. Multicoloured.

4475 7p. Type **1322** 1·00 90
4476 7p. Fountain in Luneta Park (now Rizal Park) donated by Germany 1·00 90
4477 7p. Rizal Residence in Germany 1·00 90
4478 7p. Goethe Institute anniversary emblem 1·00 90

1323 Rizal, Noli Me Tangere, Dove (by Marc Aran C. Reyes)

2011. 150th Birth Anniv of Jose Rizal. Winning Entries in Rizal@150 Art Contest. Multicoloured.

4479 7p. Type **1323** 1·00 90
4480 7p. Rizal, Philippine Flag and sun (by Lex Kempho Y. Lacar) 1·00 90
4481 7p. Rizal (blue) (by Ramon Vizmonte) 1·00 90
4482 7p. Rizal (red) (by Henritz Sales) 1·00 90
MS4483 120×175 mm. Size 21×75 mm. 7p. 1906 2c. Rizal Stamp and Rizal Monument in Daet, Camarines Norte; 7p. 1935 2c. Rizal Stamp and Rizal Monument in Guinobatan, Albay; 7p. 1941 2c. Rizal Stamp and Rizal Monument in Santa Barbara, Iloilo; 7p. 1946 2c. Rizal Stamp and Rizal Monument in Binan Laguna; 12p. 1959 6c. Rizal Stamp and Rizal Monument in San Fernando, Cebu; 13p. 1962 6p. Rizal Stamp and Rizal Monument in Lucban, Quezon; 20p. 1964 6p. Rizal Stamp and Rizal Monument in Romblon, Romblon; 30p. 1977 30p. Rizal Stamp and Rizal Monument in Jinjiang City, China; 40p. 1978 30p. Rizal Stamp and Rizal Monument in Illinois, USA (vert) 14·00 13·00

1324 Old and New YGC Complex and Centenary Emblem

2011. Centenary of Yuchengco Group of Companies (YGC)

4484 **1324** 7p. multicoloured 1·00 90

1325 President Corazon Aquino

2011. 25th Anniv of EDSA People Power Revolution. Multicoloured.

4485 7p. Type **1325** 1·00 90
4486 7p. Jaime, Cardinal Sin wearing biretta 1·00 90
4487 7p. Jaime, Cardinal Sin smiling 1·00 90
4488 7p. President Corazon Aquino, facing left 1·00 90
MS4489 120×161 mm. 7p.×8, Cory Aquino, as younger woman right; Cory Aquino with longer hair; As Type **1325**; As No. 4484; As No. 4485; Cardinal Sin wearing white facing left; Cardinal Sin fuller face facing front; As No. 4486 8·00 7·25

1326 Bajada Campus

2011. Bajada Campus Facade. Multicoloured.

4490 7p. Type **1326** 1·00 90
4491 7p. Grade School and High School buildings 1·00 90
4492 7p. Palma Gil and Mabutas halls 1·00 90
4493 7p. Babak and Camudmud campuses 1·00 90

1327 Mother Francisca and her Works

2011. 300th Death Anniv of Mother Francisca del Espiritu Santo de Fuentes

4492 **1327** 7p. multicoloured 1·00 90

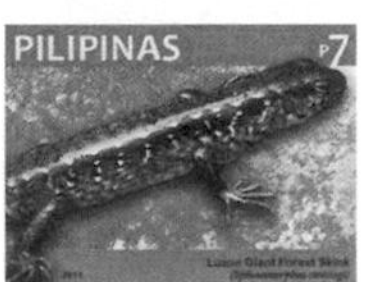

1328 Luzon Giant Forest Skink (*Sphenomorphus cumingi*)

2011. Philippine Endemic Lizards. Multicoloured.

4495 7p. Type **1328** 1·00 90
4496 7p. Luzon Karst gecko (*Gekko carusadensis*) 1·00 90
4497 7p. Southern Philippine bent-toed gecko (*Cyrtodactylus mamanwa*) 1·00 90
4498 7p. Luzon white-spotted forest skink (*Sphenomorphus leucospilos*) 1·00 90
MS4499 130×75 mm. 7p.×4, Philippine forest dragon (*Gonocephalus sophiae*); Philippine spiny stream skink (*Tropidophorus grayi*); Philippine sailfin lizard (*Hydrosuarus pustulatus*); Cordilleras slender skink (*Brachymeles elerae*) 4·00 3·50

1328a *Rhinecanthus aculeatus*

2011. Marine Biodiversity. Multicoloured.

4500 1p. Type **1328a** 1·00 90
4501 2p. *Conus marmoreus* 1·00 90
4502 5p. *Chelmon rostratus* 15 15
4503 10p. *Charonia tritonis* 20 20
4504 20p. *Oxycomanthus bennettii* 65 65
4505 30p. *Centropyge eibli* 80 80

1329 Batlag Falls in Tanay, Rizal (Prab Reyes) (First Prize)

2011. International Year of Forests. Winners in United Nations Information Centre (Manila) Photographic Competition celebrating International Year of the Forests. Multicoloured.

4506 7p. Type **1329** 35 35
4507 7p. Tree in Pansol, Laguna (Karol France) (Second Prize) 35 35

2011. Marine Biodiversity. Multicoloured.

4508 4p. Blue-faced Angelfish (*Euxiphipops xanthometapon*) 20 20
4509 7p. Murex shell 35 35
4510 100p. Regal Tang (*Paracanthurus hepatus*) (40×30 mm) 1·70 1·70

2011. Marine Biodiversity. Multicoloured.

4511 9p. Polyclad Flatworm (*Pseudoceros dimidiatus*) 45 45
4512 25p. Oriental Sweetlips (*Plectorhynchus orientalis*) 70 70
4513 35p. Kunie's Chromodoris (*Chromodoris kunei*) 80 80

1330 Galleon Ship with Map of Philippines

2011. Dia del Galeon Festival, 2011. Multicoloured.

4514 7p. Type **1330** 35 35
4515 7p. Ship with map of Mexico 35 35
4516 7p. Ship with map of Spain 35 35
MS4517 132×90 mm. As Nos. 4514/16 1·30 1·30

2011. Marine Biodiversity. Multicoloured.

4518 9p. Valentini Puffer (*Canthigaster valentini*) (inscr 'Valentine Puffer') 45 45
4519 25p. Polka-dot Grouper (*Chromileptes altivelis*) 70 70
4520 35p. Royal Empress Angelfish (*Pygoplites diacanthus*) 80 80

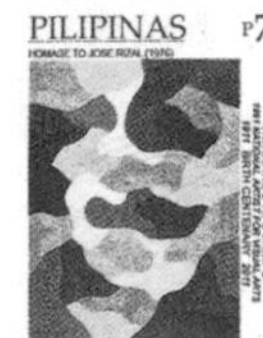

1331 Homage to Jose Rizal

2011. National Stamp Collecting Month. Paintings by H.R. Ocampo. Multicoloured.

4521 7p. Type **1331** 35 35
4522 7p. *Break of Day* 35 35
4523 7p. *Summer in September* 35 35
4524 7p. *Mother and Child* 35 35
MS4525 90×86 mm. Horiz. 7p.×4, *Fiesta; Abstraction #15, 17; Kasaysayan ng Lahi; Abstraction #22, 26* 1·40 1·40

1332 Official Seal

2011. 75th Anniv of National Bureau of Investgation (NBI). Multicoloured.

4526 7p. Type **1332** 35 35
4527 7p. Justice Yulo and President Manuel L. Quezon (forefathers of NBI) 35 35
4528 7p. President Manuel Roxas and J. Pardo de Tavera (first NBI Director) 35 35
4529 7p. Magnifying glass and laptop 35 35

1333 Bells

2011. Christmas. Multicoloured.

4530 7p. Type **1333** 35 35
4531 7p. Poinsettias 35 35
4532 7p. Presents 35 35
4533 7p. Star in a circle 35 35

1334 Dragon

2011. Chinese New Year. Year of the Dragon. Multicoloured.

4534 7p. Type **1334** 35 35
4535 30p. Dragon and 'Happy New Year' 80 80

MS4536 140×80 mm. 7p.×2, Type **1334**×2; 30p.×2, Dragon and 'Happy New Year'×2 2·00 2·00

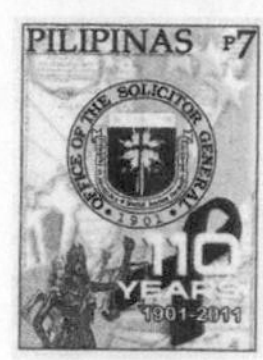

1335 Arms

2011. 110th Anniv of Office of the Solicitor General (OSG)
4537 **1335** 7p. multicoloured 35 35

1336 Spiny Cinnamon Frog (*Nyctixalus spinosus*)

2011. Frogs. Multicoloured.
4538 7p. Type **1336** 35 35
4539 7p. Pygmy forest Frog (*Platymantis pygmaeus*) 35 35
4540 7p. Flat-headed Frog (*Barbourula busuangensis*) 35 35
4541 7p. Luzon Limestone-forest Frog (inscr 'Platymantis biak') 35 35
MS4542 132×75 mm. Horiz. 7p.×4, Inscr 'Gliding tree frog' (*Rhacophorus pardalis*); Inscr 'Northern Luzon tree-hole frog' (*Kaloula kalingensis*); Inscr 'Taylor's Igarot frog' (*Sanguirana igorota*); Inscr 'Mary Inger's Wart frog' (*Ingerana mariae*) 1·40 1·40

1337 '60' and LPU Tower

2012. 60th Anniv of Lyceum of Philippines University
4543 **1337** 7p. multicoloured 35 35

1338 Grand Lodge Building and Manuel Luis Quezon

2012. Centenary of Grand Lodge of Free and Accepted Masons in Philippines. Multicoloured.
4544 7p. Type **1338** 35 35
4545 7p. Jose Rizal, Marcelo H. del Pilar, Mariano Ponce and Plaridel Masonic Temple 35 35

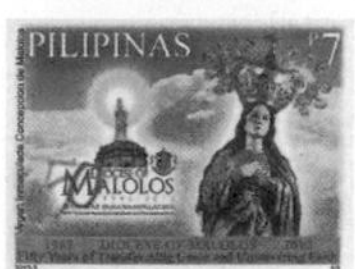

1339 Virgen Inmaculada Concepcion de Malolos and Anniversary Emblem

2012. 50th Anniv of Diocese of Malolos
4546 7p. Type **1339** 35 35
4547 7p. Façade of Immaculate Concepcion Cathedral and Minor Basilica 35 35
MS4548 110×75 mm. 40p. Virgen Inmaculada Concepcion de Malolos (vert) 1·25 1·25

1340 City Hall

2012. 75th Anniv of Davao City. Multicoloured.
4549 7p. Type **1340** 35 35
4550 7p. Kadayawan Festival 35 35
4551 7p. Waling-Waling (orchid) 35 35
4552 7p. Mount Apo and Philippine Eagle (*Pithecophaga jefferyi*) 35 35

1341 Fort Pilar Shrine

2012. Centenary of Ateneo de Zamboanga University. Multicoloured.
4553 7p. Type **1341** 35 35
4554 7p. William H. Kreutz SJ Campus 35 35
4555 7p. Ateneo Brebeuf Gymnasium 35 35
4556 7p. Saint Ignatius of Loyola 35 35
MS4557 110×85 mm. Horiz. 7p.×4, Nos. 4553/6 1·00 1·00

1342 Building Façade

2012. Centenary of St. Agnes Academy, Legazpi City. Multicoloured.
4558 7p. Type **1342** 35 35
4559 7p. Façade of Main Building as ruin during World War II 35 35
4560 7p. Façade of Main Building facing right 35 35
4561 7p. Façade of Main Building, showing entrance and gardens 35 35

1343 Maria Makiling and Deer

2012. Folklore and Legends. Maria Makiling, Guardian of the Forests
4562 **1343** 7p. multicoloured 35 35

1344 APPU Emblem and Flags of Member Countries

2012. 50th Anniv of Asian Pacific Postal Union (APPU). Multicoloured.
4563 7p. Type **1344** 35 35
4564 30p. 1977 1p.50 stamp (As. No. 1428), APPU emblem and flags of member countries (80×30 mm) 80 80

1345 Pres. Cory Aquino and Postal Service Act of 1992

2012. 20th Anniv of Philippine Postal Corporation (Philpost). Multicoloured.
4565 7p. Type **1345** 35 35
4566 7p. Main Post Office Building 35 35

1346 Inmaculada Concepcion Parish Church, Guiuan, Eastern Samar

2012. Cultural Heritage. Churches. Multicoloured.
4567 7p. Type **1346** 35 35
4568 7p. San Joaquin Parish Church, San Joaquin, Iloilo 35 35
4569 7p. Nuestra Señora de la Porteria Parish Church, Daraga, Albay. 35 35
4570 7p. San Isidro Labrador Parish Church, Lazi Siquijor 35 35
MS4571 130×70 mm. Horiz. 7p.×4, Santiago Apostol Church, Betis, Pampanga; Inmaculada Concepcion Church, Jasaan, Misamis Oriental; Our Lady of Light (Nuestra Señora de la Luz) Church, Loon, Bohol; San Gregorio Magno Church, Majayjay, Laguna 1·40 1·40

1347 Felipe Padilla De Leon and Sheet Music for *Kay Tamis ng Buhay*

2012. Birth Centenary of Felipe Padilla De Leon (composer, conductor and scholar)
4572 **1347** 7p. multicoloured 35 35

1348 Emblem

2012. 45th Annual Meeting of Board of Governors of Asian Development Bank (ADB)
4573 **1348** 7p. multicoloured 35 35

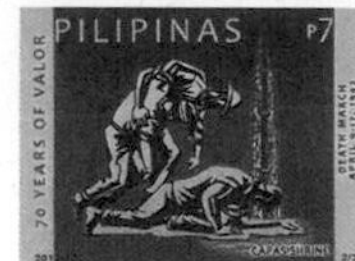

1349 Capas Shrine

2012. 70th Anniv of Day of Valor. Multicoloured.
4574 7p. Type **1349** 35 35
4575 10p. Battery Hearn, Corregidor Island 45 45
4576 30p. Shrine of Valor, Mt. Samat, Bataan 80

1350 GSIS Head Office, Solano in 1937

2012. 75th Anniv of Government Service Insurance System (GSIS). Multicoloured.
4577 7p. Type **1350** 35 35
4578 9p. GSIS Head Office, Arroceros in 1957 45 45
4579 40p. GSIS Financial Center, Pasay City (50×22 mm) 85 85

2012. Chinese New Year. Year of the Dragon. Multicoloured.
4580 7p. As Type **1334** 35 35
4581 30p. As No. 4535 80 80
MS4582 140×80 mm. 7p.×2, As Type **1334**×2; 30p.×2, As No. 4535×2 90 90

1351 'White Water Rafting, the Ultimate Advenure'

2012. White Water Rafting, Cagayan de Oro City
4583 **1351** 9p. multicoloured 45 45

1352 International Year of Forests

2012. 20th International Children's Painting Competition on the Environment. Trisha Co Reyes, Global Winner
4584 **1352** 9p. multicoloured 45 45

1353 Bonifacio Monument

2012. 50th Anniv of Caloocan City
4585 **1353** 7p. multicoloured 35 35

1354 Habagat and Birds

2012. Folklore and Legends. Habagat - God of Winds
4586 **1654** 7p. multicoloured 35 35

OFFICIAL STAMPS

1926. Commemorative issue of 1926 optd **OFFICIAL**.
O391 **49** 2c. black and green 3·75 1·50
O392 **49** 4c. black and red 3·75 1·80
O393 **49** 18c. black and brown 12·50 6·25
O394 **49** 20c. black and orange 11·00 2·75

1931. Stamps of 1906 optd **O.B.**
O413 2c. green (No. 337) 25 25
O414 4c. red (No. 338) 25 25
O415 6c. violet (No. 339) 25 25
O416 8c. brown (No. 340) 25 25
O417 10c. blue (No. 341) 35 25
O418 12c. orange (No. 342) 45 25
O419 16c. olive (No. 344) 45 25
O420 20c. orange (No. 345) 45 25
O421 26c. green (No. 346) 55 45
O422 30c. grey (No. 347) 45 45

1935. Nos. 459/68 optd **O.B.**
O473 2c. red 25 25
O474 4c. green 25 25
O475 6c. brown 25 25
O476 8c. violet 25 25
O477 10c. red 25 25
O478 12c. black 25 25
O479 16c. blue 25 25
O480 20c. bistre 25 25
O481 26c. blue 45 45
O482 30c. red 55 55

1936. Stamps of 1935 Nos. 459/68 optd **O. B. COMMON-WEALTH** (2, 6, 20c.) or **O. B. COMMONWEALTH** (others).
O538 2c. red 25 25
O539 4c. green 25 25
O540 6c. brown 25 25
O541 8c. violet 25 25
O542 10c. red 25 25
O543 12c. black 25 25
O544 16c. blue 25 25
O545 20c. bistre 45 45
O546 26c. blue 55 55
O547 30c. red 45 45

1941. Nos. 563 and 623 optd **O. B.**
O565 **104** 2c. green 25 25
O624 - 2c. brown 25 25

1948. Various stamps optd **O.B.**
O738 **147** 1c. brown 25 10
O668 **125** 2c. green 95 20
O659 4c. brown (No. 629) 25 20
O739 - 5c. red (No. 731) 35 15
O843 - 6c. blue (No. 842) 65 15
O660 **113** 10c. red 35 20
O740 - 10c. blue (No. 732) 45 20
O661 - 16c. grey (No. 632) 4·25 1·40
O669 - 20c. brown (No. 633) 1·10 25
O741 - 20c. red (No. 733) 80 25
O670 - 50c. green (No. 634) 2·30 1·00

1950. Surch **ONE CENTAVO**.
O700 **125** 1c. on 2c. green (No. O668) 45 15

1959. No. 810 optd **O B**.
O811 1c. on 5c. red 65 15

1962. Nos. 898/904 optd **G. O.**
O908 5s. red 40 10
O909 6s. brown 50 15
O910 6s. blue 50 15
O911 10s. purple 65 30
O912 20s. blue 1·00 35
O913 30s. red 1·30 55
O914 50s. violet 1·50 70

1970. Optd **G.O.**
O1182 **318** 10s. red 65 25

OFFICIAL SPECIAL DELIVERY STAMP

1931. No. E353b optd **O.B.**
EO423 **E47** 20c. violet 2·00 90·00

POSTAGE DUE STAMPS

1899. Postage Due stamps of United States of 1894 optd **PHILIPPINES.**
D268 **D87** 1c. red 9·75 2·30
D269 **D87** 2c. red 9·75 1·80
D270 **D87** 3c. red 27·00 11·00

D271	**D87**	5c. red	23·00	3·75
D272	**D87**	10c. red	30·00	8·50
D273	**D87**	30c. red	£375	£170
D274	**D87**	50c. red	£300	£150

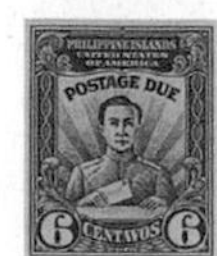

D51 Post Office Clerk

1928

D395	**D51**	4c. red	25	25
D396	**D51**	6c. red	25	45
D397	**D51**	8c. red	25	45
D398	**D51**	10c. red	25	45
D399	**D51**	12c. red	25	45
D400	**D51**	16c. red	35	45
D401	**D51**	20c. red	35	45

1937. Surch **3 CVOS. 3.**

D521	**D 51**	3c. on 4c. red	25	25

D118

1947

D644	**D 118**	3c. red	25	20
D645	**D 118**	4c. blue	60	45
D646	**D 118**	6c. green	80	65
D647	**D 118**	10c. orange	1·30	85

SPECIAL DELIVERY STAMPS

1901. Special Delivery stamp of United States of 1888 optd **PHILIPPINES.**

E268	**46**	10c. blue (No. E283)	£140	£110

1907. Special Delivery stamp of United States optd **PHILIPPINES.**

E298	**E 117**	10c. blue	£3250	

E47 Messenger running

1919. Perf (E353), perf or imperf (E353b).

E353	**E 47**	20c. blue	70	35
E353b	**E 47**	20c. violet	70	35

1939. Optd **COMMONWEALTH.** Perf.

E550	20c. violet	35	35

1945. Optd **VICTORY.**

E622	20c. violet (No. E550)	1·10	70

E120 Cyclist Messenger and Post Office

1947

E651	**E 120**	20c. purple	1·20	75

E219 G.P.O., Manila

E891	**E 219**	20c. mauve	65	45

Pt. 1

PITCAIRN ISLANDS

An island group in the Pacific Ocean, nearly midway between Australia and America.

1940. 12 pence = 1 shilling; 20 shillings = 1 pound.
1967. 100 cents = 1 New Zealand dollar.

4 Lt. Bligh and the "Bounty"

1940

1	-	½d. orange and green	1·00	60
2	-	1d. mauve and magenta	1·25	80
3	-	1½d. grey and red	1·25	50
4	**4**	2d. green and brown	2·50	1·40
5	-	3d. green and blue	1·25	1·40
5b	-	4d. black and green	23·00	12·00
6	-	6d. brown and blue	6·50	1·50
6a	-	8d. green and mauve	24·00	8·00
7	-	1s. violet and grey	6·00	3·50
8	-	2s.6d. green and brown	17·00	4·00

DESIGNS—HORIZ: ½d. Oranges; 1d. Fletcher Christian, crew and Pitcairn Is.; 1½d. John Adams and house; 3d. Map of Pitcairn Is. and Pacific; 4d. Bounty Bible; 6d. H.M.S. "Bounty"; 8d. School, 1949; 1s. Christian and Pitcairn Is.; 2s.6d. Christian, crew and Pitcairn coast.

8a Houses of Parliament, London

1946. Victory.

9	**8a**	2d. brown	70	30
10	**8a**	3d. blue	80	30

8b King George VI and Queen Elizabeth

8c King George VI and Queen Elizabeth

1949. Silver Wedding.

11	**8b**	1½d. red	2·00	1·50
12	**8c**	10s. mauve	40·00	50·00

8d Hermes, Globe and Forms of Transport

8e Hemispheres, Jet-powered Vickers Viking Airliner and Steamer

8f Hermes and Globe

8g U.P.U. Monument

1949. U.P.U.

13	**8d**	2½d. brown	1·75	4·25
14	**8e**	3d. blue	8·00	4·25
15	**8f**	6d. green	4·00	4·25
16	**8g**	1s. purple	4·00	4·25

8h Queen Elizabeth II

1953. Coronation.

17	**8h**	4d. black and green	2·00	3·75

12 Handicrafts: Bird Model

1957

33	-	½d. green and mauve	65	60
19	-	1d. black and green	4·50	1·75
20	-	2d. brown and blue	2·25	60
21	**12**	2½d. brown and orange	75	40
22	-	3d. green and blue	80	40
23	-	4d. red and blue (I)	90	40
23a	-	4d. red and blue (II)	3·50	1·50
24	**12**	6d. buff and blue	3·25	55
25	-	8d. green and red	75	40
26	-	1s. black and brown	2·25	40
27	-	2s. green and orange	11·00	10·00
28	-	2s.6d. blue and red	26·00	11·00

DESIGNS—HORIZ: ½d. "Cordyline terminalis"; 3d. Bounty Bay; 4d. Pitcairn School; 6d. Map of Pacific; 8d. Inland scene; 1s. Model of the "Bounty"; 2s.6d. Launching new whaleboat. VERT: 1d. Map of Pitcairn; 2d. John Adams and "Bounty" Bible; 2s. Island wheelbarrow.

The 4d. Type I is inscr "PITCAIRN SCHOOL"; Type II is inscr "SCHOOL TEACHER'S HOUSE".

20 Pitcairn Island and Simon Young

1961. Cent of Return of Pitcairn Islanders.

29	**20**	3d. black and yellow	50	45
30	-	6d. brown and blue	1·00	75
31	-	1s. orange and green	1·00	75

DESIGNS: 6d. Maps of Norfolk and Pitcairn Islands; 1s. Migrant brigantine "Mary Ann".

20a Protein Foods

1963. Freedom from Hunger.

32	**20a**	2s.6d. blue	4·00	2·00

20b Red Cross Emblem

1963. Cent of Red Cross.

34	**20b**	2d. red and black	1·00	1·00
35	**20b**	2s.6d. red and blue	2·00	3·00

23 Pitcairn Is. Longboat

24 Queen Elizabeth II (after Anthony Buckley)

1964. Multicoloured.

36	½d. Type **23**	10	30
37	1d. H.M.S. "Bounty"	30	30
38	2d. "Out from Bounty Bay"	30	30
39	3d. Great frigate bird	75	30
40	4d. White tern	75	30
41	6d. Pitcairn warbler	75	30
42	8d. Red-footed booby	75	30
43	10d. Red-tailed tropic birds	60	30
44	1s. Henderson Island crake	60	30
45	1s.6d. Stephen's lory	1·50	1·25
46	2s.6d. Murphy's petrel	1·50	1·50
47	4s. Henderson Island fruit dove	2·00	1·50
48	8s. Type **24**	1·25	2·00

24a I.T.U. Emblem

1965. Centenary of I.T.U.

49	**24a**	1d. mauve and brown	50	40
50	**24a**	2s.6d. turquoise and blue	1·50	2·00

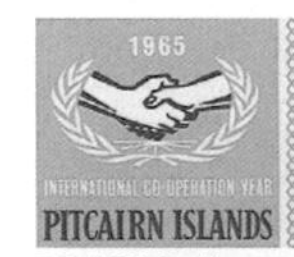

24b I.C.Y. Emblem

1965. International Co-operation Year.

51	**24b**	1d. purple and turquoise	50	40
52	**24b**	2s.6d. green and lavender	1·75	2·00

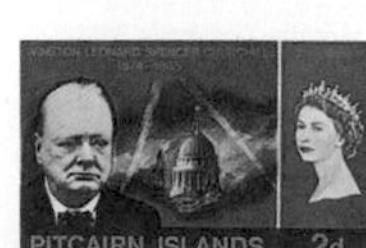

24c Sir Winston Churchill and St. Paul's Cathedral in Wartime

1966. Churchill Commemoration.

53	**24c**	2d. blue	80	85
54	**24c**	3d. green	1·50	1·00
55	**24c**	6d. brown	1·50	1·75
56	**24c**	1s. violet	1·75	2·50

25 Footballer's Legs, Ball and Jules Rimet Cup

1966. World Cup Football Championship.

57	**25**	4d. multicoloured	75	1·00
58	**25**	2s.6d. multicoloured	1·25	1·25

25a W.H.O. Building.

1966. Inauguration of W.H.O. Headquarters, Geneva.

59	**25a**	8d. black, green and blue	2·00	3·25
60	**25a**	1s.6d. black, purple and ochre	3·50	3·75

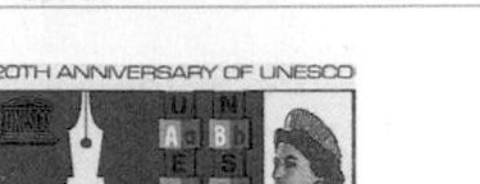

25b "Education"

25c "Science"

25d "Culture"

1966. 20th Anniv of UNESCO.

61	**25b**	½d. multicoloured	20	1·00
62	**25c**	10d. yellow, violet and olive	1·25	75
63	**25d**	2s. black, purple and orange	2·50	2·25

36 Mangarevan Canoe, c. 1325

1967. Bicentenary of Discovery of Pitcairn Islands. Multicoloured.

64	½d. Type **36**	10	20
65	1d. P. F. de Quiros and "San Pedro y San Pablo", 1606	20	20
66	8d. "San Pedro y San Pablo" and "Los Tres Reyes", 1606	25	20
67	1s. Carteret and H.M.S. "Swallow", 1767	25	25
68	1s.6d. "Hercules", 1819	25	25

1967. Decimal Currency. Nos. 36/48 surch with "Bounty" anchor and value.

69	**23**	½c. on ½d. multicoloured	10	10
70	-	1c. on 1d. multicoloured	30	1·25
71	-	2c. on 2d. multicoloured	25	1·25
72	-	2½c. on 3d. multicoloured	25	1·25
73	-	3c. on 4d. multicoloured	25	20
74	-	5c. on 6d. multicoloured	30	1·25
75	-	10c. on 8d. multicoloured	50	30
76	-	15c. on 10d. multicoloured	1·50	40
77	-	20c. on 1s. multicoloured	1·50	55
78	-	25c. on 1s.6d. multicoloured	1·50	1·25
79	-	30c. on 2s.6d. multicoloured	1·75	1·25
80	-	40c. on 4s. multicoloured	1·75	1·25
81	**24**	45c. on 8s. multicoloured	1·50	1·50

42 Bligh and "Bounty's" Launch

1967. 150th Death Anniv of Admiral Bligh.

82	42	1c. black, ultramarine & blue	10	10
83	-	8c. black, yellow and mauve	25	50
84	-	20c. black, brown and buff	25	55

DESIGNS: 8c. Bligh and followers cast adrift; 20c. Bligh's tomb.

45 Human Rights Emblem

1968. International Human Rights Year.

85	45	1c. multicoloured	10	10
86	45	2c. multicoloured	10	10
87	45	25c. multicoloured	35	35

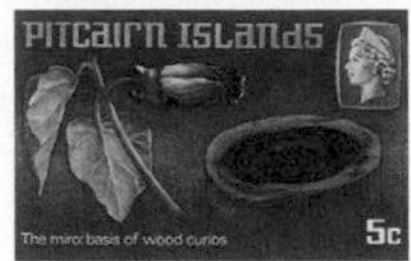

46 Moro Wood and Flower

1968. Handicrafts (1st series).

88	46	5c. multicoloured	20	30
89	-	10c. green, brown and orange	20	40
90	-	15c. violet, brown & salmon	25	40
91	-	20c. multicoloured	25	45

DESIGNS—HORIZ: 10c. flying fish model. VERT: 15c. "Hand" vases; 20c. Woven baskets.

See also Nos. 207/10.

50 Microscope and Slides

1968. 20th Anniv of World Health Organization.

92	50	2c. black, turquoise and blue	10	20
93	-	20c. black, orange and purple	40	50

DESIGN: 20c. Hypodermic syringe and jars of tablets.

52 Pitcairn Island

64b Queen Elizabeth II

1969. Multicoloured.

94	1c. Type **52**	2·25	2·00
95	2c. Captain Bligh and "Bounty" chronometer	25	15
96	3c. "Bounty" anchor (vert)	25	15
97	4c. Plans and drawing of "Bounty"	2·50	15
98	5c. Breadfruit containers and plant	70	15
99	6c. Bounty Bay	30	20
100	8c. Pitcairn longboat	2·00	20
101	10c. Ship landing point	2·00	85
102	15c. Fletcher Christian's Cave	2·25	1·75
103	20c. Thursday October Christian's house	60	40
104	25c. "Flying fox" cable system (vert)	70	40
105	30c. Radio Station, Taro Ground	55	45
106	40c. "Bounty" Bible	75	60
106a	50c. Pitcairn Coat-of-Arms	2·00	12·00
106b	$1 Type **64b**	5·50	17·00

65 Lantana

1970. Flowers. Multicoloured.

107	1c. Type **65**	15	50
108	2c. "Indian Shot"	20	65
109	5c. Pulau	25	75
110	25c. Wild gladiolus	60	2·00

69 Band-tailed Hind

1970. Fish. Multicoloured.

111	5c. Type **69**	1·50	1·00
112	10c. High-finned rudderfish	1·50	1·00
113	15c. Elwyn's wrasse	1·50	1·50
114	20c. Yellow wrasse ("Whistling daughter")	2·00	1·50

1971. Royal Visit. No. 101 optd **ROYAL VISIT 1971.**

115	10c. multicoloured	1·00	1·50

71 Polynesian Rock Carvings

1971. Polynesian Pitcairn. Multicoloured.

116	5c. Type **71**	75	75
117	10c. Polynesian artefacts (horiz)	1·00	1·00
118	15c. Polynesian stone fish-hook (horiz)	1·00	1·00
119	20c. Polynesian stone deity	1·25	1·25

72 Commission Flag

1972. 25th Anniv of South Pacific Commission. Multicoloured.

120	4c. Type **72**	40	70
121	8c. Young and elderly (Health)	40	70
122	18c. Junior school (Education)	50	90
123	20c. Goods store (Economy)	60	1·60

73 Red-tailed Tropic Birds and Longboat

1972. Royal Silver Wedding. Multicoloured, background colour given.

124	73	4c. green	30	60
125	73	20c. blue	45	90

74 Rose-apple

1973. Flowers. Multicoloured.

126	4c. Type **74**	55	55
127	8c. Mountain-apple	65	75
128	15c. "Lata"	80	1·00
129	20c. "Dorcas-flower"	80	1·25
130	35c. Guava	80	1·75

74a Princess Anne and Captain Mark Phillips

1973. Royal Wedding. Multicoloured, background colours given.

131	74a	10c. mauve	20	15
132	74a	25c. green	25	30

75 Obelisk Vertagus and Episcopal Mitre Shells

1974. Shells. Multicoloured.

147	4c. Type **75**	50	80
148	10c. Turtle dove-shell	60	1·00
149	18c. Indo-Pacific limpet, fringed false limpet and "Siphonaria normalis"	70	1·40
150	50c. "Ctena divergen"	1·00	2·00
MS151	130×121 mm. Nos. 147/50	2·75	14·00

76 Island Post Office

1974. Centenary of U.P.U.

152	76	4c. multicoloured	20	35
153	-	20c. purple, brown & black	25	60
154	-	35c. multicoloured	35	70

DESIGNS: 20c. Pre-stamp letter, 1922; 35c. Mailship and Pitcairn longboat.

77 Churchill and Text "Lift up your Hearts ..."

1974. Birth Cent of Sir Winston Churchill.

155	77	20c. olive, green and grey	30	65
156	-	35c. brown, green and grey	40	75

DESIGN: 35c. Text "Give us the tools ...".

78 H.M.S. "Seringapatam" (frigate), 1830

1975. Mailboats. Multicoloured.

157	4c. Type **78**	25	50
158	10c. "Pitcairn" (missionary schooner), 1890	30	75
159	18c. "Athenic" (liner), 1904	35	1·10
160	50c. "Gothic" (liner), 1948	60	1·75
MS161	145×110 mm. Nos. 157/60	11·00	16·00

79 "Polistes jadwigae" (wasp)

1975. Pitcairn Insects. Multicoloured.

162	4c. Type **79**	25	45
163	6c. "Euconocephalus sp." (grasshopper)	25	55
164	10c. "Anomis flavia" and "Chasmina tibialis" (moth)	30	70
165	15c. "Pantala flavescens" (skimmer)	40	1·00
166	20c. "Gnathothlibus erotus" (banana moth)	50	1·25

80 Fletcher Christian

1976. Bicent of American Revolution. Multicoloured.

167	5c. Type **80**	20	65
168	10c. H.M.S. "Bounty"	30	80
169	30c. George Washington	25	95
170	50c. "Mayflower", 1620	35	1·50

81 Chair of Homage

1977. Silver Jubilee. Multicoloured.

171	8c. Prince Philip's visit, 1971	10	15
172	20c. Type **81**	20	25
173	50c. Enthronement	40	50

82 The Island's Bell

1977. Multicoloured.

174	1c. Type **82**	10	35
175	2c. Building a longboat (horiz)	10	35
176	5c. Landing cargo (horiz)	10	35
177	6c. Sorting supplies (horiz)	10	35
178	9c. Cleaning wahoo (fish)	10	35
179	10c. Cultivation (horiz)	10	35
179a	15c. Sugar Mill (horiz)	50	1·00
180	20c. Grating coconut and bananas (horiz)	15	35
181	35c. The Island church (horiz)	15	50
182	50c. Fetching miro logs, Henderson Is. (horiz)	20	1·00
182b	70c. Burning obsolete stamp issues	50	1·25
183	$1 Prince Philip, Bounty Bay and Royal Yacht "Britannia" (horiz)	40	1·10
184	$2 Queen Elizabeth II (photograph by Reginald Davis)	50	1·25

83 Building a "Bounty" Model

1978. "Bounty" Day. Multicoloured.

185	6c. Type **83**	20	20
186	20c. The model at sea	25	25
187	35c. Burning the model	35	35
MS188	166×122 mm. Nos. 185/7	5·00	9·50

84 Coronation Ceremony

1978. 25th Anniv of Coronation. Sheet 94×78 mm.

MS189	84	$1.20 multicoloured	80	1·75

85 Harbour before Development

1978. "Operation Pallium" (Harbour Development Project). Multicoloured.

190	15c. Type **85**	25	50
191	20c. Unloading R.F.A. "Sir Geraint"	30	60
192	30c. Work on the jetty	35	70
193	35c. Harbour after development	40	80

86 John Adams and Diary Extract

1979. 150th Death Anniv of John Adams ("Bounty" mutineer). Multicoloured.

194	35c. Type **86**	30	70
195	70c. John Adams' grave and diary extract	45	90

87 Pitcairn's Island sketched from H.M.S. "Amphitrite"

1979. 19th-century Engravings.

196	**87**	6c. black, brown and stone	15	20
197	-	9c. black, violet & lt violet	15	25
198	-	20c. black, green and yellow	15	40
199	-	70c. black, scarlet and red	30	1·00

DESIGNS: 9c. Bounty Bay and Village of Pitcairn; 20c. Lookout Ridge; 70c. Church and School House.

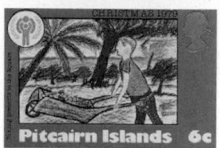

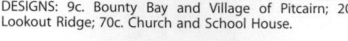

88 Taking Presents to the Square

1979. Christmas. Int Year of the Child. Multicoloured.

200	6c. Type **88**	10	20
201	9c. Decorating trees with presents	10	25
202	20c. Chosen men distributing gifts	15	40
203	35c. Carrying presents home	20	50
MS204	198×73 mm. Nos. 200/3	75	1·40

89 Loading Mail from Supply Ship to Longboats

1980. "London 1980" International Stamp Exhibition. Sheet 120×135 mm containing T **89** and similar horiz designs. Multicoloured.

MS205	35c. Type **89**; 35c. Mail being conveyed by "Flying Fox" (hoisting mechanism) to the Edge; 35c. Tractor transporting mail from the Edge to Adamstown; 35c. Mail being off-loaded at Post Office	75	1·50

90 Queen Elizabeth the Queen Mother at Henley Regatta

1980. 80th Birthday of The Queen Mother.

206	**90**	50c. multicoloured	40	70

1980. Handicrafts (2nd series). As T **46**. Multicoloured.

207	9c. Turtles (wood carvings)	10	10
208	20c. Pitcairn wheelbarrow (wood carving)	10	15
209	35c. Gamet (wood carving) (vert)	15	25
210	40c. Woven bonnet and fan (vert)	15	25

91 Part of Adamstown

1981. Landscapes. Multicoloured.

211	6c. Type **91**	10	10
212	9c. Big George	10	15
213	20c. Christian's Cave, Gannets Ridge	15	20
214	35c. Radio Station from Pawala Valley Ridge	20	30
215	70c. Tatrimoa	30	45

92 Islanders preparing for Departure

1981. 125th Anniv of Pitcairn Islanders' Migration to Norfolk Island. Multicoloured.

216	9c. Type **92**	15	30
217	35c. View of Pitcairn Island from "Morayshire"	25	50
218	70c. "Morayshire"	40	90

93 Prince Charles as Colonel-in-Chief, Cheshire Regiment

1981. Royal Wedding. Multicoloured.

219	20c. Wedding bouquet from Pitcairn Islands	20	20
220	35c. Type **93**	25	20
221	$1.20 Prince Charles and Lady Diana Spencer	75	60

94 Lemon

1982. Fruit. Multicoloured.

222	9c. Type **94**	10	10
223	20c. Pomegranate	15	20
224	35c. Avocado	20	30
225	70c. Pawpaw	40	65

95 Pitcairn Islands Coat of Arms

1982. 21st Birthday of Princess of Wales. Multicoloured.

226	6c. Type **95**	10	20
227	9c. Princess at Royal Opera House, Covent Garden, December 1981	45	20
228	70c. Balcony Kiss	55	60
229	$1.20 Formal portrait	1·00	80

96 Raphael's Angels

1982. Christmas. Raphael's Angels.

230	**96**	15c. black, silver and pink	20	20
231	-	20c. black, silver and yellow	20	20
232	-	50c. brown, silver and stone	30	30
233	-	$1 black, silver and blue	40	40

DESIGNS: 20c. to $1 Different details, the 50c. and $1 being vertical.

97 Radio Operator

1983. Commonwealth Day. Multicoloured.

234	6c. Type **97**	10	10
235	9c. Postal clerk	10	10
236	70c. Fisherman	35	65
237	$1.20 Artist	60	1·10

98 "Topaz" sights Smoke on Pitcairn

1983. 175th Anniv of Folger's Discovery of the Settlers. Multicoloured.

238	6c. Type **98**	40	20
239	20c. Three islanders approach the "Topaz"	45	30
240	70c. Capt. Mayhew Folger welcomed by John Adams	70	75
241	$1.20 Folger presented with "Bounty" chronometer	85	1·10

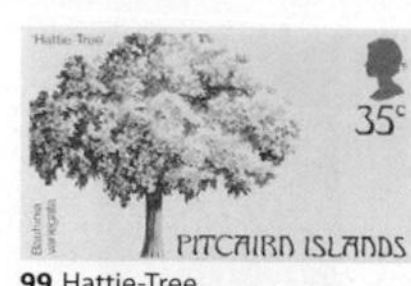

99 Hattie-Tree

1983. Trees of Pitcairn Islands (1st series). Multicoloured.

242	35c. Type **99**	25	55
243	35c. Leaves from Hattie-Tree	25	55
244	70c. Pandanus	40	90
245	70c. Pandanus and basket weaving	40	90

See also Nos. 304/7.

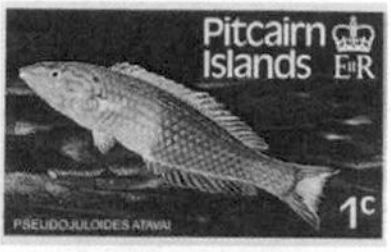

100 Atava wrasse

1984. Fish. Multicoloured.

246	1c. Type **100**	20	30
247	4c. Black-eared wrasse	30	35
248	6c. Long-finned parrotfish	30	35
249	9c. Yellow-edged lyretail	30	35
250	10c. Black-eared angelfish	30	40
251	15c. Emery's damselfish	40	40
252	20c. Smith's butterflyfish	40	50
253	35c. Crosshatched triggerfish	50	60
254	50c. Yellow damselfish	50	75
255	70c. Pitcairn angelfish	70	95
256	$1 Easter Island soldierfish	70	1·25
257	$1.20 Long-finned anthias	75	2·00
258	$2 White trevally	1·25	2·50
312	90c. As 9c.	4·00	5·00
313	$3 Wakanoura moray	5·50	8·50

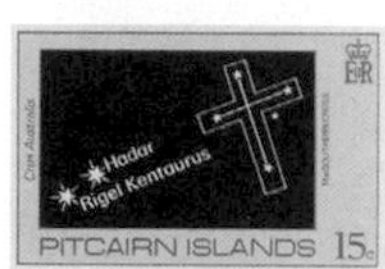

101 "Southern Cross"

1984. Night Sky.

259	**101**	15c. blue, lilac and gold	20	20
260	-	20c. blue, green and gold	30	30
261	-	70c. blue, brown and gold	75	75
262	-	$1 blue, light blue and gold	1·00	1·00

DESIGNS: 20c. "Southern Fish"; 70c. "Lesser Dog"; $1 "The Virgin".

102 Aluminium Longboat

1984. "Ausipex" International Stamp Exhibition, Melbourne. Sheet 134×86 mm containing T **102** and similar horiz design. Multicoloured.

MS263	50c. Type **102**; $2 Traditional-style wooden longboat	1·50	2·00

103 "H.M.S. "Portland" standing off Bounty Bay" (J. Linton Palmer)

1985. 19th-century Paintings (1st series). Multicoloured.

264	6c. Type **103**	40	40
265	9c. "Christian's Look Out" (J. Linton Palmer)	40	40
266	35c. "The Golden Age" (J. Linton Palmer)	75	60
267	$2 "A View of the Village, 1825" (William Smyth) (48×31 mm)	1·75	2·25

See also Nos. 308/11.

104 The Queen Mother with the Queen and Princess Margaret, 1980

1985. Life and Times of Queen Elizabeth the Queen Mother. Multicoloured.

268	6c. Receiving the Freedom of Dundee, 1964	10	25
269	35c. Type **104**	30	55
270	70c. The Queen Mother in 1983	50	85
271	$1.20 With Prince Henry at his christening (from photo by Lord Snowdon)	70	1·50
MS272	91×73 mm. $2 In coach at Ascot Races	2·75	2·75

105 "Act 6" (container ship)

1985. Ships (1st issue). Multicoloured.

273	50c. Type **105**	95	1·75
274	50c. "Columbus Louisiana" (container ship)	95	1·75
275	50c. "Essi Gina" (tanker) (48×35 mm)	95	1·75
276	50c. "Stolt Spirit" tanker (48×35 mm)	95	1·75

See also Nos. 296/9.

106 "Madonna and Child" (Raphael)

1985. Christmas. Designs showing "Madonna and Child" paintings. Multicoloured.

277	6c. Type **106**	80	50
278	9c. Krause (after Raphael)	80	50
279	35c. Andreas Mayer	1·50	70
280	$2 Unknown Austrian master	3·00	4·00

107 Green Turtle

1986. Turtles. Multicoloured.

281	9c. Type **107**	75	90
282	20c. Green turtle and Pitcairn Island	1·25	1·25
283	70c. Hawksbill turtle	2·25	3·75
284	$1.20 Hawksbill turtle and Pitcairn Island	2·75	4·25

1986. 60th Birthday of Queen Elizabeth II. As T **246a** of Papua New Guinea.

285	6c. Princess Elizabeth at Royal Lodge, Windsor, 1946	15	20
286	9c. Wedding of Princess Anne, 1973	15	20
287	20c. At Order of St. Michael and St. George service, St. Paul's Cathedral, 1961	25	30
288	$1.20 At Electrical Engineering Concert, Royal Festival Hall, 1971	60	1·25
289	$2 At Crown Agents Head Office, London 1983	75	2·00

107a Prince Andrew and Miss Sarah Ferguson

1986. Royal Wedding. Multicoloured.

290	20c. Type **107a**	50	50
291	$1.20 Prince Andrew aboard "Bluenose II" off Halifax, Canada, 1985	2·25	2·75

108 John I. Tay (pioneer missionary) and First Church

1986. Centenary of Seventh-Day Adventist Church on Pitcairn. Multicoloured.

292	6c. Type **108**	60	60
293	20c. "Pitcairn" (missionary schooner) and second church (1907)	1·50	1·00
294	35c. Baptism at Down Isaac and third church (1945)	1·75	1·50
295	$2 Islanders singing farewell hymn and present church (1954)	4·00	4·75

1987. Ships (2nd series). As T **105**. Multicoloured.

296	50c. "Samoan Reefer" (freighter)	1·10	2·50
297	50c. "Brussel" (container ship)	1·10	2·50
298	50c. "Australian Exporter" (container ship) (48×35 mm)	1·10	2·50
299	50c. "Taupo" (cargo liner) (48×35 mm)	1·10	2·50

109 Pitcairn Island Home

1987. Pitcairn Island Homes.

300	**109**	70c. black, dp violet & vio	70	60
301	-	70c. black, yellow & brn	70	60
302	-	70c. black, blue & dp blue	70	60
303	-	70c. black, green and deep green	70	60

DESIGNS: Nos. 301/3, different houses.

1987. Trees of Pitcairn Islands (2nd series). As T **99**. Multicoloured.

304	40c. Leaves and flowers from "Erythrina variegata"	1·25	1·75
305	40c. "Erythrina variegata" tree	1·25	1·75
306	$1.80 Leaves from "Aleurites moluccana" and nut torch	2·00	3·00
307	$1.80 "Aleurites moluccana" tree	2·00	3·00

1987. 19th-century Paintings (2nd series). Paintings by Lt. Conway Shipley in 1848. As T **103**. Multicoloured.

308	20c. "House and Tomb of John Adams"	75	60
309	40c. "Bounty Bay"	1·25	85
310	90c. "School House and Chapel"	2·00	2·00
311	$1.80 "Pitcairn Island" (48×31 mm)	3·00	5·50

110 *Bounty* (replica)

1988. Bicentenary of Australian Settlement. Sheet 112×76 mm.

MS314	**110** $3 multicoloured	6·00	3·00

111 H.M.S. "Swallow" (survey ship), 1767

1988. Ships. Multicoloured.

315	5c. Type **111**	50	80
316	10c. H.M.S. "Pandora" (frigate), 1791	50	80
317	15c. H.M.S. "Briton" and H.M.S. "Tagus" (frigates), 1814	55	90
318	20c. H.M.S. "Blossom" (survey ship), 1825	60	85
319	30c. "Lucy Anne" (barque), 1831	70	90
320	35c. "Charles Doggett" (whaling brig), 1831	70	90
321	40c. H.M.S. "Fly" (sloop), 1838	75	95
322	60c. "Camden" (missionary brig.), 1840	1·00	1·40
323	90c. H.M.S. "Virago" (paddle-sloop), 1853	1·00	1·75
324	$1.20 "Rakaia" (screw-steamer), 1867	1·25	2·00
325	$1.80 H.M.S. "Sappho" (screw-sloop), 1882	1·50	2·50
326	$5 H.M.S. "Champion" (corvette), 1893	3·00	5·50

112 Raising the Union Jack, 1838

1988. 150th Anniv of Pitcairn Island Constitution. Each showing different extract from original Constitution. Multicoloured.

327	20c. Type **112**	40	40
328	40c. Signing Constitution on board H.M.S. "Fly", 1838	60	60
329	$1.05 Voters at modern polling station	75	90
330	$1.80 Modern classroom	1·25	1·40

113 Angel

1988. Christmas. Multicoloured.

331	90c. Type **113**	65	70
332	90c. Holy Family	65	70
333	90c. Two Polynesian Wise Men	65	70
334	90c. Polynesian Wise Man and shepherd	65	70

114 Loading Stores, Deptford

1989. Bicentenary of Pitcairn Island Settlement (1st issue). Multicoloured.

335	20c. Type **114**	1·75	1·75
336	20c. H.M.S. "Bounty" leaving Spithead	1·75	1·75
337	20c. H.M.S. "Bounty" at Cape Horn	1·75	1·75
338	20c. Anchored in Adventure Bay, Tasmania	1·75	1·75
339	20c. Crew collecting breadfruit	1·75	1·75
340	20c. Breadfruit in cabin	1·75	1·75

See also Nos. 341/7, 356/61 and 389/94.

1989. Bicentenary of Pitcairn Island Settlement (2nd issue). As T **114**. Multicoloured.

341	90c. H.M.S. "Bounty' leaving Tahiti	3·25	3·25
342	90c. Bligh awoken by mutineers	3·25	3·25
343	90c. Bligh before Fletcher Christian	3·25	3·25
344	90c. Provisioning "Bounty's" launch	3·25	3·25
345	90c. "Mutineers casting Bligh adrift" (Robert Dodd)	3·25	3·25
346	90c. Mutineers discarding breadfruit plants	3·25	3·25
MS347	110×85 mm. 90c. No. 345; 90c. Isle of Man 1989 35p. Mutiny stamp; 90c. Norfolk Island 39c. Mutiny stamp	3·75	4·50

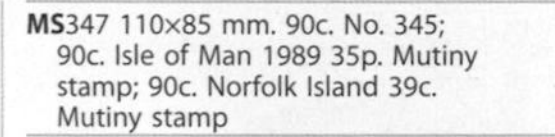

115 R.N.Z.A.F. Lockheed Orion making Mail Drop, 1985

1989. Aircraft. Multicoloured.

348	20c. Type **115**	1·50	60
349	80c. Beech 80 Queen Air on photo-mission, 1983	2·75	1·25
350	$1.05 Boeing-Vertol Chinook helicopter landing diesel fuel from U.S.S. "Breton", 1969	3·00	1·50
351	$1.30 R.N.Z.A.F. Lockheed Hercules dropping bulldozer, 1983	3·00	1·75

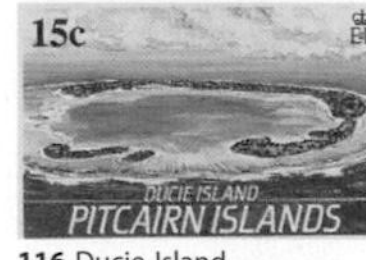

116 Ducie Island

1989. Islands of Pitcairn Group. Multicoloured.

352	15c. Type **116**	75	70
353	90c. Henderson Island	2·00	1·50
354	$1.05 Oeno Island	2·25	2·50
355	$1.30 Pitcairn Island	2·25	2·50

1990. Bicentenary of Pitcairn Island Settlement (3rd issue). As T **114**. Multicoloured.

356	40c. Mutineers sighting Pitcairn Island	1·75	1·75
357	40c. Ship's boat approaching landing	1·75	1·75
358	40c. Exploring island	1·75	1·75
359	40c. Ferrying goods ashore	1·75	1·75
360	40c. Burning of H.M.S. "Bounty"	1·75	1·75
361	40c. Pitcairn Island village	1·75	1·75

117 Ennerdale, Cumbria, and Peter Heywood

1990. "Stamp World London '90" International Stamp Exhibition, London. Designs showing English landmarks and "Bounty" crew members. Multicoloured.

362	80c. Type **117**	75	80
363	90c. St. Augustine's Tower, Hackney, and John Adams	85	90
364	$1.05 Citadel Gateway, Plymouth, and William Bligh	1·00	1·25
365	$1.30 Moorland Close, Cockermouth, and Fletcher Christian	1·25	1·40

117a Queen Elizabeth, 1937

1990. 90th Birthday of Queen Elizabeth the Queen Mother.

378	**117a**	40c. multicoloured	75	85
379	-	$3 black and red	3·00	3·75

DESIGN—29×37 mm: $3 King George VI and Queen Elizabeth on way to Silver Wedding Service, 1948.

118 "Bounty" Chronometer and 1940 1d. Definitive

1990. 50th Anniv of Pitcairn Islands Stamps. Multicoloured.

380	20c. Type **118**	80	80
381	80c. "Bounty" Bible and 1958 4d. definitive	1·60	1·75
382	90c. "Bounty" Bell and 1969 30c. definitive	1·75	1·90
383	$1.05 Mutiny on the "Bounty" and 1977 $1 definitive	2·00	2·50
384	$1.30 Penny Black and 1988 15c. definitive	2·25	2·75

119 Stephen's Lory ("Redbreast")

1990. "Birdpex '90" International Stamp Exhibition, Christchurch, New Zealand. Multicoloured.

385	20c. Type **119**	75	75
386	90c. Henderson Island fruit dove ("Wood Pigeon")	1·50	1·60
387	$1.30 Pitcairn warbler ("Sparrow")	1·75	2·75
388	$1.80 Henderson Island crake ("Chicken Bird")	2·00	3·00

1991. Bicentenary of Pitcairn Island Settlement (4th issue). Celebrations. As T **114**. Multicoloured.

389	80c. Re-enacting landing of mutineers	3·25	3·50
390	80c. Commemorative plaque	3·25	3·50
391	80c. Memorial church service	3·25	3·50
392	80c. Cricket match	3·25	3·50
393	80c. Burning model of "Bounty"	3·25	3·50
394	80c. Firework display	3·25	3·50

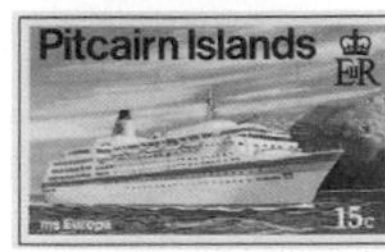

120 "Europa"

1991. Cruise Liners. Multicoloured.

395	15c. Type **120**	1·25	60
396	80c. "Royal Viking Star"	2·00	1·75
397	$1.30 "World Discoverer"	2·50	2·75
398	$1.80 "Sagafjord"	3·00	3·50

120a Queen in robes of the Order of St. George (vert)

1991. 65th Birthday of Queen Elizabeth II and 70th Birthday of Prince Philip.

399	20c. Prince Philip (vert)	75	30
400	$1.30 Type **120a**	1·50	1·25

121 Bulldozer

1991. Island Transport. Multicoloured.

401	20c. Type **121**	40	30
402	80c. Two-wheeled motorcycle	1·25	1·00
403	$1.30 Tractor	1·25	1·40
404	$1.80 Three-wheeled motorcycle	2·00	2·25

122 The Annunciation

1991. Christmas. Multicoloured.

405	20c. Type **122**	30	30
406	80c. Shepherds and lamb	90	90
407	$1.30 Holy Family	1·25	1·25
408	$1.80 Three Wise Men	1·75	1·75

122c Bounty Bay

1992. 40th Anniv of Queen Elizabeth II's Accession. Multicoloured.

409	20c. Type **122c**	25	25
410	60c. Sunset over Pitcairn	70	70
411	90c. Pitcairn coastline	90	90
412	$1 Three portraits of Queen Elizabeth	95	95
413	$1.80 Queen Elizabeth II	1·60	1·60

123 Insular Shark

1992. Sharks. Multicoloured.

414	20c. Type **123**	80	50
415	$1 Sand tiger	2·00	1·50
416	$1.50 Black-finned reef shark	2·25	2·00
417	$1.80 Grey reef shark	2·50	2·00

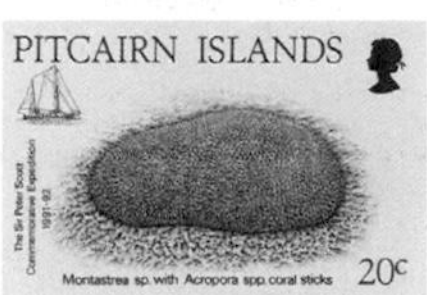

124 "Montastrea sp." and "Acropora spp." (corals)

1992. The Sir Peter Scott Memorial Expedition to Henderson Island. Multicoloured.

418	20c. Type **124**	80	60
419	$1 Henderson sandalwood	1·75	1·50
420	$1.50 Murphy's petrel	3·00	3·25
421	$1.80 Henderson hawkmoth	3·00	3·50

125 Bligh's Birthplace at St. Tudy, Cornwall

1992. 175th Death Anniv of William Bligh. Multicoloured.

422	20c. Type **125**	50	60
423	$1 Bligh on "Bounty"	1·50	1·50
424	$1.50 Voyage in "Bounty's" launch	2·00	2·75
425	$1.80 "William Bligh" (R. Combe) and epitaph	2·25	3·00

126 H.M.S. "Chichester" (frigate)

1993. Modern Royal Navy Vessels. Multicoloured

426	15c. Type **126**	75	50
427	20c. H.M.S. "Jaguar" (frigate)	75	50
428	$1.80 H.M.S. "Andrew" (submarine)	3·25	3·25
429	$3 H.M.S. "Warrior" (aircraft carrier) and Westland Dragonfly helicopter	5·75	5·50

127 Queen Elizabeth II in Coronation Robes

1993. 40th Anniv of Coronation.

430	**127**	$5 multicoloured	6·00	8·00

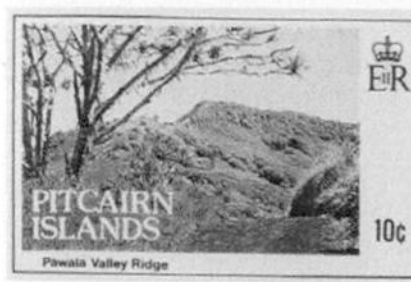

128 Pawala Valley Ridge

1993. Island Views. Multicoloured.

431	10c. Type **128**	20	20
432	90c. St. Pauls	90	90
433	$1.20 Matt's Rocks from Water Valley	1·25	1·50
434	$1.50 Ridge Rope to St. Paul's Pool	1·50	1·75
435	$1.80 Ship Landing Point	1·75	2·25

129 Indo-Pacific Tree Gecko

1993. Lizards. Multicoloured.

436	20c. Type **129**	90	50
437	45c. Stump-toed gecko	1·00	1·25
438	45c. Mourning gecko	1·00	1·25
439	$1 Moth skink	2·00	1·50
440	$1.50 Snake-eyed skink	2·50	2·75
441	$1.50 White-bellied skink	2·50	2·75

1994. "Hong Kong '94" International Stamp Exhibition. Nos. 437/8 and 440/1 optd **HONG KONG '94** and emblem.

442	45c. Stump-toed gecko	80	90
443	45c. Mourning gecko	80	90
444	$1.50 Snake-eyed skink	2·25	2·75
445	$1.50 White-bellied skink	2·25	2·75

130 Friday October Christian

1994. Early Pitcairners. Multicoloured.

446	5c. Type **130**	20	30
447	20c. Moses Young	50	40
448	$1.80 James Russell McCoy	2·25	2·75
449	$3 Rosalind Amelia Young	3·75	5·00

131 Landing Stores from Wreck of "Wildwave", Oeno Island, 1858

1994. Shipwrecks. Multicoloured.

450	20c. Type **131**	65	60
451	90c. Longboat trying to reach "Cornwallis", Pitcairn Island, 1875	1·75	1·75
452	$1.80 "Acadia" aground, Ducie Island, 1881	3·00	3·50
453	$3 Rescuing survivors from "Oregon", Oeno Island, 1883	4·25	4·50

132 Fire Coral

1994. Corals. Multicoloured.

454	20c. Type **132**	80	70
455	90c. Cauliflower coral and arc-eyed hawkfish (horiz)	2·00	2·00
456	$1 Lobe coral and high-finned rudderfish	2·00	2·00
MS457	100×70 mm. $3 Coral garden and mailed butterflyfish	4·00	5·00

133 Angel and "Ipomoea acuminata"

1994. Christmas. Flowers. Multicoloured.

458	20c. Type **133**	35	35
459	90c. Shepherds and "Hibiscus rosa-sinensis" (vert)	1·25	1·40
460	$1 Star and "Plumeria rubra"	1·25	1·40
461	$3 Holy Family and "Alpinia speciosa" (vert)	3·00	3·75

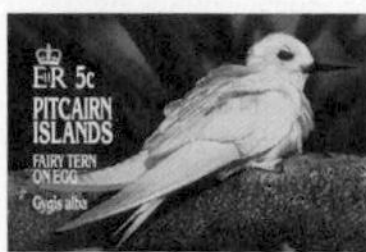

134 White ("Fairy") Tern on Egg

1995. Birds. Multicoloured.

462	5c. Type **134**	30	60
463	10c. Red-tailed tropic bird chick (vert)	30	60
464	15c. Henderson Island crake with chick	40	70
465	20c. Red-footed booby feeding chick (vert)	40	70
466	45c. Blue-grey noddy	60	80
467	50c. Pitcairn ("Henderson Reed") warbler in nest	65	90
468	90c. Common noddy	1·00	1·00
469	$1 Blue-faced ("Masked") booby and chick (vert)	1·10	1·10
470	$1.80 Henderson Island fruit dove	1·50	1·75
471	$2 Murphy's petrel	1·75	2·25
472	$3 Christmas Island shearwater	2·25	3·00
473	$5 Red-tailed tropic bird juvenile	3·50	4·50

135 Islanders in Longboats

1995. Oeno Island Holiday. Multicoloured.

474	20c. Type **135**	50	60
475	90c. Playing volleyball on beach	1·25	1·25
476	$1.80 Preparing picnic	2·25	3·25
477	$3 Singsong	3·50	5·00

136 Queen Elizabeth the Queen Mother

1995. 95th Birthday of Queen Elizabeth the Queen Mother. Sheet 75×90 mm.

MS478	**136**	$5 multicoloured	5·50	6·00

137 Guglielmo Marconi and Early Wireless, 1901

1995. Centenary of First Radio Transmission. Multicoloured.

479	20c. Type **137**	40	60
480	$1 Pitcairn radio transmitter, c. 1938	1·10	1·25
481	$1.50 Satellite Earth Station equipment, 1994	1·75	2·75
482	$3 Communications satellite in orbit, 1992	3·25	5·00

137a United Nations Float, Lord Mayor's Show

1995. 50th Anniv of United Nations. Multicoloured.

483	20c. Type **137a**	30	30
484	$1 R.F.A. "Brambleleaf" (tanker)	1·40	1·25
485	$1.50 U.N. Ambulance	2·00	2·25
486	$3 R.A.F. Lockheed L-1011 TriStar	3·50	3·75

138 Early Morning at the Jetty

1996. Supply Ship Day. Multicoloured.

487	20c. Type **138**	25	30
488	40c. Longboat meeting "America Star" (freighter)	45	55
489	90c. Loading supplies into longboats	1·00	1·10
490	$1 Landing supplies on jetty	1·10	1·25
491	$1.50 Sorting supplies at the Co-op	1·75	2·25
492	$1.80 Tractor towing supplies	1·90	2·25

1996. 70th Birthday of Queen Elizabeth II. As T **55** of Tokelau, each incorporating a different photograph of the Queen. Multicoloured.

493	20c. Bounty Bay	45	45
494	90c. Jetty and landing point, Bounty Bay	1·40	1·40
495	$1.80 Matt's Rocks	2·25	2·50
496	$3 St. Pauls	4·00	4·50

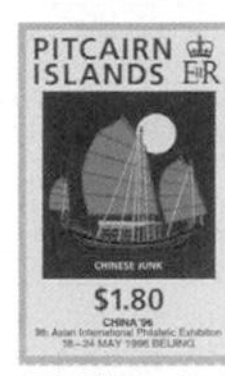

139 Chinese junk

1996. "CHINA '96" Ninth Asian International Stamp Exhibition, Peking. Multicoloured.

497	$1.80 Type **139**	2·25	2·50
498	$1.80 H.M.S. "Bounty"	2·25	2·50
MS499	80×79 mm. 90c. China 1984 8f. Year of the Rat stamp; 90c. Polynesian rat eating banana	2·00	2·00

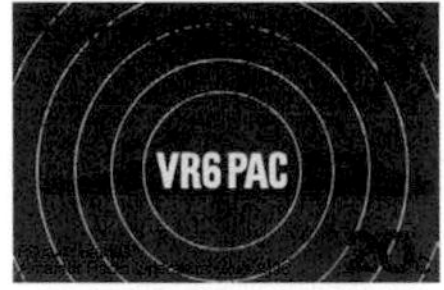

140 Island Profile and Radio Call Signs

1996. Amateur Radio Operations from Pitcairn Islands. Multicoloured.

500	20c. Type **140**	45	45
501	$1.50 Radio operator calling for medical assistance	2·00	2·50
502	$1.50 Doctors giving medical advice by radio	2·00	2·50
503	$2.50 Andrew Young (first radio operator), 1938	2·75	3·00

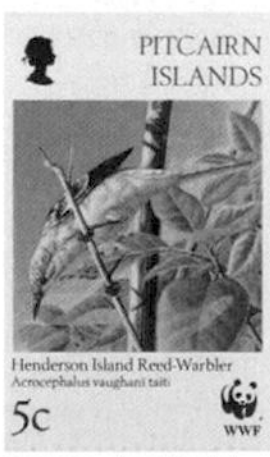

141 Pitcairn Warbler ("Henderson Island Reed Warbler")

1996. Endangered Species. Local Birds. Multicoloured.

504	5c. Type **141**	30	30
505	10c. Stephen's lory ("Stephen's Lorikeet")	30	30
506	20c. Henderson Island crake ("Henderson Island Rail")	50	50
507	90c. Henderson Island fruit dove	1·25	1·25
508	$2 White tern (horiz)	2·00	2·50
509	$2 Blue-faced booby ("Masked Booby") (horiz)	2·00	2·50

142 Coat of Arms

1997. "HONG KONG '97" International Stamp Exhibition. Chinese New Year ("Year of the Ox"). Sheet 82×87 mm.

MS510	**142** $5 multicoloured	5·00	5·50

143 "David Barker" (supply ship)

1997. 50th Anniv of South Pacific Commission. Sheet 115×56 mm, containing T **143** and similar horiz design. Multicoloured.

MS511	$2.50 Type **143**; $2.50 "McLachlan" (fishing boat)	9·50	9·50

144 Health Centre

1997. Island Health Care. Multicoloured.

512	20c. Type **144**	30	25
513	$1 Nurse treating patient	1·00	1·00
514	$1.70 Dentist treating woman	1·75	2·00
515	$3 Evacuating patient by longboat	3·00	3·75

1997. Golden Wedding of Queen Elizabeth and Prince Philip. As T **188a** of Norfolk Island. Multicoloured.

516	20c. Prince Philip driving carriage	30	40
517	20c. Queen Elizabeth	30	40
518	$1 Prince Philip at Royal Windsor Horse Show, 1996	1·00	1·25
519	$1 Queen Elizabeth with horse	1·00	1·25
520	$1.70 Queen Elizabeth and Prince Philip at the Derby, 1991	1·50	1·75
521	$1.70 Prince Charles hunting, 1995	1·50	1·75

Nos. 516/17, 518/19 and 520/21 respectively were printed together, se-tenant, with the backgrounds forming composite designs.

145 Island and Star

1997. Christmas. Multicoloured.

522	20c. Type **145**	50	40
523	80c. Hand ringing bell	1·25	80
524	$1.20 Presents in baskets	1·40	1·75
525	$3 Families outside church	3·00	3·50

146 Christian's Cave

1997. Christian's Cave. Multicoloured.

526	5c. Type **146**	15	20
527	20c. View from the beach	35	35
528	35c. Cave entrance (vert)	50	50
529	$5 Pathway through forest (vert)	3·75	5·00

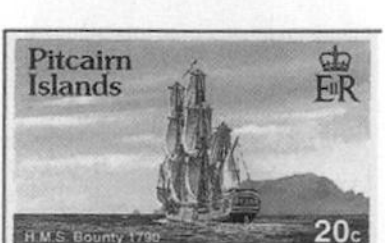

147 H.M.S. "Bounty" (Bligh), 1790

1998. Millennium Commemoration (1st issue). Sailing Ships. Multicoloured.

530	20c. Type **147**	1·00	75
531	90c. H.M.S. "Swallow" (Carteret), 1767	1·75	1·10
532	$1.80 H.M.S. "Briton" and H.M.S. "Tagus" (frigates), 1814	2·50	2·25
533	$3 H.M.S. "Fly" (sloop), 1838	3·75	4·00

See also Nos. 549/52 and 577/80.

1998. Diana, Princess of Wales Commemoration. Sheet, 145×70 mm, containing vert designs as T **194a** of Norfolk Island. Multicoloured.

MS534	90c. Wearing pearl choker and red evening dress; 90c. Wearing white hat and pearl necklace; 90c. Carrying bouquet; 90c. Wearing white dress and hat (*sold at $3.60+40c. charity premium*)	3·50	3·75

148 "Bidens mathewsii"

1998. Flowers. Multicoloured.

535	20c. Type **148**	1·25	1·00
536	90c. "Hibiscus" sp.	2·25	1·75
537	$1.80 "Osteomeles anthyllidifolia"	3·75	4·25
538	$3 "Ipomoea littoralis"	5·00	6·00

149 Fishing

1998. International Year of the Ocean. Multicoloured.

539	20c. Type **149**	1·40	1·00
540	90c. Diver at wreck of "Cornwallis" (vert)	2·50	1·75
541	$1.80 Reef fish	4·00	4·25
542	$3 Murphy's petrel and great frigate bird (vert)	5·50	6·50
MS543	86×86 mm. Nos. 539/42	13·00	13·00

150 George Nobbs and Class, 1838

1999. Development of Local Education. Multicoloured.

544	20c. Type **150**	1·00	80
545	90c. Children outside thatched school, 1893	1·90	1·60
546	$1.80 Boy in wheelbarrow outside wooden school, 1932	3·25	3·50
547	$3 Modern classroom with computer	4·50	5·00

151 H.M.S. "Bounty" and Anchor

1999. "Australia '99" World Stamp Exhibition, Melbourne. Pitcairn Archaeology Project. Sheet, 190×80 mm, containing T **151** and similar diamond-shaped designs. Multicoloured.

MS548	50c. Type **151**; $1 "Bounty" approaching Pitcairn and cannon; $1.50, "Bounty" on fire and chronometer; $2 "Bounty" sinking and metal bucket	9·50	9·50

152 John Adams (survivor of "Bounty" crew) and Bounty Bay

1999. Millennium Commemoration (2nd issue). Multicoloured.

549	20c. Type **152**	1·00	75
550	90c. "Topaz" (sealer), 1808	2·25	1·40
551	$1.80 George Hunn Nobbs and Norfolk Island	3·00	3·50
552	$3 H.M.S "Champion" (corvette), 1893	5·50	6·50

153 Prince Edward and Miss Sophie Rhys-Jones

1999. Royal Wedding. Multicoloured.

553	$2.50 Type **153**	3·75	4·25
554	$2.50 Engagement photograph	3·75	4·25

154 Bee-keepers at Work

1999. Bee-keeping. Multicoloured. Self-adhesive.

555	20c. Type **154**	1·00	1·00
556	$1 Bee on passion flower	2·25	2·25
557	$1.80 Bees in honeycomb	3·50	4·00
558	$3 Bee on flower and jar of "Mutineer's Dream" honey	5·00	6·00
MS559	74×100 mm. No. 556	5·00	6·00

No. **MS**559 includes the "China '99" International Stamp Exhibition emblem on the sheet margin.

155 Arrival of "Yankee" (schooner), 1937

2000. Protection of "Mr. Turpen" (Galapagos Tortoise on Pitcairn). Multicoloured.

560	5c. Type **155**	2·00	2·50
561	20c. Off-loading Mr. Turpen at Bounty Bay	2·75	3·25
562	35c. Mr. Turpen	3·25	3·75
563	$5 Head of Mr. Turpen	6·00	7·00

Nos. 560/3 were printed together, se-tenant, with the background forming a composite design.

156 *Guettarda speciosa* (flower)

2000. Flowers of Pitcairn Islands. Multicoloured.

564	10c. Type **156**	45	60
565	15c. *Hibiscus tiliaceus*	55	60
566	20c. *Selenicereus grandiflorus*	60	60
567	30c. *Metrosideros collina*	70	70
568	50c. *Alpinia zerumbet*	90	90
569	$1 *Syzygium jambos*	1·50	1·50
570	$1.50 *Commelina diffusa*	2·50	2·50
571	$1.80 *Canna indica*	2·75	2·75
572	$2 *Allamanda cathartica*	3·00	3·25
573	$3 *Calophyllum inophyllum*	4·00	4·50
574	$5 *Ipomea indica*	6·00	7·00
575	$10 *Bauhinia monandra* (40×40 mm)	10·00	12·00

2000. "The Stamp Show 2000" International Stamp Exhibition, London. Sheet, 120×80 mm, containing Nos. 570 and 572.

MS576	$1.50 Commelina diffusa; $2 Allamanda cathartica	7·50	8·50

157 Longboat

2000. Millennium Commemoration (3rd issue). Communications. Multicoloured.

577	20c. Type **157**	1·00	90
578	90c. Landing and Longboat House	2·25	1·40
579	$1.80 Honda quad with trailer of watermelons	3·75	4·00
580	$3 Woman with printer at Satellite Station	5·50	6·50

158 Surveyor and Helicopter

2000. "EXPO 2000" World Stamp Exhibition, Anaheim, U.S.A. Anglo-American Joint Satellite Recovery Survey Mission, Henderson Island, 1966. Sheet, 120×180 mm, containing T **158** and similar vert design. Multicoloured.

MS581	$2.50 Type **158**; $2.50 Survey team and U.S.S. *Sunnyvale* (satellite recovery vessel)	14·00	14·00

No. **MS**581 was issued folded in half horizontally with the issue title, "CLASSIFIED INFORMATION" and seal printed on the gum of the top panel. Details of the survey appear on the other side of this section.

159 Queen Elizabeth the Queen Mother

2000. Queen Elizabeth the Queen Mother's 100th Birthday. Sheet, 127×95 mm (oval-shaped), containing T **159** and similar vert design. Multicoloured.

MS582	$2 Type **159**; $3 Queen Mother wearing plum outfit	5·00	6·00

160 Wrapping Presents

2000. Christmas. Multicoloured.

583	20c. Type **160**	1·00	1·00
584	80c. Ringing island bell	2·25	2·25
585	$1.50 Making decorations	3·75	4·00
586	$3 Opening presents	5·50	6·50

161 *Europa* (liner)

2001. Cruise Ships. Multicoloured.

587	$1.50 Type **161**	3·75	4·50
588	$1.50 *Rotterdam VI*	3·75	4·50
589	$1.50 *Saga Rose*	3·75	4·50
590	$1.50 *Bremen*	3·75	4·50

162 Coconut

2001. Tropical Fruit. Multicoloured.

591	20c. Type **162**	65	65
592	80c. Pomegranate	1·25	1·25
593	$1 Passion fruit	1·50	1·50
594	$3 Pineapple	4·25	5·00
MS595	103×70 mm. Nos. 592 and 594	4·50	5·00

163 Keyboard

2001. Introduction of Pitcairn Islands Internet Domain Name. Multicoloured. Self-adhesive.

596	20c. Type **163**	70	55
597	50c. Circuit board	1·25	80
598	$1 Microchip	1·75	1·25
599	$5 Mouse	5·50	7·50

164 Ornate Butterflyfish (*Chaetodon ornatissimus*)

2001. Reef Fish. Multicoloured.

600	20c. Type **164**	1·00	1·00
601	80c. Mailed butterflyfish (*Chaetodon reticulatus*)	2·25	1·40
602	$1.50 Racoon butterflyfish (*Chaetodon lunula*)	3·00	3·50
603	$2 *Henochus chrysostomus*	4·00	4·75
MS604	87×120 mm. Nos. 600 and 603	4·25	4·75

No. **MS**604 has the paper around the outlines of fish along the upper edge of the sheet cut away.

165 Man carrying Driftwood

2001. Woodcarving. Multicoloured.

605	20c. Type **165**	1·00	1·25
606	50c. Carver at work	1·50	2·00
607	$1.50 Working on wood lathe	2·00	2·50
608	$3 Taking carvings to *World Discoverer* (cruise liner) for sale	3·00	3·50

Nos. 605/8 were printed together, se-tenant, with the backgrounds forming a composite design.

166 *Cypraea argus* Shell

2001. Cowrie Shells. Multicoloured.

609	20c. Type **166**	90	75
610	80c. *Cypraea isabella*	1·40	1·10
611	$1 *Cypraea mappa*	1·60	1·50
612	$3 *Cypraea mauritiana*	3·50	5·00

2002. Golden Jubilee. Sheet, 162×95 mm, containing designs as T **153** of Nauru.

MS613	50c. black, violet and gold; $1 multicoloured; $1.20 black, violet and gold; $1.50 multicoloured; $2 multicoloured	8·00	8·50

DESIGNS—HORIZ: 50c. Queen Elizabeth with Princesses Elizabeth and Margaret; $1 Queen Elizabeth in evening dress; $1.20 Princess Elizabeth in evening dress; $1.50 Queen Elizabeth in blue hat and coat. VERT (38×51 mm)—$2 Queen Elizabeth after Annigoni.

167 James McCoy (President of Island Council)

2002. Pitcairn Islands Celebrities. Multicoloured.

614	$1.50 Type **167**	2·75	3·00
615	$1.50 Admiral Sir Fairfax Moresby	2·75	3·00
616	$1.50 Gerald DeLeo Bliss (postmaster, Cristobal, Panama Canal Zone)	2·75	3·00
617	$1.50 Captain Arthur Jones of Shaw Savill Line	2·75	3·00

168 "Simba Christian" (cat)

2002. Pitcairn Cats. Multicoloured.

618	20c. Type **168**	70	50
619	$1 "Miti Christian"	1·50	80
620	$1.50 "Nala Brown"	2·00	2·25
621	$3 "Alicat Palau"	3·25	3·75
MS622	92×86 mm. Nos. 618 and 621	4·75	5·25

2002. Queen Elizabeth the Queen Mother Commemoration. As T **156** of Nauru.

623	40c. black, gold and purple	1·00	65
624	$1 brown, gold and purple	1·75	1·10
625	$1.50 multicoloured	2·25	2·50
626	$2 multicoloured	2·75	3·25
MS627	145×70 mm. Nos. 624 and 626	5·50	6·00

DESIGNS: 40c. Lady Elizabeth Bowes-Lyon, 1910; $1 Lady Elizabeth Bowes-Lyon, 1923; $1.50, Queen Mother at Leatherhead, 1970; $2 Queen Mother at Scrabster. Designs as Nos. 624 and 626 in No. **MS**627 omit the "1900-2002" inscription and the coloured frame.

169 Woman cutting Palm Fronds and Fan

2002. Weaving. Multicoloured.

628	40c. Type **169**	1·75	2·00
629	80c. Woman preparing leaves and woven bag	2·50	2·75
630	$1.50 Millie Christian weaving basket	3·50	4·00
631	$2.50 Thelma Brown at basket stall in the Square	4·50	5·00

Nos. 628/31 were printed together, se-tenant, with the backgrounds forming a composite design.

170 Dudwi Nut Tree (*Aleurites moluccana*)

2002. Trees. Multicoloured.

632	40c. Type **170**	80	60
633	$1 Toa (*Cordia subcordata*)	1·50	1·00
634	$1.50 Miro (*Thespesia populnea*)	2·00	2·00
635	$3 Hulianda (*Cerbera manghas*)	3·50	4·00

171 *America Star* (container ship) and Island Longboat

2003. 21 Years of Blue Star Line Service to Pitcairn Islands. Sheet 158×75 mm.

MS636	**171** $5 multicoloured	11·00	12·00

172 *Conus geographus* Shell

2003. Conus Shells. Multicoloured.

637	40c. Type **172**	1·00	65
638	80c. *Conus textile*	1·40	85
639	$1 *Conus striatus*	1·75	1·25
640	$1.20 *Conus marmoreus*	1·75	1·60
641	$3 *Conus litoglyphus*	4·00	4·75

2003. 50th Anniv of Coronation. As T **115** of Kiribati. Multicoloured.

642	40c. Queen Elizabeth II wearing tiara	80	55
643	80c. Coronation Coach drawn by eight horses	1·25	75
644	$1.50 Queen wearing tiara and white gown	2·00	2·00
645	$3 Queen with bishops and Maids of Honour	3·75	4·75
MS646	95×115 mm. 40c. As No. 642; $3 As No. 645	4·25	4·75

173 Women Storing Leaves in Earthenware Jars and *Bauhinia monandra*

2003. Art of Pitcairn (3rd series). Painted Leaves. Multicoloured.

647	40c. Type **173**	1·25	1·50
648	80c. Woman washing soaked leaves and *Bauhinia monandra*	2·00	2·25
649	$1.50 Bernice Christian with dried leaf and paints and *Sapindrus saponaria* plant	3·50	4·00
650	$3 Charlotte Christian painting leaf, Bauhinia leaf and *Bounty*	5·50	6·50

Nos. 647/50 were printed together, se-tenant with the backgrounds forming a composite design.

174 Diadem Squirrel Fish

2003. Squirrel Fish. Multicoloured.

651	40c. Type **174**	1·00	75
652	80c. Scarlet-finned squirrel fish	1·50	1·25
653	$1.50 Silver-spotted squirrel fish	2·75	2·75
654	$3 Bloodspot squirrel fish	4·50	5·50
MS655	100×80 mm. No. 654	8·00	8·50

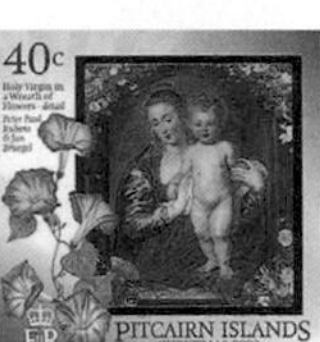

175 "Holy Virgin in a Wreath of Flowers" (detail) (Rubens and Jan Brueghel)

2003. Christmas. Multicoloured.

656	40c. Type **175**	90	60
657	$1 "Madonna della Rosa" (detail) (Raphael)	1·50	90
658	$1.50 "Stuppacher Madonna" (detail) (Matthias Grunewald)	2·50	2·00
659	$3 "Madonna with Cherries" (detail) (Titian)	4·25	5·50

176 *Terebra maculate*

2004. Terebra Shells. Multicoloured.

660	40c. Type **176**	85	65
661	80c. *Terebra subulata*	1·40	85
662	$1.20 *Terebra crenulata*	1·90	1·75
663	$3 *Terebra dimidiatai*	4·25	5·50

177 Bounty Bay and Hill of Difficulty

2004. Scenic Views. Multicoloured.

664	50c. Type **177**	1·40	1·00
665	$1 Christian's Cave on rock face (horiz)	2·50	2·00
666	$1.50 St. Paul's Pool	3·75	3·75
667	$2.50 Ridge Rope towards St. Paul's Point (horiz)	5·50	6·50

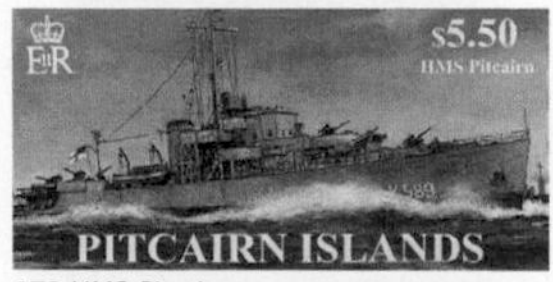

178 HMS *Pitcairn*

2004. 60th Anniv of Commission of HMS *Pitcairn*. Sheet 135×80 mm.

MS668	**178** $5.50 multicoloured	11·00	13·00

179 HMAV *Bounty* Replica

2004. HMAV Bounty Replica (three masted ship). Multicoloured.

669	60c. Type **179**	1·75	1·10
670	80c. Stern of ship	2·00	1·40
671	$1 Figurehead	2·50	2·00
672	$3.50 Ropes and HMAV *Bounty* replica sailing	7·00	9·00
MS673	103×72 mm. $3.50 As No. 672	12·00	13·00

180 Murphy's Petrels

2004. Murphy's Petrel. Multicoloured.

674	40c. Type **180**	1·00	70
675	50c. Murphy's petrel and young in nest	1·10	1·00
676	$1 Murphy's petrel from side (vert)	1·75	1·50
677	$2 Head of Murphy's petrel (vert)	2·75	3·25
678	$2.50 Murphy's petrel in flight	3·00	3·75
MS679	154×86 mm. Nos. 674/8	13·00	14·00

181 Beach, Ducie Island

2005. Scenery (1st issue). Ducie and Oeno Islands. Photographs by Dr. Michael Brooke, Cambridge, and Brian Bell, Blenheim. Multicoloured.

680	50c. Type **181**	1·10	80
681	60c. Coral reef, Ducie Island	1·25	1·00
682	80c. Low sun, Ducie Island	1·60	1·25
683	$1 Boat moored off beach, Oeno	1·90	1·75
684	$1.50 Palm trees on beach, Oeno	2·75	3·25
685	$2.50 View of Oeno from sea	4·75	5·50

See also Nos. 704/9.

182 Corona

2005. Solar Eclipse, Oeno. Sheet 144×48 mm containing T **182** and similar circular designs. Multicoloured.

MS686	$1 Type **182**; $2 Chromosphere; $3 Photosphere	10·00	13·00

183 *Hypolimnas bolina* (male)

2005. Blue Moon Butterfly. Sheet 135×51 mm containing T **183** and similar square design. Multicoloured.

MS687	$1.50 Type **183**; $4 *Hypolimnas bolina* (female)	14·00	15·00

184 Prince Charles and Mrs. Camilla Parker-Bowles

2005. Royal Wedding.

688	**184**	$5 multicoloured	15·00	15·00

185 HMS *Bounty* (Replica)

2005. HMS *Bounty* (Replica). Multicoloured.

689	40c. Type **185**	1·25	75
690	$1 Port side of ship	2·25	1·75
691	$1.20 Sailing off coast	2·50	2·25
692	$3 Bowsprit and in full sail	6·50	7·50
MS693	122×87 mm. $3 As No. 692	7·00	8·00

186 Bristle-thighed Curlews

2005. Bristle-thighed Curlew (*Numenius tahitiensis*). Multicoloured.

694	60c. Type **186**	1·75	1·10
695	$1 Back of bird	2·25	1·50
696	$1.50 Beak open (vert)	3·00	3·00
697	$1.80 Beak closed (vert)	3·50	3·75
698	$2 Perched on rock	4·00	4·50
MS699	156×86 mm. Nos. 694/8	13·00	14·00

187 Hibiscus Flower in Bauble

2005. Christmas. Designs showing baubles. Multicoloured.

700	40c. Type **187**	1·25	70
701	80c. Red-tailed tropic bird	2·25	1·40
702	$1.80 Arms	3·25	3·75
703	$2.50 Sailing ship	4·75	6·00

2005. Scenery (2nd issue). Henderson Island. As T **181** showing coastal views and line drawings of fauna. Multicoloured.

704	50c. Flying insects and misty shoreline	1·25	70
705	60c. Parrots and sandy beach	1·75	1·25
706	$1 Tropic birds and sandy bay	2·50	1·75
707	$1.20 Lobsters and shore with overhanging rock ledge	2·50	2·50
708	$1.50 Octopus and cliffs	3·00	3·50
709	$2 Turtles and sandy beach	3·50	4·00

188 Capt William Driver at Ship's Wheel and Old Glory Flag

2006. 175th Anniv of Voyage of Charles Doggett flying Old Glory (Stars and Stripes) Flag. Sheet 133×80 mm.

MS710	**188** $5 multicoloured	7·50	8·50

No. **MS**710 also commemorates the 175th anniversary of the return of the Pitcairn Islanders from Tahiti.

189 Princess Elizabeth

2006. 80th Birthday of Queen Elizabeth II. Multicoloured.

711	40c. Type **189**	80	55
712	80c. Queen wearing tiara, c. 1952	1·25	90
713	$1.80 Wearing yellow dress	2·00	2·50
714	$3.50 Wearing red hat and jacket	4·50	5·50
MS715	143×72 mm. $1.80 As No. 712; $3.50 As No. 713	7·50	8·50

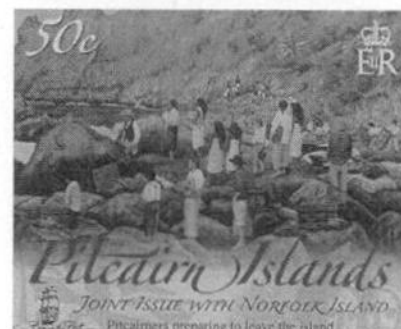

190 Pitcairn Islanders waiting to leave

2006. 150th Anniv of Migration of Pitcairn Islanders to Norfolk Island. Multicoloured.

716	50c. Type **190**	1·50	1·75
717	$1 Emigrant ship *Morayshire* leaving Pitcairn Island	2·25	2·50
718	$1.50 *Morayshire* anchored in Kingston Bay, Norfolk Island	3·00	3·50
719	$3 Arrival of Pitcairn Islanders at Kingston, Norfolk Island	5·00	6·00

Nos. 716/19 are inscribed "JOINT ISSUE WITH NORFOLK ISLAND". The Norfolk Island stamps issued on the same day have different designs.

191 Fisherman with Catch

2006. Early Civilisation (1st series). Cave Dwellers of Henderson Island. Sheet 195×82 mm containing T **191** and similar multicoloured designs.

MS720	60c. Type **191**; $1.20 Child with captive seabird; $2 Man making fish hooks; $2.50 Two women at cave entrance	7·50	8·00

The stamps and margins of No. **MS**720 form a composite design showing cave dwellers on shore of Henderson Island.

See also No. **MS**733.

192 Humpback Whale and Calf

2006. Humpback Whales (*Megaptera novaeangliae*). Multicoloured.

721	$1.50 Type **192**	3·00	3·00
722	$3.50 Tail of humpback whale	5·50	6·00
MS723	125×88 mm. Nos. 721/2	7·50	8·00

193 Sooty Tern

2007. Endangered Species. Terns and Noddies of the Pitcairn Islands. Multicoloured.

724	50c. Type **193**	1·50	1·75
725	60c. Blue-grey ternlet	1·50	1·75
726	$2 Brown noddy	3·00	3·50
727	$3 Black noddy	4·00	4·50
MS728	180×105 mm. Nos. 724/7, each ×2	16·00	18·00

194 Diver searching Seabed for Wreckage from HMS *Bounty*

2007. 50th Anniv of the Raising of the Bounty Anchor. Multicoloured.

729	60c. Type **194**	1·75	2·00
730	$1 Two divers with *Bounty* anchor	2·50	3·00
731	$1.20 Capt. Johnson on board brigantine *Yankee* winching up *Bounty* anchor	2·75	3·25
732	$2.50 *Bounty* anchor on shore	4·50	5·00

2007. Early Civilisation (2nd series). Rock Carvers of Pitcairn. Sheet 195×82 mm containing multicoloured designs as T **191**.

MS733	60c. Man carving petroglyphs into rock; $1.20 Two men carving stone god (horiz); $2 Tool-maker (horiz); $2.50 Man making stone adze	9·00	10·00

The stamps and margins of No. **MS**733 form a composite design showing rock carvers and tool-makers on shore of Pitcairn Island.

195 Salt and Pepper Moth

2007. Salt and Pepper Moth (*Utetheisa pulchelloides*). Multicoloured.

734	$2 Type **195**	4·00	4·00
735	$4 In flight	6·00	7·00
MS736	135×60 mm. Nos. 734/5	10·00	11·00

196 Crows' Nest

2007. Detail from HMS Bounty Replica. Multicoloured.

737	10c. Type **196**	10	10
738	20c. Ropes and pulleys	25	25
739	40c. Guns	50	50
740	50c. Compass	60	60
741	80c. Wheel	1·00	1·00
742	$1 Figurehead	1·20	1·20
743	$1.50 Mast	1·90	1·90
744	$2 Sail	2·25	2·25
745	$3.50 Sextant	3·00	3·00
746	$4 Lantern and stern of *Bounty*	3·50	3·50
747	$5 Bell	4·00	4·00
748	$10 Chronometer	8·75	8·75

197 *Gymnosarda unicolor* (dog tooth tuna)

2007. Ocean Fish. Multicoloured.

749	$1 Type **197**	2·50	2·50
750	$1 *Acanthocybium solandri* (wahoo)	2·50	2·50
751	$1 *Coryphaena hippurus* (dorado)	2·50	2·50
752	$1 *Thunnus albacares* (yellow fin tuna)	2·50	2·50
753	$1 *Caranx ignobilis* (giant trevally)	2·50	2·50
754	$1 *Sarda chiliensis lineolata* (bonito)	2·50	2·50

Nos. 749/54 were printed together, *se-tenant*, forming a composite background design.

198 Oeno Island

2008. Pitcairn Islands from DigitalGlobe Space Satellite. Multicoloured. Self-adhesive.

755	60c. Type **198**	1·50	1·50
756	$1 Pitcairn Island	2·25	2·25
757	$2 Henderson Island	4·00	4·50
758	$2.50 Ducie Island	4·50	5·00

199 Timber-framed Longboat under Construction

2008. Pitcairn's Longboat History. Multicoloured.

759	50c. Type **199**	1·75	2·00
760	$1 Last wooden rowing longboat, launched 1983	2·50	2·75
761	$1.50 Diesel-powered aluminium longboat, arrived 1995	3·50	3·75
762	$3.50 Longboats ashore, Oeno Island at sunset	5·00	5·50

200 Bee on Yellow Guava (*Psidium guajava*) Flower

2008. Flowers and Bees. Designs showing the Italian honey bees (*Apis mellifera ligustica*) introduced to Pitcairn on island flowers. Multicoloured.

763	$1 Type **200**	2·25	1·50
764	$1.20 Bee on portulaca (*Portulaca oleracea*)	2·75	2·25
765	$1.50 Bee approaching sunflower	3·25	3·00
766	$3 Bee on mountain chestnut tree (*Metrosideros collina*) flower	5·00	6·50
MS767	120×80 mm. Nos. 765/6	8·75	10·00

201 Sunset

2008. Pitcairn Island Sunsets. Multicoloured.

768	50c. Type **201**	1·00	1·00
769	60c. Sunset over sea, tree branches in foreground	1·10	1·10
770	80c. Setting sun reflected in ocean	1·40	1·40
771	$1 Sunset and headland	1·60	1·60
772	$2 Sunset, coast and offshore rocks	3·25	3·75
773	$2.50 Deep red sunset over coast with trees	4·00	4·50

202 Captain Mayhew Folger

2008. Bicentenary of 'the Discovery of a Community' (meeting of Capt Folger of US Topaz and surviving Bounty mutineer John Adams).

MS774	134×80 mm. **202** $5 multicoloured	6·50	7·00

203 Green Turtle

2008. Green Turtles (*Chelonia mydas*) of Henderson Island. Sheet 192×83 mm containing T **203** and similar multicoloured designs.

MS775	60c. Type **203**; $1 Turtle swimming; $2 Turtle coming ashore; $2.50 Turtle hatchlings	8·00	8·50

The stamps within **MS**775 form a composite design showing turtles coming ashore and hatchlings on a Henderson Island beach.

204 Coconut Crab

2009. Coconut Crab (Birgus latro). Multicoloured.

776	$2.80 Type **204**	5·00	5·50
777	$4 Coconut crab (side view)	7·00	8·00
MS778	109×84 mm. Nos. 776/7	11·00	13·00

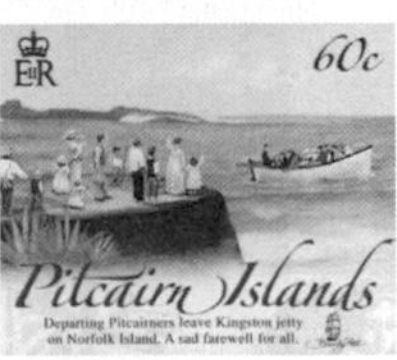

205 Departing Pitcairners leaving Kingston Jetty on Norfolk Island

2009. 150th Anniv of the Return of the Pitcairn Islanders from Norfolk Island. Multicoloured.

779	60c. Type **205**	1·75	2·00
780	$1 Pitcairners rowing out to sailing ship *Mary Ann*, 2 December 1858	2·50	3·00
781	$2 Passengers on board *Mary Ann*, approaching PItcairn Island	3·75	4·00
782	$3.50 Newly arrived Pitcairners climbing The Hill of Difficulty, 17 January 1859	5·00	5·50

Nos. 779/82 and the central stamp-size label form a composite design.

206 Giant Panda

2009. 23rd Asian International Stamp Exhibition, Hong Kong. Sheet 135×95 mm containing T **206** and T **262** of Vanuatu. Multicoloured.

MS783	$2.50 Type **206**; 150v. Type **262** of Vanuatu (sold at $5)	11·00	12·00

No. **MS**783 is identical to **MS**1054 of Vanuatu.

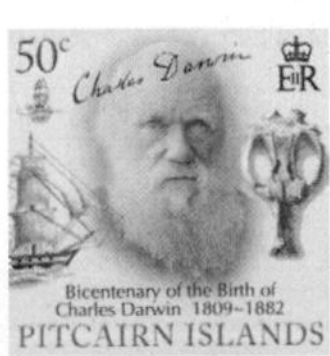

207 Charles Darwin and HMS *Bounty*

2009. Birth Bicentenary of Charles Darwin (naturalist and evolutionary theorist). Multicoloured.

784	50c. Type **207**	1·75	1·25
785	$1.50 Darwin, Galapagos giant tortoise and land iguana	3·50	3·50
786	$2 Darwin and Galapagos finches showing beak variations	4·00	4·50
787	$3.50 Darwin, *The Origin of Species* and gorilla	6·00	6·00

208 Wandering Glider Dragonfly

2009. Wandering Glider Dragonfly (Pantala flavescens). Multicoloured.

788	$2.50 Type **208**	4·50	5·00
789	$4 Perched on edge of flower	6·50	7·50
MS790	140×85 mm. Nos. 788/9	11·00	11·50

209 Walrus Amphibious Biplane, August 1937

2009. Visiting Aircraft. Multicoloured.

791	$1 Type **209**	2·50	1·75
792	$1.50 Alouette III helicopter from French cruiser *Jeanne d'Arc*, December 1971	3·75	3·25
793	$1.80 Dassault VP BMS Falcon 900, August 2002	3·75	3·75
794	$2.50 Piper Comanche 260C, March 2007	5·00	6·00

210 HMS *Actaeon*, 1837

2009. Royal Navy Visitors. Sheet 140×103 mm containing T **210** and similar horiz designs. Multicoloured.

MS795	80c. Type **210**; 80c. HMS *Calypso*, 1860; 80c. HMS *Juno*, 1855; $2 HMS *Sutlej*, 1864; $2 HMS *Shah*, 1878; $2 HMS *Pelican*, 1886	15·00	16·00

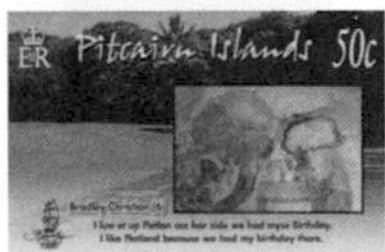

211 Flatland (Bradley Christian)

2010. Children's Art. Multicoloured.

796	50c. Type **211**	80	80
797	60c. Tedside (Torika Warren-Peu)	95	95
798	$1 St. Pauls (Jayden Warren-Peu)	1·60	1·60
799	$1.80 Beehives in Isaac's Valley (Kimiora Warren-Peu)	3·00	3·00
800	$2 Garnets Ridge (Ralph Warren-Peu)	3·25	3·25
801	$2.50 Ship Landing Point (Ariel Brown)	4·00	4·00

212 Tank

2010. ANZAC Day. T **212** and similar horiz designs, inscribed with the names of Pitcairn Islanders who fought in the World Wars. Multicoloured.

802	50c. Type **212** (Arthur Ray Lacy Young, Floyd Hasting McCoy, Colin Bruce Warren, Walma Laury Warren)	1·50	2·00
803	$1 Fighter aircraft (Boyd Christian, Clement Freeman Coffin, Ralph Chester Young, Ernest Wilfred Warren)	2·00	2·50
804	$1.80 Troopship leaving dockside (Robert Lowry Young, Edison Percy Young, Vincent Young, Burnell Young)	2·50	3·00
805	$4 Deck of warship with guns (Vivian Joe Christian, Sterling Warren, Andy Rolland Warren)	6·00	7·00

Nos. 802/3 and 804/5 were each printed together, *se-tenant*, each pair forming a composite design.

2010. London 2010 Festival of Stamps. HMAV Bounty. Sheet 148×90 mm containing Nos. 741/2 and 745

MS806	80c. Wheel; $1 Figurehead; $3.50 Sextant	7·75	7·75

213 Centropyge flavissima

2010. Endangered Species. Reef Fish of the Pitcairn Islands. Multicoloured.

807	60c. Type **213**	80	80
808	$1 *Chaetodon smithi*	1·50	1·50
809	$2 *Centropyge loricula*	3·00	3·00
810	$2.50 *Chaetodon lineolatus*	3·50	3·50
MS811	180×105 mm. Nos. 807/10, each ×2	18·00	18·00

214 Reseach Vessel L'Atalante

2010. Hotspots (submarine volcanoes). Multicoloured.

812	80c. Type **214**	1·10	1·10
813	$1.20 Submersible *Nautile*	1·90	1·90
814	$1.50 Photographing lava tube	2·75	2·75
815	$3 *Nautile* approaching Adams Volcano	4·00	4·00

Nos. 812/15 and the central stamp-size label form a composite design.

215 Orobophana solidula

2010. Endemic Snails. Multicoloured.

816	80c. Type **215**	1·10	1·10
817	$1 *Philonesia filiceti* (dark and light brown shell)	1·90	1·90
818	$1.80 *Orobophana solidula* (orange shell)	2·75	2·75
819	$2.50 *Philonesia filiceti* (striped shell)	3·75	3·75

2010. Royal Navy Visitors (2nd series). Sheet 140×103 mm containing horiz designs as T **210**. Multicoloured.

MS820	$1 HMS *Royalist*, 1898; $1 *Cambrian* & *Flora*, 1906; $1 HMS *Algerine*, 1911; $1.80 HMS *Leander*, 1937; $1.80 HMS *Monmouth*, 1995; HMS *Sutherland*, 2001	9·75	9·75

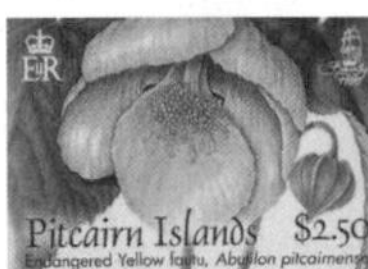

216 Yellow Fautu

2011. Endagered Species. Yellow Fautu. Multicoloured.

821	$2.50 Type **216**	3·50	3·50
822	$3 Yellow fautu flower and three buds	4·50	4·50

2011. Indipex 2011 International Stamp Exhibition, New Delhi. Sheet 137×93 mm containing No. 822 Multicoloured.

MS823	Yellow fautu flower and three buds	4·50	4·50

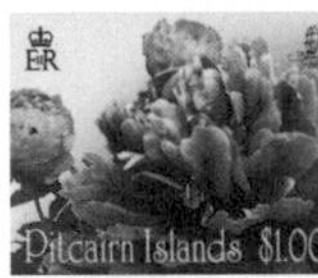

217 Pink Peony

2011. Peony Flowers. Multicoloured.

824	$1 Type **217**	1·90	1·90
825	$1 White peony with red markings	1·90	1·90

Nos. 824/5 were printed together, *se-tenant*, as horizontal pairs, each pair forming a composite design.

218 Paper Wasp

2011. Pitcairn Islands Paper Wasp (*Polistes jokahamae*). Multicoloured.

826	$2.50 Type **218**	4·50	4·50
827	$4 Paper wasp (facing left)	6·00	6·00
MS828	136×89 mm. Nos. 826/7	10·50	10·50

219 Prince William and Miss Catherine Middleton

2011. Royal Wedding. Multicoloured.

829	$2.80 Type **219**	5·25	5·25
830	$6 Wedding of Duke and Duchess of Cambridge	9·75	9·75

220 Henderson Crake (*Porzana atra*)

2011. Rare Birds of Henderson Island. Multicoloured.

831	20c. Type **220**	65	65
832	40c. Henderson fruit dove (*Ptilinopus insularis*)	95	95
833	$1.50 Henderson petrel (*Pterodroma atrata*)	2·75	2·75
834	$2.10 Henderson reed-warbler (*Acrocephalus taiti*)	4·00	4·00
835	$4.40 Henderson lorikeet (*Vini stepheni*)	6·25	6·25

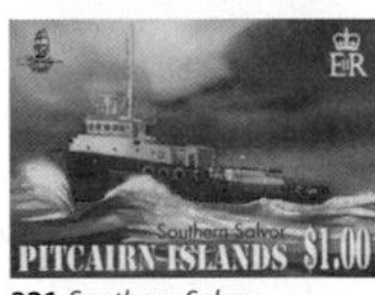

221 *Southern Salvor*

2011. Supply Ships. Multicoloured.

836	$1 Type **221**	2·00	2·10
837	$1.80 *Claymore II*	2·75	3·00
838	$2.10 Longboat approaching *Braveheart*	3·00	3·25
839	$3 Longboat leaving *Taporo VIII*	5·25	5·50

222 Parkin Christian (navigator)

2011. Prominent Pitcairners (1st series). Parkin Christian (1883–1971). Multicoloured.

840	$1.50 Type **222**	2·25	2·50
841	$1.80 Parkin Christian as 'goodwill ambassador' and globe	2·75	3·00
842	$2.10 Parkin Christian as Chief Magistrate	3·00	3·25
843	$2.40 Parkin Christian as elder of the Seventh-day Adventist Church	4·50	4·75

223 Wiseman with Gift

2011. Christmas. Multicoloured.

844	$1 Type **223**	1·90	1·90
845	$1.50 Wiseman with gift (jewelled box and mace)	2·75	2·75
846	$2.10 Wiseman with gift (gold vase)	3·50	3·50
847	$3 Nativity	4·25	4·25

224 Tapa Cloth with Rowing Boat and Turtle Designs

2012. Art of Pitcairn (4th series). Tapa. Multicoloured.

MS848	$1.80 Type **224**; $2.20 Whale design; $4.60 Sailing ship design	12·00	12·00

225 Fraser's Dolphin (*Lagenodelphis hosei*)

2012. Dolphins. Multicoloured.

849	$1 Type **225**	1·90	1·90
850	$1.50 Spinner dolphin (*Stenella longirostris*)	2·75	2·75
851	$2.10 Spotted dolphin (*Stenella attenuata*)	3·50	3·50
852	$3 Bottlenose dolphin (*Tursiops truncatus*)	4·25	4·25
MS853	139×90 mm. Nos. 850 and 852	7·00	7·00

226 Queen Elizabeth II Trooping the Colour

2012. Diamond Jubilee. Multicoloured.

854	$2.80 Type **226**	4·25	4·25
855	$4.40 Queen Elizabeth II wearing turquoise, c. 2012	6·25	6·25

227 *Bounty* Replica

2012. 'Romantic *Bounty*'. Multicoloured.

856	20c. Type **227**	40	40
857	$1 *Bounty* replica anchored offshore	1·90	1·90
858	$2.10 *Bounty* replica at sunset	3·50	3·50
859	$4.60 *Bounty* replica anchored in lagoon	6·75	6·75
MS860	120×80 mm. No. 859	6·75	6·75

2012. Prominent Pitcairners (2nd series). Roy P. Clark (1893-1980)

861	$1 Roy P. Clark holding book ('Teacher')	1·90	1·90
862	$1.50 Carrying mail sacks from post office ('Postmaster')	2·75	2·75
863	$2.20 Roy P. Clark ('Writer')	4·00	4·00
864	$2.80 With wife May Coffin ('Community and Church Elder')	4·25	4·25

228 Fluted Giant Clam (*Tridacna squamosa*)

2012. Endangered Species. Fluted Giant Clam (*Tridacna squamosa*). Multicoloured.

865	20c. Type **228**	40	40
866	$1 Fluted giant clam (yellow mantle)	1·90	1·90
867	$2.10 Fluted giant clam (blue mantle)	3·50	3·50
868	$3 Fluted giant clam (greenish mantle)	4·25	4·25
MS869	180×105 mm. Nos. 865/8, each ×2	9·50	9·50

229 Charles Dickens and Mrs. Gamp (*Martin Chuzzlewit*)

2012. Birth Bicentenary of Charles Dickens (writer). Portraits of Charles Dickens and illustrations from *Character Sketches from Charles Dickens*, c. 1890 by Joseph Clayton Clarke ('Kyd')

870	$1 Type **229**	1·90	1·90
871	$1.80 Charles Dickens and the Artful Dodger (*Oliver Twist*)	3·25	3·25
872	$2.10 Charles Dickens and Mr. Pickwick (*The Pickwick Papers*)	3·50	3·50
873	$3 Charles Dickens and Scrooge (*A Christmas Carol*)	6·25	6·25

230 *Mutiny on the Bounty*

2013. The *Bounty* Trilogy (novels by Charles Nordhoff and James Norman Hall). Multicoloured.

874	$1 Type **230**	1·90	1·90
875	$2.10 *Men against the Sea*	3·50	3·50
876	$3 *Pitcairn's Island*	4·25	4·25
MS877	110×91 mm. Nos. 874/6	9·00	9·00

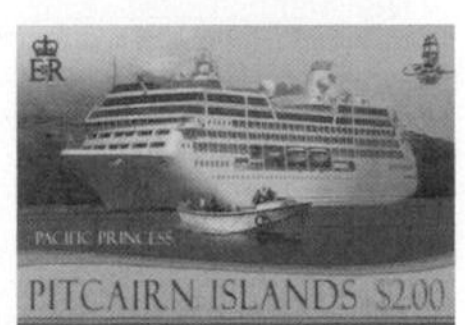

231 *Pacific Princess*

2013. Cruise Ships. Multicoloured.

878	$2 Type **231**	3·50	3·50
879	$2 MV *Marina*	3·50	3·50
880	$2 *Arcadia*	3·50	3·50
881	$2 *Costa Neo Romantica*	3·50	3·50

232 Easter Island Spiny Lobster (*Panulirus pascuensis*)

2013. Lobsters. Sheet 140×88 mm containing T **232** and similar horiz designs. Multicoloured.

MS882	$1 Type **232**; $2 Aesop Slipper Lobster (*Scyllarides haanii*); $3.40 Pronghorn Spiny Lobster (*Panulirus penicillatus*)	8·50	8·50

234 Duke and Duchess of Cambridge with Prince George

2013. Birth of Prince George of Cambridge. Multicoloured.

MS884	$3.40 Type **234**; $4.40 Prince William holding Prince George	10·50	10·50

2013. Prominent Pitcairners (3rd series). Lily Warren (1878-1969, community midwife). Multicoloured.

885	$1 Lily Warren	1·90	1·90
886	$1.50 George (navigator and boatman) and Lily Warren	2·75	2·75
887	$2.20 Lily Warren wearing her British Empire Medal	4·00	4·00
888	$2.80 Lily Warren	4·25	4·25

233 Queen Elizabeth II

2013. 60th Anniv of Coronation

883	**233**	$6 bright blue	8·50	8·50

235 Pres. Kennedy and "Ask not what your Country can do for you. Ask what you can do for your Country", 20 Jan 1961

2013. 50th Death Anniv of John F. Kennedy (1917-63, US President 1961-3). Multicoloured.

889	$1 Type **235**	1·90	1·90
890	$1.80 "WE GO TO THE MOON", 25 May 1961	3·25	3·25
891	$2.10 "KENNEDY ORDERS CUBA BLOCKADE", 18 April 1962	3·50	3·50
892	$3 "Ich bin ein Berliner", 26 June 1963	4·25	4·25

236 Ship Landing Point (seen from Bounty Bay)

2013. Ship Landing Point, Bounty Bay. Multicoloured.

893	40c. Type **236**	80	80
894	$1 Ship Landing Point seen from cliffs at Bounty Bay	1·90	1·90
895	$1 Palm trees and Ship Landing Point	1·90	1·90
896	$2 Ship Landing Point (pinnacle and ridge seen from below)	3·50	3·50
897	$2 The Nose and Bounty Bay seen from The Pinnacle	3·50	3·50
898	$2.10 Bounty Bay seen from the Pinnacle	3·50	3·50

237 Wandering Albatross (*Diomedea exulans*)

2014. Albatross. Multicoloured.

MS899	$1.80 Type **237**; $2.10 Black-browed Albatross (*Thalassarche melanophrys*); $3 Buller's Albatross (*Thalassarche bulleri*)	9·00	9·00

238 Mutineers holding Captain Bligh

2014. 225th Anniv of the Mutiny on the *Bounty*. Multicoloured.

900	$1 Type **238**	1·90	1·90
901	$2 Capt Bligh and 18 loyal crew put into *Bounty's* open boat	3·50	3·50
902	$2.10 Boat rowing away from *Bounty* with Capt Bligh in command	3·50	3·50
903	$3 *Bounty* under full sail, arriving at Pitcairn Island	4·25	4·25

Pt. 5

POLAND

A country lying between Russia and Germany, originally independent, but divided between Prussia, Austria and Russia in 1772/95. An independent republic since 1918. Occupied by Germany from 1939 to 1945.

1860. 100 kopeks = 1 rouble.
1918. 100 pfennig = 1 mark.
1918. 100 halerzy = 1 korona. 100 fenigow = 1 marka.
1924. 100 groszy = 1 zloty.

1 Russian Arms

1860

1b	1	10k. blue and red	£2000	£190

2 Sigismund III Vasa Column, Warsaw

1918. Surch **POCZTA POLSKA** and value in fen. as in T **2**.

2	**2**	5f. on 2g. brown	1·40	1·10
3	-	10f. on 6g. green	90	1·10
4	-	25f. on 10g. red	8·50	2·40
5	-	50f. on 20g. blue	7·00	6·50

DESIGNS: 6g. Arms of Warsaw; 10g. Polish eagle; 20g. Jan III Sobieski Monument, Warsaw.

1918. Stamps of German Occupation of Poland optd **Poczta Polska** or surch also.

6B	**10**	3pf. brown	31·00	22·00
7A	**10**	5pf. green	1·70	55
8A	**24**	5 on 2½pf. grey	55	20
9A	**10**	5 on 3pf. brown	5·75	2·75
10B	**10**	10pf. red	1·30	55
11A	**24**	15pf. violet	55	35
12A	**10**	20pf. blue	55	55
13A	**24**	25 on 7½pf. orange	55	20
14A	**10**	30pf. black & orange on buff	55	30
15A	**10**	40pf. black and red	1·70	1·60
16B	**10**	60pf. mauve	1·30	1·10

1918. Stamps of Austro-Hungarian Military Post (Nos. 69/71) optd **POLSKA POCZTA** and Polish eagle.

17	10h. green	11·50	11·00
18	20h. red	8·50	11·00
19	45h. blue	8·50	11·00

1918. As stamps of Austro-Hungarian Military Post of 1917 optd **POLSKA POCZTA** and Polish eagle or surch also.

20b	3h. on 3h. olive	60·00	38·00
21	3h. on 15h. red	6·75	5·00
22	10h. on 30h. green	6·75	5·50
23	25h. on 40h. olive	13·50	9·25
24	45h. on 60h. red	6·75	5·50
25	45h. on 80h. blue	9·75	7·25
26	50h. on 60h. red	16·00	13·50
28	50h. green	34·00	33·00
29	90h. violet	8·50	5·50

1919. Stamps of Austria optd **POCZTA POLSKA**, No. 49 also surch **25**.

30	**49**	3h. violet	£350	£425
31	**49**	5h. green	£425	£375
32	**49**	6h. orange	50·00	43·00
33	**49**	10h. purple	£350	£325
34	**49**	12h. blue	85·00	55·00
35	**60**	15h. red	80·00	27·00
36	**60**	20h. green	£225	£110
37	**60**	25h. blue	£1500	£1600
49	**51**	25 on 80h. brown	7·50	6·75
38	**60**	30h. violet	£400	£275
39	**51**	40h. green	25·00	26·00
40	**51**	50h. green	15·00	16·00
41	**51**	60h. blue	12·50	11·00
42	**51**	80h. brown	10·00	10·00
43	**51**	90h. purple	£1000	£1100
44	**51**	1k. red on yellow	18·00	19·00
45	**52**	2k. blue	8·25	9·50
46	**52**	3k. red	£150	£170
47	**52**	4k. green	£200	£160
48a	**52**	10k. violet	£3500	£3750

11

1919. Imperf. Re-issued without gum.

50	**11**	2h. grey	1·20	1·00
51	**11**	3h. violet	1·20	1·00
52	**11**	5h. green	70	55
53	**11**	6h. orange	22·00	27·00
54	**11**	10h. red	70	55
55	**11**	15h. brown	70	55
56	**11**	20h. olive	75	75
57	**11**	25h. red	55	55
58	**11**	50h. blue	70	70
59	**11**	70h. blue	1·20	1·00
60	**11**	1k. red and grey	1·30	1·30

15

16

17 Agriculture

18 Ploughing in peace

19 Polish Uhlan

1919. For Southern Poland. Value in halerzy or korony. Imperf or perf.

68	**15**	3h. brown	25	25
69	**15**	5h. green	25	25
70	**15**	10h. orange	25	25
71	**15**	15h. red	25	25
72	**16**	20h. brown	25	25
85	**16**	25h. blue	15	15
86	**16**	50h. brown	15	15
75	**17**	1k. green	25	25
88	**17**	1k.50 brown	80	25
89	**17**	2k. blue	1·10	55
90	**18**	2k.50 purple	1·70	75
91	**19**	5k. blue	2·30	1·10

1919. For Northern Poland. Value in fenigow or marki. Imperf or perf.

104	**15**	3f. brown	20	10
105	**15**	5f. green	20	10
179	**15**	5f. blue	30	55
106	**15**	10f. purple	20	10
129	**15**	10f. brown	25	10
107	**15**	15f. red	20	10
108	**16**	20f. blue	20	10
181	**16**	20f. red	40	1·10
109	**16**	25f. green	20	10
110	**16**	50f. green	20	10
183	**16**	50f. orange	30	1·50
137	**17**	1m. violet	25	10
112	**17**	1m.50 green	80	20
138	**17**	2m. brown	25	10
114	**18**	2m.50 brown	1·70	55
139	**18**	3m. brown	4·50	25
140	**19**	5m. purple	1·40	40
141	**19**	6m. red	1·70	20
142	**19**	10m. red	95	25
143	**19**	20m. green	4·25	35

1919. First Polish Philatelic Exhibition and Polish White Cross Fund. Surch **I POLSKA WYSTAWA MAREK**, cross and new value. Imperf or perf.

116b	**15**	5+5f. green	45	35
117b	**15**	10+5f. purple	1·40	1·60
118b	**15**	15+5f. red	45	35
119b	**16**	25+5f. olive	45	35
120	**16**	50+5f. green	1·10	1·10

20

21 Prime Minster Paderewski

22 A. Trampczynski

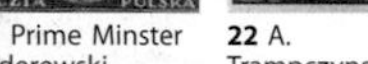

23 Eagle and Sailing Ship

1919. First Session of Parliament in Liberated Poland. Dated "1919".

121	**20**	10f. mauve	35	20
122	**21**	15f. red	35	20
123	**22**	20f. brown (21×25 mm)	1·00	55
124	**22**	20f. brown (17×20 mm)	5·75	7·50
125	-	25f. green	70	20
126	**23**	50f. blue	70	35
127	-	1m. violet	1·10	75

DESIGN—As Type **21**: 25f. Gen. Pilsudski. As Type **23**: 1m. Griffin and fasces.

24

1920

146	**24**	40f. violet	45	20
182	**24**	40f. brown	30	95
184	**24**	75f. green	40	1·50

1920. As T **15**, but value in marks ("Mk").

147	**15**	1m. red	30	20
148	**15**	2m. green	30	20
149	**15**	3m. blue	70	20
150	**15**	4m. red	30	20
151	**15**	5m. purple	30	20
152	**15**	8m. brown	1·10	35

1921. Surch **3 Mk** and bars.

153	**24**	3m. on 40f. violet	2·75	1·20

1921. Red Cross Fund. Surch with cross and **30MK**.

154	**19**	5m.+30m. purple	5·75	8·25
155	**19**	6m.+30m. red	5·75	8·25
156	**19**	10m.+30m. red	13·50	22·00
157	**19**	20m.+30m. green	£120	£110

28 Sun of Peace

29 Agriculture

1921. New Constitution.

158	**28**	2m. green	2·75	5·25
159	**28**	3m. blue	5·75	5·75
160	**28**	4m. red	1·70	75
161	**29**	6m. red	1·70	1·30
162	**29**	10m. green	1·70	1·30
163	-	25m. violet	5·75	1·30
164	-	50m. green and buff	3·50	75

DESIGN: 25, 50m. "Peace" (Seated women).

31 Sower

1921. Peace Treaty with Russia.

165	**31**	10m. blue	45	20
166	**31**	15m. brown	45	20
167	**31**	20m. red	45	20

32

1921

170	**32**	25m. violet and buff	1·10	20
171	**32**	50m. red and buff	1·10	20
172	**32**	100m. brown and orange	1·10	20
173	**32**	200m. pink and black	1·10	20
174	**32**	300m. green	55	20
175	**32**	400m. brown	80	20
176	**32**	500m. purple	1·10	20
177	**32**	1000m. orange	1·40	20
178	**32**	2000m. violet	55	20

33 Silesian Miner

1922

185	**33**	1m. black	40	95
186	**33**	1m.25 green	70	1·90
187	**33**	2m. red	30	95
188	**33**	3m. green	30	95
189	**33**	4m. blue	55	1·80
190	**33**	5m. brown	40	95
191	**33**	6m. orange	85	3·75
192	**33**	10m. brown	55	1·50
193	**33**	20m. purple	70	2·00
194	**33**	50m. olive	85	2·75
195	**33**	80m. red	1·70	12·50
196	**33**	100m. violet	1·50	9·00
197	**33**	200m. orange	3·50	20·00
198	**33**	300m. blue	7·00	29·00

34 Copernicus

1923. 450th Birth Anniv of Copernicus (astronomer) and 150th Death Anniv of Konarski (educationist).

199	**34**	1,000m. slate	1·50	75
200	-	3,000m. brown	1·50	75
201	**34**	5,000m. red	1·70	1·10

DESIGN: 3,000m. Konarski.

1923. Surch.

202	**32**	10 TYSIECY (=10000) on 25m. violet and buff	2·00	15
206	**15**	20,000m. on 2m. green (No. 148)	2·00	75
204	**31**	25,000m. on 20m. red	1·10	15
205	**31**	50,000m. on 10m. blue	5·75	15
207	**15**	100,000m. on 5m. purple (No. 151)	1·70	55

39

1924

208	**39**	10,000m. purple	3·50	55
209	**39**	20,000m. green	2·00	40
210	**39**	30,000m. red	3·50	55
211	**39**	50,000m. green	8·50	55
212	**39**	100,000m. brown	3·00	55
213	**39**	200,000m. blue	3·50	55
214	**39**	300,000m. mauve	8·50	70
215	**39**	500,000m. brown	7·00	2·75
216	**39**	1,000,000m. pink	1·00	46·00
217	**39**	2,000,000m. green	1·40	£375

40

41 President Wojciechowski

1924. New Currency.

218	**40**	1g. brown	1·70	1·60
219	**40**	2g. brown	1·70	95
220	**40**	3g. orange	1·70	95
221	**40**	5g. green	1·70	95
222	**40**	10g. green	4·50	2·50
223	**40**	15g. red	4·50	2·75
224	**40**	20g. blue	16·00	25
225	**40**	25g. red	40·00	30
226	**40**	30g. violet	55·00	55
227	**40**	40g. blue	16·00	55
228	**40**	50g. purple	5·75	40
229	**41**	1z. red	55·00	6·50

42

1925. National Fund.

230	**42**	1g.+50g. brown	17·00	33·00
231	**42**	2g.+50g. brown	17·00	33·00
232	**42**	3g.+50g. orange	17·00	33·00
233	**42**	5g.+50g. green	17·00	33·00
234	**42**	10g.+50g. green	17·00	33·00
235	**42**	15g.+50g. red	17·00	33·00
236	**42**	20g.+50g. blue	17·00	33·00
237	**42**	25g.+50g. red	17·00	33·00
238	**42**	30g.+50g. violet	17·00	33·00
239	**42**	40g.+50g. blue	£170	33·00
240	**42**	50g.+50g. purple	17·00	33·00

43 Holy Gate, Vilna

44 Town Hall, Pozan

48 Galleon

1925

241	**43**	1g. brown	55	10
242	-	2g. olive	80	25
243a	-	3g. blue	1·70	10
244a	**44**	5g. green	1·70	10
245a	-	10g. violet	1·70	10
246	-	15g. red	2·50	10
247	**48**	20g. red	34·00	10
248	**43**	24g. blue	28·00	2·20
249	-	30g. blue	5·00	10
250	-	40g. blue	4·50	10
251	**48**	45g. mauve	£100	1·60

DESIGNS—As Type **43**: VERT: 2, 30g. Jan III Sobieski Statue, Lwow. As Type **44**: 3, 10g. King Sigismund Vasa Column, Warsaw. HORIZ: 15, 40g. Wawel Castle, Cracow.

49 LVG Schneider Biplane

1925. Air.

252	**49**	1g. blue	1·40	8·25
253	**49**	2g. orange	1·40	8·25
254	**49**	3g. brown	1·40	8·25
255	**49**	5g. brown	1·80	1·10
256	**49**	10g. green	3·50	1·10
257	**49**	15g. mauve	11·50	1·60
258	**49**	20g. olive	19·00	8·25
259	**49**	30g. red	11·50	2·75
260	**49**	45g. lilac	19·00	5·50

50 Chopin

1927

261	**50**	40g. blue	28·00	4·25

51 Marshal Pilsudski

1927

262	**51**	20g. red	6·75	55
262a	**51**	25g. brown	4·00	55

52 Pres. Moscicki

1927

263	**52**	20g. red	9·75	1·30

53

1927. Educational Funds.

264	**53**	10g.+5g. purple on green	17·00	14·00
265	**53**	20g.+5g. blue on yellow	18·00	14·50

54 Dr. Karl Kaczkowki

1927. Fourth Int Military Medical Congress, Warsaw.

266	**54**	10g. green	9·50	4·25
267	**54**	25g. red	14·00	4·50
268	**54**	40g. blue	23·00	3·50

55 J. Slowacki (poet)

1927. Transfer of Slowacki's remains to Cracow.

269	**55**	20g. red	8·50	1·60

1928. Warsaw Philatelic Exhibition. Sheet 117×88 mm. T **56/7** in deep sepia.

MS270		50g. and 1z. (+1z.50)	£325	£250

See also Nos. 272/3, 328 and **MS**332a/c.

56 Marshal Pilsudski

57 Pres. Moscicki

1928

272	**56**	50g. grey	5·75	20
272a	**56**	50g. green	7·25	40
273	**57**	1z. black on cream	18·00	20

58 Gen. Joseph Bem

1928

271	**58**	25g. red	5·75	55

59 H. Sienkiewicz

1928. Henryk Sienkiewicz (author).

274	**59**	15g. blue	3·25	55

60 Slav God, "Swiatowit"

1929. National Exhibition, Poznan.

275	**60**	25g. brown	3·75	55

61

1929

276	**61**	5g. violet	45	20
277	**61**	10g. green	1·30	20
278	**61**	25g. brown	85	45

62 King Jan III Sobieski

1930. Birth Tercentenary of Jan III Sobieski.

279	**62**	75g. purple	8·75	35

63

1930. Centenary of "November Rising" (29 November 1830).

280	**63**	5g. purple	85	20
281	**63**	15g. blue	4·25	65
282	**63**	25g. lake	1·30	20
283	**63**	30g. red	11·50	5·50

64 Kosciusko, Washington and Pulaski

1932. Birth Bicentenary of George Washington.

284	**64**	30g. brown on cream	4·25	55

65

1932

284a	**65**	5g. violet	20	20
285	**65**	10g. green	20	20
285a	**65**	15g. red	20	20
286	**65**	20g. grey	55	20
287	**65**	25g. bistre	75	20
288	**65**	30g. red	2·50	20
289	**65**	60g. blue	35·00	40

67 Town Hall, Torun

1933. 700th Anniv of Torun.

290	**67**	60g. blue on cream	46·00	2·75

68 Franciszek Zwirko (airman) and Stanislaw Wigura (aircraft designer)

1933. Victory in Flight round Europe Air Race, 1932.

292	**68**	30g. green	26·00	3·25

1933. Torun Philatelic Exhibition.

293	**67**	60g. red on cream	30·00	22·00

69 Altar-piece, St. Mary's Church, Cracow

1933. Fourth Death Centenary of Veit Stoss (sculptor).

294	**69**	80g. brown on cream	22·00	2·75

70 "Liberation of Vienna" by J. Matejko

1933. 250th Anniv of Relief of Vienna.

295	**70**	1z.20 blue on cream	65·00	16·00

71 Cross of Independence

1933. 15th Anniv of Proclamation of Republic.

296	**71**	30g. red	13·00	75

1934. Katowice Philatelic Exhibition. Optd **Wyst. Filat. 1934 Katowice**.

297	**65**	20g. grey	50·00	43·00
298	**65**	30g. red	50·00	43·00

73 Marshal Pilsudski and Legion of Fusiliers Badge

1934. 20th Anniv of Formation of Polish Legion.

299	**73**	25g. blue	3·50	55
300	**73**	30g. brown	5·25	55

1934. Int Air Tournament. Optd **Challenge 1934**.

301	**49**	20g. olive	17·00	12·00
302	**68**	30g. green	22·00	5·00

1934. Surch in figures.

303	**69**	25g. on 80g. brown on cream	8·75	1·10
304	**65**	55g. on 60g. blue	6·50	55
305	**70**	1z. on 1z.20 blue on cream	30·00	8·25

77 Marshal Pilsudski

1935. Mourning Issue.

306	**77**	5g. black	1·30	35
307	**77**	15g. black	1·30	40
308	**77**	25g. black	2·50	35
309	**77**	45g. black	8·75	3·25
310	**77**	1z. black	17·00	6·50

1935. Optd **Kopiec Marszalka Pilsudskiego**.

311	**65**	15g. red	2·20	85
312	**73**	25g. blue	6·50	3·50

79 Pieskowa Skala (Dog's Rock)

80 Pres. Moscicki

1935

313	**79**	5g. blue	85	10
317	-	5g. violet	45	20
314	-	10g. green	85	10
318	-	10g. green	45	20
315	-	15g. blue	4·25	10
319	-	15g. lake	60	35
316	-	20g. black	3·00	10
320	-	20g. orange	85	55
321a	-	25g. green	1·00	10
322	-	30g. red	2·75	20
323a	-	45g. mauve	85	10
324a	-	50g. black	4·00	20
325	-	55g. blue	8·75	65
326	-	1z. brown	7·50	1·30
327	**80**	3z. brown	4·25	11·00

DESIGNS: 5g. (No. 317) Monastery of Jasna Gora, Czestochowa; 10g. (314) Lake Morskie Oko; 10g. (318) "Batory" (liner) at sea passenger terminal, Gdynia; 15g. (315) "Pilsudski" (liner); 15g. (319) University, Lwow; 20g. (316) Pieniny-Czorsztyn; 20g. (320) Administrative Buildings, Katowice; 25g. Belvedere Palace, Warsaw; 30g. Castle at Mir; 45g. Castle at Podhorce; 50g. Cloth Hall, Cracow; 55g. Raczynski Library, Poznan; 1z. Vilna Cathedral.

1936. Tenth Anniv of Moscicki Presidency. As T **57** but inscr "1926. 3. VI. 1936" below design.

328	**57**	1z. blue	8·75	7·50

1936. Gordon-Bennett Balloon Race. Optd **GORDON-BENNETT 30. VIII. 1936.**

329	30g. red (No. 322)	13·00	6·50
330	55g. blue (No. 325)	15·00	6·50

82 Marshal Smigly-Rydz

1937

331	**82**	25g. blue	60	20
332	**82**	55g. blue	85	55

1937. Visit of King of Rumania. Three sheets each 102×125 mm each containing a block of four of earlier types in new colours.

MS332a **82** 25g. sepia	21·00	32·00
MS332b **56** 50g. blue	21·00	32·00
MS332c **57** 1z. black	21·00	32·00

83 Pres. Moscicki

1938. President's 70th Birthday.

333	**83**	15g. grey	85	20
334	**83**	30g. purple	1·30	35

84 Kosciuszko, Paine and Washington

1938. 150th Anniv of U.S. Constitution.

335	**84**	1z. blue	2·75	2·20

84a Postal Coach

1938. Fifth Philatelic Exhibition, Warsaw. Sheet 130×103 mm.

MS335a **84a** 45g. (×2) green; 55g. (×2) blue	£110	85·00

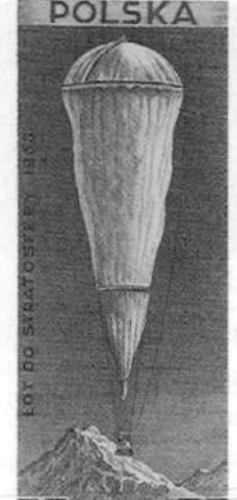

84b Stratosphere Balloon

1938. Proposed Polish Stratosphere Flight. Sheet 75×125 mm.

MS335b **84b** 75g. (+1z.25) violet	90·00	70·00

85a

86 Marshal Pilsudski

1938. 20th Anniv of Independence. (a) As T **85a** and **86**.

336	-	5g. orange	20	10
337	-	10g. green	20	10
338	**85a**	15g. brown (A)	20	20
357	**85a**	15g. brown (B)	65	35
339	-	20g. blue	65	45
340	-	25g. purple	40	10
341	-	30g. red	95	10
342	-	45g. black	1·40	90
343	-	50g. mauve	1·40	10
344	-	55g. blue	95	10
345	-	75g. green	3·75	2·20
346	-	1z. orange	3·75	2·20
347	-	2z. red	16·00	17·00
348	**86**	3z. blue	11·50	15·00

(b) 102×105 mm, containing four portraits as T **83** but with value and inscr transposed, all in purple.

MS348a 25g. Marshal Pilsudski; 25g. Pres. Narutowicz; 25g. Pres. Moscicki; 25g. Marshal Smigly-Rydz	12·00	20·00

DESIGNS—VERT: 5g. Boleslaw the Brave; 10g. Casimir the Great; 20g. Casimir Jagiellon; 25g. Sigismund August; 30g. Stefan Batory; 45g. Chodkiewicz and Zolkiewski; 50g. Jan III Sobieski; 55g. Symbol of Constitution of May 3rd, 1791; 75g. Kosciuszko, Poniatowski and Dabrowski; 1z. November Uprising 1830–31; 2z. Romuald Traugutt.

(A) Type **85a**. (B) as Type **85a** but crossed swords omitted.

87 Teschen comes to Poland

1938. Acquisition of Teschen.

349	**87**	25g. purple	3·75	55

88 "Warmth"

1938. Winter Relief Fund.

350	**88**	5g.+5g. orange	50	2·75
351	**88**	25g.+10g. purple	1·10	4·00
352	**88**	55g.+15g. blue	2·40	6·50

89 Tatra Mountaineer

1939. International Ski Championship, Zakopane.

353	**89**	15g. brown	1·40	1·30
354	**89**	25g. purple	2·40	1·60
355	**89**	30g. red	3·25	2·40
356	**89**	55g. blue	12·50	8·25

329 Ilyushin Il-14P over Steel Works

1957. Air.

1035	**329**	90g. black and pink	25	10
1036	-	1z.50 brown and salmon	25	10
1037	-	3z.40 sepia and buff	65	20
1038	-	3z.90 brown and yellow	1·40	55
1039	-	4z. blue and green	75	10
1039a	-	5z. lake and lavender	75	20
1039b	-	10z. brown and turquoise	1·30	55
1040	-	15z. violet and blue	2·75	65
1040a	-	20z. violet and yellow	2·75	1·10
1040b	-	30z. olive and buff	3·75	2·75
1040c	-	50z. blue and drab	9·00	3·75

DESIGNS—Ilyushin Il-14P over: 1z.50, Castle Square, Warsaw; 3z.40, Market, Cracow; 3z.90, Szczecin; 4z. Karkonosze Mountains; 5z. Old Market, Gdansk; 10z. Liw Castle; 15z. Lublin; 20z. Cable railway, Kasprowy Wierch; 30z. Porabka Dam; 50z. "Batory" (liner).

For stamp as No. 1039b, but printed in purple only, see No. 1095.

330a J. A. Komensky (Comenius)

1957. 300th Anniv of Publication of Komensky's "Opera Didactica Omnia".

1041	**330a**	2z.50 red	55	20

331 A. Strug

1957. 20th Death Anniv of Andrzej Strug (writer).

1042	**331**	2z.50 brown	55	20

332 Joseph Conrad and Full-rigged Sailing Ship "Torrens"

1957. Birth Centenary of Joseph Conrad (Korzeniowski) (author).

1043	**332**	60g. brown on green	20	10
1044	**332**	2z.50 blue on pink	75	30

333 Postman of 1558

1958. 400th Anniv of Polish Postal Service (1st issue).

1045	**333**	2z.50 purple and blue	55	20

For similar stamps see Nos. 1063/7.

334 Town Hall, Biecz

1958. Ancient Polish Town Halls.

1046	**334**	20g. green	20	10
1047	-	40g. brown (Wroclaw)	20	10
1048	-	60g. blue (Tarnow) (horiz)	25	10
1049	-	2z.10 lake (Gdansk)	40	10
1050	-	2z.50 violet (Zamosc)	85	35

335 Zander

1958. Fish.

1051	**335**	40g. yellow, black & blue	25	10
1052	-	60g. blue, indigo & green	40	10
1053	-	2z.10 multicoloured	75	20
1054	-	2z.50 green, black & violet	2·00	55
1055	-	6z.40 multicoloured	1·10	65

DESIGNS—VERT: 60g. Atlantic salmon; 2z.10, Northern pike; 2z.50, Brown trout. HORIZ 6z.40, European grayling.

336 Warsaw University

1958. 140th Anniv of Warsaw University.

1056	**336**	2z.50 blue	55	10

337 Fair Emblem

1958. 27th International Fair, Poznan.

1057	**337**	2z.50 red and black	55	10

338

1958. Seventh International Gliding Championships.

1058	**338**	60g. black and blue	15	10
1059	-	2z.50 black and grey	65	20

DESIGN: 2z.50, As Type **338** but design in reverse.

339 Armed Postman

1958. 19th Anniv of Defence of Gdansk Post Office.

1060	**339**	60g. blue	35	20

340 Polar Bear on Iceberg

1958. I.G.Y. Inscr as in T **340**.

1061	**340**	60g. black	20	10
1062	-	2z.50 blue	1·00	20

DESIGN: 2z.50, Sputnik and track of rocket.

341 Tomb of Prosper Prowano (First Polish Postmaster)

1958. 400th Anniv of Polish Postal Service (2nd issue).

1063	**341**	40g. purple and blue	45	10
1064	-	60g. black and lilac	20	10
1065	-	95g. violet and yellow	20	10
1066	-	2z.10 blue and grey	1·80	65
1067	-	3z.40 brown & turquoise	70	55

DESIGNS: 60g. Mail coach and Church of Our Lady, Cracow; 95g. Mail coach (rear view); 2z.10, 16th-century postman; 3z.40, Kogge.

Nos. 1064/7 show various forms of modern transport in clear silhouette in the background.

342 Envelope, Quill and Postmark

1958. Stamp Day.

1068	**342**	60g. green, red and black	1·40	75

343 Partisans' Cross

1958. 15th Anniv of Polish People's Army. Polish decorations.

1069	**343**	40g. buff, black and green	20	10
1070	-	60g. multicoloured	35	10
1071	-	2z.50 multicoloured	1·40	45

DESIGNS: 60g. Virtuti Military Cross; 2z.50, Grunwald Cross.

344 "Mail Coach in the Kielce District" (after painting by A. Kedzierskiego)

1958. Polish Postal Service 400th Anniv Exhibition.

1072	**344**	2z.50 black on buff	2·20	1·60

345 Galleon

1958. 350th Anniv of Polish Emigration to America.

1073	**345**	60g. green	20	10
1074	-	2z.50 red (Polish emigrants)	1·30	55

346 UNESCO Headquarters, Paris

1958. Inauguration of UNESCO Headquarters Building, Paris.

1075	**346**	2z.50 black and green	1·10	55

347 S. Wyspianski (dramatist and painter)

1958. Famous Poles.

1076	**347**	60g. violet	20	10
1077	-	2z.50 green	75	35

PORTRAIT: 2z.50, S. Moniuszko (composer).

348 "Human Rights"

1958. Tenth Anniv of Declaration of Human Rights.

1078	**348**	2z.50 lake and brown	1·10	20

348a Coach and Horses (after A. Kedzierski)

1958. 400th Anniv of Polish Postal Service. Sheet 86×76 mm.

MS1078a	**348a**	50z. blue	35·00	33·00

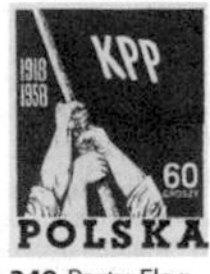

349 Party Flag

1958. 40th Anniv of Polish Communist Party.

1079	**349**	60g. red and purple	25	10

350 Yacht

1959. Sports.

1080	**350**	40g. ultramarine and blue	50	20
1081	-	60g. purple and salmon	50	20
1082	-	95g. purple and green	95	35
1083	-	2z. blue and green	50	20

DESIGNS: 60g. Archer; 95g. Footballers; 2z. Horseman.

351 The "Guiding Hand"

1959. Third Polish United Workers' Party Congress.

1084	**351**	40g. black, brown and red	20	10
1085	-	60g. multicoloured	20	10
1086	-	1z.55 multicoloured	65	30

DESIGNS—HORIZ: 60g. Hammer and ears of corn. VERT: 1z.55, Nowa Huta foundry.

352 Death Cap

1959. Mushrooms.

1087	**352**	20g. yellow, brown & green	2·00	1·10
1088	-	30g. multicoloured	95	30
1089	-	40g. multicoloured	70	15
1090	-	60g. multicoloured	70	15
1091	-	1z. multicoloured	70	15
1092	-	2z.50 brown, green & bl	1·40	35
1093	-	3z.40 multicoloured	1·90	40
1094	-	5z.60 brown, grn & yell	6·75	1·90

MUSHROOMS: 30g. Butter mushroom; 40g. Cep; 60g. Saffron milk cap; 1z. Chanterelle; 2z.50, Field mushroom; 3z.40, Fly agaric; 5z.60, Brown beech bolete.

1959. Air. 65 Years of Philately in Poland and Sixth Polish Philatelic Assn Congress, Warsaw. As No. 1039b but in one colour only.

1095	10z. purple	4·75	5·25

353 "Storks" (after Chelmonski)

1959. Polish Paintings.

1096	**353**	40g. green	20	10
1097	-	60g. purple	40	20
1098	-	1z. black	50	20
1099	-	1z.50 brown	1·10	55
1100	-	6z.40 blue	3·75	1·10

PAINTINGS—VERT: 60g. "Motherhood" (Wyspianski); 1z. "Madame de Romanet" (Roda-kowski); 1z.50, "Death" (Malczewski). HORIZ: 6z.40, "The Sandmen" (Gierymski).

354 Miner

1959. Third Int Miners' Congress, Katowice.

1101	**354**	2z.50 multicoloured	1·10	35

355 Sheaf of Wheat ("Agriculture")

1959. 15th Anniv of People's Republic.

1102	**355**	40g. green and black	10	10
1103	-	60g. red and black	10	10
1104	-	1z.50 blue and black	40	10

DESIGNS: 60g. Crane ("Building"); 1z.50, Corinthian column, and book ("Culture and Science").

356 Dr. L. Zamenhof

1959. International Esperanto Congress, Warsaw and Birth Centenary of Dr. Ludwig Zamenhof (inventor of Esperanto).

1105	**356**	60g. black & green on green	20	10
1106	-	1z.50 green, red and violet on grey	2·50	55

DESIGN: 1z.50, Esperanto Star and globe.

357 "Flowering Pink" (Map of Austria)

1959. Seventh World Youth Festival, Vienna.

1107	**357**	60g. multicoloured	20	10
1108	**357**	2z.50 multicoloured	1·10	60

358

1959. 30th Anniv of Polish Airlines "LOT".

1109	**358**	60g. blue, violet and black	30	15

359 Parliament House, Warsaw

1959. 48th Inter-Parliamentary Union Conf, Warsaw.

1110	**359**	60g. green, red and black	20	10
1111	**359**	2z.50 purple, red & black	1·10	50

1959. Baltic States' International Philatelic Exhibition, Gdansk. No. 890 optd **BALPEX I - GDANSK 1959**.

1112		45g. brown on lemon	1·10	1·10

361 Dove and Globe

1959. Tenth Anniv of World Peace Movement.

1113	**361**	60g. grey and blue	25	20

362 Nurse with Bag

1959. 40th Anniv of Polish Red Cross. Cross in red.

1114	**362**	40g. black and green	20	10
1115	-	60g. brown	20	10
1116	-	2z.50 black and red	2·00	50

DESIGNS—VERT: 60g. Nurse with bottle and bandages. SQUARE—23×23 mm: 2z.50, J. H. Dunant.

363 Emblem of Polish–Chinese Friendship Society

1959. Polish–Chinese Friendship.

1117	**363**	60g. multicoloured	95	50
1118	**363**	2z.50 multicoloured	50	35

364

1959. Stamp Day.

1119	**364**	60g. red, green & turq	20	10
1120	**364**	2z.50 blue, green and red	40	10

365 Sputnik "3"

1959. Cosmic Flights.

1121	**365**	40g. black and blue	20	10
1122	-	60g. black and lake	30	10
1123	-	2z.50 blue and green	1·90	85

DESIGNS: 60g. Rocket "Mieczta" encircling Sun; 2z.50, Moon rocket "Lunik 2".

366 Schoolgirl

1959. "1000 Schools for Polish Millennium". Inscr as in T **366**.

1124	**366**	40g. brown and green	20	10
1125	-	60g. red, black and blue	20	10

DESIGN: 60g. Children going to school.

367 Darwin

1959. Famous Scientists.

1126	**367**	20g. blue	10	10
1127	-	40g. olive (Mendeleev)	10	10
1128	-	60g. purple (Einstein)	15	10
1129	-	1z.50 brown (Pasteur)	25	10
1130	-	1z.55 green (Newton)	55	10
1131	-	2z.50 violet (Copernicus)	1·50	55

368 Costumes of Rzeszow

369 Costumes of Rzeszow

1959. Provincial Costumes (1st series).

1132	**368**	20g. black and green	10	10
1133	**369**	20g. black and green	10	10
1134	-	60g. brown and pink	15	10
1135	-	60g. brown and pink	15	10
1136	-	1z. red and blue	20	10
1137	-	1z. red and blue	20	10
1138	-	2z.50 green and grey	60	20
1139	-	2z.50 green and grey	60	20
1140	-	5z.60 blue and yellow	1·60	55
1141	-	5z.60 blue and yellow	1·60	55

DESIGNS—Male and female costumes of: Nos. 1134/5, Kurpic; 1136/7, Silesia; 1138/9, Mountain regions; 1140/1, Szamotuly.

See also Nos. 1150/9.

370 Piano

1960. 150th Birth Anniv of Chopin and Chopin Music Competition, Warsaw.

1142	**370**	60g. black and violet	50	20
1143	-	1z.50 black, red and blue	95	35
1144	-	2z.50 brown	3·25	2·20

DESIGNS—As Type **370**: 1z.50, Portion of Chopin's music. 25×39½ mm: 2z.50, Portrait of Chopin.

371 Polish 10k. Stamp of 1860 and Postmark

1960. Stamp Centenary.

1145	**371**	40g. red, blue and black	20	10
1146	-	60g. blue, black and violet	30	10
1147	-	1z.35 blue, red and grey	95	65
1148	-	1z.55 red, black & green	1·40	55
1149	-	2z.50 green, black & ol	1·90	75

DESIGNS: 1z.35, Emblem inscr "1860 1960". Reproductions of Polish stamps: 60g. No. 356; 1z.55, No. 533; 2z.50, No. 1030. With appropriate postmarks.

1960. Provincial Costumes (2nd series). As T **368/69**.

1150	40g. red and blue	10	10
1151	40g. red and blue	10	10
1152	2z. blue and yellow	20	10
1153	2z. blue and yellow	20	10
1154	3z.10 turquoise and green	30	15
1155	3z.10 turquoise and green	30	15
1156	3z.40 brown and turquoise	70	35
1157	3z.40 brown and turquoise	70	35
1158	6z.50 violet and green	1·20	55
1159	6z.50 violet and green	1·20	55

DESIGNS—Male and female costumes of: Nos. 1150/1, Cracow; 1152/3, Lowicz; 1154/5, Kujawy; 1156/7, Lublin; 1158/9, Lubusz.

372 Throwing the Discus

1960. Olympic Games, Rome. Rings and inscr in black.

1160	60g. blue (T **372**)	20	10
1161	60g. mauve (Running)	20	10
1162	60g. violet (Cycling)	20	10
1163	60g. turq (Show jumping)	20	10
1164	2z.50 blue (Trumpeters)	95	55
1165	2z.50 brown (Boxing)	95	55
1166	2z.50 red (Olympic flame)	95	55
1167	2z.50 green (Long jump)	95	55

Stamps of the same value were issued together, *se-tenant*, forming composite designs illustrating a complete circuit of the stadium track.

373 King Wladislaw Jagiello's Tomb, Wawel Castle

1960. 550th Anniv of Battle of Grunwald.

1168	**373**	60g. brown	50	20
1169	-	90g. green	95	55
1170	-	2z.50 black	4·25	1·80

DESIGNS—As Type **373**: 90g. Proposed Grunwald Monument. HORIZ: 78×35½ mm: 2z.50, "Battle of Grunwald" (after Jan Matejko).

374 1860 Stamp and Postmark

1960. International Philatelic Exn, Warsaw.

1171	**374**	10z.+10z. red, black and blue	9·50	11·00

375 Lukasiewicz (inventor of petrol lamp)

1960. Lukasiewicz Commemoration and 5th Pharmaceutical Congress. Poznan.

1172	**375**	60g. black and yellow	25	10

376 "The Annunciation"

1960. Altar Wood Carvings of St. Mary's Church, Cracow, by Veit Stoss.

1173	**376**	20g. blue	30	10
1174	-	30g. brown	30	10
1175	-	40g. violet	30	20
1176	-	60g. green	30	20
1177	-	2z.50 red	1·40	55
1178	-	5z.60 brown	7·75	7·00
MS1178a		86×107 mm. 10z. black	14·50	11·00

DESIGNS: 30g. "The Nativity"; 40g. "Homage of the Three Kings"; 60g. "The Resurrection"; 2z.50, "The Ascension"; 5z.60, "The Descent of the Holy Ghost". VERT: (72×95 mm). 10z. The Assumption of the Virgin.

377 Paderewski

1960. Birth Centenary of Paderewski.

1179	**377**	2z.50 black	50	20

1960. Stamp Day. Optd **DZIEN ZNACZKA 1960**.

1180	**371**	40g. red, blue and black	1·90	1·10

379 Gniezno

1960. Old Polish Towns as T **379**.

1181	5g. brown	10	10
1182	10g. green	10	10
1183	20g. brown	10	10
1184	40g. red	10	10
1185	50g. violet	10	10
1186	60g. lilac	15	10
1187	60g. blue	20	10
1188	80g. blue	20	10
1189	90g. brown	20	10
1190	95g. green	20	10
1191	1z. red and lilac	20	10
1192	1z.15 green and orange	20	10
1193	1z.35 mauve and green	20	10
1194	1z.50 brown and blue	20	10
1195	1z.55 lilac and yellow	20	10
1196	2z. blue and lilac	30	10
1197	2z.10 brown and yellow	30	10
1198	2z.50 violet and green	40	10
1199	3z.10 red and grey	75	40
1200	5z.60 grey and green	3·00	80

TOWNS: 10g. Cracow; 20g. Warsaw; 40g. Poznan; 50g. Plock; 60g. mauve, Kalisz; 60g. blue, Tczew; 80g. Frombork; 90g. Torum; 95g. Puck; 1z. Slupsk; 1z.15, Gdansk; 1z.35, Wroclaw; 1z.50, Szczecin; 1z.55, Opole; 2z. Kolobrzeg; 2z.10, Legnica; 2z.50, Katowice; 3z.10, Lodz; 5z.60, Walbrzych.

380 Great Bustard

1960. Birds. Multicoloured.

1201		10g. Type **380**	20	10
1202		20g. Common Raven	20	10
1203		30g. Great cormorant	20	10
1204		40g. Black stork	50	10
1205		50g. Eagle owl	50	10
1206		60g. White-tailed sea eagle	65	10
1207		75g. Golden eagle	65	10
1208		90g. Short-toed eagle	95	20
1209		2z.50 Rock thrush	4·75	2·40
1210		4z. River kingfisher	3·75	1·30
1211		5z.60 Wallcreeper	7·25	1·60
1212		6z.50 European roller	9·50	3·75

381 Front page of Newspaper "Proletaryat" (1883)

1961. 300th Anniv of Polish Newspaper Press.

1213	-	40g. green, blue and black	50	20
1214	**381**	60g. yellow, red and black	50	20
1215	-	2z.50 blue, violet & black	4·75	4·25

DESIGNS—Newspaper front page: 40g. "Mercuriusz" (first issue, 1661); 2z.50, "Rzeczpospolita" (1944).

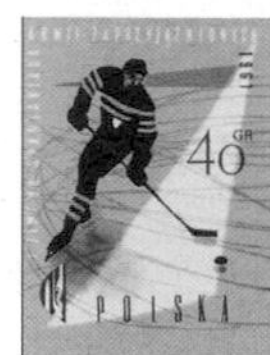

382 Ice Hockey

1961. First Winter Military Spartakiad.

1216	**382**	40g. black, yellow & lilac	50	10
1217	-	60g. multicoloured	50	20
1218	-	1z. multicoloured	9·50	3·75
1219	-	1z.50 black, yell & turq	50	55

DESIGNS: 60g. Ski jumping; 1z. Rifle-shooting; 1z.50, Slalom.

383 Congress Emblem

1961. Fourth Polish Engineers' Conference.

1220	**383**	60g. black and red	25	20

384 Yuri Gagarin

1961. World's First Manned Space Flight.

1221	**384**	40g. black, red and brown	75	20
1222	-	60g. red, black and blue	95	55

DESIGN: 60g. Globe and star.

385 Fair Emblem

1961. 30th International Fair, Poznan.

1223	**385**	40g. black, red and blue	10	10
1224	**385**	1z.50 black, blue and red	40	10

See also No. **MS**1245a.

386 King Mieszko I

1961. Famous Poles (1st issue).

1225	**386**	60g. black and blue	20	10
1226	-	60g. black and red	20	10
1227	-	60g. black and green	20	10
1228	-	60g. black and violet	95	35
1229	-	60g. black and brown	20	10
1230	-	60g. black and olive	20	10

PORTRAITS: No. 1226, King Casimire the Great; 1227, King Casmir Jagiellon; 1228, Copernicus; 1229, A. F. Modrzewski; 1230, Kosciuszko.

See also Nos. 1301/6 and 1398/1401.

387 "Leskov" (trawler support ship)

1961. Shipbuilding Industry. Multicoloured.

1231		60g. Type **387**	30	10
1232		1z.55 "Severodvinsk" (depot ship)	55	20
1233		2z.50 "Rambutan" (coaster)	95	45
1234		3z.40 "Krynica" (freighter)	1·40	55
1235		4z. "B 54" freighter	2·40	1·10
1236		5z.60 "Bavsk" (tanker)	6·25	2·75

SIZES: 2z.50, As Type **387**; 5z.60, 108×21 mm; Rest, 81×21 mm.

388 Posthorn and Telephone Dial

1961. Communications Ministers' Conference, Warsaw.

1237	**388**	40g. red, green and blue	20	10
1238	-	60g. violet, yellow & purple	20	10
1239	-	2z.50 ultram, blue & bis	85	25
MS1239a		108×66 mm. Nos. 1237/9 (sold at 5z.)	9·50	5·50

DESIGNS: 60g. Posthorn and radar screen; 2z.50, Posthorn and conference emblem.

389 Opole Seal

1961. Polish Western Provinces.

1240		40g. brown on buff	20	10
1241		40g. brown on buff	20	10
1242		60g. violet on pink	20	10
1243		60g. violet on pink	20	10
1243a		95g. green on blue	35	20
1243b		95g. green on blue	35	20
1244		2z.50 sage on green	85	55
1245		2z.50 sage on green	85	55

DESIGNS—VERT: No. 1240, Type **389**; 1242, Henry IV's tomb; 1243a, Seal of Conrad II; 1244, Prince Barnim's seal. HORIZ: No. 1241, Opole cement works; 1243, Wroclaw apartment-house; 1243b, Factory interior, Zielona Gora; 1245, Szczecin harbour.

See also Nos. 1308/13.

1961. "Intermess II" Stamp Exhibition. Sheet 121×51 mm containing pair of No. 1224 but imperf.

MS1245a		1z.50 (×2) (sold at 4z.50+2z.50)	9·00	5·00

390 Beribboned Paddle

1961. Sixth European Canoeing Championships. Multicoloured.

1246		40g. Two canoes within letter "E" (horiz)	20	10
1247		60g. Two four-seater canoes at finishing post (horiz)	20	10
1248		2z.50 Type **390**	1·90	85

391 Titov and Orbit within Star

1961. Second Russian Manned Space Flight.

1249	**391**	40g. black, red and pink	55	10
1250	-	60g. blue and black	65	20

DESIGN: 60g. Dove and spaceman's orbit around globe.

392 Monument

1961. 40th Anniv of 3rd Silesian Uprising.

1251	**392**	60g. grey and green	10	10
1252	-	1z.55 grey and blue	40	10

DESIGN: 1z.55, Cross of Silesian uprisers.

393 P.K.O. Emblem and Ant

1961. Savings Month.

1253		40g. red, yellow and black	20	10
1254	**393**	60g. brown, yellow & black	20	10
1255	-	60g. blue, violet and pink	20	10
1256	-	60g. green, red and black	35	10
1257	-	2z.50 mauve, grey & black	2·75	1·60

DESIGNS: No. 1253, Savings Bank motif; 1255, Bee; 1256, Squirrel; 1257, Savings Bank book.

394 "Mail Cart" (after J. Chelmonski)

1961. Stamp Day and 40th Anniv of Postal Museum.

1258	**394**	60g. brown	40	20
1259	**394**	60g. green	40	20

395 Congress Emblem

1961. Fifth W.F.T.U. Congress, Moscow.

1260	**395**	60g. black	25	10

396 Emblem of Kopasyni Mining Family, 1284

1961. Millenary of Polish Mining Industry.

1261	**396**	40g. purple and orange	10	10
1262	-	60g. grey and blue	10	10
1263	-	2z.50 green and black	95	25

DESIGNS: 60g. 14th-century seal of Bytom; 2z.50, Emblem of Int Mine Constructors' Congress, Warsaw, 1958.

397 Child and Syringe

1961. 15th Anniv of UNICEF.

1264	**397**	40g. black and blue	10	10
1265	-	60g. black and orange	10	10
1266	-	2z.50 black and turquoise	95	35

DESIGNS—HORIZ: 60g. Children of three races. VERT: 2z.50, Mother and child, and feeding bottle.

398 Cogwheel and Wheat

1961. 15th Economic Co-operative Council Meeting, Warsaw.

1267	**398**	40g. red, yellow and blue	20	10
1268	-	60g. red, blue & ultram	30	20

DESIGN: 60g. Oil pipeline map, E. Europe.

399 Caterpillar-hunter

1961. Insects. Multicoloured.

1269		20g. Type **399**	25	10
1270		30g. Violet ground beetle	25	10
1271		40g. Alpine longhorn beetle	25	10
1272		50g. "Cerambyx cerdo" (long-horn beetle)	25	10
1273		60g. "Carabus auronitens" (ground beetle)	25	10
1274		80g. Stag beetle	25	10
1275		1z.15 Clouded apollo (butterfly)	50	10
1276		1z.35 Death's-head hawk moth	50	10
1277		1z.50 Scarce swallowtail (butterfly)	95	10
1278		1z.55 Apollo (butterfly)	65	10
1279		2z.50 Red wood ant	1·90	70
1280		5z.60 White-tailed bumble bee	9·50	5·00

Nos. 1275/80 are square, 36½×36½ mm.

400 Worker with Flag and Dove

1962. 20th Anniv of Polish Workers' Coalition.

1281	**400**	60g. brown, black and red	15	10
1282	-	60g. bistre, black and red	15	10
1283	-	60g. blue, black and red	15	10
1284	-	60g. grey, black and red	15	10
1285	-	60g. blue, black and red	15	10

DESIGNS: No. 1282, Steersman; 1283, Worker with hammer; 1284, Soldier with weapon; 1285, Worker with trowel and rifle.

401 Two Skiers Racing

1962. F.I.S. Int Ski Championships, Zakopane.

1286	**401**	40g. blue, grey and red	20	10
1287	**401**	40g. blue, brown and red	95	20
1288	-	60g. blue, grey and red	20	10
1289	-	60g. blue, brown and red	1·40	75
1290	-	1z.50 blue, grey and red	20	20
1291	-	1z.50 violet, grey and red	2·75	1·60
MS1291a		67×80 mm. 10z. (+5z.) blue, grey and red	6·75	6·50

DESIGNS—HORIZ: 60g. Skier racing. VERT: 1z.50, Ski jumper; 10z. F.I.S. emblem.

402 Majdanek Monument

1962. Concentration Camp Monuments.

1292		40g. blue	10	10
1293	**402**	60g. black	30	10
1294	-	1z.50 violet	65	25

DESIGNS—VERT: (20×31 mm): 40g. Broken carnations and portion of prison clothing (Auschwitz camp); 1z.50, Treblinka monument.

403 Racing Cyclist

1962. 15th International Peace Cycle Race.

1295	**403**	60g. black and blue	20	10
1296	-	2z.50 black and yellow	75	20
1297	-	3z.40 black and violet	1·40	65

DESIGNS—74½×22 mm: 2z.50, Cyclists & "XV". As Type **403**: 3z.40, Arms of Berlin, Prague and Warsaw, and cycle wheel.

405 Lenin Walking

1962. 50th Anniv of Lenin's Sojourn in Poland.

1298	**405**	40g. green and light green	50	10
1299	-	60g. lake and pink	20	10
1300	-	2z.50 brown and yellow	95	45

DESIGNS: 60g. Lenin; 2z.50, Lenin wearing cap, and St. Mary's Church, Cracow.

1962. Famous Poles (2nd issue). As T **386**.

1301	60g. black and green	20	10
1302	60g. black and brown	20	10
1303	60g. black and blue	20	10
1304	60g. black and bistre	20	10
1305	60g. black and purple	20	10
1306	60g. black and turquoise	20	10

PORTRAITS: No. 1301, A. Mickiewicz (poet); 1302, J. Slowacki (poet); 1303, F. Chopin (composer); 1304, R. Traugutt (patriot); 1305, J. Dabrowski (revolutionary); 1306, Maria Konopnicka (poet).

406 Gen. K. Swierczewski-Walter (monument)

1962. 15th Death Anniv of Gen. K. Swierczewski-Walter (patriot).

1307	**406**	60g. black	25	20

1962. Polish Northern Provinces. As T **389**.

1308	60g. blue and grey	10	10
1309	60g. blue and grey	10	10
1310	1z.55 brown and yellow	30	10
1311	1z.55 brown and yellow	30	10
1312	2z.50 slate and grey	65	35
1313	2z.50 slate and grey	65	35

DESIGNS—VERT: No. 1308, Princess Elizabeth's seal; 1310, Gdansk Governor's seal; 1312, Frombork Cathedral. HORIZ: No. 1309, Insulators factory, Szczecinek; 1311, Gdansk shipyard; 1313, Laboratory of Agricultural College, Kortowo.

407 "Crocus scepusiensis" (Borb)

1962. Polish Protected Plants. Plants in natural colours.

1314	**407**	60g. yellow	20	10
1315	**A**	60g. brown	95	55
1316	**B**	60g. pink	20	10
1317	**C**	90g. green	20	10
1318	**D**	90g. olive	20	10
1319	**E**	90g. green	20	10
1320	**F**	1z.50 blue	50	20
1321	**G**	1z.50 green	50	20
1322	**H**	1z.50 turquoise	50	20
1323	**I**	2z.50 green	1·10	75
1324	**J**	2z.50 turquoise	1·40	75
1325	**K**	2z.50 blue	1·60	90

PLANTS: A, "Platanthera bifolia" (Rich); B, "Aconitum callibotryon" (Rchb.); C, "Gentiana clusii" (Perr. et Song); D, "Dictamnus albus" (L.); E, "Nymphaca alba" (L.); F, "Daphne mezereum" (L.); G, "Pulsatilla vulgaris" (Mill.); H, "Anemone silvestris" (L.); I, "Trollius europaeus" (L.); J, "Galanthus nivalis" (L.); K, "Adonis vernalis" (L.).

408 "The Poison Well", after J. Malczewski

1962. F.I.P. Day ("Federation Internationale de Philatelie").

1326	**408**	60g. black on cream	55	45

409 Pole Vault

1962. Seventh European Athletic Championships, Belgrade. Multicoloured.

1327	40g. Type **409**	10	10
1328	60g. 400 m relay	10	10
1329	90g. Throwing the javelin	10	10
1330	1z. Hurdling	10	10
1331	1z.50 High-jumping	10	10
1332	1z.55 Throwing the discus	20	10
1333	2z.50 100 m final	35	10
1334	3z.40 Throwing the hammer	1·40	25

410 "Anopheles sp."

1962. Malaria Eradication.

1335	**410**	60g. brown and turquoise	10	10
1336	-	1z.50 multicoloured	10	10
1337	-	2z.50 multicoloured	1·10	55
MS1337a		60×81 mm. 3z. multicoloured	1·90	1·30

DESIGNS: 1z.50, Malaria parasites in blood; 2z.50, Cinchona plant; 3z. Anopheles mosquito.

411 Cosmonauts "in flight"

1962. First "Team" Manned Space Flight.

1338	**411**	60g. green, black & violet	30	10
1339	-	2z.50 red, black and turquoise	75	35
MS1339a		70×94 mm. 10z. red, black and blue	3·75	3·25

DESIGN: 2z.50, Two stars (representing space-ships) in orbit.

412 "A Moment of Determination" (after painting by A. Kamienski)

1962. Stamp Day.

1340	**412**	60g. black	20	10
1341	**412**	2z.50 brown	85	35

413 Mazovian Princes' Mansion, Warsaw

1962. 25th Anniv of Polish Democratic Party.

1342	**413**	60g. black on red	25	10

414 Cruiser "Aurora"

1962. 45th Anniv of Russian Revolution.

1343	**414**	60g. blue and red	25	10

415 J. Korczak (bust after Dunikowski)

1962. 20th Death Anniv of Janusz Korczak (child educator).

1344	**415**	40g. sepia, bistre & brn	20	10
1345	-	60g. multicoloured	20	10
1346	-	90g. multicoloured	65	10
1347	-	1z. multicoloured	65	10
1348	-	2z.50 multicoloured	95	75
1349	-	5z.60 multicoloured	2·75	1·30

DESIGNS: 60g. to 5z.60, Illustrations from Korczak's children's books.

416 Old Town, Warsaw

1962. Fifth T.U. Congress, Warsaw.

1350	**416**	3z.40 multicoloured	1·10	55

417 Master Buncombe

1962. Maria Konopnicka's Fairy Tale "The Dwarfs and Orphan Mary". Multicoloured.

1351	40g. Type **417**	65	10
1352	60g. Lardie the Fox and Master Buncombe	2·75	1·10
1353	1z.50 Bluey the Frog making music	75	20
1354	1z.55 Peter's kitchen	75	55
1355	2z.50 Saraband's concert in Nightingale Valley	95	55
1356	3z.40 Orphan Mary and Subearthy	3·25	2·75

418 R. Traugutt (insurgent leader)

1963. Centenary of January (1863) Rising.

1357	**418**	60g. black, pink & turq	25	10

419 Tractor and Wheat

1963. Freedom from Hunger. Multicoloured.

1358	40g. Type **419**	20	10

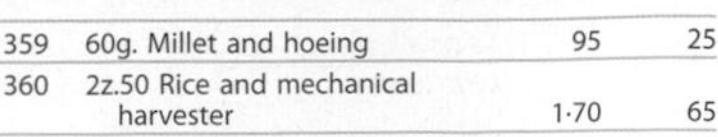

1359	60g. Millet and hoeing	95	25
1360	2z.50 Rice and mechanical harvester	1·70	65

420 Cocker Spaniel

1963. Dogs.

1361	**420**	20g. red, black and lilac	20	10
1362	-	30g. black and red	20	10
1363	-	40g. ochre, black and lilac	30	10
1364	-	50g. ochre, black and blue	30	10
1365	-	60g. black and blue	50	15
1366	-	1z. black and green	65	40
1367	-	2z.50 brown, yell & blk	1·40	65
1368	-	3z.40 black and red	3·25	1·60
1369	-	6z.50 black and yellow	6·75	5·50

DOGS—HORIZ: 30g. Sheep-dog; 40g. Boxer; 2z.50, Gundog "Ogar"; 6z.50, Great Dane. VERT: 50g. Airedale terrier; 60g. French bulldog; 1z. French poodle; 3z.40, Podhale sheep-dog.

421 Egyptian Galley (15th century B.C.)

1963. Sailing Ships (1st series).

1370	**421**	5g. brown on bistre	10	10
1371	-	10g. turquoise on green	10	10
1372	-	20g. blue on grey	10	10
1373	-	30g. black on olive	10	10
1374	-	40g. blue on blue	10	10
1375	-	60g. purple on brown	20	10
1376	-	1z. black on blue	30	10
1377	-	1z.15 green on pink	55	10

SHIPS: 10g. Phoenician merchantman (15th cent B.C.); 20g. Greek trireme (5th cent B.C.); 30g. Roman merchantman (3rd cent A.D.); 40g. "Mora" (Norman ship, 1066); 60g. Hanse kogge (14th cent); 1z. Hulk (16th cent); 1z.15, Carrack (15th cent).

See also Nos. 1451/66.

422 Insurgent

1963. 20th Anniv of Warsaw Ghetto Uprising.

1378	**422**	2z.50 brown and blue	50	20

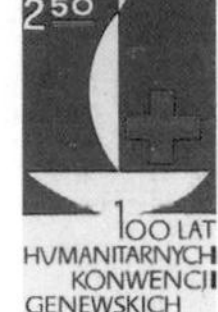

423 Centenary Emblem

1963. Red Cross Centenary.

1379	**423**	2z.50 red, blue and yellow	1·10	35

424 Lizard

1963. Protected Reptiles and Amphibians. Reptiles in natural colours: inscr in black: background colours given.

1380	**424**	30g. green	15	10
1381	-	40g. olive	15	10
1382	-	50g. brown	15	10
1383	-	60g. grey	15	10
1384	-	90g. green	20	10
1385	-	1z.15 grey	20	10
1386	-	1z.35 blue	35	10
1387	-	1z.50 turquoise	40	10

1388	-	1z.55 pale blue	50	10
1389	-	2z.50 lavender	50	20
1390	-	3z. green	1·40	55
1391	-	3z.40 purple	3·25	2·50

DESIGNS: 40g. Copperhead (snake); 50g. Marsh tortoise; 60g. Grass snake; 90g. Blindworm; 1z.15, Tree toad; 1z.35, Mountain newt; 1z.50, Crested newt; 1z.55, Green toad; 2z.50, "Bombina" toad; 3z. Salamander; 3z.40, "Natterjack" (toad).

425 Epee, Foil, Sabre and Knight's Helmet

1963. World Fencing Championships, Gdansk.

1392	**425**	20g. yellow and brown	10	10
1393	-	40g. light blue and blue	10	10
1394	-	60g. vermilion and red	10	10
1395	-	1z.15 light green & green	20	10
1396	-	1z.55 red and violet	65	10
1397	-	6z.50 yellow, pur & bis	2·10	75
MS1397a 110×93 mm. Nos. 1393/6			55·00	55·00

DESIGNS—HORIZ: Fencers with background of: 40g. Knights jousting; 60g. Dragoons in sword-fight; 1z.15, 18th-century duellists; 1z.55, Old Gdansk. VERT: 6z.50, Inscription and Arms of Gdansk.

1963. Famous Poles (3rd issue). As T **386**.

1398	60g. black and brown	20	10
1399	60g. black and brown	20	10
1400	60g. black and turquoise	20	10
1401	60g. black and green	20	10

PORTRAITS: No. 1398, L. Warynski (patriot); 1399, L. Krzywicki (economist); 1400, M. Sklodowska-Curie (scientist); 1401, K. Swierczewski (patriot).

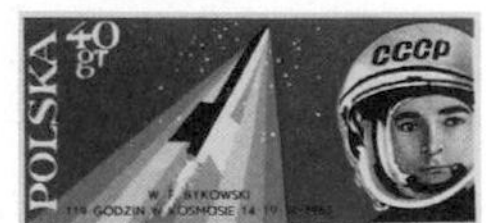

426 Bykovsky and "Vostok 5"

1963. Second "Team" Manned Space Flights.

1402	**426**	40g. black, green and blue	20	10
1403	-	60g. black, blue and green	20	10
1404	-	6z.50 multicoloured	1·60	55

DESIGNS: 60g. Tereshkova and "Vostok 6"; 6z.50, "Vostoks 5 and 6" in orbit.

427 Basketball

1963. 13th European (Men's) Basketball Championships, Wroclaw.

1405	**427**	40g. multicoloured	10	10
1406	-	50g. green, black and pink	10	10
1407	-	60g. black, green and red	10	10
1408	-	90g. multicoloured	10	10
1409	-	2z.50 multicoloured	20	10
1410	-	5z.60 multicoloured	2·10	25
MS1410a 76×86 mm. 10z. (+5z.) multicoloured			2·75	1·80

DESIGNS: 50g. to 2z.50, As Type **427** but with ball, players and hands in various positions; 5z.60, Hands placing ball in net; 10z. Town Hall, People's Hall and Arms of Wroclaw.

428 Missile

1963. 20th Anniv of Polish People's Army. Multicoloured.

1411	20g. Type **428**	10	10
1412	40g. "Blyskawica" (destroyer)	10	10
1413	60g. PZL-106 Kruk (airplane)	10	10
1414	1z.15 Radar scanner	10	10
1415	1z.35 Tank	10	10
1416	1z.55 Missile carrier	10	10
1417	2z.50 Amphibious troop carrier	50	10
1418	3z. Ancient warrior, modern soldier and two swords	95	20

429 "A Love Letter" (after Czachorski)

1963. Stamp Day.

1419	**429**	60g. brown	30	10

1963. Visit of Soviet Cosmonauts to Poland. Nos. 1402/4 optd **23-28. X. 1963** and **w Polsce** together with Cosmonauts' names.

1420	**426**	40g. black, green and blue	50	10
1421	-	60g. black, blue and green	50	10
1422	-	6z.50 multicoloured	2·40	1·60

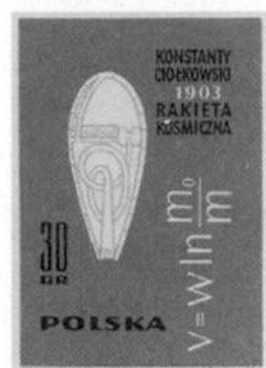

431 Tsiolkovsky's Rocket and Formula

1963. "The Conquest of Space". Inscr in black.

1423	**431**	30g. turquoise	10	10
1424	-	40g. olive	10	10
1425	-	50g. violet	10	10
1426	-	60g. brown	10	10
1427	-	1z. turquoise	10	10
1428	-	1z.50 red	10	10
1429	-	1z.55 blue	10	10
1430	-	2z.50 purple	50	10
1431	-	5z.60 green	95	20
1432	-	6z.50 turquoise	1·90	35
MS1432a 78×106 mm. Nos. 1431/2 (two of each)			60·00	60·00

DESIGNS: 40g. "Sputnik 1"; 50g. "Explorer 1"; 60g. Banner carried by "Lunik 2"; 1z. "Lunik 3"; 1z.50, "Vostok 1"; 1z.55, "Friendship 7"; 2z.50, "Vostoks 3 and 4"; 5z.60, "Mariner 2"; 6z.50, "Mars 1".

432 Mazurian Horses

1963. Polish Horse-breeding. Multicoloured.

1433	20g. Arab stallion "Comet"	10	10
1434	30g. Wild horses	10	10
1435	40g. Sokolski horse	10	10
1436	50g. Arab mares and foals	20	10
1437	60g. Type **432**	20	10
1438	90g. Steeplechasers	30	10
1439	1z.55 Arab stallion "Witez II"	65	10
1440	2z.50 Head of Arab horse (facing right)	1·10	20
1441	4z. Mixed breeds	2·75	75
1442	6z.50 Head of Arab horse (facing left)	3·75	3·50

SIZES—TRIANGULAR (55×27½ mm): 20, 30, 40g. HORIZ: (75×26 mm): 50, 90g., 4z. VERT: as Type **432**: 1z.55, 2z.50, 6z.50.

433 Ice Hockey

1964. Winter Olympic Games, Innsbruck. Multicoloured.

1443	20g. Type **433**	10	10
1444	30g. Slalom	10	10
1445	40g. Downhill skiing	20	10
1446	60g. Speed skating	20	10
1447	1z. Ski-jumping	40	10
1448	2z.50 Tobogganing	75	20
1449	5z.60 Cross-country skiing	1·60	75
1450	6z.50 Pairs, figure skating	2·40	1·10
MS1450a 110×94 mm. Nos. 1448 and 1450 (two of each)		43·00	43·00

1964. Sailing Ships (2nd series). As T **421** but without coloured backgrounds. Some new designs.

1451	**421**	5g. brown	10	10
1452	-	10g. green	10	10
1453	-	20g. blue	10	10
1454	-	30g. bronze	10	10
1455	-	40g. blue	20	10
1456	-	60g. purple	20	10
1457	-	1z. brown	20	10
1458	-	1z.15 brown	20	10
1459	-	1z.35 blue	20	10
1460	-	1z.50 purple	20	10
1461	-	1z.55 black	20	10
1462	-	2z. violet	30	10
1463	-	2z.10 green	40	10
1464	-	2z.50 mauve	50	10
1465	-	3z. olive	65	10
1466	-	3z.40 brown	1·10	10

SHIPS—HORIZ: 10g. to 1z.15, As Nos. 1370/7; 1z.50, "Ark Royal" (English galleon, 1587); 2z.10, Ship of the line (18th cent); 2z.50, Sail frigate (19th cent); 3z. "Flying Cloud" (clipper, 19th cent). VERT: 1z.35, Columbus's "Santa Maria"; 1z.55, "Wodnik" (Polish warship, 17th cent); 2z. Dutch fleute (17th cent); 3z.40, "Dar Pomorza" (cadet ship).

434 "Flourishing Tree"

1964. 20th Anniv of People's Republic (1st issue).

1467	**434**	60g. multicoloured	10	10
1468	-	60g. black, yellow and red	10	10

DESIGN: No. 1468, Emblem composed of symbols of agriculture and industry.

See also Nos. 1497/1506.

435 European Cat

1964. Domestic Cats. As T **435**.

1469	30g. black and yellow	30	10
1470	40g. multicoloured	30	10
1471	50g. black, turquoise & yellow	30	10
1472	60g. multicoloured	40	10
1473	90g. multicoloured	50	20
1474	1z.35 multicoloured	50	20
1475	1z.55 multicoloured	55	20
1476	2z.50 yellow, black and violet	95	65
1477	3z.40 multicoloured	3·75	1·30
1478	6z.50 multicoloured	5·75	3·25

CATS—European: 30, 40, 60g., 1z.55, 2z.50, 6z.50. Siamese: 50g. Persian: 90g., 1z.35, 3z.40.

Nos. 1472/5 are horiz.

436 Casimir the Great (founder)

1964. 600th Anniv of Jagiellonian University, Cracow.

1479	**436**	40g. purple	10	10
1480	-	40g. green	10	10
1481	-	60g. violet	10	10
1482	-	60g. blue	45	15
1483	-	2z.50 sepia	70	35

PORTRAITS: No. 1480, Hugo Kollataj (educationist and politician); 1481, Jan Dlugosz (geographer and historian); 1482, Copernicus (astronomer); 1483 (36×37 mm), King Wladislaw Jagiello and Queen Jadwiga.

437 Northern Lapwing

1964. Birds. Multicoloured.

1484	30g. Type **437**	20	10
1485	40g. Bluethroat	20	10
1486	50g. Black-tailed godwit	20	10
1487	60g. Osprey (vert)	25	10
1488	90g. Grey heron (vert)	50	10
1489	1z.35 Little gull (vert)	65	10
1490	1z.55 Common shoveler	65	20
1491	5z.60 Black-throated diver	1·60	75
1492	6z.50 Great crested grebe	2·50	1·30

438 Red Flag on Brick Wall

1964. Fourth Polish United Workers' Party Congress, Warsaw. Inscr "PZPR". Multicoloured.

1493	60g. Type **438**	15	10
1494	60g. Beribboned hammer	15	10
1495	60g. Hands reaching for Red Flag	15	10
1496	60g. Hammer and corn emblems	15	10

439 Factory and Cogwheel **440** Gdansk Shipyard

1964. 20th Anniv of People's Republic (2nd issue).

1497	**439**	60g. black and blue	15	10
1498	-	60g. black and green	15	10
1499	-	60g. red and orange	15	10
1500	-	60g. blue and grey	15	10
1501	**440**	60g. blue and green	15	10
1502	-	60g. violet and mauve	15	10
1503	-	60g. brown and violet	15	10
1504	-	60g. bronze and green	15	10
1505	-	60g. purple and red	15	10
1506	-	60g. brown and yellow	15	10

DESIGNS—As Type **439**: No. 1498, Tractor and ear of wheat; 1499, Mask and symbols of the arts; 1500, Atomic symbol and book. As Type **440**: No. 1502, Lenin Foundry, Nowa Huta; 1503, Cement Works, Chelm; 1504, Turoszow power station; 1505, Petro-chemical plant, Plock; 1506, Tarnobrzeg sulphur mine.

441 Battle Scene

1964. 20th Anniv of Warsaw Insurrection.

1507	**441**	60g. multicoloured	25	10

442 Relay-racing

1964. Olympic Games, Tokyo. Multicoloured.

1508	20g. Triple-jumping	10	10
1509	40g. Rowing	10	10
1510	60g. Weightlifting	10	10
1511	90g. Type **442**	10	10
1512	1z. Boxing	10	10
1513	2z.50 Football	50	10
1514	5z.60 High jumping (women)	1·40	55
1515	6z.50 High-diving	2·10	85
MS1515a 83×111 mm. Nos. 1514/15 (two of each)		60·00	55·00
MS1515b 79×106 mm. 2z.50 Rifle-shooting, 2z.50 Canoeing, 5z. Fencing, 5z. Basketball		5·25	2·40

SIZES: DIAMOND—20g. to 60g. SQUARE—90g. to 2z.50. VERT: (23½×36 mm)—5z.60, 6z.50.

443 Congress Emblem

1964. 15th Int Astronautical Congress, Warsaw.

1516	**443**	2z.50 black and violet	65	20

444 Hand holding Hammer

1964. Third Congress of Fighters for Freedom and Democracy Association, Warsaw.

1517	**444**	60g. red, black and green	25	10

445 S. Zeromski

1964. Birth Cent of Stefan Zeromski (writer).

1518	**445**	60g. brown	25	10

446 Globe and Red Flag

1964. Centenary of "First International".

1519	**446**	60g. black and red	25	10

447 18th-century Stage Coach (after Brodowski)

1964. Stamp Day.

1520	**447**	60g. green	30	10
1521	**447**	60g. brown	30	10

448 Eleanor Roosevelt

1964. 80th Birth Anniv of Eleanor Roosevelt.

1522	**448**	2z.50 brown	50	20

449 Battle of Studzianki (after S. Zoltowski)

1964. "Poland's Struggle" (World War II) (1st issue).

1523	-	40g. black	20	10
1524	-	40g. violet	20	10
1525	-	60g. blue	20	10
1526	-	60g. green	20	10
1527	**449**	60g. bronze	20	10

DESIGNS—VERT: No. 1523, Virtuti Militari Cross; 1524, Westerplatte Memorial, Gdansk; 1525, Bydogoszez Memorial. HORIZ: No. 1526, Soldiers crossing the Oder (after S. Zoltowski).

See also Nos. 1610/12.

449a W. Komarov

1964. Russian Three-manned Space Flight. Sheet 114×63 mm depicting crew.

MS1527a 60g. black and red (T **449a**); 60g. black and green (Feoktistov); 60g. black and blue (Yegorov)	1·90	1·10

450 Cyclamen

1964. Garden Flowers. Multicoloured.

1528	20g. Type **450**	10	10
1529	30g. Freesia	10	10
1530	40g. Rose	10	10
1531	50g. Peony	10	10
1532	60g. Lily	10	10
1533	90g. Poppy	10	10
1534	1z.35 Tulip	20	10
1535	1z.50 Narcissus	95	55
1536	1z.55 Begonia	30	10
1537	2z.50 Carnation	1·10	20
1538	3z.40 Iris	1·40	55
1539	5z.60 Japanese camelia	2·50	1·30

Nos. 1534/9 are smaller, 26½×37 mm.

451 Spacecraft of the Future

1964. Space Research. Multicoloured.

1540	20g. Type **451**	10	10
1541	30g. Launching rocket	10	10
1542	40g. Dog "Laika" and rocket	10	10
1543	60g. "Lunik 3" and Moon	20	10
1544	1z.55 Satelite	30	10
1545	2z.50 "Elektron 2"	55	20
1546	5z.60 "Mars 1"	1·40	65
1547	6z.50+2z. Gagarin seated in capsule	2·40	1·20

452 "Siren of Warsaw"

1965. 20th Anniv of Liberation of Warsaw.

1548	**452**	60g. green	25	10

453 Edaphosaurus

1965. Prehistoric Animals (1st series). Multicoloured.

1549	20g. Type **453**	20	10
1550	30g. Cryptocleidus (vert)	20	10
1551	40g. Brontosaurus	20	10
1552	60g. Mesosaurus (vert)	20	10
1553	90g. Stegosaurus	25	10
1554	1z.15 Brachiosaurus (vert)	30	15
1555	1z.35 Styracosaurus	30	20
1556	3z.40 Corythosaurus (vert)	1·10	45
1557	5z.60 Rhamphorhynchus (vert)	2·10	75
1558	6z.50 Tyrannosaurus	3·25	1·10

See also Nos. 1639/47.

454 Petro-chemical Works, Plock, and Polish and Soviet Flags

1965. 20th Anniv of Polish–Soviet Friendship Treaty. Multicoloured.

1559	60g. Seal (vert, 27×38½ mm)	10	10
1560	60g. Type **454**	10	10

455 Polish Eagle and Civic Arms

1965. 20th Anniv of Return of Western and Northern Territories to Poland.

1561	**455**	60g. red	25	10

456 Dove of Peace

1965. 20th Anniv of Victory.

1562	**456**	60g. red and black	25	10

457 I.T.U. Emblem

1965. Centenary of I.T.U.

1563	**457**	2z.50 black, violet & blue	75	20

458 Clover-leaf Emblem and "The Friend of the People" (journal)

1965. 70th Anniv of Peasant Movement. Multicoloured.

1564	40g. Type **458**	10	10
1565	60g. Ears of corn and industrial plant (horiz)	10	10

459 "Dragon" Dinghies

1965. World Finn Sailing Championships, Gdynia. Multicoloured.

1566	30g. Type **459**	10	10
1567	40g. "5.5 m." dinghies	10	10
1568	50g. "Finn" dinghies (horiz)	10	10
1569	60g. "V" dinghies	10	10
1570	1z.35 "Cadet" dinghies (horiz)	20	10
1571	4z. "Star" yachts (horiz)	1·10	55
1572	5z.60 "Flying Dutchman" dinghies	2·10	85
1573	6z.50 "Amethyst" dinghies (horiz)	3·00	1·20
MS1573a	79×59 mm. 15z. Finn dinghies	3·25	2·20

460 Marx and Lenin

1965. Postal Ministers' Congress, Peking.

1574	**460**	60g. black on red	30	20

461 17th-cent Arms of Warsaw

1965. 700th Anniv of Warsaw.

1575	**461**	5g. red	10	10
1576	-	10g. green	10	10
1577	-	20g. blue	10	10
1578	-	40g. brown	10	10
1579	-	60g. orange	10	10
1580	-	1z.50 black	20	10
1581	-	1z.55 blue	30	10
1582	-	2z.50 purple	55	10
MS1583		51×62 mm. 3z.40 black and bistre	1·40	1·00

DESIGNS—VERT: 10g. 13th-cent antiquities. HORIZ: 20g. Tombstone of last Masovian dukes; 40g. Old Town Hall; 60g. Barbican; 1z.50, Arsenal; 1z.55, National Theatre; 2z.50, Staszic Palace; 3z.40, T **462**.

463 I.Q.S.Y. Emblem

1965. International Quiet Sun Year. Multicoloured. Background colours given.

1584	**463**	60g. blue	10	10
1585	**463**	60g. violet	10	10
1586	-	2z.50 red	50	20
1587	-	2z.50 brown	50	20
1588	-	3z.40 orange	75	35
1589	-	3z.40 olive	75	35

DESIGNS: 2z.50, Solar scanner; 3z.40, Solar System.

464 "Odontoglossum grande"

1965. Orchids. Multicoloured.

1590	20g. Type **464**	10	10
1591	30g. "Cypripedium hibridum"	10	10
1592	40g. "Lycaste skinneri"	10	10
1593	50g. "Cattleya warzewicza"	20	10
1594	60g. "Vanda sanderiana"	20	10
1595	1z.35 "Cypripedium hibridum" (different)	50	20
1596	4z. "Sobralia"	1·40	55
1597	5z.60 "Disa grandiflora"	1·60	65
1598	6z.50 "Cattleya labiata"	2·75	1·80

465 Weightlifting

1965. Olympic Games, Tokyo. Polish Medal Winners. Multicoloured.

1599	30g. Type **465**	10	10
1600	40g. Boxing	10	10
1601	50g. Relay-racing	10	10
1602	60g. Fencing	10	10
1603	90g. Hurdling (women's 80 m)	20	10
1604	3z.40 Relay-racing (women's)	75	20
1605	6z.50 "Hop, step and jump"	1·50	75
1606	7z.10 Volleyball (women's)	1·90	1·30

466 "The Post Coach" (after P. Michalowski)

1965. Stamp Day.

1607	**466**	60g. brown	20	10
1608	-	2z.50 green	50	20

DESIGN: 2z.50, "Coach about to leave" (after P. Michalowski).

467 U.N. Emblem

1965. 20th Anniv of U.N.O.

1609	**467**	2z.50 blue	50	20

468 Memorial, Holy Cross Mountains

1965. "Poland's Struggle" (World War II) (2nd issue).

1610	**468**	60g. brown	20	10
1611	-	60g. green	20	10
1612	-	60g. brown	20	10

DESIGNS—VERT: No. 1611, Memorial Plaszow. HORIZ: No. 1612, Memorial, Chelm-on-Ner.

469 Wolf

1965. Forest Animals. Multicoloured.

1613	20g. Type **469**	20	10
1614	30g. Lynx	20	10
1615	40g. Red fox	20	10
1616	50g. Eurasian badger	20	10
1617	60g. Brown bear	20	10
1618	1z.50 Wild boar	35	10
1619	2z.50 Red deer	65	20
1620	5z.60 European bison	1·40	40
1621	7z.10 Elk	2·75	75

470 Gig

1965. Horse-drawn Carriages in Lancut Museum. Multicoloured.

1622	20g. Type **470**	20	10
1623	40g. Coupe	20	10
1624	50g. Ladies' "basket" (trap)	20	10
1625	60g. "Vis-a-vis"	20	10
1626	90g. Cab	20	10
1627	1z.15 Berlinka	30	10
1628	2z.50 Hunting brake	75	20
1629	6z.50 Barouche	2·10	75
1630	7z.10 English brake	3·00	1·80

Nos. 1627/9 are 77×22 mm and No. 1630 is 104×22 mm.

471 Congress Emblem and Industrial Products

1966. Fifth Polish Technicians' Congress, Katowice.

1631	**471**	60g. multicoloured	30	10

1966. 20th Anniv of Industrial Nationalization. Designs similar to T **471**. Multicoloured.

1632	60g. Pithead gear (vert)	30	10
1633	60g. "Henryk Jedza" (freighter)	30	10
1634	60g. Petro-chemical works, Plock	30	10
1635	60g. Combine-harvester	30	10
1636	60g. Class EN 57 electric train	30	10
1637	60g. Exhibition Hall, 35th Poznan Fair	30	10
1638	60g. Crane (vert)	30	10

1966. Prehistoric Animals (2nd series). As T **453**. Multicoloured.

1639	20g. Terror fish	20	10
1640	30g. Lobefin	20	10
1641	40g. Ichthyostega	20	10
1642	50g. Mastodonsaurus	20	10
1643	60g. Cynognathus	50	20
1644	2z.50 Archaeopteryx (vert)	65	20
1645	3z.40 Brontotherium	95	35
1646	6z.50 Machairodus	2·10	75
1647	7z.10 Mammuthus	3·25	1·30

472 H. Sienkiewicz (novelist)

1966. 50th Death Anniv of Henryk Sienkiewicz.

1648	**472**	60g. black on buff	30	20

473 Footballers (Montevideo, 1930)

1966. World Cup Football Championship. (a) Football scenes representing World Cup finals.

1649	20g. Type **473**	10	10
1650	40g. Rome, 1934	10	10
1651	60g. Paris, 1938	10	10
1652	90g. Rio de Janeiro, 1950	20	10
1653	1z.50 Berne, 1954	95	20
1654	3z.40 Stockholm, 1958	1·10	35
1655	6z.50 Santiago, 1962	1·90	1·10
1656	7z.10 "London", 1966 (elimination match, Glasgow, 1965)	2·75	2·20

(b) 61×81 mm.

MS1657 **474**	13z.50+1z.50	4·75	2·75

475 Soldier with Flag, and Dove of Peace

1966. 21st Anniv of Victory Day.

1658	**475**	60g. red and black on silver	20	10

476 Women's Relay-racing

477

1966. Eighth European Athletic Championships, Budapest. Multicoloured.

1659	20g. Runner starting race (vert)	10	10
1660	40g. Type **476**	10	10
1661	60g. Throwing the javelin (vert)	10	10
1662	90g. Women's hurdles	10	10
1663	1z.35 Throwing the discus (vert)	20	10
1664	3z.40 Finish of race	85	20
1665	6z.50 Throwing the hammer (vert)	1·50	65
1666	7z.10 High-jumping	1·70	1·00
MS1667 **477**	110×66 mm. 5z. Imperf	2·75	1·60

478 White Eagle

1966. Polish Millenary (1st issue). Each red and black on gold.

1668	60g. Type **478**	20	10
1669	60g. Polish flag	20	10
1670	2z.50 Type **478**	50	20
1671	2z.50 Polish flag	50	20

See also Nos. 1717/18.

479 Flowers and Produce

1966. Harvest Festival. Multicoloured.

1672	40g. Type **479**	50	10
1673	60g. Woman and loaf	50	10
1674	3z.40 Festival bouquet	95	65

The 3z.40 is 49×48 mm.

480 Chrysanthemum

1966. Flowers. Multicoloured.

1675	10g. Type **480**	10	10
1676	20g. Polnsettia	10	10
1677	30g. Centaury	10	10
1678	40g. Rose	10	10
1679	60g. Zinnia	20	10
1680	90g. Nasturtium	55	20
1681	5z.60 Dahlia	1·40	55
1682	6z.50 Sunflower	1·90	75
1683	7z.10 Magnolia	2·75	85

481 Tourist Map

1966. Tourism.

1684	**481**	10g. red	10	10
1685	-	20g. olive	10	10
1686	-	40g. blue	10	10
1687	-	60g. brown	10	10
1688	-	60g. black	10	10
1689	-	1z.15 green	20	10
1690	-	1z.35 red	30	10
1691	-	1z.55 violet	30	10
1692	-	2z. green	55	10

DESIGNS: 20g. Hela Lighthouse; 40g. Yacht; 60g. (No. 1687), Poniatowski Bridge, Warsaw; 60g. (No. 1688), Mining Academy, Kielee; 1z.15, Dunajee Gorge; 1z.35, Old oaks, Rogalin; 1z.55, Silesian Planetarium; 2z. "Batory" (liner).

482 Roman Capital

1966. Polish Culture Congress.

1693	**482**	60g. red and brown	25	10

483 Stable-man with Percherons

1966. Stamp Day.

1694	**483**	60g. brown	10	10
1695	-	2z.50 green	55	20

DESIGN: 2z.50, Stablemen with horses and dogs.

484 Soldier in Action

1966. 30th Anniv of Jaroslav Dabrowski Brigade.

1696	**484**	60g. black, green and red	25	10

485 Woodland Birds

1966. Woodland Birds. Multicoloured.

1697	10g. Type **485**	30	10
1698	20g. Green woodpecker	30	10
1699	30g. Jay	30	10
1700	40g. Golden oriole	30	10
1701	60g. Hoopoe	30	10
1702	2z.50 Common redstart	65	35
1703	4z. Spruce siskin	1·70	55
1704	6z.50 Chaffinch	2·10	1·20
1705	7z.10 Great tit	2·50	1·20

486 Ram (ritual statuette)

1966. Polish Archaeological Research.

1706	**486**	60g. blue	15	10
1707	-	60g. green	15	10
1708	-	60g. brown	15	10

DESIGNS—VERT: No. 1707, Plan of Biskupin settlement. HORIZ: No. 1708, Brass implements and ornaments.

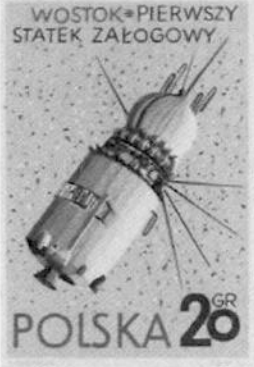

487 "Vostok 1"

1966. Space Research. Multicoloured.

1709	20g. Type **487**	15	10
1710	40g. "Gemini"	15	10
1711	60g. "Ariel 2"	15	10
1712	1z.35 "Proton 1"	20	10
1713	1z.50 "FR 1"	50	15
1714	3z.40 "Alouette"	65	20
1715	6z.50 "San Marco 1"	1·90	35
1716	7z.10 "Luna 9"	2·30	65

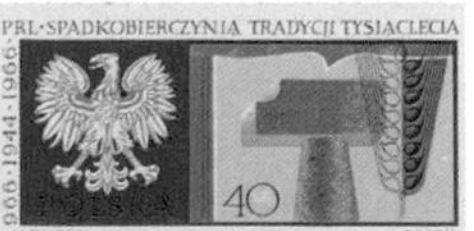

488 Polish Eagle and Hammer

1966. Polish Millenary (2nd issue).

1717	**488**	40g. purple, lilac and red	15	10
1718	-	60g. purple, green and red	15	10

DESIGN: 60g. Polish eagle and agricultural and industrial symbols.

489 Dressage

1967. 150th Anniv of Racehorse Breeding in Poland. Multicoloured.

1719	10g. Type **489**	20	10
1720	20g. Cross-country racing	20	10
1721	40g. Horse-jumping	20	10

1722	60g. Jumping fence in open country	40	10
1723	90g. Horse-trotting	50	10
1724	5z.90 Playing polo	1·40	75
1725	6z.60 Stallion "Ofir"	2·40	1·10
1726	7z. Stallion "Skowrenek"	3·75	1·30

490 Black-wedged Butterflyfish

1967. Exotic Fish. Multicoloured.

1727	5g. Type **490**	15	10
1728	10g. Emperor angelfish	15	10
1729	40g. Racoon butterflyfish	15	10
1730	60g. Clown triggerfish	15	10
1731	90g. Undulate triggerfish	15	10
1732	1z.50 Picasso triggerfish	30	10
1733	4z.50 Black-finned melon butterflyfish	1·50	20
1734	6z.60 Semicircle angelfish	2·30	1·30
1735	7z. Saddle butterflyfish	1·90	55

491 Auschwitz Memorial

1967. Polish Martyrdom and Resistance, 1939–45.

1736	**491**	40g. brown	15	10
1737	-	40g. black	15	10
1738	-	40g. violet	15	10

DESIGNS—VERT: No. 1737, Auschwitz-Monowitz Memorial; 1738, Memorial guide's emblem.

See also Nos. 1770/2, 1798/9 and 1865/9.

492 Cyclists

1967. 20th International Peace Cycle Race.

1739	**492**	60g. multicoloured	25	20

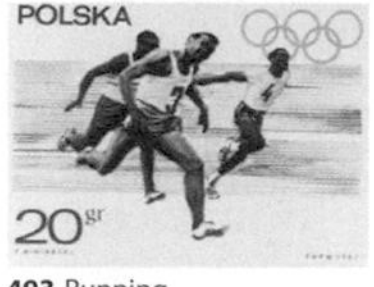

493 Running

1967. Olympic Games (1968). Multicoloured.

1740	20g. Type **493**	15	10
1741	40g. Horse-jumping	15	10
1742	60g. Relay-running	15	10
1743	90g. Weight-lifting	15	10
1744	1z.35 Hurdling	20	10
1745	3z.40 Gymnastics	85	35
1746	6z.60 High-jumping	1·10	65
1747	7z. Boxing	1·90	1·10
MS1748	65×86 mm. 10z.+5z. multicoloured	3·25	2·20

DESIGN: (30×30 mm.)—10z. Kusocinski winning 10,000 meters race at Olympic Games, Los Angeles, 1932.

494 Socialist Symbols

1967. Polish Trade Unions Congress, Warsaw.

1749	**494**	60g. multicoloured	30	20

495 "Arnica montana"

1967. Protected Plants. Multicoloured.

1750	40g. Type **495**	15	10
1751	60g. "Aquilegia vulgaris"	15	10
1752	3z.40 "Gentiana punctata"	55	15
1753	4z.50 "Lycopodium clavatum"	65	15
1754	5z. "Iris sibirica"	95	20
1755	10z. "Azalea pontica"	1·90	45

496 Katowice Memorial

1967. Inauguration of Katowice Memorial.

1756	**496**	60g. multicoloured	25	20

497 Marie Curie

1967. Birth Centenary of Marie Curie.

1757	**497**	60g. lake	15	10
1758	-	60g. brown	15	10
1759	-	60g. violet	15	10

DESIGNS: No. 1758, Marie Curie's Nobel Prize diploma; 1759, Statue of Marie Curie, Warsaw.

498 "Fifth Congress of the Deaf" (sign language)

1967. Fifth World Federation of the Deaf Congress, Warsaw.

1760	**498**	60g. black and blue	25	20

499 Bouquet

1967. "Flowers of the Meadow". Multicoloured.

1761	20g. Type **499**	15	10
1762	40g. Red poppy	15	10
1763	60g. Field bindweed	15	10
1764	90g. Wild pansy	20	10
1765	1z.15 Tansy	20	10
1766	2z.50 Corn cockle	50	20
1767	3z.40 Field scabious	85	55
1768	4z.50 Scarlet pimpernel	2·40	55
1769	7z.90 Chicory	2·50	1·10

1967. Polish Martyrdom and Resistance, 1939–45 (2nd series). As T **491**.

1770	40g. blue	15	10
1771	40g. green	15	10
1772	40g. black	15	10

DESIGNS—HORIZ: No. 1770, Stutthof Memorial. VERT: No. 1771, Walez Memorial; 1772, Lodz-Radogoszez Memorial.

500 "Wilanow Palace" (from painting by W. Kasprzycki)

1967. Stamp Day.

1773	**500**	60g. brown and blue	25	20

501 Cruiser "Aurora"

1967. 50th Anniv of October Revolution. Each black, grey and red.

1774	60g. Type **501**	15	10
1775	60g. Lenin	15	10
1776	60g. "Luna 10"	15	10

502 Peacock

1967. Butterflies. Multicoloured.

1777	10g. Type **502**	15	10
1778	20g. Swallowtail	15	10
1779	40g. Small tortoiseshell	15	10
1780	60g. Camberwell beauty	20	10
1781	2z. Purple emperor	40	15
1782	2z.50 Red admiral	50	20
1783	3z.40 Pale clouded yellow	55	35
1784	4z.50 Marbled white	2·75	1·10
1785	7z.90 Large blue	3·00	1·30

503 Kosciuszko

1967. 150th Death Anniv of Tadeusz Kosciuszko (national hero).

1786	**503**	60g. chocolate and brown	15	10
1787	**503**	2z.50 green and red	40	15

504 "The Lobster" (Jean de Heem)

1967. Famous Paintings.

1788	-	20g. multicoloured	30	10
1789	-	40g. multicoloured	30	10
1790	-	60g. multicoloured	30	10
1791	-	2z. multicoloured	55	35
1792	-	2z.50 multicoloured	65	45
1793	-	3z.40 multicoloured	95	55
1794	**504**	4z.50 multicoloured	1·60	1·10
1795	-	6z.60 multicoloured	2·40	1·30

DESIGNS (Paintings from the National Museums, Warsaw and Cracow). VERT: 20g. "Lady with a Weasel" (Leonardo da Vinci); 40g. "The Polish Lady" (Watteau); 60g. "Dog fighting Heron" (A. Hondius); 2z. "Fowler tuning Guitar" (J. B. Greuze); 2z.50, "The Tax Collectors" (M. van Reymerswaele); 3z.40, "Daria Fiodorowna" (F. S. Rokotov). HORIZ: 6z.60, "Parable of the Good Samaritan" (landscape, Rembrandt).

505 W. S. Reymont

1967. Birth Centenary of W. S. Reymont (novelist).

1796	**505**	60g. brown, red and ochre	25	20

506 J. M. Ossolinski (medallion), Book and Flag

1967. 150th Anniv of Ossolineum Foundation.

1797	**506**	60g. brown, red and blue	25	20

1967. Polish Martyrdom and Resistance, 1939–45 (3rd series). As T **491**.

1798	40g. red	15	10
1799	40g. brown	15	10

DESIGNS—VERT: No. 1798, Zagan Memorial. HORIZ: No. 1799, Lambinowice Memorial.

507 Ice Hockey

1968. Winter Olympic Games, Grenoble. Multicoloured.

1800	40g. Type **507**	15	10
1801	60g. Downhill	15	10
1802	90g. Slalom	20	10
1803	1z.35 Speed-skating	20	10
1804	1z.55 Ski-walking	20	10
1805	2z. Tobogganing	50	35
1806	7z. Rifle-shooting on skis	95	65
1807	7z.90 Ski-jumping (different)	1·90	85

508 "Puss in Boots"

1968. Fairy Tales. Multicoloured.

1808	20g. Type **508**	15	10
1809	40g. "The Raven and the Fox"	15	10
1810	60g. "Mr. Twardowski"	20	10
1811	2z. "The Fisherman and the Fish"	50	10
1812	2z.50 "Little Red Riding Hood"	55	15
1813	3z.40 "Cinderella"	85	20
1814	5z.50 "The Waif"	2·10	75
1815	7z. "Snow White"	2·50	1·10

509 "Passiflora quadrangularis"

1968. Flowers. Multicoloured.

1816	10g. "Clianthus dampieri"	10	10
1817	20g. Type **509**	10	10
1818	30g. "Strelitzia reginae"	10	10
1819	40g. "Coryphanta vivipara"	10	10
1820	60g. "Odontonia"	15	10
1821	90g. "Protea cyneroides"	20	10
1822	4z.+2z. "Abutilon"	1·50	75
1823	8z.+4z. "Rosa polyantha"	3·00	1·70

510 "Peace" (poster by H. Tomaszewski)

1968. Second Int Poster Biennale, Warsaw. Multicoloured.

1824	60g. Type **510**	15	10
1825	2z.50 Gounod's "Faust" (poster by Jan Lenica)	40	15

511 Zephyr Glider

1968. 11th World Gliding Championships, Leszno. Gliders. Multicoloured.

1826	60g. Type **511**	10	10
1827	90g. Stork	10	10
1828	1z.50 Swallow	20	10
1829	3z.40 Fly	65	35
1830	4z. Seal	1·40	45
1831	5z.50 Pirate	1·70	55

512 Child with "Stamp"

1968. "75 years of Polish Philately". Multicoloured.

1832	60g. Type **512**	15	10
1833	60g. Balloon over Poznan	15	10

513 Part of Monument

1968. Silesian Insurrection Monument, Sosnowiec.

1834	**513**	60g. black and purple	25	10

514 Relay-racing

1968. Olympic Games, Mexico. Multicoloured.

1835	30g. Type **514**	10	10
1836	40g. Boxing	10	10
1837	60g. Basketball	10	10
1838	90g. Long-jumping	15	10
1839	2z.50 Throwing the javelin	20	10
1840	3z.40 Gymnastics	40	15
1841	4z. Cycling	50	35
1842	7z.90 Fencing	95	55
1843	10z.+5z. Torch runner and Aztec bas-relief (56×45 mm)	2·75	1·10

515 "Knight on a Bay Horse" (P. Michalowski)

1968. Polish Paintings. Multicoloured.

1844	40g. Type **515**	10	10
1845	60g. "Fisherman" (L. Wyczolkowski)	10	10
1846	1z.15 "Jewish Woman with Lemons" (A. Gierymski)	10	10
1847	1z.35 "Eliza Parenska" (S. Wyspianski)	35	15
1848	1z.50 "Manifesto" (W. Weiss)	50	20
1849	4z.50 "Stanczyk" (Jan Matejko) (horiz)	65	35
1850	5z. "Children's Band" (T. Makowski) (horiz)	1·10	65
1851	7z. "Feast II" (Z. Waliszewski) (horiz)	1·90	75

516 "September, 1939" (Bylina)

1968. 25th Anniv of Polish People's Army. Designs show paintings.

1852	40g. violet and olive on yellow	10	10
1853	40g. blue and violet on lilac	10	10
1854	40g. green and blue on grey	10	10
1855	40g. black and brown on orange	10	10
1856	40g. purple & green on green	10	10
1857	60g. brown & ultram on bl	20	10
1858	60g. purple & green on green	20	10
1859	60g. olive and red on pink	20	10
1860	60g. green and brown on red	20	10
1861	60g. blue & turquoise on blue	20	10

PAINTINGS AND PAINTERS: No. 1852, Type **516**; 1853, "Partisans" (Maciag); 1854, "Lenino" (Bylina); 1855, "Monte Cassino" (Boratynski); 1856, "Tanks before Warsaw" (Garwatowski); 1857, "Neisse River" (Bylina); 1858, "On the Oder" (Mackiewicz); 1859, "In Berlin" (Bylina); 1860, "Blyskawica" (destroyer) (Mokwa); 1861, "Pursuit" (Mikoyan Gurevich MiG-17 aircraft) (Kulisiewicz).

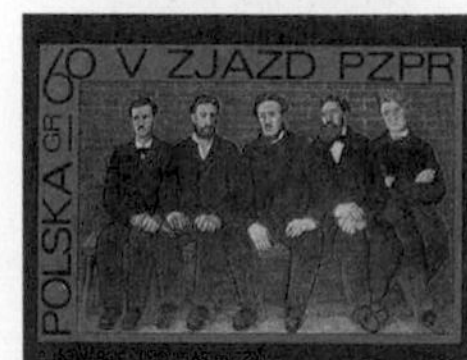

517 "Party Members" (F. Kowarski)

1968. Fifth Polish United Workers' Party Congress, Warsaw. Multicoloured designs showing paintings.

1862	60g. Type **517**	15	10
1863	60g. "Strike" (S. Lentz) (vert)	15	10
1864	60g. "Manifesto" (W. Weiss) (vert)	15	10

1968. Polish Martyrdom and Resistance, 1939–45 (4th series). As T **491**.

1865	40g. grey	15	10
1866	40g. brown	15	10
1867	40g. brown	15	10
1868	40g. blue	15	10
1869	40g. brown	15	10

DESIGNS—HORIZ: No. 1865, Tomb of Unknown Soldier, Warsaw; 1866, Guerillas' Monument, Kartuzy. VERT: No. 1867, Insurgents' Monument, Poznan; 1868, People's Guard Insurgents' Monument, Polichno; 1869, Rotunda, Zamosc.

518 "Start of Hunt" (W. Kossak)

1968. Paintings. Hunting Scenes. Multicoloured.

1870	20g. Type **518**	10	10
1871	40g. "Hunting with Falcon" (J. Kossak)	10	10
1872	60g. "Wolves' Raid" (A. Wierusz-Kowalski)	10	10
1873	1z.50 "Home-coming with a Bear" (J. Falat)	20	10
1874	2z.50 "The Fox-hunt" (T. Sutherland)	40	10
1875	3z.40 "The Boar-hunt" (F. Snyders)	55	20
1876	4z.50 "Hunters' Rest" (W. G. Pierow)	1·70	65
1877	8z.50 "Hunting a Lion in Morocco" (Delacroix)	1·90	85

519 Maltese Terrier

1969. Pedigree Dogs. Multicoloured.

1878	20g. Type **519**	20	10
1879	40g. Wire-haired fox-terrier (vert)	50	20
1880	60g. Afghan hound	50	20
1881	1z.50 Rough-haired terrier	50	20
1882	2z.50 English setter	65	25
1883	3z.40 Pekinese	95	35
1884	4z.50 Alsatian (vert)	1·90	55
1885	8z.50 Pointer (vert)	3·25	1·10

520 House Sign

1969. Ninth Polish Democratic Party Congress.

1886	**520**	60g. red, black and grey	25	10

521 "Dove" and Wheat-ears

1969. Fifth Congress of United Peasant's Party.

1887	**521**	60g. multicoloured	25	10

522 Running

1969. 75th Anniv of International Olympic Committee and 50th Anniv of Polish Olympic Committee. Multicoloured.

1888	10g. Type **522**	10	10
1889	20g. Gymnastics	10	10
1890	40g. Weightlifting	10	10
1891	60g. Throwing the javelin	10	10
1892	2z.50+50g. Throwing the discus	20	10
1893	3z.40+1z. Running	50	15
1894	4z.+1z.50 Wrestling	95	20
1895	7z.+2z. Fencing	1·40	55

523 Pictorial Map of Swietokrzyski National Park

1969. Tourism (1st series). Multicoloured.

1896	40g. Type **523**	10	10
1897	60g. Niedzica Castle (vert)	10	10
1898	1z.35 Kolobrzeg Lighthouse and yacht	20	10
1899	1z.50 Szczecin Castle and Harbour	25	15
1900	2z.50 Torun and Vistula River	30	20
1901	3z.40 Klodzko, Silesia (vert)	50	35
1902	4z. Sulejow	65	45
1903	4z.50 Kazimierz Dolny market-place (vert)	75	50

See also Nos. 1981/5.

524 Route Map and "Opty"

1969. Leonid Teliga's World Voyage in Yacht "Opty".

1904	**524**	60g. multicoloured	25	20

525 Copernicus (after woodcut by T. Stimer) and Inscription

1969. 500th Birth Anniv (1973) of Copernicus (1st issue).

1905	**525**	40g. brown, red & yellow	20	10
1906	-	60g. blue, red and green	30	15
1907	-	2z.50 olive, red & purple	65	35

DESIGNS: 60g. Copernicus (after J. Falck) and 15th-century globe; 2z.50, Copernicus (after painting by J. Matejko) and diagram of heliocentric system.

See also Nos. 1995/7, 2069/72, 2167/70, 2213/14 and 2217/21.

526 "Memory" Flame and Badge

1969. Fifth National Alert of Polish Boy Scout Association.

1908	**526**	60g. black, red and blue	15	10
1909	-	60g. red, black and green	15	10
1910	-	60g. black, green and red	15	10

DESIGN: No. 1909, "Defence" eagle and badge; 1910, "Labour" map and badge.

528 Coal-miner

1969. 25th Anniv of Polish People's Republic. Multicoloured.

1911	60g. Frontier guard and arms	15	10
1912	60g. Plock petro-chemical plant	15	10
1913	60g. Combine-harvester	15	10
1914	60g. Grand Theatre, Warsaw	15	10
1915	60g. Curie statue and University, Lublin	15	10
1916	60g. Type **528**	15	10
1917	60g. Sulphur-worker	15	10
1918	60g. Steel-worker	15	10
1919	60g. Shipbuilder	15	10

Nos. 1911/5 are vert and have white arms embossed in the top portion of the stamps.

529 Astronauts and Module on Moon

1969. First Man on the Moon.

1920	**529**	2z.50 multicoloured	1·10	65

530 "Motherhood" (S. Wyspianski)

1969. Polish Paintings. Multicoloured.

1921	20g. Type **530**	10	10
1922	40g. "Hamlet" (J. Malczewski)	10	10
1923	60g. "Indian Summer" (J. Chelmonski)	15	10
1924	2z. "Two Girls" (Olga Bonznanska) (vert)	20	10
1925	2z.50 "The Sun of May" (J. Mehoffer) (vert)	30	15
1926	3z.40 "Woman combing her Hair" (W. Slewinski)	50	45
1927	5z.50 "Still Life" (J. Pankiewicz)	1·10	55
1928	7z. "Abduction of the King's Daughter" (W. Wojtkiewicz)	1·90	75

531 "Nike" statue

1969. Fourth Congress of Fighters for Freedom and Democracy Association.

1929	**531**	60g. red, black and brown	25	10

532 Majdanek Memorial

1969. Inauguration of Majdanek Memorial.

1930	**532**	40g. black and mauve	20	10

533 Krzczonow (Lublin) Costumes

1969. Provincial Costumes. Multicoloured.

1931	40g. Type **533**	10	10
1932	60g. Lowicz (Lodz)	10	10
1933	1z.15 Rozbasrk (Katowice)	15	10
1934	1z.35 Lower Silesia (Wroclaw)	15	10
1935	1z.50 Opoczno (Lodz)	50	15
1936	4z.50 Sacz (Cracow)	75	35
1937	5z. Highlanders, Cracow	95	55
1938	7z. Kurple (Warsaw)	1·30	65

534 "Pedestrians Keep Left"

1969. Road Safety. Multicoloured.

1939 40g. Type **534** 10 10
1940 60g. "Drive Carefully" (horses on road) 20 15
1941 2z.50 "Do Not Dazzle" (cars on road at night) 40 20

535 "Welding" and I.L.O. Emblem

1969. 50th Anniv of I.L.O.

1942 **535** 2z.50 blue and gold 30 20

536 "The Bell-founder"

1969. Miniatures from Behem's Code of 1505. Multicoloured.

1943 40g. Type **536** 10 10
1944 60g. "The Painter" 15 10
1945 1z.35 "The Woodcarver" 20 10
1946 1z.55 "The Shoemaker" 30 10
1947 2z.50 "The Cooper" 40 15
1948 3z.40 "The Baker" 55 35
1949 4z.50 "The Tailor" 95 55
1950 7z. "The Bowyer" 1·60 65

537 "Angel" (19th-century)

1969. Polish Folk Sculpture. Multicoloured.

1951 20g. Type **537** 10 10
1952 40g. "Sorrowful Christ" (19th-century) 10 10
1953 60g. "Sorrowful Christ" (19th-cent) (different) 15 10
1954 2z. "Weeping Woman" (19th-century) 20 10
1955 2z.50 "Adam and Eve" (F. Czajkowski) 30 15
1956 3z.40 "Girl with Birds" (L. Kudla) 50 35
1957 5z.50+1z.50 "Choir" (A. Zegadlo) 1·30 65
1958 7z.+1z. "Organ-grinder" (Z. Skretowicz) 1·90 85

Nos. 1957/8 are larger, size 25×35 mm.

538 Leopold Staff

1969. Modern Polish Writers.

1959 **538** 40g. black, olive & green 10 10
1960 - 60g. black, red and pink 10 10
1961 - 1z.35 black, deep blue and blue 10 10
1962 - 1z.50 black, violet & lilac 15 10
1963 - 1z.55 black, deep green and green 20 10
1964 - 2z.50 black, deep blue and blue 40 15
1965 - 3z.40 black, brn & flesh 55 35

DESIGNS: 60g. Wladyslaw Broniewski; 1z.35, Leon Kruczkowski; 1z.50, Julian Tuwim; 1z.55, Konstanty Ildefons Galczynski; 2z.50, Maria Dabrowska; 3z.40, Zofia Nalkowska.

539 Nike Monument

1970. 25th Anniv of Liberation of Warsaw.

1966 **539** 60g. multicoloured 30 20

540 Early Printing Works and Colour Dots

1970. Centenary of Printers' Trade Union.

1967 **540** 60g. multicoloured 25 10

541 Mallard

1970. Game Birds. Multicoloured.

1968 40g. Type **541** 10 10
1969 60g. Common pheasant 10 10
1970 1z.15 Eurasian woodcock 15 10
1971 1z.35 Ruff 20 10
1972 1z.50 Wood pigeon 40 20
1973 3z.40 Black grouse 50 35
1974 7z. Grey partridge 3·25 1·10
1975 8z.50 Western capercaillie 3·75 1·40

542 Lenin at Desk

1970. Birth Centenary of Lenin.

1976 **542** 40g. grey and red 10 10
1977 - 60g. brown and red 20 10
1978 - 2z.50 black and red 50 20
MS1979 134×81 mm. No. 1977 ×4 3·25 1·60

DESIGNS: 60g. Lenin addressing meeting; 2z.50, Lenin at Party conference.

543 Polish and Russian Soldiers in Berlin

1970. 25th Anniv of Liberation.

1980 **543** 60g. multicoloured 20 10

1970. Tourism (2nd series). As T **523**, but with imprint "PWPW 70". Multicoloured.

1981 60g. Town Hall, Wroclaw (vert) 20 10
1982 60g. View of Opol 20 10
1983 60g. Legnica Castle 20 10
1984 60g. Bolkow Castle 20 10
1985 60g. Town Hall, Brzeg 20 10

544 Polish "Flower"

1970. 25th Anniv of Return of Western Territories.

1986 **544** 60g. red, silver and green 20 10

545 Movement Flag

1970. 75th Anniv of Peasant Movement.

1987 **545** 60g. multicoloured 20 10

546 U.P.U. Emblem and New Headquarters

1970. New U.P.U. Headquarters Building, Berne.

1988 **546** 2z.50 blue and turquoise 30 20

547 Footballers

1970. Gornik Zabrze v. Manchester City, Final of European Cup-winners Cup Championship.

1989 **547** 60g. multicoloured 50 35

548 Hand with "Lamp of Learning"

1970. 150th Anniv of Plock Scientific Society.

1990 **548** 60g. olive, red and black 25 20

549 "Olympic Runners" (from Greek amphora)

1970. Tenth Session of Int Olympic Academy.

1991 **549** 60g. red, yellow and black 20 10
1992 - 60g. violet, blue and black 20 10
1993 - 60g. multicoloured 20 10
MS1994 71×101 mm. 10z.+5z. multicoloured 3·25 1·80

DESIGNS: No. 1992, "The Archer"; 1993, Modern runners; **MS**1994, "Horse of Fame" emblem of Polish Olympic Committee.

550 Copernicus (after miniature by Bacciarelli) and Bologna

1970. 500th Birth Anniv (1973) of Copernicus (2nd issue).

1995 **550** 40g. green, orange & lilac 10 10
1996 - 60g. lilac, green & yellow 20 10
1997 - 2z.50 brown, blue & green 75 20

DESIGNS: 60g. Copernicus (after miniature by Lesseur) and Padua; 2z.50, Copernicus (by N. Zinck, after lost Goluchowska portrait) and Ferrara.

551 "Aleksander Orlowski" (self-portrait)

1970. Polish Miniatures. Multicoloured.

1998 20g. Type **551** 10 10
1999 40g. "Jan Matejko" (self-portrait) 10 10
2000 60g. "Stefan Batory" (unknown artist) 10 10
2001 2z. "Maria Leszczynska" (unknown artist) 20 10
2002 2z.50 "Maria Walewska" (Marie-Victorie Jacquetot) 30 10
2003 3z.40 "Tadeusz Kosciuszko" (Jan Rustem) 40 15
2004 5z.50 "Samuel Linde" (G. Landolfi) 1·10 65
2005 7z. "Michal Oginski" (Nanette Windisch) 2·40 75

552 U.N. Emblem within "Eye"

1970. 25th Anniv of United Nations.

2006 **552** 2z.50 multicoloured 40 20

553 Piano Keyboard and Chopin's Signature

1970. Eighth International Chopin Piano Competition.

2007 **553** 2z.50 black and violet 40 20

554 Population Pictograph

1970. National Census. Multicoloured.

2008 40g. Type **554** 20 10
2009 60g. Family in "house" 25 10

555 Destroyer "Piorun"

1970. Polish Warships, World War II.

2010 **555** 40g. brown 10 10
2011 - 60g. black 25 10
2012 - 2z.50 brown 65 20

DESIGNS: 60g. "Orzel" (submarine); 2z.50, H.M.S. "Garland" (destroyer loaned to Polish Navy).

556 "Expressions" (Maria Jarema)

1970. Stamp Day. Contemporary Polish Paintings. Multicoloured.

2013 20g. "The Violin-cellist" (J. Nowosielski) (vert) 10 10
2014 40g. "View of Lodz" (B. Liberski) (vert) 10 10

2015 60g. "Studio Concert" (W. Taranczewski) (vert) 10 10
2016 1z.50 "Still Life" (Z. Pronaszko) (vert) 15 10
2017 2z. "Hanging-up Washing" (A. Wroblewski) (vert) 20 10
2018 3z.40 Type **556** 40 20
2019 4z. "Canal in the Forest" (P. Potworowski) 95 35
2020 8z.50 "The Sun" (W. Strzeminski) 1·90 75

557 "Luna 16" landing on Moon

1970. Moon Landing of "Luna 16".
2021 **557** 2z.50 multicoloured 55 20

558 "Stag" (detail from "Daniel" tapestry)

1970. Tapestries in Wawel Castle. Multicoloured.
2022 60g. Type **558** 10 10
2023 1z.15 "White Stork" (detail) 10 10
2024 1z.35 "Panther fighting Dragon" 20 10
2025 2z. "Man's Head" (detail, "Deluge" tapestry) 40 15
2026 2z.50 "Child with Bird" (detail, "Adam Tilling the Soil" tapestry) 50 20
2027 4z. "God, Adam and Eve" (detail, "Happiness in Paradise" tapestry) 95 35
2028 4z.50 Royal Monogram tapestry 1·20 55
MS2029 Two sheets, each 62×89 mm. (a) 5z.50 Polish coat-of-arms; (b) 7z.+3z. Monogram and satyrs. Imperf. Set of 2 sheets 3·75 3·25

559 Cadet ship "Dar Pomorza"

1971. Polish Ships. Multicoloured.
2030 40g. Type **559** 10 10
2031 60g. Liner "Stefan Batory" 10 10
2032 1z.15 Ice-breaker "Perkun" 15 10
2033 1z.35 Lifeboat "R-1" 20 10
2034 1z.50 Bulk carrier "Ziemia Szczecinska" 30 15
2035 2z.50 Tanker "Beskidy" 40 20
2036 5z. Freighter "Hel" 95 45
2037 8z.50 Ferry "Gryf" 1·90 1·10

560 Checiny Castle

1971. Polish Castles. Multicoloured.
2038 20g. Type **560** 10 10
2039 40g. Wisnicz 10 10
2040 60g. Bedzin 15 10
2041 2z. Ogrodzieniec 20 10
2042 2z.50 Niedzica 30 20
2043 3z.40 Kwidzyn 40 25
2044 4z. Pieskowa Skala 65 35
2045 8z.50 Lidzbark Warminski 1·40 80

561 Battle of Pouilly, J. Dabrowski and W. Wroblewski

1971. Centenary of Paris Commune.
2046 **561** 60g. brown, blue and red 25 20

562 Plantation

1971. Forestry Management. Multicoloured.
2047 40g. Type **562** 10 10
2048 60g. Forest (27×47 mm) 10 10
2049 1z.50 Tree-felling 50 15

563 "Bishop Marianos"

1971. Fresco. Discoveries made by Polish Expedition at Faras, Nubia. Multicoloured.
2050 40g. Type **563** 10 10
2051 60g. "St. Anne" 10 10
2052 1z.15 "Archangel Michael" 10 10
2053 1z.35 "The Hermit, Anamon" 15 10
2054 1z.50 "Head of Archangel Michael" 20 10
2055 4z.50 "Evangelists' Cross" 75 25
2056 5z. "Christ protecting a nobleman" 85 45
2057 7z. "Archangel Michael" (half-length) 1·10 80

564 Revolutionaries

1971. 50th Anniv of Silesian Insurrection.
2058 **564** 60g. brown and gold 25 10
MS2059 108×106 mm. No. 2058 ×3 3·75 2·00

565 "Soldiers"

1971. 25th Anniv of UNICEF Children's Drawings. Multicoloured.
2060 20g. "Peacock" (vert) 10 10
2061 40g. Type **565** 10 10
2062 60g. "Lady Spring" (vert) 10 10
2063 2z. "Cat and Ball" 30 15
2064 2z.50 "Flowers in Jug" (vert) 40 20
2065 3z.40 "Friendship" 50 25
2066 5z.50 "Clown" (vert) 95 60
2067 7z. "Strange Planet" 1·40 80

566 Fair Emblem

1971. 40th International Fair, Poznan.
2068 **566** 60g. multicoloured 25 20

567 Copernicus's House, Torun

1971. 500th Birth Anniv (1973) of Copernicus (3rd issue). Multicoloured.
2069 40g. Type **567** 10 10
2070 60g. Collegium Naius, Jagiellonian University, Cracow (horiz) 15 10
2071 2z.50 Olsztyn Castle (horiz) 50 20
2072 4z. Frombork Cathedral 75 35

568 Folk Art Pattern

1971. Folk Art. "Paper Cut-outs" showing various patterns.
2073 **568** 20g. black, green and blue 15 10
2074 - 40g. blue, green & cream 15 10
2075 - 60g. brown, blue and grey 15 10
2076 - 1z.15 purple, brn & buff 15 10
2077 - 1z.35 green, red & yellow 15 10

569 "Head of Worker" (X. Dunikowski)

1971. Modern Polish Sculpture. Multicoloured.
2078 40g. Type **569** 15 10
2079 40g. "Foundryman" (X. Dunikowski) 15 10
2080 60g. "Miners" (M. Wiecek) 15 10
2081 60g. "Harvester" (S. Horno-Poplawski) 15 10
MS2082 158×85 mm. Nos. 2078/81 3·75 2·30

570 Congress Emblem and Computer Tapes

1971. Sixth Polish Technical Congress, Warsaw.
2083 **570** 60g. violet and red 25 20

571 "Angel" (J. Mehoffer)

1971. Stained Glass Windows. Multicoloured.
2084 20g. Type **571** 10 10
2085 40g. "Lillies" (S. Wyspianski) 10 10
2086 60g. "Iris" (S. Wyspianski) 10 10
2087 1z.35 "Apollo" (S. Wyspianski) 15 10
2088 1z.55 "Two Wise Men" (14th-century) 20 10
2089 3z.40 "The Flight into Egypt" (14th-century) 50 35
2090 5z.50 "Jacob" (14th-century) 1·00 45
2091 8z.50+4z. "Madonna" (15th-century) 1·60 1·20

572 "Mrs. Fedorowicz" (W. Pruszkowski)

1971. Contemporary Art from National Museum, Cracow. Multicoloured.
2092 40g. Type **572** 10 10
2093 50g. "Woman with Book" (T. Czyzeski) 10 10
2094 60g. "Girl with Chrysanthemums" (O. Boznanska) 15 10
2095 2z.50 "Girl in Red Dress" (J. Pankiewicz) (horiz) 20 10
2096 3z.40 "Reclining Nude" (L. Chwistek) (horiz) 50 20
2097 4z.50 "Strange Garden" (J. Mehoffer) 75 25
2098 5z. "Wife in White Hat" (Z. Pronaszko) 85 30
2099 7z.+1z. "Seated Nude" (W. Weiss) 1·10 70

573 PZL P-11C Fighters

1971. Polish Aircraft of World War II. Multicoloured.
2100 90g. Type **573** 20 10
2101 1z.50 PZL 23A Karas fighters 50 20
2102 3z.40 PZL P-37 Los bomber 65 35

574 Royal Castle, Warsaw (pre-1939)

1971. Reconstruction of Royal Castle, Warsaw.
2103 **574** 60g. black, red and gold 25 20

575 Astronauts in Moon Rover

1971. Moon Flight of "Apollo 15".
2104 **575** 2z.50 multicoloured 85 25
MS2105 122×157 mm. No. 2104 ×6 plus 2 stamp-size se-tenant labels, showing Space scenes 8·50 5·75

576 "Lunokhod 1"

1971. Moon Flight of "Lunik 17" and "Lunokhod 1".
2106 **576** 2z.50 multicoloured 85 25
MS2107 158×118 mm. No. 2106 ×6 plus 2 stamp-size se-tenant labels, showing Space scenes 8·50 5·75

577 Worker at Wheel

578 Ship-building

1971. Sixth Polish United Workers' Party Congress. (a) Party Posters.
2108 **577** 60g. red, blue and grey 15 10
2109 **577** 60g. red and grey (Worker's head) 15 10

(b) Industrial Development. Each in gold and red.
2110 60g. Type **578** 15 10
2111 60g. Building construction 15 10
2112 60g. Combine-harvester 15 10
2113 60g. Motor-car production 15 10
2114 60g. Pit-head 15 10
2115 60g. Petro-chemical plant 15 10
MS2116 102×115 mm. Nos. 2110/15 2·10 1·80

579 "Prunus cerasus"

1971. Flowers of Trees and Shrubs. Multicoloured.
2117 10g. Type **579** 10 10
2118 20g. "Malusniedzwetzskyana" 10 10
2119 40g. "Pyrus L." 10 10

2120	60g. "Prunus persica"	10	10
2121	1z.15 "Magnolia kobus"	10	10
2122	1z.35 "Crategus oxyacantha"	10	10
2123	2z.50 "Malus M."	20	10
2124	3z.40 "Aesculus carnea"	50	25
2125	5z. "Robinia pseudacacia"	1·30	60
2126	8z.50 "Prunus avium"	2·50	1·20

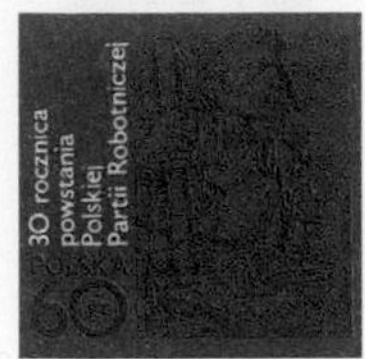

580 "Worker" (sculpture, J. Januszkiewicz)

1972. 30th Anniv of Polish Workers' Coalition.

2127	**580**	60g. black and red	25	10

581 Luge

1972. Winter Olympic Games, Sapporo, Japan. Multicoloured.

2128	40g. Type **581**	10	10
2129	60g. Slalom (vert)	15	10
2130	1z.65 Biathlon (vert)	50	20
2131	2z.50 Ski jumping	75	35
MS2132	85×68 mm. 10z.+5z. Downhill skiing	4·25	2·50

582 "Heart" and Cardiogram Trace

1972. World Heart Month.

2133	**582**	2z.50 multicoloured	40	20

583 Running

1972. Olympic Games, Munich. Multicoloured.

2134	20g. Type **583**	10	10
2135	30g. Archery	10	10
2136	40g. Boxing	10	10
2137	60g. Fencing	10	10
2138	2z.50 Wrestling	15	10
2139	3z.40 Weightlifting	20	10
2140	5z. Cycling	75	25
2141	8z.50 Shooting	1·30	60
MS2142	70×80 mm. 10z.+5z. As 30g.	2·50	1·40

584 Cyclists

1972. 25th International Peace Cycle Race.

2143	**584**	60g. multicoloured	25	10

585 Polish War Memorial, Berlin

1972. "Victory Day, 1945".

2144	**585**	60g. green	25	10

586 "Rodlo" Emblem

1972. 50th Anniv of Polish Posts in Germany.

2145	**586**	60g. ochre, red and green	25	10

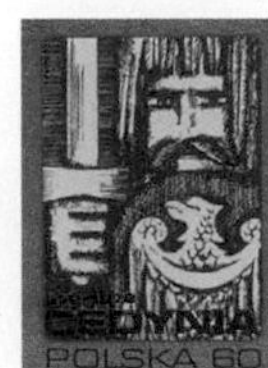

587 Polish Knight of 972 A.D.

1972. Millenary of Battle of Cedynia.

2146	**587**	60g. multicoloured	25	10

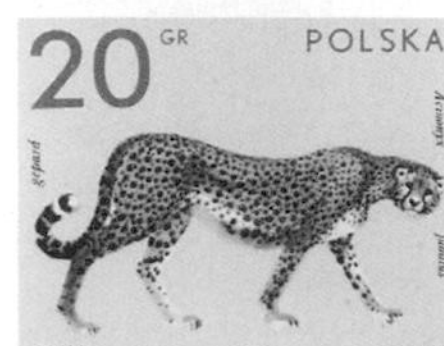

588 Cheetah

1972. Zoo Animals. Multicoloured.

2147	20g. Type **588**	15	10
2148	40g. Giraffe (vert)	20	10
2149	60g. Toco toucan	25	10
2150	1z.35 Chimpanzee	25	10
2151	1z.65 Common gibbon	50	15
2152	3z.40 Crocodile	75	25
2153	4z. Red kangaroo	1·30	70
2154	4z.50 Tiger (vert)	4·25	2·30
2155	7z. Mountain zebra	5·25	3·00

589 L. Warynski. (founder)

1972. 90th Anniv of Proletarian Party.

2156	**589**	60g. multicoloured	25	10

590 F. Dzerzhinsky

1972. 95th Birth Anniv of Feliks Dzerzhinsky (Russian politician).

2157	**590**	60g. black and red	25	10

591 Global Emblem

1972. 25th Int Co-operative Federation Congress.

2158	**591**	60g. multicoloured	25	10

592 Scene from "In Barracks" (ballet)

1972. Death Centenary of Stanislaus Moniuszko (composer). Scenes from Works.

2159		10g. violet and gold	10	10
2160		20g. black and gold	10	10
2161		40g. green and gold	10	10
2162		60g. blue and gold	10	10
2163	-	1z.15 blue and gold	15	10
2164		1z.35 blue and gold	20	10
2165		1z.55 green and gold	40	25
2166		2z.50 brown and gold	75	35

DESIGNS: 10g. Type **592**; 20g. "The Countess" (opera); 40g. "The Haunted Manor" (opera); 60g. "Halka" (opera); 1z.15, "New Don Quixote" (ballet); 1z.35, "Verbum Nobile"; 1z.55, "Ideal" (operetta); 2z.50, "Pariah" (opera).

593 "Copernicus the Astronomer"

1972. 500th Birth Anniv (1973) of Nicolas Copernicus. (4th issue).

2167	**593**	40g. black and blue	10	10
2168	-	60g. black and orange	20	10
2169	-	2z.50 black and red	65	20
2170	-	3z.40 black and green	1·00	60
MS2171		62×102 mm. 10z.+5z. multi-coloured	4·25	2·30

DESIGNS: 60g. Copernicus and Polish eagle; 2z.50, Copernicus and Medal; 3z.40, Copernicus and page of book; VERT: (29×48 mm)—10z.+5z. Copernicus charting the planets.

594 "The Amazon" (P. Michalowski)

1972. Stamp Day. Polish Paintings. Multicoloured.

2172	30g. Type **594**	15	10
2173	40g. "Ostafi Laskiewicz" (J. Metejko)	15	10
2174	60g. "Summer Idyll" (W. Gerson)	15	10
2175	2z. "The Neapolitan Woman" (A. Kotsis)	15	10
2176	2z.50 "Girl Bathing" (P. Szyndler)	15	10
2177	3z.40 "The Princess of Thum" (A. Grottger)	25	10
2178	4z. "Rhapsody" (S. Wyspianski)	1·80	40
2179	8z.50+4z. "Young Woman" (J. Malczewski) (horiz)	2·30	70

1972. Nos. 1578/9 surch.

2180	50g. on 40g. brown	20	10
2181	90g. on 40g. brown	20	10
2182	1z. on 40g. brown	20	10
2183	1z.50 on 60g. orange	20	10
2184	2z.70 on 40g. brown	20	10
2185	4z. on 60g. orange	40	10
2186	4z.50 on 60g. orange	50	10
2187	4z.90 on 60g. orange	75	20

596 "The Little Soldier" (E. Piwowarski)

1972. Children's Health Centre.

2188	**596**	60g. black and pink	25	10

597 "Royal Castle, Warsaw". (E. J. Dahlberg, 1656)

1972. Restoration of Royal Castle, Warsaw.

2189	**597**	60g. black, violet and blue	25	10

598 Chalet, Chocholowska Valley

1972. Tourism. Mountain Chalets. Multicoloured.

2190	40g. Type **598**	15	10
2191	60g. Hala Ornak (horiz)	15	10
2192	1z.55 Hala Gasienicowa	15	10
2193	1z.65 Valley of Five Lakes (horiz)	20	10
2194	2z.50 Morskie Oko	30	15

599 Trade Union Banners

1972. Seventh Polish Trade Union Congresses.

2195	**599**	60g. multicoloured	25	10

600 Congress Emblem

1972. Fifth Socialist Youth Union Congress.

2196	**600**	60g. multicoloured	25	10

601 Japanese Azalea

1972. Flowering Shrubs. Multicoloured.

2197	40g. Type **601**	10	10
2198	50g. Alpine rose	10	10
2199	60g. Pomeranian honeysuckle	15	10
2200	1z.65 Chinese quince	20	10
2201	2z.50 Korean cranberry	25	10
2202	3z.40 Pontic azalea	50	10
2203	4z. Delavay's white syringa	1·60	35
2204	8z.50 Common lilac ("Massena")	2·30	1·20

602 Piast Knight (10th-century)

1972. Polish Cavalry Through the Ages. Multicoloured.

2205	20g. Type **602**	15	10
2206	40g. 13th-century knight	15	10
2207	60g. Knight of Wladyslaw Jagiello's Army (15th-century) (horiz)	15	10
2208	1z.35 17th-century hussar	20	10

2209	4z. Lancer of National Guard (18th-century)	95	20
2210	4z.50 "Congress Kingdom" cavalry officer	1·00	25
2211	5z. Trooper of Light Cavalry (1939) (horiz)	1·70	60
2212	7z. Trooper of People's Army (1945)	2·10	95

603 Copernicus

1972. 500th Birth Anniv (1973) of Copernicus (5th issue).

2213	**603**	1z. brown	20	10
2214	**603**	1z.50 ochre	20	10

604 Couple with Hammer and Sickle

1972. 50th Anniv of U.S.S.R. Multicoloured.

2215	40g. Type **604**	20	10
2216	60g. Red star and globe	20	10

605 "Copernicus as Young Man" (Bacciarelli)

1973. 500th Birth Anniv of Copernicus (6th issue). Multicoloured.

2217	1z. Type **605**	10	10
2218	1z.50 "Copernicus" (anon)	20	10
2219	2z.70 "Copernicus" (Zinck Nor)	50	25
2220	4z. "Copernicus" (from Strasbourg clock)	65	35
2221	4z.90 "Copernicus" (Jan Matejko) (horiz)	1·00	60

606 Coronation Sword

1973. Polish Art. Multicoloured.

2222	50g. Type **606**	10	10
2223	1z. Kruzlowa Madonna (detail)	10	10
2224	1z. Armour of hussar	10	10
2225	1z.50 Carved head from Wavel Castle	10	10
2226	1z.50 Silver cockerel	10	10
2227	2z.70 Armorial eagle	50	25
2228	4z.90 Skarbimierz Madonna	1·00	60
2229	8z.50 "Portrait of Tenczynski" (anon)	1·80	1·10

607 Statue of Lenin

1973. Unveiling of Lenin's Statue, Nowa Huta.

2230	**607**	1z. multicoloured	25	10

608 Coded Letter

1973. Introduction of Postal Codes.

2231	**608**	1z. multicoloured	25	10

609 Wolf

1973. International Hunting Council Congress and 50th Anniv of Polish Hunting Association. Multicoloured.

2232	50g. Type **609**	15	10
2233	1z. Mouflon	15	10
2234	1z.50 Elk	15	10
2235	2z.70 Western capercaillie	30	10
2236	3z. Roe deer	50	10
2237	4z.50 Lynx	90	15
2238	4z.90 Red deer	2·75	75
2239	5z. Wild boar	3·25	90

610 "Salyut"

1973. Cosmic Research. Multicoloured.

2240	4z.90 Type **610**	75	35
2241	4z.90 "Copernicus" (U.S. satellite)	75	35

611 Open Book and Flame

1973. Second Polish Science Congress, Warsaw.

2242	**611**	1z.50 multicoloured	25	10

612 Ancient Seal of Poznan

1973. "Polska 73" Philatelic Exhibition, Poznan. Multicoloured.

2243	1z. Type **612**	10	10
2244	1z.50 Tombstone of N. Tomicki	10	10
2245	2z.70 Kalisz paten	20	10
2246	4z. Bronze gates, Gniezno Cathedral (horiz)	50	10
MS2247	91×66 mm. 10z.+5z. purple and olive	3·25	1·80
MS2248	91×66 mm. 10z.+5z. purple and lilac	10·50	8·75

613 M. Nowotko

1973. 80th Birth Anniv of Marceli Nowotko (party leader).

2249	**613**	1z.50 black and red	25	10

614 Cherry Blossom

1973. Protection of the Environment. Multicoloured.

2250	50g. Type **614**	15	10
2251	90g. Cattle in meadow	15	10
2252	1z. White stork on nest	15	10
2253	1z.50 Pond life	15	10
2254	2z.70 Meadow flora	30	10
2255	4z.90 Ocean fauna	65	35
2256	5z. Forest life	2·50	60
2257	6z.50 Agricultural produce	3·25	95

615 Motor-cyclist

1973. World Speedway Race Championships, Chorzow.

2258	**615**	1z.50 multicoloured	25	10

616 "Copernicus" (M. Bacciarelli)

1973. Stamp Day.

2259	**616**	4z.+2z. multicoloured	95	45

617 Tank

1973. 30th Anniv of Polish People's Army. Multicoloured.

2260	1z. Type **617**	15	10
2261	1z. Mikoyan Gurevich MiG-21D airplane	15	10
2262	1z.50 Guided missile	50	20
2263	1z.50 "Puck" (missile boat)	50	20

618 G. Piramowicz and Title Page

1973. Bicent of Nat Educational Commission.

2264	**618**	1z. brown and yellow	15	10
2265	-	1z.50 green, & light green	20	10

DESIGN: 1z.50, J. Sniadecki, H. Kollataj and J. U. Niemcewicz.

619 Pawel Strzelecki (explorer) and Red Kangaroo

1973. Polish Scientists. Multicoloured.

2266	1z. Type **619**	15	10
2267	1z. Henryk Arctowski (Polar explorer) and Adelie penguins	15	10
2268	1z.50 Stefan Rogozinski (explorer) and "Lucy-Margaret" (schooner)	15	10
2269	1z.50 Benedykt Dybowski (zoologist) and sable, Lake Baikal	15	10
2270	2z. Bronislaw Malinowski (anthropologist) and New Guinea dancers	15	10
2271	2z.70 Stefan Drzewiecki (oceanographer) and submarine	40	15
2272	3z. Edward Strasburger (botanist) and classified plants	65	25
2273	8z. Ignacy Domeyko (geologist) and Chilean desert landscape	1·90	60

620 Polish Flag

1973. 25th Anniv of Polish United Workers' Party.

2274	**620**	1z.40 red, blue and gold	40	20

621 Jelcz-Berliet Coach

1973. Polish Motor Vehicles. Multicoloured.

2275	50g. Type **621**	15	10
2276	90g. Jelcz "316" truck	15	10
2277	1z. Polski-Fiat "126p" saloon	15	10
2278	1z.50 Polski-Fiat "125p" saloon and mileage records	15	10
2279	4z. Nysa "M-521" utility van	65	35
2280	4z.50 Star "660" truck	1·00	45

622 Iris

1974. Flowers. Drawings by S. Wyspianski.

2281	**622**	50g. purple	15	10
2282	-	1z. green	15	10
2283	-	1z.50 red	15	10
2284	-	3z. violet	40	15
2285	-	4z. blue	65	25
2286	-	4z.50 green	75	35

FLOWERS: 1z. Dandelion; 1z.50, Rose; 3z. Thistle; 4z. Cornflower; 4z.50, Clover.

623 Cottage, Kurpie

1974. Wooden Architecture. Multicoloured.

2287	1z. Type **623**	15	10
2288	1z.50 Church, Sekowa	15	10
2289	4z. Town Hall, Sulmierzycc	40	25
2290	4z.50 Church, Lachowice	50	35
2291	4z.90 Windmill, Sobienie Jeziory	85	45
2292	5z. Orthodox Church, Ulucz	1·00	60

624 19th-century Mail Coach

1974. Centenary of Universal Postal Union.

2293	**624**	1z.50 multicoloured	25	10

625 Cracow Motif

1974. "SOCPHILEX IV" Int Stamp Exn, Katowice. Regional Floral Embroideries. Multicoloured.

2294	50g. Type **625**	10	10
2295	1z.50 Lowicz motif	10	10
2296	4z. Silesian motif	50	25
MS2297	69×71 mm. No. 2296 ×3	2·10	1·80

626 Association Emblem

1974. Fifth Congress of Fighters for Freedom and Democracy Association, Warsaw.

2298	**626**	1z.50 red	25	10

627 Soldier and Dove

1974. 29th Anniv of Victory over Fascism in Second World War.

2299	**627**	1z.50 multicoloured	25	10

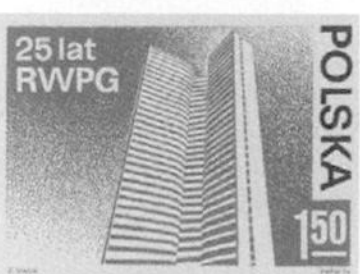

628 "Comecon" Headquarters, Moscow

1974. 25th Anniv of Council for Mutual Economic Aid.

2300	**628**	1z.50 brown, red & blue	25	10

629 World Cup Emblem

1974. World Cup Football Championship, West Germany. Multicoloured.

2301	4z.90 Type **629**	75	25
2302	4z.90 Players and Olympic Gold Medal of 1972	75	25
MS2303	116×83 mm. Nos. 2301/2	16·00	14·00

See also No. **MS**2315.

630 Model of 16th- century Galleon

1974. Sailing Ships. Multicoloured.

2304	1z. Type **630**	15	10
2305	1z.50 Sloop "Dal" (1934)	15	10
2306	2z.70 Yacht "Opty" (Teliga's circumnavigation, 1969)	20	10
2307	4z. Cadet ship "Dar Pomorza", 1972	50	20
2308	4z.90 Yacht "Polonez" (Baranowski's circumnavigation, 1973)	1·00	35

631 Title page of "Chess" by J. Kochanowski

1974. Tenth Inter-Chess Festival, Lublin. Multicoloured.

2309	1z. Type **631**	25	10
2310	1z.50 "Education" (18th-century engraving, D. Chodowiecki)	25	10

632 Lazienkowska Road Junction

1974. Opening of Lazienkowska Flyover.

2311	**632**	1z.50 multicoloured	25	10

633 Face and Map of Poland

1974. 30th Anniv of Polish People's Republic.

2312	**633**	1z.50 black, gold and red	20	10
2313	-	1z.50 multicoloured (silver background)	20	10
2314	-	1z.50 multicoloured (red background)	20	10

DESIGN—31×43 mm: Nos. 2313/14, Polish "Eagle".

1974. Poland–Third Place in World Cup Football Championship. Sheet 107×121 mm containing four stamps as No. 2301, but with inscr in silver instead of black, and two labels.

MS2315	**629**	4z.90 ×4 multicoloured	4·50	3·00

634 Strawberries

1974. 19th International Horticultural Congress, Warsaw. Fruits, Vegetables and Flowers. Multicoloured.

2316	50g. Type **634**	15	10
2317	90g. Blackcurrants	15	10
2318	1z. Apples	15	10
2319	1z.50 Cucumbers	20	10
2320	2z.70 Tomatoes	30	25
2321	4z.50 Green peas	75	35
2322	4z.90 Pansies	1·80	45
2323	5z. Nasturtiums	2·10	65

635 Civic Militia and Security Service Emblem

1974. 30th Anniv of Polish Civic Militia and Security Service.

2324	**635**	1z.50 multicoloured	25	10

636 "Child in Polish Costume" (L. Orlowski)

1974. Stamp Day. Paintings. Multicoloured.

2325	50g. Type **636**	10	10
2326	90g. "Girl with Pigeon" (anon)	10	10
2327	1z. "Portrait of a Girl" (S. Wyspianski)	10	10
2328	1z.50 "The Orphan from Poronin" (W. Slewinski)	10	10
2329	3z. "Peasant Boy" (K. Sichulski)	30	15
2330	4z.50 "Florence Page" (A. Gierymski)	50	25
2331	4z.90 "Tadeusz and Dog" (P. Michalowski)	75	35
2332	6z.50 "Boy with Doe" (A. Kotsis)	1·10	70

637 "The Crib", Cracow

1974. Polish Art. Multicoloured.

2333	1z. Type **637**	10	10
2334	1z.50 "The Flight to Egypt" (15th-century polyptych)	20	10
2335	2z. "King Sigismund III Vasa" (16th-century miniature)	30	10
2336	4z. "King Jan Olbracht" (16th-century title-page)	1·40	35

638 Angler and Fish

1974. Polish Folklore. 16th-century Woodcuts (1st series).

2337	1z. black	10	10
2338	1z.50 blue	20	10

DESIGN: 1z. Type **638**; 1z.50, Hunter and wild animals.

See also Nos. 2525/6.

639 "Pablo Neruda" (O. Guayasamin)

1974. 70th Birth Anniv of Pablo Neruda (Chilean poet).

2339	**639**	1z.50 multicoloured	25	10

640 "Nike" Memorial and National Opera House

1975. 30th Anniv of Warsaw Liberation.

2340	**640**	1z.50 multicoloured	25	10

641 Male Lesser Kestrel

1975. Birds of Prey. Multicoloured.

2341	1z. Type **641**	20	10
2342	1z. Lesser kestrel (female)	20	10
2343	1z.50 Western red-footed falcon (male)	30	10
2344	1z.50 Western red-footed falcon (female)	30	10
2345	2z. Northern hobby	50	25
2346	3z. Common kestrel	90	30
2347	4z. Merlin	2·30	1·00
2348	8z. Peregrine falcon	3·75	1·40

642 Broken Barbed Wire

1975. 30th Anniv of Auschwitz Concentration Camp Liberation.

2349	**642**	1z.50 black and red	25	10

643 Hurdling

1975. Sixth European Indoor Athletic Championships, Katowice. Multicoloured.

2350	1z. Type **643**	10	10
2351	1z.50 Pole vault	20	10
2352	4z. Triple jump	50	10
2353	4z.90 Running	75	25
MS2354	72×63 mm. 10z.+5z. green and silver (Montreal Olympics emblem) (26×31 mm)	3·75	1·80

644 "St. Anne" (Veit Stoss)

1975. "Arphila 1975" International Stamp Exhibition, Paris.

2355	**644**	1z.50 multicoloured	25	10

645 Globe and "Radio Waves"

1975. International Amateur Radio Union Conference, Warsaw.

2356	**645**	1z.50 multicoloured	25	10

646 Stone, Pine and Tatra Mountains

1975. Centenary of Mountain Guides' Association. Multicoloured.

2357	1z. Type **646**	10	10
2358	1z. Gentians and Tatra Mountains	10	10
2359	1z.50 Sudety Mountains (horiz)	20	10
2360	1z.50 Branch of yew (horiz)	20	10
2361	4z. Beskidy Mountains	50	25
2362	4z. Arnica blossoms	50	25

647 Hands holding Tulips and Rifle

1975. 30th Anniv of Victory over Fascism.

2363	**647**	1z.50 multicoloured	25	10

648 Flags of Member Countries

1975. 20th Anniv of Warsaw Treaty Organization.

2364	**648**	1z.50 multicoloured	25	10

649 Hens

1975. 26th European Zoo-technical Federation Congress, Warsaw. Multicoloured.

No.	Type	Description	Unused	Used
2365		50g. Type **649**	10	10
2366		1z. Geese	10	10
2367		1z.50 Cattle	20	10
2368		2z. Cow	25	10
2369		3z. Wielkopolska horse	30	25
2370		4z. Pure-bred Arab horses	65	25
2371		4z.50 Pigs	2·10	45
2372		5z. Sheep	2·50	1·20

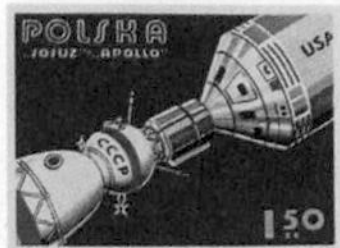

650 "Apollo" and "Soyuz" Spacecraft linked

1975. "Apollo–Soyuz" Space Project. Multicoloured.

No.	Type	Description	Unused	Used
2373		1z.50 Type **650**	20	10
2374		4z.90 "Apollo" spacecraft	95	35
2375		4z.90 "Soyuz" spacecraft	95	35
MS2376		119×156 mm. Nos. 2373 ×2, 2374 ×2 and 2375 ×2	7·50	5·75

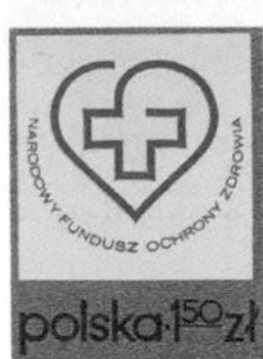

651 Organization Emblem

1975. National Health Protection Fund.

No.	Type	Description	Unused	Used
2377	**651**	1z.50 blue, black & silver	25	10

652 U.N. Emblem

1975. 30th Anniv of U.N.O.

No.	Type	Description	Unused	Used
2378	**652**	4z. multicoloured	50	25

653 Polish Flag within "E" for Europe

1975. European Security and Co-operation Conference, Helsinki.

No.	Type	Description	Unused	Used
2379	**653**	4z. red, blue and black	65	35

654 "Bolek and Lolek"

1975. Children's Television Characters. Multicoloured.

No.	Type	Description	Unused	Used
2380		50g. Type **654**	15	10
2381		1z. "Jacek" and "Agatka"	15	10
2382		1z.50 "Reksio" (dog)	25	20
2383		4z. "Telesfor" (dragon)	75	25

655 Institute Emblem

1975. 40th Session of International Statistics Institute.

No.	Type	Description	Unused	Used
2384	**655**	1z.50 multicoloured	25	10

656 Women's Faces

1975. International Women's Year.

No.	Type	Description	Unused	Used
2385	**656**	1z.50 multicoloured	25	10

657 Albatros Biplane

1975. 50th Anniv of First Polish Airmail Stamps. Multicoloured.

No.	Type	Description	Unused	Used
2386		2z.40 Type **657**	30	20
2387		4z.90 Ilyushin Il-62 airplane	65	25

658 "Mary and Margaret" and Polish Settlers

1975. Bicentenary of American Revolution. Poles in American Life. Multicoloured.

No.	Type	Description	Unused	Used
2388		1z. Type **658**	10	10
2389		1z.50 Polish glass-works, Jamestown	20	10
2390		2z.70 Helena Modrzejewska (actress)	30	10
2391		4z. K. Pulaski (soldier)	50	25
2392		6z.40 T. Kosciuzko (soldier)	85	60
MS2393		117×102 mm. 4z.90 Washington; 4z.90 Kosciuszko; 4z.90 Pulaski	2·10	1·40

659 Frederic Chopin

1975. Ninth International Chopin Piano Competition.

No.	Type	Description	Unused	Used
2394	**659**	1z.50 black, lilac & gold	30	20

660 "Self-portrait"

1975. Stamp Day. Birth Centenary of Xawery Dunikowski (sculptor). Multicoloured.

No.	Type	Description	Unused	Used
2395		50g. Type **660**	10	10
2396		1z. "Breath"	10	10
2397		1z.50 "Maternity"	20	10
2398		8z.+4z. "Silesian Insurrectionists"	1·60	70

661 Market Place, Kazimierz Dolny

1975. European Architectural Heritage Year.

No.	Type	Description	Unused	Used
2399	**661**	1z. green	20	10
2400	-	1z.50 brown	30	10

DESIGN—VERT: 1z.50, Town Hall, Zamosc.

662 "Lodz" (W. Strzeminski)

1975. "Lodz 75" National Stamp Exhibition.

No.	Type	Description	Unused	Used
2401	**662**	4z.50 multicoloured	50	25
MS2402		80×101 mm. No. 2401	2·10	1·40

663 Henry IV's Eagle Gravestone Head (14th-century)

1975. Piast Dynasty of Silesia.

No.	Type	Description	Unused	Used
2403	**663**	1z. green	10	10
2404	-	1z.50 brown	10	10
2405	-	4z. violet	50	25

DESIGNS: 1z.50, Seal of Prince Boleslaw of Legnica; 4z. Coin of last Prince, Jerzy Wilhelm.

664 Symbolized Figure "7"

1975. Seventh Congress of Polish United Workers Party.

No.	Type	Description	Unused	Used
2406	**664**	1z. multicoloured	20	10
2407	-	1z.50 red, blue and silver	20	10

DESIGN: 1z.50, Party initials "PZPR".

665 Ski Jumping

1976. Winter Olympic Games, Innsbruck. Multicoloured.

No.	Type	Description	Unused	Used
2408		50g. Type **665**	15	10
2409		1z. Ice hockey	15	10
2410		1z.50 Skiing	15	10
2411		2z. Skating	15	10
2412		4z. Tobogganing	50	10
2413		6z.40 Biathlon	1·00	30

666 Richard Trevithick and his Locomotive, 1803

1976. History of the Railway Locomotive. Multicoloured.

No.	Type	Description	Unused	Used
2414		50g. Type **666**	15	10
2415		1z. Murray and Blenkinsop's steam locomotive and carriage, 1810	15	10
2416		1z.50 George Stephenson and his locomotive "Rocket", 1829	15	10
2417		1z.50 Polish "Universal" electric locomotive No. ET22-001, 1969	15	10
2418		2z.70 Robert Stephenson and his locomotive "North Star", 1837	15	10
2419		3z. Joseph Harrison and his locomotive, 1840	20	10
2420		4z.50 Locomotive "Thomas Rogers", 1855, U.S.A.	1·30	20
2421		4z.90 A. Xiezopolski and Series Ok22 steam locomotive, 1922	1·60	30

667 Flags of Member Countries

1976. 20th Anniv of Institute for Nuclear Research (C.M.E.A.).

No.	Type	Description	Unused	Used
2422	**667**	1z.50 multicoloured	25	10

668 Early Telephone, Satellite and Radar

1976. Telephone Centenary.

No.	Type	Description	Unused	Used
2423	**668**	1z.50 multicoloured	25	10

669 Jantar Glider

1976. Air. Contemporary Aviation.

No.	Type	Description	Unused	Used
2424	**669**	5z. blue	65	25
2425	-	10z. brown	1·30	35
2425a	-	20z. olive	2·75	45
2425b	-	50z. lake	5·25	1·20

DESIGN: 10z. Mil Mi-6 helicopter; 20z. PZL-106A agricultural airplane; 50z. PZL-Mielec TS-11 Iskra jet trainer over Warsaw Castle.

670 Player

1976. World Ice Hockey Championships, Katowice. Multicoloured.

No.	Type	Description	Unused	Used
2426		1z. Type **670**	10	10
2427		1z.50 Player (different)	20	10

671 Polish U.N. Soldier

1976. Polish Troops in U.N. Sinai Force.

No.	Type	Description	Unused	Used
2428	**671**	1z.50 multicoloured	30	20

672 "Glory to the Sappers" (S. Kulon)

1976. War Memorials. Multicoloured.

No.	Type	Description	Unused	Used
2429		1z. Type **672**	10	10
2430		1z. 1st Polish Army Monument, Sandau, Laba (B. Koniuszy)	10	10

673 "Interphil 76"

1976. "Interphil '76" Int Stamp Exn, Philadelphia.

No.	Type	Description	Unused	Used
2431	**673**	8z.40 multicoloured	1·10	60

674 Wielkopolski Park and Tawny Owl

1976. National Parks. Multicoloured.

No.	Type	Description	Unused	Used
2432		90g. Type **674**	10	10
2433		1z. Wolinski Park and white-tailed sea eagle	10	10
2434		1z.50 Slowinski Park and seagull	20	10
2435		4z.50 Bieszezadzki Park and lynx	50	25
2436		5z. Ojcowski Park and bat	65	30
2437		6z. Kampinoski Park and elk	85	35

675 Peace Dove within Globe

1976. 25th Anniv of U.N. Postal Administration.

2438	**675**	8z.40 multicoloured	1·10	35

676 Fencing

1976. Olympic Games, Montreal. Multicoloured.

2439	50g. Type **676**	10	10
2440	1z. Cycling	10	10
2441	1z.50 Football	20	10
2442	4z.20 Boxing	50	20
2443	6z.90 Weightlifting	85	35
2444	8z.40 Athletics	1·10	45
MS2445	78×94 mm. 10z.+5z. black and red (Volleyball) (23×29 mm)	3·25	1·80

677 National Theatre

1976. Cent of National Theatre, Poznan.

2446	**677**	1z.50 green and orange	25	10

678 Aleksander Czekanowski and Baikal Landscape

1976. Death Centenary of Aleksander Czekanowski (geologist).

2447	**678**	1z.50 multicoloured	25	10

679 "Sphinx"

1976. Stamp Day. Corinthian Vase Paintings (7th century B.C.). Multicoloured.

2448	1z. Type **679**	10	10
2449	1z.50 "Siren" (horiz)	10	10
2450	2z. "Lion" (horiz)	20	10
2451	4z.20 "Bull" (horiz)	50	25
2452	4z.50 "Goat" (horiz)	65	35
2453	8z.+4z. "Sphinx" (different)	1·70	70

680 Warszawa "M 20"

1976. 25th Anniv of Zeran Motor-car Factory, Warsaw. Multicoloured.

2454	1z. Type **680**	10	10
2455	1z.50 Warszawa "223"	15	10
2456	2z. Syrena "104"	20	10
2457	4z.90 Polski - Fiat "125P"	65	45
MS2458	137×109 mm. Nos. 2454/7	3·25	2·30

681 Molten Steel Ladle

1976. Huta Katowice Steel Works.

2459	**681**	1z.50 multicoloured	25	10

682 Congress Emblem

1976. Eighth Polish Trade Unions Congress.

2460	**682**	1z.50 orange, bistre and brown	25	10

683 "Wirzbieto Epitaph" (painting on wood, 1425)

1976. Polish Art. Multicoloured.

2461	1z. Type **683**	10	10
2462	6z. "Madonna and Child" (painted carving, c.1410)	75	25

684 Tanker "Zawrat" at Oil Terminal, Gdansk

1976. Polish Ports. Multicoloured.

2463	1z. Type **684**	10	10
2464	1z. Ferry "Gryf" at Gdansk	10	10
2465	1z.50 Loading container ship "General Bem", Gdynia	20	10
2466	1z.50 Liner "Stefan Batory" leaving Gdynia	20	10
2467	2z. Bulk carrier "Ziemia Szczecinska" loading at Szczecin	30	15
2468	4z.20 Loading coal, Swinoujscie	65	25
2469	6z.90 Pleasure craft, Kolobrzeg	95	35
2470	8z.40 Coastal map	1·00	60

685 Nurse and Patient

1977. Polish Red Cross.

2471	**685**	1z.50 multicoloured	25	10

686 Order of Civil Defence Service

1977. Polish Civil Defence.

2472	**686**	1z.50 multicoloured	25	10

687 Ball in Road

1977. Child Road Safety Campaign.

2473	**687**	1z.50 multicoloured	25	10

688 Dewberries

1977. Wild Fruit. Multicoloured.

2474	50g. Type **688**	10	10
2475	90g. Cowberries	10	10
2476	1z. Wild strawberries	10	10
2477	1z.50 Bilberries	10	10
2478	2z. Raspberries	10	10
2479	4z.50 Sloes	50	15
2480	6z. Rose hips	75	20
2481	6z.90 Hazelnuts	1·30	35

689 Computer Tape

1977. 30th Anniv of Russian–Polish Technical Co-operation.

2482	**689**	1z.50 multicoloured	25	10

690 Pendulum Traces and Emblem

1977. Seventh Polish Congress of Technology.

2483	**690**	1z.50 multicoloured	25	10

691 "Toilet of Venus"

1977. 400th Birth Anniv of Peter Paul Rubens. Multicoloured.

2484	1z. Type **691**	10	10
2485	1z.50 "Bathsheba at the Fountain"	10	10
2486	5z. "Helena Fourment with Fur Coat"	75	20
2487	6z. "Self-portrait"	85	30
MS2488	76×62 mm. 8z.+4z. sepia ("The Stoning of St. Stephan") (21×26 mm)	2·50	1·40

692 Dove

1977. World Council of Peace Congress.

2489	**692**	1z.50 blue, yellow & black	25	10

693 Cyclist

1977. 30th International Peace Cycle Race.

2490	**693**	1z.50 multicoloured	25	10

694 Wolf

1977. Endangered Animals. Multicoloured.

2491	1z. Type **694**	25	10
2492	1z.50 Great bustard	40	10
2493	1z.50 Common kestrel	50	20
2494	6z. European otter	1·00	45

695 "The Violinist" (J. Toorenvliet)

1977. "Amphilex 77" Stamp Exhibition, Amsterdam.

2495	**695**	6z. multicoloured	75	60

696 Midsummer's Day Bonfire

1977. Folk Customs. 19th-century Wood Engravings. Multicoloured.

2496	90g. Type **696**	15	10
2497	1z. Easter cock (vert)	15	10
2498	1z.50 "Smigus" (dousing of women on Easter Monday, Miechow district) (vert)	20	10
2499	3z. Harvest Festival, Sandomierz district (vert)	25	10
2500	6z. Children with Christmas crib (vert)	75	20
2501	8z.40 Mountain wedding dance	1·30	35

697 H. Wieniawski and Music Clef

1977. Wieniawski International Music Competitions, Poznan.

2502	**697**	1z.50 black, red and gold	25	10

698 Apollo ("Parnassius apollo")

1977. Butterflies. Multicoloured.

2503	1z. Type **698**	20	10
2504	1z. Large tortoiseshell ("Nymphalis polychloros")	20	10
2505	1z.50 Camberwell beauty ("Nymphalis antiopa")	30	10
2506	1z.50 Swallowtail ("Papilio machaon")	30	10
2507	5z. High brown fritillary	1·10	30
2508	6z.90 Silver-washed fritillary	2·50	1·00

699 Keyboard and Arms of Slupsk

1977. Piano Festival, Slupsk.

2509	**699**	1z.50 mauve, blk & grn	25	10

700 Feliks Dzerzhinsky

1977. Birth Centenary of Feliks Dzerzhinsky (Russian politician).
2510 **700** 1z.50 brown and ochre 25 10

701 "Sputnik" circling Earth

1977. 60th Anniv of Russian Revolution and 20th Anniv of 1st Artificial Satellite (1st issue).
2511 **701** 1z.50 red and blue 30 20
MS2512 99×125 mm. No. 2511 ×3 plus three labels 1·60 1·20
See also No. 2527.

702 Silver Dinar (11th century)

1977. Stamp Day. Polish Coins. Multicoloured.
2513 50g. Type **702** 10 10
2514 1z. Cracow grosz, 14th-century 10 10
2515 1z.50 Legnica thaler, 17th-century 20 10
2516 4z.20 Gdansk guilder, 18th-century 55 10
2517 4z.50 Silver 5z. coin, 1936 65 25
2518 6z. Millenary 100z. coin, 1966 75 30

703 Wolin Gate, Kamien Pomorski

1977. Architectural Monuments. Multicoloured.
2519 1z. Type **703** 10 10
2520 1z. Larch church, Debno 10 10
2521 1z.50 Monastery, Przasnysz (horiz) 20 10
2522 1z.50 Plock cathedral (horiz) 20 10
2523 6z. Kornik castle (horiz) 75 25
2524 6z.90 Palace and garden, Wilanow (horiz) 85 30

1977. Polish Folklore. 16th-century woodcuts (2nd series). As T **638**.
2525 4z. sepia 50 20
2526 4z.50 brown 65 20
DESIGNS: 4z. Bird snaring; 4z.50, Bee-keeper and hives.

704 "Sputnik 1" and "Mercury" Capsule

1977. 20th Anniv of 1st Space Satellite (2nd issue).
2527 **704** 6z.90 multicoloured 85 60

705 DN Category Iceboats

1978. Sixth World Ice Sailing Championships.
2528 **705** 1z.50 black, grey & blue 25 10
2529 - 1z.50 black, grey & blue 25 10
DESIGN: No. 2529, Close-up of DN iceboat.

706 Electric Locomotive and Katowice Station

1978. Railway Engines. Multicoloured.
2530 50g. Type **706** 10 10
2531 1z. Steam locomotive No. Py27 and tender No. 721, Znin-Gasawa railway 10 10
2532 1z. Streamlined steam locomotive No. Pm36-1 (1936) and Cegielski's factory, Poznan 10 10
2533 1z.50 Electric locomotive and Otwock station 10 10
2534 1z.50 Steam locomotive No. 17 KDM and Warsaw Stalowa station 10 10
2535 4z.50 Steam locomotive No. Ty51 and Gdynia station 50 15
2536 5z. Steam locomotive No. Tr21 and locomotive works, Chrzanow 65 20
2537 6z. Cockerill steam locomotive and Vienna station 1·00 40

707 Czeslaw Tanski and Glider

1978. Aviation History and 50th Anniv of Polish Aero Club. Multicoloured.
2538 50g. Type **707** 10 10
2539 1z. Franciszek Zwirko and Stanislaw Wigura with RWD-6 aircraft (vert) 10 10
2540 1z.50 Stanislaw Skarzynski and RWD-5 bis monoplane (vert) 10 10
2541 4z.20 Mil Mi-2 helicopter (vert) 50 15
2542 6z.90 PZL-104 Wilga 35 monoplane 1·60 30
2543 8z.40 SZD-45 Ogar powered glider 1·50 35

708 Tackle

1978. World Cup Football Championship, Argentina. Multicoloured.
2544 1z.50 Type **708** 25 10
2545 6z.90 Ball on field (horiz) 75 35

709 Biennale Emblem

1978. Seventh International Poster Biennale, Warsaw.
2546 **709** 1z.50 mauve, yell & vio 25 10

710 Kazimierz Stanislaw Gzowski (bridge engineer)

1978. "Capex 78" International Stamp Exhibition, Toronto. Sheet 68×79 mm.
MS2547 **710** 8z.40+4z. multicoloured 2·10 1·20

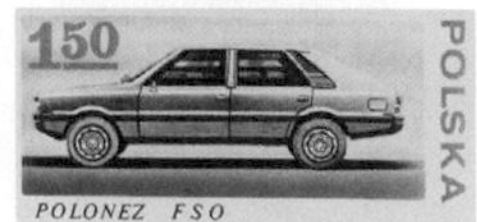

711 Polonez Saloon Car

1978. Car Production.
2548 **711** 1z.50 multicoloured 25 10

712 Fair Emblem

1978. 50th International Fair, Poznan.
2549 **712** 1z.50 multicoloured 25 10

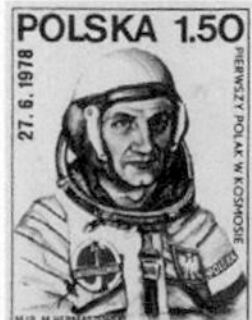

713 Miroslaw Hermaszewski

1978. First Pole in Space. Multicoloured. With or without date.
2550 1z.50 Type **713** 20 10
2551 6z.90 M. Hermaszewski and globe 85 35

714 Globe containing Face

1978. 11th World Youth and Students Festival, Havana.
2552 **714** 1z.50 multicoloured 25 10

715 Flowers

1978. 30th Anniv Polish Youth Union. Sheet 69×79 mm.
MS2553 **715** 1z.50 multicoloured 75 60

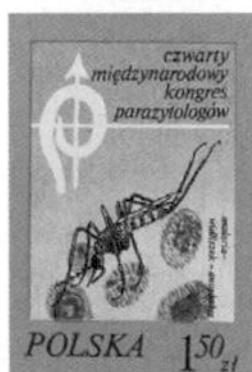

716 Mosquito and Malaria Organisms

1978. Fourth International Congress of Parasitologists, Warsaw and Cracow. Multicoloured.
2554 1z.50 Type **716** 20 10
2555 6z. Tsetse fly and sleeping sickness organism 75 35

717 Pedunculate Oak

1978. Environment Protection. Trees. Multicoloured.
2556 50g. Norway Maple 10 10
2557 1z. Type **717** 10 10
2558 1z.50 White Poplar 10 10
2559 4z.20 Scots Pine 45 15
2560 4z.50 White Willow 50 20
2561 6z. Birch 75 30

718

1978. "PRAGA 1978" International Stamp Exhibition. Sheet 69×79 mm.
MS2562 **718** 6z. multicoloured 2·10 1·20

719 Communications

1978. 20th Anniv of Socialist Countries Communications Organization.
2563 **719** 1z.50 red, lt blue & blue 25 10

720 "Peace" (Andre Le Brun)

1978
2564 **720** 1z. violet 20 10
2565 **720** 1z.50 turquoise 20 10
2565a **720** 2z. brown 20 10
2565b **720** 2z.50 blue 20 10

721 Polish Unit of U.N. Middle East Force

1978. 35th Anniv of Polish People's Army. Multicoloured.
2566 1z.50 Colour party of Tadeusz Kosciuszko 1st Warsaw Infantry Division 20 10
2567 1z.50 Mechanized Unit colour party 20 10
2568 1z.50 Type **721** 20 10

722 "Portrait of a Young Man" (Raphael)

1978. Stamp Day.
2569 **722** 6z. multicoloured 75 60

723 Janusz Korczak with Children

1978. Birth Centenary of Janusz Korczak (pioneer of children's education).
2570 **723** 1z.50 multicoloured 40 25

724 Wojciech Boguslawski

1978. Polish Dramatists. Multicoloured.
2571 50g. Type **724** 10 10
2572 1z. Aleksander Fredro 10 10
2573 1z.50 Juliusz Slowacki 15 10
2574 2z. Adam Mickiewicz 20 10
2575 4z.50 Stanislaw Wyspianski 65 20
2576 6z. Gabriela Zapolska 75 25

725 Polish Combatants' Monument and Eiffel Tower

1978. Monument to Polish Combatants in France, Paris.
2577 **725** 1z.50 brown, blue & red 25 10

726 Przewalski Horses

1978. 50th Anniv of Warsaw Zoo. Multicoloured.
2578 50g. Type **726** 10 10

2579		1z. Polar bears	10	10
2580		1z.50 Indian elephants	15	10
2581		2z. Jaguars	20	10
2582		4z.20 Grey seals	45	20
2583		4z.50 Hartebeests	50	25
2584		6z. Mandrills	1·30	35

727 Party Flag

1978. 30th Anniv of Polish Workers' United Party.

2585	**727**	1z.50 red, gold and black	25	10

728 Stanislaw Dubois

1978. Leaders of Polish Workers' Movement.

2586	**728**	1z.50 blue and red	20	10
2587	-	1z.50 lilac and red	20	10
2588	-	1z.50 olive and red	20	10
2589	-	1z.50 brown and red	20	10

DESIGNS: No. 2587, Aleksander Zawadzki; 2588, Julian Lenski; 2589, Aldolf Warski.

729 Ilyushin Il-62M and Fokker F.VIIb/3m

1979. 50th Anniv of LOT Polish Airlines.

2590	**729**	6z.90 multicoloured	85	35

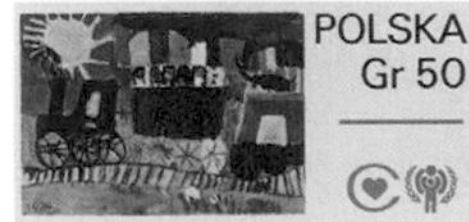

730 Steam Train

1979. International Year of the Child. Children's Paintings. Multicoloured.

2591		50g. Type **730**	10	10
2592		1z. "Mother with Children"	10	10
2593		1z.50 Children playing	20	10
2594		6z. Family Group	85	25

731 "Portrait of Artist's Wife with Foxgloves" (Karol Mondrala)

1979. Contemporary Graphics.

2595	-	50g. lilac	10	10
2596	**731**	1z. green	10	10
2597	-	1z.50 blue	20	10
2598	-	4z.50 brown	65	20

DESIGNS—HORIZ: 50g. "Lightning" (Edmund Bartlomiejezyk). VERT: 1z.50, "The Musicians" (Tadeusz Kulisiewicz); 4z.50, "Head of a Young Man" (Wladyslaw Skoczylas).

732 A. Frycz Modrzewski (political writer), King Stefan Batory and Jan Zamoyski (chancellor)

1979. 400th Anniv (1978) of Royal Tribunal in Piotrkow Trybunalski.

2599	**732**	1z.50 brown and deep brown	25	10

733 Pole Vaulting

1979. 60th Anniv of Polish Olympic Committee.

2600	**733**	1z. Lilac, brown and red	10	10
2601	-	1z.50 lilac, brown and red	20	10
2602	-	6z. lilac, brown and red	50	25
2603	-	8z.40 lilac, brown and red	85	35
MS2604		102×61 mm. 10z.+5z. brown	1·60	1·40

DESIGNS: 1z.50, High jump; 6z. Skiing; 8z.40, Horse riding; 10z. Olympic rings.

734 European Flounder

1979. Centenary of Polish Angling. Multicoloured.

2605		50g. Type **734**	10	10
2606		90g. Eurasian perch	10	10
2607		1z. European grayling	10	10
2608		1z.50 Atlantic salmon	20	10
2609		2z. Brown trout	25	10
2610		4z.50 Northern pike	50	15
2611		5z. Common carp	75	20
2612		6z. Wels	1·00	35

735 "30 Years of RWPG"

1979. 30th Anniv of Council of Mutual Economic Aid.

2613	**735**	1z.50 red, ultram & blue	25	10

736 Soldier, Civilian and Congress Emblem

1979. Sixth Congress of Association of Fighters for Liberty and Democracy.

2614	**736**	1z.50 red and black	25	10

737 St. George's Church, Sofia

1979. "Philaserdica 79" International Stamp Exhibition, Sofia, Bulgaria.

2615	**737**	1z.50 orange, brn & red	25	10

738 Pope and Auschwitz Concentration Camp Memorial

1979. Visit of Pope John Paul II. Multicoloured.

2616		1z.50 Pope and St. Mary's Church, Cracow	50	20
2617		8z.40 Type **738**	1·00	25
MS2618		68×79 mm. 50z. Framed portrait of Pope (26×35 mm)	11·50	8·75

739 River Paddle-steamer "Ksiaze Ksawery" and Old Warsaw

1979. 150th Anniv of Vistula River Navigation. Multicoloured.

2619		1z. Type **739**	15	10
2620		1z.50 River paddle-steamer "General Swierczewski" and Gdansk	20	10
2621		4z.50 River tug "Zubr" and Plock	50	10
2622		6z. Passenger launch "Syrena" and modern Warsaw	65	15

740 Statue of Tadeusz Kosciuszko (Marian Konieczny)

1979. Monument to Tadeusz Kosciuszko in Philadelphia.

2623	**740**	8z.40 multicoloured	75	45

741 Mining Machinery

1979. Wieliczka Salt Mine.

2624	**741**	1z. brown and black	10	10
2625	-	1z.50 turquoise and black	20	10

DESIGN: 1z.50, Salt crystals.

742 Heraldic Eagle

1979. 35th Anniv of Polish People's Republic.

2626		1z.50 red, silver and black	20	10
2627	**742**	1z.50 red, silver and blue	20	10
MS2628		120×84 mm. Nos. 2626/7 plus label	85	70

DESIGN: No. 2626, Girl and stylized flag.

743 Rowland Hill and 1860 Stamp

1979. Death Centenary of Sir Rowland Hill.

2629	**743**	6z. blue, black and orange	85	25

744 "The Rape of Europa" (Bernardo Stozzi)

1979. International Stamp Exhibition. Sheet 86×63 mm.

MS2630	**744**	10z. multicoloured	1·60	1·20

745 Wojciech Jastrzebowski

1979. Seventh Congress of International Ergonomic Association, Warsaw.

2631	**745**	1z.50 multicoloured	25	10

746 Monument (Wincenty Kucma)

1979. Unveiling of Monument to Defenders of Polish Post, Gdansk, and 40th Anniv of German Occupation.

2632	**746**	1z.50 grey, sepia and red	25	10
MS2633		79×69 mm. **746** 10z.+5z. grey, sepia and red. Imperf	2·10	1·80

747 Radio Mast and Telecommunications Emblem

1979. 50th Anniv of International Radio Communication Advisory Committee.

2634	**747**	1z.50 multicoloured	25	10

748 Violin

1979. Wieniawski Young Violinists' Competition, Lublin.

2635	**748**	1z.50 blue, orange & green	25	10

749 Statue of Kazimierz Pulaski, Buffalo (K. Danilewicz)

1979. Death Bicentenary of Kazimierz Pulaski (American Revolution Hero).

2636	**749**	8z.40 multicoloured	1·10	35

750 Franciszek Jozwiak (first Commander)

1979. 35th Anniv of Civic Militia and Security Force.

2637	**750**	1z.50 blue and gold	25	10

751 Post Office in Rural Area

1979. Stamp Day. Multicoloured.

2638		1z. Type **751**	10	10
2639		1z.50 Parcel sorting machinery	20	10
2640		4z.50 Loading containers on train	65	20
2641		6z. Mobile post office	75	35

752 "The Holy Family" (Ewelina Peksowa)

1979. Polish Folk Art. Glass Paintings. Multicoloured.

2642		2z. Type **752**	20	10
2643		6z.90 "The Nativity" (Zdzislaw Walczak)	75	35

753 "Soyuz 30-Salyut 6" Complex and Crystal

1979. Space Achievements. Multicoloured.

2644	1z. Type **753** (1st anniv of 1st Pole in space)	10	10
2645	1z.50 "Kopernik" and "Copernicus" satellites	15	10
2646	2z. "Lunik 2" and "Ranger 7" spacecraft (20th anniv of 1st unmanned Moon landing)	20	10
2647	4z.50 Yuri Gagarin and "Vostok 1"	50	15
2648	6z.90 Neil Armstrong, lunar module and "Apollo 11" (10th anniv of first man on Moon)	65	35
MS2649	120×103 mm. Nos. 2644/8 plus label (sold at 20z.90)	2·30	2·00

754 Coach and Four

1980. 150th Anniv of Sierakow Stud Farm. Multicoloured.

2650	1z. Type **754**	10	10
2651	2z. Horse and groom	20	10
2652	2z.50 Sulky racing	30	10
2653	3z. Hunting	40	15
2654	4z. Horse-drawn sledge	50	20
2655	6z. Haywain	70	25
2656	6z.50 Grooms exercising horses	75	30
2657	6z.90 Show jumping	85	35

755 Slogan on Map of Poland

1980. Eighth Polish United Workers' Party Congress. Multicoloured.

2658	2z.50 Type **755**	30	20
2659	2z.50 Janusz Stann (26×46 mm)	30	20

756 Horse Jumping

1980. Olympic Games, Moscow, and Winter Olympic Games, Lake Placid. Multicoloured.

2660	2z. Type **756**	20	10
2661	2z.50 Archery	30	15
2662	6z.50 Skiing	65	25
2663	8z.40 Volleyball	1·10	35

757 Town Plan and Old Town Hall

1980. 400th Anniv of Zamosc.

2665	**757**	2z.50 buff, green & brn	30	15

758 Satellite orbiting Earth

1980. "Intercosmos" Space Programme. Sheet 63×79 mm.

MS2666 **758**	6z.90+3z. multicoloured	1·60	1·30

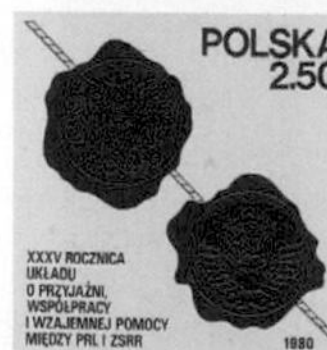

759 Seals of Poland and Russia

1980. 35th Anniv of Soviet–Polish Friendship Treaty.

2667	**759**	2z.50 multicoloured	30	15

760 "Lenin in Cracow" (Zbigniew Pronaszko)

1980. 110th Birth Anniv of Lenin.

2668	**760**	2z.50 multicoloured	30	15

761 Workers with Red Flag

1980. 75th Anniv of Revolution of 1905.

2669	**761**	2z.50 red, black & yellow	30	15

762 Dove

1980. 35th Anniv of Liberation.

2670	**762**	2z.50 multicoloured	30	15

763 Shield with Crests of Member Nations

1980. 25th Anniv of Warsaw Pact.

2671	**763**	2z. grey and red	30	15

764 Speleological Expedition, Cuba

1980. Polish Scientific Expeditions. Multicoloured.

2672	2z. Type **764**	20	10
2673	2z. Antarctic	20	10
2674	2z.50 Archaeology, Syria	25	10
2675	2z.50 Ethnology, Mongolia	25	10
2676	6z.50 Mountaineering, Nepal	75	25
2677	8z.40 Paleontology, Mongolia	1·30	35

765 School and Arms

1980. 800th Anniv of Malachowski School, Plock.

2678	**765**	2z. green and black	30	15

766 "Clathrus ruber"

1980. Fungi. Multicoloured.

2679	2z. Type **766**	20	10
2680	2z. "Xerocomus parasiticus"	20	10
2681	2z.50 Old man of the woods ("Strobilomyces floccopus")	25	10
2682	2z.50 "Phallus hadriani"	25	10
2683	8z. Cauliflower fungus	85	35
2684	10z.50 Giant puff-ball	1·00	55

767 T. Ziolowski and "Lwow"

1980. Polish Merchant Navy School. Cadet Ships and their Captains.

2685	2z. black, mauve and violet	20	10
2686	2z.50 black, light blue and blue	25	10
2687	6z. black, pale green and green	50	15
2688	6z.50 black, yellow and grey	65	25
2689	6z.90 black, grey and green	75	30
2690	8z.40 black, blue and green	1·00	35

DESIGNS: 2z. Type **767**; 2z.50, A. Garnuszewski and "Antoni Garnuszewski"; 6z. A. Ledochowski and "Zenit"; 6z.50, K. Porebski and "Jan Turleski"; 6z.90, G. Kanski and "Horyzont"; 8z.40, Maciejewicz and "Dar Pomorza".

768 Town Hall

1980. Millenary of Sandomir.

2691	**768**	2z.50 brown and black	40	20

769 "Atropa belladonna"

1980. Medicinal Plants. Multicoloured.

2692	2z. Type **769**	15	10
2693	2z.50 "Datura innoxia"	20	10
2694	3z.40 "Valeriana officinalis"	25	10
2695	5z. "Menta piperita"	50	15
2696	6z.50 "Calendula officinalis"	75	25
2697	8z. "Salvia officinalis"	1·30	35

770 Jan Kochanowski

1980. 450th Birth Anniv of Jan Kochanowski (poet).

2698	**770**	2z.50 multicoloured	40	20

771 U.N. General Assembly

1980. 35th Anniv of U.N.O.

2703	**771**	8z.40 brown, blue & red	1·10	60

772 Chopin and Trees

1980. Tenth International Chopin Piano Competition, Warsaw.

2704	**772**	6z.90 multicoloured	75	35

773 Postman emptying Post Box

1980. Stamp Day. Multicoloured.

2705	2z. Type **773**	20	10
2706	2z.50 Mail sorting	25	10
2707	6z. Loading mail onto aircraft	75	25
2708	6z.50 Letter boxes	1·00	30
MS2709	12×94 mm. Nos. 2705/8	5·25	3·50

774 Child embracing Dove

1980. United Nations Declaration on the Preparation of Societies for Life in Peace.

2710	**774**	8z.40 multicoloured	1·00	40

775 "Battle of Olszynka Grochowska" (Wojciech Kossak)

1980. 150th Anniv of Battle of Olszynka Grochowska.

2711	**775**	2z.50 multicoloured	40	20

776 Fire Engine

1980. Warsaw Horse-drawn Vehicles. Multicoloured.

2712	2z. Type **776**	15	10
2713	2z.50 Omnibus	20	10
2714	3z. Brewery dray	25	10
2715	5z. Sledge-cab	50	15
2716	6z. Horse tram	75	35
2717	6z.50 Droshky cab	1·00	55

777 "Honour to the Silesian Rebels" (statue by Jan Borowczak)

1981. 60th Anniv of Silesian Rising.

2718	**777**	2z.50 green	40	20

778 Picasso

1981. Birth Centenary of Pablo Picasso (artist).

2719 **778**	8z.40 multicoloured	1·00	45
MS2720	95×130 mm. No. 2719 ×2 plus labels (sold at 20z.80)	4·25	2·30

779 Balloon of Pilatre de Rozier and Romain, 1785

1981. Balloons. Multicoloured.

2721		2z. Type **779**	20	10
2722		2z. Balloon of J. Blanchard and J. Jeffries, 1785	20	10
2723		2z.50 Eugene Godard's quintuple "acrobatic" balloon, 1850	25	10
2724		3z. F. Hynek and Z. Burzynski's "Kosciuszko", 1933	30	10
2725		6z. Z. Burzynski and N. Wyescki's "Polonia II", 1935	75	25
2726		6z.50 Ben Abruzzo, Max Anderson and Larry Newman's "Double Eagle II", 1978	1·30	35
MS2727		59×98 mm. 10z.50 Balloon SP-BCU *L.O.P.P.* and Gordon Bennett statuette	1·60	1·40

780 "Iphigenia" (Anton Maulbertsch)

1981. "WIPA 1981" International Stamp Exhibition, Vienna.

2728	**780**	10z.50 multicoloured	1·80	60

781 Wroclaw, 1493

1981. Towns.

2729	-	4z. violet	65	25
2730	-	5z. green	85	25
2731	-	6z. orange	95	25
2732	**781**	6z.50 brown	1·00	35
2733	-	8z. blue	1·40	45

DESIGNS—VERT: 4z. Gdansk, 1652; 5z. Cracow, 1493. HORIZ: 6z. Legnica, 1744; 8z. Warsaw, 1618.

782 Sikorski

1981. Birth Centenary of General Wladyslaw Sikorski (statesman).

2744	**782**	6z.50 multicoloured	1·00	35

783 Faience Vase

1981. Pottery. Multicoloured.

2745		1z. Type **783**	20	10
2746		2z. Porcelain cup and saucer in "Baranowka" design	30	10
2747		2z.50 Porcelain jug, Korzec manufacture	40	15
2748		5z. Faience plate with portrait of King Jan III Sobieski by Thiele	85	35
2749		6z.50 Faience "Secession" vase	1·00	40
2750		8z.40 Porcelain dish, Cmielow manufacture	1·40	55

784 Congress Emblem

1981. 14th International Architects' Union Congress, Warsaw.

2751	**784**	2z. yellow, black and red	40	20

785 Wild Boar, Rifle and Oak Leaves

1981. Game Shooting. Multicoloured.

2752		2z. Type **785**	30	10
2753		2z. Elk, rifle and fir twigs	30	10
2754		2z.50 Red fox, shotgun, cartridges and fir branches	40	15
2755		2z.50 Roe deer, feeding rack, rifle and fir branches	40	15
2756		6z.50 Mallard, shotgun, basket and reeds	1·00	65
2757		6z.50 Barnacle goose, shotgun and reeds (horiz)	1·00	65

786 European Bison

1981. Protection of European Bison. Multicoloured.

2758		6z.50 Type **786**	1·00	50
2759		6z.50 Two bison, one grazing	1·00	50
2760		6z.50 Bison with calf	1·00	50
2761		6z.50 Calf Feeding	1·00	50
2762		6z.50 Two bison, both looking towards right	1·00	50

787 Tennis Player

1981. 60th Anniv of Polish Tennis Federation.

2763	**787**	6z.50 multicoloured	1·00	40

788 Boy with Model Airplane

1981. Model Making. Multicoloured.

2764		1z. Type **788**	20	10
2765		2z. Model of "Atlas 2" tug	30	10
2766		2z.50 Cars	40	15
2767		4z.20 Man with gliders	65	25
2768		6z.50 Racing cars	1·00	40
2769		8z. Boy with yacht	1·40	50

789 Disabled Pictogram

1981. International Year of Disabled Persons.

2770	**789**	8z.40 green, light green and black	1·40	50

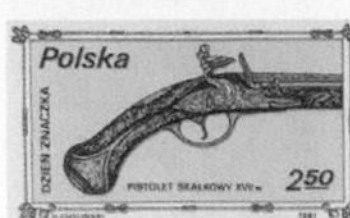

790 17th-cent Flint-lock Pistol

1981. Stamp Day. Antique Weapons. Multicoloured.

2771		2z.50 Type **790**	40	15
2772		8z.40 17th-century gala sabre (vert)	1·40	50

791 H. Wieniawski and Violin Head

1981. Wieniawski Young Violinists' Competition.

2773	**791**	2z.50 multicoloured	40	15

792 Bronislaw Wesolowski

1981. Activists of Polish Workers' Movement.

2774	**792**	50g. green and black	10	10
2775	-	2z. blue and black	30	10
2776	-	2z.50 brown and black	40	15
2777	-	6z.50 mauve and black	1·00	40

DESIGNS: 2z. Malgorzata Fornalska; 2z.50, Maria Koszutska; 6z.50, Marcin Kasprzak.

793 F.A.O. Emblem and Globe

1981. World Food Day.

2778	**793**	6z.90 brown, orange & yellow	1·10	40

794 Helena Modrzejewska (actress)

1981. Bicentenary of Cracow Old Theatre.

2779	**794**	2z. purple, grey and violet	30	10
2780	-	2z.50 blue, stone & brn	40	15
2781	-	6z.50 violet, blue & grn	1·00	25
2782	-	8z. brown, green and red	1·40	40

DESIGNS: 2z.50, Stanislaw Kozmian (politician, writer and theatre director); 6z.50, Konrad Swinarski (stage manager and scenographer); 8z. Old Theatre building.

795 Cracow and Vistula River

1981. Vistula River Project. Sheet 62×51 mm.

MS2783	**795**	10z.50 multicoloured	2·50	2·10

796 Gdansk Memorial

1981. Memorials to the Victims of the 1970 Uprisings.

2784	**796**	2z.50+1z. grey, black and red	50	25
2785	-	6z.50+1z. grey, black and blue	1·30	50

DESIGN: 6z.50, Gdynia Memorial (26×37 mm).

797 "Epiphyllopsis gaertneri"

1981. Succulent Plants. Multicoloured.

2786		90g. Type **797**	15	10
2787		1z. "Cereus tonduzii"	20	10
2788		2z. "Cylindropuntia leptocaulis"	30	10
2789		2z.50 "Cylindropuntia fulgida"	40	15
2790		2z.50 "Coralluma lugardi"	40	15
2791		6z.50 "Nopalea cochenillifera"	1·00	40
2792		6z.50 "Lithops helmutii"	1·00	40
2793		10z.50 "Cylindropuntia spinosior"	1·80	65

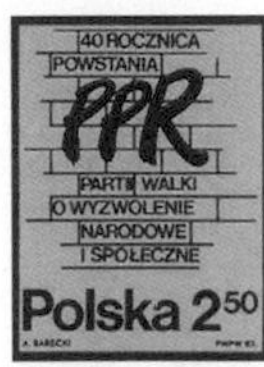

798 Writing on Wall

1982. 40th Anniv of Polish Workers' Coalition.

2794	**798**	2z.50 pink, red and black	40	15

799 Faience Plate

1982. Polish Ceramics. Multicoloured.

2795		1z. Type **799**	15	15
2796		2z. Porcelain cup and saucer, Korzec	30	15
2797		2z.50 Porcelain tureen and sauce-boat, Barnowka	40	20
2798		6z. Porcelain inkpot, Horodnica	95	40
2799		8z. Faience "Hunter's Tumbler", Lubartow	1·40	50
2800		10z.50 Faience figurine of nobleman, Biala Podlaska	1·90	75

800 Ignacy Lukasiewicz and Lamp

1982. Death Centenary of Ignacy Lukasiewicz (inventor of petroleum lamp).

2801	**800**	1z. multicoloured	15	10
2802	-	2z. multicoloured	30	10
2803	-	2z.50 multicoloured	40	15
2804	-	3z.50 multicoloured	50	15
2805	-	9z. multicoloured	1·50	50
2806	-	10z. multicoloured	1·70	65

DESIGNS: 2z. to 10z. Different designs showing lamps.

801 Karol Szymanowski

1982. Birth Centenary of Karol Szymanowski (composer).

2807	**801**	2z.50 brown and gold	40	20

802 RWD 6, 1932

1982. 50th Anniv of Polish Victory in Tourist Aircraft Challenge Competition. Multicoloured.

2808	27z. Type **802**	1·30	40
2809	31z. RWD 9 (winner of 1934 Challenge)	1·60	65
MS2810	89×101 mm. Nos. 2808/9	3·75	3·25

803 Henryk Sienkiewicz (literature, 1905)

1982. Polish Nobel Prize Winners.

2811	**803**	3z. green and black	10	10
2812	-	15z. brown and black	50	25
2813	-	25z. blue	65	30
2814	-	31z. grey and black	1·70	65

DESIGNS: 15z. Wladyslaw Reymont (literature, 1924); 25z. Marie Curie (physics, 1903, and chemistry, 1911); 31z. Czeslaw Milosz (literature, 1980).

804 Football as Globe

1982. World Cup Football Championship, Spain. Multicoloured.

2815	25z. Type **804**	1·30	65
2816	27z. Bull and football (35×28 mm)	1·40	75

805 "Maria kazimiera Sobieska"

1982. "Philexfrance 82" International Stamp Exhibition, Paris. Sheet 69×86 mm.

MS2817	**805** 65z. multicoloured	4·75	4·50

806 Stanislaw Sierakowski and Boleslaw Domanski (former Association presidents)

1982. 60th Anniv of Association of Poles in Germany.

2818	**806**	4z.50 red and green	65	25

807 Text around Globe

1982. Second U.N. Conference on the Exploration and Peaceful Uses of Outer Space, Vienna.

2819	**807**	31z. multicoloured	1·60	65

1982. No. 2732 surch **10 °°**.

2820	10z. on 6z.50 brown	50	20

809 Father Augustyn Kordecki (prior)

1982. 600th Anniv of "Black Madonna" (icon) of Jasna Gora. Multicoloured.

2821	2z.50 Type **809**	10	10
2822	25z. "Siege of Jasna Gora by Swedes, 1655" (detail) (horiz)	75	40
2823	65z. "Black Madonna"	2·10	65
MS2824	122×108 mm. No. 2823 ×2 (sold at 140z.)	13·50	16·00

The premium on No. **MS**2824 was for the benefit of the Polish Philatelic Federation.

810 Marchers with Banner

1982. Centenary of Proletarian Party.

2825	**810**	6z. multicoloured	50	25

811 Norbert Barlicki

1982. Activists of Polish Workers' Movement.

2826	**811**	5z. light blue, blue and black	10	20
2827	-	6z. deep green, green and black	15	20
2828	-	15z. pink, red and black	30	20
2829	-	20z. mauve, violet and black	50	20
2830	-	29z. light brown, brown and black	75	25

DESIGNS: 6z. Pawel Finder; 15z. Marian Buczek; 20z. Cezaryna Wojnarowska; 29z. Ignacy Daszynski.

812 Dr. Robert Koch

1982. Centenary of Discovery of Tubercle Bacillus. Multicoloured.

2831	10z. Type **812**	65	20
2832	25z. Dr. Odo Bujwid	1·70	50

813 Carved Head of Woman

813a Head of Ruler

1982. Carved Heads from Wawel Castle.

2835	**813a**	3z.50 brown	20	10
2836	-	5z. green	20	10
2837	-	5z. red	20	10
2838	-	10z. blue	25	10
2839	-	15z. brown	30	10
2840	-	20z. grey	50	15
2841	**813a**	20z. blue	20	10
2842	-	40z. brown	1·60	45
2843	-	60z. green	20	10
2833	**813**	60z. orange and brown	2·50	1·30
2834	-	100z. ochre and brown	3·50	1·90
2843a	-	200z. black	4·25	1·30

DESIGNS—As T **813**: 100z. Man. As T **813a**: 5z. (2836), Warrior; 5z. (2837), 15z. Woman wearing chaplet; 10z. Man in cap; 20z. (2840), Thinker, 40z. Man in beret; 60z. Young man; 200z. Man.

814 Maximilian Kolbe (after M. Koscielniak)

1982. Sanctification of Maximilian Kolbe (Franciscan concentration camp victim).

2844	**814**	27z. multicoloured	1·80	65

815 Polar Research Station

1982. 50th Anniv of Polish Polar Research.

2845	**815**	27z. multicoloured	1·90	65

816 "Log Floats on Vistula River" (drawing by J. Telakowski)

1982. Views of the Vistula River.

2846	**816**	12z. blue	25	10
2847	-	17z. blue	30	10
2848	-	25z. blue	40	25

DESIGNS: 17z. "Kazimierz Dolny" (engraving by Andriollo); 25z. "Danzig" (18th-cent engraving).

817 Stanislaw Zaremba

1982. Mathematicians.

2849	**817**	5z. lilac, blue and black	30	15
2850	-	6z. orange, violet and black	40	20
2851	-	12z. blue, brown and black	65	25
2852	-	15z. yellow, brown and black	1·00	40

DESIGNS: 6z. Waclaw Sierpinski; 12z. Zygmunt Janiszewski; 15z. Stefan Banach.

818 Military Council Medal

1982. First Anniv of Military Council.

2853	**818**	2z.50 multicoloured	40	20

819 Deanery Gate

1982. Renovation of Cracow Monuments (1st series).

2854	**819**	15z. black, olive & green	75	30
2855	-	25z. black, purple & mauve	1·30	45
MS2856		75×93 mm. 65z. green, purple and sepia (22×27 mm)	2·50	1·90

DESIGNS: 25z. Gateway of Collegium Iuridicum; 65z. Street plan of Old Cracow.

See also Nos. 2904/5, 2968/9; 3029/3, 3116 and 3153.

820 Bernard Wapowski Map, 1526

1982. Polish Maps.

2857	**820**	5z. multicoloured	20	10
2858	-	6z. brown, black and red	25	10
2859	-	8z. multicoloured	35	10
2860	-	25z. multicoloured	1·10	50

DESIGNS: 6z. Map of Prague, 1839; 8z. Map of Poland from Eugen Romer's Atlas, 1908; 25z. Plan of Cracow by A. Buchowiecki, 1703, and Astrolabe.

821 "The Last of the Resistance" (Artur Grottger)

1983. 120th Anniv of January Uprising.

2861	**821**	6z. brown	30	15

822 "Grand Theatre, Warsaw, 1838" (Maciej Zaleski)

1983. 150th Anniv of Grand Theatre, Warsaw.

2862	**822**	6z. multicoloured	30	15

823 Wild Flowers

1983. Environmental Protection. Multicoloured.

2863	5z. Type **823**	20	10
2864	6z. Mute swan and river fishes	35	15
2865	17z. Hoopoe and trees	95	50
2866	30z. Sea fishes	1·70	80
2867	31z. European bison and roe deer	1·80	90
2868	38z. Fruit	2·10	1·10

824 Karol Kurpinski (composer)

1983. Celebrities.

2869	**824**	5z. light brown and brown	25	10
2870	-	6z. purple and violet	30	10
2871	-	17z. light green and green	75	40
2872	-	25z. light brown and brown	1·00	50
2873	-	27z. light blue and blue	1·10	55
2874	-	31z. lilac and violet	1·60	70

DESIGNS: 6z. Maria Jasnorzewska Pawlikowska (poetess); 17z. Stanislaw Szober (linguist); 25z. Tadeusz Banachiewicz (astronomer and mathematician); 27z. Jaroslaw Iwaskiewicz (writer); 31z. Wladyslaw Tatarkiewicz (philosopher and historian).

825 3000 Metres Steeplechase

1983. Sports Achievements.

2875	**825**	5z. pink and violet	25	10

2876	-	6z. pink, brown and black	30	10
2877	-	15z. yellow and green	75	25
2878	-	27z.+5z. light blue, blue and black	1·50	65

DESIGNS: 6z. Show jumping; 1z. Football; 27z.+5z. Pole vault.

826 Ghetto Heroes Monument (Natan Rappaport)

1983. 40th Anniv of Warsaw Ghetto Uprising.

2879	**826**	6z. light brown & brown	30	15

827 Customs Officer and Suitcases

1983. 30th Anniv of Customs Co-operation Council.

2880	**827**	5z. multicoloured	20	10

828 John Paul II and Jasna Gora Sanctuary

1983. Papal Visit. Multicoloured.

2881		31z. Type **828**	1·80	65
2882		65z. Niepokalanow Church and John Paul holding crucifix	3·25	1·50
MS2883		107×81 mm. No. 2882	3·75	3·25

829 Dragoons

1983. 300th Anniv of Polish Relief of Vienna (1st issue). Troops of King Jan III Sobieski. Mult.

2884		5z. Type **829**	20	10
2885		5z. Armoured cavalryman	20	10
2886		6z. Infantry non-commissioned officer and musketeer	30	10
2887		15z. Light cavalry lieutenant	65	40
2888		27z. "Winged" hussar and trooper with carbine	1·50	75

See also Nos. 2893/6.

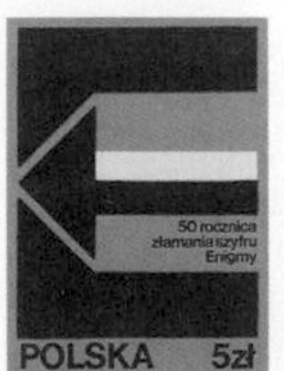

830 Arrow piercing "E"

1983. 50th Anniv of Deciphering "Enigma" Machine Codes.

2889	**830**	5z. red, grey and black	30	15

831 Torun

1983. 750th Anniv of Torun.

2890	**831**	6z. multicoloured	30	15
MS2891		142×116 mm. No. 2890 ×4	4·75	5·75

832 Child's Painting

1983. "Order of the Smile" (Politeness Publicity Campaign).

2892	**832**	6z. multicoloured	30	15

833 King Jan III Sobieski

1983. 300th Anniv of Relief of Vienna (2nd issue). Multicoloured.

2893		5z. Type **833**	25	15
2894		6z. King Jan III Sobieski (different)	30	20
2895		6z. "King Jan III Sobieski on Horseback" (Francesco Trevisani)	30	20
2896		25z. "King Jan III Sobieski" (Jerzy Eleuter)	1·60	50
MS2897		97×75 mm. 65z. +10z. "King Jan III Sobieski at Vienna" (Jan Matejko). Imperf	3·75	3·25

834 Wanda Wasilewska

1983. 40th Anniv of Polish People's Army. Multicoloured.

2898	**834**	5z. multicoloured	20	10
2899	-	5z. deep green, green and black	20	10
2900	-	6z. multicoloured	25	10
2901	-	6z. multicoloured	25	10

DESIGNS—VERT: No. 2899, General Zygmunt Berling; 2900, "The Frontier Post" (S. Poznanski). HORIZ: No. 2901, "Taking the Oath" (S. Poznanski).

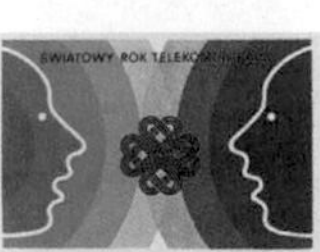

835 Profiles and W.C.Y. Emblem

1983. World Communications Year.

2902	**835**	15z. multicoloured	75	40

836 Boxing

1983. 60th Anniv of Polish Boxing Federation.

2903	**836**	6z. multicoloured	40	15

1983. Renovation of Cracow Monuments (2nd series). As T **819**.

2904		5z. brown, purple and black	15	10
2905		6z. black, green and blue	20	15

DESIGNS—HORIZ: 5z. Cloth Hall. VERT: 6z. Town Hall tower.

837 Biskupiec Costume

1983. Women's Folk Costumes. Multicoloured.

2906		5z. Type **837**	20	10
2907		5z. Rozbark	20	10
2908		6z. Warmia & Mazuria	30	10
2909		6z. Cieszyn	30	10
2910		25z. Kurpie	1·60	65
2911		38z. Lubusk	2·30	90

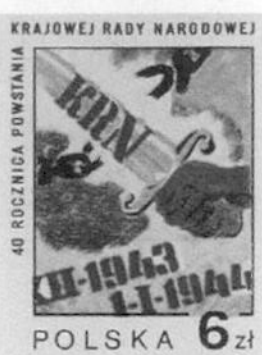

838 Hand with Sword (poster by Zakrzewski and Krolikowski, 1945)

1983. 40th Anniv of National People's Council.

2912	**838**	6z. multicoloured	25	10

839 Badge of "General Bem" Brigade

1983. 40th Anniv of People's Army.

2913	**839**	5z. multicoloured	30	10

840 Dulcimer

1984. Musical Instruments (1st series). Multicoloured.

2914		5z. Type **840**	25	10
2915		6z. Kettle drum and tambourine	30	15
2916		10z. Accordion	65	40
2917		15z. Double bass	95	50
2918		17z. Bagpipe	1·00	55
2919		29z. Country band (wood carvings by Tadeusz Zak)	1·80	80

841 Wincenty Witos

1984. 110th Birth Anniv of Wincenty Witos (leader of Peasants' Movement).

2920	**841**	6z. brown and green	30	10

842 "Clematis lanuginosa"

1984. Clematis. Multicoloured.

2921		5z. Type **842**	25	10
2922		6z. "C. tangutica"	30	1·30
2923		10z. "C. texensis"	65	25
2924		17z. "C. alpina"	1·00	40
2925		25z. "C. vitalba"	1·60	65
2926		27z. "C. montana"	1·70	70

843 "The Ecstasy of St. Francis" (El Greco)

1984. "Espana 84" International Stamp Exhibition, Madrid.

2927	**843**	27z. multicoloured	1·70	65

844 Handball

1984. Olympic Games, Los Angeles, and Winter Olympics, Sarajevo. Multicoloured.

2928		5z. Type **844**	25	10
2929		6z. Fencing	30	10
2930		15z. Cycling	85	30
2931		16z. Janusz Kusocinski winning 10,000 m race, 1932 Olympics, Los Angeles	95	40
2932		17z. Stanislawa Walasiewiczowna winning 100 m race, 1932 Olympics, Los Angeles	1·00	45
2933		31z. Women's slalom (Winter Olympics)	1·90	75
MS2934		129×78 mm. Nos. 2931/2	2·50	2·40

The 10z. premium on **MS**2934 was for the benefit of the Polish Olympic Committee.

845 Monte Cassino Memorial Cross and Monastery

1984. 40th Anniv of Battle of Monte Cassino.

2935	**845**	15z. olive and red	95	40

846 "German Princess" (Lucas Cranach)

1984. 19th U.P.U. Congress, Hamburg.

2936	**846**	27z.+10z. multicoloured	2·30	1·30

847 "Warsaw from the Praga Bank" (Canaletto)

1984. Paintings of Vistula River. Multicoloured.

2937		5z. Type **847**	25	25
2938		6z. "Trumpet Festivity" (A. Gierymski)	30	25
2939		25z. "The Vistula near Bielany District" (J. Rapacki)	1·60	75
2940		27z. "Steamship Harbour in the Powisle District" (F. Kostrzewski)	1·70	90

848 Order of Grunwald Cross

1984. 40th Anniv of Polish People's Republic. Multicoloured.

2941		5z. Type **848**	25	10
2942		6z. Order of Revival of Poland	30	15
2943		10z. Order of Banner of Labour, First Class	50	20
2944		16z. Order of Builders of People's Poland	1·00	40
MS2945		156×101 mm. Nos. 2941/4	7·25	7·50

849 Group of Insurgents

1984. 40th Anniv of Warsaw Uprising. Multicoloured.

2946	4z. Type **849**	25	10
2947	5z. Insurgent on postal duty	25	10
2948	6z. Insurgents fighting	30	15
2949	25z. Tending wounded	1·60	45

850 Defence of Oksywie Holm and Col. Stanislaw Dabek

1984. 45th Anniv of German Invasion. Multicoloured.

2950	5z. Type **850**	25	10
2951	6z. Battle of Bzura River and Gen. Tadeusz Kutrzeba	30	15

See also Nos. 3004/5, 3062, 3126/8, 3172/4 and 3240/3.

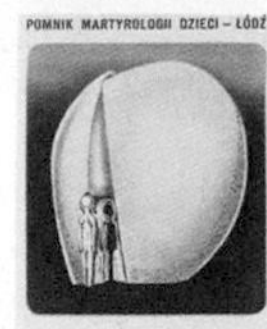

851 "Broken Heart" (monument, Lodz Concentration Camp)

1984. Child Martyrs.

2952	**851**	16z. brown, blue and deep brown	75	40

852 Militiaman and Ruins

1984. 40th Anniv of Security Force and Civil Militia. Multicoloured.

2953	5z. Type **852**	20	10
2954	6z. Militiaman in control centre	30	15

853 First Balloon Flight, 1784 (after Chostovski)

1984. Polish Aviation.

2955	**853**	5z. black, green & mauve	25	10
2956	-	5z. multicoloured	25	10
2957	-	6z. multicoloured	30	15
2958	-	10z. multicoloured	50	25
2959	-	16z. multicoloured	85	40
2960	-	27z. multicoloured	1·70	65
2961	-	31z. multicoloured	1·80	75

DESIGNS: No. 2956, Michal Scipio del Campo and biplane (1st flight over Warsaw, 1911); 2957, Balloon "Polonez" (winner, Gordon Bennett Cup, 1983); 2958, PWS 101 and Jantar gliders (Lilienthal Medal winners); 2959, PZL-104 Wilga airplane (world precise flight champion, 1983); 2960, Jan Nagorski and Farman M.F.7 floatplane (Arctic zone flights, 1914); 2961, PZL P-37 Los and PZL P-7 aircraft.

854 Weasel

1984. Fur-bearing Animals. Multicoloured.

2962	4z. Type **854**	10	10
2963	5z. Stoat	20	10
2964	5z. Beech marten	20	10
2965	10z. Eurasian beaver	30	15
2966	10z. Eurasian otter	30	15
2967	65z. Alpine marmot	2·75	90

1984. Renovation of Cracow Monuments (3rd series). As T **819**.

2968	5z. brown, black and green	20	10
2969	15z. blue, brown and black	50	25

DESIGNS—VERT: 5z. Wawel cathedral. HORIZ: 15z. Wawel castle (royal residence).

855 Protestant Church, Warsaw

1984. Religious Architecture. Multicoloured.

2970	5z. Type **855**	10	10
2971	10z. Saint Andrew's Roman Catholic church, Krakow	30	15
2972	15z. Greek Catholic church, Rychwald	50	25
2973	20z. St. Maria Magdalena Orthodox church, Warsaw	75	30
2974	25z. Tykocin synagogue, Kaczorow (horiz)	1·00	40
2975	31z. Tatar mosque, Kruszyiany (horiz)	1·30	45

856 Steam Fire Hose (late 19th century)

1985. Fire Engines. Multicoloured.

2976	4z. Type **856**	10	10
2977	10z. "Polski Fiat", 1930s	30	15
2978	12z. "Jelcz 315" fire engine	45	20
2979	15z. Manual fire hose, 1899	50	25
2980	20z. "Magirus" fire ladder on "Jelcz" chassis	75	40
2981	30z. Manual fire hose (early 18th century)	1·60	50

857 "Battle of Raclawice" (Jan Styka and Wojciech Kossak)

1985

2982	**857**	27z. multicoloured	1·00	50

858 Wincenty Rzymowski

1985. 35th Death Anniv of Wincenty Rzymowski (founder of Polish Democratic Party).

2983	**858**	10z. violet and red	40	20

859 Badge on Denim

1985. International Youth Year.

2984	**859**	15z. multicoloured	75	25

860 Boleslaw III, the Wry-mouthed, and Map

1985. 40th Anniv of Return of Western and Northern Territories to Poland. Multicoloured.

2985	5z. Type **860**	10	10
2986	10z. Wladyslaw Gomulka (vice-president of first postwar government) and map	40	20
2987	20z. Piotr Zaremba (Governor of Szczecin) and map	95	40

861 "Victory, Berlin 1945" (Joesf Mlynarski)

1985. 40th Anniv of Victory over Fascism.

2988	**861**	5z. multicoloured	25	20

862 Warsaw Arms and Flags of Member Countries

1985. 30th Anniv of Warsaw Pact.

2989	**862**	5z. multicoloured	25	20

863 Wolves in Winter

1985. Protected Animals. The Wolf. Multicoloured.

2990	5z. Type **863**	1·00	30
2991	10z. She-wolf with cubs	1·60	65
2992	10z. Close-up of wolf	1·60	65
2993	20z. Wolves in summer	3·25	1·90

1985. Musical Instruments (2nd series). As T **840**. Multicoloured.

2994	5z. Rattle and tarapata	20	10
2995	10z. Stick rattle and berlo	40	15
2996	12z. Clay whistles	50	20
2997	20z. Stringed instruments	95	40
2998	25z. Cow bells	1·10	50
2999	31z. Wind instruments	1·50	65

864 Cadet Ship "Iskra"

1985. 40th Anniv of Polish Navy.

3000	**864**	5z. blue and yellow	20	10

865 Tomasz Nocznicki

1985. Leaders of Peasants' Movement.

3001	**865**	10z. green	30	15
3002	-	20z. brown	75	30

DESIGN: 20z. Maciej Rataj.

866 Hockey Players

1985. 60th Anniv (1986) of Polish Field Hockey Association.

3003	**866**	5z. multicoloured	20	10

1985. 46th Anniv of German Invasion. As T **850**. Multicoloured.

3004	5z. Defence of Wizna and Capt. Wladyslaw Raginis	20	10
3005	10z. Battle of Mlawa and Col. Wilhelm Liszka-Lawicz	35	15

867 Type 20k Goods Wagon

1985. PAFAWAG Railway Rolling Stock. Multicoloured.

3006	5z. Type **867**	20	10
3007	10z. Electric locomotive No. ET22-001, 1969	30	15
3008	17z. Type OMMK wagon	65	30
3009	20z. Type 111A passenger carriage	75	40

868 "Madonna with Child St. John and Angel" (Sandro Botticelli)

1985. "Italia '85" International Stamp Exhibition, Rome. Sheet 81×108 mm.

MS3010	**868**	65z.+15z. multicoloured	4·25	3·75

869 Green-winged Teal

1985. Wild Ducks. Multicoloured.

3011	5z. Type **869**	20	10
3012	5z. Garganey	20	10
3013	10z. Tufted duck	50	20
3014	15z. Common goldeneye	75	30
3015	25z. Eider	1·00	40
3016	29z. Red-crested pochard	1·30	45

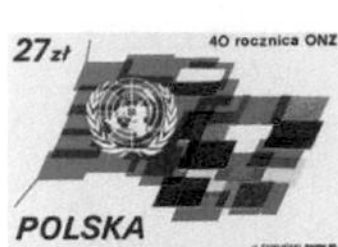

870 U.N. Emblem and "Flags"

1985. 40th Anniv of U.N.O.

3017	**870**	27z. multicoloured	1·00	50

871 Ballerina

1985. Bicentenary of Polish Ballet.

3018	**871**	5z. green, orange and red	20	10
3019	-	15z. brown, violet & orange	50	25

DESIGN: 15z. Male dancer.

872 "Marysia and Burek in Ceylon"

1985. Birth Centenary of Stanislaw Ignacy Witkiewicz (artist). Multicoloured.

3020	5z. Type **872**	20	10
3021	10z. "Woman with Fox" (horiz)	50	20
3022	10z. "Self-portrait"	50	20
3023	20z. "Compositions (1917–20)"	75	40
3024	25z. "Nena Stachurska"	1·00	50

873 Oliwa Church Organ and Bach

1985. 300th Birth Anniv of Johann Sebastian Bach (composer). Sheet 67×79 mm.

MS3025	**873**	65z. multicoloured	2·75	2·50

874 Human Profile

1986. Congress of Intellectuals for Defence of Peaceful Future of the World, Warsaw.

3026	**874**	10z. ultramarine, violet and blue	50	25

875 Michal Kamienski and Planetary and Comet's Orbits

1985. Appearance of Halley's Comet.

3027	**875**	25z. blue and brown	1·00	40
3028	-	25z. deep blue, blue and brown	1·00	40

DESIGN: No. 3028, "Vega", "Planet A", "Giotto" and "Ice" space probes and comet.

1986. Renovation of Cracow Monuments (4th series). As T **819**.

3029	5z. dp brown, brown & black	15	10
3030	10z. green, brown and black	30	15

DESIGNS: 5z. Collegium Maius (Jagiellonian University Museum); 10z. Kazimierz Town Hall.

876 Sun

1986. International Peace Year.

3031	**876**	25z. yellow, light blue and blue	75	40

877 Grey Partridge

1986. Game. Multicoloured.

3032	5z. Type **877**	10	10
3033	5z. Common rabbit	10	10
3034	10z. Common pheasants (horiz)	30	15
3035	10z. Fallow deer (horiz)	65	40
3036	20z. Hare	75	45
3037	40z. Argali	1·30	65

878 Kulczynski

1986. Tenth Death Anniv (1985) of Stanislaw Kulczynski (politician).

3038	**878**	10z. light brown and brown	30	15

879 "Warsaw Fire Brigade, 1871" (detail, Jozef Brodowski)

1986. 150th Anniv of Warsaw Fire Brigade.

3039	**879**	10z. dp brown & brown	30	15

880 Paderewski (composer)

1986. "Ameripex '86" International Stamp Exhibition, Chicago.

3040	**880**	65z. blue, black and grey	2·30	90

881 Footballers

1986. World Cup Football Championship, Mexico.

3041	**881**	25z. multicoloured	75	40

882 "Wilanow"

1986. Passenger Ferries. Multicoloured.

3042	10z. Type **882**	30	15
3043	10z. "Wawel"	30	15
3044	15z. "Pomerania"	50	25
3045	25z. "Rogalin"	75	30
MS3046	Two sheets, each 116×98 mm. (a) Nos. 3042/3 (sold at 30z.); (b) Nos. 3044/5 (sold at 55z.)	13·00	11·50

883 A. B. Dobrowolski, Map and Research Vessel "Kopernik"

1986. 25th Anniv of Antarctic Agreement.

3047	**883**	5z. green, black and red	20	20
3048	-	40z. lavender, violet and orange	2·00	50

DESIGN: 40z. H. Arctowski, map and research vessel "Profesor Siedlecki".

884 Workers and Emblem

1986. Tenth Polish United Workers' Party Congress, Warsaw.

3049	**884**	10z. blue and red	30	20

885 "The Paulinite Church on Skalka in Cracow" (detail), 1627

1986. Treasures of Jasna Gora Monastery. Multicoloured.

3050	5z. Type **885**	10	10
3051	5z. "Tree of Jesse", 17th-century	10	10
3052	20z. Chalice, 18th-century	1·70	65
3053	40z. "Virgin Mary" (detail, chasuble column), 15th-century	1·60	50

886 Precision Flying (Waclaw Nycz)

1986. 1985 Polish World Championship Successes. Multicoloured.

3054	5z. Type **886**	10	10
3055	10z. Windsurfing (Malgorzata Palasz-Piasecka)	30	15
3056	10z. Glider areobatics (Jerzy Makula)	30	15
3057	15z. Wrestling (Bogdan Daras)	50	25
3058	20z. Individual road cycling (Lech Piasecki)	75	40
3059	30z. Women's modern pentathlon (Barbara Kotowska)	1·00	50

887 "Bird" in National Costume carrying Stamp

1986. "Stockholmia '86" International Stamp Exhibition.

3060	**887**	65z. multicoloured	2·10	95
MS3061		94×80 mm. No. 3060	2·30	1·90

1986. 47th Anniv of German Invasion. As T **850**. Multicoloured.

3062	10z. Battle of Jordanow and Col. Stanislaw Maczek	30	20

888 Schweitzer

1986. Tenth Death Anniv (1985) of Albert Schweitzer (medical missionary).

3063	**888**	5z. brown, lt brown & blue	20	10

889 Airliner and Postal Messenger

1986. World Post Day.

3064	**889**	40z. brown, blue and red	1·30	65
MS3065		81×81 mm. No. 3064 ×2 (sold at 120z.)	16·00	14·50

890 Basilisk

1986. Folk Tales. Multicoloured.

3066	5z. Type **890**	20	20
3067	5z. Duke Popiel (vert)	20	20
3068	10z. Golden Duck	30	20
3069	10z. Boruta the Devil (vert)	30	20
3070	20z. Janosik the Robber (vert)	85	40
3071	50z. Lajkonik (vert)	1·80	65

891 Kotarbinski

892 20th-century Windmill, Zygmuntow

1986. Birth Centenary of Tadeusz Kotarbinski (philosopher).

3072	**891**	10z. deep brown and brown	30	15

1986. Wooden Architecture. Multicoloured.

3073	5z. Type **892**	20	10
3074	5z. 17th-century church, Baczal Dolny	20	10
3075	10z. 19th-century Oravian cottage, Zubrzyca Gorna	25	15
3076	15z. 18th-century Kashubian arcade cottage, Wdzydze	50	25
3077	25z. 19th-century barn, Grzawa	75	40
3078	30z. 19th-century watermill, Siolkowice Stare	1·00	65

893 Mieszko (Mieczyslaw) I

1986. Polish Rulers (1st series). Drawings by Jan Matejko.

3079	**893**	10z. brown and green	75	40
3080	-	25z. black and purple	1·30	90

DESIGN: 25z. Queen Dobrawa (wife of Mieszko I).

See also Nos. 3144/5, 3193/4, 3251/2, 3341/2, 3351/2, 3387/8, 3461/4, 3511/12, 3548/51, 3641/4, 3705/8, 3732/5, 3819/22 and 3887/91.

894 Star

1986. New Year.

3081	**894**	25z. multicoloured	85	45

895 Trip to Bielany, 1887

1986. Centenary of Warsaw Cyclists' Society.

3082	**895**	5z. multicoloured	20	15
3083	-	5z. brown, light brown and black	20	15
3084	-	10z. multicoloured	30	20
3085	-	10z. multicoloured	30	20
3086	-	30z. multicoloured	1·00	50
3087	-	50z. multicoloured	1·60	65

DESIGNS — VERT: No. 3083, Jan Stanislaw Skrodaki (1895 touring record holder); 3084, Dynasy (Society's headquarters, 1892–1937); 3085, Mieczyslaw Baranski (1896 Kingdom of Poland road cycling champion); 3086, Karolina Kociecka; 3087, Henryk Weiss (Race champion).

896 Lelewel

1986. Birth Bicentenary of Joachim Lelewel (historian).

3088	**896**	10z.+5z. multicoloured	50	25

897 Krill and "Antoni Garnuszewski" (cadet freighter)

1987. Tenth Anniv of Henryk Arctowski Antarctic Station, King George Island, South Shetlands. Multicoloured.

3089	5z. Type **897**	20	10
3090	5z. Antarctic toothfish, marbled rockfish and "Zulawy" (supply ship)	20	10
3091	10z. Southern fulmar and "Pogoria" (cadet brigantine)	30	15
3092	10z. Adelie penguin and "Gedania" (yacht)	30	15
3093	30z. Fur seal and "Dziunia" (research vessel)	75	40
3094	40z. Leopard seals and "Kapitan Ledochowski" (research vessel)	1·00	50

898 "Portrait of a Woman"

1987. 50th Death Anniv (1986) of Leon Wyczolkowski (artist). Multicoloured.

3095 5z. "Cineraria Flowers" (horiz) 10 10
3096 10z. Type **898** 20 10
3097 10z. "Wooden Church" (horiz) 20 10
3098 25z. "Beetroot Lifting" 50 30
3099 30z. "Wading Fishermen" (horiz) 65 40
3100 40z. "Self-portrait" (horiz) 85 50

899 "Ravage" (from "War Cycle") and Artur Grottger

1987. 150th Birth Anniv of Artur Grottger (artist).
3101 **899** 15z. brown and stone 30 15

900 Swierczewski

1987. 90th Birth Anniv of General Karol Swierczewski.
3102 **900** 15z. green and olive 30 15

901 Strzelecki

1987. 190th Birth Anniv of Pawel Edmund Strzelecki (scientist and explorer of Tasmania).
3103 **901** 65z. green 1·10 80

902 Emblem and Banner

1987. Second Patriotic Movement for National Revival Congress.
3104 **902** 10z. red, blue and brown 25 10

903 CWS "T-1" Motor Car, 1928

1987. Polish Motor Vehicles. Multicoloured.

3105 10z. Type **903** 10 10
3106 10z. Saurer-Zawrat bus, 1936 10 10
3107 15z. Ursus-A lorry, 1928 30 15
3108 15z. Lux-Sport motor car, 1936 30 15
3109 25z. Podkowa "100" motor cycle, 1939 50 30
3110 45z. Sokol "600 RT" motor cycle, 1935 1·00 65

904 Royal Palace, Warsaw

1987
3111 **904** 50z. multicoloured 1·00 65

905 Pope John Paul II

1987. Third Papal Visit. Multicoloured.

3112 15z. Type **905** 30 20
3113 45z. Pope and signature 95 55
MS3114 77×66 mm. 50z. Profile of Pope (21×27 mm) 1·60 1·30

906 Polish Settler at Kasubia, Ontario

1987. "Capex '87" International Stamp Exhibition, Toronto.
3115 **906** 50z.+20z. multicoloured 1·50 90

1987. Renovation of Cracow Monuments (5th series). As T **819**.
3116 10z. lilac, black and green 25 10
DESIGN: 10z. Barbican.

907 Ludwig Zamenhof (inventor) and Star

1987. Cent of Esperanto (invented language).
3117 **907** 5z. brown, green & black 1·00 50

908 "Poznan Town Hall" (Stanislaw Wyspianski)

1987. "Poznan 87" National Stamp Exhibition.
3118 **908** 15z. brown and orange 30 15

909 Queen Bee

1987. "Apimondia 87" International Bee Keeping Congress, Warsaw. Multicoloured.

3119 10z. Type **909** 20 10
3120 10z. Worker bee 20 10
3121 15z. Drone 30 15
3122 15z. Hive in orchard 30 15
3123 40z. Worker bee on clover flower 85 45
3124 50z. Forest bee keeper collecting honey 1·10 55

910 1984 Olympic Stamp and Laurel Wreath

1987. "Olymphilex '87" Olympic Stamps Exhibition, Rome. Sheet 83×57 mm.
MS3125 **910** 45z.+10z. multicoloured 1·60 1·50
The premium was for the benefit of the Polish Olympic Committee's fund.

1987. 48th Anniv of German Invasion. As T **850**. Multicoloured.

3126 10z. Battle of Mokra and Col. Julian Filipowicz 20 10
3127 10z. Fighting at Oleszyce and Brig.-Gen. Jozef Rudolf Kustron 20 10
3128 15z. PZL P-7 aircraft over Warsaw and Col. Stefan Pawlikowski 50 25

911 Hevelius and Sextant

1987. 300th Death Anniv of Jan Hevelius (astronomer). Multicoloured.

3129 15z. Type **911** 30 15
3130 40z. Hevelius and map of constellations (horiz) 85 45

912 High Jump (World Acrobatics Championships, France)

1987. 1986 Polish World Championship Successes. Multicoloured.

3131 10z. Type **912** 20 10
3132 15z. Two-man canoe (World Canoeing Championships, Canada) 30 15
3133 20z. Marksman (Free pistol event, World Marksmanship Championships, East Germany) 40 20
3134 25z. Wrestlers (World Wrestling Championships, Hungary) 50 25

913 "Stacionar 4" Telecommunications Satellite

1987. 30th Anniv of launch of "Sputnik 1" (first artificial satellite). Sheet 67×82 mm.
MS3135 **913** 40z. multicoloured 1·60 1·30

914 Warsaw Post Office and Ignacy Franciszek Przebendowski (Postmaster General)

1987. World Post Day.
3136 **914** 15z. green and red 30 15

915 "The Little Mermaid"

1987. "Hafnia 87" International Stamp Exhibition, Copenhagen. Hans Christian Andersen's Fairy Tales. Multicoloured.

3137 10z. Type **915** 20 10
3138 10z. "The Nightingale" 20 10
3139 20z. "The Wild Swans" 40 15
3140 20z. "The Little Match Girl" 40 15
3141 30z. "The Snow Queen" 65 40
3142 40z. "The Tin Soldier" 85 50

916 Col. Stanislaw Wieckowski (founder)

1987. 50th Anniv of Democratic Clubs.
3143 **916** 15z. black and blue 30 15

1987. Polish Rulers (2nd series). As T **893**. Drawings by Jan Matejko.

3144 10z. green and blue 30 15
3145 15z. blue and ultramarine 50 40
DESIGNS: 10z. Boleslaw I, the Brave; 15z. Mieszko (Mieczyslaw) II.

917 Santa Claus with Christmas Trees

1987. New Year.
3146 **917** 15z. multicoloured 30 15

918 Emperor Dragonfly

1988. Dragonflies. Multicoloured.

3147 10z. Type **918** 20 10
3148 15z. Four-spotted libellula ("Libellula quadrimaculata") (vert) 30 15
3149 15z. Banded agrion ("Calopteryx splendens") 30 15
3150 20z. "Condulegaster annulatus" (vert) 40 20
3151 30z. "Sympetrum pedemontanum" 65 30
3152 50z. "Aeschna viridis" (vert) 1·10 55

1988. Renovation of Cracow Monuments (6th series). As T **819**.
3153 15z. yellow, brown and black 25 10
DESIGN: 15z. Florianska Gate.

919 Composition

1988. International Year of Graphic Design.
3154 **919** 40z. multicoloured 65 50

920 17th-century Friesian Wall Clock with Bracket Case

1988. Clocks and Watches. Multicoloured.

3155 10z. Type **920** 20 10
3156 10z. 20th-century annual clock (horiz) 20 10
3157 15z. 18th-century carriage clock 25 15
3158 15z. 18th-century French rococo bracket clock 25 15
3159 20z. 19th-century pocket watch (horiz) 30 20
3160 40z. 17th-cent tile-case clock from Gdansk by Benjamin Zoll (horiz) 75 40

921 Atlantic Salmon and Reindeer

1988. "Finlandia 88" International Stamp Exhibition, Helsinki.

3161	**921**	45z.+30z. multicoloured	1·30	80

922 Triple Jump

1988. Olympic Games, Seoul. Multicoloured.

3162	15z. Type **922**	25	15
3163	20z. Wrestling	30	15
3164	20z. Canoeing	30	15
3165	25z. Judo	35	15
3166	40z. Shooting	65	20
3167	55z. Swimming	85	40

923 Kukuczka

1988. Award of Special Olympic Silver Medal to Jerzy Kukuczka for Mountaineering Achievements. Sheet 84×66 mm.

MS3168 **923**	70z.+10z. multicoloured	1·60	1·50

924 Wheat as Graph on VDU

1988. 16th European Conference of Food and Agriculture Organization, Cracow. Multicoloured.

3169	15z. Type **924**	25	15
3170	40z. Factory in forest	65	40

925 PZL P-37 Los Bomber

1988. 70th Anniv of Polish Republic (1st issue). 60th Anniv of Polish State Aircraft Works.

3171	**925**	45z. multicoloured	80	50

See also Nos. 3175, 3177, 3181/88 and 3190/2.

1988. 49th Anniv of German Invasion. As T **850**. Multicoloured.

3172	15z. Battle of Modlin and Brig.-Gen. Wiktor Thommee	40	15
3173	20z. Battle of Warsaw and Brig.-Gen. Walerian Czuma	50	20
3174	20z. Battle of Tomaszow Lubelski and Brig.-Gen. Antoni Szylling	50	20

1988. 70th Anniv of Polish Republic (2nd issue). 50th Anniv of Stalowa Wola Ironworks. As T 925. Multicoloured.

3175	15z. View of plant	25	15

926 Postal Emblem and Tomasz Arciszewski (Postal Minister, 1918–19)

1988. World Post Day.

3176	**926**	20z. multicoloured	25	15

1988. 70th Anniv of Polish Republic (3rd issue). 60th Anniv of Military Institute for Aviation Medicine. As T **925**. Multicoloured.

3177	20z. Hanriot XIV hospital aircraft (38×28 mm)	25	15

927 On the Field of Glory Medal

1988. Polish People's Army Battle Medals (1st series). Multicoloured.

3178	20z. Type **927**	30	15
3179	20z. Battle of Lenino Cross	30	15

See also Nos. 3249/50.

928 "Stanislaw Malachowski" and "Kazimierz Nestor Sapieha"

1988. Bicentenary of Four Years Diet (political and social reforms). Paintings of Diet Presidents by Jozef Peszko.

3180	**928**	20z. multicoloured	25	10

929 Ignacy Daszynski (politician)

1988. 70th Anniv of Polish Republic (4th issue). Personalities.

3181	**929**	15z. green, red and black	20	10
3182	-	15z. green, red and black	20	10
3183	-	20z. brown, red and black	25	15
3184	-	20z. brown, red and black	25	15
3185	-	20z. brown, red and black	25	15
3186	-	200z. purple, red & black	2·30	1·30
3187	-	200z. purple, red & black	2·30	1·30
3188	-	200z. purple, red & black	2·30	1·30
MS3189		102×60 mm. Nos. 3186/8	32·00	32·00

DESIGNS: No. 3182, Wincenty Witos (politician); 3183, Julian Marchlewski (trade unionist and economist); 3184, Stanislaw Wojciechowski (politician); 3185, Wojciech Korfanty (politician); 3186, Ignacy Paderewski (musician and politician); 3187; Marshal Jozef Pilsudski; 3188, Gabriel Narutowicz (President, 1922).

1988. 70th Anniv of Polish Republic (5th issue). As T **925**. Multicoloured.

3190	15z. Coal wharf, Gdynia Port (65th anniv) (38×28 mm)	30	15
3191	20z. Hipolit Cegielski (founder) and steam locomotive (142nd anniv of H. Cegielski Metal Works, Poznan) (38×28 mm)	40	25
3192	40z. Upper Silesia Tower (main entrance) (60th anniv of International Poznan Fair)	85	50

1988. Polish Rulers (3rd series). Drawings by Jan Matejko. As T **893**.

3193	10z. deep brown and brown	50	40
3194	15z. deep brown and brown	75	65

DESIGNS: 10z. Queen Rycheza; 15z. Kazimierz (Karol Odnowiciel) I.

930 Snowman

1988. New Year.

3195	**930**	20z. multicoloured	30	15

931 Flag

1988. 40th Anniv of Polish United Workers' Party.

3196	**931**	20z. red and black	30	15

932 "Blysk"

1988. Fire Boats. Multicoloured.

3197	10z. Type **932**	20	10
3198	15z. "Plomien"	25	10
3199	15z. "Zar"	25	10
3200	20z. "Strazak II"	30	15
3201	20z. "Strazak 4"	30	15
3202	45z. "Strazak 25"	80	50

933 Ardennes

1989. Horses. Multicoloured.

3203	15z. Lippizaner (horiz)	20	10
3204	15z. Type **933**	20	10
3205	20z. English thoroughbred (horiz)	35	20
3206	20z. Arab	35	20
3207	30z. Great Poland race-horse (horiz)	55	30
3208	70z. Polish horse	1·00	55

934 Wire-haired Dachshund

1989. Hunting Dogs. Multicoloured.

3209	15z. Type **934**	15	10
3210	15z. Cocker spaniel	15	10
3211	20z. Czech fousek pointer	20	10
3212	20z. Welsh terrier	20	10
3213	25z. English setter	25	15
3214	45z. Pointer	65	45

935 Gen. Wladyslaw Anders and Plan of Battle

1989. 45th Anniv of Battle of Monte Cassino.

3215	**935**	80z. multicoloured	65	65

See also Nos. 3227, 3247, 3287 and 3327.

936 Marianne

1989. Bicentenary of French Revolution.

3216	**936**	100z. black, red and blue	75	40
MS3217		93×118 mm. No. 3216 ×2 plus two labels (sold at 270z.)	2·10	1·90

937 Polonia House

1989. Opening of Polonia House (cultural centre), Pultusk.

3218	**937**	100z. multicoloured	75	40

938 Monument (Bohdan Chmielewski)

1989. 45th Anniv of Civic Militia and Security Force.

3219	**938**	35z. blue and brown	35	20

939 Xaweri Dunikowski (artist)

1989. Recipients of Order of Builders of the Republic of Poland. Multicoloured.

3220	35z. Type **939**	25	15
3221	35z. Stanislaw Mazur (farmer)	25	15
3222	35z. Natalia Gasiorowska (historian)	25	15
3223	35z. Wincenti Pstrowski (initiator of worker performance contests)	25	15

940 Astronaut

1989. 20th Anniv of First Manned Landing on Moon.

3224	**940**	100z. multicoloured	75	40
MS3225		85×85 mm. No. 3224	4·25	3·25

941 Firemen

1989. World Fire Fighting Congress, Warsaw.

3226	**941**	80z. multicoloured	55	40

1989. 45th Anniv of Battle of Falaise. As T **935**. Multicoloured.

3227	165z. Plan of battle and Gen. Stanislaw Maczek (horiz)	1·00	65

942 Daisy

1989. Plants. (a) Perf.

3229	**942**	40z. green	20	10
3230	-	60z. violet	40	15
3231	**942**	150z. red	50	25
3232	-	500z. mauve	75	40
3233	-	700z. green	20	10
3234	-	1000z. blue	1·60	65

(b) Self-adhesive. Imperf.

3297	2000z. green	1·10	70
3298	5000z. violet	1·60	1·20

DESIGNS: 60z. Juniper; 500z. Wild rose; 700z. Lily of the valley; 1000z. Blue cornflower; 2000z. Water lily; 5000z. Iris.

1989. 50th Anniv of German Invasion. As T **850**.

3240	25z. grey, orange and black	40	15
3241	25z. multicoloured	40	15
3242	35z. multicoloured	65	40
3243	35z. multicoloured	65	40

DESIGNS: No. 3240, Defence of Westerplatte and Captain Franciszek Dabrowski; 3241, Defence of Hel and Captain B. Przybyszewski; 3242, Battle of Kock and Brig.-Gen. Franciszek Kleeberg; 3243, Defence of Lwow and Brig.-Gen. Wladyslaw Langner.

943 Museum Emblem

1989. Caricature Museum.

3244	**943**	40z. multicoloured	25	15

944 Rafal Czerwiakowski (founder of first university Surgery Department)

1989. Polish Surgeons' Society Centenary Congress, Cracow.

3245	**944**	40z. blue and black	20	10
3246	-	60z. green and black	40	20

DESIGN: 60z. Ludwik Rydygier (founder of Polish Surgeons' Society).

1989. 45th Anniv of Landing at Arnhem. As T **935**. Multicoloured.

3247	210z. Gen. Stanislaw Sosabowski and plan of battle	1·30	75

945 Emil Kalinski (Postal Minister, 1933–39)

1989. World Post Day.

3248	**945**	60z. multicoloured	50	40

1989. Polish People's Army Battle Medals (2nd series). As T **927**. Multicoloured.

3249	60z. "For Participation in the Struggle for the Rule of the People"	30	20
3250	60z. Warsaw 1939–45 Medal	30	20

1989. Polish Rulers (4th series). As T **893**. Drawings by Jan Matejko.

3251	20z. black and grey	30	20
3252	30z. sepia and brown	65	40

DESIGNS: 20z. Boleslaw II, the Bold; 30z. Wladyslaw I Herman.

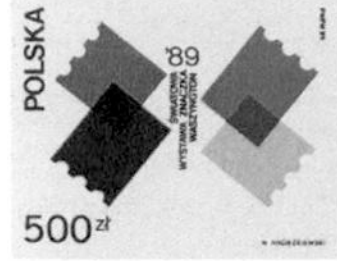

946 Stamps

1989. "World Stamp Expo '89" International Stamp Exhibition, Washington D.C.

3253	**946**	500z. multicoloured	1·80	1·30

947 Cross and Twig

1989. 70th Anniv of Polish Red Cross.

3254	**947**	200z. red, green and black	80	40

948 Ignacy Paderewski and Roman Dmowski (Polish signatories)

1989. 70th Anniv of Treaty of Versailles.

3255	**948**	350z. multicoloured	1·30	65

949 Photographer and Medal depicting Maksymilian Strasz

1989. 150th Anniv of Photography. Multicoloured.

3256		40z. Type **949**	20	10
3257		60z. Lens shutter as pupil of eye (horiz)	40	15

1989. No. 2729 surch **500**.

3258	500z. on 4z. violet	1·60	90

951 Painting by Jan Ciaglinski

1989. Flower Paintings by Artists Named. Multicoloured.

3259	25z. Type **951**	10	10
3260	30z. Wojciech Weiss	10	10
3261	35z. Antoni Kolasinski	20	10
3262	50z. Stefan Nacht-Samborski	20	10
3263	60z. Jozef Pankiewicz	20	10
3264	85z. Henryka Beyer	30	15
3265	110z. Wladyslaw Slewinski	40	25
3266	190z. Czeslaw Wdowiszewski	65	40

952 Christ

1989. Icons (1st series). Multicoloured.

3267	50z. Type **952**	20	10
3268	60z. Two saints with books	20	10
3269	90z. Three saints with books	25	15
3270	150z. Displaying scriptures (vert)	45	30
3271	200z. Madonna and child (vert)	65	40
3272	350z. Christ with saints and angels (vert)	1·30	65

See also Nos. 3345/50.

1990. No. 2839 surch **350 zl**.

3273	350z. on 15z. brown	1·00	65

954 Krystyna Jamroz

1990. Singers. Multicoloured.

3274	100z. Type **954**	20	10
3275	150z. Wanda Werminska	35	15
3276	350z. Ada Sari	55	25
3277	500z. Jan Kiepura	75	40

955 High Jumping

1990. Sports. Multicoloured.

3278	100z. Yachting	20	15
3279	200z. Rugby	20	15
3280	400z. Type **955**	20	15
3281	500z. Ice skating	45	25
3282	500z. Diving	45	25
3283	1000z. Gymnastics	75	40

956 Kozlowski

1990. Birth Centenary (1989) of Roman Kozlowski (palaeontologist).

3284	**956**	500z. brown and red	35	20

957 John Paul II

1990. 70th Birthday of Pope John Paul II.

3285	**957**	1000z. multicoloured	60	35

958 1860 10k. Stamp and Anniversary Stamp

1990. 130th Anniv of First Polish Postage Stamp. Sheet 65×68 mm.

MS3286	**958**	1000z. orange and blue	1·60	1·30

1990. 50th Anniv of Battle of Narvik. As T **935**. Multicoloured.

3287	1500z. Gen. Zygmunt Bohusz-Szyszko and plan of battle	75	40

959 Ball and Colosseum

1990. World Cup Football Championship, Italy.

3288	**959**	1000z. multicoloured	65	40

1990. No. 3230 surch **700 zl**.

3289	700z. on 60z. violet	45	20

961 Memorial

1990. 34th Anniv of 1956 Poznan Uprising.

3290	**961**	1500z. multicoloured	75	40

962 People and "ZUS"

1990. 70th Anniv of Social Insurance.

3291	**962**	1500z. blue, mauve & yellow	80	45

963 Stagnant Pond Snail

1990. Shells. No value expressed.

3292	-	B (500z.) lilac	40	15
3293	**963**	A (700z.) green	55	25

DESIGN: B, River snail.

964 Cross

1990. 50th Anniv of Katyn Massacre.

3294	**964**	1500z. black and red	80	45

965 Weather Balloon

1990. Polish Hydrology and Meteorology Service. Multicoloured.

3295	500z. Type **965**	25	15
3296	700z. Water-height gauge	45	20

966 Women's Kayak Pairs

1990. 23rd World Canoeing Championships. Multicoloured.

3305	700z. Type **966**	45	20
3306	1000z. Men's kayak singles	65	40

967 Victory Sign

1990. Tenth Anniv of Solidarity Trade Union.

3307	**967**	1500z. grey, black and red	80	45

968 Jacob's Ladder

1990. Flowers. Multicoloured.

3308	200z. Type **968**	20	10
3309	700z. Floating heart water fringe ("Nymphoides peltata")	40	20
3310	700z. Dragonhead ("Dracocephalum ruyschiana")	40	20
3311	1000z. "Helleborus purpurascens"	60	35
3312	1500z. Daphne cneorum	85	40
3313	1700z. Campion	1·00	50

969 Serving Dish, 1870–87

1990. Bicentenary of Cmieow Porcelain Works. Multicoloured.

3314	700z. Type **969**	15	10
3315	800z. Plate, 1887–90 (vert)	25	10
3316	1000z. Cup and saucer, 1887	50	15
3317	1000z. Figurine of dancer, 1941–44 (vert)	50	15
3318	1500z. Chocolate box, 1930–90	80	50
3319	2000z. Vase, 1979 (vert)	1·40	80

970 Little Owl

1990. Owls. Multicoloured.

3320	200z. Type **970**	20	10
3321	500z. Tawny owl (value at left)	40	20
3322	500z. Tawny owl (value at right)	40	20
3323	1000z. Short-eared owl	75	35
3324	1500z. Long-eared owl	1·10	65
3325	2000z. Barn owl	1·50	90

971 Walesa

1990. Lech Walesa, 1984 Nobel Peace Prize Winner and new President.

3326 **971** 1700z. multicoloured 1·10 60

1990. 50th Anniv of Battle of Britain. As T **935**. Multicoloured.

3327 1500z. Emblem of 303 Squadron, Polish Fighter Wing R.A.F. and Hawker Hurricane 80 65

972 Collegiate Church, Tum (12th century)

1990. Historic Architecture. Multicoloured.

3328 700z. Type **972** 40 20

3329 800z. Reszel Castle (11th century) 45 25

3330 1500z. Chelmno Town Hall (16th century) 85 40

3331 1700z. Church of the Nuns of the Visitation, Warsaw (18th century) 1·30 65

973 "King Zygmunt II August" (anon)

1991. Paintings. Multicoloured.

3332 500z. Type **973** 20 10

3333 700z. "Adoration of the Magi" (Pultusk Codex) 35 15

3334 1000z. "St Matthew" (Pultusk Codex) 40 20

3335 1500z. "Expelling of Merchants from Temple" (Nikolai Haberschrack) 65 35

3336 1700z. "The Annunciation" (miniature) 75 40

3337 2000z. "Three Marys" (Nikolai Haberschrack) 1·10 65

974 Silver Fir

1991. Cones. Multicoloured.

3338 700z. Type **974** 20 10

3339 1500z. Weymouth pine 55 25

See also Nos. 3483/4.

975 Radziwill Palace

1991. Admission of Poland into European Postal and Telecommunications Conference.

3340 **975** 1500z. multicoloured 95 50

1991. Polish Rulers (5th series). Drawings by Jan Matejko. As T **893** but surch.

3341 1000z. on 40z. black & green 75 40

3342 1500z. on 50z. black and red 1·00 85

DESIGNS: 1000z. Boleslaw III, the Wry Mouthed; 1500z. Wladyslaw II, the Exile.

Nos. 3341/2 were not issued unsurcharged.

977 Chmielowski

1991. 75th Death Anniv of Adam Chmielowski ("Brother Albert") (founder of Albertine Sisters).

3343 **977** 2000z. multicoloured 60 35

978 Battle (detail of miniature, Schlackenwerth Codex, 1350)

1991. 750th Anniv of Battle of Legnica.

3344 **978** 1500z. multicoloured 1·20 70

1991. Icons (2nd series). As T **952**. Multicoloured.

3345 500z. "Madonna of Nazareth" 20 10

3346 700z. "Christ the Acheirophyte" 30 15

3347 1000z. "Madonna of Vladimir" 45 30

3348 1500z. "Madonna of Kazan" 75 35

3349 2000z. "St. John the Baptist" 1·20 40

3350 2200z. "Christ the Pentocrator" 1·30 70

1991. Polish Rulers (6th series). Drawings by Jan Matejko. As T **893**.

3351 1000z. black and red 75 40

3352 1500z. black and blue 95 85

DESIGNS: 1000z. Boleslaw IV, the Curly; 1500z. Mieszko (Mieczyslaw) III, the Old.

979 Title Page of Constitution

1991. Bicentenary of 3rd May Constitution.

3353 **979** 2000z. brown, buff & red 85 40

3354 - 2500z. brown, stone & red 95 70

MS3355 85×85 mm. 3000z. multicoloured 1·80 1·70

DESIGNS: 2500z. "Administration of Oath by Gustav Taubert" (detail, Johann Friedrich Bolt); 3000z. "Constitution, 3 May 1791" (Jan Matejko).

980 Satellite in Earth Orbit

1991. Europa. Europe in Space.

3356 **980** 1000z. multicoloured 3·00 70

981 Map and Battle Scene

1991. 50th Anniv of Participation of "Piorun" (destroyer) in Operation against "Bismarck" (German battleship).

3357 **981** 2000z. multicoloured 85 40

982 Arms of Cracow

1991. European Security and Co-operation Conference Cultural Heritage Symposium, Cracow.

3358 **982** 2000z. purple and blue 1·20 70

983 Pope John Paul II

1991. Papal Visit. Multicoloured.

3359 1000z. Type **983** 50 30

3360 2000z. Pope in white robes 1·20 40

984 Bearded Penguin

1991. 30th Anniv of Antarctic Treaty.

3361 **984** 2000z. multicoloured 85 40

985 Making Paper

1991. 500th Anniv of Paper Making in Poland.

3362 **985** 2500z. blue and red 90 40

986 Prisoner

1991. Commemoration of Victims of Stalin's Purges.

3363 **986** 2500z. red and black 80 40

987 Pope John Paul II

1991. Sixth World Youth Day, Czestochowa. Sheet 70×87 mm.

MS3364 **987** 3500z. multicoloured 1·80 1·70

988 Ball and Basket

1991. Centenary of Basketball.

3365 **988** 2500z. multicoloured 85 40

989 "Self-portrait" (Leon Wyczolkowski)

1991. "Bydgoszcz '91" National Stamp Exn.

3366 **989** 3000z. green and brown 95 70

MS3367 155×92 mm. No. 3366 ×4 4·75 5·00

990 Twardowski

1991. 125th Birth Anniv of Kazimierz Twardowski (philosopher).

3368 **990** 2500z. black and grey 1·20 70

991 Swallowtail

1991. Butterflies and Moths. Multicoloured.

3369 1000z. Type **991** 25 15

3370 1000z. Dark crimson underwing ("Mormonia sponsa") 25 15

3371 1500z. Painted lady ("Vanessa cardui") 35 20

3372 1500z. Scarce swallowtail ("Iphiclides podalirius") 35 20

3373 2500z. Scarlet tiger moth ("Panaxia dominula") 85 40

3374 2500z. Peacock ("Nymphalis io") 85 40

MS3375 127×63 mm. 15000z. Black-veined white (*Aporia crataegi*) (46×33 mm) plus label for "Phila Nippon '91" International Stamp Exhibition 4·75 4·50

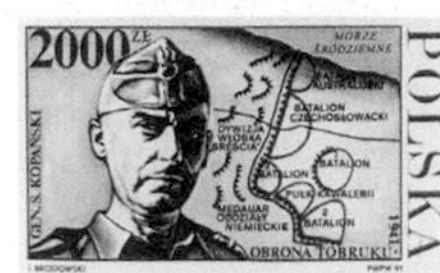

992 "The Shepherd's Bow" (Francesco Solimena)

1991. Christmas.

3376 **992** 1000z. multicoloured 60 30

993 Gen. Stanislaw Kopanski and Battle Map

1991. 50th Anniv of Participation of Polish Troops in Battle of Tobruk.

3377 **993** 2000z. multicoloured 1·20 70

994 Brig.-Gen. Michal Tokarzewski-Karaszewicz

1991. World War II Polish Underground Army Commanders.

3378 **994** 2000z. black and red 85 40

3379 - 2500z. red and violet 1·20 70

3380 - 3000z. violet and mauve 1·50 85

3381 - 5000z. brown and green 2·10 1·40

3382 - 6500z. dp brown & brn 2·75 1·70

DESIGNS: 2500z. Gen. Broni Kazimierz Sosnkowski; 3000z. Lt.-Gen. Stefan Rowecki; 5000z. Lt.-Gen. Tadeusz Komorowski; 6500z. Brig.-Gen. Leopold Okulicki.

995 Lord Baden-Powell (founder)

1991. 80th Anniv of Scout Movement in Poland.

3383 **995** 1500z. yellow and green 60 30

3384 - 2000z. blue and yellow 75 40

3385 - 2500z. violet and yellow 85 50

3386 - 3500z. brown and yellow 1·50 85

DESIGNS: 2000z. Andrzej Malkowski (Polish founder); 2500z. "Watch on the Vistula" (Wojciech Kossak); 3500z. Polish scout in Warsaw Uprising, 1944.

1992. Polish Rulers (7th series). As T **893**.

3387 1500z. brown and green 75 40

3388 2000z. black and blue 95 85

DESIGNS: 1500z. Kazimierz II, the Just; 2000z. Leszek I, the White.

996 Sebastien Bourdon

1992. Self-portraits. Multicoloured.

3389	700z. Type **996**	25	15
3390	1000z. Sir Joshua Reynolds	35	20
3391	1500z. Sir Godfrey Kneller	60	30
3392	2000z. Bartolome Esteban Murillo	75	35
3393	2200z. Peter Paul Rubens	85	40
3394	3000z. Diego de Silva y Velazquez	1·20	70

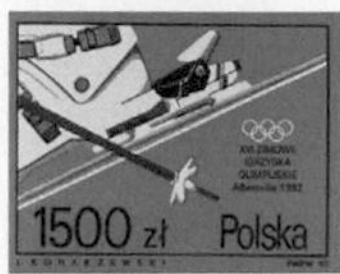

997 Skiing

1992. Winter Olympic Games, Albertville. Multicoloured.

3395	1500z. Type **997**	60	30
3396	2500z. Ice hockey	85	50

998 Manteuffel

1992. 90th Birth Anniv of Tadeusz Manteuffel (historian).

3397	**998**	2500z. brown	85	40

999 Nicolas Copernicus (astronomer)

1992. Famous Poles. Multicoloured.

3398	1500z. Type **999**	35	15
3399	2000z. Frederic Chopin (composer)	60	40
3400	2500z. Henryk Sienkiewicz (writer)	75	70
3401	3500z. Marie Curie (physicist)	1·20	85
MS3402	80×81 mm. 5000z. Kazimierz Funk (biochemist)	2·40	2·10

1000 Columbus and Left-hand Detail of Map

1992. Europa. 500th Anniv of Discovery of America by Columbus. Multicoloured.

3403	1500z. Type **1000**	45	15
3404	3000z. "Santa Maria" and right-hand detail of Juan de la Costa map, 1500	1·10	70

Nos. 3403/4 were issued together, se-tenant, forming a composite design.

1001 River Czarna Wiselka

1992. Environmental Protection. River Cascades. Multicoloured.

3405	2000z. Type **1001**	35	15
3406	2500z. River Swider	75	30
3407	3000z. River Tanew	95	40
3408	3500z. Mickiewicz waterfall	1·30	70

1002 Prince Jozef Poniatowski

1992. Bicentenary of Order of Military Virtue. Multicoloured.

3409	1500z. Type **1002**	35	15
3410	3000z. Marshal Jozef Pilsudski	60	30
MS3411	108×93 mm. 20000z. "Virgin Mary of Czestochowa" (icon) (36×57 mm)	6·00	5·75

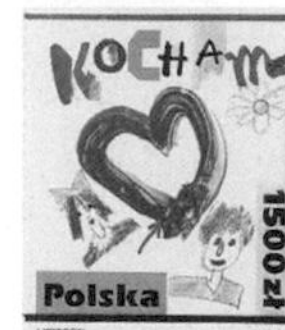

1003 Family and Heart

1992. Children's Drawings. Multicoloured.

3412	1500z. Type **1003**	35	15
3413	3000z. Butterfly, sun, bird and dog	85	70

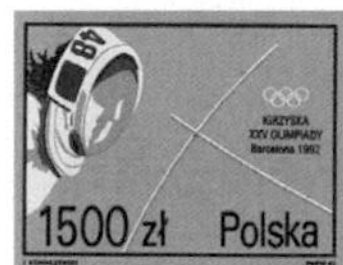

1004 Fencing

1992. Olympic Games, Barcelona. Multicoloured.

3414	1500z. Type **1004**	25	10
3415	2000z. Boxing	35	15
3416	2500z. Running	75	45
3417	3000z. Cycling	95	70

1005 Runners

1992. "Olymphilex '92" Olympic Stamps Exhibition, Barcelona. Sheet 86×81 mm.

MS3418	**1005**	20000z. multicoloured	6·00	5·75

1006 Statue of Korczak

1992. 50th Death Anniv of Janusz Korczak (educationist).

3419	**1006**	1500z. black, brown & yellow	60	40

1007 Flag and "V"

1992. Fifth Polish Veterans World Meeting.

3420	**1007**	3000z. multicoloured	95	70

1008 Wyszinski

1992. 11th Death Anniv of Stefan Wyszinski (Primate of Poland) (3421) and First Anniv of World Youth Day (3422). Multicoloured.

3421	1500z. Type **1008**	75	40
3422	3000z. Pope John Paul II embracing youth	95	85

1009 National Colours encircling World Map

1992. World Meeting of Expatriate Poles, Cracow.

3423	**1009**	3000z. multicoloured	1·10	70

1010 Polish Museum, Adampol

1992. 150th Anniv of Polish Settlement at Adampol, Turkey.

3424	**1010**	3500z. multicoloured	1·20	85

1011 18th-century Post Office Sign, Slonim

1992. World Post Day.

3425	**1011**	3500z. multicoloured	1·20	85

1012 "Dedication" (self-portrait)

1992. Birth Centenary of Bruno Schulz (writer and artist).

3426	**1012**	3000z. multicoloured	1·10	70

1013 "Seated Girl" (Henryk Wicinski)

1992. Polish Sculptures. Multicoloured.

3427	2000z. Type **1013**	60	40
3428	2500z. "Portrait of Tytus Czyzewski" (Zbigniew Pronaszko)	75	50
3429	3000z. "Polish Nike" (Edward Wittig)	85	65
3430	3500z. "The Nude" (August Zamoyski)	95	70
MS3431	107×90 mm. Nos. 3427/30	3·75	3·50

1014 "10th Theatrical Summer in Zamosc" (Jan Mlodozeniec)

1992. Poster Art (1st series). Multicoloured.

3432	1500z. Type **1014**	35	15
3433	2000z. "Red Art" (Franciszek Starowieyski)	60	40
3434	2500z. "Circus" (Waldemar Swierzy)	75	70
3435	3500z. "Mannequins" (Henryk Tomaszewski)	95	85

See also Nos. 3502/3, 3523/4, 3585/6 and 3712/15.

1015 Girl skipping with Snake

1992. "Polska '93" International Stamp Exn, Poznan (1st issue). Multicoloured.

3436	1500z. Type **1015**	35	15
3437	2000z. Boy on rocking horse with upside-down runners	60	40
3438	2500z. Boy firing bird from bow	75	70
3439	3500z. Girl placing ladder against clockwork giraffe	95	85

See also Nos. 3452, 3453/6 and 3466/9.

1016 Medal and Soldiers

1992. 50th Anniv of Formation of Polish Underground Army. Multicoloured.

3440	1500z. Type **1016**	35	15
3441	3500z. Soldiers	1·20	95
MS3442	75×95 mm. 20000z.+500z. "WP AK" (26×32 mm)	6·00	5·75

1017 Church and Star

1992. Christmas.

3443	**1017**	1000z. multicoloured	30	10

1018 Wheat

1992. International Nutrition Conference, Rome. Multicoloured.

3444	1500z. Type **1018**	35	15
3445	3500z. Glass, bread, vegetables and jug on table	95	70

1019 Arms of Sovereign Military Order

1992. Postal Agreement with Sovereign Military Order of Malta.

3446	**1019**	3000z. multicoloured	95	70

1020 Arms, 1295

1992. History of the White Eagle (Poland's arms). Each black, red and yellow.

3447	2000z. Type **1020**	60	30
3448	2500z. 15th-century arms	75	35
3449	3000z. 18th-century arms	85	40
3450	3500z. Arms, 1919	95	70
3451	5000z. Arms, 1990	1·50	85

1021 Exhibition Emblem and Stylized Stamp

1992. Centenary of Polish Philately and "Polska '93" International Stamp Exhibition, Poznan (2nd issue).

3452	**1021**	1500z. multicoloured	60	35

1022 Amber

1993. "Polska '93" International Stamp Exhibition, Poznan (3rd issue). Amber. Multicoloured.

3453	1500z. Type **1022**	25	15
3454	2000z. Pinkish amber	60	40
3455	2500z. Amber in stone	85	70
3456	3000z. Amber containing wasp	1·20	95
MS3457	82×88 mm. 20000z. Detail of map with necklace representing amber route (44×29 mm)	4·75	4·50

1023 Downhill Skier

1993. Winter University Games, Zakopane.

3458	**1023**	3000z. multicoloured	85	70

1024 Flower-filled Heart

1993. St. Valentine's Day. Multicoloured.

3459	1500z. Type **1024**	35	15
3460	3000z. Heart in envelope	85	70

1993. Polish Rulers (8th series). As T **983** showing drawings by Jan Matejko.

3461	1500z. brown and green	60	40
3462	2000z. black and mauve	85	70
3463	2500z. black and green	1·20	85
3464	3000z. deep brown and brown	1·80	1·40

DESIGNS: 1500z. Wladyslaw Laskonogi; 2000z. Henryk I; 2500z. Konrad I of Masovia; 3000z. Boleslaw V, the Chaste.

1025 Arsenal

1993. 50th Anniv of Attack by Szare Szeregi (formation of Polish Scouts in the resistance forces) on Warsaw Arsenal.

3465	**1025**	1500z. multicoloured	60	40

1026 Jousters with Lances

1993. "Polska '93" International Stamp Exhibition, Poznan (4th issue). Jousting at Golub Dobrzyn. Designs showing a modern and a medieval jouster. Multicoloured.

3466	1500z. Type **1026**	35	15
3467	2000z. Jousters	60	40
3468	2500z. Jousters with swords	75	70
3469	3500z. Officials	95	85

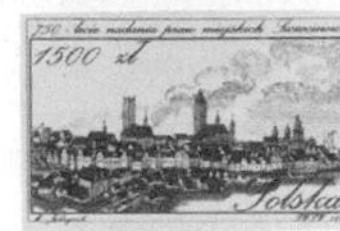

1027 Szczecin

1993. 750th Anniv of Granting of Town Charter to Szczecin.

3470	**1027**	1500z. multicoloured	60	40

1028 Jew and Ruins

1993. 50th Anniv of Warsaw Ghetto Uprising.

3471	**1028**	4000z. black, yellow & blue	1·20	85

1029 Works by A. Szapocznikow and J. Lebenstein

1993. Europa. Contemporary Art. Multicoloured.

3472	1500z. Type **1029**	60	40
3473	4000z. "CXCIX" (S. Gierawski) and "Red Head" (B. Linke)	1·20	85

1030 "King Alexander Jagiellonczyk in the Sejm" (Jan Laski, 1505)

1993. 500th Anniv of Parliament.

3474	**1030**	2000z. multicoloured	60	40

1031 Nullo

1993. 130th Death Anniv of Francesco Nullo (Italian volunteer in January 1863 Rising).

3475	**1031**	2500z. multicoloured	85	70

1032 Lech's Encounter with the White Eagle after Battle of Gniezno

1993. "Polska'93" International Stamp Exhibition, Poznan (5th issue). Sheet 103×86 mm.

MS3476	**1032**	50000z. brown	11·00	10·50

1033 Cap

1993. Third World Congress of Cadets of the Second Republic.

3477	**1033**	2000z. multicoloured	75	40

1034 Copernicus and Solar System

1993. 450th Death Anniv of Nicolas Copernicus (astronomer).

3478	**1034**	2000z. multicoloured	85	70

1035 Fiki Miki and Lion

1993. 40th Death Anniv of Kornel Makuszynski (writer of children's books). Multicoloured.

3479	1500z. Type **1035**	35	15
3480	2000z. Billy goat	60	40
3481	3000z. Fiki Miki	95	70
3482	5000z. Billy goat riding ostrich	1·50	95

1993. Cones. As T **974**. Multicoloured.

3483	10000z. Arolla pine	2·75	2·10
3484	20000z. Scots pine	5·00	3·50

1036 Eurasian Tree Sparrow

1993. Birds. Multicoloured.

3485	1500z. Type **1036**	35	15
3486	2000z. Pied wagtail	75	30
3487	3000z. Syrian woodpecker	95	70
3488	4000z. Eurasian goldfinch	1·50	95
3489	5000z. Common starling	1·60	1·40
3490	6000z. Northern bullfinch	1·90	1·70

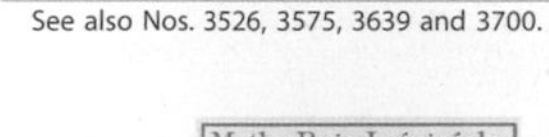

1037 Soldiers Marching

1993. Bicentenary of Dabrowski's "Mazurka" (national anthem) (1st issue).

3491	**1037**	1500z. multicoloured	60	40

See also Nos. 3526, 3575, 3639 and 3700.

1038 "Madonna and Child" (St. Mary's Basilica, Lesna Podlaska)

1993. Sanctuaries to St. Mary. Multicoloured.

3492	1500z. Type **1038**	45	35
3493	2000z. "Madonna and Child" (St. Mary's Church, Swieta Lipka)	75	70

1039 Handley Page Halifax and Parachutes

1993. The Polish Rangers (Second World War air troop).

3494	**1039**	1500z. multicoloured	60	40

1040 Trumpet Player

1993. "Jazz Jamboree '93" International Jazz Festival, Warsaw.

3495	**1040**	2000z. multicoloured	75	40

1041 Postman

1993. World Post Day.

3496	**1041**	2500z. brown, grey and blue	85	70

1042 St. Jadwiga (miniature, Schlackenwerther Codex)

1993. 750th Death Anniv of St. Jadwiga of Silesia.

3497	**1042**	2500z. multicoloured	85	70

1043 Pope John Paul II

1993. 15th Anniv of Pope John Paul II. Sheet 70×92 mm.

MS3498	**1043**	20000z. multicoloured	6·00	5·75

1044 Golden Eagle and Crown

1993. 75th Anniv of Republic. Multicoloured.

3499	4000z. Type **1044**	1·50	95
MS3500	66×89 mm. 20000z. Silhouette and shadow of flying eagle (31×38 mm)	7·25	7·00

1045 St. Nicholas

1993. Christmas.

3501	**1045**	1500z. multicoloured	60	40

1993. Poster Art (2nd series). As T **1014**. Multicoloured.

3502	2000z. "Come and see Polish Mountains" (M. Urbaniec)	85	70
3503	5000z. Production of Alban Berg's "Wozzeck" (J. Lenica)	1·50	95

1046 Daisy shedding Petals

1994. Greetings Stamp.
3504 **1046** 1500z. multicoloured 60 40

1047 Cross-country Skiing

1994. Winter Olympic Games, Lillehammer, Norway. Multicoloured.
3505 2500z. Type **1047** 85 70
3506 5000z. Ski jumping 1·50 95
MS3507 81×80 mm. 10000z. Downhill skiing 3·00 2·75

1048 Bem and Cannon

1994. Birth Bicentenary of General Jozef Bem.
3508 **1048** 5000z. multicoloured 1·50 95

1049 Jan Zamojski (founder)

1994. 400th Anniv of Zamojski Academy, Zamosc.
3509 **1049** 5000z. grey, black and brown 1·50 95

1050 Cracow Battalion Flag and Scythes

1994. Bicentenary of Tadeusz Kosciuszko's Insurrection.
3510 **1050** 2000z. multicoloured 75 40

1994. Polish Rulers (9th series). Drawings by Jan Matejko. As T **893**.
3511 2500z. black and blue 85 70
3512 5000z. black, deep violet and violet 2·10 1·40
DESIGN: 2500z. Leszek II, the Black; 5000a. Przemysl II.

1051 Oil Lamp, Open Book and Spectacles

1994. Europa. Inventions and Discoveries. Multicoloured.
3513 2500z. Type **1051** (invention of modern oil lamp by Ignacy Lukasiewicz) 75 70
3514 6000z. Illuminated filament forming "man in the moon" (astronomy) 1·70 1·40

1052 "Madonna and Child"

1994. St. Mary's Sanctuary, Kalwaria Zebrzydowska.
3515 **1052** 4000z. multicoloured 1·20 85

1053 Abbey Ruins and Poppies

1994. 50th Anniv of Battle of Monte Cassino.
3516 **1053** 6000z. multicoloured 1·50 95

1054 Mazurka

1994. Traditional Dances. Multicoloured.
3517 3000z. Type **1054** 45 35
3518 4000z. Coralski 75 60
3519 9000z. Krakowiak 1·80 1·10

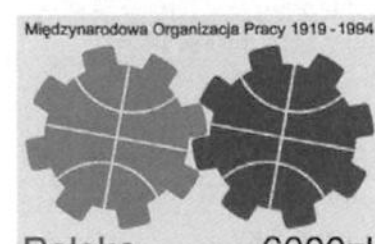

1055 Cogwheels

1994. 75th Anniv of International Labour Organization.
3520 **1055** 6000z. deep blue, blue and black 1·20 85

1056 Optic Fibre Cable

1994. 75th Anniv of Polish Electricians Association.
3521 **1056** 4000z. multicoloured 95 70

1057 Map of Americas on Football

1994. World Cup Football Championship, U.S.A.
3522 **1057** 6000z. multicoloured 1·50 95

1994. Poster Art (3rd series). As T **1014**. Multicoloured.
3523 4000z. "Monsieur Fabre" (Wiktor Gorka) 85 70
3524 6000z. "8th OISTAT Congress" (Hurbert Hilscher) (horiz) 1·50 95

1058 Znaniecki

1994. 36th Death Anniv of Professor Florian Znaniecki.
3525 **1058** 9000z. green, bistre & yellow 2·40 1·70

1994. Bicentenary of Dabrowski's Mazurka (2nd issue). As T **1037**. Multicoloured.
3526 2500z. Troops preparing to charge 85 70

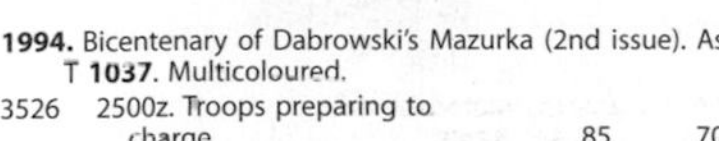

1059 Polish Eagle and Ribbon

1994. 50th Anniv of Warsaw Uprising.
3527 **1059** 2500z. multicoloured 85 70

1060 "Stamp" protruding from Pocket

1994. "Philakorea 1994" International Stamp Exhibition, Seoul.
3528 **1060** 4000z. multicoloured 95 85

1061 Basilica of St. Brigida, Gdansk

1994. Sanctuaries.
3529 **1061** 4000z. multicoloured 95 85

1062 "Nike" (goddess of Victory)

1994. Centenary of International Olympic Committee.
3530 **1062** 4000z. multicoloured 95 85

1063 Komeda and Piano Keys

1994. 25th Death Anniv of Krzysztof Komeda (jazz musician).
3531 **1063** 6000z. multicoloured 1·20 85

1064 Long-finned Bristle-mouthed Catfish

1994. Fish. Multicoloured.
3532 4000z. Type **1064** 1·10 85
3533 4000z. Freshwater angelfish ("Pterophyllum scalare") 1·10 85
3534 4000z. Red swordtail ("Xiphophorus helleri"), neon tetra ("Paracheirodon innesi") and Berlin platy 1·10 85
3535 4000z. Neon tetra ("Poecilia reticulata") and guppies 1·10 85
Nos. 3532/5 were issued together, *se-tenant*, forming a composite design.

1065 Arms of Polish Post, 1858

1994. World Post Day.
3536 **1065** 4000z. multicoloured 95 85

1066 Kolbe

1994. Maximilian Kolbe (concentration camp victim) Year.
3537 **1066** 2500z. multicoloured 85 70

1067 Pigeon

1994. Pigeons. Multicoloured.
3538 4000z. Type **1067** 75 40
3539 4000z. Friar pigeon 75 40
3540 6000z. Silver magpie pigeon 95 85
3541 6000z. Danzig pigeon (black) 95 85
MS3542 79×94 mm. 10000z. Short-tail pigeon 2·40 2·20

1068 Musicians playing Carols

1994. Christmas.
3543 **1068** 2500z. multicoloured 75 50

1069 Landscape and E.U. Flag

1994. Application by Poland for Membership of European Union.
3544 **1069** 6000z. multicoloured 1·80 1·40

1070 "I Love You" on Pierced Heart

1995. Greetings Stamp.
3545 **1070** 35g. red and blue 80 40

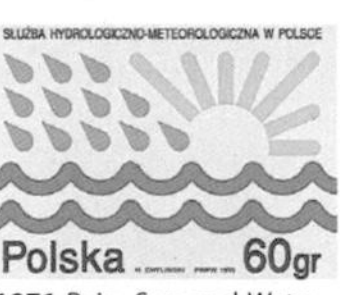

1071 Rain, Sun and Water

1995. 75th Anniv of Hydrological-Meteorological Service.
3546 **1071** 60g. multicoloured 90 70

1072 Flag and Sea

1995. 75th Anniv of Poland's "Marriage to the Sea" (symbolic ceremony commemorating renewal of access to sea).
3547 **1072** 45g. multicoloured 80 40

1995. Polish Rulers (10th series). As T **893** showing drawings by Jan Matejko.
3548 35g. deep brown, brown and light brown 40 30
3549 45g. olive, deep green and green 65 40
3550 60g. brown and ochre 90 70
3551 80g. black and blue 1·00 85
DESIGNS: 35g. Waclaw II; 45g. Wladyslaw I; 60g. Kazimierz III, the Great; 80g. Ludwik Wegierski.

1073 St. John

1995. 500th Birth Anniv of St. John of God (founder of Order of Hospitallers).
3552 **1073** 60g. multicoloured 90 70

1074 Eggs

1995. Easter. Decorated Easter eggs. Mult, background colours given.
3553 **1074** 35g. red 40 30
3554 - 35g. lilac 40 30
3555 - 45g. blue 65 45
3556 - 45g. green 65 45

1995. Cones. As T **974**. Multicoloured.
3557 45g. European larch 65 45
3558 80g. Mountain pine 1·00 70

1075 Polish Officer's Button and Leaf

1995. Katyn Commemoration Year.
3559 **1075** 80g. multicoloured 1·30 85

1076 Rose and Barbed Wire

1995. Europa. Peace and Freedom. Multicoloured.
3560 35g. Type **1076** (liberation of concentration camps) 65 45
3561 80g. Flowers in helmet 1·30 1·00

1077 Common Cranes

1995. 50th Anniv of Return of Western Territories.
3562 **1077** 45g. multicoloured 80 45

1078 Pope and Wadowice Church Font

1995. 75th Birthday of Pope John Paul II.
3563 **1078** 80g. multicoloured 1·30 85

1079 Puppets under Spotlight ("Miromagia")

1995. 50th Anniv of Groteska Fairy Tale Theatre. Multicoloured.
3564 35g. Type **1079** 50 45
3565 35g. Puppets in scene from play 50 45
3566 45g. Puppet leaning on barrel ("Thomas Fingerchen") (vert) 80 55
3567 45g. Clown ("Bumstara Circus") 80 55

1080 Cockerill Steam Locomotive and Train, 1845, Warsaw–Vienna

1995. 150th Anniv of Polish Railways. Multicoloured.
3568 35g. Type **1080** 50 45
3569 60g. "Lux-Torpedo" diesel railcar, 1927 90 70
3570 80g. Electric freight train 1·20 85
3571 1z. Eurocity "Sobieski" express, 1992, Warsaw–Vienna 1·60 1·10

1081 Symbols of Nations

1995. 50th Anniv of U.N.O.
3572 **1081** 80g. multicoloured 1·30 85

1082 Bank

1995. 125th Anniv of Warsaw Commercial Bank.
3573 **1082** 45g. multicoloured 80 45

1083 Loaf and Four-leaved Clover

1995. Centenary of Peasant Movement.
3574 **1083** 45g. multicoloured 80 45

1995. Bicentenary of Dabrowski's "Mazurka" (3rd issue). As T **1037**. Multicoloured.
3575 35g. Mounted troops 80 45

1084 Rowan Berries

1995. Fruit of Trees. No value expressed. Multicoloured.
3576 A (35g.) Type **1084** 50 30
3577 B (45g.) Acorns and sessile oak leaves 80 45

1085 Madonna and Child

1995. Basilica of the Holy Trinity, Lezajsk.
3578 **1085** 45g. multicoloured 80 45

1086 Marshal Josef Pilsudski

1995. 75th Anniv of Defence of Warsaw and of Riga Peace Conference.
3579 **1086** 45g. multicoloured 80 45

1087 Dressage

1995. World Carriage Driving Championships, Poznan. Multicoloured.
3580 60g. Type **1087** 90 70
3581 80g. Cross-country event 1·30 1·00

1088 Warsaw Technical University

1995. "Warsaw '95" National Stamp Exhibition. Multicoloured.
3582 35g. Type **1088** 65 45
MS3583 94×71 mm. 1z. Castle Place, Warsaw (horiz) 1·60 1·40

1089 Russian Space Station and U.S. Spacecraft

1995. 11th World Cosmonauts Congress, Warsaw.
3584 **1089** 80g. multicoloured 1·30 85

1995. Poster Art (4th series). As T **1014**. Multicoloured.
3585 35g. "The Crazy Locomotive" (Jan Sawka) 65 45
3586 45g. "The Wedding" (Eugeniusz Get Stankiewicz) 80 55

1090 Bar from Polonaise (Frederic Chopin)

1995. 13th International Chopin Piano Competition.
3587 **1090** 80g. multicoloured 1·40 85

1091 Postman

1995. Post Day. Multicoloured.
3588 45g. Type **1091** 65 45
3589 80g. Feather fixed to envelope by seal 1·20 85

1092 Acrobatic Pyramid

1995. World Acrobatic Sports Championships, Wroclaw.
3590 **1092** 45g. multicoloured 80 45

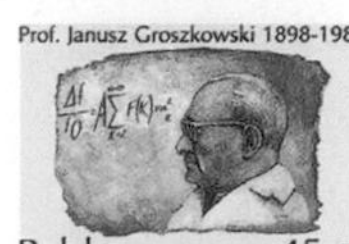

1093 Groszkowski and Formula

1995. 11th Death Anniv of Professor Janusz Groszkowski (radio-electronic scientist).
3591 **1093** 45g. multicoloured 80 45

1094 Crib

1995. Christmas. Multicoloured.
3592 35g. Type **1094** 65 45
3593 45g. Wise men, Christmas tree and star of Bethlehem 90 55

Nos. 3592/3 were issued together, se-tenant, forming a composite design.

1095 Blue Tit

1995. Song Birds. Multicoloured.
3594 35g. Type **1095** 50 45
3595 45g. Long-tailed tit 65 45
3596 60g. Great grey shrike 90 70
3597 80g. Hawfinch 1·20 85

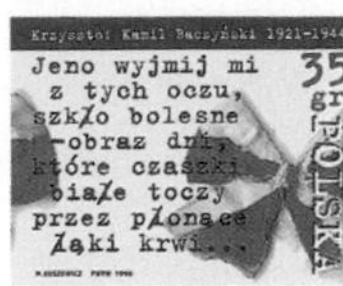

1096 Extract from Poem and Bow

1996. 75th Birth Anniv of Krzysztof Kamil Baczynski (poet).
3598 **1096** 35g. multicoloured 65 45

1097 Cherries and "I love you"

1996. Greetings Stamp.
3599 **1097** 40g. multicoloured 65 45

1098 Romanesque-style Inowlodz Church

1996. Architectural Styles. Multicoloured.
3600 40g. Type **1098** 65 55
3601 55g. Gothic-style St. Mary the Virgin's Church, Cracow 90 70
3602 70g. Renaissance-style St. Sigismund's Chapel, Wawel Castle 1·20 85
3603 1z. Baroque-style Church of the Order of the Holy Sacrament, Warsaw 1·70 1·30

1099 "Oceania"

1996. Sailing Ships. Multicoloured.
3604 40g. Type **1099** 65 55
3605 55g. "Zawisza Czarny" (cadet schooner) 90 70
3606 70g. "General Zaruski" (cadet ketch) 1·20 1·00
3607 75g. "Fryderyk Chopin" (cadet brig) 1·30 1·10

1100 16th-century Warsaw

1996. 400th Anniv of Warsaw.
3608 **1100** 55g. multicoloured 90 70

1101 Bull (Taurus)

1996. Signs of the Zodiac. Multicoloured.

3609	5g. Workman in water (Aquarius)	15	10
3610	10g. "Fish-person" holding fish (Pisces)	15	10
3611	20g. Type **1101**	20	10
3612	25g. Twins looking through keyhole (Gemini)	25	15
3613	30g. Crab smoking pipe (Cancer)	25	15
3614	40g. Maid and cogwheels (Virgo)	35	30
3615	50g. Lion in military uniform (Leo)	50	30
3616	55g. Couple with head and shoulders as scales (Libra)	60	35
3617	70g. Ram with ram-head (Aries)	65	45
3618	1z. Woman with scorpion's tail hat (Scorpio)	1·00	70
3619	2z. Archer on motor cycle (Sagittarius)	2·10	1·60
3620	5z. Office worker shielding face with paper mask (Capricorn)	5·25	3·75

1102 Hanka Ordonowna (singer)

1996. Europa. Famous Women. Multicoloured.

3621	40g. Type **1102**	65	55
3622	1z. Pola Negri (actress)	1·30	1·20

1103 Flag of Osiek and Old Photographs forming "1921"

1996. 75th Anniv of Silesian Uprising.

3623	**1103** 55g. red, green and black	90	70

1104 "On Bergamuty Islands"

1996. 50th Anniv of UNICEF. Scenes from Fairy Tales by Jan Brzechwa. Multicoloured.

3624	40g. Type **1104**	50	45
3625	40g. Waiters carrying trays of apples (nursery rhyme)	50	45
3626	55g. Vegetable characters ("At the Market Stall")	80	55
3627	55g. Chef holding duck ("Wacky Duck")	80	55
3628	70g. Woman and birdchild ("The Fibber")	1·00	70
3629	70g. Red fox ("The Impishness of Witalis Fox")	1·00	70

1105 "City Walls and Building"

1996. Paintings by Stanislaw Noakowski. Multicoloured.

3630	40g. Type **1105**	65	45
3631	55g. "Renaissance Bedroom"	80	55
3632	70g. "Rural Gothic Church"	1·00	85
3633	1z. "Renaissance Library"	1·60	1·10

1106 Discus on Ribbon

1996. Olympic Games, Atlanta, and Centenary of Modern Olympic Games. Multicoloured.

3634	40g. Type **1106** (gold medal, Halina Konopacka, 1928)	65	45
3635	55g. Tennis ball (horiz)	90	55
3636	70g. Polish Olympic Committee emblem (horiz)	1·30	85
3637	1z. Bicycle wheel	1·70	1·10

1107 Tweezers holding Stamp showing Emblem

1996. "Olymphilex '96" International Sports Stamp Exhibition, Atlanta.

3638	**1107** 1z. multicoloured	1·60	1·00

1996. Bicentenary of Dabrowski's Mazurka (4th issue). As T **1037**. Multicoloured.

3639	40g. Charge of Polish cavalry at Somosierra	80	45

1108 St. Mary of Przeczycka

1996. St. Mary's Church, Przeczycka.

3640	**1108** 40g. multicoloured	90	45

1996. Polish Rulers (11th series). As T **893**.

3641	40g. brown and bistre	65	45
3642	55g. lilac and mauve	90	60
3643	70g. deep grey and grey	1·30	75
3644	1z. deep green, green and yellow	1·70	1·00

DESIGNS: 40g. Queen Jadwiga (wife of Wladyslaw II); 55g. Wladyslaw II Jagiello; 70g. Wladyslaw III Warnenczyk; 1z. Kazimierz IV Jagiellonczyk.

1109 Mt. Giewont and Edelweiss

1996. The Tatra Mountains. Multicoloured.

3645	40g. Type **1109**	50	45
3646	40g. Mt. Krzesanica and spring gentian	50	45
3647	55g. Mt. Koscielec and leopard's bane	80	60
3648	55g. Mt. Swinica and clusius gentian	80	60
3649	70g. Mt. Rysy and ragwort	1·00	75
3650	70g. Mieguszowieckie peaks and pine trees	1·00	75

1110 Seifert

1996. 50th Birth Anniv of Zbigniew Seifert (jazz musician).

3651	**1110** 70g. multicoloured	1·30	90

1111 "Changing of Horses at Post Station" (detail, Mieczyslaw Watorski)

1996. World Post Day. 75th Anniv of Post and Telecommunications Museum, Wroclaw. Paintings. Multicoloured.

3652	40g. Type **1111**	80	45
MS3653	102×81 mm. 1z.+20g. "Mail Coach at Jagniatkowo with View over Karkonosze" (Professor Tager) (42×30 mm)	2·00	1·90

1112 Father Christmas on Horse-drawn Sleigh

1996. Christmas. Multicoloured.

3654	40g. Type **1112**	50	30
3655	55g. Carol singers with star lantern	80	45

1113 Head of Male Bison

1996. The European Bison. Multicoloured.

3656	55g. Type **1113**	80	60
3657	55g. Head of female	80	60
3658	55g. Pair of bison	80	60
3659	55g. Male	80	60

1114 Wislawa Szymborska

1996. Award of Nobel Prize for Literature to Wislawa Szymborska (poet).

3660	**1114** 1z. multicoloured	1·60	1·00

1115 "I Love You" on King of Hearts Playing Card

1997. Greetings Stamps. Multicoloured.

3661	B (40g.) Type **1115**	50	30
3662	A (55g.) Queen of hearts playing card	80	45

Nos. 3661/2 were issued together, *se-tenant*, forming a composite design.

No. 3661 was sold at the rate for postcards and No. 3662 for letters up to 20 grams.

1116 Blessing the Palms

1997. Easter. Traditional Customs. Multicoloured.

3663	50g. Type **1116**	55	45
3664	60g. Woman and child painting Easter eggs	70	55
3665	80g. Priest blessing the food	95	80
3666	1z.10 Man throwing water over woman's skirts on Easter Monday	1·40	95

1117 Long Market and Town Hall (after Mateusz Deisch)

1997. Millenary of Gdansk. Each brown, cinnamon and red.

3667	50g. Type **1117**	70	45
MS3668	94×71 mm. 1z.10 St. Mary's Church and Hall of the Main Town (after Mateusz Merian) (horiz)	2·10	2·00

1118 St. Adalbert and Monks addressing Pagans

1997. Death Millenary of St. Adalbert (Bishop of Prague).

3669	**1118** 50g. brown	55	30
3670	- 60g. green	70	45
3671	- 1z.10 lilac	1·40	95

DESIGNS—VERT: 60g. St. Adalbert and anniversary emblem; 1z.10, St. Adalbert.

1119 Mansion House, Lopuszna

1997. Polish Manor Houses. Multicoloured.

3671a	10g Lipkowie, Warsaw	15	10
3672	50g. Type **1119**	15	10
3673	55g. Henryk Sienkewicz Museum, Oblegorek	65	40
3674	60g. Zyrzyn	70	45
3675	65g. Stanislaw Wyspianski Museum, Bronowice, near Cracow	75	55
3675a	70g. Modlnica	85	65
3675b	80g. Grabonog, Gostyn	95	70
3676	90g. Obory, near Warsaw	1·10	80
3676a	1z. Krzelawice	1·20	85
3677	1z.10 Ozarow	1·30	95
3678	1z.20 Jozef Krasnewski Museum, Biala	1·40	1·00
3678a	1z.40 Winna Gora	1·50	1·10
3678b	1z.50 Sulejowku, Warsaw	1·70	1·20
3678c	1z.55 Zelazowa Wola	1·80	1·30
3678d	1z.60 Potok Zloty	1·90	1·30
3678e	1z.65 Sucha, Wegrow	2·10	1·40
3679	1z.70 Tulowice	2·20	1·50
3679a	1z.85 Kasna Dolna	2·40	1·60
3679b	1z.90 Petrykozach Mszczonowa	2·50	1·70
3680	2z.20 Kuznocin	2·75	2·00
3681	2z.65 Liwia, Wegrow	3·00	2·20
3682	3z. Janowcu, Pulaw	3·50	2·30
3683	10z. Koszuty	11·00	9·50

See also Nos. 3727/8.

1120 The Crock of Gold

1997. Europa. Tales and Legends. Multicoloured.

3685	50g. Type **1120**	70	45
3686	1z.10 Wars, Sawa and mermaid-siren	2·10	1·60

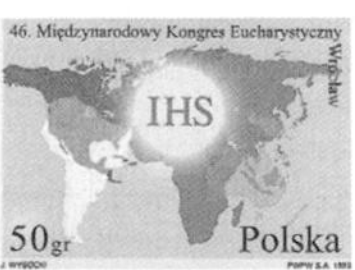

1121 World Map and Emblem

1997. 46th International Eucharistic Congress, Wroclaw.

3687	**1121** 50g. multicoloured	70	45

1122 San Francisco–Oakland Bay Bridge

1997. "Pacific 97" International Stamp Exhibition, San Francisco.

3688	**1122** 1z.30 multicoloured	1·70	1·10

1123 Pope John Paul II

1997. Fifth Papal Visit. Sheet 76×90 mm.

MS3689	**1123**	1z.10 multicoloured	1·90	1·60

1124 European Long-eared Bat

1997. Bats. Multicoloured.

3690		50g. Type **1124**	55	45
3691		60g. Common noctule	70	65
3692		80g. Brown bat	85	65
3693		1z.30 Red bat	1·50	1·10

1125 "Founding of the Main School" (Jan Matejko)

1997. 600th Anniv of Faculty of Theology, Jagiellonian University, Cracow.

3694	**1125**	80g. multicoloured	85	65

1126 Map highlighting Settled Area

1997. Centenary of Polish Migration to Argentina.

3695	**1126**	1z.40 multicoloured	1·70	1·20

1127 "Return from War to the Village"

1997. Paintings by Juliusz Kossak. Multicoloured.

3696		50g. Type **1127**	70	45
3697		60g. "Cracowian Wedding"	85	65
3698		80g. "In the Stable"	1·10	80
3699		1z.10 "Stablehand with Pair of Horses"	1·50	1·10

1997. Bicentenary of Dabrowski's "Mazurka" (5th issue). As T **1037**.

3700		50g. Dabrowski and Wybicki's arrival in Poznan, 1806	70	45
MS3701		85×77 mm. 1z.10 Manuscript of lyrics and Jozef Wybicki (composer)	1·80	1·60

1128 Strzelecki and Route Map around Australia

1997. Birth Bicentenary of Pawel Strzelecki (explorer).

3702	**1128**	1z.50 multicoloured	2·10	1·60

1129 Flooded Houses

1997. Flood Relief Fund.

3703	**1129**	60g.+30g. multicoloured	1·40	1·10

1130 "Holy Mother of Consolation" (icon)

1997. Church of the Holy Mother of Consolation and St. Michael the Archangel, Gorka Duchowa.

3704	**1130**	50g. multicoloured	70	45

1997. Polish Rulers (12th series). As T **893**.

3705		50g. agate, brown and bistre	85	45
3706		60g. purple and blue	95	65
3707		80g. green, deep green and olive	1·40	95
3708		1z.10 purple and lilac	1·80	1·30

DESIGNS: 50g. Jan I Olbracht; 60g. Aleksander Jagiellonczyk; 80g. Zygmunt I, the Old; 1z.10, Zygmunt II August.

1131 Kosz

1997. 24th Death Anniv of Mieczyslaw Kosz (jazz musician).

3709	**1131**	80g. multicoloured	95	80

1132 Globe and posthorn

1997. World Post Day.

3710	**1132**	50g. multicoloured	70	45

1133 St. Basil's Cathedral, Moscow

1997. "Moskva 97" International Stamp Exhibition, Moscow.

3711	**1133**	80g. multicoloured	95	80

1997. Poster Art (5th series). As T **1014**.

3712		50g. multicoloured	55	40
3713		50g. black	55	40
3714		60g. multicoloured	70	55
3715		60g. multicoloured	70	55

POSTERS—HORIZ: No. 3712, Advertisement for Radion washing powder (Tadeusz Gronowski). VERT: No. 3713, Production of Stanislaw Witkiewicz's play "Shoemakers" (Roman Cieslewicz); 3714, Production of Aleksander Fredro's play "A Husband and a Wife" (Andrzej Pagowski); 3715, Production of ballet "Goya" (Wiktor Sadowski).

1134 Nativity

1997. Christmas. Multicoloured.

3716		50g. Type **1134**	55	45
3717		60g. Christmas Eve feast (horiz)	70	55
3718		80g. Family going to church for Midnight Mass (horiz)	95	80
3719		1z.10 Waits (carol singers representing animals)	1·40	1·10

1135 Common Shelducks

1997. Praecocial Chicks. Multicoloured.

3720		50g. Type **1135**	70	55
3721		50g. Goosanders ("Mergus merganser")	70	55
3722		50g. Common snipes ("Gallinago gallinago")	70	55
3723		50g. Moorhens ("Gallinula chloropus")	70	55

1136 Ski Jumping

1998. Winter Olympic Games, Nagano, Japan.

3724	**1136**	1z.40 multicoloured	1·70	1·30

1137 Dog wearing Cat T-shirt inscr "I Love You"

1998. Greetings Stamps. No value expressed. Multicoloured.

3725		B (55g.) Type **1137**	55	45
3726		A (65g.) Cat wearing dog T-shirt	70	55

1998. Polish Manor Houses. No value expressed. As T **1119**. Multicoloured.

3727		B (55g.) Gluchy	55	45
3728		A (65g.) Jan Kochanwoski Museum, Czarnolas	70	55

1138 Paschal Lamb

1998. Easter. Multicoloured.

3729		55g. Type **1138**	55	45
3730		65g. The Resurrected Christ	85	65

1139 Polish National Guard and Civilians at Lvov Barricades

1998. 150th Anniv of 1848 Revolutions.

3731	**1139**	55g. brown	70	55

1998. Polish Rulers (13th series). As T **893**.

3732		55g. brown and light brown	55	45
3733		65g. purple, deep purple and mauve	70	65
3734		80g. deep green and green	95	80
3735		90g. lilac, purple and mauve	1·10	85

DESIGNS: 55g. Henryk Walezy; 65g. Queen Anna Jagiellonka (wife of Stefan I); 80g. Stefan I Batory; 90g. Zygmunt III Wasa.

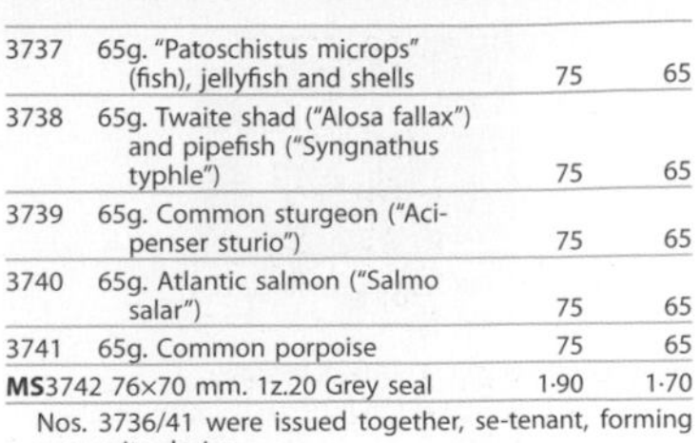

1140 Grey Seal

1998. Protection of Baltic Sea. Marine Life. Multicoloured.

3736		65g. Type **1140**	75	65
3737		65g. "Patoschistus microps" (fish), jellyfish and shells	75	65
3738		65g. Twaite shad ("Alosa fallax") and pipefish ("Syngnathus typhle")	75	65
3739		65g. Common sturgeon ("Acipenser sturio")	75	65
3740		65g. Atlantic salmon ("Salmo salar")	75	65
3741		65g. Common porpoise	75	65
MS3742		76×70 mm. 1z.20 Grey seal	1·90	1·70

Nos. 3736/41 were issued together, se-tenant, forming a composite design.

1141 Exhibition Emblem and 1948 Israeli 500 m. Stamp

1998. "Israel '98" International Stamp Exhibition, Tel Aviv.

3743	**1141**	90g. multicoloured	1·30	1·10

1142 Festival Emblem

1998. Europa. National Festivals.

3744	**1142**	55g. multicoloured	75	45
3745	-	1z.20 black, red and blue	1·80	1·60

DESIGNS: 55g. Type **1142** ("Warsaw Autumn" International Festival of Music); 1z.20, State flag and opening bars of "Welcome the May Dawn" (3rd of May Constitution Day).

1144 "Longing Holy Mother"

1998. Coronation of "Longing Holy Mother" (icon in Powsin Church).

3752	**1144**	55g. multicoloured	75	55

1145 "Triple Self-portrait"

1998. 30th Death Anniv of Nikifor (Epifan Drowniak) (artist). Multicoloured.

3753		55g. Type **1145**	75	55
3754		65g. "Cracow Office"	90	70
3755		1z.20 "Orthodox Church"	1·60	1·20
3756		2z.35 "Ucrybow Station"	3·25	2·50

1146 Anniversary Inscription

1998. 80th Anniv of Main Board of Statistics.

3757	**1146**	55g. multicoloured	75	55

1147 "Madonna and Child"

1998. Basilica of the Visitation of St. Mary the Virgin, Sejny.

3758	**1147**	55g. multicoloured	75	55

1148 Jesus (stained glass window)

1998. Bicentenary of Diocese of Warsaw.
3759 **1148** 65g. multicoloured 75 55

1998. 17th Congress of Polish Union of Stamp Collectors. Sheet 114×77 mm containing T **1141** and similar horiz design. Each blue and cream.
MS3760 65g. ×2 Composite design showing 17th-century engraving of Szczecin from Descriptio Urbis Stettinensis by Paul Feideborn 1·90 1·50

1150 Pierre and Marie Curie (physicists)

1998. Centenary of Discovery of Polonium and Radium.
3761 **1150** 1z.20 multicoloured 1·50 1·10

1151 Mazowsze Dancers

1998. 50th Anniv of Mazowsze Song and Dance Group. Multicoloured.
3762 65g. Type **1151** 80 60
3763 65g. Dancers (different) 80 60
Nos. 3762/3 were issued together, se-tenant, forming a composite design.

1152 Mniszchow Palace

1998. Belgium Embassy, Warsaw.
3764 **1152** 1z.20 multicoloured 1·60 1·20

1153 "King Sigismund" (Studio of Rubens)

1998. 400th Anniv of Battle of Stangebro.
3765 **1153** 1z.20 brown 1·60 1·20

1154 Coloured Envelopes

1998. World Post Day.
3766 **1154** 65g. multicoloured 80 60

1155 Pope John Paul II and People of Different Races

1998. 20th Anniv of Selection of Karol Wojtyla to Papacy.
3767 **1155** 65g. multicoloured 80 60

1156 State Flags and 1919 Seal

1998. 80th Anniv of Independence.
3768 **1156** 65g. black, red and gold 80 60

1157 "Nativity"

1998. Christmas. Polyptych, Grudziadz. Multicoloured.
3769 55g. Type **1157** 65 50
3770 65g. "Adoration of the Wise Men" 80 60

1158 Anniversary Emblem

1998. 50th Anniv of Universal Declaration of Human Rights.
3771 **1158** 1z.20 blue and ultramarine 1·60 1·20

1159 Maryla Wereszczakowna and Moonlit Night

1998. Birth Bicentenary of Adam Mickiewicz (poet). Multicoloured.
3772 55g. Type **1159** 65 50
3773 65g. Cranes flying over tomb of Maria Potocka 80 60
3774 90g. Burning candles and cross 1·10 85
3775 1z.20 House, field of flowers and uhlan's shako 1·40 1·10
MS3776 61×76 mm. 2z.45 Mickiewicz (bust by Jean David d'Angers) (30×38 mm) 4·00 3·75

1160 "Piorun" (destroyer), 1942–46

1999. 80th Anniv (1998) of Polish Navy. Multicoloured.
3777 55g. Type **1160** 65 50
3778 55g. "Piorun" (missile corvette), 1994 65 50

1161 Dominoes

1999. Greetings stamps. Value expressed by letter. Multicoloured.
3779 B (60g.) Type **1161** 65 50
3780 A (65g.) Dominoes (different) 80 60

1162 Ernest Malinowski and Railway Bridge over Varrugas Canyon

1999. Polish Engineers. Multicoloured.
3781 1z. Type **1162** (death cent) 1·10 85
3782 1z.60 Rudolf Modrzejewski and Benjamin Franklin Bridge over Delaware River, Philadelphia 1·90 1·50

1163 "Prayer in Ogrojec"

1999. Easter. Multicoloured.
3783 60g. Type **1163** 65 50
3784 65g. "Carrying the Cross" 70 55
3785 1z. "Pieta" 1·10 85
3786 1z.40 "Resurrection" 1·60 1·20
Nos. 3783/4 and 3786 show details of the Grudzic polyptych.

1164 Chinese Ideograms

1999. "China '99" International Stamp Exhibition, Peking. Sheet 80×96 mm.
MS3787 **1164** 1z.70 multicoloured 2·30 2·10

1165 "Victorious St. Mary of Kozielsk" (sculpture)

1999. Images of Virgin Mary made by Polish Prisoners of War. Multicoloured.
3788 60g. Type **1165** 65 50
3789 70g. "St. Mary of Katyn" (bas-relief, Stanislaw Balos) 80 60

1166 Jan Skrzetuski passing Zbara Fortress ("With Fire and Sword")

1999. "Heroes of the Trilogy" (novels) by Henryk Sienkiewicz. Multicoloured.
3790 70g. Type **1166** 80 60
3791 70g. Onufry Zagloba and 17th-century map of Poland (all three parts) 80 60
3792 70g. Longinus Podbipieta defending Zbara and three Tartars ("With Fire and Sword") 80 60
3793 70g. Bohun with Helena Kuncewiczowna on way to Czarci Jar ("With Fire and Sword") 80 60
3794 70g. Andrzej Kmicic and cannon at Jasna Gora Monastery ("The Deluge") 80 60
3795 70g. Michal Jerzy Wolodyjowski and Basia Jeziorkowska fencing ("Pan Michael") 80 60

1167 Polish Flag and N.A.T.O. Emblem

1999. 50th Anniv of North Atlantic Treaty Organization and Accession of Poland.
3796 **1167** 70g. multicoloured 95 75

1168 Anniversary Emblem and Headquarters, Strasbourg

1999. 50th Anniv of Council of Europe.
3797 **1168** 1z. multicoloured 1·60 1·20

1169 Three-toed Woodpecker

1999. Europa. Parks and Gardens. Bialowieski National Park.
3798 **1169** 1z.40 multicoloured 2·30 1·80

1170 Mountain Biking

1999. Youth Sports. Multicoloured.
3799 60g. Type **1170** 65 50
3800 70g. Snowboarding 80 60
3801 1z. Skateboarding 1·30 95
3802 1z.40 Rollerblading 1·70 1·30

1171 St. Mary's Church, Cracow, Pope John Paul II and Crowd

1999. Sixth Papal Visit to Poland. Multicoloured.
3803 60g. Type **1171** 65 50
3804 70g. Pope and crowd with crosses 80 60
3805 1z. Pope and cheering teenagers 1·30 95
3806 1z.40 Eiffel Tower (Paris), "Christ the Saviour" (statue, Rio de Janeiro), Pope and church at Fatima, Portugal 1·70 1·30

1172 Ignacy Paderewski and Roman Dmowski (signatories)

1999. 80th Anniv of Treaty of Versailles.
3807 **1172** 1z.40 multicoloured 1·70 1·30

1173 "St. Mary Carefully Listening" (icon)

1999. St. Mary's Sanctuaries. Multicoloured.
3808 60g. Type **1173** (church of St. Mary Queen of Poland, Rokitno) 65 50
3809 70g. "Mary" (statue, Ms. Jazlowiecka), Convent of Order of the Immaculate Conception, Szymanow 80 60

1174 Great Diving Beetle ("Dytiscus marginalis")

1999. Insects. Multicoloured.
3810 60g. Type **1174** 65 50
3811 60g. "Corixa punctata" 65 50
3812 70g. "Limnophilus" 80 60
3813 70g. "Perla marginata" 80 60
3814 1z.40 Emperor dragonfly ("Anax imperator") 1·70 1·30
3815 1z.40 "Ephemera vulgata" 1·70 1·30

1175 Ksiaz Castle

1999. "Walbrzych '99" 18th National Stamp Exhibition. Sheet 74×105 mm.

MS3816	**1175**	1z. blue	2·20	1·90

1176 Red Deer

1999. Eastern Carpathian Mountains International Biosphere Reserve (covering Polish, Ukrainian and Slovakian National Parks). Multicoloured.

3817	1z.40 Type **1176**	1·60	1·20
3818	1z.40 Wild cat	1·60	1·20

1999. Polish Rulers (14th series). As T **893**.

3819	60g. black and green	80	60
3820	70g. brown and light brown	95	75
3821	1z. black and blue	1·30	95
3822	1z.40 deep purple and purple	1·90	1·50

DESIGNS: 60g. Wladyslaw IV Waza; 70g. Jan II Kazimierz; 1z. Michal Korybut Wisniowiecki; 1z.40, Jan III Sobieski.

1177 U.P.U. Emblem

1999. 125th Anniv of Universal Postal Union.

3823	**1177**	1z.40 multicoloured	1·70	1·30

1178 Chopin and Academy of Fine Arts, Warsaw

1999. 150th Death Anniv of Frederic Chopin (composer).

3824	**1178**	1z.40 green	1·70	1·30

1179 Popieluszko

1999. 15th Death Anniv of Father Jerzy Popieluszko.

3825	**1179**	70g. multicoloured	80	60

1180 Barbed Wire

1999. Homage to 20th-century Heroes of Poland. Sheet 93×70 mm.

MS3826	**1180**	1z. multicoloured	1·60	1·30

1181 Angel ("Silent Night")

1999. Christmas. Inscr in Polish with the opening lines of carols. Multicoloured.

3827	60g. Type **1181**	80	60
3828	70g. Angel ("Sleep, Jesus Baby")	95	75
3829	1z. Angel ("Let's Go Everybody to the Stable")	1·30	95
3830	1z.40 Angel ("The God is Born")	1·90	1·50

1182 Polish Museum, Rapperswil Castle, Switzerland

1999. Polish Overseas Cultural Buildings. Multicoloured.

3831	1z. Type **1182**	1·30	95
3832	1z.40 Marian Priests' Museum, Fawley Court, England	1·90	1·50
3833	1z.60 Polish Library, Paris, France	2·00	1·60
3834	1z.80 Polish Institute and Gen. Sikorski Museum, London, England	2·30	1·80

1183 "Proportions of Man" (Da Vinci)

2000. New Year 2000.

3835	**1183**	A (70g.) multicoloured	95	75

1184 Bronislaw Malinowski (sociologist)

2000. Polish Personalities. Multicoloured.

3836	1z.55 Type **1184**	2·00	1·60
3837	1z.95 Jozef Zwierzycki (geologist)	2·50	1·90

1185 Otto III granting Crown to Boleslaw I

2000. 1000th Anniv of the Gniezno Summit and the Catholic Church in Poland. Multicoloured.

3838	70g. Type **1185**	80	60
3839	80g. Archbishop of Gnesna, and Bishops of Cracovina, Wratislavia and Colberga	95	75
MS3840 77×65 mm.	1z.55 Provincial representatives presenting gifts to Otto III as Roman Emperor (horiz)	2·20	1·80

1186 Jesus in Tomb

2000. Easter. Multicoloured.

3841	70g. Type **1186**	80	60
3842	80g. Resurrected Christ	95	75

1187 Saurolophus

2000. Prehistoric Animals. Multicoloured.

3843	70g. Type **1187**	80	60
3844	70g. Gallimimus	80	60
3845	80g. Saichania	95	75
3846	80g. Protoceratops	95	75
3847	1z.55 Prenocephale	1·90	1·50
3848	1z.55 Velociraptor	1·90	1·50

1188 Wajda

2000. Presentation of American Film Academy Award to Andrzej Wajda (film director).

3849	**1188**	1z.10 black	1·40	1·10

1189 Pope John Paul kneeling, St. Peter's Basilica, Rome

2000. Holy Year 2000 Opening of Holy Door, St. Peter's Basilica, Rome.

3850	**1189**	80g. multicoloured	95	75

1190 Artist and Model, Poster for *Wesele* (play), and Building

2000. Crakow, European City of Culture.

3851	**1190**	70g. multicoloured	80	60
3852	-	1z.55 multicoloured	2·30	1·80
MS3853 110×77 mm.		1z.75 blue (39×30 mm)	3·25	3·00

DESIGNS: No. 3852, Jagiellonian University, Pope John Paul II, Queen Jadwiga and Krzysztof Penderecki (composer). 38×30 mm—**MS**3853, View of Crakow (wood carving), 1489.

1191 Dying Rose

2000. "Stop Drug Addiction" Campaign.

3854	**1191**	70g. multicoloured	80	60

1192 "Building Europe"

2000. Europa.

3855	**1192**	1z.55 multicoloured	3·25	3·00

1193 Pope John Paul II

2000. 80th Birthday of Pope John Paul II.

3856	**1193**	80g. violet	1·10	85
3857	-	1z.10 multicoloured	1·40	1·10
3858	-	1z.55 green	2·00	1·60

DESIGNS: No. 3857, Holy Mother, Czestochowa; 3858, Pastoral Staff.

1194 Woman's Face and Fan

2000. "Espana 2000" International Stamp Exhibition, Madrid.

3859	**1194**	1z.55 multicoloured	2·00	1·60

1195 Family

2000. Parenthood.

3860	**1195**	70g. multicoloured	80	60

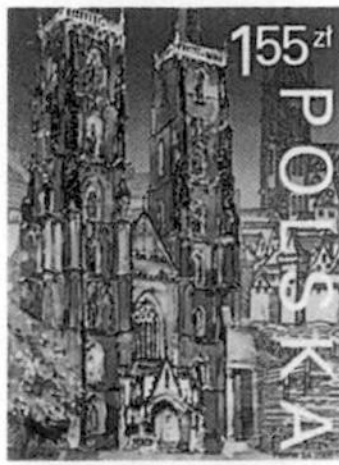

1196 Cathedral, Façade

2000. Millenary of Wroclaw. Sheet 70×90 mm.

MS3861	**1196**	1z.55 multicoloured	2·30	2·10

1197 Karol Marcinkowski

2000. Personalities. Multicoloured.

3862	70g. Type **1197** (founder of Scientific Assistance Association)	80	60
3863	80g. Josemaria Escriva de Balaguer (founder of Priests' Association of St. Cross, 1943)	95	75

1198 Gerwazy and the Count

2000. Pan Tadeusz (poem by Adam Mickiewicz). Illustrations by Michal Elwiro Andriolli from the 1882 edition.

3864	**1198**	70g. brown	80	60
3865	-	70g. brown	80	60
3866	-	80g. green	95	75
3867	-	80g. green	95	75
3868	-	1z.10 purple	1·40	1·10
3869	-	1z.10 purple	1·40	1·10

DESIGNS: No. 3865, Telimenta reclining and the Judge; 3866, Father Robak, Judge and Gerwazy; 3867, Gathering in forest; 3868, Jankiel playing musical instrument; 3869, Zosia and Tadeusz.

1199 Pope John Paul II and St. Peter's Basilica, Rome

2000. National Pilgrimage to Rome. Multicoloured.
3870 80g. Type **1199** 95 75
3871 1z.55 Cross and Colosseum 2·00 1·60

1200 "Self-portrait"

2000. Birth Bicentenary of Piotr Michalowski (artist). Multicoloured.
3872 70g. Type **1200** 80 60
3873 80g. "Portrait of a Boy in a Hat" 95 75
3874 1z.10 "Stable-boy Bridling Percherons" (horiz) 1·40 1·10
3875 1z.55 "Horses with Cart" (horiz) 2·00 1·60

1201 Mary and Jesus (painting), Rozanystok

2000. St. Mary's Sanctuaries. Multicoloured.
3876 70g. Type **1201** 80 60
3877 1z.55 Mary with crown supported by angels, Lichen 2·00 1·60

1202 John Bosco (founder of movement)

2000. Salesian Society (religious educational institution) in Poland.
3878 **1202** 80g. multicoloured 95 75

1203 Victory Sign

2000. 20th Anniv of Solidarity Trade Union. Sheet 60×78 mm.
MS3879 **1203** 1z.65 multicoloured 3·25 3·00

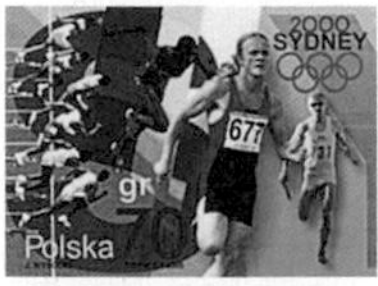

1204 Running

2000. Olympic Games, Sydney. Multicoloured.
3880 70g. Type **1204** 80 60
3881 80g. Diving, wind-surfing, sailing and kayaking 95 75
3882 1z.10 Weight lifting, high jumping and fencing 1·40 1·10
3883 1z.55 Athletics, basketball and judo 1·90 1·50

1205 Postman (Tomasz Wistuba)

2000. World Post Day. Winning Entries in Children's Painting Competition. Multicoloured.
3884 70g. Type **1205** 80 60
3885 80g. Customers and flying stork in Post Office (Katarzyna Chrzanowska) (horiz) 95 75
3886 1z.10 Post Office on "stamp" (Joanna Zbik) (horiz) 1·40 1·10
3887 1z.55 Woman at Post Office counter (Katarzyna Lonak) (horiz) 1·90 1·50

1206 Man with Postage Stamp Wings

2000. 50th Anniv of Polish Philatelic Union. Sheet 75×60 mm.
MS3888 **1206** 1z.55 multicoloured 2·30 2·10

2000. Polish Rulers (15th series). As T **893**.
3889 70g. black, green and olive 80 60
3890 80g. black and purple 95 75
3891 1z.10 black, blue and cobalt 1·40 1·10
3892 1z.55 black and brown 1·90 1·50
DESIGNS: 70g. August II; 80g. Stanislaw Leszczynski; 1z.10, August III; 1z.55, Stanislaw August Poniatowski.

1207 Priest and Cross

2000. 60th Anniv of Katyn Massacre. Multicoloured.
3893 70g. Type **1207** 80 60
3894 80g. Pope John Paul II kneeling at monument, Muranow 95 75

1208 Nativity

2000. Christmas. Multicoloured.
3895 70g. Type **1208** 80 60
3896 80g. Wedding at Cana 95 75
3897 1z.10 The Last Supper 1·40 1·10
3898 1z.55 The Ascension 1·90 1·50

1209 Building Facade

2000. Centenary of Warsaw Art Gallery.
3899 **1209** 70g. multicoloured 80 60

1210 Privately Issued Stamp

2000. Underground Post during Martial Law, 1982–89.
3900 **1210** 80g. multicoloured 1·10 85

1211 Pope John Paul II, Emblem and Crowd

2001. End of Holy Year 2000. Value expressed by letter.
3901 **1211** A (1z.10) mult 1·30 95

1212 Mountains reflected in Ski Goggles

2001. 20th University Games, Zakopane.
3902 **1212** 1z. multicoloured 1·30 95

1213 Computer Mouse

2001. The Internet.
3903 **1213** 1z. multicoloured 1·30 95

1214 Adam Malysz (ski jumper)

2001. World Classic Seniors Championships. Multicoloured.
3904 1z. Type **1214** 1·60 1·20
3905 1z. As Type **1214** but additionally inscribed "Adam Malysz" 1·30 95
3906 1z. As No. 3905 but additionally inscribed "Mistrzem Swiata" 1·30 95

1215 Tomb of the Resurrected Christ

2001. Easter. Multicoloured.
3907 1z. Type **1215** 1·40 95
3908 1z.90 Resurrected Christ and Apostles 2·50 1·80

1216 Emblem and Basketball Players

2001. 12th Salesian Youth World Championships, Warsaw.
3909 **1216** 1z. multicoloured 1·40 95

1217 Water Droplet

2001. Europa. Water Resources.
3910 **1217** 1z.90 multicoloured 2·50 1·80

1218 Man and Mermaid on Beach ("Holiday Greetings")

2001. Greetings Stamps. Multicoloured.
3911 1z. Type **1218** 1·40 95
3912 1z. Man presenting bouquet to woman ("Best Wishes") 1·40 95

1219 "Christ Blessing Children of Wrzesnia" (Marian Turwid) (stained-glass window), Parish Church, Wrzesnia

2001. Centenary of Support of Wrzesnia Schoolchildren for the Language.
3913 **1219** 1z. multicoloured 1·40 95

1220 Polish Scientific Institute and Wanda Stachiewicz Library, Montreal, Canada

2001. Polish Institutions Abroad. Multicoloured.
3914 1z. Type **1220** 1·60 1·10
3915 1z.90 Bust of Josef Pilsudski, Josef Pilsudski Institute, New York 3·00 2·10
3916 2z.10 Polonia Museum, Archives and Library, Orchard Lake, Michigan 3·25 2·30
3917 2z.20 Polish Museum, Chicago 3·50 2·40

1221 Snowdrop (*Galanthus nivalis*) and European Lynx (*Lynx lynx*)

2001. Convention on International Trade of Wild Animals and Plants Threatened with Extinction (C.I.T.E.S.). Multicoloured.
3918 1z. Type **1221** 1·60 1·10
3919 1z. Apollo butterfly (*Parnassius apollo*) and orchid (*Orchis sambucina*) 1·60 1·10
3920 1z. Northern eagle owl (*Bubo bubo*) and *Adonis vernalis* (plant) 1·60 1·10
3921 1z.90 Lady's slipper orchid (*Cypripedium calceolus*) and brown bear (*Ursus arctos*) 3·00 2·10
3922 1z.90 Peregrine falcon (*Falco peregrinus*) and *Orchis pallens* 3·00 2·10
3923 1z.90 Wide leaf orchid (*Orchis latifolia*) and European otter (*Lutra lutra*) 3·00 2·10
MS3924 90×70 mm. 2z. World map and emblem (35×28 mm) 3·50 3·25

1222 Cardinal Wyszynski and Text

2001. Birth Centenary of Cardinal Stefan Wyszynski (Primate of Poland, 1948–81).
3925 **1222** 1z. multicoloured 1·60 1·10

1223 Father Kolbe and Handwriting

2001. 60th Death Anniv of Maksymilian Maria Kolbe (founder of Knighthood of the Immaculate, and concentration camp victim).
3926 **1223** 1z. multicoloured 1·60 75

1224 "St. Mary of the Beautiful Love" (icon)

2001. St. Mary's Sanctuaries. Multicoloured.
3927 1z. Type **1224** (Cathedral of St. Martin and St. Nicolas, Bydgoszcz) 1·60 1·10
3928 1z. St. Mary of Ludzmierz, Basilica of the Assumption of St. Mary, Ludzmierz 1·60 1·10
3929 1z.90 St. Mary the Winner, Church of St. Mary in Piasek, Wroclaw 3·00 2·10

1225 Model of Sanctuary

2001. Completion of Section of God's Mercy Sanctuary at Cracow-Lagiewniki.

3930	**1225**	1z. multicoloured	1·70	1·20

1226 Ligia, Vinius and Petrinius

2001. *Quo Vadis* (film directed by Jerzy Kawalerowicz). Depicting scenes from the film. Multicoloured.

3931	1z. Type **1226**	1·70	1·20
3932	1z. Nero singing at feast	1·70	1·20
3933	1z. St. Peter in the catacombs and the baptism of Chilon Chilonides	1·70	1·20
3934	1z. Chilon Chilonides and crowd fleeing	1·70	1·20
3935	1z. Liga tied to the back of a bull and in the arms of Ursus	1·70	1·20
3936	1z. St. Peter blessing Vincius and Liga	1·70	1·20

1227 Copper Furnace

2001. "Euro Cuprum 2001" European Stamp Exhibition, Lubin. Multicoloured.

3937	1z. Type **1227**	1·70	1·20
3938	1z.90 Engraver at work and men dressing copper sheets	3·00	2·10
3939	2z. Inking plates and engraving press	3·25	2·30
MS3940	88×76 mm. 3z. 18th-century engraving of Lubin and burin (50×39 mm)	5·25	5·00

1228 "Battle of Chocim" (detail, Stanislaw Batowski-Kaczor) and Breast-plate of Stanislaw Skorkowski's Armour

2001. "One Century Passes it Over to Another Century" Exhibition, Polish Military Museum, Warsaw.

3941	**1228**	1z. multicoloured	1·70	1·20

1229 Steam and Electric Locomotives

2001. 75th Anniv of Polish State Railways.

3942	**1229**	1z. multicoloured	1·70	1·20

1230 Street Scene (Marcin Kuron)

2001. Winners of "Poland in 21st Century" (children's painting competition). Multicoloured.

3943	1z. Type **1230**	1·70	1·20
3944	1z.90 Rockets behind girl and boy (Agata Grzyb)	3·00	2·10
3945	2z. Futuristic car and house on wheels (Joanna Sadrakula)	3·25	2·20

1231 Football and Players

2001. Qualification of Poland for World Cup Football Championship, Japan and South Korea.

3946	**1231**	1z. multicoloured	1·70	1·20

1232 Children encircling Globe

2001. World Post Day. United Nations Year of Dialogue among Civilizations.

3947	**1232**	1z.90 multicoloured	3·00	2·10

1233 "100 Years Ago" (detail, Wlodzimierz Kugler)

2001. 80th Anniv of Post and Telecommunication Museum, Wroclaw. Sheet 87×70 mm.

MS3948	**1233**	3z.+75g. multicoloured	7·00	6·75

1234 Violin Peg Box and Scroll

2001. 12th Henryk Wieniawski International Violin Competition, Poznan.

3949	**1234**	1z. multicoloured	1·70	1·20

1235 Pope John Paul II

2001. Papal Day.

3950	**1235**	1z. multicoloured	1·70	1·20

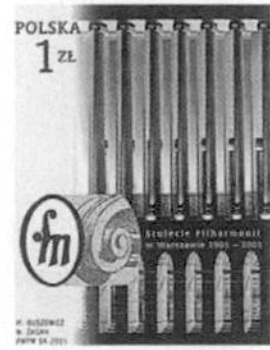
1236 Building Facade

2001. Centenary of National Philharmonic Orchestra.

3951	**1236**	1z. multicoloured	1·70	1·20

1237 Pope John Paul II

2001. New Millennium. Multicoloured.

3952	1z. Type **1237**	1·70	1·20
3953	1z. President Lech Walesa and cover of 1791 constitution	1·70	1·20
3954	1z. Covers of *Glos Wolny Wolnosc Ubespieczaiacy, Kultura, Zniewolony umysl* and *O skutecznym rad sposobie* (magazines)	1·70	1·20
3955	1z. Wojciech Boguslawski (actor and dramatist) and Jerzy Grotowski (director)	1·70	1·20
3956	1z. General Jozef Pilsudski (soldier and President 1918–22) and posters (1989)	1·70	1·20
3957	1z. N.A.T.O. emblem and General Kazimierz Pulaski (soldier)	1·70	1·20
3958	1z. Nicolaus Copernicus and Aleksander Wolszczan (astronomers)	1·70	1·20
3959	1z. Jan of Glogow (wood engraving) (mathematician and astronomer) and Tadeusz Kotarbinski (physicist)	1·70	1·20
3960	1z. "Do Broni" (poster, 1920) and "Bitwa pod Grunwaldem" (detail) (painting, Jan Matejko)	1·70	1·20
3961	1z. Leaders of November Uprising, 1830	1·70	1·20
3962	1z. Head of John the Apostle (detail) (wooden altarpiece, Wit Stwosz) and sculpture by Magdalena Abakanowicz	1·70	1·20
3963	1z. Frederik Chopin, Krzysztof Penderecki (composers) and score of *Mazurka No. 10* by Karol Szymanowski	1·70	1·20
3964	1z. Royal Castle, Warsaw and view of Cracow (wood engraving)	1·70	1·20
3965	1z. Jan III Sobieski (painting) and emblem of European Union	1·70	1·20
3966	1z. Wislawa Szymborska (Nobel Prizewinner for Literature) and Mikolaj Rej (poet)	1·70	1·20
3967	1z. Janusz Kusocinski and Robert Korzeniowski (athletes)	1·70	1·20

1238 Lower Silesian Crib

2001. Christmas. Multicoloured.

3968	1z. Type **1238**	1·60	1·10
3969	1z.90 Lower Silesian Crib (different)	3·00	2·10

1239 Radio Station Building and Virgin Mary (statue)

2001. Tenth Anniv of "Radio Maryia" (religious broadcasting station). Multicoloured.

3970	1z. Type **MS**1239	1·70	1·20
MS3971	176×78 mm. 1z. Virgin Mary (statue) and crowd; 1z. Type **1239**; 1z. Crowd and crowned Virgin Mary (statue)	4·75	4·50

1240 Pear and Apple

2002. Valentine's Day.

3972	**1240**	1z.10 multicoloured	1·70	1·20

1241 Downhill, Biathlon, Ice-skating, and Ski Jumping

2002. Winter Olympic Games, Salt Lake City, U.S.A.

3973	**1241**	1z.10 multicoloured	2·10	1·50

1242 Jan Czerski

2002. Explorers. Multicoloured.

3974	2z. Type **1242**	3·25	2·20
3975	2z. Bronislaw Pilsudski	3·25	2·20

1243 Gniezno

2002. Polish Cities.

3975a	-	5g. multicoloured	25	15
3975b	-	20g. multicoloured	35	20
3975c	-	30g. multicoloured	45	25
3975d	-	1z.20 multicoloured	1·40	75
3975e	-	1z.25 multicoloured	1·50	80
3975ea	-	1z.30 multicoloured	1·60	85
3975eb	-	1z.35 multicoloured	1·70	95
3975ec	-	1z.45 multicoloured	2·50	1·50
3975h	-	1z.80 multicoloured	2·30	1·20
3975i	-	1z.90 multicoloured	2·40	1·30
3976	**1243**	2z. multicoloured	2·50	1·50
3977	-	2z.10 multicoloured	2·75	1·60
3977a	-	2z.20 multicoloured	3·00	1·70
3977b	-	2z.40 multicoloured	3·25	1·80
3977c	-	2z.60 multicoloured	3·25	1·90
3977d	-	2z.80 multicoloured	3·50	2·10
3978	-	3z.20 multicoloured	3·75	2·20
3978a	-	3z.40 multicoloured	3·75	2·30
3978b	-	3z.45 multicoloured	4·00	2·40
3978ba	-	3z.50 green and deep green	4·25	2·50
3978bc	-	3z.55 multicoloured	4·25	2·75
3978bd	-	3z.65 multicoloured	4·50	3·00

DESIGNS: No. 3975a, Sandomierz (horiz); 3975b, Sieradz; 3975c, Katowice (horiz); 3975d, Torun; 3975e, Gdansk; 3975ea, Poznan (horiz); 3975eb, Gorzow Wielkopolski; 3975ec, Raciborz; 3975h, Kalisz (horiz); 3975i, Lodz (horiz); 3977, Krakow; 3977a, Sopot (horiz); 3977b, Czestochowa (horiz); 3977c, Pfock (horiz); 3977d, Szczecin (horiz); 3978, Warsaw; 3978a, Kazimierz Dolny; 3978b, Lublin (horiz); 3978ba, (Przemysl); 3978bc, Chorow; 3978bd, Jeleria Gora.

1244 Flowers

2002. Easter. Multicoloured.

3979	1z.10 Type **1244**	1·70	75
3980	2z. Chicks	3·00	1·20

1245 Labrador Retriever and Puppies

2002. Domestic and Wild Animals. Multicoloured.

3981	1z.10 Type **1245**	1·70	75
3982	1z.10 Cat and kittens	1·70	75
3983	1z.10 Wolf and cubs	1·70	75
3984	1z.10 Lynx and kittens	1·70	75

1246 Soldiers marching

2002. 60th Anniv of Evacuation of General Wladislaw Ander's Army from U.S.S.R.

3985	**1246**	1z.10 multicoloured	1·70	75

1247 Trees (Amanda Zejmis)

2002. Paintings. Multicoloured.

3986	1z.10 Type **1257**	1·70	75
3987	1z.10 Vase and ornaments (Henryk Paraszczuk)	1·70	75
3988	2z. Landscape (Lucjan Matula) (horiz)	3·50	1·20

3989 3z.20 Basket of flowers (Jozefa Laciak) (horiz) 5·25 2·20

1248 Stylized Figures

2002. National Census.

3990	**1248**	1z.10 multicoloured	1·70	75

1249 Radio Microphone

2002. 50th Anniv of "Radio Free Europe".

3991	**1249**	2z. multicoloured	3·25	1·20

1250 Fireman

2002. Tenth Anniv of State Fire Brigade.

3992	**1250**	1z.10 multicoloured	1·70	75

1251 Circus Artist

2002. Europa. Circus.

3993	**1251**	2z. multicoloured	3·50	1·80

1252 "Madonna with the Child, St. John the Baptist and the Angel" (Sandro Botticelli)

2002. 140th Anniv of the National Gallery, Warsaw.

3994	**1252**	1z.10 multicoloured	1·70	75

1253 Maria Konopnicka

2002. 160th Birth Anniv of Maria Konopnicka (poet and writer).

3995	**1253**	1z.10 brown, ochre and green	1·70	75

1254 Scooter

2002. Children's Games. Multicoloured.

3996		1z.10 Type **1254**	1·70	75
3997		1z.10 Flying kite	1·70	75
3998		1z.10 Badminton	1·70	75

1255 Football and Globe

2002. World Cup Football Championship, Japan and South Korea. Multicoloured.

3999	1z.10 Type **1255**	1·70	75
4000	2z. Player chasing ball	3·25	1·20

1256 Domeyko and Santiago University, Chile

2002. Birth Bicentenary of Ignacego Domeyki (scientist).

4015	**1256**	2z.60 multicoloured	4·25	2·20

1257 Hibiscus and Tulips

2002. "Philakorea 2002" International Philatelic Exhibition, Seoul and "Amphilex 2002" International Philatelic Exhibition, Amsterdam.

4016	**1257**	2z. multicoloured	3·25	1·60

1258 Pope John Paul II and Basilica of Virgin Mary of the Angel, Kalwaria Zebrzydowska

2002. Seventh Papal Visit To Poland (1st issue). Multicoloured.

4017	1z.10 Type **1258**	1·70	85
4018	1z.80 Pope John Paul II and Sanctuary of God's Mercy, Sisters of Virgin Mary's Convent, Lagiewniki	3·00	1·50

See also No. **MS**4022.

1259 "Holy Lady of Assistance"

2002. St. Mary's Sanctuaries. Multicoloured.

4019	1z.10 Type **1259** (Church of the Holy Lady of Assistance, Jaworzno)	1·70	85
4020	1z.10 "Holy Virgin of Opole" (Cathedral of Holy Cross, Opole)	1·70	85
4021	2z. "Holy Virgin of Trabki" (Church of the Assumption of the Holy Lady, Trabki Wielkie)	3·50	1·70

1260 Pope John Paul II and Wawel Castle, Cracow

2002. Seventh Papal Visit To Poland (2nd issue). Sheet 73×57 mm.

MS4022	**1260**	3z.20 black	5·25	4·75

1261 Spa Building, Ciechocinku

2002. 18th Polish Philatelic Association Convention, Ciechocinku. Sheet 74×105 mm.

MS4023	**1261**	3z.20 brown	5·25	4·75

1262 Czesnik Raptusiewicz and Dyndalski

2002. "Zemsta" (Revenge) (film directed by Andrzej Wajda). Sheet 177×137 mm containing T **1262**, Showing scenes from the film. Multicoloured.

MS4024	1z.10 Type **1262**; 1z.10 Klara and Waclaw; 1z.10 Papkin; 1z.10 Regent Milczek and Papkin; 1z.10 Regent Milczek and Czesnik Raptusiewicz; 1z.10 Podstolina and Klara	11·50	10·50

1263 Schwarzkopf Okl-359

2002. Steam Locomotives. Showing locomotives from Wolsztyn Railway Museum. Multicoloured.

4025	1z.10 Type **1263**	1·70	85
4026	1z.10 Fablok 0149-7	1·70	85
4027	2z. Krolewiec Tki3-87	3·25	1·60
4028	2z. Express locomotive Pm 36-2	3·25	1·60

1264 Hands holding Pens

2002. World Post Day.

4029	**1264**	2z. multicoloured	3·25	1·60

1265 Emblem

2002. Anti-Cancer Campaign.

4030	**1265**	1z.10 multicoloured	1·70	85

1266 Emblem

2002. 50th Anniv of Polish Television. Sheet 185×115 mm containing T **1266** Showing emblems of television programmes. Multicoloured.

MS4031	1z.10 Type **1266** (TV News); 1z.10 TV Theatre; 1z.10 "Pegaz" (cultural programme); 1z.10 "Teleranek" (children's programme)	7·00	6·50

1267 St. Stanislaw

2002. Saints. Sheet 136×165 mm containing T **1267** and similar vert designs. Multicoloured.

MS4032	1z.10 Type **1267**; 1z.10 St. Kazimierz; 1z.10 St. Faustyna Kowalska; 1z.10 St. Benedict; 1z.10 St. Cyril and St. Methody; 1z.10 St. Catherine of Siena	10·50	10·00

1268 Christmas Tree Baubles

2002. Christmas. Multicoloured.

4033	1z.10 Type **1268**	1·70	85
4034	2z. Small purple and large yellow baubles	3·00	1·50

1269 "POLSKA" superimposed on "EUROPA"

2003. Poland's Accession to European Union (1st issue). Negotiations.

4035	**1269**	1z.20 multicoloured	2·10	1·00

See also No. 4067, 4069 and 4120.

1270 Pope John Paul II on Balcony of St. Peter's Basilica, 1978

2003. 25th Anniv of the Pontificate of Pope John Paul II (1st issue). Multicoloured.

4036	1z.20 Type **1270**	1·70	85
4037	1z.20 Celebrating mass, Victory Square, Warsaw, 1979	1·70	85
4038	1z.20 Addressing young people, Parc des Princes Stadium, Paris, 1980	1·70	85
4039	1z.20 Assassination attempt, St. Peter Square, 1981	1·70	85
4040	1z.20 Giving homily surrounded by flowers, Portugal, 1982	1·70	85
4041	1z.20 Kneeling in front of Holy Doors, start of Holy Year of Redemption, 1983	1·70	85
4042	1z.20 Meeting Sandro Pertini, Pres. of Italy, 1984	1·70	85
4043	1z.20 International Youth Day, Rome, 1985	1·70	85
4044	1z.20 First visit of Pope to Synagogue, 1986	1·70	85
4045	1z.20 Inaugurating Year of Mary, 1987	1·70	85
4046	1z.20 Visiting European Parliament, Strasbourg, 1988	1·70	85
4047	1z.20 Meeting Mikhail Gorbachev, Pres. Soviet Union, 1989	1·70	85
4048	1z.20 Visiting lepers in Guinea-Bissau, 1990	1·70	85
4049	1z20 Addressing Bishop's Synod, 1991	1·70	85
4050	1z.20 Pronouncing the Catechism, 1992	1·70	85
4051	1z.20 Enthroned, Assissi, 1993	1·70	85
4052	1z.20 Celebrating Mass in the Sistine Chapel, 1994	1·70	85
4053	1z.20 Addressing the United Nations, 1995	1·70	85
4054	1z.20 Walking through the Brandenburg Gate with Chancellor Helmut Kohl, 1996	1·70	85
4055	1z.20 Celebrating Mass in Sarajevo, 1997	1·70	85
4056	1z.20 With Fidel Castro, Cuba, 1998	1·70	85
4057	1z.20 Opening door, Christmas, 1999	1·70	85
4058	1z.20 With young people, World Youth Day, Rome, 2000	1·70	85
4059	1z.20 Closing door of St. Peter's Basilica, 2001	1·70	85
4060	1z.20 Visiting the Italian Parliament, 2002	1·70	85

1271 Pope John Paul II

2003. 25th Anniv of the Pontificate of Pope John Paul II (2nd issue).

4061	**1271**	10z. silver	16·00	15·00

1272 Andrzej Modrzewski

2003. 500th Birth Anniv of Andrzej Frycz Modrzewski (writer).

4062	**1272**	1z.20 black	1·90	95

1273 "Christ Anxious"

2003. Easter. Folk Sculpture. Multicoloured.

4063	1z.20 Type **1273**	1·90	95
4064	2z.10 "Christ Vanquisher"	3·25	1·60

1274 Poznan Ancient and Modern

2003. 750th Anniv of Poznan.

4065	**1274** 1z.20 multicoloured	1·90	95
MS4066	95×72 mm 3z.40 cinnamon and black (40×31 mm)	4·75	4·25

DESIGN: 3z.40 Ancient view of city and city arms.

1275 Portico and Clouds

2003. Poland's Accession to European Union (2nd issue).

4067	**1275** 1z.20 multicoloured	2·10	1·00

1276 Poster for "Vanitas" Exhibition (Wieslaw Walkuski)

2003. Europa. Poster Art.

4068	**1276** 2z.10 multicoloured	3·50	1·70

1277 "POLSKA" superimposed on "EUROPA"

2003. Poland's Accession to European Union (3rd issue). Referendum.

4069	**1277** 1z.20 multicoloured	2·10	1·00

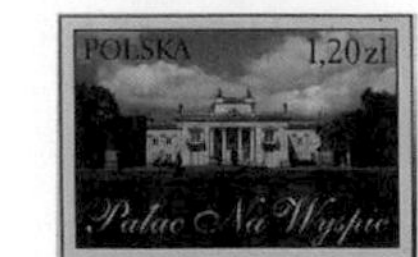

1278 Island Palace (south view)

2003. Royal Baths, Lazienki Park, Warsaw. Multicoloured.

4070	1z.20 Type **1278**	1·90	95
4071	1z.80 Island Palace (north view)	2·75	1·40
4072	2z.10 Myslewicki Palace	3·25	1·70
4073	2z.60 Amphitheatre	4·25	2·10

1279 Pyramids and Camel (Anna Golebiewska)

2003. Children's Paintings. Stamp Design Competition Winners. Designs on theme "My Dream Vacation". Multicoloured.

4074	1z.20 Type **1279**	1·90	95
4075	1z.80 Girl windsurfing (Marlena Krejpcio) (vert)	2·75	1·40
4076	2z.10 Wind-surfer and fish (Michal Korzen)	3·25	1·70
4077	2z.60 Girl and hens (Ewa Zadjdler)	4·25	2·10

1280 "Krak" (anonymous)

2003. Fairy Tales. Multicoloured.

4078	1z.20 Type **1280**	1·90	95
4079	1z.80 "Stupid Mateo" (Josef Kraszewski)	2·75	1·40
4080	2z.10 "Frog Princess" (Antoni Glinski)	3·25	1·70
4081	2z.60 "Crock of Gold" (Josef Kraszewski)	4·25	2·10

1281 Katowice Cathedral

2003. Katowice 2003 National Stamp Exhibition. Sheet 94×71 mm.

MS4082	**1281** 3z.40 black, brown and ochre	6·00	5·75

No. **MS**4082 also exists imperforate.

1282 "Self Portrait"

2003. Birth Centenary of Julian Falat (artist). Multicoloured.

4083	1z.20 Type **1282**	1·90	95
4084	1z.80 "Spear Men"	2·75	1·40
4085	2z.10 "Winter Landscape with River and Bird" (horiz)	3·25	1·70
4086	2z.60 "Aboard Ship-Merchants of Ceylon" (horiz)	4·25	2·10

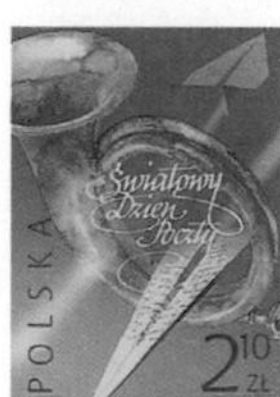

1283 Post Horn

2003. World Post Day.

4087	**1283** 2z.20 multicoloured	3·25	1·60

1284 "Holy Virgin of Czestochowa"

2003. St. Mary's Sanctuaries. Multicoloured.

4088	1z.20 Type **1284** (Church of the Holy Redeemer, Warsaw)	1·70	85
4089	1z.80 "Holy Mother Benevolent" (Basilica of Assumption of Holy Virgin, Krzeszowice)	2·50	1·30
4090	2z.10 "Holy Virgin" (Church of the Holy Virgin, Zieleniec)	3·50	1·70

1285 Motor Cycle (1903)

2003. Centenary of Motor Cycle Racing in Poland. Multicoloured.

4091	1z.20 Type **1285**	1·70	85
4092	1z.20 Rudge (c. 1930)	1·70	85
4093	1z.20 NSU (c. 1940)	1·70	85

1286 Dancers wearing Traditional Costume

2003. 50th Anniv of Folk Dance Troup "Slask". Multicoloured.

4094	1z.20 Type **1286**	1·70	85
4095	1z.20 Dancers (different)	1·70	85

Nos. 4094/5 were issued together, *se-tenant*, forming a composite design.

1287 Perching Adult holding Fish

2003. Endangered Species. Osprey (*Pandion haliaetus*). Multicoloured.

4096	1z.20 Type **1287**	1·70	85
4097	1z.20 Adult and chicks on nest	1·70	85
4098	1z.20 Adult catching fish (one wing visible)	1·70	85
4099	1z.20 Adult carrying fish (both wings visible)	1·70	85

Nos. 4096/9 were issued together, *se-tenant*, forming a composite design.

1288 Two White Storks

2003. www.poland.gov.pl (Poland on the internet).

4100	**1288** 2z.10 multicoloured	2·75	1·40

1289 The Nativity

2003. Christmas. Multicoloured.

4101	1z.20 Type **1289**	1·90	95
4102	1z.80 Three Kings	2·75	1·40
4103	2z.10 Angel appearing to Mary (vert)	3·25	1·70
4104	2z.60 Holy Family (vert)	3·75	1·90

1290 Wislawa Szymborska

2003. Polish Influence Abroad (1st series). Showing designs from other countries' stamps.

4105	**1290** 1z.20 purple, green and black	1·90	95
4106	- 1z.80 ultramarine, blue and black (horiz)	2·75	1·40
4107	- 2z.10 purple, azure and black	3·25	1·70
4108	- 2z.60 slate and black (horiz)	3·75	1·90

DESIGNS: 1z.20, Wislawa Szymborska (writer) (as Sweden No. 2120); 1z.80, Marie Sklodowska-Curie (physicist) (as France No. 1765); 2z.10, Czeslaw Milosz (writer) (as Sweden No. 1299); 2z.60, "Holy Virgin of Czestochowa" (as Vatican City No. 481).

See also Nos. 4112/13.

1291 Heart

2004. Orchestra of Holy Day Assistance (fund raising charity).

4109	**1291** 1z.25 multicoloured	1·70	85

1292 Airliner

2004. 75th Anniv of LOT (Polish airlines).

4110	**1292** 1z.25 multicoloured	1·70	85

1293 Boy and Girl with Heart-shaped Balloon

2003. St. Valentine.

4111	**1293** 1z.25 multicoloured	1·70	85

1294 Helena Paderewska

2004. Polish Influence Abroad (2nd series). Multicoloured.

4112	2z.10 Type **1294** co-founder of USA Polish White Cross (humanitarian organization)	3·25	1·60
4113	2z.10 Lucjan Bojnowski (New Britain, USA church pioneer)	3·25	1·60

1295 Chocolate Rabbit

2004. Easter. Multicoloured.

4114	1z.25 Type **1295**	1·70	85
4115	2z.10 Ceramic lamb	3·25	1·60

1296 Beaver and Frog

2004. Fauna. Multicoloured.

4116	1z.25 Type **1296**	1·70	85
4117	1z.25 Kingfisher, crayfish, roach and water beetle	1·70	85
4118	1z.25 Grayling, leech and water snail	1·70	85
4119	1z.25 Pike, grebe and roach	1·70	85

Nos. 4116/19 were issued together, *se-tenant*, forming a composite design.

1297 Map of Europe and New Members' Flags

2004. Poland's Accession to European Union (4th issue).

4120	**1297** 2z.10 multicoloured	3·25	1·60

1298 Rucksack as Landscape

2004. Europa. Holidays.
4121 **1298** 2z.10 multicoloured 3·25 1·60

1299 Figure (sculpture, St. Mariacki Square, Krakow)

2004. Tenth Government Postage Stamp Printers' Conference, Krakow.
4122 **1299** 3z.45 multicoloured 5·25 2·50

1300 Pope John Paul II

2004. Pope John Paul II visits to Poland, 1970–2002. Two sheets, each 115×185 mm containing T **1300** and similar vert designs. Multicoloured.
MS4123 (a) 1z.25 ×4, Type **1300** (1979); At prayer (1983); Holding reliquary (1987); Resting head against staff (1991). (b) 1z.25 ×4, Holding staff (1991); With raised hand (1997); Seated facing right (1999); Seated facing left (2002). Set of 2 sheets 14·00 13·00

1301 Crimson Rosella (*Platycercus elegans*)

2004. Birds. Multicoloured.
4124 1z.25 Type **1301** 1·70 85
4125 1z.25 Cockatiel (*Nymphicus hollandicus*) 1·70 85
4126 1z.25 Budgerigar (*Melopsittacus undulates*) 1·70 85
4127 1z.25 Spotted-side finch (*Poephila guttata*), Gouldian finch (*Chloebia gouldiae*) and Java sparrow (*Padda oryzivora*) 1·70 85

1302 "Self-portrait wearing White"

2004. 150th Birth Anniv of Jacek Malczewski (artist). Multicoloured.
4128 1z.25 Type **1302** 1·70 85
4129 1z.90 "Ellenai" 2·75 1·40
4130 2z.10 "Tobias with Harpy" (horiz) 3·25 1·60
4131 2z.60 "The Unknown Note" (horiz) 3·75 1·90

1303 Sun Wu-Kung (monkey king)

2004. Singapore International Stamp Exhibition. Sheet 90×70 mm.
MS4132 3z.45 multicoloured 5·25 4·75

1304 Boxer

2004. Olympic Games, Athens. Sheet 198×117 mm containing T **1304** and similar horiz designs. Multicoloured.
MS4133 1z.25 ×4, Type **1304**; Hurdler; Show jumper; Wrestler 7·00 6·50

The stamps and margin of **MS**4133 form a composite design.

1305 Witold Gombrowicz

2004. Birth Centenary of Witold Gombrowicz (writer).
4134 **1305** 1z.25 ultramarine 1·70 85

1306 "Holy Mother of Miedzna"

2004. St. Mary's Sanctuaries. Multicoloured.
4135 1z.25 Type **1306** (Church of the Annunciation of Our Lady of Miedzna) 1·70 85
4136 1z.25 "Holy Mary and Family" (John the Baptist Basilica, Studiazianna) 1·70 85
4137 1z.25 "Holy Virgin of Sianow" (Church of the Nativity of Our Lady of Sianow) 1·70 85
4138 1z.25 "Holy Mary of Rywald" (St. Sebastian and Nativity of Our Lady, Rywald) 1·70 85
4139 1z.25 "Holy Mary of Piekary" (Name of Our Lady and St. Bartholome Basilica,Piekary Slaskie) 1·70 85
4140 1z.25 "Holy Mary of Ruda" (Assumption of Our Lady Church, Ruda) 1·70 85
4141 1z.25 "Holy Mary of Lomza" (Archangel St. Michael Cathedral, Lomza) 1·70 85
4142 1z.25 "Holy Mary of Perpetual Assistance" (Barefoot Carmelite Convent,Niedzwiady) 1·70 85
4143 1z.25 "Holy Mary of Rychwald" (St. Nicholas and Our Lady of Scapular, Rychwald) 1·70 85
4144 1z.25 "Crying Holy Mary" (St. John the Baptist and Evangelist, Lublin) 1·70 85
4145 1z.25 "Holy Mary of Dzikow" (Assumption of Our Lady Convent, Tarnobrzeg) 1·70 85
4146 1z.25 "Holy Mary of Rzeszow" (Assumption of Our Lady Church, Rzeszow) 1·70 85
4147 1z.25 "Gracious Holy Mary" (St. Stanislaw, St. Peter and St. Paul, Lubaczow) 1·70 85
4148 1z.25 "Holy Mother of Fatima" (Immaculate Heart of Our Lady of Fatima,Szczecin) 1·70 85
4149 1z.25 "Pieta of Skrzatusz" (Assumption of Our lady Church, Skrzatusz) 1·70 85
4150 1z.25 "Pieta of Obory" (Visitation of Our Lady Church, Obory) 1·70 85
4151 1z.25 "Holy Mary of Jasnagora" (Queen of Poland Sanctuary, Jasnagora) 1·70 85

1307 Czeslaw Niemen

2004. Czeslaw Wydrzycki (Niemen) (musician) Commemoration.
4152 **1307** 1z.25 black 1·70 85

1308 Raft on River Dunajec

2004. Raft Men working on River Dunajec (bordering Slovakia and Poland).
4153 **1308** 2z.10 multicoloured 3·25 1·60

A stamp of the same design was issued by Slovakia.

1309 Motor Cyclists

2004. Motor Sports. Multicoloured.
4154 1z.25 Type **1309** 1·70 85
4155 1z.25 Race car 1·70 85
4156 1z.25 Kart racing 1·70 85
4157 1z.25 Motor cyclist (2004 International Six Day's Enduro) 1·70 85

Nos. 4154/7 were issued together, *se-tenant*, forming a composite design.

1310 Binary Codes forming Postman

2004. World Post Day.
4158 **1310** 2z.10 multicoloured 3·25 1·60

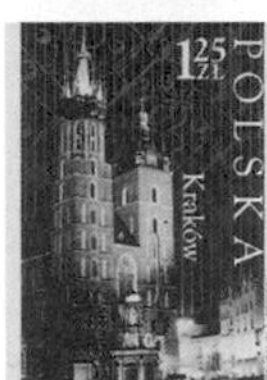

1311 Holy Mary Church, Krakow

2004. World Heritage Sites. Multicoloured.
4159 1z.25 Type **1311** 1·70 85
4160 1z.25 Tower, St. John the Baptist and Evangelist Cathedral, Torun 1·70 85
4161 1z.25 Town Hall, Zamosc 1·70 85
4162 1z.25 Riverside, Warsaw (horiz) 1·70 85
4163 1z.25 Castle, Malbork (horiz) 1·70 85

1312 People entering Church

2004. Christmas. Multicoloured.
4164 1z.25 Type **1312** 1·70 85
4165 2z.10 Decorated window (horiz) 3·25 1·60

1313 Protoplanet circling Sun

2004. History of Earth. Multicoloured.
4166 1z.25 Type **1313** 1·70 85
4167 1z.25 Asteroids bombarding earth 1·70 85
4168 1z.25 Dinosaurs 1·70 85
4169 1z.25 International space station in orbit 1·70 85

1314 "13"

2005. Orchestra of Holy Day Assistance (fund raising charity).
4170 **1314** 1z.30 multicoloured 1·90 1·10

1315 Konstanty Galczynski

2005. Birth Centenary of Konstanty Ildefons Galczynski (writer).
4171 **1315** 1z.30 multicoloured 1·90 1·10

1316 Mikolaj Rej

2005. 500th Birth Anniv of Mikolaj Rej (writer).
4172 **1316** 1z.30 black and vermilion 1·90 1·10

1317 Masked Swordsman and Carved Heart on Tree

2005. Greetings Stamp.
4173 **1317** 1z.30 multicoloured 1·90 1·10

1318 Rabbit

2005. Easter. Multicoloured.
4174 1z.30 Type **1318** 1·90 1·10
4175 2z.2 0 Chick 3·25 1·80

1319 "The Little Mermaid"

2005. Birth Bicentenary of Hans Christian Andersen (writer). Multicoloured.
4176 1z.30 Type **1319** 1·90 1·10
4177 1z.30 "The Snow Queen" 1·90 1·10

1320 Pope John Paul II

2005. Pope John Paul II Commemoration (1st issue).
4178 **1320** 1z.30 multicoloured 1·90 1·10

See also No. **MS**4184.

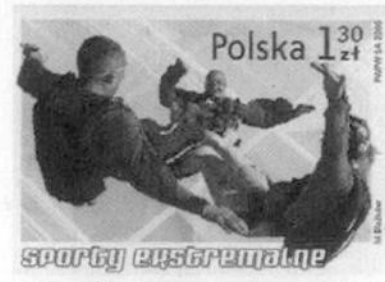

1321 Sky Diving

2005. Extreme Sports. Multicoloured.

4179	1z.30 Type **1321**	1·90	1·10
4180	1z.30 Bungee jumping	1·90	1·10
4181	1z.30 Rock climbing	1·90	1·10
4182	1z.30 White water rafting	1·90	1·10

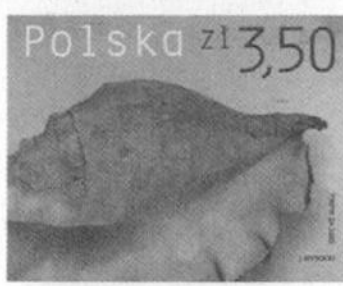

1322 Shell

2005. Pacific Explorer International Stamp Exhibition, Sydney. Sheet 90×70 mm. Perf or imperf.

MS4183 **1322** 3z.50 multicoloured 5·25 4·75

1323 Pope John Paul II

2005. Pope John Paul II Commemoration (2nd issue). Sheet 70×83 mm.

MS4184 **1323** 3z.50 multicoloured 6·00 4·75

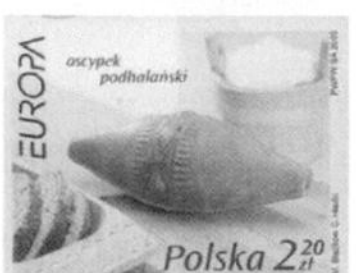

1324 Bread

2005. Europa. Gastronomy.

4185 **1324** 2z.20 multicoloured 3·50 1·90

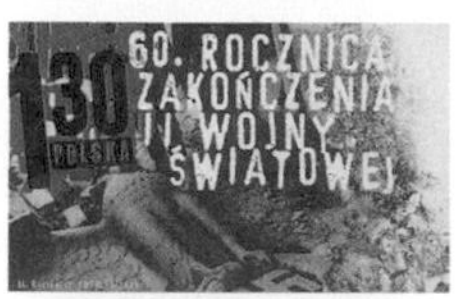

1325 Rubble

2005. 60th Anniv of End of World War II.

4186 **1325** 1z.30 black and vermilion 1·90 1·10

1326 "The Hour of the Crimson Rose" (M. Kruger)

2005. Stories. Sheet 124×124 mm containing T **1326** and similar square designs. Multicoloured.

MS4187 1z.30 Type **1326**; 2z. "The Little Prince" (Antoine de Saint-Exupery); 2z.20 "2000 Leagues under the Sea" (Jules Verne); 2z.80 "In the Desert and the Forest" (H. Sienkiewicz) 12·00 11·50

1327 "Stanislaw Kostka Potocki" (Jacques-Louis David)

2005. Bicentenary of National Museum, Wilanow. Sheet 95×130 mm containing T **1327** and similar vert designs. Multicoloured.

MS4188 1z.30 Type **1327**; 2z.17th-century Nautilus wine cup; 2z.20 Flower girl (18th-century porcelain); 2z.80 19th-century clock 12·00 11·50

1328 Embroidered Rose (Podhale)

2005. Embroidery. Designs showing embroidered roses. Multicoloured.

4189	1z.30 Type **1328**	1·90	1·10
4190	2z. Rose (Lowicz)	3·00	1·60
4191	2z.20 Rose (Podhale) (different)	3·25	1·80
4192	2z.80 Rose (Lowicz) (different)	4·25	2·30

1329 Hurdling

2005. International Athletics Championship, Helsinki. Sheet 200×115 mm containing T **1329** and similar horiz designs. Multicoloured.

MS4193 1z.30 Type **1329**; 1z.30 Shot put; 2z. Triple jump; 2z. Pole vault 9·50 9·00

1330 Jozef Pilsudski (Commander in Chief)

2005. 85th Anniv of Battle of Warsaw ("Miracle on the Vistula"). Sheet 70×90 mm.

MS4194 **1330** 3z.50 multicoloured 5·25 4·75

1331 Lech Walesa (founder)

2005. 25th Anniv of Solidarity (trade union).

4195 **1331** 2z.20 vermilion, grey and black 3·25 2·00

1332 "80"

2005. 80th Anniv of Radio.

4196 **1332** 1z.30 rosine and black 1·90 1·10

1333 Music Score and Frederick Chopin

2005. Frederick Chopin International Piano Competition.

4197 **1333** 2z.20 green, vermilion and black 3·25 2·00

1334 Lemur (Opole)

2005. Zoological Gardens. Each black.

4198	1z.30 Type **1334**	1·90	1·10
4199	2z. Siberian tiger (*Panthera tigris altaica*) (Wroclaw)	3·00	1·80
4200	2z.20 White rhinoceros (*Ceratotherium simum*) (Poznan)	3·25	2·00
4201	2z.80 Anteater (Warsaw)	4·25	2·50

1335 Post Office Building, Cracow

2005. Post Day. Architecture.

4202 **1335** 1z.30 multicoloured 1·90 1·10

1336 Gingerbread Men

2005. 60th Anniv of United Nations.

4203 **1336** 2z.20 multicoloured 3·25 2·00

1337 St. Maciej's Church and St. Stefan's Statue, Budapest

2005. European Capitals. Multicoloured.

4204	1z.30 Type **1337**	1·90	1·40
4205	1z.30 Vilnius Cathedral	1·90	1·40
4206	2z.20 Arc de Triomphe, Paris	3·25	2·30
4207	2z.20 Monument to the Discoverers Belem, Lisbon	3·25	2·30
4208	2z.80 Government building, Dublin	4·00	3·00

1338 "Ploughing in the Ukraine" (L. J. Wyczolkowski)

2005. Art. Polish Impressionists. Sheet 94×130 mm containing T **1338** and similar horiz designs. Multicoloured.

MS4209 1z.30×2, Type **1338**; "Still Life" (J. Panekiewicz); 2z.×2, "Flower Sellers" (O. Boznanska); "The Garden" (W. Podkowinski) 9·75 9·25

1339 Stethoscope in Pocket

2005. Bicentenary of Doctors' Association.

4210 **1339** 1z.30 multicoloured 1·90 1·40

1340 Trees and Angel

2005. Christmas. Multicoloured.

4211	1z.30 Type **1340**	1·90	1·40
4212	2z.20 Angel facing right	3·25	2·50

1346 *Pedicularis sudetica*

2006. Endangered Species. Flowers. Multicoloured.

4218	1z.30 Type **1346**	1·90	1·40
4219	2z.40 *Trapa antans*	3·50	2·50

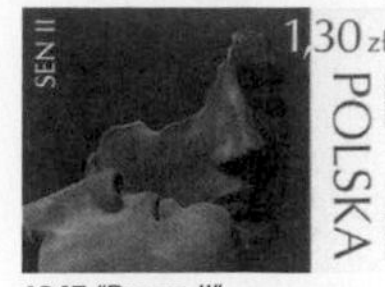

1347 "Dream II"

2006. Contemporary Sculpture. Igor Mitoraj. Multicoloured.

4220	1z.30 Type **1347**	1·90	1·40
4221	1z.30 "Lips of Eros"	1·90	1·40

1348 Floral Procession, Palm Sunday

2006. Easter. Multicoloured.

4222	1z.30 Type **1348**	1·90	1·40
4223	2z.40 Smigus-dynus (dousing with water), Easter Monday	3·50	2·50

1349 Tree, Man and Stars

2006. Europa. Integration.

4224 **1349** 2z.40 multicoloured 3·50 2·50

1350 "2006 WASHINGTON"

2006. Washington 2006 International Stamp Exhibition. Sheet 115×77 mm.

MS4225 **1350** 2z.40 blue and vermilion 3·75 3·50

1351 Pope Benedict XVI

2006. Visit of Pope Benedict XVI.

4226 **1351** 1z.30 multicoloured 1·90 1·40

1352 Stilo

2006. Lighthouses. Multicoloured.

4227	2z.40 Type **1352**	3·50	2·50
4228	2z.40 Krynica Morska	3·50	2·50
4229	2z.40 Gaski	3·50	2·50
4230	2z.40 Niechorze	3·50	2·50

1353 Spinning Top

2006. Toys. Multicoloured.

4231	1z.30 Type **1353**	1·90	1·40
4232	1z.30 Windmill	1·90	1·40

1354 Baroque Tankard

2006. Gold and Silver Ware. Multicoloured.

4233	1z.30 Type **1354**	1·90	1·40
4234	1z.30 Empire Lasting Forever Gold Cup	1·90	1·40

Stamps of the same design were issued by China.

1355 Workers Procession, Poznan

2006. 50th Anniv of Workers' Revolt, Poznan (**MS**4235a) and 30th Anniv of Workers' Revolt, Radom (**MS**4235b). Two sheets, each 90×70 mm containing T **1355** and similar horiz design.

MS4235 (a) 3z.50 blue and black. (28.6) (b) 3z.50 grey and slate 9·50 9·00

DESIGNS: (a) Type **1355**. (b) Workers on lorry, Radom.

1356 Jerzy Giedroyc

2006. Birth Centenary of Jerzy Giedroyc (journalist).

4236	**1356**	1z.30 black	1·90	1·40

1357 Edward Szczeklik

2006. Centenary of Internal Medicine Society. Multicoloured.

4237	1z.30 Type **1357**	1·90	1·40
4238	1z.30 Witold Eugeniusz Orlowskil	1·90	1·40
4239	3z. Antoni Wladyslaw Gluzinski	4·00	3·00

1358 Lubin Town Hall

2006. 19th Convention of Polish Philatelic Association. Sheet 90×70 mm.

MS4240 **1358** 3z.50 multicoloured 4·75 3·50

1363 The Nativity

2006. Christmas. Multicoloured.

4253	1z.30 Type **1363**	5·75	4·25
4254	2z.40 "Christmas"	3·50	2·50

1364 Coal bleeding

2006. 25th Anniv of End of Miners' Strike for Solidarity.

4255	**1364**	1z.30 multicoloured	1·90	1·40

1365 Heart as Planet

2007. Orchestra of Holy Day Assistance (fund raising charity).

4256	**1365**	1z.35 multicoloured	1·90	1·40

1366 Ice Dancers

2007. European Figure Skating Championships, Warsaw.

4257	**1366**	2z.40 multicoloured	3·50	2·50

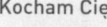

1367 Hearts as Butterflies

2007. St. Valentine's Day.

4258	**1367**	1z.35 multicoloured	1·90	1·40

1368 Straw Lamb

2007. Easter. Multicoloured.

4259	1z.35 Type **1368**	1·90	1·40
4260	2z.40 Easter egg chicken	3·50	2·50

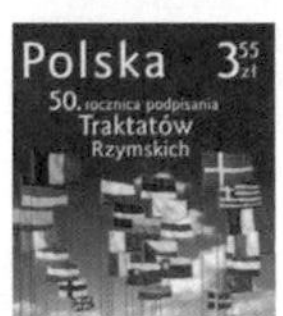

1369 Flags

2007. 50th Anniv of Treaty of Europe.

4261	**1369**	3z.55 multicoloured	5·25	3·75

1370 Cake

2007. Greetings Stamps. Multicoloured.

4262	1z.35 Type **1370**	1·90	1·40
4263	1z.35 Grapes, wine and bread	1·90	1·40
4264	1z.35 Wedding rings	1·90	1·40

1371 Recycle Emblem

2007. Earth Day.

4265	**1371**	1z.35 multicoloured	1·90	1·40

1372 Postal Wagon Type 5G c.1956

2007. Railways. Multicoloured.

4266	1z.35 Type **1372**	1·90	1·40
4267	1z.35 Carriage Type Cd21b c.1924	1·90	1·40
4268	2z.40 Carriage Type C3Pr07 c.1909	3·50	2·50
4269	2z.40 Carriage Type Ci29 c.1929	3·50	2·50

1373 Scout

2007. Europa. Centenary of Scouting.

4270	**1373**	3z. multicoloured	5·50	4·00

1374 'Little Helen with Vase of Flowers'

2007. Death Centenary of Stanislaw Wyspianski (artist and writer).

4271	**1374**	1z.35 multicoloured	1·90	1·40

1375 Karol Szymanowski

2007. 125th Birth and 70th Death Anniv of Karol Szymanowski (composer and writer).

4272	**1375**	1z.35 multicoloured	1·90	1·40

1376 Centre of Cracow, Locating Document and City Arms

2007. 750th Anniv of Cracow.

4273	**1376**	2z.40 multicoloured	3·50	2·50

1377 St. Catherine of Alexandria Church, St. Petersburg

2007. Saint Petersburg 2007 International Philatelic Exhibition. Sheet 90×70 mm.

MS4274 **1377** 3z. multicoloured 4·50 4·25

1378 Gdansk

2007. Lighthouses. Sheet 90×125 mm containing T **1378** and similar vert designs. Multicoloured.

MS4275 1z.35 Type **1378**; 2z.40 Rozewie; 3z. Kolobrzeg; 3z.55 Hel 15·00 14·50

1379 Virgin Mary and Child

2007. 300th Anniv of Lesniow Monastery.

4276	**1379**	1z.35 multicoloured	1·90	1·40

1380 Bay

2007. Arab Horses. Multicoloured.

4277	1z.35 Type **1380**	1·90	1·40
4278	3z. Grey with pink snip	4·50	3·25
4279	3z.55 Bright bay with long forelock	5·25	3·75
4280	3z.55 Dappled grey	5·25	3·75

1381 *Saguinus imperator* (emperor tamarin)

2007. Polish Zoos. Showing animals. Multicoloured.

4281	1z.35 Type **1381**	1·90	1·40
4282	3z. *Loxodonta africana* (African elephant)	3·50	2·50
4283	3z. *Ciconia nigra* (black stork)	4·50	3·25
4284	3z.55 *Uncia uncia* (snow leopard)	5·25	3·75

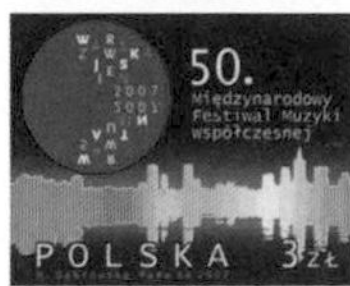

1382 Visual Interpretation of Electronic Sound as City Skyline

2007. Warsaw Autumn 2007–50th Anniv of Festival of Contemporary Music.

4285	**1382**	3z. multicoloured	4·50	3·25

1383 Performers

2007. Centenary of Theatre of Silesia, Katowice

4286	**1383**	1z.35 muulticolourd	1·90	1·40

1384 Postmarks

2007. World Post Day

4287	**1384**	1z.35 multicoloured	1·90	1·40

1385 Dragon's Bridge, Ljubljana, Slovenia

2007. Capital Cities of European Union States. Multicoloured.

4288	1z.35 Type **1385**	1·90	1·40
4289	1z.35 Roland Monument, Riga, Latvia	1·90	1·40
4290	3z. Philharmonic Hall, Luxembourg	4·00	3·00
4291	3z. Plaza de Cibeles, Madrid, Spain	4·00	3·00
4292	3z.55 Tower Bridge, London, UK	4·75	3·50

1386 Pope John Paul II

2007. 25th Anniv of Pope John Paul II Foundation

4293	**1386**	1z.35 multicoloured	1·90	1·40

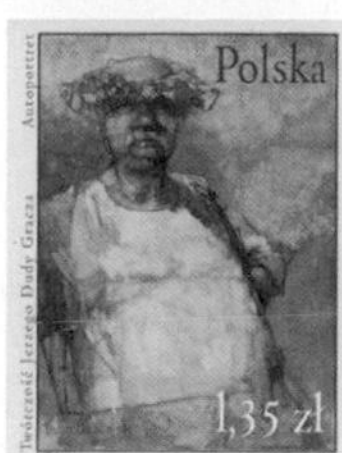

Type

2007. Jerzy Duda-Gracz (artist) Commemoration

4294	**1387**	1z.35 multicoloured	1·90	1·40

1388 Teddy and Tree

2007. Christmas. Multicoloured.

1z.35 Type **1388**	1·90	1·40
3z. *Adoration of the Magi* (Mikolaj Haberschrack)	4·00	3·00

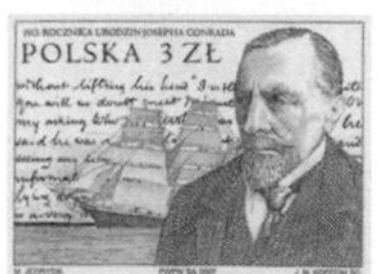

1389 Script, *Otago* and Joseph Conrad

2007. 150th Birth Anniv of Jozef Teodor Konrad Korzeniowski (Joseph Conrad) (writer and sailor).

4297	**1389**	3z. black	4·00	3·00

1390 Envelope and Quill

2008. PostEurop (Association of European Public Postal Operators) Plenary Assembly, Krakow. Sheet 70×90 mm.

MS4298	**1390**	3z. multicoloured	4·25	4·00

1391 Heart as Open Door

2008. St Valentine's Day.

4299	**1391**	1z.35 multicoloured	1·90	1·40

1392 Self Portrait, 1858

2008. History of Polish Photography. 190th Birth Anniv of Karol Beyer. Multicoloured.

4300	1z.35 Type **1392**	1·90	1·40
4301	1z.35 Street scene, Wilanow, 1866	1·90	1·40
4302	1z.35 Street scene, Warsaw, 1858	1·90	1·40
4303	1z.35 Russian army tents, 1861	1·90	1·40

1393 Easter Eggs

2008. Easter. Multicoloured.

4304	1z.35 Type **1393**	1·90	1·40
4305	2z.40 Eggs (different)	3·25	2·50

1394 Emblem

2008. 80th Anniv of Straz Graniczna (border guard).

4306	**1394**	2z.10 scarlet and black	3·00	2·20

1395 TS-11 ISKRA

2008. Polish Airforce. Multicoloured.

4307	3z. Type **1395**	4·00	3·00
4308	3z.55 F-16 JASTRZAB	4·75	3·50

1396 Sand Storm

2008. Weather Phenomena. Multicoloured.

4309	1z.35 Type **1396**	1·90	1·40
4310	1z.35 Lightning	1·90	1·40
4311	2z.40 Rainbow	3·25	2·50
4312	2z.40 Tornado	3·25	2·50

1397 Envelope as Plate

2008. Europa. The Letter.

4313	**1397**	3z. black and silver	4·00	3·00
MS4313a		90×70 mm. As No. **MS**4313. Imperf	†	†

1398 Emblem

2008. Euro 2008 European Football Championship, Austria and Switzerland.

4314	**1398**	1z.35 multicoloured	1·90	1·40

1399 Magnifier and Emblem

2008. EUROSAI Congress, Krakow.

4315	**1399**	3z.55 multicoloured	4·75	3·50

1400 Toy Train

2008. National Children's Day. Toys. Multicoloured.

4316	1z.35 Type **1400**	1·90	1·40
4317	3z. Xylophone	4·00	3·00

1401 Child and Rug

2008. Child Refugees to Esfahan, Iran during World War II.

4318	**1401**	2z.40 multicoloured	3·25	2·50

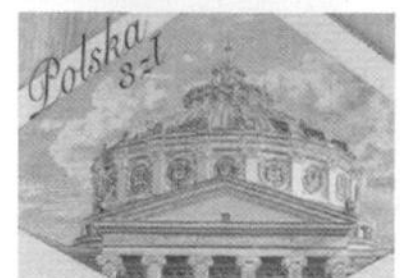

1402 Envelope enclosing Romanian Athenaeum Building

2008. EFIRO 2008 International Stamp Exhibition, Bucharest. Sheet 90×70 mm.

MS4319	**1402**	3z. multicoloured	4·25	4·00

1403 Madonna and Child

2008. St. Mary's Sanctuaries. St. Mary of the Snow.

4320	**1403**	1z.35 multicoloured	1·90	1·40

1404 Swimming

2008. Olympic Games, Beijing. Multicoloured.

4321	10g. Type **1404**	35	15
4322	10g. Volleyball	35	15
4323	1z.45 Pole vault	2·10	1·60
4324	1z.45 Fencing	2·10	1·60
MS4325	202×116 mm. Nos. 4321/4	4·75	4·50

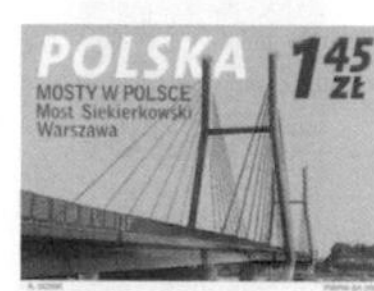

1405 Siekierkowski Bridge, Warsaw

2008. Bridges. Multicoloured.

4326	1z.45 Type **1405**	2·10	1·60
4327	1z.45 Pontiatowski Bridge, Warsaw	2·10	1·60
4328	3z. Bridge, Maurzyce	4·00	3·00
4329	3z. Ernest Malinowski Bridge, Torun	4·00	3·00

1406 Prosper Prowana

2008. 450th Anniv of Polish Postal Service. Sheet 120×80 mm containing T **1406** and similar multicoloured designs.

MS4330	1z.45×3, Type **1406**; King Zygmunt August (51×31 mm); Sebastian Montelupi	6·25	5·75

The stamps and margins of **MS**4330 form a composite design.

1407 Wladyslaw Raczkiewicz

2008. Presidents of Government in Exile. Sheet 129×125 mm containing T **1407** and similar horiz designs. Multicoloured.

MS4331	1z.45×6, Type **1407**; Edward Raczynski; August Zaleski; Kazimierz Sabbat; Stanislaw Ostrowski; Ryszard Kaczorowski	12·50	12·00

The central stamps of **MS**4331 form a composite design.

1408 Sports Men and Women

2008. Centenary of Lodz Sports Club.

4332	**1408**	1z.45 vermilion and silver	2·10	1·60

1409 Native American, Settler and Map

2008. 400th Anniv of Polish Settlers in America.

4333	**1409**	3z. multicoloured	4·25	3·25

1410 Pigeon Post

2008. World Post Day.

4334	**1410**	2z.10 multicoloured	3·25	2·30

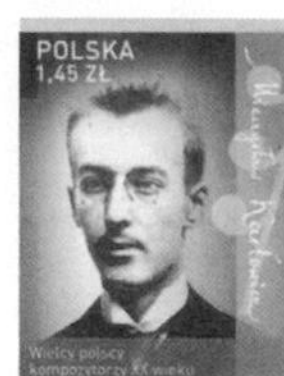

1411 Mieczyslaw Karlowicz

2008. Composers. Multicoloured.

4335	1z.45 Type **1411**	2·10	1·60
4336	1z.45 Wojciech Kilar	2·10	1·60
4337	1z.45 Henryk Mikolaj Gorecki	2·10	1·60
4338	1z.45 Witold Lutoslawski	2·10	1·60

1412 Rijksmuseum, Amsterdam

2007. Capital Cities of European Union States. Multicoloured.

4339	1z.45 Type **1412**	2·10	1·60
4340	1z.45 Royal Library, Copenhagen	2·10	1·60
4341	3z. Charles Bridge, Prague	4·25	3·25
4342	3z. Acropolis, Athens	4·25	3·25
4343	3z.65 Parliament, Vienna	5·00	3·75

1413 J. Przybora and J. Wasowski

2008. 50th Anniv of Kabaret Starszych Panów (comedy series).

4344	**1413**	1z.45 multicoloured	2·10	1·60

1414 Maria Konopnicka

2008. Centenary of Rota (the Oath (poem)) by Maria Konopnicka.

4345	**1414**	3z.65 multicoloured	5·25	4·00

1415 National Arms

2008. Centenary of Independence Day.

4346	**1415**	1z.45 carmine	2·10	1·60

1416 Stars

2008. Christmas. Multicoloured.

4347	1z.45 Type **1416**	2·10	1·60
4348	3z. Stars (different)	4·25	3·25

1417 Pope John Paul II

2008. 30th Anniv of Election of Karol Wojtyla as Pope John Paul II.

4349	**1417**	2z.40 multicoloured	3·25	2·50

1418 Zbigniew Herbert

2008. Tenth Death Anniv of Zbigniew Herbert (writer).

4350	**1418**	2z.10 multicoloured	3·00	2·20

1419 Emblem

2008. United Nations Conference on Climate Change, Poznan.

4351	**1419**	2z.40 multicoloured	3·25	2·50

1420 Postal Messenger (image scaled to 46% of original size)

2008. 450th Anniv of Polish Postal Service (2nd issue). Sheet 106×75 mm. Self-adhesive.

MS4352	**1420**	20z. multicoloured	21·00	20·00

No. **MS**4352 was screen printed on silk.
See also **MS**4330.

1421 Louis Braille

2009. Birth Bicentenary of Louis Braille (inventor of Braille writing for the blind).

4353	**1421**	1z.45 multicoloured	2·30	1·70

No. 4353 was printed with a *se-tenant* stamp size label with embossed Braille letters attached at right.

1422 Witold Pilecki (historian)

2009. Camp Survivors. Multicoloured.

4354	1z.45 Type **1422**	2·10	1·60
4355a	2z.10 Wladyslaw Wolski	3·00	2·20
4356	2z.40 Ignacy Ludwik Jez	3·25	2·50
4357	3z. Stanislawa Maria Sawicka	4·25	3·25

1423 Heart in Four-leafed Clover

2009. St Valentine's Day.

4358	**1423**	1z.45 multicoloured	2·10	1·60

1424 *Zwiastowanie*

2009. Contemporary Polish Sculpture. 10th Death Anniv of Wladyslaw Hasior. Multicoloured.

4359	1z.45 Type **1424**	2·10	1·60
4360	1z.45 *Mucha*	2·10	1·60
4361	2z.10 *Sztandar Zielonej Poetki*	3·00	2·20
4362	2z.40 *Sztandar Rozbieranie do snu*	3·25	2·50
MS4363	90×125 mm. Nos. 4359/62	10·50	10·00

1425 *Chrystus Zmartwychwstaly*

2009. Easter. Paintings by Szymon Czechowicz. Multicoloured.

4364	1z.55 Type **1425**	2·30	1·70
4365	3z. *Zlozenie do grobu* (vert)	4·25	3·25

1426 Fish

2009. China 2009 International Stamp Exhibition, Luoyang. Sheet 90×70 mm.

MS4366	**1426**	3z. multicoloured	4·50	4·00

1427 *Berek Joselewicz* (Juliusz Kossak)

2009. Polish Year in Israel. Sheet 90×70 mm.

MS4367	**1427**	3z. multicoloured	4·50	4·00

1428 Cheetahs

2009. African Animals. Sheet 124×90 mm containing T **1428** and similar horiz designs. Each black.

MS4368	1z.55 Type **1428**; 1z.95 Zebras; 2z.40 Gnu and crocodile; 3z. Elephants	13·00	12·50

1429 Numbers as Starburst

2009. Europa. Astronomy.

4369	**1429**	3z. deep turquoise-blue and new blue	4·25	3·25

No. 4369 was printed, tête-beche, in horizontal pairs within small sheets, each pair forming a composite design.

1430 Grazyna Bacewicz

2009. Birth Centenary of Grazyna Bacewicz (composer and violinist)

4370	**1430**	1z.55 multicoloured	2·30	1·70

1431 Tytus de Zoo

2009. 50th (2007) Anniv of Tytus, Romek and A'Tomek (comic created by Henryk Jerzy Chmielewski (Papcio Chmiel)). Multicoloured.

4371	1z.55 Type **1431**	2·30	1·70
4372	1z.55 Romek	2·30	1·70
4373	1z.55 A'Tomek	2·30	1·70

1432 Lech Walesa (leader Trade Union Solidarnosc)

2009. 20th Anniv of Opposition Electoral Success. Sheet 90×70 mm.

MS4374	**1432**	3z.75 multicoloured	5·50	5·25

1433 Saint Bruno

2009. Death Millennary of Saint Bruno of Querfurt (missionary and martyr).

4375	**1433**	3z. multicoloured	4·25	3·25

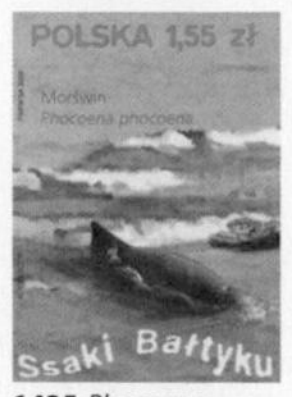
1434 *Dar Mlodziezy*(frigate of Naval Academy of Gdynia, built,1982)

2009. Tall Ships' Races–Gdynia 2009. Sheet 90×70 mm.

MS4376	**1434**	3z.75 multicoloured	5·50	5·25

1435 *Phocoena phocoena* (porpoise)

2009. Mammals of the Baltic Sea. Multicoloured.

4377	1z.55 Type **1435**	2·30	1·70
4378	1z.55 *Halichoreus grypus* (grey seal)	2·30	1·70
4379	1z.95 *Phoca vitulina* (harbour seal)	2·75	2·10
4380	1z.95 *Phoca hispida* (ringed seal)	2·75	2·10

Nos. 4377-4380 were printed, *se-tenant*, forming a composite design.

1436 Building on Fire

2009. 65th Anniv of Warsaw Uprising against German Occupation. Sheet 90×70 mm.

MS4381	**1436**	3z.75 black and rosine	4·50	4·00

1437 Cerasus avium (*Prunus avium*) (cherry)

2009. Fruit and Flowers. Multicoloured.

4382	1z.95 Type **1437**	2·75	2·10
4383	3z.75 *Calendula officinalis* (pot marigold)	5·50	4·00

1438 Jan Czochralski (specialist in metallurgy and inventor of Czochralski process)

2009. Poles in Exile. Multicoloured.

4384	1z.55 Type **1438**	2·30	1·70
4385	1z.55 Antoni Norbert Patek (watchmaker)	2·30	1·70
4386	1z.95 Ludwik Hirszfeld (micro-biologist and serologist)	2·75	2·10
4387	1z.95 Marian Rejewski, Henryk Zygalski and Jerzy Rózycki (mathematicians and cryptologists who created replica of Enigma, German encrypting machine)	2·75	2·10

1439 Juliusz Slowacki

2009. Birth Bicentenary of Juliusz Slowacki (poet, playwright and philosopher).

4388	**1439**	1z.55 multicoloured	2·30	1·70

1440 Attack on Wegierska Górka (village in Zywiec County which held out for three days)

2009. Defensive War 1939. Each black and scarlet-vermilion.

4389	1z.55 Type **1440**	2·30	1·70
4390	2z.40 Wielun (first town to come under attack)	3·25	2·50

1441 Ball and Hoop

2009. EuroBasket 2009–European Men's Basketball Championship, Poland.

4391 **1441**	3z. multicoloured	4·25	3·25

1442 Tadeusz Mazowiecki (first premier)

2009. 20th Anniv of First Non-Communist Government following Elections in June, 1989.

4392 **1442**	1z.55 multicoloured	2·30	1·70

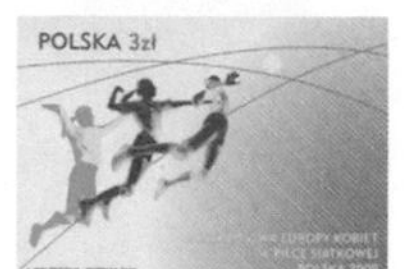
1443 Player in Motion

2009. Women's European Volleyball Championship–2009, Poland.

4393 **1443**	3z. multicoloured	4·25	3·25

2009. Capital Cities of European Union States. As T **1412**. Multicoloured.

4394	1z.55 Castle, Bratislava	2·30	1·70
4395	1z.55 Famagusta Gate, Nicosia	2·30	1·70
4396	3z. Town Hall, Brussels	5·00	3·75
4397	3z. Courtyard, Warsaw	5·00	3·75
4398	3z.75 National Museum	5·25	4·00

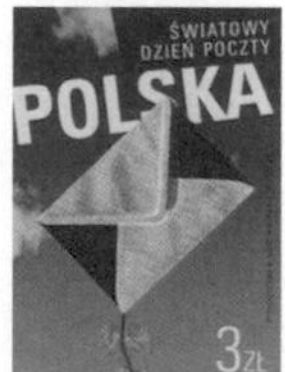
1444 Envelope as Kite

2009. World Post Day.

4399 **1444**	3z. multicoloured	5·25	4·00

1445 Jerzy Popieluszko

2009. 25th Death Anniv of Jerzy Popieluszko (priest and solidarity martyr).

4400 **1445**	1z.55 multicoloured	2·30	1·70

1446 Volunteer

2009. Centenary of Voluntary Tatra Mountains Rescue Service.

4401 **1446**	1z.55 multicoloured	2·30	1·70

1447 Pawel Jasienica

2009. Birth Centenary of Leon Lech Beynar (Pawel Jasienica) (writer and historian).

4402 **1447**	1z.55 multicoloured	2·30	1·70

1448 Jerzy Franciszek Kulczycki

2009. Polish Influence in Europe. Jerzy Franciszek Kulczycki (hero of Battle of Vienna and opened first coffee house in Vienna) Commemoration.

4403 **1448**	1z.55 multicoloured	2·50	2·00

No. 4403 was printed, *se-tenant* with a stamp size label attached at top, the whole forming a composite design.

1449 Bookplate 'Exlibris Willibald Pirkheimer' (Albrecht Durer)

2009. Lost Treasures. Art. Multicoloured.

4404	1z.55 Type **1449**	2·30	1·70
4405	1z.55 *Christ falls beneath the Cross* (Peter Paul Rubens)	2·30	1·70
4406	1z.55 *Joseph recounts his Dream* (Rembrandt)	2·30	1·70

1450 Choir

2009. Christmas. Multicoloured

4407	1z.55 Type **1450**	2·30	1·70
4408	2z.40 Holy Family	3·25	2·30

1451 Letter from Kalwaria to Warsaw, franked with 1860 10k. Stamp (As Type 1)

2010. 150th Anniv of Polish Stamps

MS4409 **1451**	4z.15 multicoloured	5·25	4·75

1452 Skiers

2010. Winter Olympic Games, Vancouver

4410 **1452**	3z. multicoloured	4·25	3·25

1453 British Shorthair

2010. Cats. Multicoloured.

MS4411	1z.55 Type **1453**; 1z.55 Siamese; 1z.95 Somali; 1z.95 Maine Coon; 3z. Persian; 3z. Tortoiseshell and white exotic	17·00	16·00

1454 Frederic Chopin

2010. Birth Bicentenary of Frederic Chopin (composer)

MS4412 **1454**	4z.15 multicoloured	5·25	4·75
MS4412a	4z.15 As Type **1454**. Imperf	19·00	18·00

1455 Lamb

2010. Easter. Multicoloured.

4413	1z.55 Type **1455**	2·30	1·70
4414	2z.40 Basket of eggs	3·50	2·50

1456 Warsaw, 1920

2010. History of Polish Photography. Jan Bulhak Commemoration. Multicoloured.

4415	1z.95 Type **1456**	2·75	2·10
4416	1z.95 Doorway, Krakow, 1921	2·75	2·10
4417	1z.95 Old Town Hall, Warsaw, 1920	2·75	2·10
4418	1z.95 Kasimir side altar, Vilnius Cathedral, 1912	2·75	2·10

1457 Anniversary Emblem

2010. 20th Anniv of Special Services

4419 **1457**	1z.55 scarlet-vermilion, indigo and silver	2·30	1·70

1458 Cross of Polish Badges

2010. 60th Anniv of Katyn Massacre

MS4420 **1458**	3z. multicoloured	4·50	4·25

1459 Tower of Belém, Lisbon

2010. Portugal 2010 International Stamp Exhibition, Lisbon

MS4421 **1459**	3z. multicoloured	4·50	4·25

1460 Boy reading

2010. Europa

4422 **1460**	3z. multicoloured	4·50	3·50

1461 Pope John Paul II and Church of Peter the Apostle, Wadowice

2010. Pope John Paul II (Karol Józef Wojtyła) Commemoration

4423 **1461**	1z.95 multicoloured	3·25	2·50

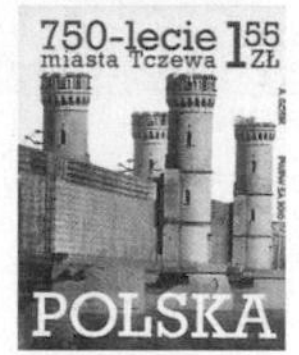
1462 Bridge over the Vistula

2010. 750th Anniv of Tczew

4424 **1462**	1z.55 multicoloured	2·40	1·80

1463 Jerzy Popieluszko

2010. Beatification of Jerzy Popiełuszko (priest and solidarity martyr)

4425 **1463**	1z.95 multicoloured	3·00	2·20

1464 Convent and Statue of Christ

2010. 750th Anniv of Dominican Ursuline Sisters Convent, Sieradtz

4426 **1464**	1z.55 multicoloured	2·40	1·80

1465 Battle Scene (Jan Matejko)

2010. 600th Anniv of Battle of Grunvald (First Battle of Tannenberg), during the Polish–Lithuanian–Teutonic War

MS4427 **1465**	8z.30 multicoloured	13·00	12·50

1466 Scouts signalling Semaphore Message, 'STO LAT' (100 YEARS)

2010. Centenary of Polish Scouts' Association

4428 **1466**	1z.95 multicoloured	3·00	2·20

1467 Forget-me-Not

2010. Flowers

4429 **1467**	4z.15 multicoloured	6·25	4·75

1468 Lech Walesa

2010. 30th Anniv of NSZZ 'Solidarnosc' (Solidarity)

4430	**1468**	3z.75 black, silver and red	5·75	4·25

1469 Sphalerite

2010. Minerals. Multicoloured.

4431	1z.55 Type **1469**	2·40	1·80
4432	1z.95 Gypsum	3·00	2·20
4433	2z.40 Agate	3·75	2·75
4434	3z. Chrysoprase	4·50	3·50

1469a Tower of Postmen

2010. World Post Day

4434	**1469a**	1z.95 multicoloured	4·50	3·50

1470 Sofia

2010. Capital Cities of European Union States. Multicoloured.

4436	1z.95 Type **1470**	3·00	2·20
4437	3z. Bucharest	4·50	3·50

1471 'A' and Floral Motif

2010. Personnal Stamp

4438	**1471**	A multicoloured	11·00	9·75

1472 Players

2010. Centenary of Widzew Lodz Football Club

4439	**1472**	1z.55 multicoloured	2·40	1·80

1473 Ignacy Paderewski

2010. 150th Birth Anniv of Ignacy Jan Paderewski (composer and Prime Minister (1919))

4440	**1473**	3z. multicoloured	5·00	3·75

1474 Shooting Star, Trail and Christmas Tree

2010. Christmas. Multicoloured.

4441	1z.55 Type **1474**	2·40	1·80
4442	2z.40 Shooting star, trail and night sky	3·75	2·75

1475 'Kocham Cie'

2010. Greeting Stamps

4443	**1475**	A multicoloured	2·40	1·80

1476 Jan Heweliusz

2011. 400th Birth Anniv of Johannes Hevelius (Jan Heweliusz) (brewer and astronomer)

4444	**1476**	3z. multicoloured	5·50	4·25

1477 Players

2011. Hockey

4445	**1477**	2z.40 multicoloured	3·75	2·75

1478 20', EU Stars and Group Colours on Hands

2011. 20th Anniv of Visegrad Group (cultural, education, science and exchange of information)

4446	**1478**	3z. multicoloured	5·00	3·75

1478a Students Demonstrating

2011. 30th Anniv of Łódź Independent Students' Association

4446a	**1478a**	1z. 95 multicoloured	3·00	2·20

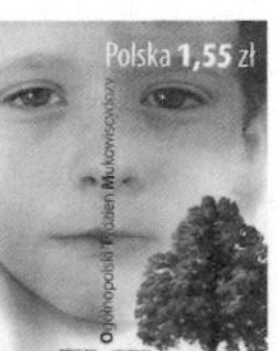

1479 Child's Face and Tree

2011. Cystic Fibrosis Awareness Week

4447	**1479**	1z.55 multicoloured	2·50	1·90

1480 Stefan Kiselewski

2011. Birth Centenary of Stefan Kiselewski (writer, composer, music critic and co-founder and member of the Union of Real Politics)

4448	**1480**	1z.95 multicoloured	3·00	2·20

1481 Chick and Flowers

2011. Easter. Multicoloured.

4449	1z.55 Type **1481**	2·50	1·90
4450	2z.40 Rabbit and flowers	3·75	2·75

1482 Cardinal Kozłowiecki

2011. Birth Centenary of Cardinal Adam Kozłowiecki

4451	**1482**	1z.95 multicoloured	3·00	2·20

1483 Boy

2011. Smile of the World (photographs by Elzbeita Dzikowska). Multicoloured.

MS4452	1z.95 Type **1483**; 1z.95 African girl with plaited hair; 2z.40 Girl with flowers in hair; 2z.40 Arab man with camel; 3z. Indian girl; 3z. Woman wearing hat	24·00	23·00

1484 Pope John Paul II

2011. Beatification of Pope John Paul II. Sheet 75×100 mm

MS4453	**1484**	8z.30 multicoloured	13·50	13·00

1485 Bison amongst Trees

2011. Europa. Forests

4454	**1485**	3z. multicoloured	5·00	3·75

1486 Guccio

2011. Cartoon Characters created by Bohdan Butenko. Multicoloured.

4455	1z.55 40 Cezar	2·50	1·90
4456	1z.55 Type **1486**	2·50	1·90
4457	2z.40 Kwapiszon	3·75	2·75
4458	2z.40 Gapiszon	3·75	2·75

1487 Arrows as Figures and Flag

2011. Polish Presidency of EU Council

4459	**1487**	3z. multicoloured	5·00	3·75

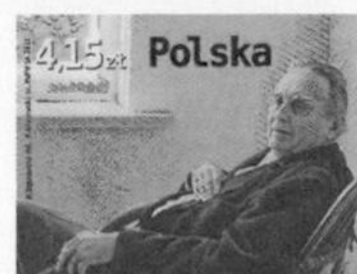

1488 Czesława Miłosz

2011. Birth Centenary of Czesława Miłosz (poet and writer). Sheet 70×90 mm

MS4460	**1488**	4z.15 black and bright rose-carmine	6·00	4·50

1489 Maximilian (Maksymilian) Maria Kolbe

2011. 60th Death Anniv of Saint Maximilian (Maksymilian) Maria Kolbe (Franciscan friar, who volunteered to die in place of a stranger in Auschwitz concentration camp)

4461	**1489**	1z.95 multicoloured	3·00	2·20

1490 Michał Sędziwój (alchemist, philosopher, and medical doctor)

2011. Personalities. Multicoloured.

4462	1z.55 Type **1490**	2·50	1·90
4463	1z.95 Jan Szczepanik (inventor)	2·50	1·90
4464	3z. Jan Józef Baranowski (astronomer)	3·75	2·75
4465	3z. Rudolf Stefan Weigl (biologist and inventor of first vacine against epidemic typhus)	3·75	2·75

1491 Jan Dzierzon

2011. Birth Bicentenary of Johan (Jan) Dzierzon (pioneering apiarist discoverer of parthenogenesis in bees and designer of first successful movable-frame beehive)

4466	**1491**	1z.55 multicoloured	2·50	1·90

1492 Saint Mary's Church, Niegowić (Karol Józef Wojtyła's first parish)

2011. Pope John Paul II (Karol Józef Wojtyła) Commemoration

4467	**1492**	1z.95 multicoloured	3·00	2·20

1493 Town Hall and Church, St. Barbar, Polkowice

2011. PZF Congress, Polkowice. Sheet 70×90 mm

MS4468	**1493**	4z.15 multicoloured	6·00	4·50

1494 *Double Portrait of Eliza Parenska* (Stanisław Wyspiański)

2011. Lost Works of Art. Multicoloured.
4469 1z.95 Type **1494** 2·50 1·90
4470 2z.40 Scene from the legend of Theophilus of Adana (late XVth century wooden carving) (Wit Stwosz) 3·75 2·75
4471 3z. *Woman standing* (Jean-Antoine Watteau) 5·00 3·75

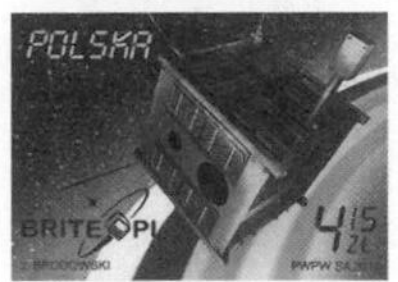

1495 Satellite

2011. First Polish Scientific Satellite. Sheet 90×70 mm
MS4472 **1495** 4z.15 multicoloured 6·00 4·50

1496 Nobel Medal

2011. Centenary of Marie Skłodowska Curie's Nobel Prize for Chemistry
MS4473 3z. Type **1496**; 7z.80 Marie Curie (40×55 mm) 10·00 6·50

1497 Santa Claus

2011. Christmas. Multicoloured.

(a) Ordinary gum
4474 1z.55 Type **1497** 2·50 1·90

(b) Self-adhesive
4475 2z.40 Holy Family 3·75 2·75

1498 School Building

2011. 30th Anniv of Strike at Higher Military Fire Service School in Warsaw. Sheet 70×90 mm
MS4476 **1498** 4z.15 multicoloured 6·00 4·50

1499 Cloth as Map of Kazakhstan

2011. 20th Anniv of Independence of Kazakhstan
4477 **1499** 2z.40 multicoloured 3·75 2·75

1500 *Rubus idaeus* (Raspberry)

2011. Flowers and Fruit
4478 **1500** 1z.55 multicoloured 2·50 1·90

1501 Heart as Globe

2012. 20th Finale of Orchestra of Holy Day Assistance (fund raising charity)
MS4479 **1501** 1z.95 multicoloured 3·00 2·20

1502 Arms

2012. 70th Anniv of National Army
4480 **1502** 1z.55 multicoloured 2·50 1·90

1503 Zygmunt Krasiński

2012. Birth Bicentenary of Count Napoleon Stanisław Adam Ludwig Zygmunt Krasiński (writer). Sheet 90×70 mm
4481 **1503** 4z.15 multicoloured 6·00 4·50

1504 Lamb and Flowers

2012. Easter. Multicoloured.
4482 1z.55 Type **1504** 2·50 1·90
4483 1z.95 Egg and flowers 3·00 2·20
4484 3z. Rabbit and flowers 5·00 3·75

1505 Leopold Kronenberg

2012. Birth Bicentenary of Baron Leopold Julian Kronenberg (banker)
4485 **1505** 2z.40 black and gold 3·75 2·75

1506 Vienna Station, Warsaw, 1890

2012. History of Polish Photography. Konrad Brandel Commemoration. Multicoloured.
4486 1z.95 Type **1506** 3·00 2·20
4487 1z.95 Krakowskie Przedmieście, 1880 3·00 2·20
4488 2z.40 Three Crosses Square, 1875 3·75 2·75
4489 2z.40 Pancera Viaduct, 1890 3·75 2·75

1507 Municipal Offices

2012. 300th Anniv of Suwałki
4490 **1507** 1z.95 multicoloured 3·00 2·20

1508 Ushebti (Funerary figurine), 4th century BC

2012. 150th Anniv of First Polish Discoveries in Egypt. Multicoloured.
MS4491 1z.55 Type **1508**; 1z.95 Blue Ushebti (Funerary figurine) 6th-7th century BC; 2z.40 Amulet figurine depicting Nefertum; 3z. Michał Tyszkiewicz (Egyptologist) 13·00 12·50

1509 Maskerada (Tadeusz Makowski)

2012. 150th Anniv of National Museum, Warsaw. Sheet 110×78 mm
MS4492 **1509** 4z.15 multicoloured 6·00 5·50

1510 Signposts showing Attractions

2012. Europa. Visit Poland
4493 **1510** 3z. multicoloured 5·00 3·75

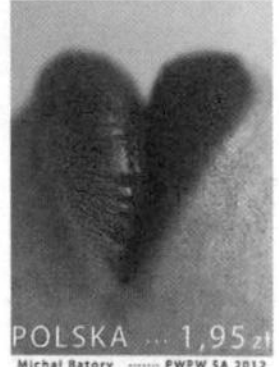

1511 Lips (poster for ARTISAN DE L' AFICHE, Musée des Arts Décoratifs at the Louvre, Paris)

2012. Art Work by Michał Batory
4494 1z.95 Type **1511** 3·00 2·20
4495 3z. Fingers (sepia) (horiz) 4·00 3·50

1512 Zajączek Parauszek

2012. Cartoon Characters created by Wojciech Próchniewicz, Anthony Bankowski and Luc Toutounghi. Sheet 90×70 mm
MS4496 **1512** 4z.15 multicoloured 6·00 5·50

1513 Municipal Stadium, Poznań

2012. Euro 2012, European Football Championships. Multicoloured.
4497 1z.55 Type **1513** 2·50 1·90
4498 1z.95 National Stadium, Warsaw 3·00 2·20
4499 2z.40 PGE Area, Gdańsk 3·25 2·50
4500 3z. Municipal Stadium, Wrocław 4·00 3·50
4501 3z. Football (39×39 mm (circular)) 4·25 3·75
MS4502 Nos. 4497/500 13·00 11·50

1514 Parkland

2012. World Heritage Site. Muskauer Park.
4503 **1514** 3z. multicoloured 4·00 3·55

1515 Sculls

2012. Olympic Games, London. Multicoloured.
MS4504 1z.55 Type **1515**; 1z.95 Handball; 2z.40 Weightlifting; 3z. Shot put 13·00 12·50

1516 Józef Kraszewski

2012. Birth Bicentenary of Józef Ignacy Kraszewski (writer, historian and journalist)
4505 **1516** 4z.15 multicoloured 5·25 4·75

1517 *Russula virescens*

2012. Fungi. Multicoloured.
MS4506 1z.55 Type **1517**; 1z.95 *Morchella esculenta*; 3z. *Macrolepiota procea*; 4z.15 *Amillaria ostoyae* 15·00 14·50

1518 Exhibition Name and National Flags of Poland and Germany

2012. Kargowa 2012 Bilateral Polish and German Philatelic Exhibiton
4507 **1518** 2z.40 multicoloured 3·50 2·50

1519 Piotr Skarga

2012. 400th Death Anniv of Piotr Skarga (Jesuit, preacher, hagiographer, polemicist and leading figure of the Counter-reformation in the Polish-Lithuanian Commonwealth)
4508 **1519** 1z.55 multicoloured 2·50 1·90

1520 Bullfinches and Dandelion Seed Heads (Piotr Kwit)

2012. Tenth Death Anniv of Piotr Kwit (artist)
4509 **1520** 1z.55 multicoloured 2·50 1·90

1521 Wawel Cathedral and Karol Wojtyła

2012. Pope John Paul II (Karol Józef Wojtyła) Commemoration. In Cracow

4510	**1521**	1z.95 multicoloured	3·50	3·00

1522 Jadwiga Smosarska (actor)

2012. Personalities of Theatre and Cinema. Multicoloured.

4511	1z.55 Type **1522**	2·50	1·90
4512	1z.95 Aleksander Zabczyński (actor)	3·00	2·20
4513	3z. Eugeniusz Bodo (film director)	5·00	3·75
MS4514	121×82 mm. Nos. 4511/13	12·00	12·00

1523 Turczynek Villa, Milanówek

2012. Garden Cities in Poland. Sheet 90×70 mm

4515	**1523**	4z.15 multicoloured	6·00	6·00

1524 Angels and Star

2012. Christmas

4516	A (1z.55) Type **1524**	2·40	1·80
4517	2z.40 Angels with Christmas gifts (horiz)	3·75	2·75

1525 Jerzy Turowicz

2012. Birth Centenary of Jerzy Turowicz (Catholic journalist and editor)

4518	**1525**	1z.55 black and yellow	2·50	1·90

1526 Emblem

2013. 21st Finale of Orchestra of Holy Day Assistance (fund raising charity)

4519	**1526**	A (1z.55) multicoloured	2·50	1·90

1527 'E' **1528** 'P'

2013. Economic and Priority Stamps. Multicoloured (blue).

4520	a 350g. Type **1527**	2·50	1·90
4521	b 350g. As Type **1527**	2·50	1·90
4522	a 350g. Type **1528**	3·75	2·75
4523	b 350g. As Type **1528**	3·75	2·75

2013. Economic and Priority Stamps. Multicoloured (green).

4524	a 1000g. As Type **1527**	5·00	3·75
4525	b 1000g. As Type **1527**	5·00	3·75
4526	a 1000g. As Type **1528**	5·25	4·50
4527	b 1000g. As Type **1528**	5·25	4·50

1529 *Alcedo atthis*

2013. Polish Birds. Kingfisher. Sheet 90×70 mm

MS4528	**1529**	4z.55 multicoloured	6·00	6·00

1530 Wiecźław Chrzanowski

2013. 90th Birth Anniv of Wiecźław Chrzanowski (politician)

4529	**1530**	3z.80 multicoloured	5·00	4·25

1531 Star

2013. 70th Anniv of Warsaw Uprising

4530	**1531**	3z.80 multicoloured	5·00	4·25

1532 Flag

2013. Flag Day of the Republic of Poland

4531	**1532**	1z.60 multicoloured	2·50	1·90

1533 Peugeot Post Van

2013. Europa. Postal Transport

4532	**1533**	4z.60 multicoloured	5·75	4·75

1534 Goofy, Minnie and Mickey

2013. Walt Disney Characters. Sheet 90×70 mm

MS4533	**1534**	4z.60 multicoloured	7·00	7·00

1535 Darłowo

2013. Lighthouses. Multicoloured.

MS4534	1z.60 Type **1535**; 2z.35 Jarosławiec; 3z.75 Ustka; 3z.80 Czołpino	16·00	16·00

2013. Economic and Priority Stamps. Multicoloured (red).

4535	a 2000g. As Type **1527**	6·00	5·75
4536	b 2000g. As Type **1527**	6·00	5·75
4537	a 2000g. As Type **1528**	7·00	6·75
4538	b 2000g. As Type **1528**	7·00	6·75

1536 Bolesław III Krzywousty (Bolesław III Wrymouth), Prince of Poland

2013. 900th Anniv of Chronicles of Gallus Anonymus. Sheet 90×70 mm

MS4539	**1536**	8z.50 black and vermilion	15·00	15·00

1537 Kashubian Strawberry

2013. Polish Regional Products - Kashubian Strawberry

4540	**1537**	4z.60 multicoloured	5·75	4·75

1538 Cyclist

2013. Polish Cycle Race - Tour de Pologne. Multicoloured.

4541	1z.55 Type **1538**	2·50	1·90
4542	1z.95 Two cyclists	3·00	2·20

1539 *Heweliusz* Satellite

2013. Poland's Second Scientific Satellite - *Heweliusz* (named after Polish astronomer Hevelius). Sheet 90×70 mm

MS4543	**1539**	4z.55 multicoloured	7·00	7·00

1540 Guitar

2013. Woodstock Free Music Festival, Kostrzyn nad Odrą, Poland (Festiwal Przystanek Woodstock)

4544	2z.35 multicoloured	3·75	2·75

1541 *Fryderyk Chopin* (Polish brig-rigged sailing ship)

2013. Tall Ships' Races, Szczecin 2013. Sheet 90×70 mm

MS4545	**1541**	8z.50 new blue and black	15·00	15·00

1542 Two General Dynamics (now Lockheed Martin) F-16 Fighting Falcons

2013. Contemporary Polish Army Weapons. Multicoloured.

4546	1z.60 Type **1542**	2·50	1·90
4547	1z.60 KTO Rosomak (Kołowy Transporter Opancerzony) wheeled armored vehicle	2·50	1·90
4548	1z.60 ORP *Kontradmiral Xawery Czernicki* (multitask logistical support ship)	2·50	1·90

1543 'E' and Mazarine Blue Butterfly **1544** 'P' and Water Strider

2013. Economic and Priority Stamps. Insects. Multicoloured (blue).

4549	a 350g. Type **1543**	2·50	1·90
4550	b 350g. As Type **1543** but with *Rosalia longicorn*	2·50	1·90
4551	a 350g. Type **1544**	3·75	2·75
4552	b 350g. As Type **1544** but with yellow-winged darter dragonfly	3·75	2·75

1545 Costumes from Bistrița-Năsăud, Romania and Kraków, Poland

2013. 20th Anniv of Poland - Romania Friendship Treaty. Traditional Folk Costumes. Sheet 70×90 mm

MS4553	**1545**	4z.60 multicoloured	7·00	7·00

1546 Halite

2013. Polish Minerals. Multicoloured.

4554	1z.60 Type **1546**	2·50	1·90
4555	1z.60 Malachite and azurite	2·50	1·90
4556	2z.35 Marcasite	3·75	2·75
4557	2z.35 Gypsum	3·75	2·75

1547 Lech Wałęsa

2013. 70th Birth Anniv of Lech Wałęsa

4558	**1547**	3z.80 multicoloured	5·00	4·25

2013. Economic and Priority Stamps. Insects. Multicoloured (green).

4559	a 1000g. As Type **1543** but with ladybird	5·00	3·75
4560	b 1000g. As Type **1543** but with Peacock butterfly	5·00	3·75
4561	a 1000g. As Type **1544** but with grasshopper	5·25	4·50
4562	b 1000g. As Type **1544** but with ant	5·25	4·50

1548 St. Mark's Church, Zagreb, Croatia

2013. Capital Cities of European Union States

4563	**1548**	4z.60 multicoloured	5·75	4·75

2013. Economic and Priority Stamps. Insects. Multicoloured (red).

4564	a 2000g. As Type **1543** but with Tiger Moth butterfly	6·00	5·75
4565	b 2000g. As Type **1543** but with stag beetle	6·00	5·75
4566	a 2000g. As Type **1544** but with honey bee	7·00	6·75
4567	b 2000g. As Type **1544** but with old world Swallowtail caterpillar	7·00	6·75

1549 Tree Rings marking Polish Postage from 16th - 21st Century

2013. World Post Day. 455th Anniv of Polish Post

4568 **1549** 4z.60 multicoloured 5·75 4·75

1550 Ludwik Solski as the Guardian in *Treasure* by Leopold Staff

2013. Lost Works of Art. Paintings of Ludwik Solski (actor) by Stanisław Wyspiański (playwright, artist and poet) in 1904. Multicoloured.

4569 1z.60 Type **1550** 2·50 1·90
4570 2z.35 As Andrew Aguecheek in William Shakespeare's *Twelfth Night* 3·75 2·75
4571 3z.80 Ludwik Solski as Veteran Defender (the old Wiarus) in *Varsovian Anthem* (Warszawianka), by Stanisław Wyspiański 5·00 3·75

2013. Personalities of Theatre and Cinema. Multicoloured.

4572 1z.60 Helena Grossówna (actress and dancer) 2·50 1·90
4573 2z.35 Adolf Dymsza (comedy actor) 3·75 2·75
4574 3z.80 Mieczysława Ćwiklińska (actor and singer) 5·00 3·75
MS4575 121×82 mm. 1z.60 Helena Grossówna (actress and dancer); 2z.55 Adolf Dymsza (comedy actor); 3z.80 Mieczysława Ćwiklińska (actor and singer) 8·00 8·00

1551 Krzysztof Penderecki

2013. 80th Birth Anniv of Krzysztof Penderecki (composer and conductor)

4576 **1551** 3z.80 multicoloured 5·00 4·25

1552 *Argiope bruennichi*

2013. Spiders protected in Poland. Multicoloured.

4577 1z.60 Type **1552** 2·50 1·90
4578 2z.35 *Atypus muralis* 3·75 2·75
4579 3z.80 *Eresus kollari* 5·00 3·75
4580 4z.55 *Philaeus chrysops* 3·75 2·75

1553 Ski Jump

2014. Winter Olympic Games, Sochi. Multicoloured.

MS4581 1z.75 Type **1553**×2; 5z. Nordic skiing×2 8·00 8·00

MILITARY POST

I. Polish Corps in Russia, 1918.

1918. Stamps of Russia optd **POCZTA Pol. Korp.** and eagle. Perf or imperf. (70k.).

M1 **22** 3k. red £130 £130
M2 **23** 4k. red £130 £130
M3 **22** 5k. red 30·00 24·00
M4 **23** 10k. blue 30·00 24·00
M5 **22** 10k. on 7k. blue (No. 151) £850 £950
M6 **10** 15k. blue and purple 8·50 8·50
M7 **14** 20k. red and blue 12·00 11·00
M8 **10** 25k. mauve and green £150 £120
M9 **10** 35k. green and purple 8·50 8·50
M10 **14** 40k. green and purple 24·00 18·00
M11 **10** 70k. orge & brn (No. 166) £475 £400

1918. Stamps of Russia surch **Pol. Korp.**, eagle and value. (a) Perf on Nos. 92/4.

M12A **22** 10k. on 3k. red 6·00 6·00
M13A **22** 35k. on 1k. orange 90·00 90·00
M14A **22** 50k. on 2k. green 6·00 6·00
M15A **22** 1r. on 3k. red £120 £110

(b) Imperf on Nos. 155/7.

M12B 10k. on 3k. red 3·75 3·75
M13B 35k. on 1k. orange 2·40 2·40
M14B 50k. on 2k. green 3·75 3·75
M15B 1r. on 3k. red 3·75 3·75

II. Polish Army in Russia, 1942

M3 "We Shall Return"

1942

M16 **M3** 50k. brown £300 £750

NEWSPAPER STAMPS

1919. Newspaper stamps of Austria optd **POCZTA POLSKA.** Imperf.

N50 **N53** 2h. brown 15·00 18·00
N51 **N53** 4h. green 9·00 9·75
N52 **N53** 6h. blue 9·00 9·75
N53 **N53** 10h. orange £225 £200
N54 **N53** 30h. red 11·50 11·50

OFFICIAL STAMPS

O24

1920

O128 **O24** 3f. red 15 50
O129 **O24** 5f. red 30 50
O130 **O24** 10f. red 30 50
O131 **O24** 15f. red 55 50
O132 **O24** 25f. red 35 50
O133 **O24** 50f. red 35 50
O134 **O24** 100f. red 35 50
O135 **O24** 150f. red 65 50
O136 **O24** 200f. red 2·00 50
O137 **O24** 300f. red 2·40 50
O138 **O24** 600f. red 4·25 90

O70

1933. (a) Inscr "ZWYCZAJNA".

O295 **O70** (No value) mauve 80 45
O306 **O70** (No value) blue 35 35

(b) Inscr "POLECONA".

O307 (No value) red 50 35

O93

1940. (a) Size 31×23 mm.

O392 **O93** 6g. brown 80 2·75
O393 **O93** 8g. grey 80 2·75
O394 **O93** 10g. green 80 2·75
O395 **O93** 12g. green 80 2·10
O396 **O93** 20g. brown 80 3·25
O397 **O93** 24g. red 13·00 2·10
O398 **O93** 30g. red 1·10 3·25
O399 **O93** 40g. violet 1·10 5·75
O400 **O93** 48g. green 3·75 5·75
O401 **O93** 50g. blue 1·10 3·25
O402 **O93** 60g. green 80 2·10
O403 **O93** 80g. purple 80 2·75

(b) Size 35×26 mm.

O404 1z. purple and grey 2·10 5·75
O405 3z. brown and grey 2·10 5·75
O406 5z. orange and grey 3·25 6·25

(c) Size 21×16 mm.

O407 6g. brown 80 1·30
O408 8g. grey 80 1·90
O409 10g. green 1·10 2·10
O410 12g. green 80 1·90
O411 20g. brown 80 1·30
O412 24g. red 80 1·30
O413 30g. red 1·10 2·10
O414 40g. violet 1·10 1·70
O415 50g. blue 1·10 2·10

O102

1943

O456 **O102** 6g. brown 20 75
O457 **O102** 8g. blue 20 75
O458 **O102** 10g. green 20 75
O459 **O102** 12g. violet 20 75
O460 **O102** 16g. orange 20 75
O461 **O102** 20g. green 20 75
O462 **O102** 24g. red 20 75
O463 **O102** 30g. purple 20 75
O464 **O102** 40g. blue 20 75
O465 **O102** 60g. green 20 75
O466 **O102** 80g. purple 20 75
O467 **O102** 100g. grey 25 1·30

O128

1945. No value. (a) With control number below design. Perf or imperf.

O534 **O128** (5z.) blue 50 20
O535 **O128** (10z.) red 95 30

(b) Without control number below design. Perf.

O748 (60g.) pale blue 45 20
O805 (60g.) indigo 70 25
O806 (1.55z.) red 95 25

The blue and indigo stamps are inscr "ZWYKLA" (Ordinary) and the red stamps "POLECONA" (Registered).

O277

1954. No value.

O871 **O277** (60g.) blue 70 20
O872 **O277** (1.55z.) red ("POLECONA") 95 20

POSTAGE DUE STAMPS

1919. Postage Due Stamps of Austria optd **POCZTA POLSKA.**

D50 **D55** 5h. red 5·50 5·00
D51 **D55** 10h. red £1750 £2750
D52 **D55** 15h. red 3·25 2·50
D53 **D55** 20h. red £700 £550
D54 **D55** 25h. red 50·00 43·00
D55 **D55** 30h. red £1900 £1700
D56 **D55** 40h. red £425 £400
D57 **D56** 1k. blue £4750 £5500
D58 **D56** 5k. blue £4750 £5500
D59 **D56** 10k. blue £19000 £22000

1919. Postage Due Provisionals of Austria optd **POCZTA POLSKA.**

D60 **50** 15 on 36h. (No. D287) £425 £500
D61 **50** 50 on 42h. (No. D289) 60·00 60·00

D20

1919. Sold in halerzy or fenigow.

D92 **D20** 2h. blue 20 10
D93 **D20** 4h. blue 20 10
D94 **D20** 5h. blue 20 10
D95 **D20** 10h. blue 20 10
D96 **D20** 20h. blue 20 10
D97 **D20** 30h. blue 20 10
D98 **D20** 50h. blue 25 10
D145 **D20** 100h. blue 20 10
D146 **D20** 200f. blue 75 10
D147 **D20** 500h. blue 75 10

The 20, 100 and 500 values were sold in both currencies.

1919. Sold in fenigow.

D128 2f. red 55 55
D129 4f. red 25 20
D130 5f. red 25 20
D131 10f. red 25 20
D132 20f. red 25 20
D133 30f. red 25 20
D134 50f. red 25 20
D135 100f. red 1·80 85
D136 500f. red 3·75 2·20

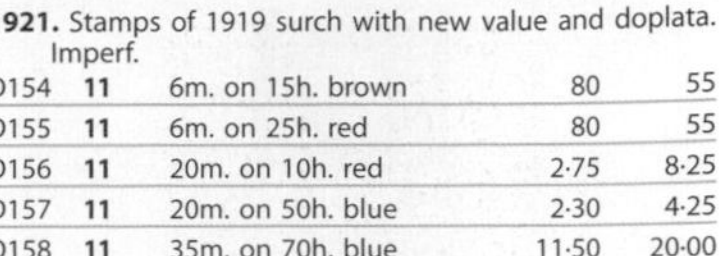

1921. Stamps of 1919 surch with new value and doplata. Imperf.

D154 **11** 6m. on 15h. brown 80 55
D155 **11** 6m. on 25h. red 80 55
D156 **11** 20m. on 10h. red 2·75 8·25
D157 **11** 20m. on 50h. blue 2·30 4·25
D158 **11** 35m. on 70h. blue 11·50 20·00

D28

1921. Value in marks. (a) Size 17×22 mm.

D159 **D28** 1m. blue 40 10
D160 **D28** 2m. blue 40 10
D161 **D28** 4m. blue 45 10
D162 **D28** 6m. blue 50 10
D163 **D28** 8m. blue 50 10
D164 **D28** 20m. blue 50 10
D165 **D28** 50m. blue 50 10
D166 **D28** 100m. blue 65 20

(b) Size 19×24 mm.

D199 50m. blue 35 10
D200 100m. blue 35 10
D201 200m. blue 35 10
D202 500m. blue 50 10
D203 1000m. blue 50 10
D204 2000m. blue 55 10
D205 10,000m. blue 50 10
D206 20,000m. blue 55 10
D207 30,000m. blue 55 10
D208 50,000m. blue 85 20
D209 100,000m. blue 55 20
D210 200,000m. blue 85 20
D211 300,000m. blue 9·75 55
D212 500,000m. blue 4·25 75
D213 1,000,000m. blue 2·50 1·10
D214 2,000,000m. blue 4·25 1·60
D215 3,000,000m. blue 6·50 1·60

1923. Surch.

D216 10,000 on 8m. blue 10 15
D217 20,000 on 20m. blue 10 35
D218 50,000 on 2m. blue 1·25 60

1924. As Type **D28** but value in "groszy" or "zloty". (a) Size 20×25½ mm.

D229 1g. brown 20 10
D230 2g. brown 30 10
D231 4g. brown 45 10
D232 6g. brown 45 10
D233 10g. brown 4·00 10
D234 15g. brown 14·00 10
D235 20g. brown 9·25 10
D236 25g. brown 16·00 10
D237 30g. brown 1·40 10
D238 40g. brown 1·80 10
D239 50g. brown 1·80 10
D240 1z. brown 1·30 10
D241 2z. brown 1·30 20
D242 3z. brown 1·70 75
D243 5z. brown 1·40 45

(b) Size 19×24 mm.

D290 1g. brown 35 10
D291 2g. brown 35 10
D292 10g. brown 1·50 10
D293 15g. brown 1·90 10
D294 20g. brown 17·00 10
D295 25g. brown 43·00 20

D63

1930

D280 **D63** 5g. brown 45 20

1934. Nos. D79/84 surch.

D301 **D28** 10g. on 2z. brown 35 25
D302 **D28** 15g. on 2z. brown 35 25
D303 **D28** 20g. on 1z. brown 35 25
D304 **D28** 20g. on 5z. brown 9·75 40
D305 **D28** 25g. on 40g. brown 1·00 40
D306 **D28** 30g. on 40g. brown 1·70 40
D307 **D28** 50g. on 40g. brown 1·70 55
D308 **D28** 50g. on 3z. brown 3·25 1·10

1934. No. 273 surch **DOPLATA** and value.

D309 10g. on 1z. black on cream 1·30 40
D310 20g. on 1z. black on cream 2·50 75
D311 25g. on 1z. black on cream 1·30 40

D88

1938

D350	**D88**	5g. green	35	10
D351	**D88**	10g. green	35	10
D352	**D88**	15g. green	35	10
D353	**D88**	20g. green	90	20
D354	**D88**	25g. green	65	20
D355	**D88**	30g. green	1·10	20
D356	**D88**	50g. green	1·70	65
D357	**D88**	1z. green	4·75	2·50

D97

1940. German Occupation.

D420	**D97**	10g. orange	40	1·30
D421	**D97**	20g. orange	40	1·30
D422	**D97**	30g. orange	40	1·30
D423	**D97**	50g. orange	1·30	2·10

D126

1945. Size 26×19½ mm. Perf.

D530	**D126**	1z. brown	25	10
D531	**D126**	2z. brown	40	10
D532	**D126**	3z. brown	55	20
D533	**D126**	5z. brown	95	45

1946. Size 29×21½ mm. Perf or imperf.

D646	1z. brown	20	10
D647	2z. brown	20	10
D572	3z. brown	20	10
D573	5z. brown	20	10
D574	6z. brown	20	10
D575	10z. brown	20	10
D649	15z. brown	1·10	35
D577	25z. brown	1·10	20
D651	100z. brown	1·70	1·00
D652	150z. brown	2·40	1·10

D190

1950

D665	**D190**	5z. red	20	20
D666	**D190**	10z. red	20	20
D667	**D190**	15z. red	25	25
D668	**D190**	20z. red	35	25
D669	**D190**	25z. red	50	30
D670	**D190**	50z. red	1·10	45
D671	**D190**	100z. red	1·40	60

1951. Value in "groszy" or "zloty".

D701	5g. red	10	10
D702	10g. red	10	10
D703	15g. red	10	10
D704	20g. red	15	10
D705	25g. red	15	10
D706	30g. red	10	10
D707	50g. red	10	10
D708	60g. red	10	10
D709	90g. red	1·60	1·10
D710	1z. red	25	10
D711	2z. red	55	20
D712	5z. purple	1·40	50

1953. As last but with larger figures of value and no imprint below design.

D804	5g. brown	10	10
D805	10g. brown	10	10
D806	15g. brown	10	10
D807	20g. brown	10	10
D808	25g. brown	10	10
D809	30g. brown	10	10
D810	50g. brown	10	10
D811	60g. brown	55	25
D812	90g. brown	50	15
D813	1z. brown	20	15
D814	2z. brown	70	45

1980. As Type D **190** but redrawn without imprint.

D2699	1z. red	10	10
D2700	2z. drab	20	10
D2701	3z. violet	40	20
D2702	5z. brown	75	45

D1143

1998

D3746	**D1143**	5g. blue, vio & yell	15	10
D3747	**D1143**	10g. blue, turq & yell	20	15
D3748	**D1143**	20g. bl, grn & yell	35	30
D3749	**D1143**	50g. black & yell	90	65
D3750	**D1143**	80g. bl, orge & yell	1·50	1·10
D3751	**D1143**	1z. blue, red & yell	2·10	1·40

Pt. 5 & 7

POLISH POST IN DANZIG

For Polish post in Danzig, the port through which Poland had access to the sea between the two Great Wars.

100 groszy = 1 zloty

Stamps of Poland optd PORT GDANSK.

1925. Issue of 1924.

R1	**40**	1g. brown	60	3·50
R2	**40**	2g. brown	60	8·25
R3	**40**	3g. orange	60	2·40
R4	**40**	5g. green	18·00	12·00
R5	**40**	10g. green	6·00	4·75
R6	**40**	15g. red	33·00	12·00
R7	**40**	20g. blue	1·80	2·40
R8	**40**	25g. red	1·80	2·40
R9	**40**	30g. violet	1·80	2·40
R10	**40**	40g. blue	1·80	2·40
R11	**40**	50g. purple	6·00	3·50

1926. Issues of 1925–28.

R14	**44**	5g. green	1·80	3·00
R15	-	10g. violet (No. 245a)	1·80	3·00
R16	-	15g. red (No. 246)	5·25	6·00
R17	**48**	20g. red	3·50	3·00
R18	**51**	25g. brown	6·00	7·00
R19	**57**	1z. black and cream	33·00	55·00

1929. Issues of 1928/9.

R21	**61**	5g. violet	1·80	3·25
R22	**61**	10g. green	1·80	3·00
R23	**59**	15g. blue	4·75	8·75
R24	**61**	25g. brown	3·50	3·00

1933. Stamp of 1928 with vert opt.

R25	**57**	1z. black on cream	90·00	£200

1934. Issue of 1932.

R26	**65**	5g. violet	4·25	9·50
R27	**65**	10g. green	41·00	£150
R28	**65**	15g. red	4·25	9·50

1936. Issue of 1935.

R29	**79**	5g. blue (No. 313)	3·50	24·00
R31	-	5g. violet (No. 317)	1·30	14·00
R30	-	15g. blue (No. 315)	3·50	24·00
R32	-	15g. lake (No. 319)	1·30	14·00
R33	-	25g. green (No. 321a)	3·50	12·00

R6 Port of Danzig

1938. 20th Anniv of Polish Independence.

R34	**R6**	5g. orange	60	21·00
R35	**R6**	15g. brown	60	21·00
R36	**R6**	25g. purple	60	21·00
R37	**R6**	55g. blue	1·80	39·00

Pt. 5

POLISH POST OFFICE IN TURKEY

Stamps used for a short period for franking correspondance handed in at the Polish Consulate, Constantinople.

100 fenigow = 1 marka

1919. Stamps of Poland of 1919 optd **LEVANT**. Perf.

1	**15**	3f. brown	80·00	£110
2	**15**	5f. green	80·00	£110
3	**15**	10f. purple	80·00	£110
4	**15**	15f. red	80·00	£110
5	**15**	20f. blue	80·00	£110
6	**15**	25f. olive	80·00	£110
7	**15**	50f. green	80·00	£110
8	**17**	1m. violet	80·00	£110
9	**17**	1m.50 green	80·00	£110
10	**17**	2m. brown	80·00	£110
11	**18**	2m.50 brown	80·00	£110
12	**19**	5m. purple	80·00	£110

Pt. 9

PONTA DELGADO

A district of the Azores, whose stamps were used from 1868, and again after 1905.

1000 reis = 1 milreis.

1892. As T **26** of Portugal but inscr "PONTA DELGADA".

6	5r. yellow	3·75	2·50
7	10r. mauve	3·75	2·50
8	15r. brown	5·00	3·50
9	20r. lilac	5·00	3·50
3	25r. green	11·00	2·50
12	50r. blue	11·00	5·25
25	75r. pink	10·50	8·75
14	80r. green	15·00	14·50
15	100r. brown on yellow	15·00	8·75
28	150r. red on pink	85·00	49·00
16	200r. blue on blue	85·00	70·00
17	300r. blue on brown	85·00	70·00

1897. "King Carlos" key-types inscr "PONTA DELGADA".

29	**S**	2½r. grey	80	50
30	**S**	5r. orange	80	50
31	**S**	10r. green	80	50
32	**S**	15r. brown	11·00	9·75
45	**S**	15r. green	2·75	1·70
33	**S**	20r. lilac	2·75	1·80
34	**S**	25r. green	4·00	1·80
46	**S**	25r. red	2·30	60
35	**S**	50r. blue	4·00	1·80
48	**S**	65r. blue	1·70	75
36	**S**	75r. pink	8·75	1·80
49	**S**	75r. brown on yellow	18·00	9·75
37	**S**	80r. mauve	2·30	1·80
38	**S**	100r. blue on blue	5·25	1·80
50	**S**	115r. brown on pink	4·50	2·00
51	**S**	130r. brown on cream	2·75	2·00
39	**S**	150r. brown on yellow	2·75	2·20
52	**S**	180r. grey on pink	2·75	2·00
40	**S**	200r. purple on pink	9·50	8·50
41	**S**	300r. blue on pink	9·50	8·50
42	**S**	500r. black on blue	20·00	16·00

Pt. 1

POONCH

A state in Kashmir, India. Now uses Indian stamps.

12 pies = 1 anna; 16 annas = 1 rupee

1

1876. Imperf.

1	**1**	6p. red	£20000	£225
2	**1**	½a. red	†	£6500

4 (1a.)

1880. Imperf.

53	**1**	1p. red	4·50	4·50
12	**4**	½a. red	5·50	5·50
50	**4**	1a. red	6·50	6·50
52	**4**	2a. red (22×22 mm)	7·00	7·50
31	**4**	4a. red (28×27 mm)	12·00	10·00

These stamps were printed on various coloured papers.

OFFICIAL STAMPS

1888. Imperf.

O1		1p. black	5·00	5·00
O7	**4**	½a. black	5·50	6·50
O3	**4**	1a. black	6·00	6·00
O4	**4**	2a. black	11·00	11·00
O5	**4**	4a. black	15·00	19·00

Pt. 6

PORT LAGOS

French Post Office in the Turkish Empire. Closed in 1898.

25 centimes = 1 piastre.

1893. Stamps of France optd **Port-Lagos** and the three higher values surch also in figures and words.

75	**10**	5c. green	14·00	11·00
76	**10**	10c. black on lilac	48·00	28·00
77	**10**	15c. blue	50·00	65·00
78	**10**	1p. on 25c. black on pink	32·00	29·00
79	**10**	2p. on 50c. red	90·00	85·00
80	**10**	4p. on 1f. green	60·00	85·00

Pt. 6

PORT SAID

French Post Office in Egypt. Closed 1931.

1902. 100 centimes = 1 franc.
1921. 10 milliemes = 1 piastre.

1899. Stamps of France optd **PORT SAID**.

101	1c. black on blue	1·30	1·70
102	2c. brown on buff	1·20	2·50
103	3c. grey	1·10	2·50
104	4c. brown on grey	90	3·25
105	5c. green	2·30	4·00
107	10c. black on lilac	5·00	7·25
109	15c. blue	6·50	11·00
110	20c. red on green	5·00	17·00
111	25c. black on pink	4·25	90
112	30c. brown	10·00	14·00
113	40c. red on yellow	12·00	16·00
115	50c. red	17·00	14·00
116	1f. green	30·00	23·00
117	2f. brown on blue	65·00	80·00
118	5f. mauve on lilac	70·00	£120

1899. No. 107 surch. (a) **25c VINGT-CINQ**.

119	25c. on 10c. black on lilac	£375	£140

(b) **VINGT-CINQ** only.

121	25c. on 10c. black on lilac	£140	30·00

1902. "Blanc", "Mouchon" and "Merson" key-types inscr "PORT SAID".

122	**A**	1c. grey	45	85
123	**A**	2c. purple	35	2·00
124	**A**	3c. red	50	3·00
125	**A**	4c. brown	55	2·30
126a	**A**	5c. green	1·90	2·30
127	**B**	10c. red	1·60	45
128	**B**	15c. red	2·50	3·50
128a	**B**	15c. orange	8·25	9·25
129	**B**	20c. brown	2·50	4·00
130	**B**	25c. blue	1·10	45
131	**B**	30c. mauve	4·25	3·25
132	**C**	40c. red and blue	3·25	5·50
133	**C**	50c. brown and lilac	4·00	3·25
134	**C**	1f. red and green	8·50	12·00
135	**C**	2f. lilac and buff	11·00	18·00
136	**C**	5f. blue and buff	32·00	60·00

1915. Red Cross. Surch **5c** and red cross.

137	**B**	10c.+5c. red	1·00	4·25

1921. Surch with value in figures and words (without bars).

151a	**A**	1m. on 1c. grey	4·00	6·75
152	**A**	2m. on 5c. green	3·50	6·50
153	**B**	4m. on 10c. red	2·50	5·00
166a	**A**	5m. on 1c. grey	11·00	21·00
167	**A**	5m. on 2c. purple	24·00	38·00
154	**A**	5m. on 3c. red	12·00	21·00
141	**A**	5m. on 4c. brown	12·00	28·00
155	**B**	6m. on 15c. orange	2·75	8·75
156	**B**	6m. on 15c. red	29·00	36·00
157	**B**	8m. on 20c. brown	3·25	6·50
168	**A**	10m. on 2c. purple	12·00	36·00
142	**A**	10m. on 4c. brown	40·00	55·00
158	**B**	10m. on 25c. blue	3·50	2·75
159	**B**	10m. on 30c. mauve	6·25	13·00
144	**B**	12m. on 30c. mauve	50·00	75·00
145	**A**	15m. on 4c. brown	15·00	20·00
169	**B**	15m. on 15c. red	50·00	80·00
170	**B**	15m. on 20c. brown	60·00	85·00
146	**C**	15m. on 40c. red and blue	70·00	£100
160	**C**	15m. on 50c. brown and lilac	5·50	9·25
161	**B**	15m. on 50c. blue	7·75	5·00
171	**C**	30m. on 50c. brown & lilac	£250	£250
162	**B**	30m. on 1f. red and green	4·50	10·00
172	**C**	60m. on 50c. brown and lilac	£275	£275
149	**C**	60m. on 2f. lilac and buff	£110	£120
164	**C**	60m. on 2f. red and green	7·50	24·00
173	**C**	150m. on 50c. brown and lilac	£300	£300
165	**C**	150m. on 5f. blue and buff	10·00	24·00

1925. Surch with value in figures and words and bars over old value.

174	**A**	1m. on 1c. grey	75	5·00
175	**A**	2m. on 5c. green	2·50	5·00
176	**B**	4m. on 10c. red	1·20	5·00
177	**A**	5m. on 3c. red	1·40	3·75
178	**B**	6m. on 15c. orange	2·30	5·75
179	**B**	8m. on 20c. brown	2·20	7·25
180	**B**	10m. on 25c. blue	2·30	3·00
181	**B**	15m. on 50c. blue	2·75	3·00
182	**C**	30m. on 1f. red and green	2·20	4·00

183	C	60m. on 2f. red and green	2·50	5·75
184	C	150m. on 5f. blue and buff	4·00	7·50

1927. Altered key-types. Inscr "Mm" below value.

185	A	3m. orange	3·75	8·50
186	B	15m. blue	2·75	4·25
187	B	20m. mauve	3·00	8·75
188	C	50m. red and green	5·00	10·50
189	C	100m. blue and yellow	3·75	14·50
190	C	250m. green and red	12·00	24·00

1927. "French Sinking Fund" issue. As No. 186 (colour changed) surch **+5 Mm Caisse d'Amortissement**.

191	B	15m.+5m. orange	2·10	11·50
192	B	15m.+5m. mauve	3·00	11·50
193	B	15m.+5m. brown	2·75	11·50
194	B	15m.+5m. lilac	6·50	17·00

POSTAGE DUE STAMPS

1921. Postage Due stamps of France surch in figures and words.

D174	D 11	2m. on 5c. blue	60·00	70·00
D175	D 11	4m. on 10c. brown	75·00	75·00
D176	D 11	10m. on 30c. red	75·00	75·00
D166	D 11	12m. on 10c. brown	60·00	70·00
D167	D 11	15m. on 5c. blue	60·00	85·00
D177	D 11	15m. on 50c. purple	85·00	85·00
D168	D 11	30m. on 20c. olive	75·00	90·00
D169	D 11	30m. on 50c. purple	£2750	£3000

For 1928 issues, see Alexandria.

Pt. 9

PORTUGAL

A country on the S.W. coast of Europe, a kingdom until 1910, when it became a republic.

1853. 1000 reis = 1 milreis.
1912. 100 centavos = 1 escudo.
2002. 100 cents = 1 euro.

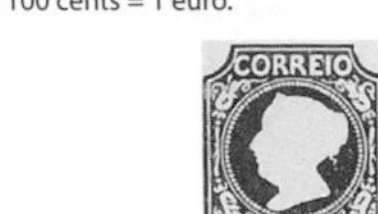

1 Queen Maria II

1853. Various frames. Imperf.

1	1	5r. brown	£4500	£1300
4	1	25r. blue	£1400	29·00
6	1	50r. green	£5500	£1500
8	1	100r. lilac	£47000	£3000

5 King Pedro V

1855. Various frames. Imperf.

18a	5	5r. brown	£650	£120
21	5	25r. blue	£600	22·00
22	5	25r. pink	£450	8·75
13	5	50r. green	£750	£110
15	5	100r. lilac	£1200	£150

9 King Luis

1862. Various frames. Imperf.

24	9	5r. brown	£200	39·00
28	9	10r. yellow	£225	70·00
30	9	25r. pink	£160	7·00
32	9	50r. green	£1100	£120
34	9	100r. lilac	£1300	£140

14 King Luis

1866. With curved value labels. Imperf.

35	14	5r. black	£170	14·50
36	14	10r. yellow	£350	£225
38	14	20r. bistre	£275	£100
39	14	25r. pink	£350	12·00
41	14	50r. green	£375	£110
43	14	80r. orange	£375	£110
45	14	100r. purple	£450	£170
46	14	120r. blue	£475	£110

1867. With curved value labels. Perf.

52		5r. black	£180	65·00
54		10r. yellow	£375	£160
56		20r. bistre	£450	£170
57		25r. pink	£100	11·50
60		50r. green	£375	£160
61		80r. orange	£550	£160
62		100r. lilac	£375	£160
64		120r. blue	£450	£110
67		240r. lilac	£1500	£700

15

1870. With straight value labels. Perf.

69	15	5r. black	80·00	8·25
70	15	10r. yellow	£110	43·00
158	15	10r. green	£200	55·00
74	15	15r. brown	£150	43·00
76	15	20r. bistre	£110	38·00
143	15	20r. red	£500	85·00
80	15	25r. red	43·00	5·50
115	15	50r. green	£225	60·00
117	15	50r. blue	£475	80·00
148	15	80r. orange	£180	28·00
153	15	100r. mauve	£100	16·00
93	15	120r. blue	£425	£110
95	15	150r. blue	£500	£180
155	15	150r. yellow	£190	22·00
99	15	240r. lilac	£2250	£1600
156	15	300r. mauve	£180	45·00
128	15	1000r. black	£450	£140

16 King Luis

17

1880. Various frames for T **16**.

185	16	5r. black	43·00	6·00
180	17	25r. grey	£475	44·00
188	16	25r. grey	44·00	5·50
190	16	25r. brown	44·00	5·50
184	16	50r. blue	£475	22·00

19 King Luis

1882. Various frames.

229	19	5r. black	19·00	1·70
231	19	10r. green	55·00	6·00
232	19	20r. red	65·00	26·00
212	19	25r. brown	42·00	3·75
234	19	25r. mauve	44·00	4·50
236	19	50r. blue	65·00	4·50
216	19	500r. black	£650	£425
217	19	500r. mauve	£400	85·00

26 King Carlos

1892

271	26	5r. orange	18·00	3·00
239	26	10r. mauve	42·00	8·25
256	26	15r. brown	42·00	6·00
242	26	20r. lilac	50·00	13·50
275	26	25r. green	60·00	4·25
244	26	50r. blue	50·00	14·50
245	26	75r. red	£100	12·00
262	26	80r. green	£130	80·00
248	26	100r. brown on buff	95·00	9·50
265	26	150r. red on pink	£250	80·00
252	26	200r. blue on blue	£250	65·00
267	26	300r. blue on brown	£275	£110

1892. Optd **PROVISORIO**.

284	19	5r. black	21·00	10·50
283	19	10r. green	24·00	13·50
297	15	15r. brown	27·00	24·00
290	19	20r. red	60·00	34·00
291	19	25r. mauve	21·00	8·25
292	19	50r. blue	£120	95·00
293	15	80r. orange	£150	£140

1893. Optd **1893 PROVISORIO** or surch also.

302	19	5r. black	35·00	32·00
303	19	10r. green	33·00	29·00
304	19	20r. red	55·00	47·00
309	19	20r. on 25r. mauve	75·00	65·00
305	19	25r. mauve	£150	£150
306	19	50r. blue	£150	£150
310	15	50r. on 80r. orange	£180	£150
312	15	75r. on 80r. orange	£100	£100
308	15	80r. orange	£150	£140

32 Prince Henry in his Caravel and Family Motto

1894. 500th Birth Anniv of Prince Henry the Navigator.

314	32	5r. orange	5·50	1·20
315	32	10r. red	5·50	1·20
316	32	15r. brown	14·50	4·50
317	32	20r. lilac	14·50	5·25
318	-	25r. green	13·50	1·70
319	-	50r. blue	43·00	9·00
320	-	75r. red	85·00	19·00
321	-	80r. green	85·00	22·00
322	-	100r. brown on buff	65·00	18·00
323	-	150r. red	£190	44·00
324	-	300r. blue on buff	£225	60·00
325	-	500r. purple	£500	£120
326	-	1000r. black on buff	£850	£180

DESIGNS: 25r. to 100r. Prince Henry directing movements of his fleet; 150r. to 1000r. Prince Henry's studies.

35 St. Anthony's Vision

37 St. Anthony ascending into Heaven

1895. 700th Birth Anniv of St. Anthony (Patron Saint). With a prayer in Latin printed on back.

327	35	2½r. black	6·00	2·00
328	-	5r. orange	6·00	2·00
329	-	10r. mauve	17·00	11·00
330	-	15r. brown	20·00	11·00
331	-	20r. lilac	20·00	12·00
332	-	25r. purple and green	17·00	2·00
333	37	50r. brown and blue	42·00	31·00
334	37	75r. brown and red	70·00	55·00
335	37	80r. brown and green	85·00	80·00
336	37	100r. black and brown	75·00	43·00
337	-	150r. red and bistre	£250	£150
338	-	200r. blue and bistre	£225	£160
339	-	300r. grey and bistre	£325	£225
340	-	500r. brown and green	£650	£475
341	-	1000r. lilac and green	£1100	£600

DESIGNS—HORIZ: 5r. to 25r. St. Anthony preaching to fish. VERT: 150r. to 1000r. St. Anthony from picture in Academy of Fine Arts, Paris.

39 King Carlos

1895. Numerals of value in red (Nos. 354 and 363) or black (others).

342	39	2½r. grey	50	20
343	39	5r. orange	50	20
344	39	10r. green	70	25
345	39	15r. green	70·00	4·00
346	39	15r. brown	£140	5·50
347	39	20r. lilac	90	55
348	39	25r. green	£100	35
349	39	25r. red	55	20
351	39	50r. blue	75	35
352	39	65r. blue	80	45
353	39	75r. red	£170	6·75
354	39	75r. brown on yellow	2·20	1·00
355	39	80r. mauve	2·75	1·60
356	39	100r. blue on blue	1·30	60
357	39	115r. brown on pink	6·50	4·50
358	39	130r. brown on cream	4·50	2·20
359	39	150r. brown on yellow	£225	34·00
360	39	180r. grey on pink	29·00	13·50
361	39	200r. puple on pink	27·00	3·75
362	39	300r. blue on pink	5·00	3·00
363	39	500r. black on blue	12·50	6·75

40 Departure of Fleet

43 Muse of History

44 Da Gama and Camoens and "Sao Gabriel" (flagship)

1898. Fourth Centenary of Discovery of Route to India by Vasco da Gama.

378	40	2½r. green	1·90	55
379	-	5r. red	1·90	55
380	-	10r. purple	12·00	2·30
381	43	25r. green	8·25	65
382	44	50r. blue	17·00	4·25
383	-	75r. brown	65·00	17·00
384	-	100r. brown	50·00	17·00
385	-	150r. brown	£110	44·00

DESIGNS—HORIZ: 5r. Arrival at Calicut; 10r. Embarkation at Rastello; 100r. Flagship "Sao Gabriel"; 150r. Vasco da Gama. VERT: 75r. Archangel Gabriel, Patron Saint of the Expedition.

48 King Manoel II

49

1910

390	48	2½r. lilac	40	35
391	48	5r. black	40	35
392	48	10r. green	70	40
393	48	15r. brown	3·75	2·50
394	48	20r. red	1·40	1·10
395	48	25r. brown	85	25
396	48	50r. blue	2·30	95
397	48	75r. brown	14·00	7·75
398	48	80r. grey	4·25	3·25
399	48	100r. brown on green	16·00	4·00
400	48	200r. green on orange	9·00	6·50
401	48	300r. black on blue	11·50	7·25
402	49	500r. brown and green	21·00	18·00
403	49	1000r. black and blue	48·00	38·00

1910. Optd **REPUBLICA**.

404	48	2½r. lilac	45	30
405	48	5r. black	45	30
406	48	10r. green	4·50	1·50
407	48	15r. brown	1·60	1·20
408	48	20r. red	6·25	2·75
409	48	25r. brown	1·20	45
410	48	50r. blue	8·75	3·25
411	48	75r. brown	15·00	6·75
412	48	80r. grey	4·50	3·50
413	48	100r. brown on green	2·75	1·40
414	48	200r. green on orange	3·25	3·00
415	48	300r. black on blue	5·75	5·00
416	49	500r. brown and green	16·00	13·50
417	49	1000r. black and blue	40·00	30·00

1911. Optd **REPUBLICA** or surch also.

441	40	2½r. green	75	30
442	D48	5r. black	1·70	75
443	D48	10r. mauve	2·10	1·20
444	-	15r. on 5r. red (No. 379)	1·30	60
445	D48	20r. orange	7·75	5·00
446	43	25r. green	90	45
447	44	50r. blue	4·50	2·10
448	-	75r. brown (No. 383)	65·00	47·00
449	-	80r. on 150r. (No. 385)	8·00	6·25
450	-	100r. brown (No. 384)	8·00	3·75
451	D48	200r. brown on buff	£180	£110
452	D48	300r. on 50r. grey	£130	65·00
453	D48	500r. on 100r. red on pink	70·00	36·00
454	-	1000r. on 10r. (No. 380)	90·00	55·00

1911. Vasco da Gama stamps of Madeira optd **REPUBLICA** or surch also.

455	2½r. green	17·00	13·50
456	15r. on 5r. red	3·75	3·75
457	25r. green	7·50	7·25
458	50r. blue	17·00	13·50
459	75r. brown	17·00	8·25
460	80r. on 150r. brown	18·00	16·00
461	100r. brown	60·00	13·50
462	1000r. on 10r. purple	60·00	38·00

56 Ceres

1912

484	56	¼c. brown	95	30
485	56	½c. black	1·00	30
486	56	1c. green	1·90	55
515	56	1c. brown	35	30
488	56	1½c. brown	10·50	4·50
516	56	1½c. green	45	30
490	56	2c. red	10·50	3·75
517	56	2c. yellow	1·80	40
702	56	2c. brown	20	20
492	56	2½c. lilac	90	30
521	56	3c. red	55	40
703	56	3c. blue	20	20
495	56	3½c. green	55	30
523	56	4c. green	35	30
704	56	4c. orange	20	20
497	56	5c. blue	10·50	1·00
705	56	5c. brown	20	20
527	56	6c. purple	1·40	65
706	56	6c. brown	20	20
815	56	6c. red	50	40
500	56	7½c. brown	19·00	3·75
529	56	7½c. blue	55	30
530	56	8c. grey	65	65
531	56	8c. green	1·10	70
532	56	8c. orange	1·20	65
503	56	10c. brown	25·00	1·60
707	56	10c. red	20	20
504	56	12c. blue	2·20	1·20
534	56	12c. green	85	55
535	56	13½c. blue	2·20	1·60
481	56	14c. blue on yellow	3·50	2·40
536	56	14c. purple	1·00	85
505	56	15c. brown	3·25	1·30
708	56	15c. black	45	20
709	56	16c. blue	45	20
474	56	20c. brown on green	26·00	2·75
475	56	20c. brown on buff	27·00	7·25
539	56	20c. brown	1·00	70
540	56	20c. green	85	55
541	56	20c. grey	1·20	65
542	56	24c. blue	1·00	65
543	56	25c. pink	85	45
710	56	25c. grey	45	20
819	56	25c. green	95	45
476	56	30c. brown on pink	£190	18·00
477	56	30c. brown on yellow	18·00	3·50
545	56	30c. brown	85	50
820	56	32c. green	95	45
548	56	36c. red	3·00	65
549	56	40c. blue	2·10	1·10
550	56	40c. brown	1·40	55
478	56	50c. orange on orange	26·00	2·20
712	56	40c. green	80	20
713	56	48c. pink	2·00	1·40
553	56	50c. yellow	3·00	1·10
824	56	50c. red	3·50	1·20
554	56	60c. blue	2·75	1·10
715	56	64c. blue	3·25	3·00
826	56	75c. red	3·00	1·30
510	56	80c. pink	2·75	1·70
558	56	80c. lilac	2·40	90
827	56	80c. green	3·00	1·30
559	56	90c. blue	3·00	1·10
717	56	96c. red	4·25	1·90
480	56	1e. green on blue	29·00	2·20
561	56	1e. lilac	6·75	3·50
565	56	1e. blue	7·50	2·20
566	56	1e. purple	7·00	2·50
829	56	1e. red	8·25	1·30
562	56	1e.10 brown	6·75	3·25
563	56	1e.20 green	3·75	2·10
830	56	1e.20 brown	6·00	1·40
831	56	1e.25 blue	5·50	1·40
568	56	1e.50 lilac	30·00	7·75
720	56	1e.60 blue	4·50	75
721	56	2e. green	28·00	1·60
833	56	2e. mauve	36·00	10·50
572	56	2e.40 green	£425	£250
573	56	3e. pink	£425	£225
722	56	3e.20 green	12·00	1·60
723	56	4e.50 yellow	12·00	1·60
575	56	5e. green	90·00	16·00
724	56	5e. brown	£150	5·75
725	56	10e. red	17·00	3·25
577	56	20e. blue	£700	£300

60 Presidents of Portugal and Brazil and Admiral Gago Coutinho, Sacadura Cabral and Fairey IIID

1923. Portugal-Brazil Trans Atlantic Flight.

578	60	1c. brown	20	1·10
579	60	2c. orange	20	1·10
580	60	3c. blue	20	1·10
581	60	4c. green	20	1·10
582	60	5c. brown	20	1·10
583	60	10c. brown	20	1·10
584	60	15c. black	20	1·10
585	60	20c. green	20	1·10
586	60	25c. red	20	1·10
587	60	30c. brown	1·00	2·75
588	60	40c. brown	70	1·10
589	60	50c. yellow	60	1·30
590	60	75c. purple	60	1·40
591	60	1e. blue	60	2·75
592	60	1e.50 grey	1·10	3·50
593	60	2e. green	1·30	8·75

62 Camoens at Ceuta

63 Saving the "Lusiad"

1924. 400th Birth Anniv of Camoens (poet). Value in black.

600	62	2c. blue	35	35
601	62	3c. orange	35	35
602	62	4c. grey	35	35
603	62	5c. green	35	35
604	62	6c. red	35	35
605	63	8c. brown	35	35
606	63	10c. violet	35	35
607	63	15c. green	35	35
608	63	16c. purple	40	40
609	63	20c. orange	50	40
610	-	25c. violet	50	40
611	-	30c. brown	50	40
612	-	32c. green	1·40	1·40
613	-	40c. blue	50	45
614	-	48c. red	2·10	2·30
615	-	50c. red	2·50	1·50
616	-	64c. green	2·50	1·50
617	-	75c. lilac	2·75	1·50
618	-	80c. brown	1·90	1·50
619	-	96c. red	1·90	1·50
620	-	1e. turquoise	1·60	1·20
621	-	1e.20 brown	9·25	6·75
622	-	1e.50 red	2·50	1·50
623	-	1e.60 blue	2·50	1·50
624	-	2e. green	9·25	6·25
625	-	2e.40 green on green	8·00	4·25
626	-	3e. blue on blue	2·75	1·40
627	-	3e.20 black on turquoise	2·75	1·30
628	-	4e.50 black on yellow	8·50	5·50
629	-	10e. brown on pink	15·00	11·00
630	-	20e. violet on mauve	18·00	11·00

DESIGNS—VERT: 25c. to 48c. Luis de Camoens; 50c. to 96c. 1st Edition of "Lusiad"; 20e. Monument to Camoens. HORIZ: 1e. to 2e. Death of Camoens; 2e.40 to 10e. Tomb of Camoens.

65 Branco's House at S. Miguel de Seide

67 Camilo Castelo Branco

1925. Birth Centenary of Camilo Castelo Branco (novelist). Value in black.

631	65	2c. orange	40	25
632	65	3c. green	40	25
633	65	4c. blue	40	25
634	65	5c. red	40	25
635	65	6c. purple	40	25
636	65	8c. brown	40	25
637	A	10c. blue	40	25
638	67	15c. green	45	35
639	A	16c. orange	55	50
640	A	20c. violet	55	50
641	67	25c. red	55	50
642	A	30c. bistre	55	50
643	A	32c. green	1·70	1·50
644	67	40c. black and green	1·20	95
645	A	48c. red	4·50	5·00
646	B	50c. green	1·20	95
647	B	64c. brown	4·75	5·00
648	B	75c. grey	1·40	1·00
649	67	80c. brown	1·40	1·10
650	B	96c. red	2·40	2·30
651	B	1e. lilac	2·20	2·30
652	B	1e.20 green	2·50	2·30
653	C	1e.50 blue on blue	46·00	22·00
654	67	1e.60 blue	9·00	5·75
655	C	2e. green on green	10·50	6·25
656	C	2e.40 red on orange	£100	50·00
657	C	3e. red on blue	£130	65·00
658	C	3e.20 black on green	60·00	50·00
659	67	4e.50 black and red	25·00	5·75
660	C	10e. brown on buff	26·00	6·00
661	D	20e. black on orange	27·00	6·00

DESIGNS—HORIZ: A, Branco's study. VERT: B, Teresa de Albuquerque; C, Mariana and Joao da Cruz; D, Simao de Botelho. Types B/D shows characters from Branco's "Amor de Peredicao".

76 Afonso I, first King of Portugal, 1140

77 Battle of Aljubarrota

1926. First Independence issue. Dated 1926. Centres in black.

671	76	2c. orange	40	40
672	-	3c. blue	40	40
673	76	4c. green	40	40
674	-	5c. brown	40	40
675	76	6c. orange	40	40
676	-	15c. green	40	40
677	76	16c. blue	1·40	1·10
678	77	20c. violet	1·40	1·10
679	-	25c. red	1·40	1·10
680	77	32c. green	1·50	1·30
681	-	40c. brown	1·00	75
682	-	46c. red	6·50	5·00
683	-	50c. bistre	6·50	5·00
684	-	64c. green	9·00	6·50
685	-	75c. brown	9·00	6·25
686	-	96c. red	13·50	10·50
687	-	1e. violet	13·50	11·00
688	77	1e.60 blue	18·00	15·00
689	-	3e. purple	50·00	43·00
690	-	4e.50 green	70·00	55·00
691	77	10e. red	£110	85·00

DESIGNS—VERT: 25, 40, 50, 75c. Philippa de Vilhena arms her sons; 64c., 1e. Don Joao IV, 1640; 96c., 3e., 4e.50, Independence Monument, Lisbon. HORIZ: 3, 5, 15, 46c. Monastery of D. Joao I.

1926. First Independence issue surch. Centres in black.

692	2c. on 5c. brown	2·00	1·80
693	2c. on 46c. red	2·00	1·80
694	2c. on 64c. green	2·30	2·10
695	3c. on 75c. brown	2·30	2·10
696	3c. on 96c. red	3·50	2·75
697	3c. on 1e. violet	3·00	2·50
698	4c. on 1e.60 blue	23·00	17·00
699	4c. on 3e. purple	8·50	7·00
700	6c. on 4e.50 green	8·50	7·00
701	6c. on 10e. red	8·75	7·00

80 Goncalo Mendes da Maia

1927. Second Independence issue. Dated 1927. Centres in black.

726	80	2c. brown	40	20
727	-	3c. blue	40	20
728	80	4c. orange	40	20
729	-	5c. brown	40	20
730	-	6c. brown	40	20
731	-	15c. brown	90	65
732	-	16c. blue	1·90	80
733	80	25c. grey	2·10	1·50
734	-	32c. green	4·75	2·40
735	-	40c. green	1·30	95
736	80	48c. red	20·00	16·00
737	-	80c. violet	14·50	11·00
738	-	96c. red	30·00	22·00
739	-	1e.60 blue	31·00	23·00
740	-	4e.50 brown	44·00	34·00

DESIGNS—HORIZ: 3, 15, 80c. Gulmaraes Castle; 6, 32c. Battle of Montijo. VERT: 5, 16c., 1e.50, Joao das Regras; 40, 96c. Brites de Aimelda; 4e.50, J. P. Ribeiro.

1928. Surch.

742	56	4c. on 8c. orange	85	50
743	56	4c. on 30c. brown	85	50
744	56	10c. on ¼c. brown	85	50
745	56	10c. on ½c. black	1·10	65
746	56	10c. on 1c. brown	1·10	65
747	56	10c. on 4c. green	85	55
748	56	10c. on 4c. orange	85	55
749	56	10c. on 5c. brown	85	55
751	56	15c. on 16c. blue	2·10	1·20
752	56	15c. on 20c. brown	65·00	50·00
753	56	15c. on 20c. grey	85	50
754	56	15c. on 24c. blue	4·00	2·50
755	56	15c. on 25c. pink	85	50
756	56	15c. on 25c. grey	85	50
757	56	16c. on 32c. green	1·60	1·20
758	56	40c. on 2c. yellow	85	50
760	56	40c. on 2c. brown	85	50
761	56	40c. on 3c. blue	85	55
762	56	40c. on 50c. yellow	85	50
763	56	40c. on 60c. blue	1·60	1·10
764	56	40c. on 64c. blue	1·60	1·20
765	56	40c. on 75c. pink	1·70	1·40
766	56	40c. on 80c. lilac	1·20	80
767	56	40c. on 90c. blue	8·25	5·00
768	56	40c. on 1e. grey	1·60	1·20
769	56	40c. on 1e.10 brown	1·60	1·20
770	56	80c. on 6c. purple	1·60	1·10
771	56	80c. on 6c. brown	1·60	1·10
772	56	80c. on 48c. pink	2·30	1·70
773	56	80c. on 1e.50 lilac	3·50	1·90
774	56	96c. on 1e.20 green	7·00	4·00
775	56	96c. on 1e.20 buff	6·75	4·50
777	56	1e.60 on 2e. green	75·00	50·00
778	56	1e.60 on 3e.20 green	19·00	11·50
779	56	1e.60 on 20e. blue	27·00	15·00

84 Storming of Santarem

1928. Third Independence issue. Dated 1928. Centres in black.

780	-	2c. blue	60	35
781	84	3c. green	60	35
782	-	4c. red	60	35
783	-	5c. green	60	35
784	-	6c. brown	60	35
785	84	15c. grey	1·20	1·10
786	-	16c. purple	1·20	1·10
787	-	25c. blue	1·20	1·10
788	-	32c. green	6·25	5·75
789	-	40c. brown	1·20	1·10
790	-	50c. red	18·00	8·50
791	84	80c. grey	18·00	11·00
792	-	96c. red	35·00	23·00
793	-	1e. mauve	60·00	44·00
794	-	1e.60 blue	23·00	17·00
795	-	4e.50 yellow	24·00	22·00

DESIGNS—VERT: 2, 25c., 1e.60, G. Paes; 6, 32, 96c. Joana de Gouveia; 4e.50, Matias de Albuquerque. HORIZ: 4, 16, 50c. Battle of Rolica; 5, 40c., 1e. Battle of Atoleiros.

1929. Optd **Revalidado.**

805	56	10c. red	85	50
806	56	15c. black	85	50
807	56	40c. brown	1·20	90
808	56	40c. green	1·10	65
810	56	96c. red	10·50	6·75
811	56	1e.60 blue	43·00	27·00

1929. Telegraph stamp surch **CORREIO 1$60** and bars.

812	1e.60 on 5c. brown	27·00	17·00

88 Camoens' Poem "Lusiad"

1931

835	88	4c. brown	45	20
836	88	5c. brown	45	20
837	88	6c. grey	45	20
838	88	10c. mauve	45	30
839	88	15c. black	45	30
840	88	16c. blue	2·30	1·00
841	88	25c. green	5·75	55
841a	88	25c. blue	6·75	65
841b	88	30c. green	3·50	65
842	88	40c. red	11·50	20
843	88	48c. brown	2·30	1·60
844	88	50c. brown	55	20
845	88	75c. red	9·75	1·80
846	88	80c. green	80	25
846a	88	95c. red	31·00	10·00
847	88	1e. purple	60·00	25
848	88	1e.20 green	4·00	1·60
849	88	1e.25 blue	3·75	35
849a	88	1e.60 blue	60·00	6·75
849b	88	1e.75 blue	1·20	35

850	**88**	2e. mauve	1·40	35
851	**88**	4e.50 orange	3·00	40
852	**88**	5e. green	3·00	40

89 St. Anthony's Birthplace

1931. 700th Death Anniv of St. Anthony.

853	**89**	15c. purple	1·60	45
854	-	25c. myrtle and green	1·80	45
855	-	40c. brown and buff	1·60	45
856	-	75c. pink	55·00	22·00
857	-	1e.25 grey and blue	£100	46·00
858	-	4e.50 purple and mauve	55·00	5·50

DESIGNS—VERT: 25c. Saint's baptismal font; 40c. Lisbon Cathedral; 75c. St. Anthony; 1e.25, Santa Cruz Cathedral, Coimbra. HORIZ: 4e.50, Saint's tomb, Padua.

90 Don Nuno Alvares Pereira

1931. Fifth Death Centenary of Pereira.

859	**90**	15c. black	1·90	1·70
860	**90**	25c. green and black	10·00	1·70
861	**90**	40c. orange	5·25	95
862	**90**	75c. red	44·00	38·00
863	**90**	1e.25 light blue and blue	50·00	33·00
864	**90**	4e.50 green and brown	£275	85·00

1933. Pereira issue of 1931 surch.

865	15c. on 40c. orange	1·30	75
866	40c. on 15c. black	6·25	3·50
867	40c. on 25c. green & black	1·60	1·20
868	40c. on 75c. red	13·50	8·00
869	40c. on 1e.25 light blue and blue	13·50	6·00
870	40c. on 4e.50 green and brown	13·50	6·00

1933. St. Anthony issue of 1931 surch.

871	-	15c. on 40c. brown and buff	1·70	75
872	**89**	40c. on 15c. purple	3·50	1·60
873	-	40c. on 25c. myrtle and green	3·00	75
874	-	40c. on 75c. pink	13·50	8·00
875	-	40c. on 1e.25 grey and blue	13·50	8·00
876	-	40c. on 4e.50 purple and mauve	13·50	8·00

94 President Carmona

1934

877	**94**	40c. violet	35·00	50

95

1934. Colonial Exhibition.

878	**95**	25c. brown	7·50	1·90
879	**95**	40c. red	36·00	60
880	**95**	1e.60 blue	75·00	20·00

96 Queen Maria

1935. First Portuguese Philatelic Exhibition.

881	**96**	40c. red	2·40	40

97 Temple of Diana at Evora

98 Prince Henry the Navigator

99 "All for the Nation"

100 Coimbra Cathedral

1935

882	**97**	4c. black	85	30
883	**97**	5c. blue	90	30
884	**97**	6c. brown	1·40	50
885	**98**	10c. green	13·50	30
886	**98**	15c. red	55	30
887	**99**	25c. blue	12·50	65
888	**99**	40c. brown	4·25	20
889	**99**	1e. red	20·00	75
890	**100**	1e.75 blue	£140	1·90
890a	**99**	10e. grey	46·00	4·50
890b	**99**	20e. blue	60·00	3·25

102 Shield and Propeller

1937. Air.

891	**102**	1e.50 blue	1·40	45
892	**102**	1e.75 red	2·10	50
893	**102**	2e.50 red	2·20	50
893a	**102**	3e. blue	31·00	17·00
893b	**102**	4e. green	40·00	25·00
894	**102**	5e. red	3·50	1·70
895	**102**	10e. purple	6·50	1·80
895a	**102**	15e. orange	30·00	11·00
896	**102**	20e. brown	17·00	4·00
896a	**102**	50e. purple	£325	£120

103 Symbol of Medicine

1937. Centenary of Medical and Surgical Colleges at Lisbon and Oporto.

897	**103**	25c. blue	19·00	1·40

104 Gil Vicente

1937. 400th Death Anniv of Gil Vicente (poet).

898	**104**	40c. brown	36·00	30
899	**104**	1e. red	4·50	30

106 Grapes

1938. Wine and Raisin Congress.

900	**106**	15c. violet	2·50	95
901	**106**	25c. brown	5·00	2·40
902	**106**	40c. mauve	17·00	50
903	**106**	1e.75 blue	55·00	40·00

107 Cross of Avis

1940. Portuguese Legion.

904	**107**	5c. buff	80	35
905	**107**	10c. violet	80	35
906	**107**	15c. blue	80	35
907	**107**	25c. brown	44·00	1·50
908	**107**	40c. green	70·00	60
909	**107**	80c. green	3·75	1·00
910	**107**	1e. red	£100	5·75
911	**107**	1e.75 blue	17·00	4·00
MS911a		155×170 mm. Nos. 904/11 (sold at 5e.50)	£700	£1200

109 Portuguese World Exhibition

1940. Portuguese Centenaries.

912	**109**	10c. purple	45	35
913	-	15c. blue	45	35
914	-	25c. green	2·20	45
915	-	35c. green	2·00	60
916	-	40c. brown	4·75	30
917	**109**	80c. purple	9·75	55
918	-	1e. red	23·00	2·40
919	-	1e.75 blue	13·50	4·00
MS919a		160×229 mm. Nos. 912/9 (sold at 10e.)	£325	£500

DESIGNS—VERT: 15, 35c. Statue of King Joao IV; 25c., 1e. Monument of Discoveries, Belem; 40c., 1e.75, King Afonso Henriques.

113 Sir Rowland Hill

1940. Centenary of First Adhesive Postage Stamps.

920	**113**	15c. purple	50	25
921	**113**	25c. red	50	25
922	**113**	35c. green	50	25
923	**113**	40c. purple	90	25
924	**113**	50c. green	36·00	6·25
925	**113**	80c. blue	3·50	1·80
926	**113**	1e. red	43·00	5·75
927	**113**	1e.75 blue	9·75	5·50
MS928		160×152 mm. Nos. 920/7 (sold at 10e.)	£150	£300

114 Fish-woman of Nazare

1941. Costumes.

932	**114**	4c. green	40	30
933	-	5c. brown	40	30
934	-	10c. purple	5·50	1·70
935	-	15c. green	40	40
936	-	25c. purple	4·50	90
937	-	40c. green	40	30
938	-	80c. blue	7·25	3·25
939	-	1e. red	21·00	2·50
940	-	1e.75 blue	22·00	7·25
941	-	2e. orange	85·00	38·00
MS941a		163×146 mm. Nos. 932/41 (sold at 10e.)	£250	£250

DESIGNS: 5c. Woman from Coimbra; 10c. Vine-grower of Saloio; 15c. Fish-woman of Lisbon; 25c. Woman of Olhao; 40c. Woman of Aveiro; 80c. Shepherdess of Madeira; 1e. Spinner of Viana do Castelo; 1e.75, Horsebreeder of Ribatejo; 2e. Reaper of Alentejo.

115 Caravel

1943

942	**115**	5c. black	35	20
943	**115**	10c. brown	35	20
944	**115**	15c. grey	35	20
945	**115**	20c. violet	35	20
946	**115**	30c. purple	35	20
947	**115**	35c. green	40	20
948	**115**	50c. purple	40	20
948a	**115**	80c. green	6·75	60
949	**115**	1e. red	14·00	20
949a	**115**	1e. lilac	4·25	35
949b	**115**	1e.20 red	6·75	45
949c	**115**	1e.50 green	55·00	55
950	**115**	1e.75 blue	40·00	20
950a	**115**	1e.80 orange	60·00	5·25
951	**115**	2e. brown	3·00	20
951a	**115**	2e. blue	8·75	65
952	**115**	2e.50 red	4·75	20
953	**115**	3e.50 blue	20·00	70
953a	**115**	4e. orange	90·00	3·75
954	**115**	5e. red	2·75	35
954a	**115**	6e. green	£170	6·00
954b	**115**	7e.50 green	60·00	5·50
955	**115**	10e. grey	5·00	35
956	**115**	15e. green	55·00	1·60
957	**115**	20e. green	£200	95
958	**115**	50e. red	£550	1·50

116 Labourer

1943. First Agricultural Science Congress.

959	**116**	10c. blue	1·50	50
960	**116**	50c. red	2·40	55

117 Mounted Postal Courier

1944. Third National Philatelic Exhibition, Lisbon.

961	**117**	10c. brown	50	25
962	**117**	50c. violet	50	25
963	**117**	1e. red	6·00	1·10
964	**117**	1e.75 blue	6·00	2·50
MS964a		82×121 mm. Nos. 961/4 (sold at 7e.50)	70·00	£350

118 Felix Avellar Brotero

1944. Birth Bicentenary of Avellar Brotero (botanist).

965	**118**	10c. brown	45	25
966	-	50c. green	2·20	25
967	-	1e. red	14·50	2·20
968	**118**	1e.75 blue	11·00	4·50
MS968a		144×195 mm. Nos. 965/8 (sold at 7e.50)	85·00	£200

DESIGN: 50c., 1e. Brotero's statue, Coimbra.

120 Vasco da Gama

1945. Portuguese Navigators.

969	-	10c. brown	45	25
970	-	30c. orange	45	25
971	-	35c. green	95	40
972	**120**	50c. green	2·75	45
973	-	1e. red	7·25	1·10
974	-	1e.75 blue	9·25	3·25
975	-	2e. black	11·00	3·75
976	-	3e.50 red	22·00	6·50
MS976a		167×173 mm. Nos. 969/76 (sold at 15e.)	75·00	£200

PORTRAITS: 10c. Gil Eanes; 30c. Joao Goncalves Zarco; 35c. Bartolomeu Dias; 1e. Pedro Alvares Cabral; 1e.75, Fernao de Magalhaes (Magellan); 2e. Frey Goncalo Velho; 3e.50, Diogo Cao.

121 President Carmona

1945

977	**121**	10c. violet	60	35

978	**121**	30c. brown	60	35
979	**121**	35c. green	55	35
980	**121**	50c. green	1·20	35
981	**121**	1e. red	24·00	2·20
982	**121**	1e.75 blue	20·00	6·00
983	**121**	2e. purple	£120	8·00
984	**121**	3e.50 grey	80·00	12·00
MS984a 136×98 mm. Nos. 977/84 (sold at 15e.)			£325	£350

122

1945. Naval School Centenary.

985	**122**	10c. brown	65	25
986	**122**	50c. green	85	25
987	**122**	1e. red	7·25	1·40
988	**122**	1e.75 blue	7·75	4·00
MS988a 115×134 mm. Nos. 985/8 (sold at 7e.50)			75·00	£200

123 Almourol Castle

1946. Portuguese Castles.

989	-	10c. purple	40	35
990	-	30c. brown	65	35
991	-	35c. green	90	35
992	-	50c. grey	1·50	35
993	**123**	1e. red	50·00	1·90
994	-	1e.75 blue	32·00	3·75
995	-	2e. green	£100	6·50
996	-	3e.50 brown	46·00	8·50
MS996a 135×102 mm. 1e.75 grey-blue on buff (block of 4) (sold at 12e.50)			£275	£450

DESIGNS: Castles at Silves (10c.); Leiria (30c.); Feira (35c.); Guimaraes (50c.); Lisbon (1e.75); Braganza (2e.) and Ourem (3e.50).

124 "Decree Founding National Bank"

1946. Centenary of Bank of Portugal.

997	**124**	50c. blue	1·20	40
MS997a 156×144 mm. No. 997 (block of four) (sold at 7e.50)			£250	£350

125 Madonna and Child

1946. Tercentenary of Proclamation of St. Mary of Castile as Patron Saint of Portugal.

998	**125**	30c. grey	75	35
999	**125**	50c. green	50	35
1000	**125**	1e. red	5·00	1·70
1001	**125**	1e.75 blue	8·00	3·25
MS1001a 108×158 mm. Nos. 998/1001 on grey paper (sold at 7e.50)			90·00	£200

126 Caramulo Shepherdess

1947. Regional Costumes.

1002	**126**	10c. mauve	40	25
1003	-	30c. red	40	25
1004	-	35c. green	80	25
1005	-	50c. brown	1·30	25
1006	-	1e. red	29·00	1·00
1007	-	1e.75 blue	31·00	6·25
1008	-	2e. blue	£110	7·25
1009	-	3e.50 green	75·00	12·00
MS1009a 135×98 mm. Nos. 1002/9 (sold at 15e.)			£325	£400

COSTUMES: 30c. Malpique timbrel player; 35c. Monsanto flautist; 50c. Woman of Avintes; 1e. Maia field labourer; 1e.75, Woman of Algarve; 2e. Miranda do Douro bastonet player; 3e.50, Woman of the Azores.

127 Surrender of the Keys of Lisbon

1947. 800th Anniv of Recapture of Lisbon from the Moors.

1010	**127**	5c. green	40	30
1011	**127**	20c. red	65	30
1012	**127**	50c. violet	95	30
1013	**127**	1e.75 blue	11·50	7·50
1014	**127**	2e.50 brown	16·00	9·50
1015	**127**	3e.50 black	31·00	20·00

128 St. Joao de Brito

1948. Birth Tercentenary of St. Joao de Brito.

1016	**128**	30c. green	40	35
1017	-	50c. brown	40	35
1018	**128**	1e. red	16·00	2·50
1019	-	1e.75 blue	20·00	4·25

DESIGN: 50c., 1e.75, St. Joao de Brito (different).

130 "Architecture and Engineering"

1948. Exhibition of Public Works and National Congress of Engineering and Architecture.

1020	**130**	50c. purple	1·60	45

131 King Joao I

1949. Portraits.

1021	**131**	10c. violet and buff	75	35
1022	-	30c. green and buff	75	35
1023	-	35c. green and olive	1·50	35
1024	-	50c. blue and light blue	2·40	35
1025	-	1e. lake and red	2·50	35
1026	-	1e.75 black and grey	45·00	18·00
1027	-	2e. blue and light blue	28·00	3·00
1028	-	3e.50 chocolate & brown	90·00	33·00
MS1028a 136×98 mm. Nos. 1021/8 (sold for 15e.)			£100	£120

PORTRAITS: 30c. Queen Philippa; 35c. Prince Fernando; 50c. Prince Henry the Navigator; 1e. Nun Alvares; 1e.75, Joao da Regras; 2e. Fernao Lopes; 3e.50, Afonso Domingues.

132 Statue of Angel

1949. 16th Congress of the History of Art.

1029	**132**	1e. red	18·00	30
1030	**132**	5e. brown	4·75	55

133 Hands and Letter

1949. 75th Anniv of U.P.U.

1031	**133**	1e. lilac	55	25
1032	**133**	2e. blue	1·60	35
1033	**133**	2e.50 green	9·25	1·60
1034	**133**	4e. brown	25·00	6·00

134 Our Lady of Fatima

1950. Holy Year.

1035	**134**	50c. green	1·10	40
1036	**134**	1e. brown	5·00	45
1037	**134**	2e. blue	10·50	3·25
1038	**134**	5e. lilac	£160	44·00

135 Saint and Invalid

1950. 400th Death Anniv of San Juan de Dios.

1039	**135**	20c. violet	75	35
1040	**135**	50c. red	1·20	45
1041	**135**	1e. green	2·75	60
1042	**135**	1e.50 orange	35·00	5·25
1043	**135**	2e. blue	28·00	4·00
1044	**135**	4e. brown	80·00	12·50

136 G. Junqueiro

1951. Birth Centenary of Junqueiro (poet).

1045	**136**	50c. brown	9·00	55
1046	**136**	1e. blue	2·75	50

137 Fisherman with Meagre

1951. Fisheries Congress.

1047	**137**	50c. green on buff	8·50	85
1048	**137**	1e. purple on buff	2·00	20

138 Dove and Olive Branch

1951. Termination of Holy Year.

1049	**138**	20c. brown and buff	85	40
1050	**138**	90c. green and yellow	20·00	2·75
1051	-	1e. purple and pink	18·00	45
1052	-	2e.30 green and blue	22·00	3·25

PORTRAIT: 1e., 2e.30, Pope Pius XII.

139 15th century Colonists

1951. 500th Anniv of Colonization of Terceira, Azores.

1053	**139**	50c. blue on flesh	5·50	75
1054	**139**	1e. brown on buff	2·75	70

140 Revolutionaries

1951. 25th Anniv of National Revolution.

1055	**140**	1e. brown	15·00	40
1056	**140**	2e.30 blue	11·50	2·00

141 Coach of King Joao VI

1952. National Coach Museum.

1057	-	10c. purple	40	30
1058	**141**	20c. green	40	30
1059	-	50c. green	1·20	30
1060	-	90c. green	4·75	2·40
1061	-	1e. orange	2·10	35
1062	-	1e.40 pink	11·00	6·50
1063	**141**	1e.50 brown	9·75	3·50
1064	-	2e.30 blue	6·25	3·25

DESIGNS (coaches of): 10, 90c. King Felippe II; 50c., 1e.40, Papal Nuncio to Joao V; 1e., 2e.30, King Jose.

142 "N.A.T.O."

1952. Third Anniv of N.A.T.O.

1065	**142**	1e. green and deep green	16·00	65
1066	**142**	3e.50 grey and blue	£500	34·00

143 Hockey Players

1952. Eighth World Roller-skating Hockey Championship.

1067	**143**	1e. black and blue	6·00	35
1068	**143**	3e.50 black and brown	10·50	3·50

144 Teixeira

1952. Birth Centenary of Prof. Gomes Teixeira (mathematician).

1069	**144**	1e. mauve and pink	1·50	35
1070	**144**	2e.30 deep blue and blue	11·50	6·50

145 Marshal Carmona Bridge

1952. Centenary of Ministry of Public Works.

1071	**145**	1e. brown on stone	1·20	40
1072	-	1e.40 lilac on stone	20·00	7·25
1073	-	2e. green on stone	12·50	4·50
1074	-	3e.50 blue on stone	21·00	6·25

DESIGNS: 1e.40, 28th May Stadium, Braga; 2e. Coimbra University; 3e.50, Salazar Barrage.

146 St. Francis Xavier

1952. Fourth Death Centenary of St. Francis Xavier.

1075	**146**	1e. blue	1·00	40
1076	**146**	2e. purple	2·75	80
1077	**146**	3e.50 blue	38·00	18·00
1078	**146**	5e. lilac	75·00	6·50

147 Medieval Knight

1953

1079	**147**	5c. green on yellow	40	20
1080	**147**	10c. grey on pink	40	20
1081	**147**	20c. orange on yellow	40	20
1081a	**147**	30c. purple on buff	50	20

1082	**147**	50c. black	40	20
1083	**147**	90c. green on yellow	29·00	1·10
1084	**147**	1e. brown on pink	70	20
1085	**147**	1e.40 red	29·00	1·60
1086	**147**	1e.50 red on yellow	90	20
1087	**147**	2e. black	1·40	20
1088	**147**	2e.30 blue	45·00	1·30
1089	**147**	2e.50 black on pink	2·50	25
1089a	**147**	2e.50 green on yellow	2·50	25
1090	**147**	5e. purple on yellow	2·50	25
1091	**147**	10e. blue on yellow	11·00	35
1092	**147**	20e. brown on yellow	22·00	50
1093	**147**	50e. lilac	15·00	70

148 St. Martin of Dume

1953. 14th Centenary of Landing of St. Martin of Dume on Iberian Peninsula.

1094	**148**	1e. black and grey	2·50	35
1095	**148**	3e.50 brown and yellow	20·00	8·25

149 G. Gomes Fernandes

1953. Birth Centenary of Fernandes (fire-brigade chief).

1096	**149**	1e. purple and cream	1·50	35
1097	**149**	2e.30 blue and cream	20·00	8·75

150 Club Emblems, 1903 and 1953

1953. 50th Anniv of Portuguese Automobile Club.

1098	**150**	1e. deep green and green	1·20	40
1099	**150**	3e.50 brown and buff	21·00	8·50

151 Princess St. Joan

1953. Fifth Centenary of Birth of Princess St. Joan.

1100	**151**	1e. black and green	2·75	35
1101	**151**	3e.50 deep blue and blue	21·00	10·00

152 Queen Maria II

1953. Centenary of First Portuguese Stamps. Bottom panel in gold.

1102	**152**	50c. red	40	35
1103	**152**	1e. brown	40	35
1104	**152**	1e.40 purple	4·00	1·40
1105	**152**	2e.30 blue	7·50	3·25
1106	**152**	3e.50 blue	7·50	3·25
1107	**152**	4e.50 green	13·00	2·40
1108	**152**	5e. green	15·00	2·10
1109	**152**	20e. violet	£110	12·50

153

1954. 150th Anniv of Trade Secretariat.

1110	**153**	1e. blue and light blue	1·10	25
1111	**153**	1e.50 brown and buff	4·75	1·00

154

1954. People's Education Plan.

1112	**154**	50c. blue and light blue	60	25
1113	**154**	1e. red and pink	60	25
1114	**154**	2e. deep green and green	55·00	1·70
1115	**154**	2e.50 brown and light brown	47·00	2·40

155 Cadet and College Banner

1954. 150th Anniv of Military College.

1116	**155**	1e. brown and green	2·50	35
1117	**155**	3e.50 blue and green	11·00	4·25

156 Father Manuel da Nobrega

1954. 400th Anniv of Sao Paulo.

1118	**156**	1e. brown	1·20	40
1119	**156**	2e.30 blue	95·00	37·00
1120	**156**	3e.50 green	25·00	4·50
1121	**156**	5e. green	80·00	7·25

157 King Sancho I, 1154–1211

1955. Portuguese Kings.

1122	-	10c. purple	45	35
1123	**157**	20c. green	45	35
1124	-	50c. blue	55	35
1125	-	90c. green	8·00	2·20
1126	-	1e. brown	2·10	40
1127	-	1e.40 red	16·00	5·50
1128	-	1e.50 green	5·25	1·70
1129	-	2e. red	18·00	4·50
1130	-	2e.30 blue	14·50	4·25

KINGS: 10c. Afonso I; 50c. Afonso II; 90c. Sancho II; 1e. Afonso III; 1e.40, Diniz; 1e.50, Afonso IV; 2e. Pedro I; 2e.30, Fernando.

158 Telegraph Poles

1955. Centenary of Electric Telegraph System in Portugal.

1131	**158**	1e. red and brown	1·10	35
1132	**158**	2e.30 blue and green	42·00	6·25
1133	**158**	3e.50 green and yellow	41·00	4·75

159 A. J. Ferreira da Silva

1956. Birth Centenary of Ferreira da Silva (teacher).

1134	**159**	1e. deep blue, blue and azure	95	35
1135	**159**	2e.30 deep green, emerald and green	25·00	7·75

160 Steam Locomotive, 1856

1956. Centenary of Portuguese Railways.

1136	**160**	1e. olive and green	85	35
1137	-	1e.50 blue and green	19·00	80
1138	-	2e. brown and bistre	50·00	2·20
1139	**160**	2e.50 brown and deep brown	70·00	3·00

DESIGN: 1e.50, 2e. Class 2500 electric locomotive, 1956.

161 Madonna and Child

1956. Mothers' Day.

1140	**161**	1e. sage and green	85	20
1141	**161**	1e.50 lt brown and brown	2·10	40

162 Almeida Garrett (after Barata Feyo)

1957. Almeida Garrett (writer) Commem.

1142	**162**	1e. brown	1·20	35
1143	**162**	2e.30 lilac	70·00	17·00
1144	**162**	3e.50 green	24·00	1·80
1145	**162**	5e. red	£130	16·00

163 Cesario Verde

1957. Cesario Verde (poet) Commem.

1146	**163**	1e. brown, buff and green	65	25
1147	**163**	3e.30 black, olive and green	3·25	1·80

164 Exhibition Emblem

1958. Brussels International Exhibition.

1148	**164**	1e. multicoloured	55	25
1149	**164**	3e.30 multicoloured	2·75	2·00

165 St. Elizabeth

1958. St. Elizabeth and St. Teotonio Commem.

1150	**165**	1e. red and cream	45	30
1151	-	2e. green and cream	85	60
1152	**165**	2e.50 violet and cream	7·25	1·30
1153	-	5e. brown and cream	12·00	1·60

PORTRAIT: 2, 5e. St. Teotonio.

166 Institute of Tropical Medicine, Lisbon

1958. Sixth Int Congress of Tropical Medicine.

1154	**166**	1e. green and grey	3·25	40
1155	**166**	2e.50 blue and grey	13·00	2·20

167 Liner

1958. Second National Merchant Navy Congress.

1156	**167**	1e. brown, ochre & sepia	7·50	40
1157	**167**	4e.50 violet, lilac and blue	10·50	3·50

168 Queen Leonora

1958. 500th Birth Anniv of Queen Leonora. Frames and ornaments in bistre, inscriptions and value tablet in black.

1158	**168**	1e. blue and brown	45	25
1159	**168**	1e.50 turquoise and blue	6·50	1·00
1160	**168**	2e.30 blue and green	5·75	2·10
1161	**168**	4e.10 blue and grey	5·75	2·10

169 Arms of Aveiro

1959. Millenary of Aveiro.

1162	**169**	1e. multicoloured	2·10	40
1163	**169**	5e. multicoloured	22·00	3·00

170

1960. Tenth Anniv of N.A.T.O.

1164	**170**	1e. black and lilac	55	35
1165	**170**	3e.50 green and grey	5·25	2·75

171 "Doorway to Peace"

1960. World Refugee Year. Symbol in black.

1166	**171**	20c. yellow, lemon & brn	25	20
1167	**171**	1e. yellow, green and blue	80	20
1168	**171**	1e.80 yellow and green	1·70	1·40

172 Glider

1960. 50th Anniv of Portuguese Aero Club. Multicoloured.

1169	1e. Type **172**	40	35
1170	1e.50 Light monoplane	1·30	45
1171	2e. Airplane and parachutes	2·10	1·10
1172	2e.50 Model glider	3·75	1·60

173 Padre Cruz (after M. Barata)

1960. Death Centenary of Padre Cruz.

1173	**173**	1e. brown	70	35
1174	**173**	4e.30 blue	13·50	10·00

174 University Seal

1960. 400th Anniv of Evora University.

1175	**174**	50c. blue	40	25
1176	**174**	1e. brown and yellow	60	25
1177	**174**	1e.40 purple	4·25	2·40

175 Prince Henry's Arms

1960. Fifth Death Centenary of Prince Henry the Navigator. Multicoloured.

1178	1e. Type **175**	55	35
1179	2e.50 Caravel	4·75	55
1180	3e.50 Prince Henry the Navigator	6·00	2·10
1181	5e. Motto	15·00	1·20
1182	8e. Barketta	6·25	1·20
1183	10e. Map showing Sagres	21·00	3·00

175a Conference Emblem

1960. Europa.

1184	**175a**	1e. light blue and blue	45	35
1185	**175a**	3e.50 red and lake	5·25	3·00

176 Emblems of Prince Henry and Lisbon

1960. Fifth National Philatelic Exhibition, Lisbon.

1186	**176**	1e. blue, black and green	60	35
1187	**176**	3e.30 blue, black and light blue	8·75	5·50

177 Portuguese Flag

1960. 50th Anniv of Republic.

1188	**177**	1e. multicoloured	50	15

178 King Pedro V

1961. Cent of Lisbon University Faculty of Letters.

1189	**178**	1e. green and brown	75	30
1190	**178**	6e.50 brown and blue	5·00	1·40

179 Arms of Setubal

1961. Centenary of Setubal City.

1191	**179**	1e. multicoloured	80	30
1192	**179**	4e.30 multicoloured	29·00	9·00

180

1961. Europa.

1193	**180**	1e. light blue, blue and deep blue	35	35
1194	**180**	1e.50 light green, green and deep green	2·00	1·80
1195	**180**	3e.50 pink, red and lake	2·30	2·10

181 Tomar Gateway

1961. 800th Anniv of Tomar.

1196	-	1e. multicoloured	35	25
1197	**181**	3e.50 multicoloured	2·10	1·70

DESIGN: 1e. As Type **181** but without ornamental background.

182 National Guardsman

1962. 50th Anniv of National Republican Guard.

1198	**182**	1e. multicoloured	35	25
1199	**182**	2e. multicoloured	3·50	1·20
1200	**182**	2e.50 multicoloured	3·25	1·00

183 St. Gabriel (Patron Saint of Telecommunications)

1962. St. Gabriel Commemoration.

1201	**183**	1e. brown, green and olive	1·00	30
1202	**183**	3e.50 green, brown & ol	1·10	60

184 Scout Badge and Tents

1962. 18th International Scout Conference (1961).

1203	**184**	20c. multicoloured	35	25
1204	**184**	50c. multicoloured	40	25
1205	**184**	1e. multicoloured	85	30
1206	**184**	2e.50 multicoloured	5·75	75
1207	**184**	3e.50 mulitcoloured	2·75	75
1208	**184**	6e.50 multicoloured	1·70	1·30

185 Children with Ball

1962. Tenth International Paediatrics Congress, Lisbon. Centres in black.

1209	-	50c. yellow and green	35	25
1210	-	1e. yellow and grey	1·30	25
1211	**185**	2e.80 yellow and brown	4·25	2·10
1212	-	3e.50 yellow and purple	7·75	2·75

DESIGNS: 50c. Children with book; 1e. Inoculating child; 3e.50, Weighing baby.

186 Europa "Honeycomb"

1962. Europa. "EUROPA" in gold.

1213	**186**	1e. ultramarine, light blue and blue	40	35
1214	**186**	1e.50 deep green, light green and green	2·00	1·30
1215	**186**	3e.50 purple, pink and claret	2·30	2·00

187 St. Zenon (the Courier)

1962. Stamp Day. Saint in yellow and pink.

1216	**187**	1e. black and purple	35	30
1217	**187**	2e. black and green	1·60	1·10
1218	**187**	2e.80 black and bistre	2·75	2·75

188 Benfica Emblem and European Cup

1963. Benfica Club's Double Victory in European Football Cup Championship (1961–62).

1219	**188**	1e. multicoloured	1·20	30
1220	**188**	4e.30 multicoloured	2·10	1·90

189 Campaign Emblem

1963. Freedom from Hunger.

1221	**189**	1e. multicoloured	35	30
1222	**189**	3e.30 multicoloured	2·00	1·60
1223	**189**	3e.50 multicoloured	2·20	1·60

190 Mail Coach

1963. Centenary of Paris Postal Conference.

1224	**190**	1e. blue, light blue and grey	35	20
1225	**190**	1e.50 multicoloured	3·00	75
1226	**190**	5e. brown, lilac & lt brown	1·30	60

191 St. Vincent de Paul

1963. 300th Death Anniv of St. Vincent de Paul. Inscr in gold.

1227	**191**	20c. ultramarine and blue	35	35
1228	**191**	1e. blue and grey	55	35
1229	**191**	2e.80 black and green	6·50	2·75
1230	**191**	5e. grey and mauve	5·75	2·00

192 Medieval Knight

1963. 800th Anniv of Military Order of Avis.

1231	**192**	1e. multicoloured	35	25
1232	**192**	1e.50 multicoloured	1·00	40
1233	**192**	2e.50 mulitcoloured	2·00	1·40

193 Europa "Dove"

1963. Europa.

1234	**193**	1e. grey, blue and black	50	35
1235	**193**	1e.50 grey, green & black	4·25	2·00
1236	**193**	3e.50 grey, red and black	6·25	3·00

194 Supersonic Flight

1963. Tenth Anniv of T.A.P. Airline.

1237	**194**	1e. blue and deep blue	30	25
1238	**194**	2e.50 light green & green	2·10	1·00
1239	**194**	3e.50 orange and red	2·50	1·80

195 Pharmacist's Jar

1964. 400th Anniv of Publication of "Coloquios dos Simples" (Dissertation on Indian herbs and drugs) by Dr. G. d'Orta.

1240	**195**	50c. brown, black & bis	80	35
1241	**195**	1e. purple, black and red	55	35
1242	**195**	4e.30 blue, black & grey	7·00	5·75

196 Bank Emblem

1964. Centenary of National Overseas Bank.

1243	**196**	1e. yellow, green and blue	35	30
1244	**196**	2e.50 yellow, olive & grn	4·00	1·60
1245	**196**	3e.50 yellow, green & brn	3·50	1·70

197 Sameiro Shrine (Braga)

1964. Centenary of Sameiro Shrine.

1246	**197**	1e. yellow, brown and red	35	25
1247	**197**	2e. yellow, light brown and brown	3·00	1·10
1248	**197**	5e. yellow, green and blue	3·50	1·70

198 Europa "Flower"

1964. Europa.

1249	**198**	1e. deep blue, light blue and blue	1·00	35
1250	**198**	3e.50 brown, light brown and purple	8·00	2·50
1251	**198**	4e.30 deep green, light green and green	9·50	4·75

199 Sun and Globe

1964. International Quiet Sun Years.

1252	**199**	1e. mulitcoloured	45	25
1253	**199**	8e. multicoloured	2·20	1·60

200 Olympic "Rings"

1964. Olympic Games, Tokyo.

1254	**200**	20c. multicoloured	35	30
1255	**200**	1e. multicoloured	45	35
1256	**200**	1e.50 multicoloured	2·50	1·60
1257	**200**	6e.50 multicoloured	4·50	3·00

201 E. Coelho (founder)

1964. Centenary of "Diario de Noticias" (newspaper).

1258	**201**	1e. multicoloured	95	20
1259	**201**	5e. multicoloured	11·50	1·60

202 Traffic Signals

1965. First National Traffic Congress Lisbon.

1260	**202**	1e. yellow, red and green	40	35
1261	**202**	3e.30 green, red & yellow	10·00	5·25
1262	**202**	3e.50 red, yellow & green	6·50	2·50

203 Dom Fernando (second Duke of Braganza)

1965. 500th Anniv of Braganza.

1263	**203**	1e. red and black	40	25
1264	**203**	10e. green and black	4·50	1·20

204 Angel and Gateway

1965. 900th Anniv of Capture of Coimbra from the Moors.

1265	**204**	1e. multicoloured	35	35
1266	**204**	2e.50 multicoloured	3·00	2·40
1267	**204**	5e. multicoloured	3·75	3·00

205 I.T.U. Emblem

1965. Centenary of I.T.U.

1268	**205**	1e. green and brown	35	35
1269	**205**	3e.50 purple and green	2·40	2·00
1270	**205**	6e.50 blue and green	2·75	1·80

206 C. Gulbenkian

1965. Tenth Death Anniv of Calouste Gulbenkian (oil industry pioneer and philanthropist).

1271	**206**	1e. multicoloured	1·00	20
1272	**206**	8e. multicoloured	1·10	75

207 Red Cross Emblem

1965. Centenary of Portuguese Red Cross.

1273	**207**	1e. red, green and black	40	35
1274	**207**	4e. red, green and black	6·50	3·25
1275	**207**	4e.30 red, light red & black	18·00	11·50

208 Europa "Sprig"

1965. Europa.

1276	**208**	1e. lt blue, black and blue	55	35
1277	**208**	3e.50 flesh, brown & red	13·50	2·40
1278	**208**	4e.30 light green, black and green	24·00	11·50

209 North American F-86 Sabre Jet Fighter

1965. 50th Anniv of Portuguese Air Force.

1279	**209**	1e. red, green and olive	45	25
1280	**209**	2e. red, green and brown	2·20	1·00
1281	**209**	5e. red, green and blue	4·50	2·75

210

1965. 500th Birth Anniv of Gil Vicente (poet and dramatist). Designs depicting characters from Vicente's poems.

1282	**210**	20c. multicoloured	25	20
1283	-	1e. multicoloured	70	20
1284	-	2e.50 multicoloured	4·75	80
1285	-	6e.50 multicoloured	2·30	1·10

211 Monogram of Christ

1966. International Committee for the Defence of Christian Civilisation Congress, Lisbon.

1286	**211**	1e. violet, gold and bistre	40	20
1287	**211**	3e.30 black, gold & pur	10·00	5·50
1288	**211**	5e. black, gold and red	7·50	3·00

212 Emblems of Agriculture, Construction and Industry

1966. 40th Anniv of National Revolution.

1289	**212**	1e. black, blue and grey	45	35
1290	**212**	3e.50 brown, light brown and bistre	4·50	2·10
1291	**212**	4e. purple, red and pink	4·50	1·70

213 Giraldo the "Fearless"

1966. 800th Anniv of Reconquest of Evora.

1292	**213**	1e. multicoloured	55	25
1293	**213**	8e. multicoloured	1·80	1·00

214 Salazar Bridge

1966. Inauguration of Salazar Bridge, Lisbon.

1294	**214**	1e. red and gold	45	25
1295	**214**	2e.50 blue and gold	2·50	1·40
1296	-	2e.80 blue and silver	3·25	2·50
1297	-	4e.30 green and silver	3·50	2·50

DESIGN—VERT: 2e.80, 4e.30, Salazar Bridge (different view).

215 Europa "Ship"

1966. Europa.

1298	**215**	1e. multicoloured	60	35
1299	**215**	3e.50 multicoloured	19·00	3·00
1300	**215**	4e.50 multicoloured	19·00	4·75

216 C. Pestana (bacteriologist)

1966. Portuguese Scientists. Portraits in brown and bistre; background colours given.

1301	**216**	20c. green	25	15
1302	-	50c. orange	25	15
1303	-	1e. yellow	35	15
1304	-	1e.50 brown	50	15
1305	-	2e. brown	2·75	25
1306	-	2e.50 green	3·00	70
1307	-	2e.80 orange	4·75	2·50
1308	-	4e.30 blue	6·25	4·75

SCIENTISTS: 50c. E. Moniz (neurologist); 1e. E. A. P. Coutinho (botanist); 1e.50, J. C. da Serra (botanist); 2e. R. Jorge (hygienist and anthropologist); 2e.50, J. L. de Vasconcelos (ethnologist); 2e.80, M. Lemos (medical historian); 4e.30, J. A. Serrano (anatomist).

217 Bocage

1966. Birth Bicentenary (1965) of Manuel M. B. du Bocage (poet).

1309	**217**	1e. black, green and bistre	25	15
1310	**217**	2e. black, green & brown	1·60	70
1311	**217**	6e. black, green and grey	2·10	1·30

218 Cogwheels

1967. Europa.

1312	**218**	1e. blue, black & lt blue	60	35
1313	**218**	3e.50 brown, black and orange	15·00	1·90
1314	**218**	4e.30 green, black and light green	21·00	3·75

219 Adoration of the Virgin

1967. 50th Anniv of Fatima Apparitions. Multicoloured.

1315	1e. Type **219**	20	15
1316	2e.80 Fatima Church	95	90
1317	3e.50 Virgin of Fatima	60	45
1318	4e. Chapel of the Apparitions	70	55

220 Roman Senators

1967. New Civil Law Code.

1319	**220**	1e. red and gold	20	15
1320	**220**	2e.50 blue and gold	3·25	1·80
1321	**220**	4e.30 green and gold	2·75	1·80

221 Lisnave Shipyard

1967. Inauguration of Lisnave Shipyard, Lisbon.

1322	**221**	1e. multicoloured	20	20
1323	-	2e.80 multicoloured	4·00	1·90
1324	**221**	3e.50 multicoloured	3·00	1·80
1325	-	4e.30 multicoloured	3·75	2·00

DESIGN: 2e.80, 4e.30, Section of ship's hull and location map.

222 Serpent Symbol

1967. Sixth European Rheumatological Congress, Lisbon.

1326	**222**	1e. multicoloured	20	20
1327	**222**	2e. multicoloured	1·90	1·00
1328	**222**	5e. multicoloured	3·00	2·00

223 Flags of EFTA Countries

1967. European Free Trade Association.

1329	**223**	1e. multicoloured	35	35
1330	**223**	3e.50 multicoloured	2·40	2·00
1331	**223**	4e.30 multicoloured	4·75	4·50

224 Tombstones

1967. Centenary of Abolition of Death Penalty in Portugal.

1332	**224**	1e. green	20	20
1333	**224**	2e. brown	2·10	1·30
1334	**224**	5e. green	3·75	3·00

225 Bento de Goes

1968. Bento de Goes Commemoration.

1335	**225**	1e. blue, brown and green	95	20
1336	**225**	8e. purple, green & brown	2·50	1·00

226 Europa "Key"

1968. Europa.

1337	**226**	1e. multicoloured	60	35
1338	**226**	3e.50 multicoloured	16·00	2·75
1339	**226**	4e.30 multicoloured	24·00	5·00

227 "Maternal Love"

1968. 30th Anniv of Organization of Mothers for National Education (O.M.E.N.).

1340	**227**	1e. black, orange and grey	35	25
1341	**227**	2e. black, orange and pink	2·75	1·00
1342	**227**	5e. black, orange and blue	5·25	2·75

228 "Victory over Disease"

1968. 20th Anniv of W.H.O.

1343	**228**	1e. multicoloured	35	35
1344	**228**	3e.50 multicoloured	2·20	1·10
1345	**228**	4e.30 multicoloured	12·00	8·50

229 Vineyard, Girao

1968. "Lubrapex 1968" Stamp Exhibition. Madeira—"Pearl of the Atlantic". Multicoloured.

1346	50c. Type **229**	25	20
1347	1e. Firework display	30	15
1348	1e.50 Landscape	60	20
1349	2e.80 J. Fernandes Vieira (liberator of Pernambuco) (vert)	3·50	2·50
1350	3e.50 Embroidery (vert)	2·75	1·60
1351	4e.30 J. Goncalves Zarco (navigator) (vert)	12·00	11·50
1352	20e. "Muschia aurea" (vert)	7·75	2·20

230 Pedro Alvares Cabral (from medallion)

1969. 500th Birth Anniv of Pedro Alvares Cabral (explorer).

1353	**230**	1e. blue	40	20
1354	-	3e.50 purple	6·25	3·50
1355	-	6e.50 multicoloured	4·50	3·50

DESIGNS—VERT: 3e.50, Cabral's arms. HORIZ: 6e.50, Cabral's fleet (from contemporary docu-ments).

231 Colonnade

1969. Europa.

1356	**231**	1e. multicoloured	60	35
1357	**231**	3e.50 multicoloured	17·00	3·50
1358	**231**	4e.30 multicoloured	26·00	5·75

232 King Joseph I

1969. Centenary of National Press.

1359	**232**	1e. multicoloured	20	20
1360	**232**	2e. multicoloured	1·70	95
1361	**232**	8e. multicoloured	1·60	1·30

233 I.L.O. Emblem

1969. 50th Anniv of I.L.O.

1362	**233**	1e. multicoloured	25	20
1363	**233**	3e.50 multicoloured	3·00	1·00
1364	**233**	4e.30 multicoloured	4·00	3·25

234 J. R. Cabrilho (navigator and colonizer)

1969. Bicentenary of San Diego, California.

1365	**234**	1e. dp green, yellow & grn	20	20
1366	**234**	2e.50 brown, light brown and blue	2·50	1·00
1367	**234**	6e.50 deep brown, green and brown	3·25	1·90

235 Vianna da Motta (from painting by C. B. Pinheiro)

1969. Birth Centenary (1968) of Jose Vianna da Motta (concert pianist).

1368	**235**	1e. multicoloured	1·20	20
1369	**235**	9e. multicoloured	1·70	1·30

236 Coutinho and Fairey IIID Seaplane

1969. Birth Centenary of Gago Coutinho (aviator). Multicoloured.

1370	1e. Type **236**	35	15
1371	2e.80 Coutinho and sextant	3·75	2·10
1372	3e.30 Type **236**	3·50	3·00
1373	4e.30 As No. 1371	3·50	3·00

237 Vasco da Gama

1969. 500th Birth Anniv of Vasco da Gama. Multicoloured.

1374	1e. Type **237**	35	25
1375	2e.50 Arms of Vasco da Gama	4·75	3·75
1376	3e.50 Route map (horiz)	3·50	1·70
1377	4e. Vasca da Gama's fleet (horiz)	3·25	1·40

238 "Flaming Sun"

1970. Europa.

1378	**238**	1e. cream and blue	60	25
1379	**238**	3e.50 cream and brown	16·00	2·10
1380	**238**	4e.30 cream and green	23·00	6·25

239 Distillation Plant and Pipelines

1970. Inauguration of Porto Oil Refinery.

1381	**239**	1e. blue and light blue	25	20
1382	-	2e.80 black and green	3·50	2·75
1383	**239**	3e.30 green and olive	2·75	2·20
1384	-	6e. brown and light brown	2·50	1·90

DESIGN: 2e.80, 6e. Catalytic cracking plant and pipelines.

240 Marshal Carmona (from sculpture by L. de Almeida)

1970. Birth Centenary of Marshal Carmona.

1385	**240**	1e. green and black	25	10
1386	**240**	2e.50 blue, red and black	2·20	90
1387	**240**	7e. blue and black	2·50	1·70

241 Station Badge

1970. 25th Anniv of Plant-breeding Station.

1388	**241**	1e. multicoloured	30	10
1389	**241**	2e.50 multicoloured	1·80	70
1390	**241**	5e. multicoloured	2·20	90

242 Emblem within Cultural Symbol

1970. Expo 70. Multicoloured.

1391	1e. Compass (postage)	25	15
1392	5e. Christian symbol	2·00	1·70
1393	6e.50 Symbolic initials	4·75	4·00
1394	3e.50 Type **242** (air)	90	45

243 Wheel and Star

1970. Centenaries of Covilha (Nos. 1395/6) and Santarem (Nos. 1397/8). Multicoloured.

1395	1e. Type **243**	30	20
1396	2e.80 Ram and weaving frame	3·50	3·00
1397	1e. Castle	20	15
1398	4e. Two knights	2·30	1·30

244 "Great Eastern" laying Cable

1970. Centenary of Portugal–England Submarine Telegraph Cable.

1399	**244**	1e. black, blue and green	30	15
1400	**244**	2e.50 black, green & buff	2·50	70
1401	-	2e.80 multicoloured	4·00	3·25
1402	-	4e. multicoloured	2·50	1·30

DESIGN: 2e.80, 4e. Cable cross-section.

245 Harvesting Grapes

1970. Port Wine Industry. Multicoloured.

1403	50c. Type **245**	15	10
1404	1e. Harvester and jug	25	10
1405	3e.50 Wine-glass and wine barge	95	25
1406	7e. Wine-bottle and casks	1·60	80

246 Mountain Windmill, Bussaco Hills

1971. Portuguese Windmills.

1407	**246**	20c. brown, black & sepia	15	10
1408	-	50c. brown, black & blue	20	10
1409	-	1e. purple, black and grey	30	10
1410	-	2e. red, black and mauve	1·00	35
1411	-	3e.30 chocolate, black and brown	3·50	2·50
1412	-	5e. brown, black & green	3·25	1·20

WINDMILLS: 50c. Beira Litoral Province; 1e. "Saloio" type Estremadura Province; 2e. St. Miguel Azores; 3e.30, Porto Santo, Madeira; 5e. Pico, Azores.

247 Europa Chain

1971. Europa.

1413	**247**	1e. green, blue and black	45	30
1414	**247**	3e.50 yellow, brn & blk	12·00	1·10
1415	**247**	7e.50 brown, green & blk	17·00	2·75

248 F. Franco

1971. Portuguese Sculptors.

1416	**248**	20c. black	15	10
1417	-	1e. red	35	10
1418	-	1e.50 brown	85	60
1419a	-	2e.50 blue	1·20	55
1420	-	3e.50 mauve	1·50	90
1421	-	4e. green	4·00	2·50

DESIGNS: 1e. A. Lopes; 1e.50, A. de Costa Mota; 2e.50, R. Gameiro; 3e.50, J. Simoes de Almeida (the Younger); 4e. F. dos Santos.

249 Pres. Salazar

1971. Pres. Antonio Salazar Commemoration.

1422	**249**	1e. brown, green & orge	25	10
1423	**249**	5e. brown, purple & orge	2·30	80
1424	**249**	10e. brown, blue & orge	3·50	1·60

250 Wolframite

1971. First Spanish–Portuguese–American Congress of Economic Geology. Multicoloured.

1425	1e. Type **250**	15	10
1426	2e.50 Arsenopyrite	2·50	60
1427	3e.50 Beryllium	90	55
1428	6e.50 Chalcopyrite	1·70	80

251 Town Gate

1971. Bicentenary of Castelo Branco. Multicoloured.

1429	1e. Type **251**	15	15
1430	3e. Town square and monument	1·80	90
1431	12e.50 Arms of Castelo Branco (horiz)	1·60	90

252 Weather Equipment

1971. 25th Anniv of Portuguese Meteorological Service. Multicoloured.

1432	1e. Type **252**	20	10
1433	4e. Weather balloon	3·00	1·40
1434	6e.50 Weather satellite	2·00	1·00

253 Drowning Missionaries

1971. 400th Anniv of Martyrdom of Brazil Missionaries.

1435	**253**	1e. black, blue and grey	15	10
1436	**253**	3e.30 black, purple & brn	2·75	1·90
1437	**253**	4e.80 black, grn & olive	2·75	1·90

254 Man and his Habitat

1971. Nature Conservation. Multicoloured.

1438	1e. Type **254**	15	10
1439	3e.30 Horses and trees ("Earth")	90	60

1440		3e.50 Birds ("The Atmosphere")	90	55
1441		4e.50 Fish ("Water")	3·50	2·10

255 Clerigos Tower, Oporto

1972. Buildings and Views.

1442	-	5c. grey, black and green	30	15
1443	-	10c. black, green & blue	20	15
1444	-	30c. sepia, brown & yell	20	15
1445p	-	50c. blue, orange & blk	55	10
1446	**255**	1e. black, brown & grn	1·20	10
1447a	-	1e.50 brown, blue & blk	75	10
1448	-	2e. black, brown & pur	3·25	10
1449p	-	2e.50 brown, light brown and grey	55	10
1450p	-	3e. yellow, black & brn	90	10
1451p	-	3e.50 green, orge & brn	55	10
1452	-	4e. black, yellow & blue	1·00	10
1453	-	4e.50 black, brn & grn	1·50	10
1454	-	5e. green, brown & black	9·25	10
1455	-	6e. bistre, green & black	3·75	25
1456	-	7e.50 black, orge & grn	2·10	20
1457	-	8e. bistre, black & green	2·75	15
1458	-	10e. multicoloured	1·30	15
1459	-	20e. multicoloured	8·75	55
1460	-	50e. multicoloured	9·25	40
1461	-	100e. multicoloured	10·00	95

DESIGNS—As T **255**: 5c. Aguas Livres aqueduct, Lisbon; 10c. Lima Bridge; 30c. Monastery interior, Alcobaca; 50c. Coimbra University; 1e.50, Belem Tower, Lisbon; 2e. Domus Municipalis, Braganza; 2e.50, Castle, Vila de Feira; 3e. Misericord House, Viana do Castelo; 3e.50, Window, Tomar Convent; 4e. Gateway, Braga; 4e.50, Dolmen of Carrazeda; 5e. Roman Temple, Evora; 6e. Monastery, Leca do Balio; 7e.50, Almourol Castle; 8e. Ducal Palace, Guimaraes. 31×22 mm: 10e. Cape Girao, Madeira; 20e. Episcopal Garden, Castelo Branco; 50e. Town Hall, Sintra; 100e. Seven Cities' Lake, Sao Miguel, Azores.

256 Arms of Pinhel

1972. Bicentenary of Pinhel's Status as a City. Multicoloured.

1464	1e. Type **256**	25	10
1465	2e.50 Balustrade (vert)	2·30	55
1466	7e.50 Lantern on pedestal (vert)	1·80	80

257 Heart and Pendulum

1972. World Heart Month.

1467	**257**	1e. red and lilac	25	15
1468	-	4e. red and green	3·50	1·60
1469	-	9e. red and brown	2·40	1·00

DESIGNS: 4e. Heart in spiral; 9e. Heart and cardiogram trace.

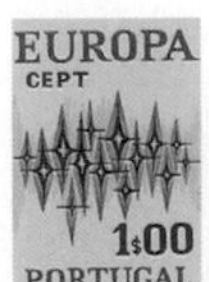

258 "Communications"

1972. Europa.

1470	**258**	1e. multicoloured	50	20
1471	**258**	3e.50 multicoloured	9·75	65
1472	**258**	6e. multicoloured	16·00	2·30

259 Container Truck

1972. 13th International Road Transport Union Congress, Estoril. Multicoloured.

1473	1e. Type **259**	25	20
1474	4e.50 Roof of taxi-cab	2·50	1·50
1475	8e. Motor-coach	2·30	1·30

260 Football

1972. Olympic Games, Munich. Multicoloured.

1476	50c. Type **260**	15	10
1477	1e. Running	20	10
1478	1e.50 Show jumping	55	25
1479	3e.50 Swimming	1·20	50
1480	4e.50 Yachting	1·80	1·40
1481	5e. Gymnastics	3·50	1·50

261 Marquis de Pombal

1972. Pombaline University Reforms. Multicoloured.

1482	1e. Type **261**	20	10
1483	2e.50 "The Sciences" (emblems)	2·10	1·20
1484	8e. Arms of Coimbra University.	2·20	1·60

262 Tome de Sousa

1972. 150th Anniv of Brazilian Independence. Multicoloured.

1485	1e. Type **262**	20	15
1486	2e.50 Jose Bonifacio	1·10	40
1487	3e.50 Dom Pedro IV	1·10	45
1488	6e. Dove and globe	2·10	1·00

263 Sacadura, Cabral, Gago, Coutinho and Fairey III D Seaplane

1972. 50th Anniv of First Lisbon–Rio de Janeiro Flight. Multicoloured.

1489	1e. Type **263**	15	10
1490	2e.50 Route map	1·20	70
1491	2e.80 Type **263**	1·50	1·10
1492	3e.80 As 2e.50	1·90	1·60

264 Camoens

1972. 400th Anniv of Camoens' "Lusiads" (epic poem).

1493	**264**	1e. yellow, brown & black	25	15
1494	-	3e. blue, green and black	1·60	95
1495	-	10e. brown, purple & blk	2·30	1·10

DESIGNS: 3e. "Saved from the Sea"; 10e. "Encounter with Adamastor".

265 Graph and Computer Tapes

1973. Portuguese Productivity Conference, Lisbon. Multicoloured.

1496	1e. Type **265**	20	10
1497	4e. Computer scale	1·60	85
1498	9e. Graphs	1·60	80

266 Europa "Posthorn"

1973. Europa.

1499	**266**	1e. multicoloured	75	30
1500	**266**	4e. multicoloured	18·00	1·40
1501	**266**	6e. multicoloured	20·00	2·40

267 Pres. Medici and Arms

1973. Visit of Pres. Medici of Brazil. Mult.

1502	1e. Type **267**	20	15
1503	2e.80 Pres. Medici and globe	1·00	85
1504	3e.50 Type **267**	1·10	80
1505	4e.80 As No. 1503	1·10	85

268 Child Running

1973. "For the Child".

1506	**268**	1e. dp blue, blue & brown	20	10
1507	-	4e. purple, mauve & brn	1·90	85
1508	-	7e.50 orange, ochre and brown	2·30	1·50

DESIGNS: 4e. Child running (to right); 7e.50, Child jumping.

269 Transport and Weather Map

1973. 25th Anniv of Ministry of Communications. Multicoloured.

1509	1e. Type **269**	15	10
1510	3e.80 "Telecommunications"	65	40
1511	6e. "Postal Services"	1·50	90

270 Child and Written Text

1973. Bicentenary of Primary State School Education. Multicoloured.

1512	1e. Type **270**	25	10
1513	4e.50 Page of children's primer	2·10	65
1514	5e.30 "Schooldays" (child's drawing) (horiz)	1·80	95
1515	8e. "Teacher and children" (horiz)	4·75	2·00

271 Electric Tramcar

1973. Centenary of Oporto's Public Transport System. Multicoloured.

1516	1e. Horse tram	30	10
1517	3e.50 Modern bus	2·75	1·90
1518	7e.50 Type **271**	3·00	1·60

Nos. 1516/17 are 31½×31½ mm.

272 League Badge

1973. 50th Anniv of Servicemen's League. Multicoloured.

1519	1e. Type **272**	20	15
1520	2e.50 Servicemen	3·00	85
1521	11e. Awards and medals	2·10	90

273 Death of Nuno Goncalves

1973. 600th Anniv of Defence of Faria Castle by the Alcaide, Nuno Goncalves.

1522	**273**	1e. green and yellow	30	15
1523	**273**	10e. purple and yellow	2·75	1·50

274 Damiao de Gois (after Durer)

1974. 400th Death Anniv of Damiao de Gois (scholar and diplomat). Multicoloured.

1524	1e. Type **274**	20	10
1525	4e.50 Title-page of "Chronicles of Prince Dom Joao"	3·00	80
1526	7e.50 Lute and "Dodecahordon" score	1·80	80

275 "The Exile" (A. Soares dos Reis)

1974. Europa.

1527	**275**	1e. green, blue and olive	90	30
1528	**275**	4e. green, red and yellow	21·00	1·40
1529	**275**	6e. dp green, green & blue	25·00	1·80

276 Light Emission

1974. Inauguration of Satellite Communications Station Network.

1530	**276**	1e.50 green	25	20
1531	-	4e.50 blue	1·80	90
1532	-	5e.30 purple	2·50	1·30

DESIGNS: 4e.50, Spiral Waves; 5e.30, Satellite and Earth.

277 "Diffusion of Hertzian Radio Waves"

1974. Birth Centenary of Guglielmo Marconi (radio pioneer). Multicoloured.

1533	1e.50 Type **277**	20	10
1534	3e.30 "Radio waves across Space"	2·50	1·10
1535	10e. "Radio waves for Navigation"	1·90	80

278 Early Post-boy and Modern Mail Van

1974. Centenary of U.P.U. Multicoloured.

1536	1e.50 Type **278**	15	10
1537	2e. Hand with letters	90	15
1538	3e.30 Sailing packet and modern liner	70	25
1539	4e.50 Dove and airliner	1·40	65
1540	5e.30 Hand with letter	1·40	75
1541	20e. Steam and electric locomotives	3·00	1·60
MS1542	106×147 mm. Nos. 1536/41 (sold at 50e.)	8·75	7·50

279 Luisa Todi

1974. Portuguese Musicians.

1543	**279**	1e.50 purple	20	15
1544	-	2e. red	1·40	35
1545	-	2e.50 brown	1·00	25
1546	-	3e. blue	1·50	50
1547	-	5e.30 green	1·20	80
1548	-	11e. red	1·30	80

PORTRAITS: 2e. Joao Domingos Bomtempo; 2e.50,Carlos Seixas; 3e. Duarte Lobo; 5e.30, Joaode Sousa Carvalho; 11e. Marcos Portugal.

280 Arms of Beja

1974. Bimillenary of Beja. Multicoloured.

1549	1e.50 Type **280**	25	10
1550	3e.50 Beja's inhabitants through the ages	3·00	1·50
1551	7e. Moorish arches	3·25	1·70

281 "The Annunciation"

1974. Christmas. Multicoloured.

1552	1e.50 Type **281**	20	10
1553	4e.50 "The Nativity"	4·00	80
1554	10e. "The Flight into Egypt"	3·50	1·10

282 Rainbow and Dove

1974. Portuguese Armed Forces Movement of 25 April.

1555	**282**	1e.50 multicoloured	15	15
1556	**282**	3e.50 multicoloured	4·00	1·90
1557	**282**	5e. multicoloured	3·00	1·10

283 Egas Moniz

1974. Birth Centenary of Professor Egas Moniz (brain surgeon).

1558	**283**	1e.50 brown and orange	35	15
1559	-	3e.30 orange and brown	3·00	80
1560	-	10e. grey and blue	6·00	1·00

DESIGNS: 3e.30, Nobel Medicine and Physiology Prize medal, 1949; 10e. Cerebral angiograph, 1927.

284 Farmer and Soldier

1975. Portuguese Cultural Progress and Citizens' Guidance Campaign.

1561	**284**	1e.50 multicoloured	25	10
1562	**284**	3e. multicoloured	2·50	85
1563	**284**	4e.50 multicoloured	3·50	1·40

285 Hands and Dove of Peace

1975. First Anniv of Portuguese Revolution. Multicoloured.

1564	1e.50 Type **285**	20	10
1565	4e.50 Hands and peace dove	3·50	90
1566	10e. Peace dove and emblem	4·25	1·50

286 "The Hand of God"

1975. Holy Year. Multicoloured.

1567	1e.50 Type **286**	20	15
1568	4e.50 Hand with cross	4·25	1·30
1569	10e. Peace dove	5·75	1·50

287 "The Horseman of the Apocalypse" (detail of 12th-cent manuscript)

1975. Europa. Multicoloured.

1570	1e.50 Type **287**	1·20	15
1571	10e. "Fernando Pessoa" (poet) (A. Negreiros)	55·00	1·90

288 Assembly Building

1975. Opening of Portuguese Constituent Assembly.

1572	**288**	2e. black, red and yellow	45	10
1573	**288**	20e. black, green & yellow	7·50	1·80

289 Hiking

1975. 36th International Camping and Caravanning Federation Rally. Multicoloured.

1574	2e. Type **289**	1·10	15
1575	4e.50 Boating and swimming	3·25	1·40
1576	5e.30 Caravanning	2·40	1·40

290 Planting Tree

1975. 30th Anniv of U.N.O. Multicoloured.

1577	2e. Type **290**	55	10
1578	4e.50 Releasing peace dove	1·80	80
1579	20c. Harvesting corn	4·75	1·60

291 Lilienthal Glider and Modern Space Rocket

1975. 26th International Astronautical Federation Congress, Lisbon. Multicoloured.

1580	2e. Type **291**	70	15
1581	4e.50 "Apollo"–"Soyuz" space link	2·30	1·10
1582	5e.30 R. H. Goddard, R. E. Pelterie, H. Oberth and K. E. Tsiolkovsky (space pioneers)	1·50	1·10
1583	10e. Astronaut and spaceships (70×32 mm)	5·75	1·60

292 Surveying the Land

1975. Centenary of National Geographical Society, Lisbon. Multicoloured.

1584	2e. Type **292**	35	10
1585	8e. Surveying the sea	2·30	90
1586	10e. Globe and people	3·50	1·50

293 Symbolic Arch

1975. European Architectural Heritage Year.

1587	**293**	2e. grey, blue & deep blue	35	25
1588	-	8e. grey and red	4·00	1·10
1589	-	10e. multicoloured	4·50	1·40

DESIGNS: 8e. Stylized building plan; 10e. Historical building being protected from development.

294 Nurse in Hospital Ward

1975. International Women's Year. Multicoloured.

1590	50c. Type **294**	30	15
1591	2e. Woman farm worker	1·10	40
1592	3e.50 Woman office worker	1·40	90
1593	8e. Woman factory worker	2·10	1·50
MS1594	104×115 mm. Nos. 1590/3 (sold at 25e.)	5·50	4·50

295 Pen-nib as Plough Blade

1976. 50th Anniv of National Writers Society.

1595	**295**	3e. blue and red	50	10
1596	**295**	20e. red and blue	5·25	1·60

296 First Telephone Set

1976. Telephone Centenary.

1597	**296**	3e. black, green & dp grn	1·10	15
1598	-	10e.50 black, red and pink	4·25	1·20

DESIGNS: 10e.50, Alexander Graham Bell.

297 "Industrial Progress"

1976. National Production Campaign.

1599	**297**	50c. red	35	10
1600	-	1e. green	55	20

DESIGN: 1e. Consumer goods.

298 Carved Olive-wood Spoons

1976. Europa. Multicoloured.

1601	3e. Type **298**	3·75	50
1602	20e. Gold ornaments	75·00	7·25

299 Stamp Designing

1976. "Interphil 76" International Stamp Exhibition, Philadelphia. Multicoloured.

1603	3e. Type **299**	35	10
1604	7e.50 Stamp being hand-cancelled	1·30	85
1605	10e. Stamp printing	2·20	90

300 King Fernando promulgating Law

1976. 600th Anniv of Law of "Sesmarias" (uncultivated land). Multicoloured.

1606	3e. Type **300**	25	15
1607	5e. Plough and farmers repelling hunters	1·90	60
1608	10e. Corn harvesting	2·75	1·00
MS1609	230×150 mm. Nos. 1606/8 (sold at 30e.)	6·00	£100

301 Athlete with Olympic Torch

1976. Olympic Games, Montreal. Multicoloured.

1610	3e. Type **301**	35	15
1611	7e. Women's relay	1·90	1·50
1612	10e.50 Olympic flame	2·50	1·40

302 "Speaking in the Country"

1976. Literacy Campaign. Multicoloured.

1613	3e. Type **302**	65	15
1614	3e. "Speaking at Sea"	65	15
1615	3e. "Speaking in Town"	65	15
1616a	3e. "Speaking at Work"	85	25
MS1617	145×104 mm. Nos. 1613/16 (sold at 25e.)	18·00	16·00

303 Azure-winged Magpie

1976. "Portucale 77" Thematic Stamp Exhibition, Oporto (1st issue). Flora and Fauna. Mult.

1618	3e. Type **303**	35	10
1619	5e. Lynx	1·50	50
1620	7e. Portuguese laurel cherry and blue tit	1·60	1·10
1621	10e.50 Little wild carnation and lizard	1·80	1·30

See also Nos 1673/8.

304 "Lubrapex" Emblem and Exhibition Hall

1976. "Lubrapex 1976" Luso-Brazilian Stamp Exhibition. Multicoloured.

1622	3e. Type **304**	45	15
1623	20e. "Lubrapex" emblem and "stamp"	3·00	2·00
MS1624	180×142 mm. Nos. 1622/3 (sold at 30e.)	5·00	5·00

305 Bank Emblem

1976. Centenary of National Trust Fund Bank.

1625	**305**	3e. multicoloured	15	10
1626	**305**	7e. multicoloured	2·75	1·20
1627	**305**	15e. multicoloured	4·00	1·40

306 Sheep Grazing

1976. Water Conservation. Protection of Humid Zones. Multicoloured.

1628	1e. Type **306**	55	10
1629	3e. Marshland	1·10	40
1630	5e. Sea trout	3·00	55
1631	10e. Mallards	4·25	1·10

307 "Liberty"

1976. Consolidation of Democratic Institutions.

1632	**307**	3e. grey, green and red	90	25

308 Examining Child's Eyes

1976. World Health Day. Detection and Prevention of Blindness. Multicoloured.

1633	3e. Type **308**	35	15
1634	5e. Welder wearing protective goggles	2·40	35
1635	10e.50 Blind person reading Braille	2·50	1·50

309 Hydro-electric Power

1976. Uses of Natural Energy. Multicoloured.

1636	1e. Type **309**	30	20
1637	4e. Fossil fuel (oil)	60	25
1638	5e. Geo-thermic sources	1·00	35
1639	10e. Wind power	1·70	1·00
1640	15e. Solar energy	3·75	1·70

310 Map of Member Countries

1977. Admission of Portugal to the Council of Europe.

1641	**310**	8e.50 multicoloured	1·60	1·60
1642	**310**	10e. multicoloured	1·80	1·70

311 Bottle inside Human Body

1977. Tenth Anniv of Portuguese Anti-Alcoholic Society. Multicoloured.

1643	3e. Type **311**	30	10
1644	5e. Broken body and bottle	1·10	55
1645	15e. Sun behind prison bars and bottle	3·00	1·60

312 Forest

1977. Natural Resources. Forests. Multicoloured.

1646	1e. Type **312**	30	20
1647	4e. Cork oaks	95	35
1648	7e. Logs and trees	2·00	1·60
1649	15e. Trees by the sea	2·00	1·70

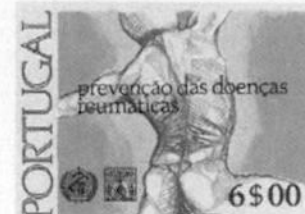

313 Exercising

1977. International Rheumatism Year.

1650	-	4e. orange, brown & blk	35	15
1651	**313**	6e. ultramarine, blue and black	1·50	1·10
1652	-	10e. red, mauve and black	1·40	95

DESIGNS: 4e. Rheumatism victim; 10e. Group exercising.

314 Southern Plains

1977. Europa. Multicoloured.

1653	4e. Type **314**	70	15
1654	8e.50 Northern terraced mountains	4·50	1·00
MS1655	148×95 mm. Nos. 1653/4 each ×3	55·00	33·00

315 John XXI Enthroned

1977. Seventh Death Centenary of Pope John XXI. Multicoloured.

1656	4e. Type **315**	30	20
1657	15e. Pope as doctor	80	65

316 Compass

1977. Camoes Day.

1658	**316**	4e. multicoloured	35	20
1659	**316**	8e.50 multicoloured	1·50	1·40

317 Child and Computer

1977. Permanent Education. Multicoloured.

1660	4e. Type **317**	55	20
1661	4e. Flautist and dancers	55	20
1662	4e. Farmer and tractor	55	20
1663	4e. Students and atomic construction	55	20
MS1664	148×96 mm. Nos. 1660/3 (sold at 20e.)	7·50	8·25

318 Pyrite

1977. Natural Resources. The Subsoil. Multicoloured.

1665	4e. Type **318**	35	15
1666	5e. Marble	1·10	45
1667	10e. Iron ore	1·20	60
1668	20e. Uranium	3·25	1·60

319 Alexandre Herculano

1977. Death Centenary of Alexandre Herculano (writer and politician).

1669	**319**	4e. multicoloured	40	15
1670	**319**	15e. multicoloured	2·00	70

320 Early Steam Locomotive and Peasant Cart (ceramic panel, J. Colaco)

1977. Centenary of Railway Bridge over River Douro. Multicoloured.

1671	4e. Type **320**	40	20
1672	10e. Maria Pia bridge (Eiffel)	3·00	2·20

321 Poviero (Northern coast)

1977. "Portucale 77" Thematic Stamp Exhibition, Oporto (2nd issue). Coastal Fishing Boats. Multicoloured.

1673	2e. Type **321**	55	15
1674	3e. Sea-going rowing boat, Furadouro	40	15
1675	4e. Rowing boat from Nazare	40	20
1676	7e. Caicque from Algarve	60	35
1677	10e. Tunny fishing boat, Algarve	1·20	75
1678	15e. Boat from Buarcos	1·60	1·10
MS1679	148×104 mm. Nos. 1673/8 (sold at 60e.)	6·00	5·00

322 "The Adoration" (Maria do Sameiro A. Santos)

1977. Christmas. Children's Paintings. Multicoloured.

1680	4e. Type **322**	40	15
1681	7e. "Star over Bethlehem" (Paula Maria L. David)	1·40	50
1682	10e. "The Holy Family" (Carla Maria M. Cruz) (vert)	1·60	75
1683	20e. "Children following the Star" (Rosa Maria M. Cardoso) (vert)	3·50	1·60

323 Medical Equipment and Operating Theatre

1978. (a) Size 22×17 mm.

1684	**323**	50c. green, black and red	15	10
1685	-	1e. blue, orange and black	15	10
1686	-	2e. blue, green & brown	15	10
1687	-	3e. brown, green and black	15	10
1688	-	4e. green, blue & brown	20	15
1689	-	5e. blue, green & brown	20	15
1690	-	5e.50 brown, buff and green	25	15
1691	-	6e. brown, yellow & grn	25	15
1692	-	6e.50 blue, deep blue and green	25	15
1693	-	7e. black, grey and blue	25	15
1694	-	8e. ochre, brown and grey	25	15
1694a	-	8e.50 brn, blk & lt brn	40	15
1695	-	9e. yellow, brown & blk	35	15
1696	-	10e. brown, black & grn	35	15
1697	-	12e.50 blue, red and black	45	15
1698	-	16e. brown, black and violet	2·75	45

(b) Size 30×21 mm.

1699	20e. multicoloured	70	15
1700a	30e. multicoloured	1·00	50
1701	40e. multicoloured	90	40
1702	50e. multicoloured	1·30	30
1703	100e. multicoloured	2·20	65
1703a	250e. multicoloured	5·75	1·00

DESIGNS: 1e. Old and modern kitchen equipment; 2e. Telegraph key and masts, microwaves and dish aerial; 3e. Dressmaking and ready-to-wear clothes; 4e. Writing desk and computer; 5e. Tunny fishing boats and modern trawler; 5e.50, Manual and mechanical weaver's looms; 6e. Plough and tractor; 6e.50, Monoplane and B.A.C. One Eleven airliner; 7e. Hand press and modern printing press; 8e. Carpenter's hand tools and mechanical tool; 8e.50, Potter's wheel and modern ceramic machinery; 9e. Old cameras and modern cine and photo cameras; 10e. Axe, saw and mechanical saw; 12e.50, Navigation and radar instruments; 16e. Manual and automatic mail sorting; 20e. Hand tools and building site; 30e. Hammer, anvil, bellows and industrial complex; 40e. Peasant cart and lorry; 50e. Alembic, retorts and modern chemical plant; 100e. Carpenter's shipyard, modern shipyard and tanker; 250e. Survey instruments.

324 Mediterranean Soil

1978. Natural Resources. The Soil. Multicoloured.

1704	4e. Type **324**	40	20
1705	5e. Rock formation	60	25
1706	10e. Alluvial soil	1·60	90
1707	20e. Black soil	3·25	1·30

325 Pedestrian on Zebra Crossing

1978. Road Safety.

1708	**325**	1e. blue, black and orange	20	20
1709	-	2e. blue, black and green	45	20
1710	-	2e.50 blue, black & lt bl	75	20
1711	-	5e. blue, black and red	1·60	25
1712	-	9e. blue, black & ultram	3·75	85
1713	-	12e.50 blue and black	4·50	2·20

DESIGNS: 2e. Motor cyclist; 2e.50, Children in back of car; 5e. Driver in car; 9e. View of road from driver's seat; 12e.50, Road victim ("Don't drink and drive").

326 Roman Tower of Centum Cellas, Belmonte

1978. Europa. Multicoloured.

1714	10e. Type **326**	1·50	35
1715	40e. Belem Monastery, Lisbon	6·00	1·80
MS1716	111×96 mm. Nos. 1714/15 each ×2 (sold at 120e.)	27·00	16·00

327 Roman Bridge, Chaves

1978. 19th Century of Chaves (Aquae Flaviae). Multicoloured.

1717	5e. Type **327**	55	20
1718	20e. Inscribed tablet from bridge	3·25	1·40

328 Running

1978. Sport for All. Multicoloured.

1719	5e. Type **328**	25	15
1720	10e. Cycling	55	35
1721	12e.50 Swimming	1·10	95
1722	15e. Football	1·10	1·10

329 Pedro Nunes

1978. 400th Death Anniv of Pedro Nunes (cosmographer). Multicoloured.

No.	Description	Mint	Used
1723	5e. Type **329**	30	10
1724	20e. Nonio (navigation instrument) and diagram	1·70	55

330 Trawler, Crates of Fish and Lorry

1978. Natural Resources. Fish. Multicoloured.

No.	Description	Mint	Used
1725	5e. Type **330**	35	15
1726	9e. Trawler and dockside cranes	90	25
1727	12e.50 Trawler, radar and lecture	1·40	1·10
1728	15e. Trawler with echo-sounding equipment and laboratory	2·50	1·60

331 Post Rider

1978. Introduction of Post Code. Multicoloured.

No.	Description	Mint	Used
1729	5e. Type **331**	45	20
1730	5e. Pigeon with letter	45	20
1731	5e. Sorting letters	45	20
1732	5e. Pen nib and post codes	45	20

332 Symbolic Figure

1978. 30th Anniv of Declaration of Human Rights. Multicoloured.

No.	Description	Mint	Used
1733	14e. Type **332**	70	50
1734	40e. Similar symbolic figure, but facing right	2·50	1·40
MS1735	120×100 mm. Nos. 1733/4 each ×2	7·75	5·25

333 Sebastiao Magalhaes Lima

1978. 50th Death Anniv of Magalhaes Lima (journalist and pacifist).

No.	Description	Mint	Used
1736	**333** 5e. multicoloured	45	20

334 Portable Post Boxes and Letter Balance

1978. Centenary of Post Museum. Multicoloured.

No.	Description	Mint	Used
1737	4e. Type **334**	65	15
1738	5e. Morse equipment	45	20
1739	10e. Printing press and Portuguese stamps of 1853 (125th anniv)	1·60	30
1740	14e. Books, bookcase and entrance to Postal Library (centenary)	2·75	1·90
MS1741	120×99 mm. Nos. 1737/40 (sold at 40e.)	7·00	5·75

335 Emigrant at Railway Station

1979. Portuguese Emigrants. Multicoloured.

No.	Description	Mint	Used
1742	5e. Type **335**	25	10
1743	14e. Emigrants at airport	85	65
1744	17e. Man greeting child at railway station	1·60	1·40

336 Traffic

1979. Fight Against Noise. Multicoloured.

No.	Description	Mint	Used
1745	4e. Type **336**	60	25
1746	5e. Pneumatic drill	90	20
1747	14e. Loud hailer	1·70	75

337 N.A.T.O. Emblem

1979. 30th Anniv of N.A.T.O.

No.	Description	Mint	Used
1748	**337** 5e. blue, red and brown	45	10
1749	**337** 50e. blue, yellow and red	3·75	3·00
MS1750	120×100 mm. Nos. 1748/9 each ×2	8·25	5·25

338 Door-to-door Delivery

1979. Europa. Multicoloured.

No.	Description	Mint	Used
1751	14e. Postal messenger delivering letter in cleft stick	1·10	50
1752	40e. Type **338**	2·20	1·10
MS1753	119×103 mm. Nos. 1751/2 each ×2	16·00	8·25

339 Children playing Ball

1979. International Year of the Child. Multicoloured.

No.	Description	Mint	Used
1754	5e.50 Type **339**	45	35
1755	6e.50 Mother, baby and dove	45	10
1756	10e. Child eating	55	50
1757	14e. Children of different races	1·10	1·00
MS1758	110×104 mm. Nos. 1754/7 (sold at 40e.)	5·00	4·00

340 Saluting the Flag

1979. Camoes Day.

No.	Description	Mint	Used
1759	**340** 6e.50 multicoloured	50	20
MS1760	148×125 mm. No. 1759 ×9	5·50	4·00

341 Pregnant Woman

1979. The Mentally Handicapped. Multicoloured.

No.	Description	Mint	Used
1761	6e.50 Type **341**	45	10
1762	17e. Boy sitting in cage	1·00	65
1763	20e. Face, and hands holding hammer and chisel	1·50	1·00

342 Children reading Book

1979. 50th Anniv of International Bureau of Education. Multicoloured.

No.	Description	Mint	Used
1764	6e.50 Type **342**	45	10
1765	17e. Teaching a deaf child	2·40	1·30

343 Water Cart, Caldas de Monchique

1979. "Brasiliana 79" International Stamp Exhibition. Portuguese Country Carts. Mult.

No.	Description	Mint	Used
1766	2e.50 Type **343**	25	25
1767	5e.50 Wine sledge, Madeira	25	25
1768	6e.50 Wine cart, Upper Douro	40	20
1769	16e. Covered cart, Alentejo	1·10	95
1770	19e. Cart, Mogadouro	1·60	1·30
1771	20e. Sand cart, Murtosa	1·70	55

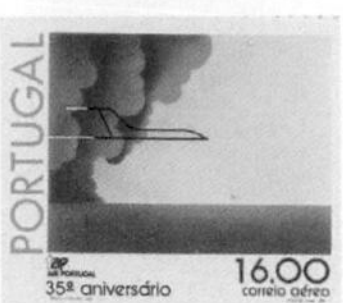

344 Aircraft flying through Storm Cloud

1979. 35th Anniv of TAP National Airline. Multicoloured.

No.	Description	Mint	Used
1772	16e. Type **344**	1·40	65
1773	19e. Aircraft and sunset	1·60	1·10

345 Antonio Jose de Almeida

1979. Republican Personalities (1st series).

No.	Description	Mint	Used
1774	**345** 5e.50 mauve, grey and red	45	15
1775	- 6e.50 red, grey and carmine	45	10
1776	- 10e. brown, grey and red	65	10
1777	- 16e. blue, grey and red	1·40	75
1778	- 19e.50 green, grey and red	1·80	1·30
1779	- 20e. purple, grey and red	2·00	65

DESIGNS: 6e. Afonso Costa; 10e. Teofilo Braga; 16e. Bernardino Machado; 19e.50, Joao Chagas; 20e. Elias Garcia.

See also Nos. 1787/92.

346 Family Group

1979. Towards a National Health Service. Multicoloured.

No.	Description	Mint	Used
1780	6e.50 Type **346**	45	10
1781	20e. Doctor examining patient	1·80	65

347 "The Holy Family"

1979. Christmas. Tile Pictures. Multicoloured.

No.	Description	Mint	Used
1782	5e.50 Type **347**	50	35
1783	6e.50 "Adoration of the Shepherds"	50	30
1784	16e. "Flight into Egypt"	1·50	1·10

348 Rotary Emblem and Globe

1980. 75th Anniv of Rotary International. Multicoloured.

No.	Description	Mint	Used
1785	16e. Type **348**	1·60	90
1786	50e. Rotary emblem and torch	3·50	2·40

349 Jaime Cortesao

1980. Republican Personalities (2nd series).

No.	Description	Mint	Used
1787	- 3e.50 orange and brown	35	15
1788	- 5e.50 green, olive and deep olive	45	25
1789	- 6e.50 lilac and violet	45	25
1790	**349** 11e. multicoloured	2·20	1·30
1791	- 16e. ochre and brown	1·20	80
1792	- 20e. green, blue & lt blue	1·20	55

DESIGNS: 3e.50, Alvaro de Castro; 5e.50, Antonio Sergio; 6e.50, Norton de Matos; 16e. Teixeira Gomes; 20e. Jose Domingues dos Santos.

350 Serpa Pinto

1980. Europa. Multicoloured.

No.	Description	Mint	Used
1793	16e. Type **350**	1·10	55
1794	60e. Vasco da Gama	2·75	1·30
MS1795	107×110 mm. Nos. 1793/4 each ×2	9·25	3·25

351 Barn Owl

1980. Protection of Species. Animals in Lisbon Zoo. Multicoloured.

No.	Description	Mint	Used
1796	6e.50 Type **351**	30	10
1797	16e. Red fox	1·20	80
1798	19e.50 Wolf	1·50	85
1799	20e. Golden eagle	1·50	80
MS1800	109×107 mm. Nos. 1796/9	5·00	4·00

352 Luis Vaz de Camoes

1980. 400th Death Anniv of Luis Vaz de Camoes (poet).

No.	Description	Mint	Used
1801	**352** 6e.50 multicoloured	55	15
1802	**352** 20e. multicoloured	1·40	65

353 Pinto in Japan

1980. 400th Anniv of Fernao Mendes Pinto's "A Peregrinacao" (The Pilgrimage). Multicoloured.

No.	Description	Mint	Used
1803	6e.50 Type **353**	45	10
1804	10e. Sea battle	1·30	75

354 Lisbon and Statue of St. Vincent (Jeronimos Monastery)

1980. World Tourism Conference, Manila, Philippines. Multicoloured.

No.	Description	Mint	Used
1805	6e.50 Type **354**	45	20
1806	8e. Lantern Tower, Evora Cathedral	65	35
1807	11e. Mountain village and "Jesus with Top-hat" (Mirando do Douro Cathedral)	1·40	75
1808	16e. Canicada dam and "Lady of the Milk" (Braga Cathedral)	1·90	1·00
1809	19e.50 Aveiro River and pulpit from Santa Cruz Monastery, Coimbra	2·20	1·10
1810	20e. Rocha beach and ornamental chimney, Algarve	1·70	80

355 Caravel

1980. "Lubrapex 80" Portuguese–Brazilian Stamp Exhibition, Lisbon. Multicoloured.

1811	6e.50 Type **355**	45	10
1812	8e. Nau	1·20	60
1813	16e. Galleon	1·70	80
1814	19e.50 Early paddle-steamer with sails	2·20	85
MS1815	132×88 mm. Nos. 1811/14 (sold at 60e.)	8·75	7·50

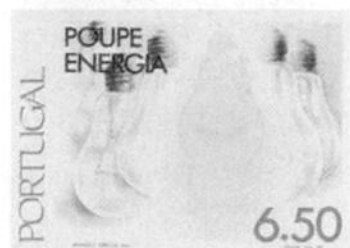

356 Lightbulbs

1980. Energy Conservation. Multicoloured.

1816	6e.50 Type **356**	45	10
1817	16e. Speeding car	2·50	90

357 Duke of Braganza and Open Book

1980. Bicentenary of Academy of Sciences, Lisbon. Multicoloured.

1818	6e.50 Type **357**	40	10
1819	19e.50 Uniformed academician, Academy and sextant	1·90	90

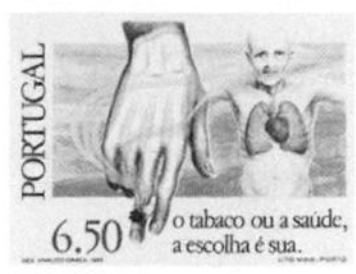

358 Cigarette contaminating Lungs

1980. Anti-Smoking Campaign. Multicoloured.

1820	6e.50 Type **358**	40	10
1821	19e.50 Healthy figure pushing away hand with cigarette	2·40	1·40

359 Head and Computer Punch-card

1981. National Census. Multicoloured.

1822	6e.50 Type **359**	45	25
1823	16e. Houses and punch-card	1·70	1·30

360 Fragata, River Tejo

1981. River Boats. Multicoloured.

1824	8e. Type **360**	40	30
1825	8e.50 Rabelo, River Douro	40	25
1826	10e. Moliceiro, Aveiro River	55	30
1827	16e. Barco, River Lima	95	60
1828	19e.50 Carocho, River Minho	1·00	60
1829	20e. Varino, River Tejo	1·00	55

361 "Rajola" Tile from Setubal Peninsula (15th century)

1981. Tiles (1st series).

1830	**361** 8e.50 multicoloured	95	15
MS1831	146×102 mm. No. 1830 ×6	6·50	80

See also Nos. 1483/**MS**1844, 1847/**MS**1848, 1862/**MS**1864, 1871/**MS**1872, 1885/**MS**1886, 1893/**MS**1894, 1902/**MS**1904, 1914/**MS**1915, 1926/**MS**1927, 1935/**MS**1936, 1941/**MS**1943, 1952/**MS**1953, 1970/**MS**1971, 1972/**MS**1973, 1976/**MS**1978, 1983/**MS**1984, 1993/**MS**1994, 2020/**MS**2021 and 2031/**MS**2033.

362 Agua Dog

1981. 50th Anniv of Kennel Club of Portugal. Multicoloured.

1832	7e. Type **362**	55	30
1833	8e.50 Serra de Aires	55	30
1834	15e. Perdigueiro	1·00	30
1835	22e. Podengo	1·90	80
1836	25e.50 Castro Laboreiro	2·40	1·40
1837	33e.50 Serra de Estrela	2·75	1·00

363 "Agriculture"

1981. May Day. Multicoloured.

1838	8e.50 Type **363**	45	10
1839	25e.50 "Industry"	1·80	1·20

364 Dancer and Tapestry

1981. Europa. Multicoloured.

1840	22e. Type **364**	1·60	65
1841	48e. Painted boat prow, painted plate and shipwright with model boat	3·25	1·70
MS1842	108×109 mm. Nos. 1840/1 each ×2	13·00	6·50

1981. Tiles (2nd series). Horiz design as T **361**.

1843	8e.50 multicoloured	95	15
MS1844	146×102 mm. No. 1843 ×6	6·25	5·00

DESIGN: 8e.50, Tracery-pattern tile from Seville (16th century).

365 St. Anthony Writing

1981. 750th Death Anniv of St. Anthony of Lisbon. Multicoloured.

1845	8e.50 Type **365**	55	15
1846	70e. St. Anthony giving blessing	4·75	2·50

1981. Tiles (3rd series). As T **361**. Multicoloured.

1847	8e.50 Arms of Jaime, Duke of Braganca (Seville, 1510)	95	15
MS1848	146×102 mm. No. 1847 ×6	6·00	5·00

366 King Joao II and Caravels

1981. 500th Anniv of King Joao II's Accession. Multicoloured.

1849	8e.50 Type **366**	55	15
1850	27e. King Joao II on horseback	3·25	1·10

367 "Dom Luiz", 1862

1981. 125th Anniv of Portuguese Railways. Multicoloured.

1851	8e.50 Type **367**	90	25
1852	19e. Pacific steam locomotive, 1925	2·75	1·30
1853	27e. Alco 1500 diesel locomotive, 1948	2·75	1·40
1854	33e.50 Alsthom BB 2600 electric locomotive, 1974	3·25	1·20

368 "Perrier" Pump, 1856

1981. Portuguese Fire Engines. Multicoloured.

1855	7e. Type **368**	95	25
1856	8e.50 Ford fire engine, 1927	85	25
1857	27e. Renault fire pump, 1914	2·40	1·30
1858	33e.50 Ford "Snorkel" combined hoist and pump, 1978	3·75	1·40

369 "Virgin and Child"

1981. Christmas. Crib Figures. Multicoloured.

1859	7e. Type **369**	1·20	40
1860	8e.50 "Nativity"	95	40
1861	27e. "Flight into Egypt"	2·50	1·50

1981. Tiles (4th series). As T **361**. Multicoloured.

1862	8e.50 "Pisana" tile, Lisbon (16th century)	95	20
MS1863	146×102 mm. No. 1862 ×6	6·00	5·00
MS1864	120×102 mm. Nos. 1830, 1843, 1847 and 1862	6·75	5·75

370 St. Francis with Animals

1982. 800th Birth Anniv of St. Francis of Assisi. Multicoloured.

1865	8e.50 Type **370**	50	30
1866	27e. St. Francis helping to build church	2·75	1·90

371 Flags of E.E.C. Members

1982. 25th Anniv of European Economic Community.

1867	**371** 27e. multicoloured	1·70	1·00
MS1868	155×88 mm. No. 1867 ×4	6·75	5·75

372 Fort St. Catherina, Lighthouse and Memorial Column

1982. Centenary of Figueira da Foz City. Mult.

1869	10e. Type **372**	60	10
1870	19e. Tagus Bridge, shipbuilding yard and trawler	2·30	1·20

1982. Tiles (5th series). As T **361**. Multicoloured.

1871	10e. Italo-Flemish pattern tile (17th century)	95	20
MS1872	146×102 mm. No. 1871 ×6	6·75	5·00

373 "Sagres I" (cadet barque)

1982. Sporting Events. Multicoloured.

1873	27e. Type **373** (Lisbon sailing races)	2·00	1·10
1874	33e.50 Roller hockey (25th World Championship)	2·75	1·80
1875	50e. "470" dinghies (World Championships)	4·00	1·90
1876	75e. Football (World Cup Football Championship, Spain)	6·25	2·20

374 Edison Gower Bell Telephone, 1883

1982. Centenary of Public Telephone Service. Multicoloured.

1877	10e. Type **374**	55	10
1878	27e. Consolidated telephone, 1887	1·80	1·40

375 Embassy of King Manuel to Pope Leo X

1982. Europa.

1879	**375** 33e.50 multicoloured	2·75	1·10
MS1880	140×114 mm. No. 1879 ×4	13·00	6·50

376 Pope John Paul II and Shrine of Fatima

1982. Papal Visit. Multicoloured.

1881	10e. Type **376**	55	10
1882	27e. Pope and Sameiro Sanctuary	2·50	1·50
1883	33e.50 Pope and Lisbon Cathedral	3·00	1·50
MS1884	138×78 mm. Nos. 1881/3 each ×2	12·00	5·75

1982. Tiles (6th series). As T **361**. Multicoloured.

1885	10e. Altar front panel depicting oriental tapestry (17th century)	95	20
MS1886	146×102 mm. No. 1885 ×6	6·00	5·00

377 Dunlin

1982. "Philexfrance 82" International Stamp Exhibition, Paris. Birds. Multicoloured.

1887	10e. Type **377**	55	15
1888	19e. Red-crested pochard	2·20	80
1889	27e. Greater flamingo	2·50	1·10
1890	33e.50 Black-winged stilt	2·75	1·60

378 Dr. Robert Koch

1982. Centenary of Discovery of Tubercle Bacillus. Multicoloured.

1891	27e. Type **378**	2·00	1·50
1892	33e.50 Lungs	2·30	1·60

1982. Tiles (7th series). As T **361**. Multicoloured.

1893	10e. Polychromatic quadrilobate pattern, 1630–40	95	15
MS1894	146×102 mm. No. 1893 ×6	6·00	5·00

379 Wine Glass and Stop Sign

1982. "Don't Drink and Drive".

1895	**379** 10e. multicoloured	70	15

380 Fairey IIID Seaplane "Lusitania"

1982. "Lubrapex 82" Brazilian–Portuguese Stamp Exhibition, Curitiba. Multicoloured.

1896	10e. Type **380**	45	30
1897	19e. Dornier Do-J Wal flying boat "Argus"	2·10	1·00
1898	33e.50 Douglas DC-7C "Seven Seas" airliner	2·50	1·00
1899	50e. Boeing 747-282B jetliner	2·75	1·30
MS1900	155×98 mm. Nos. 1896/9	8·00	6·50

381 Marquis de Pombal

1982. Death Bicentenary of Marquis de Pombal (statesman and reformer).

1901	**381** 10e. multicoloured	70	15

1982. Tiles (8th series). As T **361**. Multicoloured.

1902	10e. Monochrome quadrilobate pattern, 1670–90	95	15
MS1903	146×102 mm. No. 1902 ×6	6·00	5·00
MS1904	101×121 mm. Nos. 1871, 1885, 1893 and 1902	6·00	5·00

382 Gallic Cock and Tricolour

1983. Centenary of French Alliance (French language teaching association).

1905	**382** 27e. multicoloured	2·00	1·00

383 Lisnave Shipyard

1983. 75th Anniv of Port of Lisbon Administration.

1906	**383** 10e. multicoloured	70	15

384 Export Campaign Emblem

1983. Export Promotion.

1907	**384** 10e. multicoloured	70	15

385 Midshipman, 1782, and Frigate "Vasco da Gama"

1983. Naval Uniforms. Multicoloured.

1908	12e.50 Type **385**	1·00	15
1909	25e. Seaman and steam corvette "Estefania", 1845	1·70	40
1910	30e. Marine sergeant and cruiser "Adamastor", 1900	2·30	75
1911	37e.50 Midshipman and frigate "Joao Belo", 1982	2·50	90

386 W.C.Y. Emblem

1983. World Cummunications Year. Multicoloured.

1912	10e. Type **386**	55	25
1913	33e.50 W.C.Y. emblem (diff)	2·30	1·40

1983. Tiles (9th series). As T **361**. Multicoloured.

1914	12e.50 Hunter killing white bull (tile from Saldanha Palace, Lisbon, 17/18th century)	1·10	20
MS1915	146×102 mm. No. 1914 ×6	7·25	6·25

387 Portuguese Helmet (16th century)

1983. "Expo XVII" Council of Europe Exhibition. Multicoloured.

1916	11e. Type **387**	1·20	35
1917	12e.50 Astrolabe (16th century)	95	35
1918	25e. Portuguese caravels (from 16th-century Flemish tapestry)	2·00	65
1919	30e. Carved capital (12th century)	2·30	70
1920	37e.50 Hour glass (16th century)	2·10	1·20
1921	40e. Detail from Chinese panel painting (16th–17th century)	2·50	1·10
MS1922	115×120 mm. Nos. 1916/21	16·00	9·75

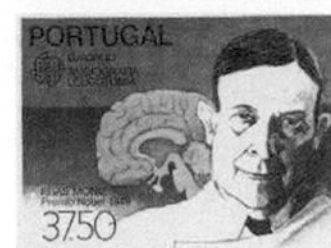

388 Egas Moniz (Nobel Prize winner and brain surgeon)

1983. Europa.

1923	**388** 37e.50 multicoloured	2·75	1·00
MS1924	140×114 mm. No. 1923 ×4	14·50	8·25

389 Passenger in Train

1983. European Ministers of Transport Conference.

1925	**389** 30e. blue, deep blue and silver	3·00	1·00

1983. Tiles (10th series). As T **361**. Multicoloured.

1926	12e.50 Tiles depicting birds (18th century)	1·10	20
MS1927	146×102 mm. No. 1926 ×6	7·25	6·25

390 Mediterranean Monk Seal

1983. "Brasiliana 83" International Stamp Exhibition, Rio de Janeiro. Marine Mammals. Multicoloured.

1928	12e.50 Type **390**	1·00	35
1929	30e. Common dolphin	3·75	60
1930	37e.50 Killer whale	3·25	1·60
1931	80e. Humpback whale	5·75	1·50
MS1932	133×81 mm. Nos. 1928/31	14·50	12·50

391 Assassination of Spanish Administrator by Prince John

1983. 600th Anniv of Independence. Multicoloured.

1933	12e.50 Type **391**	1·00	25
1934	30e. Prince John proclaimed King of Portugal	3·50	1·60

1983. Tiles (11th series). As T **361**. Multicoloured.

1935	12e.50 Flower pot by Gabriel del Barco (18th century)	1·10	20
MS1936	146×102 mm. No. 1935 ×6	7·00	5·75

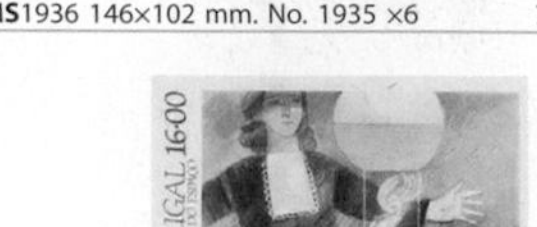

392 Bartolomeu de Gusmao and Model Balloon, 1709

1983. Bicentenary of Manned Flight. Multicoloured.

1937	16e. Type **392**	75	15
1938	51e. Montgolflier balloon, 1783	2·75	1·20

393 "Adoration of the Magi"

1983. Christmas. Stained Glass Windows from Monastery of Our Lady of Victory, Batalha. Multicoloured.

1939	12e.50 Type **393**	70	25
1940	30e. "The Flight into Egypt"	3·00	1·20

1983. Tiles (12th series). As T **361**. Multicoloured.

1941	12e.50 Turkish horseman (18th century)	1·10	20
MS1942	146×102 mm. No. 1941 ×6	7·00	5·75
MS1943	120×102 mm. Nos. 1914, 1926, 1935 and 1941	6·00	5·00

394 Siberian Tiger

1983. Centenary of Lisbon Zoo. Multicoloured.

1944	16e. Type **394**	1·80	25
1945	16e. Cheetah	1·80	25
1946	16e. Blesbok	1·80	25
1947	16e. White rhino	1·80	25

395 Fighter Pilot and Hawker Hurricane Mk II, 1954

1983. Air Force Uniforms. Multicoloured.

1948	16e. Type **395**	80	10
1949	35e. Pilot in summer uniform and Republic F-84G Thunderjet, 1960	2·50	80
1950	40e. Paratrooper in walking-out uniform and Nord 250lD Noratlas military transport plane, 1966	2·50	85
1951	51e. Pilot in normal uniform and Vought A-70 Corsair II bomber, 1966	3·00	1·20

1984. Tiles (13th series). As T **361**. Multicoloured.

1952	16e. Coat of arms of King Jose I (late 18th century)	1·10	20
MS1953	146×102 mm. No. 1952 ×6	7·25	6·25

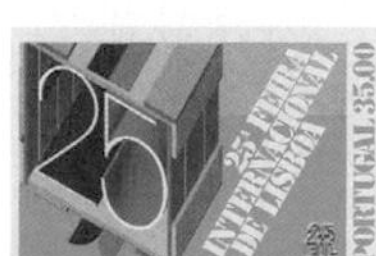

396 "25" on Crate (25th Lisbon International Fair)

1984. Events. Multicoloured.

1954	35e. Type **396**	2·50	85
1955	40e. Wheat rainbow and globe (World Food Day)	2·20	85
1956	51e. Hand holding stylized flower (15th World Congress of International Rehabilitation) (vert)	3·00	1·20

397 National Flag

1984. Tenth Anniv of Revolution.

1957	**397** 16e. multicoloured	1·40	20

398 Bridge

1984. Europa.

1958	**398** 51e. multicoloured	3·00	1·50
MS1959	140×114 mm. No. 1958 ×4	14·00	8·25

399 "Panel of St. Vincent"

1984. "Lubrapex 84" Portuguese–Brazilian Stamp Exhibition. Multicoloured.

1960	16e. Type **399**	70	25
1961	40e. "St. James" (altar panel)	3·25	90
1962	51e. "View of Lisbon" (painting)	4·00	1·20
1963	66e. "Head of Youth" (Domingos Sequeira)	4·25	1·60
MS1964	110×111 mm. Nos. 1960/3	12·50	9·75

400 Fencing

1984. Olympic Games, Los Angeles, and 75th Anniv of Portuguese Olympic Committee. Multicoloured.

1965	35e. Type **400**	2·40	70
1966	40e. Gymnastics	2·75	90
1967	51e. Running	3·25	1·30
1968	80e. Pole vaulting	3·50	1·30
MS1969	90×92 mm. 100e. Hurdling	9·75	8·25

1984. Tiles (14th series). As T **361**. Multicoloured.

1970	16e. Pictorial tile from Pombal Palace, Lisbon (late 18th century)	1·10	20
MS1971	146×102 mm. No. 1970 ×6	7·25	6·25

1984. Tiles (15th series). As T **361**. Multicoloured.

1972	16e. Four art nouveau tiles (late 19th century)	1·10	20
MS1973	146×102 mm. No. 1972 ×6	7·25	6·25

401 Gil Eanes

1984. Anniversaries. Multicoloured.

1974	16e. Type **401** (550th anniv of rounding of Cape Bojador)	55	10
1975	51e. King Pedro IV of Portugal and I of Brazil (150th death anniv)	3·25	1·30

1984. Tiles (16th series). As T **361**. Multicoloured.

1976	16e. Grasshoppers and wheat (R. Bordalo Pinheiro, 19th century)	1·10	20
MS1977	146×102 mm. No. 1976 ×6	7·25	6·25
MS1978	120×102 mm. Nos. 1952, 1970, 1972 and 1976	6·00	5·00

402 Infantry Grenadier, 1740, and Regiment in Formation

1985. Army Uniforms. Multicoloured.

1979	20e. Type **402**	80	25
1980	46e. Officer, Fifth Cavalry, 1810, and cavalry charge	3·25	85
1981	60e. Artillery corporal, 1891, and Krupp 9 mm gun and crew	3·25	1·00
1982	100e. Engineer in chemical protection suit, 1985, and bridge-laying armoured car	3·75	1·50

1985. Tiles (17th series). As T **361**. Multicoloured.

1983	20e. Detail of panel by Jorge Barrados in Lisbon Faculty of Letters (20th century)	1·10	20
MS1984	146×102 mm. No. 1983 ×6	6·75	5·75

403 Calcada R. dos Santos Kiosk

1985. Lisbon Kiosks. Multicoloured.
1985 20e. Type **403** 1·20 25
1986 20e. Tivoli kiosk, Avenida da Liberdade 1·20 25
1987 20e. Porto de Lisboa kiosk 1·20 25
1988 20e. Rua de Artilharia Um kiosk 1·20 25

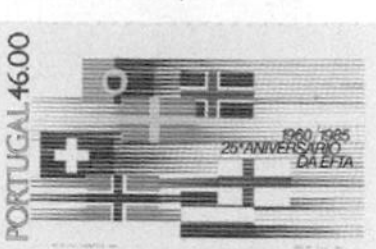

404 Flags of Member Countries

1985. 25th Anniv of European Free Trade Assn.
1989 **404** 46e. multicoloured 1·90 80

405 Profiles

1985. International Youth Year.
1990 **405** 60e. multicoloured 2·40 1·10

406 Woman holding Adufe (tambourine)

1985. Europa.
1991 **406** 60e. multicoloured 4·25 1·70
MS1992 140×114 mm. No. 1991 ×4 18·00 8·25

1985. Tiles (18th series). As T **361**. Multicoloured.
1993 20e. Detail of panel by Maria Keil on Avenida Infante Santo (20th century) 1·10 20
MS1994 146×102 mm. No. 1993 ×6 6·75 5·75

407 Knight on Horseback

1985. Anniversaries. Multicoloured.
1995 20e. Type **407** (600th anniv of Battle of Aljubarrota) 90 15
1996 46e. Queen Leonor and hospital (500th anniv of Caldas da Rainha thermal hospital) 2·75 90
1997 60e. Pedro Reinel (500th anniversary of first Portuguese sea-chart) 3·00 1·50

408 Farmhouse, Minho

1985. Architecture.
1998 - 50c. black, bistre and blue 15 15
1999 - 1e. black, yellow & green 15 15
2000 - 1e.50 black, green and emerald 15 15
2001 - 2e.50 brown, orange & bl 15 15
2002 - 10e. black, purple & pink 25 20
2003 **408** 20e. brn, yell & dp yell 40 15
2004 - 22e.50 brown, blue and ochre 40 20
2005 - 25e. brown, yellow & grn 45 15
2006 - 27e. black, grn & yell 65 15
2007 - 29e. black, yellow & orge 65 15
2008 - 30e. black, blue & brown 65 15
2009 - 40e. black, yellow & grn 90 25
2010 - 50e. black, blue & brown 1·00 20
2011 - 55e. black, yellow & grn 1·00 20
2012 - 60e. black, orange & blue 1·30 40
2013 - 70e. black, yellow & orge 1·30 40
2014 - 80e. brown, green and red 1·50 45
2015 - 90e. brown, yellow & grn 1·70 45
2016 - 100e. brown, yellow & bl 2·00 50
2017 - 500e. black, grey and blue 8·50 3·00

DESIGNS: 50e. Saloia house, Estremadura; 1e. Beira inland house; 1e.50, Ribatejo house; 2e.50, Tras-os-montes houses; 10e. Minho and Douro coast house; 22e.50, Alentejo houses; 25e. Sitio house, Algarve; 27e. Beira inland house (different); 29e. Tras-os-montes house; 30e. Algarve house; 40e. Beira inland house (different); 50e. Beira coasthouse; 55e. Tras-os-montes house (different); 60e. Beira coast house (different); 70e. Estramadura and Alentejo house; 80e. Estremadura house; 90e. Minho house; 100e. Monte house, Alentejo; 500e. Terraced houses, East Algarve.

1985. Tiles (19th series). As T **361**. Multicoloured.
2020 20e. Head of woman by Querubim Lapa (20th century) 1·10 20
MS2021 147×101 mm. No. 2020 ×6 6·75 5·75

409 Aquilino Ribeiro (writer)

1985. Anniversaries. Multicoloured.
2022 20e. Type **409** (birth centenary) 95 10
2023 46e. Fernando Pessoa (poet 50th death anniv) 2·40 85

410 Berlenga National Reserve

1985. National Parks and Reserves. Multicoloured.
2024 20e. Type **410** 55 10
2025 40e. Estrela Mountains National Park 2·40 90
2026 46e. Boquilobo Marsh National Reserve 3·00 1·10
2027 80e. Formosa Lagoon National Reserve 3·25 1·20
MS2028 100×68 mm. 100e. Jacinto Dunes National Reserve 7·75 6·50

411 "Nativity"

1985. Christmas. Illustrations from "Book of Hours of King Manoel I". Multicoloured.
2029 20e. Type **411** 60 10
2030 46e. "Adoration of the Three Wise Men" 2·40 90

1985. Tiles (20th series). As T 361. Multicoloured.
2031 20e. Detail of panel by Manuel Cargaleiro (20th century) 1·10 20
MS2032 146×102 mm. No. 2031 ×6 10·50 6·25
MS2033 120×102 mm. Nos. 1983, 1993, 2020 and 2031 6·75 5·75

412 Post Rider

1985. No value expressed.
2034 **412** (–) green and deep green 1·10 15

413 Map and Flags of Member Countries

1985. Admission of Portugal and Spain to European Economic Community. Multicoloured.
2035 20e. Flags of Portugal and Spain uniting with flags of other members 80 25
2036 57e.50 Type **413** 3·00 1·30
See also No. **MS**2056.

414 Feira Castle

1986. Castles (1st series). Multicoloured.
2037 22e.50 Type **414** 1·20 20
2038 22e.50 Beja Castle 1·20 20
See also Nos. 2040/1, 2054/5, 2065/6, 2073/4, 2086/7 2093/4, 2102/3 and 2108/9.

415 Globe and Dove

1986. International Peace Year.
2039 **415** 75e. multicoloured 3·25 1·40

1986. Castles (2nd series). As T **414**. Multicoloured.
2040 22e.50 Braganca Castle 1·20 20
2041 22e.50 Guimaraes Castle 1·20 20

416 Benz Motor Tricycle, 1886

1986. Centenary of Motor Car. Multicoloured.
2042 22e.50 Type **416** 1·50 15
2043 22e.50 Daimler motor car, 1886 1·50 15

417 Allis Shad

1986. Europa.
2044 **417** 68e.50 multicoloured 3·75 1·60
MS2045 140×114 mm. No. 2044 ×4 19·00 9·75

418 Alter

1986. "Ameripex 86" International Stamp Exn, Chicago. Thoroughbred Horses. Multicoloured.
2046 22e.50 Type **418** 80 25
2047 47e.50 Lusitano 2·75 95
2048 52e.50 Garrano 3·00 1·30
2049 68e.50 Sorraia 3·25 1·50

419 Comet

1986. Appearance of Halley's Comet. Sheet 100×68 mm.
MS2050 **419** 100e. multicoloured 15·00 12·50

420 Diogo Cao (navigator) and Monument

1986. Anniversaries. Multicoloured.
2051 22e.50 Type **420** (500th anniv of 2nd expedition to Africa) 80 15
2052 52e.50 Passos Manuel (Director) and capital (150th anniv of National Academy of Fine Arts, Lisbon) 2·10 95
2053 52e.50 Joao Baptista Ribeiro (painter and Oporto Academy Director) and drawing (150th anniv of Portuguese Academy of Fine Arts, Oporto) 2·10 95

1986. Castles (3rd series). As T **414**. Multicoloured.
2054 22e.50 Belmonte Castle 1·20 25
2055 22e.50 Montemor-o-Velho Castle 1·20 25

1986. "Europex 86" Stamp Exhibition, Lisbon. Sheet 127×91 mm.
MS2056 Nos. 2035/6 each ×2 8·00 6·50

421 Hand writing on Postcard

1986. Anniversaries. Multicoloured.
2057 22e.50 Type **421** (centenary of first Portuguese postcards) 1·10 20
2058 47e.50 Guardsman and houses (75th anniv of National Republican Guard) 2·00 95
2059 52e.50 Calipers, globe and banner (50th anniv of Order of Engineers) 2·20 1·00

422 Seasonal Mill, Douro

1986. "Luprapex 86" Portuguese–Brazilian Stamp Exhibition, Rio de Janeiro. Multicoloured.
2060 22e.50 Type **422** 80 30
2061 47e.50 Seasonal mill, Coimbra 1·80 1·10
2062 52e.50 Overshot bucket mill, Gerez 2·40 1·20
2063 90e. Permanent stream mill, Braga 3·00 1·10
MS2064 140×114 mm. Nos. 2060/3 12·00 8·25

1987. Castles (4th series). As T **414**. Multicoloured.
2065 25e. Silves Castle 1·20 20
2066 25e. Evora-Monte Castle 1·20 20

423 Houses on Stilts, Tocha

1987. 75th Anniv (1986) of Organized Tourism. Multicoloured.
2067 25e. Type **423** 80 25
2068 57e. Fishing boats, Espinho 2·75 1·20
2069 98e. Fountain, Arraiolos 3·50 2·00

424 Hand, Sun and Trees

1987. European Environment Year. Multicoloured.
2070 25e. Type **424** 80 30
2071 57e. Hands and flower on map of Europe 2·00 1·10
2072 74e.50 Hand, sea, purple dye murex shell, moon and rainbow 3·25 1·40

1987. Castles (5th series). As T **414**. Multicoloured.
2073 25e. Leiria Castle 1·20 20
2074 25e. Trancoso Castle 1·20 20

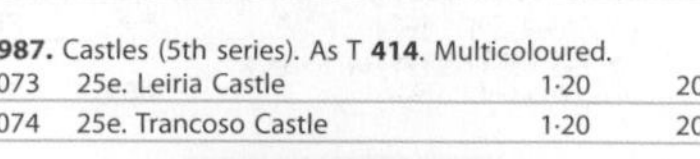

425 Bank Borges and Irmao Agency, Vila do Conde (Alvaro Siza)

1987. Europa. Architecture.
2075 **425** 74e.50 multicoloured 3·00 1·60
MS2076 140×114 mm. No. 2075 ×4 15·00 8·25

426 Cape Mondego

1987. "Capex '87" International Stamp Exhibition Toronto. Portuguese Lighthouses. Multicoloured.

2077	25e. Type **426**	1·00	35
2078	25e. Berlenga	1·00	35
2079	25e. Aveiro	1·00	35
2080	25e. Cape St. Vincent	1·00	35

427 Souza-Cardoso (self-portrait)

1987. Birth Centenary of Amadeo de Souza-Cardoso (painter).

2081	**427**	74e.50 multicoloured	2·40	1·10

428 Clipped 400 Reis Silver Coin

1987. 300th Anniv of Portuguese Paper Currency.

2082	**428**	100e. multicoloured	3·25	1·00

429 Dias's Fleet leaving Lisbon

1987. 500th Anniv of Bartolomeu Dias's Voyages (1st issue). Multicoloured.

2083	25e. Type **429**	1·20	20
2084	25e. Ships off coast of Africa	1·20	20

Nos. 2083/4 were printed together, *se-tenant*, each pair forming a composite design.

See also Nos. 2099/2100.

430 Library

1987. 150th Anniv of Portuguese Royal Library, Rio de Janeiro.

2085	**430**	125e. multicoloured	3·75	1·60

1987. Castles (6th series). As T **414**. Multicoloured.

2086	25e. Marvao Castle	1·20	20
2087	25e. St. George's Castle, Lisbon	1·20	20

431 Records and Compact Disc Player

1987. Centenary of Gramophone Record. Sheet 140×114 mm containing T **431** and similar horiz design. Multicoloured.

MS2088	75e. Type **431**; 125e. Early gramophone	12·00	9·75

432 Angels around Baby Jesus, Tree and Kings (Jose Manuel Coutinho)

1987. Christmas. Children's Paintings. Multicoloured.

2089	25e. Type **432**	1·10	25
2090	57e. Children dancing around sunburst (Rosa J. Leitao)	2·10	1·00
2091	74e.50 Santa Claus flying on dove (Sonya Alexandra Hilario)	2·30	1·30
MS2092	140×114 mm. Nos. 2089/91	6·75	5·25

1988. Castles (7th series). As T **414**. Multicoloured.

2093	27e. Fernandine Walls, Oporto	1·10	20
2094	27e. Almourol Castle	1·10	20

433 Lynx

1988. Iberian Lynx. Multicoloured.

2095	27e. Type **433**	1·40	35
2096	27e. Lynx carrying rabbit	1·40	35
2097	27e. Pair of lynxes	1·40	35
2098	27e. Mother with young	1·40	35

434 King Joao II sending Pero da Covilha on Expedition

1988. 500th Anniv of Voyages of Bartolomeu Dias (2nd issue) (2099/2100) and Pero da Covilha (2101). Multicoloured.

2099	27e. Dias's ships in storm off Cape of Good Hope	1·00	25
2100	27e. Contemporary map	1·00	55
2101	105e. Type **434**	3·25	1·50

Nos. 2099/2100 are as T **429**.

1988. Castles (8th series). As T **414**. Multicoloured.

2102	27e. Palmela Castle	1·10	20
2103	27e. Vila Nova da Cerveira Castle	1·10	20

435 19th-century Mail Coach

1988. Europa. Transport and Communications.

2104	**435**	80e. multicoloured	4·25	1·70
MS2105		139×112 mm. As No. 2104 ×4 but with cream background	16·00	9·75

436 Map of Europe and Monnet

1988. Birth Centenary of Jean Monnet (statesman). "Europex 88" Stamp Exhibition.

2106	**436**	60e. multicoloured	1·90	1·10

437 Window reflecting Cordovil House and Fountain

1988. UNESCO World Heritage Site, Evora. "Lubrapex 88" Stamp Exhibition. Sheet 112×139 mm.

MS2107	**437**	150e. multicoloured	10·50	9·25

1988. Castles (9th series). As T **414**. Multicoloured.

2108	27e. Chaves Castle	1·10	25
2109	27e. Penedono Castle	1·10	25

438 "Part of a Viola" (Amadeo de Souza-Cardoso)

1988. 20th-century Portuguese Paintings (1st series). Multicoloured.

2110	27e. Type **438**	80	30
2111	60e. "Acrobats" (Almada Negreiros)	2·00	1·00
2112	80e. "Still Life with Viola" (Eduardo Viana)	2·30	1·20
MS2113	138×112 mm. Nos. 2110/12	7·50	6·25

See also Nos. 2121/**MS**2125, 2131/**MS**2134, 2148/**MS**2152, 2166/**MS**2169 and 2206/**MS**2210.

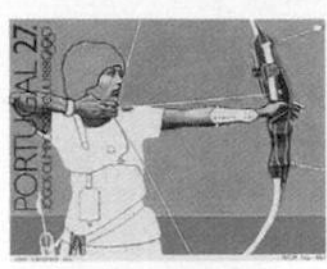

439 Archery

1988. Olympic Games, Seoul. Multicoloured.

2114	27e. Type **439**	1·00	30
2115	55e. Weightlifting	1·90	1·10
2116	60e. Judo	2·00	1·10
2117	80e. Tennis	2·50	1·10
MS2118	114×67 mm. 200e. Yachting (39×30 mm)	12·50	11·50

440 "Winter" (House of the Fountains, Coimbra)

1988. Roman Mosaics of Third Century. Multicoloured.

2119	27e. Type **440**	70	30
2120	80e. "Fish" (Baths, Faro)	2·40	1·10

1988. 20th Century Portuguese Paintings (2nd series). As T **438**. Multicoloured.

2121	27e. "Internment" (Mario Eloy)	80	20
2122	60e. "Lisbon Houses" (Carlos Botelho)	1·90	80
2123	80e. "Avejao Lirico" (Antonio Pedro)	2·20	1·10
MS2124	140×114 mm. Nos. 2121/3	7·50	6·25
MS2125	139×144 mm. Nos. 2110/12 and 2121/3	13·00	10·50

441 Braga Cathedral

1989. Anniversaries. Multicoloured.

2126	30e. Type **441** (900th anniv)	1·00	40
2127	55e. Caravel, Fischer's lovebird and S. Jorge da Mina Castle (505th anniv)	1·70	80
2128	60e. Sailor using astrolabe (500th anniv of South Atlantic voyages)	2·40	1·30

Nos. 2127/8 also have the "India 89" Stamp Exhibition, New Delhi, emblem.

442 "Greetings"

1989. Greetings Stamps. Multicoloured.

2129	29e. Type **442**	80	20
2130	60e. Airplane distributing envelopes inscribed "with Love"	1·30	70

1989. 20th-Century Portuguese Paintings (3rd series). As T **438**. Multicoloured.

2131	29e. "Antithesis of Calm" (Antonio Dacosta)	80	15
2132	60e. "Unskilled Mason's Lunch" (Julio Pomar)	1·90	90
2133	87e. "Simumis" (Vespeira)	2·20	1·20
MS2134	139×111 mm. Nos. 2131/3	7·50	6·25

443 Flags in Ballot Box

1989. Third Direct Elections to European Parliament.

2135	**443**	60e. multicoloured	1·90	1·10

444 Boy with Spinning Top

1989. Europa. Children's Games and Toys. Multicoloured.

2136	80e. Type **444**	2·50	1·50
MS2137	138×112 mm. 80e. ×2 Type **444**; 80e. ×2 Spinning tops	8·75	7·25

445 Cable Railway

1989. Lisbon Transport. Multicoloured.

2138	29e. Type **445**	80	25
2139	65e. Electric tramcar	2·30	95
2140	87e. Santa Justa lift	2·40	1·30
2141	100e. Bus	2·75	1·30
MS2142	100×50 mm. 250e. River ferry (39×29 mm)	11·00	10·00

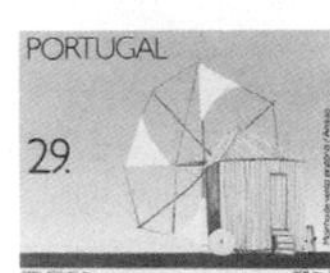

446 Gyratory Mill, Ansiao

1989. Windmills. Multicoloured.

2143	29e. Type **446**	80	25
2144	60e. Stone mill, Santiago do Cacem	2·30	95
2145	87e. Post mill, Afife	2·40	1·20
2146	100e. Wooden mill, Caldas da Rainha	2·75	1·40

447 Drummer Boy

1989. Bicentenary of French Revolution and "Philexfrance 89" International Stamp Exhibition, Paris. Sheet 111×139 mm.

MS2147	**447**	250e. multicoloured	11·00	10·00

1989. 20th-Century Portuguese Paintings (4th series). As T **438**.

2148	29e. blue, green and black	75	30
2149	60e. multicoloured	1·90	1·10
2150	87e. multicoloured	2·30	1·40
MS2151	139×111 mm. Nos. 2148/50	7·50	6·25
MS2152	138×144 mm. Nos. 231/3 and 2148/50	13·00	10·50

DESIGNS: 29e. "046-72" (Fernando Lanhas); 60e. "Spirals" (Nadir Afonso); 87e. "Sim" (Carlos Calvet).

448 Luis I (death centenary) and Ajuda Palace, Lisbon

1989. National Palaces (1st series). Multicoloured.

2153	29e. Type **448**	45	20
2154	60e. Queluz Palace	1·80	1·10

See also Nos. 2211/14.

449 "Armeria pseudarmeria"

1989. Wild Flowers. Multicoloured.

2155	29e. Type **449**	70	20
2156	60e. "Santolina impressa"	1·70	80
2157	87e. "Linaria lamarckii"	2·10	1·20
2158	100e. "Limonium multiflorum"	2·50	1·60

450 Blue and White Plate

1990. Portuguese Faience (1st series). Multicoloured.

2159	33e. Type **450**	80	30
2160	33e. Blue and white plate with man in centre	80	30
2161	35e. Vase decorated with flowers	95	35
2162	60e. Fish-shaped jug	1·50	95
2163	60e. Blue and white plate with arms in centre	1·50	95
2164	60e. Blue and white dish with lid	1·50	95
MS2165	112×140 mm. 250e. Plate with crown in centre	7·75	7·00

See also Nos. 2221/**MS**2227 and 2262/**MS**2268.

1990. 20th-Century Portuguese Paintings (5th series). As T **438**. Multicoloured.

2166	32e. "Aluenda-Tordesillas" (Joaquim Rodrigo)	55	25
2167	60e. "Painting" (Luis Noronha da Costa)	1·70	80
2168	95e. "Painting" (Vasco Costa)	2·30	1·10
MS2169	138×111 mm. Nos. 2166/8	7·50	6·25

451 Joao Goncalves Zarco

1990. Portuguese Navigators.

2170	**451**	2e. red, pink and black	15	15
2171	-	3e. green, blue and black	10	10
2172	-	4e. purple, red and black	10	10
2173	-	5e. brown, grey & black	20	15
2174	-	6e. deep green, green and black	20	15
2175	-	10e. dp red, red & black	15	10
2176	-	32e. green, brown & blk	75	15
2177	-	35e. red, pink and black	70	15
2178	-	38e. blue, lt blue & black	75	25
2179	-	42e. green, grey & black	75	20
2180	-	45e. green, yellow & blk	55	30
2181	-	60e. yellow, purple & blk	1·40	50
2182	-	65e. brown, green & blk	1·30	40
2183	-	70e. violet, mauve & blk	1·20	40
2184	-	75e. olive, green & black	1·00	65
2185	-	80e. orange, brn & blk	1·80	70
2186	-	100e. red, orange & blk	2·40	85
2187	-	200e. green, yellow & blk	3·00	90
2188	-	250e. blue, green & black	4·75	1·90
2189	-	350e. red, pink and black	5·75	2·20

DESIGNS: 3e. Pedro Lopes de Sousa; 4e. Duarto Pacheco Pereira; 5e. Tristao Vaz Teixeira; 6e. Pedro Alvares Cabral; 10e. Joao de Castro; 32e. Bartolomeu Perestrelo; 35e. Gil Eanes: 38e. Vasco da Gama; 42e. Joao de Lisboa; 45e. Joao Rodrigues Cabrilho; 60e. Nuno Tristao; 65e. Joaoda Nova; 70e. Fernao de Magalhaes (Magellan); 75e. Pedro Fernandes de Queiros; 80e. Diogo Gomes; 100e. Diogo de Silves; 200e. Estevao Gomes; 250e. Diogo Cao; 350e. Bartolomeu Dias.

452 Score and Singers

1990. Anniversaries. Multicoloured.

2191	32e. Type **452** (centenary of "A Portuguesa" (national anthem))	60	20
2192	70e. Students and teacher (700th anniv of granting of charter to Lisbon University) (vert)	2·20	1·10

453 Santo Tirso Post Office

1990. Europa. Post Office Buildings. Multicoloured.

2193	80e. Type **453**	2·10	1·10
MS2194	139×111 mm. 80e. ×2 Type **453**; 80e. ×2 19th-century Mail Coach Office	8·25	5·25

454 Stamping Letter

1990. "Stamp World London 90" International Stamp Exhibition and 150th Anniv of the Penny Black. Sheet 111×140 mm.

MS2195 **454**	250e. multicoloured	11·00	9·75

455 Street with Chairs under Trees

1990. Greetings Stamps. Multicoloured.

2196	60e. Type **455**	1·70	90
2197	60e. Hand holding bouquet out of car window	1·70	90
2198	60e. Man with bouquet crossing street	1·70	90
2199	60e. Women with bouquet behind pillar box	1·70	90

456 Camilo Castelo Branco (writer)

1990. Death Anniversaries. Multicoloured.

2200	65e. Type **456** (centenary)	1·30	90
2201	70e. Brother Bartolomeu dos Martires (Bishop of Braga, 400th anniv)	1·90	1·10

457 Barketta

1990. 15th-Century Explorers' Ships. Multicoloured.

2202	32e. Type **457**	55	25
2203	60e. Carvel-built fishing boat	1·60	80
2204	70e. Nau	1·80	1·10
2205	95e. Caravel	2·20	1·40

458 Pena Palace

1990. 20th-Century Portuguese Paintings (6th series). As T **438**. Multicoloured.

2206	32e. "Dom Sebastiao" (Costa Pinheiro)	55	30
2207	60e. "Domestic Scene with Green Dog" (Paula Rego)	1·80	1·10
2208	95e. "Homage to Magritte" (Jose de Guimaraes)	2·75	1·30
MS2209	138×112 mm. Nos. 2206/8	4·50	2·40
MS2210	138×145 mm. Nos. 2166/8 and 2206/8	13·00	10·50

1990. National Palaces (2nd series). Multicoloured.

2211	32e. Type **458**	75	25
2212	60e. Vila Palace	1·60	80
2213	70e. Mafra Palace	1·70	1·10
2214	120e. Guimaraes Palace	2·10	1·40

459 Carneiro

1990. Tenth Death Anniv of Francisco Sa Carneiro (founder of Popular Democratic Party and Prime Minister, 1980).

2215	**459**	32e. black and brown	70	25

460 Steam Locomotive No. 02, 1887

1990. Centenary of Rossio Railway Station, Lisbon. Multicoloured.

2216	32e. Type **460**	75	25
2217	60e. Steam locomotive No. 010, 1891	1·60	80
2218	70e. Steam locomotive No. 071, 1916	1·70	1·10
2219	95e. Electric train, 1956	2·10	1·40
MS2220	112×80 mm. 200e. Station clock (39×29 mm)	7·50	7·25

1991. Portuguese Faience (2nd series). As T **450**. Multicoloured.

2221	35e. Barrel of fish and plate (Rato factory Lisbon)	70	25
2222	35e. Floral vase (Bica do Sapato factory)	70	25
2223	35e. Gargoyle (Costa Briozo factory, Coimbra)	70	25
2224	60e. Dish with leaf pattern (Juncal factory)	1·30	70
2225	60e. Coffee pot (Cavaquinho factory, Oporto)	1·30	70
2226	60e. Mug (Massarelos factory, Oporto)	1·30	70
MS2227	114×140 mm. 250e. Plate with portrait in centre (Miragaia factory, Oporto)	8·25	8·00

461 Greater Flamingoes

1991. European Tourism Year. Multicoloured.

2228	60e. Type **461**	1·20	90
2229	110e. European chameleon	2·30	1·70
MS2230	112×104 mm. 250e. Red deer (39×31 mm)	7·25	7·00

462 "Eutelsat II" Satellite

1991. Europa. Europe in Space. Multicoloured.

2231	80e. Type **462**	2·50	2·00
MS2232	140×112 mm. 80e. ×2, Type **462**; 80e. ×2, "Olympus I" satellite	8·50	5·75

463 Caravel

1991. 16th-Century Explorers' Ships. Multicoloured.

2233	35e. Type **463**	55	30
2234	75e. Port view of nau	1·80	85
2235	80e. Stern view of nau	1·90	1·00
2236	110e. Galleon	2·20	1·10

464 "Isabella of Portugal and Philip the Good" (anon)

1991. "Europhalia 91 Portugal" Festival, Belgium. Sheet 140×112 mm.

MS2237 **464**	300e. multicoloured	10·50	9·50

465 Emerald and Diamond Bow

1991. "Royal Treasures" Exhibition, Ajuda Palace (1st issue). Multicoloured.

2238	35e. Type **465**	55	35
2239	60e. Royal sceptre	1·60	70
2240	70e. Sash of the Grand Cross	1·80	95
2241	80e. Hilt of sabre	1·90	1·00
2242	140e. Crown	2·40	1·20

See also Nos. 2270/4.

466 Antero de Quental (writer)

1991. Anniversaries. Multicoloured.

2243	35e. Type **466** (death centenary)	60	20
2244	110e. Arrival of expedition and baptism of Sonyo prince (500th anniv of first Portuguese missionary expedition to the Congo)	2·40	1·20

467 Faculty of Architecture, Oporto University (Siza Vieira)

1991. Architecture. Multicoloured.

2245	35e. Type **467**	55	20
2246	60e. Torre do Tombo (Arsenio Cordeiro Associates)	1·40	50
2247	80e. Maria Pia bridge over River Douro (Edgar Cardoso) and Donna Maria bridge	1·70	1·00
2248	110e. Setubal–Braga highway	2·10	1·10

468 King Manoel I creating Public Post, 1520

1991. History of Communications in Portugal. Multicoloured.

2249	35e. Type **468**	60	25
2250	60e. Woman posting letter and telegraph operator (merging of posts and telegraph operations, 1881)	1·20	65
2251	80e. Postman, mail van and switchboard operator (creation of Posts and Telecommunications administration, 1911)	1·50	85
MS2252	140×111 mm. 110e. Modern means of communications (introduction of priority mail service, 1991)	2·75	2·30

469 Show Jumping

1991. Olympic Games, Barcelona (1992) (1st issue). Multicoloured.

2253	35e. Type **469**	60	25
2254	60e. Fencing	1·30	55
2255	80e. Shooting	1·60	90
2256	110e. Yachting	2·10	1·10

See also Nos. 2295/8.

470 Peugeot "19", 1899

1991. Caramulo Automobile Museum. Multicoloured.

2257	35e. Type **470**	55	25

2258	60e. Rolls Royce "Silver Ghost", 1911	1·30	55
2259	80e. Bugatti "35B", 1930	1·60	95
2260	110e. Ferrari "1965 Inter", 1950	2·10	1·10
MS2261	140×111 mm. 70e. ×2 Mercedes Benz 380K (1934); 70e ×2 Hispano-Suiza H6b (1924)	6·00	4·50

See also Nos. 2275/**MS**2279.

1992. Portuguese Faience (3rd series). As T **450**. Multicoloured.

2262	40e. Jug (Viana do Castelo factory)	65	35
2263	40e. Plate with flower design ("Ratinho" faience, Coimbra)	65	35
2264	40e. Dish with lid (Estremoz factory)	65	35
2265	65e. Decorated violin by Wescislau Cifka (Constancia factory, Lisbon)	1·30	65
2266	65e. Figure of man seated on barrel (Calvaquinho factory, Oporto)	1·30	65
2267	65e. Figure of woman (Fervenca factory, Oporto)	1·30	65
MS2268	112×140 mm. 260e. Political figures by Rafael Bordalo Pinheiro (Caldas da Rainha factory) (44×38 mm)	5·25	5·00

471 Astrolabe (Presidency emblem)

1992. Portuguese Presidency of European Community.

2269	**471**	65e. multicoloured	1·50	1·00

1992. "Royal Treasures" Exhibition, Ajuda Palace (2nd issue). As T **465**. Multicoloured.

2270	38e. Coral diadem	55	35
2271	65e. Faberge clock	1·40	75
2272	70e. Gold tobacco box studded with diamonds and emeralds by Jacqumin	1·30	65
2273	85e. Royal sceptre with dragon supporting crown	1·40	90
2274	125e. Necklace of diamond stars by Estevao de Sousa	1·80	1·10

1992. Oeiras Automobile Museum. As T **470**. Multicoloured.

2275	38e. Citroen "Torpedo", 1922	55	25
2276	65e. Robert Schneider, 1914	1·40	65
2277	85e. Austin "Seven", 1933	1·60	85
2278	120e. Mercedes Benz armoured "770", 1938	2·00	1·10
MS2279	140×111 mm. 70e. ×2 Renault 10/14 (1911); 70e. ×2 Ford Model T (1927)	6·00	4·50

472 Portuguese Traders

1992. 450th Anniv of First Portuguese Contacts with Japan (1st issue). Details of painting attributed to Kano Domi. Multicoloured.

2280	38e. Type **472**	60	30
2281	120e. Portuguese visitors with gifts	1·90	1·30

See also Nos. 2342/4.

473 Portuguese Pavilion

1992. "Expo '92" World's Fair, Seville.

2282	**473**	65e. multicoloured	1·00	75

474 Cross-staff

1992. Nautical Instruments (1st series). Multicoloured.

2283	60e. Type **474**	95	45
2284	70e. Quadrant	1·30	70
2285	100e. Astrolabe	1·50	90
2286	120e. Compass	1·80	1·10
MS2287	140×112 mm. Nos. 2283/6	6·00	5·00

See also Nos. 2318/21.

475 Royal All Saints Hospital, Lisbon

1992. Anniversaries. Multicoloured.

2288	38e. Type **475** (500th anniv of foundation)	70	40
2289	70e. Lucia, Francisco and Jacinta (75th anniv of apparition of Our Lady at Fatima)	1·20	90
2290	120e. Crane and docks (centenary of Port of Leixoes)	2·00	1·20

476 Columbus with King Joao II

1992. Europa. 500th Anniv of Discovery of America. Multicoloured.

2291	85e. Type **476**	2·40	1·80
MS2292	Six sheets (a) 260e. brown and black (Type **479**); (b) 260e. blue and black (Columbus sighting land); (c) 260e. purple and black (Landing of Columbus); (d) 260e. lilac and black (Columbus welcomed at Barcelona); (e) 260e. black (Columbus presenting natives); (f) 260e. black ("America", Columbus and "Liberty")	41·00	29·00

478 Black-headed Gull flying over contaminated River

1992. Second United Nations Conference on Environment and Development, Rio de Janeiro. Multicoloured.

2293	70e. Type **478**	1·10	55
2294	120e. River kingfisher and butterfly beside clean river	1·90	1·10

Nos. 2293/4 were issued together, se-tenant, forming a composite design.

479 Running

1992. Olympic Games, Barcelona (2nd issue). Multicoloured.

2295	38e. Type **479**	55	35
2296	70e. Football	1·30	65
2297	85e. Hurdling	1·50	75
2298	120e. Roller hockey	1·70	1·00
MS2299	140×112 mm. 250e. Basketball	4·50	4·25

480 Bullfighter on Horse

1992. Centenary of Campo Pequeno Bull Ring, Lisbon. Multicoloured.

2300	38e. Type **480**	55	30
2301	65e. Bull charging at horse	1·30	60
2302	70e. Bullfighter attacking bull	1·40	85
2303	155e. Bullfighter flourishing hat	1·90	1·30
MS2304	140×113 mm. 250e. Entrance to ring (35×50 mm)	4·50	4·25

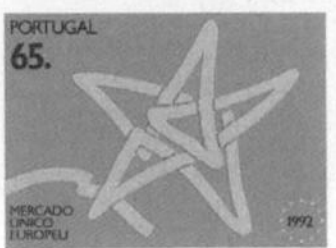

482 Star

1992. European Single Market.

2313	**482**	65e. multicoloured	1·10	75

483 Industrial Safety Equipment

1992. European Year of Health, Hygiene and Safety in the Workplace.

2314	**483**	120e. multicoloured	2·00	1·50

484 Post Office Emblem

1993. No value expressed.

2315	**484**	(–) red and black	75	35

No. 2315 was sold at the current first class inland letter rate. This was 42e. at time of issue.

485 Graphic Poem

1993. Birth Centenary of Jose de Almada Negreiros (artist and poet). Multicoloured.

2316	40e. Type **485**	70	35
2317	65e. Trawlers (painting)	1·10	85

486 Sand Clock

1993. Nautical Instruments (2nd series). Multicoloured.

2318	42e. Type **486**	55	25
2319	70e. Nocturlabio	1·10	65
2320	90e. Kamal	1·70	90
2321	130e. Back-staff	2·10	1·00

487 View from Window

1993. Europa. Contemporary Art. Untitled paintings by Jose Escada. Multicoloured.

2322	90e. Type **487**	2·00	1·40
MS2323	140×112 mm. 90e. ×2 Type **487**; 90e. × 2 Body parts	10·00	6·50

488 Rossini and "The Barber of Seville"

1993. Bicentenary of San Carlos National Theatre, Lisbon. Multicoloured.

2324	42e. Type **488**	55	35
2325	70e. Verdi and "Rigoletto"	1·20	65
2326	90e. Wagner and "Tristan and Isolde"	1·50	90
2327	130e. Mozart and "The Magic Flute"	2·30	1·00
MS2328	140×112 mm. 300e. Exterior of theatre (39×29 mm)	5·25	5·00

489 Fireman's Helmet

1993. 125th Anniv of Association of Volunteer Firemen of Lisbon.

2329	**489**	70e. multicoloured	1·30	80

490 Santos-o-Velho, Lisbon

1993. Union of Portuguese-speaking Capital Cities.

2330	**490**	130e. multicoloured	2·10	1·30
MS2331		140×112 mm. No. 2330 ×4	8·50	7·00

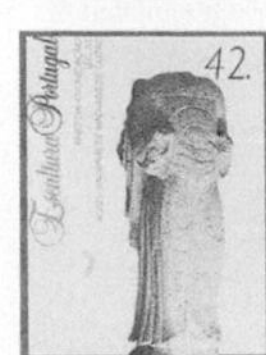

491 "Angel of the Annunciation" (from Oporto Cathedral)

1993. Sculptures (1st series). Multicoloured.

2332	42e. Type **491**	55	25
2333	70e. "St Mark" (Cornelius de Holanda) (horiz)	1·30	65
2334	75e. "Madonna and Child"	1·60	70
2335	90e. "Archangel St. Michael"	1·70	75
2336	130e. "Count of Ferreira" (Soares dos Reis)	2·10	1·10
2337	170e. "Construction" (Heldar Batista)	2·40	1·30
MS2338	112×140 mm. 75e. Marble bust of Agrippina the Elder; 75e. "Virgin of the Annunciation" (Master of the Royal Tombs); 75e. "The Widow" (Teixeira Lopes); 75e. "Love Ode" (Canto da Maya)	5·25	4·25

See also Nos. 2380/**MS**2386 and 2466/**MS**2472.

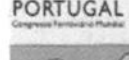

492 Road Tanker and Electric Tanker Train

1993. Int Railways Congress, Lisbon. Multicoloured.

2339	90e. Type **492**	1·20	70
2340	130e. Electric train and traffic jam	2·00	1·10
MS2341	140×112 mm. 300e. Train	4·75	4·50

493 Japanese Man with Musket

1993. 450th Anniv of First Portuguese Visit to Japan (2nd issue). Multicoloured.

2342	42e. Type **493**	55	40
2343	130e. Portuguese missionaries	2·75	1·50
2344	350e. Traders carrying goods	4·50	2·40

494 Peniche Trawler

1993. Trawlers (1st series). Multicoloured.

2345	42e. Type **494**	55	25
2346	70e. Peniche type trawler	1·00	55
2347	90e. "Germano 3" (steam trawler)	1·60	75
2348	130e. "Estrela 1" (steam trawler)	2·00	1·00

See also Nos. 2392/5.

495 Rural Post Bag, 1800

1993. Post Boxes. Multicoloured.

2349	42e. Type **495**	55	30
2350	70e. 19th-century wall-mounted box for railway travelling post office	1·00	55

2351	90e. 19th-century pillar box	1·60	70
2352	130e. Modern multi-function post box	2·00	1·00
MS2353	140×112 mm. 300e. 19th-century box for animal-drawn post wagons	4·75	4·50

496 Imperial Eagle

1993. Endangered Birds of Prey. Multicoloured.

2354	42e. Type **496**	55	30
2355	70e. Eagle owl	1·20	70
2356	130e. Peregrine falcon	2·75	1·10
2357	350e. Hen harrier	4·50	2·40

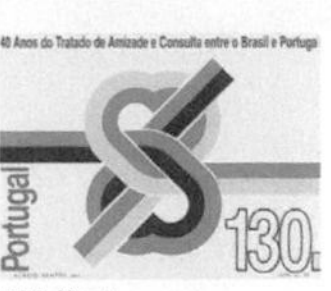

497 Knot

1993. 40th Anniv of Brazil–Portugal Consultation and Friendship Treaty.

2358	**497**	130e. multicoloured	2·00	1·20

498 Arms

1993. 850th Anniv of Zamora Conference (recognizing Afonso I as King of Portugal). Sheet 106×114 mm.

MS2359 **498**	150e. multicoloured	2·75	2·75

499 Stylized Map of Member Nations

1994. 40th Anniv of Western European Union.

2360	**499**	85e. multicoloured	1·30	85

500 Olympic Rings as Torch Flame

1994. Centenary of Int Olympic Committee. Multicoloured.

2361	100e. Type **500**	2·30	1·10
2362	100e. "100" and rings	2·30	1·10

501 Oliveira Martins (historian)

1994. Centenaries. Multicoloured.

2363	45e. Type **501** (death)	70	30
2364	100e. Florbela Espanca (poet, birth)	1·30	80

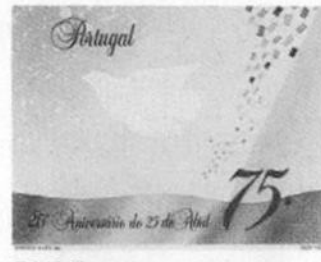

502 Map and Prince Henry

1994. 600th Birth Anniv of Prince Henry the Navigator.

2365	**502**	140e. multicoloured	2·00	1·10

503 Dove

1994. 20th Anniv of Revolution.

2366	**503**	75e. multicoloured	1·00	60

504 Mounted Knight and Explorer with Model Caravel

1994. Europa. Discoveries. Multicoloured.

2367	100e. Type **MS**504	1·60	1·10
MS2368	140×112 mm. 100e. ×2 Type **504**; 100e. ×2 Millet and explorer with model caravel	8·75	6·50

505 Emblem

1994. International Year of the Family.

2369	**505**	45e. red, black and lake	65	25
2370	**505**	140e. red, black and green	1·90	1·10

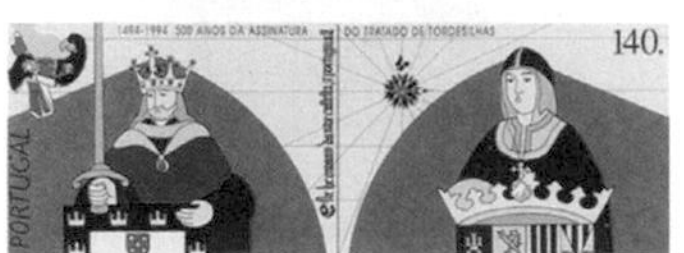

506 Footballer kicking Ball and World Map

1994. World Cup Football Championship, U.S.A. Multicoloured.

2371	100e. Type **506**	1·40	70
2372	140e. Ball and footballers' legs	2·00	1·00

507 King Joao II of Portugal and King Fernando of Spain

1994. 500th Anniv of Treaty of Tordesillas (defining Portuguese and Spanish spheres of influence).

2373	**507**	140e. multicoloured	2·00	1·10

508 Music

1994. Lisbon, European Capital of Culture. Multicoloured.

2374	45e. Type **508**	50	35
2375	75e. Photography and cinema	1·20	70
2376	100e. Theatre and dance	1·50	1·10
2377	140e. Art	1·90	1·50
MS2378	140×112 mm. Nos. 2374/7	5·75	5·75

509 Emblem

1994. Portuguese Road Safety Year.

2379	**509**	45e. red, green and black	65	30

1994. Sculptures (2nd series). As T **491**. Multicoloured.

2380	45e. Carved stonework from Citania de Briteiros (1st century) (horiz)	60	25
2381	75e. Visigothic pilaster (7th century)	80	45
2382	80e. Capital from Amorim Church (horiz)	1·00	60
2383	100e. Laying Christ's body in tomb (attr Joao de Ruao) (Monastery Church of Santa Cruz de Coimbra) (horiz)	1·20	70
2384	140e. Carved wood reliquary (Santa Maria Monastery, Alcobaca) (horiz)	1·80	1·00
2385	180e. Relief of Writers (Leopoldo de Almeida) (Lisbon National Library) (horiz)	2·40	1·20
MS2386	112×140 mm. 75e. Queen Urraca's tomb (Santa Maria Monastery, Alcobaca); 75e. Count of Ourem tomb (Colegiada de Ourem Church); 75e. Joao de Noronha and Isabel de Sousa's tomb (Santa Maria Church, Obidos); 75e. Mausoleum of Admiral Machado dos Santos (Alto de Sao Joao Cemetery, Lisbon)	4·75	4·00

510 Falconer, Peregrine Falcon and Dog

1994. Falconry. Designs showing a peregrine falcon in various hunting scenes. Multicoloured.

2387	45e. Type **510**	50	25
2388	75e. Falcon chasing duck	90	50
2389	100e. Falconer approaching falcon with dead duck	1·20	70
2390	140e. Falcons	1·60	1·00
MS2391	97×121 mm. 250e. Hooded falcon on falconer's arm	3·75	3·75

511 "Maria Arminda"

1994. Trawlers (2nd series). Multicoloured.

2392	45e. Type **511**	50	25
2393	75e. "Bom Pastor"	1·20	50
2394	100e. Aladores trawler with triplex haulers	1·30	70
2395	140e. "Sueste"	1·70	1·00

512 19th-century Horse-drawn Wagon

1994. Postal Transport. Multicoloured.

2396	45e. Type **512**	60	25
2397	75e. Travelling Post Office sorting carriage No. C7, 1910	1·00	50
2398	100e. Mercedes mail van, 1910	1·20	70
2399	140e. Volkswagen mail van, 1950	1·60	95
MS2400	140×112 mm. 250e. Daf truck, 1983A	3·50	3·00

513 Multiple Unit Set, Sintra Suburban Railway

1994. Modern Electric Locomotives (1st series). Multicoloured.

2401	45e. Type **513**	50	25
2402	75e. Locomotive No. 5611-7 (national network)	95	55
2403	140e. Lisbon Underground train	1·70	95

See also No. 2465.

514 Medal

1994. 150th Anniv of Montepio Geral Savings Bank (45e.) and World Savings Day (100e.). Multicoloured.

2404	45e. Type **514**	65	30
2405	100e. Coins and bee	1·20	65

515 St. Philip's Fort, Setubal

1994. Pousadas (hotels) in Historic Buildings. Multicoloured.

2406	45e. Type **515**	50	25
2407	75e. Obidos Castle	1·20	50
2408	100e. Convent of Loios, Evora	1·30	70
2409	140e. Santa Marinha Monastery, Guimaraes	1·60	95

516 Businessman and Tourist

1994. American Society of Travel Agents World Congress, Lisbon.

2410	**516**	140e. multicoloured	1·80	95

517 Statuette of Missionary, Mozambique

1994. Evangelization by Portuguese Missionaries. Multicoloured.

2411	45e. Type **517**	50	25
2412	75e. "Child Jesus the Good Shepherd" (carving), India	1·20	50
2413	100e. Chalice, Macao	1·30	70
2414	140e. Carving of man in frame, Angola (horiz)	1·60	95

518 Africans greeting Portuguese

1994. 550th Anniv of First Portuguese Landing in Senegal.

2415	**518**	140e. multicoloured	1·80	95

519 Battle Scene (detail of the panel, Hall of Battles, Fronteira Palace, Lisbon)

1994. 350th Anniv of Battle of Montijo. Sheet 63× 83 mm.

MS2416 **519**	150e. multicoloured	2·20	2·20

520 Adoration of the Wise Men

1994. Christmas. Sheet 140×111 mm.

MS2417 **520**	150e. multicoloured	2·20	2·20

Portugal 42·

521 Great Bustard

1995. European Nature Conservation Year. Multicoloured.

2418	42e. Type **521**	90	55
2419	90e. Osprey	1·50	1·10
2420	130e. Schreiber's green lizard	1·70	1·40
MS2421	140×112 mm. Nos. 2418/20	4·50	5·00

522 St. John and Sick Man

1995. 500th Birth Anniv of St. John of God (founder of Order of Hospitallers).

2422 **522** 45e. multicoloured 65 30

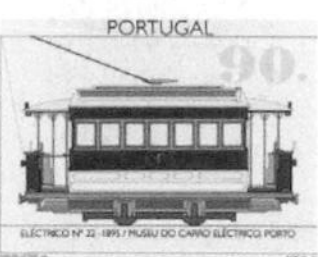

523 Electric Tramcar No. 22, 1895

1995. Centenaries of Trams and Motor Cars in Portugal. Multicoloured.

2423 90e. Type **523** 1·20 55

2424 130e. Panhard and Levassor motor car 1·50 95

524 Bread Seller

1995. 19th-century Itinerant Trades. Multicoloured.

2425 1e. Type **524** 10 10

2426 2e. Laundrywoman 10 10

2427 3e. Broker 10 10

2428 5e. Broom seller 10 10

2429 10e. Fish seller 10 10

2431 20e. Spinning-wheel and spoon seller 20 10

2432 30e. Olive oil and vinegar seller 30 20

2433 40e. Seller of indulgences 40 30

2434 45e. General street trader 50 30

2435 47e. Hot chestnut seller 40 25

2436 49e. Clothes mender 55 40

2437 50e. Fruit seller 70 40

2437a 50e. Pottery seller 65 45

2438 51e. Knife grinder 45 30

2439 75e. Whitewasher 90 60

2440 78e. Cloth seller 90 45

2440b 80e. Carrier/messenger boy 95 55

2440c 85e. Goose seller 1·00 70

2440d 86e. Bread seller 80 55

2440e 95e. Coachman 90 65

2441 100e. Mussels seller 1·30 65

2441a 100e. Milk seller 1·00 70

2442 210e. Basket seller 2·10 1·40

2443 250e. Water seller 2·75 1·60

2444 250e. Pastry seller 2·75 1·60

526 Emblem

1995. 50th Anniv of U.N.O. Multicoloured.

2449 75e. Type **526** 90 55

2450 135e. Clouds and emblem 1·60 1·00

MS2451 140×111 mm. No. 2449/50 each ×2 5·50 5·00

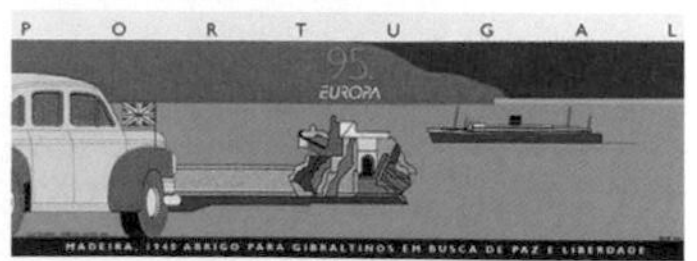

527 Evacuees from Gibraltar arriving at Madeira

1995. Europa. Peace and Freedom. Portuguese Neutrality during Second World War. Mult.

2452 95e. Type **527** 2·00 1·20

2453 95e. Refugees waiting at Lisbon for transatlantic liner and Aristides de Sousa Mendes (Portuguese Consul in Bordeaux) 2·00 1·20

528 "St. Antony holding Child Jesus" (painting)

1995. 800th Birth Anniv of St. Antony of Padua (Franciscan preacher). Multicoloured.

2454 45e. Type **528** 1·40 35

2455 75e. St. Antony with flowers (vert) 2·50 85

2456 135e. "St. Antony holding Child Jesus" (statue) 4·00 1·60

MS2457 96×110 mm. 250e. "St. Anthony holding Baby Jesus" (18th-century Madeiran statue) 17·00 10·00

529 Carpenters with Axes and Women with Water, 1395

1995. 600th Anniv of Fire Service in Portugal. Multicoloured.

2458 45e. Type **529** 50 25

2459 80e. Fire cart and men carrying barrels of water, 1834 1·00 55

2460 95e. Merryweather steam-powered fire engine, 1867 1·10 70

2461 135e. Zoost fire engine No. 1, 1908 1·50 1·00

MS2462 Two sheets, each 120×100 mm. (a) 4 ×45e. Dutch fire engine, 1701; (b) 4 ×75e. Picota fire engine, 1780 and Portuguese fire cart, 1782 5·25 5·75

530 Coronation

1995. 500th Anniv of Accession of King Manoel I.

2463 **530** 45e. brown, yellow and red 55 30

MS2464 112×140 mm. No. 2463 ×4 2·50 2·50

1995. Modern Electric Locomotives (2nd series). As T **513**.

2465 80e. multicoloured 95 55

DESIGN: 80e. Articulated trams.

1995. Sculptures (3rd series). As T **491**. Multicoloured.

2466 45e. "Warrior" (castle statue) 45 25

2467 75e. Double-headed fountain 95 55

2468 80e. "Truth" (monument to Eca de Queiros by Antonio Teixeira Lopes) 95 55

2469 95e. First World War memorial, Abrantes (Ruy Gameiro) 1·10 65

2470 135e. "Fernao Lopes" (Martins Correia) 1·60 1·00

2471 190e. "Fernando Pessoa" (Lagoa Henriques) 2·10 1·30

MS2472 112×140 mm. 75e. "Knight" (from Chapel of the Ferreiros); 75e. "King Jose I" (J. Machado de Castro), Commerce Square, Lisbon; 75e. "King Joao IV" (Francisco Franco), Vila Vicosa; 75e. "Vimara Peres" (Barata Feyo), Oporto Cathedral Square 3·75 3·25

531 "Portugal's Guardian Angel" (sculpture, Diogo Pires)

1995. Art of the Period of Discoveries (15th–16th centuries). Multicoloured.

2473 45e. Type **531** 45 25

2474 75e. Reliquary of Queen Leonor (Master Joao) 95 55

2475 80e. "Don Manuel" (sculpture, Nicolas Chanterenne) 95 55

2476 95e. "St. Anthony" (painting, Nuno Goncalves) 1·10 65

2477 135e. "Adoration of the Three Wise Men" (painting, Grao Vasco) 1·90 1·00

2478 190e. "Christ on the Way to Calvary" (painting, Jorge Afonso) 2·10 1·30

MS2479 140×112 mm. 200e. "St. Vincent" (polyptych, Nuno Goncalves) 2·50 2·00

532 Queiroz

1995. 150th Birth Anniv of Eca de Queiroz (writer).

2480 **532** 135e. multicoloured 1·50 1·00

533 Archangel Gabriel

1995. Christmas. Multicoloured. (a) With country name at foot.

2481 80e. Type **533** 1·40 1·00

MS2482 112×140 mm. No. 2481×4 6·50 5·00

(b) With country name omitted.

2483 80e. Type **533** 1·30 1·00

MS2484 112×140 mm. No. 2483 ×4 6·25 6·25

534 Airbus Industrie A340/300

1995. 50th Anniv of TAP Air Portugal.

2485 **534** 135e. multicoloured 1·50 1·00

535 King Carlos I of Portugal

1996. Centenary of Oceanographic Expeditions. Multicoloured.

2486 95e. Type **535** 1·10 65

2487 135e. Prince Albert I of Monaco 1·60 1·20

536 Books

1996. Anniversaries. Multicoloured.

2488 80e. Type **536** (bicentenary of National Library) 95 55

2489 200e. Hand writing with quill pen (700th anniv of adoption of Portuguese as official language) 2·20 1·40

537 Joao de Deus (poet and author of reading primer)

1996. Writers' Anniversaries. Multicoloured.

2490 78e. Type **537** (death centenary) 95 55

2491 140e. Joao de Barros (historian, philosopher and grammarian, 500th birth) 1·50 1·00

538 Holding Child's Hand

1996. 50th Anniv of UNICEF. Multicoloured.

2492 78e. Type **538** 1·00 55

2493 140e. Children of different races 1·60 95

539 Helena Vieira da Silva (artist, self-portrait)

1996. Europa. Famous Women.

2494 **539** 98e. multicoloured 1·70 1·20

MS2495 140×112 mm. No. 2494 ×3 5·50 6·50

540 Match Scene

1996. European Football Championship, England. Multicoloured.

2496 78e. Type **540** 1·00 55

2497 140e. Match scene (different) 1·70 95

MS2498 140×112 mm. Nos. 2496/7 2·75 2·50

541 Caravel and Arms (image scaled to 56% of original size)

1996. 500th Death Anniv of Joao Vaz Corte-Real (explorer). Multicoloured.

2499 140e. Type **541** 1·70 1·00

MS2500 90×127 mm. 315e. Close-up of caravel in Type **541** (39×30 mm) 4·25 4·25

542 Wrestling

1996. Olympic Games, Atlanta. Multicoloured.

2501 47e. Type **542** 50 25

2502 78e. Show jumping 95 55

2503 98e. Boxing 1·10 65

2504 140e. Running 1·50 95

MS2505 96×110 mm. 300e. Athletes at starting blocks 4·00 4·00

543 Hilario and Guitar

1996. Death Centenary of Augusto Hilario (fado singer).

2506 **543** 80e. multicoloured 95 55

544 Antonio Silva (actor)

1996. Centenary of Motion Pictures. Multicoloured.

2507 47e. Type **544** 50 25

2508 78e. Vasco Santana (actor) 90 55

2509 80e. Laura Alves (actress) 90 55

2510 98e. Aurelio Pais dos Reis (director) 1·10 55

2511 100e. Leitao de Barros (director) 1·10 65

2512 140e. Antonio Lopes Ribeiro (director) 1·60 90

MS2513 Two sheets, each 112×140 mm. (a) Nos. 2507/9; (b) Nos. 2510/12 6·50 5·50

MS2514 141×111 mm. Nos. 2507/12 6·50 5·75

545 King Afonso V

1996. 550th Anniv of Alphonsine Collection of Statutes.

2515 **545** 350e. multicoloured 3·75 2·20

546 Perdigao

1996. Birth Centenary of Jose de Azeredo Perdigao (lawyer and Council of State member).

2516 **546** 47e. multicoloured 65 40

547 Aveiro

1996. District Arms (1st series). Multicoloured.

2517	47e. Type **547**	55	25
2518	78e. Beja	90	60
2519	80e. Braga	90	60
2520	98e. Braganca	1·10	65
2521	100e. Castelo Branco	1·10	75
2522	140e. Coimbra	1·60	1·00
MS2523	Two sheets, each 140×112 mm. (a) Nos. 2517/19; (b) Nos. 2520/2	7·00	6·50

See also Nos. 2579/**MS**85 and 2648/**MS**54.

548 Henry of Burgundy (governor of Portucale) and his Wife Theresa

1996. 900th Anniv of Foundation of County of Portucale by King Afonso VI of Leon and Castille.

2524	**548**	47e. multicoloured	65	40

549 Rojoes (Pork dish)

1996. Traditional Portuguese Dishes (1st series). Multicoloured.

2525	47e. Type **549**	60	35
2526	78e. Boticas trout	90	50
2527	80e. Oporto tripe	90	50
2528	98e. Baked cod with jacket potatoes	1·10	55
2529	100e. Aveiro eel	1·10	70
2530	140e. Peniche lobster	1·70	90

See also Nos. 2569/74.

550 Lisbon Postman, 1821

1996. 175th Anniv of Home Delivery Postal Service. Multicoloured.

2531	47e. Type **550**	55	25
2532	78e. Postman, 1854	90	65
2533	98e. Rural postman, 1893	1·10	70
2534	100e. Postman, 1939	1·10	80
2535	140e. Modern postman, 1992	1·60	1·00

551 King Manoel I in Shipyard

1996. 500th Anniv (1997) of Discovery of Sea-route to India by Vasco da Gama (1st issue). Multicoloured.

2536	47e. Type **551**	70	35
2537	78e. Departure from Lisbon	1·30	70
2538	98e. Fleet in Atlantic Ocean	1·50	85
2539	140e. Sailing around Cape of Good Hope	1·70	1·00
MS2540	141×113 mm. 315e. "Dream of King Manuel I" (illustration from Poem IV of *The Lusiads* by Luis de Camoes)	4·25	4·25

See also Nos. 2592/**MS**96 and 2665/**MS**80.

552 "Banknote"

1996. 150th Anniv of Bank of Portugal.

2541	**552**	78e. multicoloured	90	55

553 East Timorese Couple

1996. Rights of People of East Timor. Award of 1996 Nobel Peace Prize to Don Carlos Ximenes Belo and Jose Ramos Horton.

2542	**553**	140e. multicoloured	1·50	1·10

554 Clouds forming Map of Europe

1996. Organization for Security and Co-operation in Europe Summit Meeting, Lisbon. Sheet 95×110 mm.

MS2543	**554**	200e. multicoloured	3·00	3·00

555 Portuguese Galleon

1997. Sailing Ships of the India Shipping Line. Multicoloured.

2544	49e. Type **555**	50	35
2545	80e. "Principe da Beira" (nau)	1·20	75
2546	100e. Bow view of "Don Fernando II e Gloria" (sail frigate)	1·20	95
2547	140e. Stern view of "Don Fernando II e Gloria"	1·50	1·10

556 Youth with Flower

1997. "No to Drugs – Yes to Life" (anti-drugs campaign).

2548	**556**	80e. multicoloured	90	60

557 Arms

1997. Bicent of Managing Institute of Public Credit.

2549	**557**	49e. multicoloured	65	40

558 Desman eating Worm

1997. The Pyrenean Desman. Multicoloured.

2550	49e. Type **558**	70	40
2551	49e. Diving	70	40
2552	49e. With wet fur	70	40
2553	49e. Cleaning snout	70	40

559 Moorish Girl guarding Hidden Treasure

1997. Europa. Tales and Legends.

2554	**559**	100e. multicoloured	1·70	1·40
MS2555		140×107 mm. No. 2554 ×3	6·50	6·25

560 Surfing

1997. Adventure Sports. Multicoloured.

2556	49e. Type **560**	55	35
2557	80e. Skateboarding	95	65
2558	100e. In-line skating	1·10	85
2559	140e. Paragliding	1·50	1·10
MS2560	134×113 mm. 150e. B.M.X. cycling; 150e. Hang-gliding	4·00	3·00

561 Night Attack on Santarem Fortress

1997. 850th Anniv of Capture from the Moors of Santarem and Lisbon. Multicoloured.

2561	80e. Type **561**	85	65
2562	80e. Victorious King Afonso riding past Lisbon city walls	85	65
MS2563	140×113 mm. Nos. 2561/2 each ×2	4·25	4·00

562 Frois with Japanese Man

1997. 400th Death Anniv of Father Luis Frois (author of "The History of Japan"). Multicoloured.

2564	80e. Type **562**	1·20	75
2565	140e. Father Frois and church (vert)	1·60	1·10
2566	140e. Father Frois and flowers (vert)	1·60	1·10

563 Indian Children and Jose de Anchieta

1997. Death Anniversaries of Missionaries to Brazil. Multicoloured.

2567	140e. Type **563** (400th)	1·50	1·00
2568	350e. Antonio Vieira in pulpit (300th)	4·00	2·75

1997. Traditional Portuguese Dishes (2nd series). As T **549**. Multicoloured.

2569	10e. Scalded kid, Beira Baixa	10	10
2570	49e. Fried shad with bread-pap, Ribatejo	55	35
2571	80e. Lamb stew, Alentejo	90	60
2572	100e. Rich fish chowder, Algarve	1·10	80
2573	140e. Black scabbardfish fillets with maize, Madeira	1·60	1·10
2574	200e. Stewed octopus, Azores	2·20	1·60

564 Centre of Oporto

1997. "Lubrapex 97" Portuguese–Brazilian Stamp Exhibition, Oporto. UNESCO World Heritage Site. Sheet 121×85 mm.

MS2575	**564**	350e. multicoloured	4·25	4·25

565 Couple before Clerk

1997. 700th Anniv of Mutual Assurance in Portugal.

2576	**565**	100e. multicoloured	1·20	80

566 Laboratory, Lisbon

1997. 50th Anniv of National Laboratory of Civil Engineering.

2577	**566**	80e. multicoloured	90	50

567 King Dinis and Arms of Portugal and King Fernando IV and Arms of Castile and Leon

1997. 700th Anniv of Treaty of Alcanices (defining national frontiers).

2578	**567**	80e. multicoloured	90	50

568 Evora

1997. District Arms (2nd series). Multicoloured.

2579	10e. Type **568**	10	10
2580	49e. Faro	55	30
2581	80e. Guarda	80	55
2582	100e. Leiria	1·20	65
2583	140e. Lisbon	1·40	1·00
2584	200e. Portalegre	2·10	1·30
MS2585	Two sheets, each 140×112 mm. (a) Nos. 2579, 2581 and 2583; (b) Nos. 2480, 2582 and 2584	5·00	2·75

569 Chart by Lopo Homem-Reineis, 1519

1997. Portuguese Charts. Multicoloured.

2586	49e. Type **569**	45	25
2587	80e. Chart by Joao Freire, 1546	95	70
2588	100e. Planisphere by Diogo Ribeiro, 1529	1·10	75
2589	140e. Chart showing Tropic of Capricorn (anon), 1630	1·40	95
MS2590	139×112 mm. Nos. 2586/9	4·50	4·50

570 Queen Maria I and Mail Coach

1997. Bicentenary of State Postal Service.

2591	**570**	80e. multicoloured	90	50

571 Erecting Landmark Monument, Quelimane

1997. 500th Anniv of Discovery of Portugal–India Sea Route (2nd issue). Multicoloured.

2592	49e. Type **571**	50	35
2593	80e. Arrival of fleet at Mozambique	90	50
2594	100e. Arrival of fleet in Mombasa	1·10	80
2595	140e. King of Melinde greeting Vasco da Gama	1·50	1·00
MS2596	140×113 mm. 315e. Vasco da Gama on beach at Natal	4·00	4·00

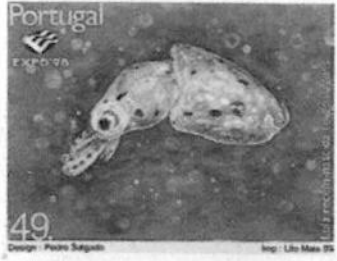

572 Squid

1997. "Expo'98" World Fair, Lisbon. Ocean Life (1st issue). Multicoloured.

2597	49e. Type **572**	50	35
2598	80e. Rock lobster larva	95	65
2599	100e. Adult "Pontellina plumata" (crustacean)	1·10	80
2600	140e. Senegal sole (pastlarva)	1·40	1·20
MS2601	110×150 mm. 100e. *Calcidiscus leptoporus*; 100e. *Tabellaria sp.* colonies	2·50	2·50

See also Nos. 2611/**MS**2615, 2621/**MS**2629 and 2630/41.

573 Sintra

1997. UNESCO World Heritage Site, Sintra. "Indepex 97" International Stamp Exhibition, New Delhi. Sheet 112×140 mm.

MS2602	**573** 350e. multicoloured	4·25	4·25

574 Officer and Plan of Almeida Fortress, 1848

1998. 350th Anniv of Portuguese Military Engineering. Multicoloured.

2603	50e. Type **574**	50	30
2604	80e. Officer and plan of Miranda do Oduro Fortress, 1834	1·10	65
2605	100e. Officer and plan of Moncao Fortress, 1797	1·30	70
2606	140e. Officer and plan of Elvas Fortress, 1806	1·50	1·10

575 Ivens and African Scene

1998. Death Centenary of Roberto Ivens (explorer).

2607	**575** 140e. multicoloured	1·50	1·00

576 Adoration of the Madonna (carving)

1998. 500th Anniv of Holy Houses Misericordia (religious social relief order).

2608	80e. Type **576**	90	50
2609	100e. Attending patient (tile mural)	1·00	85

577 Aqueduct over Alcantra

1998. 250th Anniv of Aqueduct of the Free Waters (from Sintra to Lisbon). Sheet 155×110 mm.

MS2610	**577** 350e. multicoloured	4·25	4·25

1998. "Expo '98" World's Fair, Lisbon (2nd issue). Ocean Life. As T **572**. Multicoloured.

2611	50e. Crab ("Pilumnus" sp.) larva	50	25
2612	85e. Monkfish ("Lophius piscatonis") larva	1·10	55
2613	100e. Gilthead sea bream ("Sparus aurata") larva	1·20	70
2614	140e. Medusa ("Cladonema radiatum")	1·40	1·00
MS2615	112×140 mm. 110e. Bioluminescent protozoan (*Noctiluca miliaris*); 110e. Dinoflagellate (*Dinophysis acuta*)	2·50	2·50

578 Vasco da Gama Bridge

1998. Opening of Vasco da Gama Bridge (from Sacavem to Montijo).

2616	**578** 200e. multicoloured	2·00	1·60
MS2617	125×85 mm. As No. 2616 but with background extended to edges	2·30	2·20

579 Coloured Balls

1998. 150th Anniv of Oporto Industrial Association.

2618	**579** 80e. multicoloured	90	50

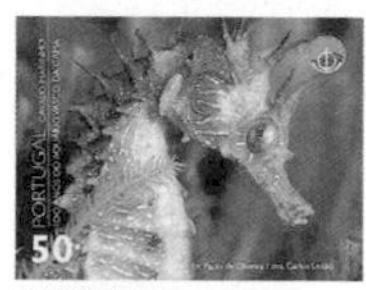

580 Seahorse

1998. International Year of the Ocean. Centenary of Vasco da Gama Aquarium. Multicoloured.

2619	50e. Type **580**	70	35
2620	80e. Angelfish and shoal	95	75

581 Diver and Astrolabe

1998. "Expo '98" World's Fair, Lisbon (3rd issue). (a) The Ocean. Multicoloured.

2621	50e. Type **581**	50	25
2622	50e. Caravel	50	25
2623	85e. Fishes and coral reef (inscr "oceanario")	90	55
2624	85e. Underwater exploration equipment observing fishes	90	55
2625	140e. Mermaid and sea anemones	1·70	1·00
2626	140e. Children with hands on globe	1·70	1·00

(b) Miniature Sheets. Designs as T **581**.

MS2627	154×116 mm. 50e. Portuguese Pavilion; 85e. Pavilion of the Future; 85e. Oceanarium; 140e. Knowledge of the Seas Pavilion; 140e. Pavilion of Utopia	6·25	6·25
MS2628	Two sheets, each 147×90 mm. (a) Nos. 2621/6; (b) 80e. Postal mascot; stamps as in No. **MS**2627	7·25	†
MS2629	148×151 mm. Nos. 2597/**MS**2601 and 2611/**MS**2615	14·50	†

(c) As Nos. 2611/14 (but with Latin names removed) and 2621/6. Size 29×23 mm. Self-adhesive.

2630	50e. As No. 2612	85	55
2631	50e. Bioluminescent protozoan	85	55
2632	50e. As No. 2611	85	55
2633	50e. As No. 2613	85	55
2634	50e. Dinoflagellate	85	55
2635	50e. As No. 2614	85	55
2636	85e. Type **581**	1·50	90
2637	85e. As No. 2624	1·50	90
2638	85e. As No. 2626	1·50	90
2639	85e. As No. 2622	1·50	90
2640	85e. As No. 2623 but inscr "Portugal e os Oceanos"	1·50	90
2641	85e. As No. 2625	1·50	90

The designers' names and printer's imprints have been removed from Nos. 2630/41.

582 Revellers before Statues of St. Antony of Padua, St. John and St. Peter

1998. Europa. National Festivals.

2642	**582** 100e. multicoloured	1·50	1·20
MS2643	140×108 mm. No. 2642 ×3	5·00	5·75

583 Marie Curie

1998. Centenary of Discovery of Radium.

2644	**583** 140e. multicoloured	1·40	90

584 Ferreira de Castro and Illustration to "The Jungle"

1998. Birth Centenary of Jose Ferreira de Castro (writer).

2645	**584** 50e. multicoloured	60	35

585 Untitled Painting

1998. Death Centenary of Bernardo Marques (artist).

2646	**585** 85e. multicoloured	90	65

586 Adam (Michelangelo) (detail from Sistine Chapel ceiling)

1998. "Juvalex '98" Stamp Exhibition. 50th Anniv of Universal Declaration of Human Rights. Sheet 90×55 mm.

MS2647	**586** 315e. multicoloured	3·50	3·50

1998. District Arms (3rd series). As T **568**. Multicoloured.

2648	50e. Vila Real	50	35
2649	85e. Setubal	1·30	80
2650	85e. Viana do Castelo (150th anniv of elevation to city)	1·30	80
2651	100e. Santarem	1·40	80
2652	100e. Viseu	1·40	80
2653	200e. Oporto	2·00	1·20
MS2654	Two sheets, each 140×113 mm. (a) Nos. 2648, 2650 and 2653; (b) Nos. 2649 and 2651/2	8·25	9·00

587 Glass Production

1998. 250th Anniv of Glass Production in Marinha Grande. Multicoloured.

2655	50e. Type **587**	50	25
2656	80e. Heating glass and finished product	95	65
2657	100e. Bottles and factory	1·00	70
2658	140e. Blue bottles and glass-maker	1·90	1·00

588 "Sagres II" (cadet barque), Portugal

1998. Vasco da Gama Regatta. Multicoloured.

2659	50e. Type **588**	50	30
2660	85e. "Asgard II" (Irish cadet brigantine)	1·20	60
2661	85e. "Rose" (American replica)	1·20	60
2662	100e. "Amerigo Vespucci" (Italian cadet ship)	1·30	80
2663	100e. "Kruzenshtern" (Russian cadet barque)	1·30	80
2664	140e. "Creoula" (Portuguese cadet schooner)	2·00	1·10

589 Da Gama with Pilot Ibn Madjid

1998. 500th Anniv (1997) of Discovery of Sea-route to India by Vasco da Gama (3rd issue). Mult.

2665	50e. Type **551**	75	45
2666	50e. As No. 2537	75	45
2667	50e. As No. 2538	75	45
2668	50e. As No. 2539	75	45
2669	50e. Type **571**	75	45
2670	50e. As No. 2593	75	45
2671	50e. As No. 2594	75	45
2672	50e. As No. 2595	75	45
2673	50e. Type **589**	95	60
2674	50e. "Sao Gabriel" (flagship) in storm	75	45
2675	50e. Fleet arriving at Calicut	75	45
2676	50e. Audience with the Samorin of Calicut	75	45
2677	80e. As No. 2674	1·00	70
2678	100e. As No. 2675	1·10	75
2679	140e. As No. 2676	1·40	90
MS2680	140×112 mm. 315e. King of Melinde listening to Vasco da Gama	4·00	4·00

590 Modern Mail Van

1998. Bicentenaries of Inauguration of Lisbon–Coimbra Mail Coach Service and of Re-organization of Maritime Mail Service to Brazil. Multicoloured.

2681	50e. Type **590**	50	35
2682	140e. Mail coach and "Postilhao da America" (brigantine)	1·80	1·10

591 Globe and Flags of participating Countries

1998. Eighth Iberian-American Summit of State Leaders and Govenors, Oporto. Sheet 90×55 mm.

MS2683	**591** 140e. multicoloured	1·70	1·60

592 Cave paintings

1998. Archeological Park, Coa Valley. Sheet 140×113 mm.

MS2684	**592** 350e. multicoloured	4·25	4·25

593 Male and Female Figures

1998. Health Awareness.
2685 **593** 100e. multicoloured 1·20 80

594 Saramago

1998. Jose Saramago (winner of Nobel prize for Literature, 1998). Sheet 140×114 mm.
MS2686 **594** 200e. multicoloured 2·40 2·40

DENOMINATION. From No. 2687 Portugal stamps are denominated both in escudos and in euros. As no cash for this latter is in circulation, the catalogue continues to use the escudo value.

595 Knife Grinder

1999. 19th-Century Itinerant Trades. Multicoloured. Self-adhesive.
2687 51e. Type **595** 50 35
2688 95e. Coachman 1·20 80

596 Flags of European Union Members and Euro Emblem

1999. Introduction of the Euro (European currency).
2696 **596** 95e. multicoloured 1·20 95

597 Galleon and Aborigines

1999. "Australia 99" International Stamp Exhibition, Melbourne. The Portuguese in Australia. Multicoloured.
2697 140e. Kangaroos and galleon 1·40 90
2698 140e. Type **597** 1·40 90
MS2699 137×104 mm. 350e. Motifs of Nos. 2697/8 (79×30 mm) 4·25 4·00
Nos. 2697/8 were issued together, se-tenant, forming a composite design.

598 Norton de Matos

1999. 50th Anniv of Candidature of General Jose Norton de Matos to Presidency of the Republic.
2700 **598** 80e. multicoloured 1·10 70

599 Almeida Garrett

1999. Birth Bicentenary of Joao Baptista Almeida Garrett (writer).
2701 **599** 95e. multicoloured 1·20 75
MS2702 130×105 mm. **599** 210e. multicoloured 2·50 2·40

600 Breguet Bre 16 Bri 2 *Patria*

1999. 25th Anniv of Sarmento de Beires and Brito Pais's Portugal–Macao Flight. Multicoloured.
2703 140e. Type **600** 1·60 1·00
2704 140e. Airco de Havilland D.H.9 biplane 1·60 1·00
MS2705 137×104 mm. Nos. 2703/4 3·25 3·25

601 Carnation

1999. 25th Anniv of Revolution. Multicoloured.
2706 51e. Type **601** 50 30
2707 80e. National Assembly building (78×29 mm) 90 60
MS2708 140×108 mm. Nos. 2706/7 1·60 1·60

602 Council Emblem

1999. 50th Anniv of Council of Europe.
2709 **602** 100e. multicoloured 1·40 1·10

603 Wolf and Iris (Peneda-Geres National Park)

1999. Europa. Parks and Gardens.
2710 **603** 100e. multicoloured 1·40 1·20
MS2711 154×109 mm. No. 2710×3 5·25 6·50

604 Marquis de Pombal

1993. 300th Birth Anniv of Marquis de Pombal (statesman and reformer). Multicoloured.
2712 80e. Type **604** 90 70
MS2713 170×135 mm. 80e. Head of Marquis and part of statue; 210e. Hand holding quill 3·50 2·75

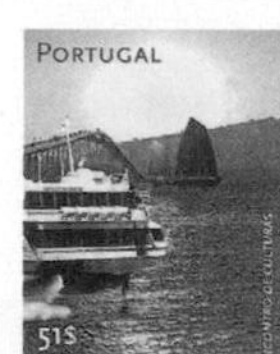

605 Harbour

1999. "Meeting of Cultures". Return of Macao to China. Multicoloured.
2714 51e. Type **605** 50 30
2715 80e. Dancers 90 55
2716 95e. Procession of the Madonna 95 80
2717 100e. Ruins of St. Paul's Basilica 1·20 80
2718 140e. Garden with bust of Luis Camoes (horiz) 1·60 95

606 de Havilland D.H.82A Tiger Moth

1999. 75th Anniv of Military Aeronautics. Multicoloured.
2719 51e. Type **606** 50 30
2720 51e. Supermarine Spitfire V6 fighter 50 30
2721 85e. Breguet Bre XIV-A2 1·20 65
2722 85e. SPAD VII-C1 1·20 65
2723 95e. Caudron G-3 1·40 75
2724 95e. Junkers Ju 52/3m 1·40 75
MS2725 150×117 mm. Nos. 2719/24 6·25 6·50

607 Portion by Antonio Pedro

1999. 50th Anniv of Surrealism (modern art movement) in Portugal. Designs showing details by artist named of collective painting "Cadavre Exquis". Multicoloured.
2726 51e. Type **607** 45 30
2727 80e. Vespeira 90 65
2728 95e. Moniz Pereira 95 70
2729 100e. Fernando de Azevedo 1·00 70
2730 140e. Antonio Domingues 1·50 1·00
MS2731 175×153 mm. Nos. 2726/30 forming a composite design of complete picture 4·75 5·25

608 Passenger Train on Bridge

1999. Inauguration of Railway Section of the 25th of April Bridge over River Tagus, Lisbon. Multicoloured.
2732 51e. Type **608** 50 30
2733 95e. Passenger train on bridge (different) 1·20 75
MS2734 Two sheets, each 140×110 mm. (a) 350e. Close-up of part of Type **608** (79×30 mm); (b) 350e. Close-up of part of No. 2733 (79×30 mm) 8·25 8·00

609 Heinrich von Stephan (founder)

1999. 125th Anniv of Universal Postal Union. Multicoloured.
2735 95e. Type **609** 95 70
2736 140e. Globe, letter and keyboard 1·40 90
MS2737 140×98 mm. 315e. Combination of motifs in Nos. 2735/6 (79×29 mm) 3·75 3·50

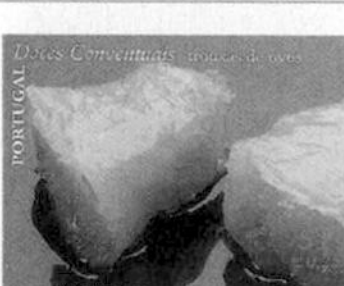

610 Egg Packs

1999. Convent Sweets (1st series). Multicoloured.
2738 51e. Type **610** 50 30
2739 80e. Egg pudding 85 50
2740 95e. Angel's purses 95 65
2741 100e. Abrantes straw 1·60 70
2742 140e. Viseu chestnuts 1·80 1·10
2743 210e. Honey cake 2·20 1·60
See also Nos. 2785/90.

611 Portuguese Troops and Moslem Ships

1999. 750th Anniv of King Afonso III's Conquest of the Algarve.
2744 **611** 100e. multicoloured 1·20 75

612 Camara Pestana (bacteriologist)

1999. Medical Anniversaries. Multicoloured.
2745 51e. Type **612** (death centenary) 50 30
2746 51e. Ricardo Jorge (founder of National Health Institute, 60th death anniv) 50 30
2747 80e. Francisco Gentil (oncologist, 35th death anniv) 85 65
2748 80e. Egas Moniz (neurosurgeon, 125th birth anniv) 85 65
2749 95e. Joao Cid dos Santos (surgeon, 23rd death anniv) 1·00 70
2750 95e. Reynaldo dos Santos (arteriography researcher, 30th death anniv (2000)) 1·00 70

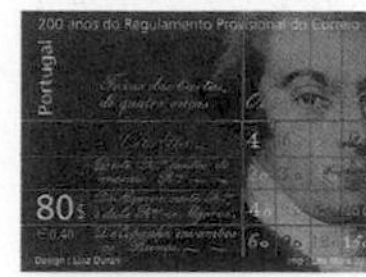

613 Jose Diogo de Mascarenhas Neto (first General Mail Lieutenant)

1999. Bicentenary of the Provisional Mail Rules (re-organization of postal system).
2751 **613** 80e. multicoloured 90 55

614 Barata, Stamps and Mural

1999. Birth Centenary of Jaime Martins Barata (artist and stamp designer).
2752 **614** 80e. multicoloured 90 55

615 Wise Men following Star (Maria Goncalves)

1999. Christmas. National Association of Art and Creativity for and by Handicapped Persons. Designs with artists name in brackets. Multicoloured.
2753 51e. Type **615** 45 30
2754 95e. Father Christmas delivering presents (Marta Silva) 95 65
2755 140e. Father Christmas (Luis Farinha) 2·00 95
2756 210e. The Nativity (Maria Goncalves) 2·40 1·30

616 Macanese Architecture

1999. Portuguese–Chinese Cultural Mix in Macao. Sheet 138×90 mm.
MS2757 **616** 140e. black and red 1·80 1·80

618 "Madonna and Child" (Alvaro Pires of Evora) Maia, Oporto)

2000. 2000th Birth Anniv of Jesus Christ.
2759 **618** 52e. multicoloured 80 40

619 Astronaut and Space Craft

2000. The Twentieth Century. Conquest of Space.
2760 **619** 86e. multicoloured 1·10 65

620 Golden Eagle

2000. Birds. (1st series). Multicoloured. (*a*) Ordinary gum. Size 30×27 mm.

2761	52e. Type **620**	50	35
2762	85e. Great crested grebe	90	65
2763	90e. Greater flamingo	90	70
2764	100e. Northern gannet	1·60	80
2765	215e. Green-winged teal	2·75	1·60

(b) Self-adhesive gum. Size 28×25 mm.

2766	52e. As No. 2761	55	35
2767	100e. As No. 2764	1·00	80

See also Nos. 2832/9.

621 Crowd and Suffragettes

2000. The Twentieth Century (2nd issue). Three sheets, each 190×220 mm, containing T **621** and similar multicoloured designs.

MS2768 (a) 52e. Type **621** (Human Rights); 52e. Fashion through the century (59×29 mm); 52e. Windmills, electricity pylon and birds (ecology) (59×39 mm); 52e. Early airplanes, car, stylised streamlined high speed train and ship (transport); 52e. As No. 2760; 52e. Space shuttle on launch pad (conquest of Space). (b) 52e. Marcel Proust and Thomas Marin (novelists), James Joyce (writer), Franz Kafka (novelist), Fernando Pessoa (poet), Jorge Luis Borges and Samuel Beckett (writers) (literature) (49×29 mm); 52e. Achille-Claude Debussy, Igor Stravinsky, Arnold Schoenberg, Bela Bartok, George Gershwin (composers), Charlie Parker (saxophonist) and William (Bill) Evans (pianist) (music) (49×29 mm); 52e. Performers (theatre); 52e. Auditorium and performers (theatre) (59×29 mm); 52e. Sculptures and paintings (art) (49×29 mm); 52e. Abstract art (29×29 mm); 52e. Charlie Chaplin on left (cinema) (49×29 mm); 52e. Woody Allen on left (cinema and television) (29×29 mm); 52e. Old and modern buildings (architecture); 52e. Modern buildings (architecture); 52e. Front and aerial views of modern buildings (architecture). (c) 52e. Edmund Husser, Ludwig Wittgenstein and Martin Heidegger (philosophy); 52e. Jules Poincare, Kurt Godel and Andrei Kolmogorov (mathematics); 52e. Max Planck, Albert Einstein and Niels Bohr (physics) (49×29 mm); 52e. Franz Boas (anthropologist), Levi Strauss (clothing manufacturer) and Margaret Mead (anthropologist) (social science and medicine); 52e. Sigmund Freud (neurologist) and Alexander Fleming (bacteriologist) (social science and medicine) (29×29 mm); 52e. Christiaan Barnard performing operation (organ transplant surgeon) (medicine); 52e. Office workers, Joseph Schumpeter and John Keynes (economics); 52e. Circuit boards (technology); 52e. Fibre optics (technology) (29×29 mm); 52e. Binary code, Alan Tuning (mathematician) and John von Neuman (mathematician) (information technology and telecommunications); 52e. Guglielmo Marconi (physicist) and satellite aerials (information technology and telecommunications); 52e. Binary code and satellite (information technology and telecommunications) (29×29 mm) 22·00 20·00

622 Members' Flags forming Stars

2000. Portuguese Presidency of European Union Council.

2769	**622**	100e. multicoloured	1·50	1·20

623 Native Indians

2000. 500th Anniv of Discovery of Brazil. Multicoloured.

2770	52e. Type **623**	60	40
2771	85e. Native Indians watching Pedro Alvares Cabral's fleet	1·10	75
2772	100e. Ship's crew and sails	1·60	95
2773	140e. Native Indians and Portuguese sailors meeting	1·80	1·30
MS2774	140×140 mm. Nos. 2770/3	5·00	3·50

624 "Building Europe"

2000. Europa.

2775	**624**	100e. multicoloured	2·00	1·70
MS2776		154×109 mm. No. 2775 ×3	6·25	7·75

625 Pope John Paul II and Children

2000. Papal Visit to Portugal. Beatification of Jacinta and Francisco Marto (Children of Fatima).

2777	**625**	52e. multicoloured	75	45

626 Draisienne Bicycle, 1817

2000. "The Stamp Show 2000" International Stamp Exhibition, London. Centenary of International Cycling Union. Bicycles. Mult.

2778	52e. Type **626**	55	40
2779	85e. Michaux, 1868	1·60	75
2780	100e. Ariel, 1871	1·20	95
2781	140e. Rover, 1888	1·90	1·30
2782	215e. BTX, 2000	3·00	1·90
2783	350e. GT, 2000	4·50	3·25
MS2784	140×112 mm. Nos. 2778/83	12·50	12·00

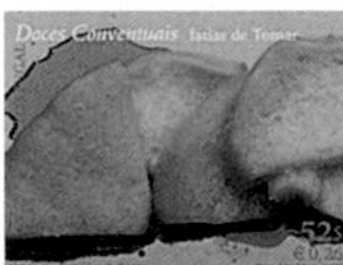
627 Slices of Tomar

2000. Convent Sweets (2nd series). Multicoloured.

2785	52e. Type **627**	55	40
2786	85e. Rodrigo's present	1·60	75
2787	100e. Sericaia	1·20	95
2788	140e. Lo bread	1·90	1·30
2789	215e. Grated bread	3·00	1·90
2790	350e. Royal paraiso cake	4·50	3·25

628 Fishing Boat and Fish

2000. Fishermen's Day.

2791	**628**	52e. multicoloured	75	45

629 Portuguese Landscapes (image scaled to 55% of original size)

2000. "EXPO 2000" World's Fair, Hanover, Germany. Humanity–Nature–Technology. Mult.

2792	100e. Type **629**	1·20	90
MS2793	140×113 mm. 350e. Portuguese Pavilion, Hanover (39×30 mm)	4·00	4·00

630 Statue and Assembly Hall

2000. 25th Anniv of Constituent Assembly.

2794	**630**	85e. multicoloured	1·10	75

631 Fishermen and Boat

2000. Cod Fishing. Multicoloured.

2795	52e. Type **631**	55	40
2796	85e. Fishing barquentine and fisherman at ship's wheel	1·10	75
2797	100e. Three fishermen and boat	1·20	90
2798	100e. Fisherman and dories on fishing schooner	1·20	90
2799	140e. Fisherman rowing and fishing barquentine	1·90	1·20
2800	215e. Fisherman and fishing schooner	2·75	1·90
MS2801	140×112 mm. Nos. 2795/2800	9·50	9·75

632 De Queiroz

2000. Death Centenary of Eca de Queiroz (author).

2802	**632**	85e. multicoloured	1·10	75

633 Running

2000. Olympic Games, Sydney. Multicoloured.

2803	52e. Type **633**	55	40
2804	85e. Show jumping	1·10	75
2805	100e. Dinghy racing	1·20	90
2806	140e. Diving	1·70	1·20
MS2807	140×112 mm. 85e. Fencing; 215e. Beach volleyball	4·50	4·25

Nos. 2803/6 are wrongly inscribed "Sidney".

634 Airbus A310 and Runway

2000. Inauguration of Madeira Airport Second Runway Extension.

2808	**634**	140e. multicoloured	1·90	1·30
MS2809		110×80 mm. 140e. multicoloured	1·90	2·00

635 Writing Letter on Computer

2000. 50th Anniv of Snoopy (cartoon character created by Charles Schulz). Postal Service. Multicoloured.

2810	52e. Type **635**	55	40
2811	52e. Posting letter	55	40
2812	85e. Driving post van	1·10	75
2813	100e. Sorting post	1·40	90
2814	140e. Delivering post	1·90	1·20
2815	215e. Reading letter	2·40	1·90
MS2816	140×112 mm. Nos. 2810/15	9·25	9·75

636 Drawing, Telescope and Sextant

2000. 125th Anniv of Lisbon Geographic Society. Multicoloured.

2817	85e. Type **636**	1·10	75
2818	100e. Sextant and drawing	1·40	1·00

Nos. 2817/18 were issued together, se-tenant, forming a composite design.

637 Carolina Michaelis de Vasconcellos (teacher)

2001. The Twentieth Century. History and Culture. Multicoloured.

2819	85e. Type **637**	1·00	80
2820	85e. Miguel Bombarda (doctor and politician)	1·00	80
2821	85e. Bernardino Machado (politician)	1·00	80
2822	85e. Tomas Alcaide (lyricist)	1·00	80
2823	85e. Jose Regio (writer)	1·00	80
2824	85e. Jose Rodrigues Migueis (writer)	1·00	80
2825	85e. Vitorino Nemesio (scholar)	1·00	80
2826	85e. Bento de Jesus Caraca (scholar)	1·00	80

638 Athletics

2001. World Indoor Athletics Championship, Lisbon. Multicoloured.

2827	85e. Type **638**	1·10	85
2828	90e. Pole vault	1·10	90
2829	105e. Shot put	1·40	95
2830	250e. High jump	3·25	2·20
MS2831	122×100 mm. 350e. hurdles	4·75	4·75

2001. Birds (2nd series). As T **620**. Multicoloured. (a) Ordinary gum. Size 27×25 mm.

2832	53e. Little bustard	60	45
2833	85e. Purple swamphen	95	75
2834	105e. Collared Pratincole	1·20	90
2835	140e. Black-shouldered kite	1·60	1·30
2836	225e. Egyptian vulture	2·75	2·10

(b) Self-adhesive gum. (i) Size 25×21 mm.

2837	53e. As No. 2832	75	45
2838	105e. As No. 2834	1·30	1·00

(ii) Size 48×22 mm.

2839	85e. Purple swamphen	1·30	85

No. 2839 is inscribed "CorreioAzul".

639 Decorated Dish

2001. Arab Artefacts. Multicoloured.

2840	53e. Type **639**	60	40
2841	90e. Painted tile	1·10	80
2842	105e. Carved stone tablet and fortress	1·40	95
2843	140e. Coin	2·40	1·30
2844	225e. Carved container	3·00	2·00
2845	350e. Jug	4·25	3·25

640 Coastal Environment (Angela M. Lopes)

2001. "Stampin' the Future". Winning Entries in Children's International Painting Competition. Multicoloured.

2846	85e. Type **640**	1·00	75
2847	90e. Earth, Sun and watering can (Maria G. Silva) (vert)	1·10	80
2848	105e. Marine life (Joao A. Ferreira)	1·20	95

641 Statue, Building Facade and Stained Glass Window

2001. Centenary of National Fine Arts Society. Multicoloured.
2849 85e. Type **641** 1·00 75
2850 105e. Painting and woman holding palette and brush 1·20 1·00
MS2851 105×80 mm. 350e. "Hen with Chicks" (detail) (Girao) 4·75 4·75

642 Congress in Session

2001. 25th Anniv of Portuguese Republic Constitution.
2852 **642** 85e. multicoloured 1·10 80

643 Fishes

2001. Europa. Water Resources.
2853 **643** 105e. multicoloured 1·70 1·40
MS2854 140×110 mm. No. 2853 ×3 5·50 6·50

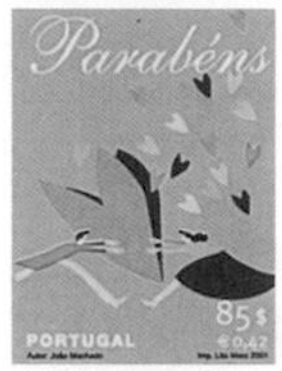

644 Couple and Heart

2001. Greetings Stamps. Multicoloured.
2855 85e. Type **644** 1·10 85
2856 85e. Birthday cake 1·10 85
2857 85e. Glasses 1·10 85
2858 85e. Bunch of flowers 1·10 85
MS2859 91×110 mm. Nos. 2855/8 4·25 4·00

645 Open Book

2001. Porto, European City of Culture. Multicoloured.
2860 53e. Type **645** 60 45
2861 85e. Bridge and Globe 1·10 70
2862 105e. Grand piano 1·20 95
2863 140e. Stage curtain 1·60 1·30
2864 225e. Picture frame 2·75 2·10
2865 350e. Firework display 4·00 3·25
MS2866 140×110 mm. Nos. 2861/6 12·00 11·00

646 Campaign Cannon, 1773

2001. 150th Anniv of Military Museum, Lisbon. Multicoloured.
2867 85e. Type **646** 1·10 80
2868 105e. 16th-century armour 1·40 1·10
MS2869 140×112 mm. 53e. Pistol of King Jose I, 1757; 53e. Cannon on carriage, 1797; 140e. Cannon "Tigre", 1533; 140e. 15th-century helmet 5·00 4·50

647 Brown Bear

2001. Lisbon Zoo. Multicoloured.
2870 53e. Type **647** 55 40
2871 85e. Emperor tamarin 1·00 75
2872 90e. Green iguana 1·00 85
2873 105e. Humboldt penguin 1·30 1·00
2874 225e. Toco toucan 2·75 2·10
2875 350e. Giraffe 4·00 3·25
MS2876 140×112 mm. 85e. Indian elephant (29×38 mm); 85e. Grevy's zebra (29×39 mm); Lion (29×38 mm); White rhinoceros (29×38 mm) 8·00 6·50

648 Emblem

2001. 47th Lion's European Forum, Oporto.
2877 **648** 85e. multicoloured 1·10 75

649 Azinhoso Pillory

2001. Pillories. Multicoloured.
2878 53e. Type **649** 60 45
2879 53e. Soajo 60 45
2880 53e. Braganca 60 45
2881 53e. Linhares 60 45
2882 53e. Arcos de Valdevez 60 45
2883 53e. Vila de Rua 60 45
2884 53e. Sernancelhe 60 45
2885 53e. Frechas 60 45

650 Faces

2001. United Nations Year of Dialogue among Civilizations.
2886 **650** 140e. multicoloured 1·60 1·20

651 Disney

2001. Birth Centenary of Walt Disney (artist and film producer).
2887 53e. Type **651** 65 50
MS2888 160×132 mm. 53e. Huey, Dewey and Louie, and 15th-century Mudejares tiles; 53e. Mickey Mouse and 16th-century tiles forming coat of arms; 53e. Minnie Mouse and 17th-century religious allegory tiles; 53e. Goofy and 18th-century tiles of birds; 53e. Type **651**; 53e. Pluto and 19th-century tile design by Rafael Bordalo Pinheiro; 53e. Donald Duck and 19th-century tiles; 53e. Scrooge McDuck and 20th-century "Querubim Lapa" tiles; 53e. Daisy Duck and 20th-century tile designs by Manuel Cargaleiro 8·00 7·00

652 Royal Police Guard, 1801

2001. Bicentenary of National Guard. Multicoloured.
2889 53e. Type **652** 60 50
2890 85e. Lisbon Municipal Guard bandsman, 1834 1·00 75
2891 90e. Infantry helmet, 1911 and modern guardsman 1·00 80
2892 105e. Mounted division helmet of 1911 and modern guardsmen 1·20 95
2893 140e. Guardsmen with motor-cycle and car 1·60 1·20
2894 350e. Customs and Excise officer and boat 4·25 3·00
MS2895 117×90 mm. 225e. Mounted division helmet and guardsman of 1911 3·00 3·00

653 Chinese Junk

2001. Ships. Multicoloured.
2896 53e. Type **653** 65 50
2897 53e. Portuguese caravel 65 50

654 1c. Coin

2002. New Currency. Multicoloured.
2898 1c. Type **654** 10 10
2899 2c. 2c. coin 10 10
2900 5c. 5c. coin 15 10
2901 10c. 10c. coin 20 15
2902 20c. 20c. coin 45 35
2903 50c. 50c. coin 1·10 90
2904 €1 €1 coin 2·50 1·80
2905 €2 €2 coin 4·75 3·50

655 Horse-rider

2002. No value expressed.
2906 **655** A (28c.) multicoloured 65 50
No. 2906 was sold at the current first class inland letter rate.

657 European Bee-eater

2002. Birds (1st series). Multicoloured. (i) Ordinary gum. Size 30×26 mm.
2914 2c. Type **657** 10 10
2915 28c. Little tern 70 50
2916 43c. Eagle owl 1·00 80
2917 54c. Pin-tailed sandgrouse 1·30 95
2918 60c. Red-necked nightjar 1·40 1·10
2919 70c. Greater spotted cuckoo 1·70 1·30

(ii) Self-adhesive gum. Size 49×23 mm.
2920 43c. Little tern (different) 1·30 85

(iii) Self-adhesive gum. Size 29×24 mm.
2921 28c. As No. 2919 75 55
2922 54c. As No. 2916 1·30 1·00

(iiii) Self-adhesive gum. Size 27×23 mm.
2923 28c. As No. 2919 1·00 70
2924 54c. As No. 2916 1·70 1·10
See also Nos. 2988/92.

658 De Gois

2002. 500th Birth Anniv of Damiao de Gois (writer).
2925 **658** 45c. multicoloured 1·10 80

659 Loxodromic Curve, Ship and Globe

2002. 500th Birth Anniv of Pedro Nunes (mathematician). Multicoloured.
2926 28c. Type **659** 65 50
2927 28c. Nonius (navigational instrument) 65 50
2928 €1.15 Portrait of Nunes 2·75 2·10
MS2929 140×105 mm Nos. 2926/8 4·25 4·00

660 Children and Flower

2002. America. Youth, Education and Literacy. Multicoloured.
2930 70c. Type **660** 1·60 1·30
2931 70c. Children, book and letters 1·60 1·30
2932 70c. Children and pencil 1·60 1·30

661 Refracting Telescope and Polytechnic School Observatory, Lisbon

2002. Astronomy. Multicoloured.
2933 28c. Type **661** 65 50
2934 28c. 16th-century astrolabe and Colegio dos Nobres, Lisbon 65 50
2935 43c. Quadrant and Solar Observatory, Coimbra 1·00 80
2936 45c. Terrestrial telescope and King Pedro V 1·00 80
2937 45c. Cassegrain telescope and King Luis 1·00 80
2938 54c. Earth, refracting telescope and Observatory, Ajuda 1·30 1·00
2939 €1.15 Cassegrain telescope and Saturn 2·75 2·10
2940 €1.75 Zeiss projector and planets 4·00 3·25
MS2941 140×111 mm. 70c. 18th-century armillary sphere; 70c. 19th-century theodolite 3·75 3·75

662 Square and Compass

2002. Bicentenary of Grande Oriente Lusitano (Masonic Grand Lodge).
2942 **662** 43c. multicoloured 1·10 80

663 Clown

2002. Europa. Circus.
2943 **663** 54c. multicoloured 2·00 1·60
MS2944 140×110 mm No. 2943×3 6·25 7·75

664 *Scabiosa nitens*

2002. Flowers of Azores. Multicoloured.
2945 28c. Type **664** 65 50
2946 45c. *Viburnum tinus subcordatum* 1·00 75
2947 54c. *Euphorbia azorica* 1·20 95
2948 70c. *Lysimachia nemorum azorica* 1·60 1·30
2949 €1.15 *Bellis azorica* 2·75 2·10
2950 €1.75 *Spergularia azorica* 4·00 3·25
MS2951 120×121 mm €1.15 *Azorina vidalli*; €1.75 *Senecio malvifolius* 6·75 6·50

665 Lockheed Martin (General Dynamics) F-16 Fighting Falcon

2002. 50th Anniv of Portuguese Air Force. Multicoloured.
2952 28c. Type **665** 65 50
2953 43c. Sud Aviation SA300 Puma helicopter 1·00 80
2954 54c. Dassault Dornier Alphajet A 1·20 95
2955 70c. Lockheed C-130 Hercules transport aircraft 1·60 1·30
2956 €1.25 Lockheed P-3P Orion reconnaissance aircraft 2·75 2·20
2957 €1.75 Fiat G-91 fighter aircraft 4·00 3·00
MS2958 140×112 mm €1.15 Four Cessna T-37; €1.75 Aerospatiale TB30 Epsilon and Cessna T-37 7·25 7·00

666 Gymnastics

2002. Sports and Sports Anniversaries. Multicoloured.

No.	Description	Unused	Used
2959	28c. Type **666** (50th anniv of Portuguese Gymnastic Federation)	60	50
2960	28c. Walking race	60	50
2961	45c. Basketball	1·00	80
2962	45c. Handball	1·00	80
2963	54c. Roller hockey (sixth Women's World Roller Hockey Championship, Pacos de Ferriera)	1·20	95
2964	54c. Fencing (World Fencing Championship, Lisbon)	1·20	95
2965	€1.75 Footballers (World Cup Football Championship, Japan and South Korea)	3·75	3·00
2966	€1.75 Golf	3·75	3·00
MS2967	140×110 mm. €1 Footballer and part of football; €2 Torsos and legs of two players	7·00	5·75

Nos. **MS**2967 was inscribed for "PHILAKOREA 2002" International Stamp Exhibition, Seoul, in the margin.

667 Globe and Emblem

2002. 13th World International Economic Association Congress.

No.	Description	Unused	Used
2968	**667** 70c. multicoloured	1·60	1·20

668 Anniversary Emblem

2002. 150th Anniv of Ministry of Public Works, Transport and Housing. Multicoloured.

No.	Description	Unused	Used
2969	43c. Type **668**	1·00	75
MS2970	144×123 mm. 43c. ×6, Ship and oil terminal; Locomotive; Stylised Boeing 737; Bridge and city skyline; Factories; Houses	6·50	5·00

669 Portrait and Symbols of Industry and Agriculture

2002. 150th Anniv of Technical Education.

No.	Description	Unused	Used
2971	**669** 43c. multicoloured	1·00	75

670 Virgin and Child (statue) and Window, Alcobaca Monastery

2002. UNESCO World Heritage Sites. Multicoloured.

No.	Description	Unused	Used
2972	28c. Type **670**	60	50
2973	28c. Lion (statue) and embossed ceiling, Jeronimos Monastery	60	50
2974	43c. Column capitals, Guimaraes	95	75
2975	43c. Cherub (statue) and vineyards, Alto Douro	95	75
2976	54c. Corbel, lake and vineyards, Alto Douro (horiz) (80×30 mm)	1·20	95
2977	54c. Houses and statues, Guimaraes (horiz) (80×30 mm)	1·20	95
2978	70c. Carved arch and statue, Jeronimos Monastery (horiz) (80×30 mm)	1·60	1·20
2979	70c. Nave and tomb, Alcobaca Monastery (horiz) (80×30 mm)	1·60	1·20
MS2980	Four sheets, each 141×114 mm. (a) €1.25 Door and statue, Alcobaca Monastery; (b) €1.25 Double doors, Jeronimos Monastery; (c) €1.25 Arches, Guimaraes; (d) €1.25 Grapes, Alto Douro	12·00	9·75

671 1870 Dress Uniform

2003. Bicentenary of Military College, Luz. Multicoloured.

No.	Description	Unused	Used
2981	20c. Type **671**	40	35
2982	30c. 1806 uniform	65	50
2983	43c. 1837 parade uniform	95	75
2984	55c. 1861 uniform (rear view)	1·20	95
2985	70c. 1866 dress uniform	1·60	1·30
2986	€2 1912 cavalry cadet uniform	4·50	3·50
MS2987	141×114 mm. €1 1802 uniform; €1 1948 Porta Guiao dress uniform	4·75	4·00

2003. Birds (2nd series). As T **657**. Multicoloured. (a) Ordinary gum.

No.	Description	Unused	Used
2988	1c. Green woodpecker	10	10
2989	30c. Rock dove	70	50
2990	43c. Blue thrush	1·00	75
2991	55c. Sub-alpine warbler	1·30	95
2992	70c. Black-eared wheatear	1·60	1·20

(b) Self-adhesive gum. Size 27×23 mm.

No.	Description	Unused	Used
2992a	30c. No. 2989	75	50
2992b	43c. No. 2990 (50×23 mm)	1·00	80
2992c	55c. No. 2991	1·80	1·20

No. 2992b is inscribed "CorreioAzul".

672 People forming Mobility Symbol

2003. European Year of the Disabled. Multicoloured.

No.	Description	Unused	Used
2993	30c. Type **672**	75	50
2994	55c. People forming head shape	1·30	95
2995	70c. As No. 2994 but with eyes, ears and mouth pink	1·60	1·20

673 1853 5r. Stamp and Queen Donna Maria II

2003. 150th Anniv of First Postage Stamp (1st issue). Designs showing 1853 stamps. Multicoloured.

No.	Description	Unused	Used
2996	30c. Type **673**	65	50
2997	43c. 25r. stamp and coin	95	75
2998	55c. 50r. stamp and portrait	1·20	95
2999	70c. 100r. stamp and arms	1·60	1·20

See also Nos. 3011 and **MS**3047.

674 *Orchis italica*

2003. Orchids. Multicoloured.

No.	Description	Unused	Used
3000	46c. *Aceras anthropophorum*	1·00	80
3001	46c. *Dactylorhiza maculate*	1·00	80
MS3002	Two sheets, each 113×140 mm. (a) 30c. Type **674**; 30c. *Ophrys tenthredinifera*; 30c. *Ophrys fusca fusca*; 30c. *Orchis papilionacea*; 30c. *Barlia robertiana*; 30c. *Ophrys lutea*; 30c. *Ophrys fusca*; 30c. *Ophrys apifera*; 30c. *Dactylorhiza ericetorum*. (b) 30c. *Orchis champagneuxii*; 30c. *Orchis morio*; 30c. *Serapias cordigera*; 30c. *Orchis coriophora*; 30c. *Ophrys bombyliflora*; 30c. *Ophrys vernixia*; 30c. *Ophrys speculum*; 30c. *Ophrys scoplopax*; 30c. *Anacamptis pyramidalis*	14·00	11·00

675 Jazz Festival (Joao Machado)

2003. Europa. Poster Art. Multicoloured.

No.	Description	Unused	Used
3003	55c. Type **675**	1·60	1·20
3004	55c. Woman wearing swimsuit ("Espimho") (Fred Kradolfer)	1·60	1·20
MS3005	140×113 mm. Nos. 3004/5	3·25	3·50

676 Lawyer and Union Seal

2003. International Lawyer's Congress, Lisbon. Multicoloured.

No.	Description	Unused	Used
3006	30c. Type **676**	65	50
3007	43c. Lawyers, arms and Court building	95	75
3008	55c. Medieval lawyer, Bishop and legal document	1·20	95
3009	70c. Lawyer's union presidential medal and female lawyer	1·60	1·20
MS3010	140×113 mm. €1 Lawyer wearing red robe and seal; €2 Seal, painted plaque and bishop	7·00	5·50

677 "150" and Stamp (Viseu)

2003. 150th Anniv of Portuguese First Stamp (2nd issue). Itinerant Exhibition.

No.	Description	Unused	Used
3011	**677** 30c. multicoloured	80	50
3012	**677** 30c. multicoloured	80	50
3013	**677** 30c. multicoloured	80	50

678 Championship Emblem

2003. Euro 2004 Football Championship, Portugal (1st issue).

No.	Description	Unused	Used
3014	**678** 30c. multicoloured	70	50
3015	**678** 43c. multicoloured	1·00	75
3016	**678** 47c. multicoloured	1·10	85
3017	**678** 55c. multicoloured	1·30	95
3018	**678** 70c. multicoloured	1·60	1·20
MS3019	(a) 140×109 mm. 55c. ×4, Parts of championship emblem. (b) 190×200 mm. Nos. 3014/18 and **MS**3019a	5·25	4·25

See also Nos. **MS**3072, 3073/4, 3084/**MS**88, 3110/17, 3119/28 and **MS**3147.

679 Open-topped Car

2003. Centenary of Portuguese Automobile Club. Multicoloured.

No.	Description	Unused	Used
3020	30c. Type **679**	65	50
3021	43c. Club engineer riding motorcycle	95	75
3022	€2 Racing cars	4·50	3·50

680 Ricardo do Espirito Santo Silva

2003. 50th Anniv of Ricardo do Espirito Santo Silva Foundation. Multicoloured.

No.	Description	Unused	Used
3023	30c. Type **680**	60	50
3024	30c. 18th-century inlaid chess table	60	50
3025	43c. Cutlery box, 1720–1750	95	75
3026	43c. 15th-century silver tray	95	75
3027	55c. 18th-century wooden container	1·20	95
3028	55c. Ming dynasty ceramic box	1·20	95
MS3029	140×112 mm. €1 17th-century cupboard; €1 18th-century tapestry	7·00	5·50

681 "Bay of Funchal" (W. G. James) (1839)

2003. Museums of Madeira. Black (No. MS3034) or multicoloured (others).

No.	Description	Unused	Used
3030	30c. Type **681**	60	50
3031	43c. Nativity (straw sculpture, Manuel Orlando Noronha Gois)	1·00	75
3032	55c. "O Largo da Fonte" (Andrew Picken) (1840)	1·30	95
3033	70c. "Le Depart" (Martha Teles) (1983)	1·50	1·20
MS3034	140×112 mm. €1 Vicente Gomes da Silva (photograph); €2 Jorge Bettencourt (photograph)	6·75	5·25

682 Curved Shape containing "EXD"

2003. ExperimentaDesign2003 (design exhibition). Sheet containing T **682** and similar curved designs. Either black (30c.) or black and red (others). Self-adhesive.

No.	Description	Unused	Used
3035	30c. Type **682**	65	50
3036	30c. "EXD" centrally	65	50
3037	30c. "EXD" bottom	65	50
3038	30c. "EXD" left	65	50
3039	43c. As No. 3038 but design reversed	95	75
3040	43c. As No. 3037 but design reversed	95	75
3041	43c. As No. 3036 but design reversed	95	75
3042	43c. As No. 3035 but design reversed	95	75
3043	55c. As No. 3035	1·20	90
3044	55c. As No. 3036	1·20	90
3045	55c. As No. 3037	1·20	90
3046	55c. As No. 3038	1·20	90

683 Queen Maria II

2003. 150th Anniv of First Portuguese Stamp (3rd issue). Four sheets, each 140×112 mm containing T **683** and similar multicoloured designs.

No.	Description	Unused	Used
MS3047	(a) 30c. Type **683**; 30c. ×4 No. 2996 ×4 (25.9); (b) €1 Queen Maria II and euro coins (90×40 mm) (12.12); (c) €2.50 Seal and postal marks (80×30 mm) (23.9); (d) €3 King Pedro V, 1853 25r. stamp and Queen Maria II (80×30 mm)	18·00	15·00

684 St. John's Well, Vila Real

2003. America. Fountains. Multicoloured.

No.	Description	Unused	Used
3048	30c. Type **684**	60	50
3049	43c. Fountain of Virtues, Porto	95	75
3050	55c. Fountain, Giraldo Square, Evora	1·20	95
3051	70c. Senora da Saude fountain, St. Marcos de Tavira	1·50	1·20
3052	€1 Town fountain, Castelo de Vide	2·20	1·70
3053	€2 St. Andreas fountain, Guarda	4·25	2·40

685 Jose I engraved Glass Tumbler (18th-century)

2003. Glass Production. Multicoloured.

3054	30c. Type **685**	60	50
3055	55c. Maria II engraved tumbler (19th-century)	1·20	95
3056	70c. Blue glass vase (Carmo Valente) (20th-century)	1·50	1·20
3057	€2 Bulbous vase (Helena Matos) (20th-century)	4·25	3·50
MS3058	140×112 mm. €1.50 Stained glass window (detail) (Fernando Santos) (19th-century)	3·50	2·75

686 Persian Medicine Jar and Roman Dropper

2003. Medicine and Pharmacy. Multicoloured.

3059	30c. Type **686**	60	50
3060	43c. Ceramic bottle and jar	95	75
3061	55c. Pestle and mortar	1·20	95
3062	70c. Still and glass bottle	1·50	1·20

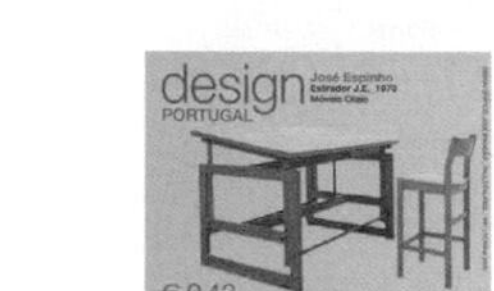

687 Drawing Board and Chair (Jose Epinho)

2003. Contemporary Design. Multicoloured.

3063	43c. Type **687**	95	75
3064	43c. Telephone point (Pedro Silva Dias) (vert)	95	75
3065	43c. Tea trolley (Cruz de Carvlho)	95	75
3066	43c. Tap (Carlos Aguiar)	95	75
3067	43c. Desk (Daciano da Costa)	95	75
3068	43c. Knives (Eduardo Afonso Dias)	95	75
3069	43c. Stacking chairs (Leonor and Antonio Sena da Silva)	95	75
3070	43c. Flask (Carlos Rocha) (vert)	95	75
3071	43c. Chair (Antonio Garcia) (vert)	95	75

688 Championship Emblem

2003. Euro 2004 Football Championship, Portugal (2nd issue). Stadiums (2nd issue). Sheet 150×165 mm containing T **688** and similar horiz designs. Multicoloured.

MS3072	30c.×10 Type **688**; Municipal stadium, Aveiro; Dr. Magalhaes Pessoa stadium, Leiria; Luz stadium, Lisbon; D. Afonso Henriques stadium, Guimaraes; Municipal stadium, Coimbra; Bessa stadium, Porto; Dragao stadium, Porto; Algarve stadium, Faro-Loule; Jose Alvalade stadium, Lisbon	12·00	6·00

689 Kinas

2004. European Football Championship 2004, Portugal (3rd series). Mascot. Multicoloured. Self-adhesive.

3073	45c. Type **689** (postage)	95	80
3074	€1.75 Kinas and football (air)	3·75	3·00

No. 3073 was inscribed "CorreioAzul". No. 3074 was inscribed "Airmail Priority".

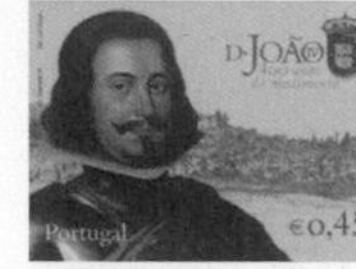

690 King Joao IV and Vila Vicosa

2004. 400th Birth Anniv of King Joao IV. Multicoloured.

3075	45c. Type **690**	95	80
3076	€1 King Joao standing	2·20	1·80

Nos. 3075/6 were issued together, se-tenant, forming a composite design.

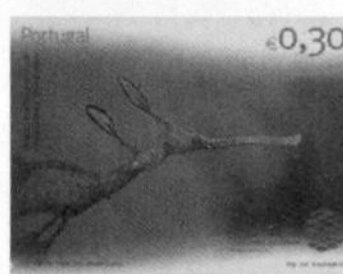

691 Seadragon (*Phyllopteryx taeniolatus*)

2004. Lisbon Oceanarium. Multicoloured.

3077	30c. Type **691**	60	50
3078	45c. Magellanic penguin (*Spheniscus magellanicus*)	95	75
3079	56c. *Hypsypops rubicundus*	1·20	95
3080	72c. Sea otter (*Enhydra lutris*)	1·60	1·30
3081	€1 Grey nurse shark (*Carcharias Taurus*)	2·10	1·70
3082	€2 Atlantic puffin (*Fratercula artica*)	4·25	3·50
MS3083	140×112 mm. €1.50 Macaroni penguin (*Eudyptes Chrysolophus*) (80×30 mm)	3·50	2·75

692 Foot kicking Ball

2004. European Football Championship 2004, Portugal (4th series). Official Match Ball. Multicoloured. Self-adhesive.

3084	10c. Type **692**	25	15
3085	20c. Ball right	45	35
3086	30c. Ball and line	70	50
3087	50c. Ball and goal post	1·10	85
MS3088	105×105 mm. Nos. 3084/7.	4·25	2·30

MS3088 is ordinary gum.

693 Portugal

2004. European Football Championship 2004, Portugal (5th series). Participating Teams. Designs showing Kinas (mascot) and country flags. Multicoloured.

3089	30c. Type **693**	70	55
3090	30c. France	70	55
3091	30c. Sweden	70	55
3092	30c. Czech Republic	70	55
3093	30c. Greece	70	55
3094	30c. UK	70	55
3095	30c. Bulgaria	70	55
3096	30c. Latvia	70	55
3097	30c. Spain	70	55
3098	30c. Switzerland	70	55
3099	30c. Denmark	70	55
3100	30c. Germany	70	55
3101	30c. Russia	70	55
3102	30c. Croatia	70	55
3103	30c. Italy	70	55
3104	30c. Netherlands	70	55

2004. Birds (3rd series). As T **657**. Multicoloured.

3105	30c. Red crossbill	60	50
3106	45c. Red-rumped swallow	95	75
3107	55c. Golden oriole	1·20	95
3108	58c. Crested lark	1·30	1·00
3109	72c. Crested tit	1·60	1·30
3109a	30c. As No. 3105 (28×23 mm)	60	50
3109b	45c. As No. 3106 (50×23 mm)	95	75
3109c	56c. As No. 3107 (28×23 mm)	1·20	95

Nos. 3105a/7a all self-adhesive.

694 "Moliceiros" Boat (Aveiro)

2004. European Football Championship 2004, Portugal (6th series). Host Cities. Multicoloured.

3110	30c. Type **694**	65	55
3111	30c. University tower (Coimbra)	65	55
3112	30c. Don Afonso Henriques (statue) (Guimaraes)	65	55
3113	30c. Castle (Leiria)	65	55
3114	30c. Tower (Faro/Loule)	65	55
3115	30c. Bom Jesus (Braga)	65	55
3116	30c. Torre di Belem (Lisbon)	65	55
3117	30c. D. Luis I Bridge (Porto)	65	55

695 Carnations

2004. 30th Anniv of 25 April (Carnation revolution).

3118	**695** 45c. multicoloured	1·00	80

696 Dr. Magalhaes Pessoa Stadium, Leiria

2004. European Football Championship 2004, Portugal (7th series). Stadiums (2nd issue). Multicoloured.

3119	30c. Type **696**	65	55
3120	30c. Municipal stadium, Coimbra	65	55
3121	30c. Municipal stadium, Braga	65	55
3122	30c. Bessa stadium, Porto	65	55
3123	30c. Luz stadium, Lisbon	65	55
3124	30c. D. Afonso Henriques stadium, Guimaraes	65	55
3125	30c. Algarve stadium, Faro-Loule	65	55
3126	30c. Jose Alvalade stadium, Lisbon	65	55
3127	30c. Dragao stadium, Porto	65	55
3128	30c. Municipal stadium, Aveiro	65	55

697 Stylized Figures

2004. European Union. Multicoloured.

3129	30c. Type **697** (EU parliamentary elections)	70	50
3130	56c. EU emblem and new members' flags (80×30 mm) (new members)	1·20	90
MS3131	140×111 mm×2 Original members' flags (80 30 mm)	4·75	4·00

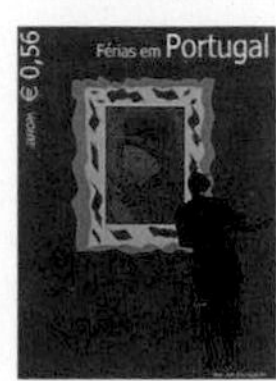

698 Picture Gallery

2004. Europa. Holidays. Multicoloured.

3132	56c. Type **698**	1·50	1·20
3133	56c. Beach	1·50	1·20
MS3134	141×112 mm. Nos. 3132/3	4·50	3·50

699 Bells of Early Telephone

2004. Centenary of Telephone Line from Porto to Lisbon. Multicoloured.

3135	30c. Type **699**	60	50
3136	45c. Insulator	95	75
3137	56c. Fibre optic cable	1·20	95
3138	72c. Video telephone	1·60	1·30
MS3139	140×112 mm. €1. ×2, No. 3135; No. 3138	6·75	4·00

700 Flower (illustration, Maimonides' Mishneh Torah)

2004. Jewish Heritage. Multicoloured.

3140	30c. Type **700**	60	50
3141	45c. Star of David (illustration, Cervera Bible)	95	75
3142	56c. Menorah (illustration, Cervera Bible)	1·20	95
3143	72c. Menorah (carved tablet)	1·60	1·30
3144	€1 Illustration, Abravanel Bible	2·10	1·70
3145	€2 Prophet (statue, de Cristo Convent, Tomar)	4·25	3·50
MS3146	140×112 mm. €1.50 Shaare Tikva Synagogue (centenary)	3·50	2·75

701 Henri Delaunay Trophy

2004. European Football Championship 2004, Portugal (8th series). Sheet 140×112 mm. Multicoloured.

MS3147	**701** €1 multicoloured	2·40	2·00

702 Stamps

2004. 50th Anniv of Portuguese Philatelic Federation. Multicoloured.

3148	30c. Type **702**	75	50
MS3149	111×79 mm €1.50 Seal	3·50	2·75

703 Footballers Past and Present (image scaled to 55% of original size)

2004. 50th Anniv of Union of European Football Associations (UEFA). Sheet 141×85 mm.

MS3150	€1 multicoloured	2·40	1·90

704 Hurdler

2004. Olympic Games, Athens 2004. Multicoloured.

3151	30c. Type **704**	65	50
3152	45c. High jump	1·10	75

705 Swimmer

2004. Paralymic Games, Athens 2004. Multicoloured.

3153	30c. Type **705**	60	50
3154	45c. Wheelchair racer	95	75
3155	56c. Cyclist	1·20	95
3156	72c. Runner	1·50	1·30

706 Pedro Homem de Melo

2004. Birth Centenary of Pedro Homem de Melo (folklorist). Sheet 140×112 mm.
MS3157 €2 multicoloured 4·75 4·00

707 Museum Facade (image scaled to 55% of original size)

2004. Inauguration of Belem Palace Museum (President of the Republic's Museum). Multicoloured.
3158 45c. Type **708** 1·00 75
MS3159 140×112 mm. €1 Museum interior 2·40 1·90

708 Quim and Manecas (Jose Stuart Carvalhais)

2004. Comic Strips. Multicoloured.
3160 30c. Type **708** 60 50
3161 45c. Guarda Abila (Julio Pinto and Nuno Saraiva) 95 75
3162 56c. Simao Infante (Raul Correia and Eduardo Teixeira Coelho) 1·20 95
3163 72c. APior Banda du Mondo (Jose Carlos Fernandes) 1·50 1·30
MS3164 141×111 mm. 50c.×4, Oespiao Acacio (Relvas); Jim del Monaco (Louro and Simoes); Tomahawk Tom (Vitor Peon); Pitanga (Arlndo Fagundes) 4·75 4·00

709 Third-century Sarcophagus and Mosaic

2004. Viticulture. Multicoloured.
3165 30c. Type **709** 70 50
3166 45c. Mosaic and 12th-century tapestry 1·10 75
3167 56c. Man carrying grapes (14th-century missal) and grape harvesting (15th-century Book of Hours) 1·30 95
3168 72c. Grape harvesting and "Grupo de Leao" (Columbano Bordalo Pine) 1·70 1·30
3169 €1 "Grupo de Leo" and 20th-century stained glass window 2·30 1·70
MS3170 140×115 mm. 50c. ×4, Fields, grapes and mechanical harvester; Harvester and amphora; Barrels in cellar, steel vats and barrels; Barrels, bottling and glass of wine 4·50 4·00
Nos. 3165/6 were issued together, se-tenant, forming a composite design.

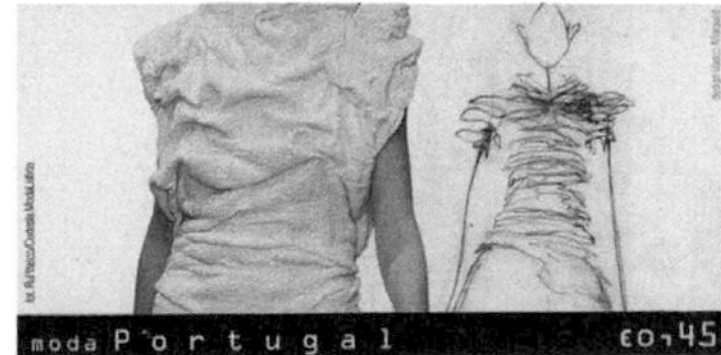

710 Ruched Dress (Alexandra Moura)

2004. Fashion. Sheet 190×200 mm containing T **710** and similar horiz designs. Multicoloured.
MS3171 45c. ×10, Type **710**; Poncho (Ana Salazar); Boned and laced dress (Filipe Faisca); Ribboned skirt (J. Branco and L. Sanchez); Wrap-over dress Antonio Tenente); Frilled front (Luis Buchinho); White top and skirted pants (Osvaldo Martins); Magenta dress with red attachments (Dino Alves); Silk-edged coat (Alves and Goncalves); Sequinned halter necked dress (Fatima Lopes) 11·00 8·50

711 "Adoration of the Magi" (Jorge Afonso)

2004. Christmas. Multicoloured.
3172 30c. Type **711** 60 50
3173 45c. "Adoration of the Magi" (16th-century Flamenga school) 95 75
3174 56c. "Escape into Egypt" (Francisco Vieira) 1·20 95
3175 72c. "Nativity" (Portuguese school) 1·50 1·30
MS3176 140×112 mm. €3 "Nativity" (detail) (Josefa de Obidos) (50×35 mm) 6·75 5·50

712 "Entrudo", Lazarim, Lamego

2005. Masks. Multicoloured. (a) Ordinary gum.
3177 10c. Type **712** 20 15
3178 30c. "Festa dos Rapazes", Salsas, Braganca 60 50
3179 45c. "Festa do Chocalheiro" Mougadouro, Braganca 90 75
3180 57c. "Cardador", Vale de Ilhavo 1·20 1·00
3181 74c. "Festa dos Rapazes", Avelada, Braganca 1·60 1·30

(b) Self-adhesive gum.
3182 30c. As No. 3178 (29×24 mm) 1·10 50
3183 45c. As No. 3179 (48×23 mm) 1·60 80
3184 57c. As No. 3180 (29×24 mm) 2·10 1·00
No. 3183 is inscribed "Correio Azul".
See also No. 3319/21.

713 Subway Train and Tram

2005. Public Transport. Multicoloured.
3185 30c. Type **713** 60 50
3186 50c. Locomotive and tram 1·00 85
3187 57c. Hovercraft 1·20 1·00
3188 €1 Coach 2·10 1·70
3189 €2 Train 4·25 3·50
Nos. 3185/9 were issued together, se-tenant, forming a composite design.

714 Sortelha

2005. Historic Villages (1st issue). Multicoloured.
3190 30c. Type **714** 65 50
3191 30c. Idanha-a-Velha 65 50
3192 30c. Castelo Novo 65 50
3193 30c. Castelo Rodrigo 65 50
3194 30c. Piodao 65 50
3195 30c. Linhares 65 50
3196 30c. Transcoso 65 50
3197 30c. Monsanto 65 50
3198 30c. Almeida 65 50
3199 30c. Belmonte 65 50
3200 30c. Marialva 65 50
3201 30c. Castelo Mendo 65 50
3202 30c. Buildings and coast, Linhares 65 50
3203 30c. Roof tops, Transcoso 65 50
3204 30c. Church, Marialva 65 50
3205 30c. Castle and houses, Castelo Rodrigo 65 50
3206 30c. Buildings and terrace, Almeida 65 50
3207 30c. Houses, Castelo Mendo 65 50
3208 30c. Rooftops, Sortelha 65 50
3209 30c. Balcony, Belmonte 65 50
3210 30c. Rooftops, Monsanto 65 50
3211 30c. Ruins, Idanha-a-Velha 65 50
3212 30c. Tower, Castelo Novo 65 50
3213 30c. Rooftops, Piodao 65 50
3214 57c. Castle, Linhares 1·30 1·00
3215 57c. Castle walls, Transcoso 1·30 1·00
3216 57c. Bells, Mariavla 1·30 1·00
3217 57c. Church, Castelo Rodrigo 1·30 1·00
3218 57c. Walls, Almeida 1·30 1·00
3219 57c. Rooftops, Castelo Mendo 1·30 1·00
3220 57c. Column, Sortelha 1·30 1·00
3221 57c. Castle walls, Belmonte 1·30 1·00
3222 57c. Tower, Monsanto 1·30 1·00
3223 57c. Doorway, Idanha-a-Velha 1·30 1·00
3224 57c. Rooftops, Castelo Novo 1·30 1·00
3225 57c. Building facade, Piodao 1·30 1·00
See also No. **MS**3247.

715 "A Beira-Mar"

2005. 150th Birth Anniv of Jose Malhoa (artist). Multicoloured.
3226 30c. Type **715** 60 50
3227 45c. "As Promessas" 95 80
MS3228 93×117 mm. €1.77 "Conversa com o Vizinho" 3·75 2·75

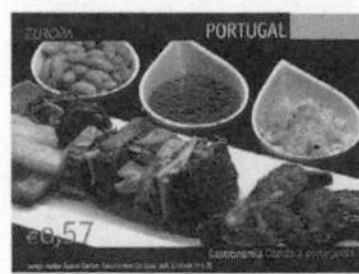

716 Cozido a Portuguesa (stew)

2005. Europa. Gastronomy. Multicoloured.
3229 57c. Type **716** 1·50 1·20
MS3230 125×95 mm. 57c.×2, Bacalhau assado com batatas a murro (cod and potatoes)×2 6·50 5·25

717 Paul Harris (founder)

2005. Centenary of Rotary International.
3231 **717** 74c. Multicoloured 1·50 1·30
MS3232 125×95 mm. **717** €1.75 multicoloured 3·75 3·00

718 19th-century Open Carriage (Carrinho de Passeio)

2005. Centenary of National Coach Museum, Lisbon. Multicoloured.
3233 30c. Type **718** 60 50
3234 30c. 19th-century closed carriage (Carruagem de Porto Covo) 60 50
3235 45c. 17th-century carriage (Coche Francisca Saboia) 95 80
3236 45c. 18th-century small carriage ("Das Plumas") 95 80
3237 57c. 18th-century sedan chair 1·20 1·00
3238 74c. 18th-century coach (Coches dos oceanos) 1·60 1·30
MS3239 125×100 mm. €1.75 Queen Amelia 3·75 3·00

719 Pegoes Aqueduct, Tomar

2005. Cultural Heritage. Multicoloured.
3240 5c. Type **719** 10 10
3241 30c. Chalice (1581) 60 50
3242 45c. Stained glass, De Christo convent, Tomar 95 80
3243 57c. Turret, Angra, Azores 1·20 1·00
3244 €1 Ship 2·10 1·70
3245 €2 St. Vincente de Fora church, Lisbon 4·25 3·50
MS3246 112×140 mm. €1.20 Crucifix, Tesauro da Se, Lisbon 3·00 2·75

2005. Historic Villages (2nd issue). 12 sheets, each 60×150 mm containing horiz designs as T **714**.
MS3247 (a) Nos. 3202 and 3214 (b) Nos. 3203 and 3215 (c) Nos. 3204 and 3216 (d) Nos. 3205 and 3217 (e) Nos. 3206 and 3218 (f) Nos. 3207 and 3219 (g) Nos. 3208 and 3220 (h) Nos. 3209 and 3221 (i) Nos. 3210 and 3222 (j) Nos. 3211 and 3223 (k) Nos. 3212 and 3224 (l) Nos. 3213 and 3225 19·00 14·00

720 Man and Cat (Raphael Bordallo Pinheiro)

2005. Caricaturists. Multicoloured.
3248 30c. Type **720** 75 50
3249 30c. Bearded man (Sebastiao Sanhudo) 75 50
3250 30c. Soldier (Celso Herminio) 75 50
3251 30c. Man wearing glasses (Leal da Camara) 75 50
3252 30c. Man holding broken pencil (Francisco Valenca) 75 50
3253 30c. Man smoking (Stuart Carvalhais) 75 50
3254 30c. Guarda Ricardo (Sam (Samuel Torres de Carvalho)) 75 50
3255 30c. Almada Negreios (Joao Abel Manta) 75 50
3256 30c. Man tie (Augusto Cid) 75 50
3257 30c. Head and pencil (Antonio Atunes) 75 50
3258 30c. Ze Povinho (Raphael Bordallo Pinheiro) 75 50

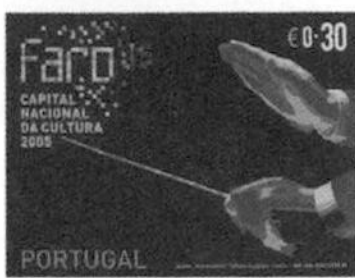

721 Conductor's Hands

2005. Faro—National Cultural Capital 2005. Multicoloured.
3259 30c. Type **721** 60 50
3260 45c. Ancient pot 95 80
3261 57c. Shell 1·20 1·00
3262 74c. Hands 1·60 1·30

722 Coastline and Bell

2005. Tourism. Multicoloured. (a) Lisbon.
3263 45c. Type **722** 95 75
3264 48c. Monument and tram 1·00 85
3265 57c. Tram, rooftops and cupola 1·40 1·00

(b) Porto e Norte.
3266 45c. Ceramic rooster, valley and church 95 75
3267 48c. Church, bay and wine glass 1·00 85
3268 57c. Wine glass, seafront and yachts 1·40 1·00
Nos. 3263/5 and 3266/8, respectively were printed together, se-tenant, each forming a composite design.

723 Harvesting Bark from protected Cork Trees

2005. Environmental Protection. Multicoloured.
3269 30c. Type **723** 60 50
3270 45c. Fire prevention officers 90 75
3271 57c. Bucaco Forest 1·20 1·00
MS3272 95×95 mm. €2 Chestnut trees (Serra de S. Mamede) 4·00 3·25

724 "50" and UN Emblem

2005. 50th Anniv of United Nations Membership. Multicoloured.
3273 30c. Type **724** 60 50
3274 45c. Dove (International Day of Peace) 90 75
3275 57c. Child (UNESCO—Children at Risk) 1·20 1·00
3276 74c. Albert Einstein (International Year of Physics) 1·50 1·30

725 Sundial, St John the Baptist Church, Sao Joao das Lampas

2005. Annular Solar Eclipse—3rd October. Multicoloured.

3277 45c. Type **725** 95 75
3278 €1 Portable sundial, 1770 2·00 1·70
MS3279 125×135 mm. €1.20×3, Partial eclipse, Lisbon; Annulus, Braganca; Partial eclipse, Faro 7·50 6·00

726 Pen Nib

2005. Communications. Multicoloured.

3280 30c. Type **726** 60 50
3281 45c. Radio microphone 90 75
3282 57c. Television camera 1·20 1·00
3283 74c. Globe and @ (internet) 1·50 1·30
MS3284 Two sheets, each 125×90 mm. (a) €1.10 Newspaper; €1.55 Radio studio. (b) €1.10 Television studio; €1.55 "http://www" (internet) 10·50 10·00

727 Fisherman and Boats, Aldeia da Carrasqueira

2005. Fishing Villages. Multicoloured.

3285 30c. Type **727** 60 50
3286 30c. Moorings and pier, Aldeia da Carrasqueira 60 50
3287 30c. Boat, Tai O, Hong Kong 60 50
3288 30c. Wrapped fish, Tai O 60 50

Nos. 3285/6 and 3287/8 respectively were issued together, se-tenant, forming a composite design.

Stamps of the same design were issued by Hong Kong.

728 Multipurpose Ship

2005. Modernisation of the Navy. Black.

3289 45c. Type **728** 90 75
3290 57c. Hydro-oceanographic ship 1·20 1·00
3291 74c. Patrol vessel 1·50 1·30
3292 €2 Submarine 4·00 3·25

729 Alvaro Cunhal, Women and Children

2005. Alvaro Barreirinhas Cunhal (politician and writer) Commemoration. Multicoloured.

3293 30c. Type **729** 1·00 50
MS3294 112×104 mm. €1 Alvaro Cunhal and girl 1·80 1·80

730 Building

2005. Serralves Foundation. Multicoloured.

3295 30c. Type **730** 60 50
3296 45c. "Projected Shadow of Adami" (Lourdes de Castro) 90 75
3297 48c. Building facade 1·00 85
3298 57c. Trowel (Claes Oldenburg Cooseje van Bruggen) 1·20 95
3299 74c. Hand and painting 1·50 1·30
3300 €1 Path, hedges and lawn 2·00 1·70
MS3301 Two sheets, each 125×150 mm. (a) 30c. As No. 3297 (horiz); 45c. Path; 45c. Columns and balustrade; 45c. Tower; 45c. Canal and evergreens (b) €1 Museum building (80×30 mm); €1 Museum displays (80×30 mm); €1 Parkland 10·50 8·25

731 Futebol Clube do Porto Emblem and Player (1993)

2005. Football Clubs' Centenaries. Showing emblem and player. Multicoloured.

3302 N (30c.) Type **731** 60 50
3303 N (30c.) Sport Lisboa e Benefica (2004) 60 50
3304 N (30c.) Sporting Clube de Portugal (2006) 60 50
MS3305 Three sheets, each 125×96 mm. (a) €1 Porto Football Club emblem and trophy; (b) €1 Sport Lisboa e Benefica emblem, player, stadium and trophy; (c) €1 Anniversary emblem 6·75 1·70

Nos. 3302/4 were for use on letters weighing 20 grams or less.

732 Scenes of Devastation (image scaled to 55% of original size)

2005. 250th Anniv of Earthquake—31 October 1755. Multicoloured.

3306 45c. Type **732** 90 75
3307 €2 Aftermath 4·00 3·25
MS3308 80×80 mm. €2.65 Survivors (40×30 mm) 5·25 4·25

733 Children's Party

2006. Greetings Stamps. Multicoloured. (a) Sheet stamps.

3309 N. Type **733** 60 50
3310 N. Girl and couples 60 50
3311 N. Mother, father and baby 60 50
3312 N. Conductor 60 50
3313 N. Couple about to kiss 60 50

(b) Size 40×29 mm.

3314 N. As No. 3309 60 50
3315 N. As No. 3310 60 50
3316 N. As No. 3311 60 50
3317 N. As No. 3312 60 50
3318 N. As No. 3313 60 50

Nos. 3314/18 were issued together, se-tenant, forming a composite design.

2006. Masks (2nd series). As T **712**. Multicoloured. Self-adhesive gum.

3319 N. "Festa dos Rapazes", Salsas, Bragança (29×24 mm) 60 50
3320 A. Lazarim carnival, Bragança (29×24 mm) 90 75
3321 E. "Dia de Ano Novo", Mogadouro, Bragança (29×24 mm) 1·20 1·00

No. 3320 is inscribed "Correio Azul".

No. 3319 was for use on normal domestic mail, up to 20 grams, 3320 was for domestic first class (blue) mail and 3321 was for European mail.

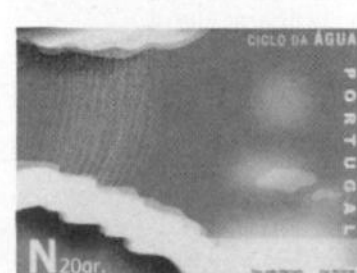

734 Rain Clouds

2006. Water. Multicoloured.

3322 N. Type **734** 60 50
3323 N. Glass of water 60 50
3324 A. Water from tap 90 75
3325 A. Water turbines 90 75
3326 E. Yacht 1·20 1·00
3327 E. Flower 1·20 1·00

Nos. 3322/3 was for use on normal domestic mail, up to 20 grams, 3324/5 was for domestic first class (blue) mail and, 3326/7 was for European mail.

735 Baptising

2006. 500th Birth Anniv of Saint Francis Xavier. Multicoloured.

3328 45c. Type **735** 95 75
3329 €1 Preaching 2·00 1·70
MS3330 85×125 mm. €2.75 Saint Francis Xavier (painting) 4·50 3·25

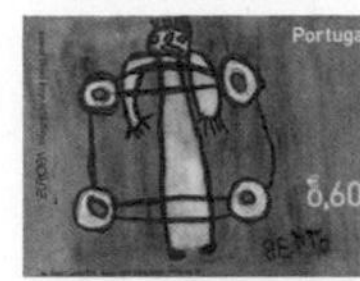

736 Enclosed Figure (Bento Luz)

2006. Europa. Integration. Winning Entries in ANACED (association for art and creativity by and for people with disabilities) Painting Competition. Multicoloured.

3331 60c. Type **736** 1·30 1·00
MS3332 125×95 mm. 60c.×2, Figure in wheelchair (David Fernandes); Aliens and humans from many nations (Ana Sofia, Renarto, Jose Luis and Alcidia) 2·50 2·00

737 Romulo de Carvalho (science writer)

2006. Birth Centenaries. Multicoloured.

3333 €1 Type **737** 2·00 1·70
3334 €1 Agostinho da Silva (philosopher) 2·00 1·70
3335 €1 Thomaz de Mello (artist) 2·00 1·70
3336 €1 Humberto Delgado (politician) 2·00 1·70
3337 €1 Lopes-Graca (composer and musician) 2·00 1·70

738 Players' Legs

2006. UEFA Under-21 Football Championship, Portugal. Sheet 125×65 mm.

MS3338 **738** €2.75 multicoloured 5·50 4·50

739 Players

2006. World Cup Football Championship, Germany. Multicoloured.

3339 45c. Type **739** 90 4·75
3340 €1 Players (different) 2·00 1·70
MS3341 125×85 mm. €2.40 Emblem and trophy 5·00 4·00

739a Mozart (etching)

2006. 250th Birth Anniv of Wolfgang Amadeus Mozart (composer). Etchings by Giovanni Antonio Sasso. Multicoloured.

3341a 60c. Type **739a** 1·20 1·00
MS3341b 90×115 mm. €2.75 Mozart facing right 5·50 4·50

740 Dunes

2006. International Year of Deserts and Desertification. Multicoloured.

3342 30c. Type **740** 60 50
3343 60c. Dead and live trees 1·20 1·00

741 Oceanus (mosaic)

2006. Roman Heritage. Multicoloured.

3344 30c. Type **741** 60 50
3345 45c. Temple, Evora 90 75
3346 50c. Patera de Lameira Larga 1·00 85
3347 60c. Two headed statue ("Herma Bifronte") 1·20 1·00
MS3348 125×95 mm. €2.40 Seahorse (mosaic) 5·00 4·00

2006. Masks (3rd series). As T **712**. Multicoloured. Ordinary gum.

3349 3c. Owl (Lazarim carnival, Bragança) 10 10
3350 5c. Scarecrow, "Festa dos Rapazes", Bacal, Braganca 10 10
3351 30c. As No. 3319 ("Festa dos Rapazes", Salsas, Braganca) 60 50
3352 45c. As No. 3320 (Lazarim carnival, Bragança) 90 75
3353 60c. As No. 3321 ("Dia de Ano Novo", Mogadouro, Braganca) 1·20 1·00
3354 75c. Devil ("Dia dos Diabos", Vinhais, Braganca) 1·50 1·30

743 Flags

2006. Tenth Anniv of Community of Portuguese Speaking Countries (CPLP). Sheet 125×65 mm.

MS3357 **743** €2.85 multicoloured 6·00 4·75

744 "Picture of a Young Woman" (Domenico Ghirlandaio)

2006. 50th Anniv of Calouste Gulbenkian Foundation. Multicoloured.

3358 30c. Type **744** 60 50
3359 45c. Brooch (Rene Lalique) 90 75
3360 60c. Tiles (Turkish c.1573) 1·20 1·00
3361 75c. "Flora" (sculpture) (Jean Baptiste Carpeaux) and Roman medallion 1·50 1·30
3362 €1 Jade jar 2·00 1·70
3363 €2 "Calouste Gulbenkian" (C. J. Watelet) 4·00 3·25
MS3364 125×95 mm. 30c.×4, Statues (art); Books (education); Spectroscope (science); Mother and child (charity) 2·50 2·00

Nos. 3358/63 when laid together form a composite design. The stamps of **MS**3364 form a composite design.

745 Jose Gomes Ferreira School, Lisbon (Raul Hestnes Ferreira)

2006. Contemporary Architecture. Multicoloured.

3365 30c. Type **745** 60 50
3366 30c. Borges & Irmao Bank, Vila do Conde (Alvaro Siza) 60 50
3367 30c. Matosinhos City Council (Alcino Soutinho) 60 50
3368 30c. Casa das Artes, Porto (Eduardo Souto Moura) 60 50
3369 30c. University campus, Santiago (Nuno Portas/CEFAUP) 60 50

3370	30c. Escola Superior de Comunicao Social (ESCS), Lisbon (Carrilho da Graca)	60	50
3371	30c. Plan for Alto do Restelo, Lisbon (Teotonio Pereira, Nuno Portas, Pedro Botelho and Joao Paciencia)	60	50
3372	30c. Order of architects, Lisbon (Manuel Graca Dias and Egas JoseVierira)	60	50
3373	30c. St. Mary's church, Forno, Marco de Canaveses (Alvaro Siza)	60	50
3374	30c. Bairro da Bouca, SAAL, Porto (Alvaro Siza)	60	50

746 Early Camera and Crew

2006. 50th Anniv of First Television Broadcast in Portugal. Multicoloured.

3375	30c. Type **746**	60	50
3376	60c. Modern camera	1·20	1·00

747 Ponte de Alcantara

2006. Bridges. Multicoloured.

3377	30c. Type **747**	60	50
3378	52c. Ponte de Vila Real de Sto. Antonio	1·10	90

Stamps of similar design were issued by Spain.

748 Grapes and Terraces (image scaled to 56% of original size)

2006. 250th Anniv of Douro Wine Demarcated Region. Sheet 125×95 mm.

MS3379	**748** €2.40 multicoloured	5·00	4·00

749 *Capros aper*

2006. Fish. Multicoloured.

3380	30c. Type **749**	60	50
3381	45c. *Anthias anthias*	90	75
3382	60c. *Lepadogaster lepadogaster*	1·20	1·00
3383	75c. *Gobiusculus flavescens*	1·50	1·30
3384	€1 *Coris julis*	2·00	1·70
3385	€2 *Calliomymus lyra*	4·00	3·25
MS3386	Two sheets, each 125×115 mm. (a) 80c.×2, *Macroramphosus scolopax; Echiichthys vipera.* (b) 80c.×2, *Thalassoma pavo; Blennius ocellaris*	7·00	5·50

750 "a"

2006. School Correspondence. Multicoloured.

3387	N Type **750**	60	50
3388	N "c, g, d"	60	50

751 Flecha de Prata (Silver Arrow)

2006. 150th Anniv of National Railways. Multicoloured.

3389	30c. Type **751**	60	50
3390	45c. Sud-Express	90	75
3391	60c. Foguette	1·20	1·00
3392	€2 Alfa Pendular	4·00	3·25
MS3393	125×95 mm. €1.60 Blessing first train (80×30 mm)	3·25	2·50

752 "A Cidade de Gale"

2006. 500th Anniv of Portuguese in Ceylon. Multicoloured.

3394	30c. Type **752**	60	50
3395	75c. "O Livro das Plantas e Todas as Fortalezas"	1·50	1·30
MS3396	125×95 mm. €2.40 As No. 3394	5·00	4·00

753 16th-century Tiles

2007. In Search of Arab Lisbon. Multicoloured.

3397	30c. Type **753**	60	50
3398	45c. 9th-century limestone carving	90	75
3399	52c. Neo-Arab door	1·00	90
3400	61c. Neo-Arab interior, National Film Library	1·20	1·00
3401	75c. Casa Alentejo	1·50	1·20
3402	€1 Palacete Ribeiro da Cunha	2·00	1·60
MS3403	130×95 mm. €2.95 11th-century Islamic jug	6·00	4·75

754 Laundress wearing Scarves ("Lavadeira") (Minho)

2007. Regional Costume. Multicoloured.

3404	30c. Type **754**	60	50
3405	30c. Bride wearing gold chains ("Noiva") (Minho)	30	50
3406	30c. Cape ("Capa de Honras") (Tras-os-Montes)	60	50
3407	30c. Embroidered tunic ("Pauliteiro") (Tras-os-Montes)	60	50
3408	30c. Fisherman's jersey ("Camisola de Pescador") (Douro Litoral)	60	50
3409	30c. Straw cape ("Coroça") (Beiras/Tras-os-Montes)	60	50
3410	30c. Embroidered apron and skirts ("Saias de Nazare") (Estremadura)	60	50
3411	30c. Horseman wearing red waistcoat ("Campino") (Ribatejo)	60	50
3412	30c. Floral apron and skirt ("Camponesa") (Algarve)	60	50
3413	30c. Cape with fur collar ("Capote") (Alentejo)	60	50
3414	30c. Hooded cloak ("Capote e Capelo") (Azores)	60	50
3415	30c. Short jacket, white shirt and red sash ("Campones") (Beira Litoral)	60	50
3416	30c. Striped dress and red cape ("Viloa") (Madeira)	60	50
3417	30c. Smoked blouse, apron and embroidered cloak ("Camponesa") (Ribatejo)	60	50

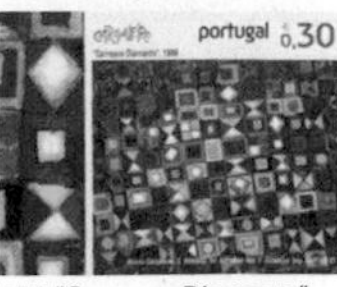

755 "Carreaux Diamants"

2007. Manuel Cargaleiro (artist and ceramist). Multicoloured.

3418	30c. Type **755**	60	50
3419	45c. "Composizione Floreale"	90	75
3420	52c. "Decorcao Mural"	1·20	1·00

756 "D. Joao i Reforca a Casa dos Contos" (painting by Jaime Martins Barata)

2007. Bicentenary of European Court of Auditors. Multicoloured.

3421	30c. Type **756**	60	50
3422	61c. Creation of Court of Auditors (painting by Almada Negreiros)	1·20	1·20
3423	€2 Headquarters of the Court, 1954–1989	4·00	3·25
MS3424	95×125 mm. €2.95 "The Auditor" (tapestry)	6·00	4·75

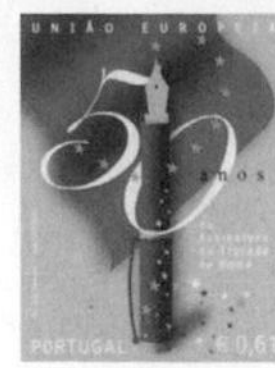

757 Pen, Flag and Stars

2007. 50th Anniv of Treaty of Rome.

3425	**757** 61c. multicoloured	1·20	1·00

758 Ox-drawn Carriage

2007. Public Transport. Multicoloured. (a) Ordinary gum.

3425a	1c. Articulated bus (8.3.10)	10	10
3425b	6c. Electric car (1927)	10	30
3425c	20c. Bus (1957)	40	30
3426	30c. Type **758**	65	35
3426a	31c. Oldsmobile taxi (1928)	60	45
3426b	32c. Triple unit electric car (1957)	65	50
3426c	32c. Articulated electric car (1995) (8.3.10)	65	50
3427	45c. Horse-drawn tram facing right ("Americano") (1872)	90	70
3427a	47c. Tram (1926)	1·00	60
3427b	47c. Carruagem ML7 (1959)	1·10	35
3427c	47c. Carruagem ML7 (1959)	1·10	35
3427d	47c. Comboio ML79 (1984) (Lisbon metro) (8.3.10)	1·00	60
3428	50c. Horse-drawn tram facing left ("Americano") (1873)	1·00	80
3429	61c. Electric tram (Eletrico No. 22) (1895)	1·20	95
3429a	67c. Coach (1944)	1·40	70
3429b	68c. Bus No. 207 (1960)	1·70	85
3429c	68c. Bus No. 207 (1960)	1·30	1·30
3429d	68c. *Madragoa* (1981) (ferry) (8.3.10)	1·30	1·30
3430	75c. Electric tram (Eletrico No. 283) (1901)	1·50	1·20
3430a	80c. Electric car (1911)	1·60	75
3430b	80c. Trolley bus (1961)	1·60	1·20
3430c	80c. Trolley bus (1961)	1·80	90
3430d	80c. Quadruple unit electric car (1992) (8.3.10)	1·60	70

(b) Size 30×22 mm. Self-adhesive gum.

3436	N As No. 3427	60	50
3436a	N Oldsmobile taxi (1928)	60	45
3436b	N (32c.) Triple electric car (1957) (As. No. 3426b)	65	50
3436c	N (32c.) Articulated electric car (1995) (inscribed Crreio Azul) (As No. 3426c) (8.3.10)	60	45
3437	A Tram with driver (Eletrico No. 22) (1895)	90	75
3437a	A Tram (1928) inauguration of electrical tractors company, Estopil	90	70
3437b	A (47c.) Carruagem ML7 (1959) (As. No. 3427b)	1·00	75
3437c	A (47c.) Comboio ML79 (1984) (Lisbon metro) (As No. 3427c) (8.3.10)	90	70
3438	E Tram with driver (Eletrico No. 283) (1901)	1·40	70
3438a	E Coach (1944) ingeration of coach company, Carris	1·40	70
3438b	E (67c.) Bus No. 207 (1960) (As No. 3429b)	1·40	70
3438c	E (67c.) *Madragoa* (1981) (ferry) (As No. 3429c) (8.3.10)	1·40	70

No. 3436/b was for use on normal domestic mail, up to 20 grams, No. 3437/b was for domestic first class (blue) mail and No. 3438/b was for European mail.

759 Castelo do Bode Dam

2007. Dams. Multicoloured. (a) Size 40×30 mm.

3445	30c. Type **759**	60	50

(b) Size 80×30 mm.

3446	30c. Aguieira	60	50
3447	61c. Valeira	1·20	1·00
3448	75c. Alto Lindoso	1·50	1·20
3449	€1 Castelo do Bode extended	2·00	1·60

760 Robert Baden Powell (founder)

2007. Europa. Centenary of Scouting Multicoloured.

3450	61c. Type **760**	1·30	1·00
MS3451	125×95 mm. 61c.×2, Compass; Scouts reading map	2·50	2·00

The stamps of **MS**3451 form a composite design.

2007. Contemporary Architecture. As T **745**. Multicoloured.

3452	30c. ESAD, Caldas da Rainha (Vitor Figueiredo)	60	50
3453	30c. Pavilion, Lisbon (Alvaro Siza)	60	50
3454	30c. VTS Tower, Lisbon Port (Goncalo Byrne)	60	50
3455	30c. Casa dos 24, Porto (Fernando Tavora)	60	50
3456	30c. Jose Saramago Library, Loures (Fernando Martins)	60	50
3457	30c. Documentation and Information Centre of President of the Republic, Lisbon (Carrilho da Graca)	60	50
3458	30c. Art Centre, Sines (Aires Mateus)	60	50
3459	30c. Municipal building, Braga (Eduardo Souto Moura)	60	50
3460	30c. Centre for Visual Arts, Coimbra (Joao Mendes Ribeiro)	60	50
3461	30c. Maritime Museum, Ilhavo (ARX Portugal)	60	50
MS3462	125×95 mm. €1.85 Pavilion, Lisbon (Alvaro Siza) (different) (Lisbon Architecture Triennale 2007)	3·75	3·00

The stamps and margins of **MS**3462 form a composite design.

761 Catamarans

2007. ISAF World Sailing Championships. Showing stylized craft. Multicoloured.

3463	61c. Type **761**	1·20	1·00
3464	61c. Two yachts, sail nos. '23' and '105'	1·20	1·00
3465	75c. Yacht, sail no. '75'	1·30	1·10
3466	75c. Two yachts, sail nos. '34' and '16'	1·30	1·10
MS3467	125×95 mm. €2.95 As No. 3465	6·00	4·75

The stamp and margin of **MS**3467 form a composite design.

762 Castelo de Guimaraes

2007. Seven Marvels of Portugal. Multicoloured.

3468	30c. Type **762**	60	50
3469	30c. Palacio de Mateus, Vila Real	60	50
3470	30c. Sao Francisco church, Porto	60	50
3471	30c. Torre dos Clerigos church, Porto	60	50
3472	30c. Clock tower, University of Coimbra	60	50
3473	30c. Ruins, Conimbriga, Condeixa-a-Nova	60	50
3474	30c. Batalha monastery	60	50
3475	30c. Convent of Christ, Tomar	60	50
3476	30c. Almourol castle, Vila Nova da Barquinha	60	50
3477	30c. Alcobaca monastery	60	50
3478	30c. Obidos castle	60	50
3479	30c. Basilica and convent of Mafra	60	50
3480	30c. Marvao castle	60	50
3481	30c. Blockhouses, Monsaraz	60	50
3482	30c. Vila Vicosa Ducal palace	60	50
3483	30c. Roman temple, Evora	60	50
3484	30c. Palacio Nacional da Pena, Sintra	60	50

3485	30c. Palacio Nacional da Queluz, Sintra	60	50
3486	30c. Mosteiro dos Jeronimos, Lisbon	60	50
3487	30c. Torre de Belem, Lisbon	60	50
3488	30c. Sagres fortress, Vila do Bispo	60	50

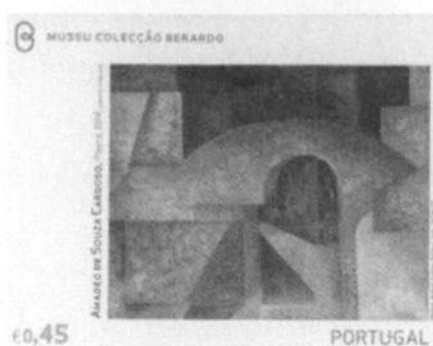

763 *Ponte* (Amadeo de Souza Cardoso)

2007. Exhibits from Berado Museum Collection. Multicoloured.

3489	45c. Type **763**	90	75
3490	61c. *Les Baigneuses* (Niki de Saint Phalle) (vert)	1·20	1·00
3491	61c. *Interior with Restful Paintings* (Roy Lichtenstein) (vert)	1·20	1·00
3492	61c. *Femme dans un Fauteuil* (Pablo Picasso) (vert)	1·20	1·00
3493	61c. *Le Couple* (Oacar Dominguez) (vert)	1·20	1·00
3494	61c. *Cafe Man Ray* (Man Ray) (vert)	1·20	1·00
3495	61c. *Nectar* (Joana Vasconcelos) (vert)	2·00	1·60
3496	61c. *Head* (Jackson Pollack) (vert)	4·00	3·25

764 Building and Stars

2007. Portugal–Presidency of European Union. Multicoloured.

3497	61c. Type **764**	1·20	1·00
MS3498	125×95 mm. €2.45 As No. 3497 but direction of stars reversed	4·50	4·50

765 SMC Nacional 500cc., 1935

2007. Motorcycles. Multicoloured.

3499	30c. Type **765**	60	50
3500	52c. Famel Fougete, 1959	1·00	90
3501	61c. Vilar Cucciolo, 1955	1·20	1·00
3502	€1 Casal Carina, 1969	2·00	1·60
MS3503	125×95 mm. 61c.×4, Qimera Alma, 1952; Cinal Pachancho, 1958; SIS Sachs V5, 1965; Casal K287, 1985	5·00	4·00

The stamps of **MS**3467 form a composite background design.

766 Globe

2007. Declaration of Winning Entries in New Seven Wonders of the World Competition–Lisbon 2007. Sheet 125×95 mm.

MS3504	**766** €2.95 multicoloured	6·00	4·75

The stamp and margin of **MS**3467 form a composite design.

767 Raul Maria Pereira and Postal Building, Peru

2007. 130th Birth Anniv of Raul Maria Pereira (artist and architect).

3505 **767**	75c. multicoloured	1·50	1·20

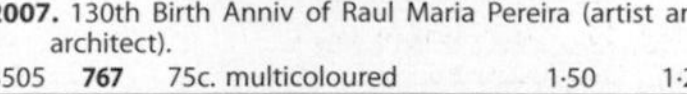

Stamp of a similar design was issued by Peru.

768 Jose Valentim Fialho de Almeida

2007. Personalities. Multicoloured.

3506	45c. Type **768** (writer) (150th birth anniv)	90	75
3507	45c. Columbano Bordalo Pinheiro (Columbano) (artist) (150th birth anniv)	90	75
3508	45c. Adolfo Correia da Rocha (Miguel Torga) (writer) (birth centenary)	90	75

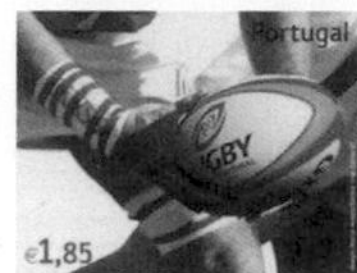

769 Hands clasping Ball

2007. Rugby World Cup, France. Sheet 125×95 mm.

MS3509	**769** €1.85 multicoloured	3·75	3·00

The stamp and margin of **MS**3509 form a composite design.

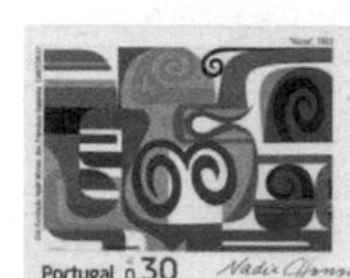

770 *Horus*, 1953

2007. Portuguese Artists. Nadir Afonso. Multicoloured.

3510	30c. Type **770**	60	50
3511	45c. *Veneza*, 1956	90	75
3512	61c. *Processao em Veneza*, 2002	1·20	1·00

771 Jacaranda

2007. Plants and Animals from the Americas. Multicoloured.

3513	30c. Type **771**	60	50
3514	30c. Potatoes	60	50
3515	30c. Maize	60	50
3516	45c. Cocoa	90	75
3517	61c. Turkeys (inscr 'Peru')	1·20	1·00
3518	75c. Passion fruit	1·50	1·20
MS3519	125×95 mm. €1.85 Humming bird and passion fruit (horiz)	3·75	3·00

The stamp and margin of **MS**3519 form a composite design.

772 Torre de Menagem, Arzila

2007. Architecture. Multicoloured.

3520	30c. Type **772**	60	50
3521	75c. Castelo de Silves, Portugal	1·50	1·20

Stamps of a similar design were issued by Morocco.

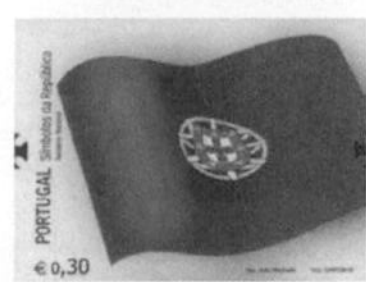

773 National Flag

2007. Symbols of the Republic. Flags. Multicoloured.

3522	30c. Type **773**	60	50
MS3523	95×125 mm. 30c.×5, As Type **773**; President of the Republic; National Assembly; Azores; Madeira	3·00	2·50

The stamps and margins of **MS**3523 form a composite background design.

774 Children and Globe (Sofia Fiteire Passeira)

2007. School Correspondence. Children's Paintings. Multicoloured.

3524	N Type **774**	60	50
3525	N Girls and flowers (Ines Filipa Navrat)	60	50
3526	N Globe enclosed in hands (Maria Correira Borges)	60	50

Nos. 3524/6 were for use on domestic mail weighing 20 grams or less.

775 Fallow Deer (*Cervus dama*)

2007. Mafra National Park. Multicoloured.

3527	30c. Type **775**	60	50
3528	45c. Wild boar (*Sus scrofa*)	90	75
3529	61c. Fox (*Vulpes vulpes*)	1·20	1·00
3530	75c. Red deer (*Cervus elaphus*)	1·50	1·20
3531	€1 Eurasian eagle owl (*Bubo bubo*)	2·00	1·25
3532	€2 Bonelli's eagle (*Hieraaetus fasciatus*)	4·00	2·50

776 Courtyard, Centro Ismali, Lisbon

2007. 50th Anniv of Ismaili Community in Portugal. Multicoloured.

3533	N Type **776**	60	50
3534	I Aerial view of courtyard	1·50	1·20

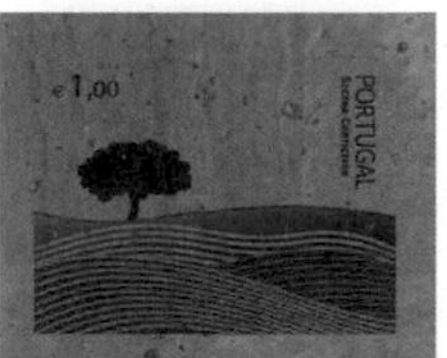

777 Cork Tree

2007. Cork Production. Self-adhesive.

3535 **777**	€1 multicoloured	2·00	1·25

No. 3535 was made of cork applied to a paper backing.

778 Motorcycle ridden by Ruben Faria

2008. 30th Anniv of Dakar Rally. Lisbon - Dakar Rally, 2007. Multicoloured.

MS3536	30c. Type **778**; 45c. Motorcycle ridden by Helder Rodrigues; 75c. Car driven by Carlos Sousa; €1.25 Lorry driven by Rainer Weigart	5·50	4·25

779 Royal Family and Entourage

2008. Bicentenary of Portuguese Royal Family's Arrival in Brazil

3537	N Type **779**	60	45
3538	I King João VI	1·50	1·20

780 Family

2008. Infertility Awareness Campaign.

3539 **780**	30c. multicoloured	60	45

781 Woodland

2008. International Year of Planet Earth. Multicoloured. each vert side).

3540	30c. Type **781**	60	45
3541	45c. Clouds	90	70
3542	61c. Volcano erupting	1·20	95
3543	75c. Under water	1·50	1·20

782 Throw

2008. Sporting Events (1st issue). European Judo Championships. Multicoloured.

3544	30c. Type **782**	60	45
3545	61c. Throw (different)	1·20	95
MS3546	125×95 mm. 45c. As Type **782** but including competition emblem; €2 As No. 3545 but including competition emblem	3·00	2·00

See also Nos. 353/6 and 3559.

783 Father Antonio Vieira

2008. Personalities. Multicoloured.

3547	30c. Type **783** (Jesuit and writer) (400th birth anniv)	60	45
3548	30c. Jose Maria Mascarenhas Relvas (politician) (150th birth anniv)	60	45
3549	30c. Aureliano de Mira Fernandes (mathematician) (50th death anniv)	60	45
3550	30c Ricardo Jorge (physician and humanist) (150th birth anniv)	60	45
3551	30c. Maria Elena Vieira da Silva (artist) (birth centenary)	60	45
3552	30c. Manoel Candido Pinto de Oliveira (film director) (birth centenary)	60	45

784 Runners

2008. Sporting Events (2nd issue). Olympic Games, Beijing. Multicoloured.

3553	30c. Type **784**	60	45
3554	30c. Cyclists	60	45
3555	75c. Long jumper	1·50	1·20
MS3556	125×95 mm. 75c.×4, Show jumper; Rower; Marksman; Gymnast	6·00	4·50

The stamps and margins of **MS**3556 form a composite design.

785 Envelope Rider

2008. Europa. The Letter. Multicoloured.

3557	61c. Type **785**	1·20	95
MS3558	125×95 mm. 61c.×2, As Type **785**; Postvan, envelope and bull	2·40	1·90

The stamps of **MS**3558 form a composite design.

786 Athletes (image scaled to 56% of original size)

2008. Sporting Events (3rd issue). European Triathlon Championship, Lisbon.

3559	**786**	€2 multicoloured	4·00	3·00

787 Mother, Child and Teacher

2008. The Rights of the Child. Right to Education. Multicoloured.

3560	30c. Type **787**	60	45
3561	45c. Teacher and pupils	90	70
3562	61c. Children reading	1·20	95
3563	75c. Child reading with parents	1·50	1·20
MS3564	95×125 mm. €2.95 Boy hugging '4'	6·00	4·50

788 Players

2008. Euro 2008–European Football Championships, Austria and Switzerland. Multicoloured.

3565	30c. Type **788**	60	45
3566	61c. Goal keeper catching ball and player	1·20	95
MS3567	125×95 mm. €1.20 Players heading ball; €1.66 Players tackling	5·75	4·50

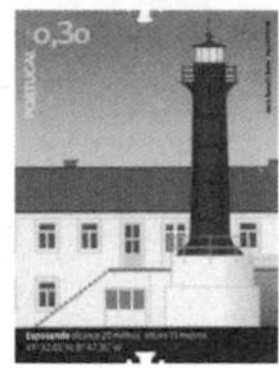

789 Esposende

2008. Lighthouses. Multicoloured.

3568	30c. Type **789**	60	50
3569	30c. Penedo da Saudade	60	50
3570	30c. Cabo Sardao (horiz)	60	50
3571	30c. Cabo da Roca (horiz)	60	50
3572	30c. Torre do Bugio (horiz)	60	50
3573	30c. Leca	60	50
3574	30c. Montedor	60	50
3575	30c. Santa Marta	60	50
3576	30c. Cabo de Sao Vincente (horiz)	60	50
3577	30c. Cabo Espichel	60	50

790 *Calidris alba* (sanderling)

2008. International Polar Year. Multicoloured.

3578	30c. Type **790**	60	45
3579	52c. *Alca torda* (razorbill)	1·00	85
3580	61c. *Oceanites oceanicus* (Wilson's storm-petrel)	1·20	95
3581	€1 *Sterna paradisea* (arctic tern)	2·00	1·60
MS3582	125×95 mm. €2.95 *Phoca hispida* (ringed seal) and *Ursus maritimus* (polar bear) (80×30 mm)	6·00	4·50

791 Vanwall 57 VW5 driven by Stirling Moss, 1958

2008. 50th Anniv of Formula I Grand Prix in Portugal. Multicoloured.

3583	31c. Type **791**	60	45
3584	67c. Cooper T53 driven by Jack Brabham, 1960	1·40	1·10
3585	80c. Cooper driven by Mark Haywood, 2005	1·60	1·20
3586	€2 McLaren M26 driven by Bobby Vernon Roe	4·00	3·00
MS3587	125×95 mm. €2.45 FI Grand Prix, 1960 (80×30 mm)	5·00	3·75

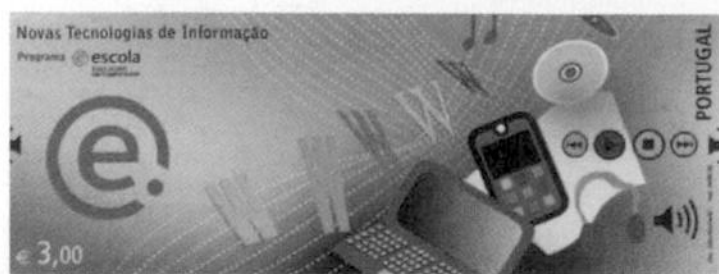

792 Symbols of Information Technology

2008. Information Technology 'E-School' Programme. Sheet 125×95 mm.

MS3588	multicoloured	6·00	4·75

793 Metal Work

2008. Centenary of Group CUF. Multicoloured.

3589	31c. Type **793**	60	45
3590	67c. Textiles	1·40	1·10
3591	€1 Naval construction	2·00	1·60
3592	€2 Chemicals	4·00	3·00
MS3593	125×95 mm. €2.45 Alfredo da Silva (founder) (vert)	5·00	4·00

794 Vases (17th century)

2008. Pharmaceutical Ceramics. Multicoloured.

3594	31c. Type **794**	60	45
3595	47c. Bottle (18th century)	1·00	80
3596	67c. Vases (17th–18th century)	1·40	1·10
3597	80c. Vases (19th century)	1·60	1·20
MS3598	125×95 mm. €2.45 Pharmacy (17th–18th century)	5·00	4·00

795 Vineyard, Dao Region

2008. Centenary of Demarcated Wine Regions. Multicoloured.

3599	31c. Type **795**	60	45
3600	31c. Barrels, Dao	60	45
3601	31c. Vineyard, Vinhos Verdes	60	45
3602	31c. Terraces, Vinhos Verdes	60	45
3603	31c. Vines, Colares	60	45
3604	31c. Barrels, Colares	60	45
3605	31c. Vineyard, Bucelas	60	45
3606	31c. Barrels, Bucelas	60	45
3607	31c. Barrels, Moscatel de Setubal	60	45
3608	31c. Vineyard, Moscatel de Setubal	60	45

Nos. 3599/600, 3601/2, 3605/6 were printed together, se-tenant, forming a composite design.

796 Centenary of First 'Executivo Republicano Camarario', Lisbon

2008. Republican Ideas. Multicoloured.

3609	31c. Type **796**	60	45
3610	31c. Republican school	60	45
3611	47c. Industrialization	1·00	80
3612	47c. Housing	1·00	80
3613	57c. State modernization	1·20	95
3614	67c. Civil register	1·30	1·00
3615	67c. Public health	1·40	1·10
3616	80c. Civic participation	1·50	1·20
MS3617	125×95 mm. €2.95 Rail–road link project over River Tejo (80×30 mm)	6·00	4·75

797 Olive Grove

2008. Olive Oil Production. Multicoloured.

3618	31c. Type **797**	60	45
3619	47c. Early harvesters	1·00	80
3620	57c. Early milling	1·20	95
3621	67c. Mill stones	1·40	1·10
3622	80c. Oil storage	1·60	1·20
3623	€2 Ready for consumption	4·00	3·00
MS3624	125×95 mm. €1.85 Hands holding olives	3·75	3·00

798 Rainbow and Symbols of Communication (Erica Bluemel Potocarrero)

2008. School Correspondence. Childrens Drawings. Multicoloured.

3625	31c. Type **798**	60	45
3626	47c. Girl and symbols of communication (Eloisa Pereira)	1·00	80
3627	67c. Postman (Joao Mario Martins Branco)	1·40	1·10

799 Ponte 25 de Abril, Lisbon

2008. Bridges. Multicoloured.

3628	31c. Type **799**	60	45
3629	47c. Arrabida, Porto	1·00	80
3630	57c. Arade, Portimao	1·20	95
3631	67c. Mosteiro, Cinfaes	1·40	1·10
3632	80c. Amizade, Vila Nova de Cerveira	1·60	1·20
3633	€1 St Clara, Coimbra	2·00	1·60
MS3634	125×95 mm. €1.85 Ponte 25 de Abril (80×30 mm)	3·75	3·00

800 Mesoamerican Bas Relief and Ceramic Plate

2008. European Year of Intercultural Dialogue. Multicoloured.

3635	31c. Type **800**	60	45
3636	47c. Asian mask and Greek head	1·00	80
3637	67c. Moorish window and feathered headdress	1·40	1·10
3638	80c. African mask and Chinese lion headdress	1·60	1·20

801 *Waiting for Success* (Henrique Cesar de Araujo Pousao)

2009. Personalities. Multicoloured.

3639	32c. Type **801** (artist) (150th birth anniv)	65	50
3640	32c. Soeiro Pereira Gomes (writer) (birth centenary) (horiz)	65	50

802 Euro Coins

2009. Tenth Anniv of Euro. Multicoloured.

3641	47c. Type **802**	1·00	75
3642	€1 €	2·00	1·50

803 Finches

2009. Birth Bicentenary of Charles Darwin (naturalist and evolutionary theorist). Multicoloured.

3643	32c. Type **803**	65	50
3644	32c. Iguana	65	50
3645	68c. Orchid	1·40	1·00
3646	68c. Diana monkey	1·40	1·00
3647	80c. Platypus	1·60	1·20
3648	80c. Skull and fossils	1·60	1·20
MS3649	125×95 mm. €2.50 *Charles Darwin* (George Richmond) (vert)	5·50	3·75

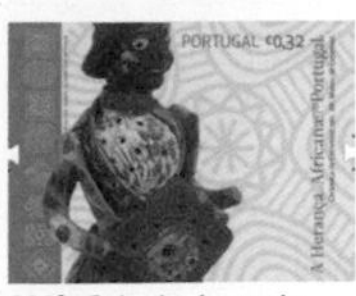

803b Guitarist (ceramic statue)

2009. African Heritage in Portugal. Multicoloured.

3649a	32c. Type **803b**	65	50
3649b	47c. Trumpeter (altarpiece, St Auta (detail))	1·00	75
3649c	57c. Three children (Conrado Roza)	1·10	75
3649d	68c. Woman	1·40	1·00
3649e	80c. Woman's head (ceramic)	1·60	1·20
3649f	€2 Three musicians (painted wood)	4·25	3·00
MS3649g	125×95 mm. €2.50 Musicians (Joaquim Marques)	4·50	3·00

Type **803a** is vacant.

804 CotA-lacase Enzyme (Nuno Micaêlo)

2009. Aquihaselo. Winning Designs in Painting Competition. Multicoloured.

3650	32c. Type **804**	65	50
3651	32c. Multiplication (Sa de Miranda School pupils)	65	50

805 St. Francis and Dog

2009. 800th Anniv of Franciscan Order. Multicoloured.

3652	32c. Type **805**	65	50
MS3653	125×95 mm. Size 31×40 mm. 50c. St. Francis kneeling; €2 Pope Innocent III giving blessing (vert)	5·50	4·00

806 Álvares Pereira

2009. Canonization of Nuno De Santa Maria (Álvares Pereira).

3654	**806**	32c. multicoloured	65	50

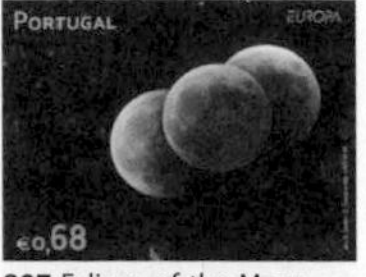

807 Eclipse of the Moon (3rd March 2007) Sequence

2009. Europa. Astronomy. Multicoloured.

3655	68c. Type **807**	1·40	1·00
MS3656	125×95 mm. 68c.×2, European Southern Observatory's 'Very Large Telescope', Chile; As Type **807**	2·75	2·10

The stamps and margins of **MS**3656 form a composite design.

808 Iznik Mosque Lamp (Turkey)

2009. Ceramics. Multicoloured.

3657	32c. Type **808**	65	50
3658	68c. Ceramic Jar (Portugal)	1·40	1·00

Stamps of a similar design were issued by Turkey.

809 Sanctuary

2009. 50th Anniv of Cristo Rei Sanctuary, South Bank of the River Tagus, near Lisbon. Multicoloured.

3659	32c. Type **809**	65	50
3660	68c. Christ (statue)	1·40	1·00
MS3661	125×95 mm. €2.48 Head of Christ, bridge and Lisbon (80×31 mm)	5·00	3·75

810 Bebinca das Sete Colinas (layered pudding) (India)

2009. Flavours of Lusophone (Portuguese speaking countries). Multicoloured.

3662	32c. Type **810**	65	50
3663	32c. Leitoa num ar de Sarapatel (meat dish) (Brazil)	65	50
3664	68c. Caldeirada de cabrito (goat stew) (Angola)	1·40	1·00
3665	68c. Balcalhau, pao, vinho e azeite (cooked dried cod, bread, wine and olive oil)	1·40	1·00
3666	80c. No caldeiro a tempura (stew and tempura) (Asia)	1·60	1·20
3667	80c. Do cozido a Cachupa (slow boiled stew of corn, beans, vegetables, spices and marinated pork or tuna) (Cape Verde Islands)	1·60	1·20
MS3668	125×95 mm. €1.85 Balcalhau, pao, vinho e azeite (detail) (vert)	3·75	2·75

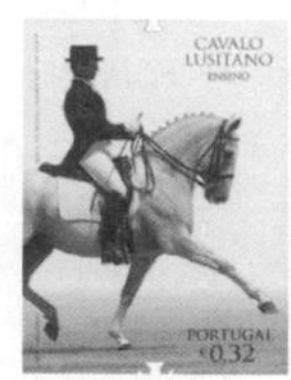

811 'Ensino' (training)

2009. The Lusitanian Horse. Multicoloured.

3669	32c. Type **811**	65	50
3670	32c. Equitacao de Trabalho	65	50
3671	57c. Toureio	1·20	90
3672	68c. Alta Escola	1·40	1·00
3673	80c. Atrelagem de Competicao	1·60	1·20
MS3674	125×95 mm. €2.50 'Alter-Real'	5·00	3·75

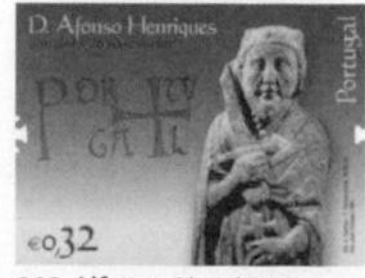

812 Alfonso Henriques (statue)

2009. 900th Birth Anniv of Alfonso Henriques (Afonso I, first king of Portugal). Multicoloured.

3675	32c. Type **812**	65	50
MS3676	95×125 mm. €3.07 On horseback	6·00	4·50

813 Trumpeter (Cascais Jazz)

2009. Jazz in Portugal. Multicoloured.

3677	32c. Type **813**	65	50
3678	47c. Trees and musicians as keyboard (Estoril Jazz Festival–Jazz On A Summer Day)	1·00	75
3679	57c. Saxophonist walking in street on instruments (Jazz in August, Calouste Gulbenkian Foundation)	1·20	90
3680	68c. Saxophonist (European Jazz Festival, Oporto)	1·40	1·00
3681	80c. Trumpeter (different) (Guimaraes Jazz Festival)	1·60	1·20
3682	€1 Fish playing saxophone (Seixal Jazz Festival)	2·00	1·50
MS3683	125×95 mm. €3.16 Hot Club of Portugal quartet	6·25	4·75

814 Pao de Centeio (rye bread)

2009. Bread. Showing loaves of bread. Multicoloured.

3684	32c. Type **814**	65	50
3685	32c. Quartos (quartered)	65	50
3686	47c. Regueifa (Arabic bread)	1·00	75
3687	68c. Chouriço (bread with sausage)	1·40	1·00
3688	68c. Testa ('brow' bread)	1·40	1·00
3689	80c. Mealhada (bread from Mealhada)	1·60	1·20

Nos. 3690/1 are vacant.

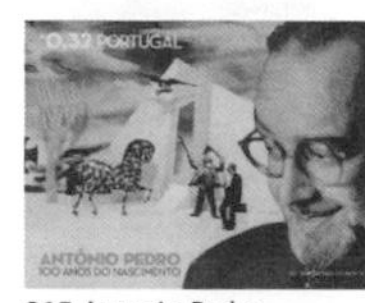

815 Antonio Pedro

2009. Birth Centenary of António Pedro da Costa (actor, writer and painter). Multicoloured.

3692	32c. Type **815**	65	50
MS3693	125×95 mm. €3.16 Facing right	6·25	4·75

816 Building Façade, 1841

2009. Belem Palace. Multicoloured.

3694	32c. Type **816**	65	50
3695	47c. Pintura das Sobreporta (painting over doorway)	1·00	75
3696	57c. Copper and silver writing equipment	1·20	90
3697	68c. Satyrs (bas relief)	1·40	1·00
3698	80c. Gold Room, detail of the ceiling molding	1·60	1·20
3699	€1 Floral allegory	2·00	1·50
MS3700	125×95 mm. €2.50 Salas das Bicas (fountain room)	5·50	3·75

817 *Pandion haliaetus* (osprey)

2009. Raptors. Multicoloured.

3701	32c. Type **817**	65	50
3702	80c. *Haliaeetus albicilla* (white-tailed eagle)	1·60	1·20

Stamps of a similar design were issued by Iran.

818 Coffee (smell)

2009. Stamps and the Senses. Birth Bicentenary of Louis Braille (inventor of Braille writing for the blind). Multicoloured.

3703	32c. Type **818**	65	50
3704	68c. Ice lolly (taste)	1·40	1·00
3705	80c. Glasses (vision)	1·60	1·20
3706	€1 Paint (touch)	2·00	1·50
3707	€2 File (Hearing)	4·00	3·00
MS3708	135×105 mm. €2.50 Louis Braille	5·00	3·75

No. **MS**3708 is embossed with Braille letters.

819 Adelaide Cabete

2009. Women of the Republic. Multicoloured.

3709	32c. Type **819**	65	50
3710	32c. Maria Veleda	65	50
3711	57c. Ana de Castro Osorio	1·20	90
3712	68c. Angelina Vidal	1·40	1·00
3713	80c. Carolina Beatriz Angelo	1·60	1·20
3714	€1 Carolina Michaelis	2·00	1·50
MS3715	125×95 mm. €1.15×2, Virginia Quaresma; Emilia de Sousa Costa	4·50	3·50

820 Children (Martina Marques Teixeira Santos)

2009. School Correspondence. Children's Drawings. Multicoloured.

3716	32c. Type **820**	65	50
3717	47c. Lets recycle to improve the world	1·00	75
3718	68c. Post boxes and recycle bins (Manuel Pedro A. B. Paiva Martins)	1·40	1·00

821 Santa and Hearts

2009. Christmas. Multicoloured.

3719	32c. Type **821**	65	50
3720	47c. Santa delivering letter through window	1·00	75
3721	68c. Christmas tree and Santa	1·30	1·00
3722	80c. Santa and reindeer	1·60	1·20
MS3723	125×95 mm. 50c. Santa riding reindeer on rocker; €1 Stocking containing Santa and parcels	3·00	2·20

822 Variato, the Lusitanian (Carlos Santos)

2010. Aqui Há Selo (your own stamp). Multicoloured.

3724	32c. Type **822**	90	70
3725	32c. Dog in a cage (animal abandonment awareness campaign) (Pedro Trindade)	90	70

823 Frédéric François Chopin

2010. Composers Birth Bicentenaries. Multicoloured.

3726	Type **823**	2·00	1·40
3727	68c. Robert Alexander Schumann	2·00	1·40
MS3728	126×95 mm. €2 Frédéric Chopin	6·00	4·50
MS3729	126×95 mm. €2 Robert Schumann	6·00	4·50

No. 3730 is vacant.

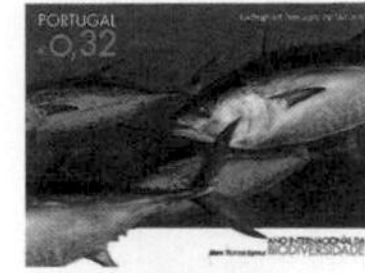

824 Thunnus thynnus (Atlantic bluefin tuna)

2010. International Year of Biodiversity. Multicoloured.

3731	32c. Type **824**	95	70
3732	47c. *Centrophorus granulosus* (gulper shark)	1·30	95
3733	68c. *Ailuropoda melanoleuca* (panda)	2·10	1·60
3734	80c. Hummingbird (Atlantic forest)	2·40	1·80
MS3735	126×95 mm. €2.50 Golden lion tamarin (Atlantic forest)	7·50	7·50

825 Floral Pin

2010. Precious Stones in Portuguese Sacred Art. Multicoloured.

3736	32c. Type **825**	95	70
3737	68c. 18th-century bodice trim	2·10	1·60
3738	€1 Processional cross of Sancho I (detail)	3·00	2·20
MS3739	126×95 mm. €2.50 Crown of Sr. de Fatima (detail)	6·75	5·00

826 Broa

2010. Bread. Multicoloured.

3740	32c. Type **826**	95	70
3741	47c. Padas	1·30	95
3742	68c. Broa de Avintes (bread from Avintes)	2·10	1·60
3743	80c. Pão Alentejano (bread from Alentejano)	2·40	1·80
MS3744	126×95 mm. 80c. Caraça; €1 Pão de Mafra (bread from Mafra)	5·50	4·00

827 Francisco Keli do Amaral (architect) (birth centenary)

2010. Historical and Cultural Personalities. Multicoloured.

3745	32c. Type **827**	95	70
3746	32c. Gomez Eanes de Azuara (writer) (600th birth anniv)	95	70
3747	32c. Fernão Mendes Pinto (explorer) (500th birth anniv)	95	70
3748	32 Alexandre Herculano (novelist and historian) (birth bicentenary)	95	70

828 Monkey

2010. Europa. Children's Books. Multicoloured.
3749 68c. Type **828** 2·00 1·50
MS3750 125×95 mm. 68c.×2, As Type **828**; Man with razor and monkey's tail 4·00 3·00

The stamps and margins of **MS**3750 form a composite design.

829 Pope Benedict XVI

2010. Visit of Pope Benedict XVI to Portugal. Multicoloured.
3751 68c. Type **829** 2·00 1·50
MS3752 125×95 mm. 80c.×3, Pope Paul VI; Pope John Paul II; Pope Benedict XVI 7·00 5·25

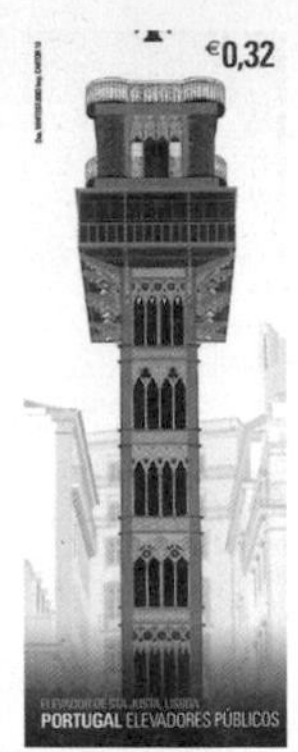

830 Santa Justa, Lisbon

2010. Public Elevators. Multicoloured.
3753 32c. Type **830** 90 70
3754 47c. Gloria, Lisbon 1·10 80
3755 57c. Guindais funicular, Porto 1·20 90
3756 68c. Bom Jesús do Monte Sanctuary, Braga 1·70 1·30
3757 80c. Santa Luzia, Viana do Castelo 2·20 1·70
3758 €1 Nazare 3·50 2·50
MS3759 95×125 mm. €1.25×2, Bica, Lisbon; Lavra, Lisbon 7·00 5·25

831 Exotic Football

2010. World Cup Football Championship, South Africa. Multicoloured.

(a) Self-adhesive.
3760 80c. Type **831** 2·30 1·70

(b) Ordinary gum
MS3761 105×105 mm (circular). €2.50 Player and cheetah (80×30 mm) 7·25 5·50

832 Estrangeiros e Vilhalpandos

2010. Theatre. Multicoloured.
3762 32c. Type **832** 95 70
3763 32c. Auto da Barca do Inferno 95 70
3764 57c. A Castro 1·20 90
3765 68c. O Fidalgo Aprendiz 1·80 1·40
3766 668c. El-Rei Seleuco 1·80 1·40
3767 80c. Guerras de Alecrim e Manjerona 2·75 2·10

833 'Republic' (Júlio Pomar)

2010. Portugal 2010–World Philatelic Exhibition. Multicoloured.
MS3768 32c. Type **833**; 32c. Francisco dos Santos; 32c. Costa Pinheiro; 32c. Bento Condado; 32c. Luis Maciera; 68c. João Abel Manta; 68c. João Machado; 80c. André Carrilho 10·00 10·00

834 Rabaçal

2010. Cheese. Multicoloured.
3769 32c. Type **834** 95 70
3770 32c. Sierra de Estrela 95 70
3771 47c. Azeitão 1·30 1·00
3772 68c. Cabra Transmontana 2·10 1·60
3773 80c. São Jorge 2·40 1·80
MS3774 95×125 mm. €2.50 Sierra de Estrela (different) 7·00 5·50

835 AzulejoTile with Seated Musician (National Museum, Lisbon)

2010. 130th Anniv of Portugal–Romania Diplomatic Relations. Multicoloured.
3775 68c. Type **835** 1·90 1·40
3776 80c. Blue tile (Peasant Life Museum, Bucharest) 2·10 1·60

Stamps of a similar design were issued by Romania.

836 Synagogue of Tomar

2010. Jewish Quarters in Portugal. Multicoloured.
3777 32c. Type **836** 90 70
3778 57c. Rua Nova de Lamego 1·30 95
3779 68c. Jewish quarter, Castelo de Vide 2·10 1·60
MS3780 125×95 mm. €2.50 Jewish construction (medieval manuscript) 7·00 5·50

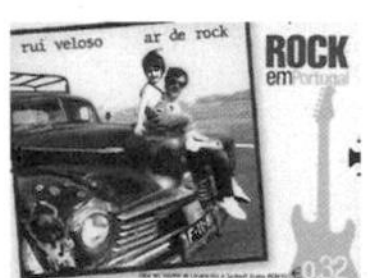

837 Rui Veluso (ar de rock)

2010. Portuguese Rock Bands. Multicoloured.
3781 32c. Type **837** 85 65
3782 47c. Herois do Mar (*Herois do Mar*) 1·10 80
3783 57c. GNR (*Pscicopatria*) 1·30 95
3784 68c. UHF (*À flor da pele*) 2·00 1·50
3785 80c. Xutos & Pontapés (*88*) 2·20 1·60
3786 €1 Moonspell (*Wolfheart*) 3·00 2·20
MS3787 125×95 mm. €2.50 Quarteto 1111 (*A Lenda de El-Rei D. Sebastião*) 7·00 5·25

838 Battle of Vimeiro

2010. Bicentenary of Peninsular War. Multicoloured.
3788 32c. Type **838** 95 70
3789 68c. Battle of Buçaco 2·10 1·60
MS3790 125×95 mm. €2.50 Battle of Pombal (80×30 mm) 7·25 5·50

839 Chamber

2010. Centenary of the Republic. Assembly of the Republic. Multicoloured.
3791 32c. Type **839** 1·70 1·30
3792 68c. Senate Chamber 3·50 2·75
MS3793 125×95 mm. €2 Assembly Building, Lisbon 5·75 4·25

840 Research Ship

2010. 50th Anniv of Hydrographic Institute. Multicoloured.
3794 32c. Type **840** 1·10 70
3795 68c. Research ship, Scientist and equipment array 1·90 1·40

Nos. 3794/5 were printed, *se-tenant*, forming a composite design.

841 Clown

2010. Chapito Circus School, Lisbon. Multicoloured.
3796 32c. Type **841** 1·10 70
3797 47c. Clown riding unicycle 1·20 90
3798 68c. Female juggler with hoops 1·90 1·40
3799 80c. Clown wearing stilts and juggling clubs 2·40 1·80
MS3800 125×95 mm. €2.50 Acrobats (30×80 mm) 7·25 5·50

842 Ceres

2010. Centenary of the Republic
3801 **842** 80c. reddish brown and yellow-ochre 2·25 1·70

843 Establishment of Republic, 1910

2010. History of Freedom. Multicoloured.
3802 32c. Type **843** 90 70
3803 32c. Female figure, symbolizing the Republic 90 70
3804 47c. Soldier with machine gun and civilian with rifle 1·20 90
3805 68c. Female symbol of French revolution and revolutionary 1·90 1·50
3806 80c. Male symbol of American revolution driving off British soldiers 2·40 1·80
3807 €1 Medieval cleric, king and peasant ('in the middle ages nobility, clergy and people had different rights and duties and the king's decisions were obeyed without question') 3·25 2·50

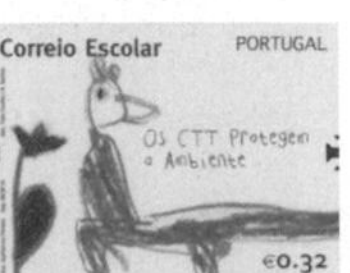

844 Protect the Environment (Guilherme Pereira)

2010. School Correspondence. Children's Drawings. Multicoloured.
3808 32c. Type **844** 1·00 90
3809 47c. Mail lorry with plug and post bicycle (Diogo Gouveia) 1·40 1·20
3810 68c. Post box as tree with letters as leaves (Ana Marques) 2·10 1·90

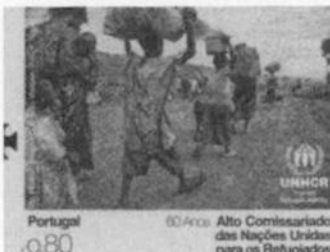

845 Refugees

2010. 60th Anniv of UNHCR (United Nations High Commissioner for Refugees)
3811 80c. black and azure 85 7·00
MS3812 125×95 mm. €2.50 multicoloured 2·40 1·80

Designs: 80c. Type **845**; €2.50 Woman in cage of sticks (vert)

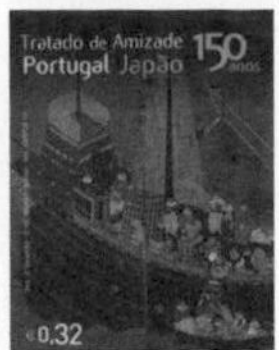

846 Nanban Byobu (detail) (Kano Naizen) (left)

2010. 150th Anniv of Portuguese - Japanese Friendship Treaty. Multicoloured.
3813 32c. Type **846**
3814 80c. Nanban Byobu (detail) (Kano Naizen) (right)

Nos. 3813/14 were printed, *se-tenant*, in horizontal pairs forming composite designs.

847 Flags as Ribbon

2010. 20th Anniv of AICEP (business development agency)
3815 **847** 80c. multicoloured 2·25 1·50

848 Messenger

2010. Ornamental Stone
3816 €1 Type **848** 3·00 2·00
MS3817 125×95 mm €2.50 Head and shoulders (detail of Type **848**) (80×30 mm) 7·50 4·75

849 Water, Wind and Solar Power Generation (Erica Barge Lopes)

2011. Aqui Há Selo (your own stamp). Environment. Multicoloured.
3818 32c. Type **849** 85 70
3819 47c. Rhino and calf on tiny airborne island (Pedro Ferreira) 1·40 1·20

850 Fireworks

2011. Traditional Festivals (1st issue). Multicoloured.
3820 10c. Type **850** 35 25
3821 32c. Three women wearing tall headdresses (Festa dos Tabuleiros, Tomar) 80 70
3822 47c. Children with flower pots (Festa de São João, Porto) 1·40 1·20
3823 68c. Men, confetti and green dragon (Carnaval, Loulé) 2·10 1·90
3824 80c. Girl surrounded by flowers (Festa de Flora, Madeira) 2·40 2·10

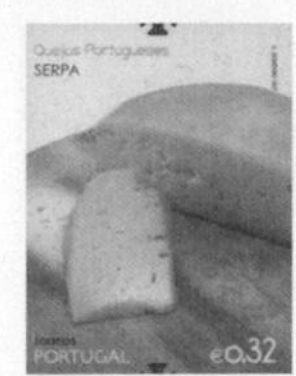

851 Serpa

2011. Cheese. Multicoloured.
3825 32c. Type **851** 80 70
3826 47c. Castelo Branco 1·40 1·20
3827 68c. Pico 2·10 1·90
3828 80c. Nisa 2·40 2·20
3829 €1 Terrincho 3·25 2·75
MS3830 125×95 mm. €2.50 Castelo Branco (different) 7·50 4·75

852 Alves Redol

2010. Personalities. Multicoloured.
3831 32c. Type **852** (birth centenary) 80 70
3832 47c. Manuel da Fonseca (Manuel Lopes Fonseca) (writer) (birth centenary) 1·40 1·20
3833 57c. Trindade Coelho (writer) (150th birth anniv) 1·60 1·30
3834 68c. Antonia Ferreira (business-woman and cultivator of Port Wine) (birth bicentenary) 2·10 1·90
3835 80c. Eugenio dos Santos (military engineer and architect) (300th birth anniv) 2·40 2·20

853 University of Lisbon

2011. Centenary of Higher Education Institutions. Multicoloured.
3836 32c. Type **853** 85 75
3837 32c. University of Porto 85 75
3838 80c. Higher Institute of Economics and Management 2·50 2·30
3839 80c. Higher Technical Institute 2·50 2·30

854 Town and Farmland

2011. Centenary of Credito Agricola (Agricultural Credit). Multicoloured.
3840 N20g. (32c.) Type **854** 80 70
3841 E20g. (68c.) Tractor and farmland 2·10 1·90

855 *Lampetra fluviatilis*

2011. Migratory Fish. Multicoloured.
3842 32c. Type **855** 85 75
3843 47c. *Alosa alosa* 1·60 1·40
3844 68c. *Platichthys flesus* 1·90 1·60
3845 80c. *Liza ramada* 2·40 2·20
MS3846 125×95 mm. €1.80 *Anguilla anguilla* 11·00 7·00
MS3846a 125×95 mm. €1.80 *Salmo salar* 11·00 7·00

856 'Turtle Ship' (Korea)

2011. 50th Anniv of Portugal - Korea Diplomatic Relations. Multicoloured.
3847 N 20g. (32c.) Type **856** 1·10 90
3848 I 20g. (80c.) *Nau* (Portugal) 2·40 2·20

857 Hats

2011. Centenary of Guarda Nacional Republicana (GNR). Multicoloured.
3849 N 20g. (32c.) Type **857** 1·00 65
MS3850 125×95 mm. €3.60 Gloved hands holding sword (detail of soldier wearing dress uniform) (horiz) 11·00 7·50

858 Cork Oak Forest

2011. Europa. Forests. Multicoloured.
3851 68c. Type **858** 2·00 1·30
MS3852 125×95 mm. 68c.×2, Deer in pine forest; As Type **858** 4·00 2·60

859 Flags as Clasped Hands

2011. Centenary of UPAEP
3853 **859** 80c. multicoloured 2·50 1·60

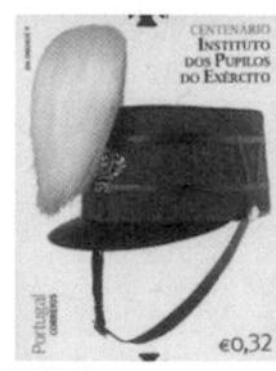

860 Cap

2011. Centenary of Pupilos do Exército (Pupils of the Army) Institute. Multicoloured.
3854 32c. Type **860** 75 65
3855 €1 Pupils 3·25 3·00
MS3856 125×95 mm. €2.50 Pupils on parade (detail, head and shoulders) (horiz) 7·50 4·75

861 Futebol Clube do Porto Emblem

2011. Portuguese Clubs in UEFA Football Championship Final, Dublin. Multicoloured.
MS3857 €1×2, Type **861**; Sporting Clube de Braga emblem 6·00 4·00

862 *A luva cinzenta* (Columbano)

2011. Centenary of the Museo Nacional de Arte (Museum of Art). Multicoloured.
3858 32c. Type **862** 80 70
3859 32c. *Triestezas, Cabeça* (Amadeo de Souza-Cardoso) 80 70
3860 47c. *A sesta* (Almada Negreiros) 1·50 1·30
3861 68c. *Cais* 44 (Fernando Lanhas) 2·20 2·00
3862 68c. *Sombra Projectada de René Bertholo* (Lourdes Castro) 2·20 2·00
3863 80c. *A esquiva* (João Maria Gusmão e Pedro Paiva) 2·50 2·30
MS3864 125×95 mm. €1.50×2, *Landscape* (Julião Sarmento); *Estrad da Vida* (Fernando Taborda) 9·00 5·75

863 Soldier in Battle Position

2011. 50th Anniv of Marine Infantry School. Multicoloured.
3865 32c. Type **863** 1·10 90
3866 80c. Soldiers in rib (rigid inflatable boat) 2·40 2·20
MS3867 125×95 mm. €2.50 Monument 7·75 5·00

864 Vila Verde

2011. Traditional Portuguese Embroideries. Multicoloured.
3868 32c. Type **864** 80 70
3869 47c. Arraiolos 1·40 1·20
3870 57c. Castelo Branco 1·60 1·30
3871 68c. Viana 2·10 1·90
3872 80c. Madeira 2·50 2·30
3873 €1 Azores 3·25 3·00
MS3874 125×95 mm. €1.75 Guimarães 5·25 3·50
MS3875 125×95 mm. €1.75 Ribatejo 5·25 3·50

865 Arrival of *Nau* (Portuguese ship) at Ayutthaya (left)

2011. 500th Anniv of Portugal - Thailand Diplomatic Relations. Multicoloured.
3876 32c. Type **865** 90 80
3877 32c. Portuguese ship and Thai landfall (left) 90 80
3878 80c. Arrival of Nau (Portuguese ship) at Ayutthaya (right) 2·50 2·30
3879 80c. Portuguese ship and Thai landfall (right) 2·50 2·30

Nos. 3876 and 3878; 3877 and 3879 were printed, *se-tenant*, in horizontal pairs forming composite designs.

866 Illuminated Letter (Leitura Nova, Além-Douro, 16th-century)

2011. Centenary of Torre do Tombo National Archives. Multicoloured.
3880 32c. Type **866** 80 70
3881 68c. Satyr (Leitura Nova, Além-Douro, 16th-century) 80 70
3882 €2 Dragon (Apocalypse Lorvão, 13th-century) 6·25 6·00
MS3883 125×95 mm. €2.30 Gargoyle (Archive building) 7·00 4·50

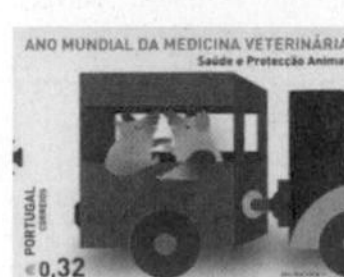

867 Pigs in Transit (Animal Health Protection)

2011. International Year of Veterinary Medicine. Multicoloured.
3884 32c. Type **867** 80 70
3885 68c. Horse (protection and animal breeding) 2·10 1·90
3886 80c. Cat (medicines and products for veterinary use) 2·40 2·20
3887 €1 Cow (veterinary public health) 3·25 3·00
MS3888 125×95 mm. €2.50 Owl (Rehabilitation Centre for Wild Animals, Lisbon) 7·25 5·50

868 Laura Alves

2011. Portuguese Theatre. Actors and Theatre Scenes. Multicoloured.
3889 32c. Type **868** 80 70
3890 32c. Amelia Rey Colaço 80 70
3891 47c. Raul Solnado 1·40 1·20
3892 68c. Armando Cortez 2·10 1·90
3893 80c. Eunice Muñoz 2·40 2·20
3894 €1 Ruy de Carvalho 3·25 3·00
MS3895 125×95 mm. €1×2, Scene from *Frei Luis de Sousa* (Almeida Garrett); Scene from *Os Velhos* (D. João Gonçalves Zarco da Câmara) 6·50 6·00

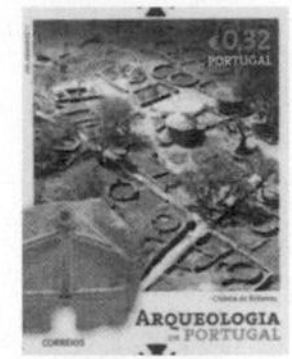

869 Citânia de Briterios

2011. Archaeology in Portugal. Multicoloured.
3896 32c. Type **869** 80 70
3897 47c. Rock carvings, Foz Coa 1·40 1·20
3898 68c. Clay lamp and mosaic, Conimbriga 2·10 1·90
3899 80c. Ruins, column and squid mosaic, Milreu 2·40 2·20
3900 €1 Stone passageway, Alcalar 3·25 3·00
MS3901 95×125 mm. €2.50 José Leite de Vasconcelos (ethnographer and director of National Archaeology Museums) 7·50 4·75

870 Quinta das Cruzes Museum

2011. Tourism. Quintas (manor houses) of Madeira. Multicoloured.
3902 32c. Type **870** 80 70
3903 68c. Quinta Jardins do Lago (botanical garden hotel) 2·10 1·90
3904 80c. Quinta Monte Palace (tropical garden) 2·40 2·50
3905 €2 Quinta (Estalagem) Serra Golf (hotel) 6·50 6·25
MS3906 125×95 mm. €1.75 Quinta Casa Velha do Palheiro (hotel) 6·00 4·00
MS3907 125×95 mm. €2.50 Quinta Vigia (official residence of President of Regional Government of Madeira) 6·00 4·00

871 Recycling

2011. Environment. Water and Waste Management. Multicoloured.
3908 32c. Hand holding glass of water and tap (tap water, confidence in water) 80 70
3909 47c. Hose pipe and sticking plaster (water saving for tomorrow) 1·40 1·40
3910 68c. Bucket, filters and flowers (treat wastewater to protect the environment) 2·10 1·90
3911 80c. Type **871** 2·40 2·20

872 Alfredo Marceneiro

2011. Fado Performers. Multicoloured.
3912 32c. Type **872** 80 70
3913 47c. Carlos Ramos 1·40 1·20
3914 57c. Herminia Silva 1·70 1·50
3915 68c. Maria Teresa de Noronha 2·10 1·00
3916 80c. Amalia Rodriguez 2·40 2·20
3917 €1 Carlos de Carmo 3·25 3·00

MS3918 125×95 mm. €2.50 Early performer (vert) 7·50 4·75

2011. Traditional Festivals (2nd issue). Multicoloured.

3919 N20g. (32c.) As No. 3820 (background colour changed to white) 80 70
3920 A20g. (47c.) As No. 3821 (background colour changed to white) 1·40 1·20
3921 E20g. (68c.) As No. 3822 (background colour changed to white) 2·10 1·90

873 Bird and Fish

2011. School Correspondence. Children's Drawings. Multicoloured.

3922 32c. Type **873** 80 70
3923 68c. Boy riding unicycle with sun and globe as wheels 2·10 1·90
3924 80c. Children of many nations 2·40 2·20

874 Marquis de Sá da Bandeira

2012. 175th Anniv of Army School. Multicoloured.

3925 32c. Type **874** 80 70
3926 68c. Arms and badges 2·10 1·90
MS3927 125×95 mm. €2.50 Sword hilt (vert) 6·00 4·00

875 Marcos António da Fonseca Portugal

2012. Historical and Cultural Personalities. Multicoloured.

3928 32c. Type **875** (composer) (250th birth anniv) 80 70
3929 68c. Manuel de Brito Camacho (writer and politician) (150th birth anniv) 2·10 1·90
3930 80c. António Vilar (actor) (birth centenary) 2·40 2·20

876 'God created Man and Woman'

2012. The Word and the Image. Multicoloured.

3931 47c. Type **876** 1·40 1·20
3932 68c. 'Moses receiving Mana in the wilderness' 2·10 1·90
3933 80c. 'Adoration of the three Magi' 2·40 2·20
3934 €1 'Last Supper' 3·25 3·00
MS3935 95×125 mm. €1.50 'Pentecost' 5·00 3·00
MS3936 95×125 mm. €1.50 'Passion of Christ' 5·00 3·00

877 Code for Orange (red and yellow), Red and Purple (red and blue)

2012. Communicating Colours for the Colour Blind (ColorADD code). Multicoloured.

3937 32c. Type **877** 80 70
3938 47c. Purple (red and blue), blue and green (yellow and blue) 1·40 1·20
3939 68c. Green (yellow and blue), yellow, orange (red and yellow) 2·10 1·90
3940 80c. Black 2·40 2·20
3941 €1 White 3·25 3·00

878 Largo da Oliveira

2012. Guimarães 2012 - European Capital of Culture. Multicoloured.

3942 32c. Type **878** 80 70
3943 47c. Vila Flor Cultural Centre 1·40 1·20
3944 68c. Drummers, Nicolinas Festival 2·10 1·90
3945 80c. Santa Marinha da Costa Inn 2·40 2·20
MS3946 125×95 mm. €3 Guimarães Castle 8·00 5·00

879 Girl on Bicycle

2012. 25th Anniv of Erasmus Programme (European Community Action Scheme for the Mobility of University Students) (EU student exchange programme). Multicoloured.

3947 68c. Type **879** 2·10 1·90
MS3948 125×95 mm. €3 Girl and boy on scooter (80×30 mm) 8·00 5·00

880 *Príncipe Perfeito*

2012. Europa. Visit Portugal. Multicoloured.

3949 68c. Type **880** 2·10 1·90
MS3950 125×95 mm. 68c.×2, Coastline; As Type **880** 5·50 4·50

881 Santarem

2012. Tourism. Route of Portuguese Cathedrals. Multicoloured.

3951 N 20g. (32c.) Type **881** 80 70
3952 N 20g. (32c.) Braga 80 70
3953 N 20g. (32c.) Viano do Castelo 80 70
3954 N 20g. (32c.) Vila Real 80 70
3955 N 20g. (32c.) Silves 80 70
3956 N 20g. (32c.) Guarda 80 70
3957 N 20g. (32c.) Lamego 80 70
3958 N 20g. (32c.) Porto 80 70
3959 N 20g. (32c.) Faro 80 70
3960 N 20g. (32c.) Viseu 80 70

882 Adérito Sedas Nunes

2012. 50th Anniv of Institute of Social Sciences, University of Lisbon (originally Social Science Research Group, Technical University of Lisbon). Multicoloured.

3961 N 20g. (32c.) Type **882** 80 70
3962 E 20g. (50c.) Building 1·50 1·30

883 Table Football Player

2012. Euro 2012 European Football Championship, Ukraine and Poland (1st issue). Multicoloured.

3963 68c. Type **883** 2·10 1·90
MS3964 125×95 mm. 68c. Subbuteo table 3·00 2·50

884 Sprinter

2012. Olympic and Paralympic Games, London. Multicoloured.

3965 N 20g. (32c.) Type **884** 80 70
3966 N 20g. (32c.) Disabled sprinters 80 70
3967 I 20g. (60c.) Fencer 2·00 1·70
3968 I 20g. (60c.) Wheelchair handball 2·00 1·70

885 Father Teodoro de Almeida

2012. Transit of Venus, 2012. Multicoloured.

3969 €2 Type **885** 6·50 6·25
MS3970 126×95 mm. €3 Lines of transit 6·75 5·00

886 Football

2012. Euro 2012 European Football Championship, Ukraine and Poland (2nd issue). 'Viva Portugal'

MS3971 **886** €1.50 multicoloured 5·00 3·00

2012. Traditional Festivals (3rd issue). Multicoloured.

3972 10c. Festival 40 30
3973 32c. Couple carrying banner (Festa de Santo António,Lisbon) 80 70
3974 47c. Child as crowned angel (Festa do Espirito Santo, Azores) 1·40 1·20
3975 68c. Masked man (Carnaval de Ílhavo) 2·10 1·90
3976 80c. Horse rider (Feira da Golegã) 2·50 2·30

887 Douro River

2012. Douro River. Multicoloured.

3977 32c. Type **887** 80 70
3978 57c. Trees sloping down to river carrying steamer 1·60 1·30
3979 68c. Vineyards on river bend 2·10 1·90
3980 80c. Mist over river 2·50 2·30
MS3981 125×95 mm. €3 Waterfront, boats and bridge (80×30 mm) 6·75 5·00

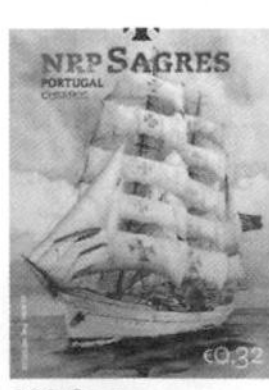

888 *Sagres*

2012. 75th Anniv of *Sagres* and *Creoula* Training Ships. Multicoloured.

3982 32c. Type **888** 80 70
3983 80c. *Creoula* 2·50 2·30
MS3984 95×125 mm. €1.75 Ship's bell, *Sagres* 5·25 3·50
MS3985 95×125 mm. €1.75 Lifeboats, *Creoula* (horiz) 5·25 3·50

CHARITY TAX STAMPS

Used on certain days of the year as an additional postal tax on internal letters. Other values in some of the types were for use on telegrams only. The proceeds were devoted to public charities. If one was not affixed in addition to the ordinary postage, postage due stamps were used to collect the deficiency and the fine.

1911. Optd **ASSISTENCIA**.

C455 **48** 10r. green (No. 406) 13·00 3·50
C484 **56** 1c. green (No. 486) 9·50 3·00

C57 "Lisbon"

1913. Lisbon Festival.

C485 **C57** 1c. green 1·80 1·30

C58 "Charity"

1915. For the Poor.

C486 **C58** 1c. red 50 45
C669 **C58** 15c. red 95 95

1924. Surch **15 ctvs.**

C594 15c. on 1c. red 2·50 1·10

C71 Muse of History

1925. Portuguese Army in Flanders, 1484 and 1918.

C662 **C71** 10c. red 1·80 1·60
C663 **C71** 10c. green 1·80 1·60
C664 **C71** 10c. blue 1·80 1·60
C665 **C71** 10c. brown 1·80 1·60

C73 Monument to De Pombal

C75 Marquis de Pombal

1925. Marquis de Pombal Commemoration.

C666 **C73** 15c. blue and black 1·80 1·10
C667 - 15c. blue and black 1·80 1·10
C668 **C 75** 15c. blue and black 65 55

DESIGN: No. C677, Planning reconstruction of Lisbon.

C81 Hurdler

1928. Olympic Games.

C741 **C81** 15c. black and red 6·00 3·50

NEWSPAPER STAMPS

N16

N17

1876

N180 **N16** 2r. black 33·00 21·00
N178 **N 17** 2½r. green 22·00 2·00
N187 **N 17** 2½r. brown 19·00 1·70

OFFICIAL STAMPS

1938. Optd **OFICIAL**.

O900 **99** 40c. brown 90 20

O144

1952. No value.

O1069 **O144** (1e.) black and stone 90 15
O1070 **O144** (1e.) black and stone 1·00 35

On No. O1069 "CORREIO DE PORTUGAL" is in stone on a black background, on No. O1070 it is in black on the stone background.

PARCEL POST STAMPS

P59

1920

P578	**P59**	1c. brown	55	45
P579	**P59**	2c. orange	55	45
P580	**P59**	5c. brown	55	45
P581	**P59**	10c. brown	55	45
P582	**P59**	20c. blue	75	45
P583	**P59**	40c. red	75	45
P584	**P59**	50c. black	1·10	80
P585	**P59**	60c. blue	1·00	80
P586	**P59**	70c. brown	6·25	3·00
P587	**P59**	80c. blue	6·50	4·75
P588	**P59**	90c. violet	6·75	3·50
P589	**P59**	1e. green	7·00	4·25
P591	**P59**	2e. lilac	20·00	5·25
P592	**P59**	3e. green	37·00	6·00
P593	**P59**	4e. blue	80·00	10·50
P594	**P59**	5e. lilac	£110	7·00
P595	**P59**	10e. brown	£170	12·50

P101

1936

P891	**P101**	50c. grey	1·10	95
P892	**P101**	1e. brown	1·10	95
P893	**P101**	1e.50 violet	1·10	95
P894	**P101**	2e. purple	4·75	1·00
P895	**P101**	2e.50 green	4·75	1·00
P896	**P101**	4e.50 purple	12·50	1·00
P897	**P101**	5e. violet	18·00	1·20
P898	**P101**	10e. orange	23·00	2·50

POSTAGE DUE STAMPS

D48 Da Gama received by the Zamorin of Calicut

1898

D386	**D48**	5r. black	5·00	3·50
D387	**D48**	10r. mauve	6·25	4·00
D388	**D48**	20r. orange	10·50	4·50
D389	**D48**	50r. grey	80·00	9·00
D390	**D48**	100r. red on pink	£120	65·00
D391	**D48**	200r. brown on buff	£130	90·00

D49

1904

D392	**D49**	5r. brown	85	80
D393	**D49**	10r. orange	4·25	1·30
D394	**D49**	20r. mauve	12·00	5·75
D395	**D49**	30r. green	8·50	4·25
D396	**D49**	40r. lilac	9·75	4·25
D397	**D49**	50r. red	65·00	7·25
D398	**D49**	100r. blue	14·50	9·50

1911. Optd **REPUBLICA**.

D418	5r. brown	80	70
D419	10r. orange	80	70
D420	20r. mauve	2·10	1·80
D421	30r. green	2·00	70
D422	40r. lilac	2·10	70
D423	50r. red	8·75	6·75
D424	100r. blue	9·25	7·25

1915. As Type **D49** but value in centavos.

D491	½c. brown	90	85
D498	1c. orange	1·10	1·00
D493	2c. purple	90	85
D499	3c. green	1·10	1·00
D500	4c. lilac	1·10	1·00
D501	5c. red	1·10	1·00
D497	10c. blue	1·10	1·00

1921

D578	½c. green	80	55
D579	4c. green	80	55
D580	8c. green	80	55
D581	10c. green	80	55
D582	12c. green	90	65
D583	16c. green	90	65
D584	20c. green	90	65
D585	24c. green	90	65
D586	32c. green	1·40	90
D587	36c. green	2·50	1·80
D588	40c. green	2·50	1·80
D589	48c. green	1·60	1·00
D590	50c. green	1·60	1·00
D591	60c. green	1·60	1·00
D592	72c. green	1·60	1·00
D593	80c. green	12·00	10·50
D594	1e.20 green	5·50	5·50

D72

1925. Portuguese Army in Flanders, 1484 and 1918.

D662	**D72**	20c. brown	95	75

1925. De Pombal types optd **MULTA**.

D663	**C73**	30c. blue	1·90	1·60
D664	-	30c. blue	1·90	1·60
D665	**C75**	30c. blue	1·90	1·60

D82

1928. Olympic Games.

D741	**D82**	30e. black and red	3·00	2·75

D91

1932

D865	**D91**	5e. buff	1·20	90
D866	**D91**	10e. blue	1·20	90
D867	**D91**	20e. pink	2·50	1·30
D868	**D91**	30e. blue	2·75	1·30
D869	**D91**	40e. green	2·75	1·30
D870	**D91**	50e. grey	3·75	1·30
D871	**D91**	60e. pink	7·50	3·50
D872	**D91**	80e. purple	14·00	7·25
D873	**D91**	1e.20 green	23·00	18·00

D108

1940

D912	**D108**	5c. brown	95	60
D922	**D108**	5e. orange	20·00	14·00
D923	**D108**	10c. lilac	50	25
D924	**D108**	20c. red	50	25
D925	**D108**	30c. violet	50	25
D926	**D108**	40c. mauve	50	25
D927	**D108**	50c. blue	50	25
D928	**D108**	60c. green	50	25
D929	**D108**	80c. red	50	25
D930	**D108**	1e. brown	50	25
D931	**D108**	2e. mauve	70	60

D218

1967

D1312	**D218**	10c. brown, yellow and orange	15	10
D1313	**D218**	20e. purple, yellow and brown	15	10
D1314	**D218**	30e. brown, light yellow and yellow	15	10
D1315	**D218**	40e. purple, yellow and bistre	15	10
D1316	**D218**	50e. indigo, blue and light blue	20	10
D1317	**D218**	60e. olive, blue and turquoise	20	10
D1318	**D218**	80e. indigo, blue and light blue	20	10
D1319	**D218**	1e. indigo, bl & ultram	20	10
D1320	**D218**	2e. olive, light green and green	20	15
D1321	**D218**	3e. deep green, light green and green	45	15
D1322	**D218**	4e. deep green, green and turquoise	45	20
D1323	**D218**	5e. brown, mauve and purple	35	20
D1324	**D218**	9e. deep lilac, lilac and violet	45	25
D1325	**D218**	10e. deep purple, grey and purple	45	25
D1326	**D218**	20e. maroon, grey and purple	1·30	35
D1327	**D218**	40e. lilac, grey and mauve	3·00	1·40
D1328	**D218**	50e. maroon, grey and purple	3·75	1·60

D481

1992. Inscr "CORREIOS DE PORTUGAL".

D2305	**D481**	1e. blue, deep blue and black	10	10
D2306	**D481**	2e. light green, green and black	10	10
D2307	**D481**	5e. yellow, brown and black	10	10
D2308	**D481**	10e. red, orange and black	20	10
D2309	**D481**	20e. green, violet and black	35	10
D2310	**D481**	50e. yellow, green and black	80	45
D2311	**D481**	100e. orange, red and black	1·50	1·00
D2312	**D481**	200e. mauve, violet and black	3·00	1·90

1995. Inscr "CTT CORREIOS".

D2445	3e. multicoloured	20	10
D2446	4e. multicoloured	20	10
D2446a	5e. multicoloured	10	10
D2447	9e. multicoloured	45	10
D2447a	10e. red, orange and black	15	10
D2447b	20e. multicoloured	25	20
D2448	40e. multicoloured	80	65
D2449	50e. multicoloured	90	60
D2450	100e. orange, red and black	1·30	90

D656

2002. Multicoloured

D2907	1c. Type D **656**	10	10
D2908	2c. "0.02"	10	10
D2909	5c. "0.05"	15	10
D2910	10c. "0.10"	30	25
D2911	25c. "0.25"	60	50
D2912	50c. "0.50"	1·30	95
D2913	€1 "1"	2·50	2·00

Pt. 9

PORTUGUESE COLONIES

General issues for the Portuguese possessions in Africa: Angola, Cape Verde Islands, Guinea, Lourenco Marques, Mozambique, Congo, St. Thomas and Prince Islands, and Zambezia.

1898. 1000 reis = 1 milreis.
1919. 100 centavos = 1 escudo.

1898. 400th Anniv of Vasco da Gama's Discovery of Route to India. As Nos. 378/85 of Portugal but inscr "AFRICA".

1	2½r. green	1·20	1·00
2	5r. red	1·20	1·00
3	10r. purple	1·20	1·00
4	25r. green	1·20	1·00
5	50r. blue	1·20	1·00
6	75r. brown	10·50	9·00
7	100r. brown	10·50	7·00
8	150r. brown	15·00	7·00

CHARITY TAX STAMPS

C1

1919. Fiscal stamps optd **TAXA DE GUERRA**.

C1	**C1**	1c. black and green	1·40	1·40
C2	**C1**	5c. black and green	1·40	1·40

POSTAGE DUE STAMPS

D1

1945. Value in black.

D1	**D1**	10c. purple	55	55
D2	**D1**	20c. purple	55	55
D3	**D1**	30c. blue	55	55
D4	**D1**	40c. brown	55	55
D5	**D1**	50c. lilac	55	55
D6	**D1**	1e. brown	2·50	2·50
D7	**D1**	2e. green	4·25	4·25
D8	**D1**	3e. red	7·00	7·00
D9	**D1**	5e. yellow	10·50	10·50

Pt. 9

PORTUGUESE CONGO

The area known as Portuguese Congo, now called Cabinda, was the part of Angola north of the River Congo. It issued its own stamps from 1894 until 1920.

1894. 1000 reis = 1 milreis.
1913. 100 centavos = 1 escudo.

1894. "Figures" key-type inscr " CONGO".

8	**R**	5r. orange	1·70	1·60
9	**R**	10r. mauve	2·50	1·70
10	**R**	15r. brown	4·25	3·50
12	**R**	20r. lilac	4·25	3·50
13	**R**	25r. green	2·75	1·00
22	**R**	50r. blue	4·75	3·00
5	**R**	75r. pink	9·00	5·50
6	**R**	80r. green	11·50	8·00
7	**R**	100r. brown on yellow	10·00	6·75
17	**R**	150r. red on pink	19·00	16·00
18	**R**	200r. blue on blue	19·00	16·00
19	**R**	300r. blue on brown	24·00	20·00

1898. "King Carlos" key-type inscr "CONGO".

24	**S**	2½r. grey	55	45
25	**S**	5r. red	55	45
26	**S**	10r. green	75	45
27	**S**	15r. brown	2·10	1·80
66	**S**	15r. green	1·30	25
28	**S**	20r. lilac	1·40	95
29	**S**	25r. green	2·00	1·30
67	**S**	25r. red	1·30	25
30	**S**	50r. blue	2·30	1·80
68	**S**	50r. brown	3·75	2·75
69	**S**	65r. blue	11·50	9·75
31	**S**	75r. pink	5·75	3·25
70	**S**	75r. purple	4·50	4·00
32	**S**	80r. mauve	4·25	3·50
33	**S**	100r. blue on blue	3·50	2·50
71	**S**	115r. brown on pink	10·50	8·25
72	**S**	130r. brown on yellow	14·00	12·00
34	**S**	150r. brown on yellow	5·75	4·00
35	**S**	200r. purple on pink	7·00	4·25
36	**S**	300r. blue on pink	8·50	4·75
73	**S**	400r. blue on cream	13·50	11·50
37	**S**	500r. black on blue	21·00	15·00
38	**S**	700r. mauve on yellow	36·00	27·00

1902. Surch.

74	**S**	50r. on 65r. blue	7·00	4·50
40	**R**	65r. on 15r. brown	6·50	5·00
41	**R**	65r. on 20r. lilac	6·50	5·00
44	**R**	65r. on 25r. green	6·50	5·00
46	**R**	65r. on 300r. blue on brn	8·25	7·75
50	**V**	115r. on 2½r. brown	6·50	5·00
47	**R**	115r. on 10r. mauve	6·50	4·75
48	**R**	115r. on 50r. blue	6·25	4·75
53	**R**	130r. on 5r. orange	6·50	5·25
54	**R**	130r. on 75r. pink	6·50	5·00
57	**R**	130r. on 100r. brn on yell	6·50	5·25
58	**R**	400r. on 80r. green	2·75	2·20
60	**R**	400r. on 150r. red on pink	4·00	3·25
61	**R**	400r. on 200r. blue on blue	4·00	3·25

1902. "King Carlos" key-type of Portuguese Congo optd **PROVISORIO**.

62	15r. brown	3·00	2·10
63	25r. green	3·00	2·10
64	50r. blue	3·00	2·10
65	75r. pink	7·00	5·00

1911. "King Carlos" key-type of Angola, optd **REPUBLICA** and **CONGO** with bar (200r. also surch).

75	2½r. grey	2·20	1·40
76	5r. red	3·00	2·20
77	10r. green	3·00	2·20
78	15r. green	3·00	2·20
79	25r. on 200r. purple on pink	3·25	2·30

1911. "King Carlos" key-type of Portuguese Congo optd **REPUBLICA**.

80	2½r. grey	45	30
81	5r. orange	65	45
82	10r. green	65	45
83	15r. green	65	45
84	20r. lilac	65	45
85	25r. red	65	45
86	50r. brown	75	45
87	75r. purple	1·30	85

88		100r. blue on blue	1·50	85
89		115r. brown on pink	2·20	1·40
90		130r. brown on yellow	2·20	1·40
143		200r. purple on pink	6·75	5·75
92		400r. blue on cream	7·50	5·75
93		500r. black on blue	7·50	6·00
94		700r. mauve on yellow	10·50	6·75

1913. Surch **REPUBLICA CONGO** and value on "Vasco da Gama" stamps of (a) Portuguese Colonies.

95		¼c. on 2½r. green	1·80	1·50
96		½c. on 5r. red	1·80	1·50
97		1c. on 10r. purple	1·80	1·50
98		2½c. on 25r. green	1·80	1·50
99		5c. on 50r. blue	2·20	2·10
100		7½c. on 75r. brown	3·75	3·50
101		10c. on 100r. brown	2·75	2·10
102		15c. on 150r. brown	2·00	2·10

(b) Macao.

103		¼c. on ½a. green	2·40	2·30
104		½c. on 1a. red	2·40	2·30
105		1c. on 2a. purple	2·40	2·30
106		2½c. on 4a. green	2·40	2·30
107		5c. on 8a. blue	2·40	2·30
108		7½c. on 12a. brown	4·75	3·25
109		10c. on 16a. brown	3·00	2·30
110		15c. on 24a. brown	3·00	2·30

(c) Portuguese Timor.

111		¼c. on ½a. green	2·40	2·30
112		½c. on 1a. red	2·40	2·30
113		1c. on 2a. purple	2·40	2·30
114		2½c. on 4a. green	2·40	2·30
115		5c. on 8a. blue	2·40	2·30
116		7½c. on 12a. brown	4·75	3·25
117		10c. on 16a. brown	3·00	2·30
118		15c. on 24a. brown	3·00	2·30

1914. "Ceres" key-type inscr "CONGO".

135	U	¼c. green	85	75
120	U	½c. black	1·10	70
121	U	1c. green	3·75	2·75
134	U	1c. green on blue	7·25	5·25
122	U	1½c. brown	2·40	1·50
136	U	2c. red	85	75
124	U	2½c. violet	75	70
125	U	5c. blue	1·10	1·10
126	U	7½c. brown	2·20	1·50
127	U	8c. grey	2·30	2·00
128	U	10c. red	2·30	2·00
129	U	15c. purple	2·40	2·00
130	U	20c. green	2·40	2·00
131	U	30c. brown on green	4·75	3·25
132	U	40c. brown on pink	4·75	3·50
133	U	50c. orange on orange	5·75	3·50

1914. "King Carlos" key-type of Portuguese Congo optd **PROVISORIO** and **REPUBLICA**.

146	S	15r. brown (No. 62)	1·60	1·10
147	S	50r. blue (No. 64)	1·60	1·10
140	S	75r. pink (No. 65)	2·20	2·00

1914. Provisional stamps of 1902 optd **REPUBLICA**.

148		50r. on 65r. blue	1·60	1·10
150	V	115r. on 2½r. brown	1·10	55
151	R	115r. on 10r. mauve	1·00	75
154	R	115r. on 50r. blue	2·50	1·60
156	R	130r. on 5r. orange	1·60	1·10
157	R	130r. on 75r. pink	2·50	1·90
160	R	130r. on 100r. brown on yellow	1·20	75

NEWSPAPER STAMPS

1894. "Newspaper" key-type inscr "CONGO".

N24	V	2½r. brown	95	80

Pt. 9

PORTUGUESE GUINEA

A former Portuguese territory, on the west coast of Africa, with adjacent islands. Used stamps of Cape Verde Islands from 1877 until 1881. In September 1974 the territory became independent and was renamed Guinea-Bissau.

1881. 1000 reis = 1 milreis.
1913. 100 centavos = 1 escudo.

1881. "Crown" key-type inscr "CABO VERDE" and optd **GUINE**.

19	P	5r. black	7·50	5·75
20	P	10r. yellow	£300	£300
31	P	10r. green	13·00	8·75
21	P	20r. bistre	6·25	4·25
32	P	20r. red	13·00	9·50
13	P	25r. pink	4·50	3·25
28	P	25r. lilac	5·75	3·50
23	P	40r. blue	£325	£225
29	P	40r. yellow	3·50	3·00
24	P	50r. green	£325	£225
30	P	50r. blue	10·50	5·00
16	P	100r. lilac	15·00	11·50
17	P	200r. orange	22·00	15·00
18	P	300r. brown	26·00	20·00

3

1886

35	3	5r. black	11·50	10·50
36	3	10r. green	14·00	7·50
37	3	20r. red	20·00	7·50
38	3	25r. purple	20·00	11·50
46	3	40r. brown	16·00	11·50
40	3	50r. blue	33·00	11·50
47	3	80r. grey	30·00	21·00
48	3	100r. brown	30·00	21·00
43	3	200r. lilac	70·00	42·00
44	3	300r. orange	90·00	65·00

1893. "Figures" key-type inscr "GUINE".

50	R	5r. yellow	3·50	2·10
51	R	10r. mauve	3·50	2·10
52	R	15r. brown	4·50	3·00
53	R	20r. lilac	4·50	3·00
54	R	25r. green	4·50	3·00
55	R	50r. blue	8·00	4·25
57	R	75r. pink	21·00	13·50
58	R	80r. green	21·00	13·50
59	R	100r. brown on buff	21·00	13·50
60	R	150r. red on pink	21·00	13·50
61	R	200r. blue on blue	36·00	28·00
62	R	300r. blue on brown	34·00	28·00

1898. "King Carlos" key-type inscr "GUINE".

65	S	2½r. grey	70	55
66	S	5r. red	70	55
67	S	10r. green	70	55
68	S	15r. brown	5·75	4·25
114	S	15r. green	3·50	1·80
69	S	20r. lilac	2·75	1·80
70	S	25r. green	3·25	2·10
115	S	25r. red	1·80	1·10
71	S	50r. blue	4·25	2·20
116	S	50r. brown	4·50	3·50
117	S	65r. blue	14·50	11·00
72	S	75r. pink	23·00	16·00
118	S	75r. purple	6·25	5·50
73	S	80r. mauve	5·75	3·50
74	S	100r. blue on blue	5·25	3·50
119	S	115r. brown on pink	16·00	11·50
120	S	130r. brown on yellow	17·00	11·50
75	S	150r. brown on yellow	17·00	7·25
76	S	200r. purple on pink	17·00	7·25
77	S	300r. blue on pink	15·00	8·75
121	S	400r. blue on yellow	18·00	12·00
78	S	500r. black on blue	23·00	13·50
79	S	700r. mauve on yellow	33·00	23·00

1902. Surch.

122	S	50r. on 65r. blue	8·75	5·75
81	3	65r. on 10r. green	12·50	7·00
84	R	65r. on 10r. mauve	10·50	5·50
85	R	65r. on 15r. brown	10·50	5·50
82	3	65r. on 20r. red	12·50	7·00
86	R	65r. on 20r. lilac	10·50	5·50
83	3	65r. on 25r. purple	12·50	7·00
88	R	65r. on 50r. blue	5·50	4·75
97	V	115r. on 2½r. brown	7·50	5·25
93	R	115r. on 5r. yellow	10·00	5·25
95	R	115r. on 25r. green	11·50	5·75
89	3	115r. on 40r. brown	11·00	6·75
91	3	115r. on 50r. blue	11·00	6·75
92	3	115r. on 300r. orange	14·00	8·75
98	3	130r. on 80r. grey	14·00	10·00
100	3	130r. on 100r. brown	14·50	10·00
102	R	130r. on 150r. red on pink	11·50	5·75
103	R	130r. on 200r. blue on blue	12·50	6·75
104	R	130r. on 300r. blue on brn	12·50	7·25
105	3	400r. on 5r. black	65·00	60·00
107	R	400r. on 75r. pink	8·25	7·25
108	R	400r. on 80r. green	5·50	3·25
109	R	400r. on 100r. brn on buff	7·00	3·25
106	3	400r. on 200r. lilac	24·00	13·50

1902. "King Carlos" key-type of Portuguese Guinea optd **PROVISORIO**.

110		15r. brown	4·50	3·00
111		25r. green	4·50	3·00
112		50r. blue	5·50	3·25
113		75r. pink	11·00	9·00

1911. "King Carlos" key-type of Portuguese Guinea optd **REPUBLICA**.

123		2½r. grey	90	65
124		5r. red	1·10	65
125		10r. green	1·20	65
126		15r. green	1·20	95
127		20r. lilac	1·20	95
128		25r. red	1·20	95
129		50r. brown	1·20	95
130		75r. purple	1·20	95
131		100r. blue on blue	3·00	1·10
132		115r. brown on pink	3·00	1·30
133		130r. brown on yellow	3·00	1·30
134		200r. purple on pink	13·00	5·25
135		400r. blue on yellow	4·25	3·25
136		500r. black on blue	4·25	3·25
137		700r. mauve on yellow	6·75	5·00

1913. Surch **REPUBLICA GUINE** and value on "Vasco da Gama" stamps. (a) Portuguese Colonies.

138		¼c. on 2½r. green	3·00	2·50
139		½c. on 5r. red	3·00	2·50
140		1c. on 10r. purple	3·00	2·50
141		2½c. on 25r. green	3·00	2·50
142		5c. on 50r. blue	3·00	2·50
143		7½c. on 75r. brown	6·50	5·00
144		10c. on 100r. brown	3·00	2·00
145		15c. on 150r. brown	8·00	6·75

(b) Macao.

146		¼c. on ½a. green	3·25	2·50
147		½c. on 1a. red	3·25	2·50
148		1c. on 2a. purple	3·25	2·50
149		2½c. on 4a. green	3·25	2·50
150		5c. on 8a. blue	3·25	2·50
151		7½c. on 12a. brown	5·75	4·00
152		10c. on 16a. brown	5·00	4·00
153		15c. on 24a. brown	6·25	4·25

(c) Portuguese Timor.

154		¼c. on ½a. green	3·25	2·50
155		½c. on 1a. red	3·25	2·50
156		1c. on 2a. purple	3·25	2·50
157		2½c. on 4a. green	3·25	2·50
158		5c. on 8a. blue	3·25	2·50
159		7½c. on 12a. brown	5·75	4·00
160		10c. on 16a. brown	5·00	4·00
161		15c. on 24a. brown	6·25	4·25

1913. "King Carlos" key-type of Portuguese Guinea optd **PROVISORIO** and **REPUBLICA**.

184		15r. brown	2·00	1·80
185		50r. blue	2·00	1·80
164		75r. pink	25·00	16·00

1914. "Ceres" key-type inscr "GUINE". Name and value in black.

204	U	¼c. green	1·40	95
209	U	½c. black	55	50
210	U	1c. green	55	50
211	U	1½c. brown	55	50
212	U	2c. red	55	50
213	U	2c. grey	55	50
214	U	2½c. violet	55	50
215	U	3c. orange	55	50
216	U	4c. red	55	50
217	U	4½c. grey	55	50
218	U	5c. blue	55	50
219	U	6c. mauve	55	50
220	U	7c. blue	75	45
221	U	7½c. brown	55	50
222	U	8c. grey	55	50
223	U	10c. red	55	50
224	U	12c. green	1·30	75
225	U	15c. red	55	50
226	U	20c. green	60	55
227	U	24c. blue	3·25	2·20
228	U	25c. brown	3·75	2·75
180	U	30c. brown on green	10·00	6·50
229	U	30c. green	1·60	75
181	U	40c. brown on pink	6·50	1·30
230	U	40c. turquoise	1·60	85
182	U	50c. orange on orange	6·50	1·30
231	U	50c. mauve	3·75	2·10
232	U	60c. blue	2·75	2·30
233	U	60c. red	3·75	1·60
234	U	80c. red	4·25	2·75
183	U	1e. green on blue	8·75	4·25
235	U	1e. blue	5·75	3·25
236	U	1e. pink	5·50	2·40
237	U	2e. purple	5·50	3·00
238	U	5e. bistre	32·00	16·00
239	U	10e. pink	46·00	17·00
240	U	20e. green	£130	65·00

1915. Provisional stamps of 1902 optd **REPUBLICA**.

186	S	50r. on 65r. blue	2·00	1·80
187	V	115r. on 2½r. brown	3·25	1·90
190	R	115r. on 5r. yellow	2·20	1·40
191	R	115r. on 25r. green	2·00	1·80
192	3	115r. on 40r. brown	1·90	1·80
194	3	115r. on 50r. blue	1·90	1·80
196	3	130r. on 80r. grey	6·00	3·75
197	3	130r. on 100r. brown	5·00	4·25
199	R	130r. on 150r. red on pink	2·00	1·80
200	R	130r. on 200r. blue on blue	2·00	1·80
201	R	130r. on 300r. blue on brn	2·00	1·80

1920. Surch.

241	U	4c. on ¼c. green	7·50	5·00
242	U	6c. on ½c. black	7·50	5·00
243	S	12c. on 115r. brown on pink (No. 132)	19·00	11·50

1925. Stamps of 1902 (Nos. 107/9) surch **Republica** and new value.

244	R	40c. on 400r. on 75r. pink	1·90	1·50
245	R	40c. on 400r. on 80r. green	1·90	1·50
246	R	40c. on 400r. on 100r. brown on buff	1·90	1·50

1931. "Ceres" key-type of Portuguese Guinea surch.

247	U	50c. on 60c. red	4·00	3·00
248	U	70c. on 80c. red	4·25	4·00
249	U	1e.40 on 2e. purple	9·75	7·00

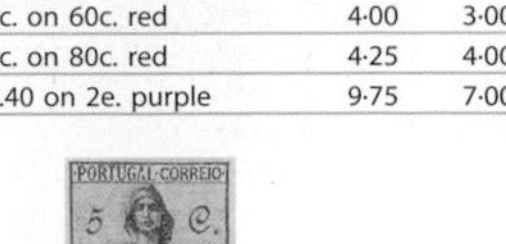

24 Ceres

1933

251	24	1c. brown	30	25
252	24	5c. brown	30	25
253	24	10c. mauve	30	25
254	24	15c. black	65	55
255	24	20c. grey	65	55
256	24	30c. green	65	55
257	24	40c. red	1·50	65
258	24	45c. turquoise	1·50	65
259	24	50c. brown	1·50	65
260	24	60c. green	1·50	95
261	24	70c. brown	1·50	95
262	24	80c. green	2·75	1·10
263	24	85c. red	4·75	2·20
264	24	1e. purple	2·30	1·50
265	24	1e.40 blue	8·00	5·00
266	24	2e. mauve	4·50	2·50
267	24	5e. green	15·00	9·00
268	24	10e. brown	27·00	12·00
269	24	20e. orange	85·00	41·00

27 Vasco da Gama

28 Mousinho de Albuquerque

1938

270	27	1c. green (postage)	25	25
271	27	5c. brown	25	25
272	27	10c. red	35	30
273	27	15c. purple	35	30
274	27	20c. grey	85	35
275	-	30c. purple	85	60
276	-	35c. green	85	65
277	-	40c. brown	85	65
278	-	50c. mauve	85	65
279	-	60c. black	85	65
280	-	70c. violet	85	65
281	-	80c. orange	1·50	75
282	-	1e. red	2·10	75
283	-	1e.75 blue	2·75	1·60
284	-	2e. red	6·75	2·40
285	-	5e. green	9·75	4·75
286	-	10e. blue	13·50	6·00
287	-	20e. brown	46·00	9·50
288	28	10c. red (air)	1·50	1·10
289	28	20c. violet	1·50	1·10
290	28	50c. orange	1·50	1·10
291	28	1e. blue	1·50	1·10
292	28	2e. red	13·00	6·50
293	28	3e. green	4·25	2·10
294	28	5e. brown	9·00	2·75
295	28	9e. red	13·00	7·00
296	28	10e. mauve	23·00	7·75

DESIGNS (postage): 30c. to 50c. Mousinho de Albuquerque; 60c. to 1e. Dam; 1e.75 to 5e. Prince Henry the Navigator; 10, 20e. Afonso de Albuquerque.

31 Cacheu Castle

1946. 500th Anniv of Discovery of Portuguese Guinea.

297	**31**	30c. black and grey	1·50	1·10
298	-	50c. green and light green	75	75
299	-	50c. purple and claret	75	75
300	-	1e.75 blue and light blue	5·00	1·90
301	-	3e.50 red and pink	8·00	3·00
302	-	5e. brown and chocolate	23·00	9·75
303	-	20e. violet and mauve	41·00	16·00

MS303a 175×221 mm. Nos. 297/303 (sold at 40e.) £130 £130

DESIGNS—VERT: 50c. Nuno Tristao; 1e.75, President Grant; 3e.50, Teixeiro Pinto; 5e. Honorio Barreto. HORIZ: 20e. Church at Bissau.

32 Native Huts

1948

304	**32**	5c. brown	25	20
305	-	10c. purple	4·75	2·75
306	-	20c. mauve	1·20	80
307	-	35c. green	1·50	80
308	-	50c. red	75	25
309	-	70c. blue	1·20	75
310	-	80c. green	1·80	75
311	-	1e. red	1·80	75
312	-	1e.75 blue	21·00	9·00
313	-	2e. blue	23·00	2·75
314	-	3e.50 brown	5·00	2·50
315	-	5e. grey	8·25	4·75
316	-	20e. violet	38·00	12·00

MS316a 176×158 mm. Nos. 304/16 (sold at 40e.) £160 £160

DESIGNS: 10c. Crowned crane; 20c., 3e.50, Youth; 35c., 5e. Woman; 50c. Musician; 70c. Man; 80c., 20e. Girl; 1, 2e. Drummer; 1e.75, Bushbuck.

33 Our Lady of Fatima

1948. Statue of Our Lady of Fatima.

317	**33**	50c. green	7·25	6·25

34 Letter and Globe

1949. 75th Anniv of U.P.U.

318	**34**	2e. orange	9·00	4·25

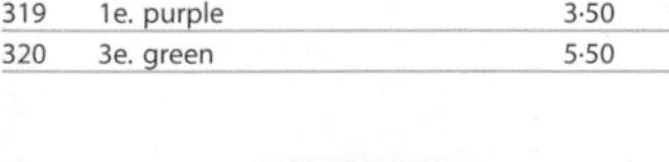

1950. Holy Year. As Nos. 425/6 of Macao.

319	1e. purple	3·50	2·10
320	3e. green	5·50	3·00

36 Our Lady of Fatima

1951. Termination of Holy Year.

321	**36**	1e. brown and buff	1·70	90

37 Doctor examining Patient

1952. First Tropical Medicine Congress, Lisbon.

322	**37**	50c. brown and purple	70	70

39 Exhibition Entrance

1953. Missionary Art Exhibition.

323	**39**	10c. red and green	20	20
324	**39**	50c. blue and brown	1·60	60
325	**39**	3e. black and orange	3·75	1·80

40 "Analeptes Trifasciata' (longhorn beetle)

1953. Bugs and Beetles. Multicoloured.

326	5c. Type **40**	20	15
327	10c. "Callidea panaethiopica kirk" (shieldbug)	20	20
328	30c. "Craspedophorus brevicollis" (ground beetle)	20	15
329	50c. "Anthia nimrod" (ground beetle)	30	15
330	70c. "Platypria luctuosa" (leaf beetle)	75	35
331	1e. "Acanthophorus maculatus" (longhorn beetle)	70	20
332	2e. "Cordylomera nitidipennis" (longhorn beetle)	1·60	30
333	3e. "Lycus latissimus" (powder-post beetle)	3·50	55
334	5e. "Cicindeia brunet" (tiger beetle)	3·75	1·40
335	10e. "Colliurus dimidiata" (ground beetle)	9·25	4·25

41 Portuguese Stamp of 1853 and Arms of Portuguese Overseas Provinces

1953. Portuguese Stamp Centenary.

336	**41**	50c. multicoloured	1·60	1·30

42 Father M. de Nobrega and View of Sao Paulo

1954. Fourth Centenary of Sao Paulo.

337	**42**	1e. multicoloured	55	30

43 Arms of Cape Verde Islands and Portuguese Guinea

1955. Presidential Visit.

338	**43**	1e. multicoloured	55	30
339	**43**	2e.50 mulitcoloured	95	65

44 Exhibition Emblem Globe and Arms

1958. Brussels International Exhibition.

340	**44**	2e.50 green	1·10	75

45 "Matenus stenegalenis"

1958. Sixth Int Congress of Tropical Medicine.

341	**45**	5e. multicoloured	4·75	2·10

46 Statue of Barreto at Bissau

1959. Death Centenary of Honorio Barreto (statesman).

342	**46**	2e.50 multicoloured	55	45

47 Astrolabe

1960. 500th Death Anniv of Prince Henry the Navigator.

343	**47**	2e.50 multicoloured	60	50

48 "Medical Service"

1960. Tenth Anniv of African Technical Co-operation Commission.

344	**48**	1e.50 multicoloured	55	45

49 Motor Racing

1962. Sports. Multicoloured.

345	50c. Type **49**	60	15
346	1e. Tennis	95	45
347	1e.50 Putting the shot	70	45
348	2e.50 Wrestling	85	50
349	3e.50 Shooting	95	50
350	15e. Volleyball	2·50	1·30

50 "Anopheles gambiae"

1962. Malaria Eradication.

351	**50**	2e.50 multicoloured	95	60

51 Common Spitting Cobra

1963. Snakes. Multicoloured.

352	20c. Type **51**	25	20
353	35c. African rock python	25	20
354	70c. Boomslang	85	50
355	80c. West African mamba	80	35
356	1e.50 Symthe's watersnake	80	25
357	2e. Common night adder	35	20
358	2e.50 Green swampsnake	3·25	50
359	3e.50 Brown house snake	60	30
360	4e. Spotted wolfsnake	75	30
361	5e. Common puff adder	90	50
362	15e. Striped beauty snake	2·20	1·50
363	20e. African egg-eating snake	3·00	2·30

The 2e. and 20e. are horiz.

52 Map of Africa, Boeing 707 and Lockheed L.1049G Super Constellation

1963. Tenth Anniv of Transportes Aereos Portugueses (airline).

364	**52**	2e.50 multicoloured	1·10	55

53 J. de A. Corvo

1964. Centenary of National Overseas Bank.

365	**53**	2e.50 multicoloured	1·20	65

54 I.T.U. Emblem and St. Gabriel

1965. Centenary of I.T.U.

366	**54**	2e.50 multicoloured	2·75	1·10

55 Soldier, 1548

1966. Portuguese Military Uniforms. Multicoloured.

367	25c. Type **55**	25	15
368	40c. Arquebusier, 1578	35	15
369	60c. Arquebusier, 1640	50	20
370	1e. Grenadier, 1721	60	20
371	2e.50 Captain of Fusiliers, 1740	1·10	20
372	4e.50 Infantryman, 1740	2·50	45
373	7e.50 Sergeant-major, 1762	5·00	2·10
374	10e. Engineers' officer, 1806	5·00	2·10

56 B. C. Lopes School and Bissau Hospital

1966. 40th Anniv of Portuguese National Revolution.

375	**56**	2e.50 multicoloured	90	65

57 O. Muzanty and Cruiser "Republica"

1967. Centenary of Military Naval Assn. Multicoloured.

376	50c. Type **57**	45	25
377	1e. A. de Cerqueira and destroyer "Guadiana"	1·40	60

58 Chapel of the Apparitions and Monument of the Holy Spirit

1967. 50th Anniv of Fatima Apparitions.

378	**58**	50c. multicoloured	30	15

63 Pres. Tomas

1968. Visit of President Tomas of Portugal.

396	**63**	1e. multicoloured	35	20

64 Cabral's Arms

1968. 500th Birth Anniv of Pedro Cabral (explorer).

397	**64**	2e.50 multicoloured	85	30

66 Admiral Coutinho's Astrolabe

1969. Birth Centenary of Admiral Gago Coutinho.

409	**66**	1e. multicoloured	45	20

67 Arms of Vasco da Gama

1969. 500th Birth Anniv of Vasco da Gama (explorer).

410	**67**	2e.50 multicoloured	50	15

68 L. A. Rebello da Silva

1969. Centenary of Overseas Administrative Reforms.

411	**68**	50c. multicoloured	35	15

69 Arms of King Manoel I

1969. 500th Birth Anniv of Manuel I.

412	**69**	2e. multicoloured	50	15

70 Ulysses Grant and Square, Bolama

1970. Centenary of Arbitral Judgment on Sovereignty of Bolama.

413	**70**	2e.50 multicoloured	60	30

71 Marshal Carmona

1970. Birth Centenary of Marshal Carmona.

414	**71**	1e.50 multicoloured	50	20

73 Camoens

1972. 400th Anniv of Camoens' "The Lusiads" (epic poem).

422	**73**	50c. multicoloured	55	30

74 Weightlifting and Hammer-throwing

1972. Olympic Games, Munich.

423	**74**	2e.50 multicoloured	75	20

75 Fairey IIID Seaplane "Lusitania" taking-off from Lisbon

1972. 50th Anniv of 1st Lisbon–Rio de Janeiro Flight.

424	**75**	1e. multicoloured	30	20

76 W.M.O. Emblem

1973. Centenary of I.M.O./W.M.O.

425	**76**	2e. multicoloured	50	30

CHARITY TAX STAMPS

The notes under this heading in Portugal also apply here.

C16

1919. Fiscal stamp optd **REPUBLICA TAXA DE GUERRA**.

C241	**C16**	10r. brown, buff & blk	7·50	5·00

1925. Marquis de Pombal Commem stamps of Portugal but inscr "GUINE".

C247	**C73**	15c. black and red	1·20	95
C248	-	15c. black and red	1·20	95
C249	**C75**	15c. black and red	1·20	95

C26

1934

C270	**C26**	50c. purple and green	17·00	9·75

C29a Arms

1938

C297	**C29a**	50c. yellow	16·00	8·00
C298	**C29a**	50c. brown and green	16·00	8·00

1942. As Type **C29a** but smaller, 20½×25 mm.

C299	50c. black and brown	30	30
C300	50c. black and yellow	4·00	2·20
C301	50c. brown and yellow	6·50	4·00
C302	2e.50 black and blue	55	55
C303	5e. black and green	85	85
C304	10e. black and blue	1·70	1·70

Nos. C302/4 were used at several small post offices as ordinary postage stamps during a temporary shortage.

C59

1967. National Defence. No gum.

C379	**C59**	50c. red, pink and black	20	20
C380	**C59**	1e. red, green and black	35	35
C381	**C59**	5e. red, grey and black	1·10	1·10
C382	**C59**	10e. red, blue and black	3·25	3·25

A 50e. in the same design was for fiscal use only.

C60

1967. National Defence. No gum.

C383	**C60**	50c. red, pink and black	1·30	1·30
C384	**C60**	1e. red, green and black	1·60	1·10
C385	**C60**	5e. red, grey and black	3·25	2·10
C386	**C60**	10e. red, blue and black	5·25	4·25

C61 Carved Statuette of Woman

1967. Guinean Artifacts from Bissau Museum. Multicoloured.

C387	50c. Type C **61**	45	25
C388	1e. "Tree of life"(carving) (horiz)	45	25
C389	2e. Cow-headed statuette	45	25
C390	2e.50 "The Magistrate" (statuette)	65	45
C391	5e. "Kneeling Servant" (statuette)	85	55
C392	10e. Stylized pelican (carving)	1·60	1·30
MSC393	149×199 mm. Nos. C387/92. Imperf. No gold (sold at 25e.)	16·00	16·00

1968. No. C389 but inscr "TOCADOR DE BOMBOLON" surch.

C394	50c. on 2e. multicoloured	45	45
C395	1e. on 2e. multicoloured	45	45

C65 Hands grasping Sword

1969. National Defence.

C398	**C65**	50c. multicoloured	45	45
C399	**C65**	1e. multicoloured	45	45
C400	**C65**	2e. multicoloured	45	45
C401	**C65**	2e.50 multicoloured	45	45
C402	**C65**	3e. multicoloured	45	45
C403	**C65**	4e. multicoloured	55	45
C404	**C65**	5e. multicoloured	65	55
C405	**C65**	8e. multicoloured	1·10	1·10
C406	**C65**	9e. multicoloured	1·30	1·30
C407	**C65**	10e. multicoloured	1·10	1·10
C408	**C65**	15e. multicoloured	1·60	1·60

NOTE—30, 50 and 100e. stamps in the same design were for fiscal use only.

C72 Mother and Children

1971

C415	**C72**	50c. multicoloured	30	25
C416	**C72**	1e. multicoloured	30	25
C417	**C72**	2e. multicoloured	30	25
C418	**C72**	3e. multicoloured	30	25
C419	**C72**	4e. multicoloured	30	25
C420	**C72**	5e. multicoloured	55	30
C421	**C72**	10e. multicoloured	1·10	65

Higher values were intended for fiscal use.

NEWSPAPER STAMP

1983. "Newspaper" key-type inscr "GUINE".

N50	**V**	2½r. brown	2·40	1·50

POSTAGE DUE STAMPS

1904. "Due" key-type inscr "GUINE". Name and value in black.

D122	**W**	5r. green	1·60	90
D123	**W**	10r. grey	1·60	90
D124	**W**	20r. brown	1·60	90
D125	**W**	30r. orange	2·50	2·10
D126	**W**	50r. brown	2·50	2·10
D127	**W**	60r. brown	7·00	5·25
D128	**W**	100r. mauve	7·00	5·25
D129	**W**	130r. blue	7·00	5·25
D130	**W**	200r. red	11·00	10·00
D131	**W**	500r. lilac	26·00	10·00

1911. "Due" key-type of Portuguese Guinea optd **REPUBLICA**.

D138	5r. green	35	25
D139	10r. grey	45	35
D140	20r. brown	70	45
D141	30r. orange	70	45
D142	50r. brown	90	45
D143	60r. brown	2·10	1·60
D208	100r. mauve	3·75	3·25
D145	130r. blue	4·25	3·25
D146	200r. red	4·25	3·25
D147	500r. lilac	3·25	2·50

1921. "Due" key-type of Portuguese Guinea. Currency changed.

D244	½c. green	50	45
D245	1c. grey	50	45
D246	2c. brown	50	45
D247	3c. orange	50	45
D248	5c. brown	50	45
D249	6c. brown	1·30	1·20
D250	10c. mauve	1·30	1·20
D251	13c. blue	1·30	1·20
D252	20c. red	1·30	1·20
D253	50c. grey	1·30	1·20

1925. Marquis de Pombal stamps, as Nos. C247/9 optd **MULTA**.

D254	**C73**	30c. black and red	1·20	1·10
D255	-	30c. black and red	1·20	1·10
D256	**C75**	30c. black and red	1·20	1·10

1952. As Type **D70** of Macao, but inscr "GUINE PORTUGUESA". Numerals in red, name in black (except 2e. in blue).

D323	10c. green and pink	25	25
D324	30c. violet and grey	25	25
D325	50c. green and lemon	25	25
D326	1e. blue and grey	25	25
D327	2e. black and olive	35	35
D328	5e. brown and orange	90	90

Pt. 9

PORTUGUESE INDIA

Portuguese territories on the west coast of India, consisting of Goa, Damao and Diu. Became part of India in December 1961.

1871. 1000 reis = 1 milreis.
1882. 12 reis = 1 tanga; 16 tangas = 1 rupia
1959. 100 centavos = 1 escudo.

1

1871. Perf.

35	**1**	10r. black	9·00	6·75
33a	**1**	15r. pink	20·00	13·50
26	**1**	20r. red	25·00	16·00
21	**1**	40r. blue	£120	90·00
22	**1**	100r. green	£100	65·00
23	**1**	200r. yellow	£300	£250
27	**1**	300r. purple	£200	£140
28	**1**	600r. purple	£250	£160
29	**1**	900r. purple	£250	£160

9

1877. Star above value. Imperf (241/3) or perf (others).

241	**9**	1½r. black	2·50	1·80
242	**9**	4½r. green	25·00	20·00
243	**9**	6r. green	20·00	15·00
48	**9**	10r. black	48·00	41·00
49	**9**	15r. pink	50·00	45·00
50	**9**	20r. red	14·50	13·50
51	**9**	40r. blue	29·00	26·00
52	**9**	100r. green	£120	95·00

53	9	200r. yellow	£120	£120
54	9	300r. purple	£170	£140
55	9	600r. purple	£170	£140
56	9	900r. purple	£170	£140

1877. "Crown" key-type inscr "INDIA PORTU-GUEZA". Perf.

65	P	5r. black	8·75	6·00
58	P	10r. buff	14·50	12·50
78	P	10r. green	18·00	14·50
67	P	20r. bistre	12·50	9·25
68	P	25r. pink	14·50	12·50
79	P	25r. grey	65·00	47·00
80	P	25r. purple	47·00	35·00
69	P	40r. blue	25·00	14·50
81	P	40r. yellow	55·00	44·00
70b	P	50r. green	44·00	29·00
82	P	50r. blue	29·00	27·00
71	P	100r. lilac	20·00	18·00
64	P	200r. orange	39·00	29·00
73	P	300r. brown	42·00	39·00

See also Nos. 204/10.

1881. Surch in figures.

213	1	1½ on 10r. black		£475
215	9	1½ on 10r. black	†	£500
90	1	1½ on 20r. red	£120	£110
91	9	1½ on 20r. red	£275	£200
217	1	4½ on 40r. blue	50·00	50·00
223	1	4½ on 100r. green	38·00	32·00
96	1	5 on 10r. black	12·50	9·75
98	9	5 on 10r. black	70·00	44·00
101	1	5 on 15r. pink	2·75	2·75
106	1	5 on 20r. red	4·00	4·00
108	9	5 on 20r. red	4·00	4·00
224	1	6 on 20r. red		
228	1	6 on 100r. green	£475	£450
231	1	6 on 200r. yellow		£225
233	9	6 on 200r. yellow	£650	£650

1881. "Crown" key-type of Portuguese India surch in figures.

199	P	1½ on 4½ on 5r. black	£120	£100
109	P	1½ on 5r. black	2·50	1·60
200	P	1½ on 6 on 10r. green	£170	£150
110	P	1½ on 10r. green	2·50	2·10
111	P	1½ on 20r. bistre	28·00	21·00
157	P	1½ on 25r. grey	65·00	50·00
158	P	1½ on 100r. lilac	£100	90·00
200a	P	1½ on 1t. on 20r. bistre		£150
201	P	2 on 4t. on 50r. green	£425	£350
114	P	4½ on 5r. black	13·00	13·00
115	P	4½ on 10r. green	£275	£275
116	P	4½ on 20r. bistre	5·75	5·25
162	P	4½ on 25r. purple	26·00	21·00
118	P	4½ on 100r. lilac	£190	£190
119a	P	6 on 10r. buff	£100	95·00
120	P	6 on 10r. green	21·00	16·00
121	P	6 on 20r. bistre	29·00	21·00
167	P	6 on 25r. grey	65·00	38·00
168	P	6 on 25r. purple	5·00	3·75
169	P	6 on 40r. blue	£130	95·00
170	P	6 on 40r. yellow	14·50	80·00
171	P	6 on 50r. green	90·00	80·00
127	P	6 on 50r. blue	£110	95·00
202	P	6 on 1t. on 10r. green	£160	
128	P	1t. on 10r. green	£225	£200
129	P	1t. on 20r. bistre	90·00	70·00
175	P	1t. on 25r. grey	60·00	48·00
176	P	1t. on 25r. purple	26·00	19·00
132	P	1t. on 40r. blue	32·00	26·00
134	P	1t. on 50r. blue	48·00	32·00
178	P	1t. on 50r. green	£100	90·00
136	P	1t. on 100r. lilac	38·00	24·00
137	P	1t. on 200r. orange	70·00	60·00
139	P	2t. on 25r. purple	26·00	17·00
182	P	2t. on 25r. grey	65·00	50·00
184	P	2t. on 40r. blue	60·00	50·00
141	P	2t. on 40r. yellow	60·00	48·00
142a	P	2t. on 50r. green	45·00	36·00
143	P	2t. on 50r. blue	£150	£130
144	P	2t. on 100r. lilac	21·00	17·00
188	P	2t. on 200r. orange	70·00	50·00
189	P	2t. on 300r. brown	65·00	60·00
190	P	4t. on 10r. green	19·00	16·00
191	P	4t. on 50r. green	19·00	16·00
148	P	4t. on 200r. orange	85·00	60·00
193	P	8t. on 20r. bistre	80·00	60·00
194	P	8t. on 25r. pink	£375	£325
151	P	8t. on 40r. blue	80·00	65·00
196	P	8t. on 100r. lilac	70·00	60·00
197	P	8t. on 200r. orange	60·00	50·00
198	P	8t. on 300r. brown	70·00	55·00

1882. "Crown" key-type of Portuguese India.

204	1½r. black	1·60	1·10
205	4½r. green	1·60	1·10
206	6r. green	1·60	1·10
207	1t. pink	1·60	95
208	2t. blue	1·60	95
209	4t. purple	1·60	1·30
210	8t. orange	5·75	5·00

1886. "Embossed" key-type inscr "INDIA PORTUGUEZA".

244	Q	1½r. black	3·75	2·00
245	Q	4½r. olive	4·50	2·20
246	Q	6r. green	5·00	2·75
247	Q	1t. red	7·75	4·50
248	Q	2t. blue	14·50	7·00
249	Q	4t. lilac	14·50	7·00
257	Q	8t. orange	13·00	7·00

1895. "Figures" key-type inscr "INDIA".

271	R	1½r. black	1·90	1·00
259	R	4½r. orange	1·90	1·20
273	R	6r. green	1·90	1·00
274	R	9r. lilac	7·75	5·50
260	R	1t. blue	2·50	1·80
261	R	2t. red	2·50	1·20
262	R	4t. blue	3·25	1·80
270	R	8t. lilac	5·75	3·50

1898. As Vasco da Gama stamps of Portugal T 40 etc, but inscr "INDIA".

275	1½r. green	1·60	70
276	4½r. red	1·60	70
277	6r. purple	1·60	1·00
278	9r. green	2·30	1·00
279	1t. blue	3·25	2·30
280	2t. brown	3·75	2·30
281	4t. brown	3·75	3·00
282	8t. brown	8·00	4·75

DESIGNS—HORIZ: 1½r. Departure of fleet; 4½r. Arrival at Calicut; 6r. Embarkation at Rastello; 4t. Flagship "Sao Gabriel"; 8t. Vasco da Gama. VERT: 9r. Muse of History; 1t. Flagship "Sao Gabriel" and portraits of Da Gama and Camoens; 2t. Archangel Gabriel, patron saint of the expedition.

1898. "King Carlos" key-type inscr "INDIA". Value in red (No. 292) or black (others).

323	S	1r. grey	55	45
283	S	1½r. orange	55	35
324	S	1½r. grey	70	35
325	S	2r. orange	55	35
326	S	2½r. brown	70	35
327	S	3r. blue	70	35
284	S	4½r. green	1·60	1·00
285	S	6r. brown	1·60	1·00
328	S	6r. green	70	35
286	S	9r. lilac	1·60	1·00
287	S	1t. green	1·60	70
329	S	1t. red	80	35
288	S	2t. blue	1·90	70
330	S	2t. brown	3·25	1·50
331	S	2½t. blue	11·50	6·00
289	S	4t. blue on blue	3·75	1·80
332	S	5t. brown on yellow	3·75	2·20
290	S	8t. purple on pink	3·75	2·00
291	S	12t. blue on pink	5·75	3·50
334	S	12t. green on pink	7·50	3·50
292	S	1rp. black on blue	11·50	5·00
335	S	1rp. blue on yellow	16·00	15·00
293	S	2rp. mauve on yellow	16·00	9·75
336	S	2rp. black on yellow	31·00	31·00

1900. No. 288 surch **1½ Reis**.

295	1½r. on 2t. blue	3·25	1·80

1902. Surch.

299	R	1r. on 6r. green	95	60
298	Q	1r. on 2t. blue	1·10	70
300	Q	2r. on 4½r. olive	75	60
301	R	2r. on 8t. lilac	95	60
302	Q	2½r. on 6r. green	95	60
303	R	2½r. on 9r. lilac	95	60
305	R	3r. on 4½r. orange	2·10	1·50
304	Q	3r. on 1t. red	75	60
306	R	3r. on 1t. blue	1·90	1·80
337	S	2t. on 2½t. blue and black	3·50	3·00
307	Q	2½t. on 1½r. black	2·50	2·00
310	R	2½t. on 1½r. black	2·50	1·80
309	Q	2½t. on 4t. lilac	2·50	1·80
315	R	5t. on 2t. red	2·50	1·80
317	R	5t. on 4t. blue	2·50	1·80
314	Q	5t. on 8t. orange	1·60	1·00

1902. 1898 "King Carlos" stamps optd **PROVISORIO**.

319	6r. brown and black	2·75	1·80
320	1t. green and black	2·75	1·80
321	2t. blue and black	2·75	1·80

1911. 1898 "King Carlos" stamps optd **REPUBLICA**. Value in black.

338	1r. grey	45	30
339	1½r. grey	45	30
340	2r. orange	45	30
341	2½r. brown	70	30
342	3r. blue	70	30
343	4½r. green	70	30
344	6r. green	55	30
345	9r. lilac	70	30
346	1t. red	1·00	30
347	2t. brown	1·10	30
348	4t. blue on blue	2·10	1·70
349	5t. brown on yellow	2·50	1·70
350	8t. purple on pink	7·50	4·25
402	12t. green on pink	9·00	7·25
352	1rp. blue on yellow	11·50	10·00
404	2rp. mauve on yellow	22·00	16·00
405	2rp. black on yellow	22·00	16·00

Both unused and used prices for the following issue (Nos. 371 etc.) are for entire stamps showing both halves.

1911. Various stamps bisected by vertical perforation, and each half surch. (a) On 1898 "King Carlos" key-type.

371	1r. on 2r. orange and black	65	60
372	1r. on 1t. red and black	65	60
378	1r. on 5t. brown and black on yellow	4·25	3·50
374	1½r. on 2½r. brown and black	1·10	90
354	1½r. on 4½r. green and black	23·00	11·00
355	1½r. on 9r. lilac and black	95	70
356	1½r. on 4t. blue and black on blue	95	70
375	2r. on 2½r. brown and black	95	70
357	2r. on 4t. blue and black on blue	1·60	90
376	3r. on 2½r. brown and black	95	70
377	3r. on 2t. brown and black	1·10	90
358	6r. on 4½r. green and black	1·30	1·00
359d	6r. on 9r. lilac and black	1·30	1·00
379	6r. on 8t. purple and black on pink	3·25	2·75

(b) On 1902 Provisional issue.

360	R	1r. on 5t. on 2t. red	11·50	9·50
361	R	1r. on 5t. on 4t. blue	9·50	7·00
363	Q	1r. on 5t. on 8t. orange	4·25	3·00
364	Q	2r. on 2½t. on 6r. green	3·75	3·50
365	R	2r. on 2½t. on 9r. lilac	27·00	21·00
366	R	3r. on 5t. on 2t. red	11·50	7·00
367	R	3r. on 5t. on 4t. blue	11·50	7·00
370	Q	3r. on 5t. on 8t. orange	3·25	2·20

(c) On 1911 issue (optd **REPUBLICA**).

380	S	1r. on 1r. grey and black	60	55
381	S	1r. on 2r. orange and black	60	55
382	S	1r. on 1t. red and black	60	55
383	S	1r. on 5t. brown and black on yellow	60	55
384	S	1½r. on 4½r. green and black	95	55
386	S	6r. on 9r. lilac and black	95	55
419	S	3r. on 2t. brown and black	9·00	6·25
420	S	6r. on 4½r. green and black	8·00	6·25
422	S	6r. on 8t. purple and black on pink	11·00	9·00

1913. Nos. 275/82 optd **REPUBLICA**.

389	1½r. green	60	40
390	4½r. red	60	40
391	6r. purple	70	55
392	9r. green	80	55
393	1t. blue	1·50	55
394	2t. brown	2·10	2·20
395	4t. brown	1·80	55
396	8t. brown	3·00	1·30

1914. Stamps of 1902 optd **REPUBLICA**.

406	R	2r. on 8t. lilac	13·50	9·00
407	Q	2½r. on 6r. green	1·80	1·40
408	R	5t. on 2t. red	9·00	7·25
410	R	5t. on 4t. blue	9·00	5·50
415	S	1t. green and black (No. 320)	22·00	12·50
458	S	2t. blue and black (No. 321)	1·80	1·70
459	S	2t. on 2½t. blue and black	2·30	1·70
460	Q	5t. on 8t. orange	2·75	2·00

1914. "King Carlos" key-type of Portuguese India optd **REPUBLICA** and surch.

423	S	1½r. on 4½r. green and black	75	70
424	S	1½r. on 9r. lilac and black	75	70
425	S	1½r. on 12t. green and black on pink	1·30	1·20
426	S	3r. on 1t. red and black	85	70
427	S	3r. on 2t. brown and black	7·25	6·25
428	S	3r. on 8t. purple and black on pink	9·00	7·25
429	S	3r. on 1rp. blue and black on yellow	1·20	75
430	S	3r. on 2rp. black on yellow	1·40	1·10

1914. Nos. 390 and 392/6 surch.

433	1½ on 4½r. red	75	60
434	1½r. on 9r. green	75	60
435	3r. on 1t. blue	75	60
436	3r. on 2t. brown	3·75	3·25
437	3r. on 4t. brown	75	60
438	3r. on 8t. brown	3·50	1·80

1914. "Ceres" key-type inscr "INDIA". Name and value in black.

439	U	1r. green	70	60
440	U	1½r. green	70	60
441	U	2r. black	1·00	65
442	U	2½r. green	1·00	65
443	U	3r. lilac	1·20	65
474	U	4r. blue	2·00	1·40
444	U	4½r. red	1·20	65
445	U	5r. green	1·20	65
446	U	6r. brown	1·20	65
447	U	9r. blue	1·30	70
448	U	10r. red	1·60	90
449	U	1t. violet	2·50	90
481	U	1½t. green	2·00	90
450	U	2t. blue	2·75	1·20
483	U	2½t. turquoise	2·00	90
451	U	3t. brown	3·75	1·50
484	U	3t. 4 brown	7·00	3·25
452	U	4t. grey	2·75	1·80
453	U	8t. purple	7·75	6·50
454	U	12t. brown on green	7·00	5·50
455	U	1rp. brown on pink	32·00	18·00
487	U	1rp. brown	26·00	20·00
456	U	2rp. orange on orange	19·00	15·00
488	U	2rp. yellow	27·00	20·00
457	U	3rp. green on blue	22·00	15·00
489	U	3rp. green	41·00	33·00
490	U	5rp. red	47·00	37·00

1922. "Ceres" key-type of Portuguese India surch with new value.

492	1½r. on 2r. black	1·50	1·40
496	1½r. on 8t. purple and black	4·00	2·75
497	2½t. on 3t. 4 brown and black	70·00	60·00

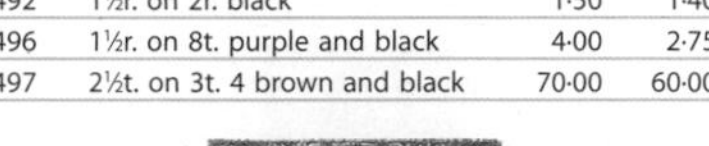

34 Vasco da Gama and Flagship "Sao Gabriel"

1925. 400th Death Anniv of Vasco da Gama. No gum.

493	34	6r. brown	7·00	4·25
494	34	1t. purple	9·50	4·75

36 The Signature of Francis

1931. St. Francis Xavier Exhibition.

498	-	1r. green	1·10	1·00
499	36	2r. brown	1·20	1·00
500	-	6r. purple	2·30	1·10
501	-	1½t. brown	8·00	5·50
502	-	2t. blue	13·50	7·75
503	-	2½t. red	19·00	8·00

DESIGNS—VERT: 1r. Monument to St. Francis; 6r. St. Francis in surplice and cassock; 1½t. St. Francis and Cross; 2½t. St. Francis's Tomb. HORIZ: 2t. Bom Jesus Church, Goa.

40 "Portugal" and Galeasse

1933

504	40	1r. brown	30	25
505	40	2r. brown	30	25
506	40	4r. mauve	30	25
507	40	6r. green	30	25
508	40	8r. black	65	50
509	40	1t. grey	65	50
510	40	1½t. red	65	50
511	40	2t. brown	65	50
512	40	2½t. blue	2·00	80
513	40	3t. turquoise	2·40	80
514	40	5t. red	3·50	80
515	40	1rp. green	8·50	3·25
516	40	2rp. purple	17·00	8·50
517	40	3rp. orange	23·00	13·00
518	40	5rp. green	48·00	31·00

1938. As T **27** and **28** of Portuguese Guinea, but inscr "ESTADO DA INDIA".

519	27	1r. green (postage)	30	25
520	27	2r. brown	30	25
521	27	3r. violet	30	25
522	27	6r. green	30	25
523	-	10r. red	65	40
524	-	1t. mauve	65	40
525	-	1½t. red	65	40
526	-	2t. orange	65	40
527	-	2½t. blue	65	40

528	-	3t. grey	1·40	50
529	-	5t. purple	2·50	65
530	-	1rp. red	6·50	1·30
531	-	2rp. green	10·00	3·75
532	-	3rp. blue	19·00	8·75
533	-	5rp. brown	38·00	10·50

DESIGNS: 10r. to 1½t. Mousinho de Albuquerque; 2t. to 3t. Prince Henry the Navigator; 5t. to 2rp. Dam; 3, 5rp. Afonso de Albuquerque.

534	**28**	1t. red (air)	2·00	95
535	**28**	2½t. violet	2·00	95
536	**28**	3½t. orange	2·00	95
537	**28**	4½t. blue	2·00	95
538	**28**	7t. red	2·40	95
539	**28**	7½t. green	2·75	95
540	**28**	9t. brown	9·25	2·75
541	**28**	11t. mauve	10·00	2·75

1942. Surch.

549	**40**	1r. on 8r. black	1·30	1·00
546	**40**	1r. on 5t. red	1·30	1·00
550	**40**	2r. on 8r. black	1·30	1·00
547	**40**	3r. on 1½t. red	1·30	1·10
551	**40**	3r. on 2t. brown	1·30	1·10
552	**40**	3r. on 3rp. orange	3·25	2·50
553	**40**	6r. on 2½t. blue	3·25	2·50
554	**40**	6r. on 3t. turquoise	3·25	2·50
542	**40**	1t. on 1½t. red	3·75	3·00
548	**40**	1t. on 2t. brown	3·25	2·50
543	**40**	1t. on 1rp. green	3·75	3·00
544	**40**	1t. on 2rp. purple	3·75	3·00
545	**40**	1t. on 5rp. green	3·75	3·00

48 St. Francis Xavier

1946. Portraits and View.

555	**48**	1r. black and grey	75	40
556	-	2r. purple and pink	75	40
557	-	6r. bistre and buff	75	40
558	-	7r. violet and mauve	3·25	1·30
559	-	9r. brown and buff	3·25	1·30
560	-	1t. green and light green	3·25	1·30
561	-	3½t. blue and light blue	3·50	1·80
562	-	1rp. purple and bistre	8·00	2·20
MS563		169×280 mm. Nos. 555/62 (sold at 1½rp.)	47·00	42·00

DESIGNS: 2r. Luis de Camoens; 6r. Garcia de Orta; 7r. Beato Joao Brito; 9r. Vice-regal Archway; 1t. Afonso de Albuquerque; 3½t. Vasco da Gama; 1rp. D. Francisco de Almeida.

50 D. Joao de Castro

1948. Portraits.

564	**50**	3r. blue and light blue	1·80	90
565	-	1t. green and light green	2·00	1·10
566	-	1½t. purple and mauve	3·00	2·10
567	-	2½t. red and orange	4·00	2·50
568	-	7½t. purple and brown	6·00	3·50
MS569		108×149 mm. Nos. 564/8 (sold at 1rp.)	49·00	44·00

PORTRAITS: 1t. St. Francis Xavier; 1½t. P. Jose Vaz; 2½t. D. Luis de Ataide; 7½t. Duarte Pacheco Pereira.

1948. Statue of Our Lady of Fatima. As T **33** of Portuguese Guinea.

570		1t. green	6·00	4·75

53 Our Lady of Fatima

1949. Statue of Our Lady of Fatima.

571	**53**	1r. light blue and blue	1·50	1·10
572	**53**	3r. yellow, orange and lemon	1·50	1·10
573	**53**	9r. red and mauve	2·20	1·30
574	**53**	2t. green and light green	8·00	2·20
575	**53**	9t. red and vermilion	7·00	3·25
576	**53**	2rp. brown and purple	13·50	4·25
577	**53**	5rp. black and green	26·00	11·00
578	**53**	8rp. blue and violet	55·00	19·00

1949. 75th Anniv of U.P.U. As T **34** of Portuguese Guinea.

579		2½t. red	7·25	3·00

1950. Holy Year. As Nos. 425/6 of Macao.

580	**65**	1r. bistre	1·70	65
588	**65**	1r. red	65	40
589	**65**	2r. green	65	40
590	-	3r. brown	65	40
591	**65**	6r. grey	65	40
592	-	9r. mauve	1·70	1·10
593	**65**	1t. blue	1·70	1·10
581	-	2t. green	2·20	1·00
594	-	2t. yellow	1·70	1·10
595	**65**	4t. brown	1·70	1·10

1950. Nos. 523 and 527 surch.

582	1real on 10r. red	65	55
583	1real on 2½t. blue	65	55
584	2reis on 10r. red	65	55
585	3reis on 2½t. blue	65	55
586	6reis on 2½t. blue	65	55
587	1tanga on 2½t. blue	65	55

1951. Termination of Holy Year. As T **36** of Portuguese Guinea.

596	1rp. blue and grey	2·40	1·70

59 Father Jose Vaz

1951. 300th Birth Anniv of Jose Vaz.

597	**59**	1r. grey and slate	25	15
598	-	2r. orange and brown	25	15
599	**59**	3r. grey and black	85	40
600	-	1t. blue and indigo	40	35
601	**59**	2t. purple and maroon	40	35
602	-	3t. green and black	70	40
603	**59**	9t. violet and blue	70	40
604	-	10t. violet and mauve	1·80	95
605	-	12t. brown and black	3·25	1·30

DESIGNS: 2r., 1, 3, 10t. Sancoale Church Ruins; 12t. Veneravel Altar.

60 Goa Medical School

1952. First Tropical Medicine Congress, Lisbon.

606	**60**	4½t. turquoise and black	7·00	3·00

1952. Fourth Death Cent of St. Francis Xavier. As Nos. 452/4 of Macao but without lined background.

607	6r. multicoloured	45	35
608	2t. multicoloured	3·00	75
609	5t. green, silver and mauve	6·00	1·70
MS610	76×65 mm. 4t. green, silver and ochre (as No. 609 but smaller); 8t. slate (T **62**)	24·00	21·00
MS611	90×100 mm. 9t. sepia and brown (T **62**)	24·00	21·00

62 St. Francis Xavier

63 Stamp of 1871

1952. Philatelic Exhibition, Goa.

612	**63**	3t. black	19·00	16·00
613	**62**	5t. black and lilac	19·00	16·00

64 The Virgin

1953. Missionary Art Exhibition.

614	**64**	6r. black and blue	30	20
615	**64**	1t. brown and buff	1·30	1·00
616	**64**	3t. lilac and yellow	4·00	2·00

1953. Portuguese Postage Stamp Centenary. As T **41** of Portuguese Guinea.

617	1t. multicoloured	1·80	1·20

66 Dr. Gama Pinto

1954. Birth Centenary of Dr. Gama Pinto.

618	**66**	3r. green and grey	40	20
619	**66**	2t. black and blue	90	50

1954. Fourth Centenary of Sao Paulo. As T **42** of Portuguese Guinea.

620	2t. multicoloured	1·00	55

67 Academy Buildings

1954. Centenary of Afonso de Albuquerque National Academy.

621	**67**	9t. multicoloured	2·50	75

68 Mgr. Dalgado

1955. Birth Centenary of Mgr. Dalgado.

622	**68**	1r. multicoloured	50	20
623	**68**	1t. multicoloured	90	35

71 M. A. de Sousa

72 F. de Almeida

73 Map of Bacaim

1956. 450th Anniv of Portuguese Settlements in India. Multicoloured. (a) Famous Men. As T **71**.

624	6r. Type **71**	45	35
625	1½t. F. N. Xavier	45	35
626	4t. A. V. Lourenco	45	40
627	8t. Father Jose Vaz	1·10	55
628	9t. M. G. de Heredia	1·10	55
629	2rp. A. C. Pacheco	4·50	2·75

(b) Viceroys. As T **72**.

630	3r. Type **72**	45	35
631	9r. A. de Albuquerque	45	35
632	1t. Vasco da Gama	65	45
633	3t. N. da Cunha	95	45
634	10t. J. de Castro	1·30	45
635	3rp. C. de Braganca	6·25	3·00

(c) Settlements. As T **73**.

636	2t. Type **73**	5·25	3·00
637	2½t. Mombaim	2·40	1·70
638	3½t. Damao	2·40	1·70
639	5t. Diu	1·10	75
640	12t. Cochim	1·80	1·40
641	1rp. Goa	4·25	2·50

74 Map of Damao. Dadra and Nagar Aveli Districts

1957. Centres multicoloured.

642	**74**	3r. grey	25	20
643	**74**	6r. green	25	20
644	**74**	3t. pink	40	30
645	**74**	6t. blue	40	30
646	**74**	11t. bistre	1·30	55
647	**74**	2rp. lilac	2·20	1·20
648	**74**	3rp. yellow	3·25	2·50
649	**74**	5rp. red	5·25	3·25

75 Arms of Vasco da Gama

1958. Heraldic Arms of Famous Men. Multicoloured.

650	2r. Type **75**	40	30
651	6r. Lopo Soares de Albergaria	40	30
652	9r. D. Francisco de Almeida	40	30
653	1t. Garcia de Noronha	45	35
654	4t. D. Afonso de Albuquerque	45	40
655	5t. D. Joao de Castro	90	40
656	11t. D. Luis de Ataide	1·50	1·20
657	1rp. Nuno da Cunha	2·30	1·30

1958. Sixth International Congress of Tropical Medicine. As T **45** of Portuguese Guinea.

658	5t. multicoloured	1·50	1·00

DESIGN: 5t. "Holarrhena antidysenterica" (plant).

1958. Brussels Int Exn. As T **44** of Portuguese Guinea.

659	1rp. multicoloured	1·00	85

1959. Surch in new currency.

660	-	5c. on 2r. (No. 650)	45	40
661	**74**	10c. on 3r. grey	45	40
662	-	15c. on 6r. (No. 651)	45	40
663	-	20c. on 9r. (No. 652)	45	40
664	-	30c. on 1t. (No. 653)	45	40
681	-	40c. on 1½t. (No. 566)	45	40
682	-	40c. on 1½t. (No. 625)	45	40
683	-	40c. on 2t. (No. 620)	45	40
665	**73**	40c. on 2t.30	45	40
666	-	40c. on 2½t. (No. 637)	1·00	75
667	-	40c. on 3½t. (No. 638)	45	40
668	**74**	50c. on 3t. pink	45	40
669	-	80c. on 3t. (No. 633)	1·70	75
684	**64**	80c. on 3t. lilac and yellow	45	40
685	-	80c. on 3½t. (No. 561)	45	40
686	-	80c. on 5t. (No. 658)	1·80	55
670	-	80c. on 10t. (No. 634)	1·00	75
687	-	80c. on 1rp. (No. 659)	3·50	1·90
671	-	80c. on 3rp. (No. 635)	1·70	75
672	-	1e. on 4t. (No. 654)	45	40
673	-	1e.50 on 5t. (No. 655)	75	40
674	**74**	2e. on 6t. blue	45	40
675	**74**	2e.50 on 11t. bistre	1·00	40
676	-	4e. on 11t. (No. 656)	1·30	75
677	-	4e.50 on 1rp. (No. 657)	1·80	1·10
678	**74**	5e. on 2rp. lilac	1·70	75
679	**74**	10e. on 3rp. yellow	2·50	1·90
680	**74**	30e. on 5rp. red	7·50	1·90

78 Coin of Manoel I

1959. Portuguese Indian Coins. Designs showing both sides of coins of various rulers. Multicoloured.

688	**74**	5c. Type **78**	25	20
689	**74**	10c. Joao III	25	20
690	**74**	15c. Sebastiao	25	20
691	**74**	30c. Filipe I	45	40
692	**74**	40c. Filipe II	45	40
693	**74**	50c. Filipe III	55	20
694	**74**	60c. Joao IV	55	20
695	**74**	80c. Afonso VI	55	20
696	**74**	1e. Pedro II	55	20
697	**74**	1e.50 Joao V	55	20
698	**74**	2e. Jose I	85	50
699	**74**	2e.50 Maria I	90	40
700	**74**	3e. Prince Regent Joao	90	50
701	**74**	4e. Pedro IV	90	55
702	**74**	4e.40 Miguel	1·20	75
703	**74**	5e. Maria II	1·20	75
704	**74**	10e. Pedro V	1·80	1·60
705	**74**	20e. Luis	4·00	3·25
706	**74**	30e. Carlos	6·00	4·00
707	**74**	50e. Portuguese Republic	9·50	5·25

79 Prince Henry's Arms

1960. 500th Death Anniv of Prince Henry the Navigator.

708	**79**	3e. multicoloured	2·40	1·00

The 1962 sports set and malaria eradication stamp similar to those for the other territories were ready for issue when Portuguese India was occupied, but they were not put on sale there.

CHARITY TAX STAMPS

The notes under this heading in Portugal also apply here.

1919. Fiscal stamp. Type **C1** of Portuguese Africa optd **TAXA DE GUERRA**.

C491	Rps. 0:00:05, 48 green	3·50	2·75
C492	Rps. 0:02:03, 43 green	7·50	4·75

1925. Marquis de Pombal Commem stamps of Portugal, but inscr "INDIA".

C495	**C73**	6r. pink	70	65
C496	-	6r. pink	70	65
C497	**C75**	6r. pink	70	65

C52 Mother and Child

1948. (a) Inscr "ASSISTENCIA PUBLICA".

C571	**C52**	6r. green	5·50	3·25
C572	**C52**	6r. yellow	3·75	2·50
C573	**C52**	1t. red	5·50	3·25
C574	**C52**	1t. orange	3·75	2·50
C575	**C52**	1t. green	6·00	3·50

(b) Inscr "PROVEDORIA DE ASSISTENCIA PUBLICA".

C607	1t. grey	6·50	3·50

1951. Surch 1 tanga.

C606	1t. on 6r. red	5·25	2·75

1953. Optd **"Revalidado" P. A. P.** and dotted line.

C617	1t. red	15·00	7·75

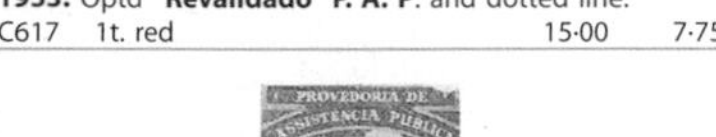

C69 Mother and Child

1953. Surch as in Type **C69**.

C624	**C69**	1t. on 4t. blue	19·00	12·00

C70 Mother and Child

1956

C625	**C70**	1t. black, green and red	1·30	65
C626	**C70**	1t. blue, orange & grn	1·10	65

1957. Surch 6 reis.

C650	6r. on 1t. black, green and red	1·80	95

1959. Surch.

C688	20c. on 1t. blue, orange and green	85	65
C689	40c. on 1t. blue, orange and green	85	65

C80 Arms and People

1960

C709	**C80**	20e. brown and red	85	65

POSTAGE DUE STAMPS

1904. "Due" key-type inscr "INDIA".

D337	**W**	2r. green	55	55
D338	**W**	3r. green	55	50
D339	**W**	4r. orange	55	50
D340	**W**	5r. grey	55	50
D341	**W**	6r. grey	55	50
D342	**W**	9r. brown	80	75
D343	**W**	1t. red	80	75
D344	**W**	2t. brown	1·50	90
D345	**W**	5t. blue	4·00	3·25
D346	**W**	10t. red	4·00	3·75
D347	**W**	1rp. lilac	18·00	8·50

1911. Nos. D337/47 optd **REPUBLICA**.

D354	2r. green	35	25
D355	3r. green	35	25
D356	4r. orange	35	25
D357	5r. grey	35	25
D358	6r. grey	45	25
D359	9r. brown	60	25
D360	1t. red	60	25
D361	2t. brown	1·00	55
D362	5t. blue	2·20	1·80
D363	10t. red	6·50	4·00
D364	1rp. lilac	6·50	4·00

1925. Marquis de Pombal stamps, as Nos. C495/7 optd **MULTA**.

D495	**C73**	1t. pink	55	55
D496	-	1t. pink	55	55
D497	**C75**	1t. pink	55	55

1943. Stamps of 1933 surch Porteado and new value.

D549	**40**	3r. on 2½t. blue	65	55
D550	**40**	6r. on 3t. turquoise	1·50	85
D551	**40**	1t. on 5t. red	2·75	2·30

1945. As Type **D1** of Portuguese Colonies, but optd **ESTADO DA INDIA**.

D555	2r. black and red	1·20	1·10
D556	3r. black and blue	1·20	1·10
D557	4r. black and yellow	1·20	1·10
D558	6r. black and green	1·20	1·10
D559	1t. black and brown	1·50	1·30
D560	2t. black and brown	1·50	1·30

1951. Surch Porteado and new value and bar.

D588	2rs. on 7r. (No. 558)	70	65
D589	3rs. on 7r. (No. 558)	70	65
D590	1t. on 1rp. (No. 562)	70	65
D591	2t. on 1rp. (No. 562)	70	65

1952. As Type **D70** of Macao, but inscr "INDIA PORTUGUESA". Numerals in red, name in black.

D606	2r. olive and brown	30	20
D607	3r. black and green	30	20
D608	6r. blue and turquoise	40	20
D609	1t. red and grey	45	35
D610	2t. orange, green and grey	1·10	75
D611	10t. blue, green and yellow	4·00	3·50

1959. Nos. D606/8 and D610/11 surch in new currency.

D688	5c. on 2r. multicoloured	40	30
D689	10c. on 3r. multicoloured	40	30
D690	15c. on 6r. multicoloured	55	45
D691	60c. on 2t. multicoloured	1·70	1·40
D692	60c. on 10t. multicoloured	5·00	4·00

Pt. 9 & 21

PORTUGUESE TIMOR

The eastern part of Timor in the Indonesian Archipelago. Administered as part of Macao until 1896, then as a separate Portuguese Overseas Province until 1975.

Following a civil war and the intervention of Indonesian forces the territory was incorporated into Indonesia on 17 July 1976.

1885. 1000 reis = 1 milreis.
1894. 100 avos = 1 pataca.
1960. 100 centavos = 1 escudo.

1885. "Crown" key-type inscr "MACAU" optd **TIMOR**.

1	**P**	5r. black	2·75	2·30
12	**P**	10r. green	6·50	5·25
3	**P**	20r. red	12·00	7·00
4	**P**	25r. lilac	2·40	1·40
5	**P**	40r. yellow	5·75	4·50
6	**P**	50r. blue	2·75	1·90
7	**P**	80r. grey	7·50	4·50
8	**P**	100r. purple	2·75	2·30
19	**P**	200r. orange	5·50	4·50
20	**P**	300r. brown	5·50	4·50

1887. "Embossed" key-type inscr "CORREIO DE TIMOR".

21	**Q**	5r. black	4·25	2·50
22	**Q**	10r. green	4·75	3·25
23	**Q**	20r. red	6·50	3·25
24	**Q**	25r. mauve	8·50	4·25
25	**Q**	40r. brown	15·00	6·00
26	**Q**	50r. blue	15·00	6·00
27	**Q**	80r. grey	17·00	7·00
28	**Q**	100r. brown	19·00	8·50
29	**Q**	200r. lilac	39·00	18·00
30	**Q**	300r. orange	44·00	22·00

1892. "Embossed" key-type inscr "PROVINCIA DE MACAU" surch **TIMOR 30 30**. No gum.

32	30 on 300r. orange	7·50	5·50

1894. "Figures" key-type inscr "TIMOR".

33	**R**	5r. orange	2·75	1·40
34	**R**	10r. mauve	2·75	1·40
35	**R**	15r. brown	3·75	1·40
36	**R**	20r. lilac	3·75	1·40
37	**R**	25r. green	4·25	2·30
38	**R**	50r. blue	6·00	4·50
39	**R**	75r. pink	8·00	6·00
40	**R**	80r. green	8·00	6·00
41	**R**	100r. brown on buff	6·25	5·25
42	**R**	150r. red on pink	26·00	12·50
43	**R**	200r. blue on blue	26·00	14·00
44	**R**	300r. blue on brown	32·00	15·00

1894. Nos. 21/30 surch **PROVISORIO** and value in European and Chinese. No gum.

46	**Q**	1a. on 5r. black	2·75	1·70
47	**Q**	2a. on 10r. green	3·00	2·50
48	**Q**	3a. on 20r. red	4·50	2·50
49	**Q**	4a. on 25r. purple	4·50	2·50
50	**Q**	6a. on 40r. brown	7·50	3·25
51	**Q**	8a. on 50r. blue	9·00	5·00
52	**Q**	13a. on 80r. grey	17·00	16·00
53	**Q**	16a. on 100r. brown	17·00	16·00
54	**Q**	31a. on 200r. lilac	45·00	34·00
55	**Q**	47a. on 300r. orange	50·00	40·00

1895. No. 32 further surch **5 avos PROVISORIO** and Chinese characters with bars over the original surch.

56	5a. on 30 on 300r. orange	10·00	6·00

1898. 400th Anniv of Vasco da Gama's Discovery of Route to India. As Nos. 1/8 of Portuguese Colonies, but inscr "TIMOR" and value in local currency.

58	½a. green	3·00	2·20
59	1a. red	3·00	2·20
60	2a. purple	3·00	2·20
61	4a. green	3·00	2·20
62	8a. blue	4·75	2·75
63	12a. brown	6·25	3·75
64	16a. brown	6·25	4·75
65	24a. brown	9·75	6·50

1898. "King Carlos" key-type inscr "TIMOR". Name and value in red (78a.) or black (others). With or without gum.

68	**S**	½a. grey	85	70
69	**S**	1a. red	85	70
70	**S**	2a. green	85	70
71	**S**	2½a. brown	2·40	1·80
72	**S**	3a. lilac	2·40	1·80
112	**S**	3a. green	3·75	2·20
73	**S**	4a. green	2·40	1·80
113	**S**	5a. red	3·00	2·20
114	**S**	6a. brown	3·00	2·20
74	**S**	8a. blue	2·40	1·80
115	**S**	9a. brown	3·00	2·20
75	**S**	10a. blue	2·40	1·80
116	**S**	10a. brown	3·00	2·20
76	**S**	12a. pink	6·50	5·75
117	**S**	12a. blue	17·00	14·00
118	**S**	13a. mauve	4·50	2·50
119	**S**	15a. lilac	7·50	4·50
78	**S**	16a. blue on blue	6·50	5·75
79	**S**	20a. brown on yellow	6·50	5·75
120	**S**	22a. brown on pink	7·50	5·50
80	**S**	24a. brown on buff	6·50	5·75
81	**S**	31a. purple on pink	6·50	5·75
121	**S**	31a. brown on cream	7·50	5·50
82	**S**	47a. blue on pink	12·50	9·00
122	**S**	47a. purple on pink	7·75	5·50
83	**S**	78a. black on blue	18·00	11·50
123	**S**	78a. blue on yellow	17·00	11·50

1899. Nos. 78 and 81 surch **PROVISORIO** and value in figures and bars.

84	10 on 16a. blue on blue	4·75	4·25
85	20 on 31a. purple on pink	4·75	4·25

1902. Surch.

88	**R**	5a. on 5r. orange	2·40	1·80
86	**Q**	5a. on 25r. mauve	4·25	2·30
89	**R**	5a. on 25r. green	2·40	1·80
90	**R**	5a. on 50r. blue	2·75	2·30
87	**Q**	5a. on 200r. lilac	6·25	3·75
95	**V**	6a. on 2½r. brown	1·50	1·30
92	**Q**	6a. on 10r. green	£275	£200
94	**R**	6a. on 20r. lilac	2·75	2·30
93	**Q**	6a. on 300r. orange	6·00	5·50
100	**R**	9a. on 15r. brown	2·75	2·30
98	**Q**	9a. on 40r. brown	7·50	5·50
101	**R**	9a. on 75r. pink	2·75	2·30
99	**Q**	9a. on 100r. brown	7·50	5·50
124	**S**	10a. on 12a. blue	4·75	3·75
104	**R**	15a. on 10r. mauve	4·50	3·25
102	**Q**	15a. on 20r. red	7·50	5·50
103	**Q**	15a. on 50r. blue	£225	£190
105	**R**	15a. on 100r. brn on buff	4·50	3·25
106	**R**	15a. on 300r. blue on brn	4·50	3·25
107	**Q**	22a. on 80r. grey	15·00	11·00
108	**R**	22a. on 80r. green	7·50	6·00
109	**R**	22a. on 200r. blue on blue	7·50	6·00

1902. Nos. 72 and 76 optd **PROVISORIO**.

110	3a. lilac	3·25	2·30
111	12a. pink	8·00	6·00

1911. Nos. 68, etc, optd **REPUBLICA**.

125	½a. grey	85	65
126	1a. red	85	65
127	2a. green	85	65
128	3a. green	85	65
129	5a. red	1·50	85
130	6a. brown	1·50	85
131	9a. brown	1·50	85
132	10a. brown	2·40	1·90
133	13a. purple	2·40	1·90
134	15a. lilac	2·40	1·90
135	22a. brown on pink	2·40	1·90
136	31a. brown on cream	2·40	1·90
163	31a. purple on pink	5·00	3·50
137	47a. purple on pink	5·00	3·75
165	47a. blue on pink	7·75	6·00
167	78a. blue on yelow	10·00	8·50
168	78a. black on blue	10·00	6·25

1911. No. 112 and provisional stamps of 1902 optd **Republica**.

139		3a. green	6·25	4·50
140	**R**	5a. on 5r. orange	2·40	2·10
141	**R**	5a. on 25r. green	2·40	2·10
142	**R**	5a. on 50r. blue	5·50	4·50
144	**V**	6a. on 2½r. brown	5·00	2·75
146	**R**	6a. on 20r. lilac	2·75	2·10
147	**R**	9a. on 15r. brown	2·75	2·10
148	**S**	10a. on 12a. blue	2·75	2·10
149	**R**	15a. on 100r. brown on buff	3·25	3·00
150	**R**	22a. on 80r. green	6·25	3·50
151	**R**	22a. on 200r. blue on blue	6·25	3·50

1913. Provisional stamps of 1902 optd **REPUBLICA**.

192	**S**	3a. lilac (No. 110)	1·20	90
194	**R**	5a. on 5r. orange	1·20	85
195	**R**	5a. on 25r. green	1·20	85
196	**R**	5a. on 50r. blue	1·20	85
200	**V**	6a. on 2½r. brown	1·20	85
201	**R**	6a. on 20r. lilac	1·20	85
202	**R**	9a. on 15r. brown	1·20	85
203	**R**	9a. on 75r. pink	1·40	85
193	**S**	10a. on 10a. blue	1·20	90
204	**R**	15a. on 10r. mauve	1·40	85
205	**R**	15a. on 100r. brown on buff	1·50	85
206	**R**	15a. on 300r. blue on brn	1·50	85
207	**R**	22a. on 80r. green	4·25	2·50
208	**R**	22a. on 200r. blue on blue	6·25	4·50

1913. Vasco da Gama stamps of Timor optd **REPUBLICA** or surch also.

169	½a. green	95	70
170	1a. red	95	70
171	2a. purple	1·00	85
172	4a. green	1·00	85
173	8a. blue	2·20	1·40
174	10a. on 12a. brown	3·75	3·00
175	16a. brown	2·75	2·20
176	24a. brown	4·50	3·50

1914. "Ceres" key-type inscr "TIMOR". Name and value in black.

211	**U**	½a. green	1·50	1·40
212	**U**	1a. black	1·50	1·40
213	**U**	1½a. green	1·30	1·20
214	**U**	2a. green	1·50	1·40
180	**U**	3a. brown	1·50	1·10
181	**U**	4a. red	1·50	1·10
182	**U**	6a. violet	1·90	1·10
216	**U**	7a. green	2·20	1·30
217	**U**	7½a. blue	2·20	1·30
218	**U**	9a. blue	2·20	1·30
183	**U**	10a. blue	1·90	1·10
219	**U**	11a. grey	3·25	2·75
184	**U**	12a. brown	2·75	1·90
221	**U**	15a. mauve	11·00	6·25
185	**U**	16a. grey	2·75	1·90
222	**U**	18a. blue	11·00	6·25
223	**U**	19a. green	11·00	6·25
186	**U**	20a. red	26·00	7·50
224	**U**	36a. turquoise	11·00	6·25
187	**U**	40a. purple	15·00	7·50
225	**U**	54a. brown	11·00	6·25
188	**U**	58a. brown on green	15·00	7·00
226	**U**	72a. red	22·00	12·50
189	**U**	76a. brown on pink	15·00	11·00

190	U	1p. orange on orange	24·00	17·00
191	U	3p. green on blue	55·00	29·00
227	U	5p. red	90·00	41·00

1920. No. 196 surch ½ **Avo P. P. n.°68 19-3-1920** and bars.

229	R	½a. on 5a. on 50r. blue	29·00	28·00

1932. Nos. 226 and 221 surch with new value and bars.

230	U	6a. on 72a. red	2·20	1·70
231	U	12a. on 15a. mauve	2·20	1·70

25a "Portugal" and Galeasse

1935

232	**25a**	½a. brown	50	35
233	**25a**	1a. brown	50	35
234	**25a**	2a. green	50	35
235	**25a**	3a. mauve	50	35
236	**25a**	4a. black	90	55
237	**25a**	5a. grey	90	55
238	**25a**	6a. brown	90	55
239	**25a**	7a. red	90	55
240	**25a**	8a. turquoise	1·40	75
241	**25a**	10a. red	1·40	75
242	**25a**	12a. blue	1·40	75
243	**25a**	14a. green	1·40	75
244	**25a**	15a. purple	1·40	75
245	**25a**	20a. orange	1·40	75
246	**25a**	30a. green	1·80	75
247	**25a**	40a. violet	5·75	2·75
248	**25a**	50a. brown	5·75	2·75
249	**25a**	1p. blue	14·00	8·25
250	**25a**	2p. brown	35·00	12·00
251	**25a**	3p. green	50·00	17·00
252	**25a**	5p. mauve	65·00	34·00

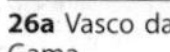

26a Vasco da Gama **26b** Airplane over globe

1938

253	**26a**	1a. green (postage)	50	45
254	**26a**	2a. brown	50	45
255	**26a**	3a. violet	50	45
256	**26a**	4a. green	50	45
257	-	5a. red	60	50
258	-	6a. grey	60	50
259	-	8a. purple	60	50
260	-	10a. mauve	60	50
261	-	12a. red	90	60
262	-	15a. orange	1·40	1·00
263	-	20a. blue	1·40	1·00
264	-	40a. black	2·20	1·30
265	-	50a. brown	3·25	2·00
266	-	1p. red	11·00	6·25
267	-	2p. olive	30·00	7·50
268	-	3p. blue	33·00	16·00
269	-	5p. brown	65·00	33·00
270	**26b**	1a. red (air)	1·20	1·10
271	**26b**	2a. violet	1·30	90
272	**26b**	3a. orange	1·30	90
273	**26b**	5a. blue	1·40	1·20
274	**26b**	10a. red	1·80	1·40
275	**26b**	20a. green	4·50	2·00
276	**26b**	50a. brown	8·75	6·00
277	**26b**	70a. red	10·50	7·75
278	**26b**	1p. mauve	21·00	11·00

DESIGNS—POSTAGE: 5a. to 8a. Mousinho de Albuquerque; 10a. to 15a. Prince Henry the Navigator; 20a. to 50a. Dam; 1p. to 5p. Afonso de Albuquerque.

1946. Stamps as above but inscr "MOCAMBIQUE" surch **TIMOR** and new value.

279	**26a**	1a. on 15c. purple (post)	8·00	5·75
280	-	4a. on 35c. green	8·00	5·75
281	-	8a. on 50c. mauve	8·00	5·75
282	-	10a. on 70c. violet	8·00	5·75
283	-	12a. on 1e. red	8·00	5·75
284	-	20a. on 1e.75 blue	8·00	5·75
285	**26b**	8a. on 50c. orange (air)	8·50	6·25
286	**26b**	12a. on 1e. blue	8·50	6·25
287	**26b**	40a. on 3e. green	8·50	6·25
288	**26b**	50a. on 5e. brown	8·50	6·25
289	**26b**	1p. on 10e. mauve	8·50	6·25

1947. Nos. 253/64 and 270/78 optd **LIBERTACAO**.

290	**26a**	1a. green (postage)	23·00	12·50
291	**26a**	2a. brown	50·00	26·00
292	**26a**	3a. violet	21·00	8·00
293	**26a**	4a. green	21·00	8·00
294	-	5a. red	9·00	3·00
295	-	8a. purple	2·30	1·00
296	-	10a. mauve	8·50	3·50
297	-	12a. red	8·50	3·50
298	-	15a. orange	8·50	3·50
299	-	20a. blue	£110	55·00
300	-	40a. black	24·00	15·00
301	**26b**	1a. red (air)	35·00	8·75
302	**26b**	2a. violet	35·00	8·75
303	**26b**	3a. orange	35·00	8·75
304	**26b**	5a. blue	35·00	8·75
305	**26b**	10a. red	8·25	3·00
306	**26b**	20a. green	8·25	3·00
307	**26b**	50a. brown	8·25	3·00
308	**26b**	70a. red	21·00	8·75
309	**26b**	1p. mauve	15·00	3·00

30 Girl with Gong

1948

310	-	1a. brown and turquoise	1·40	65
311	**30**	3a. brown and grey	3·00	1·30
312	-	4a. green and mauve	4·25	3·00
313	-	8a. grey and red	2·30	75
314	-	10a. green and brown	2·30	75
315	-	20a. ultramarine and blue	2·30	1·30
316	-	1p. blue and orange	43·00	10·00
317	-	3p. brown and violet	46·00	17·00

MS317a 130×99 mm. Nos. 310/17 (sold at 5p.) £170 £130

DESIGNS: 1a. Native woman; 4a. Girl with baskets; 8a. Chief of Aleixo de Ainaro; 10a. Timor chief; 20a. Warrior and horse; 1, 3p. Tribal chieftains.

1948. Honouring the Statue of Our Lady of Fatima. As T **33** of Portuguese Guinea.

318		8a. grey	14·00	12·50

1949. 75th Anniv of U.P.U. As T **34** of Portuguese Guinea.

319		16a. brown	33·00	18·00

31 Pottery-making

1950

320	**31**	20a. blue	1·50	1·40
321	-	50a. brown (Young girl)	4·75	1·90

1950. Holy Year. As Nos. 425/6 of Macao.

322		40a. green	3·25	2·10
323		70a. brown	5·25	3·00

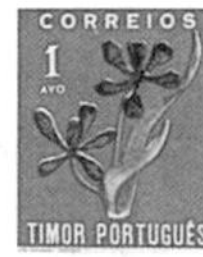

32 "Belamcanda chinensis"

1950

324	**32**	1a. red, green and grey	1·10	65
325	-	3a. yellow, green and brown	5·00	3·50
326	-	10a. pink, green and blue	5·75	3·75
327	-	16a. multicoloured	11·00	5·25
328	-	20a. yellow, green and turquoise	5·00	3·50
329	-	30a. yellow, green and blue	5·75	3·75
330	-	70a. multicoloured	7·50	4·50
331	-	1p. red, yellow and green	12·50	7·75
332	-	2p. green, yellow and red	19·00	13·00
333	-	5p. pink, green and black	30·00	24·00

FLOWERS: 3a. "Caesalpinia pulcherrima"; 10a. "Calotropis gigantea"; 16a. "Delonix regia"; 20a. "Plumeria rubra"; 30a. "Allamanda cathartica"; 70a. "Haemanthus multiflorus"; 1p. "Bauhinia"; 2p. "Eurycles amboiniensis"; 5p. "Crinum longiflorum".

1951. Termination of Holy Year. As T **36** of Portuguese Guinea.

334		86a. blue and turquoise	3·50	2·75

1952. First Tropical Medicine Congress, Lisbon. As T **37** of Portuguese Guinea.

335		10a. brown and green	1·90	1·40

DESIGN: Nurse weighing baby.

1952. 400th Death Anniv of St. Francis Xavier. Designs as No. 452/4 of Macao.

336		1a. black and grey	40	20
337		16a. brown and buff	1·80	85
338		1p. red and grey	6·50	2·75

34 Statue of The Virgin

1953. Missionary Art Exhibition.

339	**34**	3a. brown and light brown	40	20
340	**34**	16a. brown and stone	1·70	1·00
341	**34**	50a. blue and brown	3·25	2·40

1954. Portuguese Stamp Centenary. As T **41** of Portuguese Guinea.

342		10a. multicoloured	2·30	1·90

1954. 400th Anniv of Sao Paulo. As T **42** of Portuguese Guinea.

343		16a. multicoloured	1·70	1·10

35 Map of Timor

1956

344	**35**	1a. multicoloured	35	15
345	**35**	3a. multicoloured	35	15
346	**35**	8a. multicoloured	70	50
347	**35**	24a. multicoloured	75	50
348	**35**	32a. multicoloured	95	55
349	**35**	40a. multicoloured	1·40	70
350	**35**	1p. multicoloured	4·50	95
351	**35**	3p. multicoloured	11·00	5·50

1958. Sixth International Congress of Tropical Medicine. As T **45** of Portuguese Guinea.

352		32a. multicoloured	5·75	4·25

DESIGN: 32a. "Calophyllum inophyllum" (plant).

1958. Brussels International Exhibition. As T **44** of Portuguese Guinea.

353		40a. multicoloured	1·10	60

1960. New currency. Nos. 344/51 surch thus: **$05** and bars.

354		5c. on 1a. multicoloured	35	15
355		10c. on 3a. multicoloured	35	15
356		20c. on 8a. multicoloured	35	15
357		30c. on 24a. multicoloured	35	15
358		50c. on 32s. multicoloured	35	15
359		1e. on 40a. multicoloured	45	40
360		2e. on 40a. multicoloured	70	45
361		5e. on 1p. multicoloured	1·40	1·00
362		10e. on 3p. multicoloured	4·75	2·20
363		15e. on 3p. multicoloured	4·75	3·00

1960. 500th Death Anniv of Prince Henry the Navigator. As T **47** of Portuguese Guinea. Multicoloured.

364		4e.50 Prince Henry's motto (horiz)	1·10	65

38 Elephant Jar

1962. Timor Art. Multicoloured.

365		5c. Type **38**	35	15
366		10c. House on stilts	35	15
367		20c. Idol	45	30
368		30c. Rosary	65	50
369		50c. Model of outrigger canoe (horiz)	90	55
370		1e. Casket	1·10	55
371		2e.50 Archer	1·20	55
372		4e. Elephant	1·70	55
373		5e. Native climbing palm tree	2·30	55
374		10e. Statuette of woman	5·50	1·70
375		20e. Model of cockfight (horiz)	14·00	4·25
376		50e. House, bird and cat	16·00	5·00

1962. Sports. As T **49** of Portuguese Guinea. Multicoloured.

377		50c. Game shooting	45	15
378		1e. Horse-riding	1·50	50
379		1e.50 Swimming	1·40	65
380		2e. Athletes	1·70	75
381		2e.50 Football	2·00	1·00
382		15e. Big-game hunting	3·75	2·40

1962. Malaria Eradication. Mosquito design as T **50** of Portuguese Guinea. Multicoloured.

383		2e.50 "Anopheles sundaicus"	2·00	1·10

1964. Centenary of National Overseas Bank. As T **53** of Portuguese Guinea, but portrait of M. P. Chagas.

384		2e.50 multicoloured	1·30	1·10

1965. I.T.U. Centenary. As T **54** of Portuguese Guinea.

385		1e.50 multicoloured	2·00	1·20

1966. 40th Anniv of National Revolution. As T **56** of Portuguese Guinea, but showing different buildings. Multicoloured.

386		4e.50 Dr V. Machado's College and Health Centre, Dili	1·70	1·10

1967. Centenary of Military Naval Assn. As T **57** of Portuguese Guinea. Multicoloured.

387		10c. Gago Coutinho and gunboat "Patria"	45	35
388		4e.50 Sacadura Cabral and Fairey IIID seaplane "Lusitania"	3·00	1·70

39 Sepoy Officer, 1792

1967. Portuguese Military Uniforms. Multicoloured.

389		35c. Type **39**	30	20
390		1e. Infantry officer, 1815	2·50	65
391		1e.50 Infantryman 1879	45	40
392		2e. Infantryman, 1890	45	40
393		2e.50 Infantry officer, 1903	65	40
394		3e. Sapper, 1918	1·10	60
395		4e.50 Commando, 1964	1·90	60
396		10e. Parachutist, 1964	2·75	1·40

1967. 50th Anniv of Fatima Apparitions. As T **58** of Portuguese Guinea.

397		3e. Virgin of the Pilgrims	90	45

1968. 500th Birth Anniv of Pedro Cabral (explorer). As T **64** of Portuguese Guinea. Multicoloured.

398		4e.50 Lopo Homen-Reineis' map, 1519 (horiz)	1·70	90

1969. Birth Centenary of Admiral Gago Coutinho. As T **66** of Portuguese Guinea. Multicoloured.

399		4e.50 Frigate "Almirante Gago Coutinho" (horiz)	2·00	1·30

40 Pictorial Map of 1834, and Arms

1969. Bicentenary of Dili (capital of Timor).

400	**40**	1e. multicoloured	75	55

1969. 500th Anniv of Vasco da Gama (explorer). As T **67** of Portuguese Guinea. Multicoloured.

401		5e. Convert Medallion	75	55

1969. Centenary of Overseas Administrative Reforms. As T **68** of Portuguese Guinea.

402		5e. multicoloured	90	55

1969. 500th Birth Anniv of King Manoel I. As T **69** of Portuguese Guinea. Multicoloured.

403		4e. Emblem of Manoel I in Jeronimos Monastery	65	45

41 Map, Sir Ross Smith, and Arms of Britain, Timor and Australia

1969. 50th Anniv of First England–Australia Flight.

404	**41**	2e. multicoloured	1·00	75

1970. Birth Centenary of Marshal Carmona. As T **71** of Portuguese Guinea. Multicoloured.

414		1e. Portrait in civilian dress	55	35

1972. 400th Anniv of Camoens' "The Lusiads" (epic poem). As T **73** of Portuguese Guinea. Multicoloured.

415		1e. Missionaries, natives and galleon	65	45

1972. Olympic Games, Munich. As T **74** of Portuguese Guinea. Multicoloured.

416		4e.50 Football	90	55

1972. 50th Anniv of First Flight from Lisbon to Rio de Janeiro. As T **75** of Portuguese Guinea. Multicoloured.

417		1e. Aviators Gago Coutinho and Sacadura Cabral in Fairey IIID seaplane	90	75

1973. W.M.O. Centenary. As T **76** of Portuguese Guinea.

418		20e. multicoloured	3·00	2·30

CHARITY TAX STAMPS

The notes under this heading in Portugal also apply here.

1919. No. 211 surch **2 AVOS TAXA DA GUERRA**. With or without gum.

C228	**U**	2a. on ½a. green	9·25	4·25

1919. No. 196 surch **2 TAXA DE GUERRA** and bars.

C230	**R**	2 on 5a. on 50r. blue	85·00	65·00

1925. Marquis de Pombal Commem. As Nos. 666/8 of Portugal, but inscr "TIMOR".

C231	**C73**	2a. red	75	55
C232	-	2a. red	75	55
C233	**C 75**	2a. red	75	55

1934. Educational Tax. Fiscal stamps as Type **C1** of Portuguese Colonies, with values in black, optd **Instrucao D. L. n.°7 de 3-2-1934** or surch also. With or without gum.

C234		2a. green	5·25	3·50
C235		5a. green	8·00	4·25
C236		7a. on ½a. pink	8·50	5·00

1936. Fiscal stamps as Type **C1** of Portuguese Colonies, with value in black, optd **Assistencia D. L. n.°72.** With or without gum.

C253		10a. pink	5·50	3·75
C254		10a. green	4·25	3·50

C29

1948. No gum.

C310	**C29**	10a. blue	4·25	2·10
C311	**C29**	20a. green	5·25	3·50

The 20a. has a different emblem.

1960. Similar design. New currency. No gum.

C364		70c. blue	1·50	1·40
C400		1e.30 green	3·00	2·75

C42 Woman and Star

1969

C405	**C42**	30c. blue and light blue	60	55
C406	**C42**	50c. purple and orange	60	55
C407	**C42**	1e. brown and yellow	60	55

1970. Nos. C364 and C400 surch **D. L. n.° 776** and value.

C408		30c. on 70c. blue	15·00	14·50
C409		30c. on 1e.30 green	15·00	14·50
C410		50c. on 70c. blue	34·00	31·00
C411		50c. on 1e.30 green	15·00	14·50
C412		1e. on 70c. blue	20·00	17·00
C413		1e. on 1e.30 green	15·00	14·50

NEWSPAPER STAMPS

1892. "Embossed" key-type inscr "PROVINCIA DE MACAU" surch **JORNAES TIMOR 2½ 2½.** No gum.

N31	**Q**	2½ on 20r. red	3·00	2·10
N32	**Q**	2½ on 40r. brown	3·00	2·10
N33	**Q**	2½ on 80r. grey	3·00	2·10

1893. "Newspaper" key-type inscr "TIMOR".

N36	**V**	2½r. brown	1·40	1·10

1894. No. N36 surch **½ avo PROVISORIO** and Chinese characters.

N58		½a. on 2½r. brown	1·00	90

POSTAGE DUE STAMPS

1904. "Due" key-type inscr "TIMOR". Name and value in black. With or without gum (1, 2a.), no gum (others).

D124	**W**	1a. green	85	70
D125	**W**	2a. grey	85	70
D126	**W**	5a. brown	1·90	1·40
D127	**W**	6a. orange	1·90	1·40
D128	**W**	10a. brown	2·40	1·40
D129	**W**	15a. brown	4·25	3·25
D130	**W**	24a. blue	11·50	7·00
D131	**W**	40a. red	12·00	7·25
D132	**W**	50a. orange	16·00	7·75
D133	**W**	1p. lilac	34·00	19·00

1911. "Due" key-type of Timor optd **REPUBLICA.**

D139		1a. green	45	40
D140		2a. grey	45	40
D141		5a. brown	70	65
D142		6a. orange	1·00	85
D143		10a. brown	1·70	1·10
D144		15a. brown	2·10	1·30
D145		24a. blue	3·50	2·50
D146		40a. red	4·75	3·25
D147		50a. orange	6·25	3·50
D178		1p. lilac	16·00	7·75

1925. Marquis de Pombal tax stamps. As Nos. C231/3 of Timor, optd **MULTA.**

D231	**C73**	4a. red	75	60
D232	-	4a. red	75	60
D233	**C 75**	4a. red	75	60

1952. As Type **D70** of Macao, but inscr "TIMOR PORTUGUES". Numerals in red; name in black.

D336		1a. sepia and brown	30	20
D337		3a. brown and orange	30	20
D338		5a. green and turquoise	30	20
D339		10a. green and light green	35	20
D340		30a. violet and light violet	35	20
D341		1p. red and orange	1·40	85

For subsequent issues see **EAST TIMOR**.

Pt. 1

PRINCE EDWARD ISLAND

An island off the East coast of Canada, now a province of that Dominion, whose stamps it uses.

1861. 12 pence = 1 shilling.
1872. 100 cents = 1 dollar.

1

1861. Queen's portrait in various frames. Values in pence.

9	**1**	1d. orange	55·00	70·00
28	**1**	2d. red	9·50	18·00
30	**1**	3d. blue	11·00	22·00
31	**1**	4d. black	6·50	42·00
18	**1**	6d. green	£170	£120
20	**1**	9d. mauve	£120	£100

7

1870

32	**7**	4½d. (3d. stg.) brown	75·00	85·00

8

1872. Queen's portrait in various frames. Values in cents.

44	**8**	1c. orange	9·50	35·00
38	**8**	2c. blue	27·00	65·00
37	**8**	3c. red	38·00	42·00
40	**8**	4c. green	13·00	32·00
41	**8**	6c. black	8·00	32·00
42	**8**	12c. mauve	9·50	75·00

Pt. 7

PRUSSIA

Formerly a kingdom in the N. of Germany. In 1867 it became part of the North German Confederation.

1850. 12 pfennig = 1 silbergroschen; 30 silbergroschen = 1 thaler.
1867. 60 kreuzer = 1 gulden.

1 Friedrich Wilhelm IV

1850. Imperf.

14	**1**	4pf. green	£100	55·00
4	**1**	6pf. red	£120	75·00
22	**1**	½sgr. (=6pf.) red	£275	£225
5	**1**	1sgr. black on pink	£110	18·00
16	**1**	1sgr. pink	45·00	5·75
6	**1**	2sgr. black on blue	£160	23·00
18	**1**	2sgr. blue	£160	26·00
8	**1**	3sgr. black on yellow	£160	23·00
21	**1**	3sgr. yellow	£130	23·00

3

4

1861. Roul.

24	**3**	3pf. lilac	38·00	65·00
26	**3**	4pf. green	17·00	17·00
28	**3**	6pf. orange	17·00	21·00
31	**4**	1sgr. pink	5·00	2·30
35	**4**	2sgr. blue	17·00	2·30
36	**4**	3sgr. yellow	12·50	3·00

5

1866. Printed in reverse on back of specially treated transparent paper. Roul.

38	**5**	10sgr. pink	£130	£150
39	-	30sgr. blue	£160	£325

The 30 sgr. has the value in a square.

7

1867. Roul.

40	**7**	1k. green	33·00	65·00
42	**7**	2k. orange	55·00	£140
43	**7**	3k. pink	28·00	41·00
45	**7**	6k. blue	28·00	65·00
46	**7**	9k. bistre	33·00	70·00

Pt. 9, Pt. 22

PUERTO RICO

A West Indian island ceded by Spain to the United States after the war of 1898. Until 1873 stamps of Cuba were in use. Now uses stamps of the U.S.A.

1873. 100 centimos = 1 peseta.
1881. 1000 milesimas = 100 centavos = 1 peso.
1898. 100 cents = 1 dollar.

A. SPANISH OCCUPATION

(2)

1873. Nos. 53/5 of Cuba optd with T **2**.

1		25c. deep lilac	55·00	1·60
3		50c. deep brown	£160	7·75
4		1p. brown	£350	32·00

1874. No. 57 of Cuba with opt similar to T **2** (two separate characters).

5		25c. deep blue	55·00	3·50

1875. Nos. 61/3 of Cuba with opt similar to T **2** (two separate characters).

6		25c. deep blue	35·00	4·25
7		50c. deep green	50·00	5·25
8		1p. brown	£190	28·00

1876. Nos. 65a and 67 of Cuba with opt similar to T **2** (two separate characters).

9		25c. deep lilac	5·00	3·25
10		50c. deep blue	12·50	5·25
11		1p. black	70·00	23·00

1876. Nos. 65a and 67 of Cuba with opt as last, but characters joined.

12		25c. deep lilac	50·00	2·10
13		1p. black	£110	30·00

1877. As T **9** of Philippines, but inscr "PTO-RICO 1877".

14		5c. brown	9·75	4·00
15		10c. red	33·00	4·50
16		15c. green	49·00	22·00
17		25c. blue	19·00	3·25
18		50c. bistre	33·00	7·75

1878. As T **9** of Philippines, but inscr "PTO-RICO 1878".

19		5c. grey	19·00	19·00
20		10c. brown	£300	£120
21		25c. green	2·50	1·40
22		50c. blue	7·50	3·00
23a		1p. bistre	16·00	7·25

1879. As T **9** of Philippines, but inscr "PTO-RICO 1879".

24		5c. red	18·00	9·50
25		10c. brown	18·00	9·50
26		15c. grey	18·00	9·50
27		25c. blue	6·25	2·75
28		50c. green	18·00	9·50
29		1p. lilac	85·00	42·00

1880. "Alfonso XII" key-type inscr "PUERTO-RICO 1880".

30	**X**	¼c. green	34·00	27·00
31	**X**	½c. red	8·50	3·50
32	**X**	1c. purple	16·00	15·00
33	**X**	2c. grey	8·50	6·25
34	**X**	3c. buff	8·50	6·25
35	**X**	4c. black	8·50	6·25
36	**X**	5c. green	4·00	2·75
37	**X**	10c. red	4·75	3·00
38	**X**	15c. brown	8·50	4·75
39	**X**	25c. lilac	4·00	2·20
40	**X**	40c. grey	17·00	2·20
41	**X**	50c. brown	36·00	23·00
42	**X**	1p. bistre	£130	29·00

1881. "Alfonso XIII" key-type inscr "PUERTO-RICO 1881".

43		½m. red	30	20
45		1m. violet	30	20
46		2m. red	30	20
47		4m. green	30	20
48		6m. purple	30	20
49		8m. blue	30	20
50		1c. green	4·50	1·70
51		2c. red	5·75	4·75
52		3c. brown	13·50	8·00
53		5c. lilac	4·25	45
54		8c. brown	4·25	2·20
55		10c. grey	65·00	13·50
56		20c. bistre	70·00	25·00

1882. "Alfonso XII" key-type inscr "PUERTO-RICO".

57		½m. red	30	20
74		1m. red	25	20
75		1m. orange	25	20
59		2m. mauve	30	20
60		4m. purple	30	20
61		6m. brown	60	20
62		8m. green	60	20
63		1c. green	30	20
64		2c. red	1·80	20
65		3c. yellow	5·75	3·50
76		3c. brown	3·50	75
77		5c. lilac	18·00	2·50
67		8c. brown	5·25	20
68		10c. green	5·25	45
69		20c. grey	8·75	45
70		40c. blue	70·00	24·00
71		80c. bistre	95·00	35·00

1890. "Baby" key-type inscr "PUERTO-RICO".

80	**Y**	½m. black	25	20
95	**Y**	½m. grey	20	20
111	**Y**	½m. brown	20	20
124	**Y**	½m. purple	25	20
81	**Y**	1m. green	35	20
96	**Y**	1m. purple	20	20
112	**Y**	1m. blue	20	20
125	**Y**	1m. brown	25	20
82	**Y**	2m. red	25	20
97	**Y**	2m. purple	20	20
126	**Y**	2m. green	25	20
83	**Y**	4m. black	17·00	9·50
98	**Y**	4m. blue	20	20
114	**Y**	4m. brown	20	20
127	**Y**	4m. green	1·50	50
84	**Y**	6m. brown	60·00	25·00
99	**Y**	6m. red	20	20
85	**Y**	8m. bistre	44·00	37·00
100	**Y**	8m. green	20	20
86	**Y**	1c. brown	25	20
101	**Y**	1c. green	85	20
115	**Y**	1c. purple	11·50	65
128	**Y**	1c. red	95	20
87	**Y**	2c. purple	1·50	1·40
102	**Y**	2c. pink	1·40	20
116	**Y**	2c. lilac	4·25	65
129	**Y**	2c. brown	95	20
88	**Y**	3c. blue	11·50	1·70
103	**Y**	3c. orange	1·40	20
117	**Y**	3c. grey	11·50	65
131	**Y**	3c. brown	30	20
118	**Y**	4c. blue	3·00	65
132	**Y**	4c. brown	1·00	20
89	**Y**	5c. purple	18·00	65
104	**Y**	5c. green	1·40	20
133	**Y**	5c. blue	30	20
120	**Y**	6c. orange	70	20
134	**Y**	6c. lilac	30	20
90	**Y**	8c. blue	24·00	3·00
105	**Y**	8c. brown	20	20
121	**Y**	8c. purple	27·00	7·50
135	**Y**	8c. red	4·50	2·10
106	**Y**	10c. red	1·90	55
122	**Y**	20c. red	3·25	65
107	**Y**	20c. lilac	3·50	75

136	Y	20c. grey	11·00	2·10
93	Y	40c. orange	£250	85·00
108	Y	40c. blue	8·75	6·50
137	Y	40c. red	11·00	2·10
94	Y	80c. green	£700	£275
109	Y	80c. red	23·00	19·00
138	Y	80c. black	46·00	35·00

13 Landing of Columbus

1893. 400th Anniv of Discovery of America by Columbus.

110	**13**	3c. green	£300	70·00

1898. "Curly Head" key-type inscr "PTO RICO 1898 y 99".

139	Z	1m. brown	25	20
140	Z	2m. brown	25	20
141	Z	3m. brown	25	20
142	Z	4m. brown	3·25	80
143	Z	5m. brown	25	20
144	Z	1c. purple	25	20
145	Z	2c. green	25	20
146	Z	3c. brown	25	20
147	Z	4c. orange	3·25	1·50
148	Z	5c. pink	25	20
149	Z	6c. blue	25	20
150	Z	8c. brown	25	20
151	Z	10c. red	25	20
152	Z	15c. grey	25	20
153	Z	20c. purple	3·50	80
154	Z	40c. lilac	2·50	2·20
155	Z	60c. black	2·50	2·20
156	Z	80c. brown	10·00	8·25
157	Z	1p. green	25·00	18·00
158	Z	2p. blue	55·00	23·00

1898. "Baby" key-type inscr "PUERTO RICO" and optd **Habilitado PARA 1898 y '99**.

159	Y	½m. purple	23·00	13·50
160	Y	1m. brown	1·80	1·80
161	Y	2m. green	55	55
162	Y	4m. green	55	55
163	Y	1c. purple	4·50	4·50
164	Y	2c. brown	80	1·20
165	Y	3c. blue	50·00	22·00
166	Y	3c. brown	4·25	4·25
167	Y	4c. brown	1·00	1·00
168	Y	4c. blue	29·00	20·00
169	Y	5c. blue	1·00	1·00
170	Y	5c. green	13·50	11·00
172	Y	6c. lilac	1·00	65
173a	Y	8c. red	1·70	1·30
174	Y	20c. grey	1·70	1·70
175	Y	40c. red	4·25	4·25
176	Y	80c. black	50·00	32·00

WAR TAX STAMPS

1898. 1890 and 1898 stamps optd **IMPUESTO DE GUERRA** or surch also.

W177		1m. blue	3·50	2·30
W178		1m. brown	9·00	6·50
W179		2m. red	17·00	11·00
W180		2m. green	9·00	6·50
W181		4m. green	9·75	9·75
W182a		1c. brown	9·00	5·50
W183		1c. purple	15·00	14·00
W184		2c. purple	1·20	1·20
W185		2c. pink	55	35
W186		2c. lilac	55	35
W187		2c. brown	50	45
W192		2c. on 2m. red	55	35
W193c		2c. on 5c. green	3·50	2·20
W188		3c. orange	17·00	14·00
W194		3c. on 10c. red	3·00	2·20
W195		4c. on 20c. red	17·00	13·00
W189		5c. green	2·30	2·30
W196a		5c. on ½m. brown	3·75	3·75
W197		5c. on 1m. purple	35	35
W198		5c. on 1m. blue	9·00	6·50
W199	Z	5c. on 1m. brown	9·00	6·50
W200	Y	5c. on 5c. green	9·00	5·75
W191		8c. purple	26·00	22·00

B. UNITED STATES OCCUPATION

1899. 1894 stamps of United States (No. 267 etc) optd **PORTO RICO**.

202	1c. green	5·75	1·60
203	2c. red	5·00	1·40
204	5c. blue	11·50	2·75
205	8c. brown	34·00	20·00
206	10c. brown	23·00	6·75

1900. 1894 stamps of United States (No. 267 etc) optd **PUERTO RICO**.

210	1c. green	7·50	1·70
212	2c. red	6·25	2·30

POSTAGE DUE STAMPS

1899. Postage Due stamps of United States of 1894 optd **PORTO RICO**.

D207	**D87**	1c. red	26·00	6·25
D208	**D87**	2c. red	23·00	6·75
D209	**D87**	10c. red	£200	70·00

Pt. 1, Pt. 19

QATAR

An independent Arab Shaikhdom with British postal administration until 23 May 1963. The stamps of Muscat were formerly used at Doha and Urm Said. Later issues by the Qatar Post Department.

1966. 100 dirhams = 1 riyal.
1967. 100 naye paise = 1 rupee.

Stamps of Great Britain surcharged QATAR and value in Indian currency.

1957. Queen Elizabeth II and pictorials.

1	**157**	1n.p. on 5d. brown	10	15
2	**154**	3n.p. on ½d. orange	25	40
3	**154**	6n.p. on 1d. blue	25	20
4	**154**	9n.p. on 1½d. green	75	15
5	**154**	12n.p. on 2d. brown	55	3·75
6	**155**	15n.p. on 2½d. red	15	10
7	**155**	20n.p. on 3d. lilac	15	10
8	**155**	25n.p. on 4d. blue	2·00	3·25
9	**157**	40n.p. on 6d. purple	15	30
10	**158**	50n.p. on 9d. olive	80	3·50
11	**159**	75n.p. on 1s.3d. green	1·00	5·50
12	**159**	1r. on 1s.6d. blue	16·00	10
13	**166**	2r. on 2s.6d. brown	5·00	6·00
14	-	5r. on 5s. red	7·00	9·00
15	-	10r. on 10s. blue	7·00	16·00

1957. World Scout Jubilee Jamboree.

16	**170**	15n.p. on 2½d. red	35	60
17	**171**	25n.p. on 4d. blue	35	35
18	-	75n.p. on 1s.3d. green	40	40

8 Shaikh Ahmad bin All al Thani

9 Peregrine Falcon

11 Oil Derrick

1961

27	**8**	5n.p. red	15	15
28	**8**	15n.p. black	30	25
29	**8**	20n.p. purple	30	15
30	**8**	30n.p. green	35	30
31	**9**	40n.p. red	3·50	30
32	**9**	50n.p. brown	3·75	30
33	-	75n.p. blue	1·60	4·00
34	**11**	1r. red	4·25	35
35	**11**	2r. blue	4·25	2·75
36	-	5r. green	35·00	11·00
37	-	10r. black	70·00	17·00

DESIGNS—As Type **9**: 75n.p. Dhow. As Type **11**: 5r., 10r. Mosque.

1964. Olympic Games, Tokyo. Optd **1964**, Olympic rings and Arabic inscr or surch also.

38	**9**	50n.p. brown	3·00	2·40
39	-	75n.p. blue (No. 33)	4·50	3·75
40	-	1r. on 10r. black (No. 37)	6·00	1·90
41	**11**	2r. blue	12·00	3·75
42	**11**	5r. green (No. 36)	31·00	9·75

1964. Pres. Kennedy Commem. Optd **John F Kennedy 1917–1963** in English and Arabic or surch also.

43	**9**	50n.p. brown	3·00	1·30
44	-	75n.p. blue (No. 33)	4·50	1·70
45	-	1r. on 10r. black (No. 37)	6·00	2·10
46	**11**	2r. blue	13·00	6·00
47	-	5r. green (No. 36)	32·00	12·00

15 Colonnade, Temple of Isis

1965. Nubian Monuments Preservation. Multicoloured.

48	1n.p. Type **15**	2·10	55
49	2n.p. Temple of Isis, Philac	2·40	65
50	3n.p. Trajan's Kiosk, Philac	2·75	70
51	1r. As 3n.p.	4·50	2·00
52	1r.50 As 2n.p.	9·00	2·75
53	2r. Type **15**	2·75	2·50

16 Scouts on Parade

1965. Qatar Scouts.

54	-	1n.p. brown and green	55	45
55	-	2n.p. blue and brown	55	45
56	-	3n.p. blue and green	55	45
57	-	4n.p. brown and blue	55	45
58	-	5n.p. blue and turquoise	55	45
59	**16**	30n.p. multicoloured	5·25	3·50
60	**16**	40n.p. multicoloured	8·00	5·25
61	**16**	1r. multicoloured	16·00	10·50
MS61a		108×76 mm. Nos. 59/61	32·00	19·00

DESIGNS—TRIANGULAR (60×30 mm): 1, 4n.p. Qatar Scout badge; 2, 3, 5n.p. Ruler, badge, palms and camp.

17 "Telstar" and Eiffel Tower

1965. I.T.U. Centenary.

62	**17**	1n.p. brown and blue	55	15
63	-	2n.p. brown and blue	55	15
64	-	3n.p. violet and green	55	15
65	-	4n.p. blue and brown	55	15
66	**17**	5n.p. brown and violet	55	15
67	-	40n.p. black and red	6·50	1·50
68	-	50n.p. brown and green	10·00	1·80
69	-	1r. red and green	13·00	2·75
MS69a		89×89 mm. Nos. 68/9	32·00	13·00

DESIGNS: 2n.p., 1r. "Syncom 3" and pagoda; 3, 40n.p. "Relay" and radar scanner; 4, 50n.p. Post Office Tower (London), globe and satellites.

18 Jigsaw Triggerfish

1965. Fish of the Arabian Gulf. Multicoloured.

70	1n.p. Type **18**	45	30
71	2n.p. Harlequin sweetlips	45	30
72	3n.p. Saddle butterflyfish	45	30
73	4n.p. Thread-finned butterflyfish	45	30
74	5n.p. Masked unicornfish	45	30
75	15n.p. Paradise fish	45	30
76	20n.p. White-spotted surgeonfish	55	45
77	30n.p. Rio Grande cichlid	95	55
78	40n.p. Convict cichlid	1·30	95
79	50n.p. As 2n.p	1·90	1·30
80	75n.p. Type **18**	2·75	1·60
81	1r. As 30n.p.	4·00	1·90
82	2r. As 20n.p.	8·00	5·25
83	3r. As 15n.p.	15·00	6·50
84	4r. As 5n.p.	19·00	8·00
85	5r. As 4n.p.	28·00	9·00
86	10r. As 3n.p.	48·00	12·00

19 Basketball

1966. Pan-Arab Games, Cairo (1965).

87	**19**	1r. black, grey and red	4·25	2·10
88	-	1r. brown and green	4·25	2·10
89	-	1r. red and blue	4·25	2·10
90	-	1r. green and blue	4·25	2·10
91	-	1r. blue and brown	4·25	2·10

SPORTS: No. 88, Horse-jumping; No. 89, Running; No. 90, Football; No. 91, Weightlifting.

1966. Space Rendezvous. Nos. 62/9 optd with two space capsules and **SPACE RENDEZVOUS 15th. DECEMBER 1965** in English and Arabic.

92	**17**	1n.p. brown and blue	95	10
93	-	2n.p. brown and blue	95	10
94	-	3n.p. violet and green	95	10
95	-	4n.p. blue and brown	95	10
96	**17**	5n.p. brown and violet	95	10
97	-	40n.p. black and red	6·75	45
98	-	50n.p. brown and green	7·00	55
99	-	1r. red and green	14·00	95
MS100		89×89 mm. Nos. 98/9	43·00	21·00

21 Shaikh Ahmed

1966. Gold and Silver Coinage. Circular designs embossed on gold (G) or silver (S) foil, backed with "Walsall Security Paper" inscr in English and Arabic. Imperf. (a) Diameter 42 mm.

101	**21**	1n.p. bistre and purple (S)	45	15
102	-	3n.p. black and orange (S)	45	15
103	**21**	4n.p. violet and red (G)	45	15
104	-	5n.p. green and mauve (G)	45	15

(b) Diameter 55 mm.

105	**21**	10n.p. brown and violet (S)	85	20
106	-	40n.p. red and blue (S)	2·10	55
107	**21**	70n.p. blue & ultram (G)	3·25	1·30
108	-	80n.p. mauve and green (G)	3·50	1·40

(c) Diameter 64 mm.

109	**21**	1r. mauve and black (S)	6·50	1·50
110	-	2r. green and purple (S)	12·00	3·25
111	**21**	5r. purple and orange (G)	27·00	7·00
112	-	10r. blue and red (G)	55·00	17·00

The 1, 4, 10, 70n.p. and 1 and 5r. each show the obverse side of the coins as Type **21**. The remainder show the reverse side of the coins (Shaikh's seal).

22 I.C.Y. and U.N. Emblem

1966. International Co-operation Year.

113	**22**	40n.p. brown, violet & bl	4·00	2·50
114	**A**	40n.p. violet, brn & turq	4·00	2·50
115	**B**	40n.p. blue, brown & vio	4·00	2·50
116	**C**	40n.p. turquoise, vio & bl	4·00	2·50
MS117		140×87½ mm. Nos. 113/16. Imperf	55·00	43·00

DESIGNS: A, Pres. Kennedy, I.C.Y. emblem and U.N. Headquarters; B, Dag Hammarskjold and U.N. General Assembly; C, Nehru and dove.

Nos. 113/16 were issued together in blocks of four, each sheet containing four blocks separated by gutter margins. Subsequently the sheets were reissued perf and imperf with the opt **U.N. 20TH ANNIVERSARY** on the stamps. The gutter margins were also printed in various designs, face values and overprints.

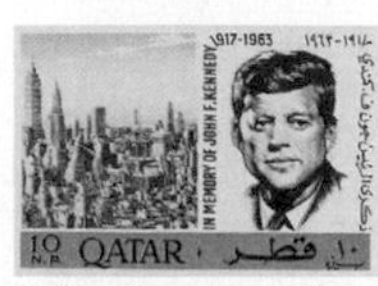

23 Pres. Kennedy and New York Skyline

1966. Pres. Kennedy Commemoration. Multicoloured.

118	10n.p. Type **23**	45	30
119	30n.p. Pres. Kennedy and Cape Kennedy	75	45
120	60n.p. Pres. Kennedy and Statue of Liberty	1·30	75
121	70n.p. Type **23**	1·60	1·20
122	80n.p. As 30n.p.	1·90	1·30
123	1r. As 60n.p.	2·75	1·90
MS124	105×70 mm. 50n.p. (As 60n.p.). Imperf	32·00	30·00

24 Horse-jumping

1966. Olympic Games Preparation (Mexico). Multicoloured.

125	1n.p. Type **24**	30	25
126	4n.p. Running	30	25
127	5n.p. Throwing the javelin	30	25
128	70n.p. Type **24**	2·40	1·30
129	80n.p. Running	2·50	1·40
130	90n.p. Throwing the javelin	2·75	1·90
MS131	105×70 mm. 50n.p. (As Type **24**)	32·00	27·00

25 J. A. Lovell and Capsule

1966. American Astronauts. Each design showing spacecraft and astronaut. Multicoloured.

132	5n.p. Type **25**	30	25
133	10n.p. T. P. Stafford	30	25
134	15n.p. A. B. Shepard	30	25
135	20n.p. J. H. Glenn	55	30
136	30n.p. M. Scott Carpenter	85	55
137	40n.p. W. M. Schirra	95	65
138	50n.p. V. I. Grissom	1·30	95
139	60n.p. L. G. Cooper	1·90	1·50
MS140	116×75 mm. **26** 50n.p. multicoloured. Imperf	43·00	34·00

Nos. 132/4 are diamond-shaped as Type **25**, the remainder are horiz designs (56×25 mm).

1966. Various stamps with currency names changed to dirhams and riyals by overprinting in English and Arabic. (i) Nos. 27/37 (Definitives).

141	**8**	5d. on 5n.p. red	10·50	7·00
142	**8**	15d. on 15n.p. black	10·50	7·00
143	**8**	20d. on 20n.p. purple	10·50	7·00
144	**8**	30d. on 30n.p. green	38·00	14·00
145	**9**	40d. on 40n.p. red	75·00	28·00
146	**9**	50d. on 50n.p. brown	85·00	33·00
147	-	75d. on 75n.p. blue	£120	39·00
148	**11**	1r. on 1r. red	£140	47·00
149	**11**	2r. on 2r. blue	£160	£110
150	-	5r. on 5r. green	£190	£140
151	-	10r. on 10r. black	£300	£225

(ii) Nos. 70/86 (Fish). Multicoloured.

152	1d. on 1n.p.	2·10	1·70
153	2d. on 2n.p.	2·10	1·70
154	3d. on 3n.p.	2·10	1·70
155	4d. on 4n.p.	2·10	1·70
156	5d. on 5n.p.	2·10	1·70
157	15d. on 15n.p.	2·40	1·70
158	20d. on 20n.p.	2·50	1·70
159	30d. on 30n.p.	2·75	1·70
160	40d. on 40n.p.	3·25	4·25
161	50d. on 50n.p.	4·25	6·50
162	75d. on 75n.p.	5·25	21·00
163	1r. on 1r.	49·00	34·00
164	2r. on 2r.	75·00	43·00
165	3r. on 3r.	85·00	55·00
166	4r. on 4r.	£140	75·00
167	5r. on 5r.	£150	95·00
168	10r. on 10r.	£190	13·00

27 National Library, Doha

1966. Education Day. Multicoloured.

169	2n.p. Type **27**	6·00	55
170	3n.p. School and playing field	6·00	55
171	5n.p. School and gardens	6·00	55
172	1r. Type **27**	14·00	4·25
173	2r. As 3n.p	24·00	9·75
174	3r. As 5n.p	32·00	14·00

28 Palace, Doha

1966. Currency expressed in naye paise and rupees. Multicoloured.

175	2n.p. Type **28**	45	25
176	3n.p. Gulf Street, Shahra Al-Khalij	45	25
177	10n.p. Doha airport	1·70	30
178	15n.p. Garden, Rayan	1·20	30
179	20n.p. Head Post Office, Doha	1·50	30
180	30n.p. Mosque Doha (vert)	2·50	45
181	40n.p. Shaikh Ahmad	4·75	65
182	50n.p. Type **28**	5·25	1·10
183	60n.p. As 3n.p.	8·50	1·60
184	70n.p. As 10n.p.	12·00	2·50
185	80n.p. As 15n.p.	12·50	2·75
186	90n.p. As 20n.p.	14·00	4·75
187	1r. As 30n.p. (vert)	15·00	5·00
188	2r. As 40n.p.	30·00	13·00

29 Hands holding Jules Rimet Trophy

1966. World Cup Football Championship, England.

189	**29**	60n.p. mult (postage)	1·70	1·30
190	-	70n.p. multicoloured	2·00	1·50
191	-	80n.p. multicoloured	2·75	1·90
192	-	90n.p. multicoloured	3·00	2·10
193	-	1n.p. blue (air)	20	20
194	-	2n.p. blue	30	20
195	-	3n.p. blue	45	30
196	-	4n.p. blue	55	45
MS197		Four sheets each 105×70 mm. Each sheet contains one design as Nos. 189/192 with face value of 25n.p. Imperf	£110	55·00

DESIGNS: No. 190, Jules Rimet Trophy and "football" globe; No. 191, Footballers and globe; No. 192, Wembley stadium; Nos. 193/6, Jules Rimet Trophy.

30 A.P.U. Emblem

1967. Admission of Qatar to Arab Postal Union.

198	**30**	70d. brown and violet	3·75	1·90
199	**30**	80d. brown and blue	4·75	1·90

31 Astronauts on Moon

1967. U.S. "Apollo" Space Missions. Multicoloured.

200	5d. Type **31**	20	10
201	10d. "Apollo" spacecraft	20	10
202	20d. Landing module on Moon	45	20
203	30d. Blast-off from Moon	85	45
204	40d. "Saturn 5" rocket	1·30	65
205	70d. Type **31**	2·75	1·70
206	80d. As 10d.	3·25	2·40
207	1r. As 20d.	3·50	2·75
208	1r.20 As 30d.	4·25	3·25
209	2r. As 40d.	5·25	4·25
MS210	100×70 mm. No. 209. Imperf	16·00	13·00

32 Traffic Lights

1967. Traffic Day.

211	**32**	20d. multicoloured	75	30
212	**32**	30d. multicoloured	1·40	65
213	**32**	50d. multicoloured	2·10	1·10
214	**32**	1r. multicoloured	4·25	2·30

33 Brownsea Island and Jamboree Camp, Idaho

1967. Diamond Jubilee of Scout Movement and World Scout Jamboree, Idaho. Multicoloured.

215	1d. Type **33**	45	10
216	2d. Lord Baden-Powell	45	10
217	3d. Pony-trekking	45	10
218	5d. Canoeing	75	15
219	15d. Swimming	2·10	55
220	75d. Rock-climbing	4·75	1·70
221	2r. World Jamboree emblem	13·00	6·00

34 Norman Ship (from Bayeux Tapestry)

1967. Famous Navigators' Ships. Multicoloured.

222	1d. Type **34**	55	10
223	2d. "Santa Maria" (Columbus)	65	10
224	3d. "Sao Gabriel" (Vasco da Gama)	95	10
225	75d. "Vitoria" (Magellan)	5·25	1·90
226	1r. "Golden Hind" (Drake)	7·50	2·75
227	2r. "Gipsy Moth IV" (Chichester)	12·00	3·75

35 Arab Scribe

1968. Tenth Anniv of Qatar Postage Stamps. Multicoloured.

228	1d. Type **35**	55	10
229	2d. Pigeon post (vert)	65	15
230	3d. Mounted postman	75	20
231	60d. Rowing boat postman (vert)	4·25	1·80
232	1r.25 Camel postman	8·00	3·00
233	2r. Letter-writing and Qatar 1n.p. stamp of 1957	14·00	4·25

36 Human Rights Emblem and Barbed Wire

1968. Human Rights Year. Multicoloured designs embodying Human Rights emblem.

234	1d. Type **36**	45	15
235	2d. Arab refugees	45	15
236	3d. Scales of justice	65	20
237	60d. Opening doors	3·75	2·10
238	1r.25 Family (vert)	5·25	4·75
239	2r. Human figures	10·50	6·50

37 Shaikh Ahmad

38 Dhow

39 Shaikh Ahmad

1968

240	**37**	5d. green and blue	20	10
241	**37**	10d. brown and blue	55	10
242	**37**	20d. red and black	85	10
243	**37**	25d. green and purple	2·10	20
244	**38**	35d. green, blue and pink	3·50	20
245	-	40d. purple, blue & orange	4·75	30
246	-	60d. brown, blue and violet	6·00	75
247	-	70d. black, blue and green	6·50	95
248	-	1r. blue, yellow and green	8·00	1·20
249	-	1r.25 blue, pink and light blue	9·00	1·40
250	-	1r.50 green, blue & purple	10·50	1·80
251	**39**	2r. blue, brown and cinnamon	15·00	2·40
252	**39**	5r. purple, green and light green	27·00	4·75
253	**39**	10r. brown, ultram & blue	55·00	9·75

DESIGNS—As Type **38**: 40d. Water purification plant; 60d. Oil jetty; 70d. Qatar mosque; 1r. Palace Doha; 1r.25, Doha fort; 1r.50, Peregrine falcon.

41 Maternity Ward

1968. 20th Anniv of W.H.O. Multicoloured.

258	1d. Type **41**	65	10
259	2d. Operating theatre	65	10
260	3d. Dental surgery	65	10
261	60d. X-ray examination table	3·50	70
262	1r.25 Laboratory	8·50	1·90
263	2r. State Hospital Qatar	13·00	3·00

42 Throwing the Discus

1968. Olympic Games, Mexico. Multicoloured.

264	1d. Type **42**	55	25
265	2d. Olympic Flame and runner	55	25
266	3d. "68", rings and gymnast	85	30
267	60d. Weightlifting and Flame	4·00	1·70
268	1r.25 "Flame" in mosaic pattern (vert)	8·00	2·75
269	2r. "Cock" emblem	13·00	3·75

43 U.N. Emblem and Flags

1968. United Nations Day. Multicoloured.

270	1d. Type **43**	20	10
271	4d. Dove of Peace and world map	65	15
272	5d. U.N. Headquarters and flags	65	15
273	60d. Teacher and class	4·50	1·30
274	1r.50 Agricultural workers	7·50	2·00
275	2r. U. Thant and U.N. Assembly	8·50	2·30

44 Trawler "Ross Rayyan"

1969. Progress in Qatar. Multicoloured.

276	1d. Type **44**	20	10
277	4d. Primary school	20	10
278	5d. Doha International Airport	65	15
279	60d. Cement factory and road-making	3·50	95
280	1r.50 Power station and pylon	8·50	2·30
281	2r. Housing estate	12·00	2·75

45 Armoured Cars

1969. Qatar Security Forces. Multicoloured.

282	1d. Type **45**	65	10
283	2d. Traffic control	65	10
284	3d. Military helicopter	75	35
285	60d. Section of military band	4·25	1·50
286	1r.25 Field gun	8·00	2·00
287	2r. Mounted police	14·00	4·00

46 Tanker "Sivella" at Mooring

1969. Qatar's Oil Industry. Multicoloured.

288	1d. Type **46**	55	10
289	2d. Training school	55	10
290	3d. "Sea Shell" (oil rig) and "Shell Dolphin" (supply vessel)	85	25
291	60d. Storage tanks, Halul	3·75	1·40
292	1r.50 Topping plant	10·50	3·00
293	2r. Various tankers, 1890–1968	16·00	4·00

47 "Guest-house" and Dhow-building

1969. Tenth Scout Jamboree, Qatar. Multicoloured.

294	1d. Type **47**	30	10
295	2d. Scouts at work	30	10
296	3d. Review and March Past	55	25
297	60d. Interior gateway	5·25	1·50
298	1r.25 Camp entrance	8·50	2·10
299	2r. Hoisting flag, and Shaikh Ahmad	12·00	3·00
MS300	128×110m. Nos. 294/7. Imperf	32·00	15·00

48 Neil Armstrong

1969. First Man on the Moon. Multicoloured.

301	1d. Type **48**	30	25
302	2d. Edward Aldrin	30	25
303	3d. Michael Collins	40	30
304	60d. Astronaut on Moon	3·00	1·20
305	1r.25 Take-off from Moon	6·00	3·00
306	2r. Splashdown (horiz)	12·00	4·75

49 Douglas DC-8 and Mail Van

1970. Admission to U.P.U. Multicoloured.

307	1d. Type **49**	30	30
308	2d. Liner "Oriental Empress"	30	30
309	3d. Loading mail-van	55	35
310	60d. G.P.O., Doha	3·25	1·50
311	1r.25 U.P.U. Building, Berne	6·50	2·30
312	2r. U.P.U. Monument, Berne	10·50	3·00

50 League Emblem, Flag and Map

1970. Silver Jubilee of Arab League.

313	**50**	35d. multicoloured	2·10	80
314	**50**	60d. multicoloured	3·75	1·40
315	**50**	1r.25 multicoloured	7·00	2·30
316	**50**	1r.50 multicoloured	9·00	4·00

51 Vickers VC-10 on Runway

1970. First Gulf Aviation Vickers VC-10 Flight, Doha–London. Multicoloured.

317	1d. Type **51**	30	25
318	2d. Peregrine falcon and VC-10	75	35
319	3d. Tail view of VC-10	75	35
320	60d. Gulf Aviation emblem on map	4·75	1·30
321	1r.25 VC-10 over Doha	9·75	2·00
322	2r. Tail assembly of VC-10	16·00	3·25

52 "Space Achievements"

1970. International Education Year.

323	**52**	35d. multicoloured	3·00	1·30
324	**52**	60d. multicoloured	6·00	2·40

53 Freesias

1970. Qatar Flowers. Multicoloured.

325	1d. Type **53**	30	15
326	2d. Azalieas	30	15
327	3d. Ixias	30	15
328	60d. Amaryllises	5·25	1·30
329	1r.25 Cinerarias	9·00	2·75
330	2r. Roses	12·00	4·00

54 Toyahama Fishermen with Giant "Fish"

1970. "EXPO 70" World Fair, Osaka. Multicoloured.

331	1d. Type **54**	30	10
332	2d. Expo emblem and map of Japan	40	15
333	3d. Fisherman on Shikoku beach	75	25
334	60d. Expo emblem and Mt. Fuji	4·00	1·30
335	1r.50 Gateway to Shinto Shrine	9·00	2·40
336	2r. Expo Tower and Mt. Fuji	13·00	4·00
MS336a	126×111 mm. Nos. 331/4. Imperf	32·00	15·00

Nos. 333, 334 and 336 are vert.

55 Globe, "25" and U.N. Emblem

1970. 25th Anniv of U.N.O. Multicoloured.

337	1d. Type **55**	55	25
338	2d. Flowers in gun-barrel	55	25
339	3d. Anniversary cake	95	35
340	35d. "The U.N. Agencies"	3·25	1·00
341	1r.50 "Trumpet fanfare"	7·50	2·40
342	2r. "World friendship"	9·75	4·00

56 Al Jahiz (philosopher) and Ancient Globe

1971. Famous Men of Islam. Multicoloured.

343	1d. Type **56**	55	35
344	2d. Saladin (soldier), palace and weapons	55	35
345	3d. Al Farabi (philosopher and musician), felucca and instruments	95	45
346	35d. Ibn Al Haithum (scientist), palace and emblems	4·25	95
347	1r.50 Al Motanabbi (poet), symbols and desert	17·00	3·75
348	2r. Ibn Sina (Avicenna) (physician and philosopher), medical instruments and ancient globe	21·00	5·00

57 Great Cormorant and Water Plants

1971. Qatar Fauna and Flora. Multicoloured.

349	1d. Type **57**	2·00	45
350	2d. Lizard and prickly pear	2·00	45
351	3d. Greater flamingos and palms	2·00	45
352	60d. Arabian oryx and yucca	9·75	2·00
353	1r.25 Mountain gazelle and desert dandelion	20·00	5·25
354	2r. Dromedary, palm and bronzed chenopod	27·00	7·50

58 Satellite Earth Station, Goonhilly

1971. World Telecommunications Day. Multicoloured.

355	1d. Type **58**	30	10
356	2d. Cable ship "Ariel"	30	10
357	3d. Post Office Tower and T.V. control-room	30	10
358	4d. Modern telephones	30	10
359	5d. Video-phone equipment	30	10
360	35d. As 3d.	3·00	95
361	75d. As 5d.	4·25	1·40
362	3r. Telex machine	17·00	3·50

59 Arab Child reading Book

1971. Tenth Anniv of Education Day.

363	**59**	35d. multicoloured	1·50	45
364	**59**	55d. multicoloured	3·00	95
365	**59**	75d. multicoloured	5·75	1·60

60 A.P.U. Emblem

1971. 25th Anniv of Arab Postal Union.

366	**60**	35d. multicoloured	1·30	35
367	**60**	55d. multicoloured	2·10	80
368	**60**	75d. multicoloured	2·75	1·30
369	**60**	1r.25 multicoloured	4·00	2·00

61 "Hammering Racism"

1971. Racial Equality Year. Multicoloured.

370	1d. Type **61**	40	10
371	2d. "Pushing back racism"	40	10
372	3d. War-wounded	40	10
373	4d. Working together (vert)	40	10
374	5d. Playing together (vert)	40	10
375	35d. Racial "tidal-wave"	3·00	95
376	75d. Type **61**	6·75	1·60
377	3r. As 2d.	14·50	3·25

62 Nurse and Child

1971. 25th Anniv of UNICEF. Multicoloured.

378	1d. Mother and child (vert)	40	10
379	2d. Child's face	40	10
380	3d. Child with book (vert)	40	10
381	4d. Type **62**	40	10
382	5d. Mother and baby	40	10
383	35d. Child with daffodil (vert)	2·20	60
384	75d. As 3d.	6·75	1·60
385	3r. As 1d.	15·00	3·00

63 Shaikh Ahmad, and Flags of Arab League and Qatar

1971. Independence.

386	**63**	35d. multicoloured	1·30	35
387	-	75d. multicoloured	2·75	80
388	-	1r.25 black, pink & brown	4·00	1·20
389	-	3r. multicoloured	12·50	3·00
MS390		80×128 mm. No. 389. Imperf	37·00	21·00

DESIGNS—HORIZ: 75d. As Type **63**, but with U.N. flag in place of Arab League flag. VERT: 1r.25, Shaikh Ahmad; 3r. Handclasp.

64 European Roller

1972. Birds. Multicoloured.

391	1d. Type **64**	1·30	55
392	2d. River kingfisher	1·30	55
393	3d. Rock thrush	1·30	55
394	4d. Caspian tern	1·50	65
395	5d. Hoopoe	1·50	65
396	35d. European bee eater	6·75	85
397	75d. Golden oriole	13·50	2·75
398	3r. Peregrine falcon	40·00	11·50

1972. Nos. 328/30 surch with value in English and Arabic.

399	10d. on 60d. multicoloured	2·75	65
400	1r. on 1r.25 multicoloured	12·50	3·25
401	5r. on 2r. multicoloured	55·00	12·50

66 Shaikh Khalifa bin Hamad al-Thani

1972

402	**66**	5d. blue and violet	65	25
403	**66**	10d. red and brown	65	65
404	**66**	35d. green and orange	1·70	80
405	**66**	55d. mauve and green	3·25	1·60
406	**66**	75d. mauve and blue	5·25	2·40
407	-	1r. black and brown	7·25	2·50
408	-	1r.25 black and green	8·25	3·25
409	-	5r. black and blue	29·00	10·50
410	-	10r. black and red	55·00	24·00

The rupee values are larger, 27×32 mm.

For similar design but with Shaikh's head turned slightly to right, see Nos. 444a/b.

67 Book Year Emblem

1972. International Book Year.

411	**67**	35d. black and blue	1·90	40
412	**67**	55d. black and brown	3·25	65
413	**67**	75d. black and green	4·75	95
414	**67**	1r.25 black and lilac	7·75	1·60

68 Football

1972. Olympic Games, Munich. Designs depicting sportsmen's hands or feet. Multicoloured.

415	1d. Type **68**	35	25
416	2d. Running (foot on starting block)	35	25
417	3d. Cycling (hand)	35	25
418	4d. Gymnastics (hand)	35	25
419	5d. Basketball (hand)	80	40
420	35d. Discus (hand)	1·90	65
421	75d. Type **68**	3·75	1·10
422	3r. As 2d.	14·50	4·00
MS423	150×108 mm. Nos. 415/20. Imperf	28·00	17·00

69 Underwater Pipeline Construction

1972. "Oil from the Sea". Multicoloured.

424	1d. Drilling (vert)	55	40
425	4d. Type **69**	55	40
426	5d. Offshore rig "Sea Shell"	55	40
427	35d. Underwater "prospecting" for oil	2·50	55
428	75d. As 1d.	5·00	1·20
429	3r. As 5d.	25·00	6·00

70 Administrative Building

1972. Independence Day. Multicoloured.

430	10d. Type **70**	1·30	25
431	35d. Handclasp and Arab League flag	3·25	55
432	75d. Handclasp and U.N. flag	6·75	1·30
433	1r.25 Shaikh Khalifa	11·00	2·00
MS434	129×103 mm. No. 433. Imperf	28·00	17·00

71 Dish Aerial, Satellite and Telephone (I.T.U.)

1972. United Nations Day. Multicoloured.

435	1d. Type **71**	65	55
436	2d. Archaeological team (UNESCO)	65	55
437	3d. Tractor, produce and helicopter (F.A.O.)	65	55
438	4d. Children with books (UNICEF)	65	55
439	5d. Weather satellite (W.M.O.)	75	65
440	25d. Construction workers (I.L.O.)	3·25	1·90
441	55d. Child care (W.H.O.)	6·25	4·00
442	1r. Airliner and van (U.P.U.)	19·00	7·25

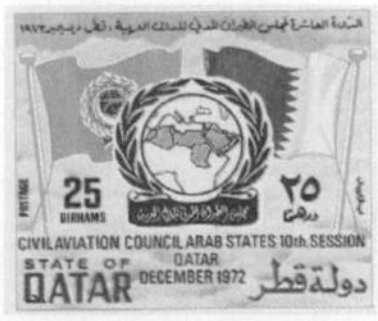
72 Emblem and Flags

1972. Tenth Session of Arab States Civil Aviation Council, Qatar.

443	**72**	25d. multicoloured	3·50	1·10
444	**72**	30d. multicoloured	5·25	1·60

72a Shaikh Khalifa

1972

444a	**72a**	10d. red and brown	£200
444b	**72a**	25d. green and purple	£200

73 Shaikh Khalifa

74 Clock Tower, Doha

1973

445	**73**	5d. multicoloured	1·00	40
446	**73**	10d. multicoloured	1·60	40
447	**73**	20d. multicoloured	2·00	40
448	**73**	25d. multicoloured	2·50	40
449	**73**	35d. multicoloured	3·25	65
450	**73**	55d. multicoloured	5·25	1·10
451	**74**	75d. purple, green and blue	7·75	2·00
452	**73**	1r. multicoloured	17·00	4·75
453	**73**	5r. multicoloured	65·00	23·00
454	**73**	10r. multicoloured	£150	55·00

Nos. 452/4 are larger, 27×32 mm.

75 Housing Development

1973. First Anniv of Shaikh Khalifa's Accession. Multicoloured.

455	2d. Road construction	35	25
456	3d. Type **75**	35	25
457	4d. Hospital operating theatre	35	25
458	5d. Telephone exchange	35	25
459	15d. School classroom	1·60	25
460	20d. Television studio	2·00	40
461	35d. Shaikh Khalifa	3·00	65
462	55d. Gulf Hotel, Doha	3·50	1·10
463	1r. Industrial plant	4·75	1·30
464	1r.35 Flour mills	6·25	2·00

76 Aerial Crop-spraying

1973. 25th Anniv of W.H.O. Multicoloured.

465	2d. Type **76**	80	55
466	3d. Drugs and syringe	80	55
467	4d. Woman in wheelchair (Prevention of polio)	80	55
468	5d. Mosquito (Malaria control)	1·60	65
469	55d. Mental patient (Mental Health Research)	12·50	1·90
470	1r. Dead trees (Anti-pollution)	25·00	3·75

77 Weather Ship

1973. Centenary of World Meteorological Organization. Multicoloured.

471	2d. Type **77**	55	40
472	3d. Launching radio-sonde balloon	55	40
473	4d. Hawker Siddeley H.S.125 weather plane	55	40
474	5d. Meteorological station	55	40
475	10d. Met airplane taking-off	1·80	55
476	1r. "Nimbus 1"	13·50	1·70
477	1r.55 Rocket on launch-pad	19·00	3·25

78 Handclasp

1973. Independence Day. Multicoloured.

478	15d. Type **78**	35	15
479	35d. Agriculture	65	25
480	55d. Government building	1·80	65
481	1r.35 View of Doha	4·00	1·50
482	1r.55 Illuminated fountain	4·50	1·70

79 Child planting Sapling (UNESCO)

1973. United Nations Day. Multicoloured.

483	2d. Type **79**	55	15
484	4d. U.N. Headquarters, New York, and flags	55	15
485	5d. Building construction (I.L.O.)	55	15
486	35d. Nurses in dispensary (W.H.O.)	1·50	55
487	1r.35 Radar control (I.T.U.)	5·50	1·60
488	3r. Inspection of wheat and cattle (F.A.O.)	14·50	5·00

80 "Open Gates"

1973. 25th Anniv of Declaration of Human Rights. Multicoloured.

489	2d. Type **80**	35	35
490	4d. Freedom marchers	35	35
491	5d. "Equality of Man"	65	35
492	35d. Primary education	2·00	65
493	1r.35 General Assembly, U.N.	6·75	2·10
494	3r. Flame emblem (vert)	12·50	3·25

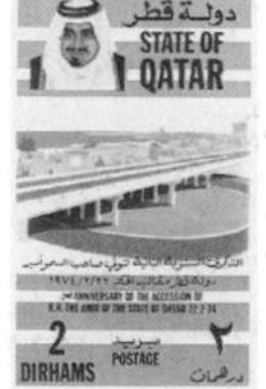
81 New Flyover, Doha

1974. Second Anniv of Shaikh Khalifa's Accession. Mult.

495	2d. Type **81**	35	25
496	3d. Education symbol	35	25
497	5d. Gas plant	35	25
498	35d. Gulf Hotel, Doha	1·90	65
499	1r.55 Space communications station	8·25	3·25
500	2r.25 Shaikh Khalifa	11·00	4·25

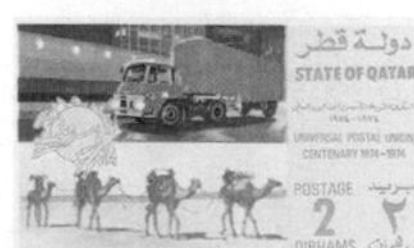
82 Camel Caravan and Articulated Mail Van

1974. Centenary of U.P.U. Multicoloured.

501	2d. Type **82**	55	25
502	3d. Early mail wagon and Japanese "Hikari" express train	55	25
503	10d. "Hindoostan" (paddle-steamer) and "Iberia" (liner)	2·00	65
504	35d. Early (Handley Page H.P.42) and modern (Vickers VC-10) mail planes	3·50	95
505	75d. Manual and mechanized mail-sorting	4·00	1·30
506	1r.25 Early and modern P.O. sales counters	6·75	2·40

83 Doha Hospital

1974. World Population Year. Multicoloured.

507	5d. Type **83**	20	20
508	10d. W.P.Y. emblem	55	20
509	15d. Emblem within wreath	55	20
510	35d. World population map	1·60	95
511	1r.75 New-born infants and clock ("a birth every minute")	5·50	3·00
512	2r.25 "Ideal Family" group	8·25	4·75

84 Television Station

1974. Independence Day. Multicoloured.

513	5d. Type **84**	45	25
514	10d. Doha palace	90	25
515	15d. Teachers' College	1·30	40
516	75d. Clock tower and mosque	3·50	55
517	1r.55 Roundabout and surroundings	6·75	1·10
518	2r.25 Shaikh Khalifa	10·00	1·60

85 Operating Theatre (W.H.O.)

1974. United Nations Day.

519	**85**	5d. orange, purple & black	55	25
520	-	10d. orange, red and black	1·10	25
521	-	20d. blue, green and black	2·20	40
522	-	25d. blue, brown and black	3·25	55
523	-	1r.75 blue, mauve & black	12·50	1·70
524	-	2r. blue, orange and black	14·50	2·00

DESIGNS: 10d. Satellite earth station (I.T.U.); 20d. Tractor (F.A.O.); 25d. Classroom (UNESCO); 1r.75, African open-air court (Human Rights); 2r. U.P.U. and U.N. emblems (U.P.U.).

86 Vickers VC-10 Airliner

1974. Arab Civil Aviation Day.

525	**86**	20d. multicoloured	2·50	55
526	-	25d. blue, green and yellow	3·50	60
527	-	30d. multicoloured	5·00	65
528	-	50d. red, green and purple	6·25	95

DESIGNS: 25d. Doha airport; 30, 50d. Flags of Qatar and the Arab League.

87 Clock Tower, Doha

1974. Tourism. Multicoloured.

529	5d. Type **87**	1·10	15
530	10d. White-cheeked terns, hoopoes and Shara'o Island (horiz)	1·50	20
531	15d. Fort Zubara (horiz)	1·80	25
532	35d. Dinghies and Gulf Hotel (horiz)	3·00	40
533	55d. Qatar by night (horiz)	3·50	65
534	75d. Arabian oryx (horiz)	5·50	1·10
535	1r.25 Khor-al-Udeid (horiz)	7·75	1·50
536	1r.75 Ruins Wakrah (horiz)	11·00	1·70

88 Traffic Roundabout, Doha

1975. Third Anniv of Shaikh Khalifa's Accession. Multicoloured.

537		10d. Type **88**	1·10	15
538		35d. Oil pipelines	1·90	40
539		55d. Laying offshore pipelines	3·00	95
540		1r. Oil refinery	6·25	1·50
541		1r.35 Shaikh Khalifa (vert)	7·75	2·10
542		1r.55 As 1r.35	9·50	3·00

89 Flintlock Pistol

1975. Opening of National Museum. Multicoloured.

543		2d. Type **89**	55	15
544		3d. Arabesque-pattern mosaic	1·00	25
545		35d. Museum buildings	2·50	40
546		75d. Museum archway (vert)	5·25	80
547		1r.25 Flint tools	8·25	1·60
548		3r. Gold necklace and pendant (vert)	18·00	3·00

90 Policeman and Road Signs

1975. Traffic Week. Multicoloured.

549		5d. Type **90**	1·50	25
550		15d. Traffic arrows and signal lights	4·00	65
551		35d. Type **90**	6·25	95
552		55d. As 15d.	10·00	1·50

91 Flag and Emblem

1975. Tenth Anniv of Arab Labour Charter.

553	**91**	10d. multicoloured	1·10	25
554	**91**	35d. multicoloured	2·75	55
555	**91**	1r. multicoloured	7·75	1·60

92 Government Building, Doha

1975. Fourth Anniv of Independence. Multicoloured.

556		5d. Type **92**	1·10	15
557		15d. Museum and clock tower, Doha	2·00	20
558		35d. Constitution – Arabic text (vert)	2·50	40
559		55d. Ruler and flag (vert)	4·00	55
560		75d. Constitution – English text (vert)	5·00	95
561		1r.25 As 55d.	7·75	1·60

93 Telecommunications Satellite (I.T.U.)

1975. 30th Anniv of U.N.O. Multicoloured.

562		5d. Type **93**	35	15
563		15d. U.N. Headquarters, New York	55	20
564		35d. U.P.U. emblem and map	1·50	40
565		1r. Doctors tending child (UNICEF)	3·50	1·50
566		1r.25 Bulldozer (I.L.O.)	6·75	2·30
567		2r. Students in class (UNESCO)	10·00	3·00

94 Fertilizer Plant

1975. Qatar Industry. Multicoloured.

568		5d. Type **94**	80	15
569		10d. Flour mills (vert)	1·30	20
570		35d. Natural gas plant	2·50	55
571		75d. Oil refinery	6·25	1·90
572		1r.25 Cement works	7·25	2·75
573		1r.55 Steel mills	11·00	3·50

95 Modern Building, Doha

1976. Fourth Anniv of Shaikh Khalifa's Accession.

574	**95**	5d. multicoloured	45	40
575	-	10d. multicoloured	55	45
576	-	35d. multicoloured	2·20	55
577	-	55d. multicoloured	3·50	95
578	-	75d. multicoloured	4·50	1·50
579	-	1r.55 multicoloured	11·00	3·75

DESIGNS: Nos. 575/6 and 579 show public buildings; Nos. 577/8 show Shaikh Khalifa with flag.

96 Tracking Aerial

1976. Opening of Satellite Earth Station. Multicoloured.

580		35d. Type **96**	2·50	80
581		55d. "Intelsat" satellite	3·25	1·30
582		75d. Type **96**	4·50	1·90
583		1r. As 55d.	6·75	2·40

97 Early and Modern Telephones

1976. Telephone Centenary.

584	**97**	1r. multicoloured	5·00	2·30
585	**97**	1r.35 multicoloured	6·25	3·00

98 Tournament Emblem

1976. Fourth Arabian Gulf Football Cup Tournament. Multicoloured.

586		5d. Type **98**	35	25
587		10d. Qatar Stadium	65	35
588		35d. Type **98**	3·25	40
589		55d. Two players with ball	5·00	95
590		75d. Player with ball	5·50	1·50
591		1r.25 As 10d.	7·75	2·00

99 Qatar Dhow

1976. Dhows.

592	**99**	10d. multicoloured	2·10	25
593	-	35d. multicoloured	4·25	40
594	-	80d. multicoloured	8·25	1·20
595	-	1r.25 multicoloured	11·00	2·00
596	-	1r.50 multicoloured	12·50	2·50
597	-	2r. multicoloured	18·00	4·00

DESIGNS: 35d. to 2r. Various craft.

100 Football

1976. Olympic Games, Montreal. Multicoloured.

598		5d. Type **100**	45	15
599		10d. Yachting	1·10	20
600		35d. Show jumping	2·75	40
601		80d. Boxing	4·50	1·10
602		1r.25 Weightlifting	6·25	1·70
603		1r.50 Basketball	8·25	2·75

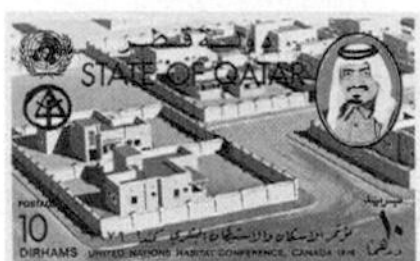
101 Urban Housing Development

1976. United Nations Conference on Human Settlements. Multicoloured.

604		10d. Type **101**	45	40
605		35d. U.N. and conference emblems	1·30	55
606		80d. Communal housing development	3·25	80
607		1r.25 Shaikh Khalifa	6·75	2·00

102 Kentish Plover

1976. Birds. Multicoloured.

608		5d. Type **102**	1·30	40
609		10d. Great cormorant	2·75	55
610		35d. Osprey	8·25	95
611		80d. Greater flamingo (vert)	17·00	2·00
612		1r.25 Rock thrush (vert)	26·00	3·00
613		2r. Saker falcon (vert)	30·00	4·00

103 Shaikh Khalifa and Flag

1976. Fifth Anniv of Independence. Multicoloured.

614		5d. Type **103**	35	15
615		10d. Type **103**	1·10	40
616		40d. Doha buildings (horiz)	2·00	55
617		80d. As 40d.	2·75	1·10
618		1r.25 "Dana" (oil rig) (horiz)	4·50	1·50
619		1r.50 United Nations and Qatar emblems (horiz)	6·25	1·70

104 U.N. Emblem

1976. United Nations Day.

620	**104**	2r. multicoloured	5·50	1·60
621	**104**	3r. multicoloured	7·75	2·40

105 Shaikh Khalifa

1977. Fifth Anniv of Amir's Accession.

622	**105**	20d. multicoloured	1·70	55
623	**105**	1r.80 multicoloured	9·50	2·40

106 Shaikh Khalifa

1977

624	**106**	5d. multicoloured	45	15
625	**106**	10d. multicoloured	65	20
626	**106**	35d. multicoloured	1·10	40
627	**106**	80d. multicoloured	2·20	55
628	**106**	1r. multicoloured	4·50	80
629	**106**	5r. multicoloured	13·50	3·25
630	**106**	10r. multicoloured	33·00	6·50

Nos. 628/30 are larger, size 25×31 mm.

107 Envelope and A.P.U. Emblem

1977. 25th Anniv of Arab Postal Union.

631	**107**	35d. multicoloured	1·60	55
632	**107**	1r.35 multicoloured	5·25	1·90

108 Shaikh Khalifa and Sound Waves

1977. International Telecommunications Day.

633	**108**	35d. multicoloured	1·00	40
634	**108**	1r.80 multicoloured	6·25	2·50

108a Shaikh Khalifa

1977

634a	**108a**	5d. multicoloured	45	45
634c	**108a**	10d. multicoloured	65	65
634d	**108a**	35d. multicoloured	90	90
634e	**108a**	80d. multicoloured	2·20	2·20

109 Parliament Building, Doha

1977. Sixth Anniv of Independence. Multicoloured.

635		80d. Type **109**	4·00	1·50
636		80d. Main business district, Doha	4·00	1·50
637		80d. Motorway, Doha	4·00	1·50

110 U.N. Emblem

1977. United Nations Day.

638	**110**	20d. multicoloured	1·10	55
639	**110**	1r. multicoloured	5·50	2·10

111 Steel Mill

1978. Sixth Anniv of Amir's Accession. Multicoloured.

640	20d. Type **111**	1·30	25
641	80d. Operating theatre	2·75	55
642	1r. Children's classroom	4·75	80
643	5r. Shaikh Khalifa	13·50	2·50

112 Oil Refinery

1978. Seventh Anniv of Independence. Multicoloured.

644	35d. Type **112**	1·00	40
645	80d. Apartment buildings	2·00	80
646	1r.35 Town centre, Doha	3·75	1·50
647	1r.80 Shaikh Khalifa	5·00	1·70

113 Man reading Alphabet

1978. International Literacy Day.

648	**113**	35d. multicoloured	1·70	65
649	**113**	80d. multicoloured	5·00	1·30

114 U.N. Emblem and Qatar Flag

1978. United Nations Day.

650	**114**	35d. multicoloured	1·30	65
651	**114**	80d. multicoloured	4·25	1·30

115 "Human Rights Flame"

1978. 30th Anniv of Declaration of Human Rights. Multicoloured.

652	35d. Type **115**	90	40
653	80d. Type **115**	2·20	1·10
654	1r.25 Flame and scales of justice	3·25	1·60
655	1r.80 As 1r.25	5·00	2·30

116 I.Y.C. Emblem

1979. International Year of the Child.

656	**116**	35d. mauve, blue and black	1·30	1·10
657	**116**	1r.80 green, blue & black	4·25	4·00

117 Shaikh Khalifa

1979

658	**117**	5d. multicoloured	20	15
659	**117**	10d. multicoloured	35	15
660	**117**	20d. multicoloured	80	20
661	**117**	25d. multicoloured	1·00	25
662	**117**	35d. multicoloured	1·50	55
663	**117**	60d. multicoloured	1·90	65
664	**117**	80d. multicoloured	2·50	80
665	**117**	1r. multicoloured	2·75	1·10
666	**117**	1r.25 multicoloured	3·00	1·20
667	**117**	1r.35 multicoloured	3·25	1·50
668	**117**	1r.80 multicoloured	5·00	1·70
669	**117**	5r. multicoloured	11·00	3·25
670	**117**	10r. multicoloured	22·00	6·75

Nos. 665/70 are larger, size 27×32½ mm.

118 Shaikh Khalifa and Laurel Wreath

1979. Seventh Anniv of Amir's Accession.

671	**118**	35d. multicoloured	1·10	40
672	**118**	80d. multicoloured	1·60	55
673	**118**	1r. multicoloured	1·80	65
674	**118**	1r.25 multicoloured	2·20	80

119 Wave Pattern and Television Screen

1979. World Telecommunications Day.

675	**119**	2r. multicoloured	4·50	2·00
676	**119**	2r.80 multicoloured	5·50	3·00

120 Two Children supporting Globe

1979. 50th Anniv of Int Bureau of Education.

677	**120**	35d. multicoloured	90	25
678	**120**	80d. multicoloured	3·50	1·10

121 Rolling Mill

1979. Eighth Anniv of Independence. Multicoloured.

679	5d. Type **121**	80	15
680	10d. Aerial view of Doha	1·10	25
681	1r.25 Qatar flag	3·75	1·20
682	2r. Shaikh Khalifa	5·50	1·50

122 U.N. Emblem and Flag of Qatar

1979. United Nations Day.

683	**122**	1r.25 multicoloured	4·00	1·10
684	**122**	2r. multicoloured	6·25	1·60

123 Mosque Minaret and Crescent Moon

1979. Third World Conference on the Prophet's Seera and Sunna.

685	**123**	35d. multicoloured	3·00	80
686	**123**	1r.80 multicoloured	8·25	1·90

124 Shaikh Khalifa

1980. Eighth Anniv of Amir's Accession.

687	**124**	20d. multicoloured	1·10	25
688	**124**	60d. multicoloured	2·75	65
689	**124**	1r.25 multicoloured	4·50	1·20
690	**124**	2r. multicoloured	9·00	2·10

125 Emblem

1980. Sixth Congress of Arab Towns Organization, Doha.

691	**125**	2r.35 multicoloured	6·75	1·60
692	**125**	2r.80 multicoloured	10·00	2·10

126 Oil Refinery

1980. Ninth Anniv of Independence. Multicoloured.

693	10d. Type **126**	65	15
694	35d. Doha	2·20	55
695	2r. Oil Rig	9·00	2·75
696	2r.35 Hospital	11·00	3·25

127 Figures supporting O.P.E.C. Emblem

1980. 20th Anniv of Organization of Petroleum Exporting Countries.

697	**127**	1r.35 multicoloured	3·25	1·20
698	**127**	2r. multicoloured	5·50	1·90

128 U.N.Emblem

1980. United Nations Day.

699	**128**	1r.35 blue, light blue and purple	2·75	1·30
700	**128**	1r.80 turquoise, green and black	4·00	1·60

129 Mosque and Kaaba, Mecca

1980. 1400th Anniv of Hegira.

701	**129**	10d. multicoloured	45	25
702	**129**	35d. multicoloured	1·10	65
703	**129**	1r.25 multicoloured	2·20	1·30
704	**129**	2r.80 multicoloured	5·50	3·75

130 I.Y.D.P. Emblem

1981. International Year of Disabled Persons.

705	**130**	2r. multicoloured	4·50	2·75
706	**130**	3r. multicoloured	6·75	3·25

131 Student

1981. 20th Anniv of Education Day.

707	**131**	2r. multicoloured	5·00	2·00
708	**131**	3r. multicoloured	6·25	2·75

132 Shaikh Khalifa

1981. Ninth Anniv of Amir's Accession.

709	**132**	10d. multicoloured	55	15
710	**132**	35d. multicoloured	1·30	25
711	**132**	80d. multicoloured	2·50	65
712	**132**	5r. multicoloured	13·50	3·75

133 I.T.U. and W.H.O. Emblems and Ribbons forming Caduceus

1981. World Telecommunications Day.

713	**133**	2r. multicoloured	4·50	1·60
714	**133**	2r.80 multicoloured	6·75	2·40

134 Torch

1981. 30th International Military Football Championship.

715	**134**	1r.25 multicoloured	5·00	1·60
716	**134**	2r.80 multicoloured	8·25	3·00

135 Qatar Flag

1981. Tenth Anniv of Independence.

717	**135**	5d. multicoloured	65	15
718	**135**	60d. multicoloured	2·10	65
719	**135**	80d. multicoloured	2·75	80
720	**135**	5r. multicoloured	17·00	5·00

136 Tractor gathering Crops

1981. World Food Day.
721 **136** 2r. multicoloured 5·50 3·25
722 **136** 2r.80 multicoloured 7·75 4·00

137 Red Crescent

1982. Qatar Red Crescent.
723 **137** 20d. multicoloured 1·10 25
724 **137** 2r.80 multicoloured 7·75 3·00

138 Shaikh Khalifa

1982. Tenth Anniv of Amir's Accession.
725 **138** 10d. multicoloured 90 15
726 **138** 20d. multicoloured 1·70 25
727 **138** 1r.25 multicoloured 6·25 1·30
728 **138** 2r.80 multicoloured 14·50 3·00

139 Hamad General Hospital

1982. Hamad General Hospital.
729 **139** 10d. multicoloured 65 25
730 **139** 2r.35 multicoloured 6·25 3·00

140 Shaikh Khalifa

1982
731 **140** 5d. multicoloured 35 15
732 **140** 10d. multicoloured 40 15
733 **140** 15d. multicoloured 45 15
734 **140** 20d. multicoloured 50 20
735 **140** 25d. multicoloured 65 25
736 **140** 35d. multicoloured 90 35
737 **140** 60d. multicoloured 1·30 40
738 **140** 80d. multicoloured 1·70 45
739 - 1r. multicoloured 2·20 65
740 - 1r.25 multicoloured 2·75 80
741 - 2r. multicoloured 4·50 2·00
742 - 5r. multicoloured 11·00 4·75
743 - 10r. multicoloured 22·00 9·50
744 - 15r. multicoloured 31·00 14·50

DESIGNS—25×32 mm: 1r. to 2r. Oil refinery; 5r. to 15r. Doha clock tower.

142 "Bar'zan" Container Ship

1982. Sixth Anniv of United Arab Shipping Company.
745 **142** 20d. multicoloured 1·10 25
746 **142** 2r.35 multicoloured 10·00 3·00

143 A.P.U. Emblem

1982. 30th Anniv of Arab Postal Union.
747 **143** 35d. multicoloured 1·10 40
748 **143** 2r.80 multicoloured 7·75 2·30

144 National Flag

1982. 11th Anniv of Independence.
749 **144** 10d. multicoloured 80 25
750 **144** 80d. multicoloured 1·90 55
751 **144** 1r.25 multicoloured 3·75 1·60
752 **144** 2r.80 multicoloured 7·25 2·30

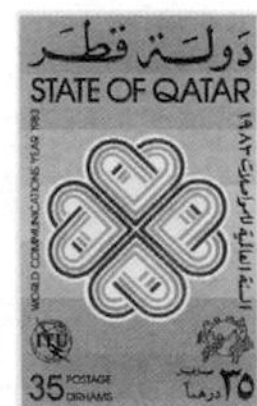

145 W.C.Y. Emblem

1983. World Communications Year.
753 **145** 35d. multicoloured 1·10 55
754 **145** 2r.80 multicoloured 6·25 2·40

146 Conference Emblem

1983. Second Gulf Postal Organization Conference.
755 **146** 1r. multicoloured 2·50 1·30
756 **146** 1r.35 multicoloured 4·25 2·00

147 Arabic Script

1983. 12th Anniv of Independence.
757 **147** 10d. multicoloured 45 25
758 **147** 35d. multicoloured 80 55
759 **147** 80d. multicoloured 1·70 80
760 **147** 2r.80 multicoloured 6·25 2·40

148 Council Emblem

1983. Fourth Session of Gulf Co-operation Council Supreme Council.
761 **148** 35d. multicoloured 1·70 55
762 **148** 2r.80 multicoloured 7·25 2·40

149 Globe and Human Rights Emblem

1983. 35th Anniv of Declaration of Human Rights. Multicoloured.
763 1r.25 Type **149** 3·25 1·60
764 2r.80 Globe and emblem in balance 7·75 2·40

150 Harbour

151 Shaikh Khalifa

1984
765 **150** 15d. multicoloured 45 15
765a **151** 25d. mult (22×27 mm) 1·00 40
766 **150** 40d. multicoloured 1·10 60
767 **150** 50d. multicoloured 1·10 65
767a **151** 75d. mult (22×27 mm) 2·50 1·50
768 **151** 1r. multicoloured 2·75 1·60
769 **151** 1r.50 multicoloured 3·25 1·70
769a **151** 2r. multicoloured 7·25 5·00
770 **151** 2r.50 multicoloured 5·50 3·00
771 **151** 3r. multicoloured 7·25 3·25
772 **151** 5r. multicoloured 13·50 6·00
773 **151** 10r. multicoloured 22·00 11·50

152 Flag and Shaikh Khalifa

1984. 13th Anniv of Independence.
774 **152** 15d. multicoloured 80 25
775 **152** 1r. multicoloured 2·50 95
776 **152** 2r.50 multicoloured 5·50 2·40
777 **152** 3r.50 multicoloured 7·75 3·00

153 Teacher and Blackboard

1984. International Literacy Day. Multicoloured, background colour behind board given.
778 **153** 1r. mauve 4·50 1·10
779 **153** 1r. orange 4·50 1·10

154 I.C.A.O. Emblem

1984. 40th Anniv of I.C.A.O.
780 **154** 20d. multicoloured 65 25
781 **154** 3r.50 multicoloured 8·25 3·00

155 I.Y.Y. Emblem

1985. International Youth Year.
782 **155** 50d. multicoloured 1·70 65
783 **155** 1r. multicoloured 4·00 1·30

156 Crossing the Road

1985. Traffic Week. Multicoloured, frame colour given.
784 **156** 1r. red 3·25 1·20
785 **156** 1r. blue 3·25 1·20

157 Emblem

1985. 40th Anniv of League of Arab States.
786 **157** 50d. multicoloured 1·60 40
787 **157** 4r. multicoloured 7·75 3·00

158 Doha

1985. 14th Anniv of Independence. Multicoloured.
788 40d. Type **158** 1·00 25
789 50d. Dish aerials and micro-wave tower 1·30 55
790 1r.50 Oil refinery 4·50 1·20
791 4r. Cement works 10·00 4·00

159 O.P.E.C. Emblem in "25"

1985. 25th Anniv of Organization of Petroleum Exporting Countries. Multicoloured, background colours given.
792 **159** 1r. red 4·50 1·30
793 **159** 1r. green 4·50 1·30

160 U.N. Emblem

1985. 40th Anniv of U.N.O.
794 **160** 1r. multicoloured 1·30 1·30
795 **160** 3r. multicoloured 4·25 3·75

161 Emblem

1986. Population and Housing Census.
796 **161** 1r. multicoloured 2·20 1·30
797 **161** 3r. multicoloured 6·75 4·00

162 "Qatari ibn al-Fuja'a" (container ship)

1986. Tenth Anniv of United Arab Shipping Company. Multicoloured.
798 1r.50 Type **162** 2·75 2·75
799 4r. "Al Wajda" (container ship) 8·25 6·00

163 Flag and Shaikh Khalifa

1986. 15th Anniv of Independence.
800 **163** 40d. multicoloured 65 55
801 **163** 50d. multicoloured 90 65

802	163	1r. multicoloured	1·90	1·30
803	163	4r. multicoloured	6·75	4·75

164 Shaikh Khalifa

1987

804	164	15r. multicoloured	17·00	12·00
805	164	20r. multicoloured	22·00	16·00
806	164	30r. multicoloured	39·00	25·00

165 Palace

1987. 15th Anniv of Amir's Accession.

807	165	50d. multicoloured	90	55
808	165	1r. multicoloured	2·00	1·10
809	165	1r.50 multicoloured	2·50	1·30
810	165	4r. multicoloured	6·25	4·75

166 Emblem

1987. 35th Anniv of Arab Postal Union.

811	166	1r. yellow, green and black	2·75	1·30
812	166	1r.50 multicoloured	4·00	2·00

167 Emblem

1987. Gulf Environment Day.

813	167	1r. multicoloured	1·90	1·30
814	167	4r. multicoloured	7·25	5·25

168 Modern Complex

1987. 16th Anniv of Independence.

815	25d. Type **168**	90	40
816	75d. Aerial view of city	2·50	95
817	2r. Modern building	4·50	2·00
818	4r. Oil refinery	9·00	4·75

169 Pens in Fist

1987. International Literacy Day.

819	169	1r.50 multicoloured	2·20	1·30
820	169	4r. multicoloured	4·50	4·00

170 Anniversary Emblem

1988. 40th Anniv of W.H.O.

821	170	1r.50 yellow, black and blue	2·75	2·50
822	170	2r. yellow, black and pink	4·00	3·75

171 State Arms, Shaikh Khalifa and Flag

1988. 17th Anniv of Independence.

823	171	50d. multicoloured	1·10	65
824	171	75d. multicoloured	1·70	95
825	171	1r.50 multicoloured	2·75	2·00
826	171	2r. multicoloured	3·50	2·40

172 Post Office

1988. Opening of New Doha General Post Office.

827	172	1r.50 multicoloured	2·00	2·00
828	172	4r. multicoloured	4·75	4·75

173 Housing Development

1988. Arab Housing Day.

829	173	1r.50 multicoloured	2·20	1·60
830	173	4r. multicoloured	6·75	3·75

174 Hands shielding Flame

1988. 40th Anniv of Declaration of Human Rights.

831	174	1r.50 multicoloured	2·75	2·50
832	174	2r. multicoloured	4·00	3·75

175 Dish Aerials and Arrows

1989. World Telecommunications Day.

833	175	2r. multicoloured	2·20	2·30
834	175	4r. multicoloured	4·50	4·00

176 Headquarters

1989. Tenth Anniv of Qatar Red Crescent Society.

835	176	4r. multicoloured	9·00	4·75

177 Palace

1989. 18th Anniv of Independence.

836	177	75d. multicoloured	1·10	80
837	177	1r. multicoloured	2·00	1·90
838	177	1r.50 multicoloured	2·50	2·10
839	177	2r. multicoloured	3·50	2·40

178 Anniversary Emblem

1990. 40th Anniv of Gulf Air.

840	178	50d. multicoloured	1·10	55
841	178	75d. multicoloured	1·70	95
842	178	4r. multicoloured	8·25	4·00

179 Map and Rising Sun

1990. 19th Anniv of Independence. Multicoloured.

843	50d. Type **179**	1·10	55
844	75d. Map and sunburst	1·70	80
845	1r.50 Musicians and sword dancer	3·25	1·60
846	2r. As No. 845	5·00	2·75

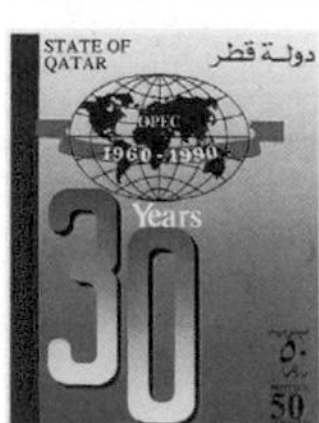
180 Anniversary Emblem

1990. 30th Anniv of Organization of Petroleum Exporting Countries. Multicoloured.

847	50d. Type **180**	1·50	55
848	1r.50 Flags of member nations	4·25	1·60

181 Emblem and Dhow

1990. 11th Session of Supreme Council of Gulf Co-operation Council. Multicoloured.

849	50d. Type **181**	1·50	55
850	1r. Council heads of state and emblem	2·50	1·10
851	1r.50 State flag and Council emblem	3·50	1·70
852	2r. State and Council emblems	4·50	2·10

182 "Glossonema edule"

1991. Plants. Multicoloured.

853	10d. Type **182**	95	40
854	25d. "Lycium shawii"	1·10	45
855	50d. "Acacia tortilis"	1·20	1·10
856	75d. "Acacia ehrenbergiana"	1·80	1·20
857	1r. "Capparis spinosa"	2·40	2·40
858	4r. "Cymbopogon parkeri"	11·00	9·50

No. 858 is wrongly inscribed "Cymhopogon".

183 Emblem

1991. 20th Anniv of Independence. Multicoloured.

859	25d. Type **183**	95	40
860	75d. As Type **183** but different Arabic inscription	1·40	65
861	1r. View of Doha (35×32 mm)	1·90	1·10
862	1r.50 Palace (35×32 mm)	3·00	1·90

184 Seabream

1991. Fish. Multicoloured.

863	10d. Type **184**	70	40
864	15d. Pennant coralfish	80	45
865	25d. Scarlet-finned squirrelfish	1·40	80
866	50d. Smooth houndshark	2·75	1·60
867	75d. Seabream	3·75	2·40
868	1r. Golden trevally	4·50	3·75
869	1r.50 Rabbitfish	7·75	6·00
870	2r. Yellow-banded angelfish	9·00	7·25

185 Shaikh Khalifa

1992. Multicoloured. (a) Size 22×28 or 28×22 mm.

871	10d. Type **185**	10	10
872	25d. North Field gas project	35	15
873	50d. Map of Qatar	60	55
874	75d. Petrochemical factory (horiz)	95	60
875	1r. Oil refinery (horiz)	1·20	80

(b) Size 25×32 or 32×25 mm.

876	1r.50 As No. 872	1·60	1·30
877	2r. As No. 873	1·90	1·60
878	3r. As No. 874	4·25	3·00
879	4r. As No. 875	4·75	3·25
880	5r. As No. 873	5·50	4·00
881	10r. As No. 875	12·00	7·25
882	15r. Shaikh Khalifa (different frame)	16·00	12·00
883	20r. As No. 882	27·00	14·50
884	30r. As No. 882	30·00	24·00

186 Shaikh Khalifa and Gateway

1992. 20th Anniv of Amir's Accession. Multicoloured.

885	25d. Type **186**	60	40
886	50d. Type **186**	1·20	55
887	75d. Archway and "20"	1·80	80
888	1r.50 As No 887	3·50	1·70

187 Heart in Centre of Flower

1992. World Health Day. "Heartbeat, the Rhythm of Health". Multicoloured.

889	50d. Type **187**	95	65
890	1r.50 Heart on clockface and cardiograph (horiz)	2·75	2·00

188 Women dancing

1992. Children's Paintings. Multicoloured.

891	25d. Type **188**	70	15
892	50d. Children's playground	1·60	55
893	75d. Boat race	3·00	65
894	1r.50 Fishing fleet	4·75	1·10
MS895	122×102 mm. Nos. 891/4	£300	£300

189 Runner and Emblems

1992. Olympic Games, Barcelona. Multicoloured.

896	50d. Type **189**	1·40	40
897	1r.50 Footballer and emblems	3·50	1·20

190 Shaikh Khalifa and Script

1992. 21st Anniv of Independence. Multicoloured.

898	50d. Type **190**	85	55
899	50d. Shaikh Kalifa and "21" in English and Arabic	85	55
900	1r. Oil well, pen and dhow (42×42 mm)	1·60	1·20
901	1r. Dhow in harbour (42×42 mm)	1·60	1·20

191 Ball, Flag and Emblem

1992. 11th Arabian Gulf Football Championship. Multicoloured.

902	50d. Type **191**	1·20	65
903	1r. Ball bursting goal net (vert)	2·40	1·30

192 Emblems and Globe

1992. International Nutrition Conference, Rome. Multicoloured.

904	50d. Type **192**	1·80	40
905	1r. Cornucopia (horiz)	3·00	65

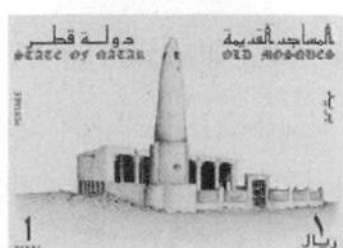
193 Mosque

1993. Old Mosques. Each sepia, yellow and brown.

906	1r. Type **193**	1·20	95
907	1r. Mosque (minaret without balcony)	1·20	95
908	1r. Mosque (minaret with wide balcony)	1·20	95
909	1r. Mosque (minaret with narrow balcony)	1·20	95

194 Presenter and Dish Aerial

1993. 25th Anniv of Qatar Broadcasting. Multicoloured.

910	25d. Type **194**	95	15
911	50d. Rocket and satellite	2·20	80
912	75d. Broadcasting House	2·75	1·10
913	1r. Journalists	4·25	1·30
MS914	123×114 mm. Nos. 910/13 forming a composite design	£180	£180

195 Oil Refinery and Sea

1993. 22nd Anniv of Independence. Multicoloured.

915	25d. Type **195**	35	25
916	50d. Flag and clock tower, Doha	70	65
917	75d. "22" in English and Arabic	1·20	1·10
918	1r.50 Flag and fort	2·75	2·30

196 Scroll, Quill and Paper

1993. International Literacy Day. Multicoloured.

919	25d. Type **196**	35	20
920	50d. Fountain pen and flags spelling "Qatar"	70	60
921	75d. Fountain pen and Arabic characters	1·20	95
922	1r.50 Arabic text on scroll and fountain pen	2·75	2·30

197 Girls playing

1993. Children's Games. Multicoloured.

923	25d. Type **197**	85	15
924	50d. Boys playing with propeller (vert)	1·60	55
925	75d. Wheel and stick race (vert)	2·40	80
926	1r.50 Skipping	4·75	1·90
MS927	Two sheets (a) 114×93 mm. Nos. 923 ×2 and 926 ×2; (b) 93×114 mm. Nos. 924 ×2 and 925 ×2	70·00	70·00

198 Lanner Falcon

1993. Falcons. Multicoloured.

928	25d. Type **198**	60	40
929	50d. Saker falcon	1·20	55
930	75d. Barbary falcon	1·80	80
931	1r.50 Peregrine falcon	3·50	1·90
MS932	122×104 mm. Nos. 928/31	£140	£140

199 Headquarters

1994. 30th Anniv of Qatar Insurance Company. Multicoloured.

933	50d. Type **199**	1·20	40
934	1r.50 Company emblem and international landmarks	3·50	1·60

200 Hands catching Drops from Tap

1994. World Water Day. Mulicoloured.

935	25d. Type **200**	1·20	40
936	1r. Hands catching raindrop, water tower, crops and United Nations emblem	2·40	1·60

201 Gavel, Scales and National Flag

1994. Qatar International Law Conference. Multicoloured.

937	75d. Type **201**	95	80
938	2r. Gavel and scales suspended from flag	2·75	2·50

202 Society Emblem

1994. Qatar Society for Welfare and Rehabilitation of the Handicapped. Multicoloured.

939	25d. Type **202**	95	55
940	75d. Handicapped symbol and hands	2·75	1·10

203 Anniversary Emblem

1994. 75th Anniv of I.L.O. Multicoloured.

941	25d. Type **203**	60	40
942	2r. Anniversary emblem and cogwheel	4·25	1·60

204 Family and Emblem

1994. International Year of the Family.

943	**204**	25d. blue and black	85	65
944	-	1r. multicoloured	2·75	1·30

DESIGN: 1r. I.Y.F. emblem and stylized family standing on U.N. emblem.

205 Scroll

1994. 23rd Anniv of Independence. Multicoloured.

945	25d. Type **205**	50	40
946	75d. Oasis	1·20	80
947	1r. Industry	1·80	1·10
948	2r. Scroll (different)	4·25	2·40

206 Map, Airplane and Emblem

1994. 50th Anniv of I.C.A.O. Multicoloured.

949	25d. Type **206**	1·20	40
950	75d. Anniversary emblem	3·50	95

207 Ship-like Carvings

1995. Rock Carvings, Jabal Jusasiyah. Multicoloured.

951	1r. Type **207**	1·10	80
952	1r. Circular and geometric patterns	1·10	80
953	1r. Six irregular-shaped carvings	1·10	80
954	1r. Carvings including three multi-limbed creatures	1·10	80
955	1r. Nine multi-limbed creatures	1·10	80
956	1r. Fishes	1·10	80

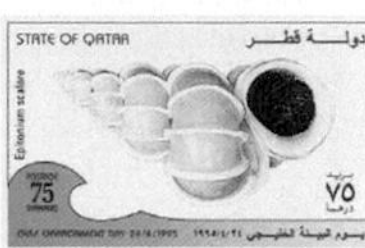
208 Precious Wentletrap ("Epitonium scalare")

1995. Gulf Environment Day. Sea Shells. Multicoloured.

957	75d. Type **208**	1·20	95
958	75d. Feathered cone ("Conus pennaceus")	1·20	95
959	75d. "Cerithidea cingulata"	1·20	95
960	75d. "Hexaplex kuesterianus"	1·20	95
961	1r. Giant spider conch ("Lambis truncata sebae")	1·40	1·30
962	1r. Woodcock murex ("Murex scolopax")	1·40	1·30
963	1r. "Thais mutabilis"	1·40	1·30
964	1r. Spindle shell ("Fusinus arabicus")	1·40	1·30

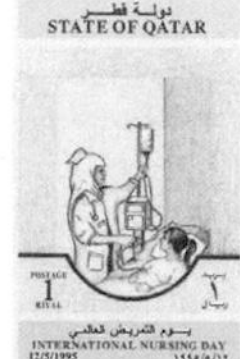
209 Nursing Patient

1995. International Nursing Day. Multicoloured.

965	1r. Type **209**	1·90	1·10
966	1r.50 Vaccinating child	3·00	1·60

210 Schoolchildren

1995. 24th Anniv of Independence. Multicoloured.

967	1r. Type **210**	95	80
968	1r. Palm trees	95	80
969	1r.50 Port	1·60	1·50
970	1r.50 Doha	1·60	1·50

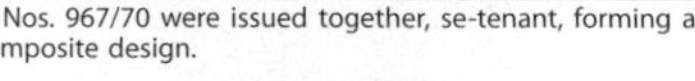
Nos. 967/70 were issued together, se-tenant, forming a composite design.

211 Anniversary Emblem

1995. 50th Anniv of U.N.O.

971	**211**	1r.50 multicoloured	2·40	1·30

212 Addra Gazelle

1996. Mammals. Multicoloured.

972	25d. Type **212**	10	10
973	50d. Beira antelope	50	35
974	75d. "Gazella dorcas pelzelni"	85	65
975	1r. Dorcas gazelle	95	80
976	1r.50 Speke's gazelle	1·80	1·50
977	2r. Soemmering's gazelle	2·40	2·40
MS978	121×81 mm. 3r. Speke's gazelle, *Gazella dorcas pelzelni* and Soemmering's gazelle. Imperf	48·00	44·00

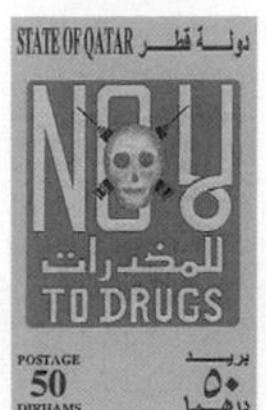
213 Syringes through Skull

1996. International Day against Drug Abuse. Multicoloured.

979	50d. Type **213**	85	55
980	1r. "No entry" sign over syringes in hand	1·60	80

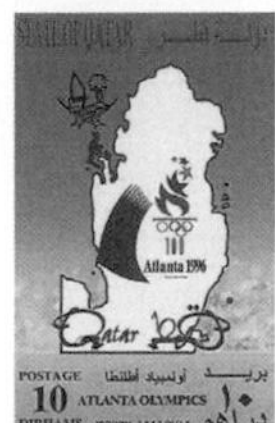
214 Map of Qatar and Games Emblem

1996. Olympic Games, Atlanta. Multicoloured.

981	10d. Type **214**	30	25
982	15d. Rifle shooting	30	25
983	25d. Bowling	30	25
984	50d. Table tennis	85	55
985	1r. Running	1·70	1·60
986	1r.50 Yachting	2·75	2·40

Nos. 981/6 were issued together, se-tenant, forming a composite design.

215 Map, National Flag and Shaikh Hamad

1996. 25th Anniv of Independence.

987	**215**	1r.50 multicoloured	2·10	1·30
988	**215**	2r. multicoloured	2·75	1·70

216 Shaikh Hamad

217 Shaikh Hamad

1996

990	**216**	25d. multicoloured	10	10
991	**216**	50d. multicoloured	50	40
992	**216**	75d. multicoloured	85	55
993	**216**	1r. multicoloured	95	65
994	**217**	1r.50 multicoloured	1·60	1·10
995	**217**	2r. multicoloured	2·10	1·30
997	**217**	4r. multicoloured	4·00	2·75
998	**217**	5r. multicoloured	4·75	5·25
999	**217**	10r. multicoloured	9·75	7·25
1001	**217**	20r. multicoloured	19·00	14·50
1002	**217**	30r. multicoloured	29·00	21·00

218 Doha Clock Tower, Dove and Heads of State

1996. 17th Session of Gulf Co-operation Council Supreme Council, Doha. Multicoloured.

1004	1r. Type **218**	1·30	80
1005	1r.50 Council emblem, dove and national flag	2·40	1·60

219 Children and UNICEF Emblem

1996. 50th Anniv of UNICEF. Multicoloured.

1006	75d. Type **219**	95	65
1007	75d. Children and emblem	95	65

220 Al-Wajbah

1997. Forts. Multicoloured.

1008	25d. Type **220**	50	25
1009	75d. Al-Zubarah (horiz)	1·10	95
1010	1r. Al-Kout Fort, Doha (horiz)	1·30	1·20
1011	3r. Umm Salal Mohammed (horiz)	4·50	4·25

221 World Map and Liquid Gas Containers (½-size illustration)

1997. Inauguration of Ras Laffan Port.

1012	**221**	3r. multicoloured	4·75	2·75

222 Palomino

1997. Arab Horses. Multicoloured.

1013	25d. Type **222**	50	25
1014	75d. Black horse	1·30	95
1015	1r. Grey	1·80	1·20
1016	1r.50 Bay	2·40	1·90
MS1017	121×81 mm. 3r. Mares and foals	£120	50·00

223 Arabic Script within Wreath, Flag and Shaikh Hamad

1997. 26th Anniv of Independence. Multicoloured.

1018	1r. Type **223**	95	80
1019	1r.50 Amir, oil refinery and Government Palace	1·40	1·20

224 Graph

1997. Middle East and Northern Africa Economic Conference, Doha.

1020	**224**	2r. multicoloured	1·60	1·30

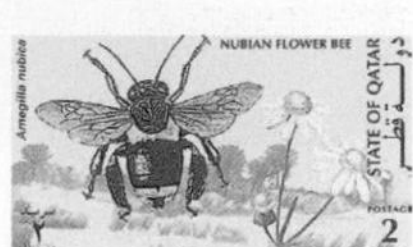
225 Nubian Flower Bee

1998. Insects. Multicoloured.

1021	2r. Type **225**	1·60	1·10
1022	2r. Domino beetle	1·60	1·10
1023	2r. Seven-spotted ladybird	1·60	1·10
1024	2r. Desert giant ant	1·60	1·10
1025	2r. Eastern death's-head hawk moth	1·60	1·10
1026	2r. Arabian darkling beetle	1·60	1·10
1027	2r. Yellow digger	1·60	1·10
1028	2r. Mole cricket	1·60	1·10
1029	2r. Migratory locust	1·60	1·10
1030	2r. Elegant rhinoceros beetle	1·60	1·10
1031	2r. Oleander hawk moth	1·60	1·10
1032	2r. American cockroach	1·60	1·10
1033	2r. Girdled skimmer	1·60	1·10
1034	2r. Sabre-toothed beetle	1·60	1·10
1035	2r. Arabian cicada	1·60	1·10
1036	2r. Pin-striped ground weevil	1·60	1·10
1037	2r. Praying mantis	1·60	1·10
1038	2r. Rufous bombardier beetle	1·60	1·10
1039	2r. Diadem	1·60	1·10
1040	2r. Shore earwig (inscr "Earwing")	1·60	1·10
MS1041	Two sheets, each 91×59 mm. (a) No. 1029; (b) No. 1039	36·00	27·00

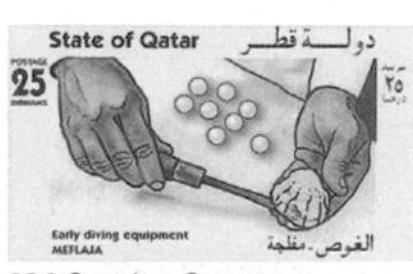
226 Opening Oysters

1998. Early Pearl-diving Equipment. Multicoloured.

1042	25d. Type **226**	50	25
1043	75d. Opened oyster with pearl	1·10	80
1044	1r. Scales for weighing pearls	1·30	1·10
1045	1r.50 Basket for keeping oysters (vert)	2·20	2·00
MS1046	106×83 mm. 2r. Pearl diver	12·00	8·75

227 Shaikh Hamad

1998. 27th Anniv of Independence. Multicoloured.

1047	1r. Type **227**	85	65
1048	1r.50 Shaikh Hamad (horiz)	1·60	1·30

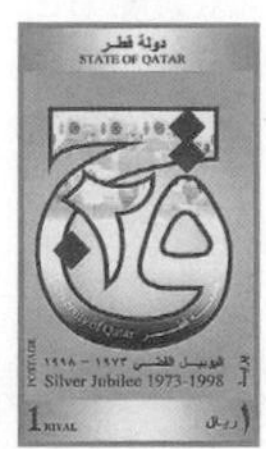
228 Anniversary Emblem

1998. 25th Anniv of University of Qatar.

1049	**228**	1r. multicoloured	85	65
1050	**228**	1r.50 multicoloured	1·60	1·30

229 Dromedaries

1999. Dromedaries. Multicoloured.

1051	25d. Type **229**	35	25
1052	75d. One dromedary	1·10	95
1053	1r. Three dromedaries	1·30	1·20
1054	1r.50 Four young dromedaries with herd	2·20	1·90
MS1055	106×83 mm. 2r. Adult and young	19·00	14·50

230 Emblem

1999. General Assembly of International Equestrian Federation, Doha.

1056	**230**	1r.50 multicoloured	2·40	2·00

231 Umayyad Dirham

1999. Coins. Multicoloured.

1057	1r. Type **231**	85	55
1058	1r. Umayyad dirham (four small circles around edge of right-hand coin)	85	55
1059	1r. Abbasid dirham (three lines of inscr on left-hand coin)	85	55
1060	1r. Abbasid dirham (six lines of inscr on left-hand coin)	85	55
1061	1r. Umayyad dirham (five small circles around edge of right-hand coin)	85	55
1062	2r. Abbasid dirham (three lines on inscr on left-hand coin)	1·60	1·30
1063	2r. Umayyad dinar	1·60	1·30
1064	2r. Abbasid dinar (five lines of inscr on left-hand coin)	1·60	1·30
1065	2r. Murabitid dinar	1·60	1·30
1066	2r. Fatimid dinar	1·60	1·30
MS1067	Two sheets, each 112×70 mm. (a) 2r. Arab Sasanian dirham; (b) 3r. Umayyad dirham	24·00	19·00

232 Shaikh Hamad

1999. 28th Anniv of Independence.

1068	**232**	1r. multicoloured	85	65
1069	**232**	1r.50 multicoloured	1·60	1·10

233 Tree of Letters

1999. 125th Anniv of Universal Postal Union. Multicoloured.

1070	1r. Type **233**	85	65
1071	1r.50 General Post Office, Doha (horiz)	1·60	1·10

234 Postal Emblems on "Stamps"

1999. Fifth Arab Gulf Countries Stamp Exhibition, Doha. Multicoloured.

1072	1r. Type **234**	85	65
1073	1r.50 Exhibition emblem (horiz)	1·60	1·10

235 Flower and Emblem

1999. National Committee for Children with Special Needs.

1074	**235**	1r.50 multicoloured	1·80	1·30

236 Clock Tower

2000. New Millennium.

1075	**236**	1r.50 gold and red	1·40	1·30
1076	**236**	2r. gold and blue	2·20	2·00

237 Emir Cup and Court

2000. New Millennium Open Tennis Championships, Qatar. Multicoloured.

1077	1r. Type **237**	1·20	1·10
1078	1r.50 Emir Cup and racquet	1·80	1·60

238 Map and Water Droplet

2000. Gulf Co-operation Council Water Week. Multicoloured.

1079	1r. Type **238**	1·20	1·10
1080	1r.50 Dried earth and water droplet	1·80	1·60

239 Bat and Ball

2000. 15th Asian Table Tennis Championship, Doha.

1081	**239**	1r.50 multicoloured	1·80	1·30

240 Shaikh Hamad, Fort and Emblem

2000. 29th Anniv of Independence. Multicoloured.

1082	1r. Type **240**	1·20	1·20
1083	1r.50 Shaikh Hamad, city and oil drilling platform	1·80	1·80

241 Emblem and Dove carrying Letter

2000. 50th Anniv of Qatar Post Office. Multicoloured.

1084	1r.50 Type **241**	1·80	1·80
1085	2r. Emblem, magnifying glass and building facade	2·40	2·40

242 Emblem

2000. Ninth Islamic Summit Conference, Doha. Multicoloured.

1086	1r. Type **242**	1·20	1·20
1087	1r.50 Emblem and olive branch (47×30 mm)	1·80	1·80

243 Gas Terminal

2001. "Clean Environment". Multicoloured.

1088	1r. Type **243**	1·20	1·10
1089	1r.50 Oryx and gas installation	1·70	1·60
1090	2r. Flamingoes and Ras Laffan city skyline	2·75	2·40
1091	3r. Earth viewed from space	3·50	3·25

244 Castle, Koran and Ship

2001. 30th Anniv of Independence.

1092	**244**	1r. multicoloured	1·20	1·20
1093	**244**	1r.50 multicoloured	1·80	1·80

245 Children encircling Globe

2001. United Nations Year of Dialogue among Civilizations. Multicoloured.

1094	1r.50 Type **245**	1·80	1·80
1095	2r. Leaves	2·75	2·75

246 Building and Emblem

2001. Fourth World Trade Organization Ministerial Conference, Doho, Qatar.

1096	**246**	1r. multicoloured	1·40	95
1097	**246**	1r.50 multicoloured	2·20	1·40

247 Door

2001. Traditional Wooden Doors. Multicoloured.

1098	25d. Type **247**	35	35
1099	75d. Small door in left-hand panel and large bolt at right	85	85
1100	1r.50 Plain doors	1·80	1·80
1101	2r. Knocker at left and smaller door in right-hand panel	2·40	2·40
MS1102	100×70 mm. 3r. As No. 1101	16·00	16·00

248 Uruguay, 1930

2002. World Cup Football Championship, Japan and South Korea. Multicoloured.

1103	2r. Type **248**	2·10	2·10
1104	2r. Italy, 1934	2·10	2·10
1105	2r. France, 1938	2·10	2·10
1106	2r. Brasil, 1950	2·10	2·10
1107	2r. Switzerland, 1954	2·10	2·10
1108	2r. Sweden, 1958	2·10	2·10
1109	2r. Chile, 1962	2·10	2·10
1110	2r. England, 1966	2·10	2·10
1111	2r. Mexico, 1970	2·10	2·10
1112	2r. West Germany, 1974	2·10	2·10
1113	2r. Argentina, 1978	2·10	2·10
1114	2r. Spain, 1982	2·10	2·10
1115	2r. Mexico, 1986	2·10	2·10
1116	2r. Italy, 1990	2·10	2·10
1117	2r. USA, 1994	2·10	2·10
1118	2r. France, 1998	2·10	2·10
1119	2r. 2002 Championship emblem	2·10	2·10
1120	2r. World Cup trophy	2·10	2·10
MS1121	133×78 mm. Nos. 2019/20	5·75	5·75

249 Championship Emblem

2002. 14th Asian Games, Busan. Sheet 133×73 mm containing T **249** and similar vert design. Multicoloured.

MS1122	1r. Type **249**; 1r. 15th (2006) Asian Games championship emblem	5·75	5·75

250 Emblem

2002. First Anniv of Global Post Code. Multicoloured.

1123	**250**	1r. multicoloured	1·20	1·00
1124	**250**	3r. multicoloured	3·50	3·25

251 Runner, Heart and No-Smoking Sign

2003. World No-Smoking Day.

1125	**251**	1r.50 multicoloured	1·50	1·50

No. 1125 was printed using thermochromatic (heat sensitive) ink. When the image is pressed parts of the design disappear leaving only the runner visible.

252 Boy and Crescent

2003. 25th Anniv of Qatar Red Crescent (humanitarian organization). Multicoloured.

1126	75d. Type **252**	1·20	80
1127	75d. Building facade	1·20	80

253 Al Mashmoom (earrings)

2003. Jewellery. Multicoloured.

1128	25d. Type **253**	35	25
1129	25d. Al Mertash (necklace)	35	25
1130	50d. Khatim (ring)	60	45
1131	50d. Ishqab (earrings)	60	45
1132	1r.50 Shmailat (bangle)	2·00	1·60
1133	1r.50 Tassa (headdress)	2·00	1·60

254 *Wright Flyer*

2003. Centenary of Powered Flight. Sheet 110×76 mm containing T **254** and similar horiz designs. Multicoloured. P 14½.

MS1134	50d. ×4 Type **254**; Otto Lilienthal's glider; Qatar Airways Boeing A330; Airplane	2·00	2·00

255 Family and Emblems

2004. Tenth Anniv of International Year of the Family.

1135	**255**	2r.50 blue and light blue	2·30	2·30

256 FIFA Emblem

2004. Centenary of FIFA (Federation Internationale de Football Association).

1136	**256**	50d. multicoloured	45	45

257 Flag, Shaikh Hamad and Book

2004. Establishment of Permanent Constitution.

1137	**257**	75d. multicoloured	70	70

258 Athens 2004 and Olympic Emblems

2004. Olympic Games, Athens 2004. Sheet 72×72 mm containing T **258** and similar vert design. Multicoloured.

MS1138	3r. ×2, Type **258**; As Type **258** but with colours and face value reversed	5·75	5·75

259 Motorcyclist

2004. MotoGP 2004 Grand Prix, Qatar. Sheet 100×131 mm containing T **259** and similar horiz design. Multicoloured.

MS1139	3r. ×2, Type **259** ×2; 3r.50 ×2, Two motorcyclists	6·50	6·50

260 Emblem

2004

1140	**260**	50d. olive	45	45
1141	**260**	50d. green	45	45
1142	**260**	50d. brown	45	45
1143	**260**	50d. purple	45	45
1144	**260**	50d. blue	45	45

261 Hand holding Olive Branch

2004. National Human Rights Committee.

1145	**261**	50d. multicoloured	45	45

262 Al Sadd Sports Club

2004. 17th Arabian Gulf Cup. Sheet 100×100 mm containing T **262** and similar multicoloured designs.

MS1146	1r.50 ×5, Type **262**; Ball and player's legs (vert); Games emblem (35×35 mm); Goalkeeper (vert); Sudaifi (games mascot)	4·50	4·50

263 Orry

2004. 15th Asian Games, 2006, Doha. Official Mascot. Showing Orry (official mascot). Multicoloured. (a) Ordinary gum.

1147	50d. Type **263**	30	30
1148	1r. Sitting in dhow (horiz)	55	55
1149	1r.50 Marking off calender (horiz)	90	90
1150	2r. Carrying flaming torch	1·20	1·20
1151	3r. Lighting flame	1·80	1·80
1152	3r.50 Waving flag at Khalifa stadium	2·00	2·00

(b) Self-adhesive.

1153	50d. Type **263**	30	30
1154	1r. No. 1148 (horiz)	55	55
1155	1r.50 No. 1149 (horiz)	90	90
1156	2r. No. 1150	1·20	1·20
1157	3r. No. 1151	1·80	1·80
1158	3r.50 No. 1152	2·00	2·00

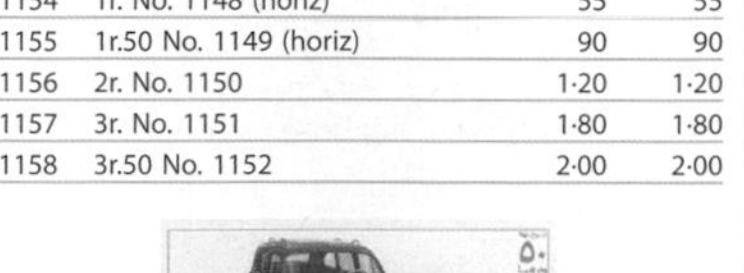

264 De Soto (1950)

2005. Classic Cars. Sheet 110×130 mm containing T **264** and similar horiz designs. Multicoloured.

MS1159	50d. ×8, Type **264**; Chevrolet (1958); Dodge Sedan (1938); Chrysler (1947); Dodge Power Wagon; Orange Chevrolet truck; Green Dodge truck; Two-tone Dodge truck	2·40	2·40

265 *Team Daedalus* Catamaran

2005. Oryx Quest 2005 (round the world sail race). Catamarans. Multicoloured.

1160	50d. Type **265**	30	30
1161	50d. With Qatar flag as sail	30	30
1162	50d. *Team Cheyenne* (vert)	30	30
1163	50d. *Team Geronimo* (vert)	30	30

266 Kiccoro and Morizo (exhibition mascots)

2005. Expo 2005 World Exposition, Aichi. Multicoloured.

1164	50d. Type **266**	30	30
1165	50d. Qatar flag	30	30

267 Emblem

2005. Doha Development Forum. Sheet 95×75 mm containing T **267** and similar horiz design. Multicoloured.

MS1166	6r.×2, Type **267**; Emblem (different)	6·50	6·50

268 Sheikh Hamad bin Khalifa al Thani

2005. Tenth Anniv of Accession of Emir Sheikh Hamad bin Khalifa al Thani. Sheet 160×53 mm.

MS1167	**268** 2r.50 multicoloured	1·60	1·60

269 Sarajevo and Doha

2005

1168	**269**	2r.50 multicoloured	1·60	1·60

270 Flag

2005. Self-adhesive.

1169	**270**	50d. purple	30	30
1170	**270**	1r. purple	55	55
1171	**270**	1r.50 purple	90	90
1172	**270**	2r.50 purple	1·50	1·50
1173	**270**	3r. purple	1·80	1·80
1174	**270**	3r.50 purple	2·00	2·00

271 Children

2005. Al Jazeera Children's Channel. Sheet 144×75 mm. Multicoloured.

MS1175	50d.×4, Type **271**; Air balloon; Runners; Family	1·20	1·20

The stamps and margins of **MS**1175 form a composite design.

272 Gold Emblem

2005. National Philatelic and Numismatic Club. Sheet 99×77 mm. Multicoloured.

MS1176	1r.×2, Type **272**; Silver emblem	1·30	1·30

273 Emblem

2005. Gulf Co-operation Council Stamp Exhibition, Doha. Multicoloured.

1177	1r. Type **273**	80	80
1178	1r. Envelope and stamp as figures	80	80

274 Fireman and Appliance

2006. International Civil Defence Day. Multicoloured.

1179	50d. Type **274**	30	30
1180	2r.50 Recuers on rope ladder and appliance	1·60	1·60
MS1181	130×146 mm. Nos. 1179/80, each×4	7·75	7·75

275 Flag

2006. 25th Anniv of Gulf Co-operation Council. Multicoloured.

1182	50d. Type **275**	30	30
MS1183	165×105 mm. 5r. Flags of member states. Imperf	3·25	3·25

Stamps of similar designs were issued by Kuwait, Oman, United Arab Emirates, Saudi Arabia and Bahrain.

276 Emblem

2006. World Cup Football Championship, Germany.

1184	**276**	2r. multicoloured	1·40	1·40

277 Torches

2006. Torch Relay. Dohar (2006).

1185	**277**	50d. multicoloured	30	30

278 Young Man and Child

2006. Volunteers. Dohar (2006).

1186	**278**	75d. multicoloured	50	50

279 Athletes Village

2006. Venues. Dohar 2006. Multicoloured.

1187	1r.50 Type **279**	95	95
1188	1r.50 Khalifa Stadium	95	95
1189	1r.50 Aspire facility	95	95
1190	1r.50 Al-dana Club	95	95
MS1191	126×179 mm. 5r. As Nos. 1187/90. Imperf	3·25	3·25

279a Runner

2006. Sports. Dohar 2006 (1st issue). Multicoloured.

1192	50d. Type **279a**	30	30
1193	50d. Judo combatants	30	30
1194	50d. Tennis player	30	30
1195	50d. Swimmer about to dive	30	30
1196	50d. Cyclist	30	30

280 Footballer and Ball

2006. Sports. Dohar 2006 (2nd issue). Multicoloured.

1197	50d. Type **280**	30	30
1198	50d. Orry cycling	30	30
1199	50d. Handball	30	30
1200	50d. Table tennis	30	30
1201	50d. Orry playing football	30	30

281 Racecourse

2007. Exceptional Meeting of General Assembly of Pan-Arab Equestrian Federation. Multicoloured.

1202	2d.50 Type **281**	1·60	1·60
MS1203	85×70 mm. 5d. Sheikh Hamad Bin Khalifa Al-Thani (vert)	3·25	3·25

282 Girl Athlete

2007. Doha 2016–Olympic and Paralympic Games Bid. Sheet 210×148 mm containing T **282** and similar square designs. Multicoloured.

MS1204	50d.×4, Type **282**; Boy crouched: Children with arms raised; Children with arms raised side view	1·40	1·40

283 Emblem and Flags of Member States

2007. Session of the Gulf Cooperation Council Supreme Council, Doha, 2007.

1205	**283**	50d. multicoloured	30	30

284 Symbol of Sheikh Jassim Bin Mohammad Bin Thani

2007. Rulers of Qatar. Sheet 140×120 mm containing T **284** and similar multicoloured designs.

MS1206	2r.50×7, Type **284**; Sheikh Hamad bin Khalifa Al-Thani (38×55 mm); As Type **284**; Sheikh Ali Bin Abdullah Al-Thani; Sheikh Abdullah Bin Qassim Al-Thani; Sheikh Khalifa bin Hamad Al-Thani; Sheikh Ahmed Bin Ali Bin Abdullah Al-Thani	9·75	9·75

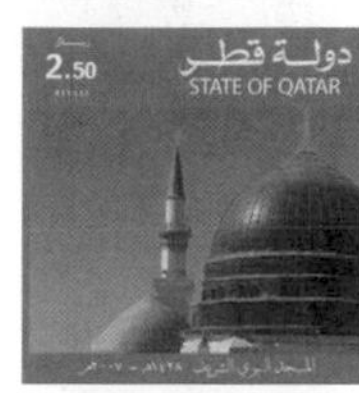
285 Green Dome, Al-Masjid al-Nabawi (Mosque of the Prophet), Medina

2007. Islamic Holy Places. Multicoloured.

1207	2r.50 Type **285**	1·60	1·60
1208	2r.50 Ka'ba and Black Stone, Mecca	1·60	1·60
1209	2r.50 Dome of the Rock (Qub-bat as-Sakhrah), Jerusalem	1·60	1·60
MS1210	95×60 mm. 5r. Composite image of Dome of the Rock, Ka'ba, Black Stone and Green Dome. Imperf	3·25	3·25

286 Emblem

2008. Arab Philatelic Exhibition, Doha. Multicoloured.

1211	50d. Type **286**	30	30
MS1212	90×115 mm. 5r. Emblem. Imperf	3·25	3·25

287 Al Marash

2008. Traditional Perfume. Sheet 181×84 mm containing T **287** and similar vert designs. Multicoloured.

MS1213	1r.50×4, Type **287**; Oud perfume oil; Agar wood; Al Moghass	3·75	3·75

The stamps and margins of **MS**1213 form a composite design and, when rubbed, release perfume .

288 Emblem

2008. Zaragoza 2008 International Water and Sustainable Development Exhibition. Sheet 210×148 mm containing T **288** and similar square designs. Multicoloured.

MS1214 50d.×4, Type **288**; As Type **288**; Fluvi (mascot); Fluvi enclosed in water droplet 1·30 1·30

289 Pigeon

2008. Arab Post Day. Sheet 170×60 mm containing T **289** and similar horiz designs. Multicoloured.

MS1215 5r.×2, Type **289**; Camels 6·50 6·50

290 Emblem

2008. Olympic Games, Beijing. Sheet 136×95 mm containing T **290** and similar multicoloured designs.

MS1216 50d.×2, Type **290**; As Type **290**; 3r. Emblem and athletes (70×36 mm) 2·50 2·50

291 Emblem

2008. 14th GCC Stamp Exhibition, Doha.

1217	**291**	50d. multicoloured	30	30

292 Emblem

2008. Police Day.

1218	**292**	50d. multicoloured (bistre)	30	30
1219	**292**	50d. multicoloured (white)	30	30

293 Museum Building

2008. Museum of Modern Art.

1220	**293**	50d. multicoloured	30	30
MS1221		100×75 mm 5r. As Type **293**	3·25	3·25

294 Waquif Souk

2008. Waquif Souk. Multicoloured.

1222	1r.50 Type **294**	1·10	1·10
1223	1r.50 Women	1·10	1·10
1224	1r.50 Man and shops	1·10	1·10
1225	1r.50 Man and tower	1·10	1·10

295 City Skyline

2009. Towards a Responsible Media.

1226	**295**	50d. multicoloured	40	40

296 Tears

2009. Tears for Gaza. Multicoloured.

1227	1r. Type **296**	70	70
MS1228	115×57 mm. 10r. Tears and wire. Imperf	7·25	7·25

297 Emblem

2009. Tenth Anniv of Democratic Elections.

1229	**297**	50d. multicoloured	40	40

298 Emblem

2009. al-Quds—2009 Capital of Arab Culture.

1230	**298**	1r. multicoloured	85	85

298a RasGas Emblem

2009. Rasgas - Celebrating Train 6 Inauguration and Tenth Annivf of LNG Sales. Multicoloured.

MS1230a 1r.×3, Type **298a**; Globe; Globe containing '6' 1·50 1·50

299 Woodchat Shrike

2009. Birds. Multicoloured.

1231	50d. Type **299**	30	30
1232	50d. Chiffchaf	30	30
1233	50d. Yellow wagtail	30	30
1234	50d. Orphean warbler	30	30
1235	50d. Isabelline shrike	30	30
1236	50d. Lesser grey shrike	30	30
1237	50d. Orphean warbler (head)	30	30
1238	50d. Woodchat shrike (head)	30	30
1239	50d. Isabelline shrike (head)	30	30
1240	50d. Lesser grey shrike (head)	30	30
1241	50d. Chiffchaf (head)	30	30
1242	50d. Yellow wagtail (head)	30	30
MS1243	98×60 mm. 5r. Cream-coloured courser	2·75	2·75

300 Anniversary Emblem

2010. 50th Anniv of Organization of Petroleum Exporting Countries (OPEC)

1244	**300**	1r. multicoloured	60	60

301 Calligraphy

2010. Mus-Haf Qatar (new printing of the Koran) - 2010

1245	**301**	3r. multicoloured	1·75	1·75

302 Census Emblem

2010. Population and Housing Census 2010

1246	**302**	1r. new blue, apple-green and grey	60	60

303 Congress Emblem

2010. 25th Universal Postal Union Congress, Doha - 2012 (1st series)

1247	**303**	50d. multicoloured	30	30

304 Cavalry and Emblem

2010. Doha - Capital of Arab Culture 2010. Multicoloured.

MS1248	125×100 mm. 1r.50×4, Type **304**; Masks and emblem; Page and emblem; Lute and emblem	3·50	3·50
MS1249	60×100 mm. 5r. Emblem as flower. Imperf	3·50	3·50

305 Museum of Islamic Art, Doha

2010. Aga Khan Award for Architecture. Sheet 135×85 mm

MS1250 **305** 1r.50 multicoloured 1·00 1·00

306 Storage enclosed in '77'

2010. Celebrating supplying 77 Million Tonnes of LNG per Annum. Multicoloured.

MS1251	1r. Type **306**	60	60
MS1252	1r. '77' enclosing calligraphy	60	60
MS1253	1r. '77' made of national flag with towers in background	60	60
MS1254	1r. '77' enclosing ship and refinery in background	60	60

307 Emblem

2010. 35th Anniv of Qatar News Agency

MS1255 **307** 1r. multicoloured 1·00 1·00

308 International Amateur Radio Union and Qatar Amateur Radio Society Emblems

2010. Qatar Amateur Radio Society

1256	**308**	50d. multicoloured	1·00	1·00

309 Emblem

2011. Arab Deaf Week

1257	**309**	1r. multicoloured	1·00	1·00

310 '50' and Umm Said

2011. 50th Anniv of First Postal Agency

1258	**310**	50d. multicoloured	1·00	1·00

2011. 25th Universal Postal Union Congress, Doha - 2012 (2nd series)

1259	**303**	1r. multicoloured (green)	1·00	1·00

311 Championship Emblem

2011. Qatar Classic Squash Championship

1260	**311**	1r. multicoloured (yellow)	60	60
1261	**311**	1r. multicoloured (green)	60	60
1262	**311**	1r. multicoloured (blue)	60	60
1263	**311**	1r. multicoloured (pink)	60	60

312 Calligraphy and 'DOHA 2011'

2011. Arab Games - Doha 2011. Multicoloured.

1264	50d. Type **312**	30	30
1265	50d. 'WHERE EVERYTHING COMES TOGETHER'	30	30
1266	50d. Calligraphy	30	30

POSTAGE DUE STAMPS

D40

1968

D254	**D40**	5d. blue	38·00	38·00
D255	**D40**	10d. red	43·00	43·00
D256	**D40**	20d. green	55·00	55·00
D257	**D40**	30d. lilac	60·00	60·00

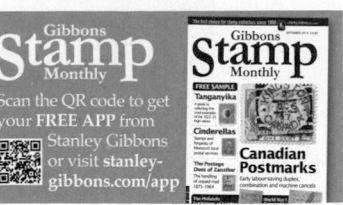

Pt. 1

QU'AITI STATE IN HADHRAMAUT

The stamps of Aden were used in Qu'aiti State in Hadhramaut from 22 April 1937 until 1942.

1937. 16 annas = 1 rupee.
1951. 100 cents = 1 shilling.
1966. 1000 fils = 1 dinar.

(I) Issues inscribed "SHIHR and MUKALLA"

1 Sultan of Shihr and Mukalla

2 Mukalla Harbour

1942

1	1	½a. green	1·75	50
2	1	¾a. brown	2·50	30
3	1	1a. blue	1·00	1·00
4	2	1½a. red	2·00	50
5	-	2a. brown	2·00	1·75
6	-	2½a. blue	50	30
7	-	3a. brown and red	1·25	1·00
8	-	8a. red	1·25	40
9	-	1r. green	7·50	4·50
10	-	2r. blue and purple	17·00	15·00
11	-	5r. brown and green	38·00	20·00

DESIGNS—VERT: 2a. Gateway of Shihr; 3a. Outpost of Mukalla; 1r. Du'an. HORIZ: 2½a. Shibam; 8a. 'Einat; 2r. Mosque in Hureidha; 5r. Meshhed.

1946. Victory. Optd **VICTORY ISSUE 8TH JUNE 1946**.

12	2	1½a. red	15	1·25
13	-	2½a. blue	15	20

1949. Royal Silver Wedding. As T **8b/c** of Pitcairn Islands.

14	1½a. red	50	4·50
15	5r. green	17·00	14·00

1949. U.P.U. As T **8d/g** of Pitcairn Islands surch.

16	2½a. on 20c. blue	15	50
17	3a. on 30c. red	1·40	2·50
18	8a. on 50c. orange	25	2·50
19	1r. on 1s. blue	30	50

1951. Stamps of 1942 surch in cents or shillings.

20	5c. on 1a. blue	15	30
21	10c. on 2a. sepia	15	30
22	15c. on 2½a. blue	15	30
23	20c. on 3a. sepia and red	30	1·00
24	50c. on 8a. red	50	2·75
25	1s. on 1r. green	2·25	55
26	2s. on 2r. blue and purple	8·50	32·00
27	5s. on 5r. brown and green	19·00	45·00

1953. Coronation. As T **8h** of Pitcairn Islands.

28	15c. black and blue	1·00	55

(II) Issues inscribed "HADHRAMAUT"

11 Metal Work

1955. Occupations. Portrait as in T **11**.

29	11	5c. blue	1·00	10
30	-	10c. black (Mat-making)	1·00	10
31a	-	15c. green (Weaving)	70	40
32	-	25c. red (Pottery)	50	10
33	-	35c. blue (Building)	1·00	10
34a	-	50c. orange (Date cultivation)	70	30
35	-	90c. brown (Agriculture)	70	15
36	-	1s. black and orange (Fisheries) (horiz)	1·00	10
37	-	1s.25 black and orange (Lime-burning) (horiz)	75	55
38	-	2s. black and blue (Dhow building) (horiz)	4·00	60
39	-	5s. black and green (Agriculture) (horiz)	5·00	2·00
40	-	10s. black and red (as No. 37) (horiz)	15·00	8·00

22 Metal Work

1963. Occupations. As Nos. 29/40 but with inset portrait of Sultan Awadh bin Saleh el Qu'aiti, as in T **22**.

41	22	5c. blue	10	1·75
42	-	10c. black	10	1·50
43	-	15c. green	10	1·75
44	-	25c. red	15	75
45	-	35c. blue	15	2·00
46	-	50c. orange	15	1·00
47	-	70c. brown (As No. 35)	20	75
48	-	1s. black and lilac	25	30
49	-	1s.25 black and orange	60	6·50
50	-	2s. black and blue	3·25	2·25
51	-	5s. black and green	15·00	30·00
52	-	10s. black and red	30·00	30·00

1966. Nos. 41/52 surch **SOUTH ARABIA** in English and Arabic, with value and bar.

53	5	5f. on 5c.	10	1·25
54	-	5f. on 10c.	1·00	1·75
55	-	10f. on 15c.	10	1·00
56	-	15f. on 25c.	10	1·75
57	-	20f. on 35c.	10	2·50
58	-	25f. on 50c.	10	1·00
59	-	35f. on 70c.	10	1·00
60	-	50f. on 1s.	65	30
61	-	65f. on 1s.25	1·50	40
62	-	100f. on 2s.	4·25	1·25
63	-	250f. on 5s.	2·25	1·50
64	-	500f. on 10s.	26·00	3·00

1966. Churchill Commemoration. Nos. 54/6 optd **1874–1965 WINSTON CHURCHILL**.

65	5f. on 10c.	8·00	17·00
66	10f. on 15c.	9·00	18·00
67	15f. on 25c.	10·00	18·00

1966. President Kennedy Commemoration. Nos. 57/9 optd **1917–63 JOHN F. KENNEDY**.

68	20f. on 35c.	1·25	6·00
69	25f. on 50c.	1·25	6·50
70	35f. on 70c.	1·25	7·50

25 World Cup Emblem

1966. World Cup Football Championship.

71	25	5f. purple and orange	2·25	25
72	-	10f. violet and green	2·50	25
73	-	15f. purple and orange	2·75	30
74	-	20f. violet and green	3·00	30
75	25	25f. green and red	3·25	30
76	-	35f. blue and yellow	3·75	35
77	-	50f. green and red	4·25	40
78	25	65f. blue and yellow	5·00	40
MS78a		110×110 mm. Nos. 77/8	48·00	7·50

DESIGNS: 10, 35f. Wembley Stadium; 15, 50f. Footballers; 20f. Jules Rimet Cup and football.

29 Mexican Hat and Basket

1966. Pre-Olympic Games, Mexico (1968).

79	29	75f. sepia and green	1·25	75

30 Telecommunications Satellite

1966. International Co-operation Year.

80	30	5f. mauve, purple and green	2·75	35
81	-	10f. multicoloured	3·00	30
82	-	15f. purple, blue and red	3·25	35
83	30	20f. blue, purple and red	3·50	40
84	-	25f. multicoloured	3·50	40
85	30	35f. purple, red and blue	4·00	40
86	-	50f. purple, green and red	4·75	45
87	30	65f. brown, violet and red	5·50	45

DESIGNS: 10f. Olympic runner (inscr "ROME 1960"); 15f. Fishes; 25f. Olympic runner (inscr "TOKIO 1964"); 50f. Tobacco plant.

APPENDIX

The following stamps have either been issued in excess of postal needs or have not been made available to the public in reasonable quantities at face value.

1967

Stampex, London. Postage 5, 10, 15, 20, 25f.; Air 50, 65f.
Amphilex International Stamp Exhibition, Amsterdam. Air 75f.
Olympic Games, Mexico (1968). 75f.
Paintings. Postage 5, 10, 15, 20, 25f.; Air 50, 65f.
Scout Jamboree, Idaho. Air 35f.
Space Research. Postage 10, 25, 35, 50, 75f.; Air 100, 250f.

The National Liberation Front is said to have taken control of Qu'aiti State in Hadhramaut on 17 September 1967.

Pt. 1

QUEENSLAND

The north eastern state of the Commonwealth of Australia whose stamps it now uses.

12 pence = 1 shilling; 20 shillings = 1 pound.

1

1860. Imperf.

1	1	1d. red	£6000	£800
2	1	2d. blue	£14000	£1700
3	1	6d. green	£10000	£800

1860. Perf.

94	1d. red	70·00	6·00
99	2d. blue	65·00	1·75
65	3d. green	£170	6·00
101	3d. brown	£110	9·50
103	4d. yellow	£1400	35·00
54	4d. grey	£375	26·00
55	4d. lilac	£375	18·00
27	6d. green	£160	12·00
29	1s. grey	£325	22·00
108	1s. purple	90·00	9·00
119	2s. blue	£140	60·00
121	2s.6d. red	£300	80·00
58	5s. red	£850	£110
123	5s. yellow	£400	£120
125	10s. brown	£750	£200
127	20s. red	£1500	£250

7

1879

134	7	1d. brown	80·00	9·00
135	7	1d. orange	60·00	9·50
136	7	1d. red	55·00	8·50
138	7	2d. blue	75·00	3·00
141	7	4d. yellow	£300	16·00
142	7	6d. green	£160	7·00
145	7	1s. mauve	£150	13·00

1880. Nos. 136 surch **Half-penny**.

151	½d. on 1d. brown	£300	£170

9

1882

152	9	2s. blue	£225	65·00
158	9	2s.6d. orange	50·00	27·00
159	9	5s. red	48·00	42·00
160	9	10s. brown	£120	50·00
161	9	£1 green	£300	85·00

13

14

12

1882. Shaded background around head.

185	13	½d. green	12·00	2·00
206	12	1d. orange	2·50	2·25
204	12	2d. blue	6·00	60
191	14	2½d. red	15·00	2·50
192	12	3d. brown	9·00	4·00
193	12	4d. yellow	16·00	3·50
196	12	6d. green	11·00	2·00
173	12	1s. mauve	22·00	6·00
197	12	2s. brown	42·00	45·00

15

16

17

1895. Head on white background.

208	15	½d. green	3·00	1·75
210	16	1d. red	3·50	50
212	16	2d. blue	32·00	50
213	17	2½d. red	23·00	5·50
215	17	5d. brown	26·00	5·00

19

1896

229	19	1d. red	18·00	70

21

1897. Same designs, but figures in all four corners, as T **21**.

286	½d. green	1·75	4·25
232	1d. red	2·50	40
234	2d. blue	7·00	40
236	2½d. red	17·00	27·00
238	2½d. purple on blue	9·50	3·25
241	3d. brown	8·00	3·00
244	4d. yellow	11·00	3·25
294	4d. black	23·00	6·50
246	5d. brown	8·50	3·00
250	6d. green	7·00	3·50
298	1s. mauve	20·00	3·50
254	2s. green	32·00	40·00

26

1899

262*a*	26	½d. green	2·50	2·50

27

1900. S. African War Charity. Inscr "PATRIOTIC FUND 1900".

264a	27	1d. (1s.) (6d.) mauve	£140	£120
264b	-	2d. (2s.) (1s.) violet (horiz)	£350	£275

28

1903

266	28	9d. brown and blue	38·00	7·00

REGISTRATION STAMP

1861. Inscr "REGISTERED"

20	1	(No value) yellow	£110	40·00

Pt. 9

QUELIMANE

A district of Portuguese E. Africa, now part of Mozambique, whose stamps it now uses.

100 centavos = 1 escudo.

1913. Surch **REPUBLICA QUELIMANE** and new value on "Vasco da Gama" stamps of (a) Portuguese Colonies.

1	¼c. on 2½r. green	2·75	2·00
2	½c. on 5r. red	2·75	2·00
3	1c. on 10r. purple	2·75	2·00
4	2½c. on 25r. green	2·75	2·00
5	5c. on 50r. blue	2·75	2·00
6	7½c. on 75r. brown	4·75	2·75
7	10c. on 100r. brown	3·00	1·50
8	15c. on 150r. brown	3·00	1·50

(b) Macao.

9	¼c. on ½a. green	2·75	2·00
10	½c. on 1a. red	2·75	2·00
11	1c. on 2a. purple	2·75	2·00
12	2½c. on 4a. green	2·75	2·00
13	5c. on 8a. blue	2·75	2·00
14	7½c. on 12a. brown	4·75	2·75
15	10c. on 16a. brown	3·00	1·50
16	15c. on 24a. brown	3·00	1·50

(c) Portuguese Timor.

17	¼c. on ½a. green	2·75	2·00
18	½c. on 1a. red	2·75	2·00
19	1c. on 2a. purple	2·75	2·00
20	2½c. on 2a. green	2·75	2·00
21	5c. on 8a. blue	2·75	2·00
22	7½c. on 12a. brown	4·75	2·75
23	10c. on 16a. brown	3·00	1·50
24	15c. on 24a. brown	3·00	1·50

1914. "Ceres" key-type inscr "QUELIMANE".

25	U	¼c. green	1·20	1·10
26	U	½c. black	2·30	1·50
42	U	1c. green	2·10	1·60
28	U	1½c. brown	3·00	1·90
29	U	2c. red	3·00	2·30
30	U	2¼c. violet	1·20	85
31	U	5c. blue	2·10	1·60
43	U	7½c. brown	2·10	1·60
33	U	8c. grey	2·50	1·90
44	U	10c. red	2·10	1·60
35	U	15c. purple	3·50	3·00
45	U	20c. green	2·10	1·60
37	U	30c. brown on green	5·25	4·00
38	U	40c. brown on pink	5·75	4·00
39	U	50c. orange on orange	5·75	4·00
40	U	1e. green on blue	6·50	4·50

Pt. 1

RAJASTHAN

Formed in 1948 from states in Rajputana, India, which included Bundi, Jaipur and Kishangarh whose separate posts functioned until 1 April 1950. Now uses Indian stamps.

12 pies = 1 anna; 16 annas = 1 rupee.

JAIPUR

(1)

1949. Nos. 86/92 of Bundi or optd with T 1.

1A	21	¼a. green	8·50	£140
2B	21	½a. violet	8·50	70·00
3A	21	1a. green	8·00	65·00
11	-	2a. red	20·00	£110
12	-	4a. orange	7·00	£110
6A	-	8a. blue	15·00	
14	-	1r. brown	8·50	

JAIPUR

राजस्थान

RAJASTHAN
(2)

1949. Stamps of Jaipur optd with T 2.

15	7	¼a. black and purple	13·00	30·00
16	7	½a. black and violet	12·00	30·00
17	7	¾a. black and orange	12·00	38·00
18	7	1a. black and blue	12·00	70·00
19	7	2a. black and orange	12·00	95·00
20	7	2½a. black and red	12·00	45·00
21	7	3a. black and green	13·00	£110
22	7	4a. black and green	12·00	£130
23	7	6a. black and blue	12·00	£170
24	7	8a. black and brown	17·00	£225
25	7	1r. black and bistre	27·00	£375

KISHANGARH

(a) On stamps of 1899

26a	2	¼a. pink	—	£500
27	2	½a. blue	£1400	
29	2	1a. lilac	20·00	60·00
30	2	4a. brown	£130	£170
31	2	1r. green	£600	£600
31a	2	2r. red	£650	£650
32	2	5r. mauve	£650	£650

(b) On stamps of 1904.

33	13	½a. brown	—	£400
33a	13	1a. blue	—	£450
34	13	4a. brown	13·00	
35	2	8a. grey	£180	£300
36	13	8a. violet	11·00	
37	13	1r. green	12·00	
38	13	2r. yellow	19·00	
39	13	5r. brown	38·00	

(c) On stamps of 1912

40	14	½a. green	£650	£400
41	14	1a. red	—	£500
43	14	2a. purple	6·00	15·00
44	14	4a. blue	—	£1200
45	14	8a. brown	5·00	
46	14	1r. mauve	10·00	
47	14	2r. green	10·00	
48	14	5r. brown	£650	

(d) On stamps of 1928

51	16	8a. violet	6·50	80·00
53	16	2r. yellow	17·00	
54	16	5r. red	16·00	

(e) On stamps of 1943

56	16	¼a. blue	80·00	80·00
57	16	½a. green	45·00	48·00
58	-	1a. red	£200	£180
59	-	2a. purple	£425	£425
61	16	4a. brown	6·00	15·00
63	16	1r. green	6·50	

Pt. 1

RAJPIPLA

A state of Bombay, India. Now uses Indian stamps.

12 pies = 1 anna; 12 annas = 1 rupee.

The Rajpipla state post was opened to the public sometime in the late 1870s. Adhesive stamps were preceded by postal stationery lettersheets which were first opened in 1879.

1 (1 pice)

2 (2a.)

1880

1	1	1p. blue	7·00	55·00
2	2	2a. green	38·00	£170
3	2	4a. red	20·00	£110

Pt. 1

RAROTONGA

Island in the South Pacific.

1 Whale-watching

2011. Tourism. Island Views. Multicoloured.

1	10c. Type **1**	25	30
2	20c. Palm trees and sailing boat	45	50
3	30c. Starfish	60	75
4	50c. Sunset (on cloudy day)	95	1·00
5	70c. Crab	1·50	1·60
6	80c. Prow of boat with Cook Islands flag	1·75	1·90
7	90c. Windsurfer off beach and aircraft	1·75	1·90
8	$1 Sunset (sun reflected in sea)	1·90	2·00
9	$1.10 Forested mountain and aircraft	1·90	2·00
10	$1.20 Promontory with beach and palm trees	2·00	2·10
11	$1.50 Goat	2·00	2·10
12	$2 Cockerel	2·25	2·50
13	$3 Beach with offshore island	2·50	2·75
14	$4 School of sergeant major fish	2·50	2·75
15	$5 Aerial view of Rarotonga and ferry	2·75	3·00
MS16	240×181 mm. Nos. 1/15	25·00	27·00

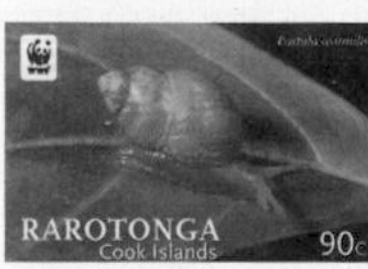

2 *Partula assimilis*

2012. Endangered Species. Land Snails. Multicoloured.

17	90c. Type **2**	1·75	1·90
18	$1.20 *Libera fratercula*	2·00	2·10
19	$1.50 *Lamprocystis globosa*	2·00	2·10
20	$2.70 *Sinployea peasei*	2·25	2·50

Pt. 19

RAS AL KHAIMA

Arab Shaikhdom in the Arabian Gulf. Ras al Khaima joined the United Arab Emirates in February 1972 and U.A.E. stamps were used in the shaikhdom from 1 January 1973.

1964. 100 naye paise = 1 rupee.
1966. 100 dirhams = 1 riyal.

1 Shaikh Saqr bin Mohamed al-Qasimi

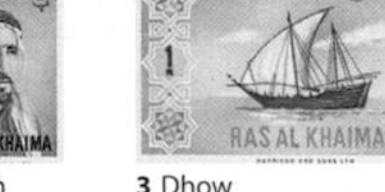

3 Dhow

1964

1	1	5n.p. brown and black	10	10
2	1	15n.p. blue and black	20	20
3	-	30n.p. brown and black	35	35
4	-	40n.p. blue and black	55	45
5	-	75n.p. red and black	1·30	90
6	3	1r. brown and green	1·90	1·30
7	3	2r. brown and violet	4·00	2·75
8	3	5r. brown and blue	12·50	8·25

DESIGNS—As Type **1**: 30n.p. to 75n.p. Seven palms.

3a Pres. Kennedy inspecting "Friendship 7"

1965. Pres. Kennedy Commemoration.

9	3a	2r. blue and brown	1·30	1·30
10	-	3r. blue and brown	2·20	2·20
11	-	4r. blue and brown	3·25	3·25

MS11a Three sheets 140×108 or 108×140 mm. 1r. stamps in block of four as Nos. 9/11 — 14·50 — 13·50

DESIGNS—HORIZ: 3r. Kennedy and wife. VERT: 4r. Kennedy and flame of remembrance.

4 Sir Winston Churchill and Houses of Parliament

1965. Churchill Commemoration.

12	4	2r. blue and brown	1·30	1·30
13	-	3r. blue and brown	2·20	2·20
14	-	4r. blue and brown	3·25	3·25

MS14a Three sheets 140×108 or 108×140 mm. 1r. stamps in blocks of four as Nos. 12/14 — 12·50 — 6·75

DESIGNS—HORIZ: 3r. Churchill and Pres. Roosevelt; 4r. Churchill, and Heads of State at his funeral.

1965. Olympic Games, Tokyo (1964). Optd **OLYMPIC TOKYO 1964** in English and Arabic and Olympic "rings".

15	3	1r. brown and green	80	80
16	3	2r. brown and violet	1·70	1·70
17	3	5r. brown and blue	4·25	4·25

1965. Death Centenary of Abraham Lincoln. Optd **ABRAHAM LINCOLN 1809-1865** in English and Arabic.

18	1r. brown and green	80	80
19	2r. brown and violet	1·70	1·70
20	5r. brown and blue	4·25	4·25

1965. 20th Death Anniv of Pres. Roosevelt. Optd **FRANKLIN D. ROOSEVELT 1882-1945** in English and Arabic.

21	1r. brown and green	80	80
22	2r. brown and violet	1·70	1·70
23	5r. brown and blue	4·25	4·25

8 Satellite and Tracking Station

1966. I.T.U. Centenary. Multicoloured.

24	15n.p. Type **8**	35	20
25	50n.p. Post Office Tower, London, "Telstar" and tracking gantry	55	35
26	85n.p. Rocket on launching-pad and "Relay"	1·20	45
27	1r. Type **8**	1·50	55
28	2r. As 50n.p.	2·50	65
29	3r. As 85n.p.	3·00	1·30
MS30	110×80 mm. 5r. Globe and satellites (53×33 mm). Imperf	5·50	3·25

9 Swimming

1966. Pan-Arab Games, Cairo (1965).

31	A	1n.p. brown, pink and green	10	10
32	B	2n.p. black, grey and green	10	10
33	C	3n.p. brown, pink and green	10	10
34	D	4n.p. brown, pink and purple	10	10
35	A	5n.p. black, grey and orange	15	10
36	9	10n.p. brown, pink and blue	20	15
37	B	25n.p. brown, pink and cinnamon	55	20
38	C	50n.p. black, grey and violet	1·10	55
39	D	75n.p. black, grey and blue	1·80	80
40	9	1r. black, grey and green	2·50	1·00

MS41 D 100×85 mm. 5r. violet, blue and yellow. Imperf — 7·25 — 6·75

DESIGNS: A, Running; B, Boxing; C, Football; D, Fencing.

10 Carpenter

1966. American Astronauts.

42	10	25n.p. black, gold and purple	20	10
43	-	50n.p. black, silver & brown	35	20
44	-	75n.p. black, silver and blue	55	30
45	-	1r. black, silver and bistre	80	35
46	-	2r. black, silver and mauve	1·70	90
47	-	3r. black, gold and green	2·50	1·20
48	-	4r. black, gold and red	3·25	1·80
49	-	5r. black, gold and blue	4·00	2·10

MS50 Two sheets each 156×106 mm containing stamps as Nos. 42/5 and 46/9 but without face values. Imperf (sold at 4e. each) — 9·50 — 4·00

ASTRONAUTS: 50n.p. Glenn; 75n.p. Shepard; 1r. Cooper; 2r. Grissom; 3r. Schirra; 4r. Stafford; 5r. Lovell.

11 Shaikh Sabah of Kuwait and Shaikh Saqr of Ras al Khaima

1966. International Co-operation Year.

51	11	1r. black and red	90	45

52	A	1r. black and lilac	90	45
53	B	1r. black and pink	90	45
54	C	1r. black and green	90	45
55	D	1r. black and green	90	45
56	E	1r. black and yellow	90	45
57	F	1r. black and orange	90	45
58	G	1r. black and blue	90	45

MS59 Two sheets each 127×115 mm. Nos. 51/4 and 55/8. Imperf 8·25 4·25

SHAIKH SAQR AND WORLD LEADERS: A, Shaikh Ahmad of Qatar; B, Pres. Nasser; C, King Hussein; D, Pres. Johnson; E, Pres. De Gaulle; F, Pope Paul VI; G, Prime Minister Harold Wilson.

NEW CURRENCY SURCHARGES. During the latter half of 1966 various issues appeared surcharged in dirhams and riyals. The 1964 definitives with this surcharge are listed below as there is considerable evidence of their postal use. Nos. 24/58 also exist with these surcharges.

In August 1966 Nos. 1/14, 24/9 and 51/8 appeared surcharged in fils and rupees. As Ras Al Khaima did not adopt this currency their status is uncertain.

1966. Nos. 1/8 with currency names changed to dirhams and riyals by overprinting in English and Arabic.

60	1	5d. on 5n.p. brown and black	10	10
60a	-	5d. on 75n.p. red and black	45	35
64b	3	5d. on 5r. brown and blue	45	35
61	1	15d. on 15n.p. blue & black	45	40
62	-	30d. on 30n.p. brown and black	90	80
63	-	40d. on 40n.p. blue & black	1·20	1·10
64	-	75d. on 75n.p. red and black	2·20	2·10
65	3	1r. on 1r. brown and green	1·80	1·70
66	3	2r. on 2r. brown and violet	3·75	3·25
67	3	5r. on 5r. brown and blue	7·25	6·25

15 W.H.O. Building and Flowers

1966. Inauguration of W.H.O. Headquarters, Geneva.

68	15	15d. multicoloured (postage)	35	15
69	-	35d. multicoloured	1·00	20
70	15	50d. multicoloured (air)	1·10	45
71	-	3r. multicoloured	3·25	1·10

MS72 79×72 mm. No. 71. Imperf 5·00 2·20

DESIGN: 35d., 3r. As Type **15** but with red instead of yellow flowers at left.

16 Queen Elizabeth II presenting Jules Rimet Cup to Bobby Moore, Captain of England Team

1966. Air. England's Victory in World Cup Football Championship. Multicoloured.

73	1r. Wembley Stadium	1·10	45
74	2r. Goalkeeper saving ball	1·90	90
75	3r. Footballers with ball	2·75	1·30
76	4r. Type **16**	3·75	2·50

MS77 Two sheets each 90×80 mm. Nos. 73 and 76. Imperf 10·00 7·75

17 Shaikh Saqr

18 Oil Rig

1971

78	17	5d. multicoloured
79	18	20d. multicoloured
80	17	30d. multicoloured

For later issues see **UNITED ARAB EMIRATES**.

APPENDIX

The following stamps have either been issued in excess of postal needs or have not been available to the public in reasonable quantities at face value. Such stamps may later be given full listing if there is evidence of regular postal use.

1967

"The Arabian Nights". Paintings. Air 30, 70d., 1, 2, 3r.
Cats. Postage 1, 2, 3, 4, 5d.; Air 3r.
Arab Paintings. 1, 2, 3, 4, 10, 20, 30d.
European Paintings. Air 60, 70d., 1, 2, 3, 5, 10r.
50th Birth Anniv of Pres. John F. Kennedy. Optd on 1965 Pres. Kennedy Commem. 2, 3, 4r.
World Scout Jamboree, Idaho. Postage 1, 2, 3, 4d.; Air 35, 75d., 1r.
U.S. "Apollo" Disaster. Optd on 1966 American Astronauts issue. 25d. on 25n.p., 50d. on 50n.p., 75d. on 75n.p., 1, 2, 3, 4, 5r.
Summer Olympics Preparation, Mexico 1968. Postage 10, 20, 30, 40d.; Air 1, 2r.
Winter Olympics Preparation, Grenoble 1968. Postage 1, 2, 3, 4, 5d.; Air 85d., 2, 3r.

1968

Mothers' Day. Paintings. Postage 20, 30, 40, 50d.; Air 1, 2, 3, 4r.
International Human Rights Year. 2r.×3.
International Museum Campaign. Paintings. 15, 15, 20, 25, 35, 40, 45, 60, 70, 80, 90d.; 1, 1r.25, 1r.50, 2r.50, 2r.75.
Winter Olympic Medal Winners, Grenoble. 50d., 1, 1r.50, 2, 2r.50, 3r.
Olympic Games, Mexico. Air 1, 2, 2, 3, 3, 4r. 5th Death Anniv of Pres. John F. Kennedy. Air. 2, 3r.
Christmas. Religious Paintings. Postage 20, 30, 40, 50, 60d., 1r.; Air 2, 3, 4r.

1969

Famous Composers (1st series). Paintings. 25, 50, 75d., 1r.50, 2r.50.
Famous Operas. 20, 40, 60, 80d., 1, 2r.
Famous Men. Postage 20, 30, 50d.; Air 1r.50, 2, 3, 4, 5r.
International Philatelic Exhibition, Mexico 1968 (EFIMEX). Postage 10, 10, 25, 35, 40, 50, 60, 70d.; Air 1, 2, 3, 5, 5r.
Int Co-operation in Olympics. 1, 2, 3, 4r.
International Co-operation in Space. Air 1r.50, 2r.50, 3r.50, 4r.50.
Birth Bicentenary of Napoleon. Paintings. Postage 1r.75, 2r.75, 3r.75; Air 75d.
"Apollo" Moon Missions. Air 2, 2r.50, 3, 3r.50, 4, 4r.50, 5, 5r.50.
"Apollo 11" Astronauts. Air 2r.25, 3r.25, 4r.25, 5r.25.
"Apollo 12" Astronauts. Air 60d., 2r.60, 3r.60, 4r.60, 5r.60.

1970

Christmas 1969. Religious Paintings. Postage 50d.; Air 3, 3r.50.
World Cup, Mexico. Air 1, 2, 3, 4, 5, 6r.
Easter. Religious Paintings. Postage 50d.; Air 3, 3r.50.
Paintings by Titian and Tiepolo. Postage 50, 50d.; Air 3, 3, 3r.50, 3r.50.
Winter Olympics, Sapporo 1972. Air 1, 2, 3, 4, 5, 6r.
Olympic Games, Munich 1972. Air 1, 2, 3, 4, 5, 6r.
Paul Gauguin's Paintings. Postage 50d.; Air 3, 3r.50.
Christmas. Religious Paintings. Postage 50d.; Air 3, 3r.50.
"World Cup Champions, Brazil". Optd on Mexico World Cup issue. Air 1, 2, 3, 4, 5, 6r.
"EXPO 70" World Fair, Osaka, Japan (1st issue). Postage 40, 45, 50, 55, 60, 65, 70, 75d.; Air 80, 85, 90, 95d., 1r.60, 1r.65, 1r.85, 2r.
"EXPO 70" World Fair, Osaka, Japan (2nd issue). Postage 55, 65, 75d.; Air 25, 85, 95d., 1r.50, 1r.75.
Space Programmes. Air 1r.×6, 2r.×6, 4r.×6.
Famous Frenchmen. Air 1r.×4, 2r.×4, 2r.50×2, 3r.×2, 4r.×4, 5r.50×2.
Int Philatelic Exn (Philympia '70). Air 1r.×4, 1r.50×4, 2r.50×4, 3r.×4, 4r.×4.
Events in the Life of Christ. Religious Paintings. 5, 10, 25, 50d., 1, 2, 5r.
"Stages of the Cross". Religious Paintings. 10, 20, 30, 40, 50, 60, 70, 80d., 1, 1r.50, 2, 2r.50, 3, 3r.50.
The Life of Mary. Religious Paintings. 10, 15, 30, 60, 75d., 3, 4r.

1971

Easter. "Stages of the Cross" (1970) but with additional inscr "EASTER". 10, 20, 30, 40, 50, 60, 70, 80d., 1, 1r.50, 2, 2r.50, 3, 3r.50.
Charles de Gaulle Memorial. Postage 50d.; Air 1, 1r.50, 2, 3, 4r.
Safe Return of "Apollo 14". Postage 50d.; Air 1, 1r.50, 2, 3, 4r.
U.S.A.–Japan Baseball Friendship. Postage 10, 25, 30, 80d.; Air 50, 70d., 1, 1r.50.
Munich Olympics, 1972. Postage 50d.; Air 1, 1r.50, 2, 3, 4r.
Cats. 35, 60, 65, 110, 120, 160d.
13th World Jamboree, Japan. Postage 30, 50, 60, 75d.; Air 1, 1r.50, 3, 4r.
Sapporo Olympic Gold Medal Winners. Optd on 1970 Winter Olympics, Sapporo 1972, issue. Air 1, 2, 3, 4, 5, 6r.
Munich Olympic Medal Winners, Optd on 1970 Summer Olympics, Munich 1972, issue. Air 1, 2, 3, 4, 5, 6r.
Japanese Locomotives. Postage 30, 35, 75d.; Air 90d., 1, 1r.75.
"Soyuz 11" Russian Cosmonauts Memorial. Air 1, 2, 3, 4r.
"Apollo 15". Postage 50d.; Air 1, 1r.50, 2, 3, 4r.
Dogs. 5, 20, 75, 85, 185, 200d.
Durer's Paintings. Postage 50d.; Air 1, 1r.50 2, 3, 4r.
Famous Composers (2nd series). Postage 50d.; Air 1, 1r.50, 2, 3, 4r.
"Soyuz 11" and "Salyut" Space Projects. Postage 50 d,; Air 1, 1r.50, 2, 3, 4r.
Butterflies. Postage 15, 20, 70d.; Air 1r.25, 1r.50, 1r.70.
Wild Animals. 10, 40, 80 d,; 1r.15, 1r.30, 1r.65.
Fishes. 30, 50, 60, 90d., 1r.45, 1r.55.
Ludwig van Beethoven. Portraits. Postage 50d.; Air 1, 1r.50, 2, 3, 4r.

1972

Birds. 50, 55, 80, 100, 105, 190d.
Winter Olympics, Sapporo (1st issue). Postage 20, 30, 50d., Air 70, 90d., 2r.50
Winter Olympics, Sapporo (2nd issue). Postage 5, 60, 80, 90d.; Air 1r.10, 1r.75
Mozart. Portraits. Postage 50d.; Air 1, 1r.50, 2, 3, 4r.
Olympic Games, Munich. Postage 50d.; Air 1, 1r.50, 2, 3, 4r.
"In Memory of Charles de Gaulle". Optd on 1971 Charles de Gaulle memorial issue. Postage 50d.; Air 1, 1r.50, 2, 3, 4r.
Winter Olympics, Sapporo (3rd issue). Postage 15, 45d.; Air 65, 75d., 1r.20, 1r.25.
Horses. Postage 10, 25, 30d.; Air 1r.40, 1r.80, 1r.95.
Parrots. 40, 45, 70, 95d., 1r.35, 1r.75.
"Apollo 16". Postage 50d.; Air 1, 1r.50, 2, 3, 4r.
European Footballers. Postage 50d.; Air 1, 1r.50, 2, 3, 4r.

A number of issues on gold or silver foil also exist, but it is understood that these were mainly for presentation purposes, although valid for postage.

In common with the other states of the United Arab Emirates the Ras al Khaima stamp contract was terminated on 1st August 1972, and any further new issues released after that date were unauthorized.

Pt. 1

REDONDA

A dependency of Antigua.

The following stamps were issued in anticipation of commercial and tourist development, philatelic mail being handled by a bureau in Antigua. Since at the present time the island is uninhabited, we do not list or stock these items. It is understood that the stamps are valid for the prepayment of postage in Antigua. Miniature sheets, imperforate stamps etc, are excluded from this section.

1979

Antigua 1976 definitive issue optd **REDONDA**. 3, 5, 10, 25, 35, 50, 75c., $1, $2.50, $5, $10.
Antigua Coronation Anniversary issue optd **REDONDA**. 10, 30, 50, 90c., $2.50.
Antigua World Cup Football Championship issue optd **REDONDA**. 10, 15c., $3.
Death Centenary of Sir Rowland Hill. 50, 90c., $2.50, $3.
International Year of the Child 25, 50c., $1, $2.
Christmas. Paintings. 8, 50, 90c., $3.

1980

Marine Life. 8, 25, 50c., $4.
75th Anniv of Rotary International. 25, 50c., $1, $2.
Birds of Redonda. 8, 10, 15, 25, 30, 50c., $1, $2, $5.
Olympic Medal Winners, Lake Placid and Moscow. 8, 25, 50c., $3.
80th Birthday of Queen Elizabeth the Queen Mother. 10c., $2.50.
Christmas Paintings. 8, 25, 50c., $4.

1981

Royal Wedding. 25, 55c., $4.
Christmas. Walt Disney Cartoon Characters. ½, 1, 2, 3, 4, 5, 10c., $2.50, $3.
World Cup Football Championship, Spain (1982). 30c.×2, 50c.×2, $1×2, $2×2.

1982

Boy Scout Annivs. 8, 25, 50c., $3, $5.
Butterflies. 8, 30, 50c., $2.
21st Birthday of Princess of Wales. $2, $4.
Birth of Prince William of Wales. Optd on Princess of Wales 21st Birthday issue. $2, $4.
Christmas. Walt Disney's "One Hundred and One Dalmatians". ½, 1, 2, 3, 4, 5, 10c., $2.50, $3.

1983

Easter. 500th Birth Anniv of Raphael. 10, 50, 90c., $5.
Bicent of Manned Flight. 10, 50, 90c., $2.50.
Christmas. Walt Disney Cartoon Characters. "Deck the Halls". ½, 1, 2, 3, 4, 5, 10c., $2.50, $3.

1984

Easter. Walt Disney Cartoon Characters. ½, 1, 2, 3, 4, 5, 10c., $2, $4.
Olympic Games, Los Angeles. 10, 50, 90c., $2.50.
Christmas. 50th Birthday of Donald Duck. 45, 60, 90c., $2, $4.

1985

Birth Bicentenary of John J. Audubon (ornithologist) (1st issue). 60, 90c., $1, $3.
Life and Times of Queen Elizabeth the Queen Mother. $1, $1.50, $2.50.
Royal Visit. 45c., $1, $4.
150th Birth Anniv of Mark Twain (author). 25, 50c., $1.50, $3.
Birth Bicentenaries of Grimm Brothers (folklorists). Walt Disney cartoon characters. 30, 60, 70c., $4.

1986

Birth Bicentenary of John J. Audubon (ornithologist) (2nd issue). 90c., $1, $1.50, $3.
Appearance of Halley's Comet. 5, 15, 55c., $4.
Centenary of Statue of Liberty (1st issue). 20, 25, 30c., $4.
60th Birthday of Queen Elizabeth II. 50, 60c., $4.
Royal Wedding. 60c., $1, $4.
Christmas (1st issue). Disney characters in Hans Andersen Stories. 30, 60, 70c., $4.
Christmas (2nd issue). "Wind in the Willows" (by Kenneth Grahame). 25, 50c., $1.50, $3.

1987

"Capex '87" International Stamp Exhibition, Toronto. Disney characters illustrating Art of Animation. 25, 30, 50, 60, 70c., $1.50, $3, $4.
Birth Centenary of Marc Chagall (artist). 10, 30, 40, 60, 90c., $1, $3, $4.
Centenary of Statue of Liberty (2nd issue). 10, 15, 25, 30, 40, 60, 70, 90c., $1, $2, $3, $4.
250th Death Anniv of Sir Isaac Newton (scientist). 20c., $2.50.
750th Anniv of Berlin. $1, $4.
Bicentenary of U.S. Constitution. 30c., $3.
16th World Scout Jamboree, Australia. 10c., $4.

1988

500th Anniv (1992) of Discovery of America by Columbus. 15, 30, 45, 60, 90c., $1, $2, $3.
"Finlandia '88" International Stamp Exhibition, Helsinki. Disney characters in Finnish scenes. 1, 2, 3, 4, 5, 6c., $5, $6.
Olympic Games, Seoul. 25, 60c., $1.25, $3.
500th Birth Anniv of Titian. 10, 25, 40, 70, 90c., $2, $3, $4.

1989

20th Anniv of First Manned Landing on Moon. Disney characters on Moon. ½, 1, 2, 3, 4, 5c., $5, $6.
500th Anniv (1992) of Discovery of America by Columbus (2nd issue). Pre-Columbian Societies. 15, 45, 45, 50c., $2, $2, $3, $3.
Christmas. Disney Characters and Cars of 1950s. 25, 35, 45, 60c., $1, $2, $3, $4.

1990

Christmas. Disney Characters and Hollywood cars. 25, 35, 40, 60c., $2, $3, $4, $5.

1991

Nobel Prize Winners. 5, 15, 25, 40, 50c., $1, $2, $4.

Pt. 6

RÉUNION

An island in the Indian Ocean, E. of Madagascar now an overseas department of France.

100 centimes = 1 franc.

1

1852. Imperf. No gum.

1	1	15c. black on blue	£35000	£23000
2	1	30c. black on blue	£33000	£22000

1885. Stamps of French Colonies surch **R** and value in figures. Imperf.

5	D	5c. on 30c. brown	55·00	50·00
7	H	5c. on 30c. brown	4·50	7·25
3	A	5c. on 40c. orange	£300	£275
6	F	5c. on 40c. orange	60·00	65·00
8	H	5c. on 40c. red on yellow	65·00	£120
9	H	10c. on 40c. red on yellow	11·00	4·50
10	H	20c. on 30c. brown	70·00	65·00
4	A	25c. on 40c. orange	60·00	55·00

1891. Stamps of French Colonies optd **REUNION**. Imperf (Types F and H) or perf (Type J).

17A	J	1c. black on blue	90	2·50
18B	J	2c. brown on buff	65	75
19A	J	4c. brown on grey	3·00	4·25
20A	J	5c. green on green	5·00	1·30
21A	J	10c. black on lilac	30·00	2·30
22A	J	15c. blue on blue	60·00	1·60
23A	J	20c. red on green	14·50	16·00
24A	J	25c. black on pink	60·00	1·40
13A	H	30c. brown	55·00	65·00
25Aa	J	35c. black on yellow	16·00	23·00
11B	F	40c. orange	£425	£425
14A	H	40c. red on yellow	34·00	21·00
26A	J	40c. red on buff	£100	95·00
15A	H	75c. red	£325	£325
27A	J	75c. red on pink	£500	£425
12B	F	80c. pink	80·00	70·00
16A	H	1f. green	70·00	60·00
28B	J	1f. green	£425	£375

1891. Stamps of French Colonies surch **REUNION** and new value.

29	02c. on 20c. red on green	4·00	6·25
31	2 on 20c. red on green	3·00	3·25
30	15c. on 20c. red on green	11·00	3·75

1892. "Tablet" key-type inscr "REUNION".

34	D	1c. black and red on blue	20	20
35	D	2c. brown and blue on buff	1·30	35
36	D	4c. brown and blue on grey	2·30	20
37	D	5c. green	1·10	20
38	D	10c. black and blue on lilac	5·75	1·20
51	D	10c. red and blue	3·25	20
39	D	15c. blue and red	55·00	45
52	D	15c. grey and red	11·00	10
40	D	20c. red and blue on green	19·00	10·00
41	D	25c. black and red on pink	23·00	2·00
53	D	25c. blue and red	25·00	38·00
42	D	30c. brown and blue on drab	27·00	11·00
43	D	40c. red and blue on yellow	55·00	14·50
44	D	50c. red and blue on pink	£100	17·00

54	D	50c. brown and red on blue	65·00	70·00
55	D	50c. brown and blue on blue	65·00	70·00
45	D	75c. brown and red on orange	65·00	65·00
46	D	1f. green and red	65·00	65·00

1893. Stamp of French Colonies, "Commerce" type, surch **2 c.**

47	J	2c. on 20c. red on green	2·50	2·50

1901. "Tablet" key-type surch in figures.

56	D	5c. on 40c. red and blue on yellow	3·25	8·50
57	D	5c. on 50c. red and blue on pink	5·25	6·00
58	D	15c. on 75c. brown and red on orange	25·00	29·00
59	D	15c. on 1f. green and red	16·00	9·00

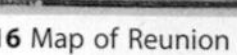

16 Map of Reunion

17 View of Saint-Denis and Arms of the Colony

18 View of St. Pierre and Crater Dolomieu

1907

60	**16**	1c. red and lilac	35	35
61	**16**	2c. blue and brown	55	1·00
62	**16**	4c. red and green	90	1·60
63	**16**	5c. red and green	2·75	35
92	**16**	5c. violet and yellow	70	35
64	**16**	10c. green and red	7·75	30
93	**16**	10c. turquoise and green	55	35
94	**16**	10c. red and lake on blue	1·00	45
65	**16**	15c. blue and black	3·75	1·60
95	**16**	15c. turquoise and green	85	50
96	**16**	15c. red and blue	3·50	1·80
66	**17**	20c. green and olive	3·50	1·80
67	**17**	25c. brown and blue	7·75	90
97	**17**	25c. blue and brown	1·50	35
68	**17**	30c. green and brown	1·30	1·00
98	**17**	30c. pink and red	3·25	4·50
99	**17**	30c. red and grey	1·80	1·70
100	**17**	30c. light green and green	3·50	5·25
69	**17**	35c. blue and brown	3·50	1·60
101	**17**	40c. brown and green	2·10	30
70	**17**	45c. pink and violet	2·75	4·75
102	**17**	45c. red and purple	2·00	4·25
103	**17**	45c. red and mauve	4·50	10·00
71	**17**	50c. blue and brown	3·00	2·30
104	**17**	50c. ultramarine and blue	2·30	2·50
105	**17**	50c. violet and yellow	2·00	35
106	**17**	60c. brown and blue	2·30	6·75
107	**17**	65c. blue and violet	4·50	4·25
72	**17**	75c. pink and red	2·50	1·00
108	**17**	75c. purple and brown	4·50	5·25
109	**17**	90c. pink and red	11·50	21·00
73	**18**	1f. blue and brown	4·00	2·75
110	**18**	1f. blue	3·25	2·20
111	**18**	1f. lilac and brown	4·75	1·80
112	**18**	1f.10 mauve and brown	4·25	4·75
113	**18**	1f.50 lt blue & blue on bl	24·00	28·00
74	**18**	2f. green and red	7·00	1·70
114	**18**	3f. mauve on pink	13·00	14·50
75	**18**	5f. brown and pink	11·00	9·25

1912. "Tablet" key-type surch.

76A	D	05 on 2c. brown and red on buff	60	35
77A	D	05 on 15c. grey and red	45	35
78A	D	05 on 20c. red and blue on green	3·50	7·25
79A	D	05 on 25c. black and red on pink	1·80	5·50
80A	D	05 on 30c. brown and blue on drab	35	2·00
81A	D	10 on 40c. red and blue on yellow	1·00	3·75
82A	D	10 on 50c. brown and blue on blue	2·30	3·75
83A	D	10 on 75c. brown and red on orange	1·90	16·00

1915. Red Cross Surch **5c** and red cross.

90	**16**	10c.+5c. green and red	1·20	5·75

1917. Surch **0,01**.

91		0,01 on 4c. chestnut and brown	4·75	3·50

1922. Surch in figures only.

115	**17**	40 on 20c. yellow and green	75	1·30
116	**17**	50 on 45c. red and purple	4·50	1·80
117	**17**	50 on 45c. red and mauve	£250	£250
118	**17**	50 on 65c. blue and violet	5·25	3·75
119	**17**	60 on 75c. carmine and red	85	55
120	**16**	65 on 15c. blue and black	3·00	8·50
121	**16**	85 on 15c. blue and black	2·50	8·25
122	**17**	85 on 75c. pink and red	2·30	8·75
123	**17**	90 on 75c. pink and red	3·25	3·25

1924. Surch in cents and francs.

124	**18**	25c. on 5f. brown and pink	1·80	8·00
125	**18**	1f.25 on 1f. blue	1·70	2·50
126	**18**	1f.50 on 1f. light blue and blue on blue	1·50	65
127	**18**	3f. on 5f. blue and red	4·75	3·50
128	**18**	10f. on 5f. red and green	23·00	44·00
129	**18**	20f. on 5f. pink and brown	26·00	46·00

1931. "Colonial Exhibition" key-types inscr "REUNION".

130	E	40c. green and black	5·50	6·00
131	F	50c. mauve and black	5·75	4·50
132	G	90c. red and black	4·50	6·75
133	H	1f.50 blue and black	8·50	9·00

30 Cascade, Salazie

31 Anchain Peak, Salazie

32 Leon Dierx Museum

1933

134	**30**	1c. purple	30	2·50
135	**30**	2c. brown	10	1·90
136	**30**	3c. mauve	75	5·50
137	**30**	4c. olive	20	3·50
138	**30**	5c. orange	35	40
139	**30**	10c. blue	40	70
140	**30**	15c. black	20	50
141	**30**	20c. blue	40	2·75
142	**30**	25c. brown	70	75
143	**30**	30c. green	80	1·00
144	**31**	35c. green	1·70	6·50
145	**31**	40c. blue	2·50	1·80
146	**31**	40c. brown	65	6·50
147	**31**	45c. mauve	1·60	7·25
148	**31**	45c. green	1·70	6·75
149	**31**	50c. red	65	10
150	**31**	55c. orange	3·00	4·50
151	**31**	60c. blue	90	6·75
152	**31**	65c. olive	4·25	2·50
153	**31**	70c. olive	3·50	7·25
154	**31**	75c. brown	7·25	12·50
155	**31**	80c. black	1·80	7·00
156	**31**	90c. red	5·50	5·25
157	**31**	90c. purple	1·70	2·00
158	**31**	1f. green	5·50	45
159	**31**	1f. red	3·00	5·50
160	**31**	1f. black	1·30	6·75
161	**32**	1f.25 brown	1·20	6·25
162	**32**	1f.25 red	3·00	7·50
163	**30**	1f.40 blue	3·00	7·25
164	**32**	1f.50 blue	65	35
165	**30**	1f.60 red	3·00	6·50
166	**32**	1f.75 olive	3·00	90
167	**30**	1f.75 blue	2·75	7·50
168	**32**	2f. red	90	2·10
169	**30**	2f.25 blue	5·25	8·75
170	**30**	2f.50 brown	2·50	3·00
171	**32**	3f. violet	1·40	1·80
172	**32**	5f. mauve	1·40	6·25
173	**32**	10f. blue	2·10	7·00
174	**32**	20f. brown	2·75	8·50

1937. Air. Pioneer Flight from Reunion to France by Laurent, Lenier and Touge. Optd **REUNION - FRANCE par avion "ROLAND GARROS"**.

174a	**31**	50c. red	£275	£250

1937. International Exhibition, Paris. As Nos. 168/73 of St.-Pierre et Miquelon.

175	20c. violet	1·60	7·50
176	30c. green	1·50	7·50
177	40c. red	90	6·00
178	50c. brown and agate	1·10	3·25
179	90c. red	1·40	4·25
180	1f.50 blue	1·80	7·50

34 Caudron C-600 "Aiglon"

1938. Air.

181	**34**	3f.65 blue and red	1·10	1·00
182	**34**	6f.65 brown and red	1·60	5·50
183	**34**	9f.65 red and blue	1·00	7·50
184	**34**	12f.65 brown and green	1·60	8·25

1938. International Anti-cancer Fund. As T **17a** of Oceanic Settlements.

185	1f.75+50c. blue	6·75	36·00

1939. New York World's Fair. As T **17b** of Oceanic Settlements.

186	1f.25 red	2·10	7·75
187	2f.25 blue	1·70	7·75

1939. 150th Anniv of French Revolution. As T **17c** of Oceanic Settlements.

188	45c.+25c. green and black (postage)	10·50	24·00
189	70c.+30c. brown and black	10·50	24·00
190	90c.+35c. orange and black	10·50	24·00
191	1f.25+1f. red and black	10·50	24·00
192	2f.25+2f. blue and black	10·50	24·00
193	3f.65+4f. blk & orge (air)	17·00	42·00

1943. Surch **1f**.

194	**31**	1f. on 65c. green	2·50	1·30

1943. Optd **France Libre**.

198	**30**	1c. purple (postage)	75	8·00
199	**30**	2c. brown	80	6·25
200	**30**	3c. purple	75	7·75
195	**16**	4c. red and green	1·80	11·50
201	**30**	4c. green	55	8·00
202	**30**	5c. red	1·20	8·00
203	**30**	10c. blue	55	3·75
204	**30**	15c. black	45	7·75
205	**30**	20c. blue	1·10	7·75
206	**30**	25c. brown	1·20	6·00
207	**30**	30c. green	85	5·00
208	**31**	35c. green	55	7·00
209	**31**	40c. blue	55	5·50
210	**31**	40c. brown	85	5·00
211	**31**	45c. mauve	55	7·00
212	**31**	45c. green	65	5·25
213	**31**	50c. red	70	3·75
214	**31**	55c. orange	55	6·75
215	**31**	60c. blue	2·30	7·75
216	**31**	65c. green	1·00	7·00
217	**31**	70c. green	1·50	7·50
196	**17**	75c. pink and red	85	7·75
218	**31**	75c. brown	2·75	10·50
219	**31**	80c. black	35	7·00
220	**31**	90c. purple	45	5·75
221	**31**	1f. green	1·10	6·25
222	**31**	1f. red	55	3·00
223	**31**	1f. black	1·40	8·75
240	**31**	1f. on 65c. green (No. 194)	75	2·50
224	**32**	1f.25 brown	75	8·00
225	**32**	1f.25 red	2·10	7·00
238	-	1f.25 red (No. 186)	90	9·50
226	**30**	1f.40 blue	1·40	7·50
227	**32**	1f.50 blue	90	6·75
228	**30**	1f.60 red	1·20	6·75
229	**32**	1f.75 green	85	7·00
230	**30**	1f.75 blue	2·30	12·00
231	**32**	2f. red	1·20	4·00
232	**30**	2f.25 blue	90	7·50
239	-	2f.25 blue (No. 187)	1·20	9·50
233	**30**	2f.50 brown	2·00	12·00
234	**32**	3f. violet	70	5·50
241	**34**	3f.65 blue and red (air)	2·75	12·00
197	**18**	5f. brown and pink	50·00	75·00
235	**32**	5f. mauve	1·20	2·50
242	**34**	6f.65 brown and red	2·75	12·00
243	**34**	9f.65 red and blue	2·75	12·00
236	**32**	10f. blue	2·10	16·00
244	**34**	12f.65 brown and green	2·75	12·00
237	**32**	20f. brown	5·25	21·00

37 Chief Products

1943. Free French Issue.

245	**37**	5c. brown	10	3·25
246a	**37**	10c. blue	1·10	2·30
247	**37**	25c. green	35	5·25
248	**37**	30c. red	70	5·00
249	**37**	40c. green	35	5·25
250	**37**	80c. mauve	85	3·75
251	**37**	1f. purple	80	35
252	**37**	1f.50 red	1·10	90
253	**37**	2f. black	55	2·10
254	**37**	2f.50 blue	1·10	4·75
255	**37**	4f. violet	1·30	1·00
256	**37**	5f. yellow	1·00	30
257	**37**	10f. brown	1·20	75
258	**37**	20f. green	1·50	1·40

1944. Air. Free French Administration. As T **19a** of Oceanic Settlements.

259	1f. orange	85	55
260	1f.50 red	55	75
261	5f. purple	70	1·30
262	10f. black	1·40	4·75
263	25f. blue	2·00	4·25
264	50f. green	1·90	1·50
265	100f. red	2·30	3·25

1944. Mutual Air and Red Cross Funds. As T **19b** of Oceanic Settlements.

266	5f.+20f. black	1·00	8·75

1945. Eboue. As T **20a** of Oceanic Settlements.

267	2f. black	35	80
268	25f. green	65	6·50

1945. Surch.

269	50c. on 5c. brown	1·00	5·50
270	60c. on 5c. brown	1·10	6·75
271	70c. on 5c. brown	55	6·75
272	1f.20 on 5c. brown	1·00	6·00
273	2f.40 on 25c. green	1·40	4·75
274	3f. on 25c. green	1·00	2·30
275	4f.50 on 25c. green	1·00	2·50
276	15f. on 2f.50 blue	75	75

1946. Air. Victory. As T **20b** of Oceanic Settlements.

277	8f. grey	65	2·30

1946. Air. From Chad to the Rhine. As T **20c** of Oceanic Settlements.

278	5f. red	1·40	7·75
279	10f. violet	1·00	7·00
280	15f. black	1·20	7·25
281	20f. red	1·40	5·00
282	25f. blue	1·50	6·00
283	50f. green	1·70	8·75

39 Cliffs

40 Banana Tree and Cliff

41 Mountain Landscape

42 Shadow of Airplane over Coast

1947

284	**39**	10c. orange & grn (postage)	20	4·25
285	**39**	30c. orange and blue	35	5·50
286	**39**	40c. orange and brown	35	6·50
287	-	50c. brown and green	35	3·75
288	-	60c. brown and blue	20	7·00
289	-	80c. green and brown	35	7·00
290	-	1f. purple and blue	45	35
291	-	1f.20 grey and green	1·00	6·50
292	-	1f.50 purple and orange	80	7·25
293	**40**	2f. blue and green	85	50
294	**40**	3f. purple and green	1·40	2·50
295	**40**	3f.60 pink and red	1·20	7·75
296	**40**	4f. blue and brown	1·80	2·30
297	**41**	5f. mauve and brown	2·30	1·10
298	**41**	6f. blue and brown	1·70	1·50
299	**41**	10f. orange and blue	2·10	3·00
300	-	15f. purple and blue	2·50	8·25
301	-	20f. blue and orange	3·25	14·00
302	-	25f. brown and mauve	2·75	5·25

303	42	50f. green and grey (air)	7·50	23·00
304	-	100f. orange and brown	13·00	36·00
305	-	200f. blue and orange	10·00	46·00

DESIGNS—20×37 mm: 50c. to 80c. Cutting sugar cane; 1f. to 1f.50, Cascade. 28×50 mm: 100f. Douglas DC-4 airplane over Reunion. 37×20 mm: 15f. to 25f. "Ville de Strasbourg" (liner) approaching Reunion. 50×28 mm: 200f. Reunion from the air.

1949. Stamps of France surch **CFA** and value. (a) Postage. (i) Ceres.

306	218	50c. on 1f. red	10	1·60
307	218	60c. on 2f. green	85	10·00

(ii) Nos. 972/3 (Arms).

308		10c. on 30c. black, red and yellow (Alsace)	35	5·25
309		30c. on 50c. brown, yellow and red (Lorraine)	20	7·50

(iii) Nos. 981, 979 and 982/a (Views).

310		5f. on 20f. blue (Finistere)	1·40	90
311		7f. on 12f. red (Luxembourg Palace)	1·00	3·75
312		8f. on 25f. blue (Nancy)	3·00	90
313		10f. on 25f. brown (Nancy)	1·00	45

(iv) Marianne.

314	219	1f. on 3f. mauve	80	10
315	219	2f. on 4f. green	50	35
316	219	2f. on 5f. green	2·75	14·50
317	219	2f. on 5f. violet	1·40	20
318	219	2f.50 on 5f. blue	2·75	40·00
319	219	3f. on 6f. red	1·10	35
320	219	3f. on 6f. green	55	45
321	219	4f. on 10f. violet	1·10	35
322	219	6f. on 12f. blue	1·80	70
323	219	6f. on 12f. orange	1·80	85
324	219	9f. on 18f. red	1·30	8·75

(v) Conques Abbey.

325	263	11f. on 18f. blue	90	2·50

(b) Air. (i) Nos. 967/70 (Mythology).

326	-	20f. on 40f. green	1·60	55
327	236	25f. on 50f. pink	2·00	30
328	237	50f. on 100f. blue	2·75	1·30
329	-	100f. on 200f. red	11·50	10·00

(ii) Nos. 1056 and 1058/9 (Cities).

330		100f. on 200f. green (Bordeaux)	40·00	36·00
331		200f. on 500f. red (Marseilles)	40·00	48·00
332		500f. on 1000f. purple and black on blue (Paris)	95·00	£160

1950. Stamps of France surch **CFA** and value. (a) Nos. 1050 and 1052 (Arms).

342		10c. on 50c. yellow, red and blue (Guyenne)	10	3·75
343		1f. on 2f. red, yellow and green (Auvergne)	1·10	9·25

(b) On Nos. 1067/8 and 1068b (Views).

344	-	5f. on 20f. red (Comminges)	1·10	50
345	284	8f. on 25f. blue (Wandrille)	70	35
346	-	15f. on 30f. blue (Arbois)	60	50

1951. Nos. 1123/4 of France (Arms) surch **CFA** and value.

347		50c. on 1f. red, yellow and blue (Bearn)	20	75
348		1f. on 2f. yellow, blue and red (Touraine)	10	20

1952. Nos. 1138 and 1144 of France surch **CFA** and value.

349	323	5f. on 20f. violet (Chambord)	55	35
350	317	8f. on 40f. violet (Bigorre)	90	35

1953. Stamps of France surch **CFA** and value. (a) Nos. 1162, 1168 and 1170 (Literary Figures and National Industries).

351		3f. on 6f. lake and red (Gargantua)	45	35
352		8f. on 40f. brown and chocolate (Porcelain)	55	10
353		20f. on 75f. red and carmine (Flowers)	1·80	80

(b) Nos. 1181/2 (Arms).

354		50c. on 1f. yellow, red and black (Poitou)	35	65
355		1f. on 2f. yellow, blue and brown (Champagne)	35	7·75

1954. Stamps of France surch **CFA** and value. (a) Postage. (i) Nos. 1188 and 1190 (Sports).

356		8f. on 40f. blue and brown (Canoeing)	2·75	2·30
357		20f. on 75f. red and orange (Horse jumping)	11·00	55·00

(ii) Nos. 1205/8 and 1210/11 (Views).

358		2f. on 6f. indigo, blue and green (Lourdes)	85	1·30
359		3f. on 8f. green and blue (Andelys)	90	7·50
360		4f. on 10f. brown and blue (Royan)	1·20	65
361		6f. on 12f. lilac and violet (Quimper)	1·50	75
362		9f. on 18f. indigo, blue and green (Cheverny)	1·70	12·00
363		10f. on 20f. brown, chestnut and blue (Ajaccio)	2·75	2·50

(iii) No. 1229 (Arms).

364		1f. on 2f. yellow, red and black (Angoumois)	10	10

(b) Air. Nos. 1194/7 (Aircraft).

365		50f. on 100f. brown and blue (Mystere IV)	2·50	90
366		100f. on 200f. purple and blue (Noratlas)	2·30	2·50
367		200f. on 500f. red and orange (Magister)	17·00	34·00
368		500f. on 1000f. indigo, purple and blue (Provence)	10·00	30·00

1955. Stamps of France surch **CFA** and value. (a) Nos. 1262/5, 1266, 1268 and 1268b (Views).

369		2f. on 6f. red (Bordeaux)	60	1·10
370		3f. on 8f. blue (Marseilles)	90	65
371		4f. on 10f. blue (Nice)	1·10	1·00
372		5f. on 12f. brown and grey (Cahors)	55	35
373		6f. on 18f. blue and green (Uzerche)	35	35
374		10f. on 25f. brown and chestnut (Brouage)	35	35
375		17f. on 70f. black and green (Cahors)	1·30	9·50

(b) No. 1273 (Arms).

376		50c. on 1f. yellow, red and blue (Comtat Venaissin)	10	35

1956. Nos. 1297/1300 of France (Sports) surch **CFA** and value.

377		8f. on 30f. black and grey (Basketball)	55	20
378		9f. on 40f. purple and brown (Pelota)	55	90
379		15f. on 50f. violet and purple (Rugby)	1·20	2·00
380		20f. on 75f. green, black and blue (Climbing)	65	1·70

1957. Stamps of France surch **CFA** and value. (a) Postage. (i) Harvester.

381	344	2f. on 6f. brown	40	10
382	344	4f. on 12f. purple	75	55
383	344	5f. on 10f. green	65	40

(ii) France.

384	362	10f. on 20f. blue	35	10
385	362	12f. on 25f. red	65	35

(iii) No. 1335 (Le Quesnoy).

386		7f. on 15f. black and green	60	35

(iv) Nos. 1351, 1352/3, 1354/5 and 1356a (Tourist Publicity).

387		3f. on 10f. chocolate and brown (Elysee)	40	40
388		6f. on 18f. brown and blue (Beynac)	65	1·50
389		9f. on 25f. brown and grey (Valencay)	60	4·50
390		17f. on 35f. mauve and red (Rouen)	80	3·25
391		20f. on 50f. brown and green (St. Remy)	45	35
392		25f. on 85f. purple (Evian-les-Bains)	1·10	60

(b) Air. Nos. 1319/20 (Aircraft).

393		200f. on 500f. black and blue (Caravelle)	6·00	10·00
394		500f. on 1000f. black, violet and brown (Alouette II)	9·25	34·00

1960. Nos. 1461, 1464 and 1467 of France (Tourist Publicity) surch **CFA** and value.

395		7f. on 15c. indigo and blue (Laon)	1·40	40
396		20f. on 50c. purple and green (Tlemcen)	7·75	1·40
397		50f. on 1f. violet, green and blue (Cilaos)	80	50

1961. Harvester and Sower stamps of France (in new currency) surch **CFA** and value.

398	344	5f. on 10c. green	65	90
400	453	10f. on 20c. red and turquoise	65	20

1961. "Marianne" stamp of France surch **12f. CFA**.

401	463	12f. on 25c. grey & purple	45	20

1961. Nos. 1457, 1457b and 1459/60 of France (Aircraft) surch **CFA** and value.

402		100f. on 2f. purple and blue (Noratlas)	4·50	1·90
403		100f. on 2f. indigo and blue (Mystere Falcon 20)	1·20	1·30
404		200f. on 5f. black and blue (Caravelle)	4·50	5·00
405		500f. on 10f. black, violet and brown (Alouette II)	14·00	9·25

1962. Red Cross stamps of France (Nos. 1593/4) surch **CFA** and value.

409	10f.+5f. on 20c.+10c.	1·30	5·00
410	12f.+5f. on 25c.+10c.	1·50	8·25

1962. Satellite Link stamps of France surch **CFA** and value.

411	12f. on 25c. (No. 1587)	90	2·75
412	25f. on 50c. (No. 1588)	50	5·25

1963. Nos. 1541 and 1545 of France (Tourist Publicity) surch **CFA** and value.

413	7f. on 15c. grey, purple and blue (Saint-Paul)	1·20	3·00
414	20f. on 45c. brown, green and blue (Sully)	80	90

1963. Nos. 1498b/9b and 1499e/f of France (Arms) surch **CFA** and value.

415	1f. on 2c. yellow, green and blue (Gueret)	35	20
416	2f. on 5c. mult (Oran)	65	35
417	2f. on 5c. red, yellow and blue (Armiens)	75	20
418	5f. on 10c. blue, yellow and red (Troyes)	1·10	20
419	6f. on 18c. multicoloured (St. Denis)	35	50
420	15f. on 30c. red and blue (Paris)	1·00	20

1963. Red Cross stamps of France Nos. 1627/8 surch **CFA** and value.

421	10f.+5f. on 20c.+10c.	2·00	10·50
422	12f.+5f. on 25c.+10c.	1·70	10·50

1964. 'PHILATEC 1964' International Stamp Exhibition stamp of France surch **CFA** and value.

423	12f. on 25c. (No. 1629)	1·10	45

1964. Nos. 1654/5 of France (Tourist Publicity) surch **CFA** and value.

431	20f. on 40c. chocolate, green and brown (Ronchamp)	85	3·00
432	35f. on 70c. purple, green and blue (Provins)	1·10	1·70

1964. Red Cross stamps of France Nos. 1665/6 surch **CFA** and value.

433	10f.+5f. on 20c.+10c.	1·70	4·25
434	12f.+5f. on 25c.+10c.	1·60	5·75

1965. No. 1621 of France (Saint Flour) surch **3F CFA.**

435	30f. on 60c. red, green & blue	1·00	1·70

1965. Nos 1684/5 and 1688 of France (Tourist Publicity) surch **CFA** and value.

436	25f. on 50c. blue, green and bistre (St. Marie)	1·50	2·00
437	30f. on 60c. brown and blue (Aix les Bains)	1·20	2·00
438	50f. on 1f. grey, green and brown (Carnac)	2·00	1·40

1965. Tercent of Colonization of Reunion. As No. 1692 of France, but additionally inscr 'CFA'.

439	15f. blue and red	1·50	40

1965. Red Cross stamps of France Nos. 1698/9 surch **CFA** and value.

440	12f.+5f. on 25c.+10c.	2·00	6·75
441	15f.+5f. on 30c.+10c.	2·00	6·75

1966. "Marianne" stamp of France surch **10f CFA.**

442	476	10f. on 20c. red and blue	2·10	4·00

1966. Launching of First French Satellite. Nos. 1696/7 (plus se-tenant label) of France surch **CFA** and value.

443	15f. on 30c. blue, turquoise and light blue	1·10	3·75
444	30f. on 60c. blue, turquoise and light blue	2·20	3·75

1966. Red Cross stamps of France Nos. 1733/4 surch **CFA** and value.

445	12f.+5f. on 25c.+10c.	1·50	6·00
446	15f.+5f. on 30c.+10c.	1·50	6·00

1967. World Fair Montreal. No. 1747 of France surch **CFA** and value.

447	30f. on 60c.	95	4·75

1967. No. 1700 of France (Arms of Auch) surch **2fCFA.**

448	2f. on 5c. red and blue	1·10	4·25

1967. 50th Anniv of Lions Int. No. 1766 of France surch **CFA** and value.

449	20f. on 40c.	1·40	4·00

1967. Red Cross. Nos. 1772/3 of France surch **CFA** and value.

450	12f.+5f. on 25c.+10c.	2·30	11·00
451	15f.+5f. on 30c.+10c.	2·30	11·00

1968. French Polar Exploration. No. 1806 of France surch **CFA** and value.

452	20f. on 40c.	2·30	5·50

1968. Red Cross stamps of France Nos. 1812/13 surch **CFA** and value.

453	12f.+5f. on 25c.+10c.	2·10	7·00
454	15f.+5f. on 30c.+10c.	2·10	7·00

1969. Stamp Day. No. 1824 of France surch **CFA** and value.

455	15f.+5f. on 30c.+10c.	2·00	6·25

1969. "Republique" stamps of France surch **CFA** and value.

456	604	15f. on 30c. green	1·60	3·50
457	604	20f. on 40c. mauve	1·30	80

1969. No. 1735 of France (Arms of Saint-Lo) surch **10F CFA.**

458	10f. on 20c. multicoloured	2·10	3·25

1969. Birth Bicent of Napoleon Bonaparte. No. 1845 of France surch **CFA** and value.

459	35f. on 70c. green, violet & bl	2·75	5·50

1969. Red Cross stamps of France Nos. 1853/4 surch **CFA** and value.

460	20f.+7f. on 40c.+15c.	2·30	6·75
461	20f.+7f. on 40c.+15c.	2·10	6·75

1970. Stamp Day. No. 1866 of France surch **CFA** and value.

462	20f.+5f. on 40c.+10c.	2·10	5·00

1970. Red Cross. Nos. 1902/3 of France surch **CFA** and value.

463	20f.+7f. on 40c.+15c.	4·00	7·25
464	20f.+7f. on 40c.+15c.	4·00	7·25

1971. "Marianne" stamp of France surch **25f CFA.**

465	668	25f. on 50c. mauve	1·30	65

1971. Stamp Day. No. 1919 of France surch **CFA** and value.

466	25f.+5f. on 50c.+10c.	1·40	5·50

1971. "Antoinette". No. 1920 of France surch **CFA** and value.

467	40f. on 80c.	2·10	6·25

1971. No. 1928 of France (Rural Aid) surch **CFA** and value.

468	678	15f. on 40c.	1·80	3·50

1971. Nos. 1931/2 of France (Tourist Publicity) surch **CFA** and value.

469	45f. on 90c. brown, green and ochre (Riquewihr)	1·60	3·25
470	50f. on 1f.10 brown, blue and green (Sedan)	1·70	2·00

1971. 40th Anniv of First Meeting of Crafts Guilds Association. No. 1935 of France surch **CFA** and value.

471	680	45c. on 90c. purple & red	1·70	4·50

63 Reunion Chameleon

1971. Nature Protection.

472	63	25f. green, brown & yellow	2·30	2·00

64 De Gaulle in Uniform (June 1940)

1971. De Gaulle Commemoration.

473	64	25f. black	2·50	4·00
474	-	25f. blue	2·50	4·00
475	-	25f. red	2·50	4·00
476	-	25f. black	2·50	4·00

DESIGNS: No. 473, De Gaulle in uniform (June, 1940); No. 474, De Gaulle at Brazzaville, 1944; No. 475, De Gaulle in Paris, 1944; No. 476, De Gaulle as President of the French Republic, 1970 (T **64**).

1971. Nos. 1942/3 of France (Red Cross Fund) surch **CFA** and value.

477	15f.+5f. on 30c.+10c.	2·50	6·50
478	25f.+5f. on 50c.+10c.	3·25	6·50

65 King Penguin, Map and Exploration Ships

1972. Bicentenary of Discovery of Crozet Islands and Kerguelen (French Southern and Antarctic Territories).

479	65	45f. black, blue and brown	7·75	14·50

1972. No. 1956 of France surch **CFA** and value.

480	**688**	25f.+5f. on 50c+10c. blue, drab and yellow	2·50	6·00

1972. No. 1966 of France (Blood Donors) surch **CFA** and value.

481	**692**	15f. on 40c. red	2·30	3·50

1972. Air. No 1890 of France (Daurat and Vanier) surch **CFA** and value.

482	**662**	200f. on 5f. brn, grn & bl	4·50	4·50

1972. Postal Codes. Nos. 1969/70 of France surch **CFA** and value.

483	**695**	15f. on 30c. red, black and green	2·00	5·25
484	**695**	25f. on 50c. yell, blk & red	1·60	1·80

1972. Red Cross Fund. Nos. 1979/80 of France surch **CFA** and value.

485	**701**	15f.+5f. on 30c.+10c.	2·10	5·25
486	**701**	25f.+5f. on 50c.+10c.	2·50	5·25

1973. Stamp Day. No. 1996 of France surch **CFA** and value.

487	**707**	25f.+5f. on 50c.+10c.	4·25	6·50

1973. No. 2011 of France surch **CFA** and value.

488	**714**	45f. on 90c. green, violet and blue	2·75	5·50

1973. No. 2008 of France surch **CFA** and value.

489	50f. on 1f. green, brown & bl	2·50	2·00

1973. No. 1960 of France surch **CFA** and value.

490	100f. on 2f. purple and green	2·75	4·75

1973. No. 2021/2 of France surch **CFA** and value.

491	**721**	15f.+5f. on 30c.+10c. green and red	3·25	6·75
492	**721**	25f.+5f. on 50c.+10c. red and black	3·25	5·00

1973. No. 2026 of France surch **CFA** and value.

494	**725**	25f. on 50c. brown, blue and purple	3·00	3·25

1974. Stamp Day. No. 2031 surch **FCFA** and value.

495	**727**	25f.+5f. on 50c.+10c.	2·75	5·25

1974. French Art. No. 2033/6 surch **FCFA** and value.

496	100f. on 2f. multicoloured	2·75	5·75
497	100f. on 2f. multicoloured	2·00	8·00
498	100f. on 2f. brown and blue	3·00	7·00
499	100f. on 2f. multicoloured	2·30	8·00

1974. French Lifeboat Service. No. 2040 surch **FCFA** and value.

500	**731**	45f. on 90c. blue, red and brown	2·50	6·50

1974. Centenary of Universal Postal Union. No. 2057 surch **FCFA** and value.

501	**741**	60f. on 1f.20 green, red and blue	2·30	6·75

1974. "Marianne" stamps of France surch **FCFA** and value.

502	**668**	30f. on 60c. green	2·30	7·25
503	**668**	40f. on 80c. red	2·50	7·50

From 1 January 1975 the CFA franc was replaced by the French Metropolitan franc, and Reunion subsequently used unsurcharged stamps of France.

1974. Red Cross Fund. "The Seasons". Nos. 2059/60 surch **FCFA** and value.

504	**743**	30f.+7f. on 60c.+15c.	3·50	6·75
505	-	40f.+7f. on 80c.+15c.	3·50	7·00

PARCEL POST STAMPS

P5

1890

P11	**P5**	10c. black on yellow (black frame)	£300	£200
P13	**P5**	10c. black on yellow (blue frame)	42·00	38·00

From 1 January 1975 the CFA franc was replaced by the French Metropolitan franc, and Reunion subsequently used unsurcharged stamps of France.

P20

1907. Receipt stamps surch as in Type **P20**.

P76	**P20**	10c. brown and black	44·00	34·00
P77	**P20**	10c. brown and red	44·00	34·00

POSTAGE DUE STAMPS

D4

1889. Imperf.

D11A	**D4**	5c. black	36·00	7·25
D12A	**D4**	10c. black	12·00	6·50
D13B	**D4**	15c. black	60·00	29·00
D14A	**D4**	20c. black	70·00	5·50
D15A	**D4**	30c. black	75·00	6·75

D19

1907

D76	**D19**	5c. red on yellow	20	35
D77	**D19**	10c. blue on blue	60	1·30
D78	**D19**	15c. black on grey	1·30	3·75
D79	**D19**	20c. pink	1·80	1·00
D80	**D19**	30c. green on green	65	5·25
D81	**D19**	50c. red on green	1·40	1·80
D82	**D19**	60c. pink on blue	1·60	5·75
D83	**D19**	1f. lilac	1·80	5·00

1927. Surch.

D130	2f. on 1f. red	5·00	26·00
D131	3f. on 1f. brown	5·75	26·00

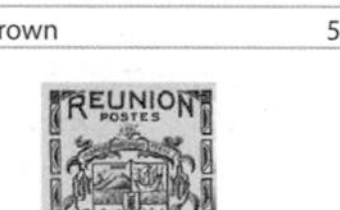

D33 Arms of Reunion

1933

D175	**D33**	5c. purple	20	4·50
D176	**D33**	10c. green	20	5·50
D177	**D33**	15c. brown	20	4·50
D178	**D33**	20c. orange	35	5·50
D179	**D33**	30c. olive	35	6·50
D180	**D33**	50c. blue	35	7·50
D181	**D33**	60c. brown	70	7·50
D182	**D33**	1f. violet	1·00	7·50
D183	**D33**	2f. blue	80	7·50
D184	**D33**	3f. red	1·00	7·50

D43

1947

D306	**D43**	10c. mauve	10	5·75
D307	**D43**	30c. brown	10	5·50
D308	**D43**	50c. green	35	6·00
D309	**D43**	1f. brown	1·30	7·25
D310	**D43**	2f. red	2·75	7·00
D311	**D43**	3f. brown	1·70	7·50
D312	**D43**	4f. blue	1·60	8·25
D313	**D43**	5f. red	1·60	8·25
D314	**D43**	10f. green	1·50	8·00
D315	**D43**	20f. blue	2·75	8·50

1949. As Type **D250** of France, but inscr "TIMBRE TAXE" surch **CFA** and value.

D333	10c. on 1f. blue	10	7·00
D334	50c. on 2f. blue	10	5·50
D335	1f. on 3f. red	40	6·00
D336	2f. on 4f. violet	80	6·75
D337	3f. on 5f. pink	1·50	8·00
D338	5f. on 10f. red	1·40	8·00
D339	10f. on 20f. brown	1·20	8·50
D340	20f. on 50f. green	3·50	17·00
D341	50f. on 100f. green	8·75	55·00

1962. Wheat Sheaves Type of France surch **CFA** and value.

D406	**D457**	1f. on 5c. mauve	1·30	6·25
D407	**D457**	10f. on 20c. brown	2·50	7·75
D408	**D457**	20f. on 50c. green	16·00	36·00

1964. Nos. D1650/4 and D1656/7 of France surch **CFA** and value.

D424	-	1f. on 5c.	35	4·50
D425	-	5f. on 10c.	35	4·50
D426	**D 539**	7f. on 15c.	40	4·75
D427	-	10f. on 20c.	2·10	5·50
D428	-	15f. on 30c.	75	5·00
D429	-	20f. on 50c.	40	5·00
D430	-	50f. on 1f.	90	6·00

Pt. 1

RHODESIA

A British territory in central Africa, formerly administered by the British South Africa Co. In 1924 divided into the territories of Northern and Southern Rhodesia which issued their own stamps (q.v.). In 1964 Southern Rhodesia was renamed Rhodesia; on becoming independent in 1980 it was renamed Zimbabwe.

1890. 12 pence = 1 shilling; 20 shillings = 1 pound.
1970. 100 cents = 1 dollar.

1 Arms of the Company

1890. The pound values are larger.

24		8d. red and ultramarine	16·00	23·00
18	**1**	½d. blue and red	3·75	4·75
1	**1**	1d. black	17·00	4·00
20	**1**	2d. green and red	26·00	7·50
21	**1**	3d. black and green	23·00	4·50
22	**1**	4d. brown and black	45·00	5·50
3	**1**	6d. blue	48·00	4·25
4	**1**	1s. brown	50·00	16·00
5	**1**	2s. orange	75·00	40·00
6	**1**	2s.6d. purple	48·00	50·00
25	**1**	3s. brown and green	£190	90·00
26	**1**	4s. black and red	48·00	50·00
8	**1**	5s. yellow	90·00	60·00
9	**1**	10s. green	£130	£100
10	-	£1 blue	£325	£170
11	-	£2 red	£550	£170
12	-	£5 green	£1600	£450
13	-	£10 brown	£2750	£700

1891. Surch in figures.

14	½d. on 6d. blue	£140	£475
15	2d. on 6d. blue	£190	£700
16	4d. on 6d. blue	£200	£800
17	8d. on 1s. brown	£225	£850

5

1896. The ends of ribbons containing motto cross the animals' legs.

41	**5**	½d. grey and mauve	4·50	3·25
42	**5**	1d. red and green	13·00	4·75
43	**5**	2d. brown and mauve	27·00	11·00
31	**5**	3d. brown and blue	10·00	2·00
44a	**5**	4d. blue and mauve	22·00	50
46	**5**	6d. mauve and red	17·00	75
34	**5**	8d. green and mauve on buff	17·00	60
35	**5**	1s. green and blue	26·00	3·25
47	**5**	2s. blue and green on buff	55·00	13·00
48	**5**	2s.6d. brown & pur on yell	90·00	65·00
36	**5**	3s. green and mauve on blue	90·00	42·00
37	**5**	4s. red and blue on green	75·00	2·75
49	**5**	5s. brown and green	65·00	13·00
50	**5**	10s. grey and red on rose	£150	75·00

1896. Surch in words.

51	**1**	1d. on 3d. black and green	£600	£750
52	**1**	1d. on 4s. black and red	£300	£350
53	**1**	3d. on 5s. yellow	£190	£250

1896. Cape of Good Hope stamps optd **BRITISH SOUTH AFRICA COMPANY.**

58	**6**	½d. black (No. 48)	18·00	23·00
59	**17**	1d. red (No. 58a)	20·00	26·00
60	**6**	2d. brown (No. 60)	27·00	14·00
61	**6**	3d. red (No. 40)	55·00	75·00
62	**6**	4d. blue (No. 51)	30·00	26·00
63	**4**	6d. purple (No. 52a)	70·00	80·00
64	**6**	1s. yellow (No. 65)	£150	£150

9

1897. The ends of motto ribbons do not cross the animals' legs.

66	**9**	½d. grey and mauve	7·00	8·50
67	**9**	1d. red and green	10·00	9·50
68	**9**	2d. brown and mauve	22·00	4·00
69	**9**	3d. brown and blue	8·50	50
70	**9**	4d. blue and mauve	28·00	4·00
71	**9**	6d. mauve and red	18·00	3·50
72	**9**	8d. green and mauve on buff	28·00	50
73	**9**	£1 black and brown on green	£450	£225

10

11

1898. Nos. 90/93a are larger (24×28½ mm).

75a	**10**	½d. green	5·50	3·50
77	**10**	1d. red	14·00	1·00
79	**10**	2d. brown	11·00	1·75
80	**10**	2½d. blue	23·00	1·75
81	**10**	3d. red	20·00	80
82	**10**	4d. olive	18·00	30
83	**10**	6d. purple	25·00	3·25
84	**11**	1s. brown	32·00	4·50
85	**11**	2s.6d. grey	75·00	2·00
86	**11**	3s. violet	32·00	4·00
87	**11**	5s. orange	70·00	25·00
88	**11**	7s.6d. black	£110	32·00
89	**11**	10s. green	65·00	2·50
90	-	£1 purple	£375	£170
91	-	£2 brown	£130	6·50
92	-	£5 blue	£3250	£2500
93	-	£10 lilac	£3500	£2250
93a	-	£20 brown	£16000	

13 Victoria Falls

1905. Visit of British Assn. and Opening of Victoria Falls Bridge across Zambesi.

94	**13**	1d. red	8·50	9·00
95	**13**	2½d. blue	18·00	11·00
96	**13**	5d. red	38·00	55·00
97	**13**	1s. green	42·00	50·00
98	**13**	2s.6d. black	£120	£170
99	**13**	5s. violet	£110	45·00

1909. Optd **RHODESIA.** or surch also.

100	**10**	½d. green	5·00	3·00
101	**10**	1d. red	10·00	1·50
102	**10**	2d. brown	5·00	7·50
103	**10**	2½d. blue	3·50	80
104	**10**	3d. red	3·50	2·25
105	**10**	4d. olive	15·00	3·75
114	**10**	5d. on 6d. purple	13·00	21·00
106	**10**	6d. purple	8·50	9·00
116	**11**	7½d. on 2s.6d. grey	5·00	3·75
117a	**11**	10d. on 2s. violet	8·00	4·00
107c	**11**	1s. brown	24·00	9·00
118	**11**	2s. on 5s. orange	15·00	8·00
108	**11**	2s.6d. grey	32·00	12·00
109	**11**	3s. violet	25·00	12·00
110	**11**	5s. orange	55·00	85·00
111	**11**	7s.6d. black	£110	30·00
112	**11**	10s. green	75·00	22·00
113	-	£1 purple	£200	£110
113d	-	£2 brown	£4000	£300
113e	-	£5 blue	£9000	£5000

17

1910

119	**17**	½d. green	15·00	2·00
123	**17**	1d. red	35·00	4·25
128	**17**	2d. black and grey	65·00	7·50
131a	**17**	2½d. blue	27·00	10·00
135	**17**	3d. purple and yellow	65·00	20·00
140	**17**	4d. black and orange	50·00	26·00
141	**17**	5d. purple and olive	65·00	75·00
145	**17**	6d. purple and mauve	65·00	24·00
148	**17**	8d. black and purple	£180	£100
149	**17**	10d. red and purple	50·00	50·00
152	**17**	1s. black and green	70·00	23·00
153	**17**	2s. black and blue	£120	75·00
157	**17**	2s.6d. black and red	£350	£425
158	**17**	3s. green and violet	£250	£200
160a	**17**	5s. red and green	£300	£200

160b	**17**	7s.6d. red and blue	£650	£425
164	**17**	10s. green and orange	£425	£500
166	**17**	£1 red and black	£1600	£375

18

1913

187	**18**	½d. green	10·00	2·25
192	**18**	1d. red	4·50	3·50
198	**18**	1½d. brown	6·50	2·25
291	**18**	2d. black and grey	15·00	9·00
200	**18**	2½d. blue	9·00	45·00
259	**18**	3d. black and yellow	19·00	3·75
261	**18**	4d. black and orange	24·00	12·00
212	**18**	5d. black and green	7·50	23·00
295	**18**	6d. black and mauve	8·50	9·00
230	**18**	8d. violet and green	20·00	75·00
247	**18**	10d. blue and red	17·00	50·00
272	**18**	1s. black and blue	12·00	14·00
273	**18**	2s. black and brown	24·00	20·00
236	**18**	2s.6d. blue and brown	85·00	60·00
304	**18**	3s. brown and blue	£130	£170
239	**18**	5s. blue and green	95·00	£100
252	**18**	7s.6d. mauve and grey	£160	£275
309	**18**	10s. red and green	£275	£325
242	**18**	£1 black and purple	£425	£650

1917. Surch **Half Penny** (without hyphen or full stop).

280	½d. on 1s. red	2·50	10·00

1917. Surch **Half-Penny**. (with hyphen and full stop).

281	½d. on 1d. red	2·00	9·50

RHODESIA

The following stamps are for the former Southern Rhodesia, renamed Rhodesia.

59 "Telecommunications"

1965. Centenary of I.T.U.

351	**59**	6d. violet and olive	1·50	40
352	**59**	1s.3d. violet and lilac	1·50	40
353	**59**	2s.6d. violet and brown	5·00	4·50

60 Bangala Dam

1965. Water Conservation. Multicoloured.

354	3d. Type **60**	30	10
355	4d. Irrigation canal	1·25	2·00
356	2s.6d. Cutting sugar cane	2·25	3·50

63 Sir Winston Churchill, Quill, Sword and Houses of Parliament

1965. Churchill Commemoration.

357	**63**	1s.3d. black and blue	70	35

64 Coat of Arms

1965. "Independence".

358	**64**	2s.6d. multicoloured	15	15

1966. Optd **INDEPENDENCE 11th November 1965**. (a) On Nos. 92/105 of Southern Rhodesia.

359	**45**	½d. yellow, green and blue	10	10
360	-	1d. violet and ochre	10	10
361	-	2d. yellow and violet	10	10
362	-	3d. brown and blue	10	10
363	-	4d. orange and green	15	10
364	**50**	6d. red, yellow and green	15	10
365	-	9d. brown, yellow and green	30	10
366	-	1s. green and ochre	40	10
367	-	1s.3d. red, violet and green	50	50
368	-	2s. blue and ochre	60	3·25
369	-	2s.6d. blue and red	60	1·00
370	**56**	5s. multicoloured	2·00	5·50
371	-	10s. multicoloured	4·50	2·25
372	-	£1 multicoloured	1·25	2·25

(b) Surch on No. 357.

373	**63**	5s. on 1s.3d. black and blue	6·00	13·00

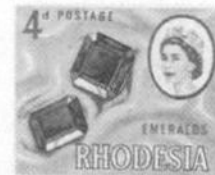

67 Emeralds

1966. As Nos. 92/105 of Southern Rhodesia, but inscr "RHODESIA" as in T **67**. Some designs and colours changed.

374	-	1d. violet and ochre	10	10
375	-	2d. orange & grn (As No. 96)	10	10
376	-	3d. brown and blue	10	10
377	**67**	4d. green and brown	1·75	10
378	**50**	6d. red, yellow and green	15	10
379	-	9d. yellow & vio (As No. 94)	60	20
380	**45**	1s. yellow, green and blue	15	10
381	-	1s.3d. bl & ochre (As No. 101)	25	15
382	-	1s.6d. brn, yell & grn (As No. 98)	2·25	25
383	-	2s. red, vio & grn (As No. 100)	60	1·50
384	-	2s.6d. blue, red & turquoise	1·50	20
385	**56**	5s. multicoloured	1·00	90
386	-	10s. multicoloured	4·25	3·50
387	-	£1 multicoloured	3·25	7·00

Nos. 379/80 are in larger format as Type **50** of Southern Rhodesia.

Stamps in these designs were later printed locally. These vary only slightly from the above in details and shade.

For Nos. 376, 380 and 382/4 in dual currency see Nos. 408/12.

68 Zeederberg Coach, c. 1895

1966. 28th Congress of Southern Africa Philatelic Federation ("Rhopex").

388	**68**	3d. multicoloured	15	10
389	-	9d. multicoloured	15	20
390	-	1s.6d. blue and black	25	30
391	-	2s.6d. pink, green and black	30	80
MS392		126×84 mm. Nos. 388/91	5·00	11·00

DESIGNS: 9d. Sir Rowland Hill; 1s.6d. The Penny Black; 2s.6d. Rhodesian stamp of 1892 (No. 12).

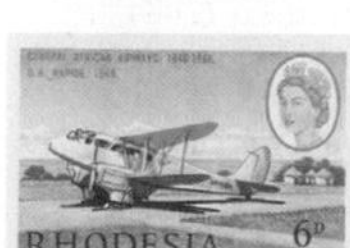

69 De Havilland Dragon Rapide (1946)

1966. 20th Anniv of Central African Airways.

393	**69**	6d. multicoloured	1·00	35
394	-	1s.3d. multicoloured	1·00	40
395	-	2s.6d. multicoloured	1·25	1·50
396	-	5s. black and blue	1·75	4·50

AIRCRAFT: 1s.3d. Douglas DC-3 (1953); 2s.6d. Vickers Viscount 748 "Matopos" (1956); 5s. B.A.C. One Eleven.

70 Kudu

1967. Dual Currency Issue. As Nos. 376, 380 and 382/4. but value in dual currency as T **70**.

408	**70**	3d./2½c. brown and blue	50	15
409	-	1s./10c. yellow, green and blue (No. 380)	50	25
410	-	1s.6d./15c. brown, yellow and green (No. 382)	4·75	40
411	-	2s./20c. red, violet and green (No. 383)	4·50	4·50
412	-	2s.6d./25c. ultramarine, red and blue (No. 384)	20·00	26·00

71 Dr. Jameson (administrator)

1967. Famous Rhodesians (1st series) and 50th Death Anniv of Dr. Jameson.

413	**71**	1s.6d. multicoloured	20	35

See also Nos. 426, 430, 457, 458, 469, 480, 488 and 513.

72 Soapstone Sculpture (Joram Mariga)

1967. Tenth Anniv of Opening of Rhodes National Gallery.

414	**72**	3d. brown, green and black	10	10
415	-	9d. blue, brown and black	20	20
416	-	1s.3d. multicoloured	20	25
417	-	2s.6d. multicoloured	25	60

DESIGNS: 9d. "The Burgher of Calais" (detail, Rodin); 1s.3d. "The Knight" (stamp design wrongly inscr) (Roberto Crippa); 2s.6d. "John the Baptist" (Mossini).

73 Baobab Tree

1967. Nature Conservation.

418	**73**	4d. brown and black	10	20
419	-	4d. green and black	25	20
420	-	4d. grey and black	25	20
421	-	4d. orange and black	10	20

DESIGNS—HORIZ: No. 419, White rhinoceros; No. 420, African elephants. VERT: No. 421, Wild gladiolus.

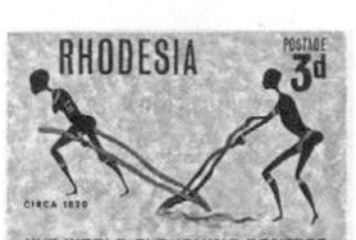

74 Wooden Hand Plough

1968. 15th World Ploughing Contest, Norton, Rhodesia.

422	**74**	3d. orange, red and brown	10	10
423	-	9d. multicoloured	15	20
424	-	1s.6d. multicoloured	20	55
425	-	2s.6d. multicoloured	20	75

DESIGNS: 9d. Early wheel plough; 1s.6d. Steam powered tractor, and ploughs; 2s.6d. Modern tractor, and plough.

75 Alfred Beit (national benefactor)

1968. Famous Rhodesians (2nd issue).

426	**75**	1s.6d. orange, black & brn	20	30

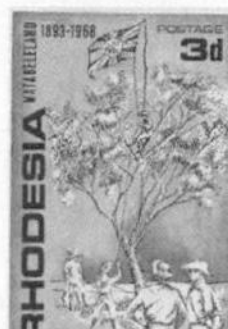

76 Raising the Flag, Bulawayo, 1893

1968. 75th Anniv of Matabeleland.

427	**76**	3d. orange, red and black	15	10
428	-	9d. multicoloured	15	20
429	-	1s.6d. green, emerald & blk	20	60

DESIGNS: 9d. View and coat of arms of Bulawayo; 1s.6d. Allan Wilson (combatant in the Matabele War).

77 Sir William Henry Milton (administrator)

1969. Famous Rhodesians (3rd issue).

430	**77**	1s.6d. multicoloured	30	40

78 2ft. Gauge Locomotive No. 15, 1897

1969. 70th Anniv of Opening of Beira–Salisbury Railway. Multicoloured.

431	3d. Type **78**	30	10
432	9d. 7th Class steam locomotive No. 43, 1903	50	40
433	1s.6d. Beyer, Peacock 15th Class steam locomotive No. 413, 1951	60	75
434	2s.6d. Class DE2 diesel-electric locomotive No. 1203, 1955	1·00	3·00

79 Low Level Bridge

1969. Bridges of Rhodesia. Multicoloured.

435	3d. Type **79**	20	10
436	9d. Mpudzi bridge	40	20
437	1s.6d. Umniati bridge	60	60
438	2s.6d. Birchenough bridge	80	1·25

80 Harvesting Wheat

81 Devil's Cataract, Victoria Falls

1970. Decimal Currency.

439	**80**	1c. multicoloured	10	10
440	-	2c. multicoloured	10	10
441	-	2½c. multicoloured	10	10
441c	-	3c. multicoloured	1·25	10
442	-	3½c. multicoloured	10	10
442b	-	4c. multicoloured	2·00	1·00
443	-	5c. multicoloured	15	10
443b	-	6c. multicoloured	4·25	4·75
443c	**81**	7½c. multicoloured	7·00	60
444	**81**	8c. multicoloured	75	20
445	-	10c. multicoloured	60	10
446	-	12½c. multicoloured	1·75	10
446a	-	14c. multicoloured	12·00	70
447	-	15c. multicoloured	1·25	15
448	-	20c. multicoloured	1·00	15
449	-	25c. multicoloured	4·00	60
450	-	50c. turquoise and blue	1·25	55
451	-	$1 multicoloured	5·50	3·00
452	-	$2 multicoloured	8·50	15·00

DESIGNS—As Type **80**: 2c. Pouring molten metal; 2½c. Zimbabwe Ruins; 3c. Articulated lorry; 3½c., 4c. Statue of Cecil Rhodes; 5c. Mine headgear; 6c. Hydrofoil "Seaflight". As Type **81**: 10c. Yachting on Lake McIlwaine; 12½c. Hippopotamus in river; 14c., 15c. Kariba Dam; 20c. Irrigation canal. 31×26 mm: 25c. Bateleurs; 50c. Radar antenna and Vickers Viscount 810; $1 "Air Rescue"; $2 Rhodesian flag.

82 Despatch Rider, c. 1890

1970. Inauguration of Posts and Telecommunications Corporation. Multicoloured.

453	2½c. Type **82**	40	10
454	3½c. Loading mail at Salisbury airport	45	50
455	15c. Constructing telegraph line, c. 1890	50	1·25
456	25c. Telephone and modern telecommunications equipment	55	2·00

83 Mother Patrick (Dominican nurse and teacher)

1970. Famous Rhodesians (4th issue).

457	**83**	15c. multicoloured	45	50

84 Fredrick Courteney Selous (big-game hunter, explorer and pioneer)

1971. Famous Rhodesians (5th issue).

458	**84**	15c. multicoloured	40	70

85 Hoopoe

1971. Birds of Rhodesia (1st series). Multicoloured.

459	2c. Type **85**	35	20
460	2½c. Half-collared kingfisher (horiz)	35	10
461	5c. Golden-breasted bunting	50	15
462	7½c. Carmine bee eater	60	15
463	8c. Red-eyed bulbul	60	20
464	25c. Senegal wattled plover (horiz)	1·00	1·25

See also Nos. 537/42.

86 Porphyritic Granite

1971. "Granite 71" Geological Symposium. Multicoloured.

465	2½c. Type **86**	30	10
466	7½c. Muscovite mica seen through microscope	40	15
467	15c. Granite seen through microscope	65	35
468	25c. Geological map of Rhodesia	65	1·25

87 Dr. Robert Moffat (missionary)

1972. Famous Rhodesians (6th issue).

469	**87**	13c. multicoloured	50	75

88 Bird ("Be Airwise")

1972. "Prevent Pollution". Multicoloured.

470	2½c. Type **88**	15	10
471	3½c. Antelope ("Be Country-wise")	15	20
472	7c. Fish ("Be Waterwise")	15	30
473	13c. City ("Be Citywise")	20	55

1972. "Rhophil '72". Nos. 439, 441 and 442 with commemorative inscr in margins.

MS474 1c. multicoloured	1·10	2·00
MS474/6 Set of 3 sheets	3·00	5·50
MS475 2½c. multicoloured	1·10	2·00
MS476 3½c. multicoloured	1·10	2·00

89 "The Three Kings"

1972. Christmas.

477	**89**	2c. multicoloured	10	10
478	**89**	5c. multicoloured	15	20
479	**89**	13c. multicoloured	30	55

90 Dr. David Livingstone

1973. Famous Rhodesians (7th issue).

480	**90**	14c. multicoloured	50	75

91 W.M.O. Emblem

1973. Centenary of I.M.O./W.M.O.

481	**91**	3c. multicoloured	10	10
482	**91**	14c. multicoloured	30	15
483	**91**	25c. multicoloured	40	75

92 Arms of Rhodesia

1973. 50th Anniv of Responsible Government.

484	**92**	2½c. multicoloured	10	10
485	**92**	4c. multicoloured	15	10
486	**92**	7½c. multicoloured	20	15
487	**92**	14c. multicoloured	35	1·00

93 George Pauling (construction engineer)

1974. Famous Rhodesians (8th issue).

488	**93**	14c. multicoloured	50	1·25

94 Greater Kudu

1974. Multicoloured. (a) Antelopes.

489	1c. Type **94**	10	10
490	2½c. Eland	75	10
491	3c. Roan antelope	10	10
492	4c. Reedbuck	20	10
493	5c. Bushbuck	20	60

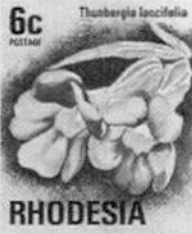

95 Thunbergia

(b) Wild Flowers.

494	6c. Type **95**	20	10
495	7½c. Flame lily	50	20
496	8c. As 7½c.	20	10
497	10c. Devil thorn	20	10
498	12c. Hibiscus	40	2·00
499	12½c. Pink sabi star	1·00	35
500	14c. Wild pimpernel	1·00	35
501	15c. As 12½c.	40	75
502	16c. As 14c.	40	30

96 "Charaxes varanes"

(c) Butterflies.

503	20c. Type **96**	1·00	35
504	24c. "Precis hierta" (sp. "cebrene")	40	40
505	25c. As 24c.	1·50	1·50
506	50c. "Colotis regina"	40	60
507	$1 "Graphium antheus"	40	60
508	$2 "Hamanumida daedalus"	40	75

97 Collecting Mail

1974. Centenary of U.P.U. Multicoloured.

509	3c. Type **97**	15	10
510	4c. Sorting mail	15	10
511	7½c. Mail delivery	20	20
512	14c. Weighing parcel	30	90

98 Thomas Baines (artist)

1975. Famous Rhodesians (9th issue).

513	**98**	14c. multicoloured	50	60

99 "Euphorbia confinalis"

1975. Int Succulent Congress, Salisbury ("Aloe '75"). Multicoloured.

514	2½c. Type **99**	10	10
515	3c. "Aloe excelsa"	10	10
516	4c. "Hoodia lugardii"	10	10
517	7½c. "Aloe ortholopha"	15	10
518	14c. "Aloe musapana"	30	10
519	25c. "Aloe saponaria"	50	2·00

100 Prevention of Head Injuries

1975. Occupational Safety. Multicoloured.

520	2½c. Type **100**	10	10
521	4c. Bandaged hand and gloved hand	15	10
522	7½c. Broken glass and eye	15	15
523	14c. Blind man and welder with protective mask	20	55

101 Telephones, 1876 and 1976

1976. Telephone Centenary.

524	**101**	3c. grey and blue	10	10
525	-	14c. black and brown	20	55

DESIGN: 14c. Alexander Graham Bell.

1976. Nos. 495, 500 and 505 surch.

526	8c. on 7½c. multicoloured	15	15
527	16c. on 14c. multicoloured	15	15
528	24c. on 25c. multicoloured	20	80

103 Roan Antelope

1976. Vulnerable Wildlife. Multicoloured.

529	4c. Type **103**	10	10
530	6c. Brown hyena	15	60
531	8c. Hunting dog	15	10
532	16c. Cheetah	20	35

104 Msasa

1976. Trees of Rhodesia. Multicoloured.

533	4c. Type **104**	10	10
534	6c. Red mahogany	10	10
535	8c. Mukwa	15	10
536	16c. Rhodesian teak	20	55

105 Garden Bulbul ("Blackeyed-Bulbul")

1977. Birds of Rhodesia (2nd series). Multicoloured.

537	3c. Type **105**	15	10
538	4c. Yellow-mantled whydah ("Yellow-mantled Wydah")	15	10
539	6c. Cape longclaw ("Orange throated longclaw")	20	60
540	8c. Magpie shrike ("Eastern Long-tailed Shrike")	20	35
541	16c. Lesser blue-eared glossy starling ("Lesser Blue-eared Starling")	25	60
542	24c. Green wood hoopoe ("Red-billed Wood hoopee")	30	1·10

106 "Lake Kyle" (Joan Evans)

1977. Landscape Paintings. Multicoloured.

543	3c. Type **106**	10	10
544	4c. "Chimanimani Mountains" (Joan Evans)	10	10
545	6c. "Rocks near Bonsor Reef" (Alice Balfour)	10	30
546	8c. "A Dwala near Devil's Pass" (Alice Balfour)	10	10
547	16c. "Zimbabwe" (Alice Balfour)	15	30
548	24c. "Victoria Falls" (Thomas Baines)	25	60

107 Virgin and Child

1977. Christmas.

549	**107**	3c. multicoloured	10	10
550	**107**	6c. multicoloured	10	20
551	**107**	8c. multicoloured	10	10
552	**107**	16c. multicoloured	15	30

108 Fair Spire

1978. Trade Fair Rhodesia, Bulawayo. Multicoloured.

553	4c. Type **108**	10	10
554	8c. Fair Spire (different)	15	25

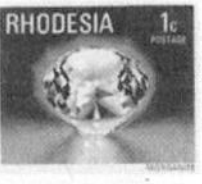

109 Morganite

1978. Gemstones, Wild Animals and Waterfalls. Multicoloured.

555	1c. Type **109**	10	10
556	3c. Amethyst	10	10
557	4c. Garnet	10	10
558	5c. Citrine	10	10
559	7c. Blue topaz	10	10
560	9c. White rhinoceros	15	10
561	11c. Lion	10	20
562	13c. Warthog	10	1·25
563	15c. Giraffe	15	20
564	17c. Common zebra	15	10
565	21c. Odzani Falls	15	40
566	25c. Goba Falls	15	15

567		30c. Inyangombi Falls	15	15
568		$1 Bridal Veil Falls	20	35
569		$2 Victoria Falls	30	60

Nos. 560/4 are 26×23 mm, and Nos. 565/9 32×27 mm.

112 Wright Flyer I

1978. 75th Anniv of Powered Flight. Multicoloured.

570		4c. Type **112**	10	10
571		5c. Bleriot XI	10	10
572		7c. Vickers Vimy "Silver Queen II"	10	10
573		9c. Armstrong Whitworth A.W.15 Atalanta	10	10
574		17c. Vickers Viking 1B "Zambezi"	10	10
575		25c. Boeing 720B	15	50

POSTAGE DUE STAMPS

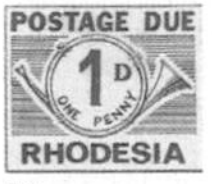

D2

1965. Roul.

D8	**D2**	1d. red	50	12·00
D9	**D2**	2d. blue	40	8·00
D10	**D2**	4d. green	50	8·00
D11	**D2**	6d. plum	50	6·00

D3 Zimbabwe Bird (soapstone sculpture)

1966

D12	**D3**	1d. red	60	3·50
D13	**D3**	2d. blue	75	1·75
D14	**D3**	4d. green	75	4·25
D15	**D3**	6d. violet	75	1·50
D16	**D3**	1s. brown	75	1·50
D17	**D3**	2s. black	1·00	5·50

1970. Decimal Currency. As Type **D3** but larger (26×22½ mm).

D18		1c. green	75	1·25
D19		2c. blue	75	60
D20		5c. violet	1·25	1·75
D21		6c. yellow	6·00	4·00
D22		10c. red	1·25	4·00

Pt. 1

RHODESIA AND NYASALAND

Stamps for the Central African Federation of Northern and Southern Rhodesia and Nysaland Protectorate. The stamps of the Federation were withdrawn on 19 February 1964 when all three constituent territories had resumed issuing their own stamps.

12 pence = 1 shilling; 20 shillings = 1 pound.

1 Queen Elizabeth II

2 Queen Elizabeth II

1954

1	**1**	½d. orange-red	15	10
2	**1**	1d. blue	15	10
3	**1**	2d. green	15	10
3a	**1**	2½d. ochre	6·50	10
4	**1**	3d. red	20	10
5	**1**	4d. brown	60	20
6	**1**	4½d. green	30	1·75
7	**1**	6d. purple	2·25	10
8	**1**	9d. violet	2·50	1·00
9	**1**	1s. grey	2·50	10
10	**2**	1s.3d. red and blue	7·00	40
11	**2**	2s. blue and brown	9·00	6·50
12	**2**	2s.6d. black and red	9·00	2·25
13	**2**	5s. violet and olive	26·00	8·00
14	-	10s. turquoise and orange	26·00	10·00
15	-	£1 olive and lake	45·00	30·00

The 10s. and £1 are as Type **2** but larger (31×17 mm) and have the name at top and foliage on either side of portrait.

4 De Havilland Comet 1 over Victoria Falls

5 Livingstone and Victoria Falls

1955. Cent of Discovery of Victoria Falls.

16	**4**	3d. blue and turquoise	1·00	30
17	**5**	1s. purple and blue	55	70

6 Tea Picking

11 Lake Bangweulu

17 Rhodes Statue

1959

18	**6**	½d. black and green	1·25	2·25
19	-	1d. red and black	30	10
20	-	2d. violet and brown	2·50	50
21	-	2½d. purple and blue	2·00	2·25
22	-	3d. black and blue	1·00	10
23	**11**	4d. purple and green	1·50	10
24	-	6d. blue and green	2·75	10
24a	-	9d. brown and violet	9·00	3·50
25	-	1s. green and blue	1·25	10
26	-	1s.3d. green and brown	4·25	10
27	-	2s. green and red	4·25	60
28	-	2s.6d. blue and brown	9·50	1·00
29	**17**	5s. brown and green	16·00	2·75
30	-	10s. brown and red	28·00	26·00
31	-	£1 black and violet	48·00	65·00

DESIGNS—VERT (as Type **6**): 1d. V.H.F. mast; 2d. Copper mining; 2½d. Fairbridge Memorial. (As Type **11**): 6d. Eastern Cataract, Victoria Falls. HORIZ (as Type **6**): 3d. Rhodes's grave. (As Type **11**): 9d. Rhodesian railway trains; 1s. Tobacco; 1s.3d. Lake Nyasa; 2s. Chirundu Bridge; 2s.6d. Salisbury Airport. (As Type **17**): 10s. Mlanje; £1 Federal Coat of Arms.

20 Kariba Gorge, 1955

1960. Opening of Kariba Hydro-electric Scheme.

32	**20**	3d. green and orange	70	10
33	-	6d. brown and bistre	1·00	20
34	-	1s. blue and green	2·50	4·00
35	-	1s.3d. blue and brown	2·75	3·50
36	-	2s.6d. purple and red	4·00	8·50
37	-	5s. violet and turquoise	11·00	12·00

DESIGNS: 6d. 330 k.V. power lines; 1s. Barrage wall; 1s.3d. Barrage and lake; 2s.6d. Interior of power station; 5s. Queen Mother and barrage wall (inscr "ROYAL OPENING").

26 Miner drilling

1961. Seventh Commonwealth Mining and Metallurgical Congress.

38	**26**	6d. green and brown	1·00	20
39	-	1s.3d. black and blue	1·25	80

DESIGN: 1s.3d. Surface installations, Nchanga Mine.

28 De Havilland Hercules "City of Basra" on Rhodesian Airstrip

1962. 30th Anniv of First London–Rhodesian Airmail Service.

40	**28**	6d. green and red	2·50	75
41	-	1s.3d. blue, black and yellow	1·75	50
42	-	2s.6d. red and violet	3·50	6·50

DESIGNS: 1s.3d. Short S.23 flying boat "Canopus" taking off from Zambesi; 2s.6d. Hawker Siddeley Comet 4 at Salisbury Airport.

31 Tobacco Plant

1963. World Tobacco Congress, Salisbury.

43	**31**	3d. green and olive	30	10
44	-	6d. green, brown and blue	40	35
45	-	1s.3d. brown and blue	1·50	45
46	-	2s.6d. yellow and brown	1·75	3·25

DESIGNS: 6d. Tobacco field; 1s.3d. Auction floor; 2s.6d. Cured tobacco.

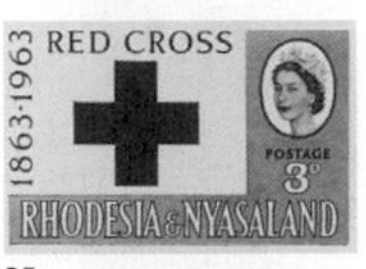

35

1963. Centenary of Red Cross.

47	**35**	3d. red	1·50	10

36 African "Round Table" Emblem

1963. World Council of Young Men's Service Clubs, Salisbury.

48	**36**	6d. black, gold and green	75	1·50
49	**36**	1s.3d. multicoloured	1·00	1·25

POSTAGE DUE STAMPS

D1

1961

D1	**D1**	1d. red	3·75	5·50
D2	**D1**	2d. blue	3·00	3·00
D3	**D1**	4d. green	3·50	9·50
D4	**D1**	6d. purple	4·50	7·50

Pt. 21

RIAU-LINGGA ARCHIPELAGO

A group of islands E. of Sumatra and S. of Singapore. Part of Indonesia.

100 cents or sen = 1 rupiah.

1954. Optd **RIAU**. (a) On stamps of Indonesia.

1	**96**	5s. red	90·00	55·00
2	**96**	7½s. green	2·20	2·50
3	**96**	10s. blue	£100	£120
4	**96**	15s. violet	4·50	4·50
5	**96**	20s. red	4·50	4·50
6	**96**	25s. green	£200	70·00
7	**97**	30s. red	9·25	8·25
8	**97**	35s. violet	1·80	2·10
9	**97**	40s. green	1·80	2·10
10	**97**	45s. purple	1·80	2·10
11	**97**	50s. brown	£750	95·00
12	**98**	60s. brown	1·80	2·50
13	**98**	70s. grey	4·50	3·75
14	**98**	75s. blue	16·00	5·25
15	**98**	80s. purple	3·25	5·75
16	**98**	90s. green	3·25	5·25

(b) On Netherlands Indies Nos. 566/71.

17		1r. violet	21·00	8·25
18		2r. green	4·50	9·50
19		3r. purple	7·00	9·50
20		5r. brown	7·00	9·50
21		10r. black	9·25	16·00
22		25r. brown	9·25	16·00

1958. Stamps of Indonesia optd **RIAU**.

26	**115**	5s. blue	1·30	1·50
27	**115**	10s. brown (No. 714)	1·30	1·50
28	**115**	15s. purple (No. 715)	1·30	1·50
29	-	20s. green (No. 716)	1·30	1·50
30	-	25s. brown (No. 717)	1·30	1·50
31	-	30s. orange (No. 718)	1·30	1·50
32	-	50s. brown (No. 722)	1·30	1·50

1960. Stamps of Indonesia optd **RIAU**.

33	**99**	1r.25 orange	6·00	10·50
34	**99**	1r.50 brown	6·00	10·50
35	**99**	2r.50 brown	9·25	16·00
36	**99**	4r. green	1·60	16·00
37	**99**	6r. mauve	1·60	16·00
38	**99**	15r. stone	1·60	16·00
39	**99**	20r. purple	1·60	21·00
40	**99**	40r. green	1·60	23·00
41	**99**	50r. violet	3·25	24·00

Pt. 9

RIO DE ORO

A Spanish territory on the West Coast of North Africa, renamed Spanish Sahara in 1924.

100 centimos = 1 peseta.

1905. "Curly Head" key-type inscr "COLONIA DE RIO DE ORO".

1	**Z**	1c. green	4·75	4·50
2	**Z**	2c. red	4·75	4·50
3	**Z**	3c. black	4·75	4·50
4	**Z**	4c. brown	4·75	4·50
5	**Z**	5c. red	4·75	4·50
6	**Z**	10c. brown	4·75	4·50
7	**Z**	15c. brown	4·75	4·50
8	**Z**	25c. blue	£120	55·00
9	**Z**	50c. green	60·00	23·00
10	**Z**	75c. violet	60·00	31·00
11	**Z**	1p. brown	41·00	12·50
12	**Z**	2p. orange	£140	85·00
13	**Z**	3p. lilac	90·00	31·00
14	**Z**	4p. green	90·00	31·00
15	**Z**	5p. blue	£120	65·00
16	**Z**	10p. red	£275	£200

1906. "Curly Head" key-type surch **HABILITADO PARA 15 CENTS** in circle.

17		15c. on 25c. blue	£300	£190

3

11

7

1907

18	**3**	1c. purple	4·25	3·75
19	**3**	2c. black	4·25	3·75
20	**3**	3c. brown	4·25	3·75
21	**3**	4c. red	4·25	3·75
22	**3**	5c. brown	4·25	3·75
23	**3**	10c. brown	4·25	3·75
24	**3**	15c. blue	4·25	3·75
25	**3**	25c. green	19·00	3·75
26	**3**	50c. purple	19·00	3·75
27	**3**	75c. brown	19·00	3·75
28	**3**	1p. buff	28·00	3·75
29	**3**	2p. lilac	7·00	3·75
30	**3**	3p. green	7·00	3·75
31	**3**	4p. blue	12·00	7·50
32	**3**	5p. red	12·00	7·50
33	**3**	10p. green	12·00	19·00

1907. Nos. 9/10 surch **1907 10 Cens**.

34	**Z**	10c. on 50c. green	£160	41·00
35	**Z**	10c. on 75c. violet	£120	41·00

1908. Nos. 12 and 26 surch **1908** and value.

36		2c. on 2p. orange	95·00	41·00
37	**3**	10c. on 50c. purple	32·00	6·25

1908. Surch **HABILITADO PARA 15 CENTS** in circle.

38		15c. on 25c. green	38·00	6·75
39		15c. on 75c. brown	50·00	13·00
40		15c. on 1p. buff	50·00	13·00
71		15c. on 3p. green	£250	36·00
72		15c. on 5p. red	16·00	15·00

1908. Large Fiscal stamp inscr "TERRITORIOS ESPANOLES DEL AFRICA OCCIDENTAL" surch **HABILITADO PARA CORREOS RIO DE ORO 5 CENS.** Imperf.

45		5c. on 50c. green	£110	47·00

1909

47	**7**	1c. orange	95	65
48	**7**	2c. orange	95	65
49	**7**	5c. green	95	65
50	**7**	10c. red	95	65
51	**7**	15c. green	95	65
52	**7**	20c. purple	2·50	1·10
53	**7**	25c. blue	2·50	1·10
54	**7**	30c. red	2·50	1·10
55	**7**	40c. brown	2·50	1·10
56	**7**	50c. purple	4·50	1·10
57	**7**	1p. brown	6·25	5·25
58	**7**	4p. red	7·50	8·00
59	**7**	10p. purple	17·00	14·00

1910. Nos. 13/16 surch **1910** and value.

60	**Z**	10c. on 5p. blue	22·00	14·00
62	**Z**	10c. on 10p. red	21·00	12·50
65	**Z**	15c. on 3p. lilac	21·00	12·50
66	**Z**	15c. on 4p. green	21·00	12·50

1911. Surch with value in figures and words.

67	**3**	2c. on 4p. blue	16·00	13·00
68	**3**	5c. on 10p. green	41·00	13·00
69	**3**	10c. on 2p. lilac	20·00	14·00
70	**3**	10c. on 3p. green	£250	80·00

1912

73	**11**	1c. pink	35	20
74	**11**	2c. lilac	35	20
75	**11**	5c. green	35	20
76	**11**	10c. red	35	20
77	**11**	15c. brown	35	20
78	**11**	20c. brown	35	20
79	**11**	25c. blue	35	20
80	**11**	30c. lilac	35	20
81	**11**	40c. green	35	20
82	**11**	50c. purple	35	20
83	**11**	1p. red	7·75	1·40
84	**11**	4p. red	8·50	7·50
85	**11**	10p. brown	13·50	12·50

12

14

15

1914

86	**12**	1c. brown	40	20
87	**12**	2c. purple	40	20
88	**12**	5c. green	40	20
89	**12**	10c. red	40	20
90	**12**	15c. red	40	20
91	**12**	20c. red	40	20
92	**12**	25c. blue	40	20
93	**12**	30c. green	40	20
94	**12**	40c. orange	40	20
95	**12**	50c. brown	40	20
96	**12**	1p. lilac	9·50	3·75
97	**12**	4p. red	12·50	3·75
98	**12**	10p. violet	12·50	11·50

1917. Nos. 73/85 optd **1917**.

99	**11**	1c. pink	18·00	1·70
100	**11**	2c. lilac	18·00	1·70
101	**11**	5c. green	3·25	1·70
102	**11**	10c. red	3·25	1·70
103	**11**	15c. brown	3·25	1·70
104	**11**	20c. brown	3·25	1·70
105	**11**	25c. blue	3·25	1·70
106	**11**	30c. lilac	3·25	1·70
107	**11**	40c. green	3·25	1·70
108	**11**	50c. purple	3·25	1·70
109	**11**	1p. red	18·00	11·00
110	**11**	4p. red	31·00	14·50
111	**11**	10p. brown	55·00	24·00

1919

112	**14**	1c. brown	1·00	70
113	**14**	2c. purple	1·00	70
114	**14**	5c. green	1·00	70
115	**14**	10c. red	1·00	70
116	**14**	15c. red	1·00	70
117	**14**	20c. orange	1·00	70
118	**14**	25c. blue	1·00	70
119	**14**	30c. green	1·00	70
120	**14**	40c. orange	1·00	70
121	**14**	50c. brown	1·00	70
122	**14**	1p. lilac	7·50	7·25
123	**14**	4p. red	12·50	14·00
124	**14**	10p. violet	18·00	24·00

1920

125	**15**	1c. purple	90	65
126	**15**	2c. pink	90	65
127	**15**	5c. red	90	65
128	**15**	10c. purple	90	65
129	**15**	15c. brown	90	65
130	**15**	20c. green	90	65
131	**15**	25c. orange	90	65
132	**15**	30c. blue	5·75	6·25
133	**15**	40c. orange	3·25	3·00
134	**15**	50c. purple	3·25	3·00
135	**15**	1p. green	50·00	3·00
136	**15**	4p. red	9·50	7·00
137	**15**	10p. brown	24·00	20·00

1921. As Nos. 14/26 of La Aguera but inscr "RIO DE ORO".

138	1c. yellow	90	60
139	2c. brown	90	60
140	5c. green	90	60
141	10c. red	90	60
142	15c. green	90	60
143	20c. blue	90	60
144	25c. blue	90	60
145	30c. pink	1·70	1·70
146	40c. violet	1·70	1·70
147	50c. orange	1·70	1·70
148	1p. mauve	5·75	2·75
149	4p. purple	16·00	11·00
150	10p. brown	24·00	25·00

For later issues see **SPANISH SAHARA**.

Pt. 9

RIO MUNI

A coastal settlement between Cameroun and Gabon, formerly using the stamps of Spanish Guinea. On 12 October 1968 it became independent and joined Fernando Poo to become Equatorial Guinea.

100 centimos = 1 peseta.

1 Native Boy reading Book

1960

1	**1**	25c. grey	30	25
2	**1**	50c. brown	30	25
3	**1**	75c. purple	30	25
4	**1**	1p. red	30	25
5	**1**	1p.50 green	30	25
6	**1**	2p. purple	30	25
7	**1**	3p. blue	55	35
8	**1**	5p. brown	1·30	45
9	**1**	10p. green	2·30	70

2 Cactus

1960. Child Welfare Fund.

10	**2**	10c.+5c. purple	55	55
11	-	15c.+5c. brown	55	55
12	-	35c. green	55	55
13	**2**	80c. green	65	65

DESIGNS: 15c. Sprig with berries; 35c. Star-shaped flowers.

3 Bishop Juan de Ribera

1960. Stamp Day.

14	**3**	10c.+5c. red	55	55
15	-	20c.+5c. green	55	55
16	-	30c.+10c. brown	55	55
17	**3**	50c.+20c. brown	65	65

DESIGNS: 20c. Portrait of man (after Velazquez); 30c. Statue.

4 Mandrill with Banana

1961. Child Welfare. Inscr "PRO-INFANCIA 1961".

18	**4**	10c.+5c. red	55	55
19	-	25c.+10c. violet	55	55
20	**4**	80c.+20c. green	65	65

DESIGN—VERT: 25c. African elephant.

5

1961. 25th Anniv of Gen. Franco as Head of State.

21	-	25c. grey	55	55
22	**5**	50c. brown	55	55
23	-	70c. green	55	55
24	**5**	1p. red	65	65

DESIGNS: 25c. Map; 70c. Government building.

6 Statuette

1961. Stamp Day. Inscr "DIA DEL SELLO 1961".

25	**6**	10c.+5c. red	55	55
26	-	25c.+10c. purple	55	55
27	**6**	30c.+10c. brown	55	55
28	-	1p.+10c. orange	65	65

DESIGN: 25c., 1p. Figure holding offering.

7 Girl wearing Headdress

1962. Child Welfare. Inscr "PRO-INFANCIA 1962".

29	**7**	25c. violet	55	55
30	-	50c. green	55	55
31	**7**	1p. brown	65	65

DESIGN: 50c. Native mask.

8 African Buffalo

1962. Stamp Day. Inscr "DIA DEL SELLO 1962".

32	**8**	15c. green	55	55
33	-	35c. purple	55	55
34	**8**	1p. red	65	65

DESIGN—VERT: 35c. Gorilla.

9 Statuette

1963. Seville Flood Relief.

35	**9**	50c. green	55	55
36	**9**	1p. brown	65	65

10 "Blessing"

1963. Child Welfare. Inscr "PRO-INFANCIA 1963".

37	-	25c. violet	55	55
38	**10**	50c. green	55	55
39	-	1p. red	65	65

DESIGN: 25c., 1p. Priest.

11 Child at Prayer

1963. "For Barcelona".

40	**11**	50c. green	55	55
41	**11**	1p. brown	65	65

12 Copal Flower

1964. Stamp Day. Inscr "DIA DEL SELLO 1963".

42	**12**	25c. violet	55	55
43	-	50c. turquoise	55	55
44	**12**	1p. red	65	65

FLOWER—HORIZ: 50c. Cinchona blossom.

13 Giant Ground Pangolin

1964. Child Welfare. Inscr "PRO-INFANCIA 1964".

45	**13**	25c. violet	55	55
46	-	50c. green (Chameleon)	55	55
47	**13**	1p. brown	65	65

1964. Wild Life. As T **13** but without "PRO INFANCIA" inscription.

48	15c. brown	20	20
49	25c. violet	20	20
50	50c. green	20	20
51	70c. green	20	20
52	1p. brown	95	20
53	1p.50 green	95	20
54	3p. blue	1·90	30
55	5p. brown	4·75	45
56	10p. green	8·50	1·20

ANIMALS: 15, 70c., 3p. Crocodile; 25c., 1, 5p. Leopard; 50c., 1p.50, 10p. Black rhinoceros.

14 "Goliath" Frog

1964. Stamp Day.

57	**14**	50c. green	55	55
58	-	1p. red	55	55
59	**14**	1p.50 green	65	65

DESIGN—VERT: 1p. Helmeted guineafowl.

15 Woman

1965. 25th Anniv of End of Spanish Civil War.

60	**15**	50c. green	55	55
61	-	1p. red	55	55
62	-	1p.50 turquoise	65	65

DESIGNS: 1p. Nurse; 1p.50, Logging.

16 Goliath Beetle

1965. Child Welfare. Insects.

63	**16**	50c. green	55	55
64	-	1p. brown	55	55
65	**16**	1p.50 black	65	65

DESIGN: 1p. "Acridoxena hewaniana".

17 Leopard and Arms of Rio Muni

1965. Stamp Day.

66	-	50c. grey	55	55
67	**17**	1p. brown	55	55
68	-	2p.50 violet	2·10	2·10

DESIGN—VERT: 50c., 2p.50, Common pheasant.

18 African Elephant and Grey Parrot

1966. Child Welfare.

69	**18**	50c. brown	55	55
70	**18**	1p. lilac	55	55
71	-	1p.50 blue	65	65

DESIGN: 1p.50, African and lion.

19 Water Chevrotain

1966. Stamp Day.

72	**19**	10c. brown and ochre	55	55
73	-	40c. brown and yellow	55	55
74	**19**	1p.50 violet and red	55	55
75	-	4p. blue and green	65	65

DESIGN—VERT: 40c., 4p. Giant ground pangolin.

20 Floss Flowers

1967. Child Welfare.

76	**20**	10c. yellow, olive and green	55	55
77	-	40c. green, black and mauve	55	55
78	**20**	1p.50 red and blue	55	55
79	-	4p. black and green	65	65

DESIGNS: 40c., 4p. Ylang-ylang (flower).

21 Bush Pig

1967. Stamp Day.

80	**21**	1p. chestnut and brown	55	55
81	-	1p.50 brown and green	55	55
82	-	3p.50 brown and green	1·10	1·10

DESIGNS—VERT: 1p.50, Potto. HORIZ: 3p.50, African golden cat.

1968. Child Welfare. Signs of the Zodiac. As T **56a** of Spanish Sahara.

83	1p. mauve on yellow	55	55
84	1p.50 brown on pink	55	55
85	2p.50 violet on yellow	95	95

DESIGNS: 1p. Cancer (crab); 1p.50, Taurus (bull); 2p.50, Gemini (twins).

Pt. 8

ROMAGNA

One of the Papal states, now part of Italy. Stamps issued prior to union with Sardinia in 1860.

100 bajocchi = 1 scudo.

1

1859. Imperf.

2	**1**	½b. black on buff	48·00	£400
3	**1**	1b. black on grey	48·00	£225
4	**1**	2b. black on buff	65·00	£250
5	**1**	3b. black on green	75·00	£400
6	**1**	4b. black on brown	£850	£225
7	**1**	5b. black on lilac	90·00	£475
8	**1**	6b. black on green	£550	£10000
9	**1**	8b. black on pink	£275	£2500
10	**1**	20b. black on green	£275	£3250

Pt. 3

ROMANIA

A republic in S.E. Europe bordering on the Black Sea, originally a kingdom formed by the union of Moldavia and Wallachia.

1858. 40 parale = 1 piastre.
1867. 100 bani = 1 leu.
2005. 10000 leu (l.) = 1 new leu (l.)

MOLDAVIA

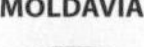

1

1858. Imperf.

1	27p. black on red	£42000	£16000
2	54p. blue on green	£21000	£6500
3	81p. blue on blue	£40000	£44000
4	108p. blue on pink	£30000	£14000

2

1858. Imperf.

12	**2**	5p. black	£200	
13	**2**	40p. blue	£200	£225
14	**2**	80p. red	£650	£400

ROMANIA

4

1862. Imperf.

29	**4**	3p. yellow	£120	£325
30	**4**	6p. red	£100	£300
31	**4**	30p. blue	75·00	85·00

5 Prince Alexander Cuza

1865. Imperf.

49a	**5**	2p. orange	75·00	£325
46	**5**	5p. blue	50·00	£325
48	**5**	20p. red	42·00	50·00

6 Prince Carol

1866. Imperf.

60	**6**	2p. black on yellow	42·00	£120
61	**6**	5p. black on blue	75·00	£900
62	**6**	20p. black on red	37·00	31·00

7 Prince Carol

1868. Imperf.

71	**7**	2b. orange	50·00	42·00
72	**7**	3b. mauve	65·00	47·00
66c	**7**	4b. blue	80·00	75·00
67	**7**	18b. red	£250	37·00

8

1869. Without beard. Imperf.

74	**8**	5b. orange	90·00	50·00
75	**8**	10b. blue	47·00	42·00
76	**8**	15b. red	47·00	42·00
77c	**8**	25b. blue and orange	45·00	31·00
78	**8**	50b. red and blue	£190	60·00

9

1871. With beard. Imperf.

83	**9**	5b. red	50·00	42·00
84	**9**	10b. orange	75·00	47·00
99	**9**	10b. blue	50·00	65·00
86	**9**	15b. red	£275	£250
87	**9**	25b. brown	65·00	60·00
100	**9**	50b. red and blue	£225	£250

1872. Perf.

93	**9**	5b. red	85·00	50·00
94	**9**	10b. blue	85·00	50·00
95	**9**	25b. brown	60·00	50·00

10

1872. Perf.

124	**10**	1¼b. black	7·75	3·25
112	**10**	1½b. green	7·75	5·25
105	**10**	3b. green	47·00	7·25
125	**10**	3b. olive	21·00	16·00
106	**10**	5b. bistre	26·00	5·75
126	**10**	5b. green	8·25	4·25
107	**10**	10b. blue	26·00	6·25
127c	**10**	10b. red	16·00	3·25
115	**10**	15b. brown	90·00	11·50
128a	**10**	15b. red	42·00	12·50
110	**10**	25b. orange	£180	23·00
130	**10**	25b. blue	£170	31·00
116	**10**	30b. red	£225	65·00
111	**10**	50b. red	£200	50·00
131	**10**	50b. bistre	£150	42·00

11 King Carol

1880

146a	**11**	15b. brown	14·50	3·25
147	**11**	25b. blue	29·00	4·25

12 King Carol

1885. On white or coloured papers.

161	**12**	1½b. black	4·25	2·10
163	**12**	3b. green	6·25	2·10
165a	**12**	3b. violet	6·25	2·10
166	**12**	5b. green	6·25	2·10
168	**12**	10b. red	6·25	3·25
169	**12**	15b. brown	18·00	3·25
171	**12**	25b. blue	21·00	7·25
186	**12**	50b. brown	95·00	26·00

14 King Carol

1890

271	**14**	1½b. lake	2·10	1·60
272a	**14**	3b. mauve	2·50	2·50
273	**14**	5b. green	4·25	2·10
274	**14**	10b. red	26·00	2·10
255	**14**	15b. brown	26·00	4·75
306	**14**	25b. blue	17·00	7·75
307	**14**	50b. orange	33·00	16·00

15

1891. 25th Anniv of Reign.

300	**15**	1½b. lake	7·25	8·25
293	**15**	3b. mauve	7·25	8·25
294	**15**	5b. green	9·50	10·50
295	**15**	10b. red	9·50	10·50
303	**15**	15b. brown	9·50	8·25

17

19

1893. Various frames as T **17** and **19**.

316	1 BANI brown	1·60	1·00
426	1 BAN brown	2·10	1·60
317	1½b. black	1·60	90
533	3b. brown	1·00	40
319	5b. blue	2·50	1·30
534	5b. green	2·10	50
320	10b. green	4·50	1·30
535	10b. red	2·10	50
332	15b. pink	6·25	1·60
400	15b. black	3·25	1·00
430	15b. brown	3·50	1·30
545	15b. violet	2·50	50

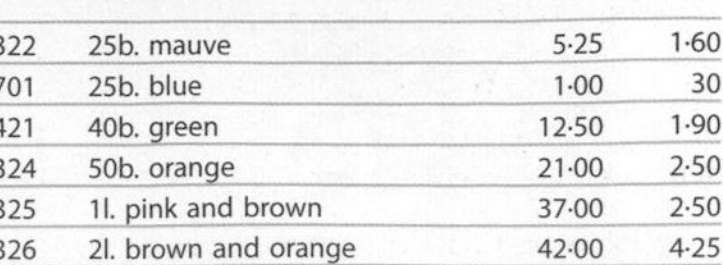

322	25b. mauve	5·25	1·60
701	25b. blue	1·00	30
421	40b. green	12·50	1·90
324	50b. orange	21·00	2·50
325	1l. pink and brown	37·00	2·50
326	2l. brown and orange	42·00	4·25

See also Nos. 532 etc.

25 Four-in-hand Postal Coach

26 New Post Office, Bucharest

1903. Opening of New Post Office in 1901.

464	**25**	1b. brown	2·10	1·80
465	**25**	3b. red	4·25	2·10
466	**25**	5b. green	7·75	3·25
467	**25**	10b. red	6·25	3·25
468	**25**	15b. black	6·25	4·25
472	**26**	15b. black	5·25	4·25
469	**25**	25b. blue	21·00	12·50
473	**26**	25b. blue	12·50	7·75
470	**25**	40b. green	31·00	16·00
474	**26**	40b. green	21·00	10·50
471	**25**	50b. orange	38·00	21·00
475	**26**	50b. orange	23·00	12·50
476	**26**	1l. brown	18·00	10·50
477	**26**	2l. red	£160	80·00
478	**26**	5l. lilac	£190	£130

See also No. 1275.

1905. Various frames as T **17** and **19**.

532	1 ban black	40	30
625b	1½b. yellow	3·25	2·50
703	40b. brown	1·80	1·00
697	50b. pink	2·10	1·00
432	1l. black and green	42·00	3·75
706	1l. green	2·40	95
433	2l. black and brown	31·00	4·75
707	2l. orange	3·25	1·00

27 Queen of Romania spinning

1906. Welfare Fund. Motto: "God guide our Hand".

481	**27**	3b.(+7) brown	7·75	5·25
482	**27**	5b.(+10) green	7·75	5·25
483	**27**	10b.(+10) red	37·00	16·00
484	**27**	15b.(+10) purple	31·00	10·50

28 Queen of Romania weaving

1906. Welfare Fund. Motto: "Woman weaves the Future of the Country".

485	**28**	3b.(+7) brown	7·75	5·25
486	**28**	5b.(+10) green	7·75	5·25
487	**28**	10b.(+10) red	42·00	16·00
488	**28**	15b.(+10) lilac	26·00	10·50

29 Queen of Romania nursing wounded Soldier

1906. Welfare Fund. Motto: "The Wounds dressed and the Tears wiped away".

489	**29**	3b.(+7) brown	7·75	5·25
490	**29**	5b.(+10) green	7·75	5·25
491	**29**	10b.(+10) red	42·00	16·00
492	**29**	15b.(+10) purple	26·00	10·50

30

1906. 25th Anniv of Kingdom.

493	30	1b. black and bistre	1·00	50
494	30	3b. black and brown	2·50	1·00
495	30	5b. black and green	1·60	75
496	30	10b. black and red	1·60	75
497	30	15b. black and violet	1·60	75
498	30	25b. black and blue	14·50	7·75
499	30	40b. black and brown	6·25	1·60
500	30	50b. black and brown	6·25	1·60
501	30	1l. black and red	6·25	1·60
502	30	2l. black and orange	6·25	1·60

31 Prince Carol at Battle of Calafat

1906. 40 Years' Rule of Prince and King. Dated "1906".

503	-	1b. black and bistre	75	50
504	-	3b. black and brown	1·60	50
505	31	5b. black and green	1·80	50
506	-	10b. black and red	1·30	50
507	-	15b. black and violet	1·30	50
508	-	25b. black and blue	7·75	6·25
508a	-	25b. black and green	9·25	6·25
509	-	40b. black and brown	2·10	1·60
510	-	50b. black and brown	2·30	1·60
511	-	1l. black and red	2·30	1·80
512	-	2l. black and orange	2·50	2·50

DESIGNS—HORIZ: 1b. Prince Carol taking oath of allegiance in 1866; 3b. Prince in carriage; 10b. Meeting of Prince and Osman Pasha, 1878; 15b. Carol when Prince in 1866 and King in 1906; 25b. Romanian Army crossing Danube, 1877; 40b. Triumphal entry into Bucharest, 1878; 50b. Prince at head of Army in 1877; 1l. King Carol at Cathedral in 1896; 2l. King at shrine of S. Nicholas, 1904.

32

1906. Welfare Fund. Motto: "But Glory, Honour and Peace to All that do Good".

513	32	3b.(+7) brown, bistre and blue	4·25	2·10
514	32	5b.(+10) green, red and bistre	4·25	2·10
515	32	10b.(+10) red, bistre and blue	6·25	4·25
516	32	15b.(+10) violet, bistre and blue	17·00	5·25

33 Peasant ploughing and Angel

1906. Jubilee Exhibition, Bucharest.

517	33	5b. black and green	5·25	1·60
518	33	10b. black and red	5·25	1·60
519	-	15b. black and violet	7·75	2·50
520	-	25b. black and blue	7·75	2·50
521	-	30b. brown and red	10·50	2·50
522	-	40b. brown and green	11·50	3·25
523	-	50b. black and orange	10·50	3·75
524	-	75b. sepia and brown	9·50	3·75
525	-	1l.50 brown and mauve	£120	50·00
526	-	2l.50 brown and yellow	42·00	31·00
527	-	3l. brown and orange	31·00	31·00

DESIGNS—HORIZ: 15, 25b. Exhibition Building. VERT: 30, 40b. Farmhouse; 50, 75b. (different), Royal Family pavilion; 1l.50, 2l.50, King Carol on horseback; 3l. Queen Elizabeth (Carmen Sylva).

34 Princess Maria and her Children receiving Poor Family conducted by an Angel

1907. Welfare Fund.

528	34	3b.(+7) brown	5·25	2·10
529	34	5b.(+10) brown and green	5·25	2·10
530	34	10b.(+10) brown and red	5·25	2·10
531	34	15b.(+10) brown and blue	5·25	2·10

35

1908

575	35	5b. green	3·25	30
562	35	10b. red	50	20
577	35	15b. violet	6·25	2·40
564	35	25b. blue	2·10	20
579	35	40b. green	75	20
702	35	40b. brown	5·75	2·50
566	35	50b. orange	75	20
705	35	50b. red	1·80	1·00
581	35	1l. brown	2·30	50
582	35	2l. red	9·50	2·50

37

1908

583	37	1b. black	50	10
590	37	3b. brown	1·00	10
585	37	5b. green	50	10
592	37	10b. red	50	10
594	37	15b. olive	1·00	10
599	37	15b. violet	11·50	10·50
692	37	15b. brown	1·00	50

38

39 Troops crossing Danube

1913. Acquisition of Southern Dobruja.

626	-	1b. black	1·00	50
627	38	3b. brown and grey	2·50	1·00
628	39	5b. black and green	2·10	50
629	-	10b. black and orange	1·00	50
630	-	15b. violet and brown	2·50	1·00
631	-	25b. brown and blue	3·75	1·60
632	39	40b. red and brown	7·25	6·25
633	38	50b. blue and yellow	16·00	8·25
634	38	1l. brown and blue	29·00	19·00
635	38	2l. red and red	42·00	26·00

DESIGNS—VERT (As Type **38**): 1b. "Dobruja" holding flag. HORIZ (As Type **39**): 10b. Town of Constanza; 25b. Church and School in Dobruja. (24×16 mm): 15b. Mircea the Great and King Carol.

1918. Surch **25. BANI**.

657	37	25b. on 1b. black	2·10	1·00

1918. Optd **1918**.

662	5b. green	75	50
663	10b. red	75	50

TRANSYLVANIA

The Eastern portion of Hungary. Union with Romania proclaimed in December 1918 and the final frontiers settled by the Treaty of Trianon on 4 June 1920.

The following issues for Transylvania (Nos. 747/858) were valid throughout Romania.

(The "F" stands for King Ferdinand and "P.T.T." for Posts Telegraphs and Telephones).

The values "BANI", "LEU" or "LEI" appear above or below the monogram.

A. Issues for Cluj (Kolozsvar or Klausenburg)

(42)

1919. Various stamps of Hungary optd as T **42**. (a) Flood Relief Charity stamps of 1913

747	7	1l. on 1f. grey	21·00	18·00
748	7	1l. on 2f. yellow	£120	85·00
749	7	1l. on 3f. orange	50·00	42·00
750	7	1l. on 5f. green	2·50	1·60
751	7	1l. on 10f. red	2·50	1·60
752	7	1l. on 12f. lilac on yellow	9·00	5·75
753	7	1l. on 16f. green	4·75	3·25
754	7	1l. on 25f. blue	50·00	42·00
755	7	1l. on 35f. purple	5·25	3·25
756	8	1l. on 1k. red	65·00	50·00

(b) War Charity stamps of 1916.

757	20	10(+2) b. red	30	20
758	-	15(+2) b. violet	30	20
759	22	40(+2) b. lake	40	30

(c) Harvesters and Parliament Types.

760	18	2b. brown	20	20
761	18	3b. red	30	20
762	18	5b. green	30	20
763	18	6b. blue	30	20
764	18	10b. red	£140	£100
765	18	15b. violet (No. 244)	5·00	3·75
766	18	15b. violet	20	10
767	18	25b. blue	20	10
768	18	35b. brown	20	10
769	18	40b. olive	20	10
770	19	50b. purple	30	20
771	19	75b. blue	40	30
772	19	80b. green	40	30
773	19	1l. lake	40	30
774	19	2l. brown	55	40
775	19	3l. grey and violet	3·50	2·50
776	19	5l. brown	2·75	2·10
777	19	10l. lilac and brown	3·50	2·50

(d) Charles and Zita stamps.

778	27	10b. red	30·00	21·00
779	27	15b. violet	11·50	7·75
780	27	20b. brown	50	30
781	27	25b. blue	85	50
782	28	40b. green	50	30

B. Issues for Oradea (Nagyvarad or Grosswardein)

(43)

1919. Various stamps of Hungary optd as T **43**. (a) "Turul" Type.

794	7	2b. yellow	5·25	4·75
795	7	3b. orange	9·75	8·50
796	7	6b. drab	95	50
797	7	16b. green	21·00	12·50
798	7	50b. lake on blue	1·30	1·00
799	7	70b. brown and green	20·00	18·00

(b) Flood Relief Charity stamps of 1913.

800	7	1l. on 1f. grey	1·20	1·10
801		1l. on 2f. yellow	4·75	4·50
802		1l. on 3f. orange	1·60	1·30
803		1l. on 5l. green	30	20
804		1l. on 6f. drab	1·20	1·10
805		1l. on 10f. red	30	20
806		1l. on 12f. lilac on yellow	50·00	46·00
807		1l. on 16f. green	1·50	1·30
808		1l. on 20f. brown	6·50	6·25
809		1l. on 25f. blue	4·50	3·25
810		1l. on 35f. purple	4·50	3·25

(c) War Charity stamp of 1915.

811	5+2b. green (No. 173)	11·50	11·50

(d) War Charity stamps of 1916.

812	20	10(+2) b. red	70	70
813	-	15(+2) b. violet	30	20
814	22	40(+2) b. lake	30	30

(e) Harvesters and Parliament Types.

815	18	2b. brown	20	20
816	18	3b. red	20	20
817	18	5b. green	30	20
818	18	6b. blue	90	65
819	18	10b. red	1·60	1·00
820	18	15b. violet (No. 244)	£130	£100
821	18	15b. violet	15	10
822	18	20b. brown	15·00	9·50
823	18	25b. blue	30	20
824	18	35b. brown	35	20
825	18	40b. olive	30	20
826	19	50b. purple	40	30
827	19	75b. blue	20	20
828	19	80b. green	30	30
829	19	1l. lake	55	40
830	19	2l. brown	20	20
831	19	3l. grey and violet	4·50	4·25
832	19	5l. brown	2·75	2·50
833	19	10l. lilac and brown	1·60	1·50

(f) Charles and Zita stamps.

834	27	10b. red	2·75	2·10
835	27	20b. brown	20	20
836	27	25b. blue	45	30
837	27	40b. green	70	50

(g) Harvesters and Parliament Types.

838	18	2b. brown	2·10	1·30
839	18	3b. red	40	30
840	18	4b. grey	30	20
841	18	5b. green	40	30
842	18	6b. blue	2·30	1·60
843	18	10b. red	21·00	17·00
844	18	20b. brown	1·90	1·30
845	18	40b. olive	40	30
846	19	1l. lake	30	20
847	19	3l. grey and violet	1·20	85
848	19	5l. brown	4·75	3·75

(h) Charles and Zita stamps.

849	27	10b. red	£130	£130
850	27	20b. brown	2·75	2·10
851	27	25b. blue	70	40
852	28	50b. purple	30	20

(k) Harvesters and Parliament Types inscr "MAGYAR POSTA".

853	18	5b. green	20	20
854	18	20b. red	20	20
855	18	20b. brown	25	20
856	18	25b. blue	1·00	50
857	18	40b. olive	1·00	75
858	19	5l. brown	8·75	6·50

(44) King Ferdinand's Monogram

1919. Optd with T **44**.

873	37	1b. black	30	20
874	37	5b. green	40	50
878a	37	10b. red	20	20

45 King Ferdinand

1920

891	45	1b. black	20	15
892	45	5b. green	20	15
893	45	10b. red	20	15
882	45	15b. brown	75	30
895	45	25b. blue	30	30
896	45	25b. brown	30	30
910	45	40b. brown	65	20
898	45	50b. pink	85	20
887	45	1l. green	1·60	30
900	45	1l. red	40	30
889	45	2l. orange	2·10	50
902	45	2l. blue	1·00	35
903	45	2l. red	3·25	2·10

46 King Ferdinand

1922

923	46	3b. black	20	10
924	46	5b. black	10	10
925	46	10b. green	20	10
926	46	25b. brown	20	10
927	46	25b. red	30	10
928	46	30b. violet	30	10
929	46	50b. yellow	50	30
930	46	60b. green	1·50	75
931	46	1l. violet	40	10
932	46	2l. red	2·10	20
933a	46	2l. green	65	20
934	46	3l. blue	3·25	1·00
935a	46	3l. brown	3·25	1·00
936a	46	3l. pink	37·00	10·50
937	46	3l. red	1·20	10
938	46	5l. green	2·75	1·00
939b	46	5l. brown	1·00	10
940	46	6l. blue	4·50	1·60
941	46	6l. red	8·25	4·25
942	46	6l. olive	4·50	1·00
943	46	7l.50 blue	4·25	50
944	46	10l. blue	4·25	50

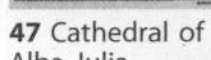

47 Cathedral of Alba Julia **48** King Ferdinand **49** State Arms

51 Michael the Brave and King Ferdinand

1922. Coronation.

1032	**47**	5b. black	50	30
1033	**48**	25b. brown	1·30	50
1034	**49**	50b. green	1·30	75
1035	-	1l. olive	1·60	1·00
1036	**51**	2l. red	1·60	1·00
1037	-	3l. blue	3·25	1·60
1050	-	6l. violet	8·75	7·00

DESIGNS—As Type **48**: 1l. Queen Marie as a nurse; 3l. Portrait of King but rectangular frame. Larger (21×33 mm): 6l. Queen Marie in coronation robes.

54 King Ferdinand

1926. King's 60th Birthday. Imperf or perf.

1051	**54**	10b. green	75	50
1052	**54**	25b. orange	75	50
1053	**54**	50b. brown	75	50
1054	**54**	1l. violet	75	50
1055	**54**	2l. green	75	50
1056	**54**	3l. red	75	1·00
1057	**54**	5l. brown	75	1·00
1058	**54**	6l. olive	75	1·00
1059	**54**	9l. grey	75	1·00
1060	**54**	10l. blue	75	1·00

55 Map of Romania

1927. 50th Anniv of Romanian Geographical Society.

1061	**55**	1+9l. violet	5·25	2·10
1062	-	2+8l. green	5·25	2·10
1063	-	3+7l. red	5·25	2·10
1064	-	5+5l. blue	5·25	2·10
1065	-	6+4l. olive	7·75	3·25

DESIGNS: 2l. Stephen the Great; 3l. Michael the Brave; 5l. Carol and Ferdinand; 6l. Adam Clisi Monument.

60 King Carol and King Ferdinand

1927. 50th Anniv of Independence.

1066	**60**	25b. red	1·00	20
1067	-	30b. black	1·00	30
1068	-	50b. green	1·00	30
1069	**60**	1l. blue	1·00	30
1070	-	2l. green	1·00	40
1071	-	3l. purple	1·00	50
1072	-	4l. brown	1·00	65
1073	-	4l.50 brown	3·25	2·10
1074	-	5l. brown	1·00	50
1075	-	6l. red	2·10	1·20
1076	**60**	7l.50 blue	1·00	50
1077	**60**	10l. blue	3·25	1·00

DESIGNS—HORIZ: 30b., 2, 3, 5l. King Ferdinand. VERT: 50b., 4l., 4l.50, 6l. King Ferdinand as in Type **60**.

63 King Michael

1928

1080	**63**	25b. black	50	20
1081	**63**	30b. pink	1·00	20
1082	**63**	50b. olive	50	20

64 King Michael

1928. (a) Size 18½×24½ mm.

1083	**64**	1l. purple	1·00	20
1084	**64**	2l. green	1·30	20
1085	**64**	3l. red	1·60	20
1086	**64**	5l. brown	2·50	20
1087	**64**	7l.50 blue	11·50	1·30
1088	**64**	10l. blue	9·50	50

(b) Size 18×23 mm.

1129	1l. purple	1·00	20
1130	2l. green	1·60	20
1131	3l. red	3·25	20
1132	7l.50 blue	6·25	1·60
1133	10l. blue	21·00	10·50

65 Bessarabian Parliament House

1928. Tenth Anniv of Annexation of Bessarabia.

1092	**65**	1l. green	2·30	1·00
1093	**65**	2l. brown	2·30	1·00
1094	-	3l. sepia	2·30	1·00
1095	-	5l. lake	2·75	1·30
1096	-	7l.50 blue	2·75	1·30
1097	-	10l. blue	7·25	3·25
1098	-	20l. violet	9·50	4·25

DESIGNS: 3, 5, 20l. Hotin Fortress; 7l.50, 10l. Fortress Cetatea Alba.

66 Bleriot SPAD 33 Biplane

1928. Air.

1099	**66**	1l. brown	7·75	5·25
1100	**66**	2l. blue	7·75	5·25
1101	**66**	5l. red	7·75	5·25

67 King Carol and King Michael

1928. 50th Anniv of Acquisition of Northern Dobruja.

1102	**67**	1l. green	1·80	65
1103	-	2l. brown	1·80	65
1104	**67**	3l. grey	2·50	65
1105	-	5l. mauve	3·25	75
1106	-	7l.50 blue	3·75	85
1107	-	10l. blue	5·25	2·10
1108	-	20l. red	9·00	2·50

DESIGNS: 2l. Constanza Harbour and Carol Lighthouse; 5l., 7l.50, Adam Clisi Monument; 10, 20l. Saligny Bridge over River Danube, Cernavoda.

68 **69** The Union

1929. Tenth Anniv of Union of Romania and Transylvania.

1109	**68**	1l. purple	4·25	2·10
1110	**69**	2l. green	4·25	2·10
1111	-	3l. brown	4·75	2·10
1112	-	4l. red	4·75	2·50
1113	-	5l. orange	6·25	2·50
1114	-	10l. blue	7·75	5·25

DESIGNS—HORIZ: 1l. Ferdinand I, Stephen the Great, Michael the Brave, Hunyadi and Brancoveanu; 10l. Ferdinand I. VERT: 2l. Union; 3l. Avram Jancu; 4l. King Michael the Brave; 5l. Bran Castle.

1930. Stamps of King Michael optd **8 IUNIE 1930** (Accession of Carol II).

1134	**63**	25b. black (postage)	50	20
1135	**63**	30b. pink	1·00	20
1136	**63**	50b. olive	1·00	20
1142	**64**	1l. purple (No. 1129)	50	20
1147	**66**	1l. brown (air)	21·00	10·50
1143	**64**	2l. green (No. 1130)	50	20
1148	**66**	2l. blue	21·00	10·50
1144	**64**	3l. red (No. 1131)	65	20
1137	**64**	5l. brown	2·10	20
1149	**66**	5l. red	21·00	10·50
1140	**64**	7l.50 blue (No. 1087)	5·25	1·00
1145	**64**	7l.50 blue (No. 1132)	4·25	85
1138	**64**	10l. blue (No. 1088)	4·25	1·00
1146	**64**	10l. blue (No. 1133)	3·50	80

72 King Carol II **73** King Carol II

1930

1172	**72**	25b. black	50	10
1173	**72**	50b. brown	1·30	65
1174	**72**	1l. violet	50	10
1175	**72**	2l. green	1·00	10
1176	**73**	3l. red	2·00	10
1177	**73**	4l. orange	2·30	10
1178	**73**	6l. red	2·75	10
1179	**73**	7l.50 blue	3·25	30
1180	-	10l. blue	7·75	10
1181	-	16l. green	18·00	30
1182	-	20l. yellow	21·00	85

DESIGN: 10l. to 20l. Portrait as Type **72**, but in plain circle, with "ROMANIA" at top.

76 King Carol II

1930. Air.

1183	**76**	1l. violet on blue	3·25	5·00
1184	**76**	2l. green on blue	4·00	5·25
1185	**76**	5l. brown on blue	7·25	5·25
1186	**76**	10l. blue on blue	15·00	6·75

77 Map of Romania **78** Woman with Census Paper

1930. National Census.

1187	**77**	1l. violet	1·80	50
1188	**78**	2l. green	3·00	60
1189	**78**	4l. orange	3·50	40
1190	**78**	6l. red	8·25	65

79 King Carol II

1931

1191	**79**	30l. blue and olive	1·40	75
1192	**79**	50l. blue and red	2·75	1·30
1193	**79**	100l. blue and green	5·75	2·75

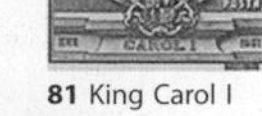

80 King Carol II **81** King Carol I

82 Kings Carol II, Ferdinand I and Carol I

1931. 50th Anniv of Romanian Monarchy.

1200	**80**	1l. violet	3·75	1·90
1201	**81**	2l. green	5·75	1·90
1202	-	6l. red	13·00	3·00
1203	**82**	10l. blue	19·00	5·75
1204	-	20l. orange	23·00	7·50

DESIGNS—As Type **80**: 6l. King Carol II, facing right. As Type **81**: 20l. King Ferdinand I.

83 Naval Cadet Ship "Mircea"

1931. 50th Anniv of Romanian Navy.

1205	**83**	6l. red	6·75	4·25
1206	-	10l. blue	9·00	4·50
1207	-	12l. green	38·00	5·00
1208	-	20l. orange	17·00	9·00

DESIGNS: 10l. Monitors "Lascar Catargiu" and "Mihail Kogaliniceaunu"; 16l. Monitor "Ardeal"; 20l. Destroyer "Regele Ferdinand".

84 Bayonet Attack **87** King Carol I **88** Infantry Attack

89 King Ferdinand I

1931. Centenary of Romanian Army.

1209	**84**	25b. black	2·30	1·10
1210	-	50b. brown	3·00	1·50
1211	-	1l. violet	3·75	1·90
1212	**87**	2l. green	6·00	2·30
1213	**88**	3l. red	13·00	6·75
1214	**89**	7l.50 blue	17·00	15·00
1215	-	16l. green	20·00	6·75

DESIGNS: 50b. Infantryman, 1870, 20×33 mm: 1l. Infantry and drummer, 1830, 23×36 mm: 16l. King Carol II in uniform with plumed helmet, 21×34 mm.

91 Scouts' Encampment

1931. Romanian Boy Scouts' Exhibition Fund.

1221	**91**	1l.+1l. red	5·75	3·75
1222	-	2l.+2l. green	7·50	4·50
1223	-	3l.+3l. blue	9·00	5·75
1224	-	4l.+4l. brown	11·50	7·50
1225	-	6l.+6l. brown	15·00	7·50

DESIGNS—VERT: As Type **91**: 3l. Recruiting, 22×37½ mm; 2l. Rescue work, 22×41½ mm; 4l. Prince Nicholas; 6l. King Carol II in scoutmaster's uniform.

92a Farman F.121 Jaribu

1931. Air.

1226	**92a**	2l. green	1·90	1·00
1227	-	3l. red	3·00	1·30
1228	-	5l. brown	3·75	1·70
1229	-	10l. blue	9·00	3·75
1230	-	20l. violet	23·00	5·25

DESIGNS—As T **92a**: 3l. Farman F.300 and biplane; 5l. Farman F.60 Goliath; 10l. Fokker F.XII. 34×20 mm: 20l. Three aircraft flying in formation.

95 Kings Carol II, Ferdinand I and Carol I

1931

1231	**95**	16l. green	15·00	90

96 Alexander the Good

1932. 500th Death Centenary of Alexander I, Prince of Moldavia.

1232	**96**	6l. red	17·00	11·50

97 King Carol II

1932

1248	**97**	10l. blue	17·00	75

98 Semaphore Signaller

1932. Boy Scouts' Jamboree Fund.

1256	-	25b.+25b. green	4·50	1·90
1257	**98**	50b.+50b. blue	5·75	3·75
1258	-	1l.+1l. green	6·50	5·75
1259	-	2l.+2l. red	11·50	7·50
1260	-	3l.+3l. blue	27·00	15·00
1261	-	6l.+6l. brown	30·00	23·00

DESIGNS—VERT: As Type **98**: 25b. Scouts in camp; 1l. On the trail; 3l. King Carol II; 6l. King Carol and King Michael when a Prince. HORIZ: 20×15 mm: 2l. Camp fire.

99 Cantacuzino and Gregory Chika

1932. Ninth International Medical Congress.

1262	**99**	1l. red	9·75	7·50
1263	-	6l. orange	24·00	11·50
1264	-	10l. blue	42·00	19·00

DESIGNS: 6l. Congress in session; 10l. Hygeia and Aesculapius.

100 Tuberculosis Sanatorium

1932. Postal Employees' Fund.

1265	**100**	4l.+1l. green	9·00	4·50
1266	-	6l.+1l. brown	10·00	5·50
1267	-	10l.+1l. blue	18·00	9·00

DESIGNS—VERT: 6l. War Memorial tablet. HORIZ: 10l. Convalescent home.

101 King Carol II

1932. International Philatelic Exhibition, Bucharest (EFIRO). Sheet 100×125 mm.

MS1267a	6l.+5l. olive	85·00	70·00

102 "Bull's head"

103 Dolphins **104** Arms

1932. 75th Anniv of First Moldavian Stamps. Imperf.

1268	**102**	25b. black	2·40	45
1269	-	1l. purple	4·00	95
1270	**103**	2l. green	4·25	1·10
1271	-	3l. red	4·75	1·40
1272	**104**	6l. red	5·75	1·60
1273	-	7l.50 blue	7·25	2·30
1274	-	10l. blue	9·75	3·75

DESIGNS—As Type **103**: 1l. Lion rampant and bridge; 3l. Eagle and castles; 7l.50, Eagle; 10l. Bull's head.

1932. 30th Anniv of Opening of G.P.O., Bucharest. As T **25** but smaller.

1275		16l. green	21·00	9·25

105 Ruins of Trajan's Bridge, Arms of Turnu-Severin and Towers of Severus

1933. Centenary of Founding of Turnu-Severin.

1279	**105**	25b. green	1·50	40
1280	-	50b. blue	1·90	60
1281	-	1l. brown	3·50	95
1282	-	2l. green	4·75	1·50

DESIGNS: 50b. Trajan at the completion of bridge over the Danube; 1l. Arrival of Prince Carol at Turnu-Severin; 2l. Trajan's Bridge.

107 Carmen Sylva and Carol I

1933. 50th Anniv of Construction of Pelesch Castle, Sinaia.

1283	**107**	1l. violet	3·50	2·40
1284	-	3l. brown	4·00	3·50
1285	-	6l. red	4·75	4·00

DESIGNS: 3l. Eagle and medallion portraits of Kings Carol I, Ferdinand I and Carol II; 6l. Pelesch Castle.

108 Wayside Shrine

1934. Romanian Women's Exhibition. Inscr "L.N.F.R. MUNCA NOASTRA ROMANEASCA".

1286	**108**	1l.+1l. brown	3·50	2·40
1287	-	2l.+1l. blue	4·75	3·00
1288	-	3l.+1l. green	6·25	4·25

DESIGNS—HORIZ: 2l. Weaver. VERT: 3l. Spinner.

1934. Mamaia Jamboree Fund. Nos. 1256/61 optd **MAMAIA 1934** and Arms of Constanza.

1289		26b.+25b. green	7·25	4·75
1290	**98**	50b.+50b. blue	9·75	5·75
1291	-	1l.+1l. green	11·50	9·25
1292	-	2l.+2l. red	14·50	10·50
1293	-	3l.+3l. blue	31·00	18·00
1294	-	6l.+6l. brown	35·00	24·00

110 King Carol II

1934

1295		50b. brown	1·90	60
1296	**110**	2l. green	3·50	60
1297	**110**	4l. orange	5·75	60
1298	-	6l. lake	14·50	60

DESIGNS: 50b. Profile portrait of King Carol II in civilian clothes; 6l. King Carol in plumed helmet.

112 "Grapes for Health"

1934. Bucharest Fruit Exhibition.

1299	**112**	1l. green	7·25	4·00
1300	-	2l. brown	7·25	4·00

DESIGN: 2l. Woman with fruit.

113 Crisan, Horia and Closca

1935. 150th Anniv of Death of Three Romanian Martyrs. Portraits inscr "MARTIR AL NEAMULUI 1785".

1301	**113**	1l. violet	1·20	70
1302	-	2l. green (Crisan)	1·60	95
1303	-	6l. brown (Closca)	4·25	1·60
1304	-	10l. blue (Horia)	7·25	3·50

114 Boy Scouts

1935. Fifth Anniv of Accession of Carol II.

1305		25b. black	5·75	4·00
1306		1l. violet	9·75	6·75
1307	**114**	2l. green	11·50	9·75
1308	-	6l.+1l. brown	14·50	11·50
1309	-	10l.+2l. blue	31·00	29·00

DESIGNS—VERT: 25b. Scout saluting; 1l. Bugler; 6l. King Carol II. HORIZ: 10l. Colour party.

1935. Portraits as T **110** but additionally inscr "POSTA".

1310		25b. black	20	10
1311		50b. brown	20	10
1312		1l. violet	50	10
1313	**110**	2l. green	95	10
1315	-	3l. red	1·50	10
1316	-	3l. blue	1·90	30
1317	**110**	4l. orange	3·00	10
1318	-	5l. red	2·40	70
1319	-	6l. lake	3·00	10
1320	-	7l.50 blue	3·50	70
1321	-	8l. purple	3·50	70
1322	**110**	9l. blue	4·75	80
1323	-	10l. blue	1·90	30
1324	-	12l. blue	3·00	1·30
1325	-	15l. brown	3·00	95
1326	-	16l. green	4·00	60
1327	-	20l. orange	2·40	80
1328	-	24l. red	4·75	95

PORTRAITS—IN PROFILE: 25b., 15l. In naval uniform; 50b., 3, 8, 10l. In civilian clothes. THREE-QUARTER FACE: 1, 5, 7l.50, In civilian clothes. FULL FACE: 6, 12, 16, 20, 24l. In plumed helmet.

118 King Carol II

1936. Bucharest Exhibition and 70th Anniv of Hohenzollern–Sigmaringen Dynasty.

1329	**118**	6l.+1l. red	2·40	1·20

119 Oltenia Peasant Girl

1936. Sixth Anniv of Accession of Carol II Inscr "O.E.T.R. 8 IUNIE 1936".

1330	**119**	50b.+50b. brown	1·90	95
1331	-	1l.+1l. violet	1·50	95
1332	-	2l.+1l. green	1·60	1·20
1333	-	3l.+1l. red	2·40	1·50
1334	-	4l.+2l. red	3·00	1·50
1335	-	6l.+3l. grey	4·00	1·90
1336	-	10l.+5l. blue	6·25	4·00

DESIGNS (costumes of following districts)—VERT: 1l. Banat; 4l. Gori; 6l. Neamz. HORIZ: 2l. Saliste; 3l. Hateg; 10l. Suceava (Bukovina).

120 Brasov Jamboree Badge

1936. National Scout Jamboree, Brasov.

1337		1l.+1l. blue	9·75	8·25
1338		3l.+3l. grey	14·50	8·25
1339	**120**	6l.+6l. red	19·00	8·25

DESIGNS: 1l. National Scout Badge; 3l. Tenderfoot Badge.

121 Liner "Transylvania"

1936. First Marine Exhibition, Bucharest.

1343	-	1l.+1l. violet	11·50	5·25
1344	-	3l.+2l. blue	9·75	5·75
1345	**121**	6l.+3l. red	12·50	8·25

DESIGNS: 1l. Submarine "Delfinul"; 3l. Naval cadet ship "Mircea".

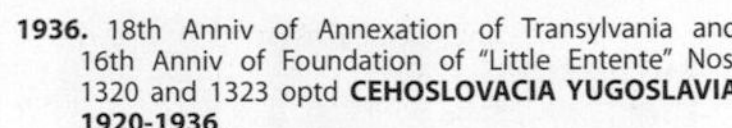

1936. 18th Anniv of Annexation of Transylvania and 16th Anniv of Foundation of "Little Entente" Nos. 1320 and 1323 optd **CEHOSLOVACIA YUGOSLAVIA 1920-1936**.

1346		7l.50 blue	7·25	5·75
1347		10l. blue	7·25	5·75

123 Creanga's Birthplace

1937. Birth Centenary of Ion Creanga (poet).

1348	**123**	2l. green	1·90	95
1349	-	3l. red	2·40	1·10
1350	**123**	4l. violet	3·00	1·40
1351	-	6l. brown	7·25	3·00

DESIGN: 3, 6l. Portrait of Creanga, 37×22 mm.

124 Footballers

1937. Seventh Anniv of Accession of Carol II.

1352	**124**	25b.+25b. olive	1·90	30
1353	-	50b.+50b. brown	1·90	50
1354	-	1l.+50b. violet	2·40	70
1355	-	2l.+1l. green	3·00	80
1356	-	3l.+1l. red	4·75	95
1357	-	4l.+1l. red	7·75	1·10
1358	-	6l.+2l. brown	9·75	1·60
1359	-	10l.+4l. blue	11·50	2·40

DESIGNS—HORIZ: 50b. Swimmer; 3 1. King Carol II hunting; 10l. U.F.S.R. Inaugural Meeting. VERT: 1l. Javelin thrower; 2l. Skier; 4l. Rowing; 6l. Steeplechaser.

Premium in aid of the Federation of Romanian Sports Clubs (U.F.S.R.).

127 Curtea de Arges Cathedral

1937. "Little Entente".

1360	**127**	7l.50 blue	3·00	1·50
1361	**127**	10l. blue	4·00	95

128 Hurdling

1937. Eighth Balkan Games, Bucharest. Inscr as in T **115**.

1362	-	1l.+1l. violet	1·90	1·20
1363	-	2l.+1l. green	2·40	1·60
1364	**128**	4l.+1l. red	3·00	2·10
1365	-	6l.+1l. brown	3·50	2·40
1366	-	10l.+1l. blue	10·50	4·25

DESIGNS: 1l. Sprinting; 2l. Throwing the javelin; 6l. Breasting the tape; 10l. High jumping.

1937. 16th Birthday of Crown Prince Michael and his promotion to Rank of Sub-lieutenant. Sheet 125×152 mm containing four stamps of 1935–40 surch.

MS1367	2l. on 20l. (No. 1327); 6l. on 10l. (No. 1323); 10l. on 6l. (No. 1319); 20l. on 2l. (No. 1313)	14·50	16·00

129 Arms of Romania, Greece, Turkey and Yugoslavia

1938. Balkan Entente.

1368	**129**	7l.50 blue	2·40	1·30
1369	**129**	10l. blue	3·50	1·10

130 King Carol II

1938. New Constitution. Profile portraits of King inscr "27 FEBRUARIE 1938". 6l. shows Arms also.

1370	**130**	3l. red	1·50	80
1371	-	6l. brown	2·40	80
1372	-	10l. blue	3·50	1·60

131 King Carol II and Provincial Arms

1938. Fund for Bucharest Exhibition celebrating 20th Anniv of Union of Provinces.

1373	**131**	6l.+1l. mauve	1·90	95

132 Dimitrie Cantemir

1938. Boy Scouts' Fund. 8th Anniv of Accession of Carol II. Inscr "STRAJA TARII 8 IUNIE 1938".

1374	**132**	25b.+25b. olive	95	60
1375	-	50b.+50b. brown	1·50	60
1376	-	1l.+1l. violet	1·50	60
1377	-	2l.+2l. green	1·60	60
1378	-	3l.+2l. mauve	1·60	60
1379	-	4l.+2l. red	1·60	60
1380	-	6l.+2l. brown	1·90	70
1381	-	7l.50 blue	2·40	95
1382	-	10l. blue	3·00	95
1383	-	16l. green	4·00	3·00
1384	-	20l. red	5·75	3·00

PORTRAITS: 50b. Maria Doamna; 1l. Mircea the Great; 2l. Constantin Brancoveanu; 3l. Stephen the Great; 4l. Prince Cuza; 6l. Michael the Brave; 7l.50, Queen Elisabeth; 10l. King Carol II; 16l. King Ferdinand I; 20l. King Carol I.

134 "The Spring"

1938. Birth Centenary of Nicholas Grigorescu (painter).

1385	**134**	1l.+1l. blue	3·00	95
1386	-	2l.+1l. green	3·00	1·90
1387	-	4l.+1l. red	3·00	1·90
1388	-	6l.+1l. red	4·00	3·00
1389	-	10l.+1l. blue	8·75	4·00

DESIGNS—HORIZ: 2l. "Escorting Prisoners" (Russo-Turkish War 1877–78); 4l. "Returning from Market". VERT: 6l. "Rodica, the Water Carrier"; 10l. Self-portrait.

135 Prince Carol in Royal Carriage

1939. Birth Centenary of King Carol I.

1390	**135**	25b. black	20	10
1391	-	50b. brown	20	10
1392	-	1l. violet	50	10
1393	-	1l.50 green	20	10
1394	-	2l. blue	20	10
1395	-	3l. red	20	10
1396	-	4l. red	20	10
1397	-	5l. black	20	10
1398	-	7l. black	20	10
1399	-	8l. blue	50	30
1400	-	10l. mauve	95	30
1401	-	12l. blue	95	30
1402	-	15l. blue	1·90	30
1403	-	16l. green	1·90	80

DESIGNS—HORIZ: 50b. Prince Carol at Battle of Calafat; 1l.50, Sigmaringen and Pelesch Castles; 15l. Carol I, Queen Elizabeth and Arms of Romania. VERT: 1l. Examining plans for restoring Curtea de Arges Monastery; 2l. Carol I and Queen Elizabeth; 3l. Carol I at age of 8; 4l. In 1866; 5l. In 1877; 7l. Equestrian statue; 8l. Leading troops in 1878; 10l. In General's uniform; 12l. Bust; 16l. Restored Monastery of Curtea de Arges.

1939. As last but in miniature sheet form. Perf or Imperf.

MS1404 141×116 mm. Nos. 1390/1 and 1393 (sold at 20l.)	4·75	14·50
MS1405 126×146 mm. Nos. 1394 and 1398/1400	4·75	14·50
MS1406 126×146 mm. Nos. 1395/6 and 1401 (sold at 50l.)	4·75	14·50

136 Romanian Pavilion N.Y. World's Fair

1939. New York World's Fair.

1407	**136**	6l. lake	1·50	80
1408	-	12l. blue	1·50	80

DESIGN: 12l. Another view of Pavilion.

137 Michael Eminescu, after painting by Joano Basarab

1939. 50th Death Anniv of Michael Eminescu (poet).

1409	**137**	5l. black	1·50	80
1410	-	7l. red	1·50	80

DESIGN: 7l. Eminescu in later years.

138 St. George and Dragon

1939. Ninth Anniv of Accession of Carol II and Boy Scouts' Fund.

1411	**138**	25b.+25b. grey	95	70
1412	**138**	50b.+50b. brown	95	70
1413	**138**	1l.+1l. blue	1·10	70
1414	**138**	2l.+2l. green	1·20	70
1415	**138**	3l.+2l. purple	1·50	70
1416	**138**	4l.+2l. orange	1·90	95
1417	**138**	6l.+2l. red	2·10	95
1418	**138**	8l. grey	2·40	95
1419	**138**	10l. blue	2·50	1·20
1420	**138**	12l. blue	3·00	1·90
1421	**138**	16l. green	4·00	2·40

139 Diesel Railcar, Class 142 Steam Locomotive (1936) and Locomotive "Calugareni" (1869)

1939. 70th Anniv of Romanian Railways.

1422	**139**	1l. violet	2·10	80
1423	-	4l. red	2·10	80
1424	-	5l. grey	2·10	80
1425	-	7l. mauve	2·10	80
1426	-	12l. blue	4·00	2·10
1427	-	15l. green	4·25	3·00

DESIGNS—HORIZ: 4l. Class 142 steam train crossing bridge, 1936; 15l. Railway Headquarters, Budapest. VERT: 5, 7l. Locomotive "Calugareni" (1869) leaving station; 12l. Diesel-mechanical twin set (1937) crossing bridge.

1940. Balkan Entente. As T **103** of Yugoslavia, but with Arms rearranged.

1428	12l. blue	1·50	95
1429	16l. blue	1·50	95

141 King Carol II

1940. Aviation Fund.

1430	**141**	1l.+50b. green	40	30
1431	**141**	2l.50+50b. green	60	50
1432	**141**	3l.+1l. red	80	60
1433	**141**	3l.50+50b. brown	85	70
1434	**141**	4l.+1l. orange	1·10	80
1435	**141**	6l.+1l. blue	1·60	50
1436	**141**	9l.+1l. blue	1·90	1·50
1437	**141**	14l.+1l. green	2·30	1·90

142 King Carol II

1940. Tenth Anniv of Accession and Aviation Fund. Portraits of King Carol II.

1438	**142**	1l.+50b. purple	1·50	50
1439	**142**	4l.+1l. brown	1·50	70
1440	-	6l.+1l. blue	1·50	95
1441	-	8l. red	1·90	1·20
1442	-	16l. blue	2·40	1·50
1443	-	32l. brown	3·50	2·40

PORTRAITS: 6, 16l. In steel helmet; 8l. In military uniform; 32l. In flying helmet.

144 The Iron Gates of the Danube

1940. Charity. Tenth Anniv of Accession of Carol II and Boy Scouts' Fund. Inscr "STRAJA TARII 8 IUNIE 1940".

1444	**144**	1l.+1l. violet	95	70
1445	-	2l.+1l. brown	1·10	80
1446	-	3l.+1l. green	1·20	95
1447	-	4l.+1l. black	1·30	1·10
1448	-	5l.+1l. orange	1·50	1·20
1449	-	8l.+1l. red	1·90	1·30
1450	-	12l.+2l. blue	2·40	1·50
1451	-	16l.+2l. grey	4·25	3·00

DESIGNS—HORIZ: 3l. Hotin Fortress; 4l. Hurez Monastery. VERT: 2l. Greco-Roman ruins; 5l. Church in Suceava; 8l. Alba Julia Cathedral; 12l. Village Church, Transylvania; 16l. Triumphal Arch, Bucharest.

1940. Armaments Fund. Nos. **MS**1404/6 optd **PRO PATRIA 1940.** Perf or Imperf.

MS1452 on No. **MS**1404	24·00	29·00
MS1453 on No. **MS**1405	29·00	48·00
MS1454 on No. **MS**1406	39·00	75·00

145 King Michael

1940

1455	**145**	25b. green	10	10
1456	**145**	50b. olive	10	10
1457	**145**	1l. violet	10	10
1458	**145**	2l. orange	10	10
1608	**145**	3l. brown	10	10
1609	**145**	3l.50 brown	10	10
1459	**145**	4l. grey	10	10
1611	**145**	4l.50 brown	10	10
1460	**145**	5l. pink	10	10
1613	**145**	6l.50 violet	10	10
1461	**145**	7l. blue	10	10
1615	**145**	10l. mauve	10	10
1616	**145**	11l. blue	10	10
1463	**145**	12l. blue	10	10
1464	**145**	13l. purple	10	10
1618	**145**	15l. blue	20	10
1619	**145**	16l. blue	10	10
1620	**145**	20l. brown	20	10
1621	**145**	29l. blue	1·60	1·30
1467	**145**	30l. green	30	10
1468	**145**	50l. brown	30	10
1469	**145**	100l. brown	95	10

146 King Michael

1940. Aviation Fund.

1470	**146**	1l.+50b. green	10	10
1471	**146**	2l.+50b. green	10	10
1472	**146**	2l.50+50b. green	10	10
1473	**146**	3l.+1l. violet	10	10
1474	**146**	3l.50+50b. pink	20	20
1475	**146**	4l.+50b. red	20	10
1476	**146**	4l.+1l. brown	10	10
1477	**146**	5l.+1l. red	1·50	50
1478	**146**	6l.+1l. blue	10	10
1479	**146**	7l.+1l. green	50	20
1480	**146**	8l.+1l. violet	30	10
1481	**146**	12l.+1l. brown	50	30
1482	**146**	14l.+1l. blue	50	10
1483	**146**	19l.+1l. mauve	1·20	50

147 Codreanu (founder)

148 Codreanu (founder)

1940. "Iron Guard" Fund.

1484	**147**	7l.+30l. grn (postage)	8·25	7·75
1485	**148**	20l.+5l. green (air)	4·75	5·75

149 Ion Mota

1941. Marin and Mota (legionaries killed in Spain).

1486	-	7l.+7l. red	4·75	4·75
1487	**149**	15l.+15l. blue	6·75	6·75
MS1487a 89×35 mm. As Nos. 1486/7 both in green. Imperf. (sold at 300l.)			£120	£150

DESIGN: 7l. Vasile Marin.

150 Library

1941. Carol I Endowment Fund. Inscr "1891 1941".

1488	-	1l.50+43l.50 violet	2·40	2·40
1489	**150**	2l.+43l. red	2·40	2·40
1490	-	7l.+38l. red	2·40	2·40
1491	-	10l.+35l. green	2·75	2·75
1492	-	16l.+29l. brown	3·00	3·00

DESIGNS: 1l.50, Ex-libris; 7l. Foundation building and equestrian statue; 10l. Foundation stone; 16l. King Michael and Carol I.

1941. Occupation of Cernauti. Nos. 1488/92 optd **CERNAUTI 5 Iulie 1941.**

1493		1l.50+43l.50 violet	4·75	4·75
1494	**150**	2l.+43l. red	4·75	4·75
1495	-	7l.+38l. red	4·75	4·75
1496	-	10l.+35l. green	4·75	4·75
1497	-	16l.+29l. brown	5·00	5·00

1941. Occupation of Chisinau. Nos. 1488/92 optd **CHISINAU 16 Iulie 1941.**

1498		1l.50+43l.50 violet	4·75	4·75
1499	**150**	2l.+43l. red	4·75	4·75
1500	-	7l.+38l. red	4·75	4·75
1501	-	10l.+35l. green	4·75	4·75
1502	-	16l.+29l. brown	5·00	5·00

153 "Charity"

1941. Red Cross Fund. Cross in red.

1503	**153**	1l.50+38l.50 violet	1·90	1·20
1504	**153**	2l.+38l. red	1·90	1·20
1505	**153**	5l.+35l. olive	1·90	1·20
1506	**153**	7l.+33l. brown	1·90	1·20
1507	**153**	10l.+30l. blue	2·40	2·20
MS1508 105×73 mm. Nos. 1506/7. Imperf. (sold at 200l.)			29·00	31·00

154 Prince Voda

1941. Conquest of Transdniestria.

1572	**154**	3l. orange	50	1·00
1509	**154**	6l. brown	50	50
1510	**154**	12l. violet	95	1·00
1511	**154**	24l. blue	1·50	1·60

155 King Michael and Stephen the Great

1941. Anti-Bolshevik Crusade. Inscr "RAZBOIUL SFANT CONTRA BOLSEVISMULUI".

1512	**155**	10l.+30l. blue	3·00	4·75
1513	-	12l.+28l. red	3·00	4·75
1514	-	16l.+24l. brown	4·00	5·25
1515	-	20l.+20l. violet	4·00	5·25
MS1516		105×73 mm. 16l. blue (emblems and angel with sword); 20l. red (helmeted soldiers and eagle). No gum. (sold at 200l.)	14·50	21·00

DESIGNS: 12l. Hotin and Akkerman Fortresses; 16l. Arms and helmeted soldiers; 20l. Bayonet charge and Arms of Romania.

1941. Fall of Odessa. Nos. 1512/15 optd **ODESA 16 Oct. 1941**.

1517	**155**	10l.+30l. blue	3·00	4·75
1518	-	12l.+28l. red	3·00	4·75
1519	-	16l.+24l. brown	4·00	5·25
1520	-	20l.+20l. violet	4·00	5·25
MS1521		(No. **MS**1516)	24·00	26·00

157 Hotin

1941. Restoration of Bessarabia and Bukovina (Suceava). Inscr "BASARABIA" or "BUCOVINA".

1522		25b. red	10	10
1523	**157**	50b. brown	10	10
1524	-	1l. violet	10	10
1525	-	1l.50 green	10	10
1526	-	2l. brown	10	10
1527	-	3l. olive	30	10
1528	-	5l. olive	50	20
1529	-	5l.50 brown	50	20
1530	-	6l.50 mauve	1·20	75
1531	**157**	9l.50 grey	1·20	75
1532	-	10l. purple	80	20
1533	-	13l. blue	85	40
1534	-	17l. brown	1·10	30
1535	-	26l. green	1·30	65
1536	-	39l. blue	2·30	85
1537	-	130l. yellow	7·25	5·25

VIEWS—VERT: 25b., 5l. Paraclis Hotin; 3l. Dragomirna; 13l. Milisauti. HORIZ: 1, 17l. Sucevita; 1l.50, Soroca; 2, 5l.50, Tighina; 6l.50, Cetatea Alba; 10, 130l. Putna; 26l. St. Nicolae, Suceava; 39l. Monastery, Rughi.

1941. Winter Relief Fund. Inscr "BASARABIA" or "BUCOVINA".

1538		3l.+50b. red	60	30
1539		5l.50+50b. orange	95	85
1540		5l.50+1l. black	95	85
1541		6l.50+1l. brown	1·20	1·20
1542		8l.+1l. blue	95	50
1543		9l.50+1l. blue	1·20	1·00
1544		10l.50+1l. blue	1·30	50
1545		16l.+1l. mauve	1·50	1·20
1546	**157**	25l.+1l. grey	1·60	1·30

VIEWS—HORIZ: 3l. Sucevita; 5l.50, (1539), Monastery, Rughi; 5l.50, (1540), Tighina; 6l.50, Soroca; 8l. St. Nicolae, Suceava; 10l.50, Putna; 16l. Cetatea Alba. VERT: 8l.50, Milisauti.

158 Titu Maiorescu

1942. Prisoners of War Relief Fund through International Education Office, Geneva.

1549	**158**	9l.+11l. violet	95	1·30
1550	**158**	20l.+20l. brown	2·40	3·25
1551	**158**	20l.+30l. blue	2·75	3·50
MS1552		128×81 mm. Nos. 1549/51. Imperf. No gum. (sold at 200l.)	11·50	13·50

159 Coat-of-Arms of Bukovina

1942. First Anniv of Liberation of Bukovina.

1553	**159**	9l.+4l. red	4·00	5·25
1554	-	18l.+32l. blue	4·00	5·25
1555	-	20l.+30l. red	4·00	5·25

ARMORIAL DESIGNS: 18l. Castle; 20l. Mounds and crosses.

160 Map of Bessarabia, King Michael, Antonescu, Hitler and Mussolini

1942. First Anniv of Liberation of Bessarabia.

1556	**160**	9l.+41l. brown	4·00	5·25
1557	-	18l.+32l. olive	4·00	5·25
1558	-	20l.+30l. blue	4·00	5·25

DESIGNS—VERT: 18l. King Michael and Marshal Antonescu below miniature of King Stephen. HORIZ: 20l. Marching soldiers and miniature of Marshal Antonescu.

161 Statue of Miron Costin

1942. First Anniv of Incorporation of Transdniestria.

1559	**161**	6l.+44l. brown	2·40	4·25
1560	**161**	12l.+38l. violet	2·40	4·25
1561	**161**	24l.+26l. blue	2·40	4·25

162 Andrei Muresanu

1942. 80th Death Anniv of A. Muresanu (novelist).

1562	**162**	5l.+5l. violet	1·50	1·60

163 Statue of Avram Iancu

1943. Fund for Statue of Iancu (national hero).

1563	**163**	16l.+4l. brown	1·50	1·70

164 Nurse and wounded Soldier

1943. Red Cross Charity. Cross in red.

1564	**164**	12l.+88l. red	1·20	1·30
1565	**164**	16l.+84l. blue	1·20	1·30
1566	**164**	20l.+80l. olive	1·20	1·30
MS1567		100×60 mm. Nos. 1565/6 (different shades). Imperf. No gum. (sold at 500l.)	9·75	12·50

165 Sword and Shield

1943. Charity. Second Year of War. Inscr "22 JUNIE 1941 22 JUNIE 1943".

1568	**165**	36l.+164l. brown	4·00	5·25
1569	-	62l.+138l. blue	4·00	5·25
1570	-	76l.+124l. red	4·00	5·25
MS1571		90×65 mm. Nos. 1569/70 (different shades). Imperf. No gum. (sold at 600l.)	24·00	26·00

DESIGNS—VERT: 62l. Sword severing chain; 76l. Angel protecting soldier and family.

167 P. Maior

1943. Transylvanian Refugees' Fund (1st issue).

1576	**167**	16l.+134l. red	95	1·00
1577	-	32l.+118l. blue	95	1·00
1578	-	36l.+114l. purple	95	1·00
1579	-	62l.+138l. red	95	1·00
1580	-	91l.+109l. brown	95	1·00

PORTRAITS—VERT: 32l. G. Sincai; 36l. T. Cipariu; 91l. G. Cosbuc. HORIZ: 62l. Horia, Closca and Crisan.

See also Nos. 1584/8.

169 King Michael and Marshal Antonescu

1943. Third Anniv of King Michael's Reign.

1581	**169**	16l.+24l. blue	3·50	3·75

170 Sports Shield

1943. Charity. Sports Week.

1582	**170**	16l.+24l. blue	1·30	1·00
1583	**170**	16l.+24l. brown	1·30	1·00

1943. Transylvanian Refugees' Fund (2nd issue) Portraits as T **167**.

1584		16l.+134l. mauve	1·00	1·00
1585		51l.+99l. orange	1·00	1·00
1586		56l.+144l. red	1·00	1·00
1587		76l.+124l. blue	1·00	1·00
1588		77l.+123l. brown	1·00	1·00

PORTRAITS—VERT: 16l. S. Micu; 51l. G. Lazar; 56l. O. Goga; 76l. S. Barnutiu; 77l. A. Saguna.

171 Calafat, 1877

1943. Centenary of National Artillery.

1596	**171**	1l.+1l. brown	50	50
1597	-	2l.+2l. violet	50	50
1598	-	3l.50+3l.50 blue	50	50
1599	-	4l.+4l. mauve	50	50
1600	-	5l.+5l. orange	1·50	1·60
1601	-	6l.50+6l.50 blue	1·50	1·60
1602	-	7l.+7l. purple	1·90	2·10
1603	-	20l.+20l. red	3·00	3·25

DESIGNS—HORIZ: (1l. to 7l. inscr battle scenes): 2l. "1916–1918"; 3l.50, Stalingrad; 4l. Crossing R. Tisza; 5l. Odessa; 6l.50, Caucasus; 7l. Sevastopol; 20l. Bibescu and King Michael.

172 Association Insignia

1943. 25th Anniv of National Engineers' Assn.

1624	**172**	21l.+29l. brown	1·50	1·60

173 Motor-cycle and Delivery Van

1944. Postal Employees' Relief Fund and Bicentenary of National Postal Service. (a) Without opt.

1625	**173**	1l.+49l. red	3·00	3·25
1626	-	2l.+48l. mauve	3·00	3·25
1627	-	4l.+46l. blue	3·00	3·25
1628	-	10l.+40l. purple	3·00	3·25
MS1629		143×86 mm. Nos. 1625/7 but in red (sold at 200l.)	9·75	10·50
MS1630		As last but in violet and imperf	9·75	10·50

(b) Optd **1744 1944**.

1631	**173**	1l+49l. red	6·25	6·75
1632	-	2l.+48l. mauve	6·25	6·75
1633	-	4l.+46l. blue	6·25	6·75
1634	-	10l.+40l. purple	6·25	6·75
MS1635		(No. **MS**1629)	24·00	31·00
MS1636		(No. **MS**1630)	24·00	31·00

DESIGNS—HORIZ: 2l. Post motorcycle, post van and eight horses; 4l. Chariot. VERT: Horseman and globe.

174 Dr. Cretzulescu

1944. Cent of Medical Teaching in Romania.

1637	**174**	35l.+65l. blue	1·50	1·60

175 Rugby Player

1944. 30th Anniv of Foundation of National Rugby Football Association.

1638	**175**	16l.+184l. red	6·25	6·75

176 Stefan Tomsa Church, Radaseni

177 Fruit Pickers

1944. Cultural Fund. Town of Radaseni. Inscr "RADASENI".

1639	**176**	5l.+145l. blue	1·30	1·30
1640	-	12l.+138l. red	1·30	1·30
1641	**177**	15l.+135l. orange	1·30	1·30
1642	-	32l.+118l. brown	1·30	1·30

DESIGNS—HORIZ: 12l. Agricultural Institution; 32l. School.

178 Queen Helen

1945. Red Cross Relief Fund. Portrait in black on yellow and Cross in red.

1643	**178**	4l.50+5l.50 violet	50	50
1644	**178**	10l.+40l. brown	70	75
1645	**178**	15l.+75l. blue	95	1·00
1646	**178**	20l.+80l. red	1·50	1·60

179 King Michael and Carol I Foundation, Bucharest

1945. King Carol I Foundation Fund.

1647	**179**	20l.+180l. orange	70	75
1648	**179**	25l.+175l. slate	70	75
1649	**179**	35l.+165l. brown	70	75
1650	**179**	76l.+125l. violet	70	75
MS1651		74×60 mm. 200l.+1000l. blue (as T **179** but portrait of King Carol I) Imperf. No gum	9·75	9·75

180 A. Saguna

181 A. Muresanu

1945. Liberation of Northern Transylvania. Inscr "1944".

1652	**180**	25b. red	95	1·00
1653	**181**	50b. orange	50	1·00
1654	-	4l.50 brown	50	1·00

1655	-	11l. blue	50	1·00
1656	-	15l. green	50	1·00
1657	-	31l. violet	50	1·00
1658	-	35l. grey	50	1·00
1659	-	41l. olive	50	1·00
1660	-	55l. brown	50	1·00
1661	-	61l. mauve	50	1·00
1662	-	75l.+75l. brown	50	1·00

DESIGNS—HORIZ: 4l.50, Samuel Micu; 31l. George Lazar; 55l. Horia, Closca and Crisan; 61l. Petru Maior; 75l. King Ferdinand and King Michael. VERT: 11l. George Sincai; 15l. Michael the Brave; 35l. Avram Iancu; 41l. Simeon Barnutiu.

182 King Michael

183 King Michael

184 King Michael

185 King Michael

1945

1663	**182**	50b. grey	10	10
1664	**183**	1l. brown	10	10
1665	**183**	2l. violet	10	10
1666	**182**	2l. brown	10	10
1667	**183**	4l. green	10	10
1668	**184**	5l. mauve	10	10
1669	**182**	10l. blue	10	10
1670	**182**	10l. brown	10	10
1671	**183**	10l. brown	10	10
1672	**182**	15l. mauve	10	10
1673	**182**	20l. blue	10	10
1674	**182**	20l. lilac	10	10
1675	**184**	20l. purple	10	10
1676	**184**	25l. red	10	10
1677	**184**	35l. brown	10	10
1678	**184**	40l. red	30	10
1679	**183**	50l. blue	10	10
1680	**183**	55l. red	30	10
1681	**184**	75l. green	50	10
1682	**185**	80l. orange	50	10
1683	**185**	80l. blue	10	10
1684	**182**	80l. blue	10	10
1685	**185**	100l. brown	10	10
1686	**182**	137l. green	50	10
1687	**185**	160l. green	10	10
1688	**185**	160l. violet	50	10
1689	**185**	200l. green	50	10
1690	**185**	200l. red	10	10
1691	**183**	200l. red	10	10
1692	**185**	300l. blue	10	10
1693	**185**	360l. brown	50	10
1694	**185**	400l. violet	10	10
1695	**183**	400l. red	10	10
1696	**185**	480l. brown	50	10
1697	**182**	500l. mauve	50	10
1698	**185**	600l. green	10	10
1699	**184**	860l. brown	80	20
1700	**185**	1000l. green	50	10
1701	**182**	1500l. green	50	10
1702	**185**	2400l. lilac	95	10
1703	**183**	2500l. blue	50	10
1704	**185**	3700l. blue	95	10
1705	**182**	5000l. grey	40	10
1706	**182**	8000l. green	95	20
1707	**185**	10000l. brown	1·20	30

186 N. Jorga

1945. War Victims' Relief Fund.

1708	-	12l.+188l. blue	95	1·00
1709	-	16l.+184l. brown	95	1·00
1710	**186**	20l.+180l. brown	95	1·00
1711	-	32l.+168l. red	95	1·00
1712	-	35l.+165l. blue	95	1·00
1713	-	36l.+164l. violet	95	1·00
MS1714 76×60 mm. Nos. 1711/12 but mauve. Imperf. (sold at 1000l.)			29·00	31·00

PORTRAITS: 12l. Ian Gheorghe Duca (Prime Minister, 1933); 16l. Virgil Madgearu (politician); 32l. Ilie Pintilie (communist); 35l. Bernath Andrei (communist); 36l. Filimon Sarbu (saboteur).

187 Books and Torch

1945. Charity. First Romanian–Soviet Congress Fund. Inscr "ARLUS".

1715	**187**	20l.+80l. olive	60	65
1716	-	35l.+165l. red	60	65
1717	-	75l.+225l. blue	60	65
1718	-	80l.+420l. brown	60	65
MS1719 60×75 mm. As Nos. 1716/17 but in red. Imperf. (sold at 900l.)			11·50	12·50

DESIGNS: 35l. Soviet and Romanian flags; 75l. Drawn curtain revealing Kremlin; 80l. T. Vladimirescu and A. Nevsky.

188 Karl Marx

1945. Trade Union Congress, Bucharest. Perf or imperf.

1720	**188**	75l.+425l. red	4·00	4·25
1723	**188**	75l.+425l. blue	11·50	12·50
1721	-	120l.+380l. blue	4·00	4·25
1724	-	120l.+380l. brown	11·50	12·50
1722	-	155l.+445l. brown	4·00	4·25
1725	-	155l.+445l. red	11·50	12·50

PORTRAITS: 120l. Engels; 155l. Lenin.

189 Postman

1945. Postal Employees. Inscr "MUNCA P.T.T.".

1726	**189**	100l. brown	95	1·00
1727	**189**	100l. olive	95	1·00
1728	-	150l. brown	1·50	1·60
1729	-	150l. red	1·50	1·60
1730	-	250l. olive	2·40	2·50
1731	-	250l. blue	2·40	2·50
1732	-	500l. mauve	19·00	21·00

DESIGNS: 150l. Telegraphist; 250l. Lineman; 500l. Post Office, Bucharest.

190 Throwing the Discus

1945. Charity. With shield inscr "O.S.P.". Perf or imperf.

1733	**190**	12l.+188l. olive (post)	3·50	3·75
1738	-	12l.+188l. orange	3·50	3·75
1734	-	16l.+184l. blue	3·50	3·75
1739	-	16l.+184l. purple	3·50	3·75
1735	-	20l.+180l. green	3·50	3·75
1740	-	20l.+180l. violet	3·50	3·75
1736	-	32l.+168l. mauve	3·50	3·75
1741	-	32l.+168l. green	3·50	3·75
1737	-	35l.+165l. blue	3·50	3·75
1742	-	35l.+165l. olive	3·50	3·75
1743	-	200l.+1000l. bl (air)	29·00	31·00

DESIGNS—As T **190**: 16l. Diving; 20l. Skiing; 32l. Volleyball; 35l. "Sport and work". 36×50 mm: 200l. Airplane and bird.

192 Agricultural and Industrial Workers

1945. First Anniv of Romanian Armistice with Russia.

1744	**192**	100l.+400l. red	1·20	1·30
1745	-	200l.+800l. blue	1·20	1·30

DESIGN: 200l. King Michael, "Agriculture" and "Industry".

193 T. Vladimirescu

1945. Charity. Patriotic Defence Fund. Inscr "APARAREA PATRIOTICA".

1746		20l.+580l. brown	8·75	11·50
1747		20l.+580l. mauve	8·75	11·50
1748		40l.+560l. blue	8·75	11·50
1749		40l.+560l. green	8·75	11·50
1750		55l.+545l. red	8·75	11·50
1751		55l.+545l. brown	8·75	11·50
1752	**193**	60l.+540l. blue	8·75	11·50
1753	**193**	60l.+540l. brown	8·75	11·50
1754	-	80l.+520l. red	8·75	11·50
1755	-	80l.+520l. mauve	8·75	11·50
1756	-	100l.+500l. green	8·75	11·50
1757	-	100l.+500l. brown	8·75	11·50

DESIGNS—HORIZ: 20l. "Political Amnesty"; 40l. "Military Amnesty"; 55l. "Agrarian Amnesty"; 100l. King Michael and "Recontruction". VERT: 80l. Nicholas Horia.

194 Destitute Children

1945. Child Welfare Fund.

1758	**194**	40l. blue	95	50

195 I. Ionescu, G. Titeica, A. G. Idachimescu and V. Cristescu

1945. 50th Anniv of Founding of Journal of Mathematics.

1759	**195**	2l. brown	20	10
1760	-	80l. blue	70	75

DESIGN: 80l. Allegory of Learning.

196 Saligny Bridge

1945. 50th Anniv of Saligny Bridge over River Danube, Cernavoda.

1761	**196**	80l. black	95	50

197 Class E.18 Electric Locomotive, 1935, Germany

198

1945. Charity. 16th Congress of Romanian Engineers. Perf or imperf. (a) Postage.

1762	**197**	10l.+490l. olive	95	1·00
1767	**197**	10l.+490l. blue	95	1·00
1763	-	20l.+480l. brown	95	1·00
1768	-	20l.+480l. violet	95	1·00
1764	-	25l.+475l. purple	95	1·00
1769	-	25l.+475l. green	95	1·00
1765	-	55l.+445l. blue	95	1·00
1770	-	55l.+445l. grey	95	1·00
1766	-	100l.+400l. brown	95	1·00
1771	-	100l.+400l. mauve	95	1·00

(b) Air. Symbolical design as T **198**. Imperf.

1772	**198**	80l.+420l. grey	2·40	2·50
1773	-	200l.+800l. blue	2·40	2·50
MS1774 75×55 mm. 80l. purple (as 1772)			14·50	19·00
MS1775 75×55 mm. 80l. green (as 1773)			24·00	27·00

DESIGNS—As Type **197**: 20l. Coats of Arms; 25l. Arterial road; 55l. Oil wells; 100l. "Agriculture". As T **198**: 200l. Icarus and Lockheed 14 Super Electra airplane.

199 Globe and Clasped Hands

1945. Charity. World Trade Union Congress, Paris. Symbolical designs inscr "CONFERINTA MONDIAL LA SINDICALA DIN PARIS 25 SEPTEMVRE 1945".

1776	**199**	80l.+920l. mauve	24·00	26·00
1777	-	160l.+1840l. brown	24·00	26·00
1778	-	320l.+1680l. violet	24·00	26·00
1779	-	440l.+2560l. green	24·00	26·00

DESIGNS: 160l. Globe and Dove of Peace; 320l. Hand and hammer; 440l. Scaffolding and flags.

1946. Nos 1444/5 surch in figures.

1780	10l.+90l. on 100l.+400l.	1·90	2·10
1781	10l.+90l. on 200l.+800l.	1·90	2·10
1782	20l.+80l. on 100l.+400l.	1·90	2·10
1783	20l.+80l. on 200l.+800l.	1·90	2·10
1784	80l.+120l. on 100l.+400l.	1·90	2·10
1785	80l.+120l. on 200l.+800l.	1·90	2·10
1786	100l.+150l. on 100l.+400l.	1·90	2·10
1787	100l.+150l. on 200l.+800l.	1·90	2·10

200 Sower

201 Distribution of Title Deeds

1946. Agrarian Reform. Inscr "REFORMA AGRARA".

1788	-	80l. blue	60	65
1789	**200**	50l.+450l. red	60	65
1790	**201**	100l.+900l. purple	60	65
1791	-	200l.+800l. orange	60	65
1792	-	400l.+1600l. green	60	65
MS1793 75×60 mm. 80l. blue (as No. 1789 but larger) (sold at 100l.) (air)			19·00	21·00

DESIGNS—VERT: 80l Blacksmith and ploughman. HORIZ: 200l. Ox-drawn farm wagon; 400l. Plough and tractor.

202

1946. 25th Anniv of Bucharest Philharmonic Orchestra.

1794	**202**	10l. blue	20	10
1795	-	20l. brown	20	10
1796	-	55l. green	20	10
1797	-	80l. violet	20	10
1798	-	160l. orange	20	10
1799	**202**	200l.+800l. red	1·50	1·60
1800	-	350l.+1650l. blue	1·90	2·10
MS1801 No. 1799×12+4 labels			60·00	65·00
MS1802 No. 1800×12+4 labels			60·00	65·00

DESIGNS: 20l., 55l., 160l. "XXV" and musical score; 80l., 350l. G. Enescu.

203 Building Worker

1946. Labour Day. Designs of workers inscr "ZIUA MUNCII".

1803	**203**	10l. red	20	10
1804	**203**	10l. green	95	1·00
1805	**203**	20l. blue	95	1·00
1806	**203**	20l. brown	20	10
1807	**203**	200l. red	50	50

204 Sky-writing

1946. Air. Labour Day. Sheet 70×63 mm.

MS1808		200l. blue and vermilion (sold at 10,000l.)	19·00	21·00

205 Sower

1946. Youth Issue.

1809	**205**	10l.+100l. red & brn	50	50
1810	-	10l.+200l. pur & blue	50	50
1811	-	80l.+200l. brn & pur	50	50
1812	-	80l.+300l. mve & brn	50	50
1813	-	200l.+400l. red & grn	50	50

DESIGNS: No. 1810, Hurdling; 1811, Student; 1812, Worker and factory; 1813, Marching with flag.

206 Aviator and Aircraft

1946. Air. Youth Issue.

1814		200l. blue and green	4·75	5·25
1815	**206**	500l. blue and orange	4·75	5·25

DESIGN: 200l. Airplane on ground.

207 Football

1946. Sports, designs inscr "O.S.P." Perf or imperf.

1816	**207**	10l. blue (postage)	50	50
1817	-	20l. red	50	50
1818	-	50l. violet	50	50
1819	-	80l. brown	50	50
1820	-	160l.+1340l. green	50	50
1821	-	300l. red (air)	1·90	2·50
1822	-	300l.+1200l. blue	1·90	2·50
MS1823		58×64 mm. 300l. crimson (as No. 1821 but larger). Imperf. (sold at 1300l.)	21·00	23·00

DESIGNS: 20l. Diving; 50l. Running; 80l. Mountaineering; 160l. Ski jumping; 300l. (both) Flying.

208 "Traditional Ties"

1946. Romanian–Soviet Friendship Pact.

1824	**208**	80l. brown	50	50
1825	-	100l. blue	50	50
1826	-	300l. grey	50	50
1827	-	300l.+1200l. red	95	1·00
MS1828		70×65 mm. 1000l. scarlet (as No. 1827) (sold at 6000l.)	9·75	10·50

DESIGNS: 100l. "Cultural ties"; 300l. "Economic ties"; 300l.+1200l. Dove.

No. 1827 also exists imperf.

209 Banat Girl holding Distaff

1946. Charity. Women's Democratic Federation.

1829		80l. olive	40	40
1830	**209**	80l.+320l. red	40	40
1831	-	140l.+360l. orange	40	40
1832	-	300l.+450l. green	40	40
1833	-	600l.+900l. blue	40	40
MS1834		80×65 mm. 500l.+9500l. vermilion and chocolate (air)	9·75	10·50

DESIGNS: 80l. Girl and handloom; 140l. Wallachian girl and wheatsheaf; 300l. Transylvanian horsewoman; 600l. Moldavian girl carrying water.

211 King Michael and Food Transport

1947. Social Relief Fund.

1845		300l. olive	50	50
1846	**211**	600l. mauve	50	50
1847	-	1500l.+3500l. orange	50	50
1848	-	3700l.+5300l. violet	50	50
MS1849		52×36 mm. **212** 5000l.+5000l. ultramarine. Imperf. No gum	9·75	10·50

DESIGNS—VERT: 300l. Loaf of bread and hungry child; 1500l. Angel bringing food and clothing to destitute people; 3700l. Loaf of bread and starving family.

213 King Michael and Chariot

1947. Peace.

1850	**213**	300l. purple	50	50
1851	-	600l. brown	50	50
1852	-	3000l. blue	50	50
1853	-	7200l. green	50	50

DESIGNS—VERT: 600l. Winged figure of Peace; 300l. Flags of four Allied Nations; 7200l. Dove of Peace.

214 Symbols of Labour and Clasped Hands

1947. Trades Union Congress.

1854	**214**	200l. blue (postage)	70	75
1855	**214**	300l. orange	70	75
1856	**214**	600l. red	70	75
1857	-	1100l. blue (air)	95	1·00

DESIGN—22×37 mm: 1100l. As Type **214** with Lockheed Super Electra airplane at top.

216 Worker and Torch

1947. Air. Trades Union Congress. Imperf.

1858	**216**	3000l.+7000l. brown	95	1·00

218 Symbolical of "Learning"

1947. Charity. People's Culture.

1859	-	200l.+200l. blue	20	30
1860	-	300l.+300l. brown	20	30
1861	-	600l.+600l. green	20	30
1862	-	1200l.+1200l. blue	20	30
1863	**218**	1500l.+1500l. red	20	30
MS1864		64×80 mm. 3700l.+3700l. blue and brown (as T **218**). Imperf	3·00	3·75

DESIGNS—HORIZ: 200l. Boys' reading class; 300l. Girls' school; 600l. Engineering classroom; 1200l. School building.

219 King Michael

1947

1865	**219**	1000l. blue	20	20
1869	**219**	3000l. blue	30	30
1866	**219**	5500l. green	30	30
1870	**219**	7200l. mauve	30	30
1871	**219**	15000l. blue	50	30
1867	**219**	20000l. brown	70	40
1872	**219**	21000l. mauve	50	30
1873	**219**	36000l. violet	95	85
1868	**219**	50000l. orange	1·30	65

Nos. 1865/8 are size 18×21½ mm and Nos. 1869/73 are 25×30 mm.

220 N. Grigorescu

221 Lisunov Li-2 Airliner

1947. Charity. Institute of Romanian–Soviet Studies.

1874	-	1500l.+1500l. purple (postage)	40	40
1875	-	1500l.+1500l. orange	40	40
1876	-	1500l.+1500l. green	40	40
1877	**220**	1500l.+1500l. blue	40	40
1878	-	1500l.+1500l. blue	40	40
1879	-	1500l.+1500l. lake	40	40
1880	-	1500l.+1500l. red	40	40
1881	-	1500l.+1500l. brown	40	40
1882	**221**	15000l.+15000l. green (air)	95	1·00

PORTRAITS: No. 1874, Petru Movila; 1875, V. Babes; 1876, M. Eminescu; 1878, P. Tchaikovsky; 1879, M. Lomonosov; 1880, A. Pushkin; 1881, I. Y. Repin.

No. 1882 is imperf.

222 Miner

1947. Charity. Labour Day.

1883	**222**	1000l.+1000l. olive	40	40
1884	-	1500l.+1500l. brown	40	40
1885	-	2000l.+2000l. blue	40	40
1886	-	2500l.+2500l. mauve	40	40
1887	-	3000l.+3000l. red	40	40

DESIGNS: 1500l. Peasant; 2000l. Peasant woman; 2500l. Intellectual; 3000l. Factory worker.

224 Douglas DC-4 Airliner over Black Sea

1947. Air. Labour Day.

1888		3000l. red	50	50
1889		3000l. green	50	50
1890		3000l. brown	50	50
1891	**224**	3000l.+12,000l. blue	95	1·00

DESIGNS—24½×30 mm: No. 1888, Four parachutes; 1889, Air Force Monument; 1890, Douglas DC-4 over landscape.

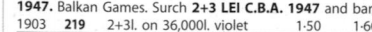

225 King Michael and Timber Barges

1947. Designs with medallion portrait of King Michael.

1892	-	50b. orange	20	10
1893	**225**	1l. brown	20	10
1894	-	2l. blue	20	10
1895	-	3l. red	50	20
1896	-	5l. blue	50	20
1897	-	10l. blue	70	30
1898	-	12l. violet	95	30
1899	-	15l. blue	1·50	30
1900	-	20l. brown	2·40	50
1901	-	32l. brown	6·25	2·50
1902	-	36l. lake	6·25	2·50

DESIGNS: 50b. Harvesting; 2l. River Danube; 3l. Reshitza Industries; 5l. Curtea de Arges Cathedral; 10l. Royal Palace, Bucharest; 12, 36l. Saligny Bridge, Cernavoda; 15, 32l. Liner "Transylvania" in Port of Constantza; 20l. Oil Wells, Prahova.

1947. Balkan Games. Surch **2+3 LEI C.B.A. 1947** and bar.

1903	**219**	2+3l. on 36,000l. violet	1·50	1·60

227

1947. 17th Congress of General Assn of Romanian Engineers. With monogram as in T **227**.

1904	**227**	1l.+1l. red (postage)	20	10
1905	-	2l.+2l. brown	20	10
1906	-	3l.+3l. violet	20	10
1907	-	4l.+4l. olive	30	30
1908	-	5l.+5l. blue (air)	1·10	1·20

DESIGNS: 2l. Sawmill; 3l. Refinery; 4l. Steel mill; 5l. Gliders over mountains.

1947. Charity. Soviet–Romanian Amity. As No. 1896 surch **ARLUS 1-7-XI. 1947 +5.** Imperf.

1909		5l.+5l. blue	95	75

229 Beehive

1947. Savings Day.

1910	**229**	12l. red	95	50

230 Food Convoy

1947. Patriotic Defence.

1911	**230**	1l.+1l. blue	50	50
1912	-	2l.+2l. brown	50	50
1913	-	3l.+3l. red	50	50
1914	-	4l.+4l. blue	50	50
1915	-	5l.+5l. red	50	50

SYMBOLIC DESIGNS—HORIZ: 2l. Soldiers' parcels ("Everything for the front"); 3l. Modern hospital ("Heal the wounded"); 4l. Hungry children ("Help famine-stricken regions"). VERT: 5l. Manacled wrist and flag.

231 Allegory of work

1947. Charity. Trades Union Congress, Bucharest. Inscr "C.G.M. 1947".

1916		2l.+10l. red (postage)	50	50
1917	**231**	7l.+10l. black	50	50
1918	-	11l. red and blue (air)	95	1·00

DESIGNS—As T **231**: 2l. Industrial and agricultural workers. 23×18 mm: 11l. Lisunov Li-2 airliner over demonstration.

233 Map of Romania

1948. Census of 1948.

1925	**233**	12l. blue	95	30

234 Printing Works and Press

1948. 75th Anniv of Romanian State Stamp Printing Works.

1926	**234**	6l. red	2·40	1·60
1927	**234**	7l.50 green	1·50	20

235 Discus Thrower

1948. Balkan Games, 1947. Inscr as in T **235**. Imperf or perf.

1928	**235**	1l.+1l. brown (postage)	70	85

1929	-	2l.+2l. red	95	1·30
1930	-	5l.+5l. blue	1·50	2·10
1931	-	7l.+7l. violet (air)	2·40	2·10
1932	-	10l.+10l. green	3·50	4·25

DESIGNS: 2l. Runner; 5l. Heads of two young athletes; 7, 10l. Airplane over running track.

1948. Nos. 1892/1902 optd **R.P.R.** (Republica Populara Romana).

1933	50b. orange	50	30
1934	1l. brown	50	20
1935	2l. blue	1·20	30
1936	3l. red	1·20	30
1937	5l. blue	1·90	40
1938	10l. blue	2·40	50
1939	12l. violet	3·00	50
1940	15l. blue	3·00	65
1941	20l. brown	4·00	75
1942	32l. brown	9·75	4·25
1943	36l. lake	9·75	4·25

237 Industrial Worker

1948. Young Workers' Union. Imperf or perf.

1954	**237**	2l.+2l. blue (postage)	50	1·00
1955	-	3l.+3l. green	60	1·00
1956	-	5l.+5l. brown	70	1·00
1957	-	8l.+8l. red	85	1·00
1958	-	12l.+12l. blue (air)	2·10	3·25

DESIGNS—As Type **237**: 3l. Peasant girl and wheatsheaf; 5l. Student and book. TRIANGULAR: 8l. Youths bearing Filimon Sarbu banner. 36×23 mm: 12l. Airplane and barn swallows.

240 "Friendship"

1948. Romanian–Bulgarian Amity.

1959	**240**	32l. brown	1·90	1·00

241 "New Constitution"

1948. New Constitution.

1960	**241**	1l. red	70	50
1961	**241**	2l. orange	95	75
1962	**241**	12l. blue	3·00	1·30

242 Globe and Banner

243 Aviator and Heinkel He 116A

1948. Labour Day.

1963	**242**	8l.+8l. red (postage)	2·40	3·75
1964	-	10l.+10l. green	3·50	5·25
1965	-	12l.+12l. brown	4·75	6·25
1966	**243**	20l.+20l. blue (air)	8·25	10·50

DESIGNS—HORIZ: 10l. Peasants and mountains. VERT: 12l. Worker and factory.

244 Barbed Wire Entanglement

1948. Army Day.

1967	-	1l.50+1l.50 red (postage)	60	65
1968	**244**	2l.+2l. purple	60	65
1969	-	4l.+4l. brown	1·10	1·20
1970	-	7l.50+7l.50 black	1·90	2·10
1971	-	8l.+8l. violet	2·10	2·30
1972	-	3l.+3l. blue (air)	9·75	10·50
1973	-	5l.+5l. blue	14·50	16·00

DESIGNS—VERT: 1l.50, Infantry; 3l. Ilyushin Stormovik fighter planes; 5l. Petlyakov Pe-2 dive bomber Il-2M3. HORIZ: 4l. Artillery; 7l.50, Tank; 8l. Destroyer.

245 Five Portraits

246 Proclamation of Islaz

1948. Cent of 1848 Revolution. Dated "1848 1948".

1974		2l.+2l. purple	60	95
1975	**245**	5l.+5l. violet	80	95
1976	**246**	11l. red	1·20	1·90
1977	-	10l.+10l. green	1·10	95
1978	-	36l.+18l. blue	2·50	4·00

DESIGNS—22×38 mm. HORIZ: 10l. Balcescu, Petofi, Iancu, Barnutiu Baritiu and Murcu. VERT: 2l. Nicolas Balcescu; 36l. Balcescu, Kogalniceanu, Alecsandri and Cuza.

247 Emblem of Republic

1948

1980	**247**	0.50l. red	50	20
2023	**247**	50b. red	50	30
1981	**247**	1l. brown	50	10
1982	**247**	2l. green	50	10
1983	**247**	3l. grey	70	20
1984	**247**	4l. brown	70	20
1985	**247**	5l. blue	70	20
2028	**247**	5l. violet	95	10
1986	**247**	10l. blue	1·90	20

No. 2023 is inscribed "BANI 0.50" (= ½ bani) and in No. 1980 this was corrected to "LEI 0.50".

248 Monimoa Gliders

249 Yachts

1948. Air Force and Navy Day. (a) Air Force (vert).

1987	**248**	2l.+2l. blue	1·90	1·90
1988	-	5l.+5l. violet	1·90	1·90
1989	-	8l.+8l. red	3·00	3·00
1990	-	10l.+10l. brown	4·00	4·00

(b) Navy (horiz).

1991	**249**	2l.+2l. green	1·90	1·90
1992	-	5l.+5l. grey	1·90	1·90
1993	-	8l.+8l. blue	3·00	3·00
1994	-	10l.+10l. red	4·00	4·00

DESIGNS—AIR FORCE: 5l. Aurel Vlaicu's No. 1 "Crazy Fly" airplane; 8l. Lisunov Li-2 airliner and tractor; 10l. Lisunov Li-2 airliner. NAVY: 5l. "Mircea" (cadet ship), 1882; 8l. "Romana Mare" (Danube river steamer); 10l. "Transylvania" (liner).

1948. Surch.

1995	**240**	31l. on 32l. brown	1·50	50

251 Newspapers and Torch

1948. Press Week. Imperf or perf.

1996	**251**	5l.+5l. red	50	10
1997	**251**	10l. brown	95	95
1998	-	10l.+10l. violet	1·50	1·50
1999	-	15l.+15l. blue	1·90	1·90

DESIGNS—HORIZ: 10l. (No. 1998), Flag, torch and ink-well. VERT: 15l. Alex Sahia (journalist).

252 Soviet Soldiers' Monument

1948. Romanian–Russian Amity.

2000	**252**	10l. red (postage)	95	95
2001	-	10l.+10l. green	4·00	4·75
2002	-	15l.+15l. blue	4·75	7·25
2003	-	20l.+20l. blue (air)	14·50	19·00

DESIGNS—VERT: 10l. (No. 2001), Badge of Arlus; 15l. Kremlin. HORIZ: 20l. Lisunov Li-2 airplane.

255 Emblem of Republic

1948. Air. Designs showing aircraft.

2004	**255**	30l. red	95	20
2005	-	50l. green	1·50	70
2006	-	100l. blue	4·75	1·90

DESIGNS: 50l. Workers in a field; 100l. Steam train, airplane and liner.

256 Lorry

1948. Work on Communications.

2007		1l.+1l. black and green	95	1·90
2008	**256**	3l.+3l. black & brown	1·30	1·90
2009	-	11l.+11l. black & blue	5·25	4·75
2010	-	15l.+15l. black and red	6·75	7·75

MS2011 110×85 mm. Nos. 2007/10 but in red, blue and red respectively. Imperf. No gum 34·00 39·00

DESIGNS: 1l. Dockers loading freighter; 11l. Lisunov Li-2 airliner on ground and in the air; 15l. Steam train.

257 Nicolas Balcescu

1948

2012	**257**	20l. red	1·50	50

258 Hands Breaking Chain

1948. First Anniv of People's Republic.

2013	**258**	5l. red	95	50

259 Runners

1948. National Sports Organization. Imperf or perf.

2014	**259**	5l.+5l. green (postage)	4·75	4·75
2017	**259**	5l.+5l. brown	4·75	4·75
2015	-	10l.+10l. violet	7·25	7·25
2018	-	10l.+10l. red	7·25	7·25
2016	-	20l.+20l. blue (air)	24·00	24·00
2019	-	20l.+20l. green	24·00	24·00

DESIGNS—HORIZ: 10l. Parade of athletes with flags. VERT: 20l. Boy flying model airplane.

260 Lenin

1949. 25th Death Anniv of Lenin. Perf or imperf.

2020	**260**	20l. black	95	50

261 Dancers

1949. 90th Anniv of Union of Romanian Principalities.

2021	**261**	10l. blue	95	50

262 I. C. Frimu and Revolutionaries

1949. 30th Death Anniv of Ion Frimu (union leader and journalist). Perf or imperf.

2022	**262**	20l. red	95	50

263 Pushkin

1949. 150th Birth Anniv of A. S. Pushkin (Russian poet).

2030	**263**	11l. red	1·50	85
2031	**263**	30l. green	1·90	95

264 Globe and Posthorn

265 Forms of Transport

1949. 75th Anniv of U.P.U.

2032	**264**	20l. brown	2·40	1·50
2033	**265**	30l. blue	4·75	2·40

266 Russians entering Bucharest

1949. Fifth Anniv of Russian Army's Entry into Bucharest. Perf or imperf.

2034	**266**	50l. brown on green	1·20	1·20

267 "Romanian–Soviet Amity"

1949. Romanian–Soviet Friendship Week. Perf or imperf.

2035	**267**	20l. red	95	50

268 Forms of Transport

1949. International Congress of Transport Unions. Perf or imperf.

2036	**268**	11l. blue	1·20	1·20
2037	**268**	20l. red	1·70	1·70

269 Stalin

1949. Stalin's 70th Birthday. Perf or imperf.

2038	**269**	31l. green	95	50

1950. Philatelic Exhibition, Bucharest. Sheet 110×80 mm comprising T **1** and **247**. Imperf. No gum.

MS2039 81 (p) blue and deep blue; 10l. carmine and rose (sold at 50l.) 7·25 4·75

270 "The Third Letter"

271 Michael Eminescu

1950. Birth Centenary of Eminescu (poet).

2040	**270**	11l. green	1·50	50
2041	-	11l. brown	2·40	95
2042	-	11l. mauve	1·50	50
2043	-	11l. violet	1·50	50
2044	**271**	11l. blue	1·50	50

DESIGNS (Scenes representing poems): No. 2041, "Angel and Demon"; 2042, "Ruler and Proletariat"; 2043, "Life".

272 "Dragaica Fair"

1950. Birth Centenary of Ion Andreescu (painter). (a) Perf.

2045	**272**	5l. olive	1·50	95
2047	-	20l. brown	3·00	1·90

(b) Perf or imperf.

2046	11l. blue	2·40	95

DESIGNS—VERT: 11l. Andreescu. HORIZ: 20l. "The Village Well".

273 Factory and Graph

1950. State Plan, 1950 Inscr "PLANUL DU STAT 1950".

2048	**273**	11l. red	60	30
2049	-	31l. violet	1·50	70

DESIGN: 31l. Tractor and factories.
No. 2048 exists imperf.

274 Worker and Flag

1950. Labour Day. Perf or imperf.

2050	**274**	31l. orange	80	10

275 Emblem of Republic

1950

2051	**275**	50b. black	30	20
2052	**275**	1l. red	20	10
2053	**275**	2l. grey	20	10
2054	**275**	3l. purple	30	10
2055	**275**	4l. mauve	20	10
2056	**275**	5l. brown	30	10
2057	**275**	6l. green	30	10
2058	**275**	7l. brown	30	10
2059	**275**	7l.50 blue	50	10
2060	**275**	10l. brown	80	10
2061	**275**	11l. red	80	10
2062	**275**	15l. blue	60	10
2063	**275**	20l. green	60	10
2064	**275**	31l. green	95	10
2065	**275**	36l. brown	1·90	80

For stamps as Type **275** but with inscriptions in white, see Nos. 2240, etc, and Nos. 2277/8.

276 Trumpeter and Drummer

1950. First Anniv of Romanian Pioneers Organization.

2074	**276**	8l. blue	1·90	95
2075	-	11l. purple	2·40	1·50
2076	-	31l. red	4·25	3·00

DESIGNS: 11l. Children reading; 31l. Youth parade.

277 Engineer

1950. Industrial Nationalization.

2077	**277**	11l. red	70	50
2078	**277**	11l. blue	1·20	50
2079	**277**	11l. brown	1·20	50
2080	**277**	11l. olive	70	30

278 Aurel Vlaicu and his Airplane No. 1 "Crazy Fly"

1950. 40th Anniv of First Flight by A. Vlaicu.

2081	**278**	3l. green	50	20
2082	**278**	6l. blue	85	30
2083	**278**	8l. blue	95	50

279 Mother and Child

1950. Peace Congress, Bucharest.

2084	**279**	11l. red	50	30
2085	-	20l. brown	60	30

DESIGN: 20l. Lathe operator and graph.

280 Statue and Flags

1950. Romanian–Soviet Amity.

2086	**280**	30l. brown	95	50

1950. Romanian–Hungarian Amity. Optd **TRAIASCA PRIETENIA ROMANO-MAGHIARAI.**

2087	**275**	15l. blue	1·60	50

282 Young People and Badge

1950. GMA Complex Sports Facilities. Designs incorporating badge.

2088	-	3l. red	1·90	1·90
2089	**282**	5l. brown	1·50	1·50
2090	**282**	5l. blue	1·50	1·50
2091	-	11l. green	1·50	1·50
2092	-	31l. olive	3·50	3·50

DESIGNS: 3l. Agriculture and Industry; 11l. Runners; 31l. Gymnasts.

283

1950. Third Congress of "ARLUS".

2093	**283**	11l. orange on orange	70	50
2094	**283**	11l. blue on blue	70	50

284 Ski-jumper

1951. Winter Sports.

2095	**284**	4l. brown	1·90	1·90
2096	-	5l. red	1·50	1·50
2097	-	11l. blue	1·50	1·50
2098	-	20l. brown	1·50	1·50
2099	-	31l. green	3·50	3·50

DESIGNS: 5l. Skater; 11l. Skier; 20l. Ice hockey; 31l. Tobogganing.

286 Peasant and Tractor

1951. Agricultural and Industrial Exhibition.

2100		11l. brown	50	50
2101	**286**	31l. blue	95	50

DESIGN—VERT: 11l. Worker and machine.

287 Star of the Republic, Class I-II

1951. Orders and Medals. Perf or imperf.

2102	-	2l. green	30	30
2103	-	4l. blue	50	50
2104	-	11l. red	80	80
2105	**287**	35l. brown	1·10	1·10

DESIGNS: 2l. Medal of Work; 4l. Star of the Republic, Class III–V; 11l. Order of Work.

288 Youth Camp

1951. Second Anniv of Romanian Pioneers Organization.

2106	**288**	1l. green	1·50	90
2107	-	11l. blue	1·50	90
2108	-	35l. red	1·90	1·30

DESIGNS—VERT: 11l. Children meeting Stalin. HORIZ: 35l. Decorating boy on parade.

289 Woman and Flags

1951. International Women's Day. Perf or imperf.

2109	**289**	11l. brown	95	45

290 Ion Negulici

1951. Death Centenary of Negulici (painter).

2110	**290**	35l. red	4·75	3·00

291 Cyclists

1951. Romanian Cycle Race.

2111	**291**	11l. brown	3·00	1·30

292 F. Sarbu

1951. Tenth Death Anniv of Sarbu (patriot).

2112	**292**	11l. brown	95	45

293 "Revolutionary Romania"

1951. Death Centenary of C. D. Rosenthal (painter).

2113	**293**	11l. green	2·40	90
2114	**293**	11l. orange	2·40	90
2115	-	11l. brown	2·40	90
2116	-	11l. violet	2·40	90

DESIGN—VERT: Nos. 2115/16, "Rumania calls to the Masses".

294 Students

1951. Third World Youth Festival, Berlin.

2117	**294**	1l. red	95	60
2118	-	5l. blue	1·90	60
2119	-	11l. purple	3·00	1·30

DESIGNS: 5l. Girl, boy and flag; 11l. Young people around globe.

295 "Scanteia" Building

1951. 20th Anniv of "Scanteia" (Communist newspaper).

2120	**295**	11l. blue	95	45

296 Soldier and Pithead

1951. Miners' Day.

2121	**296**	5l. blue	80	35
2122	-	11l. mauve	1·10	45

DESIGN: 11l. Miner and pithead.

297 Order of Defence

1951. Liberation Day.

2123	**297**	10l. red	70	45

298 Oil Refinery

1951. Five-Year Plan. Dated "1951 1955".

2124	**298**	1l. olive (postage)	95	20
2125	-	2l. red	50	20
2126	-	3l. red	95	55
2127	-	4l. brown	70	20
2128	-	5l. green	70	20
2129	-	6l. blue	2·40	1·30
2130	-	7l. green	1·50	55
2131	-	8l. brown	1·20	45
2132	-	11l. blue	1·20	35
2133	-	35l. violet	1·50	90
2134	-	30l. green (air)	4·00	2·75
2135	-	50l. brown	5·75	3·75

DESIGNS: 2l. Miner and pithead; 3l. Soldier and pylons; 4l. Steel furnace; 5l. Combine-harvester; 6l. Canal construction; 7l. Threshing machine; 8l. Sanatorium; 11l. Dam and pylons; 30l. Potato planting; 35l. Factory; 50l. Liner, steam locomotive and Lisunov Li-2 airliner.

299 Orchestra and Dancers

1951. Music Festival.

2136	**299**	11l. brown	70	45
2137	-	11l. blue (Mixed choir)	95	60
2138	-	11l. mauve (Lyre and dove) (vert)	70	45

300 Soldier and Arms

1951. Army Day.

2139	**300**	11l. blue	95	45

301 Arms of U.S.S.R. and Romania

1951. Romanian–Soviet Friendship.

2140	**301**	4l. brown on buff	50	45
2141	**301**	35l. orange	95	90

302 P. Tcancenco

1951. 25th Death Anniv of Tcancenco (revolutionary).

2142	**302**	10l. olive	95	90

303 Open Book "1907"

304 I. L. Caragiale

1952. Birth Centenary of Ion Caragiale (dramatist). (a) Unissued values surch.

2143	**303**	20b. on 11l. red	1·60	70
2144	-	55b. on 11l. green	2·10	1·00
2145	**304**	75b. on 11l. blue	3·75	1·20

(b) Without surch.

2146	**303**	55b. red	4·00	60
2147	-	55b. green	4·00	60
2148	**304**	55b. blue	4·00	60
2149	-	1l. brown	5·75	2·20

DESIGNS—HORIZ: Nos. 2144, 2147, Profile of Caragiale; 1l. Caragiale addressing assembly.

1952. Currency revalued. Surch.

2174	**275**	3b. on 1l. red	3·00	1·30
2175	**275**	3b. on 2l. grey	3·00	1·30
2176	**275**	3b. on 4l. mauve	3·00	1·30
2177	**275**	3b. on 5l. red	3·00	1·30
2178	**275**	3b. on 7l.50 blue	3·00	1·30
2179	**275**	3b. on 10l. brown	3·00	1·30
2157a	**255**	3b. on 30l. red	5·25	3·50
2158	-	3b. on 50l. (No. 2005)	2·10	1·00
2159	-	3b. on 100l. (No. 2006)	3·00	1·30
2191	**278**	10b. on 3l. green	4·00	1·30
2218	**301**	10b. on 4l. brown on buff	3·00	1·40
2192	**278**	10b. on 6l. blue	4·00	1·30
2193	**278**	10b. on 8l. blue	4·00	1·30
2220	**302**	10b. on 10l. olive	3·00	1·40
2160	**263**	10b. on 11l. red	5·25	2·00
2164	**270**	10b. on 11l. green	4·00	2·30
2165	-	10b. on 11l. (No. 2041)	4·00	2·30
2166	-	10b. on 11l. (No. 2042)	4·00	2·30
2167	-	10b. on 11l. (No. 2043)	4·00	2·30
2168	**271**	10b. on 11l. blue	4·00	2·30
2161	**263**	10b. on 30l. green	5·25	2·00
2219	**301**	10b. on 35l. orange	3·00	1·40
2199	-	20b. on 2l. (No. 2102)	6·25	2·75
2200	-	20b. on 4l. (No. 2103)	6·25	2·75
2171	**273**	20b. on 11l. red	4·75	1·50
2201	-	20b. on 11l. (No. 2104)	6·25	2·75
2194	-	20b. on 20l. (No. 2085)	4·75	2·20
2172	-	20b. on 31l. (No. 2049)	4·75	1·50
2202	**287**	20b. on 35l. brown	6·25	2·75
2206	**298**	35b. on 1l. olive	3·00	1·30
2207	-	35b. on 2l. (No. 2125)	3·00	1·30
2208	-	35b. on 3l. (No. 2126)	5·75	2·75
2209	-	35b. on 4l. (No. 2127)	6·75	3·00
2210	-	35b. on 5l. (No. 2128)	5·75	4·50
2151	**241**	50b. on 12l. blue	5·25	1·50
2180	**275**	55b. on 50b. black	8·75	2·20
2181	**275**	55b. on 3l. purple	8·75	2·20
2195	-	55b. on 3l. (No. 2088)	29·00	18·00
2169	**272**	55b. on 5l. olive	12·50	4·00
2204	**295**	55b. on 5l. blue	7·25	3·25
2182	**275**	55b. on 6l. green	8·75	2·20
2183	**275**	55b. on 7l. brown	8·75	2·20
2188	**276**	55b. on 8l. blue	11·50	5·25
2205	**297**	55b. on 10l. red	7·25	3·25
2170	-	55b. on 11l. (No. 2046)	12·50	4·00
2189	-	55b. on 11l. (No. 2075)	11·50	5·25
2150	**233**	55b. on 12l. blue	4·00	2·30
2184	**275**	55b. on 15l. blue	11·50	2·20
2185	**275**	55b. on 20l. green	8·75	2·20
2196	-	55b. on 20l. (No. 2098)	44·00	18·00
2186	**275**	55b. on 31l. green	8·75	2·20
2173	**274**	55b. on 31l. orange	6·25	4·00
2190	-	55b. on 31l. (No. 2076)	11·50	5·25
2197	-	55b. on 31l. (No. 2099)	44·00	18·00
2198	**286**	55b. on 31l. blue	7·25	4·50
2203	-	55b. on 35l. (No. 2108)	10·50	5·75
2187	**275**	55b. on 36l. brown	11·50	2·20
2211	-	1l. on 6l. (No. 2129)	7·75	6·25
2212	-	1l. on 7l. (No. 2130)	7·75	3·00
2213	-	1l. on 8l. (No. 2131)	7·75	6·25
2214	-	1l. on 11l. (No. 2132)	7·75	3·50
2216	-	1l. on 30l. (No. 2134)	12·50	2·75
2215	-	1l. on 35l. (No. 2133)	10·50	3·00
2217	-	1l. on 50l. (No. 2135)	12·50	2·75
2152	-	1l.75 on 2l.+2l. purple (No. 1974)	19·00	5·75
2153	**245**	1l.75 on 5l.+5l. violet	19·00	5·75
2154	**246**	1l.75 on 11l. red	19·00	5·75
2155	-	1l.75 on 10l.+10l. (No. 1977)	19·00	5·75
2156	-	1l.75 on 36l.+18l. (No. 1978)	19·00	5·75

1952. Air. Surch with airplane, **AERIANA** and value.

2162	**264**	3l. on 20l. brown	29·00	23·00
2163	**265**	5l. on 30l. blue	44·00	31·00

307 Railwayman

1952. Railway Day.

2229	**307**	55b. brown	4·00	45

308 Gogol and character from "Taras Bulba"

1952. Death Centenary of Nikolai Gogol (Russian writer).

2230	**308**	55b. blue	3·00	45
2231	-	1l.75 green	4·75	60

DESIGN—VERT: 1l.75, Gogol and open book.

309 Maternity Medal

1952. International Women's Day.

2232	**309**	20b. blue and purple	1·20	20
2233	-	55b. brown and chestnut	2·40	55
2234	-	1l.75 brown and red	5·75	75

MEDALS: 55b. "Glory of Maternity" medal; 1l.75, "Mother Heroine" medal.

310 I. P. Pavlov

1952. Romanian–Soviet Medical Congress.

2235	**310**	11l. red	4·00	45

311 Hammer and Sickle Medal

1952. Labour Day.

2236	**311**	55b. brown	3·50	45

312 Boy and Girl Pioneers

1952. Third Anniv of Romanian Pioneers Organization.

2237	**312**	20b. brown	1·90	20
2238	-	55b. green	4·75	30
2239	-	1l.75 blue	9·75	65

DESIGNS—VERT: 55b. Pioneer nature-study group. HORIZ: 1l.75, Worker and pioneers.

1952. As T **275** but with figures and inscriptions in white. Bani values size 20¼×24¼ mm, lei values size 24½×29½ mm.

2240	**275**	3b. orange	70	30
2241	**275**	5b. red	95	20
2242	**275**	7b. green	1·20	30
2243	**275**	10b. brown	1·50	20
2244	**275**	20b. blue	1·90	20
2245	**275**	35b. brown	3·50	20
2246	**275**	50b. green	4·00	20
2247	**275**	55b. violet	8·75	20
2248	**275**	1l.10 brown	7·75	45
2249	**275**	1l.75 violet	31·00	65
2250	**275**	2l. olive	8·25	75
2251	**275**	2l.35 brown	9·75	65
2252	**275**	2l.55 orange	11·50	65
2253	**275**	3l. green	12·50	65
2254	**275**	5l. red	16·00	1·10

For similar stamps with star added at top of emblem, see Nos. 2277/8.

314 "Smirdan" (after Grigorescu)

1952. 75th Anniv of Independence.

2255	**314**	50b. lake	1·50	10
2256	-	1l.10 blue	2·40	55

DESIGN—HORIZ: 1l.10, Romanian and Russian soldiers.

315 Leonardo da Vinci

1952. 500th Anniv of Birth of Leonardo da Vinci.

2257	**315**	55b. violet	6·75	65

316 Miner

1952. Miners' Day.

2258	**316**	20b. red	3·00	55
2259	**316**	55b. violet	3·00	55

317 Students' Union Badge

1952. Int Students' Union Council, Bucharest.

2260	**317**	10b. blue	70	10
2261	-	20b. orange	4·00	45
2262	-	55b. green	4·00	65
2263	-	1l.75 red	7·25	1·40

DESIGNS—HORIZ: 20b. Student in laboratory (35½×22 mm); 1l.75, Six students dancing (30×24 mm). VERT: 55b. Students playing football (24×30 mm).

318 Soldier, Sailor and Airman

1952. Army Day.

2264	**318**	55b. blue	2·40	45

319 Statue and Flags

320 Workers and Views of Russia and Romania (after N. Parlius)

1952. Romanian–Soviet Friendship.

2265	**319**	55b. red	1·60	10
2266	**320**	1l.75 brown	4·00	65

321 Rowing

1952. Physical Culture.

2267	**321**	20b. blue	7·75	45
2268	-	1l.75 red (Athletes)	16·00	1·20

322 N. Balcescu (after C. Tattarescu)

1952. Death Centenary of Balcescu (revolutionary).

2269	**322**	55b. grey	4·75	20
2270	**322**	1l.75 olive	11·50	1·20

323 Emblem and Flags

1952. New Constitution.

2271	**323**	55b. green	4·00	45

324

1952. Fifth Anniv of People's Republic.

2272	**324**	55b. multicoloured	4·75	65

325 Millo, Caragiale and Mme. Romanescu

1953. Centenary of Caragiale National Theatre.

2273	**325**	55b. blue	4·75	45

326 Foundry Worker

1953. Third Industrial and Agricultural Congress.

2274	**326**	55b. green	1·50	20
2275	-	55b. orange	1·50	20
2276	-	55b. brown	1·90	65

DESIGNS—HORIZ: No. 2275, Farm workers and tractor; 2276, Workman, refinery and oil wells.

1953. As Nos. 2240, etc, but with star added at top of emblem.

2277	**275**	5b. red	95	20
2278	**275**	55b. purple	1·60	30

327 "The Strikers of Grivitsa" (after Nazarev)

1953. 20th Anniv of Grivitsa Strike.

2279	**327**	55b. brown	4·00	45

328

1953. Fifth Anniv of Treaty of Friendship with Russia.

2280	**328**	55b. brown on blue	4·00	45

329 Table Tennis Badge

1953. 20th World Table Tennis Championship, Bucharest.

2281	**329**	55b. green	9·75	1·60
2282	**329**	55b. brown	9·75	1·60

330 Oltenian Carpet

1953. Romanian Art.

2283	-	10b. green	1·90	10
2284	-	20b. brown	3·00	10
2285	-	35b. violet	3·50	20
2286	-	55b. blue	6·25	20
2287	**330**	1l. purple	11·50	45

DESIGNS—VERT: 10b. Pottery; 20b. Campulung peasant girl; 55b. Apuseni Mountains peasant girl. HORIZ: 35b. National dance.

331 Karl Marx

1953. 70th Death Anniv of Karl Marx.

2288	**331**	1l.55 brown	4·75	55

332 Pioneers planting Tree

1953. Fourth Anniv of Romanian Pioneers Organization.

2289	**332**	35b. green	2·40	30
2290	-	55b. blue	3·00	35
2291	-	1l.75 brown	6·75	85

DESIGNS—VERT: 55b. Boy and girl flying model gliders. HORIZ: 1l.75, Pioneers and instructor.

333 Women and Flags

1953. Third World Congress of Women.

2292	**333**	55b. brown	3·00	45

334

1953. Fourth World Youth Festival.

2293	**334**	20b. orange	1·50	45
2294	-	55b. blue	2·40	95
2295	-	65b. red	3·50	1·40
2296	-	1l.75 purple	9·75	2·75

DESIGNS—VERT: 55b. Students releasing dove over globe. HORIZ: 65b. Girl presenting bouquet; 1l.75, Folk dancers.

335 Cornfield and Forest

1953. Forestry Month.

2297		20b. blue	1·60	20
2298	**335**	38b. green	4·75	1·40
2299	-	55b. brown	5·75	45

DESIGNS—VERT: 20b. Waterfall and trees; 55b. Forestry worker.

336 V. V. Mayakovsky

1953. 60th Birth Anniv of Vladimir Mayakovsky (Russian poet).

2300	**336**	55b. brown	3·50	65

337 Miner

1953. Miners' Day.

2301	**337**	1l.55 black	5·25	45

338 Telephonist, G.P.O. and P.O. Worker

1953. 50th Anniv of Construction of G.P.O.

2302	**338**	20b. brown	50	10
2303	-	55b. olive	95	10
2304	-	1l. blue	2·40	30
2305	-	1l.55 lake	3·50	75

DESIGNS: 55b. Postwoman and G.P.O.; 1l. G.P.O. radio transmitter and map; 1l.55, Telegraphist, G.P.O. and teletypist.

339

1953. Ninth Anniv of Liberation.

2306	**339**	55b. brown	2·40	45

340 Soldier and Flag

1953. Army Day.

2307	**340**	55b. olive	2·40	45

341 Girl and Model Glider

1953. Aerial Sports.

2308	**341**	10b. green and orange	4·25	55
2309	-	20b. olive and brown	8·75	30
2310	-	55b. purple and red	16·00	95
2311	-	1l.75 brown and purple	19·00	1·40

DESIGNS: 20b. Parachutists; 55b. Glider and pilot; 1l.75, Zlin Z-22 monoplane.

342 Workman, Girl and Flags

1953. Romanian–Soviet Friendship.

2312	**342**	55b. brown	1·30	20
2313	-	1l.55 lake	3·00	55

DESIGN: 1l.55, Spassky Tower (Moscow Kremlin) and Volga–Don canal.

343 "Unity"

1953. Third World Trades' Union Congress.

2314	**343**	55b. olive	1·20	30
2315	-	1l.25 red	3·00	95

DESIGN—VERT: 1l.25, Workers, flags and globe.

344 C. Porumbescu

1953. Birth Centenary of Porumbescu (composer).

2316	**344**	55b. lilac	11·50	45

345 Agricultural Machinery

1953. Agricultural designs.

2317	**345**	10b. olive	50	10
2318	-	35b. green	70	10
2319	-	2l.55 brown	5·75	1·20

DESIGNS: 35b. Tractor drawing disc harrows; 2l.55, Cows grazing.

346 Vlaicu and his Airplane No. 1 "Crazy Fly"

1953. 40th Death Anniv of Vlaicu (pioneer aviator).

2320	**346**	50b. blue	2·50	45

347 Lenin

1954. 30th Death Anniv of Lenin.

2321	**347**	55b. brown	3·00	45

348 Red Deer Stag

1954. Forestry Month.

2322	**348**	20b. brown on yellow	4·75	55
2323	-	55b. violet on yellow	4·00	55
2324	-	1l.75 blue on yellow	5·75	1·10

DESIGNS: 55b. Pioneers planting tree; 1l.75, Forest.

349 Calimanesti

1954. Workers' Rest Homes.

2325	**349**	5b. black on yellow	70	20
2326	-	1l.55 black on blue	3·00	30
2327	-	2l. green on pink	4·75	45
2328	-	2l.35 brown on green	4·50	1·40
2329	-	2l.55 brown on green	6·25	1·90

DESIGNS: 1l.55, Siniai; 2l. Predeal; 2l.35, Tusnad; 2l.55, Govora.

350 O. Bancila

1954. Tenth Death Anniv of Bancila (painter).

2330	**350**	55b. green and brown	5·75	2·75

351 Child and Dove of Peace

1954. International Children's Day.

2331	**351**	55b. brown	2·40	45

352 Girl Pioneer feeding Calf

1954. Fifth Anniv of Romanian Pioneer Organization.

2332	**352**	20b. black	70	20
2333	-	55b. blue	1·20	45
2334	-	1l.75 red	4·00	95

DESIGNS: 55b. Girl Pioneers harvesting; 1l.75, Young Pioneers examining globe.

353 Stephen the Great

1954. 450th Death Anniv of Stephen the Great.

2335	**353**	55b. brown	4·00	55

354 Miner operating Coal-cutter

1954. Miners' Day.

2336	**354**	1l.75 black	4·00	85

355 Dr. V. Babes

1954. Birth Centenary of Babes (pathologist).

2337	**355**	55b. red	3·00	45

356 Sailor, Flag and Destroyer "Regele Ferdinand"

1954. Navy Day.

2338	**356**	55b. blue	2·40	45

357 Dedication Tablet

1954. Fifth Anniv of Mutual Aid Organization.

2339	-	20b. violet	70	20
2340	**357**	55b. brown	1·20	45

DESIGN: 20b. Man receiving money from counter clerk.

358 Liberation Monument

1954. Tenth Anniv of Liberation.

2341	**358**	55b. violet and red	1·90	45

359 Recreation Centre

1954. Liberation Anniv Celebrations.

2342	**359**	20b. blue	70	10
2343	-	38b. violet	1·20	45
2344	-	55b. purple	1·50	30
2345	-	1l.55 brown	3·50	55

DESIGNS—38×22 mm: 55b. "Scanteia" offices. 24½×29½ mm: 38b. Opera House, Bucharest; 1l.55, Radio Station.

360 Pilot and Mikoyan Gurevich MiG-15 Jet Fighters

1954. Aviation Day.

2346	**360**	55b. blue	4·00	45

361 Chemical Plant and Oil Derricks

1954. International Chemical and Petroleum Workers Conference, Bucharest.

2347	**361**	55b. black	3·50	65

362 Dragon Pillar, Peking

1954. Chinese Culture Week.

2348	**362**	55b. black on yellow	3·50	65

363 T. Neculuta

1954. 50th Death Anniv of Dumitru Theodor Neculuta (poet).

2349	**363**	55b. violet	3·00	45

364 ARLUS Badge **365** Friendship

1954. Tenth Anniv of "ARLUS" and Romanian–Russian Friendship.

2350	**364**	55b. red	95	30
2351	**365**	65b. purple	1·50	45

366 G. Tattarescu

1954. 60th Death Anniv of Gheorghe Tattarescu (painter).

2352	**366**	55b. red	3·50	45

367 B. Iscovescu

1954. Death Centenary of Barbu Iscovescu (painter).

2353	**367**	1l.75 brown	4·75	95

368 Teleprinter

1954. Cent of Telecommunications in Romania.

2354	**368**	50b. lilac	2·40	45

369 Wild Boar

1955. Forestry Month. Inscr "LUNA PADURII 1955".

2355	**369**	35b. brown	2·10	20
2356	-	65b. blue	2·50	45
2357	-	1l.20 red	5·75	95

DESIGNS: 65b. Tree planting; 1l.20, Logging.

370 Airman

1955. Occupations.

2358		3b. blue	50	10
2359		5b. violet	30	10
2360	**370**	10b. brown	50	10
2361	-	20b. mauve	70	10
2362	-	30b. blue	1·20	30
2363	-	35b. turquoise	95	10
2364	-	40b. blue	1·90	30
2365	-	55b. olive	1·90	10
2366	-	1l. violet	2·40	10
2367	-	1l.55 lake	4·00	10
2368	-	2l.35 buff	5·25	95
2369	-	2l.55 green	7·75	65

DESIGNS: 3b. Scientist; 5b. Foundryman; 20b. Miner; 30b. Tractor driver; 35b. Schoolboy; 40b. Girl student; 55b. Bricklayer; 1l. Sailor; 1l.55, Mill girl; 2l.35, Soldier; 2l.55, Telegraph linesman.

371 Clasped Hands

1955. International Conference of Postal Municipal Workers, Vienna.

2370	**371**	25b. red	95	45

372 Lenin

1955. 85th Birth Anniv of Lenin. Portraits of Lenin.

2371	**372**	20b. brown and bistre	95	30
2372	-	55b. brown (full face)	1·90	45
2373	-	1l. lake and red (half length)	3·00	55

373 Dove and Globe

1955. Peace Congress, Helsinki.

2374	**373**	55b. blue	2·40	45

374 War Memorial, Berlin

1955. Tenth Anniv of Victory over Germany.

2375	**374**	55b. blue	1·90	45

375 Children and Dove

1955. International Children's Day.

2376	**375**	55b. brown	2·10	45

376 "Service"

1955. European Volleyball Championships.

2377	-	55b. mauve and pink	7·25	1·40
2378	**376**	1l.75 mauve and yellow	16·00	1·40

DESIGN: 55b. Volleyball players.

377 People's Art Museum

1955. Bucharest Museums.

2379	-	20b. mauve	50	20
2380	-	55b. brown	95	20
2381	**377**	1l.20 black	2·40	95
2382	-	1l.75 green	4·00	95
2383	-	2l.55 purple	6·75	1·10

MUSEUMS—30×24½ mm: 20b. Theodor Aman; 2l.55, Simu. 34×23 mm: 55b. Lenin-Stalin; 1l.75, Republican Art.

378 Mother and Child

1955. First World Mothers' Congress, Lausanne.

2384	**378**	55b. blue	2·40	45

379 "Nature Study"

1955. Fifth Anniv of Pioneer Headquarters, Bucharest.

2385	-	10b. blue	95	10
2386	**379**	20b. green	1·90	10
2387	-	55b. purple	4·25	45

DESIGNS: 10b. Model railway; 55b. Headquarters building.

380 Coxed Four

1955. Women's European Rowing Championships, Snagov.

2388	**380**	55b. green	11·50	1·10
2389	-	1l. blue (Woman sculler)	19·00	1·50

381 Anton Pann (folklorist)

1955. Romanian Writers.

2390		55b. blue	1·90	45
2391		55b. grey	1·90	45
2392	**381**	55b. olive	1·90	45
2393	-	55b. violet	1·90	45
2394	-	55b. purple	1·90	45

PORTRAITS—No. 2390, Dimitrie Cantemir (historian); 2391, Metropolitan Dosoftei (religious writer); 2393, Constantin Cantacuzino (historian); 2394, Ienachita Vacarescu (poet, grammarian and historian).

382 Marksman

1955. European Sharpshooting Championships, Bucharest.

2395	**382**	1l. brown and light brown	8·75	95

383 Fire Engine

1955. Firemen's Day.

2396	**383**	55b. red	2·50	65

384

1955. Tenth Anniv of W.F.T.U.

2397	384	55b. olive	70	20
2398	-	1l. blue	1·20	45

DESIGN: 1l. Workers and flag.

385 Spraying Fruit Trees

1955. Fruit and Vegetable Cultivation.

2399	385	10b. green	1·30	20
2400	-	20b. red	1·50	45
2401	-	55b. blue	4·00	45
2402	-	1l. lake	5·25	1·40

DESIGNS: 20b. Fruit picking; 55b. Harvesting grapes; 1l. Gathering vegetables.

386

1955. Fourth ARLUS Congress.

2403	386	20b. blue and buff	1·50	45

387 Michurin

1955. Birth Cent of Ivan Michurin (Russian botanist).

2404	387	55b. blue	2·40	45

388 Cotton

1955

2405	-	10b. purple (Sugar beet)	85	30
2406	388	20b. grey	1·20	30
2407	-	55b. blue (Linseed)	3·00	85
2408	-	1l.55 brown (Sunflower)	5·75	1·50

389 Sheep and Shepherd blowing Bucium

1955

2409	389	5b. brown and green	1·20	20
2410	-	10b. violet and bistre	1·60	30
2411	-	35b. brown and salmon	3·50	75
2412	-	55b. brown and bistre	5·75	1·00

DESIGNS: 10b. Pigs and farm girl; 35b. Cows and dairy maid; 55b. Horses and groom.

390 Johann von Schiller (novelist)

1955. Literary Anniversaries.

2413		20b. blue	70	10
2414		55b. blue	1·60	35
2415	390	1l. grey	3·00	45
2416	-	1l.55 brown	5·25	1·40
2417	-	1l.75 violet	6·25	1·40
2418	-	2l. lake	7·25	2·30

DESIGNS: 20b. Hans Christian Andersen (children's writer, 150th birth anniv); 55b. Adam Mickiewicz (poet, death centenary); 1l. Type **390** (150th death anniv); 1l.55, Baron de Montesquieu (philosopher, death bicentenary); 1l.75, Walt Whitman (centenary of publication of "Leaves of Grass"; 2l. Miguel de Cervantes (350th anniv of publication of "Don Quixote").

391 Bank and Book

1955. Savings Bank.

2419	391	55b. blue	3·00	45
2420	391	55b. violet	9·75	5·50

392 Family

1956. National Census.

2421	-	55b. orange	70	20
2422	392	1l.75 brown and green	3·00	95

DESIGNS: 55b. "21 FEBRUARIE 1956" in circle.

393 Brown Hare

1956. Wild Life.

2423	393	20b. black and green	3·00	95
2424	-	20b. black and olive	3·00	95
2425	-	35b. black and blue	3·00	95
2426	-	50b. brown and blue	3·00	95
2427	-	55b. green and bistre	3·00	95
2428	-	55b. brown and turquoise	3·00	95
2429	-	1l. lake and green	6·25	1·90
2430	-	1l.55 lake and blue	6·25	1·90
2431	-	1l.75 brown and green	6·25	1·90
2432	-	2l. brown and blue	29·00	23·00
2433	-	3l.25 black and green	29·00	23·00
2434	-	4l.25 brown and salmon	29·00	23·00

DESIGNS—VERT: No. 2424, Great bustard; 35b. Brown trout; 1l.55, Eurasian red squirrel; 1l.75, Western capercaillie; 4l.25, Red deer. HORIZ: 50b. Wild boar; No. 2427, Common pheasant; No. 2428, Brown bear; 1l. Lynx; 2l. Chamois; 3l.25, Pintail.

See also Nos. 2474/85.

394 Insurgents

1956. 85th Anniv of Paris Commune.

2435	394	55b. red	2·40	65

395 Boy and Globe

1956. International Children's Day.

2436	395	55b. violet	3·50	45

396 Red Cross Nurse

1956. Second Romanian Red Cross Congress.

2437	396	55b. olive and red	4·00	45

397 Tree

1956. Forestry Month.

2438	397	20b. grey on green	1·90	30
2439	-	55b. black on green	5·75	45

DESIGN: 55b. Lumber train.

398 Woman Speaking

1956. International Women's Congress, Bucharest.

2440	398	55b. green	2·40	45

399 Academy Buildings

1956. 90th Anniv of Romanian People's Academy.

2441	399	55b. green and buff	2·40	45

400 Vuia, Biplane, Vuia No. 1 and Yakovlev Yak-25 Fighters

1956. 50th Anniv of First Flight by Traian Vuia (pioneer airman).

2442	400	55b. brown and olive	3·00	45

401 Georgescu and Statues

1956. Birth Centenary of Ion Georgescu (sculptor).

2443	401	55b. brown and green	4·00	45

402 Farm Girl

1956. Collective Farming. (a) Inscr "1951–1956".

2444	402	55b. plum	11·50	11·00

(b) Inscr "1949–56".

2445	55b. plum	2·10	45

403 Black-veined White

1956. Insect Pests.

2446	403	10b. cream, black and violet	4·75	55
2447	-	55b. orange and brown	7·25	75
2448	-	1l.75 lake and olive	19·00	14·00
2449	-	1l.75 brown and olive	16·00	1·60

PESTS: 55b. Colorado potato beetle; 1l.75 (2), May beetle.

404 Striker

1956. 50th Anniv of Dockers' Strike at Galatz.

2450	404	55b. brown on pink	2·40	45

405

1956. 25th Anniv of "Scanteia" (Communist newspaper).

2451	405	55b. blue	1·90	45

406 Gorky

1956. 20th Death Anniv of Maksim Gorky.

2452	406	55b. brown	2·40	45

407 T. Aman

1956. 125th Birth Anniv of Aman (painter).

2453	407	55b. grey	4·00	95

408 Snowdrops and Polyanthus

1956. Flowers. Designs multicoloured. Colours of backgrounds given.

2454	408	5b. blue	95	45
2455	-	55b. black	3·50	85
2456	-	1l.75 blue	7·75	1·10
2457	-	3l. green	11·50	1·80

FLOWERS: 55b. Daffodil and violets; 1l.75, Antirrhinums and campanulas; 3l. Poppies and lilies of the valley.

409 Janos Hunyadi

1956. 500th Death Anniv of Hunyadi.

2458	409	55b. violet	2·40	55

410 Olympic Flame

1956. Olympic Games.

2459	410	20b. red	95	35
2460	-	55b. blue	1·50	40
2461	-	1l. mauve	3·00	55
2462	-	1l.55 turquoise	4·00	65
2463	-	1l.75 violet	5·25	95

DESIGNS: 55b. Water-polo; 1l. Ice-skating; 1l.55, Canoeing; 1l.75, High-jumping.

411 George Bernard Shaw (dramatist)

1956. Cultural Anniversaries.

2464	20b. blue	60	20

2465		35b. red	80	20
2466	**411**	40b. brown	85	20
2467	-	50b. brown	1·10	20
2468	-	55b. olive	1·20	20
2469	-	1l. turquoise	2·10	30
2470	-	1l.55 violet	3·00	30
2471	-	1l.75 blue	4·00	30
2472	-	2l.55 purple	5·25	45
2473	-	3l.25 blue	5·75	1·10

DESIGNS: 20b. Benjamin Franklin (U.S. statesman and journalist, 250th birth anniv); 35b. Toyo Oda (painter, 450th death anniv); 40b. Type **411** (birth centenary); 50b. Ivan Franco (writer, birth centenary); 55b. Pierre Curie (physicist, 50th death anniv); 1l. Henrik Ibsen (dramatist, 50th death anniv); 1l.55, Fyodor Dostoevsky (novelist, 75th death anniv); 1l.75, Heinrich Heine (poet, death centenary); 2l.55, Wolfgang Amadeus Mozart (composer, birth bicentenary); 3l.25, Rembrandt (artist, 350th birth anniv).

1956. Wild Life. As Nos. 2423/34 but colours changed. Imperf.

2474	20b. brown and green	6·75	6·50
2475	20b. black and blue	6·75	6·50
2476	35b. black and blue	6·75	6·50
2477	50b. black and brown	6·75	6·50
2478	55b. black and violet	6·75	6·50
2479	55b. brown and green	6·75	6·50
2480	1l. brown and blue	6·75	6·50
2481	1l.55 brown and bistre	6·75	6·50
2482	1l.75 purple and green	6·75	6·50
2483	2l. black and blue	6·75	6·50
2484	3l.25 brown and green	6·75	6·50
2485	4l.25 brown and violet	6·75	6·50

412 Ilyushin Il-18 Airliner over City

1956. Air. Multicoloured.

2486	20b. Type **412**	95	65
2487	55b. Ilyushin Il-18 over mountains	1·50	95
2488	1l.75 Ilyushin Il-18 over cornfield	4·25	1·40
2489	2l.55 Ilyushin Il-18 over seashore	6·25	2·30

413 Georgi Enescu

1956. 75th Birth Anniv of Enescu (musician).

2490	-	55b. blue	1·90	45
2491	**413**	1l.75 purple	4·00	65

DESIGN: 55b. Enescu when a child, holding violin.

414 "Rebels" (after Octav Bancila)

1957. 50th Anniv of Peasant Revolt.

2492	**414**	55b. grey	2·40	45

415 Stephen the Great

1957. 500th Anniv of Accession of Stephen the Great.

2493	**415**	55b. brown	1·90	55
2494	**415**	55b. olive	1·50	95

416 Gheorghe Marinescu (neurologist) and Institute of Medicine

1957. National Congress of Medical Sciences, Bucharest, and Centenary of Medical and Pharmaceutical Teaching in Bucharest (11.75).

2495	**416**	20b. green	70	30
2496	-	35b. brown	95	45
2497	-	55b. purple	1·60	65
2498	-	1l.75 red and blue	6·25	2·30

DESIGNS: As T **416**: 35b. Ioan Cantacuzino (bacteriologist) and Cantacuzino Institute; 55b. Victor Babes (pathologist and bacteriologist) and Babes Institute. 66×23 mm: 1l.75, Nicolae Kretzulescu and Carol Dairla (physicians) and Faculty of Medicine, Bucharest.

417 Gymnast and Spectator

1957. First European Women's Gymnastic Championships, Bucharest.

2499	**417**	20b. green	95	20
2500	-	35b. red	1·50	30
2501	-	55b. blue	3·00	45
2502	-	1l.75 purple	8·25	1·10

DESIGNS—HORIZ: 35b. On asymmetric bars; 55b. Vaulting over horse. VERT: 1l.75, On beam.

418 Emblems of Atomic Energy

1957. Second A.S.I.T. Congress.

2503	**418**	55b. brown	1·90	30
2504	**418**	55b. blue	2·40	45

419 Dove and Handlebars

1957. Tenth International Cycle Race.

2505	**419**	20b. blue	70	20
2506	-	55b. brown	1·90	45

DESIGN: 55b. Racing cyclist.

420 Rhododendron

1957. Flowers of the Carpathian Mountains.

2513	**420**	5b. red and grey	50	10
2514	-	10b. green and grey	70	20
2515	-	20b. orange and grey	80	20
2516	-	35b. olive and grey	1·50	30
2517	-	55b. blue and grey	1·60	30
2518	-	1l. red and grey	3·75	1·00
2519	-	1l.55 yellow and grey	4·00	55
2520	-	1l.75 violet and grey	7·25	65

FLOWERS: 10b. Daphne; 20b. Lily; 35b. Edelweiss; 55b. Gentian; 1l. Dianthus; 1l.55, Primula; 1l.75, Anemone.

421 N. Grigorescu

1957. 50th Death Anniv of Nicolae Grigorescu (painter).

2521		20b. green	95	20
2522	**421**	55b. brown	2·40	30
2523	-	1l.75 blue	8·75	1·10

DESIGNS—HORIZ: 20b. "Ox-cart"; 1l.75, "Attack on Smirdan".

422 Festival Visitors

423 Festival Emblem

1957. Sixth World Youth Festival, Moscow.

2524	**422**	20b. purple	30	10
2525	-	55b. green	80	20
2526	**423**	1l. orange	1·60	65
2527	-	1l.75 blue	3·00	45

DESIGNS: 55b. Girl with flags (22×38 mm); 1l.75, Dancers (49×20 mm).

424 Destroyer "Stalingrad"

1957. Navy Day.

2528	**424**	1l.75 blue	2·40	45

425 "The Trumpeter" (after N. Grigorescu)

1957. 80th Anniv of War of Independence.

2529	**425**	20b. violet	2·40	45

426 Soldiers Advancing

1957. 40th Anniv of Battle of Marasesti.

2530	**426**	1l.75 brown	3·00	45

427 Child with Dove

1957. Red Cross.

2531	**427**	55b. green and red	2·40	45

428 Sprinter and Bird

1957. Int Athletic Championships, Bucharest.

2532	**428**	20b. black and blue	70	10
2533	-	55b. black and yellow	2·10	30
2534	-	1l.75 black and red	5·75	75

DESIGNS: 55b. Javelin-thrower and bull; 1l.75, Runner and stag.

429 Ovid

1957. Birth Bimillenary of Ovid (Latin poet).

2535	**429**	1l.75 blue	4·25	95

430 Congress Emblem

1957. Fourth W.F.T.U. Congress, Leipzig.

2536	**430**	55b. blue	1·50	45

431 Oil Refinery, 1957

1957. Centenary of Romanian Petroleum Industry.

2537	**431**	20b. brown	70	10
2538	**431**	20b. blue	70	10
2539	-	55b. purple	1·50	65

DESIGN: 55b. Oil production, 1857 (horse-operated borer).

432 Lenin, Youth and Girl

1957. 40th Anniv of Russian Revolution.

2540	**432**	10b. red	50	10
2541	-	35b. purple	95	20
2542	-	55b. brown	1·50	55

DESIGNS—HORIZ: 35b. Lenin and flags; 55b. Statue of Lenin.

433 Artificial Satellite encircling Globe

1957. Air. Launching of Artificial Satellite by Russia.

2543	**433**	25b. blue	70	20
2544	-	3l.75 green	4·00	75
2545	**433**	25b. blue	70	20
2546	-	3l.75 blue	4·00	75

DESIGN: 3l.75 (2), Satellite's orbit around Globe.

See also Nos. 2593/6.

434 Peasant Soldiers

1957. 520th Anniv of Bobilna Revolution.

2547	**434**	50b. purple	60	20
2548	-	55b. grey	80	45

DESIGN—VERT: 55b. Bobilna Memorial.

435 Endre Ady

1957. 80th Birth Anniv of Endre Ady (Hungarian poet).

2549	**435**	55b. olive	1·90	45

436 Laika and "Sputnik 2"

1957. Space Flight of Laika (dog).

2550	**436**	1l.20 blue and brown	4·75	95
2551	**436**	1l.20 blue and brown	4·75	95

437 Black-winged Stilt

1957. Fauna of the Danube Delta.

No.	Type	Description	Mint	Used
2552	**437**	5b. grey & brown (postage)	30	10
2553	-	10b. orange and green	40	10
2554	-	20b. orange and red	50	10
2555	-	50b. orange and green	95	10
2556	-	55b. blue and purple	1·50	20
2557	-	1l.30 orange and violet	2·40	20
2558	-	3l.30 grey and blue (air)	4·75	1·10
2559	-	5l. orange and red	7·25	1·60

DESIGNS—VERT: 10b. Great egret; 20b. White spoonbill; 50b. Stellate sturgeon. HORIZ: 55b. Stoat; 1l.30, Eastern white pelican; 3l.30, Black-headed gull; 5l. White-tailed sea eagle.

438 Emblem of Republic and Flags

1957. Tenth Anniv of People's Republic.

No.	Type	Description	Mint	Used
2560	**438**	25b. buff, red and blue	50	20
2561	-	55b. yellow	95	30
2562	-	1l.20 red	1·90	65

DESIGNS: 55b. Emblem, Industry and Agriculture; 1l.20, Emblem, the Arts and Sports.

439 Republican Flag

1958. 25th Anniv of Strike at Grivitsa.

No.	Type	Description	Mint	Used
2563	**439**	1l. red and brown on buff	1·50	45
2564	**439**	1l. red and blue on buff	1·50	45

440 "Telecommunications"

1958. Socialist Countries' Postal Ministers Conference, Moscow.

No.	Type	Description	Mint	Used
2565	**440**	55b. violet	70	35
2566	-	1l.75 purple	1·60	45

DESIGN: 1l.75, Telegraph pole and pylons carrying lines.

441 Nicolae Balcescu (historian)

1958. Romanian Writers.

No.	Type	Description	Mint	Used
2567	**441**	5b. blue	60	20
2568	-	10b. black	70	30
2569	-	35b. blue	80	35
2570	-	55b. brown	1·10	45
2571	-	1l.75 black	2·75	65
2572	-	2l. green	4·00	75

DESIGNS: 10b. Ion Creanga (folklorist); 35b. Alexandru Vlahuta (poet); 55b. Mihail Eminescu (poet); 1l.75, Vasile Alecsandri (poet and dramatist); 2l. Barbu Delavrancea (short-story writer and dramatist).

442 Fencer

1958. World Youth Fencing Championships, Bucharest.

No.	Type	Description	Mint	Used
2573	**442**	1l.75 mauve	3·00	45

443 Symbols of Medicine and Sport

1958. 25th Anniv of Sports Doctors' Service.

No.	Type	Description	Mint	Used
2574	**443**	1l.20 red and green	3·00	45

444

1958. Fourth Int Congress of Democratic Women.

No.	Type	Description	Mint	Used
2575	**444**	55b. blue	1·60	45

445 Linnaeus (botanist)

1958. Cultural Anniversaries (1957).

No.	Type	Description	Mint	Used
2576	**445**	10b. blue	30	20
2577	-	20b. brown	60	20
2578	-	40b. mauve	95	30
2579	-	55b. blue	1·50	20
2580	-	1l. mauve	1·90	30
2581	-	1l.75 blue	2·40	55
2582	-	2l. brown	4·25	65

DESIGNS: 10b. Type **445** (250th birth anniv); 20b. Auguste Comte (philosopher, death centenary); 40b. William Blake (poet and artist, birth bicentenary); 55b. Mikhail Glinka (composer, death centenary); 1l. Henry Longfellow (poet, 150th birth anniv); 1l.75, Carlo Goldoni (dramatist, 250th birth anniv); 2l. John Komensky, Comenius (educationist, 300th death anniv).

446 Parasol Mushroom

1958. Mushrooms. As T **446**.

No.	Type	Description	Mint	Used
2583	**446**	5b. brown, lt brn & blue	30	20
2584	-	10b. brown, buff and bronze	30	20
2585	-	20b. red, yellow and grey	70	20
2586	-	30b. brown, orge & green	95	30
2587	-	35b. brown, lt brn & bl	1·10	20
2588	-	55b. brown, red and green	1·50	20
2589	-	1l. brown, buff and green	2·40	30
2590	-	1l.55 pink, drab and grey	3·50	45
2591	-	1l.75 brown, buff and green	4·00	55
2592	-	2l. yellow, brown and green	5·75	65

MUSHROOMS: 10b. "Clavaria aurea"; 20b. Caesar's mushroom; 30b. Saffron milk cap; 35b. Honey fungus; 55b. Shaggy ink cap; 1l. "Morchella conica"; 1l.55, Field mushroom; 1l.75, Cep; 2l. Chanterelle.

1958. Brussels International Exhibition. Nos. 2543/4 and 2545/6 optd **EXPOZITIA UNIVERSALA BRUXELLES 1958** and star or with star only.

No.	Type	Description	Mint	Used
2593	**433**	25b. green	4·75	1·90
2595	**433**	25b. blue	4·75	1·90
2594	-	3l.75 green	24·00	14·00
2596	-	3l.75 blue	24·00	14·00

448 Racovita and "Belgica" (Gerlache expedition, 1897)

1958. Tenth Death Anniv (1957) of Emil Racovita (naturalist and explorer).

No.	Type	Description	Mint	Used
2597	**448**	55b. indigo and blue	1·60	35
2598	-	1l.20 violet and olive	4·00	45

DESIGN: 1l.20, Racovita and grotto.

449 Sputnik encircling Globe

1958. Air. Launching of Third Artificial Satellite by Russia.

No.	Type	Description	Mint	Used
2599	**449**	3l.25 buff and blue	7·25	1·90

450 Servicemen's Statue

1958. Army Day.

No.	Type	Description	Mint	Used
2600	**450**	55b. brown (postage)	50	20
2601	-	75b. purple	70	20
2602	-	1l.75 blue	1·60	30
2603	-	3l.30 violet (air)	3·00	75

DESIGNS: 75b. Soldier guarding industrial plant; 1l.75, Sailor hoisting flag, and "Royal Ferdinand" destroyer; 3l.30, Pilot and Mikoyan Gurevich MiG-17 jet fighters.

451 Costume of Oltenia

452 Costume of Oltenia

1958. Provincial Costumes.

No.	Type	Description	Mint	Used
2604	**451**	35b. red, black and yellow (female)	50	30
2605	**452**	35b. red, black and yellow (male)	50	30
2606	-	40b. red, brown and light brown (female)	60	35
2607	-	40b. red, brown and light brown (male)	60	35
2608	-	50b. brown, red and lilac (female)	70	30
2609	-	50b. brown, red and lilac (male)	70	30
2610	-	55b. red, brown and drab (female)	95	35
2611	-	55b. red, brown and drab (male)	95	35
2612	-	1l. carmine, brown and red (female)	1·90	45
2613	-	1l. carmine, brown and red (male)	1·90	45
2614	-	1l.75 red, brown and blue (female)	2·50	65
2615	-	1l.75 red, brown and blue (male)	2·50	65

PROVINCES: Nos. 2606/7, Tara Oasului; 2608/9, Transylvania; 2610/11, Muntenia; 2612/3, Banat; 2614/5, Moldova.

453 Stamp Printer

1958. Romanian Stamp Centenary. Inscr "1858 1958".

No.	Type	Description	Mint	Used
2617	**453**	35b. blue	60	20
2618	-	55b. brown	85	20
2619	-	1l.20 blue	1·50	40
2620	-	1l.30 plum	1·90	45
2621	-	1l.55 brown	2·40	30
2622	-	1l.75 red	2·50	35
2623	-	2l. violet	3·00	65
2624	-	3l.30 brown	4·00	95
MS2625		80×89 mm. 10l. blue on pale blue	60·00	55·00
MS2626		80×89 mm. 10l. red. Imperf	80·00	75·00

DESIGNS: 55b. Scissors and Moldavian stamps of 1858; 1l.20, Driver with whip and mail coach; 1l.30, Postman with horn and mounted courier; 1l.55 to 3l.30, Moldavian stamps of 1858 (Nos. 1/4).

454 Runner

1958. Third Youth Spartacist Games.

No.	Type	Description	Mint	Used
2627	**454**	1l. brown	1·90	45

455 Revolutionary Emblem

1958. 40th Anniv of Workers' Revolution.

No.	Type	Description	Mint	Used
2628	**455**	55b. red	1·20	45

456 Boy Bugler

1958. Tenth Anniv of Education Reform.

No.	Type	Description	Mint	Used
2629	**456**	55b. red	1·20	45

457 Alexandru Cuza

1959. Centenary of Union of Romanian Provinces.

No.	Type	Description	Mint	Used
2630	**457**	1l.75 blue	2·40	45

458 First Cosmic Rocket

1959. Air. Launching of First Cosmic Rocket.

No.	Type	Description	Mint	Used
2631	**458**	3l.25 blue on salmon	16·00	2·30

1959. Air. Tenth Anniv of State Philatelic Services. No. MS2625 optd **10 ANI DE COMERT FILATELIC DE STAT 1949–1959** in red.

No.	Type	Description	Mint	Used
MS2632		10l. blue on pale blue	£225	£200

459 Charles Darwin (naturalist)

1959. Cultural Anniversaries.

No.	Type	Description	Mint	Used
2633	**459**	55b. black (postage)	95	20
2634	-	55b. blue	95	20
2635	-	55b. red	95	20
2636	-	55b. purple	95	20
2637	-	55b. brown	95	20
2638	-	3l.25 blue (air)	4·75	95

DESIGNS—No. 2633, Type **459** (150th birth anniv); 2634, Robert Burns (poet, birth bicentenary); 2635, Aleksandr Popov (radio pioneer, birth centenary); 2636, Sholem Aleichem (writer, birth centenary); 2637, Frederick Handel (composer, death bicentenary); 2638, Frederic Joliot-Curie (nuclear physicist, 10th anniv of World Peace Council).

460 Maize

1959. Tenth Anniv of Collective Farming in Romania.

No.	Type	Description	Mint	Used
2639	**460**	55b. green	60	30
2640	-	55b. orange	60	30
2641	-	55b. purple	60	30
2642	-	55b. olive	60	30
2643	-	55b. brown	60	30
2644	-	55b. bistre	60	30
2645	-	55b. blue	60	30
2646	-	55b. bistre	60	30
2647	-	5l. red	4·75	1·00

DESIGNS—VERT: No. 2640, Sunflower with bee; 2641, Sugar beet. HORIZ: No. 2642, Sheep; 2643, Cattle; 2644, Rooster and hens; 2645, Farm tractor; 2646, Farm wagon and horses; 2647 (38×26½ mm), Farmer and wife, and wheatfield within figure "10".

461 Rock Thrush

1959. Air. Birds in natural colours. Inscriptions in grey. Colours of value tablets and backgrounds given.

2648	**461**	10b. grey on buff	30	20
2649	-	20b. grey on grey	30	20
2650	-	35b. grey on deep grey	40	20
2651	-	40b. red on pink	50	20
2652	-	55b. grey on green	70	20
2653	-	55b. grey on cream	70	20
2654	-	55b. green on azure	70	20
2655	-	1l. red on yellow	2·40	30
2656	-	1l.55 red on pink	3·00	30
2657	-	5l. grey on green	7·75	2·75

BIRDS—HORIZ: No. 2649, Golden oriole; 2656, Long-tailed tit; 2657, Wallcreeper. VERT: No. 2650, Northern lapwing; 2651, Barn swallow; 2652, Great spotted woodpecker; 2653, Eurasian goldfinch; 2654, Great tit; 2655, Northern bullfinch.

462 Young Couple

1959. Seventh World Youth Festival, Vienna. Inscr "26 VII-4 VIII 1959".

2658	**462**	1l. blue	1·20	30
2659	-	1l.60 red	1·60	35

DESIGN: 1l.60, Folk-dancer in national costume.

463 Workers and Banners

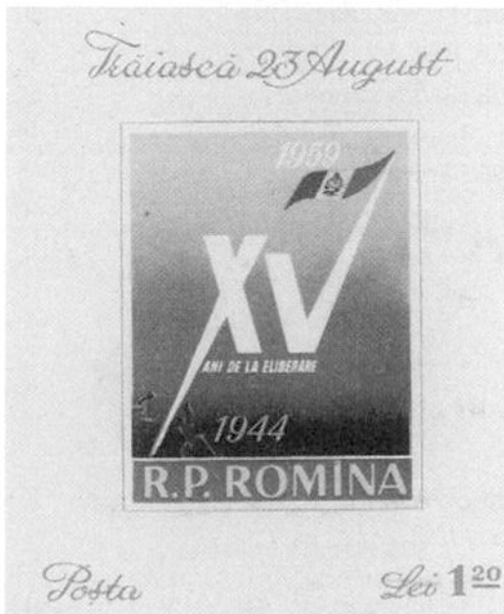

464

1959. 15th Anniv of Liberation.

2660	**463**	55b. multicoloured	95	45
MS2661		1l.20 multicoloured (39×72 mm). Imperf. No gum	3·00	1·40

1959. Air. Landing of Russian Rocket on the Moon. Surch **h. 00.02.24" 14-IX-1959 PRIMA RACHETA COSMICA IN LUNA 5 LEI** and bars.

2662	**458**	5l. on 3l.25 blue on salmon	14·50	4·25

(466)

1959. Eighth Balkan Games. Optd with T **466** in silver.

2663	**454**	1l. brown	16·00	16·00

467 Prince Vlad Tepes and Charter

1959. 500th Anniv of Bucharest.

2664	**467**	20b. black and blue	95	35
2665	-	40b. black and brown	1·80	35
2666	-	55b. black and bistre	3·00	55
2667	-	55b. black and purple	3·50	55
2668	-	1l.55 black and lilac	5·75	1·50
2669	-	1l.75 black and turquoise	6·25	2·00

DESIGNS—HORIZ: 40b. Peace Buildings, Bucharest; 55b. (No. 2666), Atheneum; 55b. (No 2667), "Scanteia" Printing House; 1l.55, Opera House; 1l.75, "23 August" Stadium.

468 Football

1959. International Sport. Multicoloured.

2671	20b. Type **468** (postage)	50	20
2672	35b. Motor-cycle racing (horiz)	60	20
2673	40b. Ice-hockey (horiz)	80	30
2674	55b. Handball	95	20
2675	1l. Horse-jumping	1·50	20
2676	1l.50 Boxing	3·00	30
2677	1l.55 Rugby football (horiz)	3·00	20
2678	1l.60 Tennis (horiz)	3·50	45
2679	2l.80 Hydroplaning (horiz) (air)	4·25	1·20

STAMP DAY ISSUES. The annual issues for Stamp Day in November together with the stamp issued on 30 March 1963 for the Romanian Philatelists' Conference are now the only stamps which carry a premium which is expressed on se-tenant labels. This was for the Association of Romanian Philatelists. These labels were at first seperated by a vertical perforation but in the issues from 1963 to 1971 the label is an integral part of the stamp.

469 "Lenin"

1959. Launching of Atomic Ice-breaker "Lenin".

2680	**469**	1l.75 violet	3·50	65

470 Stamp Album and Magnifier

1959. Stamp Day.

2681	**470**	1l.60(+40b.) blue	95	45

471 Foxglove

1959. Medicinal Flowers. Multicoloured.

2682	20b. Type **471**	30	10
2683	40b. Peppermint	60	30
2684	55b. False camomile	80	20
2685	55b. Cornflower	1·10	20
2686	1l. Meadow saffron	1·50	30
2687	1l.20 Monkshood	1·60	30
2688	1l.55 Common poppy	2·40	45
2689	1l.60 Silver lime	2·40	55
2690	1l.75 Dog rose	2·50	55
2691	3l.20 Yellow pheasant's-eye	4·00	75

472 Cuza University

1959. Centenary of Cuza University, Jassy.

2692	**472**	55b. brown	95	45

473 Rocket, Dog and Rabbit

1959. Air. Cosmic Rocket Flight.

2693	**473**	1l.55 blue	4·75	45
2694	-	1l.60 blue on cream	5·25	75
2695	-	1l.75 blue	5·25	75

DESIGNS—HORIZ: (52×29½ mm): 1l.60, Picture of "invisible" side of the Moon, with lists of place-names in Romanian and Russian. VERT—(As Type **473**): 1l.75, Lunik 3's trajectory around the Moon.

474 G. Cosbuc

1960. Romanian Authors.

2696	**474**	20b. blue	50	35
2697	-	40b. purple	95	35
2698	-	50b. brown	1·20	35
2699	-	55b. purple	1·20	35
2700	-	1l. violet	2·10	45
2701	-	1l.55 blue	3·50	55

PORTRAITS: 40b. I. L. Caragiale; 50b. G. Alexandrescu; 55b. A. Donici; 1l. C. Negruzzi; 1l.55, D. Bolintineanu.

475 Huchen

1960. Romanian Fauna.

2702	**475**	20b. blue (postage)	50	20
2703	-	55b. brown (Tortoise)	95	20
2704	-	1l.20 lilac (Common shelduck)	2·10	65
2705	-	1l.30 blue (Golden eagle) (air)	2·40	65
2706	-	1l.75 green (Black grouse)	2·40	65
2707	-	2l. red (Lammergeier)	2·50	95

476 Woman and Dove

1960. 50th Anniv of International Women's Day.

2708	**476**	55b. blue	1·50	65

477 Lenin (after painting by M. A. Gerasimov)

1960. 90th Birth Anniv of Lenin.

2709	**477**	40b. purple	80	30
2710	-	55b. blue	1·10	30
MS2711		65×75 mm. 1l.55 red	5·75	3·75

DESIGNS: 55b. Statue of Lenin by Boris Carogea; 1l.50 Lenin (sculpture by C. Baraschi).

478 "Victory"

1960. 15th Anniv of Victory.

2712	**478**	40b. blue	70	30
2714	**478**	40b. purple	3·50	3·75
2713	-	55b. blue	70	30
2715	-	55b. purple	3·50	3·75

DESIGN: 55b. Statue of soldier with flag.

479 Rocket Flight

1960. Air. Launching of Soviet Rocket.

2716	**479**	55b. blue	4·75	65

480 Diving

1960. Olympic Games, Rome (1st issue). Multicoloured.

2717	40b. Type **480**	2·40	2·30
2718	55b. Gymnastics	2·40	2·30
2719	1l.20 High jumping	2·40	2·30
2720	1l.60 Boxing	2·40	2·30
2721	2l.45 Canoeing	2·40	2·30
2722	3l.70 Canoeing	6·25	6·75

Nos. 2717/9 and 2720/1 are arranged together in "brickwork" fashion, se-tenant, in sheets forming complete overall patterns of the Olympic rings.

No. 2722 is imperf.

481 Gymnastics

1960. Olympic Games, Rome (2nd issue).

2723	-	20b. blue	20	10
2724	**481**	40b. purple	60	20
2725	-	55b. blue	85	10
2726	-	1l. red	1·20	20
2727	-	1l.60 purple	1·60	30
2728	-	2l. lilac	2·50	55
MS2729		90×69 mm. 5l. ultramarine	19·00	19·00
MS2730		90×69 mm. 6l. red. Imperf	34·00	33·00

DESIGNS: 20b. Diving; 55b. High-jumping; 1l. Boxing; 1l.60, Canoeing; 2l. Football; 5, 6l. Olympic flame and stadium.

482 Industrial Scholars

1960

2731	**482**	3b. mauve (postage)	10	10
2732	-	5b. brown	10	10
2733	-	10b. purple	20	10
2734	-	20b. blue	20	10
2735	-	30b. red	30	10
2736	-	35b. red	30	10
2737	-	40b. bistre	30	10
2738	-	50b. violet	30	10
2739	-	55b. blue	40	10
2740	-	60b. green	40	10
2741	-	75b. olive	50	10
2742	-	1l. red	70	10
2743	-	1l.20 black	60	10
2744	-	1l.50 purple	1·50	10
2745	-	1l.55 turquoise	80	10
2746	-	1l.60 blue	95	10
2747	-	1l.75 brown	1·20	10
2748	-	2l. brown	1·50	30
2749	-	2l.40 violet	1·60	20
2750	-	3l. blue	1·90	30
2751	-	3l.20 blue (air)	3·00	10

DESIGNS—VERT: 5b. Diesel train; 10b. Dam; 20b. Miner; 30b. Doctor; 35b. Textile worker; 50b. Children at play; 55b. Timber tractor; 1l. Atomic reactor; 1l.20, Petroleum refinery; 1l.50, Iron-works; 1l.75, Mason; 2l. Road-roller; 2l.40, Chemist; 3l. Radio communications and television. HORIZ: 40b. Grand piano and books; 60b. Combine harvester; 75b. Cattle-shed; 1l.55, Dock scene; 1l.60, Runner; 3l.20, Baneasa Airport, Bucharest.

483 Vlaicu and his Airplane No. 1 "Crazy Fly"

484 I.A.R. 817 Flying Ambulance

485 Pilot and Mikoyan Gurevich MiG-17 Jet Fighters

1960. 50th Anniv of First Flight by A. Vlaicu and Aviation Day.

2752	**483**	10b. brown and yellow	20	10
2753	-	20b. brown and orange	30	10
2754	**484**	35b. red	50	10
2755	-	40b. violet	70	10
2756	**485**	55b. blue	95	10
2757	-	1l.60 multicoloured	2·40	45
2758	-	1l.75 multicoloured	3·00	65

DESIGNS—As T **483**: 20b. Vlaicu in flying helmet and his No. 2 airplane; 40b. Antonov An-2 biplane spraying crops. 59×22 mm: 1l.60, Ilyushin Il-18 airliner and Baneasa airport control tower; 1l.75, Parachute descents.

486 Worker and Emblem

1960. Third Workers' Party Congress.

2759	**486**	55b. orange and red	1·50	45

487 Leo Tolstoy (writer)

1960. Cultural Anniversaries.

2760	**487**	10b. purple	20	10
2761	-	20b. brown	40	10
2762	-	35b. blue	50	10
2763	-	40b. green	60	20
2764	-	55b. brown	95	20
2765	-	1l. green	1·50	45
2766	-	1l.20 purple	1·60	20
2767	-	1l.55 grey	1·90	30
2768	-	1l.75 brown	3·00	55

DESIGNS: 10b. Type **487** (50th death anniv); 20b. Mark Twain (writer, 50th death anniv); 35b. Katsushika Hokusai (painter, birth bicentenary); 40b. Alfred de Musset (poet, 150th birth anniv); 55b. Daniel Defoe (writer, 300th birth anniv); 1l. Janos Bolyai (mathematician, death centenary); 1l,20, Anton Chekhov (writer, birth centenary); 1l.55, Robert Koch (bacteriologist, 50th death anniv); 1l.75, Frederic Chopin (composer, 150th birth anniv).

488 Tomis (Constantza)

1960. Black Sea Resorts. Multicoloured.

2769	20b. Type **488** (postage)	50	10
2770	35b. Constantza	70	10
2771	40b. Vasile Roaita	70	20
2772	55b. Mangalia	95	20
2773	1l. Eforie	1·50	45
2774	1l.60 Eforie (different)	2·40	30
2775	2l. Mamaia (air)	3·00	95

489 Globe and Flags

1960. International Puppet Theatre Festival, Bucharest. Designs (24×28½ mm, except 20b.) show puppets. Multicoloured.

2776	20b. Type **489**	30	10
2777	40b. Petrushka	50	10
2778	55b. Punch	60	10
2779	1l. Kaspar	1·10	20
2780	1l.20 Tindarica	1·30	20
2781	1l.75 Vasilache	1·90	30

490 Viennese Emperor Moth

1960. Air. Butterflies and Moths. Multicoloured.

2782	10b. Type **490**	30	10
2783	20b. Poplar admiral	30	10
2784	40b. Scarce copper	50	10
2785	55b. Swallowtail	95	20
2786	1l.60 Death's-head hawk moth	3·00	45
2787	1l.75 Purple emperor	4·00	55

SIZES: TRIANGULAR—36½×21½ mm: 20, 40b. VERT—23½×34 mm: 55b., 1l.60. HORIZ—34×23½ mm: 1l.75.

491 Children tobogganing

1960. Village Children's Games. Multicoloured.

2788	20b. Type **491**	20	10
2789	35b. "Oina" (ball-game) (horiz)	30	10
2790	55b. Ice-skating (horiz)	60	10
2791	1l. Running	1·20	20
2792	1l.75 Swimming (horiz)	2·50	30

492 Striker and Flag

1960. 40th Anniv of General Strike.

2793	**492**	55b. red and lake	95	45

493 Compass Points and Ilyushin Il-18 Airliner

1960. Air. Stamp Day.

2794	**493**	55b.(+45b.) blue	95	45

494 "XV", Globe and "Peace" Banner

1960. 15th Anniv of World Democratic Youth Federation.

2795	**494**	55b. yellow and blue	95	45

495 Black Sea Herrings

1960. Fish.

2796	-	10b. brown, yell & grn	20	10
2797	-	20b. multicoloured	50	10
2798	-	40b. brn, lt brn & yell	70	10
2799	**495**	55b. grey, blue & orge	95	10
2800	-	1l. multicoloured	1·60	20
2801	-	1l.20 multicoloured	2·40	30
2802	-	1l.60 multicoloured	3·00	45

FISHES: 10b. Common carp; 20b. Zander; 40b. Black Sea turbot; 1l. Wels; 1l.20, Sterlet; 1l.60, Beluga.

496 Woman tending Vine (Cotnari)

1960. Romanian Vineyards. Multicoloured.

2803	20b. Dragasani	20	10
2804	30b. Dealul Mare (horiz)	50	10
2805	40b. Odobesti (horiz)	70	10
2806	55b. Type **496**	95	20
2807	75b. Tirnave	1·60	30
2808	1l. Minis	2·40	45
2809	1l.20 Murfatlar	3·00	75

MS2810	95×115 mm. 5l. Antique wine jug. Imperf. No gum	5·75	3·75

497 "Furnaceman" (after I. Irimescu)

1961. Romanian Sculptures.

2811	**497**	5b. red	10	10
2812	-	10b. violet	20	10
2813	-	20b. black	30	10
2814	-	40b. bistre	70	10
2815	-	50b. brown	80	10
2816	-	55b. red	1·10	10
2817	-	1l. purple	1·50	20
2818	-	1l.55 blue	2·40	30
2819	-	1l.75 green	3·00	30

SCULPTURES—VERT: 10b. "Gh. Doja" (I. Vlad); 20b. "Reunion" (B. Caragea); 40b. "Enescu" (G. Anghel); 50b. "Eminescu" (C. Baraschi); 1l. "Peace" (I. Jalea); 1l.55, "Construc-tive Socialism" (C. Medrea); 1l.75, "Birth of an Idea" (A. Szobotka). HORIZ: 55b. "Peasant Uprising, 1907" (M. Constantinescu).

498 Slalom Racer

1961. Air. 50th Anniv of Romanian Winter Sports. (a) Perf.

2820		10b. olive and grey	30	10
2821	**498**	20b. red and grey	40	10
2822	-	25b. turquoise and grey	70	10
2823	-	40b. violet and grey	80	10
2824	-	55b. blue and grey	95	20
2825	-	1l. red and grey	1·40	30
2826	-	1l.55 brown and grey	2·10	35

(b) Imperf.

2827		10b. blue and grey	20	10
2828	**498**	20b. brown and grey	50	30
2829	-	25b. olive and grey	70	45
2830	-	40b. red and grey	80	75
2831	-	55b. turquoise and grey	95	95
2832	-	1l. violet and grey	1·50	1·40
2833	-	1l.55 red and grey	2·10	2·00

DESIGNS—HORIZ: Skier: racing (10b.), jumping (55b.), walking (1l.55). VERT: 25b. Skiers climbing slope; 40b. Toboggan; 1l. Rock-climber.

499 Petru Poni (chemist)

1961. Romanian Scientists. Inscr "1961". Portraits in sepia.

2834	**499**	10b. brown and pink	10	20
2835	-	20b. purple and yellow	30	20
2836	-	55b. red and blue	70	20
2837	-	1l.55 violet and orange	2·40	55

PORTRAITS: 20b. Anghel Saligny (engineer) and Saligny Bridge, Cernavoda; 55b. Constantin Budeanu (electrical engineer); 1l.55, Gheorghe Titeica (mathematician).

500 Yuri Gagarin in Capsule

1961. Air. World's First Manned Space Flight. Inscr "12 IV 1961". (a) Perf.

2838		1l.35 blue	1·40	35
2839	**500**	3l.20 blue	3·50	1·00

(b) Imperf.

2840		3l.20 red	11·50	4·25

DESIGN—VERT: 1l.35, Yuri Gagarin.

501 Freighter "Galati"

1961. Merchant Navy. Multicoloured.

2841	20b. Type **501**	50	10
2842	40b. "Oltenita" (Danube passenger vessel)	50	10
2843	55b. "Tomis" (hydrofoil)	70	10
2844	1l. "Arad" (freighter)	1·50	20
2845	1l.55 "N. Cristea" (tug)	2·40	30
2846	1l.75 "Dobrogea" (freighter)	3·00	45

502 Red Flag with Marx, Engels and Lenin

1961. 40th Anniv of Romanian Communist Party.

2847	**502**	35b. multicoloured	95	30
2848	-	55b. multicoloured	1·50	30
MS2849		114×80 mm. 1l. multicoloured. Imperf. No gum	3·50	1·60

DESIGNS: 55b. Two bill-posters; 1l. "Industry and Agriculture" and party emblem.

503 Eclipse over Scanteia Building and Observatory

1961. Air. Solar Eclipse.

2850		1l.60 blue	2·10	30
2851	**503**	1l.75 blue	2·50	30

DESIGN: 1l.60, Eclipse over Palace Square, Bucharest.

504 Roe Deer

1961. Forest Animals. Inscr "1961". Multicoloured.

2852	10b. Type **504**	20	20
2853	20b. Lynx (horiz)	50	20
2854	35b. Wild boar (horiz)	70	30
2855	40b. Brown bear (horiz)	1·20	30
2856	55b. Red deer	1·50	30
2857	75b. Red fox (horiz)	1·60	30
2858	1l. Chamois	1·90	30
2859	1l.55 Brown hare	2·40	45
2860	1l.75 Eurasian badger	3·00	55
2861	2l. Roe deer	3·50	95

505 George Enescu

1961. Second International George Enescu Festival.

2862	**505**	3l. lavender and brown	3·00	65

506 Yuri Gagarin and German Titov

1961. Air. Second Soviet Space Flight.

2863	-	55b. blue	95	10
2864	-	1l.35 violet	1·50	30
2865	**506**	1l.75 red	2·40	45

DESIGNS—VERT: 55b. "Vostok 2" in flight; 1l.35, G. S. Titov.

507 Iris

1961. Centenary of Bucharest Botanical Gardens. Flowers in natural colours. Background and inscription colours given. Perf or imperf.

2866	-	10b. yellow and brown	10	10
2867	-	20b. green and red	20	10
2868	-	25b. blue, green and red	30	10
2869	-	35b. lilac and grey	50	10
2870	**507**	40b. yellow and violet	70	10
2871	-	55b. blue and ultramarine	95	10

2872	-	1l. orange and blue	1·60	20
2873	-	1l.20 blue and brown	1·90	20
2874	-	1l.55 brown and lake	2·40	20
MS2875		125×92 mm. 1l.75 black, green and carmine	7·25	4·25

FLOWERS—HORIZ: 10b. Primula; 35b. Opuntia; 1l. Hepatica. VERT: 20b. Dianthus; 25b. Peony; 55b. Ranunculus; 1l.20, Poppy; 1l.55, Gentian; C. Davila, D. Brindza and Botanical Gardens buildings.

508 Cobza Player

1961. Musicians. Multicoloured.

2876		10b. Pan piper	10	10
2877		20b. Alpenhorn player (horiz)	20	10
2878		40b. Flautist	50	10
2879		55b. Type **508**	1·10	10
2880		60b. Bagpiper	1·30	20
2881		1l. Cembalo player	1·70	45

509 Heraclitus (Greek philosopher)

1961. Cultural Anniversaries.

2882	**509**	10b. purple	70	30
2883	-	20b. brown	70	30
2884	-	40b. green	70	30
2885	-	55b. mauve	1·20	30
2886	-	1l.35 blue	1·50	30
2887	-	1l.75 violet	1·90	30

DESIGNS: 20b. Sir Francis Bacon (philosopher and statesman, 400th birth anniv); 40b. Rabindradath Tagore (poet and philosopher, birth centenary); 55b. Domingo Sarmiento (writer, 150th birth anniv; 1l.35, Heinrich von Kleist (dramatist, 150th death anniv); 1l.75, Mikhail Lomonosov (writer, 250th birth anniv).

510 Olympic Flame

1961. Olympic Games 1960. Gold Medal Awards. Inscr "MELBOURNE 1956" or "ROMA 1960". Perf or imperf.

2888		10b. turquoise and ochre	20	15
2889	**510**	20b. red	20	15
2890	-	20b. grey	20	15
2891	-	35b. brown and ochre	50	15
2892	-	40b. purple and ochre	60	15
2893	-	55b. blue	70	20
2894	-	55b. blue	70	20
2895	-	55b. red and ochre	70	20
2896	-	1l.35 blue and ochre	2·40	30
2897	-	1l.75 red and ochre	3·50	40
MS2898		109×86 mm. 4l. multicoloured. Imperf. No gum	14·50	11·00

DESIGNS (Medals)—DIAMOND: 10b. Boxing; 35b. Pistol-shooting; 40b. Rifle-shooting; 55b. (No. 2895), Wrestling; 1l.35, High-jumping. VERT: as Type **510**: 20b. (No. 2890), Diving; 55b. (No. 2893), Water-polo; 55b. (No. 2894), Women's high-jumping. HORIZ—45×33 mm: 1l.75, Canoeing. Larger — 4l. Gold medals of Melbourne and Rome.

511 "Stamps Round the World"

1961. Air. Stamp Day.

2899	**511**	55b.(+45b.) blue, brown and red	1·50	65

512 Tower Building, Republic Palace Square, Bucharest

1961. Air. Modern Romanian Architecture. Multicoloured.

2900		20b. Type **512**	30	10
2901		40b. Constantza Railway Station (horiz)	50	20
2902		55b. Congress Hall, Republic Palace, Bucharest (horiz)	60	20
2903		75b. Rolling mill, Hunedoara (horiz)	70	20
2904		1l. Apartment blocks, Bucharest (horiz)	95	20
2905		1l.20 Circus Building, Bucharest (horiz)	1·20	45
2906		1l.75 Workers' Club, Mangalia (horiz)	1·90	30

513 U.N. Emblem

1961. 15th Anniv of U.N.O. Perf or imperf.

2907	-	20b. multicoloured	30	10
2908	-	40b. multicoloured	70	20
2909	**513**	55b. multicoloured	1·20	30

DESIGNS (bearing U.N. emblem): 20b. Peace dove over Eastern Europe; 40b. Peace dove and youths of three races.

514 Workers with Flags

1961. Fifth W.F.T.U. Congress, Moscow.

2910	**514**	55b. red	1·20	45

515 Cock and Savings Book

1962. Savings Day. Inscr "1962". Multicoloured.

2911		40b. Type **515**	50	30
2912		55b. Savings Bank book, bee and "honeycombs" of agriculture, housing and industry	70	30

516 Footballer

1962. European Junior Football Competition, Bucharest.

2913	**516**	55b. brown and green	1·90	45

517 Ear of Corn, Map and Tractor

1962. Completion of Agricultural Collectivisation Project. Inscr "1962".

2914	**517**	40b. red and orange	30	10
2915	-	55b. lake and yellow	50	10
2916	-	1l.55 yellow, red and blue	1·20	45

DESIGNS: 55b. Commemorative medal; 1l.55, Wheatsheaf, and hammer and sickle emblem.

518 Handball Player

1962. Women's World Handball Championships, Bucharest.

2917	**518**	55b. violet and yellow	1·90	45

519 Canoe Race

1962. Boating and Sailing. Inscr "1962". (a) Perf.

2918	**519**	10b. blue and mauve	30	10
2919	-	20b. blue and brown	40	10
2920	-	40b. blue and brown	60	10
2921	-	55b. blue and ultramarine	70	20
2922	-	1l. blue and red	1·40	20
2923	-	1l.20 blue and purple	1·60	20
2924	-	1l.55 blue and red	1·90	20
2925	-	3l. blue and violet	3·00	55

(b) Imperf. Colours changed.

2926	**519**	10b. blue and ultramarine	30	30
2927	-	20b. blue and mauve	50	30
2928	-	40b. blue and red	80	55
2929	-	55b. blue and brown	95	75
2930	-	1l. blue and brown	1·60	95
2931	-	1l.20 blue and violet	1·80	1·00
2932	-	1l.55 blue and red	2·10	1·10
2933	-	3l. blue and purple	4·00	1·90

DESIGNS: 20b. Kayak; 40b. Racing "eight"; 55b. Sculling; 1l. "Star" yachts; 1l.20, Power boats; 1l.55, "Flying Dutchman" dinghy; 3l. Canoe slalom.

520 Jean Jacques Rousseau

1962. Cultural Anniversaries (writers).

2934	**520**	40b. green	40	20
2935	-	55b. purple	50	30
2936	-	1l.75 blue	1·10	20
MS2937		91×122 mm. 3l.30 brown	7·25	5·50

DESIGNS: 40b. T **520** (250th birth anniv); 55b. Ion Caragiale (dramatist, 50th death anniv); 1l.75, Aleksandr Herzen (150th birth anniv). 32×55 mm—3l.30 Caragiale (full-length portrait).

521 Flags and Globes

1962. World Youth Festival, Helsinki.

2938	**521**	55b. multicoloured	1·50	45

522 Traian Vuia (aviator)

1962. Romanian Celebrities.

2939	**522**	15b. brown	20	20
2940	-	20b. red	30	20
2941	-	35b. purple	50	20
2942	-	40b. blue	60	20
2943	-	55b. blue	70	20
2944	-	1l. blue	1·20	20
2945	-	1l.20 red	1·50	30
2946	-	1l.35 turquoise	1·60	30
2947	-	1l.55 violet	1·90	20

PORTRAITS: 20b. Alexandru Davila (writer); 35b. Vasile Pirvan (archaeologist); 40b. Ion Negulici (painter); 55b. Grigore Cobilcescu (geologist); 1l. Dr. Gheorghe Marinescu (neurologist); 1l.20, Dr. Ion Cantacuzino (bacteriologist); 1l.35, Dr. Victor Babes (bacteriologist and pathologist; 1l.55, Dr. Constantin Levaditi (medical researcher).

523 Anglers by Pond

1962. Fishing Sport. Multicoloured.

2948		10b. Rod-fishing in fishing punts	10	10
2949		25b. Line-fishing in mountain pool	20	10
2950		40b. Type **523**	50	15
2951		55b. Anglers on beach	60	15
2952		75b. Line-fishing in mountain stream	95	15
2953		1l. Shore-fishing	1·10	20
2954		1l.75 Freshwater-fishing	1·70	20
2955		3l.25 Fishing in Danube delta	3·00	25

524 Dove and "Space" Stamps of 1957/58

1962. Air. Cosmic Flights.

2956	**524**	35b. brown	20	10
2957	-	55b. green	50	20
2958	-	1l.35 blue	1·20	30
2959	-	1l.75 red	1·90	35
MS2960		107×79 mm. Nos. 2956/9, but imperf and colours changed: 35b. blue, 55b. brown; 1l.35 red; 1l.75 green	5·25	1·90

DESIGNS—Dove and: 55b. "Space" stamps of 1959; 1l.35, "Space" stamps of 1957 ("Laika"), 1959 and 1960; 1l.75, "Spacemen" stamps of 1961.

1962. Romanian Victory in European Junior Football Competition, Bucharest. Surch **1962. Campioana Europeana 2 lei.**

2961	**516**	2l. on 55b. brown & grn	4·00	3·75

1962. Romanian Victory in Women's World Handball Championships, Bucharest. Surch **Campioana Mondiala 5 lei.**

2962	**518**	5l. on 55b. vio & yell	7·25	4·75

527 "Vostok 3" and "4" in Orbit

1962. Air. First "Team" Manned Space Flight.

2963	-	55b. violet	50	20
2964	**527**	1l.60 blue	1·50	40
2965	-	1l.75 purple	1·90	45

DESIGNS: 55b. Andrian Nikolaev (cosmonaut); 1l.75, Pavel Popovich (cosmonaut).

528 Child and Butterfly

1962. Children.

2966	**528**	20b. blue, brown and red	30	10
2967	-	30b. yellow, blue and red	35	10
2968	-	40b. blue, red & turquoise	40	10
2969	-	55b. olive, blue and red	70	10
2970	-	1l.20 red, brown & blue	1·90	25
2971	-	1l.55 ochre, blue and red	3·00	30

DESIGNS—VERT: 30b. Girl feeding dove; 40b. Boy with model yacht; 1l.20, Boy violinist and girl pianist. HORIZ: 55b. Girl teaching boy to write; 1l.55, Pioneers around camp-fire.

529 Pottery

1962. Fourth Sample Fair, Bucharest. Inscr "AL IV-LEA PAVILION DE MOSTRE BUCURESTI 1962". Multicoloured.

2972		5b. Type **529** (postage)	60	15
2973		10b. Preserved foodstuffs	70	15
2974		20b. Chemical products	80	15
2975		40b. Ceramics	85	10
2976		55b. Leather goods	1·10	10
2977		75b. Textiles	1·30	10
2978		1l. Furniture and fabrics	1·50	10
2979		1l.20 Office equipment	1·90	10
2980		1l.55 Needlework	2·50	10
2981		1l.60 Fair pavilion (horiz) (air)	3·00	30

530 Lenin and Red Flag

1962. 45th Anniv of Russian Revolution.

2982	**530**	55b. brown, red and blue	1·50	45

531 "The Coachmen" (after Szatmay)

1962. Air. Stamp Day and Centenary of 1st Romanian Stamps.

2983	**531**	55b.(+45b.) black and blue	1·90	55

532 Lamb

1962. Prime Farm Stock.

2984	**532**	20b. black and blue	20	10
2985	-	40b. brown, yellow & blue	30	10
2986	-	55b. green, buff and orange	50	10
2987	-	1l. brown, buff and grey	80	10
2988	-	1l.35 brown, black & green	1·20	20
2989	-	1l.55 brown, black & red	1·30	30
2990	-	1l.75 brown, cream & blue	1·90	65

DESIGNS—HORIZ: 40b. Ram; 1l.55, Heifer; 1l.75, Sows. VERT: 55b. Bull; 1l. Pig; 1l.35, Cow.

533 Arms, Industry and Agriculture

1962. 15th Anniv of People's Republic.

2991	**533**	1l.55 multicoloured	1·90	45

534 Strikers

1963. 30th Anniv of Grivitsa Strike.

2992	**534**	1l.75 multicoloured	1·90	45

535 Tractor-driver

1963. Freedom from Hunger.

2993	**535**	40b. blue	30	10
2994	-	55b. brown	60	10
2995	-	1l.55 red	1·50	20
2996	-	1l.75 green	1·60	30

DESIGNS (each with F.A.O. emblem): 55b. Girl harvester; 1l.55, Child with beaker of milk; 1l.75, Girl vintager.

1963. Air. Romanian Philatelists' Conference, Bucharest. No. 2983 optd **A.F.R.** surrounded by **CONFERINTA PE TARA BUCURESTI 30-III-1963** in diamond shape.

2997	**531**	55b.(+45b.) blk & bl	6·25	6·00

The opt is applied in the middle of the se-tenant pair—stamp and 45b. label.

537 Sighisoara Glass Factory

1963. Air. "Socialist Achievements".

2998	**537**	30b. blue and red	30	10
2999	-	40b. green and violet	50	15
3000	-	55b. red and blue	70	15
3001	-	1l. violet and brown	1·10	20
3002	-	1l.55 red and blue	1·30	25
3003	-	1l.75 blue and purple	1·50	30

DESIGNS: 40b. Govora soda works; 55b. Tirgul-Jiu wood factory; 1l. Savinesti chemical works; 1l.55, Hunedoara metal works; 1l.75, Brazi thermic power station.

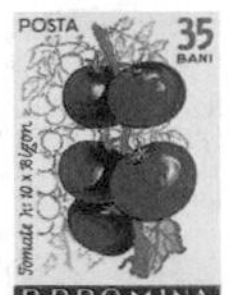

538 Tomatoes

1963. Vegetable Culture. Multicoloured.

3004		35b. Type **538**	30	10
3005		40b. Hot peppers	60	10
3006		55b. Radishes	70	15
3007		75b. Aubergines	95	20
3008		1l.20 Mild peppers	1·50	30
3009		3l.25 Cucumbers (horiz)	3·00	45

539 Moon Rocket "Luna 4"

1963. Air. Launching of Soviet Moon Rocket "Luna 4". The 1l.75 is imperf.

3010	**539**	55b. red and blue	60	30
3011	**539**	1l.75 red and violet	1·90	30

540 Chick

1963. Domestic Poultry.

3012	**540**	20b. yellow and blue	30	10
3013	-	30b. red, blue and brown	50	10
3014	-	40b. blue, orange & brn	60	10
3015	-	55b. multicoloured	70	10
3016	-	70b. blue, red and purple	80	10
3017	-	1l. red, grey and blue	95	15
3018	-	1l.35 red, blue and ochre	1·10	20
3019	-	3l.20 multicoloured	2·10	35

POULTRY: 30b. Cockerel; 40b. Duck; 55b. White Leghorn; 70b. Goose; 1l. Rooster; 1l.35, Turkey (cock); 3l.20, Turkey (hen).

541 Diving

1963. Swimming. Bodies in drab.

3020	**541**	25b. green and brown	20	10
3021	-	30b. yellow and olive	30	10
3022	-	55b. red and turquoise	50	10
3023	-	1l. red and green	80	15
3024	-	1l.35 mauve and blue	95	15
3025	-	1l.55 orange and violet	1·70	20
3026	-	2l. yellow and mauve	1·70	45

DESIGNS—HORIZ: 30b. Crawl; 55b. Butterfly; 1l. Back stroke; 1l.35, Breast stroke. VERT: 1l.55, Swallow diving; 2l. Water polo.

542 Congress Emblem

1963. International Women's Congress, Moscow.

3027	**542**	55b. blue	95	45

543 Valery Bykovsky and Globe

1963. Air. Second "Team" Manned Space Flights.

3028	**543**	55b. blue	70	20
3029	-	1l.75 red	2·40	45
MS3030		118×80 mm. 1l.20, 1l.60 blue	4·75	2·30

DESIGNS: 1l.75 Valentina Tereshkova and globe; 25×41 mm—1l.20 Bykovsky; 1l.60 Tereshkova.

The stamps in No. **MS**3030 form a composite design.

544 Class 142 Steam Locomotive, 1936

1963. Air. Transport. Multicoloured.

3031		40b. Type **544**	60	20
3032		55b. Class 060-DA diesel-electric locomotive, 1959	70	20
3033		75b. Trolley bus	95	30
3034		1l.35 "Oltenita" (Danube passenger vessel)	2·10	35
3035		1l.75 Ilyushin Il-18 airplane	3·00	45

545 William Thackeray (novelist)

1963. Cultural Anniversaries. Inscr "MARILE ANNIVERSARI CULTURALE 1963".

3036	**545**	40b. black and lilac	30	15
3037	-	50b. black and brown	60	15
3038	-	55b. black and olive	80	15
3039	-	1l.55 black and red	1·60	15
3040	-	1l.75 black and blue	1·90	30

PORTRAITS: 40b. Type **545** (death centenary); 50b. Eugene Delacroix (painter, death centenary); 55b. Gheorghe Marinescu (neurologist, birth centenary); 1l.55, Giuseppe Verdi (composer, 150th birth anniv); 1l.75, Konstantin Stanislavsky (actor and stage director, birth centenary).

546 Walnuts

1963. Fruit and Nuts. Multicoloured.

3041		10b. Type **546**	50	10
3042		20b. Plums	50	10
3043		40b. Peaches	80	10
3044		55b. Strawberries	1·10	10
3045		1l. Grapes	1·20	15
3046		1l.55 Apples	1·60	20
3047		1l.60 Cherries	2·10	30
3048		1l.75 Pears	2·50	30

1963. Air. 50th Death Anniv of Aurel Vlaicu (aviation pioneer). No. 2752 surch **1913–1963 50 ani de la moarte 1,75 lei.**

3049	**483**	1l.75 on 10b. brn & yell	4·75	1·90

548 Volleyball

1963. European Volleyball Championships.

3050	**548**	5b. mauve and grey	50	10
3051	-	40b. blue and grey	70	10
3052	-	55b. turquoise and grey	95	15
3053	-	1l.75 brown and grey	1·90	30
3054	-	3l.20 violet and grey	3·00	45

DESIGNS: 40b. to 1l.75, Various scenes of play at net; 3l.20, European Cup.

549 Romanian 1l.55 "Centenary" Stamp of 1958

1963. Air. Stamp Day and 15th U.P.U. Congress. Inscr "AL XV-LEA CONGRESS", etc.

3055	**549**	20b. brown and blue	20	10
3056	-	40b. blue and mauve	25	10
3057	-	55b. mauve and blue	30	10
3058	-	1l.20 violet and buff	70	15
3059	-	1l.55 green and red	1·10	20
3060	-	1l.60+50b. mult	2·10	45

DESIGNS (Romanian stamps): 40b. (1l.20) "Laika", 1957 (blue); 55b. (3l.20) "Gagarin", 1961; 1l.20, (55b.) "Nikolaev" and (1l.75) "Popovich", 1962; 1l.55, (55b.) "Postwoman", 1953; 1l.60, U.P.U. Monument, Berne, globe, map of Romania and aircraft (76×27 mm).

551 Ski Jumping

1963. Winter Olympic Games, Innsbruck, 1964. (a) Perf.

3061	**551**	10b. blue and red	50	20
3062	-	20b. brown and blue	70	20
3063	-	40b. brown and green	85	10
3064	-	55b. brown and violet	1·10	20
3065	-	60b. blue and brown	1·20	30
3066	-	75b. blue and mauve	1·50	45
3067	-	1l. blue and ochre	1·90	45
3068	-	1l.20 blue and turquoise	2·40	65

(b) Imperf. Colours changed.

3069	**551**	10b. brown and green	1·50	95
3070	-	20b. brown and violet	1·50	95
3071	-	40b. blue and red	1·50	95
3072	-	55b. brown and blue	1·50	95
3073	-	60b. blue and turquoise	1·50	95
3074	-	75b. blue and ochre	1·50	95
3075	-	1l. blue and mauve	1·50	95
3076	-	1l.20 blue and brown	1·50	95
MS3077		120×80 mm. 1l.50 ultramarine and red	11·50	9·25

DESIGNS: 20b. Speed skating; 40b. Ice hockey; 55b. Figure skating; 60b. Slalom; 75b. Biathlon; 1l. Bobsleighing; 1l.20 Cross-country skiing. HORIZ: 1l.55 Stadium, Innsbruck.

552 Cone, Fern and Conifer

1963. 18th Anniv of Reafforestation Campaign.

3078	**552**	55b. green	30	20
3079	-	1l.75 blue	1·20	30

DESIGN: 1l.75, Chestnut trees.

553 Silkworm Moth

1963. Bee-keeping and Silkworm-breeding. Multicoloured.

3080	10b. Type **553**	50	10
3081	20b. Moth emerging from chrysalis	70	10
3082	40b. Silkworm	85	15
3083	55b. Honey bee (horiz)	95	20
3084	60b. Honey bee on flower	1·20	30
3085	1l.20 Honey bee approaching orange flowers (horiz)	1·60	45
3086	1l.35 Honey bee approaching pink flowers (horiz)	2·10	55
3087	1l.60 Honey bee and sunflowers (horiz)	2·40	65

554 Carved Pillar

1963. Village Museum, Bucharest.

3088	**554**	20b. purple	30	10
3089	-	40b. blue (horiz)	50	10
3090	-	55b. violet (horiz)	60	10
3091	-	75b. green	80	10
3092	-	1l. red and brown	1·20	10
3093	-	1l.20 green	1·50	15
3094	-	1l.75 blue and brown	2·40	15

DESIGNS: Various Romanian peasant houses.

555 Yuri Gagarin

1964. Air. "Space Navigation". Soviet flag, red and yellow; U.S. flag, red and blue; backgrounds, light blue; portrait and inscription colours below. (a) Perf.

3095	**555**	5b. blue	30	10
3096	-	10b. violet	50	10
3097	-	20b. bronze	60	10
3098	-	35b. grey	65	10
3099	-	40b. violet	70	15
3100	-	55b. violet	85	20
3101	-	60b. brown	95	30
3102	-	75b. blue	1·20	35
3103	-	1l. purple	1·60	45
3104	-	1l.40 purple	1·90	95

(b) Imperf. Colours changed.

3105	**555**	5b. violet	10	10
3106	-	10b. blue	10	10
3107	-	20b. grey	40	15
3108	-	35b. bronze	85	45
3109	-	40b. purple	1·20	55
3110	-	55b. purple	1·60	65
3111	-	60b. blue	1·60	95
3112	-	75b. brown	2·10	1·30
3113	-	1l. violet	2·50	1·60
3114	-	1l.40 violet	3·25	2·40
MS3115		120×80 mm. 2l. multicoloured	11·50	9·25

PORTRAITS (with flags of their countries)—As Type **555**: 10b. German Titov; 20b. John Glenn; 35b. Scott Carpenter; 60b. Walter Schirra; 75b. Gordon Cooper. 35½×33½ mm: 40b. Andrian Nikolaev; 55b. Pavel Popovich; 1l. Valery Bykovsky; 1l.40, Valentina Tereshkova. 59×43 mm—2l. Globe, orbits, laurel sprigs and commemorative dates.

556 George Stephanescu (composer)

1964. Romanian Opera Singers and their stage roles. Portraits in brown.

3116	**556**	10b. olive	50	10
3117	-	20b. blue	60	10
3118	-	35b. green	70	10
3119	-	40b. light blue	80	10
3120	-	55b. mauve	95	10
3121	-	75b. violet	1·10	10
3122	-	1l. blue	1·20	20
3123	-	1l.35 violet	1·50	20
3124	-	1l.55 red	2·40	30

DESIGNS: 20b. Elena Teodorini in "Carmen"; 35b. Ion Bajenaru in "Petru Rares"; 40b. Dimitrie Popovici-Bayreuth as Alberich in "Ring of the Nibelung"; 55b. Haricled Dardee in "Tosca"; 75b. George Folescu in "Boris Godunov"; 1l. Jean Athanasiu in "Rigoletto"; 1l.35, Traian Grosarescu as Duke in "Rigoletto"; 1l.55, Nicolae Leonard as Hoffmann in "Tales of Hoffmann".

557 Prof. G. M. Murgoci

1964. Eighth International Soil Congress, Bucharest.

3125	**557**	1l.60 indigo, ochre and blue	1·20	45

558 "Ascalaphus macaronius" (owl-fly)

1964. Insects. Multicoloured.

3126	5b. Type **558**	20	10
3127	10b. "Ammophila sabulosa" (digger wasp)	30	10
3128	35b. "Scolia maculata" (dagger wasp)	50	10
3129	40b. Swamp tiger moth	60	10
3130	55b. Gypsy moth	70	15
3131	1l.20 Great banded grayling	1·10	20
3132	1l.55 "Carabus fabricii malachiticus" (ground beetle)	1·60	20
3133	1l.75 "Procerus gigas" (ground beetle)	2·10	30

559 "Nicotiana alata"

1964. Romanian Flowers. Multicoloured.

3134	10b. Type **559**	30	15
3135	20b. "Pelargonium"	50	15
3136	40b. "Fuchsia gracilis"	60	15
3137	55b. "Chrysanthemum indicum"	70	15
3138	75b. "Dahlia hybrida"	80	15
3139	1l. "Lilium croceum"	1·50	20
3140	1l.25 "Hosta ovata"	1·60	30
3141	1l.55 "Tagetes erectus"	1·90	30

560 Cross Country

1964. Horsemanship.

3142	-	40b. multicoloured	50	10
3143	**560**	55b. brown, red and lilac	70	20
3144	-	1l.35 brown, red & green	1·60	30
3145	-	1l.55 mauve, blue & bis	2·40	45

DESIGNS—HORIZ: 40b. Dressage; 1l.55, Horse race. VERT: 1l.35, Show jumping.

561 Brown Scorpionfish

1964. Constantza Aquarium. Fish designs. Multicoloured.

3146	5b. Type **561**	10	10
3147	10b. Peacock blenny	10	10
3148	20b. Black Sea horse-mackerel	20	10
3149	40b. Russian sturgeon	50	10
3150	50b. Short-snouted seahorse	60	20
3151	55b. Tub gurnard	70	20
3152	1l. Beluga	1·20	20
3153	3l.20 Common stingray	4·00	45

562 M. Eminescu (poet)

1964. Cultural Anniversaries. Portraits in brown.

3154	**562**	5b. green	20	10
3155	-	20b. red	20	10
3156	-	35b. red	50	10
3157	-	55b. bistre	70	10
3158	-	1l.20 blue	1·50	20
3159	-	1l.75 violet	1·90	45

DESIGNS: Type **562** (75th death anniv); 20b. Ion Creanga (folklorist, 75th death anniv); 35b. Emil Girleanu (writer, 50th death anniv); 55b. Michelangelo (artist, 400th death anniv); 1l.20, Galileo Galilei (astronomer, 400th birth anniv); 1l.75, William Shakespeare (dramatist, 400th birth anniv).

563 Cheile Bicazului (gorge)

1964. Mountain Resorts.

3160	**563**	40b. lake	50	10
3161	-	55b. blue	70	10
3162	-	1l. purple	95	10
3163	-	1l.35 brown	1·20	15
3164	-	1l.75 green	1·90	20

DESIGNS—VERT: 55b. Cabin on Lake Bilea; 1l. Poiana Brasov ski-lift; 1l.75, Alpine Hotel. HORIZ: 1l.35, Lake Bicaz.

564 High Jumping

1964. Balkan Games. Multicoloured.

3165	30b. Type **564**	30	10
3166	40b. Throwing the javelin	30	10
3167	55b. Running	60	10
3168	1l. Throwing the discus	1·20	15
3169	1l.20 Hurdling	1·20	15
3170	1l.55 Flags of competing countries (24×44 mm)	1·40	20

565 Arms and Flag

1964. 20th Anniv of Liberation. Multicoloured.

3171	55b. Type **565**	40	10
3172	60b. Industrial plant (horiz)	50	15
3173	75b. Harvest scene (horiz)	60	20
3174	1l.20 Apartment houses (horiz)	1·10	30

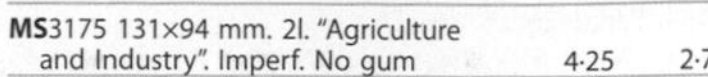

MS3175	131×94 mm. 2l. "Agriculture and Industry". Imperf. No gum	4·25	2·75

566 High Jumping

1964. Olympic Games, Tokyo. Multicoloured. (a) Perf.

3176	20b. Type **566**	30	10
3177	30b. Wrestling	50	10
3178	35b. Volleyball	60	15
3179	40b. Canoeing	70	20
3180	55b. Fencing	95	20
3181	1l.20 Gymnastics	1·10	30
3182	1l.35 Football	1·50	45
3183	1l.55 Rifle-shooting	1·90	55

(b) Imperf. Colours changed and new values.

3184	20b. Type **566**	40	10
3185	30b. Wrestling	50	10
3186	35b. Volleyball	80	15
3187	40b. Canoeing	85	20
3188	55b. Fencing	1·70	55
3189	1l.60 Gymnastics	3·50	1·50
3190	2l. Football	3·75	1·90
3191	2l.40 Rifle-shooting	4·50	2·75
MS3192	80×110 mm. 3l.25 Runner (no gum)	11·50	7·00

567 George Enescu

1964. Third International George Enescu Festival.

3193	**567**	10b. green	20	10
3194	-	55b. purple	60	20
3195	-	1l.60 purple	1·60	65
3196	-	1l.75 blue	2·10	45

DESIGNS (Portraits of Enescu): 55b. At piano; 1l.60, Medallion; 1l.75, When an old man.

568 Python

1964. Bucharest Zoo. Multicoloured.

3197	5b. Type **568**	10	10
3198	10b. Black swans	40	10
3199	35b. Ostriches	50	10
3200	40b. Crowned cranes	70	20
3201	55b. Tigers	80	20
3202	1l. Lions	1·40	20
3203	1l.55 Grevy's zebras	2·10	20
3204	2l. Bactrian camels	3·00	45

569 Brincoveanu, Cantacuzino, Lazar and Academy

1964. Anniversaries. Multicoloured.

3205	20b. Type **569**	10	10
3206	40b. Cuza and seal	20	10
3207	55b. Emblems and the Arts (vert)	30	15
3208	75b. Laboratory workers and class	50	20
3209	1l. Savings Bank building	80	45

EVENTS, etc—HORIZ: 20b. 270th Anniv of Domneasca Academy; 40b., 75b. Bucharest University centenary; 1l. Savings Bank centenary. VERT: 55b. "Fine Arts" centenary (emblems are masks, curtain, piano keyboard, harp, palette and brushes).

570 Soldier

1964. Centenary of Army Day.

3210	**570**	55b. blue and light blue	80	45

571 Post Office of 19th and 20th Centuries

1964. Air. Stamp Day.

3211	**571**	1l.60+40b. blue, red and yellow	1·90	95

No. 3211 is a two-part design, the two parts being arranged vert, imperf between.

572 Canoeing Medal (1956)

1964. Olympic Games—Romanian Gold Medal Awards. Medals in brown and bistre (Nos. 3218/19 and 3226/7 in sepia and gold). (a) Perf.

3212	**572**	20b. red and blue	50	10
3213	-	30b. green and blue	60	15
3214	-	35b. turquoise and blue	70	20
3215	-	40b. lilac and blue	95	25
3216	-	55b. orange and blue	1·20	30
3217	-	1l.20 green and blue	1·50	35
3218	-	1l.35 brown and blue	1·90	45
3219	-	1l.55 mauve and blue	2·40	45

(b) Imperf. Colours changed and new values.

3220	**572**	20b. orange and blue	20	20
3221	-	30b. turquoise and blue	50	35
3222	-	35b. green and blue	50	35
3223	-	40b. green and blue	80	55
3224	-	55b. red and blue	80	55
3225	-	1l.60 lilac and blue	2·40	1·90
3226	-	2l. mauve and blue	3·00	2·40
3227	-	2l.40 brown and blue	4·00	3·25
MS3228		140×110 mm. 10l. gold, blue and blue (no gum)	14·50	11·00

MEDALS: 30b. Boxing (1956); 35b. Pistol-shooting (1956); 40b. High-jumping (1960); 55b. Wrestling (1960); 1l.20, 1l.60, Rifle-shooting (1960); 1l.35, 2l. High-jumping (1964); 1l.55, 2l.40, Throwing the javelin (1964). HORIZ: 10l. Tokyo gold medal and world map.

573 Strawberries

1964. Forest Fruit. Multicoloured.

3229	5b. Type **573**	20	10
3230	35b. Blackberries	30	10
3231	40b. Raspberries	50	15
3232	55b. Rosehips	60	15
3233	1l.20 Blueberries	1·20	20
3234	1l.35 Cornelian cherries	1·50	20
3235	1l.55 Hazel nuts	1·60	20
3236	2l.55 Cherries	2·10	30

574 "Syncom 3"

1965. Space Navigation. Multicoloured.

3237	30b. Type **574**	30	10
3238	40b. "Syncom 3" (different)	50	10
3239	55b. "Ranger 7" (horiz)	80	15
3240	1l. "Ranger 7" (different) (horiz)	95	20
3241	1l.20 "Voskhod 1" (horiz)	1·50	20
3242	5l. Konstantin Feoktistov, Vladimir Komarov and Boris Yegorov (cosmonauts) and "Voskhod 1" (52×29 mm)	3·50	1·20

575 U.N. Headquarters, New York

1965. 20th Anniv of U.N.O.

3243	**575**	55b. gold, blue and red	70	20
3244	-	1l.60 multicoloured	1·20	45

DESIGN: 1l.60, Arms and U.N. emblem on Romanian flag.

576 Spur-thighed Tortoise

1965. Reptiles. Multicoloured.

3245	5b. Type **576**	15	10
3246	10b. Crimean lizard	20	10
3247	20b. Three-lined lizard	20	10
3248	40b. Snake-eyed skink	40	10
3249	55b. Slow worm	50	10
3250	60b. Sand viper	70	10
3251	1l. Arguta	85	20
3252	1l.20 Orsini's viper	95	20
3253	1l.35 European whip snake	1·50	20
3254	3l.25 Four-lined rat snake	3·00	45

577 Tabby Cat

1965. Domestic Cats. Multicoloured.

3255	5b. Type **577**	20	10
3256	10b. Ginger tomcat	30	10
3257	40b. White Persians (vert)	50	20
3258	55b. Kittens with shoe (vert)	70	10
3259	60b. Kitten with ball of wool (vert)	1·10	10
3260	75b. Cat and two kittens (vert)	1·50	15
3261	1l.35 Siamese (vert)	1·90	30
3262	3l.25 Heads of three cats (62×29 mm)	3·50	95

1965. Space Flight of "Ranger 9" (24.3.65). No. 3240 surch **RANGER 9 24-3-1965 5 Lei** and floral emblem over old value.

3263	5l. on 1l. multicoloured	29·00	29·00

579 Ion Bianu (philologist)

1965. Cultural Anniversaries. Portraits in sepia.

3264	**579**	40l. blue	40	10
3265	-	55b. ochre	40	10
3266	-	60b. purple	50	10
3267	-	1l. red	70	15
3268	-	1l.35 olive	95	20
3269	-	1l.75 red	1·60	45

PORTRAITS, etc: 40b. Type **579** (30th death anniv); 55b. Anton Bacalbasa (writer, birth cent); 60b. Vasile Conta (philosopher, 120th birth anniv); 1l. Jean Sibelius (composer, birth cent); 1l.35, Horace (Roman poet, birth bimillenary); 1l.75, Dante Alighieri (poet, 700th birth anniv).

580 I.T.U. Emblem and Symbols

1965. Centenary of I.T.U.

3270	**580**	1l.75 blue	1·60	45

581 Derdap Gorge (The Iron Gate)

1965. Inaug of Derdap Hydro-electric Project.

3271	**581**	30b. (25d.) green and grey	30	20
3272	-	55b. (50d.) red and grey	50	30
MS3273		103×80 mm. 80b., 1l.20, 100d., 150d. multicoloured (sold at 4l. or 500d.)	4·75	4·75

DESIGNS: 55b. Derap Dam; **MS**3273, Arms of Romania and Yugoslavia on alternate stamps with outline of dam superimposed over the four stamps.

582 Rifleman

1965. European Shooting Championships, Bucharest. Multicoloured. (a) Perf.

3274	20b. Type **582**	20	10
3275	40b. Prone rifleman	30	15
3276	55b. Pistol shooting	50	10
3277	1l. "Free" pistol shooting	95	20
3278	1l.60 Standing rifleman	1·50	20
3279	2l. Various marksmen	1·90	65

(b) Imperf. Colours changed and new values.

3280	40b. Prone rifleman	20	10
3281	55b. Pistol shooting	30	20
3282	1l. "Free" pistol shooting	70	30
3283	1l.60 Standing rifleman	1·10	45
3284	3l.25 Type **582**	1·90	95
3285	5l. Various marksmen	3·50	1·60

Apart from Type **582** the designs are horiz, the 2l. and 5l. being larger, 51½×28½ mm.

583 "Fat-Frumos and the Beast"

1965. Romanian Fairy Tales. Multicoloured.

3286	20b. Type **583**	40	10
3287	40b. "Fat-Frumos and Ileana Cosinzeana"	40	10
3288	55b. "Harap Alb" (horseman and bear)	50	10
3289	1l. "The Moralist Wolf"	95	10
3290	1l.35 "The Ox and the Calf"	1·50	20
3291	2l. "The Bear and the Wolf" (drawing a sledge)	1·90	35

584 Honey Bee on Flowers

1965. 20th International Bee-keeping Association Federation ("Apimondia") Congress, Bucharest.

3292	**584**	55b. black, red and yellow	70	20
3293	-	1l.60 multicoloured	1·70	30

DESIGN—HORIZ: 1l.60, Congress Hall.

585 Pavel Belyaev, Aleksei Leonov, "Voskhod 2" and Leonov in Space

1965. Space Achievements. Multicoloured.

3294	5b. "Proton 1"	30	15
3295	10b. "Sonda 3" (horiz)	40	30
3296	15b. "Molnia 1"	50	35
3297	1l.75 Type **585**	1·60	20
3298	2l.40 "Early Bird" satellite	2·40	30
3299	3l.20 "Gemini 3" and astronauts in capsule	4·00	45
3300	3l.25 "Mariner 4"	4·25	65
3301	5l. "Gemini 5" (horiz)	4·75	1·90

586 Marx and Lenin

1965. Socialist Countries' Postal Ministers' Congress, Peking.

3302	**586**	55b. multicoloured	95	45

587 Common Quail

1965. Migratory Birds. Multicoloured.

3303	5b. Type **587**	20	10
3304	10b. Eurasian woodcock	30	10
3305	20b. Common snipe	40	10
3306	40b. Turtle dove	50	10
3307	55b. Mallard	60	10
3308	60b. White fronted goose	70	15
3309	1l. Common crane	95	20
3310	1l.20 Glossy ibis	1·20	20
3311	1l.35 Mute swan	1·50	30
3312	3l.25 Eastern white pelican (32×73 mm)	3·00	95

588 V. Alecsandri

1965. 75th Death Anniv of Vasile Alecsandri (poet).

3313	**588**	55b. multicoloured	95	45

589 Zanzibar Water-lily

1965. Cluj Botanical Gardens. Multicoloured.

3314	5b. Bird-of-paradise flower (vert)	15	10
3315	10b. "Stanhopea tigrina" (orchid) (vert)	20	10
3316	20b. "Paphiopedilum insigne" (orchid) (vert)	25	10
3317	30b. Type **589**	30	10
3318	40b. "Ferocactus glaucescens" (cactus)	50	10
3319	55b. Tree-cotton	70	15
3320	1l. "Hibiscus rosa sinensis"	95	20
3321	1l.35 "Gloxinia hibrida" (vert)	1·50	20
3322	1l.75 Amazon water-lily	2·40	25
3323	2l.30 Hibiscus, water-lily, bird-of-paradise flower and botanical building (52×30 mm)	3·00	65

590 Running

1965. Spartacist Games. Multicoloured.

3324	55b. Type **590**	50	20
3325	1l.55 Football	1·20	30

3326 1l.75 Diving 1·40 35
3327 2l. Mountaineering (inscr "TURISM") 1·50 45
3328 5l. Canoeing (inscr "CAMPIONATELLE EUROPENE 1965") (horiz) 2·50 95

591 Pigeon and Horseman

592 Pigeon on TV Aerial

1965. Stamp Day.
3329 **591** 55b.+45b. blue & mve 70 10
3330 **592** 1l. brown and green 80 30
3331 - 1l.75 brown and green 1·90 45
DESIGN: As Type **592**: 1l.75, Pigeon in flight.

593 Chamois

1965. "Hunting Trophies".
3332 **593** 55b. brown, yell & mve 50 10
3333 - 1l. brown, green and red 95 20
3334 - 1l.60 brown, blue & orange 1·60 30
3335 - 1l.75 brown, red & green 1·90 35
3336 - 3l.20 multicoloured 2·40 85
DESIGNS—37×23 mm: 1l. Brown bear; 1l.60, Red deer stag; 1l.75, Wild boar. 49×37½ mm: 3l.20, Trophy and antlers of red deer.

594 Dachshund

1965. Hunting Dogs. Multicoloured.
3337 5b. Type **594** 10 10
3338 10b. Spaniel 20 10
3339 40b. Retriever with eurasian woodcock 40 10
3340 55b. Fox terrier 60 10
3341 60b. Red setter 95 20
3342 75b. White setter 1·50 20
3343 1l.55 Pointers 2·40 45
3344 3l.25 Duck-shooting with retriever 3·50 1·60
SIZES: DIAMOND—47½×47½ mm: 10b. to 75b. HORIZ—43½×29 mm: 1l.55, 3l.25.

595 Pawn and Globe

1966. World Chess Championships, Cuba. Multicoloured.
3345 20b. Type **595** 50 10
3346 40b. Jester and bishop 60 10
3347 55b. Knight and rook 85 15
3348 1l. As No. 3347 1·50 20
3349 1l.60 Type **595** 2·40 30
3350 3l.25 As No. 3346 4·00 1·90

596 Tractor, Corn and Sun

1966. Co-operative Farming Union Congress.
3351 **596** 55b. green and yellow 70 45

597 G. Gheorghiu-Dej

1966. First Death Anniv of Gheorghe Gheorghiu-Dej (President 1961–65).
3352 **597** 55b. black and gold 70 45
MS3353 90×100 mm. 5l. Portrait as in Type **597** 5·75 5·75

598 Congress Emblem

1966. Communist Youth Union Congress.
3354 **598** 55b. red and yellow 70 45

599 Dance of Moldova

1966. Romanian Folk-dancing.
3355 **599** 30b. black and purple 50 10
3356 - 40b. black and red 70 35
3357 - 55b. black and turquoise 95 10
3358 - 1l. black and lake 1·30 10
3359 - 1l.60 black and blue 1·90 30
3360 - 2l. black and green 4·25 2·30
DANCES OF: 40b. Oltenia; 55b. Maramures; 1l. Muntenia; 1l.60, Banat; 2l. Transylvania.

600 Footballers

1966. World Cup Football Championship, England.
3361 **600** 5b. multicoloured 30 10
3362 - 10b. multicoloured 40 10
3363 - 15b. multicoloured 60 15
3364 - 55b. multicoloured 1·10 20
3365 - 1l.75 multicoloured 2·50 45
3366 - 4l. multicoloured 4·50 4·50
MS3367 85×100 mm. 10l. gold, black and blue 11·50 11·50
DESIGNS: 10b. to 1l.75, Various footballing scenes; 4l. Jules Rimet Cup. 33×46 mm—10l. As No. 3366.

601 "Agriculture and Industry"

1966. Trade Union Congress, Bucharest.
3368 **601** 55b. multicoloured 70 45

602 Red-breasted Flycatcher

1966. Song Birds. Multicoloured.
3369 5b. Type **602** 30 10
3370 10b. Red crossbill 50 10
3371 15b. Great reed warbler 70 10
3372 20b. Common redstart 80 15
3373 55b. European robin 1·30 15
3374 1l.20 Bluethroat 1·60 20
3375 1l.55 Yellow wagtail 2·40 35
3376 3l.20 Penduline tit 4·25 2·75

603 "Venus 3"

1966. Space Achievements. Multicoloured.
3377 10b. Type **603** 50 10
3378 20b. "FR 1" satellite 60 20
3379 1l.60 "Luna 9" 3·50 30
3380 5l. "Gemini 6" and "7" 5·75 2·30

604 Urechia Nestor (historian)

1966. Cultural Anniversaries.
3381 - 5b. blue, black and green 10 10
3382 - 10b. green, black and red 10 10
3383 **604** 20b. purple, black & green 10 10
3384 - 40b. brown, black & blue 30 10
3385 - 55b. green, black & brn 40 10
3386 - 1l. violet, black and bistre 85 20
3387 - 1l.35 olive, black & blue 1·20 30
3388 - 1l.60 purple, blk & green 1·90 55
3389 - 1l.75 purple, blk & orge 1·20 30
3390 - 3l.25 lake, black and blue 1·90 55
PORTRAITS: 5b. George Cosbuc (poet, birth cent); 10b. Gheorghe Sincai (historian, 150th death anniv); 20b. Type **604** (birth cent); 40b. Aron Pumnul (linguist, death cent); 55b. Stefan Luchian (painter, 50th death anniv); 1l. Sun Yat-sen (Chinese statesman, birth cent); 1l.35, Gottfried Leibnitz (philosopher, 250th death anniv); 1l.60, Romain Rolland (writer, birth cent); 1l.75, Ion Ghica (revolutionary and diplomat, 150th birth anniv); 3l.25, Constantin Cantacuzino (historian, 250th death anniv).

605 "House" (after Petrascu)

1966. Paintings in National Gallery, Bucharest. Multicoloured.
3391 5b. Type **605** 15 15
3392 10b. "Peasant Girl" (Grigorescu) (vert) 20 15
3393 20b. "Midday Rest" (Rescu) 50 20
3394 55b. "Portrait of a Man" (Van Eyck) (vert) 1·20 30
3395 1l.55 "The 2nd Class Compartment" (Daumier) 4·75 55
3396 3l.25 "The Blessing" (El Greco) (vert) 6·75 6·00

606 "Hottonia palustris"

1966. Aquatic Flora. Multicoloured.
3397 5b. Type **606** 20 10
3398 10b. "Ceratophyllum submersum" 30 10
3399 20b. "Aldrovanda vesiculosa" 40 10
3400 40b. "Callitriche verna" 60 10
3401 55b. "Vallisneria spiralis" 70 15
3402 1l. "Elodea canadensis" 1·50 20
3403 1l.55 "Hippuris vulgaris" 2·10 35
3404 3l.25 "Myriophyllum spicatum" (28×49½ mm) 4·00 2·30

607 Diagram showing one metre in relation to quadrant of Earth

1966. Centenary of Metric System in Romania.
3405 **607** 55b. blue and brown 50 10
3406 - 1l. violet and green 80 35
DESIGN: 1l. Metric abbreviations and globe.

608 Putna Monastery

1966. 500th Anniv of Putna Monastery.
3407 **608** 2l. multicoloured 1·60 55

609 "Medicine"

1966. Centenary of Romanian Academy.
3408 **609** 40b. multicoloured 20 10
3409 - 55b. multicoloured 30 15
3410 - 1l. brown, gold and blue 60 20
3411 - 3l. brown, gold & yellow 2·10 1·40
DESIGNS—As Type **609**: 55b. "Science" (formula). 22½×33½ mm: 1l. Gold medal. 67×27 mm: 3l. Ion Radulescu (writer), Mihail Kogalniceanu (historian) and Traian Savulescu (biologist).

610 Crayfish

1966. Crustaceans and Molluscs. Multicoloured.
3412 5b. Type **610** 20 10
3413 10b. Netted nassa (vert) 30 10
3414 20b. Marbled rock crab 40 10
3415 40b. "Campylaea trizona" (snail) 50 15
3416 55b. Lucorum helix 70 20
3417 1l.35 Mediterranean blue mussel 1·70 30
3418 1l.75 Stagnant pond snail 2·10 35
3419 3l.25 Swan mussel 3·50 2·30

611 Bucharest and Mail Coach

1966. Stamp Day.
3420 **611** 55b.+45b. mult 1·50 75
No. 3420 is a two-part design arranged horiz, imperf between.

612 "Ursus spelaeus"

1966. Prehistoric Animals.
3421 **612** 5b. blue, brown and green 30 10
3422 - 10b. violet, bistre & green 40 10
3423 - 15b. brown, purple & green 50 15
3424 - 55b. violet, bistre & green 95 20
3425 - 1l.55 blue, brown & grn 2·50 30
3426 - 4l. mauve, bistre & green 4·75 2·30
ANIMALS: 10b. "Mamuthus trogontherii"; 15b. "Bison priscus"; 55b. "Archidiscodon"; 1l.55, "Megaceros eurycerus". (43×27 mm): 4l. "Deinotherium gigantissimum".

613 "Sputnik 1" orbiting Globe

1967. Ten Years of Space Achievements. Multicoloured.

3427		10b. Type **613** (postage)	20	10
3428		20b. Yuri Gagarin and "Vostok 1"	30	10
3429		25b. Valentina Tereshkova ("Vostok 6")	40	10
3430		40b. Andrian Nikolaev and Pavel Popovich ("Vostok 3" and "4")	60	10
3431		55b. Aleksei Leonov in space ("Voskhod 2")	85	15
3432		1l.20 "Early Bird" (air)	1·20	30
3433		1l.55 Photo transmission ("Mariner 4")	1·50	30
3434		3l.25 Space rendezvous ("Gemini 6" and "7")	1·90	75
3435		5l. Space link up ("Gemini 8")	3·00	2·75

614 Barn Owl

1967. Birds of Prey. Multicoloured.

3442		10b. Type **614**	50	10
3443		20b. Eagle owl	60	10
3444		40b. Saker falcon	60	10
3445		55b. Egyptian vulture	70	10
3446		75b. Osprey	80	20
3447		1l. Griffon vulture	1·60	20
3448		1l.20 Lammergeier	1·90	45
3449		1l.75 Cinereous	2·40	1·90

615 "Washerwoman" (after I. Steriadi)

1967. Paintings.

3450	-	10b. blue, gold and red	20	10
3451	**615**	20b. green, gold & ochre	30	20
3452	-	40b. red, gold and blue	60	20
3453	-	1l.55 purple, gold & blue	1·20	45
3454	-	3l.20 brown, gold & brn	3·00	65
3455	-	5l. brown, gold & orange	4·25	3·00

PAINTINGS—VERT: 10b. "Model in Fancy Dress" (I. Andreescu); 40b. "Peasants Weaving" (S. Dimitrescu); 1l.55, "Venus and Cupid" (L. Cranach); 5l. "Haman beseeching Esther" (Rembrandt). HORIZ: 3l.20, "Hercules and the Lion" (Rubens).

616 Woman's Head

1967. Tenth Anniv of C. Brancusi (sculptor). Sculptures.

3456	**616**	5b. brown, yellow and red	10	10
3457	-	10b. black, green & violet	20	10
3458	-	20b. black, green and red	25	10
3459	-	40b. black, red & green	30	20
3460	-	55b. black, olive and blue	70	30
3461	-	1l.20 brown, violet and orange	1·60	35
3462	-	3l.25 black, green and mauve	3·00	1·40

DESIGNS—HORIZ: 10b. Sleeping muse; 40b. "The Kiss"; 3l.25, Gate of Kisses, Targujiu. VERT: 20b. "The Endless Column"; 55b. Seated woman; 1l.20, "Miss Pogany".

617 Copper and Silver Coins of 1867

1967. Centenary of Romanian Monetary System.

3463	**617**	55b. multicoloured	50	45
3464	-	1l.20 multicoloured	1·10	1·00

DESIGN: 1l.20, Obverse and reverse of modern silver coin (1966).

618 "Infantryman" (Nicolae Grigorescu)

1967. 90th Anniv of Independence.

3465	**618**	55b. multicoloured	1·60	1·60

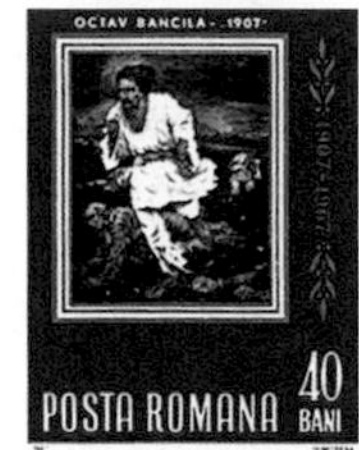

619 Peasants attacking (after Octav Bancila)

1967. 60th Anniv of Peasant Rising.

3466	**619**	40b. multicoloured	70	65
3467	-	1l.55 multicoloured	1·60	1·60

DESIGN—HORIZ: 1l.55, Peasants marching (after S. Luchian).

620 "Centaurca pinnatifida"

1967. Carpathian Flora. Multicoloured.

3468		20b. Type **620**	20	20
3469		40b. "Erysimum transsilvanicum"	30	20
3470		55b. "Aquilegia transsilvanica"	50	20
3471		1l.20 Alpine violet	1·50	10
3472		1l.75 Bellflower	1·70	20
3473		4l. Mountain avens (horiz)	4·00	2·30

621 Towers, Sibiu

1967. Historic Monuments and International Tourist Year. Multicoloured.

3474		20b. Type **621**	50	20
3475		40b. Castle at Cris	70	20
3476		55b. Wooden church, Plopis	95	20
3477		1l.60 Ruins, Neamtului	1·60	30
3478		1l.75 Mogosoaia Palace, Bucharest	1·90	35
3479		2l.25 Church, Voronet	3·00	1·90
MS3480		101×89 mm. **662** 5l. blue, black and light blue. Imperf	4·75	4·75

No. 3479 is horiz, 48½×36 mm.

623 "Battle of Marasesti" (E. Stoica)

1967. 50th Anniv of Battles of Marasesti, Marasti and Oituz.

3481	**623**	55b. brown, blue and grey	95	65

624 Dinu Lipatti (composer and pianist)

1967. Cultural Anniversaries.

3482	**624**	10b. violet, blue and black	10	10
3483	-	20b. blue, brown & black	15	10
3484	-	40b. brown, turq & blk	20	10
3485	-	55b. brown, red and black	30	10
3486	-	1l.20 brown, olive & black	50	30
3487	-	1l.75 green, blue & black	1·10	85

DESIGNS: 10b. Type **624** (50th birth anniv); 20b. Alexandru Orascu (architect, 150th birth anniv); 40b. Grigore Antipa (biologist, birth cent); 55b. Mihail Kogalniceanu (politician and historian, 150th birth anniv); 1l.20, Jonathan Swift (satirist, 300th birth anniv); 1l.75, Marie Curie (physicist, birth cent).

625 Wrestling

1967. World Wrestling Championships, Bucharest. Designs showing wrestlers and globes.

3488	**625**	10b. multicoloured	10	10
3489	-	20b. mult (horiz)	20	10
3490	-	55b. multicoloured	30	10
3491	-	1l.20 multicoloured	95	20
3492	-	2l. multicoloured (horiz)	1·60	1·00

626 Inscription on Globe

1967. International Linguists' Congress, Bucharest.

3493	**626**	1l.60 ultramarine, red and blue	1·50	45

627 Academy

1967. Centenary of Book Academy, Bucharest.

3494	**627**	55b. grey, brown and blue	1·50	45

628 Dancing on Ice

1967. Winter Olympic Games, Grenoble. Multicoloured.

3495		20b. Type **628**	10	10
3496		40b. Skiing	20	10
3497		55b. Bobsleighing	30	10
3498		1l. Downhill skiing	70	20
3499		1l.55 Ice hockey	95	30
3500		2l. Games emblem	1·50	45
3501		2l.30 Ski jumping	1·90	1·10
MS3502		80×100 mm. 5l. Bobsleighing. Imperf	6·25	6·00

629 Curtea de Arges Monastery

1967. 450th Anniv of Curtea de Arges Monastery.

3503	**629**	55b. multicoloured	95	45

630 Karl Marx and Title Page

1967. Centenary of Karl Marx's "Das Kapital".

3504	**630**	40b. black, yellow and red	70	45

631 Lenin

1967. 50th Anniv of October Revolution.

3505	**631**	1l.20 black, gold and red	1·20	45

632 Arms of Romania

633 Telephone Dial and Map

1967. (a) T **632**.

3506	**632**	40b. blue	50	10
3507	**632**	55b. yellow	70	20
3508	**632**	1l.60 red	1·60	30

(b) T **633** and similar designs.

3509	-	5b. green	10	10
3510	-	10b. red	10	10
3511	-	20b. grey	10	10
3512	-	35b. blue	10	10
3513	-	40b. blue	20	10
3514	-	50b. orange	20	10
3515	-	55b. red	30	10
3516	-	60b. brown	30	10
3517	-	1l. green	40	10
3518	-	1l.20 violet	50	10
3519	-	1l.35 blue	60	10
3520	-	1l.50 red	70	10
3521	-	1l.55 brown	80	10
3522	-	1l.75 green	85	10
3523	-	2l. yellow	95	10
3524	-	2l.40 blue	1·10	10
3525	**633**	3l. turquoise	1·20	20
3526	-	3l.20 ochre	1·40	20
3527	-	3l.25 blue	1·60	20
3528	-	4l. mauve	1·60	20
3529	-	5l. violet	1·90	20

DESIGNS—23×17 mm: 5b. "Carpati" lorry; 20b. Railway Travelling Post Office coach; 35b. Zlin Z-226A Akrobat plane; 60b. Electric parcels truck. As Type **633**: 1l.20, Motorcoach; 1l.35, Mil Mi-4 helicopter; 1l.75, Lakeside highway; 2l. Postal van; 3l.20, Ilyushin Il-18 airliner; 4l. Electric train; 5l. Telex instrument and world map. 17×23 mm: 10b. Posthorn and telephone emblem; 40b. Power pylons; 50b. Telephone handset; 55b. Dam. As T **633** but vert: 1l. Diesel-electric train; 1l.50, Trolley-bus; 1l.55, Radio station; 2l.40, T.V. relay station; 3l.25, Liner "Transylvania".

No. 3525 also commemorates the 40th anniv of the automatic telephone service.

See also Nos. 3842/57.

634 "Crossing the River Buzau" (lithograph by Raffet) (image scaled to 52% of original size)

1967. Stamp Day.

3530	**634**	55b.+45b. blue and ochre	1·50	65

635 Monorail Train and Globe

1967. World Fair, Montreal. Multicoloured.

3531	55b. Type **635**		20	10
3532	1l. Expo emblem within atomic symbol		50	10
3533	1l.60 Gold cup and world map		70	20
3534	2l. Expo emblem		1·30	75

636 Arms and Industrial Scene

1967. 20th Anniv of Republic. Multicoloured.

3535	40b. Type **636**	20	10
3536	55b. Arms of Romania	30	10
3537	1l.60 Romanian flag (34×48 mm)	95	30
3538	1l.75 Arms and cultural emblems	1·80	1·20

637 I.A.R. 817 Flying Ambulance

1968. Air. Romanian Aviation.

3539	-	40b. multicoloured	20	10
3540	**637**	55b. multicoloured	30	10
3541	-	1l. multicoloured	50	10
3542	-	2l.40 multicoloured	1·60	65

DESIGNS—VERT: 40b. Antonov An-2 biplane spraying crops; 1l. "Aviasan" emblem and airliner; 2l.40, Mircea Zorileanu (pioneer aviator) and biplane.

638 "Angelica and Medor" (S. Ricci)

1968. Paintings in Romanian Galleries. Multicoloured.

3543	40b. "Young Woman" (Misu Pop) (vert)	50	20
3544	55b. "Little Girl in Red Scarf" (N. Grigorescu) (vert)	70	30
3545	1l. "Old Nicholas, the Cobza-player" (S. Luchian) (vert)	1·20	45
3546	1l.60 "Man with Skull" (Dierick Bouts) (vert)	1·50	45
3547	2l.40 Type **638**	1·90	65
3548	3l.20 "Ecce Homo" (Titian) (vert)	4·00	5·00
MS3549	75×90 mm. 5l. As 3l.20. Imperf	11·50	11·50

See also Nos. 353/8, 3631/**MS**37, 3658/**MS**64, 3756/**MS**62 and 3779/**MS**85.

639 "Anemones" (Luchian)

1968. Birth Centenary of Stefan Luchian (painter). Sheet 90×100 mm. Imperf.

MS3550	10l. multicoloured	11·50	11·50

640 Human Rights Emblem

1968. Human Rights Year.

3551	**640**	1l. multicoloured	1·20	45

641 W.H.O. Emblem

1968. 20th Anniv of W.H.O.

3552	**641**	1l.60 multicoloured	1·60	45

642 "The Hunter" (after N. Grigorescu)

1968. Hunting Congress, Mamaia.

3553	**642**	1l.60 multicoloured	1·60	45

643 Pioneers and Liberation Monument

1968. Young Pioneers. Multicoloured.

3554	5b. Type **643**	20	10
3555	40b. Receiving scarves	25	10
3556	55b. With models	30	10
3557	1l. Operating radio sets	60	10
3558	1l.60 Folk-dancing	95	30
3559	2l.40 In camp	1·30	75

644 Prince Mircea

1968. 550th Death Anniv of Prince Mircea (the Old).

3560	**644**	1l.60 multicoloured	1·60	45

645 Ion Ionescu de la Brad (scholar)

1968. Cultural Anniversaries.

3561	**645**	40b. multicoloured	30	20
3562	-	55b. multicoloured	60	30

PORTRAITS AND ANNIVS: 40b. Type **645** (150th birth anniv); 55b. Emil Racovita (scientist, birth cent).

646 "Pelargonium zonale"

1968. Garden Geraniums. Multicoloured.

3563	10b. Type **646**	10	10
3564	20b. "Pelargonium zonale" (orange)	15	10
3565	40b. "Pelargonium zonale" (red)	20	10
3566	55b. "Pelargonium zonale" (pink)	30	10
3567	60b. "Pelargonium grandiflorum" (red)	50	10
3568	1l.20 "Pelargonium peltatum" (red)	70	20
3569	1l.35 "Pelargonium peltatum" (pink)	95	20
3570	1l.60 "Pelargonium grandiflorum" (pink)	1·50	95

647 "Nicolae Balcescu" (Gheorghe Tattarescu)

1968. 120th Anniv of 1848 Revolution. Paintings. Multicoloured.

3571	55b. Type **647**	60	10
3572	1l.20 "Avram Iancu" (B. Iscovescu)	1·10	20
3573	1l.60 "Vasile Alecsandri" (N. Livaditti)	2·10	95

648 Throwing the Javelin

1968. Olympic Games, Mexico. Multicoloured.

3574	10b. Type **648**	10	10
3575	20b. Diving	10	10
3576	40b. Volleyball	20	15
3577	55b. Boxing	40	15
3578	60b. Wrestling	60	15
3579	1l.20 Fencing	70	20
3580	1l.35 Punting	95	30
3581	1l.60 Football	1·60	45
MS3582	77×90 mm. 5l. running. Imperf	5·75	5·75

1968. Paintings in the Fine Arts Museum, Bucarest. Multicoloured.

3583	10b. "The Awakening of Romania" (G. Tattarescu) (28×49 mm)	10	10
3584	20b. "Composition" (Teodorescu Sionion)	20	10
3585	35b. "The Judgement of Paris" (H. van Balen)	30	10
3586	60b. "The Mystical Betrothal of St. Catherine" (L. Sustris)	60	20
3587	1l.75 "Mary with the Child Jesus" (J. van Bylert)	1·90	45
3588	3l. "The Summer" (J. Jordaens)	4·25	2·30

649 F.I.A.P. Emblem within "Lens"

1968. 20th Anniv of International Federation of Photographic Art (F.I.A.P.).

3589	**649**	1l.60 multicoloured	1·50	45

650 Academy and Harp

1968. Centenary of Georgi Enescu Philharmonic Academy.

3590	**650**	55b. multicoloured	80	45

651 Triumph of Trajan (Roman metope)

1968. Historic Monuments.

3591	**651**	10b. green, blue and red	20	10
3592	-	40b. blue, brown and red	30	10
3593	-	55b. violet, brown & green	50	10
3594	-	1l.20 purple, grey and ochre	95	20
3595	-	1l.55 blue, green & pur	1·50	30
3596	-	1l.75 brown, bistre and orange	1·90	95

DESIGNS—HORIZ: 40b. Monastery Church, Moldovita; 55b. Monastery. Church, Cozia; 1l.20, Tower and Church, Tirgoviste; 1l.55, Palace of Culture, Jassy; 1l.75, Corvinus Castle, Hunedoara.

652 Old Bucharest (18th-cent painting)

1968. Stamp Day.

3597	**652**	55b.+45b. multicoloured	1·70	95

653 Mute Swan

1968. Fauna of Nature Reservations. Multicoloured.

3598	10b. Type **653**	10	10
3599	20b. Black-winged stilt	20	10
3600	40b. Common shelduck	30	10
3601	55b. Great egret	50	10
3602	60b. Golden eagle	70	10
3603	1l.20 Great bustard	95	30
3604	1l.35 Chamois	1·20	30
3605	1l.60 European bison	1·90	65

654 "Entry of Michael the Brave into Alba Julia" (E. Stoica)

1968. 50th Anniv of Union of Transylvania with Romania. Multicoloured.

3606	55b. Type **654**	40	20
3607	1l. "Union Dance" (T. Aman)	80	20
3608	1l.75 "Alba Julia Assembly"	1·50	55
MS3609	121×111 mm. Nos. 3606/8. Imperf. (Sold at 4l.)	4·00	4·00

655 Neamtz Costume (female)

1968. Provincial Costumes (1st series). Multicoloured.

3610	5b. Type **655**	10	10
3611	40b. Neamtz (male)	30	10
3612	55b. Hunedoara (female)	70	15
3613	1l. Hunedoara (male)	95	20
3614	1l.60 Brasov (female)	1·50	30
3615	2l.40 Brasov (male)	2·10	1·40

See also Nos. 3617/22.

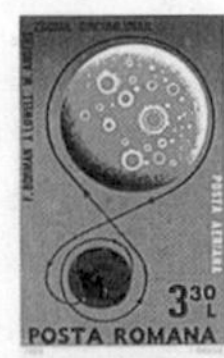

656 Earth, Moon and Orbital Track of "Apollo 8"

1969. Air. Flight of "Apollo 8" around the Moon.

3616	**656**	3l.30 black, silver & blue	2·40	2·30

1969. Provincial Costumes (2nd series). As T **655**. Multicoloured.

3617	5b. Doli (female)	10	10
3618	40b. Doli (male)	30	10
3619	55b. Arges (female)	70	15
3620	1l. Arges (male)	95	20
3621	1l.60 Timisoara (female)	1·50	30
3622	2l.40 Timisoara (male)	2·10	1·40

657 Fencing

1969. Sports.

3623	**657**	10b. grey, black & brown	10	10
3624	-	20b. grey, black and violet	10	10
3625	-	40b. grey, black and blue	15	10
3626	-	55b. grey, black and red	20	10
3627	-	1l. grey, black and green	40	10
3628	-	1l.20 grey, black and blue	50	15
3629	-	1l.60 grey, black and red	80	30
3630	-	2l.40 grey, black & green	1·50	95

DESIGNS: 20b. Throwing the javelin; 40b. Canoeing; 55b. Boxing; 1l. Volleyball; 1l.20, Swimming; 1l.60, Wrestling; 2l.40, Football.

1969. Nude Paintings in the National Gallery. As T **638**. Multicoloured.

3631	10b. "Nude" (C. Tattarescu)	10	10
3632	20b. "Nude" (T. Pallady)	10	10
3633	35b. "Nude" (N. Tonitza)	20	10
3634	60b. "Venus and Cupid" (Flemish School)	50	20
3635	1l.75 "Diana and Endymion" (M. Liberi)	1·90	95
3636	3l. "The Three Graces" (J. H. von Achen)	4·00	2·30
MS3637	73×91 mm. 5l. Designs as 1l.75	5·50	5·50

SIZES—36×49 mm: 10b., 35b., 60b., 1l.75. 27×49 mm: 3l. 49×36 mm: 20b.

658 "Soyuz 4" and "Soyuz 5"

1969. Air. Space Link-up of "Soyuz 4" and "Soyuz 5".

3638	**658**	3l.30 multicoloured	2·40	2·30

659 I.L.O. Emblem

1969. 50th Anniv of International Labour Office.

3639	**659**	55b. multicoloured	95	45

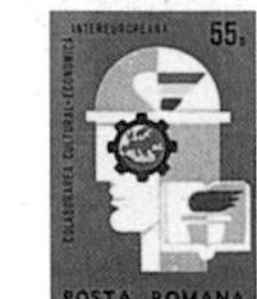

660 Stylized Head

1969. Inter-European Cultural Economic Co-operation.

3640	**660**	55b. multicoloured	50	45
3641	**660**	1l.50 multicoloured	1·90	1·90

661 Posthorn

1969. Postal Ministers' Conference, Bucharest.

3642	**661**	55b. deep blue and blue	70	45

662 Referee introducing Boxers

1969. European Boxing Championships, Bucharest. Multicoloured.

3643	35b. Type **662**	20	10
3644	40b. Sparring	30	10
3645	55b. Leading with punch	50	10
3646	1l.75 Declaring the winner	1·50	95

663 "Apollo 9" and Module over Earth

1969. Air. "Apollo" Moon Flights. Multicoloured.

3647	60b. Type **663**	30	10
3648	2l.40 "Apollo 10" and module approaching Moon (vert)	1·90	35

664 Lesser Purple Emperor

1969. Butterflies and Moths. Multicoloured.

3649	5b. Type **664**	10	10
3650	10b. Willow-herb hawk moth	10	10
3651	20b. Eastern pale clouded yellow	10	10
3652	40b. Large tiger moth	20	10
3653	55b. Pallas's fritillary	50	10
3654	1l. Jersey tiger moth	60	10
3655	1l.20 Orange-tip	95	30
3656	2l.40 Meleager's blue	2·40	1·60

665 Astronaut and Module on Moon

1969. Air. First Man on the Moon.

3657	**665**	3l.30 multicoloured	2·40	2·30

1969. Paintings in the National Gallery, Bucharest. Multicoloured. As T **638**.

3658	10b. "Venetian Senator" (School of Tintoretto)	10	10
3659	20b. "Sofia Kretzulescu" (G. Tattarescu)	10	10
3660	35b. "Philip IV" (Velasquez)	30	10
3661	35b. "Man Reading" (Memling)	70	15
3662	1l.75 "Lady D'Aguesseau" (Vigee-Lebrun)	1·50	30
3663	3l. "Portrait of a Woman" (Rembrandt)	3·50	1·90
MS3664	91×78 mm. 5l. "Return of the Prodigal Son" (Licino). Imperf	4·75	4·75

666 Communist Flag

1969. Tenth Romanian Communist Party Congress.

3665	**666**	55b. multicoloured	80	45

667 Symbols of Learning

1969. National "Economic Achievements" Exhibition, Bucharest. Multicoloured.

3666	35b. Type **667**	20	10
3667	40b. Symbols of Agriculture and Science	30	10
3668	1l.75 Symbols of Industry	1·50	35

668 Liberation Emblem

1969. 25th Anniv of Liberation. Multicoloured.

3669	10b. Type **668**	20	10
3670	55b. Crane and trowel	30	15
3671	60b. Flags on scaffolding	50	20

669 Juggling on Trick-cycle

1969. Romanian State Circus. Multicoloured.

3672	10b. Type **669**	10	10
3673	20b. Clown	10	10
3674	35b. Trapeze artists	30	10
3675	60b. Equestrian act	50	10
3676	1l.75 High-wire act	95	20
3677	3l. Performing tiger	1·90	1·10

670 Forces' Memorial

1969. Army Day and 25th Anniv of People's Army.

3678	**670**	55b. black, gold and red	70	45

671 Electric Train (1965) and Steam Locomotive "Calugareni" (1869)

1969. Centenary of Romanian Railways.

3679	**671**	55b. multicoloured	80	45

672 "Courtyard" (M. Bouquet) (⅔-size illustration)

1969. Stamp Day.

3680	**672**	55b.+45b. multicoloured	1·50	95

673 Branesti Mask

1969. Folklore Masks. Multicoloured.

3681	40b. Type **673**	30	10
3682	55b. Tudora mask	40	10
3683	1l.55 Birsesti mask	95	30
3684	1l.75 Rudaria mask	1·30	75

674 "Apollo 12" above Moon

1969. Moon Landing of "Apollo 12".

3685	**674**	1l.50 multicoloured	1·50	1·40

675 "Three Kings" (Voronet Monastery)

1969. Frescoes from Northern Moldavian Monasteries (1st series). Multicoloured.

3686	10b. Type **675**	10	10
3687	20b. "Three Kings" (Sucevita)	20	10
3688	35b. "Holy Child in Manger" (Voronet)	30	10
3689	60b. "Ship" (Sucevita) (vert)	60	15
3690	1l.75 "Walled City" (Moldovita)	1·70	35
3691	3l. "Pastoral Scene" (Voronet) (vert)	3·50	1·90

See also Nos. 3736/42 and 3872/8.

676 "Old Mother Goose", Capra

1969. New Year. Children's Celebrations. Multicoloured.

3692	40b. Type **676**	20	10
3693	55b. Decorated tree, Sorcova	30	10
3694	1l.50 Drummers, Buhaiul	1·20	20
3695	2l.40 Singer and bellringer, Plugusorul	1·50	75

677 Players and Emblem

1970. World Ice Hockey Championships (Groups B and C), Bucharest. Multicoloured.

3696	20b. Type **677**	10	10
3697	55b. Goalkeeper	30	10
3698	1l.20 Two players	85	15
3699	2l.40 Goalmouth melee	1·60	95

678 Small Pasque Flower

1970. Flowers. Multicoloured.

3700	5b. Type **678**	10	10
3701	10b. Yellow pheasant's-eye	10	10
3702	20b. Musk thistle	10	10
3703	40b. Dwarf almond	10	10
3704	55b. Dwarf bearded iris	10	10
3705	1l. Flax	50	10
3706	1l.20 Sage	70	10
3707	2l.40 Peony	3·00	1·10

679 Japanese Woodcut

1970. World Fair, Osaka, Japan. Expo 70. Multicoloured.

3714	20b. Type **679**	20	20
3715	1l. Japanese pagoda (29×92 mm)	1·20	65
MS3716	182×120 mm. 5l. As design of 1l.	5·75	5·75

The design on 1l. and 5l. is vert, 29×92 mm. On No. **MS**3716 the face value appears on the sheet and not the stamp.

680 B.A.C. One Eleven Series 475 Jetliner and Silhouettes of Aircraft

1970. 50th Anniv of Romanian Civil Aviation. Multicoloured.

3717	60b. Type **680**	50	20
3718	2l. Tail of B.A.C. One Eleven Series 475 and control tower at Otopeni Airport, Bucharest	1·20	55

681 Lenin

1970. Birth Centenary of Lenin.

3719	**681**	40b. multicoloured	70	45

682 "Camille" (Monet) and Maximum Card

1970. Maximafila Franco-Romanian Philatelic Exn, Bucharest.

3720	**682**	1l.50 multicoloured	1·90	5·50

683 "Prince Alexander Cuza" (Szathmary)

1970. 150th Birth Anniv of Prince Alexandru Cuza.

3721	**683**	55b. multicoloured	1·10	45

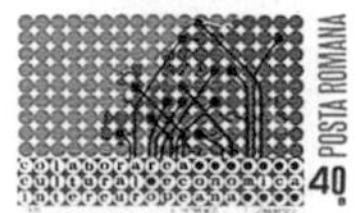
684 "Co-operation" Map

1970. Inter-European Cultural and Economic Co-operation.

3722	**684**	40b. green, brown & black	50	45
3723	**684**	1l.50 blue, brown & blk	95	95

685 Victory Monument, Bucharest

1970. 25th Anniv of Liberation.

3724	**685**	55b. multicoloured	95	45

686 Greek Silver Drachma, 5th cent B.C.

1970. Ancient Coins.

3725	**686**	10b. black and blue	10	10
3726	-	20b. black and red	20	10
3727	-	35b. bronze and green	30	10
3728	-	60b. black and brown	50	10
3729	-	1l.75 black and blue	1·20	10
3730	-	3l. black and red	2·40	1·10

DESIGNS—HORIZ: 20b. Getic-Dacian silver didrachm, 2nd—1st-cent B.C.; 35b. Copper sestertius of Trajan, 106 A.D.; 60b. Mircea ducat, 1400; 1l.75, Silver groschen of Stephen the Great, 1460. VERT: 3l. Brasov klippe-thaler, 1601.

687 Footballers and Ball

1970. World Cup Football Championship, Mexico.

3731	**687**	40b. multicoloured	20	10
3732	-	55b. multicoloured	30	10
3733	-	1l.75 multicoloured	1·20	35
3734	-	3l.30 multicoloured	2·10	1·00
MS3735		110×110 mm. 6l. Four designs with face values 1l.20, 1l.50, 1l.55 and 1l.75	4·75	4·75

DESIGNS: Nos. 3732/4, various football scenes as Type **687**.

1970. Frescoes from Northern Moldavian Monasteries (2nd series). As T **675**. Multicoloured.

3736	10b. "Prince Petru Rares and Family" (Moldovita)	10	10
3737	20b. "Metropolitan Grigore Rosca" (Voronet) (28×48 mm)	20	10
3738	40b. "Alexander the Good and Family" (Sucevita)	30	10
3739	55b. "The Last Judgement" (Voronet) (vert)	50	10
3740	1l.75 "The Last Judgement" (Voronet) (different)	1·20	30
3741	3l. "St. Anthony" (Voronet)	2·50	1·60
MS3742	90×77 mm. 5l. "Byzantine Manor" (Arbore)	4·75	4·75

688 "Apollo 13" Spashdown

1970. Air. Space Flight of "Apollo 13".

3743	**688**	1l.50 multicoloured	95	95

689 Engels

1970. 150th Birth Anniv of Friedrich Engels.

3744	**689**	1l.50 multicoloured	1·50	45

690 Exhibition Hall

1970. National Events. Multicoloured.

3745	35b. "Iron Gates" Dam	20	10
3746	55b. Freighter and flag	30	10
3747	1l.50 Type **690**	1·10	20

EVENTS: 35b. Danube navigation projects; 55b. 75th anniv of Romanian Merchant Marine; 1l.50, 1st International Fair, Bucharest.

691 New Headquarters Building

1970. New U.P.U. Headquarters Building, Berne.

3748	**691**	1l.50 blue and ultramarine	1·60	45

692 Education Year Emblem

1970. International Education Year.

3749	**692**	55b. plum, black and red	95	45

693 "Iceberg"

1970. Roses. Multicoloured.

3750	20b. Type **693**	10	10
3751	35b. "Wiener Charme"	10	10
3752	55b. "Pink Lustre"	20	10
3753	1l. "Piccadilly"	95	15
3754	1l.50 "Orange Delbard"	1·20	20
3755	2l.40 "Sibelius"	2·10	1·40

694 "Spaniel and Pheasant" (J. B. Oudry)

1970. Paintings in Romanian Galleries. Multicoloured.

3756	10b. "The Hunt" (D. Brandi) (38×50 mm)	10	10
3757	20b. Type **694**	10	10
3758	35b. "The Hunt" (Jan Fyt) (38×50 mm)	20	10
3759	60b. "After the Chase" (Jordaens) (As T **694**)	50	10
3760	1l.75 "The Game Dealer" (F. Snyders) (50×38 mm)	1·20	30
3761	3l. "The Hunt" (A. de Gryeff) (As T **694**)	2·10	95
MS3762	90×78 mm. 5l. Design as 1l.75	4·75	4·75

695 Refugee Woman and Child

1970. Danube Flood Victims (1st issue).

3763	**695**	55b. black, blue and green (postage)	20	10
3764	-	1l.50 multicoloured	80	30
3765	-	1l.75 multicoloured	1·50	75
3766	-	60b. black, drab and blue (air)	40	10

DESIGNS: 60b. Helicopter rescue; 1l.50, Red Cross post; 1l.75, Building reconstruction.

See also No. 3777.

696 U.N. Emblem

1970. 25th Anniv of United Nations.

3767	**696**	1l.50 multicoloured	1·50	45

697 Arab Horse

1970. Horses. Multicoloured.

3768	20b. Type **697**	10	10
3769	35b. American trotter	10	10
3770	55b. Ghidran	40	10
3771	1l. Hutul	95	10
3772	1l.50 Thoroughbred	1·50	30
3773	2l.40 Lippizaner	4·00	1·90

698 Beethoven

1970. Birth Bicentenary of Ludwig van Beethoven (composer).

3774	**698**	55b. multicoloured	1·60	45

699 "Mail-cart in the Snow" (E. Volkers)

1970. Stamp Day.

3775	**699**	55b.+45b. mult	1·60	1·10

700 Henri Coanda's Model Airplane

1970. Air. 60th Anniv of First Experimental Turbine-powered Airplane.

3776	**700**	60b. multicoloured	1·60	45

701 "The Flood" (abstract, Joan Miro)

1970. Danube Flood Victims (2nd issue).

3777	**701**	3l. multicoloured	3·00	2·75
MS3778		79×95 mm. **701** 5l. multicoloured. Imperf	7·25	7·25

702 "Sight" (G. Coques)

1970. Paintings from the Bruckenthal Museum, Sibiu. Multicoloured.

3779	10b. Type **702**	10	10
3780	20b. "Hearing"	10	10
3781	35b. "Smell"	20	10
3782	60b. "Taste"	50	10
3783	1l.75 "Touch"	95	20
3784	3l. Bruckenthal Museum	2·40	1·10
MS3785	90×78 mm. 5l. "View of Sibiu, 1808" (lithograph) (horiz)	5·75	5·75

Nos. 3779/83 show a series of pictures by Coques entitled "The Five Senses".

703 Vladimirescu (after Theodor Aman)

1971. 150th Death Anniv of Tudor Vladimirescu (Wallachian revolutionary).

3786	**703**	1l.50 multicoloured	1·60	45

704 "Three Races"

1971. Racial Equality Year.

3787	**704**	1l.50 multicoloured	1·60	45

705 Alsatian

1971. Dogs. Multicoloured.

3788	20b. Type **705**	10	10
3789	35b. Bulldog	10	10
3790	55b. Fox terrier	20	10
3791	1l. Setter	95	10
3792	1l.50 Cocker spaniel	1·50	45
3793	2l.40 Poodle	4·25	2·40

706 "Luna 16" leaving Moon

1971. Air. Moon Missions of "Luna 16" and "Luna 17". Multicoloured.

3794	3l.30 Type **706**	2·40	2·30
3795	3l.30 "Lunokhod 1" on Moon	2·40	2·30

707 Proclamation of the Commune

1971. Centenary of Paris Commune.

3796	**707**	40b. multicoloured	95	45

708 Astronaut and Moon Trolley

1971. Air. Moon Mission of "Apollo 14".

3797	**708**	3l.30 multicoloured	2·40	2·30

709 "Three Fists" Emblem and Flags

1971. Trade Union Congress, Bucharest.

3798	**709**	55b. multicoloured	95	45

710 "Toadstool" Rocks, Babele

1971. Tourism. Multicoloured.

3799	10b. Gorge, Cheile Bicazului (vert)	10	10
3800	40b. Type **710**	10	10
3801	55b. Winter resort, Poiana Brasov	20	10
3802	1l. Fishing punt and tourist launch, Danube delta	80	10
3803	1l.50 Hotel, Baile Sovata	1·40	20
3804	2l.40 Venus, Jupiter and Neptune Hotels, Black Sea (77×29 mm)	1·90	1·10

711 "Arrows"

1971. Inter-European Cultural Economic Co-operation. Multicoloured.

3805	55b. Type **711**	95	95
3806	1l.75 Stylized map of Europe	1·90	1·90

712 Museum Building

1971. Historical Museum, Bucharest.

3807	**712**	55b. multicoloured	70	45

713 "The Secret Printing-press" (S. Szonyi)

1971. 50th Anniv of Romanian Communist Party. Multicoloured.

3808	35b. Type **713**	20	10
3809	40b. Emblem and red flags (horiz)	20	10
3810	55b. "The Builders" (A. Anastasiu)	40	10

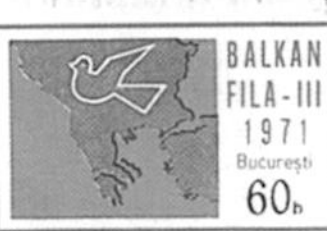

714 "Motra Tone" (Kole Idromeno)

1971. "Balkanfila III". International Stamp Exhibition, Bucharest. Multicoloured.

3811	1l.20+60b. Type **714**	1·20	1·10
3812	1l.20+60b. "Maid" (Vladimir Dimitrov-Maistora)	1·20	1·10
3813	1l.20+60b. "Rosa Botzaris" (Joseph Stieler)	1·20	1·10
3814	1l.20+60b. "Portrait of a Lady" (Katarina Ivanovic)	1·20	1·10
3815	1l.20+60b. "Agreseanca" (C. Popp de Szathmary)	1·20	1·10
3816	1l.20+60b. "Woman in Modern Dress" (Calli Ibrahim)	1·20	1·10
MS3817	90×79 mm. 5l. "Dancing the Hora" (Theodor Aman) (horiz)	4·75	4·75

Each stamp has a premium-carrying "tab" as shown in Type **714**.

715 Pomegranate

1971. Flowers. Multicoloured.

3818	20b. Type **715**	10	10
3819	35b. "Calceolus speciosum"	10	10
3820	55b. "Life jagra"	20	10
3821	1l. Blood-drop emlets	60	20
3822	1l.50 Dwarf morning glory	95	35
3823	2l.40 "Phyllocactus phyllanthoides" (horiz)	1·90	55

716 "Nude" (J. Iser)

1971. Paintings of Nudes. Multicoloured.

3824	10b. Type **716**	10	10
3825	20b. "Nude" (C. Ressu) (29×50 mm)	10	10
3826	35b. "Nude" (N. Grigorescu)	10	10
3827	60b. "Odalisque" (Delacroix) (horiz)	20	10
3828	1l.75 "Nude in a Landscape" (Renoir)	1·20	30
3829	3l. "Venus and Cupid" (Il Vecchio) (horiz)	2·10	95
MS3830	90×78 mm. 5l. "Venus and Amour" (Il Bronzino) (horiz)	7·25	7·25

717 Cosmonauts Patsaev, Dobrovolsky and Volkov (B5)

1971. Air. "Soyuz 11" Commemoration. Sheet 101×81 mm.

MS3831	6l. black and blue	11·50	11·50

718 Astronauts and Lunar Rover on Moon

1971. Air. Moon Flight of "Apollo 15".

3833	**718**	1l.50 multicoloured (blue background)	2·40	2·30

No. 3833 also exists imperforate, with background colour changed to green, from a restricted printing.

719 "Fishing Boats" (M. W. Arnold)

1971. Marine Paintings. Multicoloured.

3835	10b. "Coastal Storm" (B. Peters)	10	10
3836	20b. "Seascape" (I. Backhuysen)	10	10
3837	35b. "Boat in Stormy Seas" (A. van de Eertvelt)	30	10
3838	60b. Type **719**	50	10
3839	1l.75 "Seascape" (I. K. Aivazovsky)	1·20	35
3840	3l. "Fishing boats, Braila" (J. A. Steriadi)	2·50	75
MS3841	78×90 mm. 5l. "Venetian Fishing-boats" (N. Darascu) (vert)	5·75	5·75

1971. As Nos. 3517/29 and three new designs but in smaller format, 17×23 or 23×17 mm.

3842	1l. green	40	20
3843	1l.20 violet	50	20
3844	1l.35 blue	60	20
3845	1l.50 red	65	20
3846	1l.55 brown	70	20
3847	1l.75 green	80	20
3848	2l. yellow	85	20
3849	2l.40 blue	1·10	20
3850	3l. blue	1·30	20
3851	3l.20 brown	1·40	20
3852	3l.25 blue	1·50	20
3853	3l.60 blue	1·60	20
3854	4l. mauve	1·70	20
3855	4l.80 blue	1·90	20
3856	5l. violet	2·10	20
3857	6l. mauve	2·50	20

NEW DESIGNS—VERT: 3l.60, Clearing letter box; 4l.80, Postman on round; 6l. Postal Ministry, Bucharest.

720 "Neagoe Basarab" (fresco, Curtea de Arges)

1971. 450th Death Anniv of Prince Neagoe Basarab, Regent of Wallachia.

3858	**720**	60b. multicoloured	80	45

721 "T. Pallady" (self-portrait)

1971. Artists' Anniversaries.

3859	**721**	40b. multicoloured	10	10
3860	-	55b. black, stone and gold	20	10
3861	-	1l.50 black, stone & gold	70	10
3862	-	2l.40 multicoloured	1·60	45

DESIGNS (self-portraits: 40b. Type **721** (birth centenary); 55b. Benevenuto Cellini (400th death anniv); 1l.50, Jean Watteau (250th death anniv); 2l.40, Albrecht Durer (500th birth anniv).

722 Persian Text and Seal

1971. 2500th Anniv of Persian Empire.

3863	**722**	55b. multicoloured	95	45

723 Figure Skating

1971. Winter Olympic Games, Sapporo, Japan (1972). Multicoloured.

3864	10b. Type **723**	10	10
3865	20b. Ice-hockey	10	10
3866	40b. Biathlon	10	10
3867	55b. Bobsleighing	20	10
3868	1l.75 Downhill skiing	1·20	30
3869	3l. Games emblem	4·00	1·40
MS3870	78×90 mm. 5l. Symbolic flame (38×50 mm). Imperf	4·75	4·75

724 "Lady with Letter" (Sava Hentia)

1971. Stamp Day.

3871	**724**	1l.10+90b. mult	1·90	1·10

1971. Frescoes from Northern Moldavian Monasteries (3rd series). As T **675**. Multicoloured.

3872	10b. "St. George and The Dragon" (Moldovita) (vert)	10	10
3873	20b. "Three Kings and Angel" (Moldovita) (vert)	10	10

3874	40b. "The Crucifixion" (Moldovita) (vert)	10	10
3875	55b. "Trial" (Voronet) (vert)	20	10
3876	1l.75 "Death of a Martyr" (Voronet) (vert)	1·50	30
3877	3l. "King and Court" (Arborea)	3·00	1·90
MS3878	78×90 mm. 5l. Wall of frescoes, Voronet (vert)	4·75	4·75

725 Matei Millo (dramatist, 75th death anniv)

1971. Famous Romanians. Multicoloured.

3879	55b. Type **725**	30	20
3880	1l. Nicolae Iorga (historian, birth cent)	70	30

726 Magellan and Ships (450th death anniv)

1971. Scientific Anniversaries.

3881	**726**	40b. mauve, blue & green	20	10
3882	-	55b. blue, green and lilac	20	10
3883	-	1l. multicoloured	60	10
3884	-	1l.50 green, blue & brn	85	30

DESIGNS AND ANNIVERSARIES: 55b. Kepler and observatory (400th birth anniv); 1l. Gagarin, rocket and Globe (10th anniv of first manned space flight); 1l.50, Lord Rutherford and atomic symbol (birth cent).

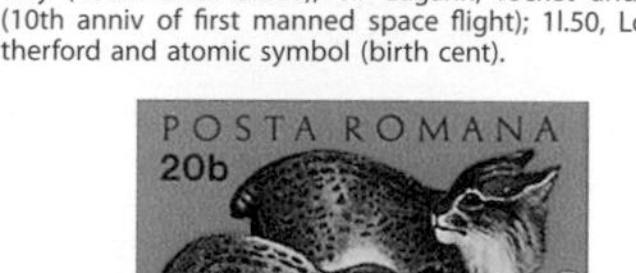

727 Lynx Cubs

1972. Young Wild Animals. Multicoloured.

3885	20b. Type **727**	10	10
3886	35b. Red fox cubs	10	10
3887	55b. Roe deer fawns	20	10
3888	1l. Wild piglets	60	20
3889	1l.50 Wolf cubs	95	20
3890	2l.40 Brown bear cubs	3·00	1·60

728 U.T.C. Emblem

1972. 50th Anniv of Communist Youth Union (U.T.C.).

3891	**728**	55b. multicoloured	70	45

729 Wrestling

1972. Olympic Games, Munich (1st issue). Multicoloured.

3892	10b. Type **729**	10	10
3893	20b. Canoeing	20	10
3894	55b. Football	30	10
3895	1l.55 High-jumping	80	15
3896	2l.90 Boxing	1·60	20
3897	6l.70 Volleyball	4·00	2·30
MS3898	100×81 mm. 6l. Runner with Olympic Torch (air)	16·00	16·00

See also Nos. 3914/**MS**3920 and 3926.

730 Stylized Map of Europe

1972. Inter-European Cultural and Economic Co-operation.

3899	**730**	1l.75 gold, black & mve	1·50	1·40
3900	-	2l.90 gold, black & green	1·90	1·90

DESIGN: 2l.90, "Crossed arrows" symbol.

731 Astronauts in Lunar Rover

1972. Air. Moon Flight of "Apollo 16".

3901	**731**	3l. blue, green and pink	1·90	1·90

732 Modern Trains and Symbols

1972. 50th Anniv of International Railway Union.

3902	**732**	55b. multicoloured	1·50	45

733 "Summer" (P. Brueghel)

1972. "Belgica 72" Stamp Exhibition, Brussels. Sheet 89×76 mm.

MS3903	6l. multicoloured	5·75	5·75

734 "Paeonia romanica"

1972. Scarce Romanian Flowers.

3904	**734**	20b. multicoloured	10	10
3905	-	40b. purple, green & brown	20	10
3906	-	55b. brown and blue	30	10
3907	-	60b. red, green and light green	50	15
3908	-	1l.35 multicoloured	95	20
3909	-	2l.90 multicoloured	2·10	65

DESIGNS: 40b. "Dianthus callizonus"; 55b. Edelweiss; 60b. Vanilla orchid; 1l.35, "Narcissus stellaris"; 2l.90, Lady's slipper.

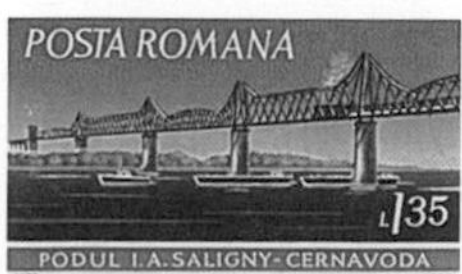

735 Saligny Bridge, Cernavoda

1972. Danube Bridges. Multicoloured.

3910	1l.35 Type **735**	60	10
3911	1l.75 Giurgeni Bridge, Vadul Oii	95	20
3912	2l.75 Friendship Bridge, Giurgiu–Ruse (Bulgaria)	1·90	45

736 North Railway Station, Bucharest, 1872

1972. Cent of North Railway Station, Bucharest.

3913	**736**	55b. multicoloured	1·20	45

737 Water-polo

1972. Olympic Games, Munich (2nd issue). Multicoloured.

3914	10b. Type **737**	10	10
3915	20b. Pistol-shooting	20	10
3916	55b. Throwing the discus	30	10
3917	1l.55 Gymnastics	85	20
3918	2l.75 Canoeing	1·90	30
3919	6l.40 Fencing	3·50	1·90
MS3920	90×78 mm. 6l. Football (air)	14·50	14·50

738 Rotary Stamp- printing Press

1972. Centenary of State Stamp-printing Works.

3921	**738**	55b. multicoloured	95	45

739 "E. Stoenescu" (Stefan Popescu)

1972. Romanian Art. Portraits. Multicoloured.

3922	55b. Type **739**	10	10
3923	1l.75 Self-portrait (Octav Bancila)	50	10
3924	2l.90 Self-portrait (Gheorghe Petrascu)	1·10	20
3925	6l.50 Self-portrait (Ion Andreescu)	2·10	65

740 Runner with Torch

1972. Olympic Games, Munich (3rd issue). Olympic Flame.

3926	**740**	55b. purple & blue on silver	1·50	45

741 Aurel Vlaicu, his Airplane No. 1 "Crazy Fly" and Silhouette of Boeing 707 Jetliner

1972. Air. Romanian Aviation Pioneers. Multicoloured.

3927	60b. Type **741**	20	10
3928	3l. Traian Vuia, Vuia No. 1 and silhouette of Boeing 707 jetliner	1·90	95

742 Cluj Cathedral

1972

3929	**742**	1l.85 violet (postage)	25	10
3930	-	2l.75 grey	50	10
3931	-	3l.35 red	70	10
3932	-	3l.45 green	70	10
3933	-	5l.15 blue	95	10
3934	-	5l.60 blue	1·10	10
3935	-	6l.20 mauve	1·20	10
3936	-	6l.40 brown	1·30	10
3937	-	6l.80 red	1·40	10
3938	-	7l.05 black	1·50	10
3939	-	8l.45 red	1·60	10
3940	-	9l.05 green	1·60	10
3941	-	9l.10 blue	1·60	10
3942	-	9l.85 green	1·90	10
3943	-	10l. brown	2·00	10
3944	-	11l.90 blue	2·10	20
3945	-	12l.75 violet	2·20	20
3946	-	13l.30 red	2·40	20
3947	-	16l.20 green	3·00	20
3948	-	14l.60 blue (air)	2·50	55

DESIGNS—HORIZ: (As Type **742**): 2l.75, Sphinx Rock, Mt. Bucegi; 3l.45, Sinaia Castle; 5l.15, Hydro-electric power station, Arges; 6l.40, Hunidoara Castle; 6l.80, Bucharest Polytechnic complex; 9l.05, Coliseum, Sarmisegtetuza; 9l.10, Hydro-electric power station, Iron Gates. (29×21 mm): 11l.90, Palace of the Republic, Bucharest; 13l.30, City Gate, Alba Julia; 14l.60, Otopeni Airport, Bucharest. VERT: (As Type **742**): 3l.35, Heroes' Monument, Bucharest; 5l.60, Iasi-Biserica; 6l.20, Bran Castle; 7l.05, Black Church, Brasova; 8l.45, Atheneum, Bucharest; 9l.85, Decebal's statue, Cetatea Deva. (20×30 mm): 10l. City Hall Tower, Sibiu; 12l.75, T.V. Building, Bucharest; 16l.20, Clock Tower, Sighisoara.

743 Satu Mare

1972. Millenium of Satu Mare.

3949	**743**	55b. multicoloured	95	45

744 Davis Cup on Racquet

1972. Final of Davis Cup Men's Team Tennis Championship, Bucharest.

3950	**744**	2l.75 multicoloured	2·40	65

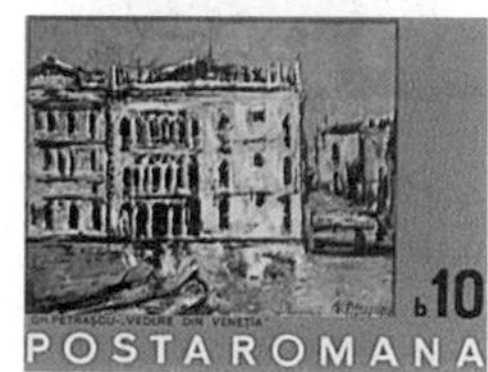

745 "Venice" (Gheorghe Petrascu)

1972. UNESCO "Save Venice" Campaign. Paintings of Venice. Multicoloured.

3951	10b. Type **745**	10	10
3952	20b. Gondolas (N. Darascu)	10	10
3953	55b. Palace (Petrascu)	20	10
3954	1l.55 Bridge (Marius Bunescu)	50	10
3955	2l.75 Palace (Darascu) (vert)	1·20	20
3956	6l.40 Canal (Bunesca)	2·50	1·20
MS3957	91×79 mm. 6l. Old houses (Petrascu)	5·75	5·75

746 Fencing and Bronze Medal

1972. Munich Olympic Games Medals. Multicoloured.

3958	10b. Type **746**	10	10
3959	20b. Handball and Bronze Medal	20	10
3960	35b. Boxing and Silver Medal	30	10
3961	1l.45 Hurdling and Silver Medal	85	10
3962	2l.75 Shooting, Silver and Bronze Medals	1·80	20
3963	6l.20 Wrestling and two Gold Medals	4·25	2·30
MS3964	90×80 mm. 6l. Gold and Silver medals (horiz) (air)	14·50	14·50

747 "Travelling Romanies" (E. Volkers)

1972. Stamp Day.

3965	**747**	1l.10+90b. mult	1·70	95

748 Flags and "25"

1972. 25th Anniv of Proclamation of Republic. Multicoloured.

3966	55b. Type **748**	30	10
3967	1l.20 Arms and "25"	70	20
3968	1l.75 Industrial scene and "25"	1·10	30

749 "Apollo 1", "2" and "3"

1972. "Apollo" Moon Flights. Multicoloured.

3969	10b. Type **749**	10	10
3970	35b. Grissom, Chaffee and White	10	10
3971	40b. "Apollo 4, 5, 6"	10	10
3972	55b. "Apollo 7, 8"	30	10
3973	1l. "Apollo 9, 10"	50	10
3974	1l.20 "Apollo 11, 12"	75	10
3975	1l.85 "Apollo 13, 14"	1·00	15
3976	2l.75 "Apollo 15, 16"	1·80	20
3977	3l.60 "Apollo 17"	3·25	1·50
MS3978	89×77 mm. 6l. Astronauts and Lunar Rover on Moon (horiz) (air)	18·00	18·00

750 European Bee Eater

1973. Protection of Nature. Multicoloured. (a) Birds.

3979	1l.40 Type **750**	50	10
3980	1l.85 Red-breasted goose	75	20
3981	2l.75 Peduline tit	1·30	50

(b) Flowers.

3982	1l.40 Globe flower	50	10
3983	1l.85 Martagon lily	75	20
3984	2l.75 Gentian	1·30	50

751 Copernicus

1973. 500th Birth Anniv of Copernicus (astronomer).

3985	**751**	2l.75 multicoloured	1·30	50

752 Suceava Costume (female)

1973. Regional Costumes. Multicoloured.

3986	10b. Type **752**	10	10
3987	40b. Suceava (male)	10	10
3988	55b. Harghila (female)	20	10
3989	1l.75 Harghila (male)	85	10
3990	2l.75 Gorj (female)	1·30	30
3991	6l.40 Gorj (male)	2·50	1·50

753 Dimitrie Paciurea (sculptor)

1973. Anniversaries. Multicoloured.

3992	10b. Type **753** (birth centenary)	10	10
3993	40b. Ioan Slavici (writer, 125th birth anniv)	10	10
3994	55b. Gheorghe Lazar (educationist, death cent)	30	10
3995	6l.40 Alexandru Flechtenmacher (composer, birth cent)	3·25	1·50

754 Map of Europe

1973. Inter-European Cultural and Economic Co-operation.

3996	**754**	3l.35 gold, blue & purple	1·00	1·00
3997	-	3l.60 gold and purple	2·10	2·00

DESIGN: 3l.60, Emblem.

755 "The Rape of Proserpine" (Hans von Achen)

1973. "iBRA 73" Stamp Exhibition, Munich. Sheet 90×78 mm.

MS3998	12l. multicoloured	12·50	12·50

756 Hand with Hammer and Sickle

1973. Anniversaries. Multicoloured.

3999	40b. Type **756**	65	30
4000	55b. Flags and bayonets	75	40
4001	1l.75 Prince Cuza	1·60	50

EVENTS: 40b. 25th anniv of Romanian Workers and Peasant Party; 55b. 40th anniv of National Anti-Fascist Committee; 1l.75, Death cent of Prince Alexandru Cuza.

757 W.M.O. Emblem and Weather Satellite

1973. Centenary of W.M.O.

4002	**757**	2l. multicoloured	1·60	50

758 "Dimitri Ralet" (anon)

1973. "Socfilex III" Stamp Exhibition, Bucharest. Portrait Paintings. Multicoloured.

4003	40b. Type **758**	10	10
4004	60b. "Enacheta Vacarescu" (A. Chladek)	20	10
4005	1l.55 "Dimitri Aman" (C. Lecca)	65	10
4006	4l.+2l. "Barbat at his Desk" (B. Iscovescu)	2·50	1·50
MS4007	78×89 mm. 6l.+2l. "The Poet Alecsandri and his Family" (N. Livaditti) (38×51 mm)	6·25	6·25

759 Prince Dimitri Cantemir

1973. 300th Birth Anniv of Dimitri Cantemir, Prince of Moldavia (writer). Multicoloured.

4008	**759**	1l.75 multicoloured	1·60	50
MS4009		77×90 mm. 6l. multicoloured	6·25	6·25

DESIGNS: (38×51 mm)—6l. Miniature of Cantemir.

760 Fibular Brooches

1973. Treasures of Pietroasa. Multicoloured.

4010	10b. Type **760**	10	10
4011	20b. Golden figurine and bowl (horiz)	10	10
4012	55b. Gold oil flask	20	10
4013	1l.55 Brooch and bracelets (horiz)	85	10
4014	2l.75 Gold platter	1·30	20
4015	6l.80 Filgree cup holder (horiz)	2·50	1·50
MS4016	78×91 mm. 12l. Jewelled breast-plate	6·25	6·25

761 Map with Flower

1973. European Security and Co-operation Conference, Helsinki. Sheet 152×81 mm containing T **761** and similar horiz design. Multicoloured.

MS4017	2l.75 ×2 Type **761**; 5l. ×2 Europe "Tree"	4·25	4·25

762 Oboga Jar

1973. Romanian Ceramics. Multicoloured.

4018	10b. Type **762**	10	10
4019	20b. Vama dish and jug	10	10
4020	55b. Maginea bowl	10	10
4021	1l.55 Sibiu Saschiz jug and dish	85	15
4022	2l.75 Pisc pot and dish	1·30	20
4023	6l.80 Oboga "bird" vessel	2·50	70

763 "Postilion" (A. Verona)

1973. Stamp Day.

4024	**763**	1l.10+90b. mult	1·00	1·00

764 "Textile Workers" (G. Saru)

1973. Paintings showing Workers. Multicoloured.

4025	10b. Type **764**	10	10
4026	20b. "Construction Site" (M. Bunescu) (horiz)	10	10
4027	55b. "Shipyard Workers" (H. Catargi) (horiz)	20	10
4028	1l.55 "Working Man" (H. Catargi)	50	15
4029	2l.75 "Miners" (A. Phoebus)	1·00	20
4030	6l.80 "The Spinner" (N. Grigorescu)	2·50	80
MS4031	90×77 mm. 12l. "Harvest Meal" (S. Popescu) (horiz)	6·25	6·25

765 Town Hall, Craiova

1974. (a) Buildings.

4032	**765**	5b. red	10	10
4033	-	10b. blue	10	10
4034	-	20b. orange	10	10
4035	-	35b. green	10	10
4036	-	40b. violet	10	10
4037	-	50b. blue	10	10
4038	-	55b. brown	20	10
4039	-	60b. red	20	10
4040	-	1l. blue	30	10
4041	-	1l.20 green	30	20

(b) Ships.

4042	1l.35 black	30	10
4043	1l.45 blue	30	10
4044	1l.50 red	30	10
4045	1l.55 blue	40	10
4046	1l.75 green	40	10
4047	2l.20 blue	50	10
4048	3l.65 lilac	95	20
4049	4l.70 purple	1·40	30

DESIGNS—VERT: 10b. "Column of Infinity", Tirgu Jiu; 40b. Romanesque church, Densus; 50b. Reformed Church, Dej; 1l. Curtea de Arges Monastery. HORIZ: 20b. Heroes' Monument, Marasesti; 35b. Citadel, Risnov; 55b. Castle, Maldarasti; 60b. National Theatre, Jassy; 1l.20, Fortress and church, Tirgu Mures; 1l.35, Danube Tug "Impingator"; 1l.45, Freighter "Dimbovita"; 1l.50, Danube passenger vessel "Muntenia"; 1l.55, Cadet barque "Mircea"; 1l.75, Liner "Transylvania"; 2l.20, Bulk carrier "Oltul"; 3l.65, Trawler "Mures"; 4l.70, Tanker "Arges".

767 "Boats at Honfleur" (Monet)

1974. Impressionist Paintings. Multicoloured.

4056	20b. Type **767**	10	10
4057	40b. "Moret Church" (Sisley) (vert)	10	10
4058	55b. "Orchard in Blossom" (Pissarro)	20	10
4059	1l.75 "Jeanne" (Pissarro) (vert)	75	10
4060	2l.75 "Landscape" (Renoir)	1·30	30
4061	3l.60 "Portrait of a Girl" (Cezanne) (vert)	2·30	60
MS4062	78×84 mm. 10l. "Women Bathing" (Renoir) (vert)	6·25	6·25

768 Trotting with Sulky

1974. Cent of Horse-racing in Romania. Multicoloured.

4063	40b. Type **768**	10	10
4064	55b. Three horses racing	20	10
4065	60b. Horse galloping	30	15
4066	1l.55 Two trotters racing	65	20
4067	2l.75 Three trotters racing	1·60	30
4068	3l.45 Two horses racing	2·30	60

769 Nicolas Titulescu (Romanian League of Nations Delegate)

1974. Interparliamentary Congress Session, Bucharest.

4069	**769**	1l.75 multicoloured	1·00	50

770 Roman Monument

1974. 1850th Anniv of Cluj (Napoca). Sheet 78×91 mm.

MS4070	10l. black and brown	6·25	6·25

771 "Anniversary Parade" (Pepene Cornelia)

1974. 25th Anniv of Romanian Pioneers Organization.

4071	**771**	55b. multicoloured	1·00	50

772 "Europe"

1974. Inter-European Cultural and Economic Co-operation. Multicoloured.

4072	2l.20 Type **772**	1·00	1·00
4073	3l.45 Satellite over Europe	2·10	2·00

1974. Romania's Victory in World Handball Championships. No. 3959 surch **ROMANIA CAMPIOANA MONDIALA 1974 175L.**

4074	1l.75 on 20b. multicoloured	5·25	5·00

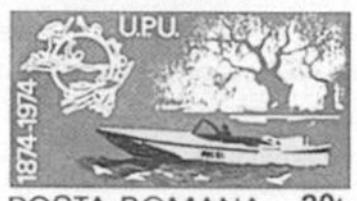

774 Postal Motor Boat

1974. U.P.U. Centenary. Multicoloured.

4075	20b. Type **774**	10	10
4076	40b. Loading mail train	10	10
4077	55b. Loading Ilyushin Il-62M mail plane	20	15
4078	1l.75 Rural postman delivering letter	95	20
4079	2l.75 Town postman delivering letter	1·20	30
4080	3l.60 Young stamp collectors	1·80	50
MS4081	90×78 mm. 4l. Postman clearing postbox; 6l. Letters and GPO, Bucharest (each 28×22 mm)	6·25	6·25

775 Footballers

1974. World Cup Football Championship, West Germany.

4082	**775**	20b. multicoloured	10	10
4083	-	40b. multicoloured	10	10
4084	-	55b. multicoloured	20	10
4085	-	1l.75 multicoloured	50	20
4086	-	2l.75 multicoloured	1·00	30
4087	-	3l.60 multicoloured	1·60	50

MS4088	90×78 mm. 10l. Three footballers (horiz, 50×38 mm)	6·25	6·25

DESIGNS: Nos. 4083/7, Football scenes similar to Type **775**.

776 Anniversary Emblem

1974. 25th Anniv of Council for Mutual Economic Aid.

4089	**776**	55b. multicoloured	85	50

777 U.N. and World Population Emblems

1974. World Population Year Conference, Bucharest.

4090	**777**	2l. multicoloured	1·30	50

778 Emblem on Map of Europe

1974. "Euromax 1974" International Stamp Exhibition, Bucharest.

4091	**778**	4l.+3l. yellow, bl & red	3·25	70

779 Hand drawing Peace Dove

1974. 25th Anniv of World Peace Movement.

4092	**779**	2l. multicoloured	1·30	50

780 Prince John of Wallachia (400th birth anniv)

1974. Anniversaries.

4093	**780**	20b. blue	10	10
4094	-	55b. red	20	10
4095	-	1l. blue	30	10
4096	-	1l.10 brown	40	10
4097	-	1l.30 purple	65	10
4098	-	1l.40 violet	75	20

DESIGNS AND ANNIVERSARIES—VERT: 1l. Iron and Steel Works, Hunedoara (220th anniv); 1l.10, Avram Iancu (revolutionary, 150th anniv); 1l.30, Dr. C. I. Parhon (birth cent); 1l.40, Dosoftel (metropolitan) (350th birth anniv). HORIZ: 55b. Soldier guarding industrial installations (Romanian People's Army, 30th anniv).

781 Romanian and Soviet Flags as "XXX"

1974. 30th Anniv of Liberation. Multicoloured.

4099	40b. Type **781**	20	10
4100	55b. Citizens and flags (horiz)	30	20

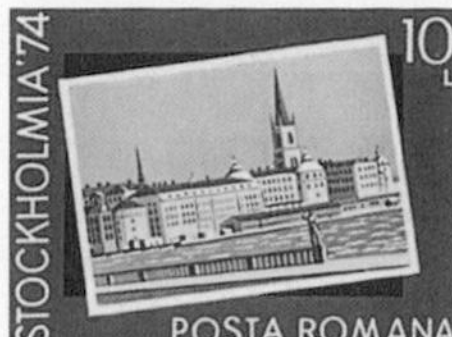

782 View of Stockholm

1974. "Stockholmia 1974" International Stamp Exhibition. Sheet 91×78 mm.

MS4101	10l. multicoloured	6·25	6·25

783 "Centaurea nervosa"

1974. Nature Conservation. Wild Flowers. Multicoloured.

4102	20b. Type **783**	10	10
4103	40b. "Fritillaria montana"	10	10
4104	55b. Yew	20	15
4105	1l.75 "Rhododendron kotschyi"	75	20
4106	2l.75 Alpine forget-me-not	1·00	30
4107	3l.60 Pink	1·60	50

784 Bust of Isis

1974. Romanian Archaeological Finds. Sculpture. Multicoloured.

4108	20b. Type **784**	10	10
4109	40b. Glykon serpent	20	10
4110	55b. Head of Emperor Decius	30	15
4111	1l.75 Romanian Woman	65	20
4112	2l.75 Mithras	1·00	30
4113	3l.60 Roman senator	1·70	50

785 Sibiu Market Place

1974. Stamp Day.

4114	**785**	2l.10+1l.90 mult	2·30	60

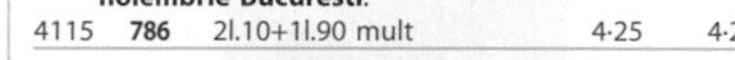

1974. "Nationala 74" Stamp Exhibition. No. 4114 optd **EXPOZITIA FILATELICA "NATIONALA '74" 15–24 noiembrie Bucuresti**.

4115	**786**	2l.10+1l.90 mult	4·25	4·25

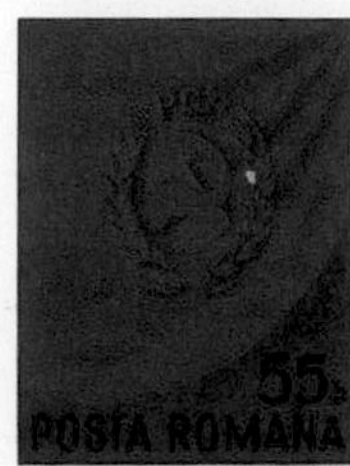

787 Party Emblem

1974. 11th Romanian Communist Party Congress, Bucharest.

4116	**787**	55b. multicoloured	20	10
4117	-	1l. multicoloured	50	30

DESIGN: 1l. Similar to Type **787**, showing party emblem and curtain.

788 "The Discus-thrower" (Myron)

1974. 60th Anniv of Romanian Olympic Committee.

4118	**788**	2l. multicoloured	1·60	50

789 "Skylab"

1974. "Skylab" Space Laboratory Project.

4119	**789**	2l.50 multicoloured	1·60	1·50

790 Dr. Albert Schweitzer

1974. Birth Centenary of Dr. Albert Schweitzer (Nobel Peace Prize-winner).

4120	**790**	40b. brown	50	50

791 Handball

1975. World Universities Handball Championships, Romania.

4121	**791**	55b. multicoloured	20	10
4122	-	1l.75 multicoloured (vert)	65	20
4123	-	2l.20 multicoloured	95	30

DESIGNS: 1l.75, 2l.20, similar designs to Type **791**.

792 "Rocks and Birches"

1975. Paintings by Ion Andreescu. Multicoloured.

4124	20b. Type **792**	10	10
4125	40b. "Peasant Woman with Green Kerchief"	10	10
4126	55b. "Winter in the Forest"	20	15
4127	1l.75 "Winter in Barbizon" (horiz)	50	20
4128	2l.75 Self-portrait	1·00	50
4129	3l.50 "Main Road" (horiz)	1·60	80

793 Torch and Inscription

1975. Tenth Anniv of Romanian Socialist Republic.

4130	**793**	40b. multicoloured	50	30

794 "Battle of the High Bridge" (O. Obedeanu)

1975. 500th Anniv of Victory over the Ottomans at High Bridge.

4131	**794**	55b. multicoloured	65	30

795 "Peasant Woman Spinning" (Nicolae Grigorescu)

1975. International Women's Year.

4132	**795**	55b. multicoloured	65	30

796 "Self-portrait"

1975. 500th Birth Anniv of Michelangelo.

4133	**796**	5l. multicoloured	2·50	50

797 Escorial Palace, Madrid

1975. "Espana 1975" International Stamp Exhibition, Madrid. Sheet 90×78 mm.

MS4134 **797**	10l. multicoloured	5·25	5·25

798 Mitsui Children's Science Pavilion, Okinawa

1975. International Exposition, Okinawa.

4135	**798**	4l. multicoloured	2·30	60

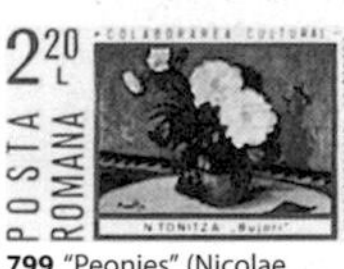
799 "Peonies" (Nicolae Tonitza)

1975. Inter-European Cultural and Economic Co-operation. Multicoloured.

4136	2l.20 Type **799**	1·00	1·00
4137	3l.45 "Chrysanthemums" (Stefan Luchian)	1·60	1·50

800 Dove with Coded Letter

1975. Introduction of Postal Coding.

4138	**800**	55b. multicoloured	65	30

801 Convention Emblem on "Globe"

1975. Centenary of International Metre Convention.

4139	**801**	1l.85 multicoloured	1·30	50

802 Mihail Eminescu and Museum

1975. 125th Birth Anniv of Mihail Eminescu (poet).

4140	**802**	55b. multicoloured	65	30

803 Roman Coins and Stone Inscription

1975. Bimillenary of Alba Julia.

4141	**803**	55b. multicoloured	65	30

804 "On the Banks of the Seine" (TH. Pallady)

1975. "Arphila 1975" International Stamp Exhibition, Paris. Sheet 76×90 mm.

MS4142 **804**	10l. multicoloured	5·25	5·25

805 Ana Ipatescu

1975. Death Cent of Ana Ipatescu (revolutionary).

4143	**805**	55b. mauve	65	30

806 Turnu-Severin

1975. European Architectural Heritage Year. Roman Antiquities.

4144	-	55b. black and brown	20	10
4145	-	1l.20 black, lt bl & bl	30	20
4146	-	1l.55 black and green	50	30
4147	-	1l.75 black and red	75	40
4148	**806**	2l. black and ochre	85	50
4149	-	2l.25 black and blue	1·60	80
MS4150		79×91 mm. 10l. multicoloured	3·25	3·25

DESIGNS—VERT: 55b. Emperor Trajan; 1l.20, Trajan's Column, Rome; 1l.55, Decebalus (sculpture); 10l. Roman remains, Gradiste. HORIZ: 1l.75, Imperial monument, Adam Clissi; 2l.25, Trajan's Bridge.

807 "Apollo" and "Soyuz" Spacecraft

1975. Air. "Apollo"–"Soyuz" Space Link. Multicoloured.

4151	1l.75 Type **807**	1·60	1·50
4152	3l.25 "Apollo" and "Soyuz" linked together	2·10	2·00

808 "Michael the Brave" (Aegidius Sadeler)

1975. 375th Anniv of First Political Union of Romanian States. Multicoloured.

4153	55b. Type **808**	20	10
4154	1l.20 "Ottoman Envoys bringing gifts to Michael the Brave" (T. Aman) (horiz)	50	10
4155	2l.75 "Michael the Brave at Calugareni" (T. Aman)	1·20	30

809 Map of Europe

1975. European Security and Co-operation Conference, Helsinki. Sheet 111×81 mm containing T **809** and similar horiz designs. Multicoloured.

MS4156 2l.75 Type **809**; 5l. Open book; 5l. Children playing Postage; 2l.75 Peace doves (air)	2·50	2·50

810 Larkspur

1975. Flowers. Multicoloured.

4157	20b. Type **810**	10	10
4158	40b. Long-headed poppy	10	10
4159	55b. Common immortelle	20	10
4160	1l.75 Common rock-rose	65	20
4161	2l.75 Meadow clary	1·30	30
4162	3l.60 Chicory	1·60	50

1975. International Philatelic Fair, Riccione (Italy). Optd **Tîrg international de mărci postale Riccione – Italia 23-25 august 1975.**

4163	**796**	5l. multicoloured	5·25	5·00

812 Policeman using Walkie-talkie

1975. Road Safety.

4164	**812**	55b. blue	65	30

813 Text on Map of Pelendava

1975. 1750th Anniv of First Documentary Attestations of Daco-Getian Settlements of Pelendava and 500th Anniv of Craiova. Multicoloured.

4165	20b. Type **813**	15	10
4166	55b. Map of Pelendava showing location of Craiova (82×33 mm)	20	10
4167	1l. Text on map of Pelendava	40	15

Nos. 4165/7 were issued together, se-tenant, forming a composite design.

814 Muntenia Carpet

1975. Romanian Traditional Carpets. Multicoloured.

4168	20b. Type **814**	10	10
4169	40b. Banat	10	10
4170	55b. Oltenia	20	10
4171	1l.75 Moldova	85	20
4172	2l.75 Oltenia (different)	1·20	30
4173	3l.60 Maramures	1·50	50

815 T.V. "12M" Minibus

1975. Romanian Motor Vehicles. Multicoloured.

4174	20b. Type **815**	10	10
4175	40b. L.K.W. "19 A.L.P." Oil tanker	10	10
4176	55b. A.R.O. "240" Field car	20	10
4177	1l.75 L.K.W. "R 8135 F" Truck	85	20
4178	2l.75 P.K.W. "Dacia 1300" Saloon car	1·20	30
4179	3l.60 L.K.W. "R 19215 D.F.K." Tipper truck	1·50	50

816 Postal Transit Centre, Bucharest

1975. Stamp Day. Multicoloured.

4180	1l.50+1l.50 Type **816**	2·10	1·00
4181	2l.10+1l.90 Aerial view of P.T.C.	3·75	1·50

817 "Winter" (Peter Brueghel)

1975. "Themabelga 1975" International Stamp Exhibition, Brussels. Sheet 90×78 mm.

MS4182 10l. multicoloured	5·75	5·75

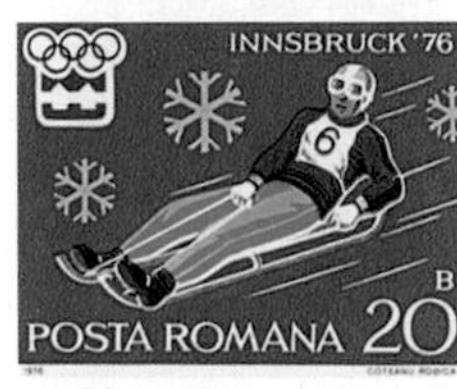
818 Tobogganing

1976. Winter Olympics Games, Innsbruck. Multicoloured.

4183	20b. Type **818**	10	10
4184	40b. Rifle-shooting (biathlon) (vert)	20	15
4185	55b. Downhill skiing (slalom)	40	20
4186	1l.75 Ski jumping	75	30
4187	2l.75 Figure skating (women's)	1·40	50
4188	3l.60 Ice hockey	1·50	1·10
MS4189	91×78 mm. 10l. Bobsleighing	9·00	9·00

819 "Washington at Valley Forge" (W. Trego)

1976. Bicent of American Revolution. Multicoloured.

4190	20b. Type **819**	10	10
4191	40b. "Washington at Trenton" (Trumbull) (vert)	10	10
4192	55b. "Washington crossing the Delaware" (Leutze)	20	10
4193	1l.75 "Capture of the Hessians" (Trumbull)	50	20
4194	2l.75 "Jefferson" (Sully) (vert)	1·00	30
4195	3l.60 "Surrender of Cornwallis at Yorktown" (Trumbull)	1·30	40
MS4196	91×78 mm. 10l. "Signing of Declaration of Independence" (J. Trumbull)	5·25	5·25

820 "Prayer"

1976. Birth Centenary of Constantin Brancusi (sculptor). Multicoloured.

4197	55b. Type **820**	20	10
4198	1l.75 Architectural Assembly, Tg. Jiu	50	30
4199	3l.60 C. Brancusi	1·80	50

821 Anton Davidoglu (mathematician) (birth cent)

1976. Anniversaries. Multicoloured.

4200	40b. Type **821**	20	10
4201	55b. Prince Vlad Tepes (500th death anniv)	20	10
4202	1l.20 Costache Negri (patriot—death centenary)	40	10
4203	1l.75 Gallery, Archives Museum (50th anniv)	65	20

822 Inscribed Tablets, Tibiscum (Banat)

1976. Daco-Roman Archaeological Finds. Multicoloured.

4204	**822**	20b. multicoloured	10	10
4205	-	40b. black, grey and red	20	10
4206	-	55b. multicoloured	30	15
4207	-	1l.75 multicoloured	85	20
4208	-	2l.75 black, grey and red	1·00	30
4209	-	3l.60 black, grey & green	1·70	70
MS4210		78×91 mm. 10l. multicoloured	6·25	6·25

DESIGNS: 40b. Sculptures (Banat); 55b. Inscribed tablet, coins and cup (Crisana); 1l.75, Pottery (Crisana); 2l.75, Altar and spears, Maramures (Banat); 3l.60, Vase and spears, Maramures.

823 Dr. Carol Davila

1976. Centenary of Romanian Red Cross. Multicoloured.

4211	55b. Type **823** (postage)	20	10
4212	1l.75 Nurse and patient	50	10
4213	2l.20 First aid	75	10
4214	3l.35 Blood donors (air)	1·30	20

824 King Decebalus Vase

1976. Inter-European Cultural and Economic Co-operation. Vases from Cluj-Napoca porcelain factory. Multicoloured.

4215	2l.20 Type **824**	50	50
4216	3l.45 Vase with portrait of King Michael the Brave	1·20	1·00

825 Romanian Arms

1976

4217	**825**	1l.75 multicoloured	1·30	50

826 de Havilland D.H.9C

1976. Air. 50th Anniv of Romanian Airline. Multicoloured.

4218	20b. Type **826**	10	10
4219	40b. I.C.A.R. Comercial	15	10
4220	60b. Douglas DC-3	20	10
4221	1l.75 Antonov An-24	75	15
4222	2l.75 Ilyushin Il-62 jetliner	1·00	30
4223	3l.60 Boeing 707 jetliner	1·60	50

827 Gymnastics

1976. Olympic Games, Montreal. Multicoloured.

4224	20b. Type **827**	10	10
4225	40b. Boxing	20	10
4226	55b. Handball	40	10
4227	1l.75 Rowing (horiz)	75	20
4228	2l.75 Gymnastics (different) (horiz)	1·00	30
4229	3l.60 Canoeing (horiz)	1·60	40
MS4230	91×78 mm. 10l. Gymnastics (55×42 mm)	6·25	6·25

828 Spiru Haret

1976. 125th Birth Anniv of Spiru Haret (mathematician).

4231	**828**	20b. multicoloured	50	30

829 Daco-Getian Sculpture on Map of Buzau

1976. 1600th Anniv of Buzau State.

4232	**829**	55b. multicoloured	65	30

1976. Philatelic Exhibition, Bucharest. No. 4199 surch **EXPOZITIA FILATELICA BUCURESTI 12–19 IX 1976 1,80+**.

4233	3l.60+1l.80 multicoloured	7·75	7·75

831 Red Deer

1976. Endangered Animals. Multicoloured.

4234	20b. Type **831**	10	10
4235	40b. Brown bear	20	10
4236	55b. Chamois	30	10
4237	1l.75 Wild boar	50	15
4238	2l.75 Red fox	1·00	30
4239	3l.60 Lynx	1·60	50

832 Cathedral, Milan

1976. "Italia '76" International Philatelic Exhibition, Milan.

4240	**832**	4l.75 multicoloured	1·80	50

833 D. Grecu (gymnast) and Bronze Medal

1976. Olympic Games, Montreal. Romanian Medal Winners. Multicoloured.

4241	20b. Type **833**	10	10
4242	40b. Fencing (Bronze Medal)	10	10
4243	55b. Javelin (Bronze Medal)	20	10
4244	1l.75 Handball (Silver Medal)	40	15
4245	2l.75 Boxing (Silver and Bronze Medals) (horiz)	85	20
4246	3l.60 Wrestling (Silver and Bronze Medals) (horiz)	1·30	50
4247	5l.70 Nadia Comaneci (gymnastics – 3 Gold, 1 Silver and 1 Bronze Medals) (27×42 mm)	3·75	1·80
MS4248	90×78 mm. 10l. D. Vasile (canoeist) and gold and silver medals (42×54 mm)	6·25	6·25

834 "Carnations and Oranges"

1976. Floral Paintings by Stefan Luchian. Multicoloured.

4249	20b. Type **834**	10	10
4250	40b. "Flower Arrangement"	10	10
4251	55b. "Immortelles"	10	10
4252	1l.75 "Roses in Vase"	50	15
4253	2l.75 "Cornflowers"	75	20
4254	3l.60 "Carnations in Vase"	1·40	30

835 "Elena Cuza" (T. Aman)

1976. Stamp Day.

4255	**835**	2l.10+1l.90 mult	2·30	1·70

836 Arms of Alba

1976. Romanian Districts' Coats of Arms (1st series). Multicoloured.

4256	55b. Type **836**	30	10
4257	55b. Arad	30	10
4258	55b. Arges	30	10
4259	55b. Bacau	30	10
4260	55b. Bihor	30	10
4261	55b. Bistrita Nasaud	30	10
4262	55b. Botosani	30	10
4263	55b. Brasov	30	10
4264	55b. Braila	30	10
4265	55b. Buzau	30	10
4266	55b. Caras-Severin	30	10
4267	55b. Cluj	30	10
4268	55b. Constanta	30	10
4269	55b. Covasna	30	10
4270	55b. Dimbovita	30	10

See also Nos. 4307/31, 4496/520 and 4542/63.

837 "Ox Cart"

1977. Paintings by Nicolae Grigorescu. Multicoloured.

4271	55b. Type **837**	20	10
4272	1l. "Self-portrait" (vert)	30	10
4273	1l.50 "Shepherdess"	40	10
4274	2l.15 "Girl with Distaff"	85	15
4275	3l.40 "Shepherd" (vert)	1·00	30
4276	4l.80 "Halt at the Well"	1·60	50

838 Telecommunications Station, Cheia

1977

4277	**838**	55b. multicoloured	50	30

839 I.C.A.R.1

1977. Air. Romanian Gliders. Multicoloured.

4278	20b. Type **839**	10	10
4279	40b. IS-3d	10	10
4280	55b. RG-5	20	10
4281	1l.50 IS-11	50	15
4282	3l. IS-29D	1·00	30
4283	3l.40 IS-28B	1·80	50

840 Red Deer

1977. Protected Animals. Multicoloured.

4284	55b. Type **840**	20	10
4285	1l. Mute swan	30	10
4286	1l.50 Egyptian vulture	50	10
4287	2l.15 European bison	75	15
4288	3l.40 White-headed duck	1·30	30
4289	4l.80 River kingfisher	1·60	50

841 "The Infantryman" (Oscar Obedeanu)

1977. Cent of Independence. Paintings. Multicoloured.

4290	55b. Type **841**	20	10
4291	1l. "Artillery Battery at Calafat" (S. Hentia) (horiz)	40	10
4292	1l.50 "Soldiers Attacking" (Stefan Luchian)	50	10
4293	2l.15 "Battle of Plevna" (horiz)	95	15
4294	3l.40 "The Artillerymen" (Nicolae Grigorescu) (horiz)	1·30	30
4295	4l.80+2l. "Battle of Rahova" (horiz)	2·75	1·20
MS4296	90×78 mm. 10l. "Battle of Grivitza"	5·25	5·25

842 Sinaia, Carpathians

1977. Inter-European Cultural and Economic Co-operation. Views. Multicoloured.

4297	2l. Type **842**	65	30
4298	2l.40 Auroa, Black Sea	85	50

843 Petru Rares, Prince of Moldavia

1977. Anniversaries. Multicoloured.

4299	40b. Type **843** (450th anniv of accession)	50	30
4300	55b. Ion Caragiale (dramatist, 125th birth anniv)	50	30

844 Nurse with Children and Emblems

1977. 23rd Int Red Cross Conference, Bucharest.

4301	**844**	1l.50 multicoloured	75	50

845 Triumphal Arch, Bucharest

1977. 60th Anniv of Battles of Marasti, Marasesti and Oituz.

4302	**845**	2l.15 multicoloured	1·40	50

846 Boeing 707 Jetliner over Bucharest Airport

1977. European Security and Co-operation Conference, Belgrade. Sheet 80×70 mm.

MS4303	**846**	10l. yellow, carmine and blue	2·50	2·50

847 Postwoman and Letters

1977. Air.

4304	20l. Type **847**	5·25	1·50
4305	30l. Douglas DC-10 jetliner and mail	7·75	2·50

848 Mount Titano Castle, San Marino

1977. Centenary of San Marino Postage Stamps.

4306	**848**	4l. multicoloured	2·30	50

1977. Romanian District Coats of Arms (2nd series). As T **836**. Multicoloured.

4307	55b. Dolj	30	10
4308	55b. Galati	30	10
4309	55b. Gorj	30	10
4310	55b. Harghita	30	10
4311	55b. Hunedoara	30	10
4312	55b. Ialomita	30	10
4313	55b. Iasi	30	10
4314	55b. Ilfov	30	10
4315	55b. Maramures	30	10
4316	55b. Mehedinti	30	10
4317	55b. Mures	30	10
4318	55b. Neamt	30	10
4319	55b. Olt	30	10
4320	55b. Prahova	30	10
4321	55b. Salaj	30	10
4322	55b. Satu Mare	30	10
4323	55b. Sibiu	30	10
4324	55b. Suceava	30	10
4325	55b. Teleorman	30	10
4326	55b. Timis	30	10
4327	55b. Tulcea	30	10
4328	55b. Vaslui	30	10
4329	55b. Vilcea	30	10
4330	55b. Vrancea	30	10
4331	55b. Romanian postal emblem	30	10

849 Gymnast on Vaulting Horse

1977. Gymnastics. Multicoloured.

4332	20b. Type **849**	10	10
4333	40b. Floor exercise	10	10
4334	55b. Gymnast on parallel bars	20	10
4335	1l. Somersault on bar	40	15
4336	2l.15 Gymnast on rings	85	30
4337	4l.80 Gymnastic exercise	2·50	1·00

850 Dispatch Rider and Army Officer

1977. Stamp Day.

4338	**850**	2l.10+1l.90 mult	2·10	2·00

851 Two Dancers with Sticks

1977. Calusarii Folk Dance. Multicoloured.

4339	20b. Type **851**	10	10
4340	40b. Leaping dancer with stick	10	10
4341	55b. Two dancers	20	10
4342	1l. Dancer with stick	40	15
4343	2l.15 Leaping dancers	85	30
4344	4l.80 Leaping dancer	2·50	1·00
MS4345	81×71 mm. 10l. Two children in costume	5·25	5·25

852 "Carpati" at Cazane

1977. European Navigation on the Danube. Multicoloured.

4346	55b. Type **852**	20	10
4347	1l. "Mircesti" near Orsova	25	10
4348	1l.50 "Oltenita" near Calafat	35	20
4349	2l.15 Hydrofoil at Giurgiu port	50	30
4350	3l. "Herculani" at Tulcea	85	40
4351	3l.40 "Muntenia" at Sulina	1·00	50
4352	4l.80 Map of Danube delta	2·10	1·00
MS4353	81×71 mm. 10l. River god Danubius (relief from Trajan's Column) (vert)	3·25	3·25

853 Arms and Flag of Romania

1977. 30th Anniv of Romanian Republic. Multicoloured.

4354	55b. Type **853**	20	15
4355	1l.20 Romanian-built computers	55	20
4356	1l.75 National Theatre, Craiova	1·10	40

854 Firiza Dam

1978. Romanian Dams and Hydro-electric Installations. Multicoloured.

4357	20b. Type **854**	10	10
4358	40b. Negovanu dam	10	10
4359	55b. Piatra Neamt power station	20	10
4360	1l. Izvorul Montelui Bicaz dam	35	10
4361	2l.15 Vidraru dam	65	20
4362	4l.80 Danube barrage and navigation system, Iron Gates	1·70	50

855 LZ-1 over Lake Constance

1978. Air. Airships. Multicoloured.

4363	60b. Type **855**	20	10
4364	1l. Santos Dumont's "Ballon No. 6" over Paris	35	10
4365	1l.50 Beardmore R-34 over Manhattan Island	55	10
4366	2l.15 N.4 "Italia" at North Pole	80	15
4367	3l.40 "Graf Zeppelin" over Brasov	1·30	30
4368	4l.80 "Graf Zeppelin" over Sibiu	2·20	65
MS4369	80×70 mm. 10l. "Graf Zeppelin" over Bucharest (50×38 mm)	5·50	5·50

856 Footballers and Emblem

1978. World Cup Football Championship, Argentina.

4370	**856**	55b. blue	20	10
4371	-	1l. orange	20	10
4372	-	1l.50 yellow	35	10
4373	-	2l.15 red	65	10
4374	-	3l.40 green	1·20	20
4375	-	4l.80 mauve	2·20	30
MS4376		80×70 mm. 10l. blue (38×50 mm)	5·50	5·50

DESIGNS: 1l.50 to 10l., Footballers and emblem, similar to Type **856**.

857 King Decebalus of Dacia

1978. Inter-European Cultural and Economic Co-operation. Multicoloured.

4377	1l.30 Type **857**	55	50
4378	3l.40 Prince Mircea the Elder	1·70	1·60

858 Worker and Factory

1978. 30th Anniv of Nationalization of Industry.

4379	**858**	55b. multicoloured	55	30

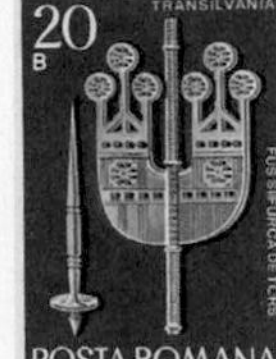

859 Spindle and Fork Handle, Transylvania

1978. Wood-carving. Multicoloured.

4380	20b. Type **859**	10	10
4381	40b. Cheese mould, Muntenia	20	10
4382	55b. Spoons, Oltenia	35	10
4383	1l. Barrel, Moldavia	45	15
4384	2l.15 Ladle and mug, Transylvania	80	20
4385	4l.80 Water bucket, Oltenia	1·70	65

860 Danube Delta

1978. Tourism. Multicoloured.

4386	55b. Type **860**	10	10
4387	1l. Bran Castle (vert)	20	10
4388	1l.50 Moldavian village	45	10
4389	2l.15 Muierii caves	65	15
4390	3l.40 Cable car at Boiana Brasov	1·10	20
4391	4l.80 Mangalia (Black Sea resort)	1·90	40
MS4392	80×70 mm. 10l. Strehaia Fortress and Monastery (37×49 mm)	6·75	6·75

861 MC-6 Electron Microscope

1978. Romanian Industry. Multicoloured.

4393	20b. Type **861**	10	10
4394	40b. Hydraulic excavator	10	10
4395	55b. Power station control room	35	10
4396	1l.50 Oil drillheads	55	15
4397	3l. C-12 combine harvester (horiz)	90	20
4398	3l.40 Petro-chemical combine, Pitesti	1·10	30

862 Polovraci Cave

1978. Caves and Caverns. Multicoloured.

4399	55b. Type **862**	10	10
4400	1l. Topolnita	20	10
4401	1l.50 Ponoare	45	10
4402	2l.15 Ratei	65	15
4403	3l.40 Closani	1·20	20
4404	4l.80 Epuran	1·90	50

863 Gymnastics

1978. "Daciada" Romanian Games. Multicoloured.

4405	55b. Type **863**	10	10
4406	1l. Running	20	10
4407	1l.50 Skiing	45	10
4408	2l.15 Horse jumping	65	15
4409	3l.40 Football	1·20	20
4410	4l.80 Handball	1·90	40

864 Zoomorphic Gold Plate

1978. Daco-Roman Archaeology. Multicoloured.

4411	20b. Type **864**	10	10
4412	40b. Gold torque	20	10
4413	55b. Gold cameo ring	35	10
4414	1l. Silver bowl	55	15
4415	2l.15 Bronze eagle (vert)	90	20
4416	4l.80 Silver armband	1·20	50
MS4417	74×89 mm. 10l. Gold helmet (38×50 mm). Imperf	19·00	19·00

865 Symbols of Equality

1978. International Anti-Apartheid Year.

4418	**865**	3l.40 black, yellow & red	1·30	1·00

866 Romulus, Remus and Wolf

1978. International Stamp Exhibition, Essen. Sheet 75×90 mm.

MS4419	10l. multicoloured	14·50	16·00

867 Ptolemaic Map of Dacia (2000th anniv of first record of Ziridava)

1978. Anniversaries in the History of Arad. Multicoloured.

4420	40b. Type **867**	10	10
4421	55b. Meeting place of National Council (60th anniv of unified Romania)	10	10
4422	1l.75 Ceramic pots (950th anniv of first documentary evidence of Arad)	55	30

868 Dacian Warrior

1978. Stamp Day.

4423	**868**	6l.+3l. multicoloured	1·70	1·00

No. 4423 was issued se-tenant with a premium- carrying tab as shown in Type **868**.

869 Assembly at Alba Julia

1979. 60th Anniv of National Unity. Multicoloured.

4424	55b. Type **869**	20	10
4425	1l. Open book, flag and sculpture	35	20

870 Wright Brothers and Wright Type A

1979. Air. Pioneers of Aviation. Multicoloured.

4426	55b. Type **870**	10	10
4427	1l. Louis Bleriot and Bleriot XI monoplane	20	10
4428	1l.50 Anthony Fokker and Fokker F.VIIa/3m "Josephine Ford"	45	10
4429	2l.15 Andrei Tupolev and Tupolev ANT-25	65	15
4430	3l. Otto Lilienthal and Lilienthal monoplane glider	80	20
4431	3l.40 Traian Vuia and Vuia No. 1	90	25
4432	4l.80 Aurel Vlaicu and No. 1 "Crazy Fly"	1·00	30
MS4433	79×70 mm. 10l. Henri Coanda and turbine-powered model airplane	5·50	5·50

871 Dacian Warrior

1979. 2050th Anniv of Independent Centralized Dacic State. Details from Trajan's Column. Multicoloured.

4434	5b. Type **871**	20	10
4435	1l.50 Dacian warrior on horseback	55	30

872 "The Heroes from Vaslui"

1979. International Year of the Child (1st issue). Children's Paintings. Multicoloured.

4436	55b. Type **872**	10	10
4437	1l. "Tica's Folk Music Band"	20	10
4438	1l.50 "Buildingsite"	45	10
4439	2l.15 "Industrial Landscape" (horiz)	55	15
4440	3l.40 "Winter Holiday" (horiz)	1·00	20
4441	4l.80 "Pioneers' Celebration" (horiz)	1·30	30

See also Nos. 4453/6.

873 Championship Emblem

1979. European Junior Ice Hockey Championship, Miercurea-Ciuc, and World Championship, Galati. Multicoloured.

4442	1l.30 Type **873**	35	10
4443	3l.40 Championship emblem (different)	1·00	30

874 Dog's tooth Violet

1979. Protected Flowers. Multicoloured.

4444	55b. Type **874**	10	10
4445	1l. Alpine violet	20	10
4446	1l.50 "Linum borzaeanum"	45	10
4447	2l.15 "Convolvulus persicus"	55	15
4448	3l.40 Auricula	1·00	20
4449	4l.80 "Aquilegia transsylvanica"	1·30	30

875 Street with Mail Coach and Post-rider

1979. Inter-European Cultural and Economic Co-operation.

4450	1l.30 Type **875** (postage)	55	30
4451	3l.40 Boeing 707 and motorcycle postman (air)	90	50

876 Oil Derrick

1979. International Petroleum Congress, Bucharest.

4452	**876**	3l.40 multicoloured	1·00	50

877 Children with Flowers

1979. International Year of the Child (2nd issue). Multicoloured.

4453	40b. Type **877**	10	10
4454	1l. Children at creative play	35	10
4455	2l. Children with hare	55	20
4456	4l.60 Young pioneers	1·50	30

878 Young Pioneer

1979. 30th Anniv of Romanian Young Pioneers.

4457	**878**	55b. multicoloured	55	30

879 "Woman in Garden"

1979. Paintings by Gh. Tattarescu. Multicoloured.

4458	20b. Type **879**	10	10
4459	40b. "Muntenian Woman"	10	10
4460	55b. "Muntenian Man"	10	10
4461	1l. "General G. Magheru"	45	15
4462	2l.15 "The Artist's Daughter"	80	20
4463	4l.80 "Self-portrait"	1·70	50

880 Brasov University

1979. Contemporary Architecture. Multicoloured.

4464	20b. State Theatre, Tirgu Mures	10	10
4465	40b. Type **880**	10	10
4466	55b. Administration Centre, Baia Mare	10	10
4467	1l. Stefan Gheorghiu Academy, Bucharest	35	15
4468	2l.15 Adminstration Centre, Botosani	65	20
4469	4l.80 House of Culture, Tirgoviste	1·50	50

881 Stefan Gheorghiu

1979. Anniversaries. Multicoloured.

4470	40b. Type **881** (birth cent)	45	20
4471	55b. Statue of Gheorghe Lazar (poet) (birth bicent)	55	30
4472	2l.15 Fallen Workers monument (Strike at Lupeni, 50th anniv)	65	40

882 Moldavian and Wallachian Women and Monuments to Union

1979. 120th Anniv of Union of Moldavia and Wallachia.

4473	**882**	4l.60 multicoloured	1·70	50

883 Party and National Flags

1979. 25th Anniv of Liberation. Multicoloured.

4474	55b. Type **883**	20	10
4475	1l. "Workers' Militia" (L. Suhar) (horiz)	45	20

884 Freighter "Galati"

1979. Ships. Multicoloured.

4476	55b. Type **884**	10	10
4477	1l. Freighter "Buchuresti"	35	10
4478	1l.50 Bulk carrier "Resita"	45	10
4479	2l.15 Bulk carrier "Tomis"	65	15
4480	3l.40 Tanker "Dacia"	1·00	20
4481	4l.80 Tanker "Independenta"	1·50	30

885 "Snapdragons"

1979. "Socflex 79" Stamp Exhibition, Bucharest. Flower Paintings by Stefan Luchian. Mult.

4482	40b. Type **885**	10	10
4483	60b. "Carnations"	20	10
4484	1l.55 "Flowers on a Stairway"	45	10
4485	4l.+2l. "Flowers of the Field"	1·90	1·00
MS4486	79×70 mm. 10l.+5l. "Roses"	6·75	6·75

886 Gymnast

1979. Fourth European Sports Conference, Berchtesgaden. Sheet 90×75 mm.

MS4487	10l. multicoloured	17·00	17·00

887 Party and National Flags

1979. 12th Romanian Communist Party Congress. Sheet 70×80 mm.

MS4488	5l. multicoloured	4·50	4·50

888 Olympic Stadium, Melbourne (1956 Games)

1979. Olympic Games, Moscow (1980). Olympic Stadia. Multicoloured.

4489	55b. Type **888**	10	10
4490	1l. Rome (1960)	35	10
4491	1l.50 Tokyo (1964)	45	10
4492	2l.15 Mexico City (1968)	65	15
4493	3l.40 Munich (1972)	1·00	20
4494	4l.80 Montreal (1978)	1·50	30
MS4495	79×69 mm. 10l. Moscow (1980)	6·75	6·50

1979. Municipal Coats of Arms. As T **836**. Multicoloured.

4496	1l.20 Alba Julia	35	10
4497	1l.20 Arad	35	10
4498	1l.20 Bacau	35	10
4499	1l.20 Baia Mare	35	10
4500	1l.20 Birlad	35	10
4501	1l.20 Botosani	35	10
4502	1l.20 Brasov	35	10
4503	1l.20 Braila	35	10
4504	1l.20 Buzau	35	10
4505	1l.20 Calarasi	35	10
4506	1l.20 Cluj	35	10
4507	1l.20 Constanta	35	10
4508	1l.20 Craiova	35	10
4509	1l.20 Dej	35	10
4510	1l.20 Deva	35	10
4511	1l.20 Drobeta Turnu Severin	35	10
4512	1l.20 Focsani	35	10
4513	1l.20 Galati	35	10
4514	1l.20 Gheorghe Gheorghiu Dej	35	10
4515	1l.20 Giurgiu	35	10
4516	1l.20 Hunedoara	35	10
4517	1l.20 Iasi	35	10
4518	1l.20 Lugoj	35	10
4519	1l.20 Medias	35	10
4520	1l.20 Odorheiu Secuiesc	35	10

889 Costumes of Maramures (female)

1979. Costumes. Multicoloured.

4521	20b. Type **889**	10	10
4522	40b. Maramures (male)	10	10
4523	55b. Vrancea (female)	10	10
4524	1l.50 Vrancea (male)	45	10
4525	3l. Padureni (female)	90	30
4526	3l.40 Padureni (male)	1·00	40

890 Post Coding Desks

1979. Stamp Day.

4527	**890**	2l.10+1l.90 mult	1·20	50

891 Figure Skating

1979. Winter Olympic Games, Lake Placid (1980). Multicoloured.

4528	55b. Type **891**	10	10
4529	1l. Downhill skiing	35	10
4530	1l.50 Biathlon	45	10
4531	2l.15 Bobsleighing	65	15
4532	3l.40 Speed skating	1·00	20
4533	4l.80 Ice hockey	1·50	30
MS4534	70×78 mm. 10l. Ice hockey (different) (37×49 mm)	5·50	5·50

892 Locomotive "Calugareni", 1869

1979. International Transport Exhibition, Hamburg. Multicoloured.

4535	55b. Type **892**	10	10
4536	1l. Steam locomotive "Orleans"	35	10
4537	1l.50 Steam locomotive No. 1059	45	10
4538	2l.15 Steam locomotive No. 150211	65	15
4539	3l.40 Steam locomotive No. 231085	1·00	20
4540	4l.80 Class 060-EA electric locomotive	1·50	30
MS4541	80×70 mm. 10l. Diesel locomotive (50×38 mm)	6·75	6·75

1980. Arms (4th series). As T **836**. Multicoloured.

4542	1l.20 Oradea	35	10
4543	1l.20 Petrosani	35	10
4544	1l.20 Piatra Neamt	35	10
4545	1l.20 Pitesti	35	10
4546	1l.20 Ploiesti	35	10
4547	1l.20 Resita	35	10
4548	1l.20 Rimnicu Vilcea	35	10
4549	1l.20 Roman	35	10
4550	1l.20 Satu Mare	35	10
4551	1l.20 Sibiu	35	10
4552	1l.20 Sighetu Marmatiei	35	10
4553	1l.20 Sighisoara	35	10
4554	1l.20 Suceava	35	10
4555	1l.20 Tecuci	35	10
4556	1l.20 Timisoara	35	10
4557	1l.20 Tirgoviste	35	10
4558	1l.20 Tirgu Jiu	35	10
4559	1l.20 Tirgu-Mures	35	10
4560	1l.20 Tulcea	35	10
4561	1l.20 Turda	35	10
4562	1l.20 Turnu Magurele	35	10
4563	1l.20 Bucharest	35	10

893 Dacian Warrior

1980. 2050th Anniv of Independent Centralized Dacian State under Burebista.

4564	55b. Type **893**	10	10
4565	1l.50 Dacian fighters with flag	45	20

894 River Kingfisher

1980. European Nature Protection Year. Multicoloured.

4566	55b. Type **894**	25	10
4567	1l. Great egret (vert)	35	10
4568	1l.50 Red-breasted goose	40	10
4569	2l.15 Red deer (vert)	50	15
4570	3l.40 Roe deer fawn	60	20
4571	4l.80 European bison (vert)	1·20	30
MS4572	90×78 mm. 10l. Eastern white pelicans ("Pelecanus onocrotallus") (38×50 mm)	3·00	3·00

895 Scarborough Lily

1980. Exotic Flowers from Bucharest Botanical Gardens. Multicoloured.

4573	55b. Type **895**	10	10
4574	1l. Floating water hyacinth	35	10
4575	1l.50 Jacobean lily	50	10
4576	2l.15 Rose of Sharon	70	15
4577	3l.40 Camellia	1·10	20
4578	4l.80 Lotus	1·60	35

896 Tudor Vladimirescu

1980. Anniversaries. Multicoloured.

4579	40b. Type **896** (revolutionary leader) (birth bicent)	10	10
4580	55b. Mihail Sadoveanu (writer) (birth cent)	10	10
4581	1l.50 Battle of Posada (650th anniv)	50	15
4582	2l.15 Tudor Arghezi (poet) (birth cent)	70	20
4583	3l. Horea (leader, Transylvanian uprising) (250th birth anniv)	95	35

897 George Enescu playing Violin

1980. Inter-European Cultural and Economic Co-operation. Two sheets, each 107×81 mm containing horiz designs as T **897**.

MS4584	(a) 1l.30 ×4 emerald (Type **897**); red (Enescu conducting); violet (Enescu at piano); blue (Enescu composing). (b) 3l.40 ×4 emerald (Beethoven at piano); red (Beethoven conducting); violet (Beethoven at piano (different); blue (Beethoven composing) Set of 2 sheets	8·50	8·50

898 Dacian Fruit Dish

1980. Bimillenary of Dacian Fortress, Petrodava (now Piatra Neamt).

4585	**898**	1l. multicoloured	60	35

899 Throwing the Javelin

1980. Olympic Games, Moscow. Multicoloured.

4586	55b. Type **899**	10	10
4587	1l. Fencing	35	10
4588	1l.50 Pistol shooting	50	10
4589	2l.15 Single kayak	70	15
4590	3l.40 Wrestling	1·10	20
4591	4l.80 Single skiff	1·60	35
MS4592	90×78 mm. 10l. Handball (38×50 mm)	4·75	4·75

900 Postman handing Letter to Woman

1980. 2050th Anniv of Independent Centralized Dacic State National Stamp Exhibition. Sheet 78×90 mm.

MS4593	5l.+5l. multicoloured	4·75	4·75

901 Congress Emblem

1980. 15th International Congress of Historical Sciences.

4594	**901**	55b. deep blue and blue	60	35

902 Fireman carrying Child

1980. Firemen's Day.

4595	**902**	55b. multicoloured	60	35

903 Chinese and Romanian Stamp Collectors

1980. Romanian–Chinese Stamp Exhibition, Bucharest.

4596	**903**	1l. multicoloured	95	55

904 National Assembly Building, Bucharest

1980. European Security and Co-operation Conference, Madrid. Sheet 78×90 mm.

MS4597	10l. multicoloured	3·00	3·00

905 Rooks and Chessboard

1980. 24th Chess Olympiad, Malta. Multicoloured.

4598	55b. Knights and chessboard	10	10
4599	1l. Type **905**	35	10
4600	2l.15 Male head and chessboard	70	15
4601	4l.80 Female head and chessboard	1·60	35

906 Dacian Warrior

1980. Military Uniforms. Multicoloured.

4602	20b. Type **906**	10	10
4603	40b. Moldavian soldier (15th century)	10	10
4604	55b. Wallachian horseman (17th century)	10	10
4605	1l. Standard bearer (19th century)	35	10
4606	1l.50 Infantryman (19th century)	50	15
4607	2l.15 Lancer (19th century)	70	20
4608	4l.80 Hussar (19th century)	1·60	45

907 Burebista (sculpture, P. Mercea)

1980. Stamp Day and 2050th Anniv of Independent Centralized Dacic State.

4609	**907**	2l. multicoloured	60	35

908 George Oprescu

1981. Celebrities' Birth Anniversaries. Multicoloured.

4610	1l.50 Type **908** (historian and art critic, centenary)	50	10
4611	2l.15 Marius Bunescu (painter, centenary)	70	15
4612	3l.40 Ion Georgescu (sculptor, 125th anniv)	1·20	20

909 St. Bernard

1981. Dogs. Multicoloured.

4613	40b. Mountain sheepdog (horiz)	10	10
4614	55b. Type **909**	10	10
4615	1l. Fox terrier (horiz)	35	10
4616	1l.50 Alsatian (horiz)	50	15
4617	2l.15 Boxer (horiz)	70	20
4618	3l.40 Dalmatian (horiz)	1·20	35
4619	4l.80 Poodle	1·80	55

910 Paddle-steamer "Stefan cel Mare"

1981. 125th Anniv of European Danube Commission. Multicoloured.

4620	55b. Type **910**	25	10
4621	1l. "Prince Ferdinand de Roumanie" steam launch	30	20
4622	1l.50 Paddle-steamer "Tudor Vladimirescu"	35	30
4623	2l.15 Dredger "Sulina"	50	35
4624	3l.40 Paddle-steamer "Republica Populara Romana"	60	45
4625	4l.80 Freighter in Sulina Channel	1·20	90
MS4626	90×78 mm. 10l. "Moldova" (tourist ship) sailing past Galati (49×38 mm)	3·00	3·00

911 Bare-neck Pigeon

1981. Pigeons. Multicoloured.

4627	40b. Type **911**	10	10
4628	55b. Orbetan pigeon	20	10
4629	1l. Craiova chestnut pigeon	35	10
4630	1l.50 Timisoara pigeon	50	15
4631	2l.15 Homing pigeon	70	20
4632	3l.40 Salonta giant pigeon	1·20	35

912 Party Flag and Oak Leaves

1981. 60th Anniv of Romanian Communist Party.

4633	**912**	1l. multicoloured	60	35

913 "Invirtita" Dance, Oas-Maramured

1981. Inter-European Cultural and Economic Co-operation. Two sheets, each 107×81 mm containing horiz designs as T **913**. Multicoloured.

MS4634	(a) 2l.50 ×4 Type **913**; "Hora" dance, Dobrogea; "Briuletul" dance, Oltenia; "Arderleana" dance, Crisana. (b) 2l.50 ×4 "Taraneasca" dance, Moldovia; "Invirtita Sibiana" dance, Transylvania; "Jocul de 2" dance, Banat; "Calusul" dance, Muntenia Set of 2 sheets	4·75	4·75

914 "Soyuz 40"

1981. Air. Soviet–Romanian Space Flight. Multicoloured.

4635	55b. Type **914**	10	10
4636	3l.40 "Soyuz"–"Salyut" link-up	1·20	45
MS4637	78×90 mm. 10l. Cosmonauts and space complex (49×38 mm)	4·75	4·75

915 Sun and Mercury

1981. Air. The Planets. Multicoloured.

4638	55b. Type **915**	10	10
4639	1l. Venus, Earth and Mars	25	20
4640	1l.50 Jupiter	50	45
4641	2l.15 Saturn	60	55
4642	3l.40 Uranus	1·10	1·00
4643	4l.80 Neptune and Pluto	1·60	1·50
MS4644	90×77 mm. 10l. Earth seen from the Moon (38×49 mm)	4·75	4·75

916 Industrial Symbols

1981. "Singing Romania" National Festival. Multicoloured.

4645	55b. Type **916**	25	10
4646	1l.50 Technological symbols	60	15
4647	2l.15 Agricultural symbols	85	20
4648	3l.40 Cultural symbols	1·20	55

917 Book and Flag

1981. "Universiada" Games, Bucharest. Multicoloured.

4649	1l. Type **917**	25	10
4650	2l.15 Games emblem	60	35
4651	4l.80 Stadium (horiz)	1·40	1·10

918 "Woman in an Interior"

1981. 150th Birth Anniv of Theodor Aman (painter). Multicoloured.

4652	40b. "Self-portrait"	10	10
4653	55b. "Battle of Giurgiu" (horiz)	10	10
4654	1l. "Family Picnic" (horiz)	25	10
4655	1l.50 "The Painter's Studio" (horiz)	60	15
4656	2l.15 Type **918**	70	20
4657	3l.10 Aman Museum, Bucharest (horiz)	1·20	30

919 "The Thinker of Cernavoda" (polished stone sculpture)

1981. 16th International Congress of Historical Sciences.

4658	**919**	3l.40 multicoloured	1·20	1·10

920 Blood Donation

1981. Blood Donor Campaign.

4659	**920**	55b. multicoloured	60	35

921 Central Military Hospital

1981. 150th Anniv of Central Military Hospital, Bucharest.

4660	**921**	55b. multicoloured	60	35

922 Paul Constantinescu

1981. Romanian Musicians and Composers. Multicoloured.

4661	40b. George Enescu	10	10
4662	55b. Type **922**	10	10
4663	1l. Dinu Lipatti	35	10
4664	1l.50 Ionel Perlea	50	15
4665	2l.15 Ciprian Porumbescu	70	20
4666	3l.40 Mihail Jora	1·20	45

923 Children at Stamp Exhibition

1981. Stamp Day.

4667	**923**	2l. multicoloured	60	35

924 Hopscotch

1981. Children's Games and Activities. Multicoloured.

4668	40b. Type **924** (postage)	10	10
4669	55b. Football	10	10
4670	1l. Children with balloons and hobby horse	25	15
4671	1l.50 Fishing	35	20
4672	2l.15 Dog looking through school window at child	60	35
4673	3l. Child on stilts	85	55
4674	4l. Child tending sick dog	1·20	90
4675	4l.80 Children with model gliders (air)	1·40	1·10

Nos. 4671/15 are from illustrations by Norman Rockwell.

925 Football Players

1981. World Cup Football Championship, Spain (1982). Multicoloured.

4676	55b. Type **925**	10	10
4677	1l. Goalkeeper saving ball	25	10
4678	1l.50 Player heading ball	35	20
4679	2l.15 Player kicking ball over head	60	35
4680	3l.40 Goalkeeper catching ball	85	55
4681	4l.80 Player kicking ball	1·20	90
MS4682	90×78 mm. 10l. Goalkeeper catching ball headed by player (38×50 mm)	4·75	4·75

926 Alexander the Good, Prince of Moldavia

1982. Anniversaries. Multicoloured.

4683	1l. Type **926** (550th death anniv)	35	15
4684	1l.50 Bodgan P. Hasdeu (historian, 75th death anniv)	50	20
4685	2l.15 Nicolae Titulescu (diplomat and politician, birth centenary)	85	35

927 Entrance to Union Square Station

1982. Inauguration of Bucharest Underground Railway. Multicoloured.

4686	60b. Type **927**	25	10
4687	2l.40 Platforms and train at Heroes' Square station	85	35

928 Dog rescuing Child from Sea

1982. Dog, Friend of Mankind. Multicoloured.

4688	55b. Type **928**	10	10
4689	1l. Shepherd and sheepdog (vert)	35	15
4690	3l. Gundog (vert)	95	20
4691	3l.40 Huskies	1·10	20
4692	4l. Dog carrying woman's basket (vert)	1·20	35
4693	4l.80 Dog guiding blind person (vert)	1·40	35
4694	5l. Dalmatian and child with doll	1·60	45
4695	6l. St. Bernard	1·80	45

929 Dove, Banner and Crowd

1982. 60th Anniv of Communist Youth Union. Multicoloured.

4696	1l. Type **929**	25	15
4697	1l.20 Construction worker	25	15
4698	1l.50 Farm workers	35	15
4699	2l. Laboratory worker and students	60	20
4700	2l.50 Labourers	85	30
4701	3l. Choir, musicians and dancers	95	35

930 Bran

1982. Inter-European Cultural and Economic Co-operation. Two sheets, each 108×80 mm containing horiz designs as T **930**. Multicoloured.

MS4702 2l.50 ×4 Type **930**; Hunedoara; Sinaia; Lasi. (b) 2l.50 ×4 Neuschwanstein; Stolzenfeis; Katz-Loreley; Linderhof Set of 2 sheets 7·25 7·25

931 Constantin Brancusi (sculptor)

1982. "Philexfrance '82" International Stamp Exhibition, Paris. Sheet 71×81 mm.

MS4703 10l. multicoloured 4·75 4·75

932 Harvesting Wheat

1982. 20th Anniv of Agricultural Co-operatives. Multicoloured.

4704	50b. Type **932** (postage)	10	10
4705	1l. Cows and milking equipment	25	10
4706	1l.50 Watering apple trees	35	15
4707	2l.50 Cultivator in vineyard	70	30
4708	3l. Watering vegetables	95	35
4709	4l. Helicopter spraying cereal crop (air)	1·20	45

MS4710 68×80 mm. 10l. Aerial view of new village (50×37 mm) 4·75 4·75

933 Vladimir Nicolae's Standard 1 Hang-glider

1982. Air. Hang-gliders. Multicoloured.

4711	50b. Type **933**	10	10
4712	1l. Excelsior D	25	10
4713	1l.50 Dedal-1	35	20
4714	2l.50 Entuziast	85	35
4715	4l. AK-22	1·20	55
4716	5l. Grifrom	1·60	65

934 Baile Felix

1982. Spas and Health Resorts. Multicoloured.

4717	50b. Type **934**	10	10
4718	1l. Predeal (horiz)	25	10
4719	1l.50 Baile Herculane	50	15
4720	2l.50 Eforie Nord (horiz)	70	30
4721	3l. Olimp (horiz)	85	35
4722	5l. Neptun (horiz)	1·60	55

935 "Legend"

1982. Paintings by Sabin Balasa. Multicoloured.

4723	1l. Type **935**	35	15
4724	1l.50 "Contrasts"	50	20
4725	2l.50 "Peace Relay"	1·30	55
4726	4l. "Genesis of the Romanian People" (vert)	1·40	65

936 Vlaicu Monument, Banesti-Prahova

1982. Air. Birth Centenary of Aurel Vlaicu (aviation pioneer). Multicoloured.

4727	50b. Vlaicu's glider, 1909 (horiz)	10	10
4728	1l. Type **936**	35	20
4729	2l.50 Air Heroes' Monument	95	55
4730	3l. Vlaicu's No. 1 airplane "Crazy Fly", 1910 (horiz)	1·10	65

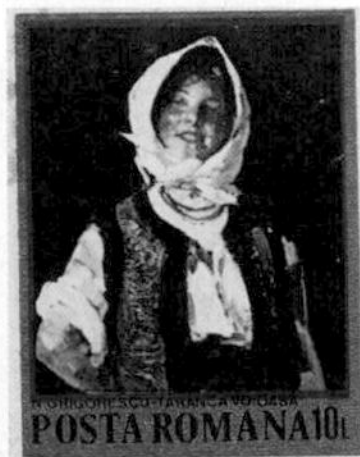

937 "Cheerful Peasant Woman"

1982. 75th Death Anniv Nicolae Grigorescu (artist). Sheet 70×80 mm.

MS4731 10l. multicoloured 4·75 4·75

938 Central Exhibition Pavilion

1982. "Tib '82" International Fair, Bucharest.

4732	**938**	2l. multicoloured	70	35

939 Young Pioneer with Savings Book and Books

1982. Savings Week. Multicoloured.

4733	1l. Type **939**	35	15
4734	2l. Savings Bank advertisement (Calin Popovici)	70	20

940 Postwoman delivering Letters

1982. Stamp Day. Multicoloured.

4735	1l. Type **940**	35	15
4736	2l. Postman	70	20

941 "Brave Young Man and the Golden Apples" (Petre Ispirescu)

1982. Fairy Tales. Multicoloured.

4737	50b. Type **941**	10	10
4738	1l. "Bear tricked by the Fox" (Ion Creanga)	25	10
4739	1l.50 Warrior fighting bird ("Prince of Tears" (Mihai Eminescu))	50	15
4740	2l.50 Hen with bag ("Bag with Two Coins" (Ion Creanga))	70	20
4741	3l. Rider fighting three-headed dragon ("Ileana Simziana" (Petre Ispirescu))	85	35
4742	5l. Man riding devil ("Danila Prepeleac" (Ion Creanga))	1·60	55

942 Symbols of Industry, Party Emblem and Programme

1982. Romanian Communist Party National Conference, Bucharest. Multicoloured.

4743	1l. Type **942**	35	15
4744	2l. Wheat symbols of industry and Party emblem and open programme	70	20

943 Wooden Canteen from Suceava

1982. Household Utensils.

4745	**943**	50b. red	10	10
4746	-	1l. blue	35	10
4747	-	1l.50 orange	60	10
4748	-	2l. blue	70	10
4749	-	3l. green	1·10	10
4750	-	3l.50 green	1·30	10
4751	-	4l. brown	1·60	10
4752	-	5l. blue	1·90	10
4753	-	6l. blue	2·30	10
4754	-	7l. purple	2·75	10
4755	-	7l.50 mauve	2·75	10
4756	-	8l. green	3·00	10
4757	-	10l. red	3·00	10
4758	-	20l. violet	4·25	20
4759	-	30l. blue	7·25	35
4760	-	50l. brown	12·00	45

DESIGNS: As T **943**—VERT: 1l. Ceramic plates from Radauti; 2l. Jug and plate from Vama-Maramures; 3l. Wooden churn and pail from North Moldavia; 4l. Wooden spoons and ceramic plate from Cluj; 5l. Ceramic bowl and pot from Marginea-Suceava. HORIZ: 1l.50, Wooden dipper from Valea Mare; 3l.50, Ceramic plates from Leheceni-Crisana. 29×23 mm: 10l. Wooden tubs from Hunedoara and Suceava; 30l. Wooden spoons from Alba. 23×29 mm: 6l. Ceramic pot and jug from Bihor; 7l. Distaff and spindle from Transylvania; 7l.50, Double wooden pail from Suceava; 8l. Pitcher and ceramic plate from Oboga and Horezu; 20l. Wooden canteen and six glasses from Horezu; 50l. Ceramic plates from Horezu.

944 Wheat, Cogwheel, Flask and Electricity Emblem

1982. 35th Anniv of People's Republic. Multicoloured.

4767	1l. Type **944**	35	15
4768	2l. National flag and oak leaves	70	35

945 H. Coanda and Diagram of Jet Engine

1983. Air. 25 Years of Space Exploration. Multicoloured.

4769	50b. Type **945**	10	10
4770	1l. H. Oberth and diagram of rocket	35	10
4771	1l.50 "Sputnik 1", 1957 (first artificial satellite)	60	15
4772	2l.50 "Vostok 1", (first manned flight)	85	20
4773	4l. "Apollo 11, 1969 (first Moon landing)	1·40	35
4774	5l. Space shuttle "Columbia"	1·80	55

MS4775 93×80 mm. 10l. Earth (41×53 mm) 7·25 7·25

946 Rombac One Eleven 500 Jetliner

1983. Air. First Romanian-built Jetliner.

4776	**946**	11l. blue	4·25	80

947 Matei Millo in "The Discontented" by Vasile Alecsandri

1983. Romanian Actors.

4777	**947**	50b. red and black	10	10
4778	-	1l. green and black	35	10
4779	-	1l.50 violet and black	60	10
4780	-	2l. brown and black	70	10
4781	-	2l.50 green and black	95	15
4782	-	3l. blue and black	1·20	20
4783	-	4l. green and black	1·40	35
4784	-	5l. lilac and black	1·80	45

DESIGNS: 1l. Mihail Pascaly in "Director Millo" by Vasile Alecsandri; 1l.50, Aristizza Romanescu in "The Dogs" by H. Lecca; 2l. C. I. Nottara in "Blizzard" by B. S. Delavrancea; 2l.50, Grigore Manolescu in "Hamlet" by William Shakespeare; 3l. Agatha Birsescu in "Medea" by Lebouvet; 4l. Ion Brezeanu in "The Lost Letter" by I. L. Caragiale; 5l. Aristide Demetriad in "The Despotic Prince" by Vasile Alecsandri.

948 Hugo Grotius

1983. 400th Birth Anniv of Hugo Grotius (Dutch jurist).

4785	**948**	2l. brown	95	55

949 Aro "10"

1983. Romanian-built Vehicles. Multicoloured.

4786	50b. Type **949**	25	10
4787	1l. Dacia "1300" Break	50	10
4788	1l.50 Aro "242"	70	15
4789	2l.50 Aro "244"	1·20	20
4790	4l. Dacia "1310"	1·90	35
4791	5l. Oltcit "Club"	2·40	55

950 Johannes Kepler (astronomer)

1983. Inter-European Cultural and Economic Co-operation. Two sheets, each 110×80 mm containing horiz designs as T **950**. Multicoloured.

MS4792 (a) 3l. ×4 Type **950**; Alexander von Humboldt (explorer) and "Pizarro" J.W. von Goethe (writer); Richard Wagner (composer). (b) 3l. ×4 Ion Andreescu (artist); George Constantinescu (engineer); Tudor Arghezi (writer); C. I. Parhon (physician) Set of 2 sheets 7·25 7·25

951 National and Communist Party Flags

1983. 50th Anniv of 1933 Workers' Revolution.

4793	**951**	2l. multicoloured	95	55

952 Loading Mail into Boeing 707

1983. Air. World Communications Year.

4794	**952**	2l. multicoloured	95	55

953 Bluethroat

1983. Birds of the Danube Delta. Multicoloured.

4795	50b. Type **953**	25	10
4796	1l. Rose-coloured starling	50	10
4797	1l.50 European roller	70	15
4798	2l.50 European bee eater	1·20	20
4799	4l. Reed bunting	1·90	35
4800	5l. Lesser grey shrike	2·40	45

954 Kayak

1983. Water Sports. Multicoloured.

4801	50b. Type **954**	25	10
4802	1l. Water polo	50	10
4803	1l.50 Canoeing	70	15
4804	2l.50 Diving	1·20	20
4805	4l. Rowing	1·90	35
4806	5l. Swimming (start of race)	2·40	45

955 Postman on Bicycle

1983. Stamp Day. Multicoloured.

4807	1l. Type **955**	35	15
4808	3l.50(+3l.) National flag as stamp	1·40	1·10

MS4809 90×79 mm. 10l. Unloading mail from Rombac One Eleven 500 at Bucharest airport (38×50 mm) (air) 7·25 7·25

No. 4808 was issued se-tenant with a premium-carrying tab showing the Philatelic Association emblem.

956 "Geum reptans"

1983. European Flora and Fauna. Multicoloured.

4810	1l. Type **956**	70	45
4811	1l. Long-headed poppy	70	45
4812	1l. Stemless carline thistle	70	45
4813	1l. "Paeonia peregrina"	70	45
4814	1l. "Gentiana excisa"	70	45
4815	1l. Eurasian red squirrel	70	45
4816	1l. "Grammia quenselii" (butterfly)	70	45
4817	1l. Middle-spotted woodpecker	70	45
4818	1l. Lynx	70	45
4819	1l. Wallcreeper	70	45

957 "Girl with Feather"

1983. Paintings by Corneliu Baba. Multicoloured.

4820	1l. Type **957**	50	15
4821	2l. "Congregation"	95	20
4822	3l. "Farm Workers"	1·40	35
4823	4l. "Rest in the Fields" (horiz)	1·90	45

958 Flag and Oak Leaves

1983. 65th Anniv of Union of Transylvania and Romania. Multicoloured.

4824	1l. Type **958**	50	20
4825	2l. National and Communist Party Flags and Parliament building, Bucharest	95	35

959 Postman and Post Office

1983. "Balkanfila IX '83" Stamp Exhibition, Bucharest. Multicoloured.

4826	1l. Type **959**	50	20
4827	2l. Postwoman and Athenaeum Concert Hall	95	35

MS4828 90×78 mm. 10l. Balkan flags and Athenaeum Concert Hall (37×50 mm) 4·75 4·75

960 "Orient Express" at Bucharest, 1883

1983. Centenary of "Orient Express". Sheet 90×78 mm.

MS4829 **960** 10l. multicoloured 7·25 7·25

961 Cross-country Skiing

1984. Winter Olympic Games, Sarajevo. Multicoloured.

4830	50b. Type **961**	10	10
4831	1l. Biathlon	35	15
4832	1l.50 Ice skating	50	20
4833	2l. Speed skating	70	35
4834	3l. Ice hockey	95	45
4835	3l.50 Bobsleighing	1·20	55
4836	4l. Luge	1·40	65
4837	5l. Downhill skiing	1·80	85

962 Prince Cuza and Arms

1984. 125th Anniv of Union of Moldova and Wallachia. Sheet 90×78 mm.

MS4838 **962** 10l. multicoloured 4·75 4·75

963 Palace of Udriste Nasturel (Chancery official)

1984. Anniversaries.

4839	50b. green, pink and silver	25	10
4840	1l. violet, green and silver	50	10
4841	1l.50 multicoloured	70	15
4842	2l. brown, blue and silver	95	20
4843	3l.50 multicoloured	1·70	40
4844	4l. multicoloured	1·90	45

DESIGNS: 50b. Type **963** (325th death anniv); 1l. Miron Costin (poet, 350th birth anniv); 1l.50, Crisan (Giurgiu Marcu) (leader of peasant revolt, 250th birth anniv); 2l. Simion Barnutiu (scientist, 175th birth anniv); 3l.50, Diuliu Zamfirescu (writer, 125th birth anniv); 4l. Nicolae Milescu at Great Wall of China (explorer, 275th death anniv).

964 Chess Game

1984. 15th Balkan Chess Championships, Baile Herculane. Sheet 107×80 mm containing T **964** and similar horiz designs. Multicoloured.

MS4845 3l. ×4 various chess games 7·25 7·25

965 Orsova Bridge

1984. Inter-European Cultural and Economic Co-operation. Two sheets each 108×81 mm containing horiz designs as T **965**. Multicoloured.

MS4846 (a) 3l. ×4 Type **965**; Arges Bridge, Basarabi Bridge; Ohaba Bridge all in Rumania. (b) 3l. ×4 Kohlbrand Bridge, Hamburg; Bosphorus Bridge, Istanbul; Europa Bridge, Innsbruck; Tower Bridge, London Set of 2 sheets 7·25 7·25

966 Sunflower

1984. Protection of Environment. Multicoloured.

4847	1l. Type **966**	50	10
4848	2l. Red deer	95	20
4849	3l. Carp	1·40	45
4850	4l. Jay	1·90	55

967 Flowering Rush

1984. Flowers of the Danube. Multicoloured.

4851	50b. Arrowhead	25	10
4852	1l. Yellow iris	50	10
4853	1l.50 Type **967**	70	15
4854	3l. White water lily	1·40	30
4855	4l. Fringed water lily (horiz)	1·90	35
4856	5l. Yellow water lily (horiz)	2·40	55

968 Crowd with Banners

1984. 45th Anniv of Anti-Fascist Demonstration.

4857	**968**	2l. multicoloured	1·20	55

969 High Jumping

1984. Olympic Games, Los Angeles (1st issue). Multicoloured.

4858	50b. Type **969**	10	10
4859	1l. Swimming	35	15
4860	1l.50 Running	50	20
4861	3l. Handball	1·10	50
4862	4l. Rowing	1·30	60
4863	5l. Canoeing	1·90	90

See also Nos. 4866/73.

970 Congress Emblem

1984. 25th Ear, Nose and Throat Association Congress, Bucharest.

4864	**970**	2l. multicoloured	95	55

971 Footballers and Romanian Flag

1984. European Cup Football Championship. Two sheets, each 109×81 mm containing horiz designs as T **971** showing footballers and national flag. Multicoloured.

MS4865	(a) 3l. ×Type **971**; West Germany; Portugal; Spain. (b) 3l. ×4 France; Belgium; Yugoslavia; Denmark Set of 2 sheets	12·00	12·00

1984. Olympic Games, Los Angeles (2nd issue). As T **969**. Multicoloured.

4866	50b. Boxing	10	10
4867	1l. Rowing	25	10
4868	1l. Handball	40	15
4869	2l. Judo	50	20
4870	3l. Wrestling	85	40
4871	3l.50 Fencing	95	45
4872	4l. Kayak	1·10	50
4873	5l. Swimming	1·40	65

972 Mihai Ciuca (bacteriologist, cent)

1984. Birth Anniversaries. Dated "1983".

4874	**972**	1l. purple, blue and silver	35	15
4875	-	2l. brown and silver	70	20
4876	-	3l. green, brown and silver	1·10	45
4877	-	4l. violet, green and silver	1·40	55

DESIGNS: 2l. Petre S. Aurelian (agronomist, 150th anniv); 3l. Alexandru Vlahuta (writer, 125th anniv); 4l. Dimitrie Leonida (engineer, centenary).

973 Lockhead 14 Super Electra

1984. Air. 40th Anniv of International Civil Aviation Organization. Multicoloured.

4878	50b. Type **973**	25	10
4879	1l.50 Britten Norman Islander	70	20
4880	3l. Rombac One Eleven 500 jetliner	1·40	45
4881	6l. Boeing 707 jetliner	3·00	55

974 Flags, Flame and Power Station

1984. 40th Anniv of Liberation.

4882	**974**	2l. multicoloured	1·20	55

975 Lippizaner

1984. Horses. Multicoloured.

4883	50b. Type **975**	25	10
4884	1l. Hutul	50	10
4885	1l.50 Bukovina	70	15
4886	2l.50 Nonius	1·20	20
4887	4l. Arab	1·90	35
4888	5l. Romanian halfbreed	2·40	45

976 V. Racila (woman's singles sculls, gold)

1984. Romanian Olympic Games Medal Winners. Two sheets, each 125×129 mm containing four designs as T **976**. Multicoloured.

MS4889	(a) 3l. ×6 Type **976**; P. Becheru and N. Vlad (weightlifting, gold); D. Melinte (800m.) and M. Puica (3000m. women's running, gold); Men's canoeing (Canadian pairs, gold); Fencing (silver); Women's modern rhythmic gymnastics (silver). (b) 3l. ×6, Women's team gymnastics (gold); Women's kayak fours (gold); A. Stanciu (women's long jump, gold); I. Draica and V. Andrei (wrestling, gold); Judo (bronze); Pistol shooting (silver) Set of 2 sheets	18·00	18·00

977 Memorial, Alba Julia

1984. Bicentenary of Horea, Closa and Crisan Uprisings.

4890	**977**	2l. multicoloured	70	45

978 "Portrait of a Child" (TH. Aman)

1984. Paintings of Children. Multicoloured.

4891	50b. Type **978**	10	10
4892	1l. "The Little Shepherd" (N. Grigorescu)	35	10
4893	2l. "Lica with an Orange" (St. Luchian)	70	15
4894	3l. "Portrait of a Child" (N. Tonitza)	1·10	20
4895	4l. "Portrait of a Boy" (S. Popp)	1·60	35
4896	5l. "Portrait of Young Girl" (I. Tuculescu)	2·00	45

979 Stage Coach and Romanian Philatelic Association Emblem

1984. Stamp Day.

4897	**979**	2l.(+1l.) multicoloured	95	55

No. 4897 was issued with premium-carrying label as shown in T **979**.

980 Flags and Party Emblem

1984. 13th Romanian Communist Party Congress, Bucharest. Sheet 90×78 mm.

MS4898	10l. multicoloured	8·50	8·50

981 Dalmatian Pelicans

1984. Protected Animals. Dalmatian Pelicans. Multicoloured.

4899	50b. Type **981**	25	15
4900	1l. Pelican on nest	60	35
4901	1l. Pelicans on lake	60	35
4902	2l. Pelicans roosting	95	55

982 Dr. Petru Groza (former President)

1984. Anniversaries. Multicoloured.

4903	50b. Type **982** (birth centenary)	10	10
4904	1l. Alexandru Odobescu (writer) (150th birth anniv)	35	10
4905	2l. Dr. Carol Davila (physician) (death centenary)	60	15
4906	3l. Dr. Nicolae Gh. Lupu (physician) (birth centenary)	1·10	20
4907	4l. Dr. Daniel Danielopolu (physician) (birth centenary)	1·30	35
4908	5l. Panait Istrati (writer) (birth centenary)	1·80	45

983 Generator

1984. Centenary of Power Station and Electric Street Lighting in Timisoara. Multicoloured.

4909	1l. Type **983**	35	20
4910	2l. Street lamp	70	35

984 Gounod and Paris Opera House

1985. Inter-European Cultural and Economic Co-operation. Composers. Two sheets, each 110×80 mm containing horiz designs as T **984**.

MS4911	(a) 3l. ×4 green and violet (Type **984**); red and blue (Strauss and Munich Opera House); violet and green (Mozart and Vienna Opera House); blue and red (Verdi and La Scala, Milan). (b) 3l. ×4 violet and green (Tchaikovsky and Bolshoi Theatre, Moscow); blue and red (Enescu and Bucharest Opera House); green and violet (Wagner and Dresden Opera House); red and blue (Moniuszko and Warsaw Opera House) Set of 2 sheets	7·25	7·25

985 August Treboniu Laurian (linguist and historian)

1985. Anniversaries. Multicoloured.

4912	50b. Type **985** (175th birth anniv)	10	10
4913	1l. Grigore Alexandrescu (writer) (death centenary)	25	10
4914	1l.50 Gheorghe Pop de Basesti (politician) (150th birth anniv)	50	15
4915	2l. Mateiu Caragiale (writer) (birth centenary)	70	20
4916	3l. Gheorghe Ionescu-Sisesti (scientist) (birth centenary)	95	35
4917	4l. Liviu Rebreanu (writer) (birth centenary)	1·40	55

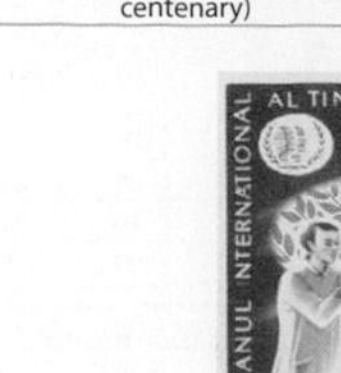

986 Students in Science Laboratory

1985. International Youth Year. Multicoloured.

4918	1l. Type **986**	35	20
4919	2l. Students on construction site	70	35
MS4920	91×79 mm. 10l. Students with banner and dove (53×41 mm)	4·75	4·75

987 Racoon Dog

1985. Protected Animals. Multicoloured.

4921	50b. Type **987**	25	10
4922	1l. Grey partridge	50	10
4923	1l.50 Snowy owl	70	10
4924	2l. Pine marten	95	15
4925	3l. Eurasian badger	1·30	20
4926	3l.50 Eurasian otter	1·40	30
4927	4l. Western Capercaillie	1·70	35
4928	5l. Great bustard	2·00	45

988 Flags and Victory Monument, Bucharest

1985. 40th Anniv of Victory in Europe Day.

4929	**988**	2l. multicoloured	1·20	55

989 Union Emblem

1985. Communist Youth Union Congress.

4930	**989**	2l. multicoloured	70	55

990 Route Map and Canal

1985. Danube–Black Sea Canal. Multicoloured.

4931	1l. Type **990**	50	10
4932	2l. Canal and bridge, Cernavoda	95	15
4933	3l. Road over Canal, Medgidia	1·40	20
4934	4l. Canal control tower, Agigea	1·80	35
MS4935	90×79 mm. 10l. Opening ceremony (53×39 mm)	9·00	9·00

991 Brown Pelican

1985. Birth Bicentenary of John J. Audubon (ornithologist). Multicoloured.

4936	50b. American robin (horiz)	25	10
4937	1l. Type **991**	50	10
4938	1l.50 Yellow-crowned night heron	70	15
4939	2l. Northern oriole	95	20
4940	3l. Red-necked grebe	1·40	35
4941	4l. Mallard (horiz)	1·90	45

992 "Fire"

1985. Paintings by Ion Tuculescu. Multicoloured.

4942	1l. Type **992**	25	10
4943	2l. "Circulation"	60	20
4944	3l. "Interior of Peasant's Home" (horiz)	85	35
4945	4l. "Sunset" (horiz)	1·20	55

993 Peacock

1985. Butterflies and Moths. Multicoloured.

4946	50b. Type **993**	10	10
4947	1l. Swallowtail	35	10
4948	2l. Red admiral	70	15
4949	3l. Emperor moth	1·20	20
4950	4l. Hebe tiger moth	1·60	35
4951	5l. Eyed hawk moth	1·90	45

994 Transfagarasan Mountain Road

1985. 20th Anniv of Election of General Secretary Nicolae Ceausescu and Ninth Communist Party Congress. Multicoloured.

4952	1l. Type **994**	60	20
4953	2l. Danube–Black Sea Canal	1·20	35
4954	3l. Bucharest underground railway	1·80	55
4955	4l. Irrigating fields	2·40	80

995 Romanian Crest, Symbols of Agriculture and "XX"

1985. 20th Anniv of Romanian Socialist Republic. Multicoloured.

4956	1l. Type **995**	60	25
4957	2l. Crest, symbols of industry and "XX"	1·20	35

996 Daimlers' Motor Cycle, 1885

1985. Centenary of Motor Cycle. Sheet 91×79 mm.

MS4958	10l. multicoloured	4·75	4·75

997 "Senecio glaberrimus"

1985. 50th Anniv of Retezat National Park. Multicoloured.

4959	50b. Type **997**	25	10
4960	1l. Chamois	50	15
4961	2l. "Centaurea retezatensis"	95	20
4962	3l. Violet	1·20	25
4963	4l. Alpine marmot	1·70	35
4964	5l. Golden eagle	2·00	55
MS4965	91×80 mm. 10l. Lynx ("Lynx lynx")	6·00	6·00

998 Universal "530 DTC"

1985. Romanian Tractors. Multicoloured.

4966	50b. Type **998**	10	10
4967	1l. Universal "550 M HC"	35	15
4968	1l.50 Universal "650 Super"	50	20
4969	2l. Universal "850"	70	25
4970	3l. Universal "S 1801 IF" tracked front loader	1·20	35
4971	4l. Universal "A 3602 IF" front loader	1·80	55

999 Costume of Muscel (female)

1985. Costumes (1st series). Multicoloured.

4972	50b. Type **999**	10	10
4973	50b. Muscel (male)	10	10
4974	1l.50 Bistrita-Nasaud (female)	50	20
4975	1l.50 Bistrita-Nasaud (male)	50	20
4976	2l. Vrancea (female)	70	35
4977	2l. Vrancea (male)	70	35
4978	3l. Vilcea (female)	95	45
4979	3l. Vilcea (male)	95	45

See also Nos. 5143/5150.

1000 Footballer attacking Goal

1985. World Cup Football Championship, Mexico (1986) (1st issue). Multicoloured.

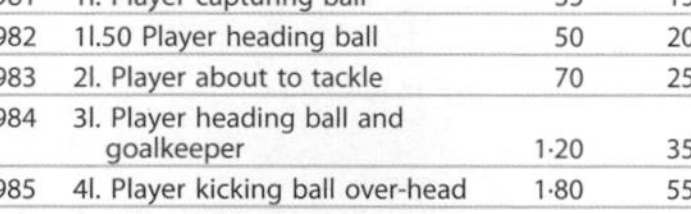

4980	50b. Type **1000**	10	10
4981	1l. Player capturing ball	35	15
4982	1l.50 Player heading ball	50	20
4983	2l. Player about to tackle	70	25
4984	3l. Player heading ball and goalkeeper	1·20	35
4985	4l. Player kicking ball over-head	1·80	55

See also Nos. 5038/43.

1001 U.N. Emblem and "40"

1985. 40th Anniv of U.N.O. (4986) and 30th Anniv of Romanian Membership (4987).

4986	2l. Type **1001**	60	45
4987	2l. U.N. building, New York, U.N. emblem and Romanian crest	60	45

1002 Copper

1985. Minerals. Multicoloured.

4988	50b. Quartz and calcite	10	10
4989	1l. Type **1002**	25	15
4990	2l. Gypsum	70	20
4991	3l. Quartz	95	25
4992	4l. Stibium	1·30	35
4993	5l. Tetrahedrite	1·80	55

1003 Posthorn

1985. Stamp Day.

4994	**1003**	2l.(+1l.) multicoloured	1·20	1·10

1004 Goofy as Hank waking to find himself at Camelot

1985. 150th Birth of Mark Twain (writer). Scenes from "A Connecticut Yankee in King Arthur's Court" (film). Multicoloured.

4995	50b. Type **1004**	3·00	2·20
4996	50b. Hank at the stake and Merlin (Mickey Mouse)	3·00	2·20
4997	50b. Hank being hoisted onto horseback in full armour	3·00	2·20
4998	50b. Pete as Sir Sagramoor on horseback	3·00	2·20
MS4999	122×96 mm. 5l. Hank at the tournament against Sir Sagramor	24·00	24·00

1985. Birth Bicentenaries of Grimm Brothers (folklorists). Scenes from "The Three Brothers". As T **1004**. Multicoloured.

5000	1l. Father (Donald Duck) bidding farewell to the brothers (Huey, Louie and Dewey)	7·25	6·75
5001	1l. Louie as fencing master brother	7·25	6·75
5002	1l. Louie keeping rain off his father with sword	7·25	6·75
5003	1l. Huey as blacksmith brother shoeing galloping horse	7·25	6·75
5004	1l. Dewey as barber brother shaving Brer Rabbit on the run	7·25	6·75
MS5005	120×95 mm. 5l. Brothers playing music	24·00	24·00

1005 Wright Brothers (aviation pioneers) and Wright Flyer 1

1985. Explorers and Pioneers. Multicoloured.

5006	1l. Type **1005**	35	10
5007	1l.50 Jacques Yves Cousteau (undersea explorer) and "Calypso"	50	10
5008	2l. Amelia Earhart (first woman trans-Atlantic flyer) and Fokker F.VIIb/3m seaplane "Friendship"	70	15
5009	3l. Charles Lindbergh (first solo trans-Atlantic flyer) and Ryan NYP Special "Spirit of St. Louis"	1·10	20
5010	3l.50 Sir Edmund Hillary (first man to reach summit of Everest)	1·20	25
5011	4l. Robert Peary and Emil Racovita (polar explorers)	1·40	30
5012	5l. Richard Byrd (polar explorer and aviator) and polar supply ship	1·80	40
5013	6l. Neil Armstrong (first man on Moon) and Moon	1·90	45

1006 Edmond Halley and Comet

1986. Air. Appearance of Halley's Comet.

5014	2l. Type **1006**	70	25
5015	4l. Comet, orbit and space probes	1·70	45

No. 5014 is wrongly inscr "Edmund".

1007 "Nina in Green"

1986. Paintings by Nicolae Tonitza. Multicoloured.

5016	1l. Type **1007**	35	10
5017	2l. "Irina"	70	20
5018	3l. "Forester's Daughter"	1·10	35
5019	4l. "Woman on Veranda"	1·40	55

1008 Wild Cat ("Felis silvestris")

1986. Inter-European Cultural and Economic Co-operation. Two sheets, each 110×81 mm containing horiz designs as T **1008**. Multicoloured.

MS5020	(a) 3l. ×4 Type **1008**; Stoat ("Mustela erminea"); Capercaillie ("Tetrao urogallus"); Brown bear ("Ursus arctos"). (b) 3l. ×4 "Dianthus callizonus"; Arolla pine ("Pinus cembra"); Willow ("Salix" sp.); "Rosa pendulina" Set of 2 sheets	7·25	7·25

1009 Goofy playing Clarinet

1986. 50th Anniv of Colour Animation. Scenes from "Band Concert" (cartoon film). Multicoloured.

5021	50b. Type **1009**	3·00	2·20
5022	50b. Clarabelle playing flute	3·00	2·20
5023	50b. Mickey Mouse conducting	3·00	2·20
5024	50b. Paddy and Peter Pig playing euphonium and trumpet	3·00	2·20
5025	1l. Conductor Mickey and flautist Donald Duck	7·25	6·75
5026	1l. Donald caught in trombone slide	7·25	6·75
5027	1l. Horace playing drums	7·25	6·75
5028	1l. Donald selling ice cream	7·25	6·75
5029	1l. Mickey and euphonium caught in tornado	7·25	6·75
MS5030	120×95 mm. 5l. Instruments and musicians in tree	24·00	24·00

1010 Hotel Diana, Baile Herculane

1986. Spa Hotels. Multicoloured.

5031	50b. Type **1010**	10	10
5032	1l. Hotel Termal, Baile Felix	25	15
5033	2l. Hotels Delfin, Meduza and Steaua de Mare, North Eforie	60	20
5034	3l. Hotel Caciulata, Calimanesti-Caciulata	95	25
5035	4l. Villa Palas, Slanic Moldova	1·30	35
5036	5l. Hotel Bradet, Sovata	1·90	55

1011 Ceausescu and Red Flag

1986. 65th Anniv of Romanian Communist Party.

5037	**1011**	2l. multicoloured	1·90	1·10

1012 Italy v. Bulgaria

1986. World Cup Football Championship, Mexico (2nd issue). Multicoloured.

5038	50b. Type **1012**	10	10
5039	1l. Mexico v. Belgium	25	15
5040	2l. Canada v. France	60	20
5041	3l. Brazil v. Spain	85	25
5042	4l. Uruguay v. W. Germany	1·40	35
5043	5l. Morocco v. Poland	1·90	55

1013 Alexandru Papanas' Bucker Bu 133 Jungmesister Biplane (Aerobatics Champion, 1936)

1986. Air. "Ameripex" '86 International Stamp Exhibition, Chicago. Sheet 120×95 mm.

MS5044	10l. multicoloured	4·75	4·75

1014 "Tulipa gesneriana"

1986. Garden Flowers. Multicoloured.

5045	50b. Type **1014**	10	10
5046	1l. "Iris hispanica"	35	15
5047	2l. "Rosa hybrida"	70	20
5048	3l. "Anemone coronaria"	1·10	25
5049	4l. "Freesia refracta"	1·40	35
5050	5l. "Chrysanthemum indicum"	1·90	55

1015 Mircea the Great and Horsemen

1986. 600th Anniv of Mircea the Great's Accession.

5051	**1015**	2l. multicoloured	70	45

1016 Thatched House with Veranda, Alba

1986. 50th Anniv of Museum of Historic Dwellings, Bucharest. Multicoloured.

5052	50b. Type **1016**	10	10
5053	1l. Stone-built house, Arges	35	15
5054	2l. House with veranda, Constanta	70	20
5055	3l. House with tiled roof and steps, Timis	1·10	25
5056	4l. House with ramp to veranda, Neamt	1·60	35
5057	5l. Two storey house with first floor veranda, Gorj	1·90	55

1017 Julius Popper (Tierra del Fuego, 1886–93)

1986. Polar Research. Multicoloured.

5058	50b. Type **1017**	10	10
5059	1l. Bazil Gh. Assan (Spitzbergen, 1896)	35	15
5060	2l. Emil Racovita and "Belgica" (barque) (Antarctic, 1897–99)	70	20
5061	3l. Constantin Dumbrava (Greenland, 1927–28)	1·10	25
5062	4l. Romanian participation in 17th Soviet Antarctic Expedition, 1971–72	1·60	35
5063	5l. 1977 "Sinoe" and 1979–80 "Tirnava" krill fishing expeditions	1·90	55

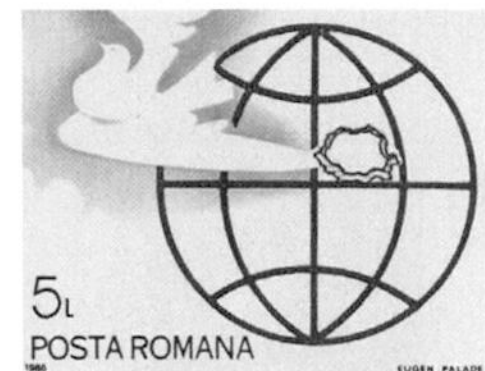

1018 Dove and map on Globe

1986. International Peace Year. Sheet 89×77 mm.

MS5064	5l. multicoloured	3·50	3·50

1019 The Blusher

1986. Fungi. Multicoloured.

5065	50b. Type **1019**	10	10
5066	1l. Oak mushroom	35	15
5067	2l. Peppery milk cap	70	20
5068	3l. Shield fungus	1·10	25
5069	4l. The charcoal burner	1·60	35
5070	5l. "Tremiscus helvelloides"	1·90	55

1020 Group of Cyclists

1986. Cycle Tour of Romania. Multicoloured.

5071	1l. Type **1020**	35	15
5072	2l. Motor cycle following cyclist	70	20
5073	3l. Jeep following cyclists	1·10	35
5074	4l. Winner	1·40	45
MS5075	90×78 mm. 10l. Cyclist (38×51 mm)	4·75	4·75

1021 Emblem

1986. 40th Anniv of UNESCO and 30th Anniv of Romanian Membership.

5076	**1021**	4l. multicoloured	1·30	55

1022 Petru Maior (historian) (225th birth anniv)

1986. Birth Anniversaries.

5077	**1022**	50b. purple, gold and green	10	10
5078	-	1b. green, gold and mauve	25	10
5079	-	2l. red, gold and blue	70	10
5080	-	3l. blue, gold and brown	1·20	20

DESIGNS: 1l. George Topirceanu (writer, centenary); 2l. Henri Coanda (engineer, centenary); 3l. Constantin Budeanu (engineer, centenary).

1023 Coach and Horses

1986. Stamp Day.

5081	**1023**	2l.(+1l.) multicoloured	1·20	1·10

No. 5081 includes the se-tenant premium-carrying tab shown in Type **1023**.

1024 F 300 Oil Drilling Rigs

1986. Industry. Multicoloured.

5082	50b. Type **1024**	10	10
5083	1l. "Promex" excavator (horiz)	35	15
5084	2l. Petrochemical refinery, Pitesti	70	20
5085	3l. Tipper "110 t" (horiz)	1·10	25
5086	4l. "Coral" computer	1·60	35
5087	5l. 350 m.w. turbine (horiz)	1·90	55

1025 "Goat"

1986. New Year Folk Customs. Multicoloured.

5088	50b. Type **1025**	10	10
5089	1l. Sorcova	35	15
5090	2l. Plugusorul	70	20
5091	3l. Buhaiul	1·10	25
5092	4l. Caiutii	1·60	35
5093	5l. Uratorii	1·90	55

1026 Tin Can and Motor Car ("Re-cycle metals")

1986. "Save Waste Materials".

5094	**1026**	1l. red and orange	35	20
5095	-	2l. light green and green	85	35

DESIGN: 2l. Trees and hand with newspaper ("Re-cycle waste paper").

1027 Flags and Young People

1987. 65th Anniv of Communist Youth Union. Multicoloured.

5096	1l. Type **1027**	35	10
5097	2l. Anniversary emblem	85	35
5098	3l. Flags and young people (different)	1·10	55

1028 Anniversary Emblem

1987. 25th Anniv of Agricultural Co-operatives.

5099	**1028**	2l. multicoloured	70	55

1029 Administrative Building, Satu Mare

1987. Inter-European Cultural and Economic Co-operation. Two sheets, each 110×80 mm containing horiz designs as T **1029**. Multicoloured.

MS5100	3l. ×4 (a) Type **1029**; House of Toung Pioneers, Bucharest; Valahia Hotel, Tirgoviste; Caciulata Hotel, Caciulata. (b) 3l. ×4 Exhibition Pavilion, Bucharest; Intercontinental Hotel, Bucharest; Europa Hotel, Eforie Nord; Polytechnic Institute, Bucharest Set of 2 sheets	8·50	8·50

1030 "Birch Trees by Lake" (Ion Andreescu)

1987. Paintings. Multicoloured.

5101	50b. Type **1030**	10	10
5102	1l. "Young Peasant Girls spinning" (N. Grigorescu)	35	15
5103	2l. "Washerwoman" (St. Luchian)	70	20
5104	3l. "Interior" (St. Dimitrescu)	1·10	25
5105	4l. "Winter Landscape" (Al. Ciucurencu)	1·60	35
5106	5l. "Winter in Bucharest" (N. Tonitza) (vert)	1·90	55

1031 "1907" and Peasants

1987. 80th Anniv of Peasant Uprising.

5107	**1031**	2l. multicoloured	70	55

1032 Players

1987. Tenth Students World Men's Handball Championship.

5108	**1032**	50b. multicoloured	10	10
5109	-	1l. multicoloured (horiz)	35	15
5110	-	2l. multicoloured	70	20
5111	-	3l. multicoloured (horiz)	1·10	25
5112	-	4l. multicoloured	1·60	35
5113	-	5l. multicoloured (horiz)	1·90	55

DESIGNS: 1l. to 5l. Various match scenes.

1033 1 Leu Coin

1987. Currency. Multicoloured.

5114 1l. Type **1033** 60 35

MS5115 90×78 mm. 10l. 10lei banknote (53×41 mm) 4·75 4·75

1034 Eastern White Pelicans in the Danube Delta

1987. Tourism. Multicoloured.

5116 50b. Type **1034** 10 10
5117 1l. Cable car above Transfagarasan mountain road 35 15
5118 2l. Cheile Bicazului 70 20
5119 3l. Ceahlau mountains 1·10 30
5120 4l. Lake Capra, Fagaras mountains 1·60 35
5121 5l. Borsa orchards 1·90 55

1035 Henri August's Glider, 1909

1987. Air. Aircraft. Multicoloured.

5122 50b. Type **1035** 10 10
5123 1l. Sky diver jumping from IS-28 B2 glider 35 15
5124 2l. IS-29 D2 glider 70 20
5125 3l. IS-32 glider 1·10 30
5126 4l. I.A.R.35 light airplane 1·60 35
5127 5l. IS-28 M2 aircraft 1·90 55

1036 Youth on Winged Horse

1987. Fairy Tales by Petre Ispirescu. Multicoloured.

5128 50b. Type **1036** 10 10
5129 1l. King and princesses ("Salt in the Food") 35 15
5130 2l. Girl on horse fighting lion ("Ileana Simziana") 70 20
5131 3l. Youth with bow and arrow aiming at bird ("The Youth and the Golden Apples") 1·10 30
5132 4l. George and dead dragon ("George the Brave") 1·60 35
5133 5l. Girl looking at sleeping youth ("The Enchanted Pig") 1·90 55

MS5134 90×79 mm. 10l. Youth holding sun and moon ("Greuceanu") (41×53 mm) 4·75 4·75

1037 Class L 45H Diesel Shunter

1987. Railway Locomotives. Multicoloured.

5135 50b. Type **1037** 10 10
5136 1l. Class LDE 125 diesel goods locomotive 35 15
5137 2l. Class LDH 70 diesel goods locomotive 70 20
5138 3l. Class LDE 2100 diesel locomotive 1·10 30
5139 4l. Class LDE 3000 diesel locomotive 1·60 35
5140 5l. Class LE 5100 electric locomotive 1·90 55

1038 Alpine Columbine ("Aquelegia alpine")

1987. Nature Reserves in Europe. Two sheets, each 150×135 mm containing horiz designs as T **1038**. Multicoloured.

MS5141 Two sheets (a) 1l. ×12 Type **1038**; Pasque flower ("Pulsatilla vernalis"); Alpine aster ("Aster alpinus"); "Soldanell pusilla"; Ornage lily ("Lilium bulbiferum"); Alpine bearberry ("Arctostaphylos uva-ursi"); "Crocus vernus"; Golden hawksbeard ("Crepis aurea"); Lady's slipper ("Cypripedium calceolus"); "Centaurea nervosa"; Mountain avens ("Dryas octopetala"); "Gentiana excisa". (b) 1l. ×12 Pine martern ("Martes Martes"); Lynx ("Felis lynx"); Polar bear ("Ursus maritimus"); European otter ("Lutra lutra"); European bison ("Bison bonasus"); Red-breasted goose ("Branta ruficollis"); Greater flamingo ("Phoenicopterus rubber"); Great bustard ("Otis tarda"); Black grouse ("Lyrurus tetrix"); Lammergeier ("Gypaetus barbatus"); Marbled polecat ("Vormela peregusna"); White-headed duck ("Oxyura leucocephala") Set of 2 sheets 16·00 16·00

1039 Bucharest Municipal Arms

1987. "Philatelia '87" International Stamp Fair, Cologne. Sheet 79×109 mm containing T **1039** and similar design. Multicoloured.

MS5142 3l. Type **1039**; 3l. Cologne arms 4·75 4·75

1987. Costumes (2nd series). As T **999**. Multicoloured.

5143 1l. Tirnave (female) 35 15
5144 1l. Tirnave (male) 35 15
5145 2l. Buzau (female) 70 20
5146 2l. Buzau (male) 70 20
5147 3l. Dobrogea (female) 1·10 30
5148 3l. Dobrogea (male) 1·10 30
5149 4l. Ilfov (female) 1·40 35
5150 4l. Ilfov (male) 1·40 35

1040 Postal Services

1987. Stamp Day.

5151 **1040** 2l.(+1l.) multicoloured 1·20 1·10

No. 5151 includes the se-tenant premium-carrying tab shown in Type **1040**, the stamp and tab forming a composite design.

1041 Honey Bee on Flower

1987. Bee-keeping. Multicoloured.

5152 1l. Type **1041** 35 15
5153 2l. Honey bee, sunflowers and hives 85 20
5154 3l. Hives in Danube delta 1·20 35
5155 4l. Apiculture Complex, Bucharest 1·70 45

1042 Car behind Boy on Bicycle

1987. Road Safety. Multicoloured.

5156 50b. Type **1042** 10 10
5157 1l. Children using school crossing 35 15
5158 2l. Driver carelessly opening car door 70 20
5159 3l. Hand holding crossing sign and children using zebra crossing 1·10 30
5160 4l. Speedometer and crashed car 1·60 35
5161 5l. Child's face and speeding car 1·90 55

1043 Red Flag and Lenin

1987. 70th Anniv of Russian Revolution.

5162 **1043** 2l. multicoloured 1·20 55

1044 Biathlon

1987. Winter Olympic Games, Calgary (1988). Multicoloured.

5163 50b. Type **1044** 10 10
5164 1l. Slalom 25 10
5165 1l.50 Ice hockey 35 10
5166 2l. Luge 50 15
5167 3l. Speed skating 85 20
5168 3l.50 Figure skating 95 35
5169 4l. Downhill skiing 1·20 40
5170 5l. Two-man bobsleigh 1·40 55

1045 Crest and National Colours

1987. 40th Anniv of People's Republic.

5171 **1045** 2l. multicoloured 95 55

1046 Pres. Ceausescu and Flags

1988. 70th Birthday and 55 Years of Revolutionary Activity of Pres. Ceausescu.

5172 **1046** 2l. multicoloured 1·40 80

1047 Wide-necked Pot, Marginea

1988. Pottery. Multicoloured.

5173 50b. Type **1047** 10 10
5174 1l. Flask, Oboga 35 15
5175 2l. Jug and saucer, Horezu 70 20
5176 3l. Narrow-necked pot, Curtea de Arges 1·10 30
5177 4l. Jug, Birsa 1·60 35
5178 5l. Jug and plate, Vama 1·90 55

1048 "Santa Maria"

1988. Inter-European Cultural and Economic Co-operation. Two sheets, each 110×80 mm containing horiz designs as T **1048**. Multicoloured.

MS5179 Two sheets (a) 3l. ×4 Type **1048**; Dish aerials, Cheia earth station; Bucharest underground train; Airbus Industrie A320 jetliner. (b) 3l. ×4 Mail coach and horses; "ECS" satellite; Oltcit motor car; "ICE" express train Set of 2 sheets 8·50 8·50

1049 Ceramic Clock

1988. Clocks in Ploiesti Museum. Multicoloured.

5180 50b. Type **1049** 10 10
5181 1l.50 Gilt clock with sun at base 35 15
5182 2l. Clock with pastoral figure 70 20
5183 3l. Gilt clock surmounted by figure 95 30
5184 4l. Vase-shaped clock 1·60 35
5185 5l. Clock surmounted by porcelain figures 1·90 55

1050 West German Flag and Player kicking Ball into Net

1988. European Football Championship, West Germany. Two sheets each 110× 80 mm containing horiz designs as T **1050**. Multicoloured.

MS5186 3l. ×4 Type **1050**; Goalkeeper diving to save ball and Spanish flag; Italian flag and player; Players and Danish flag. (b) 3l. ×4 English flag, referee and player; Players and Netherlands flag; Irish flag and players; Players and flag of U.S.S.R. Set of 2 sheets 12·00 12·00

1051 Constantin Brincoveanu

1988. 300th Anniv of Election of Constantin Brincoveanu as Ruler of Wallachia.

5187 **1051** 2l. multicoloured 70 55

1052 Gymnastics

1988. Olympic Games, Seoul (1st issue). Multicoloured.

5188 50b. Type **1052** 10 10
5189 1l.50 Boxing 35 15
5190 2l. Lawn tennis 70 20
5191 3l. Judo 95 30
5192 4l. Running 1·60 35
5193 5l. Rowing 1·90 55

See also Nos. 5197/5204.

1053 Postal Emblems and Roses

1988. Romanian–Chinese Stamp Exhibition, Bucharest.
5194 **1053** 2l. multicoloured 70 55

1054 Player and Wimbledon Centre Court

1988. "Grand Slam" Tennis Championships. Two sheets each 110×80 mm containing horiz designs as T **1054**. Multicoloured.
MS5195 (a) 3l. ×4 Type **1054**; Wimbledon match; Flushing Meadows match; Flushing Meadows centre courts, New York. (b) 3l. ×4 Melbourne centre court; Melbourne match; Roland Garros match; Roland Garros centre court, Paris Set of 2 sheets 12·00 12·00

1055 "Bowl of Flowers" (Stefan Luchian)

1988. "Praga '88" International Stamp Exhibition. Sheet 90×78 mm.
MS5196 5l. multicoloured 3·50 3·50

1056 Running

1988. Olympic Games, Seoul (2nd issue). Multicoloured.
5197 50b. Type **1056** 10 10
5198 1l. Canoeing 25 10
5199 1l.50 Gymnastics 35 10
5200 2l. Double kayak 50 15
5201 3l. Weightlifting 85 20
5202 3l.50 Swimming 95 35
5203 4l. Fencing 1·20 40
5204 5l. Double sculls 1·40 45

1057 "Oncidium lanceanum"

1988. Orchids. Two sheets, each 150×137 mm containing horiz designs as T **1057**. Multicoloured.
MS5205 (a) 1l. ×2 Type **1057**; "Cattleya trianae"; "Sophronitis cernua"; "Bulbophyllum lobbii"; "Lycaste cruenta"; "Mormolyce ringens"; "Phragmipedium schlimii"; "Angraecum atropurpurea"; "Dendrobium nobile"; "Oncidium splendidum". (b) 1l. ×12 "Brassavola perrinii"; "Paphiopedilum maudiae"; "Sophronitis coccinea"; "Vandopsis lissochiloides"; "Phalaenopsis lueddemanniana"; "Chysis bractescens"; "Cochleanthes discolor"; "Phalaenopsis amabilis"; "Pleione pricei"; "Sobralia macrantha"; "Aspasia lunata"; "Cattleya citrina" Set of 2 sheets 14·50 14·00

1058 Past and Present Postal Services

1988. Stamp Day.
5206 **1058** 2l.(+1l.) multicoloured 95 90
No. 5206 includes the se-tenant premium-carrying tab shown in T **1058**.

1059 Gymnastics and Three Gold Medals

1988. Seoul Olympic Games Romanian Medal Winners. Two sheets, each 110×80 mm containing horiz designs as T **1059**. Multicoloured.
MS5207 (a) 3l. ×4 Type **1059**; Pistol shooting and gold medal; Weightlifting and silver medal; Boxing and silver medal. (b) 3l. ×4 Athletics and silver medals; Swimming and silver medal; Wrestling and gold medal; Rowing and gold medal Set of 2 sheets 12·00 12·00

1060 State Arms

1988. 70th Anniv of Union of Transylvania and Romania.
5208 **1060** 2l. multicoloured 1·20 1·10

1061 Athenaeum Concert Hall, Bucharest (centenary)

1988. Romanian History. Multicoloured.
5209 50b. Type **1061** 10 10
5210 1l.50 Roman coin showing Drobeta Bridge 35 15
5211 2l. Ruins (600th anniv of Suceava as capital of Moldavian feudal state) 70 20
5212 3l. Scroll, arms and town (600th anniv of first documentary reference to Pitesti) 95 30
5213 4l. Dacian warriors from Trajan's Column 1·60 35
5214 5l. Thracian gold helmet from Cotofenesti-Prahova 1·90 55

1062 Zapodeni, 17th century

1989. Traditional House Architecture. Multicoloured.
5215 50b. Type **1062** 10 10
5216 1l.50 Berbesti, 18th century 35 15
5217 2l. Voitinel, 18th century 70 20
5218 3l. Chiojdu Mic, 18th century 95 30
5219 4l. Cimpanii de Sus, 19th century 1·60 35
5220 5l. Naruja, 19th century 1·90 55

1063 Red Cross Worker

1989. Life-saving Services. Multicoloured.
5221 50b. Type **1063** 10 10
5222 1l. Red Cross orderlies giving first aid to girl (horiz) 35 10
5223 1l.50 Fireman carrying child 60 10
5224 2l. Rescuing child from earthquake damaged building 70 15
5225 3l. Mountain rescue team transporting casualty on sledge (horiz) 1·10 20
5226 3l.50 Rescuing climber from cliff face 1·20 30
5227 4l. Rescuing child from river 1·30 35
5228 5l. Lifeguard in rowing boat and children playing in sea (horiz) 1·60 45

1064 Tasca Bicaz Cement Factory

1989. Industrial Achievements. Multicoloured.
5229 50b. Type **1064** 10 10
5230 1l.50 New railway bridge, Cernavoda 50 15
5231 2l. Synchronous motor, Resita 70 20
5232 3l. Bucharest underground 95 30
5233 4l. Mangalia–Constanta train ferry 1·30 35
5234 5l. "Gloria" (oil drilling platform) 1·60 55

1065 Flags and Symbols of Industry and Agriculture

1988. 50th Anniv of Anti-Fascist Demonstration.
5235 2l. Type **1065** 1·20 55
MS5236 90×78 mm. 10l. Flag and demonstrators 7·75 7·75

1066 Roses

1989. "Bulgaria '89" International Stamp Exhibition, Sofia. Sheet 90×78 mm.
MS5237 10l. multicoloured 4·75 4·75

1067 Girls playing with Dolls

1989. Inter-European Cultural and Economic Co-operation. Children. Two sheets, each 110×80 mm containing horiz designs as T **1067**.
MS5238 (a) 3l. ×4 Type **1067**; Playing football; On beach; Playing with toy cars. (b) 3l. ×4 Playing in sea; On slides; At playground; Flying kites Set of 2 sheets 8·50 8·50

1068 Ion Creanga (writer, death centenary)

1989. Anniversaries. Multicoloured.
5239 1l. Type **1068** 35 10
5240 2l. Mihai Eminescu (poet, death centenary) 85 35
5241 3l. Nicolae Teclu (scientist, 150th birth anniv) 1·20 55

1069 State and Communist Party Flags and Symbols of Industry and Agriculture

1989. 45th Anniv of Liberation.
5242 **1069** 2l. multicoloured 1·20 55

1070 "Pin-Pin"

1989. Romanian Cartoon Films. Multicoloured.
5243 50b. Type **1070** 10 10
5244 1l. "Maria" 35 10
5245 1l.50 "Gore and Grigore" 60 15
5246 2l. "Pisoiul, Balanel, Manole, Monk" 70 20
5247 3l. "Gruia lui Novac" 1·10 30
5248 3l.50 "Mihaela" 1·20 35
5249 4l. "Harap Alb" 1·30 40
5250 5l. "Homo Sapiens" 1·60 45

1071 Globe, Letter and Houses

1989. Stamp Day.
5251 **1071** 2l.(+1l.) multicoloured 1·20 1·10
No. 5251 includes the se-tenant premium-carrying tab as illustrated in T **1071**.

1072 Storming of the Bastille

1989. Bicentenary of French Revolution. Multicoloured.
5252 50b. Type **1072** 10 10
5253 1l.50 Street boy and Marianne 60 15
5254 2l. Maximilien de Robespierre 70 20
5255 3l. Rouget de Lisle singing the "Marseillaise" 1·10 30
5256 4l. Denis Diderot (encyclopaedist) 1·40 45
5257 5l. Crowd with banner 1·80 55
MS5258 90×78 mm. 10l. "Philexfrance '89" International Stamp Exhibition emblem and Eiffel Tower (50×39 mm) 6·00 6·00

1073 Conrad Haas and Diagram

1989. Air. Space Pioneers. Multicoloured.
5259 50b. Type **1073** 10 10
5260 1l.50 Konstantin Tsiolkovski and diagram 60 15
5261 2l. Hermann Oberth and equation 70 20
5262 3l. Robert Goddard and diagram 1·10 35
5263 4l. Sergei Pavlovich Korolev, Earth and satellite 1·40 45
5264 5l. Wernher von Braun and landing module 1·80 55

1074 Horse-drawn Mail Coach

1989. Air. "World Stamp Expo '89" International Stamp Exhibition, Washington D.C. Sheet 90×77 mm.
MS5265 5l. multicoloured 3·75 3·75

1075 State and Party Flags and Emblem

1989. 14th Communist Party Congress, Bucharest.

5266	**1075**	2l. multicoloured	1·20	55
MS5267		77×89 mm. 10l. multicoloured	7·25	7·25

DESIGNS: 10l. Party emblem and "XIV".

1076 Date, Flag, Victory Sign and Candles

1990. Popular Uprising (1st issue).

5268	**1076**	2l. multicoloured	85	55

See also Nos. 5294/5301.

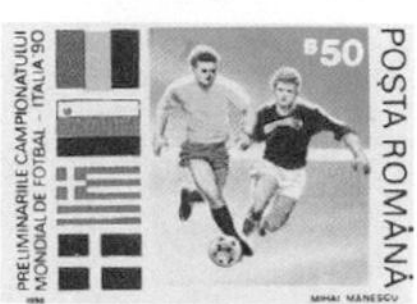

1077 Flags and Footballers

1990. World Cup Football Championship, Italy (1st issue).

5269	**1077**	50b. multicoloured	10	10
5270	-	1l.50 multicoloured	60	15
5271	-	2l. multicoloured	70	20
5272	-	3l. multicoloured	1·10	35
5273	-	4l. multicoloured	1·40	45
5274	-	5l. multicoloured	1·80	55

DESIGNS: 1l.50 to 5l. Showing flags and footballers.
See also Nos. 5276/83.

1078 Penny Black and Moldavian 27p. Stamp

1990. "Stamp World London '90" International Stamp Exhibition. Sheet 90×78 mm.

MS5275	10l. multicoloured	4·75	4·75

1079 Footballers

1990. World Cup Football Championship, Italy (2nd issue).

5276	**1079**	50b. multicoloured	10	10
5277	-	1l. multicoloured	35	10
5278	-	1l.50 multicoloured	60	15
5279	-	2l. multicoloured	70	20
5280	-	3l. multicoloured	1·10	30
5281	-	3l.50 multicoloured	1·20	35
5282	-	4l. multicoloured	1·30	40
5283	-	5l. multicoloured	1·60	45

DESIGNS: 1l. to 5l. Different football scenes.

1080 German Shepherds

1990. International Dog Show, Brno. Multicoloured.

5284	50b. Type **1080**	10	10
5285	1l. English setter	35	10
5286	1l.50 Boxers	60	10
5287	2l. Beagles	70	15
5288	3l. Dobermann pinschers	1·20	20
5289	3l.50 Great Danes	1·40	30
5290	4l. Afghan hounds	1·60	35
5291	5l. Yorkshire terriers	2·00	40

1081 Fountain, Brunnen

1990. "Riccione 90" International Stamp Fair.

5292	**1081**	2l. multicoloured	90	60

1082 Athenaeum Concert Hall, Bucharest, and Chinese Temple

1990. Romanian–Chinese Stamp Exhibition, Bucharest.

5293	**1082**	2l. multicoloured	90	60

1083 Soldiers and Crowd at Television Headquarters, Bucharest

1990. Popular Uprising (2nd issue). Multicoloured.

5294	50b.+50b. Republic Palace ablaze, Bucharest (horiz)	25	10
5295	1l.+1l. Crowd in Opera Square, Timisoara	65	15
5296	1l.50+1l. Soldiers joining crowd in Town Hall Square, Tirgu Mures (horiz)	90	20
5297	2l.+1l. Type **1083**	1·00	25
5298	3l.+1l. Mourners at funeral, Timisoara (horiz)	1·30	30
5299	3l.50+1l. Crowd celebrating, Brasov	1·50	35
5300	4l.+1l. Crowd with banners, Sibiu (horiz)	1·70	35
5301	5l.+2l. Cemetery, Bucharest (horiz)	2·20	40
MS5302	90×78 mm. 5l.+2l. Foreign aid (53×41 mm)	3·75	3·75

1084 "Nicolae Cobzarul" (Stefan Luchian)

1990. Paintings damaged during the Uprising. Multicoloured.

5303	50b. Type **1084**	15	10
5304	1l.50 "Woman in White" (Ion Andreescu)	40	10
5305	2l. "Florist" (Luchian)	65	15
5306	3l. "Vase of Flowers" (Jan Brueghel, the elder)	90	25
5307	4l. "Spring" (Pieter Brueghel, the elder) (horiz)	1·30	35
5308	5l. "Madonna and Child" (G. B. Paggi)	1·50	50

1085 Flag Stamps encircling Globe

1990. Stamp Day.

5309	**1085**	2l.(+1l.) multicoloured	1·30	1·20

No. 5309 includes the se-tenant premium-carrying tab as shown in Type **1085**.

1086 Constantin Cantacuzino (historian, 350th birth anniv)

1990. Anniversaries.

5310	**1086**	50b. brown and blue	15	10
5311	-	1l.50 green and mauve	40	10
5312	-	2l. red and blue	65	15
5313	-	3l. blue and brown	90	25
5314	-	4l. brown and blue	1·30	35
5315	-	5l. violet and green	1·50	50

DESIGNS: 1l.50, Ienachita Vacarescu (writer, 250th birth anniv); 2l. Titu Maiorescu (politician, 150th birth anniv); 3l. Nicolae Iorga (historian, 50th death anniv); 4l. Martha Bibescu (writer, birth centenary); 5l. Stefan Procupiu (scientist, birth centenary).

1087 Column of Infinity

1990. National Day.

5316	**1087**	2l. multicoloured	75	60

1990. First Anniv of Popular Uprising. No. 5268 surch **L4 UN AN DE LA VICTORIA REVOLUTIEI.**

5317	**1076**	4l. on 2l. multicoloured	1·50	60

1089 "Irises"

1991. Death Centenary of Vincent van Gogh (painter). Multicoloured.

5318	50b. Type **1089**	15	10
5319	2l. "The Artist's Room"	25	10
5320	3l. "Illuminated Coffee Terrace" (vert)	50	15
5321	3l.50 "Orchard in Blossom"	65	20
5322	5l. "Sunflowers" (vert)	90	25

1090 Greater Black- backed Gull

1991. Water Birds.

5323	**1090**	50b. blue	10	10
5324	-	1l. green	15	10
5325	-	1l.50 bistre	20	10
5326	-	2l. blue	25	10
5327	-	3l. green	40	10
5328	-	3l.50 green	50	10
5329	-	4l. violet	65	10
5330	-	5l. brown	75	10
5331	-	6l. brown	1·40	10
5332	-	7l. blue	1·50	25

DESIGNS: 1l. Common tern; 1l.50, Pied avocet; 2l. Pomarine skua; 3l. Northern lapwings; 3l.50, Red-breasted merganser; 4l. Little egret; 5l. Dunlin; 6l. Black- tailed godwit; 7l. Whiskered tern.

1091 Crucifixion

1991. Easter.

5333	**1091**	4l. multicoloured	65	60

1092 "Eutelsat 1" Communications Satellite

1991. Europa. Europe in Space.

5334	**1092**	4l.50 multicoloured	5·00	1·20

1093 Posthorn

1991

5335	**1093**	4l.50 blue	75	60

1094 Rings Exercise

1991. Gymnastics. Multicoloured.

5336	1l. Type **1094**	15	10
5337	1l. Parallel bars	15	10
5338	4l.50 Vaulting	50	10
5339	4l.50 Asymmetric bars	50	10
5340	8l. Floor exercises	90	15
5341	9l. Beam	1·20	20

For similar design to No. 5341, surcharged 90l. on 5l., see No. 5431.

1095 Curtea de Arges Monastery

1991. Monasteries. Multicoloured.

5342	1l. Type **1095**	15	10
5343	1l. Putna	15	10
5344	4l.50 Varatec	50	10
5345	4l.50 Agapia (horiz)	50	10
5346	8l. Golia (horiz)	90	10
5347	9l. Sucevita (horiz)	1·20	10

1096 Hotel Continental, Timisoara

1991. Hotels.

5349	**1096**	1l. blue	15	10
5350	-	2l. green	15	10
5351	-	4l. red	25	10
5352	-	5l. violet	50	10
5353	-	6l. brown	25	25
5354	-	8l. brown	25	25
5355	-	9l. red	1·20	35
5356	-	10l. green	1·00	35

5357	-	18l. red	1·30	35
5358	-	20l. orange	1·40	35
5359	-	25l. blue	1·70	60
5360	-	30l. purple	2·20	70
5361	-	45l. blue	1·90	50
5362	-	60l. brown	2·50	85
5363	-	80l. violet	3·25	95
5364b	-	120l. blue and grey	3·75	25
5365	-	160l. red and pink	5·00	35
5366	-	250l. blue and grey	6·50	50
5367	-	400l. brown and ochre	8·25	60
5368	-	500l. deep green & green	9·50	70
5369	-	800l. mauve and pink	11·50	95

DESIGNS—As T **1096**: HORIZ: 2l. Valea Caprei Chalet, Mt. Fagaras; 5l. Hotel Lebada, Crisan; 6l. Muntele Rosu Chalet, Mt. Ciucas; 8l. Trans-silvania Hotel, Cluj-Napoca; 9l. Hotel Orizont, Predeal; 20l. Alpin Hotel, Poiana Brasov; 25l. Constanta Casino; 30l. Miorita Chalet, Mt. Bucegi; 45l. Sura Dacilor Chalet, Poiana Brasov; 60l. Valea Draganului Tourist Complex; 80l. Hotel Florica, Venus. VERT: 4l. Intercontinental Hotel, Bucharest; 10l. Hotel Roman, Baile Herculcane; 18l. Rarau Chalet, Mt. Rarau. 26×40 mm: 120l. International Complex, Baile Felix; 160l. Hotel Egreta, Tulcea. 40×26 mm: 250l. Valea de Pesti Motel, Jiului Valley; 400l. Baisoara Tourist Complex; 500l. Bradul Hotel, Covasna; 800l. Gorj Hotel, Jiu.

Nos. 5362/9 have no frame.

1097 Gull and Sea Shore

1991. "Riccione 91" Stamp Exhibition, Riccione, Italy.

5381	**1097**	4l. multicoloured	65	60

1098 Vase decorated with Scarlet and Military Macaws

1991. Romanian–Chinese Stamp Exhibition. Multicoloured.

5382	5l. Type **1098**	50	35
5383	5l. Vase with peony decoration	50	35

1099 Academy Emblem

1991. 125th Anniv of Romanian Academy.

5384	**1099**	1l. blue	65	60

1100 "Flowers" (Nicu Enea)

1991. "Balcanfila '91" Stamp Exhibition, Bacau. Multicoloured.

5385	4l. Type **1100**	65	25
5386	5l.(+2l.) "Peasant Girl of Vlasca" (Georghe Tattarescu)	75	35

MS5387 90×77 mm. 20l. Exhibition venue (53×41 mm) 2·50 2·50

1101 Red-Billed Blue Magpie ("Casa erythorhynchai")

1991. Birds. Two sheets, each 136×150 mm containing vert designs as T **1101**. Multicoloured.

MS5388 (a) 2l. ×12 Type **1101**; Grey-headed bush shrike ("Malaconotus blanchoti"); Eastern bluebird ("Sialia sialis"); Western meadowlark ("Sturnella neglecta"); Malabar trogon ("Harpactes fasciatus"); Hoopoe ("Upupa epops"); Blue wren ("Malurus cyaneus"); Scaly ground roller ("Brachypterus squamigera"); Blue vanga ("Leptopterus madagascariensis"); White-headed wood hoopoe ("Phoeniculus bollei"); Red-headed woodpecker ("Melanerpes erythrocephalus"); Scarlet minivet ("Pericrocotus flammeus"). (b) 2l. ×12 Golden-backed honeyeater ("Melithreptus laetior"); Kagu ("Rhynochetos jubata"); American robin ("Turdus migratorius"); Magpie robin ("Copsychus saularis"); Rock thrush ("Monticola saxatilis"); Yellow-headed blackbird ("Xanthocephalus xanthocephalus"); Pel's fishing owl ("Scotopelia peli"); Long-tailed silky flycatcher ("Ptilogonys caudatus"); Puerto Rican tody ("Todus mexicanus"); White-rumped shama ("Copsychus malabaricus"); Mangrove red-headed honeyeater ("Myzomela erythrocephala"); Montezuma oropendola ("Gymnostinops montezuma") Set of 2 sheets 9·25 9·25

1102 Map with House and People

1991. Population and Housing Census.

5389	**1102**	5l. multicoloured	65	60

1103 Bridge

1991. "Phila Nippon '91" International Stamp Exhibition, Tokyo.

5390	**1103**	10l. ochre, brown & red	1·30	35
5391	-	10l. multicoloured	1·30	35

DESIGN: No. 5391, Junk.

1104 Isabel ("Graellsia isabellae")

1991. Butterflies and Moths. Two sheets, each 155×36 mm containing horiz designs as T **1104**. Multicoloured.

MS5392 (a) 3l. ×12 Type **1104**; Orange-tip ("Antocharis cardamines"); Hebe tiger moth ("Ammobiota festiva"); Comma ("Polygonia c-album"); "Catocala promisa"; Purple tiger moth ("Phyparia purpurata"); "Arctica villica"; "Polyommatus daphnis"; Southern festoon ("Zerynthia polyxena"); Oleander hawk moth ("Daphnis nerii"); "Licaena dispar rutila"; "Parage roxelana". (b) 3l. ×12 Paradise birdwing ("Ornithoptera paradisea"); Bhutan glory ("Bhutanitis lidderdalii"); "Morpho Helena"; "Ornithoptera croesus"; Red-splashed sulphur ("Phoebis avellaneda"); Queen Victoria's birdwing ("Ornithoptera victoriae"); Kaiser-i-hind ("Teinopalpus imperialis"); "Hypolimnas dexithea"; "Dabasa payeni"; "Morpho achilleana"; "Heliconius melpomene"; "Agrias claudina sardanapalus" Set of 2 sheets 13·00 13·00

1105 Running

1991. World Athletics Championships, Tokyo. Multicoloured.

5393	1l. Type **1105**	25	10
5394	4l. Long jumping	50	10
5395	5l. High jumping	65	10
5396	5l. Athlete in starting blocks	65	10
5397	9l. Hurdling	1·20	20
5398	10l. Throwing the javelin	1·30	20

1106 Mihail Kogalniceanu (policitian and historian, death cent)

1991. Anniversaries.

5399	**1106**	1l. brown, blue & dp blue	25	10
5400	-	4l. green, lilac and violet	50	10
5401	-	5l. brown, blue & ultramarine	65	10
5402	-	5l. blue, brown and red	65	10
5403	-	9l. red, blue & deep blue	1·20	20
5404	-	10l. black, lt brn & brn	1·30	20

DESIGNS: No. 5400, Nicolae Titulescu (politician and diplomat, 50th death anniv); 5401, Andrei Mureseanu (poet, 175th birth anniv); 5402, Aron Pumnul (writer, 125th death anniv); 5403, George Bacovia (writer, 110th birth anniv); 5404, Perpessicius (literature critic, birth centenary).

1107 Library Building

1991. Centenary of Central University Library.

5405	**1107**	8l. brown	1·00	60

1108 Coach and Horses

1991. Stamp Day.

5406	**1108**	8l.(+2l.) multicoloured	1·30	1·20

No. 5406 includes the se-tenant premium-carrying label shown in Type **1108**.

1109 "Nativity" (17th-century icon)

1991. Christmas.

5407	**1109**	8l. multicoloured	1·00	60

1110 Biathlon

1992. Winter Olympic Games, Albertville. Multicoloured.

5408	4l. Type **1110** (postage)	15	10
5409	5l. Downhill skiing	20	10
5410	8l. Cross-country skiing	25	10
5411	10l. Two-man luge	40	10
5412	20l. Speed skating	75	10
5413	25l. Ski-jumping	90	20
5414	30l. Ice hockey	1·20	20
5415	45l. Men's figure skating	1·50	30

MS5416 95×78 mm. 75l. Women's figure skating (37×52 mm) (air) 4·00 4·00

1112 Jug, Plate, Tray and Bowl

1992. Romanian Porcelain from Cluj Napoca. Multicoloured.

5419	4l. Type **1112**	15	10
5420	5l. Tea set	15	10
5421	8l. Jug and goblet (vert)	20	10
5422	30l. Tea set (different)	1·00	20
5423	45l. Vase (vert)	1·50	35

1113 Atlantic Mackerels

1992. Fish. Multicoloured.

5424	4l. Type **1113**	15	10
5425	5l. Tench	15	10
5426	8l. Brook charr	20	10
5427	10l. Romanian bullhead perch	25	10
5428	30l. Nase	90	25
5429	45l. Black Sea red mullet	1·40	40

1114 Vase decorated with Scarlet and Military Macaws

1992. Apollo Art Gallery. Unissued stamp surch.

5430	**1114**	90l. on 5l. multicoloured	3·25	60

1115 Gymnast on Beam

1992. Individual Gymnastic Championships, Paris. Unissued stamp surch.

5431	**1115**	90l. on 5l. multicoloured	3·25	60

For similar 9l. value, see No. 5341.

1116 Dressage

1992. Horses. Multicoloured.

5432	6l. Type **1116**	15	10
5433	7l. Racing (horiz)	15	10
5434	10l. Rearing	25	10
5435	25l. Jumping gate	75	15
5436	30l. Stamping foot (horiz)	1·00	20
5437	50l. Winged horse	1·50	25

1117 Columbus and "Santa Maria"

1992. Europa. 500th Anniv of Discovery of America by Columbus. Sheet 130×88 mm containing T **1117** and similar horiz designs. Multicoloured.

MS5438 35l. Type **1117**; 35l. Columbus (hatless) and "Nina" at sea; 35l. Columbus (in hat) and "Pinta"; 35l. Columbus, "Santa Maria" and island 38·00 38·00

1118 "Descent into Hell" (icon)

1992. Easter.

5439	**1118**	10l. multicoloured	65	50

1119 Emblem

1992. "Granada '92" International Thematic Stamp Exhibition. Sheet 122×72 mm containing T **1119** and similar vert designs.

MS5440 10l. red, emerald and black; 25l. multicoloured; 30l. multicoloured	2·50	2·50

DESIGNS: 25l. Spanish 1850 6c. and Moldavian 1858 27p. stamps; 30l. Courtyard, Alhambra.

1120 Tower and Hand Pump

1992. Centenary of Bucharest Fire Tower.

5441	**1120**	10l. multicoloured	65	50

1121 Filipino Vinta and Rook

1992. 30th Chess Olympiad, Manila, Philippines. Multicoloured.

5442	10l. Type **1121**	40	25
5443	10l. Exterior of venue and chessmen	40	25
MS5444	91×79 mm. 75l. Chessboard on beach (41×53 mm)	3·25	3·25

1122 Post Rider approaching Town

1992. Stamp Day.

5445	**1122**	10l.+4l. pink, violet and blue	65	50

1123 Pistol shooting

1992. Olympic Games, Barcelona. Multicoloured.

5446	6l. Type **1123**	10	10
5447	7l. Weightlifting	10	10
5448	9l. Two-man kayak (horiz)	15	10
5449	10l. Handball	25	10
5450	25l. Wrestling (horiz)	40	10
5451	30l. Fencing (horiz)	50	15
5452	50l. Running	90	25
5453	55l. Boxing (horiz)	1·00	30
MS5454	90×79 mm. 100l. Rowing (50×39 mm)	2·50	2·50

1124 Ion Bratianu

1992. 130th Anniv of Foreign Ministry. Designs showing former Ministers.

5455	**1124**	10l. violet, green and deep green	10	10
5456	-	25l. purple, blue & dp blue	25	10
5457	-	30l. blue, purple & brn	30	10

DESIGNS: 25l. Ion Duca; 30l. Grigore Gafencu.

1125 "The Thinker of Cernavoda" (sculpture)

1992. "Expo 92" World's Fair, Seville. "Era of Discovery". Multicoloured.

5458	6l. Type **1125**	10	10
5459	7l. Trajan's bridge, Turnu-Severin	10	10
5460	10l. House on stilts	10	10
5461	25l. Saligny Bridge, Cernavoda	25	10
5462	30l. Traian Vuia's No. 1 airplane	40	10
5463	55l. Hermann Oberth's rocket	65	20
MS5464	79×91 mm. 100l. "Kneeling Figure" (sculpture, Constantin Brancusi) (41×49 mm)	1·30	1·30

1126 Doves posting Letters in Globe

1992. World Post Day.

5465	**1126**	10l. multicoloured	65	50

1127 "Santa Maria" and Bust of Columbus

1992. 500th Anniv of Discovery of America by Columbus. Multicoloured.

5466	6l. Type **1127**	15	10
5467	10l. "Nina"	15	10
5468	25l. "Pinta"	50	15
5469	55l. Columbus claiming New World	90	25
MS5470	91×79 mm. 100l. Columbus and "Santa Maria" (38×51 mm)	2·50	2·50

1128 Post Office Emblem

1992. First Anniv of Establishment of R.A. Posta Romana (postal organization).

5471	**1128**	10l. multicoloured	65	50

1129 Jacob Negruzzi (writer, 150th birth anniv)

1992. Anniversaries.

5472	**1129**	6l. green and violet	10	10
5473	-	7l. mauve, purple and green	10	10
5474	-	9l. blue and mauve	10	10
5475	-	10l. light brown, brown and blue	10	10
5476	-	25l. blue and brown	25	10
5477	-	30l. green and blue	50	10

DESIGNS: 7l. Grigore Antipa (biologist, 125th birth anniv); 9l. Alexe Mateevici (poet, 75th death anniv); 10l. Cezar Petrescu (writer, birth centenary); 25l. Octav Onicescu (mathematician, birth centenary); 30l. Ecaterina Teodoroiu (First World War fighter, 75th death anniv).

1130 American Bald Eagle

1992. Animals. Multicoloured.

5478	6l. Type **1130**	10	10
5479	7l. Spotted owl	10	10
5480	9l. Brown bear	15	10
5481	10l. American black oyster-catcher (horiz)	15	10
5482	25l. Wolf (horiz)	25	10
5483	30l. White-tailed deer (horiz)	40	10
5484	55l. Elk (horiz)	90	25
MS5485	91×80 mm. 100l. Killer whale ("Orcinus orca") (horiz)	1·90	1·90

1131 Arms

1992. New State Arms.

5486	**1131**	15l. multicoloured	65	50

1132 Buildings and Street, Mogosoaiei

1992. Anniversaries. Multicoloured.

5487	7l. Type **1132** (300th anniv)	10	10
5488	9l. College building and statue, Roman (600th anniv)	10	10
5489	10l. Prince Basaral, monastery and Princess Despina (475th anniv of Curtea de Arges Monastery)	10	10
5490	25l. Bucharest School of Architecture (80th anniv)	20	10

1133 Nativity

1992. Christmas.

5491	**1133**	15l. multicoloured	65	50

1134 Globe and Key-pad on Telephone

1992. New Telephone Number System.

5492	**1134**	15l. black, red and blue	65	50

1135 Woman's Gymnastics (two gold medals)

1992. Romanian Medals at Olympic Games, Barcelona. Two sheets, each 110×80 mm containing horiz designs as T **1135**. Multicoloured.

MS5493 (a) 35l. ×4 Type **1135**; Rowing (two gold medals); Fencing and bronze medal; High jumping and silver medal. (b) 35l. ×4 Shooting and bronze medal; Bronze medal and wrestling; Weightlifting and bronze medal; Bronze medal and boxing. Set of 2 sheets	3·75	3·75

1136 Mihai Voda Monastery

1993. Destroyed Bucharest Buildings. Multicoloured.

5494	10l. Type **1136**	10	10
5495	15l. Vacaresti Monastery	10	10
5496	25l. Unirii Hall	20	10
5497	30l. Mina Minovici Medico-legal Institute	50	10

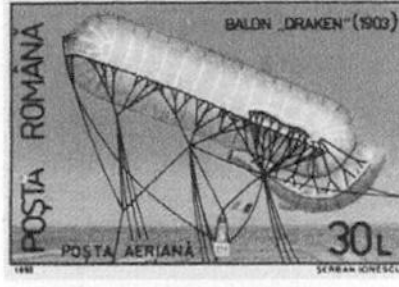

1137 Parseval Sigsfeld Kite-type Observation Balloon "Draken"

1993. Air. Balloons. Multicoloured.

5498	30l. Type **1137**	25	15
5499	90l. Caquot observation balloon, 1917	1·70	35

1138 Crucifixion

1993. Easter.

5500	**1138**	15l. multicoloured	65	50

1139 Hawthorn

1993. Medicinal Plants. Multicoloured.

5501	10l. Type **1139**	10	10
5502	15l. Gentian	10	10
5503	25l. Sea buckthorn	45	10
5504	30l. Billberry	50	10
5505	50l. Arnica	1·00	20
5506	90l. Dog rose	1·90	25

1140 Stanescu

1993. 60th Birth Anniv of Nichita Stanescu (poet).

5507	**1140**	15l. multicoloured	65	50

1141 Mounted Courier

1993. Stamp Day.

5508	**1141**	15l.+10l. multicoloured	65	50

1142 Exhibition Venue

1993. "Polska '93" International Stamp Exhibition, Poznan. Sheet 90×78 mm.

MS5509 200l. multicoloured		2·50	2·50

1143 Black-billed Magpie

1993. Birds.

5510	**1143**	5l. black and green	15	10
5511	-	10l. black and red	15	10
5512	-	15l. black and red	15	10
5513	-	20l. black and brown	25	10
5514	-	25l. black and red	25	10
5515	-	50l. black and yellow	40	10
5516	-	65l. black and red	50	10
5517	-	90l. black and red	75	10
5518	-	160l. black and blue	1·30	15
5519	-	250l. black and mauve	1·70	25

DESIGNS—HORIZ: 10l. Golden eagle. VERT: 15l. Northern bullfinch; 20l. Hoopoe; 25l. Great spotted woodpecker; 50l. Golden oriole; 65l. White winged crossbill; 90l. Barn swallows; 160l. Azure tit; 250l. Rose-coloured starling.

1144 Long-hair

1993. Cats. Multicoloured.

5520	10l. Type **1144**		25	20
5521	15l. Tabby-point long-hair		25	20
5522	30l. Red long-hair		40	20
5523	90l. Blue Persian		90	20
5524	135l. Tabby		1·20	20
5525	160l. Long-haired white Persian		1·50	25

1145 "Lola Artists' Sister" (Pablo Picasso)

1993. Europa. Contemporary Art. Sheet 75×105 mm containing T **1145** and similar vert designs. Multicoloured.

MS5526 280l. Type **1145**; 280l. "World Inception" (sculpture, Constantin Brancusi); 280l. "Girl with Idol" (sculpture, Ion Irimescu); 280l. "Woman in Grey" (Alexandru Ciucurencu)	6·50	6·50

1146 Adder

1993. Protected Animals. Multicoloured.

5527	10l. Type **1146**	25	15
5528	15l. Lynx (vert)	25	15
5529	25l. Common shelduck	40	15
5530	75l. Huchen	90	15
5531	105l. Poplar admiral	1·20	20
5532	280l. Alpine longhorn beetle	1·50	35

1147 Pine Marten

1993. Mammals.

5533	**1147**	10l. black and yellow	25	10
5534	-	15l. black and brown	25	10
5535	-	20l. red and black	25	10
5536	-	25l. black and brown	40	10
5537	-	30l. black and red	40	10
5538	-	40l. black and red	40	10
5539	-	75l. black and yellow	65	10
5540	-	105l. black and brown	1·00	10
5541	-	150l. black and orange	1·20	15
5542	-	280l. black and yellow	2·50	25

DESIGNS—HORIZ: 15l. Common rabbit; 30l. Red fox; 150l. Stoat; 280l. Egyptian mongoose. VERT: 20l. Eurasian red squirrel; 25l. Chamois; 40l. Argali; 75l. Small spotted genet; 105l. Garden dormouse.

1148 Brontosaurus

1993. Prehistoric Animals. Multicoloured.

5543	29l. Type **1148**	15	15
5544	46l. Plesiosaurus	50	15
5545	85l. Triceratops	75	15
5546	171l. Stegosaurus	1·70	20
5547	216l. Tyannosaurus	1·90	25
5548	319l. Archaeopteryx	2·50	35

1149 "Woman selling Eggs" (Marcel Iancul)

1993. "Telafila 93" Israel–Romanian Stamp Exhibition, Tel Aviv. Sheet 90×78 mm.

MS5549 535l. multicoloured	3·25	3·25

1150 St. Stefan the Great, Prince of Moldavia

1993. Icons. Multicoloured.

5550	75l. Type **1150**	25	10
5551	171l. Prince Costantin Brancoveanu of Wallachia with his sons Constantin, Stefan, Radu and Matei and Adviser Ianache Vacarescu	65	15
5552	216l. St. Antim Ivireanul, Metropolitan of Wallachia	1·50	25

1151 Mounted Officers

1993. Centenary of Rural Gendarmeric Law.

5553	**1151**	29l. multicoloured	65	50

1993. "Riccione 93" International Stamp Fair. No. 5292 surch **Riccione '93 3-5 septembrie 171L**.

5554	**1081**	171l. on 2l. multicoloured	1·30	60

1153 Temple Roof

1993. "Bangkok 1993" International Stamp Exhibition. Sheet 79×90 mm.

MS5555 535l. multicoloured	3·25	3·25

1154 George Baritiu

1993. Anniversaries.

5556	**1154**	29l. flesh, black and lilac	10	10
5557	-	46l. flesh, black and blue	15	10
5558	-	85l. flesh, black & green	40	10
5559	-	171l. flesh, black & purple	75	15
5560	-	216l. flesh, black & blue	90	20
5561	-	319l. flesh, black and grey	1·50	25

DESIGNS: 29l. Type **1154** (politician and journalist, death centenary); 46l. Horia Creanga (architect, 50th death anniv); 85l. Armand Calinescu (leader of Peasant National Party, birth centenary); 171l. Dr. Dumitru Bagdasar (neuro-surgeon, birth centenary); 216l. Constantin Brailoiu (musician, birth centenary); 319l. Iuliu Maniu (Prime Minister, 1927–30 and 1932–33, 40th death anniv).

1993. 35th Annivs of Romanian Philatelic Association and Romanian Philatelic Federation. No. 5445 surch **35 ANI DE ACTIVITATE AFR-FFR 1958–1993 70L+45L**.

5562	**1122**	70l.+45l. on 10l.+4l. pink, violet and blue	65	50

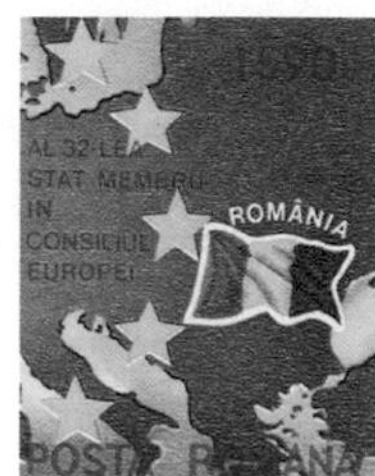

1156 Map, National Flag and Council Emblem

1993. Admission to Council of Europe. Sheet 90×78 mm.

MS5563 1590l. multicoloured	7·75	7·75

1157 Iancu Flondor (Bukovinan politician)

1993. 75th Anniv of Union of Bessarabia, Bukovina and Transylvania with Romania.

5564	**1157**	115l. brown, blue and black	65	25
5565	-	245l. violet, yellow and green	1·30	30
5566	-	255l. multicoloured	1·40	30
5567	-	325l. brown, pink and deep brown	1·90	35
MS5568 90×78 mm. 1060l. multicoloured (map in several shades of brown) (41×53 mm)			15·00	15·00

DESIGNS: 245l. Ionel Bratianu (Prime Minister 1918–19, 1922–26 and 1027; 255l. Iuliu Maniu (Prime Minister, 1927–30 and 1932–33); 325l. Pantelemon Halippa (Bessarabian politician); 1060l, King Ferdinand I and map.

1158 Emblem

1993. Anniversaries. Multicoloured.

5569	115l. Type **1158** (75th anniv of General Association of Romanian Engineers)	65	25
5570	245l. Statue of Johannes Honterus (450th anniv of Romanian Humanist School)	1·30	30
5571	255l. Bridge, arms on book spine and seal (625th anniv of first documentary reference to Slatina)	1·40	30
5572	325l. Map and town arms (625th anniv of first documentary reference to Braila)	1·50	35

1159 "Nativity" (17th-century icon)

1993. Christmas.

5573	**1159**	45l. multicoloured	65	50

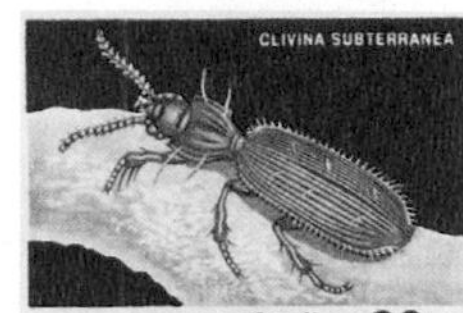

1160 "Clivina subterranea"

1993. Movile Cave Animals. Multicoloured.

5574	29l. Type **1160**	10	10
5575	46l. "Nepa anophthalma"	15	10
5576	85l. "Haemopis caeca"	50	15
5577	171l. "Lascona cristiani"	90	25
5578	216l. "Semisalsa dobrogica"	1·30	30
5579	319l. "Armadilidium tabacarui"	1·90	35
MS5580 90×78 mm. 535l. Diver exploring cave (41×53 mm)		2·50	2·50

1161 Prince Alexandru Ioan Cuza and Seal

1994. 130th Anniv of Court of Accounts.

5581	**1161**	45l. multicoloured	65	50

1162 Opera House

1994. Destroyed Buildings of Bucharest. Multicoloured.

5582	115l. Type **1162**	40	15
5583	245l. Church of Vacaresti Monastery (vert)	90	25
5584	255l. St. Vineri's Church	1·30	35
5585	325l. Cloisters of Vacaresti Monastery	1·40	40

1164 Speed Skating

1994. Winter Olympic Games, Lillehammer, Norway. Multicoloured.

5588	70l. Type **1164**	10	10
5589	115l. Skiing	50	10
5590	125l. Bobsleighing	65	10
5591	245l. Cross-country skiing	90	15
5592	255l. Ski jumping	1·00	20
5593	325l. Figure skating	1·40	25
MS5594	90×78 mm. 1590l. Single luge (41×53 mm) (air)	5·75	5·75

1165 Sarichioi Windmill, Tulcea

1994. Mills. Multicoloured.

5595	70l. Type **1165**	10	10
5596	115l. Nucarilor Valley windmill, Tulcea	25	10
5597	125l. Caraorman windmill, Tulcea	40	10
5598	245l. Romanii de Jos watermill, Valcea	75	15
5599	255l. Enisala windmill, Tulcea (horiz)	90	20
5600	325l. Nistoresti watermill, Vrancea	1·30	25

1166 Calin the Backward

1994. Fairy Tales. Multicoloured.

5601	70l. Type **1166**	25	10
5602	115l. Ileana Cosanzeana flying	60	10
5603	125l. Ileana Cosanzeana seated	65	10
5604	245l. Ileana Cosanzeana and castle	1·00	15
5605	255l. Agheran the Brave	1·20	20
5606	325l. The Enchanted Wolf carrying Ileana Cosanzeana	1·50	25

1167 "Resurrection of Christ" (17th-century icon)

1994. Easter.

5607	**1167** 60l. multicoloured	65	50

1168 "Struthiosaurus transylvanicus"

1994. Prehistoric Animals. Multicoloured.

5608	90l. Type **1168**	25	10
5609	130l. Megalosaurus	40	10
5610	150l. Parasaurolophus	65	15
5611	280l. Stenonychosaurus	1·00	20
5612	500l. Camarasaurus	1·30	25
5613	635l. Gallimimus	1·50	30

1169 Hermann Oberth (rocket designer)

1994. Europa. Inventions. Sheet 109×78 mm containing T **1169** and similar horiz design.

MS5614	240l. blue, indigo and black; 2100l. blue and black	6·50	6·50

DESIGN: 2100l. Henri Coanda (airplane designer).

1170 Silver Fir

1994. Trees. Each green and black.

5615	15l. Type **1170**	10	10
5616	35l. Scots pine	10	10
5617	45l. White poplar	15	10
5618	60l. Pedunculate oak	20	10
5619	70l. European larch	25	10
5620	125l. Beech	50	10
5621	350l. Sycamore	1·00	10
5622	940l. Ash	3·25	35
5623	1440l. Norway spruce	4·50	50
5624	3095l. Large-leaved lime	9·00	60

1171 Players and Flags of U.S.A., Switzerland, Colombia and Romania

1994. World Cup Football Championship, U.S.A. Designs showing various footballing scenes and flags of participating countries. Multicoloured.

5625	90l. Type **1171**	10	10
5626	130l. Brazil, Russia, Cameroun and Sweden (Group B)	40	10
5627	150l. Germany, Bolivia, Spain and South Korea (Group C)	65	10
5628	280l. Argentina, Greece, Nigeria and Bulgaria (Group D)	1·00	20
5629	500l. Italy, Ireland, Norway and Mexico (Group E)	1·30	25
5630	635l. Belgium, Morocco, Netherlands and Saudi Arabia (Group F)	1·50	35
MS5631	91×78 mm. 2075l. Goalkeeper stopping goal attempt (53×41 mm)	5·00	5·00

1172 Torch-bearer and Centenary Emblem

1994. Centenary of International Olympic Committee. Ancient Greek Athletes. Multicoloured.

5632	150l. Type **1172**	40	10
5633	280l. Discus-thrower and International Sports Year emblem	90	25
5634	500l. Wrestlers and Olympic Peace emblem	1·30	30
5635	635l. Arbitrator and "Paris 1994" centenary congress emblem	2·50	35
MS5636	90×78 mm. 2075l. Athletes, National Olympic Committee emblem and wreath (80th anniv of Romanian membership of Olympic movement) (53×41 mm)	5·00	5·00

1173 National History Museum (former Postal Headquarters, Bucharest)

1994. Stamp Day.

5637	**1173** 90l.+60l. multicoloured	65	50

1174 Death Trumpet ("Craterellus cornucopoiodes")

1994. Edible (**MS**5638a) and Poisonous (**MS**5638b) Fungi. Two sheets, each 155×72 mm containing vert designs as T **1174**. Multicoloured.

MS5638	(a) 30l. Type **1174**; 60l. Wood blewit ("Lepista nuda"); 150l. Cep ("Boletus edulis"); 940l. Common puff-ball ("Lycoperdon perlatum"). (b) 90l. Satan's mushroom ("Boletus satanus"); 280l. Death cap ("Amanita phalloides"); 350l. Red-staining inocybe ("Inocybe patouillardii, wrongly inscr "patonillardi"); 500l. Fly agaric ("Amanita muscaria") Set of 2 sheets	6·50	6·50

1175 Traian Vuia's Airplane No. 1, 1906

1994. Air. 50th Anniv of I.C.A.O.

5639	**1175** 110l. brown, black & blue	25	25
5640	- 350l. multicoloured	1·30	25
5641	- 500l. multicoloured	1·90	30
5642	- 635l. black, ultramarine and blue	2·50	30

DESIGNS: 350l. Rombac One Eleven; 500l. Boeing 737-300; 635l. Airbus Industrie A310.

1176 Turning Fork

1994. "Philakorea 1994" International Stamp Exhibition, Seoul.

5643	**1176** 60l. black, orange and mauve	65	50
MS5644	78×91 mm. 2075l. multicoloured	4·50	4·50

DESIGN—38×52 mm. No. 5644, Korean drummer.

1177 Beluga

1994. Environmental Protection of Danube Delta. Multicoloured.

5645	150l. Type **1177**	50	10
5646	280l. Orsini's viper	90	15
5647	500l. White-tailed sea eagle	1·50	20
5648	635l. European mink	1·70	25
MS5649	90×78 mm. 2075l. "Periploca graeca" (plant) (50×38 mm)	5·00	5·00

1994. Victory of Romanian Team in European Gymnastics Championships, Stockholm. Nos. 5338/9 surch **Echipa Romaniei Compioana Europeana Stockholm 1994** and value.

5650	150l. on 4l.50 multicoloured	65	35
5651	525l. on 4l.50 multicoloured	1·90	50

1179 Elephant

1994. The Circus. Multicoloured.

5652	90l. Type **1179**	25	10
5653	130l. Balancing bear (vert)	40	10
5654	150l. Cycling monkeys	65	15
5655	280l. Tiger jumping through hoop	1·30	20
5656	500l. Clown on tightrope balancing dogs	1·70	25
5657	635l. Clown on horseback	2·20	35

1994. World Post Day. No. 5465 surch **150LEI 1994 Posta - cea mai buna alegere**.

5658	**1126** 150l. on 10l. mult	65	50

1181 Emblem

1994. 20th International Fair, Bucharest.

5659	**1181** 525l. multicoloured	1·90	60

1182 Sterlet

1994. Sturgeons. Multicoloured.

5660	150l. Type **1182**	65	10
5661	280l. Russian sturgeon	1·30	15
5662	500l. Stellate sturgeon	1·90	20
5663	635l. Common sturgeon	2·50	25

1183 Snake

1994. Romanian–Chinese Stamp Exhibition, Timisoara and Cluj-Napoca. Multicoloured.

5664	150l. Type **1183**	65	25
5665	1135l. Dragon	4·50	50

1184 Early Steam Train, Bucharest–Giurgii Line

1994. 125th Anniv of Romanian Railway Administration.

5666	**1184** 90l. multicoloured	65	50

1185 Alexandru Orascu (architect and mathematician)

1994. Anniversaries. Multicoloured.

5667	30l. Type **1185** (death centenary)	25	15
5668	60l. Gheorghe Polizu (physician, 175th birth anniv)	40	15
5669	150l. Iulia Hasdeu (writer, 125th birth anniv)	65	15
5670	280l. S. Mehedinti (scientist, 125th birth anniv)	75	15
5671	350l. Camil Petrescu (writer, birth centenary)	1·20	25
5672	500l. N. Paulescu (physician, 125th birth anniv)	1·30	35

5673		940l. L. Grigorescu (painter, birth centenary)	3·25	50

See also No. 5684.

1186 Nativity

1994. Christmas.

5674	**1186**	60l. multicoloured	65	50

1187 St. Mary's Church, Cleveland, U.S.A.

1994

5675	**1187**	610l. multicoloured	1·90	60

1188 Anniversary Emblem

1994. 20th Anniv of World Tourism Organization.

5676	**1188**	525l. blue, orange & black	1·90	60

1189 Military Aviation Medal, 1938

1994. Military Decorations. Sheet 73×104 mm containing T **1189** and similar vert designs. Multicoloured.

MS5677	30l. Type **1189**; 60l. "For Valour" Cross, Third Class, 1916; 150l. Military Medal, First Class, 1880; 940l. Rumanian Star, 1877	3·25	3·25

1190 Kittens

1994. Young Domestic Animals. Multicoloured.

5678	90l. Type **1190**	15	25
5679	130l. Puppies	25	25
5680	150l. Kid	40	25
5681	280l. Foal	75	25
5682	500l. Rabbit kittens	1·50	35
5683	635l. Lambs	1·90	50

1994. Death Centenary of Gheorghe Tattarescu (painter). As T **1185**. Multicoloured.

5684	90l. Tattarescu	65	50

1191 Emblem

1995. Save the Children Fund.

5685	**1191**	60l. blue	65	50

1192 Tanar

1995. Brasov Youth. Neighbourhood Group Leaders. Multicoloured.

5686	40l. Type **1192**	15	25
5687	60l. Batran	25	25
5688	150l. Curcan	40	25
5689	280l. Dorobant	75	25
5690	350l. Brasovechean	1·30	25
5691	500l. Rosior	1·50	35
5692	635l. Albior	1·90	50

1193 Hand and Barbed Wire

1995. 50th Anniv of Liberation of Concentration Camps.

5693	**1193**	960l. black and red	1·30	60

1194 Emblems of French and Romanian State Airlines

1995. Air. 75th Anniv of Founding of Franco-Romanian Air Company.

5694	**1194**	60l. blue and red	25	10
5695	-	960l. blue and black	1·70	35

DESIGN: 960l. Potez IX biplane and Paris–Bucharest route map.

1195 Ear of Wheat

1995. 50th Anniversaries. Multicoloured.

5696	675l. Type **1195** (F.A.O.)	1·30	25
5697	960l. Anniversary emblem (U.N.O.)	1·90	35
5698	1615l. Hand holding pen showing members' flags (signing of U.N. Charter)	2·50	55

1196 "Resurrection" (icon)

1995. Easter.

5699	**1196**	60l. multicoloured	65	50

1197 "Youth without Age and Life without Death"

1995. Fairy Tales. Multicoloured.

5700	90l. Type **1197**	15	20
5701	130l. "The Old Man's Servant and the Old Woman's Servant" (vert)	20	20
5702	150l. "The Prince with the Golden Hair"	25	20
5703	280l. "Son of the Red King"	90	20
5704	500l. "Praslea the Brave and the Golden Apples" (vert)	1·70	20
5705	635l. "King Dafin" (drawn by golden horses)	2·50	25

1198 Enescu

1995. 40th Death Anniv of George Enescu (composer).

5706	**1198**	960l. orange and black	1·40	60

1199 Dove with Section of Rainbow

1995. Europa. Peace and Freedom. Multicoloured.

5707	150l. Type **1199**	15	10
5708	4370l. Dove wings forming "EUROPA" around rainbow	9·50	9·00

1200 Blaga

1995. Birth Centenary of Lucian Blaga (poet).

5709	**1200**	150l. multicoloured	65	50

See also Nos. 5745/9.

1201 Bucharest Underground Railway, 1979

1995. Transport.

5712	**1201**	470l. yellow and black (postage)	65	10
5713	-	630l. red and blue	90	10
5714	-	675l. red and black	90	10
5715	-	755l. blue and black	1·00	10
5716	-	1615l. green and black	1·90	50
5717	-	2300l. green and black	3·00	25
5718	-	2550l. black and red	3·25	25
5719	-	285l. green and black (air)	25	10
5720	-	715l. red and blue	90	10
5721	-	965l. black and blue	3·00	10
5722	-	1575l. green and black	2·30	35
5723	-	3410l. blue and black	4·50	60

DESIGNS—HORIZ: 285l. I.A.R. 80 aircraft (70th anniv of Romanian aeronautical industry); 630l. "Masagerul" (post boat); 715l. I.A.R. 316 Red Cross helicopter; 755l. "Razboieni" (container ship); 965l. Sud Aviation SA 330 Puma helicopter; 1575l. I.A.R. 818H seaplane; 2300l. Trolleybus, 1904; 2550l. Steam train, 1869; 3410l. Boeing 737-300 (75th anniv of Romanian air transport). VERT: 675l. Cable-car, Brasov; 1615l. Electric tram, 1894.

1202 "Dacia" (liner)

1995. Centenary of Romanian Maritime Service. Multicoloured.

5735	90l. Type **1202**	25	20
5736	130l. "Imparatul Traian" (Danube river steamer) (horiz)	25	20
5737	150l. "Romania" (Danube river steamer) (horiz)	25	20
5738	280l. "Costinesti" (tanker) (horiz)	40	20
5739	960l. "Caransebes" (container ship) (horiz)	1·30	25
5740	3410l. "Tutova" (car ferry) (horiz)	4·50	85

1203 Fallow Deer

1995. European Nature Conservation Year. Multicoloured.

5741	150l. Type **1203**	25	25
5742	280l. Great bustard	40	25
5743	960l. Lady's slipper	1·90	60
5744	1615l. Stalagmites	2·50	1·20

1995. Anniversaries. As T **1200**. Multicoloured.

5745	90l. D. Rosca (birth centenary)	25	25
5746	130l. Vasile Conta (150th birth anniv)	25	25
5747	280l. Ion Barbu (birth centenary)	25	25
5748	960l. Iuliu Hatieganu (110th birth anniv)	1·20	30
5749	1650l. Dimitrie Brandza (botanist) (death centenary)	2·00	40

1204 Youths and Torch-bearer

1995. European Youth Olympic Days.

5750	**1204**	1650l. multicoloured	2·50	60

1205 Post Wagon (image scaled to 46% of original size)

1995. Stamp Day. Centenary of Upper Rhine Local Post.

5751	**1205**	960l. (+715l.) mult	2·50	60

No. 5751 includes the se-tenant premium-carrying tab shown in Type **1205**.

1206 Saligny Bridge

1995. Centenary of Saligny Bridge, Cernavoda.

5752	**1206**	675l. multicoloured	1·30	60

1207 Mallard

1995. Domestic Birds. Multicoloured.

5753	90l. Type **1207**	25	20
5754	130l. Red junglefowl (hen)	25	20
5755	150l. Helmeted guineafowl	25	20
5756	280l. Common turkey	65	20
5757	960l. Greylag goose	1·50	25
5758	1650l. Red junglefowl (cock)	2·30	35

1208 General Dr. Victor Anastasiu

1995. 75th Anniv of Institute of Aeronautics Medicine.

5759	**1208**	960l. ultramarine, blue and red	1·90	60

1209 Battle Scene

1995. 400th Anniv of Battle of Calugareni.

5760	**1209**	100l. multicoloured	65	50

1210 Giurgiu Castle

1995. Anniversaries. Multicoloured.

5761	250l. Type **1210** (600th anniv)	40	15
5762	500l. Neamtului Castle (600th anniv) (vert)	65	15
5763	960l. Sebes-Alba Mill (700th anniv)	1·30	20
5764	1615l. Dorohoi Church (500th anniv) (vert)	1·90	30
5765	1650l. Military observatory, Bucharest (centenary) (vert)	2·30	35

1211 Moldovita Monastery

1995. UNESCO World Heritage Sites. Multicoloured.

5766	675l. Type **1211**	65	25
5767	960l. Hurez Monastery	1·30	35
5768	1615l. Biertan Castle (horiz)	1·90	50

1212 Racket

1995. Fifth Open Tennis Championships, Bucharest.

5769	**1212**	1020l. multicoloured	1·90	60

1213 Ion Ionescu (editor)

1995. Centenary of Mathematics Gazette.

5770	**1213**	100l. pink and brown	65	50

1214 "Albizzia julibrissin"

1995. Plants from Bucharest Botanical Garden. Multicoloured.

5771	50l. Type **1214**	15	10
5772	100l. Yew	15	10
5773	150l. "Paulownia tomentosa"	15	10
5774	500l. Bird of Paradise flower	75	10
5775	960l. Amazon water-lily	1·50	35
5776	2300l. Azalea	2·75	50

1215 St. John's Church

1995. 600th Anniv of First Documentary Reference to Piatra-Neamt.

5777	**1215**	250l. multicoloured	1·30	1·20

1216 George Apostu (sculptor, 10th death (1996))

1995. Anniversaries.

5778	**1216**	150l. green and black	25	20
5779	-	250l. blue and black	50	20
5780	-	500l. light brown, brown and black	75	20
5781	-	960l. rose, purple and black	1·50	25
5782	-	1650l. brown and black	2·30	50

DESIGNS: 250l. Emil Cioran (philosopher, death in 1995); 500l. Eugen Ionescu (writer, 1st death anniv); 960l. Elena Vacarescu (poetess, 130th birth (1996)); 1650l. Mircea Eliade (philosopher, 10th death (1996)).

1217 Running

1995. Olympic Games, Atlanta (1996) (1st issue). Multicoloured.

5783	50l. Type **1217**	15	15
5784	100l. Gymnastics	15	15
5785	150l. Canoeing	15	15
5786	500l. Fencing	90	15
5787	960l. Rowing	1·50	25
5788	2300l. Boxing	3·50	60
MS5789	78×92 mm. 2610l. Gymnastics (different) (41×53 mm)	3·75	3·75

See also Nos. 5829/**MS**5834.

1218 Nativity

1995. Christmas.

5790	**1218**	100l. multicoloured	65	50

1219 Masked Person

1996. Folk Masks of Maramures (250l.) and Moldavia (others).

5791	**1219**	250l. multicoloured	65	25
5792	-	500l. multicoloured	1·00	25
5793	-	960l. mult (vert)	1·70	35
5794	-	1650l. mult (vert)	2·50	50

DESIGNS: 500l. to 1650l. Different masks.

1220 Tristan Tzara

1996. Writers' Birth Anniversaries. Multicoloured.

5795	150l. Type **1220** (centenary)	25	10
5796	1500l. Anton Pann (bicentenary)	2·30	35

1221 "Resurrection" (icon)

1996. Easter.

5797	**1221**	150l. multicoloured	65	50

1222 National History Museum

1996. "Romfilex '96" Romanian–Israeli Stamp Exhibition. Sheet 124×73 mm containing T **1222** and similar vert designs.

MS5798	150l. brown and black; 370l. multicoloured; 1500l. multicoloured	10·00	10·00

DESIGNS: 370l. "On The Terrace at Sinaia" (Theodor Aman); 1500l. "Old Jerusalem" (Reuven Rubin).

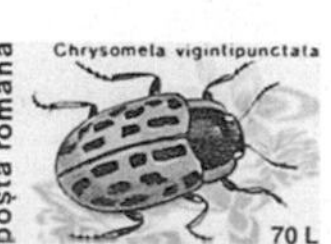

1223 "Chrysomela vigintipunctata" (leaf beetle)

1996. Beetles.

5799	**1223**	70l. yellow and black	20	10
5800	-	220l. red and black	20	10
5801	-	370l. brown and black	40	10
5802	-	650l. black, red & grey	65	10
5803	-	700l. red, black and green	75	10
5804	-	740l. black and yellow	90	10
5805	-	960l. black and red	1·20	10
5806	-	1000l. yellow and black	1·20	10
5807	-	1500l. black and brown	1·90	25
5808	-	2500l. red, black & green	2·50	50

DESIGNS: 220l. "Cerambyx cerdo" (longhorn beetle); 370l. "Entomoscelis adonidis"; 650l. Ladybird; 700l. Caterpillar-hunter; 740l. "Hedobia imperialis"; 960l. European rhinoceros beetle; 1000l. Bee chafer; 1500l. "Purpuricenus kaehleri" (longhorn beetle); 2500l. "Anthaxia salicis".

1224 Dumitru Prunariu (first Romanian cosmonaut)

1996. "Espamer" Spanish–Latin American and "Aviation and Space" Stamp Exhibitions, Seville, Spain. Sheet 91×78 mm.

MS5809	2720l. multicoloured	2·50	2·50

1225 Arbore Church

1996. UNESCO World Heritage Sites. Multicoloured.

5810	150l. Type **1225**	25	25
5811	1500l. Voronet Monastery	1·70	35
5812	2550l. Humor Monastery	3·25	60

1226 Ana Aslan (doctor)

1996. Europa. Famous Women. Multicoloured.

5813	370l. Type **1226**	40	35
5814	4140l. Lucia Bulandra (actress)	6·25	5·75

1227 "Mother and Children" (Oana Negoita)

1996. 50th Anniv of UNICEF. Prize-winning Children's Paintings. Multicoloured.

5815	370l. Type **1227**	40	35
5816	740l. "Winter Scene" (Badea Cosmin)	90	35
5817	1500l. "Children and Sun over House" (Nicoleta Georgescu)	1·50	50
5818	2550l. "House on Stilts" (Biborka Bartha) (vert)	2·30	70

1228 Goalkeeper with Ball

1996. European Football Championship, England. Multicoloured.

5819	220l. Type **1228**	10	10
5820	370l. Player with ball	25	10
5821	740l. Two players with ball	65	15
5822	1500l. Three players with ball	1·40	25
5823	2550l. Player dribbling ball	2·40	50
MS5824	90×78 mm. 4050l. Balls and two players (41×53 mm)	3·75	3·75

Nos. 5819/23 were issued together, se-tenant, forming a composite design of the pitch and stadium.

1229 Metropolitan Toronto Convention Centre (venue)

1996. "Capex '96" International Stamp Exhibition, Toronto, Canada. Multicoloured.

5825	150l. Type **1229**	65	50
MS5826	78×90 mm. 4050l. View of City (41×52 mm)	3·75	3·75

1230 Factory

1996. 225th Anniv of Resita Works.

5827	**1230**	150l. brown	65	50

1996. Fifth Anniv of Establishment of R.A. Posta Romana (postal organization). No. 5471 surch **1996 - 5 ANI DE LA INFIINTARE L150.**

5828	**1128**	150l. on 10l. multicoloured	65	60

1232 Boxing

1996. Centenary of Modern Olympic Games and Olympic Games, Atlanta (2nd issue). Multicoloured.

No.	Description		
5829	220l. Type **1232**	25	10
5830	370l. Running	40	10
5831	740l. Rowing	90	15
5832	1500l. Judo	1·70	35
5833	2550l. Gymnastics (asymmetrical bars)	2·75	50
MS5834	90×78 mm. 4050l. Gymnastics (beam) (53×41 mm) (air)	3·75	3·75

No. **MS**5834 also commemorates "Olymphilex '96" sports stamp exhibition, Atlanta.

1233 Postman, Keyboard and Stamp under Magnifying Glass

1996. Stamp Day.

No.	Type	Description		
5835	1233	1500l. (+650l.) mult	1·90	60

No. 5835 includes the se-tenant premium-carrying tab shown in Type **1233**.

1234 White Spruce

1996. Coniferous Trees. Multicoloured.

No.	Description		
5836	70l. Type **1234**	15	10
5837	150l. Serbian spruce	15	10
5838	220l. Blue Colorado spruce	15	10
5839	740l. Sitka spruce	90	10
5840	1500l. Scots pine	1·70	25
5841	3500l. Maritime pine	3·75	60

1235 Grass Snake

1996. Animals. Multicoloured.

No.	Description		
5842	70l. Type **1235**	15	10
5843	150l. Hermann's tortoise	15	10
5844	220l. Eurasian sky lark (horiz)	15	10
5845	740l. Red fox (horiz)	90	10
5846	1500l. Common porpoise	1·70	25
5847	3500l. Golden eagle (horiz)	3·75	60

1236 Madonna and Child

1996. Christmas.

No.	Type	Description		
5848	1236	150l. multicoloured	65	50

1237 Stan Golestan (composer, 40th)

1996. Death Anniversaries.

No.	Type	Description		
5849	1237	100l. pink and black	25	25
5850	-	150l. purple and black	40	35
5851	-	370l. orange and black	65	60
5852	-	1500l. red and black	2·00	1·90

DESIGNS: 150l. Corneliu Coposu (politician, 1st); 370l. Horia Vintila (writer, 4th); 1500l. Alexandru Papana (test pilot, 50th).

1238 Ford "Spider", 1930

1996. Motor Cars. Two sheets containing horiz designs as T **1238**. Multicoloured.

No.	Description		
MS5853	(a) 110×78 mm 70l. Type **1238**; 150l. Citroen (1932); 220l. Rolls Royce (1936); 280l. Mercedes Benz (1933). (b) 113×80 mm. 120l. Jaguar SS 100 (1937); 2500l. Bugatti Type 59 (1934); 2550l. Mercedes Benz 500K Roadster (1936); 2550l. Alfa Romeo 8C (1931) Set of 2 sheets	10·00	10·00

1239 Deng Xiaoping and Margaret Thatcher

1997. "Hong Kong '97" Stamp Exhibition. Sheet 92×78 mm.

No.	Description		
MS5854	1500l. multicoloured	1·90	1·90

1240 Stoat

1997. Fur-bearing Mammals. Multicoloured.

No.	Description		
5855	70l. Type **1240**	25	25
5856	150l. Arctic fox	25	25
5857	220l. Racoon-dog	25	25
5858	740l. European otter	40	30
5859	1500l. Muskrat	75	35
5860	3500l. Pine marten	1·90	60

1241 Bow

1997. 26th Anniv of Greenpeace (environmental organization). The "Rainbow Warrior" (campaign ship). Multicoloured.

No.	Description		
5861	150l. Type **1241**	25	25
5862	370l. Ship and ice	25	25
5863	1940l. Ship cruising past beach	1·00	35
5864	2500l. Rainbow and ship	1·70	35
MS5865	90×77 mm. 4050l. Ship carrying banner (49×38 mm)	3·25	3·25

1242 Thomas Edison (inventor)

1997. Birth Anniversaries. Multicoloured.

No.	Description		
5866	200l. Type **1242** (150th anniv)	25	25
5867	400l. Franz Schubert (composer, bicentenary)	40	30
5868	3600l. Miguel de Cervantes Saavedra (writer, 450th anniv)	2·50	60

1243 Emblem

1997. Inauguration of Mobile Telephone Network in Romania.

No.	Type	Description		
5869	1243	400l. multicoloured	65	50

1244 Surdesti

1997. Churches. Each brown, agate and green.

No.	Description		
5870	200l. Type **1244**	25	20
5871	400l. Plopis	25	20
5872	450l. Bogdan Voda	25	20
5873	850l. Rogoz	50	25
5874	3600l. Calinesti	1·70	30
5875	6000l. Birsana	2·75	50

1245 Al. Demetrescu Dan in "Hamlet", 1916

1997. Second Shakespeare Festival, Craiova. Multicoloured.

No.	Description		
5876	200l. Type **1245**	15	10
5877	400l. Constantin Serghie in "Othello", 1855	15	10
5878	2400l. Gheorghe Cozorici in "Hamlet", 1957	1·30	1·20
5879	3600l. Ion Manolescu in "Hamlet", 1924	1·90	1·80

1246 Vlad Tepes Dracula (Voivode of Wallachia)

1997. Europa. Tales and Legends. Dracula. Multicoloured.

No.	Description		
5880	400l. Type **1246**	25	10
5881	4250l. Dracula the myth	3·00	2·40

1247 "Dolichothele uberiformis"

1997. Cacti. Multicoloured.

No.	Description		
5882	100l. Type **1247**	25	25
5883	250l. "Rebutia"	25	25
5884	450l. "Echinofossulocactus lamellosus"	25	25
5885	500l. "Ferocactus glaucescens"	25	25
5886	650l. "Thelocactus"	25	25
5887	6150l. "Echinofossulocactus albatus"	5·00	1·20

1248 National Theatre, Cathedral and Statue of Mihai Viteazul

1997. "Balcanmax'97" Maximum Cards Exhibition, Cluj-Napoca.

No.	Type	Description		
5888	1248	450l. multicoloured	65	60

1249 19th-century Postal Transport

1997. Stamp Day.

No.	Type	Description		
5889	1249	3600l. (+1500l.) multicoloured	3·25	1·80

No. 5889 includes the se-tenant premium-carrying tab shown in Type **1249**.

1997. Nos. 5349/55 and 5357 surch.

No.	Description		
5890	250l. on 1l. blue	25	25
5891	250l. on 2l. green	25	25
5892	250l. on 4l. red	25	25
5893	450l. on 5l. violet	25	25
5894	450l. on 6l. brown	25	25
5895	450l. on 18l. red	25	25
5896	950l. on 9l. red	40	25
5897	3600l. on 8l. brown	1·90	35

1251 Archway of Vlad Tepes Dracula's House

1997. Sighisoara. Multicoloured.

No.	Description		
5898	250l. Type **1251**	25	15
5899	650l. Town Hall clocktower	40	15
5900	3700l. Steps leading to fortress and clocktower	2·00	1·20

1252 Tourism Monument

1997. Rusca Montana, Banat.

No.	Type	Description		
5901	1252	950l. multicoloured	40	25

1253 Printing Works

1997. 125th Anniv of Stamp Printing Works.

No.	Type	Description		
5902	1253	450l. red, brown and blue	65	40

1254 Emil Racovita (biologist) and "Belgica" (polar barque)

1997. Centenary of Belgian Antarctic Expedition.

5903 **1254** 450l. blue, grey and black 25 10
5904 - 650l. red, yellow and black 25 10
5905 - 1600l. green, pink and black 75 15
5906 - 3700l. brown, yellow and black 2·50 1·60

DESIGNS: 650l. Frederick Cook (anthropologist and photographer) and "Belgica" at sea; 1600l. Roald Amundsen and "Belgica" in port; 3700l. Adrien de Gerlache (expedition commander) and "Belgica" ice-bound.

1997. "Aeromfila '97" Stamp Exhibition, Brasov. No. 5334 surch **1050 L. AEROMFILA'97 Brasov** and airplane.

5907 **1292** 1050l. on 4l.50 mult 65 40

1256 Campsite

1997. Romanian Scout Association. Multicoloured.

5908 300l. Type **1256** 15 10
5909 700l. Romanian Scout Association emblem 25 15
5910 1050l. Joined hands 50 30
5911 1750l. Carvings 75 45
5912 3700l. Scouts around campfire 1·80 1·10

Nos. 5908/12 were issued together, se-tenant, forming a composite design.

1997. Ninth Romanian–Chinese Stamp Exhibition, Bucharest. No. 5293 surch **A IX-a editie a expozitiei filatelice romano-chineza 1997 500 L**.

5913 **1082** 500l. on 2l. mult 65 40

1258 Ion Mihalache (politician)

1997. Anniversaries. Multicoloured.

5914 500l. Type **1258** (34th death anniv) 25 15
5915 1050l. King Carol I (131st anniv of accession) (black inscriptions and face value) 65 40
5916 1050l. As No. 5915 but mauve inscriptions and face value 65 40
5917 1050l. As No. 5915 but blue inscriptions and face value 65 40
5918 1050l. As No. 5915 but brown inscriptions and face value 65 40

1259 Rugby

1997. Sports. Multicoloured.

5919 500l. Type **1259** 25 15
5920 700l. American football (vert) 40 25
5921 1750l. Oina (Romanian bat and ball game) 75 45
5922 3700l. Mountaineering (vert) 2·50 1·60

1260 New Building

1998. 130th Anniv of Bucharest Chamber of Commerce and Industry.

5923 **1260** 700l. multicoloured 65 40

1261 Biathlon

1998. Winter Olympic Games, Nagano, Japan. Multicoloured.

5924 900l. Type **1261** 60 40
5925 3900l. Figure skating 2·30 1·60

1262 "Romania breaking the Chains on Libertatii Plain" (C. D. Rosenthal)

1998. National Tricolour Flag Day. Sheet 78×90 mm.

MS5926 900l. multicoloured 1·20 1·20

1263 Four-leaved Clover (Good luck and Success)

1998. Europa. National Festivals.

5927 **1263** 900l. green and red 1·20 80
5928 - 3900l. red, orange and green 28·00 19·00

DESIGN: 3900l. Butterfly (youth and suaveness).

1264 Alfred Nobel

1998. The 20th-century (1st series). Multicoloured.

5929 700l. Type **1264** (establishment of Nobel Foundation, 1901) 45 30
5930 900l. Guglielmo Marconi (first radio-telegraphic trans-Atlantic link, 1901) 60 40
5931 1500l. Albert Einstein (elaboration of Theory of Relativity, 1905) 70 45
5932 3900l. Traian Vuia (his first flight, 1906) 2·30 1·60

See also Nos. 5991/5, 6056/9, 6060/3, 6128/31, 6133/6, 6205/8 and 6230/3.

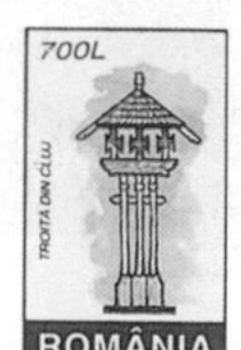

1265 Shrine, Cluj

1998. Roadside Shrines. Multicoloured.

5933 700l. Type **1265** 35 25
5934 900l. Crucifixion, Prahovac 45 30
5935 1500l. Shrine, Arges 1·20 80

1998. "Israel '98" International Stamp Exhibition, Tel Aviv. No. **MS**5798 with each stamp surch **ISRAEL '98** and the old value cancelled by Menora emblem.

MS5936 700l. on 150l. brown and black; 900l. on 370l. multicoloured; 3900l. on 1500l. multicoloured 3·50 3·50

1267 Dr. Thoma Ionescu (founder) and Coltea Hospital, Bucharest

1998. Centenary of Romanian Surgery Society.

5937 **1267** 1050l. grey, brown and red 60 40

1998. Nos. 5350/1, 5353/4 and 5357 surch, the old value cancelled by a clover leaf.

5938 50l. on 2l. green 45 30
5939 100l. on 8l. brown 45 30
5940 200l. on 4l. red 45 30
5941 400l. on 6l. brown 45 30
5942 500l. on 18l. red 45 30

1269 Player

1998. World Cup Football Championship, France. Sheet 74×104 mm containing T **1269** and similar vert designs. Each ultramarine, brown and green.

MS5943 800l. Type **1269**; 1050l. Player in air; 1850l. Player bouncing ball on knee; 4150l. Player preparing to kick ball 4·75 4·75

1998. Nos. 5615/17 and 5620 surch, the old value cancelled by a hare.

5944 - 700l. on 125l. green and black 60 40
5945 - 800l. on 35l. green and black 60 40
5946 - 1050l. on 45l. green and black 60 40
5947 **1170** 4150l. on 15l. green and black 60 40

1998. Nos. 5352 and 5355 surch, the old value cancelled by a heart.

5948 1000l. on 9l. red 60 40
5949 1500l. on 5l. violet 60 40

1272 Brown Kiwi

1998. Nocturnal Birds. Multicoloured.

5950 700l. Type **1272** 45 30
5951 1500l. Barn owl 60 40
5952 1850l. Water rail 70 45
5953 2450l. European nightjar 1·70 1·20

1998. No. 5361 surch, the old value cancelled by a sign of the zodiac.

5954 250l. on 45l. blue (Aries) 60 40
5955 350l. on 45l. blue (Taurus) 60 40
5956 400l. on 45l. blue (Gemini) 60 40
5957 450l. on 45l. blue (Cancer) 60 40
5958 850l. on 45l. blue (Leo) 60 40
5959 900l. on 45l. blue (Aquarius) 60 40
5960 1000l. on 45l. blue (Libra) 60 40
5961 1600l. on 45l. blue (Scorpio) 1·20 80
5962 2500l. on 45l. blue (Sagittarius) 4·75 3·50

1274 81p. Stamp and Waslui Cancellation

1998. 140th Anniv of Bull's Head Issue of Moldavia. Multicoloured.

5963 700l. Type **1274** 60 40
5964 1050l. 27p. stamp and Jassy cancellation 70 45

MS5965 130×80 mm. 4150l.+850l. 54 and 108p. stamps and Galatz cancellation (53×41 mm) 3·50 3·50

1275 Soldiers and Revolutionaries fighting

1998. 150th Anniv of the 1848 Revolutions.

5966 **1275** 1050l. black, yellow and red 60 40

1276 Nikolaus Lenau (poet)

1998. German Personalities of Banat.

5967 **1276** 800l. orange, black and pink 45 35
5968 - 1850l. orange, black and green 80 65
5969 - 4150l. orange, black and blue 1·70 1·40

DESIGNS: 1850l. Stefan Jager (artist); 4150l. Adam Muller-Guttenbrunn (writer).

1277 Diver and Marine Life

1998. International Year of the Ocean.

5970 **1277** 1100l. multicoloured 60 45

1998. Nos. 5336/7 surch, the old value cancelled by a sporting emblem.

5971 **1094** 50l. on 1l. multicoloured (Figure skater) 60 45
5972 - 50l. on 1l. multicoloured (Trophy) 60 45

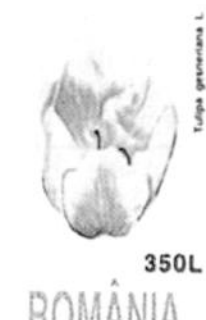

1279 "Tulipa gesneriana"

1998. Flowers. Multicoloured.

5973 350l. Type **1279** 25 20
5974 850l. "Dahlia variabilis" "Rubin" 45 35
5975 1100l. Martagon lily 60 45
5976 4450l. "Rosa centifolia" 2·30 1·90

No. 5975 commemorates the 50th anniv of the Horticulture Institute, Bucharest.

1998. Various stamps surch. (a) Nos. 5399/5404, the old value cancelled by a transport emblem.

5977 **1106** 50l. on 1l. brown, blue and deep blue (Car) 25 20
5978 - 50l. on 4l. green, lilac and violet (Steam locomotive) 25 20
5979 - 50l. on 5l. brown, blue and ultramarine (Lorry) 25 20
5980 - 50l. on 5l. blue, brown and red (Helicopter) 25 20
5981 - 50l. on 9l. red, blue and deep blue (Airplane) 25 20
5982 - 50l. on 10l. black, light brown and brown (Ship) 25 20

(b) Nos. 5472/5 and 5477, the old value cancelled by a bird.

5983 **1129** 50l. on 6l. green and violet (Cockerel) 25 20
5984 - 50l. on 7l. mauve, purple and green (Duck) 25 20
5985 - 50l. on 9l. blue and mauve (Swan) 25 20
5986 - 50l. on 10l. light brown, brown and blue (Dove) 25 20
5987 - 50l. on 30l. green and blue (Swallow) 25 20

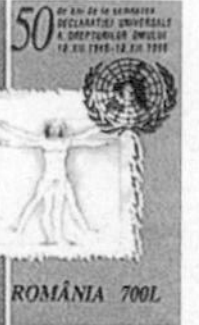

1281 "Proportions of Man" (Leonardo da Vinci)

1998. 50th Anniv of Universal Declaration of Human Rights.
5988 **1281** 700l. multicoloured 60 45

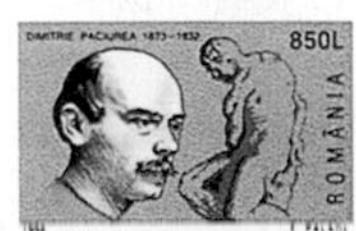

1282 Paciurea

1998. 125th Birth Anniv of Dimitrie Paciurea (sculptor).
5989 **1282** 850l. multicoloured 60 45

1283 Eclipse

1998. Total Eclipse of the Sun (1999) (1st issue).
5990 **1283** 1100l. multicoloured 60 45
See also No. 6050.

1284 Sinking of "Titanic" (liner), 1912

1998. The 20th century (2nd series).
5991 **1284** 350l. black, bl & red 25 20
5992 - 1100l. multicoloured 45 35
5993 - 1600l. multicoloured 60 45
5994 - 2000l. multicoloured 70 55
5995 - 2600l. blk, grey & red 1·40 1·10
DESIGNS: 1100l. Henri Coanda and his turbine-powered model airplane, 1910; 1600l. Louis Bleriot and his "Bleriot XI" airplane (first powered flight across English Channel, 1909); 2000l. Freighter in locks and map of American sea routes (opening of Panama Canal, 1914); 2600l. Prisoners in courtyard (Russian October revolution, 1917).

1998. Christmas. Nos. 5491 and 5674 surch with the old value cancelled by a Christmas emblem.
5996 **1133** 2000l. on 15l. multicoloured (Christmas tree) 95 75
5997 **1186** 2600l. on 60l. multicoloured (Father Christmas) 95 75

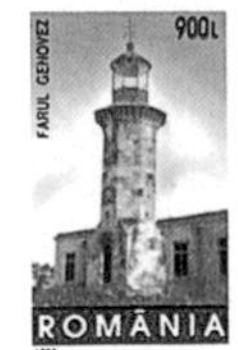

1286 Gonovez Lighthouse

1998. Lighthouses. Multicoloured.
5998 900l. Type **1286** 25 20
5999 1000l. Constanta 35 30
6000 1100l. Sfantu Gheorghe 45 35
6001 2600l. Sulina 1·60 1·30

1287 Arnota Monastery

1999. Monasteries. Multicoloured.
6002 500l. Type **1287** 25 20
6003 700l. Bistrita 35 30
6004 1100l. Dintr'un Lemn 45 35
6005 2100l. Govora 60 45
6006 4850l. Tismana 1·70 1·40

1999. No. 5492 surch with the old value cancelled by various fungi.
6007 **1134** 50l. on 15l. black, red and blue 25 20
6009 **1134** 400l. on 15l. black, red and blue 25 20
6010 **1134** 2300l. on 15l. black, red and blue 60 45
6011 **1134** 3200l. on 15l. black, red and blue 1·20 95

1999. No. 5384 surch with the old value cancelled by a musical instrument.
6012 **1099** 100l. on 1l. blue (guitar) 25 20
6013 **1099** 250l. on 1l. blue (saxophone) 35 30

1290 "Magnolia soulangiana"

1999. Shrubs. Multicoloured.
6014 350l. Type **1290** 10 10
6015 1000l. "Stewartia malacodendron" 25 20
6016 1100l. "Hibiscus rosa- sinensis" 35 30
6017 5350l. "Clematis patens" 2·30 1·90

1292 Easter Eggs

1999. Easter.
6023 **1292** 1100l. multicoloured 60 45

1999. No. 5799 surch with the old value cancelled by a dinosaur emblem.
6024 **1223** 100l. on 70l. yellow and black (Brontosaurus) 25 20
6025 **1223** 200l. on 70l. yellow and black (Iguanodon) 25 20
6026 **1223** 200l. on 70l. yellow and black (Allosaurus) 25 20
6027 **1223** 1500l. on 70l. yellow and black (Diplodocus) 30 25
6028 **1223** 1600l. on 70l. yellow and black (Tyrannosaurus) 35 30
6029 **1223** 3200l. on 70l. yellow and black (Stegosaurus) 80 65
6030 **1223** 6000l. on 70l. yellow and black (Plateosaurus) 1·50 1·20

1294 Girdle of Keys (Padureni)

1999. Jewellery. Multicoloured.
6031 1200l. Type **1294** 25 20
6032 2100l. Pendant of keys (Ilia, Hunedoara) 45 35
6033 2600l. Jewelled bib (Maramures) 60 45
6034 3200l. Necklace (Banat) (horiz) 1·70 1·40

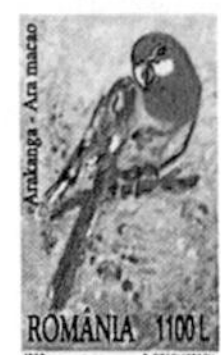

1295 Scarlet Macaw

1999. Birds. Multicoloured.
6035 1100l. Type **1295** 25 20
6036 2700l. White peafowl 60 45
6037 3700l. Common peafowl 80 65
6038 5700l. Sulphur-crested cockatoo 1·30 1·00

1296 Council Flag and Headquarters, Strasbourg

1999. 50th Anniv of Council of Europe.
6039 **1296** 2300l. multicoloured 1·20 95

1297 St. Peter's Cathedral, Rome

1999. Papal Visit.
6040 **1297** 1300l. mauve and black 95 75
6041 - 1600l. mauve and black 1·00 85
6042 - 2300l. multicoloured 1·20 95
6043 - 6300l. multicoloured 1·30 1·00
DESIGNS: 1600l. Patriarchal Cathedral, Bucharest; 2300l. Father Teoctist (patriarch of Romanian Orthodox church); 6300l. Pope John Paul II (after Dina Bellotti).

1298 Northern Shoveler

1999. Europa. Parks and Gardens: the Danube Delta Nature Reserve. Multicoloured.
6044 1100l. Type **1298** 60 45
6045 5700l. Black stork 1·70 1·40

1299 Gheorghe Cartan (historian, 150th birth anniv)

1999. Anniversaries.
6046 **1299** 600l. green, black & red 10 10
6047 - 1100l. purple, blk & red 25 20
6048 - 2600l. blue, black & red 45 35
6049 - 7300l. brown, blk & red 2·00 1·60
DESIGNS: 1100l. George Calinescu (critic and novelist, birth centenary); 2600l. Johann Wolfgang von Goethe (dramatist, 250th birth anniv); 7300l. Honore de Balzac (novelist, birth bicentenary).

1300 Moon eclipsing Sun

1999. Total Eclipse of the Sun (2nd issue).
6050 **1300** 1100l. multicoloured 60 45

1301 Cigarette and Man with Arms Crossed

1999. Public Health Awareness Campaign. Multicoloured.
6051 400l. Type **1301** (anti-smoking) 10 10
6052 800l. Bottles and man cradling glass and bottle (alcohol abuse) 25 20
6053 1300l. Cannabis leaf, pills and man injecting arm (drugs) 35 30
6054 2500l. Profiles and man on intravenous drip (HIV) 45 35

1302 Eclipse and Pavarotti (opera singer)

1999. Luciano Pavarotti's Concert on Day of Eclipse, Bucharest.
6055 **1302** 8100l. multicoloured 3·00 2·30

1303 Alexander Fleming (bacteriologist)

1999. The 20th century (3rd series). Multicoloured.
6056 800l. Type **1303** (discovery of penicillin, 1928) 25 20
6057 3000l. "Swords into Ploughshares" (sculpture) and map of Europe, Africa and Asia (foundation of League of Nations, 1920) 60 45
6058 7300l. Harold Clayton Urey (chemist) (discovery of heavy water, 1932) 1·50 1·20
6059 17000l. Deep sea drilling (first oil platform, Beaumont, Texas, 1934) 4·00 3·25

1304 Karl Landsteiner (pathologist)

1999. The 20th-century (4th series).
6060 **1304** 1500l. orange, black and yellow 25 20
6061 - 3000l. ochre, black and brown 60 45
6062 - 7300l. multicoloured 1·50 1·20
6063 - 17000l. multicoloured 4·00 3·25
DESIGNS: 1500l. Type **1304** (discovery of blood groups, 1900–02); 3000l. Nicolae Paulescu (biochemist) (discovery of insulin, 1921); 7300l. Otto Hahn (radiochemist) (discovery of nuclear fission, 1938); 17000l. Ernst Ruska (electrical engineer) (designer of first electron microscope, 1931).

1305 Posthorn in Envelope and Berne

1999. 125th Anniv of Universal Postal Union.
6064 **1305** 3100l. multicoloured 1·70 1·40

1306 Grigore Vasiliu Birlic

1999. Comic Actors. Each purple, black and red.
6065 900l. Type **1306** 25 20
6066 1500l. Toma Caragiu 35 30
6067 3100l. Constantin Tanase 60 45
6068 7950l. Charlie Chaplin 1·70 1·40
6069 8850l. Stan Laurel and Oliver Hardy (horiz) 2·30 1·90

1307 Monastery

1999. 275th Anniv of Stavropoleos Church.
6070 **1307** 2100l. brown, stone and black 60 45

1308 Snowboarding

1999. New Olympic Sports. Multicoloured.
6071 1600l. Type **1308** 50 40
6072 1700l. Softball 60 45
6073 7950l. Taekwondo 1·70 1·40

1309 Christmas Tree and Bell

1999. Christmas. Multicoloured.
6074 1500l. Type **1309** 35 30
6075 3100l. Father Christmas with presents 60 45

1310 Child as Flower (Antonela Vieriu)

1999. Tenth Anniv of U.N. Convention on the Rights of the Child. Multicoloured.
6076 900l. Type **1310** 25 20

6077 3400l. Girl writing numbers (Ana-Maria Bulete) (vert) 60 45
6078 8850l. Group of people (Maria-Luiza Rogojeanu) 2·10 1·70

1311 Diana, Princess of Wales

1999. Diana, Princess of Wales Commemoration.
6079 **1311** 6000l. multicoloured 1·70 1·40

1312 Ferrari 365 GTB/4, 1968

1999. Birth Centenary (1998) of Enzo Ferrari (car designer). Multicoloured.
6080 1500l. Type **1312** 25 20
6081 1600l. Dino 246 GT, 1970 35 30
6082 1700l. 365 GT/4BB, 1973 60 45
6083 7950l. Mondial 3.2, 1985 1·70 1·40
6084 8850l. F 355, 1994 1·90 1·50
6085 14500l. 456 MGT, 1998 3·50 2·75

1313 Child with Romanian Flag

1999. Tenth Anniv of Popular Uprising.
6086 **1313** 2100l. multicoloured 60 45

1314 European Union Flag

2000. European Union Membership Negotiations.
6087 **1314** 6100l. multicoloured 1·70 1·40

1315 Eminescu

2000. 150th Birth Anniv of Mihail Eminescu (poet). Sheet 120×92 mm containing T **1315** and similar horiz designs. Each grey, agate and black.
MS6088 3400l. Type **1315**; 3400l. Eminescu and people seated at table; 3400l. Eminescu and star shining over woman; 3400l. Eminescu and three men 4·75 4·75

1316 Cupid

2000. St. Valentine's Day. Multicoloured.
6089 1500l. Type **1316** 60 45
6090 7950l. Couple 1·70 1·40

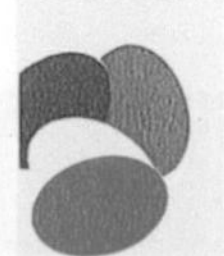

1317 Easter Eggs

2000. Easter.
6091 **1317** 1700l. blue, green and orange 60 45

2000. Nos. 5855 and 5842 surch, the old value cancelled by a different emblem.
6092 1700l. on 70l. multicoloured (crown) 60 45
6093 1700l. on 70l. multicoloured (snake) 60 45

1319 Greater Bird of Paradise

2000. Birds of Paradise. Multicoloured.
6094 1700l. Type **1319** 60 45
6095 2400l. Magnificent bird of paradise 1·20 95
6096 9050l. Superb bird of paradise 1·70 1·40
6097 10050l. King bird of paradise 2·30 1·90

2000. Nos. 5342/3 surch.
6098 1900l. on 1l. multicoloured 60 45
6099 2000l. on 1l. multicoloured 60 45

2000. Nos. 5310/14 surch, the old value cancelled by various book and quill emblems.
6100 1700l. on 50b. brown and black 45 35
6101 1700l. on 1l.50 green and mauve 45 35
6102 1700l. on 2l. red and blue 45 35
6103 1700l. on 3l. blue and brown 45 35
6104 1700l. on 4l. brown and blue 45 35

1322 Cineraria

2000. Flowers. Multicoloured.
6105 1700l. Type **1322** 25 20
6106 3100l. Indoor lily 45 35
6107 5800l. Plumeria 1·40 1·10
6108 10050l. Fuchsia 2·10 1·70

2000. Nos. 5303/7 surch, the old value cancelled by an easel with palette emblem.
6109 1700l. on 50b. multicoloured 45 35
6110 1700l. on 1l.50 multicoloured 45 35
6111 1700l. on 2l. multicoloured 45 35
6112 1700l. on 3l. multicoloured 45 35
6113 1700l. on 4l. multicoloured 45 35

1324 "Building Europe"

2000. Europa.
6114 **1324** 10150l. multicoloured 3·50 2·75

2000. Death Centenary of Vincent van Gogh (artist). Nos. 5318 and 5321 surch, the old value cancelled by paint palette emblem.
6115 1700l. on 50b. multicoloured 60 45
6116 1700l. on 3l.50 multicoloured 60 45

2000. No. 5642 surch, the old value cancelled by an airship.
6117 1700l. on 635l. black, ultramarine and blue 60 45
6118 2000l. on 635l. black, ultramarine and blue 1·20 95
6119 3900l. on 635l. black, ultramarine and blue 1·20 95
6120 9050l. on 635l. black, ultramarine and blue 1·20 95

1327 Mihai the Brave and Soldiers

2000. Anniversaries. Multicoloured.
6121 3800l. Type **1327** (400th anniv of first union of the Romanian provinces (Wallachia, Transylvania and Moldavia)) 95 75
6122 9050l. Printing press (550th anniv of the 42 line Bible (first Bible printed in Latin)) (36×23 mm) 2·00 1·60

2000. No. 5801 surch, the old value cancelled by a flower.
6123 10000l. on 37l. brown and black 1·70 1·40
6124 19000l. on 37l. brown and black 3·50 2·75
6125 34000l. on 37l. brown and black 6·50 5·00

1329 Arnhem, Players and Flags of Romania and Portugal

2000. European Football Championship, The Netherlands and Belgium. Sheet 82×121 mm containing T **1329** and similar vert designs, each showing a map of Europe pinpointing the named town. Multicoloured.
MS6126 3800l. Type **1329**; 3800l. Players, Charleroi and English and Romanian flags; 10150l. Players, Liege and Romanian and German flags; 10150l. Goalkeeper and Rotterdam 5·75 5·75

1330 Ferdinand von Zeppelin and Airship

2000. Centenary of First Zeppelin Flight.
6127 **1330** 2100l. multicoloured 60 45

1331 Enrico Fermi (physicist) and Mathematical Equation

2000. The 20th Century (5th series).
6128 **1331** 2100l. black, grey and red 45 35
6129 - 2200l. black and grey 75 60
6130 - 2400l. red and black 80 65
6131 - 6000l. multicoloured 85 70
DESIGNS: 2100l. Type **1331** (construction of first nuclear reactor, 1942); 2200l. United Nations Charter (signing of charter, 1945); 2400l. Edith Piaf (singer) (release of *La Vie en Rose* (song), 1947); 6000l. Sir Edmund Percival Hillary (mountaineer) (conquest of Mt. Everest, 1953).

2000. No. 5365 surch, the old value cancelled by a bird.
6132 1700l. on 160l. red and pink 60 45

1333 Globe and "Sputnik 1" Satellite

2000. The Twentieth Century (6th series).
6133 **1333** 1700l. multicoloured 35 30
6134 - 3900l. multicoloured 1·40 1·10
6135 - 6400l. black and red 1·50 1·20
6136 - 11300l. multicoloured 1·60 1·30
DESIGNS: 1700l. Type **1333** (launch of first man-made satellite, 1957); 3900l. Yuri Gagarin (first manned space flight, 1961); 6400l. Surgeons operating (first heart transplant operation, 1967); 11300l. Edwin E. Aldrin and Moon (first manned landing on Moon, 1969).

1334 Boxing

2000. Olympic Games, Sydney. Multicoloured.
6137 1700l. Type **1334** 45 35
6138 2200l. High jump 50 40
6139 3900l. Weight lifting 60 45
6140 6200l. Gymnastics 1·50 1·20
MS6141 89×78 mm. 11300l. Athletics (41×53 mm) 3·00 3·00

1335 Gabriela Szabo (athlete) and Emblem

2000. "Olymphilex 2000" International Olympic Stamp Exhibition, Sydney. Sheet 81×60 mm.
MS6142 14100l. multicoloured 3·50 3·50

1336 Palace of Agriculture Ministry

2000. Bucharest Palaces.
6143 **1336** 1700l. black and grey 45 35
6144 - 2200l. black and stone (horiz) 50 40
6145 - 2400l. black and green (horiz) 60 45
6146 - 3900l. black and brown (horiz) 70 55
DESIGNS: 2200l. Cantacuzino Palace (now George Enescu Museum); 2400l. Grigore Ghica Palace; 3900l. Stirbei Palace (now Museum of Ceramics and Glass).

2000. No. 5836 surch, the old value cancelled by a house.
6147 300l. on 70l. multicoloured 60 45

2000. No. 5349 surch.
6148 300l. on 1l. blue 60 45

2000. Air. No. 5695 surch.
6149 2000l. on 960l. blue & black 25 20
6150 4200l. on 960l. blue & black 60 45
6151 4600l. on 960l. blue & black 95 75
6152 6500l. on 960l. blue & black 1·20 95

1340 Ilie Ilascu (political prisoner)

2000. 50th Anniv of United Nations Convention on Human Rights.
6153 **1340** 11300l. multicoloured 3·00 2·30

2000. No. 5700 surch, the old value cancelled by an inkwell and quill emblem.
6154 2000l. on 90l. multicoloured 60 45

2000. No. 5556 surch.
6155 2000l. on 29l. flesh, blk & lil 60 45

1343 Leopard

2000. Big Cats.
6156 **1343** 1200l. multicoloured 10 10
6157 - 2000l. blue and black 25 20
6158 - 2200l. multicoloured 30 25
6159 - 2300l. multicoloured 35 30
6160 - 4200l. brown, bl & blk 60 45
6161 - 6500l. multicoloured 1·70 1·40
MS6162 90×78 mm. 14100l. multicoloured 3·50 3·50
DESIGNS: 2000l. Snow Leopard; 2200l. Lion; 2300l. Bobcat; 4200l Mountain lion; 6500l Tiger; 53×41 mm—14100l. Lions.

1344 Camil Ressu

2000. Self-portraits. Multicoloured.
6163 2000l. Type **1344** 25 20
6164 2400l. Jean Al Steriadi 35 30
6165 4400l. Nicolae Tonitza 60 45
6166 15000l. Nicolae Grigorescu 3·00 2·30

1345 Christmas Tree

2000. Christmas.
6167 **1345** 4400l. multicoloured 60 45

1346 Jesus Christ and Angel

2000. Birth Bimillenary of Jesus Christ. Multicoloured.
6168 2000l. Type **1346** 25 20
6169 7000l. Jesus Christ and dove (22×38 mm) 1·50 1·20

2000. No. 5624 surch, the previous value cancelled by different animals.
6170 7000l. on 3095l. Large-leaved lime (Pig) 2·00 1·60
6171 10000l. on 3095l. Large-leaved lime (Bear) 2·00 1·60
6172 11500l. on 3095l. Large-leaved lime (Cow) 2·00 1·60

1349 Globe and Fireworks

2001. New Millennium.
6176 **1349** 11500l. multicoloured 2·30 1·90

1350 Sculpture

2001. 125th Birth Anniv of Constantin Brancusi (sculptor). Multicoloured.
6177 4600l. Type **1350** 70 55
6178 7200l. Display of sculptures 1·00 85
Nos. 6177/8 were issued together, *se-tenant*, forming a composite design.

2001. No. 5542 surch, the previous value cancelled by different snakes.
6179 7400l. on 280l. black & yell 1·20 95
6180 13000l. on 280l. black & yell 2·30 1·90

1352 Ribbons forming Heart

2001. St. Valentine's Day. Each red and grey.
6181 2200l. Type **1352** 25 20
6182 11500l. Pierced heart 1·60 1·30

2001. Nos. 5595/6 and 5598 surch, the previous value cancelled by an ear of corn.
6183 1300l. on 245l. mult 25 20
6184 2200l. on 115l. mult 35 30
6185 5000l. on 115l. mult 70 55
6186 16500l. on 70l. mult 3·00 2·30

1354 Hortensia Papadat-Bengescu

2001. Birth Anniversaries. Multicoloured.
6187 1300l. Type **1354** 25 20
6188 2200l. Eugen Lovinescu (writer, 120th anniv) 30 25
6189 2400l. Ion Minulescu (poet, 120th anniv) 35 30
6190 4600l. Andre Malraux (writer, centenary) 60 45
6191 7200l. George H. Gallup (opinion pollster and journalist, centenary) 1·50 1·20
6192 35000l. Walt Disney (artist and film producer, centenary) 6·50 5·50

1355 Chick inside Egg

2001. Easter.
6193 **1355** 2200l. multicoloured 60 45

1356 Sloe (*Prunus spinosa*)

2001. Berries. Multicoloured.
6194 2200l. Type **1356** 25 20
6195 4600l. Red currant (*Ribes rubrum L.*) 60 45
6196 7400l. Gooseberry (*Ribes uva-crispa*) 1·70 1·40
6197 11500l. Mountain cranberry (*Vaccinium vitis-idaea L.*) 2·10 1·70

1357 Hagi

2001. Retirement of George Hagi (footballer).
6198 **1357** 2200l. multicoloured 60 45

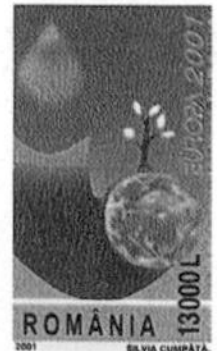

1358 Water Droplet and Globe surmounted by Tree

2001. Europa. Water Resources.
6199 **1358** 13000l. multicoloured 2·30 1·90

1359 Collie

2001. Dogs. Multicoloured.
6200 1300l. Type **1359** 25 20
6201 5000l. Basset hound 80 65
6202 8000l. Siberian husky 1·20 95
6203 13500l. Ciobanesc mioritic 2·00 1·60

1360 Goddess Europa

2001. Romanian Presidency of Organization for Security and Co-operation in Europe.
6204 **1360** 11500l. multicoloured 2·30 1·90

1361 Mariner 9 (spacecraft) and Mars

2001. The 20th Century (7th series). Multicoloured.
6205 1300l. Type **1361** (first orbit of Mars, 1979) 25 20
6206 2400l. Bull (discovery of Paleolithic cave paintings, Ardeche, 1994) 60 45
6207 5000l. Nadia Comaneci (gymnast) (first "10" for gymnastics, Olympic Games, Montreal, 1976) 95 75
6208 8000l. Wall (fall of the Berlin wall, 1989) 1·20 95

1362 George Palade (Nobel Prize winner for medicine, 1974)

2001. 50th Anniv of United Nations High Commissioner for Refugees.
6209 **1362** 13500l. multicoloured 2·30 1·90

2001. Various stamps surch the previous values cancelled by various emblems as stated.
6210 **1100** 300l. on 4l. multicoloured (candlestick) 25 20
6211 **1110** 300l. on 4l. multicoloured (biathlon) 25 20
6212 **1132** 300l. on 7l. multicoloured (harp) 25 20
6213 - 300l. on 9l. multicoloured (No. 5488) (lyre) 25 20
6214 **1168** 300l. on 90l. multicoloured (lizard) 25 20
6215 **1190** 300l. on 90l. multicoloured (computer mouse) 25 20
6216 **1202** 300l. on 90l. multicoloured (fish) 25 20
6217 - 300l. on 90l. multicoloured (No. 5745) (chess knight) 25 20
6218 **1207** 300l. on 90l. multicoloured (fungi) 25 20
6219 **1157** 300l. on 115l. brown, blue and black (scroll) 25 20
6220 **1158** 300l. on 115l. multicoloured (train) 25 20
6222 - 300l. on 115l. multicoloured (No. 5602) (kite) 25 20
6229a **1162** 300l. on 115l. multicoloured (rectangle) 25 20

2001. Nos. 5715/16 and 5720 surch, the previous values cancelled by a sign of the zodiac.
6223 2500l. on 755l. blue and black (Pisces) (postage) 35 30
6224 2500l. on 1615l. green and black (Capricorn) 35 30
6225 2500l. on 715l. red and blue (Aquarius) (air) 35 30

1365 Trap Racing

2001. Equestrian Competitive Events. Multicoloured.
6226 1500l. Type **1365** 35 30
6227 2500l. Dressage 45 35
6228 5300l. Show jumping 70 55
6229 8300l. Flat racing 1·40 1·10

1366 Augustin Maior and Drawing

2001. The 20th Century (8th series). Multicoloured.
6230 1500l. Type **1366** (invention of multiple telephony, 1906) 35 30
6231 5300l. Pioneer 10 (satellite) (launched, 1972) 80 65
6232 13500l. Microchip (introduction of first microprocessor, 1971) 1·70 1·40
6233 15500l. Hubble space telescope (launched, 1990) 2·30 1·90

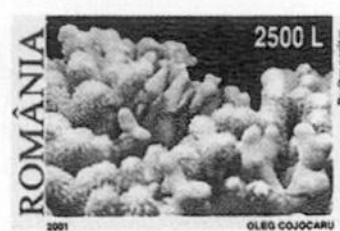

1367 Finger Coral (*Porites porites*)

2001. Corals and Sea Anemones (1st series). Multicoloured.
6234 2500l. Type **1367** 25 20
6235 8300l. Giant sea anemone (*Condylactis gigantia*) 95 75
6236 13500l. Northern red anemone (*Anemonia telia*) 1·70 1·40
6237 37500l. Common sea fan (*Gorgonia ventalina*) 4·75 4·00
See also No. **MS**6260.

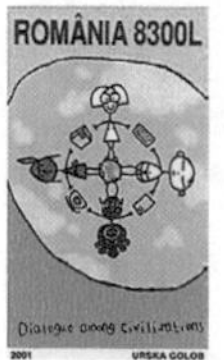

1368 Children encircling Globe

2001. United Nations Year of Dialogue among Civilizations.
6238 **1368** 8300l. multicoloured 1·20 95

1369 King, Bear and Cat

2001. Comics. Multicoloured.
6239 13500l. Type **1369** 1·50 1·20
6240 13500l. Fox beating drum and kicking cat 1·50 1·20
6241 13500l. King sleeping and fox beating drum 1·50 1·20
6242 13500l. Cat giving fox drum 1·50 1·20
6243 13500l. Drum exploding 1·50 1·20

1370 Top of Wreath with Baubles

2001. Christmas. Multicoloured.
6244 2500l. Type **1370** 60 45
6245 2500l. Bottom of wreath with stars 60 45
Nos. 6244/5 were issued together, *se-tenant*, forming a composite design of a wreath.

1371 Scorpio

2001. Signs of the Zodiac (1st series). Multicoloured.
6246 1500l. Type **1371** 25 20
6247 2500l. Libra 35 30
6248 5500l. Capricorn 60 45
6249 9000l. Pisces 1·20 95
6250 13500l. Aquarius 1·70 1·40
6251 16500l. Sagittarius 2·30 1·90
See also Nos. 6254/9.

1372 Building

2001. Centenary of Central Post Headquarters, Bucharest. Multicoloured.

6252 5500l. Type **1372** 70 55
6253 5500l. Obverse of medal showing building, 1901 (vert) 70 55

2002. Signs of the Zodiac (2nd series). As T **1371**. Multicoloured.

6254 1500l. Aries 25 20
6255 2500l. Taurus 35 30
6256 5500l. Gemini 60 45
6257 8700l. Cancer 1·00 85
6258 9000l. Leo 1·10 90
6259 23500l. Virgo 2·75 2·20

1373 Red Coral (*Corallum rubrum*)

2002. Corals and Sea Anemones (2nd series). Sheet 106×77 mm containing T **1373** and similar horiz designs. Multicoloured.

MS6260 9000l. Type **1373**; 9000l. Elkhorn coral (*Acropora palmate*); 16500l. Beadlet anemone (*Actinia equine*); 16500l. Pulmose anemone (*Metridium senile*) 6·50 6·50

1374 Emanuil Gojdu

2002. Birth Bicentenary of Emanuil Gojdu (nationalist).

6261 **1374** 2500l. black, blue and deep blue 60 45

1375 Mice

2002. St. Valentine's Day. Multicoloured.

6262 5500l. Type **1375** 70 55
6263 43500l. Elephants 5·25 4·75

1376 Ion Mincu

2002. Birth Anniversaries.

6267 **1376** 1500l. green and black 25 20
6268 - 2500l. multicoloured 35 30
6269 - 5500l. multicoloured 70 55
6270 - 9000l. multicoloured 1·00 85
6271 - 16500l. multicoloured 2·00 1·60
6272 - 34000l. multicoloured 4·00 3·50

DESIGNS: Type **1376** (architect) (150th); 2500l. Costin Nenitescu (chemist) (centenary); 5500l. Alexander Dumas (writer) (bicentenary); 9000l. Serban Cioculescu (literary historian) (centenary); 16500l. Leonardo da Vinci (artist) (550th); 34000l. Victor Hugo (writer) (bicentenary).

1377 Flag and Statue of Liberty

2002. "United We Stand". Multicoloured.

6273 25500l. Type **1377** 3·00 2·30
6274 25500l. Flags and monument 3·00 2·30

Nos. 6273/4 were issued together, *se-tenant*, forming a composite design.

1378 Fortified Church and Tower, Saschiz

2002. Germanic Fortresses and Churches in Translyvania. Multicoloured.

6275 1500l. Type **1378** 25 20
6276 2500l. Church staircase, Darjiu 35 30
6277 6500l. Fortress, Viscri (horiz) 70 55
6278 10500l. Fortified church, Vorumloc (horiz) 1·20 95
6279 13500l. Tower gate, Calnic 1·60 1·30
6280 17500l. Fortified church, Prejmer 2·00 1·60

1379 Crucifixion

2002. Easter. Showing miniatures by Picu Patrut. Multicoloured.

6281 2500l. Type **1379** 35 30
6282 10500l. Resurrection 1·40 1·10

1380 Clown

2002. Europa. Circus. Multicoloured.

6283 17500l. Type **1380** 2·30 1·90
6284 25500l. Clown (different) 3·50 2·75

1381 "Dorobantul" (Nicolae Grigorescu)

2002. 125th Anniv of Independence. Sheet 77×91 mm.

MS6285 **1381** 25500l. multicoloured 4·75 4·75

1382 Post Mark

2002. 50th Anniv of International Federation Stamp Dealers' Association (IFSDA). Sheet 105×75 mm containing T **1382** and similar horiz designs. Multicoloured.

MS6286 10000l. Type **1382**; 10000l. IFSDA emblem; 27500l. World Trade Centre, Bucharest; 27500l. Philatelic shop, Bucharest 8·75 8·75

1383 Mountains

2002. Year of Mountains (2000l.) and Year of Eco-tourism (3000l.). Multicoloured.

6287 2000l. Type **1383** 25 20
6288 3000l. Landscape and recycling symbol (32×24 mm) 35 30

1384 Cricket

2002. Sport. Multicoloured.

6289 7000l. Type **1384** 80 65
6290 11000l. Polo 1·30 1·00
6291 15500l. Golf 1·70 1·40
6292 19500l. Baseball 2·20 1·80

1385 Ion Luca Caragiale

2002. Anniversaries. Multicoloured.

6293 10000l. Type **1385** (playwright) (150th birth anniv) 1·20 95
6294 10000l. National Theatre, Bucharest (150th anniv) 1·20 95

Nos. 6293/4 were issued together, se-tenant, forming a composite design within the sheet.

1386 Financial Postal Service Emblem

2002. Postal Services.

6295 **1386** 2000l. multicoloured 25 20
6296 - 3000l. red, yellow and blue 35 30
6297 - 8000l. multicoloured 95 75
6298 - 10000l. purple and brown 1·20 95
6299 - 13000l. red, grey and black 1·40 1·10
6300 - 15500l. multicoloured 1·70 1·40
6301 - 20500l. mauve, blue and black 2·30 1·90
6302 - 27500l. multicoloured 3·25 2·50

DESIGNS: 2000l. Type **1386**; 3000l. Romania Post emblem; 8000l. Direct mailing centre emblem; 10000l. Post building (130th anniv); 13000l. Direct marketing emblem; 15500l. Rapid post emblem; 20500l. Priority post emblem; 27500l. Globe and stamp album (Romafilatelia).

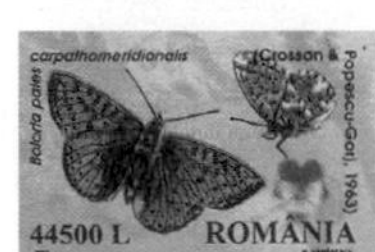

1387 *Boloria pales carpathomeridionalis*

2002. Butterflies. Sheet 101×71 mm containing T **1387** and similar horiz designs. Multicoloured.

MS6310 44500l. Type **1387**; 44500l. *Erebia pharte romaniae*; 44500l. *Peridea korbl herculana*; 44500l. *Tomares nogelii dobrogensis* 19·00 19·00

1388 Locomotive 50115 (1930)

2002. Steam Locomotives. 130th Anniv of First Locomotive made at Machine Factory, Resita (**MS**6317). Multicoloured.

6311 4500l. Type **1388** 45 35
6312 6500l. 50025 (1921) 70 55
6313 7000l. 230128 (1933) 80 65
6314 11000l. 764493 (1956) 1·20 95
6315 19500l. 142072 (1939) 2·10 1·70
6316 44500l. 704209 (1909) 4·75 4·25

MS6317 75×90 mm. 72500l. Steam locomotive (1872) (42×54 mm) 8·25 8·25

1389 Knight and Bishop

2002. 35th Chess Olympiad, Bled, Slovenia. Sheet 102×62 mm containing T **1389** and similar vert designs. Multicoloured.

MS6318 20500l. Type **1389**; 20500l. King and knight; 20500l. Queen and rook 7·00 7·00

1390 Quince (*Cydonia oblonga*)

2002. Fruit. Multicoloured.

6319 15500l. Type **1390** 1·70 1·40
6320 20500l. Apricot (*Armeniaca vulgaris*) 2·30 1·90
6321 44500l. Cherries (*Cerasus vulgaris*) 4·75 4·25
6322 73500l. Mulberry (*Morus nigra*) 8·25 7·50

1391 Father Christmas carrying Parcels

2002. Christmas. Multicoloured.

6323 3000l. Type **1391** 35 30
6324 15500l. Father Christmas and computer 1·70 1·40

1392 Eagle (Romanian emblem), Flags and NATO Emblem

2002. Romania Invitation to join North Atlantic Treaty Organization (NATO). Sheet 168×106 mm containing T **1392**.

MS6325 131000l. ×2, Type **1392** ×2 29·00 29·00

No. **MS**6325 contains a central label showing NATO emblem.

1393 "Braila Harbour" (Jean-Alexandru Steriadi)

2003. Art. Multicoloured.

6326 4500l. Type **1393** 45 35
6327 6500l. "Balcic" (Nicolae Darascu) 70 55
6328 30500l. "Conversation" (Nicolae Vermont) 3·25 2·75
6329 34000l. "Dalmatia" (Nicolae Darascu) 3·75 3·25
6330 46500l. "Fishing Boats" (Jean-Alexandru Steriadi) 5·25 4·75
6331 53000l. "Nude" (Bogdan Pietris) 5·75 5·25

MS6332 75×91 mm. 83500l. "Woman on Seashore" (Nicolae Grigorescu) (42×54 mm) 9·25 9·25

1394 Building Facade

2003. 80th Anniv of National Military Palace, Bucharest.

6333 **1394** 5000l. multicoloured 60 45

1395 Ladybird

2003. March Amulet (good luck). Multicoloured.

6334 3000l. Type **395** 45 35
6335 5000l. Chimney sweep (vert) 70 55

1396 "10"

2003. Tenth Anniv of Romania signing European Agreement (precursor to joining EU).

6336	**1396**	142000l. multicoloured	14·00	14·00

1397 Ion Irimescu

2003. Birth Anniversaries. Multicoloured.

6337	6000l. Type **1397** (sculptor) (centenary)	60	45
6338	18000l. Hector Berlioz (composer) (bicentenary)	1·70	1·40
6339	20000l. Vincent van Gogh (artist) (150th)	2·00	1·60
6340	36000l. Groeges de Bellio (doctor and art collector) (175th)	3·50	3·00

1398 Post Palace

2003. Architecture. Multicoloured.

6341	4500l. Type **1398**	45	35
6342	5500l. Central Savings House	55	45
6343	10000l. National Bank (horiz)	85	75
6344	15500l. Stock Exchange	1·40	1·20
6345	20500l. Carol I University	1·80	1·60
6346	46500l. Athenium	4·00	3·50
MS6347	76×91 mm. 73500l. Palace of Justice (42×54 mm)	6·50	6·50

1399 Map (detail) (upper left quadrant)

2003. Pieter van den Keere (Petrus Kærius Cælavit) (cartographer) Commemoration. Two sheets containing T **1399** and similar multicoloured designs.

MS6348	(a) 120×90 mm. 30500l. ×4 "Vetus description Daciarum" (description of Dacia); (b) 76×91 mm. 46500l. National Map and Book Museum (42×54 mm)	15·00	15·00

1400 Rabbit carrying Egg and Envelope

2003. Easter.

6349	**1400**	3000l. multicoloured	55	45

1401 Eurasian Scops Owl (*Otus scops*)

2003. Owls. Multicoloured.

6350	5000l. Type **1401**	45	35
6351	8000l. Ural owl (*Strix uralensis*)	65	55
6352	10000l. Eurasian pygmy owl (*Glaucidium passerinum*)	85	75
6353	13000l. Short-eared owl (*Asio flammeus*)	1·10	95
6354	15500l. Long-eared owl (*Asio otus*)	1·30	1·10
6355	20500l. Tengmalm's owl (*Aegolius funereus*)	2·20	1·90

1402 Butterfly emerging from Cocoon

2003. Europa. Poster Art. Multicoloured.

6356	20500l. Type **1402**	2·20	1·90
6357	73500l. Figure holding Painting	6·50	5·50

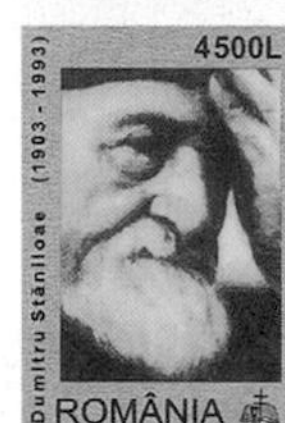

1403 Dumltru Staniloae

2003. Birth Centenaries. Multicoloured.

6358	4500l. Type **1403** (theologian)	45	35
6359	8000l. Alexandru Ciucurencu (artist)	65	55
6360	30500l. Ilarie Voronca (poet)	2·50	2·20
6361	46500l. Victor Brauner (artist)	4·00	3·50

1404 "Fantastic Animals"

2003. Birth Centenary of Victor Brauner (artist). Sheet 175×129 mm containing T **1404** and similar multicoloured designs showing paintings.

MS6362	10000l. ×12. Type **1404**; "Self Portrait" ×3 (24×33 mm); "Heron of Alexandria" (24×33 mm); "Surrealist Composition"; "Drobegea Landscape"; "Nude" (24×33 mm); "Drobegea Landscape" (different); "Courteous Passivity"; "Ion Minulescu Portrait" (abstract) (24×33 mm); "Dragon"	11·00	11·00

1405 Nostradamus and Astrolabe

2003. 500th Birth Anniv of Nostradamus (prophet). Multicoloured.

6363	73500l. Type **1405**	6·00	5·00
6364	73500l. Astrolabe, diagram and Nostradamus	6·00	5·00

1406 Magnifying Glass, Building and Emblem

2003. Post Day. Centenary of Timisoara Philatelic Association.

6365	**1406**	5000l. multicoloured	55	45

1407 Yellow Stainer (*Agaricus xanthodermus*)

2003. Fungi. Two sheets each 126×75 mm containing T **1407** and similar vert designs. Multicoloured.

MS6366	(a) 15500l. ×3 Type **1407**; Basket fungus (*Clathrus rubber*); Panther cap (*Amanita pantherina*); (b) 20500l. ×3 Red-capped scaber stalk (*Leccinum aurantiacum*); Chicken mushroom (*Laetiporus sulphurous*); *Russula xerampelina*	11·00	11·00

1408 Skydiving

2003. Extreme Sports. Multicoloured.

6367	5000l. Type **1408**	45	35
6368	8000l. Windsurfing (horiz)	65	55
6369	10000l. Motor cycle racing (horiz)	85	75
6370	30500l. Skiing	2·50	2·20

1409 Green Lizard *Lacerta viridis*

2003. Amphibians. Sheet 125×105 mm containing T **1409** and similar vert designs.

MS6371	18000l. ×4 Type **1409**; Green tree frog (*Hyla arborea*); Snake-eyed skink (*Ablepharus kitaibelii*); Common frog (*Rana temporaria*)	7·50	7·50

1410 Cobza (stringed instrument)

2003. Traditional Instruments (1st series). Multicoloured.

6372	1000l. Type **1410**	10	10
6373	4000l. Bucium (wind)	35	30
6374	6000l. Vioara cu Goarna (violin with horn)	55	45

1411 Map and Statue

2003. 125th Anniv of Berlin Treaty returning Dobrudja to Romania.

6375	**1411**	16000l. multicoloured	1·30	1·10

1412 Pope John Paul II and Teoctist, Romanian Patriarch

2003. 25th Anniv of Pontificate of Pope John Paul II. Multicoloured.

6376	16000l. Type **1412**	1·30	1·10
6377	16000l. Pope John Paul II and Teoctist (different)	1·30	1·10

1413 Father Christmas

2003. Christmas.

6378	**1413**	4000l. black, rosine and orange	45	40
6379	-	4000l. black and orange	45	40

DESIGN: No. 6379. Snowman.

Nos. 6378/9 were issued, together, se-tenant, forming a composite design.

1414 Woman wearing Suit and Cloche Hat (1921–1930)

2003. 20th-century Women's Fashion. Multicoloured.

6380	4000l. Type **1414**	45	40
6381	4000l. Wearing coat with fur collar (1931–1940)	45	40
6382	21000l. Wearing hat and carrying muff (1901–1910)	1·70	1·40
6383	21000l. Wearing caped coat and hat (1911–1920)	1·70	1·40

1415 Early Woman Footballer

2003. Centenary of FIFA (Federation Internationale de Football Association). Multicoloured.

6384	3000l. Type **1415**	25	20
6385	4000l. Players and film camera	35	30
6386	6000l. Heads and newsprint	50	40
6387	10000l. Boots, pad and ball	85	70
6388	34000l. Rule book and pitch	3·00	2·40

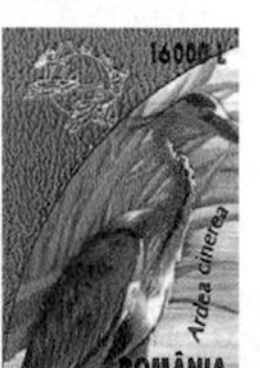

1416 Grey Heron (*Ardea cinerea*)

2004. Water Birds. Sheet 94×96 mm containing T **1416** and similar vert designs. Multicoloured.

MS6389	16000l. ×4 Type **1416**; Mallard (*Anas platyrhynchos*); Great crested grebe (*Podiceps cristatus*); Eastern white pelican (*Pelecanus onocrotalus*)	5·25	5·25

1417 Globe, Satellite and Disc

2004. Information Technology. Sheet 93×69 mm containing T **1417** and similar horiz design. Multicoloured.

MS6390	20000l. ×4 Type **1417**; Computer screen; Satellite dish; Computer keyboard	6·50	6·50

1418 Amerigo Vespucci

2004. 550th Birth Anniv of Amerigo Vespucci (explorer). Multicoloured.

6391	16000l. Type **1418**	1·30	1·10
6392	31000l. Sailing ship	2·75	2·20

1419 Couple

2004. St. Valentine.

6393	**1419**	21000l. multicoloured	1·80	1·50

1420 UPU Emblem

2004. Universal Postal Union Congress, Bucharest (1st. issues). Multicoloured.

6394	31000l. Type **1420**	2·40	2·00
6395	31000l. Bird holding envelope	2·40	2·00

Nos. 6394/5 were issued together, *se-tenant*, forming a composite design.

See also Nos. 6445/50.

1421 Easter Egg and Rabbit holding Envelope

2004. Easter.

6396	**1421**	4000l. multicoloured	60	50

1422 Bullet Locomotive, Japan

2004. Modern Locomotives. Multicoloured.

6397	4000l. Type **1422**	40	35
6398	6000l. TGV, France	55	45
6399	10000l. KTX, South Korea	90	75
6400	16000l. AVE, Spain	1·40	1·20
6401	47000l. ICE, Germany	4·00	3·25
6402	56000l. Eurostar, UK and France	5·00	4·25
MS6403	92×77 mm. 77000l. *Blue Arrow* (Sageti Albastre), Romania (54×42 mm)	6·50	6·50

1423 NATO Headquarters

2004. Romania's Accession to NATO.

6404	**1423**	40000l. multicoloured	1·00	85

1424 Pierre de Coubertin

2004. 90th Anniv of Romanian Olympic Committee. Sheet 120×86 mm containing T **1423** and similar multicoloured designs.

MS6405	16000l.+5000l. ×3, Type **1424** (founder of modern Olympics); Olympic stadium, Athens, 1896 (54×42 mm); George Bibescu (founder member)	5·00	5·00

2004. 20th-century Women's Fashion. Vert designs as T **1414** showing women's clothes. Multicoloured.

6406	4000l. Calf length suit and hat (1941–1950)	50	40
6407	4000l. Knee length coat (1951–1960)	50	40
6408	21000l. Dress and jacket (1981–1990)	1·90	1·60
6409	21000l. Sleeveless dress (1991–2000)	1·90	1·60
6410	31000l. Mini skirted coat (1961–1970)	2·75	2·20
6411	31000l. Trouser suit (1971–1980)	2·75	2·20

Nos. 6406/7, 6408/9 and 6410/11, respectively, were issued together, se-tenant, each pair forming a composite design.

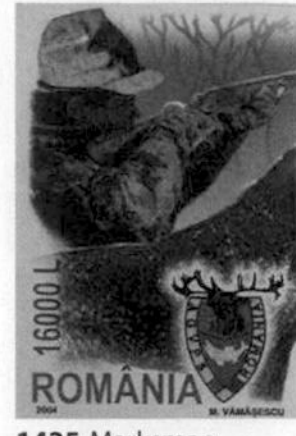

1425 Marksman

2004. 51st International Council for Game and Wildlife Conservation General Assembly. Multicoloured.

6412	16000l. Type **1425**	1·30	1·10
6413	16000l. Dog's head and pheasant	1·30	1·10
6414	16000l. Stag	1·30	1·10
6415	16000l. Ibex	1·30	1·10
6416	16000l. Bear	1·30	1·10
MS6417	99×87 mm. 16000l. Stag (54×42 mm)	1·30	1·30

Nos. 6412/16 were issued, together, *se-tenant* strips of five stamps, each strip forming a composite design.

1426 Sun and Shoreline

2004. Europa. Holidays. Multicoloured.

6418	21000l. Type **1426**	1·80	1·50
6419	77000l. Sun and snowy mountains	6·25	5·25

1427 Mihai Viteazul (Michael the Brave) (statue)

2004

6420	**1427**	3000l. multicoloured	1·00	85

1428 Facade

2004. National Philatelic Museum.

6421	**1428**	4000l. multicoloured	1·00	85

1429 Bram Stoker

2004. "Dracula" (novel by Bram Stoker). Sheet 142×84 mm containing T **1429** and similar vert designs. Multicoloured.

MS6422	31000l. ×4, Type **1429**; Dracula and cross; Dracula carrying woman; Dracula in coffin	10·00	10·00

1430 Anghel Saligny

2004. Anniversaries. Multicoloured.

6423	4000l. Type **1430** (engineer) (150th birth)	25	25
6424	16000l. Gheorgi Anghel (sculptor) (birth centenary)	1·00	95
6425	21000l. George Sand (Aurore Dupin) (writer) (birth bicentenary)	1·30	1·20
6426	31000l. Oscar Wilde (writer) (150th birth)	1·90	1·70

1431 Romainian Atheneum Bucharest

2004

6427	**1431**	10000l. olive and green	1·00	95

1432 Johnny Weissmuller

2004. Birth Centenary of Johnny Weissmuller (athlete and actor).

6428	**1432**	21000l. multicoloured	1·20	1·10

1433 Aircraft and Emblem

2004. 50th Anniv of TAROM Air Transport.

6429	**1433**	16000l. multicoloured	1·30	1·20

1434 Footballs and Anniversary Emblem

2004. Centenary of FIFA (Federation Internationale de Football Association).

6430	**1434**	31000l. multicoloured	2·30	2·10

1435 Stefan III (fresco), Dobrovat Monastery

2004. 500th Death Anniv of Stefan III (Stefan cel Mare) (Moldavian ruler). Two sheets, each 173×62 mm, containing T **1435** and similar horiz designs. Multicoloured.

MS6431	(a) 10000l. ×3, Type **1435**; Ruins of Sucevei; Stefan III (embroidered panel). (b) 16000l. pale brown; 16000l. multicoloured; 16000l. pale brown	5·75	5·75

DESIGN: **MS**6431b. 16000l. ×3, Putna monastery; Stefan III (painting); Neamt fortress.

1436 Alexandru Macedonski

2004. Anniversaries. Multicoloured.

6432	2000l. Type **1436** (writer) (150th birth)	20	20
6433	3000l. Victor Babes (scientist) (150th birth)	35	30
6434	6000l. Arthur Rimbaud (writer) (150th birth)	45	40
6435	56000l. Salvador Dali (artist) (birth centenary)	4·50	4·00

1437 King Ferdinand and First Stamp Exhibition Poster

2004. Post Day. 80th Anniv of First National Stamp Exhibition.

6436	**1437**	21000l. + 10000l. ×4 multicoloured	2·20	2·00

1438 Zeppelin LZ-127 and Buildings

2004. 75th Anniv of Zeppelin LZ-127's Flight over Brasov.

6437	**1438**	31000l. multicoloured	2·30	2·10

1439 Bank Building

2004. 140th Anniv of National Savings Bank (Casa de Economii si Consemnatiuni).

6438	**1439**	5000l. multicoloured	1·00	90

1440 Firemen and Engine

2004. 24th International CTIF (International Fire-fighters Association) Symposium, Brasov. Multicoloured.

6439	12000l. Type **1440**	85	75
6440	12000l. Firemen fighting fire	85	75

1441 Woman Rower

2004. Olympic Games, Athens. Multicoloured.

6441	7000l. Type **1441**	55	50
6442	12000l. Fencers	1·00	90
6443	21000l. Swimmer	1·80	1·60
6444	31000l.+9000l. Gymnast	3·25	2·75

1442 23rd Conference Emblem and 2004 Romania Stamp

2004. Universal Postal Union Congress, Bucharest (2nd issue). Showing emblem and stamps commemorating congresses. Multicoloured.

6445	8000l. Type **1442**	60	55
6446	10000l. 1974 Switzerland	75	65
6447	19000l. 1994 South Korea	1·70	1·50
6448	31000l. 1990 China	2·50	2·20
6449	47000l. 1989 USA	4·00	3·50
6450	77000l. 1979 Brasil	6·25	5·50

1443 "L'appel"

2004. Tenth Death Anniv of Idel Ianchelevici (sculptor). Statues. Multicoloured.

6451 21000l. Type **1443** 1·60 1·40
6452 31000l. "Perennis perdurat poeta" 2·20 2·00

Stamps of the same design were issued by Belgium.

1444 Bronze Age Cucuteni Pot

2004. Cultural Heritage. Multicoloured.

6453 5000l. Type **1444** 50 45
6454 5000l. Drum supported by phoenixes and tigers 50 45

Stamps of the same design were issued by China.

1445 Gerard Kremer (Geradus Mercator) and Jodocus Hondius

2004. European Anniversaries. Sheet 158×144 mm containing T **1445** and similar horiz designs. Multicoloured.

MS6455 118000l.×3, Type **1445** (cartographers) (450th anniv of Mercator's map of Europe and 400th anniv of Hondius—Mercator atlas); UPU monument, Berne (23rd UPU congress, Bucharest); Amerigo Vespucci (explorer) (550th birth anniv) 26·00 26·00

1446 Roman Riders and Foot Soldiers

2004. Fragments of Trajan's Column (Roman monument) (1st issue).

6456 **1446** 7000l. grey and ultramarine 55 50
6457 - 12000l. brown and ultramarine 1·00 90
6458 - 19000l. orange and ultramarine 1·60 1·40
6459 - 56000l. carmine and ultramarine 4·50 4·00

DESIGNS: Type **1446**; 12000l. Neptune and soldiers embarking on ships; 19000l. Fortress and soldier holding cauldron in stream; 56000l. Chariot in moat and soldiers attacking fortress.

See also Nos. 6468/70.

1447 "Simfonia" (Symphony) Rose

2004. Roses. Multicoloured.

6460 8000l. Type **1447** 65 60
6461 15000l. "Foc de Tabara" (Camp fire) 1·20 1·10
6462 25000l. "Golden Elegance" 2·00 1·80
6463 36000l. "Doamna in mov" (Lady in mauve) 3·00 2·50
MS6464 120×90 mm. Nos. 6460/3 6·50 6·50

1448 Ilie Nastase

2004. Ilie Nastase (tennis player). Multicoloured.

6465 10000l. Type **1448** 1·00 90
MS6466 Two sheets. (a) 110×200 mm. 72000l. Ilie Nastase (42×52 mm). (b) 91×110 mm. As No. **MS**6466a. Imperf 10·00 9·00

1449 Father Christmas

2004. Christmas.

6467 **1449** 5000l. multicoloured 1·00 90

2004. Fragments of Trajan's Column (Roman monument) (2nd issue). As T **1446**.

6468 21000l. green and ultramarine 1·70 1·50
6469 31000l. black and ultramarine 2·50 2·20
6470 145000l. vermilion and ultramarine 12·00 10·50

DESIGNS: 21000l. Ritual sacrifice; 31000l. Soldiers, trees, water and heads on posts; 145000l. Stone encampment.

1450 Scouts Emblem

2004. International Organizations. Showing emblems. Multicoloured.

6471 12000l. Type **1450** 1·00 90
6472 16000l. Lions International 1·30 1·20
6473 19000l. Red Cross and Red Crescent 1·60 1·40
MS6474 90×78 mm. 87000l. Dimitrie Cantemir (writer and linguist) (Freemasonry) (42×52 mm) 6·50 6·50

1451 Iolanda Balas-Soter

2004. Olympic Games, Athens. Women Athletes. Each black and gold.

6475 5000l. Type **1451** (high jump) 55 50
6476 33000l. Elsabeta Lipa (rowing) 3·25 2·75
6477 77000l. Ivan Patzaichin (kayaking) 6·50 5·75

1452 "Tristan Tzara" (M. H. Maxy)

2004. Modern Art. Two sheets, each 129×78 mm containing T **1452** and similar vert designs. Multicoloured.

MS6478 (a) 7000l.×3, Type **1452**; "Baroneasa" (Merica Ramniceanu); "Portret de Femeie" (Jean David). (b) 12000l.×3, "Compozitie" (Marcel Ianescu); "Femeie care viseaza II" (Victor Brauner); "Compozitie" (Hans Mattis-Teutsch) 4·50 4·50

1453 Gheorghe Magheru

2005. Anniversaries (1st issue). Multicoloured.

6479 15000l. Type **1453** (revolutionary leader) (125th death anniv) 1·20 1·10
6480 25000l. Christian Dior (dress designer) (birth centenary) 2·00 1·80
6481 35000l. Henry Fonda (actor) (birth centenary) 3·00 2·50
6482 72000l. Greta Garbo (actress) (birth centenary) 5·50 5·00
6483 77000l. George Valentin Bibescu (aviation pioneer) (125th birth anniv) 6·25 5·50

See also Nos. 6512/16.

1454 Emblem

2005. Centenary of Rotary International (charitable organization.).

6484 **1454** 21000l. multicoloured 7·00 6·25

1455 Wedding Pitcher (Oboga-Olt)

2005. Pottery (1st issue). Multicoloured.

6485 3000l. Type **1455** 35 20
6486 5000l. Jugs and pitchers (Sacel-Maramures) 45 30
6487 12000l. Pitcher (Horezu-Valcea) 1·10 90
6488 16000l. Wedding pitcher (Corund-Harghita) 1·30 1·10

See also Nos. 6498/6500, 6591/7, 6605/6, 6639/42, 6650/3, 6684/7 6781/4, 6794/7, 6817/24 and 6824/5.

1456 Elopteryx nopcsai

2005. Dinosaurs. Multicoloured.

6489 21000l. Type **1456** 2·00 1·90
6490 31000l. Telmatosaurus transylvanicus (inscr "transsylvanicus") 3·00 2·75
6491 35000l. Struthiosaurus transilvanicus 3·25 3·00
6492 47000l. Hatzegopteryx thambema 4·25 4·00
MS6493 125×120 mm. Nos. 6489/92 11·50 11·50

1457 *Carassius auratus*

2005. Fish. Multicoloured.

6494 21000l. Type **1457** 2·00 1·90
6495 31000l. *Symphysodon discus* 3·00 2·75
6496 36000l. *Labidochromis* 3·25 3·00
6497 47000l. *Betta splendens* 4·25 4·00
MS6497a 120×103 mm. Nos. 6494/7 12·00 12·00

2005. Pottery (2nd issue). As T **1455**. Multicoloured.

6498 7000l. Wedding pitchers (Romana-Olt) 65 60
6499 8000l. Jug (Vadul Crisului-Bihor) 80 75
6500 10000l. Jug (Tara Barsei-Brasov) 90 85

1458 "Castle of the Carpathians"

2005. Death Centenary of Jules Verne (writer). Multicoloured.

6501 19000l. Type **1458** 1·70 1·60
6502 21000l. "The Danube Pilot" 2·00 1·90
6503 47000l. "Claudius Bombarnac" 4·25 4·00
6504 56000l. "The Stubborn Keraban" 5·25 5·00
MS6505 120×116 mm. Nos. 6501/4 12·00 12·00

1459 Last Supper (icon) (Matei Purcariu)

2005. Easter. Multicoloured.

6506 5000l. Type **1459** 40 35
6507 5000l. Crucifixion 40 35
6508 5000l. Resurrection 40 35

1460 Pope John Paul II and Stylized Dove

2005. Pope John Paul II Commemoration. Multicoloured.

6509 5000l. Type **1460** 40 35
6510 21000l. Vatican 2·00 1·90
MS6511 106×78 mm Nos. 6509/10 each×2 4·50 4·50

2005. Anniversaries (2nd issue). As T **1453**. Multicoloured.

6512 3000l. Hans Christian Anderson (writer) (birth bicentenary) 25 25
6513 5000l. Jules Verne (writer) (death centenary) 55 50
6514 12000l. Albert Einstein (physicist) (50th death anniv) 1·10 1·00
6515 21000l. Dimitrie Gusti (sociologist and philosopher) (50th death anniv) 2·00 1·90
6516 22000l. George Enescu (musician) (50th death anniv) 2·10 2·00

1461 Map of Romania and European Stars

2005. Signing of Treaty of Accession to European Union. Multicoloured.

6517 5000l. Type **1461** 50 50
6518 5000l. As No. 6516 but map and vertical band silver 50 50

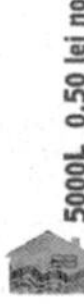

(1461a)

2005. No. 5623 surch as T **1461a**.

6519 1500l. on 1440l. 55 50

1462 Archer on Horseback and Casserole

2005. Europa. Gastronomy. Multicoloured.

6520 21000l. Type **1462** 1·80 1·70
6521 77000l. Retriever, fowl, vegetables and wine glass 6·50 6·25
MS6522 120×90 mm. Nos. 6520/1, each×2 17·00 17·00

1463 Grasa de Cotnari Grapes

2005. Viticulture. Showing grape varieties. Multicoloured.

6523	21000l. Type **1463**	1·70	1·60
6524	21000l. Feteasca neagra	1·70	1·60
6525	21000l. Feteasca alba	1·70	1·60
6526	21000l. Victoria	1·70	1·60

1464 Fire Supervision

2005. Romania Scouts. Multicoloured.

6527	22000l. Type **1464**	1·80	1·70
6528	22000l. Orienteering	1·80	1·70
6529	22000l. Trail marking	1·80	1·70
6530	22000l. Rock climbing	1·80	1·70

On 1 July 2005 the currency of Romania was simplified so that now 1 new leu equals 10000 old leu.

1465 1 bani Coin

2005. New Currency. Designs showing old and new currency. Multicoloured.

6531	30b. Type **1465**	35	30
6532	30b. As No. 6531 but design reversed	35	30
6533	50b. 1 leu bank note	55	50
6534	50b. As No. 6533 but design reversed	55	50
6535	70b. 5 bani coin	65	60
6536	70b. As No. 6535 but design reversed	65	60
6537	80b. 5 lei note	75	70
6538	80b. As No. 6537 but design reversed	75	70
6539	1l. 10 lei note	1·00	90
6540	1l. As No. 6539 but design reversed	1·00	90
6541	1l.20 50 lei note	1·10	1·00
6542	1l.20 As No. 6541 but design reversed	1·10	1·00
6543	1l.60 100 lei note	1·40	1·30
6544	1l.60 As No. 6543 but design reversed	1·40	1·30
6545	2l.10 10 bani	1·80	1·70
6546	2l.10 As No. 6545 but design reversed	1·80	1·70
6547	2l.20 500 lei note	2·10	1·90
6548	2l.20 As No. 6547 but design reversed	2·10	1·90
6549	3l.10 50 bani coin	3·00	2·75
6550	3l.10 As No. 6549 but design reversed	3·00	2·75

1466 *Constanta* (teaching ship)

2005. Stamp Day. Ships. Multicoloured.

6551	2l.20 Type **1466**	1·80	1·70
6552	2l.20 *Counter Admiral Horia Macellariu* (corvette)	1·80	1·70
6553	2l.20 *Mihail Kogalniceanu*	1·80	1·70
6554	2l.20 *Marasesti* (frigate)	1·80	1·70

1467 Rainbow and Sphinx

2005. Floods—July 2005 (1st issue).

6555	**1467** 50b. multicoloured	1·00	90

See also Nos. 6563/6.

1468 Cardinal Joseph Ratzinger

2005. Enthronement of Pontificate of Benedict XVI. Multicoloured.

6556	1l.20 Type **1468**	1·00	90
6557	2l.10 Pope Benedict XVI	1·70	1·60
MS6558	122×98 mm. Nos. 6556/7	2·75	2·75

1469 Christopher Columbus

2005. 50th Anniv of Europa Stamps. 500th Death Anniv of Christopher Columbus (2006). Multicoloured.

6559	4l.70 Type **1469**	3·75	3·50
6560	4l.70 *Santa Maria* at left and Columbus	3·75	3·50
6561	4l.70 *Santa Maria* at right and Columbus	3·75	3·50
6562	4l.70 Christopher Columbus wearing wig and hat	3·75	3·50

1470 "The Forest Mailman" (Bianca Paul)

2005. Floods—July 2005 (2nd issue). Winning Entries in Children's Design a Stamp Competition. Multicoloured.

6563	30b. Type **1470**	25	25
6564	40b. "The Road to You" (Daniel Ciornei)	35	30
6565	60b. "A Messenger of Peace" (Stefan Ghiliman) (horiz)	65	60
6566	1l. "Good News for Everybody" (Adina Elena Mocanu) (horiz)	85	80

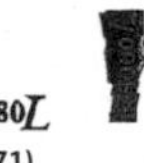

11,80L

(1471)

2005. International Philatelic Exhibition, Bucharest. No. **MS**6455 optd as T **1471**.

MS6567	11l.80×3 on 118000l.×3, multicoloured	30·00	30·00

1472 Jagd Terrier

2005. Hunting Dogs. Multicoloured.

6568	2l.20 Type **1472**	1·80	1·70
6569	2l.20 Rhodesian ridgeback	1·80	1·70
6570	2l.20 Munsterlander	1·80	1·70
6571	2l.20 Bloodhound	1·80	1·70
6572	2l.20 Copoi ardelenesc (Transylvanian hound)	1·80	1·70
6573	2l.20 Pointer	1·80	1·70

1473 Bull's Head

2005. First Anniv of National Philatelic Museum.

6574	**1473** 40b. multicoloured	1·00	90

1474 Emblem

2005. World Information Society Summit, Tunis.

6575	**1474** 5l.60 multicoloured	4·00	3·75

1475 Members Flags, Dove and UN Emblem (50th anniv of Romania's membership)

2005. United Nations Anniversaries. Multicoloured.

6576	40b. Type **1475**	55	50
6577	1l.50 Council chamber (Romania's membership of Security Council, 2004—5 and Presidency, October 2005)	1·40	1·30
6578	2l.20 UN building and dove (60th anniv of UN)	2·00	1·80
MS6579	164×76 mm. Nos. 6576/8	3·50	3·50

1476 Birthplace and Society Emblem

2005. 160th Birth Anniv of Dimitrie Butculescu (1st president of Romanian Philatelic Society). Multicoloured.

6580	50b. Type **1476**	50	45
6581	50b. Romanian Philatelic Society gazette and Dimitrie Butculescu	50	45
MS6582	114×82 mm. 9l. Dimitrie Butculescu. Imperf	7·50	7·50

1477 Library Building

2005. 110th Anniv of Central University Library (formerly Carol I University Foundation). Multicoloured.

6583	60b. Type **1477**	50	45
6584	60b. Horse and rider (statue) (21×30 mm)	50	45
MS6585	137×96 mm. Nos. 6583/4	1·00	1·00

1478 Gusat Englez (English Pouter)

2005. Domestic Pigeons. Multicoloured.

6586	2l.50 Type **1478**	2·10	1·90
6587	2l.50 Jucator pestrit (Parlour roller)	2·10	1·90
6588	2l.50 Calator tip standard (Standard carrier)	2·10	1·90
6589	2l.50 Zburator de Andaluzia (Andalusian)	2·10	1·90

1479 "Thinker of Hamangia"

2005. 60th Anniv of UNESCO.

6590	**1479** 2l.10 multicoloured	1·80	1·70

2005. Pottery (3rd issue). As T **1455**. Multicoloured.

6591	30b. Jug (Leheceni, Bihor)	35	30
6592	50b. Pitcher (Vladesti, Valcea)	55	50
6593	1l. Pitcher (Curtea de Arges, Arges)	85	80
6594	1l.20 Jug (Vama, Satu Mare)	1·10	1·00
6595	2l.20 Jug (Barsa, Arad)	1·80	1·70
6596	2l.50 Wide-necked pitcher (Corund, Harghita)	2·20	2·00
6597	14l.50 Wide-necked pitcher (Valea Izei, Maramures)	11·50	10·50

1480 The Annunciation

2005. Christmas. Designs showing icons. Multicoloured.

6598	50b. Type **1480**	40	35
6599	50b. The Nativity (48×83 mm)	40	35
6600	50b. Madonna and Child	40	35

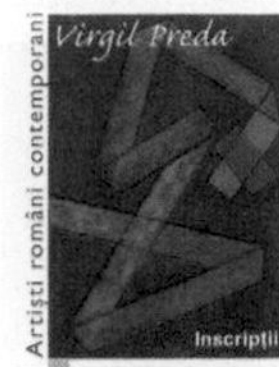

1481 "Inscripti" (Virgil Preda)

2005. Contemporary Romanian Art. Multicoloured.

6601	1l.50 Type **1481**	1·20	1·10
6602	1l.50 "Gradina suspendata" (Alin Gheorghiu) (horiz)	1·20	1·10
6603	1l.50 "Still Life" (Constantin Ceraceanu) (horiz)	1·20	1·10
6604	1l.50 "Monstru 1" (Cristian Paleologu)	1·20	1·10

2005. Pottery (4th issue). As T **1455**. Multicoloured.

6605	4l.70 Jug (Targu Neamt)	4·00	3·75
6606	5l.60 Jug and lidded jug (Poiana Deleni)	4·75	4·25

1482 Norwegian Forest Cat

2006. Cats. Multicoloured.

6607	30b. Type **1482**	25	25
6608	50b. Turkish Van	50	45
6609	70b. Siamese	60	60
6610	80b. Ragdoll	75	70
6611	1l.20 Persian	1·10	1·00
6612	1l.60 Birman (Inscr "Sacred cat of Burma")	1·50	1·40
MS6613	144×108 mm. As Nos. 6607/12. Imperf	4·25	4·25

1483 Wolfgang Amadeus Mozart (composer) (250th birth anniv)

2006. Anniversaries. Multicoloured.

6614	50b. Type **1483**	50	45
6615	1l.20 Ion Bratianu (politician) (185th birth anniv)	1·10	1·00
6616	2l.10 Grigore Moisii (mathematician) (birth centenary)	2·00	1·90

1484 Ice Dance

2006. Winter Olympic Games, Turin. Sheet 123×92 mm containing T **1484** and similar square designs. Multicoloured.

MS6617	1l.60×4, Type **1484**; 1l.60 Downhill skiing; Bobsleigh; Biathlon	6·25	6·25

No. **MS**6617 has an enlarged illustrated central gutter showing Elisabeta Lipa holding the Olympic torch.

Nos. 6618/20 are vacant.

1485 1868 Charles I 20lei

2006. Gold Coins. Multicoloured.

6621	30b. Type **1485**	25	25
6622	50b. 1906 Charles I 50lei	50	45
6623	70b. 1906 Charles I 100lei	60	60
6624	1l. 1922 Ferdinand I 50lei	1·00	95
6625	1l.20 1939 Charles II 100lei	1·10	1·00
6626	2l.20 1940 Charles II 100lei	2·10	2·00

1486 Crucifixion

2006. Easter. Icons. Multicoloured.

6627	50b. Type **1486**	50	45
6628	50b. Mary grieving	50	45
6629	50b. Mary grieving (different)	50	45
6630	50b. Removing Christ from the Cross	50	45
6631	50b. Ascension to heaven	50	45
MS6632	132×132 mm. Nos. 6627/31	2·50	2·50

1487 Traian Vuia and Drawing

2006. Centenary of Traian Vuia's First Powered Flight. Multicoloured.

6633	70b. Type **1487**	60	60
6634	80b. *Vuia I*	75	70
6635	1l.60 *Vuia II*	1·50	1·40
MS6636	114×91 mm. Nos. 6633/5	2·50	2·50
MS6637	116×84 mm. 4l.70 Traian Vuia seated on *Vuia I* (42×52 mm)	4·00	4·00

1488 Leopold Senghor

2006. Birth Centenary of Leopold Sedar Senghor (writer and president of Senegal 1960–1980).

6638	**1488**	2l.10 multicoloured	1·80	1·70

2006. Pottery (5th issue). Wedding Pots. As T **1455**. Multicoloured.

6639	60b. Jug with animal spout (Poienita Arges)	50	45
6640	70b. Complex pot with storks (Oboga Olt)	60	60
6641	80b. Jug with raised decoration (Oboga Olt)	75	70
6642	1l.60 Figure as jug (Romana Olt)	1·40	1·30

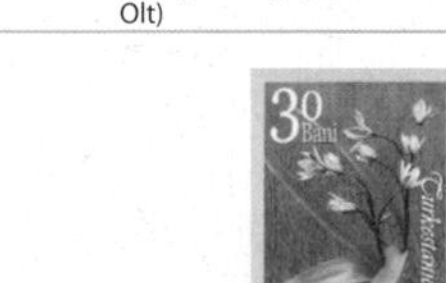

1489 "Turkestanica"

2006. Tulips. Multicoloured.

6643	30b. Type **1489**	25	25
6644	50b. "Ice Follies"	35	35
6645	1l. "Cardinal"	75	70
6646	1l.50 "Yellow Empress" (47×33 mm)	1·10	1·00
6647	2l.10 "Donna Bella"	1·70	1·60
6648	3l.60 "Don Quixot" (47×33 mm)	3·00	2·75
MS6649	112×122 mm. As Nos. 6643/8	7·50	7·50

2006. Pottery (6th issue). As T **1455**. Multicoloured.

6650	30b. Jug with snakes and frog (Oboga Olt)	35	35
6651	40b. Jug with pig's head spout (Radauti Suceava)	50	45
6652	2l.50 Jar with handle and raised decoration (Vladesti Valcea)	2·40	2·20
6653	3l.10 Jar with four handles (Jupanesti, Timis)	2·50	2·40

1490 House and Children

2006. Europa. Integration. Multicoloured.

6654	2l.10 Type **1490**	1·90	1·70
6655	3l.10 Adult and child approaching house	2·40	2·20

1491 1866 Carol I 2p. Stamp (As Type **6**)

2006. 140th Anniv of Romanian Dynasty. 125th Anniv of Proclamation of Romanian Kingdom.

6656	30b. Type **1491**	35	35
6657	1l. 1920 Ferdinand I 1b. stamp (As No. 879)	85	80
6658	2l.10 1930 Carol II 7l.50 (As No. 1179)	1·90	1·70
6659	2l.50 1940 Michael I 20l. stamp (As No. 1466)	2·40	2·20
MS6660	140×145 mm. Nos. 6656/9	5·25	5·25
MS6661	125×90 mm. 4l.70 1906 Carol I 15b. stamp (As No. 507) (horiz)	4·00	4·00

1492 Christopher Columbus (500th death anniv)

2006. Anniversaries. Multicoloured.

6662	50b. Type **1492**	45	40
6663	1l. Paul Cezanne (death centenary)	95	85
6664	1l.20 Henrik Ibsen (composer) (death centenary)	1·20	1·10

1493 Opening Ceremony

2006. Dimitrie Gusti National Village Museum.

6665	**1493**	2l.20 multicoloured	1·90	1·70

2006. 25th Anniv of First Romanian Astronaut. No. **MS**5809 surch.

MS6666	2l.10 on 2720l. mult	1·80	1·70

The margins of **MS**6666 were additionally overprinted for the anniversary.

1495 Main Entrance, Charles I Park

2006. Centenary of General Expo and Charles I Park, Bucharest. Multicoloured.

6667	30b. Type **1495**	30	30
6668	50b. Tepes Castle	45	40
6669	1l. Post Office pavilion	85	80
6670	1l.20 Danube European Commission pavilion	1·10	1·00
6671	1l.60 Palace of Industry	1·50	1·40
6672	2l.20 Roman arenas	2·10	2·00
MS6673	160×130 mm. Nos. 6667/72	5·75	5·75
MS6674	115×85 mm. 2l.20 Palace of Art	1·90	1·90

1496 Bela Bartok

2006. Composers' 125th Birth Anniversaries. Multicoloured.

6675	1l.20 Type **1496**	95	85
6676	1l.20 George Inescu	95	85
MS6677	95×82 mm. Nos. 6675/6	2·00	2·00

Stamps of a similar design were issued by Hungary.

1497 Trophy

2006. World Cup Football Championship, Germany. Multicoloured.

6678	30b. Type **1497**	35	30
6679	50b. Ball in net	45	40
6680	1l. Player	90	85
6681	1l.20 Hands holding trophy	1·10	1·00
MS6682	93×93 mm. Nos. 6678/81	2·50	2·50

1498 Young People

2006. International Day against Drug Abuse and Illegal Drug Trafficking.

6683	**1498**	2l.20 multicoloured	1·90	1·80

2006. Pottery (7th issue). As T **1455**. Multicoloured.

6684	30b. Jar with handle and central decoration (Golesti-Arges)	35	30
6685	70b. Jug with spout and raised decoration (Romana-Olt)	65	65
6686	1l. Ornate jug with bird's head spout and circular base of birds (Oboga-Olt)	90	85
6687	2l.20 White bodied jar with handle and floral decoration (Vama-Satu Mare)	1·90	1·80

1499 Woman and Accoutrements

2006. Stamp Day. 1900th Death Anniv of Decebalus (Decebal), King of Dacia. Multicoloured.

6688	30b. Type **1499**	35	30
6689	50b. Man, facing left	55	50
6690	1l.20 Helmet (c. 150 AD)	1·10	1·00
6691	3l.10 Man standing	2·75	2·50
MS6692	116×87 mm. Nos. 6688/91	4·50	4·50

1500 Fluorite

2006. Minerals. Multicoloured.

6693	30b. Type **1500**	35	30
6694	50b. Quartz	45	40
6695	1l. Agate	90	85
6696	1l.20 Zinc blende (sphalerite)	1·10	1·00
6697	1l.50 Amethyst	1·50	1·40
6698	2l.20 Stibnite	2·00	1·90
MS6699	168×85 mm. Nos. 6693/8	5·75	5·75

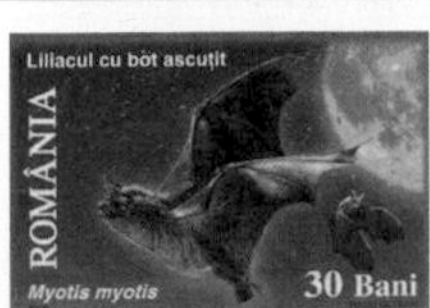

1501 *Myotis myotis*

2006. Bats. Multicoloured.

6700	30b. Type **1501**	35	30
6701	50b. *Rhinolophus hipposideros*	45	40
6702	1l. *Plecotus auritus*	90	85
6703	1l.20 *Pipistrellus pipistrellus*	1·10	1·00
6704	1l.60 *Nycatalus lasiopterus*	1·50	1·40
6705	2l.20 *Barbastella barbastella*	2·00	1·90
MS6706	116×140 mm. Nos. 6700/5	5·75	5·75

The stamps and margins of **MS**6706 form a composite design.

1502 Wartberg Type 1B-n2 (1854)

2006. 150th Anniv of First Railway Line from Oravita—Bazias. Multicoloured.

6707	30b. Type **1502**	35	30
6708	50b. Ovidiu Type C-n2 (1860)	45	40
6709	1l. Curierulu Type 1B-n2 (1869)	90	85
6710	1l.20 Berlad Type 1A1-n2 (1869)	1·10	1·00
6711	1l.50 Unirea Type 1B-n2 (1877)	1·30	1·30
6712	1l.60 Fulger King Charles I Pullman Express (1933)	1·50	1·40
MS6713	138×108 mm. 2l.20 Steyerdorf Type CB-2nf (72×33 mm)	2·00	2·00

1503 1858 27p. Stamp (As Type **1**)

2006. EFIRO 2008, International Stamp Exhibition, Bucharest. Showing first Romanian Stamps. Multicoloured.

6714	30b. Type **1503**	35	30
6715	50b. As No. 2	45	40
6716	1l.20 As No. 3	1·10	1·00
6717	1l.60 As No. 4	1·50	1·40
MS6718	100×123 mm. 2l.20 Bull's head (42×52 mm)	1·90	1·90

1504 Goddess of Fortune

2006. Centenary of National Lottery.

6719	**1504**	1l. multicoloured	1·00	95

5·60 Lei

(1505)

2006. Gymnastics. No. **MS**5834 surch as T **1505**.

6720	5l.60 on 4050l. multicoloured	4·75	4·75

1506 "Muse endormie"

2006. 130th Birth Anniv of Constantin Brancusi (sculptor). Multicoloured.

6721	2l.10 Type **1506**	1·80	1·70
6722	3l.10 "Le sommeil"	2·75	2·50
MS6723	130×94 mm. Nos. 6721/2	4·50	4·50

Stamps of a similar design were issued by France.

1507 "Thinker of Hamangia" (Neolithic sculpture)

2006. 11th La Francaphone (French speaking countries and organizations) Meeting, Bucharest.

6724	**1507**	1l.20 multicoloured	1·00	95

MS6725	90×95 mm. **1507** (42×52 mm) 5l.60 multicoloured	4·75	4·75

1508 Head Covering (Arges)

2006. Centenary of Peasant Museum. Multicoloured.

6726	40b. Type **1508**	35	30
6727	70b. Necklace (Dobruja)	65	65
6728	1l.60 Coin necklace (Bucovina)	1·50	1·40
6729	3l.10 Alexandru Tzigara-Samurcas (founder)	3·00	2·75

1509 Alexandru Ioan Cuza (ruler at time of founding of National Police force)

2006. Tenth Anniv of Romanian Membership of International Police Association. Sheet 95×95 mm.

MS6730	**1509** 8l.70 multicoloured	7·25	7·25

1510 Adult and Chicks

2006. Endangered Species. Eurasian Spoonbill (*Platalea leucorodia*). Multicoloured.

6731	80b. Type **1510**	80	75
6732	80b. Two adults feeding	80	75
6733	80b. In flight	80	75
6734	80b. Two heads facing right	80	75
MS6735	170×120 mm. Nos. 6731/4	2·75	2·75

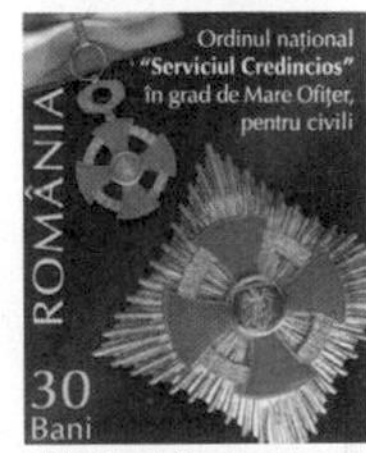

1511 Loyal Service

2006. National Orders. Multicoloured.

6736	30b. Type **1511**	20	20
6737	80b. Romanian Star	65	65
6738	2l.20 For Merit	1·90	1·80
6739	2l.50 First Class Sports Merit	2·10	2·00

1512 Radu Beligan

2006. Actors. Multicoloured.

6740	40b. Type **1512**	35	30
6741	1l. Carmen Stanescu	90	85
6742	1l.50 Dina Cocea	1·30	1·30
6743	2l.20 Colea Rautu	2·10	2·00

1513 Holy Virgin Empress

2006. Christmas. Icons. Multicoloured.

6744	50b. Type **1513**	50	45
6745	50b. Holy Virgin with Baby Jesus on the Throne	50	45
6746	50b. Worship of the Magi	50	45

1514 "EU"

2006. Romania and Bulgaria's Membership of European Union. Multicoloured.

6747	50b. Type **1514**	45	40
6748	2l.10 Ballot box and flags	1·80	1·70

Stamps of a similar design were issued by Bulgaria.

1515 "AD PERPETUAM REI MEMORIAM" (For the eternal remembrance)

2006. Contemporary Art. Works by Ciprian Paleologu. Multicoloured.

6749	30b. Type **1515**	35	30
6750	1l.50 "CUI BONO?" (Whose interest?)	1·30	1·30
6751	3l.60 "USQVE AD FINEM" (All the way)	3·25	3·25

1516 Obverse of 200 leu Banknote

2006. New Banknote. Multicoloured.

6752	50b. Type **1516**	45	40
6753	1l.20 Reverse of 200l. banknote	1·00	95

1517 Children

2006. 60th Anniv of UNICEF.

6754	**1517** 3l.10 multicoloured	2·75	2·50

1518 Sphinx, Bucegi

2007. Romania's Accession to European Union.

6755	**1518** 2l.20 multicoloured	1·90	1·80

No. 6755 has an attached label showing map of Romania and EU stars.

1519 Altar Rock Cave, Bihorului Mountains

2007. Centenary of Publication "Essay on Biospeleological Problems" (study of cave living organisms) by Emil Racovita (Romanian scientific pioneer). Multicoloured.

6756	40b. Type **1519**	35	30
6757	1l.60 Emil Racovita	1·30	1·30
6758	7l.20 *Ursus spelaeus*	6·25	5·75
6759	8l.70 Microscope and *Typhlocirolana moraguesi*	7·25	6·75
MS6760	131×112 mm. Nos. 6756/9	13·50	13·50

1520 Hand and Wire

2007. International Holocaust Remembrance Day.

6761	**1520** 3l.30 multicoloured	2·75	2·50

1521 *Hippocampus hippocampus* (Inscr "Hypocampus hypocampus")

2007. Black Sea Fauna. Multicoloured.

6762	70b. Type **1521**	65	65
6763	1l.50 *Delphinus delphis*	1·50	1·40
6764	3l.10 *Caretta caretta*	3·25	3·00
6765	7l.70 *Trigla lucerna*	6·75	6·25
MS6766	190×121 mm. Nos. 6762/5	11·00	11·00

1522 Gustave Eiffel (construction engineer)

2007. Personalities. Multicoloured.

6767	60b. Type **1522**	55	50
6768	80b. Maria Cutarida (first woman doctor)	80	75
6769	2l.10 Virginia Woolf (writer)	2·00	1·90
6770	3l.50 Nicolae Titulescu (politician)	3·25	3·00

1523 Decorated Egg, Olt

2007. Easter. Multicoloured.

6771	50b. Type **1523**	40	35
6772	50b. The Risen Christ (icon)	40	35
6773	50b. Decorated Egg, Bucovina	40	35

1524 *Cephalanthera rubra*

2007. Orchids. Multicoloured.

6774	30b. Type **1524**	35	30
6775	1l.20 *Epipactis palustris*	1·10	1·00
6776	1l.60 *Dactylorhiza maculate*	1·50	1·40
6777	2l.50 *Anacamptis pyramidalis*	2·20	2·10
6778	2l.70 *Limodorum abortivum*	2·50	2·30
6779	6l. *Ophrys scolopax*	5·50	5·00
MS6780	148×113 mm. 30b. Type **1524**; 1l.20 *Epipactis palustris*; 1l.60 *Dactylorhiza maculata*; 2l.50 *Anacamptis pyramidalis*; 2l.70 *Limodorum abortivum*; 6l. *Ophrys scolopax*	12·00	12·00

2007. Pottery (8th issue). As T **1455**. Multicoloured.

6781	70b. Brown plate with central rooster (Obaga-Olt)	70	65
6782	1l. Mottled plate inscr "1898" (Vama-Satu Mare)	95	90
6783	2l.10 Cream plate with central soldier (Valea Izea-Maramures)	2·20	2·00
6784	2l.20 Cream bodied plate with overall decoration (Fragaras-Brasov)	2·30	2·10

1525 *Accipiter nisus* (sparrow hawk)

2007. Raptors. Multicoloured.

6785	50b. Type **1525**	55	50
6786	80b. *Circus aeruginosus* (marsh harrier)	80	75
6787	1l.60 *Aquila pomarina* (lesser spotted eagle)	1·60	1·50
6788	2l.50 *Buteo buteo* (common buzzard)	2·50	2·40
6789	3l.10 *Athene noctua* (little owl)	3·25	3·00
MS6790	65×90 mm. 4l.70 *Falco subbuteo* (hobby) (42×52 mm)	4·25	4·25

1526 Scouts

2007. Europa. Centenary of Scouting. Sheet 87×117 mm containing T **1526** and similar vert designs. Multicoloured.

6791	2l.10 Type **1526**	1·80	1·70
6792	7l.70 Robert Baden Powell (founder)	6·00	5·75

1527 Curtea Veche (Principal Court)

2007. Old Bucharest. Multicoloured.

6792a	30b. Type **1527**	25	25
6792b	50b. Sturdza Palace	55	50
6792c	70b. National Military Circle	70	65
6792d	1l.60 National Theatre	1·50	1·40
6792e	3l.10 I. C. Bratianu Square	3·00	2·75
6792f	4l.70 Senate Square	4·75	4·50
MS6793	(a) 87×117 mm. 30b. As Type **1527**; 50b. As No. 6792b; 70b. As No. 6792c; 1l.60 As No. 6792d; 3l.10 As No. 6792e; 4l.70 As No. 6792f. (b) 131×111 mm. 5l.60 Romanian Athenaeum (52×42 mm)	12·00	12·00

2007. Pottery (9th issue). As T **1455**. Multicoloured.

6794	70b. Cream plate with central spiral design (Vladesti-Vdlcea)	70	65
6795	80b. Cream bodied plate with green overall decoration (Vistea-Brasov)	80	75
6796	1l.60 Brown plate with geometric design (Tansa-Iasi)	1·50	1·40
6797	3l.10 Green decorated plate (Romdana-Olt)	3·00	2·75

1528 Emblem and Medal

2007. 60th Anniv of Steaua Sports Club.

6798	**1528** 7l.70 multicoloured	7·00	6·75

1529 Palace Facade

2007. 110th Anniv of National Savings Bank Palace. Sheet 145×160 mm. Multicoloured.

6799	4l.70 Type **1529**	4·25	4·00
MS6800	5l.60 multicoloured	5·00	5·00

1530 Altemberger House

2007. Sibiu–European Capital of Culture–2007. Multicoloured.

6801	30b. Type **1530**	25	25
6802	50b. Liars' Bridge and Council Tower	55	50
6803	60b. Parochial Evangelical Church	60	60
6804	70b. Grand Square c. 1780	70	65
6805	2l.10 Brukenthal Palace and St. Nepomuk Statue c. 1935	2·00	1·90
6806	5l.60 Panorama c. 1790 (painting) (F. Neuhauser)	5·50	5·00
MS6807	(a) 190×160 mm. 30b. As Type **1530**; 50b. As No. 6802; 60b. As No. 6803; 70b. As No. 6804; 2l.10 As No. 6805; 5l.60 As No. 6806. (b) 127×102 mm. 4l.70 Sibiu Fortress c. 1650 (52×42 mm)	13·50	13·50

The stamp and margin of **MS**6807 form a composite design of Sibiu Fortress.

1530a *Anser erthyropus* (lesser white-fronted goose)

2007. Ducks and Geese. Multicoloured.

6808	40b. Type **1530a**	40	40
6809	60b. *Branta ruficollis* (red-breasted goose)	70	65
6810	1l.60 *Anas acuta* (northern pintail)	1·50	1·40
6811	2l.10 *Anser albifrons* (white-fronted goose)	2·00	1·90
6812	3l.60 *Netta rufina* (red-crested pochard)	3·75	3·50
6813	4l.70 *Anas querquedula* (garganey)	4·50	4·25
MS6814	(a) 173×124 mm. 40b. As Type **1530a**; 60b. As No. 6809; 1l.60 As No. 6810; 2l.10 As No. 6811; 3l.60 As No. 6812; 4l.70 As No. 6813. (b) 120×95 mm. 5l.60 *Anas clypeata* (northern shoveler) (52×42 mm). Imperf	16·00	16·00

1530b Bisra Local 6 Heller Stamp and Early Carriage

2007. Stamp Day. Centenary of Bisra Local Post. Multicoloured.

6815	50b. Type **1530b**	45	45
6816	2l.10 Bisra Local 2 Heller Stamp and early postman	1·90	2·40

2007. Pottery (10th and 11th issue). As T **1455**. Multicoloured.

6817	60b. Fawn plate with all over decoration (Lapus-Maramures)	70	65
6818	80b. Brown dish with yellow scrafiti designs (Luncavita-Tulcea)	80	75
6819	1l.10 Cream dish with star-shaped central decoration (Luncavita-Tulcea)	1·10	1·00
6820	1l.40 Brown bodied jar with handle and cream and green decoration (Horezu-Valcea)	1·40	1·30
6821	1l.60 Cream plate with central green and yellow flowers and border decoration (Radauti-Suceava)	1·50	1·40
6822	1l.80 Large green bodied cup with brown and white decoration (Baia Mare-Maramures)	1·80	1·70
6823	2l.90 Cream bodied cup with dark brown orange decoration (Oboga-Olt)	2·75	2·50
6824	7l.70 Wide bodied cup with brown and white dotted decoration (Baia Mare-Maramures)	7·25	7·00

1530c Father Teoctist

2007. Father Teoctist (Toader Arapasu) (Patriarch of Romanian Orthodox Church) Commemoration.

6825	**1530c** 80b. multicoloured	1·00	95

1530d 1858 5 Parale Stamp (As Type **2**)

2007. EFIRO 2008, International Stamp Exhibition, Bucharest (2nd issue). Multicoloured.

6826	1l.10 Type **1530d**	1·10	1·00
6827	2l.10 1858 40 parale stamp (As Type **3**)	2·00	1·90
6828	3l.30 1858 80 parale stamp (As No. 10)	3·25	3·00
MS6829	120×100 mm. 5l.60 Bull's Head emblem	5·50	5·50

1531 Johannes Honterus (1498–1549) (cartographer)

2007. German Personalities in Romania. Multicoloured.

6830	1l.90 Type **1531**	1·90	1·80
6831	2l.10 Herman Oberth (1894–1989) (space travel theorist)	2·00	1·90
6832	3l.90 Stephan Ludwig Roth (1796–1849) (educationalist)	3·75	3·50

1532 Luxembourg House, Sibiu

2007. Sibiu Joint European Capital of Culture—2007. Multicoloured.

6833	3l.60 Type **1532**	3·50	3·25
MS6834	123×95 mm. 4l.30 Luxembourg House, Sibiu (52×42 mm)	4·00	4·00

Stamps of a similar design were issued by Luxembourg.

1533 Obverse and Reverse of 1867 1 ban Coin

2007. 40th Anniv of Modern Currency. Multicoloured.

6835	3l.90 Type **1533**	3·75	3·50
MS6836	184×108 mm. 5l.60 1870 1 leu silver coin (30×30 mm circular)	5·50	5·50

No. 6835 is perforated around the design of the obverse of the 1 ban coin and partially perforated in the centre of the stamp.

1534 Tackle

2007. Rugby World Cup Championships, France. Multicoloured.

6837	1l.80 Type **1534**	2·00	1·90
6838	3l.10 Scrum	3·50	3·25

1535 *Sputnik* (first man made satellite)

2007. 50th Anniv of Space Exploration. Multicoloured.

6839	3l.10 Type **1535**	3·50	3·25
MS6840	85×70 mm. 5l.60 1870 1 *Sputnik* (52×42 mm)	6·25	6·25

The stamp and margin of **MS**6840 form a composite design of *Sputnik* over the Earth.

1536 *Birth of Jesus Christ* (icon)

2007. Christmas.

6841	**1536** 80b. multicoloured	1·00	95

2007. Pottery (12th issue). As T **1455**. Multicoloured.

6842	2l.10 Cream jug with green and brown garlands (Transylvania)	2·30	2·20
6843	3l.10 Cream jug with central border and green base (Horezu-Valcea)	3·50	3·25
6844	7l.20 Brown cup with blue, green and white decoration (Obarsa-Hunedoara)	8·25	7·75
6845	8l.70 Brown cup with white medallion containing flower (Baia Mare-Maramures)	9·50	9·00

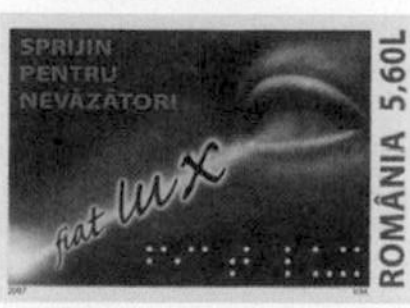

1537 Eye

2007. Support for the Blind.

6846	**1537** 5l.60 multicoloured	6·25	6·00

1538 *Orsova* (Romania)

2007. Danube Ports and Ships. Multicoloured.

6847	1l. Orsova port	1·10	1·00
6848	1l.10 Novi Sad port	1·20	1·20
MS6849	187×107 mm. 2l.10×2, Type **1538**; *Sirona* (Serbia)	5·50	5·50

No. **MS**6847 also contains two stamp size labels, showing arms of Romania and Serbia, which, with the margins, form a composite background design.

Stamps of a similar design were issued by Serbia.

1539 *Ursus maritimus* (polar bear)

2007. Polar Fauna. Multicoloured.

6850	30b. Type **1539**	30	25
6851	50b. *Pagophilus groenlandicus* (harp seal) (vert)	55	55
6852	1l.90 *Alopex lagopus* (Arctic fox) (vert)	2·20	2·00
6853	3l.30 *Aptenodytes forsteri* (emperor penguin)	4·25	4·00
6854	3l.60 *Balaenoptera musculus* (blue whale)	4·50	4·25
6855	4l.30 *Odobenus rosmarus* (walrus) (vert)	5·50	5·25

1540 *Lepiota rhacodes*

2008. Fungi. Multicoloured.

6856	1l.20 Type **1540**	1·30	1·20
6857	1l.40 *Lactarius deliciosus*	1·40	1·40
6858	2l. *Morchella esculenta*	2·20	2·00
6859	2l.40 *Paxillus involutus*	2·50	2·40
6860	3l. *Gyromitra esculenta*	3·25	3·00
6861	4l.50 *Russula emetica*	5·00	4·75
MS6862	130×116 mm. Nos. 6856/61	16·00	16·00

1541 *Voison-Farman I* and Henri Farman

2008. Centenary of First 1000m Closed Circuit Flight in One Minute.

6863	**1541** 5l. multicoloured	5·50	5·25

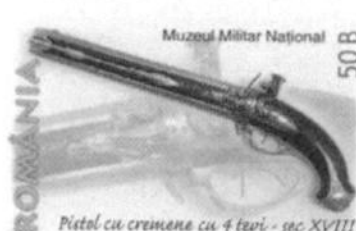

1542 18th-Century European Flint Pistol

2008. Pistols from the Collection of National Military Museum. Multicoloured.

6864	50b. Type **1542**	55	55
6865	1l. 18th-century flint pistol, Liege	1·10	1·10
6866	2l.40 7.65 mm. Mannlicher carbine pistol, 1903	2·50	2·40
6867	5l. 8 mm. Revolver, 1915	5·50	5·25
MS6868	118×75 mm. Nos. 6864/7	9·50	9·50

1543 *Explorer 1*

2008. 50th Anniv (2007) of Space Exploration. Multicoloured.

6869	1l. Type **1543**	1·10	1·10
6870	2l.40 *Sputnik 3*	2·50	2·40
6871	3l.10 *Jupiter AM-13*	3·25	3·00

1544 Resurrected Christ (iconostasis), Scaune Church, Bucharest

2008. Easter.

6872	**1544** 1l. multicoloured	1·10	1·10

2008. Pottery (13th issue). As T **1455**. Multicolored.

6873	2l. Brown mug with yellow and lower white decoration (Cosesti, Arges)	2·20	2·00
6874	2l.40 Cream bodied jug with pictorial decoration (Radauti, Suceava)	2·50	2·40
6875	6l. Brown bodied jug with central decoration (Baia Mare, Maramures)	6·50	6·00
6876	7l.60 Cream lidded pot with handles (Vladesti, Valcea)	8·25	7·75

1545 Angel and Emblems

2008. NATO Summit, Bucharest. Multicoloured.

6877	6l. Type **1545**	6·50	6·00
6878	6l. As No. 6877 but with silver emblem	6·50	6·00
6879	6l. As No. 6877 but with gold emblem	6·50	6·00

1546 *Helarctos malayanus* (sun bear)

2008. Bears. Multicoloured.

6880	60b. Type **1546**	70	70
6881	1l.20 *Ursus americanus* (American black bear) (horiz)	1·30	1·20
6882	1l.60 *Ailuropoda melanoleuca* (giant panda) (horiz)	1·90	1·80
6883	3l. *Melursus ursinus* (sloth bear) (horiz)	3·25	3·00
6884	5l. *Tremarctos ornatus* (spectacled bear)	5·50	5·25
MS6885	77×85 mm. 9l.10 *Ursus arctos* (brown bear) (42×51 mm)	9·75	9·75

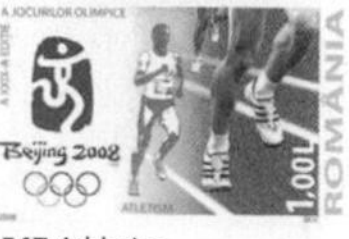

1547 Athletics

2008. Olympic Games, Beijing. Sheet 78×142 mm containing T **1547** and similar horiz designs. Multicoloured.

MS6886	1l.×4, Type **1547**; Gymnastics; Swimming; Rowing	5·00	5·00

1548 Map and Outline of Envelope

2008. Europa. The Letter. Multicoloured.

6887	1l.60 Type **1548**	1·90	1·80
6888	8l.10 A 'Priority' envelope and European stars	8·50	8·50
MS6889	122×92 mm. Nos. 6887/8, each×2	22·00	22·00

1549 Fauna

2008. Centenary of Grigore Antipa National Natural History Museum.Multicoloured.

6890	2l.40 Type **1549**	2·50	2·40
6891	3l. Grigore Antipa (founder)	3·25	3·00

1550 Building, Stars and '€'

2008. Tenth Anniv of European Central Bank.

6892	**1550**	3l.10 multicoloured	3·50	3·25

1551 1859 5p. Stamp (As Type **2**) and Emblems

2008. EFIRO 2008, International Stamp Exhibition, Bucharest (3rd issue). Designs showing early stamps and exhibition emblems. Multicoloured.

6893	50b. Type **1551**	55	55
6894	1l. 1862 6p. stamp (As No. 24)	1·10	1·10
6895	2l.40 1865 2p. stamp (As Type **5**)	2·50	2·40
6896	3l.10 1891 1½p. stamp (As Type **15**)	3·50	3·25
6897	4l.50 1903 1b. stamp (As No. 464)	5·00	4·75
6898	6l. 1932 61. stamp (As Type **96**)	6·50	6·00
MS6899	152×122 mm. 8l.10 Exhibition emblem (30×30 mm)	8·50	8·50
MS6899a	192×162 mm. Nos. 6893/8	17·00	17·00

1552 Weaving (Romania)

2008. 45th Anniv of Romania—Kuwait Diplomatic Relations. Multicoloured.

6900	2l. Type **1552**	2·20	2·00
6901	2l. Model boat builder (Kuwait)	2·20	2·00
MS6902	112×83 mm. 3l.30 Romanian fire appliance	3·50	3·50

Stamps of a similar design were issued by Kuwait.

1553 Scene from *7 Arts* (winning animated film)

2008. 50th Anniv of Ion Popescu-Gopo's Grand Prix at Film Festival, Tours. Multicoloured.

6903	1l.40 Type **1553**	1·40	1·40
6904	4l.70 Ion Popescu-Gopo and trophy	5·25	5·00
MS6905	100×125 mm. Nos. 6903/4	6·50	6·50

1554 St Gheorghe Church, Voronet Monastery (Romania)

2008. UNESCO World Heritage Sites in Romania and Russia. Multicoloured.

6906	3l. Type **1554**	3·25	3·00
6907	4l.30 St Dimitrie Church, Vladimir (Russia)	4·50	4·25
MS6908	130×105 mm. Nos. 6906/7	8·50	8·50

Stamps of a similar design were issued by Russia.

1555 Fagaras Castle

2008. Castles. Multicoloured.

6909	1l. Type **1555**	1·10	1·10
6910	2l.10 Peles	2·30	2·20
6911	3l. Huniad	3·25	3·00
6912	5l. Bethlen-Cris	5·50	5·25
MS6913	135×118 mm. Nos. 6909/12	12·00	12·00

1556 Page from Missal

2008. 500th Anniv of Printing of Macarie's Missal (first book printed in Romania). Multicoloured.

6914	4l.30 Type **1556**	5·50	5·25
MS6915	97×83 mm. 9l. 10 Two pages from missal (52×42 mm)	10·00	10·00

1557 Church of the Three Holy Hierachs

2008. 600th Anniv of Iasi City Documentary Accreditation. Multicoloured.

6916	1l. Type **1557**	1·10	1·10
6917	1l.60 Metropolitan Cathedral	1·90	1·80
6918	2l.10 Vasile Alecsandri National Theatre	2·30	2·20
6919	3l.10 Museum of Unification	3·50	3·25
MS6920	133×100 mm. 9l. 10 Palace of Culture (42×52 mm)	10·00	10·00
MS6921	182×98 mm. nos. 6916/19	8·75	8·75

1558 Queen Marie

2008. Stamp Day. 70th Death Anniv of Queen Marie of Romania. Multicoloured.

6922	1l. Type **1558**	1·10	1·10
6923	3l. Older facing left	3·25	3·00
MS6924	102×68 mm. Nos. 6921/2	4·50	4·50

1559 Moldova

2008. Heraldry. Designs showing arms. Multicoloured.

6925	60b. Type **1559**	70	70
6926	1l. Wallachia	1·10	1·10
6927	3l. Transylvania	3·25	3·00
6928	3l.10 Bucharest	3·50	3·25
MS6929	126×92 mm. Nos. 6925/8	8·50	8·50

MS6930	119×147 mm. 6l. Seal (42×52 mm)	6·50	6·50

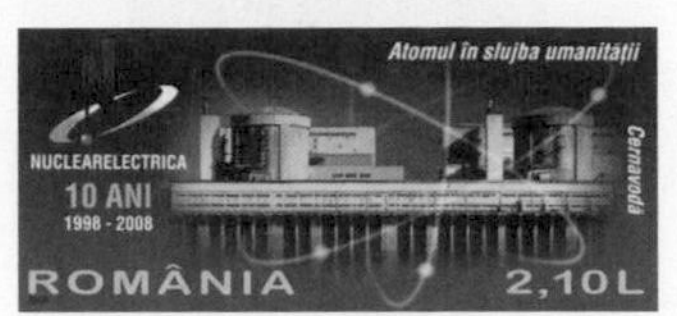

1560 Power Station

2008. Tenth Anniv of Nuclearelectrica.

6931	**1560**	2l.10 multicoloured	2·30	2·20

1561 Stylized Airwaves

2008. 80th Anniv of National Radio Broadcasting Society.

6932	**1561**	2l.40 multicoloured	2·50	2·40

1562 The Nativity

2008. Christmas. Multicoloured.

6933	1l. Type **1562**	1·10	1·10
MS6933a	As Type **1562**	1·10	1·10

1563 *Nymphaea lotus*

2008. Petea Creek Natural Reservation. Multicoloured.

6934	1l.40 Type **1563**	1·40	1·40
6935	1l.60 *Scardinius racovitzai*	1·90	1·80
6936	3l.10 *Melanopsis parreyssi*	3·50	3·25
MS6937	140×100 mm. Nos. 6934/6	6·75	6·75

The stamps and margins of **MS**6937 form a composite design.

1564 Early Coat of Arms

2009. 150th Anniv of Union. Multicoloured.

6938	2l.40 Type **1564**	2·50	2·40
MS6939	162×118 mm. 9l.10 Arms (different)	10·00	10·00

1565 '10'

2009. Tenth Anniv of Euro Currency. Multicoloured.

6940	3l. Type **1565**	3·25	3·00
6941	3l. As Type **1565**	3·25	3·00

No. 6941 has the '10' stamped in gold foil.

1566 *Crucifixion*

2009. Easter. Scenes from Iconostasis, Metropolitan Cathedral, Iasi. Multicoloured.

6942	1l. Type **1566**	1·10	1·10
6943	1l. *Resurrection*	1·10	1·10
6944	1l. *Ascension*	1·10	1·10

1567 *Alcedo atthis*

2009. Birds of Danube Delta. Multicoloured.

6945	50b. Type **1567** (kingfisher)	55	50
6946	1l.60 *Himantopus himantopus* (black-winged stilt) (48×33 mm)	1·90	1·80
6947	2l.10 *Egretta alba* (great egret) (48×33 mm)	2·30	2·20
6948	3l.10 *Falco cherrug* (Danube falcon)	3·50	3·25
MS6949	174×50 mm. Nos. 6945/8	8·25	8·25
MS6950	80×105 mm. 8l.10 *Halaeetus albicilla* (white-tailed eagle) (36×36 mm) (diamond)	8·75	8·75

1568 Penguin and Teardrop

2009. Preserve Polar Regions and Glaciers. Multicoloured.

6951	1l.60 Type **1568**	1·90	1·80
6952	8l.10 Melting Polar ice cap	8·75	8·50
MS6953	130×100 mm. Nos. 6951/2	10·00	10·00

It is reported that No. **MS**6953 also exists with silver foil printing.

1569 *Leontopodium alpinum* (eidelweiss)

2009. Flowers. Multicoloured.

6954	30b. Type **1569**	35	30
6955	60b. *Aster alpinus* (alpine aster)	70	65
6956	1l. *Dianthus superbus* (large pink)	1·10	1·00
6957	1l.20 *Silene nivalis* (pigeon's gizzard)	1·20	1·10
6958	2l.40 *Campanula persicifolia* (bell flower)	2·50	2·40
6959	3l.10 *Lilium martagon* (Turk's cap lily)	3·50	3·25

1570 Drilling Platform

2009. Centenary of Romgaz.

6960	**1570**	2l.40 multicoloured	2·50	2·40

1571 Galileo Galilei, Telescope and Tower of Pisa

2009. Europa. Astronomy.

6961	2l.40 Type **1571**	2·50	2·40
6962	9l.10 Map of constellations	9·00	8·75
MS6962a	113×91 mm. 2l.40×2, Type **1571**×2; 9l. 10×2, No. 6962×2	23·00	23·00

1572 Palace of Europe, Strasbourg

2009. 60th Anniv of Council of Europe.

6963	**1572**	6l. multicoloured	6·25	2·25

1573 Emblem (Municipal Director General of Police, Bucharest)

2009. European Capitals' Police Agencies Conference, Bucharest. Multicoloured.

6964	1l. Type **1573**	1·10	1·00
6965	1l.60 Police badge	1·70	1·60

1574 Timisoara (first European city with electric street lighting)

2009. Romania–European Source of Energy. Multicoloured.

6966	80b. Type **1574**	75	70
6967	2l.10 Turda (first European town lit with natural gas)	2·00	1·90
6968	3l. Iron Gates I hydroelectric power plant	3·00	2·75
MS6969	184×133 mm. Nos. 6966/8	3·75	3·75

1575 Symbols of First Moon Landing

2009. 40th Anniv of Moon Landing. Multicoloured.

6970	3l. Type **1575**	3·00	2·75
MS6971	128×116 mm. 14l.50 Footprint on the moon	14·00	14·00

1576 The Church on the Hill

2009. Sighisoara–UNESCO World Heritage Site. Multicoloured.

6972	1l. Type **1576**	1·10	1·00
6973	1l.60 Historic town centre	1·70	1·60
6974	6l. Clock tower	6·25	6·00
MS6975	114×100 mm. 7l.60 Old town (52×42 mm)	7·50	7·50
MS6975a	151×140 mm. Nos. 6972/4	9·00	9·00

1577 Anghel Saligny and Bridge at Cernavoda

2009. 155th Birth Anniv of Anghel Saligny (engineer). Multicoloured.

6976	2l.10 Type **1577**	2·00	1·90
6977	2l.40 Anghel Saligny and span of bridge at Cernavoda	2·50	2·40

1578 First Electric Tram, Frankfurt (1884)

2009. Electric Trams. Showing the first trams and arms of the relevant city. Multicoloured.

6978	80b. Type **1578**	75	70
6979	1l.20 Bucharest (1894)	1·10	1·00
6980	1l.60 Vienna (1897)	1·70	2·60
6981	2l.10 Braila (1899)	2·00	1·90
6982	2l.40 London (1901)	2·50	2·40
MS6983	140×100 mm. 8l.10 Berlin (1881) (48×33 mm)	8·25	8·25

1579 *Aquila chrysaetos* (golden eagle)

2009. Endangered Species. Multicoloured.

6984	30b. Type **1579**	25	20
6985	50b. *Lynx lynx* (lynx) (vert)	45	40
6986	60b. *Cervus elaphus* (red deer)	55	50
6987	1l.40 *Huso huso* (European sturgeon) (vert)	1·50	1·40
6988	3l. *Testudo graeca ibera* (Greek tortoise)	3·25	3·00
6989	6l. *Otis tarda* (great bustard) (vert)	6·50	6·25

1580 Dimtrie Cantemir (twice Prince of Moldavia, philosopher, historian, composer, musicologist, linguist, ethnographer and geographer)

2009. Romania—European Treasure. Sheet 161×137 mm containing T **1580** and similar horiz designs. Multicoloured.

MS6990	3l.×8, Type **1580**; George Enescu (composer, violinist, pianist and conductor); Three Saint Hierarchs Church, Iasi; Black Church and Johannes Honterus (humanist) (statue): *Egreta garzetta*, Retezat National Park; *Rupicapra rupicapra*, Retezat National Park; Cramposa (viticulture); Traditional crafts, Maramures	25·00	25·00

1581 Buna Vestire Church

2009. 550th Anniv of Bucharest. Multicoloured.

6991	30b. Type **1581**	25	20
6992	80b. Coltea Hospital	75	70
6993	3l. Sutu Palace	3·25	3·00
6994	4l.70 Architecture School	5·75	5·50
MS6995	140×184mm. Nos. 6991/4	10·50	10·50
MS6996	110×120mm. 8l.10 Patriarchal Cathedral, Bucharest (52×42 mm)	8·50	8·50

1582 Dove, Tears and Woman's Face

2009. International Day of Non-Violence.

6997	**1582**	3l. multicoloured	3·25	3·00

1583 Pipeline

2009. 35th Anniv of Transgaz (international natural gas transit).

6998	**1583**	5l. multicoloured	5·50	5·25

1584 Emblem

2009. 150th Anniv of Armed Forces General Staff.

6999	**1584**	7l.60 multicoloured	7·75	7·50

1585 The Nativity (icon, Buna Vestire Church (St Anthony the Great), Old Court, Bucharest))

2009. Christmas.

7000	**1585**	1l. multicoloured	1·10	1·00

1586 Building Facade and Alexandru Ioan Cuza

2009. 150th Anniv of Faculty of Law, University of Bucharest.

7001	**1586**	9l.10 multicoloured	9·50	9·25

1587 Avram Goldfaden and Stage

2009. Death Centenary of Avram Goldfaden (founder of first Yiddish theatre (1876), Iasi, Romania).

7002	**1587**	3l.10 multicoloured	3·25	2·00

1588 *Mireca* (three masted barque)

2009. Centenary of Constanta Harbour. Multicoloured.

7003	1l. Type **1588**	1·10	1·00
7004	5l. King Carol I lighthouse	5·50	5·00
MS7005	105×145 mm. Nos. 7003/4	6·50	6·50

1589 *Apis mellifera mellifera*

2010. Honey Bees. Multicoloured.

7006	50b. Type **1589**	40	35
7007	2l.10 *Apis mellifera ligustica*	2·00	1·90
7008	3l.10 *Apis mellifera carnica*	3·50	3·25
7009	4l.30 *Apis mellifera caucasica*	5·50	5·25

1590 Skiing

2010. Winter Olympic Games, Vancouver. Multicoloured.

7010	60b. Type **1590**	55	50
7011	80l. Speed skating	75	70
7012	1l. Skeleton bob (horiz)	1·10	1·00
7013	7l.60 Bobsleigh (horiz)	7·50	7·25

1591 *Brachypelma albopilosum*

2010. Tarantulas.

7014	50b. Type **1591**	45	40
7015	80b. *Haplopelma lividum*	75	70
7016	1l.20 *Brachypelma smithi*	1·10	1·00
7017	9l.10 *Grammostola rosea*	9·50	9·25

1592 Constanta Genoese Lighthouse

2010. Lighthouses. Multicoloured.

7018	60b. Type **1592**	55	50
7019	80b. Sulina	75	70
7020	1l.20 Mangalia	1·10	1·00
7021	1l.60 Tuzla	1·50	1·25
7022	8l.10 Constanta North	7·50	7·25

1593 The Resurrection (20th-century icon)

2010. Easter.

7023	**1593**	1l. multicoloured	1·10	1·00

1594 *Vlaicu I*

2010. 65th Anniv of International Civil Aviation Convention (ICAO).

7024	**1594**	8l.10 multicoloured	7·75	£750

1595 Grigore Alexandru Chica (founder) and Gendarmerie

2010. 160th Anniv of Romanian Gendarmerie.

7025	**1595**	9l.10 multicoloured	8·50	8·25

1596 Eugeniu Carada

2010. Death Centenary of Eugeniu Carada (politician).

MS7026	**1596**	9l.10 multicoloured	8·50	8·25

1597 Scene from Little Red Riding Hood

2010. Europa. Multicoloured.

7027	4l.30 Type **1597**	4·75	4·50
7028	7l.60 Boy and dragon reading	8·00	7·75
MS7029	127×108 mm. Nos. 7027/8, each×2	19·00	18·00

1598 Melk Abbey, Austria

2010. Danube Heraldry (1st issue)

7030	1l.40 Type **1598**	1·10	1·00
7031	2l.40 Bratislava Castle, Slovakia	2·50	2·25
7032	3l.10 Ilok Fortress, Croatia	3·25	3·00
7033	4l.30 Parliament Palace, Budapest, Hungary	4·75	4·50
MS7034	228×220 mm. Nos. 7030/3	11·00	10·00
MS7035	174×167 mm. 14l.50 *Mother Baar* (sculpture) (Adolf Heer) (36×36 mm)	13·00	12·00

1599 Quartz

2010. Minerals. Multicoloured.

7036	50b. Type **1599**	45	40
7037	1l.40 Gold ore	1·10	1·00
7038	1l.60 Rhodochrosite	1·50	1·40
7039	2l.40 Calcite	2·50	2·25
7040	7l.60 Red barite	8·00	7·75

1600 Hucul (Carpathian)

2010. Horses

7041	60b. Type **1600**	55	50
7042	1l. Arabian	1·10	1·00
7043	2l. Lipizzaner (vert)	1·90	1·75
7044	2l.10 Furioso North Star	2·00	1·90
7045	5l. Shagya Arabian	5·25	5·00

1601 Emblem and Children

2010. 20th Anniv of Save the Children Romania Organization

7046	**1601**	3l.10 multicoloured	3·25	3·00

1602 Vipera ursinii (meadow viper)

2010. Protected Fauna of the Danube River. Multicoloured.

7047	1l.40 Type **1602**	1·10	1·00
7048	1l.60 *Phalacrocorax pygmaeus* (pygmy cormorant)	1·50	1·40
7049	2l. *Phalacrocorax pygmaeus* (pygmy cormorant)	1·00	1·90
7050	7l.60 *Pelecanus crispus* (Dalmatian pelican)	8·00	7·75
MS7051	140×60 mm. Nos. 7047/50	11·00	10·00

1603 AzulejoTile with Seated Musician (National Museum, Lisbon)

2010. 130th Anniv of Portugal–Romania Diplomatic Relations. Multicoloured.

7052	2l.10 Type **1603**	2·00	1·90
7053	3l.10 Blue tile (Peasant Life Museum, Bucharest)	3·25	3·00

Stamps of a similar design were issued by Portugal.

1604 Arms

2010. Stamp Day. 125th Anniv of Romanian Orthodox Church Autocephaly

7054	**1604**	6l. multicoloured	6·25	6·00

1605 Clivia miniata

2010. 150th Anniv of Botanic Gardens, Bucharest

7055	1l.60 Type **1605**	1·50	1·40
7056	2l.10 *Magnolia kobus*	2·00	1·90
7057	2l.40 *Strelitzia juncea*	2·50	2·40
7058	3l. *Hepatica transsilvanica*	3·25	3·00
7059	3l.10 *Dicentra spectabilis*	3·25	3·00
MS7060	100×70 mm. 7l.60 Dimitrie Brandza (garden constructor) (36×36 mm)	8·00	7·75

1606 Carpathian Sphinx, Walker with Binoculars and 'Romania'

2010. Tourism. Multicoloured.

7061	1l. Type **1606**	1·10	1·00
7062	1l.60 Carpathian landscape and bearded figure facing left and 'Romania' at right	1·50	1·40
MS7063	108×78 mm. 1l. As Type **1606** (42×26 mm); 1l.60 As No. 7062 (42×26 mm)	1·10	1·00
MS70664	97×78 mm. 9l.10 Mountain landscape (84×26 mm)	9·25	9·00

1607 Games Emblem, Medal and Symbols of Study

2010. Youth Olympic Games, Singapore

MS7065	**1607**	8l.10 multicoloured	7·50	7·25

1608 Nahuel Huapi Lake, Argentina

2010. 80th Anniv of Argentina–Romania Diplomatic Relations. Multicoloured.

7066	2l.10 Type **1608**	2·00	1·90
7067	3l.19 Balea Lake, Romania	3·25	3·00

Stamps of a similar design were issued by Argentina.

1609 100l. Banknote

2010. 130th Anniv of National Bank. Multicoloured.

7068	2l.40 Type **1609**	2·50	2·25
7069	4l.30 100l. banknote (different)	4·75	4·50
MS7070	122×120 mm. Nos. 7068/9	7·25	7·00

1610 Steam Locomotive, Salzburg, Austria

2010. Orient Express. Multicoloured.

7071	2l.40 Type **1610**	2·50	2·40
7072	4l.70 Steam locomotive, Sinaia, Romania	7·75	7·50
MS7073	160×95 mm. Nos. 7071/2	9·75	9·50

1611 Children in Landscape (Save the Children) (Ioana Vezeanu)

2010. 20th Anniv of Ratification of UN Convention on Rights of the Child

7074	**1611**	6l. multicoloured	6·50	6·25

2010. Danube Heraldry (2nd issue). Multicoloured.

7075	1l.40 Ram Fortress, Serbia	1·50	1·40
7076	2l.40 Theatre, Ruse, Bulgaria	2·50	2·40
7077	3l.10 'Bogdan Petriceicu Hasdeu', Cahul State University, Moldova	3·25	3·00
7078	4l.30 Assumption of Virgin Mary Church, Izmail, Ukraine	4·75	4·50
MS7079	228×220 mm. Nos. 7075/8	10·00	9·00
MS7080	174×167 mm. 14l.50 Navigation Arch, Galati (designed by Petre Antonescu) (36×36 mm)	13·00	12·00

Multicoloured designs as T **1598**.

1612 Henri Coanda and Coanda Jet Aircraft

2010. Centenary of Henri Coanda's Jet Aircraft

MS7081	**1612**	14l.50 multicoloured	13·00	12·00

1613 Arms

2010. 130th Anniv of National Grand Lodge of Romania. Multicoloured.

7082	3l. Type **1613**	3·25	3·00
7083	5l. Square and Compass	5·50	5·00

1614 Wine Barrels

2010. Viticulture. Multicoloured.

7084	2l.10 Type **1614**	2·00	1·90
7085	3l.10 Grapes and decorated ceramic wine jug	3·25	3·00
MS7086	80×60 mm Horiz. 2l.10 As Type **1614**; 3l.10 As No. 7085	5·25	5·00

1615 Birth of Our Lord (icon, Gheorghe Tattarescu) (Metropolitan Cathedral, Iasi)

2010. Christmas. Multicoloured.

7087	1l. Type **1615**	90	85
7088	3l.10 *Birth of Our Lord* (Murillo School)	3·25	3·00

Stamps of the same design were issued by Vatican City.

1616

2010. Romania–World Firsts. Inventions. Multicoloured.

7089	3l. Type **1616**	3·25	3·00
7090	4l.30 Horizontal mill wheel mill (13th–14th century, precursor of turbine)	4·75	4·50
7091	5l. Fountain pen designed by Petrache Poenaru (Patent no. 3208, 1827)	5·75	5·50
7092	8l.10 Aerodynamic car, invented by Aurel Persu (German patent no. 402683, 1922)	7·50	7·25

1616a *Zamenis longissimus* (Aesculapian snake)

2011. Reptiles. Multicoloured.

7093	60b. Type **1616a**	50	45
7094	2l.40 *Podarcis taurica* (Balkan wall lizard)	2·50	2·40
7095	3l. *Vipera ammodytes ammodytes* (horned viper)	3·25	3·00
7096	9l.10 *Vipera ursinii moldavica* (Moldavian meadow viper)	9·50	9·00

1617 *Mercury* (George Demetrescu Mirea)

2011. Art. Paintings belonging to the National Bank of Romania . Multicoloured.

7097	1l.40 Type **1617**	1·10	1·00
7098	2l.10 *Marine* (Eugeniu Voinescu)	2·00	1·90
7099	3l. *Rodica* (Nicolae Grigorescu)	3·25	3·00
7100	7l.60 *Prometheus* (George Demetrescu Mirea)	7·25	7·00

1618 Ursilor

2011. Caves

7101	30b. Type **1618**	25	20
7102	50b. Closani	50	45
7103	60b. Muierii	55	50
7104	3l. Meziad (horiz)	3·25	3·00
7105	3l.10 Vantului (horiz)	3·25	3·00
7106	8l.70 Sura Mare (horiz)	7·75	7·50

1619 *Ara illiger* (Illiger's macaw)

2011. Parrots and Parakeets. Multicoloured.

7107	1l.60 Type **1619**	1·50	1·25
7108	2l.10 *Ara macao* (Scarlet macaw)	2·00	1·90
7109	2l.40 *Primolius auricollis* (yellow-collared macaw)	2·25	2·00
7110	4l.70 *Platycercus eximius* (eastern rosella)	5·25	5·00
7111	5l. *Melopsittacus undulatus* (budgerigar)	5·50	5·25
MS7112	80×103 mm. 9l.10 *Nymphicus hollandicus* (cockatiel)	9·00	8·75

1620 Globe and Child

2011. World Down Syndrome Day

7113	**1620**	3l. muulticoloured	3·25	3·00

1621 Crucifixion (icon, from Oravita Church)

2011. Easter

7114	**1621**	1l. multicoloured	1·10	1·00

1622 Peony

2011. *Paeonia peregrina* (Romanian Peony). Multicoloured.

7115	1l. Type **1622**	1·10	1·00
MS7116	100×70 mm. 2l. *Paeonia tenufolia* (Romanian Peony)	2·00	1·90

1623 *Parnasssius apollo*

2011. Butterflies and Moth. Multicoloured.

7117	50b. Type **1623**	45	50
7118	60b. *Greta oto* (vert)	55	50
7119	2l.40 *Morpho nestira*	2·50	2·40
7120	3l. *Papilio machaon*	3·35	3·00
7121	4l.50 *Attacus atlas*	4·75	4·50
7122	5l. *Inachis io*	5·00	4·75
MS7122a	105×65 mm. 8l.10 *Iphiclides podalirius*	8·00	7·75

1624 Palace of Parliament

2011. Palace of Parliament, Bucharest. Multicoloured.

7123	30b. Type **1624**	25	20
7124	50b. Senate entrance hall	45	40
7125	60b. Senate plenary hall	55	50
7126	3l. Human Rights room	3·25	3·00
7127	4l.30 Plenary hall of the Chamber of Deputies	4·75	4·50
7128	7l.60 Palace of Parliament, gate and entrance	7·75	7·50
MS7129	140×194 mm. Nos. 7123/8	17·00	17·00

1625 Deer in Forest

2011. Europa. Forests. Multicoloured.

7130	2l.40 Type **1625**	2·50	2·40
7131	9l.10 Squirrel on conifer branch	8·75	8·50
MS7131a	107×135 mm. Nos. 7130/1, each×2	11·00	11·00

1626 Aries

2011. Western Zodiac (1st issue). Multicoloured.

7132	30b. Type **1626**	25	20
7133	50b. Taurus	50	45
7134	60b. Gemini	55	50
7135	80b. Cancer	70	65
7136	1l.40 Leo	1·10	1·00
7137	14l.50 Virgo	12·00	11·00
MS7137a	130×182 mm. Nos. 7132/7	15·00	15·00

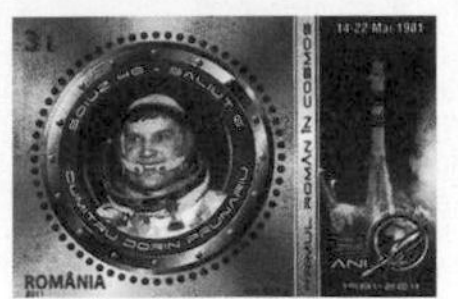

1627 Dumitru Dorin Prunariu (first Romanian cosmonaut)

2011. 50th Anniv of First Manned Space Flight, 30th Anniv of First Flight of Romanian Cosmonaut and 50th Anniv of First Session of UN Committee on the Peaceful Use of Outer Space. Multicoloured.

7138	3l. Type **1627**	3·25	3·00
7139	4l.710 Yuri Gagarin (first man in space)	5·50	5·25
MS7139a	128×116 mm. 8l.70 Globe from space (30×30 mm circular)	8·75	8·75

1628 Big Top as Clown's Face

2011. Circus. Multicoloured.

7140	50b. Type **1628**	45	40
7141	8l.10 Clown	7·50	7·25
MS7141a	118×102 mm. Nos. 7140/1	8·00	8·00

1629 Anniversary Ribbon

2011. 30th Anniv of Discovery of AIDS

7142	**1629**	3l. multicoloured	3·25	3·00

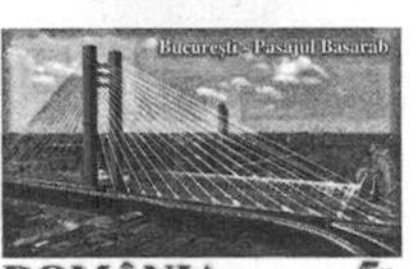

1630 Basarab Bypass

2011. Inauguration of Bucharest-Basarab Overpass

7143	**1630**	5l. multicoloured	5·00	4·75

1631 Prunus persica

2011. Flora. Peach Blossom. Multicoloured.

7144	50b. Type **1631**	45	40
7145	50b. *Prunus persica* (country name at right)	45	40

1632 Early Nurse and Patient

2011. 135th Anniv of Romanian Red Cross

7146	**1632**	3l.10 multicoloured	3·25	3·00

1633 Andre Şaguna (first President of ASTRA Association)

2011. Stamp Day. 150th Anniv of Transylvanian Association for Romanian Literature and Culture of the Romanian People (ASTRA). Multicoloured.

7147	3l. Type **1633**	3·25	3·00
7148	9l.10 ASTRA Library Building	8·75	8·50

1634 Wolf (*Canis lupus*)

2011. Fauna from Romanian Nature Reserves. Multicoloured.

7149	30b. Type **1634**	25	20
7150	4l.50 Purple heron (*Ardea purpurea*)	4·75	4·50
7151	5l. Capercaillie (*Tetrao urogallus*)	4·50	4·25
7152	8l.10 Raccoon dog (*Nyctereutes procyonoides*)	7·50	7·25
MS7153	138×138 mm. Nos. 7149/52	17·00	17·00

1635 The Artist (Austrian stained glass window, 18th century)

2011. Western Old Art Museum of Romanian Academy (Dumitru Furnica-Minovici House). Stained Glass Windows. Multicoloured.

7154	3l.60 Type **1635**	2·75	2·50
7155	4l.30 St. Katharina (Austrian stained glass window made by Gerard van Treeck, 1888)	4·75	4·50
7156	4l.50 Hunter (Tyrolese stained glass window, made by Gerard van Treeck, 19th century)	4·75	4·50
7157	4l.70 The Lady in Green (German stained glass window, 17th century)	5·00	4·75
MS7158	136×145 mm. 8l.10 St. Hieronimus, left and raising of Lazarus, right	7·50	7·25

1636 CFR 103 *Romania* Locomotive B1-n2 Egst.-1869 Type

2011. Locomotives. Multicoloured.

7159	2l. Type **1636**	2·75	2·50
7160	3l. CFR 28 *Codaesti* locomotive 2B-n2 Hart.-1887 type	3·25	3·00
7161	3l.30 CFR 185 *Domnita Maria* locomotive, C-n2 StEG. Wien -1875 type	3·50	3·25
7162	9l.10 CFR 001 *Lespezi* tender-locomotive, C-n2t Hainaut, Couillet -1884 type	8·75	8·50
MS7163	140×95 mm. 8l.10 CFR8008 8003 Type 2C-n4v Bre, (52×42 mm)	7·50	7·25

1637 George Enescu

2011. 20th 'George Enescu' International Festival and Competition (1l.40). 75th Anniv of *Oedipus* World Première) (3l.). 125th Anniv of Romanian Athenaeum (7l.60). Multicoloured.

7164	1l.40 Type **1637**	1·10	1·00
7165	3l. Score and signature	3·25	3·00
7166	7l.60 Romanian Athenaeum	11·00	10·00
MS7167	127×152 mm. Nos. 7164/6	16·00	16·00

1638 National Stadium

2011. National Areana, Bucharest

7168	5l. multicoloured	4·50	4·25
MS7169	273×107 mm. 5l.×2, As Type **1638**×2	9·00	9·00

1639 Biertan Fortified Church

2011. World Heritage Site. Fortified Church, Biertan

7170	**1639**	2l.10 multicoloured	2·75	2·50

1640 Franz Joseph Müller von Reichenstein (discoverer of Tellurium)

2011. International Year of Chemistry

7171	**1640**	5l. multicoloured	4·50	4·25

1641 Holy Gates of Chisinau

2011. 20th Anniv of Romania - Moldova Diplomatic Relations. Multicoloured.

7172	1l. Type **1641**	1·40	1·30
7173	3l.10 Arch of Triumph, Bucharest	3·25	3·00
MS7174	166×112 mm. Nos. 7172/3	4·75	4·25

2011. Western Zodiac (2nd issue). Multicoloured.

7175	50b. Libra	50	45
7176	60b. Scorpio	55	50
7177	80b. Sagittarius	70	65
7178	3l. Capricorn	3·25	3·00
7179	6l. Aquarius	6·25	6·00
7180	8l.10 Pisces	7·75	7·50
MS7180a	130×182 mm. Nos. 7175/80	5·50	5·25

As T **1626**

1642 Open Book, 'Justice' and Gavel

2011. European Day of Civil Justice

7181	**1642**	5l. multicoloured	5·25	5·00

1643 *Naşterea Domnului Iisus Hristos* (Our Lord Jesus Christ's Birth) (icon)

2011. Christmas

7182	**1643**	1l. multicoloured	1·10	1·00

1644 Lion's Head Rice Flour Figurine (Hong Kong)

2011. Handicrafts. Multicoloured.

7183 2l. Type **1644** 2·20 2·00
7184 2l. Painted egg (Romania) 2·20 2·00
MS7184a 130×82 mm. Nos 7183/4 4·75 4·75

1645 Stefan Odobleja (father of general cybernetics)

2011. Romania–World Firsts. Personalities. Multicoloured.

7185 1l.40 Type **1645** 1·60 1·50
7186 1l.60 Ioan Cantacuzino (discovered anti-cholera vaccine) 1·70 1·60
7187 2l.10 Anastase Dragomir (invented ejection seat) 2·20 2·10
7188 7l.60 Grigore Antipa (produced world's first biological diorama) 6·50 6·25

1646 Arms of Wallachia (stained glass window)

2011. Cotroceni Palace. Multicoloured.

7189 50b. Type **1646** 50 45
7190 60b. Basarab I (founder of Wallachia) 55 50
7191 80b. Arms of Moldavia 70 65
7192 1l. Bogdan I (founder of Moldavia) 1·10 1·00
7193 2l.40 Arms of Transyvania 2·50 2·20
7194 3l.10 Michael the Brave (Mihai Vitezul) (founder of first union of Romanian principalities) 3·25 3·00
MS7195 87×125 mm. 14l.50 Cotroceni Palace 13·00 12·00

1647 *Pulmonaria officinalis* and Bear

2012. Flora and Fauna (1st issue). Multicoloured.

7196 1l. Type **1647** 1·10 1·00
7197 1l.20 *Ranunculus repens* and cockerel 1·40 1·30
7198 3l.30 *Antirrhinum majus* and lion 3·75 3·50
7199 3l.60 *Oxalis acetosella* and rabbit 4·25 4·00
7200 4l.70 *Callistephus chinensis* and cow 4·75 4·50
7201 7l.60 *Convolvulus arvensis* and swallow 6·50 6·25

2012. Flora and Fauna (2nd issue). Multicoloured.

7202 50b. *Eritrichium nanum* and snake 50 45
7203 60b. *Amaranthus caudatus* and turkey 55 50
7204 1l.60 *Borago officinalis* and lamb 1·60 1·50
7205 2l. *Potentilla anserina* and crayfish 2·20 2·10

1648 Caragiale

2012. 160th Birth Anniv, and Death Centenary of Ion Luca Caragiale (playwright, short story writer, poet, theatre manager, political commentator and journalist). Caragiale Year. Multicoloured.

7206 5l. Type **1548** 5·25 5·00
MS7207 120×111 mm. 9l.10 *Caragialana* (sculpture) (Ioan Bolborea) (51×41 mm) 9·75 9·50

1649 Suţu Palace (now Municipal Museum)

2012. 150th Anniv of Bucharest as Capital City. Multicoloured.

7208 14l.50 Type **1649** 12·00 11·00
MS7209 149×121 mm. 8l.10 Alexandru Ioan Cuza (prominent figure of1848 Revolution in Moldavia and initiated reforms that contributed to modernization of society and state structures) (51×41 mm) 7·75 7·50

1650 Nicolae Iorga (historian, literary critic, playwright, poet and academician)

2012. Banknote Portraits. Multicoloured.

7210 80b. Type **1650** 75 70
7211 1l.40 George Enescu (composer, violinist, pianist and conductor) 1·60 1·50
7212 2l.10 Nicolae Grigorescu (founder of Romanian modern painting) 2·20 2·10
7213 2l.40 Aurel Vlaicu (aviation pioneer and pilot 2·50 2·40
7214 3l. Ion Luca Caragiale (playwright) 3·00 2·75
7215 3l.10 Lucian Blaga (philosopher, poet, playwright, translator, journalist, professor and diplomat) 3·25 3·00
7216 6l. Mihai Eminescu (poet) 6·25 6·00

1651 18th-century French Iron

2012. Domestic Irons. Multicoloured.

7217 50b. Type **1651** 50 45
7218 80b. 18th-century German iron 75 70
7219 1l.40 19th-century American iron 1·60 1·50
7220 4l.70 19th-century Scottish iron 4·50 4·25
7221 5l. 19th-century Romanian iron 4·75 4·50
MS7222 95×94 mm. 14l.50 Early 20th-century Romanian iron (41×51 mm) 12·00 11·00

1652 *The Resurrection of Christ* (1876), Saint Pantelimon Church, Bucharest

2012. Easter

7223 **1652** 1l. multicoloured 1·10 1·00

1653 Episcopal Roman-Catholic Cathedral

2012. Timisoara - 800th Anniv of Documentation. Multicoloured.

7224 2l.10 Type **1653** 2·50 2·00
7225 5l. Timisoara Fortress (horiz) 6·50 6·00
7226 7l.60 Hunyadi Castle (horiz) 8·50 8·00
7227 14l.50 Orthodox Metropolitan Cathedral 13·00 12·50
MS7228 130×100 mm. As No. 7227 15·00 15·00

No. 7228 is left for stamp not yet received.

1654 Heron (Danube Delta)

2012. Europa. Visit Romania. Multicoloured.

7229 1l.40 Type **1654** 1·60 1·50
7230 8l.10 Castle 5·25 5·00

No. 7231 is left for stamp not yet received.

1655 Athlete

2012. Centenary of Athletics Federation

7232 **1655** 1l.40 multicoloured 1·60 1·50

1656 Apostol Arsache (1st Minister)

2012. 150th Anniv of Ministry of Foreign Affairs. Multicoloured.

7233 2l.10 Type **1656** 2·20 2·10
MS7234 146×100 mm. 2l.10 Apostol Arsache and arms (33×48 mm) 2·20 2·10

1657 Grapes, Tomatoes and Garlic

2012. Healthy Food. Fruit and Vegetables. Multicoloured.

7235 50b. Type **1657** 50 45
7236 1L.60 Apples 1·70 1·60
7237 2l.10 Peppers 2·20 2·10

1658 Children

2012. International Children's Day

7238 **1658** 2l.40 multicoloured 2·75 2·50

1659 *Poecilia sphenops*

2012. Fish. Multicoloured.

7239 1l.40 Type **1659** 1·60 1·50
7240 3l. *Eupomotis gibbosus* 4·00 3·50
7241 3l.10 *Macropodus opercularis* 4·00 3·50
7242 14l.50 *Thorichthys meeki* 13·00 12·50

1660 *Merops apiaster* (European Bee-Eater)

2012. Ramsar Convention on Wetlands of International Importance. Multicoloured.

7243 1l. Type **1660** 1·50 1·30
7244 1l.20 *Egretta garzetta* (Little Egret) 1·50 1·30
7245 2l.10 *Ardeola ralloides* (Squacco Heron) 2·50 2·00
7246 8l.10 *Branta ruficollis* (Red-Breasted Goose) 9·00 8·50
7247 9l.10 *Pelecanus onocrotalus* (Great White Pelican) 9·00 8·50
MS7248 121×90 mm As No. 7247 10·00 10·00

1661 'Victor Babes' National Institute

2012. Stamp Day. 125th Anniv of 'Victor Babes' National Institute for Research and Development in the Field of Pathology and Biomedical Sciences. Multicoloured.

7249 3l.10 Type **1661** 4·00 3·50
7250 7l.60 Victor Babes (microbiologist and founder of Institute) 8·50 8·00
MS7250a 136×100 mm. Nos. 7249/50 10·25 10·25

1662 Gymnast

2012. Olympic Games, London. Multicoloured.

7251 1l.20 Type **1662** 10·25 10·25
7252 1l.40 Canoeing 1·60 1·50
7253 2l.10 Fencer 2·50 2·00
7254 6l. Javelin 2·50 2·00

1663 Dachshund

2012. Dogs. Multicoloured.

7255 4l.50 Type **1663** 6·00 5·50
7256 5l. Golden Retriever 6·50 6·00
7257 8l.10 Romanian Mioritic Shepherd 9·00 8·50
7258 9l.10 Romanian Carpathian Shepherd 10·00 9·50
MS7258a 127×130 mm. Nos. 7255/8 32·00 32·00

1664 Hagigadar Church, Suceava

2012. 500th Anniv of Hagigadar Monastery Church

7259 **1664** 4l.70 multicoloured 6·25 5·75

MS7259a 128×82 mm. No. 7259×2 13·00 13·00

2012. Domestic Irons. Multicoloured.

7260 80b. 19th-century Burmese iron 1·25 1·00

7261 1l. 18th-century Swedish iron 1·50 1·30

7262 1l.20 18th-century Belgian iron 1·50 1·30

7263 1l.60 18th-century Italian iron 1·75 1·50

7264 5l. 19th-century Swiss iron 6·50 6·00

7265 14l.50 19th-century pleat iron 13·00 12·50

MS7266 95×94 mm. 14l.50 As No. 7265. Imperf 15·00 15·00

1665 3p.; 6p.; 30p. Stamps of 1862 (As SG Nos. 23, 24, 25)

2012. 150th Anniv of Romanian Post. Multicoloured.

7267 1l. Type **1665** 1·50 1·30

7268 8l.10 Post Palace in Bucharest 9·00 8·50

MS7269 143×108 mm. 8l.10 As No. 7268. Imperf 10·00 10·00

1666 *Friendship* (Iftichia Georgeta Stanciu)

2012. 20th Anniv of Romanian - German Friendship Treaty. Winning Design in Children's Drawing Competition

7270 **1666** 2l.10 multicoloured 2·50 2·00

1667 Neagoe Basarab and his Family (builder) (mural paintings)

2012. 500th Anniv of Curtea de Arges Monastery Church. Multicoloured.

7271 4l.50 Type **1667** 6·00 5·50

7272 14l.50 Curtea de Arges Monastery Church 13·00 12·50

MS7272a 133×91 mm. Nos. 7271/2, each×2 15·00 15·00

1668 *Cervus elaphus*

2012. Mountain Fauna. Multicoloured.

7273 3l.10 Type **1668** (Carpathian Red Deer) 4·00 3·50

7274 3l.10 *Capra pyrenaica* (Spanish Ibex) 4·00 3·50

1669 *The Birth of our Lord* (icon (Radu Vodă Monastery, Bucharest))

2012. Christmas

7275 **1669** 1l. multicoloured 1·50 1·50

1670 Saint Nicholas Church, Densus

2012. Stone Churches from Tara Hategului. Multicoloured.

7276 3l. Type **1670** 4·00 3·50

7277 5l. Strei Church 6·50 6·00

7278 7l. Mintia Church, Vetel 8·50 8·00

7279 14l.50 Colt Church, Raul de Mori 13·00 12·50

1671 Bear Cub

2012. Fauna. Young Animals. Multicoloured.

7280 4l.30 Type **1671** 5·75 5·25

7281 5l. Fawn 6·50 6·00

7282 9l.10 Fox cub 10·00 9·50

7283 14l.50 Wolf cub 13·00 12·50

MS7283a 108×124 mm. Nos. 7280/3 15·00 15·00

1672 Arms

2012. 80th Anniv of Romania - Sovereign Military Order of Malta Diplomatic Relations. Christianity and Heraldry

7284 **1672** 8l.10 multicoloured 9·00 8·50

1673 Arms and Soldier

2012. Anti-Terrorist Brigade's Day, 24 December. Multicoloured.

7285 1l. Type **1763** 1·50 1·30

7286 8l.10 Arms and five soldiers 9·00 8·50

MS7287 130×110 mm. 8l.10 As No. 7276 10·00 10·00

1674 *Self-Portrait* (Nicolae Grigorescu)

2013. Art Anniversaries. Multicoloured.

7288 4l.50 Type **1674** (175th birth anniv) 6·00 5·50

7289 9l.10 *Self-Portrait* (Stefan Luchian) (145th birth anniv) 10·00 9·50

MS7289a 140×100 mm. No. 7289 15·00 15·00

1675 *Papaver rhoeas* (Field Poppy) (5am)

2013. Flower Clock. Multicoloured.

7290 60b. Type **1675** 1·00 75

7291 80b. *Cichorium inthybus* (Chicory) (6am.) 1·25 1·00

7292 1l. *Scorzonera rosea* (Viper's Grass) (7am.) 1·50 1·30

7293 1l.60 *Caltha palustris* (Marsh Marigold) (8am.) 1·75 1·50

7294 2l.40 *Helianthus annuus* (Sunflower) (9am.) 2·75 2·50

7295 5l. *Veronica chamaedrys* (Speedwell) (10am.) 6·50 6·00

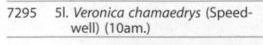

1676 Entrance

2013. 130th Anniv of Jewish Temple, Radauti. Multicoloured.

7296 8l.10 Type **1676** 9·00 8·50

7297 14l.50 Temple, side view 13·00 12·50

1677 Interior of Athenium

2013. 125th Anniv of Romanian Athenaeum (founded by Romanian Athenaeum Literary Society). Multicoloured.

7298 5l. Type **1677** 6·50 6·00

7299 9l.10 Façade 10·00 9·50

MS7300 165×123 mm. 9l.10 As No. 7299 10·50 10·50

1678 Steel Crown of King Carol I

2013. Crowns of Romania. Multicoloured.

7301 3l.30 Type **1678** 4·50 4·00

7302 4l.30 Queen Elisabeta 5·75 5·25

7303 14l.50 Queen Maria 13·00 12·50

1679 Fortified Church, Viscri

2013. Discover Romania - Transylvania

7304 3l.30 Type **1679** 4·50 4·00

7305 3l.60 Guest house, Valea Zalanului (vert) 4·50 4·00

7306 4l.30 View over Hosman (vert) 5·75 5·25

7307 5l. Saint Mihail Church, Cluj 6·50 6·00

1680 Goldmann Bellows Camera (Austria)

2013. Cameras. Multicoloured. . Multicoloured.

7308 50b. Type **1680** 80 80

7309 80b. Manufacture D`optique E. Suter camera, Bale (Switzerland) 1·50 1·50

7310 1l.40 Plaubell Makina camera (Germany) 1·80 1·80

7311 2l. Ernemann Tropen-Klapp camera (Germany 2·40 2·40

7312 2l.10 Balda Pontina camera (Germany) 2·75 2·75

7313 14kl.50 Welta camera (Germany) 13·00 13·00

1681 *Resurrection of Christ* (icon)

2013. Easter

7314 **1681** 1l. multicoloured 1·50 1·30

1682 King Carol I and Bucharest University of Economic Studies

2013. Centenary of Bucharest University of Economic Studies

7315 **1682** 8l.10 multicoloured 8·50 8·00

MS7316 110×76 mm. As Type **1682** 9·00 9·00

1683 National Bank of Romania Palace

2013. Architecture. National Bank of Romania Palace. Multicoloured. . Multicoloured.

7317 3l.10 Type **1683** 4·00 3·50

7318 3l.60 Marble Hall 4·75 4·00

7319 4l.50 Main hallway 6·00 5·50

7320 4l.70 Two monumental staircases 6·25 5·75

MS7321 160×114 mm. Nos. 7317/20 1·00 15·00

1684 Globe and Hands holding Earth and Plant

2013. Earth Day

7322 **1684** 5l. multicoloured 6·50 6·00

1685 Stefania Maracineanu (physicist)

2013. World Intellectual Property Day. Women and Inventions. Multicoloured.

7323 1l. Type **1685** 1·50 1·30

7324 3l.30 Josephine Cochrane (inventor of dishwasher) 4·50 4·00

7325 9l.10 Grace Murray Hopper (pioneer in computer programming language) 9·00 8·50

1686 Bi-plane with Envelopes as Wings

2013. Europa. Postal Transport. Multicoloured.

7326 2l.40 Type **1686** 2·75 2·50

7327 14l.30 Post car and postman riding Penny-farthing bicycle 13·00 12·50

MS7327a 112×90 mm. Nos. 7326/7, each×2 15·00 15·00

1687 Emperor Constantine and Empress Helen (his mother)

2013. 1700th Anniv of Edict of Milan. Multicoloured.

7328 4l.70 Type **1687** 6·00 5·50

7329 9l.10 Constantine and Helen (different) 9·00 8·50

1688 St George's Church, Mirauti

2013. 625th Anniv of Suceava. Multicoloured.

7330	4l.30 Type **1688**	5·50	5·50
7331	14l.50 Suceava Fortress	12·00	12·00

1689 Honey, Walnuts and Cinnamon Sticks

2013. Healthy Food. Honey, Berries and Nuts. Multicoloured.

7332	1l. Type **1689**	1·50	1·30
7333	1l.40 Honey, honeycomb and hazel nuts	1·60	1·50
7334	6l. Honey and berries	6·50	5·50
7335	8l.10 Honey, hazel nuts, berries and walnuts	8·50	8·00

2013. Flower Clock. Multicoloured.

7336	50b. *Anthericum ramosum* (3pm.)	1·00	75
7337	1l.20 *Mirabilis jalapa* (5pm.)	1·50	1·30
7338	1l.40 *Datura stramonium* (6pm.)	1·60	1·50
7339	3l. *Silene latifolia* (7pm.)	4·00	3·50
7340	3l.10 *Nicotiana alata* (8pm.)	4·00	3·50
7341	4l.70 *Oenothera biennis* (9pm.)	6·25	5·75

1690 *Athene noctua* (Little Owl)

2013. Raptors. Owls. Multicoloured.

7342	2l. Type **1690**	2·20	2·00
7343	3l.30 *Asio otus* (Long-eared Owl)	4·50	3·50
7344	4l.50 *Strix uralensis* (Ural Owl)	6·00	5·50
7345	9l.10 *Strix nbulosa* (Great Grey Owl) (horiz)	10·00	9·50

1691 Mouflon

2013. Hunting and Fishing. Multicoloured.

7346	2l. Type **1691**	2·20	2·00
7347	2l.10 Hare	2·50	2·00
7348	6l. Chamois	7·50	7·00
7349	7l.60 Trout	8·50	8·00

1692 Bolshoi Theatre and Romanian Athenaeum

2013. Tenth Anniv of Romanian - Russian Friendship and Cooperation

7350	**1692** 8l.10 multicoloured	8·50	8·50
MS7351	130×95 mm. As Type **1692**	10·00	10·00

1693 Monastery Building

2013. Stamp Day. 300th Anniv of Antim Monastery. Multicoloured.

7352	4l.30 Type **1693**	5·75	5·25
7353	14l.50 Antim Ivireanul	13·00	12·25

1694 20 Lei Gold Coin, 1870

2013. Numismatic Collection of National Bank of Romania. Multicoloured.

7354	3l.30 Type **1694**	4·00	3·50
7355	4l.30 20 lei gold coin, 1906	5·00	4·75
7356	4l.50 20 lei gold coin, 1928	5·50	5·25
7357	8l.10 20 lei gold coin, 1939	8·50	8·00

1695 *Moses* (statue) (Michelangelo)

2013. Tablets of the Law. Multicoloured.

7358	1l.20 Type **1695**	1·50	1·30
7359	1l.40 Ten Commandments, Mogosoaia Bridge Synagogue, Bucharest	1·60	1·50
7360	3l. Aron Kodesh, Great Synagogue, Bucharest	4·00	3·50
7361	14l.50 Saint Catherine's Monastery, Mount Sinai	13·00	12·50

1696 Assumption of the Virgin, Orthodox Cathedral

2013. 900th Anniv of Documentary Certification of Oradea. Multicoloured.

7362	2l.10 Type **1696**	2·50	2·00
7363	4l.30 Romano-Catholic Cathedral	5·75	5·25
7364	4l.70 Queen Marie Theatre (horiz)	6·25	5·75
7365	9l.10 Oradea City Hall (horiz)	10·00	9·50
MS7366	142×135 mm. 9l.10 As No. 7365	10·00	10·00

1697 Costumes from Bistriţa-Năsăud, Romania and Kraków, Poland

2013. 20th Anniv of Romania - Poland Friendship Treaty. Traditional Folk Costumes

7367	**1697** 8l.10 multicoloured	9·00	8·50
MS7368	70×90 mm. 8l.10 As Type **1697**	10·00	10·00

1698 Justice

2013. Architecture. National Bank of Romania Palace (2nd issue). Multicoloured.

7369	2l. Type **1698**	2·20	2·00
7370	3l.30 Commerce	4·50	4·00
7371	3l.60 Industry	4·75	4·10
7372	4l.50 Agriculture	6·00	5·50
MS7373	105×122mm. 8l.10 Eugeniu Carada (sculpture) (Ioan Bolborea) (42×52 mm)	10·00	10·00

1699 Maria Tanase

2013. Birth Centenary of Maria Tanase (singer)

7374	**1699** 9l.10 multicoloured	10·00	9·50
MS7375	75×108 mm. 9l.10 As Type **1699**	10·00	10·00

1700 Rogoz Village Church

2013. World Heritage Site. 350th Anniv of Wooden Church, Rogoz, Maramures

7376	**1700** 8l.10 multicoloured	9·00	8·50

1701 Waterwheel

2014. 50th Anniv of ASTRA (Transylvanian Association for Romanian Literature and Culture of the Romanians) Museum of Traditional Folk Civilization

7377	**1701** 14l.50 multicoloured		

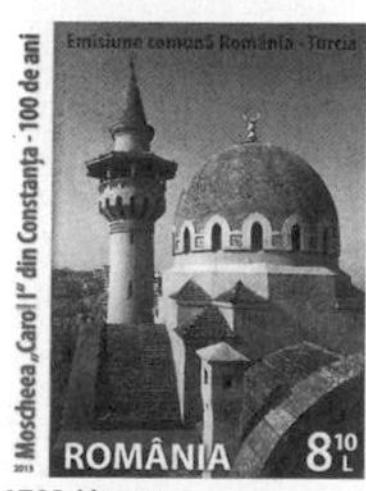

1702 Mosque

2013. 135th Anniv of Romania - Turkey Diplomatic Relations. Centenary of Carol I Mosque, Constanta

7378	**1702** 8l.10 multicoloured	9·00	8·50
MS7379	104×95 mm 8l.10 As Type **1702**	10·00	10·00

1703 *Marmota marmot* (Alpine Marmot)

2013. Romanian Fauna. Multicoloured.

7380	3l.30 Type **1703**	4·50	4·00
7381	4l.30 *Picoides tridactylus* (Eurasian Three-toed Woodpecker)	5·75	5·25
7382	4l.50 *Lynx lynx*	6·00	5·50
7383	9l.10 *Bison bonasus* (European Bison)	10·00	9·50

No. 7384 is vacant.

1704 Nicolae Iorga

2013. 85th Anniv of Romanian Radio. Golden Sound Archives of Romania. Multicoloured.

7385	1l. Type **1704**	1·50	1·30
7386	14l.50 Elena Vacărescu	13·00	12·50
MS7387	158×160mm. 1l. As Type **1704**; 14l.50 As No. 7386	15·00	15·00

1705 The Nativity (icon) (Domniţa Balaşa Church)

2013. Christmas

7388	**1705** 1l. multicoloured	1·50	1·30

1706 Emblem, Chess Pieces and Binary Numbers

2013. Strategic Intelligence - Intergrated Intelligence Office

7389	**1706** 8l.10 multicoloured	9·00	8·50

1707 Nicolae Grigorescu

2013. Art. Roses in Art. Multicoloured.

7390	1l. Type **1707**	1·10	1·00
7391	3l.60 Theodor Aman	4·50	4·00
7392	4l.50 Ştefan Luchian	6·00	5·50
7393	14l.50 Ion Andreescu	10·00	9·50

Nos. 7394/8 and Type **1708** are left for Ceramics, not yet received.

1709 Church of the Saviour, Berestovo, Ukraine

2013. World Heritage Sites. Sucevita Monastery Church and Church of the Saviour, Berestovo. Multicoloured.

7399	1l. Type **1709**	1·50	1·30
7400	9l.10 Sucevita Monastery church, Romania	10·00	9·50

1710 Mihai Eminescu

2014. National Culture Day. Mihai Eminescu (poet) Commemoration

7401	**1710** 4l.70 multicoloured	6·25	5·75
MS7402	126×160 mm. 4l.70 As Type **1710**	8·00	8·00

1711 City Hall

2014. Romanian Cities

7403	2l. Type **1711**	2·20	2·00
7404	2l.10 Old Orthodox Cathedral (vert)	2·50	2·00
7405	3l.60 Evangelical Lutherian Church (vert)	4·50	4·00
7406	14l.50 Ioan Slavici Classical Theatre	10·00	9·50

1712 *Echinocereus triglochidiatus*

2014. Flora. Desert Flowers. Multicoloured.

7407		1l. Type **1712**	1·50	1·30
7408		1l.40 *Baileya multiradiata*	1·60	1·50
7409		8l.10 *Solanum eleagnifolium*	9·00	8·50
7410		14l.50 *Hibiscus dendudatus*	10·00	9·50

1713 Map of Area and Document Seal

2014. Fifth Anniv of Maritime Delimitation of Black Sea Judgment by International Court of Justice, the Hague

7411	**1713**	9l.10 multicoloured	10·00	9·50
MS7412		136×130 mm. 9l.10 As Type **1713**	10·00	10·00

1714 Biathalon

2014. Winter Olympic Games, Sochi. Multicoloured.

7413		2l.10 Type **1714**	2·75	2·50
7414		2l.10 Bobsleigh	2·75	2·50
7415		2l.10 Skiing	2·75	2·50
7416		2l.10 Figure skating	2·75	2·50

1715 Musician (Iosef Iser)

2014. Art. Roma People in Art. Multicoloured.

MS7417	3l.30 Type **1715**; 4l.30 Girl, head and shoulders (Nicolae Grigorescu); 4l.50 Woman carrying basket (Pierre Bellet); 8l.10 Woman sleeping in chair (Nicolae Vermont)	15·00	15·00

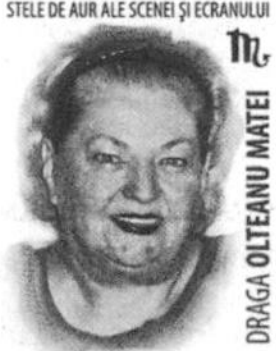

1716 Draga Olteanu Matei

2014. Golden Stars of Stage and Screen. Multicoloured.

7418	1l. Type **1716**	1·50	1·30
7419	1l. Florin Piersic	1·50	1·30
7420	1l. Olga Tudorache	1·50	1·30
7421	1l. Marin Moraru	1·50	1·30
7422	1l.40 Mircea Albulescu	1·60	1·50
7423	1l.40 Ileana Stana Ionescu	1·60	1·50
7424	1l.40 Tamara Buciuceanu-Botez	1·60	1·50
7425	8l.10 Mitica Popescu	9·00	8·50
7426	8l.10 Sebastian Papaiani	9·00	8·50
7427	8l.10 Valeria Gagealov	9·00	8·50
7428	14l.50 George Motoi	10·00	9·50
7429	14l.50 Sanda Toma	10·00	9·50
MS7430	150×220 mm. Nos. 7418/29	10·00	9·50

1717 Resurrection of Christ

2014. Easter

7431	**1717**	1l. multicoloured	1·50	1·30

1718 *Anas platyrhynchos* (Mallard)

2014. Fauna. Wild Ducks. Multicoloured.

7432	1l.20 Type **1718**	1·50	1·30
7433	1l.40 *Aythya fuligula* (Tufted duck)	1·60	1·50
7434	8l.10 *Anas clypeata* (Northern Shoveler)	9·00	8·50
7435	14l.50 *Anas crecca* (Eurasian Teal)	10·00	9·50

1719 Sphinx Rock, Romania and NATO Flags

2014. Tenth Anniv of Romanian Accession to NATO

7436	**1719**	9l.10 multicoloured	9·00	8·50

1720 Red Eggs (eaten at Easter)

2014. Healthy Food. Romanian Traditions. Multicoloured.

7437	1l. Type **1720**	1·50	1·30
7438	3l.60 Fish	4·50	4·00
7439	4l.50 Roast lamb and salads	6·00	5·50
7440	8l.10 Cheese	8·50	8·00

EXPRESS LETTER STAMPS

1919. Transylvania. Cluj Issue. No. E245 of Hungary optd as T **42**.

E784	**E18**	2b. olive and red	30	45

1919. Transylvania. Oradea Issue. No. E245 of Hungary optd as T **42**.

E860	2b. olive and red	40	70

FRANK STAMPS

F38

1913. Silistra Commemoration Committee.

F626	**F38**	(-) brown	7·75	9·50

F108 Mail Coach and Biplane

1933. For free postage on book "75th Anniv of Introduction of Rumanian Postage Stamp".

F1286	**F108**	(-) green	5·75	4·75

1946. For Internees' Mail via Red Cross. Nos. T1589/95 optd **SCUTIT DE TAXA POSTALA SERVICIUL PRIZONIERILOR DE RAZBOI** and cross.

F1809	**T171**	(-) on 50t. orange	1·50	1·60
F1810	**T171**	(-) on 1l. lilac	1·50	1·60
F1811	**T171**	(-) on 2l. brown	1·50	1·60
F1812	**T171**	(-) on 4l. blue	1·50	1·60
F1813	**T171**	(-) on 5l. violet	1·50	1·60
F1814	**T171**	(-) on 8l. green	1·50	1·60
F1815	**T171**	(-) on 10l. brown	1·50	1·60

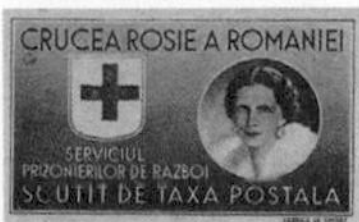

F209 Queen Helen

1946. For Internees' Mail via Red Cross. Perf or imperf.

F1829A	**F209**	(-) green and red	70	75
F1830A	**F209**	(-) purple and red	70	75
F1831A	**F209**	(-) red and carmine	70	75

F227 King Michael

F228 Torch and Book

1947. King Michael's Fund. Perf or imperf. (a) Postage.

F1904	**F227**	(-) purple	1·50	1·90
F1905	**F228**	(-) blue	1·50	1·90
F1906	-	(-) brown	1·50	1·90

(b) Air. No. F1904 overprinted "**PRIN AVION**".

F1907A	**F227**	(-) purple	70	75

DESIGN: As Type **227** but horiz—No. F1906, Man writing and couple reading.

NEWSPAPER STAMPS

1919. Transylvania. Cluj Issue. No. N136 of Hungary optd as T **42**.

N783	**N9**	2b. orange	2·50	2·10

1919. Transylvania. Oradea Issue. No. 136 of Hungary optd as T **43**.

N859	2b. orange	50	70

OFFICIAL STAMPS

O71 Rumanian Eagle and National Flag

1929

O1115	**O71**	25b. orange	20	10
O1116	**O71**	50b. brown	20	10
O1117	**O71**	1l. violet	20	10
O1118	**O71**	2l. green	20	10
O1119	**O71**	3l. red	30	10
O1120	**O71**	4l. olive	50	15
O1221	**O71**	6l. blue	1·20	20
O1222	**O71**	10l. blue	35	25
O1223	**O71**	25l. red	1·00	60
O1224	**O71**	50l. violet	3·00	1·70

1930. Optd **8 IUNIE 1930**.

O1150	25b. orange	50	20
O1151	50b. brown	50	20
O1152	1l. violet	50	20
O1153	2l. green	50	20
O1159	3l. red	50	20
O1154	4l. olive	75	20
O1155	6l. blue	85	40
O1161	10l. blue	1·60	30
O1166	25l. red	50	30
O1157	50l. violet	10·50	3·75

O80

1931

O1243	**O80**	25b. black	20	10
O1195	**O80**	1l. purple	25	25
O1196	**O80**	2l. green	55	40
O1197	**O80**	3l. red	60	40
O1247	**O80**	6l. red	1·90	75

PARCEL POST STAMPS

1895. As Type **D12** but inscr at top "TAXA DE FACTAGIU".

P353	25b. brown	8·25	1·00
P479	25b. red	6·25	2·10

1928. Surch **FACTAJ 5 LEI**.

P1078	**46**	5l. on 10b. green	2·10	85

POSTAGE DUE STAMPS

A. Ordinary Postage Due Stamps

D12

1881

D152	**D12**	2b. brown	5·25	4·25
D153	**D12**	5b. brown	26·00	6·25
D200	**D12**	10b. brown	10·50	1·00
D201	**D12**	30b. brown	10·50	1·00
D156	**D12**	50b. brown	21·00	7·25
D157	**D12**	60b. brown	26·00	10·50

1887

D448	2b. green	75	20
D449	5b. green	50	20
D450	10b. green	50	20
D451	30b. green	50	20
D371	50b. green	1·90	50
D458	60b. green	5·25	1·40

D38

1911

D617	**D38**	2b. blue on yellow	50	10
D618	**D38**	5b. blue on yellow	50	10
D619	**D38**	10b. blue on yellow	50	10
D604	**D38**	15b. blue on yellow	40	10
D621	**D38**	20b. blue on yellow	50	10
D622	**D38**	30b. blue on yellow	1·00	20
D623	**D38**	50b. blue on yellow	1·60	20
D624	**D38**	60b. blue on yellow	1·80	50
D609	**D38**	2l. blue on yellow	2·10	85

1918. Optd **TAXA DE PLATA**.

D675	**37**	5b. green	3·00	1·00
D676	**37**	10b. red	3·00	1·00

1918. Re-issue of Type **D38**. On greenish or white paper.

D1001	**D38**	5b. black	20	10
D722	**D38**	10b. black	20	10
D995	**D38**	20b. black	20	10
D735	**D38**	30b. black	75	30
D736	**D38**	50b. black	85	85
D998	**D38**	60b. black	20	10
D1007	**D38**	1l. black	40	20
D1010	**D38**	2l. black	75	30
D991	**D38**	3l. black	20	10
D992	**D38**	6l. black	50	10
D1547	**D38**	50l. black	50	20
D1548	**D38**	100l. black	70	30

1919. Transylvania. Cluj Issue. No. D190 etc of Hungary optd as T **42**.

D786	**D9**	1b. red and green	£275	£275
D787	**D9**	2b. red and green	55	55
D788	**D9**	5b. red and green	75·00	75·00
D789	**D9**	10b. red and green	30	30
D790	**D9**	15b. red and green	12·50	12·50
D791	**D9**	20b. red and green	25	25
D792	**D9**	30b. red and green	19·00	19·00
D793	**D9**	50b. red and green	13·00	13·00

1919. Transylvania. Oradea Issue. No. D190, etc of Hungary optd as T **43**.

D861	1b. red and green	26·00	26·00
D862	2b. red and green	20	20
D863	5b. red and green	5·75	5·75
D864	6b. red and green	3·75	3·75
D865	10b. red and green	30	30
D866	12b. red and green	80	80
D867	15b. red and green	80	80
D868	20b. red and green	20	20
D869	30b. red and green	85	85

1930. Optd **8 IUNIE 1930**.

D1168	**D38**	1l. black	40	20
D1169	**D38**	2l. black	40	20
D1170	**D38**	3l. black	50	40
D1171	**D38**	6l. black	1·60	1·00

D98

1932

D1249	**D98**	1l. black	10	10
D1250	**D98**	2l. black	10	10
D1251	**D98**	3l. black	20	10
D1252	**D98**	6l. black	20	10

D1835	D98	20l. black	20	10
D1839	D98	50l. black	20	15
D1840	D98	80l. black	40	20
D1841	D98	100l. black	60	30
D1842	D98	200l. black	95	65
D1843	D98	500l. black	1·50	1·00
D1844	D98	5000l. black	2·40	1·60

D233

1947. Type **D233** (without opts) perforated down centre.

D1919	2l. red	50
D1920	4l. blue	95
D1921	5l. black	1·50
D1922	10l. brown	2·40

The left half of Nos. D1919/22, showing Crown, served as a receipt and was stuck in the postman's book and so does not come postally used.

Prices for Nos. D1919/22 are for unused horizontal pairs.

1948. Nos. D1919/22, optd as in Type **D233**.

D1944	2l. red	40	20
D1945	4l. blue	60	30
D1946	5l. black	95	65
D1947	10l. brown	1·90	85

Prices for Nos. D1944 to D4055 are for unused and used horizontal pairs.

D276 Badge and Postwoman

1950

D2066	D 276	2l. red	1·50	1·50
D2067	D 276	4l. blue	1·50	1·50
D2068	D 276	5l. green	2·40	2·40
D2069	D 276	10l. brown	3·00	3·00

1952. Currency revalued. Nos. D2066/9 surch **4 Bani** on each half.

D2221	4b. on 2l. red	95	90
D2222	10b. on 4l. blue	95	90
D2223	20b. on 5l. green	2·40	2·20
D2224	50b. on 10l. brown	3·00	2·75

D420 G.P.O., Bucharest and Posthorn

1957

D2507	D 420	3b. black	20	10
D2508	D 420	5b. orange	20	10
D2509	D 420	10b. purple	20	10
D2510	D 420	20b. red	20	10
D2511	D 420	40b. green	40	20
D2512	D 420	1l. blue	95	30

D614

1967

D3436	D 614	3b. green	20	10
D3437	D 614	5b. blue	20	10
D3438	D 614	10b. mauve	20	10
D3439	D 614	20b. red	20	10
D3440	D 614	40b. brown	70	30
D3441	D 614	1l. violet	2·40	45

D766 Postal Emblems and Postman

1974

D4050	D 766	5b. blue	20	20
D4051	D 766	10b. green	20	20
D4052	-	20b. red	20	20
D4053	-	40b. violet	50	20
D4054	-	50b. brown	50	20
D4055	-	1l. orange	1·00	20

DESIGNS: 20b., 40b. Dove with letter and Hermes with posthorn; 50b., 1l. G.P.O., Bucharest and emblem with mail van.

Prices for Nos. D4050/55 are for unused horizontal pairs.

1982. As Type **D766**.

D4761		25b. violet	25	10
D4762	D 766	50b. yellow	35	10
D4763	-	1l. red	60	10
D4764	-	2l. green	1·20	15
D4765	D 766	3l. brown	1·80	15
D4766	-	4l. blue	3·00	20

DESIGNS: 25b., 1l. Dove with letter and Hermes with posthorn; 2, 4l. G.P.O., Bucharest and emblem with mail van.

D1111

1992

D5417	D 1111	4l. red	1·00	35
D5418	D 1111	8l. blue	1·30	60

D1163

1994

D5586	D 1163	10l. brown	65	50
D5587	D 1163	45l. orange	65	50

1999. Nos. D4762/4 and D4766 surch.

D6018	50l. on 50b. yellow	25	20
D6019	50l. on 1l. red	25	20
D6020	100l. on 2l. green	25	20
D6021	700l. on 1l. red	25	20
D6022	1100l. on 4l. blue	25	20

2001. Nos. D5417 and D5587 surch on both stamps in the pair.

D6173	500l. on 4l. red	10	10
D6174	1000l. on 4l. red	25	20
D6175	2000l. on 45l. orange	45	35

B. Postal Tax Due Stamps

1915. Optd **TIMBRU DE AJUTOR**.

TD643	D38	5b. blue on yellow	65	30
TD644	D38	10b. blue on yellow	85	50

TD42

1917. Green or white paper.

TD655	TD42	5b. brown	75	30
TD738	TD42	5b. red	1·00	50
TD654	TD42	10b. red	30	30
TD741	TD42	10b. brown	1·00	50

1918. Optd **TAXA DE PLATA**.

TD680	T40	5b. black	50	30
TD681	T40	10b. brown	50	30

1922. As Type **TD42** but inscr "ASSISTENTA SOCIALA". On green or white paper.

TD1028	10b. brown	20	20
TD1029	20b. brown	20	20
TD1030	25b. brown	30	30
TD1031	50b. brown	30	30

1931. Aviation Fund. Optd **TIMBRUL AVIATIEI**.

TD1219	D38	1l. black	40	25
TD1220	D38	2l. black	40	25

TD106

1932

TD1278	TD106	3l. black	1·60	95

POSTAL TAX STAMPS

Soldiers' Families Fund

The following stamps were for compulsory use at certain times on inland mail to raise money for various funds. In some instances where the stamps were not applied the appropriate Postal Tax Postage Due stamps were applied.

Other denominations exist but these were purely for revenue purposes and were not applied to postal matter.

1915. Optd **TIMBRU DE AJUTOR**.

T638	37	5b. green	30	10
T639	37	10b. red	75	30

T41 The Queen Weaving

1916

T649	T41	5b. black	30	30
T710	T41	5b. green	1·00	40
T650	T41	10b. brown	75	50
T711	T41	10b. black	1·00	40

The 50b. and 1, 2, 5 and 50l. in similar designs were only used fiscally.

1918. Optd **1918.**

T667		5b. black	1·00	50
T671	37	5b. green (No. T638)	47·00	47·00
T668		10b. brown	1·60	1·00
T672	37	10b. red (No. T639)	47·00	47·00

T47 "Charity"

1921. Social Welfare.

T978	T47	10b. green	20	10
T979	T47	25b. black	20	10

Aviation Fund

T91

1931

T1216	T91	50b. green	75	30
T1217	T91	1l. brown	1·50	30
T1218	T91	2l. blue	2·30	30

T98

1932

T1253	T98	50b. green	75	30
T1254	T98	1l. brown	1·10	30
T1255	T98	2l. blue	1·20	30

Stamps as Type **98** but inscr "FONDUL AVIATIEI" were only for fiscal use. Nos. T1253/5 could only be used fiscally after 1937.

T105

1932. Cultural Fund.

T1276	T105	2l. blue	1·50	65
T1277	T105	2l. brown	1·20	55

These were for compulsory use on postcards.

T121 "Aviation"

1936

T1340	T121	50b. green	50	40
T1341	T121	1l. brown	95	40
T1342	T121	2l. blue	95	40

Other stamps inscr "FONDUL AVIATIEI" were only for fiscal use.

T171 King Michael

1943

T1589	T171	50b. orange	40	40
T1590	T171	1l. lilac	40	40
T1591	T171	2l. brown	40	40
T1592	T171	4l. blue	40	40
T1593	T171	5l. violet	40	40
T1594	T171	8l. green	40	40
T1595	T171	10l. brown	40	40

1947. Fiscal stamps (22×18½ mm), perf vert through centre surch **IOVR** and value.

T1923	1l. on 2l. red	20	20
T1924	5l. on 1l. green	95	1·00

1948. Vert designs (approx 18½×22 mm). Inscr "I.O.V.R.".

T1948	1l. red	30	50
T1949	1l. violet	70	50
T1950	2l. blue	95	75
T1951	5l. yellow	4·75	3·25

SAVINGS BANK STAMPS

1919. Transylvania. Cluj Issue. No. B199 of Hungary optd as T **42**.

B785	B17	10b. purple	50	75

1919. Transylvania. Oradea Issue. No. B199 of Hungary optd as T **43**.

B861	10b. purple	50	70

Pt. 2

ROMANIAN OCCUPATION OF HUNGARY

100 filler = 1 korona.

A. BANAT BACSKA

The following stamps were issued by the Temesvar postal authorities between the period of the Serbian evacuation and the Romanian occupation. This area was later divided, the Western part going to Yugoslavia and the Eastern part going to Romania.

1919. Stamps of Hungary optd **Banat Bacska 1919**. (a) "Turul" Type.

1	7	50f. red on blue	16·00	16·00
		(b) War Charity stamps of 1916.		
2	20	10f.(+2f.) red	1·10	1·10
3	-	15f.(+2f.) violet	1·10	1·10
4	22	40f.(+2f.) red	1·10	1·10
		(c) Harvesters and Parliament Types.		
5	18	2f. brown	1·10	1·10
6	18	3f. purple	1·10	1·10
7	18	5f. green	1·10	1·10
8	18	6f. blue	1·10	1·10
9	18	15f. purple	1·10	1·10
10	18	35f. brown	16·00	16·00
11	19	50f. purple	16·00	16·00
12	19	75f. blue	1·10	1·10
13	19	80f. green	1·10	1·10
14	19	1k. red	1·10	1·10
15	19	2k. brown	1·10	1·10
16	19	2k. grey and violet	27·00	27·00
17	19	5k. light brown and brown	1·60	1·60
18	19	10k. mauve and brown	2·75	2·75
		(d) Charles and Zita stamps.		
19	27	10f. pink	1·10	1·10
20	27	20f. brown	1·10	1·10
21	27	25f. blue	1·10	1·10
22	28	40f. green	1·10	1·10
23	28	50f. violet	1·10	1·10
		(e) Harvesters Type inscr "MAGYAR POSTA".		
24	18	10f. red	16·00	16·00
25	18	20f. brown	16·00	16·00
26	18	25f. blue	18·00	18·00
		(f) Various Types optd KOZTARSASAG. (i) Harvesters and Parliament Types.		
27		4f. grey	1·10	1·10
28		5f. green	1·10	1·10
29		6f. blue	1·10	1·10
30		10f. red	18·00	18·00
31		20f. brown	16·00	16·00
32		40f. green	1·10	1·10
33	19	1k. red	1·10	1·10
34	19	2k. brown	16·00	16·00
35	19	3k. grey and violet	16·00	16·00
36	19	5k. light brown and brown	16·00	16·00
37	19	10k. mauve and brown	16·00	16·00
		(iii) Charles portrait stamps.		
38	27	15f. purple	16·00	16·00
39	27	25f. blue	1·10	1·10
		(g) Serbian Occupation of Temesvar stamps.		
40	18	10f. on 2f. brown	1·10	1·10
41	20	45f. on 10f.(+2f.) red	1·10	1·10
42	18	1k.50 on 15f. purple	1·10	1·10

EXPRESS LETTER STAMP

1919. No. E245 of Hungary optd **Banat Bacska 30 FILLER 1919.**

E44	E18	30f. on 2f. green and red	1·10	1·10

NEWSPAPER STAMP

1919. No. N136 of Hungary optd **Banat Bacska 1919.**

N43	N9	(2f.) orange	1·10	1·10

POSTAGE DUE STAMPS

1919. Nos. D191 etc optd as above.

D46	D9	2f. red and green	1·10	1·10
D47	D9	10f. red and green	1·10	1·10
D48	D9	15f. red and green	16·00	16·00
D49	D9	20f. red and green	1·10	1·10
D50	D9	30f. red and green	16·00	16·00
D51	D9	50f. black and green	18·00	18·00

SAVINGS BANK STAMP

1919. No. B199 of Hungary surch **Banat Bacska 50 FILLER 1919.**

B45	B17	50f. on 10f. purple	1·10	1·10

B. DEBRECEN

This area was later returned to Hungary.

(1)

1919. Stamps of Hungary optd with T **1** or surch in addition. (a) "Turul" Type.

1	**7**	2f. yellow	16·00	16·00
2	**7**	3f. orange	27·00	27·00
3	**7**	6f. brown	4·25	4·25

(b) War Charity stamps of 1915.

4	2f.+2f. yellow (No. 171)	27·00	27·00
5	3f.+2f. orange (No. 172)	27·00	27·00

(c) War Charity stamps of 1916.

6	**20**	10f.(+2f.) red	30	30
7	-	15f.(+2f.) lilac	1·60	1·60
8	**22**	40f.(+2f.) red	1·10	1·10

(d) Harvesters and Parliament Types.

9	**18**	2f. brown	20	20
10	**18**	3f. purple	20	20
11	**18**	5f. green	55	55
12	**18**	6f. blue	20	20
13	**18**	10f. red (No. 243)	43·00	43·00
14	**18**	15f. violet (No. 244)	22·00	22·00
15	**18**	15f. purple	7·00	7·00
16	**18**	20f. brown	16·00	16·00
17	**18**	25f. blue	95	95
18	**18**	35f. brown	11·00	11·00
19	**18**	35f. on 3f. purple	30	30
20	**18**	40f. green	75	75
21	**18**	45f. on 2f. brown	30	30
22	**19**	50f. purple	85	85
23	**19**	75f. blue	30	30
24	**19**	80f. green	55	55
25	**19**	1k. red	55	55
26	**19**	2k. brown	30	30
27	**19**	3k. grey and violet	7·00	7·00
28	**19**	3k. on 75f. blue	2·75	2·75
29	**19**	5k. light brown and brown	2·75	2·75
30	**19**	5k. on 75f. blue	95	95
31	**19**	10k. mauve and brown	22·00	22·00
32	**19**	10k. on 80f. green	1·80	1·80

(e) Charles and Zita stamps.

33	**27**	10f. pink	6·50	6·50
34	**27**	15f. purple	3·75	3·75
35	**27**	20f. brown	3·25	3·25
36	**27**	25f. blue	55	55
37	**28**	40f. green	60·00	60·00
38	**28**	50f. purple	30	30

(f) Harvesters and Parliament Types inscr "MAGAR POSTA".

39	**18**	5f. green	20	20
40	**18**	6f. blue	1·60	1·60
41	**18**	10f. red	20	20
42	**18**	20f. brown	20	20
43	**18**	25f. blue	20	20
44	**18**	45f. orange	1·80	1·80
45	**19**	5k. brown	£1100	

(g) Various Types optd **KOZTARSASAG**. (i) Harvesters and Parliament Types.

46	**18**	2f. brown	30	30
47	**18**	3f. purple	8·50	8·50
48	**18**	4f. grey	20	20
49	**18**	5f. green	20	20
50	**18**	10f. red	2·75	2·75
51	**18**	20f. brown	55	55
52	**18**	40f. green	30	30
53	**19**	1k. red	30	30
54	**19**	2k. brown	7·50	7·50
55	**19**	3k. grey and violet	1·80	1·80
56	**19**	5k. light brown and brown	80·00	80·00

(ii) War Charity stamps of 1916.

57	**20**	10f.(+2f.) red	2·75	2·75
58	-	15f.(+2f.) lilac	18·00	18·00
59	**22**	40f.(+2f.) red	2·75	2·75

(iii) Charles and Zita stamps.

60	**27**	10f. pink	2·20	2·20
61	**27**	15f. purple	3·75	3·75
62	**27**	20f. brown	3·25	3·25
63	**27**	25f. blue	55	55
64	**28**	50f. purple	30	30

2

4

1920. Types **2** and **4** and similar design, optd with inscr as T **1** but in circle.

65A	**2**	2f. brown	20	20
66A	**2**	3f. brown	20	20
67A	**2**	4f. violet	20	20
68A	**2**	5f. green	20	20
69A	**2**	6f. grey	20	20
70A	**2**	10f. red	20	20
71A	**2**	15f. violet	20	20
72A	**2**	20f. brown	20	20
73A	-	25f. blue	20	20
74A	-	30f. brown	20	20
75A	-	35f. purple	20	20
76A	-	40f. green	55	55
77A	-	45f. red	20	20
78A	-	50f. mauve	20	20
79A	-	60f. green	20	20
80A	-	75f. blue	20	20
81A	**4**	80f. green	20	20
82A	**4**	1k. red	30	30
83B	**4**	1k.20 orange	8·00	8·00
84A	**4**	2k. brown	55	55
85A	**4**	3k. brown	65	65
86A	**4**	5k. brown	65	65
87A	**4**	10k. purple	75	75

DESIGN: Nos. 73/80, Horseman using lasso.

5

1920. War Charity. Type **5** with circular opt, and "Segely belyeg" at top.

88	**5**	20f. green	1·10	1·10
89	**5**	20f. green on blue	30	30
90	**5**	50f. brown	1·10	1·10
91	**5**	50f. brown on mauve	55	55
92	**5**	1k. green	1·10	1·10
93	**5**	1k. green on green	55	55
94	**5**	2k. green	55	55

EXPRESS LETTER STAMP

1919. No. E245 of Hungary optd with T **1**.

E66	**E18**	2f. green and red	45	45

NEWSPAPER STAMP

1919. No. N136 of Hungary optd with T **1**.

N65	**N9**	2f. orange	20	20

POSTAGE DUE STAMPS

1919. (a) Nos. D190 etc of Hungary optd with T **1**.

D68	**D9**	1f. red and green	6·50	6·50
D69	**D9**	2f. red and green	20	20
D70	**D9**	5f. red and green	80·00	80·00
D71	**D9**	6f. red and green	8·00	8·00
D72	**D9**	10f. red and green	20	20
D73	**D9**	12f. red and green	32·00	32·00
D74	**D9**	15f. red and green	1·60	1·60
D75	**D9**	20f. red and green	1·60	1·60
D76	**D9**	30f. red and green	1·60	1·60

(b) With **KOZTARSASAG** opt.

D77	2f. red and green	5·50	5·50
D78	3f. red and green	5·50	5·50
D79	10f. red and green	5·50	5·50
D80	20f. red and green	5·50	5·50
D81	40f. red and green	5·50	5·50
D82	50f. red and green	5·50	5·50

D6

1920

D95	**D6**	5f. green	55	55
D96	**D6**	10f. green	55	55
D97	**D6**	20f. green	55	55
D98	**D6**	30f. green	55	55
D99	**D6**	40f. green	55	55

SAVINGS BANK STAMP

1919. No. B199 of Hungary optd with T **1**.

B67	**B17**	10f. purple	13·00	13·00

C. TEMESVAR

After being occupied by Serbia this area was then occupied by Romania. It later became part of Romania and was renamed Timisoara.

1919. Stamps of Hungary surch. (a) Harvesters Type.

6	**18**	30 on 2f. brown	30	30
7	**18**	1k. on 4f. grey (optd **KOZTARSASAG**)	30	30
8	**18**	150 on 3f. purple	30	30
9	**18**	150 on 5f. green	30	30

(b) Express Letter Stamp.

10	**E18**	3 KORONA on 2f. green and red	20	20

1919. Charity stamp of Hungary surch **PORTO 40**.

D11	40 on 15+(2f.) lilac (No. 265)	45	45

POSTAGE DUE STAMPS

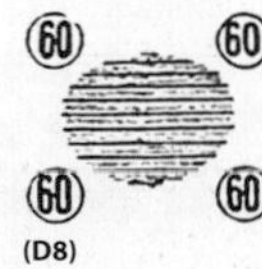

(D8)

1919. Postage Due stamps of Hungary surch with Type **D8**.

D12	**D9**	60 on 2f. red and green	9·75	9·75
D13	**D9**	60 on 10f. red and green	85	85

Pt. 16

ROMANIAN POST OFFICES IN THE TURKISH EMPIRE

Romanian P.O.s in the Turkish Empire including Constantinople. Now closed.

I. General Issues
40 paras = 1 piastre.

II. Constantinople
100 bani = 1 leu.

I. GENERAL ISSUES

1896. Stamps of Romania of 1893 surch in "PARAS".

9	10pa. on 5b. blue (No. 319)	20·00	20·00
10	20pa. on 10b. green (No. 320)	20·00	20·00
11	1pi. on 25b. mauve (No. 322)	20·00	20·00

II. CONSTANTINOPLE

(1)

1919. Stamps of Romania of 1893–1908 optd with T **1**.

1	**37**	5b. green	29·00	29·00
2	**37**	10b. red	20·00	20·00
3	**37**	15b. brown	20·00	20·00
4	-	25b. blue (No. 701)	35·00	35·00
14	-	40b. brown (No. 703)	29·00	29·00

1919. 1916 Postal Tax stamp of Romania optd with T **1**.

16	**T41**	5b. green	29·00	29·00

Pt. 1

ROSS DEPENDENCY

A dependency of New Zealand in the Antarctic on the Ross Sea.

The post office closed on 30 September 1987, but reopened in November 1994.

1957. 12 pence = 1 shilling; 20 shillings = 1 pound.
1967. 100 cents = 1 dollar.

3 Map of Ross Dependency and New Zealand

4 Queen Elizabeth II

1957

1	-	3d. blue	1·00	60
2	-	4d. red	1·00	60
3	**3**	8d. red and blue	1·00	60
4	**4**	1s.6d. purple	1·00	60

DESIGNS—HORIZ (As Type **3**): 3d. H.M.S. "Erebus"; 4d. Shackleton and Scott.

5 H.M.S. "Erebus"

1967. Nos. 1-4 with values inscr in decimal currency as T **5**.

5	**5**	2c. blue	9·00	8·00
6	-	3c. red	2·50	4·25
7	**3**	7c. red and blue	2·75	5·00
8	**4**	15c. purple	2·00	10·00

6 South Polar Skua

7 Scott Base

1972

9a	**6**	3c. black, grey and blue	70	1·75
10a	-	4c. black, blue and violet	15	1·75
11a	-	5c. black, grey and lilac	15	1·75
12a	-	8c. black, grey and brown	15	1·75
13a	**7**	10c. black, green and grey	15	1·75
14a	-	18c. black, violet and light violet	15	1·75

DESIGNS—As Type **6**: 4c. Lockheed Hercules airplane at Williams Field; 5c. Shackleton's Hut; 8c. Supply ship H.M.N.Z.S. "Endeavour". As Type **7**: 18c. Tabular ice flow.

8 Adelie Penguins and South Polar Skua

1982. Multicoloured.

15	5c. Type **8**	1·25	1·60
16	10c. Tracked vehicles	20	1·50
17	20c. Scott Base	20	75
18	30c. Field party	20	40
19	40c. Vanda Station	20	40
20	50c. Scott's hut, Cape Evans	20	40

9 South Polar Skua

1994. Wildlife. Multicoloured.

21	5c. Type **9**	50	60
22	10c. Snow petrel chick	60	70
23	20c. Black-browed albatross	80	90
24	40c. Emperor penguins	3·25	2·00
25	45c. As 40c.	1·50	1·00
26	50c. Bearded penguins ("Chinstrap Penguins")	1·50	1·25
27	70c. Adelie penguin	1·75	1·50
28	80c. Elephant seals	1·50	1·50
29	$1 Leopard seal	1·50	1·50
30	$2 Weddell seal	2·00	2·25
31	$3 Crabeater seal pup	2·75	3·25

10 Capt. James Cook with H.M.S. "Resolution" and H.M.S. "Adventure"

1995. Antarctic Explorers. Multicoloured.

32	40c. Type **10**	1·50	1·50
33	80c. James Clark Ross with H.M.S. "Erebus" and H.M.S. "Terror"	1·75	1·75
34	$1 Roald Amundsen and "Fram"	2·00	2·00
35	$1.20 Robert Scott with "Terra Nova"	2·50	2·50
36	$1.50 Ernest Shackleton with "Endurance"	2·75	2·75
37	$1.80 Richard Byrd with Ford 4-AT-B Trimotor "Floyd Bennett" (airplane)	2·75	2·75

11 Inside Ice Cave

1996. Antarctic Landscapes. Multicoloured.

38	40c. Type **11**	70	45
39	80c. Base of glacier	1·10	80
40	$1 Glacier ice fall	1·40	90
41	$1.20 Climbers on crater rim (horiz)	1·60	1·25
42	$1.50 Pressure ridges (horiz)	1·90	2·25
43	$1.80 Fumarole ice tower (horiz)	2·00	2·50

12 Snow Petrel

1997. Antarctic Seabirds. Multicoloured

(a) With "WWF" panda emblem

44	40c. Type **12**	80	60
45	80c. Pintado petrel ("Cape Petrel")	1·25	90
46	$1.20 Antarctic fulmar	1·60	1·25
47	$1.50 Antarctic petrel	1·60	1·25

(b) Without "WWF" panda emblem.

48	40c. Type **12**	2·50	2·25
49	80c. Pintado petrel ("Cape Petrel")	2·75	2·50
50	$1 Dove prion ("Antarctic Prion")	2·75	2·50
51	$1.20 Antarctic fulmar	3·00	3·00
52	$1.50 Antarctic petrel	3·00	3·25
53	$1.80 Antarctic tern	3·00	3·25

Nos. 48/53 were printed together, *se-tenant*, with the backgrounds forming a composite design.

13 Sculptured Sea Ice

1997. Ice Formation. Multicoloured.

54	40c. Type **13**	60	40
55	80c. Glacial tongue	80	70
56	$1 Stranded tabular iceberg	1·00	90
57	$1.20 Autumn at Cape Evans	1·10	1·00
58	$1.50 Sea ice in summer thaw	1·40	1·25
59	$1.80 Sunset at tubular icebergs	1·50	1·50

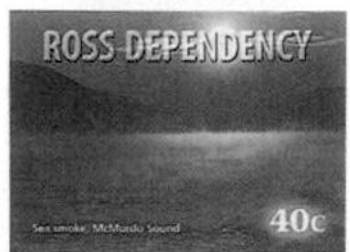

14 Sea Smoke, McMurdo Sound

1999. Night Skies. Multicoloured.

60	40c. Type **14**	1·00	65
61	80c. Alpenglow, Mount Erebus	1·50	90
62	$1.10 Sunset, Black Island	1·60	1·25
63	$1.20 Pressure ridges, Ross Sea	1·90	1·40
64	$1.50 Evening light, Ross Island	2·25	1·60
65	$1.80 Mother of pearl clouds, Ross Island	2·75	1·75

15 R.N.Z.A.F. C130 Hercules

2000. Antarctic Transport. Multicoloured.

66	40c. Type **15**	1·75	75
67	80c. Hagglunds BV206 All Terrain carrier	2·00	1·25
68	$1.10 Tracked 4×4 motorbike	2·25	1·50
69	$1.20 ASV track truck	2·25	1·50
70	$1.50 Squirrel helicopter	2·75	2·75
71	$1.80 Elan skidoo	2·75	2·75

2001. Penguins. As T **604** of New Zealand. Multicoloured.

72	40c. Two emperor penguins	1·25	75
73	80c. Two adelie penguins	1·75	1·00
74	90c. Emperor penguin leaving water	1·75	1·00
75	$1.30 Adelie penguin in water	2·00	1·40
76	$1.50 Group of emperor penguins	2·25	2·00
77	$2 Group of adelie penguins	2·75	2·25

16 British Explorers by Sledge

2002. Antarctic Discovery Expedition, 1901–1904. Each black, grey and stone.

78	40c. Type **16**	1·50	75
79	80c. H.M.S. *Discovery*, at anchor	2·50	1·25
80	90c. H.M.S. *Discovery*, trapped in ice	2·50	1·25
81	$1.30 Sledges and tents on the ice	2·75	1·90
82	$1.50 Crew of H.M.S. *Discovery*	3·25	2·25
83	$2 Scott's base at Hut Point	3·75	2·75

17 *Odontaster validus* (red seastar)

2003. Marine Life. Multicoloured.

84	40c. Type **17**	1·50	75
85	90c. *Beroe cucumis* (comb jelly)	2·50	1·25
86	$1.30 *Macroptychaster accrescens* (giant seastar)	3·00	1·75
87	$1.50 *Sterechinus neumayeri* (sea urchin)	3·25	2·25
88	$2 *Perkinsiana littoralis* (fan worm)	3·75	2·50

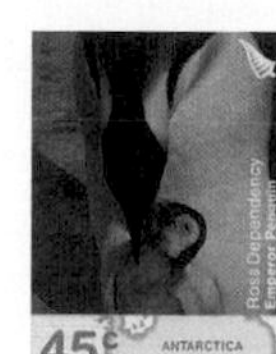

18 Penguin and Chick

2004. Emperor Penguins. Multicoloured.

89	45c. Type **18**	1·75	85
90	90c. Penguin chick	3·25	1·60
91	$1.35 Penguin feeding chick	3·75	2·00
92	$1.50 Two penguins and chick	3·75	2·50
93	$2 Group of penguins	4·25	3·25

19 Dry Valleys (Craig Potton)

2005. Photographs of Antarctica. Multicoloured.

94	45c. Type **19**	1·50	70
95	90c. Emperor penguins (Andris Apse)	2·75	1·50
96	$1.35 Antarctic fur seal (Mark Mitchell)	3·00	2·25
97	$1.50 Hut of Captain Robert F Scott (Colin Monteath)	3·50	2·75
98	$2 Antarctic minke whale (Kim Westerskov)	4·00	3·00

20 Biologist, 1957–8

2006. 50th Anniv of New Zealand Antarctic Programme. Multicoloured.

99	45c. Type **20**	1·75	1·00
100	90c. Hydrologists, 1979–80	3·00	2·00
101	$1.35 Geologist, 1984–5	3·50	3·25
102	$1.50 Meteorologists, 1994–5	3·75	4·00
103	$2 Marine biologist, 2004–5	4·25	4·50

21 Beaver Aircraft

2007. 50th Anniv of Commonwealth Trans-Antarctic Expedition. Each blue and black.

104	50c. Type **21**	1·75	1·00
105	$1 Harry Ayres and sledge	2·50	1·75
106	$1.50 Sledge dogs	3·50	3·50
107	$2 TE20 Ferguson tractor	3·75	4·00
108	$2.50 HMNZS *Endeavour*	4·75	5·00
MS109	120×80 mm. Nos. 107/8	9·00	9·00

22 Departure of *Nimrod* from Lyttelton

2008. Centenary of British Antarctic Expedition, 1907–1909. Multicoloured.

110	50c. Type **22**	1·50	1·00
111	$1 Expedition hut, Cape Royds	2·25	1·75
112	$1.50 Arrol-Johnston car (first vehicle on Antarctica)	3·00	3·00
113	$2 Professor Edgeworth David, Douglas Mawson and Alistair Mackay, first to reach South Magnetic Pole, 16 January 1909	3·50	3·75
114	$2.50 Setting out for first ascent of Mount Erebus, 1908	4·00	4·25

23 Map of Antarctica

2009. 50th Anniv of the Antarctic Treaty. Each showing silhouettes in Antarctic landscape. Multicoloured.

115	50c. Type **23**	1·40	1·00
116	$1 Penguins ('Antarctica shall be used for peaceful purposes only')	2·50	2·25
117	$1.80 Scientist ('Freedom of scientific investigation')	3·50	3·50
118	$2.30 Flags ('International co-operation in scientific investigation')	4·25	4·50
119	$2.80 Seal ('Preservation and conservation of living resources')	4·25	4·75

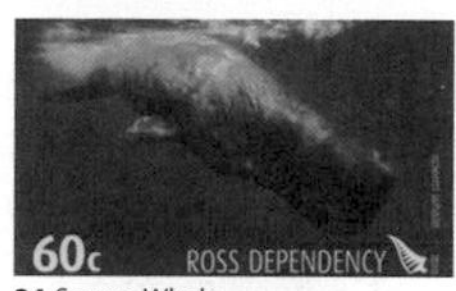

24 Sperm Whale

2010. Whales of the Southern Ocean. Multicoloured.

120	60c. Type **24**	1·40	1·10
121	$1.20 Minke whale	2·50	2·25
122	$1.90 Sei whale	3·75	3·25
123	$2.40 Killer whale	4·25	4·50
124	$2.90 Humpback whale	4·50	4·75
MS125	160×85 mm. Nos. 120/4	14·50	14·50

25 Roald Engelbregt Gravning Amundsen and *Fram*

2011. 'Race to the Pole': Centenary of the Amundsen and Scott Expeditions. Multicoloured.

126	60c. Type **25**	1·40	1·10
127	$1.20 Amundsen triumphs	2·50	2·00
128	$1.90 Robert Falcon Scott and ship *Terra Nova*	3·50	3·50
129	$2.40 Scott's party and memorial cairn at their last camp	4·00	4·25
130	$2.90 Norwegian flag and Union Jack	5·50	6·00
MS131	161×91 mm. Nos. 126/30	15·00	15·00

2012. Christchurch Philatelic Society Centennial Stamp and Postcard Exhibition. Sheet 130×90 mm. Multicoloured.

MS132	Nos. 128/9	8·50	8·50

26 Mount Erebus

2012. Landscapes. Multicoloured.

133	70c. Type **26**	1·40	1·10
134	$1.40 Beardmore Glacier	2·50	2·25
135	$1.90 Lake Vanda	3·50	3·50
136	$2.40 Cape Adare	4·00	4·25
137	$2.90 Ross Ice Shelf	4·50	4·75
MS138	134×88 mm. Nos. 133/7	14·50	14·50

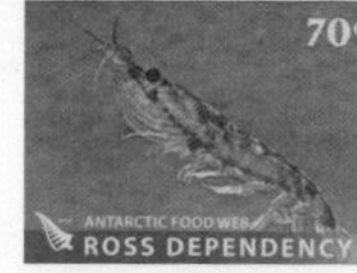

27 Antarctic Krill (*Euphausia superba*)

2013. Antarctic Food Web. Multicoloured.

139	70c. Type **27**	1·40	1·10
140	$1.40 Lesser Snow Petrel (*Pagodroma nivea*)	2·50	2·25
141	$1.90 Adelie Penguin (*Pygoscelis adeliae*)	3·50	3·50
142	$2.40 Crabeater Seal (*Lobodon carcinophaga*)	4·00	4·25
143	$2.90 Blue Whale (*Balaenoptera musculus*)	4·50	4·75
MS144	141×90 mm. Nos. 139/43	14·50	14·50

Pt. 6

ROUAD ISLAND (ARWAD)

An island in the E. Mediterranean off the coast of Syria. A French P.O. was established there during 1916.

25 centimes = 1 piastre.

1916. "Blanc" and "Mouchon" key-types inscr "LEVANT" and optd **ILE ROUAD** (vert).

1	**A**	5c. green	£450	£225
2	**B**	10c. red	£450	£225
3	**B**	1pi. on 25c. blue	£450	£225

1916. "Blanc" "Mouchon" and "Merson" key-types inscr "LEVANT" and optd **ILE ROUAD** horiz.

4	**A**	1c. grey	30	5·25
5	**A**	2c. purple	35	6·50
6	**A**	3c. red	70	6·25
7	**A**	5c. green	1·50	5·00
8	**B**	10c. red	2·30	8·50
9	**B**	15c. red	1·70	8·00
10	**B**	20c. brown	3·75	9·00
11	**B**	1p. on 25c. blue	5·00	9·50
12	**B**	30c. lilac	3·00	11·00
13	**C**	40c. red and blue	4·75	16·00
14	**C**	2p. on 50c. brown & lav	6·75	17·00
15	**C**	4p. on 1f. red and yellow	12·00	36·00
16	**C**	30p. on 5f. blue and yellow	48·00	75·00

Pt. 4

RUANDA-URUNDI

Part of German E. Africa, including Ruanda and Urundi, occupied by Belgian forces during the war of 1914–18 and a Trust Territory administered by Belgium until 1 July 1962. The territory then became two separate independent states, named Rwanda and Burundi.

100 centimes = 1 franc.

1916. Nos. 70/77 of Belgian Congo optd. (a) **RUANDA**.

1	**32**	5c. black and green	65·00	
2	**33**	10c. black and red	55·00	
3	**13**	15c. black and green	£100	
4	**34**	25c. black and blue	60·00	
5	**14**	40c. black and red	65·00	
6	-	50c. black and red	70·00	
7	-	1f. black and brown	£225	
7a	-	5f. black and orange	£3000	

(b) **URUNDI**.

8	**32**	5c. black and green	65·00	
9	**33**	10c. black and red	60·00	
10	**13**	15c. black and green	£100	
11	**34**	25c. black and blue	65·00	
12	**14**	40c. black and red	65·00	
13	-	50c. black and red	70·00	
14	-	1f. black and brown	£225	
14a	-	5f. black and orange	£3000	

1916. Stamps of Belgian Congo of 1915 optd **EST AFRICAIN ALLEMAND OCCUPATION BELGE. DUITSCH OOST AFRIKA BELGISCHE BEZETTING.**

15	**32**	5c. black and green	1·70	3·00
16	**33**	10c. black and red	2·00	3·75
17	**13**	15c. black and green	65	2·50
18	**34**	25c. black and blue	4·75	4·00
19	**14**	40c. black and lake	11·00	12·00
20	-	50c. black and lake	10·00	10·50
21	-	1f. black and olive	2·00	3·25
22	-	5f. black and orange	3·75	8·00

1918. Belgian Congo Red Cross stamps of 1918 optd **A. O.**

23	**32**	5c.+10c. blue and green	35	6·75
24	**33**	10c.+15c. blue and red	1·00	6·75
25	**13**	15c.+20c. blue and green	1·20	6·75
26	**34**	25c.+25c. blue	2·30	6·50
27	**14**	40c.+40c. blue and lake	1·20	7·50
28	-	50c.+50c. blue and lake	1·80	21·00
29	-	1f.+1f. blue and olive	3·00	12·50

30	-	5f.+5f. blue and orange	25·00	34·00
31	-	10f.+10f. blue and green	60·00	£120

1922. Stamps of 1916 surch.

32		5c. on 50c. black and lake	3·75	21·00
33	**32**	10c. on 5c. black and green	1·70	3·50
34a	**14**	25c. on 40c. black and lake	7·25	8·00
35	**33**	30c. on 10c. black and red	40	7·00
36	**34**	50c. on 25c. black and blue	3·50	6·75

1924. Belgian Congo stamps of 1923 optd **RUANDA URUNDI.**

37	**A**	5c. yellow	1·20	1·80
38	**B**	10c. green	65	1·90
39	**C**	15c. brown	35	85
40	**D**	20c. green	35	2·30
41	**E**	20c. green	40	1·40
42	**F**	25c. brown	50	15
43	**46**	30c. pink	60	1·40
44	**46**	30c. green	35	2·30
45	**D**	40c. purple	50	2·75
46	**G**	50c. blue	35	35
47	**G**	50c. orange	35	2·75
48	**E**	75c. orange	45	30
49	**E**	75c. blue	55	30
50	**H**	1f. brown	35	1·70
51	**H**	1f. blue	1·40	1·70
52	**I**	3f. brown	2·50	9·50
53	**J**	5f. grey	4·00	10·00
54	**K**	10f. black	14·50	34·00

1925. Stamp of Belgian Congo optd **RUANDA-URUNDI.** Inscriptions in French or in Flemish.

61	**55**	25c.+25c. black and red	50	7·00

1925. Native cattle type of Belgian Congo optd **RUANDA-URUNDI**.

62	**56**	45c. purple	85	7·50
63	**56**	60c. red	55	85

1927. Belgian Congo stamps of 1923 optd **RUANDA URUNDI** in two lines, wide apart.

64	**B**	10c. green	10	5·75
65	**C**	15c. brown	3·50	9·50
66	**46**	35c. green	2·50	3·75
67	**46**	75c. red	1·50	4·00
68	**H**	1f. red	3·00	3·75
69	**D**	1f.25 blue	5·50	8·25
70	**D**	1f.50 blue	1·30	4·75
71	**D**	1f.75 blue	3·00	3·00

1927. No. 144 of Belgian Congo optd **RUANDA URUNDI.**

72		1f.75 on 1f.50 blue	65	6·50

1930. Native Fund stamps of Belgian Congo (Nos. 160/8), optd **RUANDA URUNDI.**

73		10c.+5c. red	65	7·25
74		20c.+10c. brown	1·70	8·50
75		35c.+15c. green	2·75	10·50
76		60c.+30c. purple	2·30	9·50
77		1f.+50c. red	2·30	13·50
78		1f.75+75c. blue	3·75	17·00
79		3f.50+1f.50 lake	8·75	29·00
80		5f.+2f.50 brown	5·25	24·00
81		10f.+5f. black	5·00	28·00

1931. Nos. 68 and 71 surch.

82	**H**	1f.25 on 1f. red	6·75	1·20
83	**D**	2f. on 1f.75 blue	4·00	2·25

10 Mountain Scenery

1931

84	-	5c. red	1·40	3·00
85	**10**	10c. grey	75	2·30
86	-	15c. red	80	5·00
87	-	25c. purple	1·00	4·00
88	-	40c. green	2·75	6·25
89	-	50c. violet	30	1·80
90	-	60c. red	45	7·00
91	-	75c. black	1·90	5·50
92	-	1f. red	1·90	1·60
93	-	1f.25 brown	55	60
94	-	1f.50 purple	1·90	3·75
95	-	2f. blue	2·00	7·00
96	-	2f.50 blue	2·30	2·00
97	-	3f.25 purple	75	5·00
98	-	4f. red	2·75	3·00
99	-	5f. grey	4·00	3·00
100	-	10f. purple	4·25	8·50
101	-	20f. brown	10·00	19·00

DESIGNS—HORIZ: 15c. Warrior; 25c. Chieftain's kraal; 50c. Head of African buffalo; 1f. Wives of Urundi chiefs; 1f.50, 2f. Wooden pot hewer; 2f.50, 3f.25, Workers making tissues from ficus bark; 4f. Hutu Potter. VERT: 5, 60c., Native porter; 40c. Two cowherds; 75c. Native greeting; 1f.25, Mother and child; 5f. Ruanda dancer; 10f. Warriors; 20f. Native prince of Urundi.

11 King Albert I

1934. King Albert Mourning Stamp.

102	**11**	1f.50 black	2·00	1·20

11a Queen Astrid and Children

1936. Charity. Queen Astrid Fund.

103	**11a**	1f.25+5c. brown	2·75	6·25
104	**11a**	1f.50+10c. red	1·60	7·50
105	**11a**	2f.50+25c. blue	1·40	9·50

1941. Stamps of Belgian Congo optd **RUANDA URUNDI**.

106	**78**	10c. grey	40·00	36·00
107	**78**	1f.75 orange	9·25	18·00
108	**78**	2f.75 blue	12·00	17·00

1941. Ruanda-Urundi stamps of 1931 surch.

109		5c. on 40c. green	11·00	26·00
110		60c. on 50c. violet	28·00	34·00
111		2f.50 on 1f.50 purple	5·50	13·50
112		3f.25 on 2f. blue	29·00	38·00

1941. Stamps of Belgian Congo optd **RUANDA URUNDI** and surch also.

113	-	5c. on 1f.50 black and brown (No. 222)	25	2·30
114	-	75c. on 90c. brown and red (No. 221)	4·50	9·75
115	**78**	2f.50 on 10f. red	5·25	8·25

14a "Belgium shall rise Again"

1942. War Relief.

116	**14a**	10f.+40f. red	7·75	19·00
117	**14a**	10f.+40f. blue	7·25	19·00

On No. 116 the French slogan is above the Flemish, on No. 117 vice versa.

1942. Nos. 107/8 of Ruanda-Urundi surch.

118	**78**	75c. on 1f.75 orange	18·00	26·00
119	**78**	2f.50 on 2f.75 blue	25·00	29·00

15a Head of Warrior

1942

120	**A**	5c. red	10	3·25
121	**A**	10c. green	35	1·30
122	**A**	15c. brown	65	2·50
123	**A**	20c. blue	35	3·50
124	**A**	25c. purple	90	1·00
125	**A**	30c. blue	1·50	2·00
126	**A**	50c. green	95	55
127	**A**	60c. brown	1·40	1·40
128	**15a**	75c. black and lilac	2·50	90
129	**15a**	1f. black and brown	2·50	1·20
130	**15a**	1f.25 black and red	2·50	1·90
131	**B**	1f.75 brown	4·50	3·50
132	**B**	2f. orange	4·25	3·00
133	**B**	2f.50 red	2·75	15
134	**C**	3f.50 green	1·70	75
135	**C**	5f. orange	2·30	85
136	**C**	6f. blue	2·50	40
137	**C**	7f. black	1·50	1·20
138	**C**	10f. brown	2·50	2·50
139	-	20f. black and brown	4·50	5·00
140	-	50f. black and red	11·50	8·25
141	-	100f. black and green	16·00	18·00

DESIGNS—As Type **15a** (various frames): A, Oil palms; C, Askari sentry; 20f. Head of zebra. 35×24 mm: B, Leopard. 29×34 mm: 50f. Askari sentry; 100f. Head of warrior.

1944. Red Cross Fund. Nos. 126, 130, 131 and 134 surch **Au profit de la Croix Rouge Ten voordeele van het Roode Kruis** (50c., 1f.75) or with Flemish and French reversed (others) and premium.

147		50c.+50f. green	4·25	16·00
148		1f.25+100f. black and red	5·25	20·00
149		1f.75+100f. brown	6·50	16·00
150		3f.50+100f. green	4·00	20·00

17 Seated Figure

1948. Native Carvings.

151	**17**	10c. orange	35	4·50
152	**A**	15c. blue	45	5·75
153	**B**	20c. blue	1·00	3·75
154	**C**	25c. red	50	50
155	**D**	40c. purple	1·10	3·25
156	**17**	50c. brown	1·50	10
157	**A**	70c. green	1·60	3·00
158	**B**	75c. purple	2·30	2·75
159	**C**	1f. purple and orange	1·00	65
160	**D**	1f.25 red and blue	2·00	2·30
161	**E**	1f.50 red and green	4·00	3·75
162	**17**	2f. red and vermilion	80	35
163	**A**	2f.50 green and brown	2·50	35
164	**B**	3f.50 green and blue	2·75	1·70
165	**C**	5f. red and bistre	1·50	35
166	**D**	6f. green and orange	2·50	45
167	**E**	10f. brown and violet	3·50	2·75
168	**F**	20f. brown and red	4·50	4·50
169	**E**	50f. black and brown	8·25	4·75
170	**F**	100f. black and red	13·00	8·25

DESIGNS: A, Seated figure (different); B, Kneeling figure; C, Double mask; D, Mask; E, Mask with tassels; F, Mask with horns.

1949. Surch.

171		3f. on 2f.50 (No. 163)	1·20	25
172		4f. on 6f. (No. 166)	2·50	1·40
173		6f.50 on 6f. (No. 166)	3·00	35

18a St. Francis Xavier

1953. 400th Death Anniv of St. Francis Xavier.

174	**18a**	1f.50 black and blue	1·50	1·90

19 "Dissotis"

1953. Flowers Multicoloured.

175		10c. Type **19**	15	1·30
176		15c. "Protea"	15	3·25
177		20c. "Vellozia"	15	75
178		25c. "Littonia"	75	2·75
179		40c. "Ipomoea"	75	2·75
180		50c. "Angraecum"	1·00	70
181		60c. "Euphorbia"	1·80	3·50
182		75c. "Ochna"	3·00	2·50
183		1f. "Hibiscus"	2·00	70
184		1f.25 "Protea"	4·75	6·25
185		1f.50 "Schizoglossum"	55	1·00
186		2f. "Ansellia"	3·00	2·50
187		3f. "Costus"	1·80	50
188		4f. "Nymphaea"	3·25	2·00
189		5f. "Thunbergia"	3·25	2·00
190		7f. "Gerbera"	1·10	1·30
191		8f. "Gloriosa"	3·50	2·50
192		10f. "Silene"	2·30	1·30
193		20f. "Aristolochia"	9·50	2·75

20 King Baudouin and Mountains

1955

194	**20**	1f.50 black and red	5·00	3·50
195	-	3f. black and green	5·00	2·50
196	-	4f.50 black and blue	5·00	1·20
197	-	6f.50 black and purple	5·50	90

DESIGNS: 3f. Forest; 4f.50, River; 6f.50, Grassland.

20a Mozart when a Child

1956. Birth Bicentenary of Mozart.

198	**20a**	4f.50+1f.50 violet	3·25	13·00
199	-	6f.50+2f.50 purple	5·75	26·00

DESIGN—52×36 mm: 6f.50, Queen Elizabeth and Mozart sonata.

20b Nurse with Children

1957. Red Cross Fund.

200	**20b**	3f.+50c. blue	2·75	9·00
201	-	4f.50+50c. green	2·30	9·00
202	-	6f.50+50c. brown	2·00	10·50

DESIGNS: 4f.50, Doctor inoculating patient; 6f.50, Nurse in tropical kit bandaging patient.

21 Gorilla

1959. Fauna.

203	**21**	10c. black, red and brown	10	25
204	–	20c. black and green	10	20
205	–	40c. black, olive and mauve	35	1·60
206	–	50c. brown, yellow and green	65	1·90
207	–	1f. black, blue and brown	1·40	1·30
208	–	1f.50 black and orange	3·00	2·30
209	–	2f. black, brown and turquoise	1·80	1·30
210	–	3f. black, red and brown	2·75	2·50
211	–	5f. multicoloured	2·30	2·30
212	–	6f.50 brown, yellow and red	85	50
213	–	8f. black, mauve and blue	3·00	2·30
214	–	10f. multicoloured	2·75	2·00

DESIGNS—VERT: 10c., 1f. Type **21**: 40c., 2f. Eastern black and white colobus. HORIZ: 20c.1f.50, African buffaloes; 50c., 6f.50, Impala; 3, 8f. African elephants; 5, 10f. Eland and common zebras.

POSTAGE DUE STAMPS

1924. Postage Due stamps of Belgian Congo optd **RUANDA URUNDI.**

D55	**D54**	5c. brown	10	50
D56a	**D54**	10c. red	10	1·10
D57	**D54**	15c. violet	35	1·00
D58	**D54**	30c. green	35	4·00
D59a	**D54**	50c. blue	1·10	1·90
D60	**D54**	1f. grey	1·00	4·00

1943. Postage Due stamps of Belgian Congo optd **RUANDA URUNDI.**

D142	**D86**	10c. olive	80	6·75
D143	**D86**	20c. blue	15	5·50
D144	**D86**	50c. green	1·90	6·75
D145	**D86**	1f. brown	95	7·50
D146	**D86**	2f. orange	30	5·50

1959. Postage Due stamps of Belgian Congo optd **RUANDA URUNDI.**

D215	**D99**	10c. brown	1·70	7·25
D216	**D99**	20c. purple	1·60	3·00
D217	**D99**	50c. green	3·25	6·00
D218	**D99**	1f. blue	4·75	6·00
D219	**D99**	2f. red	5·00	7·75
D220	**D99**	4f. violet	4·25	9·25
D221	**D99**	6f. blue	4·50	10·00

For later issues see **BURUNDI** and **RWANDA**.

Pt. 10

RUSSIA

A country in the E. of Europe and N. Asia. An empire until 1917 when the Russian Socialist Federal Soviet Republic was formed. In 1923 this became the Union of Soviet Socialist Republics (U.S.S.R.), eventually comprising 15 constituent republics.

In 1991 the U.S.S.R. was dissolved and subsequent issues were used in the Russian Federation only.

100 kopeks = 1 rouble.

1

1858. Imperf.

1	1	10k. blue and brown	£13000	£1300

1858. Perf.

21		10k. blue and brown	75·00	3·25
22		20k. orange and blue	£150	38·00
23		30k. green and red	£200	50·00

5

1863

8	5	5k. black and blue	25·00	£650

No. 8 was first issued as a local but was later authorised for general use.

9

1864

18	9	1k. black and yellow	7·50	2·50
30	9	2k. black and red	31·00	3·75
19b	9	3k. black and green	14·00	5·00
20	9	5k. black and lilac	31·00	6·25

8

1875

31	8	7k. red and grey	25·00	2·75
32	8	8k. red and grey	31·00	3·25
33	8	10k. blue and brown	65·00	10·00
34	8	20k. orange and blue	75·00	6·25

12 No thunderbolts

1883. Posthorns in design without thunderbolts, as T **12**.

38A	9	1k. orange	6·25	1·50
39A	9	2k. green	9·50	1·50
41A	9	3k. red	9·50	1·50
42B	9	5k. purple	9·50	1·90
43B	9	7k. blue	10·00	2·50
44B	10	14k. red and blue	19·00	1·30
45C	10	35k. green and purple	£130	28·00
46C	10	70k. orange and brown	£150	23·00
47	11	3r.50 grey and black	£1100	£1000
48	11	7r. yellow and black	£1200	£1300

13 With thunderbolts **14** **15**

1889. Posthorns in design with thunderbolts as T **13**. Perf.

50	9	1k. orange	75	25
51	9	2k. green	75	25
52	9	3k. red	75	25
53	14	4k. red	90	40
54	9	5k. purple	1·30	25
55	9	7k. blue	75	25
56	14	10k. blue	1·30	25
114A	10	14k. red and blue	30	20
100	10	15k. blue and purple	5·00	1·00
116A	14	20k. red and blue	25	1·90
102	10	25k. violet and green	25	65
103	10	35k. green and purple	10·00	1·90
79	11	3r.50 grey and black	19·00	15·00
122A	11	3r.50 green and red	50	65
80	11	7r. yellow and black	15·00	19·00
124Ab	11	7r. pink and green	65	1·30

For imperf stamps, see Nos. 107B/125aB.

16 Monument to Admiral Kornilov at Sevastopol

1905. War Orphans Fund (Russo-Japanese War).

88	16	3 (6) k. brown, red and green	3·75	3·75
82	-	5 (8) k. purple and yellow	3·25	3·25
83	-	7 (10) k. blue, lt blue & pink	4·50	3·25
87	-	10 (13) k. blue, lt bl & yell	3·75	3·75

DESIGNS: 5(8) k. Monument to Minin and Pozharsky, Moscow; 7(10) k. Statue of Peter the Great, St. Petersburg; 10(13) k. Moscow Kremlin.

20

22

23

1906

107A	22	1k. orange	50	40
93	22	2k. green	1·10	25
94	22	3k. red	1·00	25
95	23	4k. red	40	15
96	22	5k. red	3·25	65
97	22	7k. blue	1·50	30
98a	23	10k. blue	10·50	4·50
123Aa	20	5r. blue and green	1·30	1·30
125Aa	20	10r. grey, red and yellow	1·90	1·90

For imperf stamps, see Nos. 107B/125aB.

25 Nicholas II

26 Elizabeth

27 The Kremlin

1913. Tercentenary of Romanov Dynasty. Views as T **27** and portraits as T **25/26**.

126		1k. orange (Peter I)	30	25
127		2k. green (Alexander II)	40	25
128		3k. red (Alexander III)	50	25
129		4k. red (Peter I)	65	25
130		7k. brown (Type **25**)	75	65
131		10k. blue (Nicholas II)	1·00	65
132		14k. green (Katherine II)	1·30	1·00
133		15k. brown (Nicholas I)	2·50	1·30
134		20k. olive (Alexander I)	3·75	1·30
135		25k. red (Alexis)	3·50	2·50
136		35k. green and violet (Paul I)	3·25	1·90
137		50k. grey and brown (T **26**)	3·50	2·50
138		70k. brown and green (Michael I, the first Russian tsar)	3·75	3·25
139		1r. green (Type **27**)	15·00	12·50
140		2r. brown	25·00	15·00
141		3r. violet	31·00	15·00
142		5r. brown	38·00	23·00

DESIGNS—As T **27**: 2r. The Winter Palace; 3r. Romanov House, Moscow (birthplace of first Romanov tsar). 23×29 mm: 5r. Nicholas II.

31 Russian hero, Ilya Murometz

1914. War Charity.

151	31	1 (2) k. green & red on yell	1·30	2·50
144	-	3 (4) k. green and red on red	1·40	3·75
145	-	7 (8) k. green and brown on buff	1·40	3·75
161	-	10 (11) k. brown and blue on blue	2·50	3·75

DESIGNS: 3k. Cossack shaking girl's hand; 7k. Symbolical of Russia surrounded by her children; 10k. St. George and Dragon.

1915. As last. Colours changed.

155	31	1 (2) k. grey and brown	1·90	3·25
156	-	3 (4) k. black and red	1·90	3·25
158	-	10 (11) k. brown and blue	2·50	3·75

35

1915. Nos. 131, 133 and 134 printed on card with inscriptions on back as T **35**. No gum.

165		10k. blue	1·50	6·25
166		15k. brown	1·50	6·25
167		20k. olive	1·90	6·25

1916. Various types surch.

168	-	10k. on 7k. brown (No. 130)	50	50
170	22	10k. on 7k. blue	50	40
169	-	20k. on 14k. green (No. 132)	50	50
171	10	20k. on 14k. red and blue	50	40

1917. Various earlier types, but imperf.

107B	22	1k. orange	1·30	25
108B	22	2k. green	30	25
109B	22	3k. red	30	25
110B	23	4k. red	1·30	6·25
111B	22	5k. lilac	30	25
113B	23	10k. blue	25·00	65·00
115B	10	15k. blue & pur (No. 100)	30	25
116B	14	20k. red and blue	30	65
117B	10	25k. vio & grn (No. 102)	1·30	5·00
118B	10	35k. grn & pur (No. 103)	25	50
119B	14	50k. green and purple	25	50
120B	10	70k. orange and brown (No. 120)	25	50
121B	15	1r. orange and brown	20	25
122B	11	3r.50 green and red	65	1·00
123Ba	20	5r. blue and green	65	1·30
124B	11	7r. pink and green	2·50	5·00
125B	20	10r. grey, red and yellow	75·00	75·00

39

41

1916. Types of 1913 printed on card with surch on back as T **39** or **41**, or optd with figure "**1**" or "**2**" in addition on front. No gum.

172	39	1k. orange (No. 126)	41·00	65·00
175	39	1 on 1k. orange (No. 126)	1·00	6·25
177	41	1 on 1k. orange (No. 126)	1·90	9·50
173	39	2k. green (No. 127)	65·00	75·00
176	39	2 on 2k. green (No. 127)	1·00	6·25
178	41	2 on 2k. green (No. 127)	1·00	5·00
174	39	3k. red (No. 128)	1·90	6·25
179	41	3k. red (No. 128)	80	3·75

45 Cutting the Fetters

1918

187	45	35k. blue	1·30	25·00
188	45	70k. brown	1·40	38·00

46 Agriculture and Industry

47 Triumph of Revolution

48 Agriculture

49 Industry

55 Science and Arts

56

64 Industry

1921. Imperf.

195	48	1r. orange	1·90	12·50
196	48	2r. brown	1·90	12·50
197	49	5r. blue	1·90	12·50
198	46	20r. blue	4·50	9·50
199	47	40r. blue	3·25	5·75
214	48	100r. yellow	20	25
215	48	200r. brown	25	40
216	55	250r. purple	20	25
217	48	300r. green	50	1·00
218	49	500r. blue	1·00	2·50
219	49	1000r. red	20	25
256	64	5000r. violet	1·00	1·90
257	46	7500r. blue	50	1·30
259	46	7500r. blue on buff	65	1·30
258	64	10000r. blue	10·50	11·50
260	64	22500r. purple on buff	65	1·30

1921. 4th Anniv of October Revolution. Imperf.

227	56	100r. orange	65	3·75
228	56	250r. violet	65	3·75
229	56	1000r. purple	65	3·75

57 Famine Relief Work

58

1921. Charity. Volga Famine. Imperf.

230	57	2250r. green	5·00	12·50
231	57	2250r. red	5·00	12·50
232	57	2250r. brown	5·00	12·50
233	58	2250r. blue	7·50	12·50

1922. Surch. Imperf.

236	49	5000r. on 5r. blue	1·60	3·75
239	48	5000r. on 1r. orange	1·60	3·25
240	48	5000r. on 2r. brown	1·60	3·25
242	46	5000r. on 20r. blue	2·50	5·00
243	47	10000r. on 40r. blue	2·00	3·75

Р. С. Ф. С. Р.
ГОЛОДАЮЩИМ
250 р.+250 р.
(62)

1922. Famine Relief. Surch as T **62**. Perf.

245	45	100r.+100r. on 70k. brown	1·10	2·50
247	45	250r.+250r. on 25k. blue	1·10	3·25

(63)

1922. Surch as T **63**. Imperf.

250	55	7500r. on 250r. purple	25	40
251	55	100000r. on 250r. purple	25	50

65

1922. Obligatory Tax. Rostov-on-Don issue. Famine Relief. Various sizes. Without gum. Imperf.

261	**65**	2T. (2000r.) green	65·00	£500
262	-	2T. (2000r.) red	65·00	£500
263	-	4T. (4000r.) red	65·00	£500
264	-	6T. (6000r.) green	65·00	£500

DESIGNS: 2T. red, Worker and family (35×42 mm); 4T. Clasped hands (triangular, 57 mm each side); 6T. Sower (29×59 mm).

РСФСР
Филателия
– детям
19 - 8 - 22

70 "Philately for the children"

1922. Optd with T **70**. Perf or imperf.

273	**22**	1k. orange	£1000	£1000
274	**22**	2k. green	44·00	£130
275	**22**	3k. red	12·50	50·00
276	**22**	5k. red	12·50	50·00
277	**23**	10k. blue	12·50	50·00

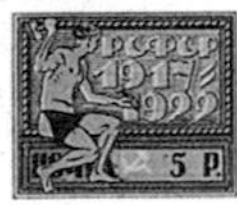
71

1922. 5th Anniv of October Revolution. Imperf.

279	**71**	5r. black and yellow	50	50
280	**71**	10r. black and brown	50	50
281	**71**	25r. black and purple	1·00	1·50
282	**71**	27r. black and red	3·50	6·25
283	**71**	45r. black and blue	2·30	3·75

1922. Air. Optd with airplane. Imperf.

284		45r. black and green	15·00	£110

73

1922. Famine Relief. Imperf.

285	**73**	20r.+5r. lilac	30	2·50
286	-	20r.+5r. violet	30	2·50
287	-	20r.+5r. blue	30	2·50
288	-	20r.+5r. blue	1·90	18·00

DESIGNS—HORIZ: No. 286, Freighter; No. 287, Steam train. VERT: No. 288, Airplane.

(77)

1922. Surch as T **77**. Imperf or perf.

289	**14**	5r. on 20k. red and blue	2·75	50·00
290	**10**	20r. on 15k. blue & purple	2·75	50·00
291	**10**	20r. on 70k. orange and brown	25	40
292a	**14**	30r. on 50k. green & pur	40	1·00
293	**10**	40r. on 15k. blue & pur	25	40
294	**10**	100r. on 15k. blue & pur	25	40
295	**10**	200r. on 15k. blue & pur	25	40

78 Worker

79 Soldier

1922. Imperf or perf.

303	**78**	10r. blue	40	1·50
304	**79**	50r. brown	25	1·00
305	**79**	70r. purple	25	1·00
310	**79**	100r. red	25	65

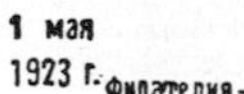

(80)

1923. Charity. Surch as T **80**. Imperf.

315	**71**	1r.+1r. on 10r. black and brown	44·00	£110
317	**55**	2r.+2r. on 250r. purple	38·00	£110
318	**64**	4r.+4r. on 5000r. violet	50·00	£130

83 Worker

84 Peasant

85 Soldier

1923. Perf.

320	**85**	3r. red	15	25
321	**83**	4r. brown	15	25
322	**84**	5r. blue	15	25
323	**85**	10r. grey	15	25
324	**85**	20r. purple	25	50

86 Reaper

88 Tractor

1923. Agricultural Exn, Moscow. Imperf or perf.

325	**86**	1r. brown and orange	3·75	12·50
326	-	2r. green and light green	3·75	12·50
327	**88**	5r. blue and light blue	3·75	12·50
328	-	7r. rose and pink	3·75	12·50

DESIGNS: As Type **86**: 2r. Sower; 7r. Exhibition buildings.

90 Worker

91 Peasant

92 Soldier

93

94

95

1923. Perf (some values also imperf).

335	**90**	1k. yellow	90	40
359	**91**	2k. green	40	25
360	**92**	3k. brown	40	25
361	**90**	4k. red	40	25
434	**90**	5k. purple	1·10	65
363	**91**	6k. blue	90	25
364	**92**	7k. brown	90	25
437	**90**	8k. olive	2·20	65
366	**91**	9k. red	1·30	65
341	**92**	10k. blue	5·00	1·30
385	**90**	14k. grey	1·50	50
386	**91**	15k. yellow	2·30	1·60
442	**92**	18k. violet	4·50	1·30
443	**90**	20k. green	4·50	1·30
444	**91**	30k. violet	6·25	1·30
445	**92**	40k. grey	10·00	1·30
343	**91**	50k. brown	7·50	1·30
447	**92**	1r. red and brown	12·50	3·75
375	**93**	2r. green and red	10·00	4·50
449	**94**	3r. green and brown	21·00	8·75
450	**95**	5r. brown and blue	25·00	10·00

96 Lenin

1924. Lenin Mourning. Imperf or perf.

413	**96**	3k. black and red	4·25	2·75
414	**96**	6k. black and red	4·50	2·10
411	**96**	12k. black and red	4·50	1·30
412	**96**	20k. black and red	3·75	8·75

97 Fokker F.III Airplane

1924. Air. Surch. Imperf.

417	**97**	5k. on 3r. blue	3·75	2·30
418	**97**	10k. on 5r. green	3·75	2·30
419	**97**	15k. on 1r. brown	3·75	2·30
420	**97**	20k. on 10r. red	3·75	2·30

С.С.С.Р.
пострадавшему
от наводнения
Ленинграду.
3 К. + 10 К.

99 Trans "For the victims of the flood in Leningrad"

1924. Leningrad Flood Relief. Surch as T **99**. Imperf.

421	**48**	3+10k. on 100r. yellow	2·50	2·30
422	**48**	7+20k. on 200r. brown	2·50	2·30
423	**48**	14+30k. on 300r. green	3·25	3·50
424	**49**	12+40k. on 500r. blue	3·25	3·50
425	**49**	20+50k. on 1000r. red	3·25	3·50

102 Lenin Mausoleum, Moscow

1925. First Death Anniv of Lenin. Imperf or perf.

426	**102**	7k. blue	3·75	3·25
427	**102**	14k. olive	10·00	6·25
428	**102**	20k. red	6·25	4·50
429	**102**	40k. brown	10·00	5·00

104 Lenin

1925

451	**104**	1r. brown	19·00	12·50
452	**104**	2r. brown	19·00	12·50
850	**104**	3r. green	3·25	2·50
851	**104**	5r. brown	6·25	6·25
852	**104**	10r. blue	7·50	10·00

106 Prof. Lomonosov and Academy of Sciences, Leningrad

1925. Bicentenary of Academy of Sciences.

456b	**106**	3k. brown	4·50	6·25
457	**106**	15k. olive	9·50	5·00

107 A. S. Popov

1925. 30th Anniv of Popov's Radio Discoveries.

458	**107**	7k. blue	3·25	2·00
459	**107**	14k. green	6·25	3·00

110 Moscow Barricade

1925. 20th Anniv of 1905 Rebellion. Imperf or perf.

463a	-	3k. green	6·25	3·75
464b	-	7k. brown	8·25	4·50
465a	**110**	14k. red	8·25	4·50

DESIGNS—VERT: 3k. Postal rioters; 7k. Orator and crowd.

111 "Decembrists in Exiles" (detail, A. Moravov)

112 Senate Square, St. Petersburg, 1825

1925. Centenary of Decembrist Rebellion. Imperf or perf.

466	**111**	3k. green	6·25	5·00
467b	**112**	7k. brown	8·75	7·50
468b	-	14k. red	9·50	10·00

DESIGN—VERT: 14k. Medallion with heads of Pestel, Ryleev, Bestuzhev-Ryumin, Muravev-Apostol and Kakhovsky.

114

1926. Sixth International Proletarian Esperanto Congress.

471	**114**	7k. red and green	5·75	3·75
472	**114**	14k. violet and green	7·50	2·50

115 Waifs

116 Lenin when a Child

1926. Child Welfare.

473B	**115**	10k. brown	1·90	1·30
474B	**116**	20k. blue	3·25	1·90

1927. Same type with new inscriptions.

475	**115**	8k.+2k. green	1·10	3·75
476	**116**	18k.+2k. red	2·50	5·00

ПОЧТОВАЯ
МАРКА
КОП. 8 КОП.
(117)

1927. Postage Due stamps surch with T **117**.

491	**D104**	8k. on 1k. red	2·00	3·75
492	**D104**	8k. on 2k. violet	2·00	3·75
493	**D104**	8k. on 3k. blue	2·00	3·75
494	**D104**	8k. on 7k. yellow	2·00	3·75
494b	**D104**	8k. on 8k. green	2·00	3·75
494d	**D104**	8k. on 10k. blue	2·00	3·75
494f	**D104**	8k. on 14k. brown	2·00	3·75

1927. Various types of 7k. surch (some values imperf or perf).

496	**92**	8k. on 7k. brown	14·00	18·00
523	**107**	8k. on 7k. blue	5·00	6·25
524	-	8k. on 7k. brn (No. 464c)	11·50	12·50
526	**114**	8k. on 7k. red and green	35·00	31·00
527	**112**	8k. on 7k. brown	14·00	19·00

119 Dr. Zamenhof

1927. 40th Anniv of Publication of Zamenhof's "Langue Internationale" (Esperanto).

498B	**119**	14k. green and brown	6·25	3·75

120 Tupolev ANT-3 Biplane and Map

1927. First Int Air Post Congress, The Hague.

499	**120**	10k. blue and brown	30·00	10·00
500	**120**	15k. red and olive	35·00	15·00

121 Worker, Soldier and Peasant

124 Sailor and Worker

122 Allegory of Revolution

1927. Tenth Anniv of October Revolution.

501	**121**	3k. red	3·25	1·50
502	**122**	5k. brown	7·50	3·75
503	-	7k. green	12·50	6·00
504	**124**	8k. black and brown	5·75	2·75
505	-	14k. red and blue	7·50	2·75
506	-	18k. blue	5·25	2·30
507	-	28k. brown	19·00	16·00

DESIGNS—HORIZ: (As Type **122**): HORIZ: 7k. Smolny Institute; 14k. Map of Russia inscr "C.C.C.P."; 18k. Various Russian races; 28k. Worker, soldier and peasant.

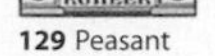

128 Worker **129** Peasant **130** Lenin

1927

508	**128**	1k. orange	1·30	65
509	**129**	2k. green	1·30	40
510	**128**	4k. blue	1·30	40
511	**129**	5k. brown	1·30	40
512	**129**	7k. red	7·00	1·60
513	**128**	8k. green	4·00	50
514	**128**	10k. brown	3·75	50
515	**130**	14k. green	4·00	75
516	**130**	18k. olive	7·00	1·30
517	**130**	18k. blue	6·00	1·30
518	**129**	20k. olive	4·50	65
519	**128**	40k. red	15·00	5·00
520	**129**	50k. blue	8·75	1·60
521	**128**	70k. olive	15·00	2·50
522	**129**	80k. orange	25·00	3·75

131 Infantryman, Lenin Mausoleum and Kremlin

1928. Tenth Anniv of Red Army.

529	**131**	8k. brown	3·50	75
530	-	14k. blue	4·00	1·30
531	-	18k. red	4·00	2·50
532	-	28k. green	6·25	5·75

DESIGNS: 14k. Sailor and cruiser "Aurora"; 18k. Cavalryman; 28k. Airman.

135 Young Factory Workers

1929. Child Welfare.

536	**135**	10k.+2k. brown & sepia	3·50	2·50
537	-	20k.+2k. blue & brown	6·25	5·00

DESIGN: 20k. Children in harvest field.

See also Nos. 567/8.

137 Trumpeter sounding the Assembly

1929. First All-Union Gathering of Pioneers.

538	**137**	10k. brown	28·00	19·00
539	**137**	14k. blue	15·00	10·00

141 Farm Girl

138 Worker (after I. Shadr) **139** Factory Girl **140** Peasant

142 Guardsman **143** Worker, Soldier and Peasant (after I. Smirnov) **144** Lenin **242a** Miner

242b Steel foundryman **242c** Infantryman **242d** Airman **242e** Arms of U.S.S.R.

149 Central Telegraph Office, Moscow **150** Lenin Hydro-electric Power Station

743a Farm Girl **743b** Architect **744** Furnaceman

1929. Perf, but some values exist imperf.

541	**138**	1k. yellow	1·50	25
542	**139**	2k. green	1·50	25
543	**140**	3k. blue	1·50	25
544	**141**	4k. mauve	1·90	40
545	**142**	5k. brown	2·50	50
847a	**242a**	5k. red	40	25
546	**143**	7k. red	2·50	65
547	**138**	10k. grey	3·25	75
727f	**139**	10k. blue	70·00	28·00
1214b	**139**	10k. black	12·00	5·50
554	**144**	14k. blue	1·90	1·00
548	**143**	15k. blue	3·75	1·00
847b	**242b**	15k. blue	2·20	1·90
847c	**242c**	15k. green	55	40
549	**140**	20k. green and blue	6·25	70
727h	**141**	20k. green	1·30	40
2252a	**743a**	20k. olive	40	25
2252b	**743b**	25k. brown	2·00	1·20
550	**139**	30k. violet and lilac	6·25	1·50
847d	**242d**	30k. blue	1·30	40
727l	**144**	40k. blue	1·50	90
727m	**141**	50k. brown and buff	1·90	5·00
847f	**242e**	60k. red	1·50	90
2253	**744**	60k. red	95	55
2253a	**744**	60k. blue	2·00	55
552	**142**	70k. red and pink	10·00	3·25
553	**140**	80k. brown and yellow	14·00	3·75
561	**149**	1r. blue	8·75	1·90
562	**150**	3r. brown and green	28·00	9·50

Nos. 727f, 1214b and 550 show the factory girl without factory in background. Nos. 549, 727m, 552, 553 have designs like those shown but with unshaded background.

151 Industry **153** "More metal more machines"

1929. Industrial Loan Propaganda.

563	**151**	5k. brown	3·25	2·50
564	-	10k. olive	9·50	7·50
565	**153**	20k. green	7·50	3·75
566	-	28k. violet	6·25	3·75

DESIGNS—HORIZ: 10k. Tractors. VERT: 28k. Blast furnace and graph of pig-iron output.

1930. Child Welfare.

567	**135**	10k.+2k. olive	3·75	5·00
568	-	20k.+2k. grn (as No. 537)	5·75	7·50

155 Cavalrymen (after M. Grekov)

1930. Tenth Anniv of 1st Red Cavalry.

569	**155**	2k. green	10·00	4·50
570	-	5k. brown	10·00	4·50
571	-	10k. olive	25·00	10·00
572	-	14k. blue and red	16·00	6·25

DESIGNS: 5k. Cavalry attack (after Yu. Merkulov); 10k. Cavalry facing left (after M. Grekov); 14k. Cavalry charge (after Yu. Merkulov).

159 Group of Soviet Pupils

1930. Educational Exhibition, Leningrad.

573	**159**	10k. green	3·50	1·30

160

1930. Air. "Graf-Zeppelin" (airship) Flight to Moscow.

574	**160**	40k. blue	65·00	31·00
575	**160**	80k. red	55·00	19·00

162 Battleship "Potemkin"

1930. 25th Anniv of 1905 Rebellion. Imperf or perf.

576b	**162**	3k. red	2·50	1·00
577b	-	5k. blue	3·75	1·80
578b	-	10k. red and green	8·75	2·50

DESIGNS—HORIZ: 5k. Barricade and rebels. VERT: 10k. Red flag at Presnya barricade.

165 From the Tundra (reindeer) to the Steppes (camel)

166 Above Dnieprostroi Dam

1931. Airship Construction Fund. Imperf or perf.

579c	**165**	10k. violet	7·50	7·00
580b	**166**	15k. blue	44·00	25·00
581c	-	20k. red	10·00	8·75
582b	-	50k. brown	12·50	7·50
583c	-	1r. green	14·00	19·00

DESIGNS—As Type **165**. VERT: 20k. Above Lenin's Mausoleum. HORIZ: 1r. Airship construction. As Type **166**: 50k. Above the North Pole.

See also No. E592.

170 "Graf Zeppelin" over Ice breaker "Malygin"

1931. Air. "Graf Zeppelin" (airship) North Pole Flight. Imperf or perf.

584	**170**	30k. purple	31·00	25·00
585b	**170**	35k. green	55·00	44·00
586	**170**	1r. black	44·00	38·00
587	**170**	2r. blue	31·00	25·00

172 Maksim Gorky

1932. 40th Anniv of Publication of "Makar Chadra".

590	**172**	15k. brown	14·00	5·00
591	**172**	35k. blue	44·00	20·00

1932. Airship Construction Fund. Imperf or perf.

592	**166**	15k. black	7·00	2·50

173 Storming the Winter Palace

1932. 15th Anniv of October Revolution.

593	-	3k. violet	3·75	2·50
594	**173**	5k. brown	3·75	2·50
595	-	10k. blue	5·25	5·00
596	-	15k. green	4·50	3·75
597	-	20k. red	8·75	6·25
598	-	30k. grey	28·00	19·00
599	-	35k. brown	£225	£275

DESIGNS—HORIZ: 10k. Dnieper Dam; 15k. Harvesting with combines; 20k. Industrial works, Magnitogorsk; 30k. Siberians listening to Moscow broadcast. VERT: 3k. Lenin's arrival in Petrograd; 35k. People of the World hailing Lenin.

175 "Liberation"

1932. Tenth Anniv of International Revolutionaries' Relief Organization.

600	**175**	50k. red	19·00	8·25

176 Museum of Fine Arts

1932. First All-Union Philatelic Exn, Moscow.

601	**176**	15k. brown	28·00	19·00
602	**176**	35k. blue	95·00	75·00

177 Trier, Marx's Birthplace

1933. 50th Death Anniv of Marx.

603	**177**	3k. green	15·00	1·60
604	-	10k. brown	19·00	3·25
605	-	35k. purple	65·00	21·00

DESIGNS—VERT: 10k. Marx's grave, Highgate Cemetery; 35k. Marx.

1933. Leningrad Philatelic Exhibition. Surch **LENINGRAD 1933** in Russian characters and premium.

606	**176**	15k.+30k. black & brn	£100	90·00
607	**176**	35k.+70k. blue	£250	£225

182 **183**

1933. Ethnographical Issue. Racial types.

608	-	1k. brown (Kazakhs)	12·50	2·50
609	**183**	2k. blue (Lesgins)	9·50	2·50
610	-	3k. green (Crimean Tatars)	16·00	3·75
611	-	4k. brown (Jews of Birobidzhan)	9·50	2·50
612	-	5k. red (Tungusians)	6·25	1·30
613	-	6k. blue (Buryats)	12·50	2·50
614	-	7k. brown (Chechens)	12·50	2·50
615	-	8k. red (Abkhazians)	12·50	2·50
616	-	9k. blue (Georgians)	12·50	2·50
617	-	10k. brown (Samoyedes)	9·50	2·50
618	-	14k. green (Yakuts)	9·50	2·50
619	-	15k. purple (Ukrainians)	9·50	2·50
620	-	15k. black (Uzbeks)	9·50	2·50
621	-	15k. blue (Tadzhiks)	9·50	2·50
622	-	15k. brown (Transcaucasians)	9·50	2·50
623	-	15k. green (Byelorussians)	9·50	2·50
624	-	15k. orange (Great Russians)	9·50	2·50
625	-	15k. red (Turkmens)	9·50	2·50
626	-	20k. blue (Koryaks)	18·00	3·75
627	-	30k. red (Bashkirs)	25·00	6·25

628	182	35k. brown (Chuvashes)	44·00	7·50

SIZES: Nos. 608, 610/11, 614/17, 626/7, As T **182**: Nos. 612/13, 618. As T **183**: Nos. 619/24, 48×22 mm. No. 625, 22×48 mm.

186 V. V. Vorovsky

1933. Communist Party Activists. Dated "1933", "1934" or "1935".

629	186	1k. green	1·90	75
718	-	2k. violet	6·25	5·75
630	-	3k. blue	3·50	1·30
719	-	4k. purple	12·50	10·00
631	-	5k. brown	9·50	2·50
632	-	10k. blue	21·00	7·50
633	-	15k. red	80·00	38·00
720	-	40k. brown	19·00	19·00

DESIGNS: 2k. M. Frunze; 3k. V. M. Volodarsky; 4k. N. E. Bauman; 5k. M. S. Uritsky; 10k. Iacov M. Sverdlov; 15k. Viktor P. Nogin; 40k. S. M. Kirov.

187 Stratosphere Balloon "U.S.S.R.-1" over Moscow

1933. Air. Stratosphere record (19000 m).

634	187	5k. blue	£190	38·00
635	187	10k. red	70·00	11·50
636	187	20k. violet	55·00	10·00

188 Massed Standard Bearers

1933. 15th Anniv of Order of Red Banner.

637	188	20k. red, yellow and black	6·25	3·25

189 Commissar Shaumyan

1934. 15th Death Anniv of 26 Baku Commissars.

638	189	4k. brown	19·00	2·50
639	-	5k. black	19·00	2·50
640	-	20k. violet	8·75	1·60
641	-	35k. blue	38·00	25·00
642	-	40k. red	31·00	6·25

DESIGNS: 5k. Commissar Dzhaparidze. HORIZ: 20k. The 26 condemned commissars; 35k. Monument in Baku; 40k. Workman, peasant and soldier dipping flags in salute.

190 Tupolev ANT-9 PS9 over Oilfield

1934. Air. Tenth Anniv of Soviet Civil Aviation and U.S.S.R. Airmail Service.

643B		5k. blue	31·00	10·00
644B	190	10k. green	31·00	10·00
645B	-	20k. red	65·00	11·50
646A	-	50k. blue	£160	50·00
647B	-	80k. violet	65·00	12·50

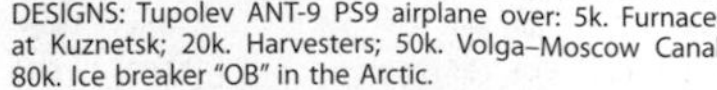

DESIGNS: Tupolev ANT-9 PS9 airplane over: 5k. Furnaces at Kuznetsk; 20k. Harvesters; 50k. Volga–Moscow Canal; 80k. Ice breaker "OB" in the Arctic.

191 New Lenin Mausoleum

1934. Tenth Death Anniv of Lenin.

648	191	5k. brown	5·00	1·40
649	191	10k. blue	38·00	5·75
650	191	15k. red	31·00	3·50
651	191	20k. green	5·00	1·40
652	191	35k. brown	50·00	4·50

192 Fyodorov Monument, Moscow, and Hand and Rotary Presses

1934. 350th Death Anniv of Ivan Fyodorov (first Russian printer).

653	192	20k. red	19·00	6·25
654	192	40k. blue	14·00	6·25

194 Dmitri Mendeleev

1934. Birth Centenary of Dmitri Mendeleev (chemist).

655	-	5k. green	10·00	2·50
656	194	10k. brown	50·00	11·50
657	194	15k. red	50·00	11·50
658	-	20k. blue	19·00	6·25

DESIGN—VERT: 5k., 20k. Mendeleev seated.

195 A. V. Vasenko and "Osoaviakhim"

1934. Air. Stratosphere Balloon "Osoaviakhim" Disaster Victims.

659		5k. purple	31·00	7·00
660	195	10k. brown	95·00	19·00
661	-	20k. violet	31·00	7·00
1042	-	1r. green	7·50	3·75
1043	195	1r. green	7·50	3·75
1044	-	1r. blue	7·50	3·75

DESIGNS: 5k., 1r. (No. 1042). I. D. Usyskin; 20k., 1r. (No. 1044), P. F. Fedoseenko.

The 1r. values, issued in 1944, commemorated the 10th anniv of the disaster.

196 Airship "Pravda"

1934. Air. Airship Travel Propaganda.

662	196	5k. red	31·00	12·50
663	-	10k. lake	31·00	12·50
664	-	15k. brown	95·00	31·00
665	-	20k. black	95·00	38·00
666	-	30k. blue	£225	38·00

DESIGNS—HORIZ: 10k. Airship landing; 15k. Airship "Voroshilov"; 30k. Airship "Lenin" and route map. VERT: 20k. Airship's gondolas and mooring mast.

199 Stalin and Marchers inspired by Lenin

1934. "Ten Years without Lenin". Portraits inscr "1924–1934".

667		1k. black and blue	9·50	2·50
668		3k. black and blue	9·50	2·50
669		5k. black and blue	19·00	7·50
670		10k. black and blue	15·00	2·50
671		20k. blue and orange	15·00	3·75
672	199	30k. red and orange	£130	55·00

DESIGN—VERT: 1k. Lenin aged 3; 3k. Lenin as student; 5k. Lenin as man; 10k. Lenin as orator. HORIZ: 20k. Red demonstration, Lenin's Mausoleum.

200 "War Clouds"

1935. Anti-War. Inscr "1914–1934".

673	200	5k. black	19·00	6·25
674	-	10k. blue	65·00	19·00
675	-	15k. green	£130	25·00
676	-	20k. brown	31·00	6·25
677	-	35k. red	£190	65·00

DESIGNS: 10k. "Flight from a burning village"; 15k. "Before war and afterwards"; 20k. "Ploughing with the sword"; 35k. "Fraternization".

202 Capt. Voronin and Ice-breaker "Chelyuskin"

1935. Air. Rescue of "Chelyuskin" Expedition.

678	202	1k. orange	12·50	2·50
679	-	3k. red	12·50	2·50
680	-	5k. green	12·50	2·50
681	-	10k. brown	31·00	3·75
682	-	15k. black	31·00	3·75
683	-	20k. purple	55·00	4·50
684	-	25k. blue	£190	38·00
685	-	30k. green	£375	65·00
686	-	40k. violet	65·00	6·25
687	202	50k. blue	£100	25·00

DESIGNS—HORIZ: 3k. Prof. Schmidt and Schmidt Camp; 50k. Schmidt Camp deserted. VERT: 5k. A. V. Lyapidevsky; 10k. S. A. Levanevsky; 15k. M. G. Slepnev; 20k. I. V. Doronin; 25k. M. V. Vodopyanov; 30k. V. S. Molokov; 40k. N. P. Kamanin.

205 Underground Station

1935. Opening of Moscow Underground.

688	-	5k. orange	31·00	4·50
689	-	10k. blue	19·00	3·75
690	205	15k. red	£225	38·00
691	-	20k. green	31·00	12·50

DESIGNS—As Type **205**: 5k. Excavating tunnel; 10k. Section of tunnel, escalator and station. 48½×23 mm: 20k. Train in station.

207 Rowing

1935. Spartacist Games.

692		1k. blue and orange	10·00	1·90
693		2k. blue and black	12·50	1·90
694	207	3k. brown and green	20·00	6·00
695	-	4k. blue and red	12·50	1·90
696	-	5k. brown and violet	12·50	1·90
697	-	10k. purple and red	24·00	4·00
698	-	15k. brown and black	£130	25·00
699	-	20k. blue and brown	25·00	8·25
700	-	35k. brown and blue	95·00	15·00
701	-	40k. red and brown	44·00	10·00

DESIGNS: 1k. Running; 2k. Diving; 4k. Football; 5k. Skiing; 10k. Cycling; 15k. Lawn tennis; 20k. Skating; 35k. Hurdling; 40k. Parade of athletes.

208 Friedrich Engels

1935. 40th Death Anniv of F. Engels.

702	208	5k. red	6·25	3·75
703	208	10k. green	7·00	5·00
704	208	15k. blue	38·00	12·50
705	208	20k. black	6·25	3·75

Перелет
Москва— 1 Р.
Сан-Франциско
через Сев. полюс
1935

(209)

1935. Air. Moscow–San Francisco via North Pole Flight. Surch with T **209**.

706	1r. on 10k. brown (No. 681)	£750	£1000

210 A "Lion Hunt" from a Sassanian Silver Plate

1935. Third International Congress of Persian Art and Archaeology, Leningrad.

707	210	5k. orange	19·00	1·90
708	210	10k. green	19·00	3·25
709	210	15k. purple	21·00	5·00
710	210	35k. brown	44·00	8·75

211 M. I. Kalinin

1935. Pres. Kalinin's 60th Birthday. Autographed portraits inscr "1875–1935".

711	-	3k. purple	90	30
712	-	5k. green	1·60	50
713	-	10k. blue	2·50	1·00
714	211	20k. brown	5·00	2·00

DESIGNS: 3k. Kalinin as machine worker; 5k. Harvester; 10k. Orator.

See also No. 1189.

212 Tolstoi

1935. 25th Death Anniv of Tolstoi (writer).

715b	-	3k. violet and black	1·90	1·40
716b	212	10k. brown and blue	5·75	2·50
717b	-	20k. brown and green	11·50	6·25

DESIGNS: 3k. Tolstoi in 1860; 20k. Monument in Moscow.

213 Pioneers securing Letter-box

1936. Pioneer Movement.

721	213	1k. green	1·00	55
722	213	2k. red	2·50	1·90
723b	-	3k. blue	3·25	2·50
724b	-	5k. red	6·25	1·60
725b	-	10k. blue	9·50	15·00
726	-	15k. brown	9·50	14·00

DESIGNS: 3, 5k. Pioneer preventing another from throwing stones; 10k. Pioneers disentangling kite line from telegraph wires; 15k. Girl pioneer saluting.

214 N. A. Dobrolyubov

1936. Birth Centenary of N. Dobrolyubov (author and critic).

727	214	10k. purple	6·25	10·00

215 Pushkin (after T. Paita)

1937. Death Centenary of A. S. Pushkin (poet).

728	215	10k. brown	80	90
729	215	20k. green	1·10	90
730	215	40k. red	2·00	1·00
731	-	50k. blue	3·75	2·00
732a	-	80k. red	7·50	2·50
733a	-	1r. green	23·00	5·75

DESIGN: 50k. to 1r. Pushkin's Monument, Moscow (A. Opekushin).

216 Pushkin Monument, Moscow (A. Operkushin)

1937. Pushkin Exn, Moscow. Sheet 105×89 mm.

MS733c **215** 10k. brown; **216** 50k. brown 31·00 £275

217 Meyerhold Theatre

1937. First Soviet Architectural Congress.

734	217	3k. red	3·25	1·00
735	-	5k. lake	3·25	50
736	217	10k. brown	5·00	65
737	-	15k. black	16·00	2·50
738	-	20k. olive	3·25	65
739	-	30k. black	3·75	90
740	-	40k. violet	3·75	1·40
741	-	50k. brown	6·25	3·25

MS741c 120×93 mm. 40k.×4 violet (as No. 740). Imperf 38·00 £150

DESIGNS—As T **217**: 5, 15k. G.P.O.; 20, 50k. Red Army Theatre. 45×27 mm: 30k. Hotel Moscow; 40k. Palace of Soviets.

218 F. E. Dzerzhinsky

1937. Tenth Death Anniv of Feliks Dzerzhinsky.

742	218	10k. brown	1·00	90
743	218	20k. green	1·60	1·90
744	218	40k. red	5·00	2·75
745	218	80k. red	9·50	4·50

219 Yakovlev Ya-7 Air 7

1937. Air. Air Force Exhibition.

746	219	10k. black and brown	2·50	65
747	-	20k. black and green	3·25	90
748	-	30k. black and brown	5·00	1·40
749	-	40k. black and purple	8·75	1·90
750	-	50k. black and violet	10·50	3·25
751	-	80k. brown and blue	31·00	3·75
752	-	1r. black, orange & brown	26·00	5·75

MS752b 165×90 mm. No. 752×4. Imperf £225 £750

DESIGNS—As T **219**: 20k. Tupolev ANT-9; 30k. Tupolev ANT-6 bomber; 40k. O.S.G.A. 101 flying boat; 50k. Tupolev ANT-4 TB-1 bomber. 60×26 mm: 80k. Tupolev ANT-20 "Maksim Gorki"; 1r. Tupolev ANT-14 "Pravda".

220 Arms of Ukraine

221 Arms of U.S.S.R.

1937. New U.S.S.R. Constitution. Arms of Constituent Republics.

753	-	20k. blue (Armenia)	4·50	2·40
754	-	20k. purple (Azerbaijan)	4·50	2·40
755	-	20k. brown (Byelorussia)	4·50	2·40
756	-	20k. red (Georgia)	4·50	2·40
757	-	20k. green (Kazakhstan)	4·50	2·40
758	-	20k. red (Kirghizia)	4·50	2·40
759	-	20k. red (Tadzhikistan)	4·50	2·40
760	-	20k. red (Turkmenistan)	4·50	2·40
761	220	20k. red (Ukraine)	4·50	2·40
762	-	20k. orange (Uzbekistan)	4·50	2·40
763	-	20k. blue (R.S.F.S.R.)	4·50	2·40
764	221	40k. red (U.S.S.R.)	9·50	4·00

222 "Worker and Collective Farmer" (sculpture, Vera Mukhina)

223 Russian Pavilion, Paris Exhibition

1938. Paris International Exhibition.

765	222	5k. red	1·50	65
766	223	20k. red	2·00	75
767	222	50k. blue	4·00	1·50

224 Shota Rustaveli

1938. 750th Anniv of Poem "Knight in Tiger Skin".

768	224	20k. green	2·00	90

225 Route of North Pole Flight

1938. North Pole Flight.

769	225	10k. black and brown	2·00	50
770	225	20k. black and grey	3·75	90
771	-	40k. red and green	14·00	4·50
772	-	80k. red and deep red	3·25	1·60

DESIGN: 40k., 80k. Soviet Flag at North Pole.

227 Infantryman

1938. 20th Anniv of Red Army.

773	227	10k. black and red	90	50
774	-	20k. black and red	1·10	50
775	-	30k. black, red and blue	1·90	65
776	-	40k. black, red and blue	2·75	1·30
777	-	50k. black and red	3·50	1·30
778a	-	80k. black and red	7·00	5·00
779	-	1r. black and red	4·00	2·75

DESIGNS—VERT: 20k. Tank driver; 30k. Sailor; 40k. Airman; 50k. Artilleryman. HORIZ: 80k. Stalin reviewing cavalry; 1r. Machine gunners.

229 G. Baidukov, V. Chkalov and A. Belyakov

1938. First Flight over North Pole.

780	229	10k. red and black	3·25	90
781	229	20k. red and black	3·25	90
782	229	40k. red and brown	6·25	2·75
783	229	50k. red and purple	9·50	5·00

230 M. Gromov, A. Yumashov and S. Danilin

1938. Second Flight over North Pole.

784	230	10k. purple	6·25	90
785	230	20k. black	5·25	1·90
786	230	50k. purple	10·50	2·50

231 Ice-breaker "Murman" approaching Survivors

1938. Rescue of Papanin's North Pole Meteorological Party.

787	231	10k. purple	5·00	80
788	231	20k. blue	5·00	1·30
789	-	30k. brown	12·50	1·90
790	-	50k. blue	16·00	3·50

DESIGNS—VERT: 30, 50k. Papanin survivors.

233 Nurse weighing Baby

234 Children visiting Statue of Lenin

1938. Soviet Union Children.

791	233	10k. blue	2·30	55
792	234	15k. blue	2·30	55
793	-	20k. purple	2·75	65
794	-	30k. red	4·00	90
795	-	40k. brown	4·50	1·00
796	-	50k. blue	12·50	2·75
797	-	80k. green	11·50	2·50

DESIGNS—HORIZ: 20, 40k. Biology class; 30k. Health camp; 50, 80k. Young inventors at play.

235 Crimean landscape

1938. Views of Crimea and Caucasus.

798	235	5k. black	3·25	1·00
799	A	5k. brown	3·25	1·00
800	B	10k. green	5·00	1·30
801	C	10k. brown	5·00	1·90
802	D	15k. black	8·75	3·75
803	A	15k. black	8·75	3·75
804	E	20k. brown	9·50	4·50
805	C	30k. black	12·50	4·50
806	F	40k. brown	14·00	4·50
807	G	50k. green	16·00	6·25
808	H	80k. brown	25·00	6·25
809	I	1r. green	44·00	8·75

DESIGNS—HORIZ: A, Yalta (two views); B, Georgian military road; E, Crimean resthouse; F, Alupka; H, Crimea; I, Swallows' Nest Castle. VERT: C, Crimea (two views); D, Swallows' Nest Castle; G, Gurzuf Park.

236 Schoolchildren and Model Tupolev ANT-6 Bomber

1938. Aviation.

810	236	5k. purple	3·25	1·30
811	-	10k. brown	3·25	1·30
812	-	15k. red	5·00	1·50
813	-	20k. blue	5·00	1·50
814	-	30k. red	6·25	2·75
815	-	40k. blue	9·50	3·00
816	-	50k. green	16·00	3·50
817	-	80k. brown	19·00	3·75
818	-	1r. green	31·00	4·50

DESIGNS—HORIZ: 10k. Glider in flight; 40k. Yakovlev VT-2 seaplane; 1r. Tupolev ANT-6 bomber. VERT: 15k. Captive observation balloon; 20k. Airship "Osoaviakhim" over Kremlin; 30k. Parachutists; 30k. Balloon in flight; 80k. Stratosphere balloon.

237 Underground Railway

1938. Moscow Underground Railway Extension.

819		10k. violet	2·50	1·60
820		15k. brown	2·75	1·90
821		20k. black	4·00	2·50
822		30k. violet	6·00	3·75
823	237	40k. black	7·50	5·00
824	-	50k. brown	12·50	10·00

DESIGNS—VERT: 10k. Mayakovskaya station; 15k. Sokol station; 20k. Kievsskaya station. HORIZ: 30k. Dynamo station; 50k. Revolutskaya station.

238 Miner and Pneumatic Drill

1938. 20th Anniv of Federation of Young Lenin Communists.

825		20k. blue	3·25	65
826	238	30k. purple	5·00	90
827	-	40k. purple	6·25	1·00
828	-	50k. red	19·00	1·90
829	-	80k. blue	31·00	2·50

DESIGNS—VERT: 20k. Girl parachutist; 50k. Students and university. HORIZ: 40k. Harvesting; 80k. Airman, sailor and battleship "Marat".

239 Diving

1938. Soviet Sports.

830	239	5k. red	2·50	65
831	-	10k. black	5·00	1·00
832	-	15k. brown	7·50	1·30
833	-	20k. green	10·00	1·90
834	-	30k. purple	16·00	2·50
835	-	40k. green	19·00	3·25
836	-	50k. blue	38·00	3·75
837	-	80k. blue	55·00	7·50

DESIGNS: 10k. Discus throwing; 15k. Tennis; 20k. Motor cycling; 30k. Skiing; 40k. Sprinting; 50k. Football; 80k. Athletic parade.

241 Council of People's Commissars Headquarters and Hotel Moscow

1939. New Moscow. Architectural designs as T **241**.

838		10k. brown	1·30	1·00
839	241	20k. green	2·10	1·50
840	-	30k. purple	2·75	1·90
841	-	40k. blue	5·00	3·25
842	-	50k. red	5·25	3·75
843	-	80k. olive	25·00	5·00

844	-	1r. blue	31·00	6·25

DESIGNS—HORIZ: 10k. Gorky Avenue; 30k. Lenin Library; 40k. Crimea suspension and 50k. Arched bridges over River Moskva; 80k. Khimki river station. VERT: 1r. Dynamo underground station.

242 Paulina Osipenko

1939. Women's Moscow–Far East Flight.

845	**242**	15k. green	3·75	1·30
846	-	30k. purple	3·75	1·90
847	-	60k. red	5·00	3·75

PORTRAITS: 30k. Marina Raskova; 60k. Valentina Grisodubova.

243 Russian Pavilion, N.Y. World's Fair

1939. New York World's Fair.

848		30k. red and black	3·25	90
849	**243**	50k. brown and blue	3·25	1·60

DESIGN—VERT: (26×41½ mm): 30k. Statue over Russian pavilion.

244 T. G. Shevchenko in early Manhood

1939. 125th Birth Anniv of Shevchenko (Ukrainian poet and painter).

853	**244**	15k. black and brown	3·75	1·00
854	-	30k. black and red	4·50	1·50
855	-	60k. brown and green	10·00	3·25

DESIGNS: 30k. Last portrait of Shevchenko; 60k. Monument to Shevchenko, Kharkov.

245 Milkmaid

1939. All Union Agricultural Fair.

856	**245**	10k. red	75	25
857	-	15k. red	75	30
858a	-	20k. grey	1·40	65
859	-	30k. orange	1·00	40
860	-	30k. violet	1·00	40
861	-	45k. green	1·60	45
862	-	50k. brown	1·60	40
863	-	60k. violet	2·50	65
864	-	80k. violet	1·30	1·00
865	-	1r. blue	3·50	1·50

DESIGNS—HORIZ: 15k. Harvesting; 20k. Sheep farming; 30k. (No. 860) Agricultural Fair Pavilion. VERT: 30k. (No. 859) Agricultural Fair Emblem; 45k. Gathering cotton; 50k. Thoroughbred horses; 60k. "Agricultural Wealth"; 80k. Girl with sugar beet; 1r. Trapper.

18 АВГУСТА
ДЕНЬ АВИАЦИИ СССР
(247)

1939. Aviation Day. As Nos. 811, 814/16 and 818 (colours changed) optd with T **247**.

866	10k. red	1·50	90
867	30k. blue	2·30	1·60
868	40k. green	2·75	2·30
869	50k. violet	3·50	2·75
870	1r. brown	7·50	5·50

1939. Surch.

871	**141**	30k. on 4k. mauve	23·00	28·00

249 Saltykov-Shchedrin

1939. 50th Death Anniv of M. E. Saltykov-Shchedrin (writer and satirist).

872	**249**	15k. red	75	40
873	-	30k. green	1·60	75
874	**249**	45k. brown	1·60	1·10
875	-	60k. blue	3·75	1·50

DESIGN: 30, 60k. Saltykov-Shchedrin in later years.

250 Kislovodsk Sanatorium

1939. Caucasian Health Resorts.

876	**250**	5k. brown	50	25
877	-	10k. red	65	40
878	-	15k. green	75	65
879	-	20k. green	1·00	65
880	-	30k. blue	1·30	1·30
881	-	50k. black	2·30	1·90
882	-	60k. purple	4·50	2·50
883	-	80k. red	5·00	3·75

DESIGNS: 10, 15, 30, 50, 80k. Sochi Convalescent Homes; 20k. Abkhazia Sanatorium, Novyi Afon; 60k. Sukumi Rest Home.

251 M. I. Lermontov

1939. 125th Birth Anniv of Lermontov (poet and novelist).

884	**251**	15k. brown and blue	2·50	1·30
885	-	30k. black and green	3·75	1·90
886	-	45k. blue and red	5·75	6·25

252 N. G. Chernyshevsky

1939. 50th Death Anniv of N. G. Chernyshevsky (writer and politician).

887B	**252**	15k. green	1·30	75
888A	**252**	30k. violet	2·75	1·40
889A	**252**	60k. green	4·50	3·25

253 A. P. Chekhov

1940. 80th Birth Anniv of Chekhov (writer).

890	**253**	10k. green	90	25
891	**253**	15k. blue	1·30	40
892	-	20k. violet	1·90	65
893	-	30k. brown	6·25	3·75

DESIGN: 20, 30k. Chekhov with hat on.

254 Welcoming Soviet Troops

1940. Occupation of Eastern Poland.

893a	**254**	10k. red	1·30	65
894	-	30k. green	1·50	1·30
895	-	50k. black	1·90	1·90
896	-	60k. blue	6·25	1·90
897	-	1r. red	9·50	3·25

DESIGNS: 30k. Villagers welcoming tank crew; 50, 60k. Soldier distributing newspapers to crowd; 1r. People waving to column of tanks.

255 Ice-breaker "Georgy Sedov" and Badigin and Trofimov

1940. Polar Research.

898		15k. green	2·20	1·30
899	**255**	30k. violet	4·50	1·90
900	-	50k. brown	7·00	3·25
901	-	1r. blue	14·00	5·75

DESIGNS: 15k. Ice-breaker "Iosif Stalin" and portraits of Papanin and Belousov; 50k. Badgin and Papanin meeting. LARGER. (46×26 mm): 1r. Route of drift of "Georgy Sedov".

256 V. Mayakovsky

1940. Tenth Death Anniv of Mayakovsky (poet).

902	**256**	15k. red	40	25
903	**256**	30k. brown	75	40
904	-	60k. violet	1·50	75
905	-	80k. blue	1·40	1·30

DESIGN—VERT: 60, 80k. Mayakovsky in profile wearing a cap.

257 Timiryazev

1940. 20th Death Anniv of K. A. Timiryazev (scientist).

906		10k. blue	75	65
907		15k. violet	75	65
908	**257**	30k. brown	1·60	1·90
909	-	60k. green	3·50	2·50

DESIGNS—HORIZ: 10k. Miniature of Timiryazev and Academy of Agricultural Sciences, Moscow; 15k. Timiryazev in laboratory. VERT: 60k. Timiryazev's statue (by S. Merkurov), Moscow.

258 Relay Runner

1940. Second All Union Physical Culture Festival.

910	**258**	15k. red	1·50	65
911a	-	30k. purple	2·50	65
912	-	50k. blue	4·50	1·30
913	-	60k. blue	4·50	2·50
914	-	1r. green	25·00	3·75

DESIGNS—HORIZ: 30k. Girls parade; 60k. Skiing; 1r. Grenade throwing. VERT: 50k. Children and sports badges.

259 Tchaikovsky and Passage from his "Fourth Symphony"

1940. Birth Cent of Tchaikovsky (composer).

915		15k. green	1·60	50
916	**259**	20k. brown	1·90	90
917	**259**	30k. blue	2·10	1·30
918	-	50k. red	7·50	1·90
919	-	60k. red	9·50	2·50

DESIGNS: 15, 50k. Tchaikovsky's house at Klin; 60k. Tchaikovsky and excerpt from "Eugene Onegin".

260 Central Regions Pavilion

ПАВИЛЬОН «ПОВОЛЖЬЕ»
No. 920

ПАВИЛЬОН «ДАЛЬНИЙ ВОСТОК»
No. 921

[illegible]
No. 922

ПАВИЛЬОН МОСКОВСКОЙ, РЯЗАНСКОЙ И ТУЛЬСКОЙ ОБЛ.
No. 923

ПАВИЛЬОН УКРАИНСКОЙ ССР
No. 924

ПАВИЛЬОН БЕЛОРУССКОЙ ССР
No. 925

ПАВИЛЬОН АЗЕРБАЙДЖАНСКОЙ ССР
No. 926

ПАВИЛЬОН ГРУЗИНСКОЙ ССР
No. 927

ПАВИЛЬОН АРМЯНСКОЙ ССР
No. 928

[illegible]
No. 929

ПАВИЛЬОН ТУРКМЕНСКОЙ ССР
No. 930

ПАВИЛЬОН КИРГИЗСКОЙ ССР
No. 931

ПАВИЛЬОН КАРЕЛО-ФИНСКОЙ ССР
No. 932

ГЛАВНЫЙ ПАВИЛЬОН
No. 933

ПАВИЛЬОН МЕХАНИЗАЦИИ
No. 934

ГЛАВНЫЙ ПАВИЛЬОН
No. 935

ПАВИЛЬОН МЕХАНИЗАЦИИ
No. 936

1940. All Union Agricultural Fair, Coloured reproductions of Soviet Pavilions in green frames as T **260**. Inscriptions at foot as illustrated.

920	10k. Volga provinces (RSFSR) (horiz)	2·30	1·60
921	15k. Far East	2·50	1·90
922	30k. Leningrad and North East RSFSR	3·25	2·50
923	30k. Three Central Regions (RSFSR)	3·25	2·50
924	30k. Ukrainian SSR	3·25	2·50
925	30k. Byelorussian SSR	3·25	2·50
926	30k. Azerbaijan SSR	3·25	2·50
927	30k. Georgian SSR (horiz)	3·25	2·50
928	30k. Armenian SSR	3·25	2·50
929	30k. Uzbek SSR	3·25	2·50
930	30k. Turkmen SSR (horiz)	3·25	2·50
931	30k. Tadzhik SSR	3·25	2·50
932	30k. Kirgiz SSR	3·25	2·50
933	30k. Karelo-Finnish SSR	3·25	2·50
934	30k. Kazakh SSR	3·25	2·50
935	50k. Main Pavilion	12·50	3·75
936	60k. Mechanization Pavilion and the statue of Stalin	16·00	5·00

261 Grenade Thrower

1940. 20th Anniv of Wrangel's Defeat at Perekop (Crimea). Perf or imperf.

937	-	10k. green	1·30	50
938	**261**	15k. red	1·30	50
939	-	30k. brown and red	1·30	1·80
940	-	50k. purple	1·60	1·10
941	-	60k. blue	1·60	1·10
942	-	1r. black	1·60	1·30

DESIGNS—VERT: 10k. Red Army Heroes Monument; 30k. Map of Perekop and portrait of M. V. Frunze; 1r. Victorious soldier. HORIZ: 50k. Soldiers crossing R. Sivash; 60k. Army H.Q. at Stroganovka.

262 Railway Bridge and Moscow–Volga Canal, Khimka

1941. Industrial and Agricultural Records.

943		10k. blue	1·30	1·00
944		15k. mauve	1·40	1·30
945	**262**	20k. blue	1·80	1·50
946	-	30k. brown	2·50	1·50
947	-	50k. brown	1·90	1·90
948	-	60k. brown	2·10	1·90
949	-	1r. green	4·50	3·25

DESIGNS—VERT: 10k. Coal-miners and pithead; 15k. Blast furnace; 1r. Derricks and petroleum refinery. HORIZ: 30k. Steam locomotives; 50k. Harvesting; 60k. Ball-bearing vehicles.

263 Red Army Ski Corps

1941. 23rd Anniv of Red Army. Designs with Hammer, Sickle and Star Symbol.

950	**263**	5k. violet	1·30	40
951	-	10k. blue	1·00	50
952	-	15k. green	75	50
953	-	20k. red	75	50
954a	-	30k. brown	90	40
955a	-	45k. green	3·25	1·00
956	-	50k. blue	1·30	1·30
957	-	1r. green	1·50	1·90
957b	-	3r. green	8·25	4·50

DESIGNS—VERT: 10k. Sailor; 20k. Cavalry; 30k. Automatic Rifle Squad; 50k. Airman; 1, 3r. Marshal's star. HORIZ: 15k. Artillery; 45k. Clearing a hurdle.

264 N. E. Zhukovsky and Air Force Academy

1941. 20th Death Anniv of Zhukovsky (scientist).

958		15k. blue	1·60	40
959	**264**	30k. red	3·25	65
960	-	50k. red	3·75	90

DESIGNS—VERT: 15k. Zhukovsky; 50k. Zhukovsky lecturing.

265 Thoroughbred Horses

1941. 15th Anniv of Kirghiz S.S.R.

961	**265**	15k. brown	3·25	90
962	-	30k. violet	3·50	1·60

DESIGN: 30k. Coal miner and colliery.

266 Arms of Karelo-Finnish S.S.R.

1941. First Anniv of Karelo-Finnish Republic.

963	**266**	30k. red	1·60	1·30
964	**266**	45k. green	1·90	1·80

267 Marshal Suvorov

1941. 150th Anniv of Battle of Izmail.

965	-	10k. green	1·30	40
966	-	15k. red	1·30	50
967	**267**	30k. blue	2·50	90
968	**267**	1r. brown	3·25	3·75

DESIGN: 10, 15k. Storming of Izmail.

268 Spassky Tower, Kremlin

1941

970	**268**	1r. red	3·25	1·00
971	-	2r. brown	5·00	2·10

DESIGN—HORIZ: 2r. Kremlin Palace.

269 "Razin on the Volga"

1941. 25th Death Anniv of Surikov (artist).

972		20k. black	4·50	2·50
973	**269**	30k. red	6·25	3·75
974	-	50k. purple	20·00	15·00
975	**269**	1r. green	30·00	19·00
976	-	2r. brown	48·00	25·00

DESIGNS—VERT: 20, 50k. "Suvorov's march through Alps, 1799"; 2r. Surikov.

270 Lenin Museum (interior)

1941. Fifth Anniv of Lenin Museum.

977	**270**	15k. red	5·00	6·25
978	-	30k. violet on mauve	44·00	38·00
979	**270**	45k. green	16·00	12·50
980	-	1r. red on rose	55·00	44·00

DESIGN: 30k., 1r. Exterior of Lenin Museum.

271 M. Yu. Lermontov

1941. Death Centenary of M. Yu. Lermontov (poet and novelist).

981	**271**	15k. grey	38·00	19·00
982	**271**	30k. violet	44·00	31·00

272 Poster by L. Lisitsky

1941. Mobilization.

983a	**272**	30k. red	25·00	44·00

273 Mass Enlistment

1941. National Defence.

984	**273**	30k. blue	£110	£130

274 Alishir Navoi

1942. Fifth Centenary of Uzbek poet Mir Ali Shir (Alishir Navoi).

985	**274**	30k. brown	55·00	65·00
986	**274**	1r. purple	41·00	50·00

275 Lt. Talalikhin ramming Enemy Bomber

289a Five Heroes

1942. Russian Heroes (1st issue).

987	**275**	20k. blue	1·30	1·10
988	**A**	30k. grey	1·30	1·10
989	**B**	30k. black	1·30	1·10
990	**C**	30k. black	1·30	1·10
991	**D**	30k. black	1·30	1·10
992	**C**	1r. green	16·00	7·50
993	**D**	2r. green	23·00	19·00
1048c	**275**	30k. green	1·40	1·10
1048d	**A**	30k. blue	1·40	1·10
1048e	**C**	30k. green	1·40	1·10
1048f	**D**	30k. purple	1·40	1·10
1048g	**289a**	30k. blue	1·40	1·10

DESIGNS: A, Capt. Gastello and burning fighter plane diving into enemy petrol tanks; B, Maj-Gen. Dovator and Cossack cavalry in action; C, Shura Chekalin guerrilla fighting; D, Zoya Kosmodemyanskaya being led to death.

See also Nos. 1072/6.

276 Anti-tank Gun

1942. War Episodes (1st series).

994	**276**	20k. brown	2·30	1·90
995	-	30k. blue	2·30	1·90
996	-	30k. green	2·30	1·90
997	-	30k. red	2·30	1·90
998	-	60k. grey	12·50	10·00
999	-	1r. brown	15·00	7·50

DESIGNS—HORIZ: 30k. (No. 996), Guerrillas attacking train; 30k. (No. 997), Munition worker; 1r. Machine gunners. VERT: 30k. (No. 995), Signallers; 60k. Defenders of Leningrad.

277 Distributing Gifts to Soldiers

1942. War Episodes (2nd series).

1000	**277**	20k. blue	2·00	1·90
1001	-	20k. purple	2·00	1·90
1002	-	30k. purple	2·75	2·50
1003	-	45k. red	7·50	8·75
1004	-	45k. blue	9·50	10·00

DESIGNS—VERT: No. 1001, Bomber destroying tank; No. 1002, Food packers; No. 1003, Woman sewing; No. 1004, Anti-aircraft gun.

See also Nos. 1013/17.

278 Munition Worker

1943. 25th Anniv of Russian Revolution.

1005	**278**	5k. brown	90	50
1006	-	10k. brown	90	50
1007	-	15k. blue	90	50
1008	-	20k. blue	90	50
1009	-	30k. brown	1·30	1·00
1010	-	60k. brown	1·90	1·80
1011	-	1r. red	8·75	2·50
1012	-	2r. brown	14·00	5·00

DESIGNS: 10k. Lorry convoy; 15k. Troops supporting Lenin's banner; 20k. Leningrad seen through an archway; 30k. Spassky Tower, Lenin and Stalin; 60k. Tank parade; 1r. Lenin speaking; 2r. Star of Order of Lenin.

279 Nurses and Wounded Soldier

1943. War Episodes (3rd series).

1013	**279**	30k. green	2·00	1·60
1014	-	30k. green (Scouts)	2·00	1·60
1015	-	30k. brown (Mine-thrower)	2·00	1·60
1016	-	60k. green (Anti-tank troops)	3·25	2·10
1017	-	60k. blue (Sniper)	3·25	2·10

280 Routes of Bering's Voyages

1943. Death Bicent of Vitus Bering (explorer).

1018		30k. blue	1·80	65
1019	**280**	60k. grey	3·25	1·30
1020	-	1r. green	8·75	3·75
1021	**280**	2r. brown	15·00	5·75

DESIGN: 30k., 1r. Mt. St. Ilya.

281 Gorky

1943. 75th Birth Anniv of Maksim Gorky (novelist).

1022	**281**	30k. green	1·60	50
1023	**281**	60k. blue	1·90	75

282 Order of the Great Patriotic War

(a) Order of Suvorov

1943. War Orders and Medals (1st series), Medals with ribbon attached.

1024	**282**	1r. black	3·50	3·75
1025	**a**	10r. olive	16·00	18·00

See also Nos. 1051/8, 1089/94, 1097/99a, 1172/86, 1197/1204 and 1776/80a.

283 Karl Marx

1943. 125th Birth Anniv of Marx.

1026	**283**	30k. blue	1·90	90
1027	**283**	60k. green	4·50	1·50

284 Naval Landing Party

1943. 25th Anniv of Red Army and Navy.

1028	**284**	20k. brown	35	40
1029	-	30k. green	45	40
1030	-	60k. green	1·30	1·00
1031	**284**	3r. blue	3·00	2·00

DESIGNS: 30k. Sailors and anti-aircraft gun; 60k. Tanks and infantry.

285 Ivan Turgenev

1943. 125th Birth Anniv of Ivan Turgenev (novelist).

1032	**285**	30k. green	31·00	38·00
1032a	**285**	60k. violet	50·00	55·00

286 Loading a Gun

1943. 25th Anniv of Young Communist League.

1033	**286**	15k. blue	65	30
1034	-	20k. orange	65	30
1035	-	30k. brown and red	65	30
1036a	-	1r. green	2·20	1·00
1037	-	2r. green	2·50	1·30

DESIGNS—As T **286**: 20k. Tank and banner; 1r. Infantrymen; 2r. Grenade thrower. 22½×28½ mm: 30k. Bayonet fighter and flag.

287 V. V. Mayakovsky

1943. 50th Birth Anniv of Mayakovsky (poet).

1038	287	30k. orange	1·10	90
1039	287	60k. blue	1·40	1·00

288 Memorial Tablet and Allied Flags

1943. Teheran Three Power Conference and 26th Anniv of Revolution.

1040	288	30k. black	1·90	65
1041	288	3r. blue	4·50	3·25

289 Defence of Odessa

1944. Liberation of Russian Towns.

1045	-	30k. brown and red	1·00	45
1046	-	30k. blue	1·00	45
1047	-	30k. green	1·00	45
1048	289	30k. green	1·00	45
MS1048b		139×105 mm. No. 1047×4. Imperf	23·00	25·00

DESIGNS: No. 1045, Stalingrad; No. 1046, Sevastopol; No. 1047, Leningrad.

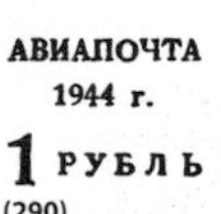
АВИАПОЧТА
1944 г.
1 РУБЛЬ
(290)

291 Order of Kutusov

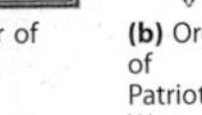
(b) Order of Patriotic War

(c) Order of Aleksandr Nevsky

(d) Order of Suvorov

(e) Order of Kutusov

1944. Air. Surch with T **290**.

1049	275	1r. on 30k. grey	2·50	1·30
1050	A	1r. on 30k. blue (No. 1048d)	2·50	1·30

1944. War Orders and Medals (2nd series). Various Stars without ribbons showing as Types **b** to **e**. Perf or imperf. (a) Frames as T **291**.

1051b	b	15k. red	45	40
1052b	c	20k. blue	45	40
1053	d	30k. green	1·30	65
1054	e	60k. red	2·10	1·10

(b) Frames as T **282**.

1055	b	1r. black	1·00	65
1056	c	3r. blue	1·60	1·90
1057	e	5r. green	4·50	3·25
1058	d	10r. red	5·25	4·50

293 Lenin Mausoleum and Red Square, Moscow

1944. "Twenty Years without Lenin". As Nos. 667/72, but inscr "1924–1944", and T **293**.

1059	-	30k. black and blue	50	40
1060	199	30k. red and orange	50	40
1061	-	45k. black and blue	65	65
1062	-	50k. black and blue	70	65
1063	-	60k. black and blue	75	65
1064	293	1r. brown and blue	3·25	1·90
1065	199	3r. black and orange	4·50	3·25

DESIGNS—VERT: Lenin at 3 years of age (No. 1059): at school (45k.); as man (50k.); as orator (60k.).

294 Allied Flags

1944. 14 June (Allied Nations' Day).

1066	294	60k. black, red and blue	1·90	1·30
1067	294	3r. blue and red	8·75	3·25

295 Rimsky-Korsakov and Bolshoi Theatre

1944. Birth Centenary of Rimsky-Korsakov (composer). Imperf or perf.

1068	295	30k. grey	45	25
1069	295	60k. green	65	40
1070	295	1r. green	1·30	50
1071	295	3r. violet	2·50	1·30

296 Nuradilov and Machine-gun

297 Polivanova and Kovshova

1944. War Heroes (3rd issue).

1072	296	30k. green	65	90
1073	-	60k. violet	1·30	90
1074	-	60k. blue	1·30	90
1075	297	60k. green	2·00	90
1076	-	60k. black	2·00	90

DESIGNS—HORIZ: No. 1073, Matrosov defending a snow-trench; 1074, Luzak hurling a hand grenade. VERT: No. 1076, B. Safonev, medals and aerial battle over the sea.

298 S. A. Chaplygin

1944. 75th Birth Anniv of S. A. Chaplygin (scientist).

1077	298	30k. grey	65	65
1078	298	1r. brown	1·80	1·90

299 V. I. Chapaev

1944. Heroes of 1918 Civil War.

1079	299	30k. green	1·10	50
1080	-	30k. black (N. Shchors)	1·10	50
1081	-	30k. green (S. Lazo)	1·10	50

For 40k. stamp as Type **299**, see No. 1531.
See also Nos. 1349/51.

300 Repin (self-portrait)

301 "Reply of the Cossacks to Sultan Mahmoud IV"

1944. Birth Centenary of Ilya Refimovich Repin (artist). Imperf or perf.

1082	300	30k. green	1·30	65
1083	301	50k. green	1·30	65
1084	301	60k. blue	1·30	65
1085	300	1r. brown	2·30	75
1086	301	2r. violet	3·50	2·50

302 I. A. Krylov

1944. Death Centenary of Krylov (fabulist).

1087	302	30k. brown	1·30	40
1088	302	1r. blue	2·50	65

(f) Partisans' Medal

(g) Medal for Bravery

(h) Order of Bogdan Chmielnitsky

(j) Order of Victory

(k) Order of Ushakov

(l) Order of Nakhimov

1945. War Orders and Medals (3rd series). Frame as T **291** with various centres as Types **f** to **l**. Perf or imperf.

1089	f	15k. black	50	40
1090	g	30k. blue	1·00	40
1091	h	45k. blue	1·60	65
1092	j	60k. red	2·50	70
1093	k	1r. blue	3·25	1·90
1094	l	1r. green	3·25	1·90

303 Griboedov (after P. Karatygin)

1945. 150th Birth Anniv of Aleksander S. Griboedov (author).

1095	303	30k. green	1·30	65
1096	303	60k. brown	2·50	1·90

1945. War Orders and Medals (4th series). Frames as T **282**. Various centres.

1097	g	1r. black	2·50	1·30
1098	h	2r. black	4·50	2·50
1098a	h	2r. purple	44·00	38·00
1098b	h	2r. olive	10·50	8·75
1099	j	3r. red	5·25	3·25
1099a	j	3r. purple	7·50	5·00

305 Soldier

1945. Relief of Stalingrad.

1100	305	60k. black and red	1·30	65
1101	305	3r. black and red	3·25	5·75
MS1101b		103×138 mm. No. 1101×4. Imperf	48·00	50·00

306 Standard Bearer

1945. Red Army Victories.

1102	306	20k. green, red and black	50	40
1103	-	30k. black and red	65	65
1104	-	1r. green and red	3·75	3·25

DESIGN—HORIZ: 30k. Infantry v. Tank; 1r. Infantry charge.

308 Attack

1945. Liberation of Russian Soil.

1105	308	30k. blue	65	65
1106	-	60k. red	1·00	1·90
1107	-	1r. green	3·75	3·25

DESIGNS: 60k. Welcoming troops; 1r. Grenade thrower.

309 Badge and Guns

1945. Red Guards Commemoration.

1108	309	60k. red	4·50	1·90

310 Barricade

1945. Battle of Moscow.

1109	-	30k. blue	50	40
1110	310	60k. black	90	75
1111	-	1r. black	1·60	1·50

DESIGNS: 30k. Tanks in Red Square, Moscow. 1r. Aerial battle and searchlights.

311 Prof. Lomonosov and Academy of Sciences, Leningrad

1945. 220th Anniv of Academy of Sciences.

1112		30k. blue	1·10	65
1113	311	2r. black	3·75	1·90

DESIGN—VERT: 30k. Moscow Academy, inscr "1725–1945".

312 Popov

1945. 50th Anniv of Popov's Radio Discoveries.

1114	312	30k. blue	95	40
1115	312	60k. red	1·30	90
1116	-	1r. brown (Popov)	2·10	1·50

314 Motherhood Medal

315 Motherhood Medal

1945. Orders and Medals of Motherhood. Imperf or perf.

1117b	314	20k. brown on blue	75	65
1118b	-	30k. brown on green	95	1·00
1119b	-	60k. red	2·20	2·00
1120	315	1r. black on green	1·90	1·00
1121	-	2r. blue	2·75	2·10
1122	-	3r. red on blue	4·00	4·50

DESIGNS: 30k., 2r. Order of Motherhood Glory; 60k., 3r. Order of Heroine-Mother.

317 Ilyushin Il-2M3 Stormovik Fighters

318 Petlyakov Pe-8 TB-7 Bomber

1945. Air. Aviation Day.

1123	316	1r. brown	3·75	1·50
1124	317	1r. brown	3·75	1·50
1125	-	1r. red	3·75	1·50
1126	-	1r. black	3·75	1·50
1127	-	1r. blue	3·75	1·50
1128	-	1r. green	3·75	1·50
1129	318	1r. grey	3·75	1·50
1130	-	1r. brown	3·75	1·50
1131	-	1r. red	3·75	1·50

DESIGNS—As Type **317**: No. 1125, Lavochkin La-7 fighter shooting tail off enemy plane; 1126, Ilyushin Il-4 DB-3 bombers dropping bombs; 1127, Tupolev ANT-60 Tu-2 bombers in flight; 1128, Polikarpov Po-2 biplane. As Type **318**: No. 1130, Yakovlev Yak-3 fighter destroying Messer-schmitt BF 109 fighter; 1131, Yakovlev Yak-9 fighter destroying Henschel Hs 129B fighter.
See also Nos. 1163/71.

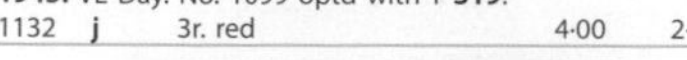

ПРАЗДНИК
ПОБЕДЫ

9 мая
1945 года

(319)

1945. VE Day. No. 1099 optd with T **319**.

1132	j	3r. red	4·00	2·50

320 Lenin

321 Lenin

1945. 75th Birth Anniv of Lenin.

1133	**320**	30k. blue	65	40
1134	-	50k. brown	1·00	50
1135	-	60k. red	1·10	65
1136	**321**	1r. black	2·00	75
1137	-	3r. brown	3·75	3·25

DESIGNS—VERT: (inscr "1870–1945"). 50k. Lenin at desk; 60k. Lenin making a speech; 3r. Portrait of Lenin.

322 Kutuzov (after R. Volkov)

1945. Birth Bicentenary of Mikhail Kutuzov (military leader).

1138	**322**	30k. blue	1·00	65
1139	**322**	60k. brown	1·80	2·50

323 A. I. Herzen

1945. 75th Death Anniv of Herzen (author and critic).

1140	**323**	30k. brown	90	65
1141	**323**	2r. black	3·00	1·30

324 I. I. Mechnikov

1945. Birth Centenary of Mechnikov (biologist).

1142	**324**	30k. brown	95	65
1143	**324**	1r. black	2·20	1·30

325 Friedrich Engels

1945. 125th Birth Anniv of Engels.

1144	**325**	30k. brown	95	65
1145	**325**	60k. green	1·90	1·60

326 Observer and Guns

327 Heavy Guns

1945. Artillery Day.

1146	**326**	30k. brown	1·90	2·50
1147	**327**	60k. black	4·25	4·50

328 Tank Production

1945. Home Front.

1148	**328**	20k. blue and brown	1·90	65
1149	-	30k. black and brown	2·30	90
1150	-	60k. brown and green	3·75	1·30
1151	-	1r. blue and brown	5·00	1·90

DESIGNS: 30k. Harvesting; 60k. Designing aircraft; 1r. Firework display.

329 Victory Medal

330 Soldier with Victory Flag

1946. Victory Issue.

1152	**329**	30k. violet	40	25
1153	**329**	30k. brown	40	25
1154	**329**	60k. black	95	40
1155	**329**	60k. brown	95	40
1156	**330**	60k. black and red	2·75	1·40

331 Arms of U.S.S.R.

332 Kremlin, Moscow

1946. Supreme Soviet Elections.

1157	**331**	30k. red	1·40	55
1158	**332**	45k. red	2·00	70
1159	**331**	60k. green	3·50	1·40

333 Tank Parade

334 Infantry Parade

1946. 28th Anniv of Red Army and Navy.

1160	**333**	60k. brown	4·00	2·75
1161	**333**	2r. violet	9·50	4·75
1162	**334**	3r. black and red	10·00	5·50

1946. Air. As Nos. 1123/31.

1163	-	5k. violet (as No. 1130)	70	40
1164	**316**	10k. red	70	45
1165	**317**	15k. red	1·10	70
1166	**318**	15k. green	1·10	70
1167	-	20k. black (as No. 1127)	1·40	1·10
1168	-	30k. violet (as No. 1127)	2·75	1·40
1169	-	30k. brown (as No. 1128)	2·75	1·40
1170	-	50k. blue (as No. 1125)	4·00	3·50
1171	-	60k. blue (as No. 1131)	5·50	4·00

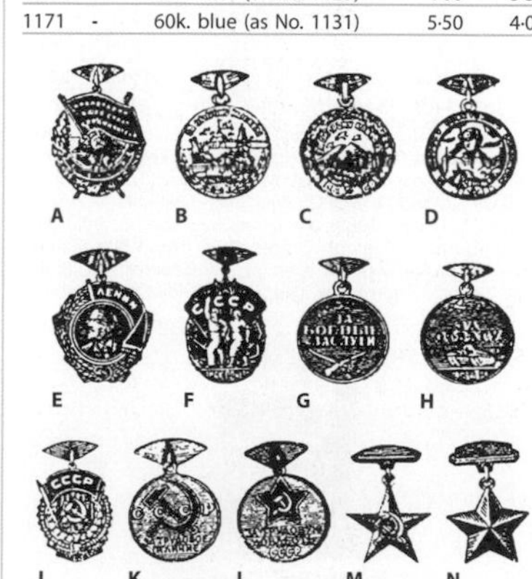

A B C D E F G H J K L M N O P

1946. War Orders with Medals (5th series). Frames as T **291** with various centres as Types **A** to **P**.

1172	**A**	60k. red	4·00	2·30
1173	**B**	60k. red	4·00	2·30
1174	**C**	60k. green	4·00	2·30
1175	**D**	60k. green	4·00	2·30
1176	**E**	60k. green	4·00	2·30
1177	**F**	60k. blue	4·00	2·30
1178	**G**	60k. blue	4·00	2·30
1179	**H**	60k. violet	4·00	2·30
1180	**J**	60k. purple	4·00	2·30
1181	**K**	60k. brown	4·00	2·30
1182	**L**	60k. brown	4·00	2·30
1183	**M**	60k. purple	4·00	2·30
1184	**N**	60k. red	4·00	2·30
1185	**O**	60k. blue	4·00	2·30
1186	**P**	60k. purple	4·00	2·30

336 P. L. Chebyshev

1946. 125th Birth Anniv of Chebyshev (mathematician).

1187	**336**	30k. brown	1·40	55
1188	**336**	60k. black	2·75	80

1946. Death of President Kalinin. As T **211**, but inscr "3-VI-1946".

1189		20k. black	4·75	2·00

337 Gorky

1946. Tenth Death Anniv of Maksim Gorky (novelist).

1190	**337**	30k. brown	1·40	70
1191	-	60k. green	2·75	1·40

DESIGN: 60k. Gorky and laurel leaves.

338 Gagry

1946. Health Resorts.

1192		15k. brown	70	25
1193	**338**	30k. green	1·40	40
1194	-	30k. green	1·40	40
1195	-	45k. brown	2·75	95

DESIGNS—HORIZ: 15k. Sukumi; 45k. Novy Afon. VERT: 30k. (No. 1194) Sochi.

339 Stalin and Parade of Athletes

1946. Sports Festival.

1196	**339**	30k. green	12·00	7·50

340 Partisan Medal

1946. War Medals (6th series). Frames as T **282** with various centres.

1197	**340**	1r. red	4·00	3·50
1198	**B**	1r. green	4·00	3·50
1199	**C**	1r. brown	4·00	3·50
1200	**D**	1r. blue	4·00	3·50
1201	**G**	1r. grey	4·00	3·50
1202	**H**	1r. red	4·00	3·50
1203	**K**	1r. purple	4·00	3·50
1204	**L**	1r. red	4·00	3·50

341 Moscow Opera House

1946. Moscow Buildings.

1205	-	5k. brown	40	25
1206	**341**	10k. grey	45	25
1207	-	15k. brown	70	40
1208	-	20k. brown	95	70
1209	-	45k. green	1·90	1·20
1210	-	50k. brown	2·00	1·40
1211	-	60k. violet	2·75	2·00
1212	-	1r. brown	4·75	3·50

DESIGNS—VERT: 5k. Church of Ivan the Great and Kremlin; 1r. Spassky Tower (larger). HORIZ: 15k. Hotel Moscow; 20k. Theatre and Sverdlov Square; 45k. As 5k. but horiz; 50k. Lenin Museum; 60k. St. Basil's Cathedral and Spassky Tower (larger).

342 Tanks in Red Square

1946. Heroes of Tank Engagements.

1213	**342**	30k. green	6·75	2·75
1214	**342**	60k. brown	3·50	2·00

343 "Iron"

1946. Fourth Stalin "Five-Year Reconstruction Plan". Agriculture and Industry.

1215	-	5k. olive	40	25
1216	-	10k. green	70	35
1217	-	15k. brown	1·10	55
1218	-	20k. violet	2·00	70
1219	**343**	30k. brown	2·75	80

DESIGNS—HORIZ: 5k. "Agriculture"; 15k. "Coal". VERT: 10k. "Oil"; 20k. "Steel".

344 Soviet Postage Stamps

1946. 25th Anniv of Soviet Postal Services.

1220	-	15k. black and red	4·00	2·00
1221	-	30k. brown and green	5·50	3·50
1222	**344**	60k. black and green	11·00	6·75
MS1222a		138×104 mm. 15k	£160	£140
MS1222b		132×104 mm. 30k	£160	£140
MS1222c		142×102 mm. 60k	£160	£140

DESIGNS: 15k. (48½×23 mm). Stamps on map of U.S.S.R.; 30k. (33×22½ mm). Reproduction of Type **47**.

345 Lenin and Stalin

1946. 29th Anniv of Russian Revolution. Imperf or Perf.

1223b	**345**	30k. orange	5·50	4·00
1224b	**345**	30k. green	5·50	4·00
MS1224c		101×134 mm. No. 1223×4. Imperf	£200	£140

346 N. A. Nekrasov

1946. 125th Birth Anniv of Nekrasov (poet).

1225	**346**	30k. black	2·00	40
1226	**346**	60k. brown	3·50	95

347 Stalin Prize Medal

1946. Stalin Prize.

1227	**347**	30k. green	6·75	1·60

348 Dnieperprostroi Dam

1946. Restoration of Dnieperprostroi Hydro-electric Power Station.

1228	**348**	30k. black	2·75	70
1229	**348**	60k. blue	6·75	2·00

349 A. Karpinsky

1947. Birth Centenary of Karpinsky (geologist).

1230	**349**	30k. green	2·00	1·10
1231	**349**	50k. black	4·00	1·60

350 N. E. Zhukovsky

1947. Birth Centenary of Zhukovsky (scientist).

1232	**350**	30k. black	2·00	95
1233	**350**	60k. blue	4·75	1·80

351 Lenin Mausoleum

352 Lenin

1947. 23rd Death Anniv of Lenin.

1234	**351**	30k. green	2·00	95
1235	**351**	30k. blue	2·00	95
1236	**352**	50k. brown	4·00	1·60

For similar designs inscr "1924/1948" see Nos. 1334/6.

353 Nikolai M. Przhevalsky

1947. Centenary of Soviet Geographical Society.

1237	-	20k. brown	2·40	1·10
1238	-	20k. blue	2·40	1·10
1239	**353**	60k. olive	6·00	4·75
1240	-	60k. brown	6·00	4·75

DESIGN: 20k. Miniature portrait of F. P. Litke and full-rigged ship "Senyavin".

354 Arms of R.S.F.S.R.

356 Arms of U.S.S.R.

1947. Supreme Soviet Elections. Arms of Constituent Republics. As T **354**.

1241	**354**	30k. red (Russian Federation)	2·40	1·60
1242	-	30k. brown (Armenia)	2·40	1·60
1243	-	30k. bistre (Azerbaijan)	2·40	1·60
1244	-	30k. green (Byelorussia)	2·40	1·60
1245	-	30k. grey (Estonia)	2·40	1·60
1246	-	30k. brown (Georgia)	2·40	1·60
1247	-	30k. purple (Karelo-Finnish S.S.R.)	2·40	1·60
1248	-	30k. orange (Kazakhstan)	2·40	1·60
1249	-	30k. purple (Kirgizia)	2·40	1·60
1250	-	30k. brown (Latvia)	2·40	1·60
1251	-	30k. green (Lithuania)	2·40	1·60
1252	-	30k. purple (Moldavia)	2·40	1·60
1253	-	30k. green (Tadzhikistan)	2·40	1·60
1254	-	30k. black (Turkmenistan)	2·40	1·60
1255	-	30k. blue (Ukraine)	2·40	1·60
1256	-	30k. brown (Uzbekistan)	2·40	1·60
1257	**356**	1r. multicoloured	9·50	4·00

A hammer and sickle in the centre of No. 1247 and at the base of No. 1249 should assist identification.

357 Russian Soldier

1947. 29th Anniv of Soviet Army. Perf or imperf.

1258b	**357**	20k. black	1·40	80
1259b	-	30k. blue	2·00	1·40
1260b	-	30k. brown	2·00	1·40

DESIGNS—VERT: No. 1259, Military cadet. HORIZ: No. 1260, Soldier, sailor and airman.

359 A. S. Pushkin

1947. 110th Death Anniv of Pushkin (poet).

1261	**359**	30k. black	1·40	1·10
1262	**359**	50k. green	3·50	1·60

360 Schoolroom

1947. International Women's Day.

1263	**360**	15k. blue	6·75	3·50
1264	-	30k. red	16·00	6·75

DESIGN—26½×39½ mm: 30k. Women students and banner.

362 Moscow Council Building

1947. 30th Anniv of Moscow Soviet. Perf or imperf.

1265b	**362**	30k. red, blue and black	6·00	2·75

363 May Day Procession

1947. May Day.

1266	**363**	30k. red	2·75	2·00
1267	**363**	1r. green	11·00	6·00

364 Yakovlev Yak-9 Fighter and Flag

1947. Air Force Day.

1268	**364**	30k. violet	1·10	55
1269	**364**	1r. blue	4·00	2·00

365 Yakhromsky Lock

1947. Tenth Anniv of Volga–Moscow Canal.

1270	-	30k. black	1·40	25
1271	**365**	30k. lake	1·40	25
1272	-	45k. red	1·90	55
1273	-	50k. blue	2·00	60
1274	-	60k. red	2·75	80
1275	-	1r. violet	4·00	1·40

DESIGNS—HORIZ: 30k. (No. 1270), Karamyshevsky Dam; 45k. Yakhromsky Pumping Station; 50k. Khimki Pier; 1r. Lock No. 8. VERT: 60k. Map of Volga–Moscow Canal.

800 лет Москвы
1147—1947 гг.
(366)

1947. 800th Anniv of Moscow (1st issue). Optd as T **366**.

1276	20k. brown (No. 1208)	1·40	70
1277	50k. brown (No. 1210)	2·75	1·10
1278	60k. violet (No. 1211)	4·00	1·40
1279	1r. brown (No. 1212)	5·50	2·75

See also Nos. 1286/1300.

367 Izmailovskaya Station

1947. Opening of New Moscow Underground Stations. Inscr "M".

1280	**367**	30k. blue	1·40	35
1281	-	30k. brown	1·40	35
1282	-	45k. brown	2·00	70
1283	-	45k. violet	2·00	70
1284	-	60k. green	2·75	1·40
1285	-	60k. red	2·75	1·40

DESIGNS—HORIZ: No. 1281, Power plant; No. 1282, Sokol underground station; No. 1283, Stalinskaya underground station; No. 1284, Kievskaya underground station. VERT: No. 1285, Maya Kovskaya underground station.

368 Crimea Bridge, Moscow

1947. 800th Anniv of Moscow (2nd issue).

1286	**368**	5k. brown and blue	45	25
1287	-	10k. black and brown	70	25
1288	-	30k. grey	2·00	70
1289	-	30k. blue	2·00	70
1290	-	30k. brown	2·00	70
1291	-	30k. green	2·00	70
1292	-	30k. green	2·00	70
1293	-	50k. green	2·75	1·40
1294	-	60k. blue	3·50	1·10
1295	-	60k. black and brown	3·50	1·10
1296	-	1r. purple	6·75	2·75
		Centre in yellow, red and blue.		
1297		1r. blue	6·75	2·75
1298		2r. red	13·50	5·50
1299		3r. blue	27·00	8·00
1300		5r. blue	41·00	20·00
MS1300b		140×175 mm. No. 1299	£100	80·00

DESIGNS—VERT: 10k. Gorky Street, Moscow; 30k. (No. 1292), Pushkin Place; 60k. (No. 1294), 2r. Kremlin; 1r. (No. 1296), "Old Moscow" after A. M. Vasnetsov; 1r. (No. 1279), St. Basil Cathedral. HORIZ: 30k. (No. 1288), Kiev railway station; 30k. (No. 1289), Kazan railway station; 30k. (No. 1290), Central Telegraph Offices; 30k. (No. 1291), Kaluga Street; 50k. Kremlin; 3r. Kremlin; 5r. Government Buildings. (54½×24½ mm): 60k. (No. 1295), Bridge and Kremlin.

369 "Ritz", Gagry

1947. U.S.S.R. Health Resorts. (a) Vertical.

1301	**369**	30k. green	1·60	55
1302	-	30k. green (Sukhumi)	1·60	55

370 "Zapadugol", Sochi

(b) Horizontal.

1303	**370**	30k. black	1·60	55
1304	-	30k. brown ("New Riviera", Sochi)	1·60	55
1305	-	30k. purple ("Voroshilov", Sochi)	1·60	55
1306	-	30k. violet ("Gulripsh", Sukhumi)	1·60	55
1307	-	30k. blue ("Kemeri", Riga)	1·60	55
1308	-	30k. brown ("Abkhazia", Novyi Afon)	1·60	55
1309	-	30k. bistre ("Krestyansky", Livadia)	1·60	55
1310	-	30k. blue ("Kirov", Kislovodsk)	1·60	55

371 1917 Revolution

1947. 30th Anniv of Revolution. Perf or imperf.

1311	**371**	30k. black and red	1·40	1·10
1312b	-	50k. blue and red	2·00	1·80
1313b	**371**	60k. black and red	2·75	2·20
1314b	-	60k. brown and red	2·75	2·20
1315b	-	1r. black and red	4·75	4·00
1316b	-	2r. green and red	10·00	8·00

DESIGNS: 50k., 1r. "Industry"; 60k. (No. 1314), 2r. "Agriculture".

372 Metallurgical Works

1947. Post-War Five Year Plan. Horiz industrial designs. All dated "1947" except No. 1324. Perf or imperf.

1317	**372**	15k. brown	70	40
1318	-	20k. brown (Foundry)	80	55
1319	**372**	30k. purple	1·40	70
1320	-	30k. green (Harvesting machines)	1·40	70
1321	-	30k. brown (Tractor)	1·40	70
1322	-	30k. brown (Tractors)	1·40	70
1323	-	60k. bistre (Harvesting machines)	2·75	2·00
1324	-	60k. purple (Builders)	2·75	2·00
1325	-	1r. orange (Foundry)	5·50	2·75
1326	-	1r. red (Tractor)	5·50	2·75
1327	-	1r. violet (Tractors)	5·50	2·75

373 Spassky Tower, Kremlin

1947

1328	**373**	60k. red	19·00	11·50
1329a	**373**	1r. red	2·75	90

374 Peter I Monument

1948. Fourth Anniv of Relief of Leningrad.

1330	-	30k. violet	1·40	40
1331	**374**	50k. green	2·40	70
1332	-	60k. black	2·75	95
1333	-	1r. violet	5·50	2·00

DESIGNS—HORIZ: 30k. Winter Palace; 60k. Peter and Paul Fortress; 1r. Smolny Institute.

1948. 24th Death Anniv of Lenin. As issue of 1947, but dated "1924 1928".

1334	**351**	30k. red	2·00	80
1335	**351**	60k. blue	3·50	1·60
1336	**352**	60k. green	4·00	2·00

376 Government Building, Kiev

1948. 30th Anniv of Ukrainian S.S.R. Various designs inscr "XXX" and "1917–1947".

1337	**376**	30k. blue	1·40	70
1338	-	50k. violet	2·50	1·20
1339	-	60k. brown	2·75	1·40
1340	-	1r. brown	4·00	2·75

DESIGNS: 50k. Dnieper hydro-electric power station; 60k. Wheatfield and granary; 1r. Metallurgical works and colliery.

377 Vasily I. Surikov

1948. Birth Centenary of Surikov (artist).

1341	**377**	30k. brown	2·00	1·00
1342	**377**	60k. green	4·75	1·80

378 Skiing

1948. R.S.F.S.R. Games.

1343	**378**	15k. blue	3·50	70
1344	-	20k. blue	4·75	95

DESIGN—VERT: 20k. Motor cyclist crossing stream.

379 Artillery

380 Bulganin and Military School

1948. 30th Anniv of Founding of Soviet Defence Forces and of Civil War. (a) Various designs with arms and inscr "1918 XXX 1948".

1345	**379**	30k. brown	2·00	95
1346	-	30k. grey	2·00	95
1347	-	30k. blue	2·00	95
1348	**380**	60k. brown	4·75	2·00

DESIGNS—VERT: No. 1346, Navy. HORIZ: No. 1347, Air Force.

(b) Portraits of Civil War Heroes as Nos. 1079/81.

1349	**299**	60k. brown (Chapaev)	3·50	2·75
1350	-	60k. green (Shchors)	3·50	2·75
1351	-	60k. blue (Lazo)	3·50	2·75

381 Karl Marx and Friedrich Engels

1948. Centenary of Publication of "Communist Manifesto".

1352	**381**	30k. black	2·30	1·10
1353	**381**	50k. brown	3·50	2·00

382 Miner

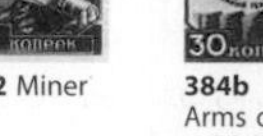
384b Arms of U.S.S.R.

384d Spassky Tower, Kremlin

1948

1354	**382**	5k. black	2·00	1·40
1355	-	10k. violet (Sailor)	3·50	2·00
1356	-	15k. blue (Airman)	5·00	3·50
1361i	**382**	15k. black	1·80	95
1357	-	20k. brown (Farm girl)	6·00	4·75
1361j	-	20k. green (Farm girl)	2·00	1·40
1361ka	-	25k. blue (Airman)	1·40	1·10
1358	**384b**	30k. brown	9·50	6·75
1361l	-	30k. brown (Scientist)	2·40	3·00
1361n	**384b**	40k. red	8·00	2·75
1359	-	45k. violet (Scientist)	20·00	9·50
1361f	**384d**	50k. blue	70·00	41·00
1361	-	60k. green (Soldier)	34·00	20·00

385 Parade of Workers

1948. May Day.

1362	**385**	30k. red	2·00	1·40
1363	**385**	60k. blue	6·75	2·75

386 Belinsky (after K. Gorbunov)

1948. Death Centenary of Vissarion Grigorievich Belinsky (literary critic and journalist).

1364	**386**	30k. brown	2·75	1·40
1365	**386**	50k. green	5·50	2·20
1366	**386**	60k. violet	6·75	2·75

387 Ostrovsky

388 Ostrovsky (after V. Perov)

1948. 125th Birth Anniv of Aleksandr Ostrovsky (dramatist).

1367	**387**	30k. green	2·75	1·40
1368	**388**	60k. brown	4·00	2·75
1369	**388**	1r. violet	7·50	5·50

389 I. I. Shishkin (after I. Kramskoi)

390 "Rye Field"

1948. 50th Death Anniv of Shishkin (landscape painter).

1370	**389**	30k. brown and green	6·75	4·00
1371	**390**	50k. yellow, red and blue	12·00	7·50
1372	-	60k. multicoloured	13·50	8·00
1373	**389**	1r. blue and brown	27·00	13·50

DESIGN—HORIZ: 60k. "Morning in the Forest".

391 Factories

1948. Leningrad Workers' Four-Year Plan.

1374	**391**	15k. brown and red	4·75	2·00
1375	-	30k. black and red	5·50	4·00
1376	**391**	60k. brown and red	8·00	5·50

DESIGN—HORIZ (40×22 mm): 30k. Proclamation to Leningrad workers.

392 Arms and People of the U.S.S.R.

1948. 25th Anniv of U.S.S.R.

1377	**392**	30k. black and red	4·00	2·00
1378	**392**	60k. olive and red	8·00	6·00

393 Caterpillar drawing Seed Drills

1948. Five Year Agricultural Plan.

1379	**393**	30k. red	2·00	80
1380	**393**	30k. green	2·00	80
1381	-	45k. brown	3·00	1·40
1382	**393**	50k. black	3·50	2·00
1383	-	60k. green	4·00	2·75
1384	-	60k. green	4·00	2·75
1385	-	1r. violet	6·75	3·50

DESIGNS: 30k. (No. 1380), 1r. Harvesting sugar beet; 45, 60k. (No. 1383), Gathering cotton; 60k. (No. 1384), Harvesting machine.

НЮЛЬ
1948
года
(394)

1948. Air Force Day. Optd with T **394**.

1386	**364**	30k. violet	6·75	4·75
1387	**364**	1r. blue	11·00	10·00

395 Miners

1948. Miners' Day.

1388	**395**	30k. blue	2·00	1·10
1389	-	60k. violet	4·00	2·00
1390	-	1r. green	7·50	3·50

DESIGNS: 60k. Inside a coal mine; 1r. Miner's emblem.

396 A. Zhdanov

1948. Death of A. A. Zhdanov (statesman).

1391	**396**	40k. blue	5·50	2·75

397 Sailor

1948. Navy Day.

1392	**397**	30k. green	4·00	2·00
1393	**397**	60k. blue	8·00	4·00

398 Football

1948. Sports.

1394	-	15k. violet	1·80	20
1395a	**398**	30k. brown	3·50	35
1396	-	45k. brown	4·00	45
1397a	-	50k. blue	5·50	45

DESIGNS—VERT: 15k. Running; 50k. Diving. HORIZ: 45k. Power boat racing.

399 Tank and Drivers

1948. Tank Drivers' Day.

1398	**399**	30k. black	5·50	2·75
1399	-	1r. red	8·00	6·75

DESIGN: 1r. Parade of tanks.

400 Horses and Groom

1948. Five Year Livestock Development Plan.

1400	**400**	30k. black	13·50	6·75
1401	-	60k. green	20·00	11·00
1402	**400**	1r. brown	34·00	16·00

DESIGN: 60k. Dairy farming.

401 Steam and Electric Locomotives

1948. Five Year Transport Plan.

1403	**401**	30k. brown	13·50	5·50
1404	**401**	50k. green	27·00	8·00
1405	-	60k. blue	47·00	13·50
1406	-	1r. violet	55·00	20·00

DESIGNS: 60k. Road traffic; 1r. Liner "Vyacheslav Molotov".

402 Iron Pipe Manufacture

1948. Five Year Rolled Iron, Steel and Machine-building Plan.

1407		30k. violet	2·75	1·60
1408		30k. purple	2·75	1·60
1409		50k. brown	4·50	2·75
1410		50k. black	4·50	2·75
1411		60k. brown	6·75	3·50
1412	**402**	60k. red	6·75	3·50
1413	**402**	1r. blue	8·00	4·75

DESIGNS—HORIZ: Nos. 1407, 1410, Foundry; No. 1408/9, Pouring molten metal; No. 1411, Group of machines.

403 Abovyan

1948. Death Centenary of Khachatur Abovyan (writer).

1414	**403**	40k. purple	5·50	4·00
1415	**403**	50k. green	11·00	6·75

404 Miner

1948. Five Year Coal Mining and Oil Extraction Plan.

1416	**404**	30k. black	19·00	1·60
1417	**404**	60k. brown	27·00	4·00
1418	-	60k. brown	27·00	4·00
1419	-	1r. green	85·00	6·75

DESIGN: Nos. 1418/19, Oil wells and tanker train.

405 Farkhadsk Power Station

1948. Five Year Electrification Plan.

1420	**405**	30k. green	9·50	5·50
1421	-	60k. red	13·00	6·00
1422	**405**	1r. red	12·50	6·50

DESIGN: 60k. Zuevsk Power Station.

406 Flying Model Aircraft

1948. Government Care of School Children's Summer Vacation.

1423	**406**	30k. green	30·00	5·50
1424	-	45k. red	50·00	20·00
1425	-	45k. violet	35·00	8·00
1426	-	60k. blue	47·00	20·00
1427	-	1r. blue	£100	27·00

DESIGNS—VERT: No. 1424, Boy and girl saluting; 60k. Boy trumpeter. HORIZ: No. 1425, Children marching; 1r. Children round camp fire.

407 Children in School

408 Flag of U.S.S.R.

1948. 30th Anniv of Lenin's Young Communist League.

1428		20k. purple	15·00	2·20
1429		25k. red	16·00	2·75
1430		40k. brown and red	22·00	4·75
1431	**407**	50k. green	30·00	5·50
1432	**408**	1r. multicoloured	85·00	22·00
1433	-	2r. violet	55·00	20·00

DESIGNS—HORIZ: 20k. Youth parade. VERT: 25k. Peasant girl; 40k. Young people and flag; 2r. Industrial worker.

409 Interior of Theatre

1948. 50th Anniv of Moscow Arts Theatre.

1434	**409**	50k. blue	9·50	8·00
1435	-	1r. purple	18·00	15·00

DESIGN: 1r. Stanislavsky and Dantchenko.

410 Searchlights over Moscow

1948. 31st Anniv of October Revolution.

1436	**410**	40k. red	8·00	5·50
1437	**410**	1r. green	15·00	11·00

411 Artillery Barrage

1948. Artillery Day.

1438	**411**	30k. blue	37·00	13·50
1439	**411**	1r. red	65·00	27·00

412 Trade Union Building (venue)

1948. 16th World Chess Championship, Moscow.

1440	**412**	30k. blue	16·00	2·00
1441	-	40k. violet	11·00	2·30
1442	**412**	50k. brown	13·50	2·75

DESIGN—VERT: 40k. Players' badge showing chessboard and rook.

413 Stasov and Building

1948. Death Centenary of Stasov (architect).

1443	-	40k. brown	5·75	4·00
1444	**413**	1r. black	13·00	5·50

DESIGN—VERT: 40k. Portrait of Stasov.

414 Yakovlev Yak-9 Fighters and Flag

1948. Air Force Day.

1445a	**414**	1r. blue	13·50	5·50

415 Statue of Ya. M. Sverdlov

1948. 225th Anniv of Sverdlovsk City. Imperf or perf.

1446b	**415**	30k. blue	3·50	70
1447b	-	40k. purple	2·75	70
1448b	**415**	1r. green	2·75	70

DESIGN: 40k. View of Sverdlovsk.

416 Sukhumi

1948. Views of Crimea and Caucasus.

1449	**416**	40k. green	5·00	75
1450	-	40k. violet	5·00	75
1451	-	40k. mauve	5·00	75
1452	-	40k. brown	5·00	75
1453	-	40k. purple	5·00	75
1454	-	40k. green	5·00	75
1455	-	40k. blue	5·00	75
1456	-	40k. green	5·00	75

DESIGNS—VERT: No. 1450, Gardens, Sochi; 1451, Eagle-topped monument, Pyatigorsk; 1452, Cliffs, Crimea. HORIZ: No. 1453, Terraced gardens, Sochi; 1454, Roadside garden, Sochi; 1455, Colonnade, Kislovodsk; 1456, Seascape, Gagry.

417 State Emblem

1949. 30th Anniv of Byelorussian Soviet Republic.

1457	**417**	40k. red	5·75	2·75
1458	**417**	1r. green	9·00	4·00

418 M. V. Lomonosov

1949. Establishment of Lomonosov Museum of Academy of Sciences.

1459	**418**	40k. brown	6·50	4·00
1460	**418**	50k. green	9·50	4·50
1461	-	1r. blue	18·00	9·75

DESIGN—HORIZ: 1r. Museum.

419 Lenin Mausoleum

1949. 25th Death Anniv of Lenin.

1462	**419**	40k. brown and green	17·00	9·75
1463	**419**	1r. brown & deep brown	32·00	24·00
MS1463a		175×132 mm. No. 1463×4	£550	£600

420 Dezhnev's Ship

1949. 300th Anniv of Dezhnev's Exploration of Bering Strait.

1464	-	40k. green	27·00	16·00
1465	**420**	1r. grey	60·00	34·00

DESIGN: 40k. Cape Dezhnev.

421 "Women in Industry"

1949. International Women's Day.

1466	**421**	20k. violet	80	25
1467	-	25k. blue	1·40	25
1468	-	40k. red	2·00	40
1469	-	50k. grey	2·75	55
1470	-	50k. brown	2·75	55
1471	-	1r. green	4·50	80
1472	-	2r. red	7·75	2·00

DESIGNS—HORIZ: 25k. Kindergarten; 50k. grey, Woman teacher; 50k. brown, Women in field; 1r. Women sports champions. VERT: 40k., 2r. Woman broadcasting.

422 Admiral S. O. Makarov

1949. Birth Centenary of Admiral S. O. Makarov (naval scientist).

1473	**422**	40k. blue	6·00	3·75
1474	**422**	1r. red	14·00	5·75

423 Soldier

1949. 31st Anniv of Soviet Army.

1475	**423**	40k. red	24·00	17·00

424 Kirov Military Medical Academy

1949. 150th Anniv of Kirov Military Medical Academy.

1476	**424**	40k. red	5·50	3·50
1477	-	50k. blue	8·75	5·50
1478	**424**	1r. green	13·00	7·50

DESIGN: 50k. Professors Botkin, Pirogov and Sechenov and Kirov Academy.

425 V. R. Williams

1949. Agricultural Reform.

1479	**425**	25k. green	6·75	4·75
1480	**425**	50k. brown	13·50	8·75

425a Three Russians with Flag

1949. Labour Day.

1481	**425a**	40k. red	4·00	2·00
1482	**425a**	1r. green	11·00	4·00

426 Newspapers and Books

1949. Press Day. Inscr "5 MAR 1949".

1483	**426**	40k. red	10·00	6·75
1484	-	1r. violet	24·00	13·50

DESIGN: 1r. Man and boy reading newspaper.

427 A. S. Popov and Radio Equipment

1949. Radio Day.

1485	**427**	40k. violet	6·75	4·00
1486	-	50k. brown	13·50	6·00
1487	**427**	1r. green	17·00	10·00

DESIGN—HORIZ: 50k. Popov demonstrating receiver to Admiral Makarov.

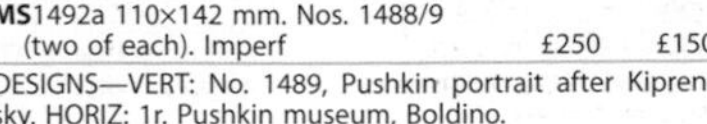

428 A. S. Pushkin

429 "Pushkin reading Poems to Southern Society" (Dmitry Kardovsky)

1949. 150th Birth Anniv of Pushkin (poet).

1488	**428**	25k. black and grey	4·00	2·00
1489	-	40k. black and brown	8·00	3·50
1490	**429**	40k. purple and red	8·00	3·50
1491	-	1r. grey and brown	19·00	9·50
1492	**429**	2r. blue and brown	37·00	20·00
MS1492a		110×142 mm. Nos. 1488/9 (two of each). Imperf	£250	£150

DESIGNS—VERT: No. 1489, Pushkin portrait after Kiprensky. HORIZ: 1r. Pushkin museum, Boldino.

430 "Boksimi Typlokod" (tug)

1949. Centenary of Krasnoe Sormovo Machine-building and Ship-building Plant, Gorky.

1493	**430**	40k. blue	24·00	9·50
1494	-	1r. brown	55·00	24·00

DESIGN: 1r. Freighter "Bolshaya Volga".

431 I. V. Michurin

1949. Agricultural Reform.

1495	**431**	40k. blue	6·50	2·00
1496	**431**	1r. green	14·00	4·50

432 Yachting

1949. National Sports.

1497	**432**	20k. blue	1·40	25
1498	-	25k. green	1·40	35
1499	-	30k. violet	2·20	35
1500	-	40k. brown	2·75	50
1501	-	40k. green	2·75	50
1502	-	50k. grey	3·00	65
1503	-	1r. red	6·50	1·50
1504	-	2r. black	13·50	2·75

DESIGNS: 25k. Canoeing; 30k. Swimming; 40k. (No. 1500), Cycling; 40k. (No. 1501), Football; 50k. Mountaineering; 1r. Parachuting; 2r. High jumping.

433 V. V. Dokuchaev

1949. Soil Research.

1505	**433**	40k. brown	3·50	70
1506	**433**	1r. green	6·75	1·40

434 V. I. Bazhenov

1949. 150th Death Anniv of V. I. Bazhenov (architect).

1507	**434**	40k. violet	4·50	80
1508	**434**	1r. brown	10·00	2·75

435 A. N. Radischev

1949. Birth Bicent of A. N. Radischev (writer).

1509	**435**	40k. green	17·00	6·00
1510	**435**	1r. grey	37·00	10·00

436 Green Cape Sanatorium, Makhindzhauri

1949. State Sanatoria. Designs showing various buildings.

1511	**436**	40k. green	1·60	40
1512	-	40k. green	1·60	40
1513	-	40k. blue	1·60	40
1514	-	40k. violet	1·60	40
1515	-	40k. red	1·60	40
1516	-	40k. orange	1·60	40
1517	-	40k. brown	1·60	40
1518	-	40k. brown	1·60	40
1519	-	40k. black	1·60	40

1520	-	40k. black	1·60	40

DESIGNS—HORIZ: No. 1512, VTsSPS No. 41, Zheleznovodsk; No. 1513, Energetics, Hosta; No. 1514, VTsSPS No. 3, Kislovodsk; No. 1515, VTsSPS No. 3, Hosta; No. 1516, State Theatre, Sochi; No. 1517, Clinical, Tskhaltubo; No. 1518, Frunze, Sochi; No. 1519, VTsSPS No. 1, Kislovodsk; No. 1520, Communication, Hosta.

437 I. P. Pavlov

1949. Birth Centenary of I. P. Pavlov (scientist).

1521	**437**	40k. brown	4·50	85
1522	**437**	1r. black	9·75	1·50

438 Globe and Letters

1949. 75th Anniv of U.P.U. Perf or imperf.

1523b	**438**	40k. blue and brown	2·75	70
1524b	**438**	50k. violet and blue	3·50	1·40

439 Tree Planting Machines

440 Map of S. W. Russia

1949. Forestry and Field Conservancy.

1525	**439**	25k. green	28·00	13·00
1526	-	40k. violet	6·50	2·75
1527	**440**	40k. green and black	11·00	5·75
1528	-	50k. blue	10·00	4·75
1529	**439**	1r. black	18·00	9·50
1530	-	2r. brown	22·00	12·50

DESIGNS—33×22½ mm: 40k. violet, Harvesters; 50k. River scene. 33×19½ mm: 2r. Old man and children.

1949. 30th Death Anniv of V. I. Chapaev (military strategist).

1531	**299**	40k. orange	44·00	28·00

442 I. S. Nikitin (after P. Borel)

1949. 125th Birth Anniv of Nikitin (poet).

1532	**442**	40k. brown	1·80	70
1533	**442**	1r. blue	3·75	95

443 Malyi Theatre, Moscow

1949. 125th Anniv of Malyi Theatre, Moscow.

1534	**443**	40k. green	3·50	55
1535	**443**	50k. orange	4·25	70
1536	-	1r. brown	11·50	2·00

DESIGN: 1r. Five portraits and theatre.

444 Crowd with Banner

1949. 32nd Anniv of October Revolution.

1537	**444**	40k. red	6·75	4·75
1538	**444**	1r. green	13·00	12·00

445 Sheep and Cows

1949. Cattle-breeding Collective Farm.

1539	**445**	40k. brown	6·50	80
1540	**445**	1r. violet	11·00	2·00

446 Lenin Hydro-electric Station, Caucasus

447 Ilyushin Il-12 Airliners and Map

1949. Air. Aerial views and map.

1541	**446**	50k. brown on yellow	4·50	1·40
1542	-	60k. brown on buff	7·00	2·00
1543	-	1r. orange on yellow	8·50	2·00
1544	-	1r. brown on buff	9·00	2·75
1545	-	1r. blue on blue	10·50	2·75
1546	**447**	1r. blue, red and grey	25·00	13·50
1547	-	2r. red on blue	31·00	13·50
1548	-	3r. green on blue	42·00	11·00

DESIGNS—Ilyushin Il-12 airplane over: HORIZ: No. 1542, Farm; 1543, Sochi. VERT: 1544, Leningrad; 1545, Aleppo; 1547, Moscow; 1548, Arctic.

448 Ski Jumping

1949. National Sports.

1549	**448**	20k. green	1·50	40
1550	-	40k. orange	3·00	70
1551	-	50k. blue	3·75	90
1552	-	1r. red	7·50	1·10
1553	-	2r. violet	15·00	2·10

DESIGNS: 40k. Girl gymnast; 50k. Ice hockey; 1r. Weight-lifting; 2r. Shooting wolves.

449 Diesel-electric Train

1949. Modern Railway Development.

1554		25k. red	3·75	80
1555	**449**	40k. violet	4·75	1·40
1556	-	50k. brown	7·00	2·00
1557	**449**	1r. green	16·00	3·50

DESIGNS: 25k. Electric tram; 50k. Steam train.

450 Arms of U.S.S.R.

1949. Constitution Day.

1558	**450**	40k. red	26·00	8·00

451 Government Buildings, Dushanbe

1949. 20th Anniv of Republic of Tadzhikstan.

1559	-	20k. blue	2·75	15
1560	-	25k. green	2·75	15
1561	**451**	40k. red	4·50	55
1562	-	50k. violet	6·50	1·10
1563	**451**	1r. black	11·50	1·50

DESIGNS: 20k. Textile mills; 25k. Irrigation canal; 50k. Medical University.

451a Stalin's Birthplace

1949. Stalin's 70th Birthday. Sheet 177×233 mm. Multicoloured.

MS1563a 40k. Type **451a**; 40k. Lenin and Stalin in Leningrad, 1917; 40k. Lenin and Stalin in Gorky; 40k. Marshal Stalin	£250	£250

452 People with Flag

1949. Tenth Anniv of Incorporation of West Ukraine and West Byelorussia in U.S.S.R.

1564	**452**	40k. red	28·00	20·00
1565	-	40k. orange	28·00	20·00

DESIGN—VERT: No. 1565, Ukrainians and flag.

453 Worker and Globe

1949. Peace Propaganda.

1566	**453**	40k. red	4·00	70
1567	**453**	50k. blue	6·75	2·00

454 Government Buildings, Tashkent

1950. 25th Anniv of Uzbek S.S.R.

1568	-	20k. blue	80	35
1569	-	25k. black	1·40	35
1570	**454**	40k. red	2·00	35
1571	-	40k. violet	2·75	35
1572	-	1r. green	5·50	1·00
1573	-	2r. brown	8·00	2·30

DESIGNS: 20k. Teachers' College; 25k. Opera and Ballet House, Tashkent; 40k. (violet) Navots Street, Tashkent; 1r. Map of Fergana Canal; 2r. Lock, Fergana Canal.

455 Dam

1950. 25th Anniv of Turkmen S.S.R.

1574		25k. black	9·50	8·00
1575	**455**	40k. brown	5·50	2·75
1576	-	50k. green	8·50	5·50
1577	**455**	1r. violet	17·00	9·50

DESIGNS: 25k. Textile factory, Ashkhabad; 50k. Carpet-making.

456 "Lenin at Rozliv" (sculpture, V. Pinchuk)

1950. 26th Death Anniv of Lenin.

1578	**456**	40k. brown and grey	4·00	45
1579	-	50k. red, brown and green	4·75	70
1580	-	1r. buff, green and brown	12·00	2·75

DESIGNS—HORIZ: 50k. Lenin's Office, Kremlin; 1r. Lenin Museum, Gorky.

457 Film Show

1950. 30th Anniv of Soviet Film Industry.

1581	**457**	25k. brown	55·00	34·00

458 Voter

1950. Supreme Soviet Elections. Inscr "12 MAPTA 1950".

1582	**458**	40k. green on yellow	24·00	11·00
1583	-	1r. red	44·00	19·00

DESIGN: 1r. Kremlin and flags.

459 Monument (I. Rabinovich)

1950. Unveiling of Monument in Moscow to Pavlik Morozov (model Soviet youth).

1584	**459**	40k. black and red	20·00	8·00
1585	**459**	1r. green and red	41·00	16·00

460 Lenin Central Museum

1950. Moscow Museums. Buildings inscr "MOCKBA 1949".

1586	**460**	40k. olive	4·00	55
1587	-	40k. red	4·00	55
1588	-	40k. turquoise	4·00	55
1589	-	40k. brown	4·00	55
1590	-	40k. mauve	4·00	55
1591	-	40k. blue (no tree)	4·00	55
1592	-	40k. brown	4·00	55
1593	-	40k. blue (with tree)	4·00	55
1594	-	40k. red	4·00	55

DESIGNS—HORIZ: (33½×23½ mm): No. 1587, Revolution Museum; 1588, Tretyakov Gallery; 1589, Timiryazev Biological Museum; No. 1591, Polytechnic Museum; 1593, Oriental Museum. (39½×26½ mm): No. 1590, Pushkin Pictorial Arts Museum. VERT: (22½×33½ mm): No. 1592, Historical Museum; 1594, Zoological Museum.

461 Hemispheres and Wireless Mast

1950. International Congress of P.T.T. and Radio Trade Unions, London.

1595	**461**	40k. green on blue	12·00	6·00
1596	**461**	50k. blue on blue	23·00	7·50

462 Three Workers

1950. Labour Day.

1597	**462**	40k. red and black	20·00	4·75
1598	-	1r. red and black	27·00	9·50

DESIGN—HORIZ: 1r. Four Russians and banner.

463 A. S. Shcherbakov

1950. Fifth Death Anniv of Shcherbakov (statesman).

1599	**463**	40k. black	13·50	2·00
1600	**463**	1r. green on pink	22·00	4·75

464 Suvorov (after N. Utkin)

1950. 150th Death Anniv of Suvorov.

1601	**464**	40k. blue on pink	13·50	5·75
1602	-	50k. brown on pink	22·00	8·00
1603	-	60k. black on blue	23·00	11·00
1604	**464**	1r. brown on yellow	29·00	16·00
1605	-	2r. green	50·00	24·00

DESIGNS—32½×47 mm: 50k. "Suvorov crossing the Alps" (V. I. Surikov). 24½×39½ mm—60k. Order of Suvorov and military parade (after portrait by N. Smdyak). 19½×33½ mm—2r. "Suvorov in the Alps" (N. Abbakumov).

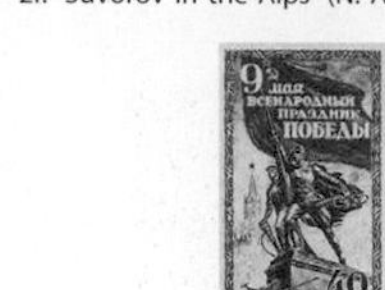

465 Statue

1950. Fifth Anniv of Victory over Germany.

1606	**465**	40k. red and brown	34·00	11·00
1607	-	1r. red	37·00	13·50

DESIGN—22½×33 mm: 1r. Medal for the Victory over Germany (profile of Stalin and Order of Victory).

466 Sowing on Collective Farm

1950. Agricultural Workers.

1608		40k. green on blue	11·00	4·00
1609	**466**	40k. brown on pink	11·00	4·00
1610	**466**	1r. blue on yellow	27·00	12·00

DESIGNS: No. 1608, Collective farmers studying.

467 G. M. Dimitrov

1950. First Death Anniv of Bulgarian Premier, Dimitrov.

1611	**467**	40k. black on yellow	11·00	4·00
1612	**467**	1r. black on orange	27·00	9·50

468 State Opera and Ballet House, Baku

1950. 30th Anniv of Azerbaijan S.S.R.

1613	**468**	25k. green on yellow	9·50	4·00
1614	-	40k. brown on red	13·50	8·00
1615	-	1r. black on orange	20·00	9·75

DESIGNS: 40k. Science Academy; 1r. Stalin Avenue, Baku.

469 Lenin Street, Stalingrad

1950. Stalingrad Reconstruction.

1616		20k. blue	2·00	2·75
1617	**469**	40k. green	2·75	4·00
1618	-	50k. orange	8·00	6·75
1619	-	1r. black	13·50	11·00

DESIGNS—VERT: 20k. Pobeda Cinema. HORIZ: 50k. Gorky Theatre; 1r. Pavlov House and Tank Memorial.

470 Kaluzhskaya Station

1950. Underground Railway Stations.

1620	**470**	40k. green on buff	4·75	1·00
1621	**A**	40k. red	4·75	1·00
1622	**B**	40k. blue on buff	4·75	1·00
1623	**C**	1r. brown on yellow	8·50	3·00
1624	**D**	1r. violet on blue	8·50	3·00
1625	**A**	1r. green on yellow	8·50	3·00
1626	**E**	1r. black on orange	8·50	3·00

DESIGNS—HORIZ: (34×22½ mm): A, Culture Park; B, Taganskaya; C, Kurskaya; D, Paveletskaya. (34×18½ mm): E, Taganskaya.

471 National Flags and Civilians

1950. Unconquerable Democracy. Flags in red, blue and yellow.

1627	**471**	40k. black	6·75	1·40
1628	**471**	50k. brown	9·50	2·00
1629	**471**	1r. green	13·50	2·75

472 Trade Union Building

1950. Tenth Anniv of Latvian S.S.R.

1630	**472**	25k. brown	3·50	2·00
1631	-	40k. red	4·75	2·30
1632	-	50k. green	20·00	5·50
1633	-	60k. blue	11·00	4·75
1634	-	1r. violet	25·00	11·00
1635	-	2r. brown	27·00	13·00

DESIGNS—VERT: 40k. Cabinet Council Offices; 50k. Monument to Jan Rainis (poet); 2r. Academy of Sciences. HORIZ: 60k. Theatre, Riga; 1r. State University, Riga.

473 Marite Melnikaite

1950. Tenth Anniv of Lithuanian S.S.R.

1636		25k. blue	13·50	4·00
1637	**473**	40k. brown	20·00	8·50
1638	-	1r. red	45·00	18·00

DESIGNS—HORIZ: 25k. Academy of Sciences; 1r. Cabinet Council Offices.

474 Stalingrad Square, Tallinn

1950. Tenth Anniv of Estonian S.S.R.

1639	**474**	25k. green	4·00	2·75
1640	-	40k. red	6·75	4·00
1641	-	50k. blue on yellow	13·50	5·50
1642	-	1r. brown on blue	41·00	15·00

DESIGNS—HORIZ: 40k. Government building; 50k. Opera and Ballet Theatre, Tallin. VERT: 1r. Viktor Kingisepp (revolutionary).

475 Signing Peace Appeal

1950. Peace Conference.

1643	**475**	40k. red on pink	4·00	3·50
1644	-	40k. black	4·00	3·50
1645	-	50k. red	7·75	4·00
1646	**475**	1r. brown on pink	22·00	8·75

DESIGNS—VERT: 40k. black, Children and teacher; 50k. Young people with banner.

476 Bellingshausan Lazarev and Globe

1950. 130th Anniv of First Antarctic Expedition.

1647	**476**	40k. red on blue	41·00	22·00
1648	-	1r. violet on blue	90·00	50·00

DESIGN—VERT: 1r. "Mirnyi" and "Vostok" (ships) and map of Antarctica.

477 Frunze (after I. Brodsky)

1950. 25th Death Anniv of M.V. Frunze (military strategist).

1649	**477**	40k. blue on pink	13·50	5·50
1650	**477**	1r. brown on blue	41·00	16·00

478 M. I. Kalinin

1950. 75th Birth Anniv of Kalinin (statesman).

1651	**478**	40k. green	4·00	2·00
1652	**478**	1r. brown	9·50	3·50
1653	**478**	5r. violet	20·00	10·00

479 Picking Grapes

1950. 30th Anniv of Armenian S.S.R.

1654	**479**	20k. blue on pink	2·75	2·00
1655	-	40k. orange on blue	5·50	4·00
1656	-	1r. black on yellow	19·00	9·50

DESIGNS—HORIZ: (33×16 mm): 40k. Government Offices. VERT: (21½×33 mm): 1r. G. M. Sundukian (dramatist).

480 Kotelnicheskaya Quay

1950. Moscow Building Projects.

1657	**480**	1r. brown on pink	70·00	47·00
1658	-	1r. black on pink	70·00	47·00
1659	-	1r. brown on blue	70·00	47·00
1660	-	1r. green on yellow	70·00	47·00
1661	-	1r. blue on pink	70·00	47·00
1662	-	1r. black	70·00	47·00
1663	-	1r. orange	70·00	47·00
1664	-	1r. green on blue	70·00	47·00

DESIGNS—HORIZ: No. 1659, Vosstaniya Square; 1660, Smolenskaya Square; 1662, Krasnye Vorota; 1664, Moscow University. VERT: No. 1658, Hotel Ukraine, Dorogomilovskaya Quay; 1661, Hotel Leningrad; 1663, Zaryade.

481 Spassky Tower, Kremlin

1950. 33rd Anniv of October Revolution.

1665	**481**	1r. red, yellow and green	55·00	20·00

482 "Golden Autumn"

1950. 50th Death Anniv of Levitan (painter).

1666	**482**	40k. multicoloured	13·50	1·40
1667	-	50k. brown	17·00	5·50

DESIGN: 50k. Portrait of Levitan by V. Serov.

483 Aivazovsky (after A. Tyranov)

1950. 50th Death Anniv of Aivazovsky (painter). Multicoloured centres.

1668		40k. brown	5·50	1·40
1669		50k. brown	8·00	2·00
1670	**483**	1r. blue	13·50	3·50

PAINTINGS—HORIZ: 40k. "Black Sea"; 50k. "Ninth Wave".

484 Newspapers "Iskra" and "Pravda"

1950. 50th Anniv of Newspaper "Iskra".

1671	-	40k. red and black	55·00	13·50
1672	**484**	1r. red and black	£120	34·00

DESIGN: 40k. Newspapers and banners.

485 Government Offices

1950. 30th Anniv of Kazakh S.S.R.

1673	**485**	40k. black on blue	12·00	7·75
1674	-	1r. brown on yellow	32·00	12·00

DESIGN: 1r. Opera House, Alma-Ata.

486 Decembrists and "Decembrist Rising in Senate Square, St. Petersburg, 14 December 1825" (K. Kolman)

1950. 125th Anniv of Decembrist Rising.

1675	**486**	1r. brown on yellow	37·00	16·00

487 Govt Offices, Tirana

1951. Friendship with Albania.

1676	**487**	40k. green on blue	55·00	31·00

488 Greeting Soviet Troops

1951. Friendship with Bulgaria.

1677	**488**	25k. black on blue	11·50	6·00
1678	-	40k. orange on pink	19·00	12·00
1679	-	60k. brown on orange	30·00	19·00

DESIGNS: 40k. Lenin Square, Sofia; 60k. Monument to Soviet fighters, Kolarovgrad.

489 Lenin at Razliv

1951. 27th Death Anniv of Lenin. Multicoloured centres.

1680	**489**	40k. green	8·00	1·40
1681	-	1r. blue	16·00	3·50

DESIGN: 1r. Lenin talking to young Communists.

490 Horses

1951. 25th Anniv of Kirghiz S.S.R.

1682	**490**	25k. brown on blue	13·50	9·50
1683	-	40k. green on blue	30·00	18·00

DESIGN—33×22½ mm: 40k. Government Offices, Frunze.

490a Gathering Lemons

1951. 30th Anniv of Georgia S.S.R.

1683a		20k. green on yellow	3·75	2·40
1683b	**490a**	25k. orange and violet	4·00	2·75
1683c	-	40k. brown on blue	19·00	13·50
1683d	-	1r. green and brown	13·50	8·00

DESIGNS—VERT: 20k. State Opera and Ballet Theatre, Tbilisi. HORIZ: 40k. Rustaveli Avenue, Tbilisi; 1r. Plucking tea.

491 University, Ulan Bator

1951. Friendship with Mongolia.

1684	**491**	25k. violet on orange	5·50	2·00
1685	-	40k. orange on yellow	8·00	2·75
1686	-	1r. multicoloured	15·00	6·75

DESIGNS—HORIZ: (37×25 mm): 40k. State Theatre, Ulan Bator. VERT: (22×33 mm): 1r. State Emblem and Mongolian Flag.

492 D. A. Furmanov

1951. 25th Death Anniv of D. A. Furmanov (writer).

1687	**492**	40k. brown on blue	25·00	8·00
1688	-	1r. black on orange	50·00	16·00

DESIGN—HORIZ: 1r. Furmanov writing.

493 Soviet Soldiers Memorial, Berlin (E. Buchetich)

1951. Stockholm Peace Appeal.

1689	**493**	40k. green and red	34·00	7·50
1690	**493**	1r. black and red	70·00	20·00

494 Factories

1951. 150th Anniv of Kirov Machine-building Factory, Leningrad.

1691	**494**	40k. brown on yellow	27·00	13·50

495 Bolshoi State Theatre

1951. 175th Anniv of State Theatre.

1692	**495**	40k. multicoloured	6·75	1·40
1693	-	1r. multicoloured	20·00	4·00

DESIGN: 1r. Theatre and medallions of Glinka, Tchaikovsky, Moussorgsky, Rimsky-Korsakov, Borodin and theatre.

496 National Museum, Budapest

1951. Hungarian Peoples' Republic. Buildings in Budapest.

1694		25k. green	5·00	2·00
1695		40k. blue	5·25	2·75
1696	**496**	60k. black	7·50	4·00
1697	-	1r. black on pink	16·00	6·75

DESIGNS—HORIZ: 25k. Liberty Bridge; 40k. Parliament buildings. VERT: 1r. Liberation Monument.

497 Harvesting

1951. Agricultural Scenes.

1698	**497**	25k. green	3·75	2·00
1699	-	40k. green on blue	4·50	2·75
1700	-	1r. brown on yellow	9·00	5·50
1701	-	2r. green on pink	34·00	9·50

DESIGNS: 40k. Apiary; 1r. Gathering citrus fruit; 2r. Harvesting cotton.

498 M. I. Kalinin

1951. Fifth Death Anniv of Pres. Kalinin.

1702		20k. black, sepia & brown	1·70	70
1703	**498**	40k. brown, dp grn & grn	2·75	1·40
1704	-	1r. black, bl & ultram	6·75	2·00

DESIGNS—HORIZ: 20k. Kalinin Museum. VERT: 1r. Statue of Kalinin (G. Alekseev).

499 F. E. Dzerzhinsky

1951. 25th Death Anniv of Dzerzhinsky (founder of Cheka).

1705	**499**	40k. red	16·00	6·75
1706	-	1r. black (Portrait in uniform)	24·00	9·50

500 P. K. Kozlov

1951. Russian Scientists.

1707	**500**	40k. orange	4·00	70
1708	-	40k. orange on pink	4·00	70
1709	-	40k. orange on blue	12·50	3·25
1710	-	40k. brown	4·00	70
1711	-	40k. brown on pink (facing left)	4·00	70
1712	-	40k. brown on pink (facing right)	4·00	70
1713	-	40k. grey	4·00	70
1714	-	40k. grey on pink	4·00	70
1715	-	40k. grey on blue	27·00	3·25
1716	-	40k. green	4·00	70
1717	-	40k. green on pink	4·00	70
1718	-	40k. blue	4·00	70
1719	-	40k. blue on pink	4·00	70
1720	-	40k. blue on blue	4·00	70
1721	-	40k. violet	4·00	70
1722	-	40k. violet on pink	4·00	70

PORTRAITS: No. 1708, N. N. Miklukho-Makai; 1709, A. M. Butlerov; 1710, N. I. Lobachevsky; 1711, K. A. Timiryazev; 1712, N. S. Kurnakov; 1713, P. N. Yablochkov; 1714, A. N. Severtsov; No. 1715, K. E. Tsiolkovsky; 1716, A. N. Lodygin; 1717, A. G. Stoletov; 1718, P. N. Lebedev; 1719, A. O. Kovalesky; 1720, D. I. Mendeleev; 1721, S. P. Krasheninnikov; 1722, S. V. Kovalevskaya.

501 Kalinnikov

1951. Russian Composers.

1723	**501**	40k. grey on pink	41·00	13·50
1724	-	40k. brown on pink	41·00	13·50

PORTRAIT: No. 1724, A. Alyabev (after N. Andreev).

502 Aviation Society Badge

1951. Aviation Developement.

1725	**502**	40k. multicoloured	3·50	25
1726	-	60k. multicoloured	7·75	1·10
1727	-	1r. multicoloured	9·00	1·40
1728	-	2r. multicoloured	17·00	2·40

DESIGNS—VERT: 60k. Boys and model gliders; 1r. Parachutists descending. HORIZ: (45×25 mm): 2r. Flight of Yakovlev Yak-18U trainers.

503 Vasnetsov (after I. Kramskoi)

1951. 25th Death Anniv of Vasnetsov (painter).

1729	**503**	40k. brown, buff and blue	15·00	2·75
1730	-	1r. multicoloured	19·00	2·75

DESIGN (47×33 mm): 1r. "Three Heroes".

504 Lenin, Stalin and Dnieperprostroi Dam

1951. 34th Anniv of October Revolution.

1731	**504**	40k. blue and red	34·00	4·00
1732	-	1r. brown and red	75·00	16·00

DESIGN: 1r. Lenin, Stalin and Spassky Tower.

505 Volga–Don Canal

1951. Construction of Hydro-electric Power Stations.

1733		20k. multicoloured	16·00	5·50
1734	**505**	30k. multicoloured	24·00	8·00
1735	-	40k. multicoloured	32·00	11·00
1736	-	60k. multicoloured	50·00	16·00
1737	-	1r. multicoloured	£150	27·00

DESIGNS—VERT: (32×47 mm): 20k. Khakhovsky power station. HORIZ: (47×32 mm); 40k. Stalingrad dam; 60k. Excavator and map of Turkmen canal; 1r. Kuibyshev power station.

506 Signing Peace Petition

1951. Third U.S.S.R. Peace Conference.

1738	**506**	40k. red and brown	47·00	20·00

507 M. V. Ostrogradsky

1951. 150th Birth Anniv of Ostrogradsky (mathematician).

1739	**507**	40k. brown on pink	30·00	24·00

508 Zhizka Monument, Prague (B. Kafka)

1951. Friendship with Czechoslovakia.

1740	**508**	20k. blue on pink	18·00	3·25
1741	-	25k. red on yellow	44·00	12·00
1742	-	40k. orange on orange	60·00	6·75
1743	-	60k. grey on pink	34·00	6·75
1744	-	1r. grey on cream	30·00	10·50

DESIGNS—VERT: 25k. Soviet Army Monument, Ostrava; 40k. J. Fucik by M. Shvabinsky; 60k. Smetana Museum, Prague. HORIZ: 1r. Soviet Soldiers Monument, Prague.

509 Volkhovsky Hydro-electric Station and Lenin Monument

1951. 25th Anniv of Lenin Volkhovsky Hydro-electric Station.

1745a	**509**	40k. yellow, indigo and blue	5·00	1·10
1746	**509**	1r. yellow, indigo and violet	11·50	2·75

510 Lenin when a Student (after V. Prager)

1952. 28th Death Anniv of Lenin. Multicoloured centres.

1747	**510**	40k. green	2·75	1·20
1748	-	60k. blue	4·25	1·50
1749	-	1r. brown	13·50	2·75

DESIGNS—HORIZ: 60k. Lenin and children (after A. Varlamov); 1r. Lenin talking to peasants (after V. Serov).

511 P. P. Semenov-Tian Shansky

1952. 125th Birth Anniv of Semenov-Tian-Shansky (scientist).

1750	**511**	1r. brown on blue	34·00	8·50

512 Skaters

1952. Winter Sports.

1751	**512**	40k. multicoloured	4·75	1·40
1752	-	60k. multicoloured (Skiers)	7·50	2·00

513 V. O. Kovalevsky

1952. Birth Centenary of Kovalevsky (scientist).

1753	**513**	40k. brown on yellow	30·00	10·50

514 Gogol (after F. Moller) and Character from "Taras Bulba"

1952. Death Centenary of Nikolai Gogol (writer).

1754	**514**	40k. black on blue	4·00	40
1755	-	60k. orange and black	5·50	55
1756	-	1r. multicoloured	11·00	2·00

DESIGNS: 60k. Gogol and Belinsky (after B. Lebedev); 1r. Gogol and Ukrainian peasants.

515 G. K. Ordzhonikidze

1952. 15th Death Anniv of Ordzhonikidze (statesman).

1757	**515**	40k. green on pink	34·00	19·00
1758	**515**	1r. black on blue	20·00	8·00

516 Workers and Flag

1952. 15th Anniv of Stalin Constitution.

1759	**516**	40k. red and black on cream	37·00	11·50
1760	-	40k. red and green on green	90·00	27·00
1761	-	40k. red and brown on blue	37·00	11·50
1762	-	40k. red and black	37·00	11·50

DESIGNS—HORIZ: No. 1760, Chess players at recreation centre; 1761, Old people and banners. VERT: No. 1762, Schoolgirl and Spassky Tower, Kremlin.

517 Novikov-Priboy and Battleship "Orel"

1952. 75th Birth Anniv of Novikov-Priboy (writer).

1763	**517**	40k. grey, yellow & green	4·75	1·60

518 Victor Hugo

1952. 150th Birth Anniv of Victor Hugo (French writer).

1764	**518**	40k. black, blue & brown	4·00	95

519 Yulaev (after T. Nechaevoi)

1952. Birth Bicent of Yulaev (Bashkirian hero).

1765	**519**	40k. red on pink	6·00	1·40

520 G. Ya. Sedov

1952. 75th Birth Anniv of Sedov (Arctic explorer).

1766	**520**	40k. brown, blue & green	47·00	12·00

521 Arms and Flag of Rumania

1952. Friendship with Rumania.

1767	**521**	40k. multicoloured	5·75	2·75
1768	-	60k. green on pink	9·00	4·00
1769	-	1r. blue	16·00	6·75

DESIGNS—VERT: 60k. Soviet Soldiers' Monument, Bucharest. HORIZ: 1r. University Square, Bucharest.

522 Zhukovsky (after K. Bryullov)

1952. Death Centenary of V. Zhukovsky (poet).

1770	**522**	40k. black on blue	10·00	1·40

523 Bryullov (after V. Tropilin)

1952. Death Centenary of K. Bryullov (artist).

1771	**523**	40k. green on blue	10·00	3·50

524 Ogarev (after M. Lemmel)

1952. 75th Death Anniv of Ogarev (revolutionary writer).

1772	**524**	40k. green	6·00	1·40

525 Uspensky (after N. Yaroshenko)

1952. 50th Death Anniv of Uspensky (writer).

1773	**525**	40k. brown and blue	6·00	2·75

526 Nakhimov (after V. Timm)

1952. 150th Birth Anniv of Admiral Nakhimov.

1774	**526**	40k. multicoloured	11·00	6·75

527 Tartu University

1952. 150th Anniv of Extension of Tartu University.

1775	**527**	40k. black on salmon	30·00	6·75

1952. War Orders and Medals (7th series). Frame as T **282** with various centres (as T **A/P** 1172).

1776	**F**	1r. brown	38·00	22·00
1777	**P**	2r. red	2·00	1·40
1778	**J**	3r. violet	1·40	1·40
1779a	**A**	5r. lake	2·40	1·40
1780	**E**	10r. red	3·75	2·00

528 Kayum Nasyri

1952. 50th Death Anniv of Nasyri (educationist).

1781	**528**	40k. brown on yellow	13·50	6·00

529 A. N. Radishchev

1952. 150th Death Anniv of Radishchev (writer).

1782	**529**	40k. black and red	23·00	5·50

530 Entrance to Volga–Don Canal

1952. 35th Anniv of Russian Revolution.

1783	**530**	40k. multicoloured	20·00	6·75
1784	-	1r. yellow, red and brown	34·00	15·00

DESIGN: 1r. Lenin, Stalin, Spassky Tower and flags.

531 P. A. Fedotov

1952. Death Centenary of Fedotov (painter).

1785	**531**	40k. brown and lake	4·75	2·75

532 Polenov (after I. Repin)

533 "Moscow Courtyard" (painting)

1952. 25th Death Anniv of Polenov (painter).

1786	**532**	40k. lake and buff	4·00	1·40
1787	**533**	1r. blue and grey	9·50	2·75

534 Odoevsky (after N. Bestuzhev)

1952. 150th Birth Anniv of A. I. Odoevsky (poet).

1788	**534**	40k. black and red	6·00	1·40

535 Mamin-Sibiryak

1952. Birth Centenary of D. N. Mamin-Sibiryak (writer).

1789	**535**	40k. green on yellow	5·50	1·40

536 V. M. Bekhterev

1952. 25th Death Anniv of Bekhterev (psychiatrist).

1790	**536**	40k. black, grey and blue	4·75	1·40

537 Komsomolskaya Koltsevaya Station

1952. Underground Stations. Multicoloured centres.

1791	-	40k. violet	4·50	95
1792	-	40k. blue	4·50	95
1793	-	40k. grey	4·50	95
1794	**537**	40k. green	4·50	95

STATIONS: No. 1791, Belorussia Koltsevaya; 1792, Botanical Gardens; 1793, Novoslo-bodskaya.

538 U.S.S.R. Arms and Flags

1952. 30th Anniv of U.S.S.R.

1795	**538**	1r. brown, red and green	27·00	8·75

539 Lenin and Flags (after A. Gerasimov)

1953. 29th Death Anniv of Lenin.

1796	**539**	40k. multicoloured	22·00	7·50

540 Peace Prize Medal

1953. Stalin Peace Prize.

1797	**540**	40k. yellow, blue & brown	22·00	9·50

541 V. V. Kuibyshev

1953. 65th Birth Anniv of Kuibyshev (statesman).

1798	**541**	40k. black and lake	6·00	2·75

542 V. V. Mayakovsky

1953. 60th Birth Anniv of Mayakovsky (poet).

1799	**542**	40k. black and red	18·00	5·50

543 N. G. Chernyshevsky

1953. 125th Birth Anniv of Chernyshevsky (writer).

1800	**543**	40k. brown and buff	18·00	5·50

544 R. Volga Lighthouse

1953. Volga–Don Canal. Multicoloured.

1801	40k. Type **544**	4·25	1·40
1802	40k. Lock No. 9	4·25	1·40
1803	40k. Lock No. 13	4·25	1·40
1804	40k. Lock No. 15	4·25	1·40
1805	40k. Tsimlyanskaya hydro-electric station	4·25	1·40
1806	1r. "Iosif Stalin" (river vessel)	6·00	2·75

545 V. G. Korolenko

1953. Birth Centenary of Korolenko (writer).

1807	**545**	40k. brown	5·50	1·40

546 Tolstoi (after N. Ge)

1953. 125th Birth Anniv of Leo Tolstoi (writer).

1808	**546**	1r. brown	20·00	8·00

547 Lomonosov University and Students

1953. 35th Anniv of "Komsomol" (Russian Youth Organization). Multicoloured.

1809	40k. Type **547**	20·00	4·00
1810	1r. Four medals and "Komsomol" badge	34·00	9·50

548 Peoples of the U.S.S.R.

1953. 36th Anniv of Russian Revolution. Multicoloured.

1811	40k. Type **548**	27·00	13·50
1812	60k. Lenin and Stalin in Smolny Institute, 1917	47·00	27·00

549 Lenin Medallion

1953. 50th Anniv of Communist Party.

1813	**549**	40k. multicoloured	13·50	8·00

550 Lenin Statue

551 Peter I Monument

1953. Views of Leningrad as T **550/1**.

1814	**550**	40k. black on yellow	6·75	2·40
1815	**550**	40k. brown on pink	6·00	2·00
1816	-	40k. brown on yellow	6·75	2·40
1817	-	40k. black on buff	6·00	2·00
1818	**551**	1r. brown on blue	14·50	6·00
1819	**551**	1r. violet on yellow	13·00	5·50
1820	-	1r. green on pink	14·50	6·00
1821	-	1r. brown on blue	13·00	5·50

DESIGNS: As Type **550**: Nos. 1816/17, Admiralty. As Type **551**: 1820/1, Smolny Institute.

552 Lenin and Book "What is to be Done?"

1953. 50th Anniv of Second Social Democratic Workers' Party Congress.

1822	**552**	1r. brown and red	27·00	16·00

553 Pioneers and Moscow University Model

1953. Peace Propaganda.

1823	**553**	40k. black, olive and grey	10·00	7·50

554 Griboedov (after I. Kramskoi)

1954. 125th Death Anniv of A. S. Griboedov (author).

1824	**554**	40k. purple on buff	4·00	2·00
1825a	**554**	1r. black on green	23·00	18·00

555 Kremlin

1954. General Election.

1826	**555**	40k. grey and red	13·50	5·50

556 V. P. Chkalov

1954. 50th Birthday of Chkalov (aviator).

1827	**556**	1r. multicoloured	31·00	4·75

557 "Lenin in Smolny Institute" (after I. Brodsky)

1954. 30th Death Anniv of Lenin. Multicoloured.

1828	40k. Lenin (after M. Rundaltsov) (26×38 mm)	7·50	4·00
1829	40k. Type **557**	7·50	4·00
1830	40k. Cottage Museum, Ulyanovsk (after I. Sokolov)	7·50	4·00
1831	40k. "Lenin proclaims Soviet Regime" (V. Serov) (48×35 mm)	7·50	4·00
1832	40k. "Lenin at Kazan University" (A. Pushnin) (48×35 mm)	7·50	4·00

558 Stalin

1954. First Death Anniv of Stalin.

1833	**558**	40k. brown	13·50	8·00

559 Supreme Soviet Buildings in Kiev and Moscow

1954. Tercentenary of Reunion of Ukraine with Russia. Multicoloured. (a) Designs as T **559** inscr "1654–1954".

1834	40k. Type **559**	2·00	70
1835	40k. Shevchenko Memorial, Kharkhov (vert)	2·00	70
1836	40k. State Opera House, Kiev	2·00	70
1837	40k. Shevchenko University, Kiev	2·00	70
1838	40k. Academy of Sciences, Kiev	2·40	1·40
1839	60k. Bogdan Chmielnitsky Memorial, Kiev (vert)	3·50	1·40
1840	1r. Flags of R.S.F.S.R. and Ukrainian S.S.R. (vert)	8·00	1·40
1841	1r. Shevchenko Monument, Kanev (vert)	4·75	4·00
1842	1r. Pereyaslavskaya Rada	8·00	1·40

(b) No. 1098b optd with five lines of Cyrillic characters as inscr at top of T **559**.

1843	**h**	2r. green	13·50	4·75

561 Running

1954. Sports. Frames in brown.

1844	**561**	40k. black and stone	2·75	45
1845	-	40k. black and blue	2·75	45
1846	-	40k. brown and buff	2·75	45
1847	-	40k. black and blue	2·75	45
1848	-	40k. black	2·75	45
1849	-	1r. grey and blue	7·00	2·00
1850	-	1r. black and blue	7·00	2·00
1851	-	1r. brown and drab	13·50	2·40

DESIGNS—HORIZ: No. 1845, "Soling" yachts; 1846, Cycling; 1847, Swimming; 1848, Hurdling; 1849, Mountaineering; 1850, Skiing. VERT: No. 1851, Basketball.

562 Cattle

1954. Agriculture.

1852	**562**	40k. blue, brown & cream	5·00	1·40
1853	-	40k. green, brown & buff	5·00	1·40
1854	-	40k. black, blue and green	5·00	1·40

DESIGNS: No. 1853, Potato cultivation; 1854, Collective farm hydro-electric station.

563 A. P. Chekhov

1954. 50th Death Anniv of Chekhov (writer).

1855	**563**	40k. brown and green	6·00	1·40

564 Bredikhin, Struve, Belopolsky and Observatory

1954. Rebuilding of Pulkov Observatory.

1856	**564**	40k. black, blue and violet	19·00	5·50

565 M. I. Glinka

1954. 150th Birth Anniv of Glinka (composer).

1857	**565**	40k. brown, pink and red	7·75	2·50
1858	-	60k. multicoloured	9·75	2·75

DESIGN—HORIZ: (38×25½ mm): 60k. "Glinka playing piano for Pushkin and Zhukovsky" (V. Artamonov).

566 Exhibition Emblem

1954. Agricultural Exhibition. Multicoloured.

1859	40k. Type **566**	2·75	1·40
1860	40k. Agricultural Pavilion	2·75	1·40
1861	40k. Cattle breeding Pavilion	2·75	1·40
1862	40k. Mechanization Pavilion	2·75	1·40
1863	1r. Exhibition Entrance	7·50	4·00
1864	1r. Main Pavilion	7·50	4·00

Nos. 1860/3 are horiz, 1860/1 being 41×30½ mm, 1862, 40×30 mm and 1863 41×33 mm. No. 1864 is vert, 29×41 mm.

567 N. A. Ostrovsky

1954. 50th Birth Anniv of Ostrovsky (writer).

1865	**567**	40k. multicoloured	9·50	2·75

568 Monument

1954. Centenary of Defence of Sevastopol.

1866	**568**	40k. black, brown & grn	4·75	1·10
1867	-	60k. black, brown & buff	8·50	1·80
1868	-	1r. multicoloured	14·00	2·20

DESIGNS—HORIZ: 60k. Heroes of Sevastopol (after V. Timm). VERT: 1r. Admiral Nakhimov (after V. Timm).

569 Marx, Engels, Lenin and Stalin

1954. 37th Anniv of October Revolution.

1869	**569**	1r. brown, red and orange	8·00	6·75

570 Kazan University

1954. 150th Anniv of Kazan University.

1870	**570**	40k. blue on blue	3·50	2·00
1871	**570**	60k. red	6·00	3·50

571 Salomea Neris

1954. 50th Birth Anniv of Salomea Neris (poetess).

1872	**571**	40k. multicoloured	8·00	2·75

572 Cultivating Vegetables

1954. Agriculture. Multicoloured.

1873	40k. Type **572**	2·75	70
1874	40k. Tractor and plough	2·75	70
1875	40k. Harvesting flax (49×25½ mm)	2·75	70
1876	60k. Harvesting sunflowers (49×25½ mm)	12·00	2·00

573 Stalin

1954. 75th Birth Anniv of Stalin.

1877	**573**	40k. purple	2·75	70
1878	**573**	1r. blue	6·75	1·40

574 Rubinstein (after I. Repin)

1954. 125th Birth Anniv of Rubinstein (composer).

1879	**574**	40k. black and purple	5·50	1·40

575 V. M. Garshin

1955. Birth Centenary of Garshin (writer).

1880	**575**	40k. black, brown & grn	5·50	2·00

576 Ilyushin Il-12 over Landscape

1955. Air.

1881	-	1r. multicoloured	4·75	70
1882	**576**	2r. black and green	9·50	1·00

DESIGN: 1r. Ilyushin Il-12 over coastline.

577 Savitsky (after N. Frandkovsky) and "Construction of Railway"

1955. 50th Death Anniv of K. Savitsky (painter).

1883	**577**	40k. brown	4·00	1·40
MS1883a		151×119 mm. No. 1883×4	47·00	47·00
MS1883b		Ditto brown inscriptions	55·00	55·00

578 Clasped Hands

1955. International Conference of Postal and Municipal Workers, Vienna.

1884	**578**	50k. multicoloured	4·00	1·40

579 Pushkin and Mickiewicz

1955. Tenth Anniv of Russo–Polish Friendship Agreement.

1885	**579**	40k. multicoloured	6·75	70
1886	-	40k. black	6·75	70
1887	-	1r. multicoloured	12·00	2·40
1888	-	1r. multicoloured	12·00	2·40

DESIGNS: No. 1886, "Brotherhood in Arms" Monument, Warsaw (26½×39 mm); No. 1887, Palace of Science, Warsaw (37½×25½ mm); No. 1888, Copernicus and Matejko (39×26½ mm).

580 Lenin at Shushenskoe (after V. Basov)

1955. 85th Birth Anniv of Lenin. Multicoloured centres.

1889	**580**	60k. red	4·00	70
1890	-	1r. red	8·00	1·80
1891	-	1r. red	8·00	1·80

DESIGNS: No. 1890, Lenin in secret printing house (after F. Golubkov) (26½×39 mm). As Type **580**: No. 1891, Lenin and Krupskaya at Gorky (after N. Sysoev).

581 Schiller

1955. 150th Death Anniv of Schiller (poet).

1892	**581**	40k. brown	4·00	2·75

582 Ilyushin Il-12 over Globe

1955. Air.

1893	**582**	2r. brown	5·50	1·80
1894	**582**	2r. blue	5·50	1·80

583 V. Mayakovsky

1955. 25th Death Anniv of Mayakovsky (poet).

1895	**583**	40k. multicoloured	5·50	1·40

584 Tadzhik S.S.R. Pavilion

1955. Agricultural Exhibition. Soviet Pavilion. Multicoloured designs with green frames.

1896	40k. R.S.F.S.R.	1·80	55
1897	40k. Byelorussian S.S.R.	1·80	55
1898	40k. Type **584**	1·80	55
1899	40k. Azerbaijan S.S.R.	1·80	55
1900	40k. Latvian S.S.R.	1·80	55
1901	40k. Lithuanian S.S.R.	1·80	55
1902	40k. Karelo-Finnish S.S.R.	1·80	55
1903	40k. Estonian S.S.R.	1·80	55
1904	40k. Armenian S.S.R.	1·80	55
1905	40k. Ukrainian S.S.R.	1·80	55
1906	40k. Georgian S.S.R.	1·80	55
1907	40k. Kazakh S.S.R.	1·80	55
1908	40k. Turkmen S.S.R.	1·80	55
1909	40k. Kirgiz S.S.R.	1·80	55
1910	40k. Uzbek S.S.R.	1·80	55
1911	40k. Moldavian S.S.R.	1·80	55
MS1911a	156×104 mm. 40k. R.S.F.S.R	30·00	30·00
MS1911b	156×104 mm. 40k. Byelorussian S.S.R.	30·00	30·00
MS1911c	156×104 mm. 40k. Ukrainian S.S.R.	30·00	30·00

585 M. V. Lomonosov and University

1955. Bicentenary of Lomonosov University. Multicoloured.

1912	40k. Type **585**	1·70	70
1913	1r. Lomonosov University	3·75	1·20
MS1913b	151×108 mm. 40k. Type **585**	16·00	16·00
MS1913c	151×109 mm. 1r. Lomonosov University	24·00	24·00

586 A. G. Venetsianov (self-portrait) and "The Labours of Spring"

1955. 175th Birth Anniv of Venetsianov (painter). Multicoloured centre.

1914	**586**	1r. black	11·00	1·40
MS1914a		151×115 mm. No. 1914 (block of four)	41·00	26·00

587 A. Lyadov

1955. Birth Centenary of Lyadov (composer).

1915	**587**	40k. multicoloured	4·75	1·40

588 A. S. Popov

1955. 60th Anniv of Popov's Radio Discoveries. Multicoloured centres.

1916	**588**	40k. blue	2·75	80
1917	**588**	1r. brown	6·00	90

589 Lenin

590 "Capture of Winter Palace" (detail, P. Sokolov-Skalya)

1955. 38th Anniv of Russian Revolution.

1918	**589**	40k. multicoloured	5·50	2·00
1919	**590**	40k. multicoloured	5·50	2·00
1920	-	1r. multicoloured	13·50	4·00

DESIGN: As T **590**: 1r. Lenin speaking to revolutionaries (after D. Nalbandyan).

„Сев. полюс" — Москва 1955 г.

(591)

1955. Air. Opening of North Pole Scientific Stations. Nos. 1881/2 optd with T **591**.

1921		1r. multicoloured	13·50	9·50
1922	**576**	2r. black and green	23·00	16·00

592 Magnitogorsk

1955. 25th Anniv of Magnitogorsk.

1923	**592**	40k. multicoloured	5·50	1·40

593 Mil Mi-4 Helicopter over Station

1955. North Pole Scientific Stations.

1924	**593**	40k. multicoloured	5·25	55
1925	**593**	60k. multicoloured	5·75	1·00
1926	-	1r. multicoloured	6·75	1·70
MS1926a		154×111 mm. No. 1926 (block of four)	47·00	41·00

DESIGN: 1r. Meteorologist taking observations.

594 Shubin (self-portrait)

1955. 150th Death Anniv of Shubin (sculptor).

1927	**594**	40k. multicoloured	2·75	70
1928	**594**	1r. multicoloured	3·50	1·40

595 A. N. Krylov

1956. Tenth Death Anniv of Krylov (scientist).

1929	595	40k. multicoloured	6·75	2·00

596 Racing

1956. International Horse Racing.

1930	596	40k. sepia and brown	5·50	55
1931	596	60k. blue and green	8·00	80
1932	-	1r. purple and blue	13·50	1·40

DESIGN—HORIZ: 1r. Trotting.

597 Badge and Stadium

1956. Fifth Spartacist Games.

1933	597	1r. purple and green	4·75	90

598 Atomic Power Station

1956. Foundation of Atomic Power Station of Russian Academy of Sciences.

1934	598	25k. multicoloured	1·50	45
1935	-	60k. yellow, turq & brn	4·00	1·10
1936	598	1r. yellow, red and blue	6·50	2·20

DESIGN: 60k. Top of atomic reactor.

599 Statue of Lenin (E. Buchetich)

1956. 20th Communist Party Congress.

1937	599	40k. multicoloured	4·00	70
1938	599	1r. multicoloured	6·75	1·60

600 Kh. Abovyan

1956. 150th Birth Anniv of Khatchatur Abovyan (Armenian writer).

1939	600	40k. black on blue	5·50	1·40

601 Revolutionaries (after N. Tereshchenko)

1956. 50th Anniv of 1905 Revolution.

1940	601	40k. multicoloured	8·00	3·50

602

ПАВИЛЬОН •УРАЛ•
No. 1941

ПАВИЛЬОН СЕВЕРО-ВОСТОЧНЫХ ОБЛАСТЕЙ
No. 1942

ПАВИЛЬОН ЦЕНТРАЛЬНЫХ ЧЕРНОЗЕМНЫХ ОБЛАСТЕЙ
No. 1943

ПАВИЛЬОН «ЛЕНИНГРАД • СЕВЕРО-ЗАПАД»
No. 1944

ПАВИЛЬОН МОСКОВСКОЙ, ТУЛЬСКОЙ, КАЛУЖСКОЙ, РЯЗАНСКОЙ И БРЯНСКОЙ ОБЛАСТЕЙ
No. 1945

ПАВИЛЬОН БАШКИРСКОЙ АССР
No. 1946

ПАВИЛЬОН ДАЛЬНЕГО ВОСТОКА
No. 1947

ПАВИЛЬОН ТАТАРСКОЙ АССР
No. 1948

ПАВИЛЬОН ЦЕНТРАЛЬНЫХ ОБЛАСТЕЙ
No. 1949

ПАВИЛЬОН ЮНЫХ НАТУРАЛИСТОВ
No. 1950

ПАВИЛЬОН СЕВЕРНОГО КАВКАЗА
No. 1951

ПАВИЛЬОН «СИБИРЬ»
No. 1952

ПАВИЛЬОН «ПОВОЛЖЬЕ»
No. 1953

1956. Agricultural Exhibition. Multicoloured. Views of Pavilions of U.S.S.R. regions as T **602**. Inscr "ВСХВ".

1941	1r. Ural	3·00	55
1942	1r. North East	3·00	55
1943	1r. Central Black Soil Region	3·00	55
1944	1r. Leningrad	3·00	55
1945	1r. Moscow-Tula-Kaluga-Ryazan-Bryansk	3·00	55
1946	1r. Bashkir	3·00	55
1947	1r. Far East	3·00	55
1948	1r. Tatar	3·00	55
1949	1r. Central Regions	3·00	55
1950	1r. Young Naturalists	3·00	55
1951	1r. North Caucasus	3·00	55
1952	1r. Siberia	3·00	55
1953	1r. Volga	3·00	55

603 N. A. Kasatkin (painter)

1956. Kasatkin Commemoration.

1954	603	40k. red	2·75	1·40

604 A. E. Arkhipov and Painting "On the Oka River"

1956. Arkhipov Commemoration.

1955	604	40k. multicoloured	4·50	40
1956	604	1r. multicoloured	7·00	1·10

605 I. P. Kulibin

1956. 220th Birth Anniv of Kulibin (inventor).

1957	605	40k. multicoloured	4·00	1·40

606 "Fowler" (after Perov)

1956. Perov Commemoration. Inscr "1956". Multicoloured centres.

1958	-	40k. green	3·00	70
1959	606	1r. brown	6·25	1·40
1960	-	1r. brown	6·25	1·40

DESIGNS—VERT: No. 1958, Self-portrait. HORIZ: No. 1960, "Hunters Resting".

607 Lenin (after P. Vasilev)

1956. 86th Birth Anniv of Lenin.

1961	607	40k. multicoloured	18·00	6·75

608 N. I. Lobachevsky (after L. Kryukov)

1956. Death Cent of Lobachevsky (mathematician).

1962	608	40k. brown	4·00	1·40

609 Student Nurses

1956. Red Cross.

1963	609	40k. red, blue and brown	3·25	70
1964	-	40k. red, olive & turquoise	3·25	70

DESIGN—37½×25½ mm: No. 1964, Nurse and textile factory.

610 Scientific Station

1956. Air. Opening of North Pole Scientific Station No. 6.

1965	610	1r. multicoloured	5·50	2·75

611 Sechenov (after I. Repin)

1956. 50th Death Anniv (1995) of I. Sechenov (naturalist).

1966	611	40k. multicoloured	4·75	1·40

612 Arsenev

1956. V. K. Arsenev (writer).

1967	612	40k. black, violet & pink	4·75	1·40

613 I. V. Michurin

1956. Birth Centenary of Michurin (naturalist). Multicoloured centres.

1968	613	25k. brown	70	25
1969	-	60k. green	1·40	45
1970	613	1r. blue	4·00	70

DESIGN—47½×26½ mm: 60k. Michurin and children.

614 Savrasov (after V. Perov)

1956. 125th Birth Anniv (1955) of A. K. Savrasov (painter).

1971	614	1r. brown and yellow	4·75	1·40

615 N. K. Krupskaya (Lenin's wife)

1956. Krupskaya Commemoration.

1972	615	40k. brown, black & blue	3·75	1·40

616 S. M. Kirov

1956. 70th Birth Anniv of Kirov (statesman).

1973	616	40k. multicoloured	2·75	1·40

617 A. A. Blok

1956. Blok (poet) Commemoration.

1974	617	40k. brown, black & olive	2·75	1·40

618 N. S. Leskov

1956. 125th Birth Anniv of Leskov (writer).

1975	618	40k. multicoloured	2·00	35
1976	618	1r. multicoloured	4·75	1·10

619 Factory Building

1956. 25th Anniv of Rostov Agricultural Machinery Works.

1977	619	40k. multicoloured	5·50	1·40

620 G. N. Fedotova (actress)

1956. Fedotova Commemoration.

1978	620	40k. multicoloured	2·00	70

For similar stamp see No. 2159.

621 P. M. Tretyakov (after I. Repin) and Art Gallery

1956. Centenary of Tretyakov Art Gallery, Moscow.

1979	621	40k. multicoloured	5·00	1·20
1980	-	40k. multicoloured	5·00	1·20

DESIGN—VERT: No. 1980, "Rooks have arrived" (painting by Savrasov).

622 Relay-race

1956. Spartacist Games.

1981	**622**	10k. red	55	15
1982	-	25k. brown	70	25
1983	-	25k. multicoloured	70	25
1984	-	25k. blue	70	25
1985	-	40k. blue	1·40	40
1986	-	40k. green	1·40	40
1987	-	40k. brown and green	1·40	40
1988	-	40k. deep brown, brown and green	1·40	40
1989	-	40k. red, green and light green	1·40	40
1990	-	40k. brown	1·40	40
1991	-	40k. multicoloured	1·40	40
1992	-	60k. violet	4·00	55
1993	-	60k. violet	4·00	55
1994	-	1r. brown	6·75	1·40

DESIGNS—VERT: No. 1982, Volleyball; 1983, Swimming; 1984, Rowing; 1985, Diving; 1989, Flag and stadium; 1990, Tennis; 1991, Medal; 1993, Boxing. HORIZ: No. 1986, Cycle racing; 1987, Fencing; 1988, Football; 1992, Gymnastics; 1994, Netball.

623 Parachutist Landing

1956. Third World Parachute-jumping Competition.

1995	**623**	40k. multicoloured	4·00	70

624 Construction Work

1956. Builders' Day.

1996a	**624**	40k. orange	2·75	70
1997	-	60k. brown	2·00	55
1998	-	1r. blue	4·00	1·00

DESIGNS: 60k. Plant construction; 1r. Dam construction.

625 Self-portrait and "Volga River Boatmen"

626 "Reply of the Cossacks to Sultan Mahmoud IV"

1956. 26th Death Anniv of I. E. Repin (artist).

1999	**625**	40k. multicoloured	8·00	1·50
2000	**626**	1r. multicoloured	20·00	4·00

627 Robert Burns

1956. 160th Death Anniv of Burns (Scots poet).

2001	**627**	40k. brown	13·50	6·75
2002	**627**	40k. brown and blue	6·00	4·75

628 Ivan Franko

1956. Birth Cent of Franko (writer) (1st issue).

2003	**628**	40k. purple	1·50	55
2004	**628**	1r. blue	2·75	80

See also No. 2037.

1956. Lesya Ukrainka Commemoration. As T **615** but portrait of Ukrainka (author).

2005	40k. black, brown and green	4·75	1·40

629 M. Aivazov (farmer)

1956. 148th Birthday of Aivazov. (a) Wrongly inscr "Muhamed" (7 characters).

2006	**629**	40k. green	80·00	70·00

(b) Corrected to "Makmud" (6 characters).

2006a	40k. green	27·00	16·00

630 Statue of Nestor (M. Antokol)

1956. 900th Birth Anniv of Nestor (historian).

2007	**630**	40k. multicoloured	1·90	55
2008	**630**	1r. multicoloured	4·00	1·10

631 Ivanov (after S. Postnikov)

1956. 150th Birth Anniv of A. A. Ivanov (painter).

2009	**631**	40k. brown and grey	2·75	70

632 Feeding Poultry

1956. Agriculture. Multicoloured.

2010	10k. Type **632**	70	25
2011	10k. Harvesting	70	25
2012	25k. Gathering maize	1·40	25
2013	40k. Maize field	2·75	70
2014	40k. Tractor station	2·75	70
2015	40k. Cattle grazing	2·75	70
2016	40k. "Agriculture and Industry"	2·75	70

SIZES: Nos. 2010, 2014/15, 37×25½ mm. Nos. 2011/13, 37×28 mm. No. 2016, 37×21 mm.

633 Mozart

1956. Cultural Anniversaries.

2017	40k. blue (Type **633**)	4·00	1·40
2018	40k. green (Curie)	4·00	1·40
2019	40k. lilac (Heine)	4·00	1·40
2020	40k. brown (Ibsen)	4·00	1·40
2021	40k. green (Dostoevsky)	4·00	1·40
2022	40k. brown (Franklin)	4·00	1·40
2023	40k. black (Shaw)	4·00	1·40
2024	40k. orange (Sessku-Toyo Oda)	4·00	1·40
2025	40k. black (Rembrandt)	4·00	1·40

Nos. 2022/5 are larger, 25×38 mm.

634 Mirnyi Base and Supply Ship "Lena"

1956. Soviet Scientific Antarctic Expedition.

2026	**634**	40k. turquoise, red & grey	4·75	1·40

1956. Julia Zhemaite Commemoration. As T **615** but portrait of Zhemaite (author).

2027	40k. green, brown and sepia	2·75	70

635 F. A. Bredikhin

1956. 125th Birth Anniv of Bredikhin (astronomer).

2028	**635**	40k. multicoloured	8·00	2·00

636 G. I. Kotovsky

1956. 75th Birth Anniv of Kotovsky (military leader).

2029a	**636**	40k. mauve	20·00	11·00

637 Shatura Electric Power Station

1956. 30th Anniv of Shatura Electric Power Station.

2030	**637**	40k. multicoloured	2·75	70

638 Marshal Suvorov (after Utkin)

1956. 225th Birth Anniv of Marshal Suvorov.

2031	**638**	40k. lake and orange	95	35
2032	**638**	1r. brown and olive	2·40	70
2033	**638**	3r. black and brown	7·50	2·00

639 Kryakutni's Ascent (after G. Savitsky)

1956. 225th Anniv of First Balloon Flight by Kryakutni.

2034	**639**	40k. multicoloured	6·00	1·40

640 Vasnetsov (after S. Malyutin) and "Dawn at the Voskresenski Gate"

1956. 30th Death Anniv of A. M. Vasnetsov (artist).

2035	**640**	40k. multicoloured	6·00	1·40

641 Y. M. Shokalsky (oceanographer)

1956. Birth Cent of Shokalsky.

2036	**641**	40k. brown and blue	4·75	1·40

642 Franko (after I. Trush)

1956. Birth Centenary of Franko (writer) (2nd issue).

2037	**642**	40k. green	2·00	70

643 Indian Temple and Books

1956. Kalidasa (Indian poet) Commemoration.

2038	**643**	40k. red	2·75	70

644 F. G. Vokov (actor) (after A. Losenko) and State Theatre

1956. Bicentenary of Leningrad State Theatre.

2039	**644**	40k. black, red and yellow	2·00	70

645 Lomonosov (after L. Miropolsky) at St. Petersburg University

1956. Russian Writers.

2040	**645**	40k. multicoloured	2·30	40
2041	-	40k. multicoloured	2·30	40
2042	-	40k. brown and blue	2·30	40
2043	-	40k. olive, brown & black	2·30	40
2044	-	40k. brown and turquoise	2·30	40
2045	-	40k. purple and brown	2·30	40
2046	-	40k. olive and blue	2·30	40

DESIGNS: No. 2041, Gorky (after V. Efanov) and scene from "Mother" (novel); 2042, Pushkin and statue of Peter the Great, Leningrad (illustrating poem "Bronze Horseman"); 2043, Rustavely and episode from "The Knight in the Tiger Skin" (poem); 2044, Tolstoy and scene from "War and Peace" (novel); 2045, V. G. Belinsky and titles of literary works; 2046, M. Y. Lermontov and Daryal Pass.

See also Nos. 2076, 2089/90, 2256, 2316/22 and 2458.

646 Vitus Bering and Routes of his Voyages

1956. 275th Birth Anniv of Bering (explorer).

2047	**646**	40k. multicoloured	3·50	2·20

647 Mendeleev

1957. 50th Death Anniv of Dmitri Mendeleev (chemist).

2048	**647**	40k. brown, grey & black	4·75	2·75

648 M. I. Glinka

1957. Death Centenary of Glinka (composer). Multicoloured.

No.	Type	Description	Mint	Used
2049a		40k. Type **648**	4·00	1·40
2050a		1r. Scene from "Ivan Susanin"	6·75	2·75

649 Youth Festival Emblem

1957. All Union Festival of Soviet Youth.

No.	Type	Description	Mint	Used
2051	**649**	40k. multicoloured	2·00	40

650 Ice Hockey Player

1957. 23rd World and 35th European Ice Hockey Championships, Moscow.

No.	Type	Description	Mint	Used
2052a	-	25k. violet	90	25
2053a	**650**	40k. blue	1·00	25
2054a	-	60k. green	1·60	40

DESIGNS: 25k. Championship emblem; 60k. Goalkeeper.

651 Youth Festival Emblem and Pigeon

1957. Sixth World Youth Festival, Moscow (1st issue). Perf or imperf.

No.	Type	Description	Mint	Used
2055	**651**	40k. multicoloured	80	25
2056	**651**	60k. multicoloured	2·75	70

See also Nos. 2084/7 and 2108/11.

652 Factory Plant

1957. Cent of "Red Proletariat" Plant. Moscow.

No.	Type	Description	Mint	Used
2057	**652**	40k. multicoloured	6·75	2·00

653 Sika Deer

1957. Russian Wildlife. Multicoloured.

No.	Description	Mint	Used
2057a	10k. Grey partridge	1·10	40
2058	15k. Black grouse	1·20	25
2058a	15k. Polar bear	1·20	55
2059	20k. Type **653**	1·20	25
2059a	20k. Brown hare	1·10	55
2059b	25k. Tiger	1·40	95
2059c	25k. Wild horse	1·40	95
2060	30k. Mallard	1·90	40
2061	30k. European bison	1·90	40
2062	40k. Elk	2·40	70
2063	40k. Sable	2·40	70
2063a	40k. Eurasian red squirrel	1·40	40
2063b	40k. Yellow-throated marten	1·40	40
2063c	60k. Hazel grouse	2·50	1·10
2063d	1r. Mute swan	3·50	2·75

Nos. 2058/a, 2059a/62, 2063a/b and 2063d are horiz.
See also Nos. 2534/6.

654 Vologda Lace-making

1957. Regional Handicrafts. Multicoloured.

No.	Description	Mint	Used
2064	40k. Moscow wood-carving	3·00	80
2065	40k. Woman engraving vase	3·00	80
2066	40k. Type **654**	3·00	80
2067	40k. Northern bone-carving	3·00	80
2067a	40k. Wood-block engraving	1·70	95
2067b	40k. Turkmen carpet-weaving	1·70	95

655 G. V. Plekhanov

1957. Birth Centenary of Plekhanov (politician).

No.	Type	Description	Mint	Used
2068	**655**	40k. plum	1·10	55

656 A. N. Bakh

1957. Birth Centenary of Bakh (biochemist).

No.	Type	Description	Mint	Used
2069a	**656**	40k. multicoloured	2·75	55

657 L. Euler

1957. 250th Birth Anniv of Euler (mathematician).

No.	Type	Description	Mint	Used
2070	**657**	40k. black and purple	2·00	70

658 Lenin in Meditation

1957. 87th Birth Anniv of Lenin. Multicoloured.

No.	Description	Mint	Used
2071	40k. Type **658**	2·20	95
2072	40k. Lenin carrying pole	2·20	95
2073	40k. Talking with soldier and sailor	2·20	95

659 Dr. William Harvey

1957. 300th Death Anniv of Dr. William Harvey (discoverer of circulation of blood).

No.	Type	Description	Mint	Used
2074	**659**	40k. brown	2·00	70

660 M. A. Balakirev

1957. 120th Birth Anniv of Balakirev (composer).

No.	Type	Description	Mint	Used
2075	**660**	40k. black	2·75	70

661 12th-century Narrator

1957. "The Tale of the Host of Igor".

No.	Type	Description	Mint	Used
2076	**661**	40k. multicoloured	2·75	70

662 Agricultural Medal

1957. Cultivation of Virgin Soil.

No.	Type	Description	Mint	Used
2077	**662**	40k. multicoloured	2·75	70

663 A. I. Herzen (after N. Ge) and N. P. Ogarev (after M. Lemmel) (founders)

1957. Centenary of Publication of Magazine "Kolokol".

No.	Type	Description	Mint	Used
2078	**663**	40k. brown, black & blue	2·75	70

664 Monument

250 лет
Ленинграда
(665)

1957. 250th Anniv of Leningrad. Vert designs as T **664** and stamps as Nos. 1818 and 1820 optd as T **665**.

No.	Type	Description	Mint	Used
2079	**664**	40k. green	1·00	70
2080	-	40k. violet	1·00	70
2081	-	40k. brown	1·00	70
2082	**551**	1r. brown on green	1·80	70
2083	-	1r. green on salmon	1·80	70

DESIGNS: No. 2080, Nevsky Prospect, Leningrad; No. 2081, Lenin Statue.

666 Youths with Banner

1957. Sixth World Youth Festival, Moscow (2nd issue). Multicoloured. Perf or imperf.

No.	Description	Mint	Used
2084	10k. Type **666**	35	15
2084c	20k. Sculptor with statue	70	40
2085	25k. Type **666**	55	20
2086	40k. Dancers	80	25
2087	1r. Festival emblem and fireworks over Moscow State University	2·20	80

667 A. M. Lyapunov

1957. Birth Centenary of Lyapunov (mathematician).

No.	Type	Description	Mint	Used
2088	**667**	40k. brown	9·50	6·75

668 T. G. Shevchenko (after I. Repin) and Scene from "Katharina"

1957. 19th-Century Writers. Multicoloured.

No.	Description	Mint	Used
2089	40k. Type **668**	1·40	70
2090	40k. N. G. Chernyshevsky and scene from "What is to be Done?"	1·40	70

669 Henry Fielding

1957. 250th Birth Anniv of Fielding (novelist).

No.	Type	Description	Mint	Used
2091	**669**	40k. multicoloured	1·40	70

670 Racing Cyclists

1957. Tenth International Cycle Race.

No.	Type	Description	Mint	Used
2092	**670**	40k. multicoloured	3·75	70

671 Interior of Observatory

1957. International Geophysical Year (1st issue).

No.	Type	Description	Mint	Used
2093	**671**	40k. brown, yellow and blue	3·50	1·10
2094	-	40k. indigo, yellow and blue	4·50	1·40
2095	-	40k. violet and lavender	3·75	1·20
2095a	-	40k. blue	2·75	55
2095b	-	40k. green	2·75	55
2095c	-	40k. yellow and blue	2·75	55

DESIGNS—As T **671**: No. 2094, Meteor in sky; 2095a, Malakhit radar scanner and balloon (meteorology); 2095b, "Zarya" (non-magnetic research schooner) (geo-magnetism); 2095c, Northern Lights and C-180 camera. 15×21 mm: No. 2095, Rocket.

See also Nos. 2371/3a.

672 Gymnast

1957. Third International Youth Games.

No.	Type	Description	Mint	Used
2096	**672**	20k. brown and blue	40	20
2097	-	25k. red and green	55	25
2098	-	40k. violet and red	40	40
2099	-	40k. olive, red and green	80	40
2100	-	60k. brown and blue	1·50	70

DESIGNS—As Type **672**: No. 2097, Wrestlers; 2098, Young athletes; 2099, Moscow Stadium; 2100, Throwing the javelin.

673 Football

1957. Russian Successes at Olympic Games, Melbourne.

No.	Type	Description	Mint	Used
2101		20k. brown, blue & black	45	15
2102		20k. red and green	45	15
2103		25k. blue and orange	55	25
2104	**673**	40k. multicoloured	80	40
2105	-	40k. brown and purple	80	40
2106	-	60k. brown and violet	1·40	55

DESIGNS—VERT: No. 2101, Throwing the javelin; 2102, Running; 2103, Gymnastics; 2105, Boxing; 2106, Weight-lifting.

674 Yanka Kupala

1957. 75th Birth Anniv of Kupala (poet).

2107	**674**	40k. brown	10·50	5·75

675 Moscow State University

1957. Sixth World Youth Festival (3rd issue). Moscow Views.

2108	-	40k. black and brown	70	15
2109	-	40k. black and purple	70	15
2110	-	1r. black and blue	2·00	55
2111	**675**	1r. black and red	2·00	55

DESIGNS—HORIZ: No. 2108, Kremlin; 2109, Stadium; 2110, Bolshoi State Theatre.

676 Lenin Library

1957. Int Philatelic Exn, Moscow. Perf or imperf.

2112	**676**	40k. turquoise	80	40
MS2112c 144×101 mm. **676** 40k.×2 blue. Imperf			47·00	70·00

677 Dove of Peace encircling Globe

1957. "Defence of Peace".

2113	**677**	40k. multicoloured	2·50	1·10
2114	**677**	1r. multicoloured	5·00	2·20

1957. Birth Centenary of Clara Zetkin (German revolutionary). As T **615** but portrait of Zetkin.

2115	40k. multicoloured	3·50	1·00

678 P. Beranger

1957. Death Centenary of Beranger (French poet).

2116	**678**	40k. green	2·75	40

679 Krengholm Factory, Narva

1957. Centenary of Krengholm Textile Factory, Narva, Estonia.

2117	**679**	40k. brown	2·75	95

680 Factory Plant and Statue of Lenin (M. Kharlamev)

1957. Centenary of Krasny Vyborzhetz Plant, Leningrad.

2118	**680**	40k. blue	1·80	95

681 Stasov (after I. Repin)

1957. 50th Death Anniv of Stasov (art critic).

2119	**681**	40k. brown	80	15
2120	**681**	1r. blue	1·60	55

682 Pigeon with Letter

1957. International Correspondence Week.

2121	**682**	40k. blue	70	25
2122	**682**	60k. purple	1·10	40

683 K. E. Tsiolkovsky

1957. Birth Centenary of Tsiolkovsky (scientist).

2123	**683**	40k. multicoloured	9·50	2·00

684 Congress Emblem

1957. Fourth World T.U.C., Leipzig.

2124	**684**	40k. blue on blue	95	55

685 Students

1957. 40th Anniv of Russian Revolution. (a) 1st issue. As T **685**. Multicoloured. Perf or imperf.

2125	10k. Type **685**	25	15
2126	40k. Railway worker (horiz)	70	25
2127	40k. Portrait of Lenin on banner	70	25
2128	40k. Lenin and workers with banners	70	25
2129	60k. Harvester (horiz)	1·40	70

686 Workers and Emblem (Ukraine)

1957. 40th Anniv of Russian Revolution (2nd issue). Multicoloured.

2130	40k. Type **686**	1·30	55
2131	40k. Estonia	1·30	55
2132	40k. Uzbekistan	1·30	55
2133	40k. R.S.F.S.R. (horiz)	1·30	55
2134	40k. Belorussia (horiz)	1·30	55
2135	40k. Lithuania (horiz)	1·30	55
2136	40k. Armenia (horiz)	1·30	55
2137	40k. Azerbaijan (horiz)	1·30	55
2138	40k. Georgia (horiz)	1·30	55
2139	40k. Kirghizia (horiz)	1·30	55
2140	40k. Turkmenistan (horiz)	1·30	55
2141	40k. Tadzhikistan (horiz)	1·30	55
2142	40k. Kazakhstan (horiz)	1·30	55
2143	40k. Latvia (horiz)	1·30	55
2144	40k. Moldavia (horiz)	1·30	55

687 Lenin (after G. Goldstein)

1957. 40th Anniv of Russian Revolution (3rd issue). As T **687**.

2145	**687**	40k. blue	2·20	95
2146	-	60k. red	3·00	1·10

DESIGN—HORIZ: 60k. Lenin at desk.

1957. 40th Anniv of Russian Revolution (4th issue). Imperf.

MS2146a 145×99 mm. Nos. 2079/80 and 1816	24·00	10·00
MS2146b 144×101 mm. Nos. 2126/7 and 2129	24·00	10·00

688 Satellite encircling Globe

1957. Launching of First Artifical Satellite.

2147	**688**	40k. indigo on blue	4·75	1·40
2148	**688**	40k. blue	4·75	1·40

689 Meteor Falling

1957. Sikhote-Alin Meteor.

2149	**689**	40k. multicoloured	4·00	1·60

690 Kuibyshev Power Station Turbine

1957. All Union Industrial Exhibition (1st issue).

2150	**690**	40k. brown	1·40	40

See also Nos. 2168.

4/X-57 г. Первый в мире искусств. спутник Земли

(691)

1957. First Artificial Satellite of the World. Optd with T **691**.

2151	**683**	40k. multicoloured	70·00	47·00

692 Soviet War Memorial, Berlin (after Ye. Bunchetich)

1957. Bicentenary of Academy of Arts, Moscow.

2152	-	40k. black on salmon	80	25
2153	**692**	60k. black	1·10	25
2154	-	1r. black on pink	1·90	55

DESIGNS—25½×37½ mm: 40k. Academy and portraits of K. Bryullov, I. Repin and V. Surikov (after I. Repin). 21½×32 mm: 1r. "Worker and Collective Farmer", Moscow (sculpture, Vera Mukhina).

693 Arms of Ukraine

1957. 40th Anniv of Ukraine S.S.R.

2155	**693**	40k. multicoloured	1·40	40

694 Garibaldi

1957. 150th Birth Anniv of Garibaldi.

2156	**694**	40k. purple, maroon and green	1·20	40

695 Edvard Grieg

1957. 50th Death Anniv of Grieg (composer).

2157	**695**	40k. black on salmon	2·75	95

696 Borovikovsky (after I. Bugaevsky-Blagodarny)

1957. Birth Bicent of Borovikovsky (painter).

2158	**696**	40k. brown	1·40	40

1967. M. N. Ermolova (actress) Commemoration. As T **620** but portrait of Ermolova.

2159	40k. brown and violet	1·40	40

698 Kolas

1957. 75th Birth Anniv of Yakyb Kolas (poet).

2160	**698**	40k. black	6·75	5·50

699 Mitskyavichyus-Kapsukas

1957. 22nd Death Anniv of V. S. Mitskyavichyus-Kapsukas (Communist Party leader).

2161	**699**	40k. brown	6·75	5·50

700 G. Z. Bashindzhagian

1957. Bashindzhagian (artist) Commemoration.

2162	**700**	40k. brown	6·75	5·50

701 Kuibyshev Hydro- electric Station

1957. 40th Anniv of Kuibyshev Hydro-electric Station.

2163	**701**	40k. blue on flesh	2·75	55

702 "To the Stars" (Ye. Buchetich)

1957. Launching of Second Artificial Satellite.

2164	**702**	20k. red and black	1·00	15
2165	**702**	40k. green and black	1·60	25
2166	**702**	60k. brown and black	2·40	35
2167	**702**	1r. blue and black	4·75	70

703 Allegory of Industry

1958. All Union Industrial Exn (2nd issue).
2168 **703** 60k. red, black & lavender 2·75 45

1958. Rosa Luxemburg Commemoration. As T **615** but portrait of Luxemburg (German revolutionary).
2169 40k. brown and blue 2·75 70

704 Tsi Bai-shi

1958. Tsi Bai-shi (Chinese artist) Commem.
2170 **704** 40k. violet 1·40 40

705 Linnaeus (Carl von Linne)

1958. 250th Birth Anniv of Linnaeus.
2171 **705** 40k. brown 7·50 6·75

706 Tolstoi

1958. 75th Birth Anniv of A. N. Tolstoi (writer).
2172 **706** 40k. bistre 95 40

707 Soldier, Sailor and Airman

1958. 40th Anniv of Red Army. Multicoloured.
2173 25k. Battle of Narva, 1918 60 35
2174 40k. Type **707** 1·10 40
2175 40k. Soldier and blast-furnace-man (vert) 1·10 40
2176 40k. Soldier and sailor (vert) 1·10 40
2177 60k. Storming the Reichstag, 1945 1·70 70

708 E. Charents

1958. Charents (Armenian poet) Commemoration.
2178 **708** 40k. brown 6·75 5·50

709 Henry W. Longfellow

1958. 150th Birth Anniv of Longfellow.
2179 **709** 40k. black 6·75 5·50

710 Blake

1958. Birth Bicentenary of William Blake (poet).
2180 **710** 40k. black 6·75 5·50

711 Tchaikovsky

1958. Tchaikovsky International Music Competition, Moscow.
2181 **711** 40k. multicoloured 1·40 40
2182 - 40k. multicoloured 1·40 40
2183a - 1r. purple and green 4·25 1·40

DESIGNS—HORIZ: No. 2182A, Scene from "Swan Lake" ballet. VERT: No. 2183Aa, Pianist, violinist and inset portrait of Tchaikovsky.

712 Admiral Rudnev and Cruiser "Varyag"

1958. 45th Death Anniv of Admiral Rudnev.
2184 **712** 40k. multicoloured 2·40 80

713 Gorky (after I. Brodsky)

1958. 90th Death Anniv of Maksim Gorky (writer).
2185 **713** 40k. multicoloured 1·40 40

714 Congress Emblem and Spassky Tower, Kremlin

1958. 13th Young Communists' League Congress, Moscow.
2186 **714** 40k. violet on pink 80 15
2187 **714** 60k. red on flesh 1·40 40

715 Russian Pavilion

1958. Brussels Int Exhibition. Perf or imperf.
2188 **715** 10k. multicoloured 45 15
2189 **715** 40k. multicoloured 80 25

716 J. A. Komensky ("Comenius")

1958. Komensky Commem.
2190 **716** 40k. green 6·75 5·50

717 Lenin

1958. Lenin Commemoration.
2191 **717** 40k. blue 80 15
2192 **717** 60k. red 1·10 25
2193 **717** 1r. brown 2·20 80

200 лет Академии
художеств СССР. 1957
(718)

1958. Bicentenary of Russian Academy of Artists. Optd with T **718**.
2194 **557** 40k. multicoloured 9·50 2·75

719 C. Goldoni

1958. 250th Birth Anniv of C. Goldoni (Italian dramatist).
2195 **719** 40k. brown and blue 1·40 40

720 Lenin Prize Medal

1958. Lenin Prize Medal.
2196 **720** 40k. red, yellow & brown 1·40 40

721 Karl Marx

1958. Karl Marx Commemoration.
2197 **721** 40k. brown 1·10 20
2198 **721** 60k. blue 1·60 25
2199 **721** 1r. red 2·75 80

722 Federation Emblem

1958. Fourth International Women's Federation Congress.
2200 **722** 40k. blue and black 80 15
2201 **722** 60k. blue and black 1·40 40

723 Radio Beacon, Airliner and Freighter

1958. Radio Day.
2202 **723** 40k. green and red 4·00 55

724 Chavchavadze (after G. Gabashvili)

1958. Chavchavadze (Georgian poet) Commem.
2203 **724** 40k. black and blue 1·40 40

725 Flags of Communist Countries

1958. Socialist Countries' Postal Ministers Conference, Moscow.
2204 **725** 40k. multicoloured (A) 27·00 9·50
2205 **725** 40k. multicoloured (B) 12·00 8·00

Central flag to left of inscription is in red, white and mauve. (A) has red at top and white at foot, (B) is vice versa.

726 Camp Bugler

1958. "Pioneers" Day. Inscr "1958".
2206 **726** 10k. multicoloured 55 15
2207 - 25k. multicoloured 70 25

DESIGN: 25k. Pioneer with model airplane.

727 Negro, European and Chinese Children

1958. International Children's Day. Inscr "1958".
2208 **727** 40k. multicoloured 1·10 25
2209 - 40k. multicoloured 1·10 25

DESIGN: No. 2209, Child with toys, and atomic bomb.

728 Fooballers and Globe

1958. World Cup Football Championship, Sweden. Perf or imperf.
2210 **728** 40k. multicoloured 1·10 25
2211 **728** 60k. multicoloured 2·30 55

729 Rimsky-Korsakov

1958. Rimsky-Korsakov (composer) Commem.
2212 **729** 40k. brown and blue 2·75 60

730 Athlete

1958. 14th World Gymnastic Championships, Moscow. Inscr "XIV". Multicoloured.
2213 40k. Type **730** 95 25
2214 40k. Gymnast 95 25

731 Young Construction Workers

1958. Russian Youth Day.
2215 **731** 40k. orange and blue 80 25
2216 **731** 60k. orange and green 1·10 35

732 Atomic Bomb, Globe, Sputniks, Atomic Symbol and "Lenin" (atomic ice-breaker)

1958. International Disarmament Conf, Stockholm.
2217 **732** 60k. black, orange & blue 7·50 1·10

733 Kiev Arsenal Uprising, 1918

1958. 40th Anniv of Ukrainian Communist Party.
2218 **733** 40k. violet and red 1·40 40

734 Silhouette of Moscow State University

1958. Fifth Int Architects Union Congress, Moscow.

2219	**734**	40k. blue and red	1·40	25
2220	-	60k. multicoloured	2·75	40

MS2220a 105×143 mm. Nos. 2219/20. Imperf 18·00 16·00

DESIGN—VERT: 60k. "U.I.A. Moscow 1958" in square panel of bricks and "V" in background.

735 Sadruddin Aini

1958. 80th Birth Anniv of Sadruddin Aini (Tadzhik writer).

2221	**735**	40k. red, black and buff	2·75	45

736 Third Artificial Satellite

1958. Launching of Third Artificial Satellite.

2222a	**736**	40k. red, blue and green	4·00	70

737 Conference Emblem

1958. First World T.U. Young Workers' Conf, Prague.

2223	**737**	40k. blue and purple	1·40	55

738 Tupolev Tu-110 Jetliner

1958. Civil Aviation. Perf or imperf.

2224	-	20k. black, red and blue	55	15
2225	-	40k. black, red and green	95	25
2226	-	40k. black, red and blue	95	25
2227	-	60k. red, buff and blue	1·10	40
2228	**738**	60k. black and red	1·10	40
2229	-	1r. black, red and orange	2·00	70
2230	-	2r. black, red and purple	3·50	1·40

DESIGNS—Russian aircraft flying across globe: No. 2224A, Ilyushin Il-14M; 2225A, Tupolev Tu-104; 2226A, Tupolev Tu-114 Rossiya; 2229A, Antonov An-10 Ukraina; 2230A, Ilyushin Il-18B; No. 2227A, Global air routes.

739 L. A. Kulik (scientist)

1958. 50th Anniv of Tunguz Meteor.

2231	**739**	40k. multicoloured	2·50	80

740 Crimea Observatory

1958. Tenth International Astronomical Union Congress, Moscow.

2232	**740**	40k. turquoise and brown	2·00	35
2233	-	60k. yellow, violet & blue	2·50	45
2234	-	1r. brown and blue	3·75	70

DESIGNS—HORIZ: 60k. Moscow University. VERT: 1r. Telescope of Moscow Observatory.

741 15th century Scribe

1958. Centenary of First Russian Postage Stamp.

2235	**741**	10k. multicoloured	25	15
2236	-	10k. multicoloured	25	15
2237	-	25k. blue, black and green	75	35
2238	-	25k. black and blue	75	35
2239	-	40k. brown, purple & sep	1·40	55
2240	-	40k. lake and brown	1·40	55
2241	-	40k. black, orange and red	1·40	55
2242	-	60k. turquoise, blk & vio	1·90	70
2243	-	60k. black, turquoise and purple	1·90	70
2244	-	1r. multicoloured	3·75	1·20
2245	-	1r. purple, black and orange	3·75	1·20

MS2245a Nos. 2235/8 and 2240. Imperf 34·00 12·00

MS2245b Nos. 2239 and 2242/3. Imperf 37·00 13·50

DESIGNS—HORIZ: No. 2236, 16th-century courier; 2237, Ordin-Nashchokin (17th-century postal administrator) (after Kh. Gusikov) and postal sleigh coach; 2238, 18th-century mail coach; 2239, Reproduction of Lenin portrait stamp of 1947; 2240, 19th-century postal troika (three-horse sleigh); 2241, Tupolev Tu-104 jetliner; 2242, Parcel post train; 2243, V. N. Podbelsky (postal administrator, 1918–20) and postal scenes; 2244, Parcel post Tupolev Tu-104; 2245, Globe and modern forms of mail transport.

741a Facade of Exhibition Building

1958. Stamp Cent Philatelic Exhibition, Leningrad.

2246	**741a**	40k. brown & lt brown	95	40

742 Vladimir Gateway

1958. 850th Anniv of Town of Vladimir. Multicoloured.

2247	40k. Type **742**	95	35
2248	60k. Street scene in Vladimir	1·50	60

743 Chigorin

1958. 50th Death Anniv of Mikhail Ivanovich Chigorin (chess player).

2249	**743**	40k. green and black	1·80	60

745 Red Cross Nurse and Patient

1958. 40th Anniv of Red Cross and Crescent Societies.

2254	**745**	40k. multicoloured	1·10	40
2255	-	40k. red, yellow and brown	1·10	40

DESIGN: No. 2255, Convalescent home.

746 Saltykov-Shchedrin (after I. Kramskoi) and Scene from his Works

1958. 69th Death Anniv of Mikhail Saltykov-Shchedrin (writer).

2256	**746**	40k. black and purple	1·10	40

For similar stamps see Nos. 2316/22 and 2458.

747 V. Kapnist (after A. Osipov)

1958. Birth Bicentenary of V. Kapnist (poet).

2257	**747**	40k. black and blue	1·80	40

748 Yerevan, Armenia

1958. Republican Capitals.

2258	40k. brown (T **748**)	95	65
2259	40k. violet (Baku, Azerbaijan)	95	65
2260	40k. brown (Minsk, Byelorussia)	95	65
2261	40k. blue (Tbilisi, Georgia)	95	65
2262	40k. green (Tallin, Estonia)	95	65
2263	40k. green (Alma-Ata, Kazakhstan)	95	65
2264	40k. blue (Frunze, Kirgizia)	95	65
2265	40k. brown (Riga, Latvia)	95	65
2266	40k. red (Vilnius, Lithuania)	95	65
2267	40k. bistre (Kishinev, Moldavia)	95	65
2268	40k. violet (Moscow, R.S.F.S.R.)	95	65
2269	40k. blue (Stalinabad, Tadzhikistan)	95	65
2270	40k. green (Ashkhabad, Turkmenistan)	95	65
2271	40k. mauve (Kiev, Ukraine)	95	65
2272	40k. black (Tashkent, Uzbekistan)	95	65

See also No. 2940.

749 Open Book, Torch, Lyre and Flowers

1958. Asian-African Writers' Conference, Tashkent.

2273	**749**	40k. orange, black and olive	2·00	45

750 Rudaki

1958. 1100th Birth Anniv of Rudaki (Tadzhik poet and musician).

2274	**750**	40k. multicoloured	1·40	25

751 Statue of Founder Vakhtang I Gorgasal (E. Amashukeli)

1958. 1500th Anniv of Founding of Tbilisi (Georgian capital).

2275	**751**	40k. multicoloured	1·80	40

752 Chelyabinsk Tractor Plant

1958. 25th Anniv of Industrial Plants.

2276	**752**	40k. green and yellow	90	25
2277	-	40k. blue and light blue	90	25
2278	-	40k. lake and light orange	90	25

DESIGNS: No. 2277, Ural machine construction plant; No. 2278, Zaporozhe foundry plant.

753 Young Revolutionary

1958. 40th Anniv of Young Communists League. Multicoloured.

2279	10k. Type **753**	40	15
2280	20k. Riveters	80	20
2281	25k. Soldier	95	25
2282	40k. Harvester	1·60	35
2283	60k. Builder	2·40	55
2284	1r. Students	4·50	1·10

754 Marx and Lenin (bas-relief)

1958. 41st Anniv of October Revolution.

2285	**754**	40k. black, yellow and red	95	25
2286	-	1r. multicoloured	1·90	55

DESIGN—HORIZ: 1r. Lenin (after N. Andreev) with student, peasant and miner.

755 "Human Rights"

1958. Tenth Anniv of Declaration of Human Rights.

2287	**755**	60k. blue, black and buff	1·40	40

756 Yesenin

1958. 30th Death Anniv of Sergei Yesenin (poet).

2288	**756**	40k. multicoloured	80	40

757 Kuan Han-ching

1958. Kuan Han-ching (Chinese playwright) Commemoration.

2289	**757**	40k. black and blue	80	40

758 Ordzhonikidze

1958. 21st Death Anniv of G. K. Ordzhonikidze (statesman).

2290	**758**	40k. multicoloured	95	40

759 John Milton

1958. 350th Birth Anniv of John Milton (poet).

2291	**759**	40k. brown	1·40	40

760 Lenin's Statue, Minsk (M. Manizer)

1958. 40th Anniv of Byelorussian Republic.

2292	**760**	40k. brown, grey and red	95	40

761 Fuzuli

1958. Fuzuli (Azerbaijan poet) Commemoration.

2293	**761**	40k. bistre and turquoise	1·40	40

762 Census Emblem

1958. All Union Census, 1959. Multicoloured.

2294	40k. Type **762**	55	25
2295	40k. Census official with worker's family	55	25

763 Eleonora Duse

1958. Birth Centenary of Eleonora Duse (Italian actress).

2296	**763**	40k. black, grey and green	1·40	40

764 Rule

1958. Death Centenary of K. F. Rule (naturalist).

2297	**764**	40k. black and blue	1·60	55

765 Atomic Ice-breaker "Lenin"

1958. All-Union Industrial Exhibition. Multicoloured.

2298	40k. Type **765**	2·50	1·90
2299	60k. Class TE 3 diesel-electric frieght locomotive	4·75	2·75

766 Moon Rocket and Sputniks

1959. 21st Communist Party Congress, Moscow.

2300	-	40k. multicoloured	1·40	55
2301	-	60k. multicoloured	2·40	1·40
2302	**766**	1r. multicoloured	9·50	3·50

DESIGNS: 40k. Lenin (after N. Andreev), Red Banner and Kremlin view; 60k. Workers beside Lenin hydro-electric plant, Volga River.

767 E. Torricelli

1959. 350th Birth Anniv of Torricelli (physicist).

2303	**767**	40k. black and green	1·40	40

768 Ice Skater

1959. Women's World Ice Skating Championships, Sverdlovsk.

2304	**768**	25k. multicoloured	70	25
2305	**768**	40k. black, blue and grey	1·10	40

769 Charles Darwin

1959. 150th Birth Anniv of Charles Darwin (naturalist).

2306	**769**	40k. brown and blue	1·20	40

770 N. Gamaleya

1959. Birth Centenary of Gamaleya (microbiologist).

2307	**770**	40k. black and red	1·20	55

771 Sholem Aleichem

1959. Birth Centenary of Aleichem (Jewish writer).

2308	**771**	40k. brown	1·40	40

Победа
баскетбольной
команды СССР.
Чили 1959 г.

(772)

1959. Russian (Unofficial) Victory in World Basketball Championships, Chile. No. 1851 optd with T **772**.

2309	1r. brown and drab	13·50	12·00

1959. Birth Bicent of Robert Burns. Optd **1759 1959**.

2310	**627**	40k. brown and blue	32·00	30·00

774 Selma Lagerlof

1959. Birth Centenary of Selma Lagerlof (Swedish writer).

2311	**774**	40k. black, brown and cream	1·40	40

775 P. Cvirka

1959. 50th Birth Anniv of Cvirka (Lithuanian poet).

2312	**775**	40k. black and red on yellow	1·40	40

776 F. Joliot-Curie (scientist)

1959. Joliot-Curie Commemoration.

2313	**776**	40k. black and turquoise	1·60	40

777 Popov and Polar Rescue by Ice-breaker "Ermak"

1959. Birth Centenary of A. S. Popov (radio pioneer).

2314	**777**	40k. brown, black & blue	1·40	55
2315	-	60k. multicoloured	2·20	80

DESIGN: 60k. Popov and radio tower.

1959. Writers as T **746**. Inscr "1959".

2316	40k. grey, black and red	1·90	1·40
2317	40k. brown, sepia and yellow	1·90	1·40
2318	40k. brown and violet	1·90	1·40
2319	40k. multicoloured	1·90	1·40
2320	40k. black, olive and yellow	1·90	1·40
2321	40k. multicoloured	1·90	1·40
2322	40k. slate and violet	1·90	1·40

PORTRAITS (with scene from works): No. 2316, Anton Chekhov; 2317, Ivan Krylov (after K. Bryullov); 2318, Aleksandr Ostrovsky; 2319, Aleksandr Griboedov (after I. Kramskoi); 2320, Nikolai Gogol (after F. Moller); 2321, Sergei Aksakov (after I. Kramskoi); 2322, Aleksei Koltsov (after K. Gorbunov).

778 Saadi (Persian poet)

1959. Saadi Commemoration.

2323	**778**	40k. black and blue	1·40	70

779 Orbeliani (Georgian writer)

1959. Orbeliani Commemoration.

2324	**779**	40k. black and red	1·10	25

780 "Hero riding Dolphin"

1959. Birth Tercentenary of Ogata Korin (Japanese artist).

2325	**780**	40k. multicoloured	4·00	2·75

781 "Rossiya" on Odessa-Batum Service

1959. Russian Liners. Multicoloured.

2326	10k. "Sovetsky Soyuz" on Vladi-vostok–Kamchatka service	40	20
2327	20k. "Feliks Dzerzhinsky" on Odessa–Latakia service	60	25
2328	40k. Type **781**	1·00	35
2329	40k. "Kooperatsiya" on Mur-mansk–Tyksi service	1·00	35
2330	60k. "Mikhail Kalinin" leaving Leningrad	1·70	55
2331	1r. "Baltika" on Leningrad–Lon-don service	2·10	1·10

782 Trajectory of Moon Rocket

1959. Launching of Moon Rocket. Inscr "2-1-1959".

2332	**782**	40k. brown and pink	1·40	45
2333	-	40k. blue and light blue	1·40	45

DESIGN: No. 2333, Preliminary route of moon rocket after launching.

783 Lenin

1959. 89th Birth Anniv of Lenin.

2334	**783**	40k. brown	1·40	70

784 M. Cachin

1959. 90th Birth Anniv of Marcel Cachin (French communist leader).

2335	**784**	60k. brown	1·40	40

785 Youths with Banner

1959. Tenth Anniv of World Peace Movement.

2336	**785**	40k. multicoloured	1·40	40

786 A. von Humboldt

1959. Death Centenary of Alexander von Humboldt (German naturalist).

2337	**786**	40k. brown and violet	1·40	55

787 Haydn

1959. 150th Death Anniv of Haydn (Austrian composer).

2338	**787**	40k. brown and blue	1·40	40

788 Mountain Climbing

1959. Tourist Publicity. Multicoloured.

2339	40k. Type **788**	1·10	40
2340	40k. Map reading	1·10	40
2341	40k. Cross country skiing	1·10	40
2342	40k. Canoeing (horiz)	1·10	40

789 Exhibition Emblem and New York Coliseum

1959. Russian Scientific, Technological and Cultural Exhibition, New York.

2343	**789**	20k. multicoloured	55	25
2344	**789**	40k. multicoloured	95	35
MS2344a		61×76 mm. As No. 2344 but larger. Imperf	10·00	6·75

790 Statue of I. Repin (painter), Moscow (M. Manizer)

1959. Cultural Celebrities. Inscr "1959". Statues in black.

2345	**790**	10k. ochre	25	15
2346	-	10k. red	25	15

2347	-	20k. lilac	40	20
2348	-	25k. turquoise	55	25
2349	-	60k. green	1·10	40
2350	-	1r. blue	2·00	80

STATUES: 10k. (No. 2346), Lenin, Ulanovsk (M. Manizer); 80k. V. Mayakosky (poet), Moscow (A. Kibalnikov); 25k Aleksandr Pushkin (writer), Leningrad, (M. Anikushin; 60k. Maksim Gorky (writer), Moscow (Vera Mukhina); Ir. Tchaikovsky (composer), Moscow (Vera Mukhina).

791 Russian Sturgeon

1959. Fisheries Protection.

2350a		20k. black and blue	55	15
2350b		25k. brown and lilac	60	25
2351	**791**	40k. black and turquoise	80	35
2351a	-	40k. purple and mauve	1·10	35
2352	-	60k. black and blue	1·50	45

DESIGNS: 20k. Zander; 25k. Northern fur seals; 40k. (No. 2351a), Common whitefish; 60k. Chum salmon and map.

792 Louis Braille

1959. 150th Birth Anniv of Braille (inventor of Braille).

2353	**792**	60k. brown, yell & turq	1·10	40

793 Musa Djalil (Tatar poet)

1959. Djalil Commemoration.

2354	**793**	40k. black and violet	1·10	40

794 Vaulting

1959. Second Russian Spartakiad. Inscr "1959".

2355	**794**	15k. grey and purple	35	15
2356	-	25k. grey, brown & green	70	20
2357	-	30k. olive and red	80	25
2358	-	60k. grey, blue and yellow	1·20	40

DESIGNS—HORIZ: 25k. Running; 60k. Water polo. VERT: 30k. Athletes supporting Spartakiad emblem.

795

1959. Second International T.U. Conference, Leipzig.

2359	**795**	40k. red, blue and yellow	1·10	40

796 Steel Worker

1959. Seven Year Plan.

2360	-	10k. red, blue and violet	25	15
2361	-	10k. lt red, dp red & yell	25	15
2362	-	15k. red, yellow & brn	35	15
2363	-	15k. brown, green & bis	35	15
2364	-	20k. red, yellow & green	40	15
2365	-	20k. multicoloured	40	15
2366	-	30k. red, flesh & purple	70	25
2366a	-	30k. multicoloured	70	25
2367	**796**	40k. orange, yellow & bl	80	35
2368	-	40k. red, pink and blue	80	35
2369	-	60k. red, blue and yellow	1·40	55
2370	-	60k. red, buff and blue	1·40	55

DESIGNS: 2360, Chemist; 2361, Spassky Tower, hammer and sickle; 2362, Builder's labourer; 2363, Farm girl; 2364, Machine minder; No. 2365, Tractor driver; 2366, Oil technician; 2366a, Cloth production; . 2368, Coal miner; 2369, Iron moulder; 2370, Power station.

797 Glaciologist

1959. International Geophysical Year (2nd issue).

2371	**797**	10k. turquoise	60	15
2372	-	25k. red and blue	1·50	25
2373	-	40k. red and blue	1·80	40
2373a	-	1r. blue and yellow	3·75	95

DESIGNS: 25k. Oceanographic survey ship "Vityaz"; 40k. Antarctic map, camp and emperor penguin; 1r. Observatory and rocket.

798 Novgorod

1959. 11th Centenary of Novgorod.

2374	**798**	40k. red, brown and blue	95	40

799 Schoolboys in Workshop

1959. Industrial Training Scheme for School-leavers. Inscr "1959".

2375	**799**	40k. violet	70	25
2376	-	1r. blue	1·50	55

DESIGN: 1r. Children at night-school.

800 Exhibition Emblem

1959. All Union Exhibition.

2377	**800**	40k. multicoloured	80	55

801 Russian and Chinese Students

1959. Tenth Anniv of Chinese Peoples' Republic.

2378	**801**	20k. multicoloured	40	25
2379	-	40k. multicoloured	95	40

DESIGN: 40k. Russian miner and Chinese foundryman.

802 Postwoman

1959. International Correspondence Week.

2380	**802**	40k. multicoloured	80	25
2381	**802**	60k. multicoloured	1·10	40

803 Mahtumkuli (after A. Khadzhiev)

1959. 225th Birth Anniv of Mahtumkuli (Turkestan writer).

2382	**803**	40k. brown	95	40

804 Arms and Workers of the German Democratic Republic

1959. Tenth Anniv of German Democratic Republic.

2383	**804**	40k. multicoloured	70	25
2384	-	60k. purple and cream	2·00	40

DESIGN—VERT: 60k. Town Hall, East Berlin.

805 Lunik 3's Trajectory around the Moon

1959. Launching of "Lunik 3" Rocket.

2385	**805**	40k. violet	2·40	55

806 Republican Arms and Emblem

1959. 30th Anniv of Tadzhikistan Republic.

2386	**806**	40k. multicoloured	1·40	40

807 Red Square, Moscow

1959. 42nd Anniv of October Revolution.

2387	**807**	40k. red	1·40	40

808 Capitol, Washington and Kremlin, Moscow

1959. Visit of Russian Prime Minister to U.S.A.

2388	**808**	60k. blue and yellow	1·50	55

809 Mil Mi-1 Helicopter

1959. Military Sports.

2389	**809**	10k. red and violet	35	15
2390	-	25k. brown and blue	55	20
2391	-	40k. blue and brown	70	25
2392	-	60k. bistre and blue	95	35

DESIGNS: 25k. Skin diver; 40k. Racing motor cyclist; 60k. Parachutist.

810 Track of Moon Rocket

1959. Landing of Russian Rocket on Moon. Inscr "14. IX.1959". Multicoloured.

2393	40k. Type **810**	1·80	40
2394	40k. Diagram of flight trajectory	1·80	40

811 Liberty Monument (Zs. Kisfaludy-Strobl), Budapest

1959. 15th Anniv of Hungarian Republic. Multicoloured.

2395	20k. Sandor Petofi (Hungarian poet) (horiz)	40	15
2396	40k. Type **811**	95	40

812 Manolis Glezos (Greek Communist)

1959. Glezos Commemoration.

2397	**812**	40k. brown and blue	18·00	10·00

813 A. Voskresensky (chemist)

1959. Voskresensky Commemoration.

2398	**813**	40k. brown and blue	1·10	40

814 River Chusovaya

1959. Tourist Publicity. Inscr "1959".

2399	**814**	10k. violet	25	15
2400	-	10k. mauve	25	15
2401	-	25k. blue	50	25
2402	-	25k. red	50	25
2403	-	25k. olive	50	25
2404	-	40k. red	95	40
2405	-	60k. turquoise	1·50	70
2406	-	1r. green	2·75	1·10
2407	-	1r. orange	2·75	1·10

DESIGNS: No. 2400, Riza Lake, Caucasus; 2401, River Lena; 2402, Iskanderkuly Lake; 2403, Coastal region; 2404, Lake Baikal; . 2405, Beluha Mountains, Altay; 2406, Khibinsky Mountains; 2407, Gursuff region, Crimea.

815 "The Trumpeters of the First Horse Army" (M. Grekov)

1959. 40th Anniv of Russian Cavalry.

2408	**815**	40k. multicoloured	4·00	2·75

816 A. P. Chekhov and Moscow Residence

1960. Birth Centenary of Chekhov (writer).

2409	**816**	20k. red, brown & vio	55	25
2410	-	40k. brown, blue & sepia	95	40

DESIGN: 40k. Chekhov and Yalta residence.

817 M. V. Frunze

1960. 75th Birth Anniv of M. V. Frunze (military leader).

2411	**817**	40k. brown	95	55

818 G. N. Gabrichevsky

1960. Birth Centenary of G. N. Gabrichevsky (microbiologist).

2412	**818**	40k. brown and violet	1·40	55

819 Vera Komissarzhevskaya

1960. 50th Death Anniv of V. F. Komissarzhevskaya (actress).

2413	**819**	40k. brown	95	40

820 Free-skating

1960. Winter Olympic Games.

2414	-	10k. blue and orange	55	15
2415	-	25k. multicoloured	80	20
2416	-	40k. orange, blue & pur	1·20	25
2417	**820**	60k. violet, brown & grn	1·90	40
2418	-	1r. blue, red and green	3·25	70

DESIGNS: 10k. Ice hockey; 25k. Ice skating; 40k. Skiing; 1r. Ski jumping.

821 Timur Frunze (fighter pilot) and Air Battle

1960. War Heroes. Multicoloured.

2419	40k. Type **821**	5·50	4·00
2420	1r. Gen. Chernyakhovksy and battle scene	4·00	1·20

822 Mil Mi-4 Helicopter over Kremlin

1960. Air.

2421	**822**	60k. blue	1·80	55

823 Women of Various Races

1960. 50th Anniv of International Women's Day.

2422	**823**	40k. multicoloured	1·40	40

824 "Swords into Ploughshares" (Ye. Buchetich)

1960. Presentation of Statue by Russia to U.N.

2423	**824**	40k. yellow, bistre and blue	95	40
MS2423a		78×115 mm. No. 2423	3·50	2·75

15 лет освобождения Венгрии
(825)

1960. 15th Anniv of Liberation of Hungary. Optd with T **825**.

2424	**811**	40k. multicoloured	8·75	7·50

826 Lenin when a Child

1960. 90th Birth Anniv of Lenin. Portraits of Lenin. Multicoloured.

2425	**826**	10k. multicoloured	25	15
2426	-	20k. multicoloured	45	20
2427	-	30k. multicoloured	70	25
2428	-	40k. multicoloured	95	35
2429	-	60k. multicoloured	1·60	45
2430	-	1r. brown, blue and red	2·40	80

DESIGNS: Lenin: 20k. holding child (after N. Zkukov); 30k. and revolutionary scenes; 40k. with party banners; 60k. and industrial scenes; 1r. with globe and rejoicing people (after A. Seral).

827 "Lunik 3" photographing Moon

1960. Flight of "Lunik 3". Inscr "7.X.1959".

2431	**827**	40k. yellow and blue	1·40	45
2432	-	60k. yellow, blue & indigo	1·90	70

DESIGN: 60k. Lunar map.

828 Government House, Baku

1960. 40th Anniv of Azerbaijan Republic.

2433	**828**	40k. brown, bistre & yell	95	40

829 "Fraternization" (K. Pokorny)

1960. 15th Anniv of Czechoslovak Republic.

2434	**829**	40k. black and blue	70	25
2435	-	60k. brown and yellow	1·10	40

DESIGN: 60k. Charles Bridge, Prague.

830 Furnaceman

1960. Completion of First Year of Seven Year Plan.

2436	**830**	40k. brown and red	80	40

831 Popov Museum, Leningrad

1960. Radio Day.

2437	**831**	40k. multicoloured	1·40	40

832 Robert Schumann

1960. 150th Birth Anniv of Schumann (composer).

2438	**832**	40k. black and blue	1·40	55

833 Sverdlov

1960. 75th Birth Anniv of Ya. M. Sverdlov (statesman).

2439	**833**	40k. sepia and brown	2·75	80

834 Magnifier and Stamp

1960. Philatelists' Day.

2440	**834**	60k. multicoloured	1·80	80

835 Petrozavodsk (Karelian Republic)

1960. Capitals of Autonomous Republic (1st issue).

2441	**835**	40k. turquoise	1·50	1·10
2442	-	40k. blue	1·50	1·10
2443	-	40k. green	1·50	1·10
2444	-	40k. purple	1·50	1·10
2445	-	40k. red	1·50	1·10
2446	-	40k. blue	1·20	55
2447	-	40k. brown	1·20	55
2448	-	40k. brown	1·20	55
2449	-	40k. red	1·20	55
2450	-	40k. brown	1·20	55

CAPITALS: Nos. 2442, Batumi (Adzharian); 2443, Izhevsk (Udmurt); 2444, Grozny (Chechen-Ingush); 2445, Cheboksary (Chuvash); 2446, Yakutsk (Yakut); 2447, Ordzhonikidze (North Ossetian); 2448, Nukus (Kara-Kalpak); 2449, Makhachkala (Daghestan); 2450, Yoshkar-Ola (Mari).

See also Nos. 2586/92 and 2703/5.

836 Children of Different Races

1960. International Children's Day. Multicoloured.

2451	10k. Type **836**	25	15
2452	20k. Children on farm (vert)	55	20
2453	25k. Children with snowman	70	25
2454	40k. Children in zoo gardens	1·20	40

1960. 40th Anniv of Karelian Autonomous Republic. Optd **40 лет КАССР 8.VI.1960.**

2455	**835**	40k. turquoise	6·25	3·00

838 Rocket

1960. Launching of Cosmic Rocket "Spacecraft 1" (first "Vostok" type spacecraft).

2456	**838**	40k. red and blue	3·00	85

839 I.F.A.C. Emblem

1960. First International Automation Control Federation Congress, Moscow.

2457	**839**	60k. brown and yellow	2·30	75

1960. Birth Centenary (1959) of Kosta Khetagurov (poet). As T **746**. Inscr "1960".

2458	40k. brown and blue	1·50	45

DESIGN: 40k. Portrait of Khetagurov and scene from his works.

840 Cement Works, Belgorod

1960. First Plant Construction of Seven Year Plan.

2459	**840**	25k. black and blue	45	15
2460	-	40k. black and red	60	30

DESIGN. 40k. Metal works, Novokrivorog.

841 Capstans and Cogwheel

1960. Industrial Mass-Production Plant.

2461	**841**	40k. turquoise	1·00	30
2462	-	40k. purple (Factory plant)	1·00	30

842 Vilnius (Lithuania)

1960. 20th Anniv of Soviet Baltic Republics. Multicoloured.

2463	40k. Type **842**	1·00	30
2464	40k. Riga (Latvia)	1·00	30
2465	40k. Tallin (Estonia)	1·00	30

843 Running

1960. Olympic Games. Inscr "1960". Multicoloured.

2466	5k. Type **843**	20	15
2467	10k. Wrestling	30	15
2468	15k. Basketball	35	15
2469	20k. Weightlifting	45	15
2470	25k. Boxing	60	20
2471	40k. High diving	85	30
2472	40k. Fencing	85	30
2473	40k. Gymnastics	85	30
2474	60k. Canoeing	1·30	45
2475	1r. Horse jumping	2·30	75

1960. 20th Anniv of Moldavian Republic. As T **842**.

2476	40k. multicoloured	1·00	30

DESIGN: 40k. Kishinev (capital).

Международная ярмарка в Риччоне
(844)

1960. International Exhibition, Riccione. No. 2471 optd with T **844**.

2477	40k. multicoloured	23·00	17·00

845 "Agriculture and Industry"

1960. 15th Anniv of Vietnam Democratic Republic.

2478	40k. Type **845**	85	30
2479	60k. Book Museum, Hanoi (vert)	1·30	30

846 G. H. Minkh

1960. 125th Birth Anniv of G. H. Minkh (epidemiologist).

2480	**846**	60k. brown and bistre	1·20	45

847 "March" (after I. Levitan)

1960. Birth Centenary of I. Levitan (painter).

2481	**847**	40k. black and olive	1·30	45

848 "Forest" (after Shishkin)

1960. Fifth World Forestry Congress, Seattle.

2482	**848**	1r. brown	3·75	1·00

849 Addressing Letter

1960. International Correspondence Week.

2483	**849**	40k. multicoloured	75	30
2484	**849**	60k. multicoloured	1·20	60

850 Kremlin, Dogs "Belka" and "Strelka" and Rocket Trajectory

1960. Second Cosmic Rocket Flight.

2485	**850**	40k. purple and yellow	1·20	30
2486	**850**	1r. blue and orange	3·00	60

851 Globes

1960. 15th Anniv of W.F.T.U.

2487	**851**	60k. blue, drab and lilac	1·20	45

852 People of Kazakhstan

1960. 40th Anniv of Kazakh Soviet Republic.

2488	**852**	40k. multicoloured	1·00	45

853 "Karl Marx"

1960. River Boats. Multicoloured.

2489	25k. Type **853**	60	15
2490	40k. "Lenin"	85	30
2491	60k. "Raketa" (hydrofoil)	1·50	60

854 A. N. Voronikhin and Leningrad Cathedral

1960. Birth Bicentenary of A. N. Voronikhin (architect).

2492	**854**	40k. black and grey	1·00	45

855 Motor Coach

1960. Russian Motor Industry.

2493	-	25k. black and blue	60	15
2494	-	40k. blue and olive	85	20
2495	-	60k. red and turquoise	1·30	30
2496	**855**	1r. multicoloured	2·00	60

DESIGNS: 25k. Lorry; 40k. "Volga" car; 60k. "Moskvich" car.

856 J. S. Gogebashvily

1960. 120th Birth Anniv of J. S. Gogebashvily (Georgian teacher).

2497	**856**	40k. black and lake	1·10	45

857 Industrial Plant and Power Plant

1960. 43rd Anniv of October Revolution.

2498	**857**	40k. multicoloured	1·10	45

858 Federation Emblem

1960. 15th Anniv of International Federation of Democratic Women.

2499	**858**	60k. red and grey	1·20	45

859 Youth of Three Races

1960. 15th Anniv of World Democratic Youth Federation.

2500	**859**	60k. multicoloured	1·20	45

40 лет Удмуртской АССР
4/XI 1960.

(860)

1960. 40th Anniv of Udmurt Autonomous Republic. No. 2443 optd with T **860**.

2501	40k. green	6·00	5·25

861 Tolstoi and his Moscow Residence

1960. 50th Death Anniv of Leo Tolstoi (writer).

2502	**861**	20k. multicoloured	45	15
2503	-	40k. brown, sepia & blue	1·10	30
2504	-	60k. multicoloured	1·50	60

DESIGNS—HORIZ: 40k. Tolstoi and his country estate. VERT: 60k. Full face portrait.

862 Government House, Yerevan

1960. 40th Anniv of Armenian Republic.

2505	**862**	40k. multicoloured	1·10	45

863 Students and University

1960. Opening of Friendship University, Moscow.

2506	**863**	40k. purple	1·10	45

864 Tulip

1960. Russian Flowers. Multicoloured.

2507	20k. Type **864**	30	15
2508	20k. Autumn crocus	30	15
2509	25k. Marsh marigold	45	25
2510	40k. Tulip	75	30
2511	40k. Panax	75	30
2512	60k. Hypericum	1·20	45
2513	60k. Iris	1·20	45
2514	1r. Wild rose	1·90	60

865 Engels

1960. 140th Birth Anniv of Engels.

2515	**865**	60k. grey	2·00	60

866 Mark Twain

1960. 125th Birth Anniv of Mark Twain.

2516	**866**	40k. bistre and orange	4·50	2·75

867 N. Pirogov

1960. 150th Birth Anniv of N. Pirogov (surgeon).

2517	**867**	40k. brown and green	1·10	45

868 Chopin (after Eugene Delacroix)

1960. 150th Birth Anniv of Chopin.

2518	**868**	40k. bistre and buff	1·80	45

869 North Korean Flag and Emblem

1960. 15th Anniv of Korean Liberation.

2519	**869**	40k. multicoloured	1·50	45

870 Lithuanian Costumes

1960. Provincial Costumes (1st issue). Inscr "1960". Multicoloured.

2520	10k. Type **870**	45	15
2521	60k. Uzbek costumes	2·10	75

See also Nos. 2537/45, 2796 and 2835/8.

871 A. Tseretely

1960. 120th Birth Anniv of A. Tseretely (Georgian poet).

2522	**871**	40k. purple and lilac	2·00	45

872 Worker

1961. Inscr "1961".

2523	**872**	1k. bistre	45	15
2524	-	2k. green	45	15
2525	-	3k. violet	2·75	30
2526	-	4k. red	95	25
2526a	-	4k. brown	23·00	21·00
2527	-	6k. red	8·25	1·10
2528	-	6k. claret	2·30	30
2529	-	10k. orange	3·50	30
2530	-	16k. blue	4·25	1·20
2533	-	12k. purple	3·50	45

DESIGNS: 2k. Combine harvester; 3k. Cosmic rocket; 4k. Soviet Arms and Flag; 6k. Spassky Tower and Kremlin; 10k. "Worker and Collective Farmer" (sculpture, Vera Mukhina); 12k. Monument to F. Minin and D. Pozharsky and Spassky Tower; 16k. Airliner over power station.

1961. Russian Wild Life. As T **653** but inscr "1961". Centres in natural colours. Frame colours given.

2534	1k. sepia (Brown bear)	60	45
2535	6k. black (Eurasian beaver)	1·50	1·40
2536	10k. black (Roe deer)	1·80	1·70

The 1k. is vert and the rest horiz.

1961. Provincial Costumes (2nd issue). As T **870** but inscr "1961".

2537	2k. red, brown and stone	30	15
2538	2k. multicoloured	30	15
2539	3k. multicoloured	55	25
2540	3k. multicoloured	55	25
2541	3k. multicoloured	55	25
2542	4k. multicoloured	70	30
2543	6k. multicoloured	90	40
2544	10k. multicoloured	1·50	45
2545	12k. multicoloured	2·30	60

COSTUMES: No. 2337, Moldavia; 2538, Georgia; 2539, Ukraine; 2540, Byelorussia; 2541, Kazakhs; 2542, Koryaks; 2543, Russia; 2544, Armenia; 2545, Estonia.

873 "Ruslan and Lyudmila" (Pushkin)

1961. Scenes from Russian Fairy Tales. Multicoloured.

2546	1k. "Geese Swans"	55	15
2547	3k. "The Fox, the Hare and the Cock"	85	30
2548	4k. "The Little Humpbacked Horse"	1·10	40
2549	6k. "The Muzhik and the Bear"	1·40	45
2550	10k. Type **873**	1·50	60

874 Lenin, Map and Power Station

1961. 40th Anniv of State Electricity Plan.

2551	**874**	4k. brown, yellow & blue	75	45
2552	**874**	10k. black, purple and salmon	1·50	60

875 Tractor

1961. Soviet Agricultural Achievements. Inscr "1961".

2553	-	3k. mauve and blue	70	25
2554	**875**	4k. black and green	90	30
2555	-	6k. brown and blue	1·10	55
2556	-	10k. purple and olive	1·50	60

DESIGNS: 3k. Dairy herd; 6k. Agricultural machinery; 10k. Fruit picking.

876 Dobrolyubov (after P. Borel)

1961. 125th Birth Anniv of N. A. Dobrolyubov (writer).

2557	**876**	4k. buff, black and blue	80	30

877 N. D. Zelinsky

1961. Birth Centenary of N. D. Zelinsky (chemist).

2558	**877**	4k. purple and mauve	75	30

878 Georgian Republic Flag

1961. 40th Anniv of Georgian Republic.

2559	**878**	4k. multicoloured	60	30

879 Sgt. Miroshnichenko and Battle

1961. War Hero.

2560	**879**	4k. blue and purple	1·10	45

See also Nos. 2664/5.

880 Self-portrait and Birthplace

1961. Death Centenary of T. G. Shevchenko (Ukrainian poet and painter).

2561	**880**	3k. brown and violet	60	30
2562	-	6k. purple and green	1·50	75

DESIGN: 6k. Shevchenko in old age (after I. Kramskoi), pen, book and candle.

See also Nos. 2956/62.

881 A. Rublev

1961. 600th Birth Anniv of Rublev (painter).

2563	**881**	4k. multicoloured	75	30

882 Statue of Shevchenko (poet), Kharkov (M. Manizer)

1961. Cultural Celebrities.

2564	-	2k. brown and blue	45	30
2565	**882**	4k. brown and black	60	40
2566	-	4k. brown and purple	60	40

DESIGNS: 2k. Shchors Monument, Kiev (M. Lysenko); 4k. (No. 2566), Kotovsky Monument, Kishinev (L. Dubinovsky).

883 N. V. Sklifosovsky

1961. 125th Birth Anniv of N. Y. Sklifosovsky (surgeon).

2567	**883**	4k. black and blue	75	30

884 Robert Koch

1961. 50th Death Anniv of Robert Koch (German microbiologist).

2568	**884**	6k. brown	1·10	45

885 Zither-player and Folk Dancers

1961. 50th Anniv of Russian National Choir.

2569	**885**	4k. multicoloured	60	30

886 "Popular Science"

1961. Cent of "Vokrug Sveta" (science magazine).

2570	**886**	6k. brown, blue and deep blue	1·80	1·10

887 Venus Rocket

1961. Launching of Venus Rocket.

2571	**887**	6k. orange and blue	1·50	30
2572	-	10k. blue and yellow	2·40	45

DESIGN: 10k. Capsule and flight route.

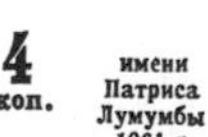

(888)

1961. Patrice Lumumba (Congolese politician) Commemoration (1st issue). Surch with T 888.

2573	**863**	4k. on 40k. purple	2·75	1·80

See also No. 2593.

889 African breaking Chains

1961. Africa Freedom Day. Inscr "1961".

2574	**889**	4k. multicoloured	45	25
2575	-	6k. purple, orange and blue	75	30

DESIGN: 6k. Hands clasping Torch of Freedom, and map.

891 Yuri Gagarin

1961. World's First Manned Space Flight. Inscr "12-IV-1961". Perf or imperf.

2576	**891**	3k. blue	90	30
2577	-	6k. blue, violet and red	1·50	90
2578	-	10k. red, green & brown	2·00	90

DESIGNS—37×26 mm: 6k. Rocket and Spassky Tower; 10k. Rocket, Gagarin and Kremlin.

892 Lenin

1961. 91st Birth Anniv of Lenin.

2579	**892**	4k. blk, salmon and red	80	30

893 Rabindranath Tagore

1961. Birth Centenary of Tagore (Indian writer).

2580	**893**	6k. black, bistre and red	1·00	45

894 Garibaldi

1961. International Labour Exhibition, Turin.

2581	-	4k. salmon and red	60	15
2582	**894**	6k. salmon and lilac	90	30

DESIGN: 4k. "To the Stars" (statue, G. Postnikov).

895 Lenin

1961

2583	**895**	20k. green and brown	2·40	2·30
2584	-	30k. blue and brown	4·00	3·75
2585	-	50k. red and brown	9·00	7·50

PORTRAITS (Lenin): 30k. In cap; 50k. Profile.

1961. Capitals of Autonomous Republics (2nd issue). As T **835**.

2586	4k. deep violet	60	45
2587	4k. blue	60	45
2588	4k. orange	60	45
2589	4k. black	60	45
2590	4k. lake	60	45
2591	4k. green	60	45
2592	4k. deep purple	60	45

CAPITALS: No. 2586, Nalchik (Kabardino-Balkar); 2587, Ulan-Ude (Buryat); 2588, Sukhumi (Abkhazia); 2589, Syktyvkar (Komi); 2590, Nakhichevan (Nakhichevan); 2591, Rodina Cinema, Elista (Kalmyk); 2592, Ufa (Bashkir).

896 Patrice Lumumba

1961. Lumumba Commemoration (2nd issue).

2593	**896**	2k. multicoloured	50	30

897 Kindergarten

1961. International Children's Day.

2594	**897**	2k. blue and orange	30	15
2595	-	3k. violet and ochre	45	30
2596	-	4k. drab and red	75	40

DESIGNS—HORIZ: 3k. Children in Pioneer camp. VERT: 4k. Children with toys and pets.

898 Chernushka and Rocket

1961. Fourth and Fifth "Spacecraft" Flights.

2597		2k. black, blue and violet	1·00	30
2598	**898**	4k. turquoise and blue	1·70	45

DESIGN—HORIZ: 2k. Dog "Zvezdochka", rocket and controller (inscr "25.III.1961").

899 Belinsky (after I. Astafev)

1961. 150th Birth Anniv of Vissarion Grigorievich Belinsky (literary critic and journalist).

2599	**899**	4k. black and red	75	30

900

1961. 40th Anniv of Soviet Hydro-meteorological Service.

2600	**900**	6k. multicoloured	1·20	45

901 D. M. Karbyshev

1961. Lieut-Gen. Karbyshev (war hero).

2601	**901**	4k. black, red and yellow	60	30

902 Glider

1961. Soviet Spartakiad.

2602	**902**	4k. red and grey	45	30
2603	-	6k. red and grey	75	45
2604	-	10k. red and grey	1·70	60

DESIGNS: 6k. Inflatable motor boat; 10k. Motor cyclists.

903 Sukhe Bator Monument and Govt. Buildings, Ulan Bator

1961. 40th Anniv of Revolution in Mongolia.

2605	**903**	4k. multicoloured	1·10	45

904 S. I. Vavilov

1961. 70th Birthday of Vavilov (scientist).

2606	**904**	4k. brown, bistre & green	75	30

905 V. Pshavela

1961. Birth Cent of Pshavela (Georgian poet).

2607	905	4k. brown and cream	75	45

906 "Youth Activities"

1961. World Youth Forum.

2608	-	2k. brown and orange	45	30
2609	-	4k. green and lilac	75	40
2610	906	6k. blue and ochre	1·10	45

DESIGNS—HORIZ: 2k. Youths pushing tank into river. VERT: 4k. "Youths and progress".

907

1961. Fifth Int Biochemical Congress, Moscow.

2611	907	6k. multicoloured	1·10	45

908

1961. Centenary of "Kalevipoeg" (Estonian Saga).

2612	908	4k. yellow, turq & blk	75	30

909 Javelin Thrower

1961. Seventh Soviet Trade Union Sports.

2613	909	6k. red	75	30

910 A.D. Zakharov (after S. Shchukin)

1961. Birth Bicentenary of Zakharov (architect).

2614	910	buff, brown and blue	70	30

911 Counter-attack (after P. Krivonogov)

1961. War of 1941–45 (1st issue). Inscr "1961".

2615	911	4k. multicoloured	70	45
2616	-	4k. multicoloured	70	45
2617	-	4k. indigo and brown	70	45

DESIGNS: No. 2616, Sailor with bayonet; No. 2617, Soldier with tommy gun.

See also Nos. 2717 and 2851/5.

912 Union Emblem

1961. 15th Anniv of International Union of Students.

2617a	912	6k. violet and red	75	30

913 Stamps commemorating Industry

1961. 40th Anniv of First Soviet Stamp. Centres multicoloured.

2618	913	2k. ochre and brown	40	30
2619	-	4k. blue and indigo	70	45
2620	-	6k. green and olive	1·10	60
2621	-	10k. buff and brown	1·70	1·10

DESIGNS (stamps commemorating): 4k. Electrification; 8k. Peace; 10k. Atomic energy.

914 Titov and "Vostok 2"

1961. Second Manned Space Flight. Perf or imperf.

2622		4k. blue and purple	75	30
2623	914	6k. orange, green & brn	1·10	45

DESIGN: 4k. Space pilot and globe.

915 Angara River Bridge

1961. Tercentenary of Irkutsk, Siberia.

2624	915	4k. black, lilac and bistre	85	30

916 Letters and Mail Transport

1961. International Correspondence Week.

2625	916	4k. black and mauve	1·40	50

917 Workers and Banners

1961. 22nd Communist Party Congress (1st issue).

2626	917	2k. brown, yellow and red	65	30
2627	-	3k. blue and orange	1·90	50
2628	-	4k. red, buff and purple	80	50
2629	-	4k. orange, black & mve	80	50
2630	-	4k. sepia, brown and red	80	50

DESIGNS: No. 2627, Moscow University and obelisk; 2628, Combine harvester; 2629, Workmen and machinery; 2630, Worker and slogan.

See also No. 2636.

918 Soviet Monument, Berlin

1961. Tenth Anniv of International Federation of Resistance Fighters.

2631	918	4k. grey and red	85	30

919 Adult Education

1961. Communist Labour Teams.

2632	-	2k. purple & red on buff	35	15
2633	919	3k. brown & red on buff	50	30
2634	-	4k. blue and red on cream	70	50

DESIGNS: 2k. Worker at machine; 4k. Workers around piano.

920 Rocket and Globes

1961. Cosmic Flights. Aluminium-surfaced paper.

2635	920	1r. red and black on silver	85·00	95·00

XXII съезд
КПСС
(921)

1961. 22nd Communist Party Congress (2nd issue). Optd with T **921**.

2636		1r. red and black on silver	70·00	80·00

922 Imanov (after A. Kasteev)

1961. 42nd Death Anniv of Amangeldy Imanov (Kazakh Leader).

2637	922	4k. sepia, brown & green	70	30

923 Liszt, Piano and Music

1961. 150th Birth Anniv of Liszt.

2638	923	4k. brown, purple & yell	1·40	40

924 Flags, Rocket and Skyline

1961. 44th Anniv of October Revolution.

2639	924	4k. red, purple and yellow	95	30

925 Congress Emblem

1961. 5th W.F.T.U. Congress, Moscow. Inscr "МОСКВА 1961".

2640	925	2k. red and bistre	35	15
2641	-	2k. violet and grey	35	15
2642	-	4k. brown, purple & blue	70	25
2643	-	4k. red, blue and violet	70	25
2644	925	6k. red, bistre and green	85	30
2645	-	6k. blue, purple and bistre	85	30

DESIGNS—HORIZ: Nos. 2641, 2645, Negro breaking chains. VERT: No. 2642, Hand holding hammer; 2643, Hands holding globe.

926 Statue of Lomonosov (N. Tomsky) and Lomonosov University

1961. 250th Birth Anniv of Mikhail Lomonosov (scientist).

2646	926	4k. brown, green and blue	70	15
2647	-	6k. blue, buff and green	1·00	30
2648	-	10k. brown, blue & pur	1·90	65

DESIGNS—VERT: 6k. Lomonosov at desk (after M. Shreier). HORIZ: 10k. Lomonosov (after L. Miropolsky), his birthplace, and Leningrad Academy of Science.

927 Power Workers

1961. Young Builders of Seven Year Plan. Inscr "1961".

2649	927	3k. grey, brown and red	45	15
2650	-	4k. brown, blue and red	50	25
2651	-	6k. grey, brown and red	1·00	30

DESIGNS: 4k. Welders; 6k. Engineer with theodolite.

928 Scene from "Romeo and Juliet" (Prokotiev)

1961. Russian Ballet (1st issue). Multicoloured.

2652	6k. Type **928**	85	30
2653	10k. Scene from "Swan Lake" (Tchaikovsky)	1·40	50

See also Nos. 2666/7.

929 Hammer and Sickle

1961. 25th Anniv of Soviet Constitution.

2654	929	4k. lake, yellow and red	70	30

930 A. Pumpur

1961. 120th Birth Anniv of Pumpur (Lettish poet).

2655	930	4k. purple and grey	55	30

1961. Air. Surch **1961 r. 6 kon.** and wavy lines.

2656	822	6k. on 60k. blue	1·40	40

932 "Bulgarian Achievements"

1961. 15th Anniv of Bulgarian Republic.

2657	932	4k. multicoloured	70	30

933 Nansen and "Fram"

1961. Birth Centenary of Nansen (explorer).

2658	933	6k. brown, blue and black	2·75	1·10

934 M. Dolivo-Dobrovolsky

1962. Birth Centenary of Dolivo-Dobrovolsky (electrical engineer).

2659	934	4k. blue and bistre	85	50

935 A. S. Pushkin (after O. Kiprensky)

1962. 125th Death Anniv of Pushkin (poet).

2660	935	4k. black, red and buff	85	50

936 Soviet Woman

1962. Soviet Women.

2661	936	4k. black, bistre & orange	70	30

937 People's Dancers

1962. 25th Anniv of Soviet People's Dance Ensemble.
2662 **937** 4k. brown and red 85 30

938 Skaters

1962. Ice Skating Championships, Moscow.
2663 **938** 4k. blue and orange 95 30

1962. War Heroes. As T **879** but inscr "1962".
2664 4k. brown and blue 1·90 95
2665 6k. turquoise and brown 2·00 1·00
DESIGNS: 4k. Lieut. Shalandin, tanks and Yakovlev Yak-9T fighters; 6k. Capt. Gadzhiev, "K-3" submarine and sinking ship.

1962. Russian Ballet (2nd issue). As T **928** but inscr "1962".
2666 2k. multicoloured 50 25
2667 3k. multicoloured 70 30
DESIGNS: Scenes from—2k. "Red Flower" (Glier); 3k. "Paris Flame" (Asafev).

СОВЕТСКИЕ КОНЬКОБЕЖЦЫ—
ЧЕМПИОНЫ
МИРА
(939)

1962. Soviet Victory in Ice Skating Championships.No 2663 Optd with T **939**.
2668 4k. blue and orange 6·75 4·75

940 Skiing

1962. First People's Winter Games, Sverdlovsk.
2669 **940** 4k. violet and red 70 30
2670 - 6k. turquoise and purple 85 50
2671 - 10k. red, black and blue 1·50 80
DESIGN: 6k. Ice Hockey; 10k. Figure skating.

941 A. I. Herzen (after N. Ge)

1962. 150th Birth Anniv of A. I. Herzen (writer).
2672 **941** 4k. flesh, black and blue 70 30

942 Lenin on Banner

1962. 14th Leninist Young Communist League Congress. Inscr "1962".
2673 **942** 4k. red, yellow and purple 50 15
2674 - 6k. purple, orange & blue 70 30
DESIGN—HORIZ: 6k. Lenin (after A. Mylnikov) on flag.

943 Rocket and Globe

1962. First Anniv of World's First Manned Space Flight. Perf or imperf.
2675 **943** 10k. multicoloured 2·10 90

944 Tchaikovsky (after sculpture by Z. M. Vilensky)

1962. Second Int Tchaikovsky Music Competition.
2676 **944** 4k. drab, black and blue 1·10 40

945 Youth of Three Races

1962. International Day of "Solidarity of Youth against Colonialism".
2677 **945** 6k. multicoloured 85 30

946 The Ulyanov (Lenin's) Family

1962. 92nd Birth Anniv of Lenin.
2678 **946** 4k. brown, grey and red 85 30
2679 - 10k. purple, red and black 2·50 65
DESIGN: 10k. Bust of Lenin (N. Sokolov).

947 "Cosmos 3"

1962. Cosmic Research.
2680 **947** 6k. black, violet and blue 1·20 50

948 Charles Dickens

1962. 150th Birth Anniv of Charles Dickens.
2681 **948** 6k. purple, turq & brn 1·00 50

949 J. J. Rousseau

1962. 250th Birth Anniv of Rousseau.
2682 **949** 6k. bistre, purple and grey 1·00 50

950 Karl Marx Monument, Moscow (L. Kerbel)

1962. Karl Marx Commemoration.
2683 **950** 4k. grey and blue 70 30

951 Lenin reading "Pravda"

1962. 50th Anniv of "Pravda" Newspaper.
2684 **951** 4k. purple, red and buff 70 50
2685 - 4k. multicoloured 70 50
2686 - 4k. multicoloured 70 50
DESIGNS—25×38 mm: No. 2685, Statuary and front page of first issue of "Pravda"; No. 2686, Lenin (after A. Mylnikov) and modern front page of "Pravda".

952 Mosquito and Campaign Emblem

1962. Malaria Eradication. Perf (6k. also imperf).
2687 **952** 4k. black, turquoise & red 75 30
2688 **952** 6k. black, green and red 1·20 65

953 Model Rocket Construction

1962. 40th Anniv of All Union Lenin Pioneer Organization. Designs embody Pioneer badge. Multicoloured.
2689 2k. Lenin and Pioneers giving Oath 35 15
2690 3k. Lenya Golikov and Valya Kotik (pioneer heroes) 50 30
2691 4k. Type **953** 85 30
2692 4k. Hygiene education 85 40
2693 6k. Pioneers marching 1·40 50

1962. 25th Anniv of First Soviet Polar Drifting Station. No. **MS**1926a optd "**1962**" in red on each stamp and with commemorative inscription optd in margin below stamps.
MS2693a 154×111 mm. No. 1926×4 £200 £200

954 M. Mashtotz

1962. 1600th Birth Anniv of Mesrop Mashtotz (author of Armenian Alphabet).
2694 **954** 4k. brown and yellow 1·30 35

955 Ski Jumping

1962. F.I.S. International Ski Championships, Zakopane (Poland).
2695 **955** 2k. red, brown and blue 50 15
2696 - 10k. blue, black and red 1·70 65
DESIGN—VERT: 10k. Skier.

956 I. Goncharov (after I. Kramskoi)

1962. 150th Birth Anniv of I. Goncharov (writer).
2697 **956** 4k. brown and grey 75 30

957 Cycle Racing

1962. Summer Sports Championships.
2698 **957** 2k. black, red and brown 35 15
2699 - 4k. black, yellow & brn 50 30
2700 - 10k. black, lemon & blue 1·50 50
2701 - 12k. brown, yellow & bl 1·70 65
2702 - 16k. multicoloured 2·40 80
DESIGN—VERT: 4k. Volleyball; 10k. Rowing; 16k. Horse jumping. HORIZ: 12k. Football (goal keeper).

1962. Capitals of Autonomous Republics. 3rd issue. As T **835**.
2703 4k. black 1·00 65
2704 4k. purple 1·00 65
2705 4k. green 1·00 65
CAPITALS: No. 2703, Kazan (Tatar); No. 2704, Kyzyl (Tuva); No. 2705, Saransk (Mordovian).

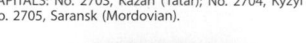

958 Lenin Library, 1862

1962. Centenary of Lenin Library.
2706 **958** 4k. black and grey 50 30
2707 - 4k. black and grey 50 30
DESIGN: No. 2707, Modern library building.

959 Fur Bourse, Leningrad and Ermine

1962. Fur Bourse Commemoration.
2708 **959** 6k. multicoloured 1·40 80

960 Pasteur

1962. Centenary of Pasteur's Sterilization Process.
2709 **960** 6k. brown and black 1·00 65

961 Youth and Girl with Book

1962. Communist Party Programme. Multicoloured.
2710 2k. Type **961** 50 15
2711 4k. Workers of three races and dove 85 30

962 Hands breaking Bomb

1962. World Peace Congress, Moscow.
2712 **962** 6k. bistre, black and blue 70 30

963 Ya. Kupala and Ya. Kolas

1962. Byelorussian Poets Commemoration.
2713 **963** 4k. brown and yellow 60 30

964 Sabir

1962. Birth Centenary of Sabir (Azerbaijan poet).

2714	**964**	4k. brown, buff and blue	70	30

965 Congress Emblem

1962. Eighth Anti-cancer Congress, Moscow.

2715	**965**	6k. red, black and blue	85	50

966 N. N. Zinin

1962. 150th Birth Anniv of N. N. Zinin (chemist).

2716	**966**	4k. brown and violet	70	30

1962. War of 1941–45 (2nd issue). As T **911** inscr "1962".

2717		4k. multicoloured	1·40	80

DESIGN: Sailor throwing petrol bomb (Defence of Sevastopol, after A. Deinekin).

967 M. V. Nesterov (painter) (after P. Korin)

1962. Russian Artists Commemoration.

2718	**967**	4k. multicoloured	85	30
2719	-	4k. brown, purple & grey	85	30
2720	-	4k. black and brown	85	30

PORTRAITS—VERT: No. 2719, I. N. Kramskoi (painter) (after N. Yovoshenko). HORIZ: No. 2220, I. D. Shadr (sculptor).

968 "Vostok-2"

1962. First Anniv of Titov's Space Flight. Perf or imperf.

2721	**968**	10k. purple, black & blue	1·70	80
2722	**968**	10k. orange, black & blue	1·70	80

969 Nikolaev and "Vostok 3"

1962. First "Team" Manned Space Flight. Perf or imperf.

2723	**969**	4k. brown, red and blue	1·50	30
2724	-	4k. brown, red and blue	1·50	30
2725	-	6k. multicoloured	2·50	50

DESIGNS: No. 2724A, As Type **969** but with Popovich and "Vostok-4"; No. 2725A (47×28½ mm), Cosmonauts in flight.

970 House of Friendship

1962. People's House of Friendship, Moscow.

2726	**970**	6k. grey and blue	75	30

971 Lomonosov University and Atomic Symbols

1962. "Atoms for Peace".

2727	**971**	4k. multicoloured	85	50
2728	-	6k. multicoloured	1·20	65

DESIGN: 6k. Map of Russia, Atomic symbol and "Peace" in ten languages.

972 Common Carp and Bream

1962. Fish Preservation Campaign.

2729	**972**	4k. yellow, violet and blue	85	30
2730	-	6k. blue, black and orange	1·20	50

DESIGN: 6k. Atlantic salmon.

973 F. E. Dzerzhinsky

1962. Birth Anniv of Feliks Dzerzhinsky (founder of Cheka).

2731	**973**	4k. blue and green	70	30

974 O. Henry

1962. Birth Cent of O. Henry (American writer).

2732	**974**	6k. black, brown & yell	1·00	50

975 Field Marshals Barclay de Tolly, Kutuzov and Bagration

1962. 150th Anniv of Patriotic War of 1812.

2733	**975**	3k. brown	50	15
2734	-	4k. blue	70	30
2735	-	6k. slate	1·00	40
2736	-	10k. violet	1·40	50

DESIGNS: 4k. D. V. Davydov and partisans; 6k. Battle of Borodino; 10k. Partisan Vasilisa Kozhina escorting French prisoners of war.

976 Lenin Street, Vinnitsa

1962. 600th Anniv of Vinnitsa.

2737	**976**	4k. black and bistre	75	30

977 Transport, "Stamp" and "Postmark"

1962. International Correspondence Week.

2738	**977**	4k. black, purple & turq	75	30

978 Cedar

1962. 150th Anniv of Nikitsky Botanical Gardens. Multicoloured.

2739	3k. Type **978**	50	15
2740	4k. "Vostok-2" canna (plant)	60	25
2741	6k. Strawberry tree (arbutus)	85	30
2742	10k. "Road to the Stars" (chrysanthemum)	1·50	50

979 Builder

1962. "The Russian People". Multicoloured.

2743	4k. Type **979**	50	30
2744	4k. Textile worker	50	30
2745	4k. Surgeon	50	30
2746	4k. Farm girl	50	30
2747	4k. P. T. instructor	50	30
2748	4k. Housewife	50	30
2749	4k. Rambler	50	30

980 "Sputnik 1"

1962. Fifth Anniv of Launching of "Sputnik 1".

2750	**980**	10k. multicoloured	2·00	95

981 Akhundov (after N. Ismailov)

1962. 150th Birth Anniv of Mirza Akhundov (poet).

2751	**981**	4k. brown and green	70	30

982 Harvester

1962. "Settlers on Virgin Lands". Multicoloured.

2752	4k. Type **982**	1·20	60
2753	4k. Surveyors, tractors and map	1·20	60
2754	4k. Pioneers with flag	1·20	60

983 N. N. Burdenko

1962. Soviet Scientists. Inscr "1962". Multicoloured.

2755	4k. Type **983**	70	30
2756	4k. V. P. Filatov (wearing beret)	70	30

984 Lenin Mausoleum

1962. 92nd Birth Anniv of Lenin.

2757	**984**	4k. multicoloured	70	30

985 Worker with Banner

1962. 45th Anniv of October Revolution.

2758	**985**	4k. multicoloured	75	30

986 "Into Space" (sculpture, G. Postnikov)

1962. Space Flights Commem. Perf or imperf.

2759	**986**	6k. black, brown and blue	1·20	50
2760	**986**	10k. ultram, bis & vio	1·50	80

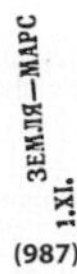

(987)

1962. Launching of Rocket to Mars (1st issue). Optd with T **987**.

2761	10k. blue, bistre and violet	6·00	4·75

See also No. 2765.

988 T. Moldo (Kirghiz poet)

1962. Poets' Anniversaries.

2762	**988**	4k. black and red	85	50
2763	-	4k. black and blue	85	50

DESIGN: No. 2763, Sayat-Nova (Armenian poet) with musical instrument (after G. Ruthkyan).

989 Hammer and Sickle

1962. 40th Anniv of U.S.S.R.

2764	**989**	4k. yellow, red and crimson	75	50

990 Mars Rocket in Space

1962. Launching of Rocket to Mars (2nd issue).

2765	**990**	10k. violet and red	2·00	95

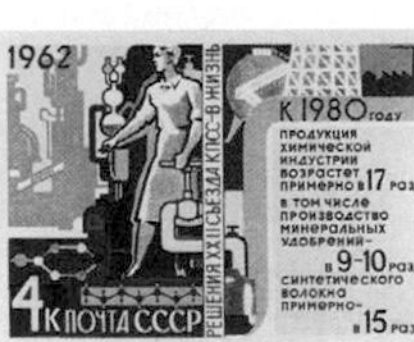

991 Chemical Industry and Statistics

1962. 22nd Communist Party Congress. "Achievements of the People". Multicoloured.

2766	4k. Type **991**	1·00	50
2767	4k. Engineering (machinery and atomic symbol)	1·00	50
2768	4k. Hydro-electric power	1·00	50
2769	4k. Agriculture (harvester)	1·00	50
2770	4k. Engineering (surveyor and welder)	1·00	50
2771	4k. Communications (telephone installation)	1·00	50
2772	4k. Heavy industry (furnace)	1·00	50
2773	4k. Transport (signalman, etc)	1·00	50
2774	4k. Dairy farming (milkmaid, etc)	1·00	50

All the designs show production targets relating to 1980.

992 Chessmen

1962. 30th Soviet Chess Championships, Yerevan.

2775	**992**	4k. black and ochre	1·70	80

993 Four Soviet Cosmonauts (image scaled to 33% of original size)

1962. Soviet Cosmonauts Commem. Perf or imperf.

2776	**993**	1r. black and blue	19·00	14·50

994 V. K. Blucher (military commander)

1962. V. K. Blucher Commemoration.

2777	**994**	4k. multicoloured	85	30

995 V. N. Podbelsky

1962. 75th Birth Anniv of V. N. Podbelsky (postal administrator, 1918–20).

2778	**995**	4k. violet and brown	85	30

996 A. Gaidar

1962. Soviet Writers.

2779	**996**	4k. buff, black and blue	90	50
2780	-	4k. multicoloured	90	50

DESIGN: No. 2780, A. S. Makharenko.

997 Dove and Christmas Tree

1962. New Year. Perf or imperf.

2781	**997**	4k. multicoloured	1·40	95

998 D. N. Pryanishnikov (agricultural chemist)

1962. D. N. Pryanishnikov Commemoration.

2782	**998**	4k. multicoloured	70	30

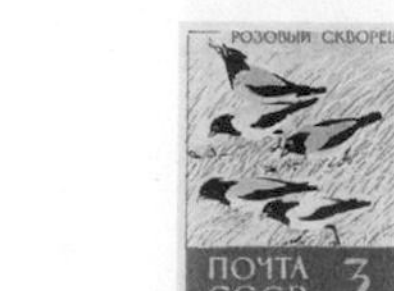

999 Rose-coloured Starlings

1962. Birds.

2783	**999**	3k. black, red and green	50	15
2784	-	4k. black, brown & orge	70	25
2785	-	6k. blue, black and red	85	30
2786	-	10k. blue, black and red	1·40	65
2787	-	16k. red, blue and black	2·20	1·10

BIRDS: 4k. Red-breasted geese; 6k. Snow geese; 10k. Great white cranes; 16k. Greater flamingos.

1000 F.I.R. Emblem and Handclasp

1962. Fourth International Federation of Resistance Heroes Congress.

2788	**1000**	4k. violet and red	50	30
2789	**1000**	6k. turquoise and red	85	50

1001 Badge and Yakovlev Yak-9 Fighters

1962. 20th Anniv of French Air Force "Normandy-Niemen" Unit.

2790	**1001**	6k. red, green and buff	1·20	50

1002 Map and Savings Book

1962. 40th Anniv of Soviet Banks.

2791	**1002**	4k. multicoloured	55	25
2792	-	6k. multicoloured	85	40

DESIGN: 6k. Savings book and map containing savers.

1003 Fertilizer Plant, Rustavi, Georgia

1962. Heavy Industries.

2793	**1003**	4k. black, lt blue & blue	70	30
2794	-	4k. black, turquoise & grn	70	30
2795	-	4k. black, blue and grey	70	30

DESIGNS: No. 2794, Construction of Bratsk hydro- electric station; 2795, Volzhskaya hydro-electric station, Volgograd.

1962. Provincial Costumes (3rd issue). As T **870**. Inscr "1962".

2796		3k. red, brown and drab	70	50

COSTUME: 3k. Latvia.

1004 K. S. Stanislavsky

1963. Russian Stage Celebrities.

2797	**1004**	4k. green on pale green	85	30
2798	-	4k. brown	85	30
2799	-	4k. brown	85	30

PORTRAITS AND ANNIVERSARIES: No. 2797, Type **1004** (actor, birth cent); 2798, M. S. Shchepkin (actor, death cent); 2799, V. D. Durov (animal trainer and circus artiste, birth cent).

1005 A. S. Serafimovich

1963. Russian Writers and Poets.

2800	**1005**	4k. brown, sepia & mve	85	30
2801	-	4k. brown and purple	85	30
2802	-	4k. brown, red and buff	85	30
2803	-	4k. brown and green	85	30
2804	-	4k. brown, sepia & mve	85	30
2805	-	4k. multicoloured	85	30

PORTRAITS AND ANNIVERSARIES: 2800, (birth cent); 2801, Demyan Bednyi (80th birth anniv); 2802, G. I. Uspensky (120th birth anniv); 2803, N. P. Ogarev (150th birth anniv); 2804, V. Ya. Bryusov (90th birth anniv); 2805, F. V. Gladkov (80th birth anniv).

1006 Children in Nursery

1963. Child Welfare.

2806	**1006**	4k. black and orange	70	50
2807	-	4k. purple, blue & orge	70	50
2808	-	4k. bistre, red and green	70	50
2809	-	4k. purple, red & orange	70	50

DESIGNS: No. 2807, Children with nurse; 2808, Young pioneers; 2809, Students at desk and trainee at lathe.

1007 Dolls and Toys

1963. Decorative Arts. Multicoloured.

2810	4k. Type **1007**	70	30
2811	6k. Pottery	85	50
2812	10k. Books	1·40	55
2813	12k. Porcelain	1·90	65

1008 Ilyushin Il-62 Jetliner

1962. 40th Anniv of "Aeroflot" Airline.

2814	**1008**	10k. black, brown & red	1·40	80
2815	-	12k. multicoloured	1·70	95
2816	-	16k. red, black and blue	2·40	1·40

DESIGNS: 12k. "Aeroflot" emblem; 16k. Tupolev Tu-124 airliner.

1009 M. N. Tukhachevsky

1963. 45th Anniv of Red Army and War Heroes.

2817	**1009**	4k. green and turquoise	50	25
2818	-	4k. black and brown	50	25
2819	-	4k. brown and blue	50	25
2820	-	4k. black and red	50	25
2821	-	4k. violet and mauve	50	25

DESIGNS (Army heroes and battle scenes): 2817, Type **1009** (70th birth anniv); 2818, U. M. Avetisyan; 2819, A. M. Matrosov; 2820, I. V. Panfilov; 2821, Ya. F. Fabricius.

1010 M. A. Pavlov (scientist)

1963. Academy of Sciences Members.

2822	**1010**	4k. blue, grey and brown	70	25
2823	-	4k. brown and green	70	25
2824	-	4k. multicoloured	70	25
2825	-	4k. brown, red and blue	70	25
2826	-	4k. multicoloured	70	25

PORTRAITS: No. 2823, I. V. Kurchatov; No. 2824, V. I. Vernadsky. LARGER (23½×30 mm): No. 2825, A. Krylov; No. 2826, V. Obruchev. All commemorate birth centenaries except No. 2823 (60th anniv of birth).

1011 Games Emblem

1963. Fifth Soviet T.U. Winter Sports.

2827	**1011**	4k. orange, black & blue	70	25

Советские
хоккеисты-
чемпионы
мира
и Европы.
Стокгольм.
1963 г.

(1012)

1963. Soviet Victory in Swedish Ice Hockey Championships. No. 2670 optd with T **1012**.

2828	6k. turquoise and purple	3·75	2·40

1013 V. Kingisepp

1963. 75th Birth Anniv of Victor Kingisepp (Estonian Communist Party Leader).

2829	**1013**	4k. brown and blue	75	30

1014 R. M. Blauman

1963. Birth Centenary of Rudolf Blauman (Latvian writer).

2830	**1014**	4k. purple and blue	75	30

1015 Globe and Flowers

1963. "World without Arms and Wars". Perf or imperf.

2831	**1015**	4k. green, blue and red	50	15
2832	-	6k. lilac, green and red	85	30
2833	-	10k. violet, blue and red	1·40	60

DESIGNS: 6k. Atomic emblem and pylon; 10k. Sun and rocket.

1016 Lenin (after I. Brodsky)

1963. 93rd Birth Anniv of Lenin.

2834	**1016**	4k. brown and red	8·50	5·00

1963. Provincial Costumes (4th issue). As T **870**. Inscr "1963". Multicoloured.

2835	3k. Tadzhikistan	85	40
2836	4k. Azerbaijan	1·10	50
2837	4k. Kirgizia	1·10	50
2838	4k. Turkmenistan	1·10	50

1017 "Luna 4" Rocket

1963. Launching of "Luna 4" Space Rocket. Perf or imperf.

2839	**1017**	6k. red, black and blue	1·20	65

See also No. 3250.

1018 Woman and Lido

1963. Fifth Anniv of World Health Day. Multicoloured.

2840	2k. Type **1018**	35	15
2841	4k. Man and stadium	50	30
2842	10k. Child and school	1·40	65

1019 Sputniks and Globe

1963. Cosmonautics Day.

2843	**1019**	10k. blue, black and purple (white figures of value)	1·70	45
2843b	**1019**	10k. blue, black and purple (blue figures)	1·70	45
2844	-	10k. purple, black and blue (white figures)	1·70	45
2844a	-	10k. purple, black and blue (purple figures)	1·70	45
2845	-	10k. red, black and yellow (white figures)	1·70	45
2845a	-	10k. red, black and yellow (yellow figures)	1·70	45

DESIGNS: Nos. 2844/a, "Vostok 1" and Moon; Nos. 2845/a, Space rocket and Sun.

1021 Cuban Horsemen with Flag

1963. Cuban-Soviet Friendship.

2846	**1021**	4k. black, red and blue	50	15
2847	-	6k. black, blue and red	85	30
2848	-	10k. blue, red and black	1·40	65

DESIGNS: 6k. Hands, weapon, book and flag; 10k. Crane, hoisting tractor and flags.

1022 J. Hasek

1963. 40th Death Anniv of Jaroslav Hasek (writer).

2849	**1022**	4k. black	75	30

1023 Karl Marx

1963. 80th Death Anniv of Karl Marx.

2850	**1023**	4k. black and brown	75	30

1963. War of 1941–45 (3rd issue). As T **911** inscr "1963".

2851	4k. multicoloured	70	30
2852	4k. multicoloured	70	30
2853	4k. multicoloured	70	30
2854	4k. sepia and red	70	30
2855	6k. olive, black and red	1·40	65

DESIGNS: No. 2851, Woman making shells (Defence of Leningrad, 1942); 2852, Soldier in winter kit with tommy gun (20th anniv of Battle of the Volga); 2853, Soldiers attacking (Liberation of Kiev, 1943); 2854, Tanks and map indicating Battle of Kursk, 1943; 2855, Tank commander and tanks.

1024 International P.O. Building

1963. Opening of Int Post Office, Moscow.

2856	**1024**	6k. brown and blue	1·20	50

1025 Medal and Chessmen

1963. World Chess Championship, Moscow. Perf or imperf.

2857	**1025**	4k. multicoloured	50	25
2858	-	6k. blue, mauve and ultramarine	85	30
2859	-	16k. black, mauve & pur	2·00	1·40

DESIGNS: 6k. Chessboard and pieces; 16k. Venue and pieces.

1026 Wagner

1963. 150th Birth Anniv of Wagner and Verdi (composers).

2860	**1026**	4k. black and red	1·20	50
2861	-	4k. purple and red	1·20	50

DESIGN: No. 2861, Verdi.

1027 Boxers on "Glove"

1963. 15th European Boxing Championships, Moscow. Multicoloured.

2862	4k. Type **1027**	75	30
2863	6k. Referee and winning boxer on "glove"	1·20	50

1028 Bykovsky and "Vostok 5"

1963. Second "Team" Manned Space Flights (1st issue). Perf or imperf.

2864	**1028**	6k. brown and purple	85	50
2865	-	6k. red and green	85	50
2866	-	10k. red and blue	2·10	70

DESIGNS: No. 2865, Tereshkova and "Vostok 6"; No. 2866, Allegory—"Man and Woman in Space".
See also Nos. 2875/7.

Всемирный
конгресс
женщин.
(1029)

1963. International Women's Congress, Moscow. Optd with T **1029**.

2867	**1015**	4k. green, blue and red	95	50

1030 Cycling

1963. Third People's Spartakiad. Multicoloured. Perf or imperf.

2868b	3k. Type **1030**	35	15
2869	4k. Athletics	50	25
2870b	6k. Swimming (horiz)	85	50
2871b	12k. Basketball	1·70	80
2872	16k. Football	2·00	80
MS2872c	152×105 mm. As Nos. 2868/9 and 2871/2 but colours changed. Imperf	6·00	2·75

1031 Globe, Film and Camera

1963. International Film Festival, Moscow.

2873	**1031**	4k. blue, black & brown	75	45

1032 V. V. Mayakovsky

1963. 70th Birth Anniv of Mayakovsky (poet).

2874	**1032**	4k. brown	85	50

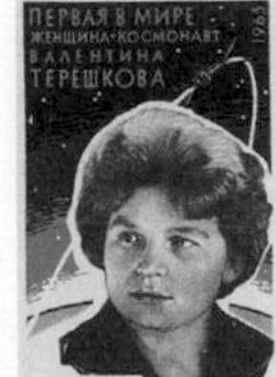

1033 Tereshkova

1963. Second "Team" Manned Space Flights (2nd issue). Multicoloured.

2875	4k. Bykovsky (horiz)	1·00	30
2876	4k. Tereshkova (horiz)	1·00	30
2877	10k. Type **1033**	2·40	95

1034 Ice Hockey Player

1963. Russian Ice Hockey Championships.

2878	**1034**	6k. blue and red	1·40	50

1035 Lenin

1963. 60th Anniv of Second Socialist Party Congress.

2879	**1035**	4k. black and red	70	30

1036 Freighter and Crate

1963. Red Cross Centenary.

2880	**1036**	6k. red and green	1·00	30
2881	-	12k. red and blue	2·20	65

DESIGN: 12k. Centenary emblem.

1037 Guibozo (polo)

1963. Regional Sports.

2882		3k. multicoloured	50	15
2883	**1037**	4k. black, red and ochre	70	30
2884	-	6k. red, brown & yellow	85	50
2885	-	10k. black, brn & olive	1·50	65

DESIGNS—HORIZ: 3k. Lapp reindeer racing; 6k. Buryat archery. VERT: 10k. Armenian wrestling.

1038 Aleksandr Mozhaisky and his Monoplane

1963. Aviation Celebrities.

2886	**1038**	6k. black and blue	85	30
2887	-	10k. black and blue	1·40	65
2888	-	16k. black and blue	2·20	1·10

DESIGNS: 10k. Pyotr Nesterov and "looping the loop"; 16k. N. E. Zhukovsky and "aerodynamics".

1039 S. S. Gulak-Artemovsky (composer, 150th birth anniv)

1040 Olga Kobilyanska (writer) (birth centenary)

1963. Celebrities.

2889	**1039**	4k. black and red	85	30
2890	-	4k. brown and purple	85	30
2891	-	4k. brown and violet	85	30
2892	**1040**	4k. mauve and brown	85	30
2893	-	4k. mauve and green	85	30

DESIGNS AND ANNIVERSARIES: As Type **1039**: No. 2893, M. I. Petraskas (Lithuanian composer) and scene from one of his works (90th birth anniv). As Type **1040**: No. 2890, G. D. Eristavi (writer, death cent, 1964); No. 2891, A. S. Dargomizhsky (composer, 150th birth anniv).

1041 Antarctic Map and Supply Ship "Ob"

1963. Arctic and Antarctic Research. Multicoloured.

2894	3k. Type **1041**	70	30
2895	4k. Convoy of snow tractors and map	1·00	50
2896	6k. Globe and aircraft at polar base	1·70	80
2897	12k. "Sovetskaya Ukraina" (whale factory ship), whale catcher and whale	3·50	1·60

1042 Letters and Transport

1963. International Correspondence Week.

2898	**1042**	4k. violet, orange & blk	70	30

1043 E. O. Paton

1963. Tenth Death Anniv of Paton (engineer).

2899	**1043**	4k. black, red and blue	70	30

1045 D. Diderot

1963. 250th Birth Anniv of Denis Diderot (French philosopher).

2900	**1045**	4k. brown, blue & bistre	1·20	50

1046 "Peace"

1963. "Peace—Brotherhood—Liberty—Labour". All black, red and lake.

2901	4k. Type **1046**	80	35
2902	4k. Worker at desk and couple consulting plan ("Labour")	80	35
2903	4k. Artist and couple ("Liberty")	80	35
2904	4k. Voters ("Equality")	80	35
2905	4k. Man shaking hands with couple with banner ("Brotherhood")	80	35
2906	4k. Family group ("Happiness")	80	35

1047 Academy of Sciences, Frunze

1963. Centenary of Union of Kirgizia and Russia.

2907	**1047**	4k. blue, yellow and red	75	30

1049 Lenin and Congress Building

1963. 13th Soviet Trade Unions' Congress, Moscow.

2908	**1049**	4k. red and black	50	15
2909	-	4k. red and black	50	15

DESIGN: No. 2909, Lenin with man and woman workers.

1050 Ilya Mechnikov

1963. 75th Anniv of Pasteur Institute, Paris.

2910	**1050**	4k. green and bistre	85	30
2911	-	6k. violet and bistre	1·20	50
2912	-	12k. blue and bistre	2·50	80

PORTRAITS: 6k. Pasteur; 12k. Calmette.

1051 Cruiser "Aurora" and Rockets

1963. 46th Anniv of October Revolution.

2913	**1051**	4k. black, orange & lake	70	30
2914	**1051**	4k. black, red and lake	1·00	65

1052 Gur Emi Mausoleum

1963. Ancient Samarkand Buildings. Multicoloured.

2915	4k. Type **1052**	85	30
2916	4k. Shachi-Zinda Mosque	85	30
2917	6k. Registan Square (55×28½ mm)	1·20	55

1053 Inscription, Globe and Kremlin

1963. Signing of Nuclear Test-ban Treaty, Moscow.

2918	**1053**	6k. violet and pale blue	1·20	50

1054 Pushkin Monument, Kiev (A. Kovalev)

1963

2919	**1054**	4k. brown	70	30

1056 Shukhov and Radio Tower, Moscow

1963. 110th Birth Anniv of V. G. Shukhov (engineer).

2920	**1056**	4k. black and green	85	30

1057 Ya. Steklov and "Izvestia"

1963. 90th Birth Anniv of Ya. M. Steklov (first editor of "Izvestia").

2921	**1057**	4k. black and mauve	85	30

1058 Buildings and Emblems of Moscow (and U.S.S.R.) and Prague (and Czechoslovakia)

1963. 20th Anniv of Soviet-Czech Friendship Treaty.

2922	**1058**	6k. red, bistre and blue	85	15

1059 F. A. Poletaev (soldier) and Medals

1963. Poletaev Commemoration.

2923	**1059**	4k. multicoloured	70	15

1062 J. Grimau (Spanish Communist)

1963. Grimau Commemoration.

2924	**1062**	6k. violet, red and cream	85	50

1063 Rockets

1963. New Year (1st issue).

2925	**1063**	6k. multicoloured	85	50

1064 "Happy New Year"

1963. New Year (2nd issue).

2926	**1064**	4k. red, blue and green	70	15
2927	**1064**	6k. red, blue and green	1·00	50

1067 Topaz

1963. "Precious Stones of the Urals". Multicoloured.

2928	2k. Type **1067**	35	25
2929	4k. Jasper	70	65
2930	6k. Amethyst	85	80
2931	10k. Emerald	1·50	1·10
2932	12k. Ruby	1·90	1·60
2933	16k. Malachite	2·40	1·90

1068 Sputnik 7

1963. "First in Space". Gold, vermilion and grey.

2934	10k. Type **1068**	1·50	65
2935	10k. Moon landing	1·50	65
2936	10k. Back of Moon	1·50	65
2937	10k. Vostok 7	1·50	65
2938	10k. Twin flight	1·50	65
2939	10k. Seagull (first woman in space)	1·50	65

1069 Dushanbe Putovsky Square

1963. Dushanbe, Capital of Tadzhikistan.

2940	**1069**	4k. blue	85	30

1071 Flame and Rainbow

1963. 15th Anniv of Declaration of Human Rights.

2941	**1071**	6k. multicoloured	85	30

1072 F. A, Sergeev ("Artem")

1963. 80th Birth Anniv of Sergeev (revolutionary).

2942	**1072**	4k. brown and red	70	15

1073 Sun and Globe

1964. International Quiet Sun Year.

2943	-	4k. black, orange & mve	50	15
2944	**1073**	6k. blue, yellow and red	70	30
2945	-	10k. violet, red and blue	1·00	50

DESIGNS—HORIZ: 4k. Giant telescope and sun; 10k. Globe and Sun.

1074 K. Donelaitis

1964. 250th Birth Anniv of K. Donelaitis (Lithuanian poet).

2946	**1074**	4k. black and myrtle	70	15

1075 Speed Skating

1964. Winter Olympic Games, Innsbruck.

2947b	**1075**	2k. black, mauve & bl	45	15
2948b	-	4k. black, blue & mve	85	30
2949b	-	6k. red, black and blue	1·20	40
2950b	-	10k. black, mve & grn	2·00	65
2951b	-	12k. black, grn & mve	2·40	80

DESIGNS: 4k. Skiing; 6k. Games emblem; 10k. Rifle shooting (biathlon); 12k. Figure skating (pairs).

See also Nos. 2969/73.

1076 Golubkina (after N. Ulyanov) and Statue, Tolstoi

1964. Birth Cent of A. S. Golubkina (sculptress).

2952	**1076**	4k. sepia and grey	70	15

1077 "Agriculture"

1964. Heavy Chemical Industries. Multicoloured.

2953	4k. Type **1077**	85	15
2954	4k. "Textiles"	85	15
2955	4k. "Tyre Production"	85	15

150 років з дня народження. 1964 р.

(1078)

1079 Shevchenko's Statue, Kiev (M. Manizer)

1964. 150th Birth Anniv of T. G. Shevchenko (Ukrainian poet and painter). No. 2561 optd with T **1078** and designs as T **1079**.

2956	**880**	3k. brown and violet	11·00	9·50
2959	**1079**	4k. green	35	15
2960	**1079**	4k. red	35	15
2961	-	6k. blue	50	30
2962	-	6k. brown	50	30
2957	-	10k. violet and brown	85	50
2958	-	10k. brown and bistre	85	50

DESIGNS: Nos. 2957/8, Portrait of Shevchenko by I. Repin; Nos. 2961/2, Self-portrait.

1080 K. S. Zaslonov

1964. War Heroes.

2963	**1080**	4k. sepia and brown	70	30
2964	-	4k. purple and blue	70	30
2965	-	4k. blue and red	70	30
2966	-	4k. brown and blue	70	30

PORTRAITS: No. 2964, N. A. Vilkov; 2965, Yu. V. Smirnov; 2966, V. Z. Khoruzhaya.

1081 Fyodorov printing the first Russian book, "Apostle"

1964. 400th Anniv of First Russian Printed Book. Multicoloured.

2967	4k. Type **1081**	60	15
2968	6k. Statue of Ivan Fyodorov, Moscow (S. Volnukin), books and newspapers	85	50

Слава советским спортсменам— победителям IX зимней Олимпиады!

(1082)

1964. Winter Olympic Games, Soviet Medal Winners. (a) Nos. 2947/51 optd with T **1082** or similarly.

2969	2k. black, mauve and blue	35	15
2970	4k. black, blue and mauve	70	30
2971	6k. red, black and blue	1·10	50
2972	10k. black, mauve and green	1·50	65
2973	12k. black, green and mauve	1·70	80

1083 Ice Hockey Player

(b) New designs.

2974 **1083** 3k. red, black & turquoise 50 30

2975 - 16k. orange and brown 2·30 1·30

DESIGN: 16k. Gold medal and inscr "Triumph of Soviet Sport–11 Gold, 8 Silver, 6 Bronze medals".

1084 Militiaman and Factory Guard

1964. "Public Security".

2976 **1084** 4k. blue, red and black 70 30

1085 Lighthouse, Odessa and Sailor

1964. 20th Anniv of Liberation of Odessa and Leningrad. Multicoloured.

2977 4k. Type **1085** 70 30

2978 4k. Lenin Statue, Leningrad 70 30

1086 Sputniks

1964. "The Way to the Stars". Imperf or perf. (a) Cosmonautics. As T **1086**.

2979b 4k. green, black and red 85 30

2980 6k. black, blue and red 1·20 1·10

2981 12k. turquoise, brown & black 2·40 2·20

DESIGNS: 6k. "Mars I" space station; 12k. Gagarin and space capsule.

1087 N. I. Kibalchich

(b) Rocket Construction Pioneers. As T **1087**.

2982b 10k. black, green and violet 1·90 80

2983b 10k. black, turquoise and red 1·90 80

2984b 10k. black, turquoise and red 1·90 80

2985b 10k. black and blue 1·70 80

DESIGNS: No. 2982B, Type **1087**; 2983B, F. A. Zander; 2984B, K. E. Tsiolkovsky; 2985B, Pioneers' medallion and Saransk memorial.

1088 Lenin

1964. 94th Birth Anniv of Lenin.

2986a **1088** 4k. black, blue & mve 6·00 5·50

1089 Shakespeare (400th Birth Anniv)

1964. Cultural Anniversaries.

2987 - 6k. yellow, brn & sepia 1·90 80

2988 **1089** 10k. brown and olive 2·20 95

2989 - 12k. green and brown 3·75 1·40

DESIGNS AND ANNIVERSARIES: 6k. Michelangelo (400th death anniv); 12k. Galileo (400th birth anniv).

1090 Crop-watering Machine and Produce

1964. "Irrigation".

2990 **1090** 4k. multicoloured 75 30

1091 Gamarnik

1964. 70th Birth Anniv of Ya. B. Gamarnik (Soviet Army commander).

2991 **1091** 4k. brown, blue & black 75 30

1092 D. I. Gulia (Abhazian poet)

1964. Cultural Anniversaries.

2992 **1092** 4k. black, green and light green 70 30

2993 - 4k. black, verm & red 70 30

2994 - 4k. black, brown & bis 70 30

2995 - 4k. black, yellow & brn 70 30

2996 - 4k. multicoloured 70 30

2997 - 4k. black, yellow & brn 70 30

DESIGNS: No. 2993, Nijazi (Uzbek writer, composer and painter); 2994, S. Seifullin (Kazakh poet); 2995, M. M. Kotsyubinsky (writer); 2996, S. Nazaryan (Armenian writer); 2997, T. Satylganov (Kirghiz poet).

1093 A. Gaidar

1964. 60th Birth Annivs of Writers A. P. Gaidar and N. A. Ostrovsky.

2998 **1093** 4k. red and blue 70 30

2999 - 4k. green and red 70 30

DESIGN: No. 2999, N. Ostrovsky and battle scene.

1094 Indian Elephant

1964. Centenary of Moscow Zoo. Multicoloured. Imperf or perf.

3000 1k. Type **1094** 15 15

3001 2k. Giant panda 35 15

3002 4k. Polar bear 70 30

3003 6k. Elk 1·00 30

3004 10k. Eastern white pelican 1·70 65

3005 12k. Tiger 2·00 80

3006 16k. Lammergeier 2·75 95

The 2k. and 12k. are horiz; the 4k. and 10k. are "square", approx 26½×28 mm.

150 лет вхождения
в состав России
1964

4
коп.

(1095)

1964. 150th Anniv of Union of Azerbaijan and Russia. Surch with T **1095**.

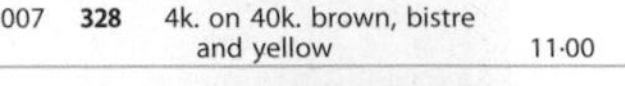

3007 **328** 4k. on 40k. brown, bistre and yellow 11·00 10·50

1096 Rumanian Woman and Emblems on Map

1964. 20th. Anniv of Rumanian–Soviet Friendship Treaty.

3008 **1096** 6k. multicoloured 85 30

1097 Maize

1964. Agricultural Crops. Multicoloured. Imperf or perf.

3009b 2k. Type **1097** 35 15

3010b 3k. Wheat 45 25

3011b 4k. Potatoes 50 30

3012b 6k. Peas 85 30

3013b 10k. Sugar beet 1·40 65

3014b 12k. Cotton 1·70 80

3015b 16k. Flax 2·20 95

1098 Flag and Obelisk

1964. 20th Anniv of Liberation of Byelorussia.

3016 **1098** 4k. multicoloured 70 30

1099 Leningrad G.P.O.

1964. 250th Anniv of Leningrad's Postal Service.

3017 **1099** 4k. black, bistre and red 70 30

1100 Map of Poland and Emblems

1964. 20th Anniv of Polish People's Republic.

3018 **1100** 6k. multicoloured 85 50

1101 Horse-jumping

1964. Olympic Games, Tokyo. Imperf or perf.

3019 **1101** 3k. multicoloured 35 15

3020b - 4k. red, black & yellow 50 25

3021b - 6k. red, black and blue 70 30

3022b - 10k. red, black & turq 1·00 50

3023b - 12k. black and grey 1·40 55

3024b - 16k. violet, red and blue 1·70 65

MS3024c 90×71 mm. 1r. green background 12·00 6·50

MS3024d 90×71 mm. 1r. red background £425 £475

DESIGNS: 4k. Weightlifting; 6k. Pole vaulting; 10k. Canoeing; 12k Gymnastics; 16k. Fencing; 1r. Gymnast and stadium.

1102 M. Thorez (French Communist leader)

1964. Maurice Thorez Commemoration.

3025 **1102** 4k. black and red 2·20 95

1103 Three Races

1964. International Anthropologists and Ethnographers Congress, Moscow.

3026 **1103** 6k. black and yellow 85 50

1104 Jawaharlal Nehru

1964. Nehru Commemoration.

3027 **1104** 4k. brown and grey 85 30

1104a

1964. World Orbit Flights. Sheet of six multicoloured stamps as T **1104a** making up composite design showing Earth, Moon, spacecraft etc.

MS3027a 140×110 mm. 10k. (×6) 13·50 9·50

1105 Globe and Banner

1964. Centenary of "First International".

3028 **1105** 4k. red, bistre and blue 60 30

3029 - 4k. red, olive and black 60 30

3030 - 4k. drab, red and lake 60 30

3031 - 4k. red, black and blue 60 30

3032 - 4k. multicoloured 60 30

DESIGNS: No. 3029, Communist Party manifesto; 3030, Marx and Engels; 3031, Chain breaker; 3032, Lenin.

1106 A. V. Vishnevsky (surgeon)

1964. "Outstanding Soviet Physicians".

3033 **1106** 4k. brown and purple 70 30

3034 - 4k. brown, red & yellow 70 30

3035 - 4k. brown, blue & bistre 70 30

DESIGNS: No. 3034, N. A. Semashko (public health pioneer). Both are 90th birth anniversaries. No. 3035, D. I. Ivanovsky and siphon (25×32 mm).

1107 Bulgarian Flag, Rose and Emblems

1964. 20th Anniv of Bulgarian People's Republic.

3036 **1107** 6k. red, green and drab 85 50

1108 P. Togliatti (Italian Communist leader)

1964. Togliatti Commemoration.

3037 **1108** 4k. black and red 70 15

1110 Globe and Letters

1964. International Correspondence Week.

3038 **1110** 4k. mauve, blue & brn 70 15

1111 Soviet and Yugoslav Soldiers

1964. 20th Anniv of Liberation of Belgrade.

3039	**1111**	6k. multicoloured	85	50

1112 East German Arms, Industrial Plants, Freighter "Havel" and Electric Goods Train

1964. 15th Anniv of German Democratic Republic.

3040	**1112**	6k. multicoloured	1·00	50

1113 Woman holding Bowl of Produce (Moldavian Republic)

1964. 40th Anniv of Soviet Republic. (a) As T **1113**.

3041	**1113**	4k. brown, green and red	85	30
3042	-	4k. multicoloured	85	30
3043	-	4k. red, purple & yellow	85	30

40 лет Советскому Таджикистану
1964 год
(**1115**)

(b) Optd with T **1115**.

3044	**1069**	4k. blue	3·75	3·00

DESIGNS—VERT: No. 3042, Woman holding Arms (Turkmenistan); 3043, Man and woman holding produce (Uzbekistan); 3044, commemorates the Tadzhikistan Republic.

1116 Yegorov

1964. Three-manned Space Flight. (a) Portraits in black, orange and turquoise.

3045	4k. Type **1116**	70	30
3046	4k. Feoktistov	70	30
3047	4k. Komarov	70	30

These can be identified by the close proximation of the Russian names on the stamps to the English versions.

(b) Designs 73½×22½ mm.

3048	6k. purple and violet	1·00	40
3049	10k. violet and blue	1·70	50
MS3049a	120×56 mm. 50k. violet, red and grey. Imperf	13·50	5·50

DESIGNS: 6k. The three cosmonauts; 10k. Space ship "Voskhod 1".

1117 Soldier and Flags

1964. 20th Anniv of Liberation of Ukraine.

3050	**1117**	4k. multicoloured	70	30

1119 Lermontov's Birthplace

1964. 150th Birth Anniv of M. Lermontov (poet).

3051	**1119**	4k. violet	70	30
3052	-	6k. black	1·00	50
3053	-	10k. brown and flesh	1·70	80

DESIGNS: 6k. Lermontov (after K. Gorbunov); 10k. Lermontov talking with V. Belinsky.

1120 Hammer and Sickle

1964. 47th Anniv of October Revolution.

3054	**1120**	4k. multicoloured	70	30

1964. 94th Birth Anniv of Lenin. Sheet 144×101 mm, comprising pair of No. 2679.

MS3054a	10k. purple, lake and black	5·00	3·25

1121 N. K. Krupskaya (Lenin's wife)

1964. Birth Anniversaries.

3055	**1121**	4k. multicoloured	70	30
3056	-	4k. multicoloured	70	30

DESIGNS: 3055 (95th anniv); 3056, A. I. Yelizarova-Ulyanova (Lenin's sister) (cent).

1122 Mongolian Woman and Lamb

1964. 40th Anniv of Mongolian People's Republic.

3057	**1122**	4k. multicoloured	85	50

1124 Butter Mushroom

1964. Mushrooms. Multicoloured.

3058	2k. Type **1124**	35	15
3059	4k. Chanterelle	50	30
3060	6k. Ceps	85	50
3061	10k. Red-capped sacker stalk	1·40	80
3062	12k. Saffron milk cap	1·70	95

1125 A. P. Dovzhenko

1964. 70th Birth Anniv of Dovzhenko (film producer).

3063	**1125**	4k. blue and grey	70	30

1126 Christmas Tree, Star and Globe

1964. New Year.

3064	**1126**	4k. multicoloured	85	50

1127 Struve

1964. Death Centenary of V. Ya. Struve (scientist).

3065	**1127**	4k. brown and blue	85	30

1128 Ivanov (after O. Braz) and "March of the Moscovites. 16th Century"

1964. Birth Centenary of S. V. Ivanov (painter).

3066	**1128**	4k. brown and black	1·00	50

1129 Scene from Film

1964. 30th Anniv of Film "Chapaev".

3067	**1129**	6k. black and green	85	50

1130 Test-tubes, Jar and Agricultural Scenes

1964. Chemistry for the National Economy.

3068	**1130**	4k. purple and olive	50	15
3069	-	6k. black and blue	85	50

DESIGN: 6k. Chemical plant.

1131 Cranberries

1964. Woodland Fruit. Multicoloured.

3070	1k. Type **1131**	25	15
3071	3k. Bilberries	35	25
3072	4k. Rowanberries	45	30
3073	10k. Blackberries	1·00	50
3074	16k. Red bilberries	1·50	95

1132 Library

1964. 250th Anniv of Academy of Sciences Library, Leningrad.

3075	**1132**	4k. black, green and red	85	30

1133 Congress Palace and Spassky Tower

1964

3076	**1133**	1r. blue	10·00	3·00

1134 Mt Khan-Tengri

1964. Mountaineering. Multicoloured.

3077	4k. Type **1134**	35	15
3078	6k. Mt Kazbek (horiz)	85	30
3079	12k. Mt Ushba	1·50	65

1136 Bowl

1964. Kremlin Treasures. Multicoloured.

3080	4k. Helmet	70	30
3081	6k. Quiver	1·00	50
3082	10k. Coronation headgear	1·70	65
3083	12k. Ladle	2·20	80
3084	16k. Type **1136**	3·00	1·10

1137 I. M. Sivko

1965. War Heroes.

3085	**1137**	4k. black and violet	50	30
3086	-	4k. brown and blue	50	30

DESIGN: No. 3086, General I. S. Polbin.

1138 Dante

1965. 700th Birth Anniv of Dante.

3087	**1138**	4k. black, bistre and purple	1·00	50

1139 Blood Donor

1965. Blood Donors. Multicoloured.

3088	4k. Type **1139**	50	30
3089	4k. Hand holding red carnation	50	30

1140 N. P. Kravkov

1965. Birth Cent of N. Kravkov (pharmacologist).

3090	**1140**	4k. multicoloured	70	30

1141 Figure Skaters

1965. European Figure Skating Championships, Moscow.

3091	**1141**	6k. red, black and green	1·00	50

See also No. 3108.

1965. World Ice Hockey Championships, Moscow. Designs similar to T **1141** but depicting ice hockey players.

3092	4k. red, blue and bistre	85	30

1142 Alsatian

1965. Hunting and Service Dogs.

3093	-	1k. black, yellow and red	25	15
3097	-	2k. brown, blue & black	35	15
3098	**1142**	3k. black, red and yellow	45	25
3099	-	4k. black, brown & grn	50	30
3100	-	4k. black, orange & grn	50	30
3101	-	6k. black, brown & blue	85	50
3102	-	6k. black, red and blue	85	50
3094	-	10k. multicoloured	1·40	80
3095	-	12k. black, brown & vio	1·50	95
3096	-	16k. multicoloured	2·00	1·30

DESIGNS—HORIZ: 1k. Hound; 2k. Setter; 4k. (3099) (value in green) Fox terrier; 4k. (3100) (value in orange) Pointer; 6k. (3101) Borzoi; 12k. Husky. VERT: 6k. (3102) Sheepdog; 10k. Collie; 16k. Caucasian sheepdog.

1143 R. Sorge

1965. Richard Sorge (Soviet secret agent) Commem.
3103 **1143** 4k. black and red 1·00 50

1144 I.T.U. Emblem and Telecommunications Symbol

1965. Centenary of I.T.U.
3104 **1144** 6k. violet and blue 1·20 50

1145 Leonov in Space

1965. Space Flight of "Voskhod 2" (1st issue). Imperf or perf.
3105 **1145** 10k. orange, black & bl 1·00 65
MS3106 1r. black, red and blue 10·00 5·50
See also Nos. 3138/9.

1965. Ice Hockey Championships. Optd **TAMIIERE 1965 r.**
3107 **1034** 6k. blue and red 5·50 4·75

Советские
фигуристы—
чемпионы мира
в парном катании

(1147)

1965. Soviet Victory in European Figure Skating Championships. Optd with T 1147.
3108 **1141** 6k. red, black and green 5·50 4·75

1148 Soldier and Woman

1965. 20th Anniversaries.
3109 **1148** 6k. multicoloured 70 30
3110 - 6k. multicoloured 70 30
3111 - 6k. ochre and red 70 30
3112 - 6k. multicoloured 70 30
3113 - 6k. multicoloured 70 30
DESIGNS: No. 3109, Type **1148** (Czech Liberation); 3110, Statue and emblems of development (Friendship with Hungary); 3111, Polish and Soviet arms (Polish–Soviet Friendship Treaty); 3112, Viennese buildings and Russian soldier (Freeing of Vienna); 3113, Liberation medal, Polish flag and building reconstruction (Freeing of Warsaw).
See also Nos. 3182 and 3232.

1149 Statue Rockets and Globe

1150 Rockets and Radio-telescope

1965. National Cosmonautics Day. Nos. 3117/18 on aluminium-surfaced paper.
3114 **1149** 4k. green, black and red 50 30
3115 - 12k. purple, red and blue 1·20 65
3116 - 16k. multicoloured 1·70 80
3117 **1150** 20k. red, black and green on silver 11·00 8·75
3118 - 20k. red, black and blue on silver 11·00 8·75
DESIGNS: 12k. Statue and Globe; 16k. Rockets and Globe; No. 3118, Globe, satellite and cosomonauts.

1151 Lenin (after bas-relief by V. Sayapin)

1965. Lenin's 95th Birth Anniv.
3119 **1151** 10k. blue, black & brn 1·40 80

1152 Poppies

1965. Flowers.
3120 **1152** 1k. red, lake and green 25 15
3121 - 3k. yellow, brown & grn 50 25
3122 - 4k. lilac, black and green 70 30
3123 - 6k. red, deep green and green 1·00 40
3124 - 10k. yellow, pur & grn 1·50 50
FLOWERS: 3k. Marguerite; 4k. Peony; 6k. Carnation; 10k. Tulips.

1153 Red Flag, Reichstag Building and Broken Swastika

1965. 20th Anniv of Victory.
3125 **1153** 1k. black, gold and red 35 15
3126 - 2k. red, black and gold 50 15
3127 - 3k. blue and gold 85 25
3128 - 4k. violet and gold 1·00 30
3129 - 4k. green and gold 1·00 30
3130 - 6k. purple, green & gold 1·70 40
3131 - 10k. purple, brn & gold 2·50 50
3132 - 12k. black, red and gold 3·00 65
3133 - 16k. red and gold 4·25 80
3134 - 20k. black, red and gold 5·00 1·10
DESIGNS: 2k. Soviet mother holding manifesto (poster by I. Toidze); 3k. "The Battle for Moscow" (V. Bogatkin); 4k. (No. 3128), "Partisan Mother" (from S. Gerasimov's film); 4k. (No. 3129), "Red Army Soldiers and Partisans" (from Yu. Neprintsev's film); 6k. Soldiers and flag (poster by V. Ivanov); 10k. "Mourning the Fallen Hero" (from F. Bogorodsky's film); 12k. Soldier and worker holding bomb (poster by V. Korestsky); 16k. Victory celebrations, Red Square, Moscow (from K. Yuon's film); 20k. Soldier and machines of war.

1153a Popov's Radio Invention

1965. 70th Anniv of A. S. Popov's Radio Discoveries. Sheet 144×100 mm comprising six stamps without face value.
MS3135 1r. multicoloured 8·50 4·75
DESIGNS: T **1153a**: Transistor radio; TV screen; Radar; Radiotelescope; Telecommunications satellite. The value is printed on the sheet.

1154 Marx and Lenin

1965. Marxism and Leninism.
3136 **1154** 6k. black and red 1·00 30
No. 3136 is similar in design to those issued by China and Hungary for the Postal Ministers' Congress, Peking, but this event is not mentioned on the stamp or in the Soviet philatelic bulletins.

1155 Bolshoi Theatre

1965. International Theatre Day.
3137 **1155** 6k. ochre, black & turq 1·00 30

1156 Leonov

1965. "Voskhod 2" Space Flight (2nd issue).
3138 **1156** 6k. violet and silver 85 30
3139 - 6k. purple and silver 85 30
DESIGN: No. 3139, Belyaev.

1157 Yakov Sverdlov (revolutionary)

1965. 80th Birth Anniversaries.
3140 **1157** 4k. black and brown 70 25
3141 - 4k. black and violet 70 25
PORTRAIT: No. 3141, J. Akhunbabaev (statesman).

1158 Otto Grotewohl (1st death anniv)

1965. Annivs of Grotewohl and Thorez (Communist leaders).
3142 **1158** 4k. black and purple 70 25
3143 - 6k. brown and red 85 30
DESIGN: 6k. Maurice Thorez (65th birth anniv).

1159 Telecommunications Satellite

1965. International Co-operation Year. Multicoloured.
3144 3k. Type **1159** 50 15
3145 6k. Star and sputnik 85 30
3146 6k. Foundry ladle, iron works and map of India 85 30
No. 3145 signifies peaceful uses of atomic energy and No. 3146 co-operation with India.

1160 Congress Emblem, Chemical Plant and Symbols

1965. 20th International Congress of Pure and Applied Chemistry, Moscow.
3147 **1160** 4k. red, black and blue 70 30

1161 V. A. Serov (after I. Repin)

1965. Birth Centenary of V. A. Serov (painter).
3148 **1161** 4k. black, brn & stone 1·70 40
3149 - 6k. black and drab 2·50 50
DESIGN: 6k. Full length portrait of Chaliapin (singer) by Serov.

1162 Vsevolod Ivanov and Armoured Train

1965. Famous Writers.
3150 **1162** 4k. black and purple 70 30
3151 - 4k. black and violet 70 30
3152 - 4k. black and blue 70 30
3153 - 4k. black and grey 70 30
3154 - 4k. black, red and green 70 30
3155 - 4k. black and brown 70 30
WRITERS AND ANNIVERSARIES: No. 3150, (70th birth anniv); 3151, A. Kunanbaev and military parade; 3152, J. Rainis (Lettish poet: 90th birth anniv); 3153, E. J. Vilde (Estonian author): 90th birth anniv); 3154, M. Ch. Abegjan (Armenian writer and critic: 90th birth anniv); 3155, M. L. Kropivnitsky and scene from play (Ukrainian playwright).

1163 Festival Emblem

1965. Film Festival, Moscow.
3156 **1163** 6k. black, gold and blue 1·00 30

1164 Concert Arena, Tallin

1965. 25th Anniv of Incorporation of Estonia, Lithuania and Latvia in the U.S.S.R.
3157 **1164** 4k. multicoloured 70 25
3158 - 4k. brown and red 70 25
3159 - 4k. brown, red and blue 70 25
DESIGNS—VERT: No. 3158, Lithuanian girl and Arms. HORIZ: No. 3159, Latvian Flag and Arms.

1165 Hand holding "Peace Flower"

1965. Peace Issue.
3160 **1165** 6k. yellow, black & blue 1·00 40

1167 "Potemkin" Sailors Monument (V. Bogdanov), Odessa

1965. 60th Anniv of 1905 Rebellion.
3161 **1167** 4k. blue and red 70 30
3162 - 4k. green, black and red 70 30
3163 - 4k. green, black and red 70 30
3164 - 4k. brown, black and red 70 30
DESIGNS: No. 3162, Demonstrator up lamp post; 3163, Defeated rebels; 3164, Troops at street barricade.

1168 G. Gheorgi-Dej (Rumanian Communist)

1965. G. Gheorgi-Dej Commemoration.
3165 **1168** 4k. black and red 70 30

1169 Power Station

1965. Industrial Progress.
3166 **1169** 1k. multicoloured 25 15
3167 - 2k. black, orange & yell 25 15
3168 - 3k. violet, yell & ochre 35 15
3169 - 4k. deep blue, blue and red 50 25
3170 - 6k. blue and bistre 85 30
3171 - 10k. brown, yellow and orange 1·40 50
3172 - 12k. turquoise and red 1·50 65
3173 - 16k. purple, blue & blk 2·00 80

DESIGNS: 2k. Steel works; 3k. Chemical works and formula; 4k. Machine tools production; 6k. Building construction; 10k. Agriculture; 12k. Communications and transport; 16k. Scientific research.

1170 Relay Racing

1965. Trade Unions Spartakiad. Multicoloured.

No.	Type	Description	Unused	Used
3174		4k. Type **1170**	70	30
3175		4k. Gymnastics	70	30
3176		4k. Cycling	70	30

1171 Gymnastics

1965. Schoolchildren's Spartakiad.

No.	Type	Description	Unused	Used
3177	**1171**	4k. red and blue	50	15
3178	-	6k. red, brown & turq	70	30

DESIGN: 6k. Cycle racing.

1172 Throwing the Javelin and Running

1965. American–Soviet Athletic Meeting, Kiev.

No.	Type	Description	Unused	Used
3179	**1172**	4k. red, brown and lilac	50	15
3180	-	6k. red, brown and green	70	30
3181	-	10k. red, brown and grey	1·00	65

DESIGNS: 6k. High jumping and putting the shot; 10k. Throwing the hammer and hurdling.

1173 Star, Palms and Lotus

1965. 20th Anniv of North Vietnamese People's Republic.

No.	Type	Description	Unused	Used
3182	**1173**	6k. multicoloured	85	30

1174 Worker with Hammer (World T.U. Federation)

1965. 20th Anniv of International Organizations.

No.	Type	Description	Unused	Used
3183	**1174**	6k. drab and plum	70	30
3184	-	6k. brown, red and blue	70	30
3185	-	6k. lt brown & turquoise	70	30

DESIGNS: No. 3184, Torch and heads of three races (World Democratic Youth Federation); No. 3185, Woman holding dove (International Democratic Women's Federation).

1176 P. K. Sternberg (astronomer: birth cent)

1965. Scientists' Anniversaries.

No.	Type	Description	Unused	Used
3186	**1176**	4k. brown and blue	85	30
3187	-	4k. black and purple	85	30
3188	-	4k. black, purple & yell	85	30

PORTRAITS: No. 3187, Ch. Valikhanov (scientific writer: death cent); 3188, V. A. Kistyakovsky (scientist: birth cent).

1177 "Battleship 'Potemkin'" (dir. Sergei Eisenshtein)

1965. Soviet Cinema Art. Designs showing scenes from films. Multicoloured.

No.	Type	Description	Unused	Used
3189		4k. Type **1177**	70	15
3190		6k. "Young Guard" (dir. S. Coesinov)	85	30
3191		12k. "A Soldier's Ballad" (dir. G. Chuthrai)	1·90	65

1178 Mounted Postman and Map

1965. History of the Russian Post Office.

No.	Type	Description	Unused	Used
3192	**1178**	1k. green, brown & vio	60	25
3193	-	1k. brown, ochre & grey	60	25
3194	-	2k. brown, blue and lilac	70	30
3195	-	4k. black, ochre & pur	85	30
3196	-	6k. black, green & brn	1·20	40
3197	-	12k. sepia, brown & blue	2·20	65
3198	-	16k. plum, red and grey	2·50	95

DESIGNS: No. 3193, Mail coach and map; 2k. Early steam train and medieval kogge; 4k. Mail lorry and map; 6k. Diesel-electric train and various transport; 12k. Moscow Post Office electronic facing sorting and cancelling machines; 16k. Airports and Lenin.

1179 "Vostok" and "Mirnyi" (Antarctic exploration vessels)

1965. Polar Research Annivs.

No.	Type	Description	Unused	Used
3199		4k. black, orange & blue	85	30
3200		4k. black, orange & blue	85	30
3201		6k. sepia and violet	1·20	50
3202	**1179**	10k. black, drab and red	1·90	80
3203	-	16k. black, violet & brn	3·00	1·30

DESIGNS—HORIZ: 37½×25½ mm: No. 3199, Ice breakers "Taimyr" and "Vaigach" in Arctic (50th anniv); 3200, Atomic ice breaker "Lenin"; 3201, Dikson settlement (50th anniv); 3203, Vostok Antarctic station. SQUARE. No. 3202, (145th anniv of Lazarev–Bellingshausen Expedition).

Nos. 3199/200 were issued together, se-tenant, forming a composite design.

1180 Basketball Players and Map of Europe

1965. European Basketball Championships, Moscow. Sheet 65×90 mm.

No.	Type	Description	Unused	Used
MS3204		1r. multicoloured	9·25	6·50

1181 Agricultural Academy

1965. Centenary of Academy of Agricultural Sciences, Moscow.

No.	Type	Description	Unused	Used
3205	**1181**	4k. violet, red and drab	50	30

1182 Lenin (after P. Vasilev)

1965. 48th Anniv of October Revolution. Sheet 64×95 mm.

No.	Type	Description	Unused	Used
MS3206	**1182**	10k. black, red and silver	4·75	3·00

1183 N. Poussin (self-portrait)

1965. 300th Death Anniv of Nicolas Poussin (French painter).

No.	Type	Description	Unused	Used
3207	**1183**	4k. multicoloured	85	50

1184 Kremlin

1965. New Year.

No.	Type	Description	Unused	Used
3208	**1184**	4k. red, silver and black	85	30

1185 M. I. Kalinin

1966. 90th Birth Anniv of Kalinin (statesman).

No.	Type	Description	Unused	Used
3209	**1185**	4k. lake and red	70	30

1186 Klyuchevski Volcano

1965. Soviet Volcanoes. Multicoloured.

No.	Type	Description	Unused	Used
3210		4k. Type **1186**	50	25
3211		12k. Karumski Volcano (vert)	1·50	65
3212		16k. Koryaski Volcano	2·00	95

1187 Oktyabrskaya Station, Moscow

1965. Soviet Metro Stations.

No.	Type	Description	Unused	Used
3213	**1187**	6k. blue	75	30
3214	-	6k. brown	75	30
3215	-	6k. brown	75	30
3216	-	6k. green	75	30

STATIONS: No. 3214, Leninksy Prospekt, Moscow; 3215, Moscow Gate, Leningrad; 3216, Bolshevik Factory, Kiev.

1188 Common Buzzard

1965. Birds of Prey. Birds in black.

No.	Type	Description	Unused	Used
3217	**1188**	1k. grey	15	15
3218	-	2k. brown	35	15
3219	-	3k. olive	50	25

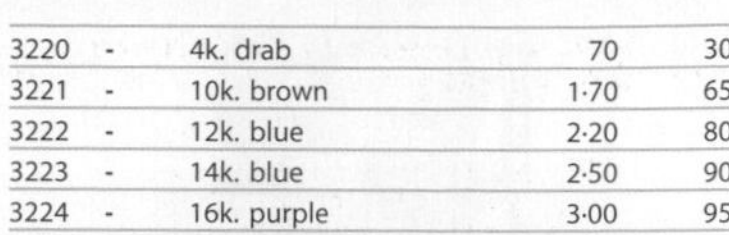

No.	Type	Description	Unused	Used
3220	-	4k. drab	70	30
3221	-	10k. brown	1·70	65
3222	-	12k. blue	2·20	80
3223	-	14k. blue	2·50	90
3224	-	16k. purple	3·00	95

BIRDS—VERT: 2k. Common kestrel; 3k. Tawny eagle; 4k. Red kite; 10k. Peregrine falcon; 16k. Gyr falcon. HORIZ: 12k. Golden eagle; 14k. Lammergeier.

1189 "Red Star" (medal) and Scenes of Odessa

1965. Heroic Soviet Towns. Multicoloured.

No.	Type	Description	Unused	Used
3225		10k. Type **1189**	85	40
3226		10k. Leningrad	85	40
3227		10k. Kiev	85	40
3228		10k. Moscow	85	40
3229		10k. Brest-Litovsk	85	40
3230		10k. Volgograd	85	40
3231		10k. Sevastopol	85	40

1190 Flag, Map and Parliament Building, Belgrade

1965. 20th Anniv of Yugoslavia Republic.

No.	Type	Description	Unused	Used
3232	**1190**	6k. multicoloured	1·50	40

1191 Tupolev Tu-134 Jetliner

1965. Soviet Civil Aviation. Multicoloured.

No.	Type	Description	Unused	Used
3233		6k. Type **1191**	1·20	30
3234		10k. Antonov An-24	1·70	50
3235		12k. Mil Mi-10 helicopter	2·00	65
3236		16k. Beriev Be-10 flying boat	2·75	80
3237		20k. Antonov An-22 Anteus	3·50	95

1192 "The Proposal of Marriage" (P. Fedotov, 150th birth anniv)

1965. Soviet Painters' Annivs.

No.	Type	Description	Unused	Used
3238	-	12k. black and red	2·75	80
3239	**1192**	16k. blue and red	4·00	1·10

DESIGN—VERT: 12k. "A Collective Farm Watchman" (S. Gerasimov, 80th birth anniv).

1193 Crystallography Congress Emblem

1966. International Congresses, Moscow.

No.	Type	Description	Unused	Used
3240	**1193**	6k. black, blue and bistre	70	30
3241	-	6k. black, red and blue	70	30
3242	-	6k. purple, grey & black	70	30
3243	-	6k. black and blue	70	30
3244	-	6k. black, red and yellow	70	30

CONGRESS EMBLEMS: No. 3241, Microbiology; 3242, Poultry-raising; 3243, Oceanography; 3244, Mathematics.

1194 Postman and Milkmaid (19th-century statuettes, des A. Venetsianov)

1966. Bicentenary of Dmitrov Ceramic Works. Multicoloured.

No.	Type	Description	Unused	Used
3245		6k. Type **1194**	70	30
3246		10k. Modern tea set	1·20	65

1195 Rolland (after A. Yar-Kravchenko)

1966. Birth Centenary of Romain Rolland (French writer) and 150th Birth Anniv of Eugene Potier (French poet).

3247	**1195**	4k. brown and blue	70	30
3248	-	4k. brown, red and black	70	30

DESIGN: No. 3248, Potier and revolutionary scene.

1196 Mongol Horseman

1966. 20th Anniv of Soviet–Mongolian Treaty.

3249	**1196**	4k. multicoloured	70	30

„ЛУНА-9" — НА ЛУНЕ!
3.2.1966

(1197)

1966. Landing of "Luna 9" Rocket on Moon. Optd with T **1197**.

3250	**1017**	6k. red, black and blue	7·75	7·25

1198 Supply Ship "Ob"

1966. Tenth Anniv of Soviet Antarctic Expedition.

3251	**1198**	10k. lake and silver	4·25	3·25
3252	-	10k. lake, silver and blue	4·25	3·25
3253	-	10k. lake, silver and blue	4·25	3·25

DESIGNS—TRIANGULAR: No. 3252, Snow vehicle. DIAMOND: No. 3253, Antarctic map. This stamp is partly perf across the centre.

1199 Mussa Dyalil and Scene from Poem

1966. Writers.

3254	**1199**	4k. black and brown	70	25
3255	-	4k. black and green	70	25
3256	-	4k. black and green	70	25

WRITERS: No. 3254 (Azerbaijan writer: 60th birth anniv); 3255, Akob Akopyan (Armenian poet: birth cent); 3256, Djalil Mamedkulizade (Azerbaijan writer: birth cent).

1200 Lenin (after bust by Kibalnikov)

1966. Lenin's 96th Birth Anniv.

3257	**1200**	10k. gold and green	2·20	95
3258	**1200**	10k. silver and red	2·20	95

1201 N. Ilin

1966. War Heroes.

3259	**1201**	4k. violet and red	50	25
3260	-	4k. lilac and blue	50	25
3261	-	4k. brown and green	50	25

PORTRAITS: No. 3260, G. P. Kravchenko; 3261, A. Uglovsky.

1202 Scene from "Alive and Dead" (dir. A. Stolper)

1966. Soviet Cinema Art.

3262	**1202**	4k. black, green and red	35	15
3263	-	10k. black and blue	1·00	50

DESIGN: 10k. Scene from "Hamlet" (dir. G. Kozintsev).

1203 Kremlin and Inscription

1966. 23rd Soviet Comunist Party Congress, Moscow (1st issue).

3264	**1203**	4k. gold, red and blue	70	25

See also Nos. 3337/41.

Учредительная конференция
Всесоюзного общества
филателистов. 1966

(1204)

1966. Philatelists All-Union Society Conference. No. 3198 optd with T **1204**.

3265	16k. plum, red and grey	6·75	3·75

1205 Ice Skating

1966. Second People's Winter Spartakiad.

3266	**1205**	4k. blue, red and olive	50	15
3267	-	6k. red, lake and lilac	70	30
3268	-	10k. lake, red and blue	1·20	65

DESIGNS: Inscription emblem and 6k. Ice hockey; 10k. Skiing.

Nos. 3266/8 are each perf across the centre.

1206 Liner "Aleksandr Pushkin"

1966. Soviet Transport.

3269		4k. multicoloured	70	25
3270		6k. multicoloured	1·00	30
3271		10k. multicoloured	1·50	65
3272	**1206**	12k. multicoloured	1·70	70
3273	-	16k. multicoloured	1·90	80

DESIGNS—HORIZ: 4k. Electric train; 6k. Map of Lenin Volga–Baltic canal system; 16k. Silhouette of liner "Aleksandr Pushkin" on globe. VERT: 10k. Canal lock (Volga–Baltic canal).

Nos. 3271/3 commemorate the inauguration of Leningrad–Montreal Sea Service.

1207 Government Building, Frunze

1966. 40th Anniv of Kirgizia.

3274	**1207**	4k. red	70	25

1208 S. M. Kirov (80th Birth Anniv)

1966. Soviet Personalities.

3275	**1208**	4k. brown	70	25
3276	-	4k. green	70	25
3277	-	4k. violet	70	25

PORTRAITS: No. 3276, G. I. Ordzhonikidze (80th birth anniv); 3277, Ion Yakir (military commander, 70th birth anniv).

1209 Lenin

1966. 23rd Soviet Communist Party Congress, Moscow (2nd issue). Sheet 119×80 mm.

MS3278	50k. red, silver and lake	6·00	1·90

1210 A. Fersman (mineralogist)

1966. Soviet Scientists. Multicoloured. Colours of name panels below.

3279	**1210**	4k. blue	70	25
3280	-	4k. brown	70	25
3281	-	4k. violet	70	25
3282	-	4k. brown and blue	70	25

PORTRAITS: No. 3280, D. K. Zabolotnyi (micro-biologist); 3281, M. A. Shatelen (electrical engineer); 3282, O. Yu. Shmidt (arctic explorer).

„Луна-10"—XXIII съезду КПСС

(1211)

1966. Launching of "Luna 10". As No. 3284, but imperf, optd with T **1211**.

3283	**1212**	10k. multicoloured	5·50	5·00

1212 Arrowheads, "Luna 9" and Orbit

1966. Cosmonautics Day. Multicoloured.

3284	10k. Type **1212**	70	25
3285	12k. Rocket launching and different orbit	85	30

1213 "Molniya I" in Orbit

1966. Launching of "Molniya I" Telecommunications Satellite.

3286	**1213**	10k. multicoloured	1·40	65

1214 Ernst Thalmann (80th birth anniv)

1966. Prominent Leaders.

3287	**1214**	6k. red	1·00	30
3288	-	6k. violet	1·00	30
3289	-	6k. brown	1·00	30

PORTRAITS: No. 3288, Wilhelm Pieck (90th birth anniv); 3289, Sun Yat-sen (birth cent).

1216 Spaceman and Soldier

1966. 15th Young Communist League Congress.

3290	**1216**	4k. black and red	70	25

1217 Ice Hockey Player

1966. Soviet Victory in World Ice Hockey Championships.

3291	**1217**	10k. multicoloured	1·20	50

1218 N. I. Kuznetsov

1966. War Heroes. Guerrilla Fighters.

3292	**1218**	4k. black and green	50	15
3293	-	4k. black and yellow	50	15
3294	-	4k. black and blue	50	15
3295	-	4k. black and purple	50	15
3296	-	4k. black and violet	50	15

PORTRAITS: No. 3293, I. Y. Sudmalis; 3294, A. A. Morozova; No. 3295, F. E. Strelets; 3296, T. P. Bumazhkov.

1219 Tchaikovsky

1966. Third International Tchaikovsky Music Competition, Moscow.

3297		4k. black, red and yellow	70	15
3298	**1219**	6k. black, red and yellow	1·00	30
3299	-	16k. black, red and blue	2·00	80

DESIGNS: 4k. Moscow State Conservatoire of Music; 16k. Tchaikovsky's house and museum, Klin.

1220 Running

1966. Sports Events.

3300	**1220**	4k. brown, olive & green	35	25
3301	-	6k. black, bistre & orge	70	30
3302	-	12k. black, bistre & blue	1·20	65

DESIGNS: 6k. Weightlifting; 12k. Wrestling.

1222 Gold Medal and Chess Pieces

1966. World Chess Championship, Moscow.

3303	**1222**	6k. multicoloured	3·00	1·40

1223 Jules Rimet Cup and Football

1966. World Cup Football Championship (England) and World Fencing Championships (Moscow).

3304	**1223**	4k. black, gold and red	50	15
3305	-	6k. multicoloured	70	30
3306	-	12k. multicoloured	1·20	50
3307	-	16k. multicoloured	1·70	65

DESIGNS: 6k. Footballers; 12k. Fencers; 16k. Fencer and fencing emblems.

1224 Sable, Lake Baikal and Animals (image scaled to 60% of original size)

1966. Barguzin Nature Reserve.

3308	**1224**	4k. black and blue	1·20	65
3309	-	6k. black and purple	1·70	80

DESIGN: 6k. Map of reserve, and brown bear.

1225 Lotus Plants

1966. 125th Anniv of Sukhumi Botanical Gardens.

3310	**1225**	3k. red, yellow and green	35	15
3311	-	6k. bistre, brown & blue	70	30
3312	-	12k. red, green & turq	1·20	50

DESIGNS: 6k. Palms and cypresses; 12k. Water lilies.

1226 "Venus 3" Medal, Globe and Flight Trajectory

1966. Space Achievements.

3313	**1226**	6k. black, silver and red	1·00	50
3314	-	6k. deep blue, blue and brown	1·00	50
3315	-	6k. ochre and blue	1·00	50
3316	-	6k. multicoloured	1·00	50
3317	-	6k. pink, mauve & black	1·00	50

DESIGNS: No. 3314, Spacedogs, Ugolek and Veterok; 3315, "Luna 10"; 3316, "Molniya I"; 3317, "Luna 2's" pennant, Earth and Moon.

1227 Itkol

1966. Tourist Resorts. Multicoloured.

3318	1k. Type **1227**	15	15
3319	4k. Cruise ship on the Volga	50	25
3320	6k. Archway, Leningrad (27½×28 mm)	85	30
3321	10k. Castle, Kislovodsk	1·20	50
3322	12k. Ismail Samani Mausoleum, Bokhara	1·50	65
3323	16k. Kavkaz Hotel, Sochi (Black Sea)	2·00	80

1229 Fencing

1966. World Sports Championships of 1966. Sheet 155×155 mm comprising four 10k. stamps as T **1229**.

MS3324 4×10k. multicoloured	20·00	7·25

DESIGNS: Type **1229**: Jules Rimet Cup (football); Chessmen; Ice Hockey.

1230 Congress Emblem

1966. Seventh Consumers' Co-operative Societies Congress, Moscow.

3325	**1230**	4k. yellow and brown	85	30

1231 Peace Dove and Japanese Crane

1966. Soviet–Japanese Meeting, Khabarovsk.

3326	**1231**	6k. black and red	1·00	50

1232 "Avtandil at a Mountain Spring", after engraving by S. Kabulazde

1233

1966. 800th Birth Anniv of Shota Rustaveli (Georgian poet).

3327	-	3k. black on green	45	15
3328	-	4k. brown on yellow	60	25
3329	**1232**	6k. black on blue	85	30
MS3330		98×68 mm. **1233** 50k. green and bistre	7·75	2·75

DESIGNS: 3k. Scene from poem "The Knight in the Tiger's Skin" (after I. Toidze); 4k. Rustaveli, (after bas-relief by Ya. Nikoladze).

1234 Arms, Moscow Skyline and Fireworks

1966. 49th Anniv of October Revolution.

3331	**1234**	4k. multicoloured	70	30

1235 Trawler, Net and Map of Lake Baikal

1966. Fish Resources of Lake Baikal. Multicoloured.

3332	2k. Baikal grayling (horiz)	35	15
3333	4k. Baikal sturgeon (horiz)	45	30
3334	6k. Type **1235**	70	65
3335	10k. Omul (horiz)	1·00	95
3336	12k. Baikal whitefish (horiz)	1·20	1·10

1236 "Agriculture and Industry"

1966. 23rd Soviet Communist Party Congress, Moscow (3rd issue).

3337	**1236**	4k. silver and brown	50	30
3338	-	4k. silver and blue	50	30
3339	-	4k. silver and red	50	30
3340	-	4k. silver and red	50	30
3341	-	4k. silver and green	50	30

DESIGN (Map as Type **1236** with symbols of): No. 3338, "Communications and Transport"; 3339, "Education and Technology"; 3340, "Increased Productivity"; 3341, "Power Resources".

1237 Government Buildings, Kishinev

1966. 500th Anniv of Kishinev (Moldavian Republic).

3342	**1237**	4k. multicoloured	70	25

1238 Clouds, Rain and Decade Emblem

1966. International Hydrological Decade.

3343	**1238**	6k. multicoloured	85	50

1239 Nikitin Monument (S. Orlov and A. Zavalor), Kalinin

1966. 50th Anniv of Afanasy Nikitin's Voyage to India.

3344	**1239**	4k. black, green & yell	70	25

1240 Scene from "Nargiz" (Muslim Magomaev)

1966. Azerbaijan Operas.

3345	**1240**	4k. ochre and black	85	30
3346	-	4k. green and black	85	30

DESIGN: No. 3346, Scene from "Kehzoglu" (Uzeir Gadzhibekov).

1241 "Luna 9" and Moon

1242 Agricultural and Chemical Symbols

1966

3347		1k. brown	15	15
3348	**1241**	2k. violet	25	15
3349	-	3k. purple	35	15
3350	-	4k. red	45	15
3351	-	6k. blue	50	25
3563	-	10k. olive	2·00	80
3353	-	12k. brown	1·00	40
3354	-	16k. blue	1·40	50
3355	-	20k. red, blue and drab	1·70	65
3566	-	20k. red	3·25	1·60
3356	**1242**	30k. green	2·50	80
3357	-	50k. ultram, blue & grey	4·25	1·10
3568	-	50k. blue	11·50	2·40
3358	-	1r. black and red	8·75	2·20
3569	-	1r. brown and black	17·00	4·75

DESIGNS—As Type **1241**: 1k. Palace of Congresses, Kremlin; 3k. Youth, girl and Lenin emblem; 4k. Arms and hammer and sickle emblem; 6k. "Communications" (Antonov An-10A Ukrainia airplane and sputnik); 10k. Soldier and star emblem; 12k. Furnaceman; 16k. Girl with dove. As Type **1242**: 20k. Workers' demonstration and flower; 50k. "Postal communications"; 1r. Lenin and industrial emblems.

1243 "Presenting Arms"

1966. 25th Anniv of People's Voluntary Corps.

3359	**1243**	4k. brown and red	70	25

1245 Campaign Meeting

1966. "Hands off Vietnam".

3360	**1245**	6k. multicoloured	70	25

1246 Servicemen

1966. 30th Anniv of Spanish Civil War.

3361	**1246**	6k. black, red and ochre	85	30

1247 Ostankino TV Tower, "Molniya I" (satellite) and "1967"

1966. New Year and "50th Year of October Revolution".

3362	**1247**	4k. multicoloured	85	50

1248 Flight Diagram

1966. Space Flight and Moon Landing of "Luna 9".

3363	**1248**	10k. black and silver	1·20	65
3364	-	10k. red and silver	1·20	65
3365	-	10k. black and silver	1·20	65

DESIGNS—SQUARE (25×25 mm): No. 3364, Arms of Russia and lunar pennant. HORIZ: No. 3365, "Lunar 9" on Moon's surface.

1249 Statue, Tank and Medal

1966. 25th Anniv of Battle of Moscow.

3366		4k. brown	50	15
3367	**1249**	6k. ochre and sepia	70	30
3368	-	10k. yellow and brown	1·20	65

DESIGNS—HORIZ: (60×28 mm): 4k. Soviet troops advancing; 10k. "Moscow at peace"– Kremlin, Sun and "Defence of Moscow" medal.

1250 Cervantes and Don Quixote

1966. 350th Death Anniv of Cervantes.

3369 **1250** 6k. brown, green and deep green 85 30

1252 Bering's Ship "Sv. Pyotr" and Map of Komandor Islands

1966. Soviet Far Eastern Territories. Multicoloured.

3370	1k. Type **1252**	35	15
3371	2k. Medny Island and map	45	25
3372	4k. Petropavlovsk Harbour, Kamchatka	70	50
3373	6k. Geyser, Kamchatka (vert)	85	65
3374	10k. Avatchinskaya Bay, Kamchatka	1·40	95
3375	12k. Northern fur seals, Bering Is	1·50	1·30
3376	16k. Common guillemot colony, Kurile Islands	2·50	1·60

1254 "The Lute Player" (Caravaggio)

1966. Art Treasures of the Hermitage Museum, Leningrad.

3377	-	4k. black on yellow	50	15
3378	-	6k. black on grey	70	30
3379	-	10k. black on lilac	1·00	40
3380	-	12k. black on green	1·40	50
3381	**1254**	16k. black on buff	1·70	65

DESIGNS—HORIZ: 4k. "Golden Stag" (from Scythian battle shield (6th cent B.C.). VERT: 6k. Persian silver jug (5th cent A.D.; 10k. Statue of Voltaire (Houdon, 1781); 12k. Malachite vase (Urals, 1840).

1255 Sea-water Distilling Apparatus

1967. World Fair, Montreal.

3382	**1255**	4k. black, silver & green	35	25
3383	-	6k. multicoloured	70	30
3384	-	10k. multicoloured	1·20	50

MS3385 127×76 mm. 30k. multicoloured 5·00 2·75

DESIGNS—VERT: 6k. "Atomic Energy" (explosion and symbol). HORIZ: 10k. Space station "Proton 1"; 30k. Soviet pavilion.

1256 Lieut. B. I. Sizov

1967. War Heroes.

3386	**1256**	4k. brown on yellow	85	50
3387	-	4k. brown on drab	85	50

DESIGN: No. 3387, Private V. V. Khodyrev.

1257 Woman's Face and Pavlov Shawl

1967. International Women's Day.

3388 **1257** 4k. red, violet and green 70 30

1258 Cine-camera and Film "Flower"

1967. Fifth International Film Festival, Moscow.

3389 **1258** 6k. multicoloured 85 30

1259 Factory Ship "Cheryashevsky"

1967. Soviet Fishing Industry. Multicoloured.

3390	6k. Type **1259**	85	80
3391	6k. Refrigerated trawler	85	80
3392	6k. Crab canning ship	85	80
3393	6k. Trawler	85	80
3394	6k. Seine-fishing boat, Black Sea	85	80

1260 Newspaper Cuttings, Hammer and Sickle

1967. 50th Anniv of Newspaper "Izvestiya".

3395 **1260** 4k. multicoloured 70 30

1261 I.S.O. Congress Emblem

1967. Moscow Congresses.

3396	6k. turquoise, black and blue	70	30
3397	6k. red, black and blue	70	30

DESIGNS: No. 3396, Type **1261** (7th Congress of Int Standards Assn "I.S.O."); 3397, "V" emblem of 5th Int Mining Congress.

1262 I.T.Y. Emblem

1967. International Tourist Year.

3398 **1262** 4k. black, silver and blue 70 30

Вена - 1967

(1263)

1967. Victory in World Ice Hockey Championship. No. 3291 optd with T **1263**.

3399 **1217** 10k. multicoloured 3·75 3·50

1264 A. A. Leonov in Space

1967. Cosmonautics Day. Multicoloured.

3400	4k. Type **1264**	50	15
3401	10k. Rocket and Earth	1·20	50
3402	16k. "Luna 10" over Moon	1·70	95

1265 "Lenin as Schoolboy" (V. Tsigal)

1967. Lenin's 97th Birth Anniv.

3403	**1265**	2k. brown, yellow & grn	50	15
3404	-	3k. brown and lake	85	30
3405	-	4k. green, yellow and olive	1·00	40
3406	-	6k. silver, black and blue	1·70	50
3407	-	10k. blue, black & silver	2·75	80
3408	-	10k. black and gold	1·40	65

SCULPTURES—VERT: 3k. Lenin's monument, Ulyanovsk; 6k. Bust of Lenin (G. and Yu. Neroda); 10k. (both) "Lenin as Leader" (N. Andreev). HORIZ: 4k. "Lenin at Razliv" (V. Pinchuk).

1266 M. F. Shmyrev

1967. War Heroes.

3409	**1266**	4k. sepia and brown	35	15
3410	-	4k. brown and blue	35	15
3411	-	4k. brown and violet	35	15

DESIGNS: No. 3410, Major-General S. V. Rudnev; 3411, First Lieut. M. S. Kharchenko.

1267 Transport crossing Ice on Lake Ladoga

1967. Siege of Leningrad, 1941–42.

3412 **1267** 4k. grey, red and cream 70 50

1268 Marshal Biryuzov

1967. Biryuzov Commemoration.

3413 **1268** 4k. green and yellow 70 30

1269 Minsk Old and New

1967. 900th Anniv of Minsk.

3414 **1269** 4k. green and black 70 30

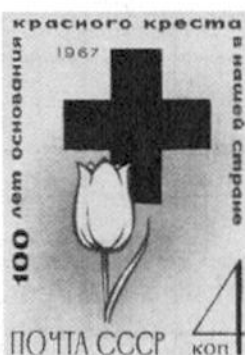

1270 Red Cross and Tulip

1967. Centenary of Russian Red Cross.

3415 **1270** 4k. red and ochre 85 30

1271 Russian Stamps of 1918 and 1967

1967. 50th Anniv of U.S.S.R. Philatelic Exn, Moscow.

3416 **1271** 20k. green and blue 2·40 1·10

MS3417 92×75 mm. **1271** 20k. green (pair). Imperf 7·25 3·25

1272 Komsomolsk-on-Amur and Map

1967. 35th Anniv of Komsomolsk-on-Amur.

3418 **1272** 4k. brown and red 1·00 65

1273 Motor Cyclist (International Motor Rally, Moscow)

1967. Sports and Pastimes. International Events.

3419	-	1k. brown, bistre & grn	25	15
3420	-	2k. brown	35	15
3421	-	3k. blue	45	15
3422	-	4k. turquoise	50	25
3423	-	6k. purple and bistre	70	30
3424	**1273**	10k. purple and lilac	1·70	50

DESIGNS AND EVENTS: 1k. Draughts board and players (World Draughts Championships); 2k. Throwing the javelin; 3k. Running; 4k. Long jumping (all preliminary events for Europa Cup Games); 6k. Gymnast (World Gymnastics Championships).

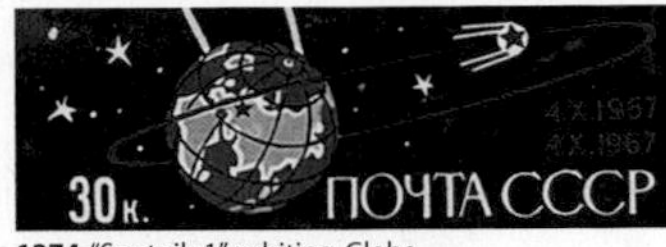

1274 "Sputnik 1" orbiting Globe

1967. Tenth Anniv of First Earth Satellite. Sheet 105×132 mm.

MS3425 **1274** 30k. multicoloured 6·00 3·25

1275 G. D. Gai (soldier)

1967. Commander G. D. Gai Commemoration.

3426 **1275** 4k. black and red 70 30

1276 Games Emblem and Cup

1967. All Union Schoolchildren's Spartakiad.

3427 **1276** 4k. red, black and silver 50 25

1277 Spartakiad Emblem and Cup

1967. Fourth People's Spartakiad.

3428	4k. black, red and silver	50	25
3429	4k. black, red and silver	50	25
3430	4k. black, red and silver	50	25
3431	4k. black, red and silver	50	25

DESIGNS: Each with Cup. No. 3428, Type **1277**; No. 3429, Gymnastics; 3430, Diving; 3431, Cycling.

1278 V. G. Klochkov (Soviet hero)

1967. Klochkov Commemoration.

3432 **1278** 4k. black and red 70 50

1279 Crest, Flag and Capital of Moldavia

No. 3433

No. 3434

БЕЛОРУССКАЯ ССР
БЕЛАРУСКАЯ ССР

No. 3435

ЭСТОНСКАЯ ССР
EESTI NSV

No. 3436

ГРУЗИНСКАЯ ССР
საქართველოს სსრ

No. 3437

КАЗАХСКАЯ ССР
ҚАЗАҚ ССР

No. 3438

КИРГИЗСКАЯ ССР
КЫРГЫЗ ССР

No. 3439

ЛАТВИЙСКАЯ ССР
LATVIJAS PSR

No. 3440

ЛИТОВСКАЯ ССР
LIETUVOS TSR

No. 3441

МОЛДАВСКАЯ ССР
РСС МОЛДОВЕНЯСКЭ

No. 3442

РОССИЙСКАЯ СОВЕТСКАЯ
ФЕДЕРАТИВНАЯ
СОЦИАЛИСТИЧЕСКАЯ РЕСПУБЛИКА

No. 3443

ТАДЖИКСКАЯ ССР
РСС ТОЧИКИСТОН

No. 3444

ТУРКМЕНСКАЯ ССР
ТУРКМЕНИСТАН ССР

No. 3445

УКРАИНСКАЯ ССР
УКРАЇНСЬКА РСР

No. 3446

УЗБЕКСКАЯ ССР
ЎЗБЕКИСТОН ССР

No. 3447

1967. 50th Anniv of October Revolution (1st issue). Designs showing crests, flags and capitals of the Soviet Republics. Multicoloured.

No.	Description		
3433	4k. Armenia	50	25
3434	4k. Azerbaijan	50	25
3435	4k. Belorussia	50	25
3436	4k. Estonia	50	25
3437	4k. Georgia	50	25
3438	4k. Kazakhstan	50	25
3439	4k. Kirgizia	50	25
3440	4k. Latvia	50	25
3441	4k. Lithuania	50	25
3442	4k. Type **1279**	50	25
3443	4k. Russia	50	25
3444	4k. Tadjikistan	50	25
3445	4k. Turkmenistan	50	25
3446	4k. Ukraine	50	25
3447	4k. Uzbekistan	50	25
3448	4k. Soviet Arms	50	25

No. 3448 is size 47×32 mm.

See also Nos. 3473/82.

1280 Telecommunications Symbols

1967. "Progress of Communism".

No.	Type	Description		
3449	**1280**	4k. red, purple and silver	5·50	3·75

1281 Manchurian Crane and Dove

1967. Soviet–Japanese Friendship.

No.	Type	Description		
3450	**1281**	16k. brown, black & red	1·70	65

1282 Karl Marx and Title Page

1967. Centenary of Karl Marx's "Das Kapital".

No.	Type	Description		
3451	**1282**	4k. brown and red	70	25

1283 Arctic Fox

1967. Fur-bearing Animals.

No.	Type	Description		
3452	**1283**	2k. blue, black & brown	25	15
3453	-	4k. blue, black and drab	50	25
3454	-	6k. ochre, black & green	70	30
3455	-	10k. brown, black & grn	1·00	40
3456	-	12k. black, ochre & vio	1·40	50
3457	-	16k. brown, black & yell	1·70	80
3458	-	20k. brown, black & turq	2·20	95

DESIGNS—VERT: 4k. Red fox; 12k. Stoat; 16k. Sable. HORIZ: 6k. Red fox; 10k. Muskrat; 20k. European mink.

1284 Ice Skating

1967. Winter Olympic Games, Grenoble (1968). Multicoloured.

No.	Description		
3459	2k. Type **1284**	25	15
3460	3k. Ski jumping	35	15
3461	4k. Games emblem (vert)	50	25
3462	10k. Ice hockey	1·00	40
3463	12k. Skiing	1·40	50

1285 Krasnodon Memorial

1967. 25th Anniv of Krasnodon Defence.

No.	Type	Description		
3464	**1285**	4k. black, yellow & pur	50	25

1285a Map and Snow Leopard (image scaled to 59% of original size)

1967. Cedar Valley Nature Reserve.

No.	Type	Description		
3465	**1285a**	10k. black and bistre	1·20	65

1286 Badge and Yakovlev Yak-9 Fighters

1967. 25th Anniv of French "Normandie-Niemen" Fighter Squadron.

No.	Type	Description		
3466	**1286**	6k. red, blue and gold	70	25

1287 Militiaman and Soviet Crest

1967. 50th Anniv of Soviet Militia.

No.	Type	Description		
3467	**1287**	4k. red and blue	70	25

1288 Cosmonauts in Space

1967. Space Fantasies. Multicoloured.

No.	Description		
3468	4k. Type **1288**	50	15
3469	6k. Men on the Moon (horiz)	70	30
3470	10k. Cosmic vehicle	1·00	40
3471	12k. Planetary landscape (horiz)	1·40	50
3472	16k. Imaginary spacecraft	1·70	65

1289 Red Star and Soviet Crest

1967. 50th Anniv of October Revolution (2nd issue). "50 Heroic Years". Designs showing paintings and Soviet Arms. Multicoloured.

No.	Description		
3473	4k. Type **1289**	50	25
3474	4k. "Lenin addressing Congress" (Serov—1955)	50	25
3475	4k. "Lenin explaining the GOE-LRO map" (Schmatko—1957)	50	25
3476	4k. "The First Cavalry" (Grekov—1924)	50	25
3477	4k. "Students" (Yoganson—1928)	50	25
3478	4k. "People's Friendship" (Karpov—1924)	50	25
3479	4k. "Dawn of the Five Year Plan" (construction work, Romas—1934)	50	25
3480	4k. "Farmers' Holiday" (Gerasimov—1937)	50	25
3481	4k. "Victory in World War II" (Korolev—1965)	50	25
3482	4k. "Builders of Communism" (Merpert and Skripkov—1965)	50	25
MS3483	93×141 mm. 40k. (2) in designs of Nos. 3474, 3482, but smaller (60×28 mm) and colours changed	7·25	2·75

1290 S. Katayama

1967. Katayama (founder of Japanese Communist Party) Commemoration.

No.	Type	Description		
3484	**1290**	6k. green	50	15

1291 Hammer, Sickle and First Earth Satellite

1967. 50th Anniv of October Revolution (3rd issue). "Conquest of Space". Sheet 129×80 mm.

No.	Description		
MS3485	1291 1r. lake	10·00	4·75

1292 T.V. Tower, Moscow

1967. Opening of Ostankino T.V. Tower, Moscow.

No.	Type	Description		
3486	**1292**	16k. black, silver & orge	1·40	65

1293 Narva-Joesuu (Estonia)

1967. Baltic Health Resorts. Multicoloured.

No.	Description		
3487	4k. Yurmala (Latvia)	35	15
3488	6k. Type **1293**	55	25
3489	10k. Druskininkai (Lithuania)	90	30
3490	12k. Zelenogradsk (Kaliningrad) (vert)	1·30	50
3491	16k. Svetlogorsk (Kaliningrad) (vert)	1·60	65

1294 K.G.B. Emblem

1967. 50th Anniv of State Security Commission (K.G.B.).

No.	Type	Description		
3492	**1294**	4k. red, silver and blue	70	25

1295 Moscow View

1967. New Year.

No.	Type	Description		
3493	**1295**	4k. brown, pink and silver	70	25

1296 Revolutionaries at Kharkov, and Monument

1967. 50th Anniv of Ukraine Republic.

No.	Type	Description		
3494	**1296**	4k. multicoloured	55	15
3495	-	6k. multicoloured	70	25
3496	-	10k. multicoloured	1·10	30

DESIGNS: 6k. Hammer and sickle and industrial and agricultural scenes; 10k. Unknown Soldier's monument, Kiev, and young Ukrainians with welcoming bread and salt.

1297 Armoury, Commandant and Trinity Towers

1967. Kremlin Buildings.

No.	Type	Description		
3497	**1297**	4k. brown, purple & grn	35	15
3498	-	6k. brown, green & yell	55	25
3499	-	10k. brown and grey	90	30
3500	-	12k. green, violet and cream	1·30	50
3501	-	16k. brown, red and light brown	1·60	55

DESIGNS—HORIZ: 6k. Cathedral of the Annunciation. VERT: 10k. Konstantino-Yelenin, Alarm and Spassky Towers; 12k. Ivan the Great's bell tower; 16k. Kutafya and Trinity Towers.

1298 Moscow Badge, Lenin's Tomb and Rockets

1967. "50 Years of Communist Development".

No.	Type	Description		
3502	**1298**	4k. lake	65	50
3503	-	4k. brown	65	50
3504	-	4k. green	65	50
3505	-	4k. blue	65	50
3506	-	4k. blue	65	50

DESIGNS—HORIZ: No. 3503, Computer-tape cogwheel and industrial scene; 3504, Ear of wheat and grain silo; 3505, Microscope, radar antennae and Moscow University. VERT: No. 3506, T.V. Tower, "Aleksandr Pushkin" (liner), railway bridge and jet airliner.

1299 Unknown Soldier's Tomb, Kremlin

1967. "Unknown Soldier" Commemoration.

3507 **1299** 4k. red 70 25

1300 "The Interrogation of Communists" (B. Ioganson)

1967. Paintings in the Tretyakov Gallery, Moscow. Multicoloured.

3508 3k. Type **1300** 35 15
3509 4k. "The Sea-shore" (I. Aivazovsky) 55 25
3510 4k. "The Lace Maker" (V. Tropinin) (vert) 55 25
3511 6k. "The Bakery" (T. Yablonskaya) (60×34 mm) 70 25
3512 6k. "Aleksandr Nevsky" (part of triptych by P. Korin) (34×60 mm) 70 25
3513 6k. "Boyarynya Morozova" (V. Surikov) (60×34 mm) 70 25
3514 10k. "The Swan Maiden" (M. Vrubel) (vert) 1·30 50
3515 10k. "The Arrest of a Propagandist" (I. Repin) 1·30 50
3516 16k. "Moscow Suburb in February" (G. Nissky) 2·30 80

1301 Congress Emblem

1968. 14th Soviet Trade Unions Congress, Moscow.

3517 **1301** 6k. red and green 70 25

1302 Lieut. S. G. Baikov

1968. War Heroes.

3518 **1302** 4k. black and blue 55 15
3519 - 4k. blue and green 55 15
3520 - 4k. black and red 55 15

PORTRAITS: No. 3519, Lieut. P. L. Guchenko; No. 3520, A. A. Pokaltchuk.

1303 Racehorses

1968. Soviet Horse Breeding.

3521 **1303** 4k. black, purple & blue 55 50
3522 - 6k. black, blue and red 70 65
3523 - 10k. black, brn & turq 1·30 1·10
3524 - 12k. black, green & brn 1·40 1·30
3525 - 16k. black, red and green 2·00 1·80

DESIGNS (each with horse's head and horses "in the field"). VERT: 6k. Show horses; 12k. Show jumpers. HORIZ: 10k. Trotters; 16k. Hunters.

1304 M. Ulyanova

1968. 90th Birth Anniv of M. I. Ulyanova (Lenin's sister).

3526 **1304** 4k. blue and green 70 25

1305 Red Star and Forces' Flags

1968. 50th Anniv of Soviet Armed Forces. Multicoloured.

3527 4k. Type **1305** 65 25
3528 4k. Lenin addressing recruits (horiz) 65 25
3529 4k. Recruiting poster (D. Moor) and volunteers (horiz) 65 25
3530 4k. Red Army entering Vladivostok, 1922, and monument (L. Shervud) (horiz) 65 25
3531 4k. Dnieper Dam and statue "On Guard" (horiz) 65 25
3532 4k. "Liberators" poster (V. Ivanov) and tanks in the Ukraine (horiz) 65 25
3533 4k. "To the East" poster and retreating Germans fording river (horiz) 65 25
3534 4k. Stalingrad battle monument and German prisoners-of-war 65 25
3535 4k. Victory parade, Red Square, Moscow, and monument, Treptow (Berlin) (horiz) 65 25
3536 4k. Rockets, tank, warships and Red Flag 65 25
MS3537 73×100 mm. 1r. Design as No. 3536 but smaller. Imperf 8·25 4·25

1306 Gorky (after Serov)

1968. Birth Centenary of Maksim Gorky (writer).

3538 **1306** 4k. brown and drab 70 25

1307 Fireman and Appliances

1968. 50th Anniv of Soviet Fire Services.

3539 **1307** 4k. black and red 70 15

1308 Linked Satellites

1968. Space Link of "Cosmos" Satellites.

3540 **1308** 6k. black, gold & purple 70 30

1309 N. N. Popudrenko

1968. War Heroes.

3541 **1309** 4k. black and green 70 25
3542 - 4k. black and lilac 70 25

DESIGN: No. 3542, P. P. Vershigora.

1310 Protective Hand

1968. "Solidarity with Vietnam".

3543 **1310** 6k. multicoloured 70 30

1311 Leonov filming in Space

1968. Cosmonautics Day. Multicoloured.

3544 4k. Type **1311** 70 25
3545 6k. "Kosmos 186" and "Kosmos 188" linking in space 1·10 40
3546 10k. "Venera 4" space probe 1·80 65

1312 Lenin

1968. Lenin's 98th Birth Anniv.

3547 **1312** 4k. multicoloured 1·40 50
3548 - 4k. black, red and gold 1·40 50
3549 - 4k. brown, red and gold 1·40 50

DESIGNS: No. 3548, Lenin speaking in Red Square; No. 3549, Lenin in peaked cap speaking from lorry during parade.

1313 Navoi (after V. Kaidalov)

1968. 525th Birth Anniv of Alisher Navoi (Uzbek poet).

3550 **1313** 4k. brown 70 25

1314 Karl Marx

1968. 150th Birth Anniv of Karl Marx.

3551 **1314** 4k. black and red 70 25

1315 Frontier Guard

1968. 50th Anniv of Soviet Frontier Guards. Multicoloured.

3552 4k. Type **1315** 70 25
3553 6k. Jubilee badge 90 30

1316 Gem and Congress Emblem

1968. "International Congresses and Assemblies".

3554 **1316** 6k. deep blue, blue and green 70 30
3555 - 6k. gold, orange & brn 70 30
3556 - 6k. gold, black and red 70 30
3557 - 6k. orange, black & mve 70 30

DESIGNS: No. 3554, Type **1316** (8th Enriched Minerals Congress); 3555, Power stations, pylon and emblem (7th World Power Conference); 3556, "Carabus schaenherri" (ground beetle) and emblem (13th Entomological Congress); 3557, Roses and emblem (4th Congress on Volatile Oils).

1317 S. Aini

1968. 90th Birth Anniv of Sadriddin Aini (Tadzhik writer).

3570 **1317** 4k. purple and bistre 70 25

1318 Congress Emblem and Postrider

1968. Meeting of U.P.U. Consultative Commission, Moscow.

3571 **1318** 6k. red and grey 80 50
3572 - 6k. red and yellow 80 50

DESIGN: No. 3572, Emblem and transport.

1319 "Kiev Uprising" (after V. Boroday)

1968. 50th Anniv of Ukraine Communist Party.

3573 **1319** 4k. red, purple and gold 55 15

1320 Athletes and "50"

1968. Young Communist League's 50th Anniv Games.

3574 **1320** 4k. red, drab and yellow 55 15

1321 Handball

1968. Various Sports Events.

3575 **1321** 2k. multicoloured 35 15
3576 - 4k. multicoloured 45 25
3577 - 6k. multicoloured 70 30
3578 - 10k. red, black & bistre 1·10 40
3579 - 12k. multicoloured 1·30 50

DESIGNS AND EVENTS—VERT: Type **1321** (World Handball Games, Moscow); 6k. Yachting (20th Baltic Regatta); 10k. Football (70th anniv of Russian soccer). HORIZ: 4k. Table tennis (All European Juvenile Competitions); 12k. Underwater swimming (European Underwater Sports Championships, Alushta, Ukraine).

1322 Girl Gymnasts

1968. Olympic Games, Mexico. Backgrounds in gold.

3580 **1322** 4k. turquoise and blue 35 15
3581 - 6k. violet and red 55 25
3582 - 10k. green and turquoise 70 30
3583 - 12k. brown and orange 90 40
3584 - 16k. blue and pink 1·30 50
MS3585 90×65 mm. 40k. multicoloured 3·50 2·10

DESIGNS: 6k. Weightlifting; 10k. Rowing; 12k. Women's hurdles; 16k. Fencing match; 40k. Running.

1323 Gediminas Tower, Vilnius (Vilna)

1968. 50th Anniv of Soviet Lithuania.

3586 **1323** 4k. red, drab and purple 70 25

1324 Tbilisi University

1968. 50th Anniv of Tbilisi University.
3587 **1324** 4k. beige and green 70 25

1325 "Death of Laocoon and his Sons" (from sculpture by Agesandre, Polidor and Asinodor)

1968. "Promote Solidarity with the Greek Democrats".
3588 **1325** 6k. drab, purple & brn 10·00 8·75

1326 Cavalryman

1968. 50th Anniv of Leninist Young Communist League (Komsomol) (1st issue). Multicoloured.
3589 2k. Type **1326** 20 15
3590 3k. Young workers 35 15
3591 4k. Army officer 45 25
3592 6k. Construction workers 55 30
3593 10k. Agricultural workers 90 50
MS3594 78×101 mm. 50k. Type **1326**. Imperf 5·50 2·40
See also No. 3654.

1327 Institute and Molecular Structure

1968. 50th Anniv of N. S. Kurnakov Institute of Chemistry.
3595 **1327** 4k. purple, black and blue 55 15

1328 Letter

1968. Int Correspondence Week and Stamp Day.
3596 **1328** 4k. brown, red and lake 55 15
3597 - 4k. blue, ochre and deep blue 55 15
DESIGN: No. 3597, Russian stamps.

1329 "The 26 Baku Commissars" (statue, S. Merkurov)

1968. 50th Anniv of Execution of 26 Baku Commissars.
3598 **1329** 4k. multicoloured 55 15

1330 T. Antikainen

1968. 70th Birthday of Toivo Antikainen (Finnish Communist leader).
3599 **1330** 6k. brown and grey 55 15

1331 Liner "Ivan Franko"

1968. Soviet Merchant Marine.
3600 **1331** 6k. red, dp blue & blue 70 25

1332 Order of the October Revolution

1968. 51st Anniv of October Revolution.
3601 **1332** 4k. multicoloured 1·30 80

1333 P. P. Postyshev (1887–1940)

1968. Soviet Personalities.
3602 **1333** 4k. black 70 25
3603 - 4k. black 70 25
3604 - 4k. black 70 25
DESIGNS: No. 3603, S. G. Shaumian (1878–1918); 3604, A. Ikramov (1898–1938).

1334 Statuette of Warrior and Ararat Mountains

1968. 2,750th Anniv of Yerevan (Armenian capital).
3605 **1334** 4k. blk & brn on grey 55 15
3606 - 12k. brn & sepia on yell 1·30 65
DESIGN: 12k. David Sasunsky Monument (Ye. Kochar).

1335 I. S. Turgenev

1968. 150th Birth Anniv of Ivan Turgenev (writer).
3607 **1335** 4k. green 55 15

1336 American Bison and Common Zebra

1968. Fauna. Soviet Wildlife Reservations. Multicoloured.
3608 4k. Type **1336** 55 15
3609 4k. Purple swamphen and lotus 55 15
3610 6k. Great egrets (vert) 70 30
3611 6k. Ostrich and golden pheasant (vert) 70 30
3612 10k. Eland and guanaco 1·10 50
3613 10k. Glossy ibis and white spoonbill 1·10 50

1337 Building and Equipment

1968. 50th Anniv of Lenin Radio-laboratory, Gorky.
3614 **1337** 4k. blue and ochre 55 15

1338 Prospecting for Minerals

1968. Geology Day. Multicoloured.
3615 4k. Type **1338** 70 30
3616 6k. "Tracking down" metals 70 30
3617 10k. Oil derrick 1·10 50

1339 Djety-Oguz Kirgizia

1968. Central Asian Spas. Multicoloured.
3618 4k. Type **1339** 55 25
3619 4k. Borovoe, Kazakhstan (horiz) 55 25
3620 6k. Issyk-kul, Kirgizia (horiz) 70 30
3621 6k. Borovoe, Kazakhstan 70 30

1340 Silver Medal, "Philatec", Paris 1964

1968. Awards to Soviet Post Office at Foreign Stamp Exhibitions.
3622 4k. black, silver and purple 35 15
3623 6k. black, gold and blue 55 25
3624 10k. black, gold and blue 70 40
3625 12k. black, silver & turquoise 90 50
3626 16k. black, gold and red 1·30 80
3627 20k. black, gold and blue 1·40 95
3628 30k. black, gold and brown 2·20 1·40
DESIGNS: 4k. Type **1340**; 6k. Plaque, "Debria", Berlin, 1959; 10k. Cup and medals, Riccione, 1952, 1968; 12k. Diploma and medal, "Thematic Biennale", Buenos Aires, 1965; 16k. Trophies and medals, Rome, 1952, 1954; 20k. Medals and plaques, "Wipa", Vienna, 1966; 30k. Glass trophies, Prague, 1950, 1955, 1962.

1341 V. K. Lebedinsky

1968. Birth Centenary of Lebedinsky (physicist).
3629 **1341** 4k. multicoloured 70 25

1342 Soldier with Flag

1968. 50th Anniv of Estonian Workers' Commune.
3630 **1342** 4k. black and red 55 15

1343 TV Satellite and Receiving Stations

1968. Satellite TV Transmissions. T **1343** and similar square designs. Multicoloured.
MS3631 96×76 mm. 16k.×3 (a) Type **1343**; (b) TV satellite; (c) Receiving station 10·00 8·00

1344 Moscow Buildings and Fir Branch

1968. New Year.
3632 **1344** 4k. multicoloured 90 35

1345 G. Beregovoi (cosmonaut)

1968. Flight of "Soyuz 3".
3633 **1345** 10k. black, red and blue 1·30 50

1346 Electric Train, Map and Emblem

1968. Soviet Railways.
3634 **1346** 4k. orange and mauve 55 25
3635 - 10k. brown and green 1·40 65
DESIGN: 10k. Track-laying train.

1347 Red Flag, Newspapers and Monument at Minsk

1968. 50th Anniv of Byelorussian Communist Party.
3636 **1347** 4k. black, brown and red 65 15

1348 "The Reapers" (A. Venetsianov)

1968. Paintings in State Museum, Leningrad. Multicoloured.
3637 1k. Type **1348** 20 15
3638 2k. "The Last Days of Pompeii" (K. Bryullov) (61×28 mm) 45 15
3639 3k. "A Knight at the Crossroads" (V. Vasentsov) (61×28 mm) 55 25
3640 4k. "Conquering a Town in Winter" (V. Surikov) (61×28 mm) 70 30
3641 6k. "The Lake" (I. Levitan) (61×28 mm) 90 25
3642 10k. "The Year 1919: Alarm" (K. Petrov-Vodkin) 1·30 30
3643 16k. "The Defence of Sevastopol" (A. Deineka) (61×28 mm) 2·00 50
3644 20k. "Homer's Bust (G. Korzhev) 2·30 65
3645 30k. "The Celebration in Uritsky Square" (B. Kustodiev) (61×28 mm) 3·50 95
3646 50k. "The Duel between Peresvet and Chelumbei" (M. Avilov) (61×28 mm) 6·00 1·60

1349 House, Onega Region

1968. Soviet Architecture.
3647 **1349** 3k. brown on buff 55 15
3648 - 4k. green on yellow 65 30
3649 - 6k. violet on grey 90 50

1403 Venus Plaque and Radio-telescope

1969. Space Exploration.

3755	**1403**	4k. red, brown and black	55	15
3756	-	6k. purple, grey & black	75	35
3757	-	10k. multicoloured	1·30	85

MS3758 117×80 mm. 50k. (2) multicoloured. Imperf 9·50 5·00

DESIGNS: 6k. "Zond 7". Smaller (27×40 mm) 50k. (a) As 10k. (b) Close-up of Moon's surface taken by "Zond 6".

1404 Soviet and Afghan Flags

1969. 50th Anniv of U.S.S.R.–Afghanistan Diplomatic Relations.

3759	**1404**	6k. red, black and green	75	25

1405 Red Star and Arms

1969. Coil Stamp.

3760	**1405**	4k. red	3·75	2·75

1406 Mikoyan Gurevich MiG-3 and MiG-23 Fighters

1969. "30 Years of MiG Aircraft".

3761	**1406**	6k. black, grey and red	1·10	50

1407 Lenin

1969. New Year.

3762	**1407**	4k. multicoloured	55	15

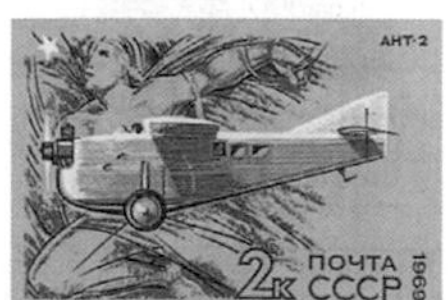

1408 Tupolev ANT-2

1969. Development of Soviet Civil Aviation.

3763	**1408**	2k. multicoloured	30	15
3764	-	3k. multicoloured	40	15
3765	-	4k. multicoloured	50	25
3766	-	6k. black, red and purple	55	35
3767	-	10k. multicoloured	95	50
3768	-	12k. multicoloured	1·30	70
3769	-	16k. multicoloured	1·70	85
3770	-	20k. multicoloured	2·10	1·00

MS3771 92×66 mm. 50k. multicoloured 5·75 3·50

AIRCRAFT: 3k. Polikarpov Po-2; 4k. Tupolev ANT-9; 6k. TsA-GI 1-EA helicopter; 10k. Tupolev ANT-20 "Maksim Gorky"; 12k. Tupolev Tu-104; 16k. Mil Mi-10 helicopter; 20k. Ilyushin Il-62; 50k. Tupolev Tu-144.

1409 Model Gliders

1969. Technical Sports.

3772	**1409**	3k. purple	40	15
3773	-	4k. green	50	25
3774	-	6k. brown	55	35

DESIGNS: 4k. Speed boat racing; 6k. Parachuting.

1410 Rumanian Arms and Soviet Memorial, Bucharest

1969. 25th Anniv of Rumanian Liberation.

3775	**1410**	6k. red and brown	75	35

1411 TV Tower, Ostankino

1969. Television Tower, Ostankino, Moscow.

3776	**1411**	10k. multicoloured	95	50

1412 "Lenin" (after N. Andreev)

1970. Birth Centenary of V. I. Lenin (1st issue). Multicoloured.

3777		4k. Type **1412**	55	25
3778		4k. "Marxist Meeting, Petrograd" (A. Moravov)	55	25
3779		4k. "Second RSDRP Congress" (Yu. Vinogradov)	55	25
3780		4k. "First Day of Soviet Power" (N. Babasyak)	55	25
3781		4k. "Visiting Lenin" (F. Modorov)	55	25
3782		4k. "Conversation with Ilich" (A. Shirokov)	55	25
3783		4k. "May Day 1920" (I. Brodsky)	55	25
3784		4k. "With Lenin" (V. Serov)	55	25
3785		4k. "Conquerors of the Cosmos" (A. Deyineka)	55	25
3786		4k. "Communism Builders" (A. Korentsov, Ye. Merkulov, V. Burakov)	55	25

See also Nos. 3812/21.

1413 F. V. Sychkov and Painting "Tobogganing"

1970. Birth Centenary of F. V. Sychkov (artist).

3787	**1413**	4k. blue and brown	75	25

1414 "Vostok", "Mirnyi" and Antarctic Map

1970. 150th Anniv of Antarctic Expedition by Bellinghausen and Lazarev.

3788	**1414**	4k. turquoise, mauve & bl	75	25
3789	-	16k. red, green & purple	2·10	85

DESIGN: 16k. Modern polar-station and map.

1415 V. I. Peshekhonov

1970. Soviet War Heroes.

3790	**1415**	4k. purple and black	40	15
3791	-	4k. brown and olive	40	15

DESIGN: No. 3791, V. B. Borsoev (1906–1945).

1416 Geographical Society Emblem

1970. 125th Anniv of Russian Geographical Society.

3792	**1416**	6k. multicoloured	75	25

1417 "The Torch of Peace" (A. Dumpe)

1970. 60th Anniv of Int Women's Solidarity Day.

3793	**1417**	6k. drab and turquoise	75	35

1418 Ivan Bazhov (folk hero) and Crafts

1970. World Fair "Expo 70", Osaka, Japan.

3794	**1418**	4k. black, red and green	40	15
3795	-	6k. silver, red and black	55	35
3796	-	10k. multicoloured	95	50

MS3797 72×97 mm. 50k. red 5·25 2·50

DESIGNS: 6k. U.S.S.R. Pavilion; 10k. Boy and model toys; 50k. Lenin in cap.

1419 Lenin

1970. Lenin Birth Centenary. All-Union Philatelic Exhibition, Moscow.

3798	**1419**	4k. black, gold and red	55	15

MS3799 73×92 mm. **1419** 20k. gold, red and black. Imperf £300 £225

1420 Friendship Tree

1970. Friendship Tree, Sochi.

3800	**1420**	10k. multicoloured	1·50	1·00

1421 Ice Hockey Players

1970. World Ice Hockey Championships, Stockholm, Sweden.

3801	**1421**	6k. green and blue	1·10	35

1422 Hammer, Sickle and Azerbaijan Emblems

1970. 50th Anniv of Soviet Republics.

3802	**1422**	4k. red and gold	55	15
3803	-	4k. brown and silver	55	15
3804	-	4k. purple and gold	55	15

DESIGNS: No. 3803, Woman and motifs of Armenia; 3804, Woman and emblem of Kazakh Republic.

1423 Worker and Book

1970. UNESCO "Lenin Centenary" Symposium.

3805	**1423**	6k. ochre and lake	95	50

1424 D. N. Medvedev

1970. Partisan War Heroes.

3806	**1424**	4k. brown	55	15
3807	-	4k. brown	55	15

PORTRAIT: No. 3807, K. P. Orlovsky.

(1425)

1970. Russian Victory in World Ice Hockey Championships, Stockholm. No. 3801 optd with T **1425**.

3808	**1421**	6k. green and blue	1·10	50

1426 Hungarian Arms and Budapest View

1970. 25th Anniv of Hungarian and Czech Liberation. Multicoloured.

3809		6k. Type **1426**	55	15
3810		6k. Czech Arms and Prague view	55	15

1427 Cosmonauts' Emblem

1970. Cosmonautics Day.

3811	**1427**	6k. multicoloured	55	15

1428 Lenin, 1891

1970. Birth Centenary of Lenin (2nd issue).

3812	**1428**	2k. green	20	15
3813	-	2k. olive	20	15
3814	-	4k. blue	40	15
3815	-	4k. lake	40	15
3816	-	6k. brown	55	25
3817	-	6k. lake	55	25
3818	-	10k. purple	95	35
3819	-	10k. brown	95	35
3820	-	12k. black and silver	1·10	50
3821	-	12k. red and gold	1·10	50

MS3822 66×102 mm. 20k. black and silver 7·50 3·50

PORTRAITS OF LENIN: No. 3813, In 1900; 3814, In 1914; 3815, In 1916; 3816, 3817, 3818, In 1918; 3819, In 1920; 3820, **MS**3822, Sculptured head by Yu. Kolesnikov; 3821, Sculptured head by N. Andreev.

1429 Order of Victory

1970. 25th Anniv of Victory in Second World War.

3823	**1429**	1k. gold, grey and purple	20	15
3824	-	2k. purple, brn & gold	30	15
3825	-	3k. red, black and gold	40	25
3826	-	4k. red, brown and gold	55	35
3827	-	10k. gold, red & purple	1·10	50
MS3828		67×97 mm. **1429** 30k. gold, grey and red. Imperf	3·75	2·20

DESIGNS: 2k. Eternal Flame; 3k. Treptow Monument, Berlin; 4k. Home Defence Order; 10k. Hero of the Soviet Union and Hero of Socialist Labour medals.

1430 Komsomol Badge

1970. 16th Congress of Leninist Young Communist League (Komsomol).

3829	**1430**	4k. multicoloured	55	15

1431 Lenin (sculpture, Yu. Kolesnikov)

1970. World Youth Meeting for Lenin Birth Centenary.

3830	**1431**	6k. red	75	25

1432 "Young Workers" and Federation Emblem

1970. 25th Anniv of World Democratic Youth Federation.

3831	**1432**	6k. black and blue	75	25

1433 Arms and Government Building, Kazan

1970. 50th Anniv of Russian Federation Autonomous Soviet Socialist Republics.

3832	**1433**	4k. blue	75	25
3833	-	4k. green	75	25
3834	-	4k. red	75	25
3835	-	4k. brown	75	25
3836	-	4k. green	75	25
3837	-	4k. brown	75	25

DESIGNS: Arms and Government Buildings. No. 3832, (Tatar Republic); 3833, Petrozavodzk (Karelian Republic); 3834, Cheboksary (Chuvash Republic); 3835, Elista (Kalmyk Republic); 3836, Izhevsk (Udmurt Republic); 3837, Ioshkar-Ola (Mari Republic).

See also Nos. 3903/7, 4052/3, 4175, 4253, 4298, 4367 and 4955.

1434 Gymnast on Bar (World Championships, Yugoslavia)

1970. International Sporting Events.

3838	**1434**	10k. red and drab	1·00	50
3839	-	16k. brown and green	1·50	70

DESIGN: 16k. Three footballers (World Cup Championship, Mexico).

1435 "Swords into Ploughshares" (sculpture by E. Vuchetich)

1970. 25th Anniv of United Nations.

3840	**1435**	12k. purple and green	1·10	50

1436 Cosmonauts and "Soyuz 9"

1970. Space Flight by "Soyuz 9".

3841	**1436**	10k. black, red & purple	95	50

1437 Engels

1970. 150th Birth Anniv of Friedrich Engels.

3842	**1437**	4k. brown and red	55	25

1438 Cruiser "Aurora"

1970. Soviet Warships.

3843	**1438**	3k. pink, lilac and black	40	35
3844	-	4k. black and yellow	55	45
3845	-	10k. blue and mauve	1·30	1·00
3846	-	12k. brown and buff	1·50	1·20
3847	-	20k. purple, blue & turq	2·75	2·20

DESIGNS: 4k. Missile cruiser "Groznyi"; 10k. Cruiser "Oktyabrskaya Revolyutsiya"; 12k. Missile cruiser "Varyag"; 20k. Nuclear submarine "Leninsky Komsomol".

1439 Soviet and Polish Workers

1970. 25th Anniv of Soviet-Polish Friendship Treaty.

3848	**1439**	6k. red and blue	55	15

1440 Allegory of the Sciences

1970. 13th Int Historical Sciences Congress, Moscow.

3849	**1440**	4k. multicoloured	55	15

1441 Mandarins

1970. Fauna of Sikhote-Alin Nature Reserve. Multicoloured.

3850		4k. Type **1441**	55	35
3851		6k. Yellow-throated marten	75	45
3852		10k. Asiatic black bear (vert)	1·10	70
3853		16k. Red deer	1·90	1·00
3854		20k. Tiger	2·50	1·40

1442 Magnifying Glass, "Stamp" and Covers

1970. Second U.S.S.R. Philatelic Society Congress, Moscow.

3855	**1442**	4k. silver and red	55	15

1443 V. I. Kikvidze

1970. 75th Birth Anniv of V. J. Kikvidze (Civil War hero).

3856	**1443**	4k. brown	55	15

1444 University Building

1970. 50th Anniv of Yerevan University.

3857	**1444**	4k. red and blue	55	15

1445 Pioneer Badge

1970. Pioneer Organization.

3858	**1445**	1k. gold, red and grey	20	15
3859	-	2k. grey and brown	30	15
3860	-	4k. multicoloured	40	15

DESIGNS: 2k. "Lenin with Children" (sculpture, N. Scherbakov), 4k. Red Star and scarf.

1446 Library Book-plate (A. Kuchas)

1970. 400th Anniv of Vilnius (Vilna) University Library (Lithuania).

3861	**1446**	4k. black, grey and silver	55	15

1447 Woman with Bouquet

1970. 25th Anniv of International Democratic Women's Federation.

3862	**1447**	6k. brown and blue	75	25

1448 Milkmaid and Cows ("Livestock")

1970. Soviet Agriculture. Multicoloured.

3863		4k. Type **1448**	55	15
3864		4k. Driver, tractor and harvester ("Mechanization")	55	15
3865		4k. Lock-operator and canal ("Irrigation and Chemical Research")	55	15

1449 Lenin addressing Meeting

1970. 53rd Anniv of October Revolution.

3866	**1449**	4k. gold and red	55	15
MS3867		107×82 mm. **1449** 30k. gold and red	4·75	2·50

50 лет
пениноному плану
ГОЭЛРО • 1970

(1450)

1970. 50th Anniv of GOELRO Electrification Plan. No. 3475 optd with T **1450**.

3868		4k. multicoloured	1·90	1·00

1451 Spassky Tower, Kremlin

1970. New Year.

3869	**1451**	6k. multicoloured	75	25

1452 A. A. Baikov

1970. Birth Centenary of A. A. Baikov (metallurgic scientist).

3870	**1452**	4k. black and brown	55	15

1453 Tsyurupa (after A. Yar-Kravchenkol)

1970. Birth Centenary of A. D. Tsyurupa (Vice-Chairman of Soviet People's Commissars).

3871	**1453**	4k. brown and yellow	55	15

1454 St. Basil's Cathedral, Red Square, Moscow

1970. Tourism.

3872	**1454**	4k. multicoloured	40	15
3873	-	6k. blue, indigo & brown	55	15
3874	-	10k. brown and green	75	25
3875	-	12k. multicoloured	95	35
3876	-	14k. blue, red and brown	1·10	45

3877 - 16k. multicoloured 1·30 50

DESIGNS: 6k. Scene from ballet "Swan Lake" (Tchaikovsky); 10k. Sika deer; 12k. Souvenir handicrafts; 14k. "Swords into Ploughshares" (sculpture by Ye. Vuchetich); 16k. Tourist and camera.

1455 Camomile

1970. Flowers. Multicoloured.

3878 4k. Type **1455** 40 15
3879 6k. Dahlia 55 25
3880 10k. Phlox 75 35
3881 12k. Aster 95 45
3882 16k. Clematis 1·30 50

1456 African Woman and Child

1970. Tenth Anniv of U.N. Declaration on Colonial Independence.

3883 **1456** 10k. brown and blue 1·10 50

1457 Beethoven

1970. Birth Bicentenary of Beethoven (composer).

3884 **1457** 10k. purple and pink 3·00 2·00

1458 "Luna 16" in Flight

1970. Flight of "Luna 16".

3885 **1458** 10k. green 75 35
3886 - 10k. purple 75 35
3887 - 10k. green 75 35
MS3888 100×76 mm. 20k.×3 as Nos. 3885/7 but change of colours 7·50 4·25

DESIGNS: No. 3886, "Luna 16" on Moon's surface; 3887, Parachute descent.

1459 Speed Skating

1970. Trade Unions' Winter Games (1971).

3889 **1459** 4k. blue, red and grey 40 15
3890 - 10k. green, brn & grey 1·10 35

DESIGN: 10k. Cross-country skiing.

1460 "The Conestabile Madonna" (Raphael)

1970. Foreign Paintings in Soviet Galleries. Multicoloured.

3891 3k. Type **1460** 30 15
3892 4k. "Saints Peter and Paul" (El Greco) 40 25
3893 10k. "Perseus and Andromeda" (Rubens) (horiz) 95 35
3894 12k. "The Return of the Prodigal Son" (Rembrandt) 1·10 45
3895 16k. "Family Portrait" (Van Dyck) 1·50 50
3896 20k. "The Actress Jeanne Samary" (Renoir) 1·70 70
3897 30k. "Woman with Fruit" (Gauguin) 2·75 1·00
MS3898 73×101 mm. 50k. "Madonna Litte" (Leonardo da Vinci). Imperf 7·50 4·75

1461 Harry Pollitt and Freighter "Jolly George"

1970. 80th Birth Anniv of H. Pollitt (British Communist).

3899 **1461** 10k. brown and purple 75 25

1462 "75" Emblem

1970. 75th Anniv of Int Co-operative Alliance.

3900 **1462** 12k. red and green 95 50

1463 Sculptured Head of Lenin (A. Belostotsky and E. Fridman)

1971. 24th Soviet Union Communist Party Congress.

3901 **1463** 4k. red and gold 55 15

1464 "50", State Emblem and Flag

1971. 50th Anniv of Georgian Soviet Republic.

3902 **1464** 4k. multicoloured 55 15

1971. 50th Anniv of Autonomous Soviet Socialist Republics. Similar designs to T **1433**, but dated "1971".

3903 4k. turquoise 55 15
3904 4k. red 55 15
3905 4k. red 55 15
3906 4k. blue 55 15
3907 4k. green 55 15

DESIGNS: No. 3903, Russian Federation Arms and Supreme Soviet building (Dagestan Republic); 3904, National emblem and symbols of agriculture and industry (Abkhazian Republic); 3905, Arms, produce and industry (Adjarian Republic); 3906, Arms and State building (Kabardino-Balkar Republic); 3907, Arms, industrial products and Government building (Komi Republic).

1465 Genua Fortress and Cranes

1971. 2500th Anniv of Feodosia (Crimean city).

3908 **1465** 10k. multicoloured 75 35

1466 Palace of Culture, Kiev

1971. 24th Ukraine Communist Party Congress, Kiev.

3909 **1466** 4k. multicoloured 55 15

1467 "Features of National Economy"

1971. 50th Anniv of Soviet State Planning Organization.

3910 **1467** 6k. red and brown 75 25

1468 N. Gubin, I. Chernykh and S. Kosinov (dive-bomber crew)

1971. Soviet Air Force Heroes.

3911 **1468** 4k. brown and green 55 15

1469 Gipsy Dance

1971. State Folk Dance Ensemble. Multicoloured.

3912 10k. Type **1469** 95 35
3913 10k. Russian "Summer" dance (women in circle) 95 35
3914 10k. Ukraine "Gopak" dance (dancer leaping) 95 35
3915 10k. Adjar "Khorumi" dance (with drummer) 95 35
3916 10k. "On the Ice" (ballet) 95 35

1470 L. Ukrainka

1971. Birth Centenary of Lesya Ukrainka (Ukrainian writer).

3917 **1470** 4k. red and brown 55 15

1471 "Luna 17" Module on Moon

1971. Soviet Moon Exploration.

3918 **1471** 10k. brown and violet 95 45
3919 - 12k. brown and blue 1·10 50
3920 - 12k. brown and blue 1·10 50
3921 - 16k. brown and violet 1·50 70
MS3922 91×69 mm. As Nos. 3918/21 but smaller 32½×21½ mm 6·00 2·75

DESIGNS: No. 3919, Control room and radio telescope; 3920, Moon trench; 3921, "Lunokhod 1" Moon-vehicle.

1472 Fighting at the Barricades

1971. Centenary of Paris Commune.

3923 **1472** 6k. black, brown and red 55 15

1473 Hammer, Sickle and Development Emblems

1971. 24th Soviet Communist Party Congress, Moscow.

3924 **1473** 6k. red, bistre & brown 55 15

1474 Gagarin Medal, Spaceships and Planets

1971. Tenth Anniv of First Manned Space Flight (1st issue) and Cosmonautics Day.

3925 **1474** 10k. olive, yellow & brn 75 35
3926 - 12k. purple, blue & grey 95 45

DESIGN: 12k. Spaceship over Globe and economic symbols.

See also No. 3974.

1475 E. Birznieks-Upitis

1971. Birth Centenary of E. Birznieks-Upitis (Lithuanian writer).

3927 **1475** 4k. red and green 55 15

1476 Honey Bee on Flower

1971. 23rd Int Bee-keeping Congress, Moscow.

3928 **1476** 6k. multicoloured 75 25

1477 "Vostok 1"

1971. Tenth Anniv of First Manned Space Flight (2nd issue). Sheet 94×77 mm containing horiz designs as T **1477**.

MS3929 10k. purple, 12k. (2) green, 16k. purple 6·00 2·75

1478 Memorial Building

1971. Lenin Memorial Building, Ulyanovsk.

3930 **1478** 4k. olive and red 55 15

1479 Lieut-Col. N. I. Vlasov

1971. 26th Anniv of Victory in 2nd World War.

3931 **1479** 4k. brown and green 55 15

1480 Khafiz Shirazi

1971. 650th Birth Anniv of Khafiz Shirazi (Tadzhik writer).

3932 **1480** 4k. multicoloured 55 15

1481 "GAZ-66" Truck

1971. Soviet Motor Vehicles.

3933	**1481**	2k. multicoloured	20	15
3934	-	3k. multicoloured	30	15
3935	-	4k. blue, black and lilac	40	15
3936	-	4k. green, purple & drab	40	15
3937	-	10k. red, black and lilac	95	35

DESIGNS: 3k. "BelAZ-540" tipper truck; 4k. (3935) "Moskvitch-412" 4-door saloon; 4k. (3936) "Zaporozhets ZAZ-968" 2-door saloon; 10k. "Volga GAZ-24" saloon.

1482 Bogomolets (after A. Yar-Kravchenko)

1971. 90th Birth Anniv of A. A. Bogomolets (medical scientist).

3938	**1482**	4k. black, pink & orange	55	15

1483 Commemorative Scroll

1971. International Moscow Congresses.

3939	**1483**	6k. brown and green	65	15
3940	-	6k. multicoloured	65	15
3941	-	6k. multicoloured	65	15

DESIGNS AND EVENTS—HORIZ: No. 3939, (13th Science History Congress); 3940, Oil derrick and symbols (8th World Oil Congress). VERT: No. 3941, Satellite over globe (15th General Assembly of Geodesics and Geophysics Union).

1484 Sukhe Bator Statue, Ulan Bator

1971. 50th Anniv of Revolution in Mongolia.

3942	**1484**	6k. grey, gold and red	55	15

1485 Defence Monument (E. Guirbulis)

1971. 30th Anniv of Defence of Liepaja, Latvia.

3943	**1485**	4k. brown, black & grey	55	15

1486 Treaty Emblem

1971. Tenth Anniv of Antarctic Treaty and 50th Anniv of Soviet Hydrometeorological Service.

3944	**1486**	6k. deep blue, black and blue	1·30	70
3945	-	10k. violet, black & red	1·90	85

DESIGN: 10k. Hydrometeorological map.

1487 "Motherland" (sculpture, Yu. Vuchetich)

1971. 20th Anniv of "Federation Internationale des Resistants".

3946	**1487**	6k. green and red	65	15

1488 Throwing the Discus

1971. Fifth Summer Spartakiad.

3947	**1488**	3k. blue on pink	30	15
3948	-	4k. green on flesh	40	15
3949	-	6k. brown on green	55	25
3950	-	10k. purple on blue	95	35
3951	-	12k. brown on yellow	1·10	50

DESIGNS: 4k. Archery; 6k. Horse-riding (dressage); 10k. Basketball; 12k. Wrestling.

1489 "Benois Madonna" (Leonardo da Vinci)

1971. Foreign Paintings in Russian Museums. Multicoloured.

3952	2k. Type **1489**	20	15
3953	4k. "Mary Magdalene confesses her Sins" (Titian)	40	35
3954	10k. "The Washerwoman" (Chardin) (horiz)	95	50
3955	12k. "Young Man with Glove" (Hals)	1·10	70
3956	14k. "Tancred and Erminia" (Poussin) (horiz)	1·20	75
3957	16k. "Girl Fruit-seller" (Murillo)	1·30	85
3958	20k. "Child on Ball" (Picasso)	1·70	1·00

1490 Lenin Badge and Kazakh Flag

1971. 50th Anniv of Kazakh Communist Youth Assn.

3959	**1490**	4k. brown, red and blue	55	15

1491 Posthorn within Star

1971. International Correspondence Week.

3960	**1491**	4k. black, blue and green	55	15

1492 A. Spendiarov (Armenian composer) (after M. Saryan)

1971. Birth Anniversaries. Multicoloured.

3961	4k. Type **1492** (cent)	55	15
3962	4k. Nikolai Nekrasov (after I. Kramskoi) (poet, 150th anniv)	55	15
3963	10k. Fyodor Dostoevsky (after V. Perov) (writer, 150th anniv)	1·30	70

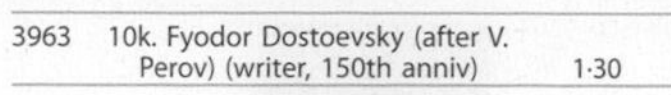

1493 Z. Paliashvili

1971. Birth Centenary of Z. Paliashvili (Georgian composer).

3964	**1493**	4k. brown	55	15

1494 Emblem, Gorky Kremlin and Hydrofoil

1971. 750th Anniv of Gorky (formerly Nizhini-Novgorod) (1st issue).

3965	**1494**	16k. multicoloured	1·30	50

See also No. 3974.

1495 Students and Globe

1971. 25th Anniv of Int Students Federation.

3966	**1495**	6k. blue, red and brown	55	15

1496 Atlantic White-sided Dolphins

1971. Marine Fauna. Multicoloured.

3967	4k. Type **1496**	55	35
3968	6k. Sea otter	75	50
3969	10k. Narwhals	1·30	85
3970	12k. Walrus	1·50	1·00
3971	14k. Ribbon seals	1·90	1·40

1497 Star and Miners' Order

1971. 250th Anniv of Coal Discovery in Donetz Basin.

3972	**1497**	4k. red, brown and black	55	15

1498 Lord Rutherford and Atomic Formula

1971. Birth Cent of Lord Rutherford (physicist).

3973	**1498**	6k. brown and purple	65	25

1499 Statue of Maksim Gorky (Vera Mukhina) and View

1971. 750th Anniv of Gorky (formerly Nizhni-Novgorod) (2nd issue).

3974	**1499**	4k. multicoloured	55	15

1500 Santa Claus in Troika

1971. New Year.

3975	**1500**	10k. red, gold and black	95	70

1501 Workers and Marx Books ("International Socialist Solidarity")

1971. 24th Soviet Union Communist Party Congress Resolutions.

3976	**1501**	4k. blue, ultram & red	55	15
3977	-	4k. red, yellow & brown	55	15
3978	-	4k. lilac, black and red	55	15
3979	-	4k. bistre, brown and red	55	15
3980	-	4k. red, green and yellow	55	15

MS3981 90×66 mm. 20k. vermilion, purple and green 3·25 1·40

DESIGNS: No. 3977, Farmworkers and wheatfield ("Agricultural Production"); 3978, Factory production line ("Increased Productivity"); 3979, Heavy industry ("Industrial Expansion"); 3980, Family in department store ("National Welfare"); (40×22 mm) 20k. Workers' demonstration.

1502 "Meeting" (V. Makovsky)

1971. Russian Paintings. Multicoloured.

3982	2k. Type **1502**	20	15
3983	4k. "Girl Student" (N. Yaroshenko)	40	25
3984	6k. "Woman Miner" (N. Kasatkin)	55	35
3985	10k. "Harvesters" (G. Myasoedov) (horiz)	95	50
3986	16k. "Country Road" (A. Savrasov)	1·50	70
3987	20k. "Pine Forest" (I. Shishkin) (horiz)	1·90	1·00

MS3988 94×68 mm. 50k. "Self-portrait" (I. Kramskoi) (31×43 mm) 4·50 2·20

See also Nos. 4064/70.

1503 V. V. Vorovsky

1971. Birth Centenary of V. V. Vorovsky (diplomat).

3989	**1503**	4k. brown	55	15

1504 Dobrovolsky, Volkov and Patsaev

1971. "Soyuz 11" Cosmonauts Commemoration.

3990	**1504**	4k. black, purple & orge	55	15

1505 Order of the Revolution and Building Construction

1971. 54th Anniv of October Revolution.

3991	**1505**	4k. multicoloured	55	15

1506 E. Vakhtangov (founder) and characters from "Princess Turandot"

1971. 50th Anniv of Vakhtangov Theatre, Moscow.

3992	**1506**	10k. red and lake	75	50
3993	-	10k. yellow and brown	75	50
3994	-	10k. orange and brown	75	50

DESIGNS—HORIZ: No. 3993, B. Shchukin (actor) and scene from "The Man with the Rifle"; 3994, R. Simonov (director) and scene from "Cyrano de Bergerac".

1507 "Dzhambul Dzhabaiev" (A. Yar-Kravchenko)

1971. 125th Anniv of Dzhambul Dzhabaiev (Kazakh poet).

3995	**1507**	4k. brown, yell & orge	55	15

1508 Pskov Kremlin

1971. Historical Buildings. Multicoloured.

3996	3k. Type **1508**	20	15
3997	4k. Novgorod kremlin	40	15
3998	6k. Smolensk fortress and Liberation Monument	50	25
3999	10k. Kolomna kremlin	55	35
MS4000	67×88 mm. 50k. Kremlin, Red Square, Moscow (22×32 mm)	4·25	1·70

1509 William Foster

1971. 90th Birth Anniv of Foster (American communist).

4001	**1509**	10k. black and brown	48·00	43·00
4002	**1509**	10k. black and brown	1·10	50

No. 4001 shows the incorrect date of death "1964"; 4002 shows the correct date, "1961".

1510 Fadeev and Scene from "The Rout" (novel)

1971. 70th Birth Anniv of Aleksandr Fadeev (writer).

4003	**1510**	4k. orange and blue	55	15

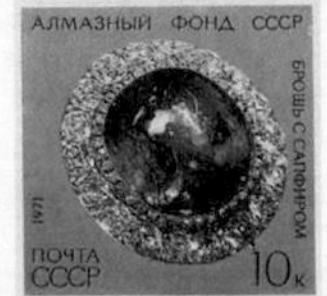

1511 Sapphire Brooch

1971. Diamonds and Jewels. Multicoloured.

4004	10k. Type **1511**	75	35
4005	10k. "Shah" diamond	75	35
4006	10k. "Narcissi" diamond brooch	75	35
4007	20k. Amethyst pendant	1·50	70
4008	20k. "Rose" platinum and diamond brooch	1·50	70
4009	30k. Pearl and diamond pendant	2·10	1·00

1512 Vanda Orchid

1971. Tropical Flowers. Multicoloured.

4010	1k. Type **1512**	20	15
4011	2k. "Anthurium scherzerianum"	30	15
4012	4k. "Cactus epiphyllum"	40	25
4013	12k. Amaryllis	1·10	70
4014	14k. "Medinilla magnifica"	1·30	85
MS4015	81×97 mm. 10k.×4 Designs as Nos. 4010 and 4012/14 but smaller (19×26 mm) and with white backgrounds	4·25	1·70

1513 Peter the Great's Imperial Barge, 1723

1971. History of the Russian Navy (1st series). Multicoloured.

4016	1k. Type **1513**	40	35
4017	4k. Galleon "Orel", 1668 (vert)	75	70
4018	10k. Ship of the line "Poltava", 1712 (vert)	1·90	1·70
4019	12k. Ship of the line "Ingermanland", 1715 (vert)	2·30	2·00
4020	16k. Steam frigate "Vladimir", 1848	3·00	2·75

See also Nos. 4117/21, 4209/13 and 4303/6.

1514 Ice Hockey Players

1971. 25th Anniv of Soviet Ice Hockey.

4021	**1514**	6k. multicoloured	95	50

1515 Baku Oil Installations

1971. Baku Oil Industry.

4022	**1515**	4k. black, red and blue	55	15

1516 G. M. Krzhizhanovsky

1972. Birth Centenary of G. M. Krzhizhanovsky (scientist).

4023	**1516**	4k. brown	55	15

1517 Scriabin

1972. Birth Centenary of Aleksandr Scriabin (composer).

4024	**1517**	4k. blue and green	55	15

1518 Red-faced Cormorant

1972. Sea Birds. Multicoloured.

4025	4k. Type **1518**	40	15
4026	6k. Ross's gull (horiz)	55	50
4027	10k. Pair of barnacle geese	95	85
4028	12k. Pair of spectacled eiders (horiz)	1·10	1·00
4029	16k. Mediterranean gull	1·50	1·40

1519 Speed Skating

1972. Winter Olympic Games, Sapporo, Japan. Multicoloured.

4030	4k. Type **1519**	20	15
4031	6k. Figure skating	40	15
4032	10k. Ice hockey	75	35
4033	12k. Ski jumping	95	50
4034	16k. Cross-country skiing	1·10	70
MS4035	67½×92 mm. 50k. "Sapporo" emblem and Olympic rings	3·75	1·70

1520 Heart Emblem

1972. World Heart Month.

4036	**1520**	4k. red and green	55	15

1521 Fair Emblem

1973. 50th Anniv of Soviet Participation in Leipzig Fair.

4037	**1521**	16k. gold and red	1·50	70

1522 Labour Emblems

1972. 15th Soviet Trade Unions Congress, Moscow.

4038	**1522**	4k. brown, red and pink	55	15

1523 "Aloe arborescens"

1972. Medicinal Plants. Multicoloured.

4039	1k. Type **1523**	20	15
4040	2k. Yellow horned poppy	20	15
4041	4k. Groundsel	30	15
4042	6k. Nephrite tea	40	25
4043	10k. Kangaroo apple	75	50

1524 Alexandra Kollontai (diplomat) (birth cent)

1972. Birth Anniversaries.

4044	**1524**	4k. brown	55	15
4045	-	4k. lake	55	15
4046	-	4k. bistre	55	15

CELEBRITIES: No. 4045, G. Chicherin (Foreign Affairs Commissar) (birth cent); 4046, "Kamo" (S. A. Ter-Petrosyan—revolutionary) (90th birth anniv).

СОВЕТСКИЕ СПОРТСМЕНЫ
ЗАВОЕВАЛИ
8 ЗОЛОТЫХ
МЕДАЛЕЙ,
5 СЕРЕБРЯНЫХ,
3 БРОНЗОВЫХ.

(1525)

1972. Soviet Medals at Winter Olympic Games, Sapporo. No. **MS**4035 optd with T **1525** on the sheet.

MS4047	50k. multicoloured	9·50	6·75

1526 "Salyut" Space-station and "Soyuz" Spacecraft

1972. Cosmonautics Day. Multicoloured.

4048	6k. Type **1526**	55	35
4049	6k. "Mars 2" approaching Mars	55	35
4050	16k. Capsule, "Mars 3"	1·30	70

1527 Factory and Products

1972. 250th Anniv of Izhora Factory.

4051	**1527**	4k. purple and silver	55	15

1972. 50th Anniv of Russian Federation Autonomous Soviet Socalist Republics. Designs similar to T **1433**, but dated "1972".

4052	4k. blue	55	15
4053	4k. mauve	55	15

DESIGNS: No. 4052, Arms, natural resources and industry (Yakut Republic); 4053, Arms, agriculture and industry (Checheno-Ingush Republic).

1528 L. Sobinov and scene from "Eugene Onegin"

1972. Birth Centenary of L. Sobinov (singer).

4054	**1528**	10k. brown	75	35

1529 Symbol of Knowledge and Children reading Books

1972. International Book Year.

4055	**1529**	6k. multicoloured	55	25

1530 Pavlik Morosov Monument (I. Rabinovich) and Pioneers Saluting

1972. 50th Anniv of Pioneer Organization.

4056	**1530**	1k. multicoloured	20	15
4057	-	2k. purple, red and green	30	15
4058	-	3k. blue, red and brown	40	15
4059	-	4k. red, blue and green	50	15
MS4060		103×82 mm. 30k. multicoloured	3·50	1·90

DESIGNS: Horiz 2k. Girl laboratory worker and Pioneers with book; 3k. Pioneer Place, Chukotka, and Pioneers at work; 4k. Pioneer parade. Vert (25×37 mm) 30k. Colour party (similar to 4k.).

1531 Pioneer Trumpeter

1972. "50th Anniv of Pioneer Organization" Youth Stamp Exhibition, Minsk.

4061	**1531**	4k. purple, red & yellow	55	15

1532 "World Security"

1972. European Security Conference, Brussels.
4062 **1532** 6k. blue, turquoise & gold 3·00 2·20

1533 M. S. Ordubady

1972. Birth Centenary of M. S. Ordubady (Azerbaijan writer).
4063 **1533** 4k. purple and orange 55 15

1972. Russian Paintings. As T **1502**, but dated "1972". Multicoloured.
4064 2k. "Cossack Hetman" (I. Nikitin) 20 15
4065 4k. "F. Volkov" (A. Lossenko) 40 25
4066 6k. "V. Majkov" (F. Rokotov) 55 35
4067 10k. "N. Novikov" (D. Levitsky) 95 50
4068 12k. "G. Derzhavin" (V. Borovikovsky) 1·10 70
4069 16k. "Peasants' Dinner" (M. Shibanov) (horiz) 1·30 85
4070 20k. "Moscow View" (F. Alexeiev) (horiz) 1·70 1·00

1534 G. Dimitrov

1972. 90th Birth Anniv of Georgi Dimitrov (Bulgarian statesman).
4071 **1534** 6k. brown and bistre 55 15

1535 Congress Building and Emblem

1972. Ninth Int Gerontology Congress, Kiev.
4072 **1535** 6k. brown and blue 55 15

1536 Fencing

1972. Olympic Games, Munich.
4073 **1536** 4k. purple and gold 40 15
4074 - 6k. green and gold 55 25
4075 - 10k. blue and gold 75 35
4076 - 14k. blue and gold 1·10 60
4077 - 16k. red and gold 1·30 70
MS4078 67×87 mm. 50k. scarlet, gold and green 3·25 2·00
DESIGNS: 6k. Gymnastics; 10k. Canoeing; 14k. Boxing; 16k. Running; 50k. Weightlifting.

1537 Amundsen, Airship N.1 "Norge" and Northern Lights

1972. Birth Centenary of Roald Amundsen (Polar explorer).
4079 **1537** 6k. blue and brown 2·50 2·20

1538 Market-place, Lvov (Lemberg)

1972. Ukraine's Architectural Monuments. Multicoloured.
4080 4k. Type **1538** 40 15
4081 6k. 17th-century house, Tchernigov (horiz) 55 25
4082 10k. Kovnirovsky building, Kiev (horiz) 75 35
4083 16k. Kamenetz-Podolsk Castle 1·10 70

1539 Indian Flag and Asokan Capital

1972. 25th Anniv of India's Independence.
4084 **1539** 6k. red, blue and green 75 25

1540 Liberation Monument, Vladivostok, and Cavalry

1972. 50th Anniv of Liberation of Far Eastern Territories.
4085 **1540** 3k. grey, orange and red 20 15
4086 - 4k. grey, yellow & ochre 40 15
4087 - 6k. grey, pink and red 55 25
DESIGNS: 4k. Labour Heroes Monument, Khabarovsk, and industrial scene; 6k. Naval statue, Vladivostok, "Vladivostok" (cruiser) and jet fighters.

1541 Miners' Day Emblem

1972. 25th Anniv of Miners' Day.
4088 **1541** 4k. red, black and violet 55 15

1542 "Boy with Dog" (Murillo)

1972. Paintings by Foreign Artists in Hermitage Gallery, Leningrad. Multicoloured.
4089 4k. "Breakfast" (Velazquez) (horiz) 40 15
4090 6k. "The Milk Seller's Family" (Le Nain) (horiz) 55 35
4091 10k. Type **1542** 95 70
4092 10k. "The Capricious Girl" (Watteau) 1·70 1·00
4093 20k. "Moroccan with Horse" (Delacroix) 2·10 1·20
MS4094 75×100 mm. 50k. Van Dyck (self-portrait) 5·25 3·00

1543 "Sputnik I"

1972. 15th Anniv of "Cosmic Era". Multicoloured.
4095 6k. Type **1543** 55 25
4096 6k. Launch of "Vostok I" 55 25
4097 6k. "Lunokhod" vehicle on Moon 55 25
4098 6k. Man in space 55 25
4099 6k. "Mars 3" module on Mars 55 25
4100 6k. Touch down of "Venera 7" on Venus 55 25

1544 Konstantin Mardzhanishvili

1972. Birth Centenary of K. Mardzhanishvili (Georgian actor).
4101 **1544** 4k. green 55 15

1545 Museum Emblem

1972. Centenary of Popov Central Communications Museum.
4102 **1545** 4k. blue, purple & green 55 15

1546 Exhibition Labels

1972. "50th Anniv of U.S.S.R." Philatelic Exhibition.
4103 **1546** 4k. red & black on yell 55 15

1547 Lenin

1972. 55th Anniv of October Revolution.
4104 **1547** 4k. red and gold 55 15

1548 Militia Badge and Soviet Flag

1972. 55th Anniv of Soviet Militia.
4105 **1548** 4k. gold, red and brown 55 15

1549 Arms of U.S.S.R.

1972. 50th Anniv of U.S.S.R.
4106 **1549** 4k. gold, purple and red 40 15
4107 - 4k. gold, red and brown 40 15
4108 - 4k. gold, purple & green 40 15
4109 - 4k. gold, purple and grey 40 15
4110 - 4k. gold, purple and grey 40 15
MS4111 127×102 mm. 30k. red and gold 4·25 1·50
DESIGNS: No. 4107, Lenin and banner; No. 4108, Arms and Kremlin; No. 4109, Arms and industrial scenes; No. 4110, Arms, worker and open book "U.S.S.R. Constitutions"; **MS**4111, Arms and Spassky Tower.

1550 Emblem of U.S.S.R.

СЛАВА
СОВЕТСКИМ ОЛИМПИЙЦАМ,
ЗАВОЕВАВШИМ
50 ЗОЛОТЫХ, 27 СЕРЕБРЯНЫХ
И 22 БРОНЗОВЫЕ НАГРАДЫ!

(1551)

1972. U.S.S.R. Victories in Olympic Games, Munich. Multicoloured.
4112 20k. Type **1550** 1·90 70
4113 30k. Olympic medals 2·75 1·20
MS4114 Sheet No. **MS**4078 optd with T **1551** in red on margin 6·50 3·50

1552 Savings Book

1972. "50 Years of Soviet Savings Bank".
4115 **1552** 4k. blue and purple 55 15

1553 Kremlin and Snowflakes

1972. New Year.
4116 **1553** 6k. multicoloured 55 15

1554 Battleship "Pyotr Veliky"

1972. History of the Russian Navy (2nd series). Multicoloured.
4117 2k. Type **1554** 30 15
4118 3k. Cruiser "Varyag" 40 15
4119 4k. Battleship "Potemkin" 55 25
4120 6k. Cruiser "Ochakov" 95 35
4121 10k. Minelayer "Amur" 1·50 70

1555 Skovoroda (after P. Meshcheryakov)

1972. 250th Birth Anniv of Grigory S. Skovoroda.
4122 **1555** 4k. blue 55 15

1556 "Pioneer Girl with Books" (N. A. Kasatkin)

1972. "History of Russian Painting". Multicoloured.
4123 2k. "Meeting of Village Party Members" (E. M. Cheptsov) (horiz) 20 15
4124 4k. Type **1556** 30 15
4125 6k. "Party Delegate" (G. G. Ryazhsky) 40 35
4126 10k. "End of Winter—Midday" (K. F. Yuon) (horiz) 75 50
4127 16k. "Partisan Lunev" (N. I. Strunnikov) 1·10 70
4128 20k. "Self-portrait in Fur Coat" (I. E. Grabar) 1·50 85
MS4129 90×70 mm. 50k. "In Blue Space" (A. A. Rylov) (horiz) 5·25 1·70

1557 Child reading Safety Code

1972. Road Safety Campaign.
4130 **1557** 4k. black, blue and red 55 15

1558 Emblem of Technology

1972. Cent of Polytechnic Museum, Moscow.
4131 **1558** 4k. red, yellow and green 55 15

1559 "Venus 8" and Parachute

1972. Space Research.
4132 **1559** 6k. blue, black and purple 65 15
MS4133 90×70 mm. 50k.×2 brown 29·00 17·00

DESIGNS—(40×20 mm): **MS**4133. (a) "Venera 8". (b) "Mars 3".

1560 Solidarity Emblem

1973. 15th Anniv of Asian and African People's Solidarity Organization.
4134 **1560** 10k. blue, red and brown 75 45

1561 Town and Gediminas Tower

1973. 650th Anniv of Vilnius (Vilna).
4135 **1561** 10k. red, black and green 75 35

1562 I. V. Babushkin

1973. Birth Cent of I. V. Babushkin (revolutionary).
4136 **1562** 4k. black 55 15

1563 Tupolev Tu-154 Jetliner

1973. 50th Anniv of Soviet Civil Aviation.
4137 **1563** 6k. multicoloured 95 50

1564 "30" and Admiralty Spire, Leningrad

1973. 30th Anniv of Relief of Leningrad.
4138 **1564** 4k. black, orange & brn 55 15

1565 Portrait and Masks (Mayakovsky Theatre)

1973. 50th Anniv of Moscow Theatres.
4139 **1565** 10k. multicoloured 75 15
4140 - 10k. red and blue 75 15

DESIGN: No. 4140, Commemorative panel (Mossoviet Theatre).

1566 Prishvin (after A. Kirillov)

1973. Birth Centenary of Mikhail Prishvin (writer).
4141 **1566** 4k. multicoloured 75 15

1567 Heroes' Square, Volgograd

1973. 30th Anniv of Stalingrad Victory. Detail from Heroes' Memorial.
4142 - 3k. black, yellow & orge 20 15
4143 **1567** 4k. yellow and black 40 15
4144 - 10k. multicoloured 75 25
4145 - 12k. black, light red and red 95 35
MS4146 93×73 mm. 20k.×2 multicoloured 4·25 2·00

DESIGNS—VERT (28×59 mm): 3k. Soldier and Allegory; 12k. Hand with torch; (18×40 mm)—Allegory, Mamai Barrow. HORIZ (59×28 mm)—Mourning mother; (40×18 mm) 20k. Mamai Barrow.

1568 Copernicus and Planetary Chart

1973. 500th Birth Anniv of Copernicus (astronomer).
4147 **1568** 10k. brown and blue 95 50

1569 Chaliapin (after K. Korovin)

1973. Birth Centenary of Fyodor Chaliapin (opera singer).
4148 **1569** 10k. multicoloured 55 35

1570 Ice Hockey Players

1973. World Ice Hockey Championships, Moscow.
4149 **1570** 10k. brown, blue & gold 1·30 50
MS4150 64×85 mm. 50k. sepia, green and gold (players) (21×32 mm) 3·50 1·50

1571 Athletes

1973. 50th Anniv of Central Red Army Sports Club.
4151 **1571** 4k. multicoloured 40 15

1572 Red Star, Tank, and Map

1973. 30th Anniv of Battle of Kursk.
4152 **1572** 4k. black, red and grey 55 35

1573 N. E. Bauman

1973. Birth Centenary of Nikolai Bauman (revolutionary).
4153 **1573** 4k. brown 75 15

1574 Red Cross and Red Crescent

1973. International Co-operation.
4154 **1574** 4k. red, black and green 40 15
4155 - 6k. light blue, red and blue 55 35
4156 - 16k. green, red and mauve 1·30 50

DESIGNS AND EVENTS: 4k. (50th anniv of Soviet Red Cross and Red Crescent Societies Union); 6k. Mask, emblem and theatre curtain (15th Int Theatre Institution Congress); 16k. Floral emblem (10th World Festival of Youth, Berlin).

1575 Ostrovsky (after V. Perov)

1973. 150th Birth Anniv of Aleksandr Ostrovsky (writer).
4157 **1575** 4k. multicoloured 55 15

1576 Satellites

1973. Cosmonautics Day. Multicoloured.
4158 6k. Type **1576** 65 15
4159 6k. "Lunokhod 2" 65 15
MS4160 75×100 mm. 20k.×3, each 51×21 mm in lake, plum and gold 5·00 2·00
MS4161 As No. **MS**4160 but in green, purple and gold 5·00 2·00

1577 "Guitarist" (V. Tropinin)

1973. "History of Russian Painting". Multicoloured.
4162 2k. Type **1577** 20 15
4163 4k. "The Young Widow" (P. Fedotov) 40 15
4164 6k. "Self-portrait" (O. Kiprensky) 55 25
4165 10k. "An Afternoon in Italy" (K. Bryullov) 75 35
4166 12k. "That's My Father's Dinner!" (boy with dog) (A. Venetsianov) 95 50
4167 16k. "Lower Gallery of Albano" (A. Ivanov) (horiz) 1·30 70
4168 20k. "Yermak conquering Siberia" (V. Surikov) (horiz) 1·70 85

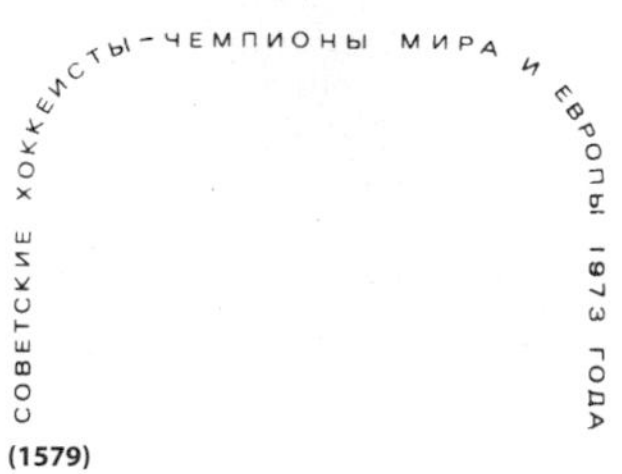

1578 Athlete and Emblems

1973. 50th Anniv of Dynamo Sports Club.
4169 **1578** 4k. multicoloured 55 15

(1579)

1973. U.S.S.R.'s Victory in World Ice-Hockey Championships. No. **MS**4150 optd with T **1579** and frame at foot in green.
MS4170 67×86 mm. 50k. sepia, green and gold 11·50 7·75

1580 Liner "Mikhail Lermontov"

1973. Inauguration of Leningrad–New York Trans-Atlantic Service.
4171 **1580** 16k. multicoloured 1·10 50

1581 E. T. Krenkel and Polar Scenes

1973. 70th Birth Anniv of E. T. Krenkel (Polar explorer).
4172 **1581** 4k. brown and blue 2·50 2·20

1582 Sports

1973. "Sport for Everyone".
4173 **1582** 4k. multicoloured 55 15

1583 Girls' Choir

1973. Centenary of Latvian Singing Festival.

4174	**1583**	10k. multicoloured	75	35

1973. 50th Anniv of Russian Federation Autonomous Soviet Socialist Republics. Design similar to T **1433**, but dated "1973".

4175	4k. blue	55	15

DESIGN: No. 4175, Arms and industries of Buryat Republic.

1584 Throwing the Hammer

1973. Universiade Games, Moscow. Multicoloured.

4176	2k. Type **1584**	20	15
4177	3k. Gymnastics	30	15
4178	4k. Swimming	40	25
4179	16k. Fencing	1·10	70
MS4180	70×88 mm. 50k. Throwing the javelin	3·50	2·00

1585 Tereshkova

1973. Tenth Anniv of Woman's First Space Flight by Valentina Nikolaieva-Tereshkova. Sheet 89×70 mm containing horiz designs as T **1585**. Multicoloured.

MS4181	20k.×3 (a) Type **1585**; (b) Tereshkova with Indian and African women; (c) Holding her baby	5·00	2·20

1586 European Bison

1973. Caucasus and Voronezh Nature Reserves. Multicoloured.

4182	1k. Type **1586**	20	15
4183	3k. Ibex	30	20
4184	4k. Caucasian snowcocks	40	35
4185	6k. Eurasian beaver with young	55	50
4186	10k. Red deer with fawns	95	85

1587 Lenin, Banner and Membership Card

1973. 70th Anniv of Second Soviet Social Democratic Workers Party Congress.

4187	**1587**	4k. multicoloured	55	15

1588 A. R. al-Biruni (after M. Nabiev)

1973. Millennium of Abu Reihan al-Biruni (astronomer and mathematician).

4188	**1588**	6k. brown	55	25

1589 Schaumberg Palace, Bonn, and Spassky Tower, Moscow

1973. General Secretary Leonid Brezhnev's Visits to West Germany, France and U.S.A. Multicoloured.

4189	**1589**	10k. mauve, brn & buff	75	35
4190	-	10k. brown, ochre and yellow	75	35
4191	-	10k. red, grey and brown	75	35
MS4192		134×139 mm. 4k.×3 as Nos. 4189/91, each crimson, flesh and deep olive	9·00	5·50

DESIGNS: No. 4189, Type **1589**; Eiffel Tower, Paris and Spassky Tower; 4191, White House, Washington and Spassky Tower.

See also Nos. 4245 and 4257.

1590 "Portrait of the Sculptor S. T. Konenkov" (P. Korin)

1973. "History of Russian Paintings". Multicoloured.

4193	2k. Type **1590**	20	15
4194	4k. "Farm-workers' Supper" (A. Plastov)	30	15
4195	6k. "Letter from the Battle-front" (A. Laktionov)	40	25
4196	10k. "Mountain Landscape" (M. Saryan)	75	35
4197	16k. "Wedding on Tomorrow's Street" (Yu. Pimenov)	1·10	50
4198	20k. "Ice Hockey" (mosaic, A. Deineka)	1·30	70
MS4199	72×92 mm. 50k. "Lenin making Speech" (B. Johanson)	4·25	1·50

1591 Lenin Museum

1973. Inaug of Lenin Museum, Tashkent.

4200	**1591**	4k. multicoloured	55	15

1592 Steklov

1973. Birth Centenary of Y. Steklov (statesman).

4201	**1592**	4k. brown, red and pink	55	15

1593 "The Eternal Pen"

1973. Afro-Asian Writers' Conference, Alma-Ata.

4202	**1593**	6k. multicoloured	65	25

1594 "Oplopanax elatum"

1973. Medicinal Plants. Multicoloured.

4203	1k. Type **1594**	20	15
4204	2k. Ginseng	30	15
4205	4k. Spotted orchid	30	15
4206	10k. Arnica	75	50
4207	12k. Lily of the valley	95	70

1595 I. Nasimi (after M. Abdullaev)

1973. 600th Birth Anniv of Imadeddin Nasimi (Azerbaijan poet).

4208	**1595**	4k. brown	75	35

1596 Cruiser "Kirov"

1973. History of Russian Navy (3rd series). Multicoloured.

4209	3k. Type **1596**	40	15
4210	4k. Battleship "Oktyabrskaya Revolyutsiya"	50	25
4211	6k. Submarine "Krasnogvardeets"	55	35
4212	10k. Destroyer "Soobrazitelnyi"	95	50
4213	16k. Cruiser "Krasnyi Kavkaz"	1·50	85

1597 Pugachev and Battle Scene

1973. Bicentenary of Peasant War.

4214	**1597**	4k. multicoloured	55	15

1598 Red Flag encircling Globe

1973. 15th Anniv of Magazine "Problems of Peace and Socialism".

4215	**1598**	6k. red, gold and green	75	25

1599 Leningrad Mining Institute

1973. Bicentenary of Leningrad Mining Institute.

4216	**1599**	4k. multicoloured	55	15

1600 Laurel and Hemispheres

1973. World Congress of "Peaceful Forces", Moscow.

4217	**1600**	6k. multicoloured	75	25

1601 Elena Stasova

1973. Birth Centenary of Yelena Stasova (party official).

4218	**1601**	4k. mauve	55	15

1602 Order of People's Friendship

1973. Foundation of Order of People's Friendship.

4219	**1602**	4k. multicoloured	65	25

1603 Marshal Malinovsky

1973. 75th Birth Anniv of Marshal R. Malinovsky.

4220	**1603**	4k. grey	55	15

1604 Workers and Red Guard

1973. 250th Anniv of Sverdlovsk.

4221	**1604**	4k. black, gold and red	55	15

1605 D. Cantemir

1973. 300th Birth Anniv of Dmitri Cantemir (Moldavian scientist and encyclopaedist).

4222	**1605**	4k. red	55	15

1606 Pres. Allende of Chile

1973. Allende Commemoration.

4223	**1606**	6k. black and brown	75	25

1607 Kremlin

1973. New Year.

4224	**1607**	6k. multicoloured	75	25

1608 N. Narimanov

1973. Birth Centenary (1970) of Nariman Narimanov (Azerbaijan politician).

4225	**1608**	4k. green	55	15

1609 "Russobalt" Touring Car (1909)

1973. History of Soviet Motor Industry (1st series). Multicoloured.

4226	2k. Type **1609**	20	15
4227	3k. "AMO-F15" lorry (1924)	30	15
4228	4k. Spartak "NAMI-1" tourer (1927)	40	25
4229	12k. Yaroslavsky "Ya-6" bus (1929)	1·10	45
4230	16k. Gorkovsky "GAZ-A" tourer (1932)	1·70	50

See also Nos. 4293/7, 4397/401 and 4512/16.

1610 "Game and Lobster" (Sneiders)

1973. Foreign Paintings in Soviet Galleries. Multicoloured.

4231	4k. Type **1610**	30	15
4232	6k. "Young Woman with Ear-rings" (Rembrandt) (vert)	40	15
4233	10k. "Sick Woman and Physician" (Steen) (vert)	55	25
4234	12k. "Attributes of Art" (Chardin)	75	35
4235	14k. "Lady in a Garden" (Monet)	95	45
4236	16k. "Village Lovers" (Bastien-Lepage) (vert)	1·10	50
4237	20k. "Girl with Fan" (Renoir) (vert)	1·30	70
MS4238	78×103 mm. 50k. "Flora" (Rembrandt) (vert)	4·50	2·50

1611 Great Sea Gate, Tallin

1973. Historical Buildings of Estonia, Latvia and Lithuania.

4239	**1611**	4k. black, red and green	40	15
4240	-	4k. brown, red and green	40	15
4241	-	4k. multicoloured	40	15
4242	-	10k. multicoloured	75	50

DESIGNS: No. 4240, Organ pipes and Dome Cathedral, Riga; 4241, Traku Castle, Lithuania; 4242, Town Hall and weather-vane, Tallin.

1612 Picasso

1973. Pablo Picasso Commemoration.

4243	**1612**	6k. green, red and gold	95	35

1613 Petrovsky

1973. I. G. Petrovsky (mathematician and Rector of Moscow University) Commemoration.

4244	**1613**	4k. multicoloured	55	15

1973. Brezhnev's Visit to India. As T **1589**, but showing Kremlin, Red Fort, Delhi and flags.

4245	4k. multicoloured	65	45

1614 Soviet Soldier and Title Page

1974. 50th Anniv of "Red Star" Newspaper.

4246	**1614**	4k. black, red and gold	55	15

1615 Siege Monument and Peter the Great Statue, Leningrad

1974. 30th Anniv of Soviet Victory in Battle for Leningrad.

4247	**1615**	4k. multicoloured	75	25

1616 Oil Workers

1974. Tenth Anniv of Tyumen Oil fields.

4248	**1616**	4k. black, red and blue	75	25

1617 "Comecon" Headquarters, Moscow

1974. 25th Anniv of Council for Mutual Economic Aid.

4249	**1617**	16k. green, red & brown	1·30	50

1618 Skaters and Stadium

1974. European Women's Ice Skating Championships, Medeo, Alma-Ata.

4250	**1618**	6k. red, blue and slate	55	15

1619 Kunstkammer Museum, Leningrad, Text and Academy

1974. 250th Anniv of Russian Academy of Sciences.

4251	**1619**	10k. multicoloured	65	25

1620 L. A. Artsimovich

1974. First Death Anniv of Academician L. A. Artsimovich (physicist).

4252	**1620**	4k. brown and green	55	15

1974. 50th Anniv of Autonomous Soviet Socialist Republics. Design similar to T **1433**, but dated "1974".

4253	4k. brown	55	15

DESIGN: No. 4253, Arms and industries of Nakhichevan ASSR (Azerbaijan).

1621 K. D. Ushinsky

1974. 150th Birth Anniv of K. D. Ushinsky (educationalist).

4254	**1621**	4k. brown and green	55	15

1622 M. D. Millionshchikov

1974. First Death Anniv of M. D. Millionshchikov (scientist).

4255	**1622**	4k. brown, pink & green	55	15

1623 Spartakiad Emblem

1974. Third Winter Spartakiad Games.

4256	**1623**	10k. multicoloured	75	25

1974. General Secretary Leonid Brezhnev's Visit to Cuba. As T **1589** but showing Kremlin, Revolution Square, Havana and Flags.

4257	4k. multicoloured	75	35

1624 Young Workers and Emblem

1974. Scientific and Technical Youth Work Review.

4258	**1624**	4k. multicoloured	55	15

1625 Theatre Facade

1974. Cent of Azerbaijan Drama Theatre, Baku.

4259	**1625**	6k. brown, red & orange	65	25

1626 Globe and Meteorological Activities

1974. Cosmonautics Day.

4260	**1626**	6k. blue, red and violet	55	15
4261	-	10k. brown, red and blue	75	50
4262	-	10k. black, red & yellow	75	50

DESIGNS: No. 4261, V. G. Lazarev and O. G. Makarov, and launch of "Soyuz 12"; 4262, P. I. Klimuk and V. V. Lebedev, and "Soyuz 13".

1627 "Odessa by Moonlight" (Aivazovsky)

1974. Marine Paintings by Ivan Aivazovsky. Multicoloured.

4263	2k. Type **1627**	20	15
4264	4k. "Battle of Chesme" (vert)	30	15
4265	6k. "St. George's Monastery"	40	15
4266	10k. "Storm at Sea"	75	25
4267	12k. "Rainbow"	95	35
4268	16k. "Shipwreck"	1·10	50
MS4269	68×91 mm. 50k. "Ivan Aivazovsky" (I. Kramskoi) (vert)	3·25	1·50

1628 Young Communists

1974. 17th Leninist Young Communist League (Komsomol) Congress (4270) and 50th Anniv of Naming League after Lenin (4271). Multicoloured.

4270	4k. Type **1628**	40	15
4271	4k. "Lenin" (from sculpture by V. Tsigal)	40	15

1629 "Lenin at the Telegraph" (I. E. Grabar)

1974. 104th Birth Anniv of Lenin. Sheet 108×82 mm.

MS4272	50k. multicoloured	3·50	1·40

1630 Swallow ("Atmosphere")

1974. "EXPO 74" World Fair, Spokane, U.S.A. "Preserve the Environment".

4273	**1630**	4k. black, red and lilac	30	15
4274	-	6k. yellow, black & blue	40	25
4275	-	10k. black, violet and red	75	35
4276	-	16k. blue, green & black	1·10	50
4277	-	20k. black, brn & orge	1·50	70
MS4278		73×93 mm. 50k. multicoloured	3·50	1·50

DESIGNS: 6k. Fish and globe ("The Sea"); 10k. Crystals ("The Earth"); 16k. Rose bush ("Flora"); 20k. Young red deer ("Fauna"); (30×42 mm) 50k. Child and Sun ("Protest the Environment").

1631 "Cobble-stone, Proletarian Weapon" (sculpture, I. Shadr)

1974. 50th Anniv of Central Museum of the Revolution.

4279	**1631**	4k. green, red and gold	55	15

1632 Congress Emblem within Lucerne Grass

1974. 12th International Congress of Meadow Cultivation, Moscow.

4280	**1632**	4k. red, green & dp green	55	15

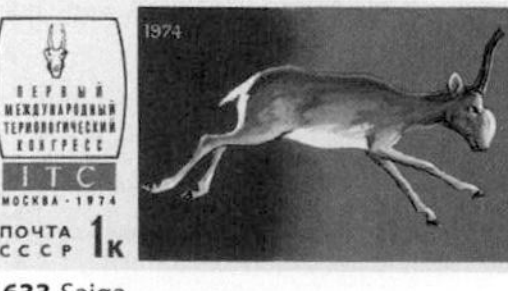

1633 Saiga

1974. First International Theriological Congress, Moscow. Fauna. Multicoloured.

4281	1k. Type **1633**	20	15
4282	3k. Asiatic wild ass	30	25
4283	4k. Russian desman	40	35
4284	6k. Northern fur seal	55	50
4285	10k. Bowhead whale	95	70

1634 Tchaikovsky and Competition Emblem

1974. Fifth Int Tchaikovsky Music Competition.

4286	**1634**	6k. black, violet & green	75	25

1635 "Puskin" (O. A. Kipernsky)

1974. 175th Birth Anniv of Aleksandr Pushkin (writer). Sheet 101×81 mm.

MS4287 50k. multicoloured	3·50	1·40

1636 Marshal F. I. Tolbukhin

1974. 80th Birth Anniv of Marshal F. I. Tolbukhin.

4288	**1636**	4k. green	55	15

1637 K. Stanislavsky, V. Nemirovich-Danchenko and Theatre Curtain

1974. 75th Anniv of Moscow Arts Festival.

4289	**1637**	10k. multicoloured	75	25

1638 Runner and Emblem

1974. 13th Soviet Schools Spartakiad, Alma Ata.

4290	**1638**	4k. multicoloured	55	15

1639 Modern Passenger Coach

1974. Centenary of Yegorov Railway Wagon Works, Leningrad.

4291	**1639**	4k. multicoloured	75	50

1640 Shield and Monument on Battle Map

1974. 30th Anniv of Liberation of Belorussia.

4292	**1640**	4k. multicoloured	55	15

See also No. 4301.

1974. History of Soviet Motor Industry (2nd series). As T **1609**. Multicoloured.

4293	2k. Gorkovsky "GAZ-AA" lorry (1932)	20	15
4294	3k. Gorkovsky "GAZ-03-30" bus (1933)	30	15
4295	4k. Moscow Auto Works "ZIS-5" lorry (1933)	40	25
4296	14k. Moscow Auto Works "ZIS-8" bus (1934)	1·30	35
4297	16k. Moscow Auto Works "ZIS-101" saloon car (1936)	1·50	50

1974. 50th Anniv of Soviet Republics. As T **1433**, dated "1974".

4298	4k. red	55	15

DESIGN: 4k. Arms and industries of North Ossetian Republic.

No. 4298 also commemorates the 200th anniv of Ossetia's merger with Russia.

1641 Liberation Monument (E. Kuntsevich) and Skyline

1974. 800th Anniv of Poltava.

4299	**1641**	4k. red and brown	55	15

1642 Flag and "Nike" Memorial, Warsaw

1974. 30th Anniv of Polish People's Republic.

4300	**1642**	6k. brown and red	75	25

1974. 30th Anniv of Liberation of Ukraine. As T **1640**, but background details and colours changed.

4301	4k. multicoloured	55	15

1644 Admiral Isakov

1974. 80th Birth Anniv of Admiral I. S. Isakov.

4302	**1644**	4k. blue	55	15

1645 Minesweeper

1974. History of the Russian Navy (4th series). Modern Warships. Multicoloured.

4303	3k. Type **1645**	20	15
4304	4k. Aligator II tank landing ship	40	35
4305	6k. "Moskova" helicopter carrier	55	50
4306	16k. Destroyer "Otvazhny"	1·30	1·20

1646 Pentathlon Sports

1974. World Modern Pentathlon Championships, Moscow.

4307	**1646**	16k. brown, gold & blue	1·10	50

1647 D. Ulyanov

1974. Birth Centenary of D. Ulyanov (Lenin's brother).

4308	**1647**	4k. green	55	15

1648 V. Menzhinsky

1974. Birth Cent of V. Menzhinsky (statesman).

4309	**1648**	4k. maroon	55	15

1649 "Lilac" (P. P. Konchalovsky)

1974. Soviet Paintings. Multicoloured.

4310	4k. Type **1649**	30	15
4311	6k. "Towards the Wind" (sailing) (E. Kalnins)	40	25
4312	10k. "Spring" (young woman) (O. Zardaryan)	75	35
4313	16k. "Northern Harbour" (G. Nissky)	1·10	45
4314	20k. "Daughter of Soviet Kirgiz" (S. Chuikov) (vert)	1·50	50

1650 S. M. Budennyi

1974. Marshal S. M. Budennyi Commemoration.

4315	**1650**	4k. green	55	15

1651 Page of First Russian Dictionary

1974. 400th Anniv of First Russian Primer.

4316	**1651**	4k. red, black and gold	55	15

1652 Flags and Soviet War Memorial, (K. Baraski), Bucharest

1974. 30th Anniv of Rumanian Liberation.

4317	**1652**	6k. blue, yellow and red	55	15

1653 Vitebsk

1974. Millenary of Vitebsk.

4318	**1653**	4k. red and green	55	15

1654 Kirgizia

1974. 50th Anniv of Soviet Republics. Flags, Agricultural and Industrial Emblems. Multicoloured. Background colours given.

4319	**1654**	4k. blue	40	15
4320	-	4k. purple	40	15
4321	-	4k. blue	40	15
4322	-	4k. yellow	40	15
4323	-	4k. green	40	15

DESIGNS: No. 4320, Moldavia; 4321, Tadzhikistan; 4322, Turkmenistan; 4323, Uzbekistan.

1655 Bulgarian Crest and Flags

1974. 30th Anniv of Bulgarian Revolution.

4324	**1655**	6k. multicoloured	65	25

1656 G.D.R. Crest and Soviet War Memorial, Treptow, Berlin

1974. 25th Anniv of German Democratic Republic.

4325	**1656**	6k. multicoloured	65	25

1657 Text and Stamp

1974. Third Soviet Philatelic Society Congress, Moscow. Sheet 111×71 mm.

MS4326 **1657** 50k. bistre, black and claret	15·00	10·00

1658 Theatre and Laurel Wreath

1974. 150th Anniv of Maly State Theatre, Moscow.

4327	**1658**	4k. gold, red and black	55	15

1659 "Guests from Overseas"

1974. Birth Centenary of Nikolai K. Rorich (painter).

4328	**1659**	6k. multicoloured	65	25

1660 Soviet Crest and U.P.U. Monument, Berne

1974. Centenary of U.P.U. Multicoloured.

4329	10k. Type **1660**	75	35
4330	10k. Ukraine crest, U.P.U. Emblem and U.P.U. H.Q., Berne	75	35
4331	10k. Byelorussia crest, U.P.U. emblem and mail transport	75	35
MS4332	122×77 mm. 30k. Ilyushin Il-62M jetliner and U.P.U. emblem; 30k. Mail coach and U.P.U. emblem; 40k. U.P.U. emblem (each 31×43 mm)	17·00	13·50

1661 Order of Labour Glory

1974. 57th Anniv of October Revolution. Multicoloured.

4333	4k. Type **1661**	40	15
4334	4k. Kamaz truck (vert)	40	15
4335	4k. Hydro-electric power station, Nurek (vert)	40	15

1662 Soviet "Space Stations" over Mars

1974. Soviet Space Exploration. Multicoloured.

4336	6k. Type **1662**	50	15
4337	10k. P. R. Popovich and Yu. P. Artyukhin ("Soyuz 14" cosomonauts)	75	35
4338	10k. I. V. Sarafanov and L. S. Demin ("Soyuz 15" cosmonauts)	75	35

SIZES—VERT: No. 4337, 28×40 mm. HORIZ: No. 4338, 40×28 mm.

1663 Mongolian Crest Flag

1974. 50th Anniv of Mongolian People's Republic.

4339	**1663**	6k. multicoloured	55	15

1664 Commemorative Inscription

1974. 30th Anniv of Estonian Liberation.

4340	**1664**	4k. multicoloured	55	15

1665 Liner "Aleksandr Pushkin", Freighter and Tanker

1974. 50th Anniv of Soviet Merchant Navy.

4341	**1665**	4k. multicoloured	55	15

1666 Spassky Clock-tower, Kremlin, Moscow

1974. New Year.

4342	**1666**	4k. multicoloured	55	15

1667 "The Market Place" (Beuckelaar)

1974. Foreign Paintings in Soviet Galleries. Multicoloured.

4343	4k. Type **1667**	40	15
4344	6k. "Woman selling Fish" (Pieters) (vert)	55	25
4345	10k. "A Goblet of Lemonade" (Terborsh) (vert)	75	35
4346	14k. "Girl at Work" (Metsu) (vert)	95	45
4347	16k. "Saying Grace" (Chardin) (vert)	1·10	50
4348	20k. "The Spoilt Child" (Greuze) (vert)	1·30	70
MS4349	77×104 mm. 50k. "Self-portrait" (David) (vert)	3·50	1·40

1668 "Ostrowskia magnifica"

1974. Flowers. Multicoloured.

4350	1k. Type **1668**	20	15
4351	2k. "Paeonia intermedia"	20	15
4352	4k. "Roemeria refracta"	40	15
4353	10k. "Tulipia dasystemon"	55	25
4354	12k. "Dianthus versicolor"	75	35

1669 Nikitin (after P. Borel)

1974. 150th Birth Anniv of I. S. Nikitin (poet).

4355	**1669**	4k. black, green & olive	55	15

1670 Leningrad Mint Building

1974. 250th Anniv of Leningrad Mint.

4356	**1670**	6k. multicoloured	65	25

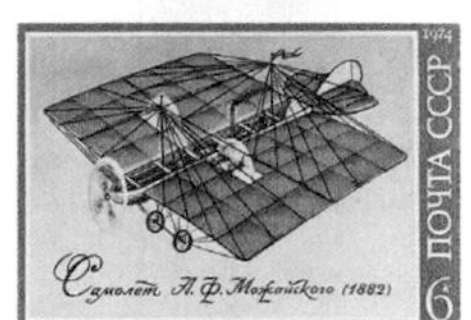
1671 Mozhaisky's Monoplane, 1884

1974. Early Russian Aircraft (1st series). Multicoloured.

4357	6k. Type **1671**	75	50
4358	6k. Grizidubov No. 2 biplane, 1910	75	50
4359	6k. Sikorsky "Russia A", 1910	75	50
4360	6k. Sikorsky Russky Vityaz, 1913	75	50
4361	6k. Grigorovich M-5 flying boat, 1914	75	50

See also Nos. 4580/4, 4661/6 and 4791/6.

1672 Gymnastics and Army Sports Palace, Moscow

1974. Sports Buildings for Olympic Games, Moscow. Sheet 95×74 mm containing T **1672** and similar horiz designs in vermilion, brown and green.

MS4362	10k. Type **1672**; 10k. Running and Znamemsky Brothers' Athletics Hall, Sokolniki; 10k. Football and Lenin Central Stadium; 10k. Canoeing and Rowing Canal, Moscow	5·00	2·75

1673 Komsomol Emblem and Rotary Press ("Komsomolskaya Pravda")

1975. 50th Anniv of Children's Newspapers.

4363	**1673**	4k. red, black and blue	55	15
4364	-	4k. red, black and silver	55	15

DESIGN—VERT: No. 4364, Pioneer emblem and newspaper sheet ("Pioneerskaya Pravda").

1674 Emblem and Skiers (8th Trade Unions' Games)

1975. Winter Spartakiads.

4365	**1674**	4k. orange, black & blue	55	15
4366	-	16k. bistre, black & blue	1·10	50

DESIGN—HORIZ: 16k. Emblem, ice hockey player and skier (5th Friendly Forces Military Games).

1975. "50th Anniv of Automomous Soviet Socialist Republics. Designs similar to T **1433**, but dated "1975".

4367	4k. green	55	25

DESIGN: No. 4367, Arms, industries and produce of Karakalpak ASSR (Uzbekistan).

1675 "David"

1975. 500th Birth Anniv of Michelangelo.

4368	**1675**	4k. deep green and green	20	15
4369	-	6k. brown and ochre	40	25
4370	-	10k. deep green & green	75	35
4371	-	14k. brown and ochre	95	50
4372	-	20k. deep green & green	1·50	70
4373	-	30k. brown and ochre	2·10	1·20
MS4374		166×74 mm. 50k. multicoloured	5·75	2·40

DESIGNS—HORIZ: 6k. "Crouching Boy"; 10k. "Rebellious Slave"; 14k. "Creation of Adam" (detail, Sistine Chapel ceiling); 20k. Staircase of Laurentiana Library, Florence; 30k. Christ and the Virgins (detail of "The Last Judgement", Sistine Chapel). VERT: 50k. Self-portrait.

1676 Mozhaisky, his Monoplane (1884) and Tupolev Tu-144 Jetliner

1975. 150th Birth Anniv of Aleksandr Mozhaisky (aircraft designer).

4375	**1676**	6k. brown and blue	75	25

1677 Convention Emblem

1975. Cent of International Metre Convention.

4376	**1677**	6k. multicoloured	55	15

1678 Games Emblem

1975. Sixth Summer Spartakiad.

4377	**1678**	6k. multicoloured	55	15

1679 Towers of Charles Bridge, Prague (Czechoslovakia)

1975. 30th Anniv of Liberation. Multicoloured.

4378	6k. Type **1679**	40	15
4379	6k. Liberation Monument and Parliament Buildings, Budapest (Hungary)	40	15

1680 French and Soviet Flags

1975. 50th Anniv of Franco-Soviet Diplomatic Relations.

4380	**1680**	6k. multicoloured	55	15

1681 Yuri Gagarin (bust by L. Kerbel)

1975. Cosmonautics Day.

4381	**1681**	6k. red, silver and blue	55	15
4382	-	10k. red, black and blue	75	25
4383	-	16k. multicoloured	95	35

DESIGNS—HORIZ: 10k. A. A. Gubarev, G. M. Grechko ("Soyuz 17") and "Salyut 4"; 16k. A. V. Filipchenko, N. N. Rukavishnikov and "Soyuz 16".

1682 Treaty Emblem

1975. 20th Anniv of Warsaw Treaty.

4384	**1682**	6k. multicoloured	40	15

1683 Emblem and Exhibition Hall, Sokolniki, Moscow

1975. "Communication 75" International Exhibition, Moscow.

4385	**1683**	6k. red, silver and blue	55	15

1684 Lenin

1975. 30th Anniv of Victory in Second World War. Multicoloured.

4386	4k. Type **1684**	40	15
4387	4k. Eternal flame and Guard of Honour	40	15
4388	4k. Woman in ammunition factory	40	15
4389	4k. Partisans	40	15
4390	4k. "Destruction of the enemy"	40	15
4391	4k. Soviet forces	40	15
MS4392	111×57 mm. 50k. Order of the Patriotic War (33×49 mm). Imperf	8·50	6·00

1685 "Lenin" (V. G. Tsyplakov)

1975. 105th Birth Anniv of Lenin.
4393 **1685** 4k. multicoloured 55 15

1686 Victory Emblems

1975. "Sozfilex 75" International Stamp Exhibition.
4394 **1686** 6k. multicoloured 55 15
4395 **1686** 6k. multicoloured 30 10
MS4395 69×95 mm. **1686** 50k. multicoloured 3·00 1·20

1687 "Apollo"–"Soyuz" Space Link

1975. "Apollo"–"Soyuz" Space Project.
4396 **1687** 20k. multicoloured 1·30 70

1975. History of Soviet Motor Industry (3rd series). As T **1609**.
4397 2k. black, orange and blue 20 15
4398 3k. black, brown and green 30 15
4399 4k. black, blue and green 40 25
4400 12k. black, buff and purple 95 35
4401 16k. black, green and olive 1·30 50
DESIGNS: 2k. Gorkovsky "GAZ-M1" saloon, 1936; 3k. Yaroslavsky "YAG-6" truck, 1936; 4k. Moscow Auto Works "ZIS-16" bus, 1938; 12k. Moscow KIM Works "KIM-10" saloon, 1940; 16k. Gorkovsky "GAZ-67B" field car, 1943.

1688 Irrigation Canal and Emblem

1975. Ninth Int Irrigation Congress, Moscow.
4402 **1688** 6k. multicoloured 55 15

1689 Flags and Crests of Poland and Soviet Union

1975. 30th Anniv of Soviet–Polish Friendship.
4403 **1689** 6k. multicoloured 55 15

1690 A. A. Leonov in Space

1975. Tenth Anniv of First Space Walk by A. A. Leonov.
4404 **1690** 6k. multicoloured 65 15

1691 Ya. M. Sverdlov

1975. 90th Birth Anniv of Ya. M. Sverdlov (statesman).
4405 **1691** 4k. brown, buff & silver 50 15

1692 Congress Emblem

1975. Eighth Int Plant Conservation Congress, Moscow.
4406 **1692** 6k. multicoloured 55 15

1693 Emblem and Plants

1975. 12th Int Botanical Congress, Leningrad.
4407 **1693** 6k. multicoloured 55 25

1694 U.N.O. Emblem

1975. 30th Anniv of United Nations Organization. Sheet 67×78 mm.
MS4408 **1694** 50k. gold, blue and light blue 3·00 1·50

1695 Festival Emblem

1975. Ninth International Film Festival, Moscow.
4409 **1695** 6k. multicoloured 55 15

1696 Crews of "Apollo" and "Soyuz"

1975. "Apollo"–"Soyuz" Space Link. Multicoloured.
4410 10k. Type **1696** 75 15
4411 12k. "Apollo" and "Soyuz 19" in docking procedure 95 35
4412 12k. "Apollo" and "Soyuz 19" linked together 95 35
4413 16k. Launch of "Soyuz 19" (vert) 1·10 50
MS4414 83×120 mm. 50k. Mission Control Centre, Moscow (55×26 mm) 3·00 1·50

1697 Russian Sturgeon

1975. Int Exposition, Okinawa. Marine Life.
4415 **1697** 3k. bistre, black and blue 20 15
4416 - 4k. lilac, black and blue 30 15
4417 - 6k. purple, black & green 40 25
4418 - 10k. brown, black & bl 55 35
4419 - 16k. green, black & purple 95 45
4420 - 20k. blue, pur & stone 1·30 50
MS4421 83×120 mm. 30k. black, lilac and blue; 30k. black, lilac and blue 3·75 1·50
DESIGNS:—SQUARE: 4k. Thomas rapa whelk; 6k. European eel; 10k. Long-tailed duck; 16k. Crab; 20k. Grey damselfish. HORIZ: (56×26 mm)—30k. (2) Common dolphin (different).

1698 "Parade in Red Square, Moscow" (K. F. Yuon)

1975. Birth Centenaries of Soviet Painters. Multicoloured.
4422 1k. Type **1698** 20 15
4423 2k. "Winter Morning in Industrial Moscow" (K. P. Yuon) 30 15
4424 6k. "Soldiers with Captured Guns" (E. E. Lansere) 55 25
4425 10k. "Excavating the Metro Tunnel" (E. E. Lansere) 75 35
4426 16k. "A. A. Pushkin and N. N. Pushkina at Palace Ball" (N. P. Ulyanov) (vert) 1·30 50
4427 20k. "Lauriston at Kutuzov's Headquarters" (N. P. Ulyanov) 1·70 70

1699 Conference Emblem

1975. European Security and Co-operation Conf, Helsinki.
4428 **1699** 6k. black, gold and blue 2·30 1·40

1700 Isaakjan (after M. Sargan)

1975. Birth Centenary of Avetic Isaakjan (Armenian poet).
4429 **1700** 4k. multicoloured 55 15

1701 M. K. Ciurlionis

1975. Birth Centenary of M. K. Ciurlionis (Lithuanian composer).
4430 **1701** 4k. gold, green & yellow 55 15

1702 J. Duclos

1975. Jacques Duclos (French communist leader) Commemoration.
4431 **1702** 6k. purple and silver 55 15

1703 Al Farabi (after L. Leontev)

1975. 1100th Birth Anniv of Al Farabi (Persian philosopher).
4432 **1703** 6k. multicoloured 55 15

1704 Ruffs

1975. 50th Anniv of Berezinsky and Stolby Nature Reserves. Multicoloured.
4433 1k. Type **1704** 20 15
4434 4k. Siberian musk deer 30 25
4435 6k. Sable 40 35
4436 10k. Western capercaillie 75 70
4437 16k. Eurasian badger 1·10 1·00

1705 Korean Crest with Soviet and Korean Flags

1975. 30th Anniversaries. Multicoloured.
4438 6k. Type **1705** (Korean liberation) 55 15
4439 6k. Vietnamese crest, Soviet and Vietnamese flags (Vietnam Democratic Republic) 55 15

1706 Cosmonauts, "Soyuz 18" and "Salyut 4" Linked

1975. Space Flight of "Soyuz 18–Salyut 4" by Cosmonauts P. Klimuk and V. Sevastyanov.
4440 **1706** 10k. black, red and blue 75 25

1707 Yesenin

1975. 80th Birth Anniv of Yesenin (poet).
4441 **1707** 6k. brown, yell & grey 55 15

1708 Standardization Emblems

1975. 50th Anniv of Soviet Communications Standardization Committee.
4442 **1708** 4k. multicoloured 40 15

1709 Astrakhan Lamb

1975. Third International Astrakhan Lamb Breeding Symposium, Samarkand.
4443 **1709** 6k. black, green & stone 55 15

1710 M. P. Konchalovsky

1975. Birth Centenary of M. P. Konchalovsky (therapeutist).
4444 **1710** 4k. brown and red 40 15

1711 Exhibition Emblem

1975. Third All-Union Philatelic Exhibition, Yerevan.
4445 **1711** 4k. red, brown and blue 40 15

1712 I.W.Y. Emblem and Rose

1975. International Women's Year.
4446 **1712** 6k. red, blue & turquoise 55 15

1713 Parliament Buildings, Belgrade

1975. 30th Anniv of Yugoslav Republic.

4447	**1713**	6k. blue, red and gold	55	15

1714 Title-page of 1938 Edition

1975. 175th Anniv of Publication of "Tale of the Host of Igor".

4448	**1714**	4k. red, grey and bistre	40	15

1715 M. I. Kalinin (statesman)

1975. Celebrities' Birth Centenaries.

4449	**1715**	4k. brown	40	15
4450	-	4k. brown	40	15

DESIGN: No. 4450, A. V. Lunacharsky (politician).

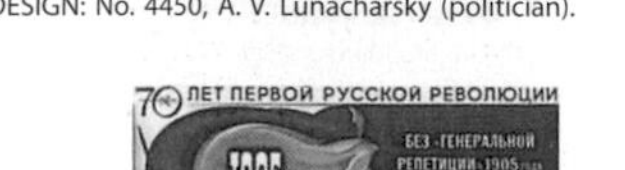

1716 Torch and Inscription

1975. 70th Anniv of Russian 1905 Revolution.

4451	**1716**	4k. red and brown	40	15

1717 Track-laying Machine and Baikal-Amur Railway

1975. 58th Anniv of October Revolution. Multicoloured.

4452	4k. Type **1717**	50	15
4453	4k. Rolling mill, Novolipetsk steel plant (vert)	50	15
4454	4k. Formula and ammonia plant, Nevynomyssk chemical works (vert)	50	15

1718 "Decembrists in Senate Square" (D. N. Kardovsky)

1975. 150th Anniv of Decembrist Rising.

4455	**1718**	4k. multicoloured	40	15

1719 Star of Spassky Tower

1975. New Year.

4456	**1719**	4k. multicoloured	40	15

1720 "Village Street"

1975. 125th Birth Anniv of F. A. Vasilev (painter). Multicoloured.

4457	2k. Type **1720**	20	15
4458	4k. "Forest Path"	30	15
4459	6k. "After the Thunderstorm"	40	15
4460	10k. "Forest Marsh" (horiz)	55	25
4461	12k. "In the Crimean Mountains"	95	35
4462	16k. "Wet Meadow" (horiz)	1·10	50
MS4463	63×94 mm. 50k. Vasilev (after I. Kramskoi)	3·00	1·40

1721 "Venus" Spacecraft

1975. Space Flights of "Venus 9" and "Venus 10".

4464	**1721**	10k. multicoloured	75	35

1722 G. Sundukyan

1975. 150th Birth Anniv of G. Sundukyan (Armenian playwright).

4465	**1722**	4k. multicoloured	40	15

1723 Iceland Poppy

1975. Flowers (1st series). Multicoloured.

4466	4k. Type **1723**	20	15
4467	6k. Globe flower	40	15
4468	10k. Yellow anemone	55	25
4469	12k. Snowdrop windflower	75	35
4470	16k. "Eminium lehemannii"	1·10	50

See also Nos. 4585/9.

1724 A. L. Mints

1975. A. L. Mints (scientist) Commemoration.

4471	**1724**	4k. brown and gold	40	15

1725 "Demon" (A. Kochupalov)

1975. Miniatures from Palekh Art Museum (1st series). Multicoloured.

4472	4k. Type **1725**	40	15
4473	6k. "Vasilisa the Beautiful" (I. Vakurov)	55	35
4474	10k. "The Snow Maiden" (T. Zubkova)	95	50
4475	16k. "Summer" (K. Kukulieva)	1·30	85
4476	20k. "Fisherman and Goldfish" (I. Vakurov) (horiz)	1·70	1·00

See also Nos. 4561/5.

1726 Pieck

1975. Birth Centenary of Wilhelm Pieck (President of German Democratic Republic).

4477	**1726**	6k. black	55	25

1727 Saltykov-Shchedrin (after I. Kramskoi)

1976. 150th Birth Anniv of M. Saltykov-Shchedrin (writer).

4478	**1727**	4k. multicoloured	40	15

1728 Congress Emblem

1976. 25th Communist Party Congress, Moscow (1st issue).

4479	**1728**	4k. gold, brown and red	40	15
MS4480	106×74 mm. **1728** 50k. gold, lake and vermilion (27×37 mm)		3·00	1·40

See also Nos. 4489 and 4556/60.

1729 Lenin (statue, S. Merkurov), Kiev

1976. 25th Ukraine Communist Party Congress, Kiev.

4481	**1729**	4k. black, red and blue	40	15

1730 Ice Hockey

1976. Winter Olympic Games, Innsbruck (1st series). Multicoloured.

4482	2k. Type **1730**	30	15
4483	4k. Skiing	40	15
4484	6k. Figure skating	55	25
4485	10k. Speed skating	75	35
4486	20k. Tobogganing	1·30	50
MS4487	90×80 mm. 50k. red, yellow and blue (Games emblem) (vert)	3·50	1·70

See also No. **MS**4492.

1731 Marshal C. E. Voroshilov

1976. 95th Birth Anniv of Marshal C. E. Voroshilov.

4488	**1731**	4k. green	40	15

1732 Congress Hall and Red Banner

1976. 25th Communist Party Congress, Moscow (2nd issue).

4489	**1732**	20k. orange, red & green	7·50	6·75

1733 "Lenin on Red Square" (P. Vasilev)

1976. 106th Birth Anniv of Lenin.

4490	**1733**	4k. multicoloured	40	15

1734 Atomic Symbol and Institute Emblem

1976. 20th Anniv of Joint Institute of Nuclear Research, Dubna.

4491	**1734**	6k. multicoloured	55	25

(1735) (1735a)

1976. Winter Olympic Games, Innsbruck (2nd issue). Dedicated to Soviet Medal Winners. No. **MS**4487 optd with Types **1735** and **1735a** in red.

MS4492	90×80 mm. 50k. red, yellow and blue	15·00	11·00

1736 Bolshoi Theatre

1976. Bicentenary of Bolshoi Theatre.

4493	**1736**	10k. blue, brn & ochre	75	45

1737 "Back from the Fair"

1976. Birth Centenary of P. P. Konchalovsky (painter). Multicoloured.

4494	1k. Type **1737**	20	15
4495	2k. "The Green Glass"	30	15
4496	6k. "Peaches"	55	35
4497	16k. "Meat, Game and Vegetables by the Window"	1·30	50
4498	20k. Self-portrait (vert)	1·50	70

1738 "Vostok", "Salyut" and "Soyuz" Spacecraft

1976. 15th Anniv of First Manned Space Flight by Yuri Gagarin.

4499	4k. Type **1738**	40	15
4500	6k. "Meteor" and "Molniya" satellites	50	25
4501	10k. Cosmonauts on board "Salyut" space-station	75	35

4502 12k. "Interkosmos" satellite and "Apollo"–"Soyuz" space link 95 45

MS4503 65×100 mm. 50k. black (Yuri Gagarin) (37×52 mm) 21·00 17·00

1739 I. A. Dzhavakhishvili

1976. Birth Centenary of I. A. Dzhavakhishvili (scientist).

4504 **1739** 4k. black, stone and green 40 15

1740 S. Vurgun

1976. 70th Birth Anniv of Samed Vurgun (Azerbaijan poet).

4505 **1740** 4k. black, brown & green 40 15

1741 Festival Emblem

1976. First All-Union Amateur Art Festival.

4506 **1741** 4k. multicoloured 40 15

1742 F. I. P. Emblem

1976. 50th Anniv of International Philatelic Federation.

4507 **1742** 6k. red and blue 55 25

1744 Dnepropetrovsk Crest

1976. Bicentenary of Dnepropetrovsk.

4509 **1744** 4k. multicoloured 40 15

1745 N. N. Burdenko

1976. Birth Centenary of N. N. Burdenko (neurologist).

4510 **1745** 4k. brown and red 40 15

1746 K. A. Trenev

1976. Birth Centenary of K. A. Trenev (playwright).

4511 **1746** 4k. multicoloured 40 15

1976. History of Soviet Motor Industry (4th series). As T **1609**.

4512 2k. black, red and green 20 15
4513 3k. black, orange and bistre 30 15
4514 4k. black, buff and blue 40 25
4515 12k. black, green and brown 75 35
4516 16k. black, red and yellow 1·10 50

DESIGNS: 2k. Moscow Auto Works "ZIS-110" saloon, 1945; 3k. Gorkovsky "GAZ-51" truck, 1946; 4k. Gorkovsky "GAZ-M20 (Pobeda)" saloon, 1946; 12k. Moscow Auto Works "ZIS-150" truck, 1947; 16k. Moscow Auto Works "ZIS-154" bus, 1947.

1747 Canoeing

1976. Olympic Games, Montreal. Multicoloured.

4517 4k. Type **1747** 20 15
4518 6k. Basketball (vert) 40 15
4519 10k. Graeco-Roman wrestling 55 25
4520 14k. Discus throwing (vert) 75 35
4521 16k. Rifle-shooting 95 45

MS4522 67×88 mm. 50k. Obverse and reverse of Gold medal 5·00 2·00

See also No. **MS**4552.

1748 Electric Railway Train

1976. 50th Anniv of Soviet Railway Electrification.

4523 **1748** 4k. black, red and green 50 15

1749 L. M. Pavlichenko

1976. 60th Birth Anniv of L. M. Pavlichenko (war heroine).

4524 **1749** 4k. brown, yellow and silver 40 15

1750 L. E. Rekabarren

1976. Birth Centenary of Luis Rekabarren (founder of Chilean Communist Party).

4525 **1750** 6k. black, red and gold 50 25

1751 "Fresh Partner"

1976. Russian Art. Paintings by P. A. Fedotov. Multicoloured.

4526 2k. Type **1751** 20 15
4527 4k. "Fastidious Fiancee" (horiz) 30 15
4528 6k. "Aristocrat's Breakfast" 40 25
4529 10k. "The Gamblers" (horiz) 95 35
4530 16k. "The Outing" 1·30 50

MS4531 70×90 mm. 50k. Self-portrait 3·50 1·40

1752 S. S. Nemetkin

1976. Birth Centenary of Sergei S. Nemetkin (chemist).

4532 **1752** 4k. black, yellow & blue 40 15

1753 Soviet Armed Forces Order

1976. (a) As T **1753**. Size 14×21½ mm.

4533 1k. olive 20 15
4534 2k. magenta 30 15
4535 3k. scarlet 40 15
4536 4k. red 55 15
4537 6k. blue 75 25
4538 10k. green 1·10 35
4539 12k. ultramarine 1·50 45
4540 16k. green 1·90 70

1754 Marx and Lenin (sculpture, Ye. Belostotsky and E. Fridman)

(b) As T **1754**.

4541 20k. lake 2·30 85
4542 30k. vermillion 3·25 1·20
4543 50k. brown 5·75 1·40
4544 1r. blue 10·50 2·75

DESIGNS: 2k. Gold Star (military) and Hammer and Sickle (labour) decorations; 3k. "Worker and Collective Farmer" (sculpture, Vera Mukhina); 4k. Soviet crest; 6k. Globe and Tupolev Tu-154 jetliner (Soviet postal communications); 10k. Soviet Reputation for Work order; 12k. Yury Gagarin and rocket (space exploration); 16k. International Lenin Prize medal (international peace and security); 30k. Council for Mutual Economic Aid building; 50k. Lenin (after P. Zhukov); 1r. Satellites orbiting globe.

See also Nos. 4669/82.

1755 Cattle Egret

1976. Water Birds. Multicoloured.

4545 1k. Type **1755** 35 30
4546 3k. Black-throated diver 70 65
4547 4k. Black coot 1·00 95
4548 6k. Atlantic puffin 1·50 1·40
4549 10k. Slender-billed gull 3·00 2·75

1756 Peace Dove with Laurel

1976. Second Stockholm World Peace Appeal.

4550 **1756** 4k. blue, yellow and gold 40 15

1757 Federation Emblem

1976. 25th Anniv of International Resistance Movement Federation.

4551 **1757** 6k. black, gold and blue 50 25

СПОРТСМЕНЫ
СССР
ЗАВОЕВАЛИ
47 ЗОЛОТЫХ,
43 СЕРЕБРЯНЫХ
И 35 БРОНЗОВЫХ
МЕДАЛЕЙ!

СОВЕТСКОМУ
СПОРТУ
СЛАВА!
(1758)

1976. Olympic Games, Montreal (2nd issue). Dedicated to Soviet Medal Winners. No. **MS**4522 optd with T **1758**.

MS4552 67×88 mm. 50k. Obverse and reverse of Gold Medal 13·50 10·00

1759 Soviet and Indian Flags

1976. Soviet–Indian Friendship.

4553 **1759** 4k. multicoloured 40 15

1760 B. V. Volynov and V. M. Zholobov

1976. Space Flight of "Soyuz 21".

4554 **1760** 10k. black, blue & brn 55 35

1761 UNESCO Emblem

1976. 30th Anniv of UNESCO.

4555 **1761** 16k. brown, bistre & blue 1·10 70

1762 "Industry"

1976. 25th Communist Party Congress (3rd issue).

4556 **1762** 4k. brown, red & yellow 40 15
4557 - 4k. green, red & orange 40 15
4558 - 4k. violet, red and pink 40 15
4559 - 4k. deep red, red and grey 40 15
4560 - 4k. violet, red and blue 40 15

DESIGNS: No. 4557, "Agriculture"; 4558, "Science and Technology"; 4559, "Transport and Communications"; 4560, "International Co-operation".

1763 "The Ploughman" (I. Golikov)

1976. Minatures from Palekh Art Museum (2nd series). Multicoloured.

4561 2k. Type **1763** 20 15
4562 4k. "The Search" (I. Markichev) (vert) 40 35
4563 12k. "The Firebird" (A. Kotukhin) 95 85
4564 14k. "Folk Festival" (A. Vatagin) (vert) 1·00 95
4565 20k. "Victory" (I. Vakurov) (vert) 1·50 1·40

1764 Shostakovich and Part of 7th Symphony

1976. 70th Birth Anniv of Dmitri Shostakovich (composer).

4566	**1764**	6k. blue	50	25

1765 G. K. Zhukov

1976. 80th Birth Anniversaries of Soviet Marshals.

4567	**1765**	4k. green	40	15
4568	-	4k. brown	40	15

DESIGN: No. 4568, K. K. Rokossovsky.

1766 "Interkosmos 14" Satellite

1976. International Co-operation in Space Research.

4569	**1766**	6k. blue, gold and black	40	15
4570	-	10k. violet, gold & black	55	25
4571	-	12k. purple, gold & black	75	35
4572	-	16k. green, gold & black	95	45
4573	-	20k. mauve, gold & black	1·10	50

DESIGNS: 10k. "Aryabhata" (Indian satellite); 12k. "Apollo"–"Soyuz" space link; 16k. "Aureole" (French satellite); 20k. Globe and spacecraft.

1767 V. I. Dal

1976. 175th Birth Anniv of V. I. Dal (scholar).

4574	**1767**	4k. green	40	15

1768 Electric Power Station

1976. 59th Anniv of October Revolution. Multicoloured.

4575	4k. Type **1768**	40	15
4576	4k. Balashovo fabrics factory	40	15
4577	4k. Irrigation ditch construction	40	15

1769 Medicine Emblem

1976. 50th Anniv of Petrov Institute of Cancer Research.

4578	**1769**	4k. lilac, gold and blue	40	15

1770 M. A. Novinsky (oncologist)

1976. Centenary of Cancer Research.

4579	**1770**	4k. brown, blue and buff	40	15

1771 Hakkel VII Biplane, 1911

1976. Early Russian Aircraft (2nd series). Multicoloured.

4580	3k. Type **1771**	20	15
4581	6k. Hakkel IX monoplane, 1912	40	35
4582	12k. Steglau No. 2, 1912	55	50
4583	14k. Dybovsky Dolphin, 1913	65	60
4584	16k. Sikorsky Ilya Mourometz, 1914	75	70

See also Nos. 4661/6 and 4791/6.

1976. Flowers (2nd series). As T **1723**. Multicoloured.

4585	1k. Safflower	20	15
4586	2k. Anemone	20	15
4587	3k. Gentian	20	15
4588	4k. Columbine	40	15
4589	6k. Fitillaria	55	25

1772 New Year Greeting

1976. New Year.

4590	**1772**	4k. multicoloured	40	15

1773 "Parable of the Vineyard"

1976. 370th Birth Anniv of Rembrandt. Multicoloured.

4591	4k. Type **1773**	20	15
4592	6k. "Danae"	40	25
4593	10k. "David and Jonathan" (vert)	55	35
4594	14k. "The Holy Family" (vert)	75	50
4595	20k. "Andrian" (vert)	1·10	85
MS4596	125×66 mm. 50k. "Artaxeres, Hamann and Esther"	16·00	14·50

1774 "Luna 24" and Emblem

1976. "Luna 24" Unmanned Space Flight to Moon.

4597	**1774**	10k. brown, yellow & blue	55	35

1775 "Pailot"

1976. Russian Ice-breakers (1st series). Multicoloured.

4598	4k. Type **1775**	55	25
4599	6k. "Ermak" (vert)	75	35
4600	10k. "Fyodor Litke"	1·10	50
4601	16k. "Vladmir Ilich" (vert)	1·50	85
4602	20k. "Krassin"	2·10	1·00

See also Nos. 4654/60, 4843/8 and 5147.

1776 "Raduga" Experiment and Cosmonauts

1976. "Soyuz 22" Space Flight by V. F. Bykovsky and V. V. Aksenov.

4603	**1776**	10k. green, blue and red	55	35

1777 Olympic Torch

1976. Olympic Games, Moscow (1980).

4604	**1777**	4k.+2k. black, red and blue	55	35
4605	-	10k.+5k. black, blue and red	95	50
4606	-	16k.+6k. black, mauve and yellow	1·50	70
MS4607		63×83 mm. 60k.+30k. black, gold and red	12·50	6·75

DESIGNS: 30×42 mm—10, 16k. Games Emblem. 27×38 mm—6k. Kemlin.

1778 Society Emblem and "Red Star"

1977. 50th Anniv of Red Banner Forces Voluntary Society.

4608	**1778**	4k. multicoloured	40	15

1779 S. P. Korolev Memorial Medallion

1977. 70th Birth Anniv of S. P. Korolev (scientist and rocket pioneer).

4609	**1779**	4k. gold, black and blue	40	15

1780 Congress Emblem

1977. World Peace Congress, Moscow.

4610	**1780**	4k. gold, ultramarine and blue	40	15

1781 Sedov and "Sv. Foka"

1977. Birth Cent of G. Y. Sedov (polar explorer).

4611	**1781**	4k. multicoloured	55	25

1782 Working Class Monument, Red Flag and Newspaper Cover

1977. 60th Anniv of Newspaper "Izvestiya".

4612	**1782**	4k. black, red and silver	40	15

1783 Ship on Globe

1977. 24th International Navigation Congress, Leningrad.

4613	**1783**	6k. blue, black and gold	50	25

1784 Kremlin Palace of Congresses, Moscow

1977. 16th Soviet Trade Unions Congress.

4614	**1784**	4k. gold, black and red	40	15

1785 L. A. Govorov

1977. 80th Birth Anniv of Marshal L. A. Govorov.

4615	**1785**	4k. brown	40	15

1786 Academy Emblem, Text and Building

1977. 150th Anniv of Grechko Naval Academy, Leningrad.

4616	**1786**	6k. multicoloured	50	25

1787 J. Labourbe

1977. Birth Centenary of Jeanne Labourbe (French communist).

4617	**1787**	4k. black, blue and red	40	15

1788 Chess Pieces

1977. Sixth European Chess Team Championship, Moscow.

4618	**1788**	6k. multicoloured	55	50

1789 "Soyuz 23" and Cosmonauts

1977. "Soyuz 23" Space Flight by V. D. Zudov and V. I. Rozhdestvensky.

4619	**1789**	10k. red, black & brown	75	35

1790 Novikov-Priboi

1977. Birth Centenary of Aleksei Novikov-Priboi (writer).

4620	**1790**	4k. black, orange & blue	40	15

1791 "Welcome" (N. M. Soloninkin)

1977. Folk Paintings from Fedoskino Village. Multicoloured.

4621	4k. Type **1791**	40	15
4622	6k. "Along the Street" (V. D. Antonov) (horiz)	50	25
4623	10k. "Northern Song" (J. V. Karapaev)	55	35
4624	12k. "Fairy Tale about Tzar Sultan" (A. I. Kozlov)	75	45
4625	14k. "Summer Troika" (V. A. Nalimov) (horiz)	95	50
4626	16k. "Red Flower" (V. D. Lipitsky)	1·10	70

1792 Congress Emblem

1977. World Electronics Congress, Moscow.
4627 **1792** 6k. red, grey and blue 40 15

1793 "In Red Square" (K. V. Filatov)

1977. 107th Birth Anniv of Lenin.
4628 **1793** 4k. multicoloured 40 15

1794 Yuri Gagarin and Spacecraft

1977. Cosmonautics Day.
4629 **1794** 6k. blue, lilac and purple 50 25

1795 N. I. Vavilov

1977. 90th Birth Anniv of N. I. Vavilov (biologist).
4630 **1795** 4k. black and brown 40 15

1796 F. E. Dzerzhinsky

1977. Birth Centenary of Feliks Dzerzhinsky (founder of Cheka).
4631 **1796** 4k. black 40 15

1797 Mountain Saxifrage

1977. Flowers. Multicoloured.

4632	2k. Type **1797**	20	15
4633	3k. Pinks	20	15
4634	4k. "Novosieversia glacialis"	30	25
4635	6k. "Cerastium maximum"	40	35
4636	16k. "Rhododendron aureum"	95	85

1798 V. V. Gorbatko and Yu. N. Glazkov (cosmonauts)

1977. "Soyuz 24–Salyut 5" Space Project.
4637 **1798** 10k. black, red and blue 75 35

1799 I. S. Konev

1977. 80th Birth Anniv of Soviet Marshals.

4638	**1799**	4k. green	40	15
4639	-	4k. black	40	15
4640	-	4k. brown	40	15

DESIGNS: No. 4639, V. D. Sokolovsky; 4640, K. A. Meretskov.

1800 Festival Emblem

1977. Tenth International Film Festival, Moscow.
4641 **1800** 6k. gold, red and lake 50 25

1801 Greco-Roman Wrestling

1977. Olympic Sports (1st series).

4642	**1801**	4k.+2k. black, ochre and gold	40	15
4643	-	6k.+3k. black, green and gold	55	25
4644	-	10k.+5k. black, mauve and gold	95	35
4645	-	16k.+6k. black, blue and gold	1·30	70
4646	-	20k.+10k. black, brown and gold	1·90	85

DESIGNS: 6k. Free-style wrestling; 10k. Judo; 16k. Boxing; 29k. Weightlifting.

See also Nos. 4684/9, 4749/53, 4820/4, 4870/4, 4896/4900, 4962/6 and 4973/7.

1802 "Portrait of a Chambermaid"

1977. 400th Birth Anniv of Rubens. Multicoloured.

4647	4k. Type **1802**	40	15
4648	6k. "The Lion Hunt" (horiz)	50	35
4649	10k. "Stone Carriers" (horiz)	75	45
4650	12k. "Water and Earth Alliance"	95	50
4651	20k. "Landscape with Rainbow" (horiz)	1·30	85

MS4652 104×74 mm. 50k. Rubens" (detail from "Portrait of Rubens and his Son") 3·50 1·40

1803 "Judith" (detail)

1977. 500th Birth Anniv of Giorgione. Sheet 77×104 mm.
MS4653 **1803** 50k. multicoloured 3·50 1·40

1977. Soviet Ice-breakers (2nd series). As T **1775**. Multicoloured.

4654	4k. "Aleksandr Sibiryakov"	40	15
4655	6k. "Georgy Sedov"	50	35
4656	10k. "Sadko"	75	70
4657	12k. "Dezhnev"	95	85
4658	14k. "Sibur"	1·10	1·00
4659	16k. "Lena"	1·30	1·20
4660	20k. "Amguema"	1·50	1·40

1977. Air. Early Soviet Aircraft (3rd series). As T **1771** but dated 1977.

4661	4k. black, brown and blue	40	15
4662	6k. black, orange and green	50	35
4663	10k. black, mauve and blue	55	50
4664	12k. black, blue and red	75	70
4665	16k. multicoloured	95	85
4666	20k. black, green and blue	1·10	1·00

DESIGNS: 4k. Porokhovshchikov P-IV bis biplane trainer, 1917; 6k. Kalinin AK-1, 1924; 10k. Tupolev ANT-3 R-3, 1925; 12k. Tupolev ANT-4 TB-1 bomber, 1929; 16k. Polikarpov R-5 biplane, 1929; 20k. Shavrov Sh-2 flying boat, 1930.

1804 Stamps and Emblem

1977. "60th Anniv of October Revolution" Philatelic Exhibition, Moscow.
4667 **1804** 4k. red, blue and brown 40 15

1805 Buildings and Arms, Stavropol

1977. Bicentenary of Stavropol.
4668 **1805** 6k. gold, red and green 50 25

1976. As Nos. 4533/44 and new value. (a) As T **1753**.

4669	1k. olive	20	15
4670	2k. mauve	20	15
4671	3k. red	20	15
4672	4k. red	40	15
4673	6k. blue	55	15
4674	10k. green	75	25
4675	12k. blue	95	35
4676	15k. blue	1·10	50
4677	16k. green	1·10	35

(b) As T **1754**.

4678	20k. red	1·30	70
4679	30k. red	1·50	75
4680	32k. blue	3·00	85
4681	50k. brown	1·90	1·40
4682	1r. blue	4·25	2·00

DESIGNS: 2k. Gold Star (military) and Hammer and Sickle (labour) decorations; 3k. "Worker and Collective Farmer" (sculpture, Vera Mukhina); 4k. Soviet crest; 6k. Globe and Tupolev Tu-154 jetliner (Soviet postal communications); 10k. Soviet Reputation for Work Order; 12k. Yuri Gagarin and rocket (space exploration); 15k. Ostankino T.V. tower and globe; 16k. International Lenin Prize medal (international peace and security); 30k. Council for Mutual Economic Aid building; 32k. Ilyushin Il-76 airplane and compass rose; 50k. Lenin (after P. Zhukov); 1r. Satellites orbiting globe.

The 6 and 32k. are airmail stamps.

1806 "Arktika"

1977. Journey to North Pole of "Arktika" (atomic ice-breaker). Sheet 107×80 mm.
MS4683 **1806** 50k. multicoloured 19·00 10·00

1977. Olympic Sports (2nd series). As T **1801**.

4684	4k.+2k. black, gold and red	40	15
4685	6k.+3k. black, gold & blue	55	35
4686	10k.+5k. black, gold & grn	95	50
4687	16k.+6k. black, gold & olive	1·50	70
4688	20k.+10k. black, gold & pur	2·30	1·00

MS4689 92×72 mm. 50k.+25k. black, gold and blue 17·00 10·00

DESIGNS—HORIZ: 4k. Cycling; 10k. Rifle-shooting; 16k. Horse-jumping; 20k. Fencing; 50k. horse-jumping and fencing (Modern pentathlon). VERT: 6k. Archery.

1807 Yuri Gagarin and "Vostok" Spacecraft

1977. 20th Anniv of Space Exploration.

4690	**1807**	10k. red, blue and brown	55	35
4691	-	10k. brown, blue & violet	55	35
4692	-	10k. red, purple & green	55	35
4693	-	20k. green, brown & red	75	45
4694	-	20k. purple, red and blue	75	45
4695	-	20k. red, blue and green	75	45

MS4696 66×86 mm. 50k. gold and lake (22×32 mm) 17·00 15·00

DESIGNS: No. 4691, Space walking; 4692, "Soyuz" spacecraft and "Salyut" space station linked; 4693, "Proton 4" satellite; 4694, "Luna Venus" and "Mars" space stations; 4695, "Intercosmos 10" satellite and "Apollo" and "Soyuz" spacecraft linked; **MS**4696, "Sputnik 1" satellite.

1808 Carving from St. Dmitri's Cathedral, Vladimir (12th-cent)

1977. Russian Art. Multicoloured.

4697	4k. Type **1808**	40	15
4698	6k. Bracelet, Ryazan (12th cent)	50	15
4699	10k. Detail of Golden Gate from Nativity Cathedral, Suzdal (13th-cent)	55	25
4700	12k. Detail from "Arch-angel Michael" (icon) (A. Rublev) (15th-cent)	75	35
4701	16k. Gold and marble chalice made by I. Fomin (15th-cent)	95	45
4702	20k. St. Basil's Cathedral, Moscow (16th-cent)	1·10	50

1809 "Snowflake and Fir Twig"

1977. New Year.
4703 **1809** 4k. multicoloured 40 15

1810 Cruiser "Aurora"

1977. 60th Anniv of October Revolution.

No.	Type	Description	Mint	Used
4704	1810	4k. multicoloured	40	15
4705	-	4k. black, red and gold	40	15
4706	-	4k. black, red and gold	40	15
4707	-	4k. multicoloured	40	15
MS4708		106×71 mm. 30k. black, vermilion and gold	2·30	85

DESIGNS: No. 4705, Statue of Lenin; 4706, Page of "Izvestiya", book by Brezhnev and crowd; 4707, Kremlin spire, star and fireworks. 26×38 mm—30k. Lenin medal.

1811 First Clause of U.S.S.R. Constitution

1977. New Constitution.

No.	Type	Description	Mint	Used
4709	1811	4k. yellow, red & brown	40	15
4710	-	4k. multicoloured	40	15
MS4711		112×82 mm. 50k. multicoloured	3·75	1·50

DESIGNS: 47×32 mm—No. 4710 People of U.S.S.R. welcoming new constitution. 69×47 mm—50k. Constitution as open book, and laurel branch.

1812 Leonid Brezhnev

1977. New Constitution (2nd issue). Sheet 143×74 mm.

No.	Type	Description	Mint	Used
MS4712	1812	50k. multicoloured	4·25	2·40

1813 Postwoman and Post Code

1977. Postal Communications. Multicoloured.

No.	Description	Mint	Used
4713	4k. Type **1813**	40	15
4714	4k. Letter collection	40	15
4715	4k. "Map-O" automatic sorting machine	40	15
4716	4k. Mail transport	40	15
4717	4k. Delivering the mail	40	15

1814 Red Fort, Delhi and Asokan Capital

1977. 30th Anniv of Indian Independence.

No.	Type	Description	Mint	Used
4718	1814	6k. gold, purple and red	55	25

1815 Monument, Kharkov

1977. 60th Anniv of Establishment of Soviet Power in the Ukraine.

No.	Type	Description	Mint	Used
4719	1815	6k. multicoloured	50	15

1816 Adder

1977. Snakes and Protected Animals. Multicoloured.

No.	Description	Mint	Used
4720	1k. Type **1816**	20	15
4721	4k. Levantine viper	30	25
4722	6k. Saw-scaled viper	40	35
4723	10k. Central Asian viper	55	50
4724	12k. Central Asian cobra	75	70
4725	16k. Polar bear and cub	95	85
4726	20k. Walrus and young	1·30	1·20
4727	30k. Tiger and cub	1·70	1·50

1817 Olympic Emblem and Arms of Vladimir

1977. 1980 Olympics. "Tourism around the Golden Ring" (1st issue). Multicoloured.

No.	Description	Mint	Used
4728	1r.+50k. Type **1817**	6·75	5·00
4729	1r.+50k. Vladimir Hotel	6·75	5·00
4730	1r.+50k. Arms of Suzdal	6·75	5·00
4731	1r.+50k. Pozharsky monument	6·75	5·00
4732	1r.+50k. Arms of Ivanovo and Frunze monument	6·75	5·00
4733	1r.+50k. Monument to Revolutionary Fighters	6·75	5·00

See also Nos. 4828/31, 4850/3, 4914/17, 4928/9, 4968/9, 4981/2 and 4990/5.

1818 Combine Harvester

1978. 50th Anniv of "Gigant" Collective Farm, Rostov.

No.	Type	Description	Mint	Used
4734	1818	4k. brown, red & yellow	40	15

1819 Kremlin Palace of Congresses

1978. 18th Leninist Young Communist League (Komsomol) Congress.

No.	Type	Description	Mint	Used
4735	1819	4k. multicoloured	40	15

1820 Globe, Obelisk and Emblem

1978. Eighth International Federation of Resistance Fighters Congress, Minsk.

No.	Type	Description	Mint	Used
4736	1820	6k. red, blue and black	50	25

1821 Red Army Detachment and Modern Sailor, Airman and Soldier

1978. 60th Anniv of Soviet Military Forces. Multicoloured.

No.	Description	Mint	Used
4737	4k. Type **1821**	40	15
4738	4k. Defenders of Moscow monument (detail), Lenin banner and Order of Patriotic War	40	15
4739	4k. Soviet soldier	40	15

1822 "Celebration in a Village"

1978. Birth Centenary of Boris M. Kustodiev (artist). Multicoloured.

No.	Description	Mint	Used
4740	4k. Type **1822**	40	15
4741	6k. "Shrovetide"	50	25
4742	10k. "Morning" (50×36 mm)	55	35
4743	12k. "Merchant's Wife drinking Tea" (50×36 mm)	75	45
4744	20k. "Bolshevik" (50×36 mm)	95	70
MS4745	92×72 mm. 50k. "Self-portrait" (36×50 mm)	3·00	1·40

1823 Gubarev and Remek at Launch Pad

1978. Soviet–Czech Space Flight. Multicoloured.

No.	Description	Mint	Used
4746	6k. Type **1823**	40	15
4747	15k. "Soyuz-28" docking with "Salyut-6" space station	75	35
4748	32k. Splashdown	1·50	70

1978. Olympic Sports (3rd series). As T **1801**. Multicoloured.

No.	Description	Mint	Used
4749	4k.+2k. Swimmer at start	40	35
4750	6k.+3k. Diving (vert)	55	50
4751	10k.+5k. Water polo	95	85
4752	10k.+6k. Canoeist	1·30	1·20
4753	20k.+10k. Single sculls	1·90	1·70
MS4754	92×71 mm. 50k.+25k. grey, black and green (Double sculls)	12·50	9·25

1824 "Soyuz" Capsules linked to "Salyut" Space Station

1978. Cosmonautics Day.

No.	Type	Description	Mint	Used
4755	1824	6k. gold, blue and deep blue	40	15

1825 Shield and Laurel Wreath

1978. Ninth World Congress of Trade Unions.

No.	Type	Description	Mint	Used
4756	1825	6k. multicoloured	50	25

1826 E. A. and M. E. Cherepanov and their Locomotive, 1833

1978. Russian Locomotives (1st series). Multicoloured.

No.	Description	Mint	Used
4757	1k. Type **1826**	20	15
4758	2k. Series D locomotive, 1845	30	25
4759	3k. Series V locomotive (first passenger train, 1845)	40	35
4760	16k. Series Gv locomotive, 1863–67	1·50	1·40
4761	20k. Series Bv locomotive, 1863–67	1·70	1·50

Nos. 4758/61 are horizontal designs.
See also Nos. 4861/5.

1827 Lenin (after V. A. Servo)

1978. 108th Birth Anniv of Lenin. Sheet 73×96 mm.

No.	Type	Description	Mint	Used
MS4762	1827	50k. multicoloured	3·75	1·70

1828 "XI" and Laurel Branch

1978. 11th World Youth and Students Festival, Havana.

No.	Type	Description	Mint	Used
4763	1828	4k. multicoloured	40	15

1829 Tulip "Bolshoi Theatre"

1978. Moscow Flowers. Multicoloured.

No.	Description	Mint	Used
4764	1k. Type **1829**	20	15
4765	2k. Rose "Moscow Morning"	20	15
4766	4k. Dahlia "Red Star"	30	15
4767	10k. Gladiolus "Moscovite"	55	35
4768	12k. Iris "To Il'ich's Anniversary"	75	45

1830 I.M.C.O. Emblem

1978. 20th Anniv of Intergovernment Maritime Consultative Organization, and World Maritime Day.

No.	Type	Description	Mint	Used
4769	1830	6k. multicoloured	50	25

1831 "Salyut-6" Space Station performing Survey Work

1978. "Salyut-6" Space Station. Multicoloured.

No.	Description	Mint	Used
4770	15k. Type **1831**	95	50
4771	15k. Yu. V. Romanenko and G. M. Grechko	95	50

Nos. 4770/1 were issued in se-tenant pairs forming a composite design.

1832 "Space Meteorology"

1978. Space Research. Multicoloured.

No.	Description	Mint	Used
4772	10k. Type **1832**	55	35

4773	10k. "Soyuz" orbiting globe ("Natural resources")	55	35
4774	10k. Radio waves, ground station and "Molniya" satellite ("Communication")	55	35
4775	10k. Human figure, "Vostok" orbiting Earth ("Medicine and biology")	55	35
MS4776	102×77 mm. "Prognoz" satellite ("Physics") (36×51 mm)	3·50	1·50

1833 Transporting Rocket to Launch Site

1978. Soviet–Polish Space Flight. Multicoloured.

4777	6k. Type **1833**	40	15
4778	15k. Crystal (Sirena experiment)	95	50
4779	32k. Space station, map and scientific research ship "Kosmonavt Vladimir Komarov"	1·90	1·00

1834 Komsomol Awards

1978. 60th Anniv of Leninist Young Communist League (Komsomol). Multicoloured.

4780	4k. Type **1834**	40	15
4781	4k. Products of agriculture and industry	40	15

1835 M. V. Zakharov

1978. 80th Birth Anniv of Marshal M. V. Zakharov.

4782	**1835**	4k. brown	40	15

1836 N. G. Chernyshevsky

1978. 150th Birth Anniv of Nikolai G. Chernyshevsky (revolutionary).

4783	**1836**	4k. brown and yellow	40	15

1837 Snow Petrel

1978. Antarctic Fauna. Multicoloured.

4784	1k. Snares Island penguin (horiz)	50	15
4785	3k. Type **1837**	55	15
4786	4k. Emperor penguin	95	15
4787	6k. Antarctic icefish	1·10	25
4788	10k. Southern elephant-seal (horiz)	1·70	35

1838 Torch and Flags

1978. Construction of Orenburg–U.S.S.R. Western Frontier Gas Pipe-line.

4789	**1838**	4k. multicoloured	40	15

1839 William Harvey

1978. 400th Birth Anniv of William Harvey (discoverer of blood circulation).

4790	**1839**	6k. green, black and blue	50	25

1978. Air. Early Russian Aircraft (3rd series). As T **1771**.

4791	4k. green, brown and black	30	15
4792	6k. multicoloured	40	35
4793	10k. yellow, blue and black	55	50
4794	12k. orange, blue and black	75	70
4795	16k. blue, deep blue and black	95	85
4796	20k. multicoloured	1·10	1·00

DESIGNS: 4k. Polikarpov Po-2 biplane, 1928; 6k. Kalinin K-5, 1929; 10k. Tupolev ANT-6 TB-3 bomber, 1930; 12k. Putilov Stal-2, 1931; 16k. Beriev Be-2 MBR-2 reconnaissance seaplane, 1932; 20k. Polikarpov I-16 fighter, 1934.

1840 "Bathing of Red Horse"

1978. Birth Centenary of K. S. Petrov-Vodkin (painter). Multicoloured.

4797	4k. Type **1840**	20	15
4798	6k. "Petrograd, 1918"	40	15
4799	10k. "Commissar's Death"	55	25
4800	12k. "Rose Still Life"	75	35
4801	16k. "Morning Still Life"	95	45
MS4802	92×72 mm. 50k. "Self-portrait" (vert)	3·00	1·70

1841 Assembling "Soyuz 31"

1978. Soviet–East German Space Flight. Multicoloured.

4803	6k. Type **1841**	40	25
4804	15k. Space photograph of Pamir mountains	75	50
4805	32k. Undocking from space station	1·90	70

1842 "Molniya 1" Satellite, "Orbita" Ground Station and Tupolev Tu-134 Jetliner

1978. "PRAGA 78" International Stamp Exhibition.

4806	**1842**	6k. multicoloured	55	35

1843 Tolstoi

1978. 150th Birth Anniv of Leo Tolstoi (novelist).

4807	**1843**	4k. green	3·00	2·20

1844 Union Emblem

1978. 14th General Assembly of International Union for the Protection of Nature and Natural Resources, Ashkhabad.

4808	**1844**	4k. multicoloured	40	15

1845 Bronze Figure, Erebuni Fortress

1978. Armenian Architecture. Multicoloured.

4809	4k. Type **1845**	40	15
4810	6k. Echmiadzin Cathedral	50	15
4811	10k. Khachkary (carved stones)	55	25
4812	12k. Matenadaran building (repository of manuscripts) (horiz)	65	35
4813	16k. Lenin Square, Yerevan (horiz)	75	50

1846 Monument (P. Kufferge)

1978. 70th Anniv of Russian Aid to Messina Earthquake Victims.

4814	**1846**	6k. multicoloured	50	25

1847 Emblem, Ostankino TV Tower and Hammer and Sickle

1978. 20th Anniv of Organization for Communications Co-operation.

4815	**1847**	4k. multicoloured	40	15

1978. "60th Anniv of Komsomol" Philatelic Exhibition. Optd with T 1848.

4816	**1834**	4k. multicoloured	2·75	2·50

1849 "Diana" (detail)

1978. 450th Birth Anniv of Paolo Veronese (artist). Sheet 76×115 mm.

MS4817	**1849**	50k. multicoloured	3·00	1·70

1850 Kremlin

1978. First Anniv of New Constitution. Sheet 160×85 mm.

MS4818	**1850**	30k. multicoloured	2·30	1·70

1851 Shaumyan

1978. Birth Centenary of Stephan Georgievich Shaumyan (Commissar).

4819	**1851**	4k. green	40	15

1852 "Star" Yacht

1978. Olympic Sports (4th series). Sailing Regatta, Tallin. Multicoloured.

4820	4k.+2k. Type **1852**	40	25
4821	6k.+3k. "Soling" yacht	55	35
4822	10k.+5k. "470" dinghy	95	70
4823	16k.+6k. "Finn" dinghy	1·50	1·00
4824	20k.+10k. "Flying Dutchman" dinghy	1·90	1·40
MS4825	71×94 mm. 50k.+25k. "Tornado" class catamaran (horiz)	13·50	9·25

1853 Industrial Structures and Flags

1978. 61st Anniv of October Revolution.

4826	**1853**	4k. multicoloured	40	15

1854 Black Sea Ferry

1978. Inauguration of Ilichevsk–Varna, Bulgaria, Ferry Service.

4827	**1854**	6k. multicoloured	50	25

1855 Zagorsk

1978. 1980 Olympics. "Tourism around the Golden Ring" (2nd issue). Multicoloured.

4828	1r.+50k. Type **1855**	5·75	4·25
4829	1r.+50k. Palace of Culture, Zagorsk	5·75	4·25
4830	1r.+50k. Kremlin, Rostov- Veliki	5·75	4·25
4831	1r.+50k. View of Rostov- Veliki	5·75	4·25

1856 Church of the Intercession on River Nerl

1978. "Masterpieces of Old Russian Culture". Multicoloured.

4832	6k. Golden crater (horiz)	40	15
4833	10k. Type **1856**	50	25
4834	12k. "St. George and the Dragon" (15th-century icon)	55	35
4835	16k. Tsar Cannon (horiz)	95	50

1857 Cup with Snake and Institute

1978. 75th Anniv of Herzen Oncology Research Institute, Moscow.
4836 **1857** 4k. gold, purple & black 40 15

1858 Nestor Pechersky and "Chronicle of Past Days"

1978. History of the Russian Posts. Multicoloured.

4837	4k. Type **1858**	30	15
4838	6k. Birch-bark letter	40	15
4839	10k. Messenger with trumpet	55	25
4840	12k. Mail sledges	65	35
4841	16k. Interior of Prikaz Post Office	75	45

1859 Spassky Tower, Kremlin

1978. New Year.
4842 **1859** 4k. multicoloured 55 35

1978. Soviet Ice breakers (3rd series). As T **1775**. Multicoloured.

4843	4k. "Vasily Pronchishchev"	40	25
4844	6k. "Kapitan Belousov" (vert)	55	35
4845	10k. "Moskva"	75	50
4846	12k. "Admiral Makarov"	95	60
4847	16k. "Lenin" atomic ice- breaker (vert)	1·10	70
4848	20k. "Arktika" atomic ice-breaker	1·30	85

1860 V. Kovalenok and A. Ivanchenkov

1978. "140 Days in Space".
4849 **1860** 10k. multicoloured 75 35

1978. 1980 Olympics "Tourism around the Golden Ring" (3rd issue). As T **1855**. Multicoloured.

4850	1r.+50k. Alexander Nevsky Monument, Pereslavl-Zalessky	5·75	4·25
4851	1r.+50k. Peter I Monument, Pereslavl-Zalessky	5·75	4·25
4852	1r.+50k. Monastery of the Transfiguration, Yaroslavl	5·75	4·25
4853	1r.+50k. Ferry terminal and Eternal Glory Monument, Yaroslavl	5·75	4·25

1861 Globe and Newspaper Titles

1978. 60th Anniv of "Soyuzpechati" State Newspaper Distribution Service. Sheet 106×82 mm.
MS4854 **1861** 30k. multicoloured 1·90 1·00

1862 Cuban Flags

1979. 20th Anniv of Cuban Revolution.
4855 **1862** 6k. multicoloured 50 25

1863 Government Building, Minsk

1979. 60th Anniv of Byelorussian Soviet Socialist Republic and Communist Party.
4856 **1863** 4k. multicoloured 40 15

1864 Flags and Reunion Monument

1979. 325th Anniv of Reunion of Ukraine with Russia.
4857 **1864** 4k. multicoloured 40 15

1865 Old and New University Buildings

1979. 400th Anniv of Vilnius University.
4858 **1865** 4k. black and pink 40 15

1866 Exhibition Hall and First Bulgarian Stamp

1979. "Philaserdica 79" International Stamp Exhibition, Sofia.
4859 **1866** 15k. multicoloured 95 50

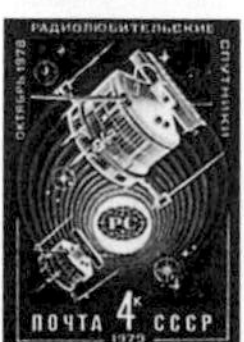
1867 Satellites "Radio 1" and "Radio 2"

1979. Launching of "Radio" Satellites.
4860 **1867** 4k. multicoloured 75 35

1868 Series A Locomotive, 1878

1979. Railway Locomotives (2nd series). Multicoloured.

4861	2k. Type **1868**	20	15
4862	3k. Class Shch steam locomotive, 1912	30	25
4863	4k. Class Lp steam locomotive, 1915	40	35
4864	6k. Class Su steam locomotive, 1925	55	50
4865	15k. Class L steam locomotive, 1947	1·50	1·40

1869 Medal and Komsomol Pass

1979. 25th Anniv of Development of Virgin and Disused Land. Sheet 99×67 mm.
MS4866 **1869** 50k. multicoloured 3·00 1·20

1870 "Venera 12" over Venus

1979. "Venera" Flights to Venus.
4867 **1870** 10k. red, lilac and purple 75 35

1871 Albert Einstein

1979. Birth Centenary of Albert Einstein (physicist).
4868 **1871** 6k. multicoloured 55 35

1872 Congress Emblem

1979. 21st World Veterinary Congress, Moscow.
4869 **1872** 6k. multicoloured 55 25

1873 Free Exercise

1979. Olympic Sports (5th series). Gymnastics.

4870	**1873**	4k.+2k. brown, stone and orange	30	15
4871	-	6k.+3k. blue, grey and violet	40	35
4872	-	10k.+5k. red, stone and brown	75	50
4873	-	16k.+6k. mauve, grey and purple	95	70
4874	-	20k.+10k. red, stone and brown	1·30	1·00

MS4875 91×71 mm. 50k.+25k. brown, stone and light brown 9·50 6·75

DESIGNS:—VERT: 6k. Parallel bars; 10k. Horizontal bar; 16k. Beam; 20k. Asymmetric bars. HORIZ: 50k. Rings.

1874 "To Arms" (poster by R. Beren)

1979. 60th Anniv of First Hungarian Socialist Republic.
4876 **1874** 4k. multicoloured 40 15

1875 Cosmonauts at Yuri Gagarin Training Centre

1979. Soviet–Bulgarian Space Flight. Multicoloured.

4877	6k. Type **1875**	50	25
4878	32k. Landing of cosmonauts	1·50	70

1876 "Intercosmos"

1979. Cosmonautics Day.
4879 **1876** 15k. multicoloured 95 50

1877 Ice Hockey

1979. World and European Ice Hockey Championship, Moscow. Sheet 85×65 mm.
MS4880 **1877** 50k. red, blue and maroon 3·75 1·70

See also **MS**4888.

1878 Exhibition Emblem

1979. U.S.S.R. Exhibition, London.
4881 **1878** 15k. multicoloured 75 35

1879 Lenin

1979. 109th Birth Anniv of Lenin. Sheet 89×71 mm.
MS4882 **1879** 50k. multicoloured 3·75 1·70

1880 Antonov An-28

1979. Air. Soviet Aircraft. Multicoloured.

4883	2k. Type **1880**	20	15
4884	3k. Yakovlev Yak-42	30	25
4885	10k. Tupolev Tu-154	75	50
4886	15k. Ilyushin Il-76	1·10	70
4887	32k. Ilyushin Il-86	2·75	1·20

СОВЕТСКИЕ ХОККЕИСТЫ—
ЧЕМПИОНЫ МИРА
И ЕВРОПЫ
(1881)

1979. Soviet Victory in European Ice Hockey Championship. No. **MS**4880 optd in margin with T **1881**.
MS4888 50k. red, blue and maroon 7·50 3·75

1882 "Tent" Monument, Mining Institute, Pushkin Theatre and Blast Furnace

1979. 50th Anniv of Magnitogorsk City.

4889	**1882**	4k. multicoloured	40	15

1883 Child and Apple Blossom

1979. International Year of the Child (1st issue).

4890	**1883**	4k. multicoloured	40	15

See also Nos. 4918/21.

1884 Bogorodsk Wood-carvings

1979. Folk Crafts. Multicoloured.

4891	2k. Type **1884**	20	15
4892	3k. Khokhloma painted dish and jars	30	15
4893	4k. Zhostovo painted tray	40	15
4894	6k. Kholmogory bone-carvings	50	25
4895	15k. Vologda lace	75	45

1885 Football

1979. Olympic Sports (6th series). Multicoloured.

4896	**1885**	4k.+2k. blue, grey and orange	40	15
4897	-	6k.+3k. yellow, orange and blue	55	25
4898	-	10k.+5k. green, red and mauve	75	35
4899	-	16k.+6k. purple, blue and green	95	50
4900	-	20k.+10k. yellow, red and green	1·30	85

DESIGNS—VERT: 6k. Basketball; 10k. Volleyball. HORIZ: 16k. Handball; 20k. Hockey.

1886 Lenin Square Underground Station

1979. Tashkent Underground Railway.

4901	**1886**	4k. multicoloured	40	15

1887 V. A. Dzhanibekov and O. G. Makarov

1979. "Soyuz 27"–"Salyut 6"–"Soyuz 26" Orbital Complex.

4902	**1887**	4k. multicoloured	40	15

1888 Council Building and Flags of Member Countries

1979. 30th Anniv of Council of Mutual Economic Aid.

4903	**1888**	16k. multicoloured	75	35

1889 Scene from "Battleship Potemkin"

1979. 60th Anniv of Soviet Films (1st issue) and 11th International Film Festival, Moscow.

4904	**1889**	15k. multicoloured	95	35

See also No. 4907.

1890 Emblem

1979. 50th Anniv of First Five Year Plan. Sheet 66×87 mm.

MS4905	**1890**	30k. multicoloured	1·90	85

1891 U.S.S.R. Philatelic Society Emblem

1979. Fourth U.S.S.R. Philatelic Society Congress. Sheet 92×66 mm.

MS4906	**1891**	50k. rose and green	3·00	1·20

1892 Exhibition Hall and Film Still

1979. 60th Anniv of Soviet Films (2nd issue).

4907	**1892**	4k. multicoloured	40	15

1893 "Lilac" (K. A. Korovin)

1979. Flower Paintings. Multicoloured.

4908	1k. "Flowers and Fruits" (I. F. Khrutsky) (horiz)	20	15
4909	2k. "Phloxes" (I. N. Kramskoi)	30	15
4910	3k. Type **1893**	40	25
4911	15k. "Bluebells" (S. V. Gerasimov)	75	35
4912	32k. "Roses" (P. P. Konchalovsky) (horiz)	1·70	85

1894 John McClean

1979. Birth Centenary of John McClean (first Soviet consul for Scotland).

4913	**1894**	4k. black and red	40	15

1979. 1980 Olympics. "Tourism around the Golden Ring" (4th issue). As T **1855**. Multicoloured.

4914	1r.+50k. Narikaly Fortress, Tbilisi	6·75	5·00
4915	1r.+50k. Georgian Philharmonic Society Concert Hall and "Muse" (sculpture), Tbilisi	6·75	5·00
4916	1r.+50k. Chir-Dor Mosque, Samarkand	6·75	5·00
4917	1r.+50k. People's Friendship Museum and "Courage" monument, Tashkent	6·75	5·00

1895 "Friendship" (Lena Liberda)

1979. International Year of the Child (2nd issue). Children's Paintings. Multicoloured.

4918	2k. Type **1895**	20	15
4919	3k. "After Rain" (Daniya Akhmetshina)	20	15
4920	4k. "Dance of Friendship" (Liliya Elistratova)	40	15
4921	15k. "On the Excursion" (Vika Smalyuk)	55	25

1896 Golden Oriole

1979. Birds. Multicoloured.

4922	2k. Type **1896**	20	15
4923	3k. Lesser spotted woodpecker	30	15
4924	4k. Crested tit	40	15
4925	10k. Barn owl	85	50
4926	15k. European nightjar	1·10	70

1897 Soviet Circus Emblem

1979. 60th Anniv of Soviet Circus.

4927	**1897**	4k. multicoloured	40	15

1979. 1980 Olympics. "Tourism around the Golden Ring" (5th issue). As T **1855**. Multicoloured.

4928	1r.+50k. Relics of Yerevan's origin	6·75	5·00
4929	1r.+50k. Armenian State Opera and Ballet Theatre, Yerevan	6·75	5·00

1898 Marx, Engels, Lenin and View of Berlin

1979. 30th Anniv of German Democratic Republic.

4930	**1898**	6k. multicoloured	55	35

1899 V. A. Lyakhov, V. V. Ryumin and "Salyut 6"

1979. Lyakhov and Ryumin's 175 Days in Space. Multicoloured.

4931	15k. Type **1899**	75	35
4932	15k. Radio telescope mounted on "Salyut 6"	75	35

Nos. 4931/2 were issued together, se-tenant, forming a composite design.

1900 Hammer and Sickle

1979. 62nd Anniv of October Revolution.

4933	**1900**	4k. multicoloured	40	15

1901 Communications Equipment and Signal Corps Emblem

1979. 60th Anniv of Signal Corps.

4934	**1901**	4k. multicoloured	40	15

1902 "Katherine" (T. G. Shevchenko)

1979. Ukrainian Paintings. Multicoloured.

4935	2k. Type **1902**	20	15
4936	3k. "Into Service" (K. K. Kostandi)	30	15
4937	4k. "To Petrograd" (A. M. Lopukhov)	40	15
4938	10k. "Return" (V. N. Kostetsky)	55	25
4939	15k. "Working Morning" (M. G. Belsky)	75	35

1903 Shabolovka Radio Mast, Moscow

1979. 50th Anniv of Radio Moscow.

4940	**1903**	32k. multicoloured	1·70	1·00

1904 Misha (Olympic mascot)

1979. New Year.

4941	**1904**	4k. multicoloured	40	15

1905 "Peace" and Hammer and Sickle

1979. "Peace Programme in Action". Multicoloured.

4942	4k. Type **1905**	40	15
4943	4k. Hand holding demand for peace	40	15
4944	4k. Hands supporting emblem of peace	40	15

1906 Traffic Policeman

1979. Road Safety. Multicoloured.

4945	3k. Type **1906**	20	15
4946	4k. Child playing in road	40	15
4947	6k. Speeding car out of control	50	25

1907 "Vulkanolog"

1979. Soviet Scientific Research Ships. Multicoloured.

4948	1k. Type **1907**	20	15
4949	2k. "Professor Bogorov"	20	15
4950	4k. "Ernst Krenkel"	30	15
4951	6k. "Kosmonavt Vladislav Volkov"	50	25
4952	10k. "Kosmonavt Yuri Gagarin"	55	35
4953	15k. "Akademik Kurchatov"	95	50

1908 Skiers at North Pole

1979. Ski Expedition to North Pole. Sheet 66×85 mm.

MS4954	**1908** 50k. multicoloured	3·75	1·70

1909 Industrial Landscape

1980. 50th Anniv of Mordovian ASSR of Russian Federation.

4955	**1909**	4k. red	40	15

1910 Speed Skating

1980. Winter Olympic Games, Lake Placid.

4956	**1910**	4k. blue, lt blue & orange	20	15
4957	-	6k. violet, blue & orange	30	25
4958	-	10k. red, blue and gold	40	35
4959	-	15k. brown, blue & turquoise	55	50
4960	-	20k. turquoise, blue and red	75	60
MS4961		60×90 mm. 50k. multicoloured	3·00	2·75

DESIGNS—HORIZ: 6k. Figure skating (pairs); 10k. Ice hockey; 15k. Downhill skiing. VERT: 20k. Luge; 50k. Cross-country skiing.

1911 Running

1980. Olympic Sports (7th series). Athletics. Multicoloured.

4962	4k.+2k. Type **1911**	40	35
4963	6k.+3k. Hurdling	50	45
4964	10k.+5k. Walking (vert)	75	70
4965	16k.+6k. High jumping	95	85
4966	20k.+10k. Long jumping	1·30	1·20

1912 N. I. Podvoisky

1980. Birth Centenary of Nikolai Ilich Podvoisky (revolutionary).

4967	**1912**	4k. brown	40	15

1980. 1980 Olympics. "Tourism around the Golden Ring" (6th issue). Moscow. As T **1855**. Multicoloured.

4968	1r.+50k. Kremlin	6·75	6·00
4969	1r.+50k. Kalinin Prospect	6·75	6·00

1913 "Rainbow" (A. K. Savrasov)

1980. Birth Annivs of Soviet Artists. Multicoloured.

4970	6k. "Harvest Summer" (A. G. Venetsianov (bicent)) (vert)	50	25
4971	6k. Type **1913** (150th anniv)	50	25
4972	6k. "Old Yerevan" (M. S. Saryan) (centenary)	50	25

1980. Olympic Sports (8th series). Athletics. As T **1911**. Multicoloured.

4973	4k.+2k. Pole vaulting	40	35
4974	6k.+3k. Discus throwing	50	45
4975	10k.+5k. Javelin throwing	75	70
4976	16k.+6k. Hammer throwing	95	85
4977	20k.+10k. Putting the shot	1·30	1·20
MS4978	92×72 mm. 50k.+25k. Relay racing	11·50	10·00

1914 Aleksei Leonov

1980. 15th Anniv of First Space Walk in Space. Sheet 111×73 mm.

MS4979	**1914** 50k. multicoloured	2·75	2·40

1915 Georg Ots

1980. 60th Birth Anniv of Georg K. Ots (artist).

4980	**1915**	4k. blue	40	15

1980. 1980 Olympics. "Tourism around the Golden Ring" (7th issue). As T **1855**. Multicoloured.

4981	1r.+50k. St. Isaac's Cathedral, Leningrad	6·75	6·00
4982	1r.+50k. Monument to the Defenders of Leningrad	6·75	6·00

1916 Order of Lenin

1980. 50th Anniv of Order of Lenin.

4983	**1916**	4k. multicoloured	40	15

1917 Cosmonauts, "Salyut", "Soyuz" Complex and Emblem

1980. Intercosmos Space Programme. Sheet 117×81 mm.

MS4984	**1917** 50k. multicoloured	3·00	2·75

1918 Lenin (after G. Nerod)

1980. 110th Birth Anniv of Lenin. Sheet 91×79 mm.

MS4985	**1918** 30k. brown, gold and vermilion	1·90	1·70

1919 "Motherland" (detail of Heroes Monument, Volgograd)

1980. 35th Anniv of World War II Victory. Multicoloured.

4986	4k. Type **1919**	40	15
4987	4k. Victory Monument, Treptow Park, Berlin	40	15
4988	4k. Victory Parade, Red Square, Moscow	40	15

1920 Government House, Arms and Flag of Azerbaijan

1980. 60th Anniv of Azerbaijan Soviet Republic.

4989	**1920**	4k. multicoloured	40	15

1980. 1980 Olympics. "Tourism around the Golden Ring" (8th issue). As T **1855**. Multicoloured.

4990	1r.+50k. Bogdan Khmelnitsky Monument and St. Sophia Monastery, Kiev	6·75	6·00
4991	1r.+50k. Underground bridge over River Dnieper, Kiev	6·75	6·00
4992	1r.+50k. Sports Palace and War Memorial, Minsk	6·75	6·00
4993	1r.+50k. House of Cinematog-rahy, Minsk	6·75	6·00
4994	1r.+50k. Old City, Tallin	6·75	6·00
4995	1r.+50k. Hotel Viru, Tallin	6·75	6·00

1921 Monument, Ivanovo

1980. 75th Anniv of First Soviet of Workers Deputies, Ivanovo.

4996	**1921**	4k. multicoloured	40	15

1922 Shield and Industrial Complexes

1980. 25th Anniv of Warsaw Treaty.

4997	**1922**	32k. multicoloured	2·30	1·70

1923 Yakovlev Yak-24 Helicopter, 1953

1980. Helicopters. Multicoloured.

4998	1k. Type **1923**	20	15
4999	2k. Mil Mi-8, 1962	20	15
5000	3k. Kamov Ka-26, 1965	30	15
5001	6k. Mil Mi-6, 1957	40	25
5002	15k. Mil Mi-10K, 1965	1·20	1·00
5003	32k. Mil Mi-V12, 1969	2·30	2·00

1924 Title Page of Book

1980. 1500th Birth Anniv of David Anacht (Armenian philosopher).

5004	**1924**	4k. multicoloured	40	15

1925 Medical Check-up of Cosmonauts

1980. Soviet–Hungarian Space Flight. Multicoloured.

5005	6k. Type **1925**	50	25
5006	15k. Crew meeting on "Salyut-6" space station	80	50
5007	32k. Press conference	1·40	1·20

1926 Red Fox

1980. Fur-bearing Animals. Multicoloured.

5008	2k. Type **1926**	20	15
5009	4k. Artic fox (horiz)	40	35
5010	6k. European mink	60	50
5011	10k. Coypu	80	70
5012	15k. Sable (horiz)	1·20	1·00

1927 Kazan

1980. 60th Anniv of Tatar Republic.

5013	**1927**	4k. multicoloured	40	15

1928 College and Emblem

1980. 150th Anniv of Bauman Technical College, Moscow.

5014	**1928**	4k. multicoloured	40	15

1929 Ho Chi Minh

1980. 90th Birth Anniv of Ho Chi Minh (Vietnamese leader).

5015	**1929**	6k. multicoloured	50	25

1930 Arms, Monument and Modern Buildings

1980. 40th Anniv of Soviet Socialist Republics of Lithuania, Latvia and Estonia. Multicoloured.

5016	**1930**	4k. Lithuania	40	15
5017	-	4k. Latvia	40	15
5018	-	4k. Estonia	40	15

1933 Crew of "Soyuz 27" at Launching Site

1980. Soviet–Vietnamese Space Flight. Multicoloured.

5019	6k. Type **1933**	60	50
5020	15k. Cosmonauts at work in space	1·20	1·00
5021	32k. Cosmonauts returning to Earth	2·10	1·90

1934 Avicenna (after E. Sokdov and M. Gerasimov)

1980. Birth Millenary of Avicenna (Arab philosopher and physician).

5022	**1934**	4k. multicoloured	40	15

1935 "Khadi-7" Gas turbine Car

1980. Racing cars designed by Kharkov Automobile and Road-building Institute. Multicoloured.

5023	2k. Type **1935**	20	15
5024	6k. "Khadi-10" piston engined car	50	35
5025	15k. "Khadi-11 E" electric car	80	70
5026	32k. "Khadi-13 E" electric car	1·40	1·20

1936 Arms, Flags, Government House and Industrial Complex

1980. 60th Anniv of Kazakh Soviet Socialist Republic.

5027	**1936**	4k. multicoloured	40	15

1937 "Self-portrait" and "The Spring"

1980. Birth Bicent of Jean Ingres (French painter).

5028	**1937**	32k. multicoloured	2·00	1·40

1938 "Morning on Kulikovo Field" (A. Bubnov)

1980. 600th Anniv of Battle of Kulikovo.

5029	**1938**	4k. multicoloured	50	20

1939 Town Hall

1980. 950th Anniv of Tartu, Estonia.

5030	**1939**	4k. multicoloured	50	20

1940 Yuri V. Malyshev and Valdimir V. Aksenov

1980. "Soyuz T-2" Space Flight.

5031	**1940**	10k. multicoloured	75	55

1941 Theoretical Training

1980. 20th Anniv of Gagarin Cosmonaut Training Centre. Multicoloured.

5032	6k. Type **1941**	50	25
5033	15k. Practical training	75	55
5034	32k. Physical endurance tests	1·30	90

1942 Crew Training

1980. Soviet–Cuban Space Flight. Multicoloured.

5035	6k. Type **1942**	25	20
5036	15k. Physical exercise on board space complex	50	35
5037	32k. Returned cosmonauts and space capsule	1·30	1·00

1943 "Bargaining" (Nevrev) (image scaled to 50% of original size)

1980. 150th Birth Anniv of N. V. Nevrev and K. D. Flavitsky (painters). Multicoloured.

5038	6k. Type **1943**	65	25
5039	6k. "Princess Tarakanova" (Flavitsky)	65	25

1944 Vasilevsky

1980. 85th Birth Anniv of Marshal A. M. Vasilevsky.

5040	**1944**	4k. green	50	20

1945 Banner

1980. 63rd Anniv of October Revolution.

5041	**1945**	4k. red, gold and purple	50	20

1946 Guramishvili

1980. 275th Birth Anniv of David Guramishvili (Georgian poet).

5042	**1946**	4k. green, silver and black	50	20

1947 Ioffe

1980. Birth Centenary of A. F. Ioffe (physicist).

5043	**1947**	4k. brown and buff	50	20

1948 Siberian Cedar

1980. Trees. Multicoloured.

5044	2k. Type **1948**	25	20
5045	4k. Pedunculate oak	25	20
5046	6k. Lime (vert)	40	25
5047	10k. Sea buckthorn	50	35
5048	15k. Ash	75	55

1949 Misha the Bear (Olympic mascot)

1980. Completion of Olympic Games, Moscow. Sheet 93×73 mm.

MS5049	**1949**	1r. multicoloured	20·00	13·50

1950 Suvorov (after N. Utkin)

1980. 250th Birth Anniv of Field Marshal A. V. Suvorov.

5050	**1950**	4k. blue	50	20

1951 State Emblem and Republican Government House

1980. 60th Anniv of Armenian Soviet Socialist Republic.

5051	**1951**	4k. multicoloured	50	20

1952 Blok (after K. Somov)

1980. Birth Cent of Aleksandr Aleksandrovich Blok (poet).

5052	**1952**	4k. multicoloured	50	20

1980. Soviet Scientific Research Ships (2nd series). As T **1907**. Multicoloured.

5053	2k. "Ayu-Dag"	25	20
5054	3k. "Valerian Uryvaev"	25	20
5055	4k. "Mikhail Somov"	50	20
5056	6k. "Akademik Sergei Korolev"	65	35
5057	10k. "Otto Schmidt"	1·00	70
5058	15k. "Akademik Mstislav Keldysh"	1·30	1·00

1953 Spassky Tower and Kremlin Palace of Congresses

1980. New Year.

5059	**1953**	4k. multicoloured	50	20

1955 Sable in Cedar

1980. Perf or imperf (2r.), perf (others).

5060	-	3k. orange	25	20
5061	-	5k. blue	75	35
5063	**1955**	35k. olive	3·00	2·20
5064	-	45k. brown	3·25	2·30
5066	-	50k. green	5·00	3·50
5067a	-	2r. black	1·50	1·10
5068	-	3r. black	18·00	12·50
5069	-	3r. green	5·00	3·50
5071	-	5r. blue	10·00	7·25

DESIGNS—14×22 mm: 3k. State flag; 5k. Forms of transport. 22×33 mm: 45k. Spassky Tower; 50k. Vodovzodny Tower and Grand Palace, Moscow Kremlin; 2r. "Arklika" atomic ice-breaker; 3r. Globe, child and olive branch; 5r. Globe and feather ("Peace").

1957 Institute Building

1980. 50th Anniv of Institute for Advanced Training of Doctors.

5075	**1957**	4k. multicoloured	50	20

1958 Lenin Monument, Leningrad, and Dneproges Hydro-electric Station

1980. 60th Anniv of GOELRO (electrification plan).
5076 **1958** 4k. multicoloured 50 20

1959 Nesmeyanov

1980. Academician A. N. Nesmeyanov (organic chemist) Commemoration.
5077 **1959** 4k. multicoloured 50 20

1960 Nagatinsky Bridge

1980. Moscow Bridges. Multicoloured.
5078 4k. Type **1960** 50 20
5079 6k. Luzhniki underground railway bridge 65 35
5080 15k. Kalininsky bridge 1·00 70

1961 Timoshenko

1980. Tenth Death Anniv of Marshal S. K. Timoshenko.
5081 **1961** 4k. purple 50 20

1962 Indian and Russian Flags with Government House, New Delhi

1980. President Brezhnev's Visit to India.
5082 **1962** 4k. multicoloured 75 55

1963 Antarctic Research Station

1981. Antarctic Exploration. Multicoloured.
5083 4k. Type **1963** 50 20
5084 6k. Antennae, rocket, weather balloon and tracked vehicle (Meteorological research) 75 55
5085 15k. Map of Soviet bases and supply ship "Ob" 1·80 1·30

1964 Arms and Symbols of Agriculture and Industry

1981. 60th Anniv of Dagestan Autonomous Soviet Socialist Republic.
5086 **1964** 4k. multicoloured 75 35

1965 Hockey Players and Emblem

1981. 12th World Hockey Championships, Khabarovsk.
5087 **1965** 6k. multicoloured 75 55

1966 Banner and Star

1981. 26th Soviet Communist Party Congress. Multicoloured.
5088 4k. Type **1966** 50 20
5089 20k. Kremlin Palace of Congresses and Lenin (51×36 mm) 3·00 2·20

1967 Lenin and Congress Building

1981. 26th Ukraine Communist Party Congress.
5090 **1967** 4k. multicoloured 75 35

1968 Keldysh

1981. 70th Birth Anniv of Academician Mtislav Vsevolodovich Keldysh (mathematician).
5091 **1968** 4k. multicoloured 75 35

1969 Banner and Kremlin Palace of Congress

1981. 26th Soviet Communist Party Congress (2nd issue). Sheet 97×74 mm.
MS5092 **1969** 50k. multicoloured 5·00 3·50

1970 Baikal–Amur Railway

1981. Construction Projects of the Tenth Five Year Plan. Multicoloured.
5093 4k. Type **1970** 50 20
5094 4k. Urengoi gas field 50 20
5095 4k. Sayano-Shushenakaya hydro-electric dam 50 20
5096 4k. Atommash Volga–Don atomic reactor 50 20
5097 4k. Syktyvkar paper mill 50 20
5098 4k. Giant excavator, Ekibastuz 50 20

1971 Freighter and Russian and Indian Flags

1981. 25th Anniv of Soviet–Indian Shipping Line.
5099 **1971** 15k. multicoloured 2·00 1·40

1972 Arms, Monument and Building

1981. 60th Anniv of Georgian Soviet Socialist Republic.
5100 **1972** 4k. multicoloured 75 35

1973 Arms and Abkhazian Scenes

1981. 60th Anniv of Abkhazian Autonomous Soviet Socialist Republic.
5101 **1973** 4k. multicoloured 75 35

1974 Institute Building

1981. 60th Anniv of Moscow Electrotechnical Institute of Communications.
5102 **1974** 4k. multicoloured 75 35

1975 Communications Equipment and Satellite

1981. 30th All-Union Amateur Radio Exhibition.
5103 **1975** 4k. multicoloured 75 35

1976 L. I. Popov and V. V. Ryumin

1981. 185 Days in Space of Cosmonauts Popov and Ryumin. Multicoloured.
5104 15k. Type **1976** 1·30 90
5105 15k. "Salyut 6"–"Soyuz" complex 1·30 90

1977 O. G. Makarov, L. D. Kizim and G. M. Strekalov

1981. "Soyuz T-3" Space Flight.
5106 **1977** 10k. multicoloured 1·30 90

1978 Rocket Launch

1981. Soviet–Mongolian Space Flight. Multicoloured.
5107 6k. Type **1978** 75 35
5108 15k. Mongolians watching space flight on television 1·30 90
5109 32k. Re-entry stages 2·50 1·80

1979 Bering

1981. 300th Birth Anniv of Vitus Bering (navigator).
5110 **1979** 4k. blue 75 35

1980 Yuri Gagarin and Globe

1981. 20th Anniv of First Manned Space Flight. Multicoloured.
5111 6k. Type **1980** 50 25
5112 15k. S. P. Korolev (spaceship designer) 1·50 1·10
5113 32k. Statue of Gagarin and "Interkosmos" emblem 3·00 2·20
MS5114 102×62 mm. 50k. Head of Gagarin (51×36 mm) 15·00 9·00

1981 "Salyut" Orbital Space Station

1981. Tenth Anniv of First Manned Space Station.
5115 **1981** 32k. multicoloured 3·25 2·30

1982 Lenin (after P. V. Vasilev)

1981. 111th Birth Anniv of Lenin. Sheet 93×91 mm.
MS5116 **1982** 50k. multicoloured 3·75 2·75

1983 Prokofiev

1981. 90th Birth Anniv of S. S. Prokofiev (composer).
5117 **1983** 4k. lilac 50 20

1984 New Hofburg Palace, Vienna

1981. "WIPA 1981" International Stamp Exhibition, Vienna.
5118 **1984** 15k. multicoloured 2·00 1·40

1985 Arms, Industrial Complex and Docks

1981. 60th Anniv of Adzharskian Autonomous Soviet Socialist Republic.
5119 **1985** 4k. multicoloured 50 20

1986 N. N. Benardos

1981. Centenary of Invention of Welding.
5120 **1986** 6k. multicoloured 65 25

1987 Congress Emblem

1981. 14th Congress of International Union of Architects, Warsaw.
5121 **1987** 15k. multicoloured 2·00 1·40

1988 "Albanian Girl in Doorway" (A. A. Ivanov)

1981. Paintings. Multicoloured.
5122 10k. Type **1988** 1·00 55
5123 10k. "Sunset over Sea at Livorno" (N. N. Ge) (horiz) 1·00 55
5124 10k. "Demon" (M. A. Vrubel) (horiz) 1·00 55
5125 10k. "Horseman" (F. A. Rubo) 1·00 55

1989 Flight Simulator

1981. Soviet–Rumanian Space Flight. Multicoloured.
5126 6k. Type **1989** 50 20
5127 15k. "Salyut"–"Soyuz" space complex 1·00 55
5128 32k. Cosmonauts greeting journalists after return 2·30 1·30

1990 "Primula minima"

1981. Flowers of the Carpathians. Multicoloured.
5129 4k. Type **1990** 25 15
5130 6k. "Carlina acaulis" 50 30
5131 10k. "Parageum montanum" 75 45
5132 15k. "Atragene alpina" 1·00 60
5133 32k. "Rhododendron kotschyi" 2·50 1·50

1991 Gyandzhevi

1981. 840th Birth Anniv of Nizami Gyandzhevi (poet and philosopher).
5134 **1991** 4k. brown, yellow & green 50 15

1992 Longo

1981. Luigi Longo (Italian politician). Commem.
5135 **1992** 6k. multicoloured 65 20

1993 Running

1981. Sports. Multicoloured.
5136 4k. Type **1993** 25 15
5137 6k. Football 50 30
5138 10k. Throwing the discus 75 45
5139 15k. Boxing 1·00 60
5140 32k. Swimmer on block 2·50 1·50

1994 Flag and Arms of Mongolia

1981. 60th Anniv of Revolution in Mongolia.
5141 **1994** 6k. multicoloured 50 15

1995 Spassky Tower and Film encircling Globe

1981. 12th International Film Festival, Moscow.
5142 **1995** 15k. multicoloured 2·00 1·20

1996 "Lenin"

1981. River Ships. Multicoloured.
5143 4k. Type **1996** 50 30
5144 6k. "Kosmonavt Gagarin" (tourist ship) 75 45
5145 15k. "Valerian Kuibyshev" (tourist ship) 1·80 1·00
5146 32k. "Baltysky" (freighter) 3·50 2·00

1981. Russian Ice-breakers (4th issue). As T **1775**. Multicoloured.
5147 15k. "Malygin" 2·30 1·30

1997 Industry

1981. Resolutions of the 26th Party Congress. Multicoloured.
5148 4k. Type **1997** 50 30
5149 4k. Agriculture 50 30
5150 4k. Energy 50 30
5151 4k. Transport and communications 50 30
5152 4k. Arts and science 50 30
5153 4k. International co-operation 50 30

1998 Ulyanov

1981. 150th Birth Anniv of I. N. Ulyanov (Lenin's father).
5154 **1998** 4k. brown, black & green 50 15

1999 Facade of Theatre

1981. 225th Anniv of Pushkin Drama Theatre, Leningrad.
5155 **1999** 6k. multicoloured 65 20

2000 Brushes, Palette and Gerasimov

1981. Birth Centenary of A. M. Gerasimov (artist).
5156 **2000** 4k. multicoloured 50 15

2001 Institute Building

1981. 50th Anniv of Institute of Physical Chemistry, Academy of Sciences, Moscow.
5157 **2001** 4k. multicoloured 50 15

2002 Severtzov's Tit Warbler

1981. Song Birds. Multicoloured.
5158 6k. Type **2002** 50 30
5159 10k. Asiatic paradise flycatcher (vert) 75 45
5160 15k. Jankowski's bunting 1·30 75
5161 20k. Vinous-throated parrotbill (vert) 1·50 85
5162 32k. Hodgson's bushchat (vert) 2·50 1·50

2003 Arms and Industrial Scenes

1981. 60th Anniv of Komi A.S.S.R.
5163 **2003** 4k. multicoloured 50 15

2004 Orbiting Satellite and Exhibition Emblem

1981. "Svyaz 81" Communications Exhibition.
5164 **2004** 4k. multicoloured 50 15

2005 Buildings, Arms and Monument

1981. 60th Anniv of Kabardino-Balkar A.S.S.R.
5165 **2005** 4k. multicoloured 50 15

2006 Soviet Soldier (monument, Treptow Park, Berlin)

1981. 25th Anniv of Soviet War Veterans Committee.
5166 **2006** 4k. multicoloured 50 15

2007 Four-masted Barque "Tovarishch"

1981. Cadet Sailing Ships. Multicoloured.
5167 4k. Type **2007** 50 15
5168 6k. Barquentine "Vega" 65 30
5169 10k. Schooner "Kodor" (vert) 75 45
5170 15k. Three-masted barque "Tovarishch" 1·00 60
5171 20k. Four-masted barque "Kruzenshtern" 1·50 85
5172 32k. Four-masted barque "Sedov" (vert) 2·00 1·20

2008 Russian and Kazakh Citizens with Flags

1981. 250th Anniv of Unification of Russia and Kazakhstan.
5173 **2008** 4k. multicoloured 50 15

2009 Lavrentev

1981. Academician Mikhail Alekseevich Lavrentev (mathematician) Commemoration.
5174 **2009** 4k. multicoloured 50 15

2010 Kremlin Palace of Congresses, Moscow, and Arch of the General Staff, Leningrad

1981. 64th Anniv of October Revolution.
5175 **2010** 4k. multicoloured 50 15

2011 Transmitter, Dish Aerial and "Ekran" Satellite

1981. "Ekran" Television Satellite.
5176 **2011** 4k. multicoloured 50 15

2012 V. V. Kovalyonok and V. P. Savinykh

1981. "Soyuz T-4"–"Salyut 6" Space Complex. Multicoloured.
5177 10k. Type **2012** 75 45
5178 10k. Microscope slide, crystal and text 75 45

2013 Picasso

1981. Birth Centenary of Pablo Picasso (artist). Sheet 101×71 mm.
MS5179 **2013** 50k. olive, sepia and blue 7·50 4·25

2014 Merkurov

1981. Birth Centenary of Sergei Dmitrievich Merkurov (sculptor).
5180 **2014** 4k. brown, green & bis 50 15

2015 "Autumn" (Nino A. Piromanashvili)

1981. Paintings by Georgian Artists. Multicoloured.
5181 4k. Type **2015** 25 15
5182 6k. "Gurian Woman" (Sh. G. Kikodze) 50 30
5183 10k. "Travelling Companions" (U. M. Dzhaparidze) (horiz) 75 45
5184 15k. "Shota Rustaveli" (S. S. Kobuladze) 1·00 60
5185 32k. "Tea Pickers" (V. D. Gudi-ashvili" (horiz)) 2·50 1·50

2016 Arms and Saviour Tower, Moscow

1981. New Year.
5186 **2016** 4k. multicoloured 50 15

2017 Horse-drawn Sleigh (19th century)

1981. Moscow Municipal Transport.
5187 **2017** 4k. brown and silver 25 15
5188 - 6k. green and silver 40 20
5189 - 10k. lilac and silver 50 30
5190 - 15k. black and silver 75 45
5191 - 20k. brown and silver 1·30 75
5192 - 32k. red and silver 2·00 1·20

DESIGNS: 6k. Horse tram (19th century); 10k. Horse-drawn cab (19th century); 15k. Taxi, 1926; 20k. British Leyland bus, 1926; 32k. Electric tram, 1912.

2018 Saviour Tower, Moscow and Rashtrapati Bhavan Palace, New Delhi

1981. Inauguration of Tropospheric Communications Link between U.S.S.R. and India. Sheet 123×67 mm.
MS5193 **2018** 50k. multicoloured 3·50 2·00

2019 Modern Kiev

1982. 1500th Anniv of Kiev.
5194 **2019** 10k. multicoloured 1·00 60

2020 S. P. Korolev

1982. 75th Birth Anniv of Academician S. P. Korolev (spaceship designer).
5195 **2020** 4k. multicoloured 50 15

2021 Arms and Industrial Complex

1982. 60th Anniv of Checheno-Ingush A.S.S.R.
5196 **2021** 4k. multicoloured 50 15

2022 Arms and Construction Sites

1982. 60th Anniv of Yakut A.S.S.R.
5197 **2022** 4k. multicoloured 50 15

2023 Hikmet

1982. 80th Birth Anniv of Nazim Hikmet (Turkish poet).
5198 **2023** 6k. multicoloured 65 20

2024 "The Oaks"

1982. 150th Birth Anniv of I. I. Shishkin (artist).
5199 **2024** 6k. multicoloured 75 45

2025 Trade Unionists and World Map

1982. Tenth World Trade Unions Congress, Havana.
5200 **2025** 15k. multicoloured 1·00 60

2026 Kremlin Palace of Congresses and Flag

1982. 17th Soviet Trade Unions Congress.
5201 **2026** 4k. multicoloured 50 15

2027 "Self-portrait"

1982. 150th Birth Anniv of Edouard Manet (artist).
5202 **2027** 32k. multicoloured 2·30 1·30

2028 Show Jumping

1982. Soviet Horse breeding. Multicoloured.
5203 4k. Type **2028** 25 15
5204 6k. Dressage 50 30
5205 15k. Racing 1·00 60

2029 Tito

1982. President Tito of Yugoslavia Commemoration.
5206 **2029** 6k. brown and black 65 20

2030 University, Book and Monument

1982. 350th Anniv of University of Tartu.
5207 **2030** 4k. multicoloured 50 15

2031 Heart on Globe

1982. Ninth Int Cardiologists Conference, Moscow.
5208 **2031** 15k. multicoloured 1·00 60

2032 Shooting and Skating

1982. Fifth Winter Spartakiad. Sheet 93×66 mm.
MS5209 **2032** 50k. multicoloured 3·25 1·90

2033 Cloudberry

1982. Wild Berries. Multicoloured.
5210 4k. Type **2033** 25 15
5211 6k. Blueberries 40 20
5212 10k. Inscr 'Stoneberry' 50 30
5213 15k. Cherry 1·00 60
5214 32k. Strawberry 2·00 1·20

2034 "Venera 13" and "14"

1982. "Venera" Space Flights to Venus.
5215 **2034** 10k. multicoloured 75 45

2035 "M. I. Lopukhina" (V. L. Borovikovsky)

1982. Paintings. Multicoloured.
5216 6k. Type **2035** 65 20
5217 6k. "E. V. Davydov" (O. A. Kiprensky) 65 20
5218 6k. "The Unequal Marriage" (V. V. Pukirev) 65 20

2036 Chukovsky

1982. Birth Cent of K. I. Chukovsky (author).
5219 **2036** 4k. black and grey 50 15

2037 Rocket, "Soyuz" Spaceship, Globe and Space Station

1982. Cosmonautics Day.
5220 **2037** 6k. multicoloured 65 20

2038 Lenin (sculpture, N. V. Tomsky)

1982. 112th Birth Anniv of Lenin. Sheet 68×87 mm.
MS5221 **2038** 50k. multicoloured 3·25 1·90

2039 Solovev-Sedoi

1982. 75th Birth Anniv of V. P. Solovev-Sedoi (composer).
5222 **2039** 4k. brown 50 15

2040 Dimitrov

1982. Birth Centenary of Georgi Dimitrov (Bulgarian statesman).
5223 **2040** 6k. green 65 20

2041 Masthead

1982. 70th Anniv of "Pravda" (Communist Party Newspaper).

5224	**2041**	4k. multicoloured	50	15

2042 Congress Emblem and Ribbons

1982. 19th Congress of Leninist Young Communist League (Komsomol).

5225	**2042**	4k. multicoloured	50	15

2043 Globe and Hands holding Seedling

1982. Tenth Anniv of U.N. Environment Programme.

5226	**2043**	6k. multicoloured	65	20

2044 Pioneers

1982. 60th Anniv of Pioneer Organization.

5227	**2044**	4k. multicoloured	50	15

2045 I.T.U. Emblem, Satellite and Receiving Station

1982. I.T.U. Delegates' Conference, Nairobi.

5228	**2045**	15k. multicoloured	1·00	60

2046 Class VL-80t Electric Locomotive

1982. Locomotives. Multicoloured.

5229	4k. Type **2046**	50	15
5230	6k. Class TEP-75 diesel	65	30
5231	10k. Class TEM-7 diesel	1·30	75
5232	15k. Class VL-82m electric	2·30	1·30
5233	32k. Class EP-200 electric	3·75	2·20

2047 Players with Trophy and Football

1982. World Cup Football Championship, Spain.

5234	**2047**	20k. lilac, yellow and brown	1·30	75

2048 Hooded Crane

1982. 18th International Ornithological Congress, Moscow. Multicoloured.

5235	2k. Type **2048**	25	15
5236	4k. Steller's sea eagle	40	20
5237	6k. Spoon-billed sandpiper	50	30
5238	10k. Bar-headed goose	1·00	45
5239	15k. Sociable plover	1·30	60
5240	32k. White stork	2·50	1·30

2049 Buildings and Workers with Picks

1982. 50th Anniv of Komsomolsk-on-Amur.

5241	**2049**	4k. multicoloured	50	15

2050 "The Cart"

1982. Birth Centenary of M. B. Grekov (artist).

5242	**2050**	6k. multicoloured	75	45

2051 U.N. Flag

1982. Second U.N. Conference on the Exploration and Peaceful Uses of Outer Space, Vienna.

5243	**2051**	15k. multicoloured	1·30	75

2052 Scientific Research in Space

1982. Soviet–French Space Flight. Multicoloured.

5244	6k. Type **2052**	65	20
5245	20k. Rocket and trajectory	1·30	75
5246	45k. Satellites and globe	2·50	1·50
MS5247	96×68 mm. 50k. Flags, space station and emblems (41×29 mm)	3·25	1·90

2053 "Legend of the Golden Cockerel" (P. I. Sosin)

1982. Lacquerware Paintings. Multicoloured.

5248	6k. Type **2053**	65	20
5249	10k. "Minin's Appeal to Count Pozharsky" (I. A. Fomichev)	75	30
5250	15k. "Two Peasants" (A. F. Kotyagin)	1·00	60
5251	20k. "The Fisherman" (N. P. Klykov)	1·50	85
5252	32k. "Arrest of the Propagandists" (N. I. Shishakov)	2·00	1·20

2054 Early Telephone, Moscow, Leningrad, Odessa and Riga

1982. Telephone Centenary.

5253	**2054**	4k. multicoloured	50	15

2055 P. Schilling (inventor)

1982. 150th Anniv of Electro-magnetic Telegraph in Russia.

5254	**2055**	6k. multicoloured	65	20

2056 Gymnast and Television Screen

1982. Intervision Cup Gymnastics Contest.

5255	**2056**	15k. multicoloured	1·00	60

2057 Mastyazhart Glider, 1923

1982. Gliders (1st series). Multicoloured.

5256	4k. Type **2057**	50	15
5257	6k. Red Star, 1930	65	30
5258	10k. TsAGI-2, 1934	1·00	60
5259	20k. Stakhanovets, 1939 (60×27 mm)	2·00	1·20
5260	32k. GR-29, 1941 (60×27 mm)	2·50	1·50

See also Nos. 5301/5.

2058 Garibaldi

1982. 175th Birth Anniv of Giuseppe Garibaldi.

5261	**2058**	6k. multicoloured	65	20

2059 Emblem

1982. 25th Anniv of International Atomic Energy Agency.

5262	**2059**	20k. multicoloured	1·30	75

2060 F.I.D.E. Emblem, Chess Symbol for Queen and Equestrian Statue

1982. World Chess Championship Interzone Tournaments for Women (Tbilisi) and Men (Moscow). Multicoloured.

5263	6k. Type **2060**	75	30
5264	6k. F.I.D.E. emblem, chess symbol for King and Kremlin tower	75	30

2061 Shaposhnikov

1982. Birth Cent of Marshal B. M. Shaposhnikov.

5265	**2061**	4k. brown	50	15

2062 Clenched Fist

1982. 70th Anniv of African National Congress.

5266	**2062**	6k. multicoloured	65	20

2063 Botkin

1982. 150th Birth Anniv of S. P. Botkin (therapeutist).

5267	**2063**	4k. green	50	15

2064 "Sputnik 1"

1982. 25th Anniv of First Artificial Satellite. Sheet 92×62 mm.

MS5268	**2064**	50k. multicoloured	3·75	2·20

А. КАРПОВ —
обладатель восьми
„Шахматных Оскаров"
(2065)

1982. Anatoly Karpov's Victory in World Chess Championship. No. 5264 optd with T **2065**.

5269	6k. multicoloured	1·00	60

2066 Submarine "S-56"

1982. Soviet Naval Ships. Multicoloured.

5270	4k Type **2066**	50	15
5271	6k. Minelayer "Gremyashchy"	65	20
5272	15k. Minesweeper "Gafel"	1·00	60
5273	20k. Cruiser "Krasnyi Krim"	1·50	85
5274	45k. Battleship "Sevastopol"	3·25	1·90

2067 Flag and Arms

1982. 65th Anniv of October Revolution.

5275	**2067**	4k. multicoloured	50	15

2068 House of the Soviets, Moscow

1982. 60th Anniv of U.S.S.R. Multicoloured.

5276	10k. Type **2068**	75	30
5277	10k. Dneiper Dam and statue	75	30
5278	10k. Soviet war memorial and resistance poster	75	30
5279	10k. Newspaper, worker holding peace text, and sun illuminating city	75	30
5280	10k. Workers' Monument, Moscow, rocket, Ilyushin Il-86 jetliner and factories	75	30
5281	10k. Soviet arms and Kremlin tower	75	30

See also No. **MS**5290.

Всесоюзная
филателистическая
выставка

(2069)

1982. All-Union Stamp Exhibition, Moscow. No. 5280 optd with T **2069**.

5282	10k. multicoloured	2·00	1·20

2070 "Portrait of an Actor" (Domenico Fetti)

1982. Italian Paintings in the Hermitage Museum, Leningrad. Multicoloured.

5283	4k. Type **2070**	50	15
5284	10k. "St. Sebastian" (Pietro Perugino)	75	45
5285	20k. "Danae" (Titian) (horiz)	1·50	85
5286	45k. "Portrait of a Woman" (Correggio)	2·50	1·50
5287	50k. "Portrait of a Young Man" (Capriolo)	3·75	2·20
MS5288	46×81 mm. 50k.×2 "Portrait of a Young Woman" (Francesco Melzi)	8·00	4·75

2072 Hammer and Sickle, Clock and Date

1982. New Year.

5289	**2072** 4k. multicoloured	50	15

2073 Lenin

1982. 60th Anniv of U.S.S.R. (2nd issue). Sheet 85×96 mm.

MS5290	**2073** 50k. green and gold	3·00	1·70

2074 Camp and Route to Summit of Mt. Everest

1982. Soviet Ascent of Mount Everest. Sheet 66×86 mm.

MS5291	**2074** 50k. multicoloured	4·00	2·30

2075 Kherson Lighthouse, Black Sea

1982. Lighthouses (1st series). Multicoloured.

5292	6k. Type **2075**	65	30
5293	6k. Vorontsov lighthouse, Odessa, Black Sea	65	30
5294	6k. Temryuk lighthouse, Sea of Azov	65	30
5295	6k. Novorossiisk lighthouse, Black Sea	65	30
5296	6k. Dneiper harbour light	65	30

See also Nos. 5362/6 and 5449/53.

2076 F. P. Tolstoi

1983. Birth Bicentenary of Fyodor Petrovich Tolstoi (artist).

5297	**2076** 4k. multicoloured	50	15

2077 Masthead of "Iskra"

1983. 80th Anniv of 2nd Social Democratic Workers' Congress.

5298	**2077** 4k. multicoloured	50	15

2078 Army Star and Flag

1983. 65th Anniv of U.S.S.R. Armed Forces.

5299	**2078** 4k. multicoloured	50	15

2079 Ilyushin Il-86 Jetliner over Globe

1983. 60th Anniv of Aeroflot (state airline). Sheet 73×99 mm.

MS5300	**2079** 50k. multicoloured	3·00	1·70

1983. Gliders (2nd series). As T **2057**. Multicoloured.

5301	2k. Antonov A-9, 1948	25	15
5302	4k. Sumonov KAU-12, 1957	50	20
5303	6k. Antonov A-15, 1960	65	30
5304	20k. SA-7, 1970	2·00	1·20
5305	45k. LAK-12, 1979	4·25	2·50

2080 "The Holy Family"

1983. 500th Birth Anniv of Raphael (artist).

5306	**2080** 50k. multicoloured	2·50	1·50

2081 B. N. Petrov

1983. 70th Birth Anniv of Academician B. N. Petrov (chairman of Interkosmos).

5307	**2081** 4k. multicoloured	50	15

2082 Tashkent Buildings

1983. 2000th Anniv of Tashkent.

5308	**2082** 4k. multicoloured	50	15

2083 Popov, Serebrov and Savitskaya

1983. "Soyuz T-7"–"Salyut 7"–"Soyuz T-5" Space Flight.

5309	**2083** 10k. multicoloured	1·00	60

2084 Globe within Posthorn

1983. World Communications Year. Sheet 72×107 mm.

MS5310	**2084** 50k. multicoloured	3·25	1·90

2085 Aleksandrov and Bars of Music

1983. Birth Centenary of A. V. Aleksandrov (composer).

5311	**2085** 4k. multicoloured	50	15

2086 "Portrait of an Old Woman"

1983. Rembrandt Paintings in Hermitage Museum, Leningrad. Multicoloured.

5312	4k. Type **2086**	50	15
5313	10k. "Portrait of a Learned Man"	1·00	60
5314	20k. "Old Warrior"	1·80	1·00
5315	45k. "Portrait of Mrs B. Martens Doomer"	3·50	2·00
5316	50k. "Sacrifice of Abraham"	3·75	2·20
MS5317	144×81 mm. 50k.×2 "Portrait of an Old Man in Red"	7·50	4·25

2087 Space Complex

1983. Cosmonautics Day. Sheet 61×91 mm.

MS5318	**2087** 50k. multicoloured	3·25	1·90

2088 "Revolution is a Storm" (N. N. Zhukov)

1983. 113th Birth Aniv of Lenin. Sheet 73×91 mm.

MS5319	**2088** 50k. brown	3·25	1·90

2089 A. N. Berezovoi and V. V. Lebedev

1983. 211 Days in Space of Berezovoi and Lebedev. Multicoloured.

5320	10k. Type **2089**	1·00	60
5321	10k. "Salyut 7"–"Soyuz T" space complex	1·00	60

2090 Marx

1983. Death Centenary of Karl Marx.

5322	**2090** 4k. multicoloured	50	15

2091 Memorial, Building and Hydrofoil

1983. Rostov-on-Don.

5323	**2091** 4k. multicoloured	50	15

2092 Kirov Theatre

1983. Bicentenary of Kirov Opera and Ballet Theatre, Leningrad.

5324	**2092** 4k. black, blue and gold	50	15

2093 Arms, Communications and Industrial Complex

1983. 60th Anniv of Buryat A.S.S.R.

5325	**2093** 4k. multicoloured	50	15

2094 Sports Vignettes

1983. Eighth Summer Spartakiad.

5326	**2094** 6k. multicoloured	65	20

2095 Khachaturyan

1983. 80th Birth Anniv of Aram I. Khachaturyan (composer).

5327	**2095** 4k. brown	50	15

2096 Tractor and Factory

1983. 50th Anniv of Lenin Tractor Factory, Chelyabinsk.

5328	**2096** 4k. multicoloured	50	15

2097 Simon Bolivar

1983. Birth Bicentenary of Simon Bolivar.

5329	**2097**	6k. deep brown, brown and black	65	20

2098 18th-century Warship and modern Missile Cruiser "Groznyi"

1983. Bicentenary of Sevastopol.

5330	**2098**	5k. multicoloured	75	30

2099 Snowdrops

1983. Spring Flowers. Multicoloured.

5331	4k. Type **2099**	40	15
5332	6k. Siberian squills	50	30
5333	10k. "Anemone hepatica"	1·00	60
5334	15k. Cyclamen	1·50	85
5335	20k. Yellow star of Bethlehem	2·00	1·20

2100 "Vostok 6" and Tereshkova

1983. 20th Anniv of First Woman Cosmonaut Valentina V. Tereshkova's Space Flight.

5336	**2100**	10k. multicoloured	75	45

2101 P. N. Pospelov

1983. 85th Birth Anniv of Pyotr Nicolaievich Pospelov (scientist).

5337	**2101**	4k. multicoloured	50	15

2102 Congress Emblem

1983. Tenth European Rheumatologists' Congress, Moscow.

5338	**2102**	4k. multicoloured	50	15

2103 Film around Globe and Festival Emblem

1983. 13th International Film Festival, Moscow.

5339	**2103**	20k. multicoloured	1·50	85

2104 Vakhtangov

1983. Birth Centenary of Ye. B. Vakhtangov (producer and actor).

5340	**2104**	5k. multicoloured	75	30

2105 Coastal Trawlers

1983. Fishing Vessels. Multicoloured.

5341	4k. Type **2105**	40	15
5342	6k. Refrigerated trawler	50	30
5343	10k. "Pulkovsky Meridian" (deep-sea trawler)	75	45
5344	15k. Refrigerated freighter	1·30	75
5345	20k. "50 Let SSR" (factory ship)	1·80	1·00

2106 "U.S.S.R.-1"

1983. 50th Anniv of Stratosphere Balloon's Record Altitude Flight.

5346	**2106**	20k. multicoloured	2·00	1·20

2107 Sockeye Salmon

1983. Fish. Multicoloured.

5347	4k. Type **2107**	40	15
5348	6k. Zerro	50	30
5349	15k. Spotted wolffish	1·00	60
5350	20k. Round goby	1·50	85
5351	45k. Starry flounder	3·25	1·90

2108 Exhibition Emblem

1983. "Sozphilex 83" Stamp Exhibition, Moscow.

5352	**2108**	6k. multicoloured	65	20
MS5353		90×69 mm. 50k. green	3·75	2·20

DESIGN: 36×22 mm—50k. Moskva River.

2109 Posthorns

1983. 125th Anniv of First Russian Postage Stamp. Sheet 78×65 mm.

MS5354	**2109**	50k. stone and black	3·75	2·20

2110 S.W.A.P.O. Flag and Emblem

1983. Namibia Day.

5355	**2110**	5k. multicoloured	75	30

2111 Palestinian with Flag

1983. Palestinian Solidarity.

5356	**2111**	5k. multicoloured	75	30

2112 Emblem and Ostankino TV Tower, Moscow

1983. First European Radio-telegraphy Championship, Moscow.

5357	**2112**	6k. multicoloured	75	30

2113 Council Session Emblem

1983. Fourth UNESCO International Communications Development Programme Council Session, Tashkent.

5358	**2113**	10k. blue, mauve & black	1·00	60

2114 Mohammed al-Khorezmi

1983. 1200th Birth Anniv of Mohammed al-Khorezmi (astonomer and mathematician).

5359	**2114**	4k. multicoloured	50	15

2115 Yegorov

1983. Birth Centenary of Marshal A. I. Yegorov.

5360	**2115**	4k. purple	50	15

2116 Treaty

1983. Bicentenary of First Russian–Georgian Friendship Treaty.

5361	**2116**	6k. multicoloured	65	20

1983. Lighthouses (2nd series). As T **2075**. Multicoloured.

5362	1k. Kipu lighthouse, Baltic Sea	25	15
5363	5k. Keri lighthouse, Gulf of Finland	50	30
5364	10k. Stirsudden lighthouse, Gulf of Finland	75	45
5365	12k. Takhkun lighthouse, Baltic Sea	1·00	60
5366	20k. Tallin lighthouse, Gulf of Finland	1·80	1·00

2117 "Wife's Portrait with Flowers" (I. F. Khrutsky)

1983. Byelorussian Paintings. Multicoloured.

5367	4k. Type **2117**	40	15
5368	6k. "Early spring" (V. K. Byalynitsky-Birulya)	50	30
5369	15k. "Young Partisan" (E. A. Zaitsev) (vert)	1·00	60
5370	20k. "Partisan Madonna" (M. A. Savitsky) (vert)	1·50	85
5371	45k. "Corn Harvest" (V. K. Tsvirko)	3·25	1·90

2118 Steel Mill

1983. Centenary of Hammer and Sickle Steel Mill.

5372	**2118**	4k. multicoloured	50	15

2119 Grain Production

1983. Food Programme. Multicoloured.

5373	5k. Type **2119**	75	30
5374	5k. Cattle breeding	75	30
5375	5k. Fruit and vegetable production	75	30

2120 Banner and Symbols of Economic Growth

1983. 66th Anniv of October Revolution.

5376	**2120**	4k. multicoloured	50	15

2121 Ivan Fyodorov

1983. 400th Death Anniv of Ivan Fyodorov (printer) and 420th Anniv of Publication of "The Apostle" (first Russian printed book).

5377	**2121**	4k. black	50	15

2122 Pipeline Construction

1983. Inaug of Urengoi-Uzhgorod Gas Pipeline.

5378	**2122**	5k. multicoloured	75	30

2123 Sidorenko

1983. Academician A. V. Sidorenko (geologist) Commemoration.

5379	**2123**	4k. multicoloured	50	15

2124 Marchers pushing Nuclear Weapons off Globe

1983. Nuclear Disarmament.
5380 **2124** 5k. multicoloured 75 30

2125 Makhtumkuli

1983. 250th Birth Anniv of Makhtumkuli (Turkmen poet).
5381 **2125** 5k. multicoloured 75 30

2126 "Madonna and Child under Apple Tree" (Cranach the Elder)

1983. German Paintings in the Hermitage Museum. Multicoloured.
5382 4k. Type **2126** 40 15
5383 10k. "Self-portrait" (Anton Raphael Mengs) 75 45
5384 20k. "Self-portrait" (Jurgens Ovens) 1·30 75
5385 45k. "On Board a Sailing Vessel" (Caspar David Friedrich) 3·25 1·90
5386 50k. "Rape of the Sabine Women" (Johann Schonfeld) (horiz) 3·50 2·00
MS5387 144×79 mm. 50k.×2 "Portrait of a Young Man" (Holbein) 7·50 4·25

2127 Sukhe Bator

1983. 90th Birth Anniv of Sukhe Bator (Mongolian statesman).
5388 **2127** 5k. multicoloured 75 30

2128 Globe and Hand holding Baby

1983. International Association of Physicians against Nuclear War.
5389 **2128** 5k. multicoloured 75 30

2129 Moscow Kremlin Tower Star

1983. New Year.
5390 **2129** 5k. multicoloured 75 30

2130 Children's Music Theatre

1983. New Buildings in Moscow.
5391 **2130** 3k. green 25 15
5392 - 4k. blue 40 20
5393 - 6k. brown 50 30
5394 - 20k. green 1·30 75
5395 - 45k. green 2·50 1·50
DESIGNS—VERT: 4k. Hotel and Tourist Centre. HORIZ: 6k. Russian Federation Soviet (parliament building); 20k. Hotel Izmailovo; 45k. Novosti News and Press Agency.

2131 Mother and Child with Flowers

1983. Environmental Protection and Peace. Sheet 81×65 mm.
MS5396 **2131** 50k. multicoloured 4·50 2·50

2132 Cuban Flag

1984. 25th Anniv of Cuban Revolution.
5397 **2132** 5k. multicoloured 75 30

2133 Broadcasting Station

1984. 50th Anniv of Moscow Broadcasting Network.
5398 **2133** 4k. multicoloured 50 15

2134 Speed Skating

1984. Women's European Skating Championship, Alma-Ata.
5399 **2134** 5k. multicoloured 75 30

2135 "T-34" Medium Tank

1984. World War II Armoured Vehicles. Multicoloured.
5400 10k. Type **2135** 75 45
5401 10k. "KV" heavy tank 75 45
5402 10k. "IS-2" heavy tank 75 45
5403 10k. "SU-100" self-propelled gun 75 45
5404 10k. "ISU-152" heavy self-propelled gun 75 45

2136 Biathlon

1984. Winter Olympic Games, Sarajevo. Multicoloured.
5405 5k. Type **2136** 25 15
5406 10k. Speed skating 50 30
5407 20k. Ice hockey 1·00 60
5408 45k. Figure skating 2·30 1·30

2137 Mandrill

1984. 120th Anniv of Moscow Zoo. Multicoloured.
5409 2k. Type **2137** 25 15
5410 3k. Blesbok 25 15
5411 4k. Snow leopard 40 15
5412 5k. South African crowned crane 50 30
5413 20k. Blue and yellow macaw 2·00 1·20

2138 Gagarin

1984. 50th Birth Anniv of Yuri Alekseevich Gagarin (first man in Space).
5414 **2138** 15k. blue 1·00 60

2139 Young Farmers

1984. 30th Anniv of Development of Unused Land. Sheet 67×86 mm.
MS5415 **2139** 50k. multicoloured 3·25 1·90

2140 "E. K. Vorontsova" (George Hayter)

1984. English Paintings in Hermitage Museum, Leningrad. Multicoloured.
5416 4k. Type **2140** 25 15
5417 10k. "Portrait of Mrs. Harriet Greer" (George Romney) 50 30
5418 20k. "Approaching Storm" (George Morland) (horiz) 1·50 85
5419 45k. "Portrait of an Unknown Man" (Marcus Gheeraerts, the younger) 2·75 1·60
5420 50k. "Cupid untying the Robe of Venus" (Joshua Reynolds) 3·00 1·70
MS5421 144×80 mm. 50k.×2 "Portrait of a Lady in Blue" (Thomas Gainsborough) 6·25 3·50

2141 Ilyushin

1984. 90th Birth Anniv of Academician S. V. Ilyushin (aircraft designer).
5422 **2141** 5k. light brown, brown and black 65 20

2142 Bubnov

1984. Birth Centenary of Andrei Sergeevich Bubnov (Communist Party Leader).
5423 **2142** 5k. light brown, brown and black 65 20

2143 Launching Site of "M-100" Meteorological Station

1984. Soviet–Indian Space Co-operation. Multicoloured.
5424 5k. Type **2143** 65 20
5425 20k. Satellite and observatory (space geodesy) 1·00 60
5426 45k. Rocket, satellites and dish aerials (Soviet–Indian space flight) 2·00 1·20
MS5427 66×86 mm. 50k. Cosmonauts abroad "Salyut 7" space station (25×36 mm) 3·25 1·90

2144 Globe and Cosmonaut

1984. Cosmonautics Day.
5428 **2144** 10k. multicoloured 75 45

2145 "Chelyuskin" (ice-breaker) and Route Map

1984. 50th Anniv of Murmansk–Vladivostok Voyage of "Chelyuskin". Multicoloured.
5429 6k. Type **2145** 50 30
5430 15k. Evacuation of sinking ship 1·30 75
5431 45k. Air rescue of crew 3·50 2·00

2146 Order of Hero of the Soviet Union

1984. 50th Anniv of Order of Hero of the Soviet Union. Sheet 105×70 mm.
MS5432 **2146** 50k. multicoloured 3·25 1·90

2147 Lenin (after Ye. N. Shirokov)

1984. 114th Birth Anniv of Lenin. Sheet 100×78 mm.
MS5433 **2147** 50k. multicoloured 3·25 1·90

2148 Lotus

1984. Aquatic Flowers. Multicoloured.
5434 1k. Type **2148** 25 15
5435 2k. Euriala 25 15
5436 3k. Yellow water lilies (horiz) 40 15
5437 10k. White water lilies (horiz) 75 45
5438 20k. Marshflowers (horiz) 1·50 85

2149 Globe and Peace March (left)

1984. Peace.

5439 **2149** 5k. multicoloured 65 20
5440 - 5k. red, gold and black 65 20
5441 - 5k. multicoloured 65 20

DESIGNS: No. 5440, Hammer and sickle and text; 5441, Globe and peace march (right).

2150 Welder

1984. 50th Anniv of E. O. Paton Institute of Electric Welding, Kiev.

5442 **2150** 10k. multicoloured 75 45

2151 Communications Emblem

1984. 25th Conference of Community for Mutual Economic Aid Electrical and Postal Communications Standing Committee, Cracow.

5443 **2151** 10k. multicoloured 75 45

2152 Emblem and Symbols of Match Venues

1984. European Youth Football Championship.

5444 **2152** 15k. multicoloured 1·00 60

2153 Maurice Bishop

1984. 40th Birth Anniv of Maurice Bishop (former Prime Minister of Grenada).

5445 **2153** 5k. brown 65 20

2154 Lenin and Museum

1984. 60th Anniv of Lenin Central Museum, Moscow.

5446 **2154** 5k. multicoloured 65 20

2155 Freighter, Monument and Aurora Borealis

1984. 400th Anniv of Archangel.

5447 **2155** 5k. multicoloured 65 20

2156 Headquarters and Spassky Tower, Moscow

1984. Council of Mutual Economic Aid Conference, Moscow.

5448 **2156** 5k. blue, red and black 65 20

1984. Lighthouses (3rd series). As T 2075. Multicoloured.

5449 1k. Petropavlovsk lighthouse, Kamchatka 25 15
5450 2k. Tokarev lighthouse, Sea of Japan 25 15
5451 4k. Basargin lighthouse, Sea of Japan 40 20
5452 5k. Kronotsky lighthouse, Kamchatka 50 30
5453 10k. Marekan lighthouse, Sea of Okhotsk 75 45

2157 Vladimir A. Lyakhov and Aleksandr Aleksandrov

1984. 150 Days in Space of "Salyut 7"–"Soyuz T-9" Cosmonauts.

5454 **2157** 15k. multicoloured 1·00 60

2158 Liner

1984. 60th Anniv of Morflot (Soviet merchant fleet).

5455 **2158** 10k. multicoloured 75 45

2159 Komsomol Badge and Banner

1984. 60th Anniv of Naming of Young Communist League (Komsomol) after Lenin.

5456 **2159** 5k. multicoloured 65 20

2160 Memorial, Minsk

1984. 40th Anniv of Byelorussian Liberation.

5457 **2160** 5k. multicoloured 65 20

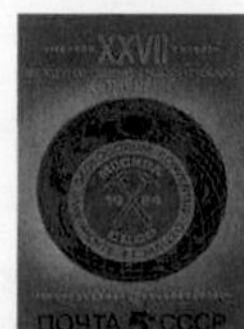
2161 Congress Emblem

1984. 27th International Geological Congress, Moscow.

5458 **2161** 5k. blue, gold and deep blue 65 20

2162 Polish Arms and Flag

1984. 40th Anniv of Republic of Poland.

5459 **2162** 5k. multicoloured 65 20

2163 Asafev

1984. Birth Centenary of Boris Vladimirovich Asafev (composer).

5460 **2163** 5k. green 65 20

2164 Russian and Mexican Flags and Scroll

1984. 60th Anniv of U.S.S.R.–Mexico Diplomatic Relations.

5461 **2164** 5k. multicoloured 65 20

2165 Title Page of "The Princess-Frog"

1984. Folk Tales. Illustration by I. Bilibin. Multicoloured.

5462 5k. Type **2165** 75 30
5463 5k. Hunter and frog in marshland 75 30
5464 5k. Old man and hunter in forest 75 30
5465 5k. Crowd and mute swans 75 30
5466 5k. Title page of "Ivan the Tsarevich, the Fire-bird and the Grey Wolf" 75 30
5467 5k. Ivan and the Fire-bird 75 30
5468 5k. Grave and Ivan on horse 75 30
5469 5k. Ivan and princess 75 30
5470 5k. Title page of "Vasilisa the Beautiful" 75 30
5471 5k. Knight on horse 75 30
5472 5k. Tree-man in forest 75 30
5473 5k. Vasilisa and skulls 75 30

2166 Basketball

1984. "Friendship 84" Sports Meetings. Multicoloured.

5474 1k. Type **2166** 25 15
5475 5k. Gymnastics (vert) 50 20
5476 10k. Weightlifting 75 45
5477 15k. Wrestling 1·00 60
5478 20k. High jumping 1·50 85

2167 Flag and Soviet Soldiers' Monument, Bucharest

1984. 40th Anniv of Rumania's Liberation.

5479 **2167** 5k. multicoloured 65 20

2168 Emblem, Chess Symbol for Queen and Motherland Statue

1984. World Chess Championship Finals for Women (Volgograd) and Men (Moscow).

5480 **2168** 15k. gold, red and black 1·50 85
5481 - 15k. multicoloured 1·50 85

DESIGN: No. 5481, Emblem, chess symbol for king and Spassky tower, Moscow Kremlin.

2169 Party House and Soviet Army Monument, Sofia, and State Emblem

1984. 40th Anniv of Bulgarian Revolution.

5482 **2169** 5k. multicoloured 65 20

2170 Arms and Flag

1984. Tenth Anniv of Ethiopian Revolution.

5483 **2170** 5k. multicoloured 65 20

2171 Excavator

1984. 50th Anniv of Lenin Machine-building Plant, Novokramatorsk.

5484 **2171** 5k. multicoloured 65 20

2172 Arms and Symbols of Industry and Agriculture

1984. 60th Anniv of Nakhichevan A.S.S.R.

5485 **2172** 5k. multicoloured 65 20

V СЪЕЗД ВОФ. МОСКВА. ОКТЯБРЬ 1984 г.
(2173)

1984. Fifth Philatelic Congress, Moscow. No. **MS**5354 optd with T **2173**.

MS5486 50k. stone and black 3·75 2·20

2174 "Luna 3" photographing Moon

1984. 25th Anniv of Photography in Space. Multicoloured.

5487 5k. Type **2174** 65 20
5488 20k. "Venera-9" and control centre 1·30 75
5489 45k. "Meteor" meteorological satellite and Earth 2·50 1·50

MS5490 60×81 mm. 50k. V. Lyakhov installing solar battery on "Salyut 7" space station (21×32 mm) 3·25 1·90

2175 Arms and Flag

1984. 35th Anniv of German Democratic Republic.

5491 **2175** 5k. multicoloured 65 20

2176 Arms and Motherland Statue, Kiev

1984. 40th Anniv of Liberation of the Ukraine.
5492 **2176** 5k. multicoloured 75 30

2177 Town, Arms and Countryside

1984. 60th Anniv of Moldavian Soviet Socialist Republic.
5493 **2177** 5k. multicoloured 65 20

2178 Arms, Power Station and Mountains

1984. 60th Anniv of Kirgizia Soviet Socialist Republic.
5494 **2178** 5k. multicoloured 65 20

2179 Arms and Symbols of Industry and Agriculture

1984. 60th Anniv of Tadzhikistan Soviet Socialist Republic.
5495 **2179** 5k. multicoloured 65 20

2180 Flags and Spassky Tower

1984. 67th Anniv of October Revolution.
5496 **2180** 5k. multicoloured 65 20

2181 Arms, State Building and Dam

1984. 60th Anniv of Uzbekistan Soviet Socialist Republic.
5497 **2181** 5k. multicoloured 65 20

2182 Arms, Flag and State Building

1984. 60th Anniv of Turkmenistan Soviet Socialist Republic.
5498 **2182** 5k. multicoloured 65 20

2183 Medal, Workers, Diesel Train and Route Map

1984. Completion of Baikal–Amur Railway.
5499 **2183** 5k. multicoloured 65 20

2184 Ilyushin Il-86 Jetliner, Rocket, "Soyuz"–"Salyut" Complex and Museum

1984. 60th Anniv of M. V. Frunze Central House of Aviation and Cosmonautics, Moscow.
5500 **2184** 5k. multicoloured 65 20

2185 "Girl in Hat" (Jean-Louis Voile)

1984. French Paintings in Hermitage Museum, Leningrad. Multicoloured.
5501 4k. Type **2185** 25 15
5502 10k. "The Stolen Kiss" (Jean-Honore Fragonard) (horiz) 50 30
5503 20k. "Woman at her Toilette" (Edgar Degas) 1·80 1·00
5504 45k. "Pygmalion and Galatea" (Francois Boucher) (horiz) 3·00 1·70
5505 50k. "Landscape with Polyphemus" (Nicolas Poussin) (horiz) 3·50 2·00
MS5506 144×79 mm. 50k.×2 "Child with Whip" (Pierre-Auguste Renoir) 7·00 4·00

2186 Mongolian Arms and Flag

1984. 60th Anniv of Mongolian People's Republic.
5507 **2186** 5k. multicoloured 65 20

2187 Spassky Tower and Snowflakes

1984. New Year.
5508 **2187** 5k. multicoloured 65 30

2188 Leaf and Urban Landscape

1984. Environmental Protection. Sheet 90×65 mm.
MS5509 **2188** 5k. multicoloured 3·75 2·20

2189 Horse-drawn Crew Wagon (19th-century)

1984. Fire Engines (1st series). Multicoloured.
5510 3k. Type **2189** 25 15
5511 5k. 19th-century horse-drawn steam pump 65 20
5512 10k. "Freze" fire engine, 1904 75 45
5513 15k. "Lessner" fire engine, 1904 1·00 60
5514 20k. "Russo-Balt" fire engine, 1913 1·50 85

See also Nos. 5608/12.

2190 Space Observatory and Flight Trajectory

1984. International Venus–Halley's Comet Space Project (1st issue).
5515 **2190** 15k. multicoloured 1·30 75

See also Nos. 5562 and 5630.

2191 Indira Gandhi

1984. Indira Gandhi (Indian Prime Minister) Commemoration.
5516 **2191** 5k. light brown & brown 65 20

2192 Heroes of December Revolution Monument, Moscow

1985. 80th Anniv of 1905 Revolution.
5517 **2192** 5k. multicoloured 65 20

2193 Jubilee Emblem

1985. 25th Anniv of Patrice Lumumba University, Moscow.
5518 **2193** 5k. multicoloured 65 20

2194 Frunze

1985. Birth Centenary of Mikhail Vasilievich Frunze (military strategist).
5519 **2194** 5k. stone, black and blue 65 20

2195 Arms and Industrial Landscape

1985. 60th Anniv of Karakalpak A.S.S.R.
5520 **2195** 5k. multicoloured 65 20

2196 Ice Hockey Player

1985. Tenth Friendly Armies Winter Spartakiad.
5521 **2196** 5k. multicoloured 65 20

2197 Dulcimer Player and Title Page

1985. 150th Anniv of "Kalevala" (Karelian poems collected by Elino Lonnrot).
5522 **2197** 5k. brown, blue & black 65 20

2198 Pioneer Badge

1985. 60th Anniv of "Pionerskaya Pravda" (children's newspaper).
5523 **2198** 5k. multicoloured 65 20

2199 Maria Aleksandrovna Ulyanova

1985. 150th Birth Anniv of Maria Aleksandrovna Ulyanova (Lenin's mother).
5524 **2199** 5k. black 65 20

2200 "Young Madonna Praying" (Francisco de Zurbaran)

1985. Spanish Paintings in Hermitage Museum, Leningrad. Multicoloured.
5525 4k. Type **2200** 25 15
5526 10k. "Still Life" (Antonio Pereda) (horiz) 50 30
5527 20k. "The Immaculate Conception" (Bartolome Esteban Murillo) 1·30 75
5528 45k. "The Grinder" (Antonio Puga) (horiz) 2·75 1·60
5529 50k. "Count Olivares" (Diego Velazquez) 3·25 1·90
MS5530 145×80 mm. 50k.×2 "Antonia Zarate" (Francisco de Goya) 8·75 5·00

2201 Cosmonauts and Globe

1985. "Expo 85" World's Fair, Tsukuba, Japan. Multicoloured.
5531 5k. Type **2201** 25 15
5532 10k. "Molniya-I" communications satellite 50 30
5533 20k. Energy sources of the future 1·30 75
5534 45k. Futuristic city 2·00 1·20
MS5535 64×85 mm. 50k. Soviet exhibition emblem, globe and tree (36×47 mm) 3·25 1·90

2202 Bach (after Hausman)

1985. 300th Birth Anniv of Johann Sebastian Bach (composer). Sheet 65×91 mm.
MS5536 **2201** 50k. black 3·25 1·90

2203 Hungarian Arms and Budapest

1985. 40th Anniv of Hungary's Liberation.

5537	**2203**	5k. multicoloured	65	20

2204 Emblem and Text

1985. 60th Anniv of Union of Soviet Societies of Friendship and Cultural Relations with Foreign Countries.

5538	**2204**	15k. multicoloured	1·00	60

2205 Cosmonauts, "Soyuz T" Training Model and Gagarin

1985. Cosmonautics Day. 25th Anniv of Yuri A. Gagarin Cosmonauts Training Centre.

5539	**2205**	15k. multicoloured	1·00	60

2206 Young People of Different Races

1985. 12th World Youth and Students' Festival, Moscow. Multicoloured.

5540	1k. Type **2206**	25	15
5541	3k. Girl with festival emblem in hair	40	20
5542	5k. Rainbow and girl	50	30
5543	20k. Youth holding camera	1·30	75
5544	45k. Festival emblem	2·75	1·60

2207 Soviet Memorial, Berlin-Treptow

1985. 40th Anniv of Victory in Second World War (1st issue). Multicoloured.

5545	5k. Type **2207**	50	20
5546	5k. Partisans	50	20
5547	5k. Lenin, soldier and Moscow Kremlin	50	20
5548	5k. Soldiers and military equipment	50	20
5549	5k. Woman worker, tank, tractor and assembly of Ilyushin Il-2M3 Stormovik fighter	50	20
MS5550	90×65 mm. 50k. Order of Patriotic War, Second Class (27×39 mm)	3·25	1·90

2208 Lenin and Paris Flat

1985. 115th Birth Anniv of Lenin. Multicoloured.

5551	5k. Type **2208**	65	20
5552	5k. Lenin and Lenin Museum, Tampere, Finland	65	20
MS5553	65×89 mm. 30k. Lenin (26×38 mm)	2·50	1·50

See also No. 5555.

Всесоюзная
филатели-
стическая
выставка

„40 лет
Великой
Победы"
(2209)

1985. "Second World War Victory" Philatelic Exhibition. No. 5545 optd with T **2209**.

5554	**2207**	5k. multicoloured	75	45

2210 Victory Order

1985. 40th Anniv of Victory in Second World War (2nd issue).

5555	**2210**	20k. multicoloured	1·30	75

2211 Czechoslovakian Arms and Prague Buildings

1985. 40th Anniv of Czechoslovakia's Liberation.

5556	**2211**	5k. multicoloured	65	20

2212 Members' Flags on Shield

1985. 30th Anniv of Warsaw Pact Organization.

5557	**2212**	5k. multicoloured	65	20

2213 Sholokhov and Books

1985. 80th Birth Anniv of Mikhail Aleksandrovich Sholokhov (writer).

5558	**2213**	5k. multicoloured	65	20
5559	-	5k. multicoloured	65	20
5560	-	5k. black, gold and brown	65	20

DESIGNS—As T **2213**. No. 5559, Sholokhov and books (different). 36×51 mm: No. 5560, Sholokhov.

2214 Sverdlov

1985. Birth Centenary of Ya. M. Sverdlov (Communist Party Leader).

5561	**2214**	5k. brown and red	65	20

1985. International Venus–Halley's Comet Space Project (2nd issue). As T **2190**. Multicoloured.

5562	15k. "Vega" space probe and Venus	1·00	60

2215 Battleship "Potemkin"

1985. 80th Anniv of Mutiny on Battleship "Potemkin".

5563	**2215**	5k. black, red and gold	65	20

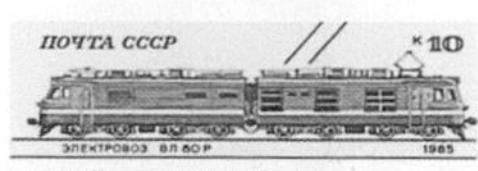
2216 Class VL-80R Electric Locomotive

1985. Locomotives and Rolling Stock.

5564	**2216**	10k. green	1·00	45
5565	-	10k. brown	1·00	45
5566	-	10k. blue	1·00	45
5567	-	10k. brown	1·00	45
5568	-	10k. blue	1·00	45
5569	-	10k. blue	1·00	45
5570	-	10k. brown	1·00	45
5571	-	10k. green	1·00	45

DESIGNS: No. 5565, Coal wagon; 5566, Oil tanker wagon; 5567, Goods wagon; 5568, Refrigerated wagon; 5569, Class TEM-2 diesel locomotive; 5570, Type SV passenger carriage; 5571, Mail van.

2217 Camp and Pioneer Badge

1985. 60th Anniv of Artek Pioneer Camp.

5572	**2217**	4k. multicoloured	50	15

2218 Leonid Kizim, Vladimir Solovyov and Oleg Atkov

1985. "237 Days in Space".

5573	**2218**	15k. multicoloured	1·00	60

2219 Youths of different Races

1985. International Youth Year.

5574	**2219**	10k. multicoloured	75	45

2220 "Beating Swords into Ploughshares" (sculpture) and U.N. Emblem

1985. 40th Anniv of U.N.O. (1st issue).

5575	**2220**	45k. blue and gold	4·00	2·30

See also No. 5601.

2221 Festival Emblem

1985. 12th World Youth and Students' Festival, Moscow (2nd issue). Sheet 64×90 mm.

MS5576	**2221**	30k. multicoloured	2·00	1·20

2222 Larkspur

1985. Plants of Siberia. Multicoloured.

5577	2k. Type **2222**	25	15
5578	3k. "Thermopsis lanceolata"	25	15
5579	5k. Rose	50	20
5580	20k. Cornflower	1·30	75
5581	45k. Bergenia	3·00	1·70

2223 V. A. Dzhanibekov, S. E. Savitskaya and I. P. Volk

1985. First Anniv of First Space-walk by Woman Cosmonaut.

5582	**2223**	10k. multicoloured	75	45

2224 Cecilienhof Palace and Flags

1985. 40th Anniv of Potsdam Conference.

5583	**2224**	15k. multicoloured	1·00	60

2225 Finland Palace

1985. Tenth Anniv of European Security and Co-operation Conference, Helsinki.

5584	**2225**	20k. multicoloured	2·00	1·20

2226 Russian and N. Korean Flags and Monument

1985. 40th Anniv of Liberation of Korea.

5585	**2226**	5k. multicoloured	65	20

2227 Pamir Shrew

1985. Protected Animals. Multicoloured.

5586	2k. Type **2227**	25	15
5587	3k. Satunin's jerboa (horiz)	25	15
5588	5k. Desert dormouse	50	30
5589	20k. Caracal (47×32 mm)	1·30	75
5590	45k. Goitred gazelle (47×32 mm)	3·00	1·70
MS5591	90×65 mm. 50k. Leopard (horiz)	3·75	2·20

2228 A. G. Stakhanov and Industrial Scenes

1985. 50th Anniv of Stakhanov Movement (for high labour productivity).

5592	**2228**	5k. yellow, red and black	65	20

2229 Cup, Football, F.I.F.A. Emblem and Kremlin Tower

1985. World Junior Football Championship, Moscow.
5593 **2229** 5k. multicoloured 65 20

2230 Chess Pieces

1985. World Chess Championship Final between Anatoly Karpov and Gary Kasparov.
5594 **2230** 10k. multicoloured 1·00 60

2231 Vietnam State Emblem

1985. 40th Anniv of Vietnamese Independence.
5595 **2231** 5k. multicoloured 65 20

2232 Immortality Monument and Buildings

1985. Millenary of Bryansk.
5596 **2232** 5k. multicoloured 65 20

2233 Title Page

1985. 800th Anniv of "Song of Igor's Campaigns".
5597 **2233** 10k. multicoloured 75 45

2234 Lutsk Castle

1985. 900th Anniv of Lutsk.
5598 **2234** 5k. multicoloured 65 20

2235 Gerasimov

1985. Birth Centenary of Sergei Vasilievich Gerasimov (artist).
5599 **2235** 5k. multicoloured 65 20

2236 Globe, Cruiser "Aurora" and 1917

1985. 68th Anniv of October Revolution.
5600 **2236** 5k. multicoloured 65 20

2237 Headquarters, New York, and Flag

1985. 40th Anniv of U.N.O. (2nd issue).
5601 **2237** 15k. green, blue and black 1·50 85

2238 Krisjanis Barons

1985. 150th Birth Anniv of Krisjanis Barons (writer).
5602 **2238** 5k. black and brown 65 20

2239 Lenin and Worker breaking Chains

1985. 90th Anniv of Petersburg Union of Struggle for Liberating the Working Class.
5603 **2239** 5k. multicoloured 65 20

2240 Telescope

1985. Tenth Anniv of World's Largest Telescope.
5604 **2240** 10k. blue 75 45

2241 Angolan Arms and Flag

1985. Tenth Anniv of Independence of Angola.
5605 **2241** 5k. multicoloured 65 20

2242 Yugoslav Arms, Flag and Parliament Building

1985. 40th Anniv of Federal People's Republic of Yugoslavia.
5606 **2242** 5k. multicoloured 65 20

2243 Troitsky Tower and Palace of Congresses

1985. New Year.
5607 **2243** 5k. multicoloured 65 20

1985. Fire Engines (2nd series). As T **2189**. Multicoloured.
5608 3k. "AMO-F15", 1926 25 15
5609 5k. "PMZ-1", 1933 40 20
5610 10k. "ATs-40", 1977 50 30
5611 20k. "AL-30" with automatic ladder, 1970 1·00 60
5612 45k. "AA-60", 1978 2·00 1·20

2244 Samantha Smith

1985. Samantha Smith (American schoolgirl peace campaigner) Commemoration.
5613 **2244** 5k. brown, blue and red 75 45

2245 N. M. Emanuel

1985. Academician N. M. Emanuel (chemist) Commemoration.
5614 **2245** 5k. multicoloured 65 20

2246 Family and Places of Entertainment

1985. Anti-alcoholism Campaign. Multicoloured.
5615 5k. Type **2246** 65 20
5616 5k. Sports centre and family 65 20

2247 Emblem

1986. International Peace Year.
5617 **2247** 20k. blue, green & silver 1·00 60

2248 Banners and Kremlin Palace of Congresses

1986. 27th Soviet Communist Party Congress.
5618 **2248** 5k. multicoloured 50 15
5619 - 20k. multicoloured 1·00 60
MS5620 95×65 mm. 50k. red, gold and black 3·25 1·90

DESIGNS—36×51 mm: 20k. Palace of Congresses, Spassky Tower and Lenin. 27×39 mm—50k. Lenin (after sculpture by N. Andreev).

2249 1896 Olympics Medal

1986. 90th Anniv of First Modern Olympic Games.
5621 **2249** 15k. multicoloured 1·00 60

2250 Tulips

1986. Plants of Russian Steppes. Multicoloured.
5622 4k. Type **2250** 25 15
5623 5k. Grass (horiz) 50 20
5624 10k. Iris 75 45
5625 15k. Violets 1·30 75
5626 20k. Cornflower 1·50 85

2251 Voronezh and Arms

1986. 400th Anniv of Voronezh.
5627 **2251** 5k. multicoloured 65 20

2252 Bela Kun

1986. Birth Centenary of Bela Kun (Hungarian Communist Party leader).
5628 **2252** 10k. blue 75 45

2253 Pozela

1986. 90th Birth Anniv of Karolis Pozela (founder of Lithuanian Communist Party).
5629 **2253** 5k. grey 65 20

2254 "Vega 1" and Halley's Comet

1986. International Venus–Halley's Comet Space Project (3rd issue). As T **2190**. Multicoloured.
5630 15k. "Vega 1" and Halley's Comet 1·00 60
MS5631 65×91 mm. 50k. Type **2254** (different) 3·25 1·90

2255 Crimson-spotted Moth

1986. Butterflies and Moths listed in U.S.S.R. Red Book (1st series). Multicoloured.
5632 4k. Type **2255** 25 15
5633 5k. Eastern festoon 50 30
5634 10k. Sooty orange-tip 75 45
5635 15k. Dark crimson underwing 1·00 60
5636 20k. "Satyrus bischoffi" 1·50 85

See also Nos. 5726/30.

2256 Globe and Model of Space Complex

1986. "Expo '86" World's Fair, Vancouver.
5637 **2256** 20k. multicoloured 1·30 75

2257 Kirov

1986. Birth Centenary of S. M. Kirov (Communist Party Secretary).
5638 **2257** 5k. black 65 20

2258 Tsiolkovsky

1986. Cosmonautics Day. Multicoloured.
5639 5k. Type **2258** 50 15
5640 10k. Sergei Pavlovich Korolev (rocket designer) and "Vostok" rocket (vert) 75 45
5641 15k. Yuri Gagarin, "Vega", sputnik and globe (25th anniv of first man in space) 1·00 60

2259 Ice Hockey Player

1986. World Ice Hockey Championship, Moscow.
5642 **2259** 15k. multicoloured 1·00 60

2260 Thalmann

1986. Birth Centenary of Ernst Thalmann (German politician).
5643 **2260** 10k. deep brown 1·00 60
5644 **2260** 10k. lake-brown 1·00 60

2261 Lenin Museum, Leipzig

1986. 116th Birth Anniv of Lenin.
5645 **2261** 5k. multicoloured 65 20
5646 - 5k. olive, brown & black 65 20
5647 - 5k. multicoloured 65 20
DESIGNS: No. 5646, Lenin (after P. Belousov) and Lenin Museum, Prague; 5647, Lenin Museum, Poronine, Poland.

2262 Tambov and Arms

1986. 350th Anniv of Tambov.
5648 **2262** 5k. multicoloured 65 20

2263 Dove with Olive Branch and Globe

1986. 25th Anniv of Soviet Peace Fund.
5649 **2263** 10k. multicoloured 75 45

2264 Emblem and Cyclists

1986. 39th Peace Cycle Race.
5650 **2264** 10k. multicoloured 75 45

2265 Death Cap

1986. Fungi. Multicoloured.
5651 4k. Type **2265** 25 15
5652 5k. Fly agaric 40 20
5653 10k. Panther cap 50 30
5654 15k. Bitter bolete 1·00 60
5655 20k. Clustered woodlover 1·30 75

2266 Globe and Wildlife

1986. UNESCO Man and Biosphere Programme.
5656 **2266** 10k. multicoloured 1·00 60

2267 Torch and Runner

1986. Ninth People's Spartakiad.
5657 **2267** 10k. multicoloured 1·00 60

2268 Kuibyshev

1986. 400th Anniv of Kuibyshev (formerly Samara).
5658 **2268** 5k. multicoloured 65 20
No. 5658 depicts the Lenin Museum, Eternal Glory and V. I. Chapaev monuments and Gorky State Theatre.

2269 Ostankino T.V. Tower

1986. "Communication 86" International Exhibition, Moscow.
5659 **2269** 5k. multicoloured 65 20

2270 Footballers

1986. World Cup Football Championship, Mexico. Multicoloured.
5660 5k. Type **2270** 50 20
5661 10k. Footballers (different) 75 45
5662 15k. Championship medal 1·30 75

2271 "Lane in Albano" (M. I. Lebedev)

1986. Russian Paintings in Tretyakov Gallery, Moscow. Multicoloured.
5663 4k. Type **2271** 25 15
5664 5k. "View of the Kremlin in foul Weather" (A. K. Savrasov) (horiz) 40 20
5665 10k. "Sunlit Pine Trees" (I. I. Shishkin) 50 30
5666 15k. "Journey Back" (A. E. Arkhipov) (69×33 mm) 75 45
5667 45k. "Wedding Procession in Moscow" (A. P. Ryabushkin) (69×33 mm) 2·30 1·30

2272 Arms and City

1986. 300th Anniv of Irkutsk City Status.
5668 **2272** 5k. multicoloured 65 20

2273 World Map, Stadium and Runners

1986. International Goodwill Games, Moscow.
5669 **2273** 10k. blue, brown & black 75 45
5670 **2273** 10k. blue, sepia & black 75 45

2274 Globe, Punched Tape and Keyboard

1986. UNESCO Programmes in U.S.S.R. Multicoloured.
5671 5k. Type **2274** 25 15
5672 10k. Landscape and geological section (geological correlation) 50 30
5673 15k. Oceanographic research vessel, albatross and ocean (Inter-governmental Oceanographic Commission) 1·00 60
5674 35k. Fluvial drainage (International Hydrological Programme) 2·30 1·30

2275 Arms and Town Buildings

1986. 400th Anniv of Tyumen, Siberia.
5675 **2275** 5k. multicoloured 65 20

2276 Olof Palme

1986. Olof Palme (Swedish Prime Minister) Commemoration.
5676 **2276** 10k. blue, black & brn 75 45

2277 Hands, Ball and Basket

1986. Tenth Women's Basketball Championship.
5677 **2277** 15k. brown, black & red 1·00 60

2278 "Ural-375D"

1986. Lorries. Multicoloured.
5678 4k. Type **2278** 25 15
5679 5k. "GAZ-53A" 40 20
5680 10k. "KrAZ-256B" 50 30
5681 15k. "MAZ-515B" 1·00 60
5682 20k. "ZIL-133GYa" 1·30 75

2279 Lenin Peak

1986. U.S.S.R. Sports Committee's International Mountaineers' Camps (1st series). Multicoloured.
5683 4k. Type **2279** 25 15
5684 5k. E. Korzhenevskaya Peak 50 30
5685 10k. Belukha Peak 75 45
5686 15k. Communism Peak 1·00 60
5687 30k. Elbrus Peak 2·00 1·20
See also Nos. 5732/5.

2280 Globe and "Red Book"

1986. Environmental Protection. Sheet 60×90 mm.
MS5688 **2280** 50k. multicoloured 3·75 2·20

2281 Lenin Monument and Drama Theatre

1986. 250th Anniv of Chelyabinsk City.
5689 **2281** 5k. multicoloured 65 20

2282 "Mukran", Maps and Flags

1986. Opening of Mukran (East Germany)–Klaipeda (U.S.S.R.) Railway Ferry.
5690 **2282** 15k. multicoloured 1·00 60

2283 Victory Monument and Buildings

1986. 750th Anniv of Siauliai, Lithuania.

5691	**2283**	5k. buff, brown and red	65	20

2284 Lenin Monument and Moscow Kremlin

1986. 69th Anniv of October Revolution.

5692	**2284**	5k. multicoloured	65	20

2285 Ice-breaker "Vladivostok", Mil Mi-4 Helicopter, Satellite and Map

1986. Antarctic Drift of "Mikhail Somov" (research vessel).

(a) As T **2285**.

5693	5k. blue, black and red	65	20
5694	10k. multicoloured	1·30	75
MS5695	70×90 mm. 50k. ultramarine and black	3·75	2·20

15.III—26.VII.1985
Дрейф во льдах Антарктики
(2286)

(b) No. 5055 optd with T **2286**.

5696	4k. multicoloured	2·50	1·50

DESIGN—As T **2285**: 10k. Map and "Mikhail Somov". 51×36 mm—"Mikhail Somov" icebound.

Nos. 5693/4 were printed together, se-tenant, forming a composite design.

2287 Class Eu No. 684-37, Slavyansk

1986. Steam Locomotive as Monuments. Multicoloured.

5697	4k. Type **2287**	25	15
5698	5k. Class FD No. 3000, Novosibirsk	65	20
5699	10k. Class Ov No. 5109, Volgograd	75	45
5700	20k. Class SO No. 17-1613, Dnepropetrovsk	1·30	75
5701	30k. Class FDp No. 20-578, Kiev	2·00	1·20

2288 G. K. Ordzhonikidze

1986. Birth Centenary of Grigory Konstantinovich Ordzhonikidze (revolutionary).

5702	**2288**	5k. grey	65	20

2289 Novikov and Score

1986. 90th Birth Anniv of Anatoli Novikov (composer).

5703	**2289**	5k. brown	65	20

2290 U.N. and UNESCO Emblem

1986. 40th Anniv of UNESCO.

5704	**2290**	10k. silver and blue	1·30	75

2291 Sun Yat-sen

1986. 120th Birth Anniv of Sun Yat-sen (first President of Chinese Republic).

5705	**2291**	5k. black and grey	65	20

2292 Lomonosov

1986. 275th Birth Anniv of Mikhail Vasilievich Lomonosov (scientist).

5706	**2292**	5k. brown	65	20

2293 Ya-1, 1927

1986. Sports Aircraft designed by Aleksandr Yakovlev. Multicoloured.

5707	4k. Type **2293**	25	15
5708	5k. VT-2 trainer, 1935	40	20
5709	10k. Yak-18, 1946	75	45
5710	20k. Yak-50, 1972	1·30	75
5711	30k. Yak-55, 1981	2·00	1·20

2294 Spassky, Senate and Nikolsky Towers, Kremlin

1986. New Year.

5712	**2294**	5k. multicoloured	65	20

2295 Computer and Terminal

1986. Resolutions of 27th Communist Party Congress. Multicoloured.

5713	5k. Type **2295** (scientific and technical progress)	65	20
5714	5k. Construction engineer and building project	65	20
5715	5k. City (welfare of people)	65	20
5716	5k. Peace demonstration at Council for Mutual Economic Aid building (peace)	65	20
5717	5k. Spassky Tower and Kremlin Palace, Moscow Kremlin (unity of party and people)	65	20

2296 Parkhomenko

1986. Birth Centenary of Aleksandr Parkhomenko (revolutionary).

5718	**2296**	5k. black	65	20

2297 Machel

1986. Samora Moizes Machel (President of Mozambique) Commemoration.

5719	**2297**	5k. brown and black	65	20

2298 Russian State Museum (Mikhailovsky Palace)

1986. Palace Museums of Leningrad.

5720	**2298**	5k. brown and green	50	30
5721	-	10k. green and blue	75	45
5722	-	15k. blue and green	1·00	60
5723	-	20k. green and brown	1·50	85
5724	-	50k. brown and blue	3·00	1·70

DESIGNS: 10k. Hermitage Museum (Winter Palace); 15k. Grand Palace Museum (Petrodvorets); 20k. Catherine Palace Museum (Pushkin); 50k. Palace Museum (Pavlovsk).

2299 Couple and Industrial Landscape

1987. 18th Soviet Trades Union Congress, Moscow.

5725	**2299**	5k. multicoloured	65	20

2300 Chinese Windmill

1987. Butterflies listed in U.S.S.R. Red Book (2nd series). Multicoloured.

5726	4k. Type **2300**	25	15
5727	5k. Swallowtail	50	20
5728	10k. Southern swallowtail	75	45
5729	15k. "Papilio maackii"	1·00	60
5730	30k. Scare swallowtail	2·00	1·20

2301 Karlis Miesnieks

1987. Birth Centenary of Karlis Miesnieks (Latvian artist).

5731	**2301**	5k. multicoloured	65	20

1987. U.S.S.R. Sports Committee's International Mountaineers' Camps (2nd series). As T **2279**. Multicoloured.

5732	4k. Chimbulak Gorge	25	15
5733	10k. Shavla Gorge	50	30
5734	20k. Donguz-Orun and Nakra-Tau, Caucasus	1·00	60
5735	35k. Kazbek, Caucasus	1·50	85

2302 Stasys Simkus

1987. Birth Centenary of Stasys Simkus (Lithuanian composer).

5736	**2302**	5k. purple and yellow	65	20

2303 V. I. Chapaev

1987. Birth Cent of Vasily Ivanovich Chapaev (revolutionary).

5737	**2303**	5k. brown	65	20

2304 Lenin

1987. 20th Leninist Young Communist League (Komsomol) Congress, Moscow. Multicoloured.

5738	5k. Type **2304**	65	20
MS5739	60×85 mm. 50k. Emblem, laurel branch, banner and decoration ribbons (23×32 mm)	3·25	1·90

2305 Heino Eller

1987. Birth Centenary of Heino Eller (Estonian composer).

5740	**2305**	5k. light brown & brown	75	30

2306 Orbeli

1987. Birth Centenary of Academician Iosif Abgarovich Orbeli (first President of Armenian Academy of Sciences).

5741	**2306**	5k. brown and pink	65	20

2307 Bears in and out of Water

1987. Polar Bears. Multicoloured.

5742	5k. Type **2307**	75	45
5743	10k. Mother and cubs	1·00	60
5744	20k. Mother and cubs (different)	2·30	1·30
5745	35k. Bears	3·50	2·00

2308 "Sputnik 1" and Globe

1987. Cosmonautics Day. Multicoloured.

5746	10k. Type **2308** (30th anniv of launching of first artificial satellite)	75	45
5747	10k. "Vostok-3", Vostok-4" and globe (25th anniv of first group space flight)	75	45

5748 10k. "Mars-1" and globe (25th anniv of launching of automatic interplanetary station) 75 45

2309 Emblem and Headquarters, Bangkok

1987. 40th Anniv of U.N. Economic and Social Commission for Asia and the Pacific Ocean.
5749 **2309** 10k. multicoloured 75 45

2310 "Birthday" (N. A. Sysoev)

1987. 117th Birth Anniv of Lenin. Multicoloured.
5750 5k. Type **2310** 50 15
5751 5k. "V. I. Lenin with Delegates to the Third Congress of the Young Communist League" (P. P. Belousov) 50 15
MS5752 130×67 mm. 10k. "Lenin's Underground Activity" (D. A. Nalnabdyan) (39×27 mm); 20k. "Lenin" (N. Andreev) (39×55 mm); 10k. "We'll Show the Earth a New Way" (A. G. Lysenko) (39×27 mm); 10k. "Before the Assault" (S. P. Viktorov) (39×27 mm); 10k. "Lenin in Smolny, October 1917" (M. G. Sokolov) (39×27 mm) 3·00 1·70

2311 Gymnast on Rings

1987. European Gymnastics Championships, Moscow.
5753 **2311** 10k. multicoloured 75 45

2312 Cyclists and "40"

1987. 40th Peace Cycle Race.
5754 **2312** 10k. multicoloured 75 45

2313 Menzbir's Marmot

1987. Mammals listed in U.S.S.R. Red Book. Multicoloured.
5755 5k. Type **2313** 50 30
5756 10k. Ratel (horiz) 75 45
5757 15k. Snow leopard (32×47 mm) 1·30 75

2314 "Maksim Gorky"

1987. River Tourist Ships. Multicoloured.
5758 5k. Type **2314** 50 30
5759 10k. "Aleksandr Pushkin" 75 45
5760 30k. "Sovetsky Soyuz" 1·50 85

2315 "Portrait of a Woman" (Lucas Cranach the Elder)

1987. West European Art in Hermitage Museum, Leningrad. Multicoloured.
5761 4k. Type **2315** 25 15
5762 5k. "St. Sebastian" (Titian) 50 30
5763 10k. "Justice" (drawing, Albrecht Durer) 75 45
5764 30k. "Adoration of the Magi" (Peter Breughel the younger) (horiz) 2·00 1·20
5765 50k. "Statue of Ceres" (Peter Paul Rubens) 3·00 1·70

2316 Car Production Line and Lenin Hydro-electric Power Station

1987. 250th Anniv of Togliatti (formerly Stavropol).
5766 **2316** 5k. multicoloured 65 20

2317 Pushkin (after T. Rait)

1987. 150th Death Anniv of Aleksandr S. Pushkin (poet).
5767 **2317** 5k. deep brown, yellow and brown 1·00 60

2318 Kovpak

1987. Birth Centenary of Major-General Sidor Artemevich Kovpak.
5768 **2318** 5k. black 65 20

2319 Congress Emblem

1987. World Women's Congress, Moscow.
5769 **2319** 10k. multicoloured 75 45

2320 Arms, Kremlin, Docks, Drama Theatre and Yermak Monument

1987. 400th Anniv of Tobolsk, Siberia.
5770 **2320** 5k. multicoloured 65 20

2321 Party Flag and Mozambican

1987. 25th Anniv of Mozambique Liberation Front (FRELIMO) (5771) and Tenth Anniv of U.S.S.R.–Mozambique Friendship and Co-operation Treaty (5772). Multicoloured.
5771 5k. Type **2321** 65 20
5772 5k. Mozambique and U.S.S.R. flags 65 20

2322 "Scolopendrium vulgare"

1987. Ferns. Multicoloured.
5773 4k. Type **2322** 25 15
5774 5k. "Ceterach officinarum" 40 20
5775 10k. "Salvinia natans" (horiz) 50 30
5776 15k. "Matteuccia struthiopteris" 1·00 60
5777 50k. "Adiantum pedatum" 3·00 1·70

2323 Moscow Kremlin and Indian Coin

1987. Indian Festival in U.S.S.R. (5778) and U.S.S.R. Festival in India (5779). Multicoloured.
5778 5k. Type **2323** 65 20
5779 5k. Hammer, sickle, open book, satellite and Red Fort, Delhi 65 20

2324 Rossiya Hotel (venue), Globe and Film

1987. 15th International Film Festival, Moscow.
5780 **2324** 10k. multicoloured 75 45

2325 Cosmonauts training

1987. Soviet–Syrian Space Flight. Multicoloured.
5781 5k. Type **2325** 25 15
5782 10k. Moscow–Damascus satellite link and cosmonauts watching television screen 50 30
5783 15k. Cosmonauts at Gagarin monument, Zvezdny 1·30 75
MS5784 90×62 mm. 50k. "Mir" space station (36×25 mm) 3·25 1·90

2326 Emblem and Vienna Headquarters

1987. 30th Anniv of Int Atomic Energy Agency.
5785 **2326** 20k. multicoloured 1·50 85

2327 14th–16th Century Messenger

1987. Russian Postal History.
5786 **2327** 4k. black and brown 25 15
5787 - 5k. black and brown 40 20
5788 - 10k. black and brown 50 30
5789 - 30k. black and brown 1·50 85
5790 - 35k. black and brown 1·80 1·00
MS5791 95×70 mm. 50k. black and yellow 3·25 1·90
DESIGNS: 5k. 17th–19th century horse-drawn sledge and 17th-century postman; 10k. 16th-century and 18th-century sailing packets; 30k. 19th-century railway mail vans; 35k. 1905 post car and 1926 "AMO-F-15" van; 50k. Mail-vans in front of Moscow Head Post Office.

2328 "V. I. Lenin" (P. V. Vasilev)

1987. 70th Anniv of October Revolution. Multicoloured.
5792 5k. Type **2328** 65 20
5793 5k. "V. I. Lenin proclaims Soviet Power" (V. A. Serov) 65 20
5794 5k. "Long Live the Socialist Revolution!" (V. V. Kuznetsov) 65 20
5795 5k. "Storming the Winter Palace" (V. A. Serov) (69×32 mm) 65 20
5796 5k. "On the Eve of the Storm" (portraying Lenin, Sverdlov and Podvoisky) (V. V. Pimenov) (69×32 mm) 65 20
MS5797 87×73 mm. 30k. (black and gold) "Lenin" (statue, V. V. Kozlov) (vert) 2·50 1·50

2329 Anniversary Emblem

1987. 175th Anniv of Battle of Borodino. Sheet 111×82 mm.
MS5798 **2329** 1r. brown, black and blue 6·50 3·75

2330 Postyshev

1987. Birth Centenary of Pavel Petrovich Postyshev (revolutionary).
5799 **2330** 5k. blue 65 20

2331 Yuri Dolgoruky (founder) Monument

1987. 840th Anniv of Moscow.
5800 **2331** 5k. brown, yell & orge 65 20

2332 Ulugh Beg (astronomer and mathematician)

1987. Scientists.
5801 **2332** 5k. multicoloured 65 30
5802 - 5k. black, green and blue 65 30

5803 - 5k. deep brown, brown and blue 65 30

DESIGNS: No. 5801, Type **2332** (550th anniv of "New Astronomical Tables"); 5802, Isaac Newton (300th anniv of "Principia Mathematica"); 5803, Marie Curie (120th birth anniv).

2333 KOSPAS Satellite

1987. Fifth Anniv of KOSPAS–SARSAT (international satellite air/sea search system). Sheet 62×80 mm.

MS5804 **2333** 50k. multicoloured 3·25 1·90

Всесоюзная
филателистическая выставка
„70 лет Великого Октября"
(2334)

1987. "70th Anniv of October Revolution" All-Union Stamp Exhibition. No. 5795 optd with T **2334**.

5805 5k. multicoloured 1·30 75

2335 "There will be Cities in the Taiga" (A. A. Yakovlev)

1987. Soviet Paintings of the 1980s. Multicoloured.

5806 4k. Type **2335** 25 15
5807 5k. "Mother" (V. V. Shcherbakov) 40 20
5808 10k. "My Quiet Homeland" (V. M. Sidorov) (horiz) 50 30
5809 30k. "In Yakutsk, Land of Pyotr Alekseev" (A. N. Osipov) (horiz) 1·80 1·00
5810 35k. "Ivan's Return" (V. I. Yerofeev) (horiz) 2·00 1·20
MS5811 92×78 mm. 50k. "Sun over Red Square" (P. P. Ossovsky) 3·25 1·90

2336 Reed

1987. Birth Centenary of John Reed (American journalist and founder of U.S. Communist Party).

5812 **2336** 10k. brown, yell & blk 75 45

2337 Marshak

1987. Birth Centenary of Samuil Yakovlevich Marshak (poet).

5813 **2337** 5k. brown 65 20

2338 Chavchavadze

1987. 150th Anniv of Ilya Grigoryevich Chavchavadze (writer).

5814 **2338** 5k. blue 65 20

2339 Indira Gandhi

1987. 70th Birth Anniv of Indira Gandhi (Indian Prime Minister, 1966–77 and 1980–84).

5815 **2339** 5k. brown and black 65 20

2340 Vadim N. Podbelsky (revolutionary)

1987. Birth Centenaries.

5816 **2340** 5k. black 65 20
5817 - 5k. blue 65 20

DESIGN: No. 5817, Academician Nikolai Ivanovich Vavilov (geneticist).

2341 Tokamak Thermonuclear System

1987. Science.

5818 **2341** 5k. brown and grey 65 20
5819 - 10k. green, blue and black 75 45
5820 - 20k. black, stone and drab 1·00 60

DESIGNS: 10k. Kola borehole; 20k. "Ratan-600" radio telescope.

2342 Bagramyan

1987. 90th Birth Anniv of Marshal Ivan Khristoforovich Bagramyan.

5821 **2342** 5k. brown 65 20

2343 Moscow Kremlin

1987. New Year.

5822 **2343** 5k. multicoloured 65 20

2344 Flags, Spassky Tower, Moscow, and Capitol, Washington

1987. Soviet–American Intermediate and Short-range Nuclear Weapons Treaty.

5823 **2344** 10k. multicoloured 75 45

2345 Grigori Andreevich Spiridov and "Tri Svyatitelya"

1987. Russian Naval Commanders (1st series).

5824 **2345** 4k. blue and deep blue 25 15
5825 - 5k. purple and blue 40 20
5826 - 10k. purple and blue 75 45
5827 - 25k. blue and deep blue 2·30 1·30
5828 - 30k. blue and deep blue 2·50 1·50

DESIGNS: 5k. Fyodor Fyodorovich Ushakov and "Sv. Pavel"; 10k. Dmitri Nikolaevich Senyavin, Battle of Afon and "Tverdyi" (battleship); 25k. Mikhail Petrovich Lazarev and "Azov"; 30k. Pavel Stepanovich Nakhimov and "Imperatritsa Maria".

See also Nos. 6091/6.

2346 Torch

1987. 30th Anniv of Asia–Africa Solidarity Organization.

5829 **2346** 10k. multicoloured 75 45

2347 Biathlon

1988. Winter Olympic Games, Calgary. Multicoloured.

5830 5k. Type **2347** 40 20
5831 10k. Cross-country skiing 50 30
5832 15k. Slalom 75 45
5833 20k. Figure skating (pairs) 1·00 60
5834 30k. Ski jumping 1·30 75
MS5835 62×80 mm. 50k. Ice hockey (horiz) 4·00 2·30

2348 1918 Stamps

1988. 70th Anniv of First Soviet Postage Stamps.

5836 **2348** 10k. blue, brown and gold 75 45
5837 **2348** 10k. brown, blue and gold 75 45

On No. 5836 the lower stamp depicted is the 35k. in blue, on No. 5837 the lower stamp is the 70k. in brown.

2349 Emblem

1988. 40th Anniv of W.H.O.

5838 **2349** 35k. gold, blue and black 2·50 1·50

2350 Byron

1988. Birth Bicentenary of Lord Byron (English poet).

5839 **2350** 15k. black, green and blue 1·00 60

2351 Exchange Activities and National Flags

1988. 30th Anniv of Agreement on Cultural, Technical and Educational Exchanges with U.S.A.

5840 **2351** 20k. multicoloured 1·30 75

2352 Lomov-Oppokov

1988. Birth Centenary of Georgy Ippolitovich Lomov-Oppokov (Communist party official).

5841 **2352** 5k. black and brown 65 20

2353 "Little Humpbacked Horse" (dir. I. Ivanov-Vano, animated L. Milchin)

1988. Soviet Cartoon Films. Multicoloured.

5842 1k. Type **2353** 25 15
5843 3k. "Winnie the Pooh" (dir. F. Khitruk, animated V. Zuikov and E. Nazarov) 25 15
5844 4k. "Gena the Crocodile" (dir. R. Kachanov, animated L. Shartsmann) 50 20
5845 5k. "Just You Wait!" (dir. V. Kotyonochkin, animated S. Rusakov) 65 30
5846 10k. "Hedgehog in a Mist" (dir. Yu. Norshtein, animated F. Yarbusova) 1·00 60
MS5847 95×75 mm. 30k. Cover and stamps ("The Post" dir. M. Tsekhanovsky) 2·50 1·50

2354 Bonch-Bruevich

1988. Birth Centenary of Mikhail Alexandrovich Bonch-Bruevich (radio engineer).

5848 **2354** 10k. black and brown 75 45

2355 Nurse and Emblems

1988. 125th Anniv of International Red Cross and Red Crescent.

5849 **2355** 15k. black, blue and red 1·30 75

2356 Skater

1988. World Speed Skating Championships, Alma-Ata.

5850 **2356** 15k. blue, violet and black 1·30 75

2357 Makarenko

1988. Birth Centenary of Anton Semenovich Makarenko (educationist and writer).

5851 **2357** 10k. green 75 45

2358 Skorina

1988. 500th Birth Anniv of Frantsisk Skorina (printer).

5852 **2358** 5k. black 65 20

2359 Banners and Globe

1988. Labour Day.
5853 **2359** 5k. multicoloured 65 20

2360 Kingisepp

1988. Birth Centenary of Victor Eduardovich Kingisepp (revolutionary).
5854 **2360** 5k. green 65 20

2361 Track and Athlete

1988. Centenary of Russian Athletics.
5855 **2361** 15k. multicoloured 1·00 60

2362 M. S. Shaginyan

1988. Birth Centenary of Marietta Sergeevna Shaginyan (writer).
5856 **2362** 10k. brown 75 45

2363 Palace of Congresses, Moscow, Finlandia Hall, Helsinki, and National Flags

1988. 40th Anniv of U.S.S.R.–Finland Friendship Treaty.
5857 **2363** 15k. multicoloured 1·00 60

2364 "Mir"–"Soyuz TM" Space Complex and "Progress" Spacecraft

1988. Cosmonautics Day.
5858 **2364** 15k. multicoloured 1·00 60

2365 Sochi

1988. 150th Anniv of Sochi.
5859 **2365** 5k. multicoloured 65 20

2366 "Victory" (P. A. Krivonogov)

1988. V. E. Day.
5860 **2366** 5k. multicoloured 65 20

2367 Lenin Museum, Moscow

1988. 118th Birth Anniv of Lenin. Designs showing branches of Lenin Central Museum.
5861 **2367** 5k. brown, deep brown and gold 65 20
5862 - 5k. red, purple and gold 65 20
5863 - 5k. ochre, brown & gold 65 20
5864 - 5k. yellow, green & gold 65 20
DESIGNS: No. 5862, Kiev; 5863, Leningrad; 5864, Krasnoyarsk.
See also Nos. 5990/2 and 6131/3.

2368 Akulov

1988. Birth Centenary of Ivan Alekseevich Akulov (Communist Party official).
5865 **2368** 5k. blue 65 20

2369 Soviet Display Emblem

1988. "Expo 88" World's Fair, Brisbane.
5866 **2369** 20k. multicoloured 1·00 60

2370 Marx

1988. 170th Birth Anniv of Karl Marx.
5867 **2370** 5k. brown 65 20

2371 Soldiers and Workers

1988. Perestroika (Reformation).
5868 **2371** 5k. multicoloured 65 20
5869 - 5k. brown, red & orange 65 20
DESIGN: No. 5869, Banner, industrial scenes and worker.

Спортсмены СССР завоевали
11 золотых, 9 серебряных
и 9 бронзовых медалей!
(2372)

1988. Winter Olympic Games Soviet Medal Winners. No. **MS**5835 optd with T **2372**.
MS5870 62×80 mm. 50k. multicoloured 3·25 1·90

2373 Shvernik

1988. Birth Centenary of Nikolai Mikhailovich Shvernik (politician).
5871 **2373** 5k. black 65 20

2374 Russian Borzoi

1988. Hunting Dogs. Multicoloured.
5872 5k. Type **2374** 50 20
5873 10k. Kirgiz borzoi 75 45
5874 15k. Russian hound 1·00 60
5875 20k. Russian spaniel 1·30 75
5876 35k. East Siberian husky 1·50 85

2375 Flags, Spassky Tower and Handshake

1988. Soviet–American Summit, Moscow.
5877 **2375** 5k. multicoloured 65 20

2376 Kuibyshev

1988. Birth Centenary of Valerian Vladimirovich Kuibyshev (politician).
5878 **2376** 5k. brown 65 20

2377 Flags, "Mir" Space Station and "Soyuz TM" Spacecraft

1988. Soviet–Bulgarian Space Flight.
5879 **2377** 15k. multicoloured 1·00 60

2378 Crowd and Peace Banners

1988. "For a Nuclear-free World".
5880 **2378** 5k. multicoloured 65 20

2379 Red Flag, Hammer and Sickle and Laurel Branch

1988. 19th Soviet Communist Party Conference, Moscow (1st issue). Multicoloured.
5881 5k. Type **2379** 65 20
5882 5k. Lenin on red flag and interior of Palace of Congresses (35×23 mm) 65 20
MS5883 100×65 mm. 50k. Palace of Congresses and Spassky Tower, Moscow, Kremlin (50×36 mm) 3·25 1·90
See also Nos. 5960/2.

2380 Flags, Skis and Globe

1988. Soviet–Canadian Transarctic Ski Expedition.
5884 **2380** 35k. multicoloured 2·50 1·50

2381 Hurdling

1988. Olympic Games, Seoul. Multicoloured.
5885 5k. Type **2381** 50 30
5886 10k. Long jumping 75 45
5887 15k. Basketball 1·00 60
5888 20k. Gymnastics 1·30 75
5889 30k. Swimming 2·00 1·20
MS5890 80×65 mm. 50k. Football 3·25 1·90

2382 Giant Bellflower

1988. Deciduous Forest Flowers. Multicoloured.
5891 5k. Type **2382** 25 15
5892 10k. Spring pea (horiz) 50 30
5893 15k. Lungwort 75 45
5894 20k. Turk's cap lily 1·00 60
5895 35k. "Ficaria verna" 1·50 85

2383 Phobos and "Phobos" Space Probe

1988. Phobos (Mars Moon) International Space Project.
5896 **2383** 10k. multicoloured 75 45

2384 Komsomol Badge

1988. 70th Anniv of Leninist Young Communist League (Komsomol).
5897 **2384** 5k. multicoloured 65 20

2385 Mandela

1988. 70th Birthday of Nelson Mandela (African nationalist).
5898 **2385** 10k. multicoloured 1·30 75

2386 "Obeyan Serebryanyi, Light Grey Arab Stallion" (N. E. Sverchkov)

1988. Paintings in Moscow Horse Breeding Museum. Multicoloured.
5899 5k. Type **2386** 25 15
5900 10k. "Konvoets" (Kabardin breed) (M. A. Vrubel) (vert) 50 30
5901 15k. "Horsewoman on Orlov-Rastopchin Horse" (N. E. Sverchkov) 1·00 60
5902 20k. "Letuchy, Grey Stallion of Orlov Trotter Breed" (V. A. Serov) (vert) 1·30 75

5903 30k. "Sardar, an Akhaltekin Stallion" (A. B. Villevalde) 2·00 1·20

Филвыставка. Москва
(2387)

1988. Stamp Exhibition, Moscow. No. 5897 optd with T **2387**.

5904 **2384** 5k. multicoloured 1·30 75

2388 Voikov

1988. Birth Centenary of Pyotr Lazarevich Voikov (diplomat).

5905 **2388** 5k. black 65 20

2389 "Portrait of O. K. Lansere" (Z. E. Serebryakova)

1988. Soviet Culture Fund. Multicoloured.

No.	Description	Mint	Used
5906	10k.+5k. Type **2389**	1·00	60
5907	15k.+7k. "Boyarynya (noblewoman) looking at Embroidery Design" (K. V. Lebedev) (horiz)	1·30	75
5908	30k.+15k. "Talent" (N. P. Bogdanov-Belsky)	2·75	1·60
MS5909	70×90 mm. 1r.+50k. "Holy Trinity" (icon, Novgorod School)	8·00	4·75

2390 Envelopes and U.P.U. Emblem

1988. International Correspondence Week.

5910 **2390** 5k. turquoise, blue & black 65 20

2391 "Mir" Space Station and "Soyuz-TM" Spacecraft

1988. Soviet–Afghan Space Flight.

5911 **2391** 15k. green, red and black 1·00 60

2392 Emblem and Open Book

1988. 30th Anniv of "Problems of Peace and Socialism" (magazine).

5912 **2392** 10k. multicoloured 75 45

2393 Kviring

1988. Birth Centenary of Emmanuil Ionovich Kviring (politician).

5913 **2393** 5k. black 65 20

2394 "Ilya Muromets" (Russia) (R. Smirnov)

1988. Epic Poems of Soviet Union (1st series). Illustrations by artists named. Multicoloured.

No.	Description	Mint	Used
5914	10k. Type **2394**	75	45
5915	10k. "Cossack Golota" (Ukraine) (M. Deregus) (horiz)	75	45
5916	10k. "Musician-Magician" (Byelorussia) (N. Poplavskaya)	75	45
5917	10k. "Koblandy Batyr" (Kazakhstan) (I. Isabaev) (horiz)	75	45
5918	10k. "Alpamysh" (Uzbekistan) (R. Khalilov)	75	45

See also Nos. 6017/21 and 6139/43.

2395 "Appeal of the Leader" (detail, I. M. Toidze)

1988. 71st Anniv of October Revolution.

5919 **2395** 5k. multicoloured 65 20

2396 Bolotov

1988. 250th Birth Anniv of Andrei Timofeevich Bolotov (agriculturalist).

5920 **2396** 10k. brown 75 45

2397 Tupolev

1988. Birth Centenary of Academician Andrei Nikolaevich Tupolev (aircraft designer).

5921 **2397** 10k. blue 75 45

2398 Bear

1988. Zoo Relief Fund. Multicoloured.

No.	Description	Mint	Used
5922	10k.+5k. Type **2398**	90	50
5923	10k.+5k. Wolf	90	50
5924	10k.+10k. Fox	1·60	95
5925	20k.+10k. Wild boar	1·60	95
5926	20k.+10k. Lynx	1·60	95

2399 "Sibir" (atomic ice-breaker)

1988. Soviet Arctic Expedition.

5927 **2399** 20k. multicoloured 2·30 1·30

2400 Ustinov

1988. 80th Birth Anniv of Marshal Dmitri Fyodorovich Ustinov.

5928 **2400** 5k. brown 65 20

2401 National Initials

1988. Tenth Anniv of U.S.S.R.–Vietnam Friendship Treaty.

5929 **2401** 10k. multicoloured 75 45

2402 Building Facade

1988. 50th Anniv of State House of Broadcasting and Sound Recording.

5930 **2402** 10k. multicoloured 75 45

2403 Emblem

1988. 40th Anniv of Declaration of Human Rights.

5931 **2403** 10k. multicoloured 75 45

2404 Life Guard of Preobrazhensky Regt. with Peter I's New Year Decree

1988. New Year.

5932 **2404** 5k. multicoloured 65 20

2405 Flags and Cosmonauts

1988. Soviet–French Space Flight.

5933 **2405** 15k. multicoloured 1·00 60

2406 "Skating Rink" (Olya Krutova)

1988. Lenin Soviet Children's Fund. Children's Paintings. Multicoloured.

No.	Description	Mint	Used
5934	5k.+2k. Type **2406**	75	45
5935	5k.+2k. "Cock" (Nasta Shcheglova)	75	45
5936	5k.+2k. "May is flying over the Meadows, May is flying over the Fields" (Larisa Gaidash)	75	45

2407 Lacis

1988. Birth Cent of Martins Lacis (revolutionary).

5937 **2407** 5k. green 65 20

★
КОСМИЧЕСКАЯ
ПОЧТА
(2408)

1988. "Space Post". No. 4682 optd with T **2408**.

5938 1r. blue 12·50 7·25

СПОРТСМЕНЫ СССР ЗАВОЕВАЛИ
55 ЗОЛОТЫХ, 31 СЕРЕБРЯНУЮ
И 46 БРОНЗОВЫХ МЕДАЛЕЙ
СЕУЛ • 1988
(2409)

1988. Olympic Games Soviet Medal. No. **MS**5890 optd with T **2409**.

MS5939 80×65 mm. 50k. multicoloured 3·75 2·20

2410 Post Messenger

1988

No.	Type	Description	Mint	Used
6072	**2410**	1k. brown	25	15
6073	-	2k. brown	25	15
6074	-	3k. green	25	15
6075	-	4k. blue	25	15
6076	-	5k. red	40	20
6077	-	7k. blue	50	30
6078	-	10k. brown	65	35
6079	-	12k. purple	75	45
6080	-	13k. violet	80	45
6081	-	15k. blue	90	50
6082	-	20k. brown	1·00	60
6083	-	25k. green	1·30	75
6084	-	30k. blue	1·50	85
6085	-	35k. brown	2·00	1·20
6086	-	50k. blue	2·75	1·60
6087	-	1r. blue	5·50	3·25

DESIGNS: 2k. Old mail transport (sailing packet, steam train and mail coach); 3k. "Aurora" (cruiser); 4k. Spassky Tower and Lenin's Tomb, Red Square, Moscow; 5k. State emblem and flag; 7k. Modern mail transport (Ilyushin Il-86 jetliner, Mil Mi-2 helicopter, "Aleksandr Pushkin" (liner), train and mail van); 10k. "The Worker and the Collective Farmer" (statue, Vera Mukhina); 12k. Rocket on launch pad; 13k. Satellite; 15k. "Orbit" dish aerial; 20k. Symbols of art and literature; 25k. "The Discus-thrower" (5th-century Greek statue by Miron); 30k. Map of Antarctica and emperor penguins; 35k. "Mercury" (statue, Giovanni da Bologna); 50k. Great white cranes; 1r. Universal Postal Union emblem.

2411 Great Cascade and Samson Fountain

1988. Petrodvorets Fountains. Each green and grey.

No.	Description	Mint	Used
5952	5k. Type **2411**	40	20
5953	10k. Adam fountain (D. Bonazza)	50	30
5954	15k. Golden Mountain cascade (Niccolo Michetti and Mikhail Zemtsov)	1·00	60
5955	30k. Roman fountains (Bartolomeo Rastrelli)	1·80	1·00
5956	50k. Oaklet trick fountain (Rastrelli)	3·00	1·70

2412 1st-cent B.C. Gold Coin of Tigran the Great

1988. Armenian Earthquake Relief. Armenian History. Multicoloured.

No.	Description	Mint	Used
5957	20k.+10k. Type **2412**	1·50	85
5958	30k.+15k. Rispsime Church	2·50	1·50
5959	50k.+25k. "Madonna and Child" (18th-century fresco, Ovnat Ovnatanyan)	4·00	2·30

2413 Hammer and Sickle

1988. 19th Soviet Communist Party Conference, Moscow (2nd issue). Multicoloured.

5960	5k. Type **2413**	65	20
5961	5k. Hammer and sickle and building girders	65	20
5962	5k. Hammer and sickle and wheat	65	20

2414 "Buran"

1988. Launch of Space Shuttle Buran. Sheet 93×63 mm.

MS5963	**2414** 50k. multicoloured	3·25	1·90

2415 "Vostok" Rocket, "Lunar 1", Earth and Moon

1989. 30th Anniv of First Russian Moon Flight.

5964	**2415**	15k. multicoloured	1·00	60

2416 Virtanen

1989. Birth Centenary of Jalmari Virtanen (poet).

5965	**2416**	5k. brown and bistre	65	20

2417 Headquarters Building, Moscow

1989. 40th Anniv of Council for Mutual Economic Aid.

5966	**2417**	10k. multicoloured	75	45

2418 Forest Protection

1989. Nature Conservation. Multicoloured.

5967	5k. Type **2418**	40	20
5968	10k. Arctic preservation	90	50
5969	15k. Anti-desertification campaign	1·10	65

2419 18th-century Samovar

1989. Russian Samovars in State Museum, Leningrad. Multicoloured.

5970	5k. Type **2419**	25	15
5971	10k. 19th-century barrel samovar by Ivan Lisitsin of Tula	50	30
5972	20k. 1830s Kabachok travelling samovar by Sokolov Brothers factory, Tula	1·30	75
5973	30k. 1840s samovar by Nikolai Malikov factory, Tula	1·80	1·00

2420 Mussorgsky (after Repin) and Scene from "Boris Godunov"

1989. 150th Birth Anniv of Modest Petrovich Mussorgsky (composer).

5974	**2420**	10k. purple and brown	75	45

2421 Dybenko

1989. Birth Centenary of Pavel Dybenko (military leader).

5975	**2421**	5k. black	65	20

2422 Shevchenko

1989. 175th Birth Anniv of Taras Shevchenko (Ukrainian poet and painter).

5976	**2422**	5k. brown, green & black	65	20

2423 "Lilium speciosum"

1989. Lilies. Multicoloured.

5977	5k. Type **2423**	40	20
5978	10k. "African Queen"	75	45
5979	15k. "Eclat du Soir"	1·00	60
5980	30k. "White Tiger"	2·00	1·20

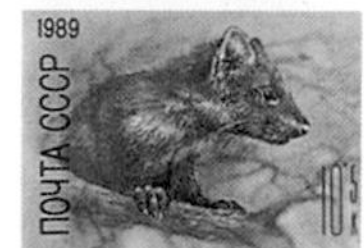

2424 Marten

1989. Zoo Relief Fund. Multicoloured.

5981	10k.+5k. Type **2424**	90	50
5982	10k.+5k. Squirrel	90	50
5983	20k.+10k. Hare	1·90	1·10
5984	20k.+10k. Hedgehog	1·90	1·10
5985	20k.+10k. Badger	1·90	1·10

2425 Red Flag, Rainbow and Globe

1989. Centenary of "Second International" Declaration of 1 May as Labour Day. Sheet 105×75 mm.

MS5986	**2425** 30k. multicoloured	2·00	1·20

2426 "Victory Banner" (P. Loginov and V. Pamfilov)

1989. Victory Day.

5987	**2426**	5k. multicoloured	65	20

2427 "Mir" Space Station

1989. Cosmonautics Day.

5988	**2427**	15k. multicoloured	1·00	60

2428 Emblem and Flags

1989. U.S.–Soviet Bering Bridge Expedition.

5989	**2428**	10k. multicoloured	75	45

1989. 119th Birth Anniv of Lenin. As T **2367**. Branches of Lenin Central Museum.

5990	5k. brown, ochre and gold	50	20
5991	5k. deep brown, brn & gold	50	20
5992	5k. multicoloured	50	20

DESIGNS: No. 5990, Frunze; 5991, Kazan; 5992, Kuibyshev.

2429 "Phobos"

1989. Launch of "Phobos" Space Probe to Mars. Sheet 89×65 mm.

MS5993	**2429** 50k. multicoloured	3·25	1·90

2430 Statue

1989. 70th Anniv of First Hungarian Soviet Republic.

5994	**2430**	5k. multicoloured	65	20

2431 "Motherland Statue"

1989. 400th Anniv of Volgograd (formerly Tsaritsyn).

5995	**2431**	5k. multicoloured	65	20

2432 Drone

1989. Honey Bees. Multicoloured.

5996	5k. Type **2432**	25	15
5997	10k. Bees, flowers and hive	50	30
5998	20k. Bee on flower	1·00	60
5999	35k. Feeding queen bee	1·80	1·00

2433 Negative and Positive Images

1989. 150th Anniv of Photography.

6000	**2433**	5k. multicoloured	65	20

2434 Map above Dove as Galley

1989. "Europe—Our Common Home". Multicoloured.

6001	5k. Type **2434**	25	15
6002	10k. Laying foundations of Peace	1·00	60
6003	15k. White storks' nest	2·00	1·20

2435 Mukhina modelling "God of Northern Wind" (after M. Nesterov)

1989. Birth Centenary of Vera Mukhina (sculptress).

6004	**2435**	5k. blue	65	20

2436 Racine

1989. 150th Birth Anniv of Jean Racine (dramatist).

6005	**2436**	15k. multicoloured	1·30	75

2437 Rabbit

1989. Lenin Soviet Children's Fund. Children's Paintings. Multicoloured.

6006	5k.+2k. Type **2437**	65	30
6007	5k.+2k. Cat	65	30
6008	5k.+2k. Nurse	65	30

See also Nos. 6162/4.

2438 Kuratov

1989. 150th Birth Anniv of Ivan Kuratov (writer).

6009	**2438**	5k. deep brown & brown	65	20

2439 Emblem

1989. 13th World Youth and Students' Festival, Pyongyang.

6010	**2439**	10k. multicoloured	75	45

2440 Common Shelduck

1989. Ducks (1st series). Multicoloured.

6011	5k. Type **2440**	40	15
6012	15k. Green-winged teal	1·00	60
6013	20k. Ruddy shelduck	1·30	75

See also Nos. 6159/61 and 6264/6.

2441 "Storming of Bastille" (Gelman after Monnet)

1989. Bicentenary of French Revolution.

6014	**2441**	5k. multicoloured	25	15
6015	-	15k. blue, black and red	75	45
6016	-	20k. blue, black and red	1·00	60

DESIGNS: 15k. Jean-Paul Marat, Georges Danton and Maximilien Robespierre; 20k. "Marseillaise" (relief by F. Rude from Arc de Triomphe).

1989. Epic Poems of Soviet Union (2nd series). Illustrations by named artists. As T **2394**. Multicoloured.

6017	10k. "Amirani" (Georgia) (V. Oniani)	75	45
6018	10k. "Koroglu" (Azerbaijan) (A. Gadzhiev)	75	45
6019	10k. "Fir, Queen of Grass Snakes" (Lithuania) (A. Makunaite)	75	45
6020	10k. "Mioritsa" (Moldavia) (I. Bogdesko)	75	45
6021	10k. "Lachplesis" (Lettish) (G. Wilks)	75	45

2442 Observatory

1989. 150th Anniv of Pulkovo Observatory.
6022 **2442** 10k. multicoloured 75 45

2443 Hemispheres, Roses in Envelope and Posthorn

1989. International Letter Week.
6023 **2443** 5k. multicoloured 65 20

2444 Lynx

1989. 50th Anniv of Tallin Zoo.
6024 **2444** 10k. multicoloured 75 45

2445 Ships and Peter I

1989. 275th Anniv of Battle of Hango Head. Sheet 95×65 mm.
MS6025 **2445** 50k. blue, black and brown 3·25 1·90

2446 Buildings, Container Ship and Bicentenary Emblem

1989. Bicentenary of Nikolaev.
6026 **2446** 5k. multicoloured 65 20

2447 Nkrumah

1989. 80th Birth Anniv of Kwame Nkrumah (first Prime Minister and President of Ghana).
6027 **2447** 10k. multicoloured 75 45

2448 1921 40r. Stamp

1989. Sixth All-Union Philatelic Society Congress, Moscow.
6028 **2448** 10k. multicoloured 1·00 60

2449 Cooper

1989. Birth Bicentenary of James Fenimore Cooper (writer) (1st issue).
6029 **2449** 15k. multicoloured 1·00 60

See also Nos. 6055/9.

2450 V. L. Durov (trainer) and Sealions

1989. 70th Anniv of Soviet Circus. Multicoloured.

6030	1k. Type **2450**	25	15
6031	3k. M. N. Rumyantsev (clown "Karandash") with donkey	25	15
6032	4k. V. I. Filatov (founder of Bear Circus) and bears on motor cycles	40	20
6033	5k. E. T. Kio (illusionist) and act	50	30
6034	10k. V. E. Lazarenko (clown and acrobat) and act	65	35
MS6035	80×65 mm. 30k. Moscow Circus building, Tsvetnoi Boulevard (33×21½ mm)	2·30	1·30

2451 Emblem on Glove

1989. International Amateur Boxing Association Championship, Moscow.
6036 **2451** 15k. multicoloured 1·00 60

2452 Li Dazhao

1989. Birth Centenary of Li Dazhao (co-founder of Chinese Communist Party).
6037 **2452** 5k. brown, stone & black 65 20

2453 Khetagurov

1989. 130th Birth Anniv of Kosta Khetagurov (Ossetian writer).
6038 **2453** 5k. brown 65 20

2454 "October Guardsmen" (M. M. Chepik)

1989. 72nd Anniv of October Revolution.
6039 **2454** 5k. multicoloured 65 20

2455 Russian Spoons, Psaltery, Balalaika, Zhaleika and Accordion

1989. Traditional Musical Instruments (1st series). Multicoloured.

6040	10k. Type **2455**	75	45
6041	10k. Ukrainian bandura, trembita, drymba, svyril (pipes) and dulcimer	75	45
6042	10k. Byelorussian tambourine, bastlya (fiddle), lera and dudka (pipe)	75	45
6043	10k. Uzbek nagors (drums), rubab, zang, karnai and gidzhak	75	45

See also Nos. 6183/6 and 6303/5.

2456 "Demonstration of First Radio Receiver, 1895" (N. A. Sysoev)

1989. 130th Birth Anniv of Aleksandr Stepanovich Popov (radio pioneer).
6044 **2456** 10k. multicoloured 75 45

2457 National Flag and Provincial Arms

1989. 40th Anniv of German Democratic Republic.
6045 **2457** 5k. multicoloured 65 20

2458 Polish National Colours forming "45"

1989. 45th Anniv of Liberation of Poland.
6046 **2458** 5k. multicoloured 65 20

2459 Kosior

1989. Birth Centenary of Stanislav Vikentievich Kosior (vice-chairman of Council of People's Commissars).
6047 **2459** 5k. black 65 20

2460 Nehru

1989. Birth Centenary of Jawaharlal Nehru (Indian statesman).
6048 **2460** 15k. brown 1·00 60

2461 "Village Market" (A. V. Makovsky)

1989. Soviet Culture Fund. Multicoloured.

6049	4k.+2k. Type **2461**	50	30
6050	5k.+2k. "Lady in Hat" (E. L. Zelenin)	75	45
6051	10k.+5k. "Portrait of the Actress Bazhenova" (A. F. Sofronova)	1·00	60
6052	20k.+10k. "Two Women" (Hugo Shaiber)	2·00	1·20
6053	30k.+15k. 19th-century teapot and plates from Popov porcelain works	2·50	1·50

2462 Berzin

1989. Birth Centenary of Yan Karlovich Berzin (head of Red Army Intelligence).
6054 **2462** 5k. black 65 20

2463 "The Hunter"

1989. Birth Bicentenary of James Fenimore Cooper (writer) (2nd issue). Illustrations of his novels. Multicoloured.

6055	20k. Type **2463**	1·00	60
6056	20k. "Last of the Mohicans"	1·00	60
6057	20k. "The Pathfinder"	1·00	60
6058	20k. "The Pioneers"	1·00	60
6059	20k. "The Prairie"	1·00	60

Nos. 6055/9 were printed together, se-tenant, forming a composite design.

2464 St. Basil's Cathedral and Minin and Pozharsky Statue, Moscow

1989. Historical Monuments (1st series). Multicoloured.

6060	15k. Type **2464**	75	45
6061	15k. Sts. Peter and Paul Cathedral and statue of Peter I, Leningrad	75	45
6062	15k. St. Sophia's Cathedral and statue of Bogdan Chmielnitsky, Kiev	75	45
6063	15k. Khodzha Ahmed Yasavi mausoleum, Turkestan	75	45
6064	15k. Khazret Khyzr Mosque, Samarkand	75	45

See also Nos. 6165/72 and 6231/3.

2465 Dymkovo Toy

1989. New Year.
6065 **2465** 5k. multicoloured 65 20

2466 Soviet Lunar Vehicle

1989. "Expo 89" International Stamp Exhibition, Washington D.C. Multicoloured.

6066	25k. Type **2466**	1·80	1·00
6067	25k. Astronaut and landing module on Moon	1·80	1·00
6068	25k. Cosmonauts on Mars	1·80	1·00
6069	25k. Flag and shield on Mars	1·80	1·00
MS6070	104×84 mm. Nos. 6066/9	8·00	4·75

2467 Barn Swallow

1989. Nature Preservation. Sheet 65×90 mm.

MS6071 20k.+10k. multicoloured 3·75 2·20

1989. Russian Naval Commanders (2nd series). As T **2345**.

6091	5k. blue and brown	25	15
6092	10k. blue and brown	75	45
6093	15k. blue and deep blue	1·00	60
6094	20k. blue and deep blue	1·50	85
6095	30k. blue and brown	2·00	1·20
6096	35k. blue and brown	2·50	1·50

DESIGNS: 5k. V. A. Kornilov and "Vladimer" (steam frigate) and "Pervaz-Bakhric" (Turkish) steam frigate); 10k. V. I. Istomin and "Parizh"; 15k. G. I. Nevelskoi and "Baikal"; 20k. G. I. Butakov and iron-clad squadron; 30k. A. A. Popov, "Pyotr Veliky" and "Vitze Admirial Popov"; 35k. S. O. Makarov, "Intibah" (Turkish warship) and "Veliky Khyaz Konstantin".

2468 Acid Rain destroying Rose

1990. Nature Conservation. Multicoloured.

6097	10k. Type **2468**	75	45
6098	15k. Oil-smeared great black-headed gull perching on globe	1·00	60
6099	20k. Blade sawing down tree	1·30	75

2469 Ladya Monument and Golden Gates, Kiev (Ukraine)

1990. Republic Capitals. Multicoloured.

6100	5k. Lenin Palace of Culture, Government House and Academy of Sciences, Alma-Ata (Kazakhstan)	50	20
6101	5k. Library, Mollanepes Theatre and War Heroes Monument, Ashkhabad (Turkmenistan)	50	20
6102	5k. Maiden's Tower and Divan-Khane Palace, Baku (Azerbaijan)	50	20
6103	5k. Sadriddin Aini Theatre and Avicenna Monument, Dushanbe (Tadzhikistan)	50	20
6104	5k. Spendyarov Theatre and David Sasunsky Monument, Yerevan (Armenia)	50	20
6105	5k. Satylganov Philharmonic Society building and Manas Memorial, Frunze (Kirgizia)	50	20
6106	5k. Type **2469**	50	20
6107	5k. Cathedral and Victory Arch, Kishinev (Moldavia)	50	20
6108	5k. Government House and Liberation Monument, Minsk (Byelorussia)	50	20
6109	5k. Konstantino-Yeleninsky Tower and Ivan the Great Bell Tower, Moscow (Russian Federation)	50	20
6110	5k. Cathedral, "Three Brothers" building and Freedom Monument, Riga (Latvia)	50	20
6111	5k. Herman the Long, Oliviste Church, Cathedral and Town hall towers and wall turret, Tallin (Estonia)	50	20
6112	5k. Kukeldash Medrese and University, Tashkent (Uzbekistan)	50	20
6113	5k. Metekh Temple and Vakhtang Gorgasal Monument, Tbilisi (Georgia)	50	20
6114	5k. Gediminas Tower and St. Anne's Church, Vilnius (Lithuania)	50	20

2470 Flag and Hanoi Monument

1990. 60th Anniv of Vietnamese Communist Party.

6115 **2470** 5k. multicoloured 65 20

2471 Ho Chi Minh

1990. Birth Cent of Ho Chi Minh (Vietnamese leader).

6116 **2471** 10k. brown and black 75 45

2472 Snowy Owl

1990. Owls. Multicoloured.

6117	10k. Type **2472**	50	30
6118	20k. Eagle owl (vert)	1·00	60
6119	55k. Long-eared owl	1·50	85

2473 Paddle-steamer, Posthorn and Penny Black

1990. 150th Anniv of the Penny Black.

6120	**2473**	10k. multicoloured	50	30
6121	-	20k. black and gold	1·00	60
6122	-	20k. black and gold	1·00	60
6123	-	35k. multicoloured	2·50	1·50
6124	-	35k. multicoloured	2·50	1·50

MS6125 87×65 mm. 1r. black and green (36×25 mm) 5·50 3·25

DESIGNS: No. 6121, Anniversary emblem and Penny Black (lettered "T P"); 6122, As No. 6121 but stamp lettered "T F"; 6123, "Stamp World London 90" International Stamp Exhibition emblem and Penny Black (lettered "V K"); 6124, As No. 6123 but stamp lettered "A H" ; 1r. Penny Black and anniversary emblem.

2474 Electric Cables

1990. 125th Anniv of I.T.U.

6126 **2474** 20k. multicoloured 1·30 75

2475 Flowers

1990. Labour Day.

6127 **2475** 5k. multicoloured 65 20

2476 "Victory, 1945" (A. Lysenko)

1990. 45th Anniv of Victory in Second World War.

6128 **2476** 5k. multicoloured 65 20

2477 "Mir" Space Complex and Cosmonaut

1990. Cosmonautics Day.

6129 **2477** 20k. multicoloured 1·50 85

2478 Lenin

1990. "Leniniana '90" All-Union Stamp Exhibition.

6130 **2478** 5k. brown 65 20

1990. 120th Birth Anniv of Lenin. Branches of Lenin Central Museum. As T **2367**.

6131	5k. red, lake and gold	65	20
6132	5k. pink, purple and gold	65	20
6133	5k. multicoloured	65	20

DESIGNS: No. 6131, Ulyanovsk; 6132, Baku; 6133, Tashkent.

2479 Scene from "Iolanta" (opera) and Tchaikovsky

1990. 150th Birth Anniv of Pyotr Ilich Tchaikovsky (composer).

6134 **2479** 15k. black 1·50 85

2480 Golden Eagle

1990. Zoo Relief Fund. Multicoloured.

6135	10k.+5k. Type **2480**	1·00	60
6136	20k.+10k. Saker falcon ("Falco cherrug")	2·00	1·20
6137	20k.+10k. Common raven ("Corvus corax")	2·00	1·20

2481 Etching by G. A. Echeistov

1990. 550th Anniv of "Dzhangar" (Kalmuk folk epic).

6138 **2481** 10k. ochre, brown & black 75 45

1990. Epic Poems of Soviet Union (3rd series). Illustrations by named artists. As T **2394**. Multicoloured.

6139	10k. "Manas" (Kirgizia) (T. Gertsen) (horiz)	75	45
6140	10k. "Gurugli" (Tadzhikistan) (I. Martynov) (horiz)	75	45
6141	10k. "David Sasunsky" (Armenia) (M. Abegyan)	75	45
6142	10k. "Gerogly" (Turkmenistan) (I. Klychev)	75	45
6143	10k. "Kalevipoeg" (Estonia) (O. Kallis)	75	45

2482 Goalkeeper and Players

1990. World Cup Football Championship, Italy. Multicoloured.

6144	5k. Type **2482**	25	15
6145	10k. Players	75	45
6146	15k. Attempted tackle	1·00	60
6147	25k. Referee and players	1·30	75
6148	35k. Goalkeeper saving ball	1·80	1·00

2483 Globe and Finlandia Hall, Helsinki

1990. 15th Anniv of European Security and Co-operation Conference, Helsinki.

6149 **2483** 15k. multicoloured 1·50 85

2484 Competitors and Target

1990. 45th World Shooting Championships, Moscow.

6150 **2484** 15k. multicoloured 1·30 75

2485 Glaciology Research

1990. Soviet–Australian Scientific Co-operation in Antarctica. Multicoloured.

6151	5k. Type **2485**	40	20
6152	50k. Krill (marine biology research)	3·50	2·00

MS6153 84×65 mm. Nos. 6151/2 5·00 3·00

2486 Emblem and Sports Pictograms

1990. Goodwill Games, Seattle.

6154 **2486** 10k. multicoloured 75 45

2487 Troops and Badge of order of Aleksandr Nevsky (B2)

1990. 750th Anniv of Battle of Neva. Sheet 94×65 mm.

MS6155 **2487** 50k. multicoloured 3·25 1·90

2488 Greylag Geese

1990. Poultry. Multicoloured.

6156	5k. Type **2488**	25	15
6157	10k. Adlers (chickens)	75	45
6158	15k. Common turkeys	1·30	75

2489 Mallards

1990. Ducks (2nd series). Multicoloured.

6159	5k. Type **2489**	25	15
6160	15k. Common goldeneyes	1·00	60
6161	20k. Red-crested pochards	1·50	85

1990. Lenin Soviet Children's Fund. Children's Paintings. As T **2437**. Multicoloured.

6162	5k.+2k. Clown	65	30
6163	5k.+2k. Ladies in crinolines	65	30
6164	5k.+2k. Children with banner	65	30

1990. Historical Monuments (2nd series). As T **2464**. Multicoloured.

6165	15k. St. Nshan's Church, Akhpat (Armenia)	75	45
6166	15k. Shirvanshah Palace, Baku (Azerbaijan)	75	45
6167	15k. Soroki Fortress and statue of Stefan III, Kishinev (Moldavia)	75	45
6168	15k. Spaso-Efrosinevsky Cathedral, Polotsk (Byelorussia)	75	45
6169	15k. St. Peter's Church and 16th-century Riga (Latvia)	75	45
6170	15k. St. Nicholas's Church and carving of city arms, Tallin (Estonia)	75	45
6171	15k. Mtatsminda Pantheon and statue of Nikoloz Baratashvili, Tbilisi (Georgia)	75	45
6172	15k. Cathedral and bell tower, Vilnius (Lithuania)	75	45

2490 Sordes

1990. Prehistoric Animals. Multicoloured.

6173		1k. Type **2490**	25	15
6174		3k. Chalicotherium (vert)	40	20
6175		5k. Indricotherium (vert)	50	30
6176		10k. Saurolophus (vert)	75	45
6177		20k. Cephalaspid ostracoderm	1·80	1·00

2491 "St. Basil's Cathedral and Kremlin, Moscow" (Sanjay Adhikari)

1990. Indo-Soviet Friendship. Children's Paintings. Multicoloured.

6178		10k. Type **2491**	75	45
6179		10k. "Life in India" (Tanya Vorontsova)	75	45

2492 Pigeon Post

1990. Letter Writing Week.

6180	**2492**	5k. blue	65	20

2493 Traffic on Urban Roads

1990. Traffic Safety Week.

6181	**2493**	5k. multicoloured	65	20

2494 Grey Heron

1990. Nature Conservation. Sheet 65×90 mm.

MS6182	**2494**	20k.+10k. multicoloured	6·25	3·75

1990. Traditional Musical Instruments (2nd series). As T **2455**. Multicoloured.

6183		10k. Azerbaijani balalian, shar and caz (stringed instruments), zurna and drum	75	45
6184		10k. Georgian bagpipes, tambourine, flute, pipes and chonguri (stringed instrument)	75	45
6185		10k. Kazakh flute, rattle, daubra and kobyz (stringed instruments)	75	45
6186		10k. Lithuanian bagpipes, horns and kankles	75	45

2495 Killer Whales

1990. Marine Mammals.

6187		25k. Type **2495**	1·50	85
6188		25k. Northern sealions	1·50	85
6189		25k. Sea otter	1·50	85
6190		25k. Common dolphin	1·50	85

2496 "Lenin among Delegates to Second Congress of Soviets" (S. V. Gerasimov)

1990. 73rd Anniv of October Revolution.

6191	**2496**	5k. multicoloured	65	20

2497 Ivan Bunin (1933)

1990. Nobel Prize Winners for Literature.

6192	**2497**	15k. brown	1·00	60
6193	-	15k. brown	1·00	60
6194	-	15k. black	1·00	60

DESIGNS: No. 6193, Mikhail Sholokhov (1965); 6194, Boris Pasternak.

2498 "Sever 2"

1990. Research Submarines. Multicoloured.

6195		5k. Type **2498**	25	15
6196		10k. "Tinro 2"	50	30
6197		15k. "Argus"	75	45
6198		25k. "Paisis"	1·80	1·00
6199		35k. "Mir"	2·30	1·30

2499 "Motherland" Statue (E. Kocher), Screen and Emblem

1990. "Armenia '90" Stamp Exhibition, Yerevan. (a) Type 2499.

6200	**2499**	10k. multicoloured	50	30

(2500)	(2501)
Филателистическая выставка „Армения-90"	**Восстановление, милосердие, помощь**

(b) Nos. 5957/9 optd with T **2500** (20k.) or as T **2501**.

6201	**2412**	20k.+10k. mult	75	45
6202	-	30k.+15k. mult	1·00	60
6203	-	50k.+25k. mult	2·00	1·20

2502 S. A. Vaupshasov

1990. Intelligence Agents.

6204	**2502**	5k. dp grn, grn and blk	40	20
6205	-	5k. dp brn, brn and blk	40	20
6206	-	5k. deep blue, blue and black	40	20
6207	-	5k. brown, buff & black	40	20
6208	-	5k. brown, bistre and black	40	20

DESIGNS: No. 6205, R. I. Abel; 6206, Kim Philby; 6207, I. D. Kudrya; 6208, Konon Molodyi (alias Gordon Lonsdale).

2503 Soviet and Japanese Flags above Earth

1990. Soviet–Japanese Space Flight.

6209	**2503**	20k. multicoloured	75	45

2504 Grandfather Frost and Toys

1990. New Year.

6210	**2504**	5k. multicoloured	50	30

2505 "Unkrada"

1990. Soviet Culture Fund. Paintings by N. K. Rerikh. Multicoloured.

6211		10k.+5k. Type **2505**	75	45
6212		20k.+10k. "Pskovo-Pechorsky Monastery"	1·30	75

2506 "Joys to all those in Need" (detail of icon) and Fund Emblem

1990. Soviet Charity and Health Fund. Sheet 90×70 mm.

MS6213	**2506**	50k.+25k. multicoloured	5·00	3·00

2507 Globe, Eiffel Tower and Flags

1990. "Charter for New Europe". Signing of European Conventional Arms Treaty, Paris.

6214	**2507**	30k. multicoloured	2·00	1·20

2508 Jellyfish

1991. Marine Animals. Multicoloured.

6215		4k. Type **2508**	25	15
6216		5k. Anemone	25	15
6217		10k. Spurdog	40	20
6218		15k. European anchovy	50	30
6219		20k. Bottle-nosed dolphin	65	35

2509 Keres

1991. 75th Birth Anniv of Paul Keres (chess player).

6220	**2509**	15k. brown	50	30

2510 Radioactive Particles killing Vegetation

1991. Fifth Anniv of Chernobyl Nuclear Power Station Disaster.

6221	**2510**	15k. multicoloured	50	30

2511 "Sorrento Coast with View of Capri" (Shchedrin)

1991. Birth Bicentenary of Silvestr Shchedrin and 150th Birth Anniv of Arkhip Kuindzhi (painters). Multicoloured.

6222		10k. Type **2511**	25	15
6223		10k. "New Rome. View of St. Angelo's Castle" (Shchedrin)	25	15
6224		10k. "Evening in the Ukraine" (Kuindzhi)	25	15
6225		10k. "Birch Grove" (Kuindzhi)	25	15

2512 White Stork

1991. Zoo Relief Fund.

6226	**2512**	10k.+5k. mult	1·30	75

2513 Sturgeon and Bell Tower, Volga

1991. Environmental Protection. Multicoloured.

6227		10k. Type **2513**	25	15
6228		15k. Sable and Lake Baikal	50	30
6229		20k. Saiga and dried bed of Aral Sea	75	45

2514 Swallowtail on Flower

1991. 25th Anniv of All-Union Philatelic Society. Sheet 90×65 mm.

MS6230	**2514**	20k.+10k. multicoloured	2·00	1·20

1991. Historical Monuments (3rd series). As T **2464**. Multicoloured.

6231		15k. Minaret, Uzgen, Kirgizia	25	20
6232		15k. Mohammed Bashar Mausoleum, Tadzhikistan	25	20
6233		15k. Talkhatan-baba Mosque, Turkmenistan	25	20

2515 G. Shelikhov and Kodiak, 1784

1991. 500th Anniv of Discovery of America by Columbus. Russian Settlements.

6234	**2515**	20k. blue and black	40	15
6235	-	30k. bistre, brown & blk	50	30
6236	-	50k. orange, brown & blk	90	45

DESIGNS: 30k. Aleksandr Baranov and Sitka, 1804; 50k. I. Kuskov and Fort Ross, California, 1812.

2516 Satellite and Liner

1991. Tenth Anniv of United Nations Transport and Communications in Asia and the Pacific Programme.

6237	**2516**	10k. multicoloured	50	30

2517 Yuri Gagarin in Uniform

1991. Cosmonautics Day. 30th Anniv of First Man in Space. Each brown.

6238		25k. Type **2517**	50	30

6239 25k. Gagarin wearing space suit 50 30
6240 25k. Gagarin in uniform with cap 50 30
6241 25k. Gagarin in civilian dress 50 30
MS6242 85×110 mm. Nos. 6238/41 2·00 1·20

(2518)

1991. "Ad Astra-91" International Stamp Exhibition, Moscow. No. **MS**6242 optd with T **2518**.
MS6243 85×119 mm. 4×25k. brown 3·75 2·20

2519 "May 1945" (A. and S. Tkachev)

1991. Victory Day.
6244 **2519** 5k. multicoloured 50 30

2520 "Lenin working on Book 'Materialism and Empirical Criticism' in Geneva Library" (P. Belousov)

1991. 121st Birth Anniv of Lenin.
6245 **2520** 5k. multicoloured 50 30

2521 Prokofiev

1991. Birth Centenary of Sergei Prokofiev (composer).
6246 **2521** 15k. brown 50 30

2522 Lady's Slipper

1991. Orchids. Multicoloured.
6247 3k. Type **2522** 25 15
6248 5k. Lady orchid 25 15
6249 10k. Bee orchid 30 15
6250 20k. Calypso 40 20
6251 25k. Marsh helleborine 50 30

2523 Ilya I. Mechnikov (medicine, 1908)

1991. Nobel Prize Winners. Each black.
6252 15k. Type **2523** 50 30
6253 15k. Ivan P. Pavlov (medicine, 1904) 50 30
6254 15k. A. D. Sakharov (peace, 1975) 50 30

2524 Soviet and British Flags in Space

1991. Soviet–British Space Flight.
6255 **2524** 20k. multicoloured 50 30

2525 Saroyan

1991. Tenth Death Anniv of William Saroyan (writer).
6256 **2525** 1r. multicoloured 2·50 1·50

2526 "The Universe"

1991. Lenin Soviet Children's Fund. Paintings by V. Lukyanets. Multicoloured.
6257 10k.+5k. Type **2526** 25 15
6258 10k.+5k. "Another Planet" 25 15

2527 Miniature from "Ostromirov Gospel" (first book written in Cyrillic), 1056–57

1991. Culture of Medieval Russia. Multicoloured.
6259 10k. Type **2527** 25 20
6260 15k. Page from "Russian Truth" (code of laws), 11th–13th century 30 20
6261 20k. Portrait of Sergy Radonezhsky (embroidered book cover), 1424 35 25
6262 25k. "The Trinity" (icon, Andrei Rublev), 1411 40 25
6263 30k. Illustration from "Book of the Apostles", 1564 50 35

2528 Pintails

1991. Ducks (3rd series). Multicoloured.
6264 5k. Type **2528** 45 30
6265 15k. Greater scaups 55 40
6266 20k. White-headed ducks 70 50

2529 Emblem

1991. European Conference on Security and Co-operation Session, Moscow.
6267 **2529** 10k. multicoloured 65 25

2530 Patroness

1991. Soviet Charity and Health Fund.
6268 **2530** 20k.+10k. mult 75 55

2531 Woman in Traditional Costume

1991. First Anniv of Declaration of Ukrainian Sovereignty.
6269 **2531** 30k. multicoloured 75 55

2532 "Albatros"

1991. Airships. Multicoloured.
6270 1k. Type **2532** 25 20
6271 3k. GA-42 30 20
6272 4k. "Norge" (horiz) 35 25
6273 5k. "Pobeda" (horiz) 40 25
6274 20k. LZ-127 "Graf Zeppelin" (horiz) 75 55

2533 "Sv. Pyotr" and Route Map

1991. 250th Anniv of Vitus Bering's and A. Chirkov's Expedition. Multicoloured.
6275 30k. Type **2533** 75 40
6276 30k. Sighting land 75 40

2534 Girl with Letter

1991. Letter Writing Week.
6277 **2534** 7k. brown 55 30

2535 Bell and Bell Towers

1991. Soviet Culture Fund.
6278 **2535** 20k.+10k. mult 75 55

The belfries depicted are from Kuliga-Drakonovo, Church of the Assumption in Pskov, Ivan the Great in Moscow and Cathedral of the Assumption in Rostov.

2536 Kayak Race and "Santa Maria"

1991. Olympic Games, Barcelona (1992) (1st issue). Multicoloured.
6279 10k. Type **2536** 25 20
6280 20k. Running and Church of the Holy Family 45 30
6281 30k. Football and stadium 50 35

See also Nos. 6362/4.

2537 Rainbow, Globe and Flags

1991. Soviet–Austrian Space Flight.
6282 **2537** 20k. multicoloured 75 35

2538 Ascension Day (Armenia)

1991. Folk Festivals. Multicoloured.
6283 15k. Type **2538** 40 25
6284 15k. Women carrying dishes of wheat (Novruz holiday, Azerbaijan) 40 25
6285 15k. Throwing garlands in water (Ivan Kupala summer holiday, Belorussia) 40 25
6286 15k. Stick wrestling and dancing round decorated tree (New Year, Estonia) (horiz) 40 25
6287 15k. Masked dancers (Berikaoba spring holiday, Georgia) 40 25
6288 15k. Riders with goat skin (Kazakhstan) (horiz) 40 25
6289 15k. Couple on horses (Kirgizia) (horiz) 40 25
6290 15k. Couple leaping over flames (Ligo (Ivan Kupala) holiday, Latvia) (horiz) 40 25
6291 15k. Family on way to church (Palm Sunday, Lithuania) (horiz) 40 25
6292 15k. Man in beribboned hat and musicians (Plugusorul (New Year) holiday, Moldova) 40 25
6293 15k. Sledge ride (Shrovetide, Russian Federation) 40 25
6294 15k. Musicians on carpet and stilt-walkers (Novruz holiday, Tajikistan) 40 25
6295 15k. Wrestlers (Harvest holiday, Turkmenistan) (horiz) 40 25
6296 15k. Dancers and couple with lute and tambourine (Christmas, Ukraine) (horiz) 40 25
6297 15k. Girls with tulips (Tulip holiday, Uzbekistan) 40 25

2539 Dimitry Komar

1991. Defeat of Attempted Coup. Multicoloured.
6298 7k. Type **2539** 40 20
6299 7k. Ilya Krichevsky 40 20
6300 7k. Vladimir Usov 40 20
MS6301 90×64 mm. 50k. Barricades around Russian Federation Government House (51×33 mm) 1·30 90

Nos. 6298/6300 depict victims killed in opposing the attempted coup.

2540 Federation Government House and Flag

1991. Election of Boris Yeltsin as President of the Russian Federation.
6302 **2540** 7k. blue, gold and red 50 35

1991. Traditional Musical Instruments (3rd series). As T **2455**. Multicoloured.
6303 10k. Kirgiz flutes, komuzes and kyyak (string instruments) 45 20
6304 10k. Latvian ganurags and stabule (wind), tambourine, duga and kokle (string instruments) 45 20
6305 10k. Moldavian flute, bagpipes, nai (pipes), kobza and tsambal (string instruments) 45 20

2541 Decorations and Gifts

1991. New Year.
6306 **2541** 7k. multicoloured 50 35

2542 Nikolai Mikhailovich Karamzin

1991. Historians' Birth Anniversaries. Multicoloured.
6307 10k. Type **2542** (225th anniv) 50 25
6308 10k. V. O. Klyuchevsky (150th anniv) 50 25
6309 10k. Sergei M. Solovyov (171st anniv) 50 25
6310 10k. V. N. Tatishchev (after A. Osipov) (305th anniv) 50 25

RUSSIAN FEDERATION

2543 Cross-country Skiing and Ski Jumping

1992. Winter Olympic Games, Albertville, France. Multicoloured.

6311		14k. Type **2543**	20	15
6312		1r. Aerobatic skiing	55	40
6313		2r. Two and four-man bob-sleighing	1·60	1·30

2544 Tiger Cubs

1992. Nature Conservation. Sheet 90×65 mm.

MS6314	**2544**	3r.+50k. multicoloured	2·30	1·80

2545 Battle Scene

1992. 750th Anniv of Battle of Lake Peipus. Sheet 95×65 mm.

MS6315	**2545**	50k. multicoloured	1·40	80

2546 Golden Gate, Vladimir

1992

6316	**2546**	10k. orange	35	15
6317	-	15k. brown	35	15
6318	-	20k. red	35	15
6344	-	25k. red	55	30
6319	-	30k. black	35	15
6320	-	50k. blue	35	15
6321	-	55k. turquoise	45	20
6322	-	60k. green	45	20
6323	-	80k. purple	55	20
6324	-	1r. brown	55	20
6325	-	1r.50 green	70	30
6326	-	2r. blue	90	35
6327	-	3r. red	1·10	55
6328	-	4r. brown	65	30
6329	-	5r. brown	1·40	70
6330	-	6r. blue	1·00	55
6331	-	10r. blue	1·80	1·10
6332	-	15r. brown	90	55
6333	-	25r. purple	2·75	1·80
6334	-	45r. black	2·20	70
6335	-	50r. violet	90	55
6336	-	75r. brown	3·50	2·10
6337	-	100r. green	6·25	2·75
6338	**2546**	150r. blue	90	55
6339	-	250r. green	1·80	1·30
6340	-	300r. red	1·80	1·10
6341	-	500r. purple	3·50	2·50
6341a	-	750r. green	1·80	1·40
6341b	-	1000r. grey	2·75	1·40
6342	-	1500r. green	2·75	2·10
6342a	-	2500r. bistre	4·50	2·75
6342b	-	5000r. blue	9·00	6·25

DESIGNS: 15k. Pskov kremlin; 20, 50k. St. George killing dragon; 25, 55k. Victory Arch, Moscow; 30, 80k. "Millennium of Russia" monument (M. Mikeshin), Novgorod; 60k., 300r. Statue of K. Minin and D. Pozharsky, Moscow; 1, 4r. Church, Kizhky; 1r.50, 6r. Statue of Peter I, St. Petersburg; 2r. St. Basil's Cathedral, Moscow; 3r. Tretyakov Gallery, Moscow; 5r. Europe House, Moscow; 10r. St. Isaac's Cathedral, St. Petersburg; 15, 45r. "The Horse-tamer" (statue), St. Petersburg; 25, 75r. Statue of Yuri Dolgoruky, Moscow; 50r. Rostov Kremlin; 100r. Moscow Kremlin; 250r. Church, Bogulyubovo; 500r. Moscow University; 750r. State Library, Moscow; 1000r. Peter and Paul Fortress, St. Petersburg; 1500r. Pushkin Museum, Moscow; 2500r. Admiralty, St. Petersburg; 5000r. Bolshoi Theatre, Moscow.

2547 "Victory" (N. Baskakov)

1992. Victory Day.

6350	**2547**	5k. multicoloured	35	15

2548 Western Capercaillie, Oak and Pine

1992. Prioksko–Terrasnyi Nature Reserve.

6351	**2548**	50k. multicoloured	35	15

2549 "Mir" Space Station, Flags and Cosmonauts

1992. Russian–German Joint Space Flight.

6352	**2549**	5r. multicoloured	1·40	1·10

2550 "Santa Maria" and Columbus

1992. 500th Anniv of Discovery of America by Columbus (1st issue). Sheet 88×65 mm.

MS6353	**2550**	3r. multicoloured	2·20	2·10

See also No. 6386.

2551 Pinocchio

1992. Characters from Children's Books (1st series). Multicoloured.

6354		25k. Type **2551**	35	15
6355		30k. Cipollino	35	15
6356		35k. Dunno	35	15
6357		50k. Karlson	35	15

See also Nos. 6391/5.

2552 Russian Cosmonaut and Space Shuttle

1992. International Space Year. Multicoloured.

6358		25r. Type **2552**	1·10	40
6359		25r. American astronaut and "Mir" space station	1·10	40
6360		25r. "Apollo" and "Vostok" spacecraft and sputnik	1·10	40
6361		25r. "Soyuz", "Mercury" and "Gemini" spacecraft	1·10	40

Nos. 6358/61 were issued together, se-tenant, forming a composite design.

2553 Handball

1992. Olympic Games, Barcelona (2nd issue).

6362	**2553**	1r. multicoloured	25	20
6363	-	2r. red, blue and black	55	30
6364	-	3r. red, green and black	1·10	35

DESIGNS—HORIZ: 2r. Fencing; 3r. Judo.

2554 L. A. Zagoskin and Yukon River, Alaska, 1842–44

1992. Expeditions. Multicoloured.

6365		55k. Type **2554**	20	15
6366		70k. N. N. Miklukho-Maklai in New Guinea, 1871–74	25	20
6367		1r. G. I. Langsdorf and route map of expedition to Brazil, 1822–28	35	30

2555 Garganeys

1992. Ducks. Multicoloured.

6368		1r. Type **2555**	35	20
6369		2r. Common pochards	55	35
6370		3r. Falcated teals	90	40

2556 "Taj Mahal Mausoleum in Agra"

1992. 150th Birth Anniv of Vasily Vasilevich Vereshchagin (painter).

6371		1r.50 Type **2556**	45	30
6372		1r.50 "Don't Touch, Let Me Approach!"	45	30

2557 "The Saviour" (icon, Andrei Rublyov)

1992

6373	**2557**	1r. multicoloured	35	20

2558 Cathedral of the Assumption

1992. Moscow Kremlin Cathedrals. Multicoloured.

6374		1r. Type **2558**	35	20
6375		1r. Cathedral of the Annunciation (15th century)	35	20
6376		1r. Archangel Cathedral (16th century)	35	20

See also Nos. 6415/17 and 6440/2.

2559 Russian "Nutcracker" Puppets

1992. Centenary of First Production of Tchaikovsky's Ballet "Nutcracker". Multicoloured.

6377		10r. Type **2559**	85	40
6378		10r. German "Nutcracker" puppets	85	40
6379		25r. Pas de deux from ballet	1·70	80
6380		25r. Dance of the toys	1·70	80

2560 "Meeting of Joachim and Anna"

1992. Icons. Multicoloured.

6381		10r. Type **2560**	1·20	90
6382		10r. "Madonna and Child"	1·20	90
6383		10r. "Archangel Gabriel" (head)	1·20	90
6384		10r. "Saint Nicholas" (½-length portrait)	1·20	90

2561 Clockface and Festive Symbols

1992. New Year.

6385	**2561**	50k. multicoloured	35	15

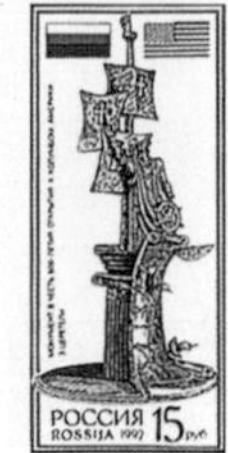
2562 "Discovery of America" Monument (Z. Tsereteli)

1992. 500th Anniv of Discovery of America by Columbus.

6386	**2562**	15r. multicoloured	2·10	1·70

2563 Petipa and Scene from "Paquita"

1993. 175th Birth Anniv of Marius Petipa (choreographer). Multicoloured.

6387		25r. Type **2563**	85	65
6388		25r. "Sleeping Beauty", 1890	85	65
6389		25r. "Swan Lake", 1895	85	65
6390		25r. "Raimunda", 1898	85	65

2564 Scrub 'n' Rub

1993. Characters from Children's Books (2nd series). Illustrations by Kornei Chukovsky. Mult.

6391		2r. Type **2564**	15	15
6392		3r. Big Cockroach	25	15
6393		10r. The Buzzer Fly	35	20
6394		15r. Doctor Doolittle	85	25
6395		25r. Barmalei	1·20	40

Nos. 6391/5 were issued together, *se-tenant*, forming a composite design.

2565 Castle

1993. 700th Anniv of Vyborg.

6396	**2565**	10r. multicoloured	50	25

2566 Part of Diorama in Belgorod Museum

1993. Victory Day. 50th Anniv of Battle of Kursk.

6397	**2566**	10r. multicoloured	50	25

2567 African Violet

1993. Pot Plants. Multicoloured.

6398	10r. Type **2567**	35	25
6399	15r. "Hibiscus rosa-sinensis"	50	40
6400	25r. "Cyclamen persicum"	85	65
6401	50r. "Fuchsia hybrida"	1·70	1·30
6402	100r. "Begonia semperflorens"	4·25	2·50

2568 "Molniya 3"

1993. Communications Satellites. Multicoloured.

6403	25r. Type **2568**	85	25
6404	45r. "Ekran M"	1·30	40
6405	50r. "Gorizont"	1·70	65
6406	75r. "Luch"	2·50	1·00
6407	100r. "Ekspress"	3·75	1·60
MS6408	88×66 mm. 250r. Earth receiving station (horiz)	6·50	4·00

2569 Snuff Box (Dmitry Kolesnikov) and Tankard

1993. Silverware. Multicoloured.

6409	15r. Type **2569**	15	15
6410	25r. Teapot	35	15
6411	45r. Vase	85	20
6412	75r. Tray and candlestick	1·20	50
6413	100r. Cream jug, coffee pot and sugar basin (Aleksandr Kordes)	1·70	80
MS6414	90×65 mm. 250r. Biscuit and sweet dishes (47×33 mm)	5·75	4·00

1993. Novgorod Kremlin. As T **2558**. Multicoloured.

6415	25r. Kukui and Knyazhaya Towers (14th–17th century)	35	25
6416	25r. St. Sophia's Cathedral (11th century)	35	25
6417	25r. St. Sophia belfry (15th–18th century)	35	25
MS6418	70×93 mm. 250r. "Our Lady of the Apparition" (icon) (41×29 mm)	3·25	2·50

2570 Map

1993. Inauguration of Denmark–Russia Submarine Cable and 500th Anniv of Friendship Treaty.

6419	**2570**	90r. green & deep green	85	40

2571 Steller's Eider

1993. Ducks. Multicoloured.

6420	90r. Type **2571**	65	20
6421	100r. Eider	85	25
6422	250r. King eider	2·00	80

2572 Ringed Seal

1993. Marine Animals. Multicoloured.

6423	50r. Type **2572**	50	15
6424	60r. "Paralithodes brevipes" (crab)	65	25
6425	90r. Japanese common squid	85	50
6426	100r. Cherry salmon	1·00	65
6427	250r. Fulmar	2·00	1·40

2573 Ceramic Candlestick, Skopino

1993. Traditional Art. Multicoloured.

6428	50r. Type **2573**	50	40
6429	50r. Painted tray with picture "Summer Troika", Zhostovo (horiz)	50	40
6430	100r. Painted box, lid and distaff, Gorodets	1·00	65
6431	100r. Enamel icon of St. Dmitry of Solun, Rostov	1·00	65
6432	250r. "The Resurrection" (lacquer miniature), Fedoskino	2·30	1·20

2574 Banknotes and Coins

1993. 175th Anniv of Goznak (State printing works and mint).

6433	**2574**	100r. multicoloured	65	25

2575 Peter I and "Goto Predestinatsiya"

1993. 300th Anniv of Russian Navy (1st issue). Multicoloured.

6434	100r. Type **2575**	35	20
6435	100r. K. A. Shilder and first all-metal submarine	35	20
6436	100r. I. A. Amosov and "Arkhimed" (frigate)	35	20
6437	100r. I. G. Bubnov and "Bars" (submarine)	35	20
6438	100r. B. M. Malinin and "Dekabrist" (submarine)	35	20
6439	100r. A. I. Maslov and "Kirov" (cruiser)	35	20

See also Nos. 6502/5, 6559/62 and 6612/18.

1993. Moscow Kremlin. As T **2558**. Multicoloured.

6440	100r. Faceted Hall (15th century)	50	25
6441	100r. Church of the Deposition of the Virgin's Robe (15th century)	50	25
6442	100r. Grand Palace (17th century)	50	25

2576 Tiger

1993. The Tiger. Multicoloured.

6443	50r. Type **2576**	15	15
6444	100r. Tiger in undergrowth	35	20
6445	250r. Two tiger cubs	85	40
6446	500r. Tiger in snow	1·70	65

2577 Splash of Blood on Figure

1993. Anti-AIDS Campaign.

6447	**2577**	90r. red, black and lilac	50	40

2578 Seasonal Decorations

1993. New Year.

6448	**2578**	25r. multicoloured	50	40

2579 Indian Elephant

1993. Animals. Multicoloured.

6449	250r. Type **2579**	65	35
6450	250r. Japanese white-naped crane	65	35
6451	250r. Giant panda	65	35
6452	250r. American bald eagle	65	35
6453	250r. Dall's porpoise	65	35
6454	250r. Koala	65	35
6455	250r. Hawaiian monk seal	65	35
6456	250r. Grey whale	65	35

2580 Rimsky-Korsakov and Scene from "Sadko"

1994. 150th Birth Anniv of Nikolai Rimsky-Korsakov (composer). Scenes from his operas. Multicoloured.

6457	250r. Type **2580**	85	65
6458	250r. "The Golden Cockerel"	85	65
6459	250r. "The Tsar's Bride"	85	65
6460	250r. "The Snow Maiden"	85	65

2581 "Epiphyllum peacockii"

1994. Cacti. Multicoloured.

6461	50r. Type **2581**	35	15
6462	100r. "Mammillaria swinglei"	50	25
6463	100r. "Lophophora williamsii"	50	25
6464	250r. "Opuntia basilaris"	85	40
6465	250r. "Selenicereus grandiflorus"	85	40

2582 York Minster, Great Britain

1994. Churches. Multicoloured.

6466	150r. Type **2582**	50	25
6467	150r. Small Metropolis church, Athens	50	25
6468	150r. Roskilde Cathedral, Denmark	50	25
6469	150r. Notre Dame Cathedral, Paris	50	25
6470	150r. St. Peter's, Vatican City	50	25
6471	150r. Cologne Cathedral, Germany	50	25
6472	150r. Seville Cathedral, Spain	50	25
6473	150r. St. Basil's Cathedral, Moscow	50	25
6474	150r. St. Patrick's Cathedral, New York	50	25

2583 "Soyuz" entering Earth's Atmosphere and "TsF-18" Centrifuge

1994. Yuri Gagarin Cosmonaut Training Centre. Multicoloured.

6475	100r. Type **2583**	35	15
6476	250r. "Soyuz"–"Mir" space complex and "Mir" simulator	1·00	40
6477	500r. Cosmonaut on space walk and hydrolaboratory	2·00	80

2584 Map and Rocket Launchers (Liberation of Russia)

1994. 50th Anniv of Liberation. Multicoloured.

6478	100r. Type **2584**	35	25
6479	100r. Map and airplanes (Ukraine)	35	25
6480	100r. Map, tank and soldiers (Belorussia)	35	25

2585 Beautiful Gate, Moscow

1994. Architects' Birth Anniversaries.

6481	**2585**	50r. sepia, black and brown	15	15
6482	-	100r. brown, black and flesh	35	20
6483	-	150r. green, black and olive	65	25
6484	-	300r. violet, black and grey	1·20	35

DESIGNS: 50r. Type **2585** (D. V. Ukhtomsky, 250th anniv); 100r. Academy of Sciences, St. Petersburg (Giacomo Quarenghi, 250th anniv); 150r. Trinity Cathedral, St. Petersburg (V. P. Stasov, 225th anniv); 300r. Church of Christ the Saviour, Moscow (K. A. Ton, bicentenary).

2586 "Christ and the Sinner"

1994. 150th Birth Anniv of Vasily Dmitrievich Polenev (painter). Multicoloured.

6485	150r. Type **2586**	50	40
6486	150r. "Golden Autumn"	50	40

2587 European Wigeon

1994. Ducks. Multicoloured.

6487	150r. Type **2587**	35	20
6488	250r. Tufted duck	65	25
6489	300r. Baikal teal	1·00	40

2588 Games Emblem and Runners

1994. Third Goodwill Games, St. Petersburg.

6490	**2588**	100r. multicoloured	35	20

2589 Pyotr Leonidovich Kapitsa

1994. Physics Nobel Prize Winners. Each sepia.

6491	150r. Type **2589** (1978)	40	25
6492	150r. Pavel Alekseevich Cherenkov (1958)	40	25

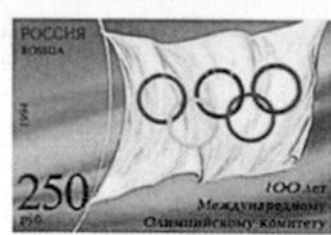
2590 Olympic Flag

1994. Cent of International Olympic Committee.

6493	**2590**	250r. multicoloured	65	35

2591 Design Motifs of First Russian Stamp

1994. Russian Stamp Day.

6494	**2591**	125r. multicoloured	35	20

2592 Snuff Box (D. Vinogradov)

1994. 250th Anniv of Imperial (now M. Lomonosov) Porcelain Factory, St. Petersburg. Multicoloured.

6495	50r. Type **2592**	15	15
6496	100r. Candlestick	15	15
6497	150r. "Water-Carrier" (statuette, after S. Pimenov)	35	15
6498	250r. Sphinx vase	50	20
6499	300r. "Lady with Mask" (statuette, after K. Somov)	85	25
MS6500	60×90 mm. 500r. Dinner service (F. Solntsev) (36×36 mm)	2·50	1·30

2593 Centre of Asia Obelisk

1994. 50th Anniv of Incorporation of Tuva into Russian Socialist Federal Soviet Republic (R.S.F.S.R.).

6501	**2593**	125r. mulitcoloured	35	20

2594 Vice-Admiral V. M. Golovnin (Kurile Islands, 1811)

1994. 300th Anniv of Russian Navy (2nd issue). Explorations. Multicoloured.

6502	250r. Type **2594**	50	25
6503	250r. Admiral I. F. Kruzenshtern (first Russain round-the-world expedition, 1803–06)	50	25
6504	250r. Admiral Ferdinand Petrovich Vrangel (Alaska, 1829–35)	50	25
6505	250r. Admiral F. P. Litke (Novaya Zemlya, 1821–24)	50	25

2595 Horses and Grandfather Frost

1994. New Year.

6506	**2595**	125r. blue, red and black	35	20

2596 Griboedov (after N. I. Utkin)

1995. Birth Bicentenary of Aleksandr Sergeevich Griboedov (dramatist and diplomat).

6507	**2596**	250r. brown, light brown and black	1·30	1·00

2597 "Sheherazade"

1995. 115th Birth Anniv of Mikhail Fokine (choreographer). Scenes from Ballets. Mult.

6508	500r. Type **2597**	50	25
6509	500r. "The Fire Bird"	50	25
6510	500r. "Petrushka"	50	25

2598 Kutuzov (after J. Doe) and Sculptures from Monument, Moscow

1995. 250th Birth Anniv of Field-Marshal Mikhail Ilarionovich Kutuzov, Prince of Smolensk.

6511	**2598**	300r. multicoloured	50	40

2599 English Yard, Varvarka Street

1995. 850th Anniv (1997) of Moscow (1st issue). Multicoloured.

6512	125r. Type **2599**	15	15
6513	250r. House of Averky Kirillov (scribe), Bersenevskaya Embankment	25	15
6514	300r. Volkov house, Bolshoi Kharitonevsky Lane	35	15

See also Nos. 6600/5, **MS**6649 and 6666/75.

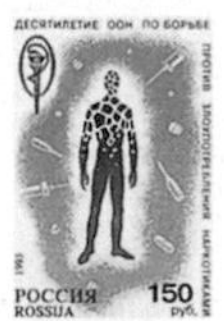

2600 Syringes and Drugs around Addict

1995. U.N. Anti-drugs Decade.

6515	**2600**	150r. multicoloured	35	15

2601 Shoreline

1995. Endangered Animals. Multicoloured.

6516	250r. Type **2601**	50	25
6517	250r. Ringed seal	50	25
6518	250r. Lynx	50	25
6519	250r. Landscape	50	25

Nos. 6516/19 were issued together, se-tenant, Nos. 6516/17 and 6518/19 respectively forming composite designs.

2602 Tomb of the Unknown Soldier, Moscow

1995. 50th Anniv of End of Second World War. Multicoloured.

6520	250r. Sir Winston Churchill, U.S. Pres. Franklin Roosevelt and Iosif Stalin (Yalta Conference) (horiz)	35	25
6521	250r. Storming of the Reichstag, Berlin (horiz)	35	25
6522	250r. Flags, map of Germany and German banners (Potsdam Conference)	35	25
6523	250r. Bombers (operation against Japanese in Manchuria (horiz))	35	25
6524	250r. Urn with victims' ashes, Auschwitz, and memorial, Sachsenhausen (liberation of concentration camps) (horiz)	35	25
6525	250r. Type **2602**	35	25
6526	500r. Victory Parade, Moscow (36×47 mm)	1·30	1·00
MS6527	64×89 mm. No. 6526	5·00	2·50

2603 Aleksandr Popov (radio pioneer) and Radio-telegraph Equipment

1995. Centenary of Radio.

6528	**2603**	250r. multicoloured	35	20

2604 Spreading Bellflower

1995. Meadow Flowers. Multicoloured.

6529	250r. Type **2604**	25	15
6530	250r. Ox-eye daisy ("Leucanthemum vulgare")	25	15
6531	300r. Red clover ("Trifolium pratense")	35	20
6532	300r. Brown knapweed ("Centaurea jacea")	35	20
6533	500r. Meadow cranesbill	1·00	40

2605 Eurasian Sky Lark ("Alauda arvensis")

1995. Songbirds. Multicoloured.

6534	250r. Type **2605**	50	25
6535	250r. Song thrush ("Turdus philomelos")	50	25
6536	500r. Eurasian goldfinch ("Carduelis carduelis")	65	40
6537	500r. Bluethroat ("Cyanosylvia svecica")	65	40
6538	750r. Thrush nightingale ("Luscinia luscinia")	1·00	65

2606 U.S. Space Shuttle "Atlantis"

1995. Russian–American Space Co-operation. Multicoloured.

6539	1500r. Type **2606**	1·50	50
6540	1500r. "Mir" space station	1·50	50
6541	1500r. "Apollo" spacecraft	1·50	50
6542	1500r. "Soyuz" spacecraft	1·50	50

Nos. 6539/42 were issued together, *se-tenant*, forming a composite design of the spacecraft over Earth.

2607 Cathedral of the Trinity, Jerusalem

1995. Russian Orthodox Churches Abroad. Multicoloured.

6543	300r. Type **2607**	35	20
6544	300r. Apostles Saints Peter and Paul Cathedral, Karlovy Vary, Czechoslovakia	35	20
6545	500r. St. Nicholas's Cathedral, Vienna	50	25
6546	500r. St. Nicholas's Cathedral, New York	50	25
6547	750r. St. Aleksei's Cathedral, Leipzig	85	40

2608 Kremlin Cathedrals

1995. 900th Anniv of Ryazan.

6548	**2608**	250r. multicoloured	35	20

2609 Easter Egg with Model of "Shtandart" (yacht)

1995. Faberge Exhibits in Moscow Kremlin Museum. Multicoloured.

6549	150r. Type **2609**	15	15
6550	250r. Goblet	35	15
6551	300r. Cross pendant	40	20
6552	500r. Ladle	50	25
6553	750r. Easter egg with model of Alexander III monument	1·30	40
MS6554	65×90 mm. 1500r. "Moscow Kremlin" easter egg (36×51 mm)	4·25	2·50

2610 Harlequin Duck

1995. Ducks. Multicoloured.

6555	500r. Type **2610**	50	20
6556	750r. Baer's pochard	85	25
6557	1000r. Goosander	1·20	50

2611 City Buildings

1995. "Singapore '95" International Stamp Exhibition Sheet 90×65 mm.

MS6558	**2611** 2500r. multicoloured	5·00	3·25

2612 "The Battle of Grengam, July 27, 1720" (F. Perrault)

1995. 300th Anniv of Russian Navy (3rd issue). Paintings. Multicoloured.

6559	250r. Type **2612**	25	15
6560	300r. "Preparations for Attacking the Turkish Fleet in the Bay of Cesme, Night of June 26, 1770" (P. Hackert)	35	20
6561	500r. "The Battle at the Revel Roadstead, May 2, 1790" (A. Bogolyubov)	50	25
6562	750r. "The Kronstadt Roadstead" (I. Aivazovsky)	85	35

2613 State Flag and Arms

1995. Constitution of the Russian Federation.

6563	**2613**	500r. multicoloured	85	65

2614 Emblem and San Francisco Conference, 1945

1995. 50th Anniv of U.N.O.

6564	**2614** 500r. brown, blue and yellow	65	40

2615 White Storks in Nest

1995. Europa. Peace and Freedom. Multicoloured.

6565	1500r. Type **2615**	2·50	1·30
6566	1500r. Stork flying over landscape	2·50	1·30

Nos. 6565/6 were issued together, *se-tenant*, forming a composite design.

2616 "Birth of Christ" (icon, Assumption Cathedral, St. Cyril's Monastery, White Sea)

1995. Christmas.

6567	**2616** 500r. multicoloured	65	30

2617 Yuri Dolgoruky (1090–1157), Kiev and Building of Moscow

1995. History of Russian State (1st series). Multicoloured.

6568	1000r. Type **2617**	1·30	60
6569	1000r. Aleksandr Nevsky (1220–63), Battle of Lake Peipus and as Grand Duke of Vladimir	1·30	60
6570	1000r. Mikhail Yaroslavich (1271–1318), Tver and torture by the Golden Horde	1·30	60
6571	1000r. Dmitry Donskoi (1350–89), Moscow Kremlin and Battle of Kulikovo	1·30	60
6572	1000r. Ivan III (1440–1505), marriage to Sophia Paleologa and Battle of Ugra River	1·30	60

See also Nos. 6640/3.

2618 Semyonov

1996. Birth Centenary of Nikolai Semyonov (Nobel Prize winner for chemistry, 1956).

6573	**2618** 750r. grey	65	30

2619 Pansies

1996. Flowers. Multicoloured.

6574	500r. Type **2619**	35	15
6575	750r. Sweet-williams ("Dianthus barbatus")	65	20
6576	750r. Sweet peas ("Lathyrus odoratus")	65	20
6577	1000r. Crown imperial ("Fritillaria imperialis")	85	45
6578	1000r. Snapdragons ("Antirrhinum majus")	85	45

2620 Tabbies

1996. Cats. Multicoloured.

6579	1000r. Type **2620**	85	75
6580	1000r. Russian blue	85	75
6581	1000r. White Persian	85	75
6582	1000r. Sealpoint Siamese	85	75
6583	1000r. Siberian	85	75

2621 Torch Bearer

1996. Centenary of Modern Olympic Games. Sheet 64×85 mm.

MS6584	**2621** 5000r. multicoloured	7·50	3·75

2622 "Laying down of Banners" (A. Mikhailov)

1996. Victory Day.

6585	**2622** 1000r. multicoloured	85	45

2623 Tula Kremlin and Monument to Peter I

1996. 850th Anniv of Tula.

6586	**2623** 1500r. multicoloured	1·20	60

2624 Putilovsky Works Tramcar, 1896

1996. Centenary of First Russian Tramway, Nizhny Novgorod. Multicoloured.

6587	500r. Type **2624**	35	20
6588	750r. Sormovo tramcar, 1912	50	30
6589	750r. 1928 Series X tramcar, 1928	50	30
6590	1000r. 1931 Series KM tramcar, 1931	1·00	60
6591	1000r. Type LM-57 tramcar, 1957	1·00	60
6592	2500r. Model 71-608K tramcar, 1973	2·00	1·00
MS6593	80×68 mm. No. 6592	3·25	3·00

2625 Ye. Dashkova (President of Academy of Sciences)

1996. Europa. Famous Women.

6594	**2625** 1500r. green and black	2·10	1·50
6595	- 1500r. purple and black	2·10	1·50

DESIGN: No. 6594, S. Kovalevskaya (mathematician).

2626 Children walking Hand in Hand

1996. 50th Anniv of UNICEF.

6596	**2626** 1000r. multicoloured	85	45

2627 "Post Troika in Snowstorm" (P. Sokolov)

1996. Post Troikas in Paintings. Mulitcoloured.

6597	1500r. Type **2627**	1·30	75
6598	1500r. "Post Troika in Summer" (P. Sokolov)	1·30	75
6599	1500r. "Post Troika" (P. Gruzinsky)	1·30	75

2628 "View of Bridge over Yauza and of Shapkin House in Moscow" (J. Delabarte)

1996. 850th Anniv (1997) of Moscow (2nd issue). Paintings. Multicoloured.

6600	500r. Type **2628**	55	25
6601	500r. "View of Moscow from Balcony of Kremlin Palace" (detail, J. Delabarte)	55	25
6602	750r. "View of Voskresenskie and Nikolskie Gates and Kamenny Bridge" (F. Ya. Alekseev)	70	40
6603	750r. "Moscow Yard near Volkhonka" (anon)	70	40
6604	1000r. "Varvarka Street" (anon)	90	45
6605	1000r. "Sledge Races in Petrovsky Park"	90	45

2629 Traffic Policeman and Pedestrian Crossing

1996. 60th Anniv of Traffic Control Department. Sheet 120×150 mm containing T **2629** and similar horiz designs. Multicoloured.

MS6606	1500r. Type **2629**; 1500r. Children learning road safety; 1500r. Examiner and learner vehicle	5·00	3·00

2630 Basketball

1996. Olympic Games, Atlanta, U.S.A. Multicoloured.

6607	500r. Type **2630**	45	25
6608	1000r. Boxing	90	45
6609	1000r. Swimming	90	45
6610	1500r. Gymnastics	1·60	75
6611	1500r. Hurdling	1·60	75

2631 "Yevstafy" (ship of the line), 1762

1996. 300th Anniv of Russian Navy (4th issue). (a) As T **2631**.

6612	**2631** 750r. brown and yellow	70	30
6613	- 1000r. deep blue, cobalt and blue	90	40
6614	- 1000r. purple, pink and rose	90	40
6615	- 1500r. multicoloured	1·40	75
6616	- 1500r. black, grey and stone	1·40	75

DESIGNS: No. 6613, "Petropavlovsk" (battleship); 6614, "Novik" (destroyer); 6615, "Tashkent" (destroyer); 6616, "S-13" (submarine).

(b) Size 35 x 24 mm. Each blue and black.

6617	1000r. "Principium" (galley)	90	40
6618	1000r. "Admiral Kuznetsov" (aircraft carrier)	90	40

Sheet size 130×65 mm containing as Nos. 6617/18 and similar horiz designs. Multicoloured (blue background).

MS6619	1000r. As No. 6617; 1000r. Nuclear-powered submarine; 1000r. "Azov" (ship of the line); 1000r. As No. 6618	5·50	3·00

2632 Gorsky and Scenes from "Gudula's Daughter" and "Salambo"

1996. 125th Birth Anniv of Aleksandr Gorsky (ballet choreographer). Multicoloured.

6620	750r. Type **2632**	70	30
6621	750r. Scene from "La Bayadere"	70	30
6622	1500r. Scene from "Don Quixote"	1·40	60
6623	1500r. Scene from "Giselle"	1·40	60

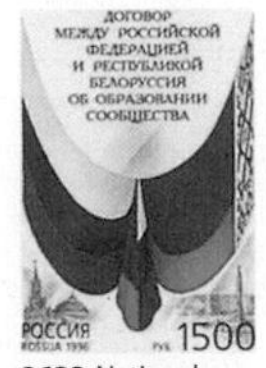

2633 National Flags

1996. Formation of Community of Sovereign Republics (union of Russian Federation and Belarus).

6624	**2633** 1500r. multicoloured	1·80	1·40

2634 Chalice

1996. Objets d'Art. Multicoloured.

6625	1000r. Type **2634**	90	40
6626	1000r. Perfume bottles	90	40
6627	1000r. Double inkwell	90	40
6628	1500r. Coffee pot	1·40	75
6629	1500r. Pendent scent containers (one ladybird-shaped)	1·40	75
MS6630	70×90 mm. 5000r. "Our Lady of Kazan" (icon) (36×51 mm)	5·00	3·00

2635 Symbols of Science and Culture on Open Book

1996. 50th Anniv of UNESCO.

6631	**2635** 1000r. black, gold and blue	90	45

2636 "Madonna and Child" (icon), Moscow

1996. Orthodox Religion. Multicoloured.

6632	1500r. Type **2636**	1·30	55
6633	1500r. Stavrovouni Monastery, Cyprus	1·30	55
6634	1500r. "St. Nicholas" (icon), Cyprus	1·30	55
6635	1500r. Voskresenkie ("Resurrection") Gate, Moscow	1·30	55

2637 Clockface of Spassky Tower, Moscow Kremlin

1996. New Year.

6636	**2637** 1000r. multicoloured	70	30

2638 First Match between U.S.S.R. and Canada, 1972

1996. 50th Anniv of Ice Hockey in Russia. Multicoloured.

6637	1500r. Type **2638**	1·10	45
6638	1500r. Goalkeeper and players (first match between Moscow and Prague, 1948)	1·10	45
6639	1500r. Players and referee (Russia versus Sweden)	1·10	45

1996. History of Russian State (2nd series). As T **2617**. Multicoloured.

6640	1500r. Basil III (1479–1533), removal of bell from Pskov and Siege of Smolensk, 1514	1·40	60
6641	1500r. Ivan IV the Terrible (1530–84), coronation in Cathedral of the Assumption (Moscow Kremlin) and executions by the Oprichnina	1·40	60
6642	1500r. Fyodor I Ivanovich (1557–98), with Cossacks and Siberian Kings, and election of love (first Russian Patriarch)	1·40	60
6643	1500r. Boris Godunov (1551–1605), as Tsar in 1598 and food distribution during famine, 1601–03	1·40	60

2639 Maule's Quince ("Chaenomeles japonica")

1997. Shrubs. Multicoloured.

6644	500r. Type **2639**	70	30
6645	500r. Ornamental almond ("Amygdalus triloba")	70	30
6646	1000r. Broom ("Cytisus scoparius")	1·40	85
6647	1000r. Burnet rose ("Rosa pimpinellifolia")	1·40	85
6648	1000r. Mock orange ("Philadelphus coronarius")	1·40	85

2640 Foundation Festival Emblem

1997. 850th Anniv of Moscow (3rd issue). Sheet 94×71 mm.

MS6649	**2640** 3000r. multicoloured	3·50	2·30

2641 Dmitri Shostakovich (composer) (from 90th birth anniv (1996) medal)

1997. "Shostakovich and World Musical Culture" International Music Festival.

6650	**2641**	1000r. multicoloured	1·30	45

2642 Russian Federation Arms

1997. 500th Anniv of Double Eagle as Russian State Emblem. Sheet 94×76 mm.

MS6651	**2642** 3000r. multicoloured	2·75	1·50

2643 Post Emblem

1997

6652	**2643**	100r. brown and black	20	15
6653	-	150r. mauve and black	35	25
6654	-	250r. green and black	55	30
6655	-	300r. green and black	1·10	45
6656	-	500r. blue and black	90	55
6657	-	750r. brown and black	1·20	60
6658	-	1000r. red and blue	1·80	75
6659	-	1500r. blue and black	2·20	1·20
6660	-	2000r. green and black	2·75	1·50
6661	-	2500r. red and black	3·25	1·80
6662	-	3000r. violet and black	3·50	2·30
6663	-	5000r. brown and black	5·50	3·00

DESIGNS: 100r. Combine harvesters in field; 150r. Oil rigs; 250r. White storks; 300r. Radio mast; 750r. St. George killing dragon; 1000r. State flag and arms; 1500r. Electric pylon inside generating machinery; 2000r. Class VL65 electric railway locomotive; 2500r. Moscow Kremlin; 3000r. Space satellite; 5000r. Pianist and theatre.

For these designs in revised currency, see Nos. 6718/35.

2644 Ioan Zlatoust Church, Sofiiski Cathedral and Admiral Barsh's House

1997. 850th Anniv of Vologda.

6664	**2644**	1000r. multicoloured	1·80	75

2645 "Volga Svyatoslavovich" (I. Bilibin)

1997. Europa. Tales and Legends.

6665	**2645**	1500r. multicoloured	3·50	1·50

2646 Jesus Christ the Saviour Cathedral

1997. 850th Anniv of Moscow (4thissue). Multicoloured.

6666	1000r. Type **2646**	1·10	90
6667	1000r. Towers and walls of Kremlin	1·10	90
6668	1000r. Grand Palace and cathedrals, Kremlin	1·10	90
6669	1000r. St. Basil's Cathedral, Spassky Tower and Trinity Church	1·10	90
6670	1000r. "St. George killing Dragon" (16th-century icon)	1·10	90
6671	1000r. First reference to Moscow in Ipatevsky Chronicle, 1147	1·10	90
6672	1000r. Prince Daniil Alexandrovich and Danilov Monastery	1·10	90
6673	1000r. "Building Moscow Kremlin, 1366" (16th-century miniature)	1·10	90
6674	1000r. Kazan cap and "Coronation of Ivan IV" (miniature)	1·10	90
6675	1000r. 16th-century plan of Moscow	1·10	90

Nos. 6666/75 were issued together, *se-tenant*, Nos. 6666/70 forming a composite design of Moscow in late 19th century.

2647 Mil Mi-14 (float)

1997. Helicopters. Multicoloured.

6676	500r. Type **2647**	90	25
6677	1000r. Mil Mi-24 (gunship)	1·80	40
6678	1500r. Mil Mi-26 (transport)	2·30	85
6679	2000r. Mil Mi-28 (gunship)	4·00	60
6680	2500r. Mil Mi-34 (patrol)	4·50	85

2648 "The Priest and Balda"

1997. Birth Bicentenary (1999) of Aleksandr Sergeevich Pushkin (poet) (1st issue). Multicoloured.

6681	500r. Type **2648**	30	25
6682	1000r. "Tsar Saltan"	80	60
6683	1500r. "The Fisherman and the Golden Fish"	1·30	95
6684	2000r. "The Dead Princess and the Seven Knights"	1·60	1·20
6685	3000r. "The Golden Cockerel"	3·25	2·40

See also Nos. 6762/6 and 6827/9.

2649 Petrodvorets (St. Petersburg) National Flags and Marble Temple, Bangkok

1997. Centenary of Russia–Thailand Diplomatic Relations and of Visit of King Rama V to St. Petersburg.

6686	**2649**	1500r. multicoloured	1·10	50

2650 Siberian Flying Squirrel

1997. Wildlife. Multicoloured.

6687	500r. Type **2650**	30	15
6688	750r. Lynx	65	30
6689	1000r. Western capercaillie	80	35
6690	2000r. European otter	1·80	75
6691	3000r. Western curlew	2·50	1·10

2651 Arkhangel Province

1997. Regions of the Russian Federation (1st series). Multicoloured.

6692	1500r. Type **2651**	1·30	55
6693	1500r. Kaliningrad Province (vert)	1·30	55
6694	1500r. Kamchatka Province	1·30	55
6695	1500r. Krasnodar Territory	1·30	55
6696	1500r. Sakha Republic (Yakutiya) (vert)	1·30	55

See also Nos. 6784/8, 6831/5, 6920/5, 6980/4, 7062/6, 7153/8, 7229/33 and 7315/20.

2652 Klyopa flying with Balloons

1997. Klyopa (cartoon character). Multicoloured.

6697	500r. Type **2652**	30	15
6698	1000r. Klyopa hang-gliding over Red Square	80	35
6699	1500r. Klyopa in troika (45×33 mm)	1·30	55

2653 Emblem, Mascot and Russian Federation 1992 and 20k. Stamp

1997. "Moscow 97" International Stamp Exhibition. Multicoloured.

6700	1500r. Russian Empire 1858 10k. and R.S.F.S.R. 1918 35k. stamps, and Spassky Tower, Moscow Kremlin	1·10	50
6701	1500r. Type **2653**	1·10	50

2654 Indian Flag and Asokan Capital

1997. 50th Anniv of Independence of India.

6702	**2654**	500r. multicoloured	50	20

2655 Presentation of Standard

1997. 325th Birth Anniv of Tsar Peter I. Multicoloured.

6703	2000r. Type **2655** (creation of regular army and navy)	1·90	85
6704	2000r. Sea battle (access to Baltic Sea)	1·90	85
6705	2000r. Peter I reviewing plans (construction of St. Petersburg)	1·90	85
6706	2000r. Council (administrative reforms)	1·90	85
6707	2000r. Boy before tutor (cultural and educational reforms)	1·90	85
MS6708	65×90 mm. 5000r. Peter I	8·00	3·50

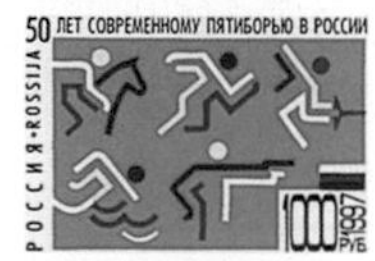

2656 Pictograms of Five Events

1997. 50th Anniv of Modern Pentathlon in Russia.

6709	**2656**	1000r. multicoloured	80	35

2657 Match Scenes

1997. Centenary of Football in Russia.

6710	**2657**	2000r. multicoloured	1·90	85

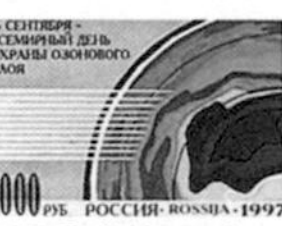

2658 Radiation and Earth

1997. World Ozone Layer Day. Tenth Anniv of Montreal Protocol (on reduction of use of chlorofluorocarbons).

6711	**2658**	1000r. multicoloured	80	35

2659 National Flag and Palace of Europe, Strasbourg

1997. Admission of Russian Federation to European Council.

6712	**2659**	1000r. multicoloured	1·60	70

2660 "Boris and Gleb" (14th-century icon)

1997. Centenary of Russian State Museum, St. Petersburg (1st issue). Multicoloured.

6713	500r. Type **2660**	65	30
6714	1000r. "Volga Boatmen" (I. Repin) (horiz)	95	40
6715	1500r. "Promenade" (Marc Chagall)	1·30	55
6716	2000r. "Merchant's Wife taking Tea" (B. Kustodiev)	1·60	70

See also Nos. 6753/**MS**6757.

2661 Sketch by Puskin of Himself and Onegin

1997. Translation into Hebrew by Abraham Shlonsky of Yevgeny Onegin (poem) by Aleksandr Pushkin. Sheet 76×60 mm.

MS6717	**2661** 3000r. black, magenta and yellow	4·00	1·80

1998. As Nos. 6652/63 but in reformed currency.

6718	10k. brown and black (as No. 6652)	15	10
6719	15k. mauve and black (as No. 6653)	15	10
6720	25k. green and black (as No. 6654)	25	10
6721	30k. green and black (as No. 6655)	25	10
6723	50k. blue and black (Type **2643**)	80	35
6726	1r. red and blue (as No. 6658)	2·50	1·10
6727	1r.50 blue and black (as No. 6659)	3·25	1·40
6728	2r. green and black (as No. 6660)	4·75	2·10
6729	2r.50 red and black (as No. 6661)	2·50	1·10
6730	3r. violet and black (as No. 6662)	3·25	1·40
6735	5r. brown and black (as No. 6663)	4·75	2·10

2662 "Menshikov in Beresovo" (detail, Surikov)

1998. 150th Birth Anniversaries of Vasily Ivanovich Surikov and V. M. Vasnetsov (artists). Multicoloured.

6741	1r.50 Type **2662**	1·10	50
6742	1r.50 "Morozov Boyar's Wife" (Surikov)	1·10	50
6743	1r.50 "Battle between Slavs and Nomads" (detail, Vasnetsov) (vert)	1·10	50
6744	1r.50 "Tsarevich Ivan on a Grey Wolf" (Vasnetsov)	1·10	50

2663 Cross-country Skiing

1998. Winter Olympic Games, Nagano, Japan. Multicoloured.

6745	50k. Type **2663**	30	15
6746	1r. Figure skating (pairs)	80	35
6747	1r.50 Biathlon	1·30	55

2664 Red-tailed Black Labeo "Epalzeorhynchus bicolor"

1998. Fish. Multicoloured.

6748	50k. Type **2664**	50	20
6749	50k. Jewel tetra ("Hyphessobrycon callistus")	50	20
6750	1r. Galina's catfish ("Synodontis galinae")	80	35
6751	1r.50 "Botia kristinae"	1·60	70
6752	1r.50 "Cichlasoma labiatum"	1·60	70

2665 "The Last Day of Pompeii" (K. P. Bryullov)

1998. Centenary of State Russian Museum, St. Petersburg (2nd issue). Multicoloured.

6753	1r.50 Type **2665**	1·30	55
6754	1r.50 "The Ninth Wave" (I. K. Aivazovsky)	1·30	55
6755	1r.50 "Pines for Masts" (I. I. Shishkin)	1·30	55
6756	1r.50 "Our Lady of Tenderness for Sick Hearts" (K. S. Petrov-Vodkin)	1·30	55
MS6757	91×70 mm. 3f. "The Milhailovsky Palace" (K.P. Beggrov) (51×36 mm)	4·75	2·10

2666 Saddleback Dolphins

1998. "Expo '98" World's Fair, Lisbon, Portugal. Sheet 91×71 mm.

MS6758	**2666** 3r. multicoloured	4·75	2·10

2667 Theatre and Characters

1998. Centenary of Moscow Art Theatre.

6759	**2667** 1r.50 multicoloured	1·60	70

2668 "End of Winter" (Shrove-tide)

1998. Europa. National Festivals.

6760	**2668** 1r.50 multicoloured	3·25	1·40

2669 War Memorial, Venets Hotel, History Museum and Goncharovsky Pavilion

1998. 350th Anniv of Ulyanovsk (formerly Simbirsk).

6761	**2669** 1r. multicoloured	2·40	1·10

2670 "The Lyceum"

1998. Birth Bicentenary (1999) of Aleksandr Sergeevich Pushkin (poet) (2nd issue). Drawings by Pushkin.

6762	**2670** 1r.50 black and blue	95	40
6763	- 1r.50 brown, stone & blk	95	40
6764	- 1r.50 brown, stone & blk	95	40
6765	- 1r.50 brown, stone & blk	95	40
6766	- 1r.50 black and blue	95	40

DESIGNS: No. 6763, "A.N. Wolf"; 6764, Self-portrait; 6765, "Tatyana" (from "Vevgeny Onegin"); 6766, Knight in armour (manuscript cover from 1830).

2671 Local History Museum and Peter I Monument

1998. 300th Anniv of Taganrog.

6767	**2671** 1r. multicoloured	80	35

2672 Games Emblem

1998. World Youth Games, Moscow. Sheet 70×90 mm.

MS6768	**2672** 3r. multicoloured	4·75	2·10

2673 Tsar Nicholas II

1998. 80th Death Anniv of Tsar Nicholas II.

6769	**2673** 3r. multicoloured	3·25	1·40

2674 Grapes

1998. Berries. Multicoloured.

6770	50k. Type **2674**	50	20
6771	75k. Raspberry	65	30
6772	1r. Magnolia vine	80	35
6773	1r.50 Cowberrry	1·30	55
6774	2r. Arctic bramble	1·60	70

2675 Landmarks

1998. 275th Anniv of Yekaterinburg.

6775	**2675** 1r. multicoloured	80	35

2676 Leontina Cohen

1998. Intelligence Agents.

6776	**2676** 1r. blue, indigo & blk	80	35
6777	- 1r. brown, yellow & blk	80	35
6778	- 1r. green, dp green & blk	80	35
6779	- 1r. purple, brown & blk	80	35

DESIGNS: No. 6777, Morris Cohen; 6778, L. R. Kvasnikov; 6779, A. A. Yatskov.

2677 Order of St. Andrew

1998. Russian Orders (1st series). Multicoloured.

6780	1r. Type **2677**	65	30
6781	1r.50 Order of St. Catherine	95	40
6782	2r. Order of St. Aleksandr Nevsky	1·30	55
6783	2r.50 Order of St. George	1·60	70

See also Nos. 6807/11 and 7242/7.

1998. Regions of the Russian Federation (2nd series). As T **2651**. Multicoloured.

6784	1r.50 Republic of Buryatiya (vert)	1·30	55
6785	1r.50 Republic of Kareliya (vert)	1·30	55
6786	1r.50 Khabarovsk Province	1·30	55
6787	1r.50 Murmansk Province	1·30	55
6788	1r.50 Primorsky Province	1·30	55

2678 Universal Postal Union Emblem

1998. World Post Day.

6789	**2678** 1r. multicoloured	80	35

2679 Anniversary Emblem

1998. 50th Anniv of Universal Declaration of Human Rights.

6790	**2679** 1r.50 multicoloured	1·40	65

2680 Headquarters, Moscow

1998. Tenth Anniv of Menatep Bank.

6791	**2680** 2r. multicoloured	1·60	70

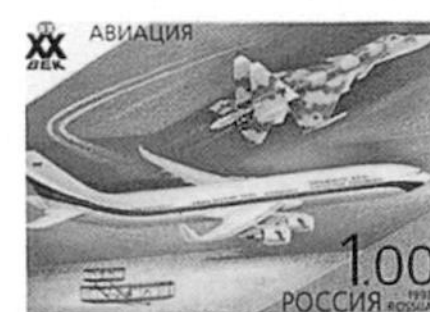

2681 Aviation

1998. Achievements of the Twentieth Century. Multicoloured.

6792	1r. Type **2681**	80	40
6793	1r. Computers	80	40
6794	1r. Genetics	80	40
6795	1r. Nuclear energy	80	40
6796	1r. Space exploration	80	40
6797	1r. Television	80	40

2682 Koshkin

1998. Birth Centenary of Mikhail Ilich Koshkin (tank designer).

6798	**2682** 1r. multicoloured	50	25

2683 Grandfather Frost

1998. New Year.

6799	**2683** 1r. multicoloured	50	25

2684 Telephone and Switchboard Operators

1999. Centenary of First Long-distance Telephone Link in Russia (between Moscow and St. Petersburg).

6800	**2684** 1r. multicoloured	50	25

2685 Western Capercaillie

1999. Hunting. Multicoloured.

No.	Description	Unused	Used
6801	1r. Type **2685**	50	25
6802	1r.50 Shooting mallard ducks from rowing boat	65	30
6803	2r. Falconry (Gyr falcon)	80	40
6804	2r.50 Wolves	95	50
6805	3r. Bears	1·10	55

2686 Russian Ship of the Line off Corfu

1999. Bicentenary of Russian Naval Expedition to Mediterranean under Command of Admiral Fyodor Ushakov. Sheet 90×70 mm.

No.	Description	Unused	Used
MS6806	5r. multicoloured	5·50	2·75

1999. Russian Orders (2nd series). As T **2677**. Multicoloured.

No.	Description	Unused	Used
6807	1r. Order of St. Vladimir	30	15
6808	1r.50 Order of St. Anne	50	25
6809	2r. Order of St. John of Jerusalem	65	30
6810	2r.50 Order of the White Eagle	80	40
6811	3r. Order of St. Stanislas	95	50

2687 18th-century Ship of the Line

1999. 300th Anniv of Adoption of St. Andrew's Flag by Tsar Peter I. Sheet 90×70 mm.

No.	Description	Unused	Used
MS6812	**2687** 7r. multicoloured	6·50	3·25

2688 "Family at Tea" (Sofya Kondrashina)

1999. Russia in the 21st Century. Children's paintings. Multicoloured.

No.	Description	Unused	Used
6813	1r.20 Type **2688**	30	15
6814	1r.20 "My Town" (Yuri Lapushkov)	30	15
6815	1r.20 "Fantasy City" (Aleksander Khudyshin) (vert)	30	15

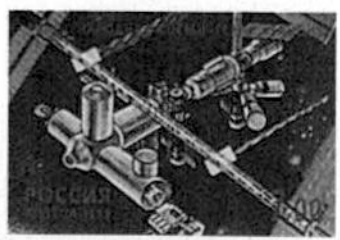

2689 "Alpha" International Space Station

1999. Space Exploration Day. Sheet 120×68 mm.

No.	Description	Unused	Used
MS6816	**2689** 7r. multicoloured	4·75	2·40

2690 Albrecht Durer's House

1999. "iBRA '99" International Stamp Exhibition, Nuremberg, Germany.

No.	Description	Unused	Used
6817	**2690** 3r. multicoloured	80	40

2691 Setting Weighted Lines

1999. Fishing. Multicoloured.

No.	Description	Unused	Used
6818	1r. Type **2691**	30	15
6819	2r. Fishing by rod and line from bank and boat	65	30
6820	2r. Fishing by rod and line from kayak	65	30
6821	3r. Fishing through holes in ice	80	40
6822	3r. Underwater fishing	80	40

2692 Council Flag and Headquarters, Strasbourg, and Spassky Tower, Moscow

1999. 50th Anniv of Council of Europe.

No.	Description	Unused	Used
6823	**2692** 3r. multicoloured	80	40

2693 Oksky State Natural Biosphere Preserve

1999. Europa. Parks and Gardens.

No.	Description	Unused	Used
6824	**2693** 5r. multicoloured	3·25	1·60

2694 Stag

1999. Red Deer. Multicoloured.

No.	Description	Unused	Used
6825	2r.50 Type **2694**	1·60	80
6826	2r.50 Doe and fawns	1·60	80

2695 Pushkin, 1815 (after S. G. Chirikov)

1999. Birth Bicentenary of Aleksandr Sergeevich Pushkin (poet) (3rd issue). Multicoloured.

No.	Description	Unused	Used
6827	1r. Type **2695**	15	10
6828	3r. Pushkin, 1826 (after I.-E. Viven)	65	30
6829	5r. Pushkin, 1836 (after Karl Bryullov)	1·10	55
MS6830	110×70 mm. 7r. Pushkin, 1827 (after V. A. Tropinin) (29×41 mm)	3·25	1·60

1999. Regions of the Russian Federation (3rd series). As T **2651**. Multicoloured.

No.	Description	Unused	Used
6831	2r. Republic of North Osetia-Alaniya	50	25
6832	2r. Republic of Bashkortostan (vert)	50	25
6833	2r. Kirov Province	50	25
6834	2r. Evenk Autonomous Region (vert)	50	25
6835	2r. Stavropol Region	50	25

2696 Rose "Carina" ("Happy Birthday")

1999. Greetings stamps. Roses. Multicoloured.

No.	Description	Unused	Used
6836	1r.20 Type **2696**	30	15
6837	1r.20 "Gloria Dei" ("From the bottom of my heart")	30	15
6838	2r. "Candia" ("Congratulations")	50	25
6839	3r. "Confidence" ("Be happy")	65	30
6840	4r. "Ave Maria" ("With love")	80	40

1999. No. 6342b surch **1.20**.

No.	Description	Unused	Used
6841	1r.20 on 5000r. blue	2·40	1·20

2698 River Station, City Arms and Nativity of the Virgin Cathedral

1999. 250th Anniv of Rostov-on-Don.

No.	Description	Unused	Used
6842	**2698** 1r.20 multicoloured	3·25	1·60

2699 Automatic Post Sorting

1999. 125th Anniv of Universal Postal Union.

No.	Description	Unused	Used
6843	**2699** 3r. multicoloured	80	40

2700 "Horsewoman"

1999. Birth Bicentenary of Karl Bryullov (painter). Multicoloured.

No.	Description	Unused	Used
6844	2r.50 Type **2700**	50	25
6845	2r.50 "Portrait of Yu. P. Samoilova and Amacilia Paccini"	50	25

2701 IZh-1 Motorcycle, 1929

1999. Russian Motor Cycles. Multicoloured.

No.	Description	Unused	Used
6846	1r. Type **2701**	15	10
6847	1r.50 L-300, 1930	30	15
6848	2r. M-72, 1941	50	25
6849	2r.50 M-1-A, 1945	65	30
6850	5r. IZ–"Planeta-5", 1987	95	50

2702 Suvorov's Vanguard passing Lake Klontal (after engraving by L. Hess)

1999. Bicentenary of General Aleksandr Suvorov's Crossing of the Alps. Multicoloured.

No.	Description	Unused	Used
6851	2r.50 Type **2702**	3·25	1·60
6852	2r.50 Schollenen Gorge Monument, Suvorov and soldiers	3·25	1·60

2703 Horse Racing

1999. Traditional Sports. Multicoloured.

No.	Description	Unused	Used
6853	2r. Type **2703**	50	30
6854	2r. Wrestling	50	30
6855	2r. Gorodki (game with stick and blocks of wood)	50	30
6856	2r. Sleigh and deer team race	50	30
6857	2r. Weightlifting (vert)	50	30

2704 Leonid Utesov

1999. Singers. Multicoloured.

No.	Description	Unused	Used
6858	2r. Type **2704**	50	30
6859	2r. Lidiya Ruslanova (in costume)	50	30
6860	2r. Klavdiya Shulzhenko (with hands clasped)	50	30
6861	2r. Mark Bernes (playing accordion)	50	30
6862	2r. Bulat Okudzhava (playing guitar in street scene)	50	30
6863	2r. Vladimir Vysotsky (with guitar and arms out wide)	50	30
6864	2r. Igor Talkov (with arm raised)	50	30
6865	2r. Victor Tsoi (playing guitar)	50	30

2705 Players chasing Ball and Club Badge

1999. Spartak-Alaniya, National Football Champions.

No.	Description	Unused	Used
6877	**2705** 2r. multicoloured	50	30

2706 Father Christmas and "2000"

1999. Christmas and New Year. Multicoloured.

No.	Description	Unused	Used
6878	1r.20 Type **2706**	30	20
6879	1r.20 "2000", globe as pearl and shell	30	20

2707 "The Raising of the Daughter of Jairus" (V. D. Polenov)

2000. Bimillenary of Christianity. Religious Paintings. Multicoloured.

No.	Description	Unused	Used
6880	3r. Type **2707**	80	50
6881	3r. "Christ in the Wilderness" (I. N. Kramskoy)	80	50
6882	3r. "Christ in the House of Mary and Martha" (G. I. Semiradsky)	80	50
6883	3r. "What is Truth?" (N. N. Ge) (vert)	80	50
MS6884	120×96 mm. 7r. "The Appearance of Christ to the People" (A. A. Ivanov) (51×36 mm)	4·00	2·50

See also Nos. **MS**6883 and **MS**6887.

2708 "The Virgin the Orans" (mosaic, St. Sophie's Cathedral, Kiev, Ukraine)

2000. Bimillenary of Christianity (2nd issue). Sheet 151×100 mm containing T **2708** and similar vert designs. Multicoloured.

No.	Description	Unused	Used
MS6885	3r. Type **2708**; 3r. "Christ Pantocrator" (fresco, Spaso-Preobrazhenskaya Church, Polotsk, Belarus); 3r. "The Virgin of Vladimir" (icon, Tretyakov State Museum, Moscow)	4·75	3·00

2709 Psurtsev and Central Telegraph Office, Moscow

2000. Birth Centenary of Nikolai D. Psurtsev (statesman).

No.	Description	Unused	Used
6886	**2709** 2r.50 multicoloured	65	40

2710 Domes of Kremlin Cathedrals, Moscow

2000. Bimillenary of Christianity (3rd issue). Sheet 151×87 mm.
MS6887 **2710** 10r. multicoloured 4·75 3·00

2711 R. L. Samoilovich

2000. Polar Explorers. Multicoloured.

6888	2r. Type **2711**	1·30	80
6889	2r. V. Yu Vize and polar station	1·30	80
6890	2r. M. M. Somov and ship	1·30	80
6891	2r. P. A. Gordienko and airplane	1·30	80
6892	2r. A. F. Treshnikov and tracked vehicles	1·30	80

2712 N. A. Panin-Kolomenkin (first Russian Olympic Ice-skating Champion, 1908)

2000. The Twentieth Century (1st issue). Sport. Multicoloured.

6893	25k. Type **2712**	15	10
6894	30k. Wrestlers (Olympic Games, Stockholm, 1912)	15	10
6895	50k. Athlete crossing finishing line (All-Russian Olympiad, 1913 and 1914)	15	10
6896	1r. Cyclists (All-Union Spartacist Games, 1928)	25	15
6897	1r.35 Emblem and parade of athletes (Sports Association for Labour and Defence, 1931)	30	20
6898	1r.50 Emblem and athletes ("Honoured Master of Sports", 1934)	40	25
6899	2r. Gymnasts and shot-putter (Olympic Games, Helsinki, 1952)	50	30
6900	2r.50 V. P. Kutz and athletes (Olympic Games, Melbourne, 1956)	80	50
6901	3r. Gold Medal, goalkeeper and player (Olympic Football Champion, Melbourne Olympic Games)	95	60
6902	4r. Mikhail Botvinnik (World Chess Champion, 1948–57, 1958–60 and 1961–63)	1·30	80
6903	5r. Soviet Union–Canada ice hockey match, 1972	1·60	1·00
6904	6r. Stadium and emblem (Olympic Games, Moscow, 1980)	2·40	1·50

See also Nos. 6926/37, 6950/61 and 6964/76.

2713 Emblem

2000. 50th Anniv of World Meteorological Society. Sheet 90×60 mm.
MS6905 **2713** 7r. multicoloured 2·40 1·50

2714 Soldier (L. F. Golovanov)

2000. 55th Anniv of End of Second World War. Posters by named artists. Multicoloured.

6906	1r.50 Type **2714**	80	50
6907	1r.50 Mother and son (N. N. Vatolina)	80	50
6908	1r.50 Soldiers celebrating (V. V. Suryaninov)	80	50
6909	1r.50 Soldier and woman (V. I. Ladyagin)	80	50
6910	5r. Soldier and emblem (V. S. Klimashin)	2·40	1·00

MS6911 100×70 mm. No. 6910 4·00 2·50

2715 "Apollo"–"Soyuz" Space Link, 1975

2000. International Space Co-operation. Multicoloured.

6912	2r. Type **2715**	80	50
6913	3r. Projected international space station and flags (horiz)	1·30	80
6914	5r. Rocket taking off from launch pad at sea	1·60	1·00

2716 Mother and Child crossing Road and Emblem

2000. World Road Safety Week.
6915 **2716** 1r.75 multicoloured 1·60 1·00

2717 Star of David, Doves and "Holocaust"

2000. Holocaust Victims' Commemoration.
6916 **2717** 2r. multicoloured 4·00 2·50

2718 Spassky Tower and President's Flag

2000. Election of President Vladimir Putin.
6917 **2718** 1r.75 multicoloured 3·25 2·00

2719 "Building Europe"

2000. Europa.
6918 **2719** 7r. multicoloured 4·50 2·75

2720 Globe, Shell, Cogs, Human Eye and Emblem

2000. "Expo 2000" International Stamp Exhibition, Hanover. Sheet 92×71 mm.
MS6919 **2720** 10r. multicoloured 4·00 2·50

2000. Regions of the Russian Federation (4th issue). As T **2651**. Multicoloured.

6920	3r. Republic of Kalmyk (vert)	80	50
6921	3r. Mari El Republic (vert)	80	50
6922	3r. Tatarstan Republic (vert)	80	50
6923	3r. Udmurt Republic (vert)	80	50
6924	3r. Chuvash Republic	80	50
6925	3r. Autonomous Republic of Yamalo Nentsky	80	50

2721 V. K. Arkadjev (Observation of Ferromagnetic Resonance, 1913)

2000. The Twentieth Century (2nd issue). Science. Multicoloured.

6926	1r.30 Type **2721** (botanist and plant geneticist)	50	30
6927	1r.30 Nikolai Ivanovich Vavilov (botanist and plant geneticist) and ears of corn (theory on plant divergence)	50	30
6928	1r.30 N. N. Luzin (founder of Moscow Mathematical School, 1920–30)	50	30
6929	1r.75 I. E. Tamm and chemical model (Phenoms Theory, 1929)	80	50
6930	1r.75 P. L. Kapitsa and diagram of experiment (discovery of liquid helium superfluidity, 1938)	80	50
6931	1r.75 Nikolai Nikolayevich Semenov (physical chemist) (chemical chain reactions theory, 1934)	80	50
6932	2r. V. I. Veksler and charged particles in accelerators, 1944–45	95	60
6933	2r. Mayan text (decipherment of Mayan language by Yu V. Knorozov, 1950s)	95	60
6934	2r. A. V. Ivanov (discovery of pogonophora, 1955–57)	95	60
6935	3r. Globe, Moon and Luna 3 (first photograph of Moon's dark side, 1959)	1·30	80
6936	3r. Scientific equipment (development of quantum electronics, 1960s)	1·30	80
6937	3r. N. J. Tolstoi (ethnolinguistic dictionary, 1995)	1·30	80

2722 Chihuahua

2000. Dogs. Multicoloured.

6938	1r. Type **2722**	15	10
6939	1r.50 Terrier	30	20
6940	2r. Poodle	50	30
6941	2r.50 French bulldog	65	40
6942	3r. Japanese chin	80	50

2723 Fencing

2000. Olympic Games, Sydney. Multicoloured.

6943	2r. Type **2723**	50	30
6944	3r. Synchronized swimming	80	50
6945	5r. Volleyball	1·10	70

2724 Charoit

2000. Minerals. Multicoloured.

6946	1r. Type **2724**	30	20
6947	2r. Haematite	50	30
6948	3r. Rock crystal	65	40
6949	4r. Gold	95	60

2725 Ballerina and Actors

2000. The Twentieth Century (3rd series). Culture. Multicoloured.

6950	30k. Type **2725** (touring ballet and opera companies, 1908–14)	15	10
6951	50k. "Black Square" (K. S. Malevich)	15	10
6952	1r. Sergi Mikhailovich Eisenstein (director) and scene from *Battleship Potemkin* (film, 1925)	15	10
6953	1r.30 Book and Aleksei Maksimovich Gorky (writer)	25	10
6954	1r.50 Sculptures and red star	30	20
6955	1r.75 Vladimir Vladimirovich Mayakovsky (poet and playwright) and propaganda posters, 1920s	40	25
6956	2r. V. E. Meierkhold and K. S. Stanislavsky (theatre producers)	50	30
6957	2r.50 Dmitri Dmitriyevich Shostakovich (composer) and musicians	55	35
6958	3r. Galina Sergeyevna Ulanova (ballerina) and dancers	65	40
6959	4r. A. T. Tvardovsky (poet)	95	60
6960	5r. Fountain and Great Palace, Petrodvorets (restoration of historical monuments)	1·10	70
6961	6r. D. S. Likhachev (literary critic)	1·30	80

2726 Zander (*Stizostedion lucioperca*) and Common Whitefish (*Coregonus lavaretus maraenoides*)

2000. Fish of Chudsko-Pskovskoye Lake. Multicoloured.

6962	2r.50 Type **2726**	65	40
6963	2r.50 European smelt (*Osmerus eperlanus spirinchus*) and European cisco (*Coregonus albula*)	65	40

2727 Doctors Operating and Medical Equipment

2000. The Twentieth Century (4th series). Technology. Multicoloured.

6964	1r.50 Type **2727**	35	20
6965	1r.50 City skyline (construction)	35	20
6966	1r.50 Bus, car and truck (transport)	50	30
6967	2r. Dam, electricity pylons and generator (engineering)	50	30
6968	2r. Telephones, televisions and rocket and satellite (communication)	50	30
6969	2r. Space stations and rocket (space technology)	70	40
6970	3r. Civil and military airplanes (aviation)	70	40
6971	3r. Steam, diesel and electric trains (rail transport)	70	40
6972	3r. Container ship, sailing ship and cruise liner (sea transport)	1·00	60
6973	4r. Furnace (metallurgy)	1·00	60
6974	4r. Oil refinery and truck (oil-refining industry)	1·00	60
6975	4r. Truck, conveyor and drill (mineral extraction)	1·00	60

2728 Moscow Kremlin, Pokrovsky Cathedral and Christmas Tree

2000. New Millennium.
6977 **2728** 2r. multicoloured 1·20 70

2729 Emblem

2000. 80th Anniv of Foreign Intelligence Service.
6978 **2729** 2r.50 multicoloured 70 40

2730 Navigation School, Moscow and Mathematical Equipment

2001. 300th Anniv of Russian Naval Education. Sheet 110×130 mm containing T **2730** and similar horiz designs. Multicoloured.

MS6979 1r.50 Type **2730**; 2r. Ship, chart of Antarctica and navigation equipment; 8r. St. Petersburg Naval Institute and statue 6·75 4·00

2001. Regions of the Russian Federation (5th issue). As T **2651**. Multicoloured.

6980	3r. Republic of Dagestan	1·00	60
6981	3r. Republic of Kabardino-Balkaskaya	1·00	60
6982	3r. Republic of Komi (vert)	1·00	60
6983	3r. Samara region	1·00	60
6984	3r. Chita region	1·00	60

2001. As Nos. 6718/35 but new designs and currency expressed as "P".

6985	10p. mauve and black	2·30	1·20
6986	25p. brown and black	6·25	2·50
6987	50p. blue and black	11·00	4·75
6988	100p. mauve and black	24·00	11·00

DESIGNS: 10p. Ballet dancer; 25p. Gymnast; 50p. Globe and computer; 100p. Universal Postal Union emblem.

2731 White Tulip ("Happy Birthday")

2001. Greetings Stamps. Tulips. Multicoloured.

7000	2r. Type **2731**	85	50
7001	2r. Deep pink tulips ("With Love")	85	50
7002	2r. Orange tulip ("Good Luck")	85	50
7003	2r. Yellow tulip ("Congratulations")	85	50
7004	2r. Magenta and white tulip ("Be Happy")	85	50

2732 I. A. Galitsin

2001. 300th Birth Anniv of Andrei Matveeich Matveev (artist) (Nos. 7005/6) and 225th Birth Anniv of Vasily Andreevich Tropinin (artist) (Nos. 7007/8). Multicoloured.

7005	3r. Type **2732**	85	50
7006	3r. A. P. Galitsina	85	50
7007	3r. P. A. Bulakhov	85	50
7008	3r. E. I. Karzinkina	85	50

2733 "Senate Square and St. Peter the Great Monument" (B. Patersen)

2001. 300th Anniv of St. Petersburg. Paintings. Multicoloured.

7009	1r. Type **2733**	15	10
7010	2r. "English embankment near Senate" (B. Patersen)	50	30
7011	3r. "Mikhailovsky Castle from Fontanka Embankment" (B. Patersen)	70	40
7012	4r. "River Moika near Stable Department" (A. E. Martynov)	1·00	60
7013	5r. "Neva from Peter and Paul Fortress" (K. P. Beggrov)	1·40	80

2734 *Pyrrhosoma numphula* (damselfly)

2001. Damselflies and Dragonflies. Multicoloured.

7014	1r. Type **2734**	15	10
7015	1r.50 *Epitheca bimaculata* (dragonfly)	35	20
7016	2r. Brown aeshna (*Aeschna grandis*)	50	30
7017	3r. *Libellula depressa* (dragonfly)	85	50
7018	5r. *Coenagrion hastulatum* (damselfly)	1·20	70

2735 Yuri Gagarin, S. P. Korolev (spaceship designer) and Baikonur Launch Site

2001. 40th Anniv of First Manned Space Flight. Multicoloured.

7019	3r. Type **2735**	85	50
7020	3r. Gagarin in uniform	85	50

Nos. 7019/20 were issued together, se-tenant, forming a composite design.

2736 Baikal Lake

2001. Europa. Water Resources.

7021 **2736** 8r. multicoloured 2·50 1·50

2737 Emblem

2001. 75th Anniv of International Philatelic Federation.

7022 **2737** 2r.50 multicoloured 70 40

2738 Russian Flag

2001. State Emblems. Multicoloured.

7023	2r.50 Type **2738**	70	40
7024	2r.50 Russian Federation national anthem	70	40
7025	5r. State Arms	1·40	80

MS7026 Sheet 150×00 mm. 2r.50 Type **2738**; 2r.50 As No. 7024; 100r. State Arms 43·00 38·00

The 100r. stamp in No. **MS**7026 has the arms embossed in gold foil.

2739 Map of Russian Federation and State Arms

2001. 11th Anniv of Declaration of State Sovereignty.

7027 **2739** 5r. multicoloured 3·50 2·00

2740 Cathedral of the Assumption, Vladimir (1189)

2001. Religious Architecture. Multicoloured.

7028	2r.50 Type **2740**	85	50
7029	2r.50 Cathedral of the Nativity of the Virgin, Zvenigorod (1405)	85	50
7030	2r.50 Cathedral of the Intercession of the Virgin of the Old Belief Community of Rogozhsk, Moscow (1792)	85	50
7031	2r.50 Roman Catholic Church of the Immaculate Conception of the Blessed Virgin Mary, Moscow (1911)	85	50
7032	2r.50 Lutheran Church of St. Peter, St. Petersburg (1838)	85	50
7033	2r.50 Prayer House of the Evangelical Christians (Pentecostal), Lesosibirsk (1999)	85	50
7034	2r.50 Revival Church of Evangelical Christians (Baptist), Bezhitsk, Bryansk (1996)	85	50
7035	2r.50 Church of Seventh Day Adventists, Ryazan (1996)	85	50
7036	2r.50 Armenian Cathedral Surb Khach, Rostov-on-Don (1792) and Monastery of St. Daniel, Moscow (13th-century)	85	50
7037	2r.50 First Mosque, Ufa (1830)	85	50
7038	2r.50 Hay Market Mosque, Kazan (1849)	85	50
7039	2r.50 Choral Synagogue, Moscow (1891)	85	50
7040	2r.50 Large Choral Synagogue, St. Petersburg (1893)	85	50
7041	2r.50 Buddhist Soskshin-Dugan, Ivolginsk Datsan (1976)	85	50

2741 "Sokol" (high speed passenger train)

2001. 150th Anniv of St. Petersburg–Moscow Railway. Sheet 90 ×80 mm.

MS7042 **2741** 12r. multicoloured 6·75 5·25

2742 G. S. Titov (cosmonaut)

2001. 40th Anniv of First Manned Space Flight.

7043 **2742** 3r. multicoloured 85 50

2743 Faina G. Ranevskaya in Cinderella

2001. Cinema Actors. Showing scenes from their films. Multicoloured.

7044	2r.50 Type **2743**	70	40
7045	2r.50 Mikhail I. Zharov in *Peter I*	70	40
7046	2r.50 Lubov P. Orlova in *Circus*	70	40
7047	2r.50 Nikolai A. Kryuchkov in *Tractor Drivers*	70	40
7048	2r.50 Yury V. Nikulin in *Diamond Arm*	70	40
7049	2r.50 Anatoly D. Papanov in *Alive and Dead*	70	40
7050	2r.50 Evgeny P. Leonov in *Stripy Voyage*	70	40
7051	2r.50 Nikolai N. Rybnikov in *Height*	70	40
7052	2r.50 Andrei A. Mironov in *Twelve Chairs*	70	40

2744 Lazarian and Institute

2001. Death Bicentenary of Horhannes Lazarian (founder of Oriental Languages Institute, Moscow).

7053 **2744** 2r.50 multicoloured 70 40

A stamp in a similar design was issued by Armenia.

2745 Arkadi Raikin

2001. 90th Birth Anniv of Arkadi I. Raikin (actor).

7054 **2745** 2r. agate and black 50 30

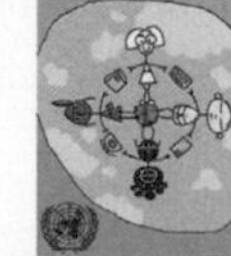
2746 Children encircling Globe

2001. United Nations Year of Dialogue among Civilizations.

7055 **2746** 5r. multicoloured 1·40 80

2747 Vladimir Dal

2001. Birth Bicentenary of Vladimir I. Dal (writer and lexicographer). Sheet 70×100 mm.

MS7056 **2747** 10r. multicoloured 6·00 5·00

2748 Court Tower

2001. Tenth Anniv of Russian Federation Constitutional Court.

7057 **2748** 3r. multicoloured 85 50

2749 Tsar Nicholas I, St. Petersburg Winter Palace and Coin

2001. 160th Anniv of Savings Bank.

7058 **2749** 2r.20 multicoloured 70 40

2750 Soldiers, Map and Red Square

2001. 60th Anniv of Battle for Moscow. Sheet 100×76 mm.

MS7059 **2750** 10r. multicoloured 6·00 4·00

2751 Union Emblem

2001. Tenth Anniv of Union of Independent States.

7060 **2751** 2r. multicoloured 3·50 2·00

2752 Father Christmas driving Troika with Three White Horses

2001. "Happy New Year".

7061 **2752** 2r.50 multicoloured 1·30 50

2002. Regions of the Russian Federation (6th issue). As T **2651**. Multicoloured.

7062 3r. Amur region 85 50

7063	3r. Republic of Karachaevo-Cherkeskaya	85	50
7064	3r. Republic of Altai (vert)	85	50
7065	3r. Sakhalin region	85	50
7066	3r. Republic of Khakassiya	85	50

2753 Skiing

2002. Winter Olympic Games, Salt Lake City. Multicoloured.

7067	3r. Type **2753**	85	50
7068	4r. Figure skating	1·20	70
7069	5r. Ski-jumping	1·40	80

2754 Dove, Rainbow and Globe

2002. "World Unity against Terrorism".

7070	**2754**	5r. multicoloured	1·40	80

2755 Locomotive emerging from Tunnel

2002. Centenary of Trans-Siberian Railway. Sheet 92×73 mm.

MS7071	**2755**	12r. multicoloured	6·75	6·00

2756 "Courtesan" (Hendrick Golzius)

2002. 150th Anniv of New Hermitage Museum, St. Petersburg. Multicoloured.

7072	2r.50 Type **2756**	1·20	70
7073	2r.50 "Ecco Homo" (Peter Paul Rubens)	1·20	70
7074	5r. 16th-century Italian Burgonet (helmet)	2·40	1·40
7075	5r. The Gonzaga Cameo	2·40	1·40
MS7076	76×106 mm. 12r. "New Hermitage" (Luigi Premazzi) (51×48 mm) (horiz)	10·00	8·00

2757 Cinnabar Lily ("Congratulations")

2002. Greetings Stamps. Lilies. Multicoloured.

7077	2r.50 Type **2757**	70	40
7078	2r.50 Orange lily ("Happy Birthday")	70	40
7079	2r.50 Pink lily ("Happiness")	70	40
7080	2r.50 Gilded lily ("From our Hearts")	70	40
7081	2r.50 Regal lily ("Love and Joy")	70	40

2758 Cane-Corso

2002. Dogs. Multicoloured.

7082	1r. Type **2758**	35	20
7083	2r. Shar pei	50	30
7084	3r. Bull mastiff	70	40
7085	4r. Brazilian mastiff (*Fila Brasileiro*)	85	50
7086	5r. Neapolitan mastiff	1·40	80
MS7087	151×152 mm. Nos. 7082×2, 7083×4 and 7084/6	8·50	7·00

2759 Cathedral of Our Lady of Kazan and Marshal Barclay de Tolli Monument

2002. 300th Anniv of St. Petersburg. Multicoloured.

7088	5r. Type **2759**	5·00	3·00
7089	5r. St. Isaak Cathedral	5·00	3·00
7090	25r. River Neva, St. Peter and Paul Fortress and gilded angel (vert)	22·00	13·00
7091	25r. Griboedov Canal, Cathedral of the Resurrection and gilded griffin	22·00	13·00
7092	25r. Gilded ship and Admiralty building	22·00	13·00

2760 Artur Artuzov

2002. Intelligence Agents. Sheet 141×91 mm containing T **2760** and similar horiz designs.

MS7093	2r.×6, Type **2760**; Nikolai Demidenko; Jan Olsky; Sergei Putzitsky; Vladimir Styrne; Grigory Syroezhkin	6·75	4·00

2761 Juggler, Trapeze Artist and Clown

2002. Europa. Circus.

7094	**2761**	8r. multicoloured	3·00	1·70

2762 Pavel Nakhimov

2002. Birth Bicentenary of Pavel S. Nakhimov (naval commander).

7095	**2762**	2r. multicoloured	60	35

2763 Congress Emblem

2002. 5th Eurosai (European Organization of Supreme Audit Institutions) Congress, Moscow.

7096	**2763**	2r. multicoloured	1·00	55

2764 Geysers

2002. Volcanoes of Kamchatka Region. Multicoloured.

7097	1r. Type **2764**	20	10
7098	2r. Caldera, Uzon volcano	60	35
7099	3r. Karymsky volcano	1·00	55
7100	5r. Troitsky acid lake, Maly Semyachic volcano	1·20	65

2765 Russian Carriage (c. 1640)

2002. Horse-drawn Carriages. Multicoloured.

7101	2r.50 Type **2765**	80	45
7102	2r.50 Enclosed sleigh, Moscow (1732)	80	45
7103	5r. Coupe carriage, Berlin (1746)	1·80	1·00
7104	5r. English carriage (c. 1770)	1·80	1·00
7105	5r. St. Petersburg Berline type carriage (1769)	1·80	1·00
MS7106	151×71 mm. 25r.×3 Nos. 7103/5	22·00	20·00

2766 Helicopter KA-10

2002. Birth Centenary of Nikolai Kamov (helicopter designer and manufacturer). Multicoloured.

7107	1r. Type **2766**	20	10
7108	1r.50 KA-22	40	20
7109	2r. KA-26	50	30
7110	2r.50 Navy helicopter KA-27	60	35
7111	5r. Army helicopter KA-50 Black Shark	1·20	65

2767 Anatoli Sobchak

2002. 65th Birth Anniv of Anatoli Sobchak (reformer and mayor of St. Petersburg).

7112	**2767**	3r.25 multicoloured	3·00	1·70

2768 Demoiselle Crane (*Anthropoides virgo*)

2002. Endangered Species. Birds. Multicoloured.

7113	2r.50 Type **2768**	1·40	75
7114	2r.50 Great black-headed gull (Pallas' Gull) (*Larus ichthyaetus Pallas*)	1·40	75

Stamps of the same design were issued by Kazakhstan.

2769 City and Emblem

2002. 850th Anniv of Kostroma.

7115	**2769**	2r. multicoloured	60	35

2770 Ministry of Internal Affairs

2002. Bicentenary of Government Ministries. Multicoloured.

7116	3r. Type **2770**	1·00	55
7117	3r. Palace Square, Alexander column, St. Petersburg and Ministry of Foreign Affairs building, Moscow	1·00	55
7118	3r. Church, Ministry of Defence building and state emblem (foreground)	1·00	55
7119	3r. Educational symbols and Moscow State University building	1·00	55
7120	3r. State emblem (centre) and Ministry of Finance building	1·00	55

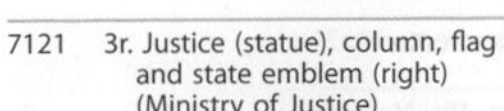

7121	3r. Justice (statue), column, flag and state emblem (right) (Ministry of Justice)	1·00	55

2771 Census Emblem surrounded by People

2002. National Census. Multicoloured. (a) Self-adhesive.

7122	3r. Type **2771**	3·00	1·70

(b) Ordinary gum.

7123	4r. Census emblem	4·00	2·20

2772 Russian Millenary Monument, Novgorod

2002. 1140th Anniv of Russian State.

7124	**2772**	3r. multicoloured	2·00	1·10

2773 Custom House, Archangelsk (19th-century engraving)

2002. Custom and Excise Service. Sheet 117×137 mm containing T **2773** and similar horiz designs. Multicoloured.

MS7125	2r. Type **2773**; 3r. Custom officers on horseback, St. Petersburg; 5r. Customs warehouse, Kalanchovsky Square	10·00	8·75

2774 The Motherland (statue)

2002. 60th Anniv of Battle for Stalingrad. Sheet 101×75 mm.

MS7126	**2774**	10r. multicoloured	8·00	7·75

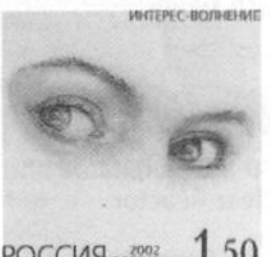

2775 Eyes

2002. Eyes. Sheet 181×107 mm containing T **2775** and similar square designs. Multicoloured.

MS7127	1r.50×10 Ten different stamps showing eyes	12·00	10·50

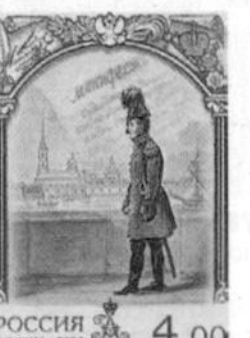

2776 Emperor Alexander I, Neva River and St. Peter and Paul Cathedral

2002. History of Russian State. Alexander I. Multicoloured.

7128	4r. Type **2776**	1·00	55
7129	4r. N. M. Karamzin (author, History of State) and Alexander I	1·00	55
7130	7r. M. Speransky handing plan for Code of Law to Alexander I	2·00	1·10

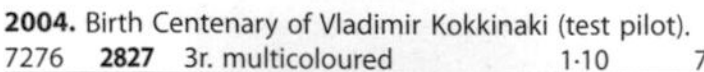

2004. Birth Centenary of Vladimir Kokkinaki (test pilot).

7276	**2827**	3r. multicoloured	1·10	70

2828 "Victory"

2004. Art. Paintings by Sergey Prisekin. Multicoloured.

7277	5r. Type **2828**	1·30	80
7278	5r. "Whosoever lives by the Sword shall perish by the Sword" (1983) (65×32 mm)	1·30	80
7279	5r. "Marshal Zhukov" (1980)	1·30	80
7280	5r. "We have honoured the Oath of Allegiance" (1991) (65×32 mm)	1·30	80

2829 Riding Habit

2004. Women's Costumes. Multicoloured.

7281	4r. Type **2829**	1·10	70
7282	4r. Two women, wearing riding habit and hat with brim and wearing walking dress, bonnet and shawl	1·10	70
7283	4r. Two women, wearing riding habit and hat with veil and wearing open-fronted dress with sash	1·10	70

2830 Runner

2004. Olympic Games, Athens. Multicoloured.

7284	3r. Type **2830**	1·10	75
7285	3r. Wrestlers	2·00	1·40

2831 Launch of Saratov Class Tanker

2004. 300th Anniv of Admiralty Wharfs (shipbuilding company). Sheet 76×96 mm.

MS7286 **2831**	12r. multicoloured	5·50	5·00

2832 Ducks using Pedestrian Crossing

2004. Children's Road Safety Campaign. Sheet 101×106 mm containing T **2832** and similar horiz designs.

MS7287 4r. ×5, Type **2832**; Crossing at traffic lights; Road closed by garden; Motor cycle stopping suddenly for girl playing ball; Car smash between teddy bears and chicken	7·25	6·75

2833 Wolverine

2004. Wolverine (Gulo gulo). Multicoloured.

7288	8r. Type **2833**	1·80	1·30
7289	8r. With prey	1·80	1·30
7290	8r. Standing on branch	1·80	1·30
7291	8r. Mother and cubs	1·80	1·30

2834 Buildings

2004. 400th Anniv of Tomsk (town).

7292	**2834**	4r. multicoloured	90	65

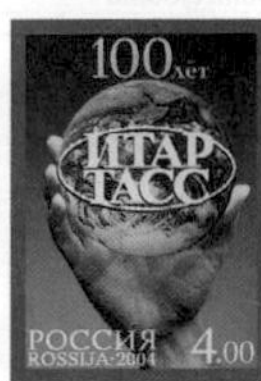

2835 Hand holding Globe

2004. Centenary of ITAR TASS (news agency).

7293	**2835**	4r. multicoloured	90	65

2836 N. L. Duhov

2004. Birth Centenaries. Multicoloured.

7294	5r. Type **2836** (military designer)	1·10	75
7295	5r. B. G. Muzrukov (manufacturer)	1·10	75

2837 Paul I

2004. 250th Birth Anniv of Emperor Paul I. Multicoloured.

7296	10r. Type **2837**	3·25	2·30
7297	10r. Wearing crown and robes	3·25	2·30
MS7298	90×75 mm. 20r. Wearing tri-corn hat	9·00	8·25

2838 Svyatoslav Rerikh

2004. Birth Centenary of Svyatoslav Nikolayevich Rerikh (artist).

7299	**2838**	4r. multicoloured	90	65

2839 Vsevolod the Big Nest

2004. History of Russian State. 850th Birth Anniv of Vsevolod III Yuryevich (Vsevolod the Big Nest).

7300	**2839**	12r. multicoloured	3·50	2·50

2840 University Building

2004. Bicentenary of Kazan State University.

7301	**2840**	5r. multicoloured	1·30	90

2841 Bowl (c. 1880—90)

2004. Silverware. Multicoloured.

7302	4r.70 Type **2841**	1·80	1·30
7304	4r.70 Ladle (c.1910)	1·80	1·30
7305	4r.70 Jug (c. 1900)	1·80	1·30
7306	4r.70 Vase (c. 1900—08) (vert)	1·80	1·30

2842 Tree

2004. Happy New Year. Self-adhesive.

7307	**2842**	5r. multicoloured	5·50	4·50

2843 Belukha Mountain

2004. Altai Mountain Range. Multicoloured.

7308	2r. Type **2843**	55	40
7309	3r. Katun River	90	65
7310	5r. Teletskoye Lake	1·30	90

2844 R-7 Intercontinental Missile

2004. 50th Anniv of Baikonur Cosmodrome. Multicoloured.

7311	2r.50 Type **2844**	55	40
7312	3r.50 Proton rocket	70	50
7313	4r. Soyuz rocket	90	65
7314	6r. Zenit rocket	1·40	1·00

2005. Regions of the Russian Federation (9th issue). As T **2651**. Multicoloured.

7315	5r. Koyrak region	1·10	75
7316	5r. Mordovia Republic	1·10	75
7317	5r. Smolensk region	1·10	75
7318	5r. Taimyr autonomous region	1·10	75
7319	5r. Tver region	1·10	75
7320	5r. Chukotski autonomous region	1·10	75

2845 University Building

2005. 250th Anniv of Lomonosov State University, Moscow.

7321	**2845**	5r. multicoloured	1·10	75

2846 Tree and Emblem

2005. EXPO 2005 World Exposition, Aichi, Japan. Sheet 91×71 mm.

MS7322 **2846**	15r. multicoloured	9·00	7·50

2847 Drinking Horn with Bull-shaped Base

2005. Sarmat (early tribe) Artefacts from Filippov Burial Ground. Multicoloured.

7323	5r. Type **2847**	1·80	1·30
7324	5r. Bear-shaped bowl	1·80	1·30
7325	7r. Camels on gold hemisphere	3·50	2·50
7326	7r. Deer-shaped ornament (vert)	3·50	2·50

2848 Type M Submarine VI-bis Series

2005. Submarines. Multicoloured.

7327	2r. Type **2848**	3·50	2·50
7328	3r. Type S submarine IX- bis series	5·50	3·75
7329	5r. Type Sch submarine X-bis series	7·25	5·00
7330	8r. Type K submarine	11·00	7·50

2849 Suyumbike Tower

2005. Kazan Millenary. Multicoloured.

7331	5r. Type **2849**	1·40	1·00
7332	5r. Kul Sharif Mosque	1·40	1·00
7333	7r. Cathedral of the Annunciation	2·75	1·90
MS7333a	143×133 mm. Nos. 7331/3	2·00	1·50

2850 Alexander with W. Schukowskij

2005. 150th Anniv of Coronation of Emperor Alexander II.

7334	10r. Type **2850**	3·25	2·20
7335	10r. Coronation in Uspenski Cathedral in the Kremlin	3·25	2·20
7336	10r. In his study	3·25	2·20
7337	10r. Mounted during Turkish—Russian war	3·25	2·20
MS7338	92×77 mm. 25r. Alexander II	8·00	7·50

2851 Russian Soldier signing Column (Berlin, 1945)

2005. 60th Anniv of End of World War II. Multicoloured.

7339	2r. Type **2851**	55	40
7340	2r. Soldiers celebrating (Berlin, 1945)	55	40
7341	3r. Soldier feeding pigeons (Kalinsky front, 1943)	70	50
7342	3r. Soldiers holding flowers (Moscow, 1945)	70	50
7343	5r. Russian soldiers with captured German banners (Kremlin, 1945)	1·10	75
MS7344	71×101 mm. 10r. Two soldiers with weapons raised	5·50	5·00

2852 City Hall

2005. 60th Anniv of Liberation of Vienna.

7345	**2852**	6r. multicoloured	1·40	1·00

2853 Greater Spotted Eagle (*Aquila clanga*)

2005. Fauna. Sheet 133×68 mm containing T **2853** and similar horiz designs. Multicoloured.

MS7346 5r.×4, Type **2853**; *Catocala sponsa*; Beaver (*Castor fiber*); Badger (*Meles meles*) 11·00 10·00

The stamps and margin of No. **MS**7346 form a composite design.

Stamps of the same design were issued by Belarus.

2854 Train and Map of First Route

2005. 70th Anniv of Moscow Metro. Sheet 91×71 mm containing T **2854** and similar horiz design. Multicoloured.

MS7347 5r. Type **2854**; 10r. Modern routes 5·50 5·00

2855 Emblem

2005. Moscow's Bid for Olympic Games—2012.

7348	**2855**	4r. multicoloured	1·10	75

2856 Blinis, Caviar and Samovar

2005. Europa. Gastronomy.

7349	**2856**	8r. multicoloured	2·75	1·90

2857 M.A. Sholokhov

2005. Birth Centenary of Mikhail Aleksandrovich Sholokhov (writer).

7350	**2857**	5r. black and brown	1·10	75

2858 Sable (*Martes zibellina*)

2005. Fauna. Multicoloured.

7351	8r. Type **2858**	1·80	1·30
7352	8r. Siberian tiger (*Panthera tigris altaica*)	1·80	1·30

Stamps of a similar design were issued by People's Democratic Republic of Korea.

2859 *Bombus armeniacus*

2005. Bees. Multicoloured.

7353	3r. Type **2859**	70	50
7354	4r. *Bombus fragrans*	1·10	75
7355	5r. *Bombus anachoreta*	1·30	90
7356	6r. *Bombus unicus*	1·40	1·00
7357	7r. *Bombus czerskii*	1·60	1·10

2860 Monuments, Gate and Towers

2005. 750th Anniv of Kaliningrad (Koenigsberg).

7358	**2860**	5r. multicoloured	1·60	1·10

2861 University Facade

2005. 175th Anniv of Moscow Technical University.

7359	**2861**	5r. multicoloured	1·30	90

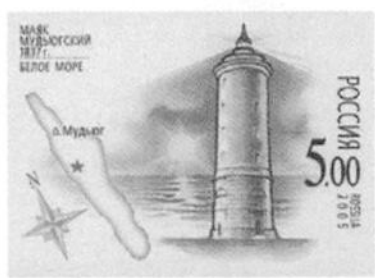

2862 Mudyugsky Lighthouse

2005. Lighthouses. Multicoloured.

7360	5r. Type **2862**	1·40	1·00
7361	6r. Solovetsky lighthouse	2·20	1·50
7362	8r. Svyatonossky lighthouse	3·50	2·50

2863 MiG-3 Fighter Aircraft

2005. Birth Centenary of Artem Ivanovich Mikoyan (aircraft designer). Multicoloured.

7363	5r. Type **2863**	1·40	1·00
7364	5r. MiG-15	1·40	1·00
7365	5r. MiG-21	1·40	1·00
7366	5r. MiG-25	1·40	1·00
7367	5r. MiG-29	1·40	1·00

2864 Priest blessing Troops

2005. 625th Anniv of Kulikovo Battle (Russian victory against the Mongols). Sheet 97×65 mm.

MS7368 **2864** 15r. multicoloured 4·50 3·75

2865 Hands

2005. Earth. Sheet 147×105 mm containing T **2865** and similar horiz designs. Multicoloured.

MS7369 3r. Type **2865**; 3r.50 Water droplets on leaf; 3r.50 Surf; 4r. Snow-topped mountain; 4r.50 Waterfall; 5r. Water droplets 6·25 5·75

2866 Alexander Suvorov

2005. 275th Birth Anniv of Alexander Vasilievich Suvorov (military commander).

7370	**2866**	4r. multicoloured	1·10	75

2867 Early Sea Infantry

2005. 300th Anniv of Sea Infantry. Multicoloured.

7371	2r. Type **2867**	70	50
7372	3r. Fighting in Crimea	90	65
7373	4r. Fighting during World War II	1·10	75
7374	5r. Modern Sea Infantry	1·30	90

2868 Ded Moroz (Father Christmas)

2005

7375	**2868**	5r. multicoloured	1·40	1·00

2869 Emblem

2005. 60th Anniv of UNESCO.

7376	**2869**	5r.60 multicoloured	1·80	1·30

2870 Trees

2005. Christmas and New Year.

7377	**2870**	5r.60 multicoloured	1·80	1·30

2871 AH-12

2006. Birth Centenary of Oleg Konstantinovich Antonov (aircraft designer). Multicoloured.

7378	5r.60 Type **2871**	1·40	1·00
7379	5r.60 AH-24	1·40	1·00
7380	5r.60 AH-124	1·40	1·00
7381	5r.60 AH-74	1·40	1·00
7382	5r.60 AH-3T	1·40	1·00

2872 Speed Skating

2006. Winter Olympic Games, Turin. Multicoloured.

7383	4r. Type **2872**	1·10	75
7384	4r. Luge	1·10	75
7385	4r. Snowboarding	1·10	75

2873 Armenian and Russian Flags and Arms

2006. Year of Armenia in Russia.

7386	**2873**	10r. multicoloured	2·20	1·60

2874 *Ob* (Icebreaker) and Mirnyi Station

2006. 50th Anniv of Antarctic Research. Multicoloured.

7387	7r. Type **2874**	1·80	1·40
7388	7r. Plane Il-76 and *Academic Fedorov* (scientific ship)	1·80	1·40
7389	7r. Transport and sea researcher	1·80	1·40

2875 "Portrait of N. N. Ge" (I. E. Repin)

2006. 175th Birth Anniv of Nikolai Nikolaevich Ge (artist). Multicoloured.

7390	5r.60 Type **2875**	1·80	1·40
7391	5r.60 "Peter I interrogating Tsarevich Aleksei" (horiz)	1·80	1·40

2876 "Self-portrait"

2006. 150th Birth Anniv of Mikhail Aleksandrovich Vrubel (artist). Multicoloured.

7392	5r.60 Type **2876**	1·80	1·40
7393	5r.60 "Tsarevna-Swan"	1·80	1·40

2877 Atomic Submarine No. 667A

2006. Centenary of Russian Submarine Navy. Atomic Submarines. Multicoloured.

7394	3r. Type **2877**	3·50	2·75
7395	4r. Submarine No. 671	4·50	3·50
7396	6r. Submarine No. 941	5·50	4·00
7397	7r. Submarine No. 949a	7·25	5·50

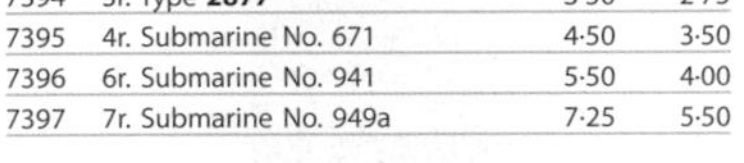
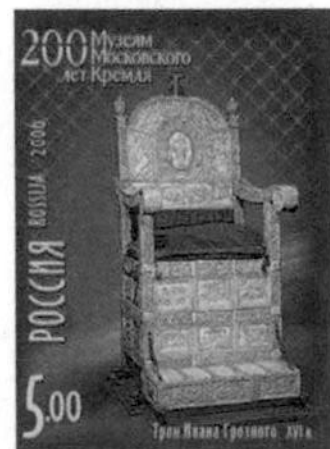

2878 Ivan Groznyi's Throne

2006. Bicentenary of Kremlin Museums, Moscow. Multicoloured.

7398	5r. Type **2878**	1·60	1·20
7399	5r. Tsar Mikhail Fyodorovich's mace	1·60	1·20
7400	5r. Tsar Mikhail Fyodorovich's helmet	1·60	1·20
7401	5r. State sword and shield	1·60	1·20
7401a	20r. Monomakh's cap	14·50	12·00
7401b	20r. As Type **2878**	14·50	12·00
7401c	20r. As No. 7399	14·50	12·00
7401d	20r. As No. 7400	14·50	12·00
7401e	20r. As No. 7401	14·50	12·00
MS7402	122×97 mm. 15r. Monomakh	5·50	5·00

2879 AIR1

2006. Birth Centenary of Alexandr Sergevich Yakovlev (aircraft designer). Multicoloured.

7403	5r. Type **2879**	1·40	1·10
7404	5r. YAK-54	1·40	1·10
7405	5r. YAK-141	1·40	1·10
7406	5r. YAK-42	1·40	1·10
7407	5r. YAK-130	1·40	1·10

2880 Arms

2006. Centenary of State Duma. Sheet 90×71 mm.
MS7408 **2880** 15r. multicoloured 5·50 5·50

2881 State Arms

2006. State Arms and Flag. Multicoloured.

7409	5r.60 Type **2881**	6·25	4·75
7410	5r.60 State flag	6·25	4·75

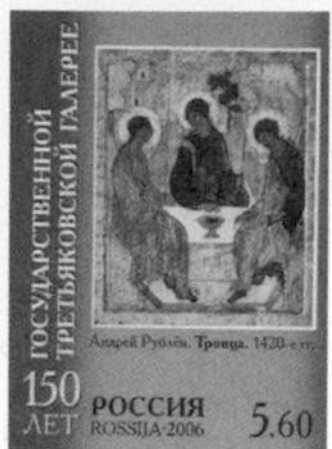
2882 "Trinity" (Andrey Rublev)

2006. 150th Anniv Tretiakov State Picture Gallery. Multicoloured.

7411	5r.60 Type **2882**	1·40	1·10
7412	5r.60 "Girl with peaches" (V.A. Serov)	1·40	1·10
7413	5r.60 "Above eternal rest" (I. I. Levitan) (horiz)	1·40	1·10
7414	5r.60 "Three Bogatyrs" (V. M. Vasnetsov) (horiz)	1·40	1·10
MS7415	90×71 mm. 15r. Gallery building (49×37 mm)	4·50	4·00

2883 Emperor Aleksandr III

2006. Emperor Aleksandr III. Multicoloured.

7416	10r. Type **2883**	3·50	2·75
7417	10r. Aleksandr III, flags and ships	3·50	2·75
MS7418	91×76 mm. 15r. Aleksandr III in close up	7·25	6·75

2884 Statue and Towers

2006. 150th Anniv of Blagoveschensk.
7419 **2884** 5r. multicoloured 1·40 1·10

2885 Ship in Dry Dock

2006. 150th Anniv of Baltic Plant. Sheet 70×90 mm.
MS7420 **2885** 12r. multicoloured 4·50 4·00

2886 Stadium at Night

2006. 50th Anniv of Luzhniki Olympic Complex, Moscow.
7421 **2886** 6r. multicoloured 1·40 1·10

2887 Summer Bouquet

2006. Flowers. Designs showing part of a seasonal bouquet. Multicoloured.

7422	7r. Type **2887**	1·60	1·20
7423	7r. Autumn	1·60	1·20
7424	7r. Winter	1·60	1·20
7425	7r. Spring	1·60	1·20

Nos. 7422/5 were issued together, se-tenant, forming a composite design.

2888 Deer

2006. 250th Anniv of Altai as Part of Russia.
7426 **2888** 5r. multicoloured 1·10 80

2006. Regions of the Russian Federation (10th issue). As T **2651**. Multicoloured.

7427	6r. Adygeja Republic (vert)	1·40	1·10
7428	6r. Vladimir region (vert)	1·40	1·10
7429	6r. Kostroma region	1·40	1·10
7430	6r. Pskov region	1·40	1·10
7431	6r. Rjazan region	1·40	1·10
7432	6r. Tula region	1·40	1·10

2889 *Kruzenshtern* (four masted training barque)

2006. Kruzenshtern's Circumnavigation of the Globe to celebrate the Bicentenary of Adam Johann Ritter von Krustenstern's Voyage.
7433 **2889** 4r. multicoloured 1·10 80

2890 Map of Spitzbergen

2006. 75th Anniv of Arcticugol Trust.
7434 **2890** 4r. multicoloured 1·10 80

2891 Left Wing Facade

2006. 250th Anniv of Tsarskoye Selo (Catherine's Palace). Sheet 166×74 mm containing T **2891** and similar horiz designs. Multicoloured.
MS7435 5r. Type **2891**; 6r. Central facade; 7r. Right wing 7·25 6·75

The stamps and margins of **MS**7435 form a composite design of the Palace facade.

2892 "A. A. Ivanov" (S. P. Postnikov)

2006. Birth Bicentenary of Alexander Andreyevich Ivanov (artist). Multicoloured.

7436	6r. Type **2892**	1·80	1·40
7437	6r. "Branch" (A. A. Ivanov) (horiz)	1·80	1·40

2893 *A. M. Vasnetsov* (N. D. Kuznetsov)

2006. 150th Birth Anniv of Apollinary Mikhailovich Vasnetsov (artist). Multicoloured.

7438	6r. Type **2893**	1·80	1·40
7439	6r. *Novodevichy Monastery* (horiz)	1·80	1·40

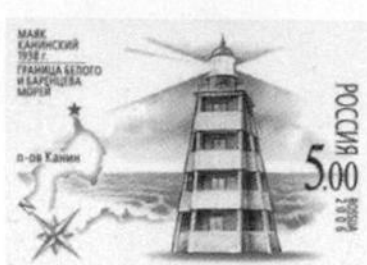
2894 Kanin Peninsula

2006. Lighthouses. Multicoloured.

7440	5r. Type **2894**	1·40	1·10
7441	6r. Kildin Island	1·80	1·40
7442	8r. Rybachiy (vert)	2·20	1·60

2895 Masks and Auditorium

2006. 250th Anniv of State Theatre. Sheet 91×71 mm.
MS7443 **2895** 15r. multicoloured 4·50 4·00

2896 *Rhodostethia rosea* (Ross's gull)

2006. Fauna of Sakha (Yakutia) Republic. Multicoloured.

7444	3r. Type **2896**	90	70
7445	4r. *Grus leucogeranus* (Siberian crane)	1·10	80
7446	5r. *Ursus maritimus* (polar bear)	1·30	95
7447	6r. *Equus caballus* (domestic horse)	1·60	1·20
7448	7r. *Rangifer tarandus* (caribou)	1·80	1·40

2897 Students

2006. Centre for Russian Language Development.
7449 **2897** 7r. multicoloured 1·80 1·40

2898 D. S. Likhachev

2006. Birth Centenary of Dmitri Sergeyevich Likhachev (writer).
7450 **2898** 5r. brown, grey and black 1·10 80

2899 Mountain Peak

2006. Natural Heritage, West Caucasus. Multicoloured.

7451	6r. Type **2899**	1·40	1·10
7452	7r. River	1·60	1·20
7453	8r. Bison	1·80	1·40

Nos. 7451/3 were issued together, se-tenant, forming a composite design of a mountain scene.

2900 Transmitter

2006. 75th Anniv of Regular Broadcasting.
7454 **2900** 7r. multicoloured 1·60 1·20

2901 Handset

2006. 15th Anniv of Mobile Telephony.
7455 **2901** 7r. multicoloured 1·60 1·20

2902 N. A. Kristofari (first investor) and Bank Facade

2006. 165th Anniv of National Saving Bank. Multicoloured.

7456	7r. Type **2902**	1·60	1·20
MS7457	96×71 mm. 15r. N. A. Kristofari (30×42 mm)	5·50	4·75

2903 Emblem

2006. Russian Membership of Council of Europe.
7458 **2903** 8r. multicoloured 1·80 1·40

2904 Emblem

2006. 15th Anniv of Regional Commonwealth in Communication.
7459 **2904** 5r. multicoloured 2·30 1·80

2905 Snowmen

2006. Ded Moroz.
7460 **2905** 7r. multicoloured 1·80 1·40

2906 Atlas

2006. National Atlas.
7461 **2906** 6r. multicoloured 1·80 1·40

2907 Snow-covered Tree

2006. New Year.

7462 **2907** 7r. multicoloured 1·80 1·40

2908 V. M. Behterev

2007. 150th Birth Anniv of Vladimir Mikhailovich Behterev (psychologist and neuropathologist).

7463 **2908** 5r. multicoloured 1·40 1·10

2909 "I. I. Shishkin" (I. N. Kramskoy)

2007. 175th Birth Anniv of Ivan Ivanovitch Shishkin (artist). Multicoloured.

7464 7r. Type **2909** 2·20 1·60

7465 7r. "In the north wild..." (I. I. Shishkin) 2·20 1·60

2910 St. George's Cross

2007. Bicentenary of Cross of St. George. Multicoloured.

7466 10r. Type **2910** 3·50 2·75

MS7467 90×126 mm. 50r. St George's Cross (different) (56×56 mm) 13·50 12·00

2911 Academy Facade

2007. Centenary of Russian Economic Academy.

7468 **2911** 5r. multicoloured 1·40 1·10

2912 "Self-portrait"

2007. 225th Birth Anniv of Orest Adamovich Kiprensky (artist). Multicoloured.

7469 7r. Type **2912** 1·80 1·40

7470 7r. "Bednaja Liza" 1·80 1·40

2913 Russian Mail Emblem

2007

7471 **2913** 6r.50 blue 1·80 1·40

2914 Research Ship and Station

2007. International Polar Year. Sheet 190×77 mm containing T **2914** and similar horiz designs. Multicoloured.

MS7472 6r. Type **2914**; 7r. Polar ice pack; 8r. Ptarmigan 12·50 11·00

The stamps of **MS**7472 form a composite design.

2915 Arseny Alexandrovich Tarkovsky

2007. Russian Cinema. Sheet 71×90 mm containing T **2915** and similar horiz designs. Multicoloured.

MS7473 8r. Type **2915** (birth centenary); 8r. Andrey Arsenyevich Tarkovsky (75th birth anniv) 7·25 6·75

2916 Sputnik

2007. 50th Anniv of Space Exploration. Sheet 110×110 mm containing T **2916** and similar square designs. Multicoloured.

MS7474 10r. Type **2916**; 20r. Sergey Pavlovich Korolyov (chief rocket designer and engineer) (birth centenary); 20r. Konstantin Eduardovitch Tsiolkovsky ('father of cosmonautics') (150th birth anniv) 12·50 12·00

The stamps and margins of **MS**7474 form a composite design.

2917 Russian and Bashkiria Leaders

2007. 450th Anniv of the Assimilation of Bashkiria into Russia.

7475 **2917** 6r.50 multicoloured 1·80 1·40

2918 *Pavel Chistyakov* (I. E. Repin)

2007. 175th Birth Anniv of Pavel Petrovich Chistyakov (artist). Multicoloured.

7476 7r. Type **2918** 1·80 1·40

7477 7r. *Pavel Chistyakov* (V. A. Serov) 1·80 1·40

2919 *Vladimir Borovikovsky* (I. V. Bugaevsky-Blagodarny)

2007. 250th Birth Anniv of Vladimir Lukich Borovikovsky (artist). Multicoloured.

7478 7r. Type **2919** 1·80 1·40

7479 7r. *Anna and Varvara Gagarina* 1·80 1·40

2920 1858 10k. Stamp (As Type 1)

2007. 150th Anniv of First Russian Stamp. Sheet 95×81 mm.

MS7480 **2920** 10r. blue and brown 3·50 3·00

The stamp and margins of **MS**7480 form a composite design.

2921 Early Handset

2007. 125th Anniv of Telephony.

7481 **2921** 5r. multicoloured 1·40 1·20

2922 Athena (statue), Cupola, Academy of Art

2007. 250th Anniv of Academy of Art. Sheet 92×76 mm.

MS7482 **2922** 25r. bistre and agate 7·25 6·50

The stamp and margins of **MS**7482 form a composite design.

2923 Exhibition Emblem

2007. St. Petersburg–2007 World Stamp Exhibition.

7483 **2923** 5r. ultramarine, gold and blue 1·10 85

2924 Launch Pad

2007. 50th Anniv of Cosmodrome, Pleseck. Sheet 91×76 mm.

MS7484 **2924** 12r. multicoloured 3·50 3·00

The stamp and margins of **MS**7484 form a composite design.

2925 Mountains

2007. 300th Anniv of the Assimilation of Hakasia into Russia.

7485 **2925** 6r.50 multicoloured 1·80 1·50

2926 N. A. Lunin

2007. Submariners' Birth Centenaries. Multicoloured.

7486 7r. Type **2926** 1·80 1·50

7487 7r. M. I. Gadjiev 1·80 1·50

Nos. 7486/7 were issued together, horizontal *se-tenant* strips of two stamps surrounding a central stamp size label, showing a submarine, the whole forming a composite design.

2927 S. P. Botkin

2007. 175th Birth Anniv of Sergei Petrovich Botkin (medical scientist).

7488 **2927** 5r. blue 1·40 1·20

2007. Regions of the Russian Federation (11th issue). As T **2651**. Multicoloured.

7489 7r. Altai region 1·60 1·30

7490 7r. Vologda region 1·60 1·30

7491 7r. Irkutsk region 1·60 1·30

7492 7r. Novosibirsk region 1·60 1·30

7493 7r. Orlov region 1·60 1·30

7494 7r. Rostov region 1·60 1·30

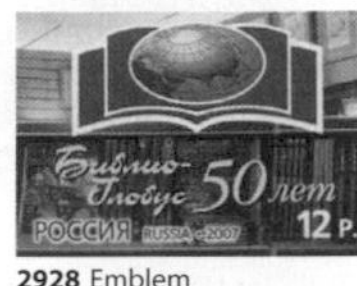

2928 Emblem

2007. 50th Anniv of Biblio-Globus Bookshop. Sheet 91×72 mm.

MS7495 **2928** 12r. multicoloured 4·50 4·00

2929 Child writing

2007. Year of Russian Language (1st issue). Sheet 92×106 mm.

MS7496 12r. multicoloured 4·50 4·00

2930 *Gladiolus gandavensis*

2007. Flora. Sheet 92×106 mm contiaining T **2930** and similar horiz designs. Multicoloured.

MS7497 6r.×4, Type **2930**; *Iris ensata*; *Rosa hybrida*; *Nelumbo nucifera* 6·25 5·75

The stamps and margins of **MS**7497 form a composite design.

2931 *Ciconia boyciana* (oriental stork)

2007. Endangered Species. Multicoloured.

7498 5r. Type **2931** 1·10 85

7499 6r. *Uncia uncia* (snow leopard) 1·30 1·00

7500 7r. *Bison bonasus* (European bison) 2·20 1·70

2932 AMO-F-15 (1924)

2007. Early Russian Lorries. Multicoloured.

7501 8r. Type **2932** 1·60 1·30

7502 8r. GAZ-AA (MM) (1932) 1·60 1·30

7503 8r. ZIS-5V (1942) 1·60 1·30

2933 Russian House of Science and Culture, Berlin

2007. Year of Russian Language (2nd issue).

7504	**2933**	8r. multicoloured	1·80	1·40

2934 Vladimirskaya Heavy Type Horse

2007. Domestic Horse Breeds. Multicoloured.

7505	6r. Type **2934**	1·30	95
7506	7r. Orlovskaya warm blood	1·40	1·10
7507	7r. Vyatskaya	1·40	1·10
7508	8r. Donskaya	1·60	1·20
MS7509	132×98 mm. As Nos. 7505/8	7·25	6·75

2935 Snowmen

2007. Happy New Year.

7510	**2935**	8r. multicoloured	1·80	1·40

2007. Arktika 2007 (first ever crewed descent to sea floor at North Pole). Multicoloured.

7511	8r. Type **2936**	1·60	1·40
7512	8r. The North Pole and Russian flag	1·60	1·40

2937 A. N. Tolstoi

2008. 125th Birth Anniv of Aleksei Nikolaevich Tolstoi (writer).

7513	**2937**	6r. multicoloured	1·30	1·10

2938 Mail Troika and Russian Empire Type **1**

2008. 150th Anniv of First Russian Stamp.

7514	**2938**	8r. multicoloured	1·80	1·50

2939 Lev Davidovich Landau

2008. Birth Centenaries of Nobel Prize Winning Physicists. Multicoloured.

7515	6r. Type **2939** (1962)	1·30	95
7516	6r. Il'ja Mikhailovich Frank (1958)	1·30	95

2940 Augustin de Betancourt

2008. 250th Birth Anniv of Augustin de Betancourt y Molina (engineer and architect).

7517	**2940**	9r. multicoloured	2·00	1·50

2941 Park

2008. 450th Anniv of Astrakhan.

7518	**2941**	9r. multicoloured	2·00	1·50

2942 Valentin Glushko

2008. Birth Centenary of Valentin Petrovich Glushko (engineer and spacecraft designer).

7519	**2942**	8r. multicoloured	1·60	1·20

2943 Buckle

2008. Archaeological Heritage. Sheet 145×70 mm containing T **2943** and similar horiz designs. Multicoloured.

MS7520	12r.×3, Type **2943**; Bronze plaque with two oxen ; Deer	9·00	8·00

The stamps and margins of **MS**7520 form a composite design.

2944 Competitors

2008. Olympic Games, Beijing. Multicoloured.

7521	8r. Type **2944**	1·60	1·20
7522	8r. Competitors, fencing and tennis central	1·60	1·20
7523	8r. Competitors, pole vault and archery central	1·60	1·20

Nos. 7521/3 were issued together, *se-tenant*, forming a composite design.

2945 Flags

2008. 225th Anniv of Black Sea Fleet. Sheet 70×90 mm.

MS7524	**2945** 15r. multicoloured	4·50	4·00

2946 Early and Modern Letters

2008. Europa. The Letter.

7525	**2946**	8r. multicoloured	1·80	1·40

2947 National Flag

2008. Inauguration of Dmitry Anatolyevich Medvedev as President.

7526	**2947**	7r. multicoloured	3·50	2·75

2008. Regions of the Russian Federation (12th issue). Multicoloured designs as T **2651**

7527	8r. Volgograd region	1·60	1·20
7528	8r. Krasnoyarsk region (vert)	1·60	1·20
7529	8r. Penza region	1·60	1·20
7530	8r. Sverdlov region (vert)	1·60	1·20
7531	8r. Yaroslavl region	1·60	1·20

2948 St Dimitry Church, Vladimir (Russia)

2008. UNESCO World Heritage Sites in Romania and Russia. Multicoloured.

7532	12r. Type **2948**	2·50	2·00
7533	12r. St Gheorghe Church, Voronet Monastery (Romania)	2·50	2·00

Stamps of a similar design were issued by Romania.

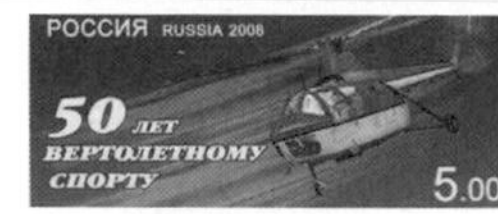

2949 Helicopter

2008. 50th Anniversary of Helicopter Sports.

7534	**2949**	5r. multicoloured	1·30	1·00

2950 Pokrovsky Cathedral

2008

7535	**2950**	7r.50 multicoloured	1·80	1·50

2951 Flags and Aircraft Carrier

2008. 75th Anniv of North Fleet. Sheet 70×90 mm.

MS7536	**2951** 15r. multicoloured	4·50	4·25

2952 Emblem

2008. 450th Anniv of Udmurtia's Assimilation into Russia.

7537	**2952**	7r.50 multicoloured	1·80	1·50

2953 Church (1714)

2008. Kizhi–World Heritage Site. Sheet 116×70 mm containing T **2953** and similar vert designs. Multicoloured.

MS7538	10r.×3, Type **2953**; Bell tower (1862); Church (1694–17)	9·00	9·50

The stamps and margins of **MS**7538 form a composite design.

2954 Emperor Nicholas I

2008. Russian History. Sheet 90×78 mm.

MS7539	**2954** 35r. multicoloured	8·00	8·00

2955 *Krasin*

2008. International Polar Year. Sheet 190×77 mm containing T **2955** and similar horiz designs. Multicoloured.

MS7540	6r. Type **2955**; 7r. *Rossija*; 8r. Small icebreaker	7·25	7·25

The stamps and margins of **MS**7540 form a composite design.

2957 Emblem

2008. 190th Anniv of GOZNAK (banknote and coin producer). Sheet 130×65 mm.

MS7556	**2957** 20r. multicoloured	5·75	5·50

2958 Squirrel and Woodpecker

2008. Fauna and Flora. Multicoloured.

7557	7r. Type **2958**	1·60	1·30
7558	7r. Fawn	1·60	1·30
7559	7r. Fungi	1·60	1·30

Nos. 7557/9 were issued together, *se-tenant*, the whole forming a composite design of a woodland scene.

2008. Regions of the Russian Federation (13th issue). As T **2651**. Multicoloured.

7560	8r. Leningrad region	4·00	3·25

2959 Medal

2008. Russian History. Cossacks. Sheet 114×148 mm containing T **2959** and similar horiz designs. Multicoloured.

MS7561	10r.×3, Type **2959**; Badge; Sabre	8·75	8·50

The stamps and margins of **MS**7561 form a composite design.

2960 Helicopter Kamov Ka-32A

2008. Helicopters. Multicoloured.

7562	7r. Type **2960**	1·60	1·30
7563	7r. Kamov Ka-226	1·60	1·30

2961 Forest and Mountains in Mist

2008. World Heritage. Central Sikhote–Alin. Multicoloured.

7564	7r. Type **2961**	1·60	1·30
7565	8r. Forest and mist	1·80	1·40
7566	9r. Forest	2·00	1·60

Nos. 7564/6 plus a stamp size label were printed, *se-tenant*, forming a composite design of forested valley.

2962 State Flag and Arms

2008. 15th Anniv of Federal Assembly of Russia. Multicoloured.

7567	10r. Type **2962**	3·00	2·40
7568	10r. State flag as map of Russia	3·00	2·40

2963 Bridge over Moscow River

2008. Bridges. Multicoloured.

7569	6r. Type **2963**	1·40	1·10
7570	7r. Bridge over Volga, Kimry	1·60	1·30
7571	8r. Bridge over Ob, Surgut	1·80	1·40
7572	9r. Bridge over Neva, St. Petersburg	2·00	1·60

2964 Swimmer

2008. Centenary of Shuvalov Swimming School.

7573	**2964** 8r. multicoloured	1·80	1·40

2965 Trophy and Player

2008. Russia—World Hockey Champions, 2008.

7574	**2965** 8r. multicoloured	1·80	1·40

2966 Leitner Bicycle (1917)

2008. Bicycles. Multicoloured.

7575	7r. Type **2966**	1·60	1·30
7576	7r. Racing cycle (1938)	1·60	1·30
7577	7r. B-22 ladies cycle (1954)	1·60	1·30

2967 Kremlin Tower and State Symbols

2008. Happy New Year.

7578	**2967** 7r.50 multicoloured	1·60	1·30

2968 Kerchief with Chain and Pendants

2008. Decorative Art of Dagestan.

7579	7r.50 Type **2968**	1·60	1·30
7580	7r.50 Headdress 'Kjukjem'	1·60	1·30
7581	7r.50 Pendant from wedding headdress 'Margjal'	1·60	1·30
7582	7r.50 Man with dagger in sheath	1·60	1·30

2009. Regions of the Russian Federation (14th issue). As T **2651**. Multicoloured.

7583	9r. Voronezh region	2·00	1·60
7584	9r. Chelyabinsk region	2·00	1·60
7585	9r. Sararov region	2·00	1·60

2969 Ernesto 'Che' Guevara and Cuban Flag

2009. 50th Anniv of Cuban Revolution.

7586	**2969** 10r. multicoloured	4·00	3·25

2970 Museum Building

2009. 300th Anniv of Naval Museum.

7587	**2970** 7r. multicoloured	1·80	1·40

2971 *Self Portrait*, 1851

2009. 175th Birth Anniv of Vasily Grigorevich Perov (artist). Multicoloured.

7588	9r. Type **2971**	2·00	1·60
7589	9r. *Tea-Party at Mytishchi near Moscow*, 1862 (horiz)	2·00	1·60

2972 Dmitri Mendeleev

2009. 175th Birth Anniv of Dmitri Ivanovich Mendeleev (chemist and creator of first version of periodic table of elements). Sheet 110×75 mm.

MS7590	**2972** 15r. multicoloured	3·50	3·25

2973 G. Bakhchivandji

2009. Birth Centenary of G.Y. Bakhchivandji (test pilot).

7591	**2973** 10r. multicoloured	2·10	1·80

2974 Yuri Gagarin and Signature

2009. 75th Birth Anniv of Yuri Alekseyevich Gagarin (cosmonaut and first man in space).

7592	**2974** 10r. multicoloured	2·10	1·80

2975 Alexander Popov

2009. 150th Birth Anniv of Alexander Stepanovich Popov (physicist). Sheet 90×70 mm.

MS7593	**2975** 20r. multicoloured	4·25	4·00

2976 Scene from *The Government Inspector*

2009. Birth Bicentenary of Nikolai Vasilievich Gogol. Two sheets containing T **2976** and similar vert designs (stamps of **MS**7594 showing scenes from his writings). Multicoloured.

MS7594	149×125 mm. 6r. Type **2976**; 7r. *Dead Souls*; 8r. *Overcoat*; 9r. *Taras Bulba*	7·75	7·25
MS7595	110×70 mm. 15r. Nikolai Gogol (painting)	3·50	3·25

The stamps and margins of No. **MS**7594 form a composite design.

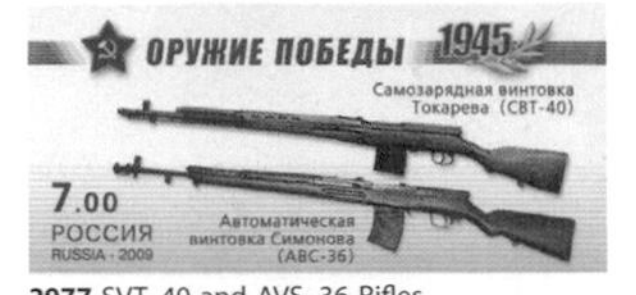

2977 SVT–40 and AVS–36 Rifles

2009. Weapons (1st issue). Multicoloured.

7596	7r. Type **2977**	1·60	1·30
7597	8r. Revolver, 1895 and TT pistol, 1933	1·80	1·40
7598	9r. PPS–43 and PPSH–41 submachine guns	2·00	1·60
7599	10r. DP and SG–43 machine guns	2·30	1·90

2978 Symbols of Astronomy

2009. Europa. Astronomy.

7600	**2978** 9r. multicoloured	2·00	1·60

2979 A. Y. Kupfer (academician–physicist instigated meteorological observations in whole territory of Russian Empire) (1779-1865)

2009. 175th Anniv of Hydrometeorologic Service. Multicoloured.

7601	8r. Type **2979**	1·60	1·30
7602	9r. Satellite and weather map	2·30	1·90

2980 Catherine I

2009. 325th Birth Anniv of Catherine I, Empress of Russia. Sheet 90×75 mm.

MS7603	**2980** 35r. multicoloured	7·75	7·25

2981 Emblem

2009. 400th Anniv of Assimulation of Kalmykia into Russian State

7604	**2981** 7r. multicoloured	1·60	1·30

2982 *Lenin*

2009. 50th Anniv of Ice Breaker Fleet. Multicoloured.

7605	7r. Type **2982**	1·60	1·30
7606	8r. *Taimyr*	2·00	1·60
7607	9r. *Yamal*	2·30	1·90
7608	10r. *50 Years of Victory*	3·00	2·40

No. 7609 is vacant

2983 *Peter I at Battle of Poltava* (I. G. Tannauer)

2009. 300th Anniv of Battle of Poltava. Sheet 83×127 mm.

MS7610	**2983** 30r. multicoloured	6·75	6·50

2984 Stylized Figures and Flag

2009. Year of Youth.

7611	**2984** 8r. multicoloured	1·80	1·40

2009. Regions of the Russian Federation (15th issue). As T **2651**. Multicoloured.

7612	9r. Ingushetiya Republic	2·00	1·60
7613	9r. Tomsk region	2·00	1·60
7614	9r. Chechen Republic	2·00	1·60

2985 Helicopter Mi-1

2009. Birth Centenary of Mikhail Leontyevich Mil (aircraft engineer). Sheet 160×100 mm containing T **2985** and similar horiz designs showing helicopters. Multicoloured.

MS7615	5r. Type **2985**; 6r. Mi-4.; 7r. Mi-8; 8r. Mi-34.; 9r. Mi-28	8·00	7·75

No. **MS**7615 also contains a stamp size label showing M. L. Mil, which with the stamps and margins, form a composite design.

2986 *Self Portrait At the Dressing-Table*

2009. 125th Birth Anniv of Zinaida Yevgenyevna Serebriakova (artist). Multicoloured.

7616	9r. Type **2986**	2·00	1·70
7617	9r. *Field in Autumn*	2·00	1·70

2987 Andrei Gromyko

2009. Birth Centenary of Andrei Andreyevich Gromyko (Soviet Union Minister for Foreign Affairs (1957–85) and Presidium of the Supreme Soviet Chairman (1985–88)).

7618	**2987**	7r. multicoloured	1·60	1·40

2988 17th-Century Monastery Complex

2009. World Heritage Site. Solovetsky Islands. Sheet 110×155 mm containing T **2988** and similar horiz designs. Multicoloured.

MS7619 12r.×4, Type **2988**; 19th-century complex; 15th-century building; Andrei Pervozvannyi church 12·00 11·00

The stamps and margins of **MS**719 form a composite design

2989 Ship on Spire of Admiralty (Symbol of St-Petersburg)

2009. Symbols of Moscow and St Petersburg. Multicoloured.

7620	6r.60 Type **2989**	1·60	1·40
7621	9r. St.Georgye (Symbol of Moscow)	2·00	1·70

2990 Bridge over the Oka, Nizhni Novgorod

2009. Bridges. Multicoloured.

7622	6r. Type **2990**	1·40	1·20
7623	7r. Bridge over the Irtysh, Khanty-Mansiysk	1·60	1·40
7624	8r. Bridge over the Matseta, Sochi	1·80	1·50
7625	9r. Bridge over the Don, Rostov on Don	2·00	1·70

2991 Belgorod

2009. Town Emblems (1st issue). Sheet 125×88 mm containing T **2991** and similar square designs. Multicoloured.

MS7626 10r.×5 Type **2991**; Kursk; Orel; Polyarny; Pzhev 11·00 10·00

2992 Church

2009. 1150th Anniv of Veliky Novgorod. Sheet 105×77 mm.

MS7627 **2992** 50r. multicoloured 11·00 10·00

2993 Ermak Timofeevich

2009. History of Russian Cossacks. Sheet 160×100 mm containing T **2993** and similar vert designs. Multicoloured.

MS7628 10r.×3, Type **2993**; Semen Ivanovich Dezhnev; Matvei Ivanovich Platov 7·25 6·75

2994 Girls Headdress, Moscow Region

2009. 19th-century Headdresses and Hat. Multicoloured.

7629	9r. Type **2994**	2·00	1·70
7630	9r. Wedding headdress, mid 19th-century, Nizhegorodskiy region	2·00	1·70
7631	9r. Woman's headdress, Yaroslavl region	2·00	1·70
7632	9r. Man's hat, Tver region	2·00	1·70

2995 Astrakhan Kremlin

2009. Kremlins. Multicoloured. Self-adhesive.

7633	1r. Type **2995**	10	10
7634	1r.50 Zaraisk	20	15
7635	2r. Kazan	40	35
7636	2r.50 Kolomna	60	50
7637	3r. Rostov	80	70
7638	4r. Nizhny Novgorod	1·00	85
7639	5r. Novgorod	1·20	1·00
7640	6r. Pskov	1·40	1·20
7641	10r. Moscow	2·40	2·00
7642	25r. Ryazan	5·00	4·25
7643	50r. Tobolsk	10·00	8·50
7644	100r. Tula	20·00	17·00

2996 WFP Emblem

2009. United Nations World Food Programme.

7645	**2996**	10r. multicoloured	2·75	2·30

2997 V. I. Istomin

2009. Birth Bicentenary of Vladimir Ivanovich Istomin (rear admiral and hero of Siege of Sevastopol).

7646	**2997**	10r. multicoloured	2·75	2·30

2998 Tyre Tracks over Traffic Sign

2009. Road Safety Campaign.

7647	**2998**	9r. multicoloured	2·40	2·10

2999 Award

2009. 75th Anniv of the Award of the Hero of Soviet Union. Gold Star.

7648	**2999**	9r. multicoloured	2·40	2·10

3000 Empress Elizaveta

2009. 300th Birth Anniv of Empress Elizaveta Petrovna. Sheet 90×75 mm.

MS7649 **3000** 40r. multicoloured 10·00 9·50

3000a Departmental Arms

2009. Bicentenary of Department of Transportation of Russia

7649a	**3000a**	9r. multicoloured	2·40	2·10

3001 School Building

2009. Bicentenary of Mikhail Shchepkin Drama School

7649b	**3001**	10r. multicoloured	2·75	2·30

3002 Researcher, Weather Equipment and Polar Vehicle

2009. 50th Anniv of Antarctic Treaty

7650	**3002**	15r. multicoloured	4·00	3·50

3003 Kremlin, Moscow enclosed in Snowflake

2009. Happy New Year

7651	**3003**	10r. multicoloured	2·75	2·30

3004 Arms, Transporter and Rocket

2009. 50th Anniv of Strategic Rocket Forces (Strategic Missile Troops) of the Russian Federation

7652	**3004**	9r. multicoloured	2·40	2·10

3005 Verkhnyaya Pyshma

2009. Fountains of Russia. Multicoloured.

7653	9r. Type **3005**	2·40	2·10
7654	10r. Nizhny Novgorod	2·75	2·30
7655	12r. Novy Urengoy (vert)	2·75	2·50
7656	15r. Yaroslavl	3·75	3·25

3006 Valentina Stepanovna Grizodubova (commander of flight of Rodina (Motherland), ANT-37 airplane, setting international women's record for straight-line distance flight)

2010. Birth Centenaries. Multicoloured.

7657	10r. Type **3006**	2·75	2·30
7658	10r. Anatoly Konstantinovich Serov (biplane fighter ace who took part in Spanish Civil War) and aircraft I-15	2·75	2·30

3007 Lady with Dog

2010. 150th Birth Anniv of Anton Pavlovich Chekhov (writer). Multicoloured.

MS7659 127×70 mm. 8r. Type **3007**; 10r. *The Seagull*; 12r. *An Artist's Story* (The House with the Mezzanine) 8·75 8·50

MS7660 73×100 mm. 20r. Anton Chekhov (36×50 mm) (oval) 5·50 5·25

3008 University Building

2010. 50th Anniv of Peoples' Friendship University

7661	**3008**	10r. multicoloured	2·75	2·30

Nos. 7662/76 are vacant.

3009 Games Emblem

2010. Winter Olympic Games, Vancouver

7677	**3009**	15r. multicoloured	4·00	3·50

3010 Prince Dmitry Mikhaylovich Golitsyn

2010. 275th Birth Anniv of Fyodor Stepanovich Rokotov (Fedor Rokotov) (artist). Multicoloured.

7678	10r.50 Type **3010**	2·75	2·30

7679 10r.50 *Countess Varvara Alekseyevna Musina–Pushkina* 2·75 2·30

2010. Regions of the Russian Federation (16th issue). Multicoloured.

7680 10r.50 Cornfield, lace and dam, Orenburg region 2·75 2·30

7681 10r.50 Yaks and pewter clasp, Tuva Republic 2·75 2·30

Horiz designs as T **2651**.

3011 Polar Researcher, Aircraft, Research Station and Eugeny Feodorov

2010. Birth Centenary of Eugeny Feodorov (geophysicist)

7682 **3011** 12r. multicoloured 3·00 2·75

3012 Malgobek

2010. Town Emblems (2nd issue). Multicoloured.

MS7683 10r.×5 Type **3012**; Elnja; Elets; Voronev; Luga 11·00 10·50

3013 Tank BT-7M

2010. 65th Anniv of Second World War (2nd issue). Tanks. Multicoloured.

7684 9r. Type **3013** 2·20 1·90

7685 10r. Tank T-70 2·40 2·10

7686 11r. T-34-85 2·50 2·20

7687 12r. Tank IS-2 2·75 2·50

3014 Victory Order

2010. 65th Anniv of Second World War (3rd issue). Sheet 80×110 mm

MS7688 **3014** 50r. multicoloured 13·00 12·50

3015 Boy reading

2010. Europa. Children's Books

7689 **3015** 10r.50 multicoloured 2·75 2·30

3016 Cyrillic Script

2010. 300th Anniv of Cyrillic Alphabet

7690 **3016** 7r.70 multicoloured 1·80 1·50

3017 Ivan Fyodorov (statue)

2010. 500th Birth Anniv of Ivan Fyodorov (Fedorovych) (Eastern Slavonic printing pioneer). Sheet 60×104 mm

MS7691 **3017** 50r. multicoloured 13·00 12·50

3018 Wooden Pocket Watch (M.S. Bronnikov and Son) (early 1900)

2010. Science and Technology. The Watch. Sheet 110×123 mm. Multicoloured.

MS7692 6r. Type **3018**; 9r. Victory wristwatch (1949); 12r. Shturmanskie wristwatch (1949); 15r. Gloriya wristwatch (1990) 11·00 10·50

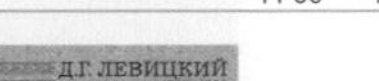

3019 Self Portrait

2010. 275th Birth Anniv of Dmitry Lewitsky (artist). Multicoloured.

7693 10r.50 Type **3019** 2·75 2·30

7694 10r.50 *G.I. Alymova* 2·75 2·30

3020 Church and Archipelago

2010. Historical and Cultural Heritage of Russia. Valaam. Sheet 95×75 mm

MS7695 **3020** 25r. multicoloured 13·00 12·50

3021 Egyptian Gates

2010. 300th Anniv of Tsarskoe Selo (Pushkin). Sheet 136×80 mm

MS7696 15r.×3, Type **3021**; A. S. Pushkin (statue) (vert); Aleksandrovsky Palace 12·00 11·50

3022 Archangel Mikhail (Andrey Rublev) (15th-century)

2010. Icons. Multicoloured.

7697 15r. Type **3022** 4·00 3·50

7698 15r. *Virgin Mary Odigitrija* (14th-century) 4·00 3·50

Stamps of a similar design were issued by Serbia.

3023 Coastline

2010. 150th Anniv of Vladivostok

7699 **3023** 15r. multicoloured 4·00 3·50

2010. Regions of the Russian Federation (17th issue). Multicoloured.

7700 10r.50 Locomotive and monument, Bryansk region 2·75 2·30

7701 10r.50 Mounment to Sholem-Aleichem, Birobidzhan, hill with TV aerial, on river Bira, Menorah fountain and Birobidzhan railway station, Jewish Autonomous Regions 2·75 2·30

3024 Sea and Dunes

2010. World Heritage Site - Kurshskaya (Curonian Spit) National Park. Multicoloured.

7702 15r. Type **3024** 3·25 2·75

7703 15r. Small tree, dunes, forest and sea 3·25 2·75

Nos. 7702/3 were printed, *se-tenant*, forming a composite design

3025 Woman's Headdress (Kalfak)

2010. Headdresses of Tatarstan. Multicoloured.

7704 11r. Type **3025** 2·75 2·50

7705 11r. Woman's embroidered cap and scarf (Kattashi) 2·75 2·50

7706 11r. Woman's fur hat and scarf (Kamchat burek) 2·75 2·50

7707 11r. Man's embroidered cap (Tyubeteika) 2·75 2·50

3026 Monastery Buildings

2010. Ferapontov Monastery. Sheet 85×71 mm

MS7708 **3026** 30r. multicoloured 8·00 7·50

3027 N.N. Zubov and Sadko (icebreaker)

2010. 125th Birth Anniv of Nikolay Zubov (naval officer, hydrographer, oceanologist and Arctic explorer). Multicoloured.

7709 **3027** 12r. multicoloured 3·00 2·75

3028 Woman and Mounted Cossack (Don)

2010. History of Russian Cossacks. Sheet 160×100 mm. Multicoloured.

MS7710 12r.×3, Type **3028**; Woman holding horse and Cossack holding sword (Kuban); Cossack couple and grazing horse (Tersk) 9·25 8·75

3029 Vladivostok

2010. Arms. Multicoloured.

7711 7r.70 Type **3029** 2·00 1·70

7712 10r.50 Yaroslavl 2·75 2·30

3030 *The Fresh Wind. The Volga*

2010. 150th Birth Anniv of Isaac Ilyich Levitan (artist). Sheet 102×82 mm

MS7713 **3030** 25r. multicoloured 6·50 6·00

3031 Monument to Returning Soldiers

2010. 65th Anniv of the End of World War II

7714 **3031** 15r. multicoloured 4·00 3·50

3032 G. S. Titov

2010. 75th Birth Anniv of Gherman Stepanovich Titov (cosmonaut and youngest person to fly in space)

7715 **3032** 10r.50 multicoloured 2·75 2·30

3034 Bogoyavleniya Church and Yarosav the Wise (statue)

2010. Yaroslavl Millenary. Sheet 92×75 mm

MS7716 **3034** 50r. multicoloured 13·00 12·50

3035 Jubilee Bridge over River Volga, Yaroslavl

2010. Bridges. Multicoloured.

7717 9r. Type **3035** 2·40 2·10

7718 10r. Viaduct over River Matsesta, Sochi 2·50 2·20

7719 12r. Bridge over Moscow canal, Khlebnikovo, Moscow region 2·75 2·50

7720 15r. Bridge across Kola Bay, Murmansk 3·00 2·75

3036 Coin with Alexander II Monogram, 1855

2010. 150th Anniv of Bank of Russia. Sheet 110×130 mm. Multicoloured.

MS7721 10r. Type **3036**; 15r. Silver 1 Ruble (with Nicholas II),1895; 20r. Revese of silver 50 kop., 1924; 25r. Reverse of gold coin (with George the Victorius), 2006 14·50 14·00

3036a Hands releasing Doves

2010. Year of the Teacher

7721a **3036a** 10r.50 multicoloured 4·50 3·75

3037 Emblem

2010. Population Census

7722	**3037**	12r. blue and scarlet	3·00	2·75

3038 Chokan Valikhanov

2010. 175th Birth Anniv of Chokan Chingisovich Valikhanov (scholar, ethnographer and historian)

7723	**3038**	15r. multicoloured	4·00	3·50

3039 Strelka and Belka

2010. 50th (2011) Anniv of Belka and Strelka's Space Flight

7724	**3039**	10r. multicoloured	2·75	2·30

2010. Regions of the Russian Federation (18th issue). Multicoloured.

7725	10r.50 Triumphal Arch, dumper truck and digger, Kursk region	2·75	2·30
7726	10r.50 Golden Woman of Ugra and troika pulled by reindeer	2·75	2·30

3040 Player

2010. 50th Anniversary of Victory in European Football Cup

7727	**3040**	12r. multicoloured	3·00	2·75

3041 Nikolay Pirogov

2010. Birth Bicentenary of Nikolay Ivanovich Pirogov (scientist, doctor, founder of field surgery, and one of first surgeons in Europe to use ether as an anaesthetic). Sheet 79×65 mm

MS7728	**3041**	20r. multicoloured	5·25	5·00

No. 7729 is vacant.

3042 Emblem of Kachino School

2010. Centenary of Kachino Aviation School

7730	**3042**	15r. multicoloured	4·00	3·50

3043 Father Frost

2010. Happy New Year

7731	**3043**	10r.50 multicoloured	2·75	2·30

3044 M. Keldysh

2011. Birth Centenary of Mstislav Vsevolodovich Keldysh (scientist)

7732	**3044**	12r. multicoloured	3·00	2·75

3045 Empress Marie Aleksandrovna

2011. 150th Anniv of Mariehamn, Aland. Sheet 103×70 mm

MS7733	**3045**	40r. multicoloured	11·00	10·50

3046 Sochi

2011. Sochi, Capital of Winter Olympic Games. Sheet 90×60 mm

MS7734 **3046** 25r. multicoloured

2011. Regions of the Russian Federation (19th issue). Multicoloured.

7735	11r.80 Crucifix, coastline and churches, Novgorod region	3·00	2·75
7736	11r.80 Apples, buildings and peasant with plough (statue), Tambov region	3·00	2·75
7737	11r.80 Oil wells and castle, Tjumen region	3·00	2·75

3047 Yuri Gagarin

2011. 50th Anniv of First Manned Space Flight. Sheet 70×80 mm

MS7738	**3047**	50r. multicoloured	14·50	14·00

3048 Vladikavkaz

2011. Town Emblems (3rd issue).Sheet 125×88 mm. Multicoloured.

MS7739 12r.×5 Vryborg; Tuapse; Type **3048**; Veliky Novgorod; Velikie Luki 19·00 18·00

3049 Emblem

2011. 50th Anniv of Russian Peace Foundation

7740	**3049**	8r.50 multicoloured	2·20	1·90

3050 Yakovlev Yak-3

2011. 65th Anniv of Second World War (2nd issue). Aircraft. Multicoloured.

7741	9r. Type **3050**	2·20	1·90
7742	10r. Lavochkin La-5	2·40	2·10
7743	11r. Ilyushin Il-2	2·50	2·20
7744	12r. Petlyakov Pe-2	2·75	2·50

3051 Birch Forest

2011. Europa. Forests

7745	**3051**	15r. multicoloured	3·75	3·25

3052 Central Telegraph Clock (Moscow)

2011. Science and Technology. Clocks. Sheet 110×115 mm. Multicoloured.

MS7746 9r. Type **3052**; 12r. Admiralty (St. Petersburg);15r. Moscow State University; 25r. Railway station, Sochi. 16·00 15·00

3053 K.I. Schelkin

2011. Birth Centenary of Kirill Ivanovich Shchelkin (physicist)

7747	**3053**	12r. multicoloured	3·00	2·75

3054 Irkutsk

2011. Arms. Multicoloured.

7748	8r.50 Type **3054**	2·20	1·90
7749	11r.80 Republic of Komi	3·00	2·75

3055 Our Lady of Kazan Cathedral, St. Petersburg

2011. Cultural Heritage. Architecture. Multicoloured.

7750	15r. Type **3055**	3·75	3·25
7751	15r. Russian Diplomatic Mission, Tsetine	3·75	3·25

3056 Valeri Bryusov

2011. Personalities. Writers. Multicoloured.

7752	12r. Type **3056**		
7753	12r. Ovanes Tumanyan		

3057 Venezuelan Flag

2011. Bicentenary of Republic of Venezuela

7754	**3057**	12r. multicoloured	3·00	2·75

3058 Arms and View of Irkutsk

2011. 350th Anniversary of Irkutsk

7755	**3058**	15r. multicoloured	4·00	3·50

3059 Arms of Buryatia

2011. 350th Anniv of Incorporation of Buryatia into Russia

7756	**3059**	11r.80 multicoloured	3·00	2·75

3060 Arms

2011. 75th Anniv of State Inspectorate for Road Safety

7757	**3060**	15r. multicoloured	4·00	3·50

3061 Order of St. Andrew the Apostle

2011. Order of St. Andrew the Apostle. Sheet 71×85 mm

MS7758	**3061**	50r. multicoloured	13·00	12·50

3062 Rock Formations, Plateau Manpupuner

2011. Pechoro-Ilych Reserve. Sheet 79×80 mm

MS7759	**3062**	25r. multicoloured	6·50	6·00

3063 Chapel of St. Makaryi

2011. Malye Korely, Open-air Museum of Wooden Architecture of Arkhangelsk Area. Sheet 151×101 mm. Multicoloured.

MS7760 10r. Type **3063**; 15r. Voznesenskaya Church; 20r. Windmill 12·00 11·50

3064 Pochtamtsky Bridge over Moika River, St. Petersburg

2011. Russian Bridges. Multicoloured.

7761	9r. Type **3064**	2·40	2·10
7762	10r. Patriarshy Bridge over Moscow River	2·75	2·30
7763	11r. Bridge over Kena River, Arkhangelsk region	3·00	2·75
7764	12r. Bridge over Vezelka River, Belgorod	4·00	3·50

3065 Horse drinking and Couple (Amur)

2011. History of Russian Cossacks. Sheet 160×100 mm. Multicoloured.

MS7765	15r.×3, Type **3065**; Woman and mounted Cossack holding spear (Astrakan); Seated Cossack couple and horse (Volga)	12·00	11·50

3066 Ludmila Georgievna Zykina (singer)

2011. Cavaliers of the Order of Saint Andrew. Multicoloured.

7766	15r. Type **3066**	4·00	3·50
7767	15r. Dmitry Sergeyevich Likhachov (Old Russian language scholar)	4·00	3·50
7768	15r. Vasily Ivanovich Petrovsky (scientist)	4·00	3·50

3067 Michael Andreas Barclay de Tolly

2011. 250th Birth Anniv of Prince Michael Andreas Barclay de Tolly (Field Marshal and Minister of War)

7769	**3067**	15r. multicoloured	4·00	3·50

3068 *Seascape*, 2007 (A. V. Adamov)

2011. Russian Modern Art. Multicoloured.

7770	14r. Type **3068**	3·75	3·25
7771	14r. *View of Borisoglebsky Monastery*, 2001 (N. I. Borovsky)	3·75	3·25
7772	14r. *Gymnasts of the USSR*, 1964-1965 (D. D. Zhilinsky) (37× 50 mm)	3·75	3·25
7773	14r. Monument to Yury Nikulin, 2000 (A. I. Rukavishnikov)	3·75	3·25
7774	14r. *Aidan*, 1967 (T. T. Salakhov) (37× 50 mm)	3·75	3·25
7775	14r. *Village Akinshino*, 1995 (V. Ya. Yukin) (50×50 mm)	3·75	3·25

3069 Naryn-kala Fortress

2011. Ancient City and Fortress Buildings of Derbent. Sheet 102×71 mm

MS7776	**3069**	50r. multicoloured	13·00	12·50

3070 Girl wearing Embroidered Headdress

2011. Headdresses of North Russia. Multicoloured.

7777	12r. Type **3070**	2·75	2·50
7778	12r. Man's fur cap	2·75	2·50
7779	12r. Woman's cap and headscarf	2·75	2·50
7780	12r. Woman's embroidered cap	2·75	2·50

3071 Panda

2011. 50th Anniv of WWF

7781	**3071**	15r. black and scarlet	3·75	3·25

3072 Ski Lift

2011. Winter Olympic Games, Sochi. Russian Black Sea Coast Tourism. Multicoloured.

7782	12r. Type **3072** (21.10.11)	3·75	3·25
7783	20r. Marine Terminal Building, Sochi (21.10.11)	5·25	4·50
7784	25r. Bolshoy Akhun Mountain and observation tower (21.10.11)	6·75	6·00
7785	30r. Volkonsky Dolmen, Sochi National Park (21.10.11)	7·75	6·75
7786	102×140 mm As Nos. 7782/5 (27.9.11)	24·00	23·00

3073 Emblem and Symbols of Innovative Biotechnologies

2011. Tenth Anniv of Eurasian Economic Community (EAEC). Innovative Biotechnologies

7787	**3073**	9r. multicoloured	2·20	1·90

3074 Cross Country Skiers

2011. Winter Olympic Games, Sochi. Multicoloured.

7788	25r. Type **3074**	6·25	5·25
7789	25r. Ski jump	6·25	5·25
7790	25r. Cross country skiing	6·25	5·25

3075 Emblem

2011. 20th Anniv of Regional Communication Community (RCC)

7791	**3075**	12r. multicoloured	2·75	2·50

3076 Cannon

2011. 300th (2012) Anniv of Tula Arms Plant (Tula Arsenal)

7792	**3076**	15r. multicoloured	3·75	3·25

Nos. 7793/6, T **3077** are vacant.

Nos. 7793/6 and Type **3077** are left for winter Olympic Games (3rd issue), not yet received.

3078 A.L. Ordin-Naschokin (founder)

2011. 300th Anniv of Moscow Post Office. Multicoloured.

7797	11r.80 Type **3078**	2·75	2·50
7798	11r.80 19th-century stagecoach	2·75	2·50
7799	11r.80 Post box, stamps mail and early post vehicle	2·75	2·50
7800	11r.80 Stamps, modern post vehicle and Post Office building	2·75	2·50
MS7801	100×66 mm 50r. Anniversary seal	13·00	12·50

3079 State Kremlin Palace

2011. 50th Anniv of State Kremlin Palace (Kremlin Palace of Congresses)

7802	**3079**	12r. multicoloured	2·75	2·50

3080 Constitutional Court of Russia

2011. 20th Anniv of Constitutional Court of Russia

7803	**3080**	12r. multicoloured	2·75	2·50

3081 Gas Street Lamp and P.G. Sobolevsky (engineer)

2011. Bicentenary of Gas Use in Russia

7804	**3081**	12r. multicoloured	2·75	2·50

3082 Flags of Member Countries

2011. 20th Anniv of Community of Independent States (CIS)

7805	**3082**	11r.80 multicoloured	2·75	2·30

3083 Lomonosov

2011. 300th Birth Anniv of Mikhail Vasilyevich Lomonosov (polymath, scientist and writer). Sheet 123×98 mm

MS7806	**3083**	100r. multicoloured	26·00	25·00

3084 *Moskvoretsky Bridge*

2011. 150th Birth Anniv of Konstantin Alekseyevich Korovin (artist). Sheet 105×77 mm

MS7807	**3084**	45r. multicoloured	12·00	11·50

3085 Emblem

2011. Centenary of Russian Olympic Committee

7808	**3085**	15r. multicoloured	4·00	3·50

3086 Catherine II (Catherine the Great)

2011. 225th Anniv of Founding of the First Russian Insurance Institution

7809	**3086**	8r.50 multicoloured	2·20	1·90

2011. Regions of the Russian Federation (20th issue). Multicoloured.

7810	11r.80 Modern building, rocket launch and river, Kaluga region	2·75	2·50

3087 Bauble

2011. Happy New Year

7811	**3087**	20r. multicoloured	5·25	4·50

3088 Emblem

2011. Year of Culture, Russia and Italy

7812	**3088**	15r. multicoloured	4·00	3·50

3089 Cathedral, Monument and Landscape

2011. Regions of the Russian Federation (21st issue). Omsk

7813	**3089**	11r.80 multicoloured	2·75	2·50

3090 Cloth, Vologda Lace

2011. Decorative and Applied Art. Lace. Multicoloured.

7814	15r. Cape (yellowish brown)	4·00	3·50
7815	15r. Type **3090**	4·00	3·50
7816	15r. Vyatka (reddish lilac)	4·00	3·50
7817	15r. Elets (pinkish brown)	4·00	3·50

3091 Arms, Shield and Weapons

2012. 300th Anniv of Tula Small Arms Factory. Sheet 70×88 mm

MS7818	**3091** 50r. multicoloured	13·00	12·50

3092 *Orcinus orca* (Killer Whale)

2012. Fauna of Russia. Whales. Multicoloured.

7819	15r. Type **3092**	4·00	3·50
7820	20r. *Megaptera novaeangliae* (Humpback Whale)	5·25	4·50

3093 P. N. Nesterov

2012. 125th Birth Anniv of Pyotr Nikolayevich Nesterov (pilot)

7821	**3093** 15r. multicoloured	4·00	3·50

3094 Snow Leopard

2012. Winter Olympic Games (**MS**7822) and Winter Paralympic Games (**MS**7823) in Sochi. Multicoloured.

MS7822	117×75 mm 15r.×3, Type **3094**; The Hare; The Polar Bear	12·00	11·50
MS7823	81×71 mm 30r. The Snow-flake and The Ray of Light	8·00	7·50

3095 Pacific Walruses, Geese in Flight and Cliffs

2012. Natural Heritage of Russia. Wrangel Island. Sheet 60×80 mm

MS7824	**3095** 45r. multicoloured	12·00	11·50

3096 Badge and Star of Order of Saint George

2012. State Awards of Russian Federation. Multicoloured.

7825	25r. Type **3096**	6·50	5·75
7826	25r. Star and Badge of the Order For Merit to the Fatherland	6·50	5·75
7827	25r. Gold Star Medal	6·50	5·75

3097 Marina Raskova

2012. Birth Centenary of Marina Mikhailovna Raskova (aviation pioneer)

7828	**3097** 15r. multicoloured	4·00	3·50

3098 P. A. Stolypin

2012. 150th Birth Anniv of Pyotr Arkadyevich Stolypin (prime minister and politician)

7829	**3098** 15r. multicoloured	4·00	3·50

3099 Lorry, GAZ-AA

2012. Military Vehicles. Multicoloured.

7830	10r. Type **3099**	2·75	2·30
7831	12r. Lorry, ZIS 5B	3·00	2·75
7832	14r. All-wheel drive car, GAZ-67B	3·75	3·25
7833	15r. Car, GAZ-M1	4·00	3·50

3100 Pskov

2012. Town Emblems. Sheet 125×88 mm. Multicoloured.

MS7834	15r.×6, Type **3100**; Vyazma, Naro-Fominsk, Tver, Kronstadt, Dmitrov	20·00	19·00

3101 Association Emblem

2012. Tenth Anniv of Veterans Association

7835	**3101** 10r. multicoloured	2·20	1·90

2012. Winter Olympic Games, Sochi. Russian Black Sea Coast Tourism. Multicoloured.

7836	12r. 'Sail' Rock, Gelendzhik	3·25	2·75
7837	20r. Railway Station, Sochi	4·50	3·75
7838	25r. Tree nursery monument	5·50	4·75
7839	30r. Orekhovsky waterfall	6·50	5·75
MS7839a	102×140 mm As Nos. 7836/9	20·00	19·00

Horiz designs as Type **3072**

3103 Girl in Traditional Dress presenting Bread and Salt

2012. Europa. Visit Russia

7840	**3103** 15r. multicoloured	3·25	2·75

3104 Regalia

2012. Inauguration of Vladimir Vladimirovich Putin for Third Term as President of Russia

7841	**3104** 15r. multicoloured	3·25	2·75

3105 Valerius Zamarev

2012. Heroes of the Russian Federation. Multicoloured.

7842	15r. Type **3105**	3·25	2·75
7843	15r. A.V. Putsykin	3·25	2·75
7844	15r. D.A. Razumovsky	3·25	2·75
7845	15r. A.B. Tsydenzhapov	3·25	2·75
7846	15r. Irina Yu. Yanina	3·25	2·75

3106 M. V. Nesterov

2012. 150th Birth Anniv of Mikhail Vasilyevich Nesterov (artist). Sheet 83×73 mm

MS7847	**3106** 30r. multicoloured	6·50	6·00

3107 *Self Portrait*

2012. 175th Birth Anniv of Ivan Nikolaevich Kramskoi (artist). Multicoloured.

7848	15r. Type **3107**	3·25	2·75
7849	15r. *The Unknown* (horiz)	3·25	2·75

3108 *I.A. Goncharov* (Ivan Kramskoi)

2012. Birth Bicentenary of Ivan Alexandrovich Goncharov (writer). Sheet 76×97 mm

MS7850	**3108** 30r. multicoloured	6·50	6·00

3109 Museum Façade

2012. Centenary of Pushkin Museum of Fine Arts. Sheet 90×110 mm

MS7851	**3109** 30r. multicoloured	6·50	6·00

3110 ANT-25 against Map of Flight

2012. 75th Anniv of First Non-stop Transpolar Flight (1st issue)

7852	**3110** 13r. multicoloured	2·75	2·50

3111 Monument to Kuzma Minin and Prince Dmitry Pozharsky, Moscow

2012. Anniversaries. 400th Anniv of Reunification of Russia (7853) or Bicentenary of Victory in War of 1812 (7854). Multicoloured.

7853	9r.20 Type **3111**	2·20	1·90
7854	13r. Triumphal Arch	3·00	2·75

3112 *Triturus cristatus* (Crested Newt)

2012. Newts. Multicoloured.

7855	13r. Type **3112**	3·00	2·75
7856	13r. *Lissotriton vulgaris* (Smooth Newt)	3·00	2·75

3113 O.E. Kutafin

2012. Oleg Emelianovich Kutafin, Holder of Order of Merit for the Fatherland, Commemoration

7857	**3113** 15r. multicoloured	3·75	3·25

3114 Patriarch Aleksei II

2012. Cavaliers of the Order of Saint Andrew. Multicoloured.

7858	15r. Type **3114**	3·75	3·25
7859	15r. Irina Arkhipova (Opera singer)	3·75	3·25
7860	15r. Valery Ivanovich Shumakov (surgeon)	3·75	3·25

3115 Arms and Aerial View of Town

2012. 1050th Anniv of Belozersk. Sheet 82×93 mm

MS7861	**3115** 30r. multicoloured	7·25	6·75

3116 Chapel and Talavskaya Tower

2012. 1150th Anniv of Izborsk. Sheet 60×100 mm

MS7862 **3116** 30r. multicoloured		7·25	6·75

(3117)

2012. No. 7574 surch as T **3117**. Russia - World Hockey Champions, 2012

7863	12r. on 8r. multicoloured	13·00	12·50

3118 ANT-25 against Map of Flight

2012. 75th Anniv of First Non-stop Transpolar Flight (2nd issue)

7864	**3118** 13r. multicoloured	3·00	2·75

3119 Episcopal Palace in Astorga (León)

2012. Cultural Heritage. Churches. Multicoloured.

7865	13r. Type **3119**	3·00	2·75
7866	13r. Church of the Saviour on Spilled Blood, St. Petersburg	3·00	2·75

3120 Emblem

2012. Millennium of Mordva in Russia

7867	**3120** 13r. multicoloured	3·00	2·75

3121 Emblem

2012. Olympic Games - 2012, London. Sheet 110×90 mm

MS7868 **3121** 50r. multicoloured		12·00	11·50

3122 Monument to F.I. Shalyapin, Kazan, 1999 (A.V. Balashov)

2012. Russian Modern Art. Multicoloured.

7869	15r. Type **3122**	3·75	3·25
7870	15r. *Kazachi provody*, 1999 (S.A. Gavrilyachenko) (horiz)	3·75	3·25
7871	15r. Mammoths, Khanty-Mansiisk, 2007 (A.N. Kovaltchuk) (50×50 mm)	3·75	3·25
7872	15r. *Kazachi provody*, 1996 (S.A. Gavrilyachenko) (horiz)	3·75	3·25
7873	15r. *Russian Madonna*, 2005 (V.I. Nesterenko) (50×50 mm)	3·75	3·25
7874	15r. *Autumn. Interior*, 1992 (A.N. Sukhovetsky)	3·75	3·25

3123 Gleb Yevgeniyevich Kotelnikov (inventor)

2012. Centenary of First Knapsack Parachute

7875	**3123** 13r. multicoloured	3·00	2·75

3124 F. A. Tsander

2012. 125th Birth Anniv of Fridrikh Arturovich Tsander (Friedrich Zander) (rocket and space flight pioneer)

7876	**3124** 9r.20 multicoloured	2·20	1·90

3125 Centenary Emblem

2012. Centenary of Russian Air Force

7877	**3125** 15r. multicoloured	3·75	3·25

3126 Rostov Kremlin

2012. 1150th Anniv of Rostov. Sheet 80×85 mm

MS7878 **3126** 30r. multicoloured		7·75	7·25

3127 Couple, Enisei

2012. History of Russian Cossacks. Multicoloured.

MS7879 15r.×3, Type **3127**; Couple, Orenburg; Couple, Ussuriysk		11·50	11·00

3128 Anniversary Emblem

2012. Bicentenary of Patriotic War of 1812. Sheet 80×90 mm

MS7880 **3128** 50r. multicoloured		13·00	12·50

3129 Monastery Buildings

2012. World Heritage Site - Trinity Lavra of St. Sergius Monastery. Sheet 71×85 mm

MS7881 **3129** 30r. multicoloured		11·50	11·00

3130 Bridge to Russky Island

2012. Asia-Pacific Economic Co-operation Summit, Vladivostok

7882	**3130** 13r. multicoloured	3·00	2·75

3131 Gavrila Romanovitch Derzhavin

2012. Personalities. Lawyers. Multicoloured.

7883	15r. Type **3131**	3·75	3·25
7884	15r. Anatolii Fedorovich Koni	3·75	3·25
7885	15r. Mikhail Mikhailovich Speransky	3·75	3·25

3132 *On a Visit* (*Away*)

2012. 150th Birth Anniv of Abram Efimovich Arkhipov (artist). Sheet 110×80 mm

MS7886 **3132** 50r. multicoloured		13·00	12·50

3133 Fort Ross

2012. Bicentenary of Fort Ross State Historic Park, California (originally Russian colony)

7887	**3133** 13r. multicoloured	3·25	2·75

3134 Quick Response Code

2012. Winter Olympic Games, Sochi, 2014

7888	**3134** 25r. multicoloured	6·50	5·50

3135 Rurik (founder of Russian dynasty) and Family

2012. 1150th Anniv of Russian Statehood

7889	**3135** 10r. multicoloured	2·75	2·30

3136 Couple, Vologda

2012. Traditional Costumes

7890	**3136** 15r. multicoloured	3·75	3·25

No. 7891, T **3137** are vacant.

3138 Steam and Diesel Locomotives

2012. 175th Anniv of Russian Railways. 110×80 mm

MS7892 **3138** 50r. vermilion and silver		13·00	12·50

3139 Anchor and Shipyard

2012. Centenary of Shipbuilding Plant 'Severnaya verf' (Northern Shipyard)

7893	**3139** 15r. multicoloured	3·75	3·25

3140 *Castro Sei* (pipe laying vessel)

2012. Building of 'Nord Stream' Gas Pipeline (export route for delivering Russian gas to Europe). Sheet 113×88 mm

MS7894 **3140** 40r. multicoloured		10·50	10·00

3141 Guards Emblem with National Flag as Map of Russia

2012. 500th Anniv of Border Guards

7895	**3141** 13r. multicoloured	3·25	2·75

2012. Winter Olympic Games, Sochi (6th issue). Multicoloured.

7896	25r. Alpine skiing	6·50	5·50
7897	25r. Luge	6·50	5·50
7898	25r. Skeleton	6·50	5·50
7899	25r. Speed skating	6·50	5·50
7900	25r. Snowboarding	6·50	5·50
7901	25r. Free style skiing	6·50	5·50

Square designs as T **3074**

3143 Kozma Minin, Dmitry Pozharsky (led militia and liberated Moscow from invaders)

2012. 400th Anniv of Restoration of Unity of Russian State. Sheet 90×90 mm

MS7902 **3143** 40r. multicoloured		10·50	10·00

3144 Cast-iron Mouldings

3145 Cast-iron Mouldings

3146 Cast-iron Mouldings

3147 Cast-iron Mouldings

2012. Kasli Cast-iron Mouldings

7903	**3144**	20r. black and mauve	5·00	4·25
7904	**3145**	20r. black and reddish brown	5·00	4·25
7905	**3146**	20r. black and light green	5·00	4·25
7906	**3147**	20r. black and lilac	5·00	4·25

3148 Arms of Moscow

2010. Arms. Multicoloured.

MS7907	50r. Type **3148**	13·00	12·50
MS7908	50r. Arms of St Petersburg	13·00	12·50

3149 Vinni Pukh (Winnie the Pooh)

2012. Russian Cartoon Characters. Multicoloured.

7909	10r. Type **3149**	2·75	2·30
7910	10r. Mowgli	2·75	2·30
7911	10r. Malish and Karlson	2·75	2·30
7912	10r. Vovka in the Thrice-Ninth Kingdom	2·75	2·30

3150 New Year Tree

2012. Happy New Year

7913	**3150**	13r. deep blue	3·50	3·00

3151 Konstantin Stanislavski

2013. 150th Birth Anniv of Konstantin Stanislavski (Konstantin Sergeyevich Alekseyev) (actor, stage director and theater educator). Sheet 90×95 mm

MS7914 **3151** 50r. multicoloured 13·00 12·50

3152 G. Flyorov

2013. Birth Centenary of Georgy Nikolayevich Flyorov (Flerov) (nuclear physicist)

7915	**3152**	15r. multicoloured	4·00	3·50

3153 Archangel (Arkhangelsk)

2013. Town Emblems (4th issue). Sheet 125×88 mm. Multicoloured.

MS7916 15.×5 Type **3153**; Bryansk; Volokolamsk; Klach-na-Donu; Kozelsk; Nalchik 24·00 23·00

3154 *Ovis nivicola* (Siberian Bighorn Sheep)

2013. Fauna of Russia. Wild Goats and Sheep. Multicoloured.

7917	15r. Type **3154**	4·00	3·50
7918	15r. *Capra aegagrus* (Wild Goat)	4·00	3·50
7919	15r. *Capra caucasica* (West Caucasian Tur)	4·00	3·50
7920	15r. *Ovis ammon* (Argali)	4·00	3·50

3155 *Pervoposelenets* (First Settler) Monument and Town Arms

2013. 350th Anniversary of Penza

7921	**3155**	15r. multicoloured	4·00	3·50

3156 Order of Saint Catherine

2013. State Awards of Russian Federation. Multicoloured.

7922	25r. Type **3156**	6·50	5·75
7923	25r. Order of Alexander Nevsky	6·50	5·75
7924	25r. Order of Suvorov	6·50	5·75

3157 A. Pokryshkin (S.N. Prisekin) and Aircraft *Aerokobra*

2013. Birth Centenary of Aleksandr Ivanovich Pokryshkin (pilot and aviation tactician)

7925	**3157**	15r. multicoloured	4·00	3·50

3158 Yu. A. Dmitriev

2013. Heroes of the Russian Federation. Multicoloured.

7926	15r. Type **3158**	4·00	3·50
7927	15r. O. G. Iliin	4·00	3·50
7928	15r. N. S. Maidanov	4·00	3·50
7929	15r. E. N. Chernyshev	4·00	3·50
7930	15r. V. I. Shkurnyi	4·00	3·50

3159 Raptor in Flight

2013. Natural Heritage of Russia. Uvs Nuur Basin. Sheet 100×75 mm

MS7931 **3159** 45r. multicoloured 11·50 11·00

3160 *Juniperus davurica*

2013. Flora of Russia. Coniferous Trees and Shrubs. Multicoloured.

7932	15r. Type **3160**	4·00	3·50
7933	15r. *Microbiota decussata*	4·00	3·50
7934	15r. *Larix cajandei*	4·00	3·50
7935	15r. *Picea obovata*	4·00	3·50

3161 *General Skobelev Mounted* (N. D. Dmitriev-Orenburgsky)

2013. 135th Anniv of Russian-Turkish War. Sheet 68×90 mm

MS7936 **3161** 35r. multicoloured 8·75 8·25

3162 V.S. Chernomyrdin

2013. Viktor Stepanovich Chernomyrdin (statesman) Commemoration

7937	**3162**	15r. multicoloured	4·00	3·50

3163 Modern Day Anti-aircraft Rocket Installation C-400 and Oboukhov Plant, 1912

2013. 150th Anniv of Obuhov Steel Works

7938	**3163**	15r. multicoloured	4·00	3·50

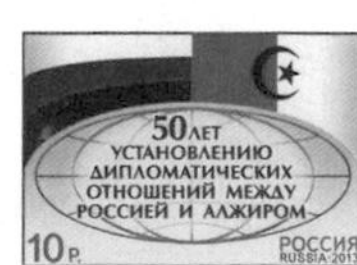
3164 Anniversary Emblem and National Flags

2013. 50th Anniv Russia - Algeria Diplomatic Relations

7939	**3164**	10r. multicoloured	2·75	2·30

3165 Winter Palace

2013. Cultural Heritage. Historical Centre of St Petersburg. Multicoloured.

7940	10r. Type **3165**	2·75	2·30
7941	15r. St. Isaac Cathedral	4·00	3·50
7942	20r. Vasilyevsky Island	5·25	4·50

3166 Delivery by Troika

2013. Europa. Postal Transport

7943	**3166**	15r. multicoloured	4·00	3·50

3167 Heydar Alirza oglu Aliyev

2013. Cavaliers of the Order of Saint Andrew

7944	**3167**	15r. multicoloured	4·00	3·50

3168 *Mina* (mine sweeper)

2013. Military Warships. Multicoloured.

7945	10r. Type **3168**	2·75	2·30
7946	12r. *Metel* (escort ship)	3·25	2·75
7947	15r. BKA-75 (armoured vessel)	4·00	3·50
7948	20r. *Usyskin* (gun boat)	5·25	4·50

3169 Alexandrovsky Kremlin (16th century)

2013. 500th Anniv of Alexandrovskaya Sloboda (Alexandrov). Sheet 104×76 mm

MS7949 **3169** 50r. multicoloured 13·00 12·50

3170 Apostles Cyril and Methodius

2013. 1150th Anniv of Arrival of Saints Cyril and Methodius to Great Moravia. Sheet 95×95 mm

MS7950 **3170** 40r. multicoloured 11·00 10·50

3171 Scientific and Research Vessel *Vyacheslav Tikhonov*

2013. Marine Fleet of Russia. Multicoloured.

7951	14r.25 Type **3171**	3·75	3·25
7952	14r.25 Ice-class tanker *Timofey Guzhenko*	3·75	3·25

3172 *Women's Summer Morning* (D.A. Belyukin)

2013. Russian Modern Art. Multicoloured.

7953	15r. Type **3172**	4·00	3·50
7954	15r. *Girl and City*, 2005 (A.A. Lyubavin)	4·00	3·50
7955	15r. *On the river Trubezh* 2008 (V.N. Polotnov) (37×50 mm)	4·00	3·50

3173
Aleksandrov

2013. Arms. Multicoloured.

7956		10r. Type **3173**	2·75	2·30
7957		14r.25 Kazan	3·75	3·25

No. 7958 and Type **3174** are left for University Games, not yet received.

3175 Rasul Gamzatov (poet)

2013. Cavaliers of the Order of Saint Andrew

7959	**3175**	15r. multicoloured	4·00	3·50

Nos. 7960/2 and Type **3176** are left for Winter Olympic Games, Sochi, not yet received.

3177 Moscow

2013. Arts and Crafts of Russia. Shawls. Multicoloured.

7963		15r. Type **3177**	4·00	3·50
7964		15r. Pavlovsky Posad (blue)	4·00	3·50
7965		15r. Orenburg (white lace)	4·00	3·50
7966		15r. Karabanovo (red)	4·00	3·50

3178 1963 10k. Stamp (Valentina Tereshkova (As T **1033**))

2013. 50th Anniv of First Woman in Space

7967	**3178**	14r.25 multicoloured	3·75	3·25

3179 *Baptism of Russia* (V. M. Vasnetsov)

2013. 1025th Anniv of Baptism of Kyivan Rus (through the baptism of Vladimir the Great). Sheet 70×85 mm

MS7968 **3179**	30r. multicoloured	8·00	6·75

3180 Arms of Penza

2013. Arms. Sheets 90×90 mm

MS7969 **3180**	50r. multicoloured	13·00	12·00

3181 St. Petersburg and the Aland Islands Passenger Ferry

2013. Passenger Ferries

7970	**3181**	14r.25 multicoloured	3·75	3·25

3182 Runners and Emblem

2013. IAAF (International Association of Athletics Federation) World Championships in Moscow

7971	**3182**	14r.25 multicoloured	3·75	3·25

3183 Tupelov Tu-2

2013. 125th Birth Anniv of Andrei Nikolayevich Tupolev. Sheet 150×98 mm. Multicoloured.

MS7972	10r. Type **3183**; 13r. Tb-7; 15r. Tu-16; 17r. Tu-22M3; 20r. Tu-95	11·00	10·50

3184 Diesel Locomotive

2013. 150th Anniv of Kolomna Locomotive Works

7973	**3184**	15r. multicoloured	4·00	3·50

3185 Express-AM Communication Satellite and RCC Emblem

2013. Regional Commonwealth in Field of Communications

7974	**3185**	14r.25 multicoloured	3·75	3·25

3186 *Hike Miniytsev* (1909)

2013. Art. Paintings by Ivan G. Myasoedova (changed name Eugene Zotov during 1930's and moved to Liechtenstein). Multicoloured.

7975		15r. Type **3186**	4·00	3·50
7976		15r. *Zilum* (1945)	4·00	3·50

3187 Icebreaker *Vaygach*

2013. Centenary of Discovery of Severnaya Zemlya Archipelago. Sheet 136×80 mm

MS7977	15r.×3, Type **3187**; B. A. Vilkitski (expedition leader) (vert); Ice braker *Taimyr*	12·00	11·50

3188 Emblem

2013. 18th Annual Conference and General Meeting of IAP (International Association of Prosecutors)

7978	**3188**	15r. multicoloured	4·00	3·50

3189 Smolensk Fortress Wall and Arms

2013. 1150th Anniv of Smolensk. Sheet 130×76 mm

MS7979 **3189**	50r. multicoloured	13·00	12·50

EXPRESS STAMPS

E171 Motor Cyclist

1932. Inscr "EXPRES".

E588	**E171**	5k. sepia	11·50	3·75
E589	-	10k. purple	17·00	6·75
E590	-	80k. green	44·00	18·00

DESIGNS—HORIZ: 10k. Express motor van; 80k. Class Ta steam locomotive.

E173 Polar Region and Kalinin K-4 Airplane over Ice-breaker "Taimyr"

1932. Air Express. Second Int Polar Year and Franz Joseph's Land to Archangel Flight.

E591	**E173**	50k. red	50·00	21·00
E592	**E173**	1r. green	£170	85·00

POSTAGE DUE STAMPS

Доплата
1 коп.
золотом.
(D96)

1924. Surch as Type **D96**.

D401b	**45**	1k. on 35k. blue	70	75
D402b	**45**	3k. on 35k. blue	70	75
D403b	**45**	5k. on 35k. blue	70	75
D404	**45**	8k. on 35k. blue	1·30	75
D405b	**45**	10k. on 35k. blue	1·30	90
D406b	**45**	12k. on 70k. brown	85	75
D407c	**45**	14k. on 35k. blue	1·30	75
D408b	**45**	32k. on 35k. blue	1·30	1·30
D409c	**45**	40k. on 35k. blue	1·30	90

ДОПЛАТА
1 коп.
(D99)

1924. Optd with Type **D99**.

D421	**48**	1k. on 100r. yellow	5·25	12·50

D104

1925

D464	**D104**	1k. red	60	1·50
D465	**D104**	2k. mauve	60	1·50
D466	**D104**	3k. blue	65	1·60
D467	**D104**	7k. yellow	70	1·60
D468	**D104**	8k. green	85	1·60
D469	**D104**	10k. blue	90	1·80
D470	**D104**	14k. brown	1·50	3·75

Pt. 17

RUSSIAN POST OFFICES IN CHINA

Russian Post Offices were opened in various towns in Manchuria and China from 1870 onwards.

1899. 100 kopeks = 1 rouble.
1917. 100 cents = 1 dollar (Chinese).

(1)

1899. Arms types (with thunderbolts) of Russia optd with T **1**.

1	**9**	1k. orange	1·00	1·75
2	**9**	2k. green	1·00	1·75
3	**9**	3k. red	1·00	1·75
9	**14**	4k. red	3·00	3·50
4	**9**	5k. purple	1·00	1·75
5	**9**	7k. blue	2·50	3·75
6	**14**	10k. blue	3·00	4·00
30	**10**	14k. red and blue	1·00	95
31	**10**	15k. blue and brown	1·00	1·50
32	**14**	20k. red and blue	75	1·20
33	**10**	25k. violet and green	1·00	2·20
34	**10**	35k. green and purple	80	75
35	**14**	50k. green and purple	70	65
36	**10**	70k. orange and brown	1·10	1·30
37	**15**	1r. orange and brown	1·50	2·20
20	**11**	3r.50 grey and black	15·00	17·00
21	**20**	5r. blue and green on green	10·20	12·00
22	**11**	7r. yellow and black	22·00	17·00
23	**20**	10r. grey and red on yellow	£100	£100

1910. Arms types of Russia optd with T **1**.

24	**22**	1k. orange	65	75
25	**22**	2k. green	65	75
26	**22**	3k. red	50	60
27	**23**	4k. red	60	55
28	**22**	7k. blue	65	75
29	**23**	10k. blue	60	55

1917. Arms types of Russia surch in "cents" and "dollars" diagonally in one line.

42	**22**	1c. on 1k. orange	1·00	7·00
43	**22**	2c. on 2k. green	1·00	7·00
44	**22**	3c. on 3k. red	1·00	7·00
45	**23**	4c. on 4k. red	2·00	5·50
46	**22**	5c. on 5k. lilac	2·00	19·00
47	**23**	10c. on 10k. blue	2·00	20·00
48	**10**	14c. on 14k. red and blue	2·20	13·00
49	**10**	15c. on 15k. blue and purple	2·20	18·00
50	**14**	20c. on 20k. red and blue	2·20	18·00
51	**10**	25c. on 25k. violet and green	2·20	18·00
52	**10**	35c. on 35k. green & purple	2·50	23·00
53	**14**	50c. on 50k. green & purple	2·20	23·00
54	**10**	70c. on 70k. orange & brn	2·20	19·00
55	**15**	1d. on 1r. orge & brn on brn	2·20	19·00
39	**10**	3d.50 on 3r.50 grey & blk	14·00	35·00
40	**20**	5d. on 5r. bl & dp bl on grn	13·00	35·00
41	**11**	7d. on 7r. yellow and black	14·00	35·00
57	**20**	10d. on 10r. grey and red on yellow	30·00	£150

1920. Arms types of Russia surch in "cents" in two lines. Perf or imperf.

65	**22**	1c. on 1k. orange	40·00	30·00
59	**22**	2c. on 2k. green	32·00	32·00
60	**22**	3c. on 3k. red	32·00	32·00
61	**23**	4c. on 4k. red	37·00	40·00
62	**22**	5c. on 5k. lilac	37·00	40·00
63	**23**	10c. on 10k. blue	£225	£200
64	**22**	10c. on 10k. on 7k. blue	£200	£220

Pt. 3

RUSSIAN POST OFFICE IN CRETE

4 metallik = 1 grosion (Turkish piastre)

(RETHYMNON PROVINCE)

The Russian Postal Service operated from 1 May to 29 July 1899.

These issues were optd with circular control marks as shown on Types **R3/4**. Prices are for stamps with these marks, but unused examples without them are known.

R1

R2

1899. Imperf.

R1	**R 1**	1m. blue	£110	55·00
R2	**R 2**	1m. green	13·50	10·00
R3	**R 2**	2m. red	£275	£225
R4	**R 2**	2m. green	13·50	10·00

R3

1899. Without stars in oval.

R5	**R 3**	1m. pink	£150	£110
R6	**R 3**	2m. pink	£150	£110
R7	**R 3**	1g. pink	£150	£110
R8	**R 3**	1m. blue	£150	£110
R9	**R 3**	2m. blue	£150	£110
R10	**R 3**	1g. blue	£150	£110
R11	**R 3**	1m. green	£150	£110
R12	**R 3**	2m. green	£150	£110
R13	**R 3**	1g. green	£150	£110

R14	**R 3**	1m. red	£150	£110
R15	**R 3**	2m. red	£150	£110
R16	**R 3**	1g. red	£150	£110
R17	**R 3**	1m. orange	£150	£110
R18	**R 3**	2m. orange	£150	£110
R19	**R 3**	1g. orange	£150	£110
R20	**R 3**	1m. yellow	£150	£110
R21	**R 3**	2m. yellow	£150	£110
R22	**R 3**	1g. yellow	£150	£110
R23	**R 3**	1m. black	£950	£800
R24	**R 3**	2m. black	£950	£800
R25	**R 3**	1g. black	£950	£800

R4

1899. Starred at each side.

R26	**R 4**	1m. pink	80·00	70·00
R27	**R 4**	2m. pink	16·00	13·50
R28	**R 4**	1g. pink	12·00	9·50
R29	**R 4**	1m. blue	47·00	27·00
R30	**R 4**	2m. blue	16·00	13·50
R31	**R 4**	1g. blue	12·00	9·50
R32	**R 4**	1m. green	47·00	27·00
R33	**R 4**	2m. green	16·00	13·50
R34	**R 4**	1g. green	12·00	9·50
R35	**R 4**	1m. red	47·00	27·00
R36	**R 4**	2m. red	16·00	13·50
R37	**R 4**	1g. red	12·00	9·50

Pt. 16

RUSSIAN POST OFFICES IN THE TURKISH EMPIRE

General issues for Russian P.O.'s in the Turkish Empire and stamps specially overprinted for use at particular offices.

1863. 100 kopeks = 1 rouble.
1900. 40 paras = 1 piastre.

1 Inscription = "Dispatch under Wrapper to the East"

1863. Imperf.

2a	**1**	6k. blue	£650	£3750

2

3

1865. Imperf.

4	**2**	(10pa.) brown and blue	£1300	£1000
5	**3**	(2pi.) blue and red	£1900	£1300

4

5

1865. Imperf.

6	**4**	(10pa.) red and blue	65·00	£100
7	**5**	(2pi.) blue and red	£150	£130

The values of 4/7 were 10pa. (or 2k.) and 2pi. (or 20k.).

6 Inscription = "Eastern Correspondence"

1868. Perf.

14	**6**	1k. brown	12·50	12·50
11	**6**	3k. green	50·00	38·00
16	**6**	5k. blue	12·50	6·25
17a	**6**	10k. red and green	£120	12·50

See also Nos. 26/35.

1876. Surch with large figures of value.

24	7k. on 10k. red and green	£190	£130
22	8k. on 10k. red and green	£150	£130

1879

26	1k. black and yellow	7·50	2·50
32	1k. orange	6·25	2·50
27	2k. black and red	12·50	3·75
33	2k. green	12·50	5·00
34	5k. purple	12·50	6·25
28	7k. red and grey	15·00	2·50
35	7k. blue	12·50	3·75

1900. Arms types of Russia surch in "**PARA**" or "**PIASTRES**".

37	**9**	4pa. on 1k. orange	15	15
50	**22**	5pa. on 1k. orange	15	15
38	**9**	10pa. on 2k. green	25	25
51	**22**	10pa. on 2k. green	15	15
201	**22**	15pa. on 3k. red	65	10·00
41	**14**	20pa. on 4k. red	40	25
52	**23**	20pa. on 4k. red	15	15
42	**9**	20pa. on 5k. purple	40	50
181	**22**	20pa. on 5k. purple	15	15
43	**14**	1pi. on 10k. blue	40	25
53	**23**	1pi. on 10k. blue	15	15
182	**10**	1½pi. on 15k. blue & purple	25	25
183	**14**	2pi. on 20k. red and blue	25	25
184	**10**	2½pi. on 25k. violet & green	25	25
185	**10**	3½pi. on 35k. green & pur	40	40
54	**14**	5pi. on 50k. green and lilac	40	65
55	**10**	7pi. on 70k. orange & brn	65	90
56	**15**	10pi. on 1r. orange and brown on brown	90	1·40
48	**11**	35pi. on 3r.50 grey & blk	10·00	10·00
202	**20**	50pi. on 5r. blue on green	6·25	£190
49	**11**	70pi. on 7r. yellow & black	18·00	18·00
203	**20**	100pi. on 10r. grey and red on yellow	25·00	£650

12

1909. As T **14**, **15**, and **11** of Russia, but ship and date in centre as T **12**, and surch in "**paras**" or "**piastres**".

57	**14**	5pa. on 1k. orange	65	65
58	**14**	10pa. on 2k. green	90	90
59	**14**	20pa. on 4k. red	1·30	1·90
60	**14**	1pi. on 10k. blue	1·90	2·50
61	**14**	5pi. on 50k. green & purple	3·25	6·25
62	**14**	7pi. on 70k. orange & brn	6·25	9·50
63	**15**	10pi. on 1r. orange & brown	12·50	15·00
64	**11**	35pi. on 3r.50 green & pur	21·00	90·00
65	**11**	70pi. on 7r. pink and green	65·00	£140

The above stamps exist overprinted for Constantinople, Jaffa, Jerusalem, Kerassunde, Mount Athos, Salonika, Smyrna, Trebizonde, Beyrouth, Dardanelles, Mytilene and Rizeh. For full list see Part 10 (Russia) of the Stanley Gibbons Catalogue.

1913. Nos. 126/42 (Romanov types) of Russia surch.

186	5pa. on 1k. orange	15	15
187	10pa. on 3k. green	15	15
188	15pa. on 3k. red	15	15
189	20pa. on 4k. red	15	15
190	1pi. on 10k. blue	25	25
191	1½pi. on 15k. brown	65	65
192	2pi. on 20k. green	65	65
193	2½pi. on 25k. purple	90	90
194	3½pi. on 35k. green and violet	1·90	1·90
195	5pi. on 50k. grey and brown	2·10	2·10
196	7pi. on 70k. brown and green	12·50	31·00
197	10pi. on 1r. green	15·00	31·00
198	20pi. on 2r. brown	9·50	12·50
199	30pi. on 3r. violet	12·50	£425
200	50pi. on 5r. brown	£190	£950

Pt. 14

RWANDA

An independent republic established in July 1962, formerly part of Ruanda-Urundi.

100 centimes = 1 franc.

1 Pres. Kayibanda and Map

1962. Independence.

1	**1**	10c. sepia and green	15	15
2	-	40c. sepia and purple	15	15
3	**1**	1f. sepia and blue	1·30	65
4	-	1f.50 sepia and brown	20	15
5	**1**	3f.50 sepia and orange	25	15
6	-	6f.50 sepia and blue	40	20
7	**1**	10f. sepia and olive	50	25
8	-	20f. sepia and red	1·00	50

DESIGN: Nos. 2, 4, 6, 8 are as Type **1** but with halo around Rwanda on map in place of "R".

1963. Admission to U.N. No. 204 of Ruanda-Urundi with coloured frame obliterating old inscr (colours below), and surch **Admission a l'O.N.U. 18-9-1962 REPUBLIQUE RWANDAISE** and new value.

9	3f.50 on 3f. grey	25	15
10	6f.50 on 3f. pink	1·90	1·70
11	10f. on 3f. blue	40	25
12	20f. on 3f. silver	1·00	80

1963. Flowers issue of Ruanda-Urundi (Nos. 178 etc) optd **REPUBLIQUE RWANDAISE** or surch also in various coloured panels over old inscription and values. Flowers in natural colours.

13	25c. orange and green	25	20
14	40c. salmon and green	25	20
15	60c. purple and green	25	20
16	1f.25 blue and green	1·90	1·60
17	1f.50 green and violet	1·60	1·30
18	2f. on 1f.50 green and violet	2·50	1·70
19	4f. on 1f.50 green and violet	3·25	2·00
20	5f. green and purple	3·25	2·00
21	7f. brown and green	3·25	2·00
22	10f. olive and purple	4·00	2·30

The coloured panels are in various shades of silver except No. 19 which is in blue.

4 Ears of Wheat and Native Implements

1963. Freedom from Hunger.

23	**4**	2f. brown and green	15	10
24	**4**	4f. mauve and blue	15	10
25	**4**	7f. red and grey	40	25
26	**4**	10f. green and yellow	1·40	1·00

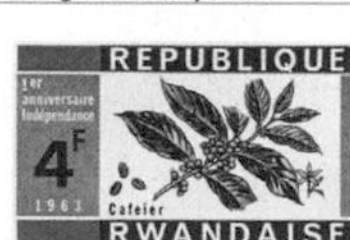

5 Coffee

1963. First Anniv of Independence.

27	**5**	10c. brown and blue	15	10
28	-	20c. yellow and blue	15	10
29	-	30c. green and orange	15	10
30	**5**	40c. brown and turquoise	15	10
31	-	1f. yellow and purple	15	10
32	-	2f. green and blue	1·90	90
33	**5**	4f. brown and red	20	15
34	-	7f. yellow and green	25	20
35	-	10f. green and violet	40	35

DESIGNS: 20c., 1, 7f. Bananas; 30c., 2, 10f. Tea.

5a "Post and Telecommunications"

1963. Second Anniv of African and Malagasy Posts and Telcommunications Union.

36	**5a**	14f. multicoloured	1·30	1·00

6 Postal Services Emblem

1963. Admission of Rwanda to U.P.U.

37	**6**	50c. blue and pink	15	10
38	**6**	1f.50 brown and blue	1·30	90
39	**6**	3f. purple and grey	15	10
40	**6**	20f. green and yellow	65	40

7 Emblem

1963. 15th Anniv of Declaration of Human Rights.

41	**7**	5f. red	25	10
42	**7**	6f. violet	90	65
43	**7**	10f. blue	40	25

8 Child Care

1963. Red Cross Centenary.

44	**8**	10c. multicoloured	15	10
45	-	20c. multicoloured	15	10
46	-	30c. multicoloured	15	10
47	-	40c. brown, red and violet	15	10
48	**8**	2f. multicoloured	1·50	1·00
49	-	7f. multicoloured	40	20
50	-	10f. brown, red and brown	50	25
51	-	20f. brown, red and orange	1·00	40

DESIGNS—HORIZ: 20c., 7f. Patient having blood test; 40, 20c. Stretcher party. VERT: 30c., 10f. Doctor examining child.

9 Map and Hydraulic Pump

1964. World Meteorological Day.

52	**9**	3f. sepia, blue and green	15	10
53	**9**	7f. sepia, blue and red	65	40
54	**9**	10f. sepia, blue and orange	90	50
MS54a		72×52 mm. 25f. sepia, blue and lilac	8·75	8·50

1964. Stamps of Ruanda-Urundi optd **REPUBLIQUE RWANDAISE** or surch also in black over coloured metallic panels obliterating old inscription or value.

55	10c. on 20c. (No. 204)	15	10
56	20c. (No. 204)	15	10
57	30c. on 1f.50 (No. 208)	15	10
58	40c. (No. 205)	15	10
59	50c. (No. 206)	15	10
60	1f. (No. 207)	15	10
61	2f. (No. 209)	15	10
62	3f. (No. 210)	15	10
63	4f. on 3f.50 on 3f. (No. 228)	65	25
64	5f. (No. 211)	65	15
65	7f.50 on 6f.50 (No. 212)	1·00	40
66	8f. (No. 213)	8·75	6·50
67	10f. (No. 214)	1·50	65
68	20f. (No. 229)	3·25	1·00
69	50f. (No. 230)	4·50	2·30

10 Boy with Crutch

1964. Gatagara Re-education Centre.

70	**10**	10c. sepia and violet	15	10
71	-	40c. sepia and blue	25	10
72	-	4f. sepia and brown	50	15
73	**10**	7f.50 sepia and green	75	25
74	-	8f. sepia and bistre	2·50	1·60
75	-	10f. sepia and purple	1·30	65

DESIGNS—HORIZ: 40c., 8f. Children operating sewing machines. VERT: 4, 10f. Crippled child on crutches.

11 Running

1964. Olympic Games, Tokyo. Sportsmen in slate.

76	11	10c. blue	15	10
77	-	20c. red	15	10
78	-	30c. turquoise	15	10
79	-	40c. brown	15	10
80	11	4f. blue	40	15
81	-	5f. green	2·75	2·50
82	-	20f. purple	75	50
83	-	50f. grey	1·90	1·40
MS83a		135×100 mm. Designs as Nos. 76/9. 10f. grey; 20f. green; 30f. green; 40f. blue	9·50	9·25

DESIGNS—VERT: 20c., 5f. Basketball; 40c., 50f. Football. HORIZ: 20f. High-jumping.

12 Faculties of "Letters" and "Sciences"

1965. National University. Multicoloured.

84	10c. Type **12**	15	10
85	20c. Student with microscope and building ("Medicine") (horiz)	15	10
86	30c. Scales of Justice, Hand of Law ("Social Sciences" and "Normal High School")	15	10
87	40c. University buildings (horiz)	15	10
88	5f. Type **12**	15	10
89	7f. As 20c.	25	15
90	10f. As 30c.	1·90	1·70
91	12f. As 40c.	65	25

13 Abraham Lincoln

1965. Death Centenary of Abraham Lincoln.

92	13	10c. green and red	15	10
93	13	20c. brown and blue	15	10
94	13	30c. violet and red	15	10
95	13	40c. blue and brown	15	10
96	13	9f. brown and purple	40	25
97	13	40f. purple and green	3·75	1·40
MS97a		65×77 mm 50f. purple and red	4·25	1·80

14 Marabou Storks

1965. Kagera National Park. Multicoloured.

98	10c. Type **14**	30	25
99	20c. Common zebras	30	25
100	30c. Impalas	30	25
101	40c. Crowned cranes, hippopotami and cattle egrets	30	25
102	1f. African buffaloes	40	25
103	3f. Hunting dogs	40	25
104	5f. Yellow baboons	8·75	2·75
105	10f. African elephant and map	75	50
106	40f. Reed cormorants and African darters	2·50	80
107	100f. Lions	5·00	1·00

SIZES—As Type **14**: VERT: 30c., 2, 5f. HORIZ: 20, 40c., 3, 10f. LARGER (45×25½ mm); 40, 100f.

15 "Telstar" Satellite

1965. Centenary of I.T.U. Multicoloured.

108	10c. Type **15**	15	10
109	40c. "Syncom" satellite	15	10
110	4f.50 Type **15**	2·10	90
111	50f. "Syncom" satellite	1·90	65
MS111a	89×65 mm. 60f. "UIT" on globe	5·00	4·75

16 "Colotis aurigineus"

1965. Rwanda Butterflies. Multicoloured.

112	10c. "Papilio bromius"	30	25
113	15c. "Papilio hesperus"	30	25
114	20c. Type **16**	30	25
115	30c. "Amphicallia pactolicus"	40	35
116	35c. "Lobobunaea phaedusa"	40	35
117	40c. "Papilio jacksoni ruandana"	40	35
118	1f.50 "Papilio dardanus"	65	40
119	3f. "Amaurina elliotti"	6·00	2·10
120	4f. "Colias electo pseudohecate"	6·25	3·25
121	10f. "Bunaea alcinoe"	1·30	50
122	50f. "Athletes gigas"	4·50	2·50
123	100f. "Charaxes ansorgei R"	5·00	2·00

The 10, 30, 35c., 3, 4 and 100f. are vert.

17 Cattle and I.C.Y. Emblem

1965. International Co-operation Year.

124	17	10c. green and yellow	15	10
125	-	40c. brown, blue and green	15	10
126	-	4f.50 green, brown & yell	2·10	90
127	-	45f. purple and brown	1·60	50

DESIGNS: 40c. Crater lake and giant plants; 4f.50, Gazelle and candelabra tree; 45f. Mt. Ruwenzori. Each with I.C.Y. emblem.

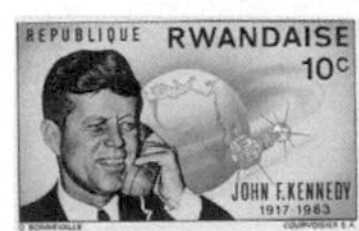

18 Pres. Kennedy, Globe and Satellites

1965. Second Anniv of Pres. Kennedy's Death.

128	18	10c. brown and green	15	10
129	18	40c. brown and red	15	10
130	18	50c. brown and blue	15	10
131	18	1f. brown and olive	15	10
132	18	8f. brown and violet	3·25	2·10
133	18	50f. brown and grey	2·50	1·60
MS133a		92×100 mm. 40f. sepia and orange; 60f. sepia and blue	15·00	14·50

19 Madonna and Child

1965. Christmas.

134	19	10c. green and gold	15	10
135	19	40c. brown and gold	15	10
136	19	50c. blue and gold	15	10
137	19	4f. black and gold	1·50	1·20
138	19	6f. violet and gold	20	15
139	19	30f. brown and gold	1·30	1·00

20 Father Damien

1966. World Leprosy Day.

140	20	10c. blue and brown	15	10
141	-	40c. red and blue	15	10
142	20	4f.50 slate and green	40	25
143	-	45f. brown and red	3·25	2·30

DESIGNS: 40c., 45f. Dr. Schweitzer.

21 Pope Paul, Rome and New York

1966. Pope Paul's Visit to U.N. Organization.

144	21	10c. blue and brown	15	10
145	-	40c. indigo and blue	15	10
146	21	4f.50 blue and purple	2·50	2·00
147	-	50f. blue and green	2·00	90

DESIGN: 40c., 50f. Pope Paul, Arms and U.N. emblem.

22 "Echinops amplexicaulis" and "E. bequaertii"

1966. Flowers. Multicoloured.

148	10c. Type **22**	15	10
149	20c. "Haemanthus multiflorus" (vert)	15	10
150	30c. "Helichrysum erici-rosenii"	15	10
151	40c. "Carissa edulis" (vert)	15	10
152	1f. "Spathodea campanulata" (vert)	15	10
153	3f. "Habenaria praestans" (vert)	15	10
154	5f. "Aloe lateritia" (vert)	8·25	4·25
155	10f. "Ammocharis tinneana" (vert)	65	40
156	40f. "Erythrina abyssinica"	1·50	80
157	100f. "Capparis tomentosa"	4·50	2·30
MS158	58×60 mm. No. 157	10·00	9·00

23 W.H.O. Building

1966. Inaug of W.H.O. Headquarters, Geneva.

159	23	2f. olive	15	10
160	23	3f. red	25	20
161	23	5f. blue	15	10

24 Football

1966. "Youth and Sports".

162	24	10c. black, blue and green	15	10
163	-	20c. black, green and red	15	10
164	-	30c. black, purple and blue	15	10
165	24	40c. black, green and bistre	25	10
166	-	9f. black, purple and grey	40	25
167	-	50f. black, blue and purple	1·50	1·40

DESIGNS: 20c., 9f. Basketball; 30c., 50f. Volleyball.

25 Mother and Child within Flames

1966. Nuclear Disarmament.

168	25	20c. brown, red and mauve	15	10
169	25	30c. brown, red and green	15	10
170	25	50c. brown, red and blue	15	10
171	25	6f. brown, red and yellow	25	10
172	25	15f. brown, red & turquoise	1·10	65
173	25	18f. brown, red and lavender	1·30	80

26 Football

1966. World Cup Football Championship.

174	26	20c. blue and turquoise	15	10
175	26	30c. blue and violet	25	10
176	26	50c. blue and green	40	15
177	26	6f. blue and mauve	1·00	25
178	26	12f. blue and brown	2·30	65
179	26	25f. indigo and blue	3·25	1·00

27 Yellow-crested Helmet Shrike and Mikeno Volcano

1966. Rwanda Scenery.

180	27	10c. green	15	10
181	-	40c. lake	15	10
182	-	4f.50 blue	75	65
183	-	55f. purple	1·10	90

DESIGNS—VERT: 40c. Nyamiranga Falls (inscr "Nyamilanga"); 55f. Rusumo Falls (inscr "Rusumu"). HORIZ: 4f.50, Gahinga and Mahubura Volcanoes, and giant plants.

28 UNESCO and Cultural Emblems

1966. 20th Anniv of UNESCO.

184	28	20c. mauve and blue	15	10
185	-	30c. turquoise and black	15	10
186	-	50c. brown and black	15	10
187	-	1f. violet and black	15	10
188	28	5f. green and brown	20	15
189	-	10f. brown and black	25	20
190	-	15f. purple and blue	90	80
191	-	50f. blue and black	1·00	90

DESIGNS: 30c., 10f. "Animal" primer; 50c., 15f. Atomic symbol and drill operator; 1, 50f. Nubian monument partly submerged in the Nile.

29 "Bitis gabonica"

1967. Snakes. Multicoloured.

192	20c. Head of mamba	20	15
193	30c. Python (vert)	20	15
194	50c. Type **29**	25	15
195	1f. "Naja melanoleuca" (vert)	40	20
196	3f. Head of python	50	25
197	5f. "Psammophis sibilans" (vert)	75	40
198	20f. "Dendroaspis jamesoni kaimosae"	3·00	1·60
199	70f. "Dasypeltis scabra" (vert)	3·75	2·30

30 Girders and Tea Flower

1967. Ntaruka Hydro-electric Project.

200	30	20c. blue and purple	15	10
201	-	30c. brown and black	15	10
202	-	50c. violet and brown	15	10
203	30	4f. purple and green	25	15
204	-	25f. green and violet	65	50
205	-	50f. brown and blue	1·90	1·70

DESIGNS: 30c., 25f. Power conductors and pyrethrum flower; 50c., 50f. Barrage and coffee beans.

31 Cogwheel

1967. Seventh Europa Stamp Exhibition, Naples. Two sheets each 90×67 mm.

MS206 (a) **31** 100f. brown on cream; (b) **31** 100f. purple on cream. Set of 2 sheets	12·50	12·00

32 Dancers

1967. "Expo 67" World Fair, Montreal (1st issue). Sheet 75×90 mm.

MS207 **32** 180f. violet	6·25	6·00

See also Nos. 222/9.

33 "St. Martin" (Van Dyck)

1967. Paintings.

208	**33**	20c. black, gold and violet	15	10
209	-	40c. black, gold and green	15	10
210	-	60c. black, gold and red	15	10
211	-	80c. black, gold and blue	15	10
212	**33**	9f. black, gold and brown	1·40	90
213	-	15f. black, gold and red	50	35
214	-	18f. black, gold and bronze	65	40
215	-	26f. black, gold and lake	75	65

PAINTINGS—HORIZ: 40c., 15f. "Rebecca and Eliezer" (Murillo); 80c., 26f. "Job and his Friends" (attributed to Il Calabrese). VERT: 60c., 18f. "St. Christopher" (D. Bouts).

34 Rwanda "Round Table" Emblem and Common Zebra's Head

1967. Rwanda "Round Table" Fund for Charitable Works. Each with "Round Table" Emblem. Mult.

216	20c. Type **34**	15	10
217	40c. African elephant's head	15	10
218	60c. African buffalo's head	15	10
219	80c. Impala's head	15	10
220	18f. Ear of wheat	50	40
221	100f. Palm	3·25	2·00

35 "Africa Place" and Dancers

1967. World Fair, Montreal.

222	**35**	20c. blue and sepia	15	10
223	-	30c. purple and sepia	15	10
224	-	50c. orange and sepia	15	10
225	-	1f. green and sepia	15	10
226	-	3f. violet and sepia	15	10
227	**35**	15f. green and sepia	40	15
228	-	34f. red and sepia	90	80
229	-	40f. turquoise and sepia	1·30	1·00

DESIGNS: "Africa Place" (two different views used alternately in order of value) and 30c., 3f. Drum and handicrafts; 50c., 40f. Dancers leaping; 1f., 34f. Spears, shields and weapons.

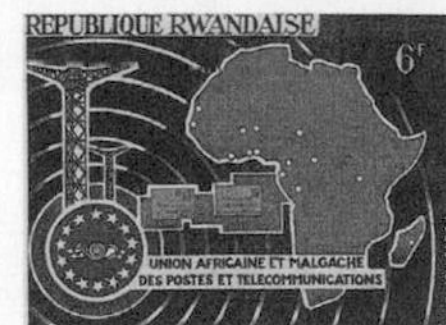

35a Map of Africa, Letters and Pylons

1967. Air. Fifth Anniv of U.A.M.P.T.

230	**35a**	6f. slate, brown and lake	25	15
231	**35a**	18f. purple and brown	90	50
232	**35a**	30f. red, green and blue	1·50	1·00

36 Common Zebra's Head and Lion's Emblem

1967. 50th Anniv of Lions International.

233	**36**	20c. black, blue and violet	15	10
234	**36**	80c. black, blue and green	15	10
235	**36**	1f. black, blue and red	15	10
236	**36**	8f. black, blue and brown	50	25
237	**36**	10f. black, blue and ultramarine	65	40
238	**36**	50f. black, blue and green	2·30	1·60

37 Red Bishop

1967. Birds of Rwanda. Multicoloured.

239	20c. Type **37**	15	10
240	40c. Woodland kingfisher (horiz)	15	10
241	60c. Red-billed quelea	15	10
242	80c. Double-toothed barbet (horiz)	15	10
243	2f. Pin-tailed whydah	25	15
244	3f. Red-chested cuckoo (horiz)	40	25
245	18f. Green wood hoopoe	1·60	1·00
246	25f. Cinnamon-chested bee eater (horiz)	2·00	1·60
247	80f. Regal sunbird	4·75	4·50
248	100f. Fan-tailed whydah (horiz)	7·00	6·50

38 Ice Skating

1968. Winter Olympic Games, Grenoble. T **38** and similar vert designs in sheet 130×90 mm.

MS249 50f. black, blue and emerald (Type **38**); 50f. black, emerald and blue (Ski-jumping)	9·50	9·25

39 Running, and Mexican Antiquities

1968. Olympic Games, Mexico (1st issue). Multicoloured.

250	20c. Type **39**	40	25
251	40c. Hammer-throwing	40	25
252	60c. Hurdling	40	25
253	80c. Javelin-throwing	40	25
MS254	8f. Football; 10f. Mexican horseman and cacti; 12f. Hockey; 18f. Cathedral; 20f. Boxing; 30f. Mexico City	12·50	12·00

The 20c. to 80c. include Mexican antiquities in their designs.

Nos. 255/9 are vacant.

40 Dr. Martin Luther King

1968. Martin Luther King Commemoration. Miniature sheet 81×81 mm.

MS260 **40** 100f. brown	3·75	2·50

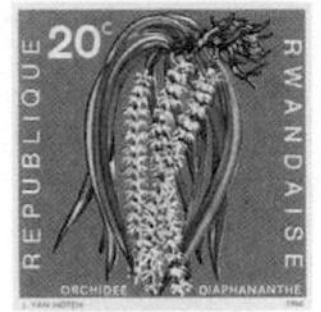

41 "Diaphananthe fragrantissima"

1968. Flowers. Multicoloured.

261	20c. Type **41**	10	10
262	40c. "Phaeomeria speciosa"	15	10
263	60c. "Ravenala madagascariensis"	15	10
264	80c. "Costus afer"	15	10
265	2f. Banana flowers	20	10
266	3f. Flowers and young fruit of pawpaw	25	15
267	18f. "Clerodendron sp."	65	25
268	25f. Sweet potato flowers	1·00	50
269	80f. Baobab flower	2·75	1·00
270	100f. Passion flower	3·50	2·00

42 Horse-jumping

1966. Olympic Games, Mexico (2nd issue).

271	**42**	20c. brown and orange	15	10
272	-	40c. brown and turquoise	15	10
273	-	60c. brown and purple	15	10
274	-	80c. brown and blue	15	10
275	-	38f. brown and red	1·00	40
276	-	60f. brown and green	2·30	90

SPORTS: 40c. Judo; 60c. Fencing; 80c. High-jumping; 38f. High-diving; 60f. Weightlifting. Each design also represents the location of previous Olympics as at left in Type **42**.

43 Tuareg (Algeria)

1968. African National Costumes (1st series). Multicoloured.

277	30c. Type **43**	15	10
278	40c. Upper Volta	15	10
279	60c. Senegal	15	10
280	70c. Rwanda	15	10
281	8f. Morocco	40	15
282	20f. Nigeria	75	25
283	40f. Zambia	1·50	65
284	50f. Kenya	1·90	1·00

See also Nos. 345/52.

44 "The Nativity" (G. Barbarelli (Giorgione))

1968. Christmas. Miniature sheet 86×86 mm.

MS285 **44** 100f.green	5·75	5·50

For annual Christmas miniature sheets see Nos. **MS**319, **MS**399, **MS**433, **MS**506, **MS**579, **MS**628, **MS**718, **MS**792 and **MS**850.

44a "Alexandre Lenoir" (J. L. David)

1968. Air. "Philexafrique" Stamp Exhibition, Abidjan (Ivory Coast, 1969) (1st issue).

286	**44a**	100f. multicoloured	4·50	2·30

45 Rwanda Scene and Stamp of Ruanda-Urundi (1953)

1969. Air. "Philexafrique" Stamp Exn (2nd issue).

287	**45**	50f. multicoloured	2·00	1·70

46 "The Musical Angels" (Van Eyck)

1969. "Paintings and Music". Multicoloured.

288	20c. Type **46** (postage)	15	10
289	40c. "The Angels' Concert" (M. Grunewald)	15	10
290	60c. "The Singing Boy" (Frans Hals)	15	10
291	80c. "The Lute player" (G. Terborch)	15	10
292	2f. "The Fifer" (Manet)	25	15
293	6f. "Young Girls at the Piano" (Renoir)	40	25
294	50f. "The Music Lesson" (Fragonard) (air)	2·10	1·80
295	100f. "Angels playing their Musical Instruments" (Memling) (horiz)	4·25	3·00
MS296	Two sheets 90×80 mm. Each 75f. Designs as (a) 60c. and (b) 6f. Pair	6·25	6·00

47 Tuareg Tribesmen

1969. African Headdresses (1st series). Multicoloured.

297	20c. Type **47**	15	10
298	40c. Young Ovambo woman	15	10
299	60c. Ancient Guinean and Middle Congo festival headdresses	15	10
300	80c. Guinean "Dagger" dancer	15	10
301	8f. Nigerian Muslims	40	15
302	20f. Luba dancer, Kabondo (Congo)	90	40
303	40f. Senegalese and Gambian women	2·10	80
304	80f. Rwanda dancer	3·50	1·40

See also Nos. 408/15.

48 "The Moneylender and his Wife" (Quentin Metsys)

1969. Fifth Anniv of African Development Bank.

305	48	30f. multicoloured on silver	1·00	90
306	-	70f. multicoloured on gold	2·50	2·20

DESIGN: 70f. "The Moneylender and his Wife" (Van Reymerswaele).

49 Astronaut with Camera

1969. First Man on the Moon. Miniature sheet 96×110 mm.

MS307	**49**	100f. blue	5·75	5·50

See also No. **MS**417.

50 Pyrethrum

1969. Medicinal Plants. Multicoloured.

308	20c. Type **50**	15	10
309	40c. Aloes	15	10
310	60c. Cola	15	10
311	80c. Coca	15	10
312	3f. Hagenia	25	15
313	75f. Cassia	3·50	2·00
314	80f. Cinchona	3·75	2·10
315	100f. Tephrosia	4·50	2·50

51 Revolutionary

1969. Tenth Anniv of Revolution.

316	**51**	6f. multicoloured	40	15
317	**51**	18f. multicoloured	90	65
318	**51**	40f. multicoloured	1·90	1·60

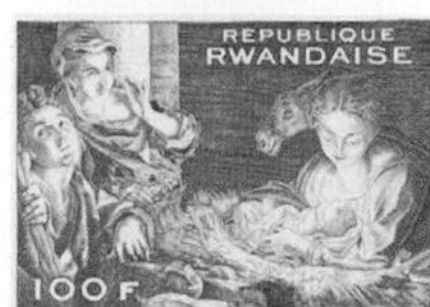

52 "The Holy Night" (Correggio)

1969. Christmas. Miniature sheet 85×85 mm.

MS319	**52**	100f. ultramarine	4·50	4·25

53 "Napoleon on Horseback" (David)

1969. Birth Bicent of Napoleon Bonaparte. Multicoloured. Portraits of Napoleon. Artist's name given.

320	20c. Type **53**	15	10
321	40c. Debret	15	10
322	60c. Gautherot	15	10
323	80c. Ingres	15	10
324	8f. Pajou	50	25
325	20f. Gros	1·30	65
326	40f. Gros	2·50	1·00
327	80f. David	4·75	2·10

54 "The Quarryman" (O. Bonnevalle)

1969. 50th Anniv of I.L.O. Multicoloured.

328	20c. Type **54**	15	10
329	40c. "Ploughing" (detail Brueghel's "Descent of Icarus")	15	10
330	60c. "The Fisherman" (C. Meunier)	15	10
331	80c. "Ostend Slipway" (J. van Noten)	15	10
332	8f. "The Cook" (P. Aertsen)	25	15
333	10f. "Vulcan's Blacksmiths" (Velazquez)	40	25
334	50f. "Hiercheuse" (C. Meunier)	2·10	80
335	70f. "The Miner" (P. Paulus)	3·25	1·30

Nos. 330, 332 and 334/5 are vert.

55 "The Derby at Epsom" (Gericault)

1970. Paintings of Horses. Multicoloured.

336	20c. Type **55**	15	10
337	40c. "Horses leaving the Sea" (Delacroix)	15	10
338	60c. "Charles V at Muhlberg" (Titian) (vert)	15	10
339	80c. "To the Races, Amateur Jockeys" (Degas)	15	10
340	8f. "Horsemen at Rest" (Wouwermans)	25	15
341	20f. "Officer of the Imperial Guard" (Gericault) (vert)	75	25
342	40f. "Horse and Dromedary" (Bonnevalle)	2·30	80
343	80f. "The Prodigal Child" (Rubens)	3·75	1·60

56 "The Fleet in the Bay of Naples" (Brueghel)

1970. Tenth "Europa" Stamp Exhibition, Naples. Miniature sheet 110×96 mm.

MS344	**56**	100f. purple	12·50	12·00

1970. African National Costumes (2nd series). As T **43**. Multicoloured.

345	20c. Tharaka Meru woman	15	10
346	30c. Niger flautist	15	10
347	50c. Tunisian water-carrier	15	10
348	1f. Kano ceremonial (Nigeria)	15	10
349	3f. Mali troubador	25	15
350	5f. Quipongo, Angola women	40	25
351	50f. Mauritanian at prayer	2·00	80
352	90f. Sinehatiali dancers, Ivory Coast	3·25	1·60

58 Footballer attacking Goal

1970. World Cup Football Championship, Mexico.

353	**58**	20c. multicoloured	15	10
354	-	30c. multicoloured	15	10
355	-	50c. multicoloured	15	10
356	-	1f. multicoloured	15	10
357	-	6f. multicoloured	25	15
358	-	18f. multicoloured	75	25
359	-	30f. multicoloured	1·50	80
360	-	90f. multicoloured	3·25	1·60

Nos. 354/60 show footballers in various positions, similar to Type **58**.

59 Flowers and Green Peafowl

1970. "EXPO 70", World Fair, Osaka, Japan. Multicoloured.

361	20c. Type **59**	15	10
362	30c. Torii gate and "Hibiscus" (Yashuda)	15	10
363	50c. Dancer and "Musician" (Katayama)	15	10
364	1f. Sun Tower and "Warrior"	15	10
365	3f. House and "Seated Buddha"	15	10
366	5f. Pagoda and "Head of Girl" (Yamakawa)	25	15
367	20f. Greeting and "Imperial Palace"	90	65
368	70f. Expo emblem and "Horseman"	2·75	1·60

60 Two Young Gorillas

1970. Gorillas of the Mountains.

369	**60**	20c. black and green	15	10
370	-	40c. black, brown & purple	25	15
371	-	60c. black, blue and brown	40	25
372	-	80c. black, orange & brown	50	35
373	-	1f. black and mauve	65	40
374	-	2f. multicoloured	1·30	65
375	-	15f. black and sepia	3·25	1·60
376	-	100f. black, brown and blue	7·50	3·00

GORILLA—VERT: 40c. Squatting; 80c. Beating chest; 2f. Eating banana; 100f. With young. HORIZ: 60c. Walking; 1f. With family; 15f. Heads.

61 Cinchona Bark

1970. 150th Anniv of Discovery of Quinine. Multicoloured.

377	20c. Type **61**	15	10
378	80c. Pharmaceutical equipment	15	10
379	1f. Anopheles mosquito	15	10
380	3f. Malaria patient and nurse	25	15
381	25f. "Attack" on mosquito	1·30	40
382	70f. Pelletier and Caventou (discoverers of quinine)	3·25	1·00

62 Rocket in Flight

1970. Moon Missions. Multicoloured.

383	20c. Type **62**	15	10
384	30c. Separation during orbit	15	10
385	50c. Spaceship above the moon	15	10
386	1f. Module and astonauts on moon	25	15
387	3f. Take-off from the moon	40	20
388	5f. Return journey to earth	65	25
389	10f. Final separation before landing	1·30	50
390	80f. Splashdown	3·50	2·00

63 F. D. Roosevelt and "Brasscattleya olympia alba"

1970. 25th Death Anniv of F. D. Roosevelt. Portraits and Orchids.

391	**63**	20c. brown, blue and black	15	10
392	-	30c. brown, red and black	15	10
393	-	50c. brown, orange & black	25	15
394	-	1f. brown, green and black	40	25
395	-	2f. green, brown and black	50	40
396	-	6f. green, purple and black	65	50
397	-	30f. green, blue and black	1·50	1·00
398	-	60f. green, red and black	2·75	1·30

ORCHIDS: 30c. "Laeliocattleya callistoglossa"; 50c. "Chondrorrhyncha chestertoni"; 1f. "Paphiopedilum"; 2f. "Cymbidium hybride"; 6f. "Cattleya labiata"; 30f. "Dendrobium nobile"; 60f. "Laelia gouldiana".

1970. Christmas. Miniature sheet 72×85 mm containing single stamp as T **52** but vert.

MS399	100f. blue DESIGN: "Adoration of the Shepherds" (Juan de Ribera)	4·50	4·25

65 Pope Paul VI

1970. Centenary of First Vatican Council.

400	**65**	10c. brown and gold	15	10
401	-	20c. green and gold	25	15
402	-	30c. lake and gold	40	20
403	-	40c. blue and gold	50	25
404	-	1f. violet and gold	65	35
405	-	18f. purple and gold	1·30	50
406	-	20f. orange and gold	1·50	65
407	-	60f. brown and gold	3·25	1·30

POPES: 20c. John XXIII; 30c. Pius XII; 40c. Pius XI; 1f. Benedict XV; 18f. Pius X; 20f. Leo XIII; 60f. Pius IX.

1971. African Headdresses (2nd series). Mult. As T **47**.

408	20c. Rendille woman	15	10
409	30c. Chad woman	15	10
410	50c. Bororo man (Niger)	15	10
411	1f. Masai man (Kenya)	25	15
412	5f. Air girl (Niger)	40	20
413	18f. Rwanda woman	75	40
414	25f. Mauritania man	1·50	50
415	50f. Rwanda girls	3·00	1·00

CHARLES de GAULLE
100F
REPUBLIQUE
RWANDAISE

66 General de Gaulle

1971. De Gaulle Commemoration. Miniature sheet 70×80 mm.

MS416	**66**	100f. blue	5·00	4·75

1971. Moon Mission of Apollo 14. As No. **MS**307 but colour changed and additionally inscr "APOLLO 14".

MS417	**49**	100f. brown and red	12·50	12·00

68 "Beethoven" (C. Horneman)

1971. Birth Cent (1970) of Beethoven. Portraits and funeral scene by various artists. Mult.

418	20c. Type **68**	15	10
419	30c. K. Stieler	15	10
420	50c. F. Schimon	15	10
421	3f. H. Best	40	25
422	6f. W. Fassbender	65	40
423	90f. "Beethoven's Burial" (Stober)	3·75	2·75

69 Horse-jumping

1971. Olympic Games, Munich (1972) (1st issue).

424	**69**	20c. gold and black	15	10
425	-	30c. gold and purple	15	10

426	-	50c. gold and violet	15	10
427	-	1f. gold and green	15	10
428	-	8f. gold and red	25	15
429	-	10f. gold and violet	40	25
430	-	20f. gold and brown	75	40
431	-	60f. gold and green	2·10	1·00

DESIGNS: 30c. Running (start); 50c. Basketball; 1f. High-jumping; 8f. Boxing; 10f. Pole-vaulting; 20f. Wrestling; 60f. Gymnastics.

See also Nos. 490/7.

70 U.A.M.P.T. H.Q. and Rwandaise Woman and Child

1971. Air. Tenth Anniv of U.A.M.P.T.

432	**70**	100f. multicoloured	3·75	3·25

1971. Christmas. Miniature sheet 63×84 mm containing single stamp as T **52**, but vert.

MS433	100f. blue	5·00	4·75

DESIGN: "The Nativity" (Van Dyck).

72 "Durer" (self-portrait)

1971. 500th Birth Anniv of Durer. Paintings. Multicoloured.

434	20c. "Adam"	15	10
435	30c. "Eve"	15	10
436	50c. "Portrait of H. Holzschuher"	15	10
437	1f. "Mourning the Dead Christ"	25	15
438	3f. "Madonna and Child"	40	20
439	5f. "St. Eustace"	65	25
440	20f. "St. Paul and St. Mark"	1·00	40
441	70f. Type **72**	2·50	2·20

73 Astronauts in Moon Rover

1972. Moon Mission of "Apollo 15".

442	**73**	600f. gold	£160

74 Participation in Sport

1972. National Guard. Multicoloured.

443	4f. Type **74**	15	10
444	6f. Transport of emergency supplies	25	15
445	15f. Helicopter transport for the sick	65	25
446	25f. Participation in health service	1·00	80
447	50f. Guard, map and emblem (vert)	2·50	2·00

75 Ice Hockey

1972. Winter Olympic Games, Sapporo, Japan. Multicoloured.

448	20c. Type **75**	15	10
449	30c. Speed-skating	15	10
450	50c. Ski-jumping	15	10
451	1f. Figure skating	15	10
452	6f. Cross-country skiing	15	10
453	12f. Slalom	40	25
454	20f. Tobogganing	75	40
455	60f. Downhill skiing	2·30	2·10

76 Savanna Monkey and Impala

1972. Akagera National Park. Multicoloured.

456	20c. Type **76**	25	15
457	30c. African buffalo	40	25
458	50c. Common zebra	50	40
459	1f. White rhinoceros	65	50
460	2f. Warthogs	75	65
461	6f. Hippopotamus	1·00	90
462	18f. Spotted hyenas	1·50	1·30
463	32f. Helmeted guineafowl	2·30	1·60
464	60f. Waterbucks	3·25	2·00
465	80f. Lion and lioness	3·50	2·30

77 Family supporting Flag

1972. Tenth Anniv of Referendum.

466	**77**	6f. multicoloured	15	10
467	**77**	18f. multicoloured	75	50
468	**77**	60f. multicoloured	2·10	2·00

78 Variable Sunbirds

1972. Rwanda Birds. Multicoloured.

469	20c. Common waxbills	15	10
470	30c. Collared sunbird	15	10
471	50c. Type **78**	15	10
472	1f. Greater double-collared sunbird	15	10
473	4f. Ruwenzori puff-back flycatcher	40	25
474	6f. Red-billed fire finch	50	40
475	10f. Scarlet-chested sunbird	65	45
476	18f. Red-headed quelea	1·00	50
477	60f. Black-headed gonolek	3·75	2·10
478	100f. African golden oriole	5·75	3·75

79 King Baudouin and Queen Fabiola with President and Mrs. Kayibanda in Rwanda

1972. "Belgica 72" Stamp Exhibition, Brussels.

479	-	18f. multicoloured	1·50	1·40
480	-	22f. multicoloured	2·30	2·20
481	**79**	40f. blue, black and gold	3·75	3·50

DESIGNS: 18f. Rwanda village; 22f. View of Bruges. Nos. 479/80 are smaller, size 39×36 mm.

80 Announcement of Independence

1972. Tenth Anniv of Independence.

482	**80**	20c. green and gold	15	10
483	-	30c. purple and gold	15	10
484	-	50c. sepia and gold	15	10
485	-	6f. blue and gold	15	10
486	-	10f. purple and gold	40	25
487	-	15f. blue and gold	50	40
488	-	18f. brown and gold	75	65
489	-	50f. green and gold	1·90	1·40

DESIGNS—HORIZ: 30c. Promotion ceremony, officers of the National Guard; 50c. Pres. Kayibanda, wife and family; 6f. Pres. Kayibanda casting vote in legislative elections; 10f. Pres. and Mrs. Kayibanda at "Festival of Justice"; 15f. President and members of National Assembly; 18f. Investiture of Pres. Kayibanda. VERT: 50f. President Kayibanda.

81 Horse-jumping

1972. Olympic Games, Munich (2nd issue).

490	**81**	20c. green and gold	15	10
491	-	30c. violet and gold	15	10
492	-	50c. green and gold	15	10
493	-	1f. purple and gold	15	10
494	-	6f. black and gold	25	15
495	-	18f. brown and gold	65	50
496	-	30f. violet and gold	1·50	90
497	-	44f. blue and gold	2·30	1·30

DESIGNS: 30c. Hockey; 50c. Football; 1f. Long-jumping; 6f. Cycling; 18f. Yachting; 30f. Hurdling; 44f. Gymnastics.

82 Runners

1972. Racial Equality Year. "Working Together". Multicoloured.

498	20c. Type **82**	15	10
499	30c. Musicians	15	10
500	50c. Ballet dancers	15	10
501	1f. Medical team in operating theatre	15	10
502	6f. Weaver and painter	25	15
503	18f. Children in class	65	50
504	24f. Laboratory technicians	1·00	80
505	50f. U.N. emblem and hands of four races	1·90	1·40

1972. Christmas. Miniature sheet 91×107 mm containing single stamp as T **52**, but vert. Perf or imperf.

MS506	100f. brown	5·00	4·75

DESIGN: "Adoration of the Shepherds" (J. Jordaens).

84 "Phymateus brunneri"

1973. Rwanda Insects. Multicoloured.

507	20c. Type **84**	15	10
508	30c. "Diopsis fumipennis" (vert)	15	10
509	50c. "Kitoko alberti"	15	10
510	1f. "Archibracon fasciatus" (vert)	15	10
511	2f. "Ornithacris cyanea imperialis"	25	15
512	6f. "Clitodaca fenestralis" (vert)	50	25
513	18f. "Senaspis oesacus"	1·00	40
514	22f. "Phonoctonus grandis" (vert)	1·50	1·00
515	70f. "Loba leopardina"	3·75	2·75
516	100f. "Ceratocoris distortus" (vert)	6·25	4·50

MS517	101×80 mm. 80f. "Phymateus brunneri" (size 44×35 mm)	9·50	9·25

85 "Emile Zola" (Manet)

1973. International Book Year. "Readers and Writers". Paintings and portraits. Multicoloured.

518	20c. Type **85**	15	10
519	30c. "Rembrandt's Mother" (Rembrandt)	15	10
520	50c. "St. Jerome removing Thorn from Lion's paw" (Colantonio)	15	10
521	1f. "St. Peter and St. Paul" (El Greco)	15	10
522	2f. "Virgin and Child" (Van der Weyden)	15	10
523	6f. "St. Jerome in his Cell" (Antonella de Messina)	25	15
524	40f. "St. Barbara" (Master of Flemalle)	1·80	1·40
525	100f. "Don Quixote" (O. Bonnevalle)	3·75	3·25

MS526	70×80 mm. 100f. Pres. Kayibanda	5·00	4·75

86 Longombe

1973. Musical Instruments. Multicoloured.

527	20c. Type **86**	15	10
528	30c. Horn	15	10
529	50c. "Xylophone"	15	10
530	1f. "Harp"	20	10
531	4f. Alur horns	25	15
532	6f. Horn, bells and drum	40	20
533	18f. Drums	65	40
534	90f. Gourds	3·75	2·75

87 "Rubens and Isabelle Brandt" (Rubens)

1973. "IBRA" Stamp Exhibition, Munich. Famous Paintings. Multicoloured.

535	20c. Type **87**	15	10
536	30c. "Portrait of a Lady" (Cranach the Younger)	15	10
537	50c. "Woman peeling Turnips" (Chardin)	15	10
538	1f. "Abduction of the Daughters of Leucippe" (Rubens)	15	10
539	2f. "Virgin and Child" (Lippi)	15	10
540	6f. "Boys eating Fruit" (Murillo)	25	15
541	40f. "The Sickness of Love" (Steen)	1·60	1·00
542	100f. "Jesus divested of His Garments" (El Greco)	3·75	3·25

MS543	75×90 mm. 100f. "Oswalt Krel" (Durer)	5·00	4·75

88 Map of Africa and Doves

1973. Tenth Anniv of O.A.U. Multicoloured.

544	6f. Type **88**	40	25
545	94f. Map of Africa and hands	3·50	3·25

1973. Pan-African Drought Relief. Nos. 308/13 and 315 optd **SECHERESSE SOLIDARITE AFRICAINE** and No. 315 additionally surch.

546	**50**	20c. multicoloured	15	10
547	-	40c. multicoloured	15	10
548	-	60c. multicoloured	15	10
549	-	80c. multicoloured	15	10
550	-	3f. multicoloured	15	10
551	-	75f. multicoloured	4·00	4·00
552	-	100f.+50f. multicoloured	8·25	8·00

90 Six-banded Distichodus

1973. Fish. Multicoloured.

553	20c. Type **90**	15	10
554	30c. Lesser tigerfish	15	10
555	50c. Angel squeaker	15	10
556	1f. Nile mouthbrooder	15	10
557	2f. African lungfish	25	15
558	6f. Mandeville's catfish	40	25
559	40f. Congo tetra	2·30	1·30
560	150f. Golden julie	7·50	5·25
MS561	90×70 mm **90** 100f.	7·00	6·75

91 Crane with Letter and Telecommunications Emblem

1973. 12th Anniv of U.A.M.P.T.

562	**91**	100f. blue, brown and mauve	4·50	2·50

1973. African Fortnight, Brussels. Nos. 408/15 optd **QUINZAINE AFRICAINE BRUXELLES 15/30 SEPT. 1973** and globe.

563	20c. multicoloured	15	10
564	30c. multicoloured	15	10
565	50c. multicoloured	15	10
566	1f. multicoloured	15	10
567	5f. multicoloured	15	10
568	18f. multicoloured	65	50
569	25f. multicoloured	1·50	1·00
570	50f. multicoloured	3·00	2·00

1973. Air. Congress of French-speaking Nations, Liege. No. 432 optd **LIEGE ACCUEILLE LES PAYS DE LANGUE FRANCAISE 1973** (No. 562) or congress emblem (No. 563).

571	100f. multicoloured	5·75	5·25
572	100f. multicoloured	5·75	5·25

1973. 13th Europa Stamp Exhibition, Naples. No. **MS**344 optd **NAPLES 1973**.

MS573	**56**	100f. purple	19·00	18·00

1973. 25th Anniv of Declaration of Human Rights. Nos. 443/7 optd with Human Rights emblem.

574	**74**	4f. multicoloured	15	10
575	-	6f. multicoloured	25	15
576	-	15f. multicoloured	65	40
577	-	25f. multicoloured	1·30	65
578	-	50f. multicoloured	2·50	1·60

1973. Christmas. Miniature sheet 102×87 mm containing single stamp as T **52**.

MS579	100f. violet	2·00	1·90

DESIGN: "Adoration of the Shepherds" (Giido Reni)

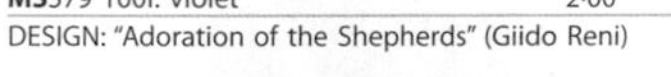

96 Copernicus and Astrolabe

1973. 500th Birth Anniv of Copernicus. Multicoloured.

580	20c. Type **96**	15	10
581	30c. Copernicus	15	10
582	50c. Copernicus and heliocentric system	15	10
583	1f. Type **96**	25	15
584	18f. As 30c.	1·30	80
585	80f. As 50c.	3·75	3·25
MS586	75×81 mm. 100f. As 30c	5·75	5·50

97 Pres. Habyarimana

1974. "New Regime".

587	**97**	1f. brown, black and buff	15	10
588	**97**	2f. brown, black and blue	15	10
589	**97**	5f. brown, black and red	15	10
590	**97**	6f. brown, black and blue	15	10
591	**97**	26f. brown, black and lilac	90	80
592	**97**	60f. brown, black and green	2·50	2·20

98 "Christ between the Two Thieves" (Rubens)

1974. Easter. Miniature sheet 92×77 mm.

MS593	**98**	100f. sepia	12·50	12·00

99 Yugoslavia v Zaire

1974. World Cup Football Championship, West Germany. Players represent specified teams. Multicoloured.

594	20c. Type **99**	15	10
595	40c. Netherlands v Sweden	15	10
596	60c. West Germany v Australia	15	10
597	80c. Haiti v Argentina	15	10
598	2f. Brazil v Scotland	25	15
599	6f. Bulgaria v Uruguay	50	25
600	40f. Italy v Poland	1·90	1·00
601	50f. Chile v East Germany	2·50	2·00

100 Marconi's Steam Yacht "Elettra"

1974. Birth Centenary of Guglielmo Marconi (radio pioneer). Multicoloured.

602	20c. Type **100**	15	10
603	30c. Cruiser "Carlo Alberto"	15	10
604	50c. Marconi's telegraph equipment	15	10
605	4f. "Global Telecommunications"	15	10
606	35f. Early radio receiver	1·40	1·00
607	60f. Marconi and Poldhu radio station	2·50	2·30
MS608	95×70 mm. 50f. Type **100**	3·25	3·00

101 "Diane de Poiters" (Fontainebleau School)

1974. International Stamp Exhibitions "Stockholmia" and "Internaba". Paintings from Stockholm and Basle. Multicoloured.

609	20c. Type **101**	15	10
610	30c. "The Flute-player" (J. Leyster)	15	10
611	50c. "Virgin Mary and Child" (G. David)	15	10
612	1f. "The Triumph of Venus" (F. Boucher)	15	10
613	10f. "Harlequin Seated" (P. Picasso)	25	15
614	18f. "Virgin and Child" (15th-century)	65	50
615	20f. "The Beheading of St. John" (H. Fries)	90	65
616	50f. "The Daughter of Andersdotter" (J. Hockert)	2·10	2·00
MS617	Six sheets each 86×73 mm. Each sheet contains two designs as Nos. 609/16 but with face values of 15f. for each stamp. Designs as Nos. 609, 611, 612 and 514 occur twice in the set of six stamps	11·50	11·00
MS618	One sheet 86×117 mm. As Nos. 610, 612, 614 and 616 but each stamp with a face value of 25f	6·25	6·00

102 Monastic Messenger

1974. Centenary of U.P.U. Multicoloured.

619	20c. Type **102**	15	10
620	30c. Inca messenger	15	10
621	50c. Moroccan postman	15	10
622	1f. Indian postman	15	10
623	18f. Polynesian postman	1·00	65
624	80f. Early Rwanda messenger with horn and drum	3·25	2·75

1974. 15th Anniv of Revolution. Nos. 316/18 optd **1974 15e ANNIVERSAIRE**.

625	**51**	6f. multicoloured	7·50	5·75
626	**51**	18f. multicoloured	7·50	5·75
627	**51**	40f. multicoloured	7·50	5·75

1974. Christmas. Miniature sheet 106×90 mm containing single stamp as T **52**.

MS628	100f. green	11·50	11·00

DESIGN: "Adoration of the Magi"

1974. Tenth Anniv of African Development Bank. Nos. 305/6 optd **1974 10e ANNIVERSAIRE**.

629	**48**	30f. multicoloured	1·50	1·40
630	-	70f. multicoloured	3·25	2·75

105 Head of Uganda Kob

1975. Antelopes. Multicoloured.

631	20c. Type **105**	25	15
632	30c. Bongo with calf (horiz)	40	20
633	50c. Roan antelope and sable antelope heads	65	25
634	1f. Young sitatungas (horiz)	1·00	40
635	4f. Great kudu	1·30	50
636	10f. Impala family (horiz)	2·50	1·00
637	34f. Waterbuck head	3·75	1·70
638	100f. Giant eland (horiz)	9·50	3·75
MS639	Two sheets each 125×90 mm. (a) 40f. Impala; (b) 60f. Great kudu	40·00	36·00

106 "The Deposition" (Raphael)

1975. Easter. Four sheets 130×89 mm each containing single stamps as T **106**. Multicoloured.

MS640	(a) 20f. Type **106**; (b) 30f. "Pieta" (Cranach the Elder); (c) 50f. "Oleta" (Van der Weyden); (d) "Pieta" (Lopez)	15·00	14·50

107 "Prince Carlos Balthezar" (Velazquez)

1975. Espana 75 International Stamp Exhibition, Madrid. Four sheets 89×130 mm each containing single stamp as T **107**. Multicoloured.

MS641	(a) 20f. Type **107**; (b) 30f. "Princess Margarita of Austria" (Velazquez); (c) 50f. "The Divine Shepherd" (Murillo); (d) 100f. "Francisco Goya" (Lopez)	15·00	14·50

108 Pyrethrum Daisies

1975. Agricultural Labour Year. Multicoloured.

642	20c. Type **108**	15	10
643	30c. Tea plant	15	10
644	50c. Coffee berries	15	10
645	4f. Bananas	15	10
646	10f. Maize	40	15
647	12f. Sorghum	50	20
648	26f. Rice	1·40	65
649	47f. Coffee cultivation	2·30	2·00
MS650	Two sheets 56×78 mm. (a) 25f. As 50c.; (b) 75f. As 47f	6·25	6·00

1975. Arphila 75 International Stamp Exhibition, Paris. Two sheets 89×130 mm each containing single stamp as T **107**. Multicoloured.

MS651	(a) 75f. "Louis XIV" (Rigaud); (b) 125f. "Hussar Officer on Horseback" (Gericault)	15·00	14·50

1975. Holy Year. Nos. 400/7 optd **1975 ANNEE SAINTE**.

652	**65**	10c. brown and gold	15	10
653	-	20c. green and gold	15	10
654	-	30c. lake and gold	15	10
655	-	40c. blue and gold	15	10
656	-	1f. violet and gold	15	10
657	-	18f. purple and gold	75	65
658	-	20f. orange and gold	1·30	1·00
659	-	60f. brown and gold	3·00	2·75

110 Eastern White Pelicans

1975. Aquatic Birds. Multicoloured.

660	20c. Type **110**	15	10
661	30c. Malachite kingfisher	15	10
662	50c. Goliath herons	15	10
663	1f. Saddle-bill stork	25	15
664	4f. African jacana	50	25
665	10f. African darter	1·00	40
666	34f. Sacred ibis	2·30	1·00
667	80f. Hartlaub's duck	5·00	3·75
MS668	Two sheets 131×89 mm each containing single stamp size 35×51 mm (a) 40f. Flamingoes; (b) 60f. Crowned cranes	29·00	28·00

111 Globe and Emblem

1975. World Population Year (1974). Multicoloured.

669	20f. Type **111**	75	65
670	26f. Population graph	1·10	1·00
671	34f. Symbolic doorway	1·50	1·30

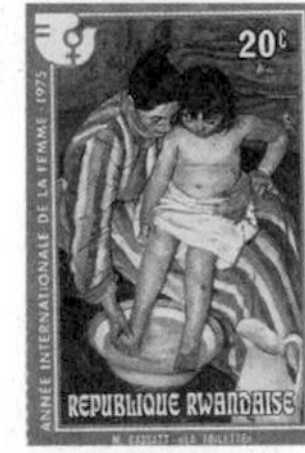

112 "La Toilette" (M. Cassatt)

1975. International Women's Year. Multicoloured.

672	20c. Type **112**	15	10
673	30c. "Mother and Child" (G. Melchers)	15	10
674	50c. "The Milk Jug" (Vermeer)	15	10
675	1f. "The Water-carrier" (Goya)	25	15
676	8f. Coffee picking	40	25
677	12f. Laboratory technician	50	40
678	18f. Rwandaise mother and child	1·00	80
679	60f. Woman carrying water jug	3·00	2·50
MS680	Two sheets each 89×130 mm. (a) 25f. "Empress Josephine" (Prud'hon); (b) 40f. "Madame Vigee-Lebrun and Daughter" (self-portrait)	£150	£140

113 "Arts"

1975. Tenth Anniv of National University. The Faculties. Multicoloured.

681	20c. Type **113**	15	10
682	30c. "Medicine"	15	10
683	1f.50 "Jurisprudence"	15	10
684	18f. "Science"	65	25

685		26f. "Commerce"	1·00	80
686		34f. University Building, Kigali	1·80	1·20

1975. 300th Death Anniv of Jan Vermeer (painter). Four sheets 130×89 mm each containing single stamp as T **107**. Multicoloured.

MS687 (a) 20f. "Man and Woman drinking Wine" (detail); (b) 30f. "Woman reading letter"; (c) 50f. "The Painter in his Studio" (detail, showing model); (d) 100f. "Young Woman playing Virginals" 15·00 14·50

114 Cattle at Pool, and "Impatiens stuhlmannii"

1975. Protection of Nature. Multicoloured.

688		20c. Type **114**	15	10
689		30c. Euphorbis "candelabra" and savannah bush	15	10
690		50c. Bush fire and "Tapinanthus prunifolius"	15	10
691		5f. Lake Bulera and "Nymphaea lotus"	15	10
692		8f. Soil erosion and "Protea madiensis"	25	15
693		10f. Protected marshland and "Melanthera brownei"	40	25
694		26f. Giant lobelias and groundsel	1·10	1·00
695		100f. Sabyinyo volcano and "Polystachya kermesina"	4·00	3·75

1975. Pan-African Drought Relief. Nos. 345/52 optd or surch **SECHERESSE SOLIDARITE 1975** (both words share same initial letter).

696		20c. multicoloured	15	10
697		30c. multicoloured	15	10
698		50c. multicoloured	15	10
699		1f. multicoloured	15	10
700		3f. multicoloured	15	10
701		5f. multicoloured	25	15
702		50f.+25f. multicoloured	3·25	3·00
703		90f.+25f. multicoloured	4·00	3·75

116 Loading Douglas DC-8F Jet Trader

1975. Year of Increased Production. Multicoloured.

704		20c. Type **116**	15	10
705		30c. Coffee-picking plant	15	10
706		50c. Lathe operator	15	10
707		10f. Farmer with hoe (vert)	40	25
708		35f. Coffee-picking (vert)	1·10	65
709		54f. Mechanical plough	2·10	1·30

117 African Woman with Basket on Head

1975. "Themabelga" Stamp Exhibition, Brussels. African Costumes.

710	**117**	20c. multicoloured	15	10
711	-	30c. multicoloured	15	10
712	-	50c. multicoloured	15	10
713	-	1f. multicoloured	25	15
714	-	5f. multicoloured	40	25
715	-	7f. multicoloured	50	40
716	-	35f. multicoloured	1·50	80
717	-	51f. multicoloured	2·30	2·30

DESIGNS: 30c. to 51f. Various Rwanda costumes.

1975. Christmas. Miniature sheet 106×90 mm containing single stamp as T **52**.

MS718 100f. mauve 7·50 7·25

DESIGN: "Adoration of the Magi".

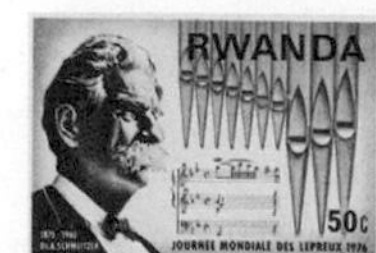

118 Dr. Schweitzer, Organ Pipes and Music Score

1976. World Leprosy Day.

719	-	20c. lilac, brown and black	15	10
720	-	30c. lilac, green and black	15	10
721	**118**	50c. lilac, brown and black	15	10
722	-	1f. lilac, purple and black	15	10
723	-	3f. lilac, blue and black	20	10
724	-	5f. lilac, brown and black	25	15
725	**118**	10f. lilac, blue and black	50	25
726	-	80f. lilac, red and black	3·75	2·75

DESIGNS: Dr. Schweitzer and: 20c. Piano keyboard and music; 30c. Lambarene Hospital; 1f. Lambarene residence; 3f. as 20c.; 5f. as 30 c; 80f. as 1f.

119 "Surrender at Yorktown"

1976. Bicentenary of American Revolution. Multicoloured.

727		20c. Type **119**	15	10
728		30c. "The Sergeant-Instructor at Valley Forge"	15	10
729		50c. "Presentation of Captured Yorktown Flags to Congress"	15	10
730		1f. "Washington at Fort Lee"	15	10
731		18f. "Washington boarding a British warship"	65	40
732		26f. "Washington studying Battle plans"	1·00	50
733		34f. "Washington firing a Cannon"	1·50	1·00
734		40f. "Crossing the Delaware"	2·00	1·60

MS735 108×90 mm. 100f. "Ships "Bonhomme", "Richard" and "Serapis" in Battle" 5·75 5·50

120 Sister Yohana

1976. 75th Anniv of Catholic Church in Rwanda. Multicoloured.

736		20c. Type **120**	15	10
737		30c. Abdon Sabakati	15	10
738		50c. Father Alphonse Brard	20	10
739		4f. Abbe Balthazar Gafuku	25	15
740		10f. Monseigneur Bigirumwami	40	25
741		25f. Save Catholic Church (horiz)	90	40
742		60f. Kabgayi Catholic Cathedral (horiz)	1·90	1·30

121 Yachting

1976. Olympic Games, Montreal (1st issue).

743	**121**	20c. brown and green	15	10
744	-	30c. blue and green	15	10
745	-	50c. black and green	15	10
746	-	1f. violet and green	20	15
747	-	10f. blue and green	40	25
748	-	18f. brown and green	65	40
749	-	29f. purple and green	1·30	80
750	-	51f. deep green and green	1·80	1·30

DESIGNS: 30c. Horse-jumping; 50c. Long jumping; 1f. Hockey; 10f. Swimming; 18f. Football; 29f. Boxing; 51f. Gymnastics.

See also Nos. 767/74.

122 Bell's Experimental Telephone and Manual Switchboard

1976. Telephone Centenary.

751	**122**	20c. brown and blue	15	10
752	-	30c. blue and violet	15	10
753	-	50c. brown and blue	15	10
754	-	1f. orange and blue	20	10
755	-	4f. mauve and blue	25	15
756	-	8f. green and blue	50	25
757	-	26f. red and blue	1·30	90
758	-	60f. lilac and blue	2·30	1·60

DESIGNS: 30c. Early telephone and man making call; 50c. Early telephone and woman making call; 1f. Early telephone and exchange building; 4f. Alexander Graham Bell and "candlestick" telephone; 8f. Rwanda subscriber and dial telephone; 26f. Dish aerial, satellite and modern handset; 60f. Rwanda PTT building, operator and push-button telephone.

1976. Bicentenary of Declaration of American Independence. Nos. 727/34 optd **INDEPENDENCE DAY** and Bicentennial Emblem.

759	**119**	20c. multicoloured	15	10
760	-	30c. multicoloured	15	10
761	-	50c. multicoloured	20	10
762	-	1f. multicoloured	25	15
763	-	18f. multicoloured	75	40
764	-	26f. multicoloured	1·00	65
765	-	34f. multicoloured	1·40	1·00
766	-	40f. multicoloured	1·50	1·30

124 Football

1976. Olympic Games, Montreal (2nd issue). Multicoloured.

767		20c. Type **124**	15	10
768		30c. Rifle-shooting	15	10
769		50c. Canoeing	20	10
770		1f. Gymnastics	25	15
771		10f. Weightlifting	40	25
772		12f. Diving	50	35
773		26f. Horse-riding	1·00	80
774		50f. Throwing the hammer	2·30	1·60

MS775 190×60 mm containing four stamps in horiz strip: 20f. Start of race; 30f. Running; 40f. leaping hurdle; 60f. Breasting tape (all horiz) 7·00 6·75

125 "Apollo" and "Soyuz" Launches and ASTP Badge

1976. "Apollo"–"Soyuz" Test Project. Multicoloured.

776		20c. Type **125**	15	10
777		30c. "Soyuz" rocket	15	10
778		50c. "Apollo" rocket	20	10
779		1f. "Apollo" after separation	25	15
780		2f. Approach to link-up	40	20
781		12f. Spacecraft docked	1·30	65
782		30f. Sectional view of interiors	2·75	1·60
783		54f. "Apollo" splashdown	3·75	2·30

126 "Eulophia cucullata"

1976. Rwandaise Orchids. Multicoloured.

784		20c. Type **126**	15	10
785		30c. "Eulophia streptopetala"	15	10
786		50c. "Disa stairsii"	20	10
787		1f. "Aerangis kotschyana"	25	15
788		10f. "Eulophia abyssinica"	75	50
789		12f. "Bonatea steudneri"	1·00	65
790		26f. "Ansellia gigantea"	2·00	1·00
791		50f. "Eulophia angolensis"	3·75	2·00

1976. Christmas. Miniature sheet 109×90 mm containing single stamp as T **52**.

MS792 100f. blue 6·25 6·00

DESIGN: "The Nativity" (Francois Boucher).

1977. World Leprosy Day. Nos. 719/26 optd with **JOURNEE MONDIALE 1977**.

793	-	20c. lilac, brown and black	15	10
794	-	30c. lilac, green and black	15	10
795	**118**	50c. lilac, brown and black	15	10
796	-	1f. lilac, purple and black	15	10
797	-	3f. lilac, blue and black	20	10
798	-	5f. lilac, brown and black	25	15
799	**118**	10f. lilac, brown and black	50	40
800	-	80f. lilac, red and black	3·00	2·50

128 Hands embracing "Cultural Collaboration"

1977. Tenth OCAM Summit Meeting, Kigali. Multicoloured.

801		10f. Type **128**	40	25
802		26f. Hands embracing "Technical Collaboration"	1·00	80
803		64f. Hands embracing "Economic Collaboration"	1·80	1·30

129 "Christ Crucified" (Rubens)

1977. Easter. Two sheets each 89×129 mm. Multicoloured.

MS804 (a) 25f. Type **129**; (b) 75f. "Christ on the Straw" (Rubens) 17·00 16·00

1977. World Water Conference. Nos. 688/95 optd **CONFERENCE MONDIALE DE L'EAU**.

805	**114**	20c. multicoloured	15	10
806	-	30c. multicoloured	15	10
807	-	50c. multicoloured	20	10
808	-	5f. multicoloured	25	15
809	-	8f. multicoloured	50	40
810	-	10f. multicoloured	65	50
811	-	26f. multicoloured	1·90	1·30
812	-	100f. multicoloured	5·75	5·25

131 Roman Signal Post and African Tam-Tam

1977. World Telecommunications Day. Multicoloured.

813		20c. Type **131**	15	10
814		30c. Chappe's semaphore and post-rider	15	10
815		50c. Morse code	15	10
816		1f. "Goliath" laying Channel cable	20	10
817		4f. Telephone, radio and television	25	15
818		18f. "Kingsport" and maritime communications satellite	75	65
819		26f. Telecommunications satellite and aerial	1·30	1·00
820		50f. "Mariner 2" satellite	2·30	2·10

1977. Amphilex 77 International Stamp Exhibition, Amsterdam. Two sheets each 129×99 mm containing vert designs as T **107**. Multicoloured.

MS822 (a) 40f. "The Night Watch" (Raphael); (b) 60f. "The Port of Amsterdam" (Willem van der Velde the Junior) 10·00 9·75

132 "The Ascent to Calvary" (detail)

1977. 400th Birth Anniv of Peter Paul Rubens. Multicoloured.

823	20c. Type **132**	15	10
824	30c. "The Judgement of Paris" (horiz)	15	10
825	50c. "Marie de Medici, Queen of France"	25	15
826	1f. "Heads of Negroes" (horiz)	40	25
827	4f. "St. Idelfonse Triptych" (detail)	50	40
828	8f. "Helene Fourment with her Children" (horiz)	65	50
829	26f. "St. Idelfonse Triptych" (different detail)	1·50	1·30
830	60f. "Helene Fourment"	2·75	2·50

133 Chateau Sassenage, Grenoble

1977. Air. Tenth Anniv of International French Language Council.

831	**133**	50f. multicoloured	2·50	2·00

134 "Viking" on Mars

1977. "Viking" Mission to Mars. Miniature sheet 129×90 mm.

MS832	**134** 100f. multicoloured	44·00	43·00

135 Long-crested Eagle

1977. Birds of Prey. Multicoloured.

833	20c. Type **135**	15	10
834	30c. African harrier hawk	15	10
835	50c. African fish eagle	20	10
836	1f. Hooded vulture	25	15
837	3f. Augur buzzard	50	20
838	5f. Black kite	1·00	25
839	20f. Black-shouldered kite	2·30	1·40
840	100f. Bateleur	8·25	5·50

1912. Dr. Wernher von Braun Commemoration. Nos. 776/83 optd with in memoriam **WERNHER VON BRAUN 1912 - 1977**.

841	20c. Type **125**	15	10
842	30c. "Soyuz" rocket	15	10
843	50c. "Apollo" rocket	15	10
844	1f. "Apollo" after separation	20	10
845	2f. Approach to link up	25	15
846	12f. Spacecraft docked	1·00	65
847	30f. Sectional view of interiors	2·30	2·00
848	54f. "Apollo" after splashdown	4·75	4·00

1977. Espamer 77 Stamp Exhibition, Barcelona. No. **MS**641 optd **ESPAMER'77**.

MS849	Four sheets each 89×130 mm. (a) 20f.; (b) 30f.; (c) 50f.; (d) 100f	20·00	19·00

1977. Christmas. Miniature sheet 88×88 mm containing single stamp as T **52** but square 37×37 mm.

MS850	100f. violet	5·00	4·75

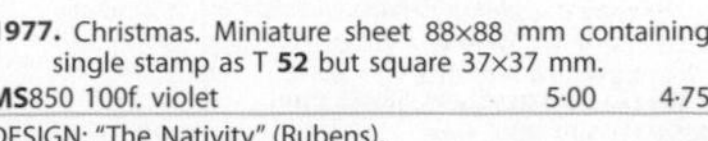
DESIGN: "The Nativity" (Rubens).

138 Scout playing Whistle

1978. Tenth Anniv of Rwanda Scout Association. Multicoloured.

851	20c. Type **138**	15	10
852	30c. Camp fire	15	10
853	50c. Scouts constructing a platform	20	10
854	1f. Two scouts	25	15
855	10f. Scouts on look-out	65	40
856	18f. Scouts in canoe	1·00	65
857	26f. Cooking at camp fire	1·50	1·00
858	44f. Lord Baden-Powell	2·50	2·00

139 Chimpanzees

1978. Apes. Multicoloured.

859	20c. Type **139**	15	10
860	30c. Gorilla	15	10
861	50c. Eastern black-and-white colobus	20	10
862	3f. Eastern needle-clawed bushbaby	25	15
863	10f. Mona monkey	80	70
864	26f. Potto	1·60	1·40
865	60f. Savanna monkey	3·75	3·50
866	150f. Olive baboon	8·00	7·75

140 "Euporus strangulatus"

1978. Beetles. Multicoloured.

867	20c. Type **140**	15	10
868	30c. "Rhina afzelii" (vert)	15	10
869	50c. "Pentalobus palini"	15	10
870	3f. "Corynodes dejeani" (vert)	20	10
871	10f. "Mecynorhina torquata"	55	15
872	15f. "Mecocerus rhombeus" (vert)	80	40
873	20f. "Macrotoma serripes"	95	50
874	25f. "Neptunides stanleyi" (vert)	1·00	55
875	26f. "Petrognatha gigas"	1·10	65
876	100f. "Eudicella gralli" (vert)	6·25	3·00

141 Poling Boat across River of Poverty

1978. National Revolutionary Development Movement. Multicoloured.

877	4f. Type **141**	15	10
878	10f. Poling boat to right	25	15
879	26f. Type **141**	95	70
880	60f. As 10f.	2·00	1·40

142 Footballers, Cup and Flags of Netherlands and Peru

1978. World Cup Football Championship, Argentina. Multicoloured.

881	20c. Type **142**	15	10
882	30c. Flags of FIFA, Sweden and Spain	15	10
883	50c. Mascot and flags of Scotland and Iran	20	10
884	2f. Emblem and flags of West Germany and Tunisia	25	15
885	3f. Cup and flags of Italy and Hungary	40	30
886	10f. Flags of FIFA, Brazil and Austria	70	40
887	34f. Mascot and flags of Poland and Mexico	1·60	1·10
888	100f. Emblem and flags of Argentina and France	4·75	3·25

No. 883 shows the Union Jack.

143 Wright Brothers and Wright Flyer I, 1903

1978. Aviation History. Multicoloured.

889	20c. Type **143**	15	10
890	30c. Alberto Santos-Dumont and biplane "14 bis", 1906	15	10
891	50c. Henri Farman and Farman Voisin No. 1 bis, 1908	20	10
892	1f. Jan Olieslagers and Bleriot XI	25	15
893	3f. General Italo Balbo and Savoia S-17 flying boat, 1919	40	30
894	10f. Charles Lindbergh and "Spirit of St. Louis", 1927	70	40
895	55f. Hugo Junkers and Junkers Ju 52/3m, 1932	2·40	1·40
896	60f. Igor Sikorsky and Vought-Sikorsky VS-300 helicopter prototype	2·75	1·70
MS897	78×95 mm. 130f. "Concorde" (46×25 mm)	6·75	6·50

143a Great Spotted Woodpecker and Oldenburg 1852⅓sgr. Stamp

1978. Air. "Philexafrique" Stamp Exhibition, Libreville, Gabon and Int Stamp Fair, Essen, West Germany. Multicoloured.

898	30f. Type **143a**	1·90	1·40
899	30f. Greater kudu and Rwanda 1967 20c. stamp	1·90	1·40

144 "Adoration of the Magi" (Durer)

1978. Christmas. Sheet 64×84 mm.

MS900	**144** 200f. sepia	9·50	9·25

1978. 15th Anniv of Organization of African Unity. Nos. 544/5 optd **1963 1978**.

901	**88**	6f. multicoloured	25	15
902	-	94f. multicoloured	3·50	3·25

146 Spur-winged Goose and Mallard

1978. Stock Rearing Year. Multicoloured.

903	20c. Type **146**	15	10
904	30c. Goats (horiz)	15	10
905	50c. Chickens	20	10
906	4f. Rabbits (horiz)	25	15
907	5f. Pigs	40	20
908	15f. Common turkey (horiz)	1·10	40
909	50f. Sheep and cattle	2·75	1·70
910	75f. Bull (horiz)	4·00	2·75

147 "Papilio demodocus"

1979. Butterflies. Multicoloured.

911	20c. Type **147**	15	10
912	30c. "Precis octavia"	20	10
913	50c. "Charaxes smaragdalis caerulea"	40	30
914	4f. "Charaxes guderiana"	70	40
915	15f. "Colotis evippe"	1·40	55
916	30f. "Danaus limniace petiverana"	2·40	70
917	50f. "Byblia acheloia"	3·00	1·40
918	150f. "Utetheisa pulchella"	8·00	3·50

148 "Euphorbia grantii" and Women weaving

1979. "Philexafrique" Exhibition, Libreville. Multicoloured.

919	40f. Type **148**	2·00	1·40
920	60f. Drummers and "Intelsat" satellite	3·00	2·10

149 "Polyscias fulva"

1979. Trees. Multicoloured.

921	20c. Type **149**	15	10
922	30c. "Entandrophragma excelsum" (horiz)	15	10
923	50c. "Ilex mitis"	15	10
924	4f. "Kigelia africana" (horiz)	20	10
925	15f. "Ficus thonningi"	70	30
926	20f. "Acacia senegal" (horiz)	80	55
927	50f. "Symphonia globulifera"	2·00	1·10
928	110f. "Acacia sieberana" (horiz)	4·75	3·00

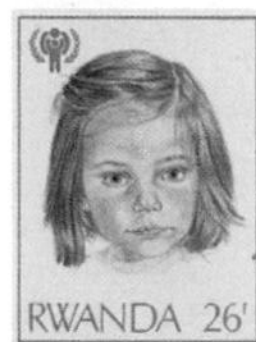

150 European Girl

1979. International Year of the Child. Each brown, gold and stone.

929	26f. Type **150**	1·20	85
930	26f. Asian	1·20	85
931	26f. Eskimo	1·20	85
932	26f. Asian boy	1·20	85
933	26f. African	1·20	85
934	26f. South American Indian	1·20	85
935	26f. Polynesian	1·20	85
936	26f. European girl (different)	1·20	85
937	42f. European and African (horiz)	2·40	1·70
MS938	62×76 mm. 100f. Children of different races (29×41 mm)	6·75	6·50

151 Basket Weaving

1979. Handicrafts. Multicoloured.

939	50c. Type **151**	15	10
940	1f.50 Wood-carving (vert)	15	10
941	2f. Metal working	20	10
942	10f. Basket work (vert)	70	30
943	20f. Basket weaving (different)	1·00	55
944	26f. Mural painting (vert)	1·40	70
945	40f. Pottery	2·75	1·40
946	100f. Smelting (vert)	5·50	2·20

152 Children lighting Christmas Tree Candle

1979. Christmas. Sheet 85×65 mm.

MS947	**152** 200f. ultramarine	10·00	9·75

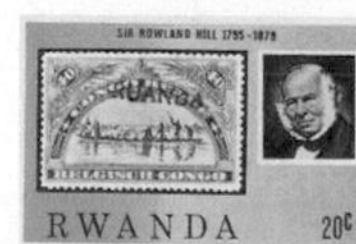

153 Rowland Hill and 40c. Ruanda Stamp of 1916

1979. Death Centenary of Sir Rowland Hill. Multicoloured.

948 20c. Type **153** 15 10
949 30c. 1916 Occupation stamp 15 10
950 50c. 1918 "A.O." overprint 15 10
951 3f. 1925 overprinted 60c. stamp 20 10
952 10f. 1931 50c. African buffalo stamp 40 15
953 26f. 1942 20f. Common zebra stamp 1·10 40
954 60f. 1953 25f. Protea stamp 2·75 1·70
955 100f. 1960 Olympic stamp 4·75 2·20

154 Strange Weaver

1980. Birds. Multicoloured.

956 20c. Type **154** 15 10
957 30c. Regal sunbird (vert) 15 10
958 50c. White-spotted crake 25 15
959 3f. Black-casqued hornbill 40 30
960 10f. Ituri owl (vert) 1·10 70
961 26f. African emerald cuckoo 2·00 1·40
962 60f. Black-crowned waxbill (vert) 3·50 2·10
963 100f. Crowned eagle (vert) 6·00 3·50

155 Armstrong's first Step on Moon

1980. Tenth Anniv of "Apollo 11" Moon Landing. Multicoloured.

964 50c. Type **155** 15 10
965 1f.50 Aldrin descending to Moon's surface 20 10
966 8f. Planting the American flag 25 15
967 30f. Placing seisometer 1·50 85
968 50f. Taking samples 2·40 1·40
969 60f. Setting-up experiment 3·00 1·50
MS970 70×58 mm. 200f. Armstrong descending to Moon's surface 10·00 9·75

156 Butare Rotary Club Banner, Globe and Chicago Club Emblem of 1905

1980. 75th Anniv of Rotary International. Multicoloured.

971 20c. Type **156** 15 10
972 30c. Kigali Rotary Club banner 15 10
973 50c. Type **156** 15 10
974 4f. As No. 972 20 10
975 15f. Type **156** 70 30
976 20f. As No. 972 80 55
977 50f. Type **156** 2·00 1·10
978 60f. As No. 972 2·75 1·70

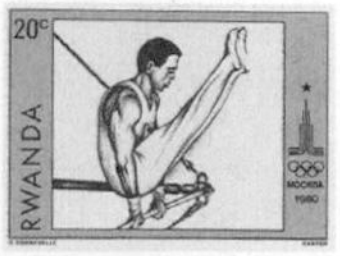

157 Gymnastics

1980. Olympic Games, Moscow.

979 **157** 20c. yellow and black 15 10
980 - 30c. green and black 15 10
981 - 50c. red and black 15 10
982 - 3f. blue and black 20 10
983 - 20f. orange and black 80 30
984 - 26f. purple and black 1·10 55
985 - 50f. turquoise and black 2·20 1·10
986 - 100f. brown and black 4·75 2·50

DESIGNS: 30c. Basketball; 50c. Cycling; 3f. Boxing; 20f. Archery; 26f. Weightlifting; 50f. Javelin; 100f. Fencing.

158 "The Amalfi Coast" (Giacinto Gigante)

1980. 20th Europa Stamp Exhibition, Naples. Sheet 117×89 mm.

MS987 **158** 200f. multicoloured 10·00 9·75

159 "Geaster"

1980. Mushrooms. Multicoloured.

988 20c. Type **159** 15 10
989 30c. "Lentinus atrobrunneus" 40 15
990 50c. "Gomphus stereoides" 55 20
991 4f. "Cantharellus cibarius" 1·40 30
992 10f. "Stilbothamnium dybowskii" 3·50 40
993 15f. "Xeromphalina tenuipes" 6·75 1·10
994 70f. "Podoscypha elegans" 12·00 3·50
995 100f. "Mycena" 16·00 7·00

160 "At the Theatre" (Toulouse-Lautrec)

1980. Impressionist Paintings. Multicoloured.

996 20c. "Still Life" (horiz) (Renoir) 15 10
997 30c. As Type **160** 15 10
998 50c. "Seaside Garden" (Monet) (horiz) 15 10
999 4f. "Mother and Child" (Mary Cassatt) 20 10
1000 5f. "Starry Night" (Van Gogh) (horiz) 25 15
1001 10f. "Three Dancers at their Toilette" (Degas) 40 30
1002 50f. "The Card Players" (Cezanne) (horiz) 2·00 1·10
1003 70f. "Tahitian Girls" (Gauguin) 2·75 1·50
1004 100f. "La Grande Jatte" (Seurat) (horiz) 4·75 2·10
MS1005 Four sheets each 137×101 mm. (a) 4f. No. 999, 26f. Type **160**; (b) 10f. As No. 998, 50f.; (c) 5f. No. 1000 75f. As No. 996; (d) 10f. No. 1001, 70f. No. 1003 13·50 13·00

161 "Virgin of the Harpies" (detail, Andrea del Sarto)

1980. Christmas. Sheet 65×84 mm.

MS1006 **161** 200f. black 10·00 9·75

162 Revolutionary Scene

1980. 150th Anniv of Belgian Independence. Scenes of the Independence War from contemporary engravings.

1007 **162** 20c. green and brown 15 10
1008 - 30c. buff and brown 15 10
1009 - 50c. blue and brown 20 10
1010 - 9f. orange and brown 25 15
1011 - 10f. mauve and brown 40 30
1012 - 20f. green and brown 70 40
1013 - 70f. pink and brown 3·00 1·10
1014 - 90f. yellow and brown 4·25 2·75

163 Draining the Marshes

1980. Soil Protection and Conservation Year. Multicoloured.

1015 20c. Type **163** 15 10
1016 30c. Bullock in pen (mixed farming and land fertilization) 15 10
1017 1f.50 Land irrigation and rice 20 10
1018 8f. Soil erosion and planting trees 25 15
1019 10f. Terrace 35 20
1020 40f. Crop fields 1·60 85
1021 90f. Bean crop 3·50 1·50
1022 100f. Picking tea 4·00 2·00

164 "Pavetta rwandensis"

1981. Flowers. Multicoloured.

1023 20c. Type **164** 15 10
1024 30c. "Cyrtorchis praetermissa" 15 10
1025 50c. "Pavonia urens" 20 10
1026 4f. "Cynorkis kassnerana" 25 15
1027 5f. "Gardenia ternifolia" 35 20
1028 10f. "Leptactina platyphylla" 55 30
1029 20f. "Lobelia petiolata" 1·10 55
1030 40f. "Tapinanthus brunneus" 2·20 1·10
1031 70f. "Impatiens niamniamensis" 3·50 2·00
1032 150f. "Dissotis rwandensis" 6·75 4·00

165 Mother and Child

1981. SOS Children's Village. Multicoloured.

1033 20c. Type **165** 15 10
1034 30c. Child with pots 15 10
1035 50c. Children drawing 15 10
1036 1f. Girl sewing 20 10
1037 8f. Children playing 40 15
1038 10f. Girl knitting 55 20
1039 70f. Children making models 3·25 1·40
1040 150f. Mother and children 6·25 2·75

166 Carol Singers

1981. Paintings by Norman Rockwell. Multicoloured.

1041 20c. Type **166** 15 10
1042 30c. People of different races 15 10
1043 50c. Father Christmas 20 10
1044 1f. Coachman 25 15
1045 8f. Man at piano 55 20
1046 20f. "Springtime" 1·10 40
1047 50f. Man making donation to girl "nurse" 2·75 1·70
1048 70f. Clown 3·75 2·20

167 Serval

1981. Carnivorous Animals. Multicoloured.

1049 20c. Type **167** 15 10
1050 30c. Black-backed jackal 25 10
1051 2f. Servaline genet 40 15
1052 2f.50 Banded mongoose 45 20
1053 10f. Zorilla 80 40
1054 15f. Zaire clawless otter 1·40 85
1055 70f. African golden cat 4·00 3·00
1056 200f. Hunting dog (vert) 10·00 7·75

168 Drummer

1981. Telecommunications and Health. Multicoloured.

1057 20c. Type **168** 15 10
1058 30c. Telephone receiver and world map 15 10
1059 2f. Airliner and radar screen 20 10
1060 2f.50 Satellite and computer tape 25 15
1061 10f. Satellite orbit and dish aerial 40 30
1062 15f. Tanker and radar equipment 70 40
1063 70f. Red Cross helicopter 3·00 2·20
1064 200f. Satellite 7·50 5·00

169 "St. Benedict leaving His Parents"

1981. 1500th Birth Anniv of St. Benedict. Multicoloured.

1065 20c. Type **169** 15 10
1066 30c. Portrait (10th century) (vert) 20 10
1067 50c. Portrait (detail from "The Virgin of the Misericord" polyptich) (vert) 25 15
1068 4f. "St. Benedict presenting the Rules of His Order" 40 20
1069 5f. "St. Benedict and His Monks at their Meal" 55 30
1070 20f. Portrait (13th century) (vert) 1·40 70
1071 70f. St. Benedict at prayer (detail from "Our Lady in Glory with Sts. Gregory and Benedict") (vert) 3·00 1·70
1072 100f. "Priest bringing the Easter Meal to St. Benedict" (Jan van Coninxlo) 4·25 3·50

170 Disabled Child painting with Mouth

1981. International Year of Disabled Persons. Multicoloured.

1073 20c. Type **170** 15 10
1074 30c. Boys on crutches playing football 15 10
1075 4f.50 Disabled girl knitting 15 10
1076 5f. Disabled child painting pot 20 10
1077 10f. Boy in wheelchair using saw 40 15
1078 60f. Child using sign language 2·20 1·00
1079 70f. Child in wheelchair playing with puzzle 3·00 1·10
1080 100f. Disabled child 4·75 2·10

171 "Adoration of the Magi" (Hugo van der Goes)

1981. Christmas. Sheet 85×85 mm.

MS1081 **171** 200f. lake 9·50 9·25

172 Kob drinking at Pool

1981. Rural Water Supplies. Multicoloured.

1082	20c. Type **172**	15	10
1083	30c. Women collecting water (vert)	15	10
1084	50c. Constructing a pipeline	20	10
1085	10f. Woman collecting water from pipe (vert)	40	15
1086	10f. Man drinking	80	30
1087	70f. Woman collecting water (vert)	2·75	1·40
1088	100f. Floating pump (vert)	3·75	2·00

173 Cattle

1982. World Food Day. Multicoloured.

1089	20c. Type **173**	15	10
1090	30c. Bee keeping	15	10
1091	50c. Fishes	15	10
1092	1f. Avocado	20	10
1093	8f. Boy eating banana	25	15
1094	20f. Sorghum	80	40
1095	70f. Vegetables	3·25	1·10
1096	100f. Three generations and balanced diet	4·50	2·75

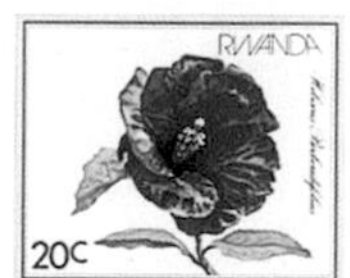

174 "Hibiscus berberidfolius"

1982. Flowers. Multicoloured.

1097	20c. Type **174**	15	10
1098	30c. "Hypericum lanceolatum" (vert)	15	10
1099	50c. "Canarina eminii"	15	10
1100	4f. "Polygala ruwenzoriensis"	40	15
1101	10f. "Kniphofia grantii" (vert)	70	20
1102	35f. "Euphorbia candelabrum" (vert)	1·90	85
1103	70f. "Disa erubescens" (vert)	3·50	1·30
1104	80f. "Gloriosa simplex"	4·00	2·75

175 Pres. Habyarimana and Flags

1982. 20th Anniv of Independence. Multicoloured.

1105	10f. Type **175**	15	15
1106	20f. Hands releasing doves (Peace)	70	55
1107	30f. Clasped hands and flag (Unity)	1·10	85
1108	50f. Building (Development)	2·00	1·40

176 Football

1982. World Cup Football Championship, Spain.

1109	**176**	20c. multicoloured	15	10
1110	-	30c. multicoloured	15	10
1111	-	1f.50 multicoloured	20	10
1112	-	8f. multicoloured	25	10
1113	-	10f. multicoloured	40	15
1114	-	20f. multicoloured	80	40
1115	-	70f. multicoloured	3·50	1·70
1116	-	90f. multicoloured	4·75	2·20

DESIGNS: 30c. to 90f. Designs show different players.

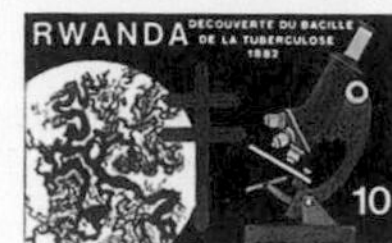

177 Microscope and Slide

1982. Centenary of Discovery of Tubercle Bacillus. Multicoloured.

1117	10f. Type **177**	40	15
1118	20f. Hand with test tube and slide	1·10	30
1119	70f. Lungs and slide	3·25	1·70
1120	100f. Dr. Robert Koch	4·75	2·75

178 "St. Anne, Virgin and Child and Donor" (detail, Van der Goes)

1982. Belgica 82 and Philexfrance 82 International Stamp Exhibitions. Four sheets each 130×90 mm. Multicoloured.

MS1121 (a) 40f. Type **178**; (b) 40f. "Portrait of Madame Recamier" (David); (c) 60f. "Pygmalion" (P. Delvaux); (d) 60f. "Liberty guiding the People" (E. Delacroix) 16·00 15·00

179 "Virgin and Child" (Murillo)

1982. Christmas. Sheet 85×85 mm.

MS1122 **179** 200f. magenta 9·50 9·25

180 African Elephants

1982. Tenth Anniv of United Nations Environment Programme. Multicoloured.

1123	20c. Type **180**	15	10
1124	30c. Lion hunting impala	15	10
1125	50c. Flower	15	10
1126	4f. African buffalo	20	10
1127	5f. Impala	25	15
1128	10f. Flower (different)	40	20
1129	20f. Common zebra	95	85
1130	40f. Crowned cranes	2·00	1·10
1131	50f. African fish eagle	2·40	1·70
1132	70f. Woman with basket of fruit	3·50	2·10

181 Scout tending Injured Kob

1982. 75th Anniv of Scout Movement. Multicoloured.

1133	20c. Type **181**	15	10
1134	30c. Tents and northern doubled-collared sunbird	15	10
1135	1f.50 Campfire	25	15
1136	8f. Scout	70	30
1137	10f. Knot	80	40
1138	20f. Tent and campfire	1·60	1·00
1139	70f. Scout cutting stake	4·75	4·00
1140	90f. Scout salute	6·50	5·25

182 Northern Double-collared Sunbird

1983. Nectar-sucking Birds. Multicoloured.

1141	20c. Type **182**	15	10
1142	30c. Regal sunbird (horiz)	15	10
1143	50c. Red-tufted malachite sunbird	20	10
1144	4f. Bronze sunbird (horiz)	25	15
1145	5f. Collared sunbird	40	30
1146	10f. Blue-headed sunbird (horiz)	70	40
1147	20f. Purple-breasted sunbird	1·40	85
1148	40f. Coppery sunbird (horiz)	2·75	2·10
1149	50f. Olive-bellied sunbird	4·00	2·75
1150	70f. Red-chested sunbird (horiz)	5·50	4·25

183 Driving Cattle

1983. Campaign Against Soil Erosion. Multicoloured.

1151	20c. Type **183**	15	10
1152	30c. Pineapple plantation	15	10
1153	50c. Interrupted ditches	15	10
1154	9f. Hedged terraces	40	30
1155	10f. Re-afforestation	45	35
1156	20f. Anti-erosion barriers	80	40
1157	30f. Contour planting	1·20	85
1158	50f. Terraces	2·20	1·40
1159	60f. River bank protection	2·40	1·50
1160	70f. Alternate fallow and planted strips	3·00	1·70

184 Feeding Ducks

1983. Birth Cent of Cardinal Cardijan (founder of Young Catholic Workers Movement). Multicoloured.

1161	20c. Type **184**	15	10
1162	30c. Harvesting bananas	15	10
1163	50c. Carrying melons	15	10
1164	10f. Wood-carving	25	15
1165	19f. Making shoes	55	30
1166	20f. Children in field of millet	70	40
1167	70f. Embroidering	3·00	1·70
1168	80f. Cardinal Cardijan	3·50	2·10

185 Young Gorillas

1983. Mountain Gorillas. Multicoloured.

1169	20c. Type **185**	15	10
1170	30c. Gorilla family	25	15
1171	9f.50 Young and adult	80	40
1172	10f. Mother with young	1·10	55
1173	20f. Heads	1·60	85
1174	30f. Adult and head	2·40	1·30
1175	60f. Adult (vert)	3·50	2·20
1176	70f. Close-up of adult (vert)	3·75	2·75

186 "Madonna del Granduca" (Raphael)

1983. Christmas. Sheet 72×85 mm.

MS1177 **186** 200f. green 9·50 9·25

187 "Hagenia abyssinica"

1984. Trees. Multicoloured.

1178	20c. Type **187**	15	10
1179	30c. "Dracaena steudneri"	15	10
1180	50c. "Phoenix reclinata"	15	10
1181	10f. "Podocarpus milanjianus"	40	15
1182	19f. "Entada abyssinica"	1·10	30
1183	70f. "Parinari excelsa"	3·00	1·40
1184	100f. "Newtonia buchananii"	4·00	2·10
1185	200f. "Acacia gerrardi" (vert)	8·75	4·25

188 "Hikari" Express Train, Japan

1984. World Communications Year. Multicoloured.

1186	20c. Type **188**	15	10
1187	30c. Liner and radar	15	10
1188	4f.50 Radio and transmitter	20	10
1189	10f. Telephone dial and cable	40	30
1190	15f. Letters and newspaper	70	40
1191	50f. Airliner and control tower	2·30	1·00
1192	70f. Television and antenna	3·00	1·50
1193	100f. Satellite and computer tape	4·75	2·20

189 "Le Martial", 1783

1984. Bicentenary of Manned Flight. Multicoloured.

1194	20c. Type **189**	15	10
1195	30c. De Rozier and Marquis d'Arlandes flight, 1783	15	10
1196	50c. Charles and Robert (1783) and Blanchard (1784) flights	15	10
1197	9f. M. and Mme. Blanchard	40	30
1198	10f. Blanchard and Jeffries, 1785	45	35
1199	50f. Demuyter (1937) and Piccard and Kipfer (1931) flights	2·20	1·40
1200	80f. Modern hot-air balloons	3·50	1·80
1201	200f. Trans-Atlantic flight, 1978	8·00	4·25

190 Equestrian

1984. Olympic Games, Los Angeles. Multicoloured.

1202	20c. Type **190**	15	10
1203	30c. Windsurfing	15	10
1204	50c. Football	15	10
1205	9f. Swimming	70	40
1206	10f. Hockey	80	55
1207	40f. Fencing	2·40	2·10
1208	80f. Running	4·00	3·50
1209	200f. Boxing	9·50	7·00

191 Mare and Foal

1984. Common Zebras and African Buffaloes. Multicoloured.

1210	20c. Type **191**	15	10
1211	30c. Buffalo and calf (vert)	15	10
1212	50c. Pair of zebras (vert)	15	10
1213	9f. Zebras fighting	40	30
1214	10f. Close-up of buffalo (vert)	55	40
1215	80f. Herd of zebras	4·00	2·10
1216	100f. Close-up of zebras (vert)	5·50	3·50
1217	200f. Buffalo charging	11·00	6·25

192 "Virgin adoring the Child" (Correggio)

1984. Christmas. Sheet 72×85 mm.

MS1218	**192** 200f. emerald	8·75	8·50

193 Gorillas at Water-hole

1985. Gorillas. Multicoloured.

1219	10f. Type **193**	4·00	1·80
1220	15f. Two gorillas in tree	6·75	3·00
1221	25f. Gorilla family	13·50	5·50
1222	30f. Three adults	16·00	6·25
MS1223	127×93 mm. 200f. As No. 1219 (35×50 mm)	13·50	13·00

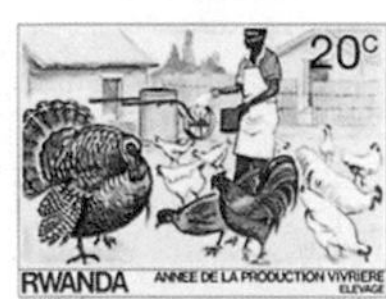

194 Man feeding Fowl

1985. Food Production Year. Multicoloured.

1224	20c. Type **194**	15	10
1225	30c. Men carrying pineapples	15	10
1226	50c. Farm animals	15	10
1227	9f. Men filling sacks with produce	40	30
1228	10f. Agricultural instruction	45	35
1229	50f. Sowing seeds	1·60	1·10
1230	80f. Storing produce	2·75	2·10
1231	100f. Working in banana plantation	3·50	2·75

195 Emblem

1985. Tenth Anniv of National Revolutionary Redevelopment Movement.

1232	**195**	10f. multicoloured	40	30
1233	**195**	30f. multicoloured	1·40	85
1234	**195**	70f. multicoloured	3·00	2·40

196 U.N. Emblem within "40"

1985. 40th Anniv of U.N.O.

1235	**196**	50f. multicoloured	2·30	2·00
1236	**196**	100f. multicoloured	4·50	3·75

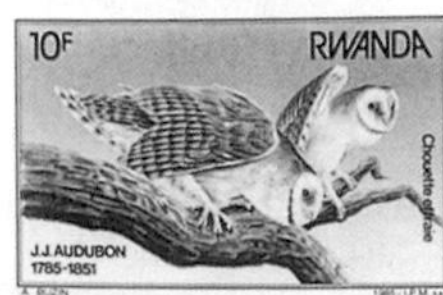

197 Barn Owls

1985. Birth Bicentenary of John J. Audubon (ornithologist). Multicoloured.

1237	10f. Type **197**	1·20	75
1238	20f. White-faced scops owls	1·80	1·40
1239	40f. Ruby-throated humming birds	3·75	2·40
1240	80f. Eastern meadowlarks	6·00	4·50

198 "Participation, Development and Peace"

1985. International Youth Year. Multicoloured.

1241	7f. Type **198**	30	15
1242	9f. Cycling	45	30
1243	44f. Youths carrying articles on head (teamwork)	2·30	1·20
1244	80f. Education	3·75	2·75

1985. 75th Anniv of Girl Guide Movement. Nos. 1133/40 optd **1910/1985** and guide emblem.

1245	20c. Type **181**	15	10
1246	30c. Tents	25	10
1247	1f.50 Campfire	30	15
1248	8f. Scout	45	30
1249	10f. Knot	60	45
1250	20f. Tent and campfire	1·80	90
1251	70f. Scout cutting stake	5·25	3·00
1252	90f. Scout salute	6·75	4·25

200 "Adoration of the Magi" (Titian)

1985. Christmas. Sheet 72×85 mm.

MS1253	**200** 200f. magenta	9·75	9·50

201 Container Lorry (Transport)

1986. Transport and Communications. Multicoloured.

1254	10f. Type **201**	45	30
1255	30f. Handstamping cover (posts)	1·50	90
1256	40f. Kigali Earth Station (telecommunication)	2·30	1·40
1257	80f. Kigali airport (aviation) (48×31 mm)	3·75	2·75

1986. Intensified Agriculture Year. Nos. 1152/60 optd **ANNEE 1986 INTENSIFICATION AGRICOLE** or surch also.

1258	9f. Hedged terraces	45	30
1259	10f. Re-afforestation	60	45
1260	10f. on 30c. Pineapple plantation	60	45
1261	10f. on 50c. Interrupted ditches	60	45
1262	20f. Anti-erosion barriers	1·20	90
1263	30f. Contour planning	1·80	1·50
1264	50f. Terraces	2·75	2·30
1265	60f. River bank protection	3·25	2·75
1266	70f. Alternate fallow and planted strips	3·75	3·00

203 Morocco v England

1986. World Cup Football Championship, Mexico. Multicoloured.

1267	2f. Type **203**	30	15
1268	4f. Paraguay v Iraq	45	30
1269	5f. Brazil v Spain	60	45
1270	10f. Italy v Argentina	1·50	90
1271	40f. Mexico v Belgium	3·25	2·00
1272	45f. France v Russia	4·25	2·30

204 Roan Antelopes

1986. Akagera National Park. Multicoloured.

1273	4f. Type **204**	30	15
1274	7f. Whale-headed storks	45	30
1275	9f. Cape eland	60	45
1276	10f. Giraffe	90	55
1277	80f. African elephant	6·00	3·00
1278	90f. Crocodile	6·75	3·75
1279	100f. Heuglin's masked weavers	7·50	4·50
1280	100f. Zebras and eastern white pelican	7·50	4·50

205 People of Different Races on Globe

1986. Christmas. International Peace Year. Multicoloured.

1281	10f. Type **205**	60	45
1282	15f. Dove and globe	90	75
1283	30f. Type **205**	1·50	1·20
1284	70f. As No. 1282	3·75	3·25

206 Mother breast-feeding Baby

1987. UNICEF Child Survival Campaign. Multicoloured.

1285	4f. Type **206**	30	15
1286	6f. Mother giving oral rehydration therapy to baby	45	30
1287	10f. Nurse immunizing baby	75	45
1288	70f. Nurse weighing baby and graph	4·25	3·25

207 Couple packing Baskets with Food

1987. Food Self-sufficiency Year. Multicoloured.

1289	5f. Type **207**	15	10
1290	7f. Woman and baskets of food	30	15
1291	40f. Man with baskets of fish and fruits	2·00	1·20
1292	60f. Fruits and vegetables	3·00	2·30

208 Pres. Habyarimana and Soldiers

1987. 25th Anniv of Independence. Multicoloured.

1293	10f. Type **208**	60	45
1294	40f. President at meeting	2·30	2·00
1295	70f. President with Pope John Paul II	3·25	3·00
1296	100f. Pres. Habyarimana (vert)	5·25	4·75

209 Bananas

1987. Fruit. Multicoloured.

1297	10f. Type **209**	45	30
1298	40f. Pineapples (horiz)	2·00	1·50
1299	80f. Papaya (horiz)	4·00	3·50
1300	90f. Avocados (horiz)	4·25	3·75
1301	100f. Strawberries	4·75	4·50

210 Mother carrying cub

1987. The Leopard. Multicoloured.

1302	50f. Type **210**	4·50	3·00
1303	50f. Leopards fighting	4·50	3·00
1304	50f. Leopards with prey	4·50	3·00
1305	50f. Leopard with prey in tree	4·50	3·00
1306	50f. Leopard leaping from tree	4·50	3·00

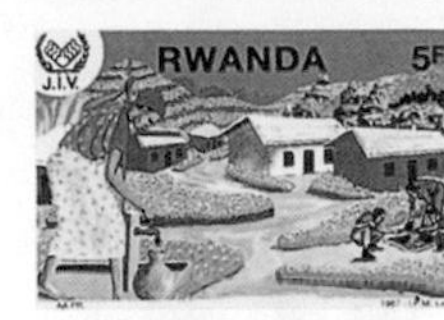

211 Village Activities

1987. International Volunteers Day. Multicoloured.

1307	5f. Type **211**	30	15
1308	12f. Pupils in schoolroom	90	60
1309	20f. View of village	1·20	90
1310	60f. Woman tending oxen	3·25	3·00

212 "Virgin and Child" (Fra Angelico)

1987. Christmas. Sheet 65×85 mm.

MS1311	**212** 200f. blue	9·75	9·50

213 Carpenter's Shop

1988. Rural Incomes Protection Year. Multicoloured.

1312	10f. Type **213**	45	30
1313	40f. Dairy farm	2·00	1·50
1314	60f. Workers in field	3·00	2·40
1315	80f. Selling baskets of eggs	4·00	3·25

214 Chimpanzees

1988. Primates of Nyungwe Forest. Multicoloured.

1316	2f. Type **214**	30	15
1317	3f. Black and white colobus	45	30
1318	10f. Lesser bushbabies	2·50	2·30
1319	90f. Monkeys	9·00	6·00

215 Boxing

1988. Olympic Games, Seoul. Multicoloured.

1320	5f. Type **215**	30	15
1321	7f. Relay race	60	30
1322	8f. Table tennis	90	45
1323	10f. Running	1·20	75
1324	90f. Hurdling	6·00	4·50

216 "25" on Map of Africa

1988. 25th Anniv of Organization of African Unity. Multicoloured.

1325	5f. Type **216**	30	15
1326	7f. Hands clasped across map	45	30
1327	8f. Building on map	60	40
1328	90f. Words forming map	4·50	3·75

217 "Virgin of the Soup" (Paul Veronese)

1988. Christmas. Sheet 65×85 mm.

MS1329 **217**	200f. turquoise	9·75	9·50

218 Newspaper Fragment and Refugees in Boat

1988. 125th Anniv of Red Cross Movement. Multicoloured.

1330	10f. Type **218**	45	30
1331	30f. Red Cross workers and patient	1·50	1·20
1332	40f. Red Cross worker and elderly lady (vert)	2·00	1·50
1333	100f. Red Cross worker and family (vert)	5·00	4·50

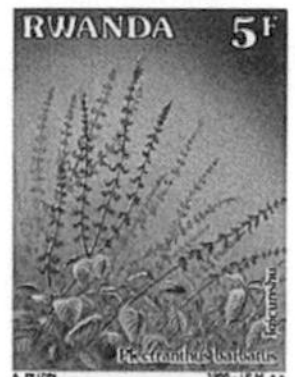

219 "Plectranthus barbatus"

1989. Plants. Multicoloured.

1334	5f. Type **219**	30	15
1335	10f. "Tetradenia riparia"	90	75
1336	20f. "Hygrophila auriculata"	1·80	1·50
1337	40f. "Datura stramonium"	4·50	3·75
1338	50f. "Pavetta ternifolia"	5·25	4·75

220 Emblem, Dates and Sunburst

1989. Centenary of Interparliamentary Union. Multicoloured.

1339	10f. Type **220**	45	30
1340	30f. Lake	1·40	1·10
1341	70f. River	3·25	3·00
1342	90f. Sun's rays	4·25	3·25

221 "Adoration of the Magi" (Peter Paul Rubens)

1989. Christmas. Sheet 70×90 mm.

MS1343 **221**	100f. black	7·50	7·25

222 Throwing Clay and Finished Pots

1989. Rural Self-help Year. Multicoloured.

1344	10f. Type **222**	45	30
1345	70f. Carrying baskets of produce (vert)	3·00	2·75
1346	90f. Firing clay pots	3·75	3·00
1347	200f. Clearing roadway	9·75	7·50

223 "Triumph of Marat" (Boilly)

1990. Bicentenary of French Revolution. Multicoloured.

1348	10f. Type **223**	60	50
1349	60f. "Rouget de Lisle singing La Marseillaise" (Pils)	3·25	2·75
1350	70f. "Oath of the Tennis Court" (Jacques Louis David)	3·75	3·00
1351	100f. "Trial of Louis XVI" (Joseph Court)	5·25	4·25

224 Old and New Lifestyles

1990. 30th Anniv of Revolution. Multicoloured.

1352	10f. Type **224**	75	60
1353	60f. Couple holding farming implements (vert)	3·00	2·40
1354	70f. Modernization	3·75	3·00
1355	100f. Flag, map and warrior	5·25	4·25

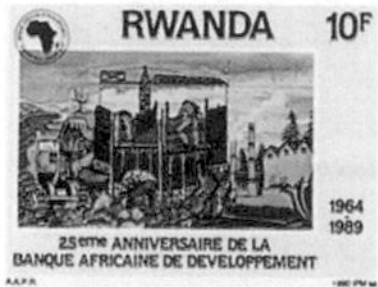

225 Construction

1990. 25th Anniv (1989) of African Development Bank. Multicoloured.

1356	10f. Type **225**	60	50
1357	20f. Tea picking	1·10	85
1358	40f. Road building	2·10	1·70
1359	90f. Tea pickers and modern housing	4·50	3·50

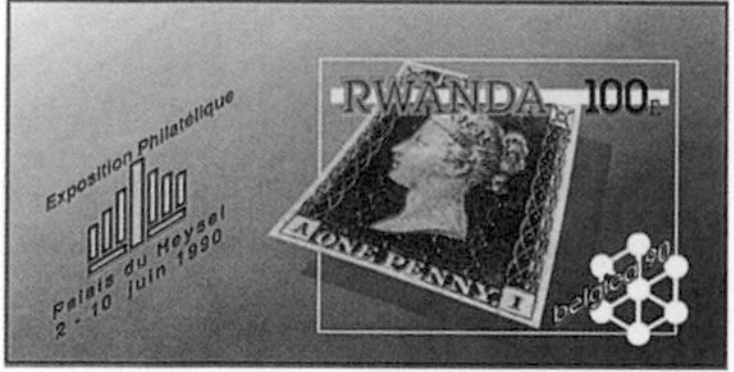

226 Penny Black (image scaled to 60% of original size)

1990. Belgica 90 International Stamp Exhibition, Brussels. Multicoloured.

MS1360	Three sheets each 82×42 mm. (a) 100f. Type **226**; (b) 100f. Belgian 1982 10f.+5f. football stamp (World Cup, Italy); (c) 100f. Rwanda 1973 30c. musician stamp	18·00	17·00

1990. World Cup Football Championship, Italy. Nos. 1267/72 optd ITALIA 90.

1361	**203**	2f. multicoloured	1·50	1·20
1362	-	4f. multicoloured	2·30	1·80
1363	-	5f. multicoloured	6·00	4·75
1364	-	10f. multicoloured	7·50	6·00
1365	-	40f. multicoloured	15·00	12·00
1366	-	45f. multicoloured	23·00	18·00

228 Pope John Paul II

1990. Papal Visits. Multicoloured.

1367	10f. Type **228**	3·00	2·40
1368	70f. Pope giving blessing	24·00	19·00
MS1369	105×110 mm. 100f. Pope praying (35×50 mm)	30·00	29·00

229 Adults learning Alphabet at School

1991. International Literacy Year (1990). Multicoloured.

1370	10f. Type **229**	60	50
1371	20f. Children reading at school	75	60
1372	50f. Lowland villagers learning alphabet in field	2·30	1·80
1373	90f. Highland villagers learning alphabet outdoors	4·50	3·50

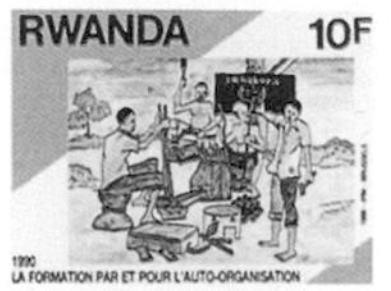

230 Tool-making

1991. Self-help Organizations. Multicoloured.

1374	10f. Type **230**	75	60
1375	20f. Rearing livestock	1·50	1·20
1376	50f. Textile manufacture	2·75	2·20
1377	90f. Construction	3·75	3·00

231 Statue of Madonna

1992. Death Centenary of Cardinal Lavigerie (founder of Orders of White Fathers and Sisters).

1378	**231**	5f. multicoloured	3·00	2·40
1379	-	15f. multicoloured	10·50	8·50
1380	-	70f. black and mauve	30·00	24·00
1381	-	110f. black and blue	50·00	42·00

DESIGNS—VERT: 15f. White Sister; 110f. Cardinal Lavigerie. HORIZ: 70f. White Fathers in Uganda, 1908.

232 Fisherman

1992. Int Nutrition Conference, Rome. Multicoloured.

1382	15f. Type **232**	1·20	95
1383	50f. Market fruit stall	4·25	3·25
1384	100f. Man milking cow	7·50	6·00
1385	500f. Woman breastfeeding	38·00	30·00

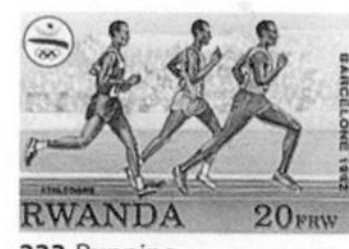

233 Running

1993. Olympic Games, Barcelona (1992). Multicoloured.

1386	20f. Type **233**	7·50	6·00
1387	30f. Swimming	12·00	9·50
1388	90f. Football	33·00	26·00
MS1389	85×124 mm. Nos. 1386/9	55·00	50·00

234 Toad

1998. Animals. Multicoloured.

1390	15f. Type **234**	3·00	2·40
1391	100f. Snail	4·50	3·50
1392	150f. Porcupine	5·25	4·25
1393	300f. Chameleon	6·00	4·75
MS1394	95×95 mm. Nos. 1390/3. Imperf	18·00	17·00

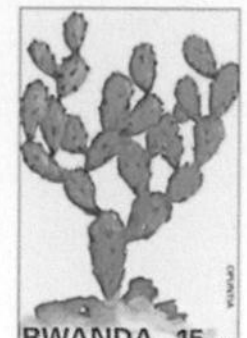

235 "Opuntia"

1998. Plants. Multicoloured.

1395	15f. Type **235**	3·00	2·40
1396	100f. "Gloriosa superba"	4·50	2·50
1397	150f. "Markhamia lutea"	5·25	4·25
1398	300f. "Hagenia abyssinica" (horiz)	6·00	4·75
MS1399	95×113 mm. Nos. 1395/8. Imperf	18·00	17·00

Pt. 18

RYUKYU ISLANDS

Group of islands between Japan and Taiwan, formerly Japanese until occupied by U.S. forces in 1945. After a period of military rule they became semi-autonomous under U.S. administration. The Amami Oshima group reverted to Japan in December 1953. The remaining islands were returned to Japan on 15 May 1972. Japanese stamps are now in use.

1948. 100 sen = 1 yen.
1958. 100 cents = 1 dollar (U.S.).

1 Cycad Palm

3 Tribute Junk

1948

1B	**1**	5s. purple	2·30	2·75
2A	-	10s. green	2·75	3·75
3A	**1**	20s. green	2·75	3·75
4B	**3**	30s. red	2·30	2·30
5B	-	40s. purple	2·30	2·30
6A	**3**	50s. blue	3·50	4·50
7B	-	1y. blue	6·50	6·50

DESIGNS: 10s., 40s. Easter lily; 1y. Farmer with hoe.

1950

8	**6**	50s. red	45	45
10	-	1y. blue	3·50	2·75
11	-	2y. purple	15·00	7·25
12	-	3y. pink	38·00	11·00
13	-	4y. grey	18·00	11·00
14	-	5y. green	11·00	6·00

DESIGNS: 1y. Shuri woman; 2y. Former Okinawa Palace, Shuri; 3y. Dragon's head; 4y. Okinawa women; 5y. Common spider and strawberry conches and radula scallop.

6 Shi-Shi Roof Tiles

12 Dove over Map of Ryukyus

1950. Air.

15	**12**	8y. blue	£120	39·00
16	**12**	12y. green	75·00	29·00
17	**12**	16y. red	23·00	23·00

14 University and Shuri Castle

1951. Inauguration of Ryukyu University.

19	**14**	3y. brown	75·00	23·00

15 Pine Tree

1951. Afforestation Week.

20	**15**	3y. green	70·00	23·00

16 Flying Goddess

1951. Air.

21	**16**	13y. blue	3·25	1·40
22	**16**	18y. green	4·50	3·50
23	**16**	30y. mauve	6·00	2·30
24	**16**	40y. purple	7·75	4·25
25	**16**	50y. orange	9·00	7·25

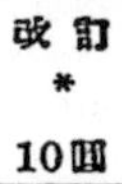

(17)

1952. Surch as T **17**.

27	**6**	10y. on 50s. red	12·00	7·00
29	-	100y. on 2y. purple (No. 11)	£2250	£1300

18 Dove and Bean Seedling

1952. Establishment of Ryukyuan Government.

30	**18**	3y. red	£170	36·00

19 Madanbashi Bridge

1952

31	**19**	1y. red	35	25
32	-	2y. green	45	25
33	-	3y. turquoise	70	35
34	-	6y. blue	4·50	3·00
35	-	10y. red	5·50	3·50
36	-	30y. green	13·50	7·25
37	-	50y. purple	17·00	11·00
38	-	100y. purple	23·00	7·25

DESIGNS: 2y. Presence Chamber, Shuri Palace; 3y. Shuri Gate; 6y. Sogenji Temple Wall; 10y. Bensaitendo Temple; 30y. Sonohyamutake Gate; 50y. Tamaudum Mausoleum, Shuri; 100y. Hosho-chai Bridge.

27 Reception at Shuri Castle

28 Perry and American Fleet at Naha Harbour

1953. Centenary of Commodore Perry's Visit to Okinawa.

39	**27**	3y. purple	16·00	7·25
40	**28**	6y. blue	2·30	3·50

29 Chofu Ota and Matrix

1953. Third Press Week.

41	**29**	4y. brown	18·00	6·00

30 Wine Flask to fit around Waist

1954

42	**30**	4y. brown	1·40	70
43	-	15y. red	3·50	3·00
44	-	20y. orange	3·25	3·25

DESIGNS: 15y. Tung Dar Bon (lacquer bowl); 20y. Kasuri (textile pattern).

33 Shigo Toma and Pen-nib

1954. Fourth Press Week.

45	**33**	4y. blue	20·00	7·25

34 Noguni Shrine and Sweet Potatoes

1955. 350th Anniv of Introduction of Sweet Potato Plant.

46	**34**	4y. blue	16·00	7·25

35 Stylized Trees

1956. Afforestation Week.

47	**35**	4y. green	12·00	6·00

38 Nidotekito Dance

1956. National Dances.

48	-	5y. purple	1·20	90
49	-	8y. violet	2·30	2·00
50	**38**	14y. brown	3·50	3·25

DESIGNS: 5y. Willow dance; 8y. Straw-hat dance.

39 Telephone and Dial

1956. Inauguration of Telephone Dialling System.

51	**39**	4y. violet	22·00	12·00

40 Floral Garland

1956. New Year.

52	**40**	2y. multicoloured	3·25	1·80

41 Flying Goddess

1957. Air.

53	**41**	15y. green	8·25	3·50
54	**41**	20y. red	13·50	7·25
55	**41**	35y. green	16·00	9·00
56	**41**	45y. brown	20·00	11·00
57	**41**	60y. grey	23·00	14·50

42 "Rocket" Pencils

1957. Seventh Press Week.

58	**42**	4y. blue	1·20	90

43 Phoenix

1957. New Year.

59	**43**	2y. multicoloured	45	25

44 Various Ryukyuan Postage Stamps

1958. Tenth Anniv of First Postage Stamps of Ryukyu Islands.

60	**44**	4y. multicoloured	1·20	90

45 Stylized Dollar Sign over Yen Symbol

1958. With or without gum (Nos. 68/69), no gum (others).

61	**45**	½c. yellow	80	70
62	**45**	1c. green	1·30	1·10
63	**45**	2c. blue	2·00	1·80
64	**45**	3c. red	1·80	1·60
65	**45**	4c. green	2·00	1·80
66	**45**	5c. brown	4·50	3·50
67	**45**	10c. blue	6·75	4·25
68	**45**	25c. blue	9·00	7·25
69	**45**	50c. grey	18·00	11·00
70	**45**	$1 purple	14·50	7·25

46 Gateway of Courtesy

1958. Restoration of Shuri Gateway.

71	**46**	3c. multicoloured	1·50	1·10

47 Lion Dance

1958. New Year.

72	**47**	1½c. multicoloured	55	25

48 Trees

1959. Afforestation Week.

73	**48**	3c. multicoloured	70	65

49 Atlas Moth

1959. Japanese Biological Teachers' Conference, Okinawa.

74	**49**	3c. multicoloured	2·75	1·20

50 Hibiscus

1959. Multicoloured. (a) Inscr as in T **50**.

75		½c. Type **50**	35	25
76		3c. Moorish idol	1·40	45
77		8c. Zebra moon, banded bonnet and textile cone (shells)	13·50	6·00
78		13c. Leaf butterfly (value at left)	3·25	2·30
79		17c. Jellyfish	23·00	11·00

(b) Inscr smaller and 13c. with value at right.

87		½c. Type **50**	55	35
88		3c. As No. 76	2·30	45
89		8c. As No. 77	5·75	2·30
90		13c. As No. 78	2·00	1·20
91		17c. As No. 79	15·00	6·00

55 Yakazi (Ryukyuan toy)

1959. New Year.

80	**55**	1½c. multicoloured	70	55

改訂 9¢

(56)

1959. Air. Surch as T **56**.

81	**41**	9c. on 15y. green	2·75	1·80
82	**41**	14c. on 20y. red	3·50	3·50
83	**41**	19c. on 35y. green	8·25	6·00
84	**41**	27c. on 45y. brown	17·00	7·75
85	**41**	35c. on 60y. grey	18·00	11·00

57 University Badge

1960. Tenth Anniv of University of the Ryukyus.

86	**57**	3c. multicoloured	1·40	70

1960. Air. Surch.

92	**30**	9c. on 4y. brown	4·50	1·50
93	-	14c. on 5y. purple (No. 48)	5·00	2·30
94	-	19c. on 15y. red (No. 43)	4·50	2·75
95	**38**	27c. on 14y. brown	8·75	4·50
96	-	35c. on 20y. orange (No. 44)	10·00	7·25

60 "Munjuru"

1960. Ryukyuan Dances. Multicoloured. (a) Inscr as in T **60**.

97		1c. Type **60**	1·80	1·10
98		2½c. "Inohabushi"	3·25	1·50
99		5c. "Hatomabushi"	1·10	1·00
100		10c. "Hanafu"	1·60	1·00

(b) As T **60** but additionally inscr "RYUKYUS".

107		1c. Type **60**	20	20
108		2½c. As No. 98	20	20
109		4c. As No. 98	25	35
110		5c. As No. 99	25	25
111		10c. As No. 100	55	45
112		20c. "Shudun"	3·25	1·30
113		25c. "Haodori"	1·10	90
114		50c. "Nobori Kuduchi"	3·25	1·30
115		$1 "Koteibushi"	6·25	45

65 Start of Race

1960. Eighth Kyushu Athletic Meeting.

101	-	3c. red, green and blue	6·75	2·75
102	**65**	8c. green and orange	1·80	1·20

DESIGN: 3c. Torch and coastal scene.

66 Little Egret and Rising Sun

1960. National Census.

103	**66**	3c. brown	6·75	3·25

67 Bull Fight

1960. New Year.

104	**67**	1½c. brown, buff and blue	3·00	1·40

68 Native Pine Tree

1961. Afforestation Week.

105	**68**	3c. deep green, red & green	2·00	1·60

69 Naha, Junk, Liner and City Seal

1961. 40th Anniv of Naha City.

106	**69**	3c. turquoise	2·75	1·80

74 Flying Goddess

1961. Air.

116	**74**	9c. multicoloured	45	20
117	-	14c. multicoloured	70	65
118	-	19c. multicoloured	1·10	80
119	-	27c. multicoloured	3·50	90
120	-	35c. multicoloured	2·30	1·60

DESIGNS: 14c. Flying goddess playing flute; 19c. Wind god; 27c. Wind god (different); 35c. Flying goddess over trees.

79 White Silver Temple

1961. Unification of Itoman District and Takamine, Kanegushiku and Miwa Villages.

121	**79**	3c. brown	2·30	1·80

80 Books and Bird

1961. Tenth Anniv of Ryukyu Book Week.

122	**80**	3c. multicoloured	1·40	1·10

81 Sunrise and Eagles

1961. New Year.

123	**81**	1½c. red, black and gold	3·50	1·80

82 Govt Building, Steps and Trees

1962. Tenth Anniv of Ryukyu Government. Multicoloured.

124	1½c. Type **82**	80	70
125	3c. Government building	1·10	90

85 Shuri Gate and Campaign Emblem

1962. Malaria Eradication. Multicoloured.

126	3c. "Anopheles hyrcanus sinensis" (mosquito)	80	70
127	8c. Type **85**	1·40	1·40

86 Windmill, Dolls and Horse

1962. Children's Day.

128	**86**	3c. multicoloured	1·50	1·10

87 "Hibiscus lilaceus"

1962. Ryukyu Flowers. Multicoloured.

129	½c. Type **87**	25	20
130	2c. "Ixora chinensis"	25	25
131	3c. "Erythrina indica"	55	20
132	3c. "Caesalpinia pulcherrima"	25	25
133	8c. "Schima mertensiana"	80	45
134	13c. "Impatiens balsamina"	1·10	65
135	15c. "Hamaomoto" (herb)	1·80	1·00
136	17c. "Alpinia speciosa"	1·40	90
142	1½c. "Etithyllum strictum"	35	25

No. 142 is smaller, 18¾×22½ mm.

95 Akaeware Bowl

1962. Philatelic Week.

137	**95**	3c. multicoloured	5·00	3·00

96 Kendo (Japanese Fencing)

1962. All-Japan Kendo Meeting.

138	**96**	3c. multicoloured	6·00	3·25

97 "Hare and Water" (textile design)

1962. New Year.

139	**97**	1½c. multicoloured	2·30	1·40

98 Reaching Maturity (clay relief)

1963. Adults' Day.

140	**98**	3c. gold, black and blue	1·10	70

99 Trees and Wooded Hills

1963. Afforestation Week.

141	**99**	3c. multicoloured	1·10	90

101 Okinawa Highway

1963. Opening of Okinawa Highway.

143	**101**	3c. multicoloured	1·50	1·20

102 Black Kites over Islands

1963. Bird Week.

144	**102**	3c. multicoloured	2·30	1·40

103 Shioya Bridge

1963. Opening of Shioya Bridge, Okinawa.

145	**103**	3c. multicoloured	1·40	1·20

104 Lacquerware Bowl

1963. Philatelic Week.

146	**104**	3c. multicoloured	3·50	2·75

105 Convair 880 Jetliner and Shuri Gate

1963. Air.

147	**105**	5½c. multicoloured	35	25
148	-	7c. black, red and blue	45	35

DESIGN: 7c. Convair 880 jetliner over sea.

107 Map and Emblem

1963. Meeting of Junior Int Chamber, Naha.

149	**107**	3c. multicoloured	1·00	90

108 Nakagusuku Castle Ruins

1963. Ancient Buildings Protection Week.

150	**108**	3c. multicoloured	1·40	90

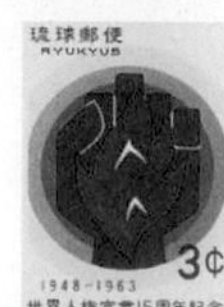

109 Flame

1963. 15th Anniv of Declaration of Human Rights.

151	**109**	3c. multicoloured	90	65

110 Bingata "dragon" (textile design)

1963. New Year.

152	**110**	1½c. multicoloured	90	45

111 Carnation

1964. Mothers' Day.

153	**111**	3c. multicoloured	90	55

112 Pineapples and Sugar-cane

1964. Agricultural Census.

154	**112**	3c. multicoloured	55	40

113 Hand-woven Sash

1964. Philatelic Week.

155	**113**	3c. brown, blue and pink	70	65

114 Girl Scout and Emblem

1964. Tenth Anniv of Ryukyu Girl Scouts.

156	**114**	3c. multicoloured	55	35

115 Transmitting Tower

1964. Inauguration of Ryukyu–Jap'an Microwave Link.

157	**115**	3c. green and black	1·10	90
158	-	8c. blue and black	1·50	1·40

DESIGN: 8c. "Bowl" receiving aerial.

Both stamps have "1963" cancelled by bars and "1964" inserted in black.

117 Shuri Gate and Olympic Torch

1964. Passage of Olympic Torch through Okinawa.

159	**117**	3c. multicoloured	45	35

118 "Naihanchi" (Karate stance)

1964. Karate ("self-defence"). Multicoloured.

160	3c. Type **118**	70	55
161	3c. "Makiwara" (karate training)	65	55
162	3c. "Kumite" exercise	55	55

121 "Miyara Dunchi" (old Ryukyuan Residence)

1964. Ancient Buildings Protection Week.

163	**121**	3c. multicoloured	45	35

122 Bingata "snake" (textile design)

1964. New Year.

164	**122**	1½c. multicoloured	55	40

123 Boy Scouts, Badge and Shuri Gate

1965. Tenth Anniv of Ryukyuan Boy Scouts.

165	**123**	3c. multicoloured	60	45

124 "Samisen" (musical instrument)

1965. Philatelic Week.

166	**124**	3c. multicoloured	60	45

125 Stadium

1965. Completion of Onoyama Sports Ground.

167	**125**	3c. multicoloured	35	25

126 Kin Power Station

1965. Completion of Kin Power Plant.

168	**126**	3c. multicoloured	45	35

127 I.C.Y. Emblem and "Globe"

1965. International Co-operation Year and 20th Anniv of United Nations.

169	**127**	3c. multicoloured	35	25

128 City Hall, Naha

1965. Completion of Naha City Hall.

170	**128**	3c. multicoloured	35	25

129 Semaruhakogame Turtle

1965. Ryukyuan Turtles. Multicoloured.

171	3c. Type **129**	80	45
172	3c. Taimai or hawksbill turtle	80	45
173	3c. Yamagame or hill tortoise	80	45

132 Bingata "horse" (textile design)

1965. New Year.

174	**132**	1½c. multicoloured	35	25

133 Pryer's Woodpecker

1966. "Natural Monument" (Wildlife). Multicoloured.

175	3c. Type **133**	65	35
176	3c. Sika deer	65	35
177	3c. Dugong	65	35

136 Pacific Swallow

1966. Bird Week.

178	**136**	3c. multicoloured	55	40

137 Lilies and Ruins

1966. Memorial Day (Battle of Okinawa).

179	**137**	3c. multicoloured	35	30

138 University of the Ryukyus

1966. Transfer of University of the Ryukyus to Government Administration.

180	**138**	3c. multicoloured	35	30

139 Lacquer Box

1966. Philatelic Week.

181	**139**	3c. multicoloured	35	30

140 Ryukyuan Tiled House

1966. 20th Anniv of UNESCO.

182	**140**	3c. multicoloured	35	30

141 "GRI" Museum, Shuri

1966. Completion of Government Museum, Shuri.

183	**141**	3c. multicoloured	35	30

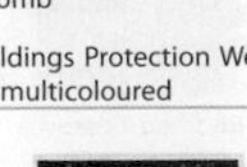

142 Nakasone-Tuimya Tomb

1966. Ancient Buildings Protection Week.

184	**142**	3c. multicoloured	35	30

143 Bingata "ram" (textile design)

1966. New Year.

185	**143**	1½c. multicoloured	55	35

144 Tomato Anemonefish

1966. Tropical Fish. Multicoloured.

186	3c. Type **144**	75	45
187	3c. Blue-spotted boxfish	75	45
188	3c. Long-nosed butterflyfish	75	45
189	3c. Clown triggerfish	75	45
190	3c. Saddle butterflyfish	75	45

149 Tsuboya Urn

1967. Philatelic Week.

191	**149**	3c. multicoloured	45	30

150 Episcopal Mitre

1967. Sea Shells. Multicoloured.

192	3c. Type **150**	65	35
193	3c. Venus comb murex ("Murex (Aranea) triremus")	65	35
194	3c. Chiragra spider conch ("Lambis (Harpago) chiragra")	70	45
195	3c. Great green turban ("Turbo (Olearia) marmoratus")	70	45
196	3c. Bubble conch ("Euprotomus bulla")	70	45

155 Roof Tiles and Emblem

1967. International Tourist Year.

197	**155**	3c. multicoloured	35	30

156 Mobile Clinic

1967. 15th Anniv of Anti-T.B. Association.

198	**156**	3c. multicoloured	35	30

157 Hojo Bridge, Enkaku

1967. Ancient Buildings Protection Week.

199	**157**	3c. multicoloured	35	30

158 Bingata "monkey" (textile design)

1967. New Year.

200	**158**	1½c. multicoloured	35	30

159 T.V. Tower and Map

1967. Opening of T.V. Broadcasting Stations in Miyako and Yaeyama.

201	**159**	3c. multicoloured	35	30

160 Dr. Nakachi and Assistant

1968. 120th Anniv of First Ryukyu Vaccination (by Dr. Kijin Nakachi).

202	**160**	3c. multicoloured	35	30

161 Medicine Case (after Sokei Dana)

1968. Philatelic Week.

203	**161**	3c. multicoloured	55	35

162 Young Man, Book, Map and Library

1968. Library Week.

204	**162**	3c. multicoloured	50	35

163 Postmen with Ryukyu Stamp of 1948

1968. 20th Anniv of First Ryukyu Islands Stamps.

205	**163**	3c. multicoloured	45	35

164 Temple Gate

1968. Restoration of Enkaku Temple Gate.

206	**164**	3c. multicoloured	45	35

165 Old Man Dancing

1968. Old People's Day.

207	**165**	3c. multicoloured	45	35

166 "Mictyris longicarpus"

1968. Crabs. Multicoloured.

208		3c. Type **166**	90	65
209		3c. "Uca dubia"	90	65
210		3c. "Baptozius vinosus"	90	65
211		3c. "Cardisoma carnifex"	90	65
212		3c. "Ocypode ceratophthalma"	90	65

171 Saraswati Pavilion

1968. Ancient Buildings Protection Week.

213	**171**	3c. multicoloured	40	30

172 Player

1968. 35th All-Japan East v West Men's Softball Tennis Tournament, Onoyama.

214	**172**	3c. multicoloured	45	35

173 Bingata "cock" (textile design)

1968. New Year.

215	**173**	1½c. multicoloured	80	35

174 Boxer

1969. 20th All-Japan Boxing Championships.

216	**174**	3c. multicoloured	45	35

175 Inkwell Screen

1969. Philatelic Week.

217	**175**	3c. multicoloured	45	25

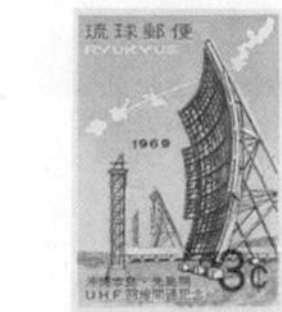

176 UHF Antennae and Map

1969. Inauguration of Okinawa–Sakishima U.H.F. Radio Service.

218	**176**	3c. multicoloured	35	25

177 Gate of Courtesy

1969. 22nd All-Japan Formative Education Study Conference, Naha.

219	**177**	3c. multicoloured	35	25

178 "Tug of War" Festival

1969. Traditional Religious Ceremonies. Multicoloured.

220		3c. Type **178**	65	45
221		3c. "Hari" canoe race	65	45
222		3c. "Izaiho" religious ceremony	65	45
223		3c. "Ushideiku" dance	65	45
224		3c. "Sea God" dance	65	45

1969. No. 131 surch.

225		½c. on 3c. multicoloured	70	65

184 Nakamura-Ke

1969. Ancient Buildings Protection Week.

226	**184**	3c. multicoloured	35	25

185 Kyuzo Toyama and Map

1969. 70th Anniv of Toyama's Ryukyu–Hawaii Emigration Project.

227	**185**	3c. multicoloured	45	35

No. 227 has "1970" cancelled by bars and "1969" inserted in black.

186 Bingata "dog and flowers" (textile design)

1969. New Year.

228	**186**	1½c. multicoloured	55	35

187 Sake Flask

1970. Philatelic Week.

229	**187**	3c. multicoloured	40	25

188 "Shushin-Kaneiri"

189 "Chu-nusudu"

190 "Mekarushi"

191 "Nidotichiuchi"

192 "Kokonomaki"

1970. "Kumi-Odori" Ryukyu Theatre. Multicoloured.

230	**188**	3c. multicoloured	75	60
231	**189**	3c. multicoloured	75	60
232	**190**	3c. multicoloured	75	60
233	**191**	3c. multicoloured	75	60
234	**192**	3c. multicoloured	75	60
MS235		94×102 mm. Nos. 230×4	6·00	6·00
MS236		94×102 mm. Nos. 231×4	6·00	6·00
MS237		94×102 mm. Nos. 232×4	6·00	6·00
MS238		94×102 mm. Nos. 233×4	6·00	6·00
MS239		94×102 mm. Nos. 234×4	6·00	6·00

193 Observatory

1970. Completion of Underwater Observatory, Busena-Misaki, Nago.

240	**193**	3c. multicoloured	80	35

194 Noboru Jahana (politician)

1970. Famous Ryukyuans.

241	**194**	3c. purple	65	65
242	-	3c. green	80	65
243	-	3c. black	65	65

PORTRAITS: No. 242, Saion Gushichan Bunjaku (statesman); 243, Choho Giwan (Regent).

197 "Population

1970. Population Census.

244	**197**	3c. multicoloured	35	30

198 "Great Cycad of Une"

1970. Ancient Buildings Protection Week.

245	**198**	3c. multicoloured	45	30

199 Ryukyu Islands, Flag and Japan Diet

1970. Election of Ryukyu Representatives to the Japanese Diet.

246	**199**	3c. multicoloured	90	65

200 "Wild Boar" (Bingata textile design)

1970. New Year.

247	**200**	1½c. multicoloured	55	35

201 "Jibata" (hand-loom)

202 "Filature" (spinning-wheel)

203 Farm-worker wearing "Shurunnu" Coat and "Kubagasa" Hat

204 Woman using "Shiri-Ushi" (rice huller)

205 Fisherman's "Umi-Fujo" (box) and "Yutui" (bailer)

1971. Ryukyu Handicrafts.

248	**201**	3c. multicoloured	45	35
249	**202**	3c. multicoloured	45	35
250	**203**	3c. multicoloured	45	35
251	**204**	3c. multicoloured	45	35
252	**205**	3c. multicoloured	45	35

206 "Taku" (container)

1971. Philatelic Week.

253	**206**	3c. multicoloured	45	30

207 Civic Emblem with Old and New City Views

1971. 50th Anniv of Naha's City Status.

254	**207**	3c. multicoloured	55	45

208 Restored Battlefield, Okinawa

1971. Government Parks. Multicoloured.

255		3c. Type **208**	35	35
256		3c. Haneji Inland Sea	35	35
257		4c. Yabuchi Island	35	35

211 Deva King, Torinji Temple

1971. Anicent Buildings Protection Week.

258	**211**	4c. multicoloured	55	45

212 "Rat" (Bingata textile pattern)

1971. New Year.

259	**212**	2c. multicoloured	70	55

213 Student-nurse and Candle

1971. 25th Anniv of Nurses' Training Scheme.

260	**213**	4c. multicoloured	55	45

214 Islands and Sunset

1972. Maritime Scenery. Multicoloured.

261		5c. Type **214**	35	70
262		5c. Coral reef (horiz)	35	70
263		5c. Island and short-tailed albatrosse	90	90

217 Dove and Flags of Japan and U.S.A

1972. Ratification of Treaty for Return of Ryukyu Islands to Japan.

264	**217**	5c. multicoloured	70	1·10

218 "Yushibin" (ceremonial sake container)

1972. Philatelic Week.

265	**218**	5c. multicoloured	55	1·10

EXPRESS DELIVERY STAMP

E13 Sea-horse

1951

E18	**E13**	5y. blue	38·00	23·00

Pt. 7

SAAR

A German territory South-east of Luxembourg. Occupied by France under League of Nations control from 1920 to 1935. Following a plebiscite, Saar returned to Germany in 1935 from when German stamps were used until the French occupation in 1945, after which Nos. F1/13 of Germany followed by Nos. 203 etc of Saar were used. The territory was autonomous under French protection until it again returned to Germany at the end of 1956 following a national referendum. Issues from 1957 were authorised by the German Federal Republic pending the adoption of German currency on 6 July 1959, after which West German stamps were used.

1920–May 1921. 100 pfennig = 1 mark.
May 1921–March 1935. 100 centimes = 1 franc.
1935–47. 100 pfennig = 1 reichsmark.
1947. 100 pfennig = 1 Saarmark.
November 1947–July 1959. 100 centimes =1 franc.
From 1959. 100 pfennig = 1 Deutsche mark.

LEAGUE OF NATIONS COMMISSION

1920. German stamps inscr "DEUTSCHES REICH" optd **Sarre** and bar.

1	**24**	2pf. grey	2·00	6·50
2c	**24**	2½pf. grey	2·20	7·75
3	**10**	3pf. brown	1·40	3·75
4c	**10**	5pf. green	65	1·30
5	**24**	7½pf. orange	90	2·40
6	**10**	10pf. red	75	1·80
7	**24**	15pf. violet	65	1·40
8	**10**	20pf. blue	65	1·40
9	**10**	25pf. black & red on yellow	13·00	27·00
10	**10**	30pf. black & orange on buff	24·00	49·00
11	**24**	35pf. brown	75	1·80
12	**10**	40pf. black and red	75	1·80
13	**10**	50pf. black & pur on cream	75	1·40
14	**10**	60pf. purple	75	1·80
15	**10**	75pf. black and green	65	1·60
16	**10**	80pf. black and red on red	£275	£375
17b	**12**	1m. red	38·00	60·00

1920. Bavarian stamps optd **Sarre** or **SARRE** (Nos. 30/1) and bars.

18	**15**	5pf. green	1·00	2·20
19	**15**	10pf. red	1·00	2·20
19a	**15**	15pf. red	1·30	2·75
21	**15**	20pf. blue	90	2·20
22	**15**	25pf. grey	15·00	22·00
23	**15**	30pf. orange	8·75	15·00
24	**15**	40pf. green	14·50	22·00
25	**15**	50pf. brown	2·20	3·75
26	**15**	60pf. green	4·50	11·00
27	**16**	1m. brown	22·00	44·00
28	**16**	2m. violet	80·00	£190
29	**16**	3m. red	£160	£225
30	-	5m. blue (No. 192)	£1100	£1200
31	-	10m. green (No. 193)	£200	£350

1920. German stamps inscr "DEUTSCHES REICH" optd **SAARGEBIET**.

32	**10**	5pf. green	35	65
33	**10**	5pf. brown	65	1·10
34	**10**	10pf. red	35	65
35	**10**	10pf. orange	65	65
36	**24**	15pf. violet	35	65
37	**10**	20pf. blue	35	65
38	**10**	20pf. green	1·30	65
39	**10**	30pf. black & orange on buff	55	65
40	**10**	30pf. blue	75	1·00
41	**10**	40pf. black and red	45	65
42	**10**	40pf. red	1·40	1·00
43	**10**	50pf. black & purple on buff	75	65
44	**10**	60pf. purple	90	65
45	**10**	75pf. black and green	1·00	65
46	**12**	1m.25 green	3·50	1·60
47	**12**	1m.50 brown	2·75	1·60
48	**13**	2m.50 purple	6·50	19·00
49	**10**	4m. red and black	12·00	31·00

1920. No. 45 of Saar surch **20** and No. 102 of Germany surch **SAARGEBIET**, arms and value.

50		20 on 75pf. black and green	55	1·60
51	**24**	5m. on 15pf. purple	7·75	22·00
52	**24**	10m. on 15pf. purple	7·75	26·00

9 Miner

11 Colliery Shafthead

12 Burbach Steelworks

1921

53	-	5pf. violet and green	45	65
54	**9**	10pf. orange and blue	45	65
55	-	20pf. grey and green	45	1·40
56	-	25pf. blue and brown	55	1·10
57	-	30pf. brown and green	55	1·00
58	-	40pf. red	55	65
59	-	50pf. black and grey	1·30	5·50
60	-	60pf. brown and red	2·20	5·00
61	-	80pf. blue	1·00	1·60
62	-	1m. black and red	1·10	2·20
63	**11**	1m.25 green and brown	1·30	2·75
64	-	2m. black and orange	3·25	5·50
65	-	3m. sepia and brown	4·50	13·00
66	-	5m. violet and yellow	13·00	31·00
67	-	10m. brown and green	16·00	33·00
68	**12**	25m. blue, black and red	44·00	£110

DESIGNS—As Type **11**. HORIZ: 5pf. Mill above Mettlach; 20pf. Pit head at Reden; 25pf. River traffic, Saarbrucken; 30pf. River Saar at Mettlach; 40pf. Slag-heap, Volklingen; 50pf. Signal gantry, Saarbrucken; 80pf. "Old Bridge", Saarbrucken; 1m. Wire-rope Railway; 2m. Town Hall, Saarbrucken; 3m. Pottery, Mettlach; 5m. St. Ludwig's Church; 10m. Chief Magistrate's and Saar Commissioner's Offices. VERT: 60pf. Gothic Chapel, Mettlach.

See also Nos. 84/97.

1921. Nos. 55/68 surch in French currency.

70		3c. on 20pf. grey and green	55	70
71		5c. on 25pf. blue and brown	55	70
72		10c. on 30pf. brown and green	55	70
73		15c. on 40pf. red	70	70
74		20c. on 50pf. black and grey	55	70
75		25c. on 60pf. brown and red	70	70
76		30c. on 80pf. blue	2·30	1·50
77		40c. on 1m. black and red	2·75	70
78		50c. on 1m.25 green & brown	4·50	1·50
79		75c. on 2m. black and orange	6·50	2·75
80		1f. on 3m. black and brown	6·75	3·50
81		2f. on 5m. violet and yellow	17·00	9·00
82		3f. on 10m. brown and green	24·00	36·00
83		5f. on 25m. blue, black and red	25·00	50·00

1922. Larger designs (except 5f.) and value in French currency.

84	3c. green (as No. 62)	55	90
85	5c. black & orange (as No. 54)	55	55
86	10c. green (as No. 61)	55	55
87	15c. brown (as No. 62)	1·70	55
98	15c. orange (as No. 62)	3·50	55
88	20c. blue & yellow (as No. 64)	19·00	55
100	25c. red and yellow (as No. 64)	3·50	55
90	30c. red and yellow (as No. 58)	2·75	3·00
91	40c. brown & yell (as No. 65)	1·40	55
92	50c. blue & yellow (as No. 56)	1·40	55
93	75c. green & yellow (as No. 65)	19·00	34·00
94	1f. brown (as No. 66)	3·50	1·10
95	2f. violet (as No. 63)	5·00	4·50
96	3f. green & orange (as No. 60)	34·00	9·00
97	5f. brown & choc (as No. 68)	34·00	65·00

14 Madonna of Blieskastel

1925

102	**14**	45c. purple	4·00	7·50
103	**14**	10f. brown (31×36 mm)	23·00	34·00

15 Army Medical Service

1926. Welfare Fund.

104	**15**	20c.+20c. green	11·50	28·00
105	-	40c.+40c. brown	11·50	28·00
106	-	50c.+50c. orange	11·50	28·00
107	-	1f.50+1f.50 blue	27·00	70·00

DESIGNS: 40c. Hospital work (nurse and patient); 50c. Child welfare (children at a spring); 1f.50, Maternity nursing service.

18 Tholey Abbey

1926

108		10c. brown	1·00	70
109		15c. green	55	1·50
110		20c. brown	55	70
111	**18**	25c. blue	1·00	70
112	-	30c. green	1·40	70
113	-	40c. brown	1·00	70
114	**18**	50c. red	1·40	70
114a	-	60c. orange	5·75	80
115	-	75c. purple	1·00	70
116	-	80c. orange	3·50	12·50
116a	-	90c. red	17·00	25·00
117	-	1f. violet	3·50	70
118	-	1f.50 blue	6·75	70
119	-	2f. red	8·00	70
120	-	3f. green	16·00	1·80
121	-	5f. brown	17·00	10·00

DESIGNS—VERT: 10, 30c. Fountain, St. Johann, Saarbrucken. HORIZ: 15, 75c. Saar Valley near Gudingen; 20, 40, 90c. View from Saarlouis fortifications; 60, 80c., 1f. Colliery shafthead; 1f.50, 2, 3, 5f. Burbach Steelworks.

1927. Welfare Fund. Optd **1927–28.**

122	**15**	20c.+20c. green	18·00	40·00
123	**15**	40c.+40c. brown	18·00	40·00
124	**15**	50c.+50c. orange	16·00	28·00
125	**15**	1f.50+1f.50 blue	25·00	90·00

19 Breguet 14 Biplane over Saarbrucken

1928. Air.

126	**19**	50c. red	5·75	5·75
127	**19**	1f. violet	9·00	6·75

20 "The Blind Beggar" by Dyckmanns

1928. Christmas Charity.

128	**20**	40c.(+40c.) brown	17·00	£100
129	**20**	50c.(+50c.) purple	17·00	£100
130	**20**	1f.(+1f.) violet	17·00	£100
131	-	1f.50(+1f.50) blue	17·00	£100
132	-	2f.(+2f.) red	20·00	£150
133	-	3f.(+3f.) green	20·00	£190
134	-	10f.(+10f.) brown	£500	£5500

DESIGNS: 1f.50, 2, 3f. "Almsgiving" by Schiestl; 10f. "Charity" by Raphael (picture in circle).

1929. Christmas Charity. Paintings. As T **20**.

135	40c.(+15c.) green	2·75	8·00
136	50c.(+20c.) red	5·75	13·50
137	1f.(+50c.) purple	5·75	16·00
138	1f.50(+75c.) blue	5·75	16·00
139	2f.(+1f.) red	5·75	16·00
140	3f.(+2f.) green	11·50	36·00
141	10f.(+8f.) brown	70·00	£190

DESIGNS: 40c. to 1f. "Orphaned" by H. Kaulbach; 1f.50, 2, 3f. "St. Ottilia" by M. Feuerstein; 10f. "The Little Madonna" by Ferruzzio.

1930. Nos. 114 and 116 surch.

141a	**18**	40c. on 50c. red	2·30	2·30
142	-	60c. on 80c. orange	2·75	3·50

1931. Christmas Charity (1930 issue). Paintings. As T **20**.

143	40c.(+15c.) brown	11·50	34·00
144	60c.(+20c.) orange	11·50	34·00
145	1f.(+50c.) red	11·50	70·00
146	1f.50(+75c.) blue	17·00	70·00
147	2f.(+1f.) brown	17·00	70·00
148	3f.(+2f.) green	28·00	70·00
149	10f.(+10f.) brown	£140	£400

DESIGNS: 40, 60c., 1f.50, "The Safetyman" (miner and lamp) by F. Zolnhofer; 1, 2, 3f. "The Good Samaritan" by J. Heinemann; 10f. "At the Window" by F. G. Waldmuller.

1931. Christmas Charity. Paintings. As T **20**.

150	40c.(+15c.) brown	18·00	50·00
151	60c.(+20c.) red	18·00	50·00
152	1f.(+50c.) purple	23·00	80·00
153	1f.50(+75c.) blue	27·00	80·00
154	2f.(+1f.) red	32·00	80·00
155	3f.(+2f.) green	40·00	£140
156	5f.(+5f.) brown	£140	£450

DESIGNS: 40c. to 1f. "St. Martin" by F. Boehle; 1f.50, 2f. "Charity" by Ridgeway-Knight; 5f. "The Widow's Mite" by Dubufe.

29 Focke Wulf A-17 Mowe over Saarbrucken Airport

1932. Air.

157	**29**	60c. red	9·00	6·75
158	**29**	5f. brown	65·00	£140

30 Kirkel Castle Ruins

1932. Christmas Charity.

159	**30**	40c.(+15c.) brown	13·50	32·00
160	-	60c.(+20c.) red	13·50	32·00
161	-	1f.(+50c.) purple	20·00	55·00
162	-	1f.50(+75c.) blue	28·00	70·00
163	-	2f.(+1f.) red	28·00	80·00
164	-	3f.(+2f.) green	80·00	£250
165	-	5f.(+5f.) brown	£170	£400

DESIGNS—VERT: 60c. Blieskastel Church; 1f. Ottweiler Church; 1f.50, St. Michael's Church, Saarbrucken; 2f. Cathedral and fountain, St. Wendel; 3f. St. John's Church, Saarbrucken. HORIZ: 5f. Kerpen Castle, Illingen.

32 Scene of the Disaster

1933. Neunkirchen Explosion Disaster.

166	**32**	60c.(+60c.) orange	23·00	28·00
167	**32**	3f.(+3f.) green	50·00	£100
168	**32**	5f.(+5f.) brown	50·00	£100

33 "Love"

1934. Christmas Charity.

169	**33**	40c.(+15c.) brown	8·00	23·00
170	-	60c.(+20c.) red	8·00	23·00
171	-	1f.(+50c.) mauve	10·00	28·00
172	-	1f.50(+75c.) blue	20·00	50·00

173	-	2f.(+1f.) red	18·00	50·00
174	-	3f.(+2f.) green	20·00	50·00
175	-	5f.(+5f.) brown	46·00	£130

DESIGNS: 60c. "Solicitude". 1f. "Peace". 1f.50, "Consolation". 2f. "Welfare". 3f. "Truth". 5f. Countess Elizabeth von Nassau.
Nos. 169/74 show statues by C. L. Pozzi in church of St. Louis, Saarbrucken.

1934. Saar Plebiscite. Optd **VOLKSABSTIMMUNG 1935**.

(a) Postage. On Nos. 108/15, 116a/21 and 103.

176		10c. brown	55	80
177		15c. green	55	80
178		20c. brown	90	1·90
179	18	25c. blue	90	1·90
180	-	30c. green	55	80
181	-	40c. brown	55	1·00
182	18	50c. red	1·00	1·90
183	-	60c. orange	55	80
184	-	75c. purple	1·00	1·90
185	-	90c. red	1·00	2·00
186	-	1f. violet	1·00	2·30
187	-	1f.50 blue	1·80	4·50
188	-	2f. red	2·75	6·75
189	-	3f. green	6·75	13·50
190	-	5f. brown	28·00	46·00
191	14	10f. brown	34·00	85·00

(b) Air. On Nos. 126/7 and 157/8.

192	19	50c. red	5·75	10·00
193	29	60c. red	4·50	4·00
194	19	1r. violet	10·00	13·50
195	29	5f. brown	13·50	20·00

1934. Christmas Charity. Nos. 169/75 optd **VOLKSABSTIMMUNG 1935**.

196	33	40c.(+15c.) brown	5·00	20·00
197	-	60c.(+20c.) red	5·00	20·00
198	-	1f.(+50c.) mauve	16·00	36·00
199	-	1f.50(+75c.) blue	10·00	36·00
200	-	2f.(+1f.) red	16·00	50·00
201	-	3f.(+2f.) green	15·00	46·00
202	-	5f.(+5f.) brown	22·00	55·00

FRENCH OCCUPATION

36 Coal-miner

37 Loop of the Saar

1947. Inscr "SAAR".

203	36	2pf. grey	35	55
204	36	3pf. orange	35	70
205	36	6pf. green	35	55
206	36	8pf. red	35	45
207	36	10pf. mauve	35	55
208	36	12pf. green	35	70
209	-	15pf. brown	35	9·00
210	-	16pf. blue	35	55
211	-	20pf. red	35	55
212	-	24pf. brown	35	55
213	-	25pf. mauve	70	32·00
214	-	30pf. green	35	1·10
215	-	40pf. brown	35	1·70
216	-	45pf. red	80	23·00
217	-	50pf. violet	80	32·00
218	-	60pf. violet	70	32·00
219	-	75pf. blue	35	55
220	-	80pf. orange	35	55
221	-	84pf. brown	35	55
222	37	1m. green	35	70

DESIGNS—As T **36**: 15pf. to 24pf. Steel workers; 25pf. to 50pf. Sugar beet harvesters; 60pf. to 80pf. Mettlach Abbey. As T **37**—VERT: 84pf. Marshal Ney.

1947. As last surch in French currency.

223B	36	10c. on 2pf. grey	35	80
224B	36	60c. on 3pf. orange	35	1·60
225B	36	1f. on 10pf. mauve	35	80
226B	36	2f. on 12pf. green	45	2·00
227B	-	3f. on 15pf. brown	45	2·00
228B	-	4f. on 16pf. blue	45	11·50
229B	-	5f. on 20pf. red	45	1·50
230B	-	6f. on 24pf. brown	45	90
231B	-	9f. on 30pf. green	55	19·00
232B	-	10f. on 50pf. violet	55	28·00
233B	-	14f. on 60pf. violet	90	19·00
234B	-	20f. on 84pf. brown	1·50	30·00
235B	37	50f. on 1m. green	2·00	30·00

42 Clasped Hands

43 Builders

44 Saar Valley

1948. Inscr "SAARPOST".

236	42	10c. red (postage)	1·00	2·75
237	42	60c. blue	1·00	2·75
238	42	1f. black	45	45
239	-	2f. red	55	45
240	-	3f. brown	55	45
241	-	4f. red	55	45
242	-	5f. violet	55	45
243	-	6f. red	1·00	45
244	-	9f. blue	6·75	70
245	-	10f. blue	4·00	1·10
246	-	14f. purple	5·75	1·60
247	43	20f. red	11·50	1·60
248	-	50f. blue	19·00	4·00
249	44	25f. red (air)	6·75	4·50
250	44	50f. blue	4·00	3·50
251	44	200f. red	40·00	50·00

DESIGNS—As Type **42**: 2, 3f. Man's head; 4, 5f. Woman's head; 6, 9f. Miner's head. As Type **43**: 10f. Blast furnace chimney; 14f. Foundry; 50f. Facade of Mettlach Abbey.

46 Floods in St. Johann, Sarbrucken

1948. Flood Disaster Relief Fund. Flood Scenes.

252	-	5f.+5f. green (postage)	6·25	50·00
253	46	6f.+4f. purple	6·25	46·00
254	-	12f.+8f. red	9·00	70·00
255	-	18f.+12f. blue	11·50	70·00
MS255a 147×104 mm. Nos. 252/5. Imperf			£1000	£3750
256	-	25f.+25f. brown (air)	34·00	£350
MS256a 90×60 mm. No. 256			£700	£2750

DESIGNS—VERT: 18f. Flooded street, Saarbrucken. HORIZ: 5f. Flooded industrial area; 12f. Landtag building, Saarbrucken; 25f. Floods at Ensdorf, Saarlouis.

47 Map of Saarland

1948. First Anniv of Constitution.

257	47	10f. red	2·75	5·75
258	47	25f. blue	4·00	11·50

48 Hikers and Ludweiler Hostel

1949. Youth Hostels Fund.

259	48	8f.+5f. brown	5·00	£150
260	-	10f.+7f. green	6·25	£150

DESIGN: 10f. Hikers and Weisskirchen hostel.

49 Chemical Research

1949. Saar University.

261	49	15f. red	10·00	70

50 Mare and Foal

1949. Horse Day.

262	50	15f.+5f. red	17·00	46·00
263	-	25f.+15f. blue	23·00	50·00

DESIGN: 25f. Two horses in steeple-chase.

51 Symbolic of Typography

52 Labourer and Foundry

1949

264		10c. purple	45	2·75
265		60c. black	45	2·75
266		1f. red	1·70	45
267		3f. brown	11·50	55
268		5f. violet	2·75	45
269		6f. green	15·00	55
270		8f. green	1·70	90
271	51	10f. orange	6·75	45
272	-	12f. green	20·00	45
273	-	15f. red	10·00	45
274	-	18f. mauve	4·00	7·50
275	52	20f. grey	2·75	45
276	-	25f. blue	28·00	45
277	-	30f. red	25·00	70
278	-	45f. purple	6·75	80
279	-	60f. green	11·50	2·75
280	-	100f. brown	15·00	3·50

DESIGNS—As Type **51**: 10c. Building trade; 60c. Beethoven; 1f. and 3f. Heavy industries; 5f. Slag heap; 6f. and 15f. Colliery; 8f. Posthorn and telephone; 12f. and 18f. Pottery. As Type **52**—VERT: 25f. Blast furnace worker; 60f. Landsweiler; 100f. Wiebelskirchen. HORIZ: 30f. St. Arnual; 45f. "Giant's Boot", Rentrisch.

53 Detail from "Moses Striking the Rock" (Murillo)

1949. National Relief Fund.

281	53	8f.+2f. blue	11·50	55·00
282	-	12f.+3f. green	13·50	70·00
283	-	15f.+5f. purple	20·00	£110
284	-	25f.+10f. blue	34·00	£180
285	-	50f.+20f. purple	50·00	£325

DESIGNS: 12f. "Our Lord healing the Paralytic" (Murillo); 15f. "The Sick Child" (Metsu); 25f. "St. Thomas of Villanueva" (Murillo); 50f. "Madonna of Blieskastel".

54 A. Kolping

1950. Honouring Adolf Kolping (miners' padre).

286	54	15f.+5f. red	36·00	£110

55 P. Wust

1950. Tenth Death Anniv of Peter Wust (philosopher).

287	55	15f. red	18·00	10·00

56 Mail Coach

1950. Stamp Day.

288	56	15f.+5f. brown and red	95·00	£160

57 "Food for the Hungry"

1950. Red Cross Fund.

289	57	25f.+10f. lake and red	39·00	90·00

58 St. Peter

1950. Holy Year.

290	58	12f. green	4·50	15·00
291	58	15f. red	6·75	13·50
292	58	25f. blue	11·50	30·00

59 Town Hall, Ottweiler

1950. 400th Anniv of Ottweiler.

293	59	10f. brown	8·50	11·50

61

1950. Saar's Admission to Council of Europe.

294	61	25f. blue (postage)	50·00	17·00
295	-	200f. red (air)	£200	£350

DESIGN: 200f. As T **61** but with dove in flight over book.

62 St. Lutwinus enters Monastery

1950. National Relief Fund. Inscr "VOLKSHILFE".

296	62	8f.+2f. brown	13·50	46·00
297	-	12f.+3f. green	12·50	46·00
298	-	15f.+5f. brown	17·00	75·00
299	-	25f.+10f. blue	18·00	£100
300	-	50f.+20f. purple	27·00	£170

DESIGNS: 12f. Lutwinus builds Mettlach Abbey; 15f. Lutwinus as Abbot; 25f. Bishop Lutwinus confirming children at Rheims; 50f. Lutwinus helping needy.

63 Orphans

1951. Red Cross Fund.

301	63	25f.+10f. green and red	27·00	90·00

64 Mail-carriers, 1760

1951. Stamp Day.

302	64	15f. purple	12·50	27·00

65 Allegory

1951. Trade Fair.

303	**65**	15f. green	4·00	9·00

66 Flowers and Building

1951. Horticultural Show, Bexbach.

304	**66**	15f. green	4·00	2·50

67 Calvin and Luther

1951. 375th Anniv of Reformation in Saar.

305	**67**	15f.+5f. brown	5·00	10·00

68 "The Good Mother" (Lepicie)

1951. National Relief Fund. Inscr "VOLKSHILFE 1951".

306	**68**	12f.+3f. green	9·00	27·00
307	-	15f.+5f. violet	11·50	27·00
308	-	18f.+7f. red	10·00	27·00
309	-	30f.+10f. blue	17·00	50·00
310	-	50f.+20f. brown	28·00	£100

PAINTINGS: 18f. "Outside the Theatre" (Kampf); 18f. "Sisters of Charity" (Browne); 30f. "The Good Samaritan" (Bassano); 50f. "St. Martin and the Poor" (Van Dyck).

69 Mounted Postman

1952. Stamp Day.

311	**69**	30f.+10f. blue	17·00	40·00

70 Athlete bearing Olympic Flame

1952. 15th Olympic Games, Helsinki. Inscr "OLYMPISCHE SPIELE 1952".

312	**70**	15f.+5f. green	8·50	17·00
313	-	30f.+5f. blue	8·50	19·00

DESIGN: 30f. Hand, laurels and globe.

71 Globe and Emblem

1952. Saar Fair.

314	**71**	15f. red	3·50	1·90

72 Red Cross and Refugees

1952. Red Cross Week.

315	**72**	15f. red	5·00	1·90

73 G.P.O., Saarbrucken

1952. (A) Without inscr in or below design. (B) With inscr.

316	-	1f. green (B)	35	35
317	-	2f. violet	35	35
318	-	3f. red	35	35
319	**73**	5f. green (A)	6·75	35
320	**73**	5f. green (B)	35	35
321	-	6f. purple	55	35
322	-	10f. brown	55	35
323	**73**	12f. green (B)	1·00	35
324	-	15f. brown (A)	11·50	35
325	-	15f. brown (B)	5·00	35
326	-	15f. red (B)	45	35
327	-	18f. purple	4·00	6·75
329	-	30f. blue	1·40	1·40
334	-	500f. red	23·00	90·00

DESIGNS—HORIZ: 1, 15f. (3) Colliery shafthead; 2, 10f. Ludwigs High School, Saarbrucken; 3, 18f. Gersweiler Bridge; 6f. Mettlach Bridge; 30f. University Library, Saarbrucken. VERT: 500f. St. Ludwig's Church, Saarbrucken.

74 "Count Stroganov as a Boy" (Greuze)

1952. National Relief Fund. Paintings inscr "VOLKSHILFE 1952".

335	**74**	15f.+5f. brown	4·50	16·00
336	-	18f.+7f. red	6·75	20·00
337	-	30f.+10f. blue	9·00	23·00

PORTRAITS: 18f. "The Holy Shepherd" (Murillo); 30f. "Portrait of a Boy" (Kraus).

75 Fair Symbol

1953. Saar Fair.

338	**75**	15f. blue	3·00	2·30

76 Postilions

1953. Stamp Day.

339	**76**	15f. blue	9·75	18·00

77 Henri Dunant

1953. Red Cross Week and 125th Anniv of Birth of Dunant (founder).

340	**77**	15f.+5f. brown and red	4·00	10·00

79 St. Benedict blessing St. Maurus

1953. Tholey Abbey Fund.

344	**79**	30f.+10f. black	3·75	11·50

80 Saar Fair

1954. Saar Fair.

345	**80**	15f. green	3·00	1·40

81 Postal Motor Coach

1954. Stamp Day.

346	**81**	15f. red	13·50	19·00

82 Red Cross and Child

1954. Red Cross Week.

347	**82**	15f.+5f. brown	4·50	10·00

83 Madonna and Child (Holbein)

1954. Marian Year.

348	**83**	5f. red	3·50	4·50
349	-	10f. green	3·50	4·50
350	-	15f. blue	4·50	8·00

DESIGNS: 10f. "Sistine Madonna" (Raphael); 15f. "Madonna and Child with Pear" (Durer).

84 "Street Urchin with a Melon" (Murillo)

1954. National Relief Fund. Paintings inscr "VOLKSHILFE 1954".

351	**84**	5f.+3f. red	1·40	2·00
352	-	10f.+5f. green	1·40	2·00
353	-	15f.+7f. violet	1·40	2·75

DESIGNS: 10f. "Maria de Medici" (A. Bronzino); 15f. "Baron Emil von Maucler" (J. F. Dietrich).

85 Cyclist and Flag

1955. World Cross-Country Cycle Race.

354	**85**	15f. blue, red and black	55	1·00

86 Rotary Emblem and Industrial Plant

1955. 50th Anniv of Rotary International.

355	**86**	15f. brown	55	1·40

87 Exhibitors' Flags

1955. Saar Fair.

356	**87**	15f. multicoloured	55	1·00

88 Nurse and Baby

1955. Red Cross Week.

357	**88**	15f.+5f. black and red	80	1·50

89 Postman

1955. Stamp Day.

358	**89**	15f. purple	2·75	3·50

1955. Referendum. Optd **VOLKSBEFRAGUNG 1955**.

359	15f. red (No. 326)	70	1·00
360	18f. purple (No. 327)	70	80
361	30f. blue (No. 329)	90	1·00

91 "Mother" (Durer)

1955. National Relief Fund. Durer paintings inscr as in T 91.

362	**91**	5f.+3f. green	90	1·80
363	-	10f.+5f. green	1·10	2·30
364	-	15f.+7f. bistre	1·60	2·75

PAINTINGS: 10f. "The Praying Hands"; 15f. "The Old Man from Antwerp".

92

1956. Saar Fair.

365	**92**	15f. green and red	55	1·40

93 Radio Tower

1956. Stamp Day.

366	**93**	15f. green and turquoise	55	1·40

94 Casualty Station

1956. Red Cross Week.

367	**94**	15f.+5f. brown	55	1·40

95

1956. Olympic Games.

368	**95**	12f.+3f. blue and green	80	1·00
369	**95**	15f.+5f. brown & purple	80	1·00

96 Winterberg Memorial

1956. Winterberg Memorial Reconstruction Fund.

370	**96**	5f.+2f. green	45	70
371	**96**	12f.+3f. purple	45	70
372	**96**	15f.+5f. brown	45	90

97 "Portrait of Lucrezia Crivelli" (da Vinci)

1956. National Relief Fund. Inscr as in T **97**.

373	**97**	5f.+3f. blue	45	45
374	-	10f.+5f. red	45	70
375	-	15f.+7f. green	45	1·10

PAINTINGS: 10f. "Saskia" (Rembrandt); 15f. "Lady Playing Spinet" (Floris).

RETURN TO GERMANY

98 Arms of the Saar

1957. Return of the Saar to Germany.

376	**98**	15f. blue and red	35	55

99 President Heuse

1957. (a) Without "F" after figure of value.

377	**99**	1f. green	35	25
378	**99**	2f. violet	35	25
379	**99**	3f. brown	35	25
380	**99**	4f. mauve	45	1·10
381	**99**	5f. green	35	25
382	**99**	6f. red	35	70
383	**99**	10f. grey	35	45
384	**99**	12f. orange	35	25
385	**99**	15f. green	35	25
386	**99**	18f. red	90	3·50
387	**99**	25f. lilac	70	1·10
388	**99**	30f. purple	70	1·10
389	**99**	45f. green	1·60	4·00
390	**99**	50f. brown	1·60	1·80
391	**99**	60f. red	2·30	4·50
392	**99**	70f. orange	4·00	6·75
393	**99**	80f. green	1·40	5·25
394	**99**	90f. grey	4·00	9·00
395	**99**	100f. red (24×29½ mm)	3·50	11·50
396	**99**	200f. lilac (24×29½ mm)	9·00	36·00

78 "Painter's Young Son" (Rubens)

1953. National Relief Fund. Paintings inscr "VOLKSHILFE 1953".

341	-	15f.+5f. violet	4·50	8·00
342	-	18f.+7f. red	4·50	8·50
343	**78**	30f.+10f. green	6·75	13·50

DESIGNS—VERT: 15f. "Clarice Strozzi" (Titian). HORIZ: 18f. "Painter's Children" (Rubens).

(b) With "F" after figure of value.

406		1f. grey	35	35
407		3f. blue	35	35
408		5f. green	35	35
409		6f. brown	35	70
410		10f. violet	35	35
411		12f. orange	35	35
412		15f. green	55	35
413		18f. grey	2·75	6·75
414		20f. green	1·70	4·50
415		25f. brown	55	55
416		30f. mauve	1·40	55
417		35f. brown	3·50	4·50
418		45f. green	2·75	5·75
419		50f. brown	1·40	2·75
420		70f. green	6·75	8·00
421		80f. blue	3·50	7·50
422		90f. red	8·00	9·00
423		100f. orange (24×29½ mm)	7·50	10·00
424		200f. green (24×29½ mm)	12·50	36·00
425		300f. blue (24 ×29½ mm)	13·50	41·00

100 Iron Foundry

1957. Saar Fair.

397	**100**	15f. red and black	35	55

101 Arms of Merzig and St. Pierre Church

1957. Centenary of Merzig.

398	**101**	15f. blue	35	55

101a "Europa" Tree

1957. Europa.

399	**101a**	20f. orange and yellow	90	1·50
400	**101a**	35f. violet and pink	1·40	2·00

101b Young Miner

1957. Humanitarian Relief Fund.

401	**101b**	6f.+4f. black & brown	35	35
402	-	12f.+6f. black & green	35	45
403	-	15f.+7f. black and red	45	55
404	-	30f.+10f. black & blue	55	1·00

DESIGNS: 12f. Miner drilling at coalface; 15f. Miner with coal-cutting machine; 30f. Operator at mine lift-shaft.

101c Carrier Pigeons

1957. International Correspondence Week.

405	**101c**	15f. black and red	35	55

101d Max and Moritz (cartoon characters)

1958. 150th Death Anniv of Wilhelm Busch (writer and illustrator).

426	**101d**	12f. green and black	35	35
427	-	15f. red and black	35	55

DESIGN: 15f. Wilhelm Busch.

101e "Prevent Forest Fires"

1958. Forest Fires Prevention Campaign.

428	**101e**	15f. black and red	35	55

101f Diesel and First Oil Engine

1958. Birth Centenary of Rudolf Diesel (engineer).

429	**101f**	12f. green	35	55

101g "The Fox who stole the Goose"

1958. Berlin Students' Fund.

430	**101g**	12f.+6f. red, black and green	25	45
431	-	15f.+7f. brown, green and red	35	55

DESIGN: 15f. "A Hunter from the Palatinate".

102 Saarbrucken Town Hall and Fair Emblem

1958. Saar Fair.

432	**102**	15f. purple	35	55

103 Homburg

1958. 400th Anniv of Homburg.

433	**103**	15f. green	35	55

103a Emblem

1958. 150th Anniv of German Gymnastics.

434	**103a**	12f. black, green and grey	35	55

103b Schulze-Delitzsch

1958. 150th Birth of Schulze-Delitzsch (pioneer of German Co-operative Movement).

435	**103b**	12f. green	35	55

103c "Europa"

1958. Europa.

436	**103c**	12f. blue and green	80	1·40
437	-	30f. red and blue	1·00	2·00

103d Friedrich Raiffeisen (philanthropist)

1958. Humanitarian Relief and Welfare Funds.

438	**103d**	6f.+4f. brn, lt brn & chest	35	35
439	-	12f.+6f. red, yell & grn	35	35
440	-	15f.+7f. blue, grn & red	70	70
441	-	30f.+10f. yellow, grn & bl	70	90

DESIGNS—Inscr "WOHLFAHRTSMARKE": 12f. Dairymaid; 15f. Vine-dresser 30f. Farm labourer.

103e Fugger

1959. 500th Birth Anniv of Jakob Fugger (merchant prince).

442	**103e**	15f. black and red	35	55

104 Hands holding Crates

1959. Saar Fair.

443	**104**	15f. red	35	55

105 Saarbrucken

1959. 50th Anniv of Greater Saarbrucken.

444	**105**	15f. blue	35	55

105a Humboldt

1959. Death Centenary of Alexander von Humboldt (naturalist).

445	**105a**	15f. blue	55	70

OFFICIAL STAMPS

1922. Nos. 84 to 94 optd **DIENSTMARKE**.

O98	3c. green	1·40	50·00
O99	5c. black and orange	55	55
O100	10c. green	55	45
O109	15c. orange	3·50	70
O101	15c. brown	55	45
O102	20c. blue and yellow	55	45
O111	25c. red and yellow	3·50	70
O104	30c. red and yellow	55	45
O105	40c. brown and yellow	80	45
O106	50c. blue and yellow	80	45
O112	75c. green and yellow	6·75	3·50
O108a	1f. brown	17·00	3·50

1927. Nos. 108/15, 117 and 119 optd **DIENSTMARKE**.

O128	10c. brown	2·75	3·50
O129	15c. green	2·75	9·00
O130	20c. brown	2·75	2·30
O131	25c. blue	3·50	9·00
O122	30c. green	8·00	1·30
O133	40c. brown	2·75	45
O134	50c. red	5·75	55
O135	60c. orange	1·70	45
O136	75c. purple	3·50	1·10
O137	1f. violet	3·50	55
O138	2f. red	3·50	55

O51 Arms

1949

O264	**O51**	10c. red	70	27·00
O265	**O51**	30c. black	70	32·00
O266	**O51**	1f. green	70	1·50
O267	**O51**	2f. red	2·75	1·70
O268	**O51**	5f. blue	3·50	1·50
O269	**O51**	10f. black	1·50	1·50
O270	**O51**	12f. mauve	12·50	16·00
O271	**O51**	15f. blue	1·50	1·50
O272	**O51**	20f. green	4·00	1·70
O273	**O51**	30f. mauve	10·00	6·75
O274	**O51**	50f. purple	3·50	5·75
O275	**O51**	100f. brown	£110	£425

Pt. 1

SABAH

Formerly North Borneo, now part of Malaysia.

100 cents = 1 Malaysian dollar.

1964. Nos. 391/406 of North Borneo optd **SABAH**.

408	1c. green and red	10	10
409	4c. olive and orange	15	50
410	5c. sepia and violet	30	10
411	6c. black and turquoise	1·25	10
412	10c. green and red	2·25	10
413	12c. brown and myrtle	20	10
414	20c. turquoise and blue	6·00	10
415	25c. black and red	1·25	90
416	30c. sepia and olive	30	10
417	35c. slate and brown	30	20
418	50c. green and bistre	30	10
419	75c. blue and purple	4·50	1·00
420	$1 brown and green	15·00	2·25
421	$2 brown and slate	17·00	3·00
422	$5 green and purple	17·00	15·00
423	$10 red and blue	20·00	38·00

138 "Vanda hookeriana"

1965. As No. 115/21 of Kedah, but with Arms of Sabah inset as T **138**.

424	**138**	1c. multicoloured	10	1·25
425	-	2c. multicoloured	10	2·00
426	-	5c. multicoloured	10	10
427	-	6c. multicoloured	30	1·50
428	-	10c. multicoloured	30	10
429	-	15c. multicoloured	3·00	10
430	-	20c. multicoloured	3·00	75

The higher values used in Sabah were Nos. 20/7 of Malaysia.

139 "Hebomoia glaucippe"

1971. Butterflies. As Nos. 124/30 of Kedah, but with Sabah Arms inset as T **139**.

432		1c. multicoloured	65	2·50
433		2c. multicoloured	75	2·50
434		5c. multicoloured	80	50
435		6c. multicoloured	1·00	2·00
436	**139**	10c. multicoloured	80	15
437	-	15c. multicoloured	1·00	10
438	-	20c. multicoloured	1·10	1·25

The higher values in use with this issue were Nos. 64/71 of Malaysia.

140 "Hibiscus rosa-sinensis"

1979. As Nos. 135/41 of Kedah, but with Arms of Sabah as T **140**.

445	1c. "Rafflesia hasseltii"	10	1·60
446	2c. "Pterocarpus indicus"	10	1·60
447	5c. "Lagerstroemia speciosa"	15	50
448	10c. "Durio zibethinus"	30	10
449	15c. Type **140**	50	10
450	20c. "Rhododendron scortechinii"	30	10
451	25c. "Etlingera elatior" (inscr "Phaeomeria speciosa")	80	20

The higher values in use with this issue were Nos. 190/7 of Malaysia.

141 Coffee

1986. As Nos. 152/8 of Kedah but with Arms of Sabah as in T **141**.

459	1c. Type **141**	10	50
460	2c. Coconuts	15	50
461	5c. Cocoa	20	15
462	10c. Black pepper	25	10
463	15c. Rubber	40	10
464	20c. Oil palm	40	10
465	30c. Rice	40	15

142 *Nelumbium nelumbo* (sacred lotus)

2007. Garden Flowers. As Nos. 210/15 of Johore, but with Arms of Sabah as in T **142**. Multicoloured.

466	5s. Type **142**	10	10
467	10s. *Hydrangea macrophylla*	15	10
468	20s. *Hippeastrum reticulatum*	25	15
469	30s. *Bougainvillea*	40	20
470	40s. *Ipomoea indica*	50	30
471	50s. *Hibiscus rosa-sinensis*	65	35
MS472	100×85 mm. Nos. 466/71	2·00	2·00

Pt. 1

ST CHRISTOPHER

One of the Leeward Is. Stamps superseded in 1890 by Leeward Islands general issue.

12 pence = 1 shilling.

1

1870

11	**1**	½d. green	5·50	3·50
6	**1**	1d. mauve	80·00	7·00
13	**1**	1d. red	3·00	2·25
14	**1**	2½d. brown	£180	60·00
16	**1**	2½d. blue	4·75	1·50
8	**1**	4d. blue	£200	15·00
18	**1**	4d. grey	1·75	1·00
9	**1**	6d. green	60·00	5·00
19	**1**	6d. olive	90·00	£400
20	**1**	1s. mauve	£100	65·00

1885. Surch in words.

23	½d. on half of 1d. red	29·00	42·00
26	1d. on ½d. green	50·00	60·00
28	1d. on 2½d. blue	70·00	70·00
24	1d. on 6d. green	20·00	45·00
22	4d. on 6d. green	65·00	50·00

1886. Surch in figures.

25	4d. on 6d. green	60·00	95·00

Pt. 1

ST HELENA

An island in the South Atlantic Ocean, west of Africa.

1856. 12 pence = 1 shilling; 20 shillings = 1 pound.
1971. 100 pence = 1 pound.

The early stamps of St. Helena, other than the 6d., were formed by printing the 6d., in various colours and surcharging it with new values in words or (in case of the 21/2d.) in figures.

1

1856. Imperf.

3	1d. on 6d. red	£150	£250
5	4d. on 6d. red	£500	£250
1	6d. blue	£500	£180

1861. Perf.

36	½d. on 6d. green	2·50	2·75
37	1d. on 6d. red	4·75	3·75
39	2d. on 6d. yellow	3·00	8·00
40	2½d. on 6d. blue	3·00	5·50
42	3d. on 6d. purple	8·00	5·00
14	4d. on 6d. red	£150	60·00
43c	4d. on 6d. brown	27·00	17·00
25	6d. blue	£500	50·00
44	6d. grey	40·00	5·00
30	1s. on 6d. green	21·00	12·00
20	5s. on 6d. yellow	60·00	70·00

11

1890

46	**11**	½d. green	2·75	6·50
47	**11**	1d. red	19·00	2·00
48	**11**	1½d. brown and green	4·50	12·00
49	**11**	2d. yellow	5·00	12·00
50	**11**	2½d. blue	18·00	12·00
51	**11**	5d. violet	11·00	32·00
52	**11**	10d. brown	25·00	70·00

12

1902. Inscr "POSTAGE POSTAGE".

53	**12**	½d. green	2·00	2·75
54	**12**	1d. red	13·00	70

13 Government House

14 The Wharf

1903

55	**13**	½d. brown and green	2·00	3·25
56	**14**	1d. black and red	1·50	35
57	**13**	2d. black and green	10·00	1·25
58	**14**	8d. black and brown	23·00	32·00
59	**13**	1s. brown and orange	26·00	40·00
60	**14**	2s. black and violet	65·00	95·00

1908. Inscr "POSTAGE & REVENUE".

64	**12**	2½d. blue	2·00	1·50
66a	**12**	4d. black and red on yellow	7·00	18·00
67a	**12**	6d. purple	10·00	14·00
70	**12**	10s. green and red on green	£425	

1912. As T **13/14** but with medallion of King George V.

72	**13**	½d. black and green	2·25	10·00
73	**14**	1d. black and red	4·75	1·75
89	**14**	1d. green	3·25	55·00
74	**14**	1½d. black and orange	3·50	9·00
90	**14**	1½d. red	12·00	48·00
75	**13**	2d. black and grey	6·00	1·75
76	**14**	2½d. black and blue	3·50	7·00
77	**13**	3d. black & purple on yellow	3·50	5·00
91	**13**	3d. blue	25·00	95·00
78	**14**	8d. black and purple	9·00	60·00
79	**13**	1s. black on green	9·00	35·00
80	**14**	2s. black and blue on blue	55·00	£100
81	**14**	3s. black and violet	75·00	£160

18

1912. Inscr "POSTAGE & REVENUE".

83	**18**	4d. black and red on yellow	15·00	26·00
84	**18**	6d. purple	4·25	5·00

1913. Inscr "POSTAGE POSTAGE".

85	4d. black and red on yellow	8·00	2·75
86	6d. purple	14·00	28·00

1916. Surch **WAR TAX ONE PENNY**.

87	1d.+1d. black and red (No. 73)	3·50	3·25

1919. Surch **WAR TAX 1d**.

88	1d.+1d. black and red (No. 73)	2·00	4·50

22 Badge of St. Helena

1922

97	**22**	½d. grey and black	4·50	4·00
98	**22**	1d. grey and green	3·75	1·60
99	**22**	1½d. red	3·25	13·00
100	**22**	2d. grey and brown	3·75	2·00
101	**22**	3d. blue	2·00	4·00
92	**22**	4d. grey and black on yellow	15·00	6·00
103	**22**	5d. green and red on green	5·00	5·50
104	**22**	6d. grey and purple	5·50	8·00
105	**22**	8d. grey and violet	4·00	8·00
106	**22**	1s. grey and brown	6·50	9·00
107	**22**	1s.6d. grey & green on grn	15·00	60·00
108	**22**	2s. purple and blue on blue	22·00	55·00
109	**22**	2s.6d. grey & red on yellow	16·00	75·00
110	**22**	5s. grey and green on yellow	42·00	90·00
111	**22**	7s.6d. grey and orange	£140	£200
112	**22**	10s. grey and green	£170	£250
113	**22**	15s. grey and purple on blue	£1100	£2750
96	**22**	£1 grey and purple on red	£450	£650

23 Lot and Lot's Wife

1934. Centenary of British Colonization.

114	**23**	½d. black and purple	1·00	80
115	-	1d. black and green	65	85
116	-	1½d. black and red	2·50	3·25
117	-	2d. black and orange	3·75	1·25
118	-	3d. black and blue	1·40	4·50
119	-	6d. black and blue	3·25	3·00
120	-	1s. black and brown	6·50	18·00
121	-	2s.6d. black and red	50·00	60·00
122	-	5s. black and brown	£100	£100
123	-	10s. black and purple	£300	£350

DESIGNS—HORIZ: 1d. The "Plantation"; 1½d. Map of St. Helena; 2d. Quay, Jamestown; 3d. James Valley; 6d. Jamestown; 1s. Munden's Promontory; 5s. High Knoll; 10s. Badge of St. Helena. VERT: 2s.6d. St. Helena.

32a Windsor Castle

1935. Silver Jubilee.

124	**32a**	1½d. blue and red	1·00	5·50
125	**32a**	2d. blue and grey	3·75	90
126	**32a**	6d. green and blue	9·50	3·25
127	**32a**	1s. grey and purple	26·00	24·00

32b King George VI and Queen Elizabeth

1937. Coronation.

128	**32b**	1d. green	40	75
129	**32b**	2d. orange	55	45
130	**32b**	3d. blue	80	50

33 Badge of St. Helena

1938

131	**33**	½d. violet	15	65
132	**33**	1d. green	11·00	2·50
132a	**33**	1d. orange	30	30
149	**33**	1d. black and green	1·50	1·50
133	**33**	1½d. red	30	40
150	**33**	1½d. black and red	1·50	1·50
134	**33**	2d. orange	30	15
151	**33**	2d. black and red	1·50	1·50
135	**33**	3d. blue	80·00	18·00
135a	**33**	3d. grey	30	30
135b	**33**	4d. blue	2·50	2·50
136	**33**	6d. blue	2·25	2·75
136a	**33**	8d. green	4·00	1·00
137	**33**	1s. brown	1·25	1·50
138	**33**	2s.6d. purple	20·00	7·00
139	**33**	5s. brown	20·00	16·00
140	**33**	10s. purple	20·00	19·00

33a Houses of Parliament, London

1946. Victory.

141	**33a**	2d. orange	40	50
142	**33a**	4d. blue	60	30

33b King George VI and Queen Elizabeth

33c King George VI and Queen Elizabeth

1948. Silver Wedding.

143	**33b**	3d. black	30	30
144	**33c**	10s. blue	28·00	42·00

33d Hermes, Globe and Forms of Transport

33e Hemispheres, Jet-powered Vickers Viking Airliner and Steamer

33f Hermes and Globe

33g U.P.U. Monument

1949. U.P.U.

145	**33d**	3d. red	25	1·00
146	**33e**	4d. blue	3·00	1·75
147	**33f**	6d. green	1·50	3·75
148	**33g**	1s. black	35	1·10

33h Queen Elizabeth II

1953. Coronation.

152	**33h**	3d. black and lilac	1·75	1·50

34 Badge of St. Helena

1953

153	**34**	½d. black and green	30	30
154	-	1d. black and green	15	20
155	-	1½d. black and purple	4·75	1·50
156	-	2d. black and red	50	30
157	-	2½d. black and red	40	30
158	-	3d. black and brown	3·25	30
159	-	4d. black and blue	40	1·00
160	-	6d. black and violet	40	30
161	-	7d. black and grey	1·50	1·75
162	-	1s. black and red	40	70
163	-	2s.6d. black and violet	20·00	8·00
164	-	5s. black and sepia	25·00	10·00
165	-	10s. black and yellow	40·00	13·00

DESIGNS—HORIZ: 1d. Flax plantation; 2d. Lace-making; 2½d. Drying flax; 3d. St. Helena sand plover; 4d. Flagstaff and The Barn (hills); 6d. Donkeys carrying flax; 7d. Map; 1s. The Castle; 2s.6d. Cutting flax; 5s. Jamestown; 10s. Longwood House. VERT: 1½d. Heart-shaped Waterfall.

45 Stamp of 1856

1956. Cent of First St. Helena Postage Stamp.

166	**45**	3d. blue and red	15	10
167	**45**	4d. blue and brown	15	20
168	**45**	6d. blue and purple	15	25

47 East Indiaman "London" off James Bay

1959. Tercentenary of Settlement.

169	-	3d. black and red	20	15
170	**47**	6d. green and blue	75	75
171	-	1s. black and orange	50	75

DESIGNS—HORIZ: 3d. Arms of East India Company; 1s. Commemoration Stone.

1961. Tristan Relief Fund. Nos. 46 and 49/51 of Tristan da Cunha surch **ST. HELENA Tristan Relief** and premium.

172	2½c.+3d. black and red	£1500	£650
173	5c.+6d. black and blue	£1800	£700
174	7½c.+9d. black and red	£3000	£1200
175	10c.+1s. black and brown	£2250	£1300

50 St. Helena Butterflyfish

63 Queen Elizabeth II with Prince Andrew (after Cecil Beaton)

1961

176	**50**	1d. multicoloured	40	20
177	-	1½d. multicoloured	50	20
178	-	2d. red and grey	15	20
179	-	3d. multicoloured	1·25	20
180	-	4½d. multicoloured	60	60
181	-	6d. red, sepia and olive	5·50	70
182	-	7d. brown, black and violet	35	70
183	-	10d. purple and blue	35	70
184	-	1s. yellow, green and brown	55	1·25
185	-	1s.6d. grey and blue	11·00	4·75
186	-	2s.6d. red, yellow & turq	2·50	2·50
187	-	5s. yellow, brown and green	14·00	5·50
188	-	10s. red, black and blue	13·00	10·00
189	**63**	£1 brown and blue	21·00	23·00

DESIGNS—VERT (as Type **50**): 1½d. Yellow canary; 3d. Queen Elizabeth II; 4½d. Red-wood flower; 6d. Madagascar red fody; 1s. Gum-wood flower; 1s.6d. White tern; 5s. Night-blooming Cereus. HORIZ (as T **50**): 2d. Brittle starfish; 7d. Trumpetfish; 10d. Feather starfish; 2s.6d. Orange starfish; 10s. Deep-water bullseye.

63a Protein Foods

1963. Freedom from Hunger.

190	**63a**	1s.6d. blue	75	40

63b Red Cross Emblem

1963. Centenary of Red Cross.

191	**63b**	3d. red and black	30	25
192	**63b**	1s.6d. red and blue	70	1·75

1965. First Local Post. Optd **FIRST LOCAL POST 4th JANUARY 1965.**

193	**50**	1d. multicoloured	10	25
194	-	3d. multicoloured (No. 179)	10	25
195	-	6d. red, sepia and olive (No. 181)	40	30
196	-	1s.6d. grey & blue (No. 185)	60	35

64a I.T.U. Emblem

1965. Centenary of I.T.U.

197	**64a**	3d. blue and brown	25	25
198	**64a**	6d. purple and green	35	25

64b I.C.Y. Emblem

1965. Centenary of I.C.Y.

199	**64b**	1d. purple and turquoise	30	15
200	**64b**	6d. green and lavender	30	15

64c Sir Winston Churchill and St. Paul's Cathedral in Wartime

1966. Churchill Commemoration.

201	**64c**	1d. blue	15	25
202	**64c**	3d. green	25	25
203	**64c**	6d. brown	40	30
204	**64c**	1s.6d. violet	45	85

64d Footballer's Legs, Ball and Jules Rimet Cup

1966. World Cup Football Championship.

205	**64d**	3d. multicoloured	50	35
206	**64d**	6d. multicoloured	75	35

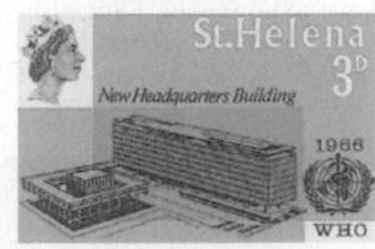
64e W.H.O. Emblem

1966. Inauguration of W.H.O. Headquarters, Geneva.

207	**64e**	3d. black, green and blue	75	20
208	**64e**	1s.6d. black, purple & ochre	2·25	1·00

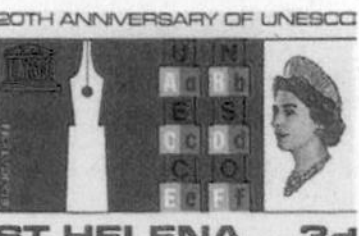
64f "Education"

64g "Science"

64h "Culture"

1966. 20th Anniv of UNESCO.

209	**64f**	3d. multicoloured	1·00	25
210	**64g**	6d. yellow, violet and olive	1·25	60
211	**64h**	1s.6d. black, purple & orge	2·25	2·25

65 Badge of St. Helena

1967. New Constitution.

212	**65**	1s. multicoloured	10	10
213	**65**	2s.6d. multicoloured	20	20

66 Fire of London

1967. 300th Anniv of Arrival of Settlers after Great Fire of London.

214	**66**	1d. red and black	15	10
215	-	3d. blue and black	20	10
216	-	6d. violet and black	20	15
217	-	1s.6d. green and black	20	20

DESIGNS: 3d. East Indiaman "Charles"; 6d. Settlers landing at Jamestown; 1s.6d. Settlers clearing scrub.

70 Interlocking Maps of Tristan and St. Helena

1968. 30th Anniv of Tristan da Cunha as a Dependency of St. Helena.

218	**70**	4d. purple and brown	10	10
219	-	8d. olive and brown	10	30
220	**70**	1s.9d. blue and brown	15	40
221	-	2s.3d. blue and brown	20	40

DESIGNS: 8d. and 2s.3d. Interlocking maps of Tristan and St. Helena (different).

72 Queen Elizabeth and Sir Hudson Lowe

1968. 150th Anniv of Abolition of Slavery in St. Helena.

222	**72**	3d. multicoloured	10	15
223	**72**	9d. multicoloured	10	20
224	-	1s.6d. multicoloured	15	30
225	-	2s.6d. multicoloured	25	45

DESIGN: Nos. 224 and 225, Queen Elizabeth and Sir George Bingham.

74 Blue Gum Eucalyptus and Road Construction

1968. Multicoloured.

226	½d. Type **74**	10	10
227	1d. Electricity development	10	10
228	1½d. Dental unit	15	10
229	2d. Pest control	15	10
230	3d. Flats in Jamestown	30	10
231	4d. Livestock improvement	20	10
232	6d. Schools broadcasting	50	10

233	8d. Country Cottages	30	10
234	10d. New school buildings	30	10
235	1s. Reafforestation	30	10
236	1s.6d. Heavy lift crane	70	3·00
237	2s.6d. Lady Field Children's Home	70	3·50
238	5s. Agricultural training	70	3·50
239	10s. New General Hospital	2·00	4·50
240	£1 Lifeboat "John Dutton"	10·00	15·00

PLANTS SHOWN: ½, 4d., 1s.6d. Blue gum eucalyptus; 1d., 6d., 2s.6d. Cabbage-tree; 1½d., 8d., 5s. St. Helena redwood; 2, 10d., 10s. Scrubweed; 3d., 1s., £1 Tree-fern.

89 Brig *Perseverance*

1969. Mail Communications. Multicoloured.

241	4d. Type **89**	20	20
242	8d. "Phoebe" (screw steamer)	25	40
243	1s.9d. "Llandovery Castle" (liner)	25	60
244	2s.3d. "Good Hope Castle" (cargo liner)	25	75

93 W.O. and Drummer of the 53rd Foot, 1815

1969. Military Uniforms. Multicoloured.

245	6d. Type **93**	15	25
246	8d. Officer and Surgeon, 20th Foot, 1816	15	25
247	1s.8d. Drum Major, 66th Foot, 1816, and Royal Artillery Officer, 1820	20	45
248	2s.6d. Private, 91st Foot, and 2nd Corporal, Royal Sappers and Miners, 1832	20	55

97 Dickens, Mr. Pickwick and Job Trotter (*Pickwick Papers*)

1970. Death Cent of Charles Dickens. Multicoloured.

249	4d. Type **97**	80	15
250	8d. Mr. Bumble and Oliver ("Oliver Twist")	90	15
251	1s.6d. Sairey Gamp and Mark Tapley ("Martin Chuzzlewit")	1·00	20
252	2s.6d. Jo and Mr. Turveydrop ("Bleak House")	1·00	25

All designs include a portrait of Dickens as Type **97**.

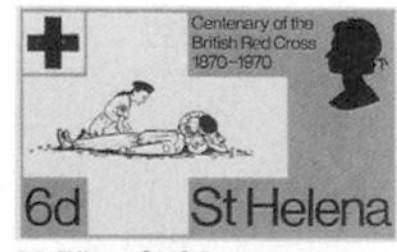

98 "Kiss of Life"

1970. Centenary of British Red Cross.

253	**98**	6d. bistre, red and black	15	15
254	-	9d. green, red and black	15	20
255	-	1s.9d. grey, red and black	20	30
256	-	2s.3d. lilac, red and black	20	45

DESIGNS: 9d. Nurse with girl in wheelchair; 1s.9d. Nurse bandaging child's knee; 2s.3d. Red Cross emblem.

99 Officer's Shako Plate (20th Foot)

1970. Military Equipment (1st issue). Multicoloured.

257	4d. Type **99**	20	20
258	9d. Officer's breast plate (66th Foot)	25	30
259	1s.3d. Officer's Full Dress shako (91st Foot)	25	40
260	2s.11d. Ensign's shako (53rd Foot)	40	60

See also Nos. 281/4, 285/8 and 291/4.

100 Electricity Development

1971. Decimal Currency. Designs as Nos. 227/40, inscr as T **100**.

261	½p. multicoloured	10	10
262	1p. multicoloured	10	10
263	1½p. multicoloured	10	10
264	2p. multicoloured	1·75	1·00
265	2½p. multicoloured	10	10
266	3½p. multicoloured	30	10
267	4½p. multicoloured	10	10
268	5p. multicoloured	10	10
269	7½p. multicoloured	40	35
270	10p. multicoloured	30	35
271	12½p. multicoloured	30	50
272	25p. multicoloured	60	1·25
273	50p. multicoloured	1·00	2·00
274	£1 multicoloured	20·00	15·00

101 St. Helena holding the "True Cross"

1971. Easter.

275	**101**	2p. multicoloured	10	10
276	**101**	5p. multicoloured	10	15
277	**101**	7½p. multicoloured	15	20
278	**101**	12½p. multicoloured	20	25

102 Napoleon (after painting by J. L. David) and Tomb on St. Helena

1971. 150th Death Anniv of Napoleon. Multicoloured.

279	2p. Type **102**	20	50
280	34p. "Napoleon at St. Helena" (H. Delaroche)	45	1·00

1971. Military Equipment (2nd issue). As T **99**. Multicoloured.

281	1½p. Artillery Private's hanger	20	30
282	4p. Baker rifle and socket bayonet	25	60
283	6p. Infantry Officer's sword	25	80
284	22½p. Baker rifle and sword bayonet	40	1·25

1972. Military Equipment (3rd issue). As T **99**. Multicoloured.

285	2p. multicoloured	15	20
286	5p. lilac, blue and black	15	40
287	7½p. multicoloured	20	50
288	12½p. sepia, brown and black	30	60

DESIGNS: 2p. Royal Sappers and Miners breast-plate, post 1823; 5p. Infantry sergeant's spontoon, c. 1830; 7½p. Royal Artillery officer's breast-plate, c. 1830; 12½p. English military pistol, c. 1800.

103 St. Helena Sand Plover and White Tern

1972. Royal Silver Wedding.

289	**103**	2p. green	20	40
290	**103**	16p. brown	30	85

1973. Military Equipment (4th issue). As T **99**. Multicoloured.

291	2p. Other Rank's shako, 53rd Foot, 1815	25	55
292	5p. Band and Drums sword, 1830	30	1·00
293	7½p. Royal Sappers and Miners Officer's hat, 1830	40	1·25
294	12½p. General's sword, 1831	45	1·50

103a Princess Anne and Captain Mark Phillips

1973. Royal Wedding. Multicoloured, background colours given.

295	**103a**	2p. blue	15	10
296	**103a**	18p. green	25	20

104 *Westminster* and *Claudine* beached, 1849

1973. Tercentenary of East India Company Charter. Multicoloured.

297	1½p. Type **104**	25	45
298	4p. "True Briton", 1790	35	65
299	6p. "General Goddard" in action, 1795	35	65
300	22½p. "Kent" burning in the Bay of Biscay, 1825	70	1·75

105 U.P.U. Emblem and Ships

1974. Centenary of U.P.U. Multicoloured.

301	5p. Type **105**	20	25
302	25p. U.P.U. emblem and letters	40	55
MS303	89×84 mm. Nos. 301/2	75	1·50

106 Churchill in Sailor Suit and Blenheim Palace

1974. Birth Cent of Sir Winston Churchill.

304	**106**	5p. multicoloured	20	20
305	-	25p. black, pink and purple	30	60
MS306		108×93 mm. Nos. 304/5	75	2·00

DESIGN: 25p. Churchill and River Thames.

107 Capt. Cook and H.M.S. *Resolution*

1975. Bicentenary of Capt. Cook's Return to St. Helena. Multicoloured.

307	5p. Type **107**	30	20
308	25p. Capt. Cook and Jamestown	40	40

108 *Mellissia begonifolia* (tree)

1975. Centenary of Publication of "St. Helena" by J. C. Melliss. Multicoloured.

310	2p. Type **108**	15	30
311	5p. "Mellissius adumbratus" (beetle)	15	35
312	12p. St. Helena sand plover (bird) (horiz)	50	80
313	25p. Melliss's scorpionfish (horiz)	50	1·00

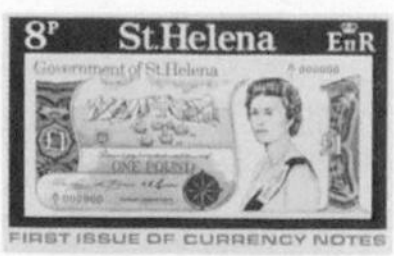

109 £1 Note

1976. First Issue of Currency Notes. Multicoloured.

314	8p. Type **109**	30	30
315	33p. £5 Note	60	80

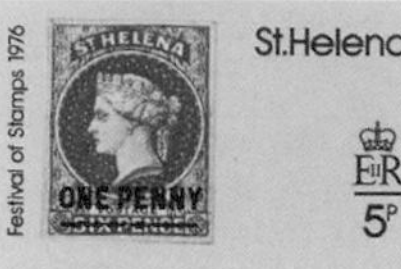

110 1d. Stamp of 1863

1976. Festival of Stamps, London.

316	**110**	5p. brown, black and pink	15	15
317	-	8p. black, green & lt green	20	30
318	-	25p. multicoloured	35	45

DESIGNS—VERT: 8p. 1d. stamp of 1922. HORIZ: 25p. Mail carrier "Good Hope Castle".

111 "High Knoll, 1806" (Capt. Barnett)

1976. Aquatints and Lithographs of St. Helena. Multicoloured.

319B	1p. Type **111**	30	75
320A	3p. "The Friar Rock, 1815" (G. Bellasis)	1·50	1·50
321A	5p. "The Column Lot, 1815" (G. Bellasis)	30	1·25
322A	6p. "Sandy Bay Valley, 1809" (H. Salt)	30	1·25
323A	8p. "Scene from Castle Terrace, 1815" (G. Bellasis)	40	1·25
324A	9p. "The Briars, 1815"	40	1·25
325A	10p. "Plantation House, 1821" (J. Wathen)	50	60
326A	15p. "Longwood House, 1821" (J. Wathen)	45	55
327A	18p. "St. Paul's Church" (V. Brooks)	45	1·50
328A	26p. "St. James's Valley, 1815" (Capt. Hastings)	45	1·50
329A	40p. "St. Matthew's Church, 1860" (V. Brooks)	70	1·75
330A	£1 "St. Helena, 1815" (G. Bellasis)	1·50	3·75
331B	£2 "Sugar Loaf Hill, 1821" (J. Wathen)	2·00	5·00

Nos. 330A and 331B are larger, 47×34 mm.

The 1 and 10p. and the £2 come with or without date imprint.

112 Duke of Edinburgh paying Homage

1977. Silver Jubilee. Multicoloured.

332	8p. Royal Visit, 1947	10	20
333	15p. Queen's sceptre with dove	20	25
334	26p. Type **112**	30	35

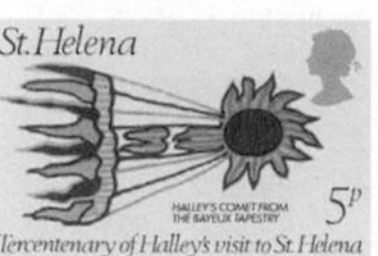

113 Halley's Comet (from Bayeux Tapestry)

1977. Tercentenary of Halley's Visit. Multicoloured.

335	5p. Type **113**	35	30
336	8p. Late 17th-century sextant	50	30
337	27p. Halley and Halley's Mount, St. Helena	1·00	75

114 Sea Lion

1978. 25th Anniv of Coronation.

338	-	25p. agate, red and silver	30	50
339	-	25p. multicoloured	30	50
340	114	25p. agate, red and silver	30	50

DESIGNS: No. 338, Black Dragon of Ulster; No. 339, Queen Elizabeth II.

115 Period Engraving of St. Helena

1978. Wreck of the "Witte Leeuw". Multicoloured.

341	3p. Type **115**	15	15
342	5p. Chinese porcelain	15	20
343	8p. Bronze cannon	15	30
344	9p. Chinese porcelain (different)	15	35
345	15p. Pewter mug and ceramic flasks	20	55
346	20p. Dutch East Indiaman	30	70

116 H.M.S. *Discovery*

1979. Bicentenary of Captain Cook's Voyages, 1768–79. Multicoloured.

347	3p. Type **116**	15	15
348	8p. Cook's portable observatory	15	25
349	12p. "Pharnaceum acidum" (sketch by Joseph Banks)	20	35
350	25p. Flaxman/Wedgwood medallion of Capt. Cook	30	90

117 Sir Rowland Hill

1979. Death Centenary of Sir Rowland Hill.

351	117	5p. multicoloured	10	15
352	-	8p. multicoloured	15	20
353	-	20p. multicoloured	30	40
354	-	32p. black, magenta & mve	40	55

DESIGNS—HORIZ: 8p. 1965 1d. First Local Post stamp; 20p. 1863 1d. on 6d. surcharged stamp; 32p. 1902 1d. stamp.

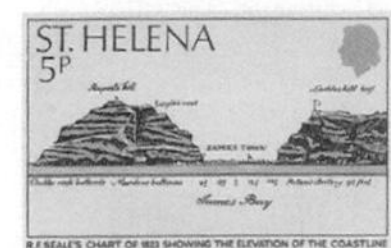
118 R. F. Seal's Chart of 1823 showing the Elevation of the Coastline

1979. 150th Anniv of Inclined Plane.

355	118	5p. black, grey and stone	15	15
356	-	8p. black, grey and stone	15	20
357	-	50p. multicoloured	60	75

DESIGNS—HORIZ: 8p. The Inclined Plane in 1829; VERT: 50p. The Inclined Plane in 1979.

119 Napoleon's Tomb, 1848

1980. Centenary of Empress Eugenie's Visit.

358	119	5p. brown, pink and gold	10	20
359	-	8p. brown, stone and gold	15	25
360	-	62p. brown, flesh and gold	65	80
MS361		180×110 mm. Nos. 358/60	80	1·10

DESIGNS: 8p. Landing at St. Helena; 62p. The Empress at Napoleon's Tomb.

120 East Indiaman

1980. "London 1980" Int Stamp Exhibition. Multicoloured.

362	5p. Type **120**	10	15
363	8p. "Dolphin" postal stone	10	15
364	47p. Postal stone outside Castle entrance, Jamestown	50	60
MS365	111×120 mm. Nos. 362/4	75	80

121 Queen Elizabeth the Queen Mother in 1974

1980. 80th Birthday of the Queen Mother.

366	121	24p. multicoloured	35	50

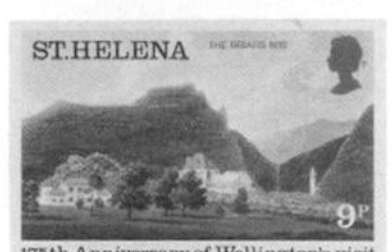
122 The Briars, 1815

1980. 175th Anniv of Wellington's Visit. Multicoloured.

367	9p. Type **122**	15	15
368	30p. "Wellington" (Goya) (vert)	45	45

123 Redwood

1981. Endemic Plants. Multicoloured.

369	5p. Type **123**	15	20
370	8p. Old father live forever	15	20
371	15p. Gumwood	20	25
372	27p. Black cabbage	35	45

124 Detail from Reinel Portolan Chart, c 1530

1981. Early Maps.

373	124	5p. multicoloured	15	15
374	-	8p. black, red and grey	15	20
375	-	20p. multicoloured	30	35
376	-	30p. multicoloured	35	50
MS377		114×83 mm. 24p. black and grey	40	65

DESIGNS: 8p. John Thornton's Map of St. Helena, c. 1700; 20p. Map of St. Helena, 1815; 24p. Part of Gastaldi's map of Africa, 16th-century; 30p. Map of St. Helena, 1817.

125 Prince Charles as Royal Navy Commander

1981. Royal Wedding. Multicoloured.

378	14p. Wedding bouquet from St. Helena	15	20
379	29p. Type **125**	25	30
380	32p. Prince Charles and Lady Diana Spencer	30	35

126 Atlantic Trumpet Triton (*Charonia variegata*)

1981. Sea Shells. Multicoloured.

381	7p. Type **126**	15	20
382	10p. St. Helena cowrie	15	20
383	25p. Common purple janthina	30	40
384	53p. Rude pen shell	50	1·00

127 Traffic Duty

1981. 25th Anniv of Duke of Edinburgh Award Scheme. Multicoloured.

385	7p. Type **127**	15	10
386	11p. Signposting	15	15
387	25p. Animal care	30	30
388	50p. Duke of Edinburgh, in Guard's uniform, on horseback	50	60

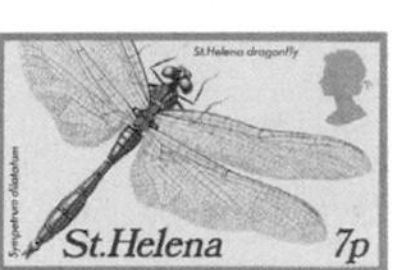
128 *Sympetrum dilatatum* (dragonfly)

1982. Insects (1st series). Multicoloured.

389	7p. Type **128**	20	20
390	10p. "Aplothorax burchelli" (beetle)	20	20
391	25p. "Ampulex compressa" (wasp)	35	35
392	32p. "Labidura herculeana" (earwig)	35	35

See also Nos. 411/14.

129 Charles Darwin

1982. 150th Anniv of Charles Darwin's Voyage. Multicoloured.

393	7p. Type **129**	20	20
394	14p. Flagstaff Hill and Darwin's hammer	25	35
395	25p. Common pheasant ("Ring-necked Pheasant") and Chukar partridge	50	70
396	29p. H.M.S. "Beagle" off St. Helena	60	80

130 Prince and Princess of Wales at Balmoral, Autumn, 1981

1982. 21st Birthday of Princess of Wales. Multicoloured.

397	7p. St. Helena coat of arms	10	15
398	11p. Type **130**	25	15
399	29p. Bride on Palace balcony	30	35
400	55p. Formal portrait	70	60

1982. Commonwealth Games, Brisbane. Nos. 326 and 328 optd **1st PARTICIPATION COMMONWEALTH GAMES 1982**.

401	15p. "Longwood House, 1821" (J. Wathen)	25	25
402	26p. "St. James's Valley, 1815" (Capt. Hastings)	45	45

132 Lord Baden-Powell

1982. 75th Anniv of Boy Scout Movement.

403	132	3p. brown, grey and yellow	15	15
404	-	11p. brown, grey and green	20	25
405	-	29p. brown, grey & orange	30	60
406	-	59p. brown, grey and green	60	1·25

DESIGNS—HORIZ: 11p. Boy Scout (drawing by Lord Baden-Powell); 59p. Camping at Thompsons Wood. VERT: 29p. Canon Walcott.

133 King and Queen Rocks

1982. Views of St. Helena by Roland Svensson. Multicoloured.

407	7p. Type **133**	15	20
408	11p. "Turk's Cap"	15	25
409	29p. Coastline from Jamestown (horiz)	35	65
410	59p. "Mundens Point" (horiz)	60	1·40

1983. Insects (2nd series). As T **128**. Multicoloured.

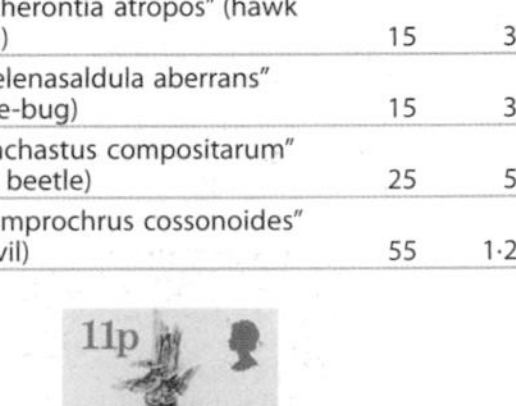

411	11p. "Acherontia atropos" (hawk moth)	15	30
412	15p. "Helenasaldula aberrans" (shore-bug)	15	35
413	29p. "Anchastus compositarum" (click beetle)	25	55
414	59p. "Lamprochrus cossonoides" (weevil)	55	1·25

134 *Trametes versicolor* ("*Coriolus versicolor*")

1983. Fungi. Multicoloured.

415	11p. Type **134**	20	25
416	15p. "Pluteus brunneisucus"	20	40
417	29p. "Polyporus induratus" (horiz)	30	60
418	59p. "Coprinus angulatus"	55	1·25

135 Java Sparrow

1983. Birds. Multicoloured.

419	7p. Type **135**	30	20
420	15p. Madagascar red fody	45	35
421	33p. Common waxbill	80	70
422	59p. Yellow canary	1·50	1·40

136 Birth of St. Helena

1983. Christmas. Life of St. Helena (1st series). Multicoloured.

423	10p. Type **136**	20	55
424	15p. St. Helena being taken to convent	20	55

See also Nos. 450/3 and 468/71.

137 1934 Centenary ½d. Stamp

1984. 150th Anniv of St. Helena as a British Colony. Multicoloured.

425	1p. Type **137**	10	20
426	3p. 1934 1d. stamp	10	20
427	6p. 1934 1½d. stamp	10	30
428	7p. 1934 2d. stamp	15	30
429	11p. 1934 3d. stamp	20	40
430	15p. 1934 6d. stamp	25	45
431	29p. 1934 1s. stamp	40	95
432	33p. 1934 5s. stamp	45	1·25
433	59p. 1934 10s. stamp	65	2·00
434	£1 1934 2s.6d. stamp	1·00	3·25
435	£2 St. Helena Coat of Arms	1·75	5·00

138 Prince Andrew and H.M.S. *Invincible* (aircraft carrier)

1984. Visit of Prince Andrew. Multicoloured.

436	11p. Type **138**	25	25
437	60p. Prince Andrew and H.M.S. "Herald" (survey ship)	75	1·40

139 *St. Helena* (schooner)

1984. 250th Anniv of *Lloyd's List* (newspaper). Multicoloured.

438	10p. Type **139**	20	20
439	18p. Solomons Facade (local agent)	25	35
440	25p. Lloyd's Coffee House, London	30	55
441	50p. "Papanui" (freighter)	75	1·00

140 Twopenny Coin and Donkey

1984. New Coinage. Multicoloured.

442	10p. Type **140**	20	35
443	15p. Five pence coin and St. Helena sand plover	20	45
444	29p. Penny coin and yellow-finned tuna	30	75
445	50p. Ten pence coin and arum lily	40	1·25

141 Mrs. Rebecca Fuller (former Corps Secretary)

1984. Centenary of Salvation Army on St. Helena. Multicoloured.

446	7p. Type **141**	15	35
447	11p. Meals-on-wheels service (horiz)	15	45
448	25p. Salvation Army Citadel, Jamestown (horiz)	25	80
449	60p. Salvation Army band at Jamestown Clock Tower	55	2·00

1984. Christmas. Life of St. Helena (2nd series). As T **136**. Multicoloured.

450	6p. St. Helena visits prisoners	15	20
451	10p. Betrothal of St. Helena	20	30
452	15p. Marriage of St. Helena to Constantius	25	40
453	33p. Birth of Constantine	50	70

142 Queen Elizabeth the Queen Mother aged Two

1985. Life and Times of Queen Elizabeth the Queen Mother. Multicoloured.

454	11p. Type **142**	20	25
455	15p. At Ascot with the Queen	20	35
456	29p. Attending Gala Ballet at Covent Garden	40	65
457	55p. With Prince Henry at his christening	60	1·00
MS458	91×73 mm. 70p. The Queen Mother with Ford "V8 Pilot"	1·75	1·60

143 Axillary Cardinalfish

1985. Marine Life. Multicoloured.

459	7p. Type **143**	15	25
460	11p. Chub mackerel	15	30
461	15p. Skipjack tuna	20	40
462	33p. Yellow-finned tuna	35	75
463	50p. Stump	50	1·25

144 John J. Audubon

1985. Birth Bicentenary of John J. Audubon (ornithologist).

464	**144**	11p. black and brown	15	25
465	-	15p. multicoloured	30	35
466	-	25p. multicoloured	40	55
467	-	60p. multicoloured	65	1·40

DESIGN—HORIZ (from original Audubon paintings): 15p. Moorhen ("Common Gallinule); 25p. White-tailed tropic bird; 68p. Common noddy.

1985. Christmas. Life of St. Helena (3rd series). As T **136**. Multicoloured.

468	7p. St. Helena jouneys to the Holy Land	20	25
469	10p. Zambres slays the bull	20	30
470	15p. The bull restored to life: conversion of St. Helena	25	40
471	60p. Resurrection of the corpse: the True Cross identified	75	1·50

145 Church Provident Society for Women Banner

1986. Friendly Societies' Banners. Multicoloured.

472	10p. Type **145**	15	25
473	11p. Working Men's Christian Association	15	25
474	25p. Church Benefit Society for Children	25	55
475	29p. Mechanics and Friendly Benefit Society	25	65
476	33p. Ancient Order of Foresters	30	70

145a Princess Elizabeth making 21st Birthday Broadcast, South Africa, 1947

1986. 60th Birthday of Queen Elizabeth II. Multicoloured.

477	10p. Type **145a**	15	20
478	15p. Silver Jubilee photograph, 1977	25	30
479	20p. Princess Elizabeth on board H.M.S. "Vanguard", 1947	30	35
480	50p. In the U.S.A., 1976	45	1·00
481	65p. At Crown Agents Head Office, London, 1983	50	1·10

146 Plaque at Site of Halley's Observatory on St. Helena

1986. Appearance of Halley's Comet. Multicoloured.

482	9p. Type **146**	35	35
483	12p. Edmond Halley	35	35
484	20p. Halley's planisphere of the southern stars	65	70
485	65p. "Unity" on passage to St. Helena, 1676	2·25	3·25

146a Prince Andrew and Miss Sarah Ferguson

1986. Royal Wedding. Multicoloured.

486	10p. Type **146a**	20	25
487	40p. Prince Andrew with Governor J. Massingham on St. Helena	80	85

147 James Ross and H.M.S. *Erebus*

1986. Explorers.

488	**147**	1p. brown and pink	30	1·50
489	-	3p. deep blue and blue	30	1·50
490	-	5p. deep green and green	30	1·50
491	-	9p. brown and red	40	1·50
492	-	10p. deep brown and brown	40	1·50
493	-	12p. green and light green	40	1·50
494	-	15p. brown and pink	50	1·50
495	-	20p. blue and light blue	55	1·50
496	-	25p. sepia and pink	55	1·50
497	-	40p. deep green and green	60	1·75
498	-	60p. deep brown and brown	70	2·00
499	-	£1 deep blue and blue	1·00	3·00
500	-	£2 deep lilac and lilac	1·50	5·00

DESIGNS: 3p. Robert FitzRoy and H.M.S. "Beagle"; 5p. Adam Johann von Krusenstern and "Nadezhda"; 9p. William Bligh and H.M.S. "Resolution"; 10p. Otto von Kotzebue and "Rurik"; 12p. Philip Carteret and H.M.S. "Swallow"; 15p. Thomas Cavendish and "Desire"; 20p. Louis-Antoine de Bougainville and "La Boudeuse"; 25p. Fyedor Petrovitch Litke and "Senyavin"; 40p. Louis Isidore Duperrey and "La Coquille"; 60p. John Byron and H.M.S. "Dolphin"; £1 James Cook and H.M.S. "Endeavour"; £2 Jules Dumont d'Urville and "L'Astrolabe".

148 Prince Edward and H.M.S. *Repulse* (battle cruiser), 1925

1987. Royal Visits to St. Helena. Multicoloured.

501	9p. Type **148**	1·75	1·25
502	13p. King George VI and H.M.S. "Vanguard" (battleship), 1947	2·25	1·50
503	38p. Prince Philip and Royal Yacht "Britannia", 1957	4·00	3·50
504	45p. Prince Andrew and H.M.S. "Herald" (survey ship), 1984	4·00	3·50

149 St. Helena Tea Plant

1987. Rare Plants (1st series). Multicoloured.

505	9p. Type **149**	65	60
506	13p. Baby's toes	80	80
507	38p. Salad plant	1·50	2·50
508	45p. Scrubwood	1·75	2·75

See also Nos. 531/4.

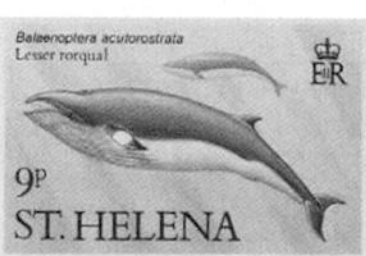

150 Lesser Rorqual

1987. Marine Mammals. Multicoloured.

509	9p. Type **150**	1·25	75
510	13p. Risso's dolphin	1·25	1·00
511	45p. Sperm whale	3·00	3·50
512	60p. Euphrosyne dolphin	3·25	4·25
MS513	102×72 mm. 75p. Humpback whale (48×31 mm)	6·50	7·00

1987. Royal Ruby Wedding. Nos. 477/81 optd **40TH WEDDING ANNIVERSARY**.

514	10p. Princess Elizabeth making 21st birthday broadcast, South Africa, 1947	20	35
515	15p. Silver Jubilee photograph, 1977	20	40
516	20p. Princess Elizabeth on board H.M.S. "Vanguard", 1947	40	55
517	50p. In the U.S.A., 1976	50	1·10
518	65p. At Crown Agents Head Office, London, 1983	50	1·50

151 *Defence* and Dampier's Signature. 1691

1988. Bicentenary of Australian Settlement. Ships and Signatures. Multicoloured.

519	9p. Type **151**	1·50	90
520	13p. H.M.S. "Resolution" (Cook), 1775	2·00	2·00
521	45p. H.M.S. "Providence" (Bligh), 1792	3·25	4·00
522	60p. H.M.S. "Beagle" (Darwin), 1836	4·25	5·50

152 "The Holy Virgin with the Child"

1988. Christmas. Religious Paintings. Multicoloured.

523	5p. Type **152**	10	30
524	20p. "Madonna"	40	50
525	38p. "The Holy Family with St. John"	75	1·50
526	60p. "The Holy Virgin with the Child"	1·25	2·00

152a Lloyds Under- writing Room, 1886

1988. 300th Anniv of Lloyd's of London.

527	**152a**	9p. deep brown and brown	40	50
528	-	20p. multicoloured	2·00	1·00
529	-	45p. multicoloured	2·50	1·75
530	-	60p. multicoloured	2·75	2·25

DESIGNS—VERT: 60p. "Spangereid" (full-rigged ship) on fire, St. Helena, 1920. HORIZ: 20p. "Edinburgh Castle" (liner); 45p. "Bosun Bird" (freighter).

153 Ebony

1989. Rare Plants (2nd series). Multicoloured.

531	9p. Type **153**	40	40
532	20p. St. Helena lobelia	70	70
533	45p. Large bellflower	1·40	2·00
534	60p. She cabbage tree	1·60	2·50

154 Private, 53rd Foot

1989. Military Uniforms of 1815. Multicoloured.

535	9p. Type **154**	65	90
536	13p. Officer, 53rd Foot	75	1·00
537	20p. Royal Marine	85	1·10
538	45p. Officer, 66th Foot	1·40	1·90
539	60p. Private, 66th Foot	1·60	2·25

1989. "Philexfrance 89" International Stamp Exhibition, Paris. Nos. 535/9 optd **PHILEXFRANCE 89** and emblem.

540	9p. Type **154**	80	1·10
541	13p. Officer, 53rd Foot	90	1·25
542	20p. Royal Marine	1·10	1·40
543	45p. Officer, 66th Foot	1·50	2·00
544	60p. Private, 66th Foot	1·60	2·25

156 Agricultural Studies

1989. New Prince Andrew Central School. Multicoloured.

545	13p. Type **156**	85	85
546	20p. Geography lesson	1·40	1·40
547	25p. Walkway and classroom block	1·50	1·50
548	60p. Aerial view of School	3·00	5·25

157 "The Madonna with the Pear" (Dürer)

1989. Christmas. Religious Paintings. Multicoloured.

549	10p. Type **157**	60	50
550	20p. "The Holy Family under the Appletree" (Rubens)	85	90
551	45p. "The Virgin in the Meadow" (Raphael)	2·00	2·50
552	60p. "The Holy Family with St. John" (Raphael)	2·50	3·50

158 Chevrolet "6" 30 cwt Lorry, 1930

1989. Early Vehicles. Multicoloured.

553	9p. Type **158**	85	80
554	20p. Austin "Seven", 1929	1·50	1·50
555	45p. Morris "Cowley" 11.9h.p., 1929	2·25	2·75
556	60p. Sunbeam 25h.p., 1932	2·75	4·25
MS557	93×74 mm. £1 Ford "Model A Fordor"	8·00	9·50

159 Sheep

1990. Farm Animals. Multicoloured.

558	9p. Type **159**	50	65
559	13p. Pigs	60	80
560	45p. Cow and calf	1·50	2·50
561	60p. Geese	2·00	3·50

160 1840 Twopence Blue

1990. "Stamp World London 90" International Stamp Exhibition, London.

562	**160**	13p. black and blue	50	50
563	-	20p. multicoloured	75	85
564	-	38p. multicoloured	1·25	2·00
565	-	45p. multicoloured	1·60	2·25

DESIGNS: 20p. 1840 Penny Black and 19th-century St. Helena postmark; 38p. Delivering mail to sub-post office; 45p. Mail van and Post Office, Jamestown.

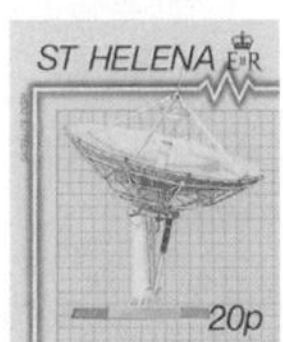

161 Satellite Dish

1990. Modern Telecommunications Links. Multicoloured.

566	20p. Type **161**	75	1·10
567	20p. Digital telephone exchange	75	1·10
568	20p. Public card phone	75	1·10
569	20p. Facsimile machine	75	1·10

161a Lady Elizabeth Bowes-Lyon, April, 1923

1990. 90th Birthday of Queen Elizabeth the Queen Mother.

570	**161a**	25p. multicoloured	1·00	75
571	-	£1 black and brown	2·25	3·50

DESIGN—29×37 mm: £1 Queen Elizabeth visiting communal kitchen, 1940.

162 *Dane* (mail ship), 1857

1990. Maiden Voyage of "St. Helena II". Multicoloured.

572	13p. Type **162**	1·25	85
573	20p. "St. Helena I" off-loading at St. Helena	1·60	1·40
574	38p. Launch of "St. Helena II"	2·25	2·75
575	45p. The Duke of York launching "St. Helena II"	2·75	3·50

MS576	100×100 mm. £1 "St. Helena II" and outline map of St. Helena	9·00	9·00

163 Baptist Chapel, Sandy Bay

1990. Christmas. Local Churches. Multicoloured.

577	10p. Type **163**	40	40
578	13p. St. Martin in the Hills Church	50	50
579	20p. St. Helena and the Cross Church	75	75
580	38p. St. James Church	1·25	2·25
581	45p. St. Paul's Cathedral	1·50	2·25

164 "Funeral Cortege, Jamestown Wharf" (detail V. Adam)

1990. 150th Anniv of Removal of Napoleon's Body.

582	**164**	13p. black, brown & green	1·75	1·25
583	-	20p. black, brown and blue	2·50	1·75
584	-	38p. black, brown & mauve	4·00	3·75
585	-	45p. multicoloured	4·00	4·00

DESIGNS: 20p. "Coffin being conveyed to the 'Belle Poule' " (detail, V. Adam); 38p. "Transfer of the Coffin to the 'Normandie', Cherbourg" (detail, V. Adam); 45p. "Napoleon's Tomb, St. Helena" (T. Sutherland).

165 Officer, Leicestershire Regiment

1991. Military Uniforms of 1897. Multicoloured.

586	13p. Type **165**	1·25	1·25
587	15p. Officer, York & Lancaster Regiment	1·25	1·25
588	20p. Colour-sergeant, Leicestershire Regiment	1·50	1·50
589	38p. Bandsman, York and Lancaster Regiment	2·50	3·00
590	45p. Lance-corporal, York and Lancaster Regiment	3·00	3·50

165a Queen Elizabeth II

1991. 65th Birthday of Queen Elizabeth II and 70th Birthday of Prince Philip. Multicoloured.

591	25p. Type **165a**	1·00	1·40
592	25p. Prince Philip in naval uniform	1·00	1·40

166 "Madonna and Child" (T. Vecellio)

1991. Christmas. Religious Paintings. Multicoloured.

593	10p. Type **166**	70	55
594	13p. "The Holy Family" (A. Mengs)	80	65
595	20p. "Madonna and Child" (W. Dyce)	1·25	1·00
596	38p. "The Two Trinities" (B. Murillo)	2·00	2·50
597	45p. "The Virgin and Child" (G. Bellini)	2·25	3·00

167 Matchless (346cc) Motorcycle, 1947

1991. "Phila Nippon '91" International Stamp Exn, Tokyo. Motorcycles. Multicoloured.

598	13p. Type **167**	1·00	80
599	20p. Triumph "Tiger 100" (500cc), 1950	1·50	1·10
600	38p. Honda "CD" (175cc), 1967	2·25	2·75
601	45p. Yamaha "DTE 400", 1976	2·50	3·00
MS602	72×49 mm. 65p. Suzuki "RM" (250cc), 1984	7·50	9·00

168 *Eye of the Wind* (cadet brig) and Compass Rose

1992. 500th Anniv of Discovery of America by Columbus and Re-enactment Voyages. Multicoloured.

603	15p. Type **168**	2·00	1·25
604	25p. "Soren Larsen" (cadet brigantine) and map of Re-enactment Voyages	2·75	2·25
605	35p. "Santa Maria", "Nina" and "Pinta"	3·50	3·50
606	50p. Columbus and "Santa Maria"	4·00	4·50

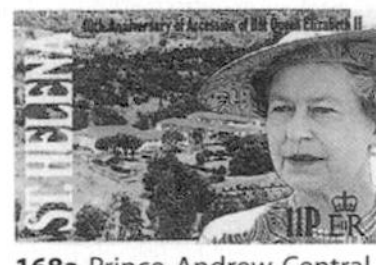

168a Prince Andrew Central School

1992. 40th Anniv of Queen Elizabeth II's Accession. Multicoloured.

607	11p. Type **168a**	40	40
608	15p. Plantation House	55	55
609	25p. Jamestown	75	95
610	35p. Three portraits of Queen Elizabeth	90	1·25
611	50p. Queen Elizabeth II	1·10	1·90

169 H.M.S. *Ledbury* (minesweeper)

1992. Tenth Anniv of Liberation of Falkland Islands. Ships. Multicoloured.

612	13p. Type **169**	80	80
613	20p. H.M.S. "Brecon" (minesweeper)	1·10	1·10
614	38p. "St. Helena I" (mail ship) off South Georgia	1·75	2·25
615	45p. Launch collecting first mail drop, 1982	2·25	3·00
MS616	116×116 mm. 13p.+3p. Type **169**; 20p.+4p. As No. 613; 38p.+8p. As No. 614; 45p.+9p. As No. 615	5·50	5·50

The premium on No. **MS**616 were for the S.S.A.F.A.

170 Shepherds and Angel Gabriel

1992. Christmas. Children's Nativity Plays. Multicoloured.

617	13p. Type **170**	1·00	85
618	15p. Shepherds and Three Kings	1·10	95
619	20p. Mary and Joseph	1·25	1·00
620	45p. Nativity scene	2·50	4·00

171 Disc Jockey, Radio St. Helena (25th anniv)

1992. Local Anniversaries. Multicoloured.

621 13p. Type **171** 75 75

622 20p. Scout parade (75th anniv of Scouting on St. Helena) 1·25 1·25

623 38p. H.M.S. "Providence" (sloop) and breadfruit (bicent of Capt. Bligh's visit) 2·25 3·25

624 45p. Governor Brooke and Plantation House (bicent) 2·25 3·50

172 Moses in the Bulrush

1993. Flowers (1st series). Multicoloured.

625 9p. Type **172** 1·00 75

626 13p. Periwinkle 1·25 90

627 20p. Everlasting flower 1·60 1·25

628 38p. Cigar plant 2·75 3·25

629 45p. "Lobelia erinus" 2·75 3·25

See also Nos. 676/80.

173 Adult St. Helena Sand Plover and Eggs

1993. Endangered Species. St. Helena Sand Plover ("Wirebird"). Multicoloured.

630 3p. Type **173** 90 90

631 5p. Male attending brooding female 90 90

632 12p. Adult with downy young 1·75 1·75

633 25p. Two birds in immature plumage 2·25 2·25

634 40p. Adult in flight 2·50 2·75

635 60p. Young bird on rocks 2·75 3·50

Nos. 634/5 are without the W.W.F. emblem.

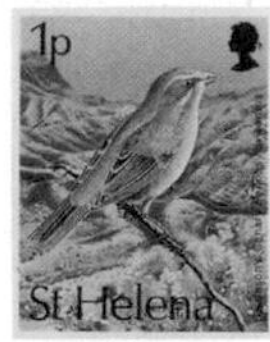

174 Yellow Canary ("Swainson's Canary")

1993. Birds. Multicoloured.

636 1p. Type **174** 50 1·25

637 3p. Rock partridge 70 1·25

638 11p. Feral rock pigeon 1·00 1·25

639 12p. Common waxbill 1·00 1·00

640 15p. Common mynah 1·10 1·00

641 18p. Java sparrow 1·25 1·00

642 25p. Red-billed tropic bird (horiz) 1·50 1·00

643 35p. Madeiran storm petrel (horiz) 2·25 1·50

644 75p. Madagascar red fody 3·00 4·00

645 £1 White tern ("Common fairy tern") (horiz) 3·25 4·00

646 £2 Giant petrel (horiz) 5·50 8·50

647 £5 St. Helena sand plover ("Wirebird") 11·00 15·00

175 Football and Teddy Bear

1993. Christmas. Toys. Multicoloured.

648 12p. Type **175** 85 85

649 15p. Yacht and doll 90 90

650 18p. Palette and rocking horse 95 95

651 25p. Model airplane and kite 1·40 1·60

652 60p. Guitar and roller skates 2·50 4·00

176 Arum Lily

1994. Flowers and Children's Art. Multicoloured.

653 12p. Type **176** 40 65

654 12p. "Arum Lily" (Delphia Mittens) 40 65

655 25p. Ebony 75 1·00

656 25p. "Ebony" (Jason Rogers) 75 1·00

657 35p. Shell ginger 95 1·10

658 35p. "Shell Ginger" (Jeremy Moyce) 95 1·10

177 Abyssinian Guinea Pig

1994. "Hong Kong '94" International Stamp Exhibition. Pets. Multicoloured.

659 12p. Type **177** 70 70

660 25p. Common tabby cat 1·40 1·40

661 53p. Plain white and black rabbits 2·25 3·00

662 60p. Golden labrador 2·50 3·25

178 Springer's Blenny

1994. Fish. Multicoloured.

663 12p. Type **178** 75 75

664 25p. St. Helena damselfish 1·50 1·50

665 53p. Melliss's scorpionfish 2·25 3·25

666 60p. St. Helena wrasse 2·75 3·50

179 *Lampides boeticus*

1994. Butterflies. Multicoloured.

667 12p. Type **179** 75 75

668 25p. "Cynthia cardui" 1·50 1·50

669 53p. "Hypolimnas bolina" 2·25 2·75

670 60p. "Danaus chrysippus" 2·75 3·25

180 "Silent Night!"

1994. Christmas. Carols. Multicoloured.

671 12p. Type **180** 55 45

672 15p. "While Shepherds watched their Flocks by Night" 60 50

673 25p. "Away in a Manger" 1·00 90

674 38p. "We Three Kings" 1·50 2·25

675 60p. "Angels from the Realms of Glory" 2·25 3·75

1994. Flowers (2nd series). As T **172**. Multicoloured.

676 12p. Honeysuckle 35 35

677 15p. Gobblegheer 40 40

678 25p. African lily 70 80

679 38p. Prince of Wales feathers 1·00 1·60

680 60p. St. Johns lily 1·75 3·25

181 Fire Engine

1995. Emergency Services. Multicoloured.

681 12p. Type **181** 1·25 75

682 25p. Lifeboat 1·40 90

683 53p. Police car 2·75 3·00

684 60p. Ambulance 3·00 3·50

182 Site Clearance

1995. Construction of Harpers Valley Earth Dam. Multicoloured.

685 25p. Type **182** 80 1·10

686 25p. Earthworks in progress 80 1·10

687 25p. Laying outlet pipes 80 1·10

688 25p. Revetment block protection 80 1·10

689 25p. Completed dam 80 1·10

Nos. 685/9 were printed together, se-tenant, forming a composite design.

182a "Lady Denison Pender" (cable ship)

1995. 50th Anniv of End of Second World War. Multicoloured.

690 5p. Type **182a** 1·00 1·40

691 5p. H.M.S. "Dragon" (cruiser) 1·00 1·40

692 12p. R.F.A. "Darkdale" (tanker) 1·75 1·90

693 12p. H.M.S. "Hermes" (aircraft carrier, launched 1919) 1·75 1·90

694 25p. Men of St. Helena Rifles 2·75 3·00

695 25p. Governor Major W. J. Bain Gray taking salute 2·75 3·00

696 53p. 6-inch coastal gun, Ladder Hill 3·25 3·50

697 53p. Flags signalling "VICTORY" 3·25 2·50

MS698 75×85 mm. £1 Reverse of 1939–45 War Medal (vert) 2·25 2·75

The two designs for each value were printed together, se-tenant, forming composite designs.

183 Blushing Snail

1995. Endemic Invertebrates. Multicoloured.

699 12p. Type **183** 1·10 1·10

700 25p. Golden sail spider 1·75 1·75

701 53p. Spiky yellow woodlouse 2·75 3·50

702 60p. St. Helena shore crab 3·00 3·75

MS703 85×83 mm. £1 Giant earwig 6·00 7·00

184 *Epidendrum ibaguense*

1995. "Singapore '95" International Stamp Exhibition. Orchids. Sheet, 122×74 mm, containing T **184** and similar vert design. Multicoloured.

MS704 50p. Type **184**; 50p. "Vanda Miss Joaquim" 6·50 7·50

185 "Santa Claus outside Market" (Jason Alex Rogers)

1995. Christmas. Children's Paintings. Multicoloured.

705 12p. Type **185** 35 35

706 15p. "Santa Claus and band" (Che David Yon) 45 45

707 25p. "Santa Claus outside Community Centre" (Leon Williams) 70 75

708 38p. "Santa Claus in decorated street" (Stacey McDaniel) 1·00 1·40

709 60p. "Make a better World" (Kisha Karla Kacy Thomas) 1·75 3·50

186 *Walmer Castle*, 1915

1996. Union Castle Mail Ships (1st series). Multicoloured.

710 12p. Type **186** 2·25 1·25

711 25p. "Llangibby Castle", 1934 3·00 1·75

712 53p. "Stirling Castle", 1940 4·00 4·50

713 60p. "Pendennis Castle", 1965 4·00 4·50

See also Nos. 757/60.

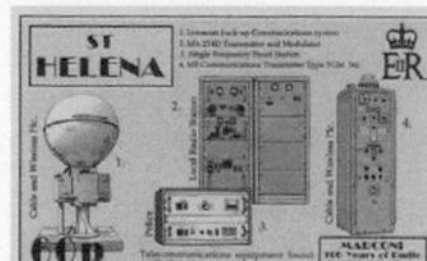

187 Early Telecommunications Equipment

1996. Centenary of Radio. Multicoloured.

714 60p. Type **187** 1·50 2·00

715 £1 Guglielmo Marconi and "Elettra" (yacht) 2·50 3·50

1996. 70th Birthday of Queen Elizabeth II. As T **55** of Tokelau, each incorporating a different photograph of the Queen. Multicoloured.

716 15p. Jamestown 50 40

717 25p. Prince Andrew School 75 65

718 53p. Castle entrance 1·50 2·25

719 60p. Plantation House 1·75 2·50

MS720 64×86 mm. £1.50 Queen Elizabeth II 3·25 4·50

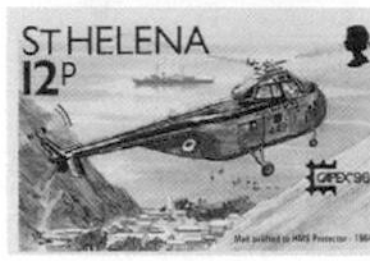

188 Helicopter Mail to H.M.S. *Protector* (ice patrol ship), 1964

1996. "CAPEX '96" International Stamp Exhibition, Toronto. Mail Transport. Multicoloured.

721 12p. Type **188** 65 60

722 25p. Postman on motor scooter, 1965 90 80

723 53p. Loading mail plane, Wideawake Airfield, Ascension Island 1·50 2·25

724 60p. "St. Helena II" (mail ship) unloading at St. Helena 1·75 2·50

MS725 98×73 mm. £1 L.M.S. No. 5624 "St. Helena" locomotive (43×27 mm) 2·75 3·75

189 "Mr. Porteous's House"

1996. Napoleonic Sites. Multicoloured.

726 12p. Type **189** 1·75 1·25

727 25p. "The Briars' Pavilion" 2·50 1·75

728 53p. "Longwood House" 4·00 4·50

729 60p. "Napoleon's Tomb" 4·00 4·50

190 Frangipani and Sandy Bay from Diana's Peak

1996. Christmas. Flowers and Views. Multicoloured.

730 12p. Type **190** 40 40

731 15p. Bougainvillaea and Upper Jamestown from Sampsons's Battery 50 50

732 25p. Jacaranda and Jacob's Ladder 75 75

733 £1 Pink periwinkle and Lot's Wife Ponds 2·75 5·00

191 Black Cabbage Tree

1997. Endemic Plants from Diana's Peak National Park. Multicoloured.

734 25p. Type **191** 1·75 2·00

735 25p. Whitewood 1·75 2·00

736 25p. Tree fern 1·75 2·00

737 25p. Dwarf jellico 1·75 2·00

738 25p. Lobelia 1·75 2·00

739 25p. Dogwood 1·75 2·00

Nos. 734/9 were printed together, se-tenant, with the backgrounds forming a composite design.

1997. "HONG KONG '97" International Stamp Exhibition. Sheet 130×90 mm, containing design as No. 644.
MS740 75p. Madagascar red fody 2·50 2·75

192 João da Nova's Lookout sighting St. Helena, 1502

1997. 500th Anniv of the Discovery of St. Helena (1st issue). Multicoloured.
741 20p. Type **192** 1·75 1·40
742 25p. Don Fernando Lopez (first inhabitant) and cockerel, 1515 1·90 1·40
743 30p. Thomas Cavendish and "Desire", 1588 2·00 1·60
744 80p. "Royal Merchant" (English galleon), 1591 4·00 5·25
See also Nos. 762/5, 786/9, 810/13, 828/31 and 857/60.

1997. Return of Hong Kong to China. Sheet 130×90 mm, containing design as No. 647, but changed face value and imprint date. W w 14 (sideways). P 14½×14.
MS745 75p. St. Helena Sand Plover ("Wirebird") 1·75 2·25

192a Royal Family's Visit, 1947

1997. Golden Wedding of Queen Elizabeth and Prince Philip. Multicoloured.
746 10p. Type **192a** 85 90
747 10p. Wedding photograph of Princess Elizabeth and Prince Philip 85 90
748 15p. Princess Elizabeth and Prince Philip, 1947 1·00 1·25
749 15p. Presenting bouquets, Royal Visit, 1947 1·00 1·25
750 50p. Prince Philip on Royal Visit, 1957 1·90 2·50
751 50p. Wedding party on balcony, 1947 1·90 2·50
MS752 111×70 mm. £1.50, Queen Elizabeth and Prince Philip in landau (horiz) 7·00 8·00

193 Flower Arrangement

1997. Christmas. 25th Anniv of the Duke of Edinburgh's Award in St. Helena. Multicoloured.
753 15p. Type **193** 1·00 65
754 20p. Calligraphy 1·25 80
755 40p. Camping 2·50 2·50
756 75p. Table laid for Christmas dinner 3·75 6·00

1998. Union Castle Mail Ships (2nd series). As T **186**. Multicoloured.
757 20p. "Avondale Castle", 1900 2·50 1·75
758 25p. "Dunnottar Castle", 1936 2·50 1·75
759 30p. "Llandovery Castle", 1943 2·75 2·00
760 80p. "Good Hope Castle", 1977 5·00 6·50

194 Wearing green and white Hat, 1983

1998. Diana, Princess of Wales Commemoration. Sheet 145×70 mm containing vert designs as T **194**.
MS761 30p. Wearing white jacket; 30p. Wearing green jacket, 1996; 30p. In evening dress, 1991 (sold at £1.20 + 20p. charity premium) 1·75 3·00

1998. 500th Anniv of the Discovery of St. Helena (2nd issue). As T **192**. Multicoloured.
762 20p. Settlers planting crops, 1659 1·75 1·25
763 25p. Dutch invasion, 1672 2·00 1·40
764 30p. Recapture by the English, 1673 2·25 2·00
765 80p. Royal Charter of 1673 4·00 5·50

195 *Desire* (Cavendish), 1588

1998. Maritime Heritage. Multicoloured.
766 10p. Type **195** 2·00 2·00
767 15p. "Witte Leeuw" (Dutch East Indiaman), 1602 2·50 2·00
768 20p. H.M.S. "Swallow" and H.M.S. "Dolphin" (Carteret), 1751 2·75 1·50
769 25p. H.M.S. "Endeavour" (Cook), 1771 3·50 1·75
770 30p. H.M.S. "Providence" (sloop), 1792 2·75 1·50
771 35p. "St. Helena" (East India Company schooner), 1815 3·00 2·25
772 40p. H.M.S. "Northumberland" (ship of the line), 1815 3·00 2·25
773 50p. "Rurik" (Von Kotzebue), 1815 3·25 3·25
774 75p. H.M.S. "Erebus" (Ross), 1826 4·50 4·50
775 80p. "Keying" (junk), 1847 4·50 4·50
776 £2 "La Belle Poule" (French frigate), 1840 8·50 11·00
777 £5 H.M.S "Rattlesnake" (screw corvette), 1861 15·00 19·00
No. 771 is inscribed "H.M.S." in error.

196 Metal Lanterns

1998. Christmas. Island Crafts. Multicoloured.
778 15p. Type **196** 70 60
779 20p. Wood-turned bowls 80 65
780 30p. Inlaid woodwork on jewellery box 1·10 90
781 85p. Hessian and seedwork bag and hat 2·75 4·50

197 H.M.S. *Endeavour* (Cook), 1771

1999. "Australia '99" World Stamp Exhibition, Melbourne. Sheet 120×80 mm.
MS782 **197** £1.50, multicoloured 8·00 9·00

197a Photographs of Prince Edward and Miss Sophie Rhys-Jones

1999. Royal Wedding. Multicoloured.
783 30p. Type **197a** 60 65
784 £1.30 Engagement photograph 2·50 3·25

1999. 500th Anniv of the Discovery of St. Helena (3rd issue). As T **192** but horiz. Multicoloured.
786 20p. Jamestown fortifications 1·50 1·10
787 25p. Roadway up Ladder Hill, 1718 1·60 1·25
788 30p. Governor Skottowe with Captain Cook at St. James Church, 1775 3·50 1·75
789 80p. Presentation of sword of honour to Governor Brooke, 1799 3·75 5·00

199 King and Queen visiting Jamestown

1999. "Queen Elizabeth the Queen Mother's Century". Multicoloured.
790 15p. Type **199** 80 65
791 25p. Viewing bomb damage, Buckingham Palace, 1940 95 75
792 30p. With Prince Andrew, 1997 1·10 90
793 80p. Presenting colour to R.A.F. Central Flying School, and with Red Arrows 2·50 3·75
MS794 145×70 mm. £1.50, Queen Elizabeth, 1937, and Royal Family on balcony after Coronation 4·00 4·50

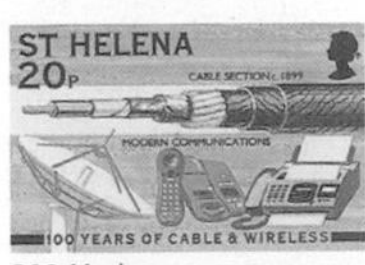

200 Modern Communications Equipment and Section of 1899 Cable

1999. Centenary of Cable & Wireless Communications plc on St. Helena.
795 **200** 20p. multicoloured 1·50 1·25
796 - 25p. black, brown and bistre 2·00 1·50
797 - 30p. black, brown and bistre 2·00 1·75
798 - 80p. multicoloured 2·75 4·50
DESIGNS: 25p. "Seine" (cable ship); 30p. "Anglia" (cable ship); 80p. Cable & Wireless Headquarters, The Briars.

201 *Victoria* (cruise liner) at St. Helena

1999. Union Castle Line Centenary Voyage. Sheet 88×72 mm.
MS799 **201** £2 multicoloured 16·00 16·00

202 King Edward VI

2000. "Stamp Show 2000" International Stamp Exhibition, London. Kings and Queens of England. Multicoloured.
800 30p. Type **202** 1·90 1·90
801 30p. King James I 1·90 1·90
802 30p. King William III and Queen Mary II 1·90 1·90
803 30p. King George II 1·90 1·90
804 30p. Queen Victoria 1·90 1·90
805 30p. King George VI 1·90 1·90

203 Distillation Plant at Ruperts

2000. Centenary of Second Boer War (1st issue). Multicoloured.
806 15p. Type **203** 1·40 1·25
807 25p. Camp at Broadbottom 2·00 1·60
808 30p. Committee of Boer prisoners 2·25 2·00
809 80p. General Cronje and family at Kent Cottage 5·00 5·75

2000. 500th Anniv of the Discovery of St. Helena (4th issue). As T **192**, but horiz. Multicoloured.
810 20p. East India Company flag with crest and Union Jack with colony badge 2·75 2·75
811 25p. Sir Hudson Lowe and Sir George Bingham with broken chains (abolition of slavery, 1832) 2·75 2·00
812 30p. Napoleon, British warship and funeral cortege 3·50 3·00
813 80p. Chief Dinizulu in exile, 1890 6·00 8·50

204 Princess Margaret

2000. Royal Birthdays. Sheet, 145×75 mm, containing T **204** and similar multicoloured designs.
MS814 25p. Type **204**; 25p. Prince William; 25p. Duke of York; 25p. Princess Royal; 50p. Queen Mother (42×56 mm) 27·00 27·00

205 *Beauty and the Beast*

2000. Christmas. Pantomimes. Multicoloured.
815 20p. Type **205** 1·40 1·75
816 20p. *Puss in Boots* 1·40 1·75
817 20p. *Little Red Riding Hood* 1·40 1·75
818 20p. *Jack and the Beanstalk* 1·40 1·75
819 20p. *Snow White and the Seven Dwarfs* 1·14 1·75

206 Chinese White Dolphin

2001. "HONG KONG 2001" Stamp Exhibition. Sheet 150×90 mm, containing T **206** and similar horiz design showing dolphins. Multicoloured.
MS820 30p. Type **206**; 40p. Striped dolphin 8·00 9·00

207 First St. Helena Postage Stamp

2001. Death Centenary of Queen Victoria. Multicoloured.
821 10p. Type **207** 1·10 1·10
822 15p. H.M.S. *Beagle* off St. Helena, 1836 1·75 1·50
823 20p. Jamestown Square (horiz) 1·25 1·25
824 25p. Queen Victoria with Prince Albert and children (horiz) 1·75 1·50
825 30p. Diamond Jubilee procession (horiz) 2·70 4·00
826 50p. Lewis Carroll and characters from *Alice in Wonderland* 4·50 5·00
MS827 105×80 mm. £1.50, Sacks of St. Helena coffee at Great Exhibition 4·00 5·00

2001. 500th Anniv of the Discovery of St. Helena (5th series). As T **192**, but horiz. Multicoloured.
828 20p. Men of St. Helena Rifles 2·75 2·25
829 25p. Prince Andrew School and Jamestown Community Centre 2·50 2·25
830 30p. Flax industry 2·50 2·50
831 80p. *St. Helena II* (mail ship) 7·00 7·50

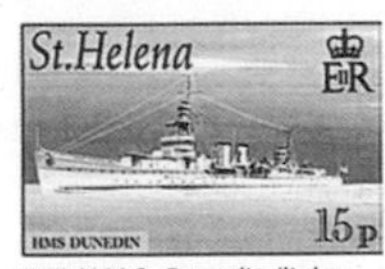

208 H.M.S. *Dunedin* (light cruiser)

2001. Royal Navy Ships of Second World War. Multicoloured.
832 15p. Type **208** 2·00 1·75
833 20p. H.M.S. *Repulse* (battle cruiser) 2·25 2·50
834 25p. H.M.S. *Nelson* (battleship) 2·50 1·75
835 30p. H.M.S. *Exmoor* (destroyer) 2·50 2·00
836 40p. H.M.S. *Eagle* (aircraft carrier, launched 1918) 3·25 3·25
837 50p. H.M.S. *Milford* (sloop) 3·75 4·25

209 Tammy Wynette and "It came upon the Midnight Clear"

2001. Christmas. Carols. Each showing carol title and Tammy Wynette ("First Lady of Country Music"). Multicoloured.
838 10p. Type **209** 60 60
839 15p. "Joy to the World" 70 70
840 20p. "Away in a Manger" 80 80
841 30p. "Silent Night" 95 95

MS842	65×99 mm. £1.50 Tammy Wynette (vert)	3·00	4·50

210 Napoleon as a Young Man

2001. 180th Death Anniv of Napoleon Bonaparte. Multicoloured.

843	20p. Type **210**	2·00	1·75
844	25p. Napoleon at military school	2·25	1·75
845	30p. Napoleon dancing	2·50	2·25
846	80p. Napoleon with children	6·00	7·00

211 Princess Elizabeth and Princess Margaret as Girl Guides

2002. Golden Jubilee.

847	**211**	20p. agate, red and gold	1·25	85
848	-	25p. multicoloured	1·40	1·00
849	-	30p. brown, red and gold	1·50	1·25
850	-	80p. multicoloured	3·50	3·75
MS851		162×95 mm. Nos. 847/50 and 50p. multicoloured	8·50	8·00

DESIGNS—HORIZ: 25p. Queen Elizabeth in evening dress, 1967; 30p. Queen Elizabeth with Prince Charles and Princess Anne, 1952; 80p. Queen Elizabeth on Remembrance Sunday, Durban, 1999. VERT (38×51 mm)— 50p. Queen Elizabeth after Annigoni.

Designs as Nos. 847/50 in No. **MS**851 omit the gold frame around each stamp and the "Golden Jubilee 1952-2002" inscription.

212 Young St. Helena Sand Plover

2002. St. Helena Sand Plover ("Wirebird"). Multicoloured.

852	10p. Type **212**	85	90
853	15p. Chick running (vert)	1·25	1·10
854	30p. Adult bird in flight	1·50	1·40
855	80p. Chick	3·25	4·00
MS856	175×80 mm. 25p. Adult bird (vert) and Nos. 852/5	7·00	8·00

213 Sir William Doveton (Council member) and Jamestown Harbour

2002. 500th Anniv of the Discovery of St. Helena (6th issue). Local Celebrities. All showing Jamestown Harbour. Multicoloured.

857	20p. Type **213**	1·25	1·25
858	25p. Canon Lawrence Walcott	1·40	1·40
859	30p. Governor Hudson Janisch	1·50	1·50
860	80p. Dr. Wilberforce Arnold	3·00	4·50

214 H.M.S. *Hermes* (aircraft carrier)

2002. Royal Navy Ships from the Falklands War. Multicoloured.

861	15p. Type **214**	1·25	1·25
862	20p. H.M.S. *Leeds Castle* (patrol vessel)	1·25	1·25
863	25p. H.M.S. *Intrepid* (assault ship)	1·40	1·25
864	30p. H.M.S. *Glasgow* (destroyer)	1·50	1·50
865	40p. St. Helena I supplying H.M.S. *Brecon* and H.M.S. *Ledbury* (minesweepers)	2·00	2·25
866	50p. H.M.S. *Courageous* (submarine)	2·25	2·75

215 Queen Mother with Prince Andrew, 1960

2002. Queen Elizabeth the Queen Mother Commemoration.

867	**215**	20p. brown, gold and purple	80	80
868	-	25p. multicoloured	90	90
869	-	30p. brown, gold and purple	1·00	1·00
870	-	50p. multicoloured	1·50	2·25
MS871		145×70 mm. 35p. black and gold; £1 multicoloured	4·00	4·50

DESIGNS: 25p. Queen Mother at Cheltenham Races; 30p. Lady Elizabeth Bowes-Lyon, 1923; 35p. Queen Elizabeth, 1945; 50p. Queen Mother at St. Patrick's Day Parade, 1984; £1 Queen Mother at Sandown Races, 1998. Designs in No. **MS**871 omit the "1900–2002" inscription and the coloured frame.

216 Sperm Whale Pod Underwater

2002. Endangered Species. Sperm Whale. Multicoloured.

872	10p. Type **216**	65	70
873	15p. Sperm whale on surface	80	90
874	20p. Two sperm whales underwater	1·00	1·25
875	30p. Tail fin of sperm whale	1·40	1·75

217 The Princess Royal in Blues and Royals' Uniform

2002. Visit of the Princess Royal to St. Helena. Sheet 62×72 mm.

MS876	**217** £2 multicoloured	7·00	8·00

218 Plantation House and Arms

2003. Tourism. Multicoloured.

877	25p. Type **218**	1·25	1·40
878	25p. *St. Helena II* (mail ship) in Jamestown harbour	1·25	1·40
879	25p. *QE2* (cruise liner) off St. Helena	1·25	1·40
880	25p. Napoleon's Tomb and Briars Pavilion	1·25	1·40
881	25p. Ebony Flower and Diana's Peak	1·25	1·40
882	25p. St. Helena sand plover ("Wirebird") and Napoleon's House	1·25	1·40
883	25p. Broadway House	1·25	1·40
884	25p. St. Helena Golf Course	1·25	1·40
885	25p. Yacht and dolphins	1·25	1·40
886	25p. Sport fishing	1·25	1·40
887	25p. Diving	1·25	1·40
888	25p. St. Helena Museum	1·25	1·40

219 Queen Elizabeth II in Coronation Robes (photograph by Cecil Beaton)

2003. 50th Anniv of Coronation. Multicoloured.

889	30p. Type **219**	1·40	1·10
890	50p. Queen and Duke of Edinburgh in Coronation Coach	2·00	2·50
MS891	95×115 mm. 30p. As Type **219**; 50p. As No. 890	2·40	3·35

220 Queen Elizabeth II

2003

892	**220**	£2.50 multicoloured	5·50	6·50

221 *Leonotis nepetifolia*

2003. Wild Flowers. Multicoloured.

893	10p. Type **221**	1·25	1·50
894	15p. *Buddleia madagascariensis*	1·60	1·50
895	20p. *Datura suaveolens*	1·75	1·25
896	25p. *Fuchsia boliviana*	1·75	1·25
897	30p. *Commelina diffusa*	2·00	1·50
898	40p. *Solanum mauritianum*	2·50	2·25
899	50p. *Tecoma stans*	2·75	2·75
900	75p. *Kalanchoe pinnata*	4·00	4·50
901	80p. *Hedychium chrysoleucum*	4·00	4·50
902	£1 *Canna indica*	4·50	5·00
903	£2 *Alpinia nutans*	7·50	9·50
904	£5 *Lantana camara*	15·00	17·00

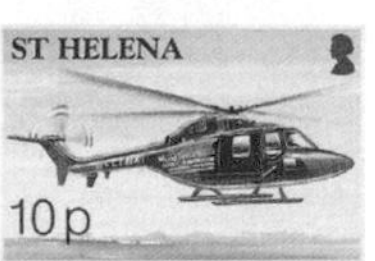

222 Westland WG-13 Lynx Helicopter

2003. Centenary of Powered Flight. Multicoloured.

905	10p. Type **222**	1·25	1·25
906	15p. Douglas C-124 Globemaster	1·40	1·40
907	20p. British Aerospace Nimrod AEW Mk 3	1·50	1·25
908	25p. Lockheed C-130 Hercules	1·60	1·25
909	30p. Lockheed L-1011 TriStar	1·75	1·60
910	50p. *Wright Flyer*	2·50	3·25
MS911	115×65 mm. £1.80 Supermarine *Walrus*	8·00	9·00

223 Large Magellanic Cloud

2003. Christmas. The Southern Sky. Multicoloured.

912	10p. Type **223**	85	1·00
913	15p. Small Magellanic cloud	1·00	1·25
914	20p. Omega Centauri globular cluster	1·25	1·25
915	25p. Eta Carinae nebula ("ETA CARRNAE")	1·40	1·40
916	30p. Southern Cross constellation	1·50	1·75

224 Christiaan Barnard (heart transplant pioneer)

2004. Medical Pioneers. Multicoloured.

917	10p. Type **224**	1·25	1·25
918	25p. Marie Curie (developer of X-radiography)	2·00	1·40
919	30p. Louis Pasteur (bacteriologist)	2·00	1·60
920	50p. Sir Alexander Fleming (discoverer of penicillin)	3·00	4·00

225 Freesia

2004. Bicentenary of Royal Horticultural Society. Multicoloured.

921	10p. Type **225**	40	50
922	15p. Bottle Brush	60	60
923	30p. Ebony	1·10	1·10
924	50p. Olive	1·50	2·00
MS925	111×111 mm. £1 Maurandya	2·50	3·00

226 St. Matthew

2004. Christmas. Stained Glass Windows. Multicoloured.

926	10p. Type **226**	45	60
927	15p. St. John	65	65
928	20p. St. Peter	80	65
929	30p. St. James	1·10	1·00
930	50p. St. Paul	2·00	3·50

227 SS *Umtata*

2004. Merchant Ships. Multicoloured.

931	20p. Type **227**	1·75	1·25
932	30p. SS *Umzinto*	2·50	1·75
933	50p. SS *Umtali*	3·50	3·50
934	80p. SS *Umbilo*	5·50	6·50

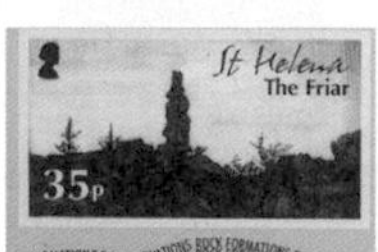

228 The Friar

2005. Rock Formations. Multicoloured.

935	35p. Type **228**	2·50	3·00
936	40p. Sugar Loaf	2·50	3·00
937	50p. The Turk's Cap	2·50	3·00
938	£1 Lot's Wife	3·50	4·00

229 HMS *Bellerophon*, *Aigle* and *Monarca*

2005. Bicentenary of the Battle of Trafalgar (1st issue). Multicoloured.

939	10p. Type **229**	1·00	1·00
940	20p. British 18 Pdr Naval Pattern canon	1·50	1·00
941	30p. HMS *Victory*	2·50	1·50
942	50p. First Lieutenant in the Royal Navy, 1805 (vert)	3·25	3·25
943	60p. HMS *Conqueror* (vert)	3·50	4·00
944	80p. Vice-Admiral Sir Horatio Nelson (vert)	4·75	6·00
MS945	120×79 mm. 75p. Admiral Cuthbert Collingwood (vert); 75p. HMS *Royal Sovereign* (vert)	8·00	8·50

Nos. 941 contains traces of powdered wood from HMS *Victory*.

See also Nos. 969/71.

230 HMS *Milford* (sloop)

2005. 60th Anniv of the End of World War II. Multicoloured.

946	20p. Type **230**	1·75	1·75
947	20p. HMS *Nelson* (battleship)	1·75	1·75
948	20p. RFA *Darkdale* (tanker)	1·75	1·75
949	20p. HMS *St Helena* (frigate)	1·75	1·75
950	20p. Atlantic Star medal	1·75	1·75
951	30p. Alan M. Turing (codebreaker) and Enigma code machine	1·75	1·75
952	30p. Captain Johnnie Walker and HMS *Starling* (sloop)	1·75	1·75
953	30p. Winston Churchill	1·75	1·75
954	30p. Churchill infantry tank	1·75	1·75
955	30p. Hawker Hurricanes	1·75	1·75

231 Pope John Paul II

2005. Pope John Paul II Commemoration.

956	**231**	50p. multicoloured	2·50	2·50

232 Sir Francis Drake

2005. Famous Elizabethans. Multicoloured.

957	10p. Type **232**	1·00	1·00
958	10p. *The Golden Hind*	1·00	1·00
959	15p. Sir Walter Raleigh	1·40	1·40
960	15p. *The Ark Royal*	1·40	1·40
961	25p. Queen Elizabeth I	1·75	1·75
962	25p. The Armada	1·75	1·75
963	£1 William Shakespeare	4·50	4·50
964	£1 The Old Globe Theatre	4·50	4·50

233 "The Little Fir Tree"

2005. Christmas and Birth Bicentenary of Hans Christian Andersen (writer). Multicoloured.

965	10p. Type **233**	55	65
966	25p. "The Ugly Duckling"	90	90
967	30p. "The Snow Queen"	1·00	1·25
968	£1 "The Little Mermaid"	3·25	4·75

234 HMS *Victory*

2005. Bicentenary of the Battle of Trafalgar (2nd issue). Multicoloured.

969	50p. Type **234**	2·75	1·75
970	80p. Ships engaged in battle (horiz)	4·00	4·00
971	£1.20 Admiral Lord Nelson	6·00	7·00

235 1961 Tristan Relief Fund stamps and Postcard

2006. 150th Anniv of the First St. Helena Postage Stamp. Treasures of the British Library. Multicoloured.

972	10p. Type **235**	1·00	1·00
973	20p. Cape of Good Hope 1855–63 1s. deep dark green triangular	1·50	1·00
974	25p. USA 1918 24c. inverted Curtiss JN-4 "Jenny" variety	1·60	1·10
975	30p. 1856 6d. blue (first St. Helena stamp)	1·60	1·25
976	80p. 1840 penny black	3·75	3·75
977	£1.20 Mauritius 1847 2d. deep blue	5·50	6·50
MS978	100×60 mm. £2 As 30p	8·00	9·50

236 Europa Stars with EU Flag

2006. 50th Anniv of the First Europa Stamps. Multicoloured.

979	10p. Type **236**	75	75
980	30p. Stars in circle and holding letter	1·00	80
981	80p. Stars and ball	2·50	2·75
982	£1.20 Stars in circle and holding stamp	3·25	4·00
MS983	122×77 mm. Nos. 979/82	6·00	6·50

237 Princess Elizabeth

2006. 80th Birthday of Queen Elizabeth II. Multicoloured.

984	10p. Type **237**	1·50	1·50
985	30p. Queen Elizabeth wearing tiara, c. 1952	2·25	1·25
986	80p. Wearing tiara and fur stole	4·75	4·75
987	£1.20 In close-up	6·00	6·50
MS988	144×75 mm. £1 Wearing tiara and pearl drop earrings, c. 1952; £1 Wearing cream sweater	7·00	8·50

238 Orange flowers (Emma-Jane Yon)

2006. St. Helena Arts and Crafts. Designs showing artwork from exhibition at Museum of St. Helena. Multicoloured.

989	30p. Type **238**	1·10	1·25
990	30p. Arum lily (Emma-Jane Yon)	1·10	1·25
991	30p. Hibiscus (Christina Stroud)	1·10	1·25
992	30p. Dolphins off coast (Christina Stroud)	1·10	1·25
993	30p. Pattern of blue flowers (Muriel Gardener)	1·10	1·25
994	30p. Wood turning by Jackie Essex	1·10	1·25
995	30p. Pottery dish by Corinda Essex	1·10	1·25
996	30p. Fish (Laura Lawrence)	1·10	1·25
997	30p. Peeled orange (Emma-Jane Yon)	1·10	1·25
998	30p. Sculptures by Sandy Walters and Johnny Drummond	1·10	1·25
999	30p. Pottery bowl by Serena Thorpe	1·10	1·25
1000	30p. Shells on beach (Christina Stroud)	1·10	1·25
1001	30p. Flower arrangement (Christina Stroud)	1·10	1·25
1002	30p. Succulent (Laura Lawrence)	1·10	1·25
1003	30p. Two fish (Laura Lawrence)	1·10	1·25
1004	30p. Pink fish (Laura Lawrence)	1·10	1·25

239 A Partridge in a Pear Tree

2006. Christmas. "The Twelve Days of Christmas" (carol) (1st issue). Multicoloured.

1005	10p. Type **239**	65	75
1006	15p. Two turtle doves	80	90
1007	25p. Three French hens	1·00	1·10
1008	30p. Four calling birds	1·10	1·25
1009	50p. Five gold rings	1·75	2·50
1010	£1 Six geese a-laying	3·00	4·25

240 Queen Victoria and First Victoria Cross Award Ceremony, 1857

2006. Exploration and Innovation. Anniversaries. Multicoloured.

1011	20p. Type **240**	2·25	2·25
1012	20p. Victoria Cross (150th anniv) and Charge of the Light Brigade	2·25	2·25
1013	25p. Charles Darwin (170th anniv of visit to St. Helena)	2·50	2·50
1014	25p. St. Helena sand plover ("Wirebird") and landscape near Sandy Bay	2·50	2·50
1015	30p. Isambard Kingdom Brunel (birth bicent) and coal railway, Cardiff Docks	2·75	2·75
1016	30p. RMS *St. Helena*, Cardiff Docks	2·75	2·75
1017	£1 Charles Dickens and Dingley Dell cricket match	5·00	5·00
1018	£1 Samuel Pickwick and cricket match (170th anniv of "The Pickwick Papers")	5·00	5·00

Nos. 1011/12, 1013/14, 1015/16 and 1017/18 were each printed together, se-tenant, each pair forming a composite background design.

241 Napoleon II (1811–32)

2007. The Napoleons. Multicoloured.

1019	25p. Type **241**	1·50	1·00
1020	30p. Napoleon I (1769–1821)	1·75	1·25
1021	£1 Napoleon III (1808–73)	4·00	5·00
MS1022	156×75 mm. Nos. 1019/21	6·50	6·50

242 Princess Elizabeth and Duke of Edinburgh

2007. Diamond Wedding of Queen Elizabeth II and Duke of Edinburgh. Multicoloured.

1023	25p. Type **242**	1·50	90
1024	35p. Princess Elizabeth on her wedding day	1·75	1·25
1025	40p. Wedding photograph	1·75	1·25
1026	£2 Princess Elizabeth getting out of car	8·50	10·00
MS1027	125×85 mm. £2 Wedding photograph (42×56 mm)	8·50	10·00

243 Black Noddy

2007. BirdLife International (2nd series). Seabirds. Multicoloured.

1028	15p. Type **243**	1·25	1·00
1029	30p. Madeiran storm petrel	2·25	1·40
1030	50p. Masked booby	3·00	2·25
1031	£2 Sooty tern	8·00	10·00

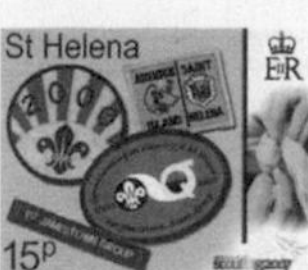

244 Scout Emblems

2007. Centenary of Scouting. Multicoloured.

1032	15p. Type **244**	90	80
1033	30p. Lord Baden-Powell inspecting scouts, May 1936	1·25	1·00
1034	50p. Lord Baden-Powell and Rev. L. C. Walcott	2·00	2·00
1035	£1 Lord Baden-Powell	3·50	5·00
MS1036	90×65 mm. £1 Badge of 1st Jamestown Scout Group (vert); £1 Lord Baden-Powell (150th birth anniv) (vert)	6·50	8·00

245 'Seven Swans a-Swimming'

2007. Christmas. 'The Twelve Days of Christmas' (carol). Multicoloured.

1037	10p. Type **245**	55	70
1038	15p. Eight Maids a-Milking	80	1·00
1039	25p. Nine Ladies Dancing	1·25	1·40
1040	30p. Ten Lords a-Leaping	1·25	1·40
1041	50p. Eleven Pipers Piping	1·75	2·00
1042	£1 Twelve Drummers Drumming	3·25	3·75

246 SS *Savannah*, (first steamship crossing), 1819

2007. Atlantic Firsts. Multicoloured.

1043	25p. Type **246**	1·75	1·10
1044	40p. Alcock and Brown's Vickers FB-27 Vimy, 1919 (first aeroplane crossing)	2·50	2·25
1045	45p. Alain Gerbault's sloop *Firecrest*, 1923 (first east-west solo sailing)	2·50	2·25
1046	£1.20 Charles Lindbergh's *Spirit of St. Louis* (first solo flight)	6·50	7·50

247 Airco D.H.9

2008. 90th Anniv of the Royal Air Force. Multicoloured.

1047	15p. Type **247**	1·50	1·40
1048	25p. Hawker Hurricane	2·00	1·40
1049	35p. Handley Page Hastings	2·75	2·25
1050	40p. English Electric Lightning	3·00	2·50
1051	50p. Harrier GR7	3·50	4·00
MS1052	110×70 mm. £1.50 Berlin Airlift, June 1948–September 1949	6·50	7·50

248 Longwood House, 1821

2008. 150th Anniv of the Purchase of Longwood House and Napoleon's Tomb. Sheet 165×95 mm containing T **248** and similar horiz designs. Multicoloured.

MS1053	90p. Type **248**; £1 Napoleon's Tomb; £1.25 Longwood House, 2008	14·00	17·00

249 Brown Booby

2008. Sea Birds (2nd series). Multicoloured.

1054	15p. Type **249**	1·25	1·00
1055	35p. Brown noddy	2·00	1·60
1056	40p. Fairy tern	2·25	1·60
1057	£1.25 Red-billed tropicbird	5·00	6·00

250 Deepwater Bullseye (*Cookeolus japonicus*)

2008. Fish. Multicoloured.

1058	5p. Type **250**	50	1·00
1059	10p. Five finger (*Abudefduf saxatilis*)	70	1·00

1060	15p. Deepwater greenfish (*Holanthias fronticinctus*)	1·25	1·25
1061	20p. Hardback soldier (*Holocentrus adscensionis*)	1·50	1·25
1062	25p. Deepwater gurnard (*Scorpaena mellissii*)	1·75	1·25
1063	35p. Red mullet (*Apogon axillaris*)	2·25	1·50
1064	40p. Softback soldier (*Myripristis jacobus*)	2·50	1·75
1065	50p. Rock bullseye (*Heteropriacanthus cruentatus*)	3·00	2·50
1066	80p. Gurnard (*Scorpaena plumieri*)	4·50	4·50
1067	£1 Cunningfish (*Chaetodon sanctaehelenae*)	5·00	6·00
1068	£2 Hogfish (*Acanthostracion notacanthus*)	9·00	11·00
1069	£5 Marmalade razorfish (*Xyrichtys blanchardi*)	16·00	18·00
MS1070	171×167 mm. Nos. 1058/69	48·00	50·00

251 St. Helena Flag

2008. St. Helena Island Flag. Self-adhesive.

1071	**251**	35p. multicoloured	2·50	2·75

252 African Lily (*Agapanthus africanus*)

2008. Flowers at Christmas. Multicoloured.

1072	15p. Type **252**	1·00	80
1073	25p. Christmas cactus (*Delosperma cooperi*)	1·50	1·00
1074	35p. Honeysuckle (*Lonicera periclymenem*)	1·75	1·40
1075	40p. St. John's lily (*Lilium longiflorum*)	1·75	1·40
1076	£1 Crucifix orchid (*Epidendrum radicans*)	3·50	5·00

253 Rupert Brooke (1914) and *The Soldier*

2008. 90th Anniv of the End of World War I. Designs showing war poets and extracts from their poems. Multicoloured.

1077	10p. Type **253**	1·00	1·25
1078	15p. Siegfried Sassoon (1919) and *Aftermath*	1·40	1·40
1079	25p. Wilfred Owen (1917) and *Anthem for Doomed Youth*	1·75	1·40
1080	35p. Laurence Binyon (1914) and *For the Fallen*	2·50	2·25
1081	40p. John McCrae (1915) and *In Flanders Fields*	2·75	2·50
1082	50p. Edward Thomas (1915) and *In Memoriam*	3·00	3·50
MS1083	110×70 mm. £2 Cenotaph, St. Helena	8·00	9·50

254 Henry VIII (as young man)

2009. 500th Birth Anniv of King Henry VIII. Multicoloured.

1084	50p. Type **254**	2·50	2·50
1085	50p. Catherine of Aragon	2·50	2·50
1086	50p. Anne Boleyn	2·50	2·50
1087	50p. Jane Seymour	2·50	2·50
1088	50p. Henry VIII (in middle age)	2·50	2·50
1089	50p. *Mary Rose* (galleon)	2·50	2·50
1090	50p. Anne of Cleves	2·50	2·50
1091	50p. Catherine Howard	2·50	2·50
1092	50p. Katherine Parr	2·50	2·50
1093	50p. Hampton Court	2·50	2·50

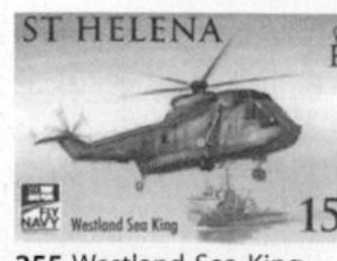

255 Westland Sea King Helicopter

2009. Centenary of Naval Aviation. Multicoloured.

1094	15p. Type **255**	2·25	1·50
1095	35p. Fairey Swordfish	3·25	2·75
1096	40p. BAe Harrier	3·25	3·00
1097	50p. Blackburn Buccaneer	3·50	4·00
MS1098	110×70 mm. £1.50 Pioneer naval aviator Lt. E. L. Gerrard in cockpit of aircraft, Central Flying School, 1913	9·00	9·00

256 The Briars Pavilion, c. 1857

2009. 50th Anniv of Donation of the Briars Pavilion (Emperor Napoleon's home 18 October to 10 December 1815) to the French Government. Sheet 95×166 mm containing T **256** and similar horiz designs. Multicoloured. W w 14 (sideways).

MS1099	90p. Type **256**; £1 Napoleon and Betsy Balcombe; £1.25 The Briars Pavilion, 2008	15·00	17·00

257 Deep Space Tracking Station, Ascension Island

2009. International Year of Astronomy. 40th Anniv of First Moon Landing. Multicoloured. W w 18 (sideways). P 13.

1100	15p. Type **257**	75	75
1101	35p. Early experiment by Dr. Robert Goddard	1·50	1·50
1102	40p. Apollo 11 launch, 1969	1·50	1·50
1103	90p. STS41: *Discovery* Landing, 1984	3·00	3·50
1104	£1.20 Working on International Space Station, 2001	3·75	5·00
MS1105	100×80 mm. £1.20 *Surveyor III, I Presume* (astronauts Pete Conrad and Alan Bean approach Surveyor III) (Alan Bean) (39×59 mm). Wmk upright	4·25	4·75

258 Father Christmas in Street Parade

2009. Christmas. Multicoloured.

1106	15p. Type **258**	75	75
1107	25p. Nativity play in church	1·00	75
1108	40p. Church lit at night	1·50	1·50
1109	£1 Street at night with Christmas tree and lights	3·25	4·50

259 St. Paul's Cathedral

2009. 150th Anniv of Diocese . Multicoloured.

1110	15p. Type **259**	75	75
1111	35p. St. Matthew's Church	1·50	1·50
1112	40p. St. James' Church	1·50	1·50
1113	£1 Piers Calveley Claughton	3·25	4·00

260 Charles I

2010. 350th Anniv of the Restoration of King Charles II. 'Revolution to Restoration'. Multicoloured.

1114	50p. Type **260**	2·50	2·50
1115	50p. Charles II	2·50	2·50
1116	50p. Prince Rupert	2·50	2·50
1117	50p. Oliver Cromwell	2·50	2·50
1118	50p. Richard Cromwell	2·50	2·50
1119	50p. Charles I arrests MPs	2·50	2·50
1120	50p. New Model Army	2·50	2·50
1121	50p. Execution of Charles I	2·50	2·50
1122	50p. Dissolution of Parliament	2·50	2·50
1123	50p. Coronation of Charles II	2·50	2·50

261 Children in Bomb Shelter

2010. 70th Anniv of the Battle of Britain. The Blitz. Multicoloured.

1124	15p. Type **261**	1·25	1·50
1125	25p. Firemen	2·50	1·50
1126	35p. Milkman	2·50	1·75
1127	40p. Wrecked bus	3·00	2·00
1128	90p. Aircraft trails over city	4·25	4·75
1129	£1 Warden with binoculars watching for enemy aircraft	4·50	5·00
MS1130	110×70 mm. £1.50 Sir Douglas Bader	7·50	8·50

262 Great Britain King George V 1912 1d. Stamp

2010. Centenary of Accession of King George V

MS1131	110×70 mm. **262** £1.50 multicoloured	6·50	8·00

263 Football Player and Globe

2010. World Cup Football Championship, South Africa. Multicoloured.

1132	40p. Type **263**	1·50	1·60
1133	40p. Globe showing South Africa	1·50	1·60
1134	40p. Two players and globe	1·50	1·60
MS1135	130×100 mm. Nos. 1132/4	4·00	4·50

264 Rainbows

2010. Centenary of Girlguiding. Multicoloured.

1136	15p. Type **264**	75	75
1137	25p. Brownies	1·25	90
1138	40p. Guides	1·75	1·75
1139	90p. Lord and Lady Baden-Powell	3·25	4·00

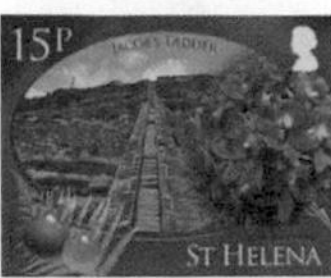

265 Crucifix Orchid and Jacob's Ladder

2010. Christmas. Multicoloured.

1140	15p. Type **265**	75	75
1141	25p. St. John's lily and Diana's Peak	1·25	90
1142	40p. Agapanthus and High Knoll Fort	1·75	1·75
1143	£1 Honeysuckle and Heart Shaped Waterfall	3·25	4·00

266 R.M.S. *St. Helena*, 2010

2010. 20th Anniv of R.M.S. *St. Helena*. Multicoloured.

1144	15p. Type **266**	1·25	1·00
1145	35p. Arrival at St. Helena on her maiden voyage	1·75	1·25
1146	40p. Launch of R.M.S. *St. Helena*, 1990	2·00	1·75
1147	90p. Captain's table	4·25	4·75

267 Queen Elizabeth II

2011. Queen Elizabeth II and Prince Philip 'A Lifetime of Service'. Multicoloured.

1148	15p. Type **267**	50	50
1149	25p. Queen Elizabeth II and Prince Philip (wearing tweed jacket), c. 1960	85	85
1150	35p. Queen Elizabeth II and Prince Philip, c. 1955	1·25	1·25
1151	40p. Queen Elizabeth II (wearing yellow) and Prince Philip, 1970s	1·40	1·60
1152	40p. Queen Elizabeth II (wearing turquoise-green jacket and hat) and Prince Philip, 1970s	1·40	1·60
1153	90p. Prince Philip, 1970s	3·00	3·50
MS1154	175×164 mm. Nos. 1148/53 and three stamp-size labels	8·00	9·00
MS1155	110×70 mm. £1.50 Queen Elizabeth II and Prince Philip, c. 2010	5·00	6·00

2011. Royal Wedding (1st issue). Multicoloured.

MS1156	£3 Prince William and Miss Catherine Middleton	11·00	12·00

2011. Royal Wedding (2nd issue). Multicoloured.

1157	15p. Miss Catherine Middleton and Maid of Honour Pippa Middleton arriving at Westminster Abbey	75	70
1158	35p. Duke and Duchess of Cambridge waving from State Landau	1·25	1·25
1159	40p. Duke and Duchess of Cambridge at Westminster Abbey after wedding ceremony (vert)	1·40	1·40
1160	60p. Duke and Duchess of Cambridge waving from Buckingham Palace balcony (vert)	2·10	2·10
1161	£1 Duke and Duchess of Cambridge kissing on Buckingham Palace balcony (vert)	3·25	3·50

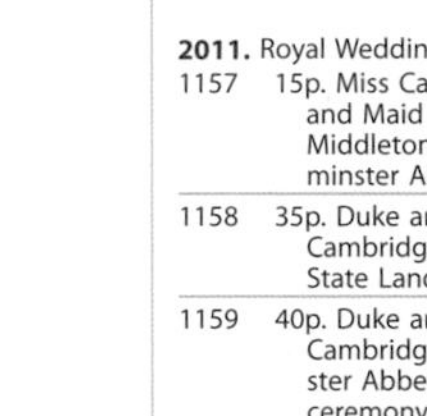

268 Island Hogfish (male)

2011. Endangered Species. Island Hogfish (*Bodianus insularis*). Multicoloured.

1162	35p. Type **268**	1·60	1·60
1163	40p. Island hogfish (juvenile)	1·75	1·75
1164	50p. Island hogfish (immature female)	2·00	2·00
1165	£1.20 Island hogfish (male, on reef)	3·50	3·50
MS1166	94×64 mm. £1.50 As No. 1165	5·00	5·00

269 RFA *Gold Rover*

2011. Christmas. Royal Fleet Auxiliary Ships. Multicoloured.

1167	35p. Type **269**	1·10	1·10
1168	50p. RFA *Black Rover*	1·75	1·75
1169	60p. RFA *Lyme Bay*	2·25	2·25
1170	£1.20 RFA *Darkdale*	3·50	3·50

270 Court House, Jamestown (seat of Legislative Council)

2011. Centenary of Commonwealth Parliamentary Association. Multicoloured.

1171	50p. Type **270**	1·60	1·60
1172	50p. Royal Charter	1·60	1·60
1173	50p. CPA Headquarters, 7 Millbank, London	1·60	1·60
MS1174	120×80 mm. Nos. 1171/3	5·00	5·00

271 Queen Elizabeth II

2012. Diamond Jubilee (1st issue). Multicoloured.

1175	20p. Type **271**	1·40	1·40
1176	35p. Queen Elizabeth II wearing tiara and diamond earrings, c. 1955	2·00	2·00
1177	40p. Queen Elizabeth II wearing mauve hat, c. 1980	2·25	2·25
1178	50p. Queen Elizabeth II, c. 1990	2·50	2·50
1179	60p. Queen Elizabeth II, c. 1975	2·75	2·75
1180	£1 Queen Elizabeth II, c. 2005	4·00	4·00
MS1181	174×164 mm. Nos. 1175/80 and three stamp-size labels	13·00	13·00
MS1182	110×71 mm. £1.50 Queen Elizabeth II wearing tiara, c. 1955	6·50	6·50

272 Union Jack over Sea

2012. Diamond Jubilee (2nd issue). Children's Paintings. Multicoloured.

1183	20p. Type **272**	1·40	1·40
1184	35p. Outline map of St. Helena, tortoise, wirebird and crown	2·00	2·00
1185	50p. Outline map of St. Helena, Queen, ship and St. James' Church	2·50	2·50
1186	£1 Union Jack on map of St. Helena, leaves, torches, heart-shaped waterfall and ship	4·00	4·00

273 Crew of RMS *St. Helena*, 1982

2012. 30th Anniv of RMS *St. Helena's* Commission for the Falklands War. Multicoloured.

1187	20p. Type **273**	1·50	1·50
1188	35p. RMS *St. Helena*, Grytviken, 1982 (winter)	2·25	2·25
1189	40p. RMS *St. Helena*, Ascension Island, 1982	2·50	2·50
1190	50p. RMS *St. Helena*, Grytviken, 1982 (summer)	2·75	2·75
1191	£1 RMS *St. Helena* under escort, 1982	4·25	4·25

274 O Little Town of Bethlehem

2012. Christmas. Carols. Multicoloured.

1192	20p. Type **274**	1·10	1·10
1193	35p. While Shepherds Watched	1·75	1·75
1194	50p. Away in a Manger	2·25	2·25
1195	£1 Silent Night Holy Night	4·25	4·25

275 Queen Victoria

2013. 60th Anniv of the Coronation. Coronation Souvenirs. Multicoloured.

1196	20p. Type **275**	75	75
1197	35p. King Edward VII and Queen Alexandra	1·25	1·25
1198	40p. King George V	1·40	1·40
1199	50p. Coronation souvenir of King George VI and Queen Elizabeth	1·60	1·60
1200	£1 Queen Elizabeth II, c. 1952 and Buckingham Palace	3·00	3·00
MS1201	111×70 mm. £2 Queen Elizabeth II in recent years (32×48 mm)	6·00	6·50

276 Margaret Thatcher

2013. Margaret Thatcher (1925-2013, Prime Minister 1979-90) Commemoration. Multicoloured.

1202	40p. Type **276**	1·75	1·50
1203	50p. Margaret Thatcher	1·75	1·50
1204	60p. Margaret Thatcher (with hand on chin)	2·00	2·00
1205	£1 Margaret Thatcher at microphone speaking	3·50	4·00
MS1206	147×82 mm. Nos. 1202/5	8·00	8·00

277 Prince William holding Prince George

2013. Birth of Prince George of Cambridge. Multicoloured.

1207	25p. Type **277**	75	75
1208	40p. Catherine, Duchess of Cambridge holding Prince George	1·40	1·40
1209	60p. Prince George	1·75	1·75
1210	£1 Duke and Duchess of Cambridge with Prince George	3·00	3·00

POSTAGE DUE STAMPS

D1 Outline Map of St. Helena

1986

D1	**D1**	1p. deep brown and brown	10	40
D2	**D1**	2p. brown and orange	15	40
D3	**D1**	5p. brown and red	20	45
D4	**D1**	7p. black and violet	20	50
D5	**D1**	10p. black and blue	25	50
D6	**D1**	25p. black and green	65	1·25

Pt. 1

ST KITTS

On 23 June 1980 separate postal administrations were formed for St. Kitts and for Nevis, although both islands remained part of the State of St. Kitts-Nevis.

100 cents = 1 West Indian dollar.

1980. As Nos. 394/406 of St. Kitts-Nevis optd **St Kitts**.

29B	5c. multicoloured	10	10
30B	10c. multicoloured	10	10
31A	12c. multicoloured	35	80
32B	15c. multicoloured	10	10
33B	25c. multicoloured	10	10
34B	30c. multicoloured	10	10
35B	40c. multicoloured	10	15
36A	45c. multicoloured	50	15
37A	50c. multicoloured	10	15
38A	55c. multicoloured	15	15
39A	$1 multicoloured	10	25
40A	$5 multicoloured	30	1·00
41A	$10 multicoloured	35	1·75

9 H.M.S. "Vanguard", 1762

1980. Ships. Multicoloured.

42	4c. Type **9**	10	10
43	10c. H.M.S. "Boreas", 1787	10	10
44	30c. H.M.S. "Druid", 1827	15	10
45	55c. H.M.S. "Winchester", 1831	15	15
46	$1.50 Harrison Line "Philosopher", 1857	30	35
47	$2 Harrison Line "Contractor", 1930	35	45

10 Queen Elizabeth the Queen Mother at Royal Variety Performance, 1978

1980. 80th Birthday of The Queen Mother.

48	**10**	$2 multicoloured	25	60

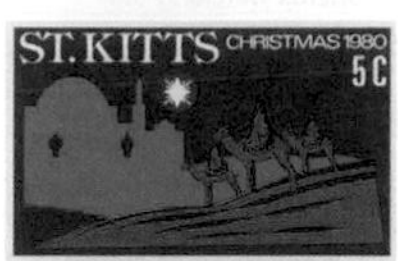

11 The Three Wise Men

1980. Christmas. Multicoloured.

49	5c. Type **11**	10	10
50	15c. The Shepherds	10	10
51	30c. Bethlehem	10	10
52	$4 Nativity scene	50	60

12 Purple-throated Carib

13 Bananaquit

1981. Birds. Multicoloured.

53A	1c. Magnificent frigate bird	25	20
54A	4c. Wied's crested flycatcher	35	20
55A	5c. Type **12**	30	20
56A	6c. Burrowing owl	60	30
57A	8c. Caribbean martin ("Purple Martin")	45	30
58A	10c. Yellow-crowned night heron	30	20
59A	15c. Type **13**	30	20
60A	20c. Scaly-breasted thrasher	30	20
61A	25c. Grey kingbird	30	20
62A	30c. Green-throated carib	30	20
63A	40c. Ruddy turnstone	35	30
64A	45c. Black-faced grassquit	35	30
65A	50c. Cattle egret	40	30
66A	55c. Brown pelican	40	30
67A	$1 Lesser Antillean bullfinch	60	60
68A	$2.50 Zenaida dove	1·25	2·25
69A	$5 American kestrel ("Sparrow Hawk")	2·25	3·50
70A	$10 Antillean crested hummingbird	4·50	6·00

The 1c. to 10c. are vertical as Type **12**. The remainder are horizontal as Type **13**.

14 Battalion Company Sergeant 3rd Regt of Foot ("The Buffs"), c. 1801

1981. Military Uniforms. Multicoloured.

71	5c. Type **14**	10	10
72	30c. Battalion Company Officer, 45th Regt of Foot, 1796–97	15	10
73	55c. Battalion Company Officer, 9th Regt of Foot, 1790	15	10
74	$2.50 Grenadier, 38th Regt of Foot, 1751	45	35

14a "Saudadoes"

14b Prince Charles and Lady Diana Spencer (image scaled to 60% of original size)

1981. Royal Wedding. Royal Yachts. Multicoloured.

75	55c. Type **14a**	10	10
77	$2.50 "Royal George"	25	30
78	$2.50 As No. 76	70	70
79	$4 "Britannia"	35	50
80	$4 As No. 76	75	1·00
MS81	120×109 mm. $5 No. 76	1·00	1·00
82	55c. Type **14b**	15	30

15 Miriam Pickard (first Guide Commissioner)

1981. 50th Anniv of St. Kitts Girl Guide Movement. Multicoloured.

84	5c. Type **15**	10	10
85	30c. Lady Baden-Powell's visit, 1964	15	10
86	55c. Visit of Princess Alice, 1960	25	10
87	$2 Thinking Day parade, 1980's	45	35

16 Stained-glass Windows

1981. Christmas.

88	**16**	5c. multicoloured	10	10
89	-	30c. multicoloured	10	10
90	-	55c. multicoloured	15	10
91	-	$3 multicoloured	50	50

DESIGNS: 30c. to $3, Various designs showing stained-glass windows.

17 Admiral Samuel Hood

1982. Bicentenary of Brimstone Hill Siege.

92	**17**	15c. multicoloured	10	10
93	-	55c. multicoloured	20	10
MS94		96×71 mm.–$5 black, orange and brown	1·10	1·10

DESIGNS: 55c. Marquis De Bouille; $5 Battle scene.

18 Alexandra, Princess of Wales, 1863

1982. 21st Birthday of Princess of Wales. Multicoloured.

95	15c. Type **18**	10	10
96	55c. Coat of arms of Alexandra of Denmark	15	15

1991. 65th Birthday of Queen Elizabeth II and 70th Birthday of Prince Philip. As T **165a** of St. Helena. Multicoloured.

336	$1.20 Prince Philip	1·00	1·25
337	$1.80 Queen holding bouquet of flowers	1·00	1·25

62 Nassau Grouper

1991. Fish. Multicoloured.

338	10c. Type **62**	50	20
339	60c. Hogfish	1·25	50
340	$1 Red hind	2·00	1·50
341	$3 Porkfish	3·50	5·50

63 School of Continuing Studies, St. Kitts and Chancellor Sir Shridath Ramphal

1991. 40th Anniv of University of West Indies. Multicoloured.

342	15c. Type **63**	40	15
343	50c. Administration Building, Barbados	70	40
344	$1 Engineering Building, Trinidad and Tobago	1·25	1·40
345	$3 Mona Campus, Jamaica and Sir Shridath Ramphal	3·00	5·00

64 Whipping The Bull

1991. Christmas. "The Bull" (Carnival play). Multicoloured.

346	10c. Type **64**	40	10
347	15c. Death of The Bull	40	10
348	60c. Cast of characters and musicians	1·25	60
349	$3 The Bull in procession	3·00	5·00

1992. 40th Anniv of Queen Elizabeth II's Accession. As T **168a** of St. Helena. Multicoloured.

350	10c. St. Kitts coastline	40	10
351	40c. Warner Park Pavilion	2·00	50
352	60c. Brimstone Hill	75	40
353	$1 Three portraits of Queen Elizabeth	1·00	1·00
354	$3 Queen Elizabeth II	1·90	2·75

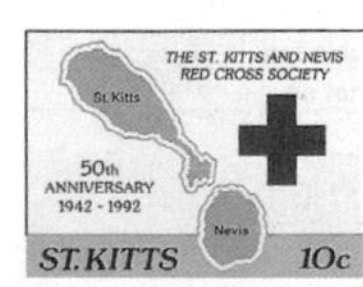

65 Map of St. Kitts-Nevis

1992. 50th Anniv of St. Kitts-Nevis Red Cross Society. Multicoloured.

355	10c. Type **65**	1·50	60
356	20c. St. Kitts-Nevis flag	2·25	45
357	50c. Red Cross House, St. Kitts	1·50	80
358	$2.40 Henri Dunant	3·50	5·50

66 Columbus meeting Amerindians

1992. Organization of East Caribbean States. 500th Anniv of Discovery of America by Columbus (2nd issue). Multicoloured.

359	$1 Type **66**	1·75	1·25
360	$2 Ships approaching island	3·50	4·00

67 Fountain, Independence Square

1992. Local Monuments. Multicoloured.

361	25c. Type **67**	25	20
362	50c. Berkeley Memorial Drinking Fountain	35	35
363	80c. Sir Thomas Warner's Tomb	55	65
364	$2 War Memorial	1·10	2·50

68 Joseph and Mary travelling to Bethlehem

1992. Christmas. Multicoloured.

365	20c. Type **68**	30	20
366	25c. Shepherds and star	30	20
367	80c. Wise Men with gifts	65	55
368	$3 Mary, Joseph and Holy Child	1·75	4·00

68a Short Singapore III

1993. 75th Anniv of Royal Air Force. Aircraft. Multicoloured.

369	25c. Type **68a**	85	20
370	50c. Bristol Beaufort Mk II	1·40	30
371	80c. Westland Whirlwind Series 3 H.A.R. 10 helicopter	3·00	1·50
372	$1.60 English Electric Canberra	3·00	3·50
MS373	110×78 mm. $2 Handley Page 0/400; $2 Fairey Long Range monoplane; $2 Vickers Wellesley; $2 Sepecat Jaguar G.R.1	11·00	11·00

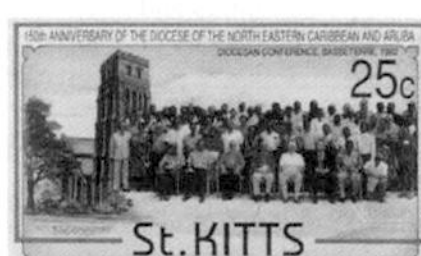

69 Members of Diocesan Conference, Basseterre, 1992

1993. 150th Anniv of Anglican Diocese of North-eastern Caribbean and Aruba. Multicoloured.

374	25c. Type **69**	15	10
375	50c. Cathedral of St. John the Divine (vert)	40	35
376	80c. Coat of arms and motto	70	85
377	$2 The Right Revd. Daniel Davis (first bishop) (vert)	1·50	3·00

70 1953 Coronation 2c. Stamp and Ampulla

1993. 40th Anniv of Coronation. Multicoloured.

378	10c. Type **70**	40	20
379	25c. 1977 Silver Jubilee $1.50 stamp and anointing spoon	50	20
380	80c. 1977 Silver Jubilee 55c. stamp and tassels	1·00	1·25
381	$2 1978 25th anniv of Coronation stamps and sceptre	2·00	3·50

71 Flags of Girls Brigade and St. Kitts-Nevis

1993. Centenary of Girls Brigade. Multicoloured.

382	80c. Type **71**	2·50	1·00
383	$3 Girls Brigade badge and coat of arms	4·00	4·50

72 Aspects of St. Kitts on Flag

1993. Tenth Anniv of Independence. Multicoloured.

384	20c. Type **72**	1·00	15
385	80c. Coat of arms and Independence anniversary logo	1·25	80
386	$3 Coat of arms and map	4·25	5·00

73 "Hibiscus sabdariffa"

1993. Christmas. Flowers. Multicoloured.

387	25c. Type **73**	25	10
388	50c. "Euphorbia pulcherrima"	60	45
389	$1.60 "Euphorbia leucocephala"	1·75	3·00

74 Mesosaurus

1994. Prehistoric Aquatic Reptiles. Multicoloured.

390	$1.20 Type **74**	1·40	1·75
391	$1.20 Placodus	1·40	1·75
392	$1.20 Liopleurodon	1·40	1·75
393	$1.20 Hydrotherosaurus	1·40	1·75
394	$1.20 Caretta	1·40	1·75

Nos. 390/4 were printed together, *se-tenant*, with the background forming a composite design.

1994. "Hong Kong '94" International Stamp Exhibition. Nos. 390/4 optd **HONG KONG '94** and emblem.

395	$1.20 Type **74**	1·90	2·25
396	$1.20 Placodus	1·90	2·25
397	$1.20 Liopleurodon	1·90	2·25
398	$1.20 Hydrotherosaurus	1·90	2·25
399	$1.20 Caretta	1·90	2·25

75 Sir Shridath Ramphal

1994. First Recipients of Order of the Caribbean Community. Multicoloured.

401	10c. Type **75**	30	50
402	10c. Star of Order	20	30
403	10c. Derek Walcott	30	50
404	10c. William Demas	30	50
405	$1 Type **75**	1·25	1·40
406	$1 As No. 402	1·00	1·00
407	$1 As No. 403	1·25	1·40
408	$1 As No. 404	1·25	1·40

76 Family singing Carols

1994. Christmas. Int Year of the Family. Multicoloured.

409	25c. Type **76**	15	10
410	25c. Family unwrapping Christmas presents	15	10
411	80c. Preparing for Christmas carnival	60	60
412	$2.50 Nativity	1·90	3·25

77 Green Turtle swimming

1995. Endangered Species. Green Turtle. Multicoloured.

427	10c. Type **77**	40	50
428	40c. Turtle crawling up beach	55	60
429	50c. Burying eggs	60	60
430	$1 Young heading for sea	75	1·00

78 St. Christopher 1d. Stamps of 1870

1995. 125th Anniv of St. Kitts Postage Stamps. Each including the St. Christopher 1870 1d. Multicoloured.

431	25c. Type **78**	15	15
432	80c. St. Kitts-Nevis 1935 Silver Jubilee 1d.	45	50
433	$2.50 St. Kitts-Nevis 1946 Victory 1d.	1·75	2·50
434	$3 St. Christopher Nevis Anguilla 1953 Coronation 2c.	2·00	2·75

1995. 50th Anniv of End of Second World War. As T **182a** of St. Helena. Multicoloured.

435	20c. Caribbean Regiment patrol, North Africa	15	15
436	50c. Grumman TBF Avengers (bombers)	35	35
437	$2 Supermarine Spitfire Mk Vb (fighter)	1·25	1·50
438	$8 U. S. Navy destroyer escort	5·00	6·50
MS439	75×85 mm. $3 Reverse of 1939–45 War Medal (vert)	1·50	2·00

79 Telecommunication Links between Islands

1995. Tenth Anniv of SKANTEL (telecommunications company). Multicoloured.

440	10c. Type **79**	25	10
441	25c. Payphone and computer link	30	15
442	$2 Telecommunications tower and dish aerial	2·25	2·75
443	$3 Silhouette of dish aerial at sunset	2·50	3·75

80 Water Treatment Works

1995. 50th Anniv of United Nations. Multicoloured.

444	40c. Type **80**	55	25
445	50c. Beach	50	30
446	$1.60 Dust cart	1·75	2·25
447	$2.50 Forest	2·75	3·75

81 F.A.O. Emblem and Vegetables

1995. 50th Anniv of F.A.O. Multicoloured.

448	25c. Type **81**	20	10
449	50c. Glazed carrots and West Indian peas with rice	35	30
450	80c. Tania and cassava plants	50	60
451	$1.50 Waterfall, Green Hill Mountain	2·50	3·00

82 Flame Helmet

1996. Sea Shells. Multicoloured.

452	$1.50 Type **82**	95	1·10
453	$1.50 Triton's trumpet	95	1·10
454	$1.50 King helmet	95	1·10
455	$1.50 True tulip	95	1·10
456	$1.50 Queen conch	95	1·10

83 L.M.S. No. 45614 Steam Locomotive "Leeward Islands" in Green Livery

1996. "CAPEX '96" International Stamp Exhibition, Toronto.

457	10c. Type **83**	75	60
MS458	110×80 mm. $10 L.M.S. No. 5614 "Leeward Islands" steam locomotive in red livery (48×31½ mm)	7·50	7·50

84 Athlete and National Flag

1996. Centennial Olympic Games, Atlanta. Multicoloured.

459	10c. Type **84**	15	15
460	25c. High jumper and U.S.A. flag	20	20
461	80c. Athlete and Olympic flag	50	55
462	$3 Poster for 1896 Olympic Games, Athens	1·75	2·50
MS463	70×64 mm. $6 Olympic torch	3·25	3·50

85 Volunteer Rifleman, 1896

1996. Centenary of Defence Force. Multicoloured.

464	10c. Type **85**	15	15
465	50c. Mounted infantryman, 1911	35	35
466	$2 Drummer, 1940–60	1·25	1·75
467	$2.50 Ceremonial uniform, 1996	1·40	2·00

86 "Holy Virgin and Child" (A. Colin)

1996. Christmas. Religious Paintings. Multicoloured.

468	15c. Type **86**	20	10
469	25c. "Holy Family" (after Rubens)	25	10
470	50c. "Madonna with the Goldfinch" (Krause after Raphael)	45	40
471	80c. "Madonna on Throne with Angels" (17th-cent Spanish)	75	1·25

1997. "HONG KONG '97" International Stamp Exhibition. Sheet 130×90 mm, containing No. 323.

MS472	$3 "Berbice" (mail steamer)	1·60	2·00

87 Princess Parrotfish

1997. Fish. Multicoloured.

473	$1 Type **87**	80	90
474	$1 Yellow-bellied hamlet	80	90
475	$1 Coney	80	90
476	$1 Fin-spot wrasse	80	90
477	$1 Doctor fish	80	90
478	$1 Squirrelfish	80	90
479	$1 Queen angelfish	80	90
480	$1 Spanish hogfish	80	90
481	$1 Red hind	80	90
482	$1 Red grouper	80	90
483	$1 Yellow-tailed snapper	80	90
484	$1 Mutton hamlet	80	90

1997. Golden Wedding of Queen Elizabeth and Prince Philip. As T **192a** of St. Helena. Multicoloured.

485	10c. Queen Elizabeth in evening dress	70	1·00
486	10c. Prince Philip and Duke of Kent at Trooping the Colour	70	1·00
487	25c. Queen Elizabeth in phaeton at Trooping the Colour	90	1·10
488	25c. Prince Philip in naval uniform	90	1·10
489	$3 Queen Elizabeth and Prince Philip	2·50	2·75
490	$3 Peter Phillips on horseback	2·50	2·75
MS491	110×70 mm. $6 Queen Elizabeth and Prince Philip in landau (horiz).	5·50	6·50

Nos. 485/6, 487/8 and 489/90 respectively were printed together, se-tenant, with the backgrounds forming composite designs.

88 C. A. Paul Southwell (first Chief Minister)

1997. National Heroes Day. Multicoloured.

492	25c. Type **88**	15	25
493	25c. Sir Joseph France (trade union leader)	15	25
494	25c. Robert Bradshaw (first Prime Minister)	15	25
495	$3 Sir Joseph France, Robert Bradshaw and C. A. Paul Southwell (horiz)	1·75	2·50

89 Wesley Methodist Church

1997. Christmas. Churches. Multicoloured.

496	10c. Type **89**	10	10
497	10c. Zion Moravian Church	10	10
498	$1.50 St. George's Anglican Church (vert)	1·00	1·00
499	$15 Co-Cathedral of the Immaculate Conception (vert)	8·50	12·00

90 Common Long-tail Skipper

1997. Butterflies. Multicoloured.

500	10c. Type **90**	20	30
501	15c. White peacock	30	30
502	25c. Caribbean buckeye	40	40
503	30c. The red rim	40	30
504	40c. Cassius blue	45	40
505	50c. The flambeau	50	40
506	60c. Lucas's blue	65	45
507	90c. Cloudless sulphur	1·00	70
508	$1 The monarch	1·10	75
509	$1.20 Fiery skipper	1·25	1·00
510	$1.60 The zebra	1·40	1·40
511	$3 Southern dagger tail	2·50	3·25
512	$5 Polydamus swallowtail	3·50	5·00
513	$10 Tropical chequered skipper	6·50	10·00

1998. Diana, Princess of Wales Commemoration. As T **62a** of Tokelau. Multicoloured.

514	30c. Wearing hat	30	30
MS515	145×70 mm. $1.60, As 30c.; $1.60, Wearing red jacket; $1.60, Wearing white jacket; $1.60, Carrying bouquets. (sold at $6.40 + 90c. charity premium)	2·25	3·25

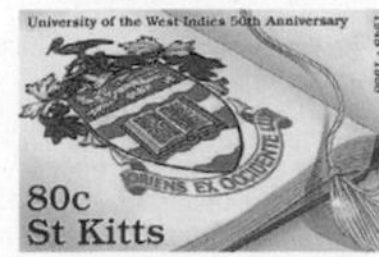

91 University Arms on Book

1998. 50th Anniv of University of West Indies. Multicoloured.

516	80c. Type **91**	45	40
517	$2 University arms and mortar-board	95	1·40

92 Santa at Carnival

1998. Christmas. Multicoloured.

518	80c. Type **92**	45	40
519	$1.20 Santa with two carnival dancers	65	1·00

93 Launching Rowing Boat

1999. 125th Anniv of Universal Postal Union. Multicoloured.

520	30c. Type **93**	25	20
521	90c. Pictorial map of St. Kitts	1·00	1·00

94 Caribbean Martin

1999. Birds of the Eastern Caribbean. Multicoloured.

522	80c. Type **94**	60	70
523	80c. Spotted sandpiper	60	70
524	80c. Sooty tern	60	70
525	80c. Red-tailed hawk	60	70
526	80c. Brown trembler	60	70
527	80c. Belted kingfisher	60	70
528	80c. Black-billed whistling duck	60	70
529	80c. Yellow warbler	60	70
530	80c. Blue-headed hummingbird	60	70
531	80c. Antillean Euphonia	60	70
532	80c. Fulvous whistling duck	60	70
533	80c. Mangrove cuckoo	60	70
534	80c. Carib grackle	60	70
535	80c. Caribbean elaenia	60	70
536	80c. Scaly-breasted ground dove	60	70
537	80c. Forest thrush	60	70

94a Lift-off

1999. 30th Anniv of First Manned Landing on Moon. Multicoloured.

538	80c. Type **94a**	60	40
539	90c. In Moon orbit	70	65
540	$1 Buzz Aldrin on Moon's surface	80	85
541	$1.20 Heat shields burning during re-entry	90	1·25
MS542	90×80 mm. $10 Earth as seen from Moon (circular, 40 mm diam)	4·75	5·00

95 Local Quartet

1999. Christmas. Musicians. Multicoloured.

543	10c. Type **95**	20	10
544	30c. Trio	30	20
545	80c. Sextet	60	45
546	$2 Quartet in green jerseys	1·10	2·25

96 "Rockets, Saturn and Earth" (A. Taylor)

1999. New Millennium. Children's Paintings. Multicoloured.

547	10c. Type **96**	30	15
548	30c. "Y2K, computer and Earth weeping" (T. Liburd)	45	25
549	50c. "Alien destroying computer" (D. Moses)	55	45
550	$1 "Technology past, present and future" (P. Liburd)	90	1·50

97 Carnival Celebrations

2000. "Carifesta VII" Arts Festival. Multicoloured.

551	30c. Type **97**	30	20
552	90c. Carifesta logo	75	75
553	$1.20 Stylized dancer with streamer (vert)	1·00	1·50

98 Steam Locomotive No. 133, U.S. Military Railroad, 1864

2001. Railways in the American Civil War. Multicoloured (except for Nos. **MS**578a and c).

554	$1.20 Type **98**	1·40	1·40
555	$1.20 Locomotive *Quigley*, Louisville and Nashville Railroad, 1860	1·40	1·40
556	$1.20 Locomotive *Colonel Holobird*, New Orleans, Opelousas and Great Western Railroad, 1865	1·40	1·40
557	$1.20 Locomotive No. 150, U.S. Military Railroad, 1864	1·40	1·40
558	$1.20 Locomotive *Doctor Thompson*, Atlanta and West Point Railroad, 1860	1·40	1·40
559	$1.20 Locomotive No. 156, U.S. Military Railroad, 1856	1·40	1·40
560	$1.20 Locomotive *Governor Nye*, U.S. Military Railroad, 1863	1·40	1·40
561	$1.20 Locomotive No. 31, Illinois Central Railroad, 1856	1·40	1·40
562	$1.20 Locomotive *C.A. Henry*, Memphis, Clarksville and Louisville Line, 1863	1·40	1·40
563	$1.20 Locomotive No. 152, Illinois Central Railroad, 1856	1·40	1·40
564	$1.20 Locomotive No. 116, U.S. Military Railroad, 1863	1·40	1·40
565	$1.20 Locomotive *Job Terry* (shown as No. 111 of the Wilmington and Weldon Railroad, 1890)	1·40	1·40
566	$1.60 Locomotive *Dover*, U.S. Military Railroad, 1856	1·40	1·40
567	$1.60 Locomotive *Scout*, Richmond to Gordonsville Line, 1861	1·40	1·40
568	$1.60 Baltimore & Ohio Railroad Locomotive, 1861	1·40	1·40
569	$1.60 Locomotive *John. M. Forbes*, Philadelphia, Wilmington and Baltimore Railroad, 1861	1·40	1·40
570	$1.60 Locomotive *Edward Kidder*, Wilmington and Weldon Railroad, 1866	1·40	1·40
571	$1.60 Locomotive *William W. Wright*, U.S. Military Railroad, 1863	1·40	1·40
572	$1.60 Locomotive No. 83, Illinois Central Railroad, 1856	1·40	1·40
573	$1.60 Locomotive *The General*, Western and Atlantic Railroad, 1855	1·40	1·40
574	$1.60 Locomotive No. 38, Louisville and Nashville Railroad, 1860	1·40	1·40
575	$1.60 Locomotive *Texas*, Western and Atlantic Railroad, 1856	1·40	1·40
576	$1.60 Locomotive No. 162, U.S. Military Railroad, 1864	1·40	1·40
577	$1.60 Locomotive *Christopher Adams Jr.*, Memphis and Littlerock Line, 1853	1·40	1·40

MS578 Four sheets, each 99×78 mm. (a) $5 Brigadier-general Herman Haupt (Federal railway chief) (brown and black) (vert). (b) $5 General George B. McClellan (vert). (c) $5 General Ulysses S. Grant (brown, grey and black) (vert). (d) $5 General Robert E. Lee (vert). Set of 4 sheets 27·00 30·00

No. 577 is inscribed "Chritopher" in error.

99 Bananaquit

2001. Caribbean Flora and Fauna. Multicoloured.

No.	Description	Unused	Used
579	$1.20 Type **99**	1·25	1·25
580	$1.20 Anthurium (face value in white)	1·25	1·25
581	$1.20 Common dolphin	1·25	1·25
582	$1.20 Horse mushroom	1·25	1·25
583	$1.20 Green anole	1·25	1·25
584	$1.20 Monarch butterfly	1·25	1·25
585	$1.20 Heliconia	1·25	1·25
586	$1.20 Anthurium (black face value)	1·25	1·25
587	$1.20 *Oncidium splendidum*	1·25	1·25
588	$1.20 Trumpet creeper	1·25	1·25
589	$1.20 Bird of paradise	1·25	1·25
590	$1.20 Hibiscus	1·25	1·25
591	$1.60 Beaugregory	1·25	1·25
592	$1.60 Banded butterflyfish	1·25	1·25
593	$1.60 Cherubfish	1·25	1·25
594	$1.60 Rock beauty	1·25	1·25
595	$1.60 Red snapper	1·25	1·25
596	$1.60 Leatherback turtle	1·25	1·25
597	$1.60 Figure-of-eight butterfly	1·25	1·25
598	$1.60 Banded king shoemaker	1·25	1·25
599	$1.60 Orange theope	1·25	1·25
600	$1.60 Grecian shoemaker	1·25	1·25
601	$1.60 Clorinde	1·25	1·25
602	$1.60 Small lace-wing	1·25	1·25
603	$1.60 Laughing gull	1·25	1·25
604	$1.60 Sooty tern	1·25	1·25
605	$1.60 Red-billed tropic bird ("White-tailed Tropicbird")	1·25	1·25
606	$1.60 Painted bunting	1·25	1·25
607	$1.60 Belted kingfisher	1·25	1·25
608	$1.60 Yellow-bellied sapsucker	1·25	1·25

MS609 Five sheets, each 82×112 mm. (a) $5 Iguana (horiz). (b) $5 *Leochilus carinatus* (orchid). (c) $5 Redband parrotfish (horiz). (d) $5 Common morpho (butterfly) (horiz). (e) $5 Ruby-throated hummingbird (horiz). Set of 5 sheets 22·00 25·00

No. 608 is inscribed "Yello-bellied" in error.

100 Symbolic Family and House

2001. Population and Housing Census. Multicoloured.

No.	Description	Unused	Used
610	30c. Type **100**	30	15
611	$3 People with Census symbol	2·00	2·75

101 Coronation of Queen Victoria

2001. Death Centenary of Queen Victoria. Multicoloured (except No. **MS**616).

No.	Description	Unused	Used
612	$2 Type **101**	1·50	2·00
613	$2 Wedding of Queen Victoria and Prince Albert	1·50	2·00
614	$2 Royal Family with Crimean War veterans	1·50	2·00
615	$2 Queen Victoria with Prince Albert	1·50	2·00

MS616 88×113 mm. $5 Queen Victoria as Empress of India. (43×52 mm) (black) 3·75 5·00

102 Mao Tse-tung, 1926

2001. 25th Death Anniv of Mao Tse-tung (Chinese leader). Multicoloured.

No.	Description	Unused	Used
617	$2 Type **102**	1·50	2·00
618	$2 Mao Tse-tung, 1945 (face value at top left)	1·50	2·00
619	$2 Mao Tse-tung, 1945 (face value at bottom left)	1·50	2·00

MS620 160×142 mm. $3 Mao Tse-tung in blue jacket 2·50 3·25

103 "On the Coast at Trouville" (Monet)

2001. 75th Death Anniv of Claude-Oscar Monet (French painter). Multicoloured.

No.	Description	Unused	Used
621	$2 Type **103**	2·00	2·50
622	$2 "Vetheuil in Summer"	2·00	2·50
623	$2 "Yellow Iris near Giverny"	2·00	2·50
624	$2 "Coastguard's Cottage at Varengeville"	2·00	2·50

MS625 137×111 mm. $5 "Poplars on Banks of Epte" (vert) 4·25 5·00

104 Queen Elizabeth carrying Bouquet

2001. 75th Birthday of Queen Elizabeth II. Multicoloured.

No.	Description	Unused	Used
626	$2 Type **104**	1·50	2·00
627	$2 Wearing cream floral hat	1·50	2·00
628	$2 Wearing blue coat and hat	1·50	2·00
629	$2 Queen in beige hat and dress	1·50	2·00

MS630 80×109 mm. $5 Queen Elizabeth riding 3·75 4·25

105 French Dragoons from *Sicilian Vespers* (opera)

2001. Death Centenary of Giuseppe Verdi (Italian composer). Designs showing Sicilian (opera). Multicoloured.

No.	Description	Unused	Used
631	$2 Type **105**	2·00	2·25
632	$2 French dragoons, drinking round table	2·00	2·25
633	$2 Original costume design	2·00	2·25
634	$2 Inhabitants of Palermo	2·00	2·25

MS635 80×108 mm. $5 Montserrat Caballe as Elena 5·50 6·00

Nos. 631/2 are inscribed "FREWNCH" and **MS**635 "MOUNTSERRAT", all in error.

106 "Hatsufunedayu as a Tatebina" (Shigenobu)

2001. "Philanippon 01" International Stamp Exhibition, Tokyo. Japanese Woodcuts. Multicoloured.

No.	Description	Unused	Used
636	50c. Type **106**	40	30
637	80c. "Samurai Kodenji as Tsuyu No Mae" (Kiyonobu I)	60	50
638	$1 "Nakamura Senya as Tokonatsu" (Kiyomasu I)	75	65
639	$1.60 "Sunida River" (Shunsho)	1·10	1·40
640	$2 "Kuemon Yoba the Wrestler" (Shune I)	1·50	2·00
641	$3 "Two actors" (Kiyonobu I/ Tori I)	2·00	3·00

MS642 78×78 mm. $5 "Actors with swords" (Shune I) 3·75 4·25

107 Submarine "A1", 1902

2001. Centenary of Royal Navy Submarine Service. Multicoloured.

No.	Description	Unused	Used
643	$1.50 Type **107**	2·25	2·25
644	$1.50 H.M.S. *Dreadnought* (battleship), 1906	2·25	2·25
645	$1.50 H.M.S. *Amethyst* (cruiser), 1903	2·25	2·25
646	$1.50 H.M.S. *Barham* (battleship), 1914	2·25	2·25
647	$1.50 H.M.S. *Exeter* (cruiser), 1929	2·25	2·25
648	$1.50 H.M.S. *Eagle* (aircraft carrier), 1918	2·25	2·25

MS649 129×90 mm. $5 H.M.S. *Dreadnought* (nuclear submarine), 1960 (43×57 mm) 9·00 9·00

Nos. 644 and **MS**649 are inscribed "DREADNAUGHT" and No. 646 "BARNHAM", both in error.

108 *Maxillaria cucullata* (orchid)

2001. . Caribbean Flora and Fauna. Multicoloured.

No.	Description	Unused	Used
650	$1.20 Type **108**	1·00	1·00
651	$1.20 *Cattleya dowiana*	1·00	1·00
652	$1.20 *Rossioglossum grande*	1·00	1·00
653	$1.20 *Aspasia epidendroides*	1·00	1·00
654	$1.20 *Lycaste skinneri*	1·00	1·00
655	$1.20 *Cattleya percivaliana*	1·00	1·00
656	$1.20 Brown trembler ("Trembler")	1·00	1·00
657	$1.20 Red-billed tropicbird	1·00	1·00
658	$1.20 Red-footed booby	1·00	1·00
659	$1.20 Red-legged thrush	1·00	1·00
660	$1.20 Painted bunting	1·00	1·00
661	$1.20 Bananaquit	1·00	1·00
662	$1.60 Killer whale (horiz)	1·00	1·00
663	$1.60 Cuvier's beaked whale (horiz)	1·00	1·00
664	$1.60 Humpback whale (horiz)	1·00	1·00
665	$1.60 Sperm whale (horiz)	1·00	1·00
666	$1.60 Blue whale (horiz)	1·00	1·00
667	$1.60 Whale shark (horiz)	1·00	1·00
668	$1.60 *Pholiota spectabilis*	1·00	1·00
669	$1.60 *Flammula penetrans*	1·00	1·00
670	$1.60 *Ungulina marginata*	1·00	1·00
671	$1.60 *Collybia iocephala*	1·00	1·00
672	$1.60 *Amanita muscaria*	1·00	1·00
673	$1.60 *Coprinus comatus*	1·00	1·00
674	$1.60 Orange-barred sulphur	1·00	1·00
675	$1.60 Giant swallowtail	1·00	1·00
676	$1.60 Orange theope butterfly	1·00	1·00
677	$1.60 Blue night butterfly	1·00	1·00
678	$1.60 Grecian shoemaker	1·00	1·00
679	$1.60 Cramer's mesene	1·00	1·00

MS680 Five sheets, each 99×69 mm (No. **MS**680c) or 69×99 mm (others). (a) $5 *Psychilis atropurpurea* (orchid). (b) $5 Ruby-throated hummingbird. (c) $5 Sei Whale (*horiz*). (d) $5 *Lepiota procera* (fungus). (e) $5 Figure-of-eight butterfly. Set of 5 sheets 22·00 24·00

No. 672 is inscribed "Aminita" and No. 673 "Corinus", both in error.

109 Christmas Tree and Angel

2001. Christmas and Carnival. Multicoloured.

No.	Description	Unused	Used
681	10c. Type **109**	35	15
682	30c. Fireworks	50	15
683	80c. Christmas wreath	1·50	60
684	$2 Steel drums	2·75	3·50

110 Coronation Coach

2002. Golden Jubilee (2nd issue). Multicoloured.

No.	Description	Unused	Used
685	$2 Type **110**	1·60	1·75
686	$2 Prince Philip after polo	1·60	1·75
687	$2 Queen Elizabeth and the Queen Mother in evening dress	1·60	1·75
688	$2 Queen Elizabeth in evening dress	1·60	1·75

MS689 76×108 mm. $5 Queen Elizabeth presenting Prince Philip with polo trophy 4·75 5·50

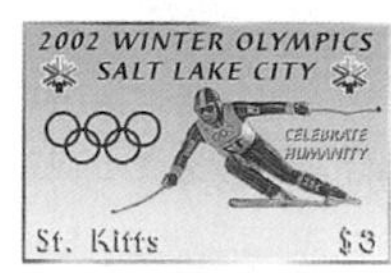

111 Downhill Ski-ing

2002. Winter Olympic Games, Salt Lake City. Multicoloured.

No.	Description	Unused	Used
690	$3 Type **111**	2·00	2·50
691	$3 Cross country ski-ing	2·00	2·50

MS692 82×102 mm. Nos. 690/1 4·00 5·00

112 Xiong Nu Tribesman and Dog

2002. Chinese New Year ("Year of the Horse"). "Wen-Gi's Return to Han" (Chang Yu). Multicoloured.

No.	Description	Unused	Used
693	$1.60 Type **112**	1·00	1·25
694	$1.60 Group of Xiong Nu tribesmen	1·00	1·25
695	$1.60 Wen-Gi (Chinese noblewoman)	1·00	1·25
696	$1.60 Standard bearer	1·00	1·25

113 World Cup Poster, Spain, 1982

2002. World Cup Football Championship, Japan and Korea (2002). Multicoloured.

No.	Description	Unused	Used
697	$1.65 Type **113**	1·00	1·10
698	$1.65 Just Fontaine, (France)	1·00	1·10
699	$1.65 American footballer	1·00	1·10
700	$1.65 Swedish footballer	1·00	1·10
701	$6 Daegu Stadium, Korea (56×42 mm)	3·50	4·00

MS702 51×3 mm. $6 Roger Milla (Cameroun), Italy, 1990 3·75 4·00

114 Policeman's Cap, Fireman's Helmet with U.S. and St. Kitts Flags

2002. "United We Stand". Support for Victims of 11 September 2001 Terrorist Attacks.

703	**114**	80c. multicoloured	1·00	1·00

115 Sakura-jima Volcano, Kyushu, Japan

2002. International Year of Mountains. Multicoloured.

704	$2 Type **115**	1·25	1·50
705	$2 Mount Assiniboine, Alberta, Canada	1·25	1·50
706	$2 Mount Asgard, Baffin Island, Canada	1·25	1·50
707	$2 Bugaboo Spire, British Columbia, Canada	1·25	1·50
MS708	75×57 mm. $6 Mount Owen, Wyoming, U.S.A.	3·75	5·00

116 Scout saluting

2002. 20th World Scout Jamboree, Thailand. Multicoloured.

709	$2 Type **116**	1·25	1·50
710	$2 Silver Award 2 badge	1·25	1·50
711	$2 Illinois Scout badge	1·25	1·50
712	$2 Scout with ceremonial sword	1·25	1·50
MS713	78×84 mm. $6 Environmental Merit badge (vert)	3·75	5·00

117 Amerigo Vespucci

2002. 500th Anniv of Amerigo Vespucci's Third Voyage. Multicoloured.

714	$3 Type **117**	2·00	2·50
715	$3 Map of the World by Waldseemüller, 1507	2·00	2·50
716	$3 Vespucci with globe	2·00	2·50
MS717	55×76 mm. $6 Vespucci as an old man (vert)	3·75	5·00

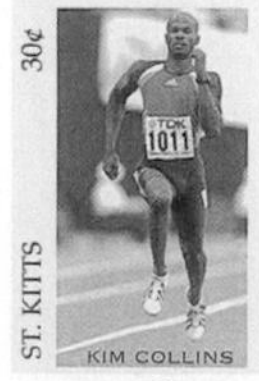

118 Kim Collins running

2002. Kim Collins (Commonwealth Games gold medallist) Commemoration. Multicoloured.

718	30c. Type **118**	50	20
719	90c. Collins with World Championship bronze medal	1·10	1·10

119 Charles Lindbergh

2002. Famous People of the 20th Century

(a) 75th Anniv of First Solo Transatlantic Flight. Sheet 130×145 mm.

MS720	$1.50 Type **119** (black, violet and red); $1.50 Lindbergh holding propellor of Ryan NYP Special *Spirit of St. Louis* (maroon, violet and red); $1.50 Lindbergh (brown, violet and red); $1.50 Lindbergh and *Spirit of St. Louis* (maroon and red); $1.50 Lindbergh wearing flying helmet (purple, violet and red); $1.50 Lindbergh (claret, violet and red)	8·00	10·00

(b) Life and Times of President John F. Kennedy. Two sheets, each 132×145 mm. Multicoloured.

MS721	$2 John Kennedy in Solomon Islands, 1942; $2 Torpedo boat commander, 1942; Naval ensign, 1941; Receiving medal for gallantry, 1944	4·00	5·00
MS722	$2 President Kennedy forming Peace Corps; $2 Promoting Space Programme; $2 With Civil Rights leaders; $2 Signing Nuclear Disarmament Treaty with Soviet Union	6·00	7·00

(c) Fifth Death Anniv of Diana, Princess of Wales. Two sheets, each 132×145 mm. Multicoloured.

MS723	$2 Princess Diana wearing jacket with mauve edged collar; $2 Wearing dress with frilled neckline; $2 Wearing pink dress; $2 Wearing mauve dress	5·00	6·00
MS724	$2 Wearing protective vest; $2 Wearing turquoise jacket; $2 Wearing yellow blouse; $2 Wearing red dress	5·00	6·00

(d) Queen Elizabeth the Queen Mother Commemoration. Sheet 200×143 mm, containing two of each design. Multicoloured.

MS725	$2×2 Duchess of York; $2×2 Queen Mother	5·50	6·50

120 Sour Sop

2002. Christmas. Island Fruit. Multicoloured.

726	10c. Type **120**	30	15
727	80c. Passion fruit	1·00	35
728	$1 Sugar apple	1·25	80
729	$2 Custard apple	2·00	3·00

121 Ram

2003. Chinese New Year ("Year of the Ram"). Multicoloured.

MS730	110×122 mm. $1×2 Type **121**; $1×2 Brown and white ram with spiral horns; $1×2 Brown ram with long horns	4·25	5·50

122 Pelican and Emblem

2003. 30th Anniv of CARICOM.

731	**122**	30c. multicoloured	1·00	65

123 Queen Victoria Bear

2003. Centenary of the Teddy Bear. Multicoloured.

MS732	135×156 mm. $2 Type **123**; $2 Teddy Roosevelt bear; $2 George Washington bear; $2 General Patton bear	5·00	6·00
MS733	90×113 mm. $5 Buffalo Bill bear	3·50	4·25

124 Queen Elizabeth II

2003. 50th Anniv of Coronation. Multicoloured.

MS734	156×94 mm. $3 Type **124**; $3 Queen wearing tiara and pink sash; $3 Wearing tiara and blue sash	6·50	7·50
MS735	106×76 mm. $6 Wearing tiara and blue robes	3·75	4·25

125 Prince William as Toddler

2003. 21st Birthday of Prince William. Multicoloured.

MS736	156×86 mm. $3 Type **125**; $3 As schoolboy; $3 As adult	6·50	7·50
MS737	106×76 mm. $5 As young boy, waving from carriage	3·50	4·00

126 Voisin LAS

2003. Centenary of Powered Flight. Multicoloured.

MS738	185×106 mm. $2 Type **126**; $2 Gotha G.V.; $2 Polikarpov I-16; $2 Bell YFM-1	5·50	7·00
MS739	106×76 mm. $5 Bristol Type 142 Blenheim Mk I	3·50	4·00

127 Miguel Indurain (1991–95)

2003. Centenary of Tour de France. Designs showing past winners. Multicoloured.

MS740	166×106 mm. $2 Type **127**; $2 Miguel Indurain (1995); $2 Bjarne Riis (1996); $2 Jan Ullrich (1997)	5·50	6·50
MS741	105×75 mm. $5 Miguel Indurain (1991–5)	3·50	4·00

128 "Child with Wooden Horse (Claude)"

2003. 30th Death Anniv of Pablo Picasso (artist). Multicoloured.

MS742	178×103 mm. $1.60 Type **128**; $1.60 "Child with a Ball (Claude)"; $1.60 "The Butterfly Catcher"; $1.60 "Boy with a Lobster"; $1.60 "Baby wearing Polka-Dot Dress"; $1.60 "El Bobo" (after Murillo)	6·50	7·50
MS743	68×86 mm. $5 Woman with baby (63×80 mm). Imperf	3·50	4·00

129 Scout and Seaman with Globe (1937)

2003. 25th Death Anniv of Norman Rockwell (artist). T **129** and similar vert designs showing illustrations from scout calendars. Multicoloured.

MS744	141×180 mm. $2 Type **129**; $2 Scouts hiking (1937); $2 Boy and dog at window (1968); $2 Scout and statue (1932)	5·50	6·50
MS745	60×83 mm. $5 Scout with cub scout (1950)	3·50	4·00

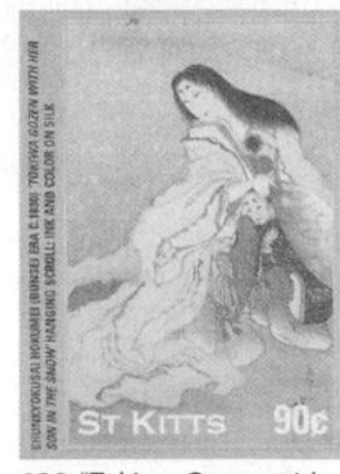

130 "Tokiwa Gozen with her Son in the Snow" (Shunkyokusai Hokumei)

2003. Japanese Art. Multicoloured.

746	90c. Type **130**	70	55
747	$1 "Courtesan and Asahina" (attrib. Eshosai Choki)	75	60
748	$1.50 "Parody of Sugawara no Michizane seated on an Ox" (Utagawa Toyokuni)	1·10	1·40
749	$3 "Visiting a Flower Garden" (detail) (Utagawa Kunisada)	2·00	3·00
MS750	147×147 mm. $2 "Akugenta Yoshihira" holding crossbow; $2 Holding painting; $2 As woman, with hand outstretched; $2 Holding sword	5·50	6·50
MS751	86×115 mm. $6 "The Courtesan Katachino under a Cherry Tree" (Utagawa Toyoharu)	3·75	4·25

No. **MS**750 shows a set of four prints of "Akugenta Yoshihira" by Utagawa Kunisada.

131 "A Family Group" (detail)

2003. Rembrandt (artist) Commemoration. Multicoloured.

752	50c. Type **131**	50	40
753	$1 "Portrait of Cornelis Claesz Anslo and Aeltje Gerritsdr Schouten" (horiz)	75	65
754	$1.60 "Portrait of a Young Woman"	1·25	1·50
755	$3 "Man in Military Costume"	2·00	3·00
MS756	181×172 mm. $2 "An Old Woman Reading"; $2 "Hendrickje Stoffels"; $2 "Rembrandt's Mother"; $2 "Saskia"	5·50	6·50
MS757	152×117 mm. $5 "Judas returning the Thirty Pieces of Silver"	3·50	4·00

132 "White Gibbon" (Giuseppe Castiglione)

2004. Chinese New Year ("Year of the Monkey").

MS758	156×141 mm. **132** $1.60×4 multicoloured	4·25	4·75
MS759	158×92 mm. **132** $3 multicoloured (30×37 mm)	2·50	2·75

133 Jiri Guth Jarkovsky

2004. Olympic Games, Athens. Multicoloured.

760	50c. Type **133**	40	35
761	90c. Olympic poster, Munich (1972)	65	55
762	$1 Medal and Eiffel Tower, Paris (1900)	75	65
763	$3 Wrestling (Greek bronze statue) (horiz)	2·00	3·00

134 12th SP Panzer Division and Map

2004. 60th Anniv of D-Day Landings.

MS764	Two sheets. (a) 178×106 mm. $2 ×4 multicoloured; purple; maroon; purple and deep purple. (b) 100×68 mm. $5 multicoloured Set of 2 sheets	12·00	12·00

DESIGNS: **MS**764 (a) $2 ×4 Type **134**; German heavy tank; Soldier aiming weapon; Soldiers and tank. (b) $5 Allied cemetery, Normandy.

135 Pope John Paul II

2004. 25th Anniv of the Pontificate of Pope John Paul II. Multicoloured.

MS765	147×105 mm. $2 ×4 Type **135**; Walking in gardens; Standing with hands crossed; Holding Pastoral Staff	8·50	9·00

136 Berti Vogts

2004. European Football Championship 2004, Portugal. Commemoration of Match between Germany and Czech Republic (1996). Multicoloured.

MS766	Two sheets (a) 147×86 mm. $2 ×4 Type **136**; Patrik Berger; Oliver Bierhoff; Empire Stadium. (b) 97×86 mm. $5 German team (1996) (51×48 mm) Set of 2 sheets	8·50	11·00

137 Deng Xiaoping

2004. Birth Centenary of Deng Xiaoping (Chinese leader, 1978–89).

MS767	**137** $5 multicoloured	3·50	4·00

138 American Standard 4-4-0

2004. Bicentenary of Steam Trains. Multicoloured.

768	$2 Type **138**	1·60	1·60
769	$2 New South Wales Government Class "79" 4-4-0	1·60	1·60
770	$2 Johnson Midland Single 4-2-2	1·60	1·60
771	$2 Union Pacific FEF-3 Class 4-8-4	1·60	1·60
772	$2 Northumbrian 0-2-2	1·60	1·60
773	$2 Prince Class 2-2-2	1·60	1·60
774	$2 Adler 2-2-2	1·60	1·60
775	$2 London and North Western Railway Webb Compound 2-4-0	1·60	1·60
776	$2 Italian State Railways Class 685 2-6-2	1·60	1·60
777	$2 Swiss Federal Railways 4-6-0	1·60	1·60
778	$2 British Engineering Standards Association Class 4-6-0	1·60	1·60
779	$2 Great Western City Class 4-4-0	1·60	1·60
MS780	Three sheets. (a) 98×68 mm. $5 CN Class U-2 4-8-4. (b) 98×68 mm. $5 Crampton 4-2-0. (c) 68×98 mm. $5 Baldwin 2-8-2	12·00	14·00

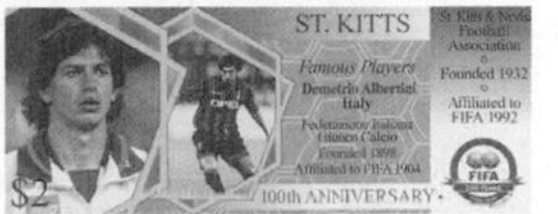

139 Demetrio Albertini

2004. Centenary of FIFA (Federation Internationale de Football Association). Multicoloured.

MS781	193×97 mm. $2×4, Type **139**; Romario; Gerd Muller; Danny Blanchflower	5·00	6·00
MS782	107×87 mm. $5 Gianfranco Zola	3·25	3·75

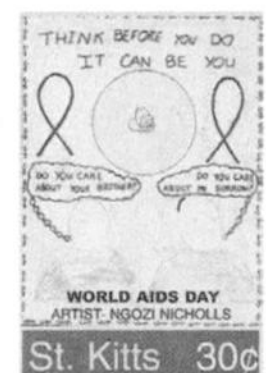

140 Couple with Thought Bubbles and (Ngozi Nicholls) AIDS Ribbons

2004. World AIDS Day. Multicoloured.

783	30c. Type **140**	50	20
784	80c. Man in shackles, fire, top of globe and characters dancing (Travis Liburd)	1·00	60
785	90c. Flag inscribed with "AIDS or LIFE" (Darren Kelly) (horiz)	1·10	90
786	$1 Red "AIDS", syringe and smiley condom (Shane Berry)	1·40	1·60

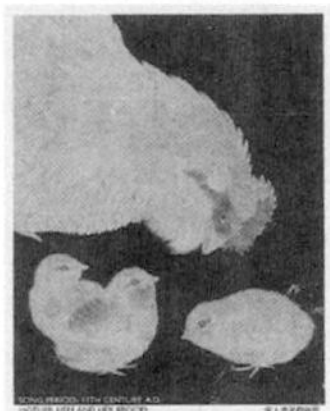

141 Hen and Three Chicks

2005. Chinese New Year ("Year of the Rooster"). Multicoloured.

787	$1.60 Type **141**	1·25	1·60
MS788	70×100 mm. $5 As No. 787 but design enlarged	3·25	3·75

142 *Papilio demoleus*

2005. Butterflies. Multicoloured.

MS789	127×151 mm. $2×4, Type **142**; *Ephemeroptera; Hamadryas februa; Aphylla caraiba*	6·00	7·00
MS790	100×70 mm. $5 *Lycaenidae cupido minimus*	4·00	4·50

143 Bahama ("White-cheeked") Pintail

2005. Ducks. Multicoloured.

791	25c. Type **143**	75	60
792	$1 Fulvous whistling duck	1·25	85
793	$2 White-faced whistling duck	2·00	2·25
794	$3 Red-billed ("Black-bellied") whistling duck	2·75	3·50

144 Ocelot

2005. Wildcats. Multicoloured.

MS795	128×152 mm. $2×4, Type **144**; Bengal leopard; Tiger; Leopard	6·00	7·00
MS796	101×70 mm. $5 Sumatran tiger	5·50	6·00

145 Australian King Parrot

2005. Parrots. Multicoloured.

MS797	128×152 mm. $2×4, Type **145**; Rose-breasted cockatoo; Pale-headed rosella; Eastern rosella	6·50	7·00
MS798	101×70 mm. $5 Two rainbow lorikeets (horiz)	4·75	5·50

146 Triceratops

2005. Prehistoric Animals. Multicoloured.

MS799	Three sheets, each 150×84 mm. (a) $3×3, Type **146**; Deinonychus; Apatosaurus. (b) $3×3, Sabre-toothed tiger; Edmontosaurus; Tyrannosaurus rex. (c) $3×3, Dimetroden; Homalocephale; Stegosaurus	19·00	23·00
MS800	Three sheets, each 100×70 mm. (a) $5 Brontosaurus (vert). (b) $5 Andrewsarchus. (c) $5 Woolly mammoth (vert)	11·00	12·00

147 *Montagne*

2005. Bicentenary of the Battle of Trafalgar. Multicoloured.

801	50c. Type **147**	1·00	55
802	90c. *San Jose*	1·25	75
803	$2 *Imperieuse*	2·25	2·50
804	$3 *San Nicolas*	2·75	3·50
MS805	69×99 mm. $5 British Navy gun crew aboard HMS *Victory*	5·50	6·50

148 Beijing Rotary

2005. Centenary of Rotary International (Humanitarian organisation). Multicoloured.

806	$3 Type **148**	2·25	2·75
807	$3 Man lying against pillow	2·25	2·75
808	$3 Man in hospital	2·25	2·75

149 US Navy Hudson PBO-1 Patrol Bombers

2005. 60th Anniv of Victory in Europe. Multicoloured.

809	$2 Type **149**	2·25	2·25
810	$2 Soldiers	2·25	2·25
811	$2 General Dwight D. Eisenhower	2·25	2·25
812	$2 German Prisoners of War	2·25	2·25
813	$2 Newspaper headline	2·25	2·25

150 Jules Verne

2005. Death Centenary of Jules Verne (writer).

814	**150**	$2 brown and bistre	2·00	2·00
815	-	$2 blue	2·00	2·00
816	-	$2 multicoloured	2·00	2·00
817	-	$2 multicoloured	2·00	2·00
MS818		99×70 mm. $5 multicoloured	5·50	6·00

DESIGNS: No. 814, Type **150**; 815, Sea monster attack; 816, Rouquayrol (breathing apparatus); 817, Modern aqualung; **MS**818, Atomic submarine.

151 "Hans Christian Anderson Fairy Tales"

2005. Birth Bicentenary of Hans Christian Anderson (artist and children's writer). Multicoloured.

MS819	115×172 mm. $3×3, Type **151**, *The Emperor's New Clothes; The Nutcracker*	6·00	7·50
MS820	70×101 mm. $5 Characters and Banner (*The Emperor's New Clothes*)	3·50	5·00

152 USS *Arizona*

2005. 60th Anniv of Victory in Japan. Multicoloured.

821	$2 Type **152**	2·25	2·25
822	$2 Captain Franklin van Valkenburgh	2·25	2·25
823	$2 Hiroshima	2·25	2·25
824	$2 Marker of first atomic bomb loading pit on Tinian Island	2·25	2·25
825	$2 Memorial cenotaph at Hiroshima Peace Park	2·25	2·25

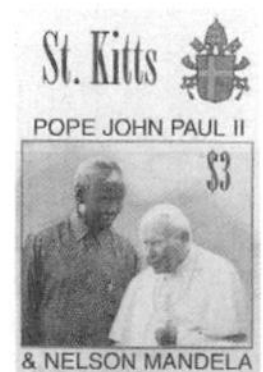

153 Pope John Paul II and Nelson Mandela

2005. Pope John Paul II Commemoration.

826	**153** $3 multicoloured	3·50	3·75

154 Junk

2005. TAIPEI 2005 International Stamp Exhibition. Multicoloured.

827	$2 Type **154**	1·50	2·00
828	$2 Junk with yellow sails	1·50	2·00
829	$2 Junk with dark orange sails	1·50	2·00
830	$2 Junk with white sails	1·50	2·00

155 "Virgin and Child" (detail) (Gerard David)

2005. Christmas. Multicoloured.

831	30c. Type **155**	50	15
832	50c. "Virgin and Child" (detail) (different) (Gerard David)	85	35
833	90c. "Virgin and Child" (detail) (different) (Gerard David)	1·40	80
834	$2 "Virgin and Child" (detail) (Bartolomeo Suardi Bramentine)	3·25	4·00
MS835	67×97 mm. $5 "The Nativity" (Martin Schongauer)	7·00	7·50

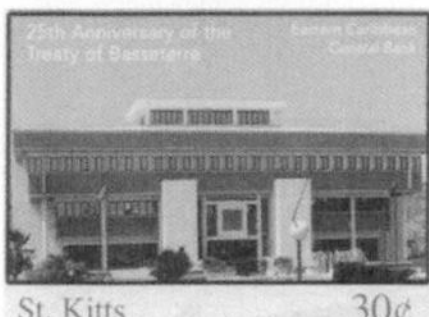

156 Eastern Caribbean Central Bank, Basseterre, St. Kitts

2006. 25th Anniv of the Treaty of Basseterre (established Organisation of Eastern Caribbean States). Multicoloured.

836	30c. Type **156**	30	15
837	90c. Flags of member countries	1·40	1·00
MS838	100×75 mm. $2.50 Inset portraits of OECS heads of government (vert)	1·75	2·00

157 "Bathsheba with King David's Letter" (detail)

2006. 400th Birth Anniv of Rembrandt Harmenszoon van Rijn (artist). Multicoloured.

839	50c. Type **157**	40	25
840	80c. "Isaac and Rebecca (The Jewish Bride)" (detail of bride)	60	40
841	90c. "Isaac and Rebecca (The Jewish Bride)" (detail of groom)	65	45
842	$1 "Samson threatening his Father-in-Law" (detail of father-in-law)	70	55
843	$1.60 "Samson threatening his Father-in-Law" (detail of Samson)	1·25	1·25
844	$2 "Equestrian Portrait" (detail)	1·50	1·75
MS845	100×70 mm. $6 "Landscape with a Stone Bridge" (detail). Imperf	4·00	4·25

158 "Mary in Adoration before the Sleeping Infant" (detail)

2006. Christmas. Showing paintings by Peter Paul Rubens. Multicoloured.

846	25c. Type **158**	35	15
847	60c. "The Holy Family under the Apple Tree" (detail, Mary and Jesus)	70	30
848	$1 "The Holy Family under the Apple Tree" (detail, Infant John the Baptist)	85	45
849	$1.20 "St. Francis of Assisi Receives the Infant Jesus from Mary" (detail, Mary and Jesus)	90	60
850	$2 Type **158**	1·40	1·75
851	$2 As No. 847	1·40	1·75
852	$2 As No. 848	1·40	1·75
853	$2 As No. 849	1·40	1·75

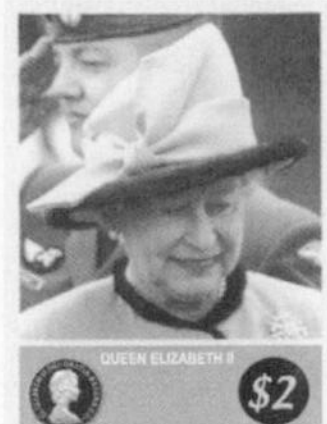

159 Queen Elizabeth II

2007. 80th Birthday of Queen Elizabeth II. Multicoloured.

854	$2 Type **159**	1·40	2·00
855	$2 Wearing tiara and Order of the Garter	1·40	2·00
856	$2 At Trooping the Colour	1·40	2·00
857	$2 On throne, wearing crown	1·40	2·00
MS858	120×120 mm. $5 Seated at desk	4·00	4·25

160 Christopher Columbus

2007. 500th Death Anniv (2006) of Christopher Columbus. Sheet 100×70 mm.

MS859	**160** $6 multicoloured	4·00	4·50

161 Dove, Emblem and Ribbon of Flags

2007. Centenary of World Scouting. Multicoloured.

860	$3 Type **161**	2·25	2·50
MS861	110×80 mm. $5 Dove, emblem and ribbon of flags (horiz)	3·25	3·50

162 Pre-Launch Tests at the Kourou Launch Site

2007. Space Anniversaries. Multicoloured

(a) 20th Anniv of Giotto Comet Probe

862	$1.60 Type **162**	1·40	1·40
863	$1.60 Halley's Comet (black background)	1·40	1·40
864	$1.60 Halley's Comet (seen from Earth's surface)	1·40	1·40
865	$1.60 *Giotto* Comet Probe	1·40	1·40
866	$1.60 *Giotto* Spacecraft mounted on Rocket Ariane	1·40	1·40
867	$1.60 Halley's Comet (blue background)	1·40	1·40

(b) 40th Anniv of Luna 9 Moon Landing.

868	$2 Molniya rocket on launch vehicle (vert)	1·50	1·50
869	$2 *Luna 9* flight apparatus (vert)	1·50	1·50
870	$2 *Luna 9* soft lander (vert)	1·50	1·50
871	$2 Image of "Ocean of Storms" on Moon's surface (vert)	1·50	1·50
MS872	100×70 mm. $5 Space Station MIR, 1986–2001	3·75	4·25

163 John Kennedy shaking hands with Peace Corps Volunteers

2007. 90th Birth Anniv of John F. Kennedy (American President 1960–3). Multicoloured.

873	$2 Type **163**	2·00	2·00
874	$2 Volunteer Ida Shoatz running school lunch programme in the Peruvian Andes	2·00	2·00
875	$2 R. Sargent Shriver, Director, Peace Corps	2·00	2·00
876	$2 John Kennedy greeting Peace Corps volunteers	2·00	2·00
877	$2 John Kennedy and map showing Guatemala, El Salvador and Honduras	2·00	2·00
878	$2 John Kennedy and South American mother and daughter	2·00	2·00
879	$2 John Kennedy and map showing Colombia	2·00	2·00
880	$2 Map showing Venezuala, Guyana, Suriname and French Guiana	2·00	2·00

Nos. 873/6 (showing Peace Corps volunteers) and 877/80 (showing "Alliance for Progress" for economic co-operation between North and South America).

164 Betty Boop

2007. Betty Boop. Multicoloured, background colours given.

881	$1.60 Type **164**	90	1·00
882	$1.60 With microphone (emerald)	90	1·00
883	$1.60 With hat and cane (white)	90	1·00
884	$1.60 With arms raised (violet)	90	1·00
885	$1.60 With arms outstretched to side (blue)	90	1·00
886	$1.60 Seated, with right leg raised (yellow)	90	1·00
MS887	100×70 mm. $3 Wearing red dress with white flower design (green heart background); $3 With right hand held out (inverted purple heart background)	3·25	3·50

165 Marilyn Monroe

2007. 80th Birth Anniv (2006) of Marilyn Monroe (actress). Multicoloured.

888	$2 Type **165**	1·60	1·60
889	$2 Wearing spectacles, hair wrapped in towel	1·60	1·60
890	$2 Facing forwards, bare shoulders	1·60	1·60
891	$2 Facing left, hand on chin	1·60	1·60

166 Elvis Presley

2007. 30th Death Anniv of Elvis Presley (1st issue). Multicoloured.

892	$2 Type **166** (inscr in blue)	1·60	1·60
893	$2 As Type **166** (inscr in magenta)	1·60	1·60
894	$2 As Type **166** (inscr in black)	1·60	1·60
895	$2 As Type **166** (inscr in lavender)	1·60	1·60
896	$2 Elvis Presley playing guitar and signature	1·60	1·60

See also Nos. 920/5.

167 Two Tiger Sharks

2007. Endangered Species. Tiger Shark (Galeocerdo cuvier). Multicoloured.

897	$1.20 Type **167**	1·00	1·00
898	$1.20 Two sharks, foreground shark with mouth open	1·00	1·00
899	$1.20 Tiger shark	1·00	1·00
900	$1.20 Three tiger sharks, showing spotted markings	1·00	1·00
MS901	115×168 mm. Nos. 897/900	3·50	3·75

168 *Rhynchostele cervantesii*

2007. Orchids. T **168** and similar vert designs. Multicoloured.

MS902	131×109 mm. $2×4 Type **168**; *Oerstedella wallisii*; *Disa uniflora*; *Pleioneformosana*	7·50	7·50
MS903	70×100 mm. $6 *Dendrobium bracteosum*	5·50	5·50

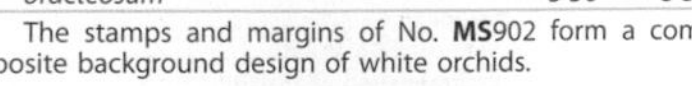
The stamps and margins of No. **MS**902 form a composite background design of white orchids.

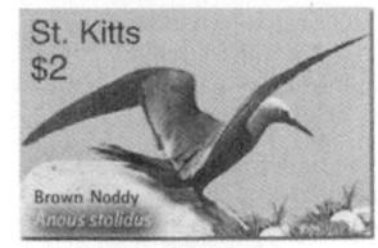

169 Brown Noddy

2007. Seabirds of the World. Multicoloured.

904	$2 Type **169**	2·25	2·25
905	$2 Royal albatross	2·25	2·25
906	$2 Masked booby	2·25	2·25
907	$2 Great cormorant	2·25	2·25
MS908	70×100 mm. $6 Rock cormorant (vert)	6·50	6·50

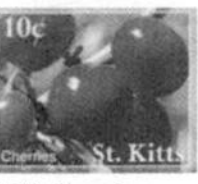

170 Cherries

2007. Fruit. Multicoloured.

909	10c. Type **170**	10	15
910	15c. Coconut	15	15
911	30c. Watermelon	25	20
912	40c. Pineapple	35	25
913	50c. Guava	40	30
914	60c. Sugar apple	50	35
915	80c. Passion fruit	65	45
916	90c. Star apple	75	50
917	$1 Tangerines	90	60
918	$5 Noni fruit	4·50	5·00
919	$10 Papaya	8·00	10·00

171 Elvis Presley

2007. 30th Death Anniv of Elvis Presley (2nd issue). Multicoloured.

920	$1.60 Type **171**	1·25	1·25
921	$1.60 Wearing white jacket with black eagle design	1·25	1·25
922	$1.60 Wearing black shirt	1·25	1·25
923	$1.60 Wearing blue shirt	1·25	1·25
924	$1.60 Wearing white shirt and red waistcoat	1·25	1·25
925	$1.60 Wearing white leather jacket	1·25	1·25

Nos. 920/5 were printed together, *se-tenant*, in sheetlets of six stamps with enlarged illustrated right margins.

172 Pope Benedict XVI

2007. 80th Birthday of Pope Benedict XVI.

926	**172** $1.10 multicoloured	1·75	1·75

173 Queen Elizabeth II

2007. Diamond Wedding of Queen Elizabeth II and Prince Philip. Multicoloured.

927	$1.60 Type **173**	1·25	1·25
928	$1.60 Princess Elizabeth and Prince Philip on wedding day, 1949	1·25	1·25
MS929	100×70 mm. $6 Queen Elizabeth and Prince Philip in recent years	6·50	7·00

174 Concorde in Flight

2007. Concorde. Multicoloured.

930	$1.60 Type **174**	1·25	1·25
931	$1.60 Concorde in flight (side view)	1·25	1·25
932	$1.60 Concorde over Singapore (panel yellow-olive at left, bright yellow-green at right)	1·25	1·25
933	$1.60 Concorde at Melbourne Airport, Australia ('Austria' in panel)	1·25	1·25
934	$1.60 As No. 932	1·25	1·25
935	$1.60 As No. 933 ('Spain' at left of panel)	1·25	1·25
936	$1.60 As No. 932 (bright yellow-green (Italy) in centre of panel)	1·25	1·25
937	$1.60 As No. 933 (bright yellow-green at left and yellow-olive (Black Sea) at right of panel)	1·25	1·25

175 Diana, Princess of Wales

2007. Tenth Death Anniv of Diana, Princess of Wales. Multicoloured.

938	$2 Type **175**	1·75	2·00
939	$2 Diana, Princess of Wales (chestnut background)	1·75	2·00
940	$2 Wearing pearl necklace	1·75	2·00
940a	$2 Wearing white and mauve brimmed hat	1·75	2·00
MS941	70×100 mm. $6 As No. 940	5·00	5·50

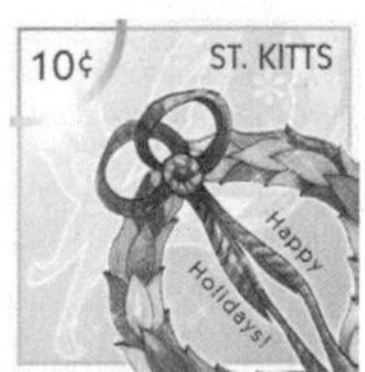

176 Door Wreath with Mauve Ribbons

2007. Christmas. Designs showing Christmas door wreaths. Multicoloured.

942	10c. Type **176**	30	20
943	30c. Wreath with cherries and red bow	55	25
944	60c. Wreath with holly and red ribbon	90	70
945	$1 Holly leaves and berries and yellow ribbon	1·25	1·50

177 Paris World's Fair, 1900

2008. Olympic Games, Beijing. Multicoloured.

946	$1.40 Type **177**	1·25	1·25
947	$1.40 Poster for Olympic Games, Paris, 1900	1·25	1·25
948	$1.40 Charlotte Cooper (Britain), tennis gold medallist, 1900	1·25	1·25
949	$1.40 Alvin Kraenzlein (USA), quadruple athletics gold medallist, 1900	1·25	1·25

178 Bethel Chapel

2008. 230th Anniv of the Moravian Church in St. Kitts. Multicoloured.

950	10c. Type **178**	30	20
951	$3 Zion Chapel	2·50	2·50
952	$10 Bethesda Chapel (vert)	6·00	7·50

179 University of the West Indies Centre, St. Kitts

2008. 60th Anniv of the University of the West Indies.

953	**179**	30c. multicoloured	40	25
954	-	90c. scarlet, yellow and black	1·25	90
955	-	$5 scarlet, yellow and black	4·00	5·00

DESIGNS—VERT: 90c. Anniversary emblem. HORIZ—$5 Anniversary emblem.

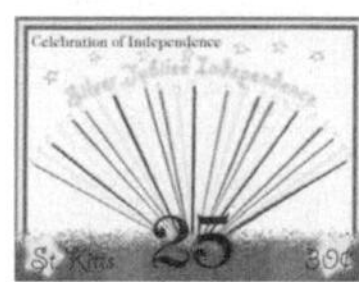

180 Emblem

2008. 25th Anniv of Independence of St. Kitts-Nevis. Multicoloured.

956	30c. Type **180** (Davern Johnson)	40	25
957	$1 Produce of St. Kitts (Yvado Simmonds)	1·25	95
958	$5 Sailing ship with national flag as sail ('Sailing Towards Our Future') (Richard Browne) (vert)	4·50	4·50
958a	$25 '25' and lifebelt ('Riding the Waves') (Dennis Richards) (vert)	12·00	14·00
958b	$30 Angel and St. Lucia Land-scape ('Past and Present') (Melvin Maynard)	13·00	15·00
958c	$50 Mrs. Ada May Edwards (vert)	21·00	25·00

Nos. 956/8*b* show winning designs from stamp design competition.

181 Elvis Presley

2008. 40th Anniv of Elvis Presley's '68 Special' (TV programme). Multicoloured.

959	$1.60 Type **181**	1·50	1·50
960	$1.60 In profile, wearing black leather jacket	1·50	1·50
961	$1.60 Wearing red shirt and black waistcoat	1·50	1·50
962	$1.60 Wearing blue shirt	1·50	1·50
963	$1.60 Wearing beige shirt	1·50	1·50
964	$1.60 Wearing white shirt and red tie	1·50	1·50

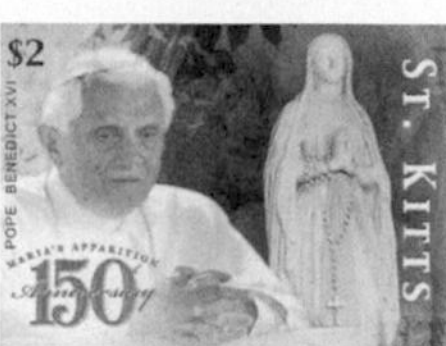

182 Pope Benedict XVI and Statue of Virgin Mary

2008. 150th Anniv of the Apparition of the Virgin Mary to St. Bernadette and Visit of Pope Benedict XVI to Lourdes. Sheet 127×178 mm containing T **182** and similar horiz designs.

MS965	$2×4 multicoloured	9·00	9·00

The four stamps within **MS**965 are as Type **182** but all have slightly different backgrounds of the church building showing in the backgrounds of the stamps.

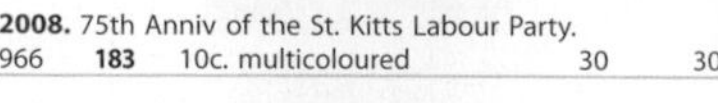

183 R. L. Bradshaw

2008. 75th Anniv of the St. Kitts Labour Party.

966	**183**	10c. multicoloured	30	30

184 Palm Trees with Christmas Baubles

2008. Christmas. Multicoloured.

967	10c. Type **184**	30	20
968	50c. Palm trees and beach house on stilts	55	40
969	60c. Palm trees and star	65	55
970	$1 Baubles on Christmas tree	1·25	1·50

185 Pres. Barack Obama

2009. Inauguration of President Barack Obama. Multicoloured.

MS971	133×100 mm. $3 Type **185**×4	14·00	15·00
MS972	80×110 mm. $10 Pres. Obama (37×37 mm, circular)	10·00	11·00

186 Princess Diana

2009. Princess Diana Commemoration. Sheet 150×100 mm containing T **186** and similar vert designs. Multicoloured. Litho.

MS973	Type **186**; Wearing mauve dress; Wearing white strapless dress; Wearing blue off the shoulder dress with ruffle	8·00	9·00

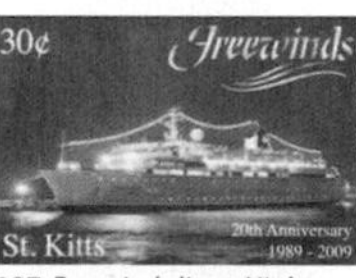

187 *Freewinds* lit at Night

2009. 20th Anniv of Freewinds (cruise ship) calling at St. Kitts. Multicoloured.

MS974	112×135 mm. 30c. Type **187**; 90c. *Freewinds* and sailing ship at St. Kitts; $3 Bow of *Freewinds* with crew on decks (42×56 mm);	4·00	4·25
MS975	144×100 mm. $2 *Freewinds* with crew on decks (79×59 mm)	2·00	2·25

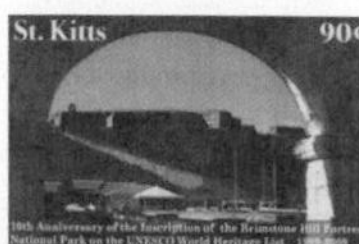

188 Brimstone Hill Fortress

2009. Tenth Anniv of Inscription of Brimstone Hill Fortress, St. Kitts on UNESCO World Heritage List. Litho.

976	**188**	90c. multicoloured	1·25	1·25

189 Michael Jackson

2009. Michael Jackson Commemoration. Multicoloured.

MS977	127×178 mm. $2.50×4 Type **189** (green inscriptions); Wearing blue shirt with white jacket, tie and hat (green inscriptions); As Type **189** (blue inscriptions); Wearing blue shirt with white jacket, tie and hat (blue inscriptions)	6·50	7·00
MS978	178×127 mm. $2.50×4 Wearing red jacket×2; With python×2	6·50	7·00

190 John Kennedy jr. as Child

2009. Tenth Death Anniv of John F. Kennedy Jr. Sheet 130×100 mm containing T **190** and similar vert designs. Multicoloured.

MS979	Type **190**; With his parents; With his mother on horseback; As adult	7·00	7·50

191 Saturn 5 Rocket

2009. 40th Anniv of the First Manned Moon Landing. International Year of Astronomy. Multicoloured.

MS980	150×100 mm. $2.50×4 Type **191**; Astronaut's bootprint on Moon; Bald Eagle, Pres. John F. Kennedy and Earth seen from Moon; Apollo 11 Command Module above Moon	8·00	8·00
MS981	100×70 mm. $6 Command Module in space	5·50	5·50

192 St. Kitts & Nevis Flag and 'MERRY CHRISTMAS'

2009. Christmas. Multicoloured.

982	10c. Type **192**	25	15
983	30c. Candy canes	50	25
984	$1.20 Outline map of St. Kitts-Nevis with Christmas trees	1·40	1·00
985	$3 St. Kitts & Nevis flag as cake decorated with candles and Christmas tree	3·25	3·75

193 Elvis Presley

2010. 75th Birth Anniv of Elvis Presley (1st issue). Sheet 120×194 mm containing T **193** and similar vert designs. Multicoloured.

MS986	Type 193; Wearing jacket and tie; Wearing white jacket; Looking to left; Wearing jacket and shirt; Wear-ing dark zipped jacket	8·50	8·50

194 Scarlet Peacock (*Anartia amathea*)

2010. Butterflies of the Caribbean. Multicoloured.

987	30c. Type **194**	50	25
988	90c. Gulf fritillary (*Agraulis vanillae*)	1·40	95
989	$3 White peacock (*Anartia jatrophae*)	3·00	3·00
990	$5 Painted lady (*Vanessa virginiensis*)	5·00	5·50
MS991	$2.50×4 Ruddy daggerwing (*Marpesia petreus*); Danaid eggfly (*Hypolimnas misippus*); Mangrove buckeye (*Junonia evarete*); Black swallowtail (*Papilio polyxenes*)	6·50	7·00
MS992	$3 Owl butterfly (*Caligo memnon*); $3 Giant swallowtail (*Papilio cresphontes*)	6·50	7·00

The stamps and margins of Nos. **MS**991/2 form composite designs.

195 Solitary Sandpiper (*Tringa solitaria*)

2010. Birds of the Caribbean. Multicoloured.

993	30c. Type **195**	60	30
994	90c. Piping plover (*Charadrius melodus*)	1·50	1·00
995	$3 Prairie warbler (*Dendroica discolor*)	3·50	3·50
996	$5 Western sandpiper (*Calidris* or *Erolia mauri*)	5·50	6·00
MS997	150×100 mm. $2.50×4 Masked booby (*Sula dactylatra*); Sooty tern (*Onychoprion fuscatus*); Brown booby (*Sula leucogaster*); Black noddy (*Anous minutus*)	7·00	7·50
MS998	110×80 mm. $3 Long-billed dowitcher (*Limnodromus scolopaceus*); $3 Willet (*Tringa semipalmata*)	6·50	7·00

196 Statue of Abraham Lincoln

2010. Birth Bicentenary of Abraham Lincoln (US President 1861–5)

MS999	$2.50×4 Type **196**	7·00	8·00

197 Red Lionfish (Pterois volitans)

2010. Reef Fish of the Caribbean. Multicoloured.

1000	30c. Type **197**	45	20
1001	90c. Stoplight parrotfish (*Sparisoma viride*)	1·25	90
1002	$3 Black Jack (*Caranx lugubris*)	3·50	3·50
1003	$5 Bermuda blue angelfish (*Holacanthus bermudensis*)	5·00	5·50
MS1004	100×140 mm. $2.50×4 Banggai cardinalfish (*Pterapognon kauderni*); Barrier reef anemonefish (*Amphipron akindynos*); Crevelle Jack (*Caranx hippos*); Lookdown fish (*Selene vomer*)	7·00	8·00
MS1005	100×70 mm. $3 Red Sea clownfish (*Amphiprion bicinctus*); $3 Saddleback clownfish (*Amphiprion polymnus*)	6·50	6·50

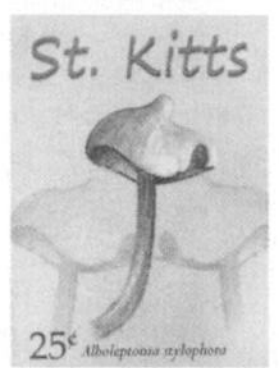

198 *Alboleptonia stylophora*

2010. Fungi of the Caribbean. Multicoloured.

1006	25c. Type **198**	45	30
1007	80c. *Cantharellus cibarius*	1·25	75
1008	$1 *Armillaria puiggarii*	1·40	1·00
1009	$5 *Battarrea phalliodes*	5·00	5·50
MS1010	106×140 mm. $2×6 *Cantharellus cinnabarinus; Collybia aurata; Collybia biformis; Amanita ocreata; Calocybe cyanea; Chroogomphus rutilus* (all horiz)	9·00	9·50

No. **MS**1010 was inscr 'ANTVERPIA 2010 09–12/04/2010 NATIONAL & EUROPEAN CHAMPIONSHIP OF PHILATELY' on the top right margin.

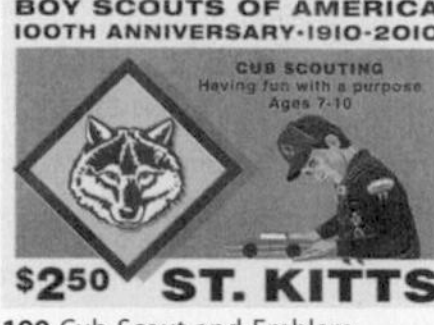

199 Cub Scout and Emblem

2010. Centenary of Boy Scouts of America. Multicoloured.

MS1011	$2.50×4 Type **199**; Scout cooking over campfire and emblem; Varsity scouts playing basketball and emblem; Venture scout kayaking and emblem	7·00	8·00
MS1012	$2.50×4 Scouts of 1910 and 2010 and emblem; Boy using pick-axe and Order of the Arrow emblem; Man painting with roller and Alpha Phi Omega emblem; Eagle scout handing out voting forms and emblem	7·00	8·00

200 Ermine

2010. Arctic Animals. Multicoloured.

MS1013	120×124 mm. $2×6 Type **200**; Arctic fox; Harp seal pup; Arctic wolf; Arctic hare; Snowy owl	8·00	8·00
MS1014	100×70 mm. $6 Polar bear	4·75	5·00

201 Czar Nicholas II

2011. Death Centenary of Henri Dunant (founder of Red Cross). Multicoloured.

MS1015	150×100 mm. $2.50×4 Type **201**; Henri Dufour; Frédéric Passy; Victor Hugo	7·00	7·50
MS1016	70×100 mm. $6 Early Red Cross nurse	4·75	5·00

202 Pedro

2011. World Cup Football, South Africa. Multicoloured.

MS1017	130×155 mm. $1.50×6 Germany vs. Spain: Type **202**; Miroslav Klose (Germany); Xavi (Spain); Piotr Trochowski (Germany); Carles Puyol (Spain); Philipp Lahm (Germany)	6·00	7·00
MS1018	$3.50 Joachim Loew (coach, Germany); $3.50 German flag on football	4·75	5·50
MS1019	$3.50 Vicente del Bosque (coach, Spain); $3.50 Spanish flag on football	2·50	2·75

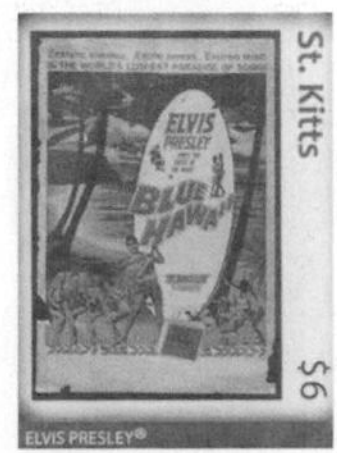

203 Poster for *Blue Hawaii*

2011. Elvis Presley in Film *Blue Hawaii*, 1961. Multicoloured.

MS1020	125×90 mm. $6 Type **203**	4·75	5·50
MS1021	90×125 mm. $6 Wearing swimming trunks	4·75	5·50
MS1022	90×125 mm. $6 Playing guitar	4·75	5·50
MS1023	125×90 mm. $6 Wearing lei and playing guitar	4·75	5·50

204 Princess Diana

2010. Princess Diana Commemoration. Multicoloured.

MS1024	170×130 mm. $2×6 Type **204**×2; Wearing pearl drop earrings, pearl necklace and white strapless dress×2; Wearing tiara×2	7·50	8·00
MS1025	90×120 mm. $2.75×4 Wearing lilac hat with white band and pearl choker×2; In profile, wearing cream hat and coat×2	7·50	8·00

205 *Journey of the Magi* (Fra Angelico)

2011. Christmas. Multicoloured.

1026	10c. Type **205**	15	15
1027	25c. *Madonna Worshipping the Child and an Angel* (Biagio d'Antonio)	20	20
1028	30c. The Nativity (Master of Vyšší Brod)	25	25
1029	90c. *The Journey of the Magi* (James Tissot)	90	90
1030	$1.80 *Worship of the Shepherds* (Agnolo di Cosimo)	1·40	1·40
1031	$3 Madonna with Child (Carlo Crivelli)	1·75	1·75

206 *Giovanna Albizi with Venus and the Graces*

2011. 500th Death Anniv (2010) of Sandro Botticelli (artist). Multicoloured.

MS1032	150×95 mm. $2.50×4 Type **206**; Lemmi frescoes from the villa near Florence; *Portrait of a Young Woman; St. Sebastian*	5·50	5·50
MS1033	70×100 mm. $6 *The Last Communion of St. Jerome* (horiz)	4·75	4·75

207 Pope John Paul II

2011. Fifth Death Anniv (2010) of Pope John Paul II. Multicoloured.

MS1034	$2.50 Type **207**×4	5·50	5·50
MS1035	$2.50 Pope John Paul II praying ×4	2·50	2·50

208 Pres. Barack Obama

2011. Pres. Barack Obama. Multicoloured.

MS1036	175×113 mm. $2.50 Type **208**×4	2·50	5·50
MS1037	113×174 mm. $2.50 Pres. Obama (blue lower border with 'THE OFFICE' inscription)×4	5·50	5·50

209 Prince William and Miss Catherine Middleton

2011. Royal Engagement (2010). Multicoloured.

MS1038	170×130 mm. $2.50×4 Type **209**; Prince William; Miss Catherine Middleton; Prince William and Miss Catherine Middleton (all horiz with blue frame)	5·50	5·50
MS1039	170×130 mm. $2.50×4 Prince William and Miss Catherine Middleton (door in background); Prince William; Miss Catherine Middleton; Prince William and Miss Catherine Middleton (gold picture frame in background) (all horiz with red frame)	5·50	5·50
MS1040	135×95 mm. $6 Prince William and Miss Catherine Middleton (vert, blue frame)	4·75	4·75
MS1041	135×95 mm. $6 Prince William and Miss Catherine Middleton (vert, red frame)	4·75	4·75

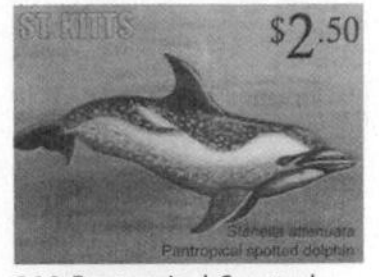

210 Pantropical Spotted Dolphin

2011. Caribbean Dolphins. Multicoloured.

MS1042	150×101 mm. $2.50×4 Type **210**; Killer whale (*Orcinus orca*); Tucuxi (*Sotalia fluviatilis*); Clymene dolphin (*Stenella clymene*)	5·50	5·50
MS1043	100×70 mm. $6 Bottlenose dolphin (*Tursiops truncatus*)	4·75	4·75
MS1044	100×70 mm. $6 Rough-toothed dolphin (*Steno bredanensis*)	4·75	4·75

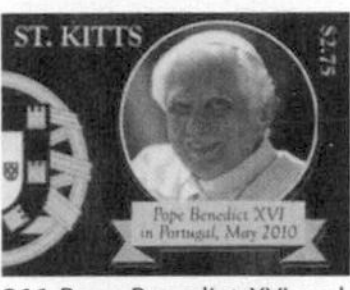

211 Pope Benedict XVI and Arms of Portugal

2011. Pope Benedict XVI visits Portugal. Multicoloured.

MS1045	170×111 mm. $2.75 Type **211**; $2.75 Portrait as Type **211** but green background and arms at right×3	5·00	5·00
MS1046	191×110 mm. $2.75 Pope Benedict XVI and Portuguese city×4	6·75	6·75

212 Ricky Ponting (Australia)

2011. Cricket World Cup. Maestros of Cricket. Multicoloured.

MS1047	212×150 mm. $1.90×14 Type **212**; Shakib Al Hasan (Bangladesh) (wrongly inscr 'Shahid Afridi'); Ashish Bagai (Canada); Mahendra Singh Dhoni (India); Andrew Strauss (England) (wrongly inscr 'Ricky Ponting'); William Porterfield (Ireland); Maurice Ouma (Kenya); Daniel Vettori (New Zealand); Shahid Afridi (Pakistan); Graeme Smith (South Africa); Kumar Sangakkara (Sri Lanka); Peter Borren (Netherlands); Elton Chigumbura (Zimbabwe); Darren Sammy (West Indies)	15·00	15·50
MS1048	212×150 mm. $1.90×14 As **MS**1047 but corrected inscriptions on stamps depicting Shakib Al Hasan and Andrew Strauss	15·00	15·50

213 Mt. Fuji, Japan

2011. Philanippon 2011 World Stamp Exhibition, Yokohama. Sites and Scenes of Japan. Multicoloured.

MS1049	$6 Type **213**	4·75	5·00
MS1050	$6 Okinawa, Japan	4·75	5·00
MS1051	$6 Tokyo, Japan	4·75	5·00

214 St. Kitts-Nevis-Anguilla National Bank, Basseterre, St. Kitts

2011. 40th Anniv of St. Kitts-Nevis-Anguilla National Bank. Multicoloured.

1052	10c. Type **214**	10	10
1053	$3 40th anniversary emblem (vert)	2·50	2·75

215 Mother Teresa with Ronald and Nancy Reagan

2011. Mother Teresa Commemoration. Multicoloured.

MS1054	150×100 mm. $2.75×4 Type **215**; Mother Teresa and nun inside convent; Mother Teresa with children; Mother Teresa with Mayor Jacques Chirac	7·50	8·00
MS1055	101×150 mm. $2.75×4 Mother Teresa (in close-up); With Prince Charles; Holding baby; With mother and baby	7·50	8·00

216 Princess Diana

2011. 50th Birth Anniv of Princess Diana. Multicoloured.

MS1056	131×80 mm. $2.75×4 Type **216**; Holding baby Prince William; Wearing red dress with white collar; Wearing check jacket, on honeymoon at Balmoral, 1981	7·00	7·50
MS1057	101×70 mm. $6 Princess Diana wearing white jacket and red top (51×38 mm)	4·75	5·50

217 Gen. Robert Lee, Gen. George Meade and Union Positions near Cemetery Ridge

2011. 150th Anniv of the American Civil War. Multicoloured.

MS1058	$2.50×4 each showing inset portraits of Gen. Robert E. Lee and Gen. George G. Meade: Type **217**; Union artillery Hazlitt's Battery in action; Union positions near Cemetery Ridge; Union Artillery Cemetery Hill in the distance	7·00	7·50
MS1059	$2.50×4 all with inset portraits of Lt. General James Longstreet and Maj. General Oliver O. Howard: Behind the breastworks on Culp's Hill; Jubal Early's attack on East Cemetery Hill; CSA 2nd Maryland Infantry at Culp's Hill; Confederate pickets at Culp's Hill	7·00	7·50
MS1060	$2.50×4 all with inset portraits of Lt. General Richard S. Ewell and Brigadier General George S. Greene: Cavalry engagement at Gettysburg; Battle of Gettysburg; Hand to hand combat at Gettysburg; Battery A, 1st Rhode Island, Cemetery Ridge	7·00	7·50

218 Duchess of Cambridge

2011. Royal Wedding. Multicoloured.

MS1061	150×100 mm. $2 Type **218**; $2 Prince William; $2 Duke and Duchess of Cambridge; $2 Duke (hand raised) and Duchess of Cambridge; $4 Miss Catherine Middleton arriving at Westminster Abbey (40×60 mm)	11·00	12·00
MS1062	150×100 mm. $2.75×4 Duke and Duchess of Cambridge (side view, Abbey wall background); Duke and Duchess of Cambridge (Abbey wall background); Duke and Duchess of Cambridge (carriage horse in background); Duke and Duchess of Cambridge (side view, carriage horse in background)	7·50	8·00
MS1063	70×100 mm. $6 Duke and Duchess of Cambridge (51×37 mm)	4·75	5·00

219 Bird of Paradise Flower (*Strelitzia reginae*)

2011. Exotic Flowers. Multicoloured.

MS1064	141×140 mm. $2×6 Type **219**; *Gardenia jasminoides*; Dutch amaryllis (*Amaryllis hippeastrum*); Ginger flower (*Etlingera elatior*); Lobster claw (*Heliconia rostrata*); Bleeding heart (*Dicentra spectabilis*)	9·50	11·00
MS1065	140×100 mm. $2.75×4 Cockscomb (*Celosia spicata*); Passion flower (*Passiflora caerulea*); Prairie Blue Eyes daylily (*Hemerocallis*); Blue water lily (*Nymphaea caerulea*) (all 30×40 mm)	7·50	8·00
MS1066	101×70 mm. $6 Painted feather (*Vriesia carinata*) (30×40 mm)	4·75	5·50
MS1067	101×70 mm. $6 Cuban lily (*Scilla peruviana*) (40×30 mm)	4·75	5·00

220 Elvis Presley

2011. 75th Birth Anniv (2010) of Elvis Presley (2nd issue). Multicoloured.

MS1068	154×174 mm. $3×4 Type **220**; Elvis Presley playing guitar; Holding microphone, seen from back; Holding microphone, side view	9·50	11·00
MS1069	154×190 mm. $3×4 Wearing white jacket with gold design on back; In profile, blue background; In close-up with microphone; Wearing black leather jacket, arms raised (all vert)	9·50	11·50

221 Wembley Stadium, London, 1948

2011. Olympic Games, London (2012). Scenes and Poster from Olympic Games, London, 1948. Multicoloured.

MS1070	$3×4 Type **221**; Robert Bruce Matthias; Maureen Gardner and Fanny Blankers-Koen; Poster for Olympic Games, London, 1948	8·25	8·25

222 Emblem

2011. CGF (Commonwealth Games Federation) General Assembly, St. Kitts. Multicoloured.

1071	25c. Type **222**	15	15
MS1072	70×100 mm. $1.20 Antoine Adams, Delwayne Delaney, Jason Rogers, Kim Collins and Bruesh Lawrence (bronze medal winning 4×100 metres relay team from Athletics World Championships, South Korea, 2011)	80	80

223 Jubilee Emblem with Flags of St. Christopher, Nevis and Anguilla and St. Kitts and Nevis

2012. Diamond Jubilee. Multicoloured.

1073	10c. Type **223**	10	10
1074	10c. Child's drawing for £2 stamp	10	10
1075	25c. Child's drawing of crown with base in colours of St. Kitts and Nevis flag	15	15
1076	30c. '60' emblem with crown on top of St. Kitts and Nevis flag and wreath of Union Jack flags	20	20
1077	$1.20 Handshake, clock towers, '60' and background of St. Kitts and Nevis and Union Jack flags	75	75
MS1078	150×100 mm. $3.50×4 Queen Elizabeth II with umbrella, 1970s; Princess Elizabeth, aged about 21; Queen Elizabeth II on Coronation day waving from doorway, 1952; Queen Elizabeth II wearing tiara and white fur stole, c. 1952 (all 35×35 mm)	9·50	9·50

MS1079	70×100 mm. $9 Sketch of Queen Elizabeth II (38×100 mm)	6·00	6·00

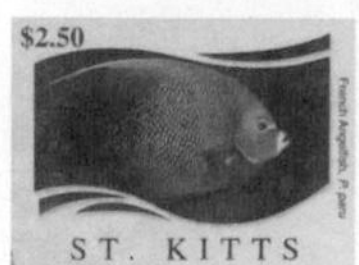

224 French Angelfish (*P. paru*)

2012. Game Fish of the Caribbean. Multicoloured.

MS1080	180×130 mm. $2.50×6 Type **224**; Barracuda (*Sphyraena*); Spotted Trunkfish (*L. bicaudalis*); Trumpetfish (*A. maculatus*); Orange-lined Triggerfish (*B. undulatus*); Eagle Ray (*Myliobatidae*)	6·00	6·00
MS1081	100×87 mm. $6 Butterfly fish (*Chaetodon semilarvatus*)	4·00	4·00

225 Abraham Lincoln

2012. Abraham Lincoln (1809-65, US President 1860-5) Commemoration. Multicoloured.

MS1082	136×87 mm. $2.75×4 Type **225**; Abraham Lincoln (three-quarter length, curtain at left); Looking left ('ha' of signature in right background); Looking left ('L' of signature in right background)	7·50	7·50
MS1083	101×70 mm. $6 Statue of Abraham Lincoln	4·00	4·00

226 Green-winged Macaw (*Ara chloropterus*)

2012. Parrots of the Caribbean. Multicoloured.

MS1084	100×151 mm. $2.75×4 Type **226**; St. Vincent Amazon (*Amazona guildingii*); Yellow-headed Amazon (*Amazona oratrix*); Orange-winged Amazon (*Amazona amazonica*)	7·50	7·50
MS1085	100×100 mm. $6 Blue and Gold Macaw (*Ara ararauna*) (51×38 mm)	4·00	4·00

227 *Turbo petholatus*

2012. Shells. Multicoloured.

MS1086	170×101 mm. $2.75×4 Type **227**; *Mitra stictica*; *Muricanthus radix*; *Murex bicolor*	7·50	7·50
MS1087	71×100 mm. $6 *Haliotis asinina* (vert 30×79 mm)	4·00	4·00

228 Princess Diana

2012. 15th Death Anniv of Princess Diana. Multicoloured.

MS1088	150×156 mm. $3 Type **228**×4	8·25	8·25
MS1089	71×101 mm. $9 Princess Diana wearing white blouse (diamond-shape)	6·00	6·00

229 Elvis Presley

2012. Elvis Presley in Documentary *That's the Way It Is* (1970). Multicoloured.

MS1090	90×125 mm. $9 Type **229**	6·00	6·00
MS1091	125×91 mm. $9 Poster for *That's the Way It Is*	6·00	6·00
MS1092	91×126 mm. $9 Elvis Presley holding microphone, singing (horiz)	6·00	6·00
MS1093	125×90 mm. $9 Elvis Presley with guitar	6·00	6·00

OFFICIAL STAMPS

1980. Nos. 32/41 optd **OFFICIAL**.

O1A	15c. multicoloured	10	10
O2A	25c. multicoloured	10	10
O3A	30c. multicoloured	10	10
O4A	40c. multicoloured	10	15
O5A	45c. multicoloured	15	15
O6A	50c. multicoloured	15	15
O7A	55c. multicoloured	15	15
O8A	$1 multicoloured	25	25
O9A	$5 multicoloured	80	1·50
O10A	$10 multicoloured	1·00	2·50

1981. Nos. 59/70 optd **OFFICIAL**.

O11	15c. Bananaquit	20	10
O12	20c. Scaly-breasted thrasher	20	10
O13	25c. Grey kingbird	25	10
O14	30c. Green-throated carib	25	10
O15	40c. Turnstone	35	15
O16	45c. Black-faced grassquit	40	20
O17	50c. Cattle egret	40	20
O18	55c. Brown pelican	50	25
O19	$1 Lesser Antillean bullfinch	75	45
O20	$2.50 Zenaida dove	1·60	1·00
O21	$5 American kestrel	2·75	2·00
O22	$10 Antillean crested hummingbird	5·00	4·25

1983. Nos. 75/80 optd **OFFICIAL** or surch also.

O23	45c. on $2.50 "Royal George"	15	15
O24	45c. on $2.50 Prince Charles and Lady Diana Spencer	25	25
O25	55c. "Saudadoes"	15	15
O26	55c. Prince Charles and Lady Diana Spencer	30	30
O27	$1.10 on $4 "Britannia"	30	40
O28	$1.10 on $4 Prince Charles and Lady Diana Spencer	60	70

1984. Nos. 145/56 optd **OFFICIAL**.

O29	15c. Red-lined cleaning shrimp	70	1·25
O30	20c. Bristleworm	80	1·50
O31	25c. Flamingo tongue	80	1·50
O32	30c. Christmas tree worm	90	1·50
O33	40c. Pink-tipped anemone	1·00	1·50
O34	50c. Small-mouthed grunt	1·00	1·50
O35	60c. Glass-eyed snapper	1·25	2·00
O36	75c. Reef squirrelfish	1·50	2·50
O37	$1 Sea fans and flamefish (vert)	2·00	2·50
O38	$2.50 Reef butterflyfish (vert)	3·75	6·00
O39	$5 Black-barred soldierfish (vert)	5·50	3·00
O40	$10 Cocoa damselfish (vert)	8·50	6·00

Pt. 1

ST KITTS-NEVIS

Islands of the Leeward Is., Br. W. Indies. The general issues for Leeward Is, were in concurrent use until 1 July 1956. From 1952 the stamps are inscribed "St. Christopher, Nevis and Anguilla". Achieved Associated Statehood on 27 February 1967. St. Kitts and Nevis had separate postal administrations from 23 June 1980.

1903. 12 pence = 1 shilling; 20 shillings = 1 pound.
1951. 100 cents = 1 West Indian dollar.

1 Christopher Columbus

2 Medicinal Spring

1903

1	1	½d. purple and green	1·75	70
12	1	½d. green	1·00	60
13	2	1d. grey and red	8·00	25
14*a*	2	1d. red	1·00	20
3	1	2d. purple and brown	2·75	11·00

16	1	2½d. black and blue	32·00	4·75
17	1	2½d. blue	2·50	50
19*ab*	1	6d. black and purple	9·50	35·00
7	1	1s. green and orange	7·50	11·00
8	1	2s. green and black	12·00	20·00
9	1	2s.6d. black and violet	18·00	48·00
10	2	5s. purple and green	65·00	55·00
22*a*		½d. green	1·00	50

1918. Optd **WAR STAMP**.

23	1½d. orange	1·75	1·00

4

5

1920

37*a*	4	½d. green	3·00	1·00
38	5	1d. red	1·25	15
39	5	1d. violet	7·50	1·00
26	4	1½d. yellow	1·25	1·75
40	4	1½d. red	6·00	1·00
40a	4	1½d. brown	1·50	30
41	5	2d. grey	1·00	60
43	4	2½d. brown	4·00	9·50
44	4	2½d. blue	1·50	1·00
45	5	3d. blue	1·00	3·50
45a	5	3d. purple on yellow	1·25	2·50
46aw	4	6d. purple and mauve	6·50	6·50
31	5	1s. black on green	3·50	4·00
47	4	2s. purple and blue on blue	12·00	32·00
33	5	2s.6d. black and red on blue	5·00	40·00
34	4	5s. green and red on yellow	5·00	40·00
35	5	10s. green and red on green	12·00	48·00
36	4	£1 purple and black on red	£300	£375

6 Old Road Bay and Mount Misery

1923. Tercentenary Commemoration.

48	6	½d. black and green	2·25	7·50
49	6	1d. black and violet	4·50	2·25
50	6	1½d. black and red	4·50	10·00
51	6	2d. black and grey	3·75	1·50
52	6	2½d. black and brown	6·00	32·00
53	6	3d. black and blue	4·75	15·00
54	6	6d. black and purple	9·50	32·00
55	6	1s. black and green	14·00	32·00
56	6	2s. black and blue on blue	50·00	80·00
57	6	2s.6d. black and red on blue	50·00	95·00
59	6	5s. black and red on yellow	90·00	£225
58	6	10s. black and red on green	£300	£500
60	6	£1 black and purple on red	£800	£1600

1935. Silver Jubilee. As T **32a** of St. Helena.

61	1d. blue and red	1·00	70
62	1½d. blue and grey	75	1·00
63	2½d. brown and blue	1·00	1·00
64	1s. grey and purple	14·00	17·00

1937. Coronation. As T **32b** of St. Helena.

65	1d. red	30	25
66	1½d. brown	40	10
67	2½d. blue	60	1·60

Nos. 61/7 are inscribed "ST. CHRISTOPHER AND NEVIS".

7 King George VI

8 King George VI and Medicinal Spring

10 King George VI and Anguilla Island

1938

68*a*	7	½d. green	10	10
69*a*	7	1d. red	2·25	50
70	7	1½d. orange	20	30
71b	8	2d. red and grey	1·50	1·25
72*a*	7	2½d. blue	70	30
73g	8	3d. purple and red	13·00	13·00
74	-	6d. green and purple	9·00	3·00
75b	8	1s. black and green	4·25	85
76ab	8	2s.6d. black and red	12·00	4·50
77b		5s. green and red	27·00	12·00
77e	10	10s. black and blue	14·00	19·00
77f	10	£1 black and brown	17·00	23·00

The 6d. and 5s. are as Type **8**, but with the Christopher Columbus device as in Type **4**.

1946. Victory. As T **33a** of St. Helena.

78	1½d. orange	10	10
79	3d. red	10	10

1949. Silver Wedding. As T **33b/c** of St. Helena.

80	2½d. blue	10	50
81	5s. red	9·50	8·00

1949. U.P.U. As T **33d/g** of St. Helena.

82	2½d. blue	15	30
83	3d. red	2·10	2·50
84	6d. mauve	20	1·75
85	1s. green	20	40

1950. Tercentary of British Settlement in Anguilla. Optd **ANGUILLA TERCENTENARY 1650–1950**.

86	7	1d. red	10	20
87	7	1½d. orange	10	50
88	7	2½d. blue	25	20
89	8	3d. purple and red	80	75
90	-	6d. green and purple (No. 74d)	45	20
91	8	1s. black and green	1·40	25

10a Arms of University

10b Princess Alice

1951. Inauguration of B.W.I. University College.

92	10a	3c. black and orange	30	15
93	10b	12c. green and mauve	30	2·00

ST. CHRISTOPHER, NEVIS AND ANGUILLA

13 Bath House and Spa

1952

94	13	1c. green and ochre	15	3·00
95	-	2c. green	1·00	1·00
96	-	3c. red and violet	30	1·25
97	-	4c. red	20	20
98	-	5c. blue and grey	30	10
99	-	6c. blue	30	15
100	-	12c. blue and brown	1·25	10
101	-	24c. black and red	30	10
102	-	48c. olive and brown	3·25	5·00
103	-	60c. ochre and green	2·25	4·50
104	-	$1.20 green and blue	7·50	5·00
105	-	$4.80 green and red	14·00	18·00

DESIGNS—HORIZ: 2c. Warner Park; 4c. Brimstone Hill; 5c. Nevis from the sea, North; 6c. Pinney's Beach, Nevis; 24c. Old Road Bay; 48c. Sea Island cotton, Nevis; 60c. The Treasury; $1.20, Salt pond, Anguilla; $4.80, Sugar factory. VERT: 3c. Map of the islands; 12c. Sir Thomas Warner's tomb.

1953. Coronation. As T **33h** of St. Helena.

106	2c. black and green	30	30

1954. As 1952 but with portrait of Queen Elizabeth II.

106a	½c. olive (as $1.20)	30	10
107	1c. green and ochre	20	10
108	2c. green	1·00	10
109	3c. red and violet	65	10
110	4c. red	15	10
111	5c. blue and grey	15	10
112	6c. blue	70	10
112b	8c. black	3·00	25
113	12c. blue and brown	15	10
114	24c. black and red	15	10
115	48c. olive and brown	1·75	1·00
116	60c. ochre and green	5·50	7·50
117	$1.20 green and blue	22·00	3·25
117b	$2.40 black and orange	20·00	14·00
118	$4.80 green and red	23·00	11·00

DESIGNS (new values)—VERT: 8c. Sombrero Lighthouse. HORIZ: $2.40, Map of Anguilla and Dependencies.

27 Alexander Hamilton and View of Nevis

1956. Birth Bicent of Alexander Hamilton.

119	27	24c. green and blue	60	25

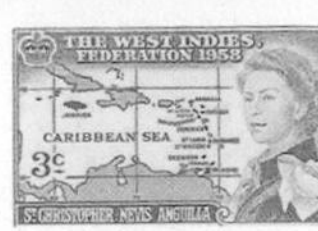

27a Federation Map

1958. British Caribbean Federation.

120	27a	3c. green	85	15
121	27a	6c. blue	1·10	2·50
122	27a	12c. red	1·10	35

28 1d. Stamp of 1861

1961. Centenary of Nevis Stamp.

123	28	2c. red and green	20	55
124	28	8c. red and blue	25	15
125	28	12c. lilac and red	30	20
126	28	24c. green and orange	35	20

The 8c., 12c. and 24c. show the original 4d., 6d. and 1s. stamps of Nevis respectively.

1963. Cent of Red Cross. As T **63b** of St. Helena.

127	3c. red and black	20	10
128	12c. red and blue	40	40

33 Loading Sugar Cane, St. Kitts

1963. Multicoloured.. Multicoloured..

129	½c. New Lighthouse, Sombrero	10	10
130	1c. Type **33**	10	10
131	2c. Pall Mall Square, Basseterre	10	10
132	3c. Gateway, Brimstone Hill Fort, St. Kitts	10	10
133	4c. Nelson's Spring, Nevis	10	10
134	5c. Grammar School, St. Kitts	3·50	10
135	6c. Crater, Mt. Misery, St. Kitts	10	10
136	10c. Hibiscus	15	10
137	15c. Sea Island cotton, Nevis	70	10
138	20c. Boat-building, Anguilla	30	10
139	25c. White-crowned pigeon	2·25	10
140	50c. St. George's Church Tower, Basseterre	60	25
141	60c. Alexander Hamilton	1·00	30
142	$1 Map of St. Kitts-Nevis	2·50	40
143	$2.50 Map of Anguilla	3·25	3·25
144	$5 Arms of St. Christopher, Nevis and Anguilla	9·00	9·50

The ½, 2, 3, 15, 25, 60c., $1 and $5 are vert, the rest horiz.

1964. Arts Festival. Optd **ARTS FESTIVAL ST KITTS 1964**.

145	3c. multicoloured (No. 132)	10	15
146	25c. multicoloured (No. 139)	20	15

1965. Cent of I.T.U. As T **64a** of St. Helena.

147	2c. bistre and red	10	10
148	50c. blue and olive	40	50

1965. I.C.Y. As T **64b** of St. Helena.

149	2c. purple and green	10	20
150	25c. green and violet	65	10

1966. Churchill Commemoration. As T **64c** of St. Helena.

151	½c. blue	10	2·75
152	3c. green	35	10
153	15c. brown	80	20
154	25c. violet	85	20

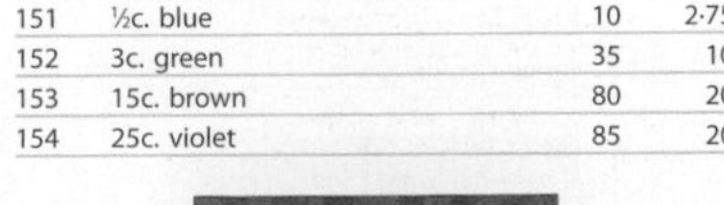

48a Queen Elizabeth and Duke of Edinburgh

1966. Royal Visit.

155	48a	3c. black and blue	25	30
156	48a	25c. black and mauve	55	30

1966. World Cup Football Championship. As T **64d** of St. Helena.

157	6c. multicoloured	40	20
158	25c. multicoloured	60	10

49 Festival Emblem

1966. Arts Festival.

159	49	3c. multicoloured	10	10
160	49	25c. multicoloured	20	10

1968. Inauguration of W.H.O. Headquarters, Geneva. As T **64e** of St. Helena.

161	3c. black, green and blue	10	10
162	40c. black, purple and brown	30	20

1966. 20th Anniv of UNESCO. As T **64f/h** of St. Helena.

163	3c. multicoloured	10	10
164	6c. yellow, violet and olive	10	10
165	40c. black, purple and orange	30	35

50 Government Headquarters, Basseterre

1967. Statehood. Multicoloured.

182	3c. Type **50**	10	10
183	10c. National flag	10	10
184	25c. Coat of arms	15	15

53 John Wesley and Cross

1967. West Indies Methodist Conference.

185	53	3c. black, red and violet	10	10
186	-	25c. black, turquoise & blue	15	10
187	-	40c. black, yellow & orange	15	15

DESIGNS: 25c. Charles Wesley and cross; 40c. Thomas Coke and cross.

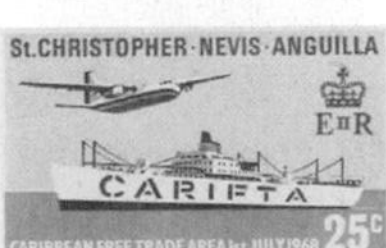

56 Handley Page Dart Herald over "Jamaica Producer" (freighter)

1968. Caribbean Free Trade Area.

188	56	25c. multicoloured	40	10
189	56	50c. multicoloured	40	20

57 Dr. Martin Luther King

1968. Martin Luther King Commemoration.

190	57	50c. multicoloured	15	10

58 "Mystical Nativity" (Botticelli)

1968. Christmas.

191	**58**	12c. multicoloured	10	10
192	-	25c. multicoloured	10	10
193	**58**	40c. multicoloured	15	10
194	-	50c. multicoloured	15	10

DESIGN: 25c., 50c. "The Adoration of the Magi" (Rubens).

60 Tarpon Snook

1968. Fish.

195	**60**	6c. multicoloured	10	10
196	-	12c. black, green and blue	15	10
197	-	40c. multicoloured	25	10
198	-	50c. multicoloured	30	15

FISHES: 12c. Needlefish; 40c. Horse-eyed jack; 50c. Black-finned snapper.

64 The Warner Badge and Islands

1969. Sir Thomas Warner Commem. Multicoloured.

199	20c. Type **64**	10	10
200	25c. Sir Thomas Warner's tomb	10	10
201	40c. Charles I's Commission	15	15

67 "The Adoration of the Kings" (Mostaert)

1969. Christmas. Multicoloured.

202	10c. Type **67**	10	10
203	25c. As 10c.	10	10
204	40c. "The Adoration of the Kings" (Geertgen)	10	10
205	50c. As 40c.	10	10

73 Portuguese Caravels (16th-cent)

1970. Multicoloured. (except ½c.).

206	½c. Pirates and treasure at Frigate Bay (black, orange and green)	10	10
207	1c. English two-decker warship, 1650	30	10
208	2c. Naval flags of colonizing nations	15	10
209	3c. Rapier hilt (17th-century)	15	10
210	4c. Type **73**	20	10
211	5c. Sir Henry Morgan and fire-ships, 1669	60	40
212	6c. L'Ollonois and pirate carrack (16th-century)	30	10
213	10c. 17th-century smugglers' ship	30	10
214	15c. "Piece of Eight"	2·50	40
215	20c. Cannon (17th-century)	35	10
216	25c. Humphrey Cole's astrolabe, 1574	40	10
217	50c. Flintlock pistol (17th-cent)	85	80
218	60c. Dutch flute (17th-cent)	1·50	70
219	$1 Capt. Bartholomew Roberts and his crew's death warrant	1·50	75
220	$2.50 Railing piece (gun) (16th-century)	1·25	5·00
221	$5 Drake, Hawkins and sea battle	1·50	4·50
280	$10 The Apprehension of Blackbeard (Edward Teach)	15·00	13·00

The ½c. to 3c., 15c., 25c., 60c. and $1 are vert designs.

85 Graveyard Scene ("Great Expectations")

1970. Death Cent of Charles Dickens.

222	**85**	4c. brown, gold and green	10	80
223	-	20c. brown, gold and purple	10	20
224	-	25c. brown, gold and green	10	20
225	-	40c. brown, gold and blue	15	35

DESIGNS—HORIZ: 20c. Miss Havisham and Pip ("Great Expectations"). VERT: 25c. Dickens' birthplace; 40c. Charles Dickens.

86 Local Steel Band

1970. Festival of Arts. Multicoloured.

226	20c. Type **86**	10	10
227	25c. Local string band	10	10
228	40c. Scene from "A Midsummer Night's Dream"	15	15

87 1d. Stamp of 1870 and Post Office, 1970

1970. Stamp Centenary.

229	**87**	½c. green and red	10	10
230	-	20c. purple, green and red	10	10
231	-	25c. purple, green and red	10	10
232	-	50c. red, green and black	30	45

DESIGNS: 20c., 25c., 1d. and 6d. stamps of 1870; 50c.6d. stamp of 1870 and early postmark.

88 "Adoration of the Shepherds" (Frans van Floris)

1970. Christmas. Multicoloured.

233	3c. Type **88**	10	10
234	20c. "The Holy Family" (Van Dyck)	10	10
235	25c. As 20c.	10	10
236	40c. Type **88**	15	50

89 Monkey Fiddle

1971. Flowers. Multicoloured.

237	½c. Type **89**	10	40
238	20c. Tropical mountain violet	15	10
239	30c. Trailing morning glory	15	15
240	50c. Fringed epidendrum	30	1·00

90 Royal Poinciana

1971. Philippe de Poincy Commem. Multicoloured.

241	20c. Type **90**	10	10
242	30c. Chateau de Poincy	10	10
243	50c. De Poincy's badge (vert)	20	15

91 The East Yorks

1971. Siege of Brimstone Hill, 1782. Multicoloured.

244	½c. Type **91**	10	10
245	20c. Royal Artillery	30	10
246	30c. French infantry	30	10
247	50c. The Royal Scots	40	20

92 "Crucifixion" (Massys)

1972. Easter.

248	**92**	4c. multicoloured	10	10
249	**92**	20c. multicoloured	10	20
250	**92**	30c. multicoloured	10	25
251	**92**	40c. multicoloured	10	25

93 "Virgin and Child" (Borgognone)

1972. Christmas. Multicoloured.

252	3c. Type **93**	10	10
253	20c. "Adoration of the Kings" (J. Bassano) (horiz)	15	10
254	25c. "Adoration of the Shepherds" (Domenichino)	15	10
255	40c. "Virgin and Child" (Fiorenzo di Lorenzo)	20	10

1972. Royal Silver Wedding. As T **103** of St. Helena, but with brown pelicans in background.

256	20c. red	35	20
257	25c. blue	35	20

95 Landing on St. Christopher, 1623

1973. 300th Anniv of Sir Thomas Warner's Landing on St. Christopher. Multicoloured.

258	4c. Type **95**	15	10
259	25c. Growing tobacco	15	10
260	40c. Building fort at Old Road	20	10
261	$2.50 "Concepcion"	80	1·10

96 "The Last Supper" (Titian)

1973. Easter. Paintings of "The Last Supper" by the artists listed. Multicoloured.

262	4c. Type **96**	10	10
263	25c. Ascribed to Roberti	10	10
264	$2.50 Juan de Juanes (horiz)	70	60

1973. Royal Visit. Nos. 258/61 optd **VISIT OF H. R. H. THE PRINCE OF WALES 1973.**

265	**95**	4c. multicoloured	10	15
266	-	25c. multicoloured	10	15
267	-	40c. multicoloured	15	15
268	-	$2.50 multicoloured	45	50

99 Harbour Scene and 2d. Stamp of 1903

1973. 70th Anniv of First St. Kitts-Nevis Stamps. Multicoloured.

285	4c. Type **99**	10	10
286	25c. Sugar-mill and 1d. stamp of 1903	15	10
287	40c. Unloading boat and ½d. stamp of 1903	35	10
288	$2.50 Rock-carvings and 3d. stamp of 1903	1·00	1·00
MS289	144×95 mm. Nos. 285/8	1·50	4·50

1973. Royal Wedding. As T **103a** of St. Helena. Multicoloured, background colours given.

290	25c. green	15	10
291	40c. brown	15	10

100 "Madonna and Child" (Murillo)

1973. Christmas. Paintings of "The Holy Family" by the artists listed. Multicoloured.

292	4c. Type **100**	10	10
293	40c. Mengs	15	10
294	60c. Sassoferrato	20	15
295	$1 Filippino Lippi (horiz)	25	30

101 "Christ carrying the Cross" (S. del Piombo)

1974. Easter. Multicoloured.

296	4c. Type **101**	10	10
297	25c. "The Crucifixion" (Goya)	15	10
298	40c. "Trinity" (Ribera)	15	10
299	$2.50 "The Deposition" (Fra Bartolomeo) (horiz)	1·00	1·00

102 University Centre, St. Kitts

1974. 25th Anniv of University of West Indies. Multicoloured.

300	10c. Type **102**	10	10
301	$1 As Type **102** but showing different buildings	20	25
MS302	99×95 mm. Nos. 300/1	35	65

103 Hands reaching for Globe

1974. Family Planning.

303	**103**	4c. brown, blue and black	10	10
304	-	25c. multicoloured	10	10
305	-	40c. multicoloured	10	10
306	-	$2.50 multicoloured	35	55

DESIGNS—HORIZ: 25c. Instruction by nurse; $2.50, Emblem and globe on scales. VERT: 40c. Family group.

104 Churchill as Army Lieutenant

1974. Birth Centenary of Sir Winston Churchill. Multicoloured.

307	4c. Type **104**	10	10
308	25c. Churchill as Prime Minister	15	10
309	40c. Churchill as Knight of the Garter	15	10
310	60c. Churchill's statue, London	25	15
MS311	99×148 mm. Nos. 307/10	75	1·25

105 Aeroplane and Map

1974. Opening of Golden Rock Airport, St. Kitts. Sheets 98×148 mm.

MS312	**105** 40c. multicoloured	20	40
MS313	45c. multicoloured	20	40

106 "The Last Supper" (Dore)

1975. Easter. Paintings by Dore. Multicoloured.

314	4c. Type **106**	10	10
315	25c. "Christ Mocked"	10	10
316	40c. "Jesus falling beneath the Cross"	10	10
317	$1 "The Erection of the Cross"	25	30

107 E.C.C.A. H.Q. Buildings, Basseterre

1975. Opening of East Caribbean Currency Authority's Headquarters.

318	**107**	12c. multicoloured	10	10
319	-	25c. multicoloured	10	10
320	-	40c. red, silver and grey	15	10
321	-	45c. multicoloured	15	15

DESIGNS: 25c. Specimen one-dollar banknote; 40c. Half-dollar of 1801 and current 4-dollar coin; 45c. Coins of 1801 and 1960.

108 Evangeline Booth (Salvation Army General)

1975. International Women's Year. Multicoloured.

338	4c. Type **108**	30	10
339	25c. Sylvia Pankhurst	35	10
340	40c. Marie Curie	2·50	80
341	$2.50 Lady Annie Allen (teacher and guider)	1·50	4·25

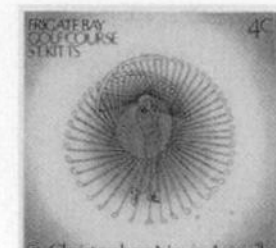

109 Golfer

1975. Opening of Frigate Bay Golf Course.

342	**109**	4c. black and red	80	10
343	**109**	25c. black and yellow	1·10	10
344	**109**	40c. black and green	1·40	20
345	**109**	$1 black and blue	1·90	2·75

110 "St. Paul" (Pier Francesco Sacchi)

1975. Christmas. Religious Paintings. Multicoloured.

346	25c. Type **110**	25	10
347	40c. "St. James" (Bonifazio di Pitati)	30	10
348	45c. "St. John the Baptist" (Mola)	30	10
349	$1 "St. Mary" (Raphael)	80	2·25

111 "Crucifixion" (detail)

1976. Easter. Stained Glass Window. Multicoloured.

350	4c. Type **111**	10	50
351	4c. Type **111**	10	50
352	4c. Type **111**	10	50
353	25c. "Last Supper"	35	10
354	40c. "Last Supper" (different)	40	10
355	$1 "Baptism of Christ"	70	80

Nos. 350/2 were printed together, se-tenant, forming a composite design, No. 350 being the left-hand stamp.

Nos. 353/5 are size 27×35 mm.

1976. West Indian Victory in World Cricket Cup. As Nos. 559/60 of Barbados.

356	12c. Map of the Caribbean	60	20
357	40c. Prudential Cup	1·40	50
MS358	95×80 mm. Nos. 356/7	4·25	3·75

112 Crispus Attucks and the Boston Massacre

1976. Bicentenary of American Revolution. Multicoloured.

359	20c. Type **112**	20	10
360	40c. Alexander Hamilton and Battle of Yorktown	25	10
361	45c. Jefferson and Declaration of Independence	25	10
362	$1 Washington and the Crossing of the Delaware	45	85

113 "The Nativity" (Sforza Book of Hours)

1976. Christmas. Multicoloured.

363	20c. Type **113**	10	10
364	40c. "Virgin and Child with St. John" (Pintoricchio)	15	10
365	45c. "Our Lady of Good Children" (Ford Maddox-Brown)	15	10
366	$1 "Little Hands Outstretched to Bless" (Margaret Tarrant)	35	50

114 Royal Visit, 1966

1977. Silver Jubilee. Multicoloured.

367	50c. Type **114**	10	10
368	55c. The Sceptre	10	10
369	$1.50 Bishops paying homage	25	50

115 "Christ on the Cross" (Niccolo di Liberatore)

1977. Easter. Paintings from National Gallery, London. Multicoloured.

370	25c. Type **115**	10	10
371	30c. "The Resurrection" (imitator of Mantegna)	10	10
372	50c. "The Resurrection" (Ugolino da Siena) (horiz)	15	10
373	$1 "Christ Rising from the Tomb" (Gaudenzio Ferrari)	25	30

116 Estridge Mission

1977. Bicentenary of Moravian Mission.

374	**116**	4c. black, green and blue	10	10
375	-	20c. black, mauve & violet	10	10
376	-	40c. black, yellow & orge	15	15

DESIGNS: 20c. Mission symbol; 40c. Basseterre Mission.

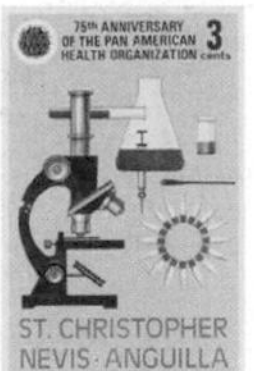

117 Laboratory Instruments

1977. 75th Anniv of Pan-American Health Organization.

377	**117**	3c. multicoloured	20	10
378	-	12c. multicoloured	35	60
379	-	20c. multicoloured	40	10
380	-	$1 brown, orange and black	1·00	1·40

DESIGNS: 12c. Fat cells, blood cells and nerve cells; 20c. "Community participation in health"; $1 Inoculation.

118 "Nativity" (West Window)

1977. Christmas. Stained-glass windows from Chartres Cathedral. Multicoloured.

381	4c. Type **118**	10	10
382	6c. "Three Magi" (west window)	10	10
383	40c. "La Belle Verriere"	35	10
384	$1 "Virgin and Child" (Rose window)	75	45

119 Savanna Monkey with Vervet

1978. The Savanna Monkey.

385	**119**	4c. brown, red and black	10	10
386	-	5c. multicoloured	10	10
387	**119**	55c. brown, green & black	30	10
388	-	$1.50 multicoloured	75	60

DESIGN: 5c., $1.50, Savanna monkeys on branch.

120 Falcon of Edward III

1978. 25th Anniv of Coronation.

389	**120**	$1 brown and red	15	20
390	-	$1 multicoloured	15	20
391	-	$1 brown and red	15	20

DESIGNS: No. 390, Queen Elizabeth II; No. 391, Brown pelican.

121 Tomatoes

1978. Tomatoes. Multicoloured.

392	1c. Type **121**	10	20
393	2c. Defence Force band	10	20
394	5c. Radio and T.V. station	10	10
395	10c. Technical college	10	10
396	12c. T.V. assembly plant	10	75
397	15c. Sugar canoe harvesting	15	20
398	25c. Crafthouse (craft centre)	15	10
399	30c. "Europa" (liner)	1·50	1·50
400	40c. Lobster and sea crab	30	10
401	45c. Royal St. Kitts Hotel and golf course	2·75	1·25
402	50c. Pinney's Beach, Nevis	30	10
403	55c. New runway at Golden Rock	1·25	10
404	$1 Cotton picking	35	30
405	$5 Brewery	75	1·25
406	$10 Pineapples and peanuts	1·00	1·75

122 Investiture

1978. 50th Anniv of Boy Scout Movement on St. Kitts and Nevis. Multicoloured.

407	5c. Type **122**	10	35
408	10c. Map reading	10	35
409	25c. Pitching tent	20	35
410	40c. Cooking	35	50
411	50c. First aid	40	60
412	55c. Rev. W. A. Beckett (founder of scouting in St. Kitts)	45	65

123 Wise Man with Gift of Gold

1978. Christmas. Multicoloured.

413	5c. Type **123**	10	10

414	15c. Wise Man with gift of Frankincense	10	10
415	30c. Wise Man with gift of Myrrh	10	10
416	$2.25 Wise Man paying homage to the Infant Jesus	35	50

124 "Canna coccinea"

1979. Local Flowers (1st series). Multicoloured.

417	5c. Type **124**	10	10
418	30c. "Heliconia bihai"	25	20
419	55c. "Ruellia tuberosa"	30	30
420	$1.50 "Gesneria ventricosa"	50	1·60

See also Nos. 430/3.

125 St. Christopher 1870 1d. Stamp and Sir Rowland Hill

1979. Death Centenary of Sir Rowland Hill. Multicoloured.

421	5c. Type **125**	10	10
422	15c. 1970 Stamp Centenary 50c. commemorative	10	10
423	50c. Great Britain 1841 2d. blue	30	35
424	$2.50 St. Kitts-Nevis 1923 300th Anniv of Colony £1 commemorative	70	1·10

126 "The Woodman's Daughter"

1979. Christmas. International Year of the Child. Paintings by Sir John Millais. Multicoloured.

425	5c. Type **126**	10	10
426	25c. "Cherry Ripe"	25	25
427	30c. "The Rescue"	25	25
428	55c. "Bubbles"	30	30

1980. Local Flowers (2nd series). As T **124**. Multicoloured.

430	4c. "Clerodendrum aculeatum"	30	10
431	55c. "Inga laurina"	30	20
432	$1.50 "Epidendrum difforme"	1·40	1·75
433	$2 "Salvia serotina"	60	2·25

127 Nevis Lagoon

1980. "London 1980" International Stamp Exhibition. Multicoloured.

434	5c. Type **127**	15	10
435	30c. Fig Tree Church (vert)	25	10
436	55c. Nisbet Plantation	45	25
437	$3 "Nelson" (Fuger) (vert)	1·75	1·60
MS438	107×77 mm. 75c. Detail of "Nelson Falling" (D. Dighton)	1·40	75

OFFICIAL STAMPS

1980. Nos. 396, 398 and 400/6 optd **OFFICIAL**.

O1	12c. multicoloured	80	1·25
O2	25c. multicoloured	15	20
O3	40c. multicoloured	40	50
O4	45c. multicoloured	2·50	2·00
O5	50c. multicoloured	30	40
O6	55c. multicoloured	1·25	50
O7	$1 multicoloured	70	2·25
O8	$5 multicoloured	80	2·50
O9	$10 multicoloured	1·00	3·50

Pt. 1

ST LUCIA

One of the Windward Islands, British West Indies. Achieved Associated Statehood on 1 March 1967.

1860. 12 pence = 1 shilling; 20 shillings = 1 pound.
1949. 100 cents = 1 West Indian dollar.

1

1860. No value on stamps.

5ax	1	(1d.) red	70·00	90·00
11a	1	(1d.) black	28·00	12·00
7	1	(4d.) blue	£130	£140
16	1	(4d.) yellow	£130	24·00
8x	1	(6d.) green	£190	£180
17a	1	(6d.) violet	£120	22·00
18a	1	(1s.) orange	£170	16·00

HALFPENNY
(3)

1881. With value added by surch as T **3**.

25	1	½d. green	30·00	45·00
26	1	1d. black	45·00	16·00
24	1	2½d. red	60·00	28·00
27	1	4d. yellow	£300	24·00
28	1	6d. violet	48·00	48·00
29	1	1s. orange	£275	£170

5

1882

43	5	½d. green	4·00	1·00
32	5	1d. red	55·00	19·00
46	5	2½d. blue	11·00	1·00
48	5	4d. brown	7·50	3·00
35	5	6d. lilac	£300	£200
36	5	1s. brown	£400	£160

1886

44	5	1d. mauve	7·00	30
45	5	2d. blue and orange	6·00	1·00
47	5	3d. mauve and green	8·00	5·50
41	5	6d. mauve and blue	7·00	18·00
50	5	1s. mauve and red	12·00	5·00
51	5	5s. mauve and orange	55·00	£160
52	5	10s. mauve and black	95·00	£160

1891. Surch in words.

56	5	½d. on 3d. mauve and green	85·00	29·00
55	5	1d. on 4d. brown	8·50	4·25

1891. Surch **½d.**

54	5	½d. on half 6d. (No. 41)	30·00	3·25

9

1902

58	9	½d. purple and green	3·50	1·50
65	9	½d. green	1·75	1·00
66	9	1d. purple and red	8·50	1·25
67	9	1d. red	4·25	30
68a	9	2½d. purple and blue	17·00	4·50
69	9	2½d. blue	3·75	1·75
70	9	3d. purple and yellow	13·00	3·00
71	9	3d. purple on yellow	3·25	19·00
72	9	6d. purple and violet	27·00	32·00
73	9	6d. purple	75·00	90·00
62	9	1s. green and black	17·00	48·00
75	9	1s. black on green	5·00	8·00
76	9	5s. green and red	85·00	£200
77	9	5s. green and red on yellow	60·00	70·00

11 The Pitons

1902. 400th Anniv of Discovery by Columbus.

63	11	2d. green and brown	15·00	1·75

12 13 14

1912

78	12	½d. green	70	50
79	12	1d. red	1·90	10
93	12	1d. brown	1·40	15
94	14	1½d. red	75	2·50
95	13	2d. grey	75	15
81a	12	2½d. blue	4·25	2·75
97	12	2½d. orange	16·00	60·00
82	12	3d. purple on yellow	1·25	2·25
99a	12	3d. blue	7·00	11·00
83a	14	4d. black and red on yellow	70	1·50
102	12	6d. purple	2·00	4·75
85	12	1s. black on green	7·00	5·00
103	12	1s. brown	7·00	3·25
104	13	2s.6d. black & red on blue	18·00	30·00
88	12	5s. green and red on yellow	25·00	85·00

1916. No. 79 optd **WAR TAX** in two lines.

89	12	1d. red	15·00	21·00

1916. No. 79 optd **WAR TAX** in one line.

90	12	1d. red	1·75	30

1935. Silver Jubilee. As T **32a** of St. Helena.

109	½d. black and green	30	2·25
110	2d. blue and grey	1·50	1·75
111	2½d. brown and blue	1·75	1·75
112	1s. grey and purple	18·00	21·00

19 Port Castries

1936. King George V.

113	19	½d. black and green	30	50
114	-	1d. black and brown	40	10
115	-	1½d. black and red	70	30
116	19	2d. black and grey	60	20
117	-	2½d. black and blue	60	15
118	-	3d. black and green	1·50	70
119	19	4d. black and brown	2·00	1·25
120	-	6d. black and orange	2·00	1·25
121	-	1s. black and blue	3·50	2·50
122	-	2s.6d. black and blue	15·00	14·00
123	-	5s. black and violet	19·00	20·00
124	-	10s. black and red	60·00	£100

DESIGNS—HORIZ: 1d., 2½d., 6d. Columbus Square, Castries (inscr "Colombus Square" in error); 1s. Fort Rodney, Pigeon Island; 5s. Government House; 10s. Badge of Colony. VERT: 1½d., 3d. Ventine Falls; 2s.6d. Inniskilling Monument.

1937. Coronation. As T **32b** of St. Helena.

125	1d. violet	30	35
126	1½d. red	55	20
127	2½d. blue	55	1·25

26 King George VI

27 Columbus Square

1938. King George VI.

128a	26	½d. green	10	10
129a	26	1d. violet	30	15
129c	26	1d. red	10	10
130	26	1½d. red	2·00	40
131a	26	2d. grey	15	10
132a	26	2½d. blue	40	10
132b	26	2½d. violet	1·00	10
133a	26	3d. orange	30	10
133b	26	3½d. blue	1·00	15
134c	26	8d. brown	3·50	30
134cb	26	8d. brown	3·75	2·25
135a	-	1s. brown	1·50	30
136	-	2s. blue and purple	10·00	1·25
136a	26	3s. purple	8·00	1·75
137	-	5s. black and mauve	22·00	16·00
138	-	10s. black on yellow	17·00	9·00
141	26	£1 sepia	15·00	10·00

DESIGNS—As Type **27**: 1s. Government House; 2s. The Pitons; 5s. "Lady Hawkins" loading bananas. VERT: 10s. Device of St. Lucia as Type **33**.

1946. Victory. As T **33a** of St. Helena.

142	1d. violet	10	30
143	3½d. blue	10	30

1948. Silver Wedding. As T **33b/c** of St. Helena.

144	1d. red	15	10
145	£1 purple	17·00	35·00

33 Device of St. Lucia

1949. New Currency.

146	26	1c. green	25	10
147	26	2c. mauve	1·00	10
148	26	3c. red	1·75	3·25
149	26	4c. grey	2·00	65
150	26	5c. violet	1·75	10
151	26	6c. orange	1·50	4·00
152	26	7c. blue	4·00	3·50
153	26	12c. red	5·50	4·75
154	26	16c. brown	5·00	50
155	33	24c. blue	50	10
156	33	48c. olive	2·00	1·25
157	33	$1.20 purple	3·75	12·00
158	33	$2.40 green	8·00	19·00
159	33	$4.80 red	14·00	18·00

1949. U.P.U. As T **33d/g** of St. Helena.

160	5c. violet	15	1·00
161	6c. orange	1·60	2·50
162	12c. mauve	20	20
163	24c. green	30	20

1951. Inauguration of B.W.I. University College. As T **10a/b** of St. Kitts-Nevis.

164	3c. black and red	45	1·50
165	12c. black and red	65	1·50

34 Phoenix rising from Burning Buildings

1951. Reconstruction of Castries.

166	34	12c. red and blue	35	1·00

1951. New Constitution. Optd **NEW CONSTITUTION 1951.**

167	26	2c. mauve	20	80
168	26	4c. grey	20	60
169	26	5c. violet	25	80
170	26	12c. red	1·00	60

1953. Coronation. As T **33h** of St. Helena.

171	3c. black and red	70	10

1953. As 1949 but portrait of Queen Elizabeth II facing left and new Royal Cypher.

172		1c. green	10	10
173		2c. purple	10	10
174		3c. red	10	10
175		4c. grey	10	10
176		5c. violet	10	10
177		6c. orange	15	1·00
178		8c. red	30	10
179		10c. blue	10	10
180		15c. brown	30	10
181	33	25c. blue	30	10
182	33	50c. olive	4·50	3·75
183	33	$1 green	4·00	6·50
184	33	$2.50 red	5·50	6·50

1958. British Caribbean Federation. As T **27a** of St. Kitts-Nevis.

185	3c. green	75	20
186	6c. blue	1·00	1·75
187	12c. red	1·00	80

38 Columbus's "Santa Maria" off the Pitons

1960. New Constitution for the Windward and Leeward Islands.

188	38	8c. red	40	45
189	38	10c. orange	40	45
190	38	25c. blue	60	50

39 Stamp of 1860

1960. Stamp Centenary.

191	**39**	5c. red and blue	25	10
192	**39**	16c. blue and green	45	90
193	**39**	25c. green and red	45	15

1963. Freedom from Hunger. As T **63a** of St. Helena.

194		25c. green	40	10

1963. Cent of Red Cross. As T **63b** of St. Helena.

195		4c. red and black	20	1·50
196		25c. red and blue	50	1·50

40 Queen Elizabeth II (after A. C. Davidson-Houston)

41 Queen Elizabeth II (after A. C. Davidson-Houston)

42 Fishing Boats

1964

197	**40**	1c. red	10	10
198	**40**	2c. violet	30	1·00
199	**40**	4c. green	1·00	30
200	**40**	5c. blue	30	10
201	**40**	6c. brown	1·00	2·50
202	**41**	8c. multicoloured	10	10
203	**41**	10c. multicoloured	1·00	10
204	**42**	12c. multicoloured	50	1·75
205	-	15c. multicoloured	20	10
206	-	25c. multicoloured	20	10
207	-	35c. blue and buff	3·00	10
208	-	50c. multicoloured	2·50	10
209	-	$1 multicoloured	1·25	2·50
210	-	$2.50 multicoloured	3·00	2·00

HORIZ (as Type **42**): 15c. Pigeon Island; 25c. Reduit Beach; 35c. Castries Harbour; 50c. The Pitons. VERT (as Type **42**): $1 Vigie Beach. (As Type **41**): $2.50, Head and shoulders portrait of Queen Elizabeth II.

The 35c. and 50c. show a royal Cypher in place of the portrait.

45a Shakespeare and Memorial Theatre, Stratford-upon-Avon

1964. 400th Birth Anniv of Shakespeare.

211	**45a**	10c. green	30	10

1965. Centenary of I.T.U. As T **64a** of St. Helena.

212		2c. mauve and purple	10	10
213		50c. lilac and green	70	90

1965. I.C.Y. As T **64b** of St. Helena.

214		1c. purple and green	10	10
215		25c. green and violet	20	20

1966. Churchill Commemoration. As T **64c** of St. Helena.

216		4c. blue	15	10
217		6c. green	70	3·75
218		25c. brown	80	15
219		35c. violet	85	20

1966. Royal Visit. As T **48a** of St. Kitts-Nevis.

220		4c. black and blue	65	25
221		25c. black and mauve	1·25	75

1966. World Cup Football Championship. As T **64d** of St. Helena.

222		4c. multicoloured	25	10
223		25c. multicoloured	75	30

1966. Inauguration of W.H.O. Headquarters, Geneva. As T **64e** of St. Helena.

224		4c. black, green and blue	15	30
225		25c. black, purple and brown	45	40

1966. 20th Anniv of U.N.E.S.C.O. As T **64f/h** of St. Helena.

226		4c. multicoloured	15	10
227		12c. yellow, violet and olive	25	65
228		25c. black, purple and orange	50	35

51 Map of St. Lucia

1967. Statehood. Nos. 198, 202/9 and 257 optd **STATEHOOD 1st MARCH 1967**.

229	**40**	2c. violet (postage)	20	20
230	**40**	5c. blue	20	10
231	**40**	6c. brown	20	20
232	**41**	8c. multicoloured	1·00	10
233	**41**	10c. multicoloured	40	10
234	**42**	12c. multicoloured	40	10
235	-	15c. multicoloured	75	1·00
236	-	25c. multicoloured	40	1·75
237	-	35c. blue and buff	2·00	35
238	-	50c. multicoloured	1·50	1·75
239	-	$1 multicoloured	65	75
240	**51**	15c. blue (air)	10	10

52 "Madonna and Child with the Infant Baptist" (Raphael)

1967. Christmas.

241	**52**	4c. multicoloured	10	10
242	**52**	25c. multicoloured	30	10

53 Batsman and Sir Frederick Clarke (Governor)

1968. M.C.C.'s West Indies Tour.

243	**53**	10c. multicoloured	20	30
244	**53**	35c. multicoloured	45	55

54 "The Crucified Christ with the Virgin Mary, Saints and the Angels" (Raphael)

1968. Easter Commemoration.

245	**54**	10c. multicoloured	10	10
246	-	15c. multicoloured	10	10
247	**54**	25c. multicoloured	15	10
248	-	35c. multicoloured	15	10

DESIGN: 15, 35c. "Noli me tangere" (detail by Titian).

56 Dr. Martin Luther King

1968. Martin Luther King Commemoration.

250	**56**	25c. blue, black and flesh	15	15
251	**56**	35c. blue, black and flesh	15	15

57 "Virgin and Child in Glory" (Murillo)

1968. Christmas.

252	**57**	5c. multicoloured	10	10
253	-	10c. multicoloured	10	10
254	**57**	25c. multicoloured	15	10
255	-	35c. multicoloured	15	10

DESIGN: 10, 35c. "Madonna with Child" (Murillo).

59 Purple-throated Carib

1969. Birds. Multicoloured.

256		10c. Type **59**	35	35
257		15c. St. Lucia amazon	40	40
258		25c. Type **59**	50	45
259		35c. As 15c.	65	50

61 "Head of Christ Crowned with Thorns" (Reni)

1969. Easter. Multicoloured.

260		10c. Type **61**	10	10
261		15c. "Resurrection of Christ" (Sodoma)	10	10
262		25c. Type **61**	15	15
263		35c. As the 15c.	15	15

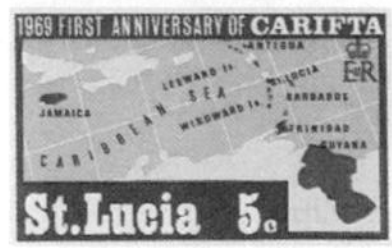

63 Map showing CARIFTA Countries

1969. First Anniv of CARIFTA.

264	**63**	5c. multicoloured	10	15
265	**63**	10c. multicoloured	10	15
266	-	25c. multicoloured	15	15
267	-	35c. multicoloured	15	15

DESIGN: 25, 35c. Handclasp and names of CARIFTA countries.

65 Emperor Napoleon and Empress Josephine

1969. Birth Bicent of Napoleon Bonaparte.

268	**65**	15c. multicoloured	10	10
269	**65**	25c. multicoloured	10	10
270	**65**	35c. multicoloured	10	10
271	**65**	50c. multicoloured	15	55

66 "Virgin and Child" (P. Delaroche)

1969. Christmas. Paintings. Multicoloured, background colours given.

272	**66**	5c. gold and purple	10	10
273	-	10c. gold and blue	10	10
274	**66**	25c. gold and red	20	10
275	-	35c. gold and green	20	10

DESIGN: 10c., 35c. "Holy Family" (Rubens).

68 House of Assembly

1970. Multicoloured.

276		1c. Type **68**	10	10
277		2c. Roman Catholic Cathedral	15	10
278		4c. The Boulevard, Castries	1·00	10
279		5c. Castries Harbour	1·50	10
280		6c. Sulphur springs	15	10
281		10c. Vigie Airport	2·00	10
282		12c. Reduit Beach	20	10
283		15c. Pigeon Island	30	10
284		25c. The Pitons and yacht	80	10
285		35c. Marigot Bay	40	10
286		50c. Diamond Waterfall	70	80
287		$1 Flag of St. Lucia	40	70
288		£2.50 St. Lucia coat of arms	55	1·75
289		$5 Queen Elizabeth II	1·00	4·00
289a		$10 Map of St. Lucia	6·00	9·00

Nos. 286/9a are vert.

69 "The Sealing of the Tomb" (Hogarth)

1970. Easter. Multicoloured.

290		25c. Type **69**	15	20
291		35c. "The Three Marys at the Tomb" (Hogarth)	15	20
292		$1 "The Ascension" (Hogarth)	30	40

The $1 is larger 39×54 mm.

Nos. 290/2 were issued in a triptych, with the $1 value 10 mm higher than the other values.

72 Charles Dickens and Dickensian Characters

1970. Death Cent of Charles Dickens.

293	**72**	1c. multicoloured	10	10
294	**72**	25c. multicoloured	20	10
295	**72**	35c. multicoloured	25	10
296	**72**	50c. multicoloured	35	1·25

73 Nurse and Emblem

1970. Cent of British Red Cross. Multicoloured.

297		10c. Type **73**	15	15
298		15c. Flags of Great Britain, Red Cross and St. Lucia	25	25
299		25c. Type **73**	35	40
300		35c. As 15c.	40	40

74 "Madonna with the Lilies" (Luca della Robbia)

1970. Christmas.

301	**74**	5c. multicoloured	10	10
302	**74**	10c. multicoloured	15	10
303	**74**	35c. multicoloured	30	10
304	**74**	40c. multicoloured	30	30

75 "Christ on the Cross" (Rubens)

1971. Easter. Multicoloured.

305	10c. Type **75**	10	10
306	15c. "Descent from the Cross" (Rubens)	15	10
307	35c. Type **75**	30	10
308	40c. As 15c.	30	40

76 Moule a Chique Lighthouse

1971. Opening of Beane Field Airport. Multicoloured.

309	5c. Type **76**	50	15
310	25c. Boeing 727-200 landing at Beane Field	50	15

77 Morne Fortune

78 Morne Fortune, Modern View

1971. Old and New Views of St. Lucia. Multicoloured.

311	5c. Type **77**	10	20
312	5c. Type **78**	10	20
313	10c. Castries City (old view)	10	20
314	10c. Castries City (modern view)	10	20
315	25c. Pigeon Island (old view)	15	30
316	25c. Pigeon Island (modern view)	15	30
317	50c. Old view from grounds of Government House	25	75
318	50c. Modern view from grounds of Government House	25	75

The old views are taken from paintings by J. H. Caddy.

79 "Virgin and Child with two Angels" (Verrocchio)

1971. Christmas. Multicoloured.

319	5c. Type **79**	10	10
320	10c. "Virgin and Child, St. John the Baptist and an Angel" (Morando)	10	10
321	35c. "Madonna and Child" (Battista)	15	10
322	40c. Type **79**	20	25

80 "St. Lucia" (Dolci School) and Coat of Arms

1971. National Day.

323	**80**	5c. multicoloured	10	10
324	**80**	10c. multicoloured	15	10
325	**80**	25c. multicoloured	25	10
326	**80**	50c. multicoloured	45	40

81 "The Dead Christ Mourned" (Carracci)

1972. Easter. Multicoloured.

327	10c. Type **81**	10	10
328	25c. "Angels weeping over the dead Christ" (Guercino)	20	10
329	35c. Type **81**	30	10
330	50c. As 25c.	40	40

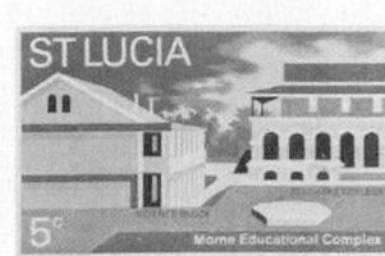

82 Science Block and Teachers' College

1972. Morne Educational Complex. Multicoloured.

331	5c. Type **82**	10	10
332	15c. University Centre	10	10
333	25c. Secondary School	10	10
334	35c. Technical College	15	10

83 Steamship Stamp and Map

1972. Centenary of First Postal Service by St. Lucia Steam Conveyance Co. Ltd.

335	**83**	5c. multicoloured	15	10
336	-	10c. blue, mauve and black	20	10
337	-	35c. red, blue and black	45	10
338	-	50c. multicoloured	75	1·00

DESIGNS: 10c. Steamship stamp and Castries Harbour; 35c. Steamship stamp and Soufriere; 50c. Steamship stamps.

84 "The Holy Family" (Sebastiano Ricci)

1972. Christmas.

339	**84**	5c. multicoloured	10	10
340	**84**	10c. multicoloured	10	10
341	**84**	35c. multicoloured	20	10
342	**84**	40c. multicoloured	25	15

1972. Royal Silver Wedding. As T **103** of St. Helena, but with Arms and St. Lucia Amazon.

343	15c. red	20	20
344	35c. green	40	40

86 Week-day Headdress

1973. Local Headdresses. Multicoloured.

345	5c. Type **86**	10	10
346	10c. Formal style	10	10
347	25c. Unmarried girl's style	15	10
348	50c. Ceremonial style	25	85

87 Coat of Arms

1973

349A	**87**	5c. green	10	75
350A	**87**	10c. blue	15	75
351A	**87**	25c. brown	15	75
953	**87**	10c. green	1·00	1·00

88 H.M.S. "St. Lucia", 1830

1973. Historic Ships. Multicoloured.

352	15c. Type **88**	20	10
353	35c. H.M.S. "Prince of Wales", 1765	30	10
354	50c. "Oliph Blossom", 1605	40	75
355	$1 H.M.S. "Rose", 1757	70	1·00
MS356	122×74 mm. Nos. 352/5	1·00	2·75

89 Plantation and Flower

1973. Banana Industry. Multicoloured.

357	5c. Type **89**	10	10
358	15c. Aerial spraying	15	10
359	35c. Boxing plant	20	10
360	50c. Loading a boat	50	40

90 "The Virgin with Child" (Maratta)

1973. Christmas. Multicoloured.

361	5c. Type **90**	10	10
362	15c. "Madonna in the Meadow" (Raphael)	10	10
363	35c. "The Holy Family" (Bronzino)	20	10
364	50c. "Madonna of the Pear" (Durer)	30	35

1973. Royal Wedding. As T **103a** of St. Helena. Multicoloured, background colours given.

365	40c. green	10	10
366	50c. lilac	10	10

91 "The Betrayal"

1974. Easter. Paintings by Ugolino da Siena. Multicoloured.

369	5c. Type **91**	60	70
370	35c. "The Way to Calvary"	80	90
371	80c. "The Deposition"	10	10
372	$1 "The Resurrection"	15	10
MS373	180×140 mm. Nos. 369/72	1·00	2·00

92 3-Escalins Coins, 1798

1974. Coins of Old St. Lucia. Multicoloured.

374	15c. Type **92**	15	15
375	35c. 6-esculins coins, 1798	20	25
376	40c. 2-livres 5-sols coins, 1813	20	10
377	$1 6-livres 15-sols coins, 1813	35	65
MS378	151×115 mm. Nos. 374/7	1·00	2·75

93 Baron de Laborie

1974. Past Governors of St. Lucia. Multicoloured.

379	5c. Type **93**	10	10
380	35c. Sir John Moore	10	10
381	80c. Sir Dudley Hill	15	10
382	$1 Sir Frederick Clarke	25	35
MS383	153×117 mm. Nos. 379/82	50	2·00

94 "Virgin and Child" (Andrea del Verrocchio)

1974. Christmas. Multicoloured.

384	5c. Type **94**	10	10
385	35c. "Virgin and Child" (Andrea della Robbia)	10	10
386	80c. "Madonna and Child" (Luca della Robbia)	15	15
387	$1 "Virgin and Child" (Rossellino)	20	25
MS388	92×140 mm. Nos. 384/7	70	2·00

95 Churchill and Montgomery

1974. Birth Centenary of Sir Winston Churchill.

389	5c. Type **95**	10	10
390	$1 Churchill and Truman	30	35

96 "Christ on the Cross" (School of Van der Weyden)

1975. Easter. Multicoloured.

391	5c. Type **96**	10	10
392	35c. "Noli me tangere" (Romano)	10	10
393	80c. "Calvary" (Gallego)	20	20
394	$1 "Noli me tangere" (Correggio)	30	35

97 "Nativity" (French Book of Hours)

1975. Christmas. Multicoloured.

399	5c. Type **97**	10	10
400	10c. "King" (stained glass window)	10	30
401	10c. "Virgin and Child" (stained glass window)	10	30
402	10c. "King and Cattle" (stained glass window)	10	30
403	40c. "Nativity" (Hastings Book of Hours)	30	10
404	$1 "Virgin and Child with Saints" (Borgognone)	70	90
MS405	105×109 mm. Nos. 399 and 403/4	75	1·00

Nos. 400/2 were printed together, *se-tenant*, forming a composite design of the Epiphany.

98 America Schooner "Hanna"

1975. Bicent of American Revolution. Ships. Multicoloured.

406	½c. Type **98**	10	30

No.	Description	Unused	Used
407	1c. "Prince of Orange" (British sailing packet)	10	30
408	2c. H.M.S. "Edward" (sloop)	15	30
409	5c. "Millern" (British merchantman)	25	10
410	15c. "Surprise" (American lugger)	40	10
411	35c. H.M.S. "Serapis" (frigate)	45	10
412	50c. "Randolph" (American frigate)	50	1·00
413	$1 "Alliance" (American frigate)	50	2·50
MS414	142×116 mm. Nos. 410/13	3·00	4·50

99 Laughing Gull

1976. Birds. Multicoloured.

No.	Description	Unused	Used
415	1c. Type **99**	30	2·00
416	2c. Little blue heron	30	2·00
417	4c. Belted kingfisher	35	1·25
418	5c. St. Lucia amazon ("St Lucia Parrot")	1·75	1·25
419	6c. St. Lucia oriole	1·25	2·00
420	8c. Grey trembler ("Trembler")	1·50	2·75
421	10c. American kestrel ("Sparrow Hawk")	1·25	35
422	12c. Red-billed tropic bird	2·00	2·50
423	15c. Moorhen ("Common Gallinule")	1·25	15
424a	25c. Common noddy ("Brown Noddy")	1·00	30
425	35c. Sooty tern	3·25	1·50
426	50c. Osprey	7·00	3·50
427	$1 White-breasted trembler ("White-breasted Thrasher")	4·00	3·50
428	$2.50 St. Lucia black finch	7·50	6·50
429	$5 Red-necked pigeon ("Ramier")	7·50	4·50
430a	$10 Caribbean elaenia	2·25	7·50

99a Caribbean Map

1976. West Indies Victory in World Cricket Cup. Multicoloured.

No.	Description	Unused	Used
431	50c. Type **99a**	1·00	1·00
432	$1 Prudential Cup	1·00	2·50
MS433	92×79 mm. Nos. 431/2	3·50	4·50

100 H.M.S. "Ceres"

1976. Royal Navy Crests. Multicoloured.

No.	Description	Unused	Used
434	10c. Type **100**	40	10
435	20c. H.M.S. "Pelican"	70	10
436	40c. H.M.S. "Ganges"	90	10
437	$2 H.M.S. "Ariadne"	2·25	2·75

101 "Madonna and Child" (Murillo)

1976. Christmas. Multicoloured.

No.	Description	Unused	Used
438	10c. Type **101**	10	10
439	20c. "Madonna and Child with Angels" (Costa)	10	10
440	50c. "Madonna and Child Enthroned" (Isenbrandt)	15	10
441	$2 "Madonna and Child with St. John" (Murillo)	50	65
MS442	105×93 mm. $2.50 As Type **101**	1·00	1·25

102 Queen Elizabeth II

1977. Silver Jubilee.

No.	Type	Description	Unused	Used
443	**102**	10c. multicoloured	10	10
444	**102**	20c. multicoloured	10	10
445	**102**	40c. multicoloured	10	15
446	**102**	$2 multicoloured	40	90
MS447		128×95 mm. **102** $2.50 multicoloured	45	1·00

103 Scouts from Tapion School

1977. Caribbean Boy Scout Jamboree. Multicoloured.

No.	Description	Unused	Used
448	½c. Type **103**	10	10
449	1c. Sea scouts	10	10
450	2c. Scout from Micoud	10	10
451	10c. Two scouts from Tapion School	20	10
452	20c. Venture scout	20	10
453	50c. Scout from Gros Islet	35	45
454	$1 Sea scouts in motor boat	50	1·00
MS455	75×85 mm. $2.50 As $1	1·10	3·00

104 "Nativity" (Giotto)

1977. Christmas. Multicoloured.

No.	Description	Unused	Used
456	½c. Type **104**	10	10
457	1c. "Perugia triptych" (Fra Angelico)	10	10
458	2c. "Virgin and Child" (El Greco)	10	10
459	20c. "Madonna of the Rosary" (Caravaggio)	15	10
460	50c. "Adoration of the Magi" (Velazquez)	20	10
461	$1 "Madonna of Carmel" (Tiepolo)	30	35
462	$2.50 "Adoration of the Magi" (Tiepolo)	45	80

105 "Susan Lunden"

1977. 400th Birth Anniv of Rubens. Multicoloured.

No.	Description	Unused	Used
463	10c. Type **105**	10	10
464	35c. "The Rape of the Sabine Women" (detail)	15	10
465	50c. "Ludovicus Nonnius"	30	10
466	$2.50 "Minerva protects Pax from Mars" (detail)	85	90
MS467	145×120 mm. Nos. 463/6	1·25	2·25

106 Yeoman of the Guard and Life Guard

1978. 25th Anniv of Coronation. Multicoloured.

No.	Description	Unused	Used
468	15c. Type **106**	10	10
469	20c. Groom and postillion	10	10
470	50c. Footman and coachman	10	10
471	$3 State trumpeter and herald	35	1·25
MS472	114×88 mm. $5 Master of the Horse and Gentleman-at-Arms	60	90

107 Queen Angelfish

1978. Fish. Multicoloured.

No.	Description	Unused	Used
473	10c. Type **107**	40	10
474	20c. Four-eyed butterflyfish	60	10
475	50c. French angelfish	90	30
476	$2 Yellow-tailed damselfish	1·10	2·75
MS477	155×89 mm. $2.50 Rock beauty	2·25	1·90

108 French Grenadier and Map of the Battle

1978. Bicent of Battle of Cul-de-Sac. Multicoloured.

No.	Description	Unused	Used
478	10c. Type **108**	60	15
479	30c. British Grenadier officer and Map of St. Lucia (Bellin), 1762	1·00	20
480	50c. Coastline from Gros Islet to Cul-de-Sac and British Fleet opposing French landings	1·10	25
481	$2.50 General James Grant, 1798, and Light Infantrymen of 46th Regiment	1·90	2·50

109 The Annunciation

1978. Christmas. Multicoloured.

No.	Description	Unused	Used
482	30c. Type **109**	10	10
483	50c. Type **109**	15	10
484	55c. The Nativity	15	10
485	80c. As 55c.	20	20

110 Hewanorra International Air Terminal

1979. Independence. Multicoloured.

No.	Description	Unused	Used
486	10c. Type **110**	10	10
487	30c. New coat of arms	10	10
488	50c. Government House and Sir Allen Lewis (first Governor-General)	15	10
489	$2 French, St. Lucia and Union flags on map of St. Lucia	30	45
MS490	127×80 mm. Nos. 486/9	50	1·00

111 Popes Paul VI and John Paul I

1979. Pope Paul VI Commemoration. Multicoloured.

No.	Description	Unused	Used
491	10c. Type **111**	10	10
492	30c. Pres. Sadat of Egypt with Pope Paul	20	10
493	50c. Pope Paul with Secretary-General U Thant	35	10
494	55c. Pope Paul and Prince Minister Golda Meir of Israel	40	25
495	$2 Martin Luther King received in audience by Pope Paul	1·00	70

112 Dairy Farming

1979. Agricultural Diversification. Multicoloured.

No.	Description	Unused	Used
496	10c. Type **112**	10	10
497	35c. Fruit and vegetables	10	10
498	50c. Water conservation	20	10
499	$3 Copra industry	75	1·10

113 Lindbergh and Sikorsky S-38A Flying Boat

1979. 50th Anniv of Lindbergh's Inaugural Airmail Flight via St. Lucia.

No.	Type	Description	Unused	Used
500	**113**	10c. black, red and orange	50	10
501	-	30c. multicoloured	60	10
502	-	50c. multicoloured	60	10
503	-	$2 multicoloured	80	85

DESIGNS: 30c. Sikorsky S-38A flying boat and route map; 50c. Arrival at La Toc, September, 1929; $2 Letters on first flight.

114 "A Prince of Saxony" (Cranach the Elder)

1979. International Year of the Child. Famous Paintings. Multicoloured.

No.	Description	Unused	Used
504	10c. Type **114**	10	10
505	50c. "The Infanta Margarita" (Velazquez)	15	10
506	$2 "Girl playing Badminton" (Chardin)	45	40
507	$2.50 "Mary and Francis Wilcox" (Stock)	45	45
MS508	113×94 mm. $5 "Two Children" (Picasso)	1·10	1·25

115 Notice of Introduction of Penny Post

1979. Death Cent of Sir Rowland Hill. Multicoloured.

No.	Description	Unused	Used
509	10c. Type **115**	10	10
510	50c. Wyon essay	15	10
511	$2 First St. Lucia stamp	25	50
512	$2.50 G.B. 1840 Penny Black	35	60
MS513	111×85 mm. $5 Sir Rowland Hill	70	90

116 "Madonna and Child" (Bernardino Fungai)

1979. Christmas. International Year of the Child. Paintings of the "Madonna and Child" by artists named. Multicoloured.

No.	Description	Unused	Used
514	10c. Type **116**	10	10
515	50c. Carlo Dolci	20	10
516	$2 Titian	50	50
517	$2.50 Giovanni Bellini	60	50
MS518	94×120 mm. Nos. 514/17	1·25	1·60

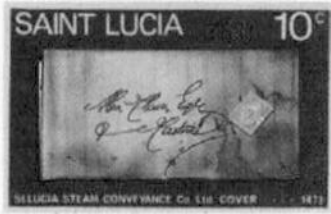

117 St. Lucia Steam Conveyance Co. Ltd. Cover, 1873

1980. "London 1980" Int Stamp Exhibition. Multicoloured.

No.	Description	Unused	Used
519	10c. Type **117**	10	10
520	30c. S.S. "Assistance" 1d. postmark, 1879	10	10
521	50c. Postage due handstamp, 1929	15	10
522	$2 Crowned-circle Paid stamp, 1844	40	55
MS523	86×76 mm. Nos. 519/22	65	90

118 Mickey Mouse astride Rocket

1980. Tenth Anniv (1979) of Moon Landing. Disney characters in Space Scenes. Multicoloured.

524	½c. Type **118**	10	10
525	1c. Donald Duck being towed by rocket (horiz)	10	10
526	2c. Minnie Mouse on Moon	10	10
527	3c. Goofy hitching lift to Mars	10	10
528	4c. Goofy and Moondog (horiz)	10	10
529	5c. Pluto burying bone on Moon (horiz)	10	10
530	10c. Donald Duck and love-sick Martian (horiz)	10	10
531	$2 Donald Duck paddling spaceship (horiz)	1·40	1·00
532	$2.50 Mickey Mouse driving moonbuggy (horiz)	1·40	1·10
MS533	102×127 mm. $5 Goofy leaping from space-ship on to Moon	3·25	2·75

119 Queen Elizabeth the Queen Mother

1980. 80th Birthday of The Queen Mother.

534	**119**	10c. multicoloured	15	10
535	**119**	$2.50 multicoloured	35	1·00
MS536	85×65 mm. **119** $3 multi-coloured		60	1·50

120 Hawker Siddeley H.S.748

1980. Transport. Multicoloured.

537	5c. Type **120**	30	30
538	10c. Douglas DC-10-30 airliner	65	30
539	15c. Local bus	35	40
540	20c. "Geestcrest" (freighter)	35	40
541	25c. Britten Norman Islander aircraft	65	30
542	30c. "Charles" (pilot boat)	40	50
543	50c. Boeing 727-200 airliner	1·00	60
544	75c. "Cunard Countess" (liner)	65	1·25
545	$1 Lockheed TriStar 500 airliner	85	1·40
546	$2 "Booker Vulcan" (cargo liner)	1·25	2·00
547	$5 Boeing 707-420 airliner	5·00	6·00
548	$10 "Queen Elizabeth 2" (liner)	5·00	8·00

121 Shot-putting

1980. Olympic Games, Moscow. Multicoloured.

549	10c. Type **121**	10	10
550	50c. Swimming	20	10
551	$2 Gymnastics	80	50
552	$2.50 Weightlifting	90	60
MS553	108×83 mm. $5 Athletes with Olympic torch	1·50	1·40

122 Coastal Landscape within Cogwheel

1980. 75th Anniv of Rotary International. Different coastal landscapes within cogwheel.

554	**122**	10c. multicoloured	10	10
555	-	50c. multicoloured	15	10
556	-	$2 black, red and yellow	40	40
557	-	$2.50 multicoloured	50	55
MS558	108×106 mm. $5 multicoloured		1·25	1·75

123 Sir Arthur Lewis

1980. Nobel Prize Winners. Multicoloured.

559	10c. Type **123**	10	10
560	50c. Martin Luther King Jnr	20	15
561	$2 Ralph Bunche	50	60
562	$2.50 Albert Schweitzer	70	80
MS563	115×91 mm. $5 Albert Einstein	2·25	2·00

1980. Hurricane Relief. Nos. 538/9 and 542 surch **$1.50 1980 HURRICANE RELIEF.**

564	$1.50 on 15c. multicoloured	30	40
565	$1.50 on 20c. multicoloured	30	40
566	$1.50 on 50c. multicoloured	30	40

125 "The Nativity" (Giovanni Battista)

1980. Christmas. Paintings. Multicoloured.

567	10c. Type **125**	10	10
568	30c. "Adoration of the Kings" (Pieter the Elder)	10	10
569	$2 "Adoration of the Shepherds" (ascribed to Murillo)	40	60
MS570	102×88 mm. $1×3, Angel with people of St. Lucia (composite design) (each 30×75 mm)	80	90

126 Brazilian Agouti

1981. Wildlife. Multicoloured.

571	10c. Type **126**	15	10
572	50c. St. Lucia amazon ("St. Lucia Parrot")	1·00	20
573	$2 Purple-throated carib	1·75	80
574	$2.50 Fiddler crab	1·25	1·00
MS575	103×87 mm. $5 "Danaus plexippus" (butterfly)	2·40	2·50

127 Prince Charles at Balmoral

1981. Royal Wedding. Multicoloured.

576	25c. Prince Charles and Lady Diana Spencer	10	10
577	50c. Clarence House	10	10
578	$4 Type **127**	40	55
MS579	96×82 mm. $5 Class Coach and coachman	50	50

128 Lady Diana Spencer

1981. Royal Wedding. Multicoloured. Self-adhesive.

580	50c. Type **128**	25	45
581	$2 Prince Charles	30	60
582	$5 Prince Charles and Lady Diana Spencer	1·50	1·75

129 "The Cock"

1981. Birth Bicentenary of Picasso. Multicoloured.

583	30c. Type **129**	25	10
584	50c. "Man with an Ice-cream"	35	10
585	55c. "Woman dressing her Hair"	35	10
586	$3 "Seated Woman"	95	85
MS587	128×102 mm. $5 "Night Fishing at Antibes"	1·75	1·75

130 "Industry"

1981. 25th Anniv of Duke of Edinburgh Award Scheme. Multicoloured.

588	10c. Type **130**	10	10
589	35c. "Community service"	15	10
590	50c. "Physical recreation"	15	10
591	$2.50 Duke of Edinburgh speaking at Caribbean Conference, 1975	45	70

131 Louis Braille

1981. International Year for Disabled People. Famous Disabled People. Multicoloured.

592	10c. Type **131**	20	10
593	50c. Sarah Bernhardt	20	10
594	$2 Joseph Pulitzer	70	70
595	$2.50 Henri de Toulouse-Lautrec	1·00	85
MS596	115×90 mm. $5 Franklin Delano Roosevelt	1·00	1·25

132 "Portrait of Fanny Travis Cochran" (Cecilia Beaux)

1981. Decade for Women. Paintings. Multicoloured.

597	10c. Type **132**	10	10
598	50c. "Women with Dove" (Marie Laurencin)	25	10
599	$2 "Portrait of a Young Pupil of David" (Aimee Duvivier)	75	70
600	$2.50 "Self-portrait" (Rosalba Carriera)	90	85
MS601	104×78 mm. "Self-portrait" (Elizabeth Vigee-le-Brun)	1·00	1·25

133 "Adoration of the Magi" (Sfoza)

1981. Christmas. Paintings. Multicoloured.

602	10c. Type **133**	10	10
603	30c. "The Adoration of the Kings" (Orcanga)	20	10
604	$1.50 "The Adoration of the Kings" (Gerard)	45	50
605	$2.50 "The Adoration of the Kings" (Foppa)	75	85

134 1860 1d. Stamp

1981. First Anniv of U.P.U. Membership. Multicoloured.

606	10c. Type **134**	20	10
607	30c. 1969 First Anniversary of Caribbean Free Trade Area 25c. commemorative	40	10
608	50c. 1979 Independence $2 commemorative	45	50
609	$2 U.P.U. emblem with U.P.U. and St. Lucia flags	1·40	2·25
MS610	128×109 mm. $5 U.P.U. Head-quarters, Berne and G.P.O. Building, Castries	1·00	1·50

135 Scene from Football Match

1982. World Cup Football Championship, Spain.

611	**135**	10c. multicoloured	60	10
612	-	50c. multicoloured	1·00	15
613	-	$2 multicoloured	1·50	90
614	-	$2.50 multicoloured	1·50	1·00
MS615	104×84 mm.–$5 multicoloured		2·50	2·25

DESIGNS: 50c. to $5, Scenes from different matches.

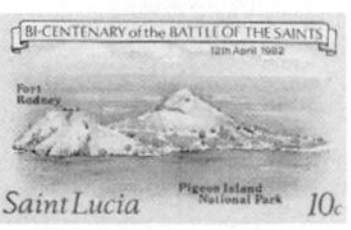

136 Pigeon Island National Park

1982. Bicent of Battle of the Saints. Multicoloured.

616	10c. Type **136**	25	15
617	35c. Battle scene	80	15
618	50c. Rodney (English admiral) and De Grasse (French admiral)	1·10	65
619	$2.50 Map of the Saints, Martinique and St. Lucia	3·75	4·50
MS620	125×75 mm. Nos. 616/19	6·50	7·00

137 Map-reading

1982. 75th Anniv of Boy Scout Movement. Multicoloured.

621	10c. Type **137**	10	10
622	50c. First Aid practice	30	15
623	$1.50 Camping	75	80
624	$2.50 Campfire singsong	1·25	1·50

138 Leeds Castle

1982. 21st Birthday of Princess of Wales. Multicoloured.

625	50c. Type **138**	30	20
626	$2 Princess Diana boarding aircraft	2·25	75
627	$4 Wedding	2·25	1·40
MS628	102×75 mm. $5 Princess of Wales	4·00	2·00

139 "Adoration of the Kings" (detail, Jan Brueghel)

1982. Christmas. Multicoloured.

629	10c. Type **139**	10	10

630	30c. "Nativity" (Lorenzo Costa)	15	10
631	50c. "Virgin and Child" (Fra Filippo Lippi)	25	15
632	80c. "Adoration of the Shepherds" (Nicolas Poussin)	40	55

140 The Pitons

1983. Commonwealth Day. Multicoloured.

633	10c. Type **140**	10	10
634	30c. Tourist beach	15	10
635	50c. Banana harvesting	20	15
636	$2 Flag of St. Lucia	1·50	2·00

141 Crown Agents Headquarters, Millbank, London

1983. 150th Anniv of Crown Agents. Multicoloured.

637	10c. Type **141**	10	10
638	15c. Road construction	10	10
639	50c. Road network map	30	25
640	$2 First St. Lucia stamp	65	1·25

142 Communications at Sea

1983. World Communications Year. Multicoloured.

641	10c. Type **142**	15	10
642	50c. Communications in the air	40	15
643	$1.50 T.V. transmission via satellite	90	75
644	$2.50 Computer communications	1·40	1·25
MS645	107×88 mm. $5 Weather satellite	1·50	1·75

143 Long-jawed Squirrelfish

1983. Coral Reef Fish. Multicoloured.

646	10c. Type **143**	10	10
647	50c. Banded butterflyfish	20	15
648	$1.50 Black-barred soldierfish	60	1·75
649	$2.50 Yellow-tailed snapper	80	1·60
MS650	122×97 mm. $5 Red hind	2·50	3·25

144 "Duke of Sutherland" (1930)

1983. Leaders of the World. Railway Locomotives (1st series).

651	**144**	35c. multicoloured	15	20
652	-	35c. multicoloured	15	20
653	-	35c. multicoloured	15	20
654	-	35c. multicoloured	15	20
655	-	50c. multicoloured	20	30
656	-	50c. multicoloured	20	30
657	-	50c. multicoloured	20	30
658	-	50c. multicoloured	20	30
659	-	$1 multicoloured	25	50
660	-	$1 multicoloured	25	50
661	-	$1 multicoloured	25	50
662	-	$1 multicoloured	25	50
663	-	$2 multicoloured	30	70
664	-	$2 multicoloured	30	70
665	-	$2 multicoloured	30	70
666	-	$2 multicoloured	30	70

DESIGNS—(The first in each pair shows technical drawings and the second the locomotive at work): Nos. 651/2, "Duke of Sutherland", Great Britain (1930); 653/4, "City of Glasgow", Great Britain (1940); 655/6, "Lord Nelson", Great Britain (1926); 657/8, "Leeds United", Great Britain (1928); 659/60, "Bodmin", Great Britain (1945); 661/2, "Eton", Great Britain (1930); 663/4, "Flying Scotsman", Great Britain (1923); 665/6, "Rocket", Great Britain (1829).

See also Nos. 715/26, 761/76, 824/31 and 858/73.

145 "The Niccolini-Cowper Madonna"

1983. Christmas. 500th Birth Anniv of Raphael. Multicoloured.

667	10c. Type **145**	10	10
668	30c. "The Holy Family with a Palm Tree"	15	10
669	50c. "The Sistine Madonna"	20	30
670	$5 "The Alba Madonna"	70	3·25

146 George III

1984. Leaders of the World. British Monarchs. Multicoloured.

671	5c. Battle of Waterloo	10	15
672	5c. Type **146**	10	15
673	10c. George III at Kew	10	15
674	10c. Kew Palace	10	15
675	35c. Coat of Arms of Elizabeth I	10	20
676	35c. Elizabeth I	10	20
677	60c. Coat of Arms of George III	20	35
678	60c. George III (different)	20	35
679	$1 Elizabeth I at Hatfield	20	40
680	$1 Hatfield Palace	20	40
681	$2.50 Spanish Armada	50	60
682	$2.50 Elizabeth I (different)	50	60

147 Clarke & Co's Drug Store

1984. Historic Buildings. Multicoloured.

683	10c. Type **147**	10	10
684	45c. Colonial architecture (horiz)	30	25
685	65c. Colonial "chattel" house (horiz)	45	35
686	$2.50 Treasury after 1906 earthquake (horiz)	1·75	1·60

148 Logwood

1984. Forestry Resources. Multicoloured.

699	10c. Type **148**	15	10
700	45c. Calabash	40	30
701	65c. Gommier (vert)	35	55
702	$2.50 Raintree	65	2·75

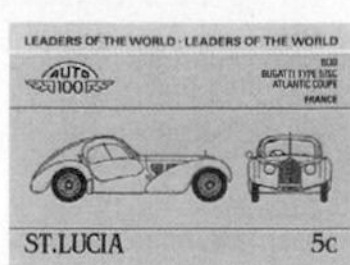

149 Bugatti Type "57SC Atlantic Coupe"

1984. Leaders of the World. Automobiles (1st series). The first in each pair showing technical drawings and the second paintings.

703	**149**	5c. black, lilac and yellow	10	10
704	-	5c. multicoloured	10	10
705	-	10c. black, blue and red	10	10
706	-	10c. multicoloured	10	10
707	-	$1 black, green and brown	15	25
708	-	$1 multicoloured	15	25
709	-	$2.50 black, pink and blue	30	40
710	-	$2.50 multicoloured	30	40

DESIGNS: Nos. 703/4, Bugatti Type "57SC Atlantic Coupe"; 705/6, Chevrolet "Bel Air Convertible"; 707/8, Alfa Romeo "1750 GS (Zagato)"; 709/10, Duesenberg "SJ Roadster".

See also Nos. 745/60, 789/96 and 902/13.

150 Pygmy Gecko

1984. Endangered Wildlife. Multicoloured.

711	10c. Type **150**	20	10
712	45c. Maria Island ground lizard	35	50
713	65c. Green iguana	40	85
714	$2.50 Couresse snake	45	3·50

1984. Leaders of the World. Railway Locomotives (2nd series). As T **144**, the first in each pair showing technical drawings and the second the locomotive at work.

715	1c. multicoloured	10	10
716	1c. multicoloured	10	10
717	15c. multicoloured	10	15
718	15c. multicoloured	10	15
719	50c. multicoloured	15	15
720	50c. multicoloured	15	15
721	75c. multicoloured	15	20
722	75c. multicoloured	15	20
723	$1 multicoloured	20	25
724	$1 multicoloured	20	25
725	$2 multicoloured	25	35
726	$2 multicoloured	25	35

DESIGNS: Nos. 715/16, "Taw", Great Britain (1897); 717/18, Class Be 6/8 "Crocodile" electric locomotive, Switzerland (1920); 719/20, "The Countess", Great Britain (1903); 721/2, Class GE 6/6 electric locomotive, Switzerland (1921); 723/4, Class P8, Germany (1906); 725/6, "Adler", Germany (1835).

151 Men's Volleyball

1984. Leaders of the World. Olympic Games, Los Angeles. Multicoloured.

727	5c. Type **151**	10	10
728	5c. Women's volleyball	10	10
729	10c. Women's hurdles	10	10
730	10c. Men's hurdles	10	10
731	65c. Show jumping	15	20
732	65c. Dressage	15	20
733	$2.50 Women's gymnastics	40	50
734	$2.50 Men's gymnastics	40	50

152 Glass of Wine and Flowers

1984. Christmas. Multicoloured.

735	10c. Type **152**	10	10
736	35c. Priest and decorated altar	10	10
737	65c. Nativity scene	15	25
738	$3 Holy Family	50	1·50
MS739	147×77 mm. Nos. 735/8	1·60	4·50

153 Slaves preparing Manioc

1984. 150th Anniv of Abolition of Slavery. Each black and brown.

740	10c. Type **153**	10	10
741	35c. Sifting and cooking cassava flour	10	10
742	55c. Cooking pot, and preparing tobacco	10	20
743	$5 Stripping tobacco leaves for twist tobacco	90	2·50
MS744	154×110 mm. As Nos. 740/3, but without dates and side inscription and with the face values in different positions	1·50	4·50

1984. Leaders of the World. Automobiles (2nd series). As T **149**, the first in each pair showing technical drawings and the second paintings.

745	10c. black, green and brown	10	10
746	10c. multicoloured	10	10
747	30c. black, blue and green	15	15
748	30c. multicoloured	15	15
749	55c. black, yellow and brown	15	30
750	55c. multicoloured	15	30
751	65c. black, grey and lilac	15	35
752	65c. multicoloured	15	35
753	75c. black, brown and red	15	35
754	75c. multicoloured	15	35
755	$1 black, brown and blue	15	40
756	$1 multicoloured	15	40
757	$2 black, green and red	20	50
758	$2 multicoloured	20	50
759	$3 black, brown and red	25	60
760	$3 multicoloured	25	60

DESIGNS: Nos. 745/6, Panhard and Levassor; 747/8, N.S.U. "RO-80" Saloon; 749/50, Abarth "Bialbero"; 751/2, TVR "Vixen 2500M"; 753/4, Ford "Mustang" Convertible; 755/6, Ford "Model T"; 757/8, Aston Martin "DB3S"; 759/60, Chrysler "Imperial CG Dual Cowl" Phaeton.

1985. Leaders of the World. Railway Locomotives (3rd series). As T **144**, the first in each pair showing technical drawings and the second the locomotive at work.

761	5c. multicoloured	10	20
762	5c. multicoloured	10	20
763	15c. multicoloured	10	20
764	15c. multicoloured	10	20
765	35c. multicoloured	15	20
766	35c. multicoloured	15	20
767	60c. multicoloured	15	25
768	60c. multicoloured	15	25
769	75c. multicoloured	15	30
770	75c. multicoloured	15	30
771	$1 multicoloured	15	30
772	$1 multicoloured	15	30
773	$2 multicoloured	25	45
774	$2 multicoloured	25	45
775	$2.50 multicoloured	30	55
776	$2.50 multicoloured	30	55

DESIGNS: Nos. 761/2, Class C53, Japan (1928); 763/4, Class L No. 39, India (1885); 765/6, Class B18¼, Australia (1926); 767/8, "Owain Glyndwr", Great Britain (1923); 769/70, "Lion", Great Britain (1838); 771/2, LNWR locomotive, Great Britain (1873); 773/4, Class Q6 No. 2238, Great Britain (1921); 775/6, Class H No. 106, Great Britain (1920).

154 Girl Guide Badge in Shield and Crest of St. Lucia

1985. 75th Anniv of Girl Guide Movement and 60th Anniv of Guiding in St. Lucia.

777	**154**	10c. multicoloured	50	10
778	**154**	35c. multicoloured	1·50	15
779	**154**	65c. multicoloured	2·00	75
780	**154**	$3 multicoloured	4·25	7·50

155 "Clossiana selene"

1985. Leaders of the World. Butterflies. Multicoloured.

781	15c. Type **155**	10	10
782	15c. "Inachis io"	10	10
783	40c. "Philaethria dido"	10	15
784	40c. "Callicore sorana"	10	15
785	60c. "Kallima inachus"	15	15
786	60c. "Hypanartia paullus"	15	15
787	$2.25 "Morpho helena"	25	50

788	$2.25 "Ornithoptera meridionalis"	25	50

1985. Leaders of the World. Automobiles (3rd series). As T **149**, the first in each pair showing technical drawings and the second paintings.

789	15c. black, blue and red	10	10
790	15c. multicoloured	10	10
791	50c. black, orange and red	15	20
792	50c. multicoloured	15	20
793	$1 black, green and orange	15	20
794	$1 multicoloured	15	20
795	$1.50 black, green and brown	20	35
796	$1.50 multicoloured	20	35

DESIGNS: 789/90, Hudson "Eight" (1940); 791/2, KdF (1937); 793/4, Kissel "Goldbug" (1925); 795/6, Ferrari "246 GTS" (1973).

156 Grenadier, 70th Regiment, c. 1775

1985. Military Uniforms. Multicoloured.

928	5c. Type **156**	40	80
798	10c. Officer, Grenadier Company, 14th Regiment, 1780	40	15
930	15c. Private, Battalion Company, 2nd West India Regiment, 1803	55	35
799	20c. Officer, Battalion Company, 46th Regiment, 1781	60	30
800	25c. Officer, Royal Artillery, c. 1782	60	15
801	30c. Officer, Royal Engineers, 1782	80	30
802	35c. Officer, Battalion Company, 54th Regiment, 1782	70	20
935	45c. Private, Grenadier Company, 14th Regiment, 1782	85	50
936	50c. Gunner, Royal Artillery, 1796	95	60
937	60c. Officer, Battalion Company, 5th Regiment, 1778	1·10	70
805	65c. Private, Battalion Company, 85th Regiment, c. 1796	90	55
806	75c. Private, Battalion Company, 76th Regiment, c. 1796	90	80
940	80c. Officer, Battalion Company, 27th Regiment, c. 1780	1·50	90
807	90c. Private, Battalion Company, 81st Regiment, c. 1796	1·00	90
808	$1 Sergeant, 74th (Highland) Regiment, 1796	1·10	90
943	$2.50 Private, Light Company, 93rd Regiment, 1803	3·50	5·00
944	$5 Private, Battalion Company, 1st West India Regiment, 1803	4·25	10·00
811	$15 Officer, Royal Artillery, 1850	8·00	20·00
946	$20 Private, Grenadier Company, 46th Regiment, 1778	18·00	28·00

157 Messerschmitt Bf 109E

1985. Leaders of the World. Military Aircraft. The first in each pair shows paintings and the second technical drawings.

812	**157**	5c. multicoloured	10	15
813	-	5c. black, blue and yellow	10	15
814	-	55c. multicoloured	25	40
815	-	55c. black, blue and yellow	25	40
816	-	60c. multicoloured	25	40
817	-	60c. black, blue and yellow	25	40
818	-	$2 multicoloured	40	75
819	-	$2 black, blue and yellow	40	75

DESIGNS: Nos. 812/13, Messerschmitt Bf 109E; 814/15, Avro Type 683 Lancaster Mk I; 816/17, North American P-51D Mustang; 818/19, Supermarine Spitfire Mk II.

158 Magnificent Frigate Birds ("Frigate Bird"), Frigate Island Bird Sanctuary

1985. Nature Reserves. Multicoloured.

820	10c. Type **158**	35	20
821	35c. Mangrove cuckoo, Scorpion Island, Savannes Bay	65	45
822	65c. Lesser yellowlegs ("Yellow Sandpiper"), Maria Island Reserve	75	85
823	$3 Audubon's shearwaters, Lapins Island Reserve	1·00	5·00

1985. Leaders of the World Railway Locomotives (4th series). As T **144**. The first in each pair shows technical drawings and the second the locomotive at work.

824	10c. multicoloured	10	10
825	10c. multicoloured	10	10
826	30c. multicoloured	15	15
827	30c. multicoloured	15	15
828	75c. multicoloured	20	25
829	75c. multicoloured	20	25
830	$2.50 multicoloured	40	70
831	$2.50 multicoloured	40	70

DESIGNS: Nos. 824/5, Tank locomotive No. 28, Great Britain (1897); 826/7, Class M No. 1621, Great Britain (1893); 828/9, Class "Dunalastair", Great Britain (1896); 830/1, "Big Bertha" type No. 2290, Great Britain (1919).

159 Queen Elizabeth the Queen Mother

1985. Leaders of the World. Life and Times of Queen Elizabeth the Queen Mother. Various portraits.

832	**159**	40c. multicoloured	10	20
833	-	40c. multicoloured	10	20
834	-	75c. multicoloured	15	25
835	-	75c. multicoloured	15	25
836	-	$1.10 multicoloured	15	35
837	-	$1.10 multicoloured	15	35
838	-	$1.75 multicoloured	20	55
839	-	$1.75 multicoloured	20	55
MS840		84×114 mm – $2 multicoloured; $2 multicoloured	60	1·40

Each value was issued in pairs showing a floral pattern across the bottom of the portraits which stops short of the left-hand edge on the first stamp and of the right-hand edge on the second.

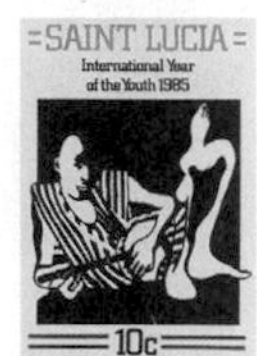

160 "Youth playing Banjo" (Wayne Whitfield)

1985. International Youth Year. Paintings by Young St. Lucians.

841	**160**	10c. black, blue and mauve	20	10
842	-	45c. multicoloured	50	25
843	-	75c. multicoloured	50	50
844	-	$3.50 multicoloured	1·00	3·00
MS845		123×86 mm. – $5 multicoloured	1·25	3·50

DESIGNS—VERT (as T **160**): 45c. "Motor-cyclist" (Mark Maragh); 75c. "Boy and Girl at Pitons" (Bartholomew Eugene); $3.50, "Abstract" (Lyndon Samuel). HORIZ (80×55 mm): $5 Young people and St. Lucia landscapes.

1985. Royal Visit. Nos. 649, 685/6, 702, 713, 778 and 836/7 optd **CARIBBEAN ROYAL VISIT 1985**.

846	**154**	35c. multicoloured	6·50	3·00
847	-	65c. mult (No. 685)	1·00	2·75
848	-	65c. mult (No. 713)	6·00	3·75
849	-	$1.10 mult (No. 836)	5·00	8·50
850	-	$1.10 mult (No. 837)	5·00	8·50
851	-	$2.50 mult (No. 649)	8·00	9·00
852	-	$2.50 mult (No. 686)	1·00	4·00
853	-	$2.50 mult (No. 702)	1·00	4·00

161 "Papa Jab"

1985. Christmas. Masqueraders. Multicoloured.

854	10c. Type **161**	30	10
855	45c. "Paille Bananne"	40	30
856	65c. "Cheval Bois"	40	1·50
MS857	70×83 mm. $4 "Madonna and Child" (Dunstan St. Omer)	1·00	1·90

1986. Leaders of the World. Railway Locomotives (5th series). As T **144**. The first in each pair shows technical drawings and the second the locomotive at work.

858	5c. multicoloured	10	15
859	5c. multicoloured	10	15
860	15c. multicoloured	15	15
861	15c. multicoloured	15	15
862	30c. multicoloured	20	30
863	30c. multicoloured	20	30
864	60c. multicoloured	25	40
865	60c. multicoloured	25	40
866	75c. multicoloured	30	50
867	75c. multicoloured	30	50
868	$1 multicoloured	35	60
869	$1 multicoloured	35	60
870	$2.25 multicoloured	45	80
871	$2.25 multicoloured	45	80
872	$3 multicoloured	45	80
873	$3 multicoloured	45	80

DESIGNS: Nos. 858/9, Cog locomotive "Tip Top", U.S.A. (1983); 860/1, Electric locomotive "Stephenson", Great Britain (1975); 862/3, Class D No. 737, Great Britain (1901); 864/5, No. 13 Class electric locomotive, Great Britain (1922); 866/7, Electric locomotive "Electra", Great Britain (1954); 868/9, "City of Newcastle", Great Britain (1922); 870/1, Von Kruckenburg propeller-driven railcar, Germany (1930); 872/3, No. 860, Japan (1893).

162 Campfire Cooking Utensils

1986. 75th Anniv of Girl Guide Movement and Boy Scouts of America. Two sheets, each 85×113 mm, containing vert designs as T **162**. Multicoloured.

MS874	$4 Type **162**; $4 Scout salute	2·75	4·25
MS875	$6 Wickerwork; $6 Lady Baden-Powell	2·75	4·25

The two stamps in each sheet were printed together, se-tenant, forming a composite design.

Nos. **MS**874/5 exist with plain or decorative margins.

Overprints on these miniature sheets commemorating "Capex '87" International Stamp Exhibition, Toronto, were not authorised by the St. Lucia administration.

162a Queen Elizabeth II

1986. 60th Birthday of Queen Elizabeth II (1st issue). Multicoloured.

876	5c. Type **162a**	10	10
877	$1 Princess Elizabeth	15	30
878	$3.50 Queen Elizabeth II (different)	40	1·10
879	$6 In Canberrra, 1982 (vert)	55	1·60
MS880	85×115 mm. $8 Queen Elizabeth II (different)	3·25	6·00

163 Queen Elizabeth and Marian Home

1986. 60th Birthday of Queen Elizabeth II (2nd issue). Multicoloured.

881	10c. Type **163**	60	15
882	45c. Queen addressing rally, Mindoo Phillip Park, 1985	1·00	35
883	50c. Queen opening Leon Hess Comprehensive School, 1985	1·10	50
884	$5 Queen Elizabeth and Government House, Castries	3·50	6·50
MS885	121×85 mm. $7 Queen Elizabeth and Royal Yacht "Britannia", Castries	4·75	7·50

164 Pope John Paul II kissing Ground, Castries Airport

1986. Visit of Pope John Paul II. Multicoloured.

886	55c. Type **164**	1·50	80
887	60c. Pope and St. Joseph's Convent	1·50	90
888	80c. Pope and Castries Catholic Cathedral (vert)	1·75	2·25
MS889	85×123 mm. $6 Pope John Paul II (vert)	9·00	10·00

164a Miss Sarah Ferguson

1986. Royal Wedding (1st issue). Multicoloured.

890	80c. Type **164a**	65	85
891	80c. Prince Andrew	65	85
892	$2 Prince Andrew and Miss Sarah Ferguson (horiz)	90	2·00
893	$2 Prince Andrew with Mrs. Nancy Reagan (horiz)	90	2·00

See also Nos. 897/901.

165 Peace Corps Teacher with Students

1986. 25th Anniv of United States Peace Corps. Multicoloured.

894	80c. Type **165**	30	40
895	$2 President John Kennedy (vert)	90	1·75
896	$3.50 Peace Corps emblem between arms of St. Lucia and U.S.A.	1·25	3·00

166 Prince Andrew in Carriage

1986. Royal Wedding (2nd issue). Multicoloured.

897	50c. Type **166**	40	30
898	80c. Miss Sarah Ferguson in coach	50	50
899	$1 Duke and Duchess of York at altar	55	60
900	$3 Duke and Duchess of York in carriage	1·00	2·75
MS901	115×85 mm. $7 Duke and Duchess of York on Palace balcony after wedding (horiz)	3·75	6·50

1986. Automobiles (4th series). As T **149**, the first in each pair showing technical drawings and the second paintings.

902	20c. multicoloured	15	15
903	20c. multicoloured	15	15
904	50c. multicoloured	15	20
905	50c. multicoloured	15	20
906	60c. multicoloured	15	20
907	60c. multicoloured	15	20
908	$1 multicoloured	15	20
909	$1 multicoloured	15	20
910	$1.50 multicoloured	20	20
911	$1.50 multicoloured	20	20
912	$3 multicoloured	30	45
913	$3 multicoloured	30	45

DESIGNS: Nos. 902/3, AMC "AMX" (1969); 904/5, Russo-Baltique (1912); 906/7, Lincoln "K.B" (1932); 908/9, Rolls-Royce "Phantom II Continental" (1933); 910/11, Buick "Century" (1939); 912/13, Chrysler "300 C" (1957).

167 Chak-Chak Band

1986. Tourism (1st series). Multicoloured.

914	15c. Type **167**	15	10
915	45c. Folk dancing	25	15
916	80c. Steel band	40	55
917	$5 Limbo dancing	1·00	3·00
MS918	157×109 mm. $10 Fire-eating	3·75	8·50

See also Nos. 988/92.

168 St. Ann Catholic Church, Mon Repos

1986. Christmas. Multicoloured.

919	10c. Type **168**	15	10
920	40c. St. Joseph the Worker Catholic Church, Gros Islet	30	15
921	80c. Holy Trinity Anglican Church, Castries	45	60
922	$4 Our Lady of the Assumption Catholic Church, Soufriere (vert)	90	3·25
MS923	120×101 mm. $7 St. Lucy Catholic Church, Micoud	2·50	6·50

169 Outline Map of St. Lucia

1987

924B	**169**	5c. black and brown	20	20
925A	**169**	10c. black and green	20	20
926A	**169**	45c. black and orange	50	50
927B	**169**	50c. black and blue	50	50
927cA	**169**	$1 black and red	75	75

170 Statue of Liberty and Flags of France and U.S.A.

1987. Cent of Statue of Liberty (1986). Multicoloured.

947	15c. Type **170**	60	10
948	80c. Statue and "Mauretania I" (liner)	1·50	55
949	$1 Statue and Concorde	2·75	1·50
950	$5 Statue and flying boat at sunset	3·00	5·50
MS951	107×88 mm. $6 Statue and Manhattan at night	3·00	4·50

171 First Cadastral Survey Map and Surveying Instruments, 1775

1987. New Cadastral Survey of St. Lucia. Multicoloured.

955	15c. Type **171**	60	15
956	60c. Map and surveying instruments, 1814	1·25	85
957	$1 Map and surveying instruments, 1888	1·50	1·50
958	$2.50 Cadastral survey map and surveying instruments, 1987	2·75	4·25

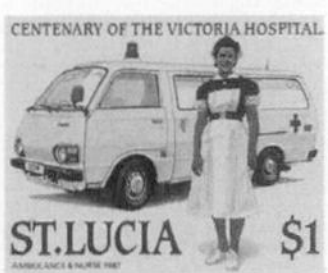

172 Ambulance and Nurse, 1987

1987. Cent of Victoria Hospital, Castries. Multicoloured.

959	**172**	$1 multicoloured	2·50	3·00
960	-	$1 blue	2·50	3·00
961	-	$2 multicoloured	3·00	3·50
962	-	$2 blue	3·00	3·50
MS963		86×68 mm. – $4.50 multicoloured	6·50	8·00

DESIGNS: No. 960, Nurse and carrying hammock, 1913; 961, $2 Victoria Hospital, 1987; 962, Victoria Hospital 1887; $4.50, Hospital gates, 1987.

173 "The Holy Family"

1987. Christmas. Paintings. Multicoloured.

964	15c. Type **173**	30	10
965	50c. "Adoration of the Shepherds"	60	30
966	60c. "Adoration of the Magi"	60	80
967	90c. "Madonna and Child"	85	2·25
MS968	82×67 mm. $6 Type **173**	3·00	5·50

174 St. Lucia Amazon perched on Branch

1987. St. Lucia Amazon. Multicoloured.

969	15c. Type **174**	2·00	40
970	35c. Pair in flight	3·00	55
971	50c. Perched on branch (rear view)	4·00	2·25
972	$1 Emerging from tree	5·50	5·00

175 Carib Clay Zemi

1988. Amerindian Artifacts. Multicoloured.

973	25c. Type **175**	15	10
974	30c. Troumassee cylinder	20	15
975	80c. Three pointer stone	45	45
976	$3.50 Dauphine petroglyph	1·75	3·50

176 East Caribbean Currency

1988. 50th Anniv of St. Lucia Co-operative Bank. Multicoloured.

977	10c. Type **176**	20	10
978	45c. Castries branch	55	35
979	60c. As 45c.	75	95
980	80c. Vieux Fort branch	1·25	1·60

177 Rural Telephone Exchange

1988. 50th Anniv of Cable and Wireless (West Indies) Ltd. Multicoloured.

981	15c. Type **177**	20	15
982	25c. Early and modern telephones	20	15
983	80c. St. Lucia Teleport dish aerial	50	45
984	$2.50 Map showing Eastern Caribbean Microwave System	3·50	2·75

178 Stained Glass Window

1988. Cent of Methodist Church in St. Lucia. Multicoloured.

985	15c. Type **178**	10	10
986	80c. Church interior	40	45
987	$3.50 Methodist Church, Castries	1·50	2·25

179 Garnished Lobsters

1988. Tourism (2nd series). Designs showing local delicacies. Multicoloured.

988	10c. Type **179**	70	1·00
989	30c. Cocktail and tourists at buffet	85	1·10
990	80c. Fresh fruits and roasted breadfruit	1·25	1·60
991	$2.50 Barbecued red snappers (fish)	2·50	2·75
MS992	80×104 mm. $5.50 Fruit stall, Castries market	2·25	3·25

Nos. 988/91 were printed together, se-tenant, forming a composite design of tourists at beach barbecue.

1988. 300th Anniv of Lloyd's of London. As T **152a** of St. Helena.

1004	10c. black, lilac and brown	45	15
1005	60c. multicoloured	1·25	75
1006	80c. multicoloured	1·60	1·25
1007	$2.50 multicoloured	3·00	4·50

DESIGNS—VERT: 10c. San Francisco earthquake; $2.50, Castries fire, 1948. HORIZ: 60c. Castries Harbour; 80c. "Lady Nelson" (hospital ship), 1942.

180 Snow on the Mountain

1988. Christmas. Flowers. Multicoloured.

1008	15c. Type **180**	30	10
1009	45c. Christmas candle	55	50
1010	60c. Balisier	70	90
1011	80c. Poinsettia	1·00	1·60
MS1012	79×75 mm. $5.50 Christmas flower arrangement	2·00	3·50

181 Princess Alexandra presenting Constitution

1989. Tenth Anniv of Independence. Multicoloured.

1013	15c. Type **181**	40	15
1014	80c. Geothermal well	1·10	60
1015	$1 Sir Arthur Lewis Community College	70	60
1016	$2.50 Pointe Seraphine shopping centre	1·25	2·25
MS1017	47×62 mm. $5 Man with national flag	2·25	3·25

182 "Gerronema citrinum"

1989. Fungi. Multicoloured.

1022	15c. Type **182**	1·25	30
1023	25c. "Lepiota spiculata"	1·50	30
1024	50c. "Calocybe cyanocephala"	2·50	1·10
1025	$5 "Russula puiggarii"	7·00	9·50

183 Local Revolutionary Declaration, 1789, and View of St. Lucia

1989. Bicentenary of the French Revolution. Designs include the "PHILEXFRANCE". International Stamp Exhibition logo. Multicoloured.

1026	10c. Type **183**	40	15
1027	60c. Hoisting Revolutionary flag, Morne Fortune, 1791 (horiz)	2·50	80
1028	$1 Declaration of Rights of Man and view of St. Lucia	2·50	1·50
1029	$3.50 Arrival of Capt. La Crosse, Gros Islet, 1792 (horiz)	8·50	9·00

184 Red Cross Headquarters, St. Lucia

1989. 125th Anniv of Int Red Cross. Multicoloured.

1030	50c. Type **184**	1·25	1·25
1031	80c. Red Cross seminar, Castries, 1987	1·75	2·00
1032	$1 Red Cross ambulance	2·00	2·25

185 Christmas Lantern

1989. Christmas.

1033	**185**	10c. multicoloured	25	10
1034	-	50c. multicoloured	65	40
1035	-	90c. multicoloured	1·00	1·25
1036	-	$1 multicoloured	1·25	1·25

DESIGNS: 50c. to $1 various decorative "building" lanterns.

186 Gwi Gwi

1990. Endangered Trees. Multicoloured.

1081	10c. Chinna	50	60
1082	15c. Latanier	50	20
1039	20c. Type **186**	1·25	1·25
1084	25c. L'encens	30	20
1085	50c. Bois lele	30	40
1042	80c. Bois d'amande	1·25	40
1043	95c. Mahot piman grand bois	2·25	1·00
1044	$1 Balata	1·50	75
1045	$1.50 Pencil cedar	3·00	2·75
1046	$2.50 Bois cendre	5·00	5·00
1047	$5 Lowye cannelle	7·00	8·00
1048	$25 Chalantier grand bois	18·00	25·00

187 Father Tapon and Original College Building

1990. International Literacy Year. Centenary of St. Mary's College, Castries. Multicoloured.

1049	30c. Type **187**	15	15
1050	45c. Brother M. C. Collins and St. Mary's College	25	25
1051	75c. Literacy class	45	55
1052	$2 Children approaching "door to knowledge"	1·50	2·25

1990. 90th Birthday of Queen Elizabeth the Queen Mother. As T **161a** of St. Helena.

1053	50c. multicoloured	1·00	35
1054	$5 black and blue	3·75	4·75

DESIGNS—(21×36 mm): 50c. Crowning of Queen Consort, 1937. (29×37 mm): $5 Queen Elizabeth arriving at New Theatre, London 1949.

1990. "EXPO 90" International Garden and Greenery Exhibition, Osaka. No. 1047 optd **EXPO '90** and emblem.

1055	$5 Lowye cannelle	3·50	4·25

189 "Adoration of the Magi" (Rubens)

1990. Christmas. Religious Paintings. Multicoloured.

1056	10c. Type **189**	50	20
1057	30c. "Adoration of the Shepherds" (Murillo)	1·25	20
1058	80c. "Adoration of the Magi" (Rubens) (different)	1·75	75
1059	$5 "Adoration of the Shepherds" (Philippe de Champaigne)	6·50	8·50

190 "Vistafjord" (liner)

1991. Cruise Ships. Multicoloured.

1060	50c. Type **190**	1·75	40
1061	80c. "Windstar" (schooner)	2·25	1·10
1062	$1 "Unicorn" (brig)	2·50	1·50
1063	$2.50 Game-fishing launch	5·50	8·50
MS1064	82×65 mm. $5 Ships in Castries Harbour	11·00	11·00

191 "Battus polydamas"

1991. Butterflies. Multicoloured.

1065	60c. Type **191**	2·00	65
1066	80c. "Strymon simaethis"	2·25	1·10
1067	$1 "Mestra cana"	2·75	1·25
1068	$2.50 "Allosmaitia piplea"	5·50	7·50

192 Mural, Jacmel Church

1991. Christmas. Paintings by Duncan St. Omer. Multicoloured.

1069	10c. Type **192**	30	10
1070	15c. "Red Madonna" (vert)	40	10
1071	80c. Mural, Monchy Church	1·50	70
1072	$5 "Blue Madonna" (vert)	4·50	7·50

193 Yacht and Map

1991. Atlantic Rally for Cruising Yachts. Multicoloured.

1073	60c. Type **193**	1·50	1·50
1074	80c. Yachts off St. Lucia	1·75	1·75

1992. Organization of East Caribbean States. 500th Anniv of Discovery of America by Columbus. As T **66** of St. Kitts. Multicoloured.

1075	$1 Columbus meeting Amerindians	2·25	1·75
1076	$2 Ships approaching island	3·25	3·50

194 Amerindian Village

1992. Discovery of St. Lucia. Multicoloured.

1077	15c. Type **194**	40	20
1078	40c. Ships of Juan de la Cosa and islands, 1499	2·00	50
1079	50c. Columbus sailing between Martinique and St. Lucia, 1502	2·50	70
1080	$5 Legendary shipwreck of Gimie	7·50	10·00

195 "Virgin and Child" (Delaroche)

1992. Christmas. Religious Paintings. Multicoloured.

1092	10c. Type **195**	65	20
1093	15c. "The Holy Family" (Rubens)	65	20
1094	60c. "Virgin and Child" (Luini)	2·50	1·75
1095	80c. "Virgin and Child" (Sassoferrato)	2·50	2·25

196 "Death" and Gravestone

1993. Anti-drugs Campaign.

1096	**196**	$5 multicoloured	6·00	7·00

197 "Gros Piton from Delcer, Choiseul" (Dunstan St. Omer)

1993. Carib Art. Multicoloured.

1097	20c. Type **197**	20	10
1098	75c. "Reduit Bay" (Derek Walcott)	75	75
1099	$5 "Woman and Child at River" (Nancy Cole Auguste)	4·25	7·00

198 "The Madonna of the Rosary" (Murillo)

1993. Christmas. Religious Paintings. Multicoloured.

1100	15c. Type **198**	20	10
1101	60c. "The Madonna and Child" (Van Dyck)	65	60
1102	95c. "The Annunciation" (Champaigne)	1·10	1·50

199 The Pitons

1994. Bicentenary of the Abolition of Slavery in St. Lucia.

1103	**199**	20c. multicoloured	65	45
MS1104		115×75 mm. $5 multicoloured	4·50	6·00

200 "Euphorbia pulcherrima"

1994. Christmas. Flowers. Multicoloured.

1105	20c. Type **200**	15	10
1106	75c. "Heliconia rostrata"	55	50
1107	95c. "Alpinia purpurata"	75	75
1108	$5.50 "Anthurium andreanum"	3·75	7·00

See also Nos. 1122/5 and 1156/9.

201 18th-century Map of St. Lucia

1995. Bicentenary of Battle of Rabot. Multicoloured.

1109	20c. Type **201**	25	15
1110	75c. Insurgent slaves	60	55
1111	95c. 9th Foot (Royal Norfolk Regiment) attacking	1·10	1·40
MS1112	150×100 mm. $5.50 Plan of battle	3·25	4·00

1995. 50th Anniv of End of Second World War. As T **182a** of St. Helena. Multicoloured.

1113	20c. St. Lucian members of the A.T.S.	55	15
1114	75c. German U-boat off St. Lucia	1·50	80
1115	95c. Bren gun-carriers of the Caribbean Regiment, North Africa	1·75	1·25
1116	$1.10 Supermarine Spitfire Mk V "St. Lucia"	2·25	2·25
MS1117	75×85 mm. $5.50 Reverse of 1939–45 War Medal (vert)	2·00	3·50

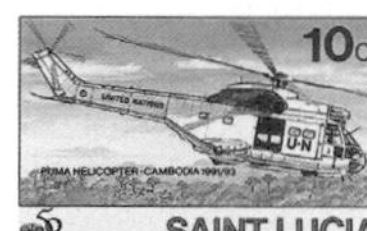

201a Sud Aviation SE 330 Puma Helicopter, Cambodia, 1991–93

1995. 50th Anniv of United Nations. Multicoloured.

1118	10c. Type **201a**	15	10
1119	65c. Renault lorry, Bosnia, 1995	50	50
1120	$1.35 Transall C-160 aircraft, Cambodia, 1991–93	95	1·40
1121	$5 Douglas DC-3 aircraft, Korea, 1950–54	3·75	6·00

1995. Christmas. Flowers. As T **200**, each including Madonna and Child. Multicoloured.

1122	15c. "Eranthemum nervosum"	15	10
1123	70c. Bougainvillea	45	45
1124	$1.10 "Allamanda cathartica"	70	90
1125	$3 "Rosa sinensis"	1·75	3·50

202 Calypso King

1996. Carnival. Multicoloured.

1126	20c. Type **202**	70	10
1127	65c. Carnival dancers	1·50	55
1128	95c. King of the Band float	2·00	85
1129	$3 Carnival Queen	4·00	6·50

203 Dry River Bed

1996. Inaug of New Irrigation Project. Multicoloured.

1130	20c. Type **203**	10	10
1131	65c. People bathing in stream	40	45
1132	$5 New dam	3·00	4·75

204 Produce Market

1996. Tourism. Multicoloured.

1133	65c. Type **204**	45	45
1134	75c. Horse-riding on beach	55	55
1135	95c. Bride and groom	70	75
1136	$5 Jazz band	2·75	4·50

205 Athlete of 1896

1996. Centenary of Modern Olympic Games. Multicoloured.

1137	15c. Type **205**	65	85
1138	15c. Athlete of 1996	65	85
1139	75c. Catamaran and dinghy	1·75	2·00
1140	75c. Sailing dinghies	1·75	2·00

Nos. 1137/8 and 1139/40 respectively were printed together, *se-tenant*, forming composite designs.

206 Spanish Royal Standard, 1502, and Caravel

1996. Flags and Ships. Multicoloured.

1141	10c. Type **206**	1·00	50
1142	15c. Skull and crossbones, 1550, and pirate carrack	1·75	50
1143	20c. Dutch royal standard, 1650, and galleon	70	20
1144	25c. Union Jack, 1739, and ship of the line	1·25	25
1145	40c. French royal standard, 1750, and ship of the line	2·75	40
1146	50c. Martinique and St. Lucia flag, 1766, and French brig	1·00	40
1147	55c. White Ensign, 1782, and frigate squadron	1·00	40
1148	65c. Red Ensign, 1782, and frigates in action	1·00	50
1149	75c. Blue Ensign, 1782, and brig	1·25	60
1150	95c. The Tricolour, 1792, and French frigate	1·25	60
1151	$1 Union Jack, 1801, and West Indies Grand Fleet	1·25	70
1152	$2.50 Confederate States of America flag, 1861, and cruiser	2·50	2·50
1153	$5 Canadian flag, 1915–19, and "V" or "W" class destroyer	4·00	4·50
1154	$10 United States flag, 1942–48, and "Fletcher" class destroyer	7·00	9·00
1155	$25 Flag of St. Lucia and "Royal Princess" (cruise liner)	14·00	19·00

The design of the $5 value is incorrect. There were no "V" or "W" class destroyers in the Canadian Navy where ships up to 1965 flew the White Ensign.

1996. Christmas. Flowers. As T **200**, each including Madonna and Child. Multicoloured.

1156	20c. "Cordia sebestena"	15	10
1157	75c. "Cryptostegia grandiflora"	50	50
1158	95c. "Hibiscus elatus"	65	65
1159	$5 "Caularthron bicornutum"	4·00	6·00

1997. Golden Wedding of Queen Elizabeth and Prince Philip. As T **192a** of St. Helena. Multicoloured.

1160	75c. Queen Elizabeth at Warwick, 1996	1·25	1·40
1161	75c. Prince Philip with carriage horses	1·25	1·40
1162	95c. Prince Philip	1·25	1·40
1163	95c. Queen in phaeton at Trooping the Colour	1·25	1·40
1164	$1 Queen Elizabeth and Prince Philip at Sandringham, 1982	1·25	1·40
1165	$1 Princess Anne show jumping	1·25	1·40
MS1166	110×70 mm. $5 Queen Elizabeth and Prince Philip in landau (horiz)	3·25	4·00

Nos. 1160/1, 1162/3 and 1164/5 respectively were printed together, *se-tenant*, with the backgrounds forming composite designs.

207 "St. George" capsized, 1935

1997. Marine Disasters. Multicoloured.

1167	20c. Type **207**	1·10	25
1168	55c. Wreck of "Belle of Bath" (freighter)	1·75	30
1169	$1 "Ethelgonda" (freighter) aground on rocks, 1897	2·75	1·50
1170	$2.50 Hurricane, 1817	3·50	6·00

208 Attack on Praslin

1997. Bicentenary of the Brigands' War. Multicoloured.

1171	20c. Type **208**	80	25
1172	55c. British troops at Battle of Dennery	1·40	40
1173	70c. Discussing peace agreement	1·40	1·00
1174	$3 Members of 1st West India Regiment	4·00	6·00

209 "Roseau Church" (detail, Dunstan St. Omer)

1997. Christmas. Paintings by Dunstan St. Omer. Multicoloured.

1175	20c. Type **209**	20	10
1176	60c. Altarpiece, Regional Seminary, Trinidad	45	35
1177	95c. "Our Lady of the Presentation", Trinidad	60	60
1178	$5 "The Four Days of Creation"	2·75	5·00

210 Diana, Princess of Wales

1998. Diana, Princess of Wales Commemoration.

1179	**210** $1 multicoloured	60	65

211 Signatories to CARICOM Treaty, 1973

1998. 25th Anniv of CARICOM. Multicoloured.

1180	20c. Type **211**	15	10
1181	75c. Flags of CARICOM and St. Lucia	85	75

212 St. Lucia Oriole

1998. Wild Life (1st series). Birds. Multicoloured.

1197	70c. Type **212**	1·00	65
1198	75c. Lesser antillean pewee	1·00	70
1199	95c. Bridled quail dove	1·25	95
1200	$1.10 Semper's warbler	2·00	2·00

See also Nos. 1212/15.

213 "Siproeta stelenes" and Chain

1998. 50th Anniv of Universal Declaration of Human Rights. Butterflies. Multicoloured.

1201	20c. Type **213**	90	20
1202	65c. "Pseudolycaena marsyas" and chain	1·50	60
1203	70c. "Heliconius melpomene" and rope	1·50	60
1204	$5 "Phoebis philea" and chain	4·25	6·00

214 "Tabebuia serratifolia"

1998. Christmas. Flowers. Multicoloured.

1205	20c. Type **214**	40	10
1206	50c. "Hibiscus sabdariffa"	75	30
1207	95c. "Euphorbia leucocephala"	1·25	50
1208	$2.50 "Calliandra slaneae"	2·25	4·00

215 "The Black Prometheus" (wall painting)

1998. 50th Anniv of University of West Indies. Multicoloured.

1209	15c. Type **215**	15	10
1210	75c. Sir Arthur Lewis College, St. Lucia	50	40
1211	$5 University arms and the Pitons, St. Lucia	2·75	5·00

216 St. Lucia Tree Lizard

1999. Wildlife (2nd series). Reptiles. Multicoloured.

1212	20c. Type **216**	25	10
1213	75c. Boa constrictor	70	45
1214	95c. Leatherback turtle	75	50
1215	$5 St. Lucia whiptail	2·75	5·00

217 "Tees" (mail steamer), 1893

1999. 125th Anniv of Universal Postal Union. Multicoloured.

1216	20c. Type **217**	75	20
1217	65c. Sikorsky S.38 (flying boat), 1929	1·25	65
1218	95c. "Lady Drake" (cargo liner), 1930	1·50	80
1219	$3 DC10 airliner, 1999	3·00	4·50
MS1220	100×84 mm. $5 Heinrich von Stephan (founder of U.P.U.) (30×37 mm)	2·75	4·00

218 The Nativity

1999. Christmas. New Millennium. Multicoloured.

1221	20c. Type **218**	20	10
1222	$1 Cathedral of the Immaculate Conception	80	1·25

219 Original Badge of the Colony

2000. 21st Anniv of Independence. Multicoloured.

1223	20c. Type **219**	15	10
1224	75c. Colonial badge, 1939	50	50
1225	95c. Coat of Arms as Associated State, 1967	65	75
1226	$1 Coat of Arms on Independence, 1979	80	1·25

220 Sugar Factory, Vieux-Fort

2000. History of St. Lucia. Multicoloured.

1227	20c. Type **220**	20	15
1228	65c. Coaling ship, Port Castries	75	45
1229	$1 Fort Rodney, Pigeon Island	85	65
1230	$5 Ruins of military hospital, Pigeon Island	3·00	4·75

221 The Old Market, Castries

2000. 150th Anniv of Castries Municipality. Multicoloured.

1231	20c. Type **221**	30	15
1232	75c. Central Library	75	55
1233	95c. Harbour	1·50	70
1234	$5 Henry H. Breen (first municipality mayor, 1851) and Joseph Desir (first city mayor, 1967)	3·00	5·00

222 Brownies and Badge

2000. 75th Anniv of Girl Guides in St. Lucia. Multicoloured.

1235	70c. Type **222**	65	40
1236	$1 Girl Guides parade	90	70
1237	$2.50 Brownies in camp and Guides with flag	2·25	3·50

223 Holy Trinity Church, Castries

2000. Christmas. Churches. Multicoloured.

1238	20c. Type **223**	30	15
1239	50c. St. Paul's Church, Vieux-Fort	50	30
1240	95c. Christ Church, Soufriere	80	55
1241	$2.50 Grace Church, River D'Oree	2·00	3·50

224 St. Lucia Black Finch

2001. Endangered Species. Birds of St. Lucia. Multicoloured.

1242	20c. Type **224**	75	65
1243	20c. White-breasted trembler ("White-breasted Thrasher")	75	65
1244	95c. St. Lucia oriole	1·10	1·25
1245	95c. Forest thrush	1·10	1·25

225 Open-air Jazz Concert

2001. Tenth Anniv of Jazz Festival. Multicoloured.

1246	20c. Type **225**	30	15
1247	$1 Jazz concert on the beach	1·00	75
1248	$5 Jazz band	4·00	6·00

226 Union Jack, Pitons and Frigate (Arrival of Civil Administrator, 1801)

2001. Bicentenary of Civil Administration. Multicoloured.

1249	20c. Type **226**	40	20
1250	65c. Napoleon, Tricolor and Conseil Superior, 1802	70	40
1251	$1.10 King George III, Union Jack and British fleet (introduction of Privy Council, 1803)	1·25	1·10
1252	$3 King George IV and island map (Treaty of Paris, 1814)	2·50	3·50

227 Three-panel Stained Glass Window

2001. Christmas. Multicoloured.

1253	20c. Type **227**	50	15
1254	95c. Circular stained glass window	1·50	55
1255	$2.50 Arched stained glass window	3·25	4·25

2002. Golden Jubilee. As T **211** of St. Helena.

1256	25c. brown, blue and gold	50	20
1257	65c. multicoloured	1·00	85
1258	75c. brown, blue and gold	1·10	1·10
1259	95c. multicoloured	1·50	1·50
MS1260	162×95 mm. Nos. 1256/9 and $5 multicoloured	4·75	5·50

DESIGNS—HORIZ: 25c. Princess Elizabeth in June 1927; 65c. Queen Elizabeth wearing striped turban; 75c. Princess Elizabeth in 1947; 95c. Queen Elizabeth arriving at St. Paul's Cathedral, 1996. VERT: (38×51 mm)—$5 Queen Elizabeth after Annigoni.

Designs as Nos. 1256/9 in No. **MS**1260 omit the gold frame around each stamp and the "Golden Jubilee 1952–2002" inscription.

228 H.M.S. *St. Lucia* (brig), 1803

2002. Royal Navy Ships. Multicoloured.

1261	15c. Type **228**	75	25
1262	75c. H.M.S. *Thetis* (frigate), 1781	1·75	70
1263	$1 H.M.S. *Berwick* (cruiser), 1903	2·00	1·10
1264	$5 H.M.S. *Victory* (Nelson), 1805	4·25	6·00

2002. Queen Elizabeth the Queen Mother Commemoration. As T **215** of St. Helena.

1265	50c. brown, gold and purple	70	45
1266	65c. multicoloured	85	65
1267	95c. brown, gold and purple	1·25	1·10
1268	$1 multicoloured	1·40	1·60
MS1269	145×70 mm. $2 black and gold; $2 multicoloured	4·00	4·25

DESIGNS: 50c. Duchess of York with Princess Elizabeth, 1926; 65c. Queen Mother at St. Peter's Church Thurso, 1992; 95c. Queen Elizabeth at Church Army services club London, 1943; $1 Queen Mother at Sandown Races, 1999; $2 (black and gold) Duchess of York, 1920s; $2 (multicoloured) Queen Mother at unveiling of S.O.E. Memorial, 1996. Designs in No. **MS**1269 omit the "1900–2002" inscription and the coloured frame.

229 Derek Walcott

2002. Tenth Anniv of Award of Nobel Literature Prize to Derek Walcott. Multicoloured.

1270 20c. Type **229** 45 20
1271 65c. Father Christmas with children (horiz) 80 50
1272 70c. Dancers 85 60
1273 $5 Outboard motor boat (cover illustration from *Omeros*) (horiz) 3·75 6·00

230 William and Catherine Booth

2002. Centenary of Salvation Army on St. Lucia. Multicoloured.

1274 20c. Type **230** 80 35
1275 $1 Early St. Lucia Salvation Army parade 2·00 1·25
1276 $2.50 Salvation Army shield symbol and crest 3·25 4·00

231 "The Adoration of the Shepherds" (Bernardino da Asola)

2003. Christmas. Religious Paintings from The National Gallery, London. Multicoloured.

1277 20c. Type **231** 40 10
1278 50c. "The Adoration of the Kings" (Girolamo da Treviso) (vert) 75 30
1279 75c. "The Adoration of the Kings" (Vincenzo Foppa) (vert) 1·10 40
1280 $5 "The Adoration of the Shepherds" (Le Nain brothers) 4·75 7·00

2003. 50th Anniv of Coronation. As T **219** of St. Helena. Multicoloured.

1281 20c. Queen Elizabeth II wearing Imperial State Crown 45 20
1282 75c. Coronation Coach passing Buckingham Palace gate 1·10 1·00
MS1283 95×115 mm. $2.50 As 75c.; $2.50 As 20c. 4·25 4·50

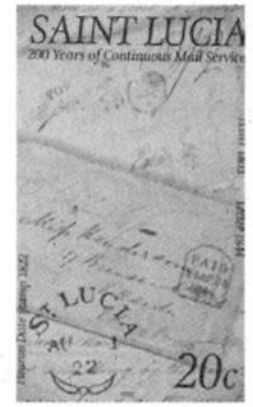

232 Letters (1803 and 1844) and Fleuron

2003. Bicentenary of Continuous Mail Service. Multicoloured.

1284 20c. Type **232** 35 25
1285 25c. Stamps of 1860 35 25
1286 65c. *Hewanorra* (steam packet), 1920 and map 90 65
1287 75c. Post Offices of 1900 and 2003 1·00 1·00

233 St. Lucia Amazon Date Stamp, 1822

2003. Coil stamps. Multicoloured.

1288 10c. Type **233** 20 20
1289 25c. The Pitons, St. Lucia 40 30

234 Sikorsky S-38 (flying boat)

2003. Centenary of Powered Flight. Multicoloured.

1290 20c. Type **234** 55 30
1291 70c. Consolidated PBY-5A Catalina (amphibian) 1·00 70
1292 $1 Lockheed Lodestar 1·40 1·25
1293 $5 Supermarine Spitfire Mk V *St. Lucia* 4·50 6·00

235 Sorrel Flowers and Ginger Root

2003. Christmas. Multicoloured.

1294 20c. Type **235** 45 15
1295 75c. Sorrel drink and ginger ale 90 50
1296 95c. Masqueraders 1·25 1·00
1297 $1 People making Christmas lanterns 1·25 1·00

236 Raising St. Lucia Flag

2004. 25th Anniv of Independence. Multicoloured.

1298 20c. Type **236** 40 15
1299 95c. Sailing ship, aircraft, cargo ship and bananas 1·00 55
1300 $1.10 Anniversary emblem (horiz) 1·00 90
1301 $5 Cruise ships, Castries harbour (horiz) 3·50 5·00

237 Antillean Crested Hummingbird

2004. Birds of the Caribbean. Multicoloured.

1302 $1 Type **237** 1·00 1·40
1303 $1 Lesser Antillian pewee ("Saint Lucia Pewee") 1·00 1·40
1304 $1 Purple-throated carib 1·00 1·40
1305 $1 Grey trembler 1·00 1·40
1306 $1 Rufous-throated solitaire 1·00 1·40
1307 $1 Adelaide's warbler ("Saint Lucia Warbler") 1·00 1·40
1308 $1 Antillean euphonia 1·00 1·40
1309 $1 Semper's warbler 1·00 1·40

Nos. 1302/9 were printed together with the backgrounds forming composite designs.

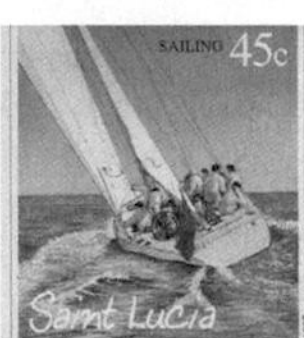

238 Sailing

2004. Tourism. Multicoloured.

1310 45c. Type **238** 60 30
1311 65c. Horse-riding 85 75
1312 70c. Scuba diving 85 85
1313 $1.10 Walking near waterfall 1·25 1·40

239 Hypodermic Needle and Couple ("Prevent")

2004. World AIDS Awareness Day. Multicoloured.

1314 30c. Type **239** 65 65
1315 30c. Two children ("Educate us") and woman 65 65

240 "The Adoration of the Kings" (Dosso)

2004. Christmas. Religious Paintings. Multicoloured.

1316 30c. Type **240** 30 15
1317 75c. "The Adoration of the Shepherds" (Poussin) (vert) 75 55
1318 95c. "The Adoration of the Kings" (Joos) (vert) 90 80
1319 $1 "The Adoration of the Shepherds" (Fabritius) 95 95

241 Convent Schoolgirls

2005. 150th Anniv of St. Joseph's Convent. Multicoloured.

1320 30c. Type **241** 35 15
1321 95c. St. Joseph's Convent 1·00 55
1322 $2.50 Street scene 2·50 3·50

2005. Bicentenary of the Battle of Trafalgar. Multicoloured. As T **229** of St. Helena.

1323 30c. HMS *Thunderer* 75 60
1324 75c. HMS *Britannia* and *Bucentaure* 1·50 1·25
1325 95c. Vice-Admiral Sir Horatio Nelson (vert) 1·75 1·50
1326 $5 HMS *Victory* 6·00 7·00
MS1327 120×79 mm. $10 HMS *Thunderer* (44×44 mm) 11·00 12·00

No. 1326 contains traces of powdered wood from HMS *Victory*.

2005. Pope John Paul II Commemoration. As T **231** of St. Helena.

1328 $2 multicoloured 2·50 2·50

242 Church of the Purification of the Blessed Virgin, Laborie

2005. Christmas. Multicoloured.

1329 30c. Type **242** 50 15
1330 $5 The Minor Basilica of the Immaculate Conception, Castries 3·75 4·50

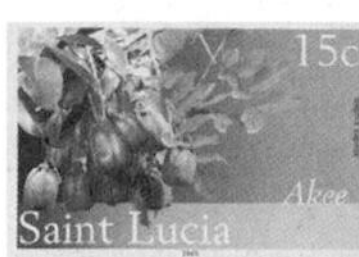

243 Akee

2005. Flowering Fruit. Multicoloured.

1331 15c. Type **243** 35 30
1332 20c. Belogen 35 20
1333 25c. Mago 35 20
1334 30c. Wezin 45 25
1335 50c. Papai 65 30
1336 55c. Pwin 70 40
1337 65c. Z'icaque 85 50
1338 70c. Chataigne 90 75
1339 75c. Cashima 90 75
1340 95c. Gwiav 1·25 75
1341 $1 Macabou 1·25 1·00
1342 $2.50 Zapoti 2·50 2·25
1343 $5 Cashew 4·75 5·50
1344 $25 Zabwico 18·00 22·00

244 Axe Head

2006. Environment Fragile. Designs showing works of art by Llewellyn Xavier. Multicoloured.

1345 20c. Type **244** 30 15
1346 30c. Stylized turtle 35 15
1347 $2.50 Pre-Columbian vase 2·00 2·50
1348 $5 Pre-Columbian zemi 3·50 5·00

245 Two Players

2006. World Cup Football Championship, Germany. Multicoloured. .

1349 95c. Type **245** 1·25 75
1350 $2 Two players (different) 2·00 2·50
MS1351 110×70 mm. Nos. 1349/50 3·25 3·50

246 LIAT Aircraft in Flight

2006. 50th Anniv of LIAT (Leeward Islands Air Transport) Airline. Multicoloured.

1352 30c. Type **246** 60 40
1353 75c. LIAT aircraft on ground 1·50 1·25

247 Sesenne Descartes and Choir

2006. Christmas. Folk Songs. Multicoloured.

1354 95c. Type **247** 1·50 60
1355 $2 Sesenne Descartes (singer) and St. Lucian folk band 2·75 3·25

248 Mindoo Phillip (cricketer)

2007. Cricket in St. Lucia. Multicoloured.

1356 30c. Type **248** 60 35
1357 75c. Outline map of St. Lucia 1·50 1·00
1358 95c. Beausejour Cricket Grounds (horiz) 2·00 1·25
MS1359 116×90 mm. $5 Beausejour Cricket Grounds (56×42 mm) 5·50 6·50

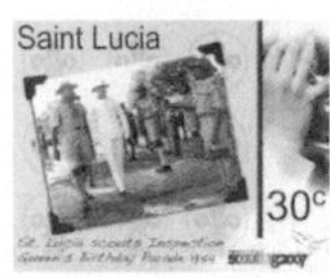

249 Scouts Inspection, Queen's Birthday Parade, 1954

2007. Centenary of Scouting. Multicoloured.

1360 30c. Type **249** 50 25
1361 $5 Cub scout laying wreath, Remembrance Day Parade, 2005 4·50 5·00
MS1362 90×65 mm. $2.50 St. Lucia Scout Association membership badge (vert); $2.50 Lord Baden-Powell (founder) (vert) 4·50 5·00

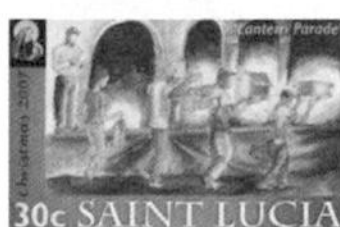

250 Lantern Parade

2007. Christmas. Multicoloured.

1363 30c. Type **250** 50 25
1364 $10 Nativity scene 7·50 9·00

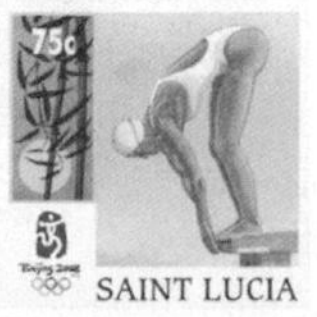

251 Swimmer

2008. Olympic Games, Beijing. Multicoloured.

1365 75c. Type **251** 70 55
1366 95c. Distance runner 80 65
1367 $1 Sprinter 90 75
1368 $2.50 High jumper 2·00 2·50

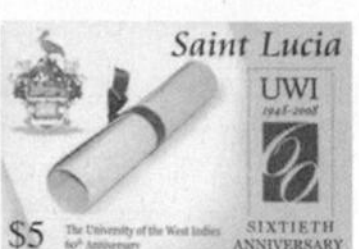

252 Scroll

2008. 60th Anniv of the University of the West Indies.

1369 **252** $5 multicoloured 4·50 5·00

253 Male Whiptail Lizard

2008. Endangered Species. St. Lucia Whiptail Lizard (Cnemidophorus vanzoi). Multicoloured.

1370	75c. Type **253**	1·25	1·25
1371	$2.50 Female lizard	1·75	1·75
1372	$5 Two male lizards	3·50	3·50
1373	$10 Male and female lizards	6·75	6·75

254 Christmas Wreath, Gift and Bell

2008. Christmas. Multicoloured.

1374	95c. Type **254**	1·50	1·00
1375	$5 Candle and nativity scene	4·50	5·00

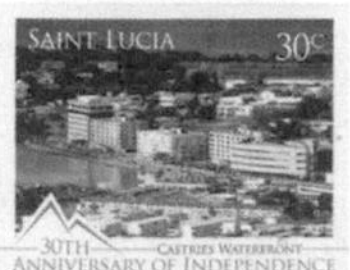

255 Castries Waterfront

2009. 30th Anniv of Independence. Multicoloured.

1376	30c. Type **255**	50	35
1377	$2.50 Roseau Dam	2·25	2·25
1378	$5 Rodney Bay Marina	3·50	4·00
1379	$10 Sir John Compton and St. Lucia flag	6·50	8·00

Nos. 1380/93 are vacant.

256 Lobelia santa-Luciae

2010. International Year of Biodiversity. Multicoloured.

1394	30c. Type **256**	35	25
1395	75c *Iguana cf. iguana*	70	55
1396	95c. Hercules beetle (*Dynastes hercules reidi*)	1·25	1·25
1397	$2.50 White breasted thrasher (*Ramphocinclus brachyurus sanctaeluciae*)	3·00	3·25

257 Township and Gros Islet

2010. 25th Anniv of Gros Islet's Township

1398	**257**	95c. multicoloured	1·00	1·00

2011. Queen Elizabeth II and Prince Philip 'A Lifetime of Service'. Multicoloured.

1399	$1.50 Formal portrait of Queen Elizabeth II (wearing tiara) and Prince Philip (in uniform), c. 1972	1·75	1·75
1400	$1.50 Prince Philip, 1960s	1·75	1·75
1401	$2 Formal portrait of Queen Elizabeth II (wearing tiara and sash) and Prince Philip, c. 1952	2·00	2·00
1402	$2 Queen Elizabeth II (wearing tiara and pale blue dress) and Prince Philip, 1960s	2·00	2·00
1403	$2.50 Queen Elizabeth II (wearing pearls), c. 1955	2·50	2·50
1404	$2.50 Queen Elizabeth II (wearing tiara, pendant and sash) and Prince Philip (wearing white uniform), c. 1955	2·50	2·50
MS1405	175×164 mm. Nos. 1399/404 and three stamp-size labels	11·00	12·00
MS1406	110×70 mm. $6 Princess Elizabeth and Prince Philip, c. 1949	6·00	6·50

Diamond-shaped designs as T **267** of St. Helena.

258 Emblem

2011. '30 Years against HIV and AIDS'

1407	**258**	30c. multicoloured	1·00	50

259 Bishop Gachet and Catholic Church, Soufriere

2011. Christmas. Birth Centenary of Bishop Charles Gachet (first Bishop of Castries 1957-74)

1408	**259**	30c. multicoloured	65	35

260 Coronation of Queen Elizabeth II, 1953

2012. Diamond Jubilee. Multicoloured.

1409	$1.50 Type **260**	1·75	1·75
1410	$1.50 Queen Elizabeth II wearing green jacket, c. 1970	1·75	1·75
1411	$2 Queen Elizabeth II, c. 2005	2·00	2·00
1412	$2 Queen Elizabeth II wearing tiara, c. 2005	2·00	2·00
1413	$2.50 Queen Elizabeth II wearing pink hat with flowers on brim, c. 1975	2·50	2·50
1414	$2.50 Queen Elizabeth II, c. 1975	2·50	2·50
MS1415	174×165 mm. Nos. 1409/14 and three stamp-size labels	11·00	12·00
MS1416	110×71 mm. $6 Queen Elizabeth II wearing tiara, c. 1960	6·00	6·50

OFFICIAL STAMPS

1983. Nos. 537/48 optd **OFFICIAL**.

O1	5c. Type **120**	20	20
O2	10c. Douglas DC-10-30	30	20
O3	15c. Local bus	40	30
O4	20c. "Geestcrest" (freighter)	50	30
O5	25c. Britten Norman Islander aircraft	60	30
O6	30c. "Charles" (pilot boat)	70	30
O7	50c. Boeing 727-200	90	40
O8	75c. "Cunard Countess" (liner)	1·10	60
O9	$1 Lockheed TriStar 500	1·50	85
O10	$2 "Booklet Vulcan" (cargo liner)	2·00	2·00
O11	$5 Boeing 707-420 airliner	3·50	3·75
O12	$10 "Queen Elizabeth 2" (liner)	6·50	7·50

1985. Nos. 797/811 optd **OFFICIAL**.

O13	5c. Type **156**	60	1·50
O14	10c. Officer, Grenadier Company, 14th Regiment, 1780	60	1·50
O15	20c. Officer, Battalion Company, 46th Regiment, 1781	70	1·00
O16	25c. Officer, Royal Artillery, c. 1782	70	90
O17	30c. Officer, Royal Engineers, 1782	80	1·00
O18	35c. Officer, Battalion Company, 54th Regiment, 1782	90	1·25
O19	45c. Private, Grenadier Company, 14th Regiment, 1782	1·00	1·25
O20	50c. Gunner, Royal Artillery, 1796	1·00	1·00
O21	65c. Private, Battalion Company, 85th Regiment, c. 1796	1·25	1·50
O22	75c. Private, Battalion Company, 76th Regiment, 1796	1·25	2·50
O23	90c. Private, Battalion Company, 81st Regiment, c. 1796	1·50	2·50
O24	$1 Sergeant 74th (Highland) Regiment, 1796	1·75	2·50
O25	$2.50 Private, Light Company, 93rd Regiment, 1803	2·75	4·00
O26	$5 Private, Battalion Company, 1st West India Regiment, 1803	4·00	4·00
O27	$15 Officer, Royal Artillery, 1850	9·00	9·00

1990. Nos. 1081/2, 1039/40, 1085 and 1042/48 optd **OFFICIAL**.

O28	10c. Chinna	45	1·25
O29	15c. Latanier	45	1·25
O30	20c. Type **186**	55	60
O31	25c. L'encens	55	60
O32	50c. Bois lele	75	75
O33	80c. Bois d'amande	1·00	1·25
O34	95c. Mahot piman grand bois	1·50	1·25
O35	$1 Balata	1·50	1·25
O36	$1.50 Pencil cedar	2·25	2·75
O37	$2.50 Bois cendre	3·50	4·25
O38	$5 Lowye cannelle	5·50	6·50
O39	$25 Chalantier grand bois	15·00	22·00

POSTAGE DUE STAMPS

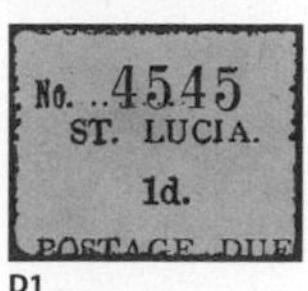

D1

1930

D1	**D1**	1d. black on blue	11·00	23·00
D2	**D1**	2d. black on yellow	23·00	50·00

D2

1933

D3	**D2**	1d. black	6·00	8·50
D4	**D2**	2d. black	24·00	11·00
D5	**D2**	4d. black	13·00	55·00
D6	**D2**	8d. black	14·00	65·00

D3

1949

D7a	**D3**	2c. black	10	9·50
D8a	**D3**	4c. black	50	14·00
D9	**D3**	8c. black	3·25	28·00
D10a	**D3**	16c. black	4·50	65·00

D4 St. Lucia Coat of Arms

1981

D13	**D4**	5c. purple	10	65
D17	**D4**	5c. red	10	25
D18	**D4**	15c. green	10	25
D19	**D4**	25c. orange	10	25
D20	**D4**	$1 blue	45	1·00

Pt. 4

SINT MAARTEN

A Netherlands colony consisting of two groups of islands in the Caribbean Sea, N. of Venezuela. Later part of Netherlands Antilles. On 10th October 2010 Sint Maarten became a constituent state within the Kingdom of the Netherlands

1 Island, Arms and Flag

2010. Constitutional Reform

1	**1**	164c. multicoloured	3·25	3·00

Pt. 6

STE MARIE DE MADAGASCAR

An island off the east coast of Madagascar. From 1898 used the stamps of Madagascar and Dependencies.

100 centimes = 1 franc.

1894. "Tablet" key-type inscr "STE MARIE DE MADAGASCAR" in red (1, 5, 15, 25, 75c., 1f.) or blue (others).

1	**D**	1c. black on blue	2·30	3·25
2	**D**	2c. brown on buff	2·50	2·50
3	**D**	4c. brown on grey	5·50	9·00
4	**D**	5c. green on green	8·75	32·00
5	**D**	10c. black on lilac	19·00	28·00
6	**D**	15c. blue	50·00	65·00
7	**D**	20c. red on green	16·00	22·00
8	**D**	25c. black on pink	9·50	10·50
9	**D**	30c. brown on drab	19·00	36·00
10	**D**	40c. red on yellow	28·00	19·00
11	**D**	50c. red on pink	65·00	70·00
12	**D**	75c. brown on orange	80·00	60·00
13	**D**	1f. green	60·00	65·00

Pt. 6

ST PIERRE ET MIQUELON

A group of French islands off the S. coast of Newfoundland. The group became an Overseas Department of France on 1 July 1976. The stamps of France were used in the islands from 1 April 1978 until 3 February 1986. Separate issues for the group were reintroduced in 1986.

1885. 100 centimes = 1 franc.
2002. 100 cents = 1 euro.

1885. Stamps of French Colonies surch **S P M** and value in figures only.

1	**J**	5 on 2c. brown on buff	£6500	£2250
4	**J**	5 on 4c. brown on grey	£375	£250
8	**J**	05 on 20c. red on green	60·00	50·00
9	**H**	05 on 35c. black on yellow	£130	£100
5	**H**	05 on 40c. red on yellow	£130	30·00
10	**H**	05 on 75c. red	£300	£200
11	**H**	05 on 1f. green	32·00	14·00
6	**H**	10 on 40c. red on yellow	30·00	18·00
7	**H**	15 on 40c. red on yellow	23·00	25·00
3	**H**	25 on 1f. green	£2750	£1600

The surcharge on No. 1 is always inverted.

1891. French Colonies "Commerce" type surch **15c. S P M.**

15	**J**	15c. on 30c. brown on drab	70·00	33·00
16	**J**	15c. on 35c. black on orange	£550	£425
17	**J**	15c. on 40c. red on yellow	£140	85·00

1891. Stamps of French Colonies "Commerce" type, optd **ST PIERRE M-on**.

23	**J**	1c. black on blue	14·50	22·00
24	**J**	2c. brown on buff	18·00	30·00
25	**J**	4c. brown on grey	21·00	26·00
26	**J**	5c. green on green	23·00	24·00
22	**J**	10c. black on lilac	50·00	36·00
28	**J**	15c. blue on blue	50·00	35·00
29	**J**	20c. red on green	£110	£100
30	**J**	25c. black on pink	50·00	14·50
31	**J**	30c. brown on drab	£140	£130
32	**J**	35c. black on orange	£450	£350
33	**J**	40c. red on yellow	£110	90·00
34	**J**	75c. red on pink	£130	£120
35	**J**	1f. green	£120	£100

1891. Stamps of French Colonies, "Commerce" type, surch **ST-PIERRE M-on** and new value in figures and words (cent.) above and below opt.

36	**J**	1c. on 5c. green and green	7·25	11·00
37	**J**	1c. on 10c. black on lilac	11·50	28·00
38	**J**	1c. on 25c. black on pink	4·50	9·25
39	**J**	2c. on 10c. black on lilac	7·25	12·00
40	**J**	2c. on 15c. blue on blue	12·00	14·00
41	**J**	2c. on 25c. black on pink	7·50	5·50
42	**J**	4c. on 20c. red on green	7·25	6·50
43	**J**	4c. on 25c. black on pink	5·50	9·25
44	**J**	4c. on 30c. brown on drab	30·00	23·00
45	**J**	4c. on 40c. red on yellow	60·00	23·00

1892. Nos. 26 and 30 surch with figure only on top of opt.

49	**J**	1c. on 5c. green on green	8·75	11·00
46	**J**	1 on 25c. black on pink	4·50	10·00
50	**J**	2 on 5c. green on green	8·25	21·00
47	**J**	2 on 25c. black on pink	2·75	11·50
51	**J**	4 on 5c. green on green	7·25	11·00
48	**J**	4 on 25c. black on pink	2·00	8·25

1892. Postage Due stamps of French Colonies optd **T ST-PIERRE M-on P.**

52	**U**	10c. black	55·00	65·00
53	**U**	20c. black	38·00	50·00
54	**U**	30c. black	32·00	50·00
55	**U**	40c. black	27·00	28·00
56	**U**	60c. black	£140	£140
57	**U**	1f. brown	£160	£160
58	**U**	2f. brown	£250	£250
59	**U**	5f. brown	£375	£375

1892. "Tablet" key-type inscr "ST PIERRE ET MIQUELON".

60	**D**	1c. black and red on blue	70	90
61	**D**	2c. brown and blue on buff	2·30	3·00
62	**D**	4c. brown and blue on grey	1·50	1·80

63	D	5c. green and red	4·50	4·00
64	D	10c. black and blue on lilac	11·50	6·75
74	D	10c. red and blue	4·75	1·80
65	D	15c. blue and red	30·00	6·50
75	D	15c. grey and red	65·00	70·00
66	D	20c. red and blue on green	26·00	32·00
67	D	25c. black and red on pink	22·00	2·30
76	D	25c. blue and red	9·25	38·00
68	D	30c. brown and blue on drab	16·00	16·00
77	D	35c. black and red on yellow	6·50	11·00
69	D	40c. red and blue on yellow	10·00	14·50
70	D	50c. red and blue on pink	50·00	32·00
78	D	50c. brown and red on blue	23·00	60·00
71	D	75c. brown and red on orange	26·00	50·00
72	D	1f. green and red	50·00	40·00

17 Fisherman

18 Glaucous Gull

19 Fishing Brigantine

1909

79	17	1c. brown and red	20	10
80	17	2c. blue and brown	20	30
81	17	4c. brown and violet	45	1·10
82	17	5c. olive and green	1·80	65
109	17	5c. black and blue	35	2·00
83	17	10c. red and pink	1·40	1·20
110	17	10c. olive and green	35	5·50
111	17	10c. mauve and bistre	1·20	1·60
84	17	15c. red and purple	1·40	2·75
85	17	20c. purple and brown	1·40	6·00
86	18	25c. blue and deep blue	4·00	4·75
112	18	25c. green and brown	2·00	1·50
87	18	30c. brown and orange	4·75	8·00
113	18	30c. red and carmine	2·30	7·25
114	18	30c. blue and red	60	6·25
115	18	30c. green and olive	2·75	5·75
88	18	35c. brown and green	2·00	7·25
89	18	40c. green and brown	4·50	6·50
90	18	45c. green and violet	1·60	7·25
91	18	50c. green and brown	5·75	8·00
116	18	50c. light blue and blue	90	4·50
117	18	50c. mauve and bistre	2·75	2·50
118	18	60c. red and blue	1·70	6·75
119	18	65c. brown and mauve	3·75	8·25
92	18	75c. green and brown	2·20	3·75
120	18	90c. red and scarlet	29·00	70·00
93	19	1f. blue and green	5·00	5·25
121	19	1f.10 red and green	5·00	12·00
122	19	1f.50 blue and ultramarine	15·00	36·00
94	19	2f. brown and violet	8·75	11·00
123	19	3f. mauve on pink	14·00	40·00
95	19	5f. green and brown	12·50	19·00

1912. "Tablet" issue surch in figures.

96A	05 on 2c. brown and blue on buff	4·00	11·00
97A	05 on 4c. brown and blue on grey	75	4·00
98A	05 on 15c. blue and red	1·00	7·25
99A	05 on 20c. red and blue on green	90	5·25
100A	05 on 25c. black and red on pink	45	4·00
101A	05 on 30c. brown and blue on drab	55	6·75
102A	05 on 35c. black and red on yellow	1·40	7·75
103A	10 on 40c. red and blue on yellow	1·10	5·75
104A	10 on 50c. red and blue	1·00	7·50
105A	10 on 75c. brown and red on orange	3·00	9·75
106A	10 on 1f. green and red	3·75	11·50

1915. Red Cross. Surch **5c** and red cross.

107	17	10c.+5c. red and pink	90	3·25
108	17	15c.+5c. red and purple	2·30	6·50

1924. Surch with new value.

124	17	25c. on 15c. red and purple	1·60	6·75
125	19	25c. on 2f. brown & violet	1·70	7·25
126	19	25c. on 5f. green & brown	1·00	7·50
127	18	65 on 45c. green and violet	3·00	9·25
128	18	85 on 75c. green and brown	2·50	9·00
129	18	90c. on 75c. red and scarlet	4·25	11·50
130	19	1f.25 on 1f. ultramarine and blue	2·40	10·00
131	19	1f.50 on 1f. blue and light blue	3·75	11·00
132	19	3f. on 5f. mauve and brown	4·75	11·00
133	19	10f. on 5f. green and red	17·00	46·00
134	19	20f. on 5f. red and violet	28·00	60·00

1931. International Colonial Exhibition, Paris, key-types inscr "ST PIERRE ET MIQUELON".

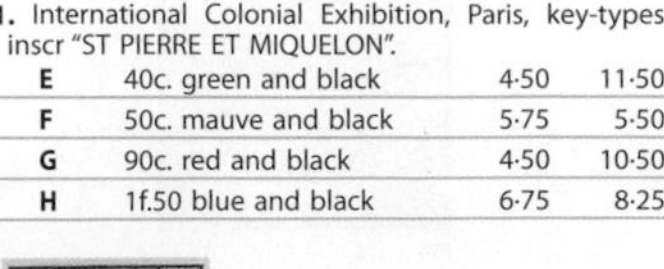

135	E	40c. green and black	4·50	11·50
136	F	50c. mauve and black	5·75	5·50
137	G	90c. red and black	4·50	10·50
138	H	1f.50 blue and black	6·75	8·25

27 Map of St. Pierre et Miquelon

28 Galantry Lighthouse

29 "Jacques Coeur" (trawler)

1932

139	27	1c. blue and purple	10	6·00
140	28	2c. green and black	10	2·00
141	29	4c. brown and red	30	5·75
142	29	5c. brown and mauve	80	2·75
143	28	10c. black and purple	70	7·00
144	28	15c. mauve and blue	1·50	7·50
145	27	20c. red and black	1·80	7·75
146	27	25c. green and mauve	4·75	2·30
147	29	30c. green and olive	5·00	8·00
148	29	40c. brown and blue	3·75	6·25
149	28	45c. green and red	4·75	7·75
150	28	50c. green and brown	3·50	1·00
151	29	65c. red and brown	6·00	4·50
152	27	75c. red and green	4·25	5·00
153	27	90c. scarlet and red	5·00	8·75
154	29	1f. scarlet and red	5·00	7·75
155	27	1f.25 red and blue	6·75	8·50
156	27	1f.50 blue and deep blue	6·50	6·75
157	29	1f.75 brown and black	7·75	8·00
158	29	2f. green and black	20·00	30·00
159	28	3f. brown and green	26·00	38·00
160	28	5f. brown and red	34·00	60·00
161	29	10f. mauve and green	65·00	£110
162	27	20f. green and red	60·00	£120

1934. 400th Anniv of Cartier's Discovery of Canada. Optd **JACQUES CARTIER 1534 - 1934**.

163	28	50c. green and brown	7·25	11·00
164	27	75c. red and green	7·50	12·00
165	27	1f.50 blue and deep blue	8·75	14·50
166	29	1f.75 brown and black	9·75	16·00
167	28	5f. brown and red	37·00	65·00

32 Commerce

1937. International Exhibition, Paris.

168	32	20c. violet	1·50	9·25
169	-	30c. green	1·50	9·25
170	-	40c. red	1·50	8·25
171	-	50c. brown and blue	1·50	4·50
172	-	90c. red	1·50	4·50
173	-	1f.50 blue	1·50	5·50
MS173a		120×100 mm. 3f. blue. Imperf	18·00	70·00

DESIGNS—VERT: 50c. Agriculture. HORIZ: 30c. Sailing ships; 40c. Women of three races; 90c., 3f. France extends Torch of Civilization; 1f.50, Diane de Poitiers.

38 Pierre and Marie Curie

1938. International Anti-cancer Fund.

174	38	1f.75+50c. blue	10·00	25·00

39 Dog Team

1938

175	39	2c. green	10	4·00
176	39	3c. brown	10	3·75
177	39	4c. purple	60	4·00
178	39	5c. red	10	4·25
179	39	10c. brown	10	4·25
180	39	15c. purple	20	4·25
181	39	20c. violet	30	5·75
182	39	25c. blue	2·50	9·75
183	-	30c. purple	30	4·00
184	-	35c. green	1·40	7·00
185	-	40c. blue	65	7·00
186	-	45c. green	1·70	7·00
187	-	50c. red	90	4·50
188	-	55c. blue	5·75	11·00
189	-	60c. violet	1·30	6·75
190	-	65c. brown	5·75	16·00
191	-	70c. orange	2·00	6·75
192	-	80c. violet	3·00	7·75
193	-	90c. blue	2·75	6·00
194	-	1f. red	12·00	28·00
195	-	1f. olive	1·30	3·75
196	-	1f.25 red	2·50	9·25
197	-	1f.40 brown	3·00	7·50
198	-	1f.50 green	85	4·75
199	-	1f.60 purple	3·00	7·25
200	-	1f.75 blue	3·75	8·25
201	-	2f. purple	1·40	5·50
202	-	2f.25 blue	2·75	7·00
203	-	2f.50 orange	2·00	4·50
204	-	3f. brown	1·10	6·25
205	-	5f. red	90	7·75
206	-	10f. blue	1·70	4·50
207	-	20f. olive	2·75	8·00

DESIGNS: 30 to 70c. St. Pierre harbour; 80c. to 1f.75, Pointe aux Canons lighthouse (wrongly inscr "PHARE DE LA TORTUE"); 2 to 20f. Soldiers' Cove, Langlade.

41

1939. New York World's Fair.

208	41	1f.25 red	1·40	9·00
209	41	2f.25 blue	1·40	9·00

42 Storming the Bastille

1939. 150th Anniv of French Revolution.

210	42	45c.+25c. green & black	13·00	20·00
211	42	70c.+30c. brown and black	13·00	18·00
212	42	90c.+35c. orange and black	13·00	18·00
213	42	1f.25+1f. red and black	13·00	18·00
214	42	2f.25+2f. blue and black	13·00	18·00

1941. Free French Plebiscite. Stamps of 1938 optd **Noel 1941 FRANCE LIBRE F.N.F.L.** or surch also.

215A	39	10c. brown	80·00	95·00
216A	39	20c. violet	85·00	£100
217A	39	25c. blue	95·00	£100
218A	-	40c. blue	95·00	95·00
219A	-	45c. green	95·00	£100
220A	-	65c. brown	£100	£100
221A	-	70c. orange	£100	£100
222A	-	80c. violet	80·00	95·00
223A	-	90c. blue	85·00	95·00
224A	-	1f. green	85·00	95·00
225A	-	1f.25 red	85·00	95·00
226A	-	1f.40 brown	85·00	95·00
227A	-	1f.60 purple	£110	£120
228A	-	1f.75 blue	£120	£120
229A	-	2f. purple	£100	£120
230A	-	2f.25 blue	£110	£120
231A	-	2f.50 orange	£110	£120
232A	-	3f. brown	£110	£120
233A	39	10f. on 10c. brown	£130	£130
234A	-	20f. on 90c. blue	£130	£130

"F.N.F.L." = Forces Navales Francaises Libres (Free French Naval Forces).

1941. Various stamps overprinted **FRANCE LIBRE F. N. F. L.** or surch also. (a) Nos. 111 and 114.

245	17	10c. mauve and bistre	£1300	£1300
246	18	30c. blue and lake	£1300	£1300

(b) On stamps of 1932.

247	28	2c. green and black	£225	£250
248	29	4c. brown and red	75·00	95·00
249	29	5c. brown and mauve	£800	£850
250	29	40c. brown and blue	19·00	38·00
251	28	45c. green and red	£180	£190
252	28	50c. green and brown	12·00	34·00
253	29	65c. red and brown	65·00	70·00
254	29	1f. red and brown	£375	£400
255	29	1f.75 brown and black	15·00	38·00
256	29	2f. green and black	25·00	40·00
257	28	5f. brown and red	£375	£375
258	29	5f. on 1f.75 brown & blk	12·00	34·00

(c) On stamps of 1938.

259	39	2c. green	£425	£475
260	39	3c. brown	£150	£150
261	39	4c. purple	£130	£130
262	39	5c. red	£850	£850
263	39	10c. brown	8·25	10·00
264	39	15c. purple	£1600	£1600
265	39	20c. violet	£170	£180
266	39	20c. on 10c. brown	10·00	25·00
267	39	25c. blue	7·50	22·00
268	39	30c. on 10c. brown	6·75	13·00
269	-	35c. green	£800	£800
270	-	40c. blue	11·00	14·00
271	-	45c. green	14·50	28·00
272	-	55c. blue	£11000	£11000
273	-	60c. violet	£600	£600
274	-	60c. on 90c. blue	11·50	12·50
275	-	65c. brown	16·00	60·00
276	-	70c. orange	60·00	70·00
277	-	80c. violet	£450	£450
278	-	90c. blue	13·00	34·00
279	-	1f. green	14·50	27·00
280	-	1f.25 red	17·00	42·00
281	-	1f.40 brown	11·00	38·00
282	-	1f.50 green	£750	£800
283	-	1f.50 on 90c. blue	18·00	15·00
284	-	1f.60 purple	14·00	34·00
285	-	2f. purple	85·00	95·00
286	-	2f.25 blue	10·50	25·00
287	-	2f.50 orange	11·00	60·00
288	7	2f.50 on 10c. brown	14·00	13·00
289	-	3f. brown	£12000	£12000
290	-	5f. red	£2250	£2250
291	7	10f. on 10c. brown	55·00	90·00
292	-	20f. olive	£900	£1000
293	-	20f. on 90c. blue	75·00	95·00

(d) On Nos. 208/9.

294	41	1f.25 red	12·00	17·00
295	41	2f.25 blue	10·50	11·00
296	41	2f.50 on 1f.25 red	12·00	32·00
297	41	3f. on 2f.25 blue	17·00	36·00

1942. Stamps of 1932 overprinted **FRANCE LIBRE F. N. F. L.** or surch also.

304	27	20c. red and black	£400	£425
305	27	75c. red and green	13·00	36·00
306	27	1f.25 red and blue	11·00	28·00
307	27	1f.50 blue and deep blue	£475	£500
308	27	10f. on 1f.25 red and blue	50·00	65·00
309	27	20f. on 75c. red and green	65·00	90·00

1942. Social Welfare Fund. Nos. 279 and 287 further surch **OEUVRES SOCIALES**, cross and premium.

320	1f.+50c. green	60·00	80·00
321	2f.50+1f. orange	60·00	80·00

47 Fishing Schooner

48 Airliner

1942. (a) Postage.

322	47	5c. blue	10	3·25
323	47	10c. pink	10	3·50
324	47	25c. green	10	4·50
325	47	30c. black	25	2·75
326	47	40c. blue	35	3·50
327	47	60c. purple	45	2·00
328	47	1f. violet	60	2·75
329	47	1f.50 red	1·00	3·00
330	47	2f. brown	1·30	3·00

331	47	2f.50 blue	1·80	2·75
332	47	4f. orange	90	5·75
333	47	5f. purple	1·00	4·50
334	47	10f. blue	90	3·25
335	47	20f. green	1·30	4·50

(b) Air.

336	48	1f. orange	65	5·00
337	48	1f.50 red	1·00	2·75
338	48	5f. purple	75	3·00
339	48	10f. black	1·10	2·75
340	48	25f. blue	1·20	7·50
341	48	50f. green	1·20	8·00
342	48	100f. red	1·40	10·00

49

1944. Mutual Aid and Red Cross Funds.

343	49	5f.+20f. blue	75	8·75

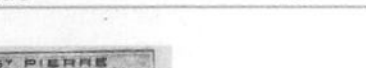

50 Felix Eboue

1945. Eboue.

344	50	2f. black	45	6·00
345	50	25f. green	90	7·75

1945. Surch.

346	47	50c. on 5c. blue	20	3·50
347	47	70c. on 5c. blue	35	7·00
348	47	80c. on 5c. blue	45	7·25
349	47	1f.20 on 5c. blue	30	5·50
350	47	2f.40 on 25c. green	40	4·25
351	47	3f. on 25c. green	55	3·50
352	47	4f.50 on 25c. green	75	7·75
353	47	15f. on 2f.50 blue	45	4·25

52 "Victory"

1946. Air. Victory.

354	52	8f. red	45	8·25

53 Legionaries by Lake Chad

1946. Air. From Chad to the Rhine.

355	53	5f. red	90	9·00
356	53	10f. lilac	90	9·00
357	53	15f. black	90	9·50
358	53	20f. violet	1·70	9·50
359	53	25f. brown	1·70	11·50
360	53	50f. black	1·80	11·50

54 Soldiers' Cove, Langlade

55 Allegory of Fishing

56 Douglas DC-4 and Wrecked Fishing Schooner

1947

361	54	10c. brown (postage)	10	1·70
362	54	30c. violet	10	3·25
363	54	40c. purple	10	3·00
364	54	50c. blue	10	2·50
365	55	60c. red	30	3·00
366	55	80c. blue	30	3·50
367	55	1f. green	55	1·80
368	-	1f.20 green	55	7·25
369	-	1f.50 black	90	2·30
370	-	2f. red	1·00	45
371	-	3f. violet	2·00	2·00
372	-	3f.60 red	2·30	4·50
373	-	4f. purple	2·75	1·20
374	-	5f. yellow	2·30	45
375	-	6f. blue	2·75	4·00
376	-	8f. sepia	5·00	1·80
377	-	10f. green	3·50	1·00
378	-	15f. green	3·25	1·30
379	-	17f. blue	6·25	5·75
380	-	20f. red	2·75	2·30
381	-	25f. blue	3·75	3·75
382	-	50f. green and red (air)	6·75	10·00
383	56	100f. green	11·00	22·00
384	-	200f. blue and red	12·00	27·00

DESIGNS—As Type **55**: 1f.20 to 2f. Cross and fishermen; 3f. to 4f. Weighing Atlantic cod; 5, 6, 10f. Trawler "Colonel Pleven"; 8, 17f. Red fox; 15, 20, 25f. Windswept mountain landscape. As Type **56**: 50f. Airplane and fishing village; 200f. Airplane and snow-bound fishing schooner.

58 People of Five Races, Aircraft and Globe

1949. Air. 75th Anniv of U.P.U.

395	58	25f. multicoloured	10·00	24·00

59 Doctor and Patient

1950. Colonial Welfare Fund.

396	59	10f.+2f. red and brown	7·25	20·00

60

1952. Centenary of Military Medal.

397	60	8f. blue, yellow and green	2·75	8·00

61 Normandy Landings, 1944

1954. Air. Tenth Anniv of Liberation.

398	61	15f. red and brown	6·00	4·50

62 Refrigeration Plant

63 Codfish

64 Dog and Coastal Scene

1955

399	62	30c. blue & dp bl (postage)	20	6·00
400	63	40c. brown and blue	35	7·00
401	62	50c. brown, grey and black	35	5·00
402	63	1f. brown and green	45	7·25
403	63	2f. indigo and blue	1·10	7·00
404	62	3f. purple	1·20	2·75
405	-	4f. purple, red and lake	3·25	7·50
406	-	10f. brown, blue & turq	3·25	2·30
407	-	20f. multicoloured	1·50	1·80
408	-	25f. brown, green and blue	2·75	8·00
409	62	40f. turquoise	2·30	6·25
410	64	50f. multicoloured (air)	30·00	60·00
411	-	100f. black and grey	12·00	34·00
412	-	500f. indigo and blue	55·00	65·00

DESIGNS—As Type **62/3**: 4, 10f. Pointe aux Canons Lighthouse and fishing dinghies; 20f. Ice hockey players; 25f. American minks. As Type **64**: 100f. Sud Aviation Caravelle airliner over St. Pierre and Miquelon; 500f. Douglas DC-3 over St. Pierre port.

65 Trawler "Galantry"

1956. Economic and Social Development Fund.

413	65	15f. sepia and brown	1·80	90

66 "Human Rights"

1958. Tenth Anniv of Declaration of Human Rights.

414	66	20f. brown and blue	55	1·00

67 "Picea"

1959

415	67	5f. multicoloured	45	8·50

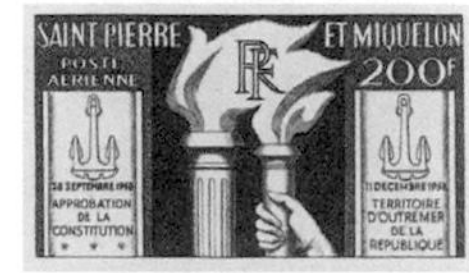

68 Flaming Torches

1959. Air. Adoption of Constitution.

416	68	200f. green, lake and violet	5·50	32·00

69 "Cypripedium acaule"

1962. Flowers.

417	69	25f. purple, orange and green (postage)	2·30	1·10
418	-	50f. red and green	3·00	14·50
419	-	100f. orange, red and green (air)	4·50	15·00

DESIGNS—VERT: 50f. "Calopogon pulchellus". HORIZ—48×27 mm: 100f. "Sarracenia purpurae".

70 Submarine "Surcouf" and Map

1962. Air. 20th Anniv of Adherence to Free French Government.

420	70	500f. black, blue and red	90·00	£130

71 "Telstar" Satellite and part of Globe

1962. Air. First Transatlantic TV Satellite Link.

421	71	50f. brown, green and sepia	2·30	14·50

72 Eiders

1963. Birds.

422	72	50c. bistre, black and blue	45	4·50
423	-	1f. brown, mauve and blue	90	5·25
424	-	2f. brown, black and blue	90	4·75
425	-	6f. bistre, blue and turquoise	2·30	7·50

DESIGNS: 1f. Rock ptarmigan; 2f. Semi-palmated plovers; 6f. Blue-winged teal.

73 Dr. A. Calmette

1963. Birth Centenary of Dr. Albert Calmette (bacteriologist).

426	73	30f. brown and blue	4·50	9·00

74 Landing of Governor from "Garonne"

1963. Air. Bicentenary of Arrival of First Governor (Dangeac) in St. Pierre and Miquelon.

427	74	200f. blue, green and brown	7·25	36·00

75 Centenary Emblem

1963. Red Cross Centenary.

428	75	25f. red, grey and blue	2·75	6·50

76 Globe and Scales of Justice

1963. 15th Anniv of Declaration of Human Rights.

429	76	20f. orange, purple and blue	3·75	10·00

77 "Philately"

1964. "PHILATEC 1964" International Stamp Exhibition, Paris.

430	77	60f. blue, green and purple	5·50	26·00

78 Common Rabbits

1964. Fauna.

431	78	3f. chocolate, brown & grn	2·00	7·00
432	-	4f. sepia, blue and green	3·00	7·25
433	-	5f. brown, sepia and blue	3·25	8·75
434	-	34f. brown, green and blue	4·50	11·00

ANIMALS: 4f. Red fox; 5f. Roe deer; 34f. Charolais bull.

79 Potez 842 Airliner and Map

1964. Air. First St. Pierre–New York Airmail Flight.

435	**79**	100f. brown and blue	6·50	23·00

80 Syncom Communications Satellite, Telegraph Poles and Morse Key

1965. Centenary of I.T.U.

436	**80**	40f. blue, brown and purple	9·25	12·00

81 Rocket "Diamant"

1966. Air. Launching of First French Satellite.

437	**81**	25f. brown, blue and red	3·50	20·00
438	**81**	30f. brown, blue and red	3·75	21·00

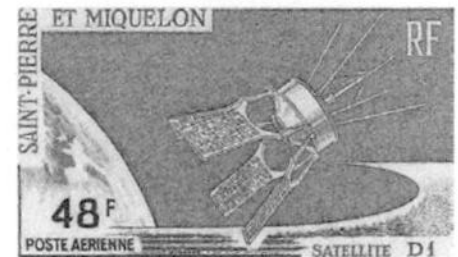

82 Satellite "D1"

1966. Air. Launching of Satellite "D1".

439	**82**	48f. blue, green and lake	3·25	8·00

83 "Revanche" and Settlers

1966. Air. 150th Anniv of Return of Islands to France.

440	**83**	100f. multicoloured	6·00	20·00

84 "Journal Officiel" and Old and New Printing Presses

1966. Air. Centenary of "Journal Officiel" Printing Works.

441	**84**	60f. plum, lake and blue	5·50	18·00

85 Map and Fishing Dinghies

1967. Air. Pres. De Gaulle's Visit.

442	**85**	25f. brown, blue and red	16·00	17·00
443	-	100f. blue, turquoise & pur	23·00	65·00

DESIGN: 100f. Maps and cruiser "Richelieu".

86 Trawler and Harbour Plan

1967. Opening of St. Pierre's New Harbour.

444	**86**	48f. brown, blue and red	8·00	10·50

87 Map and Control Tower

1967. Opening of St. Pierre Airport.

445	**87**	30f. multicoloured	4·00	8·00

88 T.V. Receiver, Aerial and Map

1967. Inauguration of Television Service.

446	**88**	40f. red, green and olive	5·50	10·50

89 Speed Skating

1968. Air. Winter Olympic Games, Grenoble. Multicoloured.

447	50f. Type **89**	6·50	14·50
448	60f. Ice-hockey goalkeeper	7·25	16·00

90 Bouquet, Sun and W.H.O. Emblem

1968. 20th Anniv of W.H.O.

449	**90**	10f. red, yellow and blue	4·50	12·50

91 J. D. Cassini (discoverer of group), Compasses and Chart

1968. Famous Visitors to St. Pierre and Miquelon (1st series).

450	**91**	4f. brown, yellow and lake	4·50	7·75
451	-	6f. multicoloured	5·75	10·50
452	-	15f. multicoloured	6·00	12·50
453	-	25f. multicoloured	7·75	13·00

CELEBRITIES: 6f. Rene de Chateaubriand and warship; 15f. Prince de Joinville, "Belle Poule" (sail frigate) and "Cassard" (survey ship); 25f. Admiral Gauchet and flagship "Provence" (Ile aux Chiens expedition).

92 Human Rights Emblem

1968. Human Rights Year.

454	**92**	20f. red, blue and yellow	7·75	18·00

93 War Memorial, St. Pierre

1968. Air. 50th Anniv of Armistice.

455	**93**	500f. multicoloured	20·00	55·00

94 Concorde in Flight

1969. Air. First Flight of Concorde.

456	**94**	34f. brown and olive	28·00	46·00

95 Mountain Stream, Langlade

1969. Tourism.

457	**95**	5f. brn, bl & grn (postage)	3·00	10·50
458	-	15f. brown, green and blue	3·25	13·00
459	-	50f. purple, olive & bl (air)	10·00	21·00
460	-	100f. brown, indigo & blue	16·00	23·00

DESIGNS: 15f. River bank, Debon, Langlade; 50f. Wild horses, Miquelon; 100f. Gathering wood, Miquelon. The 50f. and 100f. are larger 48×27 mm.

96 Treasury

1969. Public Buildings and Monuments.

461	**96**	10f. black, red and blue	2·75	8·00
462	-	25f. red, ultramarine & blue	3·75	8·25
463	-	30f. brown, green and blue	4·50	16·00
464	-	60f. black, red and blue	8·00	21·00

DESIGNS: 25f. Maritime Fisheries Scientific and Technical Institute; 30f. Unknown Sailor's Monument; 60f. St. Christopher's College.

97 "L'Estoile" and Granville, 1690

1969. Maritime Links with France.

465	**97**	34f. lake, green and emerald (postage)	8·50	13·50
466	-	40f. green, red and bistre	11·50	14·00
467	-	48f. multicoloured	12·50	16·00
468	-	200f. black, lake and green (air)	35·00	44·00

DESIGNS—As Type **97**: 40f. "La Jolie" and St. Jean de Luz, 1750; 48f. "La Juste" and La Rochelle, 1860; 48×27 mm. 200f. "L'Esperance" and St. Malo, 1600.

98 Pierre Loti, Sailing Ship and Book Titles

1969. Air. Pierre Loti (explorer and writer) Commemoration.

469	**98**	300f. multicoloured	50·00	60·00

99 Ringed Seals

1969. Marine Animals.

470	**99**	1f. brown, purple and lake	5·50	10·50
471	-	3f. blue, green and red	5·50	10·50
472	-	4f. green, brown and red	5·50	10·50
473	-	6f. violet, green and red	5·50	10·50

DESIGNS: 3f. Sperm whales; 4f. Long-finned pilot whale; 6f. Common dolphins.

100 I.L.O. Building, Geneva

1969. 30th Anniv of International Labour Organization.

474	**100**	20f. brown, slate and salmon	6·50	12·00

101 New U.P.U. Building, Berne

1970. New U.P.U. Headquarters Building, Berne.

475	**101**	25f. brown, blue and red	6·50	12·50
476	**101**	34f. slate, brown & purple	11·00	18·00

102 Rocket and Japanese Women

1970. Air. World Fair "EXPO 70", Osaka, Japan.

477	**102**	34f. brown, lake and blue	12·00	24·00
478	-	85f. blue, red and orange	20·00	44·00

DESIGN—HORIZ: 85f. "Mountain Landscape" (Y. Taikan) and Expo "star".

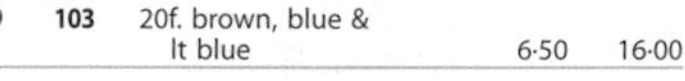

103 Rowing Fours

1970. World Rowing Championships, St. Catherine, Canada.

479	**103**	20f. brown, blue & lt blue	6·50	16·00

104 "Rubus chamaemorus"

1970. Fruit Plants.

480	**104**	3f. green, purple & brown	2·50	6·50
481	-	4f. yellow, red and green	2·50	6·50
482	-	5f. red, green and violet	2·75	8·00
483	-	6f. violet, green and purple	3·75	4·50

PLANTS: 4f. "Fragaria vesca"; 5f. "Rubus idaeus"; 6f. "Vaccinium myrtillus".

105 Ewe and Lamb

1970. Livestock Breeding.

484	**105**	15f. brown, purple & green	8·50	9·25
485	-	30f. brown, grey and green	9·25	12·50
486	-	34f. brown, purple & green	13·00	22·00
487	-	48f. purple, brown & blue	14·50	16·00

DESIGNS: 30f. Animal quarantine station; 34f. Charolais bull; 48f. Refrigeration plant and "Narrando" (trawler).

106 Etienne Francois, Duke of Choiseul, and Warships

1970. Air. Celebrities of St. Pierre and Miquelon.

488	**106**	25f. brown, blue & purple	6·50	8·25
489	-	50f. brown, purple & green	10·50	27·00
490	-	60f. brown, green & purple	12·00	29·00

DESIGNS: 50f. Jacques Cartier and "Grande Hermine"; 60f. Sebastien Le Gonard de Sourdeval and 17th-century French galleons.

107 "St. Francis of Assisi", 1900

1971. Fisheries' Protection Vessels.

491	**107**	30f. red, blue and turquoise	20·00	27·00
492	-	35f. brown, green and blue	21·00	18·00
493	-	40f. brown, blue and green	23·00	28·00
494	-	80f. black, green and blue	23·00	48·00

DESIGNS: 35f. "St. Jehanne", 1920; 40f. "L'Aventure", 1950; 80f. "Commandant Bourdais", 1970.

108 "Aconite"

1971. 30th Anniv of Allegiance to Free French Movement. British Corvettes on loan to Free French.

495	**108**	22f. black, green and blue	18·00	28·00
496	-	25f. brown, turquoise & bl	19·00	36·00
497	-	50f. black, turquoise & blue	36·00	60·00

DESIGNS: 25f. "Alyssum"; 50f. "Mimosa".

109 Ship's Bell

1971. St. Pierre Museum. Multicoloured.

498	20f. Type **109**	6·50	16·00
499	45f. Navigational instruments and charts (horiz)	10·00	14·00

110 De Gaulle in Uniform (June 1940)

1971. First Death Anniv of De Gaulle.

500	**110**	35f. black and red	7·25	13·00
501	**110**	45f. black and red	10·00	32·00

111 Haddock

1972. Ocean Fish.

502	**111**	2f. indigo, red and blue	3·75	10·00
503	-	3f. brown and green	3·75	10·00
504	-	5f. red and blue	4·50	5·50
505	-	10f. green and emerald	7·25	20·00

DESIGNS: 3f. American plaice; 5f. Deepwater redfish; 10c. Atlantic cod.

112 De Gaulle and Servicemen

1972. Air. General De Gaulle Commemoration.

506	**112**	100f. brown, green & pur	20·00	36·00

113 Long-tailed Ducks **114** Montcalm and Warships

1973. Currency Revaluation.

507	**113**	6c. brown, purple and blue (postage)	1·70	5·75
508	-	10c. black, red and blue	2·50	4·50
509	-	20c. bistre, ultram & bl	3·00	6·00
510	**113**	40c. brown, green & violet	3·50	6·00
511	-	70c. black, red and green	5·50	4·00
512	-	90c. bistre, blue and purple	9·50	27·00
513	**114**	1f.60 violet, indigo and blue (air)	12·50	12·00
514	-	2f. purple, green and violet	9·25	8·00
515	-	4f. green, mauve & brown	20·00	11·00

DESIGNS—As Type **113**: 10, 70c. Atlantic puffins; 20, 90c. Snowy owls. As Type **114**: HORIZ: 4f. La Salle, map and warships. VERT: 2f. Frontenac and various scenes.

116 Swimming Pool

1973. Inauguration of St. Pierre Cultural Centre.

521	**116**	60c. brown, blue and red	4·50	7·75
522	-	1f. purple, orange and blue	6·50	10·50

DESIGN: 1f. Centre building.

117 Transall C-160 in Flight

1973. Air.

523	**117**	10f. multicoloured	75·00	65·00

118 Met Balloon and Weather Ship

1974. World Meteorological Day.

524	**118**	1f.60 blue, green and red	11·50	21·00

119 Northern Gannet with Letter

1974. Centenary of Universal Postal Union.

525	**119**	70c. ultramarine, bl & red	4·50	9·25
526	**119**	90c. blue, red and lake	5·50	11·50

120 Clasped Hands on Red Cross

1974. Campaign for Blood Donors.

527	**120**	1f.50 multicoloured	10·00	21·00

121 Arms and Map of Islands

1974. Air.

528	**121**	2f. multicoloured	24·00	20·00

122 Banknotes in "Fish" Money-box

1974. Centenary of St. Pierre Savings Bank.

529	**122**	50c. brown, blue and black	5·00	11·50

123 Copernicus and Famous Scientists

1974. Air. 500th Birth Anniv (1973) of Nicholas Copernicus (astronomer).

530	**123**	4f. violet, red and blue	23·00	26·00

124 St. Pierre Church and Caspian Tern, Black-legged Kittiwake and Great Auk

1974. Island Churches.

531	**124**	6c. black, brown and green	5·75	7·00
532	-	10c. indigo, blue & brown	6·00	6·50
533	-	20c. multicoloured	14·00	7·25

DESIGNS: 10c. Miquelon Church and fishes; 20c. Our Lady of the Seamen Church and fishermen.

125 Red Admiral

1975. Butterflies. Multicoloured.

534	1f. Type **125**	9·25	7·00
535	1f.20 Orange tiger	12·00	9·00

126 Cod and St. Pierre et Miquelon Stamp of 1909

1975. Air. "Arphila 75" International Stamp Exhibition, Paris.

536	**126**	4f. red, indigo and blue	26·00	32·00

127 "Pottery" (Potter's wheel and products)

1975. Artisan Handicrafts.

537	**127**	50c. purple, brown & green	5·50	9·00
538	-	60c. blue and yellow	6·00	9·00

DESIGN: 60c. "Sculpture" (wood carving of Virgin and Child).

128 Pointe-Plate Lighthouse and Sea-birds

1975. Lighthouses.

539	**128**	6c. black, violet and green	3·75	7·00
540	-	10c. purple, green and slate	5·50	8·50
541	-	20c. brown, indigo & blue	13·50	9·25

DESIGNS: 10c. Galantry lighthouse, Atlantic puffin and pintail; 20c. Cap Blanc lighthouse and blue whale.

129 Judo

1975. Air. "Pre-Olympic Year". Olympic Games, Montreal (1976).

542	**129**	1f.90 blue, red and violet	11·50	15·00

130 Concorde in Flight

1976. Air. Concorde's First Commercial Flight.

543	**130**	10f. indigo, blue and red	25·00	29·00

131 President Pompidou

1976. President Pompidou Commemoration.

544	**131**	1f.10 grey and purple	6·50	16·00

132 Alexander Graham Bell and Early Telephone

1976. Air. Telephone Centenary.

545	**132**	5f. blue, orange and red	7·25	17·00

133 Washington and Lafayette

1976. Bicentenary of American Revolution.

546	**133**	1f. multicoloured	2·75	5·00

134 Basketball

1976. Olympic Games, Montreal.

547	**134**	70c. agate, blue and brown	6·00	12·50
548	-	2f.50 turquoise, green and emerald	12·00	23·00

DESIGN—HORIZ: 2f.50, Swimming.

135 Vigie Dam

1976

549	**135**	2f.20 brown, blue & turq	7·00	18·00

136 "Croix de Lorraine"

1976. Stern Trawlers. Multicoloured.

550	1f.20 Type **136**	13·00	12·00
551	1f.50 "Geolette"	29·00	24·00

1986. Nos. 2444 etc of France optd **ST-PIERRE ET MIQUELON**.

552	**916**	5c. green	20	4·00
553	**916**	10c. red	20	4·00
554	**916**	20c. green	20	4·00
555	**916**	30c. red	20	4·00
556	**916**	40c. brown	20	4·00
557	**916**	50c. mauve	20	4·00
558	**916**	1f. green	20	4·00
559	**916**	1f.80 green	35	4·25
560	**916**	2f. green	45	4·25
561	**916**	2f.20 red	55	1·80
562	**916**	2f. brown	55	5·00
563	**916**	3f.20 blue	55	5·00
564	**916**	4f. red	75	5·25
565	**916**	5f. blue	90	6·25
566	**916**	10f. violet	1·80	8·00

138 Open Book

1986. 450th Anniv of Discovery of Islands by Jacques Cartier and 1st Anniv of New Constitution.

567	**138**	2f.20 brown, deep brown and green	90	4·75

139 Statue and Harbour

1986. Centenary of Statue of Liberty.

568	**139**	2f.50 blue and red	1·10	2·40

141 Atlantic Cod and Detection Equipment

1986. Fishing.

578	**141**	1f. red	45	4·25
579	**141**	1f.10 orange	45	4·25
580	**141**	1f.30 red	55	4·25
581	**141**	1f.40 blue	55	4·25
582	**141**	1f.40 red	85	4·25
583	**141**	1f.50 blue	90	4·25
584	**141**	1f.60 green	1·00	4·25
585	**141**	1f.70 green	1·20	4·25

142 "Nativity" (stained glass window, L. Balmet)

1986. Christmas.

586	**142**	2f.20 multicoloured	1·00	4·75

143 Buff Cap ("Hygrophorus pratensis")

1987

587	**143**	2f.50 brown and ochre	1·80	5·00

See also Nos. 598, 609 and 645.

144 Dunan and Hospital

1987. Dr. Francois Dunan Commemoration.

588	**144**	2f.20 black, brown and blue	1·30	4·75

145 Ocean-racing Yachts

1987. Transatlantic Yacht Race (Lorient–St. Pierre et Miquelon–Lorient).

589	**145**	5f. brown, dp blue & blue	2·75	5·50

146 Maps

1987. Visit of President Francois Mitterand.

590	**146**	2f.20 multicoloured	1·30	5·00

147 Schooner on Slipway and Share Certificate

1987. Centenary of Marine Slipway.

591	**147**	2f.50 brown and light brown	2·00	5·00

148 Hawker Siddeley H.S. 748 (St. Pierre–Montreal first flight, 1987)

1987. Air. Airplanes named "Ville de St. Pierre".

592	**148**	5f. blue, green & turquoise	3·25	5·50
593	-	10f. dp blue, blue & orge	5·50	7·75

DESIGN: 10f. Flying boat "Ville de Saint-Pierre" (first flight, 1939).

149 "La Normande" (trawler)

1987

594	**149**	3f. multicoloured	3·00	6·25

150 "St. Christopher carrying Christ Child" (stained glass window by L. Balmet) and Scout Emblem

1987. Christmas. 50th Anniv of Scouting.

595	**150**	2f.20 multicoloured	1·80	4·50

151 Horses and Ducks

1987. Natural Heritage. Le Grand Barachois. Each orange, green and brown.

596	3f. Type **151**	2·40	5·25
597	3f. Canada geese, gulls and seals	2·40	5·25

Nos. 596/7 were printed together, *se-tenant*, with intervening half stamp size label, each strip forming a composite design.

1988. Fungi. As T **143**.

598	2f.50 black, orange and brown	1·40	4·50

DESIGN: "Russula paludosa".

152 Ice Hockey Goalkeeper

1988. Winter Olympic Games, Calgary.

599	**152**	5f. blue and red	2·00	6·00

153 Thomas and Camera

1988. Birth Centenary of Dr. Louis Thomas (photographer).

600	**153**	2f.20 brown, deep brown and blue	1·00	4·50

154 Airship "Hindenburg"

1988. Air. Aircraft. Each black, blue and purple.

601	5f. Type **154**	3·25	5·50
602	10f. Douglas DC-3	5·50	8·00

1988. "Philexfrance 89" International Stamp Exhibition, Paris. No. 2821 of France optd **ST-PIERRE ET MIQUELON**.

603	**1073**	2f.20 red, black and blue	1·70	4·75

156 "Nellie J. Banks" and Crates

1988. 50th Anniv of End of Prohibition and Last Liquor Smuggling Run from St. Pierre to Canada.

604	**156**	2f.50 ultramarine, brn & bl	2·30	5·00

157 "Le Marmouset" (stern trawler)

1988

605	**157**	3f. multicoloured	2·00	5·00

158 Ross Cove

1988. Natural Heritage. Each brown, deep blue and blue.

606	2f.20 Type **158**	2·00	4·50
607	13f.70 Cap Perce	4·50	13·50

159 Stained Glass Window

1988. Christmas.

608	**159**	2f.20 multicoloured	1·20	4·50

1989. Fungi. As T **143**.

609	2f.50 brown and red	1·40	4·50

DESIGN: 2f.50, "Tricholoma virgatum".

160 Judo

1989. 25th Anniv of Judo in St. Pierre.

610	**160**	5f. black, green and orange	2·30	5·50

161 "Liberty" (Roger Druet)

1989. Bicentenary of French Revolution and Declaration of Rights of Man. Multicoloured.

611	2f.20 Type **161**	1·10	4·50
612	2f.20 "Equality"	1·10	4·50
613	2f.20 "Fraternity"	1·10	4·50

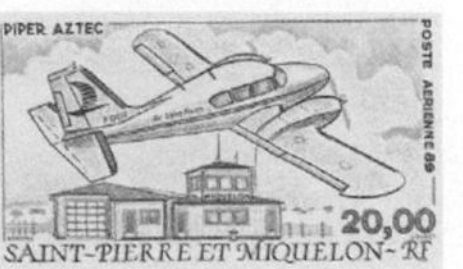

162 Piper Aztec

1989. Air.

614	**162**	20f. brown, light brown and blue	7·75	9·50

163 Tower of Bastille and Phrygian Cap on Tree

1989. "Philexfrance '89" International Stamp Exhibition, Paris (2nd issue) and Bicentenary of French Revolution (2nd issue). Sheet 150×140 mm containing T **163** and similar vert designs, each ultramarine, scarlet and black.

MS615 5f. Type **163**; 5f. Two towers of Bastille and brigantine; 5f. Raising tree of liberty; 5f. People cheering 11·00 28·00

164 Fisherman in Boat

1989. Natural Heritage. Ile aux Marins. Each brown, blue and green.

616	2f.20 Type **164**	1·80	4·50
617	13f.70 Boy flying kite from boat	5·50	13·00

165 "Le Malabar" (ocean-going tug)

1989

618	**165**	3f. multicoloured	2·10	4·50

166 Georges Landry and Emblem

1989. Centenary of Islands' Bank.

619	**166**	2f.20 blue and brown	1·30	4·50

167 "Christmas" (Magali Olano)

1989. Christmas.

620	**167**	2f.20 multicoloured	1·30	4·50

1990. Stamps of France optd **ST-PIERRE ET MIQUELON**.

621	**1118**	10c. brown	60	3·75
622	**1118**	20c. green	60	3·75
623	**1118**	50c. violet	60	3·75
624	**1118**	1f. orange	75	3·75
625	**1118**	2f. green	1·00	4·00
626	**1118**	2f. blue	1·00	4·00
627	**1118**	2f.10 green	85	4·00
628	**1118**	2f.20 green	2·00	4·00
629	**1118**	2f.30 red	1·20	3·75
630	**1118**	2f.40 green	2·10	4·25
631	**1118**	2f.50 red	1·80	4·00
632	**1118**	2f.70 green	2·00	2·75
633	**1118**	3f.20 blue	1·40	4·00
634	**1118**	3f.40 blue	2·00	4·25
635	**1118**	3f.50 green	1·60	4·50
636	**1118**	3f.80 mauve	1·40	4·00
637	**1118**	3f.80 blue	1·70	3·25
638	**1118**	4f. mauve	2·00	4·50
639	**1118**	4f.20 mauve	2·30	4·50
640	**1118**	4f.40 blue	1·80	4·50
641	**1118**	4f.50 mauve	2·00	4·00
642	**1118**	5f. blue	2·30	4·50
643	**1118**	10f. violet	3·25	5·75

The 2f.50 exists both perforated (ordinary gum) and imperforate (self-adhesive).

1990. Fungi. As T **143**.

645	2f.50 brown, black and orange	1·40	4·50

DESIGN: 2f.50, Hedgehog fungus ("Hydnum repandum").

168 "Pou du Ciel" and Gull

1990. Air.

646	**168**	5f. green, blue and brown	2·00	5·00

169 De Gaulle and Soldiers

1990. 50th Anniv of De Gaulle's Call to Resist.

647	**169**	2f.30 purple, red and blue	1·20	4·25

For design as T **169** but inscr "1890–1970", see No. 653.

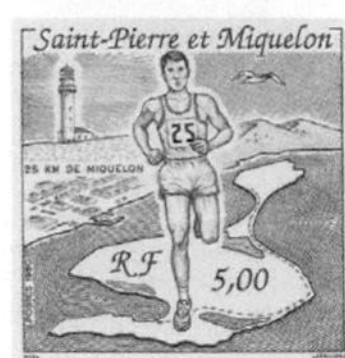

170 Runner and Map

1990. Miquelon 25 km Race.

648	**170**	5f. black, blue and brown	2·50	4·50

171 Moose, Micmac Canoe and Woman

1990

649	**171**	2f.50 orange, brown & bl	1·30	4·50

172 "Saint-Denis" and "Saint-Pierre" at Moorings

1990. Trawlers.

650	**172**	3f. multicoloured	1·90	4·50

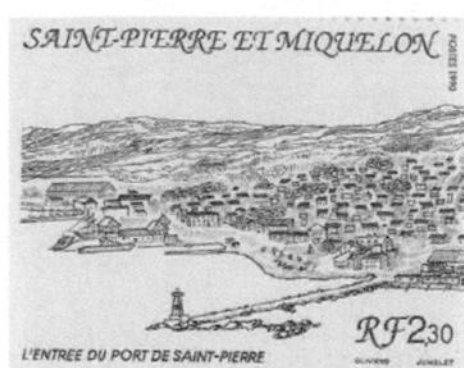

173 Entrance to Saint-Pierre Port

1990. St.-Pierre. Each brown, green and blue.

651	2f.30 Type **173**	1·60	4·50
652	14f.50 Interpeche fish factory	4·50	7·25

Nos. 651/2 were issued together, se-tenant, with intervening label, forming a composite design of part of St.-Pierre coastline.

1990. Birth Centenary of Charles de Gaulle (French statesman). As T **169** but inscr "1890–1970". Each purple, red and blue.

653	1f.70 Type **169**	1·00	1·60
654	2f.30 De Gaulle and trawler	1·20	1·80

174 Christmas Scene (Cindy Lechevallier)

1990. Christmas.

655	**174**	2f.30 multicoloured	1·40	4·50

175 Short-tailed Swallowtail on "Heracleum maximum"

1991

656	**175**	2f.50 multicoloured	1·40	4·50

176 Sail-makers' Tools and Sails

1991

657	**176**	1f.40 green and yellow	1·20	2·75
658	**176**	1f.70 red and yellow	1·40	3·25

177 Ile aux Marins

1991. Old Views.

659	**177**	1f.70 blue	90	3·25
660	-	1f.70 blue	90	3·25
661	-	1f.70 blue	90	3·25
662	-	1f.70 blue	90	3·25
663	**177**	2f.50 red	1·20	3·50
664	-	2f.50 red	1·20	3·50
665	-	2f.50 red	1·20	3·50
666	-	2f.50 red	1·20	3·50

DESIGNS: Nos. 660, 664, Langlade; 661, 665, Miquelon; 662, 666, Saint-Pierre.

178 Piper Tomahawk

1991. Air.

667	**178**	10f. blue, turquoise & brown	4·50	6·50

179 Musicians

1991. Centenary of Lyre Music Society.

668	**179**	2f.50 red, brown & orange	1·80	4·50

180 Oars

1991. St. Pierre–Newfoundland Crossing by Rowing Boat.

669	**180**	2f.50 multicoloured	1·70	4·50

181 Pelota Players

1991. Basque Sports.

670	**181**	5f. green and red	2·00	4·75

182 Fishermen

1991. Natural Heritage. Multicoloured.

671	2f.50 Type **182**	1·40	4·00
672	14f.50 Canada geese and shore	5·50	11·50

Nos. 671/2 were issued together, *se-tenant*, forming a composite design of Savoyard.

183 "Cryos" (stern trawler)

1991

673	**183**	3f. multicoloured	2·50	4·50

184 Free French Central Bank 100f. Note

1991. 50th Anniv of Central Economic Co-operation Bank.

674	**184**	2f.50 multicoloured	1·50	4·50

185 Naval Forces and Cross of Lorraine

1991. Christmas. 50th Anniv of Adherence to Free French Government.

675	**185**	2f.50 multicoloured	1·30	4·25

186 Muselier and Harbour

1992. 110th Birth Anniv of Admiral E. Muselier (commander of 1941 Free French landing force).

676	**186**	2f.50 multicoloured	1·40	4·00

187 Ice Skating

1992. Winter Olympic Games, Albertville.

677	**187**	5f. blue, ultramarine & mve	1·80	4·50

188 "Aeshna eremita" and "Nuphar variegatum"

1992

678	**188**	3f.60 multicoloured	1·70	4·25

189 Boat-building Tools and Stern of Ship

1992

679 **189** 1f.50 brown and blue 80 4·00
680 **189** 1f.80 blue and azure 90 4·00

190 Model Airplane and Remote Control

1992

681 **190** 20f. red, orange and brown 6·50 8·75

191 Ile aux Marins Lighthouse

1992. Lighthouses. Multicoloured.

682 2f.50 Type **191** 1·50 3·50
683 2f.50 Galantry 1·50 3·50
684 2f.50 Old Rouge Feu lighthouse, St. Pierre 1·50 3·50
685 2f.50 Pointe-Plate 1·50 3·50

192 Cones and Common Flicker

1992. Natural Heritage. Dolisie Valley, Langlade. Multicoloured.

686 2f.50 Type **192** 1·70 4·00
687 15f.10 Valley and berries 4·50 6·75

193 Columbus and Map on Sails

1992. 500th Anniv of Discovery of America by Columbus.

688 **193** 5f.10 multicoloured 2·30 4·75

194 Baron de l'Esperance, Map and Settlers

1992. 230th Anniv (1993) of Resettlement by French of Miquelon.

689 **194** 2f.50 brown, blue and red 1·30 4·00

195 Nativity

1992. Christmas.

690 **195** 2f.50 multicoloured 1·30 4·00

196 Birot and Free French Corvette

1993. 50th Death Anniv (1992) of Commander R. Birot.

691 **196** 2f.50 multicoloured 1·60 4·00

197 Divers and Wreck of "L'Hortense"

1993. Deep Sea Diving.

692 **197** 5f. multicoloured 2·50 4·50

198 Longhorn Beetle on "Cichorium intybus"

1993

693 **198** 3f.60 multicoloured 2·50 4·25

199 Cutting up Cod

1993

694 **199** 1f.50 multicoloured 1·40 4·00
695 **199** 1f.80 multicoloured 1·40 4·00

200 Greater Shearwater

1993. Air. Migratory Birds. Multicoloured.

696 5f. Type **200** 3·00 4·25
697 10f. American golden plover 4·00 5·50

201 Fleet of Ships

1993. Bicentenary of Settlement of Madeleine Islands.

698 **201** 5f.10 blue, green & brown 2·50 4·50

1993. No. 3121 of France optd **ST-PIERRE ET MIQUELON**.

699 **1118** (–) red 1·20 4·00

202 Short-spined Seascorpion

1993. Fish. Multicoloured.

700 2f.80 Type **202** 1·80 2·75
701 2f.80 Fishermen and capelin ("Le Capelan") 1·80 2·75
702 2f.80 Ray ("Le Raie") 1·80 2·75
703 2f.80 Atlantic halibut ("Le Fletan") 1·80 2·75

203 Pine Cones, Otter and Left Bank

1993. Natural Heritage. Sylvain Hills. Multicoloured.

704 2f.80 Type **203** 1·80 3·00
705 16f. Otter on all fours, pine cones and right bank 6·50 7·25

Nos. 704/5 were issued together, *se-tenant*, with intervening ¼ stamp-size label, forming a composite design of an otter pool.

204 Prefect's Residence

1993

707 **204** 3f.70 blue, yellow & brn 2·00 3·25

205 Father Christmas waving to Child

1993. Christmas.

708 **205** 2f.80 multicoloured 2·00 3·00

206 Blaison and "Surcouf" (Free French submarine)

1994. 50th Death Anniv (1992) of Commander Louis Blaison.

709 **206** 2f.80 multicoloured 2·00 3·25

207 Player lining up Shot

1994. First French Overseas Territories Petanque Championship.

710 **207** 5f.10 multicoloured 2·50 3·75

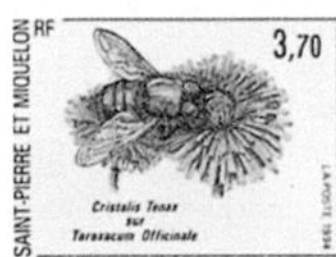

208 "Cristalis tenax" on Dandelion

1994

711 **208** 3f.70 multicoloured 1·80 3·50

209 Drying Atlantic Cod

1994

712 **209** 1f.50 black and green 85 3·00
713 **209** 1f.80 multicoloured 1·10 3·00

210 Ballot Box and Women outside Town Hall

1994. 50th Anniv of Women's Suffrage.

714 **210** 2f.80 multicoloured 1·40 3·00

211 "Saint-Pierre" (sail hospital ship)

1994. Centenary of Society of Sea Works.

715 **211** 2f.80 multicoloured 1·70 4·00

212 "Miquelon" (trawler)

1994. Ships. Multicoloured.

MS716 2f.80 Type **233**; 2f.80 "Ile de St. Pierre" (trawler); 3f.70 "St. Georges XII" (pleasure cruiser); 3f. 70"St. Eugene IV" (pleasure cruiser) 5·25 5·25

213 Poolside

1994. Natural Heritage. Miranda Pool. Multicoloured.

720 2f.80 Type **213** 1·40 2·50
721 16f. Pool 5·50 7·25

Nos. 720/1 were issued together *se-tenant* with intervening ½ stamp-size label, forming a composite design.

214 Parochial School

1994

722 **214** 3f.70 black, blue and red 1·70 3·25

215 Envelope, Magnifying Glass and Tweezers holding "Stamp"

1994. First European Stamp Salon, Flower Gardens, Paris.

723 **215** 3f.70 blue, green and yellow 2·00 3·50

216 House and Christmas Tree

1994. Christmas.

724 **216** 2f.80 multicoloured 1·70 3·00

217 Pasteur

1995. Death Centenary of Louis Pasteur (chemist).

725 **217** 2f.80 multicoloured 1·70 3·00

218 Sports Pictograms

1995. Triathlon.

726 **218** 5f.10 multicoloured 2·20 3·50

219 "Dicranum scoparium" and "Cladonia cristatella"

1995

727	**219**	3f.70 multicoloured	1·60	3·25

220 Cooper at Work

1995

728	**220**	1f.50 multicoloured	70	3·00
729	**220**	1f.80 multicoloured	90	3·00

221 Arctic Terns

1995. Air. Migratory Birds.

730	**221**	10f. multicoloured	4·50	4·50

222 Crab

1995. Crustaceans and Molluscs. Multicoloured.

731	2f.80 Winkle	2·00	3·00
732	2f.80 Type **222**	2·00	3·00
733	2f.80 Scallop	2·00	3·00
734	2f.80 Lobster	2·00	3·00

223 Geologists working at Cliff Face

1995. Geological Research. Multicoloured.

735	2f.80 Type **223**	1·80	2·75
736	16f. Geological map of Langlade	4·50	6·25

224 Sister Cesarine

1995. 150th Birth Anniv of Sister Cesarine.

737	**224**	1f.80 multicoloured	1·10	3·00

225 Building

1995. Francoforum.

738	**225**	3f.70 grey, blue and red	1·70	3·25

226 De Gaulle and French Flag

1995. 25th Death Anniv of Charles de Gaulle (French President, 1958–69).

739	**226**	14f. multicoloured	4·50	5·25

227 Shop Window

1995. Christmas.

740	**227**	2f.80 multicoloured	2·30	3·00

228 Levasseur and Free French Corvette

1996. 50th Death Anniv (1997) of Commander Jean Levasseur.

741	**228**	2f.80 multicoloured	2·50	3·25

229 Boxers

1996

742	**229**	5f.10 multicoloured	2·75	3·50

230 "Cladonia verticillata" and "Polytrichum juniperinum"

1996. Mosses and Lichens.

743	**230**	3f.70 multicoloured	2·50	3·25

231 Blacksmiths at Work

1996

744	**231**	1f.50 multicoloured	1·00	2·75
745	**231**	1f.80 multicoloured	1·10	3·00

232 Whimbrel

1996. Air. Migratory Birds.

746	**232**	15f. multicoloured	7·25	5·25

233 "Rader II" (pilot boat)

1996. Ships. Sheet 143×100 mm. containing T **233** and similar horiz designs. Multicoloured.

MS747 3f. Type **233**; 3f. "Lanelape" (ferry); 3f. "Pinta" (ferry); 3f. "Pascal-Annie" (trawler) 5·25 5·25

234 The Cape

1996. Miquelon. Multicoloured.

748	3f. Type **234**	1·30	2·50
749	15f.50 The village	4·50	5·00

Nos. 748/9 were issued together, *se-tenant*, with intervening ¾ stamp-size label, forming a composite design.

235 Customs House

1996. Centenary of Customs House, St. Pierre.

750	**235**	3f.80 blue and black	1·60	3·00

236 1947 Postage Due Design

1996. 50th Paris Autumn Stamp Show.

751	**236**	1f. multicoloured	55	2·75

237 Crib in St. Pierre Cathedral

1996. Christmas.

752	**237**	3f. multicoloured	1·60	3·00

238 Colmay

1997. 32nd Death Anniv of Commandant Constant Colmay.

753	**238**	3f. multicoloured	1·60	3·00

239 Common Cormorant and "Sedum rosea"

1997

754	**239**	3f.80 multicoloured	2·00	3·00

240 Salting House

1997

755	**240**	1f.70 multicoloured	85	3·00

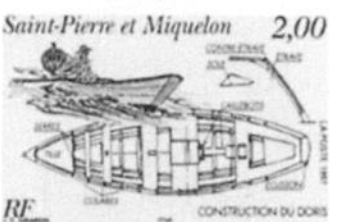
241 "Doris" (rowing boat) and Construction Plan

1997

756	**241**	2f. multicoloured	85	3·00

242 Player, Ball and Net

1997. Volleyball.

757	**242**	5f.20 multicoloured	2·00	3·25

243 Peregrine Falcon

1997. Air. Migratory Birds.

758	**243**	5f. multicoloured	2·50	3·25

244 Statue of Liberty, "L'Oiseau Blanc" and Eiffel Tower

1997. Air. 70th Anniv of Disappearance of Charles Nungesser and Francois Coli (aviators) on attempted Non-stop Flight between Paris and New York.

759	**244**	14f. black, blue and brown	4·50	5·25

245 Atlantic Salmon

1997. Fish. Multicoloured.

760	3f. Type **245**	1·30	3·00
761	3f. Lumpsucker ("Poule d'Eau")	1·30	3·00
762	3f. Atlantic mackerel ("Maquereau")	1·30	3·00
763	3f. Porbeagle ("Requin Marache")	1·30	3·00

1997. No. 3407 of France (no value expressed) optd **ST-PIERRE ET MIQUELON**. Ordinary gum or self-adhesive.

764	**1313**	(3f.) red	85	2·75

1997. Nos. 3415 etc. of France optd **ST-PIERRE ET MIQUELON**.

765	**1313**	10c. brown	1·30	2·50
766	**1313**	20c. green	1·30	2·50
767	**1313**	50c. violet	1·50	2·50
768	**1313**	1f. orange	1·60	2·75
769	**1313**	2f. blue	1·70	2·75
770	**1313**	2f.70 green	85	2·75
773	**1313**	3f.50 green	2·00	3·00
775	**1313**	3f.80 blue	1·00	3·00
776	**1313**	4f.20 red	2·30	3·00
778	**1313**	4f.40 blue	2·30	3·00
779	**1313**	4f.50 mauve	2·30	3·00
780	**1313**	5f. blue	2·30	3·25
781	**1313**	6f.70 green	2·50	3·25
782	**1313**	10f. violet	3·25	3·00

246 Cap aux Basques

1997. Multicoloured.

785	3f. Type **246**	1·60	2·50
786	15f.50 Diamant	4·50	4·00

Nos. 785/6 were issued together, *se-tenant*, with intervening ¾ stamp-size label, forming a composite design.

247 Post Office

1997. Public Buildings.

787	**247**	3f.80 multicoloured	2·00	3·00

248 Nativity

1997. Christmas.

788	**248**	3f. multicoloured	2·75	3·00

249 Savary and Building

1998. Tenth Death Anniv of Alain Savary (Governor).

789	**249**	3f. multicoloured	2·00	3·00

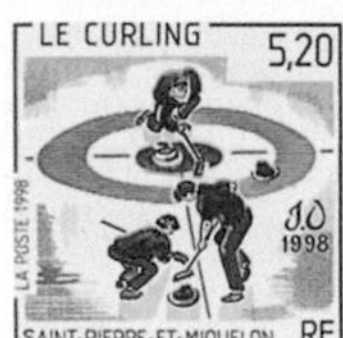
250 Curling

1998. Winter Olympic Games, Nagano, Japan.

790	**250**	5f.20 red, blue and scarlet	2·50	3·25

251 Irises and Horses

1998

791	**251**	3f.80 multicoloured	2·75	3·00

252 Lifting Blocks of Ice

1998. Work on the Ice. Multicoloured.

792	1f.70 Type **252**	1·40	2·75
793	2f. Cutting out blocks of ice	1·40	2·75

253 Head of American Bald Eagle

1998

794	**253**	10f. multicoloured	4·75	4·50

1998. "Philexfrance 99" International Stamp Exhibition, Paris. No. 3460 of France optd **ST-PIERRE ET MIQUELON**.

795	**1334**	3f. red and blue	2·00	2·75

254 Yellow House

1998. Local Houses. Multicoloured.

796	3f. Type **254**	2·00	2·75
797	3f. Pink house	2·00	2·75
798	3f. White house	2·00	2·75
799	3f. Grey house	2·00	2·75

255 Map of Gulf of St. Lawrence

1998. France in North America.

800	**255**	3f. multicoloured	1·80	2·75

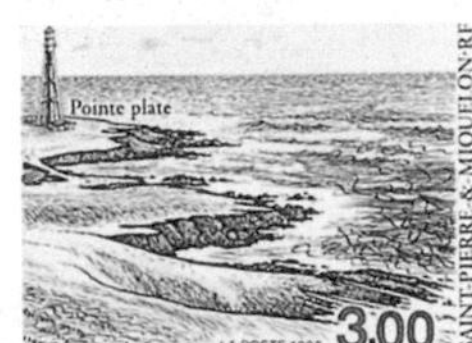
256 Pointe Plate

1998. Natural Heritage. Multicoloured.

801	3f. Type **256**	2·00	2·75
802	15f.50 Cap Bleu	5·00	3·75

Nos. 801/2 were issued together, *se-tenant*, with intervening ¾ stamp-size label, forming a composite design.

257 Map of the Americas and Map of France on Football

1998. France, World Cup Football Champion.

803	**257**	3f. multicoloured	2·75	2·75

258 War Memorial

1998

804	**258**	3f.80 purple, red and blue	3·00	3·00

259 Santa Claus delivering Presents

1998. Christmas.

805	**259**	3f. multicoloured	2·75	2·75

260 Letournel

1999. Fifth Death Anniv of Emile Letournel (orthopaedic surgeon).

806	**260**	3f. olive, green and brown	1·80	2·75

261 Ile-aux-marins Shore

1999

807	**261**	5f.20 multicoloured	2·30	3·25

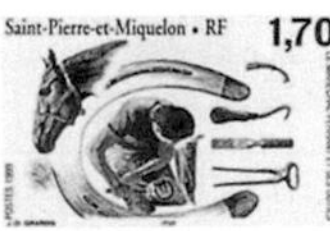
262 *Rubus chamaemorus*

1999

808	**262**	3f.80 multicoloured	2·30	3·00

1999. Nos. 3553 of France optd **ST-PIERRE ET MIQUELON.** Ordinary or self-adhesive gum.

809	**1376**	3f. red and blue	1·80	2·75

No. 809 is denominated in both French francs and euros.

263 Horseshoe, Farrier and Tools

1999. The Farrier. Multicoloured.

811	1f.70 Type **263**	1·80	2·75
812	2f. Farrier at work	2·00	3·00

264 Northern Pintail

1999. Air. Migratory Birds.

813	**264**	20f. multicoloured	10·50	7·75

265 France 1849 20c. St. Pierre et Miquelon 1885 5c. on 2c. and 1909 1c. Stamps

1999. "Philexfrance 99" International Stamp Exhibition, Paris (2nd issue). 150th Anniv of First French Postage Stamp. Sheet 132×159 mm containing T **265** and similar vert designs. Multicoloured.

MS814	3f. Type **265**; 3f. St. Pierre et Miquelon 1932 40c. and 1941 1f.25 stamps; 3f. St.Pierre et Miquelon 1957 50f. and 1967 100f. stamps; 3f. St. Pierre et Miquelon 1986 2f.20 and 1999 3f. stamps	5·00	5·00

266 "Bearn" (steam tug)

1999. Ships. Sheet 143×100m containing T **266** and similar horiz designs. Multicoloured.

MS815	3f. Type **266** ; 3f. "Pro-Patria" (mail ship); 3f. "Eminie" (deep sea fishing boat); 3f. "Colombier" (coastal patrol vessel)	4·50	4·50

267 Cars and Quayside

1999. Place du General de Gaulle. Multicoloured.

816	3f. Type **267**	2·50	3·25
817	15f.50 Boats	5·75	6·25

268 Maps of St. Pierre et Miquelon and France

1999. Visit of President Jacques Chirac of France.

818	**268**	3f. multicoloured	2·75	2·75

269 Interior

1999. Museum and Archives.

819	**269**	5f.40 mauve	3·50	3·25

270 House and Snowman (Best Wishes)

1999. Greetings Stamp.

820	**270**	3f. multicoloured	2·50	2·75

271 "Bonjour l'An 2000"

2000. New Millennium.

821	**271**	3f. multicoloured	3·00	2·75

272 Humpback Whale

2000. Whales.

822	**272**	3f. black and blue	2·50	2·75
823	-	5f.70 black and green	3·75	3·50

DESIGN: 5f.70, Fin whale.

273 "Les Graves"

2000. Art.

824	**273**	5f.20 multicoloured	4·00	3·25

274 *Vaccinium vitis-idaea*

2000

825	**274**	3f.80 multicoloured	3·25	3·00

275 Wood on Dog-sled

2000. The Collection of Wood.

826	**275**	1f.70 blue and black	2·75	2·75
827	**275**	2f. brown and black	2·75	2·75

276 Fishermen, 1904

2000. The Twentieth Century, 1900–1950 (1st issue). Multicoloured.

828	3f. Type **276** (abandonment of fishing and drying rights on French shore)	3·00	2·75
829	3f. Women carrying dried cod, 1905	3·00	2·75
830	3f. Conscripts leaving New York for Le Havre, 1915	3·00	2·75
831	3f. Assault on Souain Hill, 1915	3·00	2·75
832	3f. People on pack ice and icebound ships (isolation of St. Pierre during exceptional weather), 1923	3·00	2·75
833	3f. Unloading contraband during American prohibition era, 1925	3·00	2·75
834	3f. St. Pierre et Miquelon Pavilion at International Colonial Exhibition, Paris, 1931	3·00	2·75
835	3f. Procession flying French and American flags (end of prohibition in America), 1933	3·00	2·75
836	3f. Admiral Muselier of Free French Naval Forces inspecting seamen (loss of *Mimosa* off Terre-Neuve), 1942	3·00	2·75
837	3f. Army vehicles crossing the Rhine, 1945	3·00	2·75

See also Nos. 842/51.

Nos. 818, 820/4, 826/7 and 838 and subsequent St. Pierre et Miquelon issues are denominated both in francs and in euros. As no cash for the latter is in circulation, the catalogue continues to use the franc value.

277 *L'Inger* (wrecked galleon)

2000

838	**277**	5f.40 green	4·00	3·25

278 Houses behind Boat Sheds

2000. Salt Works. Multicoloured.

839	3f. Type **278**	3·00	2·75
840	15f.50 Church behind boat sheds	5·00	3·75

279 Angels, Village and "2000"

2000. Christmas.

841	**279**	3f. multicoloured	3·00	2·75

280 Frozen Fish Factory, 1951

2000. The Twentieth Century, 1950–2000 (2nd issue). Multicoloured.

842	2f. Type **280**	3·00	2·75
843	2f. *Ravenel* (loss of trawler and crew, 1960)	3·00	2·75
844	2f. General de Gaulle meeting ex-servicemen during visit to St. Pierre, 1967	3·00	2·75
845	2f. First television images (inauguration of local station), 1967	3·00	2·75
846	2f. Construction of new port, 1970	3·00	2·75
847	2f. Construction of new college, 1977	3·00	2·75
848	2f. View over islands (change of status to Collective Territoriale and resumption of stamp issues, 1986)	3·00	2·75
849	2f. Eric Tarbarly's racing yacht (Tarbarly's stop-off in St. Pierre during Round the World Yacht Race, 1987)	3·00	2·75
850	2f. Oil rig and map (exploitation of off-shore oil services, 1992)	3·00	2·75
851	2f. Runway extension, White Point Airport, 1999	3·00	2·75

281 Rough-legged Buzzard

2000. Air.

852	**281**	5f. multicoloured	3·75	3·25

282 "2001"

2000. New Millennium.

853	**282**	3f. multicoloured	3·00	2·75

283 Killer Whale

2001. Whales.

854	**283**	3f. black and blue	3·00	2·75
855	-	5f.70 black and green	4·00	3·50

DESIGN: 5f.70, Long-finned pilot whale.

284 "Reflections"

2001

856	**284**	5f.20 multicoloured	3·75	3·25

285 Apple

2001

857	**285**	3f.80 multicoloured	3·25	3·00

286 "Hay gathering"

2001

858	**286**	1f.70 multicoloured	2·75	2·75
859	**286**	2f. multicoloured	2·75	2·75

287 Great Blue Heron

2001. Air.

860	**287**	15f. multicoloured	6·50	3·75

288 Lake in Autumn

2001. Seasons (1st series). Multicoloured.

861	3f. Type **288**	1·80	1·60
862	3f. Lake in winter	1·80	1·60

See also Nos. 871/2.

289 Porch (Maison Jugan)

2001. Porches. Multicoloured.

863	3f. Type **289**	1·80	1·60
864	3f. Marie de L'île-aux-Marins	1·80	1·60
865	3f. Maison Voge	1·80	1·60
866	3f. Maison Guillou	1·80	1·60

290 Trees, Houses and River

2001. Landscapes. Multicoloured.

867	10f. Type **290**	3·50	2·30
868	10f. Cliff-top houses and church	3·50	2·30

291 Airport

2001. Saint-Pierre Pointe Blanche Airport.

869	**291**	5f. multicoloured	2·30	2·00

292 *Marie-Therese*

2001. Wreck of Marie-Therese off Pointe-du Diamant.

870	**292**	5f.40 green	2·50	2·10

2001. Seasons (2nd series). As T **288**. Multicoloured.

871	3f. Lake in spring	1·80	1·60
872	3f. Lake in summer	1·80	1·60

293 Commander Jacques Pepin Lehalleur and *Alysse* (corvette)

2001

873	**293**	3f. multicoloured	1·80	1·60

294 Father Christmas

2001. Christmas.

874	**294**	3f. multicoloured	1·80	1·60

2002. Nos. 3770/82 and 3784/90 of France optd **ST-PIERRE ET MIQUELON**. (a) With face value. Ordinary gum.

875	**1318**	1c. yellow	1·30	1·40
876	**1318**	2c. brown	1·30	1·40
877	**1318**	5c. green	1·30	1·40
878	**1318**	10c. violet	1·30	1·40
879	**1318**	20c. orange	1·40	1·40
880	**1318**	41c. green	1·80	1·60
881	**1318**	50c. blue	1·80	1·60
882	**1318**	53c. green	1·90	1·60
883	**1318**	58c. blue	2·00	1·70
883a	**1318**	58c. green	1·90	1·60
884	**1318**	64c. orange	2·00	1·70
885	**1318**	67c. blue	2·30	1·70
886	**1318**	69c. mauve	2·30	1·70
887	**1318**	70c. green	2·30	1·80
888	**1318**	90c. blue	2·75	1·80
889	**1318**	€1 turquoise	2·75	1·80
890	**1318**	€1.02 green	2·75	1·80
891	**1318**	€1.11 purple	3·00	2·00
892	**1318**	€1.90 purple	4·25	2·30
893	**1318**	€2 violet	4·50	2·30

(b) (i) No value expressed.

897	**1318**	(41c.) green	1·80	1·50

(ii) Self-adhesive gum.

900	**1318**	(46c.) red	1·60	1·50

295 Magnifying Glass, Birds and Map

2002. "The Archipelago and the Euro".

908	**295**	€1 multicoloured	2·50	1·80

296 Common Seal (*Phoca vitulina*)

2002. Seals (1st series).

909	**296**	46c. black and brown	1·80	1·60
910	-	87c. black and brown	2·50	2·00

DESIGN: 87c. Grey seal (*Halichoerus grypus*).

See also Nos. 926/7.

297 "La Pomme de Pre"

2002

911	**297**	58c. multicoloured	2·00	1·60

298 Laranaga Farm

2002

912	**298**	79c. green	2·50	1·90

299 Mending Nets

2002

913	**299**	26c. orange	1·50	1·60
914	**299**	30c. blue	1·60	1·60

300 Atlantic Puffin

2002

915	**300**	€2.50 multicoloured	5·50	3·00

301 West Point

2002

916	**301**	75c. multicoloured	2·30	2·00

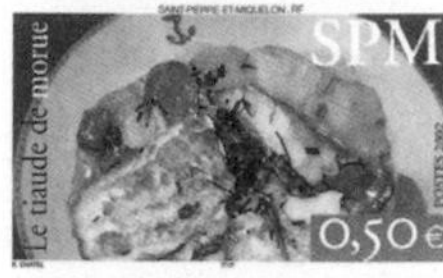

302 "Le Tiaude de Morue" (cod dish)

2002. Traditional Dishes.

917	**302**	50c. multicoloured	1·80	1·70

2002. No. 3752 of France (no value expressed) optd **ST-PIERRE ET MIQUELON**.

918	**1318**	(41c.) red	1·80	1·40

303 Arctic Hare (*Lepus timidus*)

2002

921	**303**	46c. multicoloured	1·80	1·70

304 *Le Troutpool*

2002. Wreck of *Le Troutpool* off Pointe-du Diamant.

922	**304**	84c. green	2·50	2·00

305 Grand Colombier Island and Sea Bird

2002. L'Anse a Henry Cove.

923	**305**	€2 blue, black and yellow	4·00	3·25
924	-	€2 blue and black	4·00	3·25

DESIGN: No. 924, Saint Pierre Island Nos. 923/4 were issued together, *se-tenant*, forming a composite design.

306 Yacht with Christmas Tree on Sail

2002. Christmas.

925	**306**	46c. multicoloured	1·80	1·60

307 Harp Seal (*Phoca groenlandica*)

2003. Seals (2nd series).

926	**307**	46c. black and blue	1·80	1·60
927	-	87c. black and blue	2·50	1·90

DESIGNS: Type **307**; 87c. Hooded seal (*Cystophora cristata*).

308 Francois Maurer

2003. Third Death Anniv of Monseigner Francois Maurer (bishop of St. Pierre et Miquelon).

928	**308**	46c. multicoloured	1·80	1·70

309 Capandeguy Farm

2003

929	**309**	79c. brown	2·40	1·90

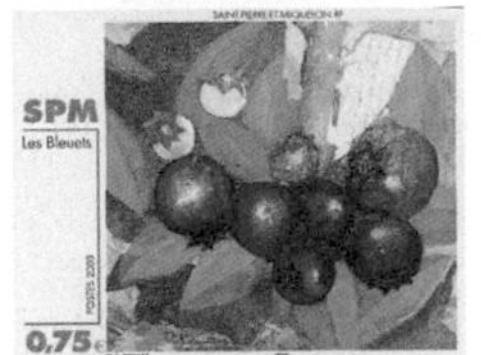
310 "Les Bleuets" (Marie-Laure Drillet)

2003

930	**310**	75c. multicoloured	2·30	1·90

311 "Le Poulieur" (the pulley man)

2003

931	**311**	30c. blue	1·60	1·60

312 Maison Patrice, Maison Jezequel and Maison Jugan (houses)

2003. International Traditional Architecture Congress. Traditional architecture. Multicoloured.

932	€2 Type **312**	5·00	3·75
933	€2 Notre-Dame des Marins and Maison Borotra	5·00	3·75

Nos. 932/3 were issued together, *se-tenant*, forming a composite design.

313 Northern Gannet

2003. Air.

934	**313**	€2.50 multicoloured	5·50	4·50

314 Player

2003. Centenary of Associations Sportives de Saint-Pierre et Miquelon (ASSP).

935	**314**	50c. multicoloured	1·80	1·70

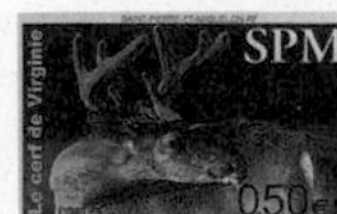
315 White-tailed Deer (*Odocoileus virginianus*)

2003

936	**315**	50c. multicoloured	1·80	1·70

316 Strawberries

2003. Langdale Strawberry Jam.

937	**316**	50c. multicoloured	1·80	1·70

317 Lions Club Emblem

2003. 50th Anniv of Lions Club (charitable organization).

938	**317**	50c. multicoloured	1·80	1·70

318 *L' Afrique*

2003. Shipwrecks (1st series). L'Afrique (1920).

939	**318**	90c. black	2·75	2·00

See also No. 953.

319 Snow-covered Trees and Icicles

2003. Christmas.

940	**319**	50c. multicoloured	1·80	1·70

320 Joseph Lehuenen

2004. Joseph Lehuenen (politician and historian) Commemoration.

941	**320**	50c. brown	1·80	1·70

321 Anse a Rodrigue

2004

942	**321**	75c. multicoloured	2·75	2·50

322 Atlantic White-sided Dolphin (*Lagenorhynchus acutus*)

2004. Dolphins.

943	**322**	50c. purple and black	1·80	1·70
944	-	€1.08 brown and black	3·25	3·25

DESIGN: €1.08 Harbour porpoise (*Phocoena phocoena*).

323 Ollivier Farm

2004

945	**323**	90c. orange	3·00	2·75

324 "Back from Fishing"

2004

946	**324**	30c. multicoloured	1·40	1·40

325 Pro Patria Postal Ship and Sail Ships

2003. St. Pierre et Miquelon Port (circa 1928).

947	€2 black, violet and magenta	6·00	6·00
948	€2 black, violet and blue	6·00	6·00

DESIGNS: €2×2 Type **325**; Sail ships and prow of schooner.

Nos. 947/8 were issued together, *se-tenant*, forming a composite design.

326 Canada Geese

2004. Air. Migrant Birds.

949	**326**	€2.50 multicoloured	8·00	7·50

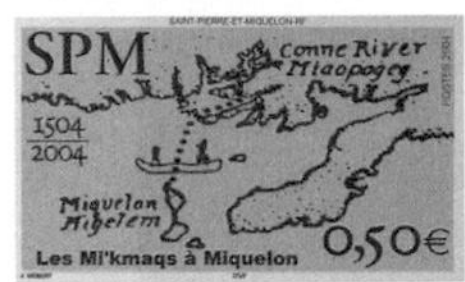
327 Map

2004. 500th Anniv of Mi'kmaq (aboriginal Indians) Village.

950	**327**	50c. multicoloured	1·90	2·00

2004. No. 950 optd **1re liason postale à la lame Miquelon - Terre Neuve Associations des Gangos**.

951	50c. multicoloured	2·00	2·10

329 Fox

2004

952	**329**	50c. multicoloured	2·10	2·30

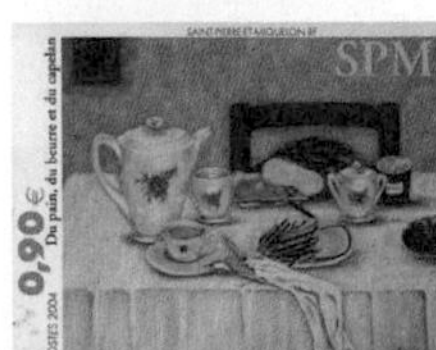
330 "Bread, Butter and Poor Cod"

2004

953	**330**	90c. multicoloured	3·00	3·25

331 Ribs of Ship

2004. Shipwrecks (2nd series). Fulwood (1828).

954	**331**	75c. lilac	2·75	3·00

332 *Le Cap Blanc*

2004. Transport Ships. Multicoloured.

MS955	170×115 mm. 50c. ×4, Type **332**; *Le Lisbet-C; Le Shamrock; L'Aldona*	8·00	8·00

333 Footballers

2004. 50th Anniv of SIAA.

956	**333**	44c. multicoloured	1·80	1·90

334 Snow Globe

2004. Christmas.

957	**334**	50c. multicoloured	2·00	2·10

2005. Nos. 4016/4028 of France optd **ST-PIERRE ET MIQUELON**. (i) With face value.

958	**1586**	1c. yellow	1·00	1·30
959	**1586**	5c. agate	1·10	1·30
960	**1586**	10c. violet	1·20	1·30
961	**1586**	60c. black	1·20	1·30
965	**1586**	55c. ultramarine	1·90	2·00
966	**1586**	58c. yellow	2·00	2·10
966a	**1586**	60c. ultramarine	2·10	2·30
967	**1586**	64c. green	2·20	2·40
968	**1586**	70c. green	2·30	2·40
968a	**1586**	70c. violet	2·30	2·40
969	**1586**	75c. blue	2·40	2·50
970	**1586**	82c. rose	2·50	2·50
970a	**1586**	85c. violet	2·75	2·75
970b	**1586**	86c. rose	2·75	2·75
972	**1586**	90c. indigo	2·75	2·75
973	**1586**	€1 orange	2·75	3·00
974	**1586**	€1.11 purple	3·00	3·25
974a	**1586**	€1.15 blue	3·75	4·00
975	**1586**	€1.22 purple	4·25	4·25
975a	**1586**	€1.30 purple	4·25	4·50
977	**1586**	€1.90 brown	5·00	5·25
981	**1586**	€1.98 purple	5·00	5·25
982a	**1586**	€2.11	7·00	7·25

(ii) Without face value.

983	(45c.) emerald	2·00	2·10
984	(50c.) scarlet	2·10	2·30

(b) Self-adhesive.

985	(50c.) As. No. 984	2·10	2·30

336 Henri Claireaux

2005. Henri Claireaux (politician).

1000	**336**	50c. purple	2·00	2·10

337 Anse a l'Allumette (Match Bay)

2005

1001	**337**	75c. multicoloured	2·75	3·00

338 Common Dolphin (*Delphinus delphis*)

2005. Dolphins.

1002	**338**	53c. black and vermilion	1·90	2·00
1003	-	€1.15 black and green	4·25	4·50

DESIGNS: Type **338**; €1.15 White beaked dolphin (*Lagenorhynchus albirostris*).

339 La Point au Cheval Farm

2005

1004	**339**	90c. olive	3·25	3·50

340 Fog

2005

1005	**340**	30c. multicoloured	1·30	1·40

341 Ferns, Rocks, Bird and Water

2005. Valley of the Seven Ponds. Multicoloured.

1006	€2 Type **341**	6·25	6·50
1007	€2 Water, rock, shrub and rabbit	6·25	6·50

342 Le pluvier siffleur (whistling plover)

2005. Air. Migrant Birds.

1008	**342**	€2.50 multicoloured	8·75	9·25

343 Le lieve variable (arctic hare)

2005

1009	**343**	53c. multicoloured	1·90	2·00

344 "Ben vous savez Madame..." (R. Goineau)

2005

1010	**344**	90c. multicoloured	3·25	3·50

345 *Transpacific*

2005. Shipwrecks.

1011	**345**	75c. blue	2·75	2·75

346 Delegates

2005. 20th Anniv of Collectivite Territoriale.

1012	**346**	53c. multicoloured	2·00	2·10

347 Snowman and Children

2005. Christmas.

1013	**347**	53c. multicoloured	2·00	2·10

348 Le poudrin de choquette (snow-covered trees)

2006

1014	**348**	53c. multicoloured	2·00	2·10

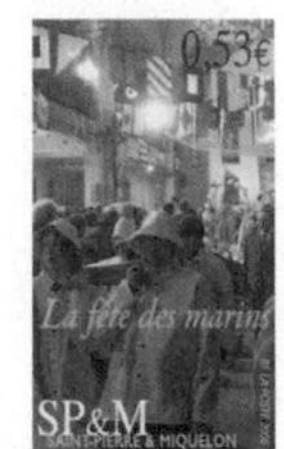
349 La fete des marins (sailors' festival)

2006. Festivals.

1015	**349**	53c. multicoloured	2·00	2·10

350 Albert Pen

2006. Albert Pen (senator) Commemoration.

1016	**350**	53c. chestnut	2·00	2·10

351 Le petit rorqual (*Balaenoptera acutorostrata*)

2006. Marine Mammals.

1017	**351**	53c. purple and black	2·00	2·10
1018	-	€1.15 green and black	4·00	4·25

DESIGNS: 53c. Type **351**; €1.15 Le cachalot (*Physeter catodon*).

352 Coastal Houses

2006. Atmosphere.

1019	**352**	30c. multicoloured	1·30	1·30

353 Le goeland arctique (arctic seagull)

2006. Air. Migrant Birds.

1020	**353**	€2.53 black and azure	9·00	9·50

354 L'Archipel au Senat (French Senate on beach)

2006

1021	**354**	53c. multicoloured	2·00	2·10

355 Hill, Houses and Beach

2006. Le Petit-Barachois. Multicoloured.

1022	€2 Type **355**	6·25	6·50
1023	€2 Cliffs, houses, boats and beach	6·25	6·50

356 "La Prohibition" (painting) (Jean-Claude Girardin)

2006. Smuggling during USA Alcohol Prohibition.

1024	**356**	75c. multicoloured	2·75	2·75

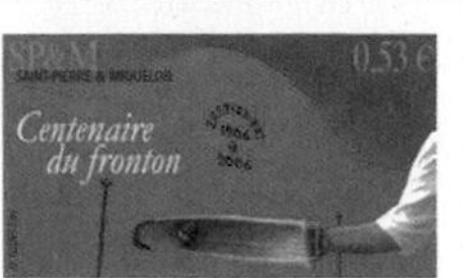
357 Pelota Bat, Ball and Wall

2006. Festivals. Centenary of Pelota Wall.

1025	**357**	53c. multicoloured	2·00	2·10

358 "Spiranthe de Romanzoff"

2006. Orchids.

1026	**358**	53c. black, green and yellow	2·00	2·10
1027	-	53c. multicoloured	2·00	2·10
1028	-	53c. black, green and red	2·00	2·10
1029	-	53c. black, green and yellow	2·00	2·10

DESIGNS: Type **358** (hooded lady's tresses); "Arethusa"; "Habenaire papillon" (small purple fringed orchid); "Habenaire laceree" (ragged fringed orchid).

359 Dugue Farm

2006

1030	**359**	95c. black	3·25	3·50

360 *Penny Fair*

2006. Shipwrecks.

1031	**360**	95c. black	3·25	3·50

361 *Anahitra*

2006. Ships. Multicoloured.

1032	54c. Type **361**	2·00	2·10
1033	54c. *Maria Galanta*	2·00	2·10
1034	54c. *Saint-Eugène V*	2·00	2·10
1035	54c. *Atlantic Jet*	2·00	2·10

362 Baubles<italic />

2006. Christmas.

1036	**362**	54c. multicoloured	2·00	2·10

363 Sister Hilarion

2007. Sister Hilarion Commemoration.

1037	**363**	54c. red and black	2·00	2·10

364 Horses and Sunset

2007

1038	**364**	€1.01 multicoloured	3·50	3·75

365 *Plactopecten magellanicus* (La Royale de Miquelon)

2007

1039	**365**	€1 multicoloured	3·50	3·75

366 Building Facade

2007. Bicentenary of Court of Auditors.

1040	**366**	54c. blue and vermilion	2·00	2·10

367 Yellow-rumped Warbler (Paruline acroupion jaune)

2007

1041	**367**	44c. multicoloured	1·80	1·90

368 Eider Ducks (L'eider)

2007. Air. Migrant Birds.

1042	**368**	€1.50 multicoloured	5·25	5·75

369 *Les Mi'Kmaqs a Miquelon* (Jean-Claude Roy)

2007

1043	**369**	80c. multicoloured	3·00	3·25

370 'La brume de capelan' (fog of small fish)

2007

1044	**370**	30c. multicoloured	1·30	1·30

371 Seagull

2007. Port Saint-Pierre Harbour. Multicoloured.

1045	**371**	€2.40 Type **371**	7·25	7·50
1046		€2.40 Cruiser, buoy and lighthouses	7·25	7·50

Nos. 1095-6 were issued *se-tenant*, with No. 1096 inverted, in strips of two stamps surrounding a central label, the wholw forming a composite design of the square.

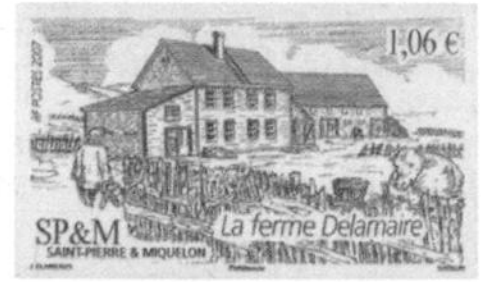

372 Delamaire Farm

2007

1047	**372**	€1.06 black	4·00	4·25

373 *Drosera intermedia* (spoon leaved sundew)

2007. Carnivorous Plants. Multicoloured.

1048	54c. Type **373**	2·00	2·10
1049	54c. *Utricularia cornuta* (horned bladderwort)	2·00	2·10
1050	54c. *Pinguicula vulgaris* (common butterwort)	2·00	2·10
1051	54c. *Sarracenia purpurea* (pitcher plant)	2·00	2·10

374 *Le Petit Miquelon*

2007. Passenger Boats. Sheet 170×115 mm containing T **374** and similar horiz designs. Multicoloured.

MS1052	54c.×4, Type **374**; *La Marguerite*; *L'Ile-aux-Marins*; *Le Mousse*	7·75	8·00

375 Hunter and White-tailed Deer (Actual size 79×25 mm)

2007

1053	**375**	€1.65 multicoloured	6·25	6·50

376 Canoeists (Amelie Poulain)

2007. Telethon.

1054	**376**	54c.+16c. multicoloured	2·75	2·75

377 Santa and Elves

2007. Christmas.

1055	**377**	54c. multicoloured	2·10	2·20

378 Rene Autin

2008. Rene Autin (member of Kieffer Commandos, 177 Free French, attached to the British commandos, who landed on Sword Beach in Normandy on D-Day, 1944) Commemoration.

1056	**378**	54c. red and black	2·30	2·40

379 'Regard envieux' (looking enviously)

2008

1057	**379**	€1.01 multicoloured	4·00	4·25

380 Cod Cages

2008. Aquaculture.

1058	**380**	€1 multicoloured	4·25	4·25

381 Tern, Shoreline and Butterfly

2008. Natural Heritage. Conservation of Littoral Zone–Langdale Dunes. Multicoloured.

1059	€2.40 Type **381**	8·50	9·00
1060	€2.40 Shore lark	8·50	9·00

Nos. 1059/60 were issued together, se-tenant, forming a composite design of the fore shore.

382 'Paruline a gorge noir'

2008. Black-throated Green Warbler.

1061	**382**	47c. multicoloured	2·30	2·40

383 Jam Jars, Bear, Ducks and Barrel

2008. Local Crafts.

1062	**383**	33c. black and olive	1·50	1·60

2008. Nos. 4407/9 and 4417/18 of France optd with T **137**. (i) With face value. Ordinary gum.

1063	**1743**	1c. yellow	1·00	1·00
1065	**1743**	5c. agate	1·00	1·00
1067	**1743**	10c. black	1·00	1·00

(ii) Without face value.

1073	(50c.) emerald	2·40	2·40
1074	(55c.) scarlet	2·75	2·75

385 Return from Fishing (Michelle Foliot)

2008

1081	**385**	80c. multicoloured	3·75	4·00

386 Arlequin plongeur (harlequin duck)

2008. Air. Migrant Birds.

1082	**386**	€1.50 multicoloured	6·50	7·00

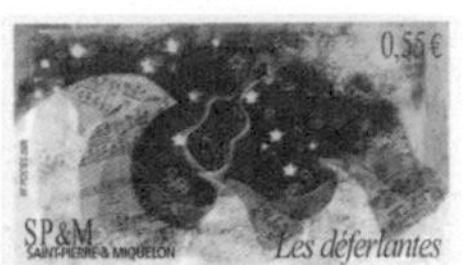

387 'Les deferlantes' (the waves)

2008

1083	**387**	55c. multicoloured	2·50	2·75

388 'Partir en degrat'

2008

1084	**388**	55c. multicoloured	2·50	2·75

389 Taekwondo

2008

1085	**389**	55c. multicoloured	2·50	2·75

390 Loading Sledge

2008. Ice Harvesting. Sheet 170×115 mm containing T **390** and similar horiz designs. Multicoloured.

MS1086	€1×4, Type **390**: Moving ice; Transporting ice; Sawing ice	16·00	17·00

391 Hunter and Hare

2008

1087	**391**	€1.65 multicoloured	7·25	7·50

392 Christmas Window

2008. Christmas.

1088	**392**	55c. multicoloured	2·75	3·00

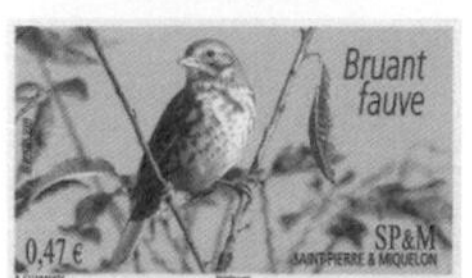

393 'Bruant fauve'

2009. Fox Sparrow.

1089	**393**	47c. multicoloured	2·40	2·50

394 'Couleurs d'hiver'

2009. Colours of Winter.

1090	**394**	€1 multicoloured	4·75	5·00

395 Henri Moraze

2009. Henri Moraze (entrepreneur) Commemoration.

1091	**395**	56c. orange-brown and black	3·00	3·25

396 ATR 42

2009. Aviation.

1092	**396**	80c. new blue and black	4·00	4·25

2009. Local Crafts. As Type **383**.

1093	33c. indigo and emerald	1·50	1·60

397 *Le banc bleu* (Raphaele Goineau)

2009

1094	**397**	56c. multicoloured	2·75	3·00

398 Place Mgr Francois Maurer

2009. Place Mgr Francois Maurer. Each reddish brown and cobalt.

1095	€2.50 Type **398**	11·00	11·50
1096	€2.50 Place Mgr Francois Maurer, right	11·00	11·50

Nos. 1095-1096 were issued *se-tenant*, with No. 1096 inverted, in strips of two stamps surrounding a central label, the whole forming a composite design of the square.

399 Tennis Racquet and Lighthouse

2009. Tennis in Saint Pierre et Miquelon.

1097	**399**	€1.05 multicoloured	4·75	5·00

400 Seaman and Ships

2009. Centenary of First Stamp.

1098	**400**	€1 multicoloured	4·50	4·75

401 Duck Shoot

2009. Duck Shoot

1099	**401**	€1.50 multicoloured	7·25	7·50

402 Moving Building

2009. The Radio Before–After.

1100	**402**	56c. multicoloured	2·75	3·00

403 Tide Hut (Maree de cabane)

2009. Tide Hut (Maree de cabane)

1101	**403**	80c. multicoloured	4·00	4·25

404 Yachts, Men and Ice Floes (les glaces dans le port de Saint-Pierre)

2009. St. Pierre Port blocked by Ice. Sheet 170×115 mm containing T **404** and similar horiz designs.

MS1102 56c.×4, Type **404**; Ship and man driving ox (La marche sue la glace); Lighthouse and ice floes (Le phare de la Point-aux-Canons); Ships caught in ice (Les bateaux de peche dans le glaces) 10·50 11·00

405 The Nativity

2009. Christmas.

1103	**405**	56c. multicoloured	2·75	3·00

406 Richard Bartlett

2010. Richard Bartlett (with Free French Forces during WW II and president of Aero Club of St Pierre et Miquelon) Commemoration.

1104	**406**	56c. salmon and black	2·75	3·00

407 'Paruline noir et blanc'

2010. Black and White Warbler.

1105	**407**	47c. multicoloured	2·40	2·50

408 'La pêche au crabe'

2010. Crab Fishing.

1106	**408**	€1 multicoloured	4·50	4·75

409 'Le cap de Miquelon' and Eider Ducks

2010. Natural Heritage. Cape of Miquelon. Multicoloured.

1107	€2.50 Type **409**	11·00	11·50
1108	€2.50 Cape and buoy	11·00	11·50

Nos. 1107/8 were issued *se-tenant*, in strips of two stamps surrounding a illustrated label, the strip forming a composite design of the Cape.

PARCEL POST STAMPS

1901. Optd **COLIS POSTAUX**.

P79	**D**	10c. black on lilac	£130	£140

1901. Optd **Colis Postaux**.

P80	**D**	10c. red	20·00	28·00

1917. Nos. 83 and 85 optd **Colis Postaux**.

P109	**17**	10c. red and pink	2·30	11·00
P110	**17**	20c. purple and brown	75	5·50

1941. Free French Plebiscite. No. P110 optd **FRANCE LIBRE F. N. F. L.**

P303	**17**	20c. purple and brown	£700	£750

POSTAGE DUE STAMPS

1892. Postage Due stamps of French Colonies optd **ST-PIERRE M-on**.

D60	**U**	5c. black	75·00	90·00
D61	**U**	10c. black	29·00	20·00
D62	**U**	15c. black	20·00	16·00
D63	**U**	20c. black	18·00	17·00
D64	**U**	30c. black	23·00	21·00
D65	**U**	40c. black	12·00	26·00
D66	**U**	60c. black	90·00	90·00
D67	**U**	1f. brown	£150	£150
D68	**U**	2f. brown	£150	£150

1925. Postage Due type of France optd **SAINT-PIERRE-ET-MIQUELON** or surch also centimes a percevoir and value in figures.

D135	**D11**	5c. blue	50	3·25
D136	**D11**	10c. brown	55	5·75
D137	**D11**	20c. olive	45	4·75
D138	**D11**	25c. red	75	4·75
D139	**D11**	30c. red	85	6·50
D140	**D11**	45c. green	1·20	6·50
D141	**D11**	50c. red	1·60	5·00
D142	**D11**	60c. on 50c. brown	1·70	9·25
D143	**D11**	1f. red	2·00	8·00
D144	**D11**	2f. on 1f. red	2·30	12·50
D145	**D11**	3f. mauve	9·25	32·00

D30 Newfoundland Dog

1932

D163	**D30**	5c. black and blue	1·00	8·00
D164	**D30**	10c. black and green	2·00	8·25
D165	**D30**	20c. black and red	3·50	9·00
D166	**D30**	25c. black and purple	4·75	9·00
D167	**D30**	30c. black and orange	6·00	11·00
D168	**D30**	45c. black and blue	8·25	13·00
D169	**D30**	50c. black and green	13·00	24·00
D170	**D30**	60c. black and red	12·00	32·00
D171	**D30**	1f. black and brown	30·00	65·00
D172	**D30**	2f. black and purple	44·00	50·00
D173	**D30**	3f. black and brown	50·00	65·00

D40 Atlantic Cod

1938

D208	**D40**	5c. black	10	5·75
D209	**D40**	10c. purple	10	7·00
D210	**D40**	15c. green	10	7·50
D211	**D40**	20c. blue	10	7·50
D212	**D40**	30c. red	30	7·25
D213	**D40**	50c. green	65	7·00
D214	**D40**	60c. blue	1·20	7·75
D215	**D40**	1f. red	1·20	7·50
D216	**D40**	2f. brown	1·50	11·50
D217	**D40**	3f. violet	2·40	11·50

1941. Free French Plebiscite. Nos. D208/17 optd **NOEL 1941 F N F L**.

D235	**D40**	5c. black	50·00	55·00
D236	**D40**	10c. purple	55·00	55·00
D237	**D40**	15c. green	55·00	55·00
D238	**D40**	20c. blue	50·00	55·00
D239	**D40**	30c. red	46·00	55·00
D240	**D40**	50c. green	65·00	70·00
D241	**D40**	60c. blue	£120	£120
D242	**D40**	1f. red	£120	£120
D243	**D40**	2f. brown	£130	£130
D244	**D40**	3f. violet	£140	£140

1941. Postage Due stamps of 1932 optd **FRANCE LIBRE F. N. F. L.** or surch also.

D298	**D30**	25c. black and purple	£325	£325
D299	**D30**	30c. black and orange	£325	£325
D300	**D30**	50c. black and green	£1100	£1100
D301	**D30**	2f. black and purple	75·00	70·00
D302	**D30**	3f. on 2f. black & pur	55·00	37·00

1941. Free French Plebiscite. Nos. D208/17 optd **FRANCE LIBRE F. N. F. L.**

D310	**D40**	5c. black	55·00	60·00
D311	**D40**	10c. purple	10·50	24·00
D312	**D40**	15c. green	10·00	24·00
D313	**D40**	20c. blue	9·75	16·00
D314	**D40**	30c. red	14·00	19·00
D315	**D40**	50c. green	9·25	29·00
D316	**D40**	60c. blue	10·00	30·00
D317	**D40**	1f. red	32·00	50·00
D318	**D40**	2f. brown	11·00	50·00
D319	**D40**	3f. violet	£450	£475

D57 Arms and Galleon

1947

D385	**D57**	10c. orange	20	2·00
D386	**D57**	30c. blue	20	1·00
D387	**D57**	50c. green	30	65
D388	**D57**	1f. red	45	6·25
D389	**D57**	2f. green	1·60	6·75
D390	**D57**	3f. violet	2·30	7·50
D391	**D57**	4f. brown	2·30	7·75
D392	**D57**	5f. green	3·00	5·50
D393	**D57**	10f. black	3·75	4·50
D394	**D57**	20f. red	3·00	4·75

D115 Newfoundland Dog and Shipwreck Scene

1973

D516	**D115**	2c. black and brown	2·75	6·00
D517	**D115**	10c. black and violet	3·25	6·50
D518	**D115**	20c. black and blue	3·75	7·75
D519	**D115**	30c. black and red	5·50	10·50
D520	**D115**	1f. black and blue	11·00	25·00

1986. Nos. D2493/2502 of France optd **ST-PIERRE ET MIQUELON**.

D569	10c. brown and black	2·00	4·00
D570	20c. black	2·00	4·00
D571	30c. red, brown and black	2·00	4·00
D572	40c. blue, brown and black	2·00	4·00
D573	50c. red and black	2·00	4·00
D574	1f. black	2·00	4·25
D575	2f. yellow and black	2·20	4·75
D576	3f. black and red	2·30	5·25
D577	4f. brown and black	2·75	6·00
D578	5f. brown, red and black	3·25	6·75

Pt. 9, Pt. 14

ST THOMAS & PRINCE ISLANDS

Two islands in the Gulf of Guinea off the west coast of Africa. A colony and then an Overseas Province of Portugal until 1975, when it became an independent republic.

1870. 1000 reis = 1 milreis.
1913. 100 centavos = 1 escudo.
1977. 100 cents = 1 dobra.

1870. "Crown" key-type inscr "S. THOME E PRINCIPE".

17	**P**	5r. black	4·50	3·00
18	**P**	10r. orange	31·00	16·00
29	**P**	10r. green	14·00	8·50
20	**P**	20r. bistre	6·75	4·25
30	**P**	20r. red	7·00	5·00
21	**P**	25r. red	3·50	2·10
31	**P**	25r. lilac	5·75	3·50
22	**P**	40r. blue	10·00	7·50
32	**P**	40r. yellow	10·00	8·50
25	**P**	50r. green	31·00	23·00
33a	**P**	50r. blue	4·50	3·50
26	**P**	100r. lilac	16·00	8·75
15	**P**	200r. orange	20·00	16·00
16	**P**	300r. brown	20·00	16·00

1887. "Embossed" key-type inscr "S. THOME E PRINCIPE".

38	**Q**	5r. black	8·25	6·50
42	**Q**	10r. green	14·00	4·75
43	**Q**	20r. red	16·00	5·00
44	**Q**	25r. mauve	9·00	5·00
45	**Q**	40r. brown	5·25	3·00
46	**Q**	50r. blue	11·50	2·75
47	**Q**	100r. brown	9·00	4·75
48	**Q**	200r. lilac	31·00	17·00
49	**Q**	300r. orange	23·00	17·00

1889. Stamps of 1887 surch. No gum.

50	5r. on 10r. green	65·00	55·00
51	5r. on 20r. red	65·00	55·00
52	50r. on 40r. brown	£250	£200

1895. "Figures" key-type inscr "S. THOME E PRINCIPE".

60	**R**	5r. yellow	3·50	1·40
61	**R**	10r. mauve	1·30	80
53	**R**	15r. brown	3·50	2·10
54	**R**	20r. lilac	3·50	2·30
62	**R**	25r. green	1·90	80
63	**R**	50r. blue	3·50	1·40
55	**R**	75r. pink	9·00	5·50
64	**R**	80r. green	20·00	16·00
56	**R**	100r. brown on buff	8·75	6·50
57	**R**	150r. red on pink	11·50	8·50
58	**R**	200r. blue on blue	16·00	13·00
59	**R**	300r. blue on brown	18·00	14·50

1898. "King Carlos" key-type inscr "S. THOME E PRINCIPE". Name and value in red (500r.) or black (others).

66	**S**	2½r. grey	50	35
67	**S**	5r. red	70	35
68	**S**	10r. green	70	50
69	**S**	15r. brown	2·10	1·70
113	**S**	15r. green	2·20	1·30
70	**S**	20r. lilac	1·30	75
71	**S**	25r. green	80	50
114	**S**	25r. red	2·20	1·10
72	**S**	50r. blue	1·20	75
115	**S**	50r. brown	9·00	5·75
116	**S**	65r. blue	17·00	10·50
73	**S**	75r. pink	21·00	11·50
117	**S**	75r. purple	4·75	2·10
74	**S**	80r. mauve	10·50	5·00
75	**S**	100r. blue on blue	3·50	3·25
118	**S**	115r. brown on pink	16·00	11·50
119	**S**	130r. brown on yellow	16·00	11·50
76	**S**	150r. brown on yellow	4·25	3·00
77	**S**	200r. purple on pink	8·00	5·75
78	**S**	300r. blue on pink	11·50	6·25
120	**S**	400r. blue on cream	23·00	13·00
79	**S**	500r. black on blue	12·50	9·00
80	**S**	700r. mauve on yellow	25·00	19·00

1902. Surch with new value.

121	**S**	50r. on 65r. blue	7·00	4·25
85	**R**	65r. on 5r. yellow	8·00	5·50
86	**R**	65r. on 10r. mauve	8·00	5·00
87	**R**	65r. on 15r. brown	8·00	5·00
81	**Q**	65r. on 20r. red	10·00	6·50
88	**R**	65r. on 20r. lilac	4·50	3·00
83	**Q**	65r. on 25r. mauve	5·75	3·75
84	**Q**	65r. on 100r. brown	10·50	6·50
90	**Q**	115r. on 10r. green	10·00	6·50
92	**R**	115r. on 25r. green	8·00	5·00
89	**P**	115r. on 50r. green	20·00	6·50
93	**R**	115r. on 150r. red on pink	8·00	5·00
94	**R**	115r. on 200r. blue on blue	8·00	5·00
91	**Q**	115r. on 300r. orange	10·00	6·50
95	**Q**	130r. on 5r. black	10·00	6·50
98	**R**	130r. on 75r. pink	8·00	5·00
99	**R**	130r. on 100r. brn on buff	8·00	5·00
97	**Q**	130r. on 200r. lilac	12·50	6·50
100	**R**	130r. on 300r. blue on brown	8·00	5·00
108	**V**	400r. on 2½r. brown	2·10	2·10
101	**P**	400r. on 10r. yellow	95·00	70·00
102	**Q**	400r. on 40r. brown	18·00	13·00
103	**Q**	400r. on 50r. blue	8·00	5·00
105	**R**	400r. on 50r. blue	2·20	2·10
107	**R**	400r. on 80r. green	4·50	3·50

1903. Stamps of 1898 optd **PROVISORIO**.

109	15r. brown	4·00	1·80
110	25r. green	4·50	1·80
111	50r. blue	2·50	1·00
112	75r. pink	10·00	7·50

1911. Stamps of 1898 optd **REPUBLICA**.

122	2½r. grey	50	45
123	5r. orange	50	25
124	10r. green	50	45
125	15r. green	50	45
126	20r. lilac	50	45
127	25r. red	50	45
128	50r. brown	50	45
129	75r. purple	50	45
130	100r. blue on blue	1·20	90
131	115r. brown on pink	2·30	1·50
132	130r. brown on yellow	2·30	1·50
267	200r. purple on pink	3·50	2·10
134	400r. blue on cream	3·25	1·30
268	500r. black on blue	2·50	2·10
136	700r. mauve on yellow	3·25	1·30

1912. "King Manoel" key type inscr "S. THOME E PRINCIPE" and optd **REPUBLICA**.

137	**T**	2½r. lilac	50	45
138	**T**	5r. black	50	45
139	**T**	10r. green	50	45
140	**T**	20r. red	2·10	1·20
141	**T**	25r. brown	1·20	75
142	**T**	50r. blue	1·20	75
143	**T**	75r. brown	1·20	80
144	**T**	100r. brown on green	2·10	1·10
145	**T**	200r. green on orange	3·25	3·00
146	**T**	300r. black on blue	5·00	2·00

1913. Nos. 109 and 111/2 optd **REPUBLICA**.

159	**S**	15r. brown	3·75	3·25
243	**S**	50r. blue	1·50	1·10
272	**S**	75r. pink	15·00	10·00

1913. Stamps of 1902 optd **REPUBLICA**.

244	**S**	50r. on 65r. blue	1·50	1·10
245	**Q**	115r. on 10r. green	4·50	3·25
246	**R**	115r. on 25r. green	1·40	70
164	**P**	115r. on 50r. green	£225	£180
247	**R**	115r. on 150r. red on pink	1·40	1·70
248	**R**	115r. on 200r. blue on blue	1·40	70
249	**Q**	115r. on 300r. orange	4·50	3·25
250	**Q**	130r. on 5r. black	9·50	5·00
251	**R**	130r. on 75r. pink	1·40	70
252	**R**	130r. on 100r. brn on buff	2·50	2·30
253	**Q**	130r. on 200r. lilac	3·00	2·10
254	**R**	130r. on 300r. blue on brown	2·20	1·30
197	**V**	400r. on 2½r. brown	4·75	2·25
198	**Q**	400r. on 50r. blue	£130	£110
200	**R**	400r. on 50r. blue	4·75	4·25
202	**R**	400r. on 80r. green	5·00	3·50

1913. Surch **REPUBLICA S. TOME E PRINCIPE** and new value on "Vasco da Gama" stamps of (a) Portuguese Colonies.

203	¼c. on 2½r. green	2·10	1·40
204	½c. on 5r. red	2·10	1·40
205	1c. on 10r. purple	2·10	1·40
206	2½c. on 25r. green	2·10	1·40
207	5c. on 50r. blue	2·10	1·40
208	7½c. on 75r. brown	4·00	3·50
209	10c. on 100r. brown	2·10	1·40
210	15c. on 150r. brown	2·30	1·70

(b) Macao.

211	¼c. on ½c. green	3·00	2·00
212	½c. on 1a. red	3·00	2·00
213	1c. on 2a. purple	3·00	2·00
214	2½c. on 4a. green	3·00	2·00
215	5c. on 8a. blue	3·25	2·75
216	7½c. on 12a. brown	5·50	4·25
217	10c. on 16a. brown	3·25	2·20
218	15c. on 24a. brown	3·25	2·20

(c) Portuguese Timor.

219	¼c. on ½a. green	3·00	2·00
220	½c. on 1a. red	3·00	2·00
221	1c. on 2a. purple	3·00	2·00
222	2½c. on 4a. green	3·00	2·00
223	5c. on 8a. blue	3·25	2·75
224	7½c. on 12a. brown	5·50	4·25
225	10c. on 16a. brown	3·25	2·20
226	15c. on 24a. brown	3·25	2·20

1914. "Ceres" key-type inscr "S. TOME E PRINCIPE" Name and value in black.

276	**U**	¼c. green	45	35
281	**U**	½c. black	45	35
282	**U**	1c. green	45	35
283	**U**	1½c. brown	2·75	2·50
284	**U**	2c. red	45	35
285	**U**	2c. grey	45	35
286	**U**	2½c. violet	45	35
287	**U**	3c. orange	45	35
288	**U**	4c. purple	45	35
289	**U**	4½c. grey	45	35
290	**U**	5c. blue	70	65
291	**U**	6c. mauve	45	35
292	**U**	7c. blue	45	35
293	**U**	7½c. brown	70	9·50
294	**U**	8c. grey	70	50
295	**U**	10c. brown	70	50
296	**U**	12c. green	85	65
297	**U**	15c. pink	85	65
298	**U**	20c. green	85	65
299	**U**	24c. blue	1·70	1·30
300	**U**	25c. brown	1·70	1·30
239	**U**	30c. brown on green	3·75	1·90
301	**U**	30c. green	1·30	85
240	**U**	40c. brown on pink	3·75	1·90
302	**U**	40c. turquoise	1·30	85
241	**U**	50c. orange on orange	9·25	6·00
303	**U**	50c. mauve	1·30	85
304	**U**	60c. blue	1·30	85
305	**U**	60c. pink	2·75	1·30
306	**U**	80c. red	3·00	1·00
242	**U**	1e. green on blue	9·25	4·75
307	**U**	1e. pink	4·25	2·10
308	**U**	1e. blue	2·30	1·50
309	**U**	2e. purple	2·75	2·30
310	**U**	5e. brown	26·00	7·00
311	**U**	10e. pink	41·00	15·00
312	**U**	20e. green	£130	55·00

1919. No. 109 surch **REPUBLICA** and new value.

255	**S**	2½r. on 15r. brown	1·50	1·10

1919. No. 122 surch with new value.

256	½c. on 2½r. grey	7·25	5·75
257	1c. on 2½r. grey	5·00	3·25
258	2½c. on 2½r. grey	2·00	1·40

1919. "Ceres" key-types of St. Thomas and Prince Islands surch.

259	**U**	½c. on ¼c. green	4·50	3·50
260	**U**	2c. on ¼c. green	4·50	3·50
261	**U**	2½c. on ¼c. green	15·00	11·00

1919. "Ceres" key-type of St. Thomas and Prince Islands surch **$04 Centavos** and with old value blocked out.

262	4c. on 2½c. violet	2·00	1·40

1923. Stamps of 1913 (optd **REPUBLICA**) surch **DEZ CENTAVOS** and bars.

313	**R**	10c. on 115r. on 25r. green	95	70
314	**R**	10c. on 115r. on 150r. red on pink	95	70
316	**R**	10c. on 115r. on 200r. blue on blue	95	70
317	**R**	10c. on 130r. on 75r. pink	95	70
318	**R**	10c. on 130r. on 100r. brown on buff	95	70
319	**R**	10c. on 130r. on 300r. blue on brown	95	70

1925. Stamps of 1902 surch **Republica 40 C.** and bars over original surcharge.

321	**V**	40c. on 400r. on 2½r. brown	1·90	90
322	**R**	40c. on 400r. on 80r. green	1·90	90

1931. Nos. 307 and 309 surch.

323	**U**	70c. on 1e. pink	4·00	2·00
324	**U**	1e.40 on 2e. purple	4·75	2·40

32 Ceres

1934

325	**32**	1c. brown	45	30
326	**32**	5c. brown	45	30
327	**32**	10c. mauve	45	30
328	**32**	15c. black	45	30
329	**32**	20c. grey	45	30
330	**32**	30c. green	45	30
331	**32**	40c. red	45	30
332	**32**	45c. turquoise	80	75
333	**32**	50c. brown	65	60
334	**32**	60c. green	1·00	60
335	**32**	70c. brown	1·00	60
336	**32**	80c. green	60	35
337	**32**	85c. red	5·00	2·00
338	**32**	1e. purple	1·50	70
339	**32**	1e.40 blue	4·00	2·00
340	**32**	2e. mauve	4·00	2·00
341	**32**	5e. green	9·00	6·00
342	**32**	10e. brown	25·00	13·50
343	**32**	20e. orange	£100	55·00

1938. As T **54** and **56** of Macao, but inscr "S. TOME".

344	**54**	1c. green (postage)	35	30
345	**54**	5c. brown	35	30
346	**54**	10c. red	35	30
347	**54**	15c. purple	35	30
348	**54**	20c. grey	35	30
349	-	30c. purple	35	30
350	-	35c. green	65	45
351	-	40c. brown	65	45
352	-	50c. mauve	65	45
353	-	60c. black	65	45
354	-	70c. violet	65	45
355	-	80c. orange	65	45
356	-	1e. red	1·30	80
357	-	1e.75 blue	2·20	1·20
358	-	2e. red	29·00	8·25
359	-	5e. green	29·00	9·25
360	-	10e. blue	34·00	10·00
361	-	20e. brown	55·00	4·00
362	**56**	10c. red (air)	£130	95
363	**56**	20c. violet	65·00	46·00
364	**56**	50c. orange	3·75	3·50
365	**56**	1e. blue	12·00	3·50
366	**56**	2e. red	9·50	6·50
367	**56**	3e. green	12·00	5·25
368	**56**	5e. brown	20·00	16·00
369	**56**	9e. red	22·00	16·00
370	**56**	10e. mauve	22·00	16·00

DESIGNS: 30 to 50c. Mousinho de Albuquerque; 60c. to 1e. Dam; 1e.75 to 5e. Prince Henry the Navigator; 10, 20e. Afonso de Albuquerque.

See also Nos. 374/400.

37 Portuguese Colonial Column

1938. President's Colonial Tour.

371	**37**	80c. green	3·75	2·10
372	**37**	1e.75 blue	13·00	7·00
373	**37**	20e. brown	80·00	41·00

1939. As Nos. 344/70 but inscr "S. TOME e PRINCIPE".

374	**54**	1c. green (postage)	35	30
375	**54**	5c. brown	35	30
376	**54**	10c. red	35	30
377	**54**	15c. purple	35	30
378	**54**	20c. grey	35	30
379	-	30c. purple	35	30
380	-	35c. green	35	30
381	-	40c. brown	45	30
382	-	50c. mauve	45	45
383	-	60c. black	95	60
384	-	70c. violet	1·10	60
385	-	80c. orange	1·10	60
386	-	1e. red	1·30	85
387	-	1e.75 blue	2·20	1·20
388	-	2e. red	3·75	2·00
389	-	5e. green	8·25	5·00
390	-	10e. blue	23·00	8·25
391	-	20e. brown	30·00	10·00
392	**56**	10c. red (air)	70	60
393	**56**	20c. violet	70	60
394	**56**	50c. orange	70	60
395	**56**	1e. blue	70	60
396	**56**	2e. red	1·70	95
397	**56**	3e. green	2·20	1·40
398	**56**	5e. brown	6·50	3·50
399	**56**	9e. red	12·50	7·00
400	**56**	10e. mauve	13·00	7·25

41 Cola Nuts

1948. Fruit.

401	**41**	5c. black and yellow	85	30
402	-	10c. black and orange	1·10	75
403	-	30c. slate and grey	5·75	3·00
404	-	50c. brown and yellow	6·50	4·75
405	-	1e. red and pink	7·25	4·75
406	-	1e.75 blue and grey	13·00	8·25
407	-	2e. black and green	11·50	4·75
408	-	5e. brown and mauve	38·00	18·00
409	-	10e. black and mauve	40	19·00
410	-	20e. black and grey	£880	60·00
MS410a 149×136 mm. Nos. 401/10 (sold at 42e.50)			£225	£250

DESIGNS: 10c. Bread-fruit; 30c. Custard-apple; 50c. Cocoa beans; 1e. Coffee; 1e.75, Dendem; 2e. Abacate; 5e. Pineapple; 10e. Mango; 20e. Coconuts.

42 Our Lady of Fatima

1948. Honouring the Statue of Our Lady of Fatima.

411	**42**	50c. violet	10·50	7·75

43 Letter and Globe

1949. 75th Anniv of U.P.U.

412	**43**	3e.50 black	11·00	7·75

44 Bells and Dove

1950. Holy Year.

413	**44**	2e.50 blue	4·00	2·50
414	**44**	4e. orange	8·25	6·00

45 Our Lady of Fatima

1951. Termination of Holy Year.

415	**45**	4e. indigo and blue	3·75	3·25

46 Doctor examining Patients

1952. First Tropical Medicine Congress, Lisbon.

416	**46**	10c. blue and brown	50	35

48 J. de Santarem

1952. Portuguese Navigators. Multicoloured.

417	10c. Type **48**	20	15

418		30c. P. Escobar	20	15
419		50c. F. de Po	35	20
420		1e. A. Esteves	45	30
421		2e. L. Goncalves	1·10	50
422		3e.50 M. Fernandes	1·10	50

49 Cloisters of Monastery

1953. Missionary Art Exhibition.

423	**49**	10c. brown and green	15	10
424	**49**	50c. brown and orange	95	75
425	**49**	3e. indigo and blue	3·25	1·80

50 Portuguese Stamp of 1853 and Arms of Portuguese Overseas Province

1953. Centenary of First Portuguese Postage Stamps.

426	**50**	50c. multicoloured	1·60	90

51 Route of President's Tour

1954. Presidential Visit.

427	**51**	15c. multicoloured	20	15
428	**51**	5e. multicoloured	1·70	1·10

52 Father M. de Nobrega and View of Sao Paulo

1954. Fourth Centenary of Sao Paulo.

429	**52**	2e.50 multicoloured	85	55

53 Exhibition Emblem, Globe and Arms

1958. Brussels International Exhibition.

430	**53**	2e.50 multicoloured	1·10	65

54 "Cassia occidentalis"

1958. Sixth International Congress of Tropical Medicine.

431	**54**	5e. multicoloured	3·75	2·30

55 Points of Compass

1960. 500th Death Anniv of Prince Henry the Navigator.

432	**55**	10e. multicoloured	1·60	85

56 "Religion"

1960. Tenth Anniv of African Technical Co-operation Commission.

433	**56**	1e.50 multicoloured	70	45

57 Fishing

1962. Sports. Multicoloured.

434		50c. Type **57**	20	15
435		1e. Gymnastics	85	20
436		1e.50 Handball	90	35
437		2e. Sailing	1·10	55
438		2e.50 Running	1·40	1·10
439		20e. Skin-diving	4·00	2·10

58 "Anopheles gambiae"

1962. Malaria Eradication.

440	**58**	2e.50 multicoloured	2·10	1·10

59 Map of Africa and Boeing 707 and Lockheed L.1049G Super Constellation Airliners

1963. Tenth Anniv of Transportes Aereos Portugueses (airline).

441	**59**	1e.50 multicoloured	95	65

60 F. de Oliveira Chamico

1964. Centenary of National Overseas Bank.

442	**60**	2e.50 multicoloured	1·00	80

61 I.T.U. Emblem and St. Gabriel

1965. Centenary of I.T.U.

443	**61**	2e.50 multicoloured	2·10	1·40

62 Infantry Officer, 1788

1965. Portuguese Military Uniforms. Multicoloured.

444		20c. Type **62**	25	20
445		35c. Infantry sergeant, 1788	25	20
446		40c. Infantry corporal, 1788	25	25
447		1e. Infantryman, 1788	2·00	80
448		2e.50 Artillery officer, 1806	2·00	85
449		5e. Light infantryman, 1811	3·00	1·90
450		7e.50 Infantry sapper, 1833	2·75	2·50
451		10e. Lancers officer, 1834	5·75	3·75

65 Arts and Crafts School and Anti-Tuberculosis Clinic

1966. 40th Anniv of National Revolution.

452	**65**	4c. multicoloured	1·10	65

66 C. Rodrigues and Steam Corvette "Vasco da Gama"

1967. Cent of Military Naval Association. Multicoloured.

453		1e.50 Type **66**	1·70	65
454		2e.50 A. Kopke, microscope and "Glossina palpalis" (insect)	2·50	1·10

67 Apparition appearing to Children and Valinhos Monument

1967. 50th Anniv of Fatima Apparitions.

455	**67**	2e.50 multicoloured	45	30

68 Medal of the Jeronimos Monastery

1968. 500th Birth Anniv of Pedro Cabral (explorer).

456	**68**	1e.50 multicoloured	90	60

69 Island Route-map and Monument

1969. Birth Centenary of Admiral Gago Coutinho.

457	**69**	2e. multicoloured	65	30

70 Da Gama's Fleet and Fireship

1969. 500th Birth Anniv of Vasco da Gama (explorer).

458	**70**	2e.50 multicoloured	85	55

71 L. A. Rebello da Silva

1969. Cent of Overseas Administrative Reforms.

459	**71**	2e.50 multicoloured	55	45

72 Manoel Gate, Guarda See

1969. 500th Birth Anniv of King Manoel I.

460	**72**	4e. multicoloured	65	55

73 Pero Escobar and Joao de Santarem

1969. 500th Anniv of Discovery of St. Thomas and Prince Islands.

461	**73**	2e.50 multicoloured	55	45

74 President A. Tomas

1970. Presidential Visit.

462	**74**	2e.50 multicoloured	60	25

75 Marshal Carmona

1970. Birth Centenary of Marshal Carmona.

463	**75**	5e. multicoloured	85	55

76 Stamps on Coffee Plant

1970. Stamp Centenary. Multicoloured.

464		1e. Type **76**	30	15
465		1e.50 Head Post Office, St. Thomas (horiz)	65	20
466		2e.50 Se Cathedral, St. Thomas	85	35

77 "Descent from the Cross" and Caravel at St. Thomas

1972. 400th Anniv of Camoens' "The Lusiads" (epic poem).

467	**77**	20e. multicoloured	2·75	1·10

78 Running and Throwing the Javelin

1972. Olympic Games, Munich.

468	**78**	1e.50 multicoloured	45	25

79 Fairey IIID Seaplane "Lusitania" and Cruiser "Gladiolus" off Rock of San Pedro

1972. 50th Anniv of 1st Flight, Lisbon–Rio de Janeiro.

469	**79**	2e.50 multicoloured	55	30

80 W.M.O. Emblem

1973. Cent of World Meteorological Organization.

470	**80**	5e. multicoloured	85	65

81 Flags of Portugal and St. Thomas and Prince Islands

1975. Independence.

471	**81**	3e. multicoloured	30	10
472	**81**	10e. multicoloured	90	40
473	**81**	20e. multicoloured	1·80	80
474	**81**	50e. multicoloured	4·40	2·20

82 National Flag

1975. Independence Proclamation.

475	**82**	1e.50 multicoloured	20	10
476	**82**	4e. multicoloured	35	15
477	**82**	7e.50 multicoloured	65	30
478	**82**	20e. multicoloured	1·80	80
479	**82**	50e. multicoloured	4·50	2·50

83 Diagram and Hand

1976. National Reconstruction Fund.

480	**83**	1e. multicoloured	10	10
481	**83**	1e.50 multicoloured	15	10
482	**83**	2e. multicoloured	20	10

1976. Optd Rep. **Democr. 12-7-75**.

483	**48**	10c. Joao de Santarem
484	**62**	20c. Infantry officer, 1788
485	-	30c. Pedro Escobar (No. 418)
486	-	35c. Infantry sergeant, 1788
487	-	40c. Infantry corporal, 1788
488	-	50c. Fernao de Po (No. 419)
489	-	1e. Alvaro Esteves (No. 420)
490	-	2e.50 Rebello da Silva (No. 459)
491	**73**	2e.50 Escobar and Santarem
492	-	3e.50 Martim Fernandes (No. 422)
493	-	4e. Manoel Gate (No. 460)
494	-	5e. W.M.O. emblem (No. 470)
495	-	7e.50 Infantry sapper, 1833 (No. 450)
496	-	10e. Compass rose (No. 432)

85 President Pinto da Costa and National Flag

1976. First Anniv of Independence.

497	2e. Type **85**	25	10
498	3e.50 Proclamation of Independence, 12 July 1975	30	15
499	4e.50 As 3e.50	45	30
500	12e.50 Type **85**	90	50

1977. Second Anniv of Independence. No. 439 optd **Rep. Democr. 12-7-77**.

501	20e. multicoloured	2·30	1·10
MS501	135×115 mm. No. 501	10·00	8·00

CHARITY TAX STAMPS

The notes under this heading in Portugal also apply here.

1925. Marquis de Pombal Commemoration. As stamps of Portugal, but additionally inscr "S. TOME E PRINCIPE".

C323	**C73**	15c. black and orange	85	45
C324	-	15c. black and orange	85	45
C325	**C75**	15c. black and orange	85	45

1946. Fiscal stamps as in Type **C1** of Portuguese Colonies surch **Assistencia** and new value.

C401	50c. on 1e. green	25·00	23·00
C402	50c. on 4e. red	30·00	30·00
C403	1e. on 4e. red	30·00	30·00
C404	1e. on 5e. red	30·00	30·00
C407	1e. on 6e. green	25·00	23·00
C408	1e. on 7e. green	32·00	23·00
C409	1e. on 10e. red	25·00	30·00
C410	1e.50 on 7e. green	29·00	23·00
C411	1e.50 on 8e. green	29·00	27·00
C412	2e.50 on 7e. green	29·00	27·00
C413	2e.50 on 9e. green	29·00	27·00
C414	2e.50 on 10e. green	25·00	23·00

40 Arms

1948. Value in black.

C415	**40**	50c. green	1·30	1·10
C416	**40**	1e. pink	3·25	2·40
C417	**40**	1e. green	1·40	1·00
C418	**40**	1e.50 brown	4·00	3·00

1965. (a) Surch **um escudo 1$00** and two heavy bars.

C452	1e. on 5e. yellow	1·80	1·30

(b) Surch **Um escudo**.

C453	1e. on 1e. green	2·30	2·20

(c) As No. C 417 but inscr "UM ESCUDO" at foot, surch **1$00**.

C454	1e. on 1e. green	1·80	1·50

(d) Previous surch "**Cinco escudos**" obliterated and further surch **Um escudo 1$00**.

C455	1e. on 5e. yellow	4·00	3·25

NEWSPAPER STAMPS

1982. Surch **2½ RS**. No gum.

N53	**Q**	2½r. on 5r. black	£880	65·00
N54	**Q**	2½r. on 10r. green	£100	95
N55	**Q**	2½r. on 20r. red	£160	£130

1893. "Newspaper" key-type inscr "S. THOME E PRINCIPE".

N59	**V**	2½r. brown	1·40	3·00

1899. No. N59 optd **PROVISORIO**.

N81	2½r. brown	75·00	35·00

POSTAGE DUE STAMPS

1904. "Due" key-type inscr "S. THOME E PRINCIPE". Name and value in black.

D121	**W**	5r. green	1·20	1·10
D122	**W**	10r. grey	1·70	1·40
D123	**W**	20r. brown	1·70	1·40
D124	**W**	30r. orange	1·70	1·40
D125	**W**	50r. brown	3·00	2·10
D126	**W**	60r. brown	4·25	4·75
D127	**W**	100r. mauve	7·00	4·25
D128	**W**	130r. blue	7·00	4·25
D129	**W**	200r. red	7·25	5·50
D130	**W**	500r. lilac	13·50	10·50

1911. As last optd **REPUBLICA**.

D137	5r. green	50	45
D138	10r. grey	50	45
D139	20r. brown	50	45
D140	30r. orange	50	45
D141	50r. brown	60	55
D142	60r. brown	1·70	1·20
D143	100r. mauve	1·70	1·20
D144	130r. blue	1·70	1·20
D145	200r. red	1·30	1·20
D146	500r. lilac	3·50	2·50

1921. "Due" key-type inscr "S. TOME E PRINCIPE". Currency changed.

D313	½c. green	65	55
D314	1c. grey	65	55
D315	2c. brown	65	55
D316	3c. orange	65	55
D317	5c. brown	65	55
D318	6c. brown	30	30
D319	10c. mauve	70	60
D320	13c. blue	70	60
D321	20c. red	70	60
D322	50c. lilac	1·80	1·40

1925. Nos. C323/5 optd **MULTA**.

D323	**C73**	30c. black and orange	85	45
D324	-	30c. black and orange	85	45
D325	**C75**	30c. black and orange	85·00	45

D14

1925. Numerals in red, name in black.

D417	**D 14**	10c. brown and yellow	25	20
D418	**D 14**	30c. brown and blue	25	20
D419	**D 14**	50c. blue and pink	25	20
D420	**D 14**	1e. blue and olive	30	25
D421	**D 14**	2e. green and orange	35	35
D422	**D 14**	5e. brown and lilac	65	45

APPENDIX

The following stamps have either been issued in excess of postal needs or have not been available to the public in reasonable quantities at face value. Such stamps may later be given full listing if there is evidence of regular postal use.

1977

400th Birth Anniv of Rubens. 1, 5, 10, 15, 20, 50e.
150th Death Anniv of Beethoven. 20, 30, 50e.
Centenary of U.P.U. Surch on Navigators and Military Uniforms issues of Portuguese administration. 1e. on 10c., 3e. on 30c., 3e.50 on 3e.50, 5e. on 50c., 10e. on 10c., 15e. on 3e.50, 20e. on 30e. on 30c., 35e. on 35c., 40e. on 40c.
Christmas. 5, 10, 25, 50, 70d.
60th Anniv of Russian Revolution. 15, 30, 40, 50d.
1st Death Anniv of Mao Tse-tung. 50d.

1978

Nobel Peace Prizes to International Organizations. Surch on Navigators and Military Uniforms issues of Portuguese administration. 3d. on 30c., 5d. on 50c., 10d. on 10c., 15d. on 3e.50, 20d. on 20c., 35d. on 35c.
3rd Anniv of Independence. 5d.×3.
3rd Anniv of Admission to United Nations. Surch on Military Uniform issue. 40d. on 40c.
International Stamp Exhibition, Essen. 10d.×5.
Centenary of U.P.U. 5d.×4, 15d.×4.
1st Anniv of New Currency. 5d.×5, 8d.×5.
World Cup Football Championship, Argentina. 3d.×4, 25d.×3.

1979

World Cup Winners. Optd on 1978 World Cup issues. 3d.×4, 25d.×3.
Butterflies. 50c., 10d., 11d.×4.
Flowers. 1d., 8d.×4, 25d.
Telecommunications Day and 50th Anniv of C.C.I.R. 1, 11, 14, 17d.
International Year of the Child. 1, 7, 14, 17d.
450th Death Anniv of Durer. 50c.×2, 1, 7, 8, 25d.
History of Aviation. 50c., 1, 5, 7, 8, 17d.
History of Navigation. 50c., 1, 3, 5, 8, 25d.
Birds. Postage 50c.×2, 1, 7, 8d.; Air 100d.

1980

Fishes. Postage 50c., 1, 5, 7, 8d.; Air 50d.
Balloons. 50c., 1, 3, 7, 8, 25d.
Airships. 50c., 1, 3, 7, 8, 17d.
Olympic Games. 50c., 11d.×4.
Death Centenary of Sir Rowland Hill. 50c., 1, 8, 20d.
10th Anniv of First Manned Moon Landing. 50c., 1, 14, 17d.

1981

Olympic Games, Moscow. Optd on 1977 Mao Tse-tung issue. 50d.
Olympic Games, Moscow. Overprint on 60th Anniv of Revolution. Either silver or black. 15; 30; 40; 50d.×2
Mammals. 50c.×2; 1; 7; 8d.
Shells. 50c.×2; 1d.; 1d.50; 11; 17d.
Philatelia 81, Frankfurt. Johann Wolfgang von Goethe Commemoration. 25d.
Josip Broz Tito Commemoration. 17d.×2
Wedding of Prince Charles and Lady Diana Spencer. Overprint in white on Ludwig von Beethoven Commemoration issues of Portuguese Administration. 20; 30; 50d.
Chess. 1d.50×4; 30d.×4
Chess. Overprint in red on Chess. 30d.×2
Birth Centenary of Pablo Picasso. 14; 17d.×4; 20d.×2
Paintings of Dogs. 1d.50×5; 50d.×2
Paintings of Cats. 1d.50×5; 50d.×2
Central African Games. 17d.×4; 50d.
Fruit. 11d.×3; 30d.×3

1982

Birth Centenary of Josip Broz Tito (1992). Overprint on Josip Broz Tito Commemoration. 17d.×2
World Cup Football Championship, Spain. 15d.×4; 25d.×2
PhilexFrance 82 International Stamp Exhibition. 15d.×2
Centenary of Robert Koch's discovery of TB Bacillus. 25d.
150th Death Anniv of Johann Wolfgang von Goethe. 50d.
21st Birth Anniv of Diana, Princess of Wales. 75d.
75th Anniv of Scouting Movement. 15d.; 30d.
Birth Centenary of Igor Strvinsky. 30d.×2
250th Birth Anniv of George Washington. 30d.×2
Dinosaurs. 6; 16d.×4; 50d.
Navigators. 50c.; 18d.×4; 50d.
Second Anniv of Trabalho Assembly. Overprint in silver on Argel Accord issues of Portuguese Administration. 3; 10; 20; 50e.
Third Trabalho Assembly. 8; 12; 16; 30d.
Pablo Picasso Commemoration. 18d.×3; 25d.×2
Railways. 9; 16d.×4; 50d.

1983

Paintings by Peter Paul Rubens. 16d.×2; 18d.
Pascoa 83. Painting by Peter Paul Rubens. 18d.
Painting by Rembrandt. 16d.×2; 18d.
Paintings by Raphael. 16d.×2
Pascoa 83. Painting by Raphael. 18d.×2
Brasiliana '83. Airships. 25d.×2
Centenary of Montgolfier Brothers' First Flight. 18d.×4; 20d.×3
UPU Congress, Hamburg. Overprint in gold on Centenary of UPU. 15d.×4
Christmas. 30d.×2
Cars. 12d×4; 20d.×4
Medicinal Plants. 50c.; 1; 5d.50; 15d.50; 16; 20; 46; 50d.
Olympic Games, Los Angeles. 16d.×4; 18d.×4
Birds. 50c.; 1d.50; 2; 3; 4; 5d.50; 7; 10; 11; 12; 14; 15d.50; 16; 17 18d.50; 20; 25; 30; 42; 46; 100d.

1984

Lubrapex 84, Lisbon. 16; 30d.
25th Anniv of UN International Maritime Organization. 50c.×3; 7d.×3; 8d.×3; 15d.×3
UPU Congress, Hamburg. Overprint in black on 25th Anniv of UN International Maritime Organization. 50c.×3;
Eradication of Malaria. 8; 16; 30d.
International Food Day. 8; 16; 46d.
Fungi. 10; 20; 30d.
Christmas. 30d.

1985

Conference of Portuguese Countries in Africa. 25d.
First Anniv of Reinstatement of Flights between Lisbon and St. Thomas. 25; 30d.
Flowers. 16; 20; 30d.

1986

Halley's Comet. 5; 6; 10; 16d.
Fungi. 6; 25; 30d.
World Cup Football Championship, Mexico. 25d.×4
Olympic Games, Seoul (1988). 25d.×4
Cars. 50c.; 6; 16; 30d.
Railways. 50c.; 6; 20d.
International Year of Peace. 8; 10; 16; 20d.
Lubrapex 86, Lisbon. 1d.×2; 2d.; 46d.
Christmas. 50c.; 1; 16; 20d.

1987

Flora and Fauna. 1d.×4; 2d.×4; 10d.×4; 20d.×4
Sport. 50c.; 20; 30d.
500th Anniv of Christopher Colombus' voyage to the Americas (1992). 15; 20d.×2
Fungi. 6; 25; 30d.
Railways. 5; 10; 20d.
Christmas. 1; 5; 15; 20d.
Scout Jamboree, Australia. 50c.

1988

70th Anniv of October Revolution. 25d.
World Cup Football Championship Winners. Overprint in gold on World Cup Football Championship, Mexico. 25d.×4
Fungi. 10d.×4; 20d.
Medicinal Plants. 5d.×3; 10d.; 20d.
Electric Locomotives. 10d.×6
150th Birth Anniv of Ferdinand Graf von Zeppelin. 10d.×5
Butterflies. 10d.×3
Automatic Telephone Exchange. 10; 25d.
Scout Jamboree, Australia. 10d.×3
125th Anniv of International Red Cross. 50c.; 5; 20d.
Sport. 50d.×4
Winter Olympic Games, Albertville. 5d.
Italia 90. 50d.×3
Christmas. 10d.×3; 30d.

1989

Fruit. 50c.; 1; 5; 10; 25; 50d.×2; 60d.; 100; 250; 500d.
Bicentenary of French Revolution. 10d.×3
Orchids. 20d.×2
Humming Birds. 20d.×3
Italia 90. 10d.×3; 20d.
Olympic Games, Barcelona (1992). 5d.×3; 35d.
Ships. 20d.×5
Railways. 20d.×5
Butterflies. 20d.×5
25th Anniv of Bank. 25d.
International Telecommunications Day. 60d.
Christmas. 25d.×4

1990

70th Anniv of Arthur Eddington Expedition to St. Thomas. 60d.×3
Orchids. 20d.×5
Railways. 5; 20d.; 25d.×3
Italia 90. 25d.×4
Butterflies. 15d.×5; 25d.
Fungi. 20d.×5
Christmas. 25d.×4
700th Anniv of Swiss Confederation. 20d.
Death Centenary of Vincent Van Gogh. 20d.
Art. 10d.×6; 25d.×2

1991

Flora and Fauna. 1; 5; 10; 50d.×2; 70d.; 75d.×; 80d.; 100; 250; 500d.
Railways. 75d.×6
Birds. 75d.×4; 200d.
Art. 50d.; 75d.×2; 100; 200d.
Fungi. 50d.×2; 75d.; 125; 200d.
Flowers. 50d.×2; 100d.×2; 200d.
500th Anniv of Christopher Colombus' voyage to the Americas (1992). 50d.×2; 75d.; 125d.; 200d.
Philanippon 91 International Stamp Exhibition. Butterflies. 125d.×2
Fauna. 25d.×6
Castles. 25d.×6
Butterflies. 125d.×4
Postal Express. 3000d.

1992

Marine Mammals. 450d.×4
Visit of Pope John Paul II. 120d.×8; 150d.×8; 180d.×4; 200d.×8; 250d.×4
Flora and Fauna. 1000d.; 1500; 2000; 2500d.
Environmental Protection Conference, Brazil. 65; 110; 150; 200; 275d.
Olympic Games, Barcelona. 50d.×6
Fungi. 75; 100; 125; 200; 500d.
Birds. 75; 100; 125; 200; 500d.
Olympic Games, Barcelona. 50; 300d.×6
Olympic Games, Barcelona 300d.×2
Railway. 75; 100; 125; 200; 500d.
Birth Centenary of Marcelo da Veiga. 10; 40; 50; 100d.
Butterflies. 75; 100; 125; 200; 500d.

1993

Fungi. 800d.×5
Butterflies and Flowers. 500d.×5

Birds. 500d.x5
Railways. 800d.x5
Flora. 500d.x5
World Cup Football Championship, Atlanta. 800d.x8
Dinosaurs. 500d.x6
UCCLA. 100d.; 150d.; 200d.; 250d.x2; 300d.; 350d.; 400d.; 500d.
Olympic Games, Atlanta. 800d.x8

1994

World Cup Football Championship, Brazil. 500d.
60th Birth Anniv of Elvis Presley. 10d.x18
Marilyn Monroe Commemoration. 10d.x9
UPU Congress. 1000d.
Butterflies. 1200d.x5
Cinema. 100d.x9
Independence. 350d.
Horses. 1000d.x9
Flowers and Fruit. 350; 370; 380; 800; 1000d.
Crafts. 350d.x2; 400d.; 500d.x2; 1000d.
United Nations. Overprint in black on Crafts. 350d.x2; 400d.; 500d.x2; 1000d.
Railways. 1000d.x6
Cats. 1000d.x9
Cats and Dogs. 1000d.x9
Dogs. 1000d.x18
Orchids. 1000d.x9
Art. 100d.x9
New Year. Year of the Rat. 1000d.x9
Fungi. 1000d.x15
Christmas. 750d.x9

Pt. 1

ST VINCENT

One of the Windward Islands, British West Indies.

1861. 12 pence = 1 shilling; 20 shillings = 1 pound.
1949. 100 cents = 1 West Indian dollar.

1

3

7

1861

36	7	½d. orange	7·00	8·50
47	7	½d. green	1·00	60
18	1	1d. black	60·00	15·00
29	1	1d. green	£180	5·00
39	1	1d. drab	75·00	3·00
48b	1	1d. red	3·00	85
61	1	2½d. blue	10·00	2·25
6	1	4d. blue	£275	£110
51	1	4d. brown	95·00	75
56	1	4d. yellow	1·75	14·00
62	1	5d. sepia	8·50	30·00
4	1	6d. green	60·00	19·00
57	1	6d. purple	2·75	24·00
11	1	1s. grey	£275	£120
13	1	1s. blue	£375	90·00
14	1	1s. brown	£500	£160
45	1	1s. red	£150	60·00
58	1	1s. orange	5·50	17·00
53	3	5s. lake	29·00	55·00

1880. Surch in figures.

33	½d. on half 6d. green	£160	£170
28	1d. on half 6d. green	£550	£375

1881. Surch in words.

34	1d. on 6d. green	£475	£350
63	3d. on 1d. mauve	5·00	25·00
60a	5d. on 6d. lake	1·75	1·75

1881. Surch in figures.

54	2½d. on 4d. brown	80·00	£120
35	4d. on 1s. orange	£1600	£800

1882. Surch in figures and words.

40	2½d. on 1d. red	25·00	1·50
55a	2½d. on 1d. blue	1·75	35
59	5d. on 4d. brown	38·00	55·00

1885. No. 40 further surch **1d** and bars.

46	1d. on 2½d. on 1d. lake	35·00	26·00

13

1899

67	13	½d. mauve and green	2·75	2·50
68	13	1d. mauve and red	4·50	1·50
69	13	2½d. mauve and blue	6·50	2·00
70	13	3d. mauve and green	4·00	20·00
71	13	4d. mauve and orange	7·00	24·00
72	13	5d. mauve and black	8·00	20·00
73	13	6d. mauve and brown	13·00	50·00
74	13	1s. green and red	17·00	60·00
75	13	5s. green and blue	95·00	£170

1902. As T 13, but portait of King Edward VII.

85a	½d. purple and green	1·25	1·25
77	1d. purple and red	4·25	30
78	2d. purple and black	6·50	6·00
79	2½d. purple and blue	5·00	3·50
80	3d. purple and green	5·00	7·00
81	6d. purple and brown	11·00	45·00
90a	1s. green and red	15·00	70·00
83	2s. green and violet	25·00	60·00
91	2s. purple and blue on blue	23·00	50·00
84	5s. green and blue	80·00	£140
92	5s. green and red on yellow	17·00	50·00
93	£1 purple and black on red	£275	£350

17 Seal of the Colony

1907

94	17	½d. green	3·25	2·25
95	17	1d. red	3·75	15
96	17	2d. orange	1·50	6·50
97	17	2½d. blue	42·00	8·50
98	17	3d. violet	8·00	17·00

18 Seal of the Colony

1909

102	18	½d. green	2·50	60
99	18	1d. red	1·25	30
104	18	2d. grey	6·50	12·00
105	18	2½d. blue	8·00	3·75
106	18	3d. purple on yellow	2·50	14·00
107	18	6d. purple	19·00	12·00
101	18	1s. black on green	4·25	10·00
139	18	2s. blue and purple	7·50	13·00
140	18	5s. red and green	18·00	35·00
141	18	£1 mauve and black	£110	£140

19

1913

108	19	½d. green	75	20
109	19	1d. red	80	50
132b	19	1½d. brown	6·00	15
133	19	2d. grey	2·50	1·00
111	19	2½d. blue	50	75
134	19	3d. blue	1·00	6·00
135	19	3d. purple on yellow	1·00	1·50
113	19	4d. red on yellow	80	2·00
136	19	5d. green	1·00	9·00
137	19	6d. purple	1·50	3·50
116	19	1s. black on green	1·50	3·75
138a	19	1s. brown	5·50	17·00

1915. Surch **ONE PENNY.**

121	1d. on 1s. black on green	10·00	40·00

1916. Optd **WAR STAMP.** in two lines.

122	1d. red	11·00	18·00

1916. Optd **WAR STAMP.** in one line.

126	1d. red	1·50	2·25

1935. Silver Jubilee. As **T 32a** of St. Helena.

142	1d. blue and red	50	5·50
143	1½d. blue and grey	1·00	4·75
144	2½d. brown and blue	2·00	6·00
145	1s. grey and purple	7·50	12·00

1937. Coronation. As **T 32b** of St. Helena.

146	1d. violet	35	1·25
147	1½d. red	40	1·25
148	2½d. blue	45	2·25

25

26 Young's Island and Fort Duvernette

1938

149	25	½d. blue and green	20	10
150	26	1d. blue and brown	20	10
151	-	1½d. green and red	20	10
152	25	2d. green and black	40	35
153	-	2½d. black and green	20	40
153a	-	2½d. green and brown	40	20
154	25	3d. orange and purple	20	10
154a	-	3½d. blue and green	75	2·50
155	25	6d. black and lake	1·50	40
156	-	1s. purple and green	1·50	80
157	25	2s. blue and purple	6·00	75
157a	25	2s.6d. brown and blue	1·25	3·50
158	25	5s. red and green	16·00	2·50
158a	25	10s. violet and brown	7·50	9·00
159	25	£1 purple and black	27·00	15·00

DESIGNS—HORIZ: 1½d. Kingstown and Fort Charlotte; 2½d. (No. 153), 3½d. Bathing beach at Villa; 2½d. (No. 153a), 1s. Victoria Park, Kingstown.

1946. Victory. As **T 33a** of St. Helena.

160	1½d. red	10	10
161	3½d. blue	10	10

1948. Silver Wedding. As **T 33b/c** of St Helena.

162	1½d. red	10	10
163	£1 mauve	27·00	38·00

1949. As 1938 issue, but values in cents and dollars.

164		1c. blue and green	20	1·75
164a		1c. green and black	30	2·50
165	26	2c. blue and brown	15	50
166	-	3c. green and red	50	1·00
166a	25	3c. orange and purple	75	2·50
167	25	4c. green and black	35	20
167a	25	4c. blue and green	30	20
168	-	5c. green and brown	15	10
169	25	6c. orange and purple	50	1·25
169a	-	6c. green and red	30	2·25
170	-	7c. black and blue	6·50	1·50
170a	-	10c. black and turquoise	75	20
171	25	12c. black and lake	35	15
172	-	24c. purple and green	35	55
173	25	48c. blue and purple	6·00	7·00
174	25	60c. brown and blue	3·00	6·50
175	25	$1.20 red and green	4·75	4·50
176	25	$2.40 violet and brown	6·00	10·00
177	25	$4.80 purple and black	15·00	20·00

DESIGNS—HORIZ: 3c. (No. 166), 6c. (No. 169a) Kingstown and Fort Charlotte; 5, 24c. Victoria Park, Kingstown; 7, 10c. Bathing beach at Villa.

1949. U.P.U. As **T 33d/g** of St. Helena.

178	5c. blue	20	20
179	6c. purple	1·50	2·25
180	12c. mauve	20	2·25
181	24c. green	20	1·00

1951. Inauguration of B.W.I. University College. As **T 10a/b** of St. Kitts-Nevis.

182	18	3c. green and red	30	65
183	19	12c. black and purple	30	1·75

1951. New Constitution. Optd **NEW CONSTITUTION 1951.**

184	-	3c. green and red (No. 166)	20	1·75
185	25	4c. green and black	20	60
186	-	5c. green & brn (No. 168)	20	60
187	25	12c. black and lake	1·25	1·25

1953. Coronation. As **T 33h** of St. Helena.

188	4c. black and green	30	20

30

31

1955

189	30	1c. orange	10	10
190	30	2c. blue	10	10
191	30	3c. grey	30	10
192	30	4c. brown	20	10
215	30	5c. red	15	10
216	30	10c. lilac	15	10
195	30	15c. blue	2·50	1·00
218	30	20c. green	45	10
197	30	25c. sepia	50	10
198a	31	50c. brown	5·50	1·50
199	31	$1 green	8·00	1·00
200	31	$2.50 blue	11·00	11·00

1958. British Caribbean Federation. As **T 27a** of St. Kitts-Nevis.

201	31	3c. green	50	20
202	31	6c. blue	55	1·25
203	31	12c. red	60	50

1963. Freedom from Hunger. As **T 63a** of St. Helena.

204	8c. violet	45	50

1963. Cent of Red Cross. As **T 63b** of St. Helena.

205	4c. red and black	15	20
206	8c. red and blue	35	50

32 Scout Badge and Proficiency Badges

1964. 50th Anniv of St. Vincent Boy Scouts Association.

221	32	1c. green and brown	10	10
222	32	4c. blue and purple	10	10
223	32	20c. yellow and violet	30	10
224	32	50c. red and green	45	70

33 Tropical Fruits

1965. Bicentenary of Botanic Gardens. Multicoloured.

225	1c. Type **33**	10	10
226	4c. Breadfruit and H.M.S. "Providence" (sloop), 1793	10	10
227	25c. Doric Temple and pond (vert)	15	10
228	40c. Talipot palm and Doric Temple (vert)	30	1·25

1965. Cent of I.T.U. As **T 64a** of St. Helena.

229	4c. blue and green	15	10
230	48c. ochre and orange	35	45

37 Boat-building, Bequia

1965. Multicoloured.

231	1c. Type **37** (inscr "BEOUIA")	10	1·00
231a	1c. Type **37** (inscr "BEQUIA")	65	40
232	2c. Friendship Beach, Bequia	10	10
233	3c. Terminal Building, Arnos Vale Airport	1·00	10
261	4c. Woman with bananas	30	30
235	5c. Crater Lake	15	10
236	6c. Carib stone	15	40
237	8c. Arrowroot	30	10
238	10c. Owia Salt Pond	30	10
239	12c. Deep water wharf	70	10
240	20c. Sea island cotton	30	10
241	25c. Map of St. Vincent and islands	35	10
242	50c. Breadfruit	50	30
243	$1 Baleine Falls	3·00	30
244	$2.50 St. Vincent amazon	18·00	11·00
245	$5 Arms of St. Vincent	3·00	14·00

Nos. 261, 236/7 and 240/5 are vert.

1966. Churchill Commem. As **T 64b** of St. Helena.

246	1c. blue	10	10
247	4c. green	20	10
248	20c. brown	35	30
249	40c. violet	55	1·00

1966. Royal Visit. As **T 48a** of St. Kitts-Nevis.

250	4c. black, green and blue	50	20
251	25c. black and mauve	1·50	80

1966. Inauguration of W.H.O. Headquarters, Geneva. As **T 64e** of St. Helena.

252	4c. black, green and blue	25	10
253	25c. black, purple and ochre	50	80

1966. 20th Anniv of UNESCO. As **T 64f/h** of St. Helena.

254	4c. multicoloured	20	10
255	8c. yellow, violet and olive	40	10
256	25c. black, purple and orange	1·00	60

38 Coastal View of Mount Coke Area

1967. Autonomous Methodist Church. Multicoloured.

257	2c. Type **38**	10	60
258	8c. Kingstown Methodist Church	10	10
259	25c. First licence to perform marriages	25	10
260	35c. Conference Arms	25	10

90 William I, William II, Henry I and Stephen

1977. Silver Jubilee. Multicoloured.

502	½c. Type **90**	10	30
503	1c. Henry II, Richard I, John, Henry III	10	30
504	1½c. Edward I, Edward II, Edward III, Richard II	10	30
505	2c. Henry IV, Henry V, Henry VI, Edward IV	10	30
506	5c. Edward V, Richard III, Henry VII, Henry VIII	10	10
507	10c. Edward VI, Lady Jane Grey, Mary I, Elizabeth I	10	10
508	25c. James I, Charles I, Charles II, James II	10	10
509	35c. William III, Mary II, Anne, George I	10	10
510	45c. George II, George III, George IV	10	10
511	75c. William IV, Victoria, Edward VII	15	25
512	$1 George V, Edward VIII, George VI	20	40
513	$2 Elizabeth II leaving Westminster Abbey	30	60
MS514	170×146 mm. Nos. 502/13	1·00	2·00

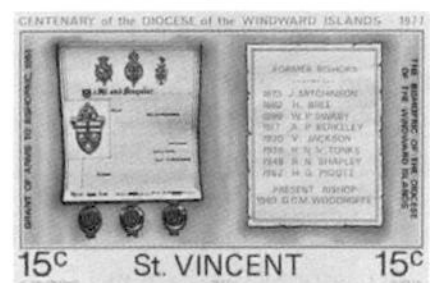

91 Grant of Arms

1977. Centenary of Windward Islands Diocese. Multicoloured.

527	15c. Type **91**	10	10
528	35c. Bishop Berkeley and mitres	10	10
529	45c. Map and arms of diocese	10	10
530	$1.25 St. George's Cathedral and Bishop Woodroffe	30	55

1977. Kingstown Carnival. Nos. 426, 429, 432/3 and 440 optd **CARNIVAL 1977 JUNE 25TH - JULY 5TH**.

531	5c. French grunt	10	10
532	10c. Sperm whale	10	10
533	15c. Skipjack tuna	10	10
534	20c. Queen angelfish	10	10
535	$1 Queen triggerfish	40	50

93 Guide and Emblem

1977. 50th Anniv of St. Vincent Girl Guides. Multicoloured.

536	5c. Type **93**	10	10
537	15c. Early uniform, ranger, guide and brownie	10	10
538	20c. Early uniform and guide	10	10
539	$2 Lady Baden-Powell	40	75

1977. Royal Visit. No. 513 optd **CARIBBEAN VISIT 1977**.

540	$2 Queen Elizabeth leaving Westminster Abbey	30	30

95 Map of St. Vincent

1977. Surch as in T **95**.

541	**95**	20c. light blue and blue	15	15
542	**95**	40c. light orange and orange	25	20
543	**95**	40c. pink and mauve	20	15

Nos. 541/3 were originally printed without face values.

96 Opening Verse and Scene

1977. Christmas. Scenes and Verses from the carol "While Shepherds Watched their Flocks by Night". Multicoloured.

544	5c. Type **96**	10	10
545	10c. Angel consoling shepherds	10	10
546	15c. View of Bethlehem	10	10
547	25c. Nativity scene	10	10
548	50c. Throng of angels	10	10
549	$1.25 Praising God	30	65
MS550	150×170 mm. Nos. 544/9	1·00	1·75

97 "Cynthia cardui" and "Bougainvillea glabra var alba"

1978. Butterflies and Bougainvilleas. Multicoloured.

551	5c. Type **97**	15	10
552	25c. "Dione juno" and "Golden Glow"	15	10
553	40c. "Anartia amathea" and "Mrs McLean"	20	10
554	50c. "Hypolimnas misippus" and "Cyphen"	25	10
555	$1.25 "Pseudolycaena marsyas" and "Thomasii"	50	80

97a Westminster Abbey

1978. 25th Anniv of Coronation. Multicoloured.

556	40c. Type **97a**	10	10
557	50c. Gloucester Cathedral	10	10
558	$1.25 Durham Cathedral	15	15
559	$2.50 Exeter Cathedral	15	25
MS560	130×102 mm. Nos. 556/9	40	1·00

98 Rotary International Emblem and Motto

1978. International Service Clubs. Emblems and Mottoes. Multicoloured.

561	40c. Type **98**	15	10
562	50c. Lions International	15	10
563	$1 Jaycees	35	50

99 "Co-operation in Education Leads to Mutual Understanding and Respect"

1978. Tenth Anniv of Project School to School (St. Vincent–Canada school twinning project). Multicoloured.

564	40c. Type **99**	10	10
565	$2 "Co-operation in Education Leads to the Elimination of Racial Intolerance" (horiz)	40	50

100 Arnos Vale Airport

1978. 75th Anniv of Powered Flight. Multicoloured.

566	10c. Type **100**	10	10
567	40c. Wilbur Wright landing Wright Flyer I	15	10
568	50c. Orville Wright in Wright Flyer III	15	10
569	$1.25 Orville Wright and Wright Flyer I airborne	45	80

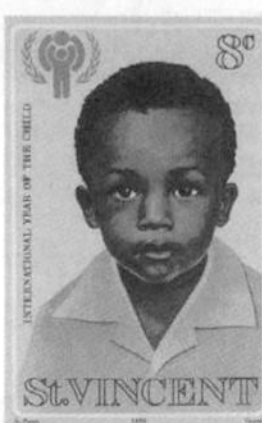

101 Young Child

1979. International Year of the Child.

570	**101**	8c. black, gold and green	10	10
571	-	20c. black, gold and lilac	10	10
572	-	50c. black, gold and blue	15	10
573	-	$2 black, gold and flesh	50	50

DESIGNS: 20, 50c., $2 Different portraits of young children.

1979. Soufriere Eruption Relief Fund. As T **95** but surch **SOUFRIERE RELIEF FUND 1979** and premium.

574	**95**	10c.+5c. blue and lilac	10	15
575	**95**	50c.+25c. brown and buff	20	20
576	**95**	$1+50c. brown and grey	25	30
577	**95**	$2+$1 green and light green	40	50

103 Sir Rowland Hill

1979. Death Cent of Sir Rowland Hill. Multicoloured.

578	40c. Type **103**	15	10
579	50c. Penny Black and Two Penny Blue stamps	15	15
580	$3 1861 1d. and 6d. stamps	40	1·10
MS581	170×123 mm. Nos. 578/80, 594/5 and 599	1·00	2·25

104 First and Latest Buccament Postmarks and Map of St. Vincent

1979. Post Office of St. Vincent. Early and modern postmarks. Multicoloured.

582	1c. Type **104**	10	10
583	2c. Sion Hill	10	10
584	3c. Cumberland	10	1·00
585	4c. Questelles	10	30
586	5c. Layou	10	10
587	6c. New Ground	10	10
588	8c. Mesopotamia	10	10
589	10c. Troumaca	10	10
590	12c. Arnos Vale	10	30
591	15c. Stubbs	10	30
592	20c. Orange Hill	10	30
593	25c. Calliaqua	10	10
594	40c. Edinboro	20	20
595	50c. Colonarie	20	25
596	80c. Biabou	30	35
597	$1 Chateaubelair	30	50
598	$2 Head P.O. Kingstown	35	80
599	$3 Barrouallie	40	1·25
600	$5 Georgetown	60	1·50
601	$10 Kingstown	1·25	2·75

1979. Opening of St. Vincent and the Grenadines Air Service. Optd **ST VINCENT AND THE GRENADINES AIR SERVICE 1979**.

602	10c. Type **100**	10	10

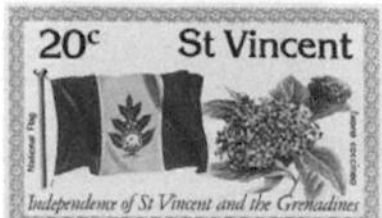

106 National Flag and "Ixora occinea" (flower)

1979. Independence. Multicoloured.

603	20c. Type **106**	15	10
604	50c. House of Assembly and "Ixora stricta" (flower)	20	10
605	80c. Prime Minister R. Milton Cato and "Ixora williamsii" (flower)	25	20

1979. Independence. Nos. 422, 425/30, 432, 437/41 and 443 optd **INDEPENDENCE 1979**.

606	1c. Type **79**	10	10
607	4c. Spanish mackerel	10	10
608	5c. French grunt	10	10
609	6c. Spotted goatfish	10	10
610	8c. Ballyhoo	10	10
611	10c. Sperm whale	15	15
612	12c. Humpback whale	15	15
613	15c. Skipjack tuna	10	15
614	25c. Princess parrotfish	10	10
615	50c. Porkfish	15	35
616	70c. Yellow-finned tuna	20	45
617	90c. Pompano	20	50
618	$1 Queen triggerfish	20	50
619	$2.50 Sailfish	35	1·00
620	$10 Blue marlin	1·10	3·25

108 Virgin and Child

1979. Christmas. Scenes and quotations from "Silent Night" (carol). Multicoloured.

621	10c. Type **108**	10	10
622	20c. Jesus sleeping	10	10
623	25c. Shepherds	10	10
624	40c. Angel	10	10
625	50c. Angels holding Jesus	10	10
626	$2 Nativity	40	45
MS627	151×170 mm. Nos. 621/6	70	1·25

109 "Polistes cinctus" (wasp) and Oleander

1979. Flowers and Insects. Different varieties of oleander. Multicoloured.

628	5c. Type **109**	10	10
629	10c. "Pyrophorus noctiluca" (click beetle)	10	10
630	25c. "Stagmomantis limbata" (mantid)	10	10
631	50c. "Psiloptera lampetis" (beetle)	10	10
632	$2 "Diaprepies abbreviatus" (weevil)	30	30

1980. Centenary of St. Vincent "Arms" Stamps. Sheet 116×72 mm containing designs as **T 31**.

MS633	116×72 mm. 50c. brown; $1 green; $2.50 blue	50	75

110 Queen Elizabeth II

1980. "London 1980" International Stamp Exhibition. Multicoloured.

634	80c. Type **110**	15	20
635	$1 Great Britain 1954 3d. and St. Vincent 1954 5c. definitives	20	30
636	$2 Unadopted postage stamp design of 1971	35	60
MS637	165×115 mm. Nos. 596/8 and 634/8	75	1·50

111 Steel Band

1980. Kingstown Carnival. Multicoloured.

638	20c. Type **111**	15	65
639	20c. Steel band (different)	15	65

112 Football

1980. "Sport for All". Multicoloured.

640		10c. Type **112**	10	10
641		60c. Cycling	30	15
642		80c. Basketball	40	40
643		$2.50 Boxing	40	1·25

1980. Hurricane Relief. Nos. 640/3 surch **HURRICANE RELIEF 50c**.

644	112	10c.+50c. multicoloured	15	20
645	-	60c.+50c. multicoloured	40	45
646	-	80c.+50c. multicoloured	45	50
647	-	$2.50+50c. mult	40	85

114 Brazilian Agouti

1980. Wildlife. Multicoloured.

648	25c. Type **114**	10	10
649	50c. Giant toad	15	10
650	$2 Small Indian mongoose	40	55

115 Map of World showing St. Vincent

1980. St. Vincent "On the Map". Maps showing St. Vincent. Multicoloured.

651	10c. Type **115**	10	10
652	50c. Western hemisphere	25	10
653	$1 Central America	40	15
654	$2 St. Vincent	60	30
MS655	143×95 mm. No. 654	75	1·50

116 "Ville de Paris" (French ship of the line), 1782

1981. Sailing Ships. Multicoloured.

656	50c. Type **116**	25	15
657	60c. H.M.S. "Ramillies" (ship of the line), 1782	25	25
658	$1.50 H.M.S. "Providence" (sloop), 1793	40	70
659	$2 "Dee" (paddle-steamer packet)	50	80

117 Arrowroot Cultivation

1981. Agriculture. Multicoloured.

660	25c. Type **117**	10	20
661	25c. Arrowroot processing	10	20
662	50c. Banana cultivation	10	30
663	50c. Banana export packaging station	10	30
664	60c. Coconut plantation	15	30
665	60c. Copra drying frames	15	35
666	$1 Cocoa cultivation	15	50
667	$1 Cocoa beans and sun drying frames	15	50

1981. Royal Wedding. Royal Yachts. As **T 14a/b** of St. Kitts. Multicoloured.

668	60c. "Isabella"	15	15
669	60c. Prince Charles and Lady Diana Spencer	30	30
670	$2.50 "Alberta" (tender)	30	30
671	$2.50 As No. 669	70	70
672	$4 "Britannia"	35	40
673	$4 As No. 669	1·00	1·25
MS674	120×109 mm. $5 As No. 669	75	75

118/19 Kingstown General Post Office

1981. U.P.U. Membership.

677	118	$2 multicoloured	40	90
678	119	$2 multicoloured	40	90

Nos. 677/8 were printed together, se-tenant, forming the composite design illustrated.

120 St. Vincent Flag with Flags of other U.N. Member Nations

1981. First Anniv of U.N. Membership. Multicoloured.

679	$1.50 Type **120**	25	25
680	$2.50 Prime Minister Robert Milton Cato	35	50

Nos. 679/80 are inscribed "ST. VINCENT and the GRENADINES".

121 Silhouettes of Figures at Old Testament Reading and Bible Extract

1981. Christmas. Designs showing silhouettes of figures. Multicoloured.

681	50c. Type **121**	25	10
682	60c. Madonna and angel	30	10
683	$1 Madonna and Bible extract	45	25
684	$2 Joseph and Mary travelling to Bethlehem	65	50
MS685	129×127 mm. Nos. 681/4	1·50	1·40

122 Sugar Boilers

1982. First Anniv of Re-introduction of Sugar Industry. Multicoloured.

686	50c. Type **122**	20	15
687	60c. Sugar drying plant	20	20
688	$1.50 Sugar mill machinery	40	75
689	$2 Crane loading sugar cane	50	1·00

123 Butterfly Float

1982. Carnival 1982 Multicoloured.

690	50c. Type **123**	20	15
691	60c. Angel dancer (vert)	20	15
692	$1.50 Winged dancer (vert)	50	80
693	$2 Eagle float	70	1·50

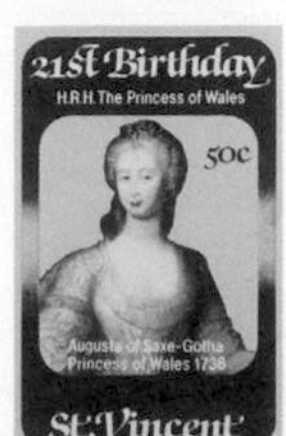

124 Augusta of Saxe-Gotha, Princess of Wales, 1736

1982. 21st Birthday of Princess of Wales. Multicoloured.

694	50c. Type **124**	15	20
695	60c. Coat of arms of Augusta of Saxe-Gotha	15	25
696	$6 Diana, Princess of Wales	1·10	1·25

125 Scout Emblem

1982. 75th Anniv of Boy Scout Movement. Multicoloured.

697	$1.50 Type **125**	70	1·00
698	$2.50 75th anniversary emblem	90	1·50

1982. Birth of Prince William of Wales. Nos. 694/6 optd **ROYAL BABY**.

699	50c. Type **124**	10	20
700	60c. Coat of arms of Augusta of Saxe-Gotha	10	25
701	$6 Diana, Princess of Wales	60	1·50

126 De Havilland Gipsy Moth, 1932

1982. 50th Anniv of Airmail Service. Multicoloured.

702	50c. Type **126**	55	30
703	60c. Grumman Goose, 1952	65	40
704	$1.50 Hawker Siddeley H.S.748, 1968	1·25	1·50
705	$2 Britten Norman "long nose" Trislander, 1982	1·40	2·00

127 "Geestport" (freighter)

1982. Ships. Multicoloured.

706	45c. Type **127**	40	25
707	60c. "Stella Oceanis" (liner)	50	40
708	$1.50 "Victoria" (liner)	80	1·50
709	$2 "Queen Elizabeth 2" (liner)	1·00	2·00

128 "Pseudocorynactis caribbeorum"

1983. Marine Life. Multicoloured.

710	50c. Type **128**	65	25
711	60c. "Actinoporus elegans" (vert)	75	40
712	$1.50 "Arachnanthus nocturnus" (vert)	1·40	2·25
713	$2 Reid's seahorse (vert)	1·60	2·50

129 Satellite View of St. Vincent

1983. Commonwealth Day. Multicoloured.

714	45c. Type **129**	15	20
715	60c. Flag of St. Vincent	20	25
716	$1.50 Prime Minister R. Milton Cato	30	65
717	$2 Harvesting bananas	45	90

Nos. 714/17 are inscribed "St. Vincent and The Grenadines".

1983. No. 681 surch **45c**.

718	121	45c. on 50c. Mult	40	30

131 Symbolic Handshake

1983. Tenth Anniv of Treaty of Chaguaramas. Multicoloured.

719	45c. Type **131**	15	20
720	60c. Commerce emblem	20	30
721	$1.50 Caribbean map	50	1·40
722	$2 Flags of member countries and map of St. Vincent	75	1·60

132 William A. Smith (founder)

1983. Centenary of Boys' Brigade. Multicoloured.

723	45c. Type **132**	20	25
724	60c. On parade	25	35
725	$1.50 Craftwork	55	1·50
726	$2 Community service	70	1·60

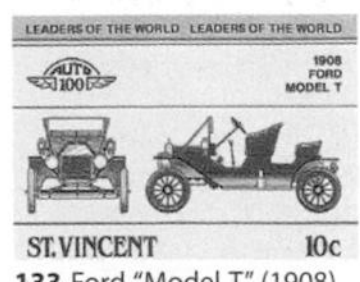

133 Ford "Model T" (1908)

1983. Leaders of the World. Automobiles (1st series).

727	133	10c. multicoloured	10	10
728	-	10c. multicoloured	10	10
729	-	60c. multicoloured	10	15
730	-	60c. multicoloured	10	15
731	-	$1.50 multicoloured	15	20
732	-	$1.50 multicoloured	15	20
733	-	$1.50 multicoloured	15	20
734	-	$1.50 multicoloured	15	20
735	-	$2 multicoloured	15	20
736	-	$2 multicoloured	15	20
737	-	$2 multicoloured	15	20
738	-	$2 multicoloured	15	20

DESIGNS: (the first in each pair shows technical drawings and the second paintings of the cars). Nos. 727/8, Ford "Model T" (1908); 729/30, Supercharged Cord "812" (1937); 731/2, Citroen "Open Tourer" (1937); 733/4, Mercedes Benz "300SL Gull-Wing" (1954); 735/6, Rolls-Royce "Phantom I" (1925); 737/8, Ferrari "Boxer 512BB" (1967).

See also Nos. 820/9, 862/7, 884/91 and 952/63.

134 Appearance of the Nativity Star

1983. Christmas. Multicoloured.

739	10c. Type **134**	10	10
740	50c. Message of the Angel	20	10
741	$1.50 The Heavenly Host	40	75
742	$2.40 Worshipping Jesus	55	1·25
MS743	130×130 mm. Nos. 739/42	1·25	1·75

135 "King Henry VIII"

1983. Leaders of the World. Railway Locomotives (1st series). First in each pair shows technical drawings and the second the locomotive at work.

744	135	10c. multicoloured	10	10
745	-	10c. multicoloured	10	10
746	-	10c. multicoloured	10	10
747	-	10c. multicoloured	10	10
748	-	25c. multicoloured	10	10
749	-	25c. multicoloured	10	10
750	-	50c. multicoloured	15	20
751	-	50c. multicoloured	15	20
752	-	60c. multicoloured	15	20
753	-	60c. multicoloured	15	20
754	-	75c. multicoloured	15	25
755	-	75c. multicoloured	15	25
756	-	$2.50 multicoloured	20	35
757	-	$2.50 multicoloured	20	35
758	-	$3 multicoloured	25	50
759	-	$3 multicoloured	25	50

See also Nos. 792/807, 834/41, 872/83, 893/904 and 1001/8.

136 Fort Duvernette

1984. Fort Duvernette. Multicoloured.

760	35c. Type **136**	20	30
761	45c. Soldiers on fortifications	25	30
762	$1 Cannon facing bay	40	60
763	$3 Map of St. Vincent and mortar	1·25	1·75

137 White Frangipani

1984. Flowering Trees and Shrubs. Multicoloured.

764	5c. Type **137**	20	10
765	10c. Genip	25	10
766	15c. Immortelle	30	10
767	20c. Pink poui	30	10
768	25c. Buttercup	30	10
769	35c. Sandbox	45	10
770	45c. Locust	45	10
771	60c. Colville's glory	50	30
772	75c. Lignum vitae	50	45
773	$1 Golden shower	50	1·00
774	$5 Angelin	1·25	6·50
775	$10 Roucou	1·75	11·00

138 Trench Warfare, First World War

1984. Leaders of the World. British Monarchs. Multicoloured.

776	1c. Type **138**	10	10
777	1c. George V and trenches	10	10
778	5c. Battle of Bannockburn	10	10
779	5c. Edward II and battle	10	10
780	60c. George V	15	20
781	60c. York Cottage, Sandringham	15	20
782	75c. Edward II	15	20
783	75c. Berkeley Castle	15	20
784	$1 Coat of arms of Edward II	15	25
785	$1 Edward II (different)	15	25
786	$4 Coat of arms of George V	35	60
787	$4 George V and Battle of Jutland	35	60

Nos. 776/7, 778/9, 780/1, 782/3, 784/5 and 786/7 were printed together, se-tenant, each pair forming a composite design.

139 Musical Fantasy Costume

1984. Carnival 1984. Costumes. Multicoloured.

788	35c. Type **139**	15	15
789	45c. African princess	15	20
790	$1 Market woman	35	40
791	$3 Carib hieroglyph	80	1·75

1984. Leaders of the World. Railway Locomotives (2nd series). As **T 135**, the first in each pair shows technical drawings and the second the locomotive at work.

792	1c. multicoloured	10	10
793	1c. multicoloured	10	10
794	2c. multicoloured	10	10
795	2c. multicoloured	10	10
796	3c. multicoloured	10	10
797	3c. multicoloured	10	10
798	50c. multicoloured	20	30
799	50c. multicoloured	20	30
800	75c. multicoloured	20	35
801	75c. multicoloured	20	35
802	$1 multicoloured	20	35
803	$1 multicoloured	20	35
804	$2 multicoloured	25	40
805	$2 multicoloured	25	40
806	$3 multicoloured	25	50
807	$3 multicoloured	25	50

DESIGNS: Nos. 792/3, Class 141-R Liberation, France (1945); 794/5, [illegible] locomotive "Dread-nought", Great Britain (1967); 796/7, No. 242A1, [illegible] (1946); 798/9, Class "Dean Goods", Great Britain (1883); 800/1, Hetton Colliery No. 1, Great Britain (1822); 802/3, "Pen-y-Darren", Great Britain (1804); 804/5, "Novelty", Great Britain (1829); 806/7, Class 44, Germany (1925).

140 Slaves tilling Field

1984. 150th Anniv of Emancipation of Slaves on St. Vincent. Multicoloured.

808	35c. Type **140**	15	20
809	45c. Sugar-cane harvesting	15	25
810	$1 Cutting sugar-cane	30	70
811	$3 William Wilberforce and African slave caravan	1·00	2·75

141 Weightlifting

1984. Leaders of the World. Olympic Games, Los Angeles. Multicoloured.

812	1c. Judo	10	10
813	1c. Type **141**	10	10
814	3c. Pursuit cycling	10	10
815	3c. Cycle road-racing	10	10
816	60c. Women's backstroke swimming	15	15
817	60c. Men's butterfly swimming	15	15
818	$3 Sprint start	40	55
819	$3 Finish of long distance race	40	55

1984. Leaders of the World. Automobiles (2nd series). As **T 133**, the first in each pair shows technical drawings and the second paintings.

820	5c. black, drab and green	10	10
821	5c. multicoloured	10	10
822	20c. black, pink and blue	10	10
823	20c. multicoloured	10	10
824	55c. black, green and brown	20	20
825	55c. multicoloured	20	20
826	$1.50 black, light turquoise and turquoise	25	30
827	$1.50 multicoloured	25	30
828	$2.50 black, turquoise and lilac	30	35
829	$2.50 multicoloured	30	35

DESIGNS: Nos. 820/1, Austin-Healey "Sprite" (1958); 822/3, Maserati "Ghibli Coupe" (1971); 824/5, Pontiac "GTO" (1964); 826/7, Jaguar "D-Type" (1957); 828/9, Ferrari "365 GTB4 Daytona" (1970).

142 Grenadier, 70th Regt of Foot, 1773

1984. Military Uniforms. Multicoloured.

830	45c. Type **142**	50	30
831	60c. Grenadier, 6th Regt of Foot, 1775	60	35
832	$1.50 Grenadier, 3rd Regt of Foot, 1768	80	1·10
833	$2 Battalion Company Officer, 14th Regt of Foot, 1780	90	1·60

1984. Leaders of the World. Railway Locomotives (3rd series). As **T 135**, the first in each pair shows technical drawings and the second the locomotive at work.

834	5c. multicoloured	10	10
835	5c. multicoloured	10	10
836	40c. multicoloured	15	15
837	40c. multicoloured	15	15
838	75c. multicoloured	15	20
839	75c. multicoloured	15	20
840	$2.50 multicoloured	50	65
841	$2.50 multicoloured	50	65

DESIGNS: Nos. 834/5, 20th Class, Rhodesia (1954); 836/7, "Southern Maid", Great Britain (1928); 838/9, "Prince of Wales", Great Britain (1911); 840/1, Class 05, Germany (1935).

143 N. S. Taylor

1985. Leaders of the World. Cricketers. The first in each pair shows a head portrait and the second the cricketer in action.

842	**143**	5c. multicoloured	10	10
843	-	5c. multicoloured	10	10
844	-	35c. multicoloured	30	20
845	-	35c. multicoloured	30	20
846	-	50c. multicoloured	30	30
847	-	50c. multicoloured	30	30
848	-	$3 multicoloured	50	1·25
849	-	$3 multicoloured	50	1·25

DESIGNS: Nos. 842/3, N. S. Taylor; 844/5, T. W. Graveney; 846/7, R. G. D. Willis; 848/9, S. D. Fletcher.

144 Eye Lash Orchid

1985. Orchids. Multicoloured.

850	35c. Type **144**	20	30
851	45c. "Ionopsis utricularioides"	20	30
852	$1 "Epidendrum secundum"	30	65
853	$3 "Oncidium altissimum"	40	2·00

145 Brown Pelican

1985. Leaders of the World. Birth Bicentenary of John J. Audubon (ornithologist). Multicoloured.

854	15c. Type **145**	10	10
855	15c. Green-backed heron ("Green Heron")	10	10
856	40c. Pileated woodpecker	15	20
857	40c. Common flicker	15	20
858	60c. Painted bunting	15	30
859	60c. White-winged crossbill	15	30
860	$2.25 Red-shouldered hawk	30	90
861	$2.25 Common caracara ("Crested Caracara")	30	90

1985. Leaders of the World. Automobiles (3rd series). As **T 133**, the first in each pair shows technical drawings and the second paintings.

862	1c. black, yellow and green	10	10
863	1c. multicoloured	10	10
864	55c. black, blue and grey	15	25
865	55c. multicoloured	15	25
866	$2 black, yellow and purple	30	70
867	$2 multicoloured	30	70

DESIGNS: Nos. 862/3, Lancia "Aprilia", (1937); 864/5, Pontiac "Firebird Trans Am", (1973); 866/7, Cunningham "C-5R", (1953).

146 Pepper

1985. Herbs and Spices. Multicoloured.

868	25c. Type **146**	10	10
869	35c. Sweet marjoram	10	15
870	$1 Nutmeg	20	65
871	$3 Ginger	60	2·50

1985. Leaders of the World. Railway Locomotives (4th series). As **T 135**, the first in each pair shows technical drawings and the second the locomotive at work.

872	1c. multicoloured	10	10
873	1c. multicoloured	10	10
874	10c. multicoloured	10	10
875	10c. multicoloured	10	10
876	40c. multicoloured	15	30
877	40c. multicoloured	15	30
878	60c. multicoloured	15	30
879	60c. multicoloured	15	30
880	$1 multicoloured	25	40
881	$1 multicoloured	25	40
882	$2.50 multicoloured	40	60
883	$2.50 multicoloured	40	60

DESIGNS: Nos. 872/3, "Glen Douglas", Great Britain (1913); 874/5, "Fenchurch", Great Britain (1872); 876/7, No. 1 Stirling "single", Great Britain (1870); 878/9, No. 158A, Great Britain (1866); 880/1, Jones Goods locomotive No. 103, Great Britain (1893); 882/3, "The Great Bear", Great Britain (1908).

1985. Leaders of the World. Automobiles (4th series). As **T 133**, the first in each pair shows technical drawings and the second paintings.

884	25c. black, grey and red	10	10
885	25c. multicoloured	10	10
886	60c. black, pink and orange	15	20
887	60c. multicoloured	15	20
888	$1 black, blue and violet	15	25
889	$1 multicoloured	15	25
890	$1.50 black, blue and red	20	30
891	$1.50 multicoloured	20	30
MS892	180×121 mm. $4 ×2 As Nos. 890/1; $5 ×2 As Nos. 888/9	1·75	4·50

DESIGNS: Nos. 884/5, Essex "Coach" (1922); 886/7, Nash "Rambler" (1950); 888/9, Ferrari "Tipo 156" (1961); 890/1, Eagle-Weslake "Type 58" (1967).

1985. Leaders of the World. Railway Locomotives (5th series). As **T 135**, the first in each pair shows technical drawings and the second the locomotive at work.

893	**151**	5c. multicoloured	10	10
894	-	5c. multicoloured	10	10
895	-	30c. multicoloured	15	20
896	-	30c. multicoloured	15	20
897	-	60c. multicoloured	20	30
898	-	60c. multicoloured	20	30
899	-	75c. multicoloured	20	30
900	-	75c. multicoloured	20	30
901	-	$1 multicoloured	25	40
902	-	$1 multicoloured	25	40
903	-	$2.50 multicoloured	30	60
904	-	$2.50 multicoloured	30	60

DESIGNS: Nos. 893/4, "Loch", Isle of Man (1874); 895/6, Class 47XX, Great Britain (1919); 897/8, Class 121, France (1876); 899/900, Class 24, Germany (1927); 901/2, Tank locomotive No. 1008, Great Britain (1889); 903/4, Class PS-4, U.S.A. (1926).

147 Bamboo Flute

1985. Traditional Musical Instruments. Multicoloured.

905	25c. Type **147**	10	15
906	35c. Quatro (four-stringed guitar)	10	25
907	$1 Ba-ha (bamboo pipe) (vert)	25	55
908	$2 Goat-skin drum (vert)	35	1·10
MS909	141×100 mm. Nos. 905/8	1·25	4·00

148 Queen Elizabeth the Queen Mother

1985. Leaders of the World. Life and Times of Queen Elizabeth the Queen Mother. Various portraits.

910	**148**	35c. multicoloured	10	25
911	-	35c. multicoloured	10	25
912	-	85c. multicoloured	10	30
913	-	85c. multicoloured	10	30
914	-	$1.20 multicoloured	15	35
915	-	$1.20 multicoloured	15	35
916	-	$1.60 multicoloured	15	35
917	-	$1.60 multicoloured	15	35
MS918		85×114 mm. $2.10 multicoloured; $2.10 multicoloured	50	1·50

Each value issued in pairs showing a floral pattern across the bottom of the portraits which stops short of the left-hand edge on the first stamp and of the right-hand edge on the second.

149 Elvis Presley

1985. Leaders of the World. Elvis Presley (entertainer). Various portraits. Multicoloured, background colours given.

919	**149**	10c. multicoloured	15	15
920	-	10c. multicoloured (blue)	15	15
921	-	60c. multicoloured (brown)	20	35

922	-	60c. multicoloured (grey)	20	35
923	-	$1 multicoloured (brown)	20	55
924	-	$1 multicoloured (blue)	20	55
925	-	$5 mult (light blue)	30	1·40
926	-	$5 multicoloured (blue)	30	1·40
MS927		Four sheets each 145×107 mm. (a) 30c. As Nos. 919/20 each ×2. (b) 50c. As Nos. 921/2 each ×2. (c) $1.50 As Nos. 923/4 each ×2. (d) $4.50 As Nos. 925/6 each ×2. Set of 4 sheets	16·00	15·00

150 Silos and Conveyor Belt

1985. St. Vincent Flour Milling Industry. Multicoloured.

928	20c. Type **150**	10	15
929	30c. Roller mills	10	20
930	75c. Administration building	20	35
931	$3 Bran finishers	50	1·40

1985. Royal Visit. Nos. 672/3, 697/8, 711, 724 and 912/13 optd **CARIBBEAN ROYAL VISIT 1985** or surch also.

932	-	60c. multicoloured (711)	1·50	2·00
933	-	60c. multicoloured (724)	1·75	2·25
934	-	85c. multicoloured (912)	4·50	6·50
935	-	85c. multicoloured (913)	4·50	6·50
936	125	$1.50 multicoloured	1·60	3·25
937	-	$1.60 on $4 mult (672)	70	2·25
938	-	$1.60 on $4 mult (673)	11·00	17·00
939	-	$2.50 multicoloured (698)	1·75	4·00

No. 938 shows a new face value only.

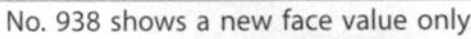

151 Michael Jackson

1985. Leaders of the World. Michael Jackson (entertainer). Various portraits. Multicoloured.

940	151	60c. multicoloured	15	30
941	-	60c. multicoloured	15	30
942	-	$1 multicoloured	15	45
943	-	$1 multicoloured	15	45
944	-	$2 multicoloured	20	60
945	-	$2 multicoloured	20	60
946	-	$5 multicoloured	30	1·00
947	-	$5 multicoloured	1·10	4·25
MS948		Four sheets, each 144×109 mm. (a) 45c. As Nos. 940/1 each ×2. (b) 90c. As Nos. 942/3 each ×2. (c) $1.50 As Nos. 944/5 each ×2. (d) $4 As Nos. 946/7 each ×2. Set of 4 sheets	3·25	7·50

Each value issued in pairs, the left-hand design showing the face value at top left (as on Type **151**) and the right-hand design at top right.

152 "The Serenaders" (Kim de Freitas)

1985. Christmas. Children's Paintings. Multicoloured.

949	25c. Type **152**	10	15
950	75c. "Poinsettia" (Jackie Douglas)	20	40
951	$2.50 "Jesus our Master" (Bernadette Payne)	55	2·00

153 "Santa Maria"

1986. 500th Anniv (1992) of Discovery of America by Columbus (1st issue). Multicoloured.

952	60c. Type **153**	40	65
953	60c. Christopher Columbus	40	65
954	$1.50 Columbus at Spanish Court	65	1·25
955	$1.50 King Ferdinand and Queen Isabella of Spain	65	1·25
956	$2.75 "Santa Maria" and fruits	90	2·00
957	$2.75 Maize and fruits	90	2·00
MS958	95×85 mm. $6 Christopher Columbus (different)	2·25	5·50

See also Nos. 1125/31, 1305/24, 1639/57, 1677/85, 1895/1901 and 1981/2.

1986. Leaders of the World. Automobiles (5th series). As **T 133**, the first in each pair shows technical drawings and the second paintings.

959	30c. black, blue and orange	10	15
960	30c. multicoloured	10	15
961	45c. black, grey and blue	10	15
962	45c. multicoloured	10	15
963	60c. black, blue and red	15	20
964	60c. multicoloured	15	20
965	90c. black, yellow and blue	15	25
966	90c. multicoloured	15	25
967	$1.50 black, lilac and mauve	20	40
968	$1.50 multicoloured	20	40
969	$2.50 black, blue and light blue	20	50
970	$2.50 multicoloured	20	50

DESIGNS: Nos. 959/60, Cadillac "Type 53" (1916); 961/2, Triumph "Dolomite" (1939); 963/4, Panther "J-72" (1972); 965/6, Ferrari "275 GTB/4" (1967); 967/8, Packard "Caribbean" (1953); 969/70, Bugatti "Type 41 Royale" (1931).

154 Guide Salute and Handclasp

1986. 75th Annivs of Girl Guide Movement and Boy Scouts of America. Two sheets, each 85×113 mm, containing vert designs as **T 154**. Multicoloured.

MS971	$5 Type **154**; $5 Palette and paintbrushes	2·00	5·00
MS972	$6 Cross-tied logs; $6 Lord Baden-Powell	2·00	6·00

The two stamps in each sheet were printed together, *se-tenant*, in horizontal pairs, each forming a composite design.

Nos. **MS**971/2 exist with plain or decorative margins.

Overprints on these miniature sheets commemorating "Capex '87" International Stamp Exhibition, Toronto, were not authorised by the St. Vincent administration.

155 Halley's Comet

1986. Appearance of Halley's Comet. Multicoloured.

973	45c. Type **155**	40	30
974	60c. Edmond Halley	40	30
975	75c. Newton's telescope and astronomers	50	55
976	$3 Amateur astronomer on St. Vincent	70	2·75
MS977	155×104 mm. Nos. 973/6	2·00	4·50

1986. 60th Birthday of Queen Elizabeth II (1st issue). As **T 162a** of St. Lucia. Multicoloured.

978	10c. Queen Elizabeth II	10	10
979	90c. Princess Elizabeth	20	30
980	$2.50 Queen gathering bouquets from crowd	35	80
981	$8 In Canberra, 1982 (vert)	1·00	2·25
MS982	85×115 mm. $10 Queen Elizabeth II (different)	3·00	6·00

See also Nos. 996/1000.

156 Mexican Player

1986. World Cup Football Championship, Mexico. Multicoloured.

983	1c. Football and world map (horiz)	10	10
984	2c. Type **156**	10	10
985	5c. Mexican player (different)	10	10
986	5c. Hungary v Scotland	10	10
987	10c. Spain v Scotland	10	10
988	30c. England v U.S.S.R. (horiz)	20	10
989	45c. Spain v France	30	10
990	75c. Mexican team (56×36 mm)	35	45
991	$1 England v Italy	35	65
992	$2 Scottish team (56×36 mm)	50	1·50
993	$4 Spanish team (56×36 mm)	75	2·75
994	$5 English team (56×36 mm)	75	3·00
MS995	Six sheets, each 84×114 mm. (a) $1.50 As Type **156**. (b) $1.50 As No. 993.(c) $2.25 As No. 992. (d) $2.50 As No. 990. (e) $3 As No. 989. (f) $5.50 As No. 994. Set of 6 sheets	6·00	11·00

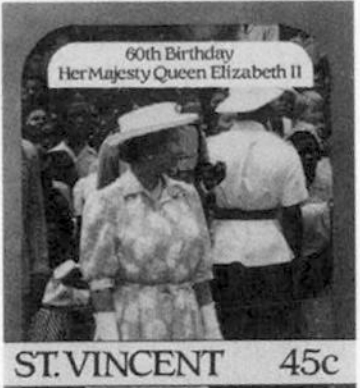

157 Queen Elizabeth at Victoria Park, Kingstown

1986. 60th Birthday of Queen Elizabeth II (2nd issue). Scenes from 1985 Royal Visit. Multicoloured.

996	45c. Type **157**	50	30
997	60c. Queen and Prime Minister James Mitchell, Bequia	65	55
998	75c. Queen, Prince Philip and Mr. Mitchell, Port Elizabeth, Bequia	75	65
999	$2.50 Queen, Prince Philip and Mr. Mitchell watching Independence Day parade, Victoria Park	1·50	2·50
MS1000	121×85 mm. $3 Queen at Victoria Park	3·50	4·50

1986. Leaders of the World. Railway Locomotives (6th series). As **T 135**. Multicoloured.

1001	30c. multicoloured	10	10
1002	30c. multicoloured	10	10
1003	50c. multicoloured	15	20
1004	50c. multicoloured	15	20
1005	$1 multicoloured	20	30
1006	$1 multicoloured	20	30
1007	$3 multicoloured	35	70
1008	$3 multicoloured	35	70

DESIGNS: Nos. 1001/2, Class ED41 BZZB electric rack and adhesion locomotive, Japan (1926); 1003/4, "The Judge", Chicago Railroad Exposition, U.S.A. (1883); 1005/6, Class E60C electric locomotive, U.S.A. (1973); 1007/8, Class SD40-2 diesel locomotive, U.S.A. (1972).

1986. Royal Wedding (1st issue). As **T 164a** of St. Lucia. Multicoloured.

1009	60c. Profile of Prince Andrew	20	25
1010	60c. Miss Sarah Ferguson	20	25
1011	$2 Prince Andrew with Mrs. Nancy Reagan (horiz)	45	75
1012	$2 Prince Andrew in naval uniform (horiz)	45	75
MS1013	115×85 mm. $10 Duke and Duchess of York in carriage after wedding (horiz)	2·50	4·50

See also Nos. 1022/5.

158 "Acrocomia aculeata"

1986. Timber Resources of St. Vincent. Multicoloured.

1014	10c. Type **158**	40	20
1015	60c. "Pithecellobium saman"	1·25	80
1016	75c. White cedar	1·60	95
1017	$3 "Andira inermis"	3·50	4·50

159 Cadet Force Emblem and Cadets of 1936 and 1986

1986. 50th Anniv of St. Vincent Cadet Force (45c., $2) and 75th Anniv of St. Vincent Girls' High School (others). Multicoloured.

1018	45c. Type **159**	40	30
1019	60c. Grimble Building, Girls' High School (horiz)	45	40
1020	$1.50 High School pupils (horiz)	1·00	1·75
1021	$2 Cadets on parade (horiz)	1·50	2·25

1986. Royal Wedding (2nd issue). Nos. 1009/12 optd **Congratulations to T.R.H. The Duke & Duchess of York.**

1022	60c. Profile of Prince Andrew	90	1·25
1023	60c. Miss Sarah Ferguson	90	1·25
1024	$2 Prince Andrew with Mrs. Nancy Reagan (horiz)	1·25	2·50
1025	$2 Prince Andrew in naval uniform (horiz)	1·25	2·50

160 King Arthur

1986. The Legend of King Arthur. Multicoloured.

1026	30c. Type **160**	30	30
1027	45c. Merlin taking baby Arthur	40	30
1028	60c. Arthur pulling sword from stone	50	50
1029	75c. Camelot	55	65
1030	$1 Arthur receiving Excalibur from the Lady of the Lake	60	70
1031	$1.50 Knights at the Round Table	80	1·50
1032	$2 The Holy Grail	90	1·75
1033	$5 Sir Lancelot jousting	1·25	2·50

161 Statue of Liberty Floodlit

1986. Centenary of Statue of Liberty. Designs showing aspects of the Statue.

1034	161	15c. multicoloured	10	10
1035	-	25c. multicoloured	10	15
1036	-	40c. multicoloured	15	25
1037	-	55c. multicoloured	20	30
1038	-	75c. multicoloured	25	45
1039	-	90c. multicoloured	25	60
1040	-	$1.75 multicoloured	35	1·10
1041	-	$2 multicoloured	35	1·25
1042	-	$2.50 multicoloured	40	1·60
1043	-	$3 multicoloured	40	1·75
MS1044		Three sheets, each 85×115 mm. $3.50; $4; $5. Set of 3 sheets	2·25	6·00

162 Fishing for Tri Tri

1986. Freshwater Fishing. Multicoloured.

1045	75c. Type **162**	25	40
1046	75c. Plumier's goby ("Tri Tri")	25	40
1047	$1.50 Crayfishing	35	80
1048	$1.50 Crayfish	35	80

163 Baby on Scales

1987. Child Health Campaign. Multicoloured.

1049	10c. Type **163**	10	10
1050	50c. Oral rehydration therapy	45	55
1051	75c. Breast feeding	55	90
1052	$1 Nurse giving injection	60	1·25

1987. World Population Control. Nos. 1049/52 optd **WORLD POPULATION 5 BILLION 11TH JULY 1987.**

1053	10c. Type **163**	10	10
1054	50c. Oral rehydration therapy	40	55
1055	75c. Breast feeding	50	90
1056	$1 Nurse giving injection	55	1·25

165 Hanna Mandlikova

1987. International Lawn Tennis Players. Multicoloured.

1057	40c. Type **165**	20	25
1058	60c. Yannick Noah	20	35
1059	80c. Ivan Lendl	20	50
1060	$1 Chris Evert	20	50
1061	$1.25 Steffi Graf	20	60
1062	$1.50 John McEnroe	20	65
1063	$1.75 Martina Navratilova with Wimbledon trophy	20	75
1064	$2 Boris Becker with Wimbledon trophy	30	85
MS1065	115×85 mm. $2.25 As No. 1063; $2.25 As No. 1064	1·40	4·00

166 Miss Prima Donna, Queen of the Bands, 1986

1987. Tenth Anniv of Carnival. Multicoloured.

1066	20c. Type **166**	10	15
1067	45c. Donna Young, Miss Carnival, 1985	15	15
1068	55c. Miss St. Vincent and the Grenadines, 1986	15	15
1069	$3.70 "Spirit of Hope" costume, 1986	50	1·60

The 45c. value is inscribed "Miss Carival" in error.

1987. Tenth Death Anniv of Elvis Presley (entertainer). Nos. 919/26 optd **THE KING OF ROCK AND ROLL LIVES FOREVER AUGUST 16TH 1977–1987.**

1070	**149**	10c. multicoloured	10	20
1071	-	10c. multicoloured (blue)	10	20
1072	-	60c. mult (brown)	15	35
1073	-	60c. multicoloured (grey)	15	35
1074	-	$1 multicoloured (brown)	15	60
1075	-	$1 multicoloured (blue)	15	60
1076	-	$5 mult (light blue)	40	1·75
1077	-	$5 multicoloured (blue)	40	1·75
MS1078		Four sheets, each 145×107 mm. (a) 30c. As Nos. 1070/1 each ×2. (b) 50c. As Nos. 1072/3 each ×2. (c) $1.50, As Nos. 1074/5 each ×2. (d) $4.50, As Nos. 1076/7 each ×2	6·00	10·00

168 Queen Victoria, 1841

1987. Royal Ruby Wedding and 150th Anniv of Queen Victoria's Accession. Multicoloured.

1079	15c. Type **168**	10	10
1080	75c. Queen Elizabeth and Prince Andrew, 1960	20	35
1081	$1 Coronation, 1953	20	40
1082	$2.50 Duke of Edinburgh, 1948	50	1·50
1083	$5 Queen Elizabeth II, c. 1980	1·50	2·25
MS1084	85×115 mm. $6 Princess Elizabeth with Prince Charles at his Christening, 1948	1·75	4·50

169 Karl Benz and Benz Three-wheeler (1886)

1987. Century of Motoring. Multicoloured.

1085	$1 Type **169**	40	60
1086	$2 Enzo Ferrari and Ferrari "Dino 206SP" (1966)	50	1·10
1087	$4 Charles Rolls and Sir Henry Royce and Rolls-Royce "Silver Ghost" (1907)	65	1·50
1088	$5 Henry Ford and Ford "Model T" (1908)	65	1·75
MS1089	Four sheets, each 144×75 mm. (a) $3 As Type **169**. (b) $5 As No. 1086. (c) $6 As No. 1087. (d) $8 As No. 1088. Set of 4 sheets	7·50	15·00

170 Everton Football Team

1987. English Football Teams. Multicoloured.

1090	$2 Type **170**	1·00	1·25
1091	$2 Manchester United	1·00	1·25
1092	$2 Tottenham Hotspur	1·00	1·25
1093	$2 Arsenal	1·00	1·25
1094	$2 Liverpool	1·00	1·25
1095	$2 Derby County	1·00	1·25
1096	$2 Portsmouth	1·00	1·25
1097	$2 Leeds United	1·00	1·25

171 Five Cent Coins

1987. East Caribbean Currency. Multicoloured.

1098	5c. Type **171**	20	10
1099	6c. Two cent coins	20	10
1100	10c. Ten cent coins	20	10
1101	12c. Two and ten cent coins	30	10
1102	15c. Five cent coins	30	10
1103	20c. Ten cent coins	35	10
1104	25c. Twenty-five cent coins	40	15
1105	30c. Five and twenty-five cent coins	40	15
1106	35c. Twenty-five and ten cent coins	40	20
1107	45c. Twenty-five and two ten cent coins	50	30
1108	50c. Fifty cent coins	50	30
1109	65c. Fifty, ten and five cent coins	60	45
1110	75c. Fifty and twenty-five cent coins	60	50
1111	$1 One dollar note (horiz)	75	65
1112	$2 Two one dollar notes (horiz)	1·25	1·75
1113	$3 Three one dollar notes (horiz)	1·25	2·50
1114	$5 Five dollar note (horiz)	2·25	5·00
1115	$10 Ten dollar note (horiz)	2·75	8·00
1115s	$20 Twenty dollar note (horiz)	13·00	19·00

172 Charles Dickens

1987. Christmas. 175th Birth Anniv of Charles Dickens. Multicoloured.

1116	6c. Type **172**	40	70
1117	6c. "Mr. Fezziwig's Ball"	40	70
1118	25c. Type **172**	45	70
1119	25c. "Scrooge's Third Visitor"	45	70
1120	50c. Type **172**	50	90
1121	50c. "The Cratchits' Christmas"	50	90
1122	75c. Type **172**	50	1·25
1123	75c. "A Christmas Carol"	50	1·25
MS1124	141×101 mm. $5 Teacher reading to class	1·75	4·50

Nos. 1116/17, 1118/19, 1120/1 and 1122/3 were printed together, *se-tenant*, each pair forming a composite design showing an open book. The first design in each pair shows Type **172** and the second a scene from "A Christmas Carol".

173 "Santa Maria"

1988. 500th Anniv (1992) of Discovery of America by Columbus (2nd issue). Multicoloured.

1125	15c. Type **173**	25	20
1126	75c. "Nina" and "Pinta"	30	60
1127	$1 Compass and hourglass	30	60
1128	$1.50 Claiming the New World for Spain	35	1·40
1129	$3 Arawak village	40	1·75
1130	$4 Blue and yellow macaw, Cuban tody, pineapple and maize	70	2·00
MS1131	114×86 mm. $5 Columbus, Arms and "Santa Maria"	1·75	3·00

174 Brown Pelican

1988

1132	**174**	45c. multicoloured	30	30

175 Windsurfing

1988. Tourism. Multicoloured.

1133	10c. Type **175**	10	10
1134	45c. Scuba diving	20	25
1135	65c. Aerial view of Young Island (horiz)	30	60
1136	$5 Cruising yacht (horiz)	2·10	3·50
MS1136a	115×85 mm. $10 Two windsurfers off St. Vincent (60×40 mm)	2·75	6·00

176 "Nuestra Senora del Rosario" (Spanish galleon) and Spanish Knight's Cross

1988. 400th Anniv of Spanish Armada. Multicoloured.

1137	15c. Type **176**	25	10
1138	75c. "Ark Royal" (galleon) and English Armada medal	45	40
1139	$1.50 English fleet and Drake's dial	60	85
1140	$2 Dismasted Spanish galleon and 16th-century shot	65	1·00
1141	$3.50 Attack of English fireships at Calais and 16th-century grenade	80	2·00
1142	$5 "Revenge" (English galleon) and Drake's Drum	90	2·25
MS1143	123×92 mm. $8 Sighting the Armada	2·25	4·50

177 D. K. Lillee

1988. Cricketers of 1988 International Season. Multicoloured.

1144	15c. Type **177**	50	30
1145	50c. G. A. Gooch	70	50
1146	75c. R. N. Kapil Dev	90	70
1147	$1 S. M. Gavaskar	1·00	85
1148	$1.50 M. W. Gatting	1·25	1·50
1149	$2.50 Imran Khan	1·25	2·00
1150	$3 I. T. Botham	1·25	2·25
1151	$4 I. V. A. Richards	1·25	2·50
MS1152	130×80 mm. $2 As $4. $3.50, As $3	2·25	5·50

178 Athletics

1988. Olympic Games, Seoul. Multicoloured.

1153	10c. Type **178**	10	10
1154	50c. Long jumping (vert)	20	25
1155	$1 Triple jumping	40	50
1156	$5 Boxing (vert)	2·10	2·75
MS1157	85×63 mm. $10 Olympic flame	4·75	6·50

179 Babe Ruth

1988. Famous Baseball Players (1st series).

1158	**179**	$2 multicoloured	1·10	1·40

See also Nos. 1264/75, 1407, 1408/88, 2152/4, 2155/6, 2426 and 3004/12.

180 Los Angeles Dodgers (National League Champions)

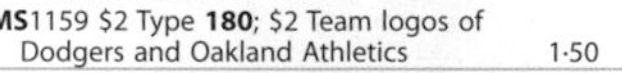

1988. 1988 Baseball World Series. Sheet 115×85 mm containing **T 180** and similar horiz design. Multicoloured.

MS1159	$2 Type **180**; $2 Team logos of Dodgers and Oakland Athletics	1·50	2·25

180a Minnie Mouse in Railway Van Loaded with Candy

1988. Christmas. "Mickey's Christmas Train". Multicoloured.

1160	1c. Type **180a**	10	10
1161	2c. Mordie and Ferdie in wagon with toys	10	10
1162	3c. Chip n' Dale in wagon with Christmas trees	10	10
1163	4c. Donald Duck's nephews riding with reindeer	10	10
1164	5c. Donald and Daisy Duck in restaurant car	10	10
1165	10c. Grandma Duck, Uncle Scrooge McDuck, Goofy and Clarabelle carol singing in carriage	10	10
1166	$5 Mickey Mouse driving locomotive	3·25	3·50
1167	$6 Father Christmas in guard's van	4·00	4·50
MS1168	Two sheets, each 127×102 mm. (a) $5 Mickey Mouse and nephews at railway station. (b) $5 Mickey and Minnie Mouse on carousel. Set of 2 sheets	7·00	8·00

181 Mickey Mouse as Snake Charmer

1989. "India-89" International Stamp Exhibition, New Delhi. Multicoloured.

1169	1c. Type **181**	10	10
1170	2c. Goofy with chowsingha antelope	10	10
1171	3c. Mickey and Minnie Mouse with common peafowl	10	10
1172	5c. Goofy with Briolette Diamond and Mickey Mouse pushing mine truck	10	10
1173	10c. Clarabelle with Orloff Diamond	10	10
1174	25c. Mickey Mouse as tourist and Regent Diamond, Louvre, Paris	20	15

1175	$4 Minnie and Mickey Mouse with Kohinoor Diamond	3·50	4·00
1176	$5 Mickey Mouse and Goofy with Indian rhinoceros	3·50	4·00
MS1177	Two sheets, each 127×102 mm. (a) $6 Mickey Mouse riding Indian elephant. (b) $6 Mickey Mouse as postman delivering Hope Diamond to Smithsonian Museum, U.S.A. (vert). Set of 2 sheets	8·50	10·00

182 Harry James

1989. Jazz Musicians. Multicoloured.

1178	10c. Type **182**	40	20
1179	15c. Sidney Bechet	50	20
1180	25c. Benny Goodman	60	20
1181	35c. Django Reinhardt	65	20
1182	50c. Lester Young	80	35
1183	90c. Gene Krupa	95	85
1184	$3 Louis Armstrong	3·00	3·00
1185	$4 Duke Ellington	3·00	3·25
MS1186	Two sheets, each 107×92 mm. (a) $5 Charlie Parker. (b) $5 Billie Holiday. Set of 2 sheets	9·00	8·00

183 Birds in Flight

1989. Wildlife Conservation. Noah's Ark. Multicoloured.

1187	40c. Type **183**	30	30
1188	40c. Rainbow (left side)	30	30
1189	40c. Noah's Ark on mountain	30	30
1190	40c. Rainbow (right side)	30	30
1191	40c. Birds in flight (different)	30	30
1192	40c. Cow elephant	30	30
1193	40c. Bull elephant	30	30
1194	40c. Top of eucalyptus tree	30	30
1195	40c. Kangaroos	30	30
1196	40c. Hummingbird	30	30
1197	40c. Lions	30	30
1198	40c. White-tailed deer	30	30
1199	40c. Koala in fork of tree	30	30
1200	40c. Koala on branch	30	30
1201	40c. Hummingbird approaching flower	30	30
1202	40c. Keel-billed toucan and flower	30	30
1203	40c. Keel-billed toucan facing right	30	30
1204	40c. Camels	30	30
1205	40c. Giraffes	30	30
1206	40c. Mountain sheep	30	30
1207	40c. Ladybirds on leaf	30	30
1208	40c. Swallowtail butterfly	30	30
1209	40c. Swallowtail butterfly behind leaves	30	30
1210	40c. Pythons	30	30
1211	40c. Dragonflies	30	30

Nos. 1187/1211 were printed together, se-tenant, forming a composite design showing Noah's Ark and animals released after the Flood.

183a "Baptism of Christ" (detail)

1989. Easter. 500th Birth Anniv of Titian (artist). Multicoloured.

1212	5c. Type **183a**	10	20
1213	30c. "Temptation of Christ"	25	15
1214	45c. "Ecce Homo"	40	25
1215	65c. "Noli Me Tangere" (fragment)	55	55
1216	75c. "Christ carrying the Cross" (detail)	60	65
1217	$1 "Christ crowned with Thorns" (detail)	70	75
1218	$4 "Lamentation over Christ" (detail)	2·50	3·50
1219	$5 "The Entombment" (detail)	2·75	4·00
MS1220	(a) 98×111 mm. $6 "Pietà" (detail). (b) 114×95 mm. $6 "The Deposition" (detail). Set of 2 sheets	7·00	8·00

184 "Ile de France"

1989. Ocean Liners. Multicoloured.

1221	10c. Type **184**	1·00	40
1222	40c. "Liberte"	1·75	30
1223	50c. "Mauretania I" (launched 1906)	1·75	50
1224	75c. "France"	2·25	1·25
1225	$1 "Aquitania"	2·25	1·25
1226	$2 "United States"	3·00	3·00
1227	$3 "Olympic"	3·50	3·75
1228	$4 "Queen Elizabeth"	3·50	4·00
MS1229	Two sheets, each 141×108 mm. (a) $6 "Queen Mary" (85×28 mm). (b) $6 "Queen Elizabeth 2" (85×28 mm). Set of 2 sheets	17·00	13·00

185 Space Shuttle deploying West German Satellite, 1983

1989. International Co-operation in Space. Multicoloured.

1230	40c. Type **185**	1·00	20
1231	60c. Vladimir Remek (Czech cosmonaut) and "Soyuz 28", 1978	1·25	50
1232	$1 Projected "Hermes" space plane and "Columbus" Space Station	1·75	1·00
1233	$4 Ulf Merbold (West German astronaut), 1983 and proposed European Spacelab	3·75	4·75
MS1234	93×67 mm. $5 Meeting in space of "Apollo/Soyuz" mission crews, 1975	3·00	4·00

186 "Mercury 9" Capsule and Astronaut L. Gordon Cooper

1989. 25th Anniv of Launching of "Telstar II" Communications Satellite (1988). Each showing satellite and T.V. screen. Multicoloured.

1235	15c. Type **186**	20	15
1236	35c. Martin Luther King addressing crowd, 1963	30	20
1237	50c. Speed skater, Winter Olympic Games, Innsbruck, 1964	45	50
1238	$3 Pope John XXIII blessing crowd	1·75	2·75
MS1239	107×77 mm. $5 Launch of "Telstar II", 1963	2·75	3·50

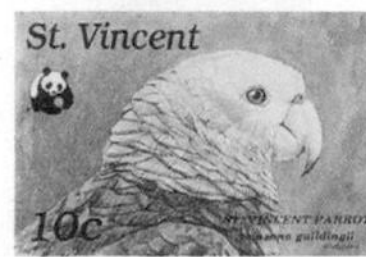

187 Head of St. Vincent Amazon

1989. Wildlife Conservation. St. Vincent Amazon ("St. Vincent Parrot"). Multicoloured.

1240	10c. Type **187**	70	30
1241	20c. St. Vincent amazon in flight	1·25	45
1242	40c. Feeding (vert)	2·00	65
1243	70c. At entrance to nest (vert)	2·75	3·25

188 Blue-hooded Euphonia ("Misletoe Bird")

1989. Birds of St. Vincent. Multicoloured.

1244	25c. Type **188**	60	25
1245	75c. Common black hawk ("Crab Hawk")	1·25	65
1246	$2 Mangrove cuckoo ("Coucou")	2·00	2·00
1247	$3 Hooded tanager ("Prince Bird")	2·25	3·00
MS1248	Two sheets. (a) 75×105 mm. $5 Rufous-throated solitaire ("Soufriere Bird") (vert). (b) 105×75 mm. $5 Purple-throated carib ("Doctor Bird"). Set of 2 sheets	5·50	7·00

188a "Autumn Flowers in Front of the Full Moon" (Hiroshige)

1989. Japanese Arts. Multicoloured.

1249	10c. Type **188a**	30	20
1250	40c. "Hibiscus" (Hiroshige)	45	25
1251	50c. "Iris" (Hiroshige)	50	30
1252	75c. "Morning Glories" (Hiroshige)	70	50
1253	$1 "Dancing Swallows" (Hiroshige)	2·50	85
1254	$2 "Sparrow and Bamboo" (Hiroshige)	3·00	2·25
1255	$3 "Yellow Bird and Cotton Rose" (Hiroshige)	3·00	2·75
1256	$4 "Judos Chrysanthemums in a Deep Ravine in China" (Hiroshige)	3·00	3·00
MS1257	Two sheets, each 102×76 mm. (a) $6 "Rural Cottages in Spring" (Sotatsu). (b) $6 "The Six Immortal Poets portrayed as Cats" (Kuniyoshi) (vert). Set of 2 sheets	7·00	9·00

189 Schooner

1989. "Philexfrance 89" International Stamp Exhibition, Paris and Bicentenary of French Revolution. 18th-century French Naval Vessels. Multicoloured.

1258	30c. Type **189**	90	30
1259	55c. Corvette	1·25	50
1260	75c. Frigate	1·60	1·10
1261	$1 Ship of the line	1·75	1·40
1262	$3 "Ville de Paris" (ship of the line)	4·50	6·00
MS1263	76×108 mm. $6 Map of St. Vincent in 18th century (vert)	3·50	4·50

190 Johnny Bench

1989. Famous Baseball Players (2nd series). Multicoloured.

1264	$2 Type **190**	70	90
1265	$2 Red Schoendienst	70	90
1266	$2 Carl Yastrzemski	70	90
1267	$2 Ty Cobb	70	90
1268	$2 Willie Mays	70	90
1269	$2 Stan Musial	70	90
1270	$2 Ernie Banks	70	90
1271	$2 Lou Gehrig	70	90
1272	$2 Jackie Robinson	70	90
1273	$2 Bob Feller	70	90
1274	$2 Ted Williams	70	90
1275	$2 Al Kaline	70	90

191 Dante Bichette, 1989

1989. Major League Baseball Rookies. Multicoloured.

1276	60c. Type **191**	30	45
1277	60c. Carl Yastrzemski, 1961	30	45
1278	60c. Randy Johnson, 1989	30	45
1279	60c. Jerome Walton, 1989	30	45
1280	60c. Ramon Martinez, 1989	30	45
1281	60c. Ken Hill, 1989	30	45
1282	60c. Tom McCarthy, 1989	30	45
1283	60c. Gaylord Perry, 1963	30	45
1284	60c. John Smoltz, 1989	30	45
1285	60c. Bob Milacki, 1989	30	45
1286	60c. Babe Ruth, 1915	30	45
1287	60c. Jim Abbott, 1989	30	45
1288	60c. Gary Sheffield, 1989	30	45
1289	60c. Gregg Jeffries, 1989	30	45
1290	60c. Kevin Brown, 1989	30	45
1291	60c. Cris Carpenter, 1989	30	45
1292	60c. Johnny Bench, 1968	30	45
1293	60c. Ken Griffey Jr. 1989	30	45

192 Chris Sabo

1989. Major League Baseball Award Winners. Multicoloured.

1294	60c. Type **192**	30	45
1295	60c. Walt Weiss	30	45
1296	60c. Willie Mays	30	45
1297	60c. Kirk Gibson	30	45
1298	60c. Ted Williams	30	45
1299	60c. Jose Canseco	30	45
1300	60c. Gaylord Perry	30	45
1301	60c. Orel Hershiser	30	45
1302	60c. Frank Viola	30	45

193 All-Star Game Line-up (image scaled to 37% of original size)

1989. American League v National League All-Star Game, 1989. Sheet 115×81 mm. Imperf.

MS1303	**193** $5 multicoloured	1·50	2·25

194 St. Vincent Amazon

1989

1304	**194**	55c. multicoloured	1·00	35

195 Queen or Pink Conch and Wide-mouthed Purpura Shells

1989. 500th Anniv (1992) of Discovery of America by Columbus (3rd issue).

1305	**195**	50c. multicoloured	45	50
1306	-	50c. multicoloured	45	50
1307	-	50c. ultramarine, blk & bl	45	50
1308	-	50c. ultramarine, blk & bl	45	50
1309	-	50c. multicoloured	45	50
1310	-	50c. multicoloured	45	50
1311	-	50c. multicoloured	45	50
1312	-	50c. black and blue	45	50
1313	-	50c. multicoloured	45	50
1314	-	50c. multicoloured	45	50
1315	-	50c. multicoloured	45	50
1316	-	50c. multicoloured	45	50
1317	-	50c. multicoloured	45	50
1318	-	50c. multicoloured	45	50
1319	-	50c. multicoloured	45	50
1320	-	50c. multicoloured	45	50
1321	-	50c. multicoloured	45	50
1322	-	50c. multicoloured	45	50
1323	-	50c. multicoloured	45	50
1324	-	50c. multicoloured	45	50

DESIGNS: No. 1306, Caribbean reef fishes; 1307, Sperm whale; 1308, Fleet of Columbus; 1309, Sharksucker (fish); 1310, Columbus planting flag; 1311, Navigational instruments; 1312, Sea monster; 1313, Kemp's ridley turtle; 1314, Magnificent frigate bird; 1315, Caribbean manatee; 1316, Caribbean monk seal; 1317, Mayan chief, dugout canoe and caravel; 1318, Blue-footed boobies ("Masked Boobies"); 1319, Venezuelan pile village; 1320, Atlantic wing oyster and lion's-paw scallop; 1321, Great hammerhead and short-finned mako; 1322, Brown pelican and hyacinth macaw ("Hyacinthine Macaw"); 1323, Venezuelan bowmen; 1324, Capuchin and squirrel monkeys.

Nos. 1305/24 were printed together, se-tenant, forming a composite design of a map of the Caribbean showing the voyages of Columbus.

196 Command Module "Columbia" returning to Earth

1989. 20th Anniv of First Manned Landing on Moon. Multicoloured.

1325	35c. Type **196**	90	30
1326	75c. Lunar module "Eagle" landing	1·75	80
1327	$1 "Apollo 11" launch	1·75	80
1328	$2 Buzz Aldrin on Moon	2·50	2·50
1329	$2 Lunar module "Eagle"	2·50	2·50
1330	$2 Earth rise from the Moon	2·50	2·50
1331	$2 Neil Armstrong	2·50	2·50
1332	$3 "Eagle" and "Columbia" in Moon orbit	2·75	2·75
MS1333	Two sheets, each 108×79 mm. (a) $3 Command Module "Columbia". $3 Lunar Module "Eagle". (b) $6 Neil Armstrong stepping on to Moon (vert). Set of 2 sheets	12·00	13·00

197 Jay Howell and Alejandro Pena

1989. Centenary of the Los Angeles Dodgers (1st issue). Baseball Players. Multicoloured.

1334	60c. Type **197**	25	40
1335	60c. Mike Davis and Kirk Gibson	25	40
1336	60c. Fernando Valenzuela and John Shelby	25	40
1337	60c. Jeff Hamilton and Franklin Stubbs	25	40
1338	60c. Aerial view of Dodger Stadium (no inscription)	25	40
1339	60c. Ray Searage and John Tudor	25	40
1340	60c. Mike Sharperson and Mickey Hatcher	25	40
1341	60c. Coaching staff	25	40
1342	60c. John Wetteland and Ramon Martinez	25	40
1343	60c. Tim Belcher and Tim Crews	25	40
1344	60c. Orel Hershiser and Mike Morgan	25	40
1345	60c. Mike Scioscia and Rick Dempsey	25	40
1346	60c. Dave Anderson and Alfredo Griffin	25	40
1347	60c. Dodgers' emblem	25	40
1348	60c. Kal Daniels and Mike Marshall	25	40
1349	60c. Eddie Murray and Willie Randolph	25	40
1350	60c. Tom Lasorda and Jose Gonzalez	25	40
1351	60c. Lenny Harris, Chris Gwynn and Billy Bean	25	40

See also Nos. 1541/58.

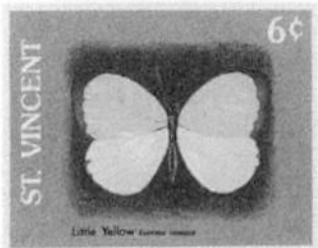

198 "Eurema venusta"

1989. Butterflies. Multicoloured.

1352	6c. Type **198**	25	15
1353	10c. "Historis odius"	30	15
1354	15c. "Cynthia virginiensis"	40	15
1355	75c. "Leptotes cassius"	80	65
1356	$1 "Battus polydamas"	90	75
1357	$2 "Astraptes talus"	2·00	2·25
1358	$3 "Danaus gilippus"	2·50	2·75
1359	$5 "Myscelia antholia"	3·50	4·00
MS1360	Two sheets, each 76×103 mm. (a) $6 "Danaus plexippus" (vert). (b) $6 "Eurema daira" (vert). Set of 2 sheets	8·00	9·00

199 Young Footballers

1989. World Cup Football Championship, Italy (1990) (1st issue). Multicoloured.

1361	10c. Type **199**	35	20
1362	55c. Youth football teams	70	30
1363	$1 St. Vincent team in training	1·00	90
1364	$5 National team with trophies	2·50	4·50
MS1365	Two sheets, each 103×73 mm. (a) $6 Youth team. (b) $6 National team. Set of 2 sheets	9·00	11·00

See also Nos. 1559/63.

200 St. Vincent Amazon ("St. Vincent Parrott")

1989. Wildlife. Multicoloured.

1366	65c. Type **200**	75	65
1367	75c. Whistling warbler	90	75
1368	$5 Black snake	4·00	5·50
MS1369	97×70 mm. $6 Volcano plant (vert)	4·50	6·50

1989. California Earthquake Relief Fund. Nos. 1276/302 surch **+10c CALIF. EARTHQUAKE RELIEF**.

1370	60c.+10c. Type **191**	60	70
1371	60c.+10c. Carl Yastrzemski	60	70
1372	60c.+10c. Randy Johnson	60	70
1373	60c.+10c. Jerome Walton	60	70
1374	60c.+10c. Ramon Martinez	60	70
1375	60c.+10c. Ken Hill	60	70
1376	60c.+10c. Tom McCarthy	60	70
1377	60c.+10c. Gaylord Perry	60	70
1378	60c.+10c. John Smoltz	60	70
1379	60c.+10c. Bob Milacki	60	70
1380	60c.+10c. Babe Ruth	60	70
1381	60c.+10c. Jim Abbott	60	70
1382	60c.+10c. Gary Sheffield	60	70
1383	60c.+10c. Gregg Jeffries	60	70
1384	60c.+10c. Kevin Brown	60	70
1385	60c.+10c. Cris Carpenter	60	70
1386	60c.+10c. Johnny Bench	60	70
1387	60c.+10c. Ken Griffey Jr	60	70
1388	60c.+10c. Type **192**	60	70
1389	60c.+10c. Walt Weiss	60	70
1390	60c.+10c. Willie Mays	60	70
1391	60c.+10c. Kirk Gibson	60	70
1392	60c.+10c. Ted Williams	60	70
1393	60c.+10c. Jose Canseco	60	70
1394	60c.+10c. Gaylord Perry	60	70
1395	60c.+10c. Orel Hershiser	60	70
1396	60c.+10c. Frank Viola	60	70

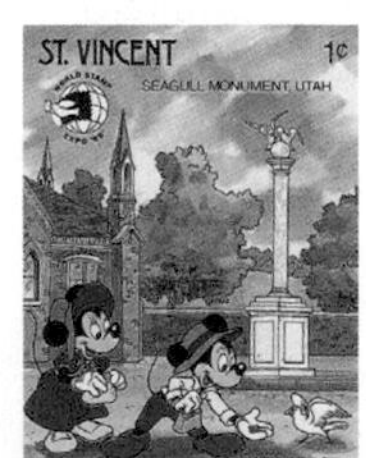

201a Mickey Mouse and Minnie Mouse by Seagull Monument, Utah

1989. "World Stamp Expo '89" International Stamp Exhibition, Washington (1st issue). Walt Disney cartoon characters and U.S. monuments. Multicoloured.

1397	1c. Type **201a**	10	10
1398	2c. Mickey Mouse and Goofy at Lincoln Memorial	10	10
1399	3c. Mickey and Minnie Mouse at Crazy Horse Memorial, South Dakota	10	10
1400	4c. Mickey Mouse saluting "Uncle Sam" Wilson statue, New York	10	10
1401	5c. Goofy and Mickey Mouse at Benjamin Franklin Memorial, Philadelphia	10	10
1402	10c. Goofy and Mickey Mouse at George Washington statue, New York	10	10
1403	$3 Mickey Mouse at John F. Kennedy's birthplace, Massachusetts	3·50	4·00
1404	$6 Mickey and Minnie Mouse at Mount Vernon, Virginia	5·50	6·00
MS1405	Two sheets, each 127×100 mm. (a) $5 Mickey and Minnie Mouse over Mount Rushmore, South Dakota. (b) $5 Mickey Mouse and Donald Duck at Stone Mountain, Georgia. Set of 2 sheets	9·00	10·00

201b Washington Monument

1989. "World Stamp Expo '89" International Stamp Exhibition, Washington (2nd issue). Sheet 61×78 mm.

MS1406	**201b** $5 multicoloured	2·10	2·50

202 Nolan Ryan

1989. Famous Baseball Players (3rd series).

1407	**202**	$2 multicoloured	70	1·00

203 Early Wynn

1989. Famous Baseball Players (4th series). As **T 203**.

1408-1488	30c.×81 30c x 81 multicoloured	13·00	18·00

204 Arms and 1979 Independence 50c. Stamp

1989. Tenth Anniv of Independence.

1489	**204**	65c. multicoloured	1·00	70
MS1490		57×77 mm. $10 multicoloured	5·00	6·50

204a Holy Family (detail, "The Adoration of the Magi") (Botticelli)

1989. Christmas. Paintings by Botticelli and Da Vinci. Multicoloured.

1491	10c. Type **204a**	15	10
1492	25c. Crowd (detail, "The Adoration of the Magi") (Botticelli)	25	15
1493	30c. "The Madonna of the Magnificat" (detail) (Botticelli)	25	15
1494	40c. "The Virgin and Child with St. Anne and St. John the Baptist" (detail) (Da Vinci)	30	20
1495	55c. Angel (detail, "The Annunciation") (Da Vinci)	40	30
1496	75c. Virgin Mary (detail, "The Annunciation") (Da Vinci)	50	50
1497	$5 "Madonna of the Carnation" (detail) (Da Vinci)	3·00	4·25
1498	$6 "The Annunciation" (detail) (Botticelli)	3·50	4·75
MS1499	Two sheets, each 70×94 mm. (a) $5 "The Virgin of the Rocks" (detail) (Da Vinci). (b) $5 Holy Family (detail, "The Adoration of the Magi") (Botticelli). Set of 2 sheets	5·50	7·00

205 Boy Scout, 1989

1989. 75th Anniv of Boy Scout and 60th Anniv of Girl Guide Movements in St. Vincent. Multicoloured.

1500	35c. Type **205**	55	50
1501	35c. Guide, ranger and brownie	55	50
1502	55c. Boy scout in original uniform	65	50
1503	55c. Mrs. Jackson (founder of St. Vincent Girl Guides)	65	50
1504	$2 Scouts' 75th Anniv logo	1·60	3·00
1505	$2 Mrs. Russell (Girl Guide leader, 1989)	1·60	3·00
MS1506	Two sheets, each 105×75 mm. (a) $5 Scout in canoe. (b) Scout and Guide with flagpoles (horiz). Set of 2 sheets	9·00	10·00

206 Man and Blind Girl

1990. 25th Anniv (1989) of Lions Club of St. Vincent. Multicoloured.

1507	10c. Type **206**	40	20
1508	65c. Handing out school books (horiz)	70	50
1509	75c. Teacher explaining diabetes (horiz)	80	60
1510	$2 Blood sugar testing machine (horiz)	1·75	2·00
1511	$4 Distributing book on drugs (horiz)	2·75	4·50

206a Scuttling of "Admiral Graf Spee" (German pocket battleship), 1939

1990. 50th Anniv of Second World War. Multicoloured.

1512	5c. Type **206a**	65	50
1513	10c. General de Gaulle and French resistance, 1940	75	30
1514	15c. British tank, North Africa, 1940	80	30
1515	25c. U.S.S. "Reuben James" (destroyer) in periscope sight, 1941	1·00	30
1516	30c. General MacArthur and map of S.W. Pacific, 1942	1·00	35
1517	40c. American parachute drop on Corregidor, 1945	1·00	40
1518	55c. H.M.S. "King George V" (battleship) engaging "Bismarck" (German battleship), 1941	1·40	70
1519	75c. American battleships entering Tokyo Bay, 1945	1·50	80
1520	$5 Hoisting the Soviet flag on the Reichstag, Berlin, 1945	4·00	4·50
1521	$6 American aircraft carriers, Battle of Philippines Sea, 1944	4·50	5·00
MS1522	100×70 mm. $6 Japanese Mitsubishi A6M Zero-Sen fighter, Battle of Java Sea, 1942	4·00	4·50

207 Two Pence Blue

1990. 150th Anniv of the Penny Black.

1523	**207**	$2 black, green and mauve	1·25	1·50
1524	-	$4 black and mauve	2·50	3·25
MS1525		130×99 mm. – $6 black, red and yellow	4·00	4·75

DESIGN: $4, $6 Penny Black.

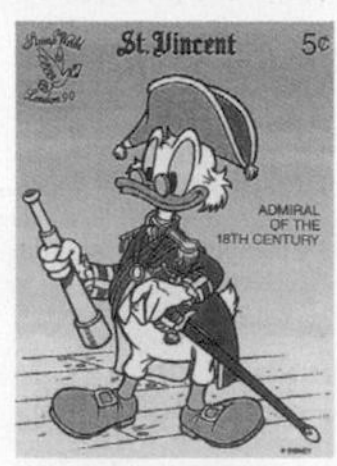

207a Scrooge McDuck as 18th-century Admiral

1990. "Stamp World London '90" International Stamp Exhibition. British Uniforms. Walt Disney cartoon characters. Multicoloured.

1526	5c. Type **207a**	20	15
1527	10c. Huey as Light Infantry bugler, 1854	25	15
1528	15c. Minnie Mouse as Irish Guards drummer, 1900	35	20
1529	25c. Goofy as Seaforth Highlanders lance-corporal, 1944	45	30
1530	$1 Mickey Mouse as 58th Regiment ensign, 1879	1·25	1·00
1531	$2 Donald Duck as Royal Engineers officer, 1813	1·90	2·00
1532	$4 Mickey Mouse as Duke of Edinburgh's Royal Regiment drum major	3·00	3·50
1533	$5 Goofy as Cameronians sergeant piper, 1918	3·00	3·50
MS1534	Two sheets, each 120×100 mm. (a) $6 Goofy as officer in King's Lifeguard of Foot, 1643. (b) $6 Mickey Mouse as Grenadier Guards drummer (vert). Set of 2 sheets	7·00	8·00

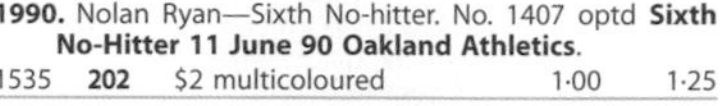

1990. Nolan Ryan—Sixth No-hitter. No. 1407 optd **Sixth No-Hitter 11 June 90 Oakland Athletics**.

1535	**202** $2 multicoloured	1·00	1·25

208a Queen Elizabeth signing Visitor's Book

1990. 90th Birthday of Queen Elizabeth the Queen Mother.

1536	**208a** $2 black, green and mauve	1·50	1·75
1537	- $2 black, green and mauve	1·50	1·75
1538	- $2 black, green and mauve	1·50	1·75
MS1539	- 90×75 mm. $6 multicoloured	3·50	4·50

DESIGNS: No. 1537, **MS**1539, Queen Elizabeth in evening dress; 1538, Queen Elizabeth the Queen Mother in Coronation robes, 1953.

1990. Nolan Ryan—300th Win. No. 1407 optd 300th Win **Milwaukee Brewers July 31, 1990**.

1540	**202** $2 multicoloured	1·00	1·25

1990. Cent of Los Angeles Dodgers (2nd issue). Baseball Players. As **T 197**. Multicoloured.

1541	60c. Mickey Hatcher and Jay Howell	30	45
1542	60c. Juan Samuel and Mike Scioscia	30	45
1543	60c. Lenny Harris and Mike Hartley	30	45
1544	60c. Ramon Martinez and Mike Morgan	30	45
1545	60c. Aerial view of Dodger Stadium (inscr "DODGER STADIUM")	30	45
1546	60c. Stan Javier and Don Aase	30	45
1547	60c. Ray Searage and Mike Sharperson	30	45
1548	60c. Tim Belcher and Pat Perry	30	45
1549	60c. Dave Walsh, Jose Vizcaino, Jim Neidlinger, Jose Offerman and Carlos Hernandez	30	45
1550	60c. Hubie Brooks and Orel Hershiser	30	45
1551	60c. Tom Lasorda and Tim Crews	30	45
1552	60c. Fernando Valenzuela and Eddie Murray	30	45
1553	60c. Kal Daniels and Jose Gonzalez	30	45
1554	60c. Dodgers emblem	30	45
1555	60c. Chris Gwynn and Jeff Hamilton	30	45
1556	60c. Kirk Gibson and Rick Dempsey	30	45
1557	60c. Jim Gott and Alfredo Griffin	30	45
1558	60c. Ron Perranoski, Bill Russell, Joe Ferguson, Joe Amalfitano, Mark Cresse, Ben Hines and Manny Mota	30	45

210 Maradona, Argentina

1990. World Cup Football Championship, Italy (2nd issue). Multicoloured.

1559	10c. Type **210**	40	15
1560	75c. Valderrama, Colombia	85	75
1561	$1 Francescoli, Uruguay	1·10	95
1562	$5 Ceulemans, Belgium	3·75	5·50
MS1563	Two sheets, each 101×85 mm. (a) $6 Klinsmann, West Germany. (b) $6 Careca, Brazil. Set of 2 sheets	6·00	8·50

1990. 95th Anniv of Rotary International. Nos. 1230/8 optd with Rotary emblem.

1564	10c. Type **186**	50	20
1565	40c. "Liberte"	1·00	40
1566	50c. "Mauretania I" (launched 1906)	75	45
1567	75c. "France"	1·00	70
1568	$1 "Aquitania"	1·00	90
1569	$2 "United States"	2·00	1·90
1570	$3 "Olympic"	2·25	1·75
1571	$4 "Queen Elizabeth"	2·25	3·00
MS1572	Two sheets, each 141×108 mm. (a) $6 "Queen Mary" (85×28 mm). (b) $6 "Queen Elizabeth 2" (85×28 mm). Set of 2 sheets	8·00	10·00

1990. Olympic Medal Winners, Seoul. Nos. 1153/6 optd.

1573	10c. Type **178** (optd **JOE DELOACH U.S.A. STEVE LEWIS U.S.A. PAUL ERANG KENYA**)	20	20
1574	50c. Long jumping (optd **CARL LEWIS U.S.A.**)	60	60
1575	$1 Triple jumping (optd **HRISTO MARKOV BULGARIA**)	90	90
1576	$5 Boxing (optd **HENRY MASKE E. GERMANY**)	3·25	4·00
MS1577	85×63 mm. $10 Olympic flame (optd **FINAL MEDAL STANDINGS**)	5·00	7·50

213 "Dendrophylax funalis" and "Dimerandra emarginata"

1990. "EXPO 90" International Garden and Greenery Exposition, Osaka. Orchids. Multicoloured.

1578	10c. Type **213**	35	20
1579	15c. "Epidendrum elongatum"	40	25
1580	45c. "Comparettia falcata"	60	30
1581	60c. "Brassia maculata"	75	60
1582	$1 "Encyclia cochleata" and "Encyclia cordigera"	90	80
1583	$2 "Cyrtopodium punctatum"	1·50	1·90
1584	$4 "Cattleya labiata"	2·50	3·50
1585	$5 "Bletia purpurea"	2·75	3·50
MS1586	Two sheets, each 108×78 mm. (a) $6 "Vanilla planifolia Jackson". (b) $6 "Ionopsis utricularioides". Set of 2 sheets	7·50	8·50

214 "Miraculous Draught of Fishes" (detail, Rubens)

1990. Christmas. 350th Death Anniv of Rubens. Multicoloured.

1587	10c. Type **214**	40	20
1588	45c. "Crowning of Holy Katherine" (detail)	65	25
1589	50c. "St. Ives of Treguier" (detail)	70	30
1590	65c. "Allegory of Eternity" (detail)	85	45
1591	$1 "St. Bavo receives Monastic Habit of Ghent" (detail)	1·25	80
1592	$2 "Crowning of Holy Katherine" (different detail)	2·00	2·00
1593	$4 "St. Bavo receives Monastic Habit of Ghent" (different detail)	3·50	3·75
1594	$5 "Communion of St. Francis" (detail)	3·50	3·75
MS1595	Four sheets. (a) 70×100 mm. $6 "Allegory of Eternity" (different detail). (b) 70×100 mm. $6 As 50c. (c) 100×70 mm. $6 As Type **214** (horiz). (d) 100×70 mm. $6 "St. Bavo receives Monastic Habit of Ghent" (different detail) (horiz). Set of 4 sheets	12·50	13·00

215 Geoffrey Chaucer

1990. International Literacy Year (1st issue). Chaucer's "Canterbury Tales". Multicoloured.

1596	40c. Type **215**	55	55
1597	40c. "When April with his showers"	55	55
1598	40c. "When Zephyr also has ..."	55	55
1599	40c. "And many little birds ..."	55	55
1600	40c. "And palmers to go seeking out ..."	55	55
1601	40c. Quill in ink well and open book	55	55
1602	40c. Green bird in tree	55	55
1603	40c. Brown bird in tree and franklin's head	55	55
1604	40c. Purple bird in tree and banner	55	55
1605	40c. Canterbury	55	55
1606	40c. Knight's head	55	55
1607	40c. Black bird in tree and squire's head	55	55
1608	40c. Friar	55	55
1609	40c. Franklin	55	55
1610	40c. Prioress and monk holding banner	55	55
1611	40c. Summoner, Oxford clerk and parson	55	55
1612	40c. Sergeant-at-Law and knight on horseback	55	55
1613	40c. Squire	55	55
1614	40c. "In fellowship ..."	55	55
1615	40c. Cockerel and horse's legs	55	55
1616	40c. Hens	55	55
1617	40c. Hen and rabbit	55	55
1618	40c. Horses' legs and butterfly	55	55
1619	40c. "And briefly, when the sun ..."	55	55

Nos. 1596/1619 were printed together, *se-tenant*, forming a composite design.

See also Nos. 1777/88 and 1790/1801.

215a Self-portrait, 1889

1990. Death Centenary of Vincent van Gogh (artist). Multicoloured.

1620	1c. Type **215a**	45	45
1621	5c. Self-portrait, 1886	45	45
1622	10c. Self-portrait with hat and pipe, 1888	45	45
1623	15c. Self-portrait at easel, 1888	45	45
1624	20c. Self-portrait, 1887	1·00	1·25
1625	45c. Self-portrait, 1889 (different)	1·25	1·25
1626	$5 Self-portrait with pipe, 1889	3·00	4·00
1627	$6 Self-portrait wearing straw hat, 1887	3·00	4·00

215b "The Photographer"

1990. Hummel Figurines. Multicoloured.

1628	10c. Type **215b**	30	15
1629	15c. "Ladder and Rope"	40	15
1630	40c. "Druggist"	60	30
1631	60c. "Hello"	75	45
1632	$1 "Boots"	1·00	80
1633	$2 "The Artist"	1·40	1·75
1634	$4 "Waiter"	2·50	3·25
1635	$5 "The Postman"	2·75	3·25
MS1636	Two sheets, each 94×121 mm. (a) Nos. 1628, 1631/2 and 1635. (b) Nos. 1629/30 and 1633/4. Set of 2 sheets	10·00	11·00

216 American Football Game

1991. 25th Anniv of Super Bowl American Football Championship (1st issue). **T 216** and similar vert designs. Multicoloured.

MS1637	Twenty-five sheets, each 127×101 mm, containing 50c. ×2 as horiz pairs forming composite designs of game scenes or 50c. ×3 (final sheet) showing Vince Lombardi Trophy and helmets of participating teams. Set of 25 sheets	12·00	16·00

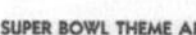

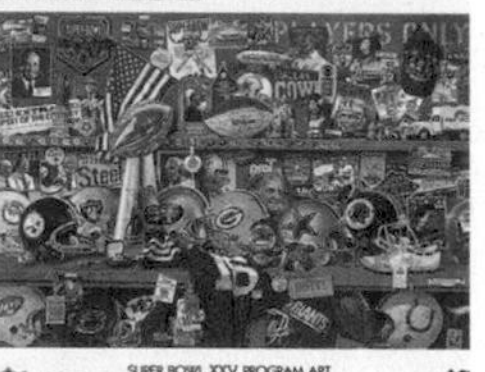

217 Programme Cover of XXV Super Bowl

1991. 25th Anniv of Super Bowl American Football Championships (2nd issue). **T 217** and similar multicoloured designs, each showing a different programme cover illustration. Imperf.

MS1638	Twenty-five sheets, 125×99 mm or 99×125 mm, each with a face value of $2. Set of 25 sheets	25·00	30·00

218 U.S.A. 1893 1c. Columbus Stamp

1991. 500th Anniv (1992) of Discovery of America by Columbus (4th issue). Designs showing U.S.A. 1893 Columbian Exposition, Chicago, stamps (Nos. 1639/54) or ships (others). Multicoloured.

1639	1c. Type **218**	90	1·00
1640	2c. Columbus 2c.	90	1·00
1641	3c. Columbus 3c.	90	1·00
1642	4c. Columbus 4c.	90	1·00
1643	5c. Columbus 5c.	90	1·00
1644	6c. Columbus 6c.	90	1·00
1645	8c. Columbus 8c.	90	1·00
1646	10c. Columbus 10c.	90	1·00
1647	15c. Columbus 15c.	90	1·00
1648	30c. Columbus 30c.	90	1·00
1649	50c. Columbus 50c.	90	1·00
1650	$1 Columbus $1	90	1·00
1651	$2 Columbus $2	1·00	1·10
1652	$3 Columbus $3	1·40	1·50
1653	$4 Columbus $4	2·00	2·10
1654	$5 Columbus $5	2·40	2·50
1655	$10 "Santa Maria", scarlet macaw and tropical flower	5·00	5·50
1656	$10 Logo, "Santa Maria" and Amerindian hut	5·00	5·50
MS1657	Two sheets, each 98×72 mm. (a) $6 Sailors on ship's fo'c'sle. (b) $6 Ship's figurehead. Set of 2 sheets	10·00	11·00

219 Pebbles and Hoppy boxing

1991. Sports. Characters from the "Flintstones" cartoons. Multicoloured.

1658	10c. Type **219**	40	10

1659 15c. Fred Flintstone and Dino playing football 55 15
1660 45c. Fred losing rowing race to Barney Rubble 75 30
1661 55c. Betty Rubble, Wilma Flintstone and Pebbles in dressage competition 1·00 50
1662 $1 Fred playing basketball 1·75 1·00
1663 $2 Bamm Bamm wrestling Barney with Fred as referee 2·00 1·75
1664 $4 Fred and Barney playing tennis 3·25 3·50
1665 $5 Fred, Barney and Dino cycling 3·75 3·50
MS1666 Two sheets, each 117×95 mm. (a) $6 Fred at the plate in baseball game. (b) $6 Fred running to home-plate. Set of 2 sheets 7·50 8·00

220 Board Meeting

1991. "The Jetsons" (cartoon film). Multicoloured.
1667 5c. Type **220** 15 10
1668 20c. Jetsons with Dog 30 15
1669 45c. Judy and Apollo Blue 50 25
1670 50c. Cosmo Spacely and George Jetson 50 35
1671 60c. George and Elroy catching cogs (horiz) 70 50
1672 $1 Judy, Apollo, Elroy and Teddy in cavern (horiz) 1·00 1·00
1673 $2 Drill destroying the cavern (horiz) 1·50 1·50
1674 $4 Jetsons celebrating with the Grungees 2·75 3·00
1675 $5 The Jetsons returning home 2·75 3·00
MS1676 Two sheets, each 114×76 mm. (a) $6 The Jetsons in spacecraft (horiz). (b) $6 The Jetsons in control room (horiz). Set of 2 sheets 7·00 8·00

220a "Sanger 2" (projected space shuttle)

1991. 500th Anniv (1992) of Discovery of America by Columbus, (5th issue). History of Exploration. Multicoloured.
1677 5c. Type **220a** 15 15
1678 10c. "Magellan" satellite, 1990 15 15
1679 25c. "Buran" space shuttle 25 25
1680 75c. Projected "Freedom" space station 65 65
1681 $1 Projected Mars mission space craft 80 80
1682 $2 "Hubble" telescope, 1990 1·60 1·75
1683 $4 Projected Mars mission "sailship" 2·50 2·75
1684 $5 Projected "Craf" satellite 2·50 2·75
MS1685 Two sheets, each 105×71 mm. (a) $6 Bow of caravel (vert). (b) $6 Caravel under full sail. Set of 2 sheets 7·00 8·25

220b Queen and Prince Philip in Spain, 1988

1991. 65th Birthday of Queen Elizabeth II. Multicoloured.
1686 5c. Type **220b** 15 15
1687 60c. Queen and Prince Philip in landau 60 45
1688 $2 Queen at Caen Hill Waterway, 1990 1·75 1·75
1689 $4 Queen at Badminton, 1983 3·00 3·25
MS1690 68×91 mm. $5 Queen Elizabeth II in 1988 and Prince Philip in 1989 4·00 4·25

1991. Tenth Wedding Anniv of the Prince and Princess of Wales. As **T 220b**. Multicoloured.
1691 20c. Prince and Princess in hard hats, 1987 75 20
1692 25c. Portraits of Prince and Princess and sons 75 20
1693 $1 Prince Henry and Prince William, both in 1988 1·25 90
1694 $5 Princess Diana in France and Prince Charles in 1987 6·00 4·75
MS1695 68×90 mm. $5 Princes Harry and William in Majorca, and Princess Diana presenting polo trophy to Prince Charles 6·00 4·25

221 Class D51 Steam Locomotive

1991. "Phila Nippon '91" International Stamp Exhibition, Tokyo. Japanese Trains. Multicoloured.
1696 75c. Type **221** 65 65
1697 75c. Class 9600 steam locomotive 65 65
1698 75c. Goods wagons and chrysanthemum emblem 65 65
1699 75c. Passenger coach 65 65
1700 75c. Decorated Class C57 steam locomotive 65 65
1701 75c. Oil tanker wagon 65 65
1702 75c. Class C53 steam locomotive 65 65
1703 75c. First Japanese steam locomotive 65 65
1704 75c. Class C11 steam locomotive 65 65
1705 $1 Class 181 electric unit 65 65
1706 $1 Class EH10 electric locomotive 65 65
1707 $1 Passenger coaches and Special Express symbol 65 65
1708 $1 Class 1 electric tramcar, Sendai City 65 65
1709 $1 Class 485 electric unit 65 65
1710 $1 Street-cleaning tram, Sendai City 65 65
1711 $1 "Hikari" express train 65 65
1712 $1 Class ED11 electric locomotive 65 65
1713 $1 Class EF66 electric locomotive 65 65
MS1714 Four sheets, each 108×77 mm. (a) $6 Class C55 steam locomotive (vert). P13×13½. (b) $6 Series 400 electric train. (c) $6 Class C62 steam locomotive (vert). (d) $6 "Super Hitachi" electric train. Set of 4 sheets 15·00 16·00

222 Marcello Mastroianni (actor)

1991. Italian Entertainers. Multicoloured.
1715 $1 Type **222** 60 70
1716 $1 Sophia Loren (actress) 60 70
1717 $1 Mario Lanza (singer) 60 70
1718 $1 Federico Fellini (director) 60 70
1719 $1 Arturo Toscanini (conductor) 60 70
1720 $1 Anna Magnani (actress) 60 70
1721 $1 Giancarlo Giannini (actor) 60 70
1722 $1 Gina Lollobrigida (actress) 60 70
1723 $1 Enrico Caruso (operatic tenor) 60 70
MS1724 117×80 mm. $6 Luciano Pavarotti (operatic tenor) (horiz) 5·50 6·00

223 Madonna

1991. Madonna (American singer). Multicoloured.
1725 $1 Type **223** 95 95
1726 $1 In strapless dress 95 95
1727 $1 Wearing necklaces, looking right 95 95
1728 $1 In green dress 95 95
1729 $1 Wearing necklaces, looking to front 95 95
1730 $1 With wrist bangles 95 95
1731 $1 With hand to face 95 95
1732 $1 In purple dress 95 95
1733 $1 With microphone 95 95

MS1734 79×118 mm. $6 Madonna (25×40 mm) 5·00 6·00

224 John Lennon

1991. John Lennon (British musician). Multicoloured.
1735 $1+2c. Type **224** 1·00 90
1736 $1+2c. With Beatle hair cut 1·00 90
1737 $1+2c. In cap 1·00 90
1738 $1+2c. In red polka-dot shirt 1·00 90
1739 $1+2c. In green polo-neck jumper and jacket 1·00 90
1740 $1+2c. In glasses and magenta jacket 1·00 90
1741 $1+2c. With long hair and glasses 1·00 90
1742 $1+2c. In black jumper 1·00 90
1743 $1+2c. In polo-neck jumper 1·00 90

225 Free French Resistance Fighters, 1944

1991. Anniversaries and Events. Multicoloured.
1744 10c. Type **225** 50 25
1745 45c. De Gaulle with Churchill, 1944 1·75 70
1746 50c. Protestor with banner 45 45
1747 65c. Tales around the camp fire (vert) 70 50
1748 75c. Liberation of Paris, 1944 70 60
1749 75c. Building Berlin Wall 70 60
1750 90c. German flag and protestors' shadows 1·25 80
1751 $1 Presidents Bush and Gorbachev shaking hands 80 80
1752 $1 "Marriage of Figaro" 2·75 1·50
1753 $1.50 British trenches and Mafeking Siege 3d. stamp 2·25 2·50
1754 $1.50 Class P-36 steam locomotive, Trans-Siberian Railway 2·25 2·50
1755 $1.50 Map of Switzerland and woman in traditional costume 2·25 2·50
1756 $1.65 Lilienthal's signature and "Flugzeug Nr. 13 Doppeldecker" 2·25 2·25
1757 $2 Street fighting, Kiev 2·50 2·75
1758 $2 Gottfried Leibniz (mathematician) 2·50 2·75
1759 $3 "The Clemency of Titus" 4·75 4·00
1760 $3.50 Angelfish and scout diver 3·00 3·50
MS1761 Four sheets. (a) 101×72 mm. $4 Arms of Berlin. (b) 77×116 mm. $4 Mozart and signature (vert). (c) 77×116 mm. $5 President De Gaulle (vert). (d) 117×89 mm. $5 Scout badge and Jamboree emblem. Set of 4 sheets 14·00 16·00

ANNIVERSARIES AND EVENTS: Nos. 1744/5, 1748, **MS**1761c, Birth centenary of Charles de Gaulle (French statesman); Nos. 1746, 1749/51, **MS**1761a, Bicentenary of Brandenburg Gate, Berlin; Nos. 1747, 1753, 1760, **MS**1761d, 50th death anniv of Lord Baden-Powell and World Scout Jamboree, Korea; Nos. 1752, 1759, **MS**1761b, Death bicentenary of Mozart; No. 1754, Centenary of Trans-Siberian Railway; No. 1755, 700th anniv of Swiss Confederation; No. 1756, Centenary of Otto Lilienthal's gliding experiments; No. 1757, 50th anniv of capture of Kiev; No. 1758, 750th anniv of Hanover.

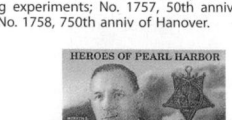

226 Myrvyn Bennion

1991. 50th Anniv of Japanese Attack on Pearl Harbor. Recipients of Congressional Medal of Honor. Multicoloured.
1762 $1 Type **226** 60 70
1763 $1 George Cannon 60 70
1764 $1 John Finn 60 70
1765 $1 Francis Flaherty 60 70
1766 $1 Samuel Fuqua 60 70
1767 $1 Edwin Hill 60 70
1768 $1 Herbert Jones 60 70
1769 $1 Isaac Kidd 60 70
1770 $1 Jackson Pharris 60 70
1771 $1 Thomas Reeves 60 70
1772 $1 Donald Ross 60 70
1773 $1 Robert Scott 60 70
1774 $1 Franklin van Valkenburgh 60 70
1775 $1 James Ward 60 70
1776 $1 Cassin Young 60 70

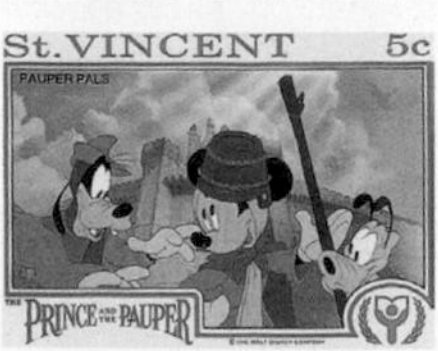

226a Mickey Mouse, Goofy and Pluto as Pauper Pals

1991. International Literacy Year (1990) (2nd issue). Scenes from Disney cartoon films. Multicoloured. (a) "The Prince and The Pauper".
1777 5c. Type **226a** 30 25
1778 10c. Mickey as the bored prince 30 25
1779 15c. Donald Duck as the valet 35 30
1780 25c. Mickey as the prince and the pauper 40 30
1781 60c. Exchanging clothes 80 55
1782 75c. Prince and pauper with suit of armour 90 65
1783 80c. Throwing food from the battlements 1·00 70
1784 $1 Pete as Captain of the Guard 1·25 85
1785 $2 Mickey and Donald in the dungeon 2·00 1·75
1786 $3 Mickey and Donald at dungeon window 2·50 2·25
1787 $4 Goofy rescuing Mickey and Donald 3·00 3·00
1788 $5 Crowning the real prince 3·00 3·00
MS1789 Four sheets, each 127×101 mm. (a) $6 Crowning the wrong prince. (b) $6 Pete holding Mickey. (c) $6 The pauper on the throne. (d) $6 Mickey telling troops to seize the guard. Set of 4 sheets 14·00 15·00

(b) "The Rescuers Down Under".
1790 5c. Miss Bianca 30 25
1791 10c. Bernard 30 25
1792 15c. Matre d'Francoise 35 30
1793 25c. Wilbur the Albatross 45 25
1794 60c. Jake the Kangaroo Mouse 80 55
1795 75c. Bernard, Bianca and Jake in the outback 90 65
1796 80c. Bianca and Bernard to the rescue 1·00 70
1797 $1 Marahute the Eagle 1·25 85
1798 $2 Cody and Marahute with eggs 2·00 1·75
1799 $3 McLeach and his pet, Joanna the Goanna 2·50 2·50
1800 $4 Frank the Frill-necked Lizard 3·00 3·00
1801 $5 Red Kangaroo, Krebbs Koala and Polly Platypus 3·00 3·25
MS1802 Four sheets, each 127×102 mm. (a) $6 The Rescuers. (b) $6 Ethiopian and Japanese mice delegates. (c) $6 Wilbur carrying Bianca and Bernard. (d) $6 Wilbur in pain. Set of 4 sheets 14·00 15·00

227 Hans-Dietrich Genscher and "Winged Victory" Statue

1991. European History. Multicoloured.
1803 $1 Type **227** 1·75 1·50
1804 $1 Destruction of Berlin Wall 1·75 1·50
1805 $1 Churchill, De Gaulle and Apeal to the French, 1940 1·75 1·50
1806 $1 Eisenhower, De Gaulle and D-Day, 1944 1·75 1·50
1807 $1 Brandenburg Gate, Berlin (bicentenary) 1·75 1·50
1808 $1 Chancellor Helmut Kohl and meeting of Berlin mayors, 1989 1·75 1·50
1809 $1 De Gaulle with Chancellor Adenauer 1·75 1·50
1810 $1 Pres. Kennedy's visit to Europe, 1961, Washington and Lafayette 1·75 1·50
MS1811 106×88 mm. $6 Casablanca Conference, 1942, and demolition of Berlin Wall (24½×39 mm) 6·00 6·50

1991. Famous Golfers. As **T 227**. Multicoloured.
1812 $1 Gary Player 1·75 1·25
1813 $1 Nick Faldo 1·75 1·25
1814 $1 Severiano Ballesteros 1·75 1·25
1815 $1 Ben Hogan 1·75 1·25
1816 $1 Jack Nicklaus 1·75 1·25
1817 $1 Greg Norman 1·75 1·25

1818	$1 Jose-Maria Olazabal	1·75	1·25
1819	$1 Bobby Jones	1·75	1·25

1991. Famous Entertainers. As **T 277**. Multicoloured.

1820	$2 Michael Jackson	1·50	1·75
1821	$2 Madonna	1·50	1·75
1822	$2 Elvis Presley	1·50	1·75
1823	$2 David Bowie	1·50	1·75
1824	$2 Prince	1·50	1·75
1825	$2 Frank Sinatra	1·50	1·75
1826	$2 George Michael	1·50	1·75
1827	$2 Mick Jagger	1·50	1·75
MS1828	Two sheets, each 110×82 mm. (a) $6 Madonna (29×43 mm). (b) $6 Elvis Presley (29×43 mm). Set of 2 sheets	7·00	10·00

1991. Famous Chess Masters. As **T 227**. Multicoloured.

1829	$1 Francoise Philidor	1·50	1·10
1830	$1 Karl Anderssen	1·50	1·10
1831	$1 Wilhelm Steinitz	1·50	1·10
1832	$1 Alexandrovich Alekhine	1·50	1·10
1833	$1 Boris Spassky	1·50	1·10
1834	$1 Robert Fischer	1·50	1·10
1835	$1 Anatoly Karpov	1·50	1·10
1836	$1 Garry Kasparov	1·50	1·10

1991. Nobel Prize Winners. As **T 227**. Multicoloured.

1837	$1 Albert Einstein (mathematical physicist)	1·60	1·10
1838	$1 Wilhelm Rontgen (physicist)	1·60	1·10
1839	$1 William Shockley (chemist)	1·60	1·10
1840	$1 Charles Townes (physicist)	1·60	1·10
1841	$1 Lev Landau (physicist)	1·60	1·10
1842	$1 Guglielmo Marconi (applied physicist)	1·60	1·10
1843	$1 Willard Libby (chemist)	1·60	1·10
1844	$1 Ernest Lawrence (nuclear physicist)	1·60	1·10

228 Walt Disney Characters decorating Christmas Tree, 1982

1991. Christmas. Walt Disney Christmas Cards. Multicoloured.

1845	10c. Type **228**	15	15
1846	45c. Mickey and Moose, 1980	40	30
1847	55c. Mickey, Pluto and Donald carrying bauble, 1970	50	40
1848	75c. Duckling and egg shell, 1943	70	70
1849	$1.50 Walt Disney characters decorating globe, 1941	1·25	1·50
1850	$2 The Lady and the Tramp by Christmas tree, 1986	1·50	1·75
1851	$4 Walt Disney characters carol singing, 1977	2·75	3·25
1852	$5 Mickey in fairy-tale castle, 1965	2·75	3·50
MS1853	Two sheets. (a) 102×128 mm. $6 Characters in balloon basket, 1966. (b) 128×102 mm. $6 Characters in national costumes, 1966. Set of 2 sheets	9·00	9·50

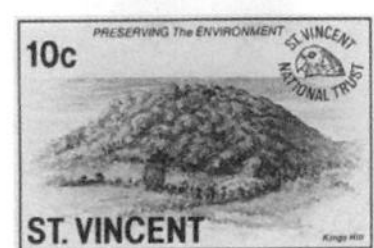

229 Kings Hill

1992. Preserving the Environment. Multicoloured.

1854	10c. Type **229**	20	20
1855	55c. Planting sapling	50	45
1856	75c. Doric Temple, Botanic Gardens	60	65
1857	$2 18th-century map of Kings Hill	1·40	2·25

229a Kingstown from the Cliffs

1992. 40th Anniv of Queen Elizabeth II's Accession. Multicoloured.

1858	10c. Type **229a**	20	15
1859	20c. Deep water wharf, Kingstown	35	15
1860	$1 Residential suburb, Kingstown	60	60
1861	$5 Kingstown from the interior	2·75	3·25
MS1862	Two sheets, each 75×92 mm. (a) $6 Deep water wharf (different). (b) $6 Beach. Set of 2 sheets	9·50	9·50

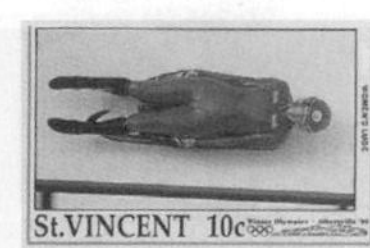

230 Women's Luge

1992. Winter Olympic Games, Albertville (1st issue). Multicoloured.

1863	10c. Type **230**	15	15
1864	15c. Women's figure skating (vert)	20	20
1865	25c. Two-man bobsleigh	25	25
1866	30c. Mogul skiing (vert)	30	30
1867	45c. Nordic combination	40	40
1868	55c. Ski jumping	55	55
1869	75c. Men's giant slalom	65	65
1870	$1.50 Women's slalom (vert)	1·10	1·10
1871	$5 Ice hockey	3·25	3·75
1872	$8 Biathlon (vert)	4·25	5·00
MS1873	Two sheets, each 100×70 mm. (a) $6 Women's speed skating (vert). (b) $6 Men's downhill skiing (vert). Set of 2 sheets	11·00	12·00

See also Nos. 1966/80.

231 Women's Synchronized Swimming

1992. Olympic Games, Barcelona. Multicoloured.

1874	10c. Type **231**	25	20
1875	15c. Men's high jump (vert)	25	20
1876	25c. Men's small-bore rifle shooting	35	20
1877	30c. Men's 200 m (vert)	35	20
1878	45c. Men's judo (vert)	40	25
1879	55c. Men's 200 m freestyle swimming	45	30
1880	75c. Men's javelin (vert)	60	50
1881	$1.50 Men's 4000 m pursuit cycling (vert)	4·50	2·00
1882	$5 Boxing	3·00	4·00
1883	$8 Women's basketball (vert)	12·00	12·00
MS1884	Two sheets, each 100×70 mm. (a) $15 Sailboarding (vert). (b) $15 Men's singles tennis (vert). Set of 2 sheets	23·00	23·00

231a The Wolf as General of Spanish Moors

1992. International Stamp Exhibitions. Walt Disney cartoon characters. Multicoloured. (a) "Granada '92", Spain. The Three Pigs in Spanish Uniforms.

1885	15c. Type **231a**	20	10
1886	40c. Pig as captain of infantry	40	25
1887	$2 Pig as halberdier	1·25	1·50
1888	$4 Pig as nobleman	2·25	3·00
MS1889	128×102 mm. $6 Nobleman at castle window	3·00	3·75

(b) "World Columbian Stamp Expo '92", Chicago Landmarks.

1890	10c. Mickey Mouse and Goofy looking at Picasso sculpture (horiz)	20	15
1891	50c. Mickey and Donald Duck admiring Robie House (horiz)	45	35
1892	$1 Calder sculpture in Sears Tower (horiz)	80	65
1893	$5 Goofy in Buckingham Memorial Fountain (horiz)	2·50	3·00
MS1894	128×102 mm. $6 Mickey painting Minnie	3·00	3·75

232 "Nina"

1992. 500th Anniv of Discovery of America by Columbus (6th issue). "World Columbian Stamp Expo '92", Chicago. Multicoloured.

1895	5c. Type **232**	40	40
1896	10c. "Pinta"	40	30
1897	45c. "Santa Maria"	75	50
1898	55c. Fleet leaving Palos, 1492	75	55
1899	$4 Christopher Columbus (vert)	3·00	3·50
1900	$5 Arms of Columbus (vert)	3·00	3·50
MS1901	Two sheets, each 115×86 mm. (a) $6 "Santa Maria" sighting land (42½×57 mm). (b) $6 Route of voyage (42½×57 mm). Set of 2 sheets	8·50	10·00

233 Elvis looking Pensive

1992. 15th Death Anniv of Elvis Presley (1st issue). Multicoloured.

1902	$1 Type **233**	1·25	1·00
1903	$1 Wearing black and yellow striped shirt	1·25	1·00
1904	$1 Singing into microphone	1·25	1·00
1905	$1 Wearing wide-brimmed hat	1·25	1·00
1906	$1 With microphone in right hand	1·25	1·00
1907	$1 In Army uniform	1·25	1·00
1908	$1 Wearing pink shirt	1·25	1·00
1909	$1 In yellow shirt	1·25	1·00
1910	$1 In jacket and bow tie	1·25	1·00
MS1911	76×107 mm. $6 In blue shirt (28½×42½ mm)	6·50	7·00

See also Nos. 2029/37, 2038/46 and 2047/9.

234 Bonnie Blair

1992. Bonnie Blair's Victories in 500 m Speed Skating at Calgary and Albertville Olympic Games. Multicoloured.

1912	$3 Type **234**	2·25	2·50
MS1913	185×127 mm. $2 Turning corner (horiz); $2 With skates in arms (43×51 mm); $2 On straight (horiz)	4·50	4·75

235 "Astraptes anaphus"

1992. "Genova '92" International Thematic Stamp Exhibition (1st issue). Butterflies. Multicoloured.

1914	5c. Type **235**	30	40
1915	10c. "Anartia jatrophae" (horiz)	30	20
1916	35c. "Danaus eresimus"	55	40
1917	45c. "Battus polydamus"	60	45
1918	55c. "Junonia evarete" (horiz)	70	50
1919	65c. "Urbanus proteus"	80	60
1920	75c. "Pyrgus oileus" (horiz)	90	65
1921	$1 "Biblis hyperia"	1·00	75
1922	$2 "Eurema daira"	1·50	1·50
1923	$3 "Leptotes cassius" (horiz)	1·75	2·00
1924	$4 "Ephyriades brunnea" (horiz)	2·25	2·50
1925	$5 "Victorina stelenes"	2·50	2·75
MS1926	Three sheets, each 98×72 mm. (a) $6 Phoebis sennae. (b) $6 Heliconius charitonius (horiz). (c) $6 Dryas julia (horiz). Set of 3 sheets	12·00	13·00

See also Nos. 1940/52.

236 "Collybia subpruinosa"

1992. Fungi. Multicoloured.

1927	10c. Type **236**	30	20
1928	15c. "Gerronema citrinum"	40	20
1929	20c. "Amanita antillana"	45	30
1930	45c. "Dermoloma atrobrunneum"	60	35
1931	50c. "Inopilus maculosus"	70	40
1932	65c. "Pulveroboletus brachyspermus"	80	55
1933	75c. "Mycena violacella"	90	60
1934	$1 "Xerocomus brasiliensis"	1·00	70
1935	$2 "Amanita ingrata"	1·50	1·75
1936	$3 "Leptonia caeruleocapitata"	1·75	2·25
1937	$4 "Limacella myochroa"	2·25	2·75
1938	$5 "Inopilus magnificus"	2·50	2·75
MS1939	Three sheets, each 101×68 mm. (a) $6 "Limacella guttata". (b) $6 "Amanita agglutinata". (c) $6 "Trogia buccinalis". Set of 3 sheets	11·00	12·00

No. 1936 is inscribed "Leptonia caeruleocaptata" in error.

237 Rufous-breasted Hermit

1992. "Genova '92" International Thematic Stamp Exhibition (2nd issue). Hummingbirds. Multicoloured.

1940	5c. Type **237**	30	40
1941	15c. Hispaniolan emerald	35	20
1942	45c. Green-throated carib	60	35
1943	55c. Jamaican mango	70	45
1944	65c. Vervain hummingbird	80	60
1945	75c. Purple-throated carib	90	70
1946	90c. Green mango	90	75
1947	$1 Bee hummingbird	1·00	80
1948	$2 Cuban emerald	1·75	1·75
1949	$3 Puerto Rican emerald	1·90	2·00
1950	$4 Antillean mango	2·40	2·75
1951	$5 Streamertail	2·75	2·75
MS1952	Three sheets, each 98×67 mm. (a) $6 Bahama woodstar. (b) $6 Antillean crested hummingbird. (c) $6 Blue-headed hummingbird. Set of 3 sheets	15·00	14·00

I 3 mm serif characters, no line through "c"
II 3 mm serif characters, line through "c"
III 3.5 mm sanserif characters, line through "c"
IV 3.5 mm broad serif characters
V 2.5 mm sanserif characters, line through "c"
VI 4.25 mm serif characters, no line through "c"
VII 3 mm thin serif numerals, sanserif "c", no line
VIII 2.5 mm sanserif characters, no line through "c"

20c	20¢	10¢	10¢
I	II	III	IV
20¢	20c	20c	20c
V	VI	VII	VIII

1993. Various issues surcharged. Original values obliterated by circle or rectangle. (a) On stamps of St. Vincent.

V1953	10c. on 2c. (No. 287) (II)	60·00	
V1954	10c. on 6c. (No. 1099)		
V1955	10c. on 12c. (No. 1101) (IV)		
V1956	10c. on 15c. (No. 1115e) (III)		
V1957	10c. on 25c. (No. 296) (II)	45·00	
V1958	10c. on 25c. (No. 1115g) (III)		15·00
V1959	10c. on 35c. (No. 1106) (II)		
V1960	10c. on 35c. (No. 788) (II)	25·00	15·00
V1961	10c. on 45c. (No. 1115j) (III)		15·00
V1962	10c. on 45c. (No. 770) (II)		
V1963	10c. on 45c. (No. 1134) (II)		
V1964	10c. on 60c. (No. 687)	13·00	
V1965	10c. on 60c. (No. 715) (II)		40·00
V1966	10c. on 60c. (No. 720) (II)	25·00	
V1967	10c. on 65c. (No. 1115l) (II)	25·00	
V1968	10c. on 70c. (No. 500) (II)	25·00	
V1969	10c. on 75c. (No. 1115m) (II)	20·00	
V1970	10c. on $1 (No. 773) (II)	25·00	
V1971	10c. on $1.25 (No. 555) (II)	20·00	

2293 $5 Willy Brandt and Robert F. Kennedy, 1967 (horiz) 2·75 3·25
2294 $5 Prince Naruhito in traditional dress and engagement photographs (horiz) 2·75 3·25
2295 $5 Pres. Clinton with school children (horiz) 2·75 3·25
2296 $6 Bogusz Church, Gozlin (horiz) 3·00 3·50
MS2297 Seven sheets. (a) 110×76 mm. $5 Copernicus. (b) 110×76 mm. $6 "Woman eating a Melon and Boy writing" (detail) (Picasso). (c) 110×76 mm. $6 Thommy Moe (U.S.A.) (downhill skiing). (d) 110×76 mm. $6 Willy Brandt at signing of Common Declaration, 1973 (horiz). (e) 110×76 mm). $6 Masako Owada. (f) 76×110 mm. $6 "Dancing" (detail) (Wladyslaw Roguski). (g) 76×110 mm. $6 Pres. Clinton wearing stetson. Set of 7 sheets 24·00 25·00

ANNIVERSARIES AND EVENTS: Nos. 2278, 2290, **MS**2297a, 450th death anniv of Copernicus (astronomer); Nos. 2279, 2285, 2291, **MS**2297b, 20th death anniv of Picasso (artist); Nos. 2280, 2292, **MS**2297c, Winter Olympic Games '94, Lillehammer; Nos. 2281, 2293, **MS**2297d, 80th birth anniv of Willy Brandt (German politician); Nos. 2282/3, 2288, 500th anniv (1990) of Thurn and Taxis postal service; Nos. 2284, 2294, **MS**2297e, Marriage of Crown Prince Naruhito of Japan; No. 2286, Marriage of Princess Stephanie of Monaco; Nos. 2287, 2289, 2296, **MS**2297f, "Polska '93" International Stamp Exhibition, Poznan; No. 2295, **MS**2297g, Inauguration of U.S. President William Clinton.

259 Supermarine Spitfire

1993. Aviation Anniversaries. Multicoloured.
2298 50c. Type **259** 75 30
2299 $1 Eckener and airship "Graf Zeppelin" over Egypt, 1931 1·25 90
2300 $1 Blanchard and Pres. Washington with balloon, 1793 1·25 90
2301 $2 De Havilland Mosquito Mk VI 1·90 2·00
2302 $2 Eckener and "Graf Zeppelin" over New York, 1928 1·90 2·00
2303 $3 Eckener and "Graf Zeppelin" over Tokyo, 1929 2·75 3·00
2304 $4 Blanchard's balloon ascending from Walnut St. Prison, Philadelphia 3·00 3·25
MS2305 Three sheets, each 100×70 mm. (a) $6 Hawker Hurricane Mk I. (b) $6 Dr. Hugo Eckener (vert). (c) $6 Blanchard's balloon (vert). Set of 3 sheets 12·00 14·00

ANNIVERSARIES: Nos. 2298, 2301, **MS**2305a, 75th anniv of Royal Air Force; Nos. 2299, 2302/3, **MS**2305b, 125th birth anniv of Hugo Eckener (airship commander); Nos. 2300, 2304, **MS**2305c, Bicentenary of first airmail flight.
No. 2303 is inscr "Toyko" in error.

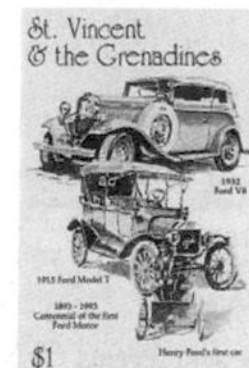

260 First Ford Car, Model "T" and "V8"

1993. Centenaries of Henry Ford's First Petrol Engine (Nos. 2306, 2309) and Karl Benz's First Four-wheeled car (others). Multicoloured.
2306 $1 Type **260** 90 60
2307 $2 Benz racing car, 1908, "Stuttgart" and "540K" 1·75 1·75
2308 $3 Benz car, 1894, "Tourenwagen" and "Blitzen Benz" 2·25 2·75
2309 $4 Ford "Runabout", 1903, Model "T" Tourer and saloon, 1935 2·50 3·00
MS2310 Two sheets, each 100×70 mm. (a) $6 Henry Ford. (b) $6 Karl Benz. Set of 2 sheets 7·00 10·00

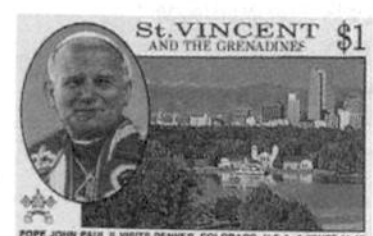

261 Pope John Paul II and Denver Skyline

1993. Papal Visit to Denver, Colorado, U.S.A.
2311 $1 Type **261** 1·00 80
MS2312 100×70 mm. $6 Pope and clock tower 4·75 5·50

262 Corvette of 1953

1993. 40th Anniv of Corvette Range of Cars. Multicoloured.
2313 $1 Type **262** 80 1·00
2314 $1 1993 model 80 1·00
2315 $1 1958 model 80 1·00
2316 $1 1960 model 80 1·00
2317 $1 "40" and symbolic chequered flag emblem 80 1·00
2318 $1 1961 model 80 1·00
2319 $1 1963 model 80 1·00
2320 $1 1968 model 80 1·00
2321 $1 1973 model 80 1·00
2322 $1 1975 model 80 1·00
2323 $1 1982 model 80 1·00
2324 $1 1984 model 80 1·00

263 Gedung Shrine, 1920

1993. Asian International Stamp Exhibitions. Multicoloured. As **T 263**. (a) "Indopex '93", Surabaya, Indonesia. Horiz designs.
2325-54 5, 10, 20, 45, 55, 75c., $1 ×2, $1.50 ×18, $2, $4, $5 ×2. Set of 30 18·00 23·00
MS2355 Three sheets. (a) 105×135 mm. $6 Relief of Sudamala epic, Mt. Lawu. (b) 105×135 mm. $6 Plaque from Banyumas, Java. (c) 135×105 mm. $6 Panel from Ramayana reliefs (vert). Set of 3 sheets 9·00 12·00
Nos. 2325/32 and 2351/4 show Indonesian scenes, Nos. 2333/50 masks (Nos. 2333/8) or paintings (Nos. 2339/50).

(b) "Taipei '93", Taiwan. Horiz designs.
2356-85 5, 10, 20, 45, 55, 75c., $1×2, $1.50×18, $2, $4, $5×2 Set of 30 18·00 23·00
MS2386 Three sheets, each 135×105 mm. (a) $6 Two Stone Guardians, Longmen Caves, Henan. (b) $6 Stone guardian, Longmen Caves, Henan (vert). (c) $6 Giant Buddha, Yungung Caves (vert). Set of 3 sheets 9·00 12·00
Nos. 2356/63 and 2382/5 show Chinese scenes, Nos. 2364/81 kites. (Nos. 2364/9) or paintings (Nos. 2370/81).

(c) "Bangkok '93", Thailand. Vert (5, 55c., $2, $4) or horiz (others).
2387-2416 5, 10, 20, 45, 55, 75c., $1×2, $1.50×18, $2, $4, $5×2 Set of 30 18·00 23·00
MS2417 Three sheets, each 105×135 mm. (a) $6 Masked dancer. (b) $6 Standing Buddha, Hua Hin (vert). (c) $6 Carved roof boss, Dusit Mahaprasad (vert). Set of 3 sheets 9·00 12·00
Nos. 2387/4 and 2413/16 show Thai scenes, Nos. 2395/2412 murals from Buddhaisawan Chapel (Nos. 2395/2400), paintings (Nos. 2401/6) or sculptures (Nos. 2407/12).

264 Players from St. Vincent and Mexico

1993. Qualifying Rounds for World Cup Football Championship, U.S.A. Multicoloured.
2418 5c. Type **264** 15 20
2419 10c. Honduras match 15 15
2420 65c. Costa Rica match 55 35
2421 $5 St. Vincent goalkeeper 3·25 4·75

265 Fish Delivery Van

1993. Japanese Aid for Fishing Industry. Multicoloured.
2422 10c. Type **265** 20 10
2423 50c. Fish aggregation device (vert) 45 30
2424 75c. Game fishing launch 60 50
2425 $5 Fish market 3·25 4·75

1993. Famous Baseball Players (7th issue). As **T 247**. Multicoloured.
2426 $2 Reggie Jackson 1·10 1·25

265a "Adoration of the Magi" (detail) (Durer)

1993. Christmas. Religious Paintings. Black, yellow and red (Nos. 2427/9, 2434) or multicoloured (others).
2427 10c. Type **265a** 20 10
2428 35c. "Adoration of the Magi" (different detail) (Durer) 40 20
2429 40c. "Adoration of the Magi" (different detail) (Durer) 45 25
2430 50c. "Holy Family with Saint Francis" (detail) (Rubens) 55 30
2431 55c. "Adoration of the Shepherds" (detail) (Rubens) 55 30
2432 65c. "Adoration of the Shepherds" (different detail) (Rubens) 65 40
2433 $1 "Holy Family" (Rubens) 90 90
2434 $5 "Adoration of the Magi" (different detail) (Durer) 2·50 4·50
MS2435 Two sheets, each 103×127 mm. (a) $6 "Adoration of the Magi" (different detail) (Dürer) (horiz). (b) $6 "Holy Family with Sts. Elizabeth and John" (detail) (Rubens). Set of 2 sheets 8·00 9·00

267 Barbra Streisand

1993. Barbra Streisand's Grand Garden Concert.
2436 **267** $2 multicoloured 1·10 1·40

268 Roy Acuff

1994. Legends of Country Music. Multicoloured.
2437 $1 Type **268** 55 70
2438 $1 Patsy Cline in pink shirt 55 70
2439 $1 Jim Reeves in dinner jacket 55 70
2440 $1 Hank Williams in brown jacket 55 70
2441 $1 Hank Williams in purple jacket 55 70
2442 $1 Roy Acuff with microphone 55 70
2443 $1 Patsy Cline wearing white scarf 55 70
2444 $1 Jim Reeves with microphone 55 70
2445 $1 Jim Reeves in orange jacket 55 70
2446 $1 Patsy Cline with microphone 55 70
2447 $1 Hank Williams in grey jacket 55 70
2448 $1 Roy Acuff in grey jacket 55 70

269 Mobile Library

1994. Centenary of Library Service. Multicoloured.
2449 5c. Type **269** 10 20
2450 10c. Old Public Library building 10 10
2451 $1 Family reading 65 85
2452 $1 Line of books joining youth and old man 65 85

270 Woman planting Breadfruit

1994. Bicent of Introduction of Breadfruit. Multicoloured.
2453 10c. Type **270** 15 10
2454 45c. Captain Bligh with breadfruit plant 75 30
2455 65c. Slice of breadfruit 50 40
2456 $5 Breadfruit growing on branch 2·75 4·75

271 Family Picnic

1994. Int Year of the Family (1st issue). Multicoloured.
2457 10c. Type **271** 15 10
2458 50c. Family in church 40 30
2459 65c. Working in the garden 50 35
2460 75c. Jogging 55 55
2461 $1 Family group (vert) 70 70
2462 $2 On the beach 1·40 1·75
See also No. 2836.

271a Hong Kong 1992 $2.30 Olympic Games stamp and "Hong Kong Harbour in 19th Century"

1994. "Hong Kong '94" International Stamp Exhibition (1st issue). Multicoloured.
2463 40c. Type **271a** 35 50
2464 40c. St. Vincent 1991 $3.50 Scouts Jamboree stamp and "Hong Kong Harbour in 19th Century" 35 50
Nos. 2463/4 were printed together, *se-tenant*, forming the complete painting.
See also Nos. 2465/94 and 2495/500.

271b Bowl with Bamboo and Sparrows

1994. "Hong Kong '94" International Stamp Exhibition (2nd issue). As **T 271b**. Multicoloured.
2465-2494 40c.×12, 45c.×12, 50c.×6 7·50 8·50
Nos. 2465/94 were printed as five *se-tenant* sheetlets, each of six different designs, depicting Ching porcelain (40c.), dragon boat races (40c.), seed-stitch purses (45c.), junks (45c.) and Qing ceramic figures (vert designs) (50c.).

272 Bird on a Flowering Spray Plate, Qianlong

1994. "Hong Kong '94" International Stamp Exhibition (3rd issue). Multicoloured.
2495 50c. Type **272** 75 75
2496 50c. Large decorated dish, Kangxi 75 75
2497 50c. Cocks on rocky ground plate, Yongzheng 75 75
2498 50c. Green decorated dish, Yuan 75 75
2499 50c. Porcelain pug dog 75 75
2500 50c. Dish decorated with Dutch ship, Qianlong 75 75
MS2501 Two sheets, each 126×95 mm. (a) $2 Dr. Sun Yat-sen. (b) $2 Chiang Kai-shek. Set of 2 sheets 3·00 3·50
No. 2497 is incorrectly inscribed "Cocks on a Rocky Groung".

273 Blue Flasher

1994. Butterflies. Multicoloured.

2502	50c. Type **273**	60	55
2503	50c. Tiger swallowtail	60	55
2504	50c. Lustrous copper	60	55
2505	50c. Tailed copper	60	55
2506	50c. Blue copper	60	55
2507	50c. Ruddy copper	60	55
2508	50c. Viceroy	60	55
2509	50c. California sister	60	55
2510	50c. Mourning cloak	60	55
2511	50c. Red passion-flower	60	55
2512	50c. Small flambeau	60	55
2513	50c. Blue wave	60	55
2514	50c. Chiricahua metalmark	60	55
2515	50c. Monarch	60	55
2516	50c. Anise swallowtail	60	55
2517	50c. Buckeye	60	55

274 Antonio Cabrini

1994. Juventus Football Club (Italy) Commemoration. Past and present players. Multicoloured.

2518	$1 Type **274**	80	90
2519	$1 Michel Platini and Roberto Baggio	80	90
2520	$1 Roberto Bettega	80	90
2521	$1 Gaetano Scirea	80	90
2522	$1 Jurgen Kohler	80	90
2523	$1 Marco Tardelli	80	90
2524	$1 Paolo Rossi	80	90
2525	$1 Giuseppe Furino	80	90
2526	$1 Dino Zoff	80	90
2527	$1 Franco Causio	80	90
2528	$1 Claudio Gentile	80	90
MS2529	100×70 mm. $6 U.E.F.A. Cup, Cup Winners Cup and European Cup trophies (all won by Juventus) (horiz)	3·25	4·00

275 "Epidendrum ibaguense"

1994. Orchids. Multicoloured.

2530	10c. Type **275**	50	30
2531	25c. "Ionopsis utricularioides"	60	30
2532	50c. "Brassavola cucullata"	75	50
2533	65c. "Enclyclia cochleata"	90	60
2534	$1 "Liparis nervosa"	1·00	75
2535	$2 "Vanilla phaeantha"	1·60	1·75
2536	$4 "Elleanthus cephalotus"	2·50	3·25
2537	$5 "Isochilus linearis"	2·50	3·25
MS2538	Two sheets, each 100×70 mm. (a) $6 "Rodriguezia lanceolata". (b) $6 "Eulophia alta". Set of 2 sheets	8·00	9·00

276 Dimorphodon

1994. Prehistoric Animals (1st series). Multicoloured.

2539	75c. Type **276**	60	65
2540	75c. Camarasaurus	60	65
2541	75c. Spinosaurus	60	65
2542	75c. Allosaurus	60	65
2543	75c. Rhamphorhynchus	60	65
2544	75c. Pteranodon and body of Allosaurus	60	65
2545	75c. Eudimorphodon	60	65
2546	75c. Ornithomimus	60	60
2547	75c. Protoavis	60	60
2548	75c. Pteranodon	60	65
2549	75c. Quetzalcoatlus	60	65
2550	75c. Lesothosaurus	60	65
2551	75c. Heterodontosaurus	60	65
2552	75c. Archaeopteryx	60	65
2553	75c. Cearadactylus	60	65
2554	75c. Anchisaurus	60	65

Nos. 2539/46 and 2547/54 respectively were printed together, *se-tenant*, forming composite designs.

See also Nos. 2556/604.

277 Triceratops

1994. "Hong Kong '94" International Stamp Exhibition (4th issue). Prehistoric Animals. Sheet 206×121 mm, containing **T 277** and similar multicoloured designs.

MS2555	$1.50, Type **277**; $1.50, Tyrannosaurus rex (vert); $1.50, Diplodocus; $1.50, Stegosaurus (vert)	4·75	5·00

278 Albertosaurus

1994. Prehistoric Animals (2nd series). As **T 278**. Multicoloured.

2556-2603	75c. ×48. Set of 48	20·00	23·00
MS2604	Four sheets, each 115×86 mm. (a) $6 Tyrannosaurus rex. (b) $6 Triceratops. (c) $6 Pteranodon and Diplodocus carnegii. (d) $6 Styracosaurus (vert). Set of 4 sheets	14·00	15·00

Nos. 2556/2603 were printed together, se-tenant, as four sheetlets of 12 with Nos. 2556/79 being horizontal and Nos. 2580/2603 vertical. The species depicted are Albertosaurus, Chasmosaurus, Brachiosaurus, Coelophysis, Deinonychus, Anatosaurus, Iguanodon, Baryonyx, Steneosaurus, Nanotyrannus, Camptosaurus, Camarasaurus, Hesperonis, Mesosaurus, Plesiosaurus Doli-chorhynchops, Squalicorax, Tylosaurus, Plesiosoar, Stenopterygius Ichthyosaurus, Steneosaurus, Eurhinosaurus Longirostris, Cryptocleidus Oxoniensis, Caturus, Protostega, Dimorphodon, Pterodactylus, Rhamphorhynchus, Pteranodon, Gallimimus, Stegosaurus, Acanthopholis, Trach-odon, Thecodonts, Ankylosaurus, Compsognathus, Protoceratops, Quetzalcoatlus, Diplodocus, Spinosaurus, Apatosaurus, Ornitholestes, Lesothosaurus, Trachodon, Protoavis, Oviraptor, Coelophysis, Ornitholestes and Archaeopteryx.

279 Mickey Mouse as Pilot

1994. 65th Anniv (1993) of Mickey Mouse. Walt Disney cartoon characters. Multicoloured.

2605	5c. Type **279**	30	30
2606	10c. Mickey in Foreign Legion	30	30
2607	15c. Mickey as frontiersman	40	40
2608	20c. Mickey, Goofy and Donald Duck	40	40
2609	35c. Horace Horsecollar and Clarabelle Cow	50	50
2610	50c. Minnie Mouse, Frankie and Figuro	60	60
2611	75c. Donald and Pluto	70	70
2612	80c. Mickey holding balloons	75	75
2613	85c. Daisy Duck and Minnie	75	75
2614	95c. Minnie	80	80
2615	$1 Mickey in red trousers	80	80
2616	$1.50 Mickey raising hat	1·40	1·40
2617	$2 Mickey with hands in pockets	1·60	1·60
2618	$3 Mickey and Minnie	2·50	2·50
2619	$4 Mickey with birthday cake	2·75	2·75
2620	$5 Mickey as Uncle Sam	2·75	2·75
MS2621	Four sheets. (a) 102×127 mm. $6 Pluto looking at portrait of Mickey. (b) 127×102 mm. $6 Mickey and camera (horiz). (c) 127×102 mm. $6 Minnie disco dancing (horiz). P 14×13½. (d) 127×102 mm. $6 Donald with Mickey's baby photo (horiz). Set of 4 sheets	18·00	18·00

280 Argentine Team

1994. World Cup Football Championship, U.S.A. Competing teams. Multicoloured.

2622	50c. Type **280**	35	45
2623	50c. Belgium	35	45
2624	50c. Bolivia	35	45
2625	50c. Brazil	35	45
2626	50c. Bulgaria	35	45
2627	50c. Cameroun	35	45
2628	50c. Colombia	35	45
2629	50c. Germany	35	45
2630	50c. Greece	35	45
2631	50c. Netherlands	35	45
2632	50c. Republic of Ireland	35	45
2633	50c. Italy	35	45
2634	50c. Mexico	35	45
2635	50c. Morocco	35	45
2636	50c. Nigeria	35	45
2637	50c. Norway	35	45
2638	50c. Rumania	35	45
2639	50c. Russia	35	45
2640	50c. Saudi Arabia	35	45
2641	50c. South Korea	35	45
2642	50c. Spain	35	45
2643	50c. Sweden	35	45
2644	50c. Switzerland	35	45
2645	50c. U.S.A.	35	45

281 Marilyn Monroe

1994. Marilyn Monroe (American film star) Commemoration. Different portraits. Multicoloured.

2646	$1 Type **281**	55	65
2647	$1 Asleep	55	65
2648	$1 With long hair style and pendulum earrings	55	65
2649	$1 Wearing striped sweater	55	65
2650	$1 With gloved hand to face	55	65
2651	$1 With bare hand to face	55	65
2652	$1 In black and white dress	55	65
2653	$1 In sequined evening dress	55	65
2654	$1 With short hair and no earrings	55	65

282 Capt. Jean-Luc Picard

1994. "Star Trek – The Next Generation" (T.V. series). Multicoloured.

2655	$2 Type **282**	1·00	1·25
2656	$2 Commander William Riker	1·00	1·25
2657	$2 Lt.-Commander Data	1·00	1·25
2658	$2 Lt. Worf	1·00	1·25
2659	$2 Crew members	1·00	1·25
2660	$2 Dr. Beverley Crusher	1·00	1·25
2661	$2 Lt. Worf and Lt. Tasha Yar	1·00	1·25
2662	$2 Q wearing hat	1·00	1·25
2663	$2 Counsellor Deanna Troi	1·00	1·25
MS2664	83×101 mm. $10 As No. 2659 (59×40 mm)	4·50	6·00

283 Shigetatsu Matsunaga (Yokohama Marinos)

284 Jef United Team

1994. Japanese Professional Football League. (a) As **T 283** showing individual players and league emblem. Multicoloured.

2665-2676	55c. ×8, $1.50 ×4	8·50	9·00

DESIGNS: 55c. Masami Ihara (Yokohama Marinos); Shunzoh Ohno (Kashima Antlers); Luiz Carlos Pereira (Verdy Kawasaki); Tetsuji Hashiratani (Verdy Kawasaki); Carlos Alberto Souza dos Santos (Kashima Antlers); Yasuto Honda (Kashima Antlers); Kazuyoshi Miura (Verdy Kawasaki); $1.50, League emblem; Takumi Horiike (Shimizu S-Pulse); Rui Ramos (Verdy Kawasaki); Ramon Angel Diaz (Yokohama Marinos).

(b) As T **284** showing teams.

2677-2688	55c. ×8, $1.50 ×4	10·00	10·00

DESIGNS: 55c. Verdy Yomiuri; Yokohama Marinos; A. S. Flugels; Bellmare; Shimizu S-Pulse; Jubilo Iwata; Panasonic Gamba Osaka; $1.50, Kashima Antlers; Red Diamonds; Nagoya Grampus Eight; Sanfrecce Hiroshima.

(c) As T **284** showing players and teams.

2689-2694	55c.×3, $1.50×2, $3 A. S. Flugels	5·00	5·00
2695-2700	55c.×3, $1.50×2, $3 Bellmare	5·00	5·00
2701-2706	55c.×3, $1.50×2, $3 Panasonic Gamba Osaka	5·00	5·00
2707-2712	55c.×3, $1.50×2, $3 Jef United	5·00	5·00
2713-2718	55c.×3, $1.50×2, $3 Jubilo Iwata	5·00	5·00
2719-2724	55c.×3, $1.50×2, $3 Kashima Antlers	5·00	5·00
2725-2730	55c.×3, $1.50×2, $3 Nagoya Grampus Eight	5·00	5·00
2731-2736	55c.×3, $1.50×2, $3 Sanfrecce Hiroshima	5·00	5·00
2737-2742	55c.×3, $1.50×2, $3 Shimizu S-Pulse	5·00	5·00
2743-2748	55c.×3, $1.50×2, $3 Red Diamonds	5·00	5·00
2749-2754	55c.×3, $1.50×2, $3 Verdy Kawasaki	5·00	5·00
2755-2760	55c.×3, $1.50×2, $3 Yokohama Marinos	5·00	5·00

Prices quoted are for se-tenant sheetlets of six stamps.

284a Fred Whipple and Halley's Comet

1994. 25th Anniv of First Manned Moon Landing. Multicoloured.

2761	$1 Type **284a**	1·10	95
2762	$1 Robert Gilruth and "Gemini 12"	1·10	95
2763	$1 George Mueller and space walk from "Gemini 4"	1·10	95
2764	$1 Charles Berry and Johnsville Centrifuge	1·10	95
2765	$1 Christopher Kraft and "Apollo 4"	1·10	95
2766	$1 James van Allen and "Explorer 1"	1·10	95
2767	$1 Robert Goddard and Goddard liquid-fuel rocket	1·10	95
2768	$1 James Webb and "Spirit of 76" flight	1·10	95
2769	$1 Rocco Patrone and "Apollo 8"	1·10	95
2770	$1 Walter Dornberger and German rocket	1·10	95
2771	$1 Alexander Lippisch and Messerschmitt ME 163B Komet (airplane)	1·10	95
2772	$1 Kurt Debus and "A4b" rocket	1·10	95
2773	$1 Hermann Oberth and projected spaceship	1·10	95
2774	$1 Hanna Reitsch and "Reichenberg" flying bomb	1·10	95

2775	$1 Ernst Stuhlinger and "Explorer 1"	1·10	95
2776	$1 Werner von Braun and rocket-powered Heinkel He 112	1·10	95
2777	$1 Arthur Rudolph and rocket motor	1·10	95
2778	$1 Willy Ley and rocket airplane	1·10	95
MS2779	Two sheets, each 131×109 mm. (a) $6 Eberhardt Rees and German rocket (50×37 mm). (b) $6 Hogler Toftoy (50×37 mm)	8·00	9·00

284b Supply Convoy

1994. 50th Anniv of D-Day. Multicoloured.

2780	40c. Type **284b**	1·00	25
2781	$5 Unloading beached supply ship	3·25	3·75
MS2782	106×76 mm. $6 Liberty ship	3·50	4·25

285 Yorkshire Terrier Bitch

1994. Chinese New Year ("Year of the Dog"). Multicoloured.

2783	10c. Type **285**	60	35
2784	25c. Yorkshire terrier dog	65	30
2785	50c. Golden retriever	75	70
2786	50c. Pomeranian	75	70
2787	50c. English springer spaniel	75	70
2788	50c. Bearded collie	75	70
2789	50c. Irish wolfhound	75	70
2790	50c. Pekingese	75	70
2791	50c. Irish setter	75	70
2792	50c. Old English sheepdog	75	70
2793	50c. Basset hound	75	70
2794	50c. Cavalier King Charles spaniel	75	70
2795	50c. Kleiner Munsterlander	75	70
2796	50c. Shetland sheepdog	75	70
2797	50c. Dachshund	75	70
2798	65c. Bernese mountain dog	1·00	65
2799	$1 Vorstehhund	1·50	80
2800	$2 Tibetan terrier	2·25	1·75
2801	$4 West Highland terrier	3·25	3·25
2802	$5 Shih tzu	3·50	3·50
MS2803	Two sheets, each 100×100 mm. (a) $6 Afghan hound with puppy. (b) $6 German shepherd. Set of 2 sheets	7·00	7·00

285a Peter Fennel (Germany) (20 km walk, 1972)

1994. Centenary of International Olympic Committee. Gold Medal Winners.

2804	45c. Type **285a**	60	25
2805	50c. Kijung Son (Japan) (marathon), 1936 (vert)	65	30
2806	75c. Jesse Owens (U.S.A.) (100 and 200 m), 1936 (vert)	90	80
2807	$1 Greg Louganis (U.S.A.) (diving), 1984 and 1988 (vert)	1·00	1·10
MS2808	106×76 mm. 86 Katja Seizinger (Germany) (women's downhill skiing), 1944 (horiz)	3·50	4·00

286 Mark Ramprakash (England) and Wisden Trophy

1994. Centenary of First English Cricket Tour to the West Indies (1995). Multicoloured.

2809	10c. Type **286**	45	20
2810	30c. Phil Simmonds (West Indies) and Wisden Trophy	65	25
2811	$2 Garfield Sobers (West Indies) (vert)	1·75	2·00
MS2812	76×96 mm. $3 First English touring team, 1895 (black and brown)	2·50	2·75

286a Oryon Waterfall

1994. "Philakorea '94" International Stamp Exhibition, Seoul. Multicoloured.

2813	10c. Type **286a**	30	20
2814	45c. Indoor sports stadium, Pyongyang (horiz)	40	25
2815	50c. Illuminated character with house at bottom right	40	50
2816	50c. Illuminated character with red dots in centre	40	50
2817	50c. Illuminated character with animal at right	40	50
2818	50c. Illuminated character with flowers at bottom right	40	50
2819	50c. Illuminated character with dragon at left	40	50
2820	50c. Illuminated character with house at top	40	50
2821	50c. Illuminated character with dragon at top	40	50
2822	50c. Illuminated character with sun at top	40	50
2823	50c. Fish and character	40	50
2824	50c. Two pheasants and character	40	50
2825	50c. Plant and cabinet	40	50
2826	50c. Vases and cabinet	40	50
2827	50c. Books on decorated cabinet	40	50
2828	50c. Pheasant, decorated cabinet and vase	40	50
2829	50c. Pheasant and lamp on table	40	50
2830	50c. Cabinet, vase and table	40	50
2831	65c. Pombong, Chonhwadae	40	50
2832	75c. Uisangdae, Naksansa	55	60
2833	$1 Buddha of the Sokkuram Grotto, Kyangju (horiz)	60	70
2834	$2 Moksogwon (horiz)	1·10	1·40
MS2835	Two sheets. (a) 70×100 mm. $4 Chongdong Mirukbul (vert). (b) 100×70 mm. Tiger hunting scene (embroidery). Set of 2 sheets	3·50	4·25

Nos. 2825/6 and 2830 are inscr "Bookshlef" in error.

287 St. Vincent Family

1994. International Year of the Family (2nd issue).

2836	**287**	75c. multicoloured	65	65

288 Sir Shridath Ramphal and Map of Guyana

1994. First Recipients of Order of the Caribbean Community. Multicoloured.

2837	$1 Type **288**	70	50
2838	$2 Derek Walcott and map of St. Lucia	2·75	2·25
2839	$5 William Demas and map of Trinidad (horiz)	3·75	5·00

No. 2838 is inscribed "Wilcott" in error.

289 Twin-engined Airliner, Bequia Airport

1994. 50th Anniv of I.C.A.O. Multicoloured.

2840	10c. Type **289**	40	40
2841	65c. Union Island Airport	80	60
2842	75c. L.I.A.T. 8-100 at E. T. Joshua Airport	85	70
2843	$1 Aircraft and logo	1·00	1·25
2844	$1 Britten Norman Islander at J. F. Mitchell Airport, Bequia	1·00	1·25

290 "The Annunciation"

1994. Christmas. Religious Paintings from Jean de Berry's "Book of Hours". Multicoloured.

2845	10c. Type **290**	25	10
2846	45c. "The Visitation"	60	25
2847	50c. "The Nativity"	65	30
2848	65c. "The Purification of the Virgin" (detail)	80	40
2849	75c. "Presentation of Jesus in the Temple"	90	45
2850	$5 "Flight into Egypt"	4·00	6·00
MS2851	110×126 mm. $6 "Adoration of the Magi" (detail)	4·00	5·50

No. 2847 is inscribed "The Annunciation" in error.

1995. Chinese New Year ("Year of the Pig") (1st issue). Designs as Nos. 2050/8, but with different face values and with Year of the Pig logo.

2852	30c. Type **245**	60	50
2853	30c. Fiddler Pig building house of sticks	60	50
2854	30c. Practical Pig building house of bricks	60	50
2855	30c. The Big Bad Wolf	60	50
2856	30c. Wolf scaring Fiddler and Fifer Pig	60	50
2857	30c. Wolf blowing down straw house	60	50
2858	30c. Wolf in sheep costume	60	50
2859	30c. Wolf blowing down stick house	60	50
2860	30c. Wolf attempting to blow down brick house	60	50
MS2861	Two sheets. (a) 103×128 mm. $3 Original sketch of Practical Pig building house of brick. (b) 128×103 mm. $3 Practical Pig playing piano (vert). Set of 2 sheets	5·50	5·50

See also Nos. 2900/3.

291 Mealy Amazon Parrot

1995. Parrots. Multicoloured.

2862	$1 Type **291**	1·10	90
2863	$1 Nanday conure	1·10	90
2864	$1 Black-headed caique	1·10	90
2865	$1 Scarlet macaw	1·10	90
2866	$1 Red-masked conure	1·10	90
2867	$1 Blue-headed parrot	1·10	90
2868	$1 Hyacinth macaw	1·10	90
2869	$1 Sun conure	1·10	90
2870	$1 Blue and yellow macaw	1·10	90
MS2871	104×76 mm. $5 White-eared conure (vert)	4·00	4·50

Nos. 2862/70 were printed together, *se-tenant*, forming a composite design.

292 Snowshoe

1995. Cats. Multicoloured.

2872	$1 Type **292**	1·10	90
2873	$1 Abyssinian	1·10	90
2874	$1 Ocicat	1·10	90
2875	$1 Tiffany	1·10	90
2876	$1 Russian blue	1·10	90
2877	$1 Siamese	1·10	90
2878	$1 Bi-colour	1·10	90
2879	$1 Malayan	1·10	90
2880	$1 Manx	1·10	90
MS2881	104×76 mm. $6 Birman (vert)	4·75	5·50

Nos. 2872/80 were printed together, *se-tenant*, forming a composite design.

293 Blue-faced Booby ("Masked Booby")

1995. Birds. Multicoloured.

2882	75c. Type **293**	70	60
2883	75c. Pair of blue-faced boobies	70	60
2884	75c. Blue-faced booby preening	70	60
2885	75c. Blue-faced booby stretching	70	60
2886	75c. Great egrets	70	60
2887	75c. Roseate spoonbills	70	60
2888	75c. Ring-billed gull	70	60
2889	75c. Ruddy quail dove	70	60
2890	75c. Royal terns	70	60
2891	75c. Killdeer plover ("Killdeer")	70	60
2892	75c. Osprey	70	60
2893	75c. Magnificent frigate bird	70	60
2894	75c. Blue-faced boobies ("Masked Booby")	70	60
2895	75c. Green-backed heron	70	60
2896	75c. Double-crested cormorants ("Cormorant")	70	60
2897	75c. Brown pelican	70	60
MS2898	Two sheets, each 100×69 mm. (a) $5 Greater flamingo ("Flamingo") (vert). (b) $6 American Purple gallinule ("Purple Gallinule") (vert). Set of 2 sheets	10·00	10·00

Nos. 2886/97 were printed together, *se-tenant*, forming a composite design.

294 Churchill, Roosevelt and Stalin at Yalta Conference

1995. 50th Anniv of V.E. Day.

2899	**294**	$1 multicoloured	1·25	1·00

295 Pig

1995. Chinese New Year ("Year of the Pig") (2nd issue). Multicoloured, central panel in colours indicated.

2900	75c. Type **295** (green)	55	65
2901	75c. Pig (brown)	55	65
2902	75c. Pig (red)	55	65
MS2903	71×101 mm. $2 Two pigs (horiz)	1·25	1·50

296 National Flag and Globe

1995. 18th World Scout Jamboree, Netherlands. Multicoloured.

2904	$1 Type **296**	70	50
2905	$4 Lord Baden-Powell	2·25	2·75
2906	$5 Handshake	2·50	3·00
MS2907	Two sheets, each 81×112 mm. (a) $6 Scout greeting. (b) $6 Scout salute. Set of 2 sheets	7·00	8·50

296a Tank of U.S. First Army

1995. 50th Anniv of End of Second World War in Europe. Multicoloured.

2908	$2 Type **296a**	1·25	1·25

2909	$2 V2 rocket	1·25	1·25
2910	$2 Consolidated B-24 Liberator bombers	1·25	1·25
2911	$2 French troops advancing to Strasbourg	1·25	1·25
2912	$2 Gloster G.41 Meteor fighter	1·25	1·25
2913	$2 Berlin on fire	1·25	1·25
2914	$2 Soviet tanks in Berlin	1·25	1·25
2915	$2 "Chicago Daily Tribune" headline	1·25	1·25
MS2916	107×77 mm. $6 Sortie markings on aircraft (57×42½)	3·50	4·00

No. 2909 is inscribed "Y2" in error.

297 Globe and Peace Dove

1995. 50th Anniv of United Nations. Multicoloured.

2917	$2 Type **297**	1·10	1·40
2918	$2 Liberty	1·10	1·40
2919	$2 U.N. Building, New York, and peace dove	1·10	1·40
MS2920	71×107 mm. $6 Asian child	2·75	3·50

Nos. 2917/19 were printed together, *se-tenant*, forming a composite design.
No. **MS**2920 is inscribed "1945–1955" in error.

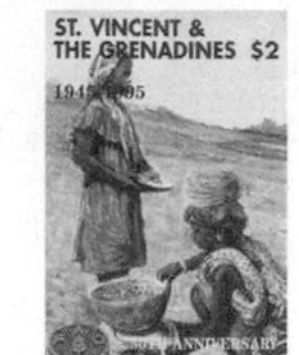

298 Women preparing Food

1995. 50th Anniv of F.A.O. Multicoloured.

2921	$2 Type **298**	1·10	1·40
2922	$2 Woman mixing food	1·10	1·40
2923	$2 Harvesting grain	1·10	1·40
MS2924	76×106 mm. 76×106 mm. $6 Baby and logo	2·75	3·50

Nos. 2921/3 were printed together, *se-tenant*, forming a composite design.
No. **MS**2924 is inscribed "1945–1955" in error.

299 Paul Harris (founder) and Logo

1995. 90th Anniv of Rotary International.

2925	**299**	$5 multicoloured	2·50	3·25
MS2926		113×79 mm. $6 National flag and logo	2·75	3·50

299a Queen Elizabeth the Queen Mother (pastel drawing)

1995. 95th Birthday of Queen Elizabeth the Queen Mother.

2927	**299a**	$1.50 brown, light brown and black	2·00	1·50
2928	-	$1.50 multicoloured	2·00	1·50
2929	-	$1.50 multicoloured	2·00	1·50
2930	-	$1.50 multicoloured	2·00	1·50
MS2931		102×127 mm. $6 multicoloured	4·75	4·75

DESIGNS: No. 2928, Wearing blue hat; 2929, At desk (oil painting); 2930, Wearing mauve dress; No. **MS**2931, wearing yellow dress.

1995. 50th Anniv of End of Second World War in the Pacific. As **T 296a**. Multicoloured.

2932	$2 Douglas Devastator torpedo bomber	1·25	1·25
2933	$2 Doolittle's North American B-25 Mitchell "Ruptured Duck"	1·25	1·25
2934	$2 Curtiss SB2C Helldiver bomber	1·25	1·25
2935	$2 U.S.S. "Yorktown" (aircraft carrier)	1·25	1·25
2936	$2 U.S.S. "Wasp" (aircraft carrier)	1·25	1·25
2937	$2 U.S.S. "Lexington" (aircraft carrier) sinking	1·25	1·25
MS2938	107×77 mm. $6 American aircraft carriers	3·75	4·50

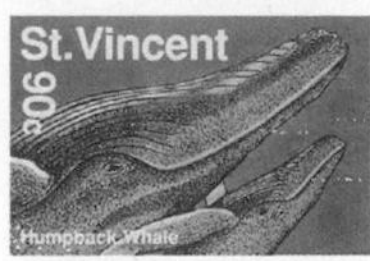

300 Head of Humpback Whale

1995. Marine Life. Multicoloured.

2939	90c. Type **300**	70	70
2940	90c. Green turtles	70	70
2941	90c. Bottlenose dolphin	70	70
2942	90c. Monk seals	70	70
2943	90c. Krill	70	70
2944	90c. Blue sharks	70	70
2945	90c. Porkfish	70	70
2946	90c. Reef butterflyfish	70	70
2947	90c. Shipwreck	70	70
2948	$1 Beaugregory (fish) (horiz)	70	70
2949	$1 Grey angelfish (horiz)	70	70
2950	$1 Yellow-tailed damselfish (horiz)	70	70
2951	$1 Four-eyed butterflyfish (horiz)	70	70
MS2952	Two sheets, each 100×70 mm. (a) $6 Sea anemones. (b) $6 "Physalia physalis" (jellyfish). Set of 2 sheets	7·00	7·50

Nos. 2939/47 were printed together, *se-tenant*, forming a composite design.

301 Symbolic Disabled Athlete

1995. Paralympic Games '95, Connecticut.

2953	**301**	$1 yellow, blue and black	1·00	1·00

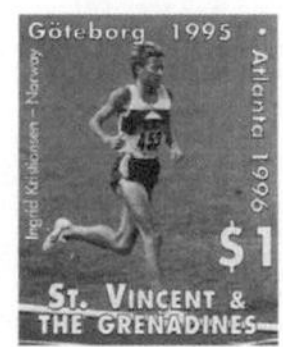

302 Ingrid Kristiansen

1995. World Athletic Championships, Gothenburg. Norwegian Athletes. Multicoloured.

2954	$1 Type **302**	70	70
2955	$1 Trine Hattestad	70	70
2956	$1 Grete Waitz	70	70
2957	$1 Vebjorn Rodal	70	70
2958	$1 Geir Moen	70	70
2959	$1 Steinar Hoen (horiz)	70	70

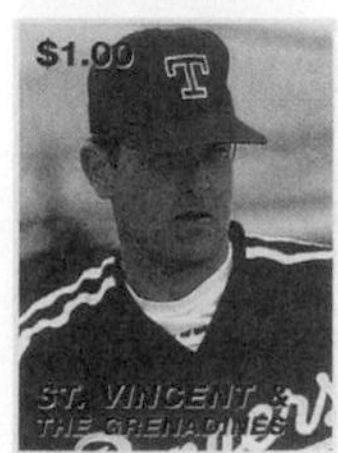

303 Nolan Ryan in Blue Jersey

1995. Retirement of Nolan Ryan (baseball player) (1993). Multicoloured.

2960	$1 Type **303**	60	80
2961	$1 With glove	60	80
2962	$1 In white jersey	60	80
2963	$1 Making pitch from left	60	80
2964	$1 Texas Rangers "All Star Game" emblem	60	80
2965	$1 Making pitch from right	60	80
2966	$1 Bleeding from blow to mouth	60	80
2967	$1 Preparing to pitch	60	80
2968	$1 Waving cap	60	80
2969	$1 Wearing "NY" cap	60	80
2970	$1 Wearing stetson with dog	60	80
2971	$1 Wearing "T" cap	60	80
2972	$1 Throwing American football	60	80
2973	$1 Nolan Ryan Foundation emblem	60	80
2974	$1 With son	60	80
2975	$1 Laughing	60	80
2976	$1 With family	60	80
2977	$1 Wearing "H" cap	60	80
MS2978	146×101 mm. $6 After final game for Texas Rangers	2·50	3·25

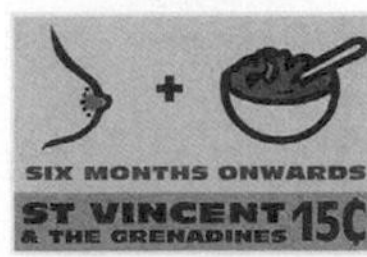

304 Breast and Bowl of Baby Food

1995. "Baby Friendly" Campaign. Multicoloured.

2979	15c. Type **304**	40	15
2980	20c. Hands squeezing milk into bowl (vert)	40	15
2981	90c. Breast-feeding (vert)	1·00	45
2982	$5 Breast-feeding emblem (vert)	3·50	4·50

305 Aerial View of Leeward Coastal Road

1995. 25th Anniv of Caribbean Development Bank. Multicoloured.

2983	10c. Type **305**	25	25
2984	15c. Feeder roads project	30	25
2985	25c. "Anthurium andraeanum" (flower)	30	25
2986	50c. Coconut palm tree (vert)	35	35
2987	65c. Fairhall Housing Scheme	45	45

306 "The God of Fire" (woodcut) (Shunichi Kadowaki)

1995. Japanese Art.

2988	**306**	$1.40 multicoloured	1·00	1·25

307 Jean Shiley (U.S.A.) (high jump)

1995. Olympic Games, Atlanta (1996) (1st issue). Multicoloured.

2989	$1 Type **307**	75	75
2990	$1 Ruth Fuchs (Germany) (javelin)	75	75
2991	$1 Alessandro Andrei (Italy) (shot put)	75	75
2992	$1 Dorando Pietri (Italy) (marathon)	75	75
2993	$1 Heide Rosendahl (Germany) (long jump)	75	75
2994	$1 Mitsuoki Watanabe (Japan) (gymnastics)	75	75
2995	$1 Yasuhiro Yamashita (Japan) (judo)	75	75
2996	$1 Dick Fosbury (U.S.A.) (high jump)	75	75
2997	$2 Long jumper and dove	1·10	1·10
2998	$2 Hurdler and deer	1·10	1·10
2999	$2 Sprinter and cheetah	1·10	1·10
3000	$2 Marathon runner and tiger	1·10	1·10
3001	$2 Gymnast and dove	1·10	1·10
3002	$2 Rower and blue-winged teal	1·10	1·10
MS3003	Two sheets. (a) 70×100 mm. $5 Magic Johnson (U.S.A.) (basketball). (b) 106×76 mm. $5 Swimmers hand (horiz). Set of 2 sheets	6·50	7·50

See also Nos. 3357/3400.

308 Frank Thomas

1995. Famous Baseball Players (8th series). Multicoloured.

3004	$1 Type **308**	60	60
3005	$1 Cal Ripken Jnr wearing "8" jersey and helmet	60	60
3006	$1 Ken Griffey Jnr wearing "S" cap	60	60
3007	$1 Ken Griffey Jnr wearing turquoise-blue jersey	60	60
3008	$1 Frank Thomas in "Sox" cap with bat on shoulder	60	60
3009	$1 Cal Ripken Jnr with ball and glove	60	60
3010	$1 Cal Ripkin Jnr wearing Orioles cap	60	60
3011	$1 Ken Griffey Jnr wearing "Seattle" jersey and helmet	60	60
3012	$1 Frank Thomas wearing "Chicago 35" jersey	60	60

309 John Lennon

1995. Centenary of Cinema. Entertainers. Multicoloured.

	Set of 51	28·00	30·00
3013-3021	$1×9 John Lennon (as T **309**)	6·00	
3022-3030	$1×9 Elvis Presley	6·00	
3031-3036	$1×6 Elvis Presley	4·50	
3037-3045	$1×9 Marilyn Monroe (with stairway in centre of sheetlet)	5·00	
3046-3054	$1×9 Marilyn Monroe (with superimposed full length portrait)	5·00	
3055-3063	$1×9 Marilyn Monroe (design with hand raised in centre of top row)	5·00	
MS3064	Four sheets. (a) 110×80 mm. $6 John Lennon. (b) 80×110 mm. $6 Elvis Presley. (c) 80×110 mm. $6 Marilyn Monroe wearing red jacket. (d) 70×100 mm. $6 Marilyn Monroe in black slip. Set of 4 sheets	11·00	14·00

310 Heinrich Boll (1972 Literature)

1995. Centenary of Nobel Prize Trust Fund. Multicoloured.

3065-3112	$1 ×48	32·00	35·00
MS3113	Four sheets, each 74×104 mm. (a) $6 Adolf Windaus (1928 Chemistry). (b) $6 Hideki Yukawa (1949 Physics). (c) $6 Bertha von Suttner (1905 Peace). (d) $6 Karl Landsteiner (1930 Medicine). Set of 4 sheets	16·00	16·00

DESIGNS: No. 3065, Type **310**; 3066, Walther Bothe (1954 Physics); 3067, Richard Kuhn (1938 Chemistry); 3068, Hermann Hesse (1946 Literature); 3069, Knut Hamsun (1920 Literature); 3070, Konrad Lorenz (1973 Medicine); 3071, Thomas Mann (1929 Literature); 3072, Fridtjof Nansen (1922 Peace); 3073, Fritz Pregl (1923 Chemistry); 3074, Christian Lange (1921 Peace); 3075, Otto Loewi (1936 Medicine); 3076, Erwin Schrodinger (1933 Physics); 3077, Giosue Carducci (1906 Literature); 3078, Wladyslaw Reymont (1924 Literature); 3079, Ivan Bunin (1933 Literature); 3080, Pavel Cherenkov (1958 Physics); 3081, Ivan Pavlov (1904 Medicine); 3082, Pyotr Kapitza (1978 Physics); 3083, Lev Landau (1962 Physics); 3084, Daniel Bovet (1957 Medicine); 3085, Henryk Sienkiewicz (1905 Literature); 3086, Aleksandr Prokhorov (1964 Physics); 3087, Julius von Jauregg (1927 Medicine); 3088, Grazia Deledda (1926 Literature); 3089, Bjornstjerne Bjornson (1903 Literature); 3090, Frank Kellogg (1929 Peace); 3091, Gustav Hertz (1925 Physics); 3092, Har Khorana (1968 Medicine); 3093, Kenichi Fukui (1981 Chemistry); 3094, Henry Kissinger (1973 Peace); 3095, Martin Luther King Jr. (1964 Peace); 3096, Odd Hassel (1969 Chemistry); 3097, Polykarp Kusch (1955 Physics); 3098, Ragnar Frisch (1969 Economics); 3099, Willis Lamb Jr. (1955 Physics); 3100, Sigrid Undset (1928 Literature); 3101, Robert Barany (1914 Medicine); 3102, Ernest Walton (1951 Physics); 3103, Alfred Fried (1911 Peace); 3104, James Franck (1925 Physics); 3105, Werner Forssmann (1956 Medicine); 3106, Yasunari Kawabata (1968 Literature); 3107, Wolfgang Pauli (1945 Physics); 3108, Jean-Paul Sartre (1964 Literature); 3109, Aleksandr Solzhenitsyn (1970 Literature); 3110, Hermann Staudinger (1953 Chemistry); 3111, Igor Tamm (1958 Physics); 3112, Samuel Beckett (1969 Literature).

311 ET4-03 Electric Train, Germany

1995. History of Transport. Modern passenger trains (Nos. 3114/19) or classic cars (Nos. 3120/5). Multicoloured.

3114	$1.50 Type **311**	1·40	1·10
3115	$1.50 TGV express train, France	1·40	1·10
3116	$1.50 Class 87 electric locomotive, Great Britain	1·40	1·10
3117	$1.50 Class "Beijing" diesel locomotive, China	1·40	1·10
3118	$1.50 Amtrak turbotrain, U.S.A.	1·40	1·10
3119	$1.50 Class RC4 electric train, Sweden	1·40	1·10
3120	$1.50 Duesenberg Model "J", 1931	1·40	1·10
3121	$1.50 Sleeve-valve Minerva, 1913	1·40	1·10
3122	$1.50 Delage "D.8. SS", 1933	1·40	1·10
3123	$1.50 Bugatti "Royale Coupe De Ville", 1931–32	1·40	1·10
3124	$1.50 Rolls Royce "Phantom I Landauette", 1926	1·40	1·10
3125	$1.50 Mercedes Benz "S236/120/180PS", 1927	1·40	1·10
MS3126	Two sheets, each 105×75 mm. (a) $5 Hispano-Suiza Type "H6B" sports car, 1924 (85×28½ mm). (b) $6 Eurostar train, Great Britain and France (85×28½ mm). Set of 2 sheets	8·00	9·00

Nos. 3120/5 also include the "Singapore '95" International Stamp Exhibition logo.

312 Grey Wolf

1995. Centenary (1992) of Sierra Club (environmental protection society). Multicoloured.

3127	$1 Type **312**	85	75
3128	$1 Grey wolf cub	85	75
3129	$1 Head of grey wolf	85	75
3130	$1 Hawaiian goose	85	75
3131	$1 Pair of Hawaiian geese	85	75
3132	$1 Head of jaguar	85	75
3133	$1 Liontail macaque	85	75
3134	$1 Sand cat kitten	85	75
3135	$1 Three sand cat kittens	85	75
3136	$1 Orang-utan in tree (horiz)	85	75
3137	$1 Orang-utan on ground (horiz)	85	75
3138	$1 Young orang-utan (horiz)	85	75
3139	$1 Jaguar lying down (horiz)	85	75
3140	$1 Head of jaguar (horiz)	85	75
3141	$1 Pair of sand cats (horiz)	85	75
3142	$1 Hawaiian goose (horiz)	85	75
3143	$1 Three liontail macaques (horiz)	85	75
3144	$1 Head of liontail macaque (horiz)	85	75

Nos. 3136/8 are inscribed "Orangutang" in error.

313 River Nile, Egypt

1995. Natural Landmarks. Multicoloured.

3145	$1.10 Type **313**	1·00	85
3146	$1.10 River Yangtze, China	1·00	85
3147	$1.10 Niagara Falls, U.S.A.–Canada border	1·00	85
3148	$1.10 Victoria Falls, Zambia–Zimbabwe border	1·00	85
3149	$1.10 Grand Canyon, U.S.A.	1·00	85
3150	$1.10 Sahara Desert, Algeria	1·00	85
3151	$1.10 Mt. Kilimanjaro, Tanzania	1·00	85
3152	$1.10 River Amazon, Brazil	1·00	85
MS3153	106×76 mm. $6 Haleakala Crater, Hawaii	4·00	4·50

314 Lionel Santa Handcar

1995. Christmas. Antique Disney Toys. Multicoloured.

3154	1c. Type **314**	10	10
3155	2c. Mickey Mouse "choo-choo"	10	10
3156	3c. Minnie Mouse pram	10	10
3157	5c. Mickey Mouse acrobats pull-toy	10	10
3158	10c. Mickey and Pluto clock-work cart	20	10
3159	25c. Mickey Mouse motorcycle	55	10
3160	$3 Lionel Mickey Mouse handcar	3·50	3·75
3161	$5 Casey Jr. Disneyland train	5·50	6·00
MS3162	Two sheets. (a) 127×100 mm. $6 Lionel streamlined locomotive and Mickey Mouse wagon. (b) 100×127 mm. $6 "Silver Link" locomotive and Mickey the Stoker tender. Set of 2 sheets	10·00	10·00

314a Croton

1996. Crotons. Multicoloured.

3162a	10c. Type **314a**	50	20
3162b	15c. *Codiaeum* "prince of monaco"	50	20
3162c	20c. *Codiaeum variagatum* "craigii"		5·00
3162d	40c. *Codiaeum variagatum* "gloriosum"	50	50
3162e	50c. *Croton* "ebureum" (vert)	50	50
3162f	60c. *Croton* "volutum ramshorn" (vert)	50	50
3162g	70c. *Codiaeum variagatum* "narrenii" (vert)	50	50
3162h	90c. *Croton* "undutatum" (vert)	1·00	1·00
3162i	$1 *Codiaeum variagatum* "carib-bean star"	1·00	1·00
3162j	$1.10 *Codiaeum variagatum* "gloriosa"	1·00	1·00
3162k	$1.40 *Codiaeum variagatum croton* "katonii"	1·50	1·50
3162l	$2 *Codiaeum variagatum* "appleleaf" ("croton")	2·00	2·00
3162m	$5 *Codiaeum variagatum tapestry* "croton"	3·00	3·00
3162n	€10 *Codiaeum variagatum* "cornutum"	5·00	5·00
3162o	$20 *Codiaeum variagatum* "punctatum aureum"	10·00	10·00

315 Symbolic Rat

1996. Chinese New Year ("Year of the Rat").

3163	**315**	75c. black, mauve and green	50	60
3164	-	75c. black, red and green	50	60
3165	-	75c. black, purple and green	50	60
MS3166		100×50 mm. $1 Type **315**; $1 As No. 3164; $1 As No. 3165	1·50	1·60
MS3167		71×102 mm. $2 black, red and green	1·25	1·50

DESIGNS: Nos. 3164/5, Different rats.

316 Spock giving Vulcan Salute

1996. 30th Anniv of "Star Trek" Television Series. Multicoloured.

3168	$1 Type **316**	60	55
3169	$1 Capt. Kirk and Spock dressed as gangsters	60	55
3170	$1 Kirk in front of computer	60	55
3171	$1 Kirk with Tribbles	60	55
3172	$1 Kirk, Spock and Lt. Uhura in front of Time Portal	60	55
3173	$1 Uhura and Lt. Sulu	60	55
3174	$1 Romulan commander and crew	60	55
3175	$1 City and planet	60	55
3176	$1 Khan	60	55
3177	$1 Spock with phaser	60	55
3178	$1 Capt. Kirk	60	55
3179	$1 Lt. Uhura	60	55
3180	$1 Lt. Sulu	60	55
3181	$1 Starship U.S.S. "Enterprise"	50	55
3182	$1 Dr. McCoy	60	55
3183	$1 Chief Engineer Scott	60	55
3184	$1 Kirk, Spock and McCoy	60	55
3185	$1 Chekov	60	55
MS3186	152×107 mm. $6 Spock and Uhura	3·25	3·50

317 Goofy the Stamp Dealer

1996. Occupations (1st series). Walt Disney Cartoon Characters at Work. Multicoloured.

3187–3195	10c. ×9 (Type **317**; Supermarket assistant; Car salesman; Florist; Fast food assistant; Street vendor; Gift shop assistant; Hobby shop assistant; Baker)	1·60	
3196–3204	50c. ×9 (Delivery man; Truck driver; Aircraft flight crew; Train crew; Bus driver; Tour guide; Cycle messenger; Tram conductor; Air traffic controller)	5·00	
3205–3213	75c. ×9 (Postal inspector; Traffic policeman; Private detectives; Highway Patrolman; Justice of the Peace; Security guard; Judge and lawyer; Sheriff; Court stenographer)	6·00	
3214–3222	90c. ×9 (Basketball player; Referee; Athletic coach; Ice skater; Golfer and caddy; Sports commentator; Tennis players; Football coach; Racing car driver)	9·00	
3223–3231	95c. ×9 (Paleontologist; Archaeologist; Inventor; Astronaut; Chemist; Engineer; Computer expert; Astronomer; Zoologist)	8·00	
3232–3239	$1.10 ×8 (Classroom teacher; Nursery school teacher; Music teacher; Electronic teacher; School psychologist; School principal; Professor; Graduate (all vert))	8·00	
3240–3248	$1.20 ×9 (Ship builders; Fisherman; Pearl diver; Underwater photographer; Bait and tackle shop owner; Swim suit models; Marine life painter; Life guard; Lighthouse keeper)	9·00	
MS3249	Seven sheets, each 127×102 mm. (a) $6 Ice cream seller. (b) $6 Tug boat captain (vert). (c) $6 Members of Jury (vert). (d) $6 Cheerleaders (vert). (e) $6 Oceanographer. (f) $6 Librarian (vert). (g) $6 Deep sea diver (vert). Set of 7 sheets	35·00	40·00

See also Nos. 3510/56.

317a "Moses striking Rock" (Abraham Bloemaert)

1996. 125th Anniv of Metropolitan Museum of Art, New York. Multicoloured.

3250–3257	75c. ×8 (Type **317a**; "The Last Communion" (Botticelli); "The Musicians" (Caravaggio); "Francesco Sassetti and Son" (Ghirlandaio); "Pepito Costa y Bunells" (Goya); "Saint Andrew" (Martini); "The Nativity" (The Dutch School); "Christ Blessing" (Solario))	4·00	
3258–3266	90c. ×9 ("Madame Cezanne"; "Still Life with Apples and Pears"; "Man in a Straw Hat"; "Still Life with a Ginger Jar"; "Madame Cezanne in a Red Dress"; "Still Life with Crockery"; "Dominique Aubert"; "Still Life with Flowers"; "The Card Players" (all by Cezanne))	4·50	
3267–3275	$1 ×9 ("Bullfight" (Goya); "Portrait of a Man" (Hals); "Mother and Son" (Sully); "Portrait of a Young Man" (Memling); "Matilde Stoughton de Jaudenes" (Stuart); "Josef de Jaudenes y Nebot" (Stuart); "Mont Sainte-Victoire" (Cezanne); "Gardanne" (Cezanne); "Empress Eugenie" (Winterhalter))	4·75	
3276–3284	$1.10 ×9 ("The Dissolute Household" (Steen); "Gerard de Lairesse" (Rembrandt); "Juan de Pareja" (Velazquez); "Curiosity" (Ter Borch); "The Companions of Rinaldo" (Poussin); "Don Gaspar de Guzman" (Velazquez); "Merry Company on a Terrace" (Steen); "Pilate washing Hands" (Rembrandt); "Portrait of a Man" (Van Dyck))	5·00	
MS3285	Four sheets, each 95×70 mm. (a) $6 "Hagar in the Wilderness" (Corot) (81×53 mm). (b) $6 "Two Young Peasant Women" (Pissarro) (81×53 mm). (c) $6 "Young Ladies from the Village" (Courbet) (81×53 mm). (d) $6 "Allegory of the Planets and Continents" (Tiepolo) (81×53 mm). Set of 4 sheets	13·00	15·00

318 Alien Band

319 Yoda

1996. "Star Wars" (film trilogy). Multicoloured. (a) As **T 318**.

3286	35c. Type **318**	1·00	90
3287	35c. Darth Vader in battle	1·00	90
3288	35c. Fighter ship	1·00	90
3289	35c. Space craft orbiting planet	1·00	90
3290	35c. Space craft and shuttle	1·00	90
3291	35c. Luke Skywalker on space bike	1·00	90

(b) As T **319**. Self-adhesive.

3292	$1 Darth Vader	1·90	1·75
3293	$1 Type **319**	1·90	1·75
3294	$1 Storm trooper	1·90	1·75
MS3295	148×71 mm. $2 ×3 Designs as Nos. 3292/4 but triangular, 65×36½ mm.	5·00	6·50

320 "Anteos menippe"

1996. Butterflies. Multicoloured.

3296	70c. Type **320**	50	40
3297	90c. "Papilio lycophron"	60	60
3298	90c. "Prepona buckleyana"	60	60
3299	90c. "Parides agavus"	60	60
3300	90c. "Papilio cacicus"	60	60
3301	90c. "Euryades duponchelli"	60	60
3302	90c. "Diaethria dymena"	60	60
3303	90c. "Orimba jansoni"	60	60
3304	90c. "Polystichtis siaka"	60	60
3305	90c. "Papilio machaonides"	60	60
3306	$1 "Eunica alcmena"	70	70
3307	$1.10 "Doxocopa lavinia"	80	80
3308	$2 "Tithorea tarricina"	1·40	1·60
MS3309	Two sheets, each 75×104 mm. (a) $5 "Adelpha albia". (b) $6 "Themone pais". Set of 2 sheets	6·50	7·50

Nos. 3297/3305 were printed together, *se-tenant*, the backgrounds forming a composite design.

321 Michael Jordan (basketball player)

1996. Sports Legends. (a) As **T 321**. Multicoloured. Perf.

3310	$2 Type **321**	1·00	1·25

3311 $2 Joe Montana (American footballer) 1·00 1·25

(b) Size 69×103 mm. Imperf.

3312 $6 Michael Jordan 5·00 7·00
3313 $10 Joe Montana 7·00 10·00

322 The Monkey King

1996. "CHINA '96" 9th Asian International Stamp Exhibition (1st issue). Chinese Animated Films – "Uproar in Heaven" (Nos. 3314/18) and "Nezha conquers the Dragon King" (Nos. 3319/23). Multicoloured.

3314 15c. Type **322** 20 25
3315 15c. Monkey King flying towards illuminated pole 20 25
3316 15c. Monkey King and flying horses 20 25
3317 15c. Monkey King picking fruit 20 25
3318 15c. Monkey King drinking from flask 20 25
3319 15c. Nezha waking up 20 25
3320 15c. Nezha swimming with fish 20 25
3321 15c. Nezha on back of sea serpent 20 25
3322 15c. Nezha with sword 20 25
3323 15c. Nezha in battle 20 25
MS3324 Two sheets, each 85×105 mm. (a) 75c. Monkey King (vert). (b) 75 c. Nezha (vert). Set of 2 sheets 1·40 1·60

323 Chongqing Dazu Buddha

1996. "CHINA '96" 9th Asian International Stamp Exhibition (2nd issue). Sheet 115×80 mm.

MS3325 **323** $2 multicoloured 1·40 1·60

323a Queen Elizabeth II

1996. 70th Birthday of Queen Elizabeth II. Showing different photographs. Multicoloured.

3326 $2 Type **323a** 1·50 1·50
3327 $2 Wearing Garter robes 1·50 1·50
3328 $2 Wearing pink hat and coat 1·50 1·50
MS3329 125×103 mm. $6 On Buckingham Palace balcony (horiz) 4·25 4·50

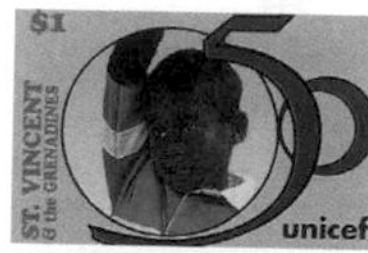

324 West Indian Boy

1996. 50th Anniv of UNICEF. Multicoloured.

3330 $1 Type **324** 60 55
3331 $1.10 European girl 70 65
3332 $2 South-east Asian girl 1·25 1·40
MS3333 104×74 mm. $5 Arab boy 2·50 3·00

325 Menorah and The Knesset

1996. 3000th Anniv of Jerusalem. Multicoloured.

3334 $1 Type **325** 1·00 55
3335 $1.10 The Montefiore Windmill 1·00 70
3336 $2 Shrine of the Book 1·40 1·60
MS3337 104×74 mm. $5 Old City, Jerusalem 4·00 3·50

The captions on Nos. 3334 and 3336 were transposed in error.

326 Walter Winchell

1996. Centenary of Radio. Entertainers. Multicoloured.

3338 90c. Type **326** 55 50
3339 $1 Fred Allen 60 55
3340 $1.10 Hedda Hopper 70 65
3341 $2 Eve Arden 1·00 1·40
MS3342 72×102 mm. $6 Major Bowes 2·50 3·25

327 Bananaquit

1996. Birds. Multicoloured.

3343 60c. Type **327** 70 45
3344 $1 Rufous-throated solitare 85 60
3345 $1 Caribbean martin (horiz) 85 80
3346 $1 Broad-winged hawk (horiz) 85 80
3347 $1 White-tailed tropic bird (horiz) 85 80
3348 $1 Black-winged stilt (horiz) 85 80
3349 $1 Bridled tern (horiz) 85 80
3350 $1 Antillean euphonia (horiz) 85 80
3351 $1 Ruddy turnstone (horiz) 85 80
3352 $1 Green-throated carib (horiz) 85 80
3353 $1 Yellow-crowned night heron (horiz) 85 80
3354 $1.10 Lesser Antillean tanager 90 85
3355 $2 Purple-throated carib 1·60 1·60
MS3356 Two sheets, each 89×92 mm. (a) $5 Red-billed whistling duck. (b) $6 St. Vincent amazon. Set of 2 sheets 8·00 8·00

Nos. 3345/53 were printed together, *se-tenant*, with the backgrounds forming a composite design.

328 Maurice King (St. Vincent) (weightlifting), Pan American Games, 1959

1996. Olympic Games, Atlanta (2nd issue). Multicoloured.

3357 20c. Type **328** 30 30
3358 70c. Eswort Coombs (St. Vincent) (400 m sprint, World University Student Games) 50 40
3359 90c. Pamenos Ballantyne (St. Vincent) (O.E.C.S. road-running) and Benedict Ballantyne (St. Vincent) (Guinness Half-marathon, 1994) 60 60
3360 90c. Ancient Greek runners, Olympia (horiz) 60 60
3361 $1 London landmarks (horiz) 60 60
3362 $1 Women's archery (Korea), 1988, 1992 60 60
3363 $1 Gymnastics (Japan),1960–76 60 60
3364 $1 Basketball (U.S.A.), 1936, 1948–68, 1976, 1984 and 1992 60 60
3365 $1 Soccer (Spain), 1992 60 60
3366 $1 Water polo (Hungary), 1956 60 60
3367 $1 Baseball (Cuba), 1992 60 60
3368 $1 Kayak (Germany), 1980 60 60
3369 $1 Fencing (France), 1980 60 60
3370 $1 Cycling (Germany), 1908, 1964, 1972–76 and 1992 60 60
3371 $1 Vitaly Shcherbo (Russia) (gymnastics), 1992 60 60
3372 $1 Fu Mingxia (China) (diving), 1992 60 60
3373 $1 Wilma Rudolph (U.S.A.) (track and field), 1960 60 60
3374 $1 Rafer Johnson (U.S.A.) (decathlon), 1960 60 60
3375 $1 Teofilo Stevenson (Cuba) (boxing), 1972–80 60 60
3376 $1 Babe Didrikson (U.S.A.) (track and field), 1932 60 60
3377 $1 Kyoko Iwasaki (Japan) (swimming), 1992 60 60
3378 $1 Yoo Namkyu (Korea) (table tennis), 1988 60 60
3379 $1 Michael Gross (Germany) (swimming), 1984–88 60 60
3380 $1 Yasuhiro Yamashita (Japan) (judo), 1984 (horiz) 60 60
3381 $1 Peter Rono (Kenya) (1500m race), 1988 (horiz) 60 60
3382 $1 Aleksandr Kourlovitch (Russia) (weightlifting), 1988 (horiz) 60 60
3383 $1 Juha Tiainen (Finland) (hammer throw), 1984 (horiz) 60 60
3384 $1 Sergei Bubka (Russia) (pole vault), 1988 (horiz) 60 60
3385 $1 Q. F. Newall (Great Britain) (archery), 1908 (horiz) 60 60
3386 $1 Nadia Comaneci (Rumania) (gymnastics), 1976 (horiz) 60 60
3387 $1 Carl Lewis (U.S.A.) (long jump), 1988 (horiz) 60 60
3388 $1 Bob Mathias (U.S.A.) (decathlon), 1948 (horiz) 60 60
3389 $1 Chuhei Nambu (Japan) (triple jump), 1932 (horiz) 60 60
3390 $1 Duncan McNaughton (Canada) (high jump), 1932 (horiz) 60 60
3391 $1 Jack Kelly (U.S.A.) (single sculls), 1920 (horiz) 60 60
3392 $1 Jackie Joyner-Kersee (U.S.A.) (heptathlon), 1988 (horiz) 60 60
3393 $1 Tyrell Biggs (U.S.A.) (super heavyweight boxing), 1984 (horiz) 60 60
3394 $1 Larisa Latynina (Russia) (gymnastics), 1964 (horiz) 60 60
3395 $1 Bob Garrett (U.S.A.) (discus), 1896 (horiz) 60 60
3396 $1 Paavo Nurmi (Finland) (5000m), 1924 (horiz) 60 60
3397 $1 Eric Lemming (Sweden) (javelin), 1908 (horiz) 60 60
3398 $1.10 Rodney Jack (St. Vincent) (1995 Caribbean Nations Football Cup) 70 70
3399 $1.10 Dorando Pietri (Italy) (marathon), 1908 70 70
3400 $2 Yachting (horiz) 1·25 1·50
MS3401 Four sheets. (a) 74×104 mm. $5 Olympic flag (horiz). (b) 74×104 mm. $5 Carl Lewis (U.S.A.) (relay). (c) 104×74 mm. $5 Hannes Kolehmainen (Finland) (marathon), 1920 (horiz). (d) 104×74 mm. $5 Alexander Ditiatin (Russia) (gymnastics), 1980 (horiz). Set of 4 sheets 11·00 12·00

No. 3371 is inscribed "GYMNASTIECS" in error.

329 Notre Dame Cathedral, Paris

1996. "The Hunchback of Notre Dame". Scenes from the Disney cartoon film. Multicoloured.

3402–3207 10c. ×6 (Type **329**; People watching puppet show; Judge Frollo on black horse; Quasimodo and his parents captured; Gargoyles; Quasimodo) 1·75
3408–3416 30c. ×9 (Captain Phoebus meets Esmeralda; Captain Phoebus and Judge Frollo; Esmeralda dancing; Esmeralda and candidates for King of Fools; Quasimodo wearing crown; Quasimodo pelted; Quasimodo carrying Esmeralda; Phoebus on black horse; Quasimodo, Esmeralda and a wounded Phoebus (all horiz)) 3·25
3417–3425 $1 ×9 (Quasimodo chained to bell tower; Three gargoyles and Quasimodo; Quasimodo pulling down pillars; Quasimodo rescuing Esmeralda; Phoebus leading citizens; Quasimodo throwing wood; Quasimodo weeping over Esmeralda; Quasimodo and Frollo fighting; Quasimodo and Esmeralda on ledge (all horiz)) 7·00
3426–3433 $1 ×8 (Quasimodo; Phoebus; Laverne and Hugo; Clopin; Frollo; Esmeralda; Victor; Djali) 6·50
MS3434 Five sheets. (a) 124×102 mm. $6 Quasimodo, Phoebus and Esmerelda (horiz). (b) 124×102 mm. $6 Esmerelda. (c) 124×102 mm. $6 Quasimodo cheering. (d) 104×126 mm. $6 Esmerelda and Quasimodo (horiz). (e) 104×126 mm. $6 Esmerelda and Phoebus (horiz). Set of 5 sheets 17·00 22·00

No. 3416 is inscribed "wonded phoebus" in error.

330 French Angelfish

1996. Fish. Multicoloured.

3435 70c. Type **330** 60 40
3436 90c. Red-spotted hawkfish 70 50
3437 $1 Barred hamlet 70 60
3438 $1 Flamefish 70 60
3439 $1 Caribbean long-nosed butterflyfish 70 60
3440 $1 Royal gramma ("Fairy Basslet") 70 60
3441 $1 Red-tailed parrotfish 70 60
3442 $1 Black-barred soldierfish 70 60
3443 $1 Three-spotted damselfish 70 60
3444 $1 Candy basslet 70 60
3445 $1 Spot-finned hogfish 70 60
3446 $1 Jackknife fish 70 60
3447 $1 Surgeon fish 70 60
3448 $1 Muttonfish 70 60
3449 $1 Seahorse 70 60
3450 $1 Comber fish 70 60
3451 $1 Angel shark 70 60
3452 $1 Moray eel 70 60
3453 $1 Bicolour parrotfish 70 60
3454 $1 "Tritonium nodiferum" (sea snail) 70 60
3455 $1.10 Balloonfish ("Spiny Puffer") 80 70
3456 $2 Grey triggerfish 1·50 1·50
MS3457 Two sheets, each 106×76 mm. (a) $5 Queen Triggerfish. (b) $6 Blue Marlin. Set of 2 sheets 6·00 7·00

Nos. 3446/54 were printed together, *se-tenant*, with the backgrounds forming a composite design.

No. 3445 is inscribed "HOFGFISH" in error.

331 "Beloperone guttata"

1996. Flowers. Multicoloured.

3458 70c. Type **331** 60 40
3459 90c. "Datura candida" 70 60
3460 90c. "Amherstia nobilis" 70 60
3461 90c. "Ipomoea acuminata" 70 60
3462 90c. "Bougainvillea glabra" 70 60
3463 90c. "Cassia alata" 70 60
3464 90c. "Cordia sebestena" 70 60
3465 90c. "Opuntia dilenii" 70 60
3466 90c. "Cryptostegia grandiflora" 70 60
3467 90c. "Rodriguezia lanceolata" 70 60
3468 $1 "Epidendrum elongatum" 80 60
3469 $1.10 "Petrea volubilis" 85 70
3470 $2 "Oncidium altissimum" 1·50 1·60
MS3471 Two sheets, each 78×64 mm. (a) $5 "Hibiscus rosa-sinensis". (b) $5 "Acalypha hispida". Set of 2 sheets 5·50 6·50

Nos. 3459/67 were printed together, *se-tenant*, with the backgrounds forming a composite design.

332 "Doric", 1923

1996. Passenger Ships. Multicoloured.

3472 $1.10 Type **332** 90 80
3473 $1.10 "Nerissa", 1926 90 80
3474 $1.10 "Howick Hall", 1910 90 80
3475 $1.10 "Jervis Bay", 1922 90 80
3476 $1.10 "Vauban", 1912 90 80
3477 $1.10 "Orinoco", 1928 90 80
3478 $1.10 "Lady Rodney", 1929 90 80
3479 $1.10 "Empress of Russia", 1913 90 80
3480 $1.10 "Providence", 1914 90 80
3481 $1.10 "Reina Victori-Eugenia", 1913 90 80
3482 $1.10 "Balmoral Castle", 1910 90 80
3483 $1.10 "Tivives", 1911 90 80
MS3484 Two sheets, each 106×76 mm. (a) $6 "Aquitania", 1914. (b) $6 "Imperator", 1913. Set of 2 sheets 8·50 9·00

394a Mahatma Gandhi and Supporters, 1930

2000. New Millennium. People and Events of Twentieth Century (1930–39). Multicoloured.

4468	60c. Type **394a**	1·00	80
4469	60c. As Type **391**, but with multicoloured frame	1·00	80
4470	60c. Empire State Building, New York (opened 1931)	1·00	80
4471	60c. Declaration of Republic, Spain, 1931	1·00	80
4472	60c. Pres. Franklin D. Roosevelt ("New Deal" inaugurated, 1933)	1·00	80
4473	60c. Reichstag on fire, 1933	1·00	80
4474	60c. Mao Tse-tung (Communist Revolution in China, 1934)	1·00	80
4475	60c. General Franco (Spanish Civil War, 1936)	1·00	80
4476	60c. King Edward VIII and Abdication document, 1936	1·00	80
4477	60c. Diego Rivera (Mexican muralist) (50th birthday, 1936)	1·00	80
4478	60c. Golden Gate Bridge, San Francisco (opened 1937)	1·00	80
4479	60c. Atomic cloud (first atomic reaction, 1939)	1·00	80
4480	60c. Troops and newspaper vendor (start of Second World War, 1939)	1·00	80
4481	60c. New York World's Fair emblem, 1939	1·00	80
4482	60c. New Dalai Lama chosen in Tibet, 1939	1·00	80
4483	60c. Explosion of *Hindenburg* (airship), 1937 (59×39 mm)	1·00	80
4484	60c. Igor Sikorsky and VS-300, first successful helicopter, 1939	1·00	80

No. 4468 is inscribed "Gahndi" in error.

394b Sigmund Freud (*Interpretation of Dreams* published, 1900)

2000. New Millennium. People and Events of Twentieth Century (1900–50). Multicoloured.

4485	20c. Type **394b**	40	40
4486	20c. Guglielmo Marconi (first long distance wireless transmission, 1901)	40	40
4487	20c. Orville and Wilbur Wright (construction of Wright *Flyer III* powered aircraft, 1903)	40	40
4488	20c. Albert Einstein (Theory of Relativity, 1905)	40	40
4489	20c. Henry Ford and Model T, 1908	40	40
4490	20c. Alfred Wegener (German meteorologist) (Theory of Continental Drift, 1912)	40	40
4491	20c. Lord Kitchener on recruiting poster (beginning of First World War, 1914)	40	40
4492	20c. Lenin (Russian Revolution, 1917)	40	40
4493	20c. James Joyce (*Ulysses*, published 1922)	40	40
4494	20c. Alexander Fleming (Scottish bacteriologist) (discovery of Penicillin, 1928)	40	40
4495	20c. Edwin Hubble (Hubble's Law on expansion of Universe, 1929)	40	40
4496	20c. Mao Tse-tung and map of Long March, 1934	40	40
4497	20c. Alan Turing (English mathematician) (Theory of digital computing, 1937)	40	40
4498	20c. Berlin researchers (discovery of frission, 1938)	40	40
4499	20c. German Troops and headline (start of Second World War, 1939)	40	40
4500	20c. Churchill, Roosevelt and Stalin (Yalta Conference, 1945)	40	40
4501	20c. Gandhi and Nehru (Independence of India, 1947)	40	40
4502	20c. William Shockley (U.S. physicist) (development of miniature transistor, 1947)	40	40

394c "Robert Rich, Earl of Warwick"

2000. 400th Birth Anniv of Sir Anthony van Dyck. Multicoloured.

4503	$1 Type **394c**	75	75
4504	$1 "James Stuart, Duke of Lennox and Richmond"	75	75
4505	$1 "Sir John Suckling"	75	75
4506	$1 "Sir Robert Shirley"	75	75
4507	$1 "Teresia, Lady Shirley"	75	75
4508	$1 "Thomas Wentworth, Earl of Strafford" (with dog)	75	75
4509	$1 "Thomas Wentworth, Earl of Strafford"	75	75
4510	$1 "Lady Anne Carr, Countess of Bedford"	75	75
4511	$1 "Portrait of a Member of the Charles Family"	75	75
4512	$1 "Thomas Howard, Earl of Arundel"	75	75
4513	$1 "Diana Cecil, Countess of Oxford"	75	75
4514	$1 "The Violincellist"	75	75
4515	$1 "The Apostle Peter"	75	75
4516	$1 "St. Matthew"	75	75
4517	$1 "St. James the Greater"	75	75
4518	$1 "St. Bartholomew"	75	75
4519	$1 "The Apostle Thomas"	75	75
4520	$1 "The Apostle Jude (Thaddeus)"	75	75
4521	$1 "The Vision of St. Anthony"	75	75
4522	$1 "The Mystic Marriage of St. Catherine"	75	75
4523	$1 "The Vision of the Blessed Herman Joseph"	75	75
4524	$1 "Madonna and Child enthroned with Sts. Rosalie, Peter and Paul"	75	75
4525	$1 "St. Rosalie interceding for the Plague stricken of Palermo"	75	75
4526	$1 "Francesco Orero in Adoration of the Crucifixion"	75	75

MS4527 Three sheets. (a) 102×127 mm. $5 "William Fielding, Earl of Denbigh". (b) 127×102 mm. $5 "The Mystic Marriage of St. Catherine". (c) 102×127 mm. $5 "St. Augustine in Ecstasy" (horiz). Set of 3 sheets 12·00 12·00

395 *Brassavola nodosa*

2000. "The Stamp Show 2000" International Stamp Exhibition, London. Orchids of the Caribbean. Multicoloured.

4528	70c. Type **395**	60	45
4529	90c. *Bletia purpurea*	70	50
4530	$1.40 *Brassavola cucullata*	1·00	90
4531	$1.50 *Brassavola cordata* (vert)	1·00	1·00
4532	$1.50 *Brassia caudata* (vert)	1·00	1·00
4533	$1.50 *Broughotnia sanguinea* (vert)	1·00	1·00
4534	$1.50 *Comparettia falcata* (vert)	1·00	1·00
4535	$1.50 *Clowesia rosea* (vert)	1·00	1·00
4536	$1.50 *Caularthron bicornutum* (vert)	1·00	1·00
4537	$1.50 *Cyrtopodium punctatum* (vert)	1·00	1·00
4538	$1.50 *Dendrophylax funalis* (vert)	1·00	1·00
4539	$1.50 *Dichaea hystricina* (vert)	1·00	1·00
4540	$1.50 *Cyrtopodium andersonii* (vert)	1·00	1·00
4541	$1.50 *Epidendrum secundum* (vert)	1·00	1·00
4542	$1.50 *Dimerandra emarginata* (vert)	1·00	1·00
4543	$1.50 *Oncidium urophyllum* (vert)	1·00	1·00
4544	$1.50 *Oeceoclades maculata* (vert)	1·00	1·00
4545	$1.50 *Vanilla planifolia* (vert)	1·00	1·00
4546	$1.50 *Isolhilus linearis* (vert)	1·00	1·00
4547	$1.50 *Ionopsis utricularioides* (vert)	1·00	1·00
4548	$1.50 *Nidema boothii* (vert)	1·00	1·00

MS4549 Two sheets, each 123×100 mm. (a) $5 *Edidendrum altissimum* (vert). (b) $5 *Neocogniauxia hexaptera* (vert). Set of 2 sheets 6·50 7·00

Nos. 4531/6, 4537/42 and 4543/8 were each printed together, se-tenant, with the backgrounds forming maps of the Caribbean.

395a In Grey Check Suit

2000. 18th Birthday of Prince William. Multicoloured.

4550	$1.40 Type **395a**	1·00	1·00
4551	$1.40 Wearing scarf	1·00	1·00
4552	$1.40 In blue suit	1·00	1·00
4553	$1.40 Wearing blue jumper	1·00	1·00

MS4554 100×80 mm. $5 Wearing Eton uniform (37×50 mm) 3·25 3·50

395b Hale Bopp Comet passing Calisto

2000. "EXPO 2000" International Stamp Exhibition, Anaheim, U.S.A. Spacecraft. Multicoloured.

4555	$1.50 Type **395b**	1·10	1·10
4556	$1.50 "Galileo" spacecraft	1·10	1·10
4557	$1.50 "Ulysse" spacecraft	1·10	1·10
4558	$1.50 "Pioneer 11"	1·10	1·10
4559	$1.50 "Voyager 1"	1·10	1·10
4560	$1.50 "Pioneer 10"	1·10	1·10
4561	$1.50 "Cassini" spacecraft	1·10	1·10
4562	$1.50 "Pioneer 11" approaching Saturn	1·10	1·10
4563	$1.50 "Voyager 1" and Ariel	1·10	1·10
4564	$1.50 "Huygens" spacecraft	1·10	1·10
4565	$1.50 "Deep Space 4 Champollion"	1·10	1·10
4566	$1.50 "Voyager 2"	1·10	1·10
4567	$1.50 "Voyager 2" passing Umbriel	1·10	1·10
4568	$1.50 "Pluto Project"	6·00	6·00
4569	$1.50 "Voyager 1" approaching Pluto	1·10	1·10
4570	$1.50 Oort Cloud (part of asteroid belt)	1·10	1·10
4571	$1.50 "Pluto Kuiper Express" spacecraft	1·10	1·10
4572	$1.50 "Voyager 2" above Neptune	1·10	1·10

MS4573 Two sheets, each 105×75 mm. (a) $5 "Pluto Project" spacecraft. (b) $5 "Stardust" spacecraft approaching Wild 2 Comet. Set of 2 sheets 6·50 7·00

Nos. 4555/60, 4561/6 and 4567/72 were each printed together, se-tenant, with the backgrounds forming composite designs.

395c *Pane, Amore e Fantasia*, 1954

2000. 50th Anniv of Berlin Film Festival. Multicoloured.

4574	$1.40 Type **395c**	80	85
4575	$1.40 Lord Olivier in *Richard III*, 1956	80	85
4576	$1.40 *Smultronstallet*, 1958	80	85
4577	$1.40 Sidney Poitier in *The Defiant Ones*, 1958	80	85
4578	$1.40 *The Living Desert*, 1954	80	85
4579	$1.40 *A Bout de Souffle*, 1960	80	85

MS4580 95×103 mm. $5 Jean-Luc Godard (director), 1960 3·25 3·50

395d George Stephenson and *Locomotion No. 1*, 1825

2000. 175th Anniv of Stockton and Darlington Line (first public railway). Multicoloured.

4581	$3 As Type **395d**	2·25	2·25
4582	$3 Camden and Amboy Railroad locomotive *John Bull*, 1831	2·25	2·25

No. 4582 is inscribed "Camoen" in error.

396 Albert Einstein

2000. Election of Albert Einstein (mathematical physicist) as Time Magazine "Man of the Century". Multicoloured.

4583	$2 Type **396**	1·75	1·75
4584	$2 Two portraits, one with hands clasped	1·75	1·75
4585	$2 Two portraits, one standing by painting	1·75	1·75

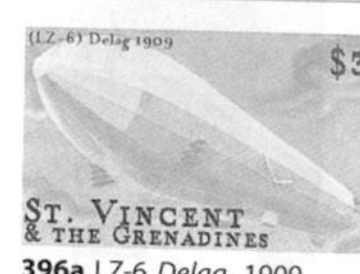

396a LZ-6 *Delag*, 1909

2000. Centenary of First Zeppelin Flight.

4586	**396a**	$3 blue, black and mauve	2·25	2·25
4587	-	$3 blue, black and mauve	2·25	2·25
4588	-	$3 green, black and mauve	2·25	2·25

MS4589 116×76 mm. $5 green, black and mauve 3·75 3·75

DESIGNS: No. 4587, LZ-127 *Graf Zeppelin*, 1928; 4588, LZ-129 *Hindenburg*, 1936. 50×38 mm: No. **MS**4589, LZ-9 ZII (*Ersatz*), 1911.

No. 4588 is inscribed "(129) Hindenberg" in error.

396b Mildred Didrikson (javelin), 1932

2000. Olympic Games, Sydney. Multicoloured.

4590	$2 Type **396b**	1·50	1·50
4591	$2 Man on vaulting horse	1·50	1·50
4592	$2 Olympic Stadium, Barcelona (1992) and Spanish flag	1·50	1·50
4593	$2 Ancient Greek horse racing	1·50	1·50

396c Ian Allen

2000. West Indies Cricket Tour and 100th Test Match at Lord's.

4594	**396c**	10c. multicoloured	30	30
4595	-	20c. black and yellow	50	25
4596	-	$1.10 multicoloured	1·25	1·00
4597	-	$1.40 multicoloured	1·50	1·50

MS4598 121×114 mm. $5 multicoloured 6·00 6·00

DESIGNS—VERT: 20c. T. Michael Findlay; $1.10, Winston Davis; $1.40, Nixon McLean. HORIZ: $5 Lord's Cricket Ground.

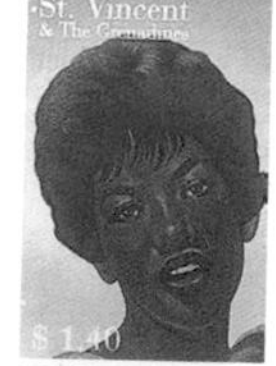

396d Member of The Chantels (value at left and hair clear of perforations)

2000. Girl Pop Groups. Multicoloured.

4599	$1.40 Type **396d**	60	80
4600	$1.40 Member of The Chantels (value at right on background)	60	80
4601	$1.40 Member of The Chantels (value at right on neck)	60	80
4602	$1.40 Member of The Chantels (value at left and hair over perforations)	60	80
4603	$1.40 Member of The Chantels (value at left on background)	60	80
4604	$1.40 Member of The Marvelettes (value on background)	60	80
4605	$1.40 Member of The Marvelettes (with curl on forehead)	60	80
4606	$1.40 Member of The Marvelettes (with gap in teeth)	60	80

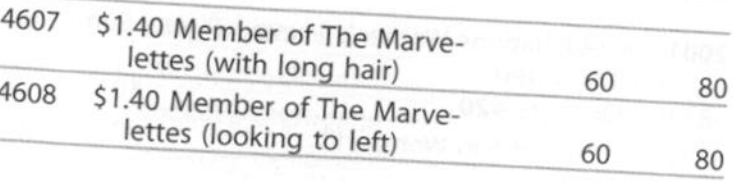

4607 $1.40 Member of The Marvelettes (with long hair) 60 80
4608 $1.40 Member of The Marvelettes (looking to left) 60 80

397 Mario Andretti in Racing Car

2000. Election of Mario Andretti as "Driver of the Century".

4609 **397** $1.10 brown and red 55 70
4610 - $1.10 multicoloured 55 70
4611 - $1.10 multicoloured 55 70
4612 - $1.10 brown and red 55 70
4613 - $1.10 brown and red 55 70
4614 - $1.10 multicoloured 55 70
4615 - $1.10 multicoloured 55 70
4616 - $1.10 brown and red 55 70
MS4617 155×114 mm. $5 black and red 3·00 3·25

DESIGNS: No. 4610, In white overalls; 4611, With hands together; 4612, During race; 4613, Standing by saloon car; 4614, With "abc" trophy; 4615, In red overalls; 4616, Watching race; **MS**4617, Holding trophy.

398 Clarinet-player

2000. The Art of Jazz. Multicoloured.

4618 $1.40 Type **398** 60 70
4619 $1.40 Pianist 60 70
4620 $1.40 Trumpeter 60 70
4621 $1.40 Guitarist 60 70
4622 $1.40 Bass-player 60 70
4623 $1.40 Saxophonist 60 70

399 Michael Palin

2000. 30th Anniv of Monty Python. Multicoloured.

4624 $1.40 Type **399** 75 80
4625 $1.40 Eric Idle 75 80
4626 $1.40 John Cleese 75 80
4627 $1.40 Graham Chapman 75 80
4628 $1.40 Terry Gilliam 75 80
4629 $1.40 Terry Jones 75 80

400 Barbara Taylor Bradford

2000. Great Writers of the 20th Century: Barbara Taylor Bradford. Sheet 128×88 mm.

MS4630 **400** $5 multicoloured 3·00 3·50

401 Betty Boop in "Jack and Jill"

2000. Betty Boop (cartoon character). Illustrating nursery rhymes. Multicoloured.

4631 $1 Type **401** 50 60
4632 $1 "Three Blind Mice" 50 60
4633 $1 "Wee Willie Winky" 50 60
4634 $1 "Hey Diddle Diddle" 50 60
4635 $1 "Mother Goose" 50 60
4636 $1 "Little Miss Muffet" 50 60
4637 $1 "Three Little Kittens" 50 60
4638 $1 "Rub-a-Dub-Dub" 50 60
4639 $1 "Little Jack Horner" 50 60
MS4640 Two sheets, each 133×91 mm. (a) $5 "Little Bo Peep". (b) $5 "Old Woman that lived in a Shoe". Set of 2 sheets 4·50 5·50

402 David Copperfield

2000. David Copperfield (conjurer). Each incorporating a similar portrait. Multicoloured.

4641 $1.40 Type **402** 75 80
4642 $1.40 David Copperfield levitating (dressed in black) 75 80
4643 $1.40 As No. 4642, but faint figure in brown 75 80
4644 $1.40 As No. 4642, but figure replaced by two large bubbles 75 80

403 Goblet or Monkey

2000. Local Utensils. Multicoloured.

4645 20c. Type **403** 20 15
4646 50c. Goose (iron) 35 25
4647 70c. Boley and calabash (vert) 45 40
4648 $1 Three flat irons 60 75

404 Pink Ginger Lily

2000. Flowers. Multicoloured.

4649 90c. Type **404** 55 60
4650 90c. *Thumbergia grandiflora* 55 60
4651 90c. Red ginger lily 55 60
4652 90c. Madagascar jasmine 55 60
4653 90c. Cluster palm 55 60
4654 90c. Red torch lily 55 60
4655 90c. *Salvia splendens* 55 60
4656 90c. Balsamapple 55 60
4657 90c. Rostrata 55 60
MS4658 Two sheets. (a) 65×82 mm. $5 Red Flamingo (b) 82×65 mm. $5 Balsamapple (horiz). Set of 2 sheets 5·50 6·00

Nos. 4649, 4651 and 4654 are all inscribed "Lilly" in error.

405 Queen Elizabeth the Queen Mother

2000. Queen Elizabeth the Queen Mother's 100th Birthday.

4659 **405** $1.40 multicoloured 1·25 1·00

2000. Faces of the Millennium: Queen Elizabeth the Queen Mother. As **T 329a** of Sierra Leone, showing collage of flower photographs. Multicoloured.

4660 $1 Top of head (face value at left) 75 65
4661 $1 Top of head (face value at right) 75 65
4662 $1 Eye and temple (face value at left) 75 65
4663 $1 Temple (face value at right) 75 65
4664 $1 Cheek (face value at left) 75 65
4665 $1 Cheek (face value at right) 75 65
4666 $1 Chin (face value at left) 75 65
4667 $1 Neck (face value at right) 75 65

Nos. 4660/7 were printed together, se-tenant, in sheetlets of 8 with the stamps arranged in two vertical columns separated by a gutter also containing miniature photographs. When viewed as a whole, the sheetlet forms a portrait of the Queen Mother.

406 Ida Cox

2000. New Millennium. "The Birth of The Blues". Showing singers and musicians. Multicoloured.

4668 $1.40 Type **406** 60 75
4669 $1.40 Lonnie Johnson 60 75
4670 $1.40 Muddy Waters 60 75
4671 $1.40 T-Bone Walker 60 75
4672 $1.40 Howlin' Wolf 60 75
4673 $1.40 Sister Rosetta Thorpe 60 75
4674 $1.40 Bessie Smith 60 75
4675 $1.40 Willie Dixon 60 75
4676 $1.40 Gertrude "Ma" Rainey 60 75
4677 $1.40 W. C. Handy 60 75
4678 $1.40 Leadbelly 60 75
4679 $1.40 Big Bill Broonzy 60 75
MS4680 Two sheets, each 80×120 mm. (a) $5 Billie Holiday. (b) $5 Robert Johnson. Set of 2 sheets 4·75 6·00

407 U.S.S. *Shaw* exploding, Pearl Harbor, 1941

2000. Wars of the Twentieth Century. Multicoloured.

4681 $1 Type **407** 1·00 1·00
4682 $1 American B-24 Liberators bombing Ploesti oil fields, 1943 1·00 1·00
4683 $1 Soviet T-34 tank, Germany, 1945 1·00 1·00
4684 $1 U.S.S. *New Jersey* (battleship) off North Korea, 1951 1·00 1·00
4685 $1 American F-86 Sabre fighter over North Korea, 1951 1·00 1·00
4686 $1 U.S.S. *Enterprise* (aircraft carrier) off Indo-China 1·00 1·00
4687 $1 American B-52 bomber over Vietnam, 1972 1·00 1·00
4688 $1 American armoured personnel carrier, Tay Ninh, 1967 1·00 1·00
4689 $1 Two Israeli F-4 Phantoms, 1967 1·00 1·00
4690 $1 Abandoned Egyptian T-72 tanks, 1967 1·00 1·00
4691 $1 SAM 6 rocket launchers, Cairo, 1973 1·00 1·00
4692 $1 Israeli M-48 tanks in desert, 1973 1·00 1·00
4693 $1 H.M.S. *Invincible* (aircraft carrier) on way to Falkland Islands, 1982 1·00 1·00
4694 $1 British Harriers and H.M.S. *Hermes* (aircraft carrier), Falkland Islands, 1982 1·00 1·00
4695 $1 Iraqi SS-1 Scud-B mobile missile launcher, 1990 1·00 1·00
4696 $1 American M1-A1 Abrams tanks, advancing, Gulf War, 1990 1·00 1·00
MS4697 Two sheets. (a) 85×110 mm. $5 Nucleur bomb test, Pershing II missile and B-52 bomber (55×40 mm). (b) 106×81 mm. $5 Israeli F-4 fighter-bomber, 1973. Set of 2 sheets 11·00 11·00

No. 4683 is inscribed "SOVIETIC", 4693 "H.M.S. HERMES" and 4696 "NOTHWARD", all in error.

408 Leopold Anthony

2000. Local Musicians.

4698 **408** $1.40 multicoloured 75 80
4699 - $1.40 black and buff 75 80
4700 - $1.40 multicoloured 75 80
4701 - $1.40 multicoloured 75 80

DESIGNS: No. 4699, "Shake" Kean (trumpeter); 4700, Olsen V. Peters (cornet-player); 4701, Patrick E. Prescod (pianist).

409 Government House

2000. 21st Anniv of Independence. Multicoloured.

4702 10c. Type **409** 20 10
4703 15c. House of Assembly in session 20 10
4704 50c. House of Assembly building 45 25
4705 $2 Government Financial Complex 1·50 2·00

410 Blue and Yellow Macaw ("Blue and Gold Macaw")

2000. Birds. Multicoloured.

4706 50c. Type **410** 60 30
4707 90c. English fallow budgerigar 75 50
4708 $1 Superb parrot ("Barraband Parakeet") 90 70
4709 $2 Dominant pied blue 1·40 1·40
4710 $2 Canary ("Stafford Canary") 1·40 1·40
4711 $2 Masked lovebird 1·40 1·40
4712 $2 Canary ("Parisian Full Canary") 1·40 1·40
4713 $2 Scarlet macaw 1·40 1·40
4714 $2 Blue-fronted amazon 1·40 1·40
4715 $2 Buffon's macaw 1·40 1·40
4716 $2 Canada goose (horiz) 1·40 1·40
4717 $2 Mandarin duck (horiz) 1·40 1·40
4718 $2 Gouldian finch (horiz) 1·40 1·40
4719 $2 English short-faced tumbler 1·40 1·40
4720 $2 Diamond dove 1·40 1·40
4721 $2 Norwich cropper 1·40 1·40
MS4722 Two sheets, each 96×67 mm. (a) $5 Budgerigar (horiz). (b) $5 Common Peafowl (horiz). Set of 2 sheets 7·50 8·00

No. 4707 is inscribed "Budgerigan", 4708 "Pazakeet", 4711 "Macked", 4713 "Searlet" and 4721 "Nozwich", all in error. There are also many mistakes in the Latin species names shown on the stamps.

411 Rebecca wearing Checked Coat in Shop

2000. Shirley Temple in Rebecca of Sunnybrook Farm. Showing scenes from the film. Multicoloured.

4723 90c. Type **411** 50 55
4724 90c. Rebecca with parents 50 55
4725 90c. Rebecca being reprimanded 50 55

437 ... Kenn... Dem... Conv...

2001. John F. K... Commemoration. ... MS5037a).

5025 $1.40 Type 437
5026 $1.40 Campaign ... York, 1959
5027 $1.40 In rockin... White House
5028 $1.40 With Rob... (brother)
5029 $1.40 Announ... Blockade, 1...
5030 $1.40 John Ke... father's fun...
5031 $1.40 With so...
5032 $1.40 With Ja...
5033 $1.40 With da...
5034 $1.40 With fa...
5035 $1.40 Sailing
5036 $1.40 Preside... Kennedy i...
MS5037 Two sheets, (a) $5 President J... olet and black). (... at Hyannis Port. ...

2001. 40th Birt... Multicolour...
5038 $1.40 Typ...
5039 $1.40 Pri... dress
5040 $1.40 Or...
MS5041 72×95 ... in evening dr...

2001. 60th A... Multicolo...
5042 $1.40 ...
5043 $1.40 ... hac...
5044 $1.40 ... Jap...
5045 $1.40 ...
5046 $1.40 ... Ak...
5047 $1.40 ... bo...
5048 $1.40 ... E...
5049 $1.4... J...
5050 $1.4... i...
5051 $1.4... ...
5052 $1....
5053 $1....
MS5054 T... Field ur... Miller r... Admira... 2 sheet...

MS5233 (a) 82×105 mm. $5 "Femme espagnole sur fond orange". Imperf. (b) 102×81 mm. $5 "Femme etendue". Imperf 7·00 8·00

466 "Portrait of Jacques de Gheyn III"

2003. Paintings by Rembrandt. Multicoloured.

5234 $1 Type **466** 80 55
5235 $1.10 "Young Man in a Black Beret" 85 65
5236 $1.40 "Hendrickje Stoffels" 1·10 1·00
5237 $2 "The Polish Rider" (horiz) 1·75 2·25
MS5238 185×175 mm. $2 "Belthazzar sees the Writing on the Wall" (detail); $2 "Portrait of a Young Man (Titus?)"; $2 "Jacob blessing the Sons of Joseph" (detail); $2 "King Uzziah stricken with Leprosy" 6·00 6·50
MS5239 158×115 mm. $5 "The Stoning of St. Stephen" 4·50 4·75

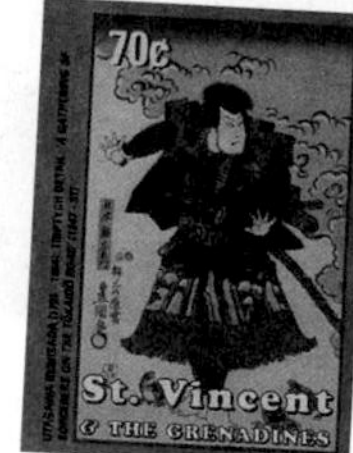

467 "A Gathering of Sorcerers on the Tokaido Road" (detail) (Utagawa Kunisada)

2003. Japanese Art. Ghosts and Demons. Multicoloured.

5240 70c. Type **467** 45 30
5241 $1.10 "Kiyohime and the Moon" (Yoshu Chikanobu) 65 50
5242 $1.40 "A Gathering of Sorcerers on the Tokaido Road" (different detail) (Utagawa Kunisada) 75 70
5243 $3 "A Gathering of Sorcerers on the Tokaido Road" (different detail) (Utagawa Kunisada) 1·75 2·25
MS5244 148×148 mm. $2 "Snake Mountain" (Utagawa Kuniyoshi); $2 "Sadanobu and Oni" (Tsukioka Yoshitoshi); $2 "Shoki" (Tsukioka Yoshitoshi); $2 "The Nightly Weeping Rock" (Utagawa Kuniyoshi) 5·00 6·00
MS5245 117×85 mm. $5 "The Ghosts of Matahachi and Kikuno" (detail) (Utagawa Kumsada) 3·50 3·75

468 Prince William as Teenager

2003. 21st Birthday of Prince William of Wales. Multicoloured.

MS5246 148×78 mm. $3 Type **468**; $3 Prince William in black and yellow polo shirt; $3 Wearing blue t-shirt 7·50 7·50
MS5247 98×68 mm. $5 Prince William as teenager (different) 4·50 4·50

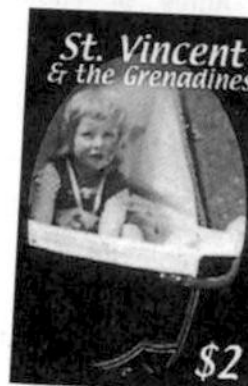

469 Lady Diana Spencer as Young Girl

2003. Fifth Death Anniv of Diana, Princess of Wales. Two sheets, each 132×146 mm, containing vert designs as **T 469**. Multicoloured.

MS5248 $2 Type **469**; $2 Princess Diana with Prince Charles on their wedding day; $2 With Prince William and baby Prince Harry; $2 Wearing mauve jacket 5·50 6·00
MS5249 $2 Princess Diana wearing tiara and yellow dress; $2 Wearing white dress; $2 Wearing mauve cardigan; $2 Wearing mauve dress 5·50 6·00

470 Antonin Magne (1931)

2003. Centenary of Tour de France Cycle Race. Multicoloured.

MS5250 157×97 mm. $2 Type **470**; $2 Andre Leducq (1932); $2 Georges Speicher (1933); $2 Antonin Magne (1934) 6·00 6·00
MS5251 157×97 mm. $2 Romain Maes (1935); $2 Silvere Maes (1936); $2 Roger Lapebie (1937); $2 Gino Bartali (1938) 6·00 6·00
MS5252 157×97 mm. $2 Silvere Maes (1939); $2 Jean Lazarides (1946) (additionally inscr "FIVE DAY RACE"); $2 Jean Robic (1947); $2 Gino Bartali (1948) 6·00 6·00
MS5253 Three sheets, each 106×78 mm. (a) $5 Antonin Magne (1931, 1934). (b) $5 Fausto Coppi (1949). (c) $5 Ferdinand Kubler (1950) Set of 3 sheets 9·50 10·00

471 Linny

2003. Centenary of Circus Clowns. Multicoloured.

MS5254 116×199 mm. $2 Type **471**; $2 Bruce Feiler; $2 Segey Provirin; $2 Weezle 4·25 4·75
MS5255 145×218 mm. $2 Mermaids (acrobats); $2 Robert Wolf (sword swallower); $2 Elbrus Pilev's Group (horsewoman); $2 Stinky (gymnast) 4·25 4·75

No. **MS**5254 is cut in the shape of a clown on a bicycle and No. **MS**5255 in the shape of a circus elephant.

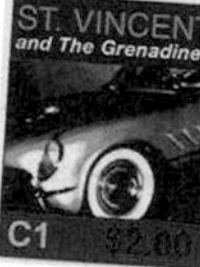

472 C1 Corvette

2003. 50th Anniv of General Motors Chevrolet Corvette. Multicoloured.

MS5256 163×202 mm. $2 Type **472**; $2 C2 Corvette; $2 C3 Corvette; $2 C4 Corvette; $2 C5 Corvette 6·00 7·00
MS5257 163×202 mm. $3 Corvette (1953); $3 Corvette (2003) (both 50×38 mm) 3·75 4·25

473 Cadillac Eldorado (1953)

2003. Centenary of General Motors Cadillac. Multicoloured.

MS5258 110×150 mm. $2 Type **473**; $2 Cadillac Eldorado (2002); $2 Cadillac Eldorado (1967); $2 Cadillac Series 62 (1962) 5·00 6·00
MS5259 102×75 mm. $5 Cadillac LaSalle (1927) 3·50 3·75

2003. Centenary of Powered Flight. As **T 126** of St. Kitts. Multicoloured.

MS5260 176×96 mm. $2 Handley Page Heyford; $2 Heinkel He 111B; $2 Gloster Gauntlet; $2 Curtiss BF2C-1 7·00 7·00
MS5261 176×96 mm. $2 Mitsubishi A6M Reisen; $2 Dewoitine D520; $2 Messerschmitt Bf 109E; $2 Republic P-47 Thunderbolt 7·00 7·00

MS5262 Two sheets, each 106×75 mm. (a) $5 Fairy Flycatcher. (b) $5 Bristol Type 142 Blenheim IV Set of 2 sheets 9·00 9·00

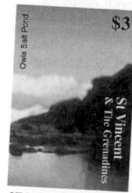

474 Owia Salt Pond

2003. International Year of Freshwater. Multicoloured.

MS5263 150×88 mm. $3 Type **474**; $3 The Soufriere; $3 Falls of Baleine 8·00 8·50
MS5264 100×70 mm. $5 Trinity Falls 4·75 5·00

475 Musicians

2003. Centenary of Salvation Army in St. Vincent. Multicoloured.

5265 70c. Type **475** 1·00 55
5266 90c. District Temple 1·25 65
5267 $1 Christmas Kettle Appeal Fund 1·40 85
5268 $1.10 Salvation Army Headquarters (horiz) 1·50 1·25

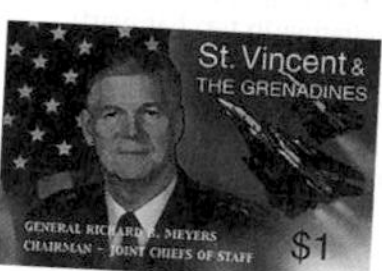

476 General Richard Meyers and Fighter Planes

2003. Operation Iraqi Freedom. Multicoloured.

MS5269 184×129 mm. $1 Type **476**; $1 Lt. General David McKiernan, troops and helicopter; $1 Lt. General Michael Moseley and bomber; $1 Vice Admiral Timothy Keating and warships; $1 Lt. General Jay Garner (retired) and troops; $1 General Tommy Franks and troops; $1 Lt. General Earl Hailston and marines in desert; $1 General John Jumper and fighter plane 6·50 6·50
MS5270 135×135 mm. $1.50 Private Jessica Lynch and rescuers; $1.50 General Tommy Franks and troops; $1.50 Troops and Spectre Gunship; $1.50 Stryker Vehicle; $1.50 USS *Constellation* (aircraft carrier); $1.50 USS *Kitty Hawk* (aircraft carrier) 6·50 6·50

477 Jean Grey

2003. X2: X-Men United (film based on Marvel comic characters). Multicoloured.

MS5271 124×165 mm. $2 Type **477**; $2 Storm; $2 Wolverine; $2 Cyclops 4·25 4·75
MS5272 124×165 mm. $2 Magneto; $2 Mystique; $2 Stryker; $2 Lady Deathstroke 4·25 4·75
MS5273 124×165 mm. $2 Nightcrawler; $2 Professor X; $2 Iceman; $2 Rogue 4·25 4·75

478 The Hulk

2003. The Hulk (film based on Marvel comic characters) Multicoloured.

MS5274 124×165 mm. $2 Type **478**; $2 The Hulk (head and shoulders, inscr "HULK" at right); $2 The Hulk (head and shoulders, inscr "HULK" at left); $2 As Type **477** (inscr "HULK" at right) 4·25 4·50
MS5275 124×165 mm. $2 The Hulk in wreckage; $2 Crouching in rubble; $2 With fists raised; $2 Punching rubble 4·25 4·50

No. **MS**5274 depicts scenes from *The Hulk* film and **MS**5275 depicts the Marvel comic character.

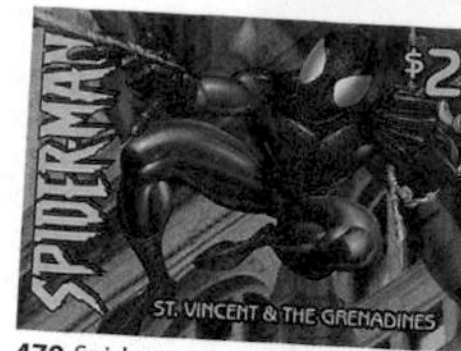

479 Spider-man

2003. Spider-Man 2 (film based on Marvel comic characters). Multicoloured.

MS5276 124×165 mm. $2 Type **479**; $2 With arm raised, brandishing weapon; $2 Suspended from building; $2 Clinging to building 4·25 4·75

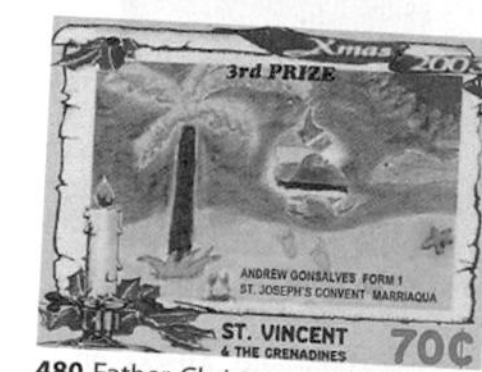

480 Father Christmas and Beach (Andrew Gonsalves)

2003. Christmas. Childrens Paintings. Multicoloured.

5277 70c. Type **480** 80 45
5278 90c. Father Christmas on raft pulled by dolphin (Georgia Gravel) 1·10 55
5279 $1.10 Father Christmas on beach (Adam Gravel) (vert) 1·40 1·10

481 *Lutjanus kasmira*

2003. Marine Life of the Caribbean. Multicoloured.

5280 70c. Type **481** 80 45
5281 90c. *Chaetadon collare* 1·10 60
5282 $1.10 *Istiophorus platypterus* 1·40 1·00
5283 $2 *Pomacanthus paru* (inscr "Pomacanthidae") 2·50 3·00
MS5284 118×106 mm. $2 *Equetus lanceolatus*; $2 *Hypoplectrus gutavariusi*; $2 *Pomacentridae*; $2 *Cichlidae* 7·50 7·50
MS5285 67×96 mm. $5 Dolphins 4·75 4·75

482 Chihuahua

2003. Dogs and Cats. Multicoloured.

5286 10c. Type **482** 35 20
5287 20c. Bulldog 50 15
5288 50c. British shorthair cat 65 25
5289 60c. Weimaraner (dog) 80 45
5290 $1 Burmese cat 1·00 70
5291 $1.40 American shorthair cat 1·25 1·00
5292 $3 Havana brown cat 2·25 2·75
5293 $5 Dalmatian 4·25 4·75
MS5294 119×109 mm. $2 Dachshund; $2 Collie; $2 Springer spaniel; $2 Hamilton hound 7·50 7·50
MS5295 119×109 mm. $2 Osicat; $2 Manx; $2 Somali; $2 Angora 7·50 7·50
MS5296 Two sheets, each 66×96 mm. (a) $5 Golden retriever. (b) $5 Abyssinian cat. Set of 2 sheets 8·50 8·50

483 *Laelia lobata*

2003. Orchids of the Caribbean. Multicoloured.

5297	40c. Type **483**	70	30
5298	90c. *Miltoniopsis phalaenopsis*	1·25	55
5299	$1 *Phalaenopsis violacea*	1·40	70
5300	$3 *Trichopilia fragrans*	3·25	3·75
MS5301	116×109 mm. $2 *Masdevallia uniflora*; $2 *Laelia flava*; $2 *Barkeria lindleyana*; $2 *Laelia tenebrosa*	8·00	8·00
MS5302	66×96 mm. $5 *Cattleya lawrenceana*	5·50	5·50

484 Daspletosaurus

2003. Prehistoric Animals. Multicoloured.

MS5303	178×118 mm. $2 Type **484**; $2 Utahraptor; $2 Scutellosaurus; $2 Scelidosaurus	7·00	7·00
MS5304	178×118 mm. $2 Syntarsus; $2 Velociraptor; $2 Mononikus; $2 Massospondylus	7·00	7·00
MS5305	Two sheets, each 98×68 mm. (a) $5 Giganotosaurus (vert). (b) $5 Pterodactylus (vert) Set of 2 sheets	8·00	8·00

485 Marilyn Monroe (1st issue)

2003. 50th Anniv of Playboy Magazine. **T 485** and similar vert designs showing Playboy magazine covers.

MS5306	240×152 mm. $1.50 Type **485** (black, grey and brown); $1.50 Playboy bunny logo; $1.50 Man with bunny's head: $1.50 Playboy model; $1.50 Woman licking stamp; $1.50 Fiftieth anniversary issue (January 2004) (black, ochre and rose)	5·50	6·50

486 Monkey

2004. Chinese New Year ("Year of the Monkey").

MS5307	75×93 mm. **486** $1.40×4 black, brown and cream	4·50	4·75
MS5308	70×100 mm. **486** $3 black, brown and pink	2·50	2·75

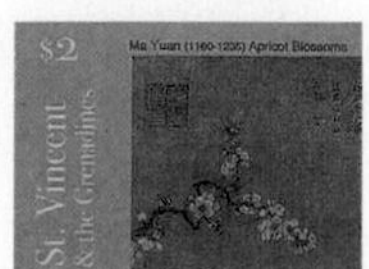

487 "Apricot Blossoms"

2004. Hong Kong 2004 International Stamp Exhibition. Paintings by Ma Yuan. Multicoloured.

MS5309	123×118 mm. $2 Type **487**; $2 "Peach Blossoms"; $2 "Watching the Deer by a Pine Shaded Stream"; $2 "Drinking in the Moonlight"	6·00	6·50
MS5310	120×80 mm. $5 "On a Mountain Path in Spring". Imperf	3·75	4·00

488 Concorde SST and Map showing Anchorage, Alaska

2004. Last Flight of Concorde (2003). Multicoloured.

MS5311	131×90 mm. $3 Type **488**; $3 Concorde SST and map showing Los Angeles; $3 Concorde SST	9·00	9·00

489 Marilyn Monroe

2004. Marilyn Monroe (actress) Commemoration. Multicoloured.

MS5312	Two sheets. (a) 127×111 mm. $2×4, Type **489**; Wearing blue dress; Wearing strapless white dress; Wearing strapless black dress. (b) 125×125 mm. $2×4, Wearing pearl earrings; Leaning head on back of hand; Looking slightly right; Wearing cluster earrings	8·00	9·00

490 Roger Lemerre

2004. European Football Championship 2004, Portugal. Commemoration of Match between France and Italy (2000). Multicoloured.

MS5313	147×85 mm. $2×4, Type **490**, Marco Delvecchio; David Trezeguet; De Kuip Stadium, Rotterdam	4·50	5·00
MS5314	98×85 mm. $5 French team, 2000 (51×38 mm)	3·50	3·75

491 Baron Pierre de Coubertin (founder of the International Olympic Committee)

2004. Olympic Games, Athens. Multicoloured.

5315	70c. Type **491**	65	40
5316	$1 Olympic pin, St Louisa (1904)	85	60
5317	$1.40 Water polo, Berlin (1936) (horiz)	1·10	1·00
5318	$3 Greek ceramic vase	2·50	3·25

492 George Herman Ruth Jr

2004. Centenary of Baseball World Series. **T 492** and similar vert designs showing George Herman Ruth Jr. ("Babe Ruth"). Multicoloured.

5319-5322	$2×4 Type **492**; From front; Leaning on bat; Swinging bat	4·00	4·50

493 Air Chief Marshal Sir Trafford Leigh-Mallory

2004. 60th Anniv of D-Day Landings.

5323	**493**	70c. multicoloured	90	55
5324	-	90c. multicoloured	1·10	65
5325	-	$1 multicoloured	1·25	80
5326	-	$1.10 multicoloured	1·25	1·00
5327	-	$1.40 multicoloured	1·40	1·40
5328	-	$1.50 multicoloured	1·50	1·75

MS5329	Two sheets each 177×107 mm. (a) $2×4, maroon and black; maroon and black; multicoloured; purple and black. (b) $2×4, multicoloured; multicoloured; indigo, ochre and black; indigo; blue and black	15·00	16·00
MS5330	Two sheets each 100×69 mm. (a) $5 maroon, blue and black. (b) $5 maroon and ultramarine	10·00	11·00

DESIGNS: No. 5323, Type **493**; 5324, Lt. Col. Maureen Gara; 5325, Gen. Omar Bradley; 5326, Jean Valentine; 5327, Jack Culshaw; 5328, Gen. Dwight Eisenhower; **MS**5329a $2×4, Rangers take Pointe du Hoc; In trenches at Pointe du Hoc; Press headlines; British liberate Hermanville. **MS**5329b $2×4, British land on Gold Beach; Landing craft on Gold Beach; Canadians at Juno Beach; Troops and tanks on Juno Beach; **MS**5330a $5 Codebreakers; **MS**5330b $5 Soldiers preparing to board landing craft.

494 Queen Juliana

2004. Queen Juliana of the Netherlands.

5331	**494**	$2 multicoloured	1·25	1·50

495 Children

2004. General Employees' Co-Operative Credit Union. Multicoloured.

5332	70c. Type **495**	50	35
5333	90c. General Employees' Co-Operative Credit Union headquarters	60	50
5334	$1.10 Calvin Nicholls (former director) (vert)	75	75
5335	$1.40 Bertrand Neehall (vert)	90	1·00

496 Ronald Reagan

2004. Ronald Reagan (President of USA 1981–89).

5336	**496**	$1.40 multicoloured	90	1·00
5337	-	$1.40 purple and black	90	1·00
5338	-	$1.40 multicoloured	90	1·00

DESIGNS: No. 5336, Type **496**; 5337, In front of flag; 5338, Giving speech.

497 2 Ct Narrow Gauge Locomotive VV12

2004. Bicentenary of Steam Locomotives. Multicoloured.

MS5339	Three sheets, each 181×123 mm. (a) $2×4, Type **497**; Gambler LNV9701; No. 4 Snowdon; *Hiawatha* 3-1. (b) $2×4, CO1604–1; CP steam locomotive N135; 6042-6; E1 Narrow gauge 0-4-0T. (c) $2×4, Standard Boston and Maine No. 410; AG locomotive; BA101 Antigua locomotive; Aster 1449	20·00	21·00
MS5340	Three sheets, each 96×67 mm. (a) $5 Union Pacific 844. (b) $5 NA12A 01-06-00. (c) *Holy War 1* (vert)	11·00	12·00

498 Halimah DeShong (former netball player)

2004. 25th Anniv of Independence. Multicoloured.

5341	10c. Type **498**	25	15
5342	20c. Winston Davis (cricket player)	1·00	35
5343	70c. Pamenoa Ballantyne (athlete) (horiz)	60	50
5344	70c. Miss Carnival (2003)	60	50
5345	70c. Flag of St Vincent (horiz)	1·25	50
5346	90c. Rodney "Chang" Jack (football player) (horiz)	70	60
5347	90c. Breadfruit	70	60
5348	90c. Cecil "Blazer" Williams (playwright)	70	60
5349	$1.10 St Vincent parrot	2·00	80
5350	$5 George McIntosh (pharmacist)	3·25	3·75
5351	$5 Ebenezer Theodore Joshua (former Chief Minister and member of Parliament) (horiz)	3·25	3·75
5352	$5 Captain Hugh Mulzac (merchant marine naval officer)	3·25	3·75
5353	$10 Robert Milton Cato (socialist political leader)	6·00	7·50
5354	$10 His Excellency Joseph Chatoyer (Carib chief)	6·00	7·50

499 Players

2004. National Football Team.

5355	**499**	90c. multicoloured	1·00	1·00

500 David Ginola (France)

2004. Centenary of FIFA (Federation Internationale de Football Association). Multicoloured.

MS5356	192×97 mm. $2 Type **500**; $2 Paul Scholes (England); $2 Jurgen Kohler (Germany); $2 Ian Rush (Wales inscr. "England")	4·50	5·00
MS5357	107×87 mm. $6 Alan Shearer (England)	3·75	4·00

501 "Lion and His Keeper" (1954)

2004. 25th Death Anniv of Norman Rockwell (artist). Multicoloured.

5358	90c. Type **501**	70	55
5359	$1 "Weighing In" (1958)	80	65
5360	$1.40 "The Young Lawyer" (1927)	1·10	1·10
5361	$2 "The Bodybuilder" (1922)	1·50	2·00
MS5362	66×88 mm. $5 "Triple Self Portrait" (1960). Imperf	3·25	3·50

502 "Head of a Young Girl" (Jean-Baptiste Greuze)

2004. 300th Anniv of St. Petersburg. "Treasures of the Hermitage". Multicoloured.

5363	10c. Type **502**	20	15
5364	20c. "Two Actresses" (Jean-Baptiste Santerre)	35	25
5365	40c. "An Allegory of History" (Jose de Ribera)	45	35
5366	60c. "A Young Woman Trying on Earrings" (Rembrandt van Rijn)	50	50
5367	$1.40 "Count N. D. Guriev" (Jean Auguste-Dominique Ingres)	90	90
5368	$1.40 "Portrait of an Actor" (Domenico Fetti)	90	90

5369 $1.40 "Napoleon Bonaparte on the Bridge and Arcole" (Baron Antoine-Jean Gros) 90 90
5370 $1.40 "A Young Man with a Glove" (Frans Hals) 90 90
5371 $1.40 "Portrait of General Alexei Yermolov" (George Dawe) 90 90
5372 $1.40 "A Scholar" (Rembrandt van Rijn) 90 90
5373 $1.40 "Landscape with Obelisk" (Hubert Robert) 90 90
5374 $1.40 "At the Hermit's" (Hubert Robert) 90 90
5375 $1.40 "Landscape with Ruins" (Hubert Robert) 90 90
5376 $1.40 "Landscape with Terrace and Cascade" (Hubert Robert) 90 90
5377 $1.40 "A Shepherdess" (Jan Siberecht) 90 90
5378 $1.40 "Landscape with a Water-fall" (Hubert Robert) 90 90
5379 $2 "The Girlhood of the Virgin" (Francisco de Zurbaran) 1·25 1·40
5380 $5 "Portrait of a Woman" (Fran Pourbus the Elder) 3·00 3·25
MS5381 Three sheets. (a) 78×83 mm. $5 "Three Men at a Table" (Diego Rodriguez De Silva). (b) 97×72 mm. $5 "The Bean King" (Jacob Jordeans). (c) 88×76 mm. $5 "Family Portrait" (Cornelis de Vos). Imperf 8·50 9·50

503 Lebron James (Cleveland Cavaliers)

2004. National Basketball Association (1st series). Multicoloured.
5382 75c. Gary Payton (Los Angeles Lakers) 1·00 80
5383 75c. Type **503** 1·00 80
5384 75c. Adonal Foyle (Golden State Warriors) 1·00 80
5385 75c. Peja Stojakovic (Sacramento Kings) 1·00 80
See also Nos. 5434/5.

504 Elvis Presley

2004. 50th Anniv of "That's Alright Mama" (record by Elvis Presley).
5386 - $2 royal blue, light green and black 1·40 1·40
5387 - $2 bright magenta, new blue and black 1·40 1·40
5388 - $2 new blue, bright magenta and black 1·40 1·40
5389 - $2 light green, royal blue and black 1·40 1·40
5390 **504** $2 multicoloured 1·40 1·40
5391 - $2 multicoloured 1·40 1·40
5392 - $2 multicoloured 1·40 1·40
5393 - $2 multicoloured 1·40 1·40
DESIGNS: Nos. 5386, Microphone touching mouth; 5387, Dancing; 5388, Dancing with guitar; 5389, Playing guitar. Nos. 5390, Type **504**; 5391, Singing (from front); 5392, Singing (from side); 5393, Kissing guitar.

505 Captain Thomas Masterman Hardy

2004. Bicentenary of the Battle of Trafalgar. Multicoloured.
5394 50c. Type **505** 75 55
5395 $1 Napoleon Bonaparte 1·25 1·00
5396 $1.50 Admiral Lord Horatio Nelson 1·75 1·60
5397 $3 Admiral Cuthbert Collingwood 3·00 3·50
MS5398 Two sheets. (a) 93×67 mm. $5 HMS *Victory*. (b) 93×74 mm. $5 Lord Nelson briefing his officers 13·00 13·00

506 Deng Xiaoping

2004. Birth Centenary of Deng Xiaoping (leader of China, 1978—89). Sheet 96×66 mm.
MS5399 **506** $5 multicoloured 3·00 3·50

507 "Santa's Helpers"

2004. Christmas. Paintings by Norman Rockwell. Multicoloured.
5400 70c. Type **507** 60 30
5401 90c. "Tiny Tim" 70 45
5402 $1.10 "Department Store Santa" 90 80
5403 $3 "The Muggleton Stage Coach" 2·25 3·00
MS5404 64×84 mm. $5 "Extra Good Boys and Girls". Imperf 3·50 4·00

508 Subway Token, New York (1953)

2004. Subways. Multicoloured (except 5419/21).
5405 $1 Type **508** 1·00 1·00
5406 $1 Kiosk on 23rd Street, New York (early 1900s) 1·00 1·00
5407 $1 Hi-V 3398 subway car, New York (1935) 1·00 1·00
5408 $1 R6 1208 subway car interior, New York (1936) 1·00 1·00
5409 $1 Construction of Harlem River tunnel, New York (1904) 1·00 1·00
5410 $1 Underground construction, New York (early 1900's) 1·00 1·00
5411 $1 Above ground construction (men on ground), New York (early 1900s) 1·00 1·00
5412 $1 Above ground construction (men on crane), New York (early 1900s) 1·00 1·00
5413 $1.40 Moscow metro 1·25 1·25
5414 $1.40 Tokyo metro 1·25 1·25
5415 $1.40 Mexico City metro 1·25 1·25
5416 $1.40 Paris metro 1·25 1·25
5417 $1.40 Hong Kong metro 1·25 1·25
5418 $1.40 Prague metro 1·25 1·25
5419 $1.40 Thames tunnel (1859) (maroon and violet) 1·25 1·25
5420 $1.40 City and South London Railway locomotives (1890) (maroon and violet) 1·25 1·25
5421 $1.40 East London line (1940) (chocolate, violet and black) 1·25 1·25
5422 $1.40 Piccadilly line (1930) 1·25 1·25
5423 $1.40 Victoria line (1960) 1·25 1·25
5424 $1.40 Jubilee line (1990) 1·25 1·25
MS5425 Three sheets, each 91×71 mm. (a) $5 "A" train, New York. (b) $5 London Underground. (c) $5 1992 Tube, Central Line, London 14·00 14·00

509 Origami Rooster

2005. Chinese New Year ("New Year of the Rooster").
5426 **509** 75c. multicoloured 1·00 1·00

510 Mahatma Gandhi

2005. International Year of Peace. Multicoloured.
5427 $3 Type **510** 4·00 4·00
5428 $3 Elie Wiesel (Nobel Peace Prize winner, 1986) 4·00 4·00
5429 $3 Rigoberta Menchu Tum (Nobel Peace Prize winner, 1992) 4·00 4·00

511 Ploughing Fields

2005. International Year of Rice (2004). Multicoloured.
5430 $3 Type **511** 2·25 2·25
5431 $3 Man and boy in rice field 2·25 2·25
5432 $3 Man in rice field 2·25 2·25
MS5433 99×67 mm. $5 Boy eating rice (vert) 3·50 4·00

512 Kirk Hinrich (Chicago Bulls)

2005. National Basketball Association (2nd series). Multicoloured.
5434 75c. Type **512** 1·25 1·00
5435 $3 Steve Francis 3·00 3·00

513 Jehanzeb Khan (disabled by polio)

2005. Centenary of Rotary International. Multicoloured.
5436 $3 Type **513** 2·25 2·25
5437 $3 Jonas Salk and polio vaccine 2·25 2·25
5438 $3 Baby receiving oral polio vaccine 2·25 2·25

514 Prince Charles and Mrs. Camilla Parker-Bowles

2005. Royal Wedding. Multicoloured.
5439 $2 Type **514** 2·25 2·25
5440 $2 Wearing dark outer coats and looking left (horiz) 2·25 2·25

515 Pope John Paul II

2005. Commemoration of Pope John Paul II.
5441 $2 Wearing evening dress 2·25 2·25
5442 **515** $3 multicoloured 3·25 3·25

516 1939 20c. Vatican City Stamp

2005. Vacant See.
5443 **516** 70c. multicoloured 1·25 1·00

517 Red Irish Lord

2005. Predatory Fish. Multicoloured.
5444 $1 Type **517** 1·25 60
5445 $1.10 Deep Sea anglerfish 1·40 85
5446 $1.40 Viperfish 1·50 1·40
5447 $2 Lionfish 2·25 2·50
MS5448 110×70 mm. $5 Gulper eel 5·00 5·50

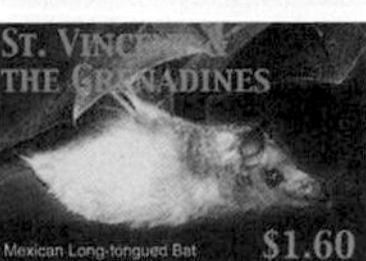

518 Mexican Long-tongued Bat

2005. Bats. Multicoloured.
MS5449 167×150 mm. $1.60×6, Type **518**; Wahlberg's fruit bat; Common vampire bat; false vampire bat; Horseshoe bat; Spear-nosed long-tongued bat 8·00 8·50
MS5450 112×83 mm. $5 Greater long-nosed bat 4·50 4·75

519 USSR T-34-85 Medium Tank

2005. 60th Anniv of Victory in Europe. Multicoloured.
5451 $2 Type **519** 2·50 2·50
5452 $2 German Tiger tank 2·50 2·50
5453 $2 USA LVT(A)-1 2·50 2·50
5454 $2 Great Britain Cruiser tank Mark VI 2·50 2·50
MS5455 100×70 mm. $5 Winston Churchill (vert) 7·00 6·00

520 Maimonides (statue)

2005. 800th Death Anniv of Moses Maimonides (Rabbi Moses Ben Maimon (Jewish scholar)) (2004).
5456 **520** $2 multicoloured 2·75 2·75

521 Field-Digger Wasp (*Mellinus arvensis*)

2005. Insects. Multicoloured.
5457 $2 Type **521** 2·00 2·00
5458 $2 Water spider (*Argyronetidae*) 2·00 2·00
5459 $2 Yellow crab spider (*Thomisus onustus*) 2·00 2·00
5460 $2 Mantid (*Empusa pennata*) 2·00 2·00
MS5461 70×100 mm. $5 Praying mantis (*Mantis religiosa*) 4·50 4·75

522 Butterwort (*Pinguicula rotundifolia*)

2005. Carnivorous Plants. Multicoloured.

5462	$2 Type **522**	2·25	2·25
5463	$2 Common sundew (*Drosera rotundifolia*)	2·25	2·25
5464	$2 Venus's flytrap (*Dionaea muscipula*)	2·25	2·25
5465	$2 Butterwort (*Pinguicula gypsicola*)	2·25	2·25
MS5466	69×99 mm. $5 Pitcher plant (*Nepenthes mixta*)	4·75	5·00

523 *The Brave Tin Soldier*

2005. Birth Bicentenary of Hans Christian Andersen (writer). Multicoloured.

5467	$3 Type **523**	1·75	2·00
5468	$3 *The Top and Ball*	1·75	2·00
5469	$3 *Ole-Luk-Oie, the Dream-God*	1·75	2·00
MS5470	100×70 mm. $5 *The Snow Queen* (50×38 mm)	3·00	3·25

524 Princess Aouda held Captive

2005. Death Centenary of Jules Verne (writer). Multicoloured.

5471-5474	$2×4 *Around the World in Eighty Days*: Type **524**; Phineas Fogg (David Niven) at train window (scene from 1956 film); Phineas Fogg; Passepartout	6·50	6·50
5475-5478	$2×4 *Twenty Thousand Leagues under the Sea*: Captain Nemo and *Nautilus* at surface; Captain Nemo looking through porthole; *Nautilus* crew watching giant octopus; Crew wearing helmets	6·50	6·50
5479-5482	$2×4 *Master of the World*: Terror (machine) on land; Terror at sea; Street scene; Terror in flight	6·50	6·50
5483-5486	$2×4 *From the Earth to the Moon*: Crew experiencing weightlessness; Space capsule on way to Moon; Take-off; Crew and space capsule	6·50	6·50
5487-5490	$2×4 *The Castle of the Carpathians*: Flying nyctalops; Crowd and ghost of La Stilla; Count Franz de Telek and Baron Rodolphe de Gortz; Orfanik (head conjuror)	6·50	6·50
MS5491	Five sheets, each 100×70 mm. (a) $5 Hot air balloon. (b) $5 Helicopter. (c) $5 Tank. (d) $5 Atomic bomb. (e) $5 Blitzkrieg of Second World War	20·00	20·00

525 Friedrich von Schiller

2005. Death Bicentenary of Friedrich von Schiller (poet and dramatist). Multicoloured.

5492	$2 Type **525**	1·75	2·00
5493	$3 In close-up (facing right)	1·75	2·00
5494	$3 In close-up (facing left)	1·75	2·00
MS5495	70×100 mm. $5 Friedrich von Schiller	3·00	3·25

526 Woolly Mammoth

2005. Expo 2005 Exhibition, Aichi, Japan. Sheet, 178×62 mm, containing **T 526** and similar horiz designs. Multicoloured.

MS5496	$2 Type **526**; $2 Woolly mammoth with long winter coat; $2 Woolly mammoth with huge upward curving tusks	5·50	6·00

527 SBD-3 *Dauntless*

2005. 60th Anniv of Victory in Japan Day. Multicoloured.

5497	$2 Type **527**	2·50	2·50
5498	$2 Mitsubishi Zero A6M5	2·50	2·50
5499	$2 USS *Yorktown* (aircraft carrier)	2·50	2·50
5500	$2 USS *Hornet* (aircraft carrier)	2·50	2·50
MS5501	100×70 mm. $5 Gen. Douglas MacArthur signing Japanese surrender	5·50	5·50

528 Panda

2005. Taipei 2005 International Stamp Exhibition. Multicoloured.

5502	$2 Type **528**	1·90	1·90
5503	$2 Formosan rock monkey	1·90	1·90
5504	$2 Formosan black bear	1·90	1·90
5505	$2 Formosan sika deer	1·90	1·90

2005. Christmas. As **T 155** of St. Kitts. Multicoloured.

5506	70c. "The Small Cowper Madonna" (detail) (Raphael)	65	30
5507	90c. "Madonna of the Grand Duke" (detail) (Raphael)	85	45
5508	$1.10 "The Sistine Madonna" (detail) (Raphael)	1·00	70
5509	$3 "The Alba Madonna" (detail) (Raphael)	2·75	3·50
MS5510	96×67 mm. $6 "Adoration of the Magi" (Rogier van der Weyden)	5·00	5·50

529 Dog

2005. Chinese New Year ("Year of the Dog").

5511	**529**	$1 multicoloured	1·40	1·25

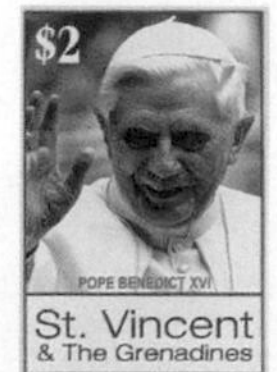

530 Pope Benedict XVI

2005. Election of Pope Benedict XVI.

5512	**530**	$2 multicoloured	2·75	2·75

531 "Panda" (Lauren Van Woy)

2006. "Kids-Did-It!" Designs. Showing children's paintings. Multicoloured.

5513	$2 Type **531**	1·40	1·40
5514	$2 "Giraffe" (Megan Albe)	1·40	1·40
5515	$2 "Orange Koala" (Holly Cramer)	1·40	1·40
5516	$2 "Red Monkey" (Roxanne Hanson)	1·40	1·40
5517	$2 "Flower Spot" (Tom Brier)	1·40	1·40
5518	$2 "Flower Vase" (Jessie Abrams)	1·40	1·40
5519	$2 "Green Flower Vase" (Nick Abrams)	1·40	1·40
5520	$2 "Red Sunflowers" (Bianca Saad)	1·40	1·40
5521	$2 "Snail" (Cortland Bobczynski)	1·40	1·40
5522	$2 "Blue Ladybug" (Jackie Wicks)	1·40	1·40
5523	$2 "Red Ladybug" (Emily Hawk)	1·40	1·40
5524	$2 "Snail Boy" (Micah Bobczynski)	1·40	1·40

532 St. Vincent Amazon Parrots

2006. 30th Anniv of the OPEC Fund for International Development. Multicoloured.

5525	$3 Type **532**	3·00	3·00
5526	$3 Waterfall in forest	3·00	3·00
5527	$3 Garden	3·00	3·00
5528	$3 Pair of St. Vincent Amazons	3·00	3·00

533 Duke and Duchess of York and Princess Elizabeth at her Christening

2006. 80th Birthday of Queen Elizabeth II. Multicoloured.

5529	$2 Type **533**	2·00	2·00
5530	$2 Princess Elizabeth making her first radio broadcast, 1940	2·00	2·00
5531	$2 Queen Elizabeth II at her Coronation, 1953	2·00	2·00
5532	$2 With Duke of Edinburgh, Princes Charles, Andrew and Edward and Princess Anne, c. 1965	2·00	2·00
5533	$2 Painting of Princesses Elizabeth and Margaret, c. 1937	2·00	2·00
5534	$2 Princess Elizabeth in ATS uniform, 1945	2·00	2·00
5535	$2 Wedding of Princess Elizabeth and Duke of Edinburgh, 1947	2·00	2·00
5536	$2 Awarding World Cup to England football captain Bobby Moore, 1966	2·00	2·00

534 Queen Angelfish

2006

5537	**534**	20c. multicoloured	15	20

535 Marilyn Monroe

2006. 80th Birth Anniv of Marilyn Monroe (actress).

5547	**535**	$3 multicoloured	1·75	2·00

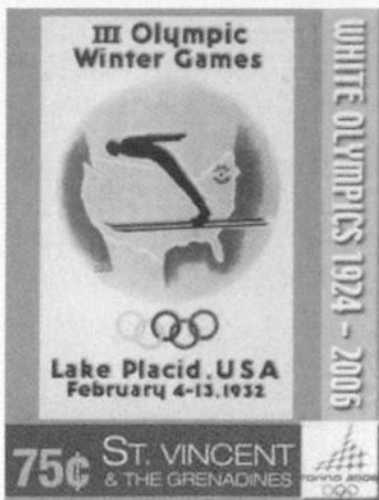

536 Poster for Winter Olympic Games, Lake Placid, 1932

2006. Winter Olympic Games, Turin. Multicoloured.

5548	75c. Type **536**	65	35
5549	90c. US 1932 Winter Olympics 2c. skiing stamp (horiz)	75	45
5550	$2 Poster for Winter Olympic Games, Chamonix, 1924	1·75	1·75
5551	$3 Letter postmarked for Winter Olympic Games, Chamonix, 1924	2·25	2·50

537 Nelson Mandela

2006. Washington 2006 International Stamp Exhibition.

5552	**537**	$3 multicoloured	2·00	2·25

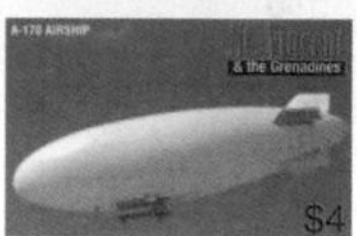

538 USS *Akron* (ZRS-4)

2006. 50th Death Anniv of Ludwig Durr (Zeppelin engineer). Multicoloured.

5553	$4 Type **538**	3·50	3·50
5554	$4 A-170 airship	3·50	3·50
5555	$4 Altair-Z experimental airship	3·50	3·50

539 "King Creole"

2006. 50th Anniv of Elvis Presley's Film Debut. Sheet 190×127 mm containing **T 539** and similar vert designs showing film posters. Multicoloured.

5556	$3 Type **539**	2·00	2·00
5557	$3 "Love Me Tender"	2·00	2·00
5558	$3 "Loving You"	2·00	2·00
5559	$3 "Roustabout"	2·00	2·00

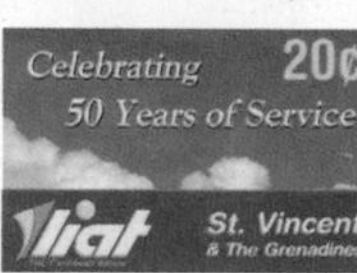

540 "Celebrating 50 Years of Service"

2006. 50th Anniv of LIAT (Leeward Islands Air Transport) Airline. Multicoloured.

5560	20c. Type **540**	35	15
5561	50c. DeHavilland DH8-300 in flight	75	45
5562	70c. HS-748 Hawker Siddely aircraft on ground	1·10	75
5563	90c. DeHavilland DH8-100 in flight	1·50	85
MS5564	99×70 mm. $5 Frank Delisle (founder) and first Beechcraft Twin Bonanza (vert)	5·50	6·00

541 Christopher Columbus

2006. 500th Death Anniv of Christopher Columbus. Multicoloured.

5565 50c. Type **541** 45 30
5566 70c. Christopher Columbus and Queen Isabella of Castile (horiz) 60 45
5567 $2 *Santa Maria* 2·25 2·25
5568 $3 *Santa Maria, Nina* and *Pinta* (horiz) 2·75 3·25
MS5569 70×100 mm. $5 *Pinta* 4·75 5·50

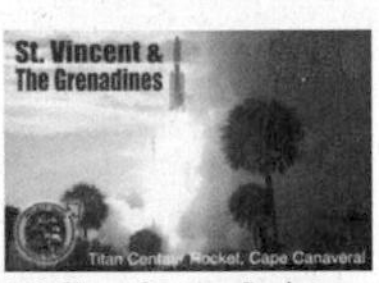

542 Titan Centaur Rocket taking-off, Cape Canaveral ("Viking I")

2006. Space Anniversaries. Multicoloured.

MS5570 Two sheets, each 150×100 mm. (a) $1.50×6 Type **542**; "Viking I", 1976; "Viking I" Lander on Mars, 1976; "Apollo XI" Landing Module on Moon, 1969; "Apollo XI" Command Module, 1969; "Apollo XI" launching by Saturn V rocket, 1969. (b) $2.50×4 S5 Mir; "Sputnik 1"; "Soyuz"; "Luna 9" 17·00 18·00
MS5571 Two sheets, each 100×70 mm. (a) $6 Artist's concept of crew exploration vehicle ("Return to the Moon"). (b) $6 Space Station MIR, 1986–81 11·00 12·00

The stamps and margins of **MS**5570(b) form a composite background design.

543 Great White Shark

2006. Endangered Species. Great White Shark (Carcharodon carcharias). Multicoloured.

5572 $1 Type **543** 1·00 1·00
5573 $1 With dolphins 1·00 1·00
5574 $1 Swimming to left 1·00 1·00
5575 $1 In close-up, showing teeth 1·00 1·00
MS5576 98×148 mm. Nos. 5572/5, each ×2 6·00 7·00

544 Princess Amalia

2006. Princess Amalia Alexia of the Netherlands. Multicoloured.

5577 $1.50 Type **544** 1·10 1·10
5578 $1.50 Princess Amalia (head and shoulders) 1·10 1·10
5579 $1.50 As baby 1·10 1·10

545 Cherub

2006. Christmas. Showing details from painting "Enthroned Madonna with Child, Encircled by Saints" by Rubens. Multicoloured.

5580 20c. Type **545** 30 10
5581 70c. Baby Jesus 60 30
5582 90c. Four saints 80 45
5583 $1.10 Virgin Mary 1·00 60
5584 $2 As Type **545** 2·00 2·25
5585 $2 As No. 5581 2·00 2·25
5586 $2 As No. 5582 2·00 2·25
5587 $2 As No. 5583 2·00 2·25

546 Captains waving Union Jack Flags

2006. Last Flights of Concorde, (2003). Multicoloured.

5588 $1.40 Type **546** 1·75 1·75
5589 $1.40 Concorde landing at Heathrow Airport 1·75 1·75
5590 $1.40 Concorde G-BOAF ("The Filton flypast") 1·75 1·75
5591 $1.40 "Concorde Comes Home to Filton" 1·75 1·75

Nos. 5588/9 show the last commercial flight on 24 October 2003 and Nos. 5590/1 show the last ever Concorde flight on 26 November 2003.

547 Pres. Chen Shui-bian of Taiwan and Ralph Gonsalves (St. Vincent Prime Minister)

2006. 25th Anniv of Diplomatic Relations with Taiwan. Multicoloured.

5592 10c. Type **547** 15 15
5593 20c. Pres. Chen, Ralph Gonsalves and woman in St. Vincent parrot costume 20 15
5594 50c. Pres. Chen and Ralph Gonsalves shaking hands 30 25
5595 70c. Pres. Chen on visit to St. Vincent, 2005 45 35
5596 90c. Ralph Gonsalves and Pres. Chen 60 45
5597 $1.10 Taiwan Premier Yu Shyi-kun and Ralph Gonsalves 75 70
5598 $1.40 St. Vincent schoolchildren waving Taiwan flags 1·00 1·10
MS5599 Three sheets, each 98×68 mm. (a) $5 Pres. Chen and Ralph Gonsalves looking at documents. (b) $5 Milton Cato (first St. Vincent Prime Minister) establishing relations with Taiwan, 1979. (c) $5 Ralph Gonsalves, his wife and Premier Yu Shyi-kun 8·00 9·50

2006. 400th Birth Anniv of Rembrandt Harmenszoon van Rijn (artist). As **T 157** of St. Kitts showing paintings. Multicoloured.

5600 50c. "The Jewish Physician Ephraim Bueno" 40 25
5601 75c. "Portrait of Ariantje Hollaer, Wife of Hendrick Martensz-Sorgh" 60 45
5602 $1 "An Old Man in a Fur Cap" 75 60
5603 $2 "Saskia van Uylenburgh" 1·40 1·50
5604 $2 "The Denial of St. Peter" (detail, woman) 1·40 1·50
5605 $2 "The Raising of Lazarus" (detail, Jesus Christ) 1·40 1·50
5606 $2 "The Denial of St. Peter" (detail, St. Peter) 1·40 1·50
5607 $2 "The Raising of Lazarus" (detail, Lazarus) 1·40 1·50
5608 $2 "Portrait of Titia van Uylenburgh" 1·40 1·50
5609 $2 "The Standing Syndic" 1·40 1·50
5610 $2 "Polish Officer" (detail) 1·40 1·50
5611 $2 "Seated Girl, in Profile to Left, Half Nude" 1·40 1·50
MS5612 Two sheets, each 70×100 mm. (a) $5 "Man Standing in Front of a Doorway". Imperf. (b) 70×100 mm. $5 "Two Young Negroes". Imperf 6·00 7·00

548 Wolfgang Amadeus Mozart

2007. 250th Birth Anniv of Wolfgang Amadeus Mozart. Sheet 100×70 mm.

MS5613 **548** $5 multicoloured 6·50 6·00

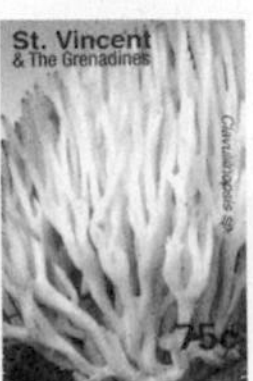

549 *Clavulilnopsis* sp.

2007. Mushrooms of the Caribbean. Multicoloured.

5614 75c. Type **549** 1·00 55
5615 90c. *Cortinarius* sp. 1·25 60
5616 $2 *Cortinarius* cf. 2·50 2·50
5617 $3 *Conocybe* spp 3·25 3·75
MS5618 100×70 mm. $6 *Galerina paludosa* 6·00 6·00

550 Lord Baden-Powell (founder) standing on Globe

2007. Centenary of Scouting. Multicoloured.

5619 $4 Type **550** 3·50 3·75
MS5620 80×110 mm. $6 Lord Baden-Powell and peace dove (horiz) 5·50 6·00

551 Congressman Kennedy

2007. 90th Birth Anniv of John F. Kennedy (US President 1960–3). Multicoloured.

5621 $3 Type **551** 2·25 2·25
5622 $3 Campaigning on crutches 2·25 2·25
5623 $3 Outdoors, wearing white t-shirt 2·25 2·25
5624 $3 Full-face portrait 2·25 2·25
5625 $3 *PT-109* 2·25 2·25
5626 $3 *PT-109* crew 2·25 2·25
5627 $3 Lieutenant Kennedy 2·25 2·25
5628 $3 Japanese destroyer 2·25 2·25

Nos. 5621/4 ("Elected to the House of Representatives 1947–53) and 5625/8 ("John Fitzgerald Kennedy Joins the Navy 1941–5).

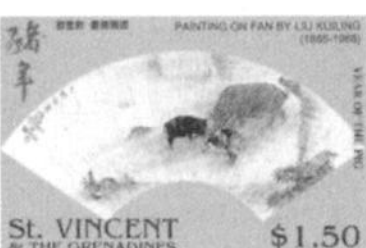

552 Pigs (painting on fan by Liu Kuiling)

2007. Chinese New Year ("Year of the Pig").

5629 **552** $1.50 multicoloured 1·75 1·75

553 Bahama Yellowthroat

2007. Birds of the Caribbean. Multicoloured.

5630 $2 Type **553** 2·75 2·75
5631 $2 Arrow-headed warbler 2·75 2·75
5632 $2 Northern jacana 2·75 2·75
5633 $2 Loggerhead kingbird 2·75 2·75
MS5634 100×70 mm. $6 Louisiana waterthrush (horiz) 7·50 7·50

554 *Ancyluris jurgensenii*

2007. Butterflies of the Caribbean. Multicoloured.

5635 $2 Type **554** 2·75 2·75
5636 $2 *Arcas cypria* 2·75 2·75
5637 $2 *Stalachtis phlegia* 2·75 2·75
5638 $2 *Xamia xami* 2·75 2·75
MS5639 100×70 mm. $5 *Theritas coronata* 7·00 7·00

555 *Stanhopea grandiflora*

2007. Orchids. Multicoloured.

5640 $2 Type **555** 2·75 2·75
5641 $2 *Psychopsis papilio* 2·75 2·75
5642 $2 *Vanilla planifolia* 2·75 2·75
5643 $2 *Tetramicra canaliculata* 2·75 2·75
MS5644 100×70 mm. $5 *Trichopilia fragrans* (horiz) 7·00 7·00

556 Cameron Cuffy

2007. World Cup Cricket, West Indies. Multicoloured.

5645 30c. Type **556** 55 40
5646 30c. Ian Allen 55 40
5647 $1.05 Neil Williams 1·50 1·00
5648 $1.35 Wilfred Slack 1·60 1·75
5649 $1.35 Michael Findlay 1·60 1·75
5650 $1.65 Winston Davis 1·75 2·00
5651 $1.65 Nixon McLean 1·75 2·00
5652 $2.10 Alphonso (Alfie) Roberts 2·40 2·50
MS5653 117×90 mm. $6 Arnos Vale Stadium, St. Vincent (horiz) 7·00 7·00

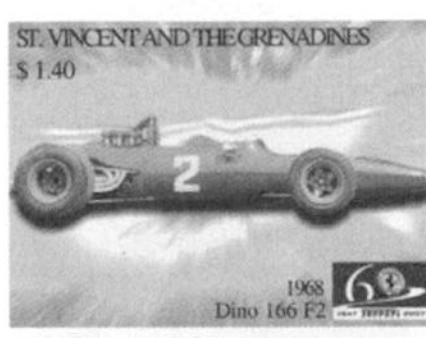

557 Dino 166 F2, 1968

2007. 60th Anniv of Ferrari Cars. Multicoloured.

5654 $1.40 Type **557** 1·25 1·25
5655 $1.40 246 F1, 1958 1·25 1·25
5656 $1.40 308 GTS, 1977 1·25 1·25
5657 $1.40 365 P Speciale, 1966 1·25 1·25
5658 $1.40 Enzo Ferrari, 2002 1·25 1·25
5659 $1.40 F40, 1987 1·25 1·25
5660 $1.40 348 Spider, 1993 1·25 1·25
5661 $1.40 212 Inter, 1951 1·25 1·25

558 Queen Elizabeth II and Duke of Edinburgh

2007. Diamond Wedding of Queen Elizabeth II and Duke of Edinburgh. Multicoloured.

5662 $1.40 Type **558** 1·50 1·50
5663 $1.40 In evening dress, in recent years 1·50 1·50
MS5664 72×102 mm. $6 In evening dress (Duke wearing military uniform), c. 1965 (vert) 6·00 6·00

559 Diana, Princess of Wales

2007. Tenth Death Anniv of Diana, Princess of Wales. Multicoloured.

5665 $2 Type **559** 2·00 2·00
5666 $2 Wearing dark blue pin-striped jacket and dress 2·00 2·00
5667 $2 Wearing black and white jacket 2·00 2·00
5668 $2 Wearing white V-necked dress 1·25 2·00
MS5669 Two sheets, each 72×102 mm. (a) $6 Wearing hat and spotted blouse. (b) $6 Wearing Red Cross uniform 11·00 12·00

560 Elvis Presley

2007. 30th Death Anniv of Elvis Presley. Multicoloured.

5670	$1.40 Type **560**	1·25	1·25
5671	$1.40 Wearing V-necked sweater	1·25	1·25
5672	$1.40 Wearing cable-knit sweater	1·25	1·25
5673	$1.40 Wearing striped shirt	1·25	1·25
5674	$1.40 Wearing jacket and tie	1·25	1·25
5675	$1.40 Wearing western shirt	1·25	1·25

561 Pope Benedict XVI

2007. 80th Birthday of Pope Benedict XVI.

5676	**561**	$1.50 multicoloured	2·25	2·25

562 Capt. Havildar Lachhiman Gurung

2007. 150th Anniv of the First Presentation of the Victoria Cross. Multicoloured.

5677	$1.40 Type **562**	1·75	1·75
5678	$1.40 Ernest Alvia ('Smokey') Smith	1·75	1·75
5679	$1.40 Nk. Yeshwant Ghadge	1·75	1·75
5680	$1.40 Lieut. Colonel Eric Charles Twelves Wilson	1·75	1·75
5681	$1.40 Warrant Officer Class 2 Keith Payne	1·75	1·75
5682	$1.40 Lance Corporal Rambahadur Limbu	1·75	1·75
MS5683	100×70 mm. $6 Piper James Richardson	7·00	7·00

563 Delano Bart, St. Kitts & Nevis

2007. Holocaust Remembrance. Multicoloured.

5684	$1.40 Type **563**	1·25	1·25
5685	$1.40 Margaret H. Ferrari, St. Vincent & the Grenadines	1·25	1·25
5686	$1.40 Ali'ioaiga F. Elisaia, Samoa	1·25	1·25
5687	$1.40 Daniele D. Bodini, San Marino	1·25	1·25
5688	$1.40 Pavle Jevremovic, Serbia	1·25	1·25
5689	$1.40 Joe R. Pemagbi, Sierra Leone	1·25	1·25
5690	$1.40 Peter Burian, Slovakia	1·25	1·25
5691	$1.40 Sanja Stiglic, Slovenia	1·25	1·25

564 *The Nativity and the Arrival of the Magi* (Giovanni di Pietro)

2007. Christmas. Multicoloured.

5692	20c. Type **564**	25	10
5693	70c. *The Annunciation* (Benozzo Gozzoli)	80	50
5694	90c. *The Nativity* (Benozzo Gozzoli)	1·00	65
5695	$1.10 *The Journey of the Magi* (Sassetta)	1·25	1·25

565 *Bombus bimaculatus* (bumble bee)

2007. Insects. Multicoloured.

5696	5c. Type **565**	15	30
5697	10c. *Stagmomantis carolina* (praying mantis)	20	30
5698	30c. *Photinus pyralis* (firefly) (vert)	45	25
5699	$1.35 *Anax junius* (green darner dragonfly) (vert)	1·75	2·00

566 Rat

2008. Chinese New Year ('Year of the Rat').

5700	**566**	$1.50 multicoloured	1·75	1·75

567 Bob Mathias (USA) (decathlon gold medallist)

2008. Olympic Games, Beijing. **T 567** and similar vert designs showing scenes from Olympic Games, Helsinki, 1952. Multicoloured.

5701	$1.40 Type **567**	6·25	6·25
5702	$1.40 Poster for Olympic Games, Helsinki, 1952	1·75	1·75
5703	$1.40 Josy Barthel (Luxembourg) winning 1500 metres	1·75	1·75
5704	$1.40 Lis Hartel (Denmark) (dressage silver medallist)	1·75	1·75

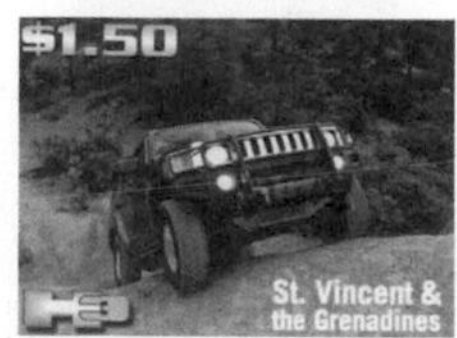

568 Hummer H3

2008. Hummer H3. Multicoloured.

5705	$1.50 Type **568**	1·50	1·50
5706	$1.50 BNE 904 off-road on rocky track	1·50	1·50
5707	$1.50 Crossing muddy water in forest	1·50	1·50
5708	$1.50 Ascending sand hill in forest	1·50	1·50
MS5709	100×70 mm. $6 In silhouette	5·50	5·50

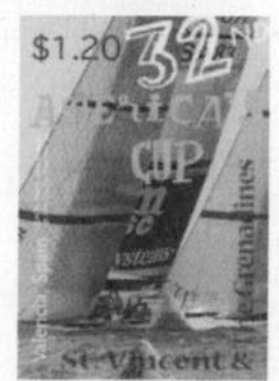

569 Yachts

2008. 32nd Americas Cup Yachting Championship, Valencia, Spain. Multicoloured.

5710	$1.20 Type **569**	1·50	2·00
5711	$1.80 Yachts from Germany and France	1·75	2·25
5712	$3 Two yachts, 'Fly Emirates' (on sail) in foreground	1·50	3·00
5713	$5 Two yachts, magenta sail at left	3·75	4·25

570 Taipei 101 Tower

2008. Taipei 2008 International Stamp Exhibition. Multicoloured.

5714	$1.50 Type **570**	1·50	1·50
5715	$1.50 Chinese pagoda	1·50	1·50
5716	$1.50 High speed railway	1·50	1·50
5717	$1.50 Lion dance	1·50	1·50
MS5718	100×70 mm. $5 National Taiwan Democracy Memorial Hall (51×37 mm)	4·00	4·50

571 Elvis Presley holding Rifle

2008. 50th Anniv of Elvis Presley's Induction into the US Army. Sheet 160×130 mm containing **T 571** and similar vert designs showing him in Army uniform. Multicoloured.

MS5719	Type **571**; In Army uniform (against wall); Seated in red car; In Army uniform (against car)	4·00	4·00

The stamps within **MS**5719 share a composite background design.

572 Machu Picchu, Peru

2008. Seven New Wonders of the World. Sheet 155×120 mm containing **T 572** and similar horiz designs. Multicoloured.

MS5720	Type **572**; Petra, Jordan; Chichén Itza, Mexico; Colosseum, Rome; Taj Mahal, India; Statue of Christ the Redeemer, Brazil; The Great Wall of China	12·00	11·00

The stamps within **MS**5720 form a composite background design.

573 *Queen Victoria*

2008. Historic meeting of 3 queens

5721	$3 Type **573**	4·00	4·00
5722	$3 *Queen Elizabeth II*	4·00	4·00
5723	$3 *Queen Mary II*	4·00	4·00

574 Pope Benedict XVI

2008. First Visit of Pope Benedict XVI to the United States.

5724	**574**	$2 multicoloured	3·25	3·25

575 Arms

2008. 60th Anniv of the University of the West Indies. Multicoloured.

5725	10c. Type **575**	20	20
5726	30c. Scroll	30	20
5727	90c. UWDEC Media Centre (horiz)	80	70
5728	$1.05 Anniversary emblem	1·00	1·25
MS5729	70×100 mm. $6 Scroll and anniversary emblem (horiz)	6·00	6·50

576 Austrian Team

2008. Eurocup 2008 European Football Championship, Austria and Switzerland. **T 576** and similar horiz designs showing teams and stadiums. Multicoloured.

MS5730	Sixteen sheets, each 187×115 mm. (a) $1.40×6 As Type **576**×4 Tivoli Stadium, Innsbruck, Austria; St. Jakob Park Stadium, Basel, Switzerland. (b) $1.40×6 Croatian team×4; Tivoli Stadium; Stade de Geneve, Geneva, Switzerland. (c) $1.40×6 Czech Republic team×4; Tivoli Stadium; Stade de Suisse, Wankdorf, Bern, Switzerland. (d) $1.40×6 French team×4; Tivoli Stadium; Letzigrund Stadium, Zurich, Switzerland. (e) $1.40×6 German team×4; Worthersee Stadium, Hypo Arena, Klagenfurt, Austria; St. Jakob Park Stadium. (f) $1.40×6 Greek team×4; Worthersee Stadium, Hypo Arena; Stade de Suisse. (g) $1.40×6 Italian team×4; Worthersee Stadium, Hypo Arena; Stade de Geneve. (h) $1.40×6 Netherlands team×4; Worthersee Stadium, Hypo Arena; Letzigrund Stadium. (i) $1.40×6 Polish team×4; Wals-Siezenheim Stadium, Salzburg, Austria; St. Jakob Park Stadium. (j) $1.40×6 Portuguese team×4; Wals-Seizenheim Stadium; Stade de Suisse. (k) Romanian team×4; Wals-Seizenheim Stadium; Stade de Geneve. (l) $1.40×6 Russian team×4; Wals-Seizenheim Stadium; Letzigrund Stadium. (m) $1.40×6 Spanish team×4; Ernst Happel Stadium, Vienna, Austria; St. Jakob Park Stadium. (n) $1.40×6 Swedish team×4; Ernst Happel Stadium; Stade de Suisse. (o) $1.40×6 Swiss team×4; Ernst Happel Stadium; Stade de Geneve. (p) $1.40×6 Turkish team×4; Ernst Happel Stadium; Letzigrund Stadium	60·00	60·00
MS5731	280×215 mm. 65c.×16 National teams: Czech Republic; Turkey; Switzerland; Portugal; Austria; Croatia; Poland; Germany; France; Netherlands; Romania; Italy; Greece; Sweden; Russia; Spain	8·00	8·00

577 Three Teenagers

2008. 50th Anniv of the Credit Union. Multicoloured.

5732	10c. Type **577**	20	20
5733	30c. Man (vert)	30	25
5734	90c. Woman (vert)	80	70
5735	$1.05 Elderly man (vert)	1·00	1·25
MS5736	100×71 mm. $6 Kingstown Co-operative Credit Union Financial Centre	6·00	6·50

578 Valentina Tereshkova (first woman in Space)

2008. 50 Years of Space Exploration and Satellites. Multicoloured.

5737	$1.40 Type **578**	1·25	1·25
5738	$1.40 Valentina Tereshkova wearing black jacket and white tie-neck blouse	1·25	1·25
5739	$1.40 *Vostok 6*	1·25	1·25
5740	$1.40 Valentina Tereshkova wearing orange space suit	1·25	1·25
5741	$1.40 Statue of Valentina Tereshkova	1·25	1·25
5742	$1.40 Valentina Tereshkova wearing space suit (without helmet)	1·25	1·25

5743	$1.40 Titan IIIE/Centaur rocket with *Viking I*	1·25	1·25
5744	$1.40 Technical drawing of *Viking I* Orbiter/Lander	1·25	1·25
5745	$1.40 *Viking I* Lander landing on Mars	1·25	1·25
5746	$1.40 *Viking I* orbiting Mars	1·25	1·25
5747	$1.40 Technical drawing of *Viking I* Lander	1·25	1·25
5748	$1.40 Picture of Mars surface from *Viking I*	1·25	1·25
5749	$1.40 *Pioneer 11* and Saturn	1·25	1·25
5750	$1.40 Atlas Centaur 27 rocket with *Pioneer 10*	1·25	1·25
5751	$1.40 Pioneer plaque	1·25	1·25
5752	$1.40 *Pioneer 10* and Jupiter	1·25	1·25
5753	$1.40 *Pioneer 10* and *11* technical drawing	1·25	1·25
5754	$1.40 Pioneer programme spacecraft	1·25	1·25
5755	$2 *Mariner 4* Mars Encounter Imaging Geometry	1·90	1·90
5756	$2 *Mariner 4*	1·90	1·90
5757	$2 Atlas Agena D rocket launching *Mariner 4*	1·90	1·90
5758	$2 *Mariner 4* passing Mars	1·90	1·90
5759	$2 *Freedom 7*	1·90	1·90
5760	$2 Astronaut Alan Shepard	1·90	1·90
5761	$2 *Vostok*	1·90	1·90
5762	$2 Cosmonaut Yuri Gagarin (first man in space)	1·90	1·90
5763	$2 *Luna 2*	1·90	1·90
5764	$2 Soviet pennants for *Luna 2*	1·90	1·90
5765	$2 *Luna 2* rocket launch aboard Luna 8K72	1·90	1·90
5766	$2 *Luna 2* above Moon	1·90	1·90

579 The Nativity

2008. Christmas. Designs showing nativity paintings.

5767	**579**	75c. multicoloured	70	45
5768	**579**	90c. multicoloured	80	55
5769	**579**	$2 multicoloured	1·90	1·90
5770	**579**	$3 multicoloured	2·75	3·25

580 Pres. Barack Obama

2009. Inauguration of Pres. Barack Obama. Multicoloured.

5771	$1.75 Type **580**	2·00	2·00
MS5772	132×94 mm. $2.75 Pres. Obama, statue of Pres. Abraham Lincoln in background (26×33 mm) ×4	8·00	9·00
MS5773	132×94 mm. $6.50 No. 5771; $6.50 Vice President Joseph Biden	11·00	12·00

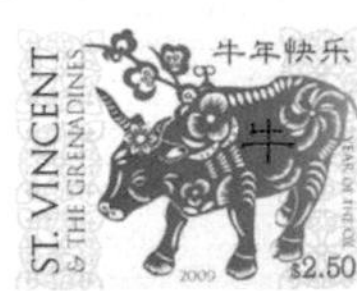

581 Ox

2009. Chinese New Year. Year of the Ox. Sheet 190×90 mm.

MS5774 $2.50 Type **581**×4 — 8·00 8·00

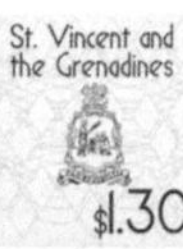

582 Arms of St. Vincent

2009

5775	**582**	$1.30 deep lilac and grey	1·00	80

583 First Inaugural Address, 1861

2009. Birth Bicentenary of Abraham Lincoln (US President 1861–5). **T 583** and similar vert designs. Multicoloured.

MS5776 126×180 mm. $2×6 Type **583**; Abraham Lincoln (older); With Union troops; Reward poster for his killer; Abraham Lincoln (younger, US flag in background); Detail from *First Reading of the Emancipation Proclamation of PresidentLincoln* by Francis Bicknell Carpenter — 10·00 11·00

MS5777 100×70 mm. $6 Head of Abraham Lincoln statue (37×50 mm) — 5·00 5·50

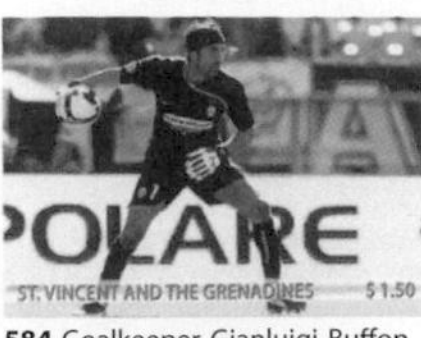

584 Goalkeeper Gianluigi Buffon

2009. Juventus Football Club, Turin, Italy. Sheet 173×134 mm containing **T 584** and similar horiz designs. Multicoloured.

MS5778 Type **584**; Mauro Camoranesi celebrating with David Trezeguet; Juventus captain Alessandro Del Piero celebrating a goal; Pavel Nedved (Czech Republic) celebrating with Mohammad Sissoko; Juventus fans inside their Stadio Olimpico di Torino; French striker David Trezeguet celebrating a goal; Zinedine Zidane (as Juventus player) celebrating; Italian striker Christian Vieri playing against Argentinian club River Plate — 9·00 10·00

585 Biplane and Astronaut on USA Ohio State Quarter

2009. International Year of Astronomy. 40th Anniv of First Moon Landing. Sheet 150×100 mm containing **T 585** and similar vert designs. Multicoloured.

MS5779 Type **585**; Apollo 11 Command Module; Apollo 11 badge; Apollo 11 Lunar Module; Diagram of Apollo 11 and Moon's surface; Astronaut Neil Armstrong — 12·00 13·00

586 Pope Benedict XVI

2009. Visit of Pope Benedict XVI to Jordan. Sheet 100×150 mm. Multicoloured.

MS5780 $1.50, $2, $2.50, $3 all As Type **586** — 13·00 13·00

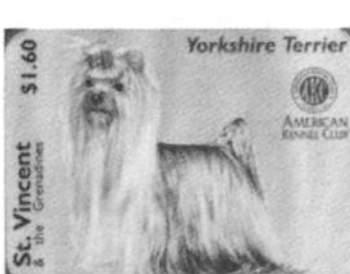

587 Yorkshire Terrier

2009. 125th Anniv of the American Kennel Club. Multicoloured.

MS5781 140×160 mm. $1.60×9 Type **587**; German shepherd dog; Golden retriever; Beagle; Dachshund; Boxer; Poodle; Shih tzu; Miniature schnauzer — 16·00 16·00

MS5782 100×120 mm. $3.25×4 Yorkshire terrier in pink basket with flowers at right; Yorkshire terrier (in front of basket); Yorkshire terrier (in close-up, white flowers at left); Yorkshire terrier (on red bench) — 15·00 15·00

588 *A Midsummer NIght's Dream* (David Scott)

2009. Birth Bicentenary of Felix Mendelssohn (composer). Sheet 164×94 mm containing **T 588** and similar vert designs. Multicoloured.

MS5783 Type **588**; *Felix Mendelssohn* (Eduard Magnus); *Cécile Jeanrenaud* (Eduard Magnus); Score for *On Wings of Song* in Mendelssohn's hand; Gewandhausorchester; Drawing of interior of Church of the Holy Ghost by Mendelssohn — 16·00 16·00

589 Michael Jackson

2009. Michael Jackson Commemoration. Multicoloured.

MS5784 120×157 mm. $2.25 Type **589**; $2.25 Wearing white; $2.75 As Type **589**; $2.75 Wearing white — 8·50 9·50

MS5785 158×112 mm. $2.50×4 Wearing pink and brown jacket; Wearing white jacket; Wearing silver jacket; Wearing white jacket with zip and black collar — 8·50 9·50

(589a)

2009. Michael Jackson Commemoration (2nd issue). As Nos. 940/8 but with new face values and optd with T **589a**.

5785a	45c. Type **151**	75	75
5785b	45c. Wearing red and blue T shirt and dark jacket and hat	1·50	1·50
5785c	90c. Wearing red and white jacket, holding microphone	75	75
5785d	90c. Wearing black T shirt over white shirt	1·40	1·40
5785e	$1.50 Wearing black, red and gold jacket and white shirt	1·40	1·40
5785f	$1.50 Wearing red and gold jacket	1·40	1·40
5785g	$4 Wearing white cap	1·40	1·40
5785h	$4 Wearing red and gold jacket and white gloves	3·25	3·25
MS5785i	144×109 mm. Nos. 5785*a*/*b*, each ×2	3·25	3·25
MS5785j	144×109 mm. Nos. 5785*c*/*d*, each ×2	3·00	3·00
MS5785k	144×109 mm. Nos. 5785*e*/*f*, each ×2	5·50	5·50
MS5785l	144×109 mm. Nos. 5785*g*/*h*, each ×2	6·50	6·50

590 Michelangelo

2009. 25th Anniv of Teenage Mutant Ninja Turtles. Sheet 107×174 mm containing **T 590** and similar horiz designs. Multicoloured.

MS5786 Type **590**; Donatello; Leonardo; Raphael — 8·00 9·00

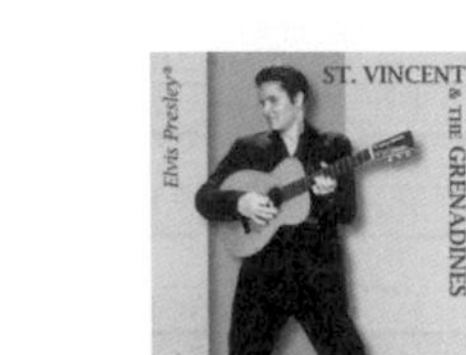

591 Elvis Presley

2009. Elvis Presley Commemoration. **T 591** and similar vert designs. Multicoloured.

MS5787 160×130 mm. $2.50×4 Type **591**; With both arms raised; With arm raised; Standing sideways — 8·00 8·00

MS5788 90×125 mm. $6 Elvis Presley as Lucky Johnson in *Viva Las Vegas*, 1964 — 8·00 8·00

MS5789 125×90 mm. $6 Poster for *Viva Las Vegas* — 8·00 8·00

MS5790 125×90 mm. $6 Elvis Presley wearing red shirt — 8·00 8·00

MS5791 90×125 mm. $6 Wearing red shirt and brown jacket — 8·00 8·00

592 Penguins swimming

2009. Philakorea 2009 International Stamp Exhibition. Preserve the Polar Regions and Glaciers. Designs showing collage of Arctic penguins made from scraps of material. Multicoloured.

MS5792 120×100 mm. $3×4 Type **592**; Penguin walking with beak open and wings raised; Penguins with wings raised; Adult and chick — 11·00 11·00

MS5793 100×70 mm. $6 Penguins with chick (37×70 mm) — 6·50 6·50

593 White-rumped Sandpiper (*Calidris fuscicollis*)

2009. Water Birds of St. Vincent. Multicoloured.

5794	$1.20 Type **593**	1·50	1·00
5795	$1.80 Tricolored heron (*Egretta tricolor*)	1·75	1·25
5796	$3 Masked booby (*Sula dactylatra*)	3·25	3·50
5797	$5 Red-footed booby (*Sula sula*) (vert)	5·50	6·50
MS5798	90×119 mm. $2.50×4 Brown pelican (*Pelecanus occidentalis*); Great blue heron (*Ardea herodias*); Snowy egret (*Egretta thula*); Pied-billed grebe (*Podilymbus podiceps*) (all vert)	11·00	11·00
MS5799	70×100 mm. $3×2 Ring-billed gull (*Larus delawarensis*); Short-billed dowitcher (*Limnodromus griseus*) (both vert)	8·00	8·00

594 Samuel de Champlain

2009. New York State's Quadricentennial Celebrations. Sheet 130×78 mm containing T **594** and similar vert designs. Multicoloured.

MS5800 Type **594** (400th anniv of his discovery of Lake Champlain); Robert Fulton (bicentenary of first New York–Albany steamboat voyage); Henry Hudson (400th anniv of his discovery of Manhattan); USA 1909 2c. Hudson-Fulton Celebration stamp — 9·00 10·00

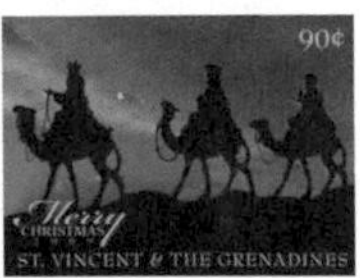

595 Journey of the Magi

2009. Christmas. Multicoloured.

5801	90c. Type **595**	75	55
5802	$1.80 Shepherds and infant Jesus	1·40	1·10
5803	$2.50 Magi and infant Jesus	2·25	2·50
5804	$3 Virgin Mary and infant Jesus	2·75	3·25

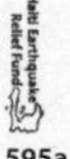

595a

2010. Haiti Earthquake Relief Fund. As No. **MS**5798 overprinted.

MS5804a $2.50×4 Brown pelican (*Pelecanus occidentalis*); Great blue heron (*Ardea herodias*); Snowy egret (*Egretta thula*); Pied-billed grebe (*Podilymbus podiceps*) — 10·00 11·00

596 Australia

2010. World Cup Football, South Africa. Designs showing teams. Multicoloured.

MS5805 170×132 mm. $1.75×8 Type **596**; Japan; North Korea; South Korea; Honduras; Mexico; United States; New Zealand 12·00 13·00

MS5806 170×132 mm. $1.75×8 Denmark; France; Greece; Portugal; Serbia; Slovakia; Slovenia; Switzerland 12·00 13·00

MS5807 170×132 mm. $1.75×8 Algeria; Cameroon; Côte D'Ivoire; Ghana; Nigeria; Chile; Paraguay; Uruguay 12·00 13·00

MS5808 170×132 mm. $1.75×8 South Africa; Brazil; Spain; Netherlands; Italy; Germany; Argentina; England 12·00 13·00

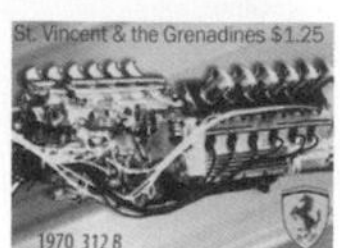

597 Engine of Ferrari 312 B, 1970

2010. Ferrari Cars. Multicoloured.

5809	$1.25 Type **597**	1·00	1·00
5810	$1.25 312 B, 1970 (car no. 25)	1·00	1·00
5811	$1.25 Engine of 126 CX, 1981	1·00	1·00
5812	$1.25 126 CX, 1981	1·00	1·00
5813	$1.25 Engine of DINO 308 GT4, 1973	1·00	1·00
5814	$1.25 DINO 308 GT4, 1973	1·00	1·00
5815	$1.25 Gears of 400 Automatic, 1976	1·00	1·00
5816	$1.25 400 Automatic, 1976	1·00	1·00

598 Oval Office

2010. 50th Anniv of Election of President John F. Kennedy. Multicoloured.

MS5817 150×100 mm. $2×6 Type **598**; John F. Kennedy; Jackie Kennedy; Lady Bird Johnson; Lyndon B. Johnson; White House 9·00 9·50

MS5818 130×100 mm. $2.75×4 John F. Kennedy (photographed indoors); John F. Kennedy Presidential Library and Museum; Statue of John F. Kennedy, Regents Park, London; Presidential Seal 8·50 9·00

599 Elvis Presley

2010. 75th Birth Anniv of Elvis Presley. Multicoloured.

MS5819 180×159 mm. $2.75×4 Wearing black leather: Type **599**; Playing guitar; Singing, holding guitar; Facing left 8·50 8·50

MS5820 168×129 mm. $2.75×4 Wearing jacket, with guitar; Wearing jacket, hands raised to face; Wearing jacket, right hand on head; Wearing T shirt 8·50 8·50

600 Leatherback Turtle (*Dermochelys coriacea*)

2010. Caribbean Marine Life. Multicoloured.

5821	25c. Type **600**	40	15
5822	80c. Caesar grunt (*Haemulon carbonarium*)	1·00	70
5823	$1 Atlantic tarpon (*Megalops atlanticus*)	1·25	80
5824	$5 Moray eel (*Strophidon sathete*)	5·00	6·00

MS5825 170×101 mm. $2×6 Caribbean reef shark (*Carcharhinus perezi*); Loggerhead sea turtle (*Caretta caretta*); Great barracuda (*Sphyraena barracuda*); Caribbean lobster (*Metanephrops binghami*); Royal gramma (*Gramma loreto*); Southern stingray (*Dasyatis americana*) 10·00 10·00

The stamps and margins of **MS**5825 form a composite background design of a coral reef

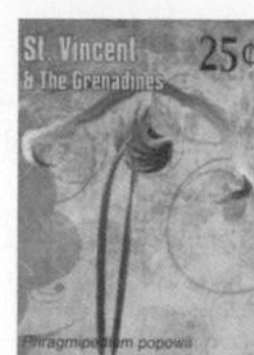

601 *Phragmipedium popowii*

2010. Orchids of the Caribbean. Multicoloured.

5826	25c. Type **601**	45	20
5827	80c. *Cattleya dowiana*	1·10	80
5828	$1 *Brassavola subulifolia*	1·40	90
5829	$5 *Brassavola acaulis*	5·50	6·50

MS5830 150×101 mm. $2×6 *Cattleya gaskelliana*; *Cattleya aurea*; *Cattleya mendelii*; *Cattleya schrodera*; *Cypripedium dickinsonianum*; *Phragmipedium longifolium* (all horiz) 12·00 12·00

The stamps and margins of **MS**5830 form a composite background design

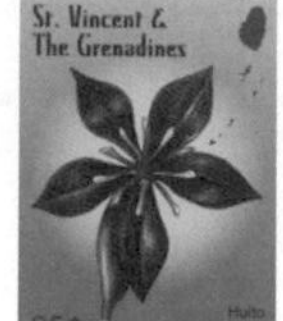

602 Huito (*Genipa americana*)

2010. Flowers of St. Vincent and the Grenadines. Multicoloured.

5831	25c. Type **602**	40	15
5832	80c. Tiny bladderwort (*Utricularia pusilla*)	1·00	70
5833	$1 Purple coral tree (*Erythrina fusca*)	1·25	80
5834	$5 Apple guava (*Psidium guajava*)	5·00	6·00

MS5835 170×100 mm. $2×6 Soufriere tree (*Spachea elegans*); Guajacum (*Guaiacum officinale*); Nipplefruit (*Solanum mammosum*); Alpine bladderworts (*Utricularia alpina*); Foetid passion flower (*Passiflora foetida*); Shoreline purslane (*Sesuvium portulacastrum*) (all horiz) 10·00 10·00

The stamps and margins of **MS**5835 form a composite background design of a forested coastline.

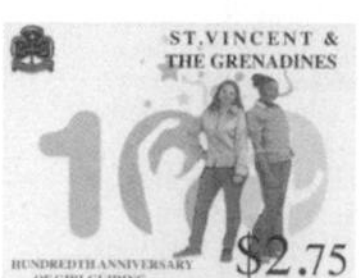

603 Two Guides

2010. Centenary of Girlguiding. Multicoloured.

MS5836 150×100 mm. $2.75×4 Type **603**; Four guides; Four guides lying in circle; Three guides 10·00 10·00

MS5837 70×100 mm. $6 Guide holding '100' placard 6·50 6·50

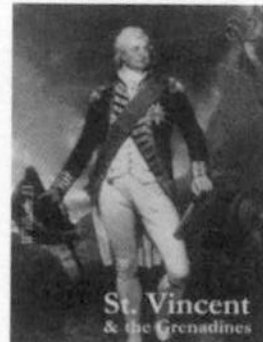

604 William IV

2011. Centenary of the Accession of King George V. Multicoloured.

MS5838 150×100 mm. $2×6 Type **604**; Queen Victoria; Edward VII; King George V medal; Portrait of King George V; Statue of King George V 11·00 11·00

605 Mother Teresa with Pope John Paul II

2010. Birth Centenary of Mother Teresa (founder of Missionaries of Charity) . Multicoloured.

MS5839 151×100 mm. $2.75×4 all with grey-brown background: Type **605**; Pope John Paul II about to kiss Mother Teresa; Pope John Paul and Mother Teresa with hands clasped; Pope John Paul II holding Mother Teresa's hands 13·00 13·00

MS5840 151×100 mm. $2.75×4 all with background of ceiling painting showing dove: Mother Teresa and Pope John Paul II (hands clasped); Pope John Paul II about to kiss Mother Teresa; Pope John Paul II (carrying staff, wearing mitre) and Mother Teresa; Pope John Paul II holding Mother Teresa's hands 13·00 13·00

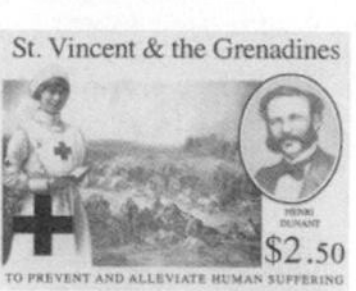

606 Early Nurse, Battlefield with Wounded Soldiers and Henri Dunant

2010. Death Centenary of Henri Dunant (founder of Red Cross). Multicoloured.

MS5841 150×100 mm. $2.50×4 Type **606**; Early nurse; Early nurse with wounded soldier; Early nurse (holding bottle) 11·00 11·00

MS5842 70×100 mm. $6 Florence Nightingale and Clara Barton 6·50 6·50

607 Abraham Lincoln

2010. Birth Bicentenary of Abraham Lincoln (US President 1861-5) . Multicoloured.

MS5843 100×140 mm. $2.75×4 Type **607**; Statue of Abraham Lincoln; Abraham Lincoln (grey background); Lincoln Memorial floodlit at dusk 8·00 9·00

MS5844 100×140 mm. $2.75×4 Abraham Lincoln (striped part of US flag at right); Aerial view of Lincoln Memorial; *Emancipation Proclamation* (F Carpenter), 1864; US 1965 4c. Lincoln stamp and portrait of Abraham Lincoln 8·00 9·00

608 Kyle Busch

2010. NASCAR (National (USA) Association for Stock Car Auto Racing). Kyle Busch. Multicoloured.

MS5845 150×140 mm. $2.75×4 Type **608**; Kyle Busch standing with arms raised in triumph; Kyle Busch (head and shoulders); Kyle Busch (half length, photo, smiling in triumph) 8·00 8·50

609 *Annunciation*

2011. 500th Death Anniv of Sandro Botticelli (artist). Multicoloured.

MS5846 150×95 mm. $2.50×4 Type **609**; *Portrait of a Young Man*; *Porträt der Simonetta Vespucci*; *Die Verstoßene* 8·00 8·00

MS5847 100×70 mm. $6 *Mystic Nativity* (51×37 mm) 4·75 4·75

610 Lt. Saavik (Kirstie Alley)

2010. *Star Trek II The Wrath of Khan* (1982) and *Star Trek III The Voyage Home* (1986) (films). Multicoloured.

MS5848 146×122 mm. $2.75×4 *Star Trek II The Wrath of Khan*: Type **610**; Capt Spock (Leonard Nimoy) and Dr. McCoy (DeForest Kelley); Admiral James T. Kirk (William Shatner); Khan Noonien Singh (Ricardo Montalban) 8·00 8·50

MS5849 143×196 mm. $2.75×4 *Star Trek IV The Voyage Home*: Montgomery Scott (James Doohan); Spock (Leonard Nimoy); Capt James T. Krik (William Shatner); Leonard McCoy (DeForest Kelley) 8·00 8·50

611 *Shûbun*

2010. Birth Centenary of Akira Kurosawa (film director). Multicoloured.

MS5850 153×133 mm. $2.50×4 Type **611**; *Subarashiki Nichiyôbi*; *Sugata Sanshirô*; *Kakushi toride no san akunin* 7·00 8·00

MS5851 154×133 mm. $2.50×4 *Kumonosu-jô*; *Waga seishun ni kuinashi*; *Tora no o wo fumu otokotachi*; *Yoidore tenshi* 7·00 8·00

MS5852 100×140 mm. $4 Toshirô Mifune as Tajomaru in *Rashômon*; $4 Machiko Kyô as Masako Kanazawa in *Rashômon* 5·00 5·00

612 Persian Cat

2010. Cats of the World. Multicoloured.

MS5853 170×130 mm. $2×6 Type **612**; Russian blue; Chartreux; Bobtail; Selkirk rex; Bengal 10·00 10·00

MS5854 100×70 mm. $6 Siamese 4·75 4·75

612a Prince William and Miss Catherine Middleton

2010. Royal Engagement. Multicoloured.

MS5854a 168×100 mm. $2.50 Type **612a**×4 8·50 8·50

MS5854b 168×100 mm. $2.50 Prince William and Miss Catherine Middleton in St. James' Palace, London ×4 8·50 8·50

MS5854c 100×70 mm. $6 Prince William and Miss Catherine Middleton 4·75 4·75

MS5854d 100×70 mm. $6 Prince William (vert) 4·75 4·75

613 Pres. Barack Obama

2010. Pres. Barack Obama. Multicoloured.

MS5855 160×110 mm. $2.75×4 Type **613**; Speaking, with hand raised (red tie); Speaking, microphone at left; Speaking, hand raised (blue tie) (all with blue borders) 8·00 8·50

MS5856 160×110 mm. $2.75×4 Speaking (black tie with white stripe); Speaking (blue tie); Smiling; Facing to right (all with red borders) 8·00 8·50

614 *Annunciation* (Domenico Di Pace Beccafumi), c. 1545

2010. Christmas. Multicoloured.

5857 90c. Type **614** 80 70

5858 $1.80 *Adoration of the Shepherds* (Gerard Van Honthorst), c. 1622 1·00 90

5859 $2.50 *Adoration of the Magi* (Guido Reni), c. 1630 2·50 2·75

5860 $3 Nativity (Domenico Ghirlandaio), c. 1492 3·00 3·50

615 Henry I (1100-1135)

2011. Kings and Queens of England. Multicoloured.

5861 $2 Type **615** 75 75

5862 $2 John (1199-1216) 75 75

5863 $2 Richard II (1377-1399) 75 75

5864 $2 Edward V (1483) 75 75

5865 $2 Edward VI (1547-1553) 75 75

5866 $2 Charles II (1660-1685) 75 75

5867 $2 George III (1760-1820) 75 75

5868 $2 George VI (1936-1952) 75 75

616 St. Vincent Flag

2011. National Stamp

5869 **616** $1 multicoloured 65 65

617

2011. Personalised Stamp

5870 **617** $1 multicoloured 65 65

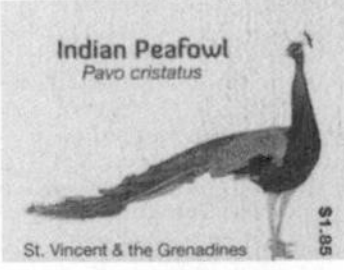

618 Indian Peafowl (*Pavo cristatus*)

619 Saffron

2011. Indipex 2011 World Philatelic Exhibition, Delhi. Animals of India and Spices of India. Multicoloured.

MS5871 147×190 mm. $1.85×7 Type **618**; Indian elephant (*Elephas maximus indicus*); Red panda (*Ailurus fulgens*); Blackbuck (*Antilope cervicapra*); King cobra (*Ophiophagus hannah*); Indian leopard (*Panthera pardus fusca*); Indian rhinoceros (*Rhinoceros unicornis*) 6·25 6·25

MS5872 100×155 mm. $1.85×6 Type **619**; Chillies (inscr 'Chilies'); Curry leaves; Turmeric; Peppercorns; Cinnamon 5·50 5·50

MS5873 70×100 mm. $5 Bengal tiger (*Panthera tigris tigris*) (white phase); $5 Bengal tiger (normal colour) 4·25 4·25

620 Ronald and Nancy Reagan

2011. Birth Centenary of Ronald Reagan (US president 1981-9). Multicoloured.

MS5874 130×170 mm. $2.75×4 Type **620**; Pres. Reagan speaking (US flag background); Pres. Reagan speaking (blue background with red stripe); Ronald Reagan (waving) and Nancy Reagan 7·50 2·75

MS5875 $6 Pres. Reagan (arms raised in triumph) (vert) 2·75 2·75

621 Pres. Barack Obama and Prime Minister Yukio Hatoyama of Japan shaking Hands

2011. Pres. Obama visits Japan. Multicoloured.

MS5876 100×151 mm. $2.75×4 Type **621**; Pres. Obama and Yukio Hatoyama (waving); Pres. Obama and Yukio Hatoyama (dark background); Pres. Obama on podium 7·50 7·50

MS5877 100×71 mm. $6 Pres. Obama waving (51×38 mm) 2·75 2·75

622 Striped Dolphin (*Stenella coeruleoalba*)

2011. Caribbean Dolphins. Multicoloured.

MS5878 151×101 mm. $2×6 Type **622**; Fraser's dolphin (*Lagenodelphis hosei*); Common dolphin (*Delphinus capensis*) (underwater); Common dolphin (*Delphinus capensis*) (leaping); Spinner dolphin (*Stenella longirostris*); Atlantic spotted dolphin (*Stenella frontalis*) 5·50 5·50

MS5879 101×72 mm. $6 Risso's dolphin (*Grampus griseus*) 2·75 2·75

623 *The Denial of St. Peter*, c. 1610

2011. 500th Death Anniv (2010) of Michelangelo Merisi da Caravaggio (artist). Multicoloured.

MS5880 150×111 mm. $2.50×4 Type **623**; *The Lute Player*, 1595; *The Fortune Teller*, c. 1594; *Supper at Emmaus*, 1601 4·50 4·50

MS5881 100×70 mm. $6 *The Cardsharps*, 1594 2·75 2·75

624 Sumo Wrestling

625 Pacific Bluefin Tuna (*Thunnus orientalis*)

2011. Philanippon 2011 World Stamp Exhibition, Yokohama, Japan. Sumo Wrestling and Fish of Japan. Multicoloured.

MS5882 150×92 mm. $2.75 Type **624**×4 7·50 7·50

MS5883 168×100 mm. $2.75×4 Type **625**; Koi (Common Carp) (*Cyprinus carpio*); Porcupinefish (*Diodon nicthemerus*); Cherry salmon (*Oncorhynchus masou*) 7·50 7·50

626 Inauguration of Pres. John F. Kennedy

2011. 50th Anniv of the Inauguration of Pres. John F. Kennedy. Multicoloured.

MS5884 $2.75 Type **626**×2; $2.75 Pres. Kennedy on telephone×2 7·50 7·50

MS5885 $2.75×4 Pres. and Mrs. Kennedy at Inauguration; John F. Kennedy (seated); John F. Kennedy (in doorway); John and Jackie Kennedy 7·50 7·50

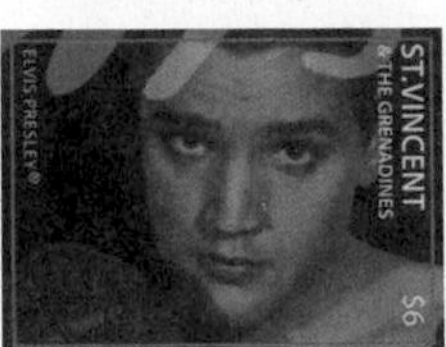

627 Elvis Presley in *Kid Galahad*, 1962

2011. Elvis Presley in Film *Kid Galahad*. Multicoloured.

MS5886 90×126 mm. $6 Type **627** 2·75 2·75

MS5887 125×91 mm. $6 Poster for *Kid Galahad* (vert) 2·75 2·75

MS5888 91×125 mm. $6 Elvis Presley as boxer Walter Gulick (vert) 2·75 2·75

MS5889 126×90 mm. $6 Elvis Presley (wearing light blue shirt) (vert) 2·75 2·75

628 Kevin Pietersen (England) batting

2011. Cricket World Cup, India, Sri Lanka and Bangladesh. Multicoloured.

MS5890 $2.25×4 Type **628**; Kevin Pietersen; England team; World Cup trophy emblem (brown-red background) 6·50 6·50

MS5891 $2.25×4 Sachin Tendulkar (India) batting; Sachin Tendulkar; Sachin Tendulkar holding trophy; World Cup trophy emblem (deep blue background) 6·50 6·50

MS5892 $2.25×4 Daniel Vettori (New Zealand) batting; Daniel Vettori; New Zealand team with Daniel Vettori holding trophy; World Cup trophy emblem (deep blue background) 6·50 6·50

MS5893 $2.25×4 Ricky Ponting (Australia) batting; Australia team with flag; Ricky Ponting holding trophy; World Cup trophy emblem (brown-red background) 6·50 6·50

MS5894 $2.25×4 Shakib Al Hasan (Bangladesh) batting; Shakib Al Hasan; Bangladesh team; World Cup trophy emblem (brown-red background) 6·50 6·50

629 Muhammad Ali

2011. 70th Birthday of Muhammad Ali (boxer). Multicoloured.

MS5895 $2.75×4 Type **629**; Muhammad Ali in ring, moving to left; Muhammad Ali walking to right; Wearing headguard 7·50 7·50

MS5896 $2.75×4 Muhammad Ali (head and shoulders portrait); Wearing bow tie; In profile; Wearing beige suit and brown tie 7·50 7·50

630 School Steel Orchestra

2011. Centenary of St. Vincent Girls' High School. Multicoloured.

5897 30c. Type **630** (first time school based Panorama champions, 2010, Junior Pan Fest) 35 35

5898 $1.05 Miss Colette Sharlene Charles (first student with 12 Grade 1 CSEC passes) 65 65

5899 $1.35 West Indies netball team, 1963 (many players GHS alumnae) (azure background) 85 85

5900 $1.35 As No. 5899 (white background) 85 85

5901 $1.65 Miss Beryl Baptiste, MBE (GHS alumna, first female director of audit in the Commonwealth) 95 95

5902 $2.10 Dame Monica Dacon (GHS alumna, Governor-General's deputy) 1·60 1·60

5903 $2.10 Mrs. Betty Boyea-King (alumna, Diplomatic Service of US Govt at UN & other international organizatons) 1·60 1·60

5904 $2.10 Grimble Building (National Heritage Building), constructed 1935 1·60 1·60

MS5905 100×70 mm. $10 Mrs. Keizer (headmistress) and Mrs. Bowman (former headmistress) 7·50 7·50

MS5906 100×70 mm. $10 Mrs. Laura Smith-Moffat, BSC (headmistress, 1940) 7·50 7·50

MS5907 100×70 mm. $10 Mrs. Susan Dougan (former headmstress, Cabinet Secretary) 7·50 7·50

631 Charles Eugene de Foucauld de Pontbriand and Pope John Paul II

2011. Beatification of Pope John Paul II. Multicoloured.

MS5908 150×100 mm. $2×6 Type **631**; Pope John Paul II and Sister Marie Simon-Pierre; Pope John XXIII and Pope John Paul II; Pope John Paul II and Pope Pius IX; Pope John Paul II with Mother Teresa; Pope John Paul II praying and Jerzy Popieluszko 5·50 2·75

MS5909 100×70 mm. $6 Pope John Paul II releasing peace dove 2·25 2·25

632 Prince William

2011. Royal Wedding. Multicoloured.

MS5910 139×154 mm. $1.20 Type **632**×2; $1.20 Duke and Duchess of Cambridge×4; Miss Catherine Middleton on wedding day×2; 5·50 5·50

MS5911 101×121 mm. $2.75 Duke and Duchess of Cambridge waving×2; $2.75 Duke and Duchess of Cambridge kissing×2 7·50 7·50

MS5912 50×121 mm. $6 Duke and Duchess of Cambridge 2·25 2·25

633 Herbert Kilpin

2011. Italian Football League. AC Milan Football Club. Multicoloured.

MS5913 173×134 mm. $1.20×9 Type **633**; Franco Baresi; Nereo Rocco (coach) and team with trophy, 1968; Intercontinental Cup match, 1969; Frank Rijkaard, Marco van Basten and Ruud Gullitt; Gianni Rivera; Italian League, 1979; Marco van Basten; UEFA Champions League, 1994 5·50 5·50

634 Pres. Abraham Lincoln

2011. 150th Anniv of the American Civil War. Multicoloured.

MS5914 $2.75×4 Type **634**; Pres. Abraham Lincoln (grey background); Battle of Fair Oaks (Union army); Battle of Fair Oaks (Confederate army) 7·50 7·50

MS5915 $2.75×4 Abraham Lincoln (brown background); Abraham Lincoln (white background, facing forwards); Battle of Opequon (Union cavalry); Battle of Opequon (Confederate army) 7·50 7·50

635 King George V

2011. Centenary of Coronation of King George V. Multicoloured.

MS5916 $$2.75×4 Type **635**; King George V in profile (wearing military uniform); King George V sitting at table; King George V wearing military unform (head and shoulders) 7·50 7·50

636 King George VI and Lady Elizabeth Bowes-Lyon

2011. 75th Anniv of Accession of King George VI. Multicoloured.

MS5917 $2.75×4 Type **636**; King George VI carrying polo mallet; King George VI (head and shoulders portrait); King George VI in military uniform inspecting troops 7·50 7·50

637 Queen Elizabeth II

2011. 85th Birthday of Queen Elizabeth II and 90th Birthday of Prince Philip. Multicoloured.

MS5918 $2.75×4 Type **637**; Princess Elizabeth at Buckingham Palace, July 1947; Princess Elizabeth, c. 1932; Queen Elizabeth II and Prince Philip, 1960s 7·50 7·50

MS5919 $2.75×4 Prince Philip, c. 2005; Prince Philip and Princess Elizabeth, 1947; Prince Philip in Buckingham Palace, 1947; Prince Philip, Queen Elizabeth II and family, 1965 7·50 7·50

638 Princess Diana

2011. 50th Birth Anniv of Princess Diana. Multicoloured.

MS5920 $2.75×4 Type **638**; Princess Diana wearing black off the shoulder dress and pearl choker; Wearing plain jacket; Wearing black V-neck dress 7·50 7·50

MS5921 $2.75×4 Princess Diana wearing red dress with black stripe, stepping off bus; Wearing red beret with black veil; Wearing red brimmed hat with black band; Wearing red brimmed hat 7·50 7·50

639 Candlelight Vigil, New York, 13 September 2001

2011. Tenth Anniv of Attack on World Trade Center, New York. Multicoloured.

MS5922 161×101 mm. $2.75×4 Type **639**; Two women at Candlelight Vigil; September 11th Memorial, The Pentagon; Flags at memorial to Flight 93, Stoneycreek Township, Pennsylvania 7·50 7·50

MS5923 110×70 mm. $6 New York building, US flag and lasers ('Never Forget') (vert) 2·25 2·25

640 Pope Benedict XVI

2011. Pope Benedict XVI visits Germany. Multicoloured.

MS5924 160×100 mm. $3×3 Type **640**; Pope Benedict XVI (wearing mitre); Pope Benedict XVI (church tower in background) 6·75 6·75

MS5925 70×120 mm. $6 Pope Benedict XVI (cathedral dome in background) (vert) 2·25 2·25

641 Chicken Turtle (*Deirochelys reticularia*)

2011. Turtles. Multicoloured.

MS5926 150×100 mm. $3×3 Type **641**; Diamondback terrapin (*Malachlemys terrapin*); Red-eared slider (*Trachemys scripta elegans*) 6·75 6·75

MS5927 100×70 mm. $9 Green sea turtle (*Chelonia mydas*) 6·75 6·75

642 *Madonna and Child* (Sandro Botticelli)

2011. Christmas. Multicoloured.

5928	30c. Type **642**	15	15
5929	90c. *Madonna Enthroned* (Giotto)	50	50
5930	$2 *Madonna and Child* (Carlo Crivelli)	1·60	1·60
5931	$3 *Mystic Nativity* (Sandro Botticelli)	2·25	2·25

643 Olympic Games at White City Stadium, London, 1908

2011. Olympic Games, London (2012). Multicoloured.

MS5932 $2.75×4 Type **643**; Dorando Pietri at marathon finish, London, 1908; Erik Lemming throwing javelin, London, 1908; Official poster for Olympic Games, London, 1908 7·50 7·50

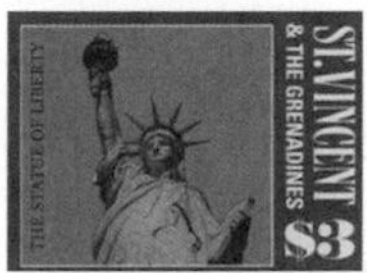

644 Barbados Anole (*Anolis extremus*)

2011. Lizards of the Caribbean. Multicoloured.

MS5933 150×100 mm. $3.50×4 Type **644**; Martinique's anole (*Anolis roquet*); Dominican anole (*Anolis oculatus*); Leopard anole (*Anolis marmoratus*) 6·75 6·75

MS5934 101×100 mm. $9 Green anole (*Anolis carolinensis*) (30×50 mm) 6·75 6·75

645 Statue of Liberty

2011. 125th Anniv of the Statue of Liberty. Multicoloured.

MS5935 181×100 mm. $3 Type **645**×3 6·75 6·75

MS5936 100×80 mm. $9 Statue of Liberty (vert) 6·75 6·75

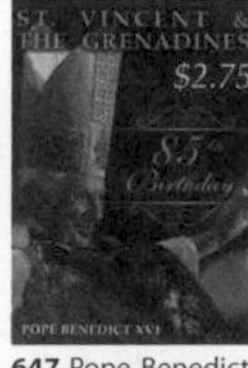

646 Engagement Photograph of Princess Elizabeth and Prince Philip, 1947

2012. Diamond Jubilee. Multicoloured.

MS5937 149×100 mm. $3.50×3 Type **646**; Queen Elizabeth II, c. 1960; Queen Elizabeth II, c. 2005 3·00 3·00

MS5938 71×100 mm. $9 Portrait of Queen Elizabeth II, 1952 (50×30 mm) 6·75 6·75

647 Pope Benedict XVI

2012. 85th Birthday of Pope Benedict XVI. Multicoloured.

MS5939 135×140 mm. $2.75 Type **647**; $2.75 Pope Benedict XVI (wearing green robes)×3 7·50 7·50

MS5940 110×75 mm. $6 Pope Benedict XVI (in profile) 2·25 2·25

648 Elvis Presley

2012. 35th Anniv of Elvis Presley. Multicoloured.

MS5941 $3×4 Type **648**; Elvis Presley wearing white jacket and turquoise and white patterned shirt; Wearing mauve striped jacket; On stage, audience in background 9·00 9·00

MS5942 $3×3 Elvis Presley wearing white catsuit (grey background); Wearing black jacket and white shirt; Wearing white catsuit (red background); Wearing red jacket 6·75 6·75

649 Benjamin Netanyahu

2012. Pres. Barack Obama meets Israeli Prime Minister Benjamin Netanyahu and Pres. Shimon Peres of Israel. Multicoloured.

MS5943 $3.50×4 Type **649**; Pres. Barack Obama; Pres. Shimon Peres; Pres. Obama and Benjamin Netanyahu 10·00 10·00

650 Spot Spacecraft

2012. 30th Anniv of Astronaut Jean-Loup Chrétien's Flight and 50th Anniv of Centre National D'Etudes Spatiales (CNES), Toulouse, France. Multicoloured.

MS5944 $3.50×4 Type **650**; SRET 2; Astronaut Jean-Loup Chrétien; Jason spacecraft 10·00 10·00

MS5945 $3.50×4 Astronaut Claudie Haigneré; SPOT spacecraft; Aureol 1; FR1 10·00 10·00

651 Lunik 3

2012. First Soft Moon Landing (Luna 9, 1966) . Multicoloured.

MS5946 $3.50×4 Type **651**; Luna 10; Lunik 2; Von Braun vehicle 10·00 10·00

MS5947 $3.50×4 Lunik 9; Russian LM; Lunar Orbiter; Imaginative spaceship 10·00 10·00

652 Prince William, Duke of Cambridge

2012. First Wedding Anniv of Duke and Duchess of Cambridge. Multicoloured.

MS5948 $2.50×4 Type **652**; Catherine, Duchess of Cambridge; Duke and Duchess of Cambridge riding in carriage; Duke and Duchess of Cambridge 7·00 7·00

653 *Danaus plexippus*

2012. Butterflies of the Caribbean. Multicoloured.

MS5949 100×100 mm. $3.50×4 Type **653**; *Euptoieta hegesia*; *Libytheana carinenta*; *Lycorea halia* 10·00 10·00

MS5950 60×60 mm. $9 *Phocides pigmalion* 6·50 6·50

654 Joan of Arc

2012. 600th Death Anniv of St. Joan of Arc. Multicoloured.

MS5951 $3.50 Type **654**×4 10·00 10·00

655 Madonna and Child with St. John and St. Nicholas

2012. Christmas. Paintings by Raphael. Multicoloured.

5952	80c. Type **655**	50	50
5953	$1 *The Holy Family with Saints Elizabeth and John*	80	80
5954	$1.70 *Madonna with Child and Saints*	1·25	1·25
5955	$2.20 *The Holy Family*	1·75	1·75
5956	$2.65 *The Aldobrandini Madonna*	1·90	1·90
MS5957	65×80 mm. $3.40 *The Visitation*	2·40	2·40

656 *Doryphora undata*

2012. Beetles of the Caribbean. Multicoloured.

MS5958 150×100 mm. $3.50×4 Type **656**; *Leptinotarsa lacerata*; *Chrysomela populi*; *Leptinotarsa decemlineata* 10·00 10·00

MS5959 70×101 mm. $9 *Leptinotarsa puncticollis* 6·50 6·50

657 Hawksbill Turtle (*Eretmochelys imbricata*)

2012. Coral Reefs. Multicoloured.

MS5960 170×100 mm. $3.50×4 Type **657**; Sea sponges and reef fish; Red Cushion Sea Star (*Oreaster reticulatus*); Close up of *Ricordea* coral 10·00 10·00

MS5961 100×100 mm. $9 Turtle, fish and coral reef (80×30 mm) 6·50 6·50

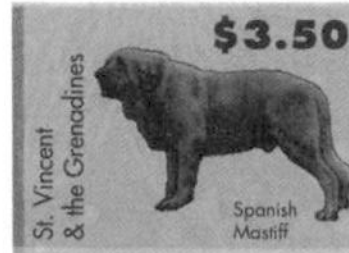

658 Spanish Mastiff

2012. Dogs. Multicoloured.

MS5962 175×100 mm. $3.50×4 Type **658**; Poodle; Dachshund (inscr 'Daschund'); Basenji 10·00 10·00

MS5963 100×70 mm. $9 German Shepherd dog 6·50 6·50

659 Dwarf Gecko (*Lygodactylus picturatus*)

2012. Reptiles of the Caribbean. Multicoloured.

MS5964 100×169 mm. $3.50×4 Type **659**; Hawksbill Turtle (*Eretmochelys imbricata*); Brown Anole (*Anolis sagrei*); Mona Boa (*Epicrates monensis*) 10·00 10·00

MS5965 99×69 mm. $9 Iguana (*Iguanidae*) 6·50 6·50

660 Clinging Crab (*Mithrax spinosissimus*)

2012. Crabs of the Caribbean. Multicoloured.

MS5966 100×122 mm. $3.50×4 Type **660**; Yellowline Arrow Crab (*Stenorhynchus seticornis*); Redeye Sponge Crab (*Dromia erythropus*); White-spotted Hermit Crab (*Dardanus megistos*) 10·00 10·00

MS5967 100×70 mm. $9 White-spotted Hermit Crab (*Dardanus megistos*) (vert) 6·50 6·50

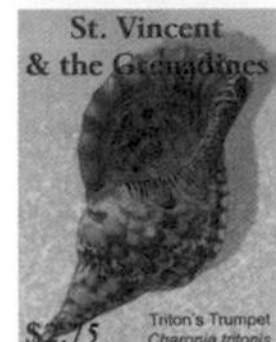

661 Triton's Trumpet (*Charonia tritonis*)

2013. Tel Aviv 2013 Multinational Stamp Exhibition. Caribbean Seashells. Multicoloured.

MS5968 $2.75×5 Type **661**; Flame Auger (*Terebra taurina*); Angular Triton (*Cymatium femorale*); Banded Tulip (*Cinctura lilium*); Lion's Paw Scallop (*Nodipecten nodosus*) 9·50 9·50

662 NGC 6302

2013. Hubble Telescope. Multicoloured.

MS5969 100×100 mm. $3.25×4 Type **662**; Galaxy M82; Orion Nebula; Scorpius Constellation 9·00 9·00

MS5970 100×100 mm. $3.25×4 Eskimo Nebula; Carina Nebula; Cat's Eye Nebula; Cone Nebula 9·00 9·00

MS5971 101×100 mm. $9 Eagle Nebula 6·50 6·50

MS5972 101×100 mm. $9 Saturn 6·50 6·50

663 *The Three Ages of Woman*, 1905 (Gustav Klimt)

2013. History of Art. Gustav Klimt (**MS**5973) and Art Nouveau (**MS**5974). Multicoloured.

MS5973 140×141 mm. $3.75×3 Type **663**; *Jurisprudence*, 1899-1907 (Gustav Klimt); *Judith and the Head of Holofernes*, 1901 (Gustav Klimt) 8·00 8·00

MS5974 140×141 mm. $3.75×3 *Absinthe Robette*, 1896 (Henri Privat-Livemont); *Tournee du Chat Noir de Rodolphe Sallis*, 1896 (Théophile Steinlen); *The Year's at the Spring*, 1920 (Harry Clarke) 8·00 8·00

MS5975 101×140 mm. $9 Advertisement for Job Cigarette Papers, 1898 (Alphonse Mucha) (horiz) 6·50 6·50

MS5976 101×140 mm. $9 *Ali Baba*, 1897 (Aubrey Beardsley) 6·50 6·50

664 Birds Pattern

2013. World Environment Day. Multicoloured.

MS5977 $3.25×4 Type **664**; Trees pattern; Fish pattern; Sun and clouds pattern 9·00 9·00

MS5978 $9 Owls and trees pattern (38×50 mm) 6·50 6·50

665 Pres. John F. Kennedy

2013. 50th Death Anniv of John F. Kennedy (1917-63, US President 1961-3). Multicoloured.

MS5979 150×135 mm. $3.25×4 Type **665**; Pres. Kennedy at desk writing; Pres. Kennedy with British Prime Minister Harold MacMillan; Pres. Kennedy at lectern speaking 9·00 9·00

MS5980 150×135 mm. $3.25×4 Pres. Kennedy holding sheet of paper; Seated in chair, sofa at left; Seated, desk in background; At lectern, right hand and arm raised 9·00 9·00

MS5981 100×90 mm. $9 Pres. Kennedy at lectern speaking (dark background) 6·50 6·50

MS5982 100×90 mm. $9 Pres. Kennedy at lectern (curtain in background) 6·50 6·50

Nos. **MS**5983/4, Type **666** are left for Margaret Thatcher Commemoration, not yet received.

Nos. **MS**5985/9, Type **667** are left for Elvis Presley Classic Hits, not yet received.

668 'She is tolerable, but not handsome enough to tempt me' (Elizabeth Bennet overhears Mr. Darcy)

2014. Bicentenary of the Publication of Jane Austen's *Pride and Prejudice*. Book illustrations by C. E. Brock from 1895 Edition. Multicoloured.

MS5990 170×120 mm. $3.25×4 Type **668**; 'I never saw anyone so shocked' (Mr. and Mrs. Bennet, both slumped in chairs); 'She went after dinner to show her ring' (Lydia and housemaids); 'Why Jane - you never dropt a word of this, you sly thing' (Mrs. Bennet sitting at tea table) 9·00 9·00

MS5991 170×120 mm. $3.25×4 'You mean to frighten me, Mr. Darcy' (Elizabeth at piano); 'Mr. Collins prefaced his speech with a solemn bow'; 'Miss Bennet, I insist on being satisfied' (Lady Catherine de Bourg confronts Elizabeth in the garden); 'On opening the door, she perceived her sister and Bingley standing together over the hearth' 9·00 9·00

MS5992 100×70 mm. $9.50 'You must allow me to tell you how ardently I admire and love you' (Mr. Darcy and Elizabeth) 6·75 6·75

MS5993 100×70 mm. $9.50 'She then told him what Mr. Darcy had voluntarily done for Lydia' (Elizabeth and her father) 6·75 6·75

669 Two-toed Sloth (*Choloepus didactylus*)

2013. Mammals of the Caribbean. Multicoloured.

MS5994 135×100 mm. $3.25×4 Type **669**; Nine-banded Armadillo (*Dasypus novemcinctus*); Leaf-nosed Bat (*Phyllostomidae*); Short-tailed Shrew (*Blarina carolinensis*) 9·00 9·00

MS5995 90×64 mm. $9 West Indian Manatee (*Trichechus manatus*) 6·50 6·50

670 Landing in Seattle

2013. Tenth Anniv of Concorde's Retirement to Museum of Flight, Seattle, USA. Multicoloured.

MS5996 115×120 mm. $3.25×4 Type **670**; Captain Bannister; 'A Crowd Gathers'; Landing in Seattle (Concorde seen from rear) 9·00 9·00

MS5997 100×71 mm. $9 Pilot and co-pilot waving from cockpit 6·50 6·50

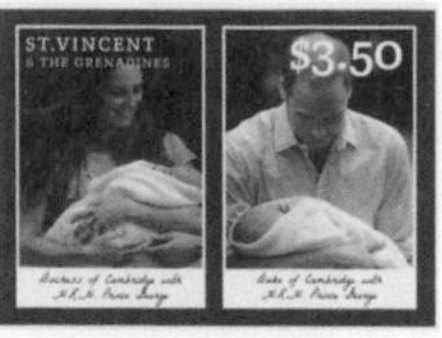

671 Photos of Duke and Duchess of Cambridge with Prince George

2013. Birth of Prince George of Cambridge. Multicoloured.

MS5998 79×150 mm. $3.50×3 Type **671**; Duke and Duchess of Cambridge holding Prince George; Duchess of Cambridge handing Prince George to Duke 7·25 7·25

MS5999 80×81 mm. $9 Duke and Duchess of Cambridge holding Prince George (colour photo) 6·25 6·25

672 Pawn

2013. Chess. Multicoloured.

MS6000 190×190 mm. $2.75×6 Type **672**; Queen; Rook; Knight; King; Bishop 11·50 11·50

MS6001 90×106 mm. $9 Wilhelm Steinitz (first World Chess Champion) 6·50 6·50

673 Princess Elizabeth

2013. 60th Anniv of the Coronation. Multicoloured.

MS6002 150×121 mm. $3.25×4 Type **673**; Coronation of Queen Elizabeth II, 1953; Princess Elizabeth and Duke of Edinburgh, c. 1949; Princess Elizabeth as Girl Guide 9·00 9·00

MS6003 71×101 mm. $9 Princess Elizabeth playing piano 6·50 6·50

OFFICIAL STAMPS

1982. Nos. 668/73 optd **OFFICIAL**.

O1	60c. "Isabella"	15	15
O2	60c. Prince Charles and Lady Diana Spencer	40	50
O3	$2.50 "Alberta" (tender)	15	25
O4	$2.50 Prince Charles and Lady Diana Spencer	55	70
O5	$4 "Britannia"	25	30
O6	$4 Prince Charles and Lady Diana Spencer	80	90

Pt. 1, Pt. 7

SAMOA

Islands in the W. Pacific administered jointly from 1889–99 by Gt. Britain, Germany and the U.S.A. In 1899 the eastern islands were assigned to the U.S.A. and the western to Germany. The latter were occupied by British forces in 1914 and were taken over by New Zealand, under mandate, in 1920. W. Samoa was under United Nations trusteeship until it became independent on 1 January 1962.

Samoa.
1877. 12 pence = 1 shilling; 20 shillings = 1 pound.
1967. 100 sene or cents = 1 tale or dollar.

German Colony.
100 pfennig = 1 mark.

INDEPENDENT KINGDOM

1

1877

15	1	1d. blue	40·00	£700
16	1	3d. red	70·00	£750

17	1	6d. violet	65·00	£500
20	1	9d. brown	80·00	£400
7b	1	1s. yellow	£100	£275
18	1	2s. brown	£275	
19	1	5s. green	£600	

The majority of the stamps of T **1** found in old collections are worthless reprints. A 2d. stamp exists but was never issued.

2 Palm Trees

3 King Malietoa Laupepa

8

1886

57*a*	2	½d. brown	4·50	1·75
88	2	½d. green	3·25	5·00
58*a*	2	1d. green	11·00	2·00
89	2	1d. brown	4·25	4·75
59*c*	2	2d. orange	6·50	11·00
60	3	2½d. red	5·00	10·00
81	3	2½d. black	2·50	3·50
61	2	4d. blue	17·00	9·50
72*a*	8	5d. red	5·50	22·00
62	2	6d. lake	18·00	3·00
63	2	1s. red	16·00	3·75
64*b*	2	2s.6d. violet	4·75	9·50

1893. Surch

(a) Surch **FIVE PENCE** and bar.

65	2	5d. on 4d. blue	75·00	50·00

(b) Surch **5d** and bar

69	2	5d. on 4d. blue	40·00	38·00

1893. Surch Surcharged and value in figures.

75	2	1½d. on 2d. orange	7·00	7·50
84	2	2½d. on 1d. green	75	3·00
85	2	2½d. on 1s. red	8·50	16·00
87	2	2½d. on 2s.6d. violet	13·00	24·00

Surch R 3d

76	2	3d. on 2d. orange	9·50	13·00

1899. Optd **PROVISIONAL GOVT**.

90	2	½d. green	3·75	5·00
91	2	1d. brown	4·50	17·00
92	2	2d. orange	2·50	12·00
93	2	4d. blue	70	16·00
94	8	5d. red	3·75	14·00
95	2	6d. lake	1·50	14·00
96	2	1s. red	1·50	45·00
97	2	2s.6d. violet	4·75	28·00

GERMAN COLONY

1900. Stamps of Germany optd **Samoa**.

G1	8	3pf. brown	12·00	16·00
G2	8	5pf. green	15·00	22·00
G3	9	10pf. red	12·00	22·00
G4	9	20pf. blue	24·00	37·00
G5	9	25pf. orange	49·00	£100
G6	9	50pf. brown	49·00	95·00

1901. "Yacht" key-type inscr "SAMOA".

G7	N	3pf. brown	1·30	1·40
G8	N	5pf. green	1·30	1·40
G9	N	10pf. red	1·30	1·40
G10	N	20pf. blue	1·30	2·75
G11	N	25pf. black & red on yell	1·40	15·00
G12	N	30pf. black & orge on buff	1·40	15·00
G13	N	40pf. black and red	1·80	15·00
G14	N	50pf. black & pur on buff	1·80	16·00
G15	N	80pf. black & red on pink	3·50	38·00
G16	O	1m. red	4·50	75·00
G17	O	2m. blue	6·00	£130
G18	O	3m. black	10·00	£190
G19	O	5m. red and black	£190	£650

NEW ZEALAND DEPENDENCY

(under Mandate from League of Nations and United Nations).

1914. "Yacht" key-types as German Cameroons, but inscr "SAMOA", surch **G.R.I.** and value in British currency.

101	N	½d. on 3pf. brown	60·00	16·00
102	N	½d. on 5pf. green	65·00	20·00
103	N	1d. on 10pf. red	£100	40·00
104	N	2½d. on 20pf. blue	60·00	14·00
105	N	3d. on 25pf. black and red on yellow	80·00	40·00
106	N	4d. on 30pf. black and orange on buff	£130	60·00
107	N	5d. on 40pf. black and red	£130	70·00
108	N	6d. on 50pf. black and purple on buff	65·00	35·00
109	N	9d. on 80pf. black and red on rose	£200	£100
110	O	1s. on 1m. red	£3250	£3500
112	O	2s. on 2m. blue	£3500	£3000
113	O	3s. on 3m. black	£1400	£1200
114	O	5s. on 5m. red and black	£1200	£1000

1914. Stamps of New Zealand (King Edward VII) optd **SAMOA**.

115	51	½d. green	1·50	30
116	50	1d. red	1·25	10
117	51	2d. mauve	1·25	1·00
118	26	2½d. blue (B)	1·75	1·75
119	51	6d. red	2·00	1·75
121	51	1s. orange	11·00	20·00

1914. Large stamps of New Zealand (Queen Victoria) optd **SAMOA**.

127	F4	2s. blue	8·00	5·50
123	F4	2s.6d. brown	5·50	15·00
129	F4	3s. violet	16·00	65·00
124	F4	5s. green	22·00	11·00
125	F4	10s. brown	40·00	28·00
126	F4	£1 red	90·00	45·00

1916. Stamps of New Zealand (King George V) optd **SAMOA**.

134	62	½d. green	1·00	1·25
135	62	1½d. grey	50	25
136	62	1½d. brown	30	50
137	62	2d. yellow	2·00	25
139a	62	2½d. blue	1·25	60
140	62	3d. brown	65	1·25
141a	62	6d. red	1·50	1·50
142	62	1s. orange	4·75	1·50

1920. Stamps of New Zealand (Victory issue. Nos. 453/8) optd **SAMOA**.

143	64	½d. green	6·50	16·00
144	65	1d. red	3·00	21·00
145	-	1½d. orange	2·00	11·00
146	-	3d. brown	8·00	10·00
147	-	6d. violet	4·50	7·50
148	-	1s. orange	13·00	11·00

16 Native Hut

1921

153	16	½d. green	4·75	1·75
150	16	1d. lake	9·00	1·75
151	16	1½d. brown	1·50	20·00
152	16	2d. yellow	3·00	3·00
157	16	2½d. blue	1·75	9·50
158	16	3d. sepia	1·75	6·00
159	16	4d. violet	1·75	3·75
160	16	5d. blue	1·75	9·00
161	16	6d. red	1·75	8·00
162	16	8d. brown	1·75	16·00
163	16	9d. olive	2·00	40·00
164	16	1s. orange	1·75	32·00

1926. Stamps of New Zealand (King George V) optd **SAMOA**.

167	71	2s. blue	5·00	18·00
168	71	3s. mauve	25·00	48·00

1932. Stamps of New Zealand (Arms type) optd **SAMOA**.

171	F6	2s.6d. brown	16·00	50·00
172	F6	5s. green	26·00	55·00
173	F6	10s. red	50·00	£100
174	F6	£1 pink	75·00	£150
175	F6	£2 violet	£1000	
176	F6	£5 blue	£2500	

1935. Silver Jubilee. Stamps of 1921 optd **SILVER JUBILEE OF KING GEORGE V 1910-1935**.

177	16	1d. lake	30	30
178	16	2½d. blue	60	65
179	16	6d. red	2·75	5·00

18 Samoan Girl

19 Apia

1935

180	18	½d. green	10	35
181	19	1d. black and red	10	10
182	-	2d. black and orange	3·50	4·25
183	-	2½d. black and blue	10	10
184	-	4d. grey and brown	70	15
205	-	5d. brown and blue	2·25	1·00
185	-	6d. mauve	50	10
186	-	1s. violet and brown	30	10
187	-	2s. green and purple	1·00	50
188	-	3s. blue and orange	2·75	3·50

DESIGNS—HORIZ: 2d. River scene; 4d. Samoan canoe and house; 5d. Apia post office; 6d. R. L. Stevenson's home, "Vailima"; 1s. Stevenson's tomb. VERT: 2½d. Samoan chief and wife; 2s. Lake Lanuto'o; 3s. Falefa Falls.

1935. Stamps of New Zealand (Arms types) optd **WESTERN SAMOA**.

207	F6	2s.6d. brown	17·00	30·00
208	F6	5s. green	21·00	16·00
209	F6	10s. red	20·00	17·00
234	F6	£1 pink	15·00	60·00
211	F6	30s. brown	£200	£300
235	F6	£2 violet	70·00	£160
213	F6	£3 green	£300	£375
194	F6	£5 blue	£225	£475

28 Coastal Scene

31 Robert Louis Stevenson

1939. 25th Anniv of New Zealand Control.

195	28	1d. olive and red	1·00	25
196	-	1½d. blue and brown	1·75	75
197	-	2½d. brown and blue	2·75	1·00
198	31	7d. violet and green	8·00	4·00

DESIGNS—HORIZ: 1½d. Map of Western Samoa; 2½d. Samoan dancing party.

32 Samoan Chief

1940. Surch.

199	32	3d. on 1½d. brown	75	20

1946. Peace stamps of New Zealand optd **WESTERN SAMOA**.

215	132	1d. green	40	15
216	-	2d. purple (No. 670)	40	15
217	-	6d. brown and orange (No. 674)	80	15
218	139	8d. black and red	40	15

35 Making Siapo Cloth

36 Native Houses and Flags

1952

219	35	½d. red and brown	10	2·00
220	36	1d. olive and green	20	40
221	-	2d. red	20	10
222	-	3d. blue and indigo	50	20
223	-	5d. brown and green	9·50	1·25
224	-	6d. blue and mauve	1·00	10
225	-	8d. red	30	30
226	-	1s. sepia and blue	20	10
227	-	2s. brown	1·00	25
228	-	3s. brown and olive	2·75	2·50

DESIGNS—VERT (as Type **35**): 2d. Seal of Samoa; 5d. Tooth-billed pigeon. (As Type **36**): 3s. Samoan chieftainess. HORIZ (as Type **35**): 1s. Thatching native hut. (As Type **36**): 3d. Malifa Falls, wrongly inscr on stamp "Aleisa Falls"; 6d. Bonito fishing canoe; 8d. Cacao harvesting; 2s. Preparing copra.

1953. Coronation. As **T 1a** of Tokelau Islands.

229	1a	2d. brown	1·25	15
230	-	6d. grey	1·25	35

DESIGN: 6d. Westminster Abbey.

48 Map of Samoa, and the Mace

1958. Inaug of Samoan Parliament. Inscr "FONO FOU 1958".

236	-	4d. red (As T **36**)	35	30
237	-	6d. violet (As No. 221)	35	30
238	48	1s. blue	85	50

INDEPENDENT STATE

49 Samoan Fine Mat

1962. Independence.

239	49	1d. brown and red	10	10
240	-	2d. multicoloured	10	10
241	-	3d. brown, green and blue	10	10
242	-	4d. multicoloured	15	20
243	-	6d. yellow and blue	80	20
261	-	8d. turquoise, green and blue	30	10
245	-	1s. brown and green	20	10
246	-	1s.3d. green and blue	1·00	45
247	-	2s.6d. red and blue	2·25	1·75
248	-	5s. multicoloured	2·50	2·25

DESIGNS—HORIZ: 2d. Samoa College; 3d. Public library; 4d. Fono house; 6d. Map of Samoa; 8d. Airport; 1s.3d. "Vailima"; 2s.6d. Samoan flag; 5s. Samoan Seal. VERT: 1s. Samoan orator.

59 Seal and Joint Heads of State

1963. First Anniv of Independence.

249	59	1d. sepia and green	10	10
250	59	4d. sepia and blue	10	10
251	59	8d. sepia and pink	15	10
252	59	2s. sepia and orange	20	15

60 Signing the Treaty

1964. Second Anniv of New Zealand–Samoa Treaty of Friendship.

253	60	1d. multicoloured	10	10
254	60	8d. multicoloured	10	10
255	60	2s. multicoloured	20	10
256	60	3s. multicoloured	25	30

62 Red-tailed Tropic Bird

1965. Air.

263	62	8d. black, orange and blue	50	10
264	-	2s. black and blue	75	20

DESIGN: 2s. Flyingfish.

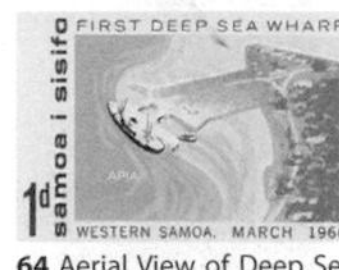

64 Aerial View of Deep Sea Wharf

1966. Opening of First Deep Sea Wharf, Apia. Multicoloured.

265		1d. Type **64**	10	10
266		8d. Aerial view of wharf and bay	15	10
267		2s. As 8d.	25	25
268		3s. Type **64**	30	35

66 W.H.O. Building

1966. Inaug of W.H.O. Headquarters, Geneva.

269	66	3d. ochre, blue and slate	35	10
270	-	4d. multicoloured	50	50
271	66	6d. lilac, green and olive	50	35
272	-	1s. multicoloured	1·25	50

DESIGN: 4d. and 1s. W.H.O. Building on flag.

1966. Hurricane Relief Fund. No. 244 surch **HURRICANE RELIEF 6d.**

273		8d. +6d. turquoise, green & bl	10	10

69 Hon. Tuatagaloa L. S. (Minister of Justice)

1967. Fifth Anniv of Independence.

274	69	3d. sepia and violet	10	10
275	-	8d. sepia and blue	10	10
276	-	2s. sepia and olive	10	10

No.	Type	Description	Mint	Used
277	-	3s. sepia and mauve	15	15

DESIGNS: 8d. Hon. F. C. F. Nelson (Minister of Works, Marine and Civil Aviation); 2s. Hon. To'omata T. L. (Minister of Lands); 3s. Hon. Fa'alava'au G. (Minister of Post Office, Radio and Broadcasting).

73 Samoan Fales (houses), 1890

1967. Centenary of Mulinu'u as Seat of Government. Multicoloured.

No.	Type	Description	Mint	Used
278		8d. Type **73**	15	10
279		1s. Fono (Parliament) House, 1967	15	10

75 Carunculated Honeyeater ("Wattled Honey-eater")

1967. Decimal Currency. Birds. Multicoloured.

No.	Type	Description	Mint	Used
280		1s. Type **75**	10	10
281		2s. Pacific pigeon	10	10
282		3s. Samoan starling	10	10
283		5s. White-vented flycatcher ("Samoan Broadbill")	10	10
284		7s. Red-headed parrot finch	10	10
285		10s. Purple swamphen	15	10
286		20s. Barn owl	1·25	40
287		25s. Tooth-billed pigeon	50	15
288		50s. Island thrush	50	30
289		$1 Samoan fantail	75	1·75
289a		$2 Black-breasted honeyeater ("Mao")	2·00	4·00
289b		$4 Savaii-white eye ("Samoan White-eye")	25·00	13·00

Nos. 289a/b are larger, 43×28 mm.

85 Nurse and Child

1967. South Pacific Health Service. Multicoloured.

No.	Type	Description	Mint	Used
290		3s. Type **85**	15	15
291		7s. Leprosarium	20	15
292		20s. Mobile X-ray unit	35	30
293		25s. Apia Hospital	40	35

89 Thomas Trood

1968. Sixth Anniv of Independence. Multicoloured.

No.	Type	Description	Mint	Used
294		2s. Type **89**	10	10
295		7s. Dr. Wilhelm Solf	10	10
296		20s. J. C. Williams	10	10
297		25s. Fritz Marquardt	15	10

93 Cocoa

1968. Agricultural Development.

No.	Type	Description	Mint	Used
298	**93**	3s. brown, green and black	10	10
299	-	5s. green, yellow and brown	10	10
300	-	10s. red, brown and yellow	10	10
301	-	20s. bistre, yellow and olive	15	15

DESIGNS: 5s. Breadfruit; 10s. Copra; 20s. Bananas.

97 Women weaving Mats

1968. 21st Anniv of South Pacific Commission. Multicoloured.

No.	Type	Description	Mint	Used
302		7s. Type **97**	10	10
303		20s. Palm trees and bay	15	10
304		25s. Sheltered cove	15	15

1968. 40th Anniv of Kingsford-Smith's Trans-Pacific Flight. No. 285 surch **1928-1968 KINGSFORD-SMITH TRANSPACIFIC FLIGHT 20 SENE**.

No.	Type	Description	Mint	Used
305		20s. on 10s. on 10s. multicoloured	10	10

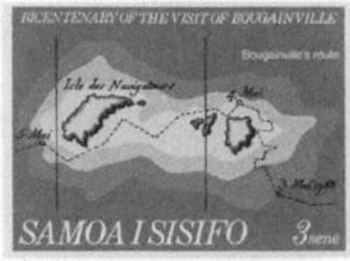

101 Bougainville's Route

1968. Bicent of Bougainville's Visit to Samoa.

No.	Type	Description	Mint	Used
306	**101**	3s. blue and black	10	20
307	-	7s. ochre and black	15	20
308	-	20s. multicoloured	45	30
309	-	25s. multicoloured	60	40

DESIGNS: 7s. Louis de Bougainville; 20s. Bougainvillea flower; 25s. Ships "La Boudeuse" and "L'Etoile".

105 Globe and Human Rights Emblem

1968. Human Rights Year.

No.	Type	Description	Mint	Used
310	**105**	7s. blue, brown and gold	10	10
311	**105**	20s. orange, green and gold	10	15
312	**105**	25s. violet, green and gold	15	15

106 Dr. Martin Luther King

1968. Martin Luther King

No.	Type	Description	Mint	Used
313	**106**	7s. black and green	15	10
314	**106**	20s. black and purple	15	10

107 Polynesian Version of Madonna and Child

1968. Christmas.

No.	Type	Description	Mint	Used
315	**107**	1s. multicoloured	10	10
316	**107**	3s. multicoloured	10	10
317	**107**	20s. multicoloured	10	10
318	**107**	30s. multicoloured	15	15

108 Frangipani "Plumeria acuminata"

1969. Seventh Anniv of Independence. Multicoloured.

No.	Type	Description	Mint	Used
319		2s. Type **108**	10	10
320		7s. Hibiscus (vert)	10	10
321		20s. Red-ginger (vert)	15	10
322		30s. Moso'oi	20	80

109 R. L. Stevenson and "Treasure Island"

1969. 75th Death Anniv of Robert Louis Stevenson. Multicoloured.

No.	Type	Description	Mint	Used
323		3s. Type **109**	15	10
324		7s. R. L. Stevenson and "Kidnapped"	20	10
325		20s. R. L. Stevenson and "Dr. Jekyll and Mr. Hyde"	20	50
326		22s. R. L. Stevenson and "Weir of Hermiston"	20	50

110 Weightlifting

1969. Third South Pacific Games, Port Moresby.

No.	Type	Description	Mint	Used
327	**110**	3s. black and green	10	10
328	-	20s. black and blue	15	15
329	-	22s. black and orange	15	15

DESIGNS: 20s. Yachting; 22s. Boxing.

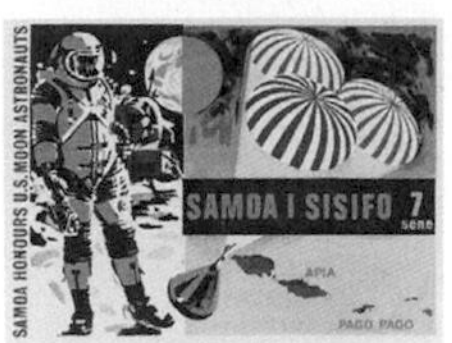

113 U.S. Astronaut on the Moon and the Splashdown near Samoan Islands

1969. First Man on the Moon.

No.	Type	Description	Mint	Used
330	**113**	7s. multicoloured	15	15
331	**113**	20s. multicoloured	15	15

114 "Virgin with Child" (Murillo)

1969. Christmas. Multicoloured.

No.	Type	Description	Mint	Used
332		1s. Type **114**	10	10
333		3s. "The Holy Family" (El Greco)	10	10
334		20s. "The Nativity" (El Greco)	20	10
335		30s. "The Adoration of the Magi" (detail) (Velazquez)	25	15
MS336		116×126 mm. Nos. 332/5	75	1·25

115 Seventh Day Adventists Sanatorium, Apia

1970. Eighth Anniv of Independence.

No.	Type	Description	Mint	Used
337	**115**	2s. brown, slate and black	10	10
338	-	7s. violet, buff and black	10	10
339	-	20s. rose, lilac and black	15	10
340	-	22s. green, buff and black	15	15

DESIGNS—HORIZ: 7s. Rev. Father Violette and Roman Catholic Cathedral, Apia; 22s. John Williams, 1797–1839, and London Missionary Society Church, Sapapali'i. VERT: 20s. Mormon Church of Latter Day Saints, Tuasivi-on-Safotulafai.

119 Wreck of "Adler" (German steam gunboat)

1970. Great Apia Hurricane of 1889. Multicoloured.

No.	Type	Description	Mint	Used
341		5s. Type **119**	30	10
342		7s. U.S.S. "Nipsic" (steam sloop)	30	10
343		10s. H.M.S. "Calliope" (steam corvette)	30	25
344		20s. Apia after the hurricane	50	75

120 Sir Gordon Taylor's Short S.25 Sandringham 7 Flying Boat "Frigate Bird III"

1970. Air. Multicoloured.

No.	Type	Description	Mint	Used
345		3s. Type **120**	45	35
346		7s. Polynesian Airlines Douglas DC-3	55	20
347		20s. Pan-American Airways Sikorsky S-42A flying boat "Samoan Clipper"	75	60
348		30s. Air Samoa Britten Norman Islander	75	2·00

121 Kendal's Chronometer and Cook's Sextant

1970. Cook's Exploration of the Pacific.

No.	Type	Description	Mint	Used
349	**121**	1s. red, silver and black	15	15
350	-	2s. multicoloured	15	15
351	-	10s. black, blue and gold	35	25
352	-	30s. multicoloured	1·00	80

DESIGN—VERT: 2s. Cook's statue, Whitby; 10s. Cook's head. HORIZ (83×25 mm): 30s. Cook, H.M.S. "Endeavour" and island.

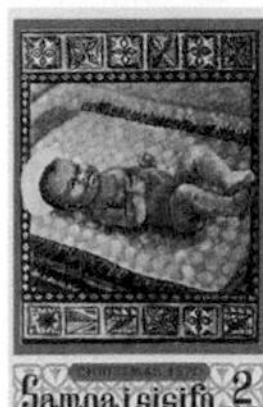

122 "Peace for the World" (F. B. Eccles)

1970. Christmas. Multicoloured.

No.	Type	Description	Mint	Used
353		2s. Type **122**	10	10
354		3s. "The Holy Family" (W. E. Jahnke)	10	10
355		20s. "Mother and Child" (F. B. Eccles)	15	10
356		30s. "Prince of Peace" (Meleane Fe'ao)	20	15
MS357		111×158 mm. Nos. 353/6	60	1·25

123 Pope Paul VI

1970. Visit of Pope Paul to Samoa.

No.	Type	Description	Mint	Used
358	**123**	8s. black and blue	15	15
359	**123**	20s. black and red	35	15

124 Native and Tree

1971. Timber Industry. Multicoloured.

No.	Type	Description	Mint	Used
360		3s. Type **124**	10	10
361		8s. Bulldozer in clearing	15	10
362		20s. Log in sawmill	30	10
363		22s. Floating logs and harbour	30	15

The 8s. and 20s. are horiz.

125 Fautasi (large canoe) in Apia Harbour and first stamps of Samoa and U.S.A. (image scaled to 57% of original size)

1971. "Interpex" Stamp Exhibition, New York. Sheet 138×80 mm.

MS364	**125** 70s. multicoloured	85	1·40

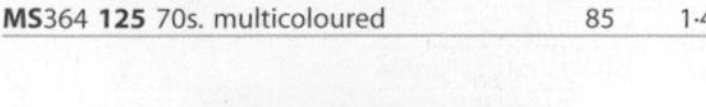

126 Siva Dance

1971. Tourism. Multicoloured.

365	5s. Type **126**	30	10
366	7s. Samoan cricket	2·25	60
367	8s. Hideaway Hotel	75	35
368	10s. Aggie Grey and her hotel	75	60

127 "Queen Salamasina"

1971. Myths and Legends of Old Samoa (1st series). Multicoloured.

369	3s. Type **127**	10	10
370	8s. "Lu and his Sacred Hens"	15	10
371	10s. "God Tagaloa fishes Samoa from the sea"	20	10
372	22s. "Mount Vaea and the Pool of Tears"	35	40

128 "The Virgin and Child" (Bellini)

1971. Christmas.

373	**128**	2s. multicoloured	10	10
374	**128**	3s. multicoloured	10	10
375	-	20s. multicoloured	30	10
376	-	30s. multicoloured	40	20

DESIGN: 20, 30s. "The Virgin and Child with St. Anne and John the Baptist" (Leonardo da Vinci).

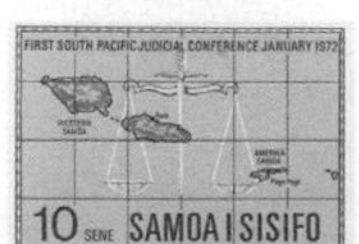

129 Map and Scales of Justice

1972. First South Pacific Judicial Conference.

377	**129**	10s. multicoloured	15	15

130 Asau Wharf, Savaii

1972. Tenth Anniv of Independence. Multicoloured.

378	1s. Type **130**	10	10
379	8s. Parliament Building	10	10
380	10s. Mothers' Centre	10	10
381	22s. "Vailima" Residence and rulers	20	25

131 Flags of Member Countries

1972. 25th Anniv of South Pacific Commission. Multicoloured.

382	3s. Type **131**	10	15
383	7s. Flag and Afoafouvale Misimoa (Secretary-General)	10	15
384	8s. H.Q. building, Noumea (horiz)	15	15
385	10s. Flags and area map (horiz)	15	15

132 Expedition Ships

1972. 250th Anniv of Sighting of Western Samoa by Jacob Roggeveen. Multicoloured.

386	2s. Type **132**	15	10
387	8s. Ships in storm (horiz)	40	10
388	10s. Ships passing island (horiz)	40	10
389	30s. Route of voyage (85×25 mm)	1·25	1·50

133 Bull Conch and Reef Heron

1972. Multicoloured.

390	1s. Type **133**	30	30
391	2s. "Oryctes rhinoceros" (beetle)	30	30
392	3s. Skipjack tuna	30	1·00
393	4s. Painted crab	30	30
394	5s. Melon butterflyfish	35	30
395	7s. "Danaus hamata" (butterfly)	2·00	1·00
396	10s. Trumpet triton	2·00	1·00
397	20s. "Chrysochroa abdominalis" (beetle)	1·25	30
398	50s. Spiny lobster	2·00	2·75
399	$1 "Gnathothlibus erotus" (moth) (29×45 mm)	6·50	4·50
399a	$2 Green turtle (29×45 mm)	4·50	2·75
399b	$4 Black marlin (29×45 mm)	2·50	7·00
399c	$5 Green tree lizard (29×45 mm)	2·50	10·00

134 "The Ascension"

1972. Christmas. Stained-glass windows. Multicoloured.

400	1s. Type **134**	10	10
401	4s. "The Blessed Virgin, and Infant Christ"	10	10
402	10s. "St. Andrew blessing Samoan canoe"	10	10
403	30s. "The Good Shepherd"	40	30
MS404	70×159 mm. Nos. 400/3	90	1·25

135 Erecting a Tent

1973. Boy Scout Movement. Multicoloured.

405	2s. Saluting the flag	10	10
406	3s. First-aid	10	10
407	8s. Type **135**	25	10
408	20s. Samoan action-song	60	85

136 Hawker Siddeley H.S.748

1973. Air. Multicoloured.

409	8s. Type **136**	45	15
410	10s. Hawker Siddeley H.S.748 in flight	55	15
411	12s. Hawker Siddeley H.S.748 on runway	60	35
412	22s. B.A.C. One Eleven	85	60

137 Apia General Hospital

1973. 25th Anniv of W.H.O. Multicoloured.

413	2s. Type **137**	10	10
414	8s. Baby clinic	15	10
415	20s. Filariasis research	30	20
416	22s. Family welfare	30	30

138 Mother and Child, and Map

1973. Christmas. Multicoloured.

417	3s. Type **138**	10	10
418	4s. Mother and child, and village	10	10
419	10s. Mother and child, and beach	10	10
420	30s. Samoan stable	55	50
MS421	144×103 mm. Nos. 417/20	65	75

139 Boxing

1973. Commonwealth Games, Christchurch. Multicoloured.

422	8s. Type **139**	10	10
423	10s. Weightlifting	10	10
424	20s. Bowls	20	10
425	30s. Athletics stadium	35	45

1974. Myths and Legends of Old Samoa (2nd series). As **T 127**. Multicoloured.

426	2s. Tigilau and sacred dove	10	10
427	8s. Pili, his sons and fishing net	10	10
428	20s. Sina and the origin of the coconut	30	10
429	30s. The warrior, Nafanua	45	55

140 Mail-van at Faleolo Airport

1974. Centenary of U.P.U. Multicoloured.

430	8s. Type **140**	35	10
431	20s. "Mariposa" (cargo liner) at Apia wharf	50	15
432	22s. Early post office, Apia and letter	50	25
433	50s. William Willis and "Age Unlimited" (sailing raft) (87×29 mm)	95	1·25
MS434	140×82 mm. No. 433	70	1·75

141 "Holy Family" (Sebastiano)

1974. Christmas. Multicoloured.

435	3s. Type **141**	10	10
436	4s. "Virgin and Child with Saints" (Lotto)	10	10
437	10s. "Madonna and Child with St. John" (Titian)	20	10
438	30s. "Adoration of the Shepherds" (Rubens)	55	45
MS439	128×87 mm. Nos. 435/8	80	1·40

142 Winged Passion Flower

1975. Tropical Flowers. Multicoloured.

440	8s. Type **142**	10	10
441	20s. Gardenia (vert)	20	15
442	22s. "Barringtonia samoensis" (vert)	20	15
443	30s. Malay apple	25	60

143 "Joyita" (inter-island coaster) loading at Apia

1975. "Interpex 1975" Stamp Exhibition, New York, and "Joyita" Mystery. Multicoloured.

444	1s. Type **143**	10	10
445	8s. "Joyita" sails for Tokelau Islands	15	10
446	20s. Taking to rafts	20	25
447	25s. "Joyita" abandoned	25	30
448	50s. Discovery of "Joyita" north of Fiji	50	1·25
MS449	150×100 mm. Nos. 444/8. Imperf	1·50	3·50

144 "Pate" Drum

1975. Musical Instruments. Multicoloured.

450	8s. Type **144**	10	10
451	20s. "Lali" drum	20	10
452	22s. "Logo" drum	20	10
453	30s. "Pu" shell horn	35	30

145 "Mother and Child" (Meleane Fe'ao)

1975. Christmas. Multicoloured.

454	3s. Type **145**	10	10
455	4s. "The Saviour" (Polataia Tuigamala)	10	10
456	10s. "A Star is Born" (Iosua To'afa)	10	10
457	30s. "Madonna and Child" (Ernesto Coter)	30	45
MS458	101×134 mm. Nos. 454/7	60	1·25

146 "The Boston Massacre, 1770" (Paul Revere)

1976. Bicent of American Revolution. Multicoloured.

459	7s. Type **146**	25	10

460	8s. "The Declaration of Independence" (John Trumbull)	25	10
461	20s. "The Ship that Sank in Victory, 1779" (J. L. G. Ferris)	35	10
462	22s. "Pitt addressing the Commons, 1782" (R. A. Hickel)	35	10
463	50s. "Battle of Princeton" (William Mercer)	60	1·00
MS464	160×125 mm. Nos. 459/63	4·00	8·00

147 Mullet Fishing

1976. Fishing. Multicoloured.

465	10s. Type **147**	10	10
466	12s. Fish traps	15	10
467	22s. Samoan fisherman	30	10
468	50s. Net fishing	85	80

148 Paul Revere's Ride

1976. "Interphil" Stamp Exhibition. Sheet 120×80 mm.

MS469	**148** $1 gold, black and green	1·00	1·00

149 Boxing

1976. Olympic Games, Montreal. Multicoloured.

470	10s. Type **149**	10	10
471	12s. Wrestling	10	10
472	22s. Javelin	15	10
473	50s. Weightlifting	45	50

150 Mary and Joseph going to Bethlehem

1976. Christmas. Multicoloured.

474	3s. Type **150**	10	10
475	5s. The Shepherds	10	10
476	22s. The Holy Family	15	10
477	50s. The Magi	55	65
MS478	124×115 mm. Nos. 474/7	80	1·75

151 Queen Elizabeth and View of Apia

1977. Silver Jubilee and Royal Visit. Multicoloured.

479	12s. Type **151**	10	10
480	26s. Presentation of Spurs of Chivalry	15	20
481	32s. Queen and Royal Yacht "Britannia"	65	25
482	50s. Queen leaving Abbey	20	60

152 Map of Flight Route

1977. 50th Anniv of Lindbergh's Transatlantic Flight. Multicoloured.

483	22s. Type **152**	25	10
484	24s. In flight	35	15
485	26s. Landing	35	15
486	50s. Col. Lindbergh	80	75
MS487	194×93 mm. Nos. 483/6	2·40	2·75

Designs show the "Spirit of St. Louis".

153 3d. Express Stamp and First Mail Notice

1977. Stamp Centenary.

488	**153**	12s. yellow, red and brown	20	10
489	-	13s. multicoloured	20	30
490	-	26s. multicoloured	30	30
491	-	50s. multicoloured	60	1·60

DESIGNS: 13s. Early cover and 6d. Express; 26s. Apia P.O. and 1d. Express; 50s. Schooner "Energy" (1877) and 6d. Express.

154 Apia Automatic Telephone Exchange

1977. Telecommunications Project. Multicoloured.

492	12s. Type **154**	15	10
493	13s. Mulinuu radio terminal	15	10
494	26s. Old and new telephones	30	20
495	50s. Global communication	50	70

155 "Samoan Nativity" (P. Feata)

1977. Christmas. Multicoloured.

496	4s. Type **155**	10	10
497	6s. "The Offering" (E. Saofaiga)	10	10
498	25s. "Madonna and Child" (F. Tupou)	20	10
499	50s. "Emmanuel" (M. Sapa'u)	35	40
MS500	117×159 mm. Nos. 496/9	55	85

156 Polynesian Airlines Boeing 737

1978. Aviation Progress. Multicoloured.

501	12s. Type **156**	15	10
502	24s. Wright brothers' Flyer I	30	20
503	26s. Kingsford Smith's Fokker F.VIIa/3m "Southern Cross"	30	20
504	50s. Concorde	75	85
MS505	150×120 mm. Nos. 501/4	1·75	2·75

157 Hatchery, Aleipata

1978. Hawksbill Turtle Conservation Project. Multicoloured.

506	24s. Type **157**	1·75	30
507	$1 Hawksbill turtle	4·25	1·60

158 Pacific Pigeon

1978. 25th Anniv of Coronation.

508	-	26s. black, brown & mauve	20	30
509	-	26s. multicoloured	20	30
510	**158**	26s. black, brown & mve	20	30

DESIGNS: No. 508, King's Lion; 509, Queen Elizabeth II.

159 Flags of Western Samoa and Canada with Canadian National Tower

1978. "Capex '78" International Stamp Exhibition, Toronto. Sheet 119×79 mm.

MS511	**159** $1 blue, red and black	75	1·40

160 Captain Cook

1978. 250th Birth Anniv of Captain Cook. Multicoloured.

512	12s. Type **160**	25	15
513	24s. Cook's Cottage, Gt. Ayton, Yorkshire	25	20
514	26s. Old drawbridge over the river Esk, Whitby	25	30
515	50s. H.M.S. "Resolution"	80	1·40

161 Thick-edged Cowrie

1978. Shells. Multicoloured.

516	1s. Type **161**	10	10
517	2s. Controversial Isabelle cowrie	10	10
518	3s. Money cowrie	15	10
519	4s. Eroded cowrie	15	10
520	6s. Honey cowrie	15	75
521	7s. Asellus or banded cowrie	15	10
522	10s. Globular or globe cowrie	15	10
523	11s. Mole cowrie	15	10
524	12s. Children's cowrie	15	10
525	13s. Flag cone	15	10
526	14s. Soldier cone	15	10
527	24s. Textile or cloth-of-gold cone	15	10
528	26s. Lettered cone	15	10
529	50s. Tesselate or tiiled cone	20	15
530	$1 Black marble cone	35	60
530a	$2 Marlin-spike auger	55	70
530b	$3 Scorpion conch	75	1·25
530c	$5 Common or major harp	1·50	2·25

Nos. 530a/c are larger, 36×26 mm.

162 "Madonna on the Crescent"

1978. Christmas. Woodcuts by Durer. Multicoloured.

531	**162**	4s. black and brown	10	10
532	-	6s. black and green	10	10
533	-	26s. black and blue	15	10
534	-	50s. black and violet	35	50
MS535		103×154 mm. Nos. 531/4	70	1·00

DESIGNS: 6s. "Nativity"; 26s. "Adoration of the Kings"; 50s. "Annunciation".

163 Boy with Coconuts

1979. International Year of the Child. Multicoloured.

536	12s. Type **163**	15	10
537	24s. White Sunday	20	15
538	25s. Children at pump	20	15
539	50s. Girl with ukulele	60	80

164 "Charles W. Morgan"

1979. Sailing Ships (1st series). Whaling Ships. Multicoloured.

540	12s. Type **164**	20	10
541	14s. "Lagoda"	20	10
542	24s. "James T. Arnold"	25	20
543	50s. "Splendid"	45	85

See also Nos. 561/4 and 584/7.

165 Launch of "Apollo 11"

1979. Tenth Anniv of Moon Landing.

544	**165**	12s. brown and red	15	10
545	-	14s. multicoloured	15	10
546	-	24s. multicoloured	15	10
547	-	26s. multicoloured	15	10
548	-	50s. multicoloured	25	35
549	-	$1 multicoloured	50	1·10
MS550		90×130 mm. No. 549	75	1·75

DESIGNS—HORIZ: 14s. Lunar module and astronaut on Moon; 26s. Astronaut on Moon; $1 Command module after splashdown. VERT: 24s. View of Earth from Moon; 50s. Lunar and Command modules in Space.

No. **MS**550 is inscribed "Spashdown" in error.

166 Sir Rowland Hill (statue) and Penny Black

1979. Death Cent of Sir Rowland Hill. Multicoloured.

551	12s. Type **166**	15	10
552	24s. Two-penny Blue with "Maltese Cross" postmark	15	15
553	26s. Sir Rowland Hill and Penny Black	15	15
554	$1 Two-penny Blue and Sir Rowland Hill	45	75
MS555	128×95 mm. Nos. 551/4	80	1·60

167 Anglican Church, Apia

1979. Christmas. Churches.

556	**167**	4s. black and blue	10	10
557	-	6s. black and yellow	10	10
558	-	26s. black and brown	15	10
559	-	50s. black and lilac	30	30
MS560		150×124 mm. Nos. 556/9	60	1·25

DESIGNS: 6s. Congregational Christian, Leulumoega; 26s. Methodist, Piula; 50s. Protestant, Apia.

1980. Sailing Ships (2nd series). Whaling Ships. As **T 164**. Multicoloured.

561	12s. "William Hamilton"	25	10
562	14s. "California"	25	10
563	24s. "Liverpool II"	25	15
564	50s. "Two Brothers"	35	75

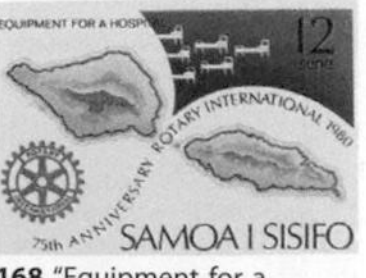

168 "Equipment for a Hospital"

1980. Anniversaries. Multicoloured.

565	12s. Type **168**	60	10
566	13s. John Williams, dove with olive twig and commemorative inscription	45	1·10
567	14s. Dr. Wilhelm Solf (instigator), flag and commemorative inscription	1·00	15
568	24s. Cairn Monument	1·00	30
569	26s. Williams Memorial, Savai'i	70	30

570	50s. Paul P. Harris (founder)	1·25	2·50

COMMEMORATIONS: 12, 50s. 75th anniv of Rotary International; 13, 26s. 150th anniv of John Williams (missionary) arrival in Samoa; 14, 24s. 80th anniv of raising of German flag.

169 Samoan Village Scene (image scaled to 58% of original size)

1980. "London 1980" International Stamp Exhibition. Sheet 140×81 mm.

MS571	**169** $1 multicoloured	60	1·00

170 Queen Elizabeth the Queen Mother in 1970

1980. 80th Birthday of The Queen Mother.

572	**170**	50s. multicoloured	30	30

171 1964 2nd Anniversary of New Zealand–Samoa Treaty of Friendship 2s. Commemorative and "Zeapex '80" Emblem

1980. "Zeapex '80" International Stamp Exhibition, Auckland. Sheet 130×80 mm.

MS573	**171** $1 multicoloured	60	1·00

172 Afiamalu Satellite Earth Station

1980. Afiamalu Satellite Earth Station. Multicoloured.

574	12s. Type **172**	15	10
575	14s. Satellite station (different)	20	10
576	24s. Satellite station and map of Savai'i and Upolu	30	15
577	50s. Satellite and globe	60	75

173 Afiamalu Satellite Earth Station 24s. Commemorative Stamp and "Sydpex 80" Emblem

1980. "Sydpex 80" International Stamp Exhibition, Sydney. Sheet 130×80 mm. Imperf.

MS578	**173** $2 multicoloured	1·00	1·00

174 "The Saviour" (J. Poynton)

1980. Christmas. Paintings. Multicoloured.

579	8s. Type **174**	10	10
580	14s. "Madonna and Child" (Lealofi F. Siaopo)	10	10
581	27s. "Nativity" (Pasila Feata)	15	10
582	50s. "Yuletide" (R. P. Aiono)	25	40
MS583	90×105 mm. Nos. 579/82	1·00	1·50

1981. Sailing Ships (3rd series). As **T 164**. Multicoloured.

584	12s. "Ocean" (whaling ship)	30	15
585	18s. "Horatio" (whaling ship)	40	20
586	27s. H.M.S. "Calliope" (screw corvette)	55	25
587	32s. H.M.S. "Calypso" (screw corvette)	60	50

175 President Franklin D. Roosevelt and Hyde Park (family home)

1981. Int Year for Disabled Persons. President Franklin D. Roosevelt Commem. Multicoloured.

588	12s. Type **175**	15	10
589	18s. Roosevelt's inauguration, 4 March 1933	15	10
590	27s. Franklin and Eleanor Roosevelt	20	15
591	32s. Roosevelt's Lend-lease Bill (Atlantic convoy, 1941)	25	20
592	38s. Roosevelt the philatelist	25	25
593	$1 Campobello House (summer home)	50	90

176 Hotel Tusitala

1981. Tourism. Multicoloured.

594	12s. Type **176**	15	10
595	18s. Apia Harbour	25	15
596	27s. Aggie Greys' Hotel	25	20
597	32s. Preparation for Ceremonial Kava	30	30
598	54s. Piula water pool	55	55

177 Wedding Bouquet from Samoa

1981. Royal Wedding. Multicoloured.

599	18s. Type **177**	15	10
600	32s. Prince Charles as Colonel-in-Chief, Gordon Highlanders	20	10
601	$1 Prince Charles and Lady Diana Spencer	30	50

178 Tattooing Instruments

1981. Tattooing. Multicoloured.

602	12s. Type **178**	30	20
603	18s. First stage of tattooing	35	25
604	27s. Progessive stage	40	30
605	$1 Completed tattoo	60	70

179 Black Marlin

1981. "Philatokyo '81" International Stamp Exhibition, Tokyo. Sheet 130×80 mm.

MS606	**179** $2 multicoloured	1·00	1·00

180 "Thespesia populnea"

1981. Christmas. Flowers. Multicoloured.

607	11s. Type **180**	15	10
608	15s. Copper leaf	15	15
609	23s. "Allamanda cathartica"	20	25
610	$1 Mango	60	1·00
MS611	86×120 mm. Nos. 607/10	1·10	2·25

181 George Washington's Pistol

1982. 250th Birth Anniv of George Washington.

612	**181**	23s. black, brown & stone	25	30
613	-	25s. black, brown & stone	25	30
614	-	34s. black, brown & stone	30	40
MS615		104×103 mm. $1 Washington taking Oath of Office as President	70	1·00

DESIGNS: 25s. Mount Vernon (Washington's home); 34s. George Washington.

182 "Forum Samoa" (container ship)

1982. 20th Anniv of Independence. Multicoloured.

616	18s. Type **182**	1·00	20
617	23s. "Air services"	1·25	30
618	25s. N.P.F. (National Provident Fund) Building, Apia	50	30
619	$1 "Telecommunications"	1·50	1·00

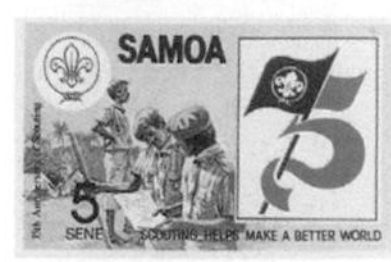

183 Scouts map-reading and "75"

1982. 75th Anniv of Boy Scout Movement. Multicoloured.

620	5s. Type **183**	10	10
621	38s. Scout salute and "75"	30	40
622	44s. Scout crossing river by rope and "75"	40	50
623	$1 "Tower" of Scouts and "75"	90	1·00
MS624	93×81 mm. $1 As No. 623 but with portrait of Lord Baden-Powell replacing emblem (47×35 mm)	1·25	1·25

184 Boxing

1982. Commonwealth Games, Brisbane. Multicoloured.

625	23s. Type **184**	20	20
626	23s. Hurdling	20	20
627	34s. Weightlifting	25	30
628	$1 Bowling	75	1·50

185 "Mary and Joseph" (Emma Dunlop)

1982. Christmas. Children's Pictures. Multicoloured.

629	11s. Type **185**	15	10
630	15s. "Mary, Joseph and Baby Jesus" (Marie Tofaeono)	15	15
631	38s. "Madonna and Child" (Ralph Laban and Fetalaiga Fareni)	40	30
632	$1 "Mother and Child" (Panapa Pouesi)	90	2·25
MS633	130×119 mm. Nos. 629/32	1·60	2·25

186 Satellite View of Australasia

1983. Commonwealth Day. Multicoloured.

634	14s. Type **186**	10	10
635	29s. Flag of Samoa	25	20
636	43s. Harvesting copra	25	25
637	$1 Head of State Malietoa Tanumafili II	50	80

187 Douglas DC-1

1983. Bicentenary of Manned Flight and 50th Anniv of Douglas Commercial Aircraft. Sheet, 215×113 mm, containing horiz designs as **T 187**. Multicoloured.

MS638	32s.×10, each design showing a different Douglas aircraft from the DC-1 to the DC-10	3·25	3·25

188 Pole vaulting

1983. South Pacific Games. Multicoloured.

639	8s. Type **188**	35	10
640	15s. Netball	45	20
641	25s. Tennis	70	50
642	32s. Weightlifting	70	50
643	35s. Boxing	75	1·00
644	46s. Football	90	1·40
645	48s. Golf	2·25	1·50
646	56s. Rugby	1·40	2·00

189 Lime

1983. Fruit. Multicoloured.

647	1s. Type **189**	10	1·00
648	2s. Starfruit	10	1·25
649	3s. Mangosteen	10	1·25
650	4s. Lychee	10	1·25
651	7s. Passion fruit	15	1·25
652	8s. Mango	15	1·25
653	11s. Pawpaw	20	1·00
654	13s. Pineapple	20	1·00
655	14s. Breadfruit	20	1·00
656	15s. Banana	30	1·00
657	21s. Cashew nut	2·00	2·00
658	25s. Guava	2·00	1·00
659	32s. Water melon	3·50	1·75
660	48s. Sasalapa	2·25	2·50
661	56s. Avocado	2·25	2·50
662	$1 Coconut	2·25	2·00
663	$2 Vi apple (25×35½ mm)	2·50	3·00
664	$4 Grapefruit (25×35½ mm)	2·50	4·50
665	$5 Orange (25×35½ mm)	3·00	4·75

190 On Parade

1983. Centenary of Boys' Brigade. Sheet 120×83 mm.

MS668	**190** $1 multicoloured	2·50	2·00

191 Togitogiga Falls, Upolu

1984. Scenic Views. Multicoloured.

669	25s. Type **191**	30	15
670	32s. Lano Beach, Savai'i	40	60
671	48s. Mulinu'u Point, Upolu	55	1·10
672	56s. Nu'utele Island	55	1·75

192 Apia Harbour

1984. 250th Anniv of "Lloyd's List" (newspaper). Multicoloured.

673	32s. Type **192**	25	20
674	48s. Apia hurricane, 1889	50	45
675	60s. "Forum Samoa" (container ship)	50	50

676	$1 "Matua" (inter-island freighter)	75	80

1984. Universal Postal Union Congress, Hamburg. No. 662 optd **19th U.P.U. CONGRESS HAMBURG 1984**.

677	$1 Coconut	1·40	80

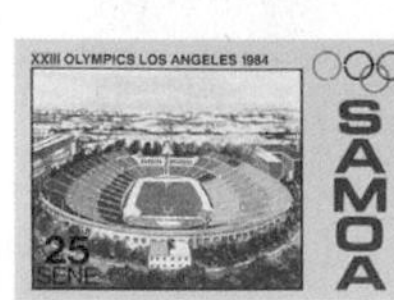

194 Olympic Stadium

1984. Olympic Games, Los Angeles. Multicoloured.

678	25s. Type **194**	20	20
679	32s. Weightlifting	20	25
680	48s. Boxing	30	45
681	$1 Running	60	80
MS682	170×120 mm. Nos. 678/81	1·40	1·60

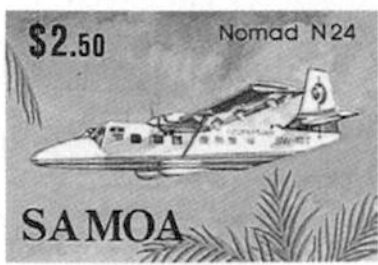

195 Government Aircraft Factory N24A Nomad

1984. "Ausipex" International Stamp Exhibition, Melbourne. Sheet 131×80 mm.

MS683	**195** $2.50 multicoloured	4·75	6·00

196 "Faith"

1984. Christmas. "The Three Virtues" (Raphael). Multicoloured.

684	25s. Type **196**	40	15
685	35s. "Hope"	50	40
686	$1 "Charity"	1·75	3·25
MS687	63×76 mm. Nos. 684/6	3·25	4·75

197 "Dendrobium biflorum"

1985. Orchids (1st series). Multicoloured.

688	48s. Type **197**	45	35
689	56s. "Dendrobium vaupelianum Kraenzl"	50	45
690	67s. "Glomera montana"	60	70
691	$1 "Spathoglottis plicata"	80	1·40

See also Nos. 818/21.

198 Ford "Model A", 1903

1985. Veteran and Vintage Cars. Multicoloured.

692	48s. Type **198**	1·50	60
693	56s. Chevrolet "Tourer", 1912	1·60	85
694	67s. Morris "Oxford", 1913	1·75	1·75
695	$1 Austin "Seven", 1923	2·25	3·25

199 "Dictyophora indusiata"

1985. Fungi. Multicoloured.

696	48s. Type **199**	1·10	55
697	56s. "Ganoderma tornatum"	1·25	85
698	67s. "Mycena chlorophos"	1·60	1·75
699	$1 "Mycobonia flava"	2·25	3·50

200 The Queen Mother at Liverpool Street Station

1985. Life and Times of Queen Elizabeth the Queen Mother. Multicoloured.

700	32s. At Glamis Castle, aged 9	50	25
701	48s. At Prince Henry's christening with other members of the Royal Family	60	35
702	56s. Type **200**	2·50	1·25
703	$1 With Prince Henry at his christening (from photo by Lord Snowdon)	80	2·25
MS704	91×73 mm. $2 Arriving at Tattenham Corner Station with the Queen	3·25	1·75

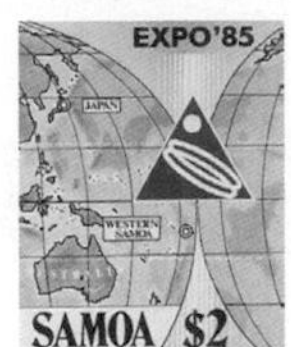

201 Map of Pacific and Exhibition Logo

1985. "Expo '85" World Fair, Japan. Sheet 70×45 mm.

MS705	**201** $2 multicoloured	1·50	2·00

202 I.Y.Y. Emblem and Map (Alaska–Arabian Gulf)

1985. International Youth Year. Designs showing background map and emblem (Nos. 706 and 710) or raised arms (others). Multicoloured.

706	60s. Type **202**	40	70
707	60s. Raised arms (Pakistan–Mexico)	40	70
708	60s. Raised arms (Central America–China)	40	70
709	60s. Raised arms (Japan–Greenland)	40	70
710	60s. Type **202** (Iceland–Siberia)	40	70

Nos. 706/10 were printed together in horizontal strips of 5, the background forming a composite design of three continuous world maps.

203 "System"

1985. Christmas. Designs showing illustrations by Millicent Sowerby for R. L. Stevenson's "A Child's Garden of Verses". Multicoloured.

711	32s. Type **203**	20	25
712	48s. "Time to Rise"	30	35
713	56s. "Auntie's Skirts"	35	40
714	$1 "Good Children"	65	2·00
MS715	87×109 mm. Nos. 711/14	2·25	4·25

204 "Hypolimnas bolina"

1986. Butterflies. Multicoloured.

716	25s. Type **204**	35	35
717	32s. "Belenois java"	40	35
718	48s. "Deudorix epijarbas"	60	50
719	56s. "Badamia exclamationis"	65	90
720	60s. "Danaus hamata"	65	90
721	$1 "Catochrysops taitensis"	1·00	2·00

205 Halley's Comet over Apia

1986. Appearance of Halley's Comet. Multicoloured.

722	32s. Type **205**	30	20
723	48s. Edmond Halley	35	35
724	60s. Comet passing Earth	45	50
725	$2 Preparing "Giotto" spacecraft	1·00	2·00

1986. 60th Birthday of Queen Elizabeth II. As **T 145a** of St. Helena. Multicoloured.

726	32s. Engagement photograph, 1947	15	20
727	48s. Queen with Liberty Bell, U.S.A., 1976	15	35
728	56s. At Apia, 1977	20	40
729	67s. At Badminton Horse Trials, 1978	30	45
730	$2 At Crown Agents Head Office, London, 1983	60	1·25

206 U.S.S. "Vincennes" (frigate)

1986. "Ameripex '86" International Stamp Exhibition, Chicago. Multicoloured.

731	48s. Type **206**	35	40
732	56s. Sikorsky S-42A flying boat	40	50
733	60s. U.S.S. "Swan" (patrol boat)	40	50
734	$2 "Apollo 10" descending	1·00	2·50

207 Vailima

1986. "Stampex '86" Stamp Exhibition, Adelaide. Sheet 158×97 mm.

MS735	**207** $3 multicoloured	4·50	5·00

208 High-finned Grouper

1986. Fish. Multicoloured.

736	32s. Type **208**	40	40
737	48s. Scarlet-finned squirrelfish	60	45
738	60s. Yellow-edged lyretail ("Lunartail grouper")	70	90
739	67s. Yellow-striped snapper	70	1·50
740	$1 Big-scaled soldierfish	90	2·25

209 Samoan Prime Ministers, American Presidents and Parliament House

1986. Christmas. 25th Anniv of United States Peace Corps. Multicoloured.

741	45s. Type **209**	25	40
742	60s. French and American Presidents, Samoan Prime Minister and Statue of Liberty	35	60
MS743	131×72 mm. Nos. 741/2	3·00	4·50

No. **MS**743 also commemorates the Centenary of the Statue of Liberty.

210 "Hibiscus rosa-sinensis" and Map of Samoa

1987. 25th Anniv of Independence. Multicoloured.

744	15s. Type **210**	20	10
745	45s. Parliament Building, Apia	25	30
746	60s. Longboat race at Independence celebration	30	40
747	70s. Peace dove and laurel wreath	35	70
748	$2 Head of State Malietoa Tanumafili II and national flag (horiz)	1·00	2·25

211 Gulper ("Eurypharynx")

1987. Deep Ocean Fish. Multicoloured.

749	45s. Type **211**	45	30
750	60s. Hatchetfish	50	60
751	70s. Bearded angelfish	60	1·00
752	$2 Swallower ("Saccopharynx")	1·00	3·25

212 Workmen trimming Logs and building Fale (traditional house)

1987. "Capex 87" International Stamp Exhibition, Toronto. Sheet 122×66 mm.

MS753	**212** $3 multicoloured	1·90	1·90

213 Lefaga Beach, Upolu

1987. Coastal Scenery. Multicoloured.

754	45s. Type **213**	70	30
755	60s. Vaisala Beach, Savaii	90	40
756	70s. Solosolo Beach, Upolu	95	75
757	$2 Neiafu Beach, Savaii	1·75	3·50

214 Abel Tasman

1987. Bicentenary of Australian Settlement (1988) (1st issue). Explorers of the Pacific. Mult.

758	40s. Type **214**	50	25
759	45s. Capt. James Cook	65	40
760	80s. Comte Louis-Antoine de Bougainville	80	80
761	$2 Comte Jean de la Perouse	1·40	3·00
MS762	90×73 mm. No. 761	1·40	1·75

See also Nos. 768/72.

1987. "Hafnia" International Stamp Exhibition, Copenhagen. No. **MS**762 optd with Hafnia emblem.

MS763	90×73 mm. $2 Comte Jean de la Perouse	2·75	2·25

216 Christmas Tree

1987. Christmas. Multicoloured.

764	40s. Type **216**	30	25
765	45s. Family going to church	40	35
766	50s. Bamboo fire-gun	45	40
767	80s. Inter-island transport	1·10	1·25

217 Samoa Coat of Arms and Australia Post Logo

1988. Bicentenary of Australian Settlement (2nd issue). Postal Services. Multicoloured.

768	45s. Type **217**	80	90
769	45s. Samoan mail van and Boeing 727 airplane	80	90
770	45s. Loading Boeing 727 mail plane	80	90
771	45s. Australian mail van and Boeing 727	80	90
772	45s. "Congratulations Australia" message on airmail letter	80	90

Nos. 768/72 were printed together, se-tenant, Nos. 769/71 forming a composite design.

218 Airport Terminal and Douglas DC-9 Airliner taking off

1988. Opening of Faleolo Airport. Multicoloured.

773	40s. Type **218**	60	40
774	45s. Boeing 727	65	40
775	60s. De Havilland D.H.C.6 Twin Otter	80	70
776	70s. Boeing 737	90	1·40
777	80s. Boeing 727 and control tower	1·00	1·50
778	$1 Douglas DC-9 over "fale" (house)	1·10	1·75

219 "Expo '88" Pacific Islands Village

1988. "Expo '88" World Fair, Brisbane. Multicoloured.

779	45s. Type **219**	30	30
780	70s. Expo Complex and monorail	1·00	1·00
781	$2 Map of Australia showing Brisbane	1·50	2·75

220 Mormon Temple, Apia

1988. Centenary of Arrival of the Latter-Day Saints in Samoa. Sheet 86×77 mm.

MS782	**220** $3 multicoloured	1·50	2·00

221 Athletics

1988. Olympic Games, Seoul. Multicoloured.

783	15s. Type **221**	10	10
784	60s. Weightlifting	30	35
785	80s. Boxing	90	45
786	$2 Olympic stadium	90	1·25
MS787	85×100 mm. Nos. 783/6	1·90	2·40

222 Spotted Triller ("Polynesian Triller")

1988. Birds. Multicoloured.

(a) Vert designs as T **222**

788	10s. Type **222**	1·25	45
789	15s. Samoan wood rail	1·50	40
790	20s. Flat-billed kingfisher	1·75	1·25
791	25s. Samoan fantail	1·75	50
792	35s. Scarlet robin	1·75	1·00
793	40s. Black-breasted honeyeater ("Mao")	1·75	1·40
794	50s. Cardinal honeyeater	2·00	50
795	65s. Yellow-fronted whistler ("Samoan Whistler")	2·00	60
796	75s. Many-coloured fruit dove	2·50	2·25
797	85s. White-throated pigeon	2·50	1·00

(b) Multicoloured designs, 25×40 mm (25s.) or 45×28 mm (others)

797a	25s. Many-coloured fruit dove (25×40 mm)	9·50	2·75
798	75s. Silver gull	2·00	1·50
799	85s. Great frigate bird	2·00	1·50
800	90s. Reef heron ("Eastern Reef Heron")	3·50	1·25
801	$3 Short-tailed albatross	1·50	1·60
802	$10 White tern ("Common Fairy Tern")	3·50	6·00
803	$20 Shy albatross	6·50	12·00

See also No. **MS**1004.

223 Forest

1988. National Conservation Campaign. Multicoloured.

807	15s. Type **223**	80	15
808	40s. Samoan handicrafts	55	30
809	45s. Forest wildlife	2·50	45
810	50s. Careful use of water (horiz)	1·00	65
811	60s. Fishing (horiz)	1·25	85
812	$1 Coconut plantation (horiz)	1·25	2·00

224 Congregational Church of Jesus, Apia

1988. Christmas. Samoan Churches. Multicoloured.

813	15s. Type **224**	25	10
814	40s. Roman Catholic Church, Leauva'a	50	25
815	45s. Congregational Christian Church, Moataa	50	30
816	$2 Baha'i Temple, Vailima	1·50	2·75
MS817	143×64 mm. Nos. 813/16	2·75	3·00

225 "Phaius flavus"

1989. Orchids (2nd series). Multicoloured.

818	15s. Type **225**	15	10
819	45s. "Calanthe triplicata"	35	30
820	60s. "Luisia teretifolia"	40	35
821	$3 "Dendrobium mohlianum"	1·75	2·00

226 "Eber" (German gunboat)

1989. Cent of Great Apia Hurricane. Multicoloured.

822	50s. Type **226**	1·75	1·75
823	65s. "Olga" (German corvette)	1·90	1·90
824	85s. H.M.S. "Calliope" (screw corvette)	2·00	2·00
825	$2 U.S.S. "Vandalia" (corvette)	2·25	2·25

227 Samoan Red Cross Youth Group on Parade

1989. 125th Anniv of Int Red Cross. Multicoloured.

826	50s. Type **227**	30	30
827	65s. Blood donors	40	45
828	75s. Practising first aid	45	55
829	$3 Red Cross volunteers carrying patient	1·60	2·25

1989. 20th Anniv of First Manned Landing on Moon. As T **50a** of St. Kitts. Multicoloured.

830	18s. Saturn rocket on mobile launcher	40	15
831	50s. Crew of "Apollo 14" (30×30 mm)	60	35
832	65s. "Apollo 14" emblem (30×30 mm)	75	45
833	$2 Tracks of lunar transporter	1·60	1·75
MS834	100×83 mm. $3 Aldrin with U.S. flag on Moon	3·50	4·00

228 Virgin Mary and Joseph

1989. Christmas. Multicoloured.

835	18s. Type **228**	30	10
836	50s. Shepherds	75	30
837	55s. Donkey and ox	80	35
838	$2 Three Wise Men	2·50	4·25

1989. "World Stamp Expo '89" International Stamp Exhibition, Washington. Sheet 91×105 mm containing designs as Nos. 824/5. Multicoloured. Imperf.

MS839	85s. H.M.S. "Calliope" $2 U.S.S. "Vandalia"	3·75	4·50

229 Pao Pao Outrigger

1990. Local Transport. Multicoloured.

840	18s. Type **229**	35	20
841	55s. Fautasi (large canoe)	85	65
842	60s. Polynesian Airlines De Havilland Twin Otter aircraft	1·75	1·40
843	$3 "Lady Samoa" (ferry)	3·75	5·50

230 Bismarck and Brandenburg Gate, Berlin

1990. Treaty of Berlin, 1889, and Opening of Berlin Wall, 1989. Multicoloured.

844	75s. Type **230**	2·00	3·00
845	$3 "Adler" (German steam gunboat)	6·00	7·00

Nos. 844/5 were printed together, se-tenant, forming a composite design showing Berliners on the Wall near the Brandenburg Gate.

231x Penny Black and Alexandra Palace, London (image scaled to 58% of original size)

1990. "Stamp World London 90" Int Stamp Exn.

846	**231** $3 multicoloured	2·50	3·00

232 Visitors' Bureau

1990. Tourism. Multicoloured.

847	18s. Type **232**	25	20
848	50s. Village resort	55	30
849	65s. Aggie's Hotel	70	60
850	$3 Swimming pool, Tusitala Hotel	2·50	4·50

233 1964 2nd Anniv of Treaty of Friendship 3s. Commemorative and "NZ 1990" Logo

1990. "New Zealand 1990" International Stamp Exhibition, Auckland. Sheet 130×85 mm.

MS851	**233** $3 multicoloured	3·00	4·00

234 "Virgin and Child" (Bellini)

1990. Christmas. Paintings. Multicoloured.

852	18s. Type **234**	30	10
853	50s. "Virgin and Child with St. Peter and St. Paul" (Bouts)	70	30
854	55s. "School of Love" (Correggio)	75	35
855	$3 "Virgin and Child" (Cima)	3·25	5·50

The 55s. value should have shown "The Madonna of the Basket" by the same artist and is so inscribed.

235 William Draper III (administrator) and 40th Anniv Logo

1990. 40th Anniv of United Nations Development Programme.

856	**235** $3 multicoloured	1·90	3·50

236 Black-capped Lory

1991. Parrots. Multicoloured.

857	18s. Type **236**	75	40
858	50s. Eclectus parrot	1·25	60
859	65s. Scarlet macaw	1·25	85
860	$3 Palm cockatoo	2·75	4·50

1991. 65th Birthday of Queen Elizabeth II and 70th Birthday of Prince Philip. As T **165a** of St. Helena. Multicoloured.

861	75s. Prince Philip in the countryside	90	1·25
862	$2 Queen wearing yellow lei	1·50	1·75

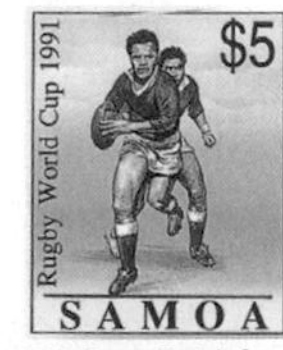

237 Peter Fatialofa (Samoan captain)

1991. World Cup Rugby Championships. Sheet 121×75 mm.

MS863	**237** $5 multicoloured	8·50	9·00

238 "O Come All Ye Faithful"

1991. Christmas. Carols (1st series). Multicoloured.

864	20s. Type **238**	55	10
865	60s. "Joy to the World"	95	40
866	75s. "Hark the Herald Angels Sing"	1·25	70
867	$4 "We wish you a Merry Christmas"	4·25	6·50

See also Nos. 886/9 and 907/11.

239 "Herse convolvuli"

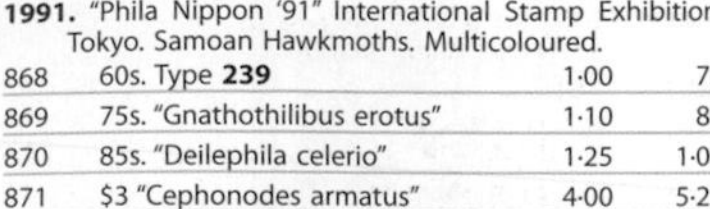

1991. "Phila Nippon '91" International Stamp Exhibition, Tokyo. Samoan Hawkmoths. Multicoloured.

868	60s. Type **239**	1·00	70
869	75s. "Gnathothilibus erotus"	1·10	80
870	85s. "Deilephila celerio"	1·25	1·00
871	$3 "Cephonodes armatus"	4·00	5·25

240 Head of State inspecting Guard of Honour

1992. 30th Anniv of Independence. Multicoloured.

872	50s. Type **240**	70	30
873	65s. Siva ceremony	75	50
874	$1 Commemorative float	1·25	1·50
875	$3 Raising Samoan flag	3·75	5·00

1992. 40th Anniv of Queen Elizabeth II's Accession. As **T 168a** of St. Helena. Multicoloured.

876	20s. Queen and Prince Philip with umbrellas	55	15
877	60s. Queen and Prince Philip on Royal Yacht	1·50	80
878	75s. Queen in multicoloured hat	1·00	75
879	85s. Three portraits of Queen Elizabeth	1·10	85
880	$3 Queen Elizabeth II	2·25	3·50

241 Samoa Express 1d. Stamp, 1877

1992. 500th Anniv of Discovery of America by Columbus. Sheet 91×70 mm.

MS881	**241** $4 multicoloured	3·00	4·00

242 Weightlifting

1992. Olympic Games, Barcelona. Multicoloured.

882	60s. Type **242**	80	70
883	75s. Boxing	90	80
884	85s. Running	1·00	1·00
885	$3 Montjuic Olympic Stadium, Barcelona	3·00	4·00

1992. Christmas. Carols (2nd series). As **T 238**. Multicoloured.

886	50s. "God rest you Merry Gentlemen"	55	30
887	60s. "While Shepherds watched their Flocks by Night"	65	55
888	75s. "Away in a Manger, no Crib for a Bed"	75	70
889	$4 "O Little Town of Bethlehem"	3·25	5·00

243 Narrow-banded Batfish

1993. Fish. Multicoloured.

890	60s. Type **243**	70	60
891	75s. Clown surgeonfish	85	85
892	$1 Black-tailed snapper	1·25	1·75
893	$3 Long-nosed emperor	2·75	4·25

244 Samoan Players performing Traditional War Dance

1993. Rugby World Cup Seven-a-Side Championship, Edinburgh. Multicoloured.

894	60s. Type **244**	1·25	65
895	75s. Two players (vert)	1·40	75
896	85s. Player running with ball and badge (vert)	1·50	1·10
897	$3 Edinburgh Castle	4·25	6·00

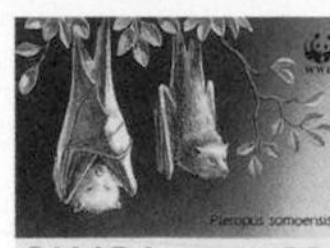

245 Flying Foxes hanging from Branch

1993. Endangered Species. Flying Foxes. Multicoloured.

898	20s. Type **245**	90	30
899	50s. Flying fox with young	1·40	70
900	60s. Flying foxes hunting for food	1·60	1·00
901	75s. Flying fox feeding from plant	1·75	1·60

246 Exhibition Emblem

1993. "Taipei '93" Asian International Stamp Exhibition, Taiwan. Sheet 137×64 mm.

MS902	**246** $5 yellow, blue and black	8·50	10·00

247 Globe, Letter and Flowers

1993. World Post Day. Multicoloured.

903	60s. Type **247**	55	45
904	75s. Post Office counter	70	80
905	85s. Hands exchanging letter	80	90
906	$4 Globe, national flags and letter	3·50	6·00

1993. Christmas Carols (3rd series). As **T 238**. Multicoloured.

907	20s. "Silent Night"	45	10
908	60s. "As with Gladness Men of Old"	85	45
909	75s. "Mary had a Baby yes, Lord"	1·00	55
910	$1.50 "Once in Royal David's City"	2·00	3·00
911	$3 "Angels from the Realms of Glory"	4·00	6·00

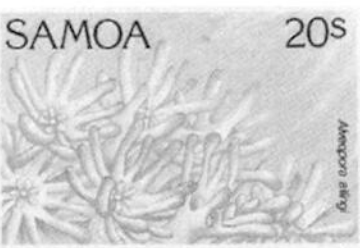

248 "Alveopora allingi"

1994. Corals. Multicoloured.

912	20s. Type **248**	30	10
913	60s. "Acropora polystoma"	65	45
914	90s. "Acropora listeri"	90	90
915	$4 "Acropora grandis"	2·75	5·00

1994. "Hong Kong '94" International Stamp Exhibition. Nos. 912/15 optd **HONG KONG '94** and emblem.

916	20s. Type **248**	35	10
917	60s. "Acropora polystoma"	65	45
918	90s. "Acrophora listeri"	90	90
919	$4 "Acropora grandis"	2·75	5·00

249 Samoan Rugby Management Team

1994. Samoan National Rugby Team. Multicoloured.

920	70s. Type **249**	70	60
921	90s. Test match against Wales	80	80
922	95s. Test match against New Zealand	80	80
923	$4 Apia Park Stadium	3·50	6·00

250 "Anaphaeis java" and "Acraea andromacha" (butterflies)

1994. "Philakorea '94" International Stamp Exhibition, Seoul. Sheet 99×82 mm.

MS924	**250** $5 multicoloured	3·00	5·00

251 Solo Singer and Choir

1994. Teuila Tourism Festival. Multicoloured.

925	70s. Type **251**	1·00	45
926	90s. Fire dancer	1·10	65
927	95s. Festival float	1·10	65
928	$4 Band outside hotel	5·50	7·00

252 "Equator" (schooner)

1994. Death Centenary of Robert Louis Stevenson (author). Multicoloured.

929	70s. Type **252**	60	50
930	90s. Robert Louis Stevenson	70	80
931	$1.20 Stevenson's tomb, Mt. Vaea	95	1·25
932	$4 Vailima House (horiz)	3·25	5·50

253 Santa Claus on House

1994. Christmas. Children's Paintings. Multicoloured.

933	70s. Type **253**	60	50
934	95s. Star over house and palm trees	70	70
935	$1.20 Family outing	95	1·25
936	$4 "Merry Christmas"	3·25	6·00

254 Lotofaga Beach, Aleipata

1995. Scenic Views. Multicoloured.

937	5s. Type **254**	15	50
938	10s. Nuutele Island	15	50
939	30s. Satuiatua, Savaii	15	40
940	50s. Sinalele, Aleipata	30	40
941	60s. Paradise Beach, Lefaga	35	40
942	70s. Houses at Piula Cave	45	50
943	80s. Taga blowholes	45	50
944	90s. View from East Coast road	45	50
945	95s. Outrigger canoes, Leulumoega	45	50
946	$1 Parliament Building	50	50

255 Under-12s Rugby Players

1995. World Cup Rugby Championship, South Africa. Multicoloured.

957	70s. Type **255**	55	55
958	90s. Secondary school players	70	70
959	$1 Samoan and New Zealand test match	75	75
960	$4 Ellis Park Stadium, Johannesburg	2·75	4·75

1995. 50th Anniv of End of Second World War. As **T 182a** of St. Helena. Multicoloured.

961	70s. Vought Sikorsky OS2U Kingfisher (seaplane)	65	55
962	90s. Chance Vought F4U Corsair (fighter)	80	70
963	95s. American transport ship and landing craft	85	75
964	$3 American marines landing on Samoa	3·00	4·50
MS965	75×85 mm. $4 Reverse of 1939–45 War Medal (vert)	1·75	2·75

256 Leatherback Turtle

1995. Year of the Sea Turtle. Multicoloured.

966	70s. Type **256**	55	55
967	90s. Loggerhead turtle	70	70
968	$1 Green turtle	75	75
969	$4 Pacific ridley turtle	2·75	4·25

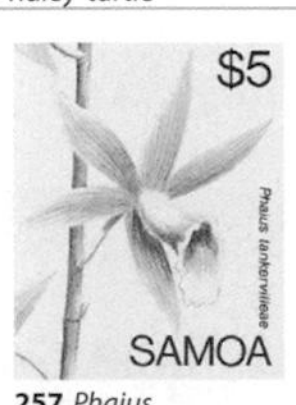

257 *Phaius tankervilleae*

1995. "Singapore '95" International Stamp Exhibition. Orchids. Sheet 76×100 mm.

MS970	**257** $5 multicoloured	3·25	4·25

See also No. **MS**1006.

1995. 50th Anniv of United Nations. As **T 201a** of St. Lucia. Multicoloured.

971	70s. Hospital lorry, Bosnia, 1995	85	55
972	90s. Bell Sioux helicopter and ambulance, Korea, 1952	1·40	85
973	$1 Bell 212 helicopter, Bosnia, 1995	1·60	1·00
974	$4 R.N.Z.A.F. Hawker Siddeley Andover, Somalia, 1995	3·50	5·00

258 Madonna and Child

1995. Christmas. Multicoloured.

975	25s. Type **258**	30	10
976	70s. Wise Man wearing green turban	65	50
977	90s. Wise Man with Child in manger	75	65
978	$5 Wise Man wearing red turban	3·50	6·50

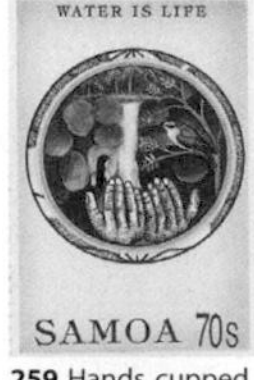

259 Hands cupped under Waterfall and Bird

1996. Environment. Water Resources. Multicoloured.

979	70s. Type **259**	50	50
980	90s. Young girl and "WATER FOR LIFE" slogan	65	65
981	$2 Village and waterfall	1·40	2·00
982	$4 Irrigation system	2·75	3·75

1996. 70th Birthday of Queen Elizabeth II. As **T 55** of Tokelau each incorporating a different photograph of the Queen. Multicoloured.

983	70s. Main Street, Apia	50	40
984	90s. Beach scene, Neiafu	65	50
985	$1 Vailima House (Head of State's residence)	75	60

986 $3 Parliament Building 2·00 3·75

MS987 64×66 mm. $5 Queen Elizabeth II 3·25 4·00

260 Moon Hare preparing Elixir of Life

1996. Moon Festival. Sheet 103×83 mm.

MS988 **260** $2.50 multicoloured 1·75 2·50

No. **MS**988 also includes the "CHINA '96" International Stamp Exhibition logo on the sheet margin.

261 Meeting Venue

1996. 63rd Session of the EU-ACP Council of Ministers. Sheet 135×71 mm.

MS989 **261** $5 multicoloured 3·25 4·50

262 Boxing

1996. Centenary of Modern Olympic Games. Multicoloured.

990 70s. Type **262** 60 40
991 90s. Running 70 55
992 $1 Weightlifting 80 60
993 $4 Throwing the javelin 2·75 5·00

263 Festival Logo

1996. Seventh Pacific Festival of Arts, Apia. Multicoloured.

994 60s. Type **263** 40 35
995 70s. Decorated pottery 50 40
996 80s. Textile pattern 55 55
997 90s. Traditional dancing 60 60
998 $1 Carved poles 70 70
999 $4 Man wearing traditional headdress and necklace 2·00 4·25

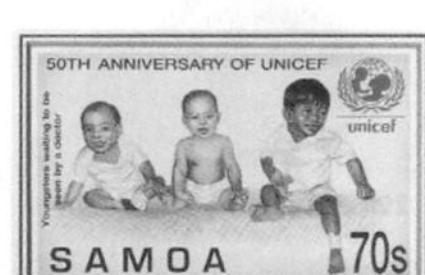

264 Young Children

1996. 50th Anniv of UNICEF. Multicoloured.

1000 70s. Type **264** 45 40
1001 90s. Children in hospital 60 60
1002 $1 Child receiving injection 70 70
1003 $4 Mothers and children 2·00 4·00

1997. "HONG KONG '97" International Stamp Exhibition. Sheet, 130×90 mm, containing No. 797a.

MS1004 $3 Many-coloured Fruit Dove 1·75 2·25

266 First U.S.A. and Samoa Postage Stamps

1997. "Pacific '97" International Stamp Exhibition, San Francisco. Sheet 96×70 mm.

MS1005 **266** $5 multicoloured 2·75 3·50

1997. Return of Hong Kong to China. Sheet 130×90 mm, containing design as **T 257**, but with new value.

MS1006 **257** $2.50, multicoloured 1·50 2·25

1997. Golden Wedding of Queen Elizabeth and Prince Philip. As **T 192a** of St. Lucia. Multicoloured.

1007 70s. Queen Elizabeth 1·00 1·25
1008 70s. Prince Philip carriage-driving at Royal Windsor Horse Show, 1996 1·00 1·25
1009 90s. Queen Elizabeth and horse 1·10 1·40
1010 90s. Prince Philip laughing 1·10 1·40
1011 $1 Prince Philip and Prince Edward with Zara Phillips on horseback, 1993 1·25 1·50
1012 $1 Queen Elizabeth and Prince William 1·25 1·50

MS1013 111×70 mm. $5 Queen Elizabeth and Prince Philip in landau (horiz) 4·00 4·50

Nos. 1007/8, 1009/10 and 1011/12 respectively were printed together, *se-tenant*, with the backgrounds forming composite designs.

267 Dolphin on Surface

1997. 26th Anniv of Greenpeace (environmental organization). Multicoloured.

1014 50s. Type **267** 45 35
1015 60s. Two dolphins swimming underwater 55 45
1016 70s. Heads of two dolphins underwater 60 65
1017 $1 Dolphin "laughing" 75 1·25

MS1018 113×91 mm. $1.25 ×4. As Nos. 1014/17 2·75 3·50

268 Christmas Bells

1997. Christmas. Multicoloured.

1019 70s. Type **268** 45 35
1020 80s. Christmas bauble 50 40
1021 $2 Candle 1·40 2·00
1022 $3 Christmas star 1·60 2·75

269 Mangrove Fruit

1998. Mangroves. Multicoloured.

1023 70s. Type **269** 40 35
1024 80s. Mangrove seedlings 45 40
1025 $2 Mangrove roots 1·25 2·00
1026 $4 Mangrove tree on seashore 2·25 3·50

1998. Diana, Princess of Wales Commemoration. As **T 98** of Tokelau. Multicoloured.

1027 50s. Wearing red jacket, 1990 30 40

MS1028 145×70 mm. $1.40 As 50s.; $1.40 Wearing tweed jacket, 1981; $1.40 Wearing red dress, 1988; $1.40 Carrying bouquets, 1993 (sold at $5.60+75s. charity premium) 1·90 3·00

270 Westland Wallace

1998. 80th Anniv of the Royal Air Force. Multicoloured.

1029 70s. Type **270** 70 35
1030 80s. Hawker Fury Mk I 70 40
1031 $2 Vickers Varsity 1·50 1·75
1032 $5 BAC Jet Provost 3·00 4·50

MS1033 110×77 mm. $2 Norman Thompson N.T.2b; $2 Nieuport 27 Scout; $2 Miles Magister; $2 Bristol Bomber 5·00 5·50

271 Christmas Star

1998. Christmas. Multicoloured.

1034 70s. Type **271** 50 35
1035 $1.05 Bell 70 60
1036 $1.40 Bauble 85 80
1037 $5 Cross 3·25 5·00

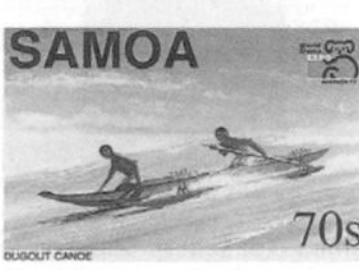

272 Outrigger Canoe

1999. "Australia '99" World Stamp Exhibition, Melbourne. Maritime Heritage. Multicoloured.

1038 70s. Type **272** 40 35
1039 90s. "Heemskerk" and "Zeehan" (Tasman), 1642 90 55
1040 $1.05 H.M.S. "Resolution" and H.M.S. "Adventure" (Cook), 1773 1·25 1·00
1041 $6 New Zealand scow schooner, 1880 3·75 5·50

1999. Royal Wedding. Vert designs as **T 197a** of St. Helena. Multicoloured.

1042 $1.50 Photographs of Prince Edward and Miss Sophie Rhys-Jones 75 75
1043 $6 Engagement photograph 3·00 4·25

1999. 30th Anniv of First Manned Landing on Moon. As **T 94a** of St. Kitts. Multicoloured.

1044 70s. Lift-off 40 35
1045 90s. Lunar lander separating from service module 45 40
1046 $3 Buzz Aldrin on Moon's surface 1·50 2·25
1047 $5 Command module descending on parachutes 2·50 3·75

MS1048 90×80 mm. $5 Earth as seen from Moon (circular, 40 mm diam) 2·75 3·50

1999. "Queen Elizabeth the Queen Mother's Century". As **T 199** of St. Helena. Multicoloured.

1049 70s. Talking to air-raid victims, 1940 60 35
1050 90s. King, Queen and Princess Elizabeth at garden party, South Africa, 1947 70 40
1051 $2 Reviewing scouts at Windsor, 1991 1·25 1·50
1052 $6 With Princess Eugenie, 1998 2·75 4·50

MS1053 145×70 mm. $5 Lady Elizabeth Bowes-Lyon, 1923, and Charlie Chaplin film 4·75 6·00

273 Hibiscus and Star

1999. Christmas and Millennium. Multicoloured.

1054 70s. Type **273** 50 35
1055 90s. Poinsettia and star 60 40
1056 $2 Christmas cactus and star 1·40 1·40
1057 $6 Southern Cross constellation and Samoan flag 4·50 6·00

274 Sunrise

2000. New Millennium. Multicoloured.

1058 70s. Type **274** 1·00 1·00
1059 70s. Sunset 1·00 1·00

274a The Count on Ladder

2000. "Sesame Street" (children's T.V. programme). Multicoloured.

1060 90s. Type **274a** 45 60
1061 90s. Ernie on trapeze 45 60
1062 90s. Grover swinging on rope 45 60
1063 90s. Cookie Monster singing and Prairie Dawn playing piano 45 60
1064 90s. Bert with bucket on his head, Elmo and Zoe 45 60
1065 90s. Big Bird dressed as tree 45 60
1066 90s. Little Bear writing and Telly 45 60
1067 90s. Mumiford coming through trap door 45 60
1068 90s. Oscar the Grouch and Slimey 45 60

MS1069 139×86 mm. $3 Cookie Monster eating popcorn 1·50 2·00

Nos. 1060/8 were printed together, *se-tenant*, with the backgrounds forming a composite design.

275 Fire Dancing

2001. Siva afi Fire Dancing. Multicoloured.

1070 25s. Type **275** 25 10
1071 50s. Dancer with torch 40 25
1072 90s. Dancer with arms crossed 65 55
1073 $1 Three dancers 70 60
1074 $4 Pati Levasa, World Fire Dance Champion 2·50 3·50

276 *Vagrans egista*

2001. Butterflies. Multicoloured. Self-adhesive.

1075 70s. Type **276** 80 1·10
1076 $1.20 *Jamides bochus* 1·00 1·40
1077 $1.40 *Papilio godeffroy* 1·00 1·40
1078 $2 *Acraea andromacha* 1·25 1·75
1079 $3 *Eurema hecabe* 1·50 2·00

277 Snorkellers

2002. U.N. Year of Eco Tourism. Multicoloured.

1080 60s. Type **277** 55 75
1081 95s. Canoeists 80 1·25
1082 $1.90 Wood-carver and children 1·10 1·50
1083 $3 Children by waterfall 1·40 1·75

Nos. 1080/3 were printed together, *se-tenant*, in horizontal strips of 4 and a central label showing the U.N. symbol, with the backgrounds forming a composite design.

278 Buses, Traditional Huts and Man with Baseball Bat

2002. 40th Anniv of Independence. Designs showing the Samoan flag in the background. Multicoloured. Self-adhesive.

1084 25s. Type **278** 50 25
1085 70s. Local dancers and conch blower 45 35
1086 95s. Ferry, aircraft and office workers 1·00 55
1087 $5 Church, police parade and rugby player 4·75 4·75

MS1088 110×85 mm. No. 1087 4·75 5·50

45 Franciscan Convent and Capuchin Church

1928. 700th Death Anniv of St. Francis of Assisi.

141	**45**	50c. red	34·00	6·50
142	**45**	1l.25 blue	8·00	7·50
143	-	2l.50 brown	8·00	7·50
144	-	5l. violet	39·00	32·00

DESIGN: 2l.50, 5l. Death of St. Francis.

46 La Rocca Fortress

47 Government Palace

48 Statue of Liberty

1929

145	**46**	5c. blue and purple	1·00	65
146	**46**	10c. mauve and blue	1·00	65
147	**46**	15c. green and orange	1·00	65
148	**46**	20c. red and blue	1·00	65
149	**46**	25c. black and green	1·00	65
150	**46**	30c. red and grey	1·00	65
151	**46**	50c. green and purple	1·00	65
152	**46**	75c. grey and red	1·00	65
153	**47**	1l. green and brown	1·00	65
154	**47**	1l.25 black and blue	1·30	65
155	**47**	1l.75 orange and green	8·75	1·60
156	**47**	2l. red and blue	2·00	1·60
157	**47**	2l.50 blue and red	2·00	1·60
158	**47**	3l. blue and orange	2·00	1·60
159	**47**	3l.70 purple and green	2·00	2·75
160	**48**	5l. green and violet	10·00	2·75
161	**48**	10l. blue and brown	20·00	10·50
162	**48**	15l. purple and green	90·00	85·00
163	**48**	20l. red and blue	£350	£375

50 Mt. Titano

1931. Air.

164	**50**	50c. green	9·00	7·50
165	**50**	80c. red	9·00	7·50
166	**50**	1l. brown	6·75	4·25
167	**50**	2l. purple	6·75	4·25
168	**50**	2l.60 blue	49·00	55·00
169	**50**	3l. grey	49·00	55·00
170	**50**	5l. green	16·00	4·25
171	**50**	7l.70 brown	16·00	8·50
172	**50**	9l. orange	18·00	10·50
173	**50**	10l. blue	£425	£400

51 G.P.O., San Marino

1932. Inauguration of New G.P.O.

174	**51**	20c. green	9·00	8·50
175	**51**	50c. red	13·50	13·00
176	**51**	1l.25 blue	£250	£130
177	**51**	1l.75 brown	£250	85·00
178	**51**	2l.75 violet	44·00	32·00

52 San Marino Railway Station

1932. Opening of San Marino Electric Railway, Rimini.

179	**52**	20c. green	3·00	2·10
180	**52**	50c. red	4·25	3·25
181	**52**	1l.25 blue	14·50	10·50
182	**52**	5l. brown	80·00	70·00

53 Garibaldi

1932. 50th Death Anniv of Garibaldi.

183	**53**	10c. brown	7·50	3·25
184	**53**	20c. violet	7·50	3·25
185	**53**	25c. green	7·50	3·25
186	**53**	50c. brown	12·00	7·50
187	-	75c. red	20·00	10·50
188	-	1l.25 blue	36·00	15·00
189	-	2l.75 orange	85·00	43·00
190	-	5l. green	£350	£350

DESIGN: 75c. to 5l. Garibaldi's arrival at San Marino.

1933. Air. LZ-127 "Graf Zeppelin". Surch **ZEPPELIN 1933** under airship and new value.

191	**50**	3l. on 50c. orange	8·25	£110
192	**50**	5l. on 80c. green	44·00	£110
193	**50**	10l. on 1l. blue	44·00	£160
194	**50**	12l. on 2l. brown	44·00	£160
195	**50**	15l. on 2l.60 red	48·00	£160
196	**50**	20l. on 3l. green	48·00	£275

1933. 20th Italian Philatelic Congress. Surch **28 MAGGIO 1933 CONVEGNO FILATELICO** and new value.

197	**51**	25c. on 2l.75 violet	13·50	10·50
198	**51**	50c. on 1l.75 brown	26·00	21·00
199	**51**	75c. on 2l.75 violet	65·00	43·00
200	**51**	1l.25 on 1l.75 brown	£400	£400

1934. Philatelic Exn. Surch 12-27 APRILE 1934 MOSTRA FILATELICA and value with wheel.

201	25c. on 1l.25 blue	1·80	2·10
202	50c. on 1l.75 brown	3·50	3·25
203	75c. on 50c. red	7·00	6·50
204	1l.25 on 20c. green	32·00	42·00

1934. Surch with value and wheel.

205	3l.70 on 1l.25 blue	90·00	75·00
206	3l.70 on 2l.75 violet	90·00	95·00

58 Ascent to Mt. Titano

1935. 12th Anniv of San Marino Fascist Party.

207	**58**	5c. black and brown	40	25
208	**58**	10c. black and violet	40	25
209	**58**	20c. black and orange	40	25
210	**58**	25c. black and green	40	25
211	**58**	50c. black and bistre	40	25
212	**58**	75c. black and red	1·20	2·75
213	**58**	1l.25 black and blue	4·75	6·00

59 Delfico

1935. Death Centenary of Melchiorre Delfico (historian of San Marino).

214	**59**	5c. black and purple	95	1·10
215	**59**	7½c. black and brown	95	1·10
216	**59**	10c. black and green	95	1·10
217	**59**	15c. black and red	24·00	7·50
218	**59**	20c. black and orange	1·90	2·10
219	**59**	25c. black and green	1·90	2·10
220	-	30c. black and violet	1·90	2·10
221	-	50c. black and green	4·75	6·50
222	-	75c. black and red	12·00	12·00
223	-	1l.25 black and blue	3·25	4·25
224	-	1l.50 black and brown	55·00	48·00
225	-	1l.75 black and orange	85·00	85·00

DESIGN—25×35 mm: 30c. to 1l.75, Statue of Delfico.

1936. Surch. (a) Postage.

226	**40**	80c. on 45c. black & violet	4·00	3·75
227	**40**	80c. on 65c. black & green	4·00	3·75
228	**45**	2l.05 on 1l.25 blue	6·50	6·50
229	-	2l.75 on 2l.50 brown (No. 143)	24·00	26·00

(b) Air.

230	**50**	75c. on 50c. green	2·20	3·75
231	**50**	75c. on 80c. red	13·50	12·50

63 St. Marinus and St. Leo

1937. Independence Monument. Sheet 125×105 mm.

MS232 **63**	5l.	16·00	21·00

64 Abraham Lincoln

1938. Dedication of Bust of Abraham Lincoln. Sheets (each 125×105 mm).

MS232a **64**	3l. blue	3·50	3·25
MS232b	5l. red	24·00	13·00

1941. Surch **10**.

233	**19**	10c. on 15c. purple	20	25
234	**19**	10c. on 30c. orange	1·30	1·10

1942. Air. Surch **Lire 10** and bars.

235	**50**	10l. on 2l.60 blue	£140	£130
236	**50**	10l. on 3l. grey	30·00	32·00

67 Gajarda Tower, Arbe, and Flags of Italy and San Marino

1942. Restoration of Italian Flag to Arbe (Rab) annexed by Italy in 1941.

237	**67**	10c. red and bistre (postage)	15	10
238	**67**	15c. red and brown	15	10
239	**67**	20c. grey and green	15	10
240	**67**	25c. blue and green	20	10
241	**67**	50c. brown and red	20	10
242	**67**	75c. grey and red	20	10
243	-	1l.25 light blue and blue	20	10
244	-	1l.75 grey and brown	45	25
245	-	2l.75 blue and bistre	65	55
246	-	5l. brown and green	4·50	4·25
247	-	25c. grey and brown (air)	30	10
248	-	50c. brown and green	30	10
249	-	75c. brown and blue	30	10
250	-	1l. brown and bistre	85	75
251	-	5l. blue and bistre	8·25	6·25

DESIGNS—HORIZ: Nos. 243/6, Galleon in Arbe Harbour. VERT: Nos. 247/51, Granda Belfry, Arbe.

1942. Italian Philatelic Congress. Surch **GIORNATA FILATELICA RIMINI - SAN MARINO 3 AGOSTO 1942 (1641 d. F. R.) C. – 30.**

252	**67**	30c. on 10c. red and bistre	20	25

1942. Surch.

253		30c. on 20c. grey and green	20	30
254	-	20l. on 75c. black and red (No. 222)	17·00	16·00

71 Printing Press

72 Newspapers

1943. Press Propaganda.

255	**71**	10c. green	15	15
256	**71**	15c. brown	15	15
257	**71**	20c. brown	15	15
258	**71**	30c. purple	15	15
259	**71**	50c. blue	15	15
260	**71**	75c. red	15	15
261	**72**	1l.25 blue	15	15
262	**72**	1l.75 violet	30	20
263	**72**	5l. blue	1·00	1·20
264	**72**	10l. brown	5·75	4·75

1943. Philatelic Exhibition. Optd **GIORNATA FILATELICA RIMINI - SAN MARINO 5 LUGLIO 1943 (1642 d. F. R.).**

265	**71**	30c. purple	10	15
266	**71**	50c. blue	10	15

74 Gateway

75 War Memorial

1943. Fall of Fascism. Unissued series for 20th Anniv of Fascism optd **28 LVGLIO 1943 1642 d. F.R.** (the "d." is omitted on T **74**) and bars cancelling commemorative inscription.

267	**74**	5c. brown (postage)	20	25
268	**74**	10c. orange	20	25
269	**74**	20c. blue	20	25
270	**74**	25c. green	20	25
271	**74**	30c. purple	20	25
272	**74**	50c. violet	20	25
273	**74**	75c. red	20	25
274	**75**	1l.25 blue	20	25
275	**75**	1l.75 orange	20	25
276	**75**	2l.75 brown	45	60
277	**75**	5l. green	1·00	1·20
278	**75**	10l. violet	1·70	2·10
279	**75**	20l. blue	6·00	4·75
280	-	25c. brown (air)	20	25
281	-	50c. purple	20	25
282	-	75c. brown	20	25
283	-	1l. purple	20	25
284	-	2l. blue	20	25
285	-	5l. orange	1·10	25
286	-	10l. green	1·80	1·40
287	-	20l. black	7·00	7·00

DESIGN—Air: Nos. 280/7, Map of San Marino.

1943. Provisional Govt. Optd **GOVERNO PROVVISORIO** over ornamentation.

288	**74**	5c. brown (postage)	20	20
289	**74**	10c. orange	20	20
290	**74**	20c. blue	20	20
291	**74**	25c. green	20	20
292	**74**	30c. purple	20	20
293	**74**	50c. violet	20	20
294	**74**	75c. red	20	20
295	**75**	1l.25 blue	20	20
296	**75**	1l.75 orange	25	20
297	**75**	5l. green	80	65
298	**75**	20l. blue	3·25	2·40
299	-	25c. brown (air)	20	25
300	-	50c. red	20	25
301	-	75c. brown	20	25
302	-	1l. purple	20	25
303	-	5l. orange	65	1·20
304	-	20l. black	4·00	3·25

78 St. Marinus

79 Mt. Titano

1944

305	**78**	20l.+10l. brown (postage)	2·75	2·75
306	**79**	20l.+10l. green (air)	2·20	2·75

80 Govt Palace

81 Govt Palace

1945. 50th Anniv of Government Palace.

307	**80**	25l. purple (postage)	27·00	8·50
308	**81**	25l. brown (air)	39·00	7·50
MS308a		180×120 mm comprising 10l. blue and15l. green (angels and crowd scene, horiz); 25l. red (Palace, vert). Perf or imperf	£375	£225

82 Arms of Montegiardino

83 Arms of San Marino

1945. Arms Types.

309	-	10c. blue	30	25
310	**82**	20c. red	30	25
311	-	40c. orange	30	25
312	**82**	60c. grey	30	25
313	-	80c. green	30	25
314	-	1l. red	55	25
315	-	1l.20 violet	55	25
316	-	2l. brown	55	25
317	-	3l. blue	55	25
317a	-	4l. orange	55	25
318	-	5l. brown	55	25
319	-	10l. red and brown	4·25	3·25
318a	-	15l. blue	5·00	3·25
320	-	20l. red and blue	9·50	4·25
321	-	20l. brown and blue	22·00	4·25
322	**82**	25l. blue and brown	21·00	7·50
323	**83**	50l. blue and green	33·00	19·00

DESIGNS (Arms of San Marino and villages in the Republic): 10c., 1l., 1l.20, 15l. Faetano; 40c., 5l. San Marino; 80c., 2, 3, 4l. Fiorentino; 10l. Borgomaggiore; 20l. (2) Serravalle.

84 U.N.R.R.A. Aid for San Marino

1946. U.N.R.R.A.

324	**84**	100l. red, purple and orange	22·00	10·50

85 Airplane and Mt. Titano

1946. Air.

325	-	25c. grey	30	25
326	**85**	75c. red	30	25
327	-	1l. brown	30	25
328	**85**	2l. green	30	25
329	**85**	3l. violet	30	25
330	-	5l. blue	55	25
331	-	10l. red	55	25
334	-	20l. purple	2·50	2·75
332	-	35l. red	13·00	7·00
335	-	50l. green	20·00	10·50
333	-	100l. brown	3·25	1·50

DESIGNS—HORIZ: 25c., 1, 10l. Wings over Mt. Titano; 100l. Airplane over globe. VERT: 5, 20, 35, 50l. Four aircraft over Mt. Titano.

1946. Stamp Day. Surch **L.10.**

336	**83**	50l.+10l. blue and green	33·00	15·00

1946. National Philatelic Convention. Nos. 329/31 but colours changed and without "POSTA AEREA" surch **CONVEGNO FILATELICO 30 NOVEMBRE 1946** and premium.

336a	**85**	3l.+25l. brown	2·20	1·10
336b	-	5l.+25l. orange	2·20	1·10
336c	-	10l.+50l. blue	18·00	9·00

87 Quotation from F.D.R. on Liberty

88 Franklin D. Roosevelt

1947. In Memory of President Franklin D. Roosevelt.

336d	**87**	1l. brn & ochre (postage)	30	25
336e	**88**	2l. brown and blue	30	25
336f	-	5l. multicoloured	30	25
336g	-	15l. multicoloured	30	25
336h	**87**	50l. brown and red	2·20	30
336i	**88**	100l. brown and violet	4·50	1·30

DESIGN—HORIZ: 5l., 15l. Roosevelt and flags of San Marino and U.S.A.

336j	1l. brown and blue (air)	30	25
336k	2l. brown and red	30	25
336l	5l. multicoloured	30	25
336m	20l. brown and purple	85	25
336n	31l. brown and orange	1·70	25
336o	50l. brown and red	4·50	1·10
336p	100l. brown and blue	6·75	2·10
336q	200l. multicoloured	44·00	22·00

DESIGNS—HORIZ: 1, 3, 50l. Roosevelt and eagle; 2, 20, 100l. Roosevelt and San Marino arms. VERT: 5, 200l. Roosevelt and flags of San Marino and U.S.A.

1947. Surch in figures.

336r	**87**	3 on 1l. brown and ochre (postage)	55	30
336s	**88**	4 on 2l. brown and blue	65	30
336t	-	6 on 5l. mult (No. 336f)	65	45
336u	-	3 on 1l. brown and blue (No. 336j) (air)	55	30
336v	-	4 on 2l. brown and red (No. 336k)	70	30
336w	-	6 on 5l. mult (No. 336l)	70	45

1947. No. 317a surch.

337	6l. on 4l. orange	35	25
338	21l. on 4l. orange	1·90	85

91 St. Marinus founding Republic

1947. Reconstruction.

339	**91**	1l. mauve & green (postage)	30	25
340	**91**	2l. green and mauve	30	25
341	**91**	4l. green and brown	30	25
342	**91**	10l. blue and orange	55	25
343	**91**	25l. mauve and red	3·50	2·10
344	**91**	50l. brown and green	48·00	20·00
345	**91**	25l. blue and orange (air)	2·20	2·40
346	**91**	50l. blue and brown	5·50	5·00

Nos. 343/6 are larger (24½×32 mm) and have two rows of ornaments forming the frame.

1947. Air. Rimini Philatelic Exhibition. No. 333 optd **Giornata Filatelica Rimini - San Marino 8 Luglio 1947.**

347	100l. brown	3·25	1·40

1947. Reconstruction. Surch + and value in figures.

348	1l.+1 mauve and green	20	20
349	1l.+2 mauve and green	20	20
350	1l.+3 mauve and green	20	20
351	1l.+4 mauve and green	20	20
352	1l.+5 mauve and green	20	20
353	2l.+1 green and mauve	20	20
354	2l.+2 green and mauve	20	20
355	2l.+3 green and mauve	20	20
356	2l.+4 green and mauve	20	20
357	2l.+5 green and mauve	20	20
358	4l.+1 green and brown	11·00	5·25
359	4l.+2 green and brown	11·00	5·25

94 Mt. Titano, Statue of Liberty and 1847 U.S.A. Stamp

95 Mt. Titano and 1847 U.S.A. Stamp

1947. Centenary of First U.S.A. Postage Stamp.

360	**94**	2l. brown & pur (postage)	30	25
361	-	3l. grey, red and blue	30	25
362	**94**	6l. green and blue	30	25
363	-	15l. violet, red and blue	1·10	55
364	-	35l. brown, red and blue	4·25	1·60
365	-	50l. green, red and blue	5·00	1·60
366	**95**	100l. brown and violet (air)	26·00	16·00

DESIGNS: 3, 35l. U.S.A. stamps, 5c. and 10c. of 1847 and 90c. of 1869 and flags of U.S.A. and San Marino; 15, 50l. Similar but differently arranged.

96 Worker and San Marino Flag

1948. Workers' Issue.

367	**96**	5l. brown	4·50	55
368	**96**	8l. green	4·50	55
369	**96**	30l. red	7·75	1·10
370	**96**	50l. brown and mauve	17·00	3·25
371	**96**	100l. blue and violet	55·00	48·00

See also Nos. 506/7.

1948. Surch **L .100** between circular ornaments.

372	**59**	100l. on 15c. black and red	£110	32·00

1948. Air. Surch **POSTA AEREA 200.**

373	**91**	200l. on 25l. mauve and red (No. 343)	70·00	29·00

99 Faetano

100 Mt. Titano

1949

374	-	1l. blue and black	55	25
375	-	2l. red and purple	55	25
376	**99**	3l. blue and violet	55	25
377	-	4l. violet and black	55	25
378	-	5l. brown and purple	55	25
379	**99**	6l. black and blue	1·70	80
380	**100**	8l. brown and deep brown	1·70	25
381	-	10l. blue and black	1·10	25
382	-	12l. violet and red	4·00	1·30
383	-	15l. red and violet	9·00	1·90
383a	**99**	20l. brown and blue	39·00	2·75
384	-	35l. violet and green	17·00	5·25
385	-	50l. brown and red	10·00	2·10
385a	-	55l. green and blue	£130	50·00
386	**100**	100l. green and brown	£140	75·00
387	-	200l. brown and blue	£140	£110

DESIGNS—HORIZ: 1, 5, 35l. Guaita Tower and walls; 2, 12, 50l. Serravalle and Mt. Titano; 4, 15, 55l. Franciscan Convent and Capuchin Church. VERT: 10, 200l. Guaita Tower.

For similar stamps see Nos. 491/5, 522a/7a and 794/9.

1949. Stamp Day. Optd **Giornata Filatelica San Marino-Riccione 28-6-1949.**

388	**91**	1l. mauve and green	55	25
389	**91**	2l. green and mauve	85	25

104 Garibaldi

1949. Centenary of Garibaldi's Retreat from Rome. (a) Postage. Portraits as T **104**. (i) Size 22×28 mm.

390	-	1l. red and black	30	25
391	-	2l. blue and brown	30	25
392	**104**	3l. green and red	30	25
393	-	4l. brown and blue	30	25

(ii) Size 27×37 mm.

394	-	5l. brown and mauve	45	25
395	-	15l. blue and red	2·20	1·20
396	-	20l. red and violet	4·00	1·90
397	**104**	50l. violet and purple	40·00	15·00

105 Garibaldi in San Marino

(b) Air. (i) Size 28×22 mm.

398	**105**	2l. blue and purple	55	25
399	**105**	3l. black and green	55	25
400	**105**	5l. green and blue	55	25

(ii) Size 37×27 mm.

401	25l. violet and green	6·00	2·40
402	65l. black and green	17·00	9·50

PORTRAITS—VERT: 1, 20l. Francesco Nullo; 2, 5l. Anita Garibaldi; 4, 15l. Ugo Bassi.

See also Nos. 538/44.

106 Mail Coach and Mt. Titano

1949. 75th Anniv of U.P.U.

403	**106**	100l. purple & blue (postage)	28·00	12·00
404	**106**	200l. blue (air)	4·50	2·10
405	**106**	300l. brown, light brown and purple	9·00	4·75

107 Mt. Titano from Serravalle

108 Second and Guaita Towers

109 Guaita Tower

1950. Air. Views.

406	**107**	2l. green and violet	55	55
407	-	3l. brown and blue	55	55
408	**108**	5l. red and brown (22×28 mm)	55	55
409	-	10l. blue and green	4·50	1·10
410	-	15l. violet and black	6·00	1·30
411	-	55l. green and blue	55·00	18·00
412	**107**	100l. black and red (37×27 mm)	44·00	14·00
413	**108**	250l. brown and violet	£225	48·00
414	**109**	500l. brown and green (37×27 mm)	£110	£100
415	**109**	500l. purple, green and blue	£325	£150

DESIGNS—As Type **107**: 3l. Distant view of Domagnano; 10l. Domagnano; 15l. San Marino from St. Mustiola. 27×37 mm: 55l. Borgo Maggiore.

1950. Air. 28th Milan Fair. As Nos. 408, 410 and 411 but in different colours, optd **XXVIII FIERA INTERNAZIONALE DI MILANO APRILE 1950**.

416	5l. green and blue	55	25
417	15l. black and red	1·10	55
418	55l. brown and violet	8·25	4·75

111 Government Palace

1951. Red Cross.

419	**111**	25l. purple, red and brown	14·50	7·50
420	-	75l. brown, red & lt brown	22·00	10·50
421	-	100l. black, red and brown	30·00	14·00

DESIGNS—HORIZ: 75l. Archway of Murata Nuova. VERT: 100l. Guaita Tower.

1951. Air. Stamp Day. No. 415 surch **Giornata Filatelica San Marino - Riccione 20-8-1951 L. 300.**

422	**109**	300l. on 500l. purple, green and blue	£100	43·00

113 Flag, Douglas DC-6 Airliner and Mt. Titano

1951. Air.

423	**113**	1000l. blue and brown	£850	£550

108 Second and Guaita Towers

1951. Air. Italian Flood Relief Fund. Surch **Pro-alluvionati italiani 1951 L. 100** and bars.

424	**108**	100l. on 250l. brown and violet	13·00	6·00

115 "Columbus at the Council of Salamanca" (after Barabino)

1952. 500th Birth Anniv (1951) of Christopher Columbus.

425	**115**	1l. orange & grn (postage)	55	25
426	-	2l. brown and violet	55	25
427	-	3l. violet and brown	55	25
428	-	4l. blue and brown	55	25
429	-	5l. green and turquoise	55	60
430	-	10l. brown and black	1·70	85
431	-	15l. red and black	2·20	1·40
432	-	20l. blue and green	3·25	1·70
433	-	25l. purple and brown	18·00	5·25
434	**115**	60l. brown and violet	28·00	10·50
435	-	80l. grey and black	60·00	27·00
436	-	200l. green and blue	£120	60·00
437	-	200l. blue and black (air)	55·00	32·00

DESIGNS—HORIZ: 2, 25l. Columbus and fleet; 3, 10, 20l. Landing in America; 4, 15, 80l. Red Indians and American settlers; 5, 200l. (No. 436) Columbus and Map of America; 200l. (No. 437) Columbus, Statue of Liberty (New York) and skyscrapers.

1952. Trieste Fair. As Columbus issue of 1952, but colours changed, optd **FIERA DI TRIESTE 1952**.

438	1l. violet and brown (postage)	30	25
439	2l. red and black	30	25
440	3l. green and turquoise	30	25
441	4l. brown and black	55	25
442	5l. mauve and violet	85	55
443	10l. blue and brown	2·20	1·10
444	15l. brown and blue	6·75	2·75
445	200l. brown and black (air)	90·00	43·00

117 Rose

118 Cyclamen, Douglas DC-6 Airliner, Rose, San Marino and Riccione

1952. Air. Stamp Day and Philatelic Exhibition.

446	-	1l. purple and violet	55	25
447	-	2l. green and blue	55	25
448	**117**	3l. red and brown	55	25
449	**118**	5l. brown and purple	1·70	25
450	**118**	25l. green and violet	4·50	1·70
451	**118**	200l. multicoloured	£100	45·00

DESIGNS—As Type **117**: 1l. Cyclamen; 2l. San Marino and Riccione.

119 Airplane over San Marino

1952. Air. Aerial Survey of San Marino.

452	**119**	25l. green and yellow	4·00	1·60
453	-	75l. violet and brown	10·00	4·75

DESIGN: 75l. Airplane over Mt. Titano.

120 "The Discus Thrower"

121 Tennis

1953. Sports.

454	**120**	1l. black & brn (postage)	15	25
455	**121**	2l. brown and black	15	25
456	-	3l. blue and black	15	25
457	-	4l. blue and green	15	25
458	-	5l. green and brown	15	25
459	-	10l. red and blue	1·40	25
460	-	25l. brown and black	6·00	1·70
461	-	100l. black and brown	19·00	7·50
462	-	200l. turquoise & grn (air)	25·00	9·75

DESIGNS—As Type **120**: 3l. Running. As Type **121**: HORIZ: 4l. Cycling; 5l. Football; 100l. Roller skating; 200l. Skiing. VERT: 10l. Model glider flying; 25l. Shooting.

See also No. 584.

1953. Stamp Day and Philatelic Exn. As No. 461 but colour changed, optd **GIORNATA FILATELICA S. MARINO - RICCIONE 24 AGOSTO 1953**.

463	100l. green and turquoise	40·00	16·00

123 Narcissus

1953. Flowers.

464	**123**	1l. blue, green and yellow	15	25
465	-	2l. blue, green and yellow	15	25
466	-	3l. blue, green and yellow	15	25
467	-	4l. blue, green and yellow	15	25
468	-	5l. green and red	15	25
469	-	10l. blue, green and yellow	1·40	60
470	-	25l. blue, green and pink	5·50	2·75
471	-	80l. blue, green and red	28·00	16·00
472	-	100l. blue, green and pink	47·00	22·00

FLOWERS: 2l. "Parrot" tulip; 3l. Oleander; 4l. Cornflower; 5l. Carnation; 10l. Iris; 25 l; Cyclamen; 80l. Geranium; 100l. Rose.

124 Douglas DC-6 Airliner over Mt. Titano and Arms

1954. Air.

473	**124**	1000l. brown and blue	75·00	38·00

125 Walking

1954. Sports.

474	**125**	1l. mauve and violet	10	15
475	-	2l. violet and green	10	15
476	-	3l. chestnut and brown	10	15
477	-	4l. blue and turquoise	10	15
478	-	5l. brown and green	10	15
479	-	8l. lilac and purple	10	15
480	-	12l. red and black	55	25
481	-	25l. green and blue	3·25	30
482	**125**	80l. green and blue	4·50	1·10
483	-	200l. brown and lilac	12·00	4·25
484	-	250l. multicoloured	90·00	43·00

DESIGNS—HORIZ: 2l. Fencing; 3l. Boxing; 5l. Motor-cycle racing; 8l. Throwing the javelin; 12l. Car racing. VERT: 4, 200, 250l. Gymnastics; 25l. Wrestling.

The 200l. measures 27×37 mm and the 250l. 28×37½ mm.

126 Statue of Liberty

1954

485	**126**	20 1. blue & brn (postage)	1·10	30
486	**126**	60l. green and red	4·00	80
487	**126**	120l. brown and blue (air)	2·20	1·30

127 Hurdling

1955. Air. First Int Exhibition of Olympic Stamps.

488	**127**	80l. black and red	3·25	1·20
489	-	120l. red and green	5·50	2·20

DESIGN—HORIZ: 120l. Relay racing.

128 Yacht

1955. Seventh International Philatelic Exhibition.

490	**128**	100l. black and blue	8·25	3·25

See also No. 518.

1955. Views as **T 99**.

491	5l. brown and blue	10	15
492	10l. green and orange	10	15
493	15l. red and green	10	15
494	25l. violet and brown	20	20
495	35l. red and lilac	20	20

DESIGNS—HORIZ: 5, 25l. Archway of Murata Nuova. VERT: 10, 35l. Guaita Tower; 15l. Government Palace.

See also Nos. 519/21 and 797/9.

129 Ice Skating

1955. Winter Olympic Games, Cortina D'Ampezzo.

496	**129**	1l. brown & yell (postage)	15	15
497	-	2l. blue and red	15	15
498	-	3l. black and brown	15	15
499	-	4l. brown and green	15	15
500	-	5l. blue and red	15	15
501	-	10l. blue and pink	15	20
502	-	25l. black and red	1·70	75
503	-	50l. brown and blue	4·00	1·30
504	-	100l. black and green	11·50	4·50
505	-	200l. black and orange (air)	55·00	21·00

DESIGNS—HORIZ: 2, 25l. Skiing; 3, 50l. Bobsleighing; 5, 100l. Ice hockey; 200l. Ski jumping. VERT: 4l. Slalom racing; 10l. Figure skating.

1956. Winter Relief Fund. As **T 96** but additionally inscr "ASSISTENZA INVERNALE".

506	50l. green	14·50	8·00

1956. 50th Anniv of "Arengo" (San Marino Parliament). As **T 96** but additionally inscr "50° ANNIVERSARIO ARENGO 25 MARZO 1906".

507	50l. blue	14·50	8·00

130 Pointer

1956. Dogs. 25l. to 100l. have multicoloured centres.

508	**130**	1l. brown and blue	10	25
509	-	2l. grey and red	10	25
510	-	3l. brown and blue	10	25
511	-	4l. grey and blue	10	25
512	-	5l. brown and red	10	25
513	-	10l. brown and blue	10	25
514	-	25l. blue	4·00	1·10
515	-	60l. red	13·00	4·75
516	-	80l. blue	17·00	6·50
517	-	100l. red	26·00	12·00

DOGS: 2l. Borzoi; 3l. Sheepdog; 4l. Greyhound; 5l. Boxer; 10l. Great Dane; 25l. Irish setter; 60l. Alsatian; 80l. Rough collie; 100l. Foxhound.

1956. Philatelic Exn. As **T 128** but inscr "1956".

518	**128**	100l. brown and green	3·25	1·70

1956. International Philatelic Congress. Designs as Nos. 491/5 but larger and new values inscr "CONGRESSO INTERNAZ. PERITI FILATELICI SAN MARINO SALSOMAGGIORE 6-8 OTTOBRE 1956".

519	20l. brown and blue	2·20	55
520	80l. red and violet	4·50	2·10
521	100l. green and orange	7·00	3·75

SIZES—26½×37 mm: 20l. Guaita Tower; 100l. Government Palace. (36½×27 mm): 8l. Archway of Murata Nuova.

1956. Air. No. 504 optd with an airplane and POSTA AEREA.

522	100l. black and green	5·00	2·75

1957. Views as **T 99**.

522a	1l. green and deep green	10	10
523	2l. red and green	10	15
524	3l. brown and blue	15	15
524a	4l. blue and brown	20	15
525	20l. green and deep green	30	15
525a	30l. violet and brown	65	30
526	60l. violet and brown	3·25	1·20
526a	115l. brown and blue	1·10	65
527	125l. blue and black	85	55
527a	500l. black and green	£170	80·00

DESIGNS—VERT: 2l. Borgo Maggiore Church; 3, 30l. Town gate, San Marino; 4, 125l. View of San Marino from southern wall; 20, 115l. Borgo Maggiore market place. HORIZ: 1, 60l. View of San Marino from Hospital Avenue. 37½×28 mm: 500l. Panorama of San Marino.

See also Nos. 794/6.

132 Marguerites

1957. Flowers. Multicoloured.

528	1l. Type **132**	10	15
529	2l. Polyanthuses	10	15
530	3l. Lilies	10	15
531	4l. Orchid	10	15
532	5l. Lilies of the valley	10	15
533	10l. Poppies	10	15
534	25l. Pansies	45	20
535	60l. Gladiolus	1·10	60
536	80l. Wild roses	2·10	90
537	100l. Anemones	3·25	1·70

1957. 150th Birth Anniv of Garibaldi. As **T 104** but inscr "COMMEMORAZIONE 150° NASCITA G. GARIBALDI 1807 1957. (a) Size 22×28 mm.

538	-	2l. blue and violet (as No. 391)	15	15
539	-	3l. green and red (as No. 390)	15	15
540	**104**	5l. drab and brown	15	15

(b) Size 26½×37 mm.

541	-	15l. violet and blue (as No. 395)	20	20
542	-	25l. black and green (as No. 396)	55	45
543	-	50l. brown and violet (as No. 394)	1·70	1·30
544	**104**	100l. violet and brown	3·25	1·60

134 St. Marinus and Fair Entrance

1958. 36th Milan Fair.

545	**134**	15l. yellow & bl (postage)	30	25
546	-	60l. green and red	55	55
547	-	125l. blue and brown (air)	4·25	3·00

DESIGNS—HORIZ: 60l. Italian pavilion and giant arch. VERT: 125l. Bristol 173 Rotocoach helicopter and airplane over fair.

135 Exhibition Emblem, Atomium and Mt. Titano

1958. Brussels International Exhibition.

548	**135**	40l. sepia and green	30	25
549	**135**	60l. lake and blue	70	45

136 View of San Marino

1958. Air.

550	**136**	200l. blue and brown	8·00	2·75
551	-	300l. violet and red	8·00	2·75

DESIGN: 300l. Mt. Titano.

137 Wheat

1958. Fruit and Agricultural Products.

552	**137**	1l. yellow and blue	10	10
553	-	2l. red and green	10	10
554	-	3l. orange and blue	10	10
555	-	4l. red and green	10	10
556	-	5l. yellow, green and blue	10	10
557	**137**	15l. yellow, brown & blue	10	10
558	-	25l. multicoloured	55	10
559	-	40l. multicoloured	1·30	45
560	-	80l. multicoloured	2·20	1·40
561	-	125l. multicoloured	6·00	3·25

DESIGNS: 2, 125l. Maize; 3, 80l. Grapes; 4, 25l. Peaches; 5, 40l. Plums.

138 Naples 10 grana stamp of 1858 and Bay of Naples

1958. Centenary of First Naples Postage Stamps.

562	**138**	25l. brown & blue (postage)	30	25
563	**138**	125l. brown and bistre (air)	4·25	2·00

The Naples stamp on No. 563 is the 50gr.

139 Mediterranean Gull

1959. Air. Native Birds.

564	**139**	5l. black and green	30	20
565	-	10l. brown, black and blue	30	20
566	-	15l. multicoloured	55	25
567	-	120l. multicoloured	2·20	75
568	-	250l. black, yellow & green	4·50	2·20

BIRDS: 10l. Common kestrel; 15l. Mallard; 120l. Feral rock dove; 250l. Barn swallow.

140 P. de Coubertin (founder)

1959. Pre-Olympic Games Issue.

569	**140**	2l. black & brn (postage)	10	10
570	-	3l. sepia and mauve	10	10
571	-	5l. green and blue	10	10
572	-	30l. black and violet	10	10
573	-	60l. sepia and green	35	20
574	-	80l. green and lake	45	20
575	-	120l. brown (air)	7·75	2·50

PORTRAITS—As Type **140**: 3l. A. Bonacossa; 5l. A. Brundage; 30l. C. Montu; 60l. J. S. Edstrom; 80l. De Baillet-Latour. HORIZ: (36×21½ mm): 120l. De Coubertin and Olympic Flame. All, except the founder, De Coubertin are executives of the Olympic Games Committee.

141 Vickers Viscount 700 Airliner over Mt. Titano

1959. Air. Alitalia Inaugural Flight, Rimini–London.

576	**141**	120l. violet	3·00	1·70

142 Abraham Lincoln and Scroll

1959. Abraham Lincoln's 150th Birth Anniv. Inscr "ABRAMO LINCOLN 1809–1959".

577	**142**	5l. brn & sepia (postage)	10	10
578	-	10l. green and blue	10	10
579	-	15k. grey and green	10	10
580	-	70k. violet	20	50
581	-	200l. blue (air)	10·50	3·75

DESIGNS—Portraits of Lincoln with: HORIZ: 10l. Map of San Marino; 15l. Govt Palace, San Marino; 200l. Mt. Titano. VERT: 70l. Mt. Titano.

143 1859 Romagna ½b. stamp and Arch of Augustus, Rimini

1959. Romagna Stamp Centenary. Inscr "1859–1959".

582	**143**	30l. brown & sepia (postage)	30	25
583	-	120l. green and black (air)	3·00	2·00

DESIGN: 120 1. 1989 Romagna 3l. stamp and view of Bologna.

1959. World University Games, Turin. Inscr "UNIVERSITY TORINO 1959".

584	**120**	30l. red	90	65

144 Portal of Messina Cathedral and ½gr. Sicily stamp

1959. Centenary of First Sicilian Postage Stamp.

585	**144**	1l. brown & yell (postage)	10	10
586	-	2l. red and green	10	10
587	-	3l. slate and blue	10	10
588	-	4l. brown and red	10	10
589	-	5l. purple and blue	10	10
590	-	25l. multicoloured	15	20
591	-	60l. multicoloured	20	25
592	-	200l. multicoloured (air)	3·50	1·40

DESIGNS—VERT: 2l. Selinunte Temple (1gr.); 3l. Erice Church (2gr.); 4l. "Concordia" Temple, Agrigento (5gr.); 5l. "Castor and Pollux" Temple, Agrigento (10gr.); 25l. "St. John of the Hermits" Church, Palermo (20gr.). HORIZ: 60l. Taormina (50gr.); 200l. Bay of Palermo (50gr.).

145 Golden Oriole

1960. Birds.

593	**145**	1l. yellow, olive and blue	20	20
594	-	2l. brown, red and green	20	20
595	-	3l. red, brown and green	20	20
596	-	4l. black, brown and green	20	20
597	-	5l. red, brown and green	20	25
598	-	10l. multicoloured	30	25
599	-	25l. multicoloured	1·10	50
600	-	60l. multicoloured	2·20	1·40
601	-	80l. multicoloured	3·50	2·75
602	-	110l. multicoloured	6·75	4·75

DESIGNS—VERT: 2l. Nightingale; 4l. Hoopoe; 10l. Eurasian goldfinch; 25l. River kingfisher; 80l. Green woodpecker; 110l. Red-breasted flycatcher. HORIZ: 3l. Eurasian woodcock; 5l. Red-legged partridge; 60l. Common pheasant.

146 Putting the Shot

1960. Olympic Games.

603	**146**	1l. violet and red (postage)	10	10
604	-	2l. orange and black	10	10
605	-	3l. violet and brown	10	10
606	-	4l. brown and red	10	10
607	-	5l. blue and brown	10	10
608	-	10l. blue and brown	10	10
609	-	15l. violet and green	10	15
610	-	25l. orange and green	10	15
611	-	60l. brown and green	45	20
612	-	110l. red, black and green	65	30
613	-	20l. violet (air)	10	30
614	-	40l. red and brown	20	25
615	-	80l. yellow and blue	30	25
616	-	125l. brown and red	55	55
MS616a 90×125 mm. 1, 2, 3, 60l. brown, green and light green			3·25	3·25
MS616b 90×127 mm. 4, 10, 20, 40l. brown, red and light red			3·25	3·25
MS616c 145×100 mm. 5, 15, 25, 80, 110, 125l. brown, deep brown and light green			5·75	5·75

DESIGNS—VERT: 2l. Gymnastics; 3l. Long-distance walking; 4l. Boxing; 10l. Cycling; 20l. Handball; 40l. Breasting the tape; 60l. Football. HORIZ: 5l. Fencing; 15l. Hockey; 25l. Rowing; 80l. Diving; 110l. Horse-jumping; 125l. Rifle shooting.

147 Melvin Jones (founder) and Lions International H.Q.

1960. Lions International Commemoration.

617		30l. brown and violet (postage)	30	30
618	**147**	45l. brown and violet	55	30
619	-	60l. red and blue	30	30
620	-	115l. green and black	55	60
621	-	150l. brown and violet	4·00	2·50
622	-	200l. blue and green (air)	21·00	8·00

DESIGNS—VERT: 30l. Mt. Titano; 60l. San Marino Government Palace. HORIZ: 115l. Pres. Clarence Sturm; 150l. Vice-Pres. Finis E. Davis; 200l. Globe. All designs except Type **147** bear the Lions emblem.

148 Riccione

1960. 12th Riccione–San Marino Stamp Day. Centres multicoloured.

623	**148**	30l. red (postage)	20	20
624	**148**	125l. blue (air)	3·00	1·40

149 "Youth with Basket of Fruit"

1960. 350th Death Anniv of Caravaggio (painter).

625	**149**	200l. multicoloured	18·00	8·00

150 Hunting Roe Deer

1961. Hunting (1st issue). Historical Scenes.

626	**150**	1l. blue and mauve	10	10
627	-	2l. red and brown	10	10
628	-	3l. black and red	10	10
629	-	4l. red and blue	10	10
630	-	5l. brown and green	10	10
631	-	10l. violet and orange	10	10
632	-	30l. blue and yellow	15	15
633	-	60l. brown, orange & black	20	20
634	-	70l. red, purple and green	30	20
635	-	115l. blue, purple & black	85	35

DESIGNS—VERT: 2l. 16th-cent falconer; 10l. 16th-cent falconer (mounted); 60l. 17th-century hunter with rifle and dog. HORIZ: 3l. 16th-cent wild boar hunt; 4l. Duck-shooting with crossbow (16th-cent); 5l. 16th-cent stag hunt with bow and arrow; 30l. 17th-cent huntsman with horn and dogs; 70l. 18th-cent hunter and beater; 115l. Duck-shooting with bow and arrow (18th-cent).

See also Nos. 679/88.

151 Bell 47J Ranger Helicopter near Mt. Titano

1961. Air.

636	**151**	1000l. red	60·00	44·00

152 Guaita Tower, Mt. Titano and 1858 Sardinian Stamp

1961. Centenary of Italian Independence Philatelic Exhibition, Turin.

637	**152**	30l. multicoloured	35	50
638	**152**	70l. multicoloured	55	70
639	**152**	200l. multicoloured	1·80	1·20

153 Mt. Titano

1961. Europe.

640	**153**	500l. green and brown	50·00	22·00

155 King Enzo's Palace, Bologna

1961. Bologna Stamp Exn. Inscr "BOLOGNA".

641	**155**	30l. black and blue	15	15
642	-	70l. black and myrtle	20	20
643	-	100l. black and brown	20	30

DESIGNS: 70l. Gateway of Merchant's Palace; 100l. Towers of Garisenda and Asinelli, Bologna.

156 Duryea, 1892

1962. Veteran Motor Cars.

644	**156**	1l. blue and brown	10	15
645	-	2l. orange and blue	10	15
646	-	3l. orange and black	10	15
647	-	4l. red and black	10	15
648	-	5l. orange and violet	10	15
649	-	10l. orange and black	10	15
650	-	15l. red and black	10	15
651	-	20l. blue and black	10	30
652	-	25l. orange and black	10	30
653	-	30l. buff and black	10	30
654	-	50l. mauve and black	15	30
655	-	70l. green and black	20	30
656	-	100l. red, yellow and black	55	50
657	-	115l. green, orange & black	80	60
658	-	150l. yellow, orange & black	1·00	90

MOTOR CARS—HORIZ: 2l. Panhard and Levassor, 1895; 3l. Peugeot "Vis-a-vis", 1895; 4l. Daimler, 1899; 10l. Decauville, 1900; 15l. Wolseley, 1901; 20l. Benz, 1902; 25l. Napier, 1903; 50l. Oldsmobile, 1904; 100l. Isotta Fraschini, 1908; 115l. Bianchi, 1910; 150l. Alfa, 1910. VERT: 5l. F.I.A.T., 1899; 30l. White, 1903; 70l. Renault, 1904.

157 Wright Type A Biplane

1962. Vintage Aircraft.

659	**157**	1l. black and yellow	10	20
660	-	2l. brown and green	10	20
661	-	3l. brown and green	10	20
662	-	4l. black and bistre	10	20
663	-	5l. red and blue	10	20
664	-	10l. brown and green	10	30
665	-	30l. bistre and blue	10	35
666	-	60l. bistre and violet	35	35
667	-	70l. black and orange	35	50
668	-	115l. bistre, black & green	1·70	1·00

DESIGNS: 2l. Archdeacon-Voisin "Boxkite" float glider; 3l. Albert and Emile Bonnet-Labranche biplane; 4l. Glenn Curtiss "June Bug"; 5l. Henri Farman H.F.III biplane; 10l. Bleriot XI, 30l. Hubert Latham's Antoinette IV; 60l. Alberto Santos-Dumont's biplane "14 bis"; 70l. Alliott Verdon Roe's Triplane II; 115l. Faccioli's airplane.

158 Roping Down

1962. Mountaineering.

669	**158**	1l. bistre and black	10	15
670	-	2l. turquoise and black	10	15
671	-	3l. purple and black	10	15
672	-	4l. blue and black	10	15
673	-	5l. orange and black	10	15
674	-	15l. yellow and black	10	15
675	-	30l. red and black	10	15
676	-	40l. blue and black	10	15
677	-	85l. green and black	20	20
678	-	115l. blue and black	65	65

DESIGNS: 2l. Sassolungo; 3l. Mt. Titano; 4l. Three Lavaredo peaks; 5l. The Matterhorn; 15l. Skier; 30l. Climber negotiating overhang; 40l. Step-cutting in ice; 85l. Aiguille du Geant; 115l. Citadel on Mt. Titano.

159 Hunter and Retriever

1962. Hunting (2nd issue). Modern scenes.

679	**159**	1l. deep purple and green	10	15
680	-	2l. blue and orange	10	15
681	-	3l. black and blue	10	15
682	-	4l. sepia and brown	10	15
683	-	5l. brown and green	10	15
684	-	15l. black and green	10	15
685	-	50l. sepia and green	30	30
686	-	70l. turquoise and red	30	30
687	-	100l. black and red	30	30
688	-	150l. green and lilac	90	55

DESIGNS—HORIZ: 3l. Marsh ducks (with decoys); 4l. Roe deer; 5l. Grey partridge; 15l. Northern lapwing; 50l. Partridge; 70l. Marsh geese; 100l. Wild boar. VERT: 2l. Huntsman and hounds; 150l. Hunter shooting pheasant.

160 Arrows encircling "Europa"

1962. Europa.

689	**160**	200l. red and black	3·25	1·40

161 Egyptian Merchant Ship, 2000 B.C.

1963. Historical Ships.

690	**161**	1l. blue and orange	10	15
691	-	2l. sepia and purple	10	15
692	-	3l. sepia and mauve	10	15
693	-	4l. dull purple and grey	10	15
694	-	5l. sepia and yellow	10	15
695	-	10l. brown and green	10	15
696	-	30l. sepia and blue	55	55
697	-	60l. blue and green	55	60
698	-	70l. red and deep grey	55	70
699	-	115l. brown and blue	3·75	2·00

DESIGNS—HORIZ: 2l. Greek trier, 5th-cent, B.C.; 3l. Roman trireme, 1st-cent, B.C.; 4l. Viking longship, 10th-cent; 5l. The "Santa Maria"; 30l. Gallery, c. 1600; 115l. "Duncan Dunbar" (full-rigged merchantman), 1550. VERT: 10l. Carrack, c. 1550; 60l. "Sovereign of the Seas" (English galleon), 1637; 70l. "Fyn" (Danish ship of the line), c. 1750.

162 "The Fornarina" (or "The Veiled Woman")

1963. Paintings by Raphael. Multicoloured.

700	30l. Type **162**	10	20
701	70l. Self portrait	15	20
702	100l. Sistine Madonna (detail of woman praying)	20	30
703	200l. "Portrait of a Young Woman" (Maddalena Strozzi)	55	80

The 200l. is larger, 27×44 mm.

163 Saracen Game, Arezzo

1963. Ancient Tournaments.

704	**163**	1l. mauve	10	15
705	-	2l. black	10	15
706	-	3l. black	10	15
707	-	4l. violet	10	15
708	-	5l. violet	10	15
709	-	10l. green	10	15
710	-	30l. red	10	15
711	-	60l. blue	15	15
712	-	70l. brown	20	20
713	-	115l. black	55	30

TOURNAMENTS—HORIZ: 2l. 14th-century, French cavaliers; 4l. 15th-century, Presenting arms to an English cavalier; 30l. Quintana game, Foligno; 70l. 15th-century, Cavaliers (from castle mural, Malpaga). VERT: 3l. Crossbow Championships, Gubbio; 5l. 16th-century, Cavaliers, Florence; 10l. Quintana game, Ascoli Piceno; 60l. Palio (horse-race), Siena; 115l. 13th-century, The Crusades: cavaliers' challenge.

164 Peacock

1963. Butterflies. Multicoloured.

714	25l. Type **164**	20	20
715	30l. "Nessaea obrinus"	20	20
716	60l. Large tortoiseshell	20	20
717	70l. Peacock (horiz)	35	45
718	115l. "Papilio blumei" (horiz)	65	55

165 Corner of Government Palace, San Marino

1963. San Marino–Riccione Stamp Fair.

719	**165**	100l. black and blue	20	20
720	-	100l. blue and sepia	20	20

DESIGN: No. 720, Fountain, Riccione.

166 Pole Vaulting

1963. Olympic Games, Tokyo (1964) (1st issue).

721		1l. purple and orange	10	10
722	**166**	2l. sepia and green	10	10
723	-	3l. sepia and blue	10	10
724	-	4l. sepia and blue	10	10
725	-	5l. sepia and red	10	10
726	-	10l. mauve and purple	10	10
727	-	30l. purple and grey	10	10
728	-	60l. sepia and yellow	10	10
729	-	70l. sepia and blue	35	10
730	-	115l. sepia and green	45	10

SPORTS—HORIZ: 1l. Hurdling; 3l. Relay-racing; 4l. High jumping (men); 5l. Football; 10l. High jumping (women); 60l. Throwing the javelin; 70l. Water polo; 115l. Throwing the hammer. VERT: 30l. Throwing the discus.

See also Nos. 743/52.

167 "E" and Flag of San Marino

1963. Europa.

731	**167**	200l. blue and brown	1·00	45

168 Tupolev Tu-104A Jetliner

1963. Air. Contemporary Aircraft.

732	**168**	5l. purple, brown and blue	15	15
733	-	10l. blue and red	15	15
734	-	15l. red, mauve and violet	15	15
735	-	25l. red, mauve and violet	15	15
736	-	50l. red and blue	20	15
737	-	75l. orange and green	20	15
738	-	120l. red and blue	35	30
739	-	200l. black and yellow	65	20
740	-	300l. black and orange	90	45
741	-	500l. multicoloured	7·25	5·50
742	-	1000l. multicoloured	4·00	2·75

DESIGNS—HORIZ: 15l. Douglas DC-8 jetliner; 25, 1000l. Boeing 707 jetliner (different views); 50l. Vickers Viscount 837 airliner; 120l. Vickers VC-10; 200l. Hawker Siddley Comet 4C jetliner; 300l. Boeing 727-100 jetliner. VERT: 10l. Boeing 707 jetliner; 75l. Sud Aviation SE 210 Caravelle jetliner; 500l. Rolls Royce Dart 527 turboprop engine.

169 Running

1964. Olympic Games, Tokyo (2nd issue).

743	**169**	1l. brown and green	15	10
744	-	2l. brown and sepia	15	10
745	-	3l. brown and black	15	10
746	-	4l. blue and red	15	10
747	-	5l. brown and blue	15	10
748	-	15l. purple and orange	15	10
749	-	30l. blue and light blue	15	10
750	-	70l. brown and green	15	10
751	-	120l. brown and blue	30	10
752	-	150l. purple and red	45	30

DESIGNS—VERT: 2l. Gymnastics; 3l. Basketball; 120l. Cycling; 150l. Fencing. HORIZ: 4l. Pistol-shooting; 5l. Rowing; 15l. Long jumping; 30l. Diving; 70l. Sprinting.

1964. "Towards Tokyo" Sports Stamp Exn, Rimini. As Nos. 749/50, but inscr "VERSO TOKIO" and colours changed.

753	30l. blue and violet	20	15
754	70l. brown and turquoise	20	15

170 Murray Blenkinsop Rack Locomotive (1812)

1964. "Story of the Locomotive".

755	**170**	1l. black and buff	10	10
756	-	2l. black and green	10	10
757	-	3l. black and violet	10	10
758	-	4l. black and yellow	10	10
759	-	5l. black and salmon	10	10
760	-	15l. black and green	15	10
761	-	20l. black and pink	15	15
762	-	50l. black and blue	20	15
763	-	90l. black and orange	30	15
764	-	110l. black and blue	45	30

LOCOMOTIVES: 2l. "Puffing Billy" (1813–14); 3l. "Locomotion" (1825); 4l. "Rocket" (1829); 5l. "Lion" (1838); 15l. "Bayard" (1839); 20l. Crampton type No. 125, France (1849); 50l. "Little England" (1851); 90l. "Spitfire", Canada (1855); 110l. Rogers, U.S.A. (c. 1865).

171 Baseball Players

1964. Seventh European Baseball Championships, Milan.

765	**171**	30l. sepia and green	20	15
766	-	70l. black and red	35	30

DESIGN: 70l. Player pitching ball.

172 "E" and Part of Globe

1964. Europa.

767	**172**	200l. red, blue & light blue	3·00	55

173 Pres. Kennedy giving Inaugural Address

1964. First Death Anniv of John F. Kennedy (President of U.S.A.). Multicoloured.

768	70l. Type **173**	20	15
769	130l. Pres. Kennedy and U.S. flag (vert)	20	30

174 Cyclists at Government Palace

1965. Cycle Tour of Italy.

770	**174**	30l. sepia	15	15
771	-	70l. purple	15	15
772	-	200l. red	30	30

DESIGNS—Cyclists passing: 70l. "The Rock"; 200l. Mt. Titano.

175 Brontosaurus

1965. Prehistoric Animals.

773	**175**	1l. purple and green	10	15
774	-	2l. black and blue	10	15
775	-	3l. yellow and green	10	15
776	-	4l. brown and blue	10	15
777	-	5l. purple and green	10	15
778	-	10l. purple and green	10	15
779	-	75l. blue and turquoise	30	20
780	-	100l. purple and green	40	55
781	-	200l. purple and green	80	60

ANIMALS—VERT: 2l. Brachyosaurus. HORIZ: 3l. Pteranodon; 4l. Elasmosaurus; 5l. Tyrannosaurus; 10l. Stegosaurus; 75l. Thamatosaurus Victor; 100l. Iguanodon; 200l. Triceratops.

176 Rooks on Chessboard

1965. Europa.

782	**176**	200l. multicoloured	50	40

177 Dante

1965. 700th Anniv of Dante's Birth.

783	**177**	40l. sepia and blue	20	15
784	-	90l. sepia and red	20	15
785	-	130l. sepia and brown	35	15
786	-	140l. sepia and blue	35	30

DESIGNS: 90l. "Hell"; 130l. "Purgatory"; 140l. "Paradise".

178 Mt. Titano and Flags

1965. Visit of Pres. Saragat of Italy.

787	**178**	115l. multicoloured	30	30

179 Trotting

1966. Equestrian Sports. Multicoloured.

788	10l. Type **179**	20	15
789	20l. Cross-country racing (vert)	20	15
790	40l. Horse-jumping	20	15
791	70l. Horse-racing	20	15
792	90l. Steeple-chasing	20	15
793	170l. Polo (vert)	35	20

1966. New values in previous designs.

794	5l. brown and blue (as No. 522a)	15	10
795	10l. green and black (as No. 524)	15	10
796	15l. violet and brown (as No. 524a)	15	10
797	40l. red and lilac (as No. 491)	15	10
798	90l. blue and black (as No. 492)	15	10
799	140l. orange and violet (as No. 493)	35	10

180 "La Bella"

1966. Paintings by Titian. Multicoloured.

800	40l. Type **180**	20	15
801	90l. "The Three Graces"	20	15
802	100l. "The Three Graces"	20	20
803	170l. "Sacred and Profane Love"	45	45

The 90 and 100l. show different details from the picture.

181 Stone Bass

1966. Sea Animals. Multicoloured.

804	1l. Type **181**	15	15
805	2l. Cuckoo wrasse	15	15
806	3l. Common dolphin	15	15
807	4l. John Dory	15	15
808	5l. Octopus (vert)	15	15
809	10l. Red scorpionfish	15	15
810	40l. Eyed electric ray (vert)	15	15
811	90l. Medusa (vert)	15	15
812	115l. Long-snouted seahorse (vert)	35	20
813	130l. Dentex seabream	35	20

182 Our Lady of Europe

1966. Europa.

814	**182**	200l. multicoloured	45	35

183 Peony

1967. Flowers. Multicoloured.

815	5l. Type **183**	10	15
816	10l. Campanula	10	15
817	15l. Pyrenean poppy	10	15
818	20l. Purple deadnettle	10	15
819	40l. Hemerocallis	10	15
820	140l. Gentian	10	15
821	170l. Thistle	35	15

Each flower has a different background view of Mt. Titano.

184 St. Marinus

1967. Paintings by Francesco Barbieri (Guercino). Multicoloured.

822	40l. Type **184**	10	20
823	170l. "St. Francis"	45	45
824	190l. "Return of the Prodigal Son" (45×37 mm)	50	45

185 Map of Europe

1967. Europa.

825	**185**	200l. green and orange	65	35

186 Caesar's Mushroom

1967. Fungi. Multicoloured.

826	5l. Type **186**	15	10
827	15l. The Miller	15	10
828	20l. Parasol mushroom	15	10
829	40l. Cep	15	10
830	50l. "Russula paludosa"	15	10
831	170l. St. George's mushroom	35	30

187 Salisbury Cathedral

1967. Gothic Cathedrals.

832	-	20l. violet on cream	15	15
833	-	40l. green on cream	15	15
834	-	80l. blue on cream	15	15
835	**187**	90l. sepia on cream	15	15
836	-	170l. red on cream	40	35

DESIGNS: 20l. Amiens; 40l. Siena; 80l. Toledo; 170l. Cologne.

188 Cimabue Crucifix, Florence

1967. Christmas.

837	**188**	300l. brown and violet	80	50

189 Arms of San Marino

1968. Arms of San Marino Villages. Multicoloured.

838	2l. Type **189**	10	15
839	3l. Penna Rossa	10	15
840	5l. Fiorentino	10	15
841	10l. Montecerreto	10	15
842	25l. Serravalle	10	15
843	35l. Montegiardino	10	15
844	50l. Faetano	10	15
845	90l. Borgo Maggiore	10	15
846	180l. Montelupo	30	15
847	500l. State crest	55	35

190 Europa "Key"

1968. Europa.

848	**190**	250l. brown	65	45

191 "The Battle of San Romano" (detail, P. Uccello)

1968. 671st Birth Anniv of Paolo Uccello (painter).

849	**191**	50l. black on lilac	10	15
850	-	90l. black on lilac (vert)	10	15
851	-	130l. black on lilac	10	15
852	-	230l. black on pink	55	35

All stamps show details of "The Battle of San Romano".

192 "The Nativity" (detail, Botticelli)

1968. Christmas.

853	**192**	50l. blue	15	15
854	**192**	90l. red	20	15
855	**192**	180l. sepia	35	30

193 "Peace"

1969. "The Good Government" (frescoes) by Ambrogio Lorenzetti.

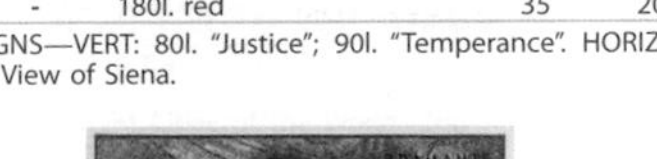

856	**193**	50l. blue	10	10
857	-	80l. sepia	15	10
858	-	90l. violet	20	10
859	-	180l. red	35	20

DESIGNS—VERT: 80l. "Justice"; 90l. "Temperance". HORIZ: 180l. View of Siena.

194 "Young Soldier" (Bramante)

1969. 525th Birth Anniv of Donato Bramante (architect and painter). Multicoloured.

860	50l. Type **194**	20	15
861	90l. "Old Soldier" (Bramante)	35	15

195 Colonnade

1969. Europa.

862	**195**	50l. green	35	20
863	**195**	180l. purple	1·00	20

196 Benched Carriage ("Char-a-banc")

1969. Horses and Carriages. Multicoloured.

864	5l. Type **196**	10	15
865	10l. Barouche	10	15
866	25l. Private drag	10	15
867	40l. Hansom cab	10	15
868	50l. Curricle	10	15
869	90l. Wagonette	10	20
870	180l. Spider phaeton	35	30

197 Mt. Titano

1969. Paintings by R. Viola. Multicoloured.

871	20l. Type **197**	20	15
872	180l. "Pier at Rimini"	45	30
873	200l. "Pier at Riccione" (horiz)	45	45

198 "Faith"

1969. Christmas. "The Theological Virtues" by Raphael.

874	**198**	20l. violet and orange	20	15
875	-	180l. violet and green	35	30
876	-	200l. violet and buff	45	45

DESIGNS: 180l. "Hope"; 200l. "Charity".

199 "Aries"

1970. Signs of the Zodiac. Multicoloured.

877	1l. Type **199**	10	10
878	2l. "Taurus"	10	10
879	3l. "Gemini"	10	10
880	4l. "Cancer"	10	10
881	5l. "Leo"	10	10
882	10l. "Virgo"	10	10

1921	41c. Prawns	1·20	90
1922	41c. Mixed seafood	1·20	90
1923	41c. Ravioli	1·20	90
1924	41c. Tagliatelle	1·20	90
1925	41c. Chicken and potatoes	1·20	90
1926	41c. Fish	1·20	90
1927	41c. Fruit tart	1·20	90
1928	41c. Chocolate pudding	1·20	90
1929	41c. Scrambled eggs	1·20	90
1930	41c. Pancetta	1·20	90
1931	41c. Pastries	1·20	90
1932	41c. Brandy snap basket	1·20	90

534 "Woman with Mango" (Paul Gauguin)

2003. Artists' Anniversaries. Multicoloured.

1933	52c. Type **534** (death centenary)	1·40	1·40
1934	62c. "Wheat-field with flight of crows" (Vincent Van Gogh) (150th birth anniv)	1·60	1·50
1935	€1.55 "Portrait of a young woman" (Parmigianino) (500th birth anniv)	4·25	4·00

535 Combination Skiing

2003. World Nordic Skiing Championship, Val di Femme. Sheet 156×116 mm containing T **535** and similar vert designs. Multicoloured.

MS1936	Type **535**; 77c. Ski jumping; 77c. Cross-country skiing	6·50	6·00

536 Molvedo (horse)

2003. Horse Racing. Showing champion race horses. Multicoloured.

1937	11c. Type **536**	25	25
1938	15c. Tornese	40	40
1939	26c. Ribot	65	65
1940	€1.55 Varenne	4·25	4·25

537 Partially submerged Woman's Head (Armando Testa)

2003. Europa. Poster Art. Multicoloured.

1941	28c. Type **537**	4·00	4·00
1942	77c. "Jane Avril" (Toulouse Latrec)	10·50	10·50

538 Girolamo Fracastoro

2003. 550th Death Anniv of Girolamo Fracastoro (writer and scientist) Centenary of Veronafil Exhibition.

1943	**538** 77c. multicoloured	2·10	2·10

539 Bridge over Winter Canal

2003. 300th Anniv of St. Petersburg. Multicoloured.

1944	15c. Type **539**	40	40
1945	26c. Bartolomeo Francesco Rastrelli (architect)	65	65
1946	36c. Trinity bridge over River Neva	95	95
1947	41c. Aleksander Sergeyevich Pushkin (writer)	1·10	1·10
1948	77c. Queen Catherine II	2·10	2·10
1949	€1.55 Tsar Peter I	4·00	4·00

540 Wright *Flyer I*

2003. Centenary of Powered Flight. Multicoloured.

1950	36c. Type **540**	95	95
1951	41c. Bleriot XI	1·10	1·10
1952	62c. Aermacchi MB339	1·70	1·70
1953	77c. Aermacchi MB339s of Frecce Tricolori (Italian acrobatic flying team)	2·10	2·10

541 Stagecoach on Road

2003. 120th Anniv of First Daily Mail Coach between Rimini and San Marino. Multicoloured.

1954	41c. Type **541**	1·10	1·10
1955	77c. Stagecoach in town	2·10	2·10

542 Chain Wheel (Tour de France)

2003. Centenary of Tour de France Cycle Race. Hamilton 2003 World Championship Road Race, Hamilton, Canada. Sheet 155×115 mm containing T **542** and similar circular design. Multicoloured.

MS1956	77c. Type **542**; 77c. Front wheel (Hamilton 2003)	4·25	4·25

543 Go-Carting

2003. Children's Games. Multicoloured.

1957	36c. Type **543**	95	95
1958	41c. Blind man's buff	1·10	1·10
1959	62c. Hoops	1·70	1·70
1960	77c. Marbles	2·10	2·10
1961	€1.24 Dance	3·25	3·25
1962	€1.55 Tug-of-war	4·00	4·00

544 Masked Puppet

2003. Puppetry. Multicoloured.

1963	41c. Type **544**	1·10	1·10
1964	41c. Blowing trumpet	1·10	1·10
1965	41c. Male puppet offering flower to female	1·10	1·10
1966	41c. Two puppets with sticks	1·10	1·10

Nos. 1963/6 were issued together, *se-tenant*, forming a composite design of a puppet theatre.

545 Two Players and Ball

2003. Rugby World Cup Championship, Australia. Multicoloured.

1967	41c. Type **545**	1·10	1·10
1968	62c. Player about to throw ball	1·70	1·70
1969	77c. Two players fighting for possession	2·10	2·10
1970	€1.55 Player with ball	4·00	4·00

546 Angel

2003. Christmas. Sheet 186×143 mm containing T **546** and similar horiz designs. Multicoloured.

MS1971	41c. ×16, Type **546** (1/2); Shepherds and three kings (3/4); Holy family (5/6); Christmas cards (7/8); Decorated tree (9); Filled stocking (10); Wreath (11/12); Child and snowman (13/14); Father Christmas (15/16); Children and toys (17/18); Toys (19); Angels singing (20/21); Children and cake (22); Girl and games (23); Cornucopia (24); San Marino arms (25)	17·00	17·00

MS1971 was arranged in the shape of a snakes and ladders board, with seven stamps (1/2; 3/4; 5/6; 7/8; 20/21; 22; 23) reversed and two (9; 10) at right angles. The numbers on the board are given in brackets.

547 Theatre Emblem

2003. Reopening of La Fenice Theatre, Venice.

1972	**547** $3.72 multicoloured	10·00	10·00

548 "Ballet" (Edgar Degas) and Tango Dancers

2004. 50th Anniv of Latin Union (inter-government organization). Multicoloured.

1973	41c. Type **548**	1·10	1·10
1974	77c. "Don Quixote" (Miguel De Cervantes) and "Donna Flor and her Two Husbands" (Jorge Amado)	2·10	2·10
1975	€1.55 "Susanna and the Elders" (Tintoretto) and "Sunday Afternoon" (Fernando Botero)	4·00	4·00

549 Building Facade and Coloured Spheres

2004. Venice Carnival. Multicoloured.

1976	77c. Type **549**	2·10	2·10
1977	€1.55 Masked woman	4·00	4·00

550 Manuel Poggiali

2004. Manuel Poggiali—2003 250cc. Motorcycle World Champion.

1978	**550** €1.55 multicoloured	4·00	4·00

See also 1889/90.

551 Bonsai Tree

2004. 20th European Bonsai Association Convention, San Marino.

1979	45c. Type **551**	1·20	1·20
1980	60c. Bonsai (different)	1·60	1·60

552 Government Palace, San Marino and Tian-An-Men Palace, China

2004. 55th Anniv of People's Republic of China. Sheet 180×166 mm containing **T 552** and similar horiz designs. Multicoloured.

MS1981	80c. ×3, Type **552**; San Marino mountain and Great Wall, China; Temple of Heaven Pagoda, China and San Marino Tower	6·25	6·25

553 Emblem

2004. Centenary of FIFA (Federation Internationale de Football Association).

1982	**553** €2.80 multicoloured	7·25	7·25

554 "Autoshipplane"

2004. Europa. Tourism. Multicoloured.

1983	45c. Type **554**	1·30	1·30
1984	80c. "Boatcampertrainbus" (horiz)	2·75	2·75

555 Chariot Racing, Boxers and Javelin Thrower

2004. Olympic Games 2004, Athens. Multicoloured.

1985	90c. Type **555**	2·40	2·40
1986	90c. Runner, discus thrower and wrestlers	2·40	2·40
1987	90c. Relay runner, cyclist and golfer	2·40	2·40
1988	90c. Racquet player, weightlifter and gymnasts	2·40	2·40

Nos. 1985/8 were issued together, *se-tenant*, forming a composite design.

556 Volkswagen Golf

2004. 50th Anniv of Volkswagen (car manufacturers). Multicoloured.

1989	€1.50 Type **556** (30th anniv of Golf)	4·00	4·00
1990	€1.50 Early and modern Beetles ("50" upright)	4·00	4·00
1991	€1.50 Early and modern Beetles ("50" diagonal)	4·00	4·00
1992	€1.50 Golf (different)	4·00	4·00

557 *Hansel and Gretel* (Jakob and Wilhelm Grimm)

2004. Fairytales.

1993	45c. Type **557**	1·20	1·20
1994	60c. *Little Red Riding Hood* (Jakob and Wilhelm Grimm)	1·60	1·60
1995	80c. *Pinocchio* (Carlo Collodi)	2·10	2·10
1996	€1 *Puss in Boots* (Charles Perrault)	2·75	2·75

558 Francesco Petrarca (Petrarch)

2004. Writers' Anniversaries. Multicoloured.

1997	45c. Type **558** (700th birth anniv)	1·20	1·20
1998	€1.50 Oscar Wilde (150th birth anniv)	4·00	4·00
1999	€2.20 Anton Chekov (death centenary)	5·75	5·75

559 Manuel de Nobrega and Josa Anchieta (founders)

2004. 450th Anniv of Founding of San Paulo, Brazil. Multicoloured.

2000	60c. Type **559**	1·60	1·60
2001	80c. Mario Andrade and Antonio Machado (writers)	2·10	2·10
2002	€1.40 Modern San Paulo and Imaculada Conceicao da Luz monastery	3·75	3·75

560 Three Men

2004. 25th Meeting for Friendship Among Peoples, Rimini, Italy (Meeting Rimini). Sheet 155×115 mm containing **T 560** and similar horiz designs. Multicoloured.

MS2003	€1 ×4 Type **560**; Two women and child; Family; Priests	10·50	10·50

The stamps and margin of No. **MS**2003 form a composite design.

561 "Rebecca at the Well" (Giovanni Battista Piazzetta)

2004. Artists' Anniversaries. Multicoloured.

2004	45c. Type **561**(250th death anniv)	1·20	1·20
2005	€1.40 "Piazza Navona" (Scipione Gino Bonichi) (birth centenary)	3·75	3·75
2006	€1.70 "The Persistence of Memory" (Salvador Dali) (birth centenary)	4·50	4·50

562 Cherubs and Musical Instruments

2004. Christmas. Designs showing cherubs. Multicoloured.

2007	60c. Type **562**	1·60	1·60
2008	60c. Holding bag of presents	1·60	1·60
2009	60c. Carrying Christmas tree	1·60	1·60
2010	60c. Holding cornucopia	1·60	1·60

563 Antonio Salieri and 18th-century Auditorium

2004. Re-opening of La Scala Theatre, Milan. Sheet 132×172 mm containing T **563** and similar horiz designs. Multicoloured.

MS2011	$1.50×3, Type **563**; 19th-century and modern theatre building facade; Ricardo Muti and modern auditorium	12·00	12·00

The stamps of No.**MS**2011 merge with the score of "Europa riconosciuta" (opera by Antonio Salieri) in the margin to form a composite design.

564 Manuel Fangio (1956)

2005. Ferrari—World Champion Racing Team. Showing World Champions and their cars. Multicoloured.

2012	1c. Type **564**	15	15
2013	4c. Niki Lauda (1975–77)	15	15
2014	5c. John Surtees (1964)	15	15
2015	45c. Michael Schumacher (2000–04)	1·20	1·20
2016	62c. Race car	1·70	1·70
2017	€1.50 Alberto Ascari (1952–3)	4·00	4·00

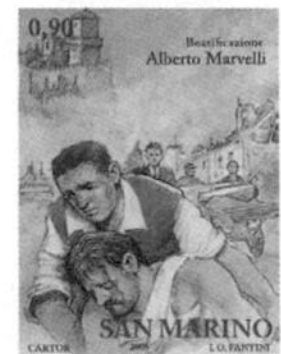

565 Carrying wounded Man

2005. Beatification of Alberto Marvelli. Multicoloured.

2018	90c. Type **565**	2·40	2·40
2019	€1.80 Pope John Paul II and Alberto Marvelli	4·75	4·75

566 "In the Hollow of a Wave off the Coast at Kanagawa" (Hokusai Katsushika) and Faces of Victims

2005. Support For Victims of the Tsunami Disaster.

2020	**566**	€1.50 multicoloured	4·00	4·00

567 Weightlifter

2005. Centenary of International Weightlifting Federation.

2021	**567**	€2.20 multicoloured	5·75	5·75

568 Soldier scaling Cliff

2005. Alpine Troops. Multicoloured.

2022	36c. Type **568**	1·10	1·10
2023	45c. Soldier picking flower	1·20	1·20
2024	62c. Soldier, mother and child	1·70	1·70
2025	€1 Map of faces	2·75	2·75

569 NCO and Third Tower

2005. Militia. Showing militia men. Multicoloured.

2026	36c. Type **569**	1·10	1·10
2027	45c. Dress uniform and Second Tower	1·20	1·20
2028	62c. Standard bearer and Palazzo Pubblico	1·70	1·70
2029	€1.50 Two militia men and First Tower	4·00	4·00

570 Bread

2005. Europa. Gastronomy. Multicoloured.

2030	62c. Type **570**	1·70	1·70
2031	€1.20 Wine	3·25	3·25

571 Ship, Courier, Letter and Train

2005. History of the Letter. Multicoloured.

2032	36c. Type **571**	1·10	1·10
2033	45c. Man reading letter	1·20	1·20
2034	60c. Three men	1·60	1·60
2035	62c. Man and woman	1·70	1·70

572 1864 5 cent Coin

2005. Coins. Multicoloured.

2036	36c. Type **572**	1·10	1·10
2037	45c. 1898 5 lira coin	1·20	1·20
2038	€1.10 and 20 lira gold coins	2·75	2·75
2039	€2.20 Modern euro coins	5·75	5·75

573 Erminio Macario

2005. Variety Performers. Multicoloured.

2040	45c. Type **573**	1·20	1·20
2041	45c. Wanda Osiris	1·20	1·20
2042	45c. Toto	1·20	1·20
2043	45c. Anna Magnani	1·20	1·20
2044	45c. Aldo Fabrizi	1·20	1·20
2045	45c. Renato Rascel	1·20	1·20
2046	45c. Nino Taranto	1·20	1·20
2047	45c. Delia Scala	1·20	1·20
2048	45c. Tino Scotti	1·20	1·20
2049	45c. Carlo Dapporto	1·20	1·20

574 Face and Kite

2005. 150th Birth Anniv of Giovanni Pascoli (writer). Multicoloured.

2050	36c. Type **574**	1·10	1·10
2051	45c. Mount Titan	1·20	1·20
2052	€1 Family home and horse	2·75	2·75
2053	€2 Tower and Giovanni Pascoli	5·25	5·25

575 Ferrari Wine Label

2005. Wine. Designs showing wine labels. Multicoloured.

2054	45c. Type **575**	1·20	1·20
2055	45c. Amarone della Valpolicella	1·20	1·20
2056	45c. Canevel	1·20	1·20
2057	45c. Biondi-Santi	1·20	1·20
2058	45c. Vecchioflorio	1·20	1·20
2059	45c. Verdicchio dei Castellidijesi	1·20	1·20
2060	45c. Sassicaia (vert)	1·20	1·20
2061	45c. Piano di Monte Vergine dei Feudi di San Gregorio (vert)	1·20	1·20
2062	45c. Tocai Friulano (vert)	1·20	1·20
2063	45c. Barolo (vert)	1·20	1·20

576 Devil and Angel as Gondoliers

2005. Venice Regatta. Multicoloured.

2064	€1.40 Type **576**	3·75	3·75
2065	€2 Gondolier wearing traditional costume (vert)	5·25	5·25

577 Dahlia

2005. Self-adhesive.

2066	**577**	(20g.) multicoloured	1·20	1·20

578 Panel, St. John the Baptist (Lorenzo Ghiberti) (550th death anniv)

2005. Anniversaries. Multicoloured.

2067	36c. Type **578**	95	95
2068	62c. "The Annunciation" (Beato Angelico) (550th death anniv)	1·70	1·70
2069	€1 Jules Verne and illustrations (writer) (death centenary)	2·75	2·75
2070	€2 Hans Christian Andersen and illustrations (writer) (birth bicentenary)	3·50	3·50

579 The Annunciation

2005. Christmas. Multicoloured.

2071	62c. Type **579**	1·70	1·70
2072	€1.55 The Nativity	4·25	4·25
2073	€2.20 Three Wise Men	6·00	6·00

580 Pope Clement XIV

2005. 300th Birth Anniv of Pope Clement XIV. Multicoloured.

2074	80c. Type **580**	2·10	2·10
2075	€1 Pope Clement XIV facing left	2·75	2·75

581 Ski Jump, Snow Board and Flags

2006. Winter Olympic Games, Turin. Multicoloured.

2076	45c. Type **581**	1·20	1·20
2077	45c. Ski run, village and flags	1·20	1·20
2078	45c. Cross-country skiing, bob-sleigh, ice hockey and finish line	1·20	1·20
2079	45c. Ice skating, cross-country skiing and chair lift	1·20	1·20

Nos. 2076/9 were issued together, *se-tenant*, forming a composite design.

582 Palazzo Pubblico

2006. Centenary of Arengo of Patriarchs (first governing body). Multicoloured.

2080	45c. Type **582**	1·20	1·20
2081	62c. Statue of Liberty, Piazza della Liberta	1·70	1·70
2082	€1.50 Basilica Del Santo Marino	4·00	4·00

583 Christopher Columbus and Native American

2006. 500th Death Anniv of Christopher Columbus (explorer). Multicoloured.

2083	90c. Type **583**	2·40	2·40
2084	€1.80 Holding globe and compasses	4·75	4·75

584 Palazzo Mentcitorio, Rome and Palazzo Pubblico, San Marino

2006. Le Due Repubbliche (two republics) Philatelic Exhibition. Sheet 121×90 mm containing **T 584** and similar horiz design. Multicoloured.

MS2085	62c.×2, Type **584**; Type **1365** of Italy	33·00	33·00

No. **MS**2085 is identical to **MS**3011 of Italy. Nos. **MS**2085 of San Marino and Nos. 3010/**MS**3011 of Italy were all issued on the same day.

585 "Bathers" (Paul Cezanne)

2006. Art. Multicoloured.

2086	36c. Type **585**	1·10	1·10
2087	45c. "Bathsheba with Letter from David" (Rembrandt)	1·20	1·20
2088	60c. "Coronation of the Virgin" (Gentile da Fabriano)	1·60	1·60
2089	€1.80 "The Room of Spouses" (Andrea Mantegna)	4·75	4·75

586 Emblem, Flag and Ball

2006. World Cup Football Championship, Germany.

2090	**586** €2.20 multicoloured	5·75	5·75

587 Flag Throwers

2006. 50th Anniv of Crossbow Federation. Multicoloured.

2091	36c. Type **587**	95	95
2092	45c. Standard bearers	1·20	1·20
2093	62c. Archer preparing to shoot	1·70	1·70
2094	€1 Two archers positioning arrows	2·75	2·75
2095	€1.50 Three flag throwers	4·00	4·00
2096	€2.80 Arms master holding target full of arrows	7·50	7·50

588 Butterfly (Sara Santolini)

2006. Europa. Integration. Multicoloured.

2097	45c. Type **588**	1·20	1·20
2098	62c. Vitruvian man (after Leonardo da Vinci) (Marco Moliari and Clementina Casadei)	1·70	1·70

589 Doctor and Child

2006. Military Order of Malta.

2099	€2.20 multicoloured	5·75	5·75

590 Hand in Ring

2006. 125th Anniv of International Gymnastic Federation. Multicoloured.

2100	15c. Type **590**	40	40
2101	€2.80 Gymnast	7·50	7·50

591 Second Tower

2006. 40th Anniv of Italian Philatelic Press Union. Multicoloured.

2102	90c. Type **591**	2·40	2·40
2103	€2.20 Archway, Palazzo Strozzi and "Gli Amanti" (sculpture) (Giacomo Maria Cavina)	5·75	5·75

592 Grandmother's Face

2006. Italy—2006 Football World Cup Champions.

2104	**592** €1 multicoloured	2·75	2·75

593 Scene from "Rome Open City" (film)

2006. Anniversaries. Multicoloured.

2105	5c. Type **593** (Roberto Rosellini (director) (birth centenary))	25	25
2106	65c. Top hat (Luchino Visconti (director) (birth centenary))	1·70	1·70
2107	85c. Friar (Iacopone da Todi (writer) (700th death anniv)	2·30	2·30
2108	€1.40 "K 551" (Wolfgang Amadeus Mozart (composer) (250th birth anniv))	3·75	3·75

594 Joseph (detail)

2006. Christmas. Showing details from "La Natività" by Giovan Battista Tiepolo. Multicoloured.

2109	60c. Type **594**	1·60	1·60
2110	60c. Angel	1·60	1·60
2111	65c. Infant Jesus	1·70	1·70
2112	65c. Virgin Mary	1·70	1·70
2113	€2.80 "La Nativita" (29×40 mm)	7·25	7·25

595 Duke Guidubaldo de Montefeltro (founder), "Ideal City" (painting) and Carlo Bo (rector, 1947–2001)

2006. 500th Anniv of Urbino University.

2119	**595** €2.20 multicoloured	5·75	5·75

596 San Marino Flag and EU Emblem

2007. San Merino's Presidency of Council of Europe Council of Ministers.

2120	**596** 65c. multicoloured	1·70	1·70

597 "Self Portrait" (painting)

2006. Gina Lollobrigida, Artist. Designs showing Gina Lollobrigida's work. Multicoloured.

2121	65c. Type **597**	1·70	1·70
2122	85c. "Potato Seller" (photograph)	2·30	2·30
2123	€1 "Esmeralda" (sculpture)	2·75	2·75
2124	€3.20 Gina Lollobrigida with Mother Teresa (as ambassador for FAO)	8·50	8·50

598 Alessandro Glaray and Philatelic Material

2007. Alessandro Glaray (philatelic expert) Commemoration.

2125	**598** €1.80 multicoloured	4·75	4·75

599 Arriving in San Marino with Anita and the Thousand

2007. Birth Bicentenary of Giuseppe Garibaldi (soldier and nationalist). Multicoloured.

2126	65c. Type **599**	1·70	1·70
2127	€1.40 Arriving in Marsala (the Kingdom of Two Sicilies war) and fighting in Uruguayan War of Independence	3·75	3·75
2128	€2 Handshake at Teano ending Italian War of Independence	5·25	5·25

600 Window Dresser's Tool

2007. Birth Centenary of Bruno Munari (artist, designer, writer, and educator).

2129	**600** 36c. yellow and black	95	95
2130	- 65c. blue and black	1·70	1·70
2131	- €1.40 magenta and black	3·75	3·75
2132	- €2 green and black	5·25	5·25

DESIGNS: 36c. Type **600**; 65c. Milk carton; €1.40 Roll-up shutter lock; €2 Garage lamp.

601 Cherubs, Church of the Immaculate Conception, Palermo

2007. San Gabriel International Philatelic Art Award, Legnago.

2133	**601** €1.50 multicoloured	4·00	4·00

602 Scouts, Globe, Compass and Brownsea Island

2007. Europa. Centenary of Scouting. Multicoloured.

2134	60c. Type **602**	1·60	1·60
2135	65c. Scout master, scout and Three Towers	1·70	1·70

603 High Jump

2007. World Athletics Championships, Osaka. Multicoloured.

2136	60c. Type **603**	1·60	1·60
2137	85c. Long jump (horiz)	2·30	2·30
2138	€1.50 Runner (horiz)	4·00	4·00

603a Striker

2007. European Baseball Cup, San Marino. Multicoloured.

2139	65c. Type **603a**	1·70	1·70
2140	€1 Pitcher	2·75	2·75

604 Cliffs and Postilion (detail from 'Theatrum civitatum et admirandorum Italiae' by Joan (Johannes) Blaeu)

2007. 400th Anniv of Mail Services. Sheet 110×83 mm.

MS2141	**604** €4.50 multicoloured	12·00	12·00

The stamp and margin of **MS**2141 form a composite design.

605 Catalogues, Albums and Magazines

2007. 30th Anniv of Constitution of ASCAT (association of philatelic editors). Riccione International Stamp Fair.

2142	**605**	65c. multicoloured	1·70	1·70

606 La Guaita (Rocca) Tower, San Marino

2007. The Oldest (San Marino–301) and Newest (Slovakia–1993) Republics of Europe. Multicoloured.

2143	65c. Type **606**	1·70	1·70
2144	65c. Orava Castle, Slovakia	1·70	1·70

Stamps of a similar design were issued by Slovakia.

607 Port (Quinta do Estanho, Portugal)

2007. European Wines. Sheet 185×143 mm. **T 607** and similar multicoloured designs.

MS2145	65c.×8, Type **607**; Champagne (Tarlant, France) (horiz); Champagne (Bauget-Jouette, France) (horiz); Zlahtina white wine (Katunar, Croatia); Reisling (Petri, Germany); Tokaji (Chateau Pajzos, Hungary) (horiz); Ribera del Duero (Carmelo Rodero, Spain) (horiz); Teodor Belo (Simcic, Slovenia)	14·00	14·00

608 Palazzo del Governo

2007. Christmas. Multicoloured.

2146	60c. Type **608**	1·60	1·60
2147	65c. Santa Claus	1·70	1·70
2148	85c. Holy Family and Three Towers, San Marino	2·30	2·30

609 Arturo Toscanni (conductor)

2007. Artistes' Anniversaries. Multicoloured.

2149	60c. Type **609** (50th death anniv)	1·60	1·60
2150	65c. *Paulina Borghese* (sculpture) (Antonio Canova) (250th birth anniv)	1·70	1·70
2151	€1 Harlequin (Carlos Goldoni) (comedic playwright) (300th birth anniv)	2·75	2·75
2152	€1.80 *Via Toscanella* (painting) (Ottone Rosai) (50th death anniv)	4·75	4·75

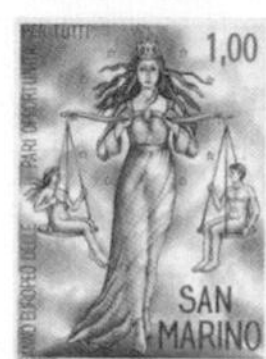

610 Woman holding Scales

2007. Equal Opportunities for All.

2153	**610**	€1 multicoloured	3·25	3·25

611 *Crocefissione* (Crucifixion) (Giovanni Bellini)

2008. Capolavori che ritornano. Multicoloured.

2154	36c. Type **611**	1·10	1·10
2155	60c. *Madonna con bambino e San Giovannino* (Madonna with Child and Saint John) (Jacopo Bassano)	1·60	1·60
2156	65c. *Venere e Amore* (Venus and Love) (Gian Antonio Pellegrini)	1·70	1·70
2157	85c. *Testa di vecchio* (Old Man's Face) (Giandomenico Tiepolo)	2·30	2·30

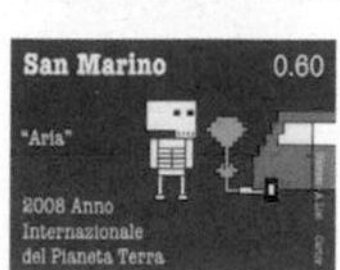

612 'Aria' (air) (Andrea Lisi)

2008. International Year of Planet Earth. Drawings by Faculty of Industrial Design Students, University of San Marino. Multicoloured.

2158	60c. Type **612**	1·60	1·60
2159	85c. Uomo	2·30	2·30
2160	€1.40 Aqua	3·75	3·75
2161	€2 Terra	5·25	5·25

613 Emblem

2008. Centenary of Inter Football Club.

2162	**613**	€1 multicoloured	2·75	2·75

614 Pianello, Old Public Palace, First Post Office and 'Affrancata' (cancellation)

2008. 175th Anniv of Post Office in San Marino.

2163	**614**	€1.80 multicoloured	4·75	4·75

615 Bernadette Soubirous and First Miracle

2008. 150th Anniv of Apparition at Lourdes. Multicoloured.

2164	36c. Type **615**	1·10	1·10
2165	60c. Pilgrims and Basilica	1·60	1·60
2166	€2 Bernadette Soubirous and Madonna	5·25	5·25

616 Globe as Pangea

2008. European Year of Intercultural Dialogue.

2167	**616**	65c. multicoloured	1·70	1·70

617 Concetto Marchesi

2008. 130th Birth Anniv of Concetto Marchesi (academic and politician).

2168	**617**	€1 multicoloured	2·75	2·75

618 Table Tennis

2008. Olympic Games, Beijing. Sheet 137×105 mm containing **T 618** and similar horiz design. Multicoloured.

MS2169	36c. Type **618**; 65c. Fencing; 85c. Swimming	5·00	5·00

619 Envelopes as Ships

2008. Europa. The Letter. Multicoloured.

2170	60c. Type **619**	1·60	1·60
2171	65c. Couple on globe releasing envelopes as doves	1·70	1·70

620 *Our Lady of Mercy*

2008. Art for Basilica of the Annunciation, Nazareth.

2172	**620**	€1 multicoloured	2·75	2·75

621 Statues of Liberty of San Marino and USA

2008. 30th Anniv of San Marino–USA Friendship Association.

2173	**621**	€1.50 multicoloured	4·00	4·00

622 Posters for *La Boheme* and *Madame Butterfly*

2008. Anniversaries. Multicoloured.

2174	60c. Type **622** (Giacomo Puccini) (composer) (150th birth anniv)	1·60	1·60
2175	€1 *Rotonda di Palmieri* and *Vita Militare* (Giovanni Fattori) (artist) (death centenary)	2·75	2·75
2176	€1.40 Book covers for *Don Camillo* and *Diario Clandestino* (Giovannino Guareschi) (writer) (birth centenary)	3·75	3·75
2177	€1.70 *The Print Collectors* and ceramic bust (Honoré Daumier) (artist) (birth bicentenary)	4·50	4·50

623 Chronometer and Cyclist

2008. World Road Cycling Championships, Varese. Multicoloured.

2178	85c. Type **623**	2·30	2·30
2179	€3.85 Rider and cycle	8·50	8·50

624 Andrea Palladio and Villa Pojana

2008. 500th Birth Anniv of Andrea Palladio (architect).

2180	**624**	€1 multicoloured	2·75	2·75

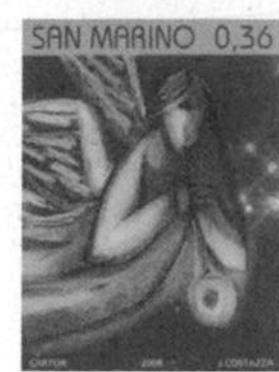

625 Angel

2008. Christmas. Multicoloured.

2181	36c. Type **625**	1·30	1·30
2182	60c. Holy Family	1·90	1·90
2183	€1 Angel carrying gift	3·25	3·25

626 Polar Landscape

2008. International Polar Year. Multicoloured.

2184	60c. Type **626**	1·90	1·90
2185	€1 Penguins	3·25	3·25
2186	€1.20 Research helicopter	4·00	4·00

627 Tamburino (character from *Cuore*)

2008. Writers. Multicoloured.

2187	60c. Type **627** (Edmondo de Amicis) (death centenary)	1·90	1·90
2188	€2.20 Scene from *La Lune e i falo* (Cesare Pavese) (birth centenary)	7·25	7·25

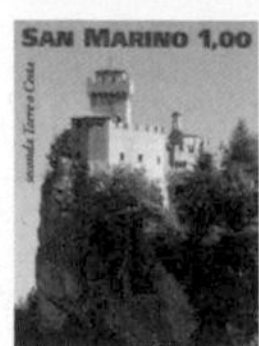

628 Second Tower (Cesta Fortress)

2008. Inclusion of Historic Centre and Mount Titano in UNESCO World Heritage Lists. Sheet 185×143 mm containing **T 628** and similar vert designs. Multicoloured.

MS2189 €1×6, Type **628**; San Marino Basilica; Piazza della Liberta, Il Palazzo Pubblico; Contrada Omerelli; Contrada delle Mura; First Tower (Guaita) 19·00 19·00

629 Two-handled Amphora (Libero Cellarosi)

2009. Sammarinese Ceramists. Multicoloured.

2190	36c. Type **629**	1·30	1·30
2191	60c. Amphora (Umberto Masi)	1·90	1·90
2192	85c. Vase (Giorgio Monti)	2·75	2·75

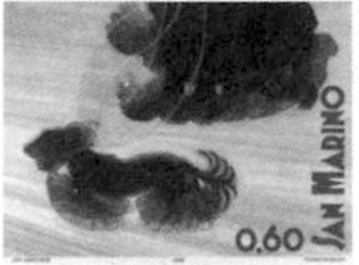

630 *Dinamismo di un cane al guinzaglio* (Giacomo Balla)

2009. Centenary of Futurist Manifesto. Sheet 185×143 mm containing **T 630** and similar multicoloured designs.

MS2193 60c.×10, Type **630**; *Treno armato* (Gino Severini) (vert); *Studio per centrale electtrica* (Antonio Sant'elia) (vert); *Zang Tumb Tumb* (Filippo Tommaso Marinetti); *Cavaliere rosso* (Carlo Carra); *Risveglio di una città* (Luigi Russolo); *Dinamismo di un ciclista* (Umberto Boccioni); *Natura morta con uvovo rosso* (Ardengo Soffici) (vert); *Forme uniche nella continuita dello spazio* (Umberto Boccioni) (vert); *Serata futurista* (Umberto Boccioni); 19·00 19·00

631 Emblem

2009. 50th Anniv of Comitato Olimpico Nazionale di San Marino (CONS) (Olympic committee).

2194	**631**	€1.80 multicoloured	5·75	5·75

632 Saturn and Astronomical Instruments

2009. Europa. Astronomy. Multicoloured.

2195	60c. Type **632**	1·90	1·90
2196	65c. Solar system	2·10	2·10

633 Hot Air Balloon and Doves

2009. World Air Games, Turin. Multicoloured.

2197	60c. Type **633**	1·90	1·90
2198	85c. Glider with a dove on each wing	2·75	2·75
2199	€1.50 Dove swinging below helicopter	4·75	4·75
2200	€1.80 Dove surfing on aircraft trail	6·00	6·00

634 Emblem

2009. ICPO–Interpol European Regional Conference, San Marino.

2201	**634**	€2 multicoloured	6·50	6·50

635 Shanghai Financial Centre and China Pavilion

2009. Expo 2010, Shanghai, China.

2202	**635**	€2.20 multicoloured	6·75	6·75

636 August Dauphin (Edgar Allan Poe)

2009. Writers' Anniversaries. Designs showing symbols of characters. Multicoloured.

2203	36c. Type **636** (birth bicentenary)	1·30	1·30
2204	85c. Sherlock Holmes (Arthur Conan Doyle) (150th birth anniv)	2·75	2·75
2205	€1.40 Philip Marlowe (Raymond Chandler) (50th death anniv)	4·50	4·50

637 Tessano

2009. Wines of San Marino. Sheet 137×105 mm containing **T 637** and similar horiz designs showing wine bottles. Multicoloured.

MS2206 60c.×6, Type **637**; Brugneto; Riserva Titano; Caldese; Roncale; Moscato Spumante 9·50 9·50

638 Athletics

2009. Mediterranean Games, Pescara. Multicoloured.

2207	60c. Type **638**	1·90	1·90
2208	€1.40 Cycling	4·50	4·50
2209	€1.70 Wrestling	5·25	5·25

639 'Braille'

2009. Birth Bicentenary of Louis Braille (inventor of Braille writing for the blind).

2210	**639**	€1.50 multicoloured	4·75	4·75

No. 2210 is embossed with Braille writing.

640 '30' enclosing Dove

2009. 30th (2010) Meeting for Friendship Among Peoples, Rimini.

2211	**640**	€1.80 multicoloured	6·00	6·00

641 Centenary Emblem, Club Colours and Player

2009. Centenary of Bologna Football Club.

2212	**641**	€1 multicoloured	3·25	3·25

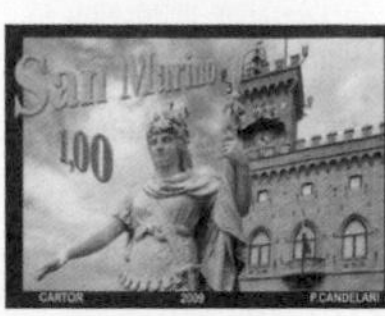

642 Statue of Liberty

2009. European Year of Creativity and Innovation. Stereoscopic Stamps. Three sheets, each 150×43 mm containing **T 642** and similar horiz designs. Multicoloured.

MS2213 €1×2, Type **642**×2 6·50 6·50

MS2214 €1×2, Palazzo Pubblico interior×2 6·50 6·50

MS2215 €1×2, Statue of St. Marinus×2 6·50 6·50

The stamps of Nos. **MS**2213/**MS**2215, whilst showing the same image, differ slightly.

643 Cat (Natascia Stefanelli)

2009. Pet Photograph Competition Winners. Multicoloured.

2216	36c. Type **643**	1·30	1·30
2217	60c. Cocker spaniel (Tina Woodcock)	1·90	1·90
2218	65c. Duck (Ettore Zonzini)	2·10	2·10
2219	75c. Goat, foal and dog (Anna Rosa Francioni)	2·50	2·50
2220	85c. Tiny tortoise (Maria Eleonora Vaglio)	2·75	2·75
2221	€1.20 Basset hound (Lorenzo Zamagni)	3·75	3·75

644 Dante and Virgil and Three Wild Beasts (from 15th-century Codex Urbinate Latino 365, Vatican Apostolic Library)

2009. Italia 2009 International Stamp Exhibition, Rome. Italian Language.

2222	**644**	60c. multicoloured	1·90	1·90

A stamp of a similar design was issued by Italy and Vatican City.

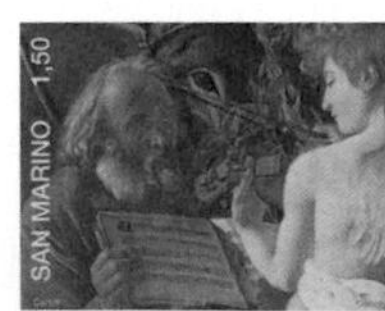

645 Joseph

2009. Christmas. Rest on the Flight into Egypt (Caravaggio). Sheet 137×105 mm containing **T 645** and similar multicoloured design.

MS2223 €1.50 Type **645**; €2 Virgin and Child (vert) 4·75 4·75

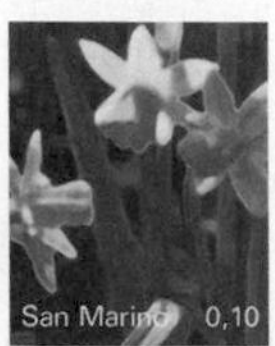

646 Narcissi

2010. Flowers. Multicoloured.

2224	10c. Type **646**	20	20
2225	85c. Hyacinth	2·50	2·50
2226	€1 Muscari	3·50	3·50
2227	€1.50 Tulips	3·75	3·75

647 Ski Jump, Snowboarding, Ice Hockey and Speed Skating

2010. Winter Olympic Games, Vancouver. Multicoloured.

MS2228 65c. Type **647**; 85c. Downhill skiing, Nordic skiing, Curling and Bob sleigh; €1 Speed skating (different), Ice dance and Grand Slalom 7·50 7·50

648 Third Tower

2010. Expo 2010, Shanghai. Multicoloured.

MS2229 65c. Type **648**; €1 Second tower; €1.50 First Tower; €1.80 Government Building and the Statue of Liberty (36×51 mm) 15·00 15·00

649 La Republica (V. Pochini) and First Tower (Guaita)

2010. 50th Anniv of Association of Blood and Organ Donors (AVSSO)

2230	**649**	€1.80 multicoloured	5·25	5·25

650 Flying Girl with Open Book as Wings

2010. Europa. Multicoloured.

2231	60c Type **650**	3·50	3·50
2232	65c. Girl sleeping on open book, amongst clouds containing characters and planets	3·75	3·74

651 Gino Bartali (10th death anniv)

2010. Cyclists' Anniversaries. Multicoloured.

2233	€1.40 Type **651**	4·25	4·25
2234	€1.50 Fausto Coppi (50th death anniv)	4·25	2·25

Nos. 2233/4 were printed, *se-tenant*, forming a composite design

652 Player and Net

2010. World Men's Volleyball Championship, Italy

2235	**652**	€1 multicoloured	3·00	3·00

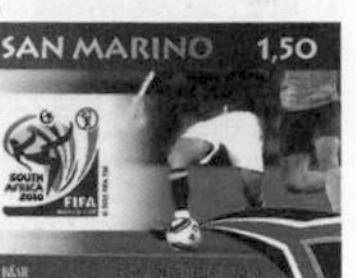

653 Emblem and Players

2010. World Cup Football Championships, South Africa

2236	**653**	€1.50 multicoloured	8·50	8·50

654 La Republica (V. Pochini) and First Tower (Guaita)

2010. San Marino–Japan. Multicoloured.
MS2237 €1.50×4, Type **654**; Himej Castle; *Apparizione di San Marino al suo popolo* (E. Retrosi) (mural); *Tokaido-Gojyusantugi* (Nihonbashi in the Morning) 18·00 18·00
Stamps of a similar design were issued by Japan

655 San Marino from East

2010. 50th Anniv of San Marino Lions Club. Multicoloured.

2238	36c. Type **655**	90	90
2239	60c. San Marino, aerial view	1·90	1·90

656 'inter', Italian Flag and Football

2010. Inter Football Club, winners of Italian Football League, Italian Cup and European Champions League. Multicoloured.

2240	€1 Type **656**	3·00	3·00
2241	€1 '3 volte', Italian shield enclosing '18'	3·00	3·00
2242	€1 'campione' and 'Campione d'Europa'	3·00	3·00

657 *The Birth of Venus* (Sandro Botticelli)

2010. Art. Multicoloured.

2243	€1 Type **657**	3·00	3·00
2244	€1.40 *The Tempest* (Giorgione da Castelfranco Veneto)	3·75	3·75
2245	€1.45 *Supper at Emmaus* (Michelangelo Merisi da Caravaggio)	4·25	4·25
2246	€1.50 *The Football Players* (Henri Rousseau)	5·00	5·00

658 Second Tower

2010. San Marino–Gibraltar. Multicoloured.
MS2247 €1.50×4, Type **658**; Moresco Castle, Gibraltar; Mount Titano; Rock of Gibraltar 16·00 16·00
Stamps of a similar design were issued by Gibraltar

659 Christmas Tree

2010. Christmas

2248	**659**	60c. multicoloured	1·80	1·80
2249	**659**	65c. multicoloured	2·00	2·00
2250	**659**	85c. multicoloured	2·40	2·40

660 Hands and Keyboard (Fryderyk Chopin (birth bicentenary))

2010. Artistes Anniversaries. Multicoloured.

2251	60c. Type **660**	1·80	1·80
2252	65c. Scenes from films (Akira Kurosawa (film director, producer, screenwriter and editor) (birth centenary))	2·00	2·00
2253	85c. Orchestra (Gustav Mahler (composer and conductor) (150th birth anniv))	2·20	2·20
2254	€4.95 Mark Twain and scenes from his novels (death centenary)	15·00	15·00

661 Luciano Pavarotti

2010. 75th Birth Anniv of Luciano Pavarotti

2255	**661**	€2.20 multicoloured	6·75	6·75

662 *Self-portrait with Beret* (Paul Cezanne)

2011. French Painters. Multicoloured.

2256	10c. Type **662**	40	40
2257	50c. *Horse Race at Longchamp* (Edgar Degas)	1·90	1·90
2258	85c. *View from the Artist's Window* (Camille Pissarro)	2·75	2·75
2259	€1 *Flower Beds at Vetheuil* (Claude Monet)	3·25	3·25
2260	€2.50 *Jacques Bergeret as Child* (Auguste Renoir)	8·00	8·00

663 Athletes

2011. San Marino 2011 Exhibition. Sport in San Marino Stamps

2261	**663**	€1.50 multicoloured	4·50	4·50

664 Anniversary Emblem

2011. 50th Anniv of San Marino Choir

2262	**664**	€2.20 multicoloured	6·75	6·75

665 Luigi Einaudi

2011. 50th Death Anniv of Luigi Einaudi (politician, economist and second President of Italian Republic, 1948-1955)

2263	**665**	€3.30 multicoloured	10·00	10·00

666 Yuri Alekseyevich Gagarin and USSR Flag

2011. 50th Anniv of First Manned Space Flight. Multicoloured.

2264	50c. Type **666**	2·00	2·00
2265	€2.40 Alan Bartlett Shepard and USA flag	6·75	6·75

667 Healthy Forest

2011. Europa. Forests. Multicoloured.

2266	60c. Type **667**	1·90	1·90
2267	65c. Stack of logs	1·90	1·90

668 Guaita (First Tower)

2011. Tourism. Sites of San Marino. Multicoloured.
MS2268 65c.×6, Type **668**; Basilica of Holy Parish (horiz); St. Quirinus Capuchin Church (horiz); Government Palace; San Francesco Church; Porta del Loco, San Francesco Port 12·00 12·00

669 *Delphinium belladonna*

2011. Flowers of Republic of San Marino. Multicoloured.
MS2269 €1.50×3, Type **669**; Dianthus 'Agatha' (associated with Saint Agatha, Patroness of San Marino); Rose hybrid tea 'Republic of San Marino' 13·50 13·50

670 Venetian Set

2011. World Theatre Day. Multicoloured.
MS2270 85c.×6, Type **670**; Columbine mask; Actor declaiming; Three Towers and tragic mask; Women dancing leaning left; Women dancing leaning right 15·00 15·00

671 Pope Benedict XVI

2011. Visit of Pope Benedict XVI to San Marino

2271	**671**	€1 multicoloured	3·00	3·00

672 Club Arms

2011. Centenary of Company Brescia Calcio

2272	**672**	€1 multicoloured	3·00	3·00

673 Anita and Giuseppe Garibaldi, and Three Towers on Mount Titano

2011. 150th Anniv of Re-unification of Italy. 150th Anniv of Conferment of Honorary Citizenship of San Marino to Giuseppe Garibaldi. Sheet 80×60 mm
MS2273 **673** €1.50 multicoloured 4·50 4·50

674 Alcide De Gasperi and *Social Justice* (Renato Garrasi)

2011. Alcide De Gasperi (politician) Commemoration. Multicoloured.

2274	50c. Type **674**	1·90	1·70
2275	€2.64 A. de Gaspari, *The Torch of Freedom* (Paolo Paschetto) and map of Europe	10·00	9·00

675 San Francesco Bell Tower and Piazzetta Giuseppe Garibaldi Market

2011. 30th Anniv of Statute of the Azienda Autonoma di Stato Filatelica e Numismatica. Multicoloured.
MS2276 65c. Type **675**; 85c. Piazzetta Giuseppe Garibaldi Market 5·75 5·50

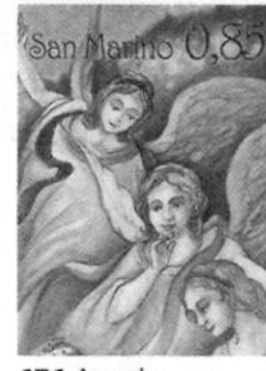

676 Angels

2011. Christmas. Multicoloured.
MS2277 85c. Type **676**; €1 Magi; €1.50 Mary and Joseph; €2 Infant Jesus 22·00 21·00

677 Club Emblems

2011. AC Milan - Champions of Italy 2010 - 2011

2278	**677**	€1 multicoloured	3·75	3·50

678 Pushing Wheelchair

2011. European Year of Volunteering. Sheet 80×60 mm

2279	**678**	€4.95 multicoloured	19·00	18·00

679 Arms

2012. Arms of San Marino
MS2280 60c. blue; 85c. silver; €4.95 gold 24·00 23·00
Designs: 60c., 85c, €4.95 As Type **679**

680 *The Embrace*

2012. 150th Birth Anniv of Gustav Klimt (artist). Multicoloured.
MS2281 85c. Type **680**; €1 *The Kiss*; €1.40 *The Three Ages of Woman*; €1.50 *Hope II* 18·00 17·00

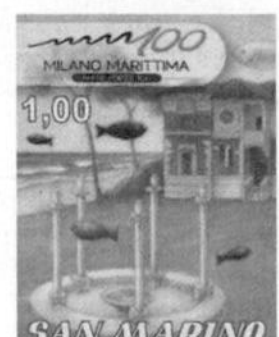

681 Symbols of Milano Marittima

2012. Centenary of Milano Marittima Holiday Resort

2282	**681**	€1 multicoloured		

682 Solar Energy

2012. International Year of Sustainable Energy for All. Multicoloured.

2283	50c. Type **682**	1·90	1·70
2284	50c. Water and wave electricity generation	1·90	1·70
2285	50c. Biomass energy	1·90	1·70
2286	50c. Geothermal energy	1·90	1·70

683 Solar Energy

2012. Made in San Marino. Ceramica Faetano

2287	**683**	65c. multicoloured	2·40	2·20

684 Emblem

2012. Centenary of Santos Football Club, Brazil

2288	**684**	€1 multicoloured	3·75	3·50

685 Mount Titano

2012. 40th Anniv of UNESCO World Heritage Convention. Multicoloured.

MS2289 €1.50×4, Type **685**; Pyramid, Nefertiti and symbols of Egyptian heritage; Darwin, Giant Tortoise and symbols of Galapagos Islands; Scroll inscribed 'GALAPAGOS', Eiffel Tower and Louvre Museum	23·00	22·00

686 Club Emblem and Stadium

2012. Juventus - Champions of Italy 2011 - 2012

2290	**686**	€1 multicoloured	3·75	3·50

687 Olympic Torch

2012. Olympic Games, London. Multicoloured.

2291	50c. Type **687**	1·90	1·70
2292	50c. Female swimmer wearing swim hat and goggles	1·90	1·70
2293	50c. Male athlete	1·90	1·70
2294	50c. Female shooting competitor wearing cap, glasses and ear defenders	1·90	1·70

688 Ball and Net

2012. 25th 'San Marino CEPU Open' International Tennis Championship

2295	**688**	60c. multicoloured	2·30	2·10

689 Cable Car and Hands

2012. Europa. Visit San Marino

2296	**689**	65c. multicoloured	2·40	2·20

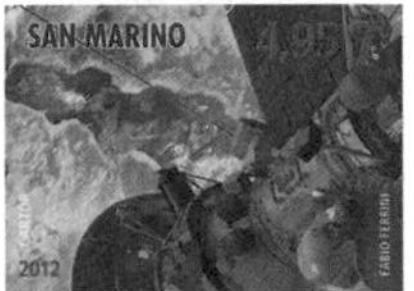

690 SM TV Satellite

2012. First Anniv of San Marino RTV on Satellite. Sheet 95×85 mm

MS2297 **690** €4.95 multicoloured	19·00	18·00

691 Green 'Fingers' holding Brick

2012. Earthquake Relief for Finale Emilia and San Felice sul Panaro

2298	**691**	€1 multicoloured	3·75	3·50

692 *Madonna con Bambino* (Our Lady with Child) (Marco Ventura)

2012. Christmas

2299	**692**	multicoloured	3·25	3·00

693 Women's Traditional Costume, San Marino

2012. 20th Anniv of Croatia - San Marino Diplomatic Relations. St. Marino, stone-cutter from Rab Island, Croatia, founder of San Marino. Multicoloured.

MS2300 85c.×2, Type **693**; Men's costume, Rab Island	6·50	6·25

694 Kendall-Jackson Chardonnay

2012. Wines of the World. Multicoloured.

MS2301 €1×7, Type **694**; Casillero del Diablo; Mission Hill; Octagon; Jacob's Creek; Luigi Bosca; Groot Constantia	26·00	25·00

695 Filippo Turati

2012. Freedom Masters. Filippo Turati and Giacomo Matteotti (socialist anti-fascist campaigners) Commemoration. Multicoloured.

2302	€1.74 Type **695**	6·50	6·00
2303	€2.64 Giacomo Matteotti	10·00	9·00

696 Train

2012. 80th Anniv of San Marino - Rimini Electric Railway

2304	**696**	€2.64 multicoloured	10·00	9·00

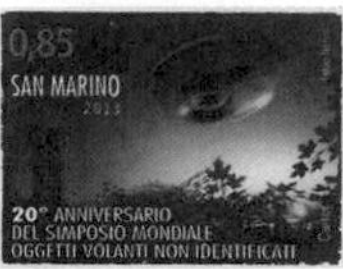

697 UFO

2013. 20th Anniv of World Symposium on Unidentified Flying Objects

2305	**697**	85c. multicoloured	3·25	3·00

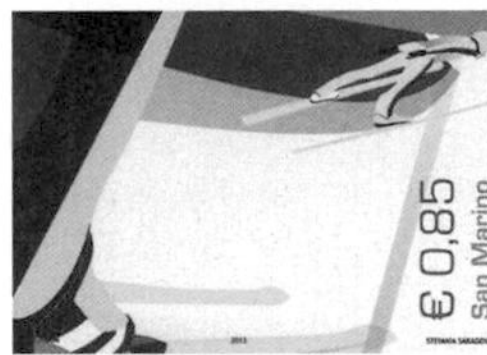

698 Ski and Boot

2013. Nordic World Ski Championships, Val di Fiemme. .

MS2306 85c. Type **698**; €1.74 Ski boot, heel raised; €2.64 Skiers (vert)	17·00	16·00

699 Constantine (left) and Licinio (right) enthroned (bas-relief from Dome of Milan)

2013. 1700th Anniv of Edict of Milan. Multicoloured.

MS2307 €2.50×2, Type **699**; Medallion showing Emperor Constantine and map of Europe	20·00	19·00

EXPRESS LETTER STAMPS

E22 Mt. Titano and "Liberty"

1907

E53	**E22**	25c. pink	27·00	10·50

1923. Optd **ESPRESSO**.

E92	**19**	60c. violet	55	55

1923. Surch **Cent. 60**.

E93	**E22**	60c. on 25c. pink	55	55

E34

1923. Red Cross.

E101	**E34**	60c.+5c. red	2·20	2·10

1926. No. E92 surch **Lire 1.25**.

E134	**E19**	1l.25 on 60c. violet	1·10	1·10

1927. No. E93 surch **L. 1.25** and bars over old surch.

E138	**E22**	1l.25 on 60c. on 25c. pink	80	85

E50 Statue of Liberty and View of San Marino

1929. As Type **E50** but without "UNION POSTALE UNIVERSELLE" and inscr "ESPRESSO".

E164	**E50**	1l.25 green	30	20

1929. Optd **UNION POSTALE UNIVERSELLE** as in Type **E50**.

E165		2l.50 blue	70	80

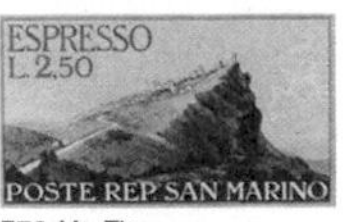

E78

1943

E305	**E78**	1l.25 green	15	15
E306	**E78**	2l.50 orange	15	15

E79 Mt. Titano

1945

E307	**E79**	2l.50 green	20	15
E308	**E79**	5l. orange	20	15
E309	**E79**	5l. red	1·40	60
E310	**E79**	10l. blue	3·25	1·90
E419	**E79**	60l. red	15·00	5·50

E87 Pegasus and Mt. Titano

1946

E337	**E87**	30l. blue	7·25	4·25
E420	**E87**	80l. blue	24·00	9·50

1947. Surch.

E339	**E79**	15l. on 5l. red	60	25
E340	**E79**	15l. on 10l. blue	60	25
E374	**E 87**	35l. on 30l. blue	46·00	31·00
E341	**E 87**	60l. on 30l. blue	5·50	5·50
E545	**E 79**	75l. on 60l. red	4·25	2·50
E375	**E 87**	80l. on 30l. blue	49·00	22·00
E546	**E 87**	100l. on 80l. blue	4·25	2·50
E783	**E 180**	120l. on 75l. black and yellow	15	15
E784	**E 180**	135l. on 100l. black and orange	15	15

E180 Crossbow and Three "Castles"

1966

E800	**E180**	75l. black and yellow	15	15
E801	**E180**	80l. black and purple	15	15
E802	**E180**	100l. black and orange	15	15

No. E800 has crossbow in white without "shadows".

PARCEL POST STAMPS

Unused and used prices are for complete pairs

P46

1928

P145	**P46**	5c. purple and blue	30	25
P146	**P46**	10c. blue and light blue	30	25
P147	**P46**	20c. black and blue	30	25
P148	**P46**	25c. red and blue	30	25
P149	**P46**	30c. ultramarine & blue	40	25
P150	**P46**	30c. orange and blue	40	25
P151	**P46**	60c. red and blue	40	25
P152	**P46**	1l. violet and red	40	25
P153	**P46**	2l. green and red	80	1·30
P154	**P46**	3l. bistre and red	1·30	2·10
P155	**P46**	4l. grey and red	1·60	2·75
P156	**P46**	10l. mauve and red	4·75	4·25
P157	**P46**	12l. lake and red	13·50	12·00
P158	**P46**	15l. green and red	21·00	21·00
P159	**P46**	20l. purple and red	34·00	34·00

1945

P309	5c. purple and red	20	15
P310	10c. brown and black	20	15
P311	20c. red and green	20	15
P312	25c. yellow and black	20	15
P313	30c. mauve and red	20	15
P314	50c. violet and black	20	15
P315	60c. red and black	20	15
P316	1l. brown and blue	35	15
P317	2l. brown and blue	35	15
P318	3l. grey and brown	35	15
P319	4l. green and brown	35	15
P320	10l. grey and violet	80	15
P770	10l. green and red	15	15
P321	12l. green and blue	4·25	4·75
P322	15l. green and violet	3·00	2·40
P323	20l. violet and brown	3·00	2·40
P324	25l. red and blue	80·00	37·00
P771	50l. yellow and red	15	15
P455	300l. violet and red	£275	£170
P773	300l. violet and brown	35	35
P526	500l. brown and red	3·25	5·25
P775	1000l. green and brown	1·10	1·10

1948. Nos. P324 and P771 surch in figures and wavy lines on each half of design.

P524	100l. on 50l. yellow and red	85	1·70
P375	200l. on 25l. red & blue	£350	£180

POSTAGE DUE STAMPS

D18

1897

D38	**D18**	5c. brown and green	1·10	55
D39	**D18**	10c. brown and green	1·10	55
D40	**D18**	30c. brown and green	2·75	1·10
D41	**D18**	50c. brown and green	7·25	2·10
D42	**D18**	60c. brown and green	29·00	7·50
D43	**D18**	1l. brown and pink	13·50	6·50
D44	**D18**	3l. brown and pink	40·00	20·00
D45	**D18**	5l. brown and pink	£250	65·00
D46	**D18**	10l. brown and pink	80·00	36·00

1924

D102	5c. brown and red	80	1·10
D103	10c. brown and red	80	1·10
D104	30c. brown and red	1·30	1·10
D105	50c. brown and red	1·90	1·30
D106	60c. brown and red	10·00	7·25
D107	1l. brown and green	16·00	12·00
D108	3l. brown and green	50·00	37·00
D109	5l. brown and green	70·00	55·00
D110	10l. brown and green	£400	£350

1925

D112	5c. brown and red	40	25
D113	10c. brown and blue	85	60
D114	15c. brown and blue	40	25
D115	20c. brown and blue	40	25
D116	25c. brown and blue	65	60
D117	30c. brown and blue	85	55
D118	40c. brown and blue	4·00	3·75
D119	50c. brown and blue	1·90	2·10
D120	60c. brown and blue	4·00	1·10
D121	1l. brown and orange	7·75	1·60
D122	2l. brown and orange	2·30	2·10
D123	3l. brown and orange	£110	46·00
D124	5l. brown and orange	28·00	7·50
D125	10l. brown and orange	44·00	16·00
D126	15l. brown and orange	3·50	2·10
D127	25l. brown and orange	55·00	34·00
D128	30l. brown and orange	10·50	14·00
D129	50l. brown and orange	14·00	14·00

1931. As Type **D18** but with centre obliterated in black and new value superimposed in silver.

D164	15c. on 5c. blue	55	55
D165	15c. on 10c. blue	55	55
D166	15c. on 30c. blue	55	55
D167	20c. on 5c. blue	55	55
D168	20c. on 10c. blue	65	55
D169	20c. on 30c. blue	65	55
D170	25c. on 5c. blue	2·40	1·60
D171	25c. on 10c. blue	2·40	1·60
D172	25c. on 30c. blue	21·00	13·00
D173	40c. on 10c. blue	2·50	1·10
D174	40c. on 10c. blue	3·00	1·60
D175	40c. on 30c. blue	3·00	1·60
D176	2l. on 5c. blue	80·00	46·00
D177	2l. on 10c. blue	£150	85·00
D178	2l. on 30c. blue	£110	70·00

1936. Surch in figures and words and bars. Nos. D233/8 and D242 are brown and blue; the rest brown and orange.

D233	10c. on 5c.	55	55
D234	25c. on 30c.	16·00	16·00
D235	50c. on 5c.	4·00	1·60
D237	1l. on 30c.	60·00	9·50
D238	1l. on 40c.	12·00	9·50
D239	1l. on 3l.	60·00	2·25
D240	1l. on 25l.	£120	28·00
D241	2l. on 15l.	55·00	33·00
D242	3l. on 20c.	42·00	28·00
D243	25l. on 50l.	3·00	3·00

D82

1945

D309	**D82**	5c. green	30	15
D310	**D82**	10c. brown	30	15
D311	**D82**	15c. red	30	15
D312	**D82**	20c. blue	30	15
D313	**D82**	25c. violet	30	15
D314	**D82**	30c. mauve	30	15
D315	**D82**	40c. yellow	30	15
D316	**D82**	50c. grey	30	15
D317	**D82**	60c. brown	30	15
D318	**D82**	1l. orange	30	15
D319	**D82**	2l. red	30	15
D320	**D82**	5l. violet	30	15
D321	**D82**	10l. blue	1·10	80
D322	**D82**	20l. green	18·00	12·00
D323	**D82**	25l. brown	18·00	12·00
D324	**D82**	50l. brown	18·00	12·00

Pt. 20

SANTANDER

One of the states of the Granadine Cofederation.

A department of Columbia from 1886, now uses Colombian stamps.

100 centavos = 1 peso.

1

1884. Imperf.

1	**1**	1c. blue	35	30
2	**1**	5c. red	65	65
3	**1**	10c. violet	2·40	2·30

2

1886. Imperf.

4	**2**	1c. blue	1·20	1·20
5	**2**	5c. red	45	45
6	**2**	10c. lilac	65	65

1887. As T **1** but inscr "REPUBLICA DE COLOMBIA". Imperf.

7	1c. blue	35	30
8	5c. red	2·20	2·10
9	10c. violet	7·25	7·00

3

4

5

1890. Perf.

10	**3**	1c. blue	45	45
11	**4**	5c. red	1·70	1·60
12	**5**	10c. violet	55	55

6

1895

14	**6**	5c. red on buff	1·30	1·20

7

1895

15	**7**	5c. brown	90	85
16	**7**	5c. green	90	85

8

9

10

1899

17	**8**	1c. black on green	45	45
18	**9**	5c. black on red	45	45
19	**10**	10c. blue	1·00	95

F11

1903. Fiscal stamp as Type **F11** optd Provisional. Correos de Santander. Imperf.

21	**F11**	50c. red	75	75

Pt. 1

SARAWAK

Formerly an independent state on the north coast of Borneo under British protection. Under Japanese occupation from 1941 until 1945. A Crown Colony from 1946 until September 1963, when it became a state of the Federation of Malaysia.

100 centes = 1 dollar (Malayan or Malaysian)

1 Sir James Brooke

1869

1	**1**	3c. brown on yellow	55·00	£225

2 Sir Charles Brooke

1871

3	**2**	2c. mauve on lilac	24·00	17·00
4	**2**	4c. brown on yellow	6·50	3·00
5	**2**	6c. green on green	5·00	4·50
6	**2**	8c. blue on blue	5·50	6·50
7	**2**	12c. red on red	11·00	6·50

4 Sir Charles Brooke

1888

8	**4**	1c. purple and black	5·50	1·50
9	**4**	2c. purple and red	7·00	3·25
10	**4**	3c. purple and blue	9·00	5·00
11	**4**	4c. purple and yellow	40·00	65·00
12	**4**	5c. purple and green	35·00	5·00
13	**4**	6c. purple and brown	28·00	65·00
14	**4**	8c. green and red	19·00	5·50
15	**4**	10c. green and purple	55·00	15·00
16	**4**	12c. green and blue	19·00	15·00
17	**4**	16c. green and orange	65·00	90·00
18	**4**	25c. green and brown	75·00	50·00
19	**4**	32c. green and black	55·00	70·00
20	**4**	50c. green	80·00	£120
21	**4**	$1 green and black	£110	£110

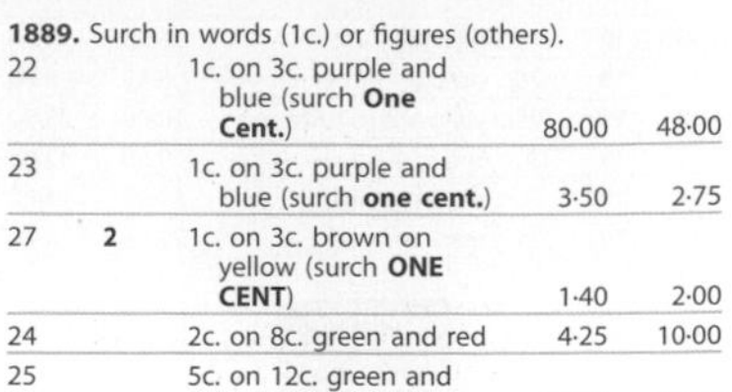

1889. Surch in words (1c.) or figures (others).

22		1c. on 3c. purple and blue (surch **One Cent.**)	80·00	48·00
23		1c. on 3c. purple and blue (surch **one cent.**)	3·50	2·75
27	**2**	1c. on 3c. brown on yellow (surch **ONE CENT**)	1·40	2·00
24		2c. on 8c. green and red	4·25	10·00
25		5c. on 12c. green and blue	35·00	55·00

11 Sir Charles Brooke

1895. Various frames.

28	**11**	2c. red	17·00	9·00
29	**11**	4c. black	17·00	3·50
30	**11**	6c. violet	20·00	9·00
31	**11**	8c. green	45·00	6·00

1889. Surch in figures and words.

32	**2**	2c. on 3c. brown on yellow	3·75	1·75
33	**2**	2c. on 12c. red on red	3·50	4·50
34	**2**	4c. on 6c. green on green	60·00	£110
35	**2**	4c. on 8c. blue on blue	9·00	14·00

1899. As T **4**, but inscr "POSTAGE POSTAGE".

36	1c. blue and red	1·50	1·25
37	2c. green	2·00	90
38	3c. purple	24·00	65
39*a*	4c. red	2·50	15
40	8c. yellow and black	2·75	80
41	10c. blue	5·50	1·00
42	12c. mauve	7·00	4·50
43	16c. brown and green	8·50	1·75
44	20c. brown and mauve	7·00	7·50
45	25c. brown and blue	11·00	7·00
46	50c. green and red	30·00	40·00
47	$1 red and green	£100	£120

17 Sir Charles Vyner Brooke

1918

76	**17**	1c. blue and red	1·50	50
51	**17**	2c. green	2·50	1·50
77	**17**	2c. purple	2·25	1·25
52	**17**	3c. purple	3·25	2·75
64	**17**	3c. green	4·50	1·25
53	**17**	4c. red	9·00	4·25
79	**17**	4c. purple	1·75	10
66	**17**	5c. orange	3·00	2·75
81	**17**	6c. purple	1·25	30
54	**17**	8c. yellow and black	16·00	70·00
82	**17**	8c. red	3·25	32·00
55	**17**	10c. blue	6·50	6·50
83	**17**	10c. black	1·75	1·25
56	**17**	12c. purple	21·00	50·00
84	**17**	12c. blue	3·25	42·00
85	**17**	16c. brown and green	3·50	4·00
86	**17**	20c. bistre and violet	3·50	9·00
87	**17**	25c. brown and blue	7·00	8·50
71	**17**	30c. brown and grey	3·75	4·25
89	**17**	50c. green and red	15·00	24·00
90	**17**	$1 pink and green	21·00	24·00

1923. Surch in words.

72	1c. on 10c. blue	12·00	65·00
73	2c. on 12c. purple	7·00	55·00

19 Sir Charles Vyner Brooke

1932

91	**19**	1c. blue	80	1·00
92	**19**	2c. green	1·00	2·25
93	**19**	3c. violet	4·00	1·00
94	**19**	4c. orange	12·00	75
95	**19**	5c. lake	6·50	1·25
96	**19**	6c. red	7·00	11·00
97	**19**	8c. yellow	11·00	8·50
98	**19**	10c. black	2·25	3·25
99	**19**	12c. blue	4·00	9·50

100	**19**	15c. brown	6·50	13·00
101	**19**	20c. orange and violet	6·50	8·00
102	**19**	25c. yellow and brown	10·00	25·00
103	**19**	30c. brown and red	9·50	42·00
104	**19**	50c. red and olive	14·00	13·00
105	**19**	$1 green and red	22·00	35·00

21 Sir Charles Vyner Brooke

1934

106	**21**	1c. purple	1·25	10
107	**21**	2c. green	1·50	10
107a	**21**	2c. black	4·75	1·60
108	**21**	3c. black	1·25	10
108a	**21**	3c. green	7·50	4·50
109	**21**	4c. purple	2·00	15
110	**21**	5c. violet	2·00	10
111	**21**	6c. red	2·75	60
111a	**21**	6c. brown	8·50	8·00
112	**21**	8c. brown	2·25	10
112a	**21**	8c. red	9·00	10
113	**21**	10c. red	5·00	40
114	**21**	12c. blue	3·00	25
114a	**21**	12c. orange	7·50	4·75
115	**21**	15c. orange	8·00	10·00
115a	**21**	15c. blue	9·00	15·00
116	**21**	20c. green and red	8·00	1·25
117	**21**	25c. violet and orange	8·00	1·50
118	**21**	30c. brown and violet	8·00	2·50
119	**21**	50c. violet and red	12·00	75
120	**21**	$1 red and brown	6·00	75
121	**21**	$2 purple and violet	30·00	30·00
122	**21**	$3 red and green	50·00	55·00
123	**21**	$4 blue and red	50·00	80·00
124	**21**	$5 red and brown	75·00	85·00
125	**21**	$10 black and yellow	35·00	85·00

1945. Optd **B M A**.

126	1c. purple	1·25	60
127	2c. black	5·50	1·50
128	3c. green	1·25	2·00
129	4c. purple	4·75	1·00
130	5c. violet	6·50	1·50
131	6c. brown	6·00	75
132	8c. red	19·00	25·00
133	10c. red	2·75	70
134	12c. orange	7·00	3·75
135	15c. blue	11·00	40
136	20c. green and red	7·00	5·50
137	25c. violet and orange	7·50	3·50
138	30c. brown and violet	12·00	4·25
139	50c. violet and red	2·50	50
140	$1 red and brown	3·50	5·00
141	$2 purple and violet	12·00	23·00
142	$3 red and green	42·00	£100
143	$4 blue and red	38·00	70·00
144	$5 red and brown	£200	£300
145	$10 black and yellow	£225	£275

23 Sir James Brooke, Sir Charles Vyner Brooke and Sir Charles Brooke

1946. Centenary Issue.

146	**23**	8c. red	4·75	1·75
147	**23**	15c. blue	5·00	2·25
148	**23**	50c. black and red	5·00	2·50
149	**23**	$1 black and brown	5·00	45·00

1947. Optd with the Royal Cypher.

150	**21**	1c. purple	20	30
151	**21**	2c. black	25	15
152	**21**	3c. green	25	15
153	**21**	4c. purple	30	15
154	**21**	6c. brown	50	90
155	**21**	8c. red	1·00	10
156	**21**	10c. red	50	20
157	**21**	12c. orange	70	1·00
158	**21**	15c. blue	50	40
159	**21**	20c. green and red	2·25	50
160	**21**	25c. violet and orange	65	30
161	**21**	50c. violet and red	1·25	40
162	**21**	$1 red and brown	1·50	90
163	**21**	$2 purple and violet	4·00	6·50
164	**21**	$5 red and brown	8·50	3·25

1948. Silver Wedding. As T **33b/c** of St. Helena.

165	8c. red	30	30
166	$5 brown	48·00	60·00

1949. U.P.U. As T **33d/g** of St. Helena.

167	8c. red	1·25	60
168	15c. blue	3·50	2·50
169	25c. green	2·00	2·00
170	50c. violet	2·00	7·00

25 "Trogonoptera brookiana"

26 Western Tarsier

27 Kayan Tomb

1950

171	**25**	1c. black	75	30
172	**26**	2c. orange	45	40
173	**27**	3c. green	60	1·25
174	-	4c. brown	1·00	20
175	-	6c. blue	75	20
176	-	8c. red	1·00	30
177	-	10c. orange	3·25	6·00
178	-	12c. violet	3·50	1·50
179	-	15c. blue	4·50	15
180	-	20c. brown and orange	2·75	30
181	-	25c. green and red	3·75	30
182	-	50c. brown and violet	8·50	45
183	-	$1 green and brown	27·00	4·50
184	-	$2 blue and red	45·00	17·00
185	-	$5 multicoloured	35·00	17·00

DESIGNS—VERT: 4c. Kayan boy and girl; 6c. Beadwork; 50c. Iban woman. HORIZ: 8c. Dayak dancer; 10c. (No. 177) Malayan Pangolin; 10c. (No. 186) Map of Sarawak; 12c. Kenyah boys; 15c. Fire-making; 20c. Kelemantan rice barn; 25c. Pepper vines; $1 Kelabit smithy; $2 Map of Sarawak; $5 Arms of Sarawak.

1953. Coronation. As T **33h** of St. Helena.

187	10c. black and blue	2·25	1·75

47 Barong Panau (sailing prau)

51 Queen Elizabeth II

52 Queen Elizabeth II (after Annigoni)

1955

188	-	1c. green	10	30
189	-	2c. orange	30	55
190	-	4c. brown	1·50	60
191	-	6c. blue	3·75	3·25
192	-	8c. red	40	30
193	-	10c. green	30	10
194	**47**	12c. plum	3·75	55
195	-	15c. blue	2·25	30
196	-	20c. olive and brown	1·00	10
197	-	25c. sepia and green	6·50	20
198	**51**	30c. brown and lilac	9·00	30
199	**51**	50c. black and red	2·50	30
200	**52**	$1 green and brown	16·00	2·50
201	**52**	$2 violet and green	26·00	3·75
202	-	$5 multicoloured	40·00	23·00

DESIGNS—VERT (as Type **47**): 1c. Logging; 2c. Young orang-utan; 4c. Kayan dancing. HORIZ: 6c. Malabar pied hornbill ("Hornbill"); 8c. Shield with spears; 10c. Kenyah ceremonial carving; 15c. Turtles; 20c. Melanau basket-making; 25c. Astana, Kuching; $5 Arms of Sarawak.

1963. Freedom from Hunger. As T **63a** of St. Helena.

203	12c. sepia	1·75	2·25

53 "Vanda hookeriana"

1965. As Nos. 155/21 of Kedah, but with Arms of Sarawak inset as in T **53**.

212	**53**	1c. multicoloured	10	1·10
213	-	2c. multicoloured	1·25	2·50
214	-	5c. multicoloured	1·75	10
215	-	6c. multicoloured	1·25	2·00
216	-	10c. multicoloued	1·25	10
217	-	15c. multicoloured	1·50	10
218	-	20c. multicoloured	2·00	50

The higher values used in Sarawak were Nos. 20/7 of Malaysia (National issues).

54 "Precis orithya"

1971. Butterflies. As Nos. 124/30 of Kedah, but with Sarawak Arms as in T **54**.

219		1c. multicoloured	65	2·25
220		2c. multicoloured	70	2·25
221		5c. multicoloured	2·00	10
222		6c. multicoloured	2·00	2·50
223		10c. multicoloured	2·00	10
224	**54**	15c. multicoloured	3·00	10
225	-	20c. multicoloured	3·00	1·25

The higher values in use with this issue were Nos. 64/71 of Malaysia (National issues).

55 "Precis orithya" (different crest at right)

1977. As Nos. 219/21 and 223/5, but showing new State Crest.

226		1c. multicoloured	5·50	13·00
227		2c. multicoloured	14·00	10·00
228		5c. multicoloured	80	70
230		10c. multicoloured	50	30
231	**55**	15c. multicoloured	1·25	20
232	-	20c. multicoloured	4·00	2·25

56 "Rhododendron scortechinii"

1979. As Nos. 135/41 of Kedah, but with Arms of Sarawak as in T **56**.

233	1c. "Rafflesia hasseltii"	10	50
234	2c. "Pterocarpus indicus"	10	50
235	5c. "Lagerstroemia speciosa"	20	70
236	10c. "Durio zibethinus"	20	10
237	15c. "Hibiscus rosa-sinensis"	20	10
238	20c. Type **56**	60	10
239	25c. "Etlingera elatior" (inscr "Phaeomeria speciosa")	65	70

57 Coffee

1986. As Nos. 152/8 of Kedah, but with Arms of Sarawak as in T **57**.

247	1c. Type **57**	10	50
248	2c. Coconuts	15	50
249	5c. Cocoa	20	20
250	10c. Black pepper	25	10
251	15c. Rubber	40	10
252	20c. Oil palm	40	10
253	30c. Rice	40	15

Nos. 247/53 exist with slightly different versions to state arms at right.

58 *Nelumbium nelumbo* (sacred lotus)

2007. Garden Flowers. As Nos. 210/15 of Johore, but with Arms of Sarawak as in T **58**. Multicoloured.

261	5s. Type **58**	10	10
262	10s. *Hydrangea macrophylla*	15	10
263	20s. *Hippeastrum reticulatum*	25	15
264	30s. *Bougainvillea*	40	20
265	40s. *Ipomoea indica*	50	30
266	50s. *Hibiscus rosa-sinensis*	65	35
MS267	100×85 mm. Nos. 261/6	2·00	2·00

JAPANESE OCCUPATION

府政国帝本日大

(1) "Imperial Japanese Government"

1942. Stamps of Sarawak optd with T **1**.

J1	**21**	1c. purple	45·00	85·00
J2	**21**	2c. green	£170	£200
J3	**21**	2c. black	£170	£180
J4	**21**	3c. black	£550	£550
J5	**21**	3c. green	95·00	£120
J6	**21**	4c. purple	£130	£140
J7	**21**	5c. violet	£160	£170
J8	**21**	6c. red	£225	£225
J9	**21**	6c. brown	£150	£160
J10	**21**	8c. brown	£500	£500
J11	**21**	8c. red	75·00	£120
J12	**21**	10c. red	£130	£150
J13	**21**	12c. blue	£250	£250
J14	**21**	12c. orange	£200	£200
J15	**21**	15c. orange	£600	£600
J16	**21**	15c. blue	£180	£190
J17	**21**	20c. green and red	90·00	£110
J18	**21**	25c. violet and orange	£130	£150
J19	**21**	30c. brown and violet	95·00	£120
J20	**21**	50c. violet and red	85·00	£110
J21	**21**	$1 red and brown	£160	£180
J22	**21**	$2 purple and violet	£325	£475
J23	**21**	$3 red and green	£3750	£3750
J24	**21**	$4 blue and red	£325	£550
J25	**21**	$5 red and brown	£325	£550
J26	**21**	$10 black and yellow	£325	£550

Pt. 8

SARDINIA

A former Italian kingdom, including the island of Sardinia, a large part of the mainland and parts of what is now south-east France. The kingdom of Italy was formed by the adhesion of other Italian states to Sardinia, whose king became the first ruler of united Italy.

100 centesimi = 1 lira.

1 Victor Emmanuel II

1851. Imperf.

1	**1**	5c. black	£13000	£2500
3	**1**	20c. blue	£12000	£300
7	**1**	40c. pink	£21000	£5000

1853. Embossed on coloured paper. Imperf.

9	5c. on green	£20000	£1400
10	20c. on blue	£22000	£250
11	40c. on pink	£13000	£1200

1854. Embossed on white paper. Imperf.

13	5c. green	£41000	£750
15	20c. blue	£21000	£225
18	40c. red	£119000	£3750

2 Victor Emmanuel II

1855. Head embossed. Imperf.

28	**2**	5c. green	8·50	21·00
35	**2**	10c. grey	37·00	£130
39	**2**	10c. brown	£140	£120
40	**2**	10c. bistre	9·00	32·00
47	**2**	20c. blue	£250	32·00
55	**2**	40c. red	32·00	70·00
59	**2**	80c. yellow	37·00	£450
61	**2**	3l. bronze	£650	£3500

For Type **2** perf, see Italy Nos. 1/4.

NEWSPAPER STAMPS

N3

1861. Numerals embossed. Imperf.

N62	**N3**	1c. black	10·50	21·00
N63	**N3**	2c. black	£225	£140

For 2c. stamps of similar types in yellow see Italy No. N5.

Pt. 3

SASENO

An island off the W. coast of Albania, temporarily occupied by Italy.

100 centesimi = 1 lira.

1923. Stamps of Italy optd **SASENO**.

1	**38**	10c. red	23·00	43·00
2	**38**	15c. grey	23·00	43·00
3	**41**	20c. orange	23·00	43·00
4	**39**	25c. blue	23·00	43·00
5	**39**	30c. brown	23·00	43·00
6	**39**	50c. mauve	23·00	43·00
7	**39**	60c. red	23·00	43·00
8	**34**	1l. brown and green	23·00	43·00

Pt. 19

SAUDI ARABIA

Formerly under Turkish rule, the Hejaz became an independent kingdom in 1916 but was conquered in 1925 by the Sultan of Nejd. In 1926 the two kingdoms were combined. In 1932 the name of the state was changed to the Saudi Arabian Kingdom.

1916. 40 paras = 1 piastre.
1929. 110 guerche = 10 riyal = 1 gold sovereign.
1952. 440 guerche = 40 riyal = 1 gold sovereign.
1960. 100 halalah = 20 guerche = 1 riyal.
(1 piastre = 1 guerche.)

A. HEJAZ

5 From Stucco Work over Entrance to Cairo Railway Station

1916. As T **5** (various Arabic designs). Perf or roul.

11	**5**	1pa. purple	6·25	2·20
12	-	⅛pi. yellow	6·75	3·25
13	-	¼pi. green	6·75	3·25
14	-	½pi. red	7·75	4·75
15	-	1pi. blue	8·00	4·75
16	-	2pi. purple	37·00	16·00

7 "1340 Hashemite Kingdom 1340"

1921. Optd with T **7**.

21	1pa. purple	50·00	26·00
22	⅛pi. yellow	95·00	28·00
23	¼pi. green	20·00	10·00
24	½pi. red	23·00	12·50
26	1pi. blue	20·00	11·00
28	2pi. purple	28·00	16·00

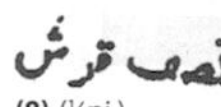

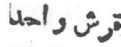

(8) (½pi.) **(9)** (1pi.)

1921. No. 21 surch with T **8** or **9**.

29	**5**	½pi. on 1pa. purple	£550	£250
30	**5**	1pi. on 1pa. purple	£550	£250

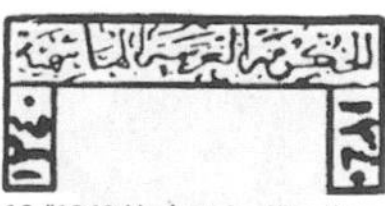

10 "1340 Hashemite Kingdom 1340"

1922. Nos. 11 to 16 optd with T **10**.

31		1pa. purple	5·00	4·75
32	-	⅛pi. yellow	16·00	13·50
33	-	¼pi. green	6·25	4·75
34	-	½pi. red	4·00	3·50
35	-	1pi. blue	4·00	1·50
36	-	2pi. claret	11·00	10·50

1922. No. 31 surch with T **8** or **9**.

37	**5**	½pi. on 1pa. purple	42·00	23·00
38	**5**	1pi. on 1pa. purple	4·00	1·60

11 Meccan Sherifian Arms

1922

39	**11**	⅛pi. brown	3·25	90
57	**11**	¼pi. green	10·00	10·00
41	**11**	½pi. red	3·25	65
42	**11**	1pi. blue	3·25	65
43	**11**	1½pi. lilac	3·25	90
44	**11**	2pi. orange	3·50	1·00
45	**11**	3pi. brown	3·25	90
46	**11**	5pi. green	3·25	90
58	-	10pi. purple and mauve	7·75	7·75

DESIGN: 10pi. As T **11** but with different corner ornaments in the centre motif.

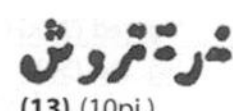

(12) (¼pi.) **(13)** (10pi.)

1923. Surch with T **12** or **13**.

47	**11**	¼pi. on⅛pi. brown	60·00	55·00
49	**11**	10pi. on 5pi. olive	90·00	47·00

(14)

1924. Proclamation of King Hussein as Caliph. Optd with T 14.

50	⅛pi. brown	7·75	5·00
51	½pi. red	5·00	2·20
52	1pi. blue	7·75	5·00
53	1½pi. lilac	7·75	5·00
54	2pi. orange	7·75	5·00
55	3pi. brown	7·75	5·00
56	5pi. green	9·00	7·75

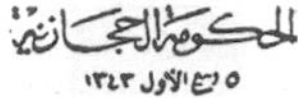

15 "Hejaz Government. 4th October, 1924"

1924. Optd with T **15**.

66	1pa. purple (No. 11)	21·00	21·00
77	1pa. purple (No. 31)	£275	£275
59	⅛pi. yellow (No. 12)	28·00	28·00
78	⅛pi. yellow (No. 32)	£4000	£3250
68	¼pi. green (No. 13)	33·00	33·00
79	¼pi. green (No. 33)	£110	£110
71	½pi. red (No. 14)	50·00	50·00
76	½pi. red (No. 24)	£4500	
80	½pi. red (No. 34)	£160	£150
86	½pi. red (No. 41)	£1700	£1700
84	½pi. on 1pa. purple (No. 37)	£160	£160
73	1pi. blue (No. 15)	55·00	55·00
81	1pi. blue (No. 35)	£225	£180
85	1pi. on 1pa. purple (No. 38)	£120	£120
74	2pi. purple (No. 16)	60·00	55·00
83	2pi. purple (No. 36)	£275	£275
87	10pi. purple and mauve (No. 58)	£3250	£3250

16 "Hejaz Government, 4th October, 1924"

1924. Optd with T **16** (or smaller size). (a) On No. 13.

90		¼pi. green	£110	£110
		(b) On Nos. 39 etc.		
105	**11**	⅛pi. brown	7·75	7·75
96	**11**	¼pi. green	28·00	28·00
116	**11**	½pi. red	7·75	7·75
98	**11**	1pi. blue	14·50	14·50
99	**11**	1½pi. lilac	7·75	7·75
119	**11**	2pi. orange	12·50	12·50
120	**11**	3pi. brown	12·50	10·00
103	**11**	5pi. green	21·00	12·50
104	-	10pi. purple and mauve	28·00	28·00
		(c) On Nos. 50/6.		
136		⅛pi. brown	65·00	65·00
137		½pi. red	£150	£150
138		1pi. blue	£100	90·00
139		1½pi. lilac	£120	£110
134		2pi. orange	£180	£160
146		3pi. brown	£180	£180
142		5pi. green	65·00	65·00

For similar overprint see Nos. 172/6.

(17)

1925. Stamps of 1922 surch as Type **17**.

148	¼pi. on⅛pi. brown	£170
149	¼pi. on ½pi. red	£170
150	1pi. on 2pi. orange	£170
151	1pi. on 3pi. brown	£170
153	10pi. on 5pi. green	£170

(18)

1925. Nos. 148/53 further surch with values in larger type as Type **18**.

154	¼pi. on ¼pi. on⅛pi. brown	85·00	85·00
155	¼pi. on ¼pi. on ½pi. red	50·00	50·00
157	1pi. on 1pi. on 2pi. orange	50·00	50·00
158	1pi. on 1pi. on 3pi. brown	39·00	39·00
160	10pi. on 10pi. on 5pi. green	28·00	28·00

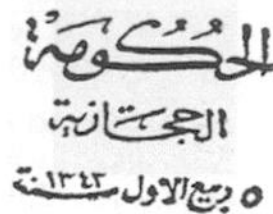

(19)

1925. Stamps of 1922 surch as T **19**.

165	⅛pi. on ½pi. red	23·00	18·00
166	¼pi. on ½pi. red	23·00	18·00
167	1pi. on ½pi. red	23·00	18·00
173c	1pi. on 1½pi. lilac	14·50	14·50
174	1pi. on 2pi. orange	14·50	14·50
175	1pi. on 3pi. brown	14·50	14·50
176	10pi. on 5pi. green	23·00	23·00

20 **(24)**

1925. As T **20** (various Arabic designs) optd with T **24**.

177C	⅛pi. brown	2·75	2·75
178C	¼pi. blue	2·75	2·75
179C	½pi. red	3·25	3·25
180C	1pi. green	3·25	3·25
181C	1½pi. orange	3·25	3·25
182C	2pi. blue	4·00	4·00
183B	3pi. green	3·25	3·25
184A	5pi. brown	6·50	6·50
185C	10pi. green and red	8·75	8·75

B. NEJDI OCCUPATION OF HEJAZ

(25) "Nejd Sultanate Post 1343"

1925. Various stamps optd with T **25**. (A.) Stamps of Turkey.

190	**30**	5pa. bistre (No. 583)	36·00	22·00
191	**30**	10pa. green (No. 503)	25·00	19·00

26

(B.) Hejaz Fiscal stamps. (i) Notarial stamps.

192	**26**	1pi. violet	31·00	31·00
193a	**26**	1pi. blue	39·00	39·00

27

(ii) Bill stamp.

194	**27**	1pi. violet	22·00	22·00

28

(iii) Railway Tax stamps.

195	**28**	1pi. blue	25·00	25·00
196	**28**	2pi. orange	33·00	33·00
197	**28**	3pi. lilac	39·00	39·00

(C.) Hejaz Postage stamps (1922 issue).

198	**11**	⅛pi. brown	33·00	33·00
198ca	**11**	¼pi. red	39·00	39·00
199a	**11**	½pi. red	25·00	25·00
200	**11**	1½pi. lilac	33·00	33·00
201	**11**	2pi. orange	55·00	55·00
202	**11**	3pi. red	33·00	33·00

(30) "Wednesday"

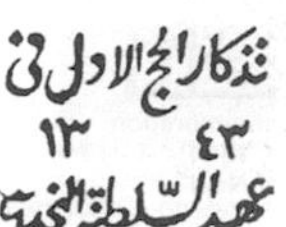

(29) "1343 Commemoration of First Pilgrimage under Sultan of Nejd"

(31)

1925. Pilgrimage Commemoration. Various stamps optd with T **29** and **30** and surch as T **31**. (a) 1914 pictorial stamps of Turkey.

210	1pi. on 10pa. green (No. 503)	£110	85·00
211	5pi. on 1pi. blue (No. 518)	£110	85·00
	(b) 1916 stamps of Hejaz.		
212	2pi. on 1pa. purple	£150	£110
213	4pi. on⅛pi. yellow	£500	£250
	(c) Railway Tax stamp of Hejaz.		
214	**28** 3pi. lilac	£375	£130

(32) "Nejd Sultanate Post"

1925. Various stamps optd with T **32**. (A.) Stamps of Turkey.

215	**30**	5pa. bistre	17·00	16·00
216	-	10pa. green (No. 503)	22·00	19·00
		(B.) Hejaz Fiscal stamps. (i) Notarial stamp.		
217	**26**	2pi. blue	31·00	25·00
		(ii) Railway Tax Stamps.		
218	**28**	1pi. blue	36·00	16·00
219	**28**	2pi. orange	39·00	16·00
220	**28**	3pi. lilac	33·00	22·00
221	**28**	5pi. green	31·00	19·00

28

(C.) Hejaz Postage stamps. (i) Nos. 35/6.

222		1pi. blue	60·00	60·00
223		2pi. purple	85·00	85·00
		(ii) Stamps of 1922 (some in new colours).		
224	**11**	⅛pi. brown	£6000	
225	**11**	½pi. red	22·00	10·00
226	**11**	1pi. violet	25·00	22·00
227	**11**	1½pi. pink	45·00	28·00
228	**11**	2pi. orange	£130	85·00
229	**11**	2pi. purple	85·00	65·00
230	**11**	3pi. red	33·00	25·00
231	**11**	5pi. red	45·00	39·00

(33) (1pi.) **(34)** (1½pi.) **(35)** (2pi.)

1925. Stamps optd with T **32** further surch with T **33/5**.

239	1pi. on ½pi. red	11·00	3·25
241	1½pi. on ½pi. red	13·50	3·25
243	2pi. on 3pi. red	22·00	4·50

(36) "Postage of Nejd, 1344, Commemoration of Medina"

1925. Capture of Medina. Railway Tax stamps of Hejaz optd with T **36**.

244	**28**	1pi. on 10pi. mauve and violet	£110	80·00
245	**28**	2pi. on 50pi. red and blue	£110	80·00

194 Tractor

1981. World Food Day.
1277 **194** 20h. multicoloured 3·25 35
For similar design see No. 1343.

195 Conference Emblem

1981. Second Session of Gulf Co-operation Council Summit Conference, Riyadh.
1278 **195** 20h. multicoloured 1·00 35
1279 **195** 80h. multicoloured 3·25 80

196 University Emblem

1982. 25th Anniv of King Saud University.
1280 **196** 20h. multicoloured 1·20 35
1281 **196** 50h. multicoloured 2·75 60

1982. As T 149/150 but in smaller size, 25×20 mm. (a) Type **149**.
1283 10h. black and lilac 35 35
1284 15h. black and orange 35 35
1285d 20h. black and blue 35 35
1291c 50h. black and red 45 35
1294c 65h. black and blue 1·00 35
1301c 1r. black and green 2·20 35

(b) Type **150**.
1306a 5h. blue and orange 35 35
1307c 10h. green and orange 35 35
1308c 15h. brown and orange 35 35
1309c 20h. green and orange 35 35
1310 25h. purple and orange 35 35
1315c 50h. red and orange 45 35
1318c 65h. brown and orange 55 35
1325c 1r. green and orange 80 45

197 Riyadh Postal Building

1982. New Postal Buildings. Multicoloured.
1330 20h. Type **197** 55 35
1331 65h. Jeddah 1·50 60
1332 80h. Dammam 2·10 60
1333 115h. Postal mechanized sorting 2·75 95
MS1334 Four sheets, each 8×70 mm. (a) No. 1330; (b) No. 1331; (c) No. 1332; (d) No. 1333. Imperf (each sold at 3000h.) £130 £130

198 Riyadh Television Centre

1982. Riyadh Television Centre.
1335 **198** 20h. multicoloured 1·70 35

199 Football and King's Cup

1982. 25th Anniv of King's Cup Football Championship.
1336 **199** 20h. multicoloured 1·20 35
1337 **199** 65h. multicoloured 2·50 60

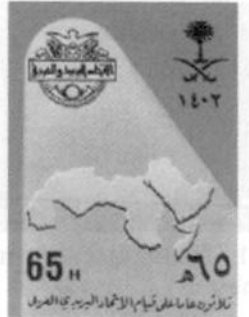
200 A.P.U. Emblem and Map

1982. 30th Anniv of Arab Postal Union. Multicoloured.
1338 20h. A.P.U. Emblem and Arabic "30" 1·00 35
1339 65h. Type **200** 2·75 60

201 Pilgrims at Muzdalefa looking for Stones to stone the Devil

1982. Pilgrimage to Mecca.
1340 **201** 20h. multicoloured 1·00 35
1341 **201** 50h. multicoloured 2·75 60

202 Saudi Arabian and World Standards Organizations Emblems

1982. World Standards Day.
1342 **202** 20h. multicoloured 2·00 45

203 Tractor

1982. World Food Day.
1343 **203** 20h. multicoloured 1·70 35
For similar design see No. 1277.

204 King Fahd

1983. Installation of King Fahd.
1344 **204** 20h. multicoloured 45 25
1345 **204** 50h. multicoloured 1·00 45
1346 **204** 65h. multicoloured 1·50 60
1347 **204** 80h. multicoloured 1·70 80
1348 **204** 115h. multicoloured 2·75 1·00

205 Crown Prince Abdullah

1983. Installation of Crown Prince.
1349 **205** 20h. multicoloured 45 25
1350 **205** 50h. multicoloured 1·00 45
1351 **205** 65h. multicoloured 1·50 60
1352 **205** 80h. multicoloured 1·70 80
1353 **205** 115h. multicoloured 2·75 1·00

206 Dome of the Rock, Jerusalem

1983. Solidarity with Palestinians.
1354 **206** 20h. multicoloured 1·00 45
For similar design but inscribed "K.S.A." see No. 1226.

207 Container Ship "Bar'zan"

1983. Sixth Anniv of United Arab Shipping Company. Multicoloured.
1355 20h. Type **207** 80 35
1356 65h. "Al Drieya" (container ship) 2·75 95

208 Stoning the Devil

1983. Pilgrimage to Mecca.
1357 **208** 20h. multicoloured 55 35
1358 **208** 65h. multicoloured 2·00 45

209 Saudi Arabia Post and U.P.U. Emblems

1983. World Communications Year. Multicoloured.
1359 20h. Type **209** 45 35
1360 80h. Saudi Arabia telephone and I.T.U. emblems 2·00 45

210 Terminal Building

1983. Opening of King Khaled International Airport, Riyadh. Multicoloured.
1361 20h. Type **210** 80 25
1362 65h. Embarkation wing of terminal 2·20 95

211 Wheat and F.A.O. Emblem

1983. World Food Day.
1363 **211** 20h. multicoloured 2·00 45

212 Al Aqsa Mosque, Jerusalem

1983. Solidarity with Palestinians.
1364 **212** 20h. brown, blue & green 80 35

213 Riyadh

1984. Saudi Cities. (a) Riyadh.
1365 **213** 20h. multicoloured 35 35
1366 **213** 50h. multicoloured 45 35
1370 **213** 75h. multicoloured 1·00 60
1371 **213** 150h. multicoloured 2·50 1·30

214 Shobra Palace, Taif

(b) Taif.
1367 **214** 20h. multicoloured 35 35
1368 **214** 50h. multicoloured 1·00 60
1374 **214** 75h. multicoloured 1·00 60
1375 **214** 150h. multicoloured 2·50 1·30

215 Jeddah

(c) Jeddah.
1377 **215** 50h. multicoloured 1·50 80
1378 **215** 75h. multicoloured 1·50 80
1379 **215** 150h. multicoloured 2·50 1·30

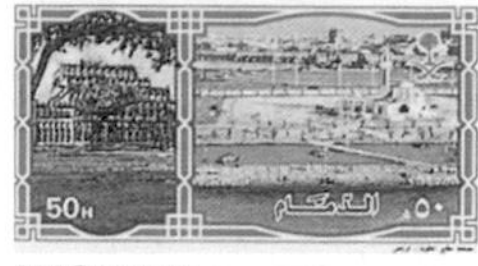
216 Dammam

(d) Dammam.
1380 **216** 50h. multicoloured 80 45
1381 **216** 75h. multicoloured 1·00 60
1382 **216** 150h. multicoloured 2·00 1·00

217 Abha

(e) Abha.
1383 **217** 1r. multicoloured 1·10 1·20
1384 **217** 2r. multicoloured 2·20 2·30

223 Family and House

1984. Tenth Anniv of Estate Development Fund.
1385 **223** 20h. multicoloured 80 35

224 Solar Panels and Symbols

1984. Al-Eyenah Solar Village. Multicoloured.
1386 20h. Type **224** 55 35
1387 80h. Sun and solar panels 1·70 45
MS1388 Two sheets, each 80×80 mm. Imperf. (a) 100h. As Type **224**; (b) As No. 1387, but both larger 85·00 85·00

225 Al-Kheef Mosque, Mina

1984. Pilgrimage to Mecca. Multicoloured.
1389 20h. Type **225** 80 25
1390 65h. Al-Kheef Mosque, Mina (different) 2·20 45

226 Olympic and Saudi Football Federation Emblems

1984. Qualification of Saudi Football Team for Olympic Games.
1391 **226** 20h. multicoloured 1·90 45

1392 **226** 115h. multicoloured 7·75 1·50

Nos. 1391/2 have the incorrect spellings "Gamos" and "Olympied".

227 Wheat and F.A.O. Emblem

1984. World Food Day.

1393 **227** 20h. green, buff and black 80 35

228 Olympic Rings and "90"

1984. 90th Anniv of Int Olympic Committee.

1394 **228** 20h. multicoloured 1·50 45
1395 **228** 50h. multicoloured 3·50 80

229 "Arabsat" and Globe

1985. Launch of "Arabsat" Satellite.

1396 **229** 20h. multicoloured 2·75 35

230 Emblem and Koran

1985. International Koran Reading Competition.

1397 **230** 20h. multicoloured 55 35
1398 **230** 65h. multicoloured 1·50 60

231 King Fahd and Jubail Industrial Complex

1985. Five Year Plan. Multicoloured.

1399 20h. Type **231** 55 35
1400 50h. King Fahd, T.V. tower, dish aerial and microwave tower 1·50 35
1401 65h. King Fahd and agricultural landscape 1·70 35
1402 80h. King Fahd and Yanbu industrial complex 2·50 45

232 I.Y.Y. Emblem

1985. International Youth Year.

1403 **232** 20h. multicoloured 45 35
1404 **232** 80h. multicoloured 1·70 45

233 Map and Wheat

1985. "Self Sufficiency in Wheat Production".

1405 **233** 20h. multicoloured 80 35

234 Loading Berth, Yanbu

1985. Abqaiq–Yanbu Oil Pipeline. Multicoloured.

1406 20h. Type **234** 80 35
1407 65h. Pipeline and map 2·00 60

235 "Arabsat 2" Satellite and Launch of "Discovery" (space shuttle)

1985. First Arab Astronaut, Prince Sultan Ibn Salman Al-Saud. Multicoloured.

1408 20h. Type **235** 1·20 60
1409 115h. Space shuttle and mission emblem (51×26 mm) 6·75 3·25

236 "40" and U.N. Emblem

1985. 40th Anniv of U.N.O.

1410 **236** 20h. light blue, blue and green 90 35

237 Highway and Map of Route

1985. Mecca–Medina Highway.

1411 **237** 20h. multicoloured 55 35
1412 **237** 65h. multicoloured 1·70 45

238 Coded Envelope and Post Emblem

1985. Post Code Publicity.

1413 **238** 20h. multicoloured 80 35

239 Trophy and Football

1985. Victory in Eighth (1984) Asian Football Cup Championship.

1414 **239** 20h. multicoloured 55 25
1415 **239** 65h. multicoloured 1·90 60
1416 **239** 115h. multicoloured 3·25 1·20

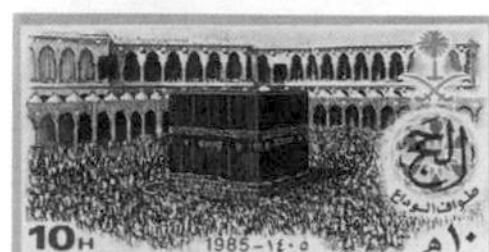

240 Pilgrims around Kaaba

1985. Pilgrimage to Mecca.

1417 **240** 10h. multicoloured 35 35
1418 **240** 15h. multicoloured 35 35
1419 **240** 20h. multicoloured 45 35
1420 **240** 65h. multicoloured 1·10 35

241 Olympic Rings and Council Emblem

1985. First Arabian Gulf Co-operation Council Olympic Day.

1421 **241** 20h. multicoloured 60 40
1422 **241** 115h. multicoloured 3·00 65

242 Irrigation System

1985. World Food Day.

1423 **242** 20h. multicoloured 1·30 65
1424 **242** 65h. multicoloured 4·00 1·40

243 King Abdulaziz and Horsemen

1985. International Conference on King Abdulaziz.

1425 **243** 15h. multicoloured 25 25
1426 **243** 20h. multicoloured 35 25
1427 **243** 65h. multicoloured 1·20 65
1428 **243** 80h. multicoloured 1·60 90
MS1429 120×100 mm. Nos. 1425/8. Imperf (sold at 10r.) 34·00 34·00

244 Building within Roll of Printed Paper

1985. King Fahd Holy Koran Press Compound, Medina. Multicoloured.

1430 20h. Type **244** 35 35
1431 65h. Open book sculpture within roll of printed paper 1·80 50

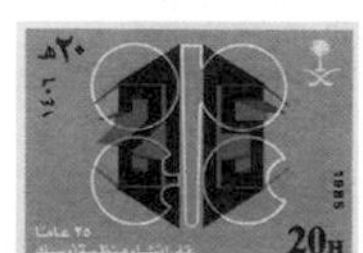

245 O.P.E.C. Emblem and "25"

1985. 25th Anniv of Organization of Petroleum Exporting Countries.

1432 **245** 20h. sepia, brown and black 50 35
1433 **245** 65h. multicoloured 2·40 50

246 Doves and I.P.Y. Emblem

1986. International Peace Year.

1434 **246** 20h. multicoloured 1·60 65

1986. As T **149** but size 29×19 mm.

1435 10h. black and violet 9·75 9·75
1436 20h. black and blue 16·00 16·00
1437 50h. black and red 33·00 28·00

247 Riyadh

1986. 50th Anniv of Riyadh Municipality.

1438a **247** 20h. multicoloured 60 50
1439 **247** 65h. multicoloured 1·80 65

248 Child in Droplet

1986. World Health Day.

1440 **248** 20h. multicoloured 60 50
1441 **248** 50h. multicoloured 1·80 65

249 Electricity Pylon and Flashes

1986. Tenth Anniv of General Electricity Corporation.

1442 **249** 20h. multicoloured 60 50
1443 **249** 65h. multicoloured 1·80 65

250 Route Map of Cable

1986. Inauguration of Singapore–Marseilles Communications Cable.

1444 **250** 20h. blue, black and green 95 50
1445 **250** 50h. multicoloured 1·80 65

251 Houses and Soldier

1986. National Guards Housing Project, Riyadh.

1446 **251** 20h. multicoloured 60 50
1447 **251** 65h. multicoloured 1·80 65

252 Holy Kaaba

1986. Holy Kaaba

1448 **252** 30h. black and green 75 50
1449 **252** 40h. black and mauve 1·00 75
1450 **252** 50h. black and green 1·50 1·00
1451a **252** 75h. black and blue 1·75 1·50
1451b **252** 100h. black and green 2·75 2·20
1451c **252** 100h. black and orange 2·75 2·20
1452a **252** 150h. black and mauve 3·10 1·80
1454 **252** 2r. black and blue 5·25 4·50

253 Mount Arafat, Pilgrims and Kaaba

1986. Pilgrimage to Mecca. Multicoloured.

1460 20h. Type **253** 2·75 2·30
1461 20h. Pilgrims leaving jet airliner 2·75 2·30
1462 20h. Stoning the Devil 2·75 2·30
1463 20h. Pilgrims at Muzdalefa looking for stones to stone the Devil 2·75 2·30
1464 20h. Pilgrims passing through Almasa'a Arcade 2·75 2·30
1465 20h. Kaaba, Mecca 2·75 2·30
1466 20h. Pilgrims around Kaaba 2·75 2·30
1467 20h. Al-Kheef Mosque, Mina 2·75 2·30

254 Refinery

444 Building Facade

2001. King Abdul Aziz History Centre. Multicoloured.

2033 1r. Type **444** 2·75 2·20
2034 1r. Corner of building 2·75 2·20
2035 1r. Towers and wall 2·75 2·20
2036 1r. Aerial view of complex 2·75 2·20

445 Buildings

2001. Folk Art. Multicoloured.

2037 1r. Type **445** 2·75 2·20
2038 1r. Horse 2·75 2·20
2039 1r. Doorways 2·75 2·20
2040 1r. Desert 2·75 2·20
2041 1r. Gate 2·75 2·20

446 Handshake

2001. World Teachers' Day.

2042 **446** 1r. multicoloured 2·75 2·20

447 Symbols of Industry

2002. Seventh Five Year Plan.

2043 **447** 1r. multicoloured 2·75 2·20

448 Islamic Education, Scientific and Culture Organization (ISESCO) Emblem

2002. First Conference of Islamic Ministers of Higher Education and Scientific Research.

2044 **448** 1r. multicoloured 2·75 2·20

449 Tents and Pilgrims

2002. Pilgrimage to Mecca.

2045 **449** 1r. multicoloured 2·75 2·20

450 King Fahd

2002. 20th Anniv of King Fahd's Accession to the Throne. Multicoloured.

2046 1r. Type **450** 2·75 2·20
MS2047 98×128 mm. 3r. As Type **450** plus a montage of other stamps issued during his reign. Imperf 8·00 8·00

451 King Fahd Port, Yanbu

2002. King Fahd Port

2048 **451** 1r. multicoloured 2·75 2·20
2049 **451** 2r. multicoloured 5·25 4·50

452 Ship at Dockside, King Fahd Port, Jubail

2002. King Fahd Port, Jubail.

2050 **452** 1r. multicoloured 2·75 2·20
2051 **452** 2r. multicoloured 5·25 4·50

453 Pilgrims and Tunnel, Mecca

2003. Pilgrimage to Mecca.

2052 **453** 1r. multicoloured 2·75 2·20

454 Water Droplet

2003. Water Conservation. Multicoloured.

2053 1r. Type **454** 2·75 2·20
2054 1r. Two droplets (vert) 2·75 2·20

455 Fire Fighters

2003. Civil Defence.

2055 **455** 1r. multicoloured 2·75 2·20

456 Emblem and Red Crescent Workers

2003. Saudi Red Crescent (aid organization).

2056 **456** 1r. multicoloured 2·75 2·20

457 *Cirrhilabrus rubriventralis*

2003. Red Sea Fish. Multicoloured.

2057 1r. Type **457** 2·75 2·20
2058 1r. *Cryptocentrus caeruleopunctatus* 2·75 2·20
2059 1r. *Plesiops nigricans* 2·75 2·20
2060 1r. Arabian angelfish (*Pomacanthus asfur*) 2·75 2·20
2061 1r. *Cheilinus abudjubbe* 2·75 2·20
2062 1r. *Pomacentrus albicaudatus* 2·75 2·20
2063 1r. *Caesio suevicus* 2·75 2·20
2064 1r. *Chaetodon austriacus* 2·75 2·20
2065 1r. *Thalassoma klumzinger* (inscr "klumzingeri") 2·75 2·20
2066 1r. *Oxymonacanthus halli* 2·75 2·20
2067 1r. Two-banded anemonefish (*Amphiprion bicinctus*) 2·75 2·20
2068 1r. *Canthigaster pygmaea* 2·75 2·20
2069 2r. *Cirrhilabrus rubriventralis* 2·75 2·20
2070 2r. *Cryptocentrus caeruleopunctatus* 2·75 2·20
2071 2r. *Plesiops nigricans* 2·75 2·20
2072 2r. Arabian angelfish (*Pomeacanthus asfur*) 2·75 2·20
2073 2r. *Cheilinus abudjubbe* 2·75 2·20
2074 2r. *Pomacentrus albicaudatus* 2·75 2·20
2075 2r. *Caesio suevicus* 2·75 2·20
2076 2r. *Chaetodon austriacus* 2·75 2·20
2077 2r. *Thalassoma klumzingeri* 2·75 2·20
2078 2r. *Oxymonacanthus halli* 2·75 2·20
2079 2r. Two-banded anemonefish (*Amphiprion bicinctus*) 2·75 2·20
2080 2r. *Canthigaster pygmaea* 2·75 2·20

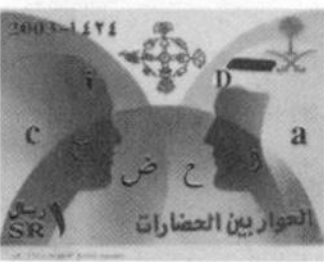
458 Faces

2003. Dialogue among Civilzations.

2081 **458** 1r. multicoloured 2·75 2·20

459 Hands enclosing Light Bulb

2003. Electricity Consumption Campaign.

2082 **459** 1r. multicoloured 2·75 2·20

460 Envelope and Postman

2003. Post Day.

2083 **460** 1r. multicoloured 2·75 2·20

461 "9" enclosing Emblem and Fireworks

2003. Ninth Gulf Co-operation Council Philatelic Exhibition, Riyadh.

2084 **461** 1r. multicoloured 2·75 2·20

462 1930 Hedjaz and Nedjde 5g. Stamp

2003. 75th Anniv of First Saudi Stamp.

2085 **462** 1r. multicoloured 3·25 2·75

463 Adult and Child

2003. Council for the Disabled.

2086 **463** 1r. multicoloured 2·75 2·20

464 Horse Race

2003. King Abdul Aziz Equestrian Centre, Riyadh.

2087 **464** 1r. multicoloured 2·75 2·20

465 Pilgrims at Airport

2003. Pilgrimage to Mecca.

2088 **465** 1r. multicoloured 2·75 2·20

466 Mosque

467 Mosque

468 Mosque

469 Mosque

470 Mosque

471 Mosque

472 Mosque

473 Mosque

2003. Mosques of Saudi Arabia.

2089 **466** 1r. multicoloured 2·75 2·20
2090 **467** 1r. multicoloured 2·75 2·20
2091 **468** 1r. multicoloured 2·75 2·20
2092 **469** 1r. multicoloured 2·75 2·20
2093 **470** 1r. multicoloured 2·75 2·20
2094 **471** 1r. multicoloured 2·75 2·20
2095 **472** 1r. multicoloured 2·75 2·20
2096 **473** 1r. multicoloured 2·75 2·20
2097 **466** 2r. multicoloured 5·25 4·50
2098 **467** 2r. multicoloured 5·25 4·50
2099 **468** 2r. multicoloured 5·25 4·50
2100 **469** 2r. multicoloured 5·25 4·50
2101 **470** 2r. multicoloured 5·25 4·50
2102 **471** 2r. multicoloured 5·25 4·50
2103 **472** 2r. multicoloured 5·25 4·50
2104 **473** 2r. multicoloured 5·25 4·50

474 McDonnell-Douglas MD 11-F

2004. Aircraft. Multicoloured.

2105 1r. Type **474** 2·75 2·20
2106 1r. Boeing 747-400 2·75 2·20
2107 1r. Boeing 777-268 2·75 2·20
2108 1r. McDonnell-Douglas MD-90-30 2·75 2·20

475 Rose and Town Square

2004. Tabuk.

2109 **475** 1r. multicoloured 2·75 2·20
2110 **475** 2r. multicoloured 5·25 4·50

476 Scales and Book

2004. Legal System.

2111	**476**	1r. multicoloured	2·75	2·20

477 Tower and City Walls

2004. Hail City.

2112	**477**	1r. multicoloured	2·75	2·20
2113	**477**	2r. multicoloured	5·25	4·50

478 World Map and Binary Code

2004. World Conferences on Information Technology, Geneva and Tunis.

2114	**478**	1r. multicoloured	2·75	2·20

479 Dunes

2004. Tourism. Multicoloured.

2115	2r. Type **479**	5·25	4·50
2116	2r. Cable cars	5·25	4·50
2117	2r. Coastline	5·25	4·50
2118	2r. Mountains	5·25	4·50

480 Clasped Hands

2004. Peace.

2119	**480**	2r. multicoloured	5·25	4·50

481 Pilgrims

2005. Pilgrimage to Mecca.

2120	**481**	1r. multicoloured	3·25	2·75

482 Emblem

2005. Municipal Elections.

2121	**482**	1r. multicoloured	3·25	2·75

483 Emblem

2005. First Islamic Solidarity Games, Makkah, Madinah, Jeddah and Taif.

2122	**483**	1r. multicoloured	2·75	2·20

484 Emblem

2005. National Anti-Terrorism Campaign. Multicoloured.

2123	1r. Type **484**	2·75	2·20
MS2124	108×74 mm. 1r. As Type **484**. Imperf	13·50	13·50

485 Towers

2005. Arar City.

2125	**485**	1r. multicoloured	2·75	2·20

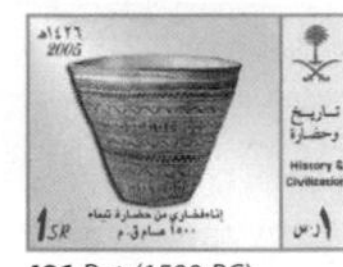
486 Pot (1500 BC)

2005. Cultural Heritage. Multicoloured.

2126	1r. Type **486**	2·75	2·20
2127	1r. Bronze lion head (500 BC)	2·75	2·20
2128	1r. Gold mask	2·75	2·20
2129	1r. Inscribed tablet	2·75	2·20
2130	2r. Castleb	5·25	4·50
2131	2r. Omar bin al Khattab Mosque	5·25	4·50
2132	2r. Palace	5·25	4·50
2133	2r. Zaa'bal Fortress	5·25	4·50

487 King Fahd

2005. King Fahd Bin Abdul Aziz Commemoration. Multicoloured.

2134	2r. Type **487**	4·25	3·50
2135	3r. As No. 2134	6·50	5·25
MS2136	80×106 mm. 5r. King Fahd facing left. Imperf	27·00	27·00

488 Mecca

2005. Pilgrimage to Mecca.

2137	**488**	2r. multicoloured	5·25	4·50

489 King Abdullah Bin Abdul Aziz

2005. Accession of King Abdullah Bin Abdul Aziz and Installation of Sultan bin Abdul Aziz al-Saud as Heir Apparent. Multicoloured.

2138	2r. Type **489**	5·25	4·50
2139	2r. Sultan bin Abdul Aziz al-Saud	5·25	4·50
2140	3r. As Type **489**	6·50	5·25
2141	3r. As No. 2139	6·50	5·25
MS2142	106×81 mm. 5r. King Abdullah Bin Abdul Aziz and Sultan bin Abdul Aziz al-Saud. Imperf	42·00	42·00

490 Emblem

2005. Mecca—Capital of Islamic Culture. Multicoloured.

2143	3r. Type **490**	7·75	6·50
MS2144	80×105 mm. 5r. Ka'ba. Imperf	40·00	40·00

491 Emblem

2005. National Society for Human Rights. Multicoloured.

2145	2r. Type **491**	5·25	4·50
MS2146	80×105 mm. 5r. Emblem (different). Imperf	40·00	40·00

492 Emblem

2006. 30th Anniv of OPEC Development Fund.

2147	**492**	2r. multicoloured	5·25	4·50

493 Medals and King Faisal

2006. King Faisal International Prize.

2148	**493**	2r. multicoloured	5·25	4·50
2149	**493**	3r. multicoloured	7·25	6·25

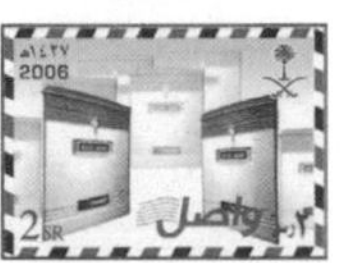
494 Post Boxes

2006. Postal Address System.

2150	**494**	2r. multicoloured	5·25	4·50

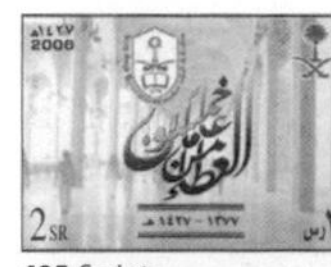
495 Script

2006. 50th Anniv of King Saud University.

2151	**495**	2r. multicoloured	5·25	4·50

496 Stylized Players

2006. World Cup Football Championship, Germany. Multicoloured.

2152	2r. Type **496**	5·25	4·50
2153	3r. Championship emblem	7·25	6·25

497 Flag

2006. 25th Anniv of Gulf Co-operation Council. Multicoloured.

2154	**497** 2r. multicoloured	5·25	4·50
MS2155	165×105 mm. 5r. Flags of member states. Imperf	42·00	42·00

Stamps of similar designs were issued by Kuwait, Oman, Qatar, United Arab Emirates and Bahrain.

497a Emblem

2006. Centre for Organ Transplantation.

2155a	**497a**	2r. multicoloured	5·25	4·50

498 City Centre

2006. Al Medina Al Munawarah. Multicoloured.

2156	2r. Type **498**	5·25	4·50
MS2157	105×80 mm. 5r. As No. 2156 and doorway. Imperf	42·00	42·00

499 Open Book

2006. International Book Fair, Riyadh.

2158	**499**	2r. multicoloured	5·25	4·50

500 Child's Face enclosed in Map

2006. National Day.

2159	**500**	2r. multicoloured	5·25	4·50

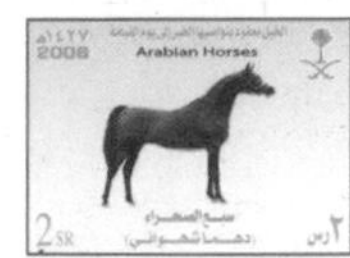

501 Horse

2006. Arabian Horse. Multicoloured.

2160	2r. Type **501**	5·25	4·50
2161	2r. Bay facing left	5·25	4·50
2162	2r. Chestnut facing right	5·25	4·50
2163	2r. Roan facing left	5·25	4·50
2164	2r. Grey cantering	5·25	4·50
2165	2r. Mare and foal	5·25	4·50

502 King Abdullah Bin Abdul Aziz and Mecca

2006. Pilgrimage to Mecca.

2166	**502**	2r. multicoloured	5·25	4·50

503 Abdullah bin Abdul Aziz Al Saud and Patients

2007. Kingdom of Humanity. Multicoloured.

2167	2r. Type **503**	5·25	4·50
MS2168	105×80 mm. 5r. Abdullah bin Abdul Aziz Al Saud and patients (different)	42·00	42·00

504 Emblem

2007. KSA—Winner of Football Cup for Mentally Disabled Championship.

2169	**504**	2r. multicoloured	5·25	4·50

505 Map and Immunization Campaign Emblem

2007. Polio Free Saudi Arabia Campaign.

2170	**505**	2r. multicoloured	5·25	4·50

506 *Junonia hierta*

2007. Butterflies. Multicoloured.

2171	2r. Type **506**	5·25	4·50
2172	2r. *Melitaea deserticola*	5·25	4·50
2173	2r. *Funonia orithya cheesmani*	5·25	4·50
2174	2r. *Eyrema hecabe*1	5·25	4·50
2175	2r. *Papilio demoleus*	5·25	4·50
2176	2r. Inscr 'Colotis calas'	5·25	4·50
2177	2r. *Colotis phisadia*	5·25	4·50
2178	2r. *Vanessa cardui*	5·25	4·50
2179	3r. *Junonia hierta*	7·25	6·25
2180	3r. *Melitaea deserticola*	7·25	6·25
2181	3r. *Funonia orithya cheesmani*	7·25	6·25
2182	3r. *Eyrema hecabe*	7·25	6·25
2183	3r. *Papilio demoleus*	7·25	6·25
2184	3r. Inscr 'Colotis calas'	7·25	6·25
2185	3r. *Colotis phisadia*	7·25	6·25
2186	3r. *Vanessa cardui*	7·25	6·25

507 Emblem

2007. Postal Events. Multicoloured.

2187	2r. Type **507** (PosTech 2007 (global conference on technology), Jeddah)	5·25	4·50
2188	2r. Flags of member countries (Steering Committee of GCC countries)	5·25	4·50
2189	2r. 13	5·25	4·50
2190	2r. UPU emblem (Arab Regional Postal Roundtable, Jeddah)	5·25	4·50

508 Woman teaching

2007. Female Participation in Science and Education Campaign. Multicoloured.

2191	2r. Type **508**	5·25	4·50
2192	2r. Woman using microscope	5·25	4·50
2193	2r. Women students	5·25	4·50
2194	2r. Women using computers	5·25	4·50

509 '3' and Flags of Member States

2007. Third OPEC Summit, Riyadah.

2195	**509**	2r. multicoloured	5·25	4·50

510 Map Outline enclosing People and Symbols of Saudi Arabia

2007. National Day.

2196	**510**	2r. multicoloured	5·25	4·50

511 King Abdullah Bin Abdul Aziz and Mecca

2007. Pilgrimage to Mecca.

2197	**511**	2r. multicoloured	5·25	4·50

512 Emblem

2007. King Abdullah Bin Abdul Aziz Centre for National Dialogue.

2198	**512**	2r. multicoloured	5·75	4·75

513 Al majaheem

2008. Camels. Multicoloured.

2199	2r. Type **513**	5·25	4·50
2200	2r. Al wad'h	5·25	4·50
2201	2r. Al shog'h	5·25	4·50
2202	2r. Al shoe'l	5·25	4·50
MS2203	105×75 mm. Size 23×17 mm. Nos 2199/202. Imperf	42·00	42·00

No. **MS**2203 was sold for 5r.

514 Refinery

2008. 75th Anniv of Saudi Aramco. Multicoloured.

2204	2r. Type **514**	5·25	4·50
2205	2r. Diver	5·25	4·50
2206	2r. Refinery (child's drawing)	5·25	4·50
2207	2r. Men with flags (child's drawing)	5·25	4·50

515 King Abdullah bin Abdul Aziz Al Saud and City

2008. Riyadh–50 Years of Development.

2208	**515**	2r. multicoloured	5·75	4·75

515a Emblem

2008. Centenary of International Electrotechnical Commission.

2209	**515a**	2r. multicoloured	5·75	4·75

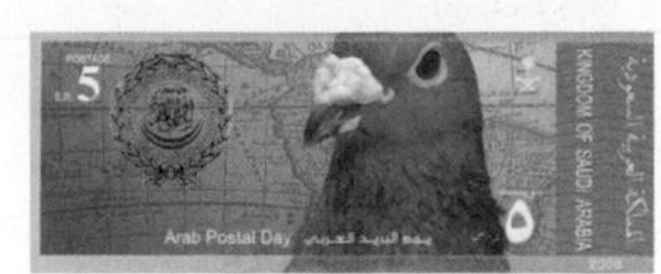

516 Pigeon

2008. Arab Post Day. Sheet 170×60 mm containing T **516** and similar horiz design. Multicoloured.

MS2210	5r.×2, Type **516**; Camels	60·00	60·00

517 King Abdullah Bin Abdul Aziz and Mecca

2008. Pilgrimage to Mecca.

2211	**517**	2r. multicoloured	5·75	4·75

518 King Abdullah Bin Abdul Aziz and KAUST Breakwater Beacon

2009. King Abdullah University of Science and Technology (KAUST). Multicoloured.

2212	2r. Type **518**	5·25	4·50
MS2212a	105×75 mm. 5r. King Abdullah. Imperf	22·00	22·00

519 Emblem

2009. Al Quds—Capital of Arab Culture.

2213	**519**	2r. multicoloured	5·75	4·75

520 King Abdullah Bin Abdul Aziz and Flags

2009. 79th National Day.

2214	**520**	2r. multicoloured	5·75	4·75

521 Pilgrims and Mecca

2009. Pilgrimage to Mecca.

2215	**521**	2r. multicoloured	5·75	4·75

522 '50'

2010. 50th Anniv of OPEC.

2216	**522**	2r. multicoloured	5·75	4·75

524 Pilgrims and Hajj Train

2010. Pilgrimage to Mecca. Multicoloured.

MS2218	2r.×3, Type **524**; Pilgrims and Abraj Al-Bait Towers; Abraj Al-Bait Towers and Mecca Royal Hotel Clock Tower	22·00	22·00

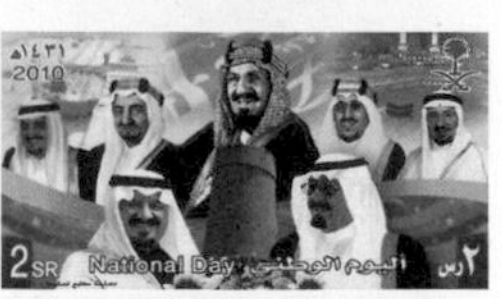

525 King Abdullah and Royal Family

2010. National Day

2219	**525**	2r. multicoloured	22·00	22·00

526 Bracelet

2010. Traditional Saudi Jewellery (1st issue). Multicoloured.

2220	2r. Type **526**	5·25	4·50
2221	2r. Deep gold bracelet with raised decoration	5·25	4·50
2222	2r. Three bracelets inscribed 'Horseshoe Bracelets'	5·25	4·50
2223	2r. Inscribed 'Silver Armlets'	5·25	4·50
2224	2r. Two silver bangles with decorated surface	5·25	4·50
2225	2r. Two silver bracelets inset with blue stones	5·25	4·50

2011. Traditional Saudi Jewellery (2nd issue). Multicoloured.

2226	2r. Tasselled head dress ornament	5·25	4·50
2227	2r. Wide earrings with pendants	5·25	4·50
2228	2r. Tasselled earrings	5·25	4·50
2229	2r. Circular pendant on chain, inscribed 'Head Ornament'	5·25	4·50
2230	2r. Two rings	5·25	4·50
2231	2r. Inscribed 'Forehead Ornament'	5·25	4·50

2011. Traditional Saudi Jewellery (3rd issue). Multicoloured.

2232	2r. Inscribed 'Gold, Cornelian & Ruby Necklace'	5·25	4·50
2233	2r. 'Silver Necklace'	5·25	4·50
2234	2r. Necklace with large wedge-shaped pendant	5·25	4·50
2235	2r. Belt	5·25	4·50
2236	2r. Multidrop necklace with central pendant	5·25	4·50
2237	2r. Silver necklace with three large square frontal pendants and one at clasp	5·25	4·50

527 King Abdullah Haram Expansion Project

2011. Pilgrimage to Mecca

2238	**527**	2r. multicoloured	5·25	4·50

528 Dove of Peace

2011. Scout Jamboree 2011, Sweden

2239	**528**	2r. multicoloured	5·25	4·50

NEWSPAPER STAMPS
NEJDI OCCUPATION OF HAJAZ

(N29)

1925. Nos. 198 and 199a optd with Type **N29**.

N208	**11**	⅛pi. brown	£2250
N209	**11**	½pi. red	£5500

OFFICIAL STAMPS
SAUDI ARABIA

O52

1939

O347	**O52**	3g. blue	5·50	3·25
O348	**O52**	5g. mauve	9·00	4·00
O349	**O52**	20g. brown	14·50	8·25
O350	**O52**	50g. turquoise	33·00	16·00
O351	**O52**	100g. olive	£120	65·00
O352	**O52**	200g. purple	95·00	49·00

O72

1961. Size 18½×22½ mm.

O449	**O72**	1p. black	1·60	45
O450	**O72**	2p. green	2·50	65
O451	**O72**	3p. bistre	3·50	1·10
O452	**O72**	4p. blue	4·75	1·30
O453	**O72**	5p. red	5·50	1·80
O454	**O72**	10p. purple	7·75	3·50
O455	**O72**	20p. violet	16·00	6·75
O456	**O72**	50p. brown	39·00	18·00
O457	**O72**	100p. green	80·00	36·00

1964. Size 21×26 mm.

O497	1p. black	2·00	65
O498	2p. green	3·50	1·20
O504	3p. ochre	6·75	2·75
O505	4p. blue	6·75	2·75
O501	5p. red	9·50	3·25
O507	6p. purple	13·50	3·25
O508	7p. green	13·50	3·25
O509	8p. red	13·50	3·25
O510	9p. red	£300	
O511	10p. brown	55·00	3·25
O512	11p. green	£100	
O513	12p. violet	£550	
O514	13p. blue	18·00	5·00
O515	14p. violet	18·00	5·00
O516	15p. orange	£325	
O517	16p. black	£325	
O518	17p. green	£325	
O519	18p. yellow	£325	
O520	19p. purple	£325	
O520a	20p. blue		
O521	23p. blue	£450	
O522	24p. green	£325	
O523	26p. bistre	£325	
O524	27p. lilac	£325	
O525	31p. brown	£450	
O526	33p. green	£325	
O527	50p. green	£650	
O528	100p. green	£1500	

O111

1970

O1040	**O111**	1p. brown	5·25	1·70
O1041	**O111**	2p. green	5·25	1·70
O1042	**O111**	3p. mauve	6·75	2·75
O1043	**O111**	4p. blue	8·25	3·25
O1044	**O111**	5p. red	8·25	3·25
O1045	**O111**	6p. orange	8·25	3·25
O1046	**O111**	7p. red	£200	
O1047	**O111**	8p. violet		
O1048	**O111**	9p. blue		
O1049	**O111**	10p. blue	11·00	5·25
O1050	**O111**	11p. green		
O1050a	**O111**	12p. brown		
O1051	**O111**	20p. blue	27·00	8·25
O1051b	**O111**	23p. brown	£450	
O1052	**O111**	31p. purple	85·00	36·00
O1053	**O111**	50p. brown		
O1054	**O111**	100p. green		

POSTAGE DUE STAMPS
A. HEJAZ

D7 From Old Door at El Ashra Barsbai, Shari El Ashrafuga, Cairo

(D11)

1917

D17	**D7**	20pa. red	4·75	3·25
D18	**D7**	1pi. blue	4·75	3·25
D19	**D7**	2pi. purple	4·75	3·25

1921. Nos. D17/19 optd with T **7**.

D31	20pa. red	31·00	4·75
D33	1pi. blue	10·00	6·25
D34	2pi. purple	17·00	12·50

1922. Nos. D17/19 optd with T **10**.

D39	20pa. red	39·00	45·00
D40	1pi. blue	5·50	5·50
D41	2pi. purple	5·50	5·50

1923. Optd with Type **D11**.

D47A	**11**	½pi. red	6·25	2·30
D48A	**11**	1pi. blue	11·00	2·50
D49A	**11**	2pi. orange	6·25	3·25

1924. Nos. D47/9 optd with T **14**.

D57	½pi. red	£3750	
D58	1pi. blue	£3750	
D59	2pi. orange	£3750	

1925. Nos. D17/19 optd with T **15**.

D88a	20pa. red	£550	£550
D91	1pi. blue	49·00	42·00
D92	2pi. purple	23·00	23·00

1925. Nos. D17/19 optd with T **16**.

D93a	20pa. red	£375	
D94	1pi. blue	39·00	39·00
D96	2pi. claret	31·00	45·00

No. D93a has the overprint inverted.

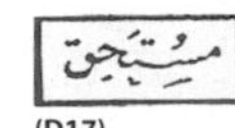
(D17)

1925. Stamps of 1924 (optd T **16**) optd with Type **D17**.

D149	½pi. red (No. 116)	£130	
D150	1½pi. lilac (No. 99)	£130	
D151	2pi. orange (No. 119)	£190	
D152	3pi. brown (No. 120)	£130	
D153	5pi. green (No. 103)	£130	

(D18)

1925. Stamps of 1922 optd with Type **D18**.

D154		⅛pi. brown	60·00
D155		½pi. red	65·00
D156		1pi. blue	65·00
D157		1½pi. lilac	65·00
D158		2pi. orange	65·00
D160		3pi. brown	65·00
D161		5pi. green	95·00
D162	-	10pi. purple and mauve	95·00

1925. Nos. D154/62 optd with Type **D17**.

D163	**11**	⅛pi. brown	33·00	31·00
D164	**11**	½pi. red	42·00	42·00
D165	**11**	1pi. blue	31·00	31·00
D166	**11**	1½pi. lilac	33·00	31·00
D167	**11**	2pi. orange	33·00	32·00
D168	**11**	3pi. brown	33·00	32·00
D170	**11**	5pi. green	33·00	32·00
D171	-	10pi. purple and mauve	49·00	42·00

D25

1925. Optd with T **24**.

D186	**D 25**	½pi. blue	5·00
D187	**D 25**	1pi. orange	5·00
D188	**D 25**	2pi. brown	5·00
D189	**D 25**	3pi. pink	5·00

These stamps without overprint were not officially issued.

B. NEJDI OCCUPATION OF HEJAZ

1925. Nos. D47/9 of Hejaz optd with T **25**.

D203A	**11**	½pi. red	39·00
D204Ac	**11**	1pi. blue	£110
D205Ac	**11**	2pi. orange	£110

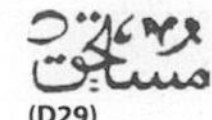
(D29)

(D33)

1925. Hejaz Postage Stamps of 1922 optd with Type **D29**.

D206	½pi. red	45·00
D207	3pi. red	45·00

1925. Postage stamps optd with T **32** further optd with Type **D33**.

D232	**28**	1pi. blue	33·00
D233	**28**	2pi. orange	33·00
D234	**11**	3pi. red	25·00
D236	**28**	5pi. green	55·00

1925. No. D40 of Hejaz optd with T **32**.

D238	**D 7**	1pi. blue	£150

C. HEJAZ AND NEJD

D40

1926

D267	**D 40**	½pi. red	5·50	2·20
D270	**D 40**	2pi. orange	5·50	2·20
D272	**D 40**	6pi. brown	5·50	2·20

1926. Pan-Islamic Congress, Cairo. Optd with T **40**.

D281	½pi. red	11·00	7·75
D282	2pi. orange	11·00	7·75
D283	6pi. brown	11·00	7·75

D42 Tougra of Ibn Saud

1927

D292	**D 42**	1pi. grey	16·00	2·20
D293	**D 42**	2pi. violet	19·00	2·20

D. SAUDI ARABIA

1935. No. 331a optd **T** in a circle.

D343	**49**	½g. red	£325

D52

1937

D347	**D52**	½g. brown	23·00	23·00
D348	**D52**	1g. blue	23·00	23·00
D349	**D52**	2g. purple	32·00	14·50

D72

1961

D449	**D72**	1p. violet	9·50	9·50
D450	**D72**	2p. green	17·00	7·25
D451	**D72**	4p. red	19·00	19·00

Pt. 7

SAXONY

A former kingdom in S. Germany. Stamps superseded in 1868 by those of the North German Federation.

10 pfennige = 1 neugroschen;
30 neugroschen = 1 thaler.

1

1850. Imperf.

1	**1**	3pf. red	£10000	£9500

2

1851. Imperf.

7	**2**	3pf. green	£180	£140

3 Friedrich August II

1851. Imperf.

10	**3**	½ngr. black on grey	£100	18·00
12	**3**	1ngr. black on pink	£130	14·00
13	**3**	2ngr. black on blue	£350	£110
14	**3**	3ngr. black on yellow	£225	35·00

4 King Johann I

1855. Imperf.

16	**4**	½ngr. black on grey	55·00	5·75
18	**4**	1ngr. black on pink	17·00	5·75
20	**4**	2ngr. black on blue	28·00	28·00
23	**4**	3ngr. black on yellow	33·00	23·00
24	**4**	5ngr. red	£120	95·00
28	**4**	10ngr. blue	£325	£325

5

6

1863. Perf.

31	**5**	3pf. green	2·75	60·00
36	**5**	½ngr. orange	2·75	4·00
39	**6**	1ngr. pink	1·70	3·50
40	**6**	2ngr. blue	4·00	11·50
42	**6**	3ngr. brown	5·50	18·00
45	**6**	5ngr. blue	28·00	70·00
46	**6**	5ngr. purple	45·00	70·00
47	**6**	5ngr. grey	33·00	£400

Pt. 7

SCHLESWIG-HOLSTEIN

Two former Duchies of the King of Denmark which, following a revolt, established a Provisional Government in 1848. Danish stamps were in use from 1851 in Schleswig and 1853 in Holstein.

The Duchies were invaded by Prussia and Audtria in 1864 and, by the Convention of Gastein in 1865, were placed under joint sovereignty of those countries, with Holstein administered by Austria.

The Duchies were annexed by Prussia in 1867 adn from 1868 used the stamps of the North German Confederation.

96 skilling = 1 Rigsbankdaler (Danish).
16 schilling = 1 mark.

SCHLESWIG-HOLSTEIN

1

2

1850. Imperf.

2a	**1**	1s. blue	£450	£8000
4	**1**	2s. pink	£800	£11000

1865. Inscr "SCHLESWIG-HOLSTEIN". Roul.

6	**2**	½s. pink	50·00	65·00
7	**2**	1¼s. green	25·00	29·00
8	**2**	1⅓s. mauve	60·00	£180
9	**2**	2s. blue	65·00	£350
10	**2**	4s. bistre	90·00	£1900

SCHLESWIG

1864. Inscr "HERZOGTH. SCHLESWIG". Roul.

24	½s. green	45·00	80·00
21	1¼s. green	65·00	29·00
25	1¼s. lilac	80·00	35·00
27	1⅓s. pink	40·00	95·00
28	2s. blue	40·00	80·00
22	4s. red	£130	£700
29	4s. bistre	45·00	£120

HOLSTEIN

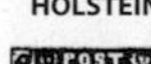

6

1864. Imperf.

51	**6**	1¼s. blue	80·00	80·00

9

1864. Roul.

59	**9**	1¼s. blue	60·00	29·00

10

1865. Roul.

61	**10**	½s. green	90·00	£140
62	**10**	1¼s. mauve	65·00	35·00
63	**10**	1⅓s. pink	85·00	65·00
64	**10**	2s. blue	70·00	70·00
65	**10**	4s. bistre	80·00	£120

On the 1⅓s. and 4s. the word "SCHILLING" is inside the central oval.

1868. Inscr "HERZOGTH. HOLSTEIN". Roul.

66	**2**	1¼s. purple	£100	35·00
67	**2**	2s. blue	£200	£225

Pt. 1

SELANGOR

A state of the Federation of Malaya, incorporated in Malaysia in 1963.

100 cents = 1 dollar (Straits or Malayan).

1881. Stamps of Straits Settlements optd **SELANGOR**.

3	**5**	2c. brown	£170	£190
35	**5**	2c. red	22·00	2·75

1882. Straits Settlements stamp optd **S**.

8	2c. brown	—	£4000

1891. Stamp of Straits Settlements surch **SELANGOR Two CENTS**.

44	2c. on 24c. green	50·00	70·00

40

1891

49	**40**	1c. green	1·50	25
50	**40**	2c. red	3·50	1·75
51	**40**	2c. orange	2·50	1·75
52	**40**	5c. blue	24·00	6·50

1894. Surch **3 CENTS**.

53	3c. on 5c. red	6·00	50

42

43

1895

54	**42**	3c. purple and red	6·50	30
55	**42**	5c. purple and yellow	13·00	50
56	**42**	8c. purple and blue	50·00	8·50
57	**42**	10c. purple and orange	13·00	3·50
58	**42**	25c. green and red	80·00	60·00
59	**42**	50c. purple and black	95·00	32·00
60	**42**	50c. green and black	£425	£120
61	**43**	$1 green	70·00	£160
62	**43**	$2 green and red	£275	£325
63	**43**	$3 green and yellow	£650	£650
64	**43**	$5 green and blue	£325	£425
65	**43**	$10 green and purple	£850	£1400
66	**43**	$25 green and orange	£4750	£4750

1900. Surch in words.

66a	**42**	1c. on 5c. purple & yellow	70·00	£130
66b	**42**	1c. on 50c. green and black	5·00	38·00
67	**42**	3c. on 50c. green and black	6·00	30·00

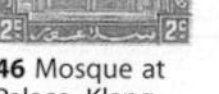
46 Mosque at Palace, Klang

47 Sultan Suleiman

1935

68	**46**	1c. black	30	10
69	**46**	2c. green	90	10
70	**46**	2c. orange	6·00	75
71	**46**	3c. green	4·00	9·00
72	**46**	4c. orange	50	10
73	**46**	5c. brown	70	10
74	**46**	6c. red	11·00	10
75	**46**	8c. grey	60	10
76	**46**	10c. purple	60	10
77	**46**	12c. blue	1·50	10
78	**46**	15c. blue	12·00	32·00
79	**46**	25c. purple and red	1·00	60
80	**46**	30c. purple and orange	1·00	85
81	**46**	40c. red and purple	1·50	1·00
82	**46**	50c. black on green	1·00	15
83	**47**	$1 black and red on blue	14·00	90
84	**47**	$2 green and red	38·00	9·50
85	**47**	$5 green and red on green	£110	23·00

48 Sultan Hisamud-din Alam Shah

1941

86	**48**	$1 black and red on blue	24·00	6·50
87	**48**	$2 green and red	50·00	48·00

1948. Silver Wedding. As T **33b/c** of St. Helena.

88	10c. violet	20	30
89	$5 green	27·00	22·00

49 Sultan Hisamud-din Alam Shah

1949

90	**49**	1c. black	10	60
91	**49**	2c. orange	30	1·50
92	**49**	3c. green	4·50	1·50
93	**49**	4c. brown	60	10
94a	**49**	5c. purple	50	2·00
95	**49**	6c. grey	30	40
96	**49**	8c. red	3·25	1·00
97	**49**	8c. green	1·25	1·75
98	**49**	10c. purple	20	10
99	**49**	12c. red	2·00	3·75
100	**49**	15c. blue	9·00	10
101	**49**	20c. black and green	9·00	35
102	**49**	20c. blue	1·00	10
103	**49**	25c. purple and orange	2·00	20
104	**49**	30c. red and purple	3·00	2·25
105	**49**	35c. red and purple	1·25	1·50
106	**49**	40c. red and purple	16·00	8·00
107	**49**	50c. black and blue	3·50	10
108	**49**	$1 blue and purple	3·50	60
109	**49**	$2 green and red	15·00	60
110	**49**	$5 green and brown	48·00	3·50

1949. U.P.U. As T **33d/g** of St. Helena.

111	10c. purple	30	10
112	15c. blue	2·50	2·50
113	25c. orange	35	4·50
114	50c. black	1·00	6·50

1953. Coronation. As T **33h** of St. Helena.

115	10c. black and purple	2·00	10

1957. As Nos. 92-102 of Kedah but inset portrait of Sultan Hisamud-din Alam Shah.

116	1c. black	10	2·25
117	2c. red	30	1·00
118	4c. sepia	10	10
119	5c. lake	10	10
120	8c. green	4·25	3·00
121	10c. sepia	2·50	10
122	10c. purple	15·00	10
123	20c. blue	2·75	20
124	50c. black and blue	40	10
125	$1 blue and purple	9·50	10
126	$2 green and red	9·50	3·00
127a	$5 brown and green	16·00	2·50

50 Sultan Salahuddin Abdul Aziz Shah

1961. Coronation of the Sultan.

128	**50**	10c. multicoloured	20	10

51 Sultan Salahuddin Abdul Aziz Shah

1961. As Nos. 116 etc but with inset portrait of Sultan Salahuddin Abdul Aziz as in T **51**.

129	1c. black	1·50	3·25
130	2c. red	2·25	3·00
131	4c. sepia	2·25	10
132	5c. lake	2·25	10
133	8c. green	7·50	7·50
134	10c. purple	1·50	10
135	20c. blue	11·00	2·25

52 "Vanda hookeriana"

1965. As Nos. 115-121 of Kedah but with inset portrait of Sultan Salahuddin Abdul Aziz Shah as in T **52**.

136	**52**	1c. multicoloured	10	20
137	-	2c. multicoloured	10	1·75
138	-	5c. multicoloured	1·50	10
139	-	6c. multicoloured	15	10
140	-	10c. multicoloured	15	10
141	-	15c. multicoloured	1·25	10
142	-	20c. multicoloured	1·90	70

The higher values used in Selangor were Nos. 20-7 of Malaysia (National issues).

53 "Parthenos sylvia"

1971. Butterflies. As Nos. 124-130 of Kedah, but with portrait of Sultan Salahuddin Abdul Aziz Shah as in T **53**.

146		1c. multicoloured	75	2·00
147		2c. multicoloured	1·50	2·00
148	**53**	5c. multicoloured	1·50	20
149	-	6c. multicoloured	1·50	2·00
150	-	10c. multicoloured	1·50	10
151	-	15c. multicoloured	1·50	10
152	-	20c. multicoloured	1·50	50

The higher values in use with this issue were Nos. 64-71 of Malaysia (National issues).

54 "Lagerstroemia speciosa"

1979. Flowers. As Nos. 135-141 of Kedah but with portrait of Sultan Salahuddin Abdul Aziz Shah as in T **54**.

158	1c. "Rafflesia hasseltii"	10	1·00
159	2c. "Pterocarpus indicus"	10	1·00
160	5c. Type **54**	10	10
161	10c. "Durio zibethinus"	15	10
162	15c. "Hibiscus rosa sinensis"	15	10
163	20c. "Rhododendron scortechinii"	20	10
164	25c. "Etlingera elatior" (inscr "Phaeomeria speciosa")	40	10

55 Sultan Salahuddin Abdul Aziz Shah and Royal Crest

1985. Silver Jubilee of Sultan.

173	**55**	15c. multicoloured	1·75	10
174	**55**	20c. multicoloured	1·75	15
175	**55**	$1 multicoloured	6·50	9·00

56 Black Pepper

1986. As Nos. 152-158 of Kedah but with portrait of Sultan Salahuddin Abdul Aziz Shah as in T **56**.

176	1c. Coffee	10	40
177	2c. Coconuts	10	40
178	5c. Cocoa	15	15
179	10c. Type **56**	20	10
180	15c. Rubber	40	10
181	20c. Oil palm	40	15
182	30c. Rice	40	15

2003. As Type **56** but redenominated 'sen'. Multicoloured.

183	30s. Rice	1·25	10

57 *Nelumbium nelumbo* (sacred lotus)

2007. Garden Flowers. As Nos. 210-215 of Johore, but with portrait of Sultan Sharafuddin Idris Shah and Arms of Selangor as in T **57**. Multicoloured.

184	5s. Type **57**	10	10
185	10s. *Hydrangea macrophylla*	15	10
186	20s. *Hippeastrum reticulatum*	25	15
187	30s. *Bougainvillea*	40	20
188	40s. *Ipomoea indica*	50	30
189	50s. *Hibiscus rosa-sinensis*	65	35
MS190	100×85 mm. Nos. 184/9	2·00	2·00

Pt. 6, Pt. 14

SENEGAL

A French colony incorporated in French West Africa in 1944. In 1958 Senegal became an autonomous State within the French Community and in 1959 joined the Sudan to form the Mali Federation. In 1960 the Federation broke up with Mali and Senegal becoming independent republics.

100 centimes = 1 franc.

1887. Stamps of French Colonies, "Commerce" type, surch in figures.

1	**J**	5 on 20c. red on green	£170	£180
2	**J**	5 on 30c. brown on drab	£225	£225
3	**J**	10 on 4c. brown on green	£100	85·00
4c	**J**	10 on 20c. red on green	£425	£425
5a	**J**	15 on 20c. red on green	80·00	80·00

1892. Stamps of French Colonies, "Commerce" type, surch **SENEGAL** and new value.

6	75 on 15c. blue on blue	£425	£150
7	1f. on 5c. green on green	£425	£170

1892. "Tablet" key-type inscr "SENEGAL ET DEPENDANCES".

8	**D**	1c. black and red on blue	90	75
9	**D**	2c. brown and blue on buff	4·50	4·25
10	**D**	4c. red and blue on grey	1·00	1·20
21	**D**	5c. green and red	4·25	35
12	**D**	10c. black and blue on lilac	10·00	4·50
22	**D**	10c. red and blue	6·50	20
13	**D**	15c. blue and red	17·00	90
23	**D**	15c. grey and red	6·50	50
14	**D**	20c. red and blue on green	7·50	8·00
15	**D**	25c. black and red on pink	4·25	1·00
24	**D**	25c. blue and red	32·00	70·00
16	**D**	30c. brown & blue on drab	11·50	13·00
17	**D**	40c. red and blue on yellow	48·00	50·00
18	**D**	50c. red and blue on pink	12·50	23·00
25	**D**	50c. brown and red on blue	60·00	75·00
19	**D**	75c. brown & red on orange	14·00	30·00
20	**D**	1f. green and red	17·00	25·00

1903. Surch.

26	5 on 40c. red & blue on yell	12·00	36·00
27	10 on 50c. red and blue on pink	20·00	50·00
28	10 on 75c. brown and red on orange	50·00	38·00
29	10 on 1f. green and red	£120	£120

1906. "Faidherbe". "Palms" and "Balay" key types inscr "SENEGAL".

33	I	1c. grey and red	1·80	75
34	I	2c. brown and blue	1·60	75·00
34	I	2c. brown and red	1·60	75
35	I	4c. brown and red on blue	2·50	1·40
36	I	5c. green and red	3·75	35
37	I	10c. pink and blue	13·50	35
38	I	15c. violet and red	11·00	4·25
39	J	20c. black and red on blue	4·00	3·25
40	J	25c. blue and red	2·30	85
41	J	30c. brown and red on pink	5·00	6·00
42	J	35c. black and red on yellow	14·00	1·40
43	J	40c. red and blue on blue	8·25	11·00
44	J	45c. brown & red on green	13·50	17·00
45	J	50c. violet and red	9·75	7·75
46	J	75c. green & red on orange	5·75	7·75
47	K	1f. black and red on blue	16·00	55·00
48	K	2f. blue and red on pink	21·00	60·00
49	K	5f. red and blue on yellow	60·00	95·00

1912. Surch.

58A	05 on 15c. grey and red	45	90
59A	05 on 20c. red and blue on green	1·90	8·50
60A	05 on 30c. brown and blue on drab	1·40	7·00
61A	10 on 40c. red and blue on yellow	1·70	6·00
62A	10 on 50c. red and blue	4·00	12·00
63A	10 on 75c. brown and red on orange	8·25	22·00

33 Market

1914

64	33	1c. violet and brown	35	10
65	33	2c. blue and black	35	50
66	33	4c. brown and grey	50	90
67	33	5c. green and light green	1·40	75
91	33	5c. red and black	35	55
68	33	10c. pink and red	2·00	80
92	33	10c. green and light green	85	1·30
113	33	10c. blue and purple	55	55
69	33	15c. purple and brown	80	55
70	33	20c. grey and brown	1·10	1·00
114	33	20c. green	65	2·50
115	33	20c. blue and grey	1·80	10
71	33	25c. blue and ultramarine	3·75	1·00
93	33	25c. black and red	1·90	60
72	33	30c. pink and black	1·00	80
94	33	30c. carmine and red	3·00	7·50
116	33	30c. blue and grey	80	35
117	33	30c. green and olive	2·30	90·00
73	33	35c. violet and orange	1·50	2·75
74	33	40c. green and violet	2·50	60
75	33	45c. brown and blue	2·30	7·50
95	33	45c. blue and red	3·00	6·50
118	33	45c. red and carmine	80	1·20
119	33	45c. red and brown	6·00	13·00
76	33	50c. blue and purple	4·00	5·50
96	33	50c. blue and ultramarine	1·80	1·90
120	33	50c. green and red	2·00	30·00
121	33	60c. violet on pink	1·00	6·50
122	33	65c. green and red	4·50	7·25
77	33	75c. pink and grey	2·00	3·25
123	33	75c. light blue and blue	1·20	1·10
124	33	75c. blue and pink	2·30	65
125	33	90c. carmine and red	4·00	4·25
78	33	1f. black and violet	2·50	1·30
126	33	1f. blue	70	60
127	33	1f. blue and black	2·00	45
128	33	1f.10 black and green	6·25	12·50
129	33	1f.25 red and green	1·50	1·40
130	33	1f.50 light blue and blue	4·00	90
131	33	1f.75 green and brown	14·50	1·20
79	33	2f. blue and pink	3·75	9·00
97	33	2f. brown and blue	4·75	85
132	33	3f. mauve on pink	4·25	75
80	33	5f. violet and green	5·00	1·40

1915. Surch **5c** and red cross.

89	10c.+5c. pink and red	1·80	2·75
90	15c.+5c. purple & brown	1·50	9·00

1922. Surch.

102	0.01 on 15c. purple & brn	45	6·25
103	0.02 on 15c. purple & brn	45	7·00
104	0.04 on 15c. purple & brn	45	5·50
105	0.05 on 15c. purple & brn	45	7·00
106	25c. on 5f. violet on green	1·20	7·50
98	60 on 15c. purple and pink	55	35
99	65 on 15c. purple & brown	2·30	6·75
100	85 on 15c. purple & brown	1·90	8·25
101	85 on 75c. pink and grey	2·00	8·25
107	90c. on 75c. pink and red	1·80	3·50
108	1f.25 on 1f. blue	55	3·50
109	1f.50 on 1f. lt blue & blue	1·30	45
110	3f. on 5f. brown and purple	1·40	55
111	10f. on 5f. red and blue	5·50	2·50
112	20f. on 5f. brown & mauve	10·00	8·25

1931. "Colonial Exhibition" key-types.

135	E	40c. green and black	3·75	4·25
136	F	50c. mauve and black	4·00	5·75
137	G	90c. red and black	3·75	4·25
138	H	1f.50 blue and black	6·50	5·50

38 Faidherbe Bridge, Dakar

39 Senegalese Girl

1935

139	38	1c. blue (postage)	35	2·50
140	38	2c. brown	20	3·00
141	38	3c. violet	55	6·75
142	38	4c. blue	45	5·75
143	38	5c. orange	40	1·10
144	38	10c. purple	65	1·50
145	38	15c. black	70	90
146	38	20c. red	80	2·10
147	38	25c. brown	1·30	40
148	38	30c. green	1·20	3·00
149	39	35c. green	1·90	3·00
150	38	40c. red	65	1·00
151	38	45c. green	1·50	2·50
152	A	50c. orange	85	20
153	39	55c. brown	3·00	3·25
154	A	60c. violet	1·00	3·25
155	A	65c. violet	1·90	35
156	A	70c. brown	2·75	6·50
157	A	75c. brown	2·75	1·80
158	39	80c. violet	3·25	2·50
159	A	90c. red	2·50	2·75
160	39	90c. violet	2·30	3·25
161	A	1f. violet	17·00	5·50
162	39	1f. red	2·50	1·40
163	39	1f. brown	70	75
164	A	1f.25 brown	1·80	4·25
165	A	1f.25 red	1·70	5·75
166	A	1f.40 green	1·90	5·50
167	A	1f.50 blue	1·30	55
168	A	1f.60 blue	2·30	4·50
169	A	1f.75 green	2·30	1·70
170	39	1f.75 blue	2·50	3·50
171	A	2f. blue	2·50	60
172	39	2f.25 blue	2·75	3·50
173	39	2f.50 black	2·30	3·00
174	A	3f. green	1·40	1·50
175	A	5f. brown	2·50	1·30
176	A	10f. red	3·75	3·00
177	A	20f. grey	2·50	1·80
178	B	25c. brown (air)	2·30	5·25
179	B	50c. red	2·00	4·50
180	B	1f. purple	1·30	80
181	B	1f.25 green	1·30	2·75
182	B	1f.90 blue	1·70	4·50
183	B	2f. blue	2·30	75
184	B	2f.90 red	1·20	5·50
185	B	3f. green	1·60	1·90
186	C	3f.50 violet	2·75	1·50
187	B	4f.50 green	1·10	3·25
188	C	4f.75 orange	1·90	3·75
189	B	4f.90 brown	2·30	4·00
190	C	6f.50 blue	1·50	3·25
191	B	6f.90 orange	1·80	4·75
192	C	8f. black	3·25	4·00
193	C	15f. red	3·25	3·50

DESIGNS—HORIZ: A, Djourbel Mosque; B, Airplane over village; C, Airplane over camel caravan.

1937. International Exhibition, Paris. As Nos. 168/73 of St.-Pierre and Miquelon.

194	20c. violet	2·00	6·25
195	30c. green	1·30	3·75
196	40c. red	1·30	3·25
197	50c. brown	90	3·50
198	90c. red	1·50	2·00
199	1f.50 blue	1·30	4·50
MS200	120×100 mm. 3f. purple. Imperf	12·00	36·00

1938. International Anti-cancer Fund. As T **38** of St.-Pierre et Miquelon.

201	1f.75+50c. blue	5·50	24·00

40 René Caillié (explorer)

1939. Death Centenary of René Caillié (explorer).

202	40	90c. orange	50	35
203	40	2f. violet	55	45
204	40	2f.25 blue	65	55

1939. New York World's Fair. As T **41** of St.-Pierre et Miquelon.

205	1f.25 red	85	3·75
206	2f.25 blue	1·20	4·50

1939. 150th Anniv of French Revolution. As T **42** of St.-Pierre et Miquelon.

207	45c.+25c. green and black (postage)	9·25	19·00
208	70c.+30c. brown and black	9·25	19·00
209	90c.+35c. orange and black	9·25	19·00
210	1f.25+1f. red and black	9·50	19·00
211	2f.25+2f. blue and black	9·50	19·00
212	4f.75+4f. black & orge (air)	16·00	20·00

1941. National Defence Fund. Surch **SECOURS NATIONAL** and value.

213	+1f. on 50c. (No. 152)	2·75	2·30
214	+2f. on 80c. (No. 158)	8·50	14·50
215	+2f. on 1f.50 (No. 167)	11·00	20·00
216	+3f. on 2f. (No. 171)	8·50	17·00

1942. Air. Colonial Child Welfare Fund. As Nos. **98g/i** of Niger.

216a	1f.50+3f.50 green	65	2·30
216b	2f.+6f. brown	80	4·25
216c	3f.+9f. red	65	2·30

40c "Vocation"

1942. Air. "Imperial Fortnight".

216d	40c	1f.20+1f.80 blue and red	65	4·50

40d Aeroplane over Camel Caravan

1942. Air. As T **40d**, but inscr "SENEGAL" and similar design.

217	40d	50f. green and yellow	2·30	4·50
218	-	100f. blue and red	2·50	5·50

DESIGN—48×26 mm: 100f. Twin-engined airliner landing.

1944. Stamps of 1935 surch.

219	38	1f.50 on 15c. black	1·70	60
220	A	1f.50 on 65c. violet	75	55
221	38	4f.50 on 15c. black	1·00	1·40
222	38	5f.50 on 2c. brown	1·80	1·80
223	A	5f.50 on 65c. violet	1·40	1·00
224	38	10f. on 15c. black	1·80	75
225	A	50f. on 65c. violet	1·50	1·80

1944. No. 202 surch.

226	20f. on 90c. orange	1·80	3·75
227	50f. on 90c. orange	5·25	3·75

42 African Buffalo

1960. Niokolo-Koba National Park.

228	-	5f. purple, black and green	20	10
229	42	10f. purple, black and green	45	15
230	-	15f. purple, brown and sepia	50	30
231	-	20f. brown, green & chest	70	30
232	-	25f. brown, choc & green	1·00	40
233	-	85f. multicoloured	2·25	1·00

ANIMALS—VERT: 5f. Roan antelope; 15f. Warthog; 20f. Giant eland; 85f. Waterbuck. HORIZ: 25f. Bushbuck.

43 African Fish Eagle

1960. Air.

234		50f. multicoloured	2·50	90
235		100f. multicoloured	5·50	1·40
236		200f. multicoloured	10·50	4·50
237		250f. multicoloured	13·50	5·50
238	43	500f. multicoloured	29·00	7·50

BIRDS—VERT: 50f. Carmine bee-eater; 200f. Violet turaco; 250f. Red bishop. HORIZ: 100f. Abyssinian roller.

44 Mother and Child

1961. Independence Commemoration.

239	44	25f. brown, blue and green	55	20

45 Pirogue Race

1961. Sports.

240	-	50c. brown, blue and sepia	10	10
241	45	1f. purple, turquoise & green	10	10
242	-	2f. sepia, bistre and blue	10	10
243	-	30f. purple and red	90	55
244	-	45f. black, blue and brown	1·50	65

DESIGNS: 50c. African wrestling; 2f. Horse race; 30f. African dancers; 45f. Lion game.

46 Senegal Flag, U.N. Emblem and H.Q. Building

1962. First Anniv of Admission of Senegal to U.N.O.

245	46	10f. red, ochre and green	15	15
246	46	30f. green, ochre and red	30	25
247	46	85f. multicoloured	1·10	55

47 I.T.U. Emblems, African Map and Telephonist

1962. First I.T.U. African Plan Sub-Committee Meeting, Dakar.

248	47	25f. multicoloured	55	20

47a European, African and Airliners

1962. Air. "Air Afrique" Airline.

249	47a	25f. purple, brown & green	35	20

47b Campaign Emblem

1962. Malaria Eradication.

250	47b	25f.+5f. turquoise	40	35

47c Union Flag

1962. First Anniv of Union of African and Malagasy States.

251	**47c**	30f. turquoise	40	35

47d Globe and Emblem

1963. Freedom from Hunger.

252	**47d**	25f.+5f. olive, brn & vio	35	35

48 Boxing

1963. Dakar Games. Inscr as in T **48**. Centres brown; inscr and frame colours given.

253	**48**	10f. red and green	15	10
254	-	15f. ochre and blue	20	15
255	-	20f. red and blue	25	15
256	-	25f. green and blue	40	20
257	-	30f. red and green	85	25
258	-	85f. blue	1·75	1·00

DESIGNS—HORIZ: 15f. Diving; 20f. High- jumping. VERT: 25f. Football; 30f. Basketball; 85f. Running.

49 Main Motif of U.P.U. Monument, Berne

1963. Second Anniv of Admission to U.P.U.

259	**49**	10f. red and green	20	15
260	**49**	15f. brown and blue	20	20
261	**49**	30f. blue and brown	45	25

50 "Charaxes varanes"

1963. Butterflies. Butterflies in natural colours; inscr in black; background colours given.

262	**50**	30f. blue	1·00	40
263	-	45f. orange	1·75	60
264	-	50f. yellow	1·75	1·00
265	-	85f. red	4·25	1·75
266	-	100f. blue	5·50	2·50
267	-	500f. green	17·00	7·50

BUTTERFLIES: 45f. "Papilio nireus"; 10f. "Colotis danae"; 85f. "Epiphora bauhiniae"; 100f. "Junonia hierta"; 500f. "Danaus chrysippus".

1963. Air. Second Anniv of African and Malagasian Posts and Telecommunications Union. As No. 36 of Rwanda.

268		85f. multicoloured	1·10	55

51 G. Berger, Owl and "Prospective" (book)

1963. Third Death Anniv of Prof. Gaston Berger (educationalist).

269	**51**	25f. multicoloured	55	20

51a Airline Emblem

1963. Air. First Anniv of "Air Afrique" and "DC-8" Service Inauguration.

270	**51a**	50f. multicoloured	1·25	55

52 Globe, Scales of Justice and Flag

1963. 15th Anniv of Declaration of Human Rights.

271	**52**	60f. multicoloured	90	40

53 Mother and Child

1963. Senegalese Red Cross.

272	**53**	25f. multicoloured	55	25

54 Temple Gods, Abu Simbel

1964. Air. Nubian Monument Preservation Fund.

273	**54**	25f.+5f. brown, green and turquoise	1·40	70

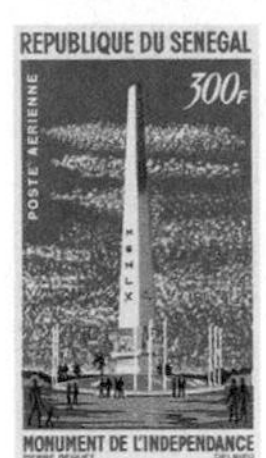

55 Independence Monument

1964. Air.

274	**55**	300f. multicoloured	4·00	2·00

56 Allegorical Figures of Twin Towns

1964. Air. World Twin Towns Federation Congress, Dakar.

275	**56**	150f. brown, black & turq	3·25	1·40

57 Titanium Sand Dredger

1964. Senegal Industries.

276	**57**	5f. brown, turquoise & lake	15	15
277	-	10f. blue, brown and green	15	10
278	-	15f. brown, green and blue	20	10
279	-	20f. purple, bistre and blue	25	10
280	-	25f. black, ochre and blue	65	10
281	-	85f. brown, blue and red	2·25	1·10

DESIGNS: 10f. Titanium sorting works; 15f. Rufisque cement works; 20f. Loading phosphate at Pallo; 25f. Working phosphate at Taiba; 85f. Mineral wharf, Dakar.

58 "Supporting the Globe"

1964. Air. "Europafrique".

282	**58**	50f. multicoloured	1·25	55

59 Basketball

1964. Air. Olympic Games, Tokyo.

283	**59**	85f. brown and blue	2·00	70
284	-	100f. purple and green	2·25	90

DESIGN: 100f. Pole-vaulting.

60 "Syncom 2" Satellite and Rocket

1964. Air. Space Telecommunications.

285	**60**	150f. blue, brown and green	2·25	1·25

60a "Co-operation"

1964. French, African and Malagasy Co-operation.

286	**60a**	100f. brown, red and green	1·75	90

61 Church of Ste. Therese, Dakar

1964. Religious Buildings.

287	**61**	5f. lake, green and blue	10	10
288	-	10f. brown, black and blue	15	10
289	-	15f. slate, brown and blue	45	15

DESIGNS—HORIZ: 10f. Touba Mosque. VERT: 15f. Dakar Mosque.

62 Pres. Kennedy

1964. Air. Pres. Kennedy Commemoration.

290	**62**	100f. brown, yellow & green	2·00	1·00
MS291		90×129 mm. No. 290 (×4)	8·00	4·00

63 Child and Microscope

1965. Anti-leprosy Campaign.

292	**63**	20f. black, green and brown	25	20
293	-	65f. multicoloured	90	45

DESIGN: 65f. Peycouk Village.

64 Haute Casamance

1965. Senegal Landscapes.

294	**64**	25f. green, brown and blue (postage)	25	15
295	-	30f. blue, green and brown	30	15
296	-	45f. turquoise, green & brown	75	55
297	-	100f. black, green and bistre (air)	1·50	1·10

DESIGNS: 30f. Sangalkam; 45f. Senegal River forest region; 100f. Banks of Gambia River, East Senegal (48×27 mm).

65 A. Seck (Director of Posts, 1873–1931)

1965. Postal Services Commemoration.

298	**65**	10f. black and brown	15	15
299	-	15f. brown and green	20	15

DESIGN—HORIZ: 15f. P.T.T. Headquarters, Dakar.

66 Berthon-Ader Telephone

1965. I.T.U. Centenary.

300	**66**	50f. brown, bistre and green	50	30
301	-	60f. red, green and blue	1·00	60
302	-	85f. purple, red and blue	1·10	50

DESIGNS: 60f. Cable-ship "Alsace"; 85f. Picard's submarine telegraph cable relay apparatus.

67 Ploughing with Oxen

1965. Rural Development.

303	**67**	25f. brown, violet and green	35	25
304	-	60f. multicoloured	90	45
305	-	85f. black, red and green	1·25	55

DESIGNS—VERT: 50f. Millet cultivation. HORIZ: 85f. Rice cultivation, Casamance.

68 Goree Pirogue under Sail

1965. Senegal Pirogues. Multicoloured.

306	10f. Type **68**	20	15
307	20f. Large pirogue at Se-umbedioune	35	15
308	30f. One-man pirogue at Fadiouth Island	85	20
309	45f. One-man pirogue on Senegal River	1·50	65

69 Woman holding Child and U.N. Emblems

1965. Air. International Co-operation Year.

310	**69**	50f. brown, green and blue	90	30

70 "Fruit of Cashew Tree"

1965. Fruit. Multicoloured.

311		10f. Type **70**	15	10
312		15f. Papaw	20	15
313		20f. Mango	25	10
314		30f. Groundnuts	65	15

71 "The Gentleman of Fashion"

1966. Goree Puppets.

315	**71**	1f. blue, brown and red	10	10
316	-	2f. orange, brown and blue	10	10
317	-	3f. blue, brown and red	10	10
318	-	4f. green, brown and violet	10	10

PUPPETS: 2f. "The Lady of Fashion"; 3f. "The Pedlar"; 4f. "The Pounder".

72 Tom-tom Player

1966. World Festival of Negro Arts, Dakar ("Announcement").

319	**72**	30f. brown, red and green	75	15

See also Nos. 327/30.

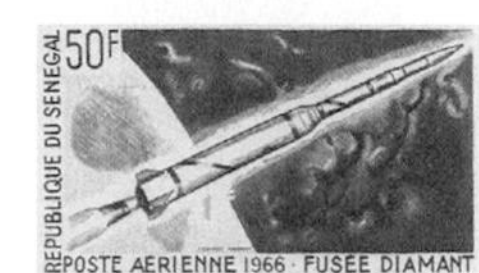

73 Rocket "Diamant"

1966. Air. French Satellites.

320	**73**	50f. red, blue and brown	70	40
321	-	50f. black, brown and green	70	40
322	-	90f. blue, brown and slate	1·75	75

DESIGNS: No. 321, Satellite "A1"; 322, Rocket "Scout" and satellite "FR1".

74 Little Tuna

1966. Senegal Fish. Multicoloured.

323		20f. Type **74**	50	25
324		30f. White grouper	90	35
325		50f. Peacock wrasse	1·90	65
326		100f. West African parrotfish	3·50	1·25

1966. World Festival of Negro Arts, Dakar. As T **72**.

327		15f. lake, orange and blue	15	15
328		30f. lake, yellow and blue	35	20
329		75f. black, lake and blue	1·25	55
330		90f. lake, black and orange	1·40	65
MS331		140×110 mm. Nos. 327/30	3·25	1·60

DESIGNS: 15f. Statuette ("Sculpture"); 30f. Musical instrument ("Music"); 75f. Carving ("Dance"); 90f. Ideogram.

75 Satellite "D 1"

1966. Air. Launching of Satellite "D 1".

332	**75**	100f. blue, lake and violet	1·50	65

76 Arms of Senegal

1966

333	**76**	30f. multicoloured	55	15

76a Douglas DC-8F Jet Trader and "Air Afrique" Emblem

1966. Air. Inauguration of DC-8F Air Services.

334	**76a**	30f. yellow, black & brown	55	20

77 "Argemone mexicana"

1966. Flowers. Multicoloured.

335		45f. Type **77**	1·00	20
336		55f. "Dichrostachys glomerata"	1·00	25
337		60f. "Haemanthus multiflorus"	1·25	35
338		90f. "Adansonia digitata"	1·75	50

78 Couzinet 70 "Arc en Ciel"

1966. Air. 30th Anniv of Disappearance of Jean Mermoz (aviator).

339	**78**	20f. slate, purple and blue	70	20
340	-	35f. slate, brown and green	85	20
341	-	100f. lake, emerald & green	1·50	45
342	-	150f. lake, black and blue	3·00	1·00

DESIGNS—HORIZ: 35f. Latecoere 300 flying boat "Croix du Sud"; 100f. Map of Mermoz's last flight across Atlantic Ocean. VERT: 150f. Jean Mermoz.

79 Port of Ile de Goree

1966. Tourism.

343	**79**	20f. lake, blue and black	20	15
344	-	25f. sepia, green and red	1·75	30
345	-	30f. blue, red and green	30	10
346	-	50f. blue, green and red	50	20
347	-	90f. black, green and blue	1·10	45

DESIGNS: 25f. Liner "France" at Dakar; 30f. N'Gor Hotel and tourist cabins; 50f. N'Gor Bay and Hotel; 90f. Town Hall, Dakar.

80 Laying Water Mains

1967. International Hydrological Decade.

348	**80**	10f. blue, green and brown	15	15
349	-	20f. brown, green and blue	30	20
350	-	30f. blue, orange and black	35	20
351	-	50f. lake, flesh and blue	75	20

DESIGNS—HORIZ: 20f. Cattle at trough. VERT: 30f. Decade emblem; 50f. Obtaining water from primitive well.

81 Terminal Building, Dakar-Yoff Airport

1967. Air.

352	**81**	200f. indigo, blue & brown	2·75	1·00

82 Lions Emblem

1967. 50th Anniv of Lions International.

353	**82**	30f. multicoloured	65	45

83 Blaise Diagne

1967. 95th Birth Anniv of Blaise Diagne (statesman).

354	**83**	30f. brown, green & purple	55	20

84 Spiny Mimosa

1967. Air. Flowers. Multicoloured.

355		100f. Type **84**	2·50	75
356		150f. Barbary fig	3·50	1·40

85 "Les Demoiselles d'Avignon" (Picasso)

1967. Air.

357	**85**	100f. multicoloured	3·00	1·10

86 Carved Eagle and Kudu's Head

1967. "EXPO 67" World Fair, Montreal.

358	**86**	90f. black and red	1·50	50
359	-	150f. multicoloured	2·00	75

DESIGN: 150f. Maple leaf and flags.

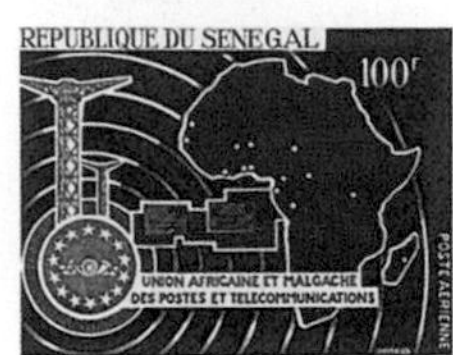

86a Map, Letters and Pylons

1967. Air. Fifth Anniv of UAMPT.

360	**86a**	100f. red, green and violet	90	50

87 I.T.Y. Emblem

1967. International Tourist Year.

361	**87**	50f. black and blue	80	35
362	-	100f. black, green & orange	2·75	1·00

DESIGN: 100f. Tourist photographing hippo-potamus.

88 Currency Tokens

1967. Fifth Anniv of West African Monetary Union.

363	**88**	30f. violet, purple and grey	25	15

89 "Lyre" Stone, Kaffrine

1967. Sixth Pan-American Prehistory Congress, Dakar.

364	**89**	30f. red, blue and green	90	15
365	-	70f. red, brown and blue	1·60	90

DESIGN: 70f. Ancient bowl, Bandiala.

90 Nurse feeding Baby

1967. Senegalese Red Cross.

366	**90**	50f. lake, red and green	50	25

91 Human Rights Emblem

1968. Human Rights Year.

367	**91**	30f. gold and green	35	20

92 Chancellor Adenauer

1968. Air. Adenauer Commemoration.

368	**92**	100f. sepia, red and green	1·40	55
MS369		120×171 mm. No. 368×4	5·50	2·20

93 Weather Balloon, Flourishing Plants and W.M.O. Emblem

1968. Air. World Meteorological Day.

370	**93**	50f. green, blue and black	90	40

94 Parliament Building, Dakar

1968. Inter-Parliamentary Union Meeting, Dakar.

371	**94**	30f. red	55	15

95 Spiny Lobster

1968. Marine Crustacea. Multicoloured.

372		10f. Type **95**	15	10
373		20f. Sea crawfish	25	15
374		35f. Prawn	75	20
375		100f. Gooseneck barnacle	2·40	1·00

96 Lesser Pied Kingfisher

1968. Birds. Multicoloured.

376		5f. Type **96** (postage)	35	10
377		15f. African jacana	65	10
378		70f. African darter	2·25	1·10
379		250f. Village weaver (air)	6·75	1·50
380		300f. Comb duck	10·50	2·50
381		500f. Bateleur	18·00	6·75

Nos. 379/81 are 45½×26 mm.

97 Ox and Syringe

1968. Campaign for Prevention of Cattle Plague.

382	**97**	30f. red, green and blue	55	20

98 Hurdling

1968. Air. Olympic Games, Mexico.

383	**98**	20f. brown, green and blue	45	15
384	-	30f. brown, ochre & purple	65	15
385	-	50f. lake, brown and blue	1·25	35
386	-	75f. bistre, brown and green	2·00	60

DESIGNS: 30f. Throwing the javelin; 50f. Judo; 75f. Basketball.

98a "Young Girl reading a Letter" (J. Raoux)

1968. Air. "Philexafrique". Stamp Exhibition, Abidjan (1st issue) (1969).

387	**98a**	100f. multicoloured	3·00	2·25

99 Senegalese Boy

1968. 20th Anniv of W.H.O.

388	**99**	30f. black, red and green	25	25
389	**99**	45f. black, green and brown	60	20

101 Faculty Building

1969. Faculty of Medicine and Pharmaceutics, and Sixth "Medical Days", Dakar.

391	**101**	30f. blue and green	55	20
392	-	50f. green, red and brown	60	25

DESIGN—VERT: 50f. Emblem of "Medical Days".

101a Modern Dakar and Senegal Stamp of 1935

1969. Air. "Philexafrique". Stamp Exhibition, Abidjan, Ivory Coast (2nd issue).

393	**101a**	50f. violet, slate and green	1·25	1·25

102 Panet, Camels and Route-map

1969. 150th Birth Anniv of Leopold Panet, first Explorer of the Mauritanian Sahara.

394	**102**	75f. brown and blue	1·50	75

103 AITY Emblem

1969. Air. African International Tourist Year.

395	**103**	100f. red, green and blue	1·10	45

104 I.L.O. Emblem

1969. 50th Anniv of I.L.O.

396	**104**	30f. black and turquoise	25	15
397	**104**	45f. black and red	40	20

105 Pres. Lamine Gueye

1969. Air. President Gueye Memorial.

398	**105**	30f. black, buff and brown	25	15
399	-	45f. black, blue and brown	65	20
MS400		120×160 mm. Nos. 398/9×2	1·90	80

DESIGN: 45f. Pres. Lamine Gueye (different).

106 Arms of Casamance

1969. Senegal Arms. Multicoloured.

401		15f. Type **106**	15	10
402		20f. Arms of Ile de Goree	45	15

107 Bank Emblem

1969. Fifth Anniv of African Development Bank.

403	**107**	30f. brown, green and slate	25	15
404	**107**	45f. brown and green	35	20

108 Mahatma Gandhi

1969. Birth Centenary of Mahatma Gandhi.

405	**108**	50f. multicoloured	45	25
MS406		100×129 mm. No. 405 in block of 4	1·90	1·20

109 "Transmission of Thought" (O. Faye)

1969. Air. Tapestries. Multicoloured.

407		25f. Type **109**	60	20
408		30f. "The Blue Cock" (Mamadou Niang)	35	20
409		45f. "The Fairy" (Papa Sidi Diop)	1·25	50
410		50f. "Fari" (A. N'Diaye)	1·50	75
411		75f. "Lunaris" (J. Lurcat)	2·00	70

SIZES—VERT: 30f., 45f. 37×49 mm. HORIZ: 50f. 49×37 mm.

110 Baila Bridge

1969. Air. Europafrique.

412	**110**	100f. multicoloured	1·25	45

111 Rotary Emblem and "Sailing Ship"

1969. 30th Anniv of Dakar Rotary Club.

413	**111**	30f. yellow, black and blue	35	20

112 Airliner, Map and Airport

1969. Tenth Anniv of ASECNA.

414	**112**	100f. slate	90	35

113 Cape Skiring, Casamance

1969. Tourism.

415	**113**	20f. green, lake and blue	45	15
416	-	30f. lake, brown and blue	65	15
417	-	35f. black, brown and blue	2·50	65
418	-	45f. lake and blue	1·10	55

DESIGNS: 30f. Tourist camp, Niokolo-Koba; 35f. Herd of African elephants, Niokolo-Koba Park; 45f. Millet granaries on stilts, Fadiouth Island.

114 Lecrivain, Latecoere 25 Airplane and Route

1970. Air. 40th Anniv of Disappearance of Emile Lecrivain (aviator).

419	**114**	50f. lake, slate and green	1·00	40

115 Bottle-nosed Dolphins

1970

420	**115**	50f. multicoloured	2·50	1·10

116 R. Maran (Martinique)

1970. Air. Negro Celebrities (1st series).

421	**116**	30f. brown, green and lake	25	15
422	-	45f. brown, blue and pink	65	25
423	-	50f. brown, green & yellow	75	35

PORTRAITS: 45f. M. Garvey (Jamaica); 50f. Dr. P. Mars (Haiti).

See also Nos. 457/60.

117 Sailing Pirogue and Obelisk

1970. Air. Tenth Anniv of Independence.

424	**117**	500f. multicoloured	6·50	3·25
MS425		72×104 mm. No. 424 (sold at 600f.)	7·75	3·75

118 Lenin

1970. Birth Centenary of Lenin.

426	**118**	30f. brown, stone and red	1·40	55
MS427		67×97 mm. 50f. As No. 426 but larger	2·20	90

119 Bay of Naples, and Post Office, Dakar

1970. Air. Tenth "Europa" Stamp Exn, Naples.

428	**119**	100f. multicoloured	1·25	55

1970. New U.P.U. Headquarters Building, Berne. As T **101** of St. Pierre et Miquelon.

429		30f. plum, blue and lake	25	15
430		45f. brown, lake and green	45	20

121 Nagakawa and Mt. Fuji

1970. Air. World Fair "EXPO 70", Osaka, Japan.

431	-	25f. red, green and lake	45	15
432	**121**	75f. red, blue and green	1·25	30
433	-	150f. red, brown and blue	1·90	70

DESIGNS—VERT: 25f. "Woman playing guitar" (Hokusai) and Sun tower; 150f. "Nanboku Beauty" (Shuncho).

122 Harbour Quayside, Dakar

1970. Air. Industrial and Urban Development.

434	**122**	30f. blue, black and red	75	15
435	-	100f. brown, green & slate	1·40	45

DESIGN: 100f. Aerial view of city centre, Dakar.

123 Beethoven, Napoleon and "Evocation of Eroica" Symphony

1970. Air. Birth Bicentenary of Beethoven.

436	**123**	50f. brown, orange and green	1·25	35
437	-	100f. red and blue	2·50	1·25

DESIGN: 100f. Beethoven with quillpen and scroll.

124 Heads of Four Races

1970. Air. 25th Anniv of U.N.O.

438	**124**	100f. multicoloured	1·60	90

125 Looms and Textile Works, Thies

1970. "Industrialization".

439	**125**	30f. red, blue and green	30	15
440	-	45f. blue, brown and red	65	20

DESIGN: 45f. Fertilizer plant, Dakar.

126 Scouts in Camp

1970. First African Scouting Conference, Dakar. Multicoloured.

441		30f. Type **126**	30	20
442		100f. Scout badge, Lord Baden-Powell and map	1·40	45

127 Three Heads and Sun

1970. International Education Year.

443	**127**	25f. brown, blue & orange	25	15
444	-	40f. multicoloured	45	20

DESIGN: 40f. Map of Africa on Globe, and two heads.

128 Arms of Senegal

1970

445	**128**	30f. multicoloured	35	15
446	**128**	35f. multicoloured	35	15
446a	**128**	50f. multicoloured	35	15
446b	**128**	65f. multicoloured	35	15
803	**128**	95f. multicoloured	35	30

129 De Gaulle, Map, Ears of Wheat and Cogwheel

1970. Air. "De Gaulle the De-colonizer". Multicoloured.

447		50f. Type **129**	1·25	90
448		100f. De Gaulle, and map within "sun"	3·00	1·90

130 Refugees

1971. 20th Anniv of U.N. High Commissioner for Refugees. Multicoloured.

449		40f. Type **130** (postage)	65	20
450		100f. Building house (air)	1·10	80

No. 450 is 46×27 mm.

131 "Mbayang" Horse

1971. Horse-breeding Improvement Campaign.

451		25f. "Madjiguene"	65	40
452		40f. Type **131**	90	45
453		100f. "Pass"	2·25	1·50
454		125f. "Pepe"	2·75	1·60

132 European Girl and African Boy

1971. Racial Equality Year. Multicoloured.

455		30f. Type **132**	25	15
456		50f. People of four races (horiz) (37×30 mm)	80	25

133 Phillis Wheatley

1971. Air. Negro Celebrities (2nd series). Multicoloured.

457		25f. Type **133**	20	15
458		40f. J. E. K. Aggrey	35	20
459		60f. A. Le Roy Locke	80	25
460		100f. Booker T. Washington	1·10	45

134 "Telephones"

1971. World Telecommunications Day.

461	**134**	30f. brown, green & purple	25	15
462	-	40f. brown, red and blue	65	20

DESIGN: 40f. "Telecommunications" theme.

135 "Napoleon as First Consul" (Ingres)

1971. Air. 150th Death Anniv of Napoleon. Multicoloured.

463		15f. Type **135**	55	25
464		25f. "Napoleon in 1809" (Lefevre)	70	30
465		35f. "Napoleon on his Death-bed" (Rouget)	1·25	45
466		50f. "The Awakening to Immortality" (bronze by Rude)	2·25	1·10

136 Pres. Nasser

1971. Air. Nasser Commemoration.

467	**136**	50f. multicoloured	45	25

137 Hayashida (drummer)

1971. 13th World Scout Jamboree, Asagiri, Japan. Multicoloured.

468		35f. Type **137**	65	15
469		50f. Japonica	90	45
470		65f. Judo	1·25	55
471		75f. Mt. Fuji	1·60	90

138 A. Nobel

1971. Air. 75th Death Anniv of Alfred Nobel (scientist and philanthropist).

472	**138**	100f. multicoloured	1·50	60

139 Persian Flag and Senegal Arms

1971. Air. 2500th Anniv of Persian Empire.

473	**139**	200f. multicoloured	2·25	1·00

140 Map and Emblem

1971. 25th Anniv of UNICEF. Multicoloured.

474		35f. Type **140**	35	20
475		100f. Nurse, children and UNICEF emblem	1·25	55

141 UAMPT Headquarters, Brazzaville, and arms of Senegal

1971. Air. Tenth Anniv of UAMPT.

476	**141**	100f. multicoloured	1·10	40

142 Louis Armstrong

1971. Air. Louis Armstrong Commemoration.

477	**142**	150f. brown and gold	3·75	1·60

143 Trying for Goal

1971. Sixth African Basketball Championships, Dakar. Multicoloured.

478		35f. Type **143**	55	15
479		40f. Players reaching for ball	75	25
480		75f. Championships emblem	1·25	60

144 Ice-skating

1971. Air. Winter Olympic Games, Sapporo, Japan. Multicoloured.

481		5f. Type **144**	15	10
482		10f. Bobsleighing	15	10
483		125f. Alpine skiing	1·75	60

145 "Il Fonteghetto della Farina" (detail, Canaletto)

1972. Air. UNESCO "Save Venice" Campaign. Multicoloured.

484		50f. Type **145**	90	55
485		100f. "Giudecca e S. Giorgio Maggiore" (detail, Guardi) (vert)	1·90	1·10

146 "Albouri and Queen Seb Fall" (scene from "The Exile of Albouri")

1972. International Theatre Day. Multicoloured.

486		35f. Type **146** (postage)	65	20
487		40f. Scene from "The Merchant of Venice"	65	25
488		150f. Daniel Sorano as "Shylock" ("The Merchant of Venice") (vert) (air)	3·25	1·50

147 Human Heart

1972. World Heart Month.

489	**147**	35f. brown and blue	25	15
490	-	40f. purple, green & emerald	55	20

DESIGN: 40f. Doctor and patient.

148 Vegetation in Desert

1972. U.N. Environmental Conservation Conf, Stockholm. Multicoloured.

491		35f. Type **148** (postage)	65	20
492		100f. Oil slick on shore (air)	1·60	60

149 Tartarin of Tarascon shooting Lion

1972. 75th Death Anniv of Alphonse Daudet (writer).

493	**149**	40f. red, green and brown	1·10	30
494	-	100f. brown, lt blue & blue	1·25	50

DESIGN: 100f. Daudet and scene from "Tartarin de Tarascon".

150 Musical Instruments

1972. Belgica 72 Stamp Exhibition, Brussels. Sheet 111×95 mm.

MS495	**150**	150f. red	2·20	75

151 Wrestling

1972. Olympic Games, Munich. Multicoloured.

496		15f. Type **151**	20	15
497		20f. Running (100 m)	45	15
498		100f. Basketball	1·40	45
499		125f. Judo	1·75	55
MS500		91×71 mm. 240f. Torch runner	2·50	1·10

152 Emperor Haile Selassie and Flags

1972. Air. Emperor Haile Selassie's 80th Birthday.

501	**152**	100f. multicoloured	1·25	55

153 Children reading Book

1972. International Book Year.

502	**153**	50f. multicoloured	45	20

154 "Senegalese Elegance"

1972. (1st issue).

502a	**154**	5f. blue	10	10
502b	**154**	10f. red	15	10
502c	**154**	15f. orange	15	10
502d	**154**	20f. purple	15	10
503	**154**	25f. black	20	10
503a	**154**	30f. brown	15	10
504	**154**	40f. blue	55	10
504a	**154**	45f. orange	10	10
504b	**154**	50f. red	35	10
504c	**154**	60f. green	60	10
504d	**154**	75f. purple	55	35
504e	**154**	90f. red	65	35
504f	**154**	125f. blue	80	20
504g	**154**	145f. orange	90	25
504h	**154**	180f. blue	1·10	45

See also Nos. 1334/45 and 1544/6.

155 Alexander Pushkin

1972. Pushkin (writer) Commemoration.

505	**155**	100f. purple and pink	1·50	50

156 Africans and 500f. Coin

1972. Tenth Anniv of West African Monetary Union.

506	**156**	40f. brown, grey and blue	60	15

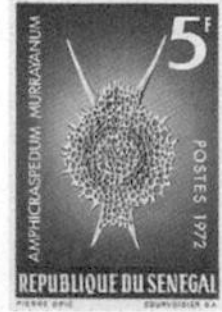

157 "Amphicraspedum murrayanum"

1972. Protozoans and Marine Life. Multicoloured.

507		5f. Type **157** (postage)	10	10
508		10f. "Pterocanium tricolpum"	15	10
509		15f. "Ceratospyris polygona"	75	10
510		20f. "Cortiniscus typicus"	20	10
511		30f. "Theopera cortina"	75	10
512		50f. Swordfish (air)	1·40	50
513		65f. Killer whale	1·75	65
514		75f. Whale shark	2·50	1·25
515		125f. Fin whale	4·25	1·50

Nos. 512/15 are size 45×27 mm.

1972. No. 353 surch 1872-1972 and value.

516	**83**	100f. on 30f. brown, green and chestnut	1·40	60

159 Melchior

1972. Christmas. Nativity Scene and Three Kings. Multicoloured.

517		10f. Type **159**	15	15
518		15f. Gaspard	20	15
519		40f. Balthazar	90	20
520		60f. Joseph	1·10	40
521		100f. Mary and Baby Jesus (African representation)	1·50	65

160 "Sharing the Load"

1973. Europafrique.

522	**160**	65f. black and green	1·00	30

161 Palace of the Republic

1973. Air.

523	**161**	100f. multicoloured	1·10	60

162 Station and Aerial

1973. Inauguration of Satellite Earth Station, Gandoul.

524	**162**	40f. multicoloured	35	20

163 Hotel Teranga

1973. Air. Opening of Hotel Teranga, Dakar.

525	**163**	100f. multicoloured	1·10	60

164 "Lions" African Emblem

1973. Air. 15th Lions International District 403 Congress, Dakar.

526	**164**	150f. multicoloured	1·75	85

165 Stages of Eclipse

1973. Eclipse of the Sun. Multicoloured.

527		35f. Type **165**	55	15
528		65f. Eclipse in diagramatic form	90	25
529		150f. Eclipse and "Skylab 1"	1·90	75

166 Symbolic Torch

1973. Tenth Anniv of Organization of African Unity.

530	**166**	75f. multicoloured	80	40

1973. "Drought Relief". African Solidarity. No. 451 surch **SECHERESSE SOLIDARITE AFRICAINE** and value.

531		100f. on 25f. multicoloured	1·50	75

168 "Couple with Mimosa" (Chagall)

1973. Air.

532	**168**	200f. multicoloured	5·00	2·25

169 "Riccione 1973"

1973. Air. Int Stamp Exhibition, Riccione (Italy).

533	**169**	100f. violet, green and red	1·50	55

170 Crane with Letter and Telecommunications Emblem

1973. 12th Anniv of African and Malagasy Posts and Telecommunications Union.

534	**170**	100f. violet, green and red	1·10	35

171 W.H.O. Emblem and Child

1973. Centenary of W.M.O.

535	**171**	50f. multicoloured	35	15

172 Interpol H.Q., Paris

1973. 50th Anniv of International Criminal Police Organization (Interpol).

536	**172**	75f. brown, blue and green	1·00	40

173 Pres. Kennedy

1973. Tenth Death Anniv of President Kennedy. Sheet 90×106 mm.

MS537	**173**	150f. blue	1·75	50

174 Flame Emblem and People

1973. 25th Anniv of Declaration of Human Rights. Multicoloured.

538		35f. Type **174**	55	15
539		65f. Emblem and drummer	70	25

175 R. Follereau (rehabilitation pioneer) and Map

1973. Air. Cent of Discovery of Leprosy Bacillus.

540	**175**	40f. brown, green & violet	75	15
541	-	100f. purple, red and green	1·50	50

DESIGN: 100f. Dr. G. Hansen (discoverer of leprosy bacillus) and laboratory equipment.

176 "Key" Emblem

1973. Air. World Twinned Towns Congress, Dakar. Multicoloured.

542		50f. Type **176**	75	20
543		125f. Arms of Dakar and meeting of citizens (horiz)	1·50	50

177 Amilcar Cabral and Weapons

1974. Amilcar Cabral (Guinea Bissau guerilla leader) Commemoration.

544	**177**	75f. multicoloured	90	40

178 Peters's Finfoot

1974. Air. Birds of Djoudj Park. Multicoloured.

545	1f. Type **178**	15	10
546	2f. White spoonbills	15	10
547	3f. Crowned cranes	15	10
548	4f. Little egret	30	10
549	250f. Greater flamingos (gold value)	6·50	2·25
550	250f. Greater flamingos (black value)	6·50	2·25

179 "Tiger attacking Wild Horse"

1974. Air. Paintings by Delacroix. Multicoloured.

551	150f. Type **179**	2·25	80
552	200f. "Tiger-hunting"	2·75	1·25

180 Athletes on Podium

1974. National Youth Week. Multicoloured.

553	35f. Type **180**	50	15
554	40f. Dancer with mask	50	20

181 World Cup, Footballers and "Munich"

1974. World Cup Football Championship. Footballers and locations.

555	25f. Type **181**	15	10
556	40f. "Hamburg"	40	15
557	65f. "Hanover"	60	20
558	70f. "Stuttgart"	1·00	25

182 U.P.U. Emblem, Letters and Transport

1974. Centenary of U.P.U.

559	**182**	100f. green, blue and lilac	1·75	75

183 Archway, and Africans at Work

184 Dakar, "Gateway to Africa"

1974. First Dakar International Fair.

560	**183**	100f. brown, orange and blue (postage)	1·00	35
561	**184**	350f. silver (air)	4·50	
562	**184**	1500f. gold	20·00	

Nos. 561/2 are embossed on foil.

1975. West Germany's Victory in World Cup Football Championship, Munich. No. 566 surch **200F ALLEMAGNE RFA–HOLLANDE 2 – 1.**

563	200f. on 40f. multicoloured	2·00	1·25

186 Pres. Senghor and King Baudouin

1975. Visit of King Baudouin of the Belgians.

564	**186**	65f. blue and purple	50	25
565	**186**	100f. green and orange	1·25	45

187 I.L.O. Emblem

1975. Labour Day.

566	**187**	125f. multicoloured	1·10	45

188 "Apollo" and "Soyuz" Spacecraft

1975. Air. "Apollo"–"Soyuz" Space Co-operation Project.

567	**188**	125f. green, blue and red	1·25	60

189 Spanish "Stamp", Globe and Letters

1975. "Espana 75" (Madrid) and "Arphila 75" (Paris) International Stamp Exhibitions.

568	**189**	55f. red, blue and green	85	30
569	-	95f. light brown and brown	2·00	70

DESIGN: 95f. Head of Apollo and "Arphila" Emblem.

190 Classroom and Tractor

1975. Technical Education.

570	**190**	85f. brown, blue and black	75	30

191 Dr. Schweitzer

1975. Birth Centenary of Dr. Albert Schweitzer.

571	**191**	85f. lilac and green	90	55

192 Soldier, Flag and Map of Sinai Desert 1973–74

1975. Senegalese Battalion with U.N.

572	**192**	100f. multicoloured	90	40

193 Stamps and Map of Italy

1975. Air. Riccione Stamp Exhibition.

573	**193**	125f. brown, red and lilac	1·25	75

194 Woman pounding Maize

1975. International Women's Year. Multicoloured.

574	55f. Type **194**	65	20
575	75f. Mother and child with woman doctor (horiz)	90	25

1975. Air. "Apollo"–"Soyuz" Space Link. Optd **JONCTION 17 Juil. 1975.**

576	**188**	125f. green, blue and red	1·40	60

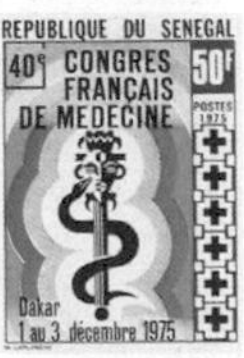

196 Stylized Caduceus

1975. French Medical Congress, Dakar.

577	**196**	50f. multicoloured	55	15

197 "Massacre of Boston" (A. Chappel)

1975. Air. Bicentenary of American Revolution. (1st issue).

578	**197**	250f. brown, red and blue	2·75	1·00
579	-	500f. red and blue	5·50	2·75

DESIGN: 500f. Siege of Yorktown.

See also No. 593.

198 Emblem on Map of Africa

1976. International "Rights of Man" and Namibia Conferences, Dakar.

580	**198**	125f. multicoloured	60	30

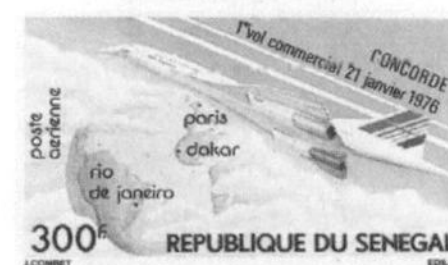

199 Concorde and Flight Locations

1976. Air. Concorde's First Commercial Flight.

581	**199**	300f. multicoloured	4·50	2·25

See also No. 646.

200 Deep-sea Fishing

1976. "Expo", Okinawa. Multicoloured.

582	140f. Type **200**	3·25	1·60
583	200f. Yacht-racing	2·25	1·25

201 Serval

1976. Basse Casamance National Park. Fauna. Multicoloured.

584	2f. Type **201**	10	10
585	3f. Bar-tailed godwit (marsh bird)	60	10
586	4f. Bush pig	10	10
587	5f. African fish eagle	1·60	30
588	250f. Sitatunga (males)	3·25	1·50
589	250f. Sitatunga (females)	3·25	1·50

202 Alexander Graham Bell

1976. Telephone Centenary.

590	**202**	175f. multicoloured	1·40	85

203 Map of Africa

1976. G.A.D.E.F. Scientific and Cultural Days.

591	**203**	60f. multicoloured	35	20

204 Heads on Graphs

1976. First Population Census.

592	**204**	65f. multicoloured	65	25

205 Jefferson reading Independence Declaration

1976. Bicentenary of American Revolution (2nd issue).

593	**205**	50f. black, red and blue	65	20

206 Plant Cultivation

1976. Operation "Sahel Vert".

594	**206**	60f. multicoloured	35	20

207 Scouts around Campfire

1976. First All African Scouts Jamboree, Jos, Nigeria. Multicoloured.

595	80f. Type **207**	45	35
596	100f. Emblem and map (vert)	90	45

208 Swimming 209 Basketball

1976. Olympic Games, Montreal. Multicoloured.

597	5f. Type **208** (postage)	10	10
598	10f. Weightlifting	10	10
599	15f. Hurdling (horiz)	15	10
600	20f. Horse-jumping (horiz)	15	10
601	25f. Steeplechasing (horiz)	15	10
602	50f. Wrestling (horiz)	55	15
603	60f. Hockey	55	20
604	65f. Running	65	20
605	70f. Gymnastics	75	25
606	100f. Cycling (horiz)	1·10	30
607	400f. Boxing (horiz) (air)	3·75	40
607a	500f. Judo	4·50	1·10
608	1000f. Basketball (41×41 mm)	7·25	3·75
608a	1500f. Running (41×41 mm)	11·00	5·50
MS609	Two sheets (a) 121×83 mm. 400f. Aerial view of stadium (58×40 mm); (b) 118×81 mm. 500f. Front view of stadium (58×40 mm)	8·50	1·70
MS609a	Two sheets. As T **209**. (a) 120×90 mm. 1000f. Boxing; (b) 90×120 mm. 1500f. Long Jump	18·00	9·50

210 Emblem and Map

1976. President Senghor's 70th Birthday. Multicoloured.

610	40f. Type **210**	25	20
611	60f. Star over world map	35	25
612	70f. Technicians and symbol	75	30
613	200f. President Senghor and extended hands	1·90	75

211 Harvesting Tomatoes

1976. Tomato Production.

614	**211**	180f. multicoloured	2·25	1·25

212 Concorde and Route Plan

1976. Air. Dakar International Fair.

615	**212**	500f. silver	5·50	
616	**212**	1500f. gold	20·00	

213 Black Peoples' "Charter"

1977. Black Peoples' Day.

617	**213**	60f. multicoloured	65	25

214 Mohammed Ali and Joe Frazier

1977. World Boxing Championship.

618	**214**	60f. black and blue	50	15
619	-	150f. black and green	1·75	50

DESIGN—HORIZ: 150f. Mohammed Ali landing punch.

215 Dancer and Musicians

1977. Second World Black and African Festival of Arts and Culture, Lagos (Nigeria). Multicoloured.

620	50f. Type **215**	40	20
621	75f. Statuette and masks	85	25
622	100f. Statuette and dancers	1·00	45

216 Cog Wheels

1977. First Anniv of Dakar Industrial Zone.

623	**216**	70f. brown and green	40	20

217 Hauling in Net

1977. Fishing. Multicoloured.

624	25f. Type **217** (postage)		
625	5f. Fishing by trawl-line (air)		
626	10f. Harpooning		
627	15f. Pirogue breasting wave		
628	20f. Displaying prize catch		

218 Burnt Tree in "Flame"

1977. Fight Against Forest Fires. Multicoloured.

629	40f. Type **218**	55	15
630	60f. Firefighting vehicle (horiz)	1·00	55

219 Industrial and Pre-Industrial Communication

1977. World Telecommunications Day. Multicoloured.

631	80f. Type **219**	45	35
632	100f. Printed circuit (vert)	70	45

220 Arms of Senegal

1977. Tenth Anniv of International French Language Council. Multicoloured.

633	65f. Type **220**	35	20
634	250f. As No. 831 of Rwanda	2·00	1·00

221 Woman rowing on River

1977. "Amphilex 1977" International Stamp Exhibition, Amsterdam. Multicoloured.

635	50f. Type **221**	30	25
636	125f. Senegalese woman	1·00	45

222 "Viking" and Control Centre

1977. Air. "Viking" Space Mission to Mars.

637	**222**	300f. multicoloured	2·25	1·25

223 Class in Front of Blackboard

1977. Literacy Week. Multicoloured.

638	60f. Type **223**	35	25
639	65f. Man with alphabet table	35	25

224 "Mercury and Argus" (Rubens)

1977. Paintings. Multicoloured.

640	20f. Type **224**	10	10
641	25f. "Daniel and the Lions" (Rubens)	15	10
642	40f. "The Empress" (Titian)	20	15
643	60f. "Flora" (Titian)	55	20
644	65f. "Jo la belle Irlandaise" (Courbet)	75	20
645	100f. "The Painter's Studio" (Courbet)	1·40	55

1977. Air. First Paris–New York Commercial Flight of Concorde. Optd **22.11.77 PARIS NEW-YORK**.

646	**199**	300f. multicoloured	4·25	2·25

226 "Adoration of the Kings"

1977. Christmas. Multicoloured.

647	20f. Type **226**	10	10
648	25f. Fanal (celebration)	15	10
649	40f. Family Christmas tree	55	15
650	100f. "Three Wise Men" (horiz)	1·00	40

227 Wrestler

1978. Tourism. Multicoloured.

651	10f. Type **227**	10	10
652	30f. Soumbedioun Regatta (canoes)	20	15
653	65f. Soumbedioun Regatta (race) (horiz)	45	25
654	100f. Dancers (horiz)	95	50

228 Dakar Cathedral and Parthenon, Athens

1978. UNESCO Campaign for Protection of Monuments.

655	**228**	75f. multicoloured	35	25

229 Solar Pump

1978. Sources of Energy. Multicoloured.

656	50f. Type **229**	25	15
657	95f. Electricity power station	75	30

230 Caspian and Royal Terns

1978. Saloum Delta National Park. Multicoloured.

658	5f. Type **230**	20	15
659	10f. Pink-backed pelicans	50	15
660	15f. Grey Heron and warthog	1·00	40
661	20f. Greater flamingoes	1·00	40
662	150f. Grey heron and royal terns	5·00	1·50
663	150f. Abyssinian ground hornbill and warthog	5·00	1·50

231 Dome of the Rock

1978. Palestine Freedom-Fighters.

664	**231**	60f. multicoloured	55	20

232 Mahatma Gandhi

1978. Apostles of Non-violence. Multicoloured.

665	125f. Type **232**	85	50
666	150f. Martin Luther King	1·25	60
MS667	85×73 mm. 200f.×2 As Nos. 665/6	2·20	1·20

233 Jenner and Vaccination of Children

1978. Global Eradication of Smallpox.

668	**233**	60f. multicoloured	55	20

234 Players, and Flags of Group 1 Countries

1978. World Cup Football Championship, Argentina. Multicoloured.

669	25f. Type **234**	15	10
670	40f. Players and flags of Group 2 countries	30	15
671	65f. Players and flags of Group 3 countries	45	20
672	100f. Players and flags of Group 4 countries	85	30
MS673	Two sheets, each 99×82 mm. (a) 100f. As No. 670, 150f. Type **234**; (b) 75f. As No. 672, 125f. As No. 671	3·75	1·50

235 Symbols of Technology, Equipment and Industrialization

1978. Third International Fair, Dakar.

674	**235**	110f. multicoloured	75	30

236 Wright Brothers and Wright Type A

1978. Conquest of Space. Multicoloured.

675	75f. Type **236** (75th anniv of first powered flight)	65	20
676	100f. Yuri Gagarin (10th death anniv of first cosmonaut)	1·00	30
677	200f. "Apollo 8" (10th anniv of first manned moon orbit)	1·60	85
MS678	96×160 mm. 150f. Type **236**; 250f. As No. 676; 300f. As No. 677	7·25	2·30

237 Henri Dunant and Children's Ward

1978. 150th Birth Anniv of Henri Dunant (founder of the Red Cross).

679	**237**	5f. blue, black and red	10	10
680	-	20f. multicoloured	15	10

DESIGN: 20f. Henri Dunant and scenes of Red Cross aid.

237a Western Capercaillie and Schleswig-Holstein 1850 1s. stamp

1978. Air. "Philexafrique" Stamp Exhibition, Libreville, Gabon and International Stamp Fair, Essen, West Germany. Multicoloured.

681	100f. Type **237a**	2·25	1·60
682	100f. Lion and Senegal 1960 200f. Violet turaco stamp	2·25	1·60

238 Telecommunications

1978. Post Office Achievements. Multicoloured.

683	50f. Type **238**	25	15
684	60f. Social welfare	30	20
685	65f. Travelling post offce	55	20

239 Doctor with Students

1979. Ninth Medical Days, Dakar. Multicoloured.

686	50f. Type **239**	25	15
687	100f. Problems of pollution	70	45

240 Agriculture

1979. Professional Pride. Multicoloured.

688	30f. Type **240**	15	10
689	150f. Symbols of progress	1·00	45

241 Open Air Class

1979. S.O.S. Children's Village. Multicoloured.

690	40f. Type **241**	20	15
691	60f. View of village	30	20

242 Young Child

1979. International Year of the Child. Multicoloured.

692	60f. Type **242**	30	20
693	65f. Children with book	30	20

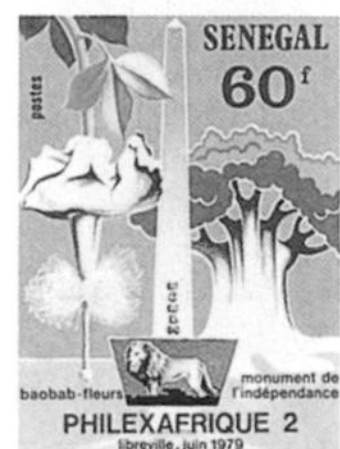

243 Baobab Flower and Tree and Independence Monument

1979. "Philexafrique" Stamp Exhibition, Libreville, Gabon. Multicoloured.

694	60f. Type **243**	1·25	90
695	150f. Drum, early telegraph apparatus and dish aerial (square, 36×36 mm)	2·50	1·60

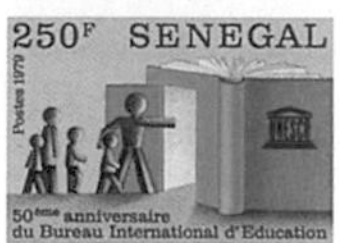

244 Children ushered into Open Book

1979. 50th Anniv of International Bureau of Education.

696	**244**	250f. multicoloured	1·40	80

245 Hill and Senegal 100f. Stamp of 1960

1979. Death Centenary of Sir Rowland Hill.

697	**245**	500f. multicoloured	4·75	2·75

246 "Black Trees"

1979. Paintings by Friedensreich Hundertwasser. Multicoloured.

698	60f. Type **246**	1·10	65
699	100f. "Head"	2·25	1·00
700	200f. "Rainbow Windows"	3·25	1·60
MS701	Three sheets each 190×260 mm. (a) No. 698×4; (b) No. 699×4; (c) No. 700×4	27·00	14·00

247 Start of Race

1980. First African Athletic Championships. Multicoloured.

702	20f. Type **247**	15	10
703	25f. Javelin	15	10
704	50f. Passing the relay baton	25	10
705	100f. Discus	75	30

248 Musicians

1980. Mudra African Arts Festival.

706	50f. Type **248**	40	15
707	100f. Dancers	85	25
708	200f. Dancers and drummer	1·50	70

249 Lions Emblem

1980. 22nd Congress of Lions' Club District 403, Dakar.

709	**249**	100f. multicoloured	75	25

250 Chimpanzees

1980. Niokolo-Koba National Park. Multicoloured.

710	40f. Type **250**	25	10
711	60f. African elephants	45	20
712	65f. Giant elands	75	20
713	100f. Spotted hyenas	1·00	30
714	200f. Wildlife on the savannah	3·00	70
715	200f. Simenti Hotel	3·00	70
MS716	133×98 mm. 125f.×4, As No. 710/13	2·50	85

Nos. 714/15 were issued together, se-tenant, forming a composite deisgn.

251 Watering Sapling

1980. Tree Planting Year.

717	**251**	60f. multicoloured	75	25
718	**251**	65f. multicoloured	95	30

252 Women with Bowls of Rice Flour and Electric Mill

1980. Rural Women. Multicoloured.

719	50f. Street market (horiz)	25	15
720	100f. Type **252**	90	30
721	200f. Drawing water (horiz)	1·50	70

253 Wrestling

1980. Olympic Games, Moscow. Multicoloured.

722	60f. Type **253**	30	20
723	65f. Running	30	20
724	70f. Games emblems	35	25
725	100f. Judo	45	30
726	200f. Basketball	1·25	70
MS727	Two sheets each 76×62 mm. (a) 75f. Type **253**; 125f. As No. 723; (b) 75f. As No. 725, 125f. As No. 726	2·75	1·50

254 Dabry, Gimie, Mermoz and Seaplane "Comte de la Vaulx"

1980. Air. 50th Anniv of First South Atlantic Airmail Flight.

728	**254**	300f. multicoloured	2·50	1·00

255 Caspian Tern, Eastern White Pelicans and Grey-headed Gulls (Pointe Kalissaye Bird Sanctuary)

1981. National Parks. Multicoloured.

729	50f. Type **255**	2·25	50
730	70f. Slender-billed gulls and gull-billed tern (Langue de Barbarie)	2·25	75
731	85f. Turtle and crab (Madeline Islands)	50	25
732	150f. White-breasted cormorant and red-billed tropic bird (Madeline Islands)	4·75	1·60
MS733	127×115 mm. 125f.×4, As Nos. 729/32	9·50	3·00

256 Healthy Activities

1981. Anti-smoking Campaign. Multicoloured.

734	75f. Type **256**	30	30
735	80f. Cancerous mouth with pipe	35	35

257 Fair Visitors beneath Tree

1981. Fourth International Fair, Dakar.

736	**257**	80f. multicoloured	35	35

258 Lat Dior Damel Teigne

1982. National Heroes. Lat Dior. Multicoloured.

737	80f. Type **258**	35	25
738	500f. Lat Dior on horseback	3·25	1·25

259 "Nymphaea lotus"

1982. Flowers. Multicoloured.

739	50f. Type **259**	50	20
740	75f. "Strophanthus sarmentosus"	75	30
741	200f. "Crinum moorei"	1·75	75
742	225f. "Cochlospermum tinctorium"	2·00	1·00

260 "Euryphrene senegalensis" (male and female)

1982. Butterflies. Multicoloured.

743	45f. Type **260**	60	35

744 55f. "Hypolimnas salmacis, Precis octavia" and "Salamis cytora" 75 45
745 75f. "Cymothoe caenis" and "Cyrestis camillus" 90 55
746 80f. "Precis cebrene, Junonia terea" and "Salamis parhassus" 1·10 70
MS747 124×95 mm. 100f. As No. 743; 150f. As No. 744; 200f. As No. 745; As No. 746

261 "Rhaguva albipunctella"

1982. Harmful Insects. Multicoloured.
748 75f. Type **261** 75 45
749 80f. "Amsacta moloneyi, Tolyposporium penicillariae" and "Sclerospore graminicola" (horiz) 1·50 45
750 100f. "Amsacta moloneyi" 1·10 60

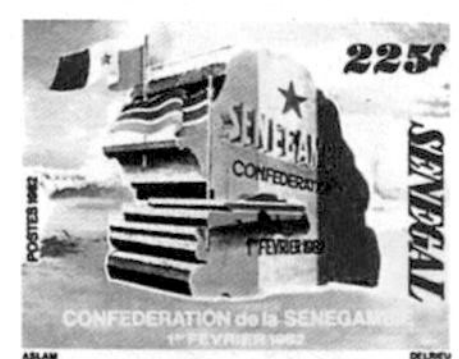

262 Flags and Three-dimensional Map of Senegambia

1982. Senegambia Confederation. Multicoloured.
751 225f. Type **262** 1·60 60
752 350f. Arms of Senegal and Gambia 2·25 90

263 Black-tailed Godwit

1982. Birds. Multicoloured.
753 45f. Type **263** 45 30
754 75f. Saddle-bill stork 95 40
755 80f. Double-spurred francolin 1·10 45
756 500f. Tawny eagle 5·75 3·25

264 Footballer and Emblem

1982. World Cup Football Championship, Spain. Multicoloured.
757 30f. Type **264** 15 15
758 50f. Footballer 20 20
759 75f. Football 55 30
760 80f. World Cup and emblem 60 35
MS761 Four sheets each 90×80 mm. (a) 75f. Type **264**; (b) 100f. As No. 758; (c) 150f. As No. 759; (d) 200f. As No. 760

265 Flag "Stamp" and Ribbon

1982. "Philexfrance 82" International Stamp Exhibition, Paris. Multicoloured.
762 100f. Type **265** 40 25
763 500f. Arms "stamp" between circling arrows 3·25 1·50

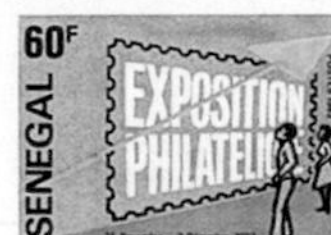

266 Exhibition Poster

1983. Stamp Exhibition, Dakar. Multicoloured.
764 60f. Type **266** 25 20
765 70f. Butterfly stamps 65 20
766 90f. Stamps and magnifying glass 75 25
767 95f. Exhibition hall and Dakar arms on stamp 75 30

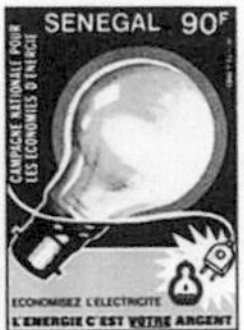

267 Light Bulb

1983. Energy Conservation. Multicoloured.
768 90f. Type **267** 90 30
769 95f. Cars queueing for petrol 1·00 30
770 260f. Woman cooking 1·60 85

268 Torch on Map of Africa

1983. "For Namibian Independence". Multicoloured.
771 90f. Type **268** 55 30
772 95f. Clenched fist and broken chain on map of Africa 60 30
773 260f. Woman with torch on map of Africa 2·25 85

269 Agency Building, Ziguinchor

1983. 20th Anniv of West African Monetary Union. Multicoloured.
774 60f. Type **269** 25 20
775 65f. Headquarters building, Dakar (vert) 25 25

270 Dakar Rotary Banner

1983. First Anniv of Dakar Alizes Rotary Club.
776 **270** 70f. multicoloured 50 25
777 **270** 500f. multicoloured 3·50 1·75

271 Customs Council Headquarters

1983. 30th Anniv of Customs Co-operation Council.
778 **271** 90f. multicoloured 30 30
779 **271** 300f. multicoloured 2·25 1·00

272 Anniversary Emblem

1984. 25th Anniv of Economic Commission for Africa.
780 **272** 90f. multicoloured 60 30
781 **272** 95f. multicoloured 60 30

273 Village

1984. S.O.S. Children's Village. Multicoloured.
782 90f. Type **273** 55 30
783 95f. Foster-mother and child (vert) 65 30
784 115f. Foster-family 80 40
785 260f. House (vert) 2·00 85

274 Scout Salute

1984. 75th Anniv of Boy Scout Movement. Multicoloured.
786 60f. Type **274** 45 15
787 70f. Scout badge 55 20
788 90f. Scouts of different nations 60 30
789 95f. Lord Baden-Powell (founder) 65 35

275 Javelin-throwing

1984. Olympic Games, Los Angeles. Multicoloured.
790 90f. Type **275** 35 30
791 95f. Hurdling 65 35
792 165f. Football 1·10 70
MS793 120×90 mm. 125f. Type **275**; 175f. As No. 791; 250f. As No. 792

276 Basket of Food, Fishing and Farming

1984. World Food Day. Multicoloured. Inscr "16 OCTOBRE 1983".
794 65f. Type **276** 25 20
795 70f. Woman cooking and child (vert) 60 20
796 225f. Group and food 1·90 1·25

1984. Drought Aid. No. 785 optd **Aide au Sahel 84**.
797 260f. multicoloured 2·00 1·25

278 William Ponty School

1984. World Heritage. Goree Island.
798 **278** 90f. multicoloured 75 30
799 - 95f. black and blue 90 35
800 - 250f. multicoloured 2·25 85
801 - 500f. multicoloured 4·50 2·25
MS802 120×110 mm. 125f. multicoloured; 150f. black and blue; 325f. multicoloured; 675f. multicoloured 11·00 5·00
DESIGNS—VERT: 90, 120f. Type **278**; 250, 325f. Goree Historical Museum. HORIZ: 95, 150f. Map of Goree; 500, 650f. Slaves House.

279 Pump and Sprinkler

1985. Irrigation Project. Multicoloured.
810 40f. Type **279** 45 15
811 50f. Tap and dam 55 15
812 90f. Storage tanks and cattle 1·00 55
813 250f. Women at water pump 2·40 1·10

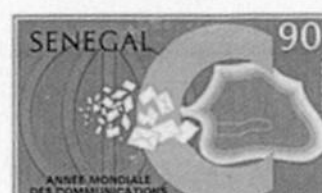

280 Globe, Envelopes and Map

1985. World Communication Year (1984).
814 **280** 90f. multicoloured 55 25
815 - 95f. blue, green and brown 60 30
816 - 350f. multicoloured 2·75 1·50
DESIGNS: 95f. Maps of Africa and Senegal and aerial; 350f. Globe, dove and map of Senegal.

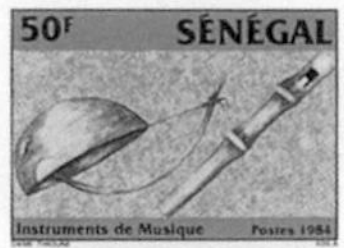

281 Stringed Instrument and Flute

1985. Musical Instruments. Multicoloured.
817 50f. Type **281** 65 15
818 85f. Drums and stringed instrument 1·00 25
819 125f. Musician, stringed instruments, xylophone and drums 1·50 40
820 250f. Stringed instruments 2·50 1·10

282 Seaplane "Comte de la Vaulx" and Map

1985. Air. 55th Anniv of First Airmail Flight across South Atlantic.
821 **282** 250f. multicoloured 2·50 1·10

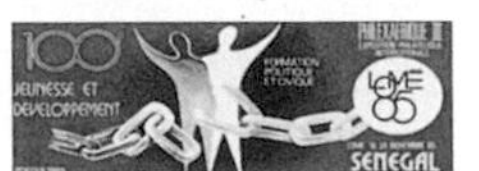

283 People and Broken Chain

1985. "Philexafrique" Int Stamp Exn, Lome, Togo. "Youth and Development". Multicoloured.
822 100f. Type **283** (political and civic education) 45 40
823 125f. Carpenter and draughtsman (professional education) 75 45
824 150f. Couple looking at planets (general education) 90 60
825 175f. Farm workers (food self-sufficiency) 1·40 80

284 Laboratory and Farm Workers

1985. International Youth Year. Multicoloured.
826 40f. Type **284** 20 15
827 50f. Young people, forms of communication and globe 20 15
828 90f. Youth building "Peace" monument 65 35
829 125f. Youth, football and globe 90 45

285 Man, Woman and Boy

1985. National Costumes. Multicoloured.
830 40f. Type **285** 20 15
831 95f. Man in straw hat and striped gown (vert) 65 35
832 100f. Seated gown (vert) 75 40
833 150f. Man and woman (vert) 1·25 60

286 Men bringing Boat Ashore

1986. Fishing at Kayar. Multicoloured.
834 40f. Type **286** 20 15
835 50f. Women waiting on shore 20 15
836 100f. Man with large fish (vert) 1·00 55

837	125f. Sorting the catch (vert)	1·50	65
838	150f. View of beach	1·75	90

287 Perruque and Ceeli

1986. Hairstyles. Multicoloured.

839	90f. Type **287**	40	30
840	125f. Ndungu, Kearly and Rasta	75	40
841	250f. Jamono, Kura and Kooraa	1·50	60
842	300f. Mbaram and Jeere	2·00	70

288 Flags and Football

1986. African Football Cup, Cairo. Multicoloured.

843	115f. Type **288**	70	35
844	125f. Footballer and map	75	45
845	135f. Lion rampant with torch ascending pyramid (horiz)	1·10	50
846	165f. Lions rampant beneath flag (horiz)	1·25	65

1986. Fifth Convention of District 403 of Lions Int. No. 818 surch **Ve CONVENTION MULTI-DISTRICT 8-10 MAI 1988**.

847	165f. on 85f. Drums and stringed instrument	1·00	65

290 Doe and Calf

1986. Ndama Gazelle. Multicoloured.

848	15f. Type **290**	10	10
849	45f. Group of gazelle resting	75	15
850	85f. Gazelle among dead trees	1·25	30
851	125f. Gazelle running	1·75	90

291 Immunizing Child

1986. UNICEF Child Survival Campaign. Multicoloured.

852	50f. Type **291**	20	15
853	85f. Child drinking from bowl	40	35

292 Trophy, Footballers and Terracotta Offertory Vessel

1986. World Cup Football Championship, Mexico. Multicoloured. (a) As T **292**.

854	125f. Type **292**	75	45
855	135f. Trophy, footballers and stucco Maya head from Palenque	80	50
856	165f. Gold breastplate, footballers and trophy	1·00	65
857	340f. Teotihuacan porcelain mask, footballers and trophy	2·00	90

(b) Nos. 854/7 optd **ARGENTINA 3 R.F.A. 2**.

858	125f. Type **292**	75	45
859	135f. Trophy, footballers and stucco Maya head from Palenque	80	50
860	165f. Gold breastplate, footballers and trophy	1·00	65
861	340f. Teotihuacan porcelain mask, footballers and trophy	2·00	90

294 Ostriches

1986. Guembeul Nature Reserve. Multicoloured.

862	50f. Type **294**	1·25	35
863	65f. Gazelles	55	20
864	85f. Giraffes	60	30
865	100f. Ostrich, buffalo, gazelle and giraffe	2·00	75
866	150f. Buffalo	1·40	60

295 Man with Puppet (Xuusmaanapaa)

1986. Christmas. Customs. Multicoloured.

867	70f. Type **295**	25	20
868	85f. Setting up fanal (Fente) (horiz)	65	25
869	150f. Decorating fanal (Jebele)	90	55
870	250f. Boy praying before candle and Nativity scene (horiz)	1·50	75

296 Statue of Liberty

1986. Centenary of Statue of Liberty.

871	**296**	225f. multicoloured	1·50	80

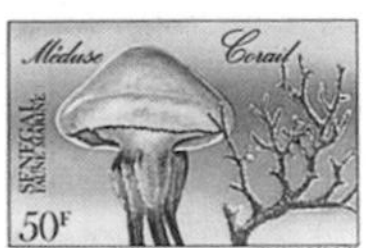

297 Jellyfish and Coral

1987. Marine Fauna. Multicoloured.

872	50f. Type **297**	30	15
873	85f. Sea urchin and starfish	75	25
874	100f. Norway lobster	1·10	35
875	150f. Common dolphin	1·50	55
876	200f. Octopus	2·25	1·10

298 Motor Cyclist and Lorry

1987. Paris–Dakar Rally. Multicoloured.

877	115f. Type **298**	1·10	40
878	125f. Thierry Sabine, helicopter, motor cyclist, lorry and car (horiz)	1·50	60
879	135f. Sabine and motor car (horiz)	1·50	45
880	340f. Eiffel Tower, car and huts	2·75	1·10

299 Hands over Antelope

1987. Endangered Fauna in Ferlo National Park. Multicoloured.

881	55f. Type **299**	20	15
882	70f. Ostriches	1·25	35
883	85f. Warthog	75	25
884	90f. Elephant	75	30

300 Spacecraft above Earth

1987. Tenth Anniv of "Gemini 8"–Agena Flight.

885	**300**	320f. multicoloured	2·25	1·40

301 International Express Mail Emblem

1987. Centenary of First Senegal Stamp. Multicoloured.

887	100f. Type **301**	65	35
888	130f. 1892 4c. Senegal and Dependencies stamp	75	45
889	140f. 1961 Senegal independence stamp	80	50
890	145f. 1935 30c. and 1f.25 Senegal stamps	85	50
891	320f. Senegal 1887 15c. on 20c. stamp and cancellation	2·25	1·10

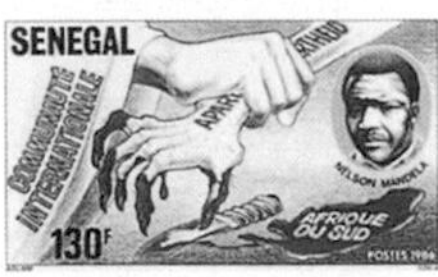

302 Hand gripping Bloodied Claw above Map of South Africa

1987. Anti-Apartheid Campaign. Multicoloured.

892	130f. Type **302**	80	45
893	140f. Broken and bloodied chain in fist (vert)	85	50
894	145f. Skeleton with scythe, dove and globe	85	50

303 Emblem

1987. 20th Anniv of Intelsat. Multicoloured.

895	50f. Type **303**	20	15
896	125f. Satellite and emblem	75	45
897	150f. Emblem and globe	90	55
898	200f. Globe and satellite	1·25	75

304 Emblem and Crowd

1987. West African Cities Organization. Multicoloured.

899	40f. Type **304**	15	15
900	125f. Emblem and clasped hands	75	45

305 Yacht and Sun

1987. 45th Anniv of Dakar Rotary Club.

901	**305**	500f. multicoloured	4·00	1·50

306 U.N. Building, New York

1987. 40th Anniv (1985) of U.N.O. Multicoloured.

902	85f. Type **306**	60	25
903	95f. Emblem	65	35
904	150f. Hands of different races and emblem	90	55

307 Fr. Daniel Brottier (founder) and Angel

1987. 50th Anniv of Cathedral of African Remembrance. Multicoloured.

905	130f. Type **307**	85	45
906	140f. Cathedral in 1936 and 1986	85	50

308 Hand pouring Grain into Globe

1987. World Food Day. Multicoloured.

907	130f. Type **308**	80	45
908	140f. Ear of wheat and F.A.O. emblem rising as sun (horiz)	1·10	50
909	145f. Emblem	1·25	50

309 Servals

1987. Basse Casamance National Park. Multicoloured.

910	115f. Type **309**	1·00	40
911	135f. Demidoff's galagos	1·40	45
912	150f. Bush pig	1·50	55
913	250f. Leopards	2·75	1·25
914	300f. Little egrets	11·00	3·50
915	300f. Carmine bee eaters	11·00	3·50

310 Wrestlers

1987. Senegalese Wrestling. Multicoloured.

916	115f. Type **310**	80	40
917	125f. Wrestlers and musicians	80	45
918	135f. Wrestlers (vert)	1·00	45
919	165f. Referee, wrestlers and crowd (vert)	1·25	55

311 African Open-bill Stork

1987. Djoudj National Park. Multicoloured.

920	115f. Type **311**	1·75	85
921	125f. Greater flamingos (horiz)	1·75	1·25
922	135f. Pink-backed pelican and greater flamingos (horiz)	2·60	1·25
923	300f. Pink-backed pelicans	4·75	2·00
924	350f. As No. 921	5·00	2·50
925	350f. As No. 922	5·00	2·50

312 Boy dreaming of Father Christmas's Visit

1987. Christmas. Multicoloured.

No.	Type	Description	Mint	Used
926		145f. Type **312**	85	50
927		150f. Star behind Virgin gazing at Child	90	55
928		180f. Nativity scene above people praying in church	1·25	65
929		200f. Nativity scene in candle glow	1·25	75

313 Battle of Dekhele

1988. Death Centenary of Lat-Dior. Multicoloured.

No.	Type	Description	Mint	Used
930		130f. Type **313**	1·00	45
931		160f. Lat-Dior on his horse "Maalaw"	1·00	60

314 10th Anniv Emblem and Map

1988. Dakar International Fair.

No.	Type	Description	Mint	Used
932	**314**	125f. multicoloured	75	45

315 Brown Bullhead

1988. Fish. Multicoloured.

No.	Type	Description	Mint	Used
933		5f. Type **315**	10	10
934		100f. Pennant coralfish	50	45
935		145f. Common barberfish	1·10	70
936		180f. Common carp	1·90	1·25

316 W.M.O. Emblem and Means of Conveying Information

1988. World Meteorology Day.

No.	Type	Description	Mint	Used
937	**316**	145f. multicoloured	90	30

317 Motor Cyclist

1988. Tenth Anniv of Paris–Dakar Rally. Multicoloured.

No.	Type	Description	Mint	Used
938		145f. Type **317**	1·25	50
939		180f. Rally car and emblem	1·50	65
940		200f. Rally cars and man	1·75	70
941		410f. Thierry Sabine and motor cyclist	3·50	1·90

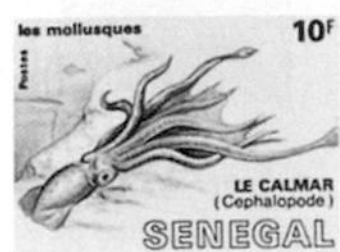

318 Squid

1988. Molluscs. Multicoloured.

No.	Type	Description	Mint	Used
942		10f. Type **318**	15	10
943		20f. Truncate donax (bivalve)	15	10
944		145f. Giant East African snail	1·40	65
945		165f. Banded snail	1·75	75

319 Football, Cup and Map

1988. Africa Cup Football Championship, Rabat. Multicoloured.

No.	Type	Description	Mint	Used
946		80f. Type **319**	55	25
947		100f. Player's leg and ball (vert)	75	35
948		145f. Match scene and map of Africa (vert)	90	50
949		180f. Emblem and cup (vert)	1·25	65

320 Corps Member and Children

1988. 25th Anniv of American Peace Corps in Senegal.

No.	Type	Description	Mint	Used
950	**320**	190f. multicoloured	1·25	65

321 "Dictyota atomaria"

1988. Marine Flora. Multicoloured.

No.	Type	Description	Mint	Used
951		10f. Type **321**	10	10
952		65f. "Agarum gmelini"	75	20
953		145f. "Saccorrhiza bulbosa"	1·10	55
954		180f. "Rhodymenia palmetta"	1·75	65

1988. Riccione Stamp Fair. No. 891 optd **RICCIONE 88 27-29-08-89.**

No.	Type	Description	Mint	Used
955		320f. multicoloured	2·25	1·25

323 Hodori (mascot) and Stadium

1988. Olympic Games, Seoul. Multicoloured.

No.	Type	Description	Mint	Used
956		5f. Type **323**	10	10
957		75f. Athletics, swimming and football	55	25
958		300f. Hodori, flame and sports pictograms	2·10	1·00
959		410f. Emblem and athletics pictogram	2·75	1·40

324 Thierno Saidou Nourou Tall Centre

1988

No.	Type	Description	Mint	Used
960	**324**	125f. multicoloured	70	60

325 Thies Phosphate Mine

1988. Senegal Industries. Multicoloured.

No.	Type	Description	Mint	Used
961		5f. Type **325**	1·00	50
962		20f. Chemical industry	10	10
963		145f. Diourbel factory	85	50
964		410f. Mbao refinery	3·00	1·75

326 Children and Government Palace

1988. Postcards of 1900. Multicoloured.

No.	Type	Description	Mint	Used
965		20f. Type **326**	10	10
966		145f. Wrestlers and St. Louis Grand Mosque	1·10	50
967		180f. Old Dakar railway station and young woman	2·25	1·25
968		200f. Goree Governor's residence and young woman	1·60	70

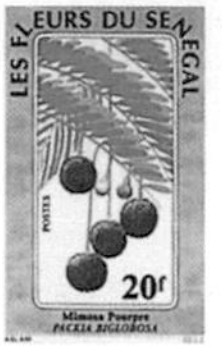

327 "Packia biglobosa"

1988. Flowers. Multicoloured.

No.	Type	Description	Mint	Used
969		20f. Type **327**	10	10
970		60f. "Euphorbia pulcherrima"	20	15
971		65f. "Cyrtosperma senegalense"	25	20
972		410f. "Bombax costatum"	3·00	1·40

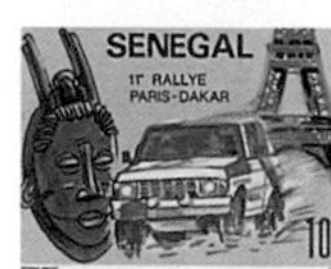

328 Mask, Rally Car and Eiffel Tower

1989. 11th Paris–Dakar Rally. Multicoloured.

No.	Type	Description	Mint	Used
973		10f. Type **328**	10	10
974		145f. Crash helmet and sand dunes	1·25	55
975		180f. Turban and motor cyclist	1·50	70
976		220f. Motor cyclist and Thierry Sabine	2·00	85

329 Teranga Hotel

1989. Tourism (1st series). Multicoloured.

No.	Type	Description	Mint	Used
977		10f. Type **329**	10	10
978		80f. Thatched hut and shades on beach	55	25
979		100f. Saly hotel	65	35
980		350f. Dior hotel	2·50	1·25

330 Senegal Tourism Emblem

1989. Tourism (2nd series). Multicoloured.

No.	Type	Description	Mint	Used
981		130f. Type **330**	75	45
982		140f. Rural tourism (horiz)	85	50
983		145f. Fishing (horiz)	1·40	70
984		180f. Water sports (horiz)	1·25	70

331 Saint-Exupery and Scene from "Courrier Sud"

1989. 45th Anniv of Disappearance of Antoine de Saint-Exupery (pilot and writer).

No.	Type	Description	Mint	Used
985	**331**	180f. black, orange and grey	1·40	50
986	-	220f. black, blue and grey	1·75	75
987	-	410f. multicoloured	3·50	1·25

DESIGNS: 220f. Scene from "Vol de Nuit"; 410f. Scene from "Pilote de Guerre".

332 Presentation of Lists of Grievances by People of St. Louis

1989. Bicentenary of French Revolution. Multicoloured.

No.	Type	Description	Mint	Used
988		180f. Type **332**	1·25	1·00
989		220f. Declaration of Rights of Man, quill pen in hand and phrygian cap (vert)	1·25	1·10
990		300f. Revolutionaries and flag	2·75	1·50

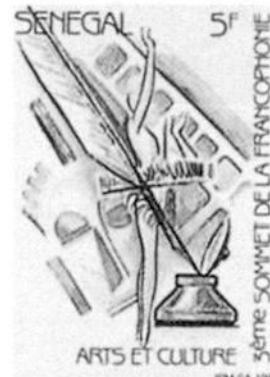

333 Arts and Culture

1989. Third Francophone Summit. Multicoloured.

No.	Type	Description	Mint	Used
991		5f. Type **333**	10	10
992		30f. Education (horiz)	15	10
993		100f. Communication (horiz)	65	35
994		200f. Development (horiz)	1·25	75

1989. No. 960 surch.

No.	Type	Description	Mint	Used
995		555f. on 125f. multicoloured	3·50	1·25

335 Stamps

1989. "Philexfrance 89" International Stamp Exhibition, Paris. Multicoloured.

No.	Type	Description	Mint	Used
996		10f. Type **335**	10	10
997		25f. Stamp on map of France (vert)	10	10
998		75f. Couple viewing stamp on easel (vert)	55	25
999		145f. Sticking stamp on envelope (vert)	1·10	55

336 "30" Dish Aerial and Envelope

1989. 30th Anniv Meeting of West African Post and Telecommunications Administrations Conference, Dakar. Multicoloured.

No.	Type	Description	Mint	Used
1000		25f. Type **336**	10	10
1001		30f. Telephone handset, punched tape and map on stamp	15	10
1002		180f. Map of Africa, stamp and telephone earpiece	1·40	70
1003		220f. Stamp, satellite, globe and map of Africa	1·50	85

337 Record Stacks and 1922 Postcard

1989. 75th Anniv (1988) of Senegal Archives. Multicoloured.
1004 15f. Type **337** 10 10
1005 40f. 1825 document 15 10
1006 145f. 1825 document and archive building 1·10 55
1007 180f. Bound volume 1·25 70

338 Jar with Lid

1989. Pottery. Multicoloured.
1008 15f. Type **338** 10 10
1009 30f. Potter at work 15 10
1010 75f. Stacked pots 65 25
1011 145f. Woman carrying pots 1·25 55

339 Nehru

1989. Birth Centenary of Jawaharlal Nehru (Indian statesman).
1012 **339** 220f. multicoloured 1·25 85
1013 - 410f. black, red & yellow 2·75 1·40
DESIGN—HORIZ: 410f. Nehru (different).

340 Swimming Crab

1989. Marine Life. Multicoloured.
1014 10f. Type **340** 10 10
1015 60f. Long-snouted seahorse (vert) 60 25
1016 145f. Barnacles 1·25 55
1017 220f. Sand-hopper 1·50 85

341 Clasped Hand and People of Different Races

1989. World AIDS Day. Multicoloured.
1018 5f. Type **341** 10 10
1019 100f. People under umbrella 40 35
1020 145f. Fist smashing AIDS virus 85 55
1021 180f. Hammer smashing AIDS virus 1·10 70

342 Pilgrims

1989. Centenary of Pilgrimage to Our Lady of Popenguine. Multicoloured.
1022 145f. Type **342** 90 55
1023 180f. Our Lady of Popenguine Church 1·40 70

343 White-breasted Cormorant and African Darter, Djoudj

1989. National Parks. Multicoloured.
1024 10f. Type **343** 25 15
1025 45f. Grey-headed gulls, Langue de Barbarie 90 35
1026 100f. Blue-checked bee eater and long-crested eagle, Basse Casamance 1·50 85
1027 180f. Western reef herons, Saloum 4·25 1·75

344 Boy looking at Christmas Tree

1989. Christmas. Multicoloured.
1028 10f. Type **344** 10 10
1029 25f. Teddy bear and bauble hanging from tree 10 10
1030 30f. Animals around Baby Jesus 15 10
1031 200f. Madonna and Child 1·25 75

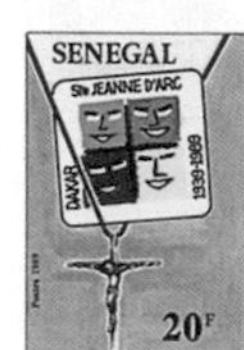

345 Crucifix and Anniversary Emblem

1989. 50th Anniv of St. Joan of Arc Institute, Dakar. Multicoloured.
1032 20f. Type **345** 10 10
1033 500f. Emblem and Institute building 3·50 1·40

346 "Hydravion"

1989. 79th Anniv of First Flight of Henri Fabre's Seaplane. Multicoloured.
1034 125f. Type **346** 75 55
1035 130f. Fabre working on engine of "Hydravion" 1·10 55
1036 475f. Technical drawings and Fabre (vert) 3·50 1·00
MS1037 141×101 mm. 700f. As No. 1036 5·50 2·75

347 Basketball

1990. Olympic Games, Barcelona (1992). Multicoloured.
1038 10f. Type **347** 10 10
1039 130f. High jumping 50 20
1040 180f. Throwing the discus 1·00 35
1041 190f. Running 1·10 45
1042 315f. Lawn tennis 2·00 55
1043 475f. Show jumping 2·75 65
MS1044 85×85 mm. 600f. Football 3·75 1·00

348 Rally Car

1990. 12th Paris–Dakar Rally. Multicoloured.
1045 20f. Type **348** 10 10
1046 25f. Motor cycle and sidecar 10 10
1047 180f. Crowd cheering winning driver 1·40 70
1048 200f. Thierry Sabine and car 1·40 75

349 Piazza della Signoria, Florence, and Footballer

1990. World Cup Football Championship, Italy. Multicoloured.
1049 45f. Type **349** 20 15
1050 140f. Piazza Navona, Rome 1·00 25
1051 180f. "Virgin with St. Anne and Infant Jesus" (Leonardo da Vinci) 1·25 30
1052 220f. "Giuseppe Garibaldi" (oil painting) 1·40 55
1053 300f. "Sistine Madonna" (Raphael) 2·00 75
1054 415f. "Virgin and Child" (Danielle da Volterra) 2·75 1·10
MS1055 83×78 mm. 700f. Christopher Columbus statue, Milan (51×39 mm) 4·00 1·90

350 Footballer

1990. African Nations Cup Football Championship, Algeria. Multicoloured.
1056 20f. Type **350** 10 10
1057 60f. Goalkeeper 25 20
1058 100f. Clasped hands and pennants 75 35
1059 500f. Trophy 3·50 1·75

351 Facsimile Telegraphy

1990. Postal Services. Multicoloured.
1060 5f. Type **351** 10 10
1061 15f. Express mail service 10 10
1062 100f. Postal cheques 65 35
1063 180f. Savings 1·25 40

352 Hands and Umbrella protecting Children

1990. Louga S.O.S. Children's Village. Multicoloured.
1064 5f. Type **352** 10 10
1065 500f. Children under umbrella 3·25 1·25

353 Envelopes on Map

1990. 20th Anniv of Multinational Postal Training School, Abidjan. Multicoloured.
1066 145f. Type **353** 1·00 55
1067 180f. Man carrying wreath containing envelope 1·25 70

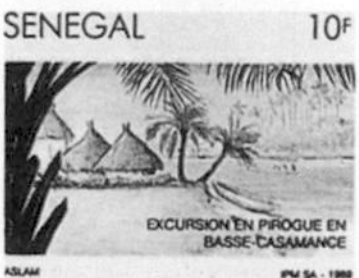

354 Excursion by Pirogue, Basse-Casamance

1990. Tourism. Multicoloured.
1068 10f. Type **354** 10 10
1069 25f. Hotel and beach, Goree 10 10
1070 30f. Houses on stilts, Fadiouth 15 10
1071 40f. Rose Lake and salt drying 15 10

355 Camp

1990. Scouting. Multicoloured.
1072 30f. Type **355** 15 10
1073 100f. Scouts trekking alongside lake 75 35
1074 145f. Scouts trekking through hilly landscape 1·00 55
1075 200f. Scout and emblem (vert) 1·25 75

356 "Cassia tora"

1990. Medicinal Plants. Multicoloured.
1076 95f. Type **356** 65 35
1077 105f. "Tamarind" 75 40
1078 125f. "Cassia occidentalis" 90 45
1079 175f. "Leptadenia hastata" 1·25 65

357 Angels and Tree

1990. Christmas.
1080 **357** 25f. multicoloured 10 10
1081 - 145f. multicoloured 1·00 55
1082 - 180f. orange, red & black 1·25 70
1083 - 200f. multicoloured 1·40 75
DESIGNS: 145f. Angel trumpeting stars; 180f. Adoration of Three Kings; 200f. Donkey and cow gazing at Child.

358 Anniversary Emblem

1991. 125th Anniv (1988) of International Red Cross and 25th Anniv of Senegal Red Cross.
1084 **358** 180f. multicoloured 1·25 45

359 Rally Car

1991. 13th Paris–Dakar Rally. Multicoloured.
1085 15f. Type **359** 10 10
1086 15f. Car and motor cycle at night 75 35
1087 180f. Rally car (different) 1·25 75
1088 220f. Motor cycles 1·60 90

360 African Python

1991. Reptiles. Multicoloured.
1089 15f. Type **360** 10 10
1090 60f. Common green turtle 65 15
1091 100f. Nile crocodile 1·10 25
1092 180f. Senegal chameleon 1·75 90

361 Sphinx, House of Slaves, Frescoes, Kirdi Houses and Mohammed's Tomb

1991. "Fespaco". 12th Pan-African Cinema and Television Festival. Multicoloured.

1093	30f. Type **361**	10	10
1094	60f. Dogon mask, B. Dioulasso Mosque, drawing of Osiris, and camel rider	25	15
1095	100f. Rabat, "Seated Scribe" (Egyptian statue), drum and camels	75	25
1096	180f. Pyramids of Egypt, Djenne Mosque, Guinean mask, Moroccan architecture and Moorish door decorations	1·25	75

362 Nobel

1991. 95th Death Anniv of Alfred Nobel (founder of Nobel prizes). Multicoloured. Self-adhesive.

1097	145f. Type **362**	1·00	75
1098	180f. Nobel and prize presentation (horiz)	1·25	90

363 Oribi

1991. National Parks. Multicoloured.

1099	5f. Type **363**	10	10
1100	10f. Dorcas gazelle	10	10
1101	180f. Kob	1·25	45
1102	555f. Hartebeest	4·50	2·25

364 Cashew

1991. Trees and their Fruit. Multicoloured.

1103	90f. Type **364**	65	25
1104	100f. Mango	75	25
1105	125f. Sugar-palm (vert)	90	35
1106	145f. Oil palm (vert)	1·00	45

365 Ader, Motor Car and Telephone

1991. Air. Centenary (1990) of First Heavier than Air Powered Flight. Multicoloured.

1107	145f. Type **365**	1·10	40
1108	180f. Clement Ader and his monoplane "Eole"	1·25	55
1109	615f. "Eole" and Ader (vert)	4·25	2·00
MS1110	132×96 mm. 940f. As No. 1105	6·25	2·75

366 Columbus and Haitians

1991. 500th Anniv (1992) of Discovery of America by Columbus. Multicoloured.

1111	100f. Type **366**	65	25
1112	145f. Arms of Castile and Leon (vert)	90	40
1113	180f. "Santa Maria" and Columbus	1·10	45
1114	200f. Vicente Yanez Pinzon and "Nina"	1·25	55
1115	220f. Martin Alonzo Pinzon and "Pinta"	1·40	60
1116	500f. Details of charts	3·25	1·25
1117	625f. Compass rose and Columbus with charts	4·00	1·75

367 Armstrong

1991. 20th Death Anniv of Louis Armstrong (musician). Multicoloured.

1118	10f. Type **367**	10	10
1119	145f. Armstrong singing	90	40
1120	180f. Armstrong and trumpets	1·40	45
1121	220f. Armstrong playing trumpet	2·00	90

368 Yuri Gagarin and "Vostok 1"

1991. 30th Anniv of First Man in Space. Multicoloured.

1125	15f. Type **368**	10	10
1126	145f. "Vostok 1" and Gagarin in spacesuit	90	40
1127	180f. Gagarin in spacesuit and "Vostok 1" (different)	1·25	45
1128	220f. Globe, "Vostok 1" and Gagarin in flying kit	1·50	90

369 Flags and Water dripping into Bowl

1991. "Water, Source of Life". Senegal–Saudi Arabia Rural Water Supply Co-operation. Multicoloured.

1129	30f. Type **369**	10	10
1130	145f. Tap and village	90	40
1131	180f. Tap dripping and flags	1·25	45
1132	220f. Water tower and village	1·50	90

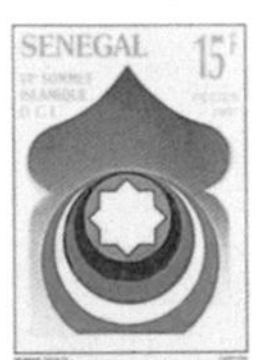

370 Star and Crescents

1991. Sixth Summit Meeting of Islamic Conference Organization, Dakar. Multicoloured.

1133	15f. Type **370**	10	10
1134	145f. Hands	90	40
1135	180f. Conference centre and accommodation	1·25	45
1136	220f. Grand Mosque, Dakar	1·50	90

371 Player shooting at Basket

1991. Centenary of Basketball. Multicoloured.

1137	125f. Type **371**	75	35
1138	145f. Player approaching basket	1·00	40
1139	180f. King and Queen of the Basket	1·10	45
1140	220f. Lion, trophies and ball	1·50	60

372 Giving Blessing

1991. Christmas. Multicoloured.

1141	5f. Type **372**	10	10
1142	145f. Madonna and Child	90	40
1143	160f. Angels and star	1·25	45
1144	220f. Animals and Baby Jesus	1·50	90

373 Bust of Mozart and Score

1991. Death Bicentenary of Wolfgang Amadeus Mozart (composer). Multicoloured.

1145	5f. Type **373**	10	10
1146	150f. Mozart conducting	1·00	40
1147	180f. Mozart at keyboard	1·25	45
1148	220f. Mozart and score	1·50	90

374 Flags on Player's Sock

1992. 18th African Nations Cup Football Championship. Multicoloured.

1149	10f. Type **374**	10	10
1150	145f. Footballs forming "92"	70	45
1151	200f. Cup and mascot	1·25	65
1152	220f. Players	1·50	1·00

1992. Papal Visit. No. 1143 surch **VISITE DU PAPE JEAN PAUL II AU SENEGAL 19-23/02/92 180F**.

1153	180f. on 160f. multicoloured	1·60	1·10

376 Saloum Delta

1992. National Parks. Multicoloured.

1154	10f. Type **376**	35	15
1155	125f. Djoudj	1·50	60
1156	145f. Niokolo-Koba	2·10	65
1157	220f. Basse Casamance	3·00	1·75

377 Oil Wells, Flag and Bombs

1992. Participation of Senegal Contingent in Gulf War. Multicoloured.

1158	30f. Type **377**	15	10
1159	145f. Senegalese officer	70	45
1160	180f. Kaaba and Senegalese guard	1·10	55
1161	220f. Map, dove and flag	1·50	75

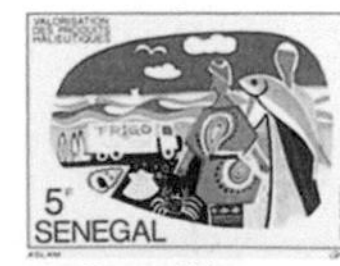

378 Frozen Fish

1992. Fish Products. Multicoloured.

1162	5f. Type **378**	10	10
1163	60f. Sandwich seller and platters of fish	40	20
1164	100f. Woman filleting fish	1·10	40
1165	150f. Women packing prawns	1·10	75

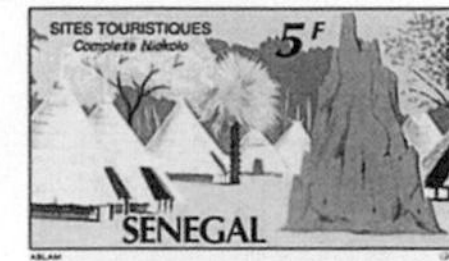

379 Niokolo Complex

1992. Tourist Sites. Multicoloured.

1166	5f. Type **379**	10	10
1167	10f. Basse Casamance	10	10
1168	150f. Dakar	1·10	45
1169	200f. Saint-Louis	1·60	80

380 Teacher and Pupils carrying Saplings

1992. Reforestation by School children. Multicoloured.

1170	145f. Type **380**	1·00	45
1171	180f. Planting sapling	1·25	55
1172	200f. Planting saplings (different)	1·40	90
1173	220f. Watering-in sapling (vert)	1·75	1·10

381 People with Cleaning Materials

1992. Manpower Services Operation, Setal. Multicoloured.

1174	25f. Type **381**	10	10
1175	145f. Clearing road	70	45
1176	180f. Sweeping streets (vert)	1·10	55
1177	220f. Painting kerbstones (vert)	1·50	1·00

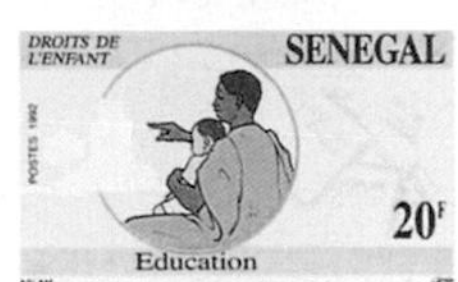

382 Education

1992. Rights of the Child. Multicoloured.

1178	20f. Type **382**	10	10
1179	45f. Vocational training	20	15
1180	165f. Instruction	1·10	55
1181	180f. Health	1·25	55

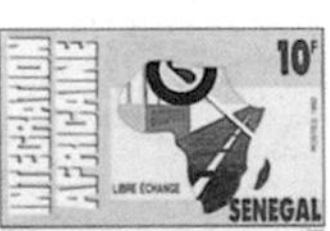

383 Customs Post (Free Trade)

1992. African Integration. Multicoloured.

1182	10f. Type **383**	10	10
1183	30f. Silhouettes (youth activities)	15	10
1184	145f. Communications equipment	1·10	45
1185	220f. Women's movements	1·50	75

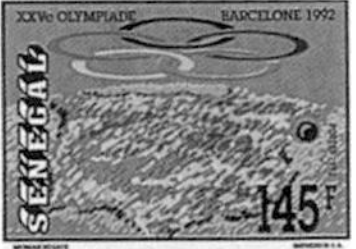

384 Rings and Map of Spain

1992. Olympic Games, Barcelona. Multicoloured.

1186	145f. Type **384**	70	45
1187	180f. Runner (vert)	1·10	55
1188	200f. Sprinter	1·40	90
1189	300f. Athlete carrying torch (vert)	2·00	1·50

385 Passenger Carriages

1992. "The Blue Train". Multicoloured.

1190	70f. Type **385**	45	30
1191	145f. Diesel locomotives and carriages	1·00	55
1192	200f. Train and track on map	1·40	90
1193	220f. Railway station	1·50	1·00

386 Sealife around Map of Antarctic

1992. International Maritime Heritage Year.

1194	**386**	25f. black, blue & yellow	10	10
1195	-	100f. multicoloured	70	25
1196	-	180f. multicoloured	1·25	55

1197	-	220f. multicoloured	1·50	75

DESIGNS—VERT: 100f. Marine life caught in sun ray; 180f. United Nations seminar; 220f. Fish, ship, flags and hands holding globe.

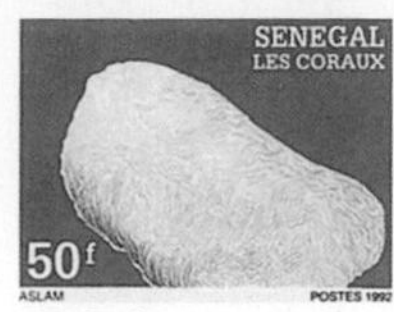

387 Coral

1992. Corals.

1198	**387**	50f. multicoloured	35	15
1199	-	100f. multicoloured	90	25
1200	-	145f. multicoloured (vert)	1·25	45
1201	-	220f. multicoloured	2·00	1·00

DESIGNS: 100f. to 220f. Different corals.

388 Adenauer

1992. 25th Death Anniv of Konrad Adenauer (German statesman). Multicoloured.

1202	5f. Type **388**	10	10
1203	145f. Schaumburg Palace and flags (horiz)	1·00	45
1204	180f. German flag and handshake (horiz)	1·25	55
1205	220f. Map, flag and emblem of Germany (horiz)	1·50	75

389 Crab

1992. Crustaceans. Multicoloured.

1206	20f. Type **389**	10	10
1207	30f. Sea spider	25	10
1208	180f. Crayfish	1·50	55
1209	200f. King prawn	1·75	1·00

390 "Parkia biglobosa"

1992. Flowers and their Fruit. Multicoloured.

1210	10f. Type **390**	10	10
1211	50f. Desert date	35	15
1212	200f. "Parinari macrophylla"	1·50	65
1213	220f. Cactus	1·75	1·00

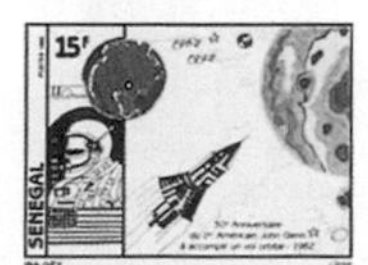

391 Rocket and Earth

1992. 30th Anniv of First American Manned Orbit of the Earth. Multicoloured.

1214	15f. Type **391**	10	10
1215	145f. American flag and John Glenn	1·00	55
1216	180f. Rocket launch and globe	1·25	90
1217	200f. Astronaut and rocket on launch-pad (vert)	1·40	1·00

392 Bakari II and Map from 14th-century Catalan Atlas

1992. Bakari II. Multicoloured.

1218	100f. Type **392**	65	25
1219	145f. Giant Mexican carved head and map from 15th-century atlas	1·00	45

393 Picture Frame and Obelisk

1992. Dakar Biennale. Multicoloured.

1220	20f. Type **393**	10	10
1221	50f. Mask hanging from window frame	35	10
1222	145f. Open book	1·00	65
1223	220f. Traditional string instrument	1·75	1·00

394 Children dancing round Decorated Globe

1992. Christmas. Multicoloured.

1224	15f. Type **394**	10	10
1225	145f. People around tree (vert)	1·00	55
1226	180f. Jesus (vert)	1·25	65
1227	200f. Father Christmas (vert)	1·40	90

1993. 15th Paris–Dakar Rally. Nos. 941 and 975 surch **Dakar le 17-01-93** and new value.

1228	145f. on 180f. multicoloured	1·10	90
1229	220f. on 410f. multicoloured	1·60	1·10

396 First Aid Post

1993. Accident Prevention Campaign. Multicoloured.

1230	20f. Type **396** (prevention, security and first aid)	10	10
1231	25f. The Sonacos incident (reinforcement of preventative measures) (36×28 mm)	10	10
1232	145f. Chemical accident (need for vigilance and security) (36×28 mm)	1·00	55
1233	200f. Helicopter rescue (rapid and efficient intervention at air disasters)	1·25	90

397 Seck

1993. 120th Birth Anniv of Abdoulaye Seck (Director of Posts and Telecommunications).

1234	**397**	220f. multicoloured	1·50	65

398 Spotted Hyena

1993. Wild Animals. Multicoloured.

1235	30f. Type **398**	10	10
1236	50f. Lioness	10	10
1237	70f. Leopard	25	10
1238	150f. Giraffe (vert)	50	25
1239	180f. Stag	75	30

399 Decorated Tree, Children playing and Father Christmas

1993. Christmas. Multicoloured.

1240	5f. Type **399**	10	10
1241	80f. Children decorating tree and Father Christmas	20	15
1242	145f. Children visiting Father Christmas	35	25
1243	150f. Girl tugging Father Christmas's beard	35	25

400 U.S. Flag and Kennedy

1993. 30th Anniv of Assassination of President John F. Kennedy of the United States. Multicoloured.

1244	80f. Type **400**	20	15
1245	555f. Kennedy and White House	1·90	95

402 Vehicles and Tree at Sunset

1994. 16th Anniv of Paris–Dakar Rally. Multicoloured.

1250	145f. Type **402**	50	25
1251	180f. Boys with camel	60	30
1252	220f. Rally cars	75	35

403 Diplodocus

1994. Prehistoric Animals. Multicoloured.

1253	100f. Type **403**	25	15
1254	175f. Brontosaurus	40	25
1255	215f. Triceratops	50	35
1256	290f. Stegosaurus	1·25	45
1257	300f. Tyrannosaurus	1·75	1·10

404 Black-headed Herons

1994. Birds of Kalissaye National Park. Multicoloured.

1258	100f. Type **404**	50	20
1259	275f. Caspian terns	1·10	45
1260	290f. Little egrets	1·25	45
1261	380f. Pink-backed pelicans (horiz)	1·75	1·10

405 Dried Moray Fat

1994. Produce of the Sea. Multicoloured.

1262	5f. Type **405**	10	10
1263	90f. Sifting shellfish	20	15
1264	100f. Salted shark	40	25
1265	200f. Smoking small fry	70	40

406 "Stop Sand Extraction"

1994. Coastal Protection. Multicoloured.

1266	5f. Type **406**	10	10
1267	75f. Prevention of sand dunes	20	15
1268	100f. Horizontal and vertical barrages	25	15
1269	200f. Cleanliness of beaches	50	35

407 Water Store, Goree, and Railway Station, Rufisque

1994. Preservation of Heritage Sites. Multicoloured.

1270	100f. Type **407**	30	20
1271	175f. Soudan House	40	25
1272	215f. Goree Island	50	35
1273	275f. Pinet Laprade Fort, Sedhiou	90	45

408 Red-flowered Kapok

1994. Flowers. Multicoloured.

1274	30f. Type **408**	10	10
1275	75f. Golden trumpet	20	15
1276	100f. Rose periwinkle	25	15
1277	1000f. Glory-bower	3·50	2·10

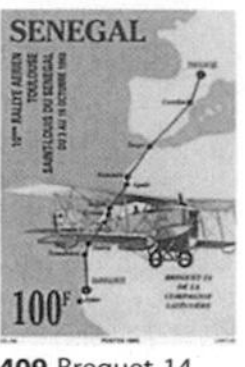

409 Breguet 14 Biplane over Route Map

1994. Tenth Toulouse–Saint-Louis Aerial Rally (1993). Multicoloured.

1278	100f. Type **409**	40	15
1279	145f. Henri Guillaumet and route map	50	25
1280	180f. Jean Mermoz and route map	60	30
1281	220f. Antoine Saint-Exupery and route map	75	35

410 Head of Elephant with Ear forming Map of Africa

1994. S.O.S. Elephant Conservation Programme. Multicoloured.

1282	30f. Type **410**	20	10
1283	60f. Elephant within "SOS"	25	10
1284	90f. Pair of elephants with trunks forming "SOS"	40	15
1285	145f. Dead elephant and tusks	50	25

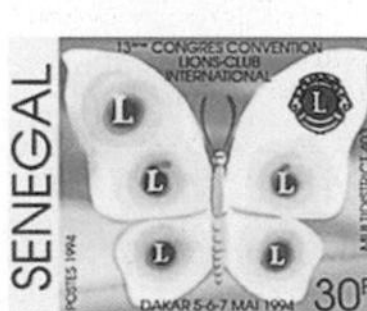

411 Emblems on Butterfly

1994. 13th Congress of District 403 of Lions Clubs International, Dakar. Multicoloured.

1286	30f. Type **411**	20	10
1287	60f. Emblem over butterfly	30	10
1288	175f. "L's and emblem	60	25
1289	215f. Emblem on rainbow	90	35

412 "Stamp" showing Children playing

1994. African Children's Day. Children's Drawings. Multicoloured.

1290	175f. Type **412**	40	25
1291	215f. Preparing meal outside house	50	35

413 Flags and Football

1994. World Cup Football Championship, U.S.A. Multicoloured.

1292	45f. Type **413**	10	10
1293	175f. World map forming part of football	65	25
1294	215f. Player dribbling ball (horiz)	75	35
1295	665f. Players with ball (horiz)	2·10	1·10

414 Slave House

1994. World Heritage Site, Goree.

1296	**414**	500f. multicoloured	1·60	1·10

415 Rainbow over Globe

1994. 21st Universal Postal Union Congress and "Philakorea 1994" International Stamp Exhibition, Seoul. Multicoloured.

1297	10f. Type **415**	10	10
1298	175f. "Stamp" forming wing of dove	40	25
1299	260f. "Stamp" forming sail of boat	65	45
1300	300f. Globe, hands and airmail envelope	75	50

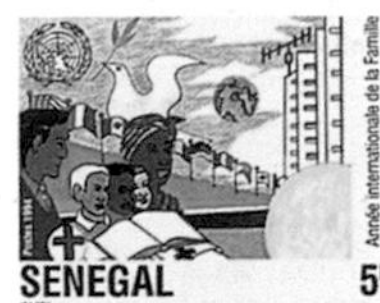

416 Peace Dove, People of Different Cultures and Flags

1994. International Year of the Family. Multicoloured.

1301	5f. Type **416**	10	10
1302	175f. People of different cultures, flags and globe	65	25
1303	215f. Globe and mothers with children	75	35
1304	290f. Globe, dove and family	1·00	45

417 "Murex saxatilis"

1994. Shells. Multicoloured.

1305	20f. Type **417**	10	10
1306	45f. "Nerita senegalensis" (vert)	10	10
1307	75f. "Polymita picea"	20	15
1308	175f. "Scalaria pretiosa" (vert)	65	25
1309	215f. Glory of the sea cone (vert)	75	65

418 Golden Jackal

1994. Animals. Multicoloured.

1310	60f. Type **418**	25	10
1311	70f. African clawless otter	25	10
1312	100f. Egyptian mongoose	40	15
1313	175f. Giant ground pangolin	90	25
1314	215f. Nile monitor	1·00	35

419 Pierre de Coubertin (founder) and Anniversary Emblem

1994. Centenary of International Olympic Committee. Multicoloured.

1315	175f. Type **419**	40	25
1316	215f. Coubertin within wreath and anniversary emblem	50	35
1317	275f. Coubertin over anniversary emblem (vert)	90	45
1318	290f. Coubertin within anniversary emblem and Olympic rings (vert)	1·10	45

420 Africans greeting Portuguese

1994. 550th Anniv of First Portuguese Landing in Senegal.

1319	**420**	175f. multicoloured	65	25

421 Father Christmas and Children with Presents

1994. Christmas. Multicoloured.

1320	175f. Type **421**	40	25
1321	215f. Madonna and Child and Christmas trees	50	35
1322	275f. Adoration of the Wise Men (horiz)	90	45
1323	290f. Madonna and Child	1·10	45

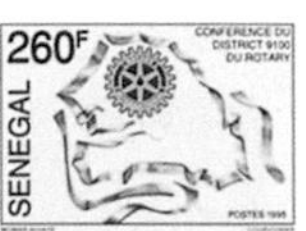

422 Emblem and Ribbons

1995. Conference of District 9100 of Rotary International. Multicoloured.

1324	260f. Type **422**	90	45
1325	275f. Emblem and dove in flight	90	45

423 Sudan and Xylophone

1995. Centenary of Formation of French Governate-General of French West Africa. Map highlighting featured country. Multicoloured.

1326	10f. Type **423**	10	10
1327	15f. Dahomey and canoes	10	10
1328	30f. Ivory Coast and elephant	10	10
1329	70f. Mauritania and camel	15	10
1330	175f. Guinea, stringed instrument and plants	40	25
1331	180f. Upper Volta, cow and produce	45	30
1332	215f. Niger and Cross of Agadez	75	35
1333	225f. Senegal and lions	80	35

1995. As Nos. 502a/504h but size 21×26 mm.

1334	**154**	5f. orange	10	10
1335	**154**	10f. green	10	10
1336	**154**	20f. red	10	10
1337	**154**	25f. green	10	10
1338	**154**	30f. green	10	10
1339	**154**	40f. green	10	10
1340	**154**	50f. green	10	10
1341	**154**	60f. green	10	10
1342	**154**	70f. green	15	10
1343	**154**	80f. green	15	10
1344	**154**	100f. blue	25	15
1345	**154**	150f. blue	35	25
1346	**154**	175f. brown	40	25
1347	**154**	190f. green	40	30
1348	**154**	200f. black	50	35
1349	**154**	215f. blue	45	30
1350	**154**	225f. blue	45	30
1351	**154**	240f. brown	50	35
1352	**154**	250f. red	60	40
1353	**154**	260f. brown	50	35
1354	**154**	275f. red	65	45
1355	**154**	300f. purple	60	40
1356	**154**	320f. mauve	60	40
1357	**154**	350f. brown	70	50
1358	**154**	410f. red and brown	80	55
1363	**154**	500f. purple	1·00	70
1366	**154**	1000f. red	2·00	1·40

424 Communications, Map of West Africa and Energy Sources

1995. First Economic Community of West African States Trade Fair. Multicoloured.

1370	175f. Type **424**	40	25
1371	215f. Members' flags, banknotes and crops (horiz)	50	35

425 Pasteur developing Rabies Vaccine

1995. Death Centenary of Louis Pasteur (chemist). Multicoloured.

1372	275f. Type **425**	1·10	45
1373	500f. Pasteur working on pasteurization	1·60	85

426 Scene from "L'Arroseur Arrose" (dir. Lumiere Brothers)

1995. Centenary of Motion Pictures. Multicoloured.

1374	100f. Type **426**	25	15
1375	200f. First public film screening by Lumiere brothers	75	35
1376	250f. Auguste and Louis Lumiere watching screening of "Arrival by Train"	90	40
1377	275f. Presentation on cinematography by Antoine Lumiere, 1895	1·25	90

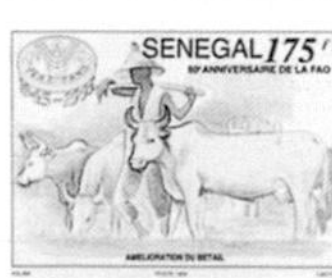

427 Animal Welfare

1995. 50th Anniv of F.A.O. Multicoloured.

1378	175f. Type **427**	40	25
1379	215f. Teaching new skills to rural communities	50	35
1380	260f. Aquaculture	1·00	45
1381	275f. Nourishment of children	1·10	90

428 People of Different Cultures

1995. 50th Anniv of U.N.O.

1382	**428**	275f. blue, violet and black	1·10	45
1383	-	1000f. multicoloured	3·25	2·10

DESIGN: 1000f. "ONU 50" and U.N. Headquarters, New York.

429 Figures dancing around Book

1995. 25th Anniv of Agency for Cultural and Technical Co-operation in French-speaking Countries. Multicoloured.

1384	150f. Type **429**	35	25
1385	500f. Panels of contestants (victory of St. Louis Military Academy in 1994 competition)	1·60	1·10

430 African buffalo

1995. Animals. Multicoloured.

1386	90f. Type **430**	20	15
1387	150f. Warthog	50	25
1388	175f. Bushbuck	1·00	25
1389	275f. African spurred tortoise	1·25	45
1390	300f. North African crested porcupine	1·25	50

431 Caspian Tern

1995. Endangered Birds. Terns. Multicoloured.

1391	90f. Type **431**	20	15
1392	145f. Gull-billed tern	35	25
1393	150f. Royal tern	65	25
1394	180f. Common tern	75	55

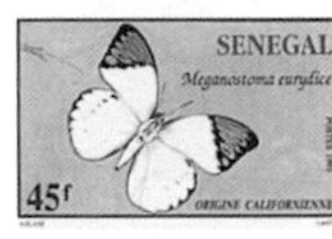

432 "Meganostoma eurydice"

1995. Butterflies. Multicoloured.

1395	45f. Type **432**	10	10
1396	100f. "Luehdorfia japonica"	40	15
1397	200f. Great orange-tip	1·00	35
1398	220f. Small tortoiseshell	1·25	65

433 Bassari Festivals

1995. Cultural Tourism. Multicoloured.

1399	100f. Type **433**	25	15
1400	175f. "Baawnann" (vert)	40	25
1401	220f. Pyramid-roofed houses	55	35
1402	500f. Turu Dance	1·60	1·10

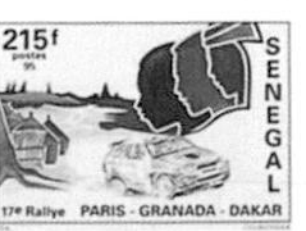

434 Rally Car and Profiles

1996. Paris–Granada–Dakar Motor Rally. Multicoloured.

1403	215f. Type **434**	50	35
1404	275f. Motor cyclists (vert)	65	45
1405	290f. Landmarks and vehicles	65	45
1406	665f. Rally cars	1·75	1·10

435 Sea-island Cotton

1996. Flowers. Multicoloured.

1407	175f. Type **435**	40	30
1408	275f. Sorrel	75	45
1409	290f. Wood sorrel	75	45
1410	500f. Lotus water-lily	1·25	75

436 Diop in Youth and "Sphinx" (Dominique Denon)

1996. Tenth Death Anniv of Cheikh Anta Diop. Mult.

1411	175f. Type **436**	40	30
1412	215f. Diop engaged in Carbon 14 dating tests	50	35

437 Saloum Delta National Park

1996. National Parks. Multicoloured.

1413	175f. Type **437**	40	30
1414	200f. Niokolo Koba	45	30
1415	220f. Madeleine Islands	50	35
1416	275f. Basse Casamance	65	45

438 Boxing

1996. Sport. Multicoloured.

1417	125f. Type **438**	30	20
1418	215f. Judo	50	35
1419	275f. Throwing the javelin	65	45
1420	320f. Throwing the discus	75	55

439 Woman

1996. Improvement of World. Multicoloured.

1421	215f. Type **439** (campaign against poverty)	50	35
1422	500f. "Drop of Hope" (balloon) over landscape (Rio de Janeiro, 1992–Dakar, 1996)	1·10	75

440 "Choose Corridor 1"

1996. "Hall of Pearls" by Serge Correa (painter). Multicoloured.

1423	260f. Type **440**	60	40
1424	320f. "Choose Symphony 1"	75	55

441 Man with Globe rejecting Drugs

1996. United Nations Decade against the Abuse and Trafficking of Drugs. Multicoloured.

1425	175f. Type **441**	40	30
1426	215f. U.N. emblem and hand holding up stop sign to drugs	50	35

442 Competitors and Statue

1996. Centenary of Modern Olympic Games.

1427	**442**	215f. multicoloured	50	35

443 Swimming

1996. Olympic Games, Atlanta, U.S.A. Multicoloured.

1428	10f. Type **443**	10	10
1429	80f. Gymnastics	30	15
1430	175f. Running	60	30
1431	260f. Hurdling	75	40

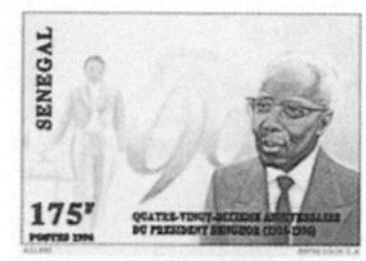

444 "90" and Senghor

1996. 90th Birthday of Leopold Senghor (President, 1960–81). Multicoloured.

1432	175f. Type **444**	40	30
1433	275f. Senghor as young and older man (vert)	65	45

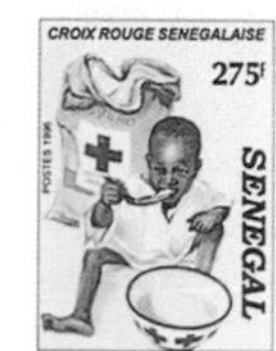

445 Sack of Food and Boy eating

1996. Senegalese Red Cross.

1434	**445**	275f. multicoloured	65	45

446 Savanna Monkey

1996. Primates. Multicoloured.

1435	10f. Type **446**	20	10
1436	30f. Patas monkey	25	10
1437	90f. Campbell's monkey	40	15
1438	215f. Chimpanzee	75	35
1439	260f. Guinea baboon	1·00	40

447 Sad and Injured Boys (child victims of armed conflicts)

1996. 50th Anniv of UNICEF. Multicoloured.

1440	75f. Type **447**	15	10
1441	275f. Nurse and child, mother feeding baby, smiling boy and boy at tap (primary health care) and breast-feeding	65	45

448 Lorry

1997. Dakar–Agades–Dakar Motor Rally. Multicoloured.

1442	25f. Type **448**	25	10
1443	75f. Man pushing car	50	10
1444	215f. Rally car	75	30
1445	300f. Motor cyclist	1·00	45

449 Praying Mantis

1997. Insects. Multicoloured.

1446	10f. Type **449**	20	10
1447	50f. Common earwig	20	10
1448	75f. Desert locust	25	10
1449	215f. Sand tiger beetle	75	30
1450	220f. European field cricket	75	30

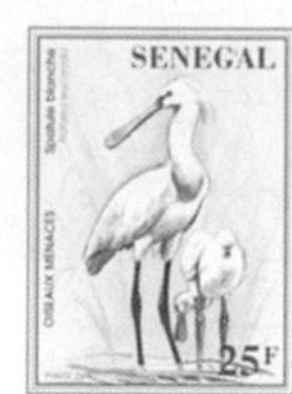

450 White Spoonbill

1997. Endangered Birds. Multicoloured.

1451	25f. Type **450**	10	10
1452	70f. Marabou stork	25	10
1453	175f. Western curlew	50	25
1454	215f. Saddle-bill stork	1·00	30
1455	220f. Crowned crane	1·00	30

The French and Latin inscriptions on Nos. 1453 and 1455 have been transposed.

451 Acacia

1997. Trees and their Fruit. Multicoloured.

1456	80f. Type **451**	40	10
1457	175f. Eucalyptus	50	25
1458	220f. "Khaya senegalensis"	75	30
1459	260f. Horse-tail tree	1·00	40

452 Goree Island

1997. Unissued stamp with part of inscription deleted by bar as in T **452**.

1460	**452**	180f. multicoloured	85	30

453 African Buffaloes

1997. Mammals. Multicoloured.

1461	25f. Type **453**	20	10
1462	90f. Antelopes	35	15
1463	100f. Gnus	40	15
1464	200f. African hunting dogs	75	30
1465	240f. Cheetahs	1·00	35

454 African Fish Eagle

1997. Niokolo-Badiar National Park. Multicoloured.

1466	30f. Type **454**	50	10
1467	90f. Hippopotamus	50	15
1468	240f. African elephant	75	35
1469	300f. Giant eland	1·00	45

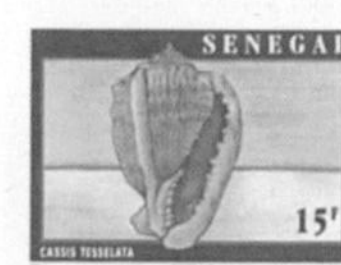

455 West African Helmet

1997. Shells. Multicoloured.

1470	15f. Type **455**	20	10
1471	40f. "Pugilina meria"	30	10
1472	190f. Map cowrie	60	30
1473	200f. "Natica adansoni"	75	30
1474	300f. "Bullia miran"	1·00	45

There are errors of spelling in the Latin inscriptions.

456 Von Stephan

1997. Death Centenary of Heinrich von Stephan (founder of U.P.U.).

1475	**456**	310f. multicoloured	75	45

457 Cereal Stockpiles

1997. Security of Food Supplies. Multicoloured.

1476	190f. Type **457**	70	30
1477	200f. Woman weighing herself (post-weaning nutritional vulnerability)	90	30

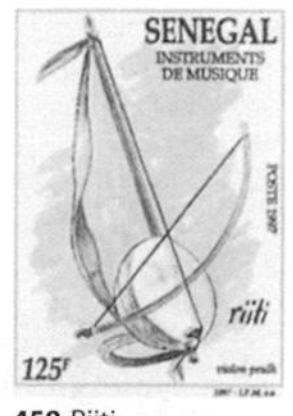

458 Riiti

1997. Musical Instruments. Multicoloured.

1478	125f. Type **458**	40	20
1479	190f. Kora (stringed instrument)	70	30
1480	200f. Tama (double-ended drum)	75	30
1481	240f. Dioung dioung (royal ceremonial drum)	1·00	35

459 Da Gama and Ship's Hold containing Spices (Spice Route)

1997. 500th Anniv of Vasco da Gama's Voyage to India via the Cape of Good Hope. Multicoloured.

1482	40f. Type **459**	20	10
1483	75f. Map of Africa, scales and Da Gama (port of call at Zanzibar)	25	10
1484	190f. "Sao Gabriel" (flagship) and Da Gama (development of caravel)	90	30
1485	200f. Compass rose over map of Africa and printing press (introduction of compass and printed maps)	90	30

460 Planche Mask, Burkina Faso

1997. Traditional Masks. Multicoloured.

1486	45f. Type **460**	25	10
1487	90f. Kpeliyehe mask, Senufo, Ivory Coast	40	15
1488	200f. Nimba mask, Baga, Guinea	80	30
1489	240f. Walu mask, Dogon, Mali	90	35
1490	300f. Dogon mask, Bandiagara, Mali	1·00	45

461 Series CC2400 Diesel-electric Locomotive

1997. Trains. Multicoloured.

1491	15f. Type **461**	25	10
1492	90f. Diesel goods locomotive	45	15
1493	100f. Mountain steam locomotive	50	15

1494	240f. Maquinista diesel locomotive	85	35
1495	310f. Series 151-A steam locomotive and goods wagons	1·00	45

462 Cat

1997. The African Golden Cat. Multicoloured.

1496	45f. Type **462**	25	10
1497	100f. Standing on branch	50	15
1498	240f. Lying on branch	75	35
1499	300f. One cat grooming another	1·00	45

463 Lorry crossing Sahara

1998. Dakar–Dakar Motor Rally. Multicoloured.

1500	20f. Type **463**	20	10
1501	45f. Motor cycle at Lac Rose	40	10
1502	190f. Off-road vehicle crossing Mauritanian desert	75	30
1503	240f. Rally car by River Senegal	1·00	35

464 Hut and Children

1998. 25th Anniv of Aldiana Club. Multicoloured.

1504	290f. Type **464**	90	55
1505	320f. Canoe, woman and fish	95	60

465 Children

1998. SOS Children's Village, Ziguinchor. Multicoloured.

1506	190f. Type **465**	60	35
1507	240f. Girl and huts	95	60

466 Diana, Princess of Wales

1998. Diana, Princess of Wales Commemoration. Multicoloured.

1508	240f. Diana wearing hat with veil	95	60
MS1509	Five sheets. (a) 141×198 mm. 200f. T **466** and different designs showing Diana, Princess of Wales; (b) 141×198 mm. 25f. As No. 1508 and 8 different designs showing Diana; (c) 131×94 mm. 1000f. With head on hand; (d) 131×94 mm. 1500f. With Princes William and Harry (e) 138×100 mm. 2000f. Wearing tiara Set of 5 sheets	26·00	14·00

467 Slave House, Goree Island

1998. 150th Anniv of Abolition of Slavery. Multicoloured.

1510	20f. Type **467**	15	10
1511	40f. Frederick Douglas (American abolitionist)	15	10
1512	190f. Mother, child and slave ship	60	35
1513	290f. Victor Schoelcher (French abolitionist and politician)	90	55

468 Museum Emblem, Museum Building and Reyane Henriette Bathily (founder)

1998. Fourth Anniv of Henriette Bathily Women's Museum. Multicoloured.

1514	190f. Type **468**	60	25
1515	270f. Emblem, building and Henriette Bathily (different)	95	60

469 Brazilian Player with Football

1998. World Cup Football Championships, France. Multicoloured.

1516	25f. Type **469**	15	10
1517	50f. Mascot, legs, ball and trophy	15	10
1518	150f. Mascot, trophy and ball	45	25
1519	300f. Flags of competing countries	95	60

470 House and Car

1998. Children's Paintings. SOS Children's Village, Ziguinchor. Multicoloured.

1520	30f. Type **470**	10	10
1521	50f. Trees and rainbow	15	10
1522	180f. Sunrise and flowers	60	35
1523	300f. House, road and eyes	95	60

471 Buoy with Siren

1998. Lighthouses and Buoys. Multicoloured.

1524	50f. Type **471**	15	15
1525	100f. Mammelles lighthouse	30	20
1526	190f. Luminescent buoy	60	35
1527	240f. Port entrance lighthouse	75	45

472 Alberto Ascari

1998. Ferrari Formula I Racing Team. Two sheets containing T **472** and similar horiz designs. Multicoloured.

MS1528	(a) 158×125 mm. 100f.×6 Type **472**, Guiseppe Farina, Ricardo Patrese, Michele Alboreto, Elio de Angelis, Andrea de Cesaris; (b) 81×100 mm. 1000f. Ferrari race car Set of two sheets	7·75	4·50

473 Leaning Tower, Pisa

1998. Italia '98 International Stamp Exhibition, Milan (1st issue).

1529	**473**	290f. multicoloured	95	60

See also No. **MS**1559 and **MS**1607.

474 Seagull, Dolphin and Undersea Fauna

1998. International Year of the Ocean. Multicoloured.

1530	190f. Type **474**	60	35
1531	790f. Fish	2·60	1·50

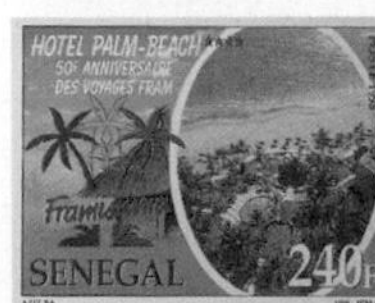

475 Emblem and Beach

1998. Palm Beach Hotel. 50th Anniv of FRAM (travel company). Multicoloured.

1532	240f. Type **475**	75	45
1533	300f. Women and beach scene	95	60

476 Woman wearing Turban

1998. Women's Hair Styles and Headdresses.

1534	**476**	40f. brown, chocolate and black	10	10
1535	-	100f. green, deep green and black	30	20
1536	-	240f. violet, deep violet and black	75	45
1537	-	300f. blue, deep blue and black	95	60

DESIGNS: Type **476**; 100f. Long braided hair; 240f. Braided hair with beads; 300f. Turban tied in front.

477 Figure behind Bars and United Nations Emblem

1998. 50th Anniv of United Nations Declaration of Human Rights. Multicoloured.

1538	200f. Type **477**	60	35
1539	350f. Women and emblem	1·00	60

478 Seagull, Fish and Net

1998. Marine Protection. Multicoloured.

1540	50f. Type **478**	15	10
1541	100f. Fish and effluent pipe	30	20
1542	310f. Dynamite and dead fish	90	55
1543	365f. Fish and oil pollution	1·00	60

479 Smiling Woman

1998. "Senegalese Elegance" (3rd series).

1544	**479**	125f. olive	45	25
1545	**479**	290f. purple	90	55
1546	**479**	310f. purple	95	60

480 Repairing Rally Car

1999. 21st Paris—Dakar Rally. Multicoloured.

1555	150f. Type **480**	45	25
1556	175f. Digging out of sand dune	50	30
1557	240f. Motorcycle crash	75	45
1558	290f. Motorcycle and car sunk in sand	95	60

481 Romy Schneider

1999. Italia '98 International Stamp Exhibition, Milan (2nd issue). Film Actors. Three sheets containing T **481** and similar horiz designs. Multicoloured.

MS1559	(a) 140×195 mm. 200f.×9, Type **481**; Yves Montand; Catherine Deneuve; Gina Lollobrigida; Marcello Mastroianni; Sophia Loren; Frank Sinatra; Dean Martin; Marilyn Monroe; (b) 144×116 mm. 1500f. Marilyn Monroe (different); (c) 144×116 mm. 2000f. Marcello Masstroianni (different)	4·50	2·75

482 Black Coupe

1999. 40th Anniv of De Tomaso (car manufacturer). Sheet 153×103 mm containing T **482** and similar horiz designs. Multicoloured.

MS1560	250f.×4, Type **482**; White coupe; Dark blue coupe; Red coupe	3·00	1·75

483 Elvis Presley

1999. Elvis Presley (entertainer) Commemoration. Sheet 130×175 mm containing T **483** and similar vert designs. Multicoloured.

MS1561	250f. Type **483** and 8 designs showing Elvis Presley	6·00	3·50

484 Stamp and Flags

1999. PhilexFrance '99 International Stamp Exhibition, Paris. 150th Anniv of First French Stamp.

1562	**484**	240f. multicoloured	95	60

485 Ayrton Senna

1999. Formula 1 Racing Drivers. Multicoloured.

1563	200f. Type **485**	80	50
MS1564	(a) 157×120 mm. 200f.×9, Juan Manuel Fangio; Alberto Ascari; Graham Hill; Jim Clark; Jack Brabham; Jackie Stewart; Niki Lauda; Type **485** (design enlarged); Alain Prost; (b) 112×82 mm. 2000f. Ayrton Senna (different) (50×36 mm)	6·00	3·50

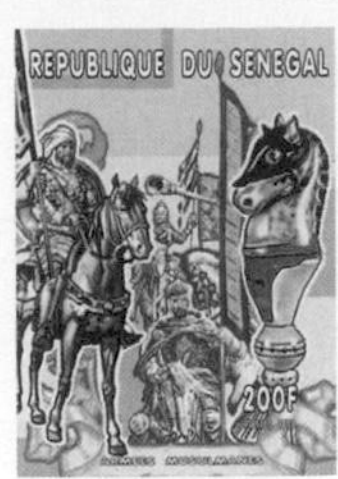

486 Knight on Horseback and Knight (chess piece)

1999. Chess. Multicoloured.

1565 250f. Knight and chess piece (different) 95 60

MS1566 Three sheets, each 140×200 mm. (a) 200f. Type **486** and 8 different designs showing soldiers of the Crusades and chess pieces; (b) 250f.×9 Soldiers and chess pieces; (c) 400f.×9 Soldiers and chess pieces (different) Set of 3 sheets 25·00 15·00

487 Jackie Robinson

1999. Jackie Robinson (baseball player) Commemoration. Multicoloured.

1567 250f. Type **487** 95 60

MS1568 Three sheets. (a) 132×177 mm. 1000f. Type **487** and 8 different designs showing Jackie Robinson; (b) 88×138 mm. 1500f. Looking left (36×42 mm); (c) 88×138 mm. 2000f. With raised bat Set of 3 sheets 7·50 4·50

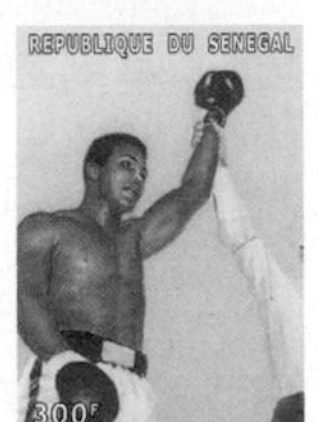

488 Ludger Beerbaum (show jumper)

1999. Equestrian Competitors. Multicoloured.

1569 300f. Type **488** 1·10 65

MS1570 Two sheets. (a) 120×156 mm. 300f.×9, Martin Schaudi; Klaus Balkenhols; Nadine Capellmann Bifar; Willi Melliger; Type **488**; Ulrich Kircchnoff; Sally Clark; Bettina Overesch Boker; Karen O' Connor; (b) 112×82 mm. 1500f. German equestrian team (50×36 mm) Set of 2 sheets 8·50 5·00

489 Mohammed Ali

1999. 25th Anniv of Mohammed Ali—George Forman Boxing Match. Multicoloured.

1571 300f. Type **489** 95 60

MS1572 Three sheets. (a) 132×177 mm. 300f. Type **489** and 8 different designs showing Mohammed Ali; (b) 88×138 mm. 1000f. Wearing robe (36×42 mm) (c) 88×138 mm. 2000f. With raised fists (36×42 mm) 7·50 4·50

490 Pete Sampras

1999. Racquet Sports. Multicoloured.

1573 400f. Type **490** 1·30 80

MS1574 Two sheets. (a) 120×156 mm. 400f.×9, Liu Guoliang (tennis player); Martina Hingis (tennis); Deng Yaping (table tennis player); Andre Agassi (tennis); Jean-Philippe Gatien (table tennis); Anna Kournikova (tennis); Mikael Appelgren (table tennis); Type **490** (tennis); Jan-Ove Waldner (table tennis); (b) 112×82 mm. 2000f. Vladimir Samsonov, Deng Yaping and Jörg Rosskopf (table tennis players) (50×36 mm) Set of 2 sheets 12·00 7·00

491 Racing Yachts

1999. Transport. Multicoloured.

1575 250f. Type **491** 95 60

1576 325f. Bentley coupe 1·00 60

1577 350f. Prussian locomotive S10 1·10 65

1578 375f. Ducati 900 SS motorbike 1·20 70

1579 500f. Concorde super sonic aircraft 1·50 90

MS1580 Ten sheets. (a) 155×119 mm. Ships:—250f.×9, *France* (liner); United States (liner); *Finnjet* (ferry); *Chusan* ` (liner); *Cheers* (inscr "Sheers") (catamaran); *Vendredi 13* (racing yacht); Type **491**; *Pen Duick II* (transatlantic ketch); *Jester* (transatlantic yacht); (b) 155×119 mm. Cars:—325f.×9, Duryea (1893); Menon (1897); Renault; Fiat Zero (1912); Inscr "Spa" (1913); Packard; As No. 1525; Mercedes Benz; Morris Minor (1930); (c) 155×119 mm Steam trains:—350f.×9, *Mikado*; French locomotive 241 P (1948); French locomotive 230 K; The Milwaukee road class A locomotive (1935) Russian locomotive class 1.5; Prussian locomotive G12; As No. 1526; Inscr "Austrian locomotive KK SEB series 310"; French locomotive *Outrance* (1877) (d) 155×119 mm. 375f.×9, Zenith motorcycle and sidecar (1913) Brough Superior motor cycle (1920); Motor cycle racing, 1903; As No. 1257; Dave Thorpe (motocross rider); Suzuki 500 motorcycle; Michaux bicycle (1865); Modern solid wheel racing cycle; Woman cyclist (e) 155×119 mm. High speed trains:—450f.×9, Acela, USA; Class 332 Britain; I.C.E., Germany; Trans Europe Express locomotive, Luxembourg; California–Nevada Super Speed monorail, USA; Inter City 250, Britain; Korean high speed locomotive; Eurostar locomotive, Britain; TGV Thalys PBA, France (f) 155×119 mm. Aircraft:—500f.×9, USA; USA Maglifter launch catapult; Inscr "S.M." (USA); Concorde; Inscr "T.U. 144" (URSS); Inscr "Futur X USA"; USA X 33; Type **491**; USA X 34 space vehicle (g) 121×92 mm. 1000f. Eric Tabarly and *Pen Duick VI* (51×36 mm) (h) 121×92 mm.1500f. Walter Chrysler and Chrysler (1924) (i) 122×92 mm. 1500f. Marc Seguin and steam locomotive (36×51 mm) (j) 112×82 mm. 2000f. Bobby Julich (cycle racer) (51×36 mm) (k) 122×92 mm. TGV locomotive *Atlantique*, TGV *Mediterranee* and *Etienne Chambron* (l) 122×92 mm. 2000f. Concorde (51×36 mm) Set of 10 sheets 65·00 38·00

492 Evacuation of Sinking Ship

1999. Sinking of *Titanic* (liner), 1912. Multicoloured.

1581 300f. Type **492** 95 60

MS1582 155×119 mm. 300f.×9, In shipyard; At the dockside; Pulled by tugboat; At sea; Collision with iceberg; Type **492**; Expedition to wreck; Couple lost in accident; Captain John Smith 9·00 5·00

493 Russian R.D. 107 Rocket

1999. Spacecraft. Two sheets containing T **493** and similar multicoloured designs.

MS1583 (a) 140×200 mm. 400f.×9, Type **493**; Russian Soyuz; Russian Proton; USA Atlas-Centaur; USA Atlas-Agena; USA Atlas-mercury; USA Titan 2; USA Juno 2; USA Saturn I; (b) 122×92 mm. Neil Armstrong (51×36 mm) Set of 2 sheets 12·00 7·00

494 Book, Men and National Colours

1999. International Year of the Elderly. Multicoloured.

1584 30f. Type **494** 15 10

1585 150f. Blacksmith 45 25

1586 290f. Musicians 90 55

1587 300f. Scientist (vert) 95 60

495 Death Cap (*Amanita phalloides*) (inscr "Amanite phalloide")

1999. Fungi. Senegal Scouts. Multicoloured.

1588 60f. Type **495** 20 10

1589 175f. Common ink cap (*Coprinus atramantarius*) 60 35

1590 220f. Destroying angel (*Amanita virosa*) (inscr "Amanite vireuse") 75 45

1591 250f. Field mushroom (*Agaricus campestri*) (inscr "campester") 95 60

496 Astronauts and Flag on Moon

1999. 30th Anniv of First Moon Landing. Multicoloured.

1592 25f. Type **496** 15 10

1593 145f. Neil Armstrong, flag and astronaut (vert) 45 25

1594 180f. Astronaut, flag and rocket (vert) 55 30

1595 500f. Astronaut and space shuttle (vert) 1·50 90

497 Roan Antelope (*Hippotragus equines*)

1999. Fauna. Multicoloured.

1596 60f. Type **497** 20 10

1597 90f. Oyster catcher (*Haematopus ostralegus*) 30 20

1598 300f. White-face whistling duck (*Dendrocygna viduata*) (inscr "viduada") 95 60

1599 320f. Leatherback turtle (*Dermochelys coriacea*) 95 60

498 Mother Teresa and Child

1999. 20th Anniv of Award of Nobel Peace Prize to Mother Teresa (humanitarian). Multicoloured.

1600 75f. Type **498** 20 10

1601 100f. With children 45 25

1602 290f. With priest 80 50

1603 300f. Holding laughing child 1·00 60

499 Emblem and Rainbows

1999. 125th Anniv of Universal Postal Union. Multicoloured.

1604 270f. Type **499** 90 55

1605 300f. Emblem 1·10 65

500 "Mont Sainte-Victoire seen from Bibemus Quarry"

1999. Art. Four sheets containing T **500** and similar multicoloured designs showing paintings by artists named.

MS1606 (a) Horiz. 195×141 mm. Paul Cezanne. 200f. ×9, Type **500**; "Sea at l'Estaque"; "Landscape"; "Still Life"; "Still Life with Basket"; "Still Life with Apples and Peaches"; "Bibemus Quarry"; "Woods with Millstone"; "Lake Annecy". (b) Vert. 113×163 mm. Paul Gauguin. 250f. ×4, "Te Faaturuma (Brooding Woman)"; "The Cellist (Portrait of Upaupa Scheklud)"; "Self-portrait with Halo"; "When are you getting Married?". (c) Vert. 113×163 mm. Pablo Picasso. 375f. ×4, "Cavalier with Pipe"; "Rembrandt Figure and Eros"; "Female Nude and Smoker"; "The Doves". (d) Vert. 156×120 mm. Vincent van Gogh. 2000f. "Dr. Paul Gachet" Set of 4 sheets 12·50 7·50

501 Clark Gable

1999. Italia '98 International Stamp Exhibition, Milan (3rd issue). Film Actors. Four sheets containing T **501** and similar vert designs. Multicoloured.

MS1607 (a) 136×196 mm. 250f. ×9, Type **501**; Rudolph Valentino; Errol Flynn; Cary Grant; Robert Taylor; Gary Cooper; James Dean; Humphrey Bogart; Marlon Brando. (b) 136×196 mm. 425f. ×9, Grace Kelly; Marilyn Monroe; Audrey Hepburn; Greta Garbo; Jean Harlow; Loretta Young; Jane Russell; Dorothy Lamour; Veronica Lake. (c) 140×200 mm. 450f. ×9, Ginger Rogers and Fred Astaire; Cary Grant, Katherine Hepburn and James Stewart; Melvyn Douglas and Greta Garbo; Vivien Leigh and Clark Gable; Burt Lancaster and Deborah Kerr; Humphrey Bogart and Lauren Bacall; Steve McQueen and Jacqueline Bisset; Gene Kelly and Rita Hayworth; Ingrid Bergman and Cary Grant. (d) 116×143 mm. 2000f. Grace Kelly (different) Set of 4 sheets 24·00 14·50

502 Betty Boop holding Microphone

1999. Betty Boop (cartoon character created by Max Fleischer). Multicoloured.

1608 250f. Type **502** 50 30

1609 250f. Holding guitar 50 30

1610 400f. Seated 80 50

MS1611 Five sheets. (a) 132×177 mm. 250f. ×9, Holding saxophone; Playing tambourine; 1609; Playing guitar; Wearing top hat; Holding drum sticks; Wearing headphones; 1608; Wearing patterned trousers. (b) 132×177 mm. 400f. ×9, Wearing red dress; Wearing flowered earrings, bracelets and belt; Wearing ruffled blouse and waistcoat; Wearing purple dress; 1610; Wearing black outfit; Wearing fringed waistcoat; Wearing black sleeveless dress; Wearing purple jacket and trousers. (c) 89×140 mm. 1000f. Head and shoulders. (d) 89×140 mm. 1500f. With folded arms. (e) 89×140 mm. 2000f. Wearing purple jacket Set of 5 sheets — 20·00 — 12·00

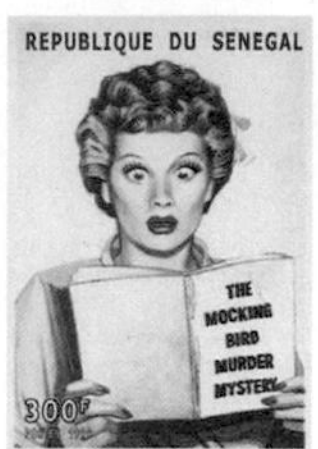

503 Lucy (Lucille Ball)

1999. *I Love Lucy* (Television comedy series). Multicoloured.

1612	300f. Type **503**	60	40
1613	300f. Fred Mertz (William Fawley), Ethel Mertz (Vivian Vance) and Lucy	60	40

MS1614 Four sheets. (a) Vert. 137×182 mm. 330f. ×9, Lucy holding telephone; No. 1612; Wearing green dress with black tie; With hand raised; Wearing pearl necklace and black hat; Holding medicine bottle; Wearing hat, glasses and fur stole; Wearing purple hat; Wearing top hat. (b) Horiz. 177×132 mm. 330f. ×9, With Ethel holding boxes; Desi Arnaz, Lucy, Fred and Ethel; Fred, Ethel and Lucy wearing headscarf; Lucy and chicks; Fred, Ethel, Lucy and Desi seated at table; Ethel and Lucy; Lucy dancing wearing rolled up trousers; As No. 1613; Lucy, Ethel and Fred seated at table. (c) 89×127 mm. 1000f. Lucy holding box (36×51 mm). (d) 117×89 mm. 2000f. Lucy holding paper bag (36×51 mm) Set of 4 sheets — 18·00 — 11·00

504 Three Stooges

1999. *The Three Stooges* (comedy series starring Moe Howard, Larry Fine and Curly Howard). Multicoloured.

1615	400f. Type **504**	80	50

MS1616 Three sheets. (a) Horiz. 175×140 mm. 400f. ×9, Moe and Larry lying on bed; Moe, Larry and Curly; Moe and Larry listening to telephone ("False Alarms"); Holding scissors; As No. 1615; With surgical trolley ("Dizzy Doctors"); Larry and Curly holding Moe down; Holding step ladder; Holding plank ("Tassels in the Air"). (b) Vert. 140×89 mm. 1000f. Curly and Moe with feathers. (c) Vert. 140×89 mm. 1500f. Curly as cowboy Set of 3 sheets — 12·00 — 7·25

505 Participants and Pyramids

2001. 22nd Paris—Dakar Rally. Multicoloured.

1617	75f. Type **505**	15	10
1618	100f. Truck, four-wheel drive and rally car	20	10
1619	220f. Truck and motorcycle	45	25
1620	320f. Camel and motorcycle	65	40

506 Motorcyclist and Rally Emblem

2001. 23rd Paris—Dakar Rally. Multicoloured.

1621	190f. Type **506**	40	25
1622	220f. Emblem as face (vert)	45	25
1623	240f. Emblem containing camel (vert)	50	30
1624	790f. Emblem and four-wheel drive car	1·60	95

507 Festival of Arts and Culture Emblem

2001. Third Millennium. Multicoloured.

1625	20f. Type **507**	10	10
1626	100f. Pan African Plastic Arts festival emblem	20	10
1627	150f. National Heritage Day emblem	30	20
1628	300f. Memorial, Goree Island (anti-slavery memorial) (horiz)	60	35

508 Swimmer and Weightlifter

2001. Olympic Games, Sydney (2000). Multicoloured.

1629	40f. Type **508**	10	10
1630	80f. Taekwondo	15	10
1631	240f. Runners finishing 200m race	50	30
1632	290f. Handball match	60	35

509 Flower Seller

2001. Craft Market, Kermel. Multicoloured.

1633	50f. Type **509**	10	10
1634	90f. Wooden carvings	20	10
1635	250f. Bowls and pendants (horiz)	50	30
1636	350f. Carvings and flower seller	70	40

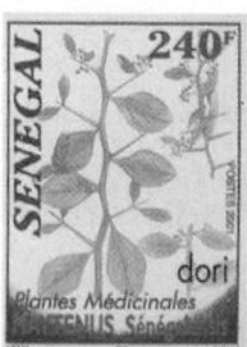

510 Satellite Dish, Globe and Weather Station

2001. 50th Anniv of World Meteorological Organization. Multicoloured.

1637	100f. Type **510**	20	10
1638	790f. Weather station (vert)	1·60	95

511 *Maytenus senegalensis*

2001. Medicinal Plants. Multicoloured.

1639	240f. Type **511**	50	30
1640	320f. *Boscia senegalensis*	65	40
1641	350f. *Euphorbia hirta*	70	40
1642	500f. *Guiera senegalensis*	1·00	60

512 Outline of Senegal

2001. 19th Lions International District 403 Congress, Dakar. Multicoloured.

1643	190f. Type **512**	40	25
1644	300f. Lion (vert)	60	35

513 Emblem, Tank and Runners

2001. 50th Anniv of United Nations High Commissioner for Refugees. Multicoloured.

1645	240f. Type **513**	50	30
1646	320f. Emblem, globe and runner (vert)	65	40

514 Hands holding Book

2001. International Teachers' Day. Multicoloured.

1647	225f. Type **514**	45	25
1648	290f. Man writing and world map (horiz)	60	35

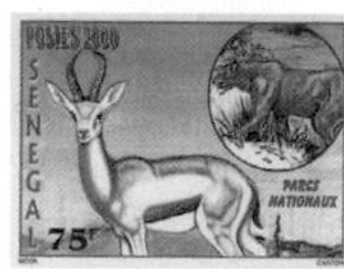

515 Drummer

2001. Tourism. Multicoloured.

1649	145f. Type **515**	30	20
1650	290f. Tree, windsurfer, and beach (vert)	60	35

516 Antelope and Lioness

2001. National Parks. Multicoloured.

1651	75f. Type **516**	15	10
1652	125f. Heron and marabou stork	25	15
1653	275f. Crowned cranes and elephant	55	35
1654	300f. Zebra (vert)	60	35

517 Motorcyclists

2002. 24th Paris—Dakar Rally (inscr "2001"). Multicoloured.

1655	250f. Type **517**	50	30
1656	360f. Four-wheel drive race cars	75	45
1657	370f. Eiffel tower and motorcyclist (vert)	80	50
1658	425f. Motorcyclist (vert)	90	55

518 Trophy, Footballers and Flags

2002. African Nations Football Championship. Multicoloured.

1659	250f. Type **518**	50	30
1660	380f. Players in front of goal	80	50
1661	425f. Saving goal	90	55
1662	440f. Trophy and player (vert)	90	55

519 Peulh Woman

520 Linguere Woman

2002. Senegalese Women.

1663	519	5f. magenta	10	10
1664	519	10f. yellow	10	10
1665	519	20f. orange	10	10
1666	519	25f. red	10	10
1667	519	40f. magenta	10	10
1668	519	50f. blue	10	10
1669	519	60f. green	15	10
1670	519	70f. green	15	10
1671	519	100f. green	20	10
1672	519	150f. olive	30	20
1673	519	175f. brown	35	20
1674	520	200f. olive	40	25
1675	520	250f. orange	50	30
1676	520	290f. red	60	35
1677	520	300f. purple	60	35
1678	520	360f. violet	75	45
1679	520	390f. blue	80	50
1680	520	425f. green	90	55
1681	520	500f. bistre	1·00	60
1682	520	800f. black	1·70	1·00
1683	520	1000f. blue	2·10	1·30

521 Map of Africa

2002. Proclamation of African Union Act. Multicoloured.

1684	330f. Type **521**	70	40
1685	390f. Flags, hands and map (horiz)	80	50

522 Gate of the Third Millennium, Dakar

2002. New Millennium. Showing the Millennium Gate. Multicoloured.

1686	200f. Type **522**	40	25
1687	290f. Front of gate	60	35
1688	390f. Rear of gate	80	50
1689	725f. Rocks and gate	1·50	90

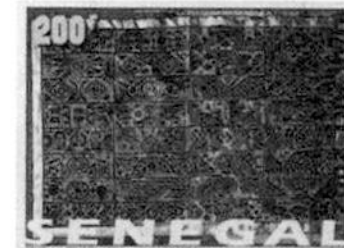

523 Woven Hanging (Zehum Yetmgeta)

2002. Dak'Art 2002 Biennial Art Exhibition. Multicoloured.

1690	200f. Type **523**	40	25
1691	330f. Sculpture (Moustapha Dime) (vert)	70	40
1692	400f. Woven Hanging (Abdoulaye Konate)	85	50
1693	425f. Two figures (painting) (Gora Mbengue)	90	55

524 Trophy and Football

2002. World Cup Football Championship, Japan and South Korea. Multicoloured.

1694	75f.+100f. Type **524**	35	20
1695	200f.+100f. Trophy and emblem (36×27 mm)	60	35
1696	290f.+50f. Stadium and football (36×27 mm)	70	40
1697	360f.+50f. Hands holding trophy and goalposts (36×27 mm)	85	50

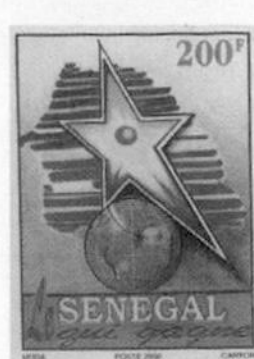

525 Map, Star and Globe

2002. Culture and Sport. "Senegal Wins".

1698	**525**	200f. multicoloured	40	25
1699	**525**	380f. multicoloured	80	50

526 Globe, Rainbow, Skyscraper and Traditional Dwellings

2002. United Nations Year of Dialogue among Civilizations. Multicoloured.

1700	290f. Type **526**	60	35
1701	380f. Children surrounding globe	80	50

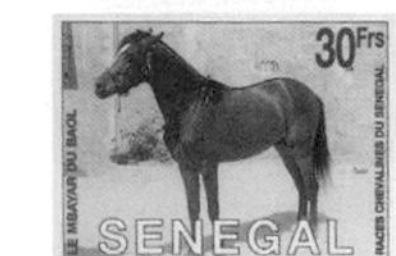

527 "Le Mbayar du Baol" (race horse)

2002. Senegalese Race Horses. Multicoloured.

1702	30f. Type **527**	10	10
1703	200f. "Le Mpar du Cayor"	40	25
1704	250f. "Le Narougor"	50	30
1705	300f. "Le Foutanke"	60	35

528 Sacred Baobab Tree

2002. International Year of Eco-Tourism. Multicoloured.

1706	90f. Type **528**	20	10
1707	250f. Pelican, Du Djoudj National Park	50	30
1708	300f. Mangroves	60	35
1709	380f. Rope bridge	80	50

529 Gorillas

2002. Fauna. Multicoloured.

1710	75f. Type **529**	15	10
1711	290f. Black rhinoceros	60	35
1712	360f. Ostrich and tortoise	75	45
1713	380f. Giraffes (vert)	80	50

530 Four-wheel Drive Race Cars

2003. 25th Paris–Dakar Rally. Multicoloured.

1714	360f. Type **530**	75	45
1715	425f. Motorcyclists	90	55

531 Hands holding Document and Rose

2003. New Partnership for Africa's Development (NEPAD). Multicoloured.

1716	200f. Type **531**	40	25
1717	250f. Map of Africa and symbols of renewal	50	30
1718	290f. Gannet and map	60	35

532 Animal Sacrifice

2003. Art. Multicoloured.

1719	250f. Type **532**	50	30
1720	360f. Faces	75	45

533 "Le Cailcedrat Mort"

2003. Sculpture. Multicoloured.

1721	200f. Type **533**	40	25
1722	300f. "Tete d'un Sorcier"	60	35
1723	380f. "Le Laard"	80	50
1724	440f. "Le Thioury"	90	55

534 Le Goumbe Lebon

2003. Traditional Costumes. Multicoloured.

1725	250f. Type **534**	50	30
1726	360f. La Badiaranke	75	45
1727	390f. Le Grand Boubou	80	50
1728	500f. Le Bowede	1·00	60

535 *Cymbium cymbium*

2003. Marine Fauna. Multicoloured.

1729	290f. Type **535**	60	35
1730	370f. Herrings	80	50
1731	380f. Catfish	80	50
1732	400f. *Chelonia mydas*	85	50

536 Motorcyclists

2004. 26th Paris–Dakar Rally (inscr "2003"). Multicoloured.

1733	390f. Type **536**	80	50
1734	500f. Four-wheel drive race car and motorcyclist	1·00	60

537 Emblem

2004. African Nations Cup Football Championship. Multicoloured.

1735	200f. Type **537**	20	10
1736	300f. Trophy, stadium, football and television (horiz)	60	35
1737	400f. Shaking hands (horiz)	85	50
1738	425f. Match play (horiz)	90	55

2004. Senegalese Women.

1739	**519**	125f. silver	25	15
1740	**520**	350f. violet	75	45
1741	**520**	600f. black	1·20	70
1742	**520**	700f. violet	1·40	85

See also Nos. 1739-1742

538 Dakar Railway Station

2004. Cultural Heritage. Architecture. Multicoloured.

1743	240f. Type **538**	50	30
1744	370f. Podor fort	80	50
1745	390f. Town Hall	80	50
1746	500f. Notre Dame de Victoires Cathedral	1·00	60

539 Mosque, Omarienne de Guede

2004. Places of Worship. Multicoloured.

1747	200f. Type **539**	40	25
1748	225f. Popenguine Basilica (vert)	50	30
1749	250f. Grand Mosque, Touba	50	30
1750	300f. Grand Mosque, Tivaouane	60	35

540 Millet

2004. Local Cereals. Multicoloured.

1751	100f. Type **540**	20	10
1752	150f. Millet and maize (horiz)	30	20
1753	200f. Maize	40	25
1754	300f. Rice (horiz)	60	35

541 Race Truck and Motorcyclist

2005. 27th Paris–Dakar Rally. Multicoloured.

1755	450f. Type **541**	95	60
1756	550f. Emblem and dunes (vert)	1·10	65

542 Hands (Mbaye Gnilane)

2005. Children's Drawings. Multicoloured.

1757	50f. Type **542**	20	20
1758	75f. Village (Pape Cheick Diack) (*horiz*)	30	30
1759	100f. Dove carrying leaf (Aly Gueye) (*horiz*)	35	35
1760	425f. School (Abdourahim Diallo) (*horiz*)	1·50	1·50

543 Tents and Race Car

2006. 28th Paris—Dakar Rally. Multicoloured.

1761	500f. Type **543**	1·00	1·80
1762	1000f. Repair to race car and men carrying vehicle doors	3·50	3·50

544 Family Discussion

2006. AIDS Awareness Campaign. Multicoloured.

1763	200f. Type **544**	75	75
1764	250f. Virus (*vert*)	90	90
1765	290f. Couples (fidelity)	1·10	1·10
1766	425f. Adults in circle	1·50	1·50

545 'Toorodo Penlh' (inscr '2005')

2006. African Dolls. Multicoloured.

1767	200f. Type **545**	75	75
1768	250f. La Reine Signare	90	90
1768a	375f. Zulu Afrique du Sud	1·30	1·30
1768b	425f. Femme Woloff–Senegal	1·50	1·50

546 Symbols of Communication

2006. World Numerical Solidarity Day. Multicoloured.

1769	200f. Type **546**	75	75
1770	250f. Globe, speaking over telephone and four clasped hands	90	90
1771	370f. Satellite, computer circuits and map of Senegal (*horiz*)	1·30	1·30
1772	380f. Hand, cable, satellite and computer (*horiz*)	1·40	1·40

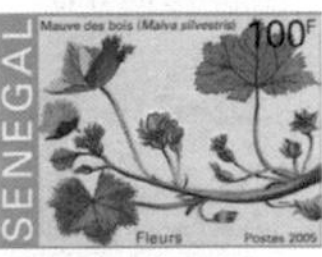

547 *Malva silvestris* (mallow)

2006. Flowering Plants. Multicoloured.

1773	100f. Type **547**	35	35
1774	150f. *Moringa oleifera* (*vert*)	55	55
1775	300f. *Cichorum intybus* (chicory) (*vert*)	1·10	1·10
1776	450f. Dandelion (*Taraxacum*)	1·60	1·60

548 Combatants sparring

2006. Traditional Wrestling. Multicoloured.

1777	100f. Type **548**	35	35
1778	200f. Wrestling	75	75
1779	250f. Mud covered wrestler (*vert*)	90	90
1780	500f. Drummers and wrestler (preparation mystique) (*vert*)	1·80	1·80

549 'Demba & Dupont' (statue of Senegalese and French soldier)

2006. Tirailleur Senegalais Day. Multicoloured.

1781	200f. Type **549**	75	75
1782	450f. Demba & Dupont	1·60	1·60

550 Leopold Senghor

2006. Birth Centenary of Leopold Sedar Senghor (poet and politician) (first president 1960—80).

1783	**550**	200f. multicoloured	75	75
1784	**550**	450f. multicoloured	1·60	1·60

551 Women struggling

2006. Campaign against Female Excision. Multicoloured.

1785	50f. Type **551**	20	20
1786	200f. Women and children	75	75
1787	350f. Health workers and woman	1·20	1·20
1788	370f. Women and girl	1·30	1·30

551a *Luscinia phoenicurus*

2006. Birds. Multicoloured.

1788a	30f. Type **551a**	10	10
1788b	75f. Inscr 'Rouge gorge bleu' (vert)	25	25
1788c	200f. *Pica pica* (magpie) (vert)	75	75
1788d	400f. Crow (vert)	1·40	1·40

552 Competitors

2007. 29th Paris—Dakar Rally. Multicoloured.

1789	450f. Type **552**	1·60	1·60
1790	550f. Motorcyclist	1·40	1·40

553 Hands Exchanging Book and Sharing Food

2007. National Solidarity Day. Multicoloured.

1791	50f. Type **553**	20	20
1792	100f. Hands holding star and map outline	35	35
1793	200f. Map outline and hands placing goods in bowl	75	75
1794	500f. Map outline and symbols of prosperity	1·80	1·80

554 Emblem

2007. Gorée Diaspora Cutural Festival. Multicoloured.

1795	50f. Type **554**	20	20
1796	200f. Art installation (horiz)	75	75
1797	450f. Building and hands writing with quill	1·60	1·60
1798	525f. Sail ship	1·90	1·90

554a *Strichnos nux vomica*

2007. Flora. Multicoloured.

1798a	200f. Type **554a**	75	75
1798b	290f. *Conium macultum*	1·10	1·10
1798c	300f. Succulent	1·20	1·20
1798d	450f. Pitcher Plant	1·60	1·60

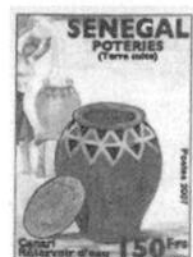
554b Water Reservoir Pot

2007. Terracotta Pottery. Multicoloured.

1798e	150f. Type **554b**	65	65
1798f	200f. Libation pot	80	80
1798g	225f. Cooking fireplace	85	85
1798h	425f. Varnished incense burner	1·70	1·70

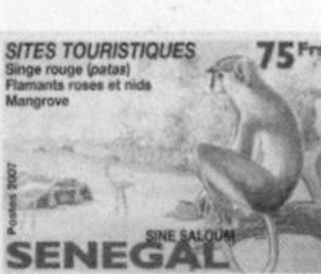
555 Flamingoes and Monkey (Sine Saloum Delta)

2008. Tourism. Multicoloured.

1799	75f. Type **555**	25	25
1800	125f. Cockatoo, Roan antelope and cheetah (Niokolo-Koba Park)	45	45
1801	200f. Lion, giraffe and elephant (Niokolo-Koba Park)	75	75
1802	450f. Pelicans and Faidherbe Bridge (Saint Louis)	1·60	1·60

556 Preventing Tree Felling

2008. Protection of the Environment. Multicoloured.

1803	100f. Type **556**	35	35
1804	200f. No bonfires (vert)	75	75
1805	300f. Boy collecting litter	1·10	1·10
1806	450f. Trees with guards	1·60	1·60

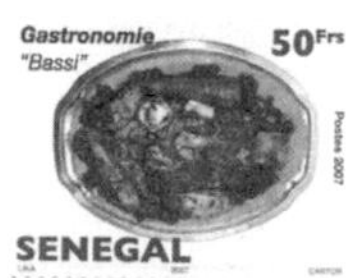
557 Bassi

2008. Gastronomy. Sheet 120×90 mm containing T **557** and similar horiz designs. Multicoloured.

MS1807	50f. Type **557**; 200f. Yassa poulet; 250f. Thieboudiene; 500f. Yassa poisson	3·50	3·50

558 Motor Cyclist and Camel

2009. 30th Paris–Dakar Rally. Multicoloured.

1808	450f. Type **558**	1·60	1·60
1809	550f. Motor cyclist and rally car (horiz)	1·90	1·90

559 Child reading Braille Book

2009. Birth Centenary of Louis Braille (inventor of Braille writing for the blind). Multicoloured.

1810	200f. Type **559**	75	75
1811	450f. Braille letters	1·60	1·60

560 Mother receiving Bouquet

2009. Mothers' Day. Multicoloured.

1812	200f. Type **560**	75	75
1813	450f. Mother and daughter hugging (vert)	1·60	1·60

560a African Sacred Ibis (*Threskiornis aethiopicus*) (inscr 'Ibis blanche' 'Ibis religionas')

2010. Birds. Multicoloured.

1813a	10f. Type **560a**	15	15
1813b	200f. *Ardea pavonia* (crowned crane) (vert)	80	80
1813c	450f. Roseate Spoonbill (*Platalea ajaja*) (inscr 'Spatule' 'Spatula') (vert)	1·70	1·70
1813d	500f. *Himantopus himantopus* (common stilt) (vert)	1·80	1·80

Nos. 1813a/d are inscribed '2009'.

560b Independence Monument, Flag of Senegal and Lion

2010. 50th Anniv of Independence. Multicoloured.

1813e	300f. Type **560b**	1·10	1·10
1813f	500f. As Type **560b**	1·60	1·60

561 Demonstrators (freedom of expression)

2010. Democracy and Liberty. Multicoured.

1814	150f. Type **561**	60	60
1815	250f. Woman with voting registration card (right to voter registration card)	80	80
1816	400f. Woman voting (right to vote freely and democratically)	1·20	1·20
1817	450f. Symbols of communication (freedom of press, radio and television)	1·60	1·60

Nos. 1814/17 are inscribed '2006'.

562 Coin and BCEAO Emblem

2010. Economic and Monetary Union of West Africa. Multicoloured.

1818	500f. Type **562**	10	10
1819	790f. Central Bank of States of West Africa (BCEAO) building, Dakar, UEMOA emblem and BCEAO emblem (horiz)	2·75	2·75

Nos. 1818/19 are inscribed for 11th anniversary of UEMOA.

Nos. 1818/19 are inscribed '2006'

563 Ndaw rabine

2010. Traditional Dances. Multicoloured.

1820	100f. Type **563**	75	75
1821	200f. Niary gorom (horiz)	85	85
1822	250f. Dagathe	90	90
1823	450f. Ndaa daly	1·60	1·60

Nos. 1820/3 are inscribed '2009'.

564 Praying Mantis

2010. Insects. Multicoloured.

1824	150f. Type **564**	60	60
1825	200f. Wasp	80	80
1826	250f. Grasshopper	90	90
1827	500f. Ant	1·70	1·70

565

2010. Great Offensive for Food and Agricultural Abundance (GOANA). Multicoloured.

1828	100f. Type **565**	65	65
1829	200f. Man holding sweet potatoes, peanuts, tomatoes and man harrowing (horiz)	80	80
1830	250f. Men stacking bags of produce and vegetable crops	90	90
1831	500f. Women, children and an abundance of food	1·90	1·90

Nos. 1828/31 are inscribed '2009'.

566 Children holding hands in Circle

2010. SOS Children's Villages. Multicoloured.

1832	300f. Type **566**	1·10	1·10
1833	400f. As Type **566**		

567 Musician, Slaves' House and Aimé Fernand David Césaire (one of founders of the négritude movement in Francophone literature)

2010. Gorée Diaspora Cultural Festival, 2010. Multicoloured.

1834	190f. Type **567**	65	65
1835	200f. Dancers, Gorée Island and Aimé Césaire	85	85
1836	250f. Young girls dancing at 2008 festival	95	95
1837	450f. Freed slaves (statue) and Gorée Island	1·70	1·70

568 Statue

2010. International Negro Arts Festival, Dakar. Multicoloured.

1838	200f. Type **568**	85	85
1839	300f. Map of Africa enclosing cultural symbols and Festival emblem (horiz)	1·20	1·20
1840	450f. Emblem and globe	1·90	1·90
1841	500f. Statue with pipe	2·10	2·10

Nos. 1838/41 are inscribed '2007'.

OFFICIAL STAMPS

O45 Arms of Dakar

1961. Figures of value in black.

O240	**O45**	1f. black and blue	10	10
O241	**O45**	2f. blue and yellow	10	10
O242	**O45**	5f. lake and green	10	10
O243	**O45**	10f. red and blue	10	10

O244	**O45**	25f. blue and red	45	15
O245	**O45**	50f. red and grey	75	30
O246	**O45**	85f. purple and orange	1·40	45
O247	**O45**	100f. red and green	2·25	1·10

O78 Baobab Tree

1966

O339	**O78**	1f. black and yellow	10	10
O340	**O78**	5f. black and orange	10	10
O341	**O78**	10f. black and red	10	10
O342	**O78**	20f. black and purple	15	10
O342a	**O78**	25f. black and mauve	15	10
O343	**O78**	30f. black and blue	15	10
O344	**O78**	35f. black and blue	45	10
O344a	**O78**	40f. black and blue	20	10
O1122	**O78**	50f. black and red	20	15
O345	**O78**	55f. black and green	65	20
O345a	**O78**	60f. black and green	45	20
O346	**O78**	90f. black and green	1·00	35
O347	**O78**	100f. black & brown	1·10	40
O1123	**O78**	145f. black and green	1·00	35
O1124	**O78**	180f. black & orange	1·10	45

1969. No. O345 surch.

O390	60f. on 55f. black & grn	1·10	10

POSTAGE DUE STAMPS

1903. Postage Due stamps of French Colonies surch.

D30	**U**	10 on 50c. purple	£120	£110
D31	**U**	10 on 60c. brown on buff	£110	£120
D32	**U**	10 on 1f. pink on buff	£325	£325

1906. "Natives" key-type.

D50	**L**	5c. green and red	2·00	3·25
D51	**L**	10c. purple and blue	4·50	3·75
D52	**L**	15c. blue and red on blue	3·75	10·00
D53	**L**	20c. black & red on yellow	5·50	2·75
D54	**L**	30c. red and blue on cream	8·25	12·00
D55	**L**	50c. violet and red	7·25	22·00
D56	**L**	60c. black and red on buff	10·00	17·00
D57	**L**	1f. black and red on pink	12·00	60·00

1915. "Figure" key-type.

D81	**M**	5c. green	1·00	5·00
D82	**M**	10c. red	55	2·75
D83	**M**	15c. grey	85	5·25
D84	**M**	20c. brown	90	3·50
D85	**M**	30c. blue	1·80	3·00
D86	**M**	50c. black	2·50	3·75
D87	**M**	60c. orange	3·25	9·75
D88	**M**	1r. violet	3·00	1·80

1927. Surch in figures.

D133	2f. on 1f. purple	3·25	17·00
D134	3f. on 1f. brown	3·75	14·50

D40

1935

D194	**D40**	5c. green	35	5·75
D195	**D40**	10c. orange	30	6·75
D196	**D40**	15c. violet	30	7·00
D197	**D40**	20c. olive	30	5·75
D198	**D40**	30c. brown	40	7·00
D199	**D40**	50c. purple	55	6·75
D200	**D40**	60c. yellow	1·70	7·25
D201	**D40**	1f. black	1·00	7·00
D202	**D40**	2f. blue	2·50	9·50
D203	**D40**	3f. red	1·60	8·25

D43

1961

D239	**D43**	1f. orange and red	10	10
D240	**D43**	2f. blue and red	10	10
D241	**D43**	5f. brown and red	10	10
D242	**D43**	20f. green and red	25	25
D243	**D43**	25f. purple and red	65	65

D77 Lion's Head

1966. Head in gold and black; value in black.

D339	**D77**	1f. red	15	15
D340	**D77**	2f. brown	15	15
D341	**D77**	5f. violet	20	20
D342	**D77**	10f. blue	40	40
D343	**D77**	20f. green	50	50
D344	**D77**	30f. grey	65	65
D345	**D77**	60f. blue	65	65
D346	**D77**	90f. purple	75	75

Pt. 6

SENEGAMBIA AND NIGER

A French colony later re-named Upper Senegal and Niger, and later French Sudan.

100 centimes = 1 franc.

1903. "Tablet" key-type inscr "SENEGAMBIE ET NIGER" in red (1, 5, 15, 25, 75c., 1f.) or blue (others).

22	**D**	1c. black on blue	2·00	5·75
23	**D**	2c. brown on buff	65	3·00
24	**D**	4c. brown on grey	3·00	6·50
25	**D**	5c. green	6·00	3·75
26	**D**	10c. red	8·50	4·00
27	**D**	15c. grey	30·00	18·00
28	**D**	20c. red on green	21·00	44·00
29	**D**	25c. blue	28·00	55·00
30	**D**	30c. brown on drab	14·00	55·00
31	**D**	40c. red on yellow	22·00	65·00
32	**D**	50c. brown on blue	60·00	85·00
33	**D**	75c. brown on orange	55·00	95·00
34	**D**	1f. green	70·00	£120

Pt. 3

SERBIA

A kingdom in the Balkans, S.E. Europe. Part of Yugoslavia since 1918, except during the Second World War when stamps were issued by a German sponsored Government.

1866. 40 para = 1 grosch.
1880. 100 para = 1 dinar.

2 Prince Michael (Obrenovic III)

1866. Perf.

12	**2**	10p. orange	£130	£170
15	**2**	20p. red	22·00	34·00
14	**2**	40p. blue	85·00	55·00

3 Prince Milan (Obrenovic IV)

1869. Perf.

42	**3**	10p. brown	13·50	7·25
45	**3**	10p. orange	3·25	9·00
31c	**3**	15p. orange	£100	45·00
46	**3**	20p. blue	2·20	4·00
39b	**3**	25p. red	3·25	9·00
34c	**3**	35p. green	6·75	8·00
47	**3**	40p. mauve	3·25	11·00
36	**3**	50p. green	13·50	22·00

5 King Milan I

1880. Perf.

54a	**5**	5p. green	2·20	55
55	**5**	10p. red	3·25	55
56	**5**	20p. orange	1·70	1·10
57a	**5**	25p. blue	2·20	1·70
58	**5**	50p. brown	2·20	7·25
59	**5**	1d. violet	16·00	17·00

6 King Alexander (Obrenovic V)

1890

60	**6**	5p. green	55	20
61	**6**	10p. red	1·90	20
62	**6**	15p. lilac	1·70	20
63	**6**	20p. orange	1·10	20
64	**6**	25p. blue	2·20	55
65	**6**	50p. brown	4·50	4·50
66	**6**	1d. lilac	17·00	13·50

7 King Alexander (Obrenovic V)

1894

75	**7**	1p. red	45	20
76	**7**	5p. green	5·50	20
68	**7**	10p. red	8·50	20
69	**7**	15p. lilac	13·50	35
79	**7**	20p. orange	8·50	35
80	**7**	25p. blue	4·25	35
81a	**7**	50p. brown	14·00	1·00
73	**7**	1d. green	2·20	4·50
74	**7**	1d. brown on blue	28·00	4·50

1900. Surch.

82	10p. on 20p. red	8·50	1·10
84	15p. on 1d. brown on blue	7·75	2·20

10 King Alexander (Obrenovic V)

1901

85a	**10**	5p. green	55	35
86	**10**	10p. red	55	35
87	**10**	15p. purple	55	35
88	**10**	20p. yellow	55	35
89	**10**	25p. blue	55	35
90	**10**	50p. yellow	1·10	85
91	-	1d. brown	1·70	2·75
92a	-	3d. pink	17·00	22·00
93a	-	5d. violet	17·00	22·00

The 1d. to 5d. are larger.

12 King Alexander 1 (Obrenovic V)

1903. Optd with shield.

94	**12**	1p. black and red	1·30	1·70
95	**12**	5p. black and green	1·10	55
96	**12**	10p. black and red	80	55
97	**12**	15p. black and grey	80	55
98	**12**	20p. black and yellow	1·10	55
99	**12**	25p. black and blue	1·10	55
100	**12**	50p. black and grey	6·75	1·70
101	**12**	1d. black and green	17·00	6·75
102	**12**	3d. black and lilac	4·75	5·00
103	**12**	5d. black and brown	4·75	5·50

1903. Surch with arms and new value.

104	1p. on 5d. black and brown	3·25	17·00

14 Karageorge and Petar 1

1904. Coronation. Centenary of Karageorgevic Dynasty. Dated "1804 1904".

108	**14**	5p. green	1·10	55
109	**14**	10p. red	1·10	55
110	**14**	15p. purple	1·10	55
111	**14**	25p. blue	2·00	1·10
112	**14**	50p. brown	2·20	2·20
113	-	1d. bistre	3·25	7·75
114	-	3d. green	4·50	11·00
115	-	5d. violet	5·50	13·50

DESIGN: 1, 3, 5d. Karageorge and insurgents, 1804.

16 Petar I

1905

116	**16**	1p. black and grey	35	10
117	**16**	5p. black and green	1·70	20
118	**16**	10p. black and red	4·00	20
119	**16**	15p. black and mauve	4·50	20
120	**16**	20p. black and yellow	7·75	35
121	**16**	25p. black and blue	11·00	35
122	**16**	30p. black and green	6·75	35
123	**16**	50p. black and brown	8·50	80
135	**16**	1d. black and bistre	1·30	55
136	**16**	3d. black and green	1·30	1·30
137	**16**	5d. black and violet	5·50	4·00

17 Petar I

1911

146	**17**	1p. black	20	10
147	**17**	2p. violet	20	10
169	**17**	5p. green	20	10
170	**17**	10p. red	20	10
150	**17**	15p. purple	45	10
171	**17**	15p. black	20	10
151	**17**	20p. yellow	45	10
172	**17**	20p. brown	80	45
173	**17**	25p. blue	20	10
153	**17**	30p. green	45	35
173a	**17**	30p. bronze	20	45
154	**17**	50p. brown	80	55
174	**17**	50p. red	65	55
155	**17**	1d. orange	34·00	65·00
175	**17**	1d. green	5·50	11·00
156	**17**	3d. lake	45·00	£130
176	**17**	3d. yellow	£225	£1700
177	**17**	5d. violet	9·00	29·00

19 King Petar I on the Battlefield

1915

178	**19**	5p. green	55	
179	**19**	10p. red	55	
179a	**19**	15p. grey	8·50	
179b	**19**	20p. brown	2·20	
179c	**19**	25p. blue	17·00	
179d	**19**	30p. green	11·00	
179e	**19**	50p. brown	45·00	

20 King Petar I and Prince Alexander

1918

194	**20**	1p. black	10	10
195	**20**	2p. olive	10	10
196	**20**	5p. green	10	10
197	**20**	10p. red	10	10
198	**20**	15p. sepia	10	10
199	**20**	20p. brown	10	10
208	**20**	20p. mauve	5·25	1·30
200	**20**	25p. blue	10	10
201	**20**	30p. olive	10	10
202	**20**	50p. mauve	10	10
220	**20**	1d. brown	35	15
204	**20**	3d. slate	1·70	1·30
205	**20**	5d. brown	2·75	1·70

These issues were only for sale within Serbia.

(S22a)

2003. Cancer Awareness Campaign. Un-issued stamp surch **8d**
S234a **S22a** multicoloured 70 70

2003. No. 2864, Nos. 2927, 2928 and 2930 surch.
S235 1d. on R ultramarine 95 95
S236 12d. on 1p. violet and bistre 1·00 1·00
S236a 12d. on 20p. purple and brown-lilac 1·80 1·80
S236b 32d. on 5p. deep dull blue and orange 2·50 2·50

S24 Father Christmas and Reindeer

2003. Christmas. Multicoloured.
S237 10d. Type S **24** 90 90
S238 13d.50 Baubles 1·10 1·10
S239 26d.20 Snowflakes 1·70 1·70

S24a St Sava and Temple

2003. OBLIGATORY TAX. St. Sava's Temple
S239a **S24a** 8d. multicoloured 70 70

S24b St Sava

2004. OBLIGATORY TAX. St. Sava's Temple
S239b **S24b** 8d. multicoloured 70 70

S24c Ancient Stadium and Warrior

2004. Olympic Committee
S239c **S24c** 8d. multicoloured 70 70

S24d Long Jumpers and the Acropolis

2004. Olympic Committee
S239d **S24d** 8d. multicoloured 70 70

S24e Dr Predraga Brzakovića

2004. Cancer Awareness Campaign
S239e **S24e** 8d. multicoloured 70 70

S24f Balls

2004. Sport
S239f **S24f** 8d. multicoloured 70 70

S24g Condom with Wings

2004. AIDS Awareness Campaign
S239g **S24g** 8d. multicoloured 70 70

S24h Dr Slobodana Čikarića

2005. Cancer Awareness Campaign
S239h **S24h** 8d. multicoloured 70 70

S25 Bat and Virus as Ball

2005. AIDS Awareness Campaign.
S240 **S25** 8d. multicoloured 55 55

S26 Children

2006. OBLIGATORY TAX. Red Cross. Each vermilion and blue.
S241 8d. Type S **26** 55 55
S242 8d. Elderly couple 55 55

S27 **S28**

2006. Monasteries.
S243 **S27** 8d. multicoloured 55 55
S244 **S28** 8d. multicoloured 55 55

S29 Glass containing Virus

2006. AIDS Awareness Campaign.
S245 **S29** 8d. multicoloured 55 55

On 3rd of June 2006 Montenegro resigned from the Alliance (Serbia & Montenegro) and Serbia reverted to a single unit.

30 National Flag

2006. National Symbols. Multicoloured.
246 16d.50 Type **30** 55 55
247 20d. Arms (vert) 65 65

31 Battle Scene (detail) (Paja Jovanovic)

2006. Bicentenary of Battle of Misar.
248 **31** 46d. multicoloured 1·50 1·50

32 Net, Ball and Players

2006. Water Polo Championships, Belgrade. Multicoloured.
249 **32** 46d. multicoloured 1·50 1·50

2006. Serbia—2006 Water Polo Champions. As T **32**. Multicoloured.
250 46d. Medal, players and ball 1·50 1·50

33 Train

2006. 38th "Joy in Europe" Meeting. Children's Day. Multicoloured.
251 46d. Type **33** 1·50 1·50
252 73d. Girl and bird 2·40 2·40

34 Zica Monastery

2006
253 **34** 8d. multicoloured 25 25

35 1866 1p. Stamp (As Type **1**)

2006. Stamp Day. 140th Anniv of First Serbian Stamp.
254 **35** 46d. multicoloured 1·50 1·50

36 Crown

2006. Museum Exhibits. Bridal Jewellery. Multicoloured.
255 16d.50 Type **36** 55 55
256 16d.50 Ring 55 55
257 46d. Earrings 1·50 1·50
258 46d. Necklace 1·50 1·50

37 Actors and Theatre Facade

2006. 50th Anniv of Theatre ATELJE 212.
259 **37** 46d. multicoloured 1·50 1·50

38 Wolfgang Amadeus Mozart

2006. Birth Anniversaries. Multicoloured.
260 46d. Type **38** (composer) (250th) 1·50 1·50
261 46d. Rembrandt Harmenszoon van Rijn (artist) (400th) 1·50 1·50

39 Wine, Apples, Bread and Candle

2006. Christmas. Multicoloured.
262 16d.50 Type **39** 55 55
263 46d. Candle and decoration 1·50 1·50

39a Athletes

2006. European Olympic Youth Festival Games, Belgrade.
263a **39a** 8d. multicoloured 25 25

40 Santa Claus and Presents

2006. New Year.
264 **40** 46d. multicoloured 1·50 1·50

41 Children

2006. 60th Anniv of UNICEF.
265 **41** 16d.50 multicoloured 65 65

42 Battle Scene

2006. Bicentenary of the Liberation of Belgrade.
266 **42** 16d.50 multicoloured 65 65

43 Dahlia

2007. Flora. Multicoloured.
267 50p. Type **43** 15 15
268 1d. Sunflowers (horiz) 15 15
269 5d. Apple tree (horiz) 25 25

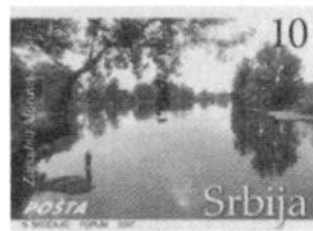

44 Western Moravia

2007. Tourism. Multicoloured.
270 10d. Type **44** 40 40
271 13d. Field and woods, Coc (37×29 mm) 55 55
272 33d. Lake and trees, Zlatibov (37×29 mm) 1·20 1·20
273 50d. Winter sports centre, Kopaomk (37×29 mm) 1·70 1·70
274 100d. National Theatre, Belgrade (29×37 mm) 3·50 3·50

45 Combatants

2007. European Judo Championships, Belgrade.
275 **45** 8d. multicoloured 25 25

46 Map and Milutin Milankovic (engineer and geophysicist)

2007. International Polar Year.
276 **46** 46d. multicoloured 1·60 1·60

47 Petar Dubrinovic

2007. Actors and Actresses. Multicoloured.
277 16d.50 Type **47** 65 65
278 16d.50 Milka Grgurova Aleksic 65 65

279 16d.50 Ljubisa Jovanovic 65 65
280 16d.50 Rahela Farari 65 65
281 16d.50 Miodrag Petrovic Skalja 65 65
282 16d.50 Branko Plesa 65 65
283 16d.50 Ljuba Tadic 65 65
284 16d.50 Danilo Bata Stojkovic 65 65

48 Crucifixion (icon)

2007. Easter. Multicoloured.
285 20d. Type **48** 65 65
286 46d. Crucifixion 1·60 1·60

49 Hand, Paddle and Balls

2007. European Table Tennis Championship, Belgrade. Multicoloured.
287 46d. Type **49** 1·60 1·60
MS288 99×71 mm. 112d. Emblem, net and player 4·00 4·00

The stamp and margin of **MS**288 form a composite design.

49a Fresco

2007. OBLIGATORY TAX. St Sava's Temple.
288a **49a** 10d. multicoloured 50 50

50 Rose

2007
289 **50** 40d. multicoloured 1·50 1·50

51 Black Woodpecker

2007. Endangered Species. Black Woodpecker (*Dryocopus martius*). Multicoloured.
290 20d. Type **51** 80 80
291 20d. Feeding young facing right 80 80
292 40d. Feeding young facing left 1·50 1·50
293 40d. Black wood pecker facing right 1·50 1·50

52 City Park, Vrnjacka Banja

2007. Nature Protection. Multicoloured.
294 40d. Type **52** 1·30 1·30
295 46d. Fountain, Pionirski Park, Belgrade 1·60 1·60

52a Hand enclosing Elderly Couple

2007. Senior Care Programme.
295a **52a** 10d. vermilion and black 60 60

53 Scouts

2007. Europa. Centenary of Scouting. Multicoloured.
296 20d. Type **53** 65 65
297 20d. Milos Popovic (founder of Serbian Scouting) 65 65
298 20d. Robert Baden Powell (original founder) 65 65
299 46d. Scouts canoeing 1·60 1·60

54 Emblem and Map

2007. Serbia's Chairmanship of Council of Europe's Ministers' Committee, May–November 2007.
300 **54** 20d. multicoloured 65 65

55 Amelia Earhart and Lockheed *Vega 5b*

2007. 75th Anniv of Amelia Earhart's Transatlantic Flight.
301 **55** 50d. multicoloured 1·60 1·60

56 *Dositej Obradovic* (Uros Predic)

2007. Dositej Obradovic (writer, philosopher and linguist) Commemoration. Bicentenary of Return to Serbia.
302 **56** 20d. multicoloured 65 65

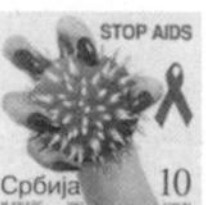

56a Hand crushing Virus

2007. AIDS Awareness Campaign.
302a **56a** 10d. multicoloured 1·00 1·00

57 Jovan Zmaj

2007. 50th Anniv of Zmaj's Children's Games (youth cultural event).
303 **57** 20d. multicoloured 65 65

58 Prince Stefan Lazarevic (Despot 1402–1427) (fresco) and Arms

2007. Srbijafila 2007 Philatelic Exhibition. Sheet 95×53 mm containing T **58** and similar horiz design. Multicoloured.
MS304 20d. Type **58**; 46d. Court at Kalemegdan and seal 2·20 2·20

The stamps of **MS**304 form a composite background design.

59 Swimmer

2007. European Olympic Youth Festival, Belgrade. Sheet 95×53 mm containing T **59** and similar horiz design. Multicoloured.
MS305 46d.×2 Type **59**; Runner 3·25 3·25

The stamps and margins of **MS**305 form a composite background design.

60 Eventing

2007. Equestrian Sports. Multicoloured.
306 20d. Type **60** 65 65
307 20d. Carriage driving 65 65
308 40d. Dressage 1·30 1·30
309 40d. Show jumping 1·30 1·30

61 William Thomas Kelvin

2007. Scientists' Centenaries. Multicoloured.
310 40d. Type **61** (developed second law of thermodynamics and formulated the Kelvin temperature scale) (death centenary) 1·30 1·30
311 46d. Giuseppe Occhialini (expert on cosmic radiation) (birth centenary) 1·60 1·60
312 46d. Dmitrij Ivanovitch Mendeleev (developed Periodic Table) (death centenary) 1·60 1·60

62 Peter Lubarda and *Horses' Game* (1960)

2007. Birth Centenary of Peter Lubarda (artist).
313 **62** 20d. multicoloured 65 65

63 Monastery Building

2007. 600th Anniv of Kalenic Monastery.
314 **63** 20d. multicoloured 65 65

64 *Haliaeetus albicilla* (white-tailed eagle)

2007
315 **64** 46d. multicoloured 1·60 1·60

A stamp of the same design was issued by Austria.

65 Hands

2007. International Ozone Layer Protection Day.
316 **65** 20d. multicoloured 65 65

66 Ruins

2007. UNESCO World Heritage Site. Felix Romuliana, Gamzigrad. Multicoloured.
317 46d. Type **66** 1·60 1·60
318 46d. Columns surrounding tiled area with bowl 1·60 1·60

67 Emblem

2007. OBLIGATORY TAX. Red Cross. Roma Week.
319 **67** 10d. multicoloured 35 35

68 Children

2007. 39th 'Joy in Europe' Meeting. Children's Day.
320 **68** 46d. multicoloured 1·60 1·60

69 *Sputnik I*

2007. 50th Anniv of Space Exploration.
321 **69** 46d. multicoloured 1·60 1·60

70 Observatory and Medal showing Milan Nedeljkovic

2007. 120th Anniv of Astronomical Observatory, Belgrade. 150th Birth Anniv of Milan Nedeljkovic (founder).
322 **70** 20d. multicoloured 65 65

71 Erzen Derocco

2007. Stamp Day. Erzen Derocco (philatelist) Commemoration.
323 **71** 46d. multicoloured 1·60 1·60

72 *Rest after Battle* (Djura Jaksic)

2007. Artists' Anniversaries. Multicoloured.
324 20d. Type **72** (175th birth anniv) 65 65
325 46d. *Self Portrait* (Frida Kahlo) (birth centenary) 1·60 1·60
326 46d. *Boy at Window* (Uros Predic) (150th birth anniv) 1·60 1·60

73 *The Nativity* (Eremija Profeta)

2007. Christmas. Multicoloured.
327 20d. Type **73** 65 65
328 46d. *The Nativity* ('XVIII century') 1·60 1·60

74 Novi Sad Port

2007. Danube Ports and Ships. Multicoloured.
329 20d. Type **74** 65 65
330 46d. Orsova port 1·60 1·60

MS331 95×53 mm. 40d. *Sirona* (Serbia); 50d. *Orsova* (Romania) 3·00 3·00

Stamps of a similar design were issued by Romania.

75 King Milan I Obrenovic and Emperor Meiji of Japan

2007. 125th Anniv of Serbia–Japan Bi-lateral Relations.

332	**75**	46d. multicoloured	1·60	1·60

76 Ladu of Vinca (statue) and Ruins of Neolithic House

2008. Centenary of First Archaeological Dig, Vinca.

333	**76**	20d. multicoloured	65	65

77 *Cluny Museum, Paris*

2008. Art. Birth Centenary of Peda Milosavljevic. Multicoloured.

334	20d. Type **77**	65	65
335	46d. *Notre Dame, Paris*	1·60	1·60

78 Swimmer and Emblem

2008. Centenary of Swimming Federation (Fina).

336	**78**	50d. multicoloured	1·70	1·70

79 Tennis Player

2008. Olympic Games, Beijing. Multicoloured.

337	46d. Type **79**	1·60	1·60
338	50d. Hurdlers	2·00	2·00

80 Christ enclosed (detail) (King Milutin's plastanica (13th–14th century textile))

2008. Easter. Multicoloured.

339	20d. Type **80**	65	65
340	46d. Christ enclosed (detail) (15th century icon)	1·60	1·60

81 Janko Tipsarevic

2008. Olympic Tennis Team. Designs showing players. Multicoloured.

341	20d. Type **81**	65	65
342	30d. Nenad Zimonjic	90	90
343	30d. Jelena Jankovic	90	90
344	40d. Ana Ivanovic	1·30	1·30
345	46d. Novak Dokovic	1·50	1·50

82 *Cervus elaphus* (red deer)

2008. Fauna. Multicoloured.

346	20d. Type **82**	65	65
347	20d. *Meles meles* (European badger)	65	65
348	46d. *Felis silvestris* (wildcat)	1·60	1·60
349	46d. *Sus scrofa* (wild boar)	1·60	1·60

83 Singer

2008. Eurovision Song Contest, Belgrade. Sheet 95×53 mm.

MS350	**83** 177d. multicoloured	5·75	5·75

83a Clasped Hands

2008. Senior Care Programme.

350a	**83a**	10d. multicoloured	35	35

84 Quill and Envelope

2008. Europa. The Letter. Multicoloured.

351	46d. Type **84**	1·60	1·60
352	50d. Letter opener	2·00	2·00

85 Vlasina Plateau

2008. European Protection. Multicoloured.

353	20d. Type **85**	65	65
354	46d. Djavolija varos (devil's town)	1·60	1·60

86 Train and Eiffel Tower

2008. 125th Anniv of Orient Express. Multicoloured.

355	20d. Type **86**	65	65
356	50d. Train and mosque	1·60	1·60

87 Camera and Film

2008. 50th Anniv of Television Belgrade.

357	**87**	46d. multicoloured	1·60	1·60

88 Dositej Obradovic and Building

2008. Bicentenary of Grand School, Belgrade.

358	**88**	20d. multicoloured	65	65

89 Green Grapes

2008. Wine Growing. Multicoloured.

359	20d. Type **89**	65	65
360	20d. White grapes	65	65
361	46d. Black grapes	1·60	1·60
362	46d. Crimson grapes	1·60	1·60

90 Children

2008. 40th 'Joy in Europe' Meeting. Children's Day.

363	**90**	46d. multicoloured	1·60	1·60

91 Panta Mihajlovic, Early Handset and Telephone Wires

2008. Stamp Day. 125th Anniv of First Telephone in Serbia.

364	**91**	46d. multicoloured	1·60	1·60

92 Sumadija

2008. Museum Exhibits. Traditional Children's Costumes. Multicoloured.

365	46d. Type **92**	1·60	1·60
366	50d. Kumodraz	1·60	1·60

93 Danube

2008. 60th Anniv of Danube Commission.

367	**93**	46d. multicoloured	1·60	1·60

94 The Nativity (18th–century)

2008. Christmas. Multicoloured.

368	20d. Type **94**	65	65
369	46d. *The Nativity* (Dimitrije Bacevic)	1·60	1·60

95 Anniversary Emblem

2008. 50th Anniv of Dadov Theatre, Belgrade.

370	**95**	20d. multicoloured	65	65

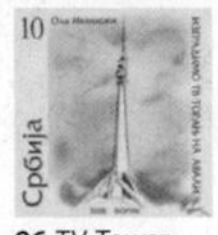
96 TV Tower, Avala

2008

371	**96**	10d. multicoloured	35	35

97 St. Sava

2008. OBLIGATORY TAX. St. Sava's Temple.

372	**97**	10d. multicoloured	35	35

98 Don Quixote

2009. 75th Anniv of Osisani Jez (magazine).

373	**98**	20d. multicoloured	65	65

99 Louis Braille and Writing

2009. Birth Bicentenary of Louis Braille (inventor of Braille writing for the Blind).

374	**99**	46d. multicoloured	1·60	1·60

100 Buckle

2009. Cultural Heritage. Multicoloured.

375	11d. Type **100**	40	40
376	22d. Ring	75	75

No. 377 has been left for stamp not yet received.

22
(101)

2009. No. 247 surch as T **101.**

378	22d. on 20c. multicoloured	80	80

102 Kalemegdan Fortress

2009. Tourism.

379	**102**	55d. multicoloured	1·70	1·70

103 *Mustela erminea* (stoat)

2009. Fauna. Multicoloured.

380	22d. Type **103**	65	65
381	22d. *Micromys minutus* (harvest mouse)	65	65
382	46d. *Sicista subtilis* (southern birch mouse)	1·60	1·60
383	46d. *Spermophilus citellus* (inscr 'citelluss') (European ground squirrel)	1·60	1·60

104 Dikan an Uncle Vu Koje (from *Dikan* (cartoon by Lazo Sredanovic))

2009. 70th Anniv of Politikin Zabavnik (magazine).

384	**104**	22d. multicoloured	65	65

105 *Scolopax rusticola* (Eurasian woodcock)

2009. Ecology—Balkan Mountains. Multicoloured.

385	22d. Type **105**	65	65
386	46d. *Monticola saxatilis* (rufous-tailed rock thrush)	1·60	1·60
MS387	127×67 mm. Nos. 385/6	2·30	2·30

Stamps of a similar design were issued by Bulgaria.

106 The Last Supper

2009. Easter. Design showing wood carving. Multicoloured.

388	22d. Type **106**	65	65
389	46d. Entombment of Christ	1·60	1·60

107 Vela Nigrinova

2009. Actors and Actresses. Multicoloured.

390	22d. Type **107**	65	65
391	22d. Milan Ajvaz	65	65
392	22d. Nevenka Urbanova	65	65
393	22d. Stevo Zigon	65	65
394	22d. Slobodan Perovic	65	65
395	22d. Stevan Salajic	65	65
396	22d. Neda Spasojevic	65	65
397	22d. Milos Zutic	65	65

108 Birds as Footballers

2009. 25th Summer Universiade (games), Belgrade. Multicoloured.

398	22d. Type **108**	65	65
399	46d. Birds as athletes	1·60	1·60

108a St. Sava's Temple

2009. OBLIGATORY TAX

399a	**108a**	10d. multicoloured	1·00	1·00

109 *Self Portrait with Veil* (Milena Barelli) (birth centenary)

2009. Artists' Anniversaries. Multicoloured.

400	22d. Type **109**	65	65
401	46d. *Dead Nature with Parrot* (Jovan Bijelic) (125th birth anniv)	1·60	1·60
402	46d. *Young Woman in Pink Dress* (Paja Jovanovic) (150th birth anniv)	1·60	1·60

110 Urania (muse of astrology) (statue), Galileo's Telescope and Milky Way

2009. Europa. Astronomy. Multicoloured.

403	46d Type **110**	1·60	1·60
404	50d. Radio telescope and Horsehead nebula	1·70	1·70

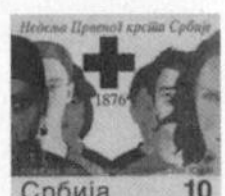

110a People of Many Nations

2009. OBLIGATORY TAX. Red Cross Week.

404a	**110a**	10d. multicoloured	1·00	1·00

111 Saint Sava's Panagia and Temple of Saint Sava

2009. 70th Anniv of Laying of Saint Sava's Temple Foundation Stone on Vracar.

405	**111**	22d. multicoloured	65	65

112 Griffon Vulture (*Gyps fulvus*) over Uvac River Gorge

2009. European Nature Protection. Multicoloured

406	22d. Type **112**	65	65
407	46d. Pcinja Valley	1·60	1·60

113 Kornelije Stankovic

2009. Musical Personalities. Sheet 116×126 containing T **113** and similar vert designs. Multicoloured.

MS408	22d.×8, Type **113**; Josef Marinkovic; Petar Konjovic; Stefan Hristic; Miloje Milojevic; Mihovil Logar; Ljubica; Vasilije Mokranjac	5·25	5·25

The stamps and margins of **MS**407 share a common background design.

114 *Battle at Cegar* (Boza Ilic)

2009. Bicentenary of Battle at Cegar during First Serbian Uprising. Multicoloured.

409	22d. Type **114**	65	65
410	46d. *Stevan Sindelic and Skull Tower* (lithograph by Konstantin Nenadovic)	1·60	1·60

115 *The Virgin of Studenica*

2009. 800th Anniv of Frescoes, Church of the Virgin, Studenica Monastery.

411	**115**	22d. multicoloured	65	65

116 Dimitrije Putnikovi

2009. Scientific Personalities' Anniversaries. Multicoloured.

412	22c. Type **116** (educator) (150th birth anniv)	65	65
413	22c. Pavle Savic (physicist and chemist) (birth centenary)	65	65
414	46d. Pierre Curie (chemist) (birth centenary)	1·60	1·60
415	46d. Charles Robert Darwin (naturalist and evolutionary theorist) (birth bicentenary)	1·60	1·60

117 CS No.1 (first steam locomotive) and Belgrade Railway Station

2009. 125th Anniv of Serbian Railways. Multicoloured.

416	22d. Type **117**	65	65
417	46d. Electric locomotive JZ 441and Nis Station	1·60	1·60

118 Hands and '50'

2009. 50th Golden Pen of Belgrade and Tenth International Biennial of Illustration–2009 Exhibition, Art Pavillion Cvijeta Zuzoric, Kalemegdan, Belgrade.

418	**118**	22d. bronze and black	65	65

119 Children

2009. 41st 'Joy in Europe' Meeting. Children's Day.

419	**119**	46d. multicoloured	1·60	1·60

120 Mother and Child

2009. OBLIGATORY TAX. Red Cross Week.

420	**120**	10d. multicoloured	1·00	1·00

121 Nada Higl

2009. FINA International Swimming Championship, Rome. Gold Medallists. Multicoloured.

421	46d. Type **121**	1·60	1·60
422	46d. Milorad Cavic	1·60	1·60
423	50d. Serbian water polo team	1·70	1·70

122 Front Cover and George Hugo Paul Michel (founder)

2009. Stamp Day. Centenary (2010) of Michel Stamp Catalogues.

424	**122**	46d. multicoloured	1·60	1·60

123 *Herrerasaurus ischigualastensis*

2009. Museum Exhibition. Dinosaurs of Argentina–Giants of Patagonia. Multicoloured.

425	22d. Type **123**	65	65
426	46d. *Giganotosaurus carolinii*	1·60	1·60

124 Front Pages

2010. 75th Anniv of NIN (weekly magazine).

427	**124**	22d. multicoloured	65	65

125 Tiger

2010. Chinese New Year. Year of the Tiger. Multicoloured.

428	22d. Type **125**	65	65
429	50d. Tiger to left of horoscope circle	1·60	1·60

126 Peony

2010. European Nature Protection. Paeonia officinalis. Multicoloured.

430	22d. Type **126**	65	65
431	46d. Pink double-flowered peony	1·60	1·60
MS432	96×78 mm. Nos. 430/1	2·30	2·30

No. **MS**432 forms a composite design of peonies in a landscape.

127 Nordic Skiers

2010. Winter Olympic Games, Vancouver. Multicoloured.

433	22d. Type **127**	65	65
434	50d. Skier	1·60	1·60

128 Athletes as '100'

2010. Centenary of Serbian Olympic Committee.

435	**128**	22d. multicoloured	65	65

128a Pavilion, interior

2010. Expo 2010, Shanghai. Multicoloured.

435a	22d. Type **128a**	65	65
435b	50d. Pavilion, exterior	1·60	1·60

129 Frederic Chopin

2010. Birth Bicentenary of Fryderyk Franciszek Chopin (Frederic Francois Chopin) (composer).

436 **129** 50d. multicoloured 1·60 1·60

130 The Crucifixion

2010. Easter. Multicoloured.

437 22d. Type **130** 65 65

438 46d. Resurrected Christ on Easter egg 1·60 1·60

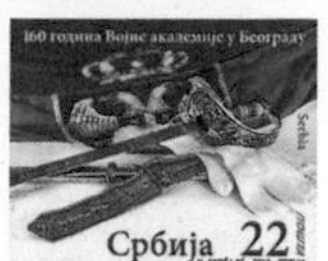

131 Mlitary Artefacts

2010. 160th Anniv of Military Academy, Belgrade

439 **131** 22d. multicoloured 85 85

132 Zastava 750

2010. 55th Anniv of Zastava 750 (car made by Zavod Crvena Zastava)

440 **132** 22d. multicoloured 85 85

133 *Passer domesticus* (house sparrow)

2010. Birds. Multicoloured.

441 22d. Type **133** 65 65

442 33d. *Phoenicurus ochruros* (black redstart) 95 95

443 46d. *Columba livia* (rock pigeon) 2·30 2·30

444 50d. *Parus major* (great tit) 2·40 2·40

134 'K', Factory and Townscape

2010. 140th Anniv of Industrialization

445 **134** 22d. multicoloured 85 85

135 Beanstalk, White Rabbit, Girl reading and Giraffe

2010. Europa. Multicoloured.

446 66d. Type **135** 2·50 2·50

447 77d. Pumpkin, boy in hammock hanging from moon, fairy, elves and girl reading for star 3·00 3·00

136 Players and Map of Africa

2010. World Cup Football Championships, South Africa. Multicoloured.

448 22d. Type **136** 1·10 1·10

449 50d. Players and South African and Serbian flags 2·20 2·20

MS450 85×78 mm. 177d. Players legs and football (42×35 mm) 8·00 8·00

137 Cyclists

2010. 50th Anniv of Tour de Serbie Cycle Race

451 **137** 50d. multicoloured 2·00 2·00

138 The Virgin Odigitrija (19th-century, Belgrade)

2010. Icons. Multicoloured.

452 50d. Type **138** 2·20 2·20

453 50d. The Archangel Mikhail (Andrey Rublev, 15th-century) 2·20 2·20

139 Trumpeteers and Trumpets

2010. 50th Anniv of Trumpet Festival, Guca

454 **139** 44d. multicoloured 2·00 2·00

140 Athletes

2010. Youth Olympic Games, Singapore

455 **140** 51d. multicoloured 2·30 2·30

141 Mother Teresa

2010. Birth Centenary of Agnes Gonxha Bojaxhiu (Mother Teresa) (founder of Missionaries of Charity)

456 **141** 50d. multicoloured 2·00 2·00

142 Laza Kostic (1841-1910)

2010. Literary Personalities. Multicoloured.

457 22d. Type **142** 1·40 1·40

458 22d. Branislav Nusic (1864-1938) 1·40 1·40

459 22d. Borisav Stankovi (1876-1927) 1·40 1·40

460 22d. Ivo Andric (1892-1975) 1·40 1·40

461 22d. Milos Crnjanski (1893-1977) 1·40 1·40

462 22d. Mesa Selimovic (1910-1982) 1·40 1·40

463 22d. Borislav Peki (1930-1992) 1·40 1·40

464 22d. Danilo Kis (1935-1989) 1·40 1·40

143 Decorated Plate (16th-century)

2010. 60th Anniv of Art Museum, Belgrade. Multicoloured.

465 22d. Type **143** 1·00 1·00

466 44d. Musical figurine (19th-century) 3·25 3·25

144 Postman, Letter, Pen and Main Post Office, Belgrade

2010. 170th Anniv of Serbian Post

467 **144** 46d. multicoloured 2·00 2·00

145 Pig

2010. Joy of Europe

468 **145** 46d. multicoloured 3·00 3·00

146 Birth of Christ (Arsenije Teodorovic)

2010. Christmas. Icons from Mother of God Church, Zemin. Multicoloured.

469 22d. Type **146** 1·30 1·30

470 46d. Birth of Christ (unknown) 3·25 3·25

147 Novak Djokovic, Vitor 'Troiki, Nenad Zimonjic and Janko Tipsarevi

2010. Serbian Davis Cup Team - World Champions 2010

471 **147** 50d. multicoloured 6·75 6·75

148 Ivan Saric and Saric I

2010. Centenary of Aviation in Serbia. Ivan Sarić Commemoration. Multicoloured.

472 22d. Type **148** 80 80

473 44d. Inscr 'Брезе 14' 1·20 1·20

474 55d. Inscr 'Spartan Kruzer' 2·00 2·00

475 66d. Inscr 'MK-3' 3·25 3·25

476 77d. McDonnell Douglas DC-9 3·75 3·75

149 Large Ice Floe

2011. Preserve Polar Regions and Glaciers. Multicoloured.

MS477 46d. Type **149**; 66d. Smaller ice floe 4·00 4·00

150 Rabbit

2011. Chinese New Year. Year of the Rabbit. Multicoloured.

478 22d. Type **150** 80 80

479 55d. Rabbit, facing forward (pinkish background) 2·10 2·10

151 ITU Emblem

2011. 145th Anniv of Serbia as Member of International Telecommunications Union (ITU)

480 **151** 46d. multicoloured 1·70 1·70

152 Avala Tower

2011. Architecture

481 **152** 44d. multicoloured 4·00 4·00

153 Katarina Ivanovic (self-portrait, 1836)

2011. Serbian Artist's Anniversaries. Multicoloured.

482 22d. Type **153** (birth bicentenary) 80 80

483 33d. Uros Knezevic (birth bicentenary) 1·10 1·10

484 44d. Dorde Jovanovic (150th birth anniv) 1·30 1·30

485 66d. Bora Baruh (birth centenary) 2·75 2·75

154 Stevan Stojanović Mokranjac

2011. Centenary of Stankovic Music School

486 **154** 22d. multicoloured 1·00 1·00

155 *Entering Jerusalem*

2011. Easter. Paintings by Arsenije Teodorović. Multicoloured.

487 22d. Type **155** 1·10 1·10

488 112d. *Resurrection of Christ* 3·50 3·50

156 'END POLIO NOW'

2011. 'Polio Plus' Project - Eradication of Polio

489 **156** 50d. multicoloured 4·00 4·00

156a Dimitrije Miodragovic

2011. OBLIGATORY TAX. Cancer Awareness Campaign

489a **156a** 10d. black and scarlet 90 90

157 Pygmy Cormorants

2011. Endangered Species. Pygmy Cormorant (*Phalacrocorax pygmeus*). Multicoloured.

490	22d. Type **157**	80	80
491	33d. Facing left with wings spread	1·10	1·10
492	44d. Two in flight	1·30	1·30
493	66d. Female swimming and male with wings spread	2·75	2·75

158 'IYB'

2011. International Year of Biodiversity

494	**158**	50d. multicoloured	1·90	1·90

159 Early and Modern Buildings

2011. 150th Anniv of Founding of First Serbian Theatre in Novi Sad

495	**159**	22d. multicoloured	1·00	1·00

160 Healthy Trees

2011. Europa. Forests. Multicoloured.

496	22d. Type **160**	80	80
497	66d. Diseased trees	2·75	2·75

161 '100' and Symbols of Scouting

2011. Centenary of Scout Association in Serbia

498	**161**	22d. multicoloured	1·00	1·00

2011. OBLIGATORY TAX. Red Cross Week

498a	10d. As Type **110a**	90	90

162 Borisav (Bora) Stanković and Building Façade

2011. 130th Anniv of the 'Bora Stankovic' Secondary School

499	**162**	22d. multicoloured	1·00	1·00

163 Laza Lazarevic

2011. Birth Centenary of Laza Lazarevic (writer, psychiatrist, and neurologist)

500	**163**	22d. multcoloured	1·00	1·00

164 *Rubus idaeus*

2011. Fruit. Berries. Multicoloured.

501	22d. Type **164** (Raspberry)	80	80
502	33d. *Fragaria vesca* (Wild Strawberry)	1·10	1·10
503	44d. *Ribes rubrum* (Redcurrant)	1·30	1·30
504	66d. *Vaccinium macrocarpon* (Cranberry)	2·75	2·75

165 '30' containing Stylized Virus

2011. 30th Anniv of AIDS Prevention Campaign

505	**165**	50d. multicoloured	1·90	1·90

165a St. Sava Cathedral and Bells

2011. OBLIGATORY TAX. St. Sava Cathedral

505a	**165a**	10d. multicoloured	90	90

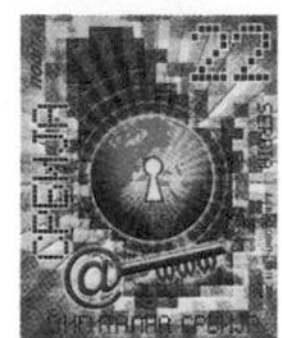
166 Pixilated Globe with Keyhole and Key

2011. Digital Serbia (1st issue). Multicoloured.

506	22d. Type **166**	1·10	1·10
507	33d. Pixilated eye	1·30	1·30

167 Waterfall on the Sikolska River (Mokranjska stena)

2011. European Nature Protection. Waterfalls. Multicoloured.

508	22d. Type **167**	1·10	1·10
509	46d. Waterfall on the Šaška river (Beli izvorac)	1·40	1·40

168 Bridge across Danube River, Beška, (1975)

2011. Science. Bridges. Multicoloured.

510	22d. Type **168**	1·10	1·10
511	44d. New railway bridge across Sava river in Belgrade, (1979)	1·50	1·50
512	46d. 'Most Slobode' road bridge across Danube river in Novi Sad, (1981)	1·50	1·50

169 Franz Liszt

2011. Birth Bicentenary of Franz Liszt (composer)

513	**169**	50d. multicoloured	1·90	1·90

170 Dom Gospodnji Church, Subotica

2011. Centenary of Celebration of 'Duzijanca' Festival. Museum Exhibits. Multicoloured.

514	22d. Type **170**	1·10	1·10
515	55d. Crown	1·70	1·70

171 *Panthera tigris* (white Tiger)

2011. 75th Anniv of Belgrade Zoo. Multicoloured.

516	33d. Type **171**	1·10	1·10
517	44d. *Neophron percnopterus* (Egyptian vulture)	1·30	1·30
518	46d. *Macropus rufogriseus* (red-necked wallaby)	1·50	1·50
519	50d. *Panthers leo* (white lion)	2·00	2·00

172 Digital Mice and Connectors as Flower

2011. Digital Serbia (2nd issue)

520	**172**	22d. multicoloured	1·00	1·00

173 Soko G-2 Galeb Aircraft

2011. 50th Anniv of Soko G-2 *Galeb* Aircraft

521	**173**	50d. multicoloured	1·90	1·90

174 Globe showing Non-Aligned Countries and Clasped Hands

2011. 50th Anniv of First Non-Aligned Countries Conference

522	**174**	22d. multicoloured	1·00	1·00

174a Red Cross and Damaged Buildings

2011. OBLIGATORY TAX. Solidarity Week

522a	**174a**	10d. multicoloured	90	90

175 Players

2011. European CEV Volleyball Women's Championships - 2011, Italy and Serbia

523	**175**	46d. multicoloured	1·60	1·60

176 Fantastic Creatures (Child's drawing)

2011. Joy of Europe

524	**176**	46d. multicoloured	1·60	1·60

176a Children

2011. OBLIGATORY TAX. Children's Week

524a	**176a**	10d. multicoloured	90	90

177 Scene from *Life and Deeds of the Immortal Duke Karadjordje*

2011. Centenary of First Serbian Film. *Life and Deeds of the Immortal Duke Karadjordje*

525	**177**	22d. multicoloured	1·60	1·60

178 Exhibition Emblem

2011. Stamp Day. Beogradfila Philatlelic Exhibition

526	**178**	46d. multicoloured	1·00	1·00

179 Rachel de Queiroz (Brazil)

2011. Literary Personalities. 50th Anniv of Ivo Andric's Nobel Prize for Literature (No. 528). Multicoloured.

527	22d. Type **179**	1·00	1·00
528	46d. Ivo Andric (Serbia)	1·50	1·50

180 The Nativity

2011. Christmas. Icons. Multicoloured.

529	22d. Type **180**	80	80
530	112d. Birth of Christ	3·25	3·25

181 Emblem

2011. OBLIGATORY TAX. United Nations Children's Fund (UNICEF)

531	**181**	10d. new blue and black	90	90

182 Typewriter and Laptop

2011. 130th Anniv of Journalist Association

532	**182**	22d. multicoloured	80	80

183 Women Competitors and Medal

2011. Serbia - European Volleyball Champions 2011. Multicoloured.

533		22d. Type **183**	80	80
534		22d. Male competitors and medal	80	80

184 Construction

2011. 130th Anniv of Moravica Hydroelectric Power Station

535	**184**	22d. multicoloured	80	80

185 Nelson Mandela, Flag and Emblem

2012. Centenary of African National Congress (ANC)

536	**185**	46d. multicoloured	1·40	1·40

186 Emblem

2012. OBLIGATORY TAX. European Handball Championship

537	**186**	10d. multicoloured	90	90

187 Dragon

2012. Chinese New Year. Year of the Dragon. Multicoloured.

538		22d. Type **187**	80	80
539		55d. Green dragon seated on decorative ledge	2·00	2·00

188 Wrestlers and Championship Emblem

2012. OBLIGATORY TAX. European Senior Wrestling Championship

540	**188**	10d. multicoloured	90	90

189 Robni Magazin on Kralja Petra 16, Belgrade

2012. Architecture. Secessionist (Art Nouveau) Buildings. Multicoloured.

541		22d. Type **189**	80	80
542		33d. Telephone Exchange, Belgrade (horiz)	1·10	1·10
543		46d. Moskva Hotel, Belgrade (horiz)	1·40	1·40
544		55d. Town Hall, Subotica (horiz)	2·00	2·00

190 Theatre Façade

2012. 125th Anniv of National Theatre, Niš

545	**190**	22d. multicoloured	80	80

191 Cross

2012. Easter. Multicoloured.

546		22d. Type **191**	80	80
547		46d. Risen Christ	1·40	1·40

192 Aleksije Milosavljevic

2012. OBLIGATORY TAX. Cancer Awareness Campaign

548	**192**	10d. multicoloured	90	90

193 Woman holding Horn

2012. Anniversaries. Multicoloured.

549		22d. Type **193** (75th anniv of Faculty of Music, Belgrade)	80	80
550		33d. Woman holding brush and palette (75th anniv of Faculty of Fine Arts, Belgrade)	1·10	1·10
551		44d. Woman holding compass and book (150th anniv of Požarevac Grammar School)	1·30	1·30

194 *John the Baptist*

2012. 60th Death Anniv of Jan Koniarek (sculptor)

552	**194**	50d. multicoloured	1·90	1·90

195 Runners Legs and Emblem

2012. 25th Belgrade Marathon

553	**195**	22d. multicoloured	80	80

196 Symbols of Historical Serbia

2012. Europa. Visit Serbia. Multicoloured.

554		44d. Type **196**	1·40	1·40
555		77d. Symbols of outdoor adventures and scenery	3·75	3·75

2012. OBLIGATORY TAX. Red Cross Week

556		10d. As Type **110a**	90	90

197 *Coronella austriaca*

2012. Fauna. Reptiles. Multicoloured.

557		22d. Type **197**	80	80
558		33d. *Podarcis taurica*	1·10	1·10
559		44d. *Lacerta viridis*	1·30	1·30
560		66d. *Emys orbicularis*	2·75	2·75

198 *Pinus nigra* and Forest

2011. European Nature Protection. Forests. Multicoloured.

561		22d. Type **198**	80	80
562		46d. *Acer heldreichii* and ash trees	1·40	1·40

199 Wheelchair Racer

2012. OBLIGATORY TAX. Paralympic Games, London

563	**199**	10d. multicoloured	90	90

200 Cathedral Interior

2012. OBLIGATORY TAX. St. Sava Cathedral

564	**200**	10d. multicoloured	90	90

NEWSPAPER STAMPS

1 State Arms

1866. Imperf.

N7	**1**	1p. green and pink	85·00	
N2	**1**	2p. green and blue	£3250	
N6	**1**	2p. brown and blue	£325	

1867. Perf.

N17	**2**	1p. green	28·00	£850
N18	**2**	2p. brown	45·00	£850

1868. Imperf.

N19	1p. green	80·00	
N20	2p. brown	£110	

1869. Perf.

N49a	**3**	1p. yellow	4·00	£275

4 King Milan

1872. Imperf.

N51		1p. yellow	10·00	28·00
N53	**4**	2p. black	2·20	1·10

POSTAGE DUE STAMPS

D8

1895

D87	**D8**	5p. mauve	80	55
D83	**D8**	10p. blue	8·50	55
D91	**D8**	20p. brown	55	1·10
D85	**D8**	30p. green	85	1·10
D86	**D8**	50p. red	85	1·50

D21

1918

D227	**D21**	5p. red	55	1·10
D228	**D21**	10p. green	55	1·10
D229	**D21**	20p. brown	55	1·10
D230	**D21**	30p. blue	55	1·10
D231	**D21**	50p. brown	1·30	2·20
D232	**D21**	5p. brown	55	1·10
D233	**D21**	30p. grey	1·30	1·90

GERMAN OCCUPATION

1941. Stamps of Yugoslavia on paper with coloured network optd **SERBIEN** reading downwards.

G1	**99**	25p. black	55	10·50
G2	**99**	50p. orange	55	5·25
G3	**99**	1d. green	55	5·25
G4	**99**	1d.50 red	55	5·25
G5	**99**	2d. red	55	5·25
G6	**99**	3d. brown	1·90	42·00
G7	**99**	4d. blue	1·30	8·50
G8	**99**	5d. blue	1·90	21·00
G9	**99**	5d.50 violet	1·90	21·00
G10	**99**	6d. blue	1·90	21·00
G11	**99**	8d. brown	3·25	32·00
G12	**99**	12d. violet	3·25	32·00
G13	**99**	16d. purple	4·25	£110
G14	**99**	20d. blue	10·50	£375
G15	**99**	30d. pink	32·00	£1400

1941. Air. Stamps of Yugoslavia on paper with coloured network, optd **SERBIEN.**

G16	**80**	50p. brown	9·50	£200
G17	-	1d. green (No. 361)	9·50	£200
G18	-	2d. blue (No. 362)	9·50	£200
G19	-	2d.50 red (No. 363)	9·50	£200
G20	**80**	5d. violet	9·50	£200
G21	-	10d. red (No. 365)	9·50	£200
G22	-	20d. green (No. 366)	13·00	£225
G23	-	30d. blue (No. 367)	13·00	£225
G24	-	40d. green (No. 443)	16·00	£850
G25	-	50d. blue (No. 444)	26·00	£1500

1941. Air. As last, but without network opt, surch **SERBIEN** and value.

G26	1d. on 10d. red (No. 365)	8·00	£275
G27	3d. on 20d. grn (No. 366)	8·00	£275
G28	6d. on 30d. blue (No. 367)	8·00	£275
G29	8d. on 40d. grn (No. 443)	13·00	£550
G30	12d. on 50d. blue (No. 444)	19·00	£1200

1941. As Nos. G1/15, but with **SERBIEN** reading upwards.

G31	**99**	25p. black	55	32·00
G32	**99**	50p. orange	55	7·50
G33	**99**	1d. green	55	7·50
G34	**99**	1d.50 red	55	7·50
G35	**99**	2d. red	55	7·50
G36	**99**	3d. brown	1·10	27·00
G37	**99**	4d. blue	1·10	7·50
G38	**99**	5d. blue	1·10	13·50
G39	**99**	5d.50 violet	2·10	27·00
G40	**99**	6d. blue	2·40	27·00
G41	**99**	8d. brown	2·75	42·00
G42	**99**	12d. violet	3·00	42·00
G43	**99**	16d. purple	3·25	£140
G44	**99**	20d. blue	3·25	£425
G45	**99**	30d. pink	19·00	£1400

G4 Smederovo Fortress

1941. Smederovo Explosion Relief Fund. (a).

G46	**G4**	0.50d.+1d. brown	1·10	2·75
G47	-	1d.+2d. green (Refugees)	1·10	3·25
G48	-	1.50d.+3d. purple (Refugees)	1·90	4·75
G49	**G4**	2d.+4d. blue	1·90	7·50

(b) Sheets 149×109 mm comprising Nos. G47 and G49, colours changed and with high premiums.

MSG49a 1d.+49d. red; 2d.+48d. green. P 11½	£110	£900
MSG49b 1d.+49d. green; 2d.+48d. red. Imperf	£110	£900

G6 Christ and the Virgin Mary

1941. Prisoners of War Fund.

G50	**G6**	0.50d.+1.50d. red	70	8·50
G51	**G6**	1d.+3d. green	70	8·50
G52	**G6**	2d.+6d. red	70	8·50
G53	**G6**	4d.+12d. blue	70	8·50

This set also exists with an optd network, both plain and incorporating a large "E", this letter being either normal or reversed.

G7

G8

1942. Anti-Masonic Exn. Dated "22.X.1941".

G54	**G7**	0.50d.+1.50d. brown	1·10	4·75
G55	-	1d.+1d. green	1·10	4·75
G56	**G8**	2d.+2d. red	1·10	8·50
G57	-	4d.+4d. blue	1·10	8·50

DESIGNS—HORIZ: 1d. Hand grasping snake. VERT: 4d. Peasant demolishing masonic symbols.

G9 Kalenic

1942. Monasteries.

G58		0d.50 violet	25	65
G59	**G9**	1d. red	25	65
G60	-	1d.50 brown	1·30	8·50
G61	-	1d.50 green	25	65
G62	-	2d. purple	25	65
G63	-	3d. blue	1·30	8·50
G64	-	3d. pink	25	65
G65	-	4d. blue	25	65
G66	-	7d. green	25	65
G67	-	12d. red	25	4·25
G68	-	16d. black	1·60	4·75

DESIGNS—VERT: 0d.50, Lazarica; 1d.50, Ravanica; 12d. Gornjak; 16d. Studenica. HORIZ: 2d. Manasija; 3d. Ljubostinja; 4d. Sopocani; 7d. Zica.

1942. As Nos. G50/53, colours changed.

G68a	**G6**	0.50d.+1.50d. brown	1·60	5·25
G68b	**G6**	1d.+3d. green	1·60	5·25
G68c	**G6**	2d.+6d. red	1·60	5·25
G68d	**G6**	4d.+12d. blue	1·60	5·25

1942. Air. 1939 issue of Yugoslavia surch with airplane, "**SERBIA**" in cyrillic characters and new value.

G69	**99**	2 on 2d. mauve	35	2·75
G70	**99**	4 on 4d. blue	35	2·75
G71	**99**	10 on 12d. violet	35	5·25
G72	**99**	14 on 20d. blue	35	5·25
G73	**99**	20 on 30d. pink	65	21·00

G11 Mother and Children

1942. War Orphans Fund.

G74	**G11**	2d.+6d. violet	9·00	19·00
G75	**G11**	4d.+8d. blue	9·00	19·00
G76	**G11**	7d.+13d. green	9·00	19·00
G77	**G11**	20d.+40d. red	9·00	19·00

G12 Broken Sword

1943. War Invalids' Relief Fund.

G78	**G12**	1.50d.+1.50d. brown	2·10	4·25
G79	-	2d.+3d. green	2·10	5·25
G80	-	3d.+5d. mauve	3·25	7·50
G81	-	4d.+10d. blue	3·25	8·50

MSG81a Two sheets, each 149×110 mm. Thick paper. P 11½. (a) 1d.50+48d.50, 4d.+46d. (b) 2d.+48d., 3d.+47d. £200 £8500

DESIGNS—HORIZ: 2d. Fallen standard bearer; 3d. Wounded soldier (seated). VERT: 4d. Nurse tending soldier.

G13 Post Rider

1943. Postal Centenary. Inscr "15.X.1843–15.X.1943".

G82	**G13**	3d. red and lilac	1·60	7·50
G83	-	8d. red and green	1·60	7·50
G84	-	9d. green and brown	1·60	7·50
G85	-	30d. brown and green	1·60	7·50
G86	-	50d. blue and red	1·60	7·50

DESIGNS: 8d. Horse wagon; 9d. Railway mail van; 30d. Postal motor van; 50d. Junkers Ju 52/3m mail plane.

1943. Bombing of Nish Relief Fund. Monasteries issue of 1942 on paper with network, surch with Serbian inscr 20-X-1943 and value.

G87		0d.50+2d. violet	55	65·00
G88		1d.+3d. red	55	65·00
G89		1d.50+4d. green	55	65·00
G90		2d.+5d. purple	55	65·00
G91		3d.+7d. pink	55	65·00
G92		4d.+9d. blue	55	65·00
G93		7d.+15d. green	1·10	65·00
G94		12d.+25d. red	1·10	£300
G95		16d.+33d. black	1·90	£475

OFFICIAL STAMP

GO12

1943

GO78	**GO12**	3d. red	1·30	3·25

POSTAGE DUE STAMPS

GD2

GD3

1941. Unissued Postage Due stamps optd **SERBIEN**.

GD16	**GD2**	0d.50 violet	1·60	55·00
GD17	**GD2**	1d. red	1·60	55·00
GD18	**GD2**	2d. blue	1·60	55·00
GD19	**GD2**	3d. red	1·60	80·00
GD20	**GD3**	4d. blue	2·40	£190
GD21	**GD3**	5d. orange	2·40	£190
GD22	**GD3**	10d. violet	4·25	£475
GD23	**GD3**	20d. green	13·00	£1300

1942. Types **GD2** and **GD3** without opt. Bottom inscription on white background.

GD69	**GD2**	1d. red and green	1·60	10·50
GD70	**GD2**	2d. blue and red	1·60	10·50
GD71	**GD2**	3d. red and blue	1·60	16·00
GD72	**GD3**	4d. blue and red	1·60	16·00
GD73	**GD3**	5d. orange and blue	2·40	42·00
GD74	**GD3**	10d. violet and red	2·40	42·00
GD75	**GD3**	20d. green and red	13·00	£190

GD13

1943

GD82	**GD13**	0d.50 black	2·10	10·50
GD83	**GD13**	3d. violet	2·10	10·50
GD84	**GD13**	4d. blue	2·10	10·50
GD85	**GD13**	5d. green	2·10	10·50
GD86	**GD13**	6d. orange	2·10	42·00
GD87	**GD13**	10d. red	3·75	42·00
GD88	**GD13**	20d. blue	10·50	85·00

Pt. 3

SERBIA AND MONTENEGRO

On 4 February 2003 Yugoslavia became Serbia & Montenegro. See Yugoslavia for previous issues.

2003. 100 para = 1 dinar.

1 "e", Stars and Map of Europe

2003. Accession to the Council of Europe. Multicoloured.

1	16d. Type **1**	1·30	1·30
2	28d.70 Smaller "e", stars and map of Europe	2·20	2·20

2 The Descent from the Cross (16th-century icon)

2003. Easter. Multicoloured.

3	12d. Type **2**	90	90
4	16d. Resurrection (Dimitrije Bacevic)	1·10	1·10
5	26d.20 Mourning Christ (icon, St. Paul's Monastery, Athos) (1616)	2·00	2·00
6	28d.70 Transfiguration of Christ (Giovanni Bellini)	2·20	2·20

3 Document and Emblem

2003. 150th Anniv of First Belgrade Singers' Society.

7	**3**	16d. multicoloured	3·25	3·25

4 Pasting up Poster

2003. Europa. Poster Art. Multicoloured.

8	28d.70 Type **4**	2·20	2·20
9	50d. Pasting up poster for Balkan Express	5·50	5·50

5 *Galanthus nivalis*

2003. Flowers. Multicoloured.

10	16d. Type **5**	1·30	1·30
11	24d. *Erythronium dens canis*	1·80	1·80
12	26d.20 *Hepatica nobilis*	2·00	2·00
13	28d.70 *Anemone runculoides*	2·20	2·20

6 Ilija Stanojevic

2003. Actors and Actresses. Multicoloured.

14	16d. Type **6**	1·30	1·30
15	16d. Zivana Stokic	1·30	1·30
16	16d. Radomir Plaovic	1·30	1·30
17	16d. Milosav Aleksic	1·30	1·30
18	16d. Dobrivoje Milotinovic	1·30	1·30
19	16d. Lubinka Bobic	1·30	1·30
20	16d. Milivoje Zivanovic	1·30	1·30
21	16d. Zoran Radmilovic	1·30	1·30

7 Early Car

2003. Centenary of First Motor Vehicle in Belgrade.

22	**7**	16d. multicoloured	13·50	13·50

8 Tree overhanging River

2003. Nature Protection. Zasavica Park. Multicoloured.

23	28d.70 Type **8**	2·00	2·00
24	50d. Boat and river	3·50	3·50

9 Magnifying Glass and Stamp

2003. Communications. Multicoloured.

25	1d. Type **9**	45	45
26	8d. Parcels in post van	65	65
27	12d. Telephonist (vert)	1·00	1·00
28	16d. Post van	1·50	1·50
29	32d. Television screen	3·25	3·25

10 Prince Milan Obrenovic (military reformer)

2003. 125th Anniv of Belgrade Military Museum.

30	**10**	16d. multicoloured	1·10	1·10

11 Delfa Ivanic (founder)

2003. Centenary of Serbian Sisters (humanitarian organization).

31	**11**	16d. multicoloured	1·10	1·10

12 Serbia State Arms

2003. 125th Anniversary of Serbia and Montenegro State. Multicoloured.

32	16d. Type **12**	1·10	1·10
33	16d. Montenegro state arms	1·10	1·10

13 Model Rockets

2003. European Model Rocket Building Championship.

34	**13**	16d. multicoloured	1·10	1·10

14 Neolithic Carved Figure

2003. Philatelica Danubiana Stamp Exhibition, Belgrade. Multicoloured.

35	16d. Type **14**	1·10	1·10
36	16d. Circular head	1·10	1·10

15 17th-century Belgrade

2003. 13th Srbijafila Stamp Exhibition, Belgrade. Sheet 84×57 mm containing T **15** and similar vert design. Multicoloured.

MS37	32d.×2, Type **15**; "Serbia" as woman (sculpture) (Djordje Jovanovic)	9·00	9·00

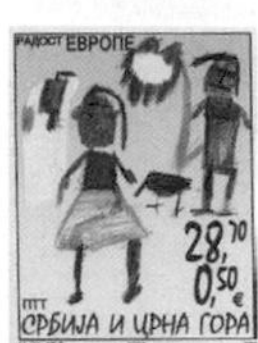
16 Children

2003. 35th "Joy in Europe" Meeting. Children's Day. Multicoloured.

38	28d.70 Type **16**	2·20	2·20
39	50d. Stylized rabbit (horiz)	3·50	3·50

17 Newspaper Vendor

2003. 50th Anniv of the Vecernje Novost Newspaper.

40	**17**	32d. multicoloured	2·20	2·20

18 Stamp Catalogues

2003. Stamp Day.

41	**18**	16d. multicoloured	4·50	4·50

19 Emblem

2003. 50th Anniv of ULUPUDS (Fine and Applied Artists and Designers of Serbia Association).

42	**19**	16d. multicoloured	1·10	1·10

20 Actors and Theatre Building

2003. 50th Anniv of Montenegro National Theatre, Podgorica.

43	**20**	50d. multicoloured	2·20	2·20

21 Early City

2003. 850th Anniv of Pancevo City.

44	**21**	32d. multicoloured	2·20	2·20

22 Saint John the Baptist (1645)

2003. Russian Orthodox Museum Exhibits. Multicoloured.

45	16d. Type **22**	1·10	1·10
46	24d. Cross (1602)	1·60	1·60
47	26d.20 Embroidered mitre (15th-century)	1·80	1·80
48	28d.70 Iron work tabernacle (1550)	2·20	2·20

23 Nativity (Oropos) (1983)

2003. Christmas. Icons. Multicoloured.

49	12d. Type **23**	90	90
50	16d. Nativity (Belgrade) (18th-century)	1·10	1·10
51	26d.20 (Panagiota Fourka) (2000)	1·80	1·80
52	28d.70 Wise men bearing gifts (Albrecht Durer)	2·20	2·20

24 Submarine

2003. 75th Anniv of Submarine Shipping.

53	**24**	32d. multicoloured	2·10	2·10

25 Wilbur and Orville Wright and *Wright Flyer I*

2003. Centenary of Powered Flight. Multicoloured.

54	16d. Type **25**	90	90
55	28d.70 *Wright Flyer I* and horse-drawn carriages	2·10	2·10

26 Building Facade

2004. Centenary of Politika Newspaper. Multicoloured.

56	16d. Type **26**	1·10	1·10
57	16d. Typewriter (horiz)	1·10	1·10

27 *Parnassius Apollo*

2004. Endangered Species. Butterflies and Insects. Multicoloured.

58	12d. Type **27**	65	65
59	16d. *Rosalia alpine*	80	80
60	26d.20 *Aeshna viririds*	1·80	1·80
61	28d.70 *Saga pedo*	2·10	2·10

28 Karadorde (Dorde Petrovic) (leader)

2004. Bicentenary of Serbian Rebellion against Turkey (1st issue). Multicoloured.

62	16d. Type **28**	1·10	1·10
63	16d. Children and globe	1·10	1·10

See also Nos. 70/3.

29 *Ramonda serbica*

2004. Fauna and Flora. Multicoloured.

64	16d. Type **29**	1·00	1·00
65	24d. *Ramonda nathaliae*	1·40	1·40
66	26d.20 *Heodes virgaureae*	1·60	1·60
67	28d.70 *Lysandra bellargus*	2·00	2·00

30 Early Greek and Modern Runners

2004. Olympic Games, Athens (1st issue). Multicoloured.

68	32d. Type **30**	2·30	2·30
69	56d. Early Greek and modern wrestlers	3·25	3·25

See also Nos. 90/3.

2004. Bicentenary of Serbian Rebellion against Turkey (2nd issue). As T **28**. Multicoloured.

70	12d. Freedom fighters	85	85
71	16d. Pistol and flag (vert)	1·00	1·00
72	28d.70 Karadorde (vert)	1·90	1·90
73	32d. Children and globe (vert)	2·10	2·10

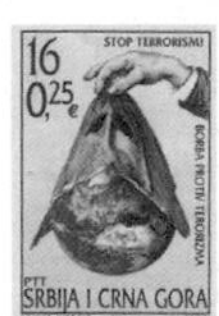
31 Lifting Mask from Globe

2004. Anti-Terrorism Campaign.

74	**31**	16d. multicoloured	1·00	1·00

32 Crucified Christ and Angels

2004. Easter. Multicoloured.

75	16d. Type **32**	1·10	1·10
76	28d.70 Risen Christ	2·20	2·20

33 Globes and Milutin Milankovic (geophysicist)

2004. 125th Birth Anniversaries. Multicoloured.

77	16d. Type **33**	1·00	1·00
78	16d. Albert Einstein (physicist) (vert)	1·00	1·00

34 South (Gurdich) Gate and Beskutcha Family Portal (detail)

2004. 25th Anniv of Kotor as UNESCO World Heritage Site.

79	**34**	16d. multicoloured	1·00	1·00

35 Vasiliji Petrovic (author)

2004. 250th Anniv of Publication of First History of Montenegro.

80	**35**	16d. multicoloured	1·00	1·00

36 Paragliding

2004. Europa. Holidays. Multicoloured.

81	16d. Type **36**	1·30	1·30
82	56d. Sail boat and water-skier in water (horiz)	3·50	3·50
MS83	97×55 mm. 32d. Yacht (35×29 mm); 56d. Rowing boats (35×29 mm)	6·00	6·00

37 Mosaic and Church Facade

2004. Saint Sava's Church, Belgrade. Multicoloured.

84	16d. Type **37**	1·10	1·10
85	28d.70 Church facade and statue (horiz)	2·20	2·20

38 Michael Pupin

2004. 150th Birth Anniv of Michael Idvorsky Pupin (Serbian–American physicist).

86	**38**	16d. lilac	1·00	1·00

39 Emblem

2004. Centenary of FIFA (Federation Internationale de Football).

87	**39**	28d.70 multicoloured	2·30	2·30

40 River, Ravnjak

2004. Nature Protection. Multicoloured.

88	32d. Type **40**	2·30	2·30
89	56d. Mountains, Sara	3·50	3·50

41 Early and Modern Runners and Gate of Athene Archgetis

2004. Olympic Games, Athens (2nd issue). Multicoloured.

90	16d. Type **41**	1·20	1·20
91	28d.70 Runners and Parthenon	2·40	2·40
92	32d. Long jumpers and Olympieion	2·50	2·50
93	57d.40 Hurdlers and Temple of Hephaistos	4·00	4·00

42 Guilielmo Marconi (inventor) and Antenna

2004. Establishment of First Radio Telegraph Stations in Volujica and Bar.

94	**42**	16d. multicoloured	1·00	1·00

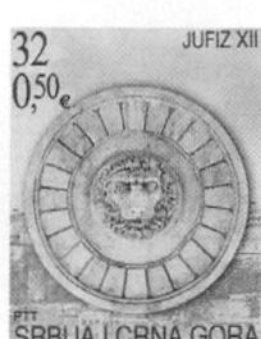

43 Lions Head Medallion

2004. Jufiz XII, National Philatelic Exhibition, Belgrade. Sheet 88×65 mm containing T **43** and similar vert design. Multicoloured.

MS95	32d.×2, Type **43**; Monument	4·25	4·25

44 Bridge (Angelka Misurovic)

2004. 35th "Joy in Europe" Meeting. Children's Day. Multicoloured.

96	32d. Type **44**	2·50	2·50
97	56d. Houses and church (Karol Sackievicz) (vert)	3·75	3·75

45 Boats

2004. 125th Anniv of Bar (Montenegrin port).

98	**45**	32d. multicoloured	2·30	2·30

46 Stamp and Magnifier

2004. Stamp Day.

99	**46**	16d. multicoloured	1·00	1·00

47 Bank Building Facade

2004. 120th Anniv of Serbian National Bank.

100	**47**	16d. indigo, black and cobalt	1·10	1·10
101	-	32d. multicoloured	2·20	2·20

DESIGNS: 16d. Type **47**; 32d. Mr Djordje Vajfert (Governor of the National Bank of the Kingdom of Serbia, the first Governor of the Kingdom of Serbs, Croats and Slovenes).

48 Fruit Stand

2004. Museum Exhibits. Silverware. Multicoloured.

102	16d. Type **48**	1·00	1·00
103	24d. Box	1·50	1·50
104	26d.20 Pierced bowl	1·70	1·70
105	28d.70 Cup with handles and lid	2·10	2·10

49 Lombardic Palace

2004. Architecture. Kotor Palaces. Multicoloured.

106	16d. Type **49**	1·00	1·00
107	24d. Pima Palace	1·50	1·50
108	26d.20 Grgurina Palace	1·70	1·70
109	28d.70 Bizanti Palace	2·10	2·10

50 Mary and Jesus (painting)

2004. Christmas. Multicoloured.

110	16d. Type **50**	1·00	1·00
111	28d.70 Mary and Jesus (painting) (different)	2·30	2·30

51 *Capparis spinosa*

2005. Endangered Species. Mammals and Flowers. Multicoloured.

112	16d.50 Type **51**	1·00	1·00
113	33d. *Mustela erminea*	1·70	1·70
114	41d.50 *Trollius europaeus*	2·10	2·10
115	49d.50 *Rupicapra rupicapra*	2·75	2·75

51a Stamps and Tweezers

2005. Philately

115a	**51a**	50p. multicoloured	70	70

52 Great Egret (*Egretta alba*)

2005. Birds. Multicoloured.

116	16d.50 Type **52**	1·00	1·00
117	33d. Black-necked grebe (*Podiceps nigricollis*)	1·70	1·70
118	41d.50 Ferruginous duck (*Aythya nyroca*)	2·10	2·10
119	49d.50 Black stork (*Ciconia nigra*)	2·75	2·75

53 Bat, Balls and Net

2005. 50th Anniv of Montenegrin Table Tennis Association.

120	**53**	16d.50 multicoloured	1·00	1·00

54 18th-century Fresco

2005. Easter. Multicoloured.

121	16d.50 Type **54**	1·00	1·00
122	28d.70 Crucifixion (carving) (1602)	2·30	2·30

55 University Facade, Belgrade

2005. Centenary of First Serbian University.

123	**55**	16d.50 multicoloured	1·00	1·00

56 Jovan Djordjevic

2005. Actors and Actresses. Multicoloured.

124	16d. Type **56**	1·10	1·10
125	16d. Milan Predic	1·10	1·10
126	16d. Milan Grol	1·10	1·10
127	16d. Mira Trailovic	1·10	1·10
128	16d. Soja Jovanovic	1·10	1·10
129	16d. Hugo Klajn	1·10	1·10
130	16d. Mata Milosevic	1·10	1·10
131	16d. Bojan Stupica	1·10	1·10

57 Colonnade (As No. 1407)

2005. 50th Anniv of Europa Stamps. Multicoloured.

132	16d.50 Type **57**	1·20	1·20
133	16d.50 Flaming sun (As No. 1425)	1·20	1·20
134	16d.50 Europa chain (As No. 1455)	1·20	1·20
135	16d.50 Communications (As No. 1514)	1·20	1·20
136	41d.50 Europa posthorn (As No. 1553)	2·40	2·40
137	41d.50 "Widow and Child" (sculpture, Ivan Mestrovic) (As No. 1604)	2·40	2·40
138	41d.50 Bridge (As No. 2138)	2·40	2·40
139	41d.50 Combined design (As No. 132, 134 and 137)	2·40	2·40
MS140	Two sheets, each 90×69 mm. (a) Nos. 132/5 (b) Nos. 136/139	13·00	13·00

58 *The Little Mermaid*

2005. Birth Bicentenary of Hans Christian Andersen (writer). Multicoloured.

141	41d.50 Type **58**	2·10	2·10
142	58d. *Snow Queen*	3·25	3·25

59 Bread and Bowl

2005. Europa. Gastronomy. Multicoloured.

143	41d.50 Type **59**	2·10	2·10
144	73d. Fish	4·00	4·00
MS145	93×50 mm. 41d.50 Cake; 73d. Tart	6·00	6·00

60 Marko Ivanovic

2005. Boka Kotorska Sea Captains. Multicoloured.

146	16d.50 Type **60**	1·00	1·00
147	33d. Petar Zelalic	1·70	1·70
148	41d.50 Matija Balovic	2·10	2·10
149	49d.50 Ivan Bronza	2·75	2·75

61 Crvena Zvezda (Red Star Football Club, Belgrade)

2005. Sports Associations' 60th Anniversaries. Multicoloured.

150	16d.50 Type **61**	1·10	1·10
151	16d.50 Partizan Football Club, Belgrade	1·10	1·10
MS152	94×53 mm. 16d.50×2, Crvena Zvezda; Partizan	2·10	2·10

The stamps and margins of No. **MS**152 form a composite design of knights jousting.

62 Boats and River Bank

2005. 50th Anniv of Danube Regatta. Sheet 97×49 mm containing T **62** and similar horiz design. Multicoloured.

MS153	41d.50 Type **62**; 49d.50 Boats, bridge and trees	4·75	4·75

The stamps and margins of No. **MS**153 form a composite design of the start of a boat race.

63 Rings surrounding Globe

2005. International Year of Physics (154) and Centenary of Publication of Theory of Special Relativity by Albert Einstein (155). Multicoloured.

154	41d.50 Type **63**	2·10	2·10
155	58d. Albert Einstein	3·25	3·25

64 Flowering Tree and Water

2005. Nature Protection. Koviljsko Petrovaradinski Rit Special Nature Reserve. Multicoloured.

156	41d.50 Type **64**	2·10	2·10
157	58d. Reeds, shrubs and water	3·25	3·25

65 Hands, Net and Ball

2005. European Volleyball Championships, Belgrade and Rome.

158	**65**	16d.50 multicoloured	1·30	1·30

66 Ball and Emblem

2005. European Basketball Championship (Eurobasket 2005), Belgrade.

159	**66**	16d.50 multicoloured	1·00	1·00

67 Parrot

2005. 36th "Joy in Europe" Meeting. Children's Day. Multicoloured.

160	41d.50 Type **67**	2·10	2·10
161	58d. Figure with raised arms (horiz)	3·25	3·25

68 Heart-shaped Graffiti

2005. World Youth Day.

162	**68**	41d.50 multicoloured	2·10	2·10

69 Roadway and Stars

2005. Initiation of Stabilization and Association Agreement with European Union.

163	**69**	16d.50 multicoloured	1·00	1·00

70 Early Airplane and Air Balloon

2005. Centenary of International Airline Federation. Multicoloured.

164	49d.50 Type **70**	2·50	2·50
165	58d. Glider, parachute and hang glider	3·25	3·25

71 Anniversary Emblem

2005. 60th Anniv of United Nations.

166	**71**	16d.50 multicoloured	1·10	1·10

72 Envelope and Aircraft

2005. Stamp Day.

167	**72**	16d.50 multicoloured	1·10	1·10

73 Petar I

2005. 175th Death Anniv of Valdika Petar I Petrovic (St Peter Cetinjski (bishop and leader)).

168	**73**	16d.50 multicoloured	1·10	1·10

74 Nicholas I

2005. Centenary of Montenegro's First Constitution.

169	**74**	16d.50 multicoloured	1·10	1·10

75 Stevan Sremac

2005. 150th Birth Anniv of Stevan Sremac (writer).

170	**75**	16d.50 multicoloured	1·10	1·10

76 Sudenica (Djorde Krstic)

2005. Paintings of Monasteries. Multicoloured.

171	16d.50 Type **76**	1·00	1·00
172	33d. Sopocani (Paja Jovanovic)	1·70	1·70
173	41d.50 Zica (Djorde Krstic)	2·30	2·30
174	49d.50 Gracanica (Milan Milanovic)	2·75	2·75

77 "Girl with Blue Ribbon" (F. X. Winterhalter)

2005. Paintings. Multicoloured.

175	16d.50 Type **77**	1·00	1·00
176	33d. "Adoration of the Child" (Andrea Alovidi)	1·70	1·70
177	41d.50 "Madonna with the Saints" (Biagio d'Antonio)	2·30	2·30
178	49d.50 "Remorse" (Vlaho Bukovaa)	2·75	2·75

78 The Nativity

2005. Christmas. Multicoloured.

179	16d.50 Type **78**	1·00	1·00
180	46d. The Nativity (different)	2·10	2·10

79 Footprints in Snow

2005. Tourism. Multicoloured.

181	5d. Type **79**	30	30
182	13d. Frozen lake	85	85
183	16d.50 Snow covered house and trees	1·00	1·00
184	33d. Snow covered hills	1·70	1·70

80 Jovan Sterija Popovic (birth bicentenary)

2006. Writers' Anniversaries. Multicoloured.

185	33d. Type **80**	1·70	1·70
186	46d. Stevan Stojanovic Mokranjac (150th birth anniv)	2·10	2·10

81 Ski Jump

2006. Winter Olympic Games, Turin. Multicoloured.

187	53d. Type **81**	2·50	2·50
188	73d. Skier	3·25	3·25

82 Easter Egg

2006. Easter. Multicoloured.

189	16d.50 Type **82**	85	85
190	46d. Basket of eggs	2·20	2·20

83 Bridge, Novi Sad

2006. 150th Anniv of Danube Commission. Multicoloured.

191	16d.50 Type **83**	85	85
192	16d.50 Castle, Smederevo	85	85
193	46d. Belgrade from river	2·20	2·20
194	46d. Tabula Traiana	2·20	2·20

84 *Canis lupus*

2006. Fauna. Multicoloured.

195	16d.50 Type **84**	85	85
196	16d.50 *Otis tarda*	85	85
197	46d. *Vormela peregusna*	2·20	2·20
198	46d. *Ursus arctos*	2·20	2·20

85 Two Players

2006. World Cup Football Championship, Germany. Multicoloured.

199	33d. Type **85**	1·70	1·70
200	33d. Goalkeeper	2·20	2·20
MS201	95×55 mm. 46d.×2, Left of stadium (horiz); Right of stadium (horiz)	8·75	8·75

The stamps and margins of **MS**201 form a composite design.

86 Eskimo and Penguin on Beach

2006. Europa. Integration. Multicoloured.

202	46d. Type **86**	2·20	2·20
203	73d. Lion and lamb	3·50	3·50
MS204	95×55 mm. 46d. Women in park; 73d. Couple entering house	5·75	5·75

The stamps and margins of **MS**204 form a composite design.

87 Nikola Tesla

2006. 150th Birth Anniv of Nikola Tesla (inventor). Multicoloured.

205	16d.50 Type **87**	85	85
206	46d. Nikola Tesla and coil	2·20	2·20
MS207	124×70 mm. 46d. Nikola Tesla (horiz); 112d. Engine (horiz)	7·75	7·75

The stamps and margins of **MS**207 form a composite design.

88 Aqua

2006. Roses. Multicoloured.

208	16d.50 Type **88**	85	85
209	16d.50 Vendela	85	85
210	46d. Sphinx	2·20	2·20
211	46d. Red Berlin	2·20	2·20

89 Belgrade

2006

212	**89**	46d. multicoloured	2·20	2·20

90 Parkland

2006. Nature Protection. Multicoloured.

213	46d. Type **90**	2·20	2·20
214	58d. Graddski park	2·50	2·50

Pt. 2

SERBIAN OCCUPATION OF HUNGARY

100 filler = 1 korona.

BARANYA

1919. Stamps of Hungary optd **1919 Baranya** or surch also. (a) "Turul" Type.

1	**7**	6f. drab	30	30
2	**7**	50f. red on blue	20	20
3	**7**	60f. green on red	55	55
4	**7**	70f. brown on green	20	20
5	**7**	80f. violet	2·75	2·75

(b) War Charity stamp of 1915.

6		50+2f. red on blue	8·50	8·50

(c) War Charity stamps of 1916.

8	**20**	10f. (+ 2f.) red	20	20
9	-	15f. (+ 2f.) violet	20	20

(d) Harvesters and Parliament Types.

10	**18**	2f. brown	20	20
11	**18**	3f. purple	30	30
12	**18**	5f. green	55	55
13	**18**	6f. blue	30	30
14	**18**	15f. purple	20	20
15	**18**	20f. brown	16·00	16·00
16	**18**	25f. blue	2·75	2·75
17	**18**	35f. brown	5·50	5·50
18	**18**	40f. green	22·00	22·00
19	**18**	50f. purple	55	55
20	**18**	75f. blue	20	20
21	**18**	80f. green	30	30
22	**19**	1k. lake	30	30
23	**19**	2k. brown	30	30
24	**19**	3k. grey and violet	30	30
25	**19**	5k. pale brown and brown	1·10	1·10
26	**19**	10k. magenta and brown	6·50	6·50

(e) Charles and Zita stamps.

27		10f. rose	20	20
28		20f. brown	20	20
29		25f. blue	1·10	1·10
30	**27**	40f. green	13·00	13·00
31	**27**	2f. brown	8·00	6·00
32	**27**	40f. green	18·00	18·00
33	**18**	45f. on 2f. brown	55	55
34		45f. on 5f. green	20·00	20·00
35		45k. on 15f. plum	20	20

(ii) Zita stamp.

36	**28**	45f. on 2f. brown	1·10	1·10

1919. Stamps of Hungary surch **BARANYA** and value. (a) Harvesters and Parliament Types.

42	**18**	20 on 2f. brown	8·00	8·00
43	**18**	50 on 5f. green	4·25	4·25
44	**18**	150 on 15f. purple	75	75
45	**19**	200 on 75f. blue	75	75

(b) Harvesters Type inscr "MAGYAR POSTA".

46	**18**	20 on 2f. brown	20	20
47	**18**	30 on 6f. blue	45	45
48	**18**	50 on 5f. green	10	10
49	**18**	100 on 25f. blue	10	10
50	**18**	100 on 40f. green	10	10
51	**18**	100 on 45f. orange	55	55
52	**18**	150 on 20f. brown	30	30

(c) Charles stamp optd **KOZTARSASAG**.

53	**27**	150 on 15f. purple	1·60	1·60

EXPRESS LETTER STAMPS

1919. No. E245 of Hungary surch 1919 **Baranya 105.**

E37	**E 18**	105 on 2f. green and red	1·10	1·10

1919. No. E245 of Hungary surch **BARANYA 10.**

E55	10 on 2f. olive and red	45	45

NEWSPAPER STAMP

1919. No. N136 of Hungary surch **BARANYA 10.**

N54	**N 9**	10 on 2(f). orange	10	10

POSTAGE DUE STAMPS

1919. Nos. D191 etc of Hungary optd **1919 BARANYA** or surch also.

D38	**D9**	2f. red and green	4·25	4·25
D39	**D9**	10f. red and green	75	75
D40	**D9**	20f. red and geen	75	75
D41	**D9**	40 on 2f. red and green	75	75

SAVINGS BANK STAMP

1919. No. B199 of Hungary surch **BARANYA 10.**

B56	**B 17**	10 on 10f. purple	55	55

TEMESVAR

Temesvar was later occupied by Romania which issued stamps for this area. It was then incorporated in Romania and renamed Timosoara.

1919. Stamps of Hungary surch. (a) War Charity stamps of 1916.

1	**20**	45f. on 10f.(+2f.) red	20	20

(b) Harvesters Type.

2	**18**	10f. on 2f. brown	20	20
3	**18**	30f. on 2f. brown	30	30
4	**18**	1k.50 on 15f. purple	45	45

(c) Charles Stamp.

5	**27**	50f. on 20f. brown	30	30

POSTAGE DUE STAMPS

1919. No. D191 of Hungary surch.

D6	**D 9**	40f. on 2f. red and green	55	55
D7	**D 9**	60f. on 2f. red and green	55	55
D8	**D 9**	100f. on 2f. red and green	55	55

Pt. 1

SEYCHELLES

A group of islands in the Indian Ocean, east of Africa.

100 cents = 1 rupee.

1

1890

9	1	2c. green and red	2·50	1·00
28	1	2c. brown and green	2·00	2·50
22	1	3c. purple and orange	1·50	50
10	1	4c. red and green	2·50	1·75
29	1	6c. red	3·50	50
11	1	8c. purple and blue	15·00	1·75
12	1	10c. blue and brown	15·00	3·25
23	1	12c. brown and green	2·50	60
13	1	13c. grey and black	6·50	1·75
24	1	15c. olive and lilac	8·00	2·00
30	1	15c. blue	11·00	7·00
6	1	16c. brown and blue	14·00	4·25
31	1	18c. blue	12·00	1·50
32	1	36c. brown and red	45·00	7·00
25	1	45c. brown and red	25·00	35·00
7	1	48c. bistre and green	25·00	10·00
33	1	75c. yellow and violet	55·00	70·00
8	1	96c. mauve and red	65·00	48·00
34	1	1r. mauve and red	14·00	7·50
35	1	1r.50 grey and red	85·00	95·00
36	1	2r.25 mauve and green	£110	85·00

1893. Surch in figures and words in two lines.

15	3c. on 4c. red and green	1·10	1·50
16	12c. on 16c. brown and blue	6·50	7·50
19	15c. on 16c. brown and blue	25·00	3·00
20	45c. on 48c. brown and green	35·00	7·00
21	90c. on 96c. mauve and red	70·00	50·00

1896. Surch in figures and words in one line.

26	18c. on 45c. brown and red	9·00	3·25
27	36c. on 45c. brown and red	10·00	60·00

1901. Surch in figures and words.

41	2c. on 4c. red and green	4·50	2·75
37	3c. on 10c. blue and brown	3·00	75
38	3c. on 16c. brown and blue	6·00	8·50
39	3c. on 36c. brown and red	1·75	80
40	6c. on 8c. purple and blue	6·00	3·25
42	30c. on 75c. yellow and violet	2·50	6·50
43	30c. on 1r. mauve and red	18·00	48·00
44	45c. on 1r. mauve and red	8·50	50·00
45	45c. on 2r.25 mauve and green	50·00	£110

6

1903

46	6	2c. brown and green	1·75	2·00
47	6	3c. green	1·00	1·25
62	6	6c. red	2·00	80
49	6	12c. brown and green	4·50	2·50
64	6	15c. blue	3·00	2·00
65	6	18c. olive and red	3·00	6·50
66	6	30c. violet and green	6·00	8·00
67	6	45c. brown and red	3·00	12·00
54	6	75c. yellow and violet	10·00	32·00
69	6	1r.50 black and red	60·00	60·00
70	6	2r.25 purple and green	55·00	65·00

1903. Surch **3 cents.**

57	3c. on 15c. blue	1·00	3·25
58	3c. on 18c. olive and red	2·75	45·00
59	3c. on 45c. brown and red	3·00	3·75

9

1912. Inscr "POSTAGE POSTAGE".

71	9	2c. brown and green	1·00	8·00
72	9	3c. green	5·50	60
73	9	6c. red	4·25	2·50
74	9	12c. brown and green	1·50	6·00
75	9	15c. blue	4·25	2·25
76	9	18c. olive and red	3·25	11·00
77	9	30c. violet and green	12·00	2·25
78	9	45c. brown and red	2·75	50·00
79	9	75c. yellow and violet	2·75	6·00
80	9	1r.50 black and red	11·00	1·00
81	9	2r.25 purple and green	75·00	2·50

11

1917. Inscr "POSTAGE & REVENUE".

98	11	2c. brown and green	25	15
99	11	3c. green	1·75	15
100	11	3c. black	1·00	30
101	11	4c. green	1·00	2·50
102	11	4c. olive and red	6·50	19·00
103	11	5c. brown	75	5·50
85	11	6c. red	4·25	1·00
105	11	6c. mauve	1·50	10
106	11	9c. red	3·50	4·25
107	11	12c. grey	2·75	20
108	11	12c. red	1·75	30
87	11	15c. blue	1·75	1·50
111	11	15c. yellow	1·00	2·75
112	11	18c. purple on yellow	2·50	19·00
113	11	20c. blue	1·50	35
89b	11	25c. black and red on yellow	4·75	17·00
90	11	30c. purple and olive	1·50	14·00
116	11	45c. purple and orange	1·25	5·50
117	11	50c. purple and black	2·50	2·25
93a	11	75c. black on green	1·40	23·00
119	11	1r. purple and red	28·00	18·00
121	11	1r.50 purple & blue on bl	15·00	22·00
122	11	2r.25 green and violet	19·00	14·00
123	11	5r. green and blue	£120	£170

1935. Silver Jubilee. As T **32a** of St. Helena.

128	6c. blue and black	1·25	2·25
129	12c. green and blue	4·75	1·50
130	20c. brown and blue	3·50	5·50
131	1r. grey and purple	7·50	28·00

1937. Coronation. As T **32b** of St. Helena.

132	6c. green	75	15
133	12c. orange	75	50
134	20c. blue	1·00	1·00

14 Coco-de-mer Palm

1938

135	14	2c. brown	1·50	40
136	-	3c. green	12·00	2·75
136ab	-	3c. orange	55	1·50
137	-	6c. orange	17·00	3·50
137ab	-	6c. green	2·00	2·25
138	14	9c. red	18·00	4·00
138ac	-	9c. blue	8·00	3·25
139	-	12c. mauve	50·00	1·25
139ab	-	15c. red	9·00	4·75
139c	14	18c. red	14·00	60
140	-	20c. blue	45·00	6·00
140ab	-	20c. yellow	£500	£150
141	14	25c. brown	50·00	14·00
142	-	30c. red	50·00	11·00
142ab	-	30c. blue	2·50	6·50
143a	-	45c. brown	4·50	2·75
144a	14	50c. violet	1·75	3·25
145	-	75c. blue	85·00	50·00
145ab	-	75c. mauve	4·00	8·50
146	-	1r. green	£150	90·00
146ab	-	1r. black	5·50	7·00
147a	14	1r.50 blue	8·00	17·00
148a	-	2r.25 olive	32·00	40·00
149	-	5r. red	30·00	15·00

DESIGNS—VERT: 3, 12, 15, 30, 75c., 2r.25, Giant tortoise. HORIZ: 6, 20, 45c., 1, 5r. Fishing pirogue.

1946. Victory. As T **33a** of St. Helena.

150	9c. blue	10	10
151	30c. blue	30	20

1948. Silver Wedding. As T **33b/c** of St. Helena.

152	9c. blue	15	60
153	5r. red	15·00	48·00

1949. U.P.U. As T **33d/g** of St. Helena.

154	18c. mauve	20	25
155	50c. purple	1·75	3·00
156	1r. grey	50	40
157	2r.25 olive	35	1·25

17 Sailfish

1952. Full face portrait.

158	17	2c. lilac	75	70
159	-	3c. orange	1·00	30
160	-	9c. blue	60	1·75
161	-	15c. green	50	1·00
162	-	18c. lake	1·75	20
163	-	20c. yellow	3·00	1·50
164	-	25c. red	70	3·25
165	17	40c. blue	1·25	2·75
166	-	45c. brown	2·00	30
167	-	50c. violet	1·50	1·75
168	-	1r. black	6·50	4·50
169	-	1r.50 blue	13·00	18·00
170	-	2r.25 olive	19·00	21·00
171	-	5r. red	20·00	22·00
172	17	10r. green	28·00	50·00

DESIGNS—VERT: 2, 25c., 2r.25, Giant tortoise; 9, 50c., 1r.50, Coco-de-mer palm. HORIZ: 15, 20, 45c. Fishing pirogue; 18c., 1, 5r. Map of Indian Ocean.

1953. Coronation. As T **33h** of St. Helena.

173	9c. black and blue	60	70

1954. Designs as 1952 but with portrait of Queen Elizabeth II.

174	2c. lilac	10	10
175	3c. orange	10	10
175a	5c. violet	2·75	30
176	9c. blue	10	10
176a	10c. blue (as 9c.)	1·00	2·25
177	15c. green	2·50	30
178	18c. lake	30	10
179	20c. yellow	1·50	20
180	25c. red	2·25	1·00
180a	35c. lake (as 18c.)	6·50	1·75
181	40c. blue	1·00	25
182	45c. brown	20	15
183	50c. violet	30	80
183a	70c. brown (as 45c.)	6·50	2·25
184	1r. black	1·75	40
185	1r.50 blue	9·50	14·00
186	2r.25 olive	8·50	10·00
187	5r. red	18·00	9·00
188	10r. green	28·00	18·00

NEW DESIGN: 5c. Seychelles flying fox.

21 "La Pierre de Possession"

1956. Bicent of "La Pierre de Possession".

189	**21**	40c. blue	20	15
190	**21**	1r. black	30	20

1957. No. 182 surch **5 cents** and bars.

191	5c. on 45c. brown	15	10

23 Mauritius 6d. Stamp with Seychelles "B 64" Cancellation

1961. Cent of First Seychelles Post Office.

193	**23**	10c. blue, black and purple	25	10
194	**23**	35c. blue, black and green	40	10
195	**23**	2r.25 blue, black & brown	70	45

24 Black Parrot

40 Colony's Badge

1962. Multicoloured.. Multicoloured..

233	5c. Type **24**	35	2·25
234	10c. Vanilla vine	30	15
198	15c. Fisherman	30	10
199	20c. Denis Is. Lighthouse	1·50	10
200	25c. Clock Tower, Victoria	50	10
200a	30c. Anse Royale Bay	8·50	5·50
201	35c. Anse Royale Bay	1·75	1·50
202	40c. Government House	20	1·50
203	45c. Fishing pirogue	3·50	5·00
204	50c. Cascade Church	40	25
236	60c. red, blue and brown (Flying fox)	1·75	45
205	70c. ultramarine and blue (Sailfish)	7·00	3·00
206	75c. Coco-de-mer palm	2·75	4·25
237	85c. ultramarine and blue (Sailfish)	1·00	40
207	1r. Cinnamon	1·00	10
208	1r.50 Copra	5·50	6·50
209	2r.25 Map	5·50	10·00
210	3r.50 Land settlement	2·25	6·50
211	5r. Regina Mundi Convent	8·00	2·50
212	10r. Type **40**	16·00	4·00

The 30, 35, 40, 85c., 1, 1r.50, 2r.25, 3r.50 and 5r. are horiz.

No. 236 is 23×25 mm.

1963. Freedom from Hunger. As T **63a** of St. Helena.

213	70c. violet	60	25

1963. Cent of Red Cross. As T **63b** of St. Helena.

214	10c. red and black	25	10
215	75c. red and blue	75	1·25

1965. Surch.

216	45c. on 35c. (No. 201)	15	15
217	75c. on 70c. (No. 205)	35	15

1965. Cent of I.T.U. As T **64a** of St. Helena.

218	5c. orange and blue	10	10
219	1r.50 mauve and green	50	25

1965. I.C.Y. As T **64b** of St. Helena.

220	5c. purple and turquoise	15	10
221	40c. green and lavender	35	30

1966. Churchill Commemoration. As T **64c** of St. Helena.

222	5c. blue	15	75
223	15c. green	45	10
224	75c. brown	1·25	45
225	1r.50 violet	1·40	3·75

1966. World Cup Football Championship. As T **64d** of St. Helena.

226	15c. multicoloured	20	25
227	1r. multicoloured	35	40

1966. Inauguration of W.H.O. Headquarters, Geneva. As T **64e** of St. Helena.

228	20c. black, green and blue	20	10
229	30c. black, purple and ochre	40	20

1966. 20th Anniv of UNESCO. As T **64f** of St. Helena.

230	15c. multicoloured	20	10
231	1r. yellow, violet and olive	35	10
232	5r. black, purple and orange	80	1·00

1967. Universal Adult Suffrage. Nos. 198, 203, 206 and 210 optd **UNIVERSAL ADULT SUFFRAGE 1967**.

238	15c. multicoloured	10	10
239	45c. multicoloured	10	10
240	75c. multicoloured	10	10
241	3r.50 multicoloured	20	50

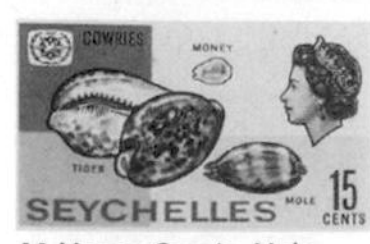
44 Money Cowrie, Mole Cowrie and Tiger Cowrie

1967. International Tourist Year. Multicoloured.

242	15c. Type **44**	20	10
243	40c. Beech cone, textile or cloth of gold cone and Virgin cone	25	10
244	1r. Arthritic spider conch	35	10
245	2r.25 Subulate auger and trumpet triton shells	60	1·25

1968. Nos. 202-203 and 206 surch.

246	30c. on 40c. multicoloured	15	50
247	60c. on 45c. multicoloured	20	30
248	85c. on 75c. multicoloured	20	30

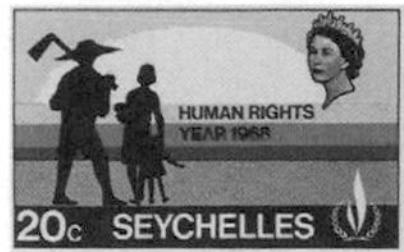
49 Farmer with Wife and Children at Sunset

1968. Human Rights Year.

249	**49**	20c. multicoloured	10	10
250	**49**	50c. multicoloured	10	10
251	**49**	85c. multicoloured	10	10
252	**49**	2r.25 multicoloured	25	1·60

50 Expedition landing at Anse Possession

1968. Bicent of First Landing on Praslin. Multicoloured.

253	20c. Type **50**	35	10
254	50c. French warships at anchor (vert)	40	15
255	85c. Coco-de-mer and Black parrot (vert)	90	25
256	2r.25 French warships under sail	90	3·00

54 Apollo Launch

1969. First Man on the Moon. Multicoloured.

257	5c. Type **54**	10	50
258	20c. Module leaving mother ship for the Moon	15	10
259	50c. Astronauts and Space Module on the Moon	20	15
260	85c. Tracking station	25	15
261	2r.25 Moon craters with Earth on the "Horizon"	45	1·60

59 Picault's Landing, 1742

1969. Multicoloured

262	5c. Type **59**	10	10
263	10c. U.S. satellite-tracking station	10	10
264	15c. "Konigsberg I" (German cruiser) at Aldabra, 1914	3·00	2·00
265	20c. Fleet re-fuelling off St. Anne, 1939–45	1·75	10
266	25c. Exiled Ashanti King, Prempeh	20	10
267	30c. Laying Stone of Possession, 1756	1·00	4·00
268a	40c. As 30c.	1·60	1·60
269	50c. Pirates and treasures	30	15
270	60c. Corsairs attacking merchantman	1·00	1·50
271	65c. As 60c.	6·00	8·00
272	85c. Impression of proposed airport	3·50	1·75
273a	95c. As 85c.	6·50	3·25
274	1r. French Governor capitulating to British naval officer, 1794	35	15
275	1r.50 H.M.S. "Sybille" (frigate) and "Chiffone" (French frigate) in battle, 1801	1·75	2·00
276	3r.50 Visit of the Duke of Edinburgh, 1956	1·00	2·25
277	5r. Chevalier Queau de Quincy	1·00	2·75
278	10r. Indian Ocean chart, 1574	2·75	8·00
279	15r. Badge of Seychelles	4·00	14·00

NOTE: The design of No. 264 incorrectly shows the vessel "Konigsberg II" and date "1915".

74 White Terns, French Warship and Island

1970. Bicentenary of First Settlement, St. Anne Island. Multicoloured.

280	20c. Type **74**	1·40	10
281	50c. Spot-finned flyingfish, ship and island	45	10
282	85c. Compass and chart	45	10
283	3r.50 Anchor on sea-bed	70	1·25

78 Girl and Optician's Chart

1970. Centenary of British Red Cross. Multicoloured.

284	20c. Type **78**	30	10
285	50c. Baby, scales and milk bottles	30	10
286	85c. Woman with child and umbrella (vert)	30	10
287	3r.50 Red Cross local headquarters building	1·25	2·75

79 Pitcher Plant

1970. Flowers. Multicoloured.

288	20c. Type **79**	25	15
289	50c. Wild vanilla	30	15
290	85c. Tropic-bird orchid	80	30
291	3r.50 Vare hibiscus	1·00	2·25
MS292	81×133 mm. Nos. 288-291	2·75	13·00

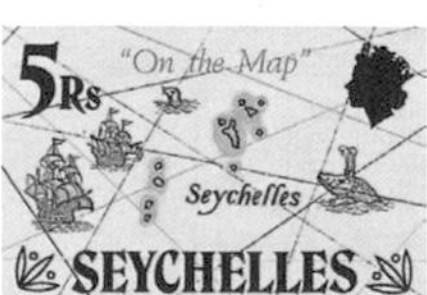
80 Seychelles "On the Map"

1971. "Putting Seychelles on the Map". Sheet 152×101 mm.

MS293	**80** 5r. multicoloured	1·75	9·00

81 Piper Navajo

1971. Airport Completion. Multicoloured.

294	5c. Type **81**	30	50
295	20c. Westland Wessex HAS-1 helicopter	65	10
296	50c. Consolidated Catalina amphibian (horiz)	70	10
297	60c. Grumman Albatross	75	10
298	85c. Short "G" Class flying boat "Golden Hind" (horiz)	80	10
299	3r.50 Vickers Supermarine Walrus Mk I amphibian (horiz)	2·25	3·50

82 Santa Claus delivering Gifts (Jean-Claude Waye Hive)

1971. Christmas. Multicoloured.

300	10c. Type **82**	10	10
301	15c. Santa Claus seated on turtle (Edison Theresine)	10	10
302	3r.50 Santa Claus landing on island (Isabelle Tirant)	40	2·25

1971. Nos. 267, 270 and 272 surch.

303	40c. on 30c. on 30c. multicoloured	30	55
304	65c. on 60c. on 60c. multicoloured	40	75
305	95c. on 85c. on 85c. multicoloured	45	1·00

1972. Royal Visit. Nos. 265 and 277 optd **ROYAL VISIT 1972**.

306	20c. multicoloured	15	20
307	5r. multicoloured	1·00	3·00

85 Seychelles Brush Warbler

1972. Rare Seychelles Birds. Multicoloured.

308	5c. Type **85**	60	70
309	20c. Bare-legged scops owl ("Seychelles Scoops Owl")	2·25	70
310	50c. Seychelles blue pigeon	2·25	70
311	65c. Seychelles magpie robin	2·75	75
312	95c. Seychelles paradise flycatcher ("Black Paradise Flycatcher")	3·00	2·50
313	3r.50 Seychelles kestrel	8·00	12·00
MS314	144×162 mm. Nos. 308/13	22·00	28·00

86 Fireworks Display

1972. "Festival '72". Multicoloured.

315	10c. Type **86**	10	10
316	15c. Pirogue race (horiz)	10	10
317	25c. Floats and costumes	10	10
318	5r. Water skiing (horiz)	60	1·25

1972. Royal Silver Wedding. As T **103** of St. Helena, but with Giant Tortoise and Sailfish in background.

319	95c. blue	15	10
320	1r.50 brown	15	10

1973. Royal Wedding. As T **103a** of St. Helena. Multicoloured, background colours given.

321	95c. brown	10	10
322	1r.50 blue	10	10

88 Seychelles Squirrelfish

1974. Fish. Multicoloured.

323	20c. Type **88**	25	15
324	50c. Harlequin filefish	35	15
325	95c. Pennant coralfish ("Papillon")	40	40
326	1r.50 Oriental sweetlips ("Peau d'ane canal")	85	2·50

89 Globe and Letter

1974. Centenary of U.P.U. Multicoloured.

327	20c. Type **89**	10	10
328	50c. Globe and radio beacon	20	10
329	95c. Globe and postmark	35	40
330	1r.50 Emblems within "UPU"	50	1·25

90 Sir Winston Churchill

1974. Birth Centenary of Sir Winston Churchill. Multicoloured.

331	95c. Type **90**	20	20
332	1r.50 Profile portrait	35	80
MS333	81×109 mm. Nos. 331/2	60	1·75

1975. Visit of Liner "Queen Elizabeth II". Nos. 265, 269, 273a and 275 optd **VISIT OF Q.E. II** and silhouette of liner.

334	20c. multicoloured	15	15
335	50c. multicoloured	20	20
336	95c. multicoloured	25	40
337	1r.50 multicoloured	35	1·75

1975. Internal Self-Government. Nos. 265, 271, 274 and 276 optd **INTERNAL SELF-GOVERNMENT OCTOBER 1975**.

338	20c. multicoloured	15	15
339	65c. multicoloured	25	30
340	1r. multicoloured	30	35
341	3r.50 multicoloured	75	2·50

93 Queen Elizabeth I

1975. International Women's Year. Multicoloured.

342	10c. Type **93**	10	50
343	15c. Gladys Aylward	10	50
344	20c. Elizabeth Fry	10	10
345	25c. Emmeline Pankhurst	10	10
346	65c. Florence Nightingale	25	20
347	1r. Amy Johnson	40	35
348	1r.50 Joan of Arc	50	1·50
349	3r.50 Eleanor Roosevelt	1·00	3·50

94 Map of Praslin and Postmark

1976. Rural Posts. Multicoloured.

350	20c. Type **94**	20	10
351	65c. La Digue	30	20
352	1r. Mahe with Victoria postmark	35	25
353	1r.50 Mahe with Anse Royale postmark	55	2·00
MS354	166×127 mm. Nos. 350/3	1·50	3·00

Nos. 350-353 show maps and postmarks.

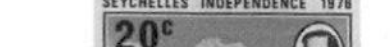

95 First Landing, 1609 (inset portrait of Premier James Mancham)

1976. Independence. Multicoloured.

355	20c. Type **95**	15	15
356	25c. The Possession Stone	15	15
357	40c. First settlers, 1770	15	15
358	75c. Chevalier Queau de Quincy	15	60
359	1r. Sir Bickham Sweet-Escott	15	20
360	1r.25 Legislative Building	20	1·00
361	1r.50 Seychelles badge	20	1·00
362	3r.50 Seychelles flag	80	2·25

96 Flags of Seychelles and U.S.A.

1976. Seychelles Independence and American Bicent of Independence. Multicoloured.

363	1r. Type **96**	30	15
364	10r. Statehouses of Seychelles and Philadelphia	70	3·00

97 Swimming

1976. Olympic Games, Montreal.

365	**97**	20c. blue, lt blue & brown	10	10
366	-	65c. lt green, green & grey	35	10
367	-	1r. brown, blue and grey	35	10
368	-	3r.50 light red, red & grey	50	2·75

DESIGNS: 65c. Hockey; 1r. Basketball; 3r.50, Football.

98 Seychelles Paradise Flycatcher

1976. Fourth Pan-African Ornithological Congress, Seychelles. Multicoloured.

369	20c. Type **98**	40	20
370	1r.25 Seychelles sunbird (horiz)	1·40	1·00
371	1r.50 Seychelles brown white eye ("The Seychelles White-eye") (horiz)	1·50	1·50
372	5r. Black parrot ("The Seychelles Black Parrot")	2·50	4·50
MS373	161×109 mm. Nos. 369-372	6·50	9·00

1976. Independence. Nos. 265, 269, 271, 273a, 274 and 276-279 optd **Independence 1976** or surch also.

374	20c. Fleet re-fuelling off St. Anne, 1939–45	70	2·50
375	50c. Pirates and treasure	60	2·50
376	95c. Impression of proposed airport	2·25	2·25
377	1r. French Governor capitulating to British naval officer, 1794	55	2·25
378	3r.50 Visit of Duke of Edinburgh, 1956	2·75	4·50
379	5r. Chevalier Queau de Quincy	1·75	7·50
380	10r. Indian Ocean chart, 1574	2·50	12·00
381	15r. Badge of Seychelles	2·75	12·00
382	25r. on 65c. on 65c. Corsairs attacking merchantman	3·00	16·00

100 Inauguration of George Washington

1976. Bicentenary of American Revolution.

383	**100**	1c. deep red and red	10	10
384	-	2c. violet and lilac	10	10
385	-	3c. light blue and blue	10	10
386	-	4c. brown and yellow	10	10
387	-	5c. green and yellow	10	10
388	-	1r.50 brown & light brown	30	35
389	-	3r.50 blue and green	35	70
390	-	5r. brown and yellow	40	80
391	-	10r. blue and light blue	65	1·50
MS392		141×141 mm. 25r. purple and mauve	2·50	6·50

DESIGNS: 2c. Jefferson and Louisiana Purchase; 3c. William Seward and Alaska Purchase; 4c. Pony Express, 1860; 5c. Lincoln's Emancipation Proclamation; 1r.50, Trans-continental Railroad, 1869; 3r.50, Wright Brothers flight, 1903; 5r. Henry Ford's assembly-line, 1913; 10r. J. F. Kennedy and 1969 Moon-landing; 25r. Signing Independence Declaration, 1776.

101 Silhouette of the Islands

1977. Silver Jubilee. Multicoloured.

393	20c. Type **101**	10	10
394	40c. Silhouette (different)	10	10
395	50c. The Orb (vert)	10	10
396	1r. St. Edward's Crown (vert)	10	10
397	1r.25 Ampulla and Spoon (vert)	10	15
398	1r.50 Sceptre with Cross (vert)	10	15
399	5r. Silhouette (different)	25	30
400	10r. Silhouette (different)	45	60
MS401	133×135 mm. 20c., 50c., 1r., 10r.	55	1·40

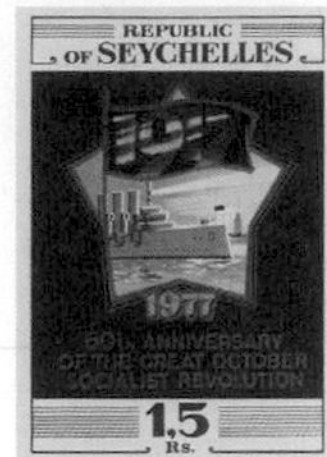

102 Cruiser "Aurora" and Flag

1977. 60th Anniv of Russian Revolution.

402	**102**	1r.50 multicoloured	55	30
MS403		101×129 mm. No. 402	80	1·10

103 Coral Scene

1977. Marine Life. Rupee face values shown as "Re" or "Rs". Multicoloured.

404A	5c. Reef fish	30	2·00
405B	10c. Hawksbill turtle	20	10
406B	15c. Coco-de-mer	20	15
407A	20c. Wild vanilla orchid	1·50	20
408A	25c. "Hypolimnas misippus" (butterfly)	1·50	1·75
409B	40c. Type **103**	20	10
410A	50c. Giant tortoise	30	10
411A	75c. Crayfish	40	10
412A	1r. Madagascar red fody ("Madagascar Fody")	1·25	10
413A	1r.25 White tern ("Fairy Tern")	1·25	20
414A	1r.50 Seychelles flying fox	1·00	20
736	3r. Green gecko	6·50	7·00
415A	3r.50 As 3r.	75	3·25
416A	5r. Octopus	1·50	40
417A	10r. Tiger cowrie	1·50	2·50
418A	15r. Pitcher plant	1·50	2·50
419A	20r. Coat of arms	1·50	2·50

The 40c., 1r., 1r.25 and 1r.50 values are horizontal, 31×27 mm. The 5, 10, 15 and 20r. are vertical, 28×36 mm. The others are horizontal, 29×25 mm.

Nos. 405-412 and 414 exist with or without imprint date at foot.

For similar designs with rupee face values shown as "R" see Nos. 487a-494.

104 St. Roch Roman Catholic Church, Bel Ombre

1977. Christmas. Multicoloured.

420	20c. Type **104**	10	10
421	1r. Anglican cathedral, Victoria	10	10
422	1r.50 Roman Catholic cathedral, Victoria	15	10
423	5r. St. Mark's Anglican church, Praslin	30	45

105 Liberation Day ringed on Calendar

1978. Liberation Day. Multicoloured.

424	40c. Type **105**	10	10
425	1r.25 Hands holding bayonet, torch and flag	15	10
426	1r.50 Fisherman and farmer	15	15
427	5r. Soldiers and rejoicing people	35	40

106 Stamp Portraits of Edward VII, George V and George VI

1978. 25th Anniv of Coronation. Multicoloured.

428	40c. Type **106**	10	10
429	1r.50 Queen Victoria and Elizabeth II	15	10
430	3r. Queen Victoria Monument	25	25
431	5r. Queen's Building, Victoria	35	35
MS432	87×129 mm. Nos. 428-431	75	85

107 Gardenia

1978. Wildlife. Multicoloured.

433	40c. Type **107**	15	10
434	1r.25 Seychelles magpie robin ("Magpie Robin of Fregate Island")	1·25	50
435	1r.50 Seychelles paradise flycatcher	1·25	50
436	5r. Green turtle	75	1·10

108 Possession Stone

1978. Bicentenary of Victoria. Multicoloured.

437	20c. Type **108**	10	10
438	1r.25 Plan of 1782 "L' Etablissement"	15	15
439	1r.50 Clock Tower	15	15
440	5r. Bust of Pierre Poivre	40	75

109 Seychelles Fody

1979. Birds (1st series). Multicoloured.

441	2r. Type **109**	55	50
442	2r. Green-backed heron	55	50
443	2r. Thick-billed bulbul ("Seychelles Bulbul")	55	50
444	2r. Seychelles cave swiftlet	55	50
445	2r. Grey-headed lovebird	55	50

See also Nos. 463-467, 500-504 and 523-527.

110 Patrice Lumumba

1979. Africa Liberation Heroes.

446	**110**	40c. black, violet and lilac	10	10
447	-	2r. black, blue & light blue	20	25
448	-	2r.25 black, brown & orange	20	30
449	-	5r. black, olive and green	45	1·25

DESIGNS: 2r. Kwame Nkrumah; 2r.25, Dr. Eduardo Mondlane; 5r. Hamilcar Cabral.

111 1978 5r. Liberation Day Commemorative and Sir Rowland Hill

1979. Death Cent of Sir Rowland Hill. Multicoloured.

450	40c. Type **111**	10	10
451	2r.25 1972 50c. Seychelles blue pigeon commemorative	25	70
452	3r. 1962 50c. definitive	35	95
MS453	112×88 mm. 5r. 1892 4c. definitive	50	55

112 Child with Book

1979. International Year of the Child. Multicoloured.

454	40c. Type **112**	10	10
455	2r.25 Children of different races	15	30
456	3r. Young child with ball (vert)	20	50
457	5r. Girl with glove puppet (vert)	35	70

113 The Herald Angel

1979. Christmas. Multicoloured.

458	20c. Type **113**	10	10
459	2r.25 The Virgin and Child	30	40
460	3r. The Three Kings (horiz)	40	60
MS461	87×75 mm. 5r. The Flight into Egypt (horiz)	50	70

1980. No. 415 surch **R.1.10**.

462	1r.10 on 3r.50 Green gecko	30	50

115 Seychelles Kestrel

1980. Birds (2nd series). Seychelles Kestrel. Multicoloured.

463	2r. Type **115**	80	60
464	2r. Pair of Seychelles kestrels	80	60
465	2r. Seychelles kestrel with eggs	80	60
466	2r. Seychelles kestrel on nest with chick	80	60
467	2r. Seychelles kestrel chicks in nest	80	60

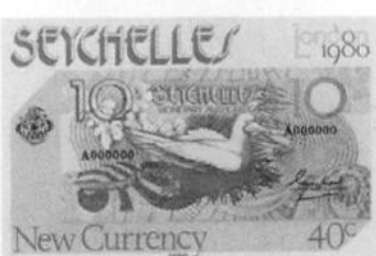

116 10 Rupees Banknote

1980. "London 1980" International Stamp Exhibition. Currency Notes. Multicoloured.

468	40c. Type **116**	15	10
469	1r.50 25 rupees	30	15
470	2r.25 50 rupees (vert)	40	25
471	5r. 100 rupees (vert)	80	75
MS472	119×102 mm. Nos. 468-471	2·00	1·60

117 Sprinting

1980. Olympic Games, Moscow. Multicoloured.

473	40c. Type **117**	10	10
474	2r.25 Weightlifting	20	20
475	3r. Boxing	30	30
476	5r. Sailing	60	50
MS477	90×121 mm. Nos. 473-476	1·40	2·25

118 Boeing 747-200 Airliner

1980. Int Tourism Conference, Manila. Multicoloured.

478	40c. Type **118**	10	10
479	2r.25 Bus	25	30
480	3r. Cruise liner	35	40
481	5r. "La Belle Coralline" (tourist launch)	55	65

119 Female Palm

1980. Coco-de-mer (palms). Multicoloured.

482	40c. Type **119**	10	10
483	2r.25 Male palm	25	20
484	3r. Artefacts	40	35
485	5r. Fisherman's gourd	55	55
MS486	82×140 mm. Nos. 482/5	1·60	1·60

1981. As Nos. 412-414, 415 (with new value), and 416-419 but face values redrawn as "R" instead of "Re" or "Rs".

487	1r. Madagascar red fody ("Madagascar Fody")	1·00	60
488	1r.10 Green gecko	70	1·00
489	1r.25 White tern ("Fairy Tern")	2·75	1·75
490	1r.50 Seychelles flying fox	50	75
491	5r. Octopus	1·25	1·40
492	10r. Tiger cowrie	3·25	3·50
493	15r. Pitcher plant	4·00	4·50
494	20r. Seychelles coat of arms	5·00	6·00

120 Vasco da Gama's "Sao Gabriel", 1497

1981. Ships. Multicoloured.

495	40c. Type **120**	15	10
496	2r.25 Mascarenhas' caravel, 1505	50	55
497	3r.50 Darwin's H.M.S. "Beagle", 1831	55	1·00
498	5r. "Queen Elizabeth 2" (liner), 1968	60	1·40
MS499	141×91 mm. Nos. 495/8	1·50	3·50

121 Male White Tern

1981. Birds (3rd series). White Tern. Multicoloured.

500	2r. Type **121**	1·00	65
501	2r. Pair of white terns	1·00	65
502	2r. Female white tern	1·00	65
503	2r. Female white tern on nest and egg	1·00	65
504	2r. White tern and chick	1·00	65

1981. Royal Wedding. Royal Yachts. As T **14a/b** of St. Kitts. Multicoloured.

505	1r.50 "Victoria and Albert I"	15	25
506	1r.50 Prince Charles and Lady Diana Spencer	65	75
507	5r. "Cleveland"	35	60
509	10r. "Britannia"	60	1·50
510	10r. As No. 506	1·75	3·00
MS511	120×109 mm. 7r.50 As No. 506	1·00	1·00

122 Britten Norman Islander

1981. Tenth Anniv of Opening of Seychelles International Airport. Aircraft. Multicoloured.

514	40c. Type **122**	15	10
515	2r.25 Britten Norman "long nose" Trislander	40	45
516	3r.50 Vickers Super VC-10 airliner	60	70
517	5r. Boeing 747-100 airliner	75	1·00

123 Seychelles Flying Foxes in Flight

1981. Seychelles Flying Fox (Roussette). Multicoloured.

518	40c. Type **123**	10	10
519	2r.25 Flying fox eating	30	45
520	3r. Flying fox climbing across tree branch	45	70
521	5r. Flying fox hanging from tree branch	55	1·00
MS522	95×130 mm. Nos. 518-521	1·50	3·75

124 Chinese Little Bittern (male)

1982. Birds (4th series). Chinese Little Bittern. Multicoloured.

523	3r. Type **124**	2·00	1·50
524	3r. Chinese little bittern (female)	2·00	1·50
525	3r. Hen on nest	2·00	1·50
526	3r. Nest and eggs	2·00	1·50
527	3r. Hen with chicks	2·00	1·50

125 Silhouette Island and La Digue

1982. Modern Maps. Multicoloured.

528	40c. Type **125**	15	10
529	1r.50 Denis and Bird Islands	20	25
530	2r.75 Praslin	30	65
531	7r. Mahe	50	2·25
MS532	92×128 mm. Nos. 528-531	1·10	5·00

126 "Education"

1982. Fifth Anniv of Liberation. Multicoloured.

533	40c. Type **126**	10	10
534	1r.75 "Health"	25	25
535	2r.75 "Agriculture"	30	45
536	7r. "Construction"	80	1·40
MS537	128×120 mm. Nos. 533-536	2·25	6·50

127 Tourist Board Emblem

1982. Tourism. Multicoloured.

538	1r.75 Type **127**	20	35
539	1r.75 Northolme Hotel	20	35
540	1r.75 Reef Hotel	20	35
541	1r.75 Barbarous Beach Hotel	20	35
542	1r.75 Coral Strand Hotel	20	35
543	1r.75 Beau Vallon Bay Hotel	20	35
544	1r.75 Fisherman's Cove Hotel	20	35
545	1r.75 Mahe Beach Hotel	20	35

128 Tata Bus

1982. Land Transport. Multicoloured.

546	20c. Type **128**	10	10
547	1r.75 Mini-Moke	20	30
548	2r.75 Ox-cart	25	65
549	7r. Truck	80	2·75

129 Radio Seychelles Control Room

1983. World Communications Year. Multicoloured.

550	40c. Type **129**	10	10
551	2r.75 Satellite Earth station	30	60
552	3r.50 Radio Seychelles television control room	45	90
553	5r. Postal services sorting office	60	1·50

130 Agricultural Experimental Station

1983. Commonwealth Day. Multicoloured.

554	40c. Type **130**	10	10
555	2r.75 Food processing plant	25	40
556	3r.50 Unloading fish catch	40	60
557	7r. Seychelles flag	65	1·40

131 Denis Island Lighthouse

1983. Famous Landmarks. Multicoloured.

558	40c. Type **131**	10	10
559	2r.75 Victoria Hospital	30	45
560	3r.50 Supreme Court	35	65
561	7r. State House	55	1·40
MS562	110×98 mm. Nos. 558-561	2·75	7·00

132 "Royal Vauxhall" Balloon, 1836

1983. Bicentenary of Manned Flight. Multicoloured.

563	40c. Type **132**	15	10
564	1r.75 De Havilland D.H.50J	30	30
565	2r.75 Grumman Albatros flying boat	35	55
566	7r. Swearingen Merlin IIIA	55	1·75

133 Douglas DC-10-30

1983. First International Flight of Air Seychelles.

567	**133** 2r. multicoloured	1·75	2·00

134 Swamp Plant and Moorhen

1983. Centenary Visit to Seychelles by Marianne North (botanic artist). Multicoloured.

568	40c. Type **134**	35	10
569	1r.75 "Wormia flagellaria"	50	30
570	2r.75 Asiatic pancratium	60	75
571	7r. Pitcher plant	1·10	2·50
MS572	90×121 mm. Nos. 568-571	2·75	6·50

1983. Nos. 505-507, 509-510 and 513 surch.

573	50c. on 1r.50 "Victoria and Albert I"	15	30
574	50c. on 1r.50 Prince Charles and Lady Diana Spencer	40	1·50
575	2r.25 on 5r. "Clevland"	45	70
576	2r.25 on 5r. As No. 574	1·25	3·00
577	3r.75 on 10r. "Britannia"	75	1·10
578	3r.75 on 10r. As No. 574	1·60	3·50

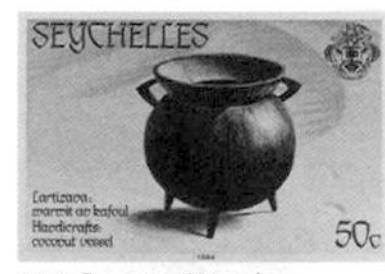

136 Coconut Vessel

1984. Traditional Handicrafts. Multicoloured.

579	50c. Type **136**	15	10
580	2r. Scarf and doll	30	70
581	3r. Coconut-fibre roses	35	1·00
582	10r. Carved fishing boat and doll	90	4·50

137 Victoria Port

1984. 250th Anniv of "Lloyd's List" (newspaper). Multicoloured.

583	50c. Type **137**	25	10
584	2r. "Boissevain" (cargo liner)	65	55
585	3r. "Sun Viking" (liner)	90	90
586	10r. Loss of R.F.A. "Ennerdale II" (tanker)	2·40	3·50

138 Old S.P.U.P. Office

1984. 20th Anniv of Seychelles People's United Party. Multicoloured.

587	50c. Type **138**	10	10
588	2r. Liberation statue (vert)	25	50
589	3r. New S.P.U.D. office	35	85
590	10r. President Rene (vert)	1·00	4·00

139 1949 U.P.U. 2r 25 Stamp

1984. Universal Postal Union Congress, Hamburg. Sheet 70×85 mm.

MS591	**139** 5r. green, pink and black	1·40	2·50

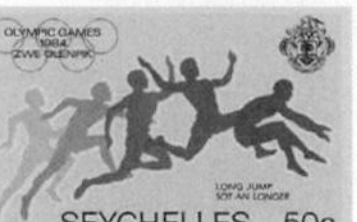

140 Long Jumping

1984. Olympic Games, Los Angeles. Multicoloured.

592	50c. Type **140**	10	10
593	2r. Boxing	40	45
594	3r. Swimming	60	75

595 10r. Weightlifting 1·75 2·50
MS596 100×100 mm. Nos. 592-595 3·00 5·50

141 Sub-aqua Diving

1984. Water Sports. Multicoloured.
597 50c. Type **141** 30 10
598 2r. Paraskiing 90 45
599 3r. Sailing 1·00 75
600 10r. Water-skiing 2·40 2·50

142 Humpback Whale

1984. Whale Conservation. Multicoloured.
601 50c. Type **142** 1·50 20
602 2r. Sperm whale 2·75 1·75
603 3r. Black right whale 3·00 2·50
604 10r. Blue whale 6·00 9·00

143 Two Bare-legged Scops Owls in Tree

1985. Birth Bicentenary of John J. Audubon (ornithologist). Bare-legged Scops Owl. Multicoloured.
605 50c. Type **143** 2·00 50
606 2r. Owl on branch 3·00 2·25
607 3r. Owl in flight 3·00 2·75
608 10r. Owl on ground 6·00 8·50

144 Giant Tortoises

1985. "Expo '85" World Fair, Japan. Multicoloured.
609 50c. Type **144** 70 30
610 2r. White terns ("Fairy Tern") 2·00 1·75
611 3r. Windsurfing 2·00 2·25
612 5r. Coco-de-mer 2·00 5·00
MS613 130×80 mm. Nos. 609-612 9·00 11·00
See also No. **MS**650.

145 The Queen Mother with Princess Anne and Prince Andrew, 1970

1985. Life and Times of Queen Elizabeth the Queen Mother. Multicoloured.
614 50c. The Queen Mother in 1930 25 10
615 2r. Type **145** 60 50
616 3r. On her 75th Birthday 80 75
617 5r. With Prince Henry at his christening (from photo by Lord Snowdon) 1·10 1·50
MS618 91×73 mm. 10 r. Arriving at Blenheim Palace by Westland Wessex helicopter 3·00 3·25

146 Boxing

1985. Second Indian Ocean Islands Games. Multicoloured.
619 50c. Type **146** 15 10
620 2r. Football 55 50
621 3r. Swimming 75 75
622 10r. Windsurfing 2·40 2·75

1985. Acquisition of First Air Seychelles "Airbus". As No. 413A, but additionally inscribed "AIR SEYCHELLES FIRST AIRBUS".
623 1r.25 White tern ("Fairy Tern") 3·00 2·75

147 Agriculture Students

1985. International Youth Year. Multicoloured.
624 50c. Type **147** 10 10
625 2r. Construction students building wall 55 50
626 3r. Carpentry students 70 1·00
627 10r. Science students 2·25 5·00

148 Ford "Model T" (1919)

1985. Vintage Cars. Multicoloured.
628 50c. Type **148** 50 20
629 2r. Austin "Seven" (1922) 1·25 1·00
630 3r. Morris "Oxford" (1924) 1·40 1·75
631 10r. Humber "Coupe" (1929) 2·50 6·50

149 Five Foot Transit Instrument

1986. Appearance of Halley's Comet. Multicoloured.
632 50c. Type **149** 40 10
633 2r. Eight foot quadrant 85 70
634 3r. Comet's orbit 85 95
635 10r. Edmond Halley 1·25 3·00

150 Ballerina

1986. Visit of Ballet du Louvre Company, "Giselle". Multicoloured.
636 2r. Type **150** 50 75
637 3r. Male dancer 60 1·50
MS638 80×90 mm. 10r. Pas de deux 1·40 2·40

1986. 60th Birthday of Queen Elizabeth II. As T **145a** of St. Helena. Multicoloured.
639 50c. Wedding photograph, 1947 10 10
640 1r.25 At State Opening of Parliament, 1982 25 35
641 2r. Queen accepting bouquet, Seychelles, 1972 30 50
642 3r. On board Royal Yacht "Britannia", Qatar, 1979 40 75
643 5r. At Crown Agents Head Office, London, 1983 60 1·25

151 Ferry to La Digue

1986. "Ameripex '86" Int Stamp Exhibition, Chicago. Inter-island Communications. Multicoloured.
644 50c. Type **151** 60 10
645 2r. Telephone kiosk (vert) 1·25 70
646 3r. Post Office counter, Victoria (vert) 1·40 1·10
647 7r. Air Seychelles Britten Norman "short nose" Trislander aircraft 4·00 3·50

152 Crests of Seychelles and Knights of Malta

1986. Seychelles Knights of Malta Day.
648 **152** 5r. multicoloured 1·10 1·60
MS649 101×81 mm. No. 648 2·50 4·00

1986. Seychelles Philatelic Exhibition, Tokyo. Miniature sheet, 130×80 mm, containing stamps as Nos. 609-612, but without "Expo '85" inscription and emblem.
MS650 As Nos. 609-612 1·75 3·00

1986. Royal Wedding. As T **146a** of St. Helena. Multicoloured.
651 2r. Prince Andrew and Miss Sarah Ferguson 35 50
652 10r. Prince Andrew boarding Wessex helicopter, 1983 1·40 3·00

1986. International Creole Day. No. 487 optd **LAZOURNEN ENTERNASYONAL KREOL**.
653 1r. Madagascar red fody 2·75 3·00

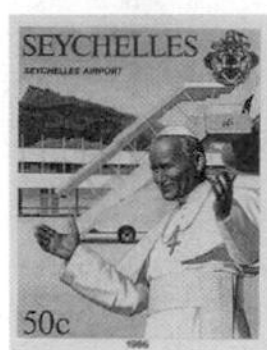

154 Pope John Paul at Seychelles Airport

1986. Visit of Pope John Paul II. Designs showing Pope and Seychelles scenes. Multicoloured.
654 50c. Type **154** 75 30
655 2r. Catholic Cathedral, Victoria 2·00 1·25
656 3r. Baie Lazare Parish Church 2·50 2·25
657 10r. Aerial view of People's Stadium 4·25 8·50
MS658 95×106 mm. Nos. 654-657 11·00 13·00

155 "Melanitis leda"

1987. Butterflies. Multicoloured.
659 1r. Type **155** 1·00 30
660 2r. "Phalanta philiberti" 1·60 1·25
661 3r. "Danaus chrysippus" 1·90 2·25
662 10r. "Euploea mitra" 5·00 8·50

156 Royal Oak Scallop

1987. Sea Shells. Multicoloured.
663 1r. Type **156** 1·25 30
664 2r. Golden thorny oyster 2·00 1·00
665 3r. Ventral or single harp and ornate pitar venus 2·25 1·60
666 10r. Silver conch 5·50 8·00

157 Statue of Liberation

1987. Tenth Anniv of Liberation. Multicoloured.
667 1r. Type **157** 20 25
668 2r. Seychelles hospital (horiz) 35 50
669 3r. Orphanage village (horiz) 45 75
670 10r. Proposed Sail-fish Monument 1·00 2·50

158 Seychelles Savings Bank, Praslin

1987. Centenary of Banking in Seychelles.
671 **158** 1r. deep green and green 20 25
672 - 2r. brown and orange 35 50
673 - 10r. deep blue and blue 1·00 2·50
DESIGNS: 2r. Development Bank; 10r. Central Bank.

1987. Royal Ruby Wedding. Nos. 639-643 optd **40TH WEDDING ANNIVERSARY**.
674 50c. Wedding photograph, 1947 15 15
675 1r.25 At State Opening of Parliament, 1982 25 65
676 2r. Queen accepting bouquet, Seychelles, 1972 30 65
677 3r. On board Royal Yacht "Britannia", Qatar, 1979 40 1·10
678 5r. At Crown Agents Head Office, London, 1983 60 2·00

159 Tuna-canning Factory

1987. Seychelles Fishing Industry. Multicoloured.
679 50c. Type **159** 15 15
680 2r. Trawler 45 55
681 3r. Weighing catch 70 1·00
682 10r. Unloading net 2·25 3·50

160 Water Sports

1988. Tourism. Multicoloured.
683 1r. Type **160** 65 25
684 2r. Speedboat and yachts 1·00 65
685 3r. Yacht at anchor 1·60 1·40
686 10r. Hotel at night 3·50 6·50

161 Young Turtles making for Sea

1988. The Green Turtle. Multicoloured.
687 2r. Type **161** 1·50 2·00
688 2r. Young turtles hatching 1·50 2·00
689 3r. Female turtle leaving sea 1·75 2·25
690 3r. Female laying eggs 1·75 2·25
Nos. 687-688 and 689-690 were printed together, se-tenant, each pair forming a composite design.

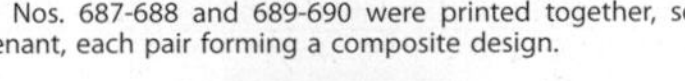

162 Shot Put

1988. Olympic Games, Seoul. Multicoloured.
691 1r. Type **162** 30 25
692 2r. Type **162** 55 90
693 2r. High jump 55 90
694 2r. Gold medal winner on podium 55 90
695 2r. Athletics 55 90
696 2r. Javelin 55 90
697 3r. As No. 694 60 90
698 4r. As No. 695 80 1·10
699 5r. As No. 696 1·00 1·25
MS700 121×52 mm. 10r. Tennis 4·00 6·50

1988. 300th Anniv of Lloyd's of London. As T **152a** of St. Helena. Multicoloured.

701	1r. Leadenhall Street, 1928	60	25
702	2r. "Cinq Juin" (travelling post office) (horiz)	1·60	75
703	3r. "Queen Elizabeth 2" (liner) (horiz)	3·00	1·50
704	10r. Loss of "Hindenburg" (airship), 1937	6·00	5·00

163 Police Motorcyclists

1988. First Anniv of Defence Forces Day. Multicoloured.

705	1r. Type **163**	2·75	50
706	2r. Hindustan Aircraft Chetak helicopter	4·00	2·25
707	3r. "Andromanche" (patrol boat)	4·00	2·75
708	10r. BRDM armoured car	7·50	10·00

164 Father Christmas with Basket of Presents

1988. Christmas. Multicoloured.

709	50c. Type **164**	15	10
710	2r. Bird and gourd filled with presents	70	70
711	3r. Father Christmas basket weaving	90	90
712	10r. Christmas bauble and palm tree	2·50	5·00

165 "Dendrobium sp."

1988. Orchids (1st series). Multicoloured.

713	1r. Type **165**	1·25	25
714	2r. Arachnis" hybrid (horiz)	1·75	70
715	3r. "Vanda caerulea"	2·00	1·25
716	10r. "Dendrobium phalaenopsis" (horiz)	4·00	6·50

See also Nos. 767-770 and 795-798.

166 India 1976 25p. Nehru Stamp

1989. Birth Centenary of Jawaharlal Nehru (Indian statesman). Each showing flags of Seychelles and India. Multicoloured.

724	2r. Type **166**	1·25	50
725	10r. Jawaharlal Nehru	3·25	5·50

167 Pres. Rene addressing Rally at Old Party Office

1989. 25th Anniv of Seychelles People's United Party. Multicoloured.

742	1r. Type **167**	25	25
743	2r. Women with Party flags and Maison du Peuple	60	50
744	3r. President Rene making speech and Torch of Freedom	70	80
745	10r. President Rene, Party flag and Torch of Freedom	2·25	5·00

1989. 20th Anniv of First Manned Landing on Moon. As T **50a** of St. Kitts. Multicoloured.

746	1r. Lift off of "Saturn 5" rocket	45	25
747	2r. Crew of "Apollo 15" (30×30 mm)	75	75
748	3r. "Apollo 15" emblem (30×30 mm)	90	1·10
749	5r. James Irwin saluting U.S. flag on Moon	1·50	2·25
MS750	100×83 mm. 10r. Aldrin alighting from "Apollo 11" on Moon	5·00	6·50

168 British Red Cross Ambulance, Franco-Prussian War, 1870

1989. 125th Anniv of International Red Cross.

751	**168**	1r. black and red	3·00	35
752	-	2r. black, green and red	3·25	1·50
753	-	3r. black and red	3·75	2·50
754	-	10r. black and red	10·00	12·00

DESIGNS: 2r. "Liberty" (hospital ship), 1914–18; 3r. Sunbeam "Standard" army ambulance, 1914–18; 10r. "White Train" (hospital train), South Africa, 1899–1902.

169 Black Parrot and Map of Praslin

1989. Island Birds. Multicoloured.

755	50c. Type **169**	2·50	55
756	2r. Sooty tern and Ile aux vaches	3·50	1·75
757	3r. Seychelles magpie robin ("Magpie Robin") and Fregate	4·25	3·00
758	5r. Roseate tern and Aride	4·75	7·50
MS759	83×109 mm. Nos. 755-758	14·00	15·00

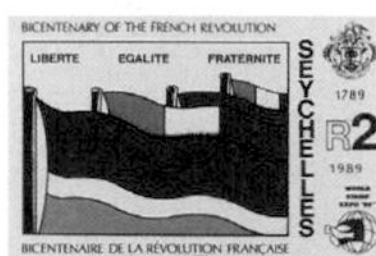

170 Flags of Seychelles and France

1989. Bicentenary of French Revolution and "World Stamp Expo '89". International Stamp Exhibition, Washington.

760	**170**	2r. multicoloured	3·50	1·50
761	-	5r. black, blue and red	4·00	6·00
MS762		78×100 mm. 10r. mult	5·00	7·00

DESIGN: 5r. Storming the Bastille, Paris, 1789; 10r. Reading Revolutionary proclamation, Seychelles, 1791.

171 Beau Vallon School

1989. 25th Anniv of African Development Bank. Multicoloured.

763	1r. Type **171**	45	25
764	2r. Seychelles Fishing Authority Headquarters	80	1·00
765	3r. "Variola" (fishing boat) (vert)	2·75	2·50
766	10r. "Deneb" (fishing boat) (vert)	6·50	10·00

172 "Disperis tripetaloides"

1990. Orchids (2nd series). Multicoloured.

767	1r. Type **172**	2·50	50
768	2r. "Vanilla phalaenopsis"	3·00	1·50
769	3r. "Angraecum eburneum" subsp. "superbum"	3·50	2·50
770	10r. "Polystachya concreta"	7·00	11·00

173 Seychelles 1903 2c. and Great Britain 1880 1½d. Stamps

1990. "Stamp World London '90" International Stamp Exhibition. Each showing stamps. Multicoloured.

771	1r. Type **173**	75	25
772	2r. Seychelles 1917 25c. and G.B. 1873 1s.	1·25	1·25
773	3r. Seychelles 1917 2c. and G.B. 1874 6d.	1·75	2·25
774	5r. Seychelles 1890 2c. and G.B. 1841 1d. red	2·50	4·50
MS775	88×60 mm. 10r. Seychelles 1961 Post Office Centenary 2r.25 and G.B. 1840 Penny Black	10·00	11·00

174 Fumiyo Sako

1990. "EXPO 90" International Garden and Greenery Exhibition, Osaka. Multicoloured.

776	2r. Type **174**	1·75	1·00
777	3r. Male and female coco-de-mer palms	2·00	1·50
778	5r. Pitcher plant and Aldabra lily	3·00	3·50
779	7r. Arms of Seychelles and gardenia	3·75	6·00
MS780	130×85 mm. Nos. 776-779	8·50	11·00

175 Air Seychelles Boeing 767-200ER over Island

1990. Air Seychelles "Boeing 767-200ER" World Record-breaking Flight (1989).

781	**175**	3r. multicoloured	4·25	4·00

1990. 90th Birthday of Queen Elizabeth the Queen Mother. As T **161a** of St. Helena.

782	2r. multicoloured	1·25	75
783	10r. black and violet	3·25	4·50

DESIGNS—(21×36 mm): 2r. Queen Elizabeth in Coronation robes, 1937. (29×37 mm): 10r. Queen Elizabeth visiting Lord Roberts Workshops, 1947.

176 Adult Class

1990. International Literacy Year. Multicoloured.

784	1r. Type **176**	75	25
785	2r. Reading a letter	1·50	1·25
786	3r. Following written instructions	2·00	2·00
787	10r. Typewriter, calculator and crossword	5·00	8·50

177 Sega Dancers

1990. Kreol Festival. Sega Dancing. Multicoloured.

788	2r. Type **177**	2·50	2·75
789	2r. Dancing couple (girl in yellow dress)	2·50	2·75
790	2r. Female Sega dancer	2·50	2·75
791	2r. Dancing couple (girl in floral pattern skirt)	2·50	2·75
792	2r. Dancing couple (girl in red patterned skirt)	2·50	2·75

178 Beach

1990. First Indian Ocean Regional Seminar on Petroleum Exploration. Multicoloured.

793	3r. Type **178**	1·75	1·50
794	10r. Geological map	5·75	7·50

1991. Orchids (3rd series). As T **172**. Multicoloured.

795	1r. "Bullbophyllum intertextum"	1·75	45
796	2r. "Agrostophyllum occidentale"	2·25	1·75
797	3r. "Vanilla planifolia"	2·50	2·50
798	10r. "Malaxis seychellarum"	6·00	7·50

1991. 65th Birthday of Queen Elizabeth II and 70th Birthday of Prince Philip. As T **165a** of St. Helena. Multicoloured.

799	4r. Queen in evening dress	1·60	2·25
800	4r. Prince Philip in academic robes	1·60	2·25

179 "Precis rhadama"

1991. "Phila Nippon '91" International Stamp Exhibition, Tokyo. Butterflies. Multicoloured.

801	1r.50 Type **179**	2·00	85
802	3r. "Lampides boeticus"	2·50	2·25
803	3r.50 "Zizeeria knysna"	2·75	2·50
804	10r. "Phalanta phalantha"	7·25	7·50
MS805	78×81 mm. 10r. "Eagris sabadius"	7·00	7·50

180 "The Holy Virgin, Joseph, The Holy Child and St. John" (S. Vouillemont after Raphael)

1991. Christmas. Woodcuts.

806	**180**	50c. black, brown and red	50	15
807	-	1r. black, brown and green	90	25
808	-	2r. black, brown and blue	1·75	1·10
809	-	7r. black, brown and blue	4·50	7·00

DESIGNS: 1r. "Holy Virgin, the Child and Angel" (A. Blooting after Van Dyck); 2r. "The Holy Family, St. John and St. Anna" (L. Vorsterman after Rubens); 7r. "The Holy Family, Angel and St. Cathrin" (C. Bloemaert).

1992. 40th Anniv of Queen Elizabeth II's Accession. As T **168a** of St. Helena. Multicoloured.

810	1r. Seychelles coastline	65	25
811	1r.50 Clock Tower, Victoria	80	40
812	3r. Victoria harbour	1·50	1·50
813	3r.50 Three portraits of Queen Elizabeth	1·60	1·75
814	5r. Queen Elizabeth II	1·75	2·75

181 Seychelles Brush Warbler ("Bush Warbler")

1993. Flora and Fauna. Multicoloured.

815	10c. Type **181**	1·50	1·25
816	25c. Bronze gecko (vert)	1·00	15
817	50c. Seychelles tree frog	1·00	20
818	1r. Seychelles splendid palm (vert)	70	25
819	1r.50 Seychelles skink (vert)	1·25	80
820	2r. Giant tenebrionid beetle	1·00	45
821	3r. Seychelles sunbird	2·00	1·25
822	3r.50 Seychelles killifish	1·25	1·00
823	4r. Seychelles magpie robin ("Magpie Robin")	2·75	1·75
824	5r. Seychelles vanilla (plant) (vert)	1·75	1·75
825	10r. Tiger chameleon	3·50	3·00
826	15r. Coco-de-mer (vert)	4·50	5·50

827 25r. Seychelles paradise flycatcher ("Paradise Flycatcher") (vert) 12·00 12·00
828 50r. Giant tortoise 17·00 23·00

182 Archbishop George Carey and Anglican Cathedral, Victoria

1993. First Visit of an Archbishop of Canterbury to Seychelles. Multicoloured.
834 3r. Type **182** 2·50 1·50
835 10r. Archbishop Carey with Air France Boeing 747-400 and Air Seychelles Boeing 737-200 airliners 6·00 8·50

183 Athletics

1993. Fourth Indian Ocean Island Games. Multicoloured.
836 1r.50 Type **183** 65 55
837 3r. Football 1·25 1·00
838 3r.50 Cycling 2·00 1·75
839 10r. Sailing 3·25 6·00

184 "Scotia" (cable ship) off Victoria, 1893

1993. Century of Telecommunications. Multicoloured.
840 1r. Type **184** 1·75 60
841 3r. Eastern Telegraph Co office, Victoria, 1904 2·50 1·75
842 4r. HF Transmitting Station, 1971 2·75 3·00
843 10r. New Telecoms House, Victoria, 1993 5·00 7·50

1994. "Hong Kong '94" Int Stamp Exhibition. Nos. 62, 64 and 66-67 of Zil Elwannyen Sesel surch **HONG KONG '94**, emblem and value.
844 1r. on 2r.10 on 2r.10 Souimanga sunbird 50 30
845 1r.50 on 2r.75 on 2r.75 Sacred ibis 75 60
846 3r.50 on 7r. on 7r. Seychelles kestrel (vert) 1·60 2·25
847 10r. on 15r. on 15r. Comoro blue pigeon (vert) 3·00 5·00

186 "Eurema floricola"

1994. Butterflies. Multicoloured.
848 1r.50 Type **186** 1·75 75
849 3r. "Coeliades forestan" 2·50 2·00
850 3r.50 "Borbo borbonica" 2·75 2·75
851 10r. "Zizula hylax" 5·50 7·50

187 Lady Elizabeth Bowes-Lyon

1995. 95th Birthday of Queen Elizabeth the Queen Mother. Multicoloured.
852 1r.50 Type **187** 75 40
853 3r. Duchess of York on wedding day, 1923 1·40 1·00
854 3r.50 Queen Elizabeth 1·60 1·40
855 10r. Queen Elizabeth the Queen Mother 3·50 6·50

188 Female Seychelles Paradise Flycatcher feeding Chick

1996. Endangered Species. Seychelles Paradise Flycatcher. Multicoloured.
856 1r. Type **188** 70 95
857 1r. Male bird in flight 70 95
858 1r. Female bird on branch 70 95
859 1r. Male bird on branch 70 95
MS860 60×53 mm. 10r. Pair on branch 5·00 6·50

189 Swimming

1996. Centenary of Modern Olympic Games. Multicoloured.
861 50c. Type **189** 40 20
862 1r.50 Running 60 45
863 3r. Sailing 1·25 1·50
864 5r. Boxing 1·90 3·00

190 Archbishop Makarios at Table

1996. 40th Anniv of Exile of Archbishop Makarios of Cyprus to Seychelles. Multicoloured.
865 3r. Type **190** 1·50 1·00
866 10r. Archbishop Makarios in priest's robes 3·25 6·00

191 Comoro Blue Pigeon

1996. Birds. Multicoloured.
867 3r. Type **191** 1·50 1·75
868 3r. Seychelles blue pigeon 1·50 1·75
869 3r. Souimanga sunbird 1·50 1·75
870 3r. Seychelles sunbird 1·50 1·75
871 3r. Mascarene fody ("Aldabra Red-headed Fody") 1·50 1·75
872 3r. Seychelles fody 1·50 1·75
873 3r. Madagascar white eye 1·50 1·75
874 3r. Seychelles brown white-eye ("Seychelles White eye") 1·50 1·75

Nos. 867/8, 869/70, 871/2 and 873/4 respectively were printed together, *se-tenant*, with the background of each pair forming a composite design showing a regional map.

1997. "HONG KONG '97" International Stamp Exhibition. No. 226 of Zil Elwannyen Sesel surch **R1.50** and emblem.
875 1r.50 on 2r. on 2r. Little egret ("Dimorphic Little Egret") 2·50 2·50

1997. Golden Wedding of Queen Elizabeth and Prince Philip. As T **192a** of St. Helena. Multicoloured.
876 1r. Queen Elizabeth wearing red and white suit 65 90
877 1r. Prince Philip driving carriage 65 90
878 1r.50 Prince Philip 75 1·10
879 1r.50 Queen Elizabeth with horse 75 1·10
880 3r. Prince Charles and Princess Anne on horseback 1·40 1·75
881 3r. Prince Philip and Queen Elizabeth 1·40 1·75
MS882 110×70 mm. 10r. Queen Elizabeth and Prince Philip in landau (horiz) 4·00 4·50

Nos. 876/7, 878/9 and 880/1 respectively were printed together, se-tenant, with the backgrounds forming composite designs.

1998. Diana, Princess of Wales Commemoration. Sheet, 145×70 mm, containing vert designs as T **62a** of Tokelau. Multicoloured.
MS883 3r. Wearing red jacket, 1992; 3r. Wearing floral dress, 1981; 3r. Wearing blue and black jacket, 1993; 3r. Wearing white dress, Nepal 1993 (sold at 12r.+2r. charity premium) 2·50 3·75

193 Powderblue Surgeonfish

1998. International Year of the Ocean. Multicoloured.
884 3r. Type **193** 90 1·25
885 3r. Shoal of soldierfish 90 1·25
886 3r. Lionfish 90 1·25
887 3r. School of fish 90 1·25
888 3r. Coral 90 1·25
889 3r. Turtle 90 1·25

194 "Vierge du Cap" (galleon), 1721

1999. 18th-century Ships. Multicoloured.
890 1r.50 Type **194** 65 35
891 3r. "L'Elizabeth" (corvette), 1741 1·40 1·00
892 3r.50 "Curieuse" (sloop), 1768 1·40 1·75
893 10r. "La Fleche" (frigate), 1801 3·00 5·00
MS894 105×70 mm. 20r. "Le Cheval Marin" (French merchantman), 1774 (vert) 7·00 9·00

No. **MS**894 also includes the "Australia '99" World Stamp Exhibition, Melbourne, emblem on the sheet margin.

195 Royal Couple on Steps of Chapel Royal, Windsor

1999. Royal Wedding. Multicoloured.
895 3r. Type **195** 1·25 75
896 15r. In landau 4·75 7·00

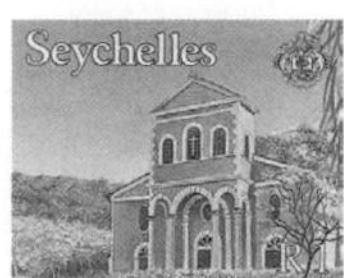

196 Cathedral of the Immaculate Conception

1999. New Millennium. Multicoloured.
897 1r. Type **196** 40 30
898 1r.50 White tern at sunrise 1·50 1·00
899 2r.50 Dolphin and island 1·75 1·50
900 10r. Comet over beach 4·00 6·00

197 Lady Elizabeth Bowes-Lyon

2000. Queen Elizabeth the Queen Mother's 100th Birthday.
901 **197** 3r. multicoloured 1·40 70
902 - 5r. black and brown 1·90 1·75
903 - 7r. black and lilac 2·50 3·00
904 - 10r. multicoloured 3·00 3·75

DESIGNS: 5r. Queen Elizabeth in East End of London during Second World War; 7r. Visiting Seychelles with King George VI and Princess Elizabeth; 10r. Wearing blue hat and outfit.

198 Arrival of Jacobin Deportees (Bicentenary)

2001. Milestones in Seychelles History. Multicoloured.
905 1r. Type **198** 65 30
906 1r.50 Victoria (160th anniv as capital) 75 40
907 3r. Father Leon des Avanchers (150th anniv of arrival) 1·40 1·00
908 3r.50 Victoria Fountain (centenary) (vert) 1·40 1·25
909 5r. Botanical Gardens (centenary) 2·00 2·25
910 10r. Independence monument (25th anniv) (vert) 2·75 4·00

199 Ruddy Shelduck

2001. Bird Life World Bird Festival. Migrant Ducks and Bare-legged Scops Owl (No. **MS**915). Multicoloured.
911 3r. Type **199** 2·25 2·25
912 3r. White-faced whistling duck 2·25 2·25
913 3r. Northern Shoveler 2·25 2·25
914 3r. Garganey 2·25 2·25
MS915 171×78 mm. 3r. Bare-legged scops owl ("Seychelles Scops Owl") in flight (35×30 mm); 3r. Chick in tree hole (35×30 mm); 3r. Adult tufts down (30×35 mm); 3r. Adult tufts erect (30×35 mm); 3r. Immature (35×30 mm) 9·50 10·00

2002. Queen Elizabeth the Queen Mother Commemoration. Sheet, 145×70 mm, containing vert designs as T **215** of St. Helena.
MS916 5r. brown, gold and black; 10r. multicoloured 4·75 6·00

DESIGNS: 5r. Lady Elizabeth Bowes-Lyon, 1923; 10r. Queen Mother on her birthday, 1986.

200 Seychelles Frog

2003. Endangered Species. Frogs. Multicoloured.
917 1r. Type **200** 75 85
918 1r. Palm frog 75 85
919 1r. Thomasset's frog 75 85
920 1r. Gardiner's frog 75 85
MS921 65×65 mm. 20r. Seychelles tree frog 7·50 9·50

201 Seychelles Blenny

2003. Marine Life. Multicoloured.
922 10c. Type **201** 40 60
923 25c. African pygmy angelfish 1·00 75
924 50c. Seychelles anemonefish 60 20
925 1r. Indian butterflyfish 1·00 25
926 1r.50 Goldbar wrasse 1·25 35
927 2r. Picasso triggerfish 2·00 70
928 3r. Seychelles squirrelfish 1·50 1·00
929 3r.50 Palette surgeonfish 2·50 1·00
930 4r. Longfin batfish 2·50 1·50
931 5r. Green-beaked parrotfish ("Greenthroat Parrotfish") 2·00 1·75
932 10r. Masked moray 4·50 3·50
933 15r. Lyretail grouper 6·50 7·00
934 25r. Emperor snapper 9·50 11·00
935 50r. Whale shark 17·00 20·00

202 Emblem

2004. 20th Anniv of the Indian Ocean Commission.
936 **202** 15r. multicoloured 4·75 6·00

2004. Flora and Fauna. Nos. 819, 821 and 824-828 surch.
937 1r. on 1r.50 Seychelles skink (vert) 1·00 30

938	2r. on 3r. Seychelles sunbird	1·50	65
939	3r.50 on 5r. Seychelles vanilla (vert)	2·25	2·25
940	3r.50 on 10r. Tiger chameleon	2·25	2·25
941	3r.50 on 15r. Coco-de-mer (vert)	2·25	2·25
942	4r. on 25r. Paradise flycatcher (vert)	2·50	2·50
943	4r. on 50r. Giant tortoise	2·50	2·50

2005. Pope John Paul II Commemoration. As T **231** of St. Helena.

944	5r. multicoloured	1·75	2·00

204 Archbishop Makarios in Exile, 1956

2006. 50th Anniv of Exile of Archbishop Makarios of Cyprus to the Seychelles. Multicoloured.

945	3r.50 Type **204**	1·75	1·50
946	15r. Archbishop Makarios	4·75	6·00

205 Possession Stone (250th anniv of naming of Seychelles)

2006. 30th Anniv of Independence. Multicoloured.

947	50c. Type **205**	35	15
948	1r. National flag and national flags of 1977–96 and 1976	80	30
949	1r.50 Vallee de Mai, Praslin (World Heritage Site)	90	45
950	2r. School children	1·00	65
951	3r.50 Jacob Marie (musician) with bonm (musical arc)	1·75	1·50
952	4r. *Seychelles Progress* (tanker)	2·00	1·75
953	15r. "Selebre Sesel" emblem	4·25	6·50

206 *Solanum aldabrensis*

2007. 25th Anniv of Aldabra as a World Heritage Site. Multicoloured.

954	2r. Type **206**	1·25	1·10
955	3r.50 Dugong	1·75	1·75
956	10r. Giant tortoise	4·00	5·00

207 Kayaking

2008. Olympic Games, Beijing. Multicoloured.

957	1r. Type **207**	60	30
958	1r.50 Swimming	85	75
959	2r. Sailing	95	95
960	3r.50 Javelin throwing	1·50	2·00

208 Pair of Aldabra Drongos

2008. Endangered Species. Aldabra Drongo (*Dicrurus aldabranus*) and Aldabra Red-headed Fody (*Foudiaeminentissima aldabrana*). Multicoloured.

961	1r. Type **208**	75	80
962	1r. Pair of Aldabra red-headed fodies (in tree with foliage, looking to left)	75	80
963	1r. Pair of Aldabra red-headed fodies (on bare branch, looking to right)	75	80
964	1r. Pair of Aldabra drongos (left hand bird facing forwards)	75	80
MS965	84×60 mm. 20r. Aldabra red-headed fody and Aldabra drongo	9·00	9·50

209 Ferdinand Magellan

2009. Seafaring and Exploration. Multicoloured.

966	1r.50 Type **209**	30	30
967	3r.50 Sir Martin Frobisher	1·75	1·60
968	6r.50 Sir Francis Drake	2·75	2·75
969	8r. Henry Hudson	3·00	3·25
970	15r. Abel Tasman	5·75	6·50
971	27r. Sir John Franklin	9·25	11·00
MS972	110×70 mm. 7r. *Ascension* (East Indiaman), 1609 (400th anniv of first European landing on the Seychelles)	3·75	3·75

Nos. 966-971 were each printed in sheetlets of six stamps with enlarged illustrated margins.

2009. International Year of Astronomy. 40th Anniv of First Moon Landing. As T **257** of St. Helena. Multicoloured.

973	3r.50 X1 being loaded under Superfortress, 1951	1·75	1·60
974	7r. Lunar Landing Research Vehicle, 1964	3·25	3·25
975	8r. Apollo 11 Launch Site, 1969	3·75	4·00
976	13r. Space Transportation System 86, 1997	5·25	5·75
977	20r. Soyuz TMA-13 rolls out to Launch Pad, 2008	6·75	7·50
MS978	100×80 mm. 24r. *An American Success Story* (astronaut John Young) (Alan Bean) (39×59 mm). Wmk upright	11·00	11·00

2010. As Nos. 929/35 and new values (6r.50, 7r., 8r., 100r.). Multicoloured.

989	6r.50 Queen Coris	1·75	1·75
990	7r. White-lined goatfish	2·10	2·10
991	8r. Three-spot angelfish	2·20	2·50
996	100r. Coral grouper	25·00	25·00

Nos. 979/85 are left for possible additions to this definitive series.

210 Duke and Duchess of Cambridge waving from State Landau

2011. Royal Wedding. Multicoloured.

997	3r.50 Type **210**	1·75	1·60
998	4r. Duke and Duchess of Cambridge kissing on Buckingham Palace balcony (vert)	2·00	1·75
999	7r. Duke and Duchess of Cambridge waving from Buckingham Palace balcony (vert)	3·25	3·25
1000	25r. Duke and Duchess of Cambridge at Westminster Abbey after wedding ceremony (vert)	9·50	11·00

211 State House, Victoria

2011. Centenary of the State House of Seychelles, Victoria

1001	**211**	3r.50 multicoloured	1·75	1·60

212 New Post Office, Victoria, 2011

2011. 150th Anniv of the Seychelles Post Office. Multicoloured.

1002	3r.50 Type **212**	1·75	1·75
1003	7r. The Old Post Office, Victoria, 1900s	3·25	3·25

POSTAGE DUE STAMPS

D1

1951. Value in red.

D1	**D1**	2c. red and carmine	80	1·50
D2	**D1**	3c. red and green	2·75	1·50
D3	**D1**	6c. red and bistre	2·25	1·25
D4	**D1**	9c. red and orange	2·50	1·25
D5	**D1**	15c. red and violet	2·25	12·00
D6	**D1**	18c. red and blue	2·25	12·00
D7	**D1**	20c. red and brown	2·25	12·00
D8	**D1**	30c. red and claret	2·25	7·50

1980. As Type **D1** but 18×22 mm.

D11	5c. red and mauve	15	1·00
D12	10c. red and green	15	1·00
D13	15c. red and bistre	20	1·00
D14	20c. red and brown	20	1·00
D15	25c. red and violet	20	1·00
D16	75c. red and maroon	30	1·00
D17	80c. red and blue	30	1·00
D18	1r. red and purple	30	1·00

Pt. 1

SHAHPURA

One of the Indian Feudatory States. Now uses Indian stamps.

12 pies = 1 anna; 16 annas = 1 rupee.

RAJ
SHAHPURA
Postage 1 pice
1

1914. Perf (No. 1) or imperf (No. 2).

1	**1**	1p. red on grey	—	£800
2	**1**	1p. red on brown	—	£1100

1920. As T **1** but "Postage" omitted. Imperf.

3	1p. red on brown	—	£1300
4	1a. black on pink	—	£1500

Pt. 17

SHANGHAI

A seaport on the E. coast of China, which for a time had a separate postal system.

1865. 10 cash = 1 candareen. 100 candareens = 1 tael.
1890. 100 cents = 1 dollar (Chinese).

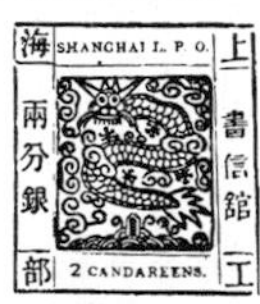

1 Dragon

1865. Value in candareens. Imperf. (a) "CANDAREEN" in singular.

28	1ca. blue	£250	£5000
12	2ca. black	£700	£8500
29	3ca. brown	£300	£6000
13	4ca. yellow	£850	£9000
14	8ca. green	£750	
15	16ca. red	£800	

(b) "CANDAREENS" in plural.

30	2ca. black	£250	
31	3ca. brown	£275	£4500
3	4ca. yellow	£1000	£6500
18	6ca. brown	£450	
20	6ca. red	£650	
4	8ca. green	£750	£7000
21	12ca. brown	£500	
22	16ca. red	£500	

2

1866. Value in cents. Frames differ. Perf.

32	**2**	2c. red	25·00	35·00
33	**2**	4c. lilac	60·00	75·00
34	**2**	8c. blue	75·00	£100
35	**2**	16c. green	£120	£160

6

1867. Value in candareens. Frames differ.

37	**6**	1ca. brown	11·00	16·00
59	**6**	1ca. yellow on yellow	50·00	45·00
62	**6**	1ca. yellow	25·00	32·00
73	**6**	1ca. red	£3250	£4250
38	**6**	3ca. yellow	55·00	65·00
60	**6**	3ca. pink on pink	50·00	45·00
63	**6**	3ca. red	£130	£120
39	**6**	6ca. grey	65·00	80·00
64	**6**	6ca. green	£225	£250
65	**6**	9ca. grey	£375	£425
40	**6**	12ca. brown	£110	£130

1873. Surch with value in English and Chinese.

41	**2**	1ca. on 2c. red	90·00	90·00
44	**2**	1ca. on 4c. lilac	25·00	32·00
46	**2**	1ca. on 8c. blue	50·00	60·00
48	**2**	1ca. on 16c. green	£6000	£5500
50	**2**	3ca. on 2c. red	£375	£325
52	**2**	3ca. on 16c. green	£6000	£4750

1873. Surch with value in English and Chinese.

53	**6**	1ca. on 3ca. yellow	£45000	£28000
67	**6**	1ca. on 3ca. red	£225	£200
68	**6**	1ca. on 3ca. pink on pink	£700	£500
54	**6**	1ca. on 6ca. grey	£950	£750
69	**6**	1ca. on 6ca. green	£400	£350
70	**6**	1ca. on 9ca. grey	£700	£650
56	**6**	1ca. on 12ca. brown	£1700	£1700
58	**6**	3ca. on 12ca. brown	£8000	£8000

1877. Value in cash.

74	20 cash blue	18·00	17·00
75	20 cash lilac	14·00	11·00
93	20 cash green	9·00	6·00
114	20 cash grey	5·50	3·25
81	40 cash pink	25·00	22·00
94	40 cash brown	16·00	14·00
107	40 cash black	12·00	9·50
82	60 cash green	30·00	27·00
95	60 cash violet	22·00	20·00
108	60 cash red	22·00	18·00
83	80 cash blue	32·00	30·00
96	80 cash brown	27·00	26·00
109	80 cash green	14·00	12·00
84	100 cash brown	32·00	30·00
97	100 cash yellow	27·00	26·00
110	100 cash blue	20·00	20·00

1879. Surch in English and Chinese.

89	20 cash on 40 cash pink	40·00	35·00
103	20 cash on 40 cash brown	38·00	32·00
105	20 cash on 80 cash brown	20·00	18·00
111	20 cash on 80 cash green	18·00	18·00
112	20 cash on 100 cash blue	18·00	18·00
100	40 cash on 80 cash brown	20·00	18·00
101	40 cash on 100 cash yellow	25·00	25·00
90	60 cash on 80 cash blue	55·00	55·00
88	60 cash on 100 cash brown	£100	95·00
102	60 cash on 100 cash yellow	28·00	25·00

1886. Surch **20 CASH** in English and Chinese in double-lined frame.

104	20 cash on 40 cash brown	40·00	38·00

1889. Surch **100 CASH** over 20 CASH in English and Chinese in double-lined frame.

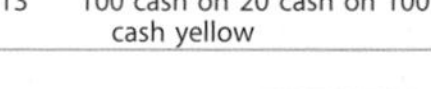

113	100 cash on 20 cash on 100 cash yellow	£300	£325

16

1890. Value in cents.

119	**16**	2c. brown	4·00	4·25
142	**16**	2c. green	2·75	2·50
120	**16**	5c. pink	15·00	9·00
143	**16**	5c. red	8·00	7·25
122	**16**	10c. black	28·00	26·00
144	**16**	10c. orange	26·00	25·00
123	**16**	15c. blue	32·00	24·00
145	**16**	15c. mauve	15·00	13·00
124	**16**	20c. mauve	25·00	22·00
146	**16**	20c. brown	18·00	15·00

1892. Surch **2 Cts** and in Chinese.

141	2c. on 5c. pink	£250	80·00

1893. Surch in words in English and Chinese.

147	½c. on 15c. mauve	20·00	13·00
148	1c. on 20c. brown	20·00	13·00

1893. Surch **½Ct.** or **1 Ct.**

149	½c. on half of 5c. pink	12·00	10·00
152	½c. on half of 5c. red	12·00	10·00
155	1c. on half of 2c. brown	3·25	3·00
156	1c. on half of 2c. green	15·00	12·00

25

1893. Inscriptions in outer frame in black.

165	**25**	½c. orange	50	50
166	**25**	1c. brown	50	50
187	**25**	2c. red	25	1·60
188	**25**	4c. orange on yellow	6·50	5·50
161	**25**	5c. blue	1·00	55
189	**25**	6c. red on pink	7·50	8·50
167	**25**	10c. green	2·50	3·00
163	**25**	15c. yellow	1·00	75
168	**25**	20c. mauve	2·50	4·25

26

1893. Jubilee of First Settlement.

176	**26**	2c. red and black	1·25	1·25

1893. Optd **1843 Jubilee 1893**. Inscriptions in outer frame in black.

177	**25**	½c. orange	40	40
178	**25**	1c. brown	55	55
179	**25**	2c. red	75	75
180	**25**	5c. blue	3·25	4·25
181	**25**	10c. green	13·00	12·00
182	**25**	15c. yellow	7·50	6·50
183	**25**	20c. mauve	10·00	10·00

1896. Surch in English and Chinese.

184	4c. on 15c. yellow	10·00	8·00
185	6c. on 20c. mauve	10·00	8·00

POSTAGE DUE STAMPS

1892. T **16** optd **Postage Due**.

D134	2c. brown	3·00	2·75
D135	5c. pink	18·00	10·00
D130	10c. black	50·00	50·00
D138	10c. orange	26·00	18·00
D131	15c. blue	38·00	32·00
D139	15c. mauve	38·00	38·00
D132	20c. mauve	30·00	25·00
D140	20c. brown	38·00	35·00

D26

1893. Inscriptions in outer frame in black.

D169	**D26**	½c. orange	50	50
D170	**D26**	1c. brown	60	50
D171	**D26**	2c. red	60	50
D172	**D26**	5c. blue	90	90
D173	**D26**	10c. green	5·50	1·80
D174	**D26**	15c. yellow	4·25	3·75
D175	**D26**	20c. mauve	1·60	1·60

Pt. 19

SHARJAH

One of the Trucial States on the Persian Gulf. Embodies the principalities of Dibbah, Khor Fakkan and Khor al-Kalba.

On 2 December 1971, Sharjah, together with six other Gulf Shaikdoms, formed the United Arab Emirates.

1963. 100 naye paise = 1 rupee.
1966. 100 dirhams = 1 riyal.

IMPERFORATE STAMPS. Some sets also exist imperf in limited quantities.

1 Shaikh Saqr bin Sultan al Qasimi, Flag and Map

1963. Multicoloured.

1	**1**	1n.p. (postage) multicoloured	10	10
2	**1**	2n.p. multicoloured	10	10
3	**1**	3n.p. multicoloured	10	10
4	**1**	4n.p. multicoloured	10	10
5	**1**	5n.p. multicoloured	10	10
6	**1**	6n.p. multicoloured	10	10
7	**1**	8n.p. multicoloured	10	10
8	**1**	10n.p. multicoloured	25	25
9	**1**	16n.p. multicoloured	50	25
10	**1**	20n.p. multicoloured	60	25
11	**1**	30n.p. multicoloured	85	35
12	**1**	40n.p. multicoloured	95	60
13	**1**	50n.p. multicoloured	1·30	70
14	**1**	75n.p. multicoloured	2·40	1·60
15	**1**	100n.p. multicoloured	3·25	2·40
16	**1**	1r. (air) multicoloured	1·40	70
17	**1**	2r. multicoloured	2·75	1·20
18	**1**	3r. multicoloured	3·00	1·90
19	**1**	4r. multicoloured	5·00	2·75
20	**1**	5r. multicoloured	6·75	3·50
21	**1**	10r. multicoloured	12·00	7·25

The air stamps are as T **1** but additionally inscr "AIR-MAIL" in English and Arabic, and with a hawk in flight.

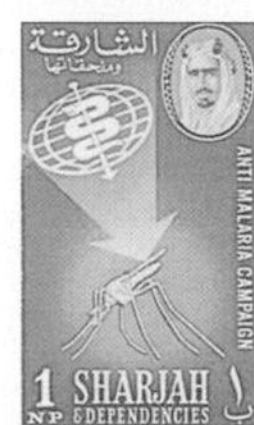

2 Mosquito and W.H.O. Emblem

1963. Malaria Eradication.

22	**2**	1n.p. turquoise	10	10
23	**2**	2n.p. blue	10	10
24	**2**	3n.p. blue	25	10
25	**2**	4n.p. green	35	25
26	**2**	90n.p. brown	3·75	1·80
MS26a 64×90 mm. **2** 100n.p. greenish blue (40×67 mm). Imperf			7·50	2·40

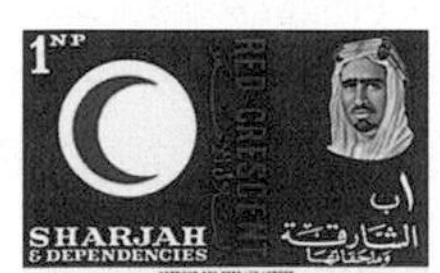

3 "Red Crescent"

1963. Red Cross Centenary.

27	**3**	1n.p. red and purple	10	10
28	**3**	2n.p. red and turquoise	10	10
29	**3**	3n.p. red and blue	10	10
30	**3**	4n.p. red and green	10	10
31	**3**	5n.p. red and brown	10	10
32	**3**	85n.p. red and green	2·40	1·20
MS32a 90×64 mm. **3** 100n.p. red and purple (67×40 mm). Imperf			5·50	3·00

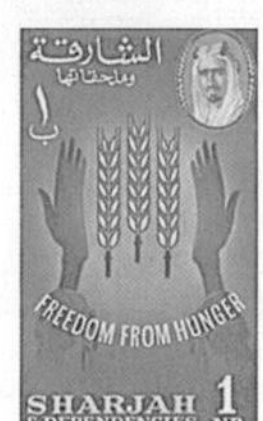

4 Campaign Emblem between Hands

1963. Freedom from Hunger.

33	**4**	1n.p. green	10	10
34	**4**	2n.p. brown	10	10
35	**4**	3n.p. green	10	10
36	**4**	4n.p. blue	10	25
37	**4**	90n.p. red	2·75	1·20
MS37a 64×90 mm. **4** 100n.p. plum (40×67 mm). Imperf			3·50	2·40

1963. Surch.

38	**4**	10n.p. on 1n.p. green	35	35
39		20n.p. on 2n.p. brown	70	60
40		30n.p. on 3n.p. green	1·20	95
41		40n.p. on 4n.p. blue	1·60	1·40
42		75n.p. on 90n.p. red	3·00	2·40
43		80n.p. on 90n.p. red	3·50	2·75
44	**2**	1r. on 90n.p. brown	4·75	4·00

1964. Air. Pres. Kennedy Memorial Issue (1st issue). Nos. 16-21 optd **In Memoriam John F Kennedy 1917-1963** in English and Arabic, and emblems.

45	**1**	1r. multicoloured	3·50	3·50
46	**1**	2r. multicoloured	7·25	7·25
47	**1**	3r. multicoloured	12·00	12·00
48	**1**	4r. multicoloured	14·50	14·50
49	**1**	5r. multicoloured	22·00	22·00
50	**1**	10r. multicoloured	31·00	31·00

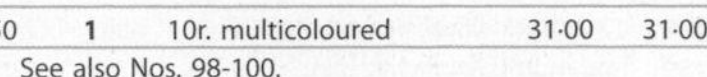

See also Nos. 98-100.

7 Orbiting Astronomical Observatory

1964. Scientific Space Research.

51	**7**	1n.p. blue	10	10
52	**7**	2n.p. green and brown	10	10
53	**7**	3n.p. blue and black	10	10
54	**7**	4n.p. black and bistre	10	10
55	**7**	5n.p. bistre and violet	10	10
56	**7**	35n.p. violet and blue	1·20	95
57	**7**	50n.p. brown and green	2·40	1·40
MS57a 112×80 mm. 100n.p. multicoloured (Various satellites). Imperf			8·50	2·40

DESIGNS: 2n.p. "Nimbus" weather satellite; 3n.p. "Pioneer V" space probe; 4n.p. "Explorer XIII" satellite; 5n.p. "Explorer XII" satellite; 35n.p. Project "Relay" satellite; 50n.p. Orbiting solar observatory.

8 Running

1964. Olympic Games, Tokyo (1st issue).

58	**8**	1n.p. blue, green and yellow	10	10
59	-	2n.p. red and turquoise	10	10
60	-	3n.p. brown and green	10	10
61	-	4n.p. green and brown	10	10
62	-	20n.p. blue and brown	60	25
63	-	30n.p. bistre and pink	95	50
64	-	40n.p. violet and yellow	1·20	60
65	-	1r. brown and blue	3·00	1·80
MS65a 102×102 mm. 1r. sepia and cobalt (67×67 mm) (As No. 65). Imperf			12·00	9·75

DESIGNS: 2n.p. Throwing the discus; 3n.p. Hurdling; 4n.p. Putting the shot; 20n.p. High jumping; 30n.p. Weightlifting; 40n.p. Throwing the javelin; 1r. High diving.

See also Nos. 90-7.

9 Flame and World Map

1964. Air. Human Rights Day.

66	**9**	50n.p. brown	70	35
67	**9**	1r. violet	1·40	85
68	**9**	150n.p. green	2·75	1·40
MS68a 90×64 mm. **9** 3r. rosine (67×40 mm). Imperf			4·75	3·00

10 Girl Scouts Marching

1964. Sharjah Girl Scouts.

69	**10**	1n.p. green	10	10
70	**10**	2n.p. green	10	10
71	**10**	3n.p. blue	25	25
72	**10**	4n.p. violet	25	25
73	**10**	5n.p. mauve	35	25
74	**10**	2r. brown	4·00	2·75
MS74a 103×76 mm. **10** 2r. vermilion (67×40 mm). Imperf			6·00	4·25

11 Khor Fakkan

1964. Air. Multicoloured.

75	10n.p. Type **11**	25	25
76	20n.p. Bedouin camp, Beni Qatab	35	25
77	30n.p. Dhaid oasis	50	25
78	40n.p. Kalba Castle	60	35
79	75n.p. Street and Wind tower, Sharjah	1·30	50
80	100n.p. Fortress	2·40	60

12 "Mr. Gus" (oil rig)

1964. Air. New York World's Fair. Multicoloured.

81	20n.p. Type **12**	70	25
82	40n.p. Unisphere	1·20	35
83	1r. New York skyline (85½×44½ mm)	3·00	85
MS83a 76×108 mm. 40n.p. multicoloured (40×67 mm) (As No. 82). Imperf		4·75	2·10

13 Scout at Attention

1964. Sharjah Boy Scouts.

84	**13**	1n.p. green	10	10
85	-	2n.p. green	10	10
86	-	3n.p. blue	10	10
87	**13**	4n.p. violet	60	50
88	-	5n.p. mauve	70	60
89	-	2r. brown	2·75	1·80
MS89a 77×103 mm. 2r. vermilion (40×67 mm) (As No. 86). Imperf			6·00	4·25

DESIGNS—HORIZ: 2, 5n.p. Scouts marching. VERT: 3n.p., 2r. Boy scout.

14 Olympic Torch

1964. Olympic Games, Tokyo (2nd issue).

90	**14**	1n.p. green	10	10
91	**14**	2n.p. blue	10	10
92	**14**	3n.p. brown	10	10
93	**14**	4n.p. turquoise	10	10
94	**14**	5n.p. violet	10	10
95	**14**	40n.p. blue	50	10
96	**14**	50n.p. brown	85	35
97	**14**	2r. brown	4·25	2·20
MS97a 108×76 mm. **14** 2r. green (57×82 mm). Imperf			12·00	9·75

15 Pres. Kennedy and Statue of Liberty

1964. Air. Pres. Kennedy Commemoration (2nd issue). Inscr in gold.

98	**15**	40n.p. blue, brown & green	2·40	1·20

99	15	60n.p. brown, green & blue	2·40	1·20
100	15	100n.p. green, blue & brown	2·40	1·20
MS100a		108×76 mm. Nos. 98-100. Imperf	12·00	9·75

16 Feral Rock Pigeon ("Rock Dove")

1965. Air. Birds. Multicoloured.

101	30n.p. Type **16**	95	25
102	40n.p. Red junglefowl	1·20	35
103	75n.p. Hoopoe	1·80	60
104	150n.p. Type **16**	3·50	1·20
105	2r. Red junglefowl	4·75	1·40
106	3r. Hoopoe	6·00	2·40

17 Early Telephone

1965. "Science, Transport and Communications".

107	**17**	1n.p. black and red	10	10
108	**A**	1n.p. black and red	10	10
109	**B**	2n.p. blue and orange	10	10
110	**C**	2n.p. blue and orange	10	10
111	**D**	3n.p. brown and green	10	10
112	**E**	3n.p. brown and green	10	10
113	**F**	4n.p. violet and green	10	10
114	**G**	4n.p. violet and green	10	10
115	**H**	5n.p. brown and green	10	10
116	**I**	5n.p. brown and green	10	10
117	**J**	30n.p. indigo and blue	25	25
118	**K**	30n.p. indigo and blue	25	25
119	**L**	40n.p. blue and yellow	50	25
120	**M**	40n.p. blue and yellow	50	25
121	**N**	50n.p. brown and blue	60	35
122	**O**	50n.p. brown and blue	60	35
123	**P**	75n.p. brown and green	60	35
124	**Q**	75n.p. brown and green	60	35
125	**R**	1r. blue and yellow	3·00	1·20
126	**S**	1r. blue and yellow	3·00	1·20
MS126a		Two sheets each 153×77 mm. Nos. 119-20 and 125-6. Imperf	9·00	5·00

DESIGNS: A, Modern teleprinter; B, 1895 Car; C, 1964 American car; D, Early X-ray apparatus; E, T.V. X-ray machine; F, Early mail coach; G, "Telstar" satellite; H, Medieval ship; I, Nuclear- powered freighter "Savannah"; J, Early astronomers; K, Jodrell Bank radio-telescope; L, Greek messengers; M, "Relay" satellite; N, "Man's early flight" (Lilienthal biplane glider); O, Sud Aviation Caravelle jetliner; P, Persian waterwheel; Q, Hydro-electric dam; R, Locomotive "Fitzwilliam", 1849, Great Britain; S, Modern diesel train.

1965. Air. Churchill Commemoration (1st issue). Optd **In Memoriam Sir Winston Churchill 1874-1965** in English and Arabic.

127	**15**	40n.p. multicoloured	1·20	50
128	**15**	60n.p. multicoloured	1·80	60
129	**15**	100n.p. multicoloured	2·40	70
MS129a		108×76 mm. Nos. 127-9. Imperf	14·50	12·00

See also Nos. 201-4.

18a A.P.U. Emblem

1965. Tenth Anniv (1964) of Arab Postal Union's Permanent Office.

130	**18a**	5n.p. blue and yellow	10	10
131	**18a**	30n.p. blue and red	70	35
132	**18a**	65n.p. green and orange	1·80	1·10

1965. Various issues of Shaikh Saqr with portrait obliterated with bars. (a) Postage. Nos. 5, 8/13.

150	**1**	5n.p. multicoloured	10	10
151	**1**	10n.p. multicoloured	10	10
152	**1**	16n.p. multicoloured	25	25
153	**1**	20n.p. multicoloured	35	25
154	**1**	30n.p. multicoloured	50	25
155	**1**	40n.p. multicoloured	50	35
156	**1**	50n.p. multicoloured	60	50

(b) Air. (i) Nos. 16, 18-21.

157	1r. multicoloured	95	70
158	3r. multicoloured	3·00	2·40
159	4r. multicoloured	3·75	3·00
160	5r. multicoloured	5·00	3·50
161	10r. multicoloured	10·00	6·00

(ii) Nos. 75-80.

144	**11**	10n.p. multicoloured	35	25
145	-	20n.p. multicoloured	50	25
146	-	30n.p. multicoloured	60	25
147	-	40n.p. multicoloured	70	35
148	-	75n.p. multicoloured	95	35
149	-	100n.p. multicoloured	1·20	50

22 Rameses II in War Chariot

1965. Nubian Monuments Preservation.

162	**22**	5n.p. blue and yellow	10	10
163	**22**	10n.p. green and brown	10	10
164	**22**	30n.p. blue and orange	70	60
165	**22**	55n.p. violet and blue	1·20	85

23 Cable Ship "Monarch IV" and COMPAC Cable Route Map

1965. I.T.U. Centenary. Country name in gold.

166	**23**	1n.p. brown and blue	10	10
167	-	2n.p. brown and blue	10	10
168	-	3n.p. violet and green	10	10
169	-	4n.p. brown and blue	10	10
170	**23**	5n.p. brown and violet	25	10
171	-	50n.p. purple and black	60	25
172	-	1r. green and brown	1·20	50
173	-	120n.p. red and green	1·80	70

DESIGNS: 2, 120n.p. "Relay 1" satellite and tracking station, Goonhilly Down; 3, 50n.p. "Telstar" satellite and Atlas-Agena rocket on launching pad; 4n.p., 1r. "Syncom" satellite, Post Office Tower (London) and horn paraboloid reflector aerial.

24 Running

1965. Pan-American Games, Cairo.

174	**24**	50n.p. turquoise and lilac	85	35
175	-	50n.p. green and brown	85	35
176	-	50n.p. lilac and brown	85	35
177	-	50n.p. brown and green	85	35
178	-	50n.p. brown and turquoise	85	35

SPORTS: No. 175, Pole vaulting; 176, Boxing; 177, High jumping; 178, Long jumping.

25 Flags (reverse of 5r. coin)

1966. Arabian Gulf Area Monetary Conf. Circular designs on silver foil, backed with paper inscr "Walsall Security Paper" in English and Arabic. Imperf. (a) Diameter 41 mm.

179	**25**	50n.p. black	1·20	1·20
180	-	75n.p. violet	1·30	1·30

(b) Diameter 52 mm.

181	**25**	1r. purple	1·40	1·40
182	-	3r. blue	4·00	4·00

(c) Diameter 64 mm.

183	**25**	4r. green	6·00	6·00
184	-	5r. orange	6·75	6·75

COINS: 75n.p., 3r. and 5r. show the obverse (Pres. Kennedy).

1966. Rendezvous in Space. Nos. 33-6 optd 15–12–1965 Rendezvous in SPACE, two space capsules and four bars obliterating portrait or surch also in English and Arabic.

185	**4**	1n.p. green	10	10
186	**4**	2n.p. brown	10	10
187	**4**	3n.p. green	10	10
188	**4**	4n.p. blue	10	10
189	**4**	15n.p. on 1n.p. green	35	25
190	**4**	30n.p. on 2n.p. brown	50	35
191	**4**	50n.p. on 3n.p. green	1·30	85
192	**4**	1r. on 4n.p. blue	1·70	95

27 I.C.Y. Emblem and Prime Minister Harold Wilson

1986. International Co-operation Year.

193	**27**	80n.p. brown and violet	70	25
194	-	80n.p. brown and green	70	25
195	-	80n.p. green and red	70	25
196	-	80n.p. purple and blue	70	25
197	-	80n.p. blue and orange	70	25
198	-	80n.p. purple and green	70	25
199	-	80n.p. blue and grey	70	25
200	-	80n.p. purple and brown	70	25

DESIGNS—I.C.Y. emblem and "World Leaders": No. 194, Chancellor Erhard (West Germany); 195, Pres. Nasser (Egypt); 196, Pres. Johnson (U.S.A.); 197, Pope Paul VI; 198, Pres. De Gaulle (France); 199, Shaikh Isa bin Sulman al-Khalifa (Bahrain); 200, King Faisal (Saudi Arabia).

28 Sir Winston Churchill, Pen and Ink, and Books

1966. Churchill Commemoration (2nd issue). Multicoloured, printed on gold foil, backed with paper.

201	2r. Type **28**	1·20	60
202	3r. Churchill and Houses of Parliament, pen and ink	1·40	70
203	4r. Churchill and St. Paul's Cathedral	2·20	95
204	5r. Churchill and "Big Ben" (clock tower, Houses of Parliament) and Tower Bridge	2·40	1·20
MS205	102×71 mm. 1, 2, 3, and 4r. stamps in colours and designs of Nos. 201-2, 204 and 203 but smaller	16·00	11·00

29 Pennant Coralfish

1966. Fish. Multicoloured.

206	1n.p. Type **29**	35	25
207	2n.p. Sail-finned tang	35	25
208	3n.p. Young emperor angelfish	35	25
209	4n.p. African mouthbrooder	35	25
210	5n.p. Undulate triggerfish	35	25
211	15n.p. Diamond fingerfish	1·10	25
212	20n.p. Ornate butterflyfish	1·40	25
213	30n.p. Moorish idol	1·40	25
214	40n.p. Regal angelfish	1·80	25
215	50n.p. African mouthbrooder	1·80	25
216	75n.p. Undulate triggerfish	2·20	35
217	1r. Regal angelfish	3·00	35
218	2r. Moorish idol	4·25	65
219	3r. Ornate butterflyfish	5·50	70
220	4r. Diamond fingerfish	7·25	1·30
221	5r. Young emperor angelfish	11·00	1·70
222	10r. Type **29**	22·00	3·25

30 Arms of Munich and "Souvenir Sheet"

1966. International Philatelic Federation and International Philatelic Journalists Association Congresses, Munich. Multicoloured.

223	80n.p. Type **30**	60	25
224	120n.p. Frauenkirche, Munich	85	35
225	2r. Statue and Hall of Fame, Munich (81×41 mm)	1·60	70

NEW CURRENCY SURCHARGES. During the latter half of 1966 various issues appeared surcharged in dirhams and riyals. The 1966 definitives with this surcharge are listed below as there is evidence of their postal use. Nos. 102, 107-126, 135, 145, 150-161, 174-184 and 190 also exist with these surcharges.

Earlier in 1966 Nos. 98-100, 171-173, 193-194, 196, 198 and 200-205 appeared surcharged in piastres and rials. As Sharjah did not adopt this currency their status is uncertain.

1966. Nos. 206-22 with currency names changed by overprinting in English and Arabic. (a) Optd. **Dirham** or **Riyal**.

226	**29**	1d. on 1n.p. multicoloured	25	25
227	-	2d. on 2n.p. multicoloured	25	25
228	-	3d. on 3n.p. multicoloured	25	25
229	-	4d. on 4n.p. multicoloured	25	25
230	-	5d. on 5n.p. multicoloured	25	25
231	-	15d. on 15n.p. mult	25	25
232	-	20d. on 20n.p. mult	25	25
233	-	30d. on 30n.p. mult	50	50
234	-	40d. on 40n.p. mult	70	50
235	-	50d. on 50n.p. mult	95	70
236	-	75d. on 75n.p. mult	1·40	95
237	-	1r. on 1r. multicoloured	1·90	1·40
238	-	2r. on 2r. multicoloured	4·00	3·00
239	-	3r. on 3r. multicoloured	5·75	4·00
240	-	4r. on 4r. multicoloured	7·75	5·25
241	-	5r. on 5r. multicoloured	8·50	6·00
242	**29**	10r. on 10r. multicoloured	16·00	13·50

(b) Optd **Dh**.

242b	2d. on 2n.p. multicoloured	25	25
242c	3d. on 3n.p. multicoloured	25	25
242f	15d. on 15n.p. mult	40	25
242g	20d. on 20n.p. mult	50	30
242h	30d. on 30n.p. mult	60	25
242i	40d. on 40n.p. mult	70	25
242j	50d. on 50n.p. mult	70	50
242k	75d. on 75n.p. mult	1·10	70

33 Greek 6th-cent Ball-player

1966. World Cup Football Championship, England. Printed on coloured metal foil-surfaced paper. Multicoloured.

243	½r. Type **33**	1·60	25
244	½r. Tsu-chu "Kick-ball" game, China, c. 175 B.C.	1·60	25
245	½r. 14th-cent ball game	1·60	25
246	½r. Blowing up ball-bladder (17th-cent)	1·60	25
247	½r. Football game, Barnet, England, c. 1750	1·60	25
248	½r. England v. Scotland game, Kennington Oval (London), 1879	1·60	25
249	½r. Victorious England team, Wembley, 1966 (56×55½ mm)	1·60	25
MS250	Six sheets comprising Nos. 243-248, but smaller, 31×36 mm, each block of four	14·50	14·50

34 Pres. Kennedy

1966. Third Death Anniv of Pres. Kennedy and Inauguration of Arlington Memorial.

251	50d. Type **34**	50	25
252	2r. Sharjah 50n.p. Kennedy stamp of 1964	1·90	60
253	2r.50 Pres. Kennedy's grave (77×40 mm)	2·40	95
MS254	102×126 mm. 3r. President Kennedy's grave (55×42 mm)	8·50	8·50

35 Shaikh Khalid bin Mohammed al Qasimi and Arms

1968. Multicoloured.. Multicoloured..

255		5d. Type **35** (postage)	25	25
256		10d. Flag	25	25
257		15d. Flag and arms (vert)	35	25
258		20d. Decorative pattern (vert)	35	25
259		35d. Type **35** (air)	60	35
260		40d. As 10d.	60	35
261		60d. As 15d.	85	35
262		75d. As 20d.	1·10	50
263		1r. Type **35**	1·40	50
264		2r. As 10d.	3·00	1·20
265		3r. As 15d.	4·25	2·20
266		4r. As 20d.	5·50	3·00
267		5r. Type **35**	6·75	3·00
268		10r. As 10d.	12·00	7·25

36 Freighter at Wharf

1970. Fifth Anniv of Ruler's Accession. "Progress in Sharjah".

285	**36**	5d. deep violet and violet	25	25
286	**A**	5d. deep blue and blue	25	25
287	**B**	5d. brown and red	25	25
288	**C**	5d. brown and green	25	25
289	**D**	5d. brown and light brown	25	25
290	**D**	20d. brown and light brown	25	25
291	**36**	35d. deep violet and violet	35	35
292	**A**	35d. deep blue and blue	35	35
293	**B**	35d. brown and red	35	35
294	**C**	35d. brown and green	35	35
295	**D**	35d. brown and light brown	35	35
296	**36**	40d. deep violet and violet	50	35
297	**A**	40d. deep blue and blue	50	35
298	**B**	40d. brown and red	50	35
299	**C**	40d. brown and green	50	35
300	**D**	40d. brown and light brown	50	35
301	**36**	60d. deep violet and violet	70	50
302	**A**	60d. deep blue and blue	70	50
303	**B**	60d. brown and red	70	50
304	**C**	60d. brown and green	70	50
305	**D**	60d. brown and light brown	70	50

DESIGNS: A, Airport; B, Oil derrick; C, Modern building; D, Shaikh Khalid.

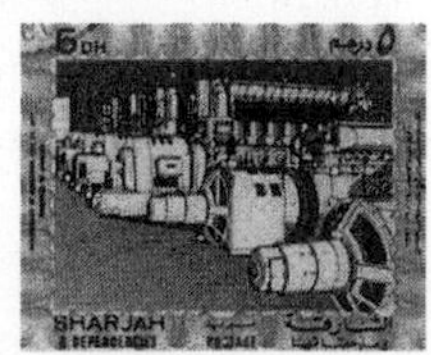

37 Turbines

1971. Sixth Anniv of Ruler's Accession. "Progress in Sharjah".

306	**37**	5d. bl, vio & grn (postage)		
307	**A**	5d. mauve, brown & vio		
308	**B**	5d. multicoloured		
309	**C**	5d. multicoloured		
310	**B**	35d. multicoloured (air)		
311	**37**	75d. blue, violet and green		
312	**A**	75d. mauve, brown and violet		
313	**B**	75d. multicoloured		
314	**C**	75d. multicoloured		
315	**37**	1r. blue, violet and green		
316	**A**	1r. mauve, brown and violet		
317	**B**	1r. multicoloured		
318	**C**	1r. multicoloured		
319	**A**	2r. mauve, brown and violet		
320	**37**	3r. blue, violet and green		
321	**A**	3r. mauve, brown and violet		
322	**B**	3r. multicoloured		
323	**C**	3r. multicoloured		
324	**C**	5r. multicoloured		

DESIGNS—HORIZ: A, Mosque. VERT: B, Clock fountain; C, Shaikh Khalid.

38 Shaikh Rashid of Dubai and Shaikh Khalid

1971. Air. Proclamation of United Arab Emirates. Multicoloured.

325		25d. Type **38**		
326		35d. Shaikh Ahmed of Umm al Qiwain and Shaikh Khalid		
327		65d. United Nations and Arab League emblems		
328		75d. Shaikh Rashid of Ajman and Shaikh Khalid		
329		1r. Shaikh Mohamed of Fujeira and Shaikh Khalid		
330		2r. Shaikh Zaid of Abu Dhabi and Shaikh Khalid		

1971. Various stamps surcharged. (a) 1968 Winter Olympics issue (Appendix).

331		35d. on 5d. multicoloured		
		(b) Nos. 255 and 262.		
332	**35**	35 on 5d. mult (postage)		
334	-	60 on 75d. multicoloured		
		(c) 5th Anniv of Ruler's Accession (Nos. 296-300).		
335	**36**	5 on 40d. dp vio & vio		
336	**A**	5 on 40d. dp blue & blue		
337	**B**	5 on 40d. brown and red		
338	**C**	5 on 40d. brown and green		
339	**D**	5 on 40d. brn & lt brn		
		(d) Air. Proclamation of United Arab Emirates (Nos. 325 and 328-330).		
340	**38**	65d. on 25d. multicoloured		
341	-	65d. on 75d. multicoloured		
342	-	65d. on 1r. multicoloured		
343	-	65d. on 2r. multicoloured		

OFFICIAL STAMPS

1966. Optd **ON STATE SERVICE** in English and Arabic. Multicoloured.

O101	**1**	8n.p.	10	10
O102	**1**	10n.p.	10	10
O103	**1**	16n.p.	25	25
O104	**1**	20n.p.	35	35
O105	**1**	30n.p.	35	35
O106	**1**	40n.p.	60	60
O107	**1**	50n.p.	1·60	1·60
O108	**1**	75n.p.	4·00	4·00
O109	**1**	100n.p.	7·25	7·25

1968. As Nos. 258 and 261 but colours changed and inscr "OFFICIAL".

O269		20d. multicoloured		
O270		60d. multicoloured		

For later issues see **UNITED ARAB EMIRATES**.

APPENDIX

The following stamps have either been issued in excess of postal needs or have not been made available to the public in reasonable quantities at face value. Such stamps may later be given full listing if there is evidence of regular postal use.

1967

Post Day. Japanese Paintings. 1r.x3.
22nd Anniv of United Nations. 10, 30, 60d.
Olympics Preparation, Mexico, 1968. Postage 1, 2, 3, 10 d; Air 30, 60d., 2r.
Flowers and Butterflies. Postage 1, 2, 3, 4, 5, 10, 20d.; Air 30, 60d., 1, 2r.
Famous Paintings. Postage 1, 2, 3, 4, 5, 30, 40, 60, 75d.; Air 1, 2, 3, 4, 5r.

1968

Winter Olympic Games, Grenoble. Postage 1, 2, 3, 4, 5d.; Air 1, 2, 3r.
12th World Jamboree. Postage 1, 2, 3, 4, 5, 10d.; Air 30, 50, 60d., 1r.50.
Grenoble Olympic Medal Winners. Optd on Winter Olympics, Grenoble issue. Postage 1, 2, 3, 4, 5d.; Air 1, 2, 3r.
Mothers' Day. Paintings. Postage 10, 20, 30, 40d.; Air 1, 2, 3, 4r.
American Paintings. Postage 20, 30, 40, 50, 60d.; Air 1, 4, 5r.
Egyptian Art. 15, 25, 35, 45, 55, 65, 75, 95d.
Martyrs of Liberty. Air 35d.x4, 60d.x4, 1r.x4.
Olympic Games, Mexico. 10, 20, 30d., 2r., 2r. 40, 5r.
Previous Olympic Games. Air 25, 50, 75d., 1r. 50, 3, 4r.
Sportsmen and Women. Postage 20, 30, 40, 60d., 1r. 50, 2r. 50; Air 25, 50d., 1, 2r., 3r. 25, 4, 4r.
Robert Kennedy Memorial. Optd on American Paintings issue. Air 4r.
Olympic Medal Winners, Mexico. 35, 50, 60d., 1, 2, 4r.

1969

Famous Men and Women. Postage 10, 20, 25, 35, 50, 60d.; Air 1, 2, 3, 4, 5, 6r.
"Apollo 8" Moon Mission. Postage 5d.x6; Air 10, 15, 20d., 2, 3, 4r.
"Apollo 11" Moon Mission (1st series). Postage 5d.x8; Air 75d.x8, 1r.x8.
Post Day. Famous Ships. Postage 5d.x8; Air 90d.x8.
"Apollo 12" Moon Mission. Optd on Famous Ships issue. 5d.x8.

1970

UNICEF. Paintings of Children. Postage 5d.x9; Air 20, 25, 35, 40, 50, 60, 75d., 1, 3r.
Animals. Postage 3d.x14, 10, 10, 15, 15d.; Air 20, 20, 35, 35d., 1, 1, 2, 2r.
"Expo 70" World Fair, Osaka, Japan (1st series). Japanese Paintings. Postage 3d.x4; Air 1r.x4.
"Expo 70" World Fair, Osaka, Japan (2nd series). Pavilions. Postage 2, 2, 3, 3d.; Air 40d.x4.
Paintings of Napoleon. Postage 3d.x5; Air 20, 30, 40, 60d., 2r.
De Gaulle Commemoration. Postage 3d.x5; Air 20, 30, 40, 60d., 2r.
"Mercury" and "Vostok" Moon Missions. Postage 1, 2, 3, 4, 5d.; Air 25, 40, 85d., 1, 2r.
"Gemini" Space Programme. Postage 1, 2, 3, 4, 5d.; Air 25, 40, 85d., 1, 2r.
"Apollo", "Voskhod" and "Soyuz" Projects. Postage 1, 2, 3, 4, 5d.; Air 25, 40, 85d., 1, 2r.
Events of 1970. Postage 1d.x5, 5d.; Air 75d., 1, 2, 3r.
200th Birth Anniv of Beethoven. Postage 3d.x5; Air 35, 40, 60d., 1, 2r.
Mozart. Postage 3d.x5; Air 35, 40, 60d., 1, 2r.
The Life of Christ (1st series). Postage 1, 2, 3, 4, 5d.; Air 25, 40, 60d., 1, 2r.

1971

"Apollo 14" Moon Mission. Optd on 1969 "Apollo 11" issue. Postage 5d.x4; Air 75d.x4.
Post Day 1970. Cars. Postage 1, 2, 3, 4, 5d.; Air 25, 50, 60d., 2, 3r.
Post Day (1st series). American Cars. Postage 1, 2, 3, 4, 5d.; Air 35, 50d., 1, 2, 3r.
Post Day (2nd series). Trains. Postage 1, 2, 3, 4, 5d.; Air 25, 50, 60d., 1, 2r.
Pres. Nasser Commemoration. Postage 5d.x5; Air 20, 35, 40, 60d., 2r.
Safe return of "Apollo 13". Optd on 1969 "Apollo 8" issue. Air 10, 15, 20d., 2, 3, 4r.
De Gaulle Memorial. Postage 3, 4, 5, 6, 7d.; Air 40, 60, 75d., 1, 2r.
Olympics Preparation, Munich, 1972. Postage 2, 3, 4, 5, 6d.; Air 35, 40, 60d., 1, 2r.
Miracles of Christ. Postage 1, 2, 3, 4, 5d.; Air 25, 40, 60d., 1, 2r.

1972

Sport. Postage 2, 3, 4, 5, 6d.; Air 35, 40, 60d., 1, 2r.
The Life of Christ (2nd series). Postage 1, 2, 3, 4, 5d.; Air 25, 40, 60d., 1, 2r.
Winter Olympics Preparation, Sapporo. Postage 2, 3, 4, 5, 6d.; Air 35, 40, 60d., 1, 2r.
Safe Return of "Apollo 14". Optd on 1969 "Apollo 11" issue. Postage 5d.x4; Air 1r.x4.
Previous World Cup Winners. Postage 5, 10, 15, 20, 25d.; Air 35, 75d., 1, 2, 3r.
Sapporo Olympic Medal Winners. Paintings. Postage 5, 10, 15, 20, 25d.; Air 35, 75d., 1, 2, 3r.
Famous People, Churchill, De Gaulle and John Kennedy. Postage 5d.x4, 10d.x4, 35d.x4; Air 75d.x4, 1r.x4, 3r.x4.
Olympic Games, Munich. Postage 5, 10, 15, 20, 25d.; Air 35, 75d., 1, 2, 3r.
Cats. Postage 20, 25d.; Air 75d., 1, 2r.
Birds (1st series). Postage 20, 25, 75d., Air 1, 2r.
"Apollo 11" Moon Mission (2nd series). Postage 1, 1r. Air 1r.x3.
"Apollo 16" Moon Mission. Postage 1, 1r.; Air 1r.x3.
Dogs. Postage 20, 25d.; Air 75d., 1, 2r.
"Apollo 17" Moon Mission. Postage 1, 1r.; Air 1r.x3.
Munich Olympic Medal Winners. Air 5r.x20.
Horses. Postage 20, 25d.; Air 75d., 1, 2r.
"Apollo 17" Astronauts. Postage 1, 1r.; Air 1r.x3.
Butterflies. Postage 20, 25d.; Air 75d., 1, 2r.
"Luna 9" Soviet Space Programme. Postage 1, 1r.; Air 1r.x3.
Monkeys. Postage 20, 25d.; Air 75d., 1, 2r.
Birds (2nd series). Air 25, 25, 35, 35, 50, 50, 65, 65d., 1r.x6, 3, 3r.
Fish. Air 25, 35, 50, 65d., 1r.x5, 3r.
Insects. Air 25, 35, 50, 65d., 1, 3r.
Flowers. Postage 25, 35, 50, 65d., 1, 3r.; Air 1r.x4.
Fruit. Air 1r.x4.
Children. Air 1r.x4.
Eastern Antiquities. Air 25, 35, 40, 65, 75d., 1r.x4, 3r.
Planetary Exploration. Postage 1r.x3; Air 1, 1r.
13th World Jamboree. Postage 2d.x3, 3d.x3, 4d.x3, 5d.x3, 6d.x3; Air 35d.x3, 75d.x3, 1r.x3, 2r.x3, 3r.x3.

A number of issues on gold or silver foil also exist, but it is understood that these were mainly for presentation purposes, although valid for postage.

In common with the other states of the United Arab Emirates the Sharjah stamp contract was terminated on 1 August 1972, and further new issues released after that date were unauthorized.

Pt. 10

SIBERIA

Various Anti-Bolshevist governments existed in this area, culminating in Kolchak's assumption of power as "Supreme Ruler". The Kolchak Government fell in January 1920, provincial issues followed until the area was incorporated into the Soviet Union in 1922.

100 kopeks = 1 rouble.

1919. Admiral Kolchak Govt. Arms types of Russia surch in figures, or in figures and words (rouble values). Imperf or perf.

5	**22**	35 on 2k. green	65	3·25
6	**22**	50 on 3k. red	65	3·25
3	**22**	70 on 1k. orange	90	6·50
8	**23**	1r. on 4k. red	1·60	4·00
9	**22**	3r. on 7k. blue	5·75	10·00
10	**10**	5r. on 14k. red and blue	8·50	25·00

1920. Transbaikal Province. Ataman Semyonov regime. Arms types of Russia surch **p. 1 p.** Perf.

11	**23**	1r. on 4k. red	39·00	£100
12	**14**	2r.50 on 20k. red and blue	27·00	60·00
13	**22**	5r. on 5k. red	20·00	46·00
14	**10**	10r. on 70k. orange & brn	27·00	60·00

6

1920. Amur Province. Imperf.

15	**6**	2r. red	3·50	9·75
16	**6**	3r. green	3·50	9·75
17	**6**	5r. blue	3·50	9·75
18	**6**	15r. brown	5·25	14·50
19	**6**	30r. mauve	5·25	14·50

FAR EAST REPUBLIC

1920. Vladivostok issue. Optd DBP in fancy letters or surch also. Imperf or perf. (a) On Arms types of Russia.

32	**22**	1k. orange	9·75	12·00
33	**22**	2k. green	5·00	6·50
21	**22**	3k. red	6·50	6·50
39	**10**	3k. on 35k. green and purple	10·50	13·00
22	**23**	4k. red	10·50	14·50
40	**10**	4k. on 70k. orange & brown	5·00	9·00
41	**10**	7k. on 15k. blue and purple	4·00	6·50
23	**23**	10k. blue	£120	£120
44	**11**	10k. on 3r.50 green & brn	11·00	20·00
24	**10**	14k. red and blue	42·00	39·00
25	**10**	15k. blue and purple	11·00	14·50
26	**14**	20k. red and blue	£130	£130
27	**10**	20k. on 14k. red and blue	6·50	9·00
28	**10**	25k. mauve and green	16·00	20·00
29	**10**	35k. green and purple	39·00	46·00
30	**14**	50k. green and purple	16·00	20·00
35	**15**	1r. orange and brown	23·00	33·00
		(b) On Nos. 5 and 3 of Siberia.		
37	**22**	35k. on 2k. green	5·00	9·00
38	**22**	70k. on 1k. orange	6·50	11·50
		(c) On Postal Savings Bank stamps of Russia.		
45		1k. on 5k. green on buff	10·50	16·00
46		2k. on 10k. brown on buff	19·00	21·00

10

11

1921. Chita issue. Imperf.

47	**10**	1k. orange	1·30	2·00
48	**10**	3k. red	65	90
49	**11**	4k. brown and red	65	90
50	**10**	5k. brown	65	90
51b	**10**	7k. blue	1·30	2·50
52	**11**	10k. red and blue	90	1·40
53	**10**	15k. red	1·30	2·00
54	**11**	20k. red and blue	1·30	2·00
55	**11**	30k. red and green	1·70	2·30
56	**11**	50k. red and black	2·50	3·25

13

1922. Vladivostok issue. 5th Anniv of Russian October Revolution. Optd **1917 7-XI 1922.** Imperf.

57	**13**	2k. green	10·50	20·00
58	**13**	4k. red	13·00	23·00
59	**13**	5k. brown	17·00	29·00
60	**13**	10k. blue	20·00	29·00

PRIAMUR AND MARITIME PROVINCES

Anti-Bolshevist Government

1921. Vladivostok issue. Imperf.

61		2k. green	1·30	1·30
62		4k. red	1·60	1·60
63		5k. purple	2·00	2·00
64		10k. blue	3·25	3·25

(15)

1922. Anniv of Priamur Provisional Govt. Optd with T **15**.

89		2k. green	33·00	33·00
90		4k. red	33·00	33·00
91		5k. purple	33·00	33·00
92		10k. blue	33·00	33·00

16 Trans. "Priamur Territory"

1922. Optd or surch as T **16**.

93		1k. on 2k. green	5·25	7·25
94		2k. green	6·50	10·00
95		3k. on 4k. red	5·75	8·75
96		4k. red	6·75	10·00
97		5k. purple	6·25	10·00
98		10k. blue	5·00	10·00

1922. Optd as T **16**. Imperf or perf. (a) On Arms types of Russia.

114	**22**	1k. orange	7·25	13·00
115	**22**	2k. green	8·25	13·50
116	**22**	3k. red	11·00	26·00
102	**23**	4k. red	7·75	13·00
118	**22**	5k. red	18·00	42·00
104	**22**	7k. blue	36·00	65·00
105	**23**	10k. blue	36·00	75·00
106	**10**	14k. red and blue	£120	£200
107	**10**	15k. blue and purple	7·75	13·00
108	**14**	20k. red and blue	9·75	20·00
109	**10**	20k. on 14k. red and blue	£160	£250
110	**10**	25k. mauve and green	29·00	50·00
111	**10**	35k. green and purple	5·75	13·00
112	**14**	50k. green and purple	9·25	16·00
113	**10**	70k. orange and brown	20·00	39·00
121	**15**	1r. orange and brown	14·50	34·00

(b) On Nos. 5 and 3 of Siberia.

122	**22**	35k. on 2k. green	80·00	£120
123	**22**	70k. on 1k. orange	85·00	£130

1922. Nos. 37 and 38 optd II.3.K. and three bars. Imperf and perf.

125		35k. on 2k. green	5·25	10·50
126		70k. on 1k. orange	7·75	15·00

SOVIET UNION ISSUE FOR THE FAR EAST

А. В.
коп. 1 коп.
ЗОЛОТОМ
(18)

1923. Stamps of Russia surch as T **18**. Imperf or perf.

131	**79**	1k. on 100r. red	85	1·30
128	**79**	2k. on 70r. purple	45	65
129	**78**	5k. on 10r. blue	45	65
130	**79**	10k. on 50r. brown	65	90

Pt. 8

SICILY

An island to the south of Italy, which, with Naples, formed the Kingdom of the Two Sicilies, until incorporated in the Kingdom of Italy.

100 grano = 1 ducato.

1 King "Bomba"

1859. Imperf.

1c	**1**	½g. yellow	£850	£1300
2b	**1**	1g. olive	£900	£225
3	**1**	2g. blue	£250	£180
4	**1**	5g. red	£850	£650
5	**1**	10g. blue	£800	£325
6	**1**	20g. grey	£1200	£750
7	**1**	50g. brown	£1200	£6000

Pt. 1

SIERRA LEONE

A British colony on the west coast of Africa. Achieved independence within the British Commonwealth in 1961. By vote of the Assembly on 19 April 1971, Sierra Leone was proclaimed a republic.

1859. 12 pence = 1 shilling; 20 shillings = 1 pound.
1964. 100 cents = 1 leone.

1

2

1859

16	**2**	½d. brown	5·00	14·00
27	**2**	½d. green	3·00	2·75
28	**2**	1d. red	14·00	1·25
29	**2**	1½d. lilac	3·50	7·50
25	**2**	2d. mauve	75·00	8·50
30	**2**	2d. grey	60·00	4·00
31	**2**	2½d. blue	17·00	1·75
32	**2**	3d. yellow	3·50	13·00
21	**2**	4d. blue	£225	6·50
33	**2**	4d. brown	2·50	3·50
37	**1**	6d. purple	2·75	8·50
22	**2**	1s. green	90·00	6·50
34	**2**	1s. brown	26·00	19·00

1893. Surch **HALF PENNY**.

39	**2**	½d. on 1½d. lilac	8·50	3·75

4

1896

41	**4**	½d. mauve and green	2·50	3·00
42	**4**	1d. mauve and red	5·00	1·75
43	**4**	1½d. mauve and black	4·00	22·00
44	**4**	2d. mauve and orange	2·50	5·00
45	**4**	2½d. mauve and blue	2·50	1·25
46	**4**	3d. mauve and grey	8·50	7·00
47	**4**	4d. mauve and red	9·50	13·00
48	**4**	5d. mauve and black	13·00	15·00
49	**4**	6d. mauve	8·00	27·00
50	**4**	1s. green and black	6·00	24·00
51	**4**	2s. green and blue	32·00	75·00
52	**4**	5s. green and red	90·00	£250
53	**4**	£1 purple on red	£325	£600

6

1897. T **6** optd **POSTAGE AND REVENUE**.

54	**6**	1d. purple and green	7·50	3·75

1897. T **6** optd **POSTAGE AND REVENUE** and surch 2½d. and bars.

55		2½d. on 3d. purple and green	11·00	21·00
59		2½d. on 6d. purple and green	8·50	21·00
63		2½d. on 1s. lilac	£110	70·00
67		2½d. on 2s. lilac	£2000	£3000

15

1903

73	**15**	½d. purple and green	3·00	6·50
87	**15**	1d. purple and red	1·50	1·00
88	**15**	1½d. purple and black	3·00	16·00
89	**15**	2d. purple and orange	4·25	4·00
90	**15**	2½d. purple and blue	6·50	2·00
78	**15**	3d. purple and grey	15·00	17·00
92	**15**	4d. purple and red	11·00	8·00
93	**15**	5d. purple and black	13·00	35·00
94	**15**	6d. purple	7·50	3·75
95	**15**	1s. green and black	7·50	9·00
96	**15**	2s. green and blue	30·00	32·00
97	**15**	5s. green and red	48·00	65·00
98	**15**	£1 purple on red	£375	£325

1907

99		½d. green	1·00	50
100a		1d. red	18·00	60
101		1½d. orange	3·00	2·00
102		2d. grey	2·75	1·50
103		2½d. blue	3·75	3·00
104		3d. purple on yellow	13·00	2·75
105		4d. black and red on yellow	2·25	1·60
106		5d. purple and green	22·00	6·50
107		6d. purple and light purple	20·00	8·00
108		1s. black on green	6·00	5·00
109		2s. purple and blue on blue	25·00	19·00
110		5s. green and red on yellow	48·00	70·00
111		£1 purple and black on red	£300	£250

17

20

1912

131	**17**	½d. green	2·25	1·00
113	**17**	1d. red	2·25	30
132a	**17**	1d. violet	7·00	20
114	**17**	1½d. orange	2·00	2·50
133	**17**	1½d. red	2·00	1·25
134	**17**	2d. grey	1·25	20
116a	**17**	2½d. blue	1·25	1·00
116b	**20**	3d. purple on yellow	5·00	3·25
136	**17**	3d. blue	1·75	1·25
137	**17**	4d. black and red on yellow	4·75	3·25
138	**17**	5d. purple and green	1·50	1·25
139	**17**	6d. purple and light purple	1·50	2·75
120	**17**	7d. purple and orange	3·00	10·00
121	**17**	9d. purple and black	5·00	12·00
122	**17**	10d. purple and red	3·00	18·00
124a	**20**	1s. black on green	8·50	3·50
125	**20**	2s. blue and purple on blue	26·00	6·00
126	**20**	5s. red and green on yellow	24·00	35·00
127	**20**	10s. red and green on green	£110	£150
128	**20**	£1 black and purple on red	£225	£300
147	**20**	£2 blue and purple	£850	£1200
148	**20**	£5 orange and green	£2750	£4000

21 Rice Field

22 Palms and Cola Tree

1932

155	**21**	½d. green	25	50
156	**21**	1d. violet	40	30
157	**21**	1½d. red	50	2·25
158	**21**	2d. brown	50	30
159	**21**	3d. blue	1·75	2·75
160	**21**	4d. orange	1·50	13·00
161	**21**	5d. green	2·50	7·50
162	**21**	6d. blue	1·50	4·75
163	**21**	1s. lake	6·50	13·00
164	**22**	2s. brown	6·00	8·00
165	**22**	5s. blue	19·00	26·00
166	**22**	10s. green	90·00	£140
167	**22**	£1 purple	£180	£250

23 Arms of Sierra Leone

1933. Cent of Abolition of Slavery and of Death of William Wilberforce. Dated "1833 1933".

168	**23**	½d. green	1·00	1·25
169	-	1d. black and brown	65	10
170	-	1½d. brown	7·50	4·50
171	-	2d. purple	3·25	20
172	-	3d. blue	6·50	1·75
173	-	4d. brown	6·50	10·00
174	-	5d. green and brown	7·00	11·00
175	-	6d. black and orange	12·00	7·00
176	-	1s. violet	4·75	18·00
177	-	2s. brown and blue	40·00	50·00
178	-	5s. black and purple	£160	£190
179	-	10s. black and olive	£300	£475
180	-	£1 violet and orange	£650	£800

DESIGNS—VERT: 1d. "Freedom"; 1½d. Map of Sierra Leone; 4d. Government sanatorium; 5s. African elephant. HORIZ: 2d. Old Slave Market, Freetown; 3d. Native fruit seller; 5d. Bullom canoe; 6d. Punting near Banana Is; 1s. Government buildings, Freetown; 2s. Bunce Is; 10s. King George V; £1 Freetown Harbour.

1935. Silver Jubilee. As T **32a** of St. Helena.

181	1d. blue and black	2·00	2·50
182	3d. brown and blue	3·25	8·50
183	5d. green and blue	4·50	25·00
184	1s. grey and purple	24·00	22·00

1937. Coronation. As T **32b** of St. Helena.

185	1d. orange	70	1·00
186	2d. purple	1·00	1·25
187	3d. blue	2·00	4·50

30 Freetown from the Harbour

1938. King George VI.

188	**30**	½d. black and green	15	40
189	**30**	1d. black and lake	40	60
190	-	1½d. red	20·00	1·00
190a	-	1½d. mauve	30	60
191	-	2d. mauve	50·00	3·00
191a	-	2d. red	30	2·00
192	**30**	3d. black and blue	65	50
193	**30**	4d. black and brown	2·50	4·50
194	-	5d. green	3·25	4·25
195	-	6d. grey	1·50	50
196	**30**	1s. black and green	3·75	70
196a	-	1s.3d. orange	75	60
197	**30**	2s. black and brown	4·50	2·75
198	-	5s. brown	10·00	17·00
199	-	10s. green	35·00	19·00
200	**30**	£1 blue	21·00	35·00

DESIGNS: 1½, 2, 5, 6d., 1s.3d., 5s., 10s. Rice harvesting.

1946. Victory. As T **33a** of St. Helena.

201	1½d. lilac	20	10
202	3d. blue	20	30

1948. Silver Wedding. As T **33b/c** of St. Helena.

203	1½d. mauve	15	15
204	£1 blue	20·00	28·00

1949. 75th Anniv of U.P.U. As T **33d/g** of St. Helena.

205	1½d. purple	20	50
206	3d. blue	2·00	5·50
207	6d. grey	50	7·50
208	1s. green	35	1·00

1953. Coronation. As T **33h** of St. Helena.

209	1½d. black and lilac	75	30

32 Cape Lighthouse

1956. Centres in black.

210	**32**	½d. lilac	1·00	2·75
211	-	1d. olive	90	40
212	-	1½d. blue	1·60	6·50
213	-	2d. brown	70	40
214	-	3d. blue	1·25	10
215	-	4d. slate	2·50	2·25
216	-	6d. violet	1·00	30
217	-	1s. red	1·25	50
218	-	1s.3d. sepia	11·00	30
219	-	2s.6d. brown	15·00	13·00
220	-	5s. green	6·00	3·75
221	-	10s. mauve	4·00	2·75
222	-	£1 orange	26·00	35·00

DESIGNS—HORIZ: 1d. Queen Elizabeth II Quay; 1½d. Piassava workers; 4d. Iron ore production, Marampa; 6d. Whale Bay, York Village; 1s.3d. Bristol 170 Freighter Mk 31 airplane and map; 10s. Law Courts, Freetown; £1 Government House. VERT: 2d. Cotton tree, Freetown; 3d. Rice harvesting; 1s. Bullom canoe; 2s.6d. Orugu railway bridge; 5s. Kuranko chief.

46 Licensed Diamond Miner

1961. Independence.

223		½d. brown and turquoise	20	30
224	**46**	1d. brown and green	1·50	10
225	-	1½d. black and green	20	30
226	-	2d. black and blue	20	10
227	-	3d. brown and blue	20	10
228	-	4d. blue and red	20	10
229	-	6d. black and purple	20	10

230	-	1s. brown and orange	20	10
231	-	1s.3d. blue and violet	20	10
232	**46**	2s.6d. green and black	2·75	30
233	-	5s. black and red	1·00	1·25
234	-	10s. black and green	1·00	1·25
235	-	£1 red and yellow	9·00	20·00

DESIGNS—VERT: ½d., 1s. Palm fruit gathering; 1½d., 5s. Bundu mask; 2d., 10s. Bishop Crowther and Old Fourah Bay College; £1 Forces bugler. HORIZ: 3d., 6d. Sir Milton Margai; 4d., 1s.3d. Lumley Beach, Freetown.

53 Royal Charter, 1799

55 Old House of Representatives, Freetown, 1924

1961. Royal Visit.

236	**53**	3d. black and red	15	10
237	-	4d. black and violet	15	1·75
238	**55**	6d. black and orange	20	10
239	-	1s.3d. black and blue	3·50	1·75

DESIGNS—VERT: 4d. King's Yard Gate, Freetown, 1817. HORIZ: 1s.3d. Royal Yacht "Britannia" at Freetown.

57 Campaign Emblem

1962. Malaria Eradication.

240	**57**	3d. red	10	10
241	**57**	1s.3d. green	20	10

58 Fireball Lily

1963. Flowers in natural colours; background colours given below.

242	**58**	½d. bistre	10	50
243	-	1d. red	10	10
244	-	1½d. green	20	25
245	-	2d. olive	20	10
246	-	3d. green	20	10
247	-	4d. blue	20	30
248	-	6d. blue	30	10
249	-	1s. green	40	10
250	-	1s.3d. green	1·50	20
251	-	2s.6d. purple	1·25	50
252	-	5s. violet	1·25	80
253	-	10s. purple	4·00	1·50
254	-	£1 blue	6·00	11·00

FLOWERS—VERT: 1½d. Stereospermum; 3d. Beniseed; 4d. Blushing hibiscus; 1s. Beautiful crinum; 2s.6d. Broken hearts; 5s. Ra-ponthi; 10s. Blue plumbago. HORIZ: 1d. Jina-gbo; 2d. Black-eyed Susan; 6d. Climbing lily; 1s.3d. Blue bells; £1 African tulip tree.

71 Threshing Machine and Corn Bins

1963. Freedom from Hunger.

255	**71**	3d. black and ochre	30	10
256	-	1s.3d. sepia and green	35	10

DESIGN: 1s.3d. Girl with onion crop.

1963. Second Anniv of Independence. Stamps of 1956 surch **2ND YEAR OF INDEPENDENCE PROGRESS DEVELOPMENT 1963** and value (except 2s.6d.). Centres in black. (a) Postage.

257		3d. on ½d. lilac	40	10
258		4d. on 1½d. blue	15	10
259		6d. on ½d. lilac	30	10
260		10d. on 3d. blue	50	10
261		1s.6d. on 3d. blue	30	20
262		3s.6d. on 3d. blue	40	20

(b) Air. Optd **AIR MAIL** in addition.

263		7d. on 1½d. blue	20	10
264		1s.3d. on 1½d. blue	20	10
265		2s.6d. brown	2·50	40
266		3s. on 3d. blue	40	20
267		6s. on 3d. blue	1·00	20
268		11s. on 10s. mauve	2·75	3·00
269		11s. on £1 orange	£750	£250

75 Centenary Emblem

1963. Centenary of Red Cross.

270	**75**	3d. red and violet	50	10
271	-	6d. red and black	50	15
272	-	1s.3d. red and green	65	20

DESIGNS: 6d. Red Cross emblem; 1s.3d. As T **75** but with lined background and value on left.

1963. Postal Commemorations. (a) Postage. Optd or surch **1853–1859–1963 Oldest Postal Service Newest G.P.O. in West Africa** and value.

273		3d. (No. 214)	10	10
274		4d. on 1½d. (No. 212)	10	10
275		9d. on 1½d. (No. 212)	10	10
276		1s. on 1s.3d. (No. 231)	10	10
277	**32**	1s.6d. on ½d	15	10
278	-	2s. on 3d. (No. 214)	15	10

(b) Air. Optd or surch as above but Postage Stamp instead of Postal Service and **AIRMAIL** in addition.

279	**53**	7d. on 3d.	20	1·00
280	-	1s.3d. (No. 239)	2·00	1·50
281	-	2s.6d. on 4d. (No. 228)	1·25	60
282	**52**	3s. on 3d.	2·50	3·25
283	**55**	6s. on 6d.	1·00	2·25
284	-	£1 (No. 222)	38·00	40·00

Commemoration dates:—
1853—"First Post Office".
1859—"First Postage Stamps".
1963—"Newest G.P.O. in West Africa".

80 Lion Emblem and Map **81** Globe and Map

1964. World's Fair, New York. Imperf. Self-adhesive.

285	**80**	1d. multicoloured (postage)	10	10
286	**80**	3d. multicoloured	10	10
287	**80**	4d. multicoloured	10	10
288	**80**	6d. multicoloured	10	10
289	**80**	1s. multicoloured	15	10
290	**80**	2s. multicoloured	40	30
291	**80**	5s. multicoloured	60	85
292	**81**	7d. multicoloured (air)	10	10
293	**81**	9d. multicoloured	10	10
294	**81**	1s.3d. multicoloured	30	10
295	**81**	2s.6d. multicoloured	40	15
296	**81**	3s.6d. multicoloured	40	25
297	**81**	6s. multicoloured	65	85
298	**81**	11s. multicoloured	80	1·75

WARNING:—These self-adhesive stamps should be kept mint on their backing paper and used on cover or piece.

82 Inscription and Map **83** Pres. Kennedy and Map

1964. President Kennedy Memorial Issue. Imperf. Self-adhesive.

299	**82**	1d. multicoloured (postage)	10	10
300	**82**	3d. multicoloured	10	10
301	**82**	4d. multicoloured	10	10
302	**82**	6d. multicoloured	10	10
303	**82**	1s. multicoloured	15	10
304	**82**	2s. multicoloured	40	1·25
305	**82**	5s. multicoloured	60	2·25
306	**83**	7d. multicoloured (air)	10	10
307	**83**	9d. multicoloured	10	10
308	**83**	1s.3d. multicoloured	25	10
309	**83**	2s.6d. multicoloured	40	40
310	**83**	3s.6d. multicoloured	40	55
311	**83**	6s. multicoloured	65	1·75
312	**83**	11s. multicoloured	80	3·00

The note below No. 298 applies also to the above issue.

1964. Decimal Currency. Various stamps surch. (i) First issue. Surch in figures. (a) Postage.

313	-	1c. on 6d. (No. 248)	10	10
314	**53**	2c. on 3d. (No. 236)	10	10
315	-	3c. on 3d. (No. 246)	10	10
316	-	5c. on ½d. (No. 223)	10	10
317	**71**	8c. on 3d. (No. 255)	15	10
318	-	10c. on 1s.3d. (No. 250)	15	10
319	-	15c. on 1s. (No. 249)	50	10
320	**55**	25c. on 6d. (No. 238)	30	25
321	**46**	50c. on 2s.6d. (No. 232)	2·50	1·50

(b) Air. Nos. 322/5 additonally optd **AIRMAIL**.

322	-	7c. on 1s.3d. (No. 256)	15	10
323	-	20c. on 4d. (No. 228)	25	20
324	-	30c. on 10s. (No. 234)	40	45
325	-	40c. on 5s. (No. 233)	50	60
326	**83**	1l. on 1s.3d. (No. 308)	75	2·00
327	**83**	2l. on 11s. (No. 312)	1·25	3·50

(ii) Second issue. Surch in figures or figures and words (Nos. 332/3).

328	-	1c. on 3d. (No. 227) (postage)	10	10
329	**82**	2c. on 1d. (No. 299)	10	10
330	**82**	4c. on 3d. (No. 300)	10	10
331	-	5c. on 2d. (No. 245)	10	10
332	-	1l. on 5s. (No. 252)	1·75	3·50
333	-	2l. on £1 (No. 235)	4·00	5·50
334	**83**	7c. on 7d. (No. 306) (air)	15	10
335	**83**	60c. on 9d. (Nos. 307)	1·00	1·50

(iii) Third issue. Surch in figures.

336	-	1c. on 1½d. (No. 225) (postage)	10	20
337	**82**	2c. on 3d. (No. 300)	10	25
338	**80**	2c. on 4d. (No. 287)	10	25
339	-	3c. on 1d. (No. 243)	10	25
340	-	3c. on 2d. (No. 226)	10	25
341	-	5c. on 1s.3d. (No. 231)	10	10
342	**82**	15c. on 6d. (No. 302)	1·00	50
343	**82**	15c. on 1s. (No. 303)	1·50	90
344	-	20c. on 6d. (No. 229)	40	15
345	-	25c. on 6d. (No. 248)	45	20
346	-	50c. on 3d. (No. 227)	1·25	70
347	**80**	60c. on 5s. (No. 291)	4·25	2·50
348	**82**	1l. on 4d. (No. 301)	4·50	5·50
349	-	2l. on £1 (No. 235)	14·00	14·00
350	**81**	7c. on 9d. (air)	25	10

(iv) Fourth issue. Surch in figures.

351	**80**	1c. on 6d. (postage)	3·25	8·50
352	**80**	1c. on 2s.	3·25	8·50
353	**82**	1c. on 2s.	3·25	8·50
354	**82**	1c. on 5s.	3·25	8·50
355	**81**	2c. on 1s.3d. (air)	3·25	8·50
356	**83**	2c. on 1s.3d.	3·25	8·50
357	**83**	2c. on 3s.6d.	3·25	8·50
358	**81**	3c. on 7d.	3·25	8·50
359	**83**	3c. on 9d.	3·25	8·50
360	**81**	5c. on 2s.6d.	3·25	8·50
361	**83**	5c. on 2s.6d.	3·25	8·50
362	**81**	5c. on 3s.6d.	3·25	8·50
363	**81**	5c. on 6s.	3·25	8·50
364	**83**	5c. on 6s.	3·25	8·50

(v) Fifth issue. No. 374 further surch **TWO Leones**.

365		2l. on 30c. on 6d. (air)	2·50	2·00

91 Margai and Churchill

1965. Sir Milton Margai and Sir Winston Churchill Commem. Flower stamps of 1963 surch as T **91** on horiz designs or with individual portraits on vert designs as indicated. Multicoloured. (a) Postage.

366	2c. on 1d.	65	30
367	3c. on 3d. Margai	10	20
368	10c. on 1s. Churchill	1·50	20
369	20c. on 1s.3d.	1·60	20
370	50c. on 4d. Margai	90	45
371	75c. on 5s. Churchill	4·50	1·25

(b) Air. Additionally optd **AIRMAIL**.

372	-	7c. on 2d.	1·25	20
373	**58**	15c. on ½d. Margai	45	20
374	-	30c. on 6d.	2·50	35
375	-	1l. on £1	6·50	1·50
376	-	2l. on 10s. Churchill	13·00	5·50

92 Cola Plant and Nut

1965. Various shapes, backed with paper bearing advertisements. Imperf. Self-adhesive. A. Printed in green, yellow and red on silver foil. Values in colours given.

377	**92**	1c. green (postage)	25	10
378	**92**	2c. red	25	10
379	**92**	3c. yellow	25	10
380	**92**	4c. silver on green	30	10
381	**92**	5c. silver on red	30	10

B. Designs 45×49 mm showing Arms of Sierra Leone.

382	20c. mult on cream (postage)	2·25	60
383	50c. multicoloured on cream	4·00	4·00
384	40c. mult on cream (air)	4·00	4·00

C. Designs 48×44½ mm showing inscription and necklace.

385	7c. multicoloured (air)	80	15
386	15c. multicoloured	1·50	90

1966. Fifth Anniv of Independence. Surch **FIVE YEARS INDEPENDENCE 1961-1966** and value. (a) Postage.

387	1c. on 6d. (No. 248)	10	20
388	2c. on 4d. (No. 247)	10	20
389	3c. on 1½d. (No. 212)	10	20
390	8c. on 1s. (No. 249)	1·00	20
391	10c. on 2s.6d. (No. 251)	25	10
392	20c. on 2d. (No. 213)	40	10

(b) Air. Surch **AIRMAIL** also.

393	**75**	7c. on 3d.	25	10
394	-	15c. on 1s. (No. 249)	1·50	20
395	-	25c. on 2s.6d. (No. 251)	75	60
396	-	50c. on 1½d. (No. 244)	1·75	1·50
397	-	1l. on 4d. (No. 247)	2·00	2·75

97 Lion's Head

1966. First Sierra Leone Gold Coinage Commem. Circular designs, embossed on gold foil, backed with paper bearing advertisements. Imperf. (a) Postage. (i) ¼ golde coin. Diameter 1½ in.

398	**97**	2c. mauve and orange	10	10
399	-	3c. green and purple	10	10

(ii) ½ golde coin. Diameter 218in.

400	**97**	5c. red and blue	10	10
401	-	8c. turquoise and black	20	20

(iii) 1 golde coin. Diameter 3¼ in.

402	**97**	25c. violet and green	40	35
403	-	1l. orange and red	2·75	3·25

(b) Air. (i) ¼ golde coin. Diameter 1½ in.

404	**97**	7c. orange and red	15	10
405	-	30c. purple and black	20	25

(ii) ½ golde coin. Diameter 218in.

406	**97**	15c. orange and red	35	35
407	-	30c. purple and black	50	60

(iii) 1 golde coin. Diameter 3¼ in.

408	**97**	50c. green and purple	1·00	1·00
409	-	2l. black and green	4·00	4·50

DESIGN: Nos. 399, 401, 403, 405, 407 and 409, Map of Sierra Leone.

1967. Decimal Currency Provisionals. Nos. 347/8, 369/71 and 383/4 surch.

410	6½c. on 75c. on 5s. (postage)	50	25
411	7½c. on 75c. on 5s.	50	25
412	9½c. on 50c. on 4d.	35	25
413	12½c. on 20c. on 1s.3d.	65	35
414	17½c. on 50c. on 1l. on 4d.	2·25	3·00
415	17½c. on 1l. on 4d.	2·25	3·00
416	18½c. on 1l. on 4d.	2·25	3·00
417	18½c. on 60c. on 5s.	6·00	8·50
418	25c. on 50c.	1·00	1·25
419	11½c. on 40c. (air)	45	40
420	25c. on 40c.	1·00	1·25

1967. Decimal Currency. Imperf. Self-adhesive. As T **92**, but embossed on white paper, backed with paper bearing advertisements. Background colours given first, and value tablet colours in brackets.

421	**92**	½c. red (red on white)	10	50
422	**92**	1c. red (red on white)	15	20

423	**92**	1½c. yellow (green on white)	20	30
424	**92**	2c. red (green on white)	35	10
425	**92**	2½c. green (yellow on white)	60	60
426	**92**	3c. red (white on red)	35	10
427	**92**	3½c. purple (white on green)	60	60
428	**92**	4c. red (white on green)	60	15
429	**92**	4½c. green (green on white)	60	60
430	**92**	5c. red (yellow on white)	60	15
431	**92**	5½c. red (green on white)	60	90

102 Eagle

1967. T **102** embossed on black paper, backed with paper bearing advertisements, or as No. 382 also with advertisements (No. 433/b).

432	**102**	9½c. red and gold on black	8·00	1·00
432a	**102**	9½c. blue & gold on black	9·50	9·50
433	-	10c. mult (red frame)	80	80
433b	-	10c. mult (black frame)	10·00	10·00
434	**102**	15c. green & gold on black	1·25	1·25
434a	**102**	15c. red and gold on black	11·00	11·00

See also Nos. 538/44.

1968. No advertisements on back and colours in value tablet reversed. Background colours given first, and value tablet colours in brackets.

435	**92**	½c. red (white on green)	10	50
436	**92**	1c. red (white on red)	20	50
437	**92**	2c. red (white on green)	6·00	7·50
438	**92**	2½c. green (white on yellow)	6·50	8·00
439	**92**	3c. red (red on white)	3·00	1·00

On Nos. 435 and 438 the figure "½" is larger than on Nos. 421 and 425.

1968. No advertisements on back, colours changed and new value (7c.). Background colours given.

440	2c. pink (postage)	2·75	2·75
441	2½c. green	2·75	2·75
442	3½c. yellow	3·00	3·50
442a	7c. yellow (air)	9·00	4·00

On Nos. 441/2 the fraction "½" is larger than on Nos. 425 and 427.

103 Outline Map of Africa

1968. Human Rights Year. Each value comes in six types showing the following territories: Portuguese Guinea; South Africa; Mozambique; Rhodesia; South West Africa and Angola. Imperf. Self-adhesive.

443	**103**	½c. multicoloured (postage)	10	10
444	**103**	2c. multicoloured	10	10
445	**103**	2½c. multicoloured	10	10
446	**103**	3½c. multicoloured	10	10
447	**103**	10c. multicoloured	25	15
448	**103**	11½c. multicoloured	30	20
449	**103**	15c. multicoloured	40	25
450	**103**	7½c. multicoloured (air)	25	15
451	**103**	9½c. multicoloured	30	20
452	**103**	14½c. multicoloured	40	25
453	**103**	18½c. multicoloured	50	30
454	**103**	25c. multicoloured	60	40
455	**103**	1l. multicoloured	3·25	5·50
456	**103**	2l. multicoloured	9·00	12·00

Nos. 443/56 were issued in sheets of 30 (6×5) on backing paper depicting diamonds or the coat-of-arms on the reverse. The six types occur once in each horiz row.

1968. Mexico Olympics Participation. Nos. 383/4 optd **OLYMPIC PARTICIPATION MEXICO 1968** or surch also.

457	6½c. on 50c. mult (postage)	40	30
458	17½c. on 50c. multicoloured	45	35
459	22½c. on 50c. multicoloured	65	50
460	28½c. on 50c. multicoloured	85	1·50
461	50c. multicoloured	1·25	2·50
462	6½c. on 40c. mult (air)	45	30
463	17½c. on 40c. multicoloured	55	35
464	22½c. on 40c. multicoloured	70	50
465	28½c. on 40c. multicoloured	85	1·50
466	40c. multicoloured	1·25	2·50

105 1859 6d. Stamp

111 1965 15c. Self-adhesive

1969. Fifth Anniv of World's First Self-adhesive Postage Stamps. Multicoloured. Self-adhesive. Imperf.

467	1c. Type **105** (postage)	10	10
468	2c. 1965 2c. self-adhesive	10	10
469	3½c. 1961 Independence £1	10	10
470	5c. 1965 20c. self-adhesive	10	10
471	12½c. 1948 Royal Silver Wedding £1	30	15
472	1l. 1923 £2	2·50	1·50
473	7½c. Type **111** (air)	20	10
474	9½c. 1967 9½c. self-adhesive	20	10
475	20c. 1964 1s.3d. self-adhesive	40	25
476	30c. 1964 President Kennedy Memorial 6s. self-adhesive	55	35
477	50c. 1933 Centenary of Abolition of Slavery £1	1·50	75
478	2l. 1963 2nd Anniv of Independence 11s.	9·00	8·00

DESIGNS—As Type **105**, Nos. 468/72; As Type **111**, Nos. 474/8.

All values are on white backing paper with advertisement printed on the reverse.

117 Ore Carrier, Globe and Flags of Sierra Leone and Japan

118 Ore Carrier, Map of Europe and Africa and Flags of Sierra Leone and Netherlands

1969. Pepel Port Improvements. Imperf. Self-adhesive, backed with paper bearing advertisements.

479	**117**	1c. multicoloured (postage)	20	10
480	**118**	2c. multicoloured	30	10
481	-	3½c. multicoloured	35	10
482	-	10c. multicoloured	55	10
483	**118**	18½c. multicoloured	85	25
484	-	50c. multicoloured	1·50	1·00
485	**117**	7½c. multicoloured (air)	70	10
486	-	9½c. multicoloured	70	10
487	**117**	15c. multicoloured	80	25
488	**118**	25c. multicoloured	1·00	35
489	-	1l. multicoloured	2·00	2·00
490	-	2l. multicoloured	2·50	4·50

The 3½, 9½c., 2l., 10, 50c., 1l. show respectively the flags of Great Britain and West Germany instead of the Netherlands.

119 African Development Bank Emblem

1969. Fifth Anniv of African Development Bank. Imperf. Self-adhesive, backed with paper bearing advertisements.

491	**119**	3½c. green, gold and black (postage)	25	40
492	**119**	9½c. violet, gold & grn (air)	35	70

120 Boy Scouts Emblem in "Diamond"

1969. Boy Scouts Diamond Jubilee. Imperf. Self-adhesive.

493	**120**	1c. multicoloured (postage)	10	10
494	**120**	2c. multicoloured	10	10
495	**120**	3½c. multicoloured	15	10
496	**120**	4½c. multicoloured	15	15
497	**120**	5c. multicoloured	15	15
498	**120**	75c. multicoloured	5·50	2·75
499	-	7½c. multicoloured (air)	35	20
500	-	9½c. multicoloured	45	25
501	-	15c. multicoloured	70	50
502	-	22c. multicoloured	90	70
503	-	55c. multicoloured	4·00	2·00
504	-	3l. multicoloured	50·00	38·00

DESIGN—OCTAGONAL (65×51 mm): Nos. 499/504, Scout saluting, Baden-Powell and badge.

1970. Air. No. 443 surch **AIRMAIL** twice and new value.

505	**103**	7½c. on ½c. multicoloured	60	20
506	**103**	9½c. on ½c. multicoloured	60	20
507	**103**	15c. on ½c. multicoloured	1·00	40
508	**103**	28c. on ½c. multicoloured	1·50	75
509	**103**	40c. on ½c. multicoloured	2·00	2·00
510	**103**	2l. on ½c. multicoloured	7·50	18·00

122 Expo Symbol and Maps of Sierra Leone and Japan

1970. World Fair, Osaka. Imperf. Self-adhesive.

511	**122**	2c. multicoloured (postage)	10	10
512	**122**	3½c. multicoloured	15	10
513	**122**	10c. multicoloured	25	10
514	**122**	12½c. multicoloured	25	10
515	**122**	20c. multicoloured	30	10
516	**122**	45c. multicoloured	60	45
517	-	7½c. multicoloured (air)	20	10
518	-	9½c. multicoloured	25	10
519	-	15c. multicoloured	30	10
520	-	25c. multicoloured	55	20
521	-	50c. multicoloured	75	50
522	-	3l. multicoloured	2·00	5·50

DESIGN—CHRYSANTHEMUM (43×42 mm): Nos. 517/22, Maps of Sierra Leone and Japan.

123 Diamond **124** Palm Nut

1970. Imperf. Self-adhesive.

523	**123**	1c. multicoloured	55	40
524	**123**	1½c. multicoloured	55	40
525	**123**	2c. multicoloured	55	10
526	**123**	2½c. multicoloured	55	10
527	**123**	3c. multicoloured	65	10
528	**123**	3½c. multicoloured	65	10
529	**123**	4c. multicoloured	70	10
530	**123**	5c. multicoloured	80	20
531	**124**	6c. multicoloured	50	20
532	**124**	7c. multicoloured	55	20
533	**124**	8½c. multicoloured	70	25
534	**124**	9c. multicoloured	70	25
535	**124**	10c. multicoloured	75	25
536	**124**	11½c. multicoloured	1·25	30
537	**124**	18½c. multicoloured	2·25	85

1970. Air. As T **102**, but on white paper.

538	**102**	7½c. gold and red	60	10
539	**102**	9½c. silver and green	70	10
540	**102**	15c. silver and blue	2·00	20
541	**102**	25c. gold and purple	3·00	50
542	**102**	50c. green and orange	6·50	3·50
543	**102**	1l. blue and silver	13·00	16·00
544	**102**	2l. blue and gold	20·00	32·00

126 Jewellery Box and Sewa Diadem

1970. Diamond Industry. Imperf. Self-adhesive.

545	**126**	2c. multicoloured (postage)	45	20
546	**126**	3½c. multicoloured	45	20
547	**126**	10c. multicoloured	70	20
548	**126**	12½c. multicoloured	1·00	30
549	**126**	40c. multicoloured	2·50	1·25
550	**126**	1l. multicoloured	12·00	11·00
551	-	7½c. multicoloured (air)	75	20
552	-	9½c. multicoloured	85	20
553	**126**	15c. multicoloured	1·50	35
554	-	25c. multicoloured	2·00	60
555	-	75c. multicoloured	7·00	6·00
556	-	2l. multicoloured	27·00	27·00

DESIGN—HORIZ (63×61 mm): Nos. 551/6, Diamond and curtain.

127 "Traffic Changeover"

1971. Changeover to Driving on the Right of the Road. Imperf. Self-adhesive.

557	**127**	3½c. orange, blue and black (postage)	1·50	1·00
558	**127**	9½c. blue, orge & blk (air)	2·00	2·50

1971. Air. Various stamps surch **AIRMAIL** and value (Nos. 559/61) or value only (Nos. 562/3).

559	10c. on 2d. (No. 226)	40	20
560	20c. on 1s. (No. 230)	70	45
561	50c. on 1d. (No. 243)	1·25	1·50
562	70c. on 30c. (No. 476)	2·00	4·00
563	1l. on 30c. (No. 476)	3·00	5·00

129 Flag and Lion's Head

1971. Tenth Anniv of Independence. Imperf. Self-adhesive.

564	**129**	2c. multicoloured (postage)	15	10
565	**129**	3½c. multicoloured	15	10
566	**129**	10c. multicoloured	25	10
567	**129**	12½c. multicoloured	35	10
568	**129**	40c. multicoloured	1·10	40
569	**129**	1l. multicoloured	1·90	2·50
570	-	7½c. multicoloured (air)	15	10
571	-	9½c. multicoloured	15	10
572	-	15c. multicoloured	25	10
573	-	25c. multicoloured	35	35
574	-	75c. multicoloured	1·10	1·50
575	-	2l. multicoloured	3·00	6·50

DESIGN—"Map" shaped as Type **129**: Nos. 570/5, Bugles and lion's head.

130 Pres. Siaka Stevens

1972. Multicoloured. Background colour given.

576	**130**	1c. lilac	10	10
577	**130**	2c. lavender	10	10
578	**130**	4c. blue	10	10
579	**130**	5c. brown	10	10
580	**130**	7c. pink	15	10
581	**130**	10c. brown	15	10
582	**130**	15c. green	25	15
583	**130**	18c. yellow	25	15
584	**130**	20c. blue	30	15
585	**130**	25c. orange	35	15
586	**130**	50c. green	1·00	55
587	**130**	1l. mauve	1·50	1·00
588	**130**	2l. pink	2·25	3·50
589	**130**	5l. cream	3·75	8·50

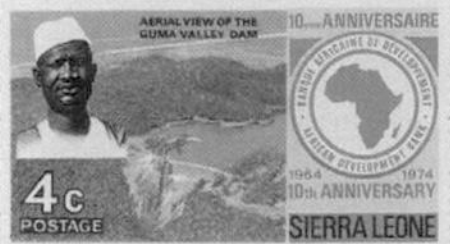

131 Guma Valley Dam and Bank Emblem

1975. Tenth Anniv of African Development Bank.

590	**131**	4c. multicoloured (postage)	60·00	28·00
591	**131**	15c. multicoloured (air)	1·00	80

132 Opening Ceremony

1975. New Congo Bridge Opening and 70th Birthday of President Stevens.

592	**132**	5c. multicoloured (postage)	1·60	85
593	**132**	20c. multicoloured (air)	40	25

133 Presidents Tolbert and Stevens, and Handclasp

1975. First Anniv of Mano River Union.

594	**133**	4c. multicoloured (postage)	30	40
595	**133**	15c. multicoloured (air)	20	20

134 "Quaid-i-Azam" (Mohammed Ali Jinnah)

1977. Birth Centenary of Mohammed Ali Jinnah (Quaid-i-Azam).

596	**134**	30c. multicoloured	1·25	30

135 Queen Elizabeth II

1977. Silver Jubilee.

597	**135**	5c. multicoloured	10	10
598	**135**	1l. multicoloured	65	80

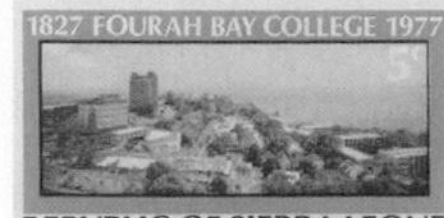

136 College Buildings

1977. 150th Anniv of Fourah Bay College. Multicoloured.

599	5c. Type **136**	10	10
600	20c. The old college (vert)	35	60

137 St. Edward's Crown and Sceptres

1978. 25th Anniv of Coronation. Multicoloured.

601	5c. Type **137**	10	10
602	50c. Queen Elizabeth II in Coronation Coach	20	40
603	1l. Queen Elizabeth II and Prince Philip	35	60

138 "Myrina silenus"

1979. Butterflies (1st series). Multicoloured.

604	5c. Type **138**	10	10
605	15c. "Papilio nireus"	25	15
606	25c. "Catacroptera cloanthe"	40	15
607	1l. "Druryia antimachus"	1·00	1·50

See also Nos. 646/9.

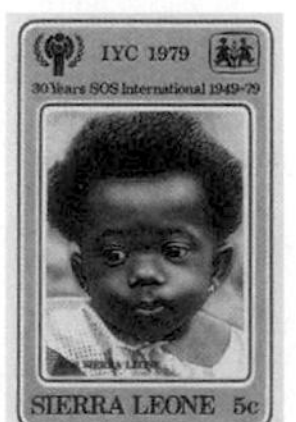

139 Young Child's Face

1979. International Year of the Child. 30th Anniv of S.O.S. International. Multicoloured.

608	5c. Type **139**	10	10
609	27c. Young child with baby	20	25
610	1l. Mother with young child	50	1·10
MS611	114×84 mm. No. 610	75	1·75

140 Presidents Stevens (Sierra Leone) and Tolbert (Liberia), Dove with Letter and Bridge

1979. Fifth Anniv of Mano River Union and 1st Anniv of Postal Union.

612	**140**	5c. brown, orange & yellow	10	10
613	**140**	22c. brown, yellow & violet	10	15
614	**140**	27c. brown, blue & orange	10	15
615	**140**	35c. brown, green and red	15	20
616	**140**	1l. brown, violet and blue	50	1·00
MS617		144×73 mm. No. 616	55	1·00

141 Great Britain 1848 10d. Stamp

1979. Death Centenary of Sir Rowland Hill.

618	**141**	10c. black, brown and blue	15	10
619	-	15c. black, brown and blue	25	15
620	-	50c. black, red and yellow	60	70
MS621		90×99 mm. 1l. black, red and pink	60	80

DESIGNS: 15c. 1872 4d. stamp; 50c. 1961 £1 Independence commemorative; 1l. 1912 £1.

142 Green Turaco ("Sierra Leone Turaco")

1980. Birds. Multicoloured.

622B	1c. Type **142**	30	1·75
623B	2c. Olive-bellied sunbird ("Sierra Leone Olive-billed Sunbird")	40	1·75
624B	3c. Western black-headed oriole ("Sierra Leone Black-headed Oriole")	40	1·75
625B	5c. Spur-winged goose	40	75
626A	7c. Didric cuckoo ("White-bellied Didric Cuckoo")	1·25	60
627B	10c. Grey parrot ("Sierra Leone Grey Parrot") (vert)	40	80
628B	15c. Indian Blue quail ("African Blue Quail") (vert)	50	2·00
629B	20c. African wood owl ("West African Wood Owl") (vert)	50	2·25
630B	30c. Greater blue turaco ("Blue Plantain eater") (vert)	50	2·25
631B	40c. Blue-breasted kingfisher ("Nigerian Blue-breasted kingfisher") (vert)	60	2·50
632B	50c. African black crake ("Black Crake") (vert)	60	2·50
633A	1l. Hartlaub's duck	1·40	2·50
634A	2l. Black bee eater	2·00	4·00
635B	5l. Denham's Bustard	1·00	11·00

143 Paul P. Harris (founder), President Stevens of Sierra Leone and Rotary Emblem

1980. 75th Anniv of Rotary International.

636	**143**	5c. multicoloured	10	10
637	**143**	27c. multicoloured	10	10
638	**143**	50c. multicoloured	20	25
639	**143**	1l. multicoloured	40	55

144 "Maria", 1844

1980. "London 1980" Int Stamp Exhibition. Multicoloured.

640	6c. Type **144**	30	10
641	31c. "Tarquah", 1902	40	35
642	50c. "Aureol", 1951	50	70
643	1l. "Africa Palm", 1974	60	1·60

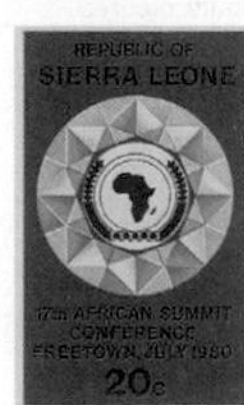

145 Organization for African Unity Emblem

1980. African Summit Conference, Freetown.

644	**145**	20c. black, blue and purple	10	10
645	**145**	1l. black, purple and blue	45	45

146 "Graphium policenes"

1980. Butterflies (2nd series). Multicoloured.

646	5c. Type **146**	10	10
647	27c. "Charaxes varanes"	25	15
648	35c. "Charaxes brutus"	25	25
649	1l. "Euphaedra zaddachi"	75	1·40

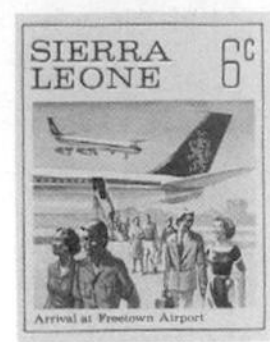

147 Arrival at Freetown Airport

1980. Tourism. Multicoloured.

650	6c. Type **147**	10	10
651	26c. Welcome to tourists	10	20
652	31c. Freetown cotton tree	10	25
653	40c. Beinkongo Falls	20	30
654	50c. Sports facilities	20	40
655	1l. African elephant	1·10	95

148 Servals

1981. Wild Cats. Multicoloured.

656	6c. Type **148**	35	10
657	6c. Serval cubs	35	10
658	31c. African golden cats	60	30
659	31c. African golden cat cubs	60	30
660	50c. Leopards	75	45
661	50c. Leopard cubs	75	45
662	1l. Lions	1·00	80
663	1l. Lion cubs	1·00	80

The two designs of each value were printed together, *se-tenant*, in horizontal pairs, forming composite designs.

149 Soldiers (Defence)

1981. 20th Anniv of Independence and Tenth Anniv of Republic. National Services. Multicoloured.

664	6c. Type **149**	65	10
665	31c. Nurses administering first aid, and ambulance (Health) (horiz)	1·75	30
666	40c. Traffic (Police Force)	3·00	1·00
667	1l. Patrol boat (Coastguard) (horiz)	3·25	3·00

150 Wedding Bouquet from Sierra Leone

1981. Royal Wedding (1st issue). Multicoloured.

668	31c. Type **150**	10	10
669	45c. Prince Charles as helicopter pilot	15	20
670	1l. Prince Charles and Lady Diana Spencer	20	90

151 Sandringham

1981. Royal Wedding (2nd issue). Multicoloured.

671	35c. Type **151**	10	15
672	60c. Prince Charles in outdoor clothes	15	25
673	1l.50 Prince Charles and Lady Diana Spencer	25	90

MS674 96×83 mm. 3l. Royal landau 65 65
675 70c. Type **151** 75 90
676 1l.30 As 60c. 75 90
677 2l. As 1l.50 1·50 2·00

152 "Physical Recreation"

1981. 25th Anniv of Duke of Edinburgh Award Scheme and President's Award Scheme Publicity. Multicoloured.
678 6c. Type **152** 10 10
679 31c. "Community service" 15 10
680 1l. Duke of Edinburgh 30 40
681 1l. President Siaka Stevens 30 40

153 Pineapples

1981. World Food Day. Multicoloured.
682 6c. Type **153** 10 10
683 31c. Ground nuts 15 10
684 50c. Cassava fruits 20 15
685 1l. Rice plants 50 50

154 Groundnut

1981. World Food Day (2nd issue). Agricultural Industry. Multicoloured.
686 6c. Type **154** 10 10
687 31c. Cassava 25 10
688 50c. Rice 40 25
689 1l. Pineapples 65 70

155 Scouts with Cattle

1982. 75th Anniv of Boy Scout Movement. Multicoloured.
690 20c. Type **155** 25 10
691 50c. Scouts picking flowers 50 40
692 1l. Lord Baden-Powell 90 1·00
693 2l. Scouts fishing 1·90 2·00
MS694 101×70 mm. 3l. Scouts raising flag 1·75 3·25

1982. Nos. 668/74 surch.
695 50c. on 31c. Type **150** 1·00 70
696 50c. on 35c. Type **151** 1·00 70
697 50c. on 45c. Prince Charles as helicopter pilot 1·00 70
698 50c. on 60c. Prince Charles in outdoor clothes 1·00 70
699 90c. on 1l. Prince Charles and Lady Diana Spencer 2·00 85
699a 1l.30 on 60c. Prince Charles in outdoor clothes 2·25 2·75
699b 2l. on 35c. Type **151** 3·25 3·75
700 2l. on 1l.50 Prince Charles and Lady Diana Spencer 1·75 2·00
700a 8l. on 1l.50 Prince Charles and Lady Diana Spencer 11·00 13·00
MS701 95×83 mm. 3l.50 on 3l. Royal landau 1·00 1·00

157 Heading

1982. World Cup Football Championship, Spain. Multicoloured.
702 20c. Type **157** 45 15
703 30c. Dribbling 70 20
704 1l. Tackling 2·25 2·50
705 2l. Goalkeeping 3·50 4·25
MS706 92×75 mm. 3l. Shooting 4·75 3·00

158 Prince and Princess of Wales

1982. 21st Birthday of Princess of Wales. Multicoloured.
707 31c. Caernarvon Castle 20 15
708 50c. Type **158** 40 15
709 2l. Princess of Wales 2·50 80
MS710 103×75 mm. 3l. Princess of Wales (different) 1·40 1·00

1982. Birth of Prince William of Wales. Nos. 707/9 optd **ROYAL BABY 21.6.82.**
711 31c. Caernarvon Castle 15 15
712 50c. Type **158** 30 15
713 2l. Princess of Wales 1·00 80
MS714 103×75 mm. 3l. Princess of Wales (different) 1·25 1·00

159 Washington with Troops

1982. 250th Birth Anniv of George Washington. Multicoloured.
715 6c. Type **159** 10 10
716 31c. Portrait of Washington (vert) 20 20
717 50c. Washington with horse 35 35
718 1l. Washington standing on battlefield (vert) 65 80
MS719 103×71 mm. 2l. Washington at home 75 1·25

160 Temptation of Christ

1982. Christmas. Stained-glass Windows. Multicoloured.
720 6c. Type **160** 10 10
721 31c. Baptism of Christ 15 20
722 50c. Annunciation 20 40
723 1l. Nativity 55 90
MS724 74×104 mm. 2l. Mary and Joseph 70 1·10

1982. World Cup Football Championship Winners. Nos. 702/5 optd **WORLD CUP WINNERS ITALY (3) vs. W. GERMANY (1).**
725 20c. Type **157** 30 20
726 30c. Dribbling 30 30
727 1l. Tackling 80 75
728 2l. Goalkeeping 1·25 1·75
MS729 91×75 mm. 3l. Shooting 1·00 2·00

162 Long Snouted Crocodile

1982. Death Cent of Charles Darwin. Multicoloured.
730 6c. Type **162** 1·50 20
731 31c. Rainbow lizard 2·25 75
732 50c. River turtle 2·75 2·50
733 1l. Chameleon 3·75 6·00
MS734 90×70 mm. 2l. Royal python (vert) 1·75 3·00

163 Diogenes

1983. 500th Birth Anniv of Raphael. Details from painting "The School of Athens". Multicoloured.
735 6c. Type **163** 20 10
736 31c. Euclid, Ptolemy, Zoroaster, Raphael and Sodoma 40 30
737 50c. Euclid and his pupils 55 45
738 2l. Pythagoras, Francesco Maria della Rovere and Heraclitus 1·25 1·40
MS739 101×126 mm. 3l. Plato and Aristolle (vert) 1·50 2·00

164 Agricultural Training

1983. Commonwealth Day. Multicoloured.
740 6c. Type **164** 10 10
741 10c. Tourism development 10 10
742 50c. Broadcasting training 45 45
743 1l. Airport services 1·50 1·25

165 Map of Africa and Flag of Sierra Leone

1983. 25th Anniv of Economic Commission for Africa.
744 **165** 1l. multicoloured 80 1·10

166 Chimpanzees in Tree

1983. Endangered Species. Multicoloured.
745 6c. Type **166** 1·50 20
746 10c. Three chimpanzees (vert) 1·75 30
747 31c. Chimpanzees swinging in tree (vert) 3·25 90
748 60c. Group of chimpanzees 5·50 7·50
MS749 115×80 mm. 3l. African elephant 3·00 2·25

167 Traditional Communications

1983. World Communications Year. Multicoloured.
750 6c. Type **167** 10 10
751 10c. Mail via Mano River 15 10
752 20c. Satellite ground station 15 10
753 1l. British packet, c. 1805 90 65
MS754 115×85 mm. 2l. Telecommunications 80 1·25

168 Montgolfier Balloon, Paris, 1783

1983. Bicentenary of Manned Flight. Multicoloured.
755 6c. Type **168** 35 10
756 20c. Wolfert's airship "Deutschland", Berlin, 1879 (horiz) 1·00 30
757 50c. Amundsen's airship N.1 "Norge", North Pole, 1926 (horiz) 2·75 2·25
758 1l. "Cap Sierra" sport balloon, Freetown, 1983 2·25 3·00

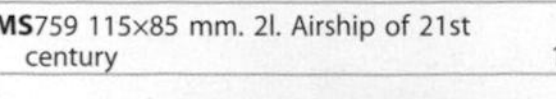

MS759 115×85 mm. 2l. Airship of 21st century 1·00 1·75

169 Mickey Mouse

1983. Space Ark Fantasy. Walt Disney Cartoon Characters. Multicoloured.
774 1c. Type **169** 10 10
775 1c. Huey, Dewey and Louie 10 10
776 3c. Goofy in spaceship 10 10
777 3c. Donald Duck 10 10
778 10c. Ludwig von Drake 10 10
779 10c. Goofy 10 10
780 2l. Mickey Mouse and Giraffe in spaceship 1·00 1·25
781 3l. Donald Duck floating in space 1·25 1·75
MS782 140×116 mm. 5l. Mickey Mouse leaving spaceship 3·00 3·50

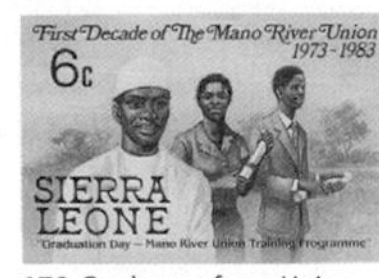

170 Graduates from Union Training Programme

1984. Tenth Anniv of Mano River Union. Multicoloured.
783 6c. Type **170** 10 10
784 25c. Intra-Union trade 10 10
785 31c. Member Presidents on map 10 10
786 41c. Signing ceremony marking Guinea's accession 20 20
MS787 75×113 mm. No. 786 35 90

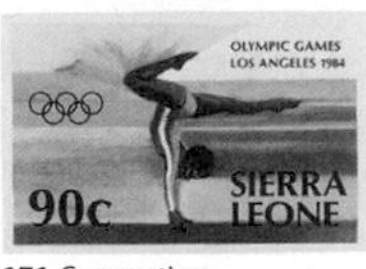

171 Gymnastics

1984. Olympic Games, Los Angeles. Multicoloured.
788 90c. Type **171** 30 40
789 1l. Hurdling 30 40
790 3l. Javelin-throwing 75 1·25
MS791 104×71 mm. 7l. Boxing 1·10 2·00

172 "Apollo 11" Liftoff

1984. 15th Anniv of First Moonwalk. Multicoloured.
792 50c. Type **172** 20 20
793 75c. Lunar module 30 30
794 1l.25 First Moonwalk 45 45
795 2l.50 Lunar exploration 85 85
MS796 99×69 mm. 5l. Family watching Moonwalk on television (horiz) 1·60 2·25

173 Concorde

1984. Universal Postal Union Congress, Hamburg. Multicoloured.
797 4l. Type **173** 3·00 1·75
MS798 100×70 mm. 4l. Heinrich von Stephan (founder of U.P.U.) 1·25 1·75

174 Citroen "Traction Avante"

1984. United Nations Decade of African Transport. Multicoloured.
799 12c. Type **174** 50 20
800 60c. Locomotive 80 45

801 90c. A.C. "Ace" 95 65
802 1l. Vauxhall "Prince Henry" 95 65
803 1l.50 Delahaye "135" 1·00 1·50
804 2l. Mazda "1105" 1·00 1·50
MS805 107×75 mm. 6l. Volkswagen "Beetle" 3·75 4·50

1984. Nos. 625, 627 and 634 surch.
811 25c. on 10c. Grey parrot (vert) 75 85
812 40c. on 10c. Grey parrot (vert) 50 70
813 50c. on 2l. Black bee eater 50 70
814 70c. on 5c. Spur-winged goose 50 70
815 10l. on 5c. Spur-winged goose 2·25 3·50

1984. "Ausipex" International Stamp Exhibition, Melbourne. Nos. 632 and 635 optd **AUSIPEX 84.**
818 50c. African black crake (vert) 1·50 75
819 5l. Denham's bustard 3·50 2·00

177 Portuguese Caravel

1984. History of Shipping. Multicoloured.
820B 2c. Type **177** 55 1·50
821B 5c. "Merlin" of Bristol 55 80
822B 10c. "Golden Hind" 75 70
823A 15c. "Mordaunt" 1·75 90
824B 20c. "Atlantic" (sail transport) 80 60
825B 25c. H.M.S. "Lapwing" (frigate), 1785 80 60
826B 30c. "Traveller" (brig) 80 60
827B 40c. "Amistad" (schooner) 90 60
828B 50c. H.M.S. "Teazer" (gun vessel), 1868 1·00 60
829B 70c. "Scotia" (cable ship) 1·75 2·00
830B 1l. H.M.S. "Alecto" (paddle-steamer), 1882 1·75 2·00
831B 2l. H.M.S. "Blonde" (cruiser), 1889 2·00 3·00
832B 5l. H.M.S. "Fox" (cruiser), 1895 2·75 4·50
833B 10l. "Accra" (liner) 3·25 5·50
833cA 15l. H.M.S. "Favourite" (sloop), 1829 3·00 4·00
833dA 25l. H.M.S. "Euryalus" (screw frigate), 1883 3·00 4·50

Nos. 820/2 and 824/33 come both with and without imprint dates.

178 Mail Runner approaching Mano River Depot, c. 1843

1984. 125th Anniv of First Postage Stamps. Multicoloured.
834 50c. Type **178** 35 15
835 2l. Isaac Fitzjohn, first Postmaster, receiving letters, 1855 1·25 85
836 3l. 1859 packet franked with four 6d. stamps 1·75 1·50
MS837 100×70 mm. 5l. Sierra Leone 1859 6d. purple and Great Britain 1840 Penny Black stamps 1·50 1·60

179 "Madonna and Child" (Pisanello)

1984. Christmas. Madonna and Child Paintings by artists named. Multicoloured.
838 20c. Type **179** 10 10
839 1l. Memling 40 40
840 2l. Raphael 75 90
841 3l. Van der Werff 1·10 1·40
MS842 100×69 mm. 6l. Picasso 2·75 2·75

180 Donald Duck in "The Wise Little Hen"

1984. 50th Birthday of Donald Duck. Walt Disney Cartoon Characters. Multicoloured.
843 1c. Type **180** 10 10
844 2c. Mickey Mouse and Donald Duck in "Boat Builders" 10 10
845 3c. Panchito, Donald Duck and Jose Carioca in "The Three Caballeros" 10 10
846 4c. Donald Duck meeting Pythagoras in "Mathmagic Land" 10 10
847 5c. Donald Duck and nephew in "The Mickey Mouse Club" 10 10
848 10c. Mickey Mouse, Goofy and Donald Duck in "Donald on Parade" 10 10
849 1l. Donald Duck riding donkey in "Don Donald" 1·00 1·00
850 2l. Donald Duck in "Donald Gets Drafted" 2·00 2·00
851 4l. Donald Duck meeting children in Tokyo Disneyland 3·25 3·25
MS852 126×102 mm. 5l. Style sheet for Donald Duck 4·50 2·50

181 Fischer's Whydah

1985. Birth Bicentenary of John J. Audubon (ornithologist). Songbirds of Sierra Leone. Multicoloured.
853 40c. Type **181** 1·75 55
854 90c. Spotted flycatcher 3·00 1·75
855 1l.30 Garden warbler 3·25 3·50
856 3l. Speke's weaver 5·50 7·50
MS857 100×70 mm. 5l. Great grey shrike 3·50 3·00

182 Fishing

1985. International Youth Year. Multicoloured.
858 1l.15 Type **182** 45 55
859 1l.50 Sawing timber 60 75
860 2l.15 Rice farming 75 95
MS861 100×70 mm. 5l. Polishing diamonds 1·75 1·50

183 Eddie Rickenbacker and Spad "XIII", 1918

1985. 40th Anniv of I.C.A.O. Multicoloured.
862 70c. Type **183** 1·50 75
863 1l.25 Samuel P. Langley and "Aerodrome A", 1903 2·00 1·75
864 1l.30 Orville and Wilbur Wright with Wright Flyer I, 1903 2·00 1·75
865 2l. Charles Lindbergh and "Spirit of St. Louis", 1927 2·25 2·75
MS866 100×69 mm. 5l. Sierra Leone Airlines Boeing 707-384C 2·00 1·75

184 "Temptation of Christ" (Botticelli)

1985. Easter. Religious Paintings. Multicoloured.
867 45c. Type **184** 30 15
868 70c. "Christ at the Column" (Velasquez) 55 35
869 1l.55 "Pieta" (Botticelli) (vert) 90 75
870 10l. "Christ on the Cross" (Velasquez) (vert) 4·75 5·00
MS871 106×76 mm. 12l. "Man of Sorrows" (Botticelli) 4·00 4·00

185 The Queen Mother at St. Paul's Cathedral

1985. Life and Times of Queen Elizabeth the Queen Mother. Multicoloured.
872 1l. Type **185** 20 25
873 1l.70 With her racehorse, "Double Star", at Sandown (horiz) 30 40
874 10l. At Covent Garden, 1971 1·75 2·50
MS875 56×85 mm. 12l. With Princess Anne at Ascot 1·75 2·25

1985. 75th Anniv of Girl Guide Movement. Nos. 690/3 surch **75th ANNIVERSARY OF GIRL GUIDES**.
876 70c. on 20c. Type **155** 30 30
877 1l.30 on 50c. Scouts picking flowers 55 55
878 5l. on 1l. Lord Baden-Powell 1·60 1·60
879 7l. on 2l. Scouts fishing 2·25 2·25
MS880 101×70 mm. 15l. on 3l. Scouts raising flag 3·75 4·00

1985. Olympic Gold Medal Winners, Los Angeles. Nos. 788/90 surch.
881 2l. on 90c. Type **171** (surch **Le2 MA YANHONJG CHINA GOLD MEDAL**) 50 55
882 4l. on 1l. Hurdling (surch **Le4 E. MOSES U.S.A. GOLD MEDAL**) 1·00 1·25
883 8l. on 3l. Javelin-throwing (surch **Le8 A. HAERKOENEN FINLAND GOLD MEDAL**) 2·00 2·10
MS884 104×71 mm. 15l. on 7l. Boxing (surch **M. TAYLOR U.S.A. GOLD MEDAL**) 3·25 3·75

188 Chater-Lea (1905) at Hill Station House

1985. Centenary of Motor Cycle and Decade for African Transport. Multicoloured.
885 1l.40 Type **188** 1·00 1·00
886 2l. Honda "XR 350 R" at Queen Elizabeth II Quay, Freetown 1·40 1·40
887 4l. Kawasaki "Vulcan" at Bo Clock Tower 2·50 2·50
888 5l. Harley-Davidson "Electra-Glide" in Makeni village 2·75 2·75
MS889 104×71 mm. 12l. Millet (1893) 4·75 4·25

189a Viola Pomposa

1985. 300th Birth Anniv of Johann Sebastian Bach (composer). Multicoloured (except No. **MS**894).
890 70c. Type **189a** 1·00 25
891 3l. Spinet 2·50 80
892 4l. Lute 2·50 1·10
893 5l. Oboe 2·50 1·40
MS894 103×77 mm. 12l. "Johann Sebastian Bach" (Toby E. Rosenthal) (black) 5·00 3·50

1985. Nos. 707/10 and 711/14 surch.
895 70c. on 3l. Caernarvon Castle (No. 707) 30 30
896 4l. on 50c. Type **158** (No. 708) 2·00 2·50
897 5l. on 2l. Princess of Wales (No. 709) 2·75 3·00
MS898 103×75 mm. 15l. on 3l. Princess of Wales (different) (No. **MS**710) 8·00 6·00
899 1l.30 on 3lc. Caernarvon Castle (No. 711) 2·00 1·25
900 5l. on 50c. Type **158** (No. 712) 4·00 3·50
901 7l. on 2l. Princess of Wales (No. 713) 6·50 4·50
MS902 103×75 mm. 15l. on 3l. Princess of Wales (different) (No. **MS**714) 8·00 6·00

190 "Madonna and Child" (Crivelli)

1985. Christmas. "Madonna and Child" Paintings by artists named. Multicoloured.
903 70c. Type **190** 25 10
904 3l. Bouts 80 40
905 4l. Da Messina 95 55
906 5l. Lochner 1·10 65
MS907 113×85 mm. 12l. Miniature from Book of Kells 1·50 1·60

190a Snow White and Bashful

1985. 150th Birth Anniv of Mark Twain (author). Walt Disney cartoon characters illustrating Mark Twain quotations. Multicoloured.
908 1l.50 Type **190a** 1·25 1·00
909 3l. Three Little Pigs 1·50 1·60
910 4l. Donald Duck and nephew 1·60 1·75
911 5l. Pinocchio and Figaro the cat 1·75 2·00
MS912 126×101 mm. 15l. Winnie the Pooh 4·25 2·50

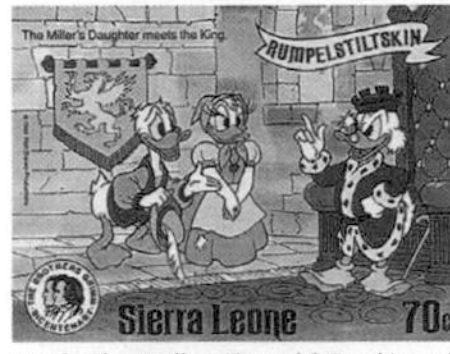

190b The Miller (Donald Duck) and his daughter (Daisy Duck) meet the King (Uncle Scrooge)

1985. Birth Bicentenaries of Grimm Brothers (folklorists). Walt Disney cartoon characters in scenes from "Rumpelstiltskin". Multicoloured.
913 70c. Type **190b** 20 25
914 1l. The King puts the Miller's daughter to work 35 40
915 2l. Rumpelstiltskin demands payment 50 55
916 10l. The King with gold spun from straw 2·75 3·50
MS917 126×100 mm. 15l. The King and Queen with baby 5·50 4·50

190c John Kennedy and 1954 Human Rights 8c. Stamp

1985. 40th Anniv of U.N.O. Showing United Nations (New York) stamps. Multicoloured.
918 2l. Type **190c** 50 70
919 4l. Albert Einstein (scientist) and 1958 Atomic Energy 3c. 1·00 1·60
920 7l. Maimonides (physician) and 1956 W.H.O. 8c. 3·50 4·25
MS921 110×85 mm. 12l. Martin Luther King (civil rights leader) (vert) 1·25 1·75

191 Player kicking Ball

1986. World Cup Football Championship, Mexico. Multicoloured.
922 70c. Type **191** 55 10
923 3l. Player controlling ball 1·00 50
924 4l. Player chasing ball 1·25 70
925 5l. Player kicking ball (different) 1·50 80
MS926 105×74 mm. 12l. Player kicking ball (different) 1·50 1·75

191a Times, Square, 1905

1986. Centenary of Statue of Liberty. Multicoloured.
927 40c. Type **191a** 10 10
928 70c. Times Square, 1986 15 10

929 1l. "Tally Ho" coach, c. 1880 (horiz) 35 15
930 10l. Express bus, 1986 (horiz) 2·00 1·90
MS931 105×75 mm. 12l. Statue of Liberty 2·50 2·25

191b Johannes Kepler (astronomer) and Paris Observatory

1986. Appearance of Halley's Comet (1st issue). Multicoloured.
932 15c. Type **191b** 30 10
933 50c. N.A.S.A. Space Shuttle landing, 1985 40 10
934 70c. Halley's Comet (from Bayeux Tapestry) 40 15
935 10l. Comet of 530 A.D. and Merlin predicting coming of King Arthur 2·75 1·60
MS936 101×70 mm. 12l. Halley's Comet 1·50 1·60
See also Nos. 988/91.

191c Princess Elizabeth Inspecting Guard of Honour, Cranwell, 1951

1986. 60th Birthday of Queen Elizabeth II.
937 **191c** 10c. black and yellow 20 10
938 - 1l.70 multicoloured 55 35
939 - 10l. multicoloured 2·50 2·75
MS940 120×85 mm. 12l. black and brown 2·25 2·00
DESIGNS: 1l.70, In Garter robes; 10l. At Braemar Games, 1970; 12l. Princess Elizabeth, Windsor Castle, 1943.

192 Chicago–Milwaukee "Hiawatha Express"

1986. "Ameripex" International Stamp Exhibition, Chicago. American Trains. Multicoloured.
941 50c. Type **192** 90 40
942 2l. Rock Island Line "The Rocket" 1·75 1·75
943 4l. Rio Grande "Prospector" 2·75 3·25
944 7l. Southern Pacific "Daylight Express" 3·50 5·00
MS945 105×85 mm. 12l. Pennsylvania "Broadway Limited" 3·25 2·25

192c Prince Andrew and Miss Sarah Ferguson

1986. Royal Wedding. Multicoloured.
946 10c. Type **192c** 10 10
947 1l.70 Prince Andrew at clay pigeon shoot 30 35
948 10l. Prince Andrew in naval uniform 1·40 1·75
MS949 88×88 mm. 12l. Prince Andrew and Miss Sarah Ferguson (different) 2·25 1·60

193 "Monodora myristica"

1986. Flowers of Sierra Leone. Multicoloured.
950 70c. Type **193** 15 10
951 1l.50 "Gloriosa simplex" 20 15
952 4l. "Mussaenda erythrophylla" 35 25
953 6l. "Crinum ornatum" 50 40
954 8l. "Bauhinia purpurea" 60 60
955 10l. "Bombax costatum" 70 70
956 20l. "Hibiscus rosasinensis" 1·25 1·50
957 30l. "Cassia fistula" 1·75 2·00
MS958 Two sheets, each 101×92 mm. (a) 40l. "Clitoria ternatea" (b) 40l. "Plumbago auriculata" Set of 2 sheets 6·00 6·00

194 Handshake and Flags of Sierra Leone and U.S.A.

1986. 25th Anniv of United States Peace Corps.
959 **194** 4l. multicoloured 70 70

195 Transporting Goods by Canoe

1986. International Peace Year. Multicoloured.
960 1l. Type **195** 30 15
961 2l. Teacher and class 40 25
962 5l. Rural post office 80 50
963 10l. Fishermen in longboat 1·60 1·25

1986. Various stamps surch.
964 30l. on 2c. Type **177** (No. 820) 3·75 3·75
965 40l. on 30c. "Traveller" (brig) (No. 826) 4·25 4·25
966 45l. on 40c. "Amistad" (schooner) (No. 827) 4·50 4·50
967 50l. on 70c. "Scotia" (cable ship) (No. 829) 4·50 4·50
968 70c. on 10c. Type **191c** (No. 937) 1·25 30
969 45l. on 10l. Queen at Braemar Games, 1970 (No. 934) 6·00 2·50
MS970 120×85 mm. 50l. on 12l. black and brown (No. **MS**940) 2·50 3·00
971 70c. on 10c. Prince Andrew and Miss Sarah Ferguson (No. 946) 20 20
972 45l. on 10l. Prince Andrew in naval uniform (No. 948) 3·00 2·50
MS973 88×88 mm. 50l. on 12l. Prince Andrew and Miss Sarah Ferguson (different) (No. **MS**949) 2·50 3·00

1986. World Cup Football Championship Winners, Mexico. Nos. 922/5 optd **WINNERS Argentina 3 W.Germany 2** or surch also.
974 70c. Type **191** 35 10
975 3l. Player controlling ball 75 30
976 4l. Player chasing ball 80 40
977 40l. on 5l. Player kicking ball (different) 6·50 4·50
MS978 105×74 mm. 40l. on 12l. Player kicking ball (different) 2·75 2·50

198 Mickey and Minnie Mouse as Jack and Jill

1986. "Stockholmia '86" International Stamp Exn, Sweden. Walt Disney cartoon characters in scenes from nursery rhymes. Multicoloured.
979 70c. Type **198** 10 10
980 1l. Donald Duck as Wee Willie Winkie 15 15
981 2l. Minnie Mouse as Little Miss Muffet 20 20
982 4l. Goofy as Old King Cole 40 40
983 5l. Clarabelle as Mary Quite Contrary 50 50
984 10l. Daisy Duck as Little Bo Peep 90 1·00
985 25l. Daisy Duck and Minnie Mouse in "Polly put the Kettle on" 2·00 2·75
986 35l. Goofy, Mickey Mouse and Donald Duck as the Three Men in a Tub 2·50 3·25
MS987 Two sheets, each 127×102 mm. (a) 40l. Aunt Matilda as the Old Woman in the Shoe. (b) 40l. Goofy as Simple Simon Set of 2 sheets 6·50 6·50

(198a)

1986. Appearance of Halley's Comet (2nd issue). Nos. 932/5 optd as T **198a**.
988 50c. N.A.S.A. Space Shuttle landing, 1985 30 10
989 70c. Halley's Comet (from Bayeux Tapestry) 30 10
990 1l.50 on 15c. Johannes Kepler (astronomer) and Paris Observatory 30 10
991 45l. on 10l. Comet of 530 A.D. and Merlin predicting coming of King Arthur 6·00 3·75
MS992 101×70 mm. 50l. on 12l. Halley's Comet 3·25 3·75

199 "Virgin and Child with St. Dorothy"

1986. Christmas. Paintings by Titian. Multicoloured.
993 70c. Type **199** 10 10
994 1l.50 "The Gypsy Madonna" (vert) 15 10
995 20l. "The Holy Family" 2·25 2·50
996 30l. "Virgin and Child in an Evening Landscape" (vert) 2·75 3·25
MS997 76×102 mm. 40l. "Madonna with the Pesaro Family" (vert) 7·50 7·00

200 Nomoli (soapstone figure)

1987. Bicentenary of Sierra Leone. Multicoloured.
998 2l. Type **200** 20 20
999 5l. King's Yard Gate, Royal Hospital, 1817 80 60
MS1000 100×70 mm. 60l. Early 19th-century British warship at Freetown 3·25 3·75

201 Removing Top of Statue's Torch

1987. Centenary of Statue of Liberty (1986) (2nd issue). Multicoloured.
1001 70c. Type **201** 10 10
1002 1l.50 View of Statue's torch and New York harbour (horiz) 10 10
1003 2l. Crane lifting torch 10 10
1004 3l. Workman steadying torch 10 15
1005 4l. Statue's crown (horiz) 15 20
1006 5l. Statue of Liberty (side view) and fireworks 20 25
1007 10l. Statue of Liberty and fireworks 40 45
1008 25l. Bedloe Island, statue and fireworks (horiz) 1·00 1·40
1009 30l. Statue's face 1·25 1·75

202 Emblem, Mother and Child and Syringe

1987. 40th Anniv of UNICEF.
1010 **202** 10l. multicoloured 50 55

203 "U.S.A.", 1987

1987. America's Cup Yachting Championship. Multicoloured.
1011 1l. Type **203** 15 10
1012 1l.50 "New Zealand II", 1987 (horiz) 15 10
1013 2l.50 "French Kiss", 1987 15 10
1014 10l. "Stars and Stripes", 1987 (horiz) 75 45
1015 15l. "Australia II", 1983 1·00 75
1016 25l. "Freedom", 1980 1·75 1·40
1017 30l. "Kookaburra", 1987 (horiz) 1·75 1·60
MS1018 100×70 mm. 50l. "Constellation", 1964 2·25 2·50

204 Mickey Mouse as Mountie and Parliament Building, Ottawa

1987. "Capex '87" International Stamp Exhibition, Toronto. Walt Disney cartoon characters in Canada. Multicoloured.
1019 2l. Type **204** 20 20
1020 5l. Goofy dressed as Mountie and totem poles 35 35
1021 10l. Goofy windsurfing and Donald Duck fishing off Perce Rock 60 45
1022 20l. Goofy with mountain goat in Rocky Mountains 1·00 1·25
1023 25l. Donald Duck and Mickey Mouse in Old Quebec 1·25 1·40
1024 45l. Goofy emerging from igloo and "Aurora Borealis" 1·75 2·50
1025 50l. Goofy as gold prospector and post office, Yukon 2·00 3·00
1026 75l. Dumbo flying over Niagara Falls 3·25 4·50
MS1027 Two sheets, each 127×101 mm. (a) 100l. Mickey Mouse driving chuckwagon in Calgary Stampede. (b) 100l. Mickey Mouse and Goofy as Vikings in Newfoundland Set of 2 sheets 8·00 12·00

205 "Salamis temora"

1987. Butterflies. Multicoloured. "Sierra Leone" in black.
1028A 10c. Type **205** 1·25 40
1029B 20c. "Stugeta marmorea" 1·00 1·00
1030B 40c. "Graphium ridleyanus" 1·00 65
1031A 1l. "Papilio bromius" 1·25 40
1032Ac 2l. "Iterus zalmoxis" 1·25 60
1033A 3l. "Cymothoe sangaris" 1·50 60
1033Bd 3l. As 40c. 5·00 2·75
1034A 5l. "Graphium tynderaeus" 1·50 40
1034Bc 9l. As 3l. (No. 1033) 6·00 3·75
1035Ac 10l. "Graphium policenes" 1·25 30
1035Bc 12l. Type **205** 7·00 4·00
1035Bd 16l. As 20c. 7·00 4·00
1036Ac 20l. "Tanuetheira timon" 1·50 60
1037Ac 25l. "Danaus limniace" 1·50 30
1038Ac 30l. "Papilio hesperus" 1·75 65
1039Ac 45l. "Charaxes smaragdalis" 2·25 30
1040Ac 60l. "Charaxes lucretius" 2·00 2·25
1041Ac 75l. "Antanartia delius" 2·25 2·75
1042A 100l. "Abisara talantus" 3·25 6·00
For similar stamps but with "Sierra Leone" in blue, see Nos. 1658/72.

206 Cycling

1987. Olympic Games, Seoul (1988) (1st series). Multicoloured.
1043 5l. Type **206** 20 25
1044 10l. Three-day eventing 40 50
1045 45l. Athletics 1·75 2·00
1046 50l. Tennis 2·00 2·40
MS1047 73×84 mm. 100l. Olympic gold medal 4·00 4·50
See also Nos. 1137/41.

206a "The Quarrel"

1987. Birth Centenary of Marc Chagall (artist). Multicoloured.

1048	3l. Type **206a**	15	15
1049	5l. "Rebecca giving Abraham's Servant a Drink"	20	25
1050	10l. "The Village"	40	45
1051	20l. "Ida at the Window"	60	65
1052	25l. "Promenade"	1·00	1·10
1053	45l. "Peasants"	2·00	2·25
1054	50l. "Turquoise Plate" (ceramic)	2·25	2·25
1055	75l. "Cemetery Gate"	3·25	3·75
MS1056	Two sheets, each 110×95 mm. (a) 100l. "Wedding Feast" (stage design) (104×78 mm). (b) 100l. "The Falling Angel" (104×78 mm). Imperf Set of 2 sheets	9·00	10·00

206b "Apollo 8" Spacecraft (first manned Moon orbit), 1968

1987. Milestones of Transportation. Multicoloured.

1057	3l. Type **206b**	40	30
1058	5l. Blanchard's balloon (first U.S. balloon flight), 1793	40	30
1059	10l. Amelia Earhart's Lockheed Vega 5B (first solo transatlantic flight by woman), 1932	1·25	60
1060	15l. Vicker's Vimy (first non-stop transatlantic flight), 1919	1·50	80
1061	20l. British "Mk 1" tank (first combat tank), 1916	1·75	1·25
1062	25l. Vought-Sikorsky VS-300 (first U.S. helicopter flight), 1939	2·00	1·60
1063	30l. Wright brothers Flyer I (first powered flight), 1903	2·00	1·60
1064	35l. Bleriot XI (first cross Channel flight), 1909	2·00	2·00
1065	40l. Paraplane (first flexible-wing ultralight), 1983	2·00	2·25
1066	50l. Daimler's first motorcycle, 1885	2·00	2·50
MS1067	114×83 mm. 100l. "Rhinegold Express" (first electric express service) (horiz)	3·75	6·50

Nos. 1058/64 are horiz.

207 Evonne Goolagong

1987. Wimbledon Tennis Champions. Multicoloured.

1068	2l. Type **207**	35	35
1069	5l. Martina Navratilova	55	55
1070	10l. Jimmy Connors	85	85
1071	15l. Bjorn Borg	1·25	1·25
1072	30l. Boris Becker	2·25	2·25
1073	40l. John McEnroe	2·50	2·50
1074	50l. Chris Evert Lloyd	2·75	2·75
1075	75l. Virginia Wade	3·50	3·50
MS1076	Two sheets, each 105×75 mm. (a) 100l. Boris Becker (different). (b) 100l. Steffi Graf Set of 2 sheets	13·00	13·00

208 Ducats, "Santa Maria" and Isaac Abravanel (financier)

1987. 500th Anniv (1992) of Discovery of America by Columbus. Multicoloured.

1077	5l. Type **208**	80	20
1078	10l. Astrolabe, "Pinta" and Abraham Zacuto (astronomer)	90	35
1079	45l. Maravedis (coins), "Nina" and Luis de Santangel (financier)	2·75	3·00
1080	50l. Carib and Spaniard with tobacco plant and Luis de Torres (translator)	3·00	3·25
MS1081	101×70 mm. 100l. Christopher Columbus and map	3·00	3·50

209 Cotton Tree

1987. Flora and Fauna. Multicoloured.

1082	3l. Type **209**	15	15
1083	5l. Dwarf crocodile	35	25
1084	10l. Kudu	40	35
1085	20l. Yellowbells	65	65
1086	25l. Hippopotamus and calf	1·75	1·25
1087	45l. Comet orchid	3·25	2·50
1088	50l. Baobab tree	2·25	2·50
1089	75l. Elephant and calf	4·25	5·00
MS1090	Two sheets, each 100×70 mm. (a) 100l. Bananas, Coconut Palm, Papayas and Pineapple. (b) 100l. Leopard Set of 2 sheets	5·75	7·00

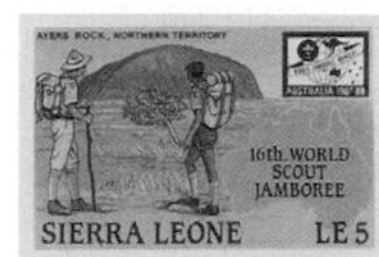

210 Scouts at Ayers Rock

1987. World Scout Jamboree, Australia. Multicoloured.

1091	5l. Type **210**	30	20
1092	15l. Scouts sailing yacht	65	65
1093	40l. Scouts and Sydney skyline	1·75	2·50
1094	50l. Scout, Sydney Harbour Bridge and Opera House	3·25	2·75
MS1095	114×78 mm. 100l. Flags of Sierra Leone, Australia and Boy Scouts	3·00	3·50

210a White House

1987. Bicentenary of U.S. Constitution. Multicoloured.

1096	5l. Type **210a**	15	20
1097	10l. George Washington (Virginia delegate) (vert)	30	35
1098	30l. Patrick Henry (statesman) (vert)	80	95
1099	65l. State Seal, New Hampshire	1·60	2·40
MS1100	105×75 mm. 100l. John Jay (jurist) (vert)	1·50	3·00

210b Mickey and Minnie Mouse on Space Mountain

1987. 60th Anniv of Mickey Mouse (Walt Disney cartoon character). Cartoon characters at Tokyo Disneyland. Multicoloured.

1101	20c. Type **210b**	10	10
1102	40c. Mickey Mouse at Country Bear Jamboree	10	10
1103	80c. Mickey Mouse as bandleader and Minnie Mouse, Goofy and Pluto as musicians	10	10
1104	1l. Goofy, Mickey Mouse and children in canoe and Mark Twain's river boat	10	10
1105	2l. Mickey Mouse, Goofy and Chip n'Dale on Western River Railroad	10	10
1106	3l. Goofy and Mickey Mouse as Pirates of the Caribbean	15	15
1107	10l. Mickey Mouse, Goofy and children aboard Big Thunder Mountain train	55	55
1108	20l. Mickey Mouse, Morty and Ferdie in boat and Goofy on flying carpet	1·25	1·50
1109	30l. Mickey and Minnie Mouse in kimonos at Disneyland entrance	1·75	2·00
MS1110	127×102 mm. 65l. Mickey and Minnie Mouse in kimonos at Cinderella's Castle	5·50	4·50

211 "The Annunciation" (detail) (Titian)

1987. Christmas. Religious Paintings by Titian. Multicoloured.

1111	2l. Type **211**	20	10
1112	10l. "Madonna and Child with Saints"	60	35
1113	20l. "Madonna and Child with Saints Ulfus and Brigid"	1·10	1·25
1114	35l. "The Madonna of the Cherries"	1·90	2·75
MS1115	70×100 mm. 65l. "The Pesaro Altarpiece" (vert)	3·50	4·00

211a Wedding of Princess Elizabeth and Duke of Edinburgh, 1947

1988. Royal Ruby Wedding.

1116	**211a**	2l. brown, black and grey	40	10
1117	-	3l. multicoloured	40	10
1118	-	10l. brown, black and orange	60	35
1119	-	50l. multicoloured	2·75	2·50
MS1120		76×100 mm. 65l. mult	3·00	2·50

DESIGNS: 3l. Prince Charles's christening photograph, 1949; 10l. Queen Elizabeth II with Prince Charles and Princess Anne, c. 1951; 50l. Queen Elizabeth, c. 1960; 65l. Wedding photograph, 1947.

212 "Russula cyanoxantha"

1988. Fungi. Multicoloured.

1121	3l. Type **212**	45	30
1122	10l. "Lycoperdon perlatum"	1·10	70
1123	20l. "Lactarius deliciosus"	1·90	2·00
1124	30l. "Boletus edulis"	2·25	2·75
MS1125	100×70 mm. 65l. "Amanita muscaria"	5·50	4·75

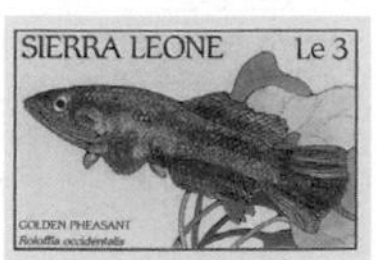

213 Golden Pheasant Panchax

1988. Fish of Sierra Leone. Multicoloured.

1126	3l. Type **213**	15	15
1127	10l. Banded panchax	30	30
1128	20l. Jewel cichlid	50	75
1129	35l. Freshwater butterflyfish	75	1·40
MS1130	99×69 mm. 65l. Long-finned tetra	2·50	4·00

1988. Stamp Exhibitions. Nos. 1016, 1072 and 1079 optd.

1131	25l. "Freedom", 1980 (optd **INDEPENDENCE 40**, Israel)	1·10	1·40
1132	30l. Boris Becker (optd **OLYMPHILEX '88**, Seoul)	1·25	1·75
1133	45l. Maravedis (coins), "Nina" and Luis de Santangel (financier) (optd **PRAGA 88**, Prague)	1·75	2·25

214 Hands holding Coffee Beans and Woman with Cocoa

1988. International Fund for Agricultural Development. Multicoloured.

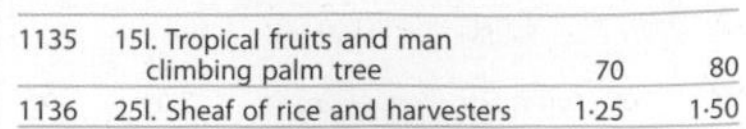

1134	3l. Type **214**	20	20
1135	15l. Tropical fruits and man climbing palm tree	70	80
1136	25l. Sheaf of rice and harvesters	1·25	1·50

215 Basketball

1988. Olympic Games, Seoul (2nd issue). Multicoloured.

1137	3l. Type **215**	10	10
1138	10l. Judo	30	35
1139	15l. Gymnastics	45	55
1140	40l. Synchronized swimming	1·25	1·75
MS1141	73×101 mm. 65l. Sierra Leone athlete	1·90	2·50

216 Swallow-tailed Bee Eater

1988. Birds. Multicoloured.

1142	3l. Type **216**	85	75
1143	5l. Double-toothed barbet ("Tooth-billed Barbet")	1·10	1·00
1144	8l. African golden oriole	1·40	1·25
1145	10l. Red bishop	1·40	1·25
1146	12l. Red-billed shrike	1·40	1·25
1147	20l. European bee eater	1·60	1·40
1148	35l. Common gonolek ("Barbary Shrike")	2·25	2·00
1149	40l. Western black-headed oriole ("Black-headed Oriole")	2·25	2·25
MS1150	Two sheets, each 111×82 mm. (a) 65l. Purple heron. (b) 65l. Saddle-bill stork Set of 2 sheets	3·75	4·50

217 "Aureol" (liner)

1988. Ships. Multicoloured.

1151	3l. Type **217**	75	30
1152	10l. "Dunkwa" (freighter)	1·75	80
1153	15l. "Melampus" (container ship)	2·50	1·60
1154	30l. "Dumbaia" (freighter)	3·25	3·00
MS1155	95×95 mm. 65l. Loading container ship, Freetown	2·25	2·50

1988. 500th Birth Anniv of Titian (artist). As T **183a** of St. Vincent. Multicoloured.

1156	1l. "The Concert" (detail)	15	10
1157	2l. "Philip II of Spain"	20	15
1158	3l. "Saint Sebastian" (detail)	20	20
1159	5l. "Martyrdom of St. Peter Martyr"	30	30
1160	15l. "St. Jerome"	90	85
1161	20l. "St. Mark enthroned with Saints"	1·10	1·10
1162	25l. "Portrait of a Young Man"	1·25	1·40
1163	30l. "St. Jerome in Penitence"	1·40	1·50
MS1164	Two sheets, each 110×95 mm. (a) 50l. "Self Portrait". (b) 50l. "Orpheus and Eurydice" Set of 2 sheets	4·00	4·50

218 Sikorsky S-58 Helicopter lowering "Mercury" Capsule to Flight Deck

1988. 25th Death Anniv of John F. Kennedy (American statesman). U.S. Space Achievements. Multicoloured.

1165	3l. Type **218**	1·25	30
1166	5l. "Liberty Bell 7" capsule descending (vert)	1·00	20
1167	15l. Launch of first manned American capsule (vert)	1·25	70
1168	40l. "Freedom 7" orbiting Earth	3·00	2·00
MS1169	98×69 mm. 65l. President Kennedy and quotation	1·90	2·25

219 Famine Relief Convoy crossing Desert

1988. 125th Anniv of Int Red Cross. Multicoloured.

1170 3l. Type **219** 1·00 40
1171 10l. Rifle and map of Battle of Solferino, 1859 2·50 90
1172 20l. World War II hospital ship in Pacific 3·00 2·00
1173 40l. Red Cross tent and World War I German biplanes 3·75 3·25
MS1174 100×70 mm. 65l. Henri Dunant (founder), Alfred Nobel and Peace Prize scroll (horiz) 2·40 3·00

219a Donald Duck's Nephews playing as Band

1988. Christmas. "Mickey's Christmas Dance". Walt Disney cartoon characters. Multicoloured.

1175 10l. Type **219a** 80 80
1176 10l. Clarabelle 80 80
1177 10l. Goofy 80 80
1178 10l. Scrooge McDuck and Grandma Duck 80 80
1179 10l. Donald Duck 80 80
1180 10l. Daisy Duck 80 80
1181 10l. Minnie Mouse 80 80
1182 10l. Mickey Mouse 80 80
MS1183 Two sheets, each 127×102 mm. (a) 70l. Mickey Mouse dancing the Charleston. (b) 70l. Mickey Mouse jiving Set of 2 sheets 6·50 6·50

Nos. 1175/82 were printed together, *se-tenant*, forming a composite design.

220 "Adoration of the Magi" (detail)

1988. Christmas. Religious Paintings by Rubens. Multicoloured.

1184 3l. Type **220** 25 15
1185 3l.60 "Adoration of the Shepherds" (detail) 25 15
1186 5l. "Adoration of the Magi" (detail) 40 25
1187 10l. "Adoration of the Shepherds" (different detail) 60 40
1188 20l. "Virgin and Child surrounded by Flowers" 1·00 75
1189 40l. "St. Gregory the Great and Other Saints" (detail) 1·75 1·75
1190 60l. "Adoration of the Magi" (detail) 2·25 2·75
1191 80l. "Madonna and Child with Saints" (detail) 2·75 3·25
MS1192 Two sheets, each 76×113 mm. (a) 100l. "Virgin and Child enthroned with Saints". (b) 100l. "St. Gregory the Great and Other Saints" Set of 2 sheets 6·00 9·00

1989. Steffi Graf's "Grand Slam" Tennis Victories. No. **MS**1076b optd **GOLD MEDALIST** (No. **MS**1193e) or (others), each with different inscription on sheet margin, all in gold.

MS1193 105×75 mm. 100l. Steffi Graf. (a) Optd **AUSTRALIAN OPEN JANUARY 11–24, 1988 GRAFv EVERET**. (b) Optd **FRENCH OPEN MAY 23–JUNE 5, 1988 GRAFv ZVERENA**. (c) Optd **WIMBLEDON JUNE 20–JULY 4, 1988 GRAFv NAVRATILOVA**. (d) Optd **U.S. OPEN AUGUST 29–SEPTEMBER 11, 1988 GRAFv SABATINI**. (e) Optd **SEOUL OLYMPICS 1988 GRAFv SABBATINI** Set of 5 sheets 17·00 15·00

Each marginal overprint includes score of match involved.

No. **MS**1193a overprinted "EVERET" in error for "EVERT".

222 Brazil v. Sweden, 1958

1989. World Cup Football Championship, Italy (1st issue). Designs showing action from previous World Cup finals. Multicoloured.

1194 3l. Type **222** 40 30
1195 6l. West Germany v. Hungary, 1954 50 40
1196 8l. England v. West Germany, 1966 60 45
1197 10l. Argentina v. Netherlands, 1978 70 50
1198 12l. Brazil v. Czechoslovakia, 1962 75 75
1199 20l. West Germany v. Netherlands, 1974 1·00 1·00
1200 30l. Italy v. West Germany, 1982 1·40 1·60
1201 40l. Brazil v. Italy, 1970 1·75 1·90
MS1202 Two sheets, each 73×104 mm. (a) 100l. Argentina v. West Germany, 1986. (b) 100l. Uruguay v. Brazil, 1950 Set of 2 sheets 6·75 6·75

See also Nos. 1455/74.

223 Decathlon (Gold, C. Schenk, East Germany)

1989. Olympic Medal Winners, Seoul (1988). Multicoloured.

1203 3l. Type **223** 70 30
1204 6l. Men's heavyweight judo (Gold, H. Saito, Japan) 1·00 40
1205 10l. Women's cycle road race (Silver, J. Niehaus, West Germany) 3·00 75
1206 15l. Men's single sculls (Gold, T. Lange, East Germany) 1·50 80
1207 20l. Men's 50 metres freestyle swimming (Gold, M. Biondi, U.S.A.) 1·50 1·00
1208 30l. Men's 100 m (Gold, C. Lewis, U.S.A.) 1·50 1·50
1209 40l. Dressage (Gold, West Germany) 2·75 2·00
1210 50l. Greco-Roman wrestling (57 kg) (Gold, A. Sike, Hungary) 2·50 2·75
MS1211 Two sheets, each 70×100 mm. (a) 100l. Olympic gold medal. (b) 100l. Olympic torch and rings Set of 2 sheets 6·75 6·75

224 Map of Union States, Mail Lorry and Post Office

1989. 15th Anniv of Mano River Union. Multicoloured.

1212 1l. Type **224** 1·00 65
1213 3l. Map of West Africa and Presidents Momoh, Conte and Doe 1·25 40
1214 10l. Construction of Freetown–Monrovia Highway 1·75 1·00
MS1215 96×68 mm. 15l. Presidents signing anniversary metting communique 1·00 1·00

225 "Richard III"

1989. 425th Birth Anniv of Shakespeare. Multicoloured.

1216 15l. Type **225** 60 60
1217 15l. "Othello" (Iago) 60 60
1218 15l. "Two Gentlemen of Verona" 60 60
1219 15l. "Macbeth" (Lady Macbeth) 60 60
1220 15l. "Hamlet" 60 60
1221 15l. "The Taming of the Shrew" 60 60
1222 15l. "The Merry Wives of Windsor" 60 60
1223 15l. "Henry IV" (Sir John Falstaff) 60 60
1224 15l. "Macbeth" (The Witches) 60 60
1225 15l. "Romeo and Juliet" 60 60
1226 15l. "Merchant of Venice" 60 60
1227 15l. "As You Like It" 60 60
1228 15l. "The Taming of the Shrew" (banquet scene) 60 60
1229 15l. "King Lear" 60 60
1230 15l. "Othello" (Othello and Desdemona) 60 60
1231 15l. "Henry IV" (Justice Shallow) 60 60
MS1232 Two sheets, each 117×82 mm. (a) 100l. Shakespeare and arms (49×36 mm). (b) 100l. Shakespeare (49×36 mm) Set of 2 sheets 8·00 8·50

226 Centenary Logo

1989. Cent of Ahmadiyya Muslim Society.

1233 **226** 3l. black and blue 30 30

1989. Japanese Art (1st series). Paintings by Seiho. As T **188a** of St. Vincent. Multicoloured.

1234 3l. "Lapping Waves" 60 35
1235 6l. "Hazy Moon" (vert) 70 45
1236 8l. "Passing Spring" (vert) 70 45
1237 10l. "Mackerels" 70 45
1238 12l. "Calico Cat" 70 45
1239 30l. "The First Time to be a Model" (vert) 2·00 80
1240 40l. "Kingly Lion" 2·25 1·10
1241 75l. "After a Shower" (vert) 2·75 2·00
MS1242 Two sheets, each 102×77 mm. (a) 150l. "Dozing in the midst of all the Chirping" (Detail) (vert). (b) 150l. "Domesticated Monkeys and Rabbits" (detail) Set of 2 sheets 8·50 8·50

See also Nos. 1321/50.

227 Robespierre and Bastille

1989. "Philexfrance '89" International Stamp Exhibition, Paris and Bicentenary of French Revolution. Multicoloured.

1243 6l. Type **227** 45 35
1244 20l. Danton and Louvre 90 80
1245 45l. Queen Marie Antoinette and Notre Dame 1·40 1·25
1246 80l. Louis XVI and Palace of Versailles 2·00 2·75
MS1247 77×107 mm. 150l. Celebrating crowd, Paris (vert) 3·25 4·00

228 Sputnik Satellite in Orbit, 1957

1989. History of Space Exploration. As T **228**. Multicoloured.

1248–1301 10l.×27, 15l.×27 Set of 54 22·00 23·00
MS1302 Three sheets, each 112×90 mm. 100l.×3 Set of 3 sheets 12·00 13·00

229 "Bulbophyllum barbigerum"

1989. Orchids of Sierra Leone. Multicoloured.

1303 3l. Type **229** 55 40
1304 6l. "Bulbophyllum falcatum" 85 60
1305 12l. "Habenaria macrara" 1·25 90
1306 20l. "Eurychone rothchildiana" 1·60 1·40
1307 50l. "Calyptrochilum christyanum" 2·25 2·25
1308 60l. "Bulbophyllum distans" 2·50 2·75
1309 70l. "Eulophia guineensis" 2·50 2·75
1310 80l. "Diaphananthe pellucida" 2·75 3·25
MS1311 Two sheets, each 112×80 mm. (a) 100l. "Cyrtorchis arcuata" and Pagoda, Kew Gardens. (b) 100l. "Eulophia cucullata" Set of 2 sheets 17·00 17·00

230 "Salamis temora"

1989. Butterflies. Multicoloured.

1312 6l. Type **230** 85 75
1313 12l. "Pseudacraea lucretia" 1·25 1·10
1314 18l. "Charaxes boueti" (vert) 1·60 1·40
1315 30l. "Graphium antheus" (vert) 2·25 2·00
1316 40l. "Colotis protomedia" 2·50 2·25
1317 60l. "Asterope pechueli" (vert) 3·00 2·75
1318 72l. "Coenyra aurantiaca" 3·25 3·00
1319 80l. "Precis octavia" (vert) 3·25 3·00
MS1320 Two sheets, each 100×70 mm. (a) 100l. "Charaxes cithaeron" (vert). (b) 100l. "Euphaedra themis" Set of 2 sheets 14·00 14·00

1989. Japanese Art (2nd series). Paintings by Hiroshige of "The Fifty-three Stations on the Tokaido Road". As T **188a** of St. Vincent. Multicoloured.

1321 25l. "Ferry-boat to Kawasaki" 1·00 1·00
1322 25l. "The Hilly Town of Hodogaya" 1·00 1·00
1323 25l. "Lute Players at Fujisawa" 1·00 1·00
1324 25l. "Mild Rainstorm at Oiso" 1·00 1·00
1325 25l. "Lake Ashi and Mountains of Hakone" 1·00 1·00
1326 25l. "Twilight at Numazu" 1·00 1·00
1327 25l. "Mount Fuji from Hara" 1·00 1·00
1328 25l. "Samurai Children riding through Yoshiwara" 1·00 1·00
1329 25l. "Mountain Pass at Yui" 1·00 1·00
1330 25l. "Harbour at Ejiri" 1·00 1·00
1331 25l. "Halt at Fujieda" 1·00 1·00
1332 25l. "Misty Kanaya on the Oi River" 1·00 1·00
1333 25l. "The Bridge to Kakegawa" 1·00 1·00
1334 25l. "Teahouse at Fukuroi" 1·00 1·00
1335 25l. "The Ford at Mistuke" 1·00 1·00
1336 25l. "Coolies warming themselves at Hamamatsu" 1·00 1·00
1337 25l. "Imakiri Ford at Maisaka" 1·00 1·00
1338 25l. "Pacific Ocean from Shirasuka" 1·00 1·00
1339 25l. "Futakawa Street-singers" 1·00 1·00
1340 25l. "Repairing Yoshida Castle" 1·00 1·00
1341 25l. "The Inn at Akasaka" 1·00 1·00
1342 25l. "The Bridge to Okazaki" 1·00 1·00
1343 25l. "Samurai's Wife entering Narumi" 1·00 1·00
1344 25l. "Harbour at Kuwana" 1·00 1·00
1345 25l. "Autumn in Ishiyakushi" 1·00 1·00
1346 25l. "Snowfall at Kameyama" 1·00 1·00
1347 25l. "The Frontier-station of Seki" 1·00 1·00
1348 25l. "Teahouse at Sakanoshita" 1·00 1·00
1349 25l. "Kansai Houses at Minakushi" 1·00 1·00
1350 25l. "Kusatsu Station" 1·00 1·00
MS1351 Two sheets, each 102×75 mm. (a) 120l. "Nihom Bridge, Edo". (b) 120l. "Sanjo Bridge, Kyoto" Set of 2 sheets 8·00 8·50

The English captions of the two miniature sheets of No. **MS**1351 are transposed. The sheet showing the Nihom Bridge, Edo, has a group of fishmongers in the left foreground.

231 Formosan Sika Deer

1989. "World Stamp Expo '89" International Stamp Exhibition, Washington (2nd issue). Endangered Fauna. Multicoloured.

1353 6l. Humpback whale 50 40
1354 9l. Type **231** 40 40
1355 16l. Spanish lynx 65 60
1356 20l. Goitred gazelle 60 60
1357 30l. Japanese sea lion 65 65
1358 50l. Long-eared owl 1·50 1·25
1359 70l. Lady Amherst's ("Chinese Copper") pheasant 1·50 1·50
1360 100l. Siberian tiger 2·25 2·50
MS1361 Two sheets, each 103×75 mm. (a) 150l. Mauritius kestrel (vert). (b) 150l. Japanese crested ibis (vert) Set of 2 sheets 12·00 13·00

231a Mickey Mouse and Goofy in Rolls-Royce "Phantom II Roadstar", 1934

1989. Christmas. Walt Disney cartoon characters with cars. Multicoloured.

1362	3l. Type **231a**	55	30
1363	6l. Mickey and Minnie Mouse in Mercedes-Benz "500K", 1935	70	40
1364	10l. Mickey and Minnie Mouse with Jaguar "SS-100", 1938	80	45
1365	12l. Mickey Mouse and Goofy with U.S. army jeep, 1941	90	55
1366	20l. Mickey and Minnie Mouse with Buick Roadmaster Sedan "Model 91", 1937	1·25	90
1367	30l. Mickey Mouse driving 1948 Tucker	1·50	1·25
1368	40l. Mickey and Minnie Mouse in Alfa Romeo, 1933	1·60	1·40
1369	50l. Mickey and Minnie Mouse with 1937 Cord	1·75	1·60
MS1370	Two sheets, each 127×101 mm. (a) 100l. Mickey in Fiat Topolino, 1938. (b) 100l. Mickey Mouse with gifts and Pontiac "Model 401", 1931 Set of 2 sheets	6·50	7·00

1989. Christmas. Paintings by Rembrandt. As T **204a** of St. Vincent. Multicoloured.

1371	3l. "The Adoration of the Magi"	50	30
1372	6l. "The Holy Family with a Cat"	60	40
1373	10l. "The Holy Family with Angels"	70	45
1374	15l. "Simeon in the Temple"	85	55
1375	30l. "The Circumcision"	1·50	1·10
1376	90l. "The Holy Family"	3·00	3·25
1377	100l. "The Visitation"	3·00	3·25
1378	120l. "The Flight into Egypt"	3·25	3·50
MS1379	Two sheets, each 70×95 mm. (a) 150l. "The Adoration of the Shepherds" (detail). (b) 150l. "The Presentation of Jesus in the Temple" (detail) Set of 2 sheets	8·50	8·50

232 Johann Kepler (astronomer)

1990. Exploration of Mars. Designs as T **232** showing astronomers, spacecraft and Martian landscapes.

1380-1415	175l.×36 multicoloured	65·00	75·00
MS1416	Two sheets, each 105×85 mm. (a) 150l. The "Face" on Mars. (b) 150l. Section of space station Set of 2 sheets	11·00	12·00

1990. 50th Anniv of Second World War. American Aircraft. As T **206a** of St. Vincent. Multicoloured.

1417	1l. Dolittle's North American B-25 Mitchell "Ruptured Duck", 1942	30	30
1418	2l. Consolidated B-24 Liberator	40	30
1419	3l. Douglas A20J Boston attacking Japanese convoy, Bismark Sea, 1943	40	30
1420	9l. Lockheed P-38 Lightning	60	35
1421	12l. Martin B-26 Marauder	75	40
1422	16l. Boeing B-17F Flying Fortress bombers	85	55
1423	50l. North American B-25D Mitchell bomber	2·50	1·75
1424	80l. Boeing B-29 Superfortress	2·75	2·75
1425	90l. Boeing B-17G Flying Fortress bomber	2·75	3·00
1426	100l. Boeing B-29 Superfortress "Enola Gay"	3·00	3·00
MS1427	Two sheets, each 106×77 mm. (a) 150l. North American B-25 Mitchell "Ruptured Duck" taking off from U.S.S. "Hornet" 1942. (b) 150l. Boeing B-17G Flying Fortress of 447th Bomber Group Set of 2 sheets	7·50	8·00

233 Mickey Mouse at Bauxite Mine

1990. Sierra Leone Sites and Scenes. Walt Disney cartoon characters. Multicoloured.

1428	3l. Type **233**	30	15
1429	6l. Scrooge McDuck panning for gold	30	15
1430	10l. Minnie Mouse at Lungi Airport	40	20
1431	12l. Mickey Mouse at Old Fourah Bay College	40	20
1432	16l. Mickey Mouse mining bauxite	60	25
1433	20l. Huey, Dewey and Louie harvesting rice	60	30
1434	30l. Mickey and Minnie Mouse admire the Freetown Cotton Tree	70	40
1435	100l. Mickey Mouse flying over Rutile Mine	3·00	3·25
1436	200l. Mickey Mouse fishing at Goderich	3·75	4·25
1437	225l. Mickey and Minnie Mouse at Bintumani Hotel	3·75	4·25
MS1438	Two sheets, each 130×100 mm. (a) 250l. Dwarfs with diamonds. (b) 250l. Mickey and Minnie Mouse at King Jimmy Market (vert) Set of 2 sheets	9·00	9·50

234 Olivier as Antony in "Antony and Cleopatra", 1951

1990. Sir Laurence Olivier (actor) Commem. Multicoloured.

1439	3l. Type **234**	55	20
1440	9l. As King Henry V in "Henry V", 1943	65	30
1441	16l. As Oedipus in "Oedipus", 1945	80	35
1442	20l. As Heathcliffe in "Wuthering Heights", 1939	85	40
1443	30l. As Szell in "Marathon Man", 1976	1·00	55
1444	70l. As Othello in "Othello", 1964	2·25	1·40
1445	175l. As Michael in "Beau Geste", 1929	3·00	3·00
1446	200l. As King Richard III in "Richard III", 1956	3·25	3·25
MS1447	Two sheets, each 98×68 mm. (a) 250l. As Hamlet in "Hamlet", 1947. (b) 250l. As Sir Hugh Dowding in "The Battle of Britain", 1969 Set of 2 sheets	9·50	9·50

235 Penny Black

1990. 150th Anniv of the Penny Black.

1448	**235**	50l. blue	2·25	1·50
1449	**235**	100l. brown	3·00	2·75
MS1450		145×106 mm. **235** 250l. black	4·00	4·50

236 Cameroons World Cup Team

1990. World Cup Football Championship, Italy (2nd issue). Finalists. Multicoloured.

1451-1474	15l.×8 (Type **236**, Colombia, Costa Rica, Egypt, Rumania, South Korea, U.A.E., Yugoslavia) 30l.×8 (Austria, Belgium, Czechoslovakia, Netherlands, Scotland, Sweden, Uruguay, U.S.S.R.) 45l.×8 (Argentina, Brazil, England, Ireland, Italy, Spain, U.S.A., West Germany)	14·00	15·00

No. 1452 is inscr "COLUMBIA" and No. 1465 "URAGUAY", both in error.

237 Great Crested Grebe

1990. Birds. Multicoloured.

1475	3l. Type **237**	20	20
1476	6l. Green wood hoopoe	25	25
1477	10l. African jacana	30	30
1478	12l. Pied avocet ("Avocet")	35	35
1479	20l. Peter's finfoot	40	40
1480	80l. Glossy ibis	1·25	1·50
1481	150l. Hammerkop	1·75	2·00
1482	200l. Black-throated honey-guide	2·00	2·50
MS1483	Two sheets, each 100×70 mm. (a) 250l. African palm swift. (b) 250l. Painted snipe Set of 2 sheets	7·00	8·00

1990. "Stamp World London '90" International Stamp Exhibition. British Costumes. As T **207a** of St. Vincent showing Walt Disney cartoon characters. Multicoloured.

1484	3l. Mickey Mouse as a Yeoman Warder	20	15
1485	6l. Scrooge McDuck as a lamplighter	20	15
1486	12l. Goofy as a medieval knight	30	20
1487	15l. Clarabelle as Ann Boleyn	30	20
1488	75l. Minnie Mouse as Queen Elizabeth I	2·50	2·00
1489	100l. Donald Duck as a chimney sweep	2·75	2·25
1490	125l. Pete as King Henry VIII	3·00	2·50
1491	150l. Clarabell, Minnie Mouse and Daisy Duck as May dancers	3·00	2·50
MS1492	Two sheets, each 127×102 mm. (a) 250l. Donald Duck as a lawyer (vert). (b) 250l. Minnie Mouse as Queen Boadicea Set of 2 sheets	7·50	8·50

1990. 90th Birthday of Queen Elizabeth the Queen Mother. As T **208a** of St. Vincent. Multicoloured.

1493	75l. Queen Mother on Remembrance Sunday	1·75	1·25
1494	75l. Queen Mother in yellow hat	1·75	1·25
1495	75l. Waving to crowds on 85th birthday	1·75	1·25
MS1496	90×75 mm. 250l. As No. 1495	3·50	3·50

238 Golden Cat

1990. Wildlife. Multicoloured.

1497	25l. Type **238**	75	75
1498	25l. White-backed night heron	75	75
1499	25l. Bateleur ("Bateleur Eagle")	75	75
1500	25l. Marabou stork	75	75
1501	25l. White-faced whistling duck	75	75
1502	25l. Aardvark	75	75
1503	25l. Royal antelope	75	75
1504	25l. Pygmy hippopotamus	75	75
1505	25l. Leopard	75	75
1506	25l. Sacred ibis	75	75
1507	25l. Mona monkey	75	75
1508	25l. African darter	75	75
1509	25l. Chimpanzee	75	75
1510	25l. African elephant	75	75
1511	25l. Potto	75	75
1512	25l. African manatee	75	75
1513	25l. African fish eagle	75	75
1514	25l. African spoonbill	75	75
MS1515	106×76 mm. 150l. Crowned eagle (vert)	7·00	7·50

239 Rabbit

1990. Fairground Carousel Animals. Multicoloured.

1516	5l. Type **239**	15	15
1517	10l. Horse with panther saddle	20	20
1518	20l. Ostrich	30	30
1519	30l. Zebra	40	40
1520	50l. Horse	55	55
1521	80l. Sea monster	80	80
1522	100l. Giraffe	1·00	1·00
1523	150l. Armoured horse	1·40	1·40
1524	200l. Camel	1·75	1·75
MS1525	Two sheets (a) 98×68 mm. 300l. Masked horse. (b) 68×98 mm. 300l. Baden-Powell as Centaur Set fo 2 sheets	8·50	9·50

239a Start of Men's 100 m

1990. Olympic Games, Barcelona (1992). Multicoloured.

1526	5l. Type **239a**	20	15
1527	10l. Men's 4×400 m relay	25	20
1528	20l. Men's 100 m in progress	40	30
1529	30l. Weightlifting	50	40
1530	40l. Freestyle wrestling	55	45
1531	80l. Water polo	80	90
1532	150l. Women's gymnastics	1·40	1·75
1533	200l. Cycling	3·75	3·00
MS1534	Two sheets, each 103×75 mm. (a) 400l. Boxing (horiz). (b) 400l. Olympic flag (horiz) Set of 2 sheets	8·00	9·00

240 Morty assembling Bicycle by Christmas Tree

1990. Christmas. "The Night before Christmas". As T **240** showing Walt Disney cartoon characters in scenes from Clement Moore's poem. Multicoloured.

1535-1558	50l.×8, 75l.×8, 100l.×8	20·00	22·00
MS1559	Six sheets, each 129×107 mm. 400l.×6 multicoloured	20·00	22·00

Of the stamps in No. **MS**1559 four are horizontal and two vertical.

241 "Holy Family with St. Elizabeth" (Mantegna)

1990. Christmas. Paintings. Multicoloured.

1560	10l. "Holy Family resting" (Rembrandt)	40	15
1561	20l. Type **241**	55	20
1562	30l. "Virgin and Child with an Angel" (Correggio)	70	30
1563	50l. "Annunciation" (Bernardo Strozzi)	85	45
1564	100l. "Madonna and Child appearing to St. Anthony" (Lippi)	2·00	80
1565	175l. "Virgin and Child" (Giovanni Boltraffio)	3·00	3·25
1566	200l. "Esterhazy Madonna" (Raphael)	3·25	3·25
1567	300l. "Coronation of Mary" (Andrea Orcagna)	3·75	4·25
MS1568	Two sheets, each 75×114 mm. (a) 400l. "Adoration of the Shepherds" (Bronzino). (b) 400l. "Adoration of the Shepherds" (Gerard David) Set of 2 sheets	9·00	9·50

241a Helena Fourment as "Hagar in the Wilderness" (detail)

1990. 350th Death Anniv of Rubens (1st issue). Multicoloured.

1569	5l. Type **241a**	15	10
1570	10l. "Isabella Brant"	20	15
1571	20l. "Countess of Arundel and her Party" (detail)	30	20
1572	60l. "Countess of Arundel and her Party" (different detail)	70	70

1573	80l. "Nicolaas Rockox"	90	90
1574	100l. "Adriana Perez"	1·00	1·00
1575	150l. "George Villiers, Duke of Buckingham" (detail)	1·75	2·00
1576	300l. "Countess of Buckingham"	2·50	2·75
MS1577	Two sheets, each 71×100 mm. (a) 350l. "Giovanni Carlo Dorio" (detail). (b) 350l. "Veronica Spinola Dorio" (detail) Set of 2 sheets	8·00	8·50

See also Nos. 1595/602.

242 "Chlorophyllum molybdites"

1990. Fungi. Multicoloured.

1578	3l. Type **242**	30	15
1579	5l. "Lepista nuda"	30	15
1580	10l. "Clitocybe nebularis"	40	20
1581	15l. "Cyathus striatus"	50	30
1582	20l. "Bolbitius vitellinus"	55	35
1583	25l. "Leucoagaricus naucinus"	55	40
1584	30l. "Suillus luteus"	60	45
1585	40l. "Podaxis pistillaris"	70	55
1586	50l. "Oudemansiella radicata"	80	60
1587	60l. "Phallus indusiatus"	90	70
1588	80l. "Macrolepiota rhacodes"	1·00	1·10
1589	100l. "Mycena pura"	1·25	1·25
1590	150l. "Volvariella volvacea"	1·60	1·75
1591	175l. "Omphalotus olearius"	1·90	2·25
1592	200l. "Sphaerobolus stellatus"	2·00	2·50
1593	250l. "Schizophyllum commune"	2·25	2·75
MS1594	Four sheets, each 101×70 mm. (a) 350l. "Hypholoma fasciculare" (b) 350l. "Psilocybe coprophila" (c) 350l. "Agaricus campestris" (d) 350l. "Suillus granulatus" Set of 4 sheets	15·00	15·00

243 "The Flight of St. Barbara" (detail) (Rubens)

1991. Easter. 350th Death Anniv (1990) of Rubens (2nd issue). Multicoloured.

1595	10l. Type **243**	55	15
1596	20l. "The Last Judgement" (detail)	75	20
1597	30l. "St. Gregory of Nazianzus"	85	30
1598	50l. "Doubting Thomas"	1·25	45
1599	80l. "The Way to Calvary" (detail)	2·00	1·10
1600	100l. "St. Gregory with Sts. Domitilla, Maurus and Papianus"	2·25	1·25
1601	175l. "Sts. Gregory, Maurus and Papianus"	3·50	3·75
1602	300l. "Christ and the Penitent Sinners"	5·00	6·50
MS1603	Two sheets, each 70×101 mm. (a) 400l. "The Last Judgement" (different detail). (b) 400l. "The Way to Calvary" (different detail) Set of 2 sheets	8·50	9·00

244 Krauss Class 1400 Steam Locomotive, 1895

1991. "Phila Nippon '91" International Stamp Exhibition, Tokyo. Japanese Trains. Multicoloured.

1604	10l. Type **244**	35	20
1605	20l. Class C55 streamline steam locomotive, 1935	50	25
1606	30l. Class ED17 electric locomotive, 1931	70	40
1607	60l. Class EF13 electric locomotive, 1944	1·00	85
1608	100l. Baldwin Mikado steam locomotive, 1897	1·25	1·25
1609	150l. Class C62 steam locomotive, 1948	1·75	2·00
1610	200l. Class Kiha 81 diesel multiple unit, 1960	2·00	2·25
1611	300l. Schenectady Class 8550 steam locomotive, 1899	2·25	2·75
MS1612	Four sheets, each 106×76 mm. (a) 400l. Class 9600 steam locomotive, 1913. (b) 400l. Class D51 steam locomotive, 1936. (c) 400l. Class 7000 electric multiple unit. (d) 400l. "Hikari" express train Set of 4 sheets	15·00	15·00

245 Turquoise Killifish

1991. Fish. Multicoloured.

1613	10l. Type **245**	45	20
1614	20l. Red-chinned panchax	65	25
1615	30l. Peters' killifish	80	40
1616	60l. Micro-walkeri killifish	1·40	90
1617	100l. Freshwater butterflyfish	1·60	1·25
1618	150l. Green panchax	2·00	2·25
1619	200l. Six-banded lyretail	2·25	2·50
1620	300l. Nile pufferfish	2·25	2·50
MS1621	Two sheets, each 96×70 mm. (a) 400l. Spot-finned squeaker. (b) 400l. Two-striped panchax Set of 2 sheets	8·50	8·50

1991. Death Centenary of Vincent van Gogh (artist). As T **215a** of St. Vincent. Multicoloured.

1622	10c. "The Langlois Bridge at Arles" (horiz)	10	30
1623	50c. "Tree in Garden at Saint-Paul Hospital"	10	30
1624	1l. "Wild Flowers and Thistles in a Vase"	10	30
1625	2l. "Still Life: Vase with Oleanders and Books" (horiz)	15	30
1626	5l. "Farmhouses in a Wheatfield near Arles" (horiz)	20	20
1627	10l. "Self-portrait, September 1889"	30	15
1628	20l. "Patience Escalier"	55	20
1629	30l. "Doctor Felix Rey"	70	30
1630	50l. "The Iris"	1·00	45
1631	60l. "The Shepherdess"	1·25	65
1632	80l. "Vincent's House in Arles" (horiz)	1·60	1·00
1633	100l. "The Road Menders" (horiz)	1·75	1·10
1634	150l. "The Garden of Saint-Paul Hospital"	3·00	3·25
1635	200l. "View of the Church, Saint-Paul-de-Mausole" (horiz)	3·25	3·50
1636	250l. "Seascape at Saintes-Maries" (horiz)	3·50	3·75
1637	300l. "Pieta"	3·50	3·75
MS1638	Six sheets. (a) 102×76 mm. 400l. "Haystacks in Provence" (96×70 mm). (b) 102×76 mm. 400l. "The Trinquetaille Bridge" (96×70 mm). (c) 102×76 mm. 400l. "Vineyards with a View of Auvers" (96×70 mm). (d) 102×76 mm. 400l. "The Garden of Saint-Paul Hospital" (96×107 mm). (e) 76×102 mm. 400l. "Church at Auvers-sur-Dise" (70×96 mm). (f) 76×102 mm. 400l. "Two Poplars on a Road through the Hills" (70×96 mm). Imperf Set of 6 sheets	17·00	17·00

1991. 65th Birthday of Queen Elizabeth II. As T **220b** of St. Vincent. Multicoloured.

1639	10l. The Queen and Prince Charles at polo match	25	10
1640	30l. The Queen at Windsor, 1989	35	20
1641	200l. The Queen and Princess Diana in Nigeria, 1989	2·00	2·00
1642	250l. The Queen and Prince Philip	2·25	2·25
MS1643	68×90 mm. 400l. Separate photographs of the Queen and Prince Philip in 1987 and 1988	4·25	3·75

1991. Tenth Wedding Anniv of Prince and Princess of Wales. As T **220b** of St. Vincent. Multicoloured.

1644	20l. Prince and Princess of Wales in August, 1987	90	15
1645	80l. Separate photographs of Prince, Princess and sons	2·25	85
1646	100l. Prince Henry in Majorca and Prince William on his first day at school	2·00	95
1647	300l. Prince Charles at Caister, April, 1988 and Princess Diana in Hyde Park, May, 1989	4·50	4·00
MS1648	68×90 mm. 400l. Prince, Princess and Prince Henry in Majorca and Prince William going to school	5·00	4·50

246 "Graphium latreillianus" and "Ancistrochilus rothschildianus"

1991. Butterflies and Flowers. Multicoloured.

1649	10l. Type **246**	75	30
1650	30l. "Euphraedra eleus" and "Clitoria ternatea"	1·25	45
1651	50l. "Graphium antheus" and "Gloriosa simplex"	1·50	60
1652	60l. "Salamis cacta" and "Stenandriopsis guineensis"	1·75	85
1653	80l. "Kallima rumia" and "Cassia fistula"	2·25	1·25
1654	100l. "Hypolimnas salmacis" and "Amorphophallus abyssinicus"	2·25	1·50
1655	200l. "Danaus formosa" and "Nephthytis afzelii"	3·75	3·75
1656	300l. "Graphium leonidas" and "Clappertonia ficifolia"	4·50	5·50
MS1657	Four sheets, each 102×74 mm. (a) 400l. "Charaxes cynthia" and "Plumbago auriculata" (b) 400l. "Colias electo" and "Combretum grandiflorum" (c) 400l. "Cynandra opis" and "Bombax costatum" (d) 400l. "Eurema brigitta" and "Monodora myristica" Set of 4 sheets	14·00	14·00

1991. Butterflies. As Nos. 1028/42 but "Sierra Leone" in blue. Multicoloured.

1658	10c. "Danaus limniace"	7·50	75
1660	50c. "Graphium ridleyanus"	7·50	60
1661	1l. "Papilio bromius"	7·50	60
1662	2l. "Iterus ("Papilio") zalmoxis"	7·50	60
1663	5l. "Graphium tynderaeus"	24·00	80
1665	10l. "Graphium policenes"	7·50	50
1666	20l. "Tanuetheira ("Iolaus") timon"	24·00	70
1667	30l. "Cymothoe sangaris"	24·00	70
1668	50l. Type **205**	7·50	55
1669	60l. "Charaxes lucretius"	7·50	70
1670	80l. "Stugeta ("Iolaus") marmorea"	14·00	1·00
1671	100l. "Abisara talantus"	24·00	1·00
1672	300l. "Papilio hesperus"	14·00	2·75

247 Audie Murphy in "To Hell and Back"

1991. Films of Second World War. Multicoloured.

1675	2l. Type **247**	15	10
1676	5l. Jack Palance in "Attack"	20	15
1677	10l. Greer Garson and Walter Pidgeon in "Mrs. Miniver"	20	20
1678	20l. Heavy artillery from "The Guns of Navarone"	40	30
1679	30l. Charlie Chaplin and Paulette Goddard in "The Great Dictator"	75	40
1680	50l. Steam locomotive from "The Train"	80	60
1681	60l. Diary and fountain pen from "The Diary of Anne Frank"	90	70
1682	80l. William Holden in "The Bridge on the River Kwai"	1·25	90
1683	100l. Tallulah Bankhead in "Lifeboat" and Alfred Hitchcock (director)	1·25	1·00
1684	200l. John Wayne in "Sands of Iwo Jima"	2·25	2·25
1685	300l. Van Johnson and Spencer Tracy in "Thirty Seconds over Tokyo"	3·00	3·25
1686	350l. Humphrey Bogart and Ingrid Bergman in "Casablanca"	3·25	3·50
MS1687	Three sheets, each 116×76 mm. (a) 450l. George C. Scott in "Patton". (b) 450l. Gregory Peck in "Twelve O'clock High". (c) 450l. Burning American cruiser from "Tora! Tora! Tora!" Set of 3 sheets	11·00	11·00

248 Meissen China Parrot Ornament, Munich Botanic Garden

1991. Botanical Gardens of the World. Multicoloured.

1688-1735	60l.×48 Type **248**	24·00	25·00
MS1736	Three sheets, each 97×69 mm. (a) 600l. Munich Botanic Garden. (b) 600l. Kyoto Botanic Garden. (c) 600l. Brooklyn Botanic Garden	13·00	15·00

Issued in 3 sheetlets of 16 stamps, depicting features and plants from Munich (Nos. 1688/1703), Kyoto (Nos. 1704/19) and Brooklyn (Nos. 1720/35).

The single designs in the three miniature sheets of No. **MS**1736 are horiz.

248a "Mary being Crowned by Two Angels"

1991. Christmas. Drawings and Paintings by Albrecht Durer.

1737	**248a**	6l. black and mauve	15	10
1738	-	60l. black and blue	35	30
1739	-	80l. multicoloured	45	40
1740	-	100l. multicoloured	65	65
1741	-	200l. multicoloured	1·60	1·60
1742	-	300l. multicoloured	2·00	2·00
1743	-	700l. multicoloured	4·75	5·00
MS1744		Two sheets, each 102×127 mm. (a) 600l. multicoloured. (b) 600l. multicoloured Set of 2 sheets	7·50	7·50

DESIGNS: 60l. "St. Christopher"; 80l. "Virgin and Child with St. Anne" (detail); 100l. "Virgin with the Pear" (detail); 200l. "Madonna and Child" (detail); 300l. "The Virgin in Half-Length" (detail); 700l. "The Madonna with the Siskin" (detail); 600l. (No. **MS**1744a) "Virgin and Child with St. Anne"; 600l. (No. **MS**1744b) "The Feast of the Rose Garlands" (detail).

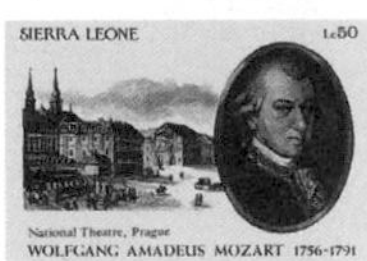

249 National Theatre, Prague

1991. Anniversaries and Events. Multicoloured.

1745	50l. Type **249**	50	20
1746	100l. St. Peter's Abbey, Salzburg	70	35
1747	250l. Sea Scouts learning sailing	1·00	1·00
1748	300l. Sierra Leone scouts emblem and Lord Baden-Powell	1·00	1·00
1749	400l. Scouts playing baseball at Mt. Sorak Jamboree	1·40	1·60
1750	500l. Scene from "Idomeneo"	2·75	3·25
MS1751	Two sheets. (a) 75×105 mm. 600l. Bust of Mozart (vert). (b) 89×117 mm. 750l. 17th World Scout Jamboree emblem (vert) Set of 2 sheets	10·00	10·00

ANNIVERSARIES AND EVENTS: Nos. 1745/6, 1750, Death bicentenary of Mozart; 1747/9, 50th death anniv of Lord Baden-Powell and World Scout Jamboree, Korea.

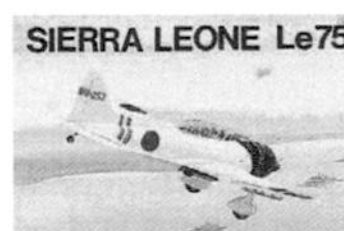

250 Aichi D3A "Val" Dive Bomber

1991. 50th Anniv of Japanese Attack on Pearl Harbor. Multicoloured.

1752	75l. Type **250**	75	75
1753	75l. Japanese Aichi D3A "Val" dive bomber and smoke	75	75
1754	75l. Battleship Row burning	75	75
1755	75l. Planes and burning dockyard	75	75
1756	75l. Burning installations	75	75
1757	75l. Two Japanese Aichi D3A "Val" dive bombers	75	75
1758	75l. Burning ships and hangars	75	75
1759	75l. Airfield under attack	75	75
1760	75l. American Curtiss P-40C fighter	75	75
1761	75l. Japanese Mitsubishi A6M Zero-Sen fighter-bombers	75	75
1762	75l. Japanese Mitsubishi A6M Zero-Sen fighter-bombers over suburb	75	75
1763	75l. Japanese Nakajima B5N "Kate" bombers attacking ships	75	75
1764	75l. Japanese Nakajima B5N "Kate" aircraft on fire	75	75
1765	75l. Japanese Nakajima B5N "Kate" bombers over jungle	75	75
1766	75l. Mitsubishi A6M Zero-Sen fighters	75	75

1991. Christmas. Walt Disney Christmas Cards. As T **228** of St. Vincent. Multicoloured.

No.	Description	Unused	Used
1767	12l. Mickey Mouse, Donald Duck and characters from "Peter Pan", 1952 (horiz)	35	10
1768	30l. Disney characters reading "Alice in Wonderland", 1950 (horiz)	45	10
1769	60l. Sleepy and animals, 1938 (horiz)	65	25
1770	75l. Mickey, Minnie, Donald and Pluto posting card, 1936 (horiz)	75	30
1771	100l. Disney cartoon characters, 1984 (horiz)	1·00	45
1772	125l. Mickey and Donald singing carols with Donald's nephews and Pluto reading, 1954 (horiz)	1·40	90
1773	150l. "101 Dalmatians", 1960 (horiz)	1·60	1·10
1774	200l. Mickey and Donald opening presents, 1948 (horiz)	2·00	1·40
1775	300l. Mickey, Minnie, Morte and Ferdie decorating tree, 1983 (horiz)	2·50	2·50
1776	400l. Donald decorating tree and nephews watching television, 1956 (horiz)	2·75	3·00
1777	500l. Characters from Disney films, 1972 (horiz)	2·75	3·00
1778	600l. Mickey, Donald, Pluto and friends singing, 1964 (horiz)	2·75	3·25
MS1779	Three sheets, each 128×102 mm. (a) 900l. Mad Hatter's tea party, 1950; (b) 900l. Disneyland, 1955. (c) 900l. Seven Dwarfs in toboggan, 1959 Set of 3 sheets	12·00	13·00

250a Minnie Mouse as Chiquita with Pluto, Cuba

1992. Mickey's World Tour. Walt Disney cartoon characters in different countries. Multicoloured.

No.	Description	Unused	Used
1780	6l. Type **250a**	20	10
1781	10l. Goofy as Olympic discus champion, Greece	20	10
1782	20l. Donald and Daisy Duck as flamenco dancers, Spain	30	15
1783	30l. Goofy and Donald as guardsman, England	40	15
1784	50l. Mickey and Minnie at Paris fashion show, France	50	25
1785	100l. Goofy in the Alps, Switzerland	80	50
1786	200l. Daisy and Minnie in grass skirts, Hawaii	1·50	1·75
1787	350l. Mickey, Donald and Goofy as ancient Egyptians (horiz)	2·00	2·25
1788	500l. Daisy and Minnie as can-can dancers, France (horiz)	2·25	2·50
MS1789	Three sheets, each 83×105 mm. (a) 700l. Mickey playing bagpipes, Scotland. (b) 700l. Donald the gondolier, Italy. (c) 700l. Mickey and Goofy smashing plates, Greece Set of 3 sheets	12·00	13·00

1992. 40th Anniv of Queen Elizabeth II's Accession. As T **229a** of St. Vincent. Multicoloured.

No.	Description	Unused	Used
1790	60l. State House	80	20
1791	100l. Beach	1·40	40
1792	300l. Parliament Building	3·00	2·50
1793	400l. Canoe on beach	3·00	3·00
MS1794	Two sheets, each 75×97 mm. (a) 700l. Jungle hillside. (b) 700l. Freetown Set of 2 sheets	12·00	13·00

250b "Visit of St. Thomas Aquinas to St. Bonaventure"

1992. "Granada '92" International Stamp Exhibition, Spain. Paintings by Francisco Zurbaran. Multicoloured.

No.	Description	Unused	Used
1795	1l. Type **250b**	10	10
1796	10l. "St. Gregory"	15	10
1797	30l. "St. Andrew"	30	20
1798	50l. "St. Gabriel the Archangel"	40	30
1799	60l. "The Blessed Henry Suso"	40	30
1800	100l. "St. Lucy"	65	40
1801	300l. "St. Casilda"	1·75	1·25
1802	400l. "St. Margaret of Antioch"	2·00	1·75
1803	500l. "St. Apollonia"	3·25	2·25
1804	600l. "St. Bonaventure at Council of Lyons"	2·50	2·75
1805	700l. "St. Bonaventure on his Bier"	2·75	3·00
1806	800l. "The Martyrdom of St. James" (detail)	3·00	3·25
MS1807	Three sheets. (a) 95×112 mm. 900l. "The Martyrdom of St. James". (b) 95×112 mm. 900l. "The Young Virgin". (c) 112×95 mm. 900l. "St. Hugh in the Refectory". Imperf Set of 3 sheets	10·00	11·00

250c Rhamphorhynchus

1992. Prehistoric Animals. Multicoloured.

No.	Description	Unused	Used
1808	50l. Type **250c**	60	60
1809	50l. Pteranodon	60	60
1810	50l. Dimorphodon	60	60
1811	50l. Pterodactyl	60	60
1812	50l. Archaeopteryx	60	60
1813	50l. Iguanodon	60	60
1814	50l. Hypsilophodon	60	60
1815	50l. Nothosaurus	60	60
1816	50l. Brachiosaurus	60	60
1817	50l. Kentrosaurus	60	60
1818	50l. Plesiosaurus	60	60
1819	50l. Trachodon	60	60
1820	50l. Hesperornis	60	60
1821	50l. Henodus	60	60
1822	50l. Steneosaurus	60	60
1823	50l. Stenopterygius	60	60
1824	50l. Eurhinosaurus	60	60
1825	50l. Placodus	60	60
1826	50l. Mosasaurus	60	60
1827	50l. Mixosaurus	60	60
MS1828	106×76 mm. No. 1820	1·75	2·00

Nos. 1808/27 were printed together, *se-tenant*, forming a composite design.

No. 1811 is inscribed "Pteradactyl" and No. 1826 "Mosasaurs", both in error.

251 Greater Flamingo

1992. Birds. Multicoloured.

No.	Description	Unused	Used
1829	30l. Type **251**	60	50
1830	50l. African white-crested hornbill ("White-crested Hornbill")	75	50
1831	100l. Crested touraco ("Verreaux's Touraco")	1·40	65
1832	170l. Yellow-spotted barbet	2·00	1·25
1833	200l. African spoonbill	2·25	1·25
1834	250l. Saddle-bill stork	2·25	1·50
1835	300l. Red-faced lovebird ("Red Headed Lovebird")	2·50	2·50
1836	600l. Yellow-billed barbet	7·75	7·00
MS1837	Two sheets, each 72×101 mm. (a) 1000l. Fire-bellied woodpecker. (b) 1000l. Swallow-tailed bee eater Set of 2 sheets	11·00	11·00

251a Marathon

1992. Olympic Games, Albertville and Barcelona. Multicoloured.

No.	Description	Unused	Used
1838	10l. Type **251a**	25	20
1839	20l. Men's parallel bars	30	25
1840	30l. Men's discus	30	25
1841	50l. Men's 110 m hurdles (horiz)	40	30
1842	60l. Women's long jump	40	30
1843	100l. Men's floor exercise (horiz)	55	45
1844	200l. Windsurfing	1·00	80
1845	250l. Women's biathlon	1·25	1·00
1846	300l. Cycle road race	4·50	2·75
1847	400l. Weightlifting	3·00	3·25
1848	500l. Men's speed skating	3·50	3·50
1849	600l. Men's downhill skiing (horiz)	4·50	5·00
MS1850	Three sheets, each 102×71 mm. (a) 900l. Football (horiz). (b) 900l. Men's single luge (horiz). (c) 900l. Pairs ice dancing Set of 3 sheets	14·00	15·00

252 Minnie Mouse and Chip decorating Christmas Tree

1992. Christmas. Walt Disney cartoon characters. Multicoloured.

No.	Description	Unused	Used
1851	10l. Type **252**	25	10
1852	20l. Goofy as Father Christmas	35	10
1853	30l. Daisy Duck and Minnie decorating Christmas tree	35	10
1854	50l. Mickey Mouse, and Goofy lighting candle	50	20
1855	80l. Big Pete as Father Christmas	80	40
1856	100l. Donald Duck as Father Christmas	90	40
1857	150l. Morty and Ferdie decorating cake	1·75	1·25
1858	200l. Mickey and bauble	1·90	1·40
1859	300l. Goofy and toy Father Christmas	2·25	1·75
1860	500l. Chip and Dale with sledge	2·75	2·75
1861	600l. Donald and Dale with musical instruments	2·75	3·25
1862	800l. Huey, Dewey and Louie making patterns in snow	3·25	4·25
MS1863	Three sheets, each 128×102 mm. (a) 900l. Mickey as Father Christmas. (b) 900l. Chip and Christmas tree fairy (horiz). (c) 900l. Mickey and Minnie (horiz) Set of 3 sheets	14·00	15·00

253 Toy Pennsylvania Railroad GG-1 Electric Locomotive No. 6-18306, 1992

1992. "Genova '92" International Thematic Stamp Exhibition. Toy Trains. Designs showing electric locomotives and rolling stock manufactured by Lionel. Multicoloured.

No.	Description	Unused	Used
1864	150l. Type **253**	1·25	1·25
1865	150l. Wabash Railroad Hudson locomotive No. 8610, 1985	1·25	1·25
1866	150l. Locomotive No. 1911, 1911	1·25	1·25
1867	150l. Chesapeake & Ohio locomotive No. 6-18627, 1992	1·25	1·25
1868	150l. Gang car No. 50, 1954	1·25	1·25
1869	150l. Rock Island & Peoria locomotive No. 8004, 1980	1·25	1·25
1870	150l. Western Maryland Railroad Shay locomotive No. 6-18023, 1992	1·25	1·25
1871	150l. Boston & Albany Railroad Hudson locomotive No. 784, 1986	1·25	1·25
1872	150l. Locomotive No. 6, 1906	1·25	1·25
1873	170l. Special F-3 diesel locomotive, 1947	1·25	1·25
1874	170l. Pennsylvania Railroad diesel switcher locomotive No, 6-18905, 1992	1·25	1·25
1875	170l. No. 1 Trolley, 1913	1·25	1·25
1876	170l. Seaboard Railroad diesel freight locomotive No. 602, 11008	1·25	1·25
1877	170l. Pennsylvania Railroad S-2 turbine locomotive, 1991	1·25	1·25
1878	170l. Western Pacific GP-9 diesel locomotive No. 6-18822, 1992	1·25	1·25
1879	170l. Locomotive No. 10, 1929	1·25	1·25
1880	170l. Locomotive No. 400E, 1931	1·25	1·25
1881	170l. Locomotive No. 384E, 1928	1·25	1·25
1882	170l. Pennsylvania Railroad "Torpedo" locomotive No. 238EW, 1936	1·25	1·25
1883	170l. Denver & Rio Grande Western Type PA diesel locomotive, 1992	1·25	1·25
1884	170l. Locomotive No. 408E, 1930	1·25	1·25
1885	170l. Mickey Mouse 60th Birthday boxcar No. 19241, 1991	1·25	1·25
1886	170l. Polished brass locomotive No. 54, 1913	1·25	1·25
1887	170l. Pennsylvania Railroad "Broadway Limited" locomotive No. 392E, 1936	1·25	1·25
1888	170l. Great Northern Railroad EP-5 electric locomotive No. 18302, 1988	1·25	1·25
1889	170l. Locomotive No. 6, 1918	1·25	1·25
1890	170l. Locomotive No. 400E, 1933	1·25	1·25
MS1891	Three sheets, each 119×90 mm. (a) 1000l. Joshua Lionel Cowen commemorative locomotive (50×37 mm). (b) 1000l. Trolley No. 300 (50×37 mm). (c) 1000l. Locomotive No. 381E, 1928 (50×37 mm) Set of 3 sheets	17·00	17·00

Nos. 1874 and 1877 are inscribed "Pennsylvannia" in error.

254 African Pygmy Goose ("Pigmy Goose")

1992. Birds. Multicoloured.

No.	Description	Unused	Used
1892B	50c. Type **254**	25	10
1893A	1l. Spotted eagle owl	70	60
1894A	2l. Crested touraco ("Verraux's Toucan")	70	60
1895A	5l. Saddle-bill stork	70	60
1896A	10l. African golden oriole	70	50
1897A	20l. Malachite kingfisher	1·00	50
1898A	30l. Red-crowned bishop ("Fire-crowned Bishop")	1·00	50
1899A	40l. Fire-bellied woodpecker	1·00	50
1900B	50l. Red-billed fire finch	10	10
1901A	80l. Blue flycatcher ("Blue Fairy Flycatcher")	1·00	50
1902B	100l. Crested malimbe	25	10
1903B	150l. Vitelline masked weaver	10	10
1904A	170l. Great blue turaco ("Blue Plantain-eater")	1·50	40
1905B	200l. Superb sunbird	10	10
1906B	250l. Swallow-tailed bee eater	10	15
1907B	300l. Cabanis's yellow bunting ("Cabanis's Yellow Bunting")	10	10
1908B	500l. Egyptian plover ("Crocodile Bird")	20	25
1909A	750l. White-faced scops owl ("White-faced Owl")	1·25	75
1910B	1000l. African blue cuckoo shrike (Blue Cuckoo-shrike")	40	45
1911B	2000l. White-necked bald crow ("Bare-headed Rock fowl")	80	85
1912B	3000l. African red-tailed buzzard ("Red-tailed Buzzard")	1·25	1·40
1913A	4000l. Grey-headed bush shrike	1·60	1·75
1914A	5000l. Black-backed puffback	1·90	2·00
1915A	6000l. Burchell's gonolek ("Crimson-breasted Shrike)	2·25	2·40
1915Ac	10000l. Northern shrike	4·00	4·25

1992. Christmas. Religious Paintings. As T **241a** of St. Vincent. Multicoloured.

No.	Description	Unused	Used
1916	1l. "Virgin and Child" (Fiorenzo di Lorenzo)	10	10
1917	10l. "Madonna and Child on a Wall" (School of Bouts)	15	15
1918	20l. "Virgin and Child with the Flight into Egypt" (Master of Hoogstraeten)	25	20
1919	30l. "Madonna and Child before Firescreen" (Robert Campin)	30	20
1920	50l. "Mary in a Rosegarden" (detail) (Hans Memling)	50	25
1921	100l. "Virgin Mary and Child" (Lucas Cranach the Elder)	90	45
1922	170l. "Virgin and Child" (Rogier van der Weyden)	1·60	1·25
1923	200l. "Madonna and Saints" (detail) (Perugino)	1·75	1·25
1924	250l. "Madonna Enthroned with Sts. Catherine and Barbara" (Master of Hoogstraeten)	1·90	1·25
1925	300l. "The Virgin in a Rose Arbour" (Stefan Lochner)	2·25	1·75
1926	500l. "Madonna with Child and Angels" (Botticelli)	3·50	3·75
1927	1000l. "Madonna and Child with young St. John the Baptist" (Fra Bartolommeo)	6·00	7·50
MS1928	Three sheets, each 76×102 mm. (a) 900l. "Virgin and Child" (detail) (Jan Gossaert). (b) 900l. "Virgin and Child (detail) (Lucas Cranach the Younger). (c) 900l. "The Virgin with the Green Cushion" (detail) (Anrea Solario) Set of 3 sheets	16·00	16·00

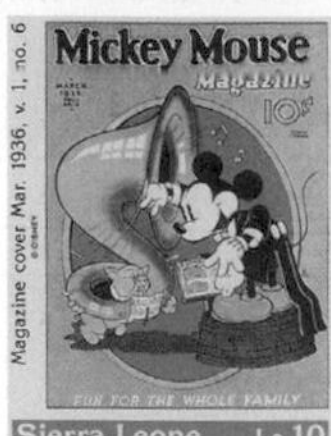

255 Mickey Mouse and Sousaphone (magazine cover, 1936)

1992. Mickey Mouse in Literature. Designs showing Walt Disney cartoon characters on magazine or book covers. Multicoloured.

1929	10l. Type **255**	25	10
1930	20l. Mickey and Minnie Mouse, 1936	30	10
1931	30l. Mickey and Donald Duck, 1936	30	10
1932	40l. Mickey, Minnie and Goofy in car, 1936	30	15
1933	50l. Mickey as Ringmaster, 1937	35	15
1934	60l. Mickey as Father Christmas, 1937	40	25
1935	70l. Donald and Goofy representing 1937 and 1938	45	25
1936	150l. Mickey and Minnie steering ship, 1935	1·25	1·10
1937	170l. Mickey and Tanglefoot the horse, 1936	1·40	1·10
1938	200l. Mickey tied up	1·60	1·25
1939	300l. Mickey and Goofy in Jungle	2·00	1·75
1940	400l. Mickey and Goofy on submarine	2·25	2·25
1941	500l. Mickey and Minnie singing and dancing, 1931	2·50	2·75
MS1942	Three sheets. (a) 127×102 mm. 900l. Mickey reading to Morty and Ferdie, 1933 (horiz). (b) 102×127 mm. 900l. Mickey with book, 1935 (horiz). (c) 102×127 mm. 900l. Mickey the hunter, 1948 Set of 3 sheets	12·00	13·00

256 Emblems

1993. Anniversaries and Events. Multicoloured.

1943	150l. Type **256**	70	70
1944	170l. Cow and cereal with emblems	80	90
1945	170l. Airship LZ-127 "Graf Zeppelin"	1·50	90
1946	200l. Starving child with W.H.O. emblem	1·00	1·00
1947	250l. Summit emblem and cottonwood tree	1·25	1·25
1948	250l. Lions Club emblem and World map	1·25	1·25
1949	300l. Emblem and African elephant	3·00	2·00
1950	300l. Columbus, King Ferdinand and Queen Isabella	2·50	2·00
1951	500l. Landing in the New World	3·25	3·00
1952	600l. American space shuttle	3·50	3·75
1953	700l. Construction drawings of "Graf Zeppelin"	3·75	4·00
MS1954	Three sheets. (a) 100×70 mm. 900l. Count Ferdinand von Zeppelin (vert). (b) 97×67 mm. 900l. Christopher Columbus (vert). (c) 100×70 mm. 900l. American astronaut on space walk Set of 3 sheets	10·50	11·50

ANNIVERSARIES AND EVENTS: Nos. 1943/4, International Conference on Nutrition, Rome; 1945, 1953, **MS**1954a, 75th death anniv of Count Ferdinand von Zeppelin (airship pioneer); 1946, United Nations World Health Organization Projects; 1947, 1949, Earth Summit '92, Rio; 1948, 75th anniv of International Association of Lions Clubs; 1950/1, **MS**1954b, 500th anniv of discovery of America by Columbus; 1952, **MS**1954c, International Space Year.

257 Joe Louis

1993. Centenary of Modern Boxing (1st issue). World Champions. Multicoloured.

1955	200l. Type **257**	1·40	1·40
1956	200l. Archie Moore	1·40	1·40
1957	200l. Muhammad Ali	1·40	1·40
1958	200l. George Foreman	1·40	1·40
1959	200l. Joe Frazier	1·40	1·40
1960	200l. Marvin Hagler	1·40	1·40
1961	200l. Sugar Ray Leonard	1·40	1·40
1962	200l. Evander Holyfield	1·40	1·40
MS1963	128×102 mm. 1000l. Muhammad Ali (different)	4·25	4·75

1993. Centenary of Modern Boxing (2nd issue). Boxing Films. As T **257**. Multicoloured.

1964	200l. Wallace Beery ("The Champ")	1·40	1·40
1965	200l. William Holden ("Golden Boy")	1·40	1·40
1966	200l. John Garfield ("Body and Soul")	1·40	1·40
1967	200l. Kirk Douglas ("Champion")	1·40	1·40
1968	200l. Robert Ryan ("The Set-Up")	1·40	1·40
1969	200l. Anthony Quinn ("Requiem for a Heavyweight")	1·40	1·40
1970	200l. Elvis Presley ("Kid Galahad")	1·40	1·40
1971	200l. Jeff Bridges ("Fat City")	1·40	1·40
MS1972	Two sheets, each 128×102 mm. (a) 1000l. Errol Flynn "Gentleman Jim" (b) 1000l. Sylvester Stallone "Rocky III" Set of 2 sheets	7·00	7·50

1993. Bicentenary of the Louvre, Paris. Paintings by Delacroix. As T **255a** of St. Vincent. Multicoloured.

1973	70l. "Young Orphan at a Cemetery"	45	50
1974	70l. "Algerian Women in their Apartment" (left detail)	45	50
1975	70l. "Algerian Women in their Apartment" (right detail)	45	50
1976	70l. "Dante and Virgil"	45	50
1977	70l. "Self-portrait"	45	50
1978	70l. "Massacre of Chios" (left detail)	45	50
1979	70l. "Massacre of Chios" (right detail)	45	50
1980	70l. "Frederic Chopin"	45	50
1981	70l. "Entry of the Crusaders into Constantinople" (left detail)	45	50
1982	70l. "Entry of the Crusaders into Constantinople" (right detail)	45	50
1983	70l. "Jewish Wedding, Morocco" (left detail)	45	50
1984	70l. "Jewish Wedding, Morocco" (right detail)	45	50
1985	70l. "Death of Sardanopoulous" (left detail)	45	50
1986	70l. "Death of Sardanopoulous" (right detail)	45	50
1987	70l. "Liberty leading the People" (left detail)	45	50
1988	70l. "Liberty leading the People" (right detail)	45	50
MS1989	100×70 mm. 900l. "The Sabine Women" (Louis David) (85×53 mm)	6·00	6·50

258 "Amanita flammeola"

1993. Mushrooms. Multicoloured.

1990	30l. Type **258**	40	20
1991	50l. "Cantharellus pseudocibarius"	50	20
1992	100l. "Volvariella volvacea"	70	40
1993	200l. "Termitomyces microcarpus"	1·10	90
1994	300l. "Auricularia auricula-judae"	1·60	1·50
1995	400l. "Lentinus tuber-regium" ("Pleurotus tuberregium")	1·75	2·00
1996	500l. "Schizophyllum commune"	1·90	2·25
1997	600l. "Termitomyces robustus"	2·00	2·50
MS1998	Two sheets, each 106×76 mm. (a) 1000l. "Daldinia concentrica" (b) 1000l. "Phallus rubicundus" Set of 2 sheets	11·00	12·00

259 "Pseudacraea boisduvali"

1993. Butterflies. Multicoloured.

1999	20l. Type **259**	60	20
2000	30l. "Salamis temora"	65	25
2001	50l. "Charaxes jasius"	70	30
2002	100l. "Amblypodia anita"	1·00	40
2003	150l. "Papilio nireus"	1·25	70
2004	170l. "Danaus chrysippus"	1·25	85
2005	200l. "Meneris tulbaghia"	1·40	90
2006	250l. "Precis octavia"	1·50	1·00
2007	300l. "Palla ussheri"	1·60	1·40
2008	500l. "Catacroptera cloanthe"	1·90	1·90
2009	600l. "Cynthia cardui"	2·00	2·50
2010	700l. "Euphaedra neophron"	2·25	2·75
MS2011	Three sheets, each 100×70 mm. (a) 1000l. "Papilio zalmoxis" (b) 1000l. "Hypolimnas salmacts" (c) 1000l. "Kallimoides rumia" Set of 3 sheets	11·00	11·00

260 Black Persian

1993. Cats. Multicoloured.

2012	150l. Type **260**	90	80
2013	150l. Blue-point Siamese	90	80
2014	150l. American wirehair	90	80
2015	150l. Birman	90	80
2016	150l. Scottish fold	90	80
2017	150l. American shorthair red tabby	90	80
2018	150l. Blue and white Persian bicolour	90	80
2019	150l. Havana brown	90	80
2020	150l. Norwegian forest cat	90	80
2021	150l. Brown tortie Burmese	90	80
2022	150l. Angora	90	80
2023	150l. Exotic shorthair	90	80
2024	150l. Somali	90	80
2025	150l. Egyptian mau smoke	90	80
2026	150l. Chocolate-point Siamese	90	80
2027	150l. Mi-Ke Japanese bobtail	90	80
2028	150l. Chinchilla	90	80
2029	150l. Red Burmese	90	80
2030	150l. British shorthair brown tabby	90	80
2031	150l. Blue Persian	90	80
2032	150l. British silver classic tabby	90	80
2033	150l. Oriental ebony	90	80
2034	150l. Red Persian	90	80
2035	150l. British calico shorthair	90	80
MS2036	Two sheets, each 108×65 mm. (a) 1000l. American shorthair blue tabby. (B) 1000l. Seal-point colourpoint Set of 2 sheets	11·00	11·00

261 Gorilla

1993. Wildlife. Multicoloured.

2037	30l. Type **261**	50	30
2038	100l. Bongo	60	35
2039	150l. Potto	70	60
2040	170l. Chimpanzee	90	90
2041	200l. Dwarf galago	1·00	1·00
2042	300l. African linsang	1·25	1·25
2043	500l. Banded duiker	1·75	2·00
2044	750l. Diana monkey	2·25	3·75
MS2045	Two sheets, each 106×77 mm. (a) 1200l. African elephant. (b) 1200l. Leopard Set of 2 sheets	12·00	12·00

262 "Clerodendrum thomsonae"

1993. Flowers. Multicoloured.

2046	30l. Type **262**	40	20
2047	40l. "Passiflora quadrangularis"	45	25
2048	50l. "Hydrangea macrophylla"	45	25
2049	60l. "Begonia semperflorens"	55	30
2050	100l. "Hibiscus rosa-sinensis"	75	40
2051	150l. "Lagerstroemia indica"	1·00	75
2052	170l. "Bougainvillea glabra"	1·10	85
2053	200l. "Plumbago capensis"	1·25	1·00
2054	250l. "Gerbera jamesonae"	1·50	1·25
2055	300l. "Thunbergia alata"	1·75	1·75
2056	500l. "Gloriosa superba"	2·00	2·50
2057	900l. "Viola odorata"	3·00	4·75
MS2058	Three sheets, each 72×102 mm. (a) 1200l. "Hibiscus rosa-sinensis" (different). (b) 1200l. "Passiflora quadrangularis" (different). (c) 1200l. "Gloriosa superba" (different) Set of 3 sheets	12·00	13·00

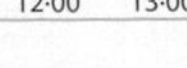

263 Royal Family

1993. Anniversaries and Events. Black (No. 2061) or multicoloured (others).

2059	100l. Type **263**	1·25	40
2060	170l. "Woman with Hat" (Picasso)	1·50	1·00
2061	200l. Coronation procession	1·50	1·25
2062	200l. "Buste de Femme" (Picasso)	1·50	1·25
2063	250l. Early telescope	3·75	2·00
2064	600l. Queen Elizabeth II in Coronation robes (from photograph by Cecil Beaton)	3·25	3·50
2065	800l. "Maya with a Doll" (Picasso)	4·00	6·00
2066	800l. Craters on Moon	6·00	6·00
MS2067	Two sheets. (a) 100×70 mm. 1000l. "Woman of Algiers" (detail) (Picasso). (b) 73×103 mm. 1500l. "Queen Elizabeth II" (detail) (Pietro Annigoni) Set of 2 sheets	13·00	14·00

ANNIVERSARIES AND EVENTS: Nos. 2059, 2061, 2064, **MS**2067b, 40th anniv of Coronation; 2060, 2062, 2065, **MS**2067a, 20th death anniv of Picasso (artist); 2063, 2066, 450th death anniv of Copernicus (astronomer).

1993. Christmas. Religious Paintings. As T **265a** of St. Vincent. Black, yellow and red (Nos. 2071/4) or multicoloured (others).

2068	50l. "Madonna of the Fish" (detail) (Raphael)	30	10
2069	100l. "Madonna of the Fish" (different detail) (Raphael)	50	20
2070	150l. "Madonna and Child enthroned with Five Saints" (detail) (Raphael)	75	30
2071	200l. "The Circumcision" (detail) (Durer)	85	55
2072	250l. "The Circumcision" (different detail) (Durer)	95	75
2073	300l. "The Circumcision" (different detail) (Durer)	1·00	1·00
2074	500l. "Holy Family with Saints and Two Angels playing Music" (detail) (Durer)	1·90	2·25
2075	800l. "The Holy Family with the Lamb" (detail) (Raphael)	2·50	4·00
MS2076	Two sheets. (a) 102×127 mm. 1200l. "Madonna of the Fish" (different detail) (Raphael). (b) 127×102 mm. 1200l. "Holy Family with Saints and Two Angels playing Music" (different detail) (Durer) Set of 2 sheets	8·50	9·00

265 Donald Duck and Toy Train

1993. Christmas. Walt Disney cartoon characters in Christmas scenes. Multicoloured.

2077	50l. Type **265**	50	10
2078	100l. Disney carol singers	75	20
2079	170l. Mickey drinking punch	1·40	70
2080	200l. Pluto with cream-covered bones	1·60	85
2081	250l. Goofy eating angel cakes	1·75	1·25
2082	500l. Donald's nephews decorating Christmas tree	3·00	3·00
2083	600l. Donald dropping Christmas cake on foot	3·25	3·75
2084	800l. Uncle Scrooge and Daisy under mistletoe	3·75	4·75
MS2085	Four sheets. (a) 127×102 mm. 1200l. Father Christmas in sleigh. (b) 102×127 mm. 1200l. Disney carol singers in wood (horiz). (c) 127×102 mm. 1200l. Father Christmas (horiz). (d) 127×102 mm. 1200l. Mickey and Minnie with turkey (horiz) Set of 4 sheets	15·00	16·00

265a Jose Brown with Goalkeeper (Agentina)

1993. World Cup Football Championship, U.S.A. (1994) (1st issue). Multicoloured.

2086 30l. Type **265a** 50 20
2087 50l. Gary Lineker (England) 75 30
2088 100l. Carlos Valderrama (Colombia) 85 35
2089 250l. Tomas Skuhravy (Czechoslovakia) and Hector Marchena (Costa Rica) 1·60 1·40
2090 300l. Butragueno (Spain) 1·75 1·75
2091 400l. Roger Milla (Cameroun) 2·25 2·50
2092 500l. Roberto Donadoni (Italy) 2·50 2·75
2093 700l. Enzo Scifo (Belgium) 2·75 3·25
MS2094 Two sheets. (a) 70×100 mm. 1200l. Mark Wright (England) and Stephane Demol (Belgium). (b) 100×70 mm. 1200l. Socrates (Brazil) Set of 2 sheets 13·00 13·00

See also Nos. 2130/5.

1994. "Hong Kong '94" International Stamp Exhibition (1st issue). As T **271a** of St. Vincent. Multicoloured.

2095 200l. Hong Kong 1985 $1.70 Bauhinia stamp and Pagoda, Tiger Baum Garden 65 75
2096 200l. Sierra Leone 1989 70l. Orchid stamp and Aw Par Gardens 65 75

See also Nos. 2097/2102 and 2103/4.

1994. "Hong Kong '94" International Stamp Exhibition (2nd issue). Ching Dynasty Carved Lacquerware. As T **271b** of St. Vincent. Multicoloured.

2097 100l. Bowl 55 70
2098 100l. Four-wheeled box 55 70
2099 100l. Flower container 55 70
2100 100l. Box with human figure design 55 70
2101 100l. Shishi dog 55 70
2102 100l. Box with persimmon design 55 70

1994. "Hong Kong '94" International Stamp Exhibition (3rd issue). Nos. 2013 and 2025 optd **HONG KONG '94** and emblem.

2103 150l. Blue-point Siamese 75 75
2104 150l. Egyptian mau smoke 75 75
MS2105 Two sheets, each 108×65 mm. (a) 1000l. American shorthair blue tabby. (b) 1000l. Seal-point colourpoint Set of 2 sheets 7·00 7·50

On No. **MS**2105 the overprint only appears on the margins of the miniature sheet.

267 Pekingese

1994. Chinese New Year ("Year of the Dog"). Multicoloured.

2106 100l. Type **267** 85 1·10
2107 150l. Dobermann pinscher 1·10 1·25
2108 200l. Tibetan terrier 1·25 1·40
2109 250l. Weimaraner 1·25 1·40
2110 400l. Rottweiler 1·40 1·60
2111 500l. Akita 1·40 1·60
2112 600l. Schnauzer 1·50 1·75
2113 1000l. Tibetan spaniel 1·75 1·90
MS2114 Two sheets, each 116×88 mm. (a) 1200l. Wire-haired pointing griffon. (b) 1200l. Shih Tzu Set of 2 sheets 6·00 7·00

1994. 50th Anniv of D-Day. As T **284b** of St. Vincent. Multicoloured.

2115 500l. British paratroop drop 1·50 1·50
2116 750l. U.S. paratrooper jumping from aircraft 2·00 2·00
MS2117 106×76 mm. 1000l. U.S. paratrooper preparing to jump from Douglas C-47 Dakota 3·00 3·50

1994. "Philakorea '94" International Stamp Exn, Seoul. As T **286a** of St. Vincent. Multicoloured.

2118 100l. Traditional wedding 40 25
2119 200l. Tiger and cubs 70 70
2120 200l. Munsa-pasal 70 70
2121 200l. Extinct Korean tiger 70 70
2122 200l. Tiger and bamboo 70 70
2123 200l. Tiger, three cubs and magpies 70 70
2124 200l. Tiger, two cubs and black-billed magpies 70 70
2125 200l. Mountain spirit 70 70
2126 200l. Tiger and black-billed magpie 70 70
2127 400l. Royal tombs, Kaesong 1·00 1·00
2128 600l. Terraced fields, Chungmu 1·50 1·75
MS2129 100×70 mm. 1200l. Tiger hunt 5·00 5·00

No. **MS**2129 is inscribed "Sierre Leone" in error.

268 Kim Ho (South Korea)

1994. World Cup Football Championship, U.S.A. (2nd issue). Multicoloured.

2130 250l. Type **268** 95 85
2131 250l. Cobi Jones (U.S.A.) ("No. 13") 95 85
2132 250l. Claudio Suarez (Mexico) ("No. 2") 95 85
2133 250l. Tomas Brolin (Sweden) ("No. 11") 95 85
2134 250l. Ruud Gullit (Holland) (red shirt without number) 95 85
2135 250l. Andreas Herzog (Austria) (white shirt without number) 95 85
MS2136 Two sheets. (a) 70×100 mm. 1500l. Player and Giant Stadium, New Jersey. (b) 100×70 mm. 1500l. Sierra Leone national team Set of 2 sheets 8·00 9·00

1994. 25th Anniv of First Manned Moon Landing. As T **284a** of St. Vincent. Multicoloured.

2137 200l. Buzz Aldrin gathering Moon samples 65 65
2138 200l. Lunar Module "Eagle" on Moon's surface 65 65
2139 200l. Tranquility Base 65 65
2140 200l. Aldrin with U.S. flag 65 65
2141 200l. Plaque 65 65
2142 200l. "Apollo 11" crew with stamps 65 65
2143 200l. Edwin Aldrin 65 65
2144 200l. Michael Collins 65 65
2145 200l. Neil Armstrong 65 65
2146 200l. "Apollo 11" lift off 65 65
2147 200l. Aldrin descending to Moon's surface 65 65
2148 200l. Reflection in Aldrin's face shield 65 65
MS2149 103×73 mm. 1000l. First lunar footprint (vert) 3·00 3·50

269 White-necked Bald Crow ("Picathartes") feeding Chicks

1994. Birds. Multicoloured.

2150 50l. Type **269** 65 65
2151 100l. Adult white-necked bald crow 75 75
2152 150l. Pair of white-necked bald crows 85 85
2153 200l. Young white-necked bald crow 90 90
2154 250l. Black kite 1·00 1·00
2155 300l. Superb sunbird 1·10 1·10
2156 500l. Martial eagle 1·60 2·00
2157 800l. Red bishop 2·00 2·75
MS2158 Two sheets, each 90×65 mm. (a) 1200l. Greater flamingo (vert). (b) 1200l. White-necked bald crow (vert) Set of 2 sheets 10·00 10·00

270 "Aerangis kotschyana"

1994. Orchids. Multicoloured.

2159 50l. Type **270** 40 20
2160 100l. "Brachycorythis kalbreyeri" 50 30
2161 150l. "Diaphananthe pellucida" 65 55
2162 200l. "Eulophia guineensis" 75 65
2163 300l. "Eurychone rothschildiana" 1·00 85
2164 500l. "Tridactyle tridactylites" 1·60 1·60
2165 750l. "Cyrtorchis arcuata" 2·25 3·00
2166 900l. "Ancistrochilus rothschildianus" 2·50 3·50
MS2167 Two sheets, each 117×78 mm. (a) 1500l. "Plectrelminthus caudatus". (b) 1500l. "Polystachaya affinis" Set of 2 sheets 8·50 9·50

1994. Christmas. Religious Paintings. As T **290** of St. Vincent. Multicoloured.

2168 50l. "The Birth of the Virgin" (Murillo) 35 10
2169 100l. "Education of the Virgin" (Murillo) 45 20
2170 150l. "Annunciation" (detail) (Filippino Lippi) 75 55
2171 200l. "Marriage of the Virgin" (Bernard van Orley) 85 70
2172 250l. "The Visitation" (Nicolas Vleughels) 1·00 90
2173 300l. "Castelfranco Altarpiece" (detail) (Giorgione) 1·25 1·25
2174 400l. "Adoration of the Magi" (workshop of Bartholome Zeitblom) 1·60 1·75
2175 600l. "Presentation of Infant Jesus in the Temple" (Master of the Prado) 2·00 3·25
MS2176 Two sheets, each 115×95 mm. (a) 1500l. "Nativity Altarpiece" (detail) (Lorenzo Monaco). (b) 1500l. "Allendale Nativity" (detail) (Giorgione) Set of 2 sheets 8·00 9·00

271 Family working in Field

1994. International Year of the Family. Multicoloured.

2177 300l. Type **271** 75 80
2178 350l. Family on beach 75 80

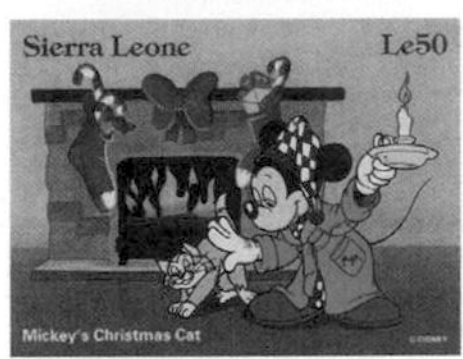

272 Mickey Mouse stroking Cat

1995. Christmas. Walt Disney cartoon characters. Multicoloured.

2179 50l. Type **272** 40 10
2180 100l. Goofy with Christmas tree and axe (vert) 50 20
2181 150l. Donald Duck giving Daisy Duck a plant 80 45
2182 200l. Donald finding Chipmunk in stocking (vert) 90 60
2183 250l. Minnie Mouse in airplane 1·10 85
2184 300l. Goofy in snowball (vert) 1·40 1·00
2185 400l. Goofy with Chip N' Dale at mail box 1·60 1·50
2186 500l. Mickey and Donald on sledge (vert) 1·75 1·75
2187 600l. Mickey and Minnie making snowmouse 2·00 2·50
2188 800l. Mickey and Pluto with cake (vert) 2·50 3·50
MS2189 Two sheets. (a) 108×133 mm. 1500l. Goofy caught up in Christmas lights. (b) 130×108 mm. 1500l. Mickey asleep in armchair (vert) Set of 2 sheets 9·50 10·00

273 "Madonna Duck" (after Da Vinci)

1995. Donald's Gallery of Old Masters. Donald and Daisy Duck in portraits inspired by famous paintings. Multicoloured.

2190 50l. Type **273** 25 15
2191 100l. "Portrait of a Venetian Duck" (after Tintoretto) 35 25
2192 150l. "Duck with a Glove" (after Frans Hals) 50 50
2193 200l. "Donald with a Pink" (after Massys) 60 60
2194 250l. "Pinkie Daisy" (after Lawrence) 70 70
2195 300l. "Donald's Whistling Mother" (after Whistler) 80 80
2196 400l. "El Quacko" (after El Greco) 90 90
2197 500l. "The Noble Snob" (after Rembrandt) 1·00 1·00
2198 600l. "The Blue Duck" (after Gainsborough) 1·25 1·50
2199 800l. "Modern Quack" (after Picasso) 1·40 1·60
MS2200 Two sheets, each 133×108 mm. (a) 1500l. "Soup's On" (detail) (after Brueghel). (b) 1500l. "Two Duck Dancers" (detail) (after Degas) (horiz) Set of 2 sheets 8·50 9·00

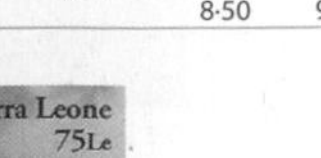
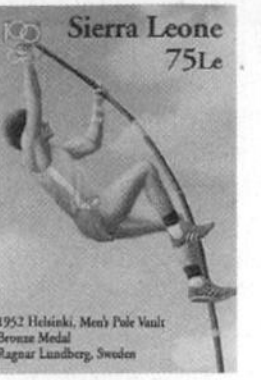

274 Ragnar Lundberg (Sweden) (1952 pole vault bronze medal)

1995. Centenary of International Olympic Committee. Medal Winners. Multicoloured.

2201 75l. Type **274** 45 45
2202 75l. Karin Janz (Germany) (1972 gymnastics silver) 45 45
2203 75l. Matthias Volz (Germany) (1936 gymnastics bronze) 45 45
2204 75l. Carl Lewis (U.S.A.) (1988 long jump gold) 45 45
2205 75l. Sara Simeoni (Italy) (1976 high jump silver) 45 45
2206 75l. Daley Thompson (Great Britain) (1980 decathlon gold) 45 45
2207 75l. Japan and Britain (1964 football) 45 45
2208 75l. Gabriella Dorio (Italy) (1984 1500 m gold) 45 45
2209 75l. Daniela Hunger (Germany) (1988 swimming gold) 45 45
2210 75l. Kyoko Iwasaki (Japan) (1992 swimming bronze) 45 45
2211 75l. Italian team (1960 water polo gold) 45 45
2212 75l. David Wilkie (Great Britain) (1976 swimming gold) 45 45
2213 200l. Katja Seizinger (Germany) (1994 alpine skiing gold) 55 55
2214 200l. Hot air balloon showing Olympic Rings 55 55
2215 200l. Elvis Stojko (Canada) (1994 figure skating silver) 55 55
2216 200l. Jans Weissflog (Germany) (1994 ski jumping gold) 55 55
2217 200l. Bjorn Daehlie (Norway) (1994 cross-country skiing gold) 55 55
2218 200l. German team (1994 four-man bobsled gold) 55 55
2219 200l. Markus Wasmeier (Germany) (1994 alpine skiing gold) 55 55
2220 200l. Georg Hacki (Germany) (1994 luge gold) 55 55
2221 200l. Jayne Torvill and Christopher Dean (Great Britain) (1994 ice dancing bronze) 55 55
2222 200l. Bonnie Blair (U.S.A.) (1994 speed skating gold) 55 55
2223 200l. Nancy Kerrigan (U.S.A.) (1994 figure skating silver) 55 55
2224 200l. Sweden team (1994 ice hockey gold) 55 55
MS2225 Two sheets, each 100×70 mm. (a) 1000l. Medal winners (1994 women's figure skating) (horiz). (b) 100l. Athlete holding Olympic Torch (horiz) Set of 2 sheets 5·50 6·50

275 Ceratosaurus

1995. Prehistoric Animals. Multicoloured.

2226 200l. Type **275** 75 75
2227 200l. Brachiosaurus 75 75
2228 200l. Pteranodon 75 75
2229 200l. Stegoceras 75 75
2230 200l. Saurolophus 75 75
2231 200l. Ornithomumus 75 75
2232 200l. Compsognathus 75 75
2233 200l. Deinonychus 75 75
2234 200l. Ornitholestes 75 75
2235 200l. Archaeopteryx 75 75
2236 200l. Heterodontosaurus 75 75
2237 200l. Lesothosaurus 75 75
MS2238 130×58 mm. 100l. Triceratops (vert); 250l. Protoceratops (vert); 400l. Monoclonius (vert); 800l. Styracosaurus (vert) 3·50 3·50
MS2239 Two sheets, each 99×79 mm. (a) 2500l. Rhamphorynchus (vert). (b) 2500l. Deinonychus (vert) Set of 2 sheets 5·50 6·00

Nos. 2226/37 were printed together, *se-tenant*, forming a composite design.

276 Pig (on red panel)

1995. Chinese New Year ("Year of the Pig"). Multicoloured.

2240	100l. Type **276**	50	50
2241	100l. Pig facing right (on green panel)	50	50
2242	100l. Pig facing left (on green panel)	50	50
2243	100l. Pig facing right (on red panel)	50	50
MS2244	77×105 mm. 500l. Two pigs (vert)	2·00	2·75

276a Black-faced Impalas

1995. Centenary (1992) of Sierra Club (environmental protection society). Endangered Species. Multicoloured.

2245	150l. Type **276a**	50	50
2246	150l. Herd of black-faced impalas	50	50
2247	150l. Black-faced impalas drinking	50	50
2248	150l. Bonobo with young	50	50
2249	150l. Black-footed cat in foliage	50	50
2250	150l. Close-up of black-footed cat	50	50
2251	150l. L'Hoest's monkey on all fours	50	50
2252	150l. L'Hoest's monkey squatting	50	50
2253	150l. Pair of mandrills	50	50
2254	150l. L'Hoest's monkey (vert)	50	50
2255	150l. Black-footed cat (vert)	50	50
2256	150l. Head of colobus monkey (vert)	50	50
2257	150l. Colobus monkey in tree fork (vert)	50	50
2258	150l. Head of mandrill (vert)	50	50
2259	150l. Bonobo with young (vert)	50	50
2260	150l. Bonobo asleep on log (vert)	50	50
2261	150l. Mandrill facing right (vert)	50	50
2262	150l. Colobus monkey on log (vert)	50	50

277 Denver and Rio Grande Western Railroad

1995. Railways of the World. Multicoloured.

2263-2274	200l.×12 (Type **277**; Central of Georgia; Seaboard Air Line; Missouri Pacific Lines; Atchison, Topeka and Santa Fe; Chicago, Milwaukee, St. Paul and Pacific; Texas and Pacific; Minneapolis, St. Paul and Sault Ste. Marie; Western Pacific; Great Northern; Baltimore and Ohio; Chicago, Rock Island and Pacific)	7·00	7·50
2275-2286	200l.×12 (Southern Pacific; Belgian National; Indian; Southern Australian; Union Pacific; British Railways; German Federal; Japanese National; Pennsylvania; East African; Milwaukee; Paris-Orleans)	7·00	7·50
2287-2298	250l.×12 (Eurostar; E.T.R. 401 Pendolino express; British Rail Intercity 125; Talgo "Virgen" express, Spain; French National TGV; Amtrak "South-west Chief" express; French National TGV "Atlantique" express; Greek "Peloponnese Express"; Japanese "Hikari" express train; Canadian National Turbotrain; Australian XPT high-speed train; Chinese SS1 electric locomotive)	7·50	8·00
2299-2310	300l.×12 (Canadian National U1-f locomotive; Union Pacific steam locomotive No. 119; LNER Class A4 No. 4468 "Mallard"; New York Central Class J3a steam locomotive; Canadian National Class U4 locomotive; Australian Class 38 locomotive; Canadian Pacific Class G3c locomotive; Southern Railway Class "West Country" locomotive; Norfolk & Western Class J locomotive; China Class RM locomotive; Russia Class P-36 locomotive; GWR Class "King" locomotive)	7·50	8·00
MS2311	Five sheets, each 107×79 mm. containing larger designs, 56½×42½ mm. (a) 1500l. British Railways No. 45627 "Sierra Leone" locomotive. (b) 1500l. China Railways Class QJ locomotive. (c) 1500l. Denver and Rio Grande Western Railroad "California Zephyr" express. (d) 1500l. China Railways Beijing-Shanghai express. (e) 1500l. China Railways first train across Yangtze Bridge, 1968 Set of 5 sheets	16·00	18·00

No. 2290 is inscribed "VIRGIN", No. 2300 "CENTRAL PACIFIC RAILWAY" and No. 2302 "J-32", all in error.

278 National Flag and Scout Emblems

1995. 18th World Scout Jamboree, Netherlands. Multicoloured.

2312	400l. Type **278**	90	1·00
2313	500l. Lord Baden-Powell	1·00	1·25
2314	600l. Scout sign	1·10	1·40
MS2315	80×111 mm. 1500l. Scout saluting	2·75	3·25

1995. 50th Anniv of End of Second World War in Europe. As T **296a** of St. Vincent, showing warships. Multicoloured.

2316	250l. U.S.S. "Idaho" (battleship)	75	75
2317	250l. H.M.S. "Ark Royal" (aircraft carrier)	75	75
2318	250l. Admiral "Graf Spee" (German pocket battleship)	75	75
2319	250l. American destroyer	75	75
2320	250l. H.M.S. "Nelson" (battleship)	75	75
2321	250l. U.S.S. "PT 109" (motor torpedo boat)	75	75
2322	250l. U.S.S. "Iowa" (battleship)	75	75
2323	250l. "Bismarck" (German battleship)	75	75
MS2324	105×74 mm. 1500l. H.M.S. "Indomitable" (aircraft carrier) (57×42½ mm)	4·00	4·50

No. 2323 is wrongly inscr "BISMARK".

278a U.N. Emblem above Podium

1995. 50th Anniv of the United Nations. Multicoloured.

2325	300l. Type **278a**	60	70
2326	400l. U Thant (Secretary-General, 1961–71)	70	1·00
2327	500l. Peace dove and U.N. Building, New York	80	1·10
MS2328	105×74 mm. 1500l. Dag Hammarskjold (Secretary-General, 1953-61)	2·00	2·50

Nos. 2325/7 were printed together, se-tenant, forming a composite design.

1995. 50th Anniv of F.A.O. As T **298** of St. Vincent. Multicoloured.

2329	300l. Fisherman in boat (horiz)	60	70
2330	400l. Boy carrying wood (horiz)	70	1·00
2331	500l. Woman with fruit (horiz)	80	1·10
MS2332	76×106 mm. 1500l. Mother and child	2·00	2·50

1995. 90th Anniv of Rotary International. As T **299** of St. Vincent. Multicoloured.

2333	500l. National flag and Rotary logo	1·10	1·50
MS2334	105×75 mm. 1000l. Paul Harris (founder) and logo	1·60	1·75

1995. 95th Birthday of Queen Elizabeth the Queen Mother. As T **323a** of St. Vincent.

2335	400l. brown, lt brown & blk	90	1·00
2336	400l. multicoloured	90	1·00
2337	400l. multicoloured	90	1·00
2338	400l. multicoloured	90	1·00
MS2339	102×127 mm. 1500l. multicoloured	3·50	3·50

DESIGNS: No. 2335, Queen Elizabeth the Queen Mother (pastel drawing); 2336, Holding bouquet of flowers; 2337, At desk (oil painting); . 2338, Wearing pink evening dress; **MS**2339, wearing blue hat.

1995. 50th Anniv of End of Second World War in the Pacific. As T **296a** of St. Vincent. Multicoloured.

2340	300l. American B-179 bomber	80	80
2341	300l. American B-25 bomber	80	80
2342	300l. American Consolidated B-24 Liberator bomber	80	80
2343	300l. U.S.S. "Missouri" (battleship)	80	80
2344	300l. American Douglas A-20 Boston bomber	80	80
2345	300l. American battle fleet in Lingayen Gulf	80	80
MS2346	108×76 mm. 1500l. Nose of B-29 Superfortress	3·00	3·50

279 Black-spotted Pufferfish

1995. "Singapore '95" International Stamp Exhibition (1st issue). Marine Life. Multicoloured.

2347	300l. Type **279**	65	65
2348	300l. Coral hind	65	65
2349	300l. Hawksbill turtle	65	65
2350	300l. Hogfish	65	65
2351	300l. Emperor angelfish	65	65
2352	300l. Red-tailed butterflyfish	65	65
2353	300l. Lemon butterflyfish	65	65
2354	300l. Green-beaked parrotfish	65	65
2355	300l. Spotted reef moray	65	65
2356	300l. Pintado petrel ("Cape Pigeons")	65	65
2357	300l. Eastern white pelican ("Pelican")	65	65
2358	300l. Atlantic puffin ("Puffin")	65	65
2359	300l. Humpback whale	65	65
2360	300l. Greater shearwater	65	65
2361	300l. Bottlenose dolphin	65	65
2362	300l. Gurnards	65	65
2363	300l. Atlantic salmon	65	65
2364	300l. John Dory	65	65
MS2365	Two sheets. (a) 71×101 mm. 1500l. Ocean surgeonfish. (b) 101×71 mm. 1500l. Pennant coralfish ("Angelfish") (vert) Set of 2 sheets	6·00	6·50

Nos. 2347/55 and 2356/64 were printed together, *se-tenant*, forming composite designs.

280 Flame Lily

1995. "Singapore '95" International Stamp Exhibition (2nd issue). African Flora and Fauna. Multicoloured.

2366	300l. Type **280**	1·00	1·00
2367	300l. Grant's gazelle	1·00	1·00
2368	300l. Dogbane	1·00	1·00
2369	300l. Gold-banded forester	1·00	1·00
2370	300l. Horned chameleon	1·00	1·00
2371	300l. Malachite kingfisher	1·00	1·00
2372	300l. Leaf beetle	1·00	1·00
2373	300l. Acanthus	1·00	1·00
2374	300l. African tulip tree	1·00	1·00
2375	300l. Senegal bush locust	1·00	1·00
2376	300l. Killfish	1·00	1·00
2377	300l. Bird of paradise (flower)	1·00	1·00
2378	300l. Mandrill	1·00	1·00
2379	300l. Painted reed frog	1·00	1·00
2380	300l. Large spotted acraea	1·00	1·00
2381	300l. Carmine bee eater	1·00	1·00
MS2382	Two sheets, each 103×73 mm. (a) 1500l. Elephant. (b) 1500l. Lion Set of 2 sheets	6·50	7·00

281 School Building and Emblem

1995. 150th Anniv of Sierra Leone Grammar School.

2383	**281**	300l. brown, mauve and black	70	70

281a "Holy Family" (detail) (Beccafumi)

1995. Christmas. Religious Paintings. Multicoloured.

2384	50l. Type **281a**	25	10
2385	100l. "The Rest on the Flight into Egypt" (detail) (Federico Barocci)	30	10
2386	150l. "The Virgin" (Jacopo Bellini)	40	15
2387	200l. "The Flight" (Cavaliere d'Arpino)	50	25
2388	600l. "Adoration of the Magi" (detail) (Francken)	1·60	2·25
2389	800l. "The Annunciation" (Cima de Conegliano)	1·75	2·50
MS2390	Two sheets, each 102×127 mm. (a) 1500l. "Virgin and Child" (detail) (Cranach). (b) 1500l. "Madonna and Child" (detail) (Berlinghiero) Set of 2 sheets	6·00	6·50

282 Mickey Mouse Doll

1995. Christmas. Disney Toys. Multicoloured.

2391	5l. Type **282**	10	10
2392	10l. Donald Duck drum-major doll	10	10
2393	15l. Donald Duck wind-up toy	15	10
2394	20l. Donald Duck toothbrush holder	15	10
2395	25l. Mickey Mouse telephone	15	10
2396	30l. Mickey Mouse walking toy	15	10
2397	800l. Toy film projector	2·50	3·25
2398	1000l. Goofy tricycle toy	2·75	3·50
MS2399	Two sheets, each 133×107 mm. (a) 1500l. Black Mickey Mouse doll. (b) 1500l. First Mickey Mouse book Set of 2 sheets	6·00	6·50

283 Andrew Huxley (1963 Medicine)

1995. Cent of Nobel Prize Trust Fund. Multicoloured.

2400-2408	250l.× 9 (Type **283**; Nelson Mandela (1993 Peace); Gabriela Mistral (1945 Literature); Otto Diels (1950 Chemistry); Hannes Alfven (1970 Physics); Wole Soyinka (1986 Literature); Hans Dehmelt (1989 Physics); Desmond Tutu (1984 Peace); Leo Esaki (1973 Physics))	7·50	7·50
2409-2417	250l.× 9 (Tobias Asser (1911 Peace); Andrei Sakharov (1975 Peace); Frederic Passy (1901 Peace); Dag Hammarskjold (1961 Peace); Aung San Suu Kyi (1991 Peace); Ludwig Quidde (1927 Peace); Elie Wiesel (1986 Peace); Bertha von Suttner (1905 Peace); The Dalai Lama (1989 Peace))	7·50	7·50
2418-2426	50l.× 9 (Richard Zsigmondy (1925 Chemistry); Robert Huber (1988 Chemistry); Wilhelm Ostwald (1909 Chemistry); Johann Deisenhofer (1988 Chemistry); Heinrich Wieland (1922 Chemistry); Gerhard Herzberg (1971 Chemistry); Hans von Euler-Chelpin (1929 Chemistry); Richard Willsatter (1915 Chemistry); Fritz Haber (1918 Chemistry))	7·50	5·50
2427-2435	250l.× 9 (Maria Goeppert Mayer (1963 Physics); Irene Joliot-Curie (1935 Chemistry); Mother Teresa (1979 Peace); Selma Lagerlof (1909 Literature); Rosalyn Yalow (1977 Medicine); Dorothy Hodgkin (1964 Chemistry); Rita Levi-Montalcini (1986 Medicine); Mairead Corrigan (1976 Peace); Betty Williams (1976 Peace))	7·50	5·50
MS2436	Three sheets, each 80×110 mm. (a) 1500l. Albert Einstein (1921 Physics). (b) 1500l. Wilhelm Rontgen (1901 Physics). (c) 1500l. Sin-Itiro Tomonaga (1965 Physics) Set of 3 sheets	9·00	11·00

284 Rat

1996. Chinese New Year ("Year of the Rat"). Background colour given.

2437	**284**	200l. multicoloured (brown background)	50	55
2438	-	200l. multicoloured (pink background)	50	55
2439	-	200l. multicoloured (red background)	50	55
2440	-	200l. multicoloured (blue background)	50	55

MS2441 110×84 mm. Nos. 2437/40 2·00 2·50

MS2442 76×106 mm. 500l. multicoloured (orange background) (vert) 2·00 2·50

285 Mickey Mouse as Magician

1996. Disney Circus Performers. Cartoon Characters. Multicoloured.

2443	100l. Type **285**	50	20
2444	200l. Clarabelle Cow walking tightrope	70	50
2445	250l. Donald Duck and nephews as clowns	80	60
2446	300l. Donald as lion tamer	1·00	75
2447	800l. Minnie Mouse riding bareback	2·50	3·25
2448	1000l. Goofy on trapeze	2·75	3·50

MS2449 Two sheets, each 104×125 mm. (a) 1500l. Mickey with dinosaur (horiz). (b) 1500l. Pluto balancing ball on nose (horiz) Set of 2 sheets 7·00 8·00

286 Lumiere Brothers (cine camera inventors) and Train

1996. Centenary of Cinema. Multicoloured.

2450	250l. Type **286**	70	75
2451	250l. Georges Melies (director)	70	75
2452	250l. Toshiro Mefune (director)	70	75
2453	250l. David O. Selznick (director)	70	75
2454	250l. Character from "Metropolis"	70	75
2455	250l. Akira Kurosawa (director)	70	75
2456	250l. Charlie Chaplin (actor)	70	75
2457	250l. Marlene Dietrich (actress)	70	75
2458	250l. Steven Spielberg (director)	70	75
2459	250l. Film camera	70	75
2460	250l. Pete (dog)	70	75
2461	250l. Silver (horse)	70	75
2462	250l. Rin-Tin-Tin (dog)	70	75
2463	250l. King Kong (gorilla)	70	75
2464	250l. Flipper (dolphin)	70	75
2465	250l. Great White Shark from "Jaws"	70	75
2466	250l. Elsa (lioness)	70	75
2467	250l. Whale from "Moby Dick"	70	75

MS2468 Two sheets, each 109×80 mm. (a) 1500l. Cecil B. De Mille (producer). (b) 1500l. Lassie (dog) Set of 2 sheets 6·50 7·00

Nos. 2450/8 and 2459/67 respectively were printed together, *se-tenant*, forming composite designs.

1996. 125th Anniv of Metropolitan Museum of Art, New York. As T **317a** of St. Vincent. Multicoloured.

2469-76	200l.× 8 ("Honfleur" (detail) (Jongkind); "A Boat on the Shore" (detail) (Courbet); "Barges at Pontoise" (detail) (Pissarro); "The Dead Christ with Angels" (Manet); "Salisbury Cathedral" (detail) (Constable); "Lady with a Setter Dog" (detail) (Eakins); "Tahitian Women Bathing" (detail) (Gauguin); "Majas on a Balcony" (detail) (Goya))	4·00	4·25
2477-84	200l.× 8 ("In the Meadow"; "By the Seashore" (detail); "Still Life with Peaches and Grapes" (detail); "Marguerite Berard"; "Young Girl in Pink and Black Hat"; "Waitress at Duval's Restaurant" (detail); "A Road in Louveciennes" (detail); "Two Young Girls at the Piano" (detail) (all by Renoir))	4·00	4·25
2485-92	200l.× 8 ("Morning, An Overcast Day, Rouen" (detail) (Pissarro); "The Horse Fair" (detail) (Bonheur); "High Tide: The Bathers" (detail) (Homer); "The Dance Class" (Degas); "The Brioche" (detail) (Manet); "The Grand Canal, Venice" (detail) (Turner); "St. Tecia interceding for plague-stricken Este" (detail) (G. B. Tiepolo); "Bridge at Villeneuve" (detail) (Sisley))	4·00	4·25
2493-2500	200l.× 8 ("Madame Charpentier" (detail) (Renoir); "Head of Christ" (detail) (Rembrandt); "The Standard-bearer" (detail) (Rembrandt); "Girl Asleep" (Vermeer); "Lady with a Lute" (Vermeer); "Portrait of a Woman" (detail) (Rembrandt); "La Grenouillere" (detail) (Monet); "Woman with Chrysanthemums" (detail) (Degas))	4·00	4·25

MS2501 Four sheets, each 95×70 mm. (a) 1500l. "The Death of Socrates" (J. L. David) 85×56 mm). (b) 1500l. "Battle of Constantine and Licinius" (detail) (rubens) (85×56 mm). (c) 1500l. "Samson and Delilah" (detail) (rubens) (85×56 mm). (d) 1500l. "The Emblem of Christ appearing to Constantine" (detail) (Rubens) (85×56 mm) Set of 4 sheets 6·50 7·50

287 Olympic Stadium, Los Angeles, 1932

1996. Olympic Games, Atlanta. Multicoloured.

2502	100l. Type **287**	30	20
2503	150l. Archery	50	50
2504	300l. Hockey	80	90
2505	300l. Swimming	80	90
2506	300l. Equestrian	80	90
2507	300l. Boxing	80	90
2508	300l. Pommel horse exercises	80	90
2509	300l. 100 m running	80	90
2510	500l. Rings exercises	1·25	1·40
2511	600l. Pole vault	1·40	1·60

MS2512 104×75 mm. 1500l. Running (vert) 3·50 4·00

288 "Cantharellus cinnabarinus"

1996. Fungi. Multicoloured.

2513	50l. Type **288**	35	20
2514	250l. "Poronidulus conchifer" and "Aphyllophorales polyporaceae"	80	85
2515	250l. "Ceratiomyxa fruticulosa"	80	85
2516	250l. "Cortinarius semisanguineus" and "Cortinariaceae agaricales"	80	85
2517	250l. "Volvamella surrecta" and "Pluteaceae agricales"	80	85
2518	250l. "Lepiota cepaestipes"	80	85
2519	250l. "Amanita rubescans"	80	85
2520	250l. "Phyllotopsis nidulans" and "Tricholomataceas agaricales"	80	85
2521	250l. "Lysyrus gardneri" and "Clathraceae phallales"	80	85
2522	250l. "Lactarius indigo"	80	85
2523	250l. "Coprinus quadrifidus"	80	85
2524	250l. "Geopyxis carbonaria"	80	85
2525	250l. "Astraeus hygrometricus"	80	85
2526	250l. "Agaicaceae agaricales"	80	85
2527	250l. "Mycena maculata"	80	85
2528	250l. "Lactarius delciosus"	80	85
2529	250l. "Amanita fulva"	80	85
2530	300l. "Suillus grevillci"	90	95
2531	400l. "Morchella esculenta"	1·10	1·25
2532	500l. "Cortinamaceae agaricales"	1·25	1·40

MS2533 Two sheets, each 110×80 mm. (a) 1500l. "Psathyrella epimyces" (horiz). (b) 1500l. "Rhodotus parmatus" (horiz) Set of 2 sheets 6·00 6·50

289 Abyssinian Cat

1996. Cats. Multicoloured.

2534	200l. Type **289**	65	60
2535	200l. British tabby	65	60
2536	200l. Norwegian forest cat	65	60
2537	200l. Maine coon	65	60
2538	200l. Bengal	65	60
2539	200l. Asian	65	60
2540	200l. American curl	65	60
2541	200l. Devon rex	65	60
2542	200l. Tonkinese	65	60
2543	200l. Egyptian mau	65	60
2544	200l. Burmese	65	60
2545	200l. Siamese	65	60
2546	200l. British shorthair	65	60
2547	200l. Tiffany	65	60
2548	200l. Birman	65	60
2549	200l. Somali	65	60
2550	200l. Malayan	65	60
2551	200l. Japanese bobtail	65	60
2552	200l. Himalayan	65	60
2553	200l. Tortoiseshell	65	60
2554	200l. Oriental	65	60
2555	200l. Ocicat	65	60
2556	200l. Chartreux	65	60
2557	200l. Ragdoll	65	60

MS2558 Two sheets, each 110×80 mm. (a) 2000l. Persian. (b) 2000l. Burmilla Set of 2 sheets 6·50 7·00

1996. 70th Birthday of Queen Elizabeth II. As T **323a** of St. Vincent. Different photographs. Multicoloured.

2559	600l. Queen Elizabeth II	1·40	1·50
2560	600l. Receiving posy	1·40	1·50
2561	600l. Carrying bouquets	1·40	1·50

MS2562 125×103 mm. 1500l. Waving from balcony 3·75 4·00

290 Three Asian Girls reading

1996. 50th Anniv of UNICEF. Multicoloured.

2563	300l. Type **290**	80	80
2564	400l. African children reading	90	1·00
2565	500l. Children in class	95	1·10

MS2566 104×74 mm. 1500l. Children's faces 3·00 3·50

291 "Pioneer" Spacecraft in Venus Orbit, 1986–1992

1996. Space Exploration. Multicoloured.

2567	300l. Type **291**	80	75
2568	300l. Hubble space telescope	80	75
2569	300l. "Voyager" space probe	80	75
2570	300l. Space Shuttle "Challenger"	80	75
2571	300l. "Pioneer II" space probe	80	75
2572	300l. "Viking I" Mars lander	80	75

MS2573 104×74 mm. 1500l. Space shuttle "Challenger" landing 3·75 4·00

Nos. 2567/72 were printed together, *se-tenant*, the background forming a composite design.

292 Rat

1996. Chinese Lunar Calendar. Multicoloured.

2574	150l. Type **292**	70	70
2575	150l. Ox	70	70
2576	150l. Tiger	70	70
2577	150l. Hare	70	70
2578	150l. Dragon	70	70
2579	150l. Snake	70	70
2580	150l. Horse	70	70
2581	150l. Sheep	70	70
2582	150l. Monkey	70	70
2583	150l. Cockerel	70	70
2584	150l. Dog	70	70
2585	150l. Pig	70	70

293 "Charaxes pleione"

1996. Butterflies. Multicoloured.

2586	150l. Type **293**	50	35
2587	200l. "Eurema brigitta"	70	50
2588	250l. "Precis orithya"	75	80
2589	250l. "Palla ussheri"	75	80
2590	250l. "Junonia orithya"	75	80
2591	250l. "Cymothoe sangaris"	75	80
2592	250l. "Cyrestis camillus"	75	80
2593	250l. "Precis rhadama"	75	80
2594	250l. "Precis cebrene"	75	80
2595	250l. "Hypolimnas misippus"	75	80
2596	250l. "Colotis danae"	75	80
2597	300l. "Charaxes ameliae"	80	85
2598	500l. "Kallimoides rumia"	1·25	1·40

MS2599 Two sheets, each 100×70 mm. (a) 1500l. "Papilio antimachus" (b) 1500l. "Charaxes bohemani" Set of 2 sheets 6·50 7·00

294 "Begonia multiflora" "Rambouillet"

1996. Flowers. Multicoloured.

2600	150l. "Tulipa" "Georgette"	40	30
2601	200l. "Helichrysum bracteatum" "Monstrosum"	55	60
2602	200l. Fountain	55	60
2603	200l. Type **294**	55	60
2604	200l. Narcissus "Trumpet Daffodil"	55	60
2605	200l. "Crocus speciosus"	55	60
2606	200l. "Chrysanthemum frutescens" "Marguerite"	55	60
2607	200l. Petunia "Polaris" and "Danaus gilippus" (butterfly)	55	60
2608	200l. "Cosmos pipinnatus" "Sensation" and "Papilio calguanabus" (butterfly)	55	60
2609	200l. "Anemone coronaris"	55	60
2610	200l. "Convolvulus minor"	55	60
2611	300l. "Paphiopedilum" "Claire de Lune"	80	85
2612	300l. "Cymbidium" "Peach Bloom"	80	85
2613	300l. Yacht	80	85
2614	300l. "Mitonia" "Peach Blossom"	80	85
2615	300l. "Parides gundalachianus" (butterfly)	80	85
2616	300l. "Laeliocattleya" "Grand Gate"	80	85
2617	300l. "Lycaste aromatica"	80	85
2618	300l. "Brassolaeliocattleya" "Golden Land"	80	85
2619	300l. "Cymbidium" "Southern Lace" and "Catastica teutila" (butterfly)	80	85
2620	400l. Vida "Pansy"	90	1·00
2621	500l. "Phalaenopsis" "Pink Beauty"	1·10	1·25

MS2622 Two sheets, each 80×110 mm. (a) 1500l. "Helianthus annuus" (b) 1500l. "Cymbidium" "Lucifer" Set of 2 sheets 6·00 7·00

Nos. 2602/10 and 2611/19 respectively were printed together, *se-tenant*, with the backgrounds forming composite designs.

295 Greek War Galley (4th-century B.C.)

1996. History of Ships. Multicoloured.

2623	300l. Type **295**	90	90

2624	300l. Roman war galley (A.D. 50)	90	90
2625	300l. Viking longship (9th-century)	90	90
2626	300l. Flemish carrack (15th-century)	90	90
2627	300l. Merchantman (16th-century)	90	90
2628	300l. Tudor galleon (16th-century)	90	90
2629	300l. Elizabethan galleon (17th-century)	90	90
2630	300l. Dutch warship (17th-century)	90	90
2631	300l. "Maestrale" (18th-century Maltese galley)	90	90
2632	300l. "Cutty Sark" (19th-century clipper)	90	90
2633	300l. "Great Britain", 1846 (steam/sail liner)	90	90
2634	300l. H.M.S. "Dreadnought", 1906 (battleship)	90	90
2635	300l. "Queen Elizabeth", 1940 (liner)	90	90
2636	300l. Ocean-going yacht, 1962	90	90
2637	300l. "United States", 1952 (liner)	90	90
2638	300l. Nuclear-powered submarine, 1950s	90	90
2639	300l. Super tanker, 1960s	90	90
2640	300l. U.S.S. "Enterprise", 1961 (aircraft carrier)	90	90

MS2641 Two sheets, each 96×66 mm. (a) 1500l. Egyptian ship (1480 B.C.) (56×42 mm). (b) 1500l. "Legend of the Seas" 1996 (cruise ship) (56×42 mm) Set of 2 sheets 8·50 9·00

No. 2634 is inscribed "Dreadnaught" in error.

1996. Christmas. Religious Paintings. As T **337** of St.Vincent. Multicoloured.

2642	200l. "Madonna of Humility" (Filippo Lippi)	60	15
2643	250l. "Coronation of the Virgin" (Lippi)	70	25
2644	400l. "The Annunciation" (Lippi)	1·25	1·10
2645	500l. "Annunciation" (different) (Lippi)	1·40	1·40
2646	600l. "Barbadori Altarpiece" (Lippi)	1·60	2·25
2647	800l. "Coronation of the Virgin" (different) (Lippi)	2·00	3·00

MS2648 Two sheets, each 76×106 mm. (a) 2000l. "Adoration of the Magi" (Rubens). (b) 2000l. "Holy Family with St. Anne" (Rubens) Set of 2 sheets 6·50 7·00

No. 2646 is inscribed "Alterpiece" in error.

296 "The Sea Dragon's Daughter"

1996. Legends of the Seas. Forty sheets, each 105×75 mm, containing T **296** and similar multicoloured designs.

MS2649 (a) 1500l. Type **296**; (b) 1500l. "Homo aquaticus"; (c) 1500l. Chinese sea fairy; (d) 1500l. Sea totem pole; (e) 1500l. "Turtle" (fantasy submarine) (horiz); (f) 1500l. Mermaid (horiz); (g) 1500l. "How the Whale got its throat" (horiz); (h) 1500l. Killer Whale crest; (i) 1500l. Odysseus and siren (horiz); (j) 1500l. "The Little Mermaid" (Hans Christian Andersen) (horiz); (k) 1500l. Squamish Indians (horiz); (l) 1500l. Boy on Dolphin; (m) 1500l. Atlantis airship (horiz); (n) 1500l. Sea Bishop (horiz); (o) 1500l. "Twenty Thousand Leagues Under the Sea" (Jules Verne); (p) 1500l. "Whale Song" (horiz); (q) 1500l. Arion (horiz); (r) 1500l. Dragonrider of Pern (horiz); (s) 1500l. Kelpie (horiz); (t) 1500l. Natsihlane on Sea Lion (horiz); (u) 1500l. Triton; (v) 1500l. Lang (dragon) (horiz); (w) 1500l. "The Flying Dutchman" (horiz); (x) 1500l. Lilith; (y) 1500l. "Queen of the Orkney Islands"; (z) 1500l. Merman; (za) 1500l. Sea Centaur; (zb) 1500l. Albatross (horiz); (zc) 1500l. "The Rime of the Ancient Mariner" (Samuel Coleridge); (zd) 1500l. Haida Eagle (horiz); (ze) 1500l. Poseidon; (zf) 1500l. Captain Ahab "Moby Dick"; (zg) 1500l. Underwater City; (zh) 1500l. Jonah and the Whale; (zi) 1500l. Waskos (horiz); (zj) 1500l. Tom Swift (horiz); (zk) 1500l. Arthropod sea monsters; (zl) 1500l. Sea Serpant; (zm) 1500l. Aphrodite (horiz); (zn) 1500l. Ship's figurehead Set of 40 sheets 48·00 55·00

297 Ox

1997. Chinese New Year ("Year of the Ox"). Multicoloured.

2650	250l. Type **297** (on purple panel)	40	50
2651	250l. Ox (on green panel)	40	50
2652	250l. Ox (on blue panel)	40	50
2653	250l. Ox (on brown panel)	40	50
MS2654	106×76 mm. Nos. 2650/3	1·60	1·75
MS2655	106×76 mm. 800l. Ox (vert)	1·40	1·75

298 Aladdin and Jasmine

1997. Christmas. Aladdin. Disney Cartoon Characters. Multicoloured.

2656	10l. Type **298**	25	10
2657	15l. Genie and Santa Claus	25	10
2658	20l. Aladdin and Jasmine on magic carpet	30	10
2659	25l. Genie as a Christmas tree	30	10
2660	30l. Genie as Santa Claus and Aladdin	30	10
2661	100l. Aladdin, Jasmine and Genie on magic carpet	1·25	30
2662	800l. Genie writing letter to Santa Claus	3·50	3·75
2663	1000l. Genie with four heads	3·75	4·25

MS2664 Two sheets, each 127×101 mm. (a) 2000l. Aladdin under a pile of gold; (b) 2000l. Aladdin and Jasmine on magic carpet (horiz) Set of 2 sheets 7·50 8·00

299 Hong Kong Skyline by Day

1997. "Hong Kong '97" International Stamp Exhibition. Two sheets, each 125×68 mm, containing T **299** and similar vert designs. Multicoloured.

MS2665 (a) 500l.×4 forming panorama of central Hong Kong by day. (b) 500l.×4 forming panorama of central Hong Kong by night Set of 2 sheets 7·50 8·00

1997. 50th Anniv of UNESCO. As T **342a** of St. Vincent. Multicoloured.

2666	60l. Church, Kizhi Pogost, Russia	15	10
2667	200l. Durmitor National Park, Yugoslavia	40	15
2668	250l. Nessebar, Bulgaria	60	35
2669	300l. Roros, Norway	75	80
2670	300l. Varsovia city gate, Poland	75	80
2671	300l. Nuestra Senora Cathedral, Luxembourg	75	80
2672	300l. Tower, Vilnius, Lithuania	75	80
2673	300l. Jelling, Denmark	75	80
2674	300l. Petajavesi Church, Finland	75	80
2675	300l. Round house, Sweden	75	80
2676	300l. Berne Cathedral, Switzerland	75	80
2677	300l. Slopes of Mount Kilimanjaro, Tanzania	75	80
2678	300l. Tombs, Fasil Ghebbi, Ethiopia	75	80
2679	300l. Mount Ruwenzori National Park, Uganda	75	80
2680	300l. Nubia Monument, Abu Simbel, Egypt	75	80
2681	300l. Tsingy of Bemaraha Nature Reserve, Madagascar	75	80
2682	300l. House, Djenne, Mali	75	80
2683	300l. Traditional house, Ghana	75	80
2684	300l. House, Abomey, Benin	75	80
2685	400l. Gateway, Bukhara, Uzbekistan	85	90
2686	500l. Monastery, Petchersk, Ukraine	95	1·10
2687	500l. Tower, Himeji-jo, Japan (horiz)	95	1·10
2688	500l. Gateway, Himeji-jo, Japan (horiz)	95	1·10
2689	500l. Outer wall and turrets, Himeji-jo, Japan (horiz)	95	1·10
2690	500l. Village, Himeji-jo, Japan (horiz)	95	1·10
2691	500l. Ornate gables, Himeji-jo, Japan (horiz)	95	1·10
2692	800l. Mountains, Slovakia	1·40	1·60

MS2693 Two sheets, each 127×102 mm. (a) 2000l. Djudj National Bird Sanctuary, Senegal (horiz). (b) 2000l. The Acropolis, Athens, Greece (horiz) Set of 2 sheets 7·50 8·00

No. 2676 is inscribed "BERNA", No. 2677 "KILIMANDJARO" and No. 2686 "MONESTRY", all in error.

1997. 300th Anniv of Mother Goose Nursery Rhymes. Two sheets, each 72×102 mm, containing horiz designs as T **346a** of St. Vincent.

MS2694 (a) 1500l. "Three Blind Mice". (b) 1500l. Woman in pink dress ("Myself") Set of 2 sheets 5·50 6·00

1997. Tenth Anniv of Chernobyl Nuclear Disaster. As T **347** of St. Vincent. Multicoloured.

2695	1000l. Child's face and UNESCO emblem	2·00	2·50
2696	1500l. As 1000l., but inscribed "CHABAD'S CHILDREN OF CHERNOBYL" at foot	2·50	3·00

1997. Golden Wedding of Queen Elizabeth and Prince Philip. As T **347a** of St. Vincent. Multicoloured (except Nos. 2699/2700).

2697	400l. Queen Elizabeth II	1·50	1·50
2698	400l. Royal coat of arms	1·50	1·50
2699	400l. Queen Elizabeth with Prince Philip in military uniform (black)	1·50	1·50
2700	400l. Queen Elizabeth with Prince Philip in naval mess dress (black)	1·50	1·50
2701	400l. St. James's Palace	1·50	1·50
2702	400l. Prince Philip	1·50	1·50

MS2703 100×70 mm. 1500l. Queen Elizabeth with Prince Philip in naval uniform 2·75 3·00

1997. Birth Bicentenary of Hiroshige (Japanese painter). "One Hundred Famous Views of Edo". As T **347d** of St. Vincent. Multicoloured.

2704	400l. "Hatsune Riding Grounds, Bakuro-cho"	85	85
2706	400l. "Ryogoku Bridge and the Great Riverbank"	85	85
2707	400l. "Asakusa River, Great Riverbank, Miyato River"	85	85
2708	400l. "Silk-goods Lane, Odenma-cho"	85	85
2709	400l. "Mokuboji Temple, Uchigawa Inlet, Gozensaihata"	85	85
2710	400l. "Mannen Bridge, Fukagawa"	85	85

MS2710 Two sheets, each 102×127 mm. (a) 1500l. "Nihonbashi Bridge and Edobashi Bridge". (b) 1500l. "Tsukudajima from Eitai Bridge" Set of 2 sheets 5·00 5·50

300 Hong Kong Skyline

1997. Return of Hong Kong to China.

2711	**300**	400l. multicoloured	85	90
2712	-	500l. multicoloured	95	1·00
2713	-	550l. multicoloured	1·00	1·10
2714	-	600l. multicoloured	1·10	1·25
2715	-	650l. multicoloured	1·25	1·40
2716	-	800l. multicoloured	1·50	1·60

DESIGNS: 500l. to 650l. Different views of modern Hong Kong; 800l. Deng Xiaoping.

301 Calgary Stadium, 1988

1997. Winter Olympic Games, Nagano, Japan (1998). Multicoloured.

2717	250l. Type **301**	60	40
2718	300l. Freestyle Skiing Aerials, 1994 (vert)	75	80
2719	300l. Peggy Fleming (U.S.A.) (figure skating, 1968) (vert)	75	80
2720	300l. Japanese competitor (Nordic combined-ski jump, 1992/4) (vert)	75	80
2721	300l. German team (two-man luge, 1968 to 1992) (vert)	75	80
2722	300l. Frank-Peter Roetsch (East Germany) (biathlon, 1988) (vert)	75	80
2723	500l. Ice Hockey (vert)	1·25	1·40
2724	800l. Dan Jansen (U.S.A.) (speed skating, 1994) (vert)	1·50	1·60

MS2725 Two sheets. (a) 106×76 mm. 1500l. Jamaican bobsleigh team (vert). (b) 76×106 mm. 1500l. Johann Olav Koss (Norway) (speed skating, 1992/4) (vert) Set of 2 sheets 5·00 5·50

301a Stabile, Uruguay

1997. World Cup Football Championship, France (1998).

2726	**301a**	100l. black	30	20
2727	-	150l. black	40	30
2728	-	200l. black	50	30
2729	-	250l. black	60	40
2730	-	300l. multicoloured	80	85
2731	-	300l. multicoloured	80	85
2732	-	300l. multicoloured	80	85
2733	-	300l. multicoloured	80	85
2734	-	300l. multicoloured	80	85
2735	-	300l. multicoloured	80	85
2736	-	300l. multicoloured	80	85
2737	-	300l. multicoloured	80	85
2738	-	500l. black	95	1·10
2739	-	600l. black	1·10	1·25

MS2740 Two sheets, each 127×102 mm. (a) 1500l. brown (b) 1500l. multicoloured Set of 2 sheets 8·00 8·00

DESIGNS—VERT: No. 2727, Schavio, Italy; 2728, Kocsis, Hungary; 2729, Nejedly, Czechoslovakia; 2730, Dwight Yorke, Trinidad and Tobago; 2731, Dennis Bergkamp, Netherlands; 2732, Steve McManaman, England; 2733, Ryan Giggs, Wales; 2734, Romario, Brazil; 2735, Faustino Asprilla, Colombia; 2736, Roy Keane, Republic of Ireland; 2737, Peter Schmeichel, Denmark; 2738, Leonidas, Brazil; 2739, Ademir, Brazil. HORIZ: No. **MS**2740a, Pele, Brazil; **MS**2740b, Lato, Poland.

302 "Vindula erota"

1997. Butterflies of the World. Multicoloured.

2741	150l. Type **302**	50	20
2742	200l. "Pereute leucodrosime"	65	20
2743	250l. "Dynastor napolean"	70	25
2744	300l. "Thauria aliris"	80	50
2745	500l. "Lycaena dispar"	1·10	1·25
2746	500l. "Graphium sarpedon"	1·10	1·25
2747	500l. "Euploe core"	1·10	1·25
2748	500l. "Papilio cresphontes"	1·10	1·25
2749	500l. "Colotis danae"	1·10	1·25
2750	500l. "Battus philenor"	1·10	1·25
2751	600l. "Papilio aegeus"	1·25	1·40
2752	600l. "Mylothris chloris"	1·25	1·40
2753	600l. "Argynnis lathonia"	1·25	1·40
2754	600l. "Elymnias agondas"	1·25	1·40
2755	600l. "Palla ussheri"	1·25	1·40
2756	600l. "Papilio glaucus"	1·25	1·40
2757	600l. "Cercyonis pegala"	1·25	1·40
2758	800l. "Amblypodia anita"	1·75	1·90
2759	1500l. "Kallimoides rumia"	3·00	3·50
2760	2000l. "Papilio dardanas"	3·50	4·00

MS2761 Two sheets, each 74×103 mm. (a) 3000l. "Hebomoia glaucippe" (horiz). (b) 3000l. "Colias eurytheme" (horiz) Set of 2 sheets 10·00 11·00

Nos. 2745/50 and 2752/7 respectively were printed together, se-tenant, with the backgrounds forming composite designs.

303 Lon Chaney in "Phantom of the Opera", 1925

1997. Famous Films. Horror classics (Nos. 2762/70) or the films of Alfred Hitchcock (Nos. 2771/9). Multicoloured.

2762	300l. Type **303**	80	80

No.	Description	Mint	Used
2763	300l. Boris Karloff in "The Mummy", 1932	80	80
2764	300l. Fredric March in "Dr. Jekyll and Mr Hyde", 1932	80	80
2765	300l. Lon Chaney Jr. in "The Wolf Man", 1941	80	80
2766	300l. Charles Laughton in "Island of Lost Souls", 1933	80	80
2767	300l. Lionel Atwill in "Mystery of the Wax Museum", 1933	80	80
2768	300l. Bela Lugosi in "Dracula", 1931	80	80
2769	300l. Vincent Price in "The Haunted Palace", 1963	80	80
2770	300l. Elsa Lanchester in "Bride of Frankenstein", 1935	80	80
2771	350l. Ray Milland in "Dial M for Murder", 1954	80	80
2772	350l. James Stewart and Kim Novak in "Vertigo", 1958	80	80
2773	350l. Cary Grant, Ingrid Bergman and Claude Rains in "Notorious", 1946	80	80
2774	350l. Farley Granger and John Dall in "Rope", 1948	80	80
2775	350l. Cary Grant in "North by Northwest", 1959	80	80
2776	350l. James Stewart and Grace Kelly in "Rear Window", 1954	80	80
2777	350l. Joan Fontaine and Laurence Olivier in "Rebecca", 1940	80	80
2778	350l. Tippi Hedren in "The Birds", 1963	80	80
2779	350l. Janet Leigh in "Psycho", 1960	80	80
MS2780	Two sheets. (a) 72×102 mm. 1500l. Alfred Hitchcock. (b) 82×82 mm. 3000l. Boris Karloff in "Son of Frankenstein" 1939 Set of 2 sheets	8·50	9·00

Nos. 2762/70 and 2771/9 respectively were printed together, *se-tenant*, with the backgrounds forming composite designs.

304 Shetland Sheepdog

1997. Dogs and Cats. Multicoloured.

No.	Description	Mint	Used
2781	100l. Type **304**	40	15
2782	150l. American shorthair tabby cat	50	25
2783	250l. British shorthair cat	70	55
2784	250l. Alaskan husky	70	55
2785	400l. Basset hound	90	90
2786	400l. Irish setter	90	90
2787	400l. St. Bernard	90	90
2788	400l. German shepherd	90	90
2789	400l. Dalmatian	90	90
2790	400l. Cocker spaniel	90	90
2791	400l. Chartreux cat	90	90
2792	400l. Abyssinian cat	90	90
2793	400l. Burmese cat	90	90
2794	400l. White angora cat	90	90
2795	400l. Japanese bobtail cat	90	90
2796	400l. Cymric cat	90	90
2797	500l. Turkish angora cat	95	95
2798	600l. Jack Russell terrier	1·10	1·25
MS2799	Two sheets, each 106×75 mm. (a) 1500l. Boxer (31×63 mm). (b) 1500l. Egyptian mau cat (63×31 mm) Set of 2 sheets	6·50	7·00

305 "Ansellia africana"

1997. Orchids of the World. Multicoloured.

No.	Description	Mint	Used
2800	150l. Type **305**	60	25
2801	200l. "Maxillaria praestans"	70	30
2802	250l. "Cymbidium mimi"	70	35
2803	300l. "Dendrobium bigibbum"	80	40
2804	400l. "Laelia anceps"	90	95
2805	400l. "Paphiopedilum fairrieanum"	90	95
2806	400l. "Restrepia lansbergii"	90	95
2807	400l. "Yamadara cattleya"	90	95
2808	400l. "Cleistes divaricata"	90	95
2809	400l. "Calypso bulbosa"	90	95
2810	500l. "Encyclia vitellina"	1·00	1·00
2811	800l. "Epidendrum prismatocarpum"	1·75	2·00

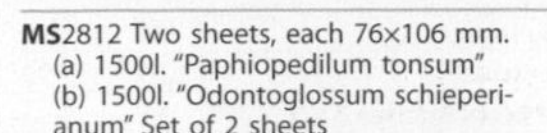

No.	Description	Mint	Used
MS2812	Two sheets, each 76×106 mm. (a) 1500l. "Paphiopedilum tonsum" (b) 1500l. "Odontoglossum schieperianum" Set of 2 sheets	5·50	5·50

306 Daisy Duck

1997. Christmas. Disney Holidays. Multicoloured.

No.	Description	Mint	Used
2813	50l. Type **306**	20	20
2814	50l. Huey, Dewey and Louie	20	20
2815	50l. Donald Duck	20	20
2816	50l. Minnie Mouse	20	20
2817	50l. Morty and Ferdie	20	20
2818	50l. Mickey Mouse	20	20
2819	150l. As No. 2814	60	60
2820	200l. As No. 2817	75	75
2821	250l. Type **306**	90	90
2822	300l. As No. 2816	1·10	1·10
2823	400l. As No. 2818	1·25	1·40
2824	500l. As No. 2815	1·50	1·60
2825	600l. Pluto	1·75	2·00
2826	800l. Goofy	2·25	2·50
MS2827	Two sheets. (a) 114×140 mm. 2000l. Mickey Mouse in sleigh. (b) 140×114 mm. 2000l. Mickey, Donald and Daisy (horiz) Set of 2 sheets	11·00	12·00

307 Benoist Type XIV

1997. Development of the Civil Airliner. Multicoloured.

No.	Description	Mint	Used
2828	600l. Type **307**	1·50	1·50
2829	600l. Douglas DC-3	1·50	1·50
2830	600l. Junkers JU52/3m seaplane	1·50	1·50
2831	600l. Sikorsky S-42 flying boat	1·50	1·50
2832	600l. Sud Caravelle 6	1·50	1·50
2833	600l. Boeing 707	1·50	1·50
2834	600l. De Havilland Comet	1·50	1·50
2835	600l. Airbus Industrie A300	1·50	1·50
MS2836	Two sheets, each 121×96 mm. (a) 2000l. Lockheed L.1649A Starliner (91×34 mm). (b) 2000l. Concorde (91×34 mm) Set of 2 sheets	8·00	8·50

308 "The Annunciation" (Titian)

1997. Christmas. Religious Paintings. Multicoloured.

No.	Description	Mint	Used
2837	100l. Type **308**	35	10
2838	150l. "The Annunciation" (Titian) (different)	40	20
2839	200l. "Madonna of Foligno" (Raphael)	50	20
2840	250l. "The Annunciation" (Michelino)	60	25
2841	500l. "The Prophet Isaiah" (Michelangelo)	1·10	1·50
2842	600l. "Three Angels" (Master of the Rhenish Housebook)	1·40	1·75
MS2843	Two sheets, each 105×95 mm. (a) 2000l. "The Fall of the Rebel Angels" (Bruegel the Elder) (horiz). (b) 2000l. Angel and Monk (Anon) (horiz) Set of 2 sheets	6·00	7·00

308a With Daffodils

1998. Diana, Princess of Wales Commemoration. Multicoloured (except Nos. 2844, 2849, 2854 and 2856).

No.	Description	Mint	Used
2844	400l. Type **308a** (violet and black)	80	80
2845	400l. Carrying bouquet	80	80
2846	400l. With Mother Teresa	80	80
2847	400l. Wearing green and black jacket	80	80
2848	400l. With shawl over head	80	80
2849	400l. In evening dress (red and black)	80	80
2850	400l. Wearing choker and earrings	80	80
2851	400l. With Prince William	80	80
2852	400l. Wearing blue jacket and hat	80	80
2853	400l. Wearing white jacket	80	80
2854	400l. Wearing hat (brown and black)	80	80
2855	400l. Wearing black evening dress	80	80
2856	400l. Laughing (blue and black)	80	80
2857	400l. Wearing blue and white jacket and hat	80	80
2858	400l. Wearing green jacket with arms folded	80	80
2859	400l. Wearing black and white hat	80	80
2860	400l. Wearing open white shirt	80	80
2861	400l. Getting out of car	80	80
MS2862	Three sheets. (a) 100×70 mm. 1500l. Spooning food into bowl. (b) 100×70 mm. 1500l. Wearing grey-blue hat and jacket. (c) 70×100 mm. 1500l. Inspecting guard of honour Set of 3 sheets	8·50	9·00

309 Tiger

1998. Chinese New Year ("Year of the Tiger"). Designs with the tiger in the colour given.

No.	Type	Description	Mint	Used
2863	**309**	250l. mult (mauve)	40	50
2864	-	250l. mult (lake)	40	50
2865	-	250l. mult (purple)	40	50
2866	-	250l. mult (red)	40	50
MS2867		76×106 mm. 800l. multicoloured (vert)	1·25	1·50

310 "Metagyrphus nitens"

1998. Fauna and Flora. Multicoloured.

No.	Description	Mint	Used
2868	200l. Type **310**	35	15
2869	250l. Lord Derby's parakeet	50	25
2870	300l. Narcissus	55	20
2871	400l. "Barbus tetrazona" (fish) (horiz)	75	60
2872	450l. Japanese white-eyes (bird) (horiz)	80	85
2873	450l. Rhododendron (horiz)	80	85
2874	450l. Slow loris (horiz)	80	85
2875	450l. Gentiana (flower) (horiz)	80	85
2876	450l. "Orthetrum albistylum" (dragonfly) (horiz)	80	85
2877	450l. "Coluber jugularis" (snake) (horiz)	80	85
2878	450l. Cheetah (horiz)	80	85
2879	450l. "Ornithogalum thyrsoides" (plant) (horiz)	80	85
2880	450l. Ostrich (horiz)	80	85
2881	450l. Common chameleon (horiz)	80	85
2882	450l. Fennec fox (horiz)	80	85
2883	450l. "Junonia hierta cebrene" (butterfly) (horiz)	80	85
2884	500l. "Agalychnis callidryas" (frog) (horiz)	80	85
2885	600l. Wolverine (horiz)	95	95
MS2886	Two sheets (a) 70×100 mm. 2000l. Louisiana heron ("Tricoloured Heron") (b) 100×70 mm. 2000l. "Atheris squamiger" (snake) (horiz) Set of 2 sheets	6·50	7·00

Nos. 2872/7 and 2878/83 respectively were printed together, *se-tenant*, with the backgrounds forming composite designs.

311 Hypsilophodon

1998. Prehistoric Animals. Multicoloured.

No.	Description	Mint	Used
2887	200l. Type **311**	40	15
2888	400l. Lambeosaurus	75	50
2889	500l. Corythosaurus	80	85
2890	500l. Tyrannosaurus (horiz)	80	85
2891	500l. Tenontosaurus (horiz)	80	85
2892	500l. Deinonychus (horiz)	80	85
2893	500l. Triceratops (horiz)	80	85
2894	500l. Maiasaura with eggs (horiz)	80	85
2895	500l. Struthiomimus (horiz)	80	85
2896	500l. Plateosaurus	80	85
2897	500l. Tyrannosaurus	80	85
2898	500l. Brachiosaurus	80	85
2899	500l. Iguanodon	80	85
2900	500l. Styracosaurus	80	85
2901	500l. Hadrosaurus	80	85
2902	600l. Stegosaurus	85	90
2903	800l. Antrodemus (horiz)	1·25	1·40
MS2904	Two sheets. (a) 73×103 mm. 2000l. Triceratops (horiz). (b) 83×108 mm. 2000l. Tyrannosaurus (horiz) Set of 2 sheets	6·50	7·00

Nos. 2890/5 and 2896/2901 respectively were printed together, *se-tenant*, with the backgrounds forming composite designs.

312 Phoenician Galley

1998. Ships of the World. Multicoloured.

No.	Description	Mint	Used
2905	300l. Type **312**	90	90
2906	300l. Viking longship	90	90
2907	300l. Carrack	90	90
2908	300l. Venetian galley	90	90
2909	300l. Galeasse	90	90
2910	300l. Chebeck	90	90
2911	300l. Junk	90	90
2912	300l. H.M.S. "Victory" (ship of the line, 1765)	90	90
2913	300l. "Savannah" (paddle-steamer)	90	90
2914	300l. Gaissa (sailing canoe)	90	90
2915	300l. H.M.S. "Warrior" (ironclad)	90	90
2916	300l. "Preussen" (full-rigged ship)	90	90
MS2917	Two sheets, each 108×83 mm. (a) 2000l. "Santa Maria" (Columbus) (56×41 mm). (b) 2000l. "Titanic" (liner) (56×41 mm) Set of 2 sheets	7·00	7·50

1998. 70th Birthday of Mickey Mouse. Nos. 2813/18 and **MS**2827. Optd with Mickey Mouse and **HAPPY BIRTHDAY 1998**.

No.	Description	Mint	Used
2918	50l. Type **306**	90	80
2919	50l. Huey, Dewey and Louie	90	80
2920	50l. Donald Duck	90	80
2921	50l. Minnie Mouse	90	80
2922	50l. Morty and Ferdie	90	80
2923	50l. Mickey Mouse	90	80
MS2924	Two sheets. (a) 114×140 mm. 2000l. Mickey Mouse in sleigh. (b) 140×114 mm. 2000l. Mickey, Donald and Daisy (horiz) Set of 2 sheets	11·00	12·00

No. **MS**2924 are overprinted on the sheet margins which are additionally overprinted "MICKEY & MINNIE — 70th ANNIVERSARY".

314 Kiara and Butterfly

1998. Disney's "Lion King" (cartoon film). Multicoloured.

No.	Description	Mint	Used
2925	500l. Type **314**	1·25	1·25
2926	500l. Timon and Pumbaa	1·25	1·25
2927	500l. Kiara	1·25	1·25
2928	500l. Kiara and Kovu lying down	1·25	1·25
2929	500l. Kovu with bird	1·25	1·25
2930	500l. Kiara sitting with Kovu	1·25	1·25
2931	500l. Kiara and bird	1·25	1·25

2932 500l. Pumbaa 1·25 1·25
2933 500l. Kiara and Kovu side by side 1·25 1·25
2934 500l. Kovu 1·25 1·25
2935 500l. Kiara and Kovu back to back 1·25 1·25
2936 500l. Timon 1·25 1·25
MS2937 Two sheets, each 130×104 mm. (a) 2500l. Pumbaa and Timon. (b) 2500l. Kiara, Kovu and butterflies (horiz). 12·00 13·00

315 "Mary Magdalen Penitent" (Titian)

1998. Christmas. Religious Paintings. Multicoloured.
2938 200l. Type **315** 35 15
2939 500l. "Lamentation of Christ" (Veronese) 75 30
2940 1500l. "Building of Noah's Ark" (Guido Reni) 2·00 2·50
2941 2000l. "Abraham and Isaac" (Rembrandt) 2·50 3·00
MS2942 Two sheets, each 70×100 mm. (a) 3000l. "The Assumption of the Virgin" (Murillo). (b) 3000l. "Adoration of the Shepherds" (Murillo) Set of 2 sheets 7·50 8·50

1998. 25th Death Anniv of Pablo Picasso (painter). As T **373** of St. Vincent. Multicoloured.
2943 400l. "Man with Straw Hat and Ice Cream Cone" (vert) 70 50
2944 600l. "Woman in a Red Arm-chair" (vert) 1·00 1·10
2945 800l. "Nude in a Garden" 1·25 1·50
MS2946 101×127 mm. 2000l. "Girl holding a Dove" (vert) 2·50 3·00

315a Dan Beard and Lord Baden-Powell, 1937

1998. 19th World Scout Jamboree, Chile. Multicoloured (except No. 2950).
2947 1500l. Type **315a** 1·75 1·90
2948 1500l. Kuwaiti Scouts 1·75 1·90
2949 1500l. Scout leader feeding bear cub 1·75 1·90
2950 1500l. William D. Boyce (founder of Lone Scouts) (purple, brown and black) (vert) 1·75 1·90
2951 1500l. Guion S. Bluford (astronaut and former Eagle scout) (vert) 1·75 1·90
2952 1500l. Ellison S. Onizuka (astronaut and former Eagle scout) (vert) 1·75 1·90
MS2953 Two sheets, each 70×100 mm. (a) 3000l. Lord and Lady Baden-Powell, 1932. (b) 3000l. Feeding bear cub from bottle Set of 2 sheets 8·00 9·00

315b Mahatma Gandhi

1998. 50th Death Anniv of Mahatma Gandhi.
2954 **315b** 600l. multicoloured 2·75 2·25
MS2955 98×59 mm. 2000l. brown and black (horiz) 3·25 3·50

1998. 80th Anniv of Royal Air Force. As T **373d** of St. Vincent. Multicoloured.
2956 800l. McDonnell Douglas FRG2 Phantom 2·00 2·00
2957 800l. Pair of Panavia Tornado GR1s 2·00 2·00
2958 800l. Sepecat Jaguar GR1A 2·00 2·00
2959 800l. Lockheed C-130 Hercules 2·00 2·00
MS2960 Two sheets, each 92×70 mm.(a) 2000l. Lysander (reconnaissance) and Eurofighter EF-2000. (b) 2000l. Common buzzard and Bristol F2B fighter Set of 2 sheets 7·00 7·00

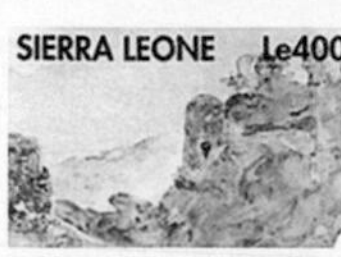

316 "Rocks and a Small Valley"

1998. Birth Bicentenary of Eugene Delacroix (painter). Multicoloured.
2961 400l. Type **316** 1·25 1·25
2962 400l. "Jewish Musicians from Magador" 1·25 1·25
2963 400l. "Moroccans travelling" 1·25 1·25
2964 400l. "Women of Algiers in their Apartment" 1·25 1·25
2965 400l. "Moroccan Military Training" 1·25 1·25
2966 400l. "Arabs skirmishing in the Mountains" 1·25 1·25
2967 400l. "Arab Chieftain reclining on a Carpet" 1·25 1·25
2968 400l. "Procession in Tangier" 1·25 1·25
MS2969 85×100 mm. 400l. "Self-portrait" (vert) 2·00 2·25

316a Diana, Princess of Wales

1998. First Death Anniv of Diana, Princess of Wales. Multicoloured.
2970 **316a** 600l. multicoloured 1·25 1·40

317 Rabbit

1998. Chinese New Year ("Year of the Rabbit"). Designs with the rabbit in the colour given.
2971 **317** 700l. mult (red) 1·10 1·25
2972 - 700l. mult (purple) 1·10 1·25
2973 - 700l. mult (blue) 1·10 1·25
2974 - 700l. mult (violet) 1·10 1·25
MS2975 76×106 mm. 1500l. multicoloured (vert) 2·25 2·75

318 Powder-blue Surgeonfish

1999. International Year of the Ocean. Multicoloured.
2976 150l. Type **318** 35 15
2977 250l. Frilled anemone 50 20
2978 400l. Reef heron ("Eastern Reef Heron") 80 85
2979 400l. Dolphins 80 85
2980 400l. Humpback whale and sailing ship 80 85
2981 400l. Green-winged macaw ("Red and Green Macaw") 80 85
2982 400l. Blue tangs 80 85
2983 400l. Guitarfish and blue-striped pipefish 80 85
2984 400l. Manatees 80 85
2985 400l. Hammerhead shark 80 85
2986 400l. Blue shark 80 85
2987 400l. Lemon goby and moorish idol 80 85
2988 400l. Ribbon moray ("Ribbon Eels") 80 85
2989 400l. Loggerhead turtle 80 85
2990 500l. Blue shark 85 90
2991 500l. Tiger shark 85 90
2992 500l. Bull shark 85 90
2993 500l. Great white shark 85 90
2994 500l. Scalloped hammerhead shark 85 90
2995 500l. Oceanic white-tipped shark 85 90
2996 500l. Zebra shark 85 90
2997 500l. Leopard shark 85 90
2998 500l. Horn shark 85 90
2999 500l. Hector's dolphin 85 90
3000 500l. Tucuxi 85 90
3001 500l. Hourglass dolphin 85 90
3002 500l. Bottlenose dolphin 85 90
3003 500l. Gray's beaked whale 85 90
3004 500l. Bowhead whale 85 90
3005 500l. Fin whale 85 90
3006 500l. Gray whale 85 90
3007 500l. Blue whale 85 90
3008 600l. Red beard sponge 95 1·00
3009 800l. Dusky batfish ("Red-finned Batfish") 1·25 1·40
MS3010 Three sheets, each 110×85 mm. (a) 3000l. Purple fire goby ("Purple Fire-fish"). (b) 3000l. Spotted eagle ray. (c) 3000l. Leather-back turtle Set of 3 sheets 15·00 16·00

Nos. 2978/89, 2990/8 and 2999/3007 were each printed together, *se-tenant*, with the backgrounds forming composite designs.

319 Grumman X-29

1999. Aircraft. Multicoloured.
3011 200l. Type **319** 40 20
3012 300l. Bell XS-1 rocket aircraft 50 20
3013 400l. Mikoyan Gurevich MiG-21 60 30
3014 600l. Bleriot XI 80 85
3015 600l. Nieuport 11 "Bebe" 80 85
3016 600l. D.H.100 Vampire 80 85
3017 600l. Aerospatiale/Aeritalia ATR 72 80 85
3018 600l. Fiat CR-32 80 85
3019 600l. Curtiss P-6E Hawk 80 85
3020 600l. SAAB JA 37 Viggen 80 85
3021 600l. Piper PA-46 Malibu 80 85
3022 600l. Grumman F-14 Tomcat 80 85
3023 600l. Grumman F3F-1 80 85
3024 600l. North American F-86A Sabre 80 85
3025 600l. Cessna 377 Super Skymaster 80 85
3026 600l. General Dynamics F-16 Fighting Falcon 80 85
3027 600l. "Voyager" experimental aircraft 80 85
3028 600l. Fairchild A10A Thunderbolt II 80 85
3029 600l. Wiley Post's Lockheed Vega, 1933 80 85
3030 600l. Amelia Earhart's Lockheed Vega, 1930 80 85
3031 600l. Sopwith Tabloid 80 85
3032 600l. Vickers F.B.5 "Gun Bus" 80 85
3033 600l. Savoia-Marchetti S.M. 79-II Sparviero 80 85
3034 600l. Mitsubishi A6M3 "Zero Sen" 80 85
3035 600l. Morane-Saulnier L 80 85
3036 600l. Shorts 360 80 85
3037 600l. Tupolev TU-160 80 85
3038 600l. Mikoyan-Gurevich MiG-15 80 85
3039 800l. Fokker F.VIIa/3m "Southern Cross" 1·25 1·40
3040 1500l. Supermarine S6B (seaplane) 2·00 2·50
MS3041 Two sheets, each 98×68 mm. (a) 3000l. Ryan NYP Special "Spirit of St. Louis" (56×42 mm). (b) 3000l. Canadair CL-215 (fire-fighting amphibian) (56×42 mm) Set of 2 sheets 8·50 9·00

No. 3023 is inscribed "GUMMAN F3F-1", No. 3027 "NICK" and No. 3030 "Amelia Earhart", all in error.

320 "Geranium wallichianum"

1999. "Australia '99" World Stamp Exhibition, Melbourne. Flowers. Multicoloured.
3042 150l. Type **320** 30 15
3043 200l. "Osmanthus x burkwoodii" 40 20
3044 250l. "Iris pallida dalmatica" (vert) 40 20
3045 500l. Rhododendron (vert) 70 30
3046 600l. Rose (vert) 80 80
3047 600l. "Clematis hybrida" (vert) 80 80
3048 600l. "Cardiospermum halicacabum" (vert) 80 80
3049 600l. "Fritillaria imperialis" (vert) 80 80
3050 600l. "Iris foetidiissima" (vert) 80 80
3051 600l. Pyracantha (vert) 80 80
3052 600l. "Hepatica transsilvanica" (vert) 80 80
3053 600l. "Aquilegia olympica" 80 80
3054 600l. Lilium (orange) 80 80
3055 600l. "Magnolia grandiflora" 80 80
3056 600l. "Polygonatum x hybridum" 80 80
3057 600l. "Clematis montana" 80 80
3058 600l. "Vinca minor" 80 80
3059 600l. "Jack Snipe" 80 80
3060 600l. "Alstroemeria ligtu" 80 80
3061 600l. Lilium (yellow) 80 80
3062 600l. "Marjorie fair" 80 80
3063 600l. "Anemone coronaria" 80 80
3064 600l. "Clematis ranncu lanaceae" 80 80
3065 600l. "Colchicum speciosum" 80 80
3066 600l. "Scandere" 80 80
3067 600l. "Helianthus annuus" 80 80
3068 600l. "Lady Kerkrade" 80 80
3069 600l. "Clematis x durandii" 80 80
3070 600l. "Lilium regale" 80 80
3071 800l. Papoose (vert) 1·25 1·40
3072 1500l. "Viola labradorica" (vert) 1·75 2·00
3073 2000l. "Rosa banksiae lutea" (vert) 2·25 2·50
MS3074 Four sheets. (a) 100×74 mm. 4000l. "Clerodendrum trichotomum fargesii" (b) 75×100 mm. 4000l. "Rubus fruitcosus" (vert). (c) 75×100 mm. 4000l. "Crocus angustifolius" (vert). (d) 75×100 mm. 4000l. "Holboellia" Set of 4 sheets 18·00 20·00

Nos. 3047/52, 3053/8 and 3071/3 were printed together, *se-tenant*, with the backgrounds forming a composite design.

Only Nos. 3042/6 and 3071/3 show the "Australia '99" emblem actually printed on the stamp.

No. 3043 is inscribed "Osmanthus burkwoodu" and No. 3069 "Clematix x durandii", both in error.

321 Red-headed Malimbe

1999. Birds of Africa. Multicoloured.
3075 400l. Type **321** 50 25
3076 500l. Common kestrel 60 30
3077 600l. Little owl 70 75
3078 600l. Eastern white pelican ("Great White Pelican") 70 75
3079 600l. Superb starling 70 75
3080 600l. Red-throated bee eater 70 75
3081 600l. Woodland kingfisher 70 75
3082 600l. Purple swamphen 70 75
3083 600l. Lesser pied kingfisher ("Pied Kingfisher") 70 75
3084 600l. African spoonbill 70 75
3085 600l. Egyptian plover ("Crocodilebird") 70 75
3086 600l. Cattle egret 70 75
3087 600l. White-fronted bee eater 70 75
3088 600l. Gray parrot ("African Grey Parrot") 70 75
3089 600l. Cinnamon-chested bee eater 70 75
3090 600l. Malachite kingfisher 70 75
3091 600l. White-throated bee eater 70 75
3092 600l. Yellow-billed stork 70 75
3093 600l. Hildebrandt's starling 70 75
3094 600l. White-faced whistling duck (horiz) 70 75
3095 600l. Black-headed heron (horiz) 70 75
3096 600l. Black-headed gonolek (horiz) 70 75
3097 600l. Malachite kingfisher (horiz) 70 75
3098 600l. African fish eagle ("Fish-eagle") (horiz) 70 75
3099 600l. African spoonbill (horiz) 70 75
3100 600l. African skimmer (horiz) 70 75
3101 600l. Black heron (horiz) 70 75
3102 600l. Allen's gallinule (horiz) 70 75
3103 600l. Montagu's harrier (horiz) 70 75
3104 600l. Booted eagle (horiz) 70 75
3105 600l. Yellow-crested helmet shrike (horiz) 70 75
3106 600l. Red-tufted malachite sunbird ("Scarlet-tufted Malachite Sunbird") (horiz) 70 75
3107 600l. Pin-tailed whydah (horiz) 70 75
3108 600l. Red-headed weaver ("Red-headed Malimbe") (horiz) 70 75
3109 600l. Violet-backed sunbird (horiz) 70 75
3110 600l. Yellow white eye (horiz) 70 75
3111 600l. Brubru shrike (horiz) 70 75
3112 600l. African paradise flycatcher ("African Paradise Monarch") (horiz) 70 75
3113 600l. Lilac-breasted roller (horiz) 70 75
3114 600l. Scops owl ("European Scops Owl") (horiz) 70 75
3115 600l. African emerald cuckoo (horiz) 70 75
3116 600l. Blue flycatcher ("Blue Monarch") (horiz) 70 75
3117 600l. African golden oriole (horiz) 70 75
3118 600l. White-throated bee eater (horiz) 70 75
3119 600l. Black-bellied seedcracker (horiz) 70 75

No.	Description	Mint	Used
3120	600l. Hoopoe (horiz)	70	75
3121	600l. Scimitar-bill (horiz)	70	75
3122	600l. Bateleur (horiz)	70	75
3123	600l. Village weaver ("Black-headed Weaver") (horiz)	70	75
3124	600l. Variable sunbird (horiz)	70	75
3125	600l. Blue swallow (horiz)	70	75
3126	600l. Red-crowned bishop ("Black-winged Red Bishop") (horiz)	70	75
3127	600l. Namaqua dove (horiz)	70	75
3128	600l. Golden-breasted bunting (horiz)	70	75
3129	600l. Hartlaub's bustard (horiz)	70	75
MS3130	Six sheets, each 85×110 mm (3000l.) or 73×98 mm (4000l.). (a) 3000l. African fish eagle. (b) 3000l. Baglafecht weaver ("Richenow's Weaver"). (c) 4000l. African Pygmy kingfisher. (d) 4000l. Ruwenzori turaco. (e) 4000l. Crowned crane ("Grey Crowned Crane") (f) 4000l. Whale-headed stork ("Shoebill") Set of 6 sheets	23·00	25·00

Nos. 3078/85, 3086/93, 3094/102, 3103/11, 3112/20 and 3121/9 were each printed together, *se-tenant*, with the backgrounds forming composite designs.

No. 3077 is inscribed "LITLE OWL", No. 3087 "BMerops bullockoides", No. 3112 "Terpsiphonevirdis", No. 3121 "Scimitarbill", No. 3124 "Nectarina", No. 3126 "hordeaceus" and No. **MS**3130d ("Rwenzori"), all in error.

322 Diana Monkey

1999. Wildlife. Multicoloured.

No.	Description	Mint	Used
3131	300l. Type **322**	60	20
3132	800l. Bush pig	1·25	1·25
3133	900l. Flap-necked chameleon	1·50	1·60
3134	900l. Golden oriole	1·50	1·60
3135	900l. European bee eater	1·50	1·60
3136	900l. Leopard	1·50	1·60
3137	900l. Lion	1·50	1·60
3138	900l. Chimpanzee	1·50	1·60
3139	900l. Senegal galago	1·50	1·60
3140	900l. Hoopoe	1·50	1·60
3141	900l. Long-tailed pangolin	1·50	1·60
3142	900l. Hippopotamus	1·50	1·60
3143	900l. African elelphant	1·50	1·60
3144	900l. Red-billed hornbill	1·50	1·60
3145	1500l. Lioness	2·25	2·50
MS3146	Two sheets, each 85×110 mm. (a) 3000l. Grey parrot. (b) 3000l. West African linsang Set of 2 sheets	9·00	10·00

Nos. 3133/8 and 3139/44 were each printed together, *se-tenant*, forming composite designs.

SIERRA LEONE Le150
323 Steam Locomotive, Benguela Railway, Angola

1999. Famous Trains. Multicoloured.

No.	Description	Mint	Used
3147	100l. The "Rocket" (vert)	30	15
3148	150l. Type **323**	35	20
3149	200l. Class 310 steam locomotive, Sudan	40	25
3150	250l. Steam locomotive, Chicago, Burlington and Quincy Railway, U.S.A.	40	25
3151	300l. Class "Terrier" tank locomotive, Great Britain	50	30
3152	400l. Dublin to Cork express train, Ireland	60	40
3153	500l. Steam locomotive "George Stephenson", Scotland	70	55
3154	600l. Shay steam locomotive	75	65
3155	800l. Class 19D, Africa	90	90
3156	800l. Double-headed train on viaduct over Kaaiman River, Africa	90	90
3157	800l. Bo-Bo electric locomotive, Egypt	90	90
3158	800l. Gmam Garratt steam locomotive, South Africa	90	90
3159	800l. Passenger train at Rabat, Morocco	90	90
3160	800l. Class 14A Garratt, Rhodesia	90	90
3161	800l. Western type steam locomotive, U.S.A.	90	90
3162	800l. "The Flying Scotsman" express, Scotland	90	90
3163	800l. Steam locomotive "Lord Nelson"	90	90
3164	800l. Steam locomotive "Mallard"	90	90
3165	800l. Steam locomotive "Evening Star"	90	90
3166	800l. Indian Railways Class WP steam locomotive No. 7418	90	90
3167	1500l. "South Wind" express, U.S.A. (horiz)	1·60	1·75
MS3168	Two sheets. (a) 76×106 mm. 3000l. Railcar on an Alpine rack railway (vert). (b) 106×76 mm. 3000l. Royal train, Rhodesia Set of 2 sheets	8·50	8·50

No. 3166 is inscribed "THE BRITIANIA" and No. **MS**3168a "MOUNTAIN CLASS GARRATT/AFRICA", both in error.

1999. "iBRA '99" International Stamp Exhibition, Nuremburg. As T **384a** of St. Vincent. Multicoloured.

No.	Description	Mint	Used
3169	1500l. "Claud Hamilton" steam locomotive, Germany	2·25	2·50
3170	2000l. "Borsig" steam locomotive, 1835, Germany	2·75	3·00

1999. 150th Death Anniv of Katsushika Hokusai (Japanese artist). As T **384b** of St. Vincent. Multicoloured.

No.	Description	Mint	Used
3171	1000l. "People admiring Mount Fuji from a Tea House"	1·25	1·25
3172	1000l. "People on a Temple Balcony"	1·25	1·25
3173	1000l. "Sea Life" (shrimp)	1·25	1·25
3174	1000l. "Sea Life" (shells)	1·25	1·25
3175	1000l. "The Pontoon Bridge at Sano in Winter"	1·25	1·25
3176	1000l. "A Shower below the Summit"	1·25	1·25
3177	1000l. "The Hanging Cloud Bridge"	1·25	1·25
3178	1000l. "The Timber Yard by the Tate River"	1·25	1·25
3179	1000l. "Bird Drawings" (owl)	1·25	1·25
3180	1000l. "Bird Drawings" (ducks)	1·25	1·25
3181	1000l. "Travellers crossing the Oi River"	1·25	1·25
3182	1000l. "Travellers on the Tokaido Road at Hodogaya"	1·25	1·25
MS3183	Two sheets, each 100×70 mm. (a) 3000l. "A view of Mount Fuji and Travellers by a Bridge" (vert). (b) 3000l. "A Sudden Gust of Wind at Ejiri" (vert) Set of 2 sheets	8·00	8·50

1999. Tenth Anniv of United Nations Rights of the Child Convention. As T **348d** of St. Vincent. Multicoloured.

No.	Description	Mint	Used
3184	1600l. Japanese girl holding candle	1·75	2·00
3185	1600l. Two Japanese children	1·75	2·00
3186	1600l. Japanese girl in kimono	1·75	2·00
MS3187	110×85 mm. 3000l. Baby boy (horiz)	3·75	4·25

1999. "PhilexFrance '99" International Stamp Exhibition, PAris. railway Locomotives. Two sheets, each 106×76 mm containing horiz designs as T **385d** of St. Vincent. Multicoloured.

No.	Description	Mint	Used
MS3188	(a) 3000l. Crampton locomotive, French Eastern Railway. (b) 3000l. De Glehn Compund locomotive, French Northern Railway Set of 2 sheets	9·00	10·00

1999. 250th Birth Anniv of Johann von Goethe (German writer). As T **384c** of St. Vincent.

No.	Description	Mint	Used
3189	1600l. multicoloured	2·00	2·25
3190	1600l. blue, lilac and black	2·00	2·25
3191	1600l. multicoloured	2·00	2·25
3192	1600l. blue, black and green	2·00	2·25
3193	1600l. light blue, blue and black	2·00	2·25
MS3194	Two sheets. (a) 106×76 mm. 3000l. brown and black. (b) 76×106 mm. 3000l. brown and black Set of 2 sheets	8·00	8·50

DESIGNS—HORIZ: No. 3189, Helena with her Chorus; 3190, Goethe and Schiller; 3191, Faust seated beside Helena; 3192, The Witch beseeching Faust to drink her fiery brew; 3193, Margaret placing flowers before the niche of Mater Dolorosa; No. **MS**3191a, Angelic spirit. VERT: No. **MS**3194b, Ariel.

No. 3192 is inscribed "BESEIGES" in error.

1999. "Queen Elizabeth the Queen Mother's Century". As T **386b** of St. Vincent.

No.	Description	Mint	Used
3195	1300l. black and gold	1·75	1·75
3196	1300l. multicoloured	1·75	1·75
3197	1300l. black and gold	1·75	1·75
3198	1300l. multicoloured	1·75	1·75
MS3199	153×157 mm. 4000l. multicoloured	6·50	7·00

DESIGNS: No. 3195, Duke and Duchess of York and Princess Elizabeth, 1926; 3196, Queen Mother, 1979; 3197, Queen Mother visiting Nairobi, 1959; 3198, Queen Mother holding bouquet, 1991. 37×50 mm: No. **MS**3199, Queen Elizabeth in Coronation robes, 1937.

No. **MS**3199 also shows the Royal Arms embossed in gold.

324 "Interpretation of a Poem of Shi-Tao" (Fu Baoshi)

1999. "China '99" International Stamp Exhibition, Beijing. Paintings of Fu Baoshi (Chinese artist). Multicoloured.

No.	Description	Mint	Used
3200	400l. Type **324**	65	75
3201	400l. "Autumn of Ho-Pao"	65	75
3202	400l. "Landscape in Rain" (bridge at bottom right)	65	75
3203	400l. "Landscape in Rain" (mountain peaks)	65	75
3204	400l. "Landscape in Rain" (mountain rest house)	65	75
3205	400l. "Portrait of To-Fu"	65	75
3206	400l. "Classic Lady" (amongst green trees)	65	75
3207	400l. "Portrait of Li-Pai"	65	75
3208	400l. "Sprite of the Mountain"	65	75
3209	400l. "Classic Lady" (amongst bare trees)	65	75
MS3210	138×105 mm. 800l. "Four Seasons–Winter" (51×39 mm) (vert); 1500l. "Four Seasons–Summer" (51×39 mm) (vert)	3·25	3·75

325 Macao Skyline inside "MACAU"

1999. Return of Macao to China.

No.	Type	Description	Mint	Used
3211	**325**	1200l. multicoloured	1·25	1·40

326 Sophie Rhys-Jones

1999. Royal Wedding. Multicoloured.

No.	Description	Mint	Used
3212	2000l. Type **326**	2·00	2·25
3213	2000l. Prince Edward (wearing striped shirt and black jacket)	2·00	2·25
3214	2000l. Sophie Rhys-Jones (different)	2·00	2·25
3215	2000l. Prince Edward	2·00	2·25
MS3216	117×115 mm. 4000l. Sophie Rhys-Jones and Prince Edward (horiz)	7·00	7·50

327 Dragon

2000. Chinese New Year ("Year of the Dragon"). Multicoloured.

No.	Description	Mint	Used
3217	1500l. Type **327**	1·75	1·90
3218	1500l. Dragon ("LUNAR NEW YEAR" bottom right)	1·75	1·90
3219	1500l. Dragon ("LUNAR NEW YEAR" bottom left)	1·75	1·90
3220	1500l. Dragon ("LUNAR NEW YEAR" top right)	1·75	1·90
MS3221	76×106 mm. 4000l. Dragon (vert)	5·00	6·00

328 Sammy Davis Jr.

2000. 75th Birth Anniv of Sammy Davis Jr. (American entertainer).

No.	Type	Description	Mint	Used
3222	-	1000l. brown and black	1·00	1·10
3223	-	1000l. brown and black	1·00	1·10
3224	**328**	1000l. multicoloured	1·00	1·10
3225	-	1000l. multicoloured	1·00	1·10
3226	-	1000l. red and black	1·00	1·10
3227	-	1000l. red and black	1·00	1·10
MS3228		130×130 mm. 5000l. brown and black	5·00	5·50

DESIGNS: No. 3222, As young boy; 3223, Arms outstretched in front of motorcycle; 3225, Holding microphone and singing; 3226, With foot on chair: 3227, Singing with cigarette. **MS**3228, Wearing sunglasses, white shirt and waistcoat.

329 Betty Boop

2000. Betty Boop (cartoon character). Multicoloured.

No.	Description	Mint	Used
3229	800l. Wearing short flowered dress	85	90
3230	800l. Out shopping	85	90
3231	800l. Wearing baseball cap	85	90
3232	800l. Type **329**	85	90
3233	800l. Sitting on chair	85	90
3234	800l. In duffle coat and carrying book	85	90
3235	800l. Playing guitar	85	90
3236	800l. As cowgirl with lasso	85	90
3237	800l. Holding flower	85	90
MS3238	Two sheets (a) 140×101 mm. 5000l. Riding bicycle. (b) 101×140 mm. 5000l. Wearing purple coat Set of 2 sheets	9·00	10·00

Nos. 3229/37 were printed, *se-tenant*, with the backgrounds forming a composite design.

330 Lucille Ball in Hotel Uniform

2000. "I Love Lucy" (American T.V. comedy series). Multicoloured.

No.	Description	Mint	Used
3239	800l. Type **330**	85	90
3240	800l. Behind medicine counter with hands crossed	85	90
3241	800l. In bed	85	90
3242	800l. Poking tongue out	85	90
3243	800l. Inside television set	85	90
3244	800l. Behind counter with bottle in left hand	85	90
3245	800l. Behind medicine counter with hands by sides	85	90
3246	800l. Leaning on counter holding bottle in right hand	85	90
3247	800l. Tipping medicine away	85	90
MS3248	Two sheets, each 101×140 mm. (a) 5000l. Lucy inside television set. (b) 5000l. Lucy pinching man's face Set of 2 sheets	6·00	6·25

330a Tsar Michael Romanov of Russia (elected 1613)

2000. New Millennium. People and Events of Seventeenth Century (1600–1650). Multicoloured.

No.	Description	Mint	Used
3249	400l. Type **330a**	70	70
3250	400l. William Shakespeare ("Hamlet", published 1603)	70	70
3251	400l. "Thousand Peaks and Myriad Ravines" (Kung Hsien, 1620–89)	70	70
3252	400l. Francis Bacon and title page (works published 1605)	70	70
3253	400l. Captain John Smith and colonists (Jamestown, founded 1607)	70	70

3254 400l. Versailles and courtiers (succession of Louis XIV, 1643) 70 70
3255 400l. Flag, map and waterfall (French foundation of Quebec, 1608) 70 70
3256 400l. Isaac Newton (born 1642) 70 70
3257 400l. "The Rape of the Sabine Women" (Nicolas Poussin), 1636 70 70
3258 400l. Johannes Kepler ("The New Astronomy" published 1609) 70 70
3259 400l. Colonists at Cape Cod (arrival of "Mayflower" in America, 1620) 70 70
3260 400l. King James I of England and title page of Bible (King James Bible, published 1611) 70 70
3261 400l. Activities of Dutch East India Company (introduction of tea to Europe, 1610) 70 70
3262 400l. Rene Descartes and sketch of boy (doctrine "I think, therefore I am", 1641) 70 70
3263 400l. Galileo (proves Earth orbits Sun, 1632) 70 70
3264 400l. Queen Elizabeth I (died 1603) (59×39 mm) 70 70
3265 400l. Miguel de Cervantes and title page (publication of "Don Quixote", 1605) 70 70

330b Flowers forming Top of Head

2000. Faces of the Millennium: Diana, Princess of Wales. Showing collage of miniature flower photographs. Multicoloured.

3266 800l. Type **330b** (face value at left) 85 90
3267 800l. Top of head (face value at right) 85 90
3268 800l. Ear (face value at left) 85 90
3269 800l. Eye and temple (face value at right) 85 90
3270 800l. Cheek (face value at left) 85 90
3271 800l. Cheek (face value at right) 85 90
3272 800l. Blue background (face value at left) 85 90
3273 800l. Chin (face value at right) 85 90

Nos. 3266/73 were printed together, *se-tenant*, in sheetlets of 8 with the stamps arranged in two vertical columns separated by a gutter also containing miniature photographs. When viewed as a whole, the sheetlet forms a portrait of Diana, Princess of Wales.

331 Colonel Lloyd (Lionel Barrymore) and his Granddaughter (Shirley Temple)

2000. Shirley Temple in "The Little Colonel". Showing scenes from the film. Multicoloured.

3274 1200l. Type **331** 1·00 1·10
3275 1200l. Lloyd (Shirley Temple) and Walker (Bill Robinson) 1·00 1·10
3276 1200l. Lloyd with Henry Clay and May Lily 1·00 1·10
3277 1200l. Lloyd with soldiers 1·00 1·10
3278 1200l. Lloyd with her mother and Mom Beck 1·00 1·10
3279 1200l. Lloyd hugging her grandfather 1·00 1·10
3280 1500l. Lloyd with her grandfather's servants 1·25 1·40
3281 1500l. Walker and Lloyd tap dancing 1·25 1·40
3282 1500l. Lloyd standing in bushes 1·25 1·40
3283 1500l. Lloyd and the Colonel 1·25 1·40
MS3284 107×76 mm. 5000l. Lloyd saluting 3·00 3·25

332 Mario Andretti in Saloon Car

2000. 60th Birthday of Mario Andretti (U.S. racing driver). Multicoloured (except Nos. 3285 and 3288).

3285 600l. Type **332** (black, yellow and red) 70 75
3286 600l. Wearing racing helmet 70 75
3287 600l. Being congratulated 70 75
3288 600l. In car number 26 (black and red) 70 75
3289 600l. Changing wheel 70 75
3290 600l. Wearing white T-shirt 70 75
3291 600l. Shirtless 70 75
3292 600l. Driving GT Ferrari 70 75
MS3293 128×151 mm. 5000l. As young man with friends and first car 6·00 6·50

2000. 400th Birth Anniv of Sir Anthony Van Dyck (Flemish painter). As T **394c** of St. Vincent. Multicoloured.

3294 1000l. "Taking of Christ" (detail) 90 1·00
3295 1000l. "Ecce Homo" (1625–26) 90 1·00
3296 1000l. "Christ carrying the Cross" (soldier in black helmet) 90 1·00
3297 1000l. "Raising of Christ on the Cross" 90 1·00
3298 1000l. "The Crucifixion" (c. 1627) 90 1·00
3299 1000l. "The Lamentation" (c. 1616) 90 1·00
3300 1000l. "Taking of Christ" (complete painting) 90 1·00
3301 1000l. "The Mocking of Christ" 90 1·00
3302 1000l. "Ecce Homo" (1628–32) 90 1·00
3303 1000l. "Christ carrying the Cross" (soldier in red helmet) 90 1·00
3304 1000l. "The Crucifixion" (1629–30) 90 1·00
3305 1000l. "The Lamentation" (1618–20) 90 1·00
3306 1000l. "Portrait of a Man" 90 1·00
3307 1000l. "Anna Wake, Wife of Peeter Stevens" 90 1·00
3308 1000l. "Peeter Stevens" 90 1·00
3309 1000l. "Adriaen Stevens" 90 1·00
3310 1000l. "Maria Bosschaerts, Wife of Adriaen Stevens" 90 1·00
3311 1000l. "Portrait of a Woman" 90 1·00
3312 1000l. "Self-portrait" (1617–18) 90 1·00
3313 1000l. "Self-portrait" (1620–21) 90 1·00
3314 1000l. "Self-portrait" (1622–23) 90 1·00
3315 1000l. "Andromeda chained to the Rock" 90 1·00
3316 1000l. "Self-portrait" (late 1620s–early 1630s) 90 1·00
3317 1000l. "Mary Ruthven" 90 1·00
3318 1000l. "The Duchess of Croy with her Son" 90 1·00
3319 1000l. "Susanna Fourment and her Daughter" 90 1·00
3320 1000l. "Geronima Brignole-Sale with her Daughter Maria Aurelia" 90 1·00
3321 1000l. "Woman with her Daughter" 90 1·00
3322 1000l. "Genoese Noblewoman with her Child" 90 1·00
3323 1000l. "Paola Adorno and her Son" 90 1·00
MS3324 Six sheets. (a) 102×127 mm. 5000l. "Young Woman with a Child". (b) 102×127 mm. 5000l. "Pozia Imperiale and her Daughter Maria Frencesca". (c) 102×127 mm. 5000l. "Portrait of Mother and Daughter". (d) 127×102 mm. 5000l. "Self-portrait with Endymion Porter". (e) 127×102 mm. 5000l. "Self-portrait with Sunflower". (f) 102×127 mm. 5000l. "Woman and Child" (horiz) Set of 6 sheets 26·00 29·00

No. 3311 is inscribed "Protrait of a Women" in error.

333 Grey Parrot ("African Grey Parrot")

2000. "The Stamp Show 2000" International Stamp Exhibition, London. Parrots and Parakeets. Multicoloured.

3325 200l. Type **333** 35 15
3326 800l. Monk parakeet 1·10 1·10
3327 800l. Lesser sulphur-crested cockatoo ("Citron-crested Cockatoo") 1·10 1·10
3328 800l. Golden conure ("Queen of Bavaria Conure") 1·10 1·10
3329 800l. Budgerigar 1·10 1·10
3330 800l. Canary-winged parakeet ("Yellow-chevroned Parakeet") 1·10 1·10
3331 800l. Cockatiel 1·10 1·10
3332 800l. Green-checked amazon ("Amazon Parrot") 1·10 1·10
3333 800l. Sun conure 1·10 1·10
3334 800l. Malabar parakeet 1·10 1·10
3335 800l. Eclectus parrot ("Grand Eclectus Parrot") 1·10 1·10
3336 800l. Jandaya conure ("Sun Parakeet") 1·10 1·10
3337 800l. Hawk-headed parrot ("Red fan Parakeet") 1·10 1·10
3338 800l. Fischer's lovebird 1·10 1·10
3339 800l. Masked lovebird ("Blue-masked Lovebird") 1·10 1·10
3340 800l. White-bellied caique ("White-bellied Rosella") 1·10 1·10
3341 800l. Plum-headed parakeet 1·10 1·10
3342 800l. Striated lorikeet 1·10 1·10
3343 800l. Eastern rosella ("Gold-mantled Rosella") 1·10 1·10
3344 1500l. Sulphur-crested cockatoo 1·90 2·25
MS3345 120×81 mm. 4000l. Blue and yellow macaw ("Blue and Gold Macaw") (37×50 mm) 7·00 7·50

Nos. 3326/34 and 3335/43 were each printed together, *se-tenant*, with the backgrounds forming composite designs.

No. 3327 is inscribed "Cockatto" and No. 3344 "Sulfur Crested Cockatto", both in error.

334 Herring Gull

2000. Seabirds of the World. Multicoloured.

3346 400l. Type **334** 65 35
3347 600l. Caspian tern (standing by rock) 90 60
3348 800l. Grey phalarope ("Red Phalarope") 1·10 90
3349 1000l. Wandering albatross 1·25 1·40
3350 1000l. Fork-tailed storm petrel 1·25 1·40
3351 1000l. Greater shearwater 1·25 1·40
3352 1000l. Blue-footed booby 1·25 1·40
3353 1000l. Great cormorant 1·25 1·40
3354 1000l. Atlantic puffin 1·25 1·40
3355 1000l. Caspian tern (fishing) 1·25 1·40
3356 1000l. Glaucous gull 1·25 1·40
3357 1000l. Northern gannet 1·25 1·40
3358 1000l. Long-tailed skua ("Long-tailed Jaeger") 1·25 1·40
3359 1000l. Brown pelican 1·25 1·40
3360 1000l. Great skua 1·25 1·40
3361 2000l. Magnificent frigate bird 2·25 2·50
MS3362 Two sheets, each 56×66 mm. (a) 5000l. red-billed tropic bird ("Red-tailed Tropic Bird") (vert). (b) 5000l. Brown booby (vert) Set of 2 sheets 11·00 12·00

No. **MS**3362b is inscribed "Brown Boobie" in error.

Nos. 3349/54 and 3355/60 were each printed together, *se-tenant*, with the backgrounds forming composite designs.

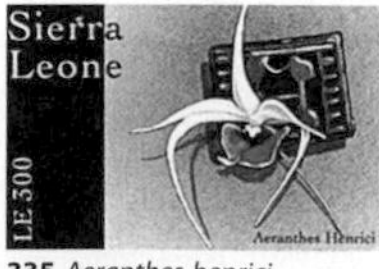

335 *Aeranthes henrici*

2000. Orchids. Multicoloured.

3363 300l. Type **335** 50 20
3364 500l. *Ophrys apifera* 70 35
3365 600l. *Disa crassicornis* 80 55
3366 1100l. *Oeleoclades maculata* (vert) 1·25 1·40
3367 1100l. *Polystachya campyloglossa* (vert) 1·25 1·40
3368 1100l. *Polystachya pubescens* (vert) 1·25 1·40
3369 1100l. *Tridactyle bicaudata* (vert) 1·25 1·40
3370 1100l. *Angraecum veitcii* (vert) 1·25 1·40
3371 1100l. *Sobennikoffia robusta* (vert) 1·25 1·40
3372 1100l. *Aerangis curnowiana* (vert) 1·25 1·40
3373 1100l. *Aerangis fastudsa* (vert) 1·25 1·40
3374 1100l. *Angraecum magdalenae* (vert) 1·25 1·40
3375 1100l. *Angraecum sororium* (vert) 1·25 1·40
3376 1100l. *Eulophia speciosa* (vert) 1·25 1·40
3377 1100l. *Ansellia africana* (vert) 1·25 1·40
3378 2000l. *Aeranthes grandiflora* 2·25 2·50
MS3379 Two sheets, each 74×64 mm. (a) 4000l. *Angraecum eburneum* (vert). (b) 4000l. *Angraecum compactum* (vert) Set of 2 sheets 11·00 12·00

Nos. 3366/71 and 3372/7 were each printed together, *se-tenant*, with the backgrounds forming composite designs.

No. 3367 is inscribed "Ploystachya" in error.

2000. 18th Birthday of Prince William. As T **395a** of St. Vincent. Multicoloured.

3380 1100l. Prince William laughing 1·40 1·40
3381 1100l. Wearing blue shirt and grey suit 1·40 1·40
3382 1100l. In dark jacket and red-patterned tie 1·40 1·40
3383 1100l. Wearing white shirt and blue suit 1·40 1·40
MS3384 100×80 mm. 5000l. Holding bouquet of flowers (37×50 mm) 7·00 7·50

335a "Apollo 18"

2000. 25th Anniv of "Apollo–Soyuz" Joint Project. Multicoloured.

3385 1200l. Type **335a** 1·25 1·40
3386 1200l. "Soyuz 19" 1·25 1·40
3387 1200l. "Apollo 18" and "Soyuz 19" docked in orbit 1·25 1·40
MS3388 94×84 mm. 5000l. "Apollo 18" and "Soyuz 19" docking 6·50 7·00

2000. 50th Anniv of Berlin Film Festival. As T **395c** of St. Vincent. Showing film scenes. Multicoloured.

3389 1100l. *Las Palabras de Max*, 1978 1·25 1·40
3390 1100l. *Ascendancy*, 1983 1·25 1·40
3391 1100l. *Deprisa, Deprisa*, 1981 1·25 1·40
3392 1100l. *Die Sehnsucht der Veronika Voss*, 1982 1·25 1·40
3393 1100l. *Heartland*, 1980 1·25 1·40
3394 1100l. *La Colmena*, 1983 1·25 1·40
MS3395 97×103 mm. 5000l. *Las Truches*, 1978 6·50 7·00

2000. 175th Anniv of Stockton and Darlington Line (first public railway). As T 395d of St. Vincent. Multicoloured.

3396 3000l. George Stephenson and *Locomotion No. 1* 3·50 3·75
3397 3000l. James Watt's original design for separate condenser engine, 1789 3·50 3·75

No. 3397 is inscribed "comdensor" in error.

335b Johann Sebastian Bach

2000. 250th Death Anniv of Johann Sebastian Bach (German composer). Sheet, 104×101 mm.

MS3398 **335b** 5000l. multicoloured 7·00 7·50

335c Albert Einstein holding Pipe

2000. Election of Albert Einstein (mathematical physicist) as Time Magazine "Man of the Century". Sheet 117×91 mm.

MS3399 **335c** 5000l. multicoloured 6·00 6·50

2000. Centenary of First Zeppelin Flight. As T **396a** of St. Vincent. Multicoloured.

3400 2000l. LZ-129 *Hindenburg*, 1936 2·00 2·25
3401 2000l. LZ-4, 1908 2·00 2·25
3402 2000l. LZ-6 *Delag*, 1909 2·00 2·25

MS3403 116×76 mm. 4000l. LZ-127 *Graf Zeppelin*, 1928 (50×37 mm) 6·00 6·50

No. 3400 is inscribed "Hindenberg" in error.

2000. Olympic Games, Sydney. As T **396b** of St. Vincent. Multicoloured.

3404	1500l. Forrest Smithson (hurdling), London (1908)	1·75	2·00
3405	1500l. Football	1·75	2·00
3406	1500l. Olympic Stadium, Helsinki (1952) with Finnish flag	1·75	2·00
3407	1500l. Ancient Greek wrestlers	1·75	2·00

336 Richard Petty sitting on Car with Trophy

2000. Richard Petty (stock car driver) Commem. Multicoloured.

3408	800l. Type **336**	75	85
3409	800l. In cream overalls and cap	75	85
3410	800l. In stetson and sunglasses (blue collar)	75	85
3411	800l. In plain white shirt (blue background)	75	85
3412	800l. In stetson and sunglasses (red collar)	75	85
3413	800l. Squatting with cap alongside No. 43	75	85
3414	800l. Leaning on car	75	85
3415	800l. Crouching with arm in car	75	85
3416	800l. Looking out of car No. 43	75	85
3417	800l. Car in pits	75	85
3418	800l. Standing with family	75	85
3419	800l. Standing by car with helmet on door	75	85
3420	800l. In Pontiac cap	75	85
3421	800l. In white stetson and sunglasses (green background)	75	85
3422	800l. In STP cap	75	85
3423	800l. Standing up in blue car	75	85
3424	800l. In white stetson (with STP epaulettes)	75	85
3425	800l. Sitting watching race	75	85
3426	800l. Being interviewed	75	85
3427	800l. In plain white shirt (brown background)	75	85
3428	800l. Wearing orange cap and sunglasses	75	85
3429	800l. Sitting in car (interior view)	75	85
3430	800l. Timing a race	75	85
3431	800l. In blue and red helmet	75	85
3432	800l. In white stetson and sunglasses (blue overalls)	75	85
3433	800l. Holding trophy in blue, red and white overalls	75	85
3434	800l. Sitting in white stetson and sunglasses	75	85

MS3435 Two sheets, each 110×76 mm. (a) 5000l. As No. 3423. (b) 5000l. Car No. 43 during race (horiz) Set of 2 sheets 9·00 10·00

337 Worns (German player)

2000. "Euro 2000" Football Championship. Multicoloured.

3436	1300l. Type **337**	1·10	1·25
3437	1300l. German team	1·10	1·25
3438	1300l. Babbel (German player)	1·10	1·25
3439	1300l. Franz Beckenbauer, 1972	1·10	1·25
3440	1300l. Selessin Stadium, Liege	1·10	1·25
3441	1300l. Stefan Kuntz, (German player), 1996	1·10	1·25
3442	1300l. Walter Zenga (Italian player)	1·10	1·25
3443	1300l. Italian team	1·10	1·25
3444	1300l. Roberto Bettega (Italian player), 1980	1·10	1·25
3445	1300l. Totti (Italian player)	1·10	1·25
3446	1300l. Philips Stadium, Eindhoven	1·10	1·25
3447	1300l. Vieri (Italian player)	1·10	1·25
3448	1300l. Dimas (Portuguese player)	1·10	1·25
3449	1300l. Portuguese team	1·10	1·25
3450	1300l. Pinto (Portuguese player)	1·10	1·25
3451	1300l. Santos (Portuguese player)	1·10	1·25
3452	1300l. Gelredome Stadium, Arnhem	1·10	1·25
3453	1300l. Sousa (Portuguese player)	1·10	1·25
3454	1300l. Munteanu (Romanian player)	1·10	1·25
3455	1300l. Romanian team	1·10	1·25
3456	1300l. Petre (Romanian player)	1·10	1·25
3457	1300l. Petrescu (Romanian player)	1·10	1·25
3458	1300l. Popescu (Romanian player)	1·10	1·25

MS3459 Four sheets, each 145×95 mm. (a) 5000l. Erich Ribbeck (German trainer) (vert). (b) 5000l. Dino Zoff (Italian trainer) (vert). (c) 5000l. Humberto Coelho (Portuguese trainer) (vert). (d) 5000l. Emerich Jenei (Romanian trainer) (vert) Set of 4 sheets 15·00 17·00

337a Emperor Hung-Wu of China

2000. Monarchs of the Millennium.

3460	**337a**	1100l. multicoloured	1·10	1·25
3461	-	1100l. multicoloured	1·10	1·25
3462	-	1100l. multicoloured	1·10	1·25
3463	-	1100l. black, stone & brn	1·10	1·25
3464	-	1100l. multicoloured	1·10	1·25
3465	-	1100l. black, stone & brn	1·10	1·25

MS3466 116×131 mm.–5000l. multicoloured 6·00 6·50

DESIGNS: No. 3461, Emperor Hsuan-Te of China; 3462, King Sejong of Korea; 3463, Emperor T'ung Chin of China; 3464, Emperor T'ai-Tsu of China; 3465, Empress Yung Ching of China; **MS**3466, Kublai Khan, Great Khan of the Mongols.

2000. Popes of the Millennium. As T **337a**. Each black, yellow and green (Nos. 3467/78 or black, yellow and brown (No. **MS**3479).

3467	1100l. Gregory VI	1·40	1·40
3468	1100l. Celestine V	1·40	1·40
3469	1100l. Honorius IV	1·40	1·40
3470	1100l. Innocent IV	1·40	1·40
3471	1100l. Innocent VII	1·40	1·40
3472	1100l. John XXII	1·40	1·40
3473	1100l. Martin IV	1·40	1·40
3474	1100l. Nicholas II	1·40	1·40
3475	1100l. Nicholas IV	1·40	1·40
3476	1100l. Urban IV	1·40	1·40
3477	1100l. Urban V	1·40	1·40
3478	1100l. Urban VI	1·40	1·40

MS3479 Two sheets, each 116×136 mm. (a) 5000l. Nicholas IV. (b) 5000l. Clement XI Set of 2 sheets 12·00 13·00

338 Bulldog

2000. Dogs and Cats. Multicoloured.

3480	500l. Type **338**	70	30
3481	800l. Brown tabby	85	60
3482	1000l. Red tabby stumpy manx	1·00	1·00
3483	1000l. Red self	1·00	1·00
3484	1000l. Maine coon	1·00	1·00
3485	1000l. Black smoke	1·00	1·00
3486	1000l. Chinchilla	1·00	1·00
3487	1000l. Russian blue cat	1·00	1·00
3488	1000l. Beagle	1·00	1·00
3489	1000l. Scottish terrier	1·00	1·00
3490	1000l. Bloodhound	1·00	1·00
3491	1000l. Greyhound	1·00	1·00
3492	1000l. German shepherd	1·00	1·00
3493	1000l. Cocker spaniel	1·00	1·00
3494	1100l. Singapura	1·00	1·00
3495	1100l. Himalayan	1·00	1·00
3496	1100l. Abyssinian	1·00	1·00
3497	1100l. Black cat	1·00	1·00
3498	1100l. Siamese	1·00	1·00
3499	1100l. North African wild cat	1·00	1·00
3500	1100l. Pointer	1·00	1·00
3501	1100l. Doberman pinscher	1·00	1·00
3502	1100l. Collie	1·00	1·00
3503	1100l. Chihuahua	1·00	1·00
3504	1100l. Afghan hound	1·00	1·00
3505	1100l. Boxer	1·00	1·00
3506	1500l. Burmese	1·40	1·50
3507	2000l. Dachshund	1·90	2·25

MS3508 Two sheets, each 48×62 mm. (a) 5000l. Calico cat (vert). (b) 5000l. Fox terrier (vert) Set of 2 sheets 12·00 13·00

Nos. 3482/7 (cats), 3489/93 (dogs), 3494/9 (cats) and 3500/505 (dogs) were printed together, *se-tenant*, with the backgrounds forming composite designs.

339 "Adam" (Durer)

2000. "Espana 2000" International Stamp Exhibition, Madrid. Paintings from the Prado. Multicoloured.

3509	1000l. Type **339**	80	90
3510	1000l. "Moor" (M. Vives)	80	90
3511	1000l. "Eve" (Durer)	80	90
3512	1000l. "Gypsy" (R. de Madrazo y Garreta)	80	90
3513	1000l. "Maria Guerrero" (J. Sorolla y Bastida)	80	90
3514	1000l. "Aline Masson with a White Mantilla" (R. de Madrazo y Garreta)	80	90
3515	1000l. "Madonna and Child between Sts. Catherine and Ursula" (G. Bellini) (left detail)	80	90
3516	1000l. "Madonna and Child between Sts. Catherine and Ursula" (centre detail)	80	90
3517	1000l. "Madonna and Child between Sts. Catherine and Ursula" (right detail)	80	90
3518	1000l. "Giovanni Mateo Ghiberti" (B. India)	80	90
3519	1000l. "The Marchioness of Santa Cruz" (A. Esteve)	80	90
3520	1000l. "Self Portrait" (O. Borgianni)	80	90
3521	1000l. "The Transport of Mary Magdalen" (J. Antolinez)	80	90
3522	1000l. "The Holy Family" (Goya)	80	90
3523	1000l. "Our Lady of the Immaculate Conception" (J. Antolinez)	80	90
3524	1000l. "Charles IV as Prince" (A. Mengs)	80	90
3525	1000l. "Louis XIII of France" (P. de Champaigne)	80	90
3526	1000l. "Prince Ferdinand VI" (J. Ranc)	80	90
3527	1000l. "Feliciana Bayeu" (F. Bayeu)	80	90
3528	1000l. "Tomas de Iriarte" (J. Inza)	80	90
3529	1000l. "St. Elizabeth of Portugal" (F. de Zurbaran)	80	90
3530	1000l. "The Vision of St. Francis at Porziuncola" (Murillo) (Christ with cross)	80	90
3531	1000l. "The Vision of St. Francis at Porziuncola" (St. Francis)	80	90
3532	1000l. "The Vision of St. Francis at Porziuncola" (Two women)	80	90
3533	1000l. "The Holy Family with a Little Bird" (Murillo) (Virgin Mary)	80	90
3534	1000l. "The Holy Family with a Little Bird" (Holy Child)	80	90
3535	1000l. "The Holy Family with a Little Bird" (St. Joseph)	80	90
3536	1000l. "Cardinal Carlos de Borja" (A. Procaccini)	80	90
3537	1000l. "St. Dominic de Guzman" (C. Coello)	80	90
3538	1000l. "The Dead Christ Supported by an Angel" (A. Cano)	80	90
3539	1000l. "The Seller of Fans" (woman) (J. del Castillo)	80	90
3540	1000l. "Allegory of Summer" (M. Maella)	80	90
3541	1000l. "The Seller of Fans" (man)	80	90
3542	1000l. "Portrait of a Girl" (C. de Ribera y Fieve)	80	90
3543	1000l. "The Poultry Keeper" (Il Pensionante del Saraceni)	80	90
3544	1000l. "The Death of Cleopatra" (G. Reni)	80	90

MS3545 Six sheets, each 110×91 mm. (a) 5000l. "The Two Friends" (J. Agrasot y Juan) (horiz). (b) 5000l. "The Finding of Joseph's Cup in Benjamin's Sack" (J. Amiconi). (c) 5000l. "The Execution of Tprrijos and His Companions" (A. Gisbert Pirez). (d) 5000l. "The Concert" (V. Palmaroli Gonzalez). (e) 5000l. "Lot and His Daughters" (F. Furini). (f) 5000l. "Vulcan's Forge" (Velazquez) Set of 6 sheets 25·00 28·00

2000. Faces of the Millennium: Pope John Paul II. As T **330b**, showing collage of miniature religious photographs. Multicoloured.

3546	900l. Top of head (face value at left)	1·25	1·40
3547	900l. Top of head (face value at right)	1·25	1·40
3548	900l. Ear (face value at left)	1·25	1·40
3549	900l. Eye and temple (face value at right)	1·25	1·40
3550	900l. Back of neck (face value at left)	1·25	1·40
3551	900l. Cheek (face value at right)	1·25	1·40
3552	900l. Collar and top of cassock (face value at left)	1·25	1·40
3553	900l. Hand (face value at right)	1·25	1·40

Nos. 3546/53 were printed together, se-tenant, in sheetlets of 8 with the stamps arranged in two vertical columns separated by a gutter also containing miniature photographs. When viewed as a whole, the sheetlet forms a portrait of Pope John Paul II.

2000. Faces of the Millennium: Queen Elizabeth, The Queen Mother. As T **330b**, showing collage of miniature flower photographs. Multicoloured.

3554	800l. Top of forehead and hat (face value at left)	1·10	1·25
3555	800l. Hat (face value at right)	1·10	1·25
3556	800l. Eye (face value at left)	1·10	1·25
3557	800l. Side of face and hat (face value at right)	1·10	1·25
3558	800l. Cheek (face value at left)	1·10	1·25
3559	800l. Cheek (face value at right)	1·10	1·25
3560	800l. Chin (face value at left)	1·10	1·25
3561	800l. Chin and neck (face value at right)	1·10	1·25

Nos. 3554/61 were printed together, *se-tenant*, in sheetlets of 8 with the stamps arranged in two vertical columns separated by a gutter also containing miniature photographs. When viewed as a whole, the sheetlet forms a portrait of The Queen Mother.

340 *Tuberus polypore*

2001. Fungi. Multicoloured.

3562	600l. Type **340**	75	40
3563	900l. *Cultivated agaricus*	95	85
3564	1000l. Armed stinkhorn (vert)	1·00	1·00
3565	1000l. *Red-staining inocybe* (vert)	1·00	1·00
3566	1000l. Grisette (*Amanitopsis vaginata*) (vert)	1·00	1·00
3567	1000l. *Inocybe jurana* (vert)	1·00	1·00
3568	1000l. *Xerula longipes* (vert)	1·00	1·00
3569	1000l. Matsu-take mushroom (*Tricholoma matsutake*) (vert)	1·00	1·00
3570	1000l. Orange-staining mycena (vert)	1·00	1·00
3571	1000l. *Russula amoema* (vert)	1·00	1·00
3572	1000l. *Cinnabar chanterelle*(vert)	1·00	1·00
3573	1000l. *Calodon aurantiacum* (vert)	1·00	1·00
3574	1000l. Scaly lentinus (*Lentinus lepideus*) (vert)	1·00	1·00
3575	1000l. *Gomphidius roseus* (vert)	1·00	1·00
3576	1200l. Scarlet wax cap	1·25	1·40
3577	2500l. Blue-green psilocybe	2·25	2·50

MS3578 Two sheets. (a) 98×74 mm. 5000l. Orange latex lactarius. (b) 74×98 mm. 5000l. Common morel (vert) Set of 2 sheets 11·00 12·00

Nos. 3564/9 and 3570/575 were each printed together, *se-tenant*, with the backgrounds forming a composite design.

No. 3567 is inscribed "Inoeybe" in error.

341 Kahat Shor (shooting coach)

2000. Israel Olympic Team Members killed at Munich (1972) Commemoration. Multicoloured.

3579	500l. Type **341**	80	80
3580	500l. Andrei Schpitzer (fencing referee)	80	80
3581	500l. Joseph Romano (weightlifter)	80	80
3582	500l. Yaakov Springer (weightlifting referee)	80	80
3583	500l. Eliazer Halffin (wrestler)	80	80
3584	500l. Amitsur Shapira (athletics coach)	80	80
3585	500l. Moshe Weinberg (wrestling referee)	80	80
3586	500l. Mark Slavin (wrestler)	80	80
3587	500l. Flag and runner with Olympic Torch	80	80
3588	500l. Joseph Gottfreund (wrestling referee)	80	80

3589 500l. Ze'ev Friedman (weightlifter) 80 80
3590 500l. David Berger (weightlifter) 80 80
MS3591 116×80 mm. 5000l. Runner with Olympic Torch (vert) 7·50 8·00

342 Tightrope Cyclist

2000. Circus. Multicoloured.
3592 800l. Type **342** 1·25 70
3593 1000l. Bear with ball 1·25 1·00
3594 1100l. Polar bear 1·25 1·25
3595 1100l. Gorilla 1·25 1·25
3596 1100l. Clown (green background) 1·25 1·25
3597 1100l. Tightrope walker 1·25 1·25
3598 1100l. Sealions 1·25 1·25
3599 1100l. Camel 1·25 1·25
3600 1100l. Clown (brown background) 1·25 1·25
3601 1100l. Tiger on tightropes 1·25 1·25
3602 1100l. Chimpanzee 1·25 1·25
3603 1100l. Dancing dogs 1·25 1·25
3604 1100l. Bear on skates with hockey stick 1·25 1·25
3605 1100l. Trapeze artists 1·25 1·25
3606 1100l. Acrobat (vert) 1·25 1·25
3607 1100l. Giraffe (vert) 1·25 1·25
3608 1100l. Bear on stilts (vert) 1·25 1·25
3609 1100l. Elephant (vert) 1·25 1·25
3610 1100l. Rearing horse (vert) 1·25 1·25
3611 1100l. Fire-eater (vert) 1·25 1·25
3612 1500l. Tiger on ball 1·60 1·75
3613 2000l. Camels 2·25 2·50
MS3614 Three sheets, each 70×90 mm. (a) 5000l. Tiger leaping through flames (vert). (b) 5000l. Human cannonball (vert). (c) 5000l. Ringmaster standing on elephant (vert) Set of 3 sheets 20·00 20·00

2000. Queen Elizabeth the Queen Mother's 100th Birthday. As T **405** of St. Vincent. Multicoloured.
3615 1100l. Queen Mother in blue hat 2·25 2·25

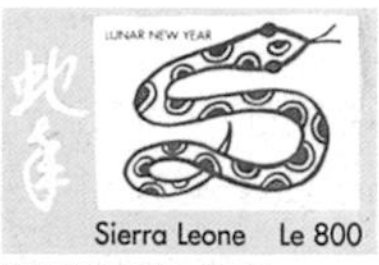

343 Decorative Snake

2001. Chinese New Year. "Year of the Snake". Decorative snakes. Multicoloured.
3616 800l. Type **343** (blue frame) 90 1·00
3617 800l. Snake (pink frame) 90 1·00
3618 800l. Snake (lilac frame) 90 1·00
3619 800l. Snake (green frame) 90 1·00
MS3620 65×95 mm. 2500l. Snake (vert) 2·50 3·00

344 Natal Mixands Dwarf Chameleon

2001. African Reptiles. Multicoloured.
3621 250l. Type **344** 40 15
3622 400l. Cape cobra 50 30
3623 500l. Western sand lizard 55 30
3624 600l. Pan-hinged terrapin 65 40
3625 800l. Many-horned adder 85 65
3626 1200l. Reticulated desert lizard 1·10 1·25
3627 1200l. Ball python 1·10 1·25
3628 1200l. Gabon viper 1·10 1·25
3629 1200l. Dumeril's boa 1·10 1·25
3630 1200l. Common egg-eater 1·10 1·25
3631 1200l. Helmet turtle 1·10 1·25
3632 1200l. Saw-scaled viper 1·10 1·25
3633 1200l. Namibian sand snake 1·10 1·25
3634 1200l. Angolan gartersnake 1·10 1·25
3635 1200l. Striped skaapsteker 1·10 1·25
3636 1200l. Brown housesnake 1·10 1·25
3637 1200l. Shield-nosed cobra 1·10 1·25
3638 1500l. Hawequa flat gecko 1·40 1·50
MS3639 Two sheets, each 86×56 mm. (a) 5000l. Flat-necked chameleon. (b) 5000l. Green water snake Set of 2 sheets 10·00 11·00

Nos. 3626/31 and 3632/7 were each printed together, *se-tenant*, with the backgrounds forming a composite map of Africa.

No. 3621 is inscribed "Chamaeleon" in error.

345 Sleeping Car No. 507, 1897

2001. "The Orient Express". Multicoloured.
3640 1000l. First sleeping car, 1872 1·00 1·00
3641 1000l. Dining car No. 193, 1886 1·00 1·00
3642 1000l. Dining car No. 2422, 1913 1·00 1·00
3643 1000l. Sleeping car Type S1 1·00 1·00
3644 1000l. Metal sleeping car No. 2645, 1922 1·00 1·00
3645 1000l. Metal sleeping car No. 2644, 1922 1·00 1·00
3646 1000l. Dining car series No. 8341 1·00 1·00
3647 1000l. Dining car series No. 3342 1·00 1·00
3648 1000l. Sleeping car series Type Z, No. 3312 1·00 1·00
3649 1000l. Sleeping car series No. 3879, 1950 1·00 1·00
3650 1000l. Sleeping car series, Type Z, No. 3311 1·00 1·00
3651 1000l. Dining car series No. 3785, 1932 1·00 1·00
3652 1100l. Type **345** 1·00 1·00
3653 1100l. Sleeping car No. 438, 1894 1·00 1·00
3654 1100l. Sleeping car No. 313, 1880 1·00 1·00
3655 1100l. Sleeping car No. 190, 1886 1·00 1·00
3656 1100l. Sleeping car No. 102, 1882 1·00 1·00
3657 1100l. Sleeping car No. 77, 1881 1·00 1·00
3658 1100l. Steam locomotive, Ostend–Vienna Express, 1910 5·50 5·50
3659 1100l. Steam locomotive East 230 No. 3175 1·00 1·00
3660 1100l. Dual-cylinder steam locomotive 1·00 1·00
3661 1100l. Steam locomotive, Simplon Orient Express, 1919 1·00 1·00
3662 1100l. Steam locomotive East 220 No. 2405 1·00 1·00
3663 1100l. Brake van of Simplon Express, c. 1906 1·00 1·00
MS3664 Four sheets, each 106×81 mm. (a) 5000l. Agatha Christie (author) (vert). (b) 5000l. Georges Nagelmackers (company founder) (vert). (c) 5000l. Mata Hari (spy) (vert). (d) 5000l. "Orient Express" leaving Constantinople Set of 4 sheets 16·00 17·00

346 Candle-bearers from "David playing the Harp" (Jan de Bray)

2001. Bicentenary of Rijksmuseum, Amsterdam. Dutch Paintings. Multicoloured.
3665 1100l. Type **346** 90 1·00
3666 1100l. Women and children from "St. Paul healing the Cripple at Lystra" (Karel Dujardin) 90 1·00
3667 1100l. Two pikemen (one wearing hat) from "The Meagre Company" (Frans Hals and Pieter Codde) 90 1·00
3668 1100l. "The Grey" (Philips Wouwermans) 90 1·00
3669 1100l. "Elegant Couple in an Interior" (Eglon van der Neer) 90 1·00
3670 1100l. "The Hut" (Adriaen van der Velde) 90 1·00
3671 1100l. "Lady reading a Letter" (Gabriel Metsu) 90 1·00
3672 1100l. "Portrait of Titus" (Rembrandt) 90 1·00
3673 1100l. "Gerard de Lairesse" (Rembrandt) 90 1·00
3674 1100l. "Family in an Interior" (Emanuel de Witte) 90 1·00
3675 1100l. "The Letter" (Gerard ter Borch) 90 1·00
3676 1100l. "Three Women and a Man in a Courtyard" (Pieter de Hooch) 90 1·00
3677 1100l. "Gentleman writing a Letter" (Gabriel Metsu) 90 1·00
3678 1100l. "Self-portrait" (Carel Fabritius) 90 1·00
3679 1100l. "Windmill at Wijk bij Duurstede" (Jacob van Ruisdael) 90 1·00
3680 1100l. "Bentheim Castle" (Jacob van Ruisdael) 90 1·00
3681 1100l. "Ships on a Stormy Sea" (Willem van der Velde the Younger) 90 1·00
3682 1100l. David from "David playing the Harp" (Jan de Bray) 90 1·00
3683 1100l. St. Paul from "St. Paul healing the Cripple at Lystra" (Karel Dujardin) 90 1·00
3684 1100l. Two pikemen (both bareheaded) from "The Meagre Company" (Frans Hals and Pieter Codde) 90 1·00
3685 1100l. Man from "Elegant Couple in an Interior" (Eglon van der Neer) 90 1·00
3686 1100l. "Laid Table with Cheese and Fruit" (Floris van Dijck) 90 1·00
3687 1100l. "Bacchanal" (Moses van Uyttenbroeck) 90 1·00
3688 1100l. The cripple from "St. Paul healing the Cripple at Lystra" (Karel Dujardin) 90 1·00
MS3689 Four sheets. (a) 118×73 mm. 5000l. "Road in the Dunes with a Coach" (Salomon van Ruysdael) (horiz) (b) 118×73 mm. 5000l. "Cows in the Meadow" (Albert Gerard Bilders) (horiz). (c) 118×78 mm. 5000l. "Lot and his Daughters" (Hendrick Goltzius) (horiz). (d) 118×83 mm. 5000l. "Arrival of Queen Wilhelmina at the Frederiksplein, Amsterdam (Otto Eerelman) (horiz) Set of 4 sheets 16·00 17·00

347a "Song of Simeon"

2001. Biblical Drawings and Paintings by Rembrandt.
3723 **347a** 1000l. deep brown, brown and grey 1·00 1·00
3724 - 1000l. deep brown, brown and grey 1·00 1·00
3725 - 1000l. deep brown, brown and grey 1·00 1·00
3726 - 1000l. blue, brown and grey 1·00 1·00
3727 - 1000l. deep brown, brown and grey 1·00 1·00
3728 - 1000l. blue and brown 1·00 1·00
3729 - 1000l. red, brown and grey 1·00 1·00
3730 - 1000l. deep brown, brown and red 1·00 1·00
3731 - 1000l. deep brown, brown and red 1·00 1·00
3732 - 1000l. deep brown, brown and grey 1·00 1·00
3733 - 1000l. deep brown, brown and grey 1·00 1·00
3734 - 1000l. deep brown, brown and grey 1·00 1·00
MS3735 Four sheets 86×110 mm. (a) 5000l. multicoloured. (b) 5000l. multicoloured. (c) 5000l. multicoloured. (d) 5000l. multicoloured Set of 4 sheets 16·00 17·00

DESIGNS—HORIZ: No. 3723, Type **347a**; 3724, Study for "Adoration of the Magi"; 3725, "Mary with the Child by a Window"; 3726, "The Rest on the Flight into Egypt"; 3727, "The Circumcision"; 3728, "The Shepherds worship the Child"; 3729, "The Angel rises up in the Flame of Manoah's Sacrifice"; 3730, "Tobias frightened by the Fish"; 3731, "The Angel of the Lord stands in Balaam's Path"; 3732, "The Angel appears to Hagar in the Desert"; 3733, "Jacob's Dream"; 3734, "The Healing of Tobit"; **MS**3735a, "The Angel prevents the Sacrifice of Isaac"; **MS**3735b, "Simeon's Prophecy to Mary". VERT: No. **MS**3735c, "The Adoration of the Magi"; **MS**3735d, "The Angel leaves Tobit and His Family".

2001. 60th Anniv of the Battle of Britain. As T **413** of St. Vincent. Multicoloured.
3690 1000l. St. Paul's Cathedral, London 1·25 1·25
3691 1000l. Evacuating bombed building 1·25 1·25
3692 1000l. Winston Churchill being cheered by British troops 1·25 1·25
3693 1000l. Rescuing British pilot by boat 1·25 1·25
3694 1000l. Boy Scout and children 1·25 1·25
3695 1000l. British anti-aircraft gun 1·25 1·25
3696 1000l. Searchlight and crew 1·25 1·25
3697 1000l. Royal Observer Corps post 1·25 1·25
3698 1000l. Bombed houses 1·25 1·25
3699 1000l. Sheltering in underground station 1·25 1·25
3700 1000l. Firemen 1·25 1·25
3701 1000l. Home Guard at drill 1·25 1·25
3702 1000l. ARP warden and blackout sign 1·25 1·25
3703 1000l. Pilots on stand-by 1·25 1·25
3704 1000l. Brendan "Paddy" Finucane (fighter pilot) 1·25 1·25
3705 1000l. Hawk 75 (fighter) 1·25 1·25
3706 1000l. Tower Bridge, London 1·25 1·25
3707 1000l. Surrey Home Guard 1·25 1·25
3708 1000l. Cruiser tank MK III 1·25 1·25
3709 1000l. Newfoundland gun crew 1·25 1·25
3710 1000l. Bomb damage in Plymouth 1·25 1·25
3711 1000l. Winston Churchill 1·25 1·25
3712 1000l. Bomb damage at Westminster Hall 1·25 1·25
3713 1000l. Radar screen 1·25 1·25
3714 1000l. Female telephone engineer and W.A.A.F. 1·25 1·25
3715 1000l. Women munitions workers 1·25 1·25
3716 1000l. Winston Churchill at desk 1·25 1·25
3717 1000l. Dornier DO17 (German bomber) 1·25 1·25
3718 1000l. Church fire 1·25 1·25
3719 1000l. Searchlights over London 1·25 1·25
3720 1000l. Lunch in the underground 1·25 1·25
3721 1000l. Sing song in the underground 1·25 1·25
MS3722 Four sheets. (a) 76×106 mm. 6000l. London skyline. (b) 76×106 mm. 6000l. Winston Churchill and his wife, Clementine. (c) 106×76 mm. 6000l. Supermarine Spitfire. (d) 106×76 mm. 6000l. British bomber crew preparing for mission (vert) Set of 4 sheets 32·00 35·00

No. 3706 is inscribed "LONDON BRIDGE", 3707 "SURRY", 3714 "WAFF", 3716 "DEFINSE" and **MS**3722c "SUBMARINE SPITFIRE", all in error.

348 "Piebald" from National Velvet (Enid Bagnold)

2001. Horses from Literature and Mythology. Multicoloured.
3736 1100l. Type **348** 1·40 1·40
3737 1100l. "Strider" (Tolstoy) 1·40 1·40
3738 1100l. "Black Beauty" (Anna Sewell) 1·40 1·40
3739 1100l. "Red Pony" (John Steinbeck) 1·40 1·40
3740 1100l. "Black Stallion" (Walter Farley) 1·40 1·40
3741 1100l. "Misty" from *Misty of Chincoteague* (Marguerite Henry) 1·40 1·40
3742 1100l. "Arvak" and "Alsvid" pulling Sun (Norse myth) 1·40 1·40
3743 1100l. "Pegasus" (Greek myth) 1·40 1·40
3744 1100l. Odin on "Sleipnir" (Norse myth) 1·40 1·40
3745 1100l. Roland on "Veillantif" from the "Song of Roland" 1·40 1·40
3746 1100l. Sigurd with "Grani" (Norse myth) 1·40 1·40
3747 1100l. Hector on "Galathe" from *Troilus and Cressida* (Shakespeare) 1·40 1·40
MS3748 Two sheets, each 97×67 mm. (a) 5000l. Don Quixote on "Rocinante" (Cervantes). (b) 5000l. "Xanthus" and "Balius" pulling Achilles chariot (greek myth) Set of 2 sheets 13·00 14·00

Nos. 3736/41 and 3742/7 were each printed together, *se-tenant*, the backgrounds forming composite designs.

No. 3745 is inscribed "Veillanfif" and No. 3747 "Truilus", both in error.

349 "Native Dancer", 1950 (racehorse)

2001. Racehorses. Multicoloured.
3749 200l. Type **349** 55 20
3750 500l. "Citation", 1945 85 40
3751 1200l. "Arkle", 1957 1·40 1·40
3752 1200l. "Golden Miller", 1927 1·40 1·40
3753 1200l. "Phar Lap", 1927 1·40 1·40
3754 1200l. "Battleship", 1927 1·40 1·40
3755 1200l. "Kelso", 1957 1·40 1·40
3756 1200l. "Nijinski", 1967 1·40 1·40
3757 1200l. "Red Rum", 1965 1·40 1·40
3758 1200l. "Sir Ken", 1947 1·40 1·40
3759 1200l. "War Admiral", 1934 1·40 1·40
3760 1200l. "Troytown", 1913 1·40 1·40

3761	1200l. "Shergar", 1981	1·40	1·40
3762	1200l. "Allez France", 1970	1·40	1·40
3763	1500l. "Spectre", 1899	1·40	1·40
3764	2000l. "Carbine", 1885	1·40	1·40
MS3765	Four sheets. (a) 100×74 mm. 5000l. "Cigar". (b) 100×74 mm. 5000l. Racing trophy. (c) 100×74 mm. 5000l. French racecourse. (horiz) (d) 74×100 mm. 5000l. "Desert Orchid" Set of 4 sheets	21·00	21·00

350 Acrocanthosaurus

2001. "Hong Kong 2001" International Stamp Exhibition. Dinosaurs. Multicoloured.

3766	1000l. Type **350**	1·25	1·25
3767	1000l. Edmontosaurus	1·25	1·25
3768	1000l. Archaeopteryx	1·25	1·25
3769	1000l. Hadrosaurus	1·25	1·25
3770	1000l. Mongolian avimimus	1·25	1·25
3771	1000l. Pachyrhinosaurus	1·25	1·25
3772	1000l. Iguanadons and log	1·25	1·25
3773	1000l. Iguanadons	1·25	1·25
3774	1000l. Albertosaurus (horiz)	1·25	1·25
3775	1000l. Pteranadon ingens (horiz)	1·25	1·25
3776	1000l. Asiatic Iguanadon (horiz)	1·25	1·25
3777	1000l. Sordes (horiz)	1·25	1·25
3778	1000l. Coelophysis (horiz)	1·25	1·25
3779	1000l. Saichania (horiz)	1·25	1·25
3780	1000l. Bactrosaurus (horiz)	1·25	1·25
3781	1000l. Triceratops (horiz)	1·25	1·25
MS3782	Five sheets. (a) 85×110 mm. 5000l. Dryosaurus. (b) 110×85 mm. 5000l. Diplodocus. (c) 110×85 mm. 5000l. Allosaurus (horiz). (d) 71×90 mm. 5000l. Stenonychosaurus. (e) 71×90 mm. 5000l. Corythosaurus Set of 5 sheets	28·00	30·00

Nos. 3771, 3774 and **MS**3782b are inscribed "PACHYRMINOSAURUS", "ALBERTO-SAUR" or "DIPLODOCIDS", all in error.

351 Benz Velo, 1898

2001. Cars. Multicoloured.

3783	1000l. Type **351**	1·25	1·25
3784	1000l. Rolls-Royce Silver Ghost, 1909	1·25	1·25
3785	1000l. Ford Model T, 1912	1·25	1·25
3786	1000l. Duesenberg SJ, 1937	1·25	1·25
3787	1000l. Grosse Mercedes, 1938–40	1·25	1·25
3788	1000l. Citroën Light 15, 1938	1·25	1·25
3789	1000l. Lincoln Zephyr, 1939	1·25	1·25
3790	1000l. Volkswagen Beetle, 1947	1·25	1·25
3791	1000l. Jaguar Mark II, 1959	1·25	1·25
3792	1000l. Ford Mustang GT500, 1968	1·25	1·25
3793	1000l. Opel/Vauxhall Senator, 1987-94	1·25	1·25
3794	1000l. Mercedes Maybach, 2002	1·25	1·25
MS3795	Two sheets, each 110×75 mm. (a) 5000l. 3-Litre Bentley Short Chassis Tourer, 1928. (b) 5000l. Ferrari 360 Modena, 1999 Set of 2 sheets	13·00	14·00

No. 3783 is inscribed "Bena" in error.

352 *Teinopalpus imperialis*

2001. Butterflies of the World. Multicoloured.

3796	1100l. Type **352**	1·50	1·50
3797	1100l. *Papilio mochaon*	1·50	1·50
3798	1100l. *Heliconius doris*	1·50	1·50
3799	1100l. *Delias argenthona*	1·50	1·50
3800	1100l. *Danaus formosa*	1·50	1·50
3801	1100l. *Precis octavia*	1·50	1·50
3802	1100l. *Danaus chrysippus*	1·50	1·50
3803	1100l. *Tithorea harmonia*	1·50	1·50
3804	1100l. *Morpho cypris*	1·50	1·50
3805	1100l. *Castnia licusi*	1·50	1·50
3806	1100l. *Dismorphia nemesis*	1·50	1·50
3807	1100l. *Saintpaulia ionanthe*	1·50	1·50
MS3808	Two sheets, each 75×55 mm. (a) 5000l. *Iphiclides podalirius*. (b) 5000l. *Colias crocea* (vert) Set of 2 sheets	13·00	14·00

Nos. 3796/8001 and 3802/7 were each printed together, *se-tenant*, with the backgrounds forming composite designs.

No. **MS**3808a is inscribed "podoliruis" in error.

353 *Eurema floricola*

2001. Butterflies of Africa. Multicoloured.

3809	250l. Type **353**	65	25
3810	400l. *Papilio dardanus*	85	40
3811	800l. *Amauris nossima*	1·25	80
3812	1100l. *Charaxes lucretia*	1·50	1·50
3813	1100l. *Euxanthe crossleyi*	1·50	1·50
3814	1100l. *Charaxes phoenix*	1·50	1·50
3815	1100l. *Charaxes acraeades*	1·50	1·50
3816	1100l. *Charaxes protoclea*	1·50	1·50
3817	1100l. *Charaxes lydiae*	1·50	1·50
3818	1100l. *Papilio dardanus*	1·50	1·50
3819	1100l. *Cymothoe sangaris*	1·50	1·50
3820	1100l. *Epiphora albida*	1·50	1·50
3821	1100l. African giant swallowtail	1·50	1·50
3822	1100l. *Papilio nobilis*	1·50	1·50
3823	1100l. *Charaxes hadrianus*	1·50	1·50
3824	1500l. *Gideona lucasi*	1·50	1·50
MS3825	Two sheets, each 110×85 mm. (a) 5000l. *Colotis zoe*. (b) 5000l. *Acraea ranaualona* (vert) Set of 2 sheets	13·00	14·00

Nos. 3812/17 and 3818/23 were each printed together, *se-tenant*, with the backgrounds forming composite designs based on the map of Africa.

Nos. 3813, 3814, 3819, 3823 and **MS**3825a are inscribed "CLOSSEX", "PHENIX", "CYMOTOE", "HADNANUS" and "CLOTIS", all in error.

2001. 25th Death Anniv of Mao Tse-tung (Chinese leader). As T **426** of St. Vincent. Multicoloured.

3826	1100l. Young Mao wearing blue	1·00	1·10
3827	1100l. Mao in green People's Army uniform	1·00	1·10
3828	1100l. Mao in blue cap	1·00	1·10
3829	1100l. Mao in khaki uniform	1·00	1·10
3830	1100l. Mao in open-necked shirt	1·00	1·10
3831	1100l. Mao in grey cap	1·00	1·10
MS3832	Two sheets, each 90×119 mm. (a) 5000l. Mao in traditional robe. (b) 5000l. Mao in blue tunic Set of 2 sheets	10·00	11·00

2001. 75th Death Anniv of Claude-Oscar Monet (French painter). As T **427** of St. Vincent. Multicoloured.

3833	1500l. "Road to Vetheuil, Winter, 1879"	1·75	1·90
3834	1500l. "Church at Vetheuil, 1879"	1·75	1·90
3835	1500l. "Breakup of Ice near Vetheuil, 1880"	1·75	1·90
3836	1500l. "Boulevard de Pontoise, Argenteuil, 1875"	1·75	1·90
MS3837	137×110 mm. 5000l. "Irises by Pool, 1914–17" (vert)	6·50	7·00

2001. 75th Birthday of Queen Elizabeth II. As T **428** of St. Vincent. Multicoloured.

3838	2000l. Princess Elizabeth in A.T.S. uniform	2·50	2·75
3839	2000l. Princess Elizabeth and Prince Charles	2·50	2·75
3840	2000l. Coronation portrait	2·50	2·75
3841	2000l. Princess Elizabeth in Girl Guide uniform	2·50	2·75
MS3842	80×110 mm. 5000l. Queen Elizabeth in evening dress (37×50 mm)	7·50	8·00

2001. Golden Jubilee (1st issue). As T **429** of St. Vincent. Multicoloured.

3843	1000l. Queen Elizabeth II	1·50	1·75

See also Nos. 3960/4.

No. 3843 was printed in sheetlets of 8, containing two vertical rows of four, separated by a large illustrated central gutter. Both the stamp and the illustration on the central gutter are made up of a collage of miniature flower photographs.

2001. Death Centenary of Giuseppe Verdi (Italian composer). As T **430** of St. Vincent showing scenes from Aida (opera). Multicoloured.

3844	1700l. Vladimir Popov	2·50	2·50
3845	1700l. Enrico Caruso	2·50	2·50
3846	1700l. Rudolf Bockelmann	2·50	2·50
3847	1700l. Scene from *Aida*	2·50	2·50
MS3848	79×110 mm. 5000l. Aprile Millo as Aida and Barseq Tumayan as Amonasro	8·50	8·50

2001. Death Centenary of Henri de Toulouse-Lautrec (French painter). As T **431** of St. Vincent. Multicoloured.

3849	2200l. "A la Mie"	2·25	2·50
3850	2200l. "Corner of the Moulin de la Galette"	2·25	2·50
3851	2200l. "Start of the Quadrille"	2·25	2·50
MS3852	68×109 mm. 5000l. "La Gouloue" (vert)	7·00	8·00

2001. Centenary of Royal Navy Submarine Service. As T **107** of St. Kitts. Multicoloured.

3853	1100l. C29 (submarine)	1·75	1·75
3854	1100l. H.M.S. *Spartan* (submarine)	1·75	1·75
3855	1100l. H.M.S. *Exeter*(cruiser)	1·75	1·75
3856	1100l. H.M.S. *Chatham* (frigate)	1·75	1·75
3857	1100l. H.M.S. *Verdun* (destroyer)	1·75	1·75
3858	1100l. H.M.S. *Marlborough* (frigate)	1·75	1·75
MS3859	70×55 mm. 5000l. H.M.S. *Vanguard* (missle submarine)	8·00	8·50

Nos. 3854 and 3857 are inscribed "SPARTON" or "VERDUM",both in error.

354 Marlene Dietrich in Black Dress

2001. Birth Centenary of Marlene Dietrich (actress and singer).

3860	**354**	2000l. black, purple and red	1·75	2·00
3861	-	2000l. multicoloured	1·75	2·00
3862	-	2000l. black, purple and red	1·75	2·00
3863	-	2000l. black, purple and red	1·75	2·00

DESIGNS: No. 3861, Marlene Dietrich in evening dress; 3862, Wearing white fur coat; 3863, Smoking.

2001. "Philanippon '01" International Stamp Exhibition, Tokyo. Japanese Art. As T **432** of St. Vincent. Multicoloured.

3864	50l. "Iziu Chinuki No Hi" (Hokkei) (horiz)	20	20
3865	100l. "Visit to Enoshima" (Torii Kiyonaga) (horiz)	20	20
3866	150l. "Inn on a Harbour" (Sadahide) (horiz)	30	20
3867	200l. "Entrance to Foreigners' Establishment" (Sadahide) (horiz)	35	25
3868	250l. "Courtesans at Cherry Blossom Time" (Kiyonaga) (horiz)	35	25
3869	300l. "Cherry Blossom Viewing at Ueno" (Toyohara Chikanobu) (horiz)	40	25
3870	400l. "Summer Evening at Restaurant by the Sumida River" (Kiyonaga) (horiz)	45	30
3871	500l. "Ichikana Yaozo I as Samurai" (Buncho)	50	30
3872	600l. "Nakamura Noshoi II as Street Walker" (Katsukawa Shunzan)	50	30
3873	800l. "Arashi Sangoro II Hosoban" (Shokosai)	60	40
3874	1500l. "Bando Mitsuguro I" (Shunko)	85	60
3875	2000l. "Matsumoto Koshiro II" (Masanobu)	1·40	1·50
3876	2000l. "Young Woman attended by Maid" (Suzuki Harunobu)	1·75	1·90
3877	2000l. "Lovers by Lespedeza Bush" (Harunobu)	1·75	1·90
3878	2000l. "Girl contemplating a Landscape" (Harunobu)	1·75	1·90
3879	2000l. "Young Man unrolling a Hanging Scroll" (Harunobu)	1·75	1·90
3880	2000l. "Promenade" (Harunobu)	1·75	1·90
3881	2000l. "Wine Tasters" (Harunobu)	1·75	1·90
3882	2000l. "Rain in May" (Harunobu)	1·75	1·90
3883	2000l. "Lovers by the Wall" (Harunobu)	1·75	1·90
3884	2000l. "Six Girls" (standing figure with orange sash) (Eisho)	1·75	1·90
3885	2000l. "Courtesan on a Bench" (Eiri)	1·75	1·90
3886	2000l. "Courtesan and her Two Kamuro" (Harunobu)	1·75	1·90
3887	2000l. "Clearing Weather at Awazu" (Shigemasa)	1·75	1·90
3888	2000l. "Nakamura Shikan II and Nakamura Baiko" (Shigeharu)	1·75	1·90
3889	2000l. "Women making Rice Cakes" (Shunsho)	1·75	1·90
3890	2000l. "Youth sending Letter by Arrow" (Harushige)	1·75	1·90
3891	2000l. "Six Girls" (standing figure with green sash) (Eisho)	1·75	1·90
MS3892	Five sheets, each 85×120 mm. (a) 5000l. "Courtesan and Two Kamuro". (b) 5000l. "Searching for the Hermit". (c) 5000l. "Girl contemplating a Landscape" (different). (d) 5000l. "Drying Clothes". (e) 5000l. "Komachi praying for Rain". All by Harunobu Set of 5 sheets	24·00	26·00

355 General Ulysses S. Grant

2001. American Civil War. Multicoloured.

3893	2000l. Type **355**	2·00	2·25
3894	2000l. General John Hood	2·00	2·25
3895	2000l. General Jeb Stuart	2·00	2·25
3896	2000l. General Robert E. Lee	2·00	2·25
3897	2000l. General Joshua Chamberlain	2·00	2·25
3898	2000l. General "Stonewall" Jackson	2·00	2·25
3899	2000l. General George McClellan	2·00	2·25
3900	2000l. Admiral David Farragut	2·00	2·25
3901	2000l. Battle of Fredericksburg, 1862	2·00	2·25
3902	2000l. Battle of Gettysburg, 1863	2·00	2·25
3903	2000l. Naval Battle of Mobile Bay, 1864	2·00	2·25
3904	2000l. Bombardment of Fort Sumter, 1861	2·00	2·25
3905	2000l. Battle of Shiloh, 1862	2·00	2·25
3906	2000l. Battle of Bull Run, 1861 and 1862	2·00	2·25
3907	2000l. Battle of Fair Oaks, 1863	2·00	2·25
3908	2000l. Battle of Chattanooga, 1863	2·00	2·25
MS3909	Four sheets. (a) 109×157 mm. 5000l. General George Custer. (b) 109×157 mm. 5000l. General William T. Sherman. (c) 109×157 mm. 5000l. Battle of Vicksburg, 1863. (d) 157×109 mm. 5000l. Battle of Antietam, 1862 Set of 4 sheets	21·00	23·00

No. 3900 is inscribed "ADMRIAL" in error.

356 Ferrari 360 Challenge, 2001

2001. Ferrari Racing Cars. Multicoloured.

3910	100l. Type **356**	35	20
3911	500l. 712 Can Am, 1971	75	35
3912	600l. 512M, 1970	85	65
3913	1000l. F40, 1988	1·40	1·50
3914	1500l. 365 GT4/BB, 1982	1·90	2·25
3915	2000l. 365 GTB/4, 1972	2·25	2·50

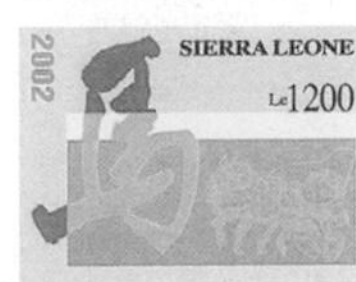

357 Chinese Character with Symbolic Horse ("2002" in green)

2001. Chinese New Year ("Year of the Horse"). Each incorporating the same character and a symbolic horse. Multicoloured.

3916	1200l. Type **357**	1·60	1·75
3917	1200l. "2002" in red	1·60	1·75
3918	1200l. "2002" in orange	1·60	1·75
3919	1200l. "2002" in blue	1·60	1·75
MS3920	97×69 mm. 1200l. European toy horse on wheels (37×24 mm); 1200l. Chinese toy horse and rider (37×24 mm)	3·00	3·50

358 British Newspaper Article, Brazil, 1950

2001. World Cup Football Championship, Japan and Korea (2002). Multicoloured.

3921 1400l. Type **358** 1·60 1·60
3922 1400l. Jules Rimet (F.I.F.A. President), Switzerland, 1954 1·60 1·60
3923 1400l. Pele and other members of Brazilian team, Sweden, 1958 1·60 1·60
3924 1400l. Vava (Brazil) and Schroiff (Czechoslovakia), Chile, 1962 1·60 1·60
3925 1400l. Bobby Charlton (England), England, 1966 1·60 1·60
3926 1400l. Pele (Brazil), Mexico, 1970 1·60 1·60
3927 1400l. Daniel Passarella (Argentina) with World Cup, Argentina, 1978 1·60 1·60
3928 1400l. Karl-Heinz Rummenigge (West Germany), Spain, 1982 1·60 1·60
3929 1400l. Diego Maradona (Argentina), Mexico, 1986 1·60 1·60
3930 1400l. Roger Milla (Cameroon), Italy, 1990 1·60 1·60
3931 1400l. Romario (Brazil), U.S.A., 1994 1·60 1·60
3932 1400l. Zinedine Zidane (France), France, 1998 1·60 1·60
MS3933 Two sheets, each 88×75 mm. (a) 5000l. Detail of Jules Rimet Trophy, Uruguay, 1930. (b) 5000l. Detail of World Cup Trophy, Japan/Korea 2002 Set of 2 sheets 13·00 14·00

No. 3922 is inscribed "Rimmet" in error.

359 "Madonna of Humility" (Filippo Lippi)

2001. Christmas. Religious Paintings by Filippo Lippi. Multicoloured.

3934 300l. Type **359** 60 20
3935 600l. "Annunciation" 90 35
3936 1500l. "Annunciation" (different) (vert) 2·00 2·50
3937 2000l. "Adoration of the Child and Saints" (vert) 2·50 3·00
MS3938 136×106 mm. 5000l. "Barbadori Altarpiece" (vert) 5·50 6·50

No. **MS**3938 is inscribed "Alterpiece" in error.

360 Early Steam Fire Engine

2002. Technological Development from Steam to Electricity. Multicoloured.

3939 1100l. Type **360** 1·50 1·50
3940 1100l. Dial telephone 1·50 1·50
3941 1100l. Luxury liner 1·50 1·50
3942 1100l. Electrical battery 1·50 1·50
3943 1100l. Steam carriage, 1770 1·50 1·50
3944 1100l. Modern electric locomotive 1·50 1·50
3945 1100l. Robert Fulton and early steam ship 1·50 1·50
3946 1100l. Thomas Edison and early electric light bulb 1·50 1·50
3947 1100l. Class T9 steam locomotive, 1899 1·50 1·50
3948 1100l. Early radio and transmitting masts 1·50 1·50
3949 1100l. James Watt and diagram of steam engine 1·50 1·50
3950 1100l. Alexander Graham Bell and early telephone 1·50 1·50
3951 1100l. *The Rocket* (steam locomotive), 1829 1·50 1·50
3952 1100l. Modern TGV train 1·50 1·50
3953 1100l. Firefighting steam pump, 1863 1·50 1·50
3954 1100l. Early electric tram 1·50 1·50
3955 1100l. Steam car, 1893 1·50 1·50
3956 1100l. Modern electric monorail 1·50 1·50
MS3957 Three sheets, each 70×100 mm (a) 5000l. Class T9 steam locomotive, 1899. (b)5000l. Telephone, radio and light bulb. (c) 5000l. Benjamin Franklin (vert) Set of 3 sheets 20·00 22·00

361 S.O.S. Children's Village Logo

2002. S.O.S. Children's Villages (Kinderdorf International).

3958 **361** 2000l. multicoloured 1·75 2·00

2002. "United We Stand". Support for Victims of 11 September 2001 Terrorist Attacks. As T **445** of St. Vincent. Multicoloured.

3959 2000l. U. S. flag as Statue of Liberty and Sierra Leone flag 2·00 2·50

2002. Golden Jubilee (2nd issue). As T **110** of St. Kitts Multicoloured.

3960 2000l. Queen Elizabeth with Prince Charles and Princess Anne 2·75 3·00
3961 2000l. Queen Elizabeth in red dress and fur stole 2·75 3·00
3962 2000l. Queen Elizabeth wearing tiara and fur 2·75 3·00
3963 2000l. Queen Elizabeth wearing beige hat and coat 2·75 3·00
MS3964 76×108 mm. 5000l. Queen Elizabeth wearing grey hat and coat 7·00 7·50

362 Curling

2002. Winter Olympic Games, Salt Lake City. Multicoloured.

3965 2000l. Type **362** 2·75 3·00
3966 2000l. Ice hockey 2·75 3·00
MS3967 88×118 mm. Nos. 3965/6 5·50 6·00

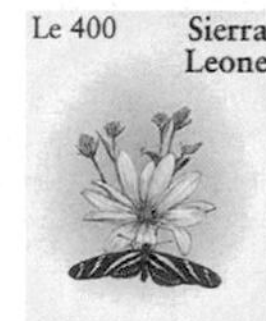

363 Jerusalem Artichoke Flower and Butterfly

2002. Flowers of Sierra Leone. Multicoloured.

3968 400l. Type **363** 55 30
3969 500l. Painted trillium and bee 70 35
3970 600l. Bell flower ("Bluebells") and moth 90 45
3971 1000l. Rough-fruited cinquefoil and moth 1·25 90
3972 1300l. Laevigata iris (43×29 mm) 1·40 1·50
3973 1300l. Wild iris ("Dietes") (43×29 mm) 1·40 1·50
3974 1300l. Day lily (43×29 mm) 1·40 1·50
3975 1300l. Cardinal flower (43×29 mm) 1·40 1·50
3976 1300l. Mountain pink (43×29 mm) 1·40 1·50
3977 1300l. Seaside gentian (43×29 mm) 1·40 1·50
3978 1300l. Hepatica americana (43×29 mm) 1·40 1·50
3979 1300l. Star of Bethlehem (43×29 mm) 1·40 1·50
3980 1300l. Wood lily (43×29 mm) 1·40 1·50
3981 1300l. Wild geranium (43×29 mm) 1·40 1·50
3982 1300l. Hedge bindweed (43×29 mm) 1·40 1·50
3983 1300l. Gloxinia (43×29 mm) 1·40 1·50
3984 1500l. Wake-robin and wasp 1·40 1·50
3985 2000l. Seashore mallow and butterfly 1·40 1·50
MS3986 Two sheets, each 117×107 mm. (a) 5000l. Dame's rocket (29×43 mm). (b) 5000l. Pinxter flower (29×43 mm) Set of 2 sheets 13·00 14·00

Nos. 3972/7 and 3978/83 were each printed together, *se-tenant*, with the backgrounds forming composite designs.

364 African Buffalo

2002. Sierra Leone Wildlife. Multicoloured.

3987 200l. Giraffe (vert) 75 30
3988 400l. L'Host's guenon (vert) 70 35
3989 1100l. Type **364** 1·40 1·50
3990 1100l. Wild dog 1·40 1·50
3991 1100l. Black-backed jackal 1·40 1·50
3992 1100l. Aardvark 1·40 1·50
3993 1100l. Impala 1·40 1·50
3994 1100l. Waterbuck 1·40 1·50
3995 1100l. Kudu 1·40 1·50
3996 1100l. Caracal 1·40 1·50
3997 1100l. Oribis 1·40 1·50
3998 1100l. Aardwolf 1·40 1·50
3999 1100l. Bushpig 1·40 1·50
4000 1100l. Meerkat ("Suricates") 1·40 1·50
4001 1500l. Jentink's duiker 1·40 1·50
MS4002 Two sheets, each 117×107 mm. (a) 8000l. Springbok (vert). (b) 8000l. Vervet monkey (vert) Set of 2 sheets 18·00 20·00

Nos. 3989/94 and 3995/4000 were each printed together, *se-tenant*, with the backgrounds forming composite designs. Nos. 3991, 3997 and 4001 are inscribed "Jackel", "Orbis" and "Jentik's", all in error.

2002. Queen Elizabeth the Queen Mother Commemoration. Nos. 2335/9 surch.

4003 800l. on 400l. Queen Mother (brown, light brown and black) 1·60 1·75
4004 800l. on 400l. Holding bouquet 1·60 1·75
4005 800l. on 400l. Sitting at desk 1·60 1·75
4006 800l. on 400l. Wearing pink evening dress 1·60 1·75
MS4007 103×127 mm. 5000l. on 1500l. Wearing blue hat 7·50 8·00

2002. Shirley Temple in Wee Willie Winkie. As T **411** of St. Vincent showing scenes from the film. Multicoloured.

4008 1100l. Meeting Khoda Khan 90 1·00
4009 1100l. Priscilla looking in mirror 90 1·00
4010 1100l. With drummer boy 90 1·00
4011 1100l. Priscilla being admonished by Indian servant 90 1·00
4012 1100l. Priscilla with grandfather 90 1·00
4013 1100l. Exchanging letter with Khoda Khan in prison 90 1·00
4014 1300l. Priscilla and mother (vert) 1·00 1·10
4015 1300l. Examining Khoda Khan's locket (vert) 1·00 1·10
4016 1300l. Priscilla with mother and grandfather (vert) 1·00 1·10
4017 1300l. Priscilla with colour sergeant, holding rifle (vert) 1·00 1·10
MS4018 106×76 mm. 5000l. Priscilla on parade (vert) 5·50 6·00

2002. International Year of Mountains. As T **115** of St. Kitts. Multicoloured.

4019 2000l. Mount Etna, Italy 2·50 2·50
4020 2000l. Mount Cotopaxi, Ecuador 2·50 2·50
4021 2000l. Mount Everest, Nepal 2·50 2·50
4022 2000l. Mount Popocatepetl, Mexico 2·50 2·50
MS4023 118×68 mm. 5000l. Mount Machhapuchare, Nepal 7·00 7·50

2002. U.N. Year of Eco Tourism. As T **449** of St.Vincent, but horiz. Multicoloured.

4024 1300l. Bullom boats 1·60 1·60
4025 1300l. Dinkongor Falls 1·60 1·60
4026 1300l. Sailing canoe on River Rokel 1·60 1·60
4027 1300l. Pigmy hippopotamus 1·60 1·60
4028 1300l. Soa Chiefdom hills 1·60 1·60
4029 1300l. Long Beach 1·60 1·60
MS4030 88×103 mm. 5000l. Photo safari 6·50 7·50

366 *Spirit of St. Louis* (aircraft)

2002. 75th Anniv of First Solo Transatlantic Flight, by Charles Lindbergh.

4031 **366** 2500l. lake and red 3·00 3·25
4032 - 2500l. green and red 3·00 3·25
4033 - 2500l. lilac and red 3·00 3·25
MS4034 116×85 mm. 2500l. multicoloured (vert) 3·00 3·25

DESIGNS—HORIZ: No. 4032, *Spirit of St. Louis*, Curtisfield, 1927; 4033, Taking off from Roosevelt Field, 1927. VERT: No. **MS**4034, Charles Lindbergh.

367 Chiune Sugihara

2002. Chiune Sugihara, Japanese Consul-general to Lithuania, 1939–40, Commemoration.

4035 **367** 2000l. multicoloured 2·75 3·00

2002. 20th World Scout Jamboree, Thailand. As T **116** St. Kitts, but vert. Multicoloured.

4036 2000l. Scouts on rocks 2·50 2·50
4037 2000l. Scouts of all nations 2·50 2·50
4038 2000l. Two scouts in river, holding fish 2·50 2·50
4039 2000l. Watching demonstration 2·50 2·50
MS4040 107×122 mm. 5000l. Sailing on lake 7·00 7·50

2002. "Pokemon" (children's cartoon series). As T **417** of St. Vincent. Multicoloured.

4041 1500l. "Sudowoodo No. 185" 1·10 1·40
4042 1500l. "Aipom No. 190" 1·10 1·40
4043 1500l. "Shuckle No. 213" 1·10 1·40
4044 1500l. "Miltank No. 241" 1·10 1·40
4045 1500l. "Hitmontop No. 237" 1·10 1·40
4046 1500l. "Ledian No. 166" 1·10 1·40
MS4047 67×91 mm. 5000l. "Lugia No. 249" 5·50 6·00

368 Popeye and Olive Oyl at Helm

2002. "Popeye" (cartoon character) in New York. Multicoloured.

4048 1300l. Type **368** 1·10 1·25
4049 1300l. Popeye giving Olive Oyl spinach 1·10 1·25
4050 1300l. By Brooklyn Bridge 1·10 1·25
4051 1300l. Popeye near Statue of Liberty 1·10 1·25
4052 1300l. At the Flatiron building 1·10 1·25
4053 1300l. In front of Empire State Building 1·10 1·25
MS4054 128×89 mm. 5000l. Popeye and Olive Oyl ice skating (78×51 mm) 6·00 6·50

369 Elvis Presley

2002. 25th Death Anniv of Elvis Presley (American entertainer). Each black and brown.

4055 1000l. Type **369** 1·40 1·40
4056 1000l. Playing bi-coloured guitar 1·40 1·40
4057 1000l. Sitting in director's chair 1·40 1·40
4058 1000l. Wearing polo neck jumper 1·40 1·40
4059 1000l. In Hispanic suit 1·40 1·40
4060 1000l. Playing dark guitar 1·40 1·40

370 Michael Ballack (Germany)

2002. World Cup Football Championship, Japan and Korea. Multicoloured.

4061 1400l. Type **370** 1·10 1·10
4062 1400l. Oliver Kahn (Germany) 1·10 1·10
4063 1400l. Miroslav Klose (Germany) 1·10 1·10
4064 1400l. Diego Gavilan (Paraguay) 1·10 1·10
4065 1400l. Jose Luis Chilavert (Paraguay) 1·10 1·10
4066 1400l. Guido Alvarenga (Paraguay) 1·10 1·10
4067 1400l. Rafael Marquez (Mexico) 1·10 1·10
4068 1400l. Oscar Perez (Mexico) 1·10 1·10
4069 1400l. Jared Borgetti (Mexico) 1·10 1·10
4070 1400l. Landon Donovan (U.S.A.) 1·10 1·10
4071 1400l. Brad Friedel (U.S.A.) 1·10 1·10
4072 1400l. DaMarcus Beasley (U.S.A.) 1·10 1·10
4073 1400l. Jesper Gronkjaer (Denmark) 1·10 1·10
4074 1400l. Thomas Helveg (Denmark) 1·10 1·10
4075 1400l. Dennis Rommedahl (Denmark) 1·10 1·10
4076 1400l. Michael Owen (England) 1·10 1·10
4077 1400l. David Seaman (England) 1·10 1·10

4078 1400l. Rio Ferdinand (England) 1·10 1·10
4079 1400l. Ryuzo Morioka (Japan) 1·10 1·10
4080 1400l. Kazuyuki Toda (Japan) 1·10 1·10
4081 1400l. Atsushi Yanagisawa (Japan) 1·10 1·10
4082 1400l. Fatih Akyel (Turkey) 1·10 1·10
4083 1400l. Yildiray Basturk (Turkey) 1·10 1·10
4084 1400l. Umit Davala (Turkey) 1·10 1·10
MS4085 Eight sheets, each 82×82 mm. (a) 2500l. Rudi Voeller (coach) (Germany); 2500l. Dietmar Hamann (Germany). (b) 2500l. Julio Cesar Caceres (Paraguay); 2500l. Cesare Maldini (coach) (Paraguay). (c) 2500l. Javier Aguirre (coach) (Mexico); 2500l. Jesus Arellano (Mexico). (d) 2500l. Brian McBride (U.S.A.); 2500l. Bruce Arena (coach) (U.S.A.). (e) 2500l. Morten Olsen (coach) (Denmark); 2500l. Jon Dahl Tomasson (Denmark). (f) 2500l. David Beckham (England); 2500l. Sven Goran Eriksson (coach) (England). (g) 2500l. Philippe Troussier (coach) (Japan); 2500l. Junichi Inamoto (Japan). (h) 2500l. Vildiray Basturk (Turkey); 2500l. Senol Gunes (coach) (Turkey) Set of 8 sheets 17·00 20·00

371 "Madonna and Child between Sts. John the Baptist and Catherine of Alexandria" (Perugino)

2002. Christmas. Religious Paintings. Multicoloured.
4086 50l. Type **371** 20 15
4087 100l. "Madonna and Child enthroned between Angels and Saints" (Ghirlandaio) 25 15
4088 150l. "The Virgin" (Giovanni Bellini) 30 15
4089 500l. "The Birth of Mary" (Ghirlandaio) 80 25
4090 5000l. "Adoration of the Magi" (Ghirlandaio) 6·50 7·50
MS4091 100×76 mm. 6000l. "Madonna enthroned with Saints" (Ghirlandaio) 7·50 8·50

372 Teddy Bear with Green and Gold Bow

2002. Centenary of the Teddy Bear (1st issue). Two sheets containing T **372** and similar vert designs. Multicoloured.
MS4092 107×115 mm. 1700l. Type **372**; 1700l. Jester teddy bear; 1700l. Bear with red and gold headband; 1700l. Bear with sash 6·00 7·00
MS4093 148×158 mm. 2000l. Baby girl bear; 2000l. School girl bear; 2000l. Bear in denim overalls; 2000l. Bear in pyjamas 6·50 7·50
See also Nos. **MS**4128/9.

373 Princess Diana

2002. Fifth Death Anniv of Diana, Princess of Wales. Two sheets, each 120×130 mm, containing T **373** and similar vert design. Multicoloured.
MS4094 1700l. ×4 Type **373** 7·50 8·00
MS4095 1700l. ×4 Princess Diana (wearing tiara) 7·50 8·00

374 President John F. Kennedy

2002. Presidents John F. Kennedy (Commemoration) and Ronald Reagan. Miniature sheets containing vert designs as T **374**. Multicoloured.
MS4096 122×135 mm. 1700l. Type **374**; 1700l. John Kennedy reading newspaper; 1700l. John Kennedy (looking ahead); 1700l. John Kennedy (looking left) 6·00 7·00
MS4097 114×129 mm. 1700l. John and Jacqueline Kennedy in evening dress; 1700l. John and Jacqueline Kennedy; 1700l. With John Jnr; 1700l. Jacqueline Kennedy in pink hat and coat 6·00 7·00
MS4098 143×110 mm. 1700l. ×4 containing two different portraits of Ronald Reagan 6·00 7·00
MS4099 137×165 mm. 1700l. ×4 containing two different portraits of Ronald Reagan 6·00 7·00

375 Great Blue Turaco

2003. Fauna and Flora of Africa. Miniature sheets containing T **375** and similar multicoloured designs.
MS4100 139×100 mm. 1300l. Type **375**; 1300l. Helmet bird ("Helmet Vanga"); 1300l. Red-tufted malachite sunbird ("Scarlet-tufted Malachite Sunbird"); 1300l. African pitta; 1300l. African jacana; 1300l. Carmine bee eater 10·00 11·00
MS4101 139×100 mm. 1300l. *Ancistrochilus rothschildianus*; 1300l. *Oeceoclades maculate*; 1300l. *Eulophia guineensis*; 1300l. *Angraecum distichum*; 1300l. *Disa uniflora*; 1300l. *Vanilla imperialis* 10·00 11·00
MS4102 139×100 mm. 1300l. Panther-spotted grasshopper; 1300l. Basker moth; 1300l. *Charaxes samagdalis* (butterfly); 1300l. Carpenter ant; 1300l. Worker bee; 1300l. *Libellula pulchella* (ten-spot dragonfly) 10·00 11·00
MS4103 Three sheets. (a) 63×87 mm. 5000l. European robin. (b) 87×63 mm. 5000l. *Bulbophyllum lepidum*. (c) 87×63 mm. 5000l. Common dotted border (butterfly) (horiz) Set of 3 sheets 20·00 21·00
No. **MS**4100 shows birds, **MS**4101 shows flowers and **MS**4102 insects.

376 Green Symbolic Ram

2003. Chinese New Year ("Year of the Ram"). Sheet 109×128 mm, containing T **376** and similar vert designs. Multicoloured.
MS4104 900l. Type **376**; 900l.×3 Carved ram; 900l. Red symbolic ram. 900l. Magenta symbolic ram 4·25 4·75

377 David Brown

2003. Columbia Space Shuttle Commemoration. Sheet 184×145 mm, containing T **377** and similar vert designs showing crew members. Multicoloured.
MS4105 1000l. Type **377**; 1000l. Commander Rick Husband; 1000l. Laurel Clark; 1000l. Kalpana Chawla; 1000l. Payload Commander Michael Anderson; 1000l. Pilot William McCool; 1000l. Ilan Ramon 8·00 9·00

2003. Centenary of the Teddy Bear (2nd issue). Embroidered Fabric Teddy Bears. As T **464** of St. Vincent. Self-adhesive. Imperf.
4106 12000l. ochre, silver and black 3·50 3·75
MS4107 126×157 mm. No. 4106 ×4 14·00 14·50

378 "Priest Raigo tranformed into a Rat" (Tsukioka Yoshitoshi)

2003. Japanese Art. Ghosts and Demons. Multicoloured.
4108 800l. Type **378** 1·00 60
4109 1000l. "The Spirit of Tamichi as a Great Snake" (Tsukioka Yoshitoshi) 1·25 85
4110 1500l. "The Gathering and Gossiping of Various Tools" (Utagawa Kuniyoshi) 1·75 2·00
4111 2500l. "Caricatures of Actors as Three Animals playing Ken" (Utagawa Kuniyoshi) 2·75 3·25
MS4112 148×148 mm. 2000l. "The Fox Woman leaving her Child"; 2000l. "Fox Cry"; 2000l. "The Lucky Teakettle of Morin Temple"; 2000l. "The Ghost of Okiku" (all Tsukioka Yoshitoshi) 8·50 9·50
MS4113 88×118 mm. 5000l. "Fox in a Thunderstorm" (Utagawa Kunisada) 6·00 6·50

2003. 30th Death Anniv of Pablo Picasso (artist). As T **465** of St. Vincent, but vert. Multicoloured.
4114 400l. "Verres Pipe, Carte a Jouer" 70 45
4115 500l. "Gueridon devant un Balcon" 80 50
4116 600l. "Femme au Chapeau a Plumes" 90 65
4117 700l. "Gueridon et Guitare" 1·00 1·00
4118 1000l. "Femme en Pied" 1·25 1·25
4119 3000l. "Femme Acrobate" 3·50 4·00
MS4120 205×140 mm. 2000l. "Portrait de Face"; 2000l. "Femme au Fauteuil Rouge"; 2000l. "Femme au Petit Chapeau Rond, Assise (Dora Maar)"; 2000l. "Femme aux Mains Croisees" 8·00 8·50
MS4121 (a) 82×105 mm. 5000l. "Garcon au Calecon noir". Imperf. (b) 102×81 mm. 5000l. "Les Baigneuses". Imperf 12·00 13·00

2003. Paintings by Rembrandt. As T **466** of St. Vincent. Multicoloured.
4122 800l. "Young Man with Pointed Beard" 1·00 75
4123 1000l. "Old Man with Book" 1·25 95
4124 1200l. "The Shipbuilder Jan Rijcksen and his Wife, Griet Jans" (horiz) 1·40 1·40
4125 2000l. "Portrait of a Young Jew" 2·40 3·00
MS4126 185×183 mm. 1700l. "Juno"; 1700l. "Bellona, Goddess of War"; 1700l. "Artemisia" (detail); 1700l. "Esther preparing to Intercede with Ahasuerus" (detail) (all 35×47 mm) 8·00 8·50
MS4127 110×130 mm. 5000l. "Two Scholars Disputing" 6·50 7·00

379 Teddy Bear wearing Apron and Hat

2003. Centenary of the Teddy Bear (3rd issue). German Teddy Bears. Multicoloured.
MS4128 183×129 mm. 1500l. Type **379**; 1500l. Bear wearing waistcoat, hat and water bottle; 1500l. Bear wearing pink dress 1500l. Bear with trumpet and score 6·00 7·00
MS4129 98×72 mm. 5000l. Bear in Volkswagen Beetle car (horiz) 5·00 6·00

2003. 50th Anniv of Coronation. As T **462** of St. Vincent. Multicoloured.
4130 1500l. Queen Elizabeth II holding Sovereign's Sword 1·90 1·90
4131 1500l. Ampulla and spoon 1·90 1·90
4132 1500l. Queen presented with Holy Bible 1·90 1·90
4133 1500l. Crowning of Queen 1·90 1·90
4134 1500l. Queen signing Oath 1·90 1·90
4135 1500l. Anointing of Queen 1·90 1·90
4136 1500l. Orb and Sceptre 1·90 1·90
4137 1500l. Crowd at Palace gates and Royal Family on balcony 1·90 1·90
MS4138 9×67 mm. 5000l. Queen Elizabeth II (38×50 mm) 7·50 8·00

380 Prince William

2003. 21st Birthday of Prince William of Wales. Multicoloured.
MS4139 146×85 mm. 2500l. Type **380**; 2500l. Prince William (wearing black jacket and tie); 2500l. Wearing grey sweatshirt 10·00 11·00
MS4140 96×67 mm. 5000l. Prince William 7·50 8·00

381 Peggy Williams

2003. Centenary of Circus Clowns. Multicoloured.
MS4141 116×196 mm. 2000l. Type **381**; 2000l. Nico; 2000l. Steve TJ Tatter Smith; 2000l. Uncle Dippy 7·00 7·50
MS4142 145×217 mm. 2000l. Caracal (cat) ; 2000l. Chairs (gymnast); 2000l. Elena Panova on trapeze; 2000l. Chinese Circus performer 7·00 7·50

382 "Mona Lisa"

2003. 500th Anniv of "Mona Lisa" (painting, Da Vinci).
MS4143 100×77 mm. 2000l. Type **382** (black and grey); 2000l. "Mona Lisa" (black, deep brown and brown); 2000l. "Mona Lisa" (multicoloured) 7·00 8·00
MS4144 67×97 mm. 5000l. "Mona Lisa" (detail) (multicoloured) 6·50 7·00

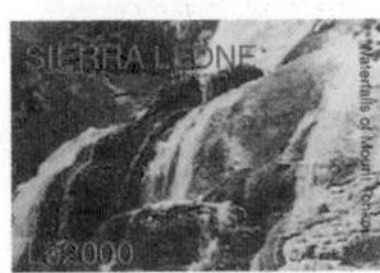

383 Waterfalls of Mount Tonkour

2003. International Year of Freshwater. Multicoloured.
MS4145 96×138 mm. 2000l. Type **383**; 2000l. Tagbaladougou Falls; 2000l. Cascades d,Ouzoud 7·00 8·00
MS4146 67×97 mm. 5000l. Little Scarcies 6·50 7·00

384 Rotarian and People in Canoe

2003. 40th Anniv of Rotary Club in Sierra Leone. Multicoloured.
MS4147 105×77 mm. 2500l. Type **384**; 2500l. People of Sierra Leone and cacheted first day cover; 2500l. Paul Harris (founder) and girl with flowers 8·00 9·00
MS4148 97×67 mm. 6000l. Bhichai Rattakul (Rotary President) 7·00 8·00

385 Wright Brothers First Plane (USA), 1903

2003. Centenary of Powered Flight. Multicoloured.

MS4149 176×96 mm. 150l. Wright Brothers' First Plane (U.S.A.), 1903; 150l. Voisin-Farmin (France), 1907 (grey background); 150l. Levavasseur Antoinette (France), 1909 (No. 29 on fuselage); 150l. Nieuport (France) 1910 7·50 8·50

MS4150 176×96 mm. 150l. Curtiss Triad, 1911 (inscr "Wright Brothers First Plane (U.S.A.) 1903"; 150l. Avro Biplane, 1911 (inscr "Voisin-Farmin (France) 1907") (blue-grey background); 150l. Curtiss America, 1913 (inscr "Levavasseur Antoinette (France) 1909"); 150l. Farnborough Be-2, 1913 (inscr "Nieuport (France) 1910") (No. 345 on tail) 7·50 8·50

MS4150a 176×96 mm. 150l. Curtiss Triad (U.S.A.), 1911; 150l. Avro Biplane (British), 1911; 150l. Curtiss America (U.S.A.), 1913; 150l. Farnborough Be-2 (British), 1913 7·50 8·50

MS4151 Two sheets, each 106×76 mm. (a) 5000l. Voisin-Farman plane crossing finish line, Aero Club, 1908. (b) 500l. Roland Garros and Morane-Saulnier monoplane after first non-stop Mediterranean crossing, 1913 Set of 2 sheets 7·50 8·50

No. **MS**4150 was issued with the incorrect aircraft inscriptions and **MS**4150a was issued subsequently with the correct inscriptions.

2003. Centenary of Tour de France Cycle Race. As T **470** of St.Vincent. Multicoloured.

MS4152 157×97 mm. 150l. Ferdinand Kubler (1950); 150l. Hugo Koblet (1951); 150l. Fausto Coppi (1952); 150l. Louison Bobet (1953) 7·50 8·00

MS4153 157×97 mm. 150l. Louison Bobet 1954); 150l. Louison Bobet (1955); 150l. Roger Walkowiak (1956); 150l. Jacques Anquetil (1957) 7·50 8·00

MS4154 157×97 mm. 150l. Eddy Merckx (1970); 150l. Eddy Merckx (1971); 150l. Eddy Merckx (1972); 150l. Luis Ocana (1973) 7·50 8·00

MS4155 Two sheets, each 106×77 mm. (a) 500l. Louison Bobet (1953, 1954, 1955). (b) 500l. Jacques Anquetil (1957). (c) 500l. Bernard Hinault (1978) Set of 2 Sheets 12·00 13·00

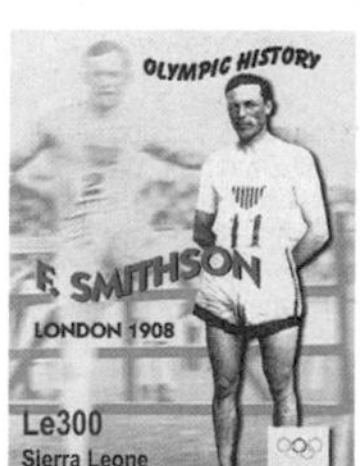

386 Forrest Smithson (110 metre hurdles), USA, 1908

2003. Olympic History. Gold Medal Winners. Multicoloured.

4156 300l. Type **386** 50 25

4157 400l. Hannes Kolehmainen (10000 metres, 5000 metres and cross-country), Finland, 1912 60 30

4158 500l. Larisa Latynina (gymnastics–floor exercises), URS, 1964 65 35

4159 800l. Klaus Dibiasi (10 metre platform diving), Italy, 1976 1·00 70

4160 1000l. Archie Hahn (100 metres and 200 metres), USA, 1904 1·25 95

4161 1500l. Marcus Hurley (cycling), USA, 1904 2·00 2·00

4162 2000l. Ray Ewry (standing high jump, standing long jump and standing triple jump), USA, 1900 2·25 2·50

4163 3000l. Henry Taylor (swimming–1500 metres and 400 metres freestyle), Great Britain, 1908 3·25 3·75

387 "Madonna and Child with St. Anne and Four Saints" (detail)

2003. Christmas. Paintings by Fiorentino. Multicoloured.

4164 100l. Type **387** 25 15

4165 150l. "Madonna and Child with Two Saints" (detail) 30 15

4166 500l. "Madonna and Child enthroned with Four Saints" (detail) (Ognissanti Altarpiece) 75 30

4167 4000l. "Madonna enthroned between Two Saints" (detail) 5·00 6·00

MS4168 99×110 mm. 5000l. "Madonna with Saints" 6·50 7·50

388 Camarasaurus

2004. Prehistoric Animals. Multicoloured.

MS4169 138×99 mm. 2000l. Type **388**; 2000l. lystrosaurus; 2000l. Ankylosaurus; 2000l. Herrerasaurus 8·50 9·50

MS4170 125×106 mm. 2000l. Apatosaurus (vert); 2000l. Styracosaurus (vert); 2000l. Plateosaurus (vert); 2000l. Pachyrhinosaurus (vert) 8·50 9·50

MS4171 Two sheets (a) 97×67 mm. 5000l. Archaeopteryx. (b) 67×96 mm. 5000l. Dunklosteus (vert) 11·00 12·00

No. **MS**4171a is incorrectly inscr "Archaeopterxy".

389 Monkey eating Fruit

2004. Chinese New Year ("Year of the Monkey"). Multicoloured.

MS4173 85×70 mm. 1200l. Type **389** (ochre background); 1200l. Type **389** (blue background); 1200l. Monkey eating fruit (facing right, mauve background); 1200l. Monkey eating fruit (facing right, orange background) 4·50 4·75

MS4174 66×96 mm. 2500l. Monkey holding fruit (42×28 mm) 4·25 4·50

390 "Taoist Ritual at the Imperial Court"

2004. Hong Kong 2004 International Stamp Exhibition. Paintings by Chiao Ping-chen. Multicoloured.

MS4175 136×139 mm. 2000l. Type **390**; 2000l. Landscape of mountains, river and lake; 2000l. "Court Ladies" (by pavilion); 2000l. "Court Ladies" (poling raft) 7·00 8·00

MS4176 90×90 mm. 5000l. "The Beauty of Traditional Chinese Architecture in Painting". Imperf 5·00 5·50

391 Cabani's Yellow Bunting

2004. 60th Anniv of British Council in Sierra Leone.

4177 **391** 500l. multicoloured 85 30

4178 **391** 1000l. multicoloured 1·25 90

4179 **391** 2000l. multicoloured 2·25 2·50

4180 **391** 3000l. multicoloured 3·00 3·75

392 Lion Emblem and Map

2004. 40th Anniv of First Self-adhesive Stamps. As T **80** (World's Fair, New York of 1964) but redrawn with face value in leones as T **392**. Self-adhesive. Imperf.

4181 **392** 1000l. multicoloured 1·25 1·40

393 "Ice Cream Carrier"

2004. 25th Death Anniv of Norman Rockwell (artist) (2003). Multicoloured.

MS4182 150×180 mm. 2000l. Type **393**; 2000l. "The Voyeur"; 2000l. "Teacher's Birthday"; 2000l. Fisk Tires advertisement, 1919 7·50 8·50

MS4183 90×97 mm. 5000l. "Cousin Reginald plays Pirate" 6·00 7·00

394 Concorde over River, Rio de Janeiro

2004. Last Flight of Concorde (2003). Multicoloured.

MS4184 90×131 mm. 3000l. Type **394**; 3000l. Concorde over Brazil flag (top left of blue circle); 3000l. Concorde over Brazil flag (bottom left of blue circle) 12·00 12·00

MS4185 90×129 mm. 3000l. Concorde (pink background); 3000l. Concorde and pyramid (red background); 3000l. Concorde and pyramid (dark brown background) 12·00 12·00

MS4186 131×90 mm. 3000l. Concorde and Nairobi skyline; 3000l. Concorde over Kenyan bush (black and red background) 3000l. Concorde over Kenyan bush (red and green background) 12·00 12·00

No. **MS**4184 shows Concorde 206 G-BOAA over Rio de Janeiro, **MS**4185 Concorde G-AXDN and Egyptian pyramid and **MS**4186 Concorde G-AXDN Aircraft No. 101 over Kenya.

395 "The Birth of John the Baptist" (detail) (Tintoretto)

2004. 300th Anniv of St. Petersburg. "Treasures of the Hermitage". Multicoloured.

MS4187 144×144 mm. 1400l. Type **395**; 1400l. "Penitent Mary Magdalen" (Titian); 1400l. "The Death of St. Petronilla" (Simone Pignoni); 1400l. "The Assumption of the Virgin" (Murillo); 1400l. "St. Jerome Hears the Trumpet" (Jusepe de Ribera); 1400l. "St. George and the Dragon" (Tintoretto) 7·50 8·50

MS4187a 160×140 mm. 2000l. "Countess A. S. Stroganova and Her Son" (Louise-Elisabeth Vigee-Lebrun); 2000l. "Count G. I. Chernyshev Holding a Mask (Louise-Elisabeth Vigee-Lebrun)"; 2000l. "Self Portrait" (Louise-Elisabeth Vigee-Lebrun); 2000l. "Baron G. A. Stroganov" (Louise-Elisabeth Vigee-Lebrun) 7·50 8·50

MS4188 Two sheets. (a) 62×81 mm. 5000l. "The Apostles Peter and Paul" (El Greco). (b) 100×69 mm. 5000l. "A Visit to the Priest" (Jean-Baptiste Greuze). Both imperf 11·00 12·00

396 Marilyn Monroe

2004. Marilyn Monroe (actress) Commemoration. Multicoloured.

4189 1000l. Type **396** 1·00 1·10

4190 1000l. With short hair and sparkly earrings (cobalt background) 1·00 1·10

4191 1000l. As No. 4190 but with lavender background 1·00 1·10

4192 1000l. Wearing pink patterned shirt 1·00 1·10

MS4193 113×112 mm. 2000l. Wearing strapless top; 2000l. With arms above head; 2000l. Leaning back with shoulders hunched; 2000l. Wearing scoop-necked top 7·00 8·00

397 Yang Liwei (Chinese Astronaut)

2004. Astronauts. Multicoloured.

4194 900l. Type **397** 1·25 1·25

4195 900l. Yang Liwei wearing uniform 1·25 1·25

4196 900l. Yang Liwei wearing space suit 1·25 1·25

4197 900l. Yang Liwei showing "victory" sign 1·25 1·25

4198 1200l. "Vostok 1" (vert) 1·40 1·40

4199 1200l. John Glenn (American astronaut) (vert) 1·40 1·40

4200 1200l. Launch of "Friendship 7" (vert) 1·40 1·40

4201 1200l. Yuri Gagarin (Russian astronaut) (vert) 1·40 1·40

4202 1200l. Launch of "Shenzhou 5" (vert) 1·40 1·40

4203 1200l. Yang Liwei (vert) 1·40 1·40

MS4204 Two sheets, each 100×70 mm. (a) 5000l. John Glenn. (b) 5000l. Yang Liwei Set of 2 sheets 12·00 13·00

398 Lo Moth

2004. Butterflies and Moths. Multicoloured.

4205 200l. Type **398** 50 20

4206 300l. Hackberry butterfly 70 30

4207 400l. Red admiral 80 45

4208 4000l. Spangled fritillary 5·50 6·50

MS4209 Two sheets. (a) 144×118 mm. 1700l. Pearl crescent; 1700l. Pipevine swallowtail; 1700l. Alfalfa looper; 1700l. Tiger swallowtail. (b) 66×65 mm. 5000l. Cecropia moth Set of 2 sheets 15·00 16·00

399 *Catasetum pileatum*

2004. Orchids. Multicoloured.

4210 150l. Type **399** 60 20

4211 400l. *Cattleya araguainsis* 80 70

4212 400l. *Barkeria spectabilis* 80 70

4213 1700l. *Odontonia vesta* 2·00 2·25

4214 1700l. *Ancistro rothschildianus* 2·00 2·25

4215 1700l. *Ansellia Africana* 2·00 2·25

4216 1700l. *Aspasia epidendroides* 2·00 2·25

4217 3500l. *Catasetum fimbriatum* 2·00 2·25

MS4218 68×73 mm. 5000l. *Bulbophyllum lobbii* 7·00 8·00

400 Banded Sculpin

2004. Marine Life. Multicoloured.

4219 800l. Type **400** 1·00 60
4220 1100l. Black durgon 1·40 1·25
4221 1400l. Atlantic spadefish 1·50 1·75
4222 1400l. Queen triggerfish 1·50 1·75
4223 1700l. Peacock flounder 1·75 1·90
4224 1700l. Northern puffer 1·75 1·90
4225 1700l. Sea raven 1·75 1·90
4226 1700l. Tiger shark 1·75 1·90
MS4227 68×74 mm. 5000l. Sea lamprey (vert) 7·00 8·00

401 Ruddy Somali

2004. Cats. Multicoloured.

4228 100l. Type **401** 30 20
4229 800l. Bombay (walking right) 1·00 60
4230 1200l. Burmese (walking left) 1·40 1·25
4231 1700l. Persian (vert) 1·75 1·90
4232 1700l. Colorpoint shorthair (vert) 1·75 1·90
4233 1700l. Cornish Rex (vert) 1·75 1·90
4234 1700l. Blue Point Balinese (vert) 1·75 1·90
4235 3000l. Blue British shorthair 1·75 1·90
MS4236 83×63 mm. 5000l. Devon Rex 7·00 8·00

402 Great Pyrenees

2004. Dogs. Multicoloured.

4237 250l. Type **402** 60 25
4238 600l. Kerry blue terrier 85 50
4239 1300l. Mastiff 1·50 1·25
4240 1700l. Sealyham terrier 1·75 1·90
4241 1700l. Norwich terrier 1·75 1·90
4242 1700l. Wheaton terrier 1·75 1·90
4243 1700l. Bull terrier 1·75 1·90
4244 1800l. English sheepdog 1·75 1·90
MS4245 70×79 mm. 5000l. Greyhound 7·00 8·00

403 Belted Kingfisher

2004. Birds. Multicoloured.

4246 500l. Type **403** 85 45
4247 1000l. Burrowing owl 1·60 1·25
4248 1500l. Crested caracara 1·75 1·75
4249 1700l. Snail kite (horiz) 1·75 1·90
4250 1700l. Avocet (horiz) 1·75 1·90
4251 1700l. Greater flamingo (horiz) 1·75 1·90
4252 1700l. Bald eagle (horiz) 1·75 1·90
4253 2000l. Red headed finch 2·25 2·50
MS4254 84×64 mm. 5000l. Ring neck pheasant 7·50 8·00

404 Pope John Paul II

2004. 25th Anniv of the Pontificate of Pope John Paul II. Sheet 95×118 mm containing T **404** and similar horiz designs. Multicoloured.

MS4255 2000l. Type **404**; 2000l. Pope and John Bonica (President of International Association for the Study of Pain); 2000l. Pope in Croatia; 2000l. Pope presiding over Mass 9·50 10·00

405 Deng Xiaoping

2004. Birth Centenary of Deng Xiaoping (leader of China, 1978–89). Sheet 96×67 mm.

MS4256 5000l. multicoloured 5·00 6·00

406 Marathon, 1908

2004. Olympic Games, Athens. Multicoloured.

4257 250l. Type **406** 45 25
4258 300l. Demetrius Vikelas (President of International Olympic Committee 1894–1896) 50 25
4259 1500l. Detail of gold medal, Athens (1896) 1·75 2·00
4260 2000l. Discobolus (Greek sculpture) 2·00 2·25

407 General Dwight D. Eisenhower

2004. 60th Anniv of D-Day Landings. Multicoloured.

4261 1400l. Type **407** 1·60 1·60
4262 1400l. Rear Admiral Don. P. Moon 1·60 1·60
4263 1400l. Lieutenant General Omar N. Bradley 1·60 1·60
4264 1400l. Rear Admiral Alan G. Kirk 1·60 1·60
4265 1400l. Major General Clarence R. Huebner 1·60 1·60
4266 1400l. Major General Maxwell D. Taylor 1·60 1·60
MS4267 Six sheets each 200×117 mm. (a) 950l. ×8, LST landing craft; M4 Sherman tank; US soldier on tank; Gun of tank; 70th Tank Battalion patch; Soldier aiming rifle; 743rd Tank Battalion patch; 741st Tank Battalion patch. (b) 1000l. ×8, P-51 Mustang; Parachutists; Map of troop movements; P-38 Lightning; M4 Sherman tank and explosion; Soldiers; LCM landing craft; U.S. light cruiser. (c) 1000l. ×8, Spitfire; Typhoon; Tail of Typhoon; P-51 Mustang; C-47 Skytrain; War plane and wing of Typhoon; P-38 Lightning; U.S. Airforce patch. (d) 1000l. ×8, P-47 Thunderbolt; Parachutists, map and planes; Tank and map of troop movements; Map showing Dieppe and soldier aiming rifle; U.S. heavy cruiser; U.S. light cruiser and bow of heavy cruiser; Destroyer and bow and stern of ships; U.S. Destroyer escort. (e) 1100l. ×8 U.S. light cruiser and airships; LST landing craft and airships; Bow of LST landing craft; Hull of LST landing craft; U.S. armoured car; Soldiers; U.S. medical transport; U.S. armoured car and landing craft. (f) 1100l. ×8 Soldier aiming rifle and map of parachutists' descent; Badge of 101st Airborne "Screaming Eagles"; Parachutist and tail of plane; Cockpit of plane; General Dwight D. Eisenhower; Bernard Montgomery; 82nd Airborne Division; C-47 Skytrain and parachutists Set of 6 sheets 45·00 50·00

408 "Mona Lisa"

2004. 500th Anniv of the "Mona Lisa".

4268 **408** 2000l. multicoloured 2·00 2·25

409 Peace Dove carrying Olive Branch

2004. United Nations International Year of Peace. Sheet 143×83 mm, containing T **409** and similar designs. Multicoloured.

MS4269 3000l. ×3 Type **409**; Dove facing left; Dove with legs tucked up 8·25 8·50

410 The Smalls Lighthouse

2004. Lighthouses of Great Britain. Multicoloured.

4270 1800l. Type **410** 2·00 2·00
4271 2000l. Needles Rock lighthouse 2·00 2·00
4272 2500l. St. John's Point lighthouse 2·25 2·50
4273 3500l. Bell Rock lighthouse 3·00 3·50
4274 4000l. Eddystone lighthouse 3·50 4·00

411 Arapaho Pipe Bag

2004. American Indians. Multicoloured.

4275–83 Decorative Artifacts. 1000l. ×9, Type **411**; Apache basket; Blackfoot parfleche; Crow Elkhide robe; Iroquois moccasins; Hopi canteen; Sioux parfleche; Navajo rug; Nez Perce cradle 8·00 9·00
4284–9 Chiefs and Warriors. 1500l. ×6, Ne-O-Mon-Ne; Ma-Has-Kah; Moa-Na-Hon-Ga; Tah-Ro-Hon; Not-Chi-Mi-Ne; Shau-Hau-Napo-Tinia 8·00 9·00

412 Patas Monkeys

2004. Endangered Species. Patas Monkey. Multicoloured.

4290 1000l. Type **412** 1·25 1·25
4291 1000l. Feeding 1·25 1·25
4292 1000l. With baby 1·25 1·25
4293 1000l. Monkey 1·25 1·25

413 Carmelo Anthony (Denver Nuggets)

2004. National Basketball Association (1st series). Multicoloured.

4294 700l. Type **413** 1·00 1·00
4295 700l. Yao Ming (Houston Rockets) 1·00 1·00
4296 700l. Jermaine O'Neal (Indiana Pacers) 1·00 1·00
4297 700l. Kobe Bryant (Los Angeles Lakers) 1·00 1·00

See also Nos. 4320/1.

414 George Herman Ruth Jr

2004. Centenary of Baseball World Series.

4298 **414** 500l. multicoloured 45 50

415 LMS 8F 2-8-0, Great Central Railway

2004. Bicentenary of Steam Locomotives. Multicoloured.

MS4299 Four sheets, each 148×176 mm. (a) 1000l.×9, Type **413**; Rhodesia Railways 12 Class 4-8-2; DR German Railways 01 Class Pacific; Indian Railways Metre Gauge McArthur 2-8-2; USATC 0-6-0 T, Greece; China Railways KD6 2-8-0; Polish Feldbahn 0-8-0 T; Indian Railways MAWD 2-8-2; North British 2-10-0. (b) 1000l.×9 (horiz), Stephenson's Rocket; Indonesian State Railway B50 Class 2-4-0; Eurostar; China Railways SY Class 2-8-2; Baldwin 0-6-0, Philippines; Hunsle 0-4-2 T, Java; Bagnall 0-6-0 ST Progress; North British built 4-8-2 T; Baldwin 0-6-2 ST, Brazil. (c) 1000l.×9, B12 Class 4-6-0; Uruguay Railways Beyer Peacock Mogul 2-6-0; Ghana Railways Diesel Electric, 1950s; Bagnall 0-4-0, St. Assam; Ledo Brickworks, Upper Assam; Metregauge 2 gauge operation; Carbon converter, China; Timbre loading, China; Loading clay at Bagnall, Saddletank. (d) 1000l.×9, GWR Mogul, Severn Valley Railway; Litson Meyer 0-6-6-0, Chile; China Railways SL7 Class Pacific; Firing a Yugoslav 20-2-6-0; Lookout man warning of approaching train; Filling sandboxes, Midland Railway; Taking water; Indian Railways; Indian Railways 2′6″ Gauge ZP Pacific Pulgeon; Smokebox cleaning, Wankaner 35·00 40·00
MS4300 Four sheets, each 98×68 mm. (a) 5000l. The Bullet Train. (b) 5000l. The Blue Train. (c) 5000l. The Ghan. (d) 5000l. The Hudson Line 22·00 24·00

416 Players

2004. National Football Team.

4301 **416** 2000l. multicoloured 2·00 2·25

417 Diego Simeone (Argentina)

2004. Centenary of FIFA (Federation Internationale de Football Association). Multicoloured.

MS4302 193×97 mm. 2000l.×4, Type **417**; Carcea (Brazil); Oliver Bierhoff (Germany); Kevin Keegan (England) 7·00 8·00
MS4303 108×87 mm. 5000l. David Ginola (France) 4·25 4·50

418 Elvis

2004. 50th Anniv of First Record by Elvis Presley. Multicoloured.

4304 2000l. Type **418** 2·25 2·25
4305 2000l. Holding guitar upright 2·25 2·25
4306 2000l. Leaning on guitar 2·25 2·25
4307 2000l. Playing guitar 2·25 2·25
4308 2000l. Singing into microphone (from front) 2·25 2·25
4309 2000l. Holding microphone on stand 2·25 2·25
4310 2000l. Holding microphone without stand 2·25 2·25
4311 2000l. Singing into microphone (from side) 2·25 2·25

419 *Paris*

2004. Ocean Liners. Multicoloured.
4312 600l. Type **419** 85 55
4313 800l. *Statendam* 1·10 80
4314 1000l. *Stavengerfjords* 1·25 1·10
4315 1500l. *Campania* 1·75 1·75
4316 2000l. *Drottningholm* 2·25 2·50
4317 3000l. *Lusitania* 3·25 3·75
MS4318 82×76 mm. 5000l. *United States* (horiz) 6·50 7·00

420 *Tokyo Story*

2004. Birth Centenary of Ozu Yasujiro (Japanese film director). Sheet, 190×203 mm, containing T **420** and similar vert designs. Multicoloured.
MS4319 1400l.×6, Type **420**; *Late Spring; Early Summer; Equinox Flower; Good Morning; An Autumn Afternoon* 7·00 8·00

2004. National Basketball Association (2nd series). As T 413. Multicoloured.
4320 700l. Vlade Divac (Sacramento Kings) 1·00 1·00
4321 700l. Leandro Barbosa (Phoenix Suns) 1·00 1·00

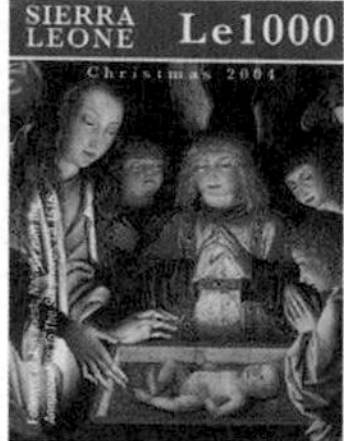

421 "Nativity with the Annunciation to the Shepherds" (Jan Joest)

2004. Christmas. Paintings. Multicoloured.
4322 1000l. Type **421** 1·25 70
4323 1500l. "Christmas Snow" (Norman Rockwell) 1·75 1·60
4324 2000l. "The Christmas Tree" (E. Osborn) 2·25 2·25
4325 5000l. "The Spirit of Christmas" (Norman Rockwell) 5·50 6·50
MS4326 55×110 mm. 8000l. "Madonna and Child Enthroned with Two Angels" (Fra Filippo Lippi) 8·50 9·50

422 Ronald and Nancy Reagan with Queen Elizabeth and Prince Philip

2004. Ronald Reagan (President of USA, 1981–1989) Commemoration. Sheet, 153×144 mm, containing T **422** and similar horiz designs. Multicoloured.
MS4327 2000l.×3, Type **422**; 2000l.×3, President Reagan and Queen Elizabeth II 9·50 11·00

423 Rooster

2005. Chinese New Year ("Year of the Rooster"). Multicoloured.
4328 600l. Type **423** 80 80
4329 600l. As Type **423** but with country name and value in different colours 80 80

424 Pres. Roosevelt addressing Congress

2005. 60th Anniv of Victory in Japan. Multicoloured.
MS4330 174×83 mm. 2000l.×4, Type **424**; Little Boy (Hiroshima bomb); Fat Man (Nagasaki bomb); Foreign Minister Shigemitsu signing surrender instrument aboard *Missouri* (battleship) 8·00 9·00
MS4331 70×80 mm. 5000l. Newspaper headlines 6·00 6·50

425 Handshake

2005. Centenary of Rotary International. Sheet, 114×103 mm, containing T **425** and similar vert designs. Multicoloured.
MS4332 1800l.×4, Type **425**; Two people shaking hands over map; Rotary emblem; Paul Harris (founder of Rotary) 7·00 8·00

426 Ships Lined Up

2005. Bicentenary of the Battle of Trafalgar. Multicoloured.
4333 500l. Type **426** 1·00 60
4334 1000l. Surrounded ship on fire 1·60 1·10
4335 2000l. Fleets of ships 2·50 2·25
4336 5000l. Line of ships shrouded in smoke 6·00 7·00
MS4337 84×119 mm. 8000l. Ships engaged in battle 9·50 10·00

427 *Little Claus and Big Claus*

2005. Birth Bicentenary of Hans Christian Andersen (artist and children's writer).
4338 **427** 3000l. multicoloured 2·75 3·25
4339 - 3000l. multicoloured 2·75 3·25
4340 - 3000l. green and black 2·75 3·25
MS4341 100×70 mm. 5000l. multicoloured 5·50 6·50
DESIGNS: No. 4338, Type **427**; 4339, *Little Ida's Flowers*; 4340, *The Tinder-Box*. **MS**4341, *The Princess and The Pea* (50×38 mm).

428 Luftwaffe Air Strikes

2005. Battle of Britain. Multicoloured.
4342 2000l. Type **428** 2·50 2·50
4343 2000l. Civilians sheltering in Underground station 2·50 2·50
4344 2000l. Pilots running to planes 2·50 2·50
4345 2000l. Fighting planes 2·50 2·50
MS4346 107×97 mm. 5000l. Winston Churchill, pilot and plane (vert) 7·00 7·50

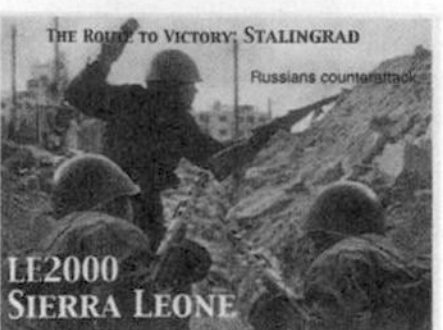

429 Russian Soldiers

2005. Battle for Stalingrad.
4347 **429** 2000l. grey and black 2·50 2·50
4348 - 2000l. grey 2·50 2·50
4349 - 2000l. grey, stone and black 2·50 2·50
4350 - 2000l. grey, stone and blue 2·50 2·50
MS4351 107×97 mm. 5000l. grey, blue and black 6·50 7·00
DESIGNS: No. 4347, Type **429**; 4348, Destroyed German tank; 4349, Remains of German 6th Army; 4350, German Prisoners of War; **MS**4351, Russian victory at Stalingrad.

430 Pope John Paul II and French Pres. Jacques Chirac

2005. Pope John Paul II Commemoration.
4352 **430** 1800l. multicoloured 2·50 2·50

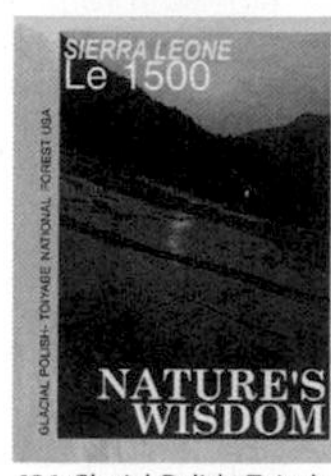

431 Glacial Polish, Toiyabe National Forest, USA

2005. Expo. World Exposition, Aichi, Japan. Multicoloured.
4353/8 1500l×6, Type **431**; African gorilla; Rock climbing, Yosemite Valley, USA; Nassau groupers; Ladybirds; Evolution Valley, USA 7·50 8·50

432 Pres. Franklin D. Roosevelt and Prime Minister Winston Churchill

2005. 60th Anniv of Victory in Europe. Multicoloured.
4359 2000l. Type **432** 2·50 2·50
4360 2000l. Louis Johnson (Secretary of Defence), Gen. Douglas Macarthur and Gen. Omar Bradley 2·50 2·50
4361 2000l. Top commanders of Allied Expeditionary Forces, 1944 2·50 2·50
4362 2000l. Prime Minister Winston Churchill 2·50 2·50
MS4363 70×80 mm. 5000l. Winston Churchill at VE Day celebrations 7·00 7·50

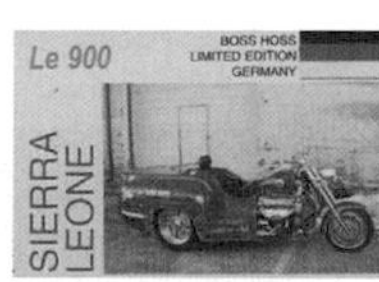

433 Boss Hoss Limited Edition, Germany

2005. Fire Engines. Multicoloured.
4364 900l. Type **433** 1·40 1·25
4365 1200l. Pumper 8 by 10, Austria 1·75 1·50
4366 1500l. Hydraulic platform 2·00 1·75
4367 1800l. Scania fire appliance, Australia 2·25 2·00
4368 2000l. Fire engine, Japan 2·25 2·25
4369 2000l. Fire engine, Germany 2·25 2·25
4370 2000l. Fire engine, Canada 2·25 2·25
4371 2000l. Fire engine, Ireland 2·25 2·25
4372 2000l. Mercedes Benz 2635 Thoma, Germany 2·25 2·25
4373 2000l. Dennis Sabre water tender, Ireland 2·25 2·25
4374 2000l. Microscopic fire truck, Japan 2·25 2·25
4375 2000l. Scania fire appliance, Australia 2·25 2·25
4376 2000l. Chevy fire truck 2·25 2·25
4377 2000l. 1914 International fire truck 2·25 2·25
4378 2000l. 1884 chemical fire engine 2·25 2·25
4379 2000l. 1963 Mason FD1 fire engine 2·25 2·25
MS4380 Two sheets, each 100×70 mm. (a) 5000l. 1890 Horse driven fire truck, UK. (b) 5000l. Fire engine, USA 13·00 14·00

434 Jules Verne's Tomb, Amiens

2005. Death Centenary of Jules Verne (writer). Multicoloured (except No. 4382).
4381 3000l. Type **434** 3·25 3·75
4382 3000l. Michael Arden (sepia, green and black) 3·25 3·75
4383 3000l. Jules Verne and lunar surface 3·25 3·75
MS4384 100×75 mm. 5000l. Pencil sketch of Jules Verne and hot air balloon 5·50 6·00

435 Moses Maimonides

2005. 800th Death Anniv of Moses Maimonides (Jewish rabbi, physician and philosopher) (2004).
4385 **435** 2000l. multicoloured 2·25 2·25

436 Playhouse Square Memorial, Berlin

2005. 200th Death Anniv of Friedrich Von Schiller (poet and dramatist). Multicoloured.
4386 3000l. Type **436** 3·00 3·50
4387 3000l. Statue, Munich 3·00 3·50
4388 3000l. Statue of Friedrich Von Schiller and Johann Wolfgang von Goethe 3·00 3·50
MS4389 100×70 mm. 5000l. Friedrich Von Schiller 5·50 6·00

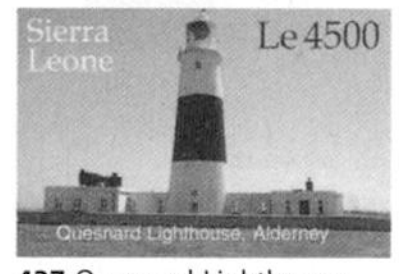

437 Quesnard Lighthouse, Alderney

2005. Lighthouses (2nd series).
4390 **437** 4500l. multicoloured 6·00 7·00

2005. Royal Wedding. Multicoloured designs as T **514** of St. Vincent. Multicoloured.
4391 2000l. Prince Charles and Mrs. Camilla Parker-Bowles during wedding ceremony 2·50 2·50
4392 2000l. Prince Charles and Duchess of Cornwall holding posy 2·50 2·50
4393 2000l. Prince Charles and Duchess of Cornwall with their families (horiz) 2·50 2·50

438 Man and Woman in Workshop

2005. International Year of Microcredit. Each showing portrait of woman at left. Multicoloured.
MS4394 105×105 mm. 2500l. Type **438**; 2500l. Man in workshop; 2500l. Man with scales; 2500l. Woman feeding fodder to cattle 11·00 12·00
The stamps within No. **MS**4394 have a composite background design showing part of the UN emblem.

2005. Christmas. As T **155** of St. Kitts. Multicoloured.
4395 500l. "The Virgin with Grapes" (detail) (Pierre Mignard) 75 35
4396 1500l. "Adoration of the Shepherds (detail) (Murillo) 1·60 1·60

4397	2000l. "Madonna with the Child" (detail) (Murillo)	2·25	2·50
4398	3000l. "Fountain of Life" (detail) (Holbein the Elder)	3·25	3·50
MS4399	100×70 mm. 6000l. "Adoration of the Shepherds" (different) (Murillo)	7·00	8·00

439 Elvis Presley playing Guitar

2005. 70th Birth Anniv of Elvis Presley. Multicoloured.

4400	2000l. Type **439** (blue background)	2·50	2·50
4401	2000l. Holding guitar (black background)	2·50	2·50
4402	2000l. As No. 4401 (black background)	2·50	2·50
4403	2000l. Type **439** (lilac background)	2·50	2·50
4404	2000l. Elvis singing (blue silhouette)	2·50	2·50
4405	2000l. As No. 4404 (emerald silhouette)	2·50	2·50
4406	2000l. As No. 4404 (yellow silhouette)	2·50	2·50
4407	2000l. As No. 4404 (purple and magenta silhouette)	2·50	2·50

440 "In It's Position" (Xu Beihong)

2006. Chinese New Year ("Year of the Dog"). Multicoloured.

4408	600l. Type **440**	45	45
MS4409	70×100 mm. 2000l. As Type **440** but 29×64 mm	2·50	2·50

The stamp within **MS**4409 is as Type **440** but shows more of the foreground of the painting.

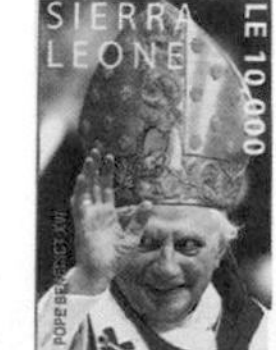

441 Pope Benedict XVI

2006. Election of Pope Benedict XVI.

4410	**441** 10000l. multicoloured	12·00	13·00

2006. "Kids-Did-It!" Designs. Vert designs as T **531** of St. Vincent showing children's paintings.

4411	2000le. "Monkey" (Andrew Heye)	2·25	2·25
4412	2000le. "Red Toed Elephant" (Conrad Mazur)	2·25	2·25
4413	2000le. "Colored Giraffe" (Adeline Longstreth)	2·25	2·25
4414	2000le. "Colored Bird" (Sarah Bowen)	2·25	2·25
4415	2000le. "Green Gecko" (Nick Abrams)	2·25	2·25
4416	2000le. "Froggy" (Brett Walker)	2·25	2·25
4417	2000le. "Spots" (Maya Barba)	2·25	2·25
4418	2000le. "Orange Lizard" (Nick Abrams)	2·25	2·25
4419	2000le. "Yellow Flowers" (Christina Miller)	2·25	2·25
4420	2000le. "Poppies" (Trevor Nielsen)	2·25	2·25
4421	2000le. "Orange Flowers" (Christina Miller)	2·25	2·25
4422	2000le. "Lilies" (Lauren Van Woy)	2·25	2·25

442 Chief Medicine Crow (Crow)

2006. Great Indian Chiefs. Multicoloured.

4423	1250le. Type **442**	1·25	1·25
4424	1250le. Chief Quanah Parker (Comanche)	1·25	1·25
4425	1250le. Chief Garfield (Jicarilla)	1·25	1·25
4426	1250le. Chief Pretty Eagle (Crow)	1·25	1·25
4427	1250le. Chief Plenty Coups (Crow)	1·25	1·25
4428	1250le. Chief He Dog (Oglala)	1·25	1·25
4429	1250le. Chief Crow King (Hunkpapa)	1·25	1·25
4430	1250le. Chief Pontiac (Ottawa)	1·25	1·25
4431	1250le. Chief Naiche (Chiricahua Apache)	1·25	1·25
4432	1250le. Chief Gall (Hunkpapa)	1·25	1·25

443 Pope John Paul II, Madrid, 2003

2006. Visits of Pope John Paul II, 2003–2004. Multicoloured.

4433	2500le. Type **443**	3·00	3·00
4434	2500le. Croatia, 2003	3·00	3·00
4435	2500le. Banja Luka, Bosnia Herzegovina	3·00	3·00
4436	2500le. Slovakia, 2003	3·00	3·00
4437	2500le. Pompeii, Italy, 2003	3·00	3·00
4438	2500le. Shaking hands with Swiss President Joseph Deiss, Bern, 2004	3·00	3·00
4439	2500le. Praying at Lourdes, France, 2004	3·00	3·00
4440	2500le. Loreto, Italy, 2004	3·00	3·00

2006. Winter Olympic Games, Turin. As T **536** of St. Vincent. Multicoloured.

4441	1000le. US 1960 Winter Olympics 4c. stamp	1·25	1·00
4442	1300le. Canada 1987 Winter Olympics 36c. cross-country skiing stamp	1·60	1·60
4443	2000le. Poster for Winter Olympic Games, Calgary, 1988	2·25	2·25
4444	3000le. Poster for Winter Olympic Games, Squaw Valley, California, 1960	3·00	3·50

444 Michael Douglas (actor)

2006. Michael Douglas, "UN Messenger of Peace". Multicoloured.

4445	2000le. Type **444**	2·00	2·00
4446	2000le. UN Building, New York	2·00	2·00

445 US 1903 Stamp and Benjamin Franklin

2006. Washington 2006 International Stamp Exhibition. Sheet 91×116 mm.

MS4447	**445** 6000le. Multicoloured	5·00	6·00

446 Queen Elizabeth II

2006. 80th Birthday of Queen Elizabeth II. Multicoloured.

4448	3000le. Type **446**	3·50	3·50
4449	3000le. Wearing dark blue hat and coat	3·50	3·50
4450	3000le. Wearing blue blouse	3·50	3·50
4451	3000le. With parasol and bouquet	3·50	3·50
MS4452	125×126 mm. 6000le. Wearing diadem, 1950s	7·00	7·50

447 Zeppelin L30

2006. 50th Death Anniv of Ludwig Durr (Zeppelin engineer). Multicoloured.

4453	4000le. Type **447**	4·00	4·50
4454	4000le. Airship *Hindenburg*	4·00	4·50
4455	4000le. *Graf Zeppelin*	4·00	4·50

2006. 400th Birth Anniv of Rembrandt Harmenszoon van Rijn (artist). As T **157** of St. Kitts showing paintings. Multicoloured.

4456	800le. "Abraham Frans" (detail)	1·10	65
4457	1000le. "The Rat Catcher" (detail)	1·25	80
4458	2000le. "Young Man with Velvet Cap" (detail)	2·25	2·00
4459	3000le. "The Night Watch" (detail of man with black hat)	2·75	3·00
4460	3000le. "The Night Watch" (detail of man with brown hat)	2·75	3·00
4461	3000le. "The Night Watch" (detail of man with pale hat	2·75	3·00
4462	3000le. "The Night Watch" (detail of man with brown hat and ruffed collar)	2·75	3·00
4463	3000le. "Abraham and Isaac" (detail)	2·75	3·00
4464	3000le. "Abraham entertaining the Angels" (detail)	2·75	3·00
4465	3000le. "Return of the Prodigal Son" (detail)	2·75	3·00
4466	3000le. "Adam and Eve" (detail)	2·75	3·00
4467	8000le. "The Flute Player" (detail)	2·75	3·00
MS4468	Three sheets, each 70×100 mm. (a) 6000le. "Homer dictating to a Scribe" (detail). (b) 6000le. "Portrait of an Amsterdam Citizen as a Militiaman" (detail). (c) 6000le. "Maria Trip, Daughter of Alottte Adriaensdr" (detail). All imperf	14·00	16·00

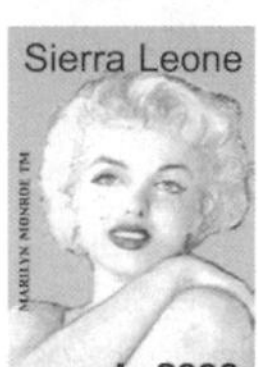

448 Marilyn Monroe

2006. 80th Birth Anniv of Marilyn Monroe (actress). Multicoloured.

4469	2000l. Type **448**	1·90	2·00
4470	2000l. Wearing brown patterned dress with narrow straps	1·90	2·00
4471	2000l. Wearing white, with hand behind head	1·90	2·00
4472	2000l. In half profile, wearing pendant earrings	1·90	2·00

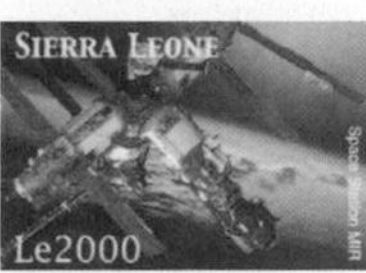

449 Space Station MIR

2006. Space Anniversaries. Multicoloured. (a) "Conquering our Universe".

4473	2000le. Type **449**	2·25	2·25
4474	2000le. Space Shuttle *Challenger*	2·25	2·25
4475	2000le. *Giotto* Comet Probe	2·25	2·25
4476	2000le. Luna 9, first soft lander	2·25	2·25
4477	2000le. Viking 1 Mars Lander	2·25	2·25
4478	2000le. International Space Station	2·25	2·25

(b) International Space Station.

4479	3000le. ISS 3 June 1999 (vert)	3·00	3·00
4480	3000le. ISS 2 December 2000 (vert)	3·00	3·00
4481	3000le. ISS 15 June 2002 (vert)	3·00	3·00
4482	3000le. ISS 6 August 2005 (vert)	3·00	3·00

(c) Artist's Concept of "Journey's to the Moon".

4483	3000le. NASA's "Crew Launch" (vert)	3·00	3·00
4484	3000le. New spacecraft to rendezvous with International Space Station (vert)	3·00	3·00
4485	3000le. New lunar lander on lunar surface (vert)	3·00	3·00
4486	3000le. Parachutes deployed after re-entry (vert)	3·00	3·00

(d) CloudSat/Calipso Satellites.

4487	3000le. Launch vehicle: Boeing Delta II Rocket	3·00	3·00
4488	3000le. *Calipso* Spacecraft	3·00	3·00
4489	3000le. *CloudSat* Spacecraft	3·00	3·00
4490	3000le. Six satellites of the "A-Train": *Aura*, *Parasol*, *Calipso*, *CloudSat*, *Aqua* and *OCO 2*	3·00	3·00
MS4491	Four sheets, each 100×70 mm. (a) 6000le. Impactor with Deep Impact Probe, 2005. (b) 6000le. Apollo 11 Lunar Module *Eagle* in a landing configuration, 1969. (c) 6000le. Mars Reconnaissance Orbiter, 2005. (d) 6000le. Space Shuttle *Columbia*, 1981 (vert)	23·00	25·00

450 Mozart as Young Boy playing Piano

2006. 250th Birth Anniv of Wolfgang Amadeus Mozart (composer). Sheet 100×70 mm.

MS4492	**450** 7000le. Multicoloured	8·50	8·50

451 Angel

2006. Christmas. Multicoloured.

4493	1000l. Type **451**	1·10	75
4494	1500l. Madonna and Child	1·75	1·50
4495	2000l. Angel (facing to right)	2·25	2·00
4496	3000l. Angel (looking to left)	3·00	3·25
MS4497	150×100 mm. 2000l.×4 As Nos. 4493/6	6·50	7·50

The stamps and margins of **MS**4497 form a composite design showing the Crown of the Main Altar of the Jesuit Church in Antwerp, Belgium, by Peter Paul Rubens. Nos. 4493/6 show portions of the design.

452 John F. Kennedy making Speech, 20 January 1961

2006. 90th Birth Anniv of John F. Kennedy (US President 1960–3). Multicoloured.

4498	2000l. Type **452**	1·90	2·00
4499	2000l. John Kennedy and Official Inaugural Program	1·90	2·00
4500	2000l. Coin with profile of John Kennedy	1·90	2·00
4501	2000l. Robert Frost and words of "The Gift Outright" recited at Inauguration, 1961	1·90	2·00
4502	2000l. Pres. Kennedy and map of Cuba (Missile Crisis 22 October 1962)	1·90	2·00
4503	2000l. Soviet Premier Khrushchev and map showing range of Soviet R-12 medium range missile	1·90	2·00
4504	2000l. Pres. Kennedy and Soviet Foreign Minister Andrei Gromyko, 22 October 1962	1·90	2·00
4505	2000l. Cuban Pres. Fidel Castro and Pres. Kennedy at the White House	1·90	2·00

453 Elvis Presley

2006. 30th Death Anniv of Elvis Presley. Multicoloured.
4506 2000l. Type **453** 2·00 2·00
4507 2000l. Wearing black and silver patterned cape 2·00 2·00
4508 2000l. In uniform in front of US flag 2·00 2·00
4509 2000l. Wearing blue jacket 2·00 2·00

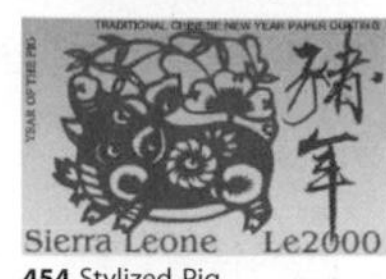

454 Stylized Pig

2007. Chinese New Year ("Year of the Pig").
4510 **454** 2000l. multicoloured 2·00 2·00

455 Peace Dove and "One World One Promise" Text

2007. Centenary of Scouting and 21st World Scout Jamboree, England. Multicoloured.
MS4511 175×160 mm. 3000l. Type **455**×4 8·00 9·00
MS4512 110×80 mm. 6000l. Peace dove, text and symbols of scouting 6·00 7·00

456 Speedometer (Mach 2.23 Speed Record, 26 March 1974)

2007. Concorde. Multicoloured.
4513 2000l. Type **456** 2·25 2·25
4514 2000l. Concorde silhouette and "MACH 2.23" 2·25 2·25
4515 2000l. Concorde with RAF Red Arrows in Golden Jubilee Flypast 2·25 2·25
4516 2000l. Golden Jubilee Flypast over London, 4 June 2002 2·25 2·25

457 Diana, Princess of Wales

2007. Tenth Death Anniv of Diana, Princess of Wales. Multicoloured.
4517 1500le. Type **457** 1·75 1·75
4518 1500le. Wearing pendant and blue off-the-shoulder evening dress 1·75 1·75
4519 1500le. Wearing white blouse with pie-frill neck (olive background) 1·75 1·75
4520 1500le. Wearing yellow dress (green background) 1·75 1·75
4521 1500le. Seen in half-profile (pink background) 1·75 1·75
4522 1500le. Wearing white blouse with ruffled layers (turquoise background) 1·75 1·75
MS4523 100×70 mm. 7000le. Wearing bright blue jacket and hat (horiz) 6·50 6·50

458 166 Inter, 1948

2007. 60th Anniv of Ferrari. Multicoloured.
4524 1400le. Type **458** 1·60 1·60
4525 1400le. 612 Scaglietti 1·60 1·60
4526 1400le. F50, 1995 1·60 1·60
4527 1400le. 550 Barchetta Pininfarina, 2000 1·60 1·60
4528 1400le. 250 GT Cabriolet, 1957 1·60 1·60
4529 1400le. 250 P, 1963 1·60 1·60
4530 1400le. 246 SP, 1961 1·60 1·60
4531 1400le. 126 CK, 1981 1·60 1·60

459 Pope Benedict XVI

2007. 80th Birthday of Pope Benedict XVI.
4532 **459** 1500le. Multicoloured 2·00 2·00

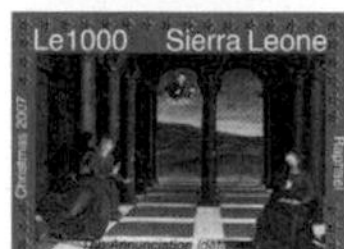

460 *The Annunciation* (detail) (Raphael)

2007. Christmas. Multicoloured.
4533 1000le. Type **460** 1·00 75
4534 1500le. *The Adoration of the Magi* (detail) (Raphael) 1·50 1·40
4535 2000le. *The Presentation of the Christ Child in the Temple* (detail) (Raphael) 1·90 2·00
4536 3000le. *The Nativity and the Arrival of the Magi* (detail) (Giovanni di Pietro) 2·50 3·00

461 Murray Rose (Australia) (swimming 400m & 1500m freestyle gold medallist)

2008. Olympic Games, Beijing. Designs showing scenes from 1956 Olympic Games, Melbourne. Multicoloured.
4537 1500l. Type **461** 1·50 1·60
4538 1500l. Poster for Olympic Games, Melbourne, 1956 1·50 1·60
4539 1500l. Vladimir Kuts (USSR) (10000m & 5000m gold medallist) winning race 1·50 1·60
4540 1500l. Laszlo Papp (Hungary) winning light middleweight boxing gold medal 1·50 1·60

2008. Nos. 1142/4, 1147/8, 2745/50 and 2752/7, 2905/10, 2950/2, 3086/93, 2150/4, 2954, 3112/20, 745/8, 2911/16 and 4290/3 surch

(a) Nos. 1142/4 and 1147/8
4541 800l. on 3l. Type **216** 75 75
4542 800l. on 5l. Double-toothed barbet 75 75
4543 800l. on 8l. African golden oriole 75 75
4544 800l. on 20l. European bee eater 75 75
4545 800l. on 35l. Common gonolek ('Barbary shrike') 75 75

(b) Nos. 2745/50 and 2752/7
4546 2500l. on 500l. *Lycaena dispar* 2·25 2·25
4547 2500l. on 500l. *Graphium sarpedon* 2·25 2·25
4548 2500l. on 500l. *Euploe core* 2·25 2·25
4549 2500l. on 500l. *Papilio cresphontes* 2·25 2·25
4550 2500l. on 500l. *Colotis danae* 2·25 2·25
4551 2500l. on 500l. *Battus philenor* 2·25 2·25
4552 2500l. on 600l. *Mylothis chloris* 2·25 2·25
4553 2500l. on 600l. *Argynnis lathonia* 2·25 2·25
4554 2500l. on 600l. *Elymnias agendas* 2·25 2·25
4555 2500l. on 600l. *Palla ussheri* 2·25 2·25
4556 2500l. on 600l. *Papilio glaucus* 2·25 2·25
4557 2500l. on 600l. *Cercyonis pegala* 2·25 2·25

(c) Nos. 2905/10
4558 2800l. on 300l. Type **312** 2·50 2·50
4559 2800l. on 300l. Viking longship 2·50 2·50
4560 2800l. on 300l. Carrack (surch reading downwards) 2·50 2·50
4561 2800l. on 300l. Venetian galley (surch reading downwards) 2·50 2·50
4562 2800l. on 300l. Galeasse (surch reading downwards) 2·50 2·50
4563 2800l. on 300l. Chebeck (surch reading downwards) 2·50 2·50

(d) Nos. 2950/2
4564 2800l. on 1500l. William D. Boyce (founder of Lone Scouts) (brown-purple, yellow-brown and black) (vert) 2·50 2·50
4565 2800l. on 1500l. Guion S. Bluford (astronaut and former Eagle scout) (vert) 2·50 2·50
4566 2800l. on 1500l. Ellison S. Onizuka (astronaut and former Eagle scout) (vert) (surch at top left, reading upwards) 2·50 2·50

(e) Nos. 3086/93
4567 2800l. on 600l. Cattle egret 2·50 2·50
4568 2800l. on 600l. White-fronted bee eater
4569 2800l. on 600l. Gray parrot 2·50 2·50
4570 2800l. on 600l. Cinnamon-chested bee eater 2·50 2·50
4571 2800l. on 600l. Malachite kingfisher 2·50 2·50
4572 2800l. on 600l. White-throated bee eater 2·50 2·50
4573 2800l. on 600l. Yellow-billed stork 2·50 2·50
4574 2800l. on 600l. Hildebrandt's starling 2·50 2·50

(f) Nos. 2150/4
4575 3500l. on 50l. Type **269** (surch at right of obliterator) 3·00 3·00
4576 3500l. on 100l. Adult white-necked bald crow 3·00 3·00
4577 3500l. on 150l. Pair of white-necked bald crows 3·00 3·00
4578 3500l. on 200l. Young white-necked bald crow 3·00 3·00

(g) No. 2954
4579 3500l. on 600l. Gandhi as a young man 3·00 3·00

(h) Nos. 3112/20
4580 3500l. on 600l. African paradise flycatcher ('Monarch') (horiz) 3·00 3·00
4581 3500l. on 600l. Lilac-breasted roller (horiz) 3·00 3·00
4582 3500l. on 600l. Scops owl (horiz) 3·00 3·00
4583 3500l. on 600l. African emerald cuckoo (horiz) 3·00 3·00
4584 3500l. on 600l. Blue flycatcher ('Monarch') (horiz) 3·00 3·00
4585 3500l. on 600l. African golden oriole (horiz) 3·00 3·00
4586 3500l. on 600l. White-throated bee eater (horiz) (surch at right, reading downwards) 3·00 3·00
4587 3500l. on 600l. Black-bellied seedcracker (horiz) (surch at right, reading downwards) 3·00 3·00
4588 3500l. on 600l. Hoopoe (horiz) 3·00 3·00

(i) Nos. 745/8
4589 4000l. on 6c. Type **166** (surch at right of country name) 3·75 3·75
4590 4000l. on 10c. Three chimpanzees (vert) 3·75 3·75
4591 4000l. on 31c. Chimpanzees swinging in tree (vert) 3·75 3·75
4592 4000l. on 60c. Group of chimpanzees (surch at top right) 3·75 3·75

(j) Nos. 2911/16
4593 4000l. on 300l. Junk 3·75 3·75
4594 4000l. on 300l. HMS *Victory* (ship of the line, 1765) 3·75 3·75
4595 4000l. on 300l. *Savannah* (paddle-steamer) 3·75 3·75
4596 4000l. on 300l. Gaissa (sailing canoe) 3·75 3·75
4597 4000l. on 300l. HMS *Warrior* (ironclad) 3·75 3·75
4598 4000l. on 300l. *Preussen* (full-rigged ship) 3·75 3·75

(k) Nos. 4290/3
4599 4000l. on 1000l. Type **412** 3·75 3·75
4600 4000l. on 1000l. Feeding (surch at bottom right) 3·75 3·75
4601 4000l. on 1000l. With baby (surch at centre right) 3·75 3·75
4602 4000l. on 1000l. Patas monkey 3·75 3·75

472 King David's Harp at Entrance to City of David, Jerusalem (image scaled to 48% of original size)

2008. Israel 2008 World Stamp Championship. Sheet 100×110 mm.
MS4603 **472** 7500l. multicoloured 7·50 7·50

473 Joel Palmer locates Pass through the Cascades

2008. Oregon Discovery and Exploration. Multicoloured.
4604 1500l. Type **473** 1·50 1·60
4605 1500l. Ship, coastline and Sir Francis Drake (first European to view Oregon coast) (40×25 mm) 1·50 1·60
4606 1500l. Multnomah Falls and Lewis and Clark (explorers) 1·50 1·60
4607 1500l. Ship in river estuary and Capt. Robert Gray (discovery of the Columbia River) (40×25 mm) 1·50 1·60

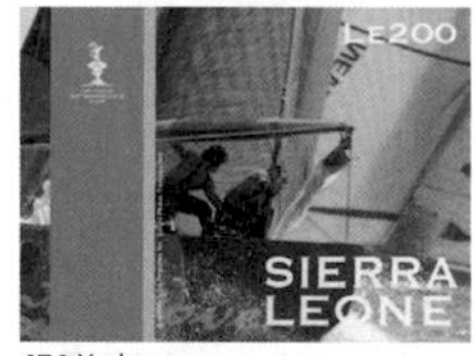

474 Yacht

2008. 32nd Americas Cup Yachting Championship, Valencia, Spain. Multicoloured.
4608 200l. Type **474** 30 25
4609 500l. *Shosholoza* (South Africa) and another yacht 50 40
4610 1000l. Yacht *Prada* (crew in white) 1·00 75
4611 10000l. Yachts ('Espresso' and 'Toyota' on sails) 10·00 11·00

475 Queen Elizabeth II and Prince Philip

2008. Diamond Wedding of Queen Elizabeth II and Prince Philip (2007). Multicoloured.
4612 1500l. Type **475** 1·50 1·60
4613 1500l. Queen Elizabeth II 1·50 1·60

476 Statue of Christ the Redeemer, Rio de Janeiro, Brazil

2008. Seven New Wonders of the World. Multicoloured.

4614	1500l. Type **476**	1·50	1·60
4615	1500l. Colosseum, Rome, Italy	1·50	1·60
4616	1500l. Great Wall of China	1·50	1·60
4617	1500l. Machu Picchu, Peru	1·50	1·60
4618	1500l. Petra, Jordan	1·50	1·60
4619	1500l. Chichén Itza, Mexico	1·50	1·60
MS4620	70×100 mm. 7000l. Taj Mahal, India (horiz)	6·50	6·50

477 World Map and Minaret

2008. Centenary of Khilafat Ahmadiyya.

4621	**477**	800l. multicoloured	90	65
4622	**477**	1000l. multicoloured	1·00	75
4623	**477**	2000l. multicoloured	1·90	2·00
4624	**477**	3000l. multicoloured	2·50	3·00

478 Elvis Presley

2008. Elvis Presley. Multicoloured.

4625	1500l. Type **478**	1·50	1·60
4626	1500l. Facing to left	1·50	1·60
4627	1500l. Facing towards left, holding microphone	1·50	1·60
4628	1500l. As No. 4626, but signature at top left and country inscr at bottom right	1·50	1·60
4629	1500l. Wearing mauve shirt (37×50 mm)	1·50	1·60
4630	1500l. In full-face close-up (37×50 mm)	1·50	1·60
4631	1500l. Wearing white jacket and red shirt (37×50 mm)	1·50	1·60
4632	1500l. Wearing green jacket, seen from back (37×50 mm)	1·50	1·60
4633	1500l. Seen in black/white, hands raised (37×50 mm)	1·50	1·60
4634	1500l. In close-up, wearing glasses (37×50 mm)	1·50	1·60

Nos. 4625/8 commemorate the 35th anniversary of Elvis Presley's Aloha from Hawaii Concert.

479 Mother Penguin and Two Chicks

2008. Penguins. Designs showing cartoon penguins. Multicoloured.

4635	3000l. Type **479**	2·50	3·00
4636	3000l. Penguin karaoke	2·50	3·00
4637	3000l. Four penguin chicks	2·50	3·00
4638	3000l. Mother penguin with hat, spade and red patterned skirt and two young penguins	2·50	3·00
MS4639	100×70 mm. 7000l. Penguin couple on iceberg	7·00	7·00

480 Nativity Scene

2008. Christmas. Multicoloured.

4640	1000l. Type **480**	1·00	75
4641	1500l. Mary and baby Jesus in manger	1·50	1·60
4642	2000l. Joseph and baby Jesus in manger	1·90	2·00
4643	3000l. Angels and baby Jesus in manger	2·50	3·00

No. 4640 shows the complete scene and Nos. 4641/3 details from it.

481 Pres. Barack Obama

2009. Inauguration of Pres. Barack Obama. Sheet 133×94 mm.

MS4644 3000l. Type **481**×4 — 10·00 10·00

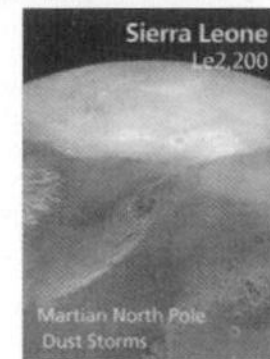

482 Dust Storms at Martian North Pole

2009. 50 Years of Space Exploration. Multicoloured.

MS4645 150×100 mm. 2200le.×6 Type **482**; Saturn; Jupiter's atmosphere; Craters on Mercury's surface; Venus; Mercury — 13·00 13·00

MS4646 150×100 mm. 2200le.×6 Spitzer Space Telescope; Galaxy M81; Hubble Space Telescope; Galaxy M64; The Cat's Eye Nebula; Hoag's Object (all horiz) — 13·00 13·00

MS4647 130×100 mm. 3000le.×4 Astronaut and sun shining in a dark sky in low earth orbit; South Pole of the Sun; Solar eruption; Solar eclipse (all horiz) — 10·00 10·00

MS4648 100×130 mm. 3000le.×4 Apollo 11 Lunar Module *Eagle*; Mercury-Redstone rocket; Space shuttle *Atlantis* on Launch Pad; Space shuttle *Endeavour* — 10·00 10·00

483 Pope John Paul II

2009. Pope John Paul II Commemoration. Sheet 127×194 mm containing T **483** and similar vert designs.

MS4649 3000l.×4 Type **483**; Wearing white; Wearing mitre and green robes; Wearing mitre and gold robes — 10·00 10·00

484 Yi Jianlian

2009. National Basketball Association. Yi Jianlian (New Jersey Nets). Sheet 139×202 mm containing T **484** and similar vert designs. Multicoloured.

MS4650 1500le. Type **484**×2; 1500le. Wearing dark blue×2; 1500le. Facing left×2 — 3·00 3·00

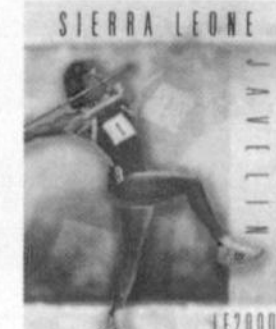

485 Javelin

2009. Olympic Games, Beijing (2008). Sheet 157×79 mm containing T **485** and similar vert designs. Multicoloured.

MS4651 2000l.×4 Type **485**; Fencing; Football; Weightlifting — 7·50 7·50

The stamps and margins of No. **MS**4651 form a composite design.

486 *Landscape of Yangshuo*

2009. China 2009 World Stamp Exhibition, Luoyang (1st issue). Paintings by Chang Dai-shien. Multicoloured.

MS4652 120×150 mm. 1500l.×4 Type **486**; *Scholar admiring Plum Blossoms; The Golden Summit ofMount Emei; Lotuses after the Rain* — 5·00 5·00

487 Temple of Heaven, Beijing

2009. China 2009 World Stamp Exhibition (2nd issue). Sites and Scenes of China. Multicoloured.

MS4653 100×130 mm. 1500l.×4 Type **487**; Dalian Exhibition Centre; Xian South Gate, Shaanxi Province; National Grand Theatre, Beijing — 5·00 5·00

488 Pink and Red Peonies

2009. China 2009 International Stamp Exhibition and Peony Festival, Luoyang

4654	**488**	1500l. multicoloured	1·60	1·75

489 Elvis Presley

2009. Elvis Presley Commemoration. Sheet 154×124 mm containing T **489** and similar vert designs. Multicoloured.

MS4655 3000l.×4 Type **489**; Singing (gold borders); In close-up (yellow-green borders); In profile (dull violet borders) — 10·00 10·00

490 Abraham Lincoln taking the Oath at his Second Inauguration

2009. Birth Bicentenary of Abraham Lincoln (US President 1861–5) and Inauguration of President Barack Obama. Sheet 100×130 mm containing T **490** and similar horiz designs. Multicoloured.

MS4656 3000l.×4 Type **490**; Barack Obama sworn in as 44th President; Barack Obama places his hand on the Lincoln bible; Abraham Lincoln's Inauguration Bible — 10·00 10·00

The stamps within **MS**4656 each contain a portion of the US President's seal, so that the four stamps show the whole seal.

491 Handel's Birthplace, Halle

2009. 250th Death Anniv of George Frideric Handel (composer). Sheet 164×94 mm containing T **491** and similar vert designs. Multicoloured.

MS4657 2500l.×6 Type **491**; Handel concert at The Foundling Hospital, London; Portrait by Thomas Hudson; Handel music at Ranelagh Gardens, London; Marble statue of Handel by Louis-Francois Roubiliac; Singers Farinelli and Senesino in Handel's opera *Flavio* — 11·00 11·00

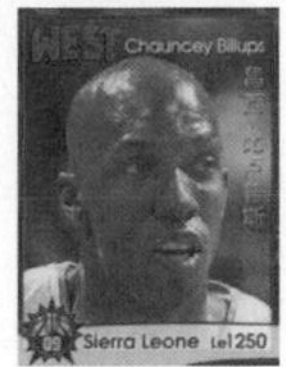

492 Chauncey Billups

2009. National Basketball Association All-Star Tournament, Phoenix. Two sheets, each 150×200 mm, containing T **492** and similar vert designs. Multicoloured.

MS4658 1250l.×12 West: Type **492**; Kobe Bryant; Tim Duncan; Pau Gasol; Yao Ming; Dirk Nowitzki; Shaquille O'Neal; Tony Parker; Chris Paul; Brandon Roy; Amare Stoudemire; David West — 18·00 18·00

MS4659 1250l.×12 East: Ray Allen; Kevin Garnett; Danny Granger; Devin Harris; Dwight Howard; Allen Iverson; LeBron James; Joe Johnson; Rashard Lewis; Paul Pierce; Dwyane Wade; Mo Williams — 18·00 18·00

493 Ferrari 312 T2, 1977

2009. Ferrari Race Cars. Sheet 120×100 mm containing T **493** and similar horiz designs. Multicoloured.

MS4660 3000l.×4 Type **493**; 126 C2, 1982; 126 C3, 1983; F2007, 2007 — 3·00 3·00

494 Apollo 11

2009. 40th Anniv of First Manned Moon Landing. Sheet 150×100 mm containing T **494** and similar vert designs. Multicoloured.

MS4661 2500l.×6 Type **494**; Astronaut Neil Armstrong; Apollo 11 plaque; Apollo 11 Command Module; Apollo 11 Lunar Module; Apollo 11 crew in quarantine — 11·00 11·00

495 Cavalier King Charles Spaniel

2009. 125th Anniv of American Kennel Club. Two sheets, each 100×120 mm, containing T **495** and similar horiz designs showing Cavalier King Charles spaniels (**MS**4662) or English springer spaniels (**MS**4663). Multicoloured.

MS4662 3000l.×4 Type **495**; Laying on grass in front of hat; In close-up, laying with head on paw; Close-up, in garden — 5·00 5·00

MS4663 3000l.×4 Springer spaniel sat on decking; Close-up of head; Standing; Sat in front of overturned tub — 10·00 10·00

496 Pres. Barack Obama and Italian Prime Minister Silvio Berlusconi

2009. Meeting of Pres. Barack Obama with Italian Prime Minister Silvio Berlusconi at G8 Summit, L'Aquila, Italy.

MS4664	**496**	8000l. multicoloured	7·25	5·25

497 Fringed Panaeolus (*Panaeolus papilionaceus*)

2009. Fungi of the World. Multicoloured.

4665	1000l. Type **497**	1·00	75
4666	1500l. Orange latex lactarius (*Lactarius deliciosus*)	1·50	1·60
4667	2000l. Purple laccaria (*Laccaria amethystina*)	1·90	2·00
4668	3000l. Liver lactarius (*Lactarius hepaticus*)	2·50	2·75
MS4669	1700l.×6 Death cap amanita (*Amanita phalloides*); Cinnabar polypore (*Pycnoporus cinnabarinus*); King bolete (*Boletus edulis*); Panther amanita (*Amanita pantherina*); Fly amanita (*Amanita muscaria*); Mica inky cap (*Coprinus micaceus*) (all horiz)	9·50	9·50

498 Birman–lilac point

2009. Cats of the World. Multicoloured.

4670	1000l. Type **498**	1·00	75
4671	1500l. Singapura–sepia agouti	1·50	1·60
4672	2000l. Scottish fold–blue tortie tabby and white	1·90	2·00
4673	3000l. Asian shaded–lilac shaded silver	2·50	2·75
MS4674	130×100 mm. 2000l.×4 Somali–lilac; British Angora–red shaded silver; Maine coon–Maine wave; Turkish van–tortie and white	10·00	10·00

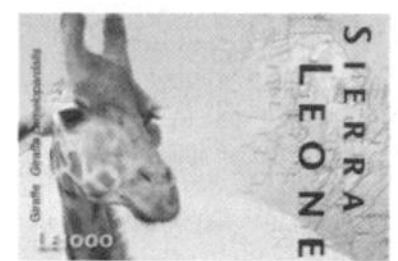

499 Giraffe

2009. Sierra Leone Wildlife. Multicoloured.

4675	1000l. Type **499**	1·00	75
4676	1500l. Bonobo	1·50	1·60
4677	2000l. African bush elephant	1·90	2·00
4678	3000l. Zebra	2·75	2·50
MS4679	185×88 mm. 2000l.×4 Cheetah; Red colobus monkey; Hippopotamus; Lion	7·50	7·50

500 *Penthea filicornis*

2009. Orchids of Africa. Multicoloured.

4680	1000l. Type **500**	1·00	75
4681	1500l. *Herchelia graminfolia*	1·50	1·60
4682	2000l. *Satyrium princeps*	1·90	2·00
4683	3000l. *Herschelia charpentieriana*	2·75	2·50
MS4684	150×100 mm. 1500l.×6 *Eulophia quartiniana*; *Ansellia gigantea* var. *azanica*; *Angraecum infundibulare*; *Disperis capensis*; *Bartholina burmanniana*; *Disa uniflora* (all horiz)	8·75	8·75

501 Pied Kingfisher (*Ceryle rudis*)

2009. Birds of Africa. Multicoloured.

4685	1000l. Type **501**	1·00	75
4686	1500l. House sparrow (*Passer domesticus*)	1·10	1·60
4687	2000l. Skylark (*Alauda arvensis*)	1·90	2·00
4688	3000l. Black-chested snake-eagle (*Circaetus pectoralis*)	2·75	2·50
MS4689	151×109 mm. 2000l.×4 Greenfinch (*Carduelis chloris*); Pangani longclaw (*Macronyx aurantiigula*); Barn swallow (*Hirundo rustica*); Namaqua sandgrouse (*Pterocles namaqua*) (all vert)	7·50	7·50

502 Pope Benedict XVI giving Blessing

2009. Visit of Pope Benedict XVI to Israel. Sheet 150×100 mm containing T **502** and similar vert designs showing Pope at Latin Patriarch Church, Jerusalem. Multicoloured.

MS4690	2600l. Type **502**; 2600l. Benedict XVI (different); 2800l. As Type **502**; 2800l. As 2600l.	8·75	8·75

503 Feng Ru (first Chinese aircraft designer and aviator) and Newspaper Article, 1909

2009. Centenary of Chinese Aviation and Aeropex 2009 Exhibition, Beijing. Multicoloured.

MS4691	145×95 mm. 2700l.×4 Type **503**; Feng Ru with early aircraft, Auckland; Feng Ru in aircraft, 1912; *Feng Ru II* in flight	9·25	9·25
MS4692	120×80 mm. 7500l. Feng Ru and his assistants with early aircraft and statue of Feng Ru (51×38 mm)	5·75	5·75

504 The Three Stooges

2009. The Three Stooges. Sheet 104×130 mm containing T **504** and similar horiz designs. Multicoloured. Litho.

MS4693	2700l.×4 Type **504**; With bottles of liquor; Curly with hands in mangle and Larry turning handle; With glasses of beer	9·25	9·25

505 Tower Bridge, London

2009. Bridges of the World. T **505** and similar horiz designs. Multicoloured.

MS4694	140×110 mm. 2000l.×6 Type **505**; Hangzhou Bay Bridge, Zhejiang, China; Juscelino Kubitschek Bridge, Brasilia, Brazil; Sydney Harbour Bridge; Ponte Vecchio, Florence, Italy; Bosphorus Bridge, Istanbul, Turkey	11·00	11·00
MS4695	110×80 mm. 7000l. Golden Gate Bridge, San Francisco	6·25	6·25

505a Rat

2010. Chinese Lunar Calendar. 30th Anniv of Chinese Zodiac Stamps. Multicoloured.

MS4695a	800l.×12 Type **505a**; Ox; Tiger; Rabbit; Dragon; Snake; Horse; Ram; Monkey; Cock; Dog; Pig	9·00	9·00

505b Tiger

2010. Chinese New Year. Year of the Tiger. Multicoloured.

MS4695b	8000l.×2 Type **505b**; Tiger (walking to left)	1·50	1·50

The stamps and margins of **MS**4696 form a composite background design showing a tiger's head.

506 Abraham Lincoln

2010. Birth Bicentenary (2009) of Abraham Lincoln. Multicoloured.

MS4696	2700l. Type **506**×4	9·25	9·25

507 Elvis Presley

2010. 75th Birth Anniv of Elvis Presley. Multicoloured.

MS4697	2700l.×4 Type **507**; Playing guitar; With hand resting on guitar; Wearing white, hand raised to face	9·25	9·25

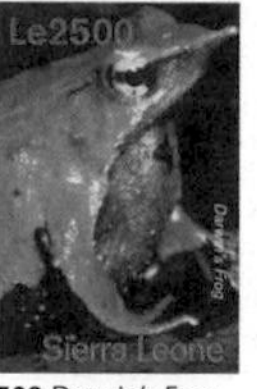

508 Darwin's Frog

2010. Birth Bicentenary (2009) of Charles Darwin (biologist and evolutionary theorist). Multicoloured.

MS4698	2500l.×4 Type **508**; Darwin's fox; Galapagos tortoise; Galapagos marine iguana	9·25	9·25

509 Pres. John F. Kennedy

2010. 50th Anniv of Election of President John F. Kennedy. Multicoloured.

MS4699	4000l.×4 Type **509**; Pres. Kennedy with arm raised; Seated, smiling; Profile and 'KENNEDY FOR PRESIDENT'	3·50	3·50

510 Elvis Presley as Walter Hale in *The Trouble with Girls*, 1969

2010. Elvis Presley in *The Trouble with Girls*. Multioloured.

MS4700	90×125 mm. 8000l. Type **510**	7·50	7·50
MS4701	125×90 mm. 8000l. Poster for *The Trouble with Girls*	7·50	7·50
MS4702	90×125 mm. 8000l. Wearing black jacket, smiling	7·50	7·50
MS4703	125×90 mm. 8000l. Standing beside train	7·50	7·50

511 Mexico

2010. World Cup Football Championship, South Africa. Multicoloured.

4704	1900l. Type **511**	1·75	1·75
4705	1900l. Switzerland	1·75	1·75
4706	1900l. Honduras	1·75	1·75
4707	1900l. Greece	1·75	1·75
4708	1900l. Nigeria	1·75	1·75
4709	1900l. Germay	1·75	1·75
4710	1900l. New Zealand	1·75	1·75
4711	1900l. Chile	1·75	1·75
4712	1900l. North Korea	1·75	1·75
4713	1900l. Cameroon	1·75	1·75
4714	1900l. South Korea	1·75	1·75
4715	1900l. Algeria	1·75	1·75
4716	1900l. Argentina	1·75	1·75
4717	1900l. Slovakia	1·75	1·75
4718	1900l. France	1·75	1·75
4719	1900l. South Africa	1·75	1·75
4720	1900l. Japan	1·75	1·75
4721	1900l. Netherlands	1·75	1·75
4722	1900l. Spain	1·75	1·75
4723	1900l. United States	1·75	1·75
4724	1900l. Paraguay	1·75	1·75
4725	1900l. Brazil	1·75	1·75
4726	1900l. Serbia	1·75	1·75
4727	1900l. Slovenia	1·75	1·75
4728	1900l. Ghana	1·75	1·75
4729	1900l. England	1·75	1·75
4730	1900l. Italy	1·75	1·75
4731	1900l. Uruguay	1·75	1·75
4732	1900l. Denmark	1·75	1·75
4733	1900l. Côte d'Ivoire	1·75	1·75
4734	1900l. Australia	1·75	1·75
4735	1900l. Portugal	1·75	1·75

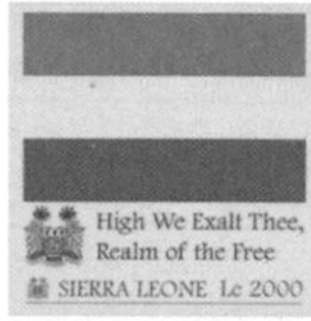

512 National Flag and Arms

2010. National Stamp.

4736	**512**	2000l. multicoloured	1·80	1·90

513

2010. Personalised Stamp

4737	**513**	2000l. multicoloured	1·80	1·90

514 Michael Jackson

2010. Michael Jackson (singer) Commemoration. Multicoloured.

MS4738	4000l.×4 Type **514**; Wearing cream jacket with black lapel; In profile, facing right, head tilted back; Wearing black and gold jacket, holding microphone close to mouth	12·00	12·00
MS4739	4000l.×4 Wearing black, facing to right; Wearing white collared shirt; Wearing white T shirt and shirt; Wearing black and red roll-neck	12·00	12·00

515 Scout holding Badge and Olive Branch

2010. Centenary of Boy Scouts of America. Multicoloured.

MS4740	182×134 mm. 4000l. ×4 Type **515**×2; Eagle scout medal and merit badges for dog care, small-boat sailing, law and plant science; Scout medal and merit badges for astronomy, energy, theatre and home repairs	12·00	12·00
MS4741	150×154 mm. 4000l.×4 Two eagle scout badges and 'Be prepared' badge; Scout holding badge and olive branch×2; Eagle scout badge and eagle badges with star and heart backgrounds (all horiz)	12·00	12·00

516 Pope John Paul II

2010. Fifth Death Anniv of Pope John Paul II (1st issue). Multicoloured.

MS4742 4000l.×4 Type **516**; Wearing red cassock and gold robes; With hands raised in blessing; Wearing mitre	14·00	14·00
MS4743 4000l.×4 With hand raised; With mitre and staff (at right of stamp); With mitre and staff (at left of stamp); Wearing white zucchetto (skullcap) (candlestick at right)	14·00	14·00

The stamps and margins of **MS**4742 form a composite design.

517 *Protogoniomorpha parhassus*

2010. Butterflies of Sierra Leone. Multicoloured.

MS4744 170×100 mm. 4000l.×4 Type **517**; *Kallimoides rumia rumia*; *Précis pelarga*; *Salamis cacta cacta*	12·00	12·00
MS4745 100×70 mm. 6000l. *Junonia sophia sophia*; 6000l. *Junonia oenone*	12·00	12·00
MS4746 100×70 mm. 6000l. *Hypolimnas misippus*; 6000l. *Hypolimnas salmacis salmacis*	12·00	12·00

The stamps and margins of Nos. **MS**4744 and **MS**4746 form composite background designs of a poppy field (**MS**4744) or silhouettes of white flowers (**MS**4746).

518 Three Modern Guides and Four Early Guides

2010. Centenary of Girlguiding. Multicoloured.

MS4747 150×100 mm. 2700l.×4 Type **518**; Three modern guides blowing bubbles and troop of early guides; Four modern guides and five early guides; Group of modern guides, some with arms raised in triumph and early guides	9·25	9·25
MS4748 70×100 mm. 8000l. Brownie saluting	9·25	9·25

519 Harriet Beecher Stowe and Henri Dunant

2010. Death Centenary of Henri Dunant (founder of the Red Cross). Multicoloured.

MS4749 150×100 mm. 4000l.×4 Type **519**; Charles Dickens; Bertha Von Suttner; Victor Hugo	6·00	6·00
MS4750 70×100 mm. 10000le. Frédéric Passy	6·00	6·00

520 Mother Teresa with Children

2010. Birth Centenary of Mother Teresa (founder of the Missionaries of Charity). Multicoloured.

MS4751 151×100 mm. 4000l.×4 Type **520**; Mother Teresa with women; Mother Teresa with children (carrying young girl); Mother Teresa carrying baby and village family outside their home	5·00	5·00
MS4752 151×100 mm. 4000l.×4 Mother Teresa and three girls and two boys; Mother Teresa and two boys; Mother Teresa and five girls; Mother Teresa and four girls	5·00	5·00

The stamps within **MS**4751/2 were all wrongly inscr 'Mother Tersesa'.

The stamps within **MS**4752 all have an inset portrait of Mother Teresa at left.

521 Princess Diana

2010. Princess Diana Commemoration. Multicoloured.

MS4753 150×110 mm. 4000l.×4 Type **521**; Wearing blue jacket and white blouse; Wearing white sleeveless dress; Wearing pearl necklace and earrings	19·00	19·00
MS4754 99×71 mm. 10000l. Wearing grey and black jacket	8·50	8·50
MS4755 99×71 mm. 10000l. Wearing white hat	8·50	8·50

522 'EMPEROR GAOZU HAN DYNASTY'

2010. Beijing 2010 International Stamp and Coin Exposition. Multicoloured.

MS4756 95×170 mm. 3000l. Type **522**; 3000l. Emperor Gaozu (Han Dynasty)×3	3·75	3·75
MS4757 95×171 mm. 3000l.×4 Inscription 'EMPEROR HONGWU MING DYNASTY'; Painting of Emperor Hongwu; Drawing of Emperor Hongwu; Empress Ma (Ming Dynasty)	3·75	3·75
MS4758 95×170 mm. 3000l.×4 'EMPEROR KANGXI'; Emperor Kangxi (Qing Dynasty) (wearing blue); Emperor Kangxi (Qing Dynasty) (on throne); Emperor Kangxi (Qing Dynasty) (at writing desk)	3·75	3·75

523 Rabbit

2010. Chinese New Year. Year of the Rabbit. Multicoloured.

MS4759 6000l.×2 Type **523**; Rabbit (with head raised)	3·75	3·75

2010. Fifth Death Anniv of Pope John Paul II (2nd issue). Multicoloured.

MS4760 150×100 mm. 2700l.×4 Pope John Paul II: Holding staff with crucifixion carving at top; With hand raised; Wearing red cassock and gold robes; Praying	3·50	3·50
MS4761 150×100 mm. 2700l.×4 Pope John Paul II: Wearing mitre, head inclined to left; Wearing red cassock and gold robes, smiling; Smiling, eyes closed; Hands raised in blessing		

524 Pope Benedict XVI

2010. Visit of Pope Benedict XVI to the United Kingdom. Multicoloured.

MS4762 130×175 mm. 4500l.×4 Type **524**; Pope Benedict XVI at Hyde Park, London; Pope Benedict XVI at Westminister Cathedral, London; Pope Benedict XVI at Westminster Abbey, London	5·75	5·75
MS4763 130×175 mm. 4500l.×4 Pope Benedict XVI seated in red chair with arms raised; Pope Benedict XVI with Dr. Rowan Williams, Archbishop of Canterbury; Pope Benedict XVI with Chief Rabbi Jonathan Sacks; Pope Benedict XVI with Prime Minister David Cameron	5·75	5·75

525 Southern Minke Whale (*Balaenoptera bonaerensis*)

2011. Whales of the World. Multicoloured.

MS4764 171×100 mm. 4000le.×4 Type **525**; Common minke whale (*Balaenoptera acutorostrata*); Blue whale (*Balaenoptera musculus*); Sei whale (*Balaenoptera borealis*)	13·00	13·00
MS4765 101×71 mm. 8000l. Bryde's whale (*Balaenoptera brydei*)	7·00	7·00
MS4766 101×71 mm. 8000l. Fin whale (*Balaenoptera physalus*)	7·00	7·00

526 Lotus Flower

2011. Indipex International Stamp Exhibition, New Delhi. Lotus Flowers (*Nelumbo nucifera*)

MS4767 169×98 mm. 4000l.×4 Type **526**; Lotus Flower (*Nelumbo nucifera*) inscription at top, country inscription at left; Country inscription at top; Country inscription at right	12·00	12·00
MS4768 110×75 mm. 10000l. Lotus flower (vert)	8·50	9·00

527 Ray Alexander

2011. Legendary Heroes of Africa. Jewish Anti-Apartheid Campaigners. Multicoloured.

MS4769 4500l.×4 Type **527**; Baruch Hirson; Norma Kitson; Yetta Barrenblatt	13·00	13·00

528 Elvis Presley

2011. 75th Birth Anniv of Elvis Presley (2nd issue). Multicoloured.

MS4770 101×173 mm. 3300l.×6 Type **528**; Elvis Presley wearing black leather jacket in profile; Wearing white suit, facing left; Wearing black leather jacket, singing; Wearing white suit, standing upright with right arm outstretched; Wearing black leather jacket, playing guitar	14·00	14·00
MS4771 163×127 mm. 4100l.×5 Elvis Presley singing, right hand playing guitar, left arm outstretched; Head and shoulders, microphone in left foreground; Half-length photo, with guitar; Half length photo, in profile with guitar; On stage playing guitar and singing, side view	14·00	14·00

529 Prince William and Miss Catherine Middleton

2011. Royal Engagement. Multicoloured.

MS4772 4000l. Type **529**×4	13·00	13·00
MS4773 4000l.×4 Prince William; Miss Catherine Middleton; Prince William and Miss Catherine Middleton (three quarter length); Prince William and Miss Catherine Middleton (head and shoulders) (all vert)	13·00	13·00
MS4774 5000l. Miss Catherine Middleton (wearing black hat); 5000l. Prince William	8·50	8·50
MS4775 5000l. Miss Catherine Middleton wearing feathered fascinator; 5000l. Prince William wearing beret (both vert)	8·50	8·50

530 *Portrait of a Young Man*

2011. 500th Death Anniv of Sandro Botticelli (artist). Multicoloured.

MS4776 4000l.×4 Type **530**; *Flight into Egypt*; Crucifixion (Museo dell 'Opera dell Duomo); *Three Miracles of Saint Zenobius*	13·00	13·00
MS4777 100×71 mm. 8000l. *The Annunciation* (50×38 mm)	7·00	7·00

531 Pres. Barack Obama

2011. Pres. Barack Obama holds Summit with Afghan Pres. Hamid Karzai, May 12 2010, and Meets Congressional Leaders, June 10 2010. Multicoloured.

MS4778 4000l.×4 Pres. Hamid Karzai; Pres. Barack Obama talking to Pres. Karzai; Presidents Obama and Karzai shaking hands; Pres. Barack Obama speaking, looking to left	12·00	12·00
MS4779 4000l.×4 Type **531**; Pres. Obama and House Speaker Nancy Pelosi; Pres. Obama and Senator Harry Reid; Pres. Obama speaking	12·00	12·00

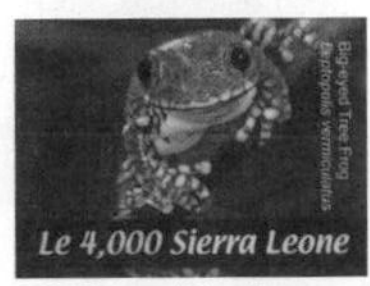

532 Big-eyed Tree Frog (*Leptopelis vermiculatus*)

2011. Frogs and Reptiles of Africa. Multicoloured.

MS4780 168×99 mm. 4000l.×4 Type **532**; Marbled reed frog (*Hyperolius marmoratus*); African red toad (*Schismaderma carens*); Afrcian clawed frog (*Xenopus laevis*)	13·00	13·00
MS4781 168×99 mm. 4000l.×4 Nile crocodile (*Crocodylus niloticus*); African clawed gecko (*Holodactylus*); African spurred tortoise (*Geochelone sulcata*); Rainbow agama (*Agama agama*)	13·00	13·00
MS4782 100×70 mm. 8000l. African bullfrog (*Pyxicephalus adspersus*)	7·00	7·00
MS4783 100×70 mm. 8000l. Eastern green mamba (*Dendroaspis angusticeps*)	7·00	7·00

533 Mikhail Gorbachev

2011. 80th Birthday of Mikhail Gorbachev (General Secretary of the Communist Party 1985-95). Multicoloured.

MS4784 5000l. Type **533**×2; 5000l. Mikhail Gorbachev and US President Ronald Reagan; 5000l. Mikhail Gorbachev and Ronald Reagan shaking hands;	11·00	11·00
MS4785 5000l.×4 Mikhail Gorbachev in front of microphone, speaking; In profile; Mikhail Gorbachev and Ronald Reagan (seated in front of desk); Mikhail Gorbachev and US President George H. W. Bush	11·00	11·00

534 Prince William

2011. Royal Wedding. Multicoloured.

MS4786 160×210 mm. 3500l.×6 Type **534**; Miss Catherine Middleton; Prince Charles; Princess Diana; Prince Philip; Queen Elizabeth II and five stamp-size labels	14·00	14·00
MS4787 160×95 mm. 5500l. Prince William; 5500l. Duke and Duchess of Cambridge riding in carriage on wedding day	9·00	9·00
MS4788 160×95 mm. 5500l. Duchess of Cambridge on wedding day; 5500l. Duke and Duchess of Cambridge kissing on Buckingham Palace balcony	9·00	9·00

535 Pink-backed Pelican (*Pelecanus rufescens*)

2011. Seabirds of West Africa. Multicoloured.
MS4789 135×90 mm. 4000l.×4 Type **535**; Abdim's stork (*Ciconia abdimii*); Western reef-heron (*Egretta gularis*); African spoonbill (*Platalea alba*) 14·00 14·00
MS4790 135×90 mm. 4000l.×4 Greater flamingo (*Phoenicopterus roseus*); Fulvous whistling-duck (*Dendrocygna bicolor*); Cory's shearwater (*Calonectris diomedea*); Purple heron (*Ardea purpurea*) 14·00 14·00
MS4791 95×96 mm. 10000l. Squacco heron (*Ardeola ralloides*) (horiz) 9·00 9·00
MS4792 95×96 mm. 10000l. African sacred ibis (*Threskiornis aethiopicus*) (horiz) 9·00 9·00

536 Rat

2011. Chinese Lunar Calendar. Zodiac Animals (on medallions). Multicoloured.
MS4793 1250l.×12 Type **536**; Ox; Tiger; Snake; Dragon; Rabbit; Horse; Ram; Monkey; Boar; Dog; Rooster 11·00 11·00

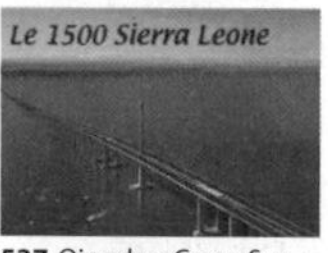

537 Qingdao Cross-Sea Bridge

2011. Bridges and Tunnels of the World. Multicoloured.
MS4794 150×140 mm. 1500l. Type **537**×3; 1500l. Distant view of Qingdao Cross-Sea Bridge and near and far coastlines×3 3·75 3·75
MS4795 108×133 mm. 2500l. Qingdao Jiaozhouwan Undersea Tunnel×2; 2500l. Tunnel entrance×2 7·00 7·00

538 Forest

2011. International Year of Forests. Multicoloured.
MS4796 100×165 mm. 2500l.×6 Type **538** ('Forests cover 31% of total land area'); Boy in forest ('Forests are home to 300 million people around the world'); Red-eyed treefrog (*Agalychnis callidryas*); Red-crested turaco (*Tauraco erythrolophus*); Logger ('30% of forests are used for production of wood and non-wood products'); Ban Ki Moon, Secretary General of the United Nations 12·00 12·00
MS4797 70×72 mm. 5000l.×2 Man in tree emblem; Forest ('Primary forests account for 36% of forest area') 8·50 8·50

539 Forest Puff Adder

2011. Endangered Species. Forest Puff Adder (*Bitis gabonica*). Multicoloured.
4798 3100l. Type **539** 2·50 2·50
4799 3100l. Forest puff adder swimming 2·50 2·50
4800 3100l. Close-up of head (side view) 2·50 2·50
4801 3100l. Close-up of head (seen from above) 2·50 2·50
MS4802 190×125 mm. Nos. 4798/801, each ×2 11·00 11·00

540 *Bolusiella imbricata*

2011. Orchids of West Africa. Multicoloured.
MS4803 150×100 mm. 3400l.×6 Type **540**; *Bulbophyllum scaberulum*; *Oeceoclades maculata*; *Ancistrochilus rothschildianus*; *Sarracenia flava*; *Phaius* 15·00 15·00
MS4804 150×100 mm. 4800l.×4 *Ancistrochilus rothshildianus* (different); *Angraecum subulatum*; *Eulophia guieensis*; *Eurychone rothschildiana* 20·00 20·00
MS4805 100×71 mm. 11000l. *Polystachya galeata* 10·00 10·00
MS4806 100×71 mm. 11000l. *Monodora myristica* 10·00 10·00

541 Memorial to Firefighters

2011. Tenth Anniv of Attack on World Trade Center, New York. Multicoloured.
MS4807 150×100 mm. 3400l.×6 Type **541**; New York skyline with tribute in lights; Pentagon memorial; Commemorative flag; American flags as memorial; Ground Zero (site of World Trade Center) 15·00 15·00
MS4808 100×70 mm. 11000l. Tribute in lights (38×51 mm) 10·00 10·00

542 Vostok Rocket

2011. 50th Anniv of the First Man in Space. Multicoloured.
MS4809 150×100 mm. 4000l.×4 Type **542**; Vostok capsule; Gagarin mission patch; Astronaut Gordon Cooper and Gemini 5 capsule 13·00 13·00
MS4810 150×100 mm. 4000l.×4 Vostok rocket on launch pad; Mig 15; Yuri Gagarin; Astronaut Alan Shepard 13·00 13·00
MS4811 100×70 mm. 8000l. Yuri Gagarin (vert) 7·50 7·50
MS4812 100×70 mm. 8000l. Vostok (vert) 7·50 7·50

543 Bronze Statue of Abraham Lincoln

2011. President Abraham Lincoln and 150th Anniv of the American Civil War. Multicoloured.
MS4813 98×150 mm. 4000l. Type **543**×2; 4000l. Painting of Abraham Lincoln×2 12·00 12·00
MS4814 130×120 mm. 6000l.×3 Union soldier's hat; Pres. Abraham Lincoln's hat; Confederate soldier's hat 13·00 13·00

544 Sun Yat-sen

2011. China 2011 International Stamp Exhibition, Wuxi, China. Sheet 150×116 mm. Multicoloured.
MS4815 4000l. Type **544**×4 11·00 11·00

545 Pope John Paul II

2011. Beatification of Pope John Paul II. Multicoloured.
MS4816 5000l. Type **545**×2; 5000l. Pope John Paul II (facing right)×2 9·00 9·00

546 Jane Goodall

2011. 50th Anniv of the Arrival of Jane Goodall (primatologist) at Gombe, Tanzania. Multicoloured.
MS4817 188×108 mm. 5000l.×4 Type **546**; Jane Goodall with young champanzee; Jane Goodall with chimpanzee (tent in background); Jane Goodall looking over forested landscape of Gombe 15·00 15·00
MS4818 108×189 mm. 5000l.×4 Jane Goodall writing; Jane Goodall looking at adult chimpanzee at base of tree trunk; Jane Goodall with female chimpanzee and baby; Jane Goodall watching sunset 15·00 15·00

547 Dumbo Octopus (*Grimpoteuthis innominata*)

2011. Deep Ocean Creatures. Multicoloured.
MS4819 91×140 mm. 5000l.×4 Type **547**; Vampire squid (*Vampyroteuthis internalis*); Gulper eel (*Eurypharynx pelecanoides*); Ping pong tree sponge (*Chondrochladia lampadiglobus*) 14·00 14·00
MS4820 180×100 mm. 5000l.×4 Comb jelly (*Bathocyroe fosteri*); *Benthocodon pedunculata*; Glowing sucker octopus (*Stauroteuthis syrtensis*); Hatchetfish (*Argyropelecus gigas*) (all horiz) 14·00 14·00
MS4821 70×110 mm. 11000l. Anglerfish (*Himantolophus paucifilosus*) (38×51 mm) 14·00 14·00
MS4822 70×110 mm. 11000l. Dana octopus squid (*Taningia danae*) (38×51 mm) 14·00 14·00

548 Princess Diana

2011. 50th Birth Anniv of Princess Diana. Multicoloured.
MS4823 201×70 mm. 5000l.×4 Type **548**; Lady Diana Spencer as girl wearing black hat; Princess Diana with baby Prince William; Princess Diana facing right wearing white hat 14·00 14·00
MS4824 100×70 mm. 11000l. Princess Diana in profile facing right wearing white 9·00 9·00

549 Freddy Will

2011. Freddy Will (musician and author). Multicoloured.
MS4825 4000l.×4 Type **549**; Freddy Will (wearing bow tie); Wearing bow tie, looking down; Wearing T shirt (wire fence in background) 12·00 12·00

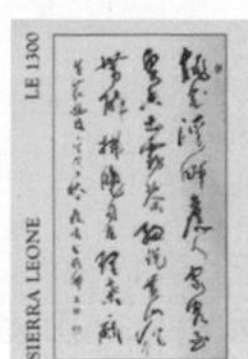

550 Calligraphy

2011. Chinese Modern Art (5th series). Lu Lv Jun. Multicoloured.
MS4826 1300l.×12 Type **550**; Two birds on branch; Forest (60×40 mm); Still life of flowers, Two birds on ground and bamboo; Calligraphy (different); Bamboo; Spring blossom; Cat (60×40 mm); Woman; Flowers (calligraphy at top); Flowers 11·00 11·00

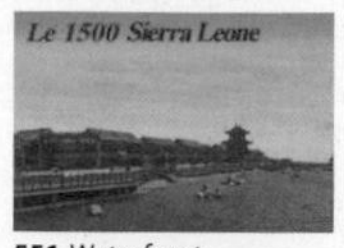

551 Waterfront

2011. Binhai New Area, Tianjin, China. Multicoloured.
MS4827 1500l.×6 Type **551**; Financial area and harbour; Aircraft carrier *Kiev*; Housing; Construction site; Pavilion 8·00 8·00

552 *The Adoration of the Magi* (Stefano da Verona)

2011. Christmas. Nativity Paintings. Multicoloured.
4828 1000l. Type **552** 1·00 75
4829 2000l. *Madonna and Child* (Taddeo di Bartolo) 1·75 1·25
4830 3000l. *Madonna* (Don Lorenzo Monaco) 2·50 2·75
4831 3500l. *Virgin and Child* (Gentile da Fabriano) 2·75 3·00

553 Mao Tse-tung

2012. Mao Tse-tung Commemoration. Multicoloured.
4832 1100l. Type **553** 1·00 1·00
4833 1100l. Mao Tse-tung as young man (head and shoulders) 1·00 1·00
4834 1100l. Mao Tse-tung seated at table 1·00 1·00
4835 1100l. Mao Tse-tung with hat raised 1·00 1·00
MS4836 150×100 mm. 5200l.×3 As Nos. 4832/4 4·00 4·50
MS4837 91×91 mm. 10000l. As No. 4835 7·00 8·00

554 Freize of Five Ancient Greek Athletes (left portion)

2012. Olympic Games, London. Multicoloured.
MS4838 3600l.×4 Type **554**; Athletes (right portion); Athletes in red (left portion); Athletes in red (right portion) 12·00 12·00

555 Poland Team

2012. UEFA Euro 2012 European Football Championship, Poland and Ukraine. Multicoloured.
MS4839 150×126 mm. 2500l.×9 Type **555**; Greece team; Russian team; Netherlands team; Football emblem and 'UEFA EURO 2012'; Czech Republic team; Denmark team; Germany team; Portugal team 15·00 15·00
MS4840 150×126 mm. 2500l.×9 Spain team; Italy team; Ireland team; Ukraine team; Football emblem and 'UEFA EURO 2012'; Croatia team; Sweden team; France team; England team 15·00 15·00

MS4841 150×101 mm. 2500l. Poland teamx4; 2500l. National Stadium, Poland; 2500l. Municipal Stadium, Poland	15·00	15·00
MS4842 150×101 mm. 2500l. Greece teamx4; 2500l. Municipal Stadium, Poland; 2500l. National Stadium, Poland	15·00	15·00
MS4843 150×101 mm. 2500l. Russia teamx4; 2500l. National Stadium, Poland; 2500l. PGE Arena, Poland	15·00	15·00
MS4844 150×101 mm. 2500l. Netherlands teamx4; 2500l. Metalist Stadium, Ukraine; 2500l. PGE Arena, Poland	15·00	15·00
MS4845 150×101 mm. 2500l. Czech Republic teamx4; 2500l. National Stadium, Poland; 2500l. Municipal Stadium, Poland	15·00	15·00
MS4846 150×101 mm. 2500l. Denmark teamx4; 2500l. Arena Lviv, Ukraine; 2500l. National Stadium, Poland	15·00	15·00
MS4847 150×101 mm. 2500l. Germany teamx4; 2500l. Arena Lviv, Ukraine; 2500l. Metalist Stadium, Ukraine	15·00	15·00
MS4848 150×101 mm. 2500l. Portugal teamx4; 2500l. Metalist Stadium, Ukraine; 2500l. Arena Lviv, Ukraine	15·00	15·00
MS4849 150×101 mm. 2500l. Spain teamx4; 2500l. Donbass Arena, Ukraine; 2500l. PGE Arena, Poland	15·00	15·00
MS4850 150×101 mm. 2500l. Italy teamx4; 2500l. Municpal Stadium, Poland; 2500l. Olympic Stadium, Ukraine	15·00	15·00
MS4851 150×101 mm. 2500l. Ireland teamx4; 2500l. Municpal Stadium, Poland; 2500l. PGE Arena, Poland	15·00	15·00
MS4852 150×101 mm. 2500l. Ukraine teamx4; 2500l. Olympic Stadium, Ukraine; 2500l. Donbass Arena, Ukraine	15·00	15·00
MS4853 150×101 mm. 2500l. Croatia teamx4; 2500l. National Stadium, Poland; 2500l. Municipal Stadium, Poland	15·00	15·00
MS4854 150×101 mm. 2500l. Sweden teamx4; 2500l. Olympic Stadium, Ukraine; 2500l. National Stadium, Poland	15·00	15·00
MS4855 150×101 mm. 2500l. France teamx4; 2500l. Donbass Arena, Ukraine; 2500l. Olympic Stadium, Ukraine	15·00	15·00
MS4856 150×101 mm. 2500l. England teamx4; 2500l. Olympic Stadium, Ukraine; 2500l. Donbass Arena, Ukraine	15·00	15·00

556 African Honey Bee (*Apis mellifera scutellata*)

2012. Bees of Africa. Multicoloured.

MS4857 5000l.×5 Type **556**; Honey bee (*Apis mellifera*); Leafcutter bee (*Megachile latreille*); Maranga bee (*Meliponula cockerell*); Stingless bee (*Hypotrigona cockerell*)	16·00	16·00

Pt. 1

SINGAPORE

An island to the south of the Malay peninsula, formerly part of the Straits Settlement but became a separate Crown Colony on 1 April 1946. From 1 August 1958 an internally self-governing territory designated the State of Singapore. From 16 September 1963 part of the Malaysian Federation until 9 August 1965, when it became an independent republic within the Commonwealth.

100 cents = 1 dollar.

1948. As T **58** of Straits Settlements, but inscr "MALAYA SINGAPORE".

1	1c. black	30	1·50
2	2c. orange	20	1·00
3	3c. green	50	2·25
19	4c. brown	2·25	10
19a	5c. mauve	5·50	2·25
5	6c. grey	1·00	1·00
6	8c. red	50	1·00
21a	8c. green	11·00	5·50
7	10c. purple	30	10
22a	12c. red	14·00	18·00
8	15c. blue	11·00	10
9	20c. black and green	5·50	1·25
24a	20c. blue	12·00	10
25	25c. purple and orange	5·00	10
25a	35c. red and purple	10·00	1·00
11	40c. red and purple	9·50	6·00
12	50c. black and blue	3·25	10
13	$1 blue and purple	11·00	4·25
14	$2 green and red	48·00	6·50
15	$5 green and brown	£110	8·50

1948. Silver Wedding. As T **32a** of St. Helena.

31	10c. violet	75	1·00
32	$5 brown	£110	50·00

1949. 75th Anniv of U.P.U. As T **33d/g** of St Helena.

33	10c. purple	75	70
34	15c. blue	6·00	4·75
35	25c. orange	6·00	3·00
36	50c. black	6·00	3·25

1953. Coronation. As T **33h** of St. Helena.

37	10c. black and purple	3·00	30

1 Chinese Sampan

3 Singapore River

1955

38	**1**	1c. black	10	1·00
39	-	2c. orange	2·50	1·50
40	-	4c. brown	1·50	15
41	-	5c. purple	65	50
42	-	6c. blue	65	70
43	-	8c. turquoise	1·25	2·00
44	-	10c. lilac	3·00	10
45	-	12c. red	5·00	3·00
46	-	20c. blue	2·25	10
47	-	25c. orange and violet	7·00	1·50
48	-	30c. violet and lake	3·75	10
49	-	50c. blue and black	2·25	10
50	-	$1 blue and purple	38·00	30
51	**3**	$2 green and red	42·00	1·75
52	-	$5 multicoloured	42·00	5·00

DESIGNS—HORIZ (as Type **1**) (2c. to 20c. are sailing craft): 2c. Malay kolek; 4c. Twa-kow lighter; 5c. Lombok sloop; 6c. Trengganu pinas; 8c. Palari schooner; 10c. Timber tongkong; 12c. Hainan junk; 20c. Cocos-Keeling schooner; 25c. Douglas DC-4M2 "Argonaut" aircraft; 30c. Oil tanker; 50c. "Chusan III" (liner). VERT (as Type **3**): $1 Raffles statue; $5 Arms of Singapore.

16 The Singapore Lion

1959. New Constitution. Lion in yellow and sepia.

53	**16**	4c. red	65	75
54	**16**	10c. purple	1·00	40
55	**16**	20c. blue	2·25	3·00
56	**16**	25c. green	2·50	2·25
57	**16**	30c. violet	2·50	3·25
58	**16**	50c. slate	3·25	3·25

17 State Flag

1960. National Day.

59	**17**	4c. red, yellow and blue	1·50	1·75
60	**17**	10c. red, yellow and grey	2·75	30

18 Clasped Hands

1961. National Day.

61	**18**	4c. black, brown and yellow	1·00	2·00
62	**18**	10c. black, green and yellow	1·25	10

19 "Arachnis" "Maggie Oei" (orchid)

20 Yellow Seahorse

1962. Orchids, Fish and Birds.

63	**19**	1c. multicoloured	30	1·00
64	**20**	2c. brown and green	30	2·00
65	-	4c. black and red	30	1·25
66	-	5c. red and black	20	10
67	-	6c. black and yellow	55	1·25
68	-	8c. multicoloured	1·25	3·50
69	-	10c. orange and black	40	10
70	-	12c. multicoloured	1·25	3·50
70a	-	15c. multicoloured	4·50	10
71	-	20c. orange and blue	1·25	10
72	-	25c. black and orange	75	10
73	-	30c. multicoloured	1·25	40
74	-	50c. multicoloured	1·25	10
75	-	$1 multicoloured	21·00	60
76	-	$2 multicoloured	9·00	1·00
77	-	$5 multicoloured	19·00	9·00

DESIGNS—HORIZ (as Type **20**): 4c. Six-banded Tiger barb; 5c. Orange clownfish; 10c. Harlequinfish; 25c. Three-spotted gourami. (As Type **19**): 50c. White-rumped shama; $1 White-throated kingfisher.VERT (as Type **20**): 6c. Archer-fish; 20c. Copper-banded butterflyfish. (As Type **19**): 8c. "Vanda" "Tan Chay Yan" (orchid); 12c. "Grammatophyllum speciosum" (orchid); 15c. Black-naped tern; 30c. "Vanda" "Miss Joaquim" (orchid); $2 Yellow-bellied sunbird; $5 White-bellied sea eagle.

34 "The Role of Labour in Nation-Building"

1962. National Day.

78	**34**	4c. yellow, red and black	1·25	2·25
79	**34**	10c. yellow, blue and black	1·50	75

35 Blocks of Flats, Singapore

1963. National Day.

80	**35**	4c. multicoloured	50	1·50
81	**35**	10c. multicoloured	1·75	20

36 Dancers in National Costume

1963. South East Asia Cultural Festival.

82	**36**	5c. multicoloured	50	50

37 Workers

1966. First Anniv of Republic.

89	**37**	15c. multicoloured	75	30
90	**37**	20c. multicoloured	1·00	1·25
91	**37**	30c. multicoloured	1·25	2·00

38 Flag Procession

1967. National Day.

92	**38**	6c. red, brown and slate	50	90
93	**38**	15c. purple, brown and slate	80	10
94	**38**	50c. blue, brown and slate	1·50	1·60

Nos. 92/4 are respectively inscr "Build a Vigorous Singapore" in Chinese, Malay and Tamil, in additon to the English inscr.

39 Skyscrapers and Afro-Asian Map

1967. Second Afro-Asian Housing Congress.

95	**39**	10c. multicoloured	30	10
96	**39**	25c. multicoloured	75	1·00
97	**39**	50c. multicoloured	1·40	1·60

40 Symbolical Figure wielding Hammer and Industrial Outline of Singapore

1968. National Day. Inscription at top in Chinese (6c.), Malay (15c.) or Tamil (50c.).

98	**40**	6c. red, black and gold	35	65
99	**40**	15c. green, black and gold	45	15
100	**40**	50c. blue, black and gold	1·00	1·25

43 Mirudhangam

45 Sword Dance

1968

101	**43**	1c. multicoloured	15	2·25
102	-	4c. multicoloured	60	3·75
103	**45**	5c. multicoloured	60	1·75
104	-	6c. black, lemon and orange	1·75	2·25
105	-	10c. multicoloured	20	10
106	-	15c. multicoloured	60	10
107	-	20c. multicoloured	1·00	1·75
108	-	25c. multicoloured	1·25	1·75
109	-	30c. multicoloured	40	1·50
110	-	50c. black, red and brown	50	1·00
111	-	75c. multicoloured	3·00	3·75
112	-	$1 multicoloured	4·50	1·25
113	-	$2 multicoloured	3·50	1·00
114	-	$5 multicoloured	14·00	1·50
115	-	$10 multicoloured	38·00	15·00

DESIGNS—VERT (as Type **43**): 4c. Pi Pa; $2 Rebab; $10 Ta Ku. (As Type **45**): 6c. Lion Dance; 10c. Bharatha Natyam; 15c. Tari Payong; 20c. Kathak Kali; 25c. Lu Chih Shen and Lin Chung; 50c. Tari Lilin; 75c. Tarian Kuda Kepang; $1 Yao Chi. HORIZ (as Type **43**): $5 Vine. (As Type **45**): 30c. Dragon dance.

58 E.C.A.F.E. Emblem

1969. Plenary Session of Economic Commission for Asia and the Far East.

116	**58**	15c. black, silver and blue	35	20
117	**58**	30c. black, silver and red	65	1·25
118	**58**	75c. black, silver and violet	1·00	2·50

59 "100000" and Slogan as Block of Flats

1969. Completion of "100000 Homes for the People" Project.

119	**59**	25c. black and green	1·00	50
120	**59**	50c. black and blue	1·25	1·25

60 Aircraft over Silhouette of Singapore Docks

1969. 150th Anniv of Founding of Singapore.

121	**60**	15c. black, red and yellow	2·50	70
122	-	30c. black and blue	2·50	1·00

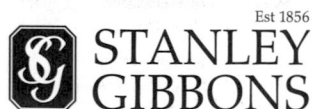

123	-	75c. multicoloured	4·50	1·00
124	-	$1 black and red	9·00	10·00
125	-	$5 red and black	18·00	45·00
126	-	$10 black and green	27·00	45·00
MS127		120×120 mm. Nos. 121/6	£375	£400

DESIGNS: 30c. U.N. emblem and outline of Singapore; 75c. Flags and outline of Malaysian Federation; $1 Uplifted hands holding crescent and stars; $5 Tail of Japanese aircraft and searchlight beams; $10 Bust from statue of Sir Stamford Raffles.

61 Sea Shells

1970. World Fair, Osaka. Multicoloured.

128	15c. Type **61**	1·00	15
129	30c. Veil-tailed guppys	1·50	70
130	75c. Greater flamingo and helmeted hornbill	4·00	2·75
131	$1 Orchid	4·50	5·50
MS132	94×154 mm. Nos. 128×31	24·00	24·00

62 "Kindergarten"

1970. Tenth Anniv of People's Association.

133	**62**	15c. brown and orange	75	20
134	-	50c. blue and orange	1·75	2·25
135	-	75c. purple and black	2·75	5·00

DESIGNS: 50c. "Sport"; 75c. "Culture".

63 Soldier charging

1970. National Day. Multicoloured.

136	15c. Type **63**	1·25	20
137	50c. Soldier on assault course	3·00	2·75
138	$1 Soldier jumping	4·00	9·50

64 Sprinters

1970. Festival of Sports.

139	**64**	10c. mauve, black and blue	2·00	3·25
140	-	15c. black and orange	2·50	3·50
141	-	25c. black, orange and green	2·75	3·75
142	-	50c. black, green and mauve	3·00	3·75

DESIGNS: 15c. Swimmers; 25c. Tennis players; 50c. Racing cars.

65 "Neptune Aquamarine" (freighter)

1970. Singapore Shipping.

143	**65**	15c. multicoloured	2·50	65
144	-	30c. yellow and blue	4·50	4·25
145	-	75c. yellow and red	8·00	9·50

DESIGNS: 30c. Container berth; 75c. Shipbuilding.

66 Country Names in Circle

1971. Commonwealth Heads of Government Meeting, Singapore. Multicoloured.

146	15c. Type **66**	90	20
147	30c. Flags in circle	1·25	80
148	75c. Commonwealth flags	2·25	4·00
149	$1 Commonwealth flags linked to Singapore (63×61 mm)	3·00	7·00

67 Bicycle Rickshaws

1971. Tourism. ASEAN Year. (ASEAN = Association of South East Asian Nations).

150	**67**	15c. black, violet and orange	80	25
151	-	20c. indigo, orange & blue	95	80
152	-	30c. red and purple	1·25	1·40
153	-	50c. multicoloured	3·75	7·00
154	-	75c. multicoloured	4·50	9·00

DESIGNS—SQUARE: 20c. Houseboat "village" and boats; 30c. Bazaar. HORIZ (68×18 mm): 50c. Modern harbour skyline; 75c. Religious buildings.

68 Chinese New Year

1971. Singapore Festivals. Multicoloured.

155	15c. Type **68**	1·25	15
156	30c. Hari Raya	2·00	1·75
157	50c. Deepavali	3·00	5·00
158	75c. Christmas	4·00	6·50
MS159	150×125 mm. Nos. 155/8	75·00	48·00

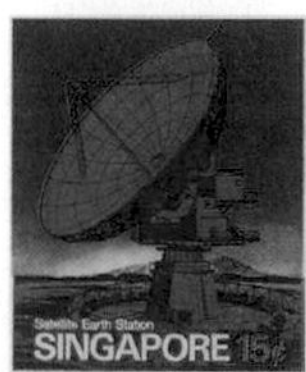

69 "Dish" Aerial

1971. Opening of Satellite Earth Station.

160	**69**	15c. multicoloured	2·50	1·25
161	-	30c. multicoloured	7·00	7·50
162	-	30c. multicoloured	7·00	7·50
163	-	30c. multicoloured	7·00	7·50
164	-	30c. multicoloured	7·00	7·50

DESIGNS: Nos. 161/4 were printed in *se-tenant* blocks of four throughout the sheet, the four stamps forming a composite design similar to Type **69**. They can be identified by the colour of the face values which are: yellow (No. 161), green (No. 162), red (No. 163) or orange (No. 164).

70 "Singapore River and Fort Canning, 1843–7" (Lieut. E. A. Porcher)

1971. Art. Multicoloured.

165	10c. Type **70**	2·00	2·00
166	15c. "The Padang, 1851" (J. T. Thomson)	2·75	3·00
167	20c. "Singapore Waterfront, 1848–9"	3·00	3·50
168	35c. "View from Fort Canning 1846" (J. T. Thomson)	6·00	7·00
169	50c. "View from Mt. Wallich, 1857" (P. Carpenter)	9·00	13·00
170	$1 "Singapore Waterfront, 1861" (W. Gray)	11·00	18·00

The 50c. and $1 are larger, 69×47 mm.

71 One Dollar of 1969

1972. Coins.

171	-	15c. orange, black and green	1·00	35
172	**71**	35c. black and red	2·25	2·50
173	-	$1 yellow, black and blue	4·00	7·00

DESIGNS: 15c. One-cent coin of George V; $1 One hundred and fifty dollar gold coin of 1969.

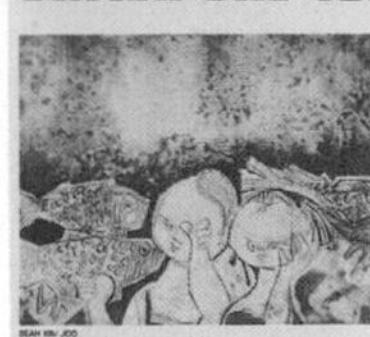

72 "Moon Festival" (Seah Kim Joo)

1972. Contemporary Art. Multicoloured.

174	15c. Type **72**	65	30
175	35c. "Complimentary Forces" (Thomas Yeo) (36×54 mm)	1·25	2·00
176	50c. "Rhythm in Blue" (Yusman Aman) (36×54 mm)	1·50	3·50
177	$1 "Gibbons" (Chen Wen Hsi)	3·25	6·50

73 Lanterns and Fish

1972. National Day. Designs symbolizing Festivals. Multicoloured.

178	15c. Type **73**	50	20
179	35c. Altar and candles	80	1·75
180	50c. Jug, bowl and gifts	1·00	2·50
181	75c. Candle	1·50	3·75

74 Student Welding

1972. Youth.

182	**74**	15c. multicoloured	65	30
183	-	35c. multicoloured	1·50	2·75
184	-	$1 orange, violet and green	2·75	6·50

DESIGNS: 35c. Sport; $1 Dancing.

75 "Maria Rickmers" (barque)

1972. Shipping. Multicoloured.

185	15c. "Neptune Ruby" (container ship) (42×29 mm)	2·00	80
186	75c. Type **75**	6·00	7·00
187	$1 Chinese junk	6·50	8·00
MS188	152×84 mm. Nos. 185/7	40·00	45·00

76 P.Q.R. Slogan

1973. "Prosperity Through Quality and Reliability" Campaign. Multicoloured.

189	15c. Type **76**	50	15
190	25c. Badge	1·25	2·50
191	75c. Text (different)	1·40	2·75
192	$1 Seal	1·40	4·00

77 Jurong Bird Park

1973. Singapore Landmarks.

193	**77**	15c. black and orange	80	15
194	-	35c. black and green	1·50	2·25
195	-	50c. black and brown	2·25	3·25
196	-	$1 black and purple	3·00	5·00

DESIGNS: 35c. National Theatre; 50c. City Hall; $1 Fullerton Building and Singapore River.

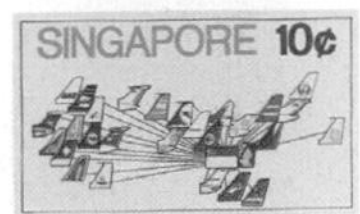

78 Aircraft Tail-fins

1973. Aviation. Multicoloured.

197	10c. Type **78**	50	10
198	35c. Emblems of Singapore Airlines and destinations	1·25	1·75
199	75c. Emblem on tail-fin	1·50	2·25
200	$1 Emblems encircling the globe	2·00	3·25

79 "Culture"

1973. National Day.

201	**79**	10c. orange and black	90	1·75
202	-	35c. orange and black	1·00	2·00
203	-	50c. orange and black	1·10	2·25
204	-	75c. orange and black	1·40	2·75

Nos. 201/4 were printed in *se-tenant* blocks of four within the sheet, and form a composite design representing Singapore's culture.

80 Athletics, Judo and Boxing

1973. Seventh S.E.A.P.* Games.

205	**80**	10c. gold, silver and blue	55	20
206	-	15c. gold and black	1·75	1·25
207	-	25c. gold, silver and black	1·25	1·50
208	-	35c. gold, silver and blue	2·25	3·00
209	-	50c. multicoloured	1·50	3·50
210	-	$1 silver, blue and green	2·50	6·00
MS211		130×111 mm. Nos. 205/10	32·00	35·00

DESIGNS—SQUARE (as Type **80**): 15c. Cycling, weightlifting, pistol-shooting and sailing; 25c. Footballs; 35c. Table-tennis bat, shuttlecock, tennis ball and hockey stick. HORIZ (41×25 mm): 50c. Swimmers; $1 Stadium.

*S.E.A.P. = South East Asian Peninsula.

81 Agave

82 Mangosteen

1973. Multicoloured

(a) Flowers and plants as T **81**.

212	1c. Type **81**	1·00	1·50
213	5c. "Coleus blumei"	10	50
214	10c. "Vinca rosea"	15	10
215	15c. "Helianthus angustifolius"	1·50	10
216	20c. "Licuala grandis"	45	60
217	25c. "Wedelia trilobata"	3·75	55
218	35c. "Chrysanthemum frutescens"	1·00	1·00
219	50c. "Costus malorticanus"	1·00	55
220	75c. "Gerbera jamesonii"	2·50	1·00

(b) Fruits as T **82**.

221	$1 Type **82**	1·50	40
222	$2 Jackfruit	1·75	1·25
223	$5 Coconut	1·75	4·50
224	$10 Pineapple	3·00	7·00

83 Tiger and Orang-Utans

1973. Singapore Zoo. Multicoloured.

No.	Description		
225	5c. Type **83**	75	85
226	10c. Leopard and waterbuck	80	45
227	35c. Leopard and thamin	2·75	4·50
228	75c. Horse and lion	4·00	7·00

84 Delta Guppy

1974. Tropical Fish. Multicoloured.

No.	Description		
229	5c. Type **84**	50	60
230	10c. Half-black delta guppy	50	15
231	35c. Delta guppy (different)	1·75	3·00
232	$1 Black delta guppy	3·00	8·50

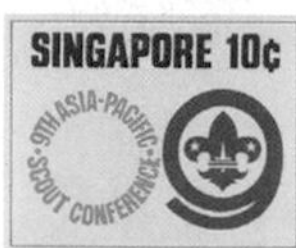

85 Scout Badge within "9"

1974. Ninth Asian-Pacific Scout Conference.

No.	Type	Description		
233	**85**	10c. multicoloured	30	10
234	**85**	75c. multicoloured	1·00	2·00

86 U.P.U. Emblem and Multiple "Centenary"

1974. Centenary of U.P.U.

No.	Type	Description		
235	**86**	10c. brown, purple and gold	15	10
236	-	35c. blue, deep blue & gold	40	1·60
237	-	75c. multicoloured	80	2·75

DESIGNS: 35c. U.P.U. emblem and multiple U.N. symbols; 75c. U.P.U. emblem and multiple peace doves.

87 Family Emblem

1974. World Population Year. Multicoloured.

No.	Description		
238	10c. Type **87**	30	10
239	35c. Male and female symbols	80	1·40
240	75c. World population map	1·25	2·75

88 "Tree and Sun" (Chia Keng San)

1974. Universal Children's Day. Multicoloured.

No.	Description		
241	5c. Type **88**	40	65
242	10c. "My Daddy and Mummy" (Angeline Ang)	40	20
243	35c. "A Dump Truck" (Si-Hoe Yeen Joong)	1·25	2·75
244	50c. "My Aunt" (Raymond Teo)	1·40	3·50
MS245	138×100 mm. Nos. 241/4	23·00	28·00

89 Street Scene

1975. Singapore Views. Multicoloured.

No.	Description		
246	15c. Type **89**	65	20
247	20c. Singapore River	1·25	1·25
248	$1 "Kelong" (fish-trap)	3·25	7·00

90 Emblem and Lighters' Prows

1975. Ninth Biennial Conference of Int Association of Ports and Harbours, Singapore. Multicoloured.

No.	Description		
249	5c. Type **90**	30	15
250	25c. Freighter and ship's wheel	1·50	1·00
251	50c. Oil-tanker and flags	2·00	2·50
252	$1 Container-ship and propellers	2·75	5·50

91 Satellite Earth Station, Sentosa

1975. "Science and Industry". Multicoloured.

No.	Description		
253	10c. Type **91**	35	10
254	35c. Oil refineries (vert)	2·00	2·50
255	75c. "Medical Sciences"	2·25	3·75

92 "Homes and Gardens"

1975. Tenth National Day. Multicoloured.

No.	Description		
256	10c. Type **92**	20	10
257	35c. "Shipping and Shipbuilding"	1·25	1·75
258	75c. "Communications and Technology"	1·40	2·75
259	$1 "Trade, Commerce and Industry"	1·40	2·75

93 South African Crowned Cranes

1975. Birds. Multicoloured.

No.	Description		
260	5c. Type **93**	1·50	80
261	10c. Great Indian hornbill	1·50	30
262	35c. White-throated kingfishers and white-collared kingfisher	8·00	8·50
263	$1 Sulphur-crested cockatoo and blue and yellow macaw	10·00	15·00

94 "Equality"

1975. International Women's Year. Multicoloured.

No.	Description		
264	10c. Type **94**	25	10
265	35c. "Development"	1·40	2·75
266	75c. "Peace"	1·75	5·00
MS267	128×100 mm. Nos. 264/6	15·00	20·00

95 Yellow Flame

1976. Wayside Trees. Multicoloured.

No.	Description		
268	10c. Type **95**	60	10
269	35c. Cabbage tree	1·50	2·50
270	50c. Rose of India	1·75	2·50
271	75c. Variegated coral tree	2·25	4·75

96 "Arachnis hookeriana x Vanda" Hilo Blue

1976. Singapore Orchids. Multicoloured.

No.	Description		
272	10c. Type **96**	1·25	10
273	35c. "Arachnis Maggie Oei x Vanda insignis"	3·00	3·50
274	50c. "Arachnis Maggie Oei x Vanda" Rodman	3·25	3·75
275	75c. "Arachnis hookeriana x Vanda" Dawn Nishimura	4·50	7·00

97 Festival Symbol and Band

1976. Tenth Anniv of Singapore Youth Festival. Multicoloured.

No.	Description		
276	10c. Type **97**	20	10
277	35c. Athletes	1·25	1·75
278	75c. Dancers	1·40	2·75

98 "Queen Elizabeth Walk"

1976. Paintings of Old Singapore. Multicoloured.

No.	Description		
279	10c. Type **98**	50	20
280	50c. "The Padang"	1·50	3·25
281	$1 "Raffles Place"	3·00	5·50
MS282	164×91 mm. Nos. 279/81	15·00	23·00

99 Chinese Costume

1976. Bridal Costumes. Multicoloured.

No.	Description		
283	10c. Type **99**	55	10
284	35c. Indian costume	1·40	2·00
285	75c. Malay costume	2·25	4·75

100 Radar, Missile and Soldiers

1977. Tenth Anniv of National Service. Multicoloured.

No.	Description		
286	10c. Type **100**	65	10
287	50c. Tank and soldiers	2·00	2·00
288	75c. Soldiers, wireless operators, pilot and Douglas A-4 Skyhawk aircraft	3·00	4·25

101 Lyrate Cockle

102 Spotted Hermit Crab

1977. Multicoloured

(a) Shells as T **101**

No.	Description		
289	1c. Type **101**	1·00	2·00
290	5c. Folded or plicate scallop	20	10
291	10c. Marble cone	20	10
292	15c. Scorpion conch	1·00	40
293	20c. Amplustre or royal paper bubble	1·00	10
294	25c. Spiral babylon	1·25	2·50
295	35c. Royal thorny or spiny oyster	1·50	1·50
296	50c. Maple-leaf triton or winged frog shell	2·00	10
297	75c. Troschel's murex	3·00	20

(b) Fish and Crustaceans as T **102**.

No.	Description		
298	$1 Type **102**	2·00	15
299	$2 Zuge's stingray	2·00	75
300	$5 Cuttlefish	2·00	3·00
301	$10 Lionfish	3·00	5·50

103 Shipbuidling

1977. Labour Day. Multicoloured.

No.	Description		
302	10c. Type **103**	30	10
303	50c. Building construction	1·25	2·00
304	75c. Road construction	1·75	2·50

104 Keyhole and Banknotes

1977. Cent of Post Office Savings Bank. Multicoloured.

No.	Description		
305	10c. Type **104**	30	10
306	35c. On-line banking service	75	50
307	75c. GIRO service	1·75	1·50

105 Flags of Member Nations

1977. Tenth Anniv of ASEAN (Association of South-East Asian Nations). Multicoloured.

No.	Description		
308	10c. Type **105**	30	10
309	35c. "Agriculture"	75	75
310	75c. "Industry"	1·75	1·90

106 "Chingay Procession" (Liang Yik Yin)

1977. Children's Art. Multicoloured.

No.	Description		
311	10c. Type **106**	25	10
312	35c. "At the Bus Stop" (Chong Khing Ann) (horiz)	75	50
313	75c. "Playground" (Yap Li Hwa) (horiz)	2·00	2·50
MS314	160×97 mm. Nos. 311/13	10·00	17·00

107 "Life Sciences"

1977. Singapore Science Centre. Multicoloured.

No.	Description		
315	10c. Type **107**	20	10
316	35c. "Physical sciences"	45	30
317	75c. "Science and technology"	1·25	1·75
318	$1 Singapore Science Centre	1·50	1·75

108 Botanical Gardens and Esplanade, Jurong Bird Park

1978. Parks and Gardens. Multicoloured.

No.	Description		
319	10c. Type **108**	20	10
320	35c. Lagoon, East Coast Park (vert)	80	80
321	75c. Botanical Gardens (vert)	1·50	2·25

109 Red-whiskered Bulbul

1978. Singing Birds. Multicoloured.
322 10c. Type **109** 50 20
323 35c. Oriental white-eye ("White eye") 1·50 1·25
324 50c. White-rumped shama 1·75 2·00
325 75c. White-crested laughing thrush and melodious laughing thrush ("China Thrush") 2·00 3·25

110 Thian Hock Keng Temple

1978. National Monuments. Multicoloured.
326 10c. Type **110** 65 80
327 10c. Hajjah Fatimah Mosque 65 80
328 10c. Armenian Church 65 80
329 10c. Sri Mariamman Temple 65 80
MS330 173×86 mm. 35c.×4, as Nos. 326/9 3·50 3·75

Stamps from No. **MS**330 are similar in design to Nos. 326/9 but have no borders and the inscriptions are slightly larger.

111 Map of South East Asia showing Cable Network

1978. A.S.E.A.N. Submarine Cable (1st issue). Philippines–Singapore Section.
331 **111** 10c. multicoloured 15 10
332 **111** 35c. multicoloured 60 85
333 **111** 50c. multicoloured 80 1·50
334 **111** 75c. multicoloured 90 2·00

See also Nos. 385/8 and 458/61.

112 "Neptune Spinel" (bulk carrier)

1978. Tenth Anniv of Neptune Orient Shipping Lines. Multicoloured.
335 10c. Type **112** 70 20
336 35c. "Neptune Aries" (tanker) 1·50 1·50
337 50c. "Anro Temasek" (container ship) 1·75 2·25
338 75c. "Neptune Pearl" (container ship) 2·25 3·75

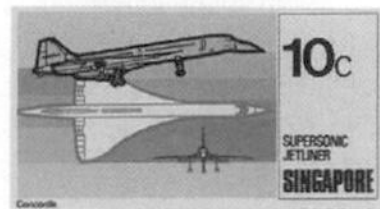

113 Concorde

1978. Aviation. Multicoloured.
339 10c. Type **113** 1·00 30
340 35c. Boeing 747-200 1·00 1·25
341 50c. Vickers Vimy 1·25 2·50
342 75c. Wright Brothers' Flyer I 1·50 4·00

114 10-Kilometre Marker

1979. Metrication. Multicoloured.
343 10c. Type **114** 15 10
344 35c. Tape measure 30 50
345 75c. Weighing scales 65 1·25

115 Vanda Hybrid

1979. Orchids.
346 **115** 10c. multicoloured 30 10
347 - 35c. multicoloured 60 75
348 - 50c. multicoloured 70 1·00
349 - 75c. multicoloured 80 1·40

DESIGNS—HORIZ: 35c. VERT: 50, 75c. Different varieties of vanda hybrid.

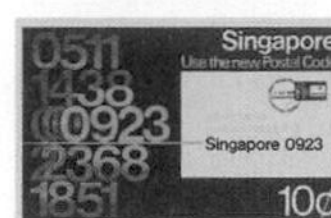

116 Envelope with new Singapore Postcode

1979. Postal Code Publicity.
350 **116** 10c. multicoloured 10 10
351 - 50c. multicoloured 60 90

The 50c. design is as Type **116**, but the envelope is addressed to the Philatelic Bureau, General Post Office and has the postcode "Singapore 0104".

117 Early Telephone and Overhead Cables

1979. Centenary of Telephone Service.
352 **117** 10c. brown and blue 15 10
353 - 35c. orange and violet 30 40
354 - 50c. blue, turquoise & grn 45 70
355 - 75c. green and orange 65 1·25

DESIGNS: 35c. Telephone dial and world map; 50c. Modern telephone and city scene; 75c. Latest computerized telephone and circuit diagram.

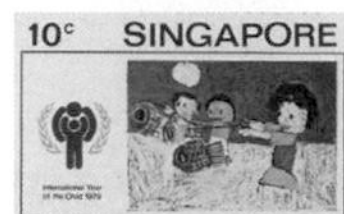

118 "Lantern Festival" (Eng Chun-Ngan)

1979. International Year of the Child. Children's Drawings. Multicoloured.
356 10c. Type **118** 10 10
357 35c. "Singapore Harbour" (Wong Chien Chien) 30 40
358 50c. "Use Your Hands" (Leong Choy Yeen) 40 70
359 75c. "Soccer" (Tan Cheong Hin) 60 1·25
MS360 154×98 mm. Nos. 356/9 3·75 4·25

119 View of Gardens

1979. 120th Anniv of Botanic Gardens.
361 **119** 10c. multicoloured 30 10
362 - 50c. multicoloured 1·00 1·50
363 - $1 multicoloured 1·50 2·50

DESIGNS: 50c., $1 Different views of Botanic Gardens.

120 Hainan Junk

1980. Ships. Multicoloured.
364 1c. Type **120** 1·00 2·00
365 5c. Full-rigged clipper 30 55
366 10c. Fujian junk 30 10
367 15c. Golekkan (sailing craft) 40 15
368 20c. Palari (sailing craft) 70 40
369 25c. East Indiaman 80 50
370 35c. Galleon 90 50
371 50c. Caravel 60 70
372 75c. Jiangsu trading junk 1·00 1·50
373 $1 "Kedah" (coaster) 70 1·00
374 $2 "Murex" (tanker) 1·00 1·60
375 $5 "Chusan" (screw steamer) 1·50 2·75
376 $10 "Braganza" (paddle-steamer) 4·00 5·00

Nos. 373/6 are 42×25 mm.

121 Straits Settlements 1867 1½c. Stamp and Map of Singapore, 1843

1980. "London 1980" International Stamp Exn. Multicoloured.
377 10c. Type **121** 20 10
378 35c. Straits Settlements 1906 $500 stamp and treaty between Johore and British Colony of Singapore 35 25
379 $1 1948 $2 stamp and map of Malaysia 60 1·10
380 $2 1969 150th Anniv of Singapore $10 commemorative and letter to Col. Addenbrooke from Sir Stamford Raffles 1·00 2·25
MS381 148×104 mm. Nos. 377/80 2·00 4·50

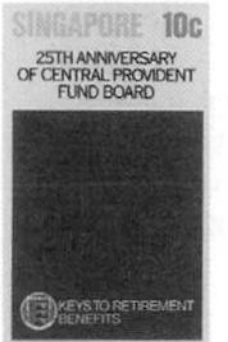

122 C.P.F. Emblem and "Keys to Retirement Benefits"

1980. 25th Anniv of Central Provident Fund Board. Multicoloured.
382 10c. Type **122** 10 10
383 50c. "C.P.F. savings for home ownership" 40 40
384 $1 "C.P.F. savings for old-age" 75 1·25

123 Map of South East Asia showing Cable Network

1980. A.S.E.A.N. (Association of South-East Asian Nations) Submarine Cable Network (2nd issue). Completion of Indonesia–Singapore Section.
385 **123** 10c. multicoloured 10 10
386 **123** 35c. multicoloured 50 50
387 **123** 50c. multicoloured 60 1·10
388 **123** 75c. multicoloured 75 2·00

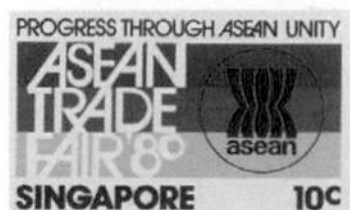

124 A.S.E.A.N. Trade Fair Emblem

1980. A.S.E.A.N. (Association of South-East Asian Nations) Trade Fair.
389 **124** 10c. multicoloured 15 10
390 **124** 35c. multicoloured 35 30
391 **124** 75c. multicoloured 60 1·00

125 Ixora

1980. National Tree Planting Day. Flowers. Multicoloured.
392 10c. Type **125** 10 10
393 35c. Allamanda 40 45
394 50c. Sky vine 50 70
395 75c. Bougainvillea 60 1·10

126 International Currency Symbols

1981. Tenth Anniv of Singapore Monetary Authority.
396 **126** 10c. black, red and yellow 10 10
397 **126** 35c. multicoloured 30 30
398 **126** 75c. multicoloured 55 1·25

1981. No. 65 surch **10 CENTS**.
399 10c. on 4c. black and red 30 40

128 Woodwork

1981. Technical Training. Multicoloured.
400 10c. Type **128** 10 10
401 35c. Building construction 25 25
402 50c. Electronics 40 60
403 75c. Precision machining 50 1·10

129 Figures representing various Sports

1981. "Sports for All".
404 **129** 10c. multicoloured 30 10
405 - 75c. multicoloured 2·00 2·50
406 - $1 multicoloured 2·50 3·50

DESIGNS: 75c. and $1 Figures representing different sports.

130 "The Right to Environmental Aids"

1981. International Year for Disabled Persons. Multicoloured.
407 10c. Type **130** 10 10
408 35c. "The right to social integration" 30 25
409 50c. "The right to education" 45 50
410 75c. "The right to work" 60 90

131 Control Tower and Passenger Terminal Building, Changi Airport

1981. Opening of Changi Airport.
411 **131** 10c. multicoloured 10 10
412 **131** 35c. multicoloured 20 30
413 **131** 50c. multicoloured 30 75
414 **131** 75c. multicoloured 40 1·50
415 **131** $1 multicoloured 45 1·60
MS416 154×105 mm. Nos. 411/15 2·25 4·50

The background emblem differs for each value.

132 "Parthenos sylvia"

1982. Butterflies. Multicoloured.
417 10c. Type **132** 40 15
418 50c. "Danaus vulgaris" 1·00 75
419 $1 "Trogonoptera brookiana" 1·40 1·75

133 A.S.E.A.N. Emblem

1982. 15th Anniv of A.S.E.A.N. (Association of South-East Asian Nations).

420	**133**	10c. multicoloured	10	10
421	**133**	35c. multicoloured	30	35
422	-	50c. multicoloured	40	65
423	-	75c. multicoloured	60	1·00

The 50 and 75c. values are as Type **133** but are inscribed "15th ASEAN Ministerial Meeting".

134 Football and Stylized Player

1982. World Cup Football Championship, Spain.

424	**134**	10c. black, light blue & bl	20	10
425	-	75c. multicoloured	75	1·50
426	-	$1 multicoloured	95	1·50

DESIGNS: 75c. Football and World Cup, Asian Four emblem; $1 Football and globe.

135 Sultan Shoal Lighthouse, 1896

1982. Lighthouses of Singapore. Multicoloured.

427	10c. Type **135**	50	15
428	75c. Horsburgh Lighthouse, 1855	1·40	1·75
429	$1 Raffles Lighthouse, 1855	1·50	2·00
MS430	148×104 mm. Nos. 427/9	5·50	6·00

136 Yard Gantry Cranes

1982. Tenth Anniv of Container Terminal. Multicoloured.

431	10c. Type **136**	10	10
432	35c. Computer	25	40
433	50c. Freightlifter	35	85
434	75c. Straddle carrier	65	1·75

137 Scouts on Parade

1982. 75th Anniv of Boy Scout Movement. Multicoloured.

435	10c. Type **137**	15	10
436	35c. Scouts hiking	30	25
437	50c. Scouts building tower	50	35
438	75c. Scouts canoeing	60	80

138 Productivity Movement Slogans

1983. Productivity Movement.

439	**138**	10c. orange and green	10	10
440	-	35c. brown and blue	25	50
441	-	50c. red, yellow and grey	40	90
442	-	75c. red and yellow	55	1·25

DESIGNS: 35c. Family and housing ("Benefits of Productivity"); 50c. Works meeting ("Quality Control Circles"); 75c. Aspects of Singapore business ("Everybody's Business").

139 Commonwealth Logo and Country Names

1983. Commonwealth Day.

443	**139**	10c. multicoloured	10	10
444	**139**	35c. multicoloured	20	35
445	**139**	75c. multicoloured	45	1·10
446	**139**	$1 multicoloured	65	1·40

140 Soccer

1983. 12th South-East Asia Games. Multicoloured.

447	10c. Type **140**	10	10
448	35c. Racket games	20	25
449	75c. Athletics	45	50
450	$1 Swimming	65	70

141 Policeman and Family

1983. Neighbourhood Watch Scheme. Multicoloured.

451	10c. Type **141**	15	10
452	35c. Policeman and children	55	55
453	75c. Policeman and inhabitants with linked arms	1·00	2·00

142 1977 A.S.E.A.N. Stamps and Statue of King Chulalongkorn

1983. Bangkok Int Stamp Exhibition. Multicoloured.

454	10c. Type **142**	20	10
455	35c. 1980 A.S.E.A.N. stamps and map of South-east Asia	55	50
456	$1 1982 A.S.E.A.N. stamps and signatures of Heads of State	1·25	1·60
MS457	147×104 mm. Nos. 454/6	3·50	6·00

143 Map of South-East Asia showing Cable Network

1983. A.S.E.A.N. (Association of South-East Asian Nations) Submarine Cable Network (3rd issue). Completion of Malaysia–Singapore–Thailand section.

458	**143**	10c. multicoloured	15	10
459	**143**	35c. multicoloured	55	75
460	**143**	50c. multicoloured	80	1·25
461	**143**	75c. multicoloured	1·25	2·00
MS462		146×100 mm. Nos. 331, 388, 458/61	4·75	6·00

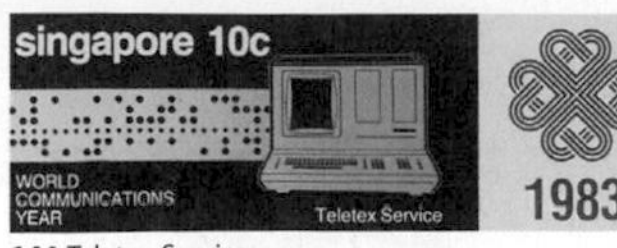

144 Teletex Service

1983. World Communications Year.

463	**144**	10c. yellow, green & black	20	15
464	-	35c. yellow, red and brown	55	75
465	-	75c. green, blue & dp blue	1·10	1·75
466	-	$1 yellow, brown and black	1·50	2·75

DESIGNS: 35c. World telephone numbering plan; 75c. Satellite transmission; $1 Sea communications.

145 Blue-breasted Banded Rail ("Slaty-breasted Rail")

1984. Coastal Birds. Multicoloured.

467	10c. Type **145**	60	15
468	35c. Black bittern	1·50	1·50
469	50c. Brahminy kite	1·75	2·25
470	75c. Moorhen ("Common Moorhen")	2·00	3·25

146 House of Tan Yeok Nee

1984. National Monuments. Multicoloured.

471	10c. Type **146**	15	10
472	35c. Thong Chai building	40	65
473	50c. Telok Ayer market	55	1·10
474	$1 Nagore Durgha shrine	80	2·50

147 1970 $1 National Day Stamp

1984. "25 Years of Nation Building". Multicoloured.

475	10c. Type **147**	15	10
476	35c. 1981 $1 "Sports for All" stamp	50	70
477	50c. 1969 25c. "100, 000 Homes for the People" stamp	60	1·00
478	75c. 1976 10c. Wayside Trees stamp	70	1·25
479	$1 1981 $1 Opening of Changi Airport stamp	80	1·75
480	$2 1981 10c. Monetary Authority stamp	1·40	4·00
MS481	132×106 mm. Nos. 475/80	6·00	7·50

148 Schoolchildren

1984. "Total Defence".

482	**148**	10c. brown and red	25	40
483	-	10c. brown, olive and blue	25	40
484	-	10c. brown, violet and salmon	25	40
485	-	10c. brown, light brown and mauve	25	40
486	-	10c. brown, yellow & olive	25	40

DESIGNS: No. 483, People of Singapore; 484, Indus-trial workers; 485, Civil Defence first aid worker; 486, Anti-aircraft gun crew.

149 Coleman Bridge

1985. Bridges of Singapore.

487	10c. black (Type **149**)	15	10
488	35c. black (Cavenagh Bridge)	30	40
489	75c. black (Elgin Bridge)	55	70
490	$1 black (Benjamin Sheares Bridge)	70	90

150 "Ceriagrion cerinorubellum" (damselfly)

1985. Insects. Multicoloured.

491	5c. Type **150**	1·25	50
492	10c. "Apis javana" (bee)	1·25	65
493	15c. "Delta arcuata" (wasp)	1·50	1·50
494	20c. "Xylocopa caerulea" (bee)	1·00	1·75
495	25c. "Donacia javana" (water beetle)	1·00	1·50
496	35c. "Heteroneda reticulata" (ladybird)	1·50	30
497	50c. "Catacanthus nigripes" (bug)	1·50	1·25
498	75c. "Chremistica pontianaka" (cicada)	1·50	2·50
499	$1 "Homoexipha lycoides" (cricket) (35×30 mm)	2·75	60
500	$2 "Traulia azureipennis" (grass-hopper) (35×30 mm)	1·50	1·50
501	$5 "Trithemis aurora" (dragon-fly) (35×30 mm)	2·00	3·50
502	$10 "Scambophyllum sanguinolentum" (grasshopper) (35×30 mm)	3·50	7·00

151 Tennis, Canoeing, Judo and Children Playing

1985. 25th Anniv of People's Assn. Multicoloured.

503	10c. Type **151**	25	10
504	35c. Lion dance, martial arts and athletes with flags	30	35
505	50c. Tae-kwon-do, Indian dance and Dragon dance	40	50
506	75c. Boxing, table tennis, basketball and dancing	1·00	90

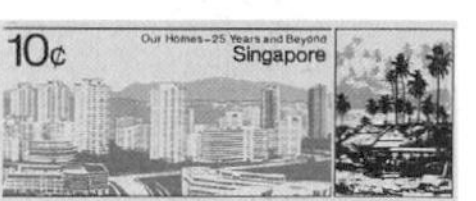

152 Modern Housing Estate and Squatter Settlement

1985. 25th Anniv of Housing and Development Board. Designs show different aspects of housing at left. Multicoloured.

507	10c. Type **152**	15	10
508	35c. Singapore family (home-ownership)	40	45
509	50c. Group of residents (community development)	50	1·00
510	75c. Construction workers (building technology)	60	1·75
MS511	126×105 mm. Nos. 507/10	3·25	5·00

153 Brownies

1985. 75th Anniv of Girl Guide Movement. Multicoloured.

512	10c. Type **153**	15	10
513	35c. Guides practising first aid	45	40
514	50c. Senior Branch	55	60
515	75c. Adult leaders and guides	75	90

154 Badges and Emblems of Singapore Youth Organizations

1985. International Youth Year. Multicoloured.

516	10c. Type **154**	20	10
517	75c. Hand protecting sapling	90	75
518	$1 Stylized figures and dove	1·10	1·10

155 Guava

1986. Singapore Fruit. Multicoloured.

519	10c. Type **155**	30	10
520	35c. Jambu air	85	65
521	50c. Rambutan	1·10	1·25
522	75c. Ciku	1·40	2·00

156 Laboratory Technician and Salesmen with Bar Graph

1986. 25th Anniv of National Trades Union Congress. Multicoloured.

523	10c. Type **156**	30	50
524	10c. Computer operator and welder	30	50
525	10c. Draughtsmen and surveyors	30	50
526	10c. Group of workers	30	50
MS527	148×100 mm. As Nos. 523/6, but each stamp with a face value of 35c.	4·00	6·00

157 Calligraphy

1986. "Expo '86" World Fair, Vancouver. Multicoloured.

528	50c. Type **157**	55	75
529	75c. Garland maker	70	95
530	$1 Batik printer	85	1·25

158 Industrial Automation

1986. 25th Anniv of Economic Development Board. Multicoloured.

531	10c. Type **158**	15	10
532	35c. Manufacture of aircraft components	30	30
533	50c. Electronics industry	40	50
534	75c. Biotechnology industry	55	90

159 Map showing Route of Cable and "Vercors" (cable ship)

1986. SEA-ME-WE Submarine Cable Project.

535	**159** 10c. multicoloured	40	10
536	**159** 35c. multicoloured	85	55
537	**159** 50c. multicoloured	1·10	90
538	**159** 75c. multicoloured	1·40	2·00

160 Stylized Citizens

1986. 21st Anniv of Citizens' Consultative Committees.

539	**160** 10c. multicoloured	30	45
540	- 35c. multicoloured	45	60
541	- 50c. multicoloured	55	70
542	- 75c. multicoloured	75	85

DESIGN: 35c. to 75c. Citizens.

Nos. 539/42 were printed together, *se-tenant*, forming a composite design.

161 Peace Doves and People of Different Races

1986. International Peace Year. Multicoloured.

543	10c. Type **161**	15	10
544	35c. Doves and map of A.S.E.A.N. countries	50	70
545	$1 Doves and globe	1·25	3·00

162 Orchard Road

1987. Singapore Skyline. Multicoloured.

546	10c. Type **162**	15	10
547	50c. Central Business District	50	65
548	75c. Marina Centre and Raffles City	75	1·50

163 Flags of Members Nations and Logo

1987. 20th Anniv of Association of South-east Asian Nations.

549	**163** 10c. multicoloured	15	10
550	**163** 35c. multicoloured	35	40
551	**163** 50c. multicoloured	55	65
552	**163** 75c. multicoloured	65	90

164 Soldier with Rocket Launcher and Tank

1987. 20th Anniv of National Service. Multicoloured (except No. MS557).

553	10c. Type **164**	55	70
554	10c. Radar operator and patrol boat	55	70
555	10c. Fighter pilot and General Dynamics Fighting Falcon and Douglas A-4 Skyhawk aircraft	55	70
556	10c. Servicemen pledging allegiance	55	70
MS557	148×100 mm. 35c.×5. As Nos. 553/6 and Singapore lion symbol (red and black)	4·75	6·00

165 Singapore River and Dragon Boats

1987. River Conservation. Multicoloured.

558	10c. Type **165**	30	10
559	50c. Kallang Basin, canoe and fishing punt	80	1·25
560	$1 Kranji Reservoir, athletes and cyclist	2·75	4·25

166 Majapahit Gold Bracelet and Museum

1987. Centenary of National Museum. Each showing different drawings of Museum. Multicoloured.

561	10c. Type **166**	30	10
562	75c. Ming fluted kendi (water vessel)	1·25	1·75
563	$1 Patani hulu pekakak keris (sword)	1·40	3·00

167 Omni-theatre

1987. Tenth Anniv of Singapore Science Centre. Multicoloured.

564	10c. Type **167**	15	10
565	35c. Omni planetarium	1·50	1·25
566	75c. Model of body cell	1·50	2·75
567	$1 Physical sciences exhibits	1·50	3·25

168 Modern Anti-aircraft Gun

1988. Centenary of Singapore Artillery. Multicoloured.

568	10c. Type **168**	55	15
569	35c. 25-pounder field gun firing salute	1·40	1·25
570	50c. Gunner and 12-pounder gun, c. 1920	1·50	2·00
571	$1 Gunner and Maxim gun, 1889	2·25	4·50

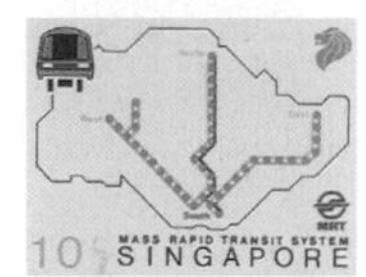

169 Route Map

1988. Singapore Mass Rapid Transit System. Multicoloured.

572	10c. Type **169**	1·25	15
573	50c. Train on elevated section	2·50	2·25
574	$1 Train in tunnel	4·00	5·00

170 Camera, Film and Outside Broadcast Van

1988. 25th Anniv of Television in Singapore. Multicoloured.

575	10c. Type **170**	40	10
576	35c. Camera, studio lights and microphone	80	75
577	75c. Television set and transmitter	1·00	1·50
578	$1 Globe on TV screen and dish aerial	1·50	2·25

171 Water Droplet and Blocks of Flats

1988. 25th Anniv of Public Utilities Board. Multicoloured.

579	10c. Type **171**	20	10
580	50c. Electric light bulb and city centre	1·10	1·00
581	$1 Gas flame and factories	2·00	2·50
MS582	116×75 mm. Nos. 579/81	4·75	6·50

172 Greeting Neighbours

1988. Tenth Anniv of National Courtesy Campaign. Each showing campaign mascot "Singa". Multicoloured.

583	10c. Type **172**	20	10
584	30c. Queueing at checkout	50	55
585	$1 Helping the elderly	1·50	2·75

173 Modern 30 Metre Turntable Fire Appliance

1988. Centenary of Fire Service. Multicoloured.

586	10c. Type **173**	1·00	25
587	$1 Steam fire engine, c. 1890	3·25	3·25

174 Container Ships and Warehouses

1989. 25th Anniv of Singapore Port Authority. Multicoloured.

588	10c. Type **174**	55	10
589	30c. Shipping and oil storage depot	1·00	50
590	75c. Container ships and Singapore skyline	1·50	1·50
591	$1 Container port at night	1·60	1·60

175 "Sago Street"

1989. Paintings of Chinatown by Choo Keng Kwang. Multicoloured.

592	10c. Type **175**	40	15
593	35c. "Pagoda Street"	1·25	1·00
594	75c. "Trengganu Street"	2·00	2·75
595	$1 "Temple Street"	2·25	3·25

176 North-west Singapore City, 1920

1989. Maps of Singapore. Multicoloured.

596	15c. Type **176** (top left)	1·50	1·75
597	15c. North-east Singapore (top right)	1·50	1·75
598	15c. South-west Singapore (bottom left)	1·50	1·75
599	15c. South-east Singapore (bottom right)	1·50	1·75
600	50c. Singapore Island and Dependencies, 1860s	2·25	2·00
601	$1 British Settlement of Singapore, 1820s	3·00	3·50

Nos. 596/9 were printed together, *se-tenant*, forming a composite design.

Individual stamps can be identifed by the position of the lion emblem which is quoted in brackets.

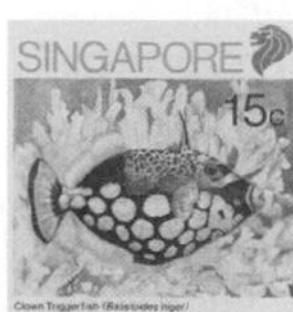

177 Clown Triggerfish

1989. Fish. Multicoloured.

602	15c. Type **177**	1·75	20
603	30c. Blue-girdled angelfish	2·75	1·50
604	75c. Emperor angelfish	4·25	5·00
605	$1 Regal angelfish	4·75	6·50

178 "Hari Raya Puasa" (Loke Yoke Yum)

1989. Festivals of Singapore Children's Drawings. Multicoloured.

606	15c. Type **178**	40	10
607	35c. "Chinese New Year" (Simon Koh)	70	65
608	75c. "Thaipusam" (Henry Setiono)	1·40	1·40
609	$1 "Christmas" (Wendy Ang Lin Min)	1·75	1·75
MS610	126×75 mm. Nos. 606/9	4·00	4·00

179 North Entrance of Stadium

1989. Opening of Singapore Indoor Stadium. Multicoloured.

611 30c. Type **179** 85 30
612 75c. Arena 1·75 1·50
613 $1 East entrance 2·00 1·75
MS614 104×104 mm. Nos. 611/13 4·50 4·50

180 "Singapore River, 1839" (Louis le Breton)

1990. Lithographs of 19th-century Singapore. Multicoloured.

615 15c. Type **180** 70 15
616 30c. "Chinatown, 1837" (Barthelemy Lauvergne) 1·25 70
617 75c. "Singapore Harbour, 1837" (Barthelemy Lauvergne) 2·25 2·25
618 $1 "View from the French Resident's House, 1824" (Deroy) 2·50 2·75

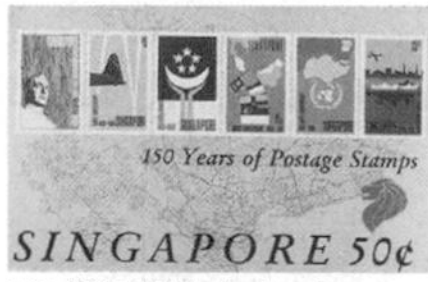

181 1969 150th Anniv of Singapore Stamp Issue

1990. 150th Anniv of the Penny Black. Multicoloured.

619 50c. Type **181** 1·00 60
620 75c. Indian stamps, including bisect, used from Singapore in 1859 1·25 1·50
621 $1 Indian stamps used from Singapore in 1854 1·90 1·90
622 $2 Penny Black and Two Pence Blue 3·00 5·00
MS623 134×90 mm. Nos. 619/22 8·50 7·50

No. **MS**623 also commemorates the "Stamp World London 90" international stamp exhibition.

182 Zoological Gardens

183 Chinese Opera Singer and Siong Lim Temple

1990. Tourism. Multicoloured

(a) As T **182**

624 5c. Type **182** 30 40
625 15c. Sentosa Island 30 10
626 20c. Singapore River 30 20
627 25c. Dragon Boat Festival 55 75
628 30c. Raffles Hotel 70 30
629 35c. Coffee shop bird singing contest 1·25 75
630 40c. Jurong Bird Park 2·00 1·00
631 50c. Chinese New Year boat float 1·25 45
632 75c. Peranakan Place 1·75 70

(b) As T **183**.

633 $1 Type **183** 4·50 1·25
634 $2 Malay dancer and Sultan Mosque 7·00 2·25
635 $5 Indian dancer and Sri Mariamman Temple 9·00 7·00
636 $10 Ballet dancer and Victoria Memorial Hall 13·00 11·00

184 Armed Forces Personnel

1990. 25th Anniv of Independence. Multicoloured.

637 15c. Type **184** 1·25 20
638 35c. Inhabitants of Singapore 1·75 1·00
639 75c. Workers and technological achievements 2·50 2·75
640 $1 Cultural activities 3·25 5·00

185 Stag's Horn Fern

1990. Ferns. Multicoloured.

641 15c. Type **185** 25 10
642 35c. Maiden hair fern 60 75
643 75c. Bird's nest fern 1·25 2·00
644 $1 Rabbit's foot fern 1·60 2·50

186 Carved Dragon Pillar, Hong San See Temple

1991. National Monuments. Multicoloured.

645 20c. Type **186** 50 80
646 20c. Hong San See Temple (40×25 mm) 50 80
647 50c. Interior of dome, Abdul Gaffoor Mosque 80 1·10
648 50c. Abdul Gaffoor Mosque (40×25 mm) 80 1·10
649 75c. Statue of Vishnu, Sri Perumal Hindu Temple 1·10 1·50
650 75c. Sri Perumal Temple (40×25 mm) 1·10 1·50
651 $1 Stained glass window, St. Andrew's Cathedral 1·25 1·75
652 $1 St. Andrew's Cathedral (40×25 mm) 1·25 1·75

187 "Vanda Miss Joaquim"

1991. "Singapore '95" International Stamp Exhibition. Orchids (1st issue). Mult.

653 $2 Type **187** 4·00 5·00
654 $2 "Dendrobium anocha" 4·00 5·00
MS655 123×80 mm. Nos. 653/4 11·00 12·00

See also Nos. 674/5, 725/6, 755/6, 795/6 and **MS**817.

188 Changi Airport Terminal II, 1991, and Boeing 747-400

1991. Singapore Civil Aviation. Multicoloured.

656 20c. Type **188** 1·25 25
657 75c. Changi Airport Terminal I, 1981, and Boeing 747-200 2·50 2·00
658 $1 Paya Lebar Airport, 1955–1981, and Concorde 2·50 2·25
659 $2 Kallang Airport, 1937–1955, and Douglas DC-2 3·75 6·00

189 "Arachnopsis Eric Holttum"

1991. Orchid Dress Motifs. Multicoloured.

660 20c. Type **189** 1·00 25
661 30c. "Cattleya meadii" 1·25 1·50
662 $1 "Calanthe vestita" 3·00 5·00

190 Long-tailed Tailor Bird ("Common Tailorbird")

1991. Garden Birds. Multicoloured.

663 20c. Type **190** 45 25
664 35c. Scarlet-backed flower-pecker 1·50 1·50
665 75c. Black-naped oriole 2·25 3·25
666 $1 Common iora 2·50 3·75

191 Productivity Discussion

1991. Tenth Anniv of Productivity Movement. Multicoloured.

667 20c. Type **191** 40 30
668 $1 Construction workers 1·10 2·50

192 Railway Creeper

1992. "Phila Nippon '91" International Stamp Exhibition, Tokyo. Wild Flowers. Multicoloured.

669 30c. Type **192** 75 25
670 75c. Asystasia 1·25 1·25
671 $1 Singapore rhododendron 1·50 2·00
672 $2 Coat buttons 2·50 5·25
MS673 132×90 mm. Nos. 669/72 7·50 8·50

1992. "Singapore '95" International Stamp Exn. Orchids (2nd issue). As T **187**. Multicoloured.

674 $2 "Dendrobium Sharifah Fatimah" 2·75 4·25
675 $2 "Phalaenopsis Shim Beauty" 2·75 4·25
MS676 123×80 mm. Nos. 674/5 11·00 12·00

193 "Singapore Waterfront" (Georgette Chen Liying)

1992. Local Artists (1st series). Multicoloured.

677 20c. Type **193** 40 20
678 75c. "Kampung Hut" (Lim Cheng Hoe) 85 1·25
679 $1 "The Bridge" (Poh Siew Wah) 1·10 1·40
680 $2 "Singapore River" (Lee Boon Wang) 2·25 4·50

See also Nos. 818/21.

194 Football

1992. Olympic Games, Barcelona. Multicoloured.

681 20c. Type **194** 25 20
682 35c. Athletics 35 30
683 50c. Swimming 55 65
684 75c. Basketball 1·25 1·25
685 $1 Tennis 1·50 1·50
686 $2 Sailing 2·00 2·75
MS687 132×90 mm. Nos. 681/6 9·50 11·00

195 Chinese Family and Samfu Pattern

1992. Singapore Costumes of 1910. Multicoloured.

688 20c. Type **195** 50 20
689 35c. Malay family and sarong pattern 65 45
690 75c. Indian family and sari pattern 1·25 1·25
691 $2 Straits Chinese family and belt pattern 2·25 3·50

196 Infantryman, Air Force Pilot and Navy Gunner

1992. 25th Anniv of National Service. Multicoloured.

692 20c. Type **196** 1·00 30
693 35c. Navy diver, General Dynamics F-16 Fighting Falcon and FH-88 155 mm howitzer 1·50 1·00
694 $1 General Dynamics F-16 Fighting Falcon in flight, corvette and AMX-13SM1 tank 4·00 5·50

197 Crafts from A.S.E.A.N. Countries

1992. 25th Anniv of A.S.E.A.N. (Association of South-East Asian Nations). Multicoloured.

695 20c. Type **197** 50 20
696 35c. National dances 1·25 1·00
697 $1 National landmarks 2·25 3·75

198 Mosaic Crab

1992. Crabs. Multicoloured.

698 20c. Type **198** 55 25
699 50c. Johnson's freshwater crab 1·00 1·25
700 75c. Singapore freshwater crab 1·50 2·25
701 $1 Swamp forest crab 1·75 3·00

199 Coins

1992. 25th Anniv of Singapore Currency. Multicoloured.

702 20c. Type **199** 1·25 1·75
703 75c. Currency note from "orchid" series 2·75 2·75
704 $1 Currency note from "ship" series 2·25 3·00
705 $2 Currency note from "bird" series 3·00 3·75

Nos. 702/5 were printed together, *se-tenant*, forming a composite design.

200 Sun Bear

1993. South-East Asian Mammals. Multicoloured.

706 20c. Type **200** 30 20
707 30c. Orang-utan 60 65
708 75c. Slow loris 1·10 1·40
709 $2 Greater Malay chevrotain ("Large Mouse Deer") 2·25 3·75

201 "Thank You"

1993. Greetings Stamps. Multicoloured.

710 20c. Type **201** 60 90
711 20c. "Congratulations" 60 90
712 20c. "Best Wishes" 60 90
713 20c. "Happy Birthday" 60 90
714 20c. "Get Well Soon" 60 90

202 Shophouses

1993. Conservation of Tanjong Pagar District. Multicoloured.

715	20c. Type **202**	50	20
716	30c. Jinrikisha Station	2·50	70
717	$2 View of Tanjong Pagar	3·75	4·00

203 "Cranes" (painting) (Chen Wen Hsi)

1993. "Indopex '93" International Stamp Exhibition, Surabaya.

718	**203**	$2 multicoloured	2·25	3·50

204 Football

1993. 17th South-East Asian Games, Singapore. Multicoloured.

719	20c. Type **204**	30	20
720	35c. Basketball	70	60
721	50c. Badminton	90	1·25
722	75c. Athletics	1·00	1·50
723	$1 Water polo	1·40	2·00
724	$2 Yachting	2·25	4·00

1993. "Singapore '95" International Stamp Exhibition. Orchids (3rd issue). As T **187** but 25×35 mm. Multicoloured.

725	$2 "Phalaenopsis amabilis"	3·00	4·00
726	$2 "Vanda sumatrana"	3·00	4·00
MS727	123×80 mm. Nos. 725/6	7·50	8·00

No. **MS**727 also commemorates "Taipei '93" Asian International Stamp Exhibition, Taiwan.

205 "Danaus chrysippus"

1993. Butterflies. Multicoloured.

728	20c. Type **205**	30	30
729	50c. "Cethosia hypsea"	65	65
730	75c. "Amathusia phidippus"	90	1·50
731	$1 "Papilio demolion"	1·25	2·00

206 Papaya

1993. "Bangkok '93" International Stamp Exhibition. Local Fruit. Multicoloured.

732	20c. Type **206**	40	20
733	35c. Pomegranate	60	50
734	75c. Starfruit	1·25	1·50
735	$2 Durian	2·25	4·00
MS736	120×89 mm. Nos. 732/5	4·00	5·50

207 Egrets drinking

1993. Endangered Species. Swinhoe's Egret ("Chinese Egret"). Multicoloured.

737	20c. Type **207**	50	1·10
738	25c. Egrets eating	55	1·10
739	30c. Egrets searching for fish	65	1·10
740	35c. Egrets in flight	70	1·10

Nos. 737/40 were printed together, *se-tenant*, with the background forming a composite design.

208 Palm Tree

1993. Self-adhesive. Imperf.

741	**208**	(20c.) multicoloured	30	50

No. 741 was only valid for use on mail to local addresses and was initially sold at 20c.

209 Tiger Cowrie

1994. Reef Life (1st series). Multicoloured.

742	5c. Type **209**	30	30
743	20c. Sea-fan	60	75
744	25c. Tunicate	65	25
745	30c. Clown anemonefish	70	50
746	35c. Ruppell's nudibranch	75	75
747	40c. Sea-urchin	1·00	1·50
748	50c. Soft coral	1·00	50
749	75c. Pin cushion star	1·50	70
750	$1 Knob coral (31×27 mm)	4·50	1·75
751	$2 Mushroom coral (31×27 mm)	7·00	3·50
752	$5 Bubble coral (31×27 mm)	10·00	7·50
753	$10 Octopus coral (31×27 mm)	15·00	12·00

See also No. 784.

1994. "Singapore '95" International Stamp Exhibition. Orchids (4th issue). As T **187** but each 25×35 mm. Multicoloured.

755	$2 "Paphiopedilum victori-aregina"	4·00	4·50
756	$2 "Dendrobium smillieae"	4·00	4·50
MS757	123×80 mm. Nos. 755/6	7·50	8·00

No. **MS**757 also commemorates "Hong Kong'94" International Stamp Exhibition.

210 Dancers

1994. Singapore Festival of Arts. Multicoloured.

758	20c. Type **210**	45	20
759	30c. Actors and puppet	65	55
760	50c. Musicians	1·00	1·00
761	$1 Artists	1·75	3·00

211 Civilian taking Pledge, National Day Parade and Soldier with Anti-tank Missile

1994. 25th Anniv of Operationally-ready National Servicemen. Multicoloured.

762	20c. Type **211**	90	30
763	30c. Serviceman on beach with family and on jungle patrol	1·10	1·25
764	35c. Serviceman relaxing at home and with machine gun	1·25	1·25
765	75c. National Service officer at work and commanding patrol	2·00	3·00

212 Black-crowned Night Heron

1994. Care for Nature. Herons. Multicoloured.

766	20c. Type **212**	50	60
767	50c. Green-heron ("Little Heron")	70	85
768	75c. Purple heron	85	1·00
769	$1 Grey heron	95	1·25

Nos. 766/9 were printed together, se-tenant, forming a composite design.

213 Traditional and Modern Education

1994. 175th Anniv of Modern Singapore. Multicoloured.

770	20c. Type **213**	25	25
771	50c. Rickshaws and Mass Rapid Transit train	70	75
772	75c. Sampans and modern container port	1·00	1·40
773	$1 Victorian buildings and modern skyline	1·25	2·00
MS774	135×95 mm. Nos. 770/3	3·50	4·00

214 Balloons

1994. Self-adhesive Greetings Stamps. Multicoloured.

775	(20c.) Type **214**	55	80
776	(20c.) Fireworks	55	80
777	(20c.) Gift-wrapped parcel	55	80
778	(20c.) Bouquet of flowers	55	80
779	(20c.) Birthday cake	55	80

215 Logo and Globe

1994. 50th Anniv of I.C.A.O. Multicoloured.

780	20c. Type **215**	20	20
781	35c. Boeing 747 and Changi Airport control tower	60	60
782	75c. Projected hypersonic aircraft over airport	85	1·25
783	$2 Control tower, satellite and Boeing 747	2·00	3·25

1994. Reef Life (2nd series). Multicoloured design as T **209**, but inscr "FOR LOCAL ADDRESSES ONLY".

784	(20c.) Blue-spotted stingray	35	30

No. 784 exists with either ordinary or self-adhesive gum.

216 Singapore International Convention and Exhibition Centre, Suntec City

1995. Opening of Singapore International Convention and Exhibition Centre. Multicoloured.

786	(20c.) Type **216**	20	20
787	75c. Suntec City skyline	85	85
788	$1 Temasek Boulevard	1·10	1·40
789	$2 Fountain Terrace	1·75	2·75

No. 786 is inscr "FOR LOCAL ADDRESSES ONLY".

217 "Love, LOVE, Love"

1995. Self-adhesive Greetings Stamps.

790	**217**	(20c.) multicoloured	90	1·00
791	-	(20c.) red and black	90	1·00
792	-	(20c.) multicoloured	90	1·00
793	-	(20c.) multicoloured	90	1·00
794	-	(20c.) multicoloured	90	1·00

DESIGNS: No. 791, "LOVE" forming spiral around heart; No. 792, "LOVE, LOVE"; No. 793, "Love" in four different languages; No. 794, Geometric symbols.

1995. "Singapore '95" International Stamp Exhibition. Orchids (5th issue). As T **187**. Multicoloured.

795	$2 Vanda "Marlie Dolera"	2·00	3·00
796	$2 "Vanda limbata"	2·00	3·00
MS797	123×80 mm. Nos. 795/6 with sheet margins showing animals from Singapore Zoo	10·00	10·00

See also No. **MS**817.

218 Ribbons and "My Singapore, My Country, Happy Birthday"

1995. 30th Anniv of Independence. Multicoloured.

798	(22c.) Type **218**	20	20
799	50c. Chinese inscr and 1985 Housing and Development 50c. stamp (horiz)	65	80
800	75c. National anthem, Civil Aviation 20c. and inscr in Malay (horiz)	90	1·50
801	$1 National flag, 1986 Economic Development Board and inscr in Tamil	1·25	2·25
MS802	120×78 mm. Nos. 798/801	5·50	6·50

No. 798 is inscribed "For Local Addresses Only".

219 Rejoicing Crowd and 1945 B.M.A. $5 Stamp

1995. 50th Anniv of End of Second World War. Multicoloured.

803	(22c.) Type **219**	30	20
804	60c. Lord Mountbatten accepting Japanese surrender at Singapore and 1945 B.M.A. 15c. stamp	1·50	1·00
805	70c. Emergency food kitchen (horiz)	80	1·25
806	$2 Police road block during State of Emergency (horiz)	3·00	4·00

No. 803 is inscribed "For Local Addresses Only".

220 Yellow-faced Angelfish

1995. Marine Fish. Multicoloured.

807	(22c.) Type **220**	35	25
808	60c. Harlequin sweetlips	80	1·00
809	70c. Lionfish	90	1·50
810	$1 Pennant coralfish ("Longfin bannerfish")	1·25	2·25

No. 807 is inscribed "For Local Addresses Only".

221 Envelope, Stamps and Museum

1995. Opening of Singapore Philatelic Museum. Each showing Museum. Multicoloured.

811	(22c.) Type **221**	50	25
812	50c. Stamps and stamp booklet	1·10	65
813	60c. Stamps and philatelic equipment	1·25	1·25
814	$2 Museum displays	3·25	5·50

No. 811 is inscribed "FOR LOCAL ADDRESSES ONLY".

222 Two, Four and Six Digit Post Codes

1995. Introduction of Six Digit Postal Codes. Multicoloured.

815	(22c.) Type **222**	30	25
816	$2 Six empty post code boxes	2·25	3·50

No. 815 is inscribed "For local addresses only".

1995. "Singapore '95" International Stamp Exhibition. Orchids (6th issue). Sheet 123×80 mm, containing Nos. 795/6 with sheet margins showing Sentosa Gardens.

MS817	$2×2 multicoloured	8·00	9·00

223 "Tropical Fruits" (Georgette Chen Liying)

1995. Local Artists (2nd series). Multicoloured.

818	(22c.) Type **223**	30	25
819	30c. "Bali Beach" (Cheong Soo Pieng)	40	40

820 70c. "Gibbons" (Chen Wen Hsi) 80 1·25
821 $2 "Shi (Lion)" (Pan Shou) (22½×38½ mm) 2·25 3·75

No. 818 is inscribed "FOR LOCAL ADDRESSES ONLY".

224 Bukit Pasoh, Chinatown

1996. Architectural Conservation. Multicoloured.
822 (22c.) Type **224** 35 25
823 35c. Jalan Sultan, Kampong Glam 50 50
824 70c. Dalhousie Lane, Little India 80 1·25
825 $1 Supreme Court, Civic District 1·10 2·25

No. 822 is inscribed "FOR LOCAL ADDRESSES ONLY".

225 Pair of Rats

1996. Chinese New Year ("Year of the Rat"). Multicoloured.
826 (22c.) Type **225** 30 25
827 $2 Rat holding orange 2·25 3·50

No. 826 is inscribed "FOR LOCAL ADDRESSES ONLY".
See also Nos. **MS**832/3 and **MS**838.

226 The Straits of Singapore, 1794 (Thomas Jefferys)

1996. Old Maps. Multicoloured.
828 (22c.) Type **226** 45 25
829 60c. Singapore (19th-century) 75 75
830 $1 Singapore by James Duncan, 1835 1·25 1·50
831 $2 Singapore by J. B. Tassin, 1839 2·00 3·25

No. 828 is inscribed "FOR LOCAL ADDRESSES ONLY".

1996. "Indonesia 96" International Youth Stamp Exhibition, Bandung. Sheet 123×80 mm.
MS832 22c. As Type **225**; $2 No. 827 14·00 16·00

1996. "CHINA '96" 9th Asian International Stamp Exhibition, Peking. Sheet 123×80 mm.
MS833 22c. As Type **225**; $2 No. 827 14·00 16·00

227 17th-century Chinese Calligraphy by Zhang Ruitu and Museum Building

1996. Inauguration of Asian Civilizations Museum. Each including museum building. Multicoloured.
834 (22c.) Type **227** 35 25
835 60c. Javanese divination manuscript, 1842 70 70
836 70c. 19th-century temple hanging, South India 80 1·00
837 $2 17th to 19th-century calligraphic implements, Iran and Turkey 2·00 3·50

No. 834 is inscribed "FOR LOCAL ADDRESSES ONLY".

1996. "CAPEX '96" International Stamp Exhibition, Toronto. Sheet 123×80 mm.
MS838 22c. As Type **225**; $2 No. 827 15·00 16·00

228 "Children in Library" (Ivan Chang)

1996. Self-adhesive Greetings Stamps. "Courtesy". Children's Drawings. Multicoloured.
839 (22c.) Type **228** 30 30
840 35c. "Children crossing Road" (Cheong Kah Yin) 50 60
841 50c. "Waiting for Bus" (Jeannie Fong) 65 80
842 60c. "In the Rain" (Liew Cai Yun) 75 95
843 $1 "On the Train" (Yong Wan Quan) 1·25 1·60
MS844 200×130 mm. 22c. As Type **228** and Nos. 840/3 4·75 5·50

No. 839 is inscribed "For Local Addresses Only".

229 Wind Surfing and Dinghy Sailing

1996. Olympic Games, Atlanta. Multicoloured.
845 (22c.) Type **229** 35 25
846 60c. Tennis and football 90 80
847 70c. Pole vaulting and hurdling 90 1·10
848 $2 Diving and swimming 2·25 4·00
MS849 120×70 mm. 22c. As Type **229** and Nos. 846/8 4·00 5·50

No. 845 is inscribed "For Local Addresses Only".

230 "Cinnamomum iners"

1996. Singapore Trees. Multicoloured.
850 (22c.) Type **230** 30 25
851 60c. "Hibiscus tiliaceus" 70 90
852 70c. "Parkia speciosa" 80 1·25
853 $1 "Terminalia catappa" 1·25 1·75

No. 850 is inscribed "FOR LOCAL ADDRESSES ONLY".

231 Panmen Gate, Suzhou, China

1996. Singapore–China Joint Issue. Multicoloured.
854 (22c.) Type **231** 30 25
855 60c. Singapore waterfront 80 1·25
MS856 120×78 mm. 22c. As Type **231** and No. 855 1·40 2·00

No. 854 is inscribed "FOR LOCAL ADDRESSES ONLY".

232 Conference Logo

1996. Inaugural Ministerial Conference of World Trade Organization.
857 **232** (22c.) multicoloured 30 30
858 **232** 60c. multicoloured 70 1·25
859 **232** $1 multicoloured 1·25 1·90
860 **232** $2 multicoloured 2·25 3·75

No. 857 is inscribed "For local addresses Only".

233 Ox

1997. Chinese New Year ("Year of the Ox").
861 **233** (22c.) multicoloured 15 20
862 - $2 multicoloured 1·75 2·50

DESIGN: $2 Stylized ox.
No. 861 is inscribed "FOR LOCAL ADDRESSES ONLY".

1997. "HONG KONG '97" International Stamp Exhibition. Chinese New Year ("Year of the Ox"). sheet 123×80 mm.
MS863 22c. As Type **233**; $2 No. 862 6·00 7·00

234 Shuttlecock

1997. "SINGPEX '97" International Stamp Exhibition. Traditional Games. Multicoloured.
864 (22c.) Type **234** 20 20
865 35c. Marbles 40 40
866 60c. Tops 55 75
867 $1 Fivestones 80 1·50
MS868 140×75 mm. 22c. As Type **234** and Nos. 865/7 1·75 2·50

No. 864 is inscribed "For Local Addresses Only".

235 Bullock Cart **236** Taxi

1997. Transportation. Multicoloured. Ordinary or self-adhesive gum (No. 871), ordinary gum (others)

(a) As T **235**
869 5c. Type **235** 30 50
870 20c. Bicycle (vert) 1·00 1·00
871 (22c.) Jinrickshaw (vert) 40 20
872 30c. Electric tram 1·00 30
873 35c. Trolley bus 1·25 30
874 40c. Trishaw (vert) 70 50
875 50c. Vintage car (vert) 1·00 45
876 60c. Horse-drawn carriage 1·50 50
877 70c. Fire engine 2·25 60
MS878 132×76 mm. 22c. As No. 871 and Nos. 869/70, 872/7 8·00 8·00

(b) As T **236**.
879 $1 Type **236** 1·50 80
880 $2 Bus (43×24 mm) 3·50 1·60
881 $5 Mass Rapid Transit train 6·00 4·50
882 $10 Light Rapid Transit carriages (43×24 mm) 9·00 9·50
MS883 119×71 mm. Nos. 879/82 17·00 20·00

No. 871 is inscribed "For Local Addresses Only".

237 Man's Head

1997. Self-adhesive Greeting Stamps. "Friends". Multicoloured.
885 (22c.) Type **237** 45 60
886 (22c.) Hands holding umbrella 45 60
887 (22c.) Two emperor penguins 45 60
888 (22c.) Two butterflies 45 60
889 (22c.) Cup and saucer 45 60
890 (22c.) Large flower 45 60
891 (22c.) Candle 45 60
892 (22c.) Tree 45 60
893 (22c.) Jar with stars 45 60
894 (22c.) Simple telephone 45 60

Nos. 885/94 are inscribed "FOR LOCAL ADDRESSES ONLY".

1997. "Pacific '97" International Stamp Exhibition, San Francisco. sheet 123×80 mm, containing designs as Nos. 861/2.
MS895 22c. As Type **233**; $2 No. 862 8·00 9·00

238 Family with Car

1997. Renovation of Housing and Development Board Estates. Multicoloured.
896 (22c.) Type **238** 25 20
897 30c. Family at playground 35 35
898 70c. Couple walking through garden 70 80
899 $1 Family on balcony 95 1·50

No. 896 is inscribed "FOR LOCAL ADDRESSES ONLY".

239 Globe and Hand Clasp

1997. 30th Anniv of A.S.E.A.N. (Association of Southeast Asian Nations). Multicoloured.
900 (22c.) Type **239** 25 20
901 35c. Dancers, kite flying and decorated truck 40 40
902 60c. Dish aerial and map 65 70
903 $1 National landmarks 95 2·00

No. 900 is inscribed "FOR LOCAL ADDRESSES ONLY".

240 Flower and Tree ("Clean Environment")

1997. 25th Anniv of the Ministry of the Environment. Multicoloured.
904 (22c.) Type **240** 20 20
905 60c. Fish and river ("Clean Waters") 65 60
906 70c. Bird and sky ("Clean Air") 70 70
907 $1 Dustbin and block of flats ("Clean Homes") 95 1·25

No. 904 is inscribed "FOR LOCAL ADDRESSES ONLY".

241 "Drupa morum"

1997. Singapore—Thailand Joint Issue. Sea Shells. Multicoloured.
908 (22c.) Type **241** 25 20
909 35c. "Nerita chamaeleon" 35 40
910 60c. "Littoraria melanostoma" 55 60
911 $1 "Cryptospira elegans" 90 2·00
MS912 125×80 mm. 22c. As Type **241** and Nos. 909/11 2·00 2·50

No. 908 is inscribed "FOR LOCAL ADDRESSES ONLY".

1997. "Shanghai '97" International Stamp and Coin Exhibition. Sheet 123×80 mm.
MS913 22c. As Type **233**; $2 No. 862 4·25 5·50

242 Tiger

1998. Chinese New Year ("Year of the Tiger").
914 **242** (22c.) multicoloured 30 20
915 - $2 multicoloured 1·75 2·00

DESIGN: $2 Stylized tigers.
No. 914 is inscribed "FOR LOCAL ADDRESSES ONLY".

243 Pentaceratops

1998. Dinosaurs. Multicoloured. Self-adhesive. Imperf.
916 (22c.) Type **243** 35 45
917 (22c.) Apatosaurus 35 45
918 (22c.) Albertosaurus 35 45

Nos. 916/18 are inscribed "For Local Addresses Only".

244 Lesser Green Leafbird

1998. Songbirds. Multicoloured.
919 (22c.) Type **244** 45 20
920 60c. Magpie robin 80 65
921 70c. Straw-crowned bulbul ("Straw-headed bulbul") 90 80
922 $2 Yellow-bellied prinia 1·75 2·25

No. 919 is inscribed "For Local Addresses Only".

1998. "Israel 98" International Stamp Exhibition. Sheet 122×80 mm.
MS923 22c. As Type **242**; $2 No. 915 2·75 3·25

245 "Hello" in Yellow and Orange Bubble

1998. Self-adhesive Greetings Stamps. Multicoloured.
924 (22c.) Type **245** 50 65
925 (22c.) "hello" in red and yellow bubble 50 65
926 (22c.) "hello" in yellow and green bubble 50 65
927 (22c.) "Hello" in violet and blue bubble 50 65
928 (22c.) "Hello" in black, red and yellow bubble 50 65
Nos. 924/8 are inscribed "FOR LOCAL ADDRESSES ONLY".

246 Rhino Beetle

1998. 25th Anniv of Singapore Zoological Gardens and Launch of New "Fragile Forest" Display. Multicoloured. Self-adhesive.
929 (22c.) Type **246** 50 65
930 (22c.) Surinam horned frog 50 65
931 (22c.) Green iguana 50 65
932 (22c.) Atlas moth 50 65
933 (22c.) Giant scorpion 50 65
934 (22c.) Hissing cockroach 50 65
935 (22c.) Two-toed sloth 50 65
936 (22c.) Cobalt blue tarantula 50 65
937 (22c.) Archer fish 50 65
938 (22c.) Greater mousedeer 50 65
Nos. 929/38 are inscribed "FOR LOCAL ADDRESSES ONLY".

247 Students and Workers Demonstrating, 1955–59

1998. "The Singapore Story" Exhibition. Multicoloured.
939 (22c.) Type **247** 25 20
940 60c. Self-government, 1959–63 55 55
941 $1 Creation of Malaysian Federation, 1961–65 80 90
942 $2 Celebrating Independence, 1965 1·60 2·25
MS943 214×105 mm. 22c. As Type **247** and Nos. 940/2 (sold at $7) 9·00 10·00
No. **MS**943, which also commemorates "SINGPEX '98" National Stamp Exhibition, was only available in a special folder.
No. 939 is inscribed "FOR LOCAL ADDRESSES ONLY".

248 "Phalaenopsis rosenstromii"

1998. Singapore–Australia Joint Issue. Orchids. Multicoloured.
944 (22c.) Type **248** 35 20
945 70c. "Arundina graminifolia" 80 65
946 $1 "Grammatophyllum speciosum" 85 90
947 $2 "Dendrobium phalaenopsis" 1·60 2·25
MS948 134×73 mm. 22c. As Type **248** and Nos. 945/7 3·75 4·50
No. 944 is inscribed "For Local Addresses Only".

249 "Canna" Hybrid

1998. Flowers of Singapore. Multicoloured.
949 (22c.) Type **249** 35 45
950 (22c.) "Caesalpinia pulcherrima" 35 45
951 (22c.) "Wedilia trilobata" 35 45
952 (22c.) "Dillenia suffruticosa" 35 45
953 35c. "Zephyranthes rosea" 50 70
954 35c. "Cassia alata" 50 70
955 60c. "Heliconia rostrata" 65 80
956 60c. "Allamanda cathartica" 65 80
MS957 206×82 mm. Nos. 949/56 2·25 2·75
Nos. 949/52 are inscribed "FOR LOCAL ADDRESSES ONLY".

250 Hari Raya Aidilfitri (Muslim)

1998. Festivals. Multicoloured.
958 (22c.) Type **250** 35 45
959 (22c.) Christmas 35 45
960 (22c.) Chinese New Year 35 45
961 (22c.) Deepavali (Hindu) 35 45
962 30c. Boy and decorations (Hari Raya Aidilfitri) (20×39 mm) 45 60
963 30c. Girl with holly (Christmas) (20×39 mm) 45 60
964 30c. Boy with lanterns (Chinese New Year) (20×39 mm) 45 60
965 30c. Girl with oil lamps (Deepavali) (20×39 mm) 45 60
Nos. 958/61 are inscribed "For Local Addresses Only" and come with either ordinary or self-adhesive gum.
Nos. 958/61 were printed together, se-tenant, forming a composite design.

1998. "Italia 98" International Stamp Exhibition, Milan. Sheet 123×80 mm.
MS970 22c. As Type **242**; $2 No. 915 2·50 3·50

251 Parliament House, 1827

1998. Historical Buildings. Multicoloured.
971 (22c.) Type **251** 35 20
972 70c. Chapel of former Convent of the Holy Infant Jesus, 1903 80 65
973 $1 Hill Street Building, 1934 95 95
974 $2 Sun Yat Sen Nanyang Memorial Hall, 1900 1·75 2·25
No. 971 is inscribed "For Local Addresses Only".

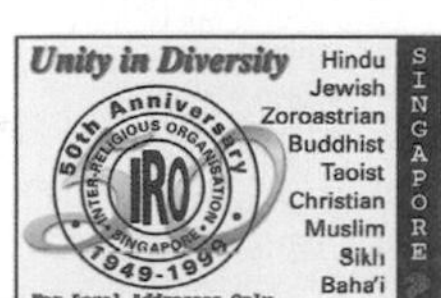

252 Anniversary Logo and List of Religions

1999. 50th Anniv of Inter-Religious Organization.
975 **252** (22c.) multicoloured 35 20
976 **252** 60c. multicoloured 65 65
977 **252** $1 multicoloured 95 1·40
No. 975 is inscribed "For Local Addresses Only".

253 Rabbit

1999. Chinese New Year ("Year of the Rabbit").
978 **253** (22c.) multicoloured 35 20
979 - $2 multicoloured 1·75 2·00
DESIGN: $2 Stylized rabbits.
No. 978 is inscribed "FOR LOCAL ADDRESSES ONLY".

254 Clipper, Tank Locomotive and Tongkang Junk

1999. Maritime Heritage. Multicoloured.
980 (22c.) Type **254** 40 20
981 70c. Twakow (barge) and Sampan Kotek (vert) 85 65
982 $1 Fujian junk (vert) 1·25 1·10
983 $2 Maduran golekkan (sailing vessel) 1·75 2·25
MS984 200×67 mm. 22c. As Type **254** and Nos. 981/3 3·50 4·00
No. **MS**984 also includes the "Australia '99" World Stamp Exhibition, Melbourne, emblem on the sheet margin.
No. 980 is inscribed "For Local Addresses Only".

1999. "iBRA '99" International Stamp Exhibtion, nuremberg. Sheet 123×80 mm.
MS985 22c. As Type **253**; $2 No. 979 2·00 2·75

255 Washing Lines ("Think of others")

1999. Self-adhesive Greeting Stamps. "Try a Little Kindness". Multicoloured.
986 (22c.) Type **255** 35 55
987 (22c.) Man throwing litter ("Do not litter") 35 55
988 (22c.) Girl feeding cat and dog ("Be kind to animals") 35 55
989 (22c.) Man watching television ("Be considerate") 35 55
990 (22c.) Boy putting money in collection tin ("Be generous") 35 55
Nos. 986/90 are inscribed "FOR LOCAL ADDRESSES ONLY".

256 Hong Kong Harbour

1999. Singapore–Hong Kong, China Joint Issue. Multicoloured.
991 (22c.) Type **256** 25 20
992 35c. Singapore skyline 45 40
993 50c. Giant Buddha, Lantau Island, Hong Kong 60 55
994 60c. Merlion statue, Sentosa Island, Singapore 70 75
995 70c. Street scene, Hong Kong 75 80
996 $1 Bugis Junction, Singapore 1·00 1·10
MS997 125×93 mm. 22c. As Type **256** and Nos. 992/6 3·25 4·00
No. 991 is inscribed "FOR LOCAL ADDRESSES ONLY".

1999. "PhilexFrance '99" International Stamp Exhibtion, Paris. Sheet 123×80 mm.
MS998 22c. As Type **253**; $2 No. 979 2·00 2·50

257 Peacock Butterfly

1999. Singapore–Sweden Joint Issue. Butterflies. Multicoloured.
999 (22c.) Type **257** 55 20
1000 70c. Blue pansy 1·00 65
1001 $1 Great egg-fly 1·25 95
1002 $2 Red admiral 2·00 2·50
MS1003 129×75 mm. 22c. As Type **257** and Nos. 1000/2 4·25 4·50
No. 999 is inscribed "FOR LOCAL ADDRESSES ONLY".

1999. "China '99" International Stamp Exhibition, Peking. sheet 123×80 mm.
MS1004 22c. As Type **253**; $2 As No. 979 2·25 2·75

258 Pres. Yusof bin Ishak

1999. Yusof bin Ishak (first President of Singapore) Commemoration.
1005 **258** $2 multicoloured 2·50 2·00

259 Green Turtle

1999. Amphibians and Reptiles. Multicoloured.
1006 (22c.) Type **259** 35 20
1007 60c. Green crested lizard 70 60
1008 70c. Copper-cheeked frog 80 70
1009 $1 Water monitor 1·00 1·25
No. 1006 is inscribed "For Local Addresses Only".

260 New Parliament House from North

1999. Opening of New Parliament House. Multicoloured.
1010 (22c.) Type **260** 30 20
1011 60c. North-east view 60 60
1012 $1 South-east view 90 1·00
1013 $2 West view 1·60 2·25
No. 1010 is inscribed "For Local Addresses Only".
The lion's head emblem on these stamps is printed in optically variable ink which changes colour when viewed from different angles.

261 Sir Stamford Raffles and Sir Frank Swettenham (British Governers) and Raffles Museum

1999. New Millennium (1st issue). 20th Century Singapore. Multicoloured.
1014 (22c.) Type **261** 35 35
1015 (22c.) Past and present schooling 35 35
1016 35c. Street scene, 1900, and Samsui woman 45 55
1017 35c. Parliament (Government) 45 55
1018 60c. British surrender, 1942, and Lord Mountbatten celebrating Japanese surrender, 1945 1·25 1·23
1019 60c. Soldiers firing missile and fighter aircraft 1·25 1·25
1020 70c. Singapore River, 1902, and modern forms of transportation 1·25 1·40
1021 70c. Festival scenes 1·25 1·40
1022 $1 Housing, past and present 1·25 1·50
1023 $1 Skyscrapers 1·25 1·50
Nos. 1014/15 are inscribed "for Local addresses only".
See also Nos. 1027/30.

262 Dragon

2000. Chinese New Year ("Year of the Dragon"). Multicoloured.
1024 (22c.) Type **262** 25 20
1025 $2 Dragon curled around spheres 1·75 2·25
MS1026 105×65 mm. $10 As No. 1025 9·00 12·00
No. 1024 is inscribed "FOR LOCAL ADDRESSES ONLY".
No. **MS**1026 was only sold in a decorative hongbao (envelope).

263 Information Technology Equipment

2000. New Millennium (2nd issue). Singapore in 2000. Multicoloured.
1027 (22c.) Type **263** 20 20
1028 60c. Symbols of Arts and Culture 60 60
1029 $1 Heritage artifacts 95 1·10
1030 $2 Modern global communications 1·60 2·25
MS1031 140×75 mm. 22c. As Type **263** and Nos. 1028/30 2·75 3·75
No. 1027 is inscribed "For local addresses only".

264 Post Office from across Singapore River, 1854

2000. Opening of Singapore Post Centre. Postal Landmarks. Multicoloured.

1032	(22c.) Type **264**	25	20
1033	60c. General Post Office, c. 1873	60	60
1034	$1 G.P.O. Fullerton Building, 1928	95	1·00
1035	$2 Singapore Post Centre, 2000	1·90	2·25
MS1036	110×94 mm. 22c. As Type **264** and Nos. 1033/5	3·00	3·75

No. 1032 is inscribed "FOR LOCAL ADDRESSES ONLY".

2000. "Bangkok 2000" International Stamp Exhibition. Sheet 123×75 mm. Multicoloured.

MS1037	22c. As Type **262**; $2 No. 1025	1·75	2·25

265 "yipee"

2000. Self-adhesive Greetings Stamps. Multicoloured.

1038	(22c.) Type **265**	45	60
1039	(22c.) "yeah"	45	60
1040	(22c.) "hurray"	45	60
1041	(22c.) "yes"	45	60
1042	(22c.) "happy"	45	60

Nos. 1038/42 are inscribed "For Local Addresses Only".

2000. "The Stamp Show 2000" International Stamp Exhibition, London. Sheet, 123×75 mm, containing Nos. 1024/5. Multicoloured.

MS1043	22c. As Type **262**; $2 No. 1025	1·90	2·40

2000. "naba 2000" National Stamp Exhibition, St. Gallen, Switzerland. Sheet, 123×75 mm, containing Nos. 1024/5. Multicoloured.

MS1044	22c. As Type **262**; $2 No. 1025	1·90	2·40

266 Singapore River, 1920s

2000. "A Century on Singapore River". Showing scenes and common map section. Multicoloured.

1045	(22c.) Type **266**	35	40
1046	(22c.) South Boat Quay, 1930s	35	40
1047	(22c.) Social gathering, 1950s	35	40
1048	(22c.) Skyscrapers, 1980s	35	40
1049	(22c.) River Regatta, 1900s	35	40
1050	60c. Sampans at river mouth, 1990s	70	80
1051	60c. Stevedores, 1910s	70	80
1052	60c. Lighters, 1940s	70	80
1053	60c. Men at work on junk, 1960s	70	80
1054	60c. Unloading with crane, 1970s	70	80

Nos. 1045/9 are inscribed "For local addresses only".
Nos. 1045/54 were printed together, *se-tenant*, with the backgrounds forming a composite design.

267 "Future Lifestyle" (Liu Jiang Wen)

2000. "Stampin' the Future" (children's stamp design competition). Multicoloured.

1055	(22c.) Type **267**	25	20
1056	60c. "Future Homes" (Shaun Yew Chuan Bin)	60	60
1057	$1 "Home Automation" (Gwendolyn Soh)	90	1·00
1058	$2 "Floating City" (Dawn Koh)	1·60	2·25
MS1059	125×80 mm. Nos. 1055/8	3·00	3·50

No. 1055 is inscribed "FOR LOCAL ADDRESSES ONLY".

268 Archer Fish

2000. Wetland Wildlife. Multicoloured.

1060	(22c.) Type **268**	35	30
1061	(22c.) Smooth otter and cubs	35	30
1062	$1 White-collared kingfisher ("Collared Kingfisher")	1·40	1·50
1063	$1 Orange fiddler crab	1·40	1·50
MS1064	294×210 mm. Nos. 1060/3, both perf and imperf in se-tenant blocks of 4	7·00	8·50

Nos. 1060/1 are inscribed "For Local Addresses Only".
Nos. 1060/3 were printed together, *se-tenant*, with the backgrounds forming composite designs.

269 High Jump and Swimming

2000. Olympic Games, Sydney. Designs showing a sport within the outline of another. Multicoloured.

1065	(22c.) Type **269**	25	20
1066	60c. Discus and badminton	60	60
1067	$1 Hurdles and football	90	1·00
1068	$2 Gymnastics and table tennis	1·75	2·25

No. 1065 is inscribed "For local addresses only".

270 Chinese New Year

2000. Festivals. Multicoloured

(a) Normal gum

1069	(22c.) Type **270**	55	55
1070	(22c.) Hari Raya Aidilfitri	55	55
1071	(22c.) Deepavali	55	55
1072	(22c.) Christmas	55	55
1073	30c. Chinese New Year (different) (diamond, 36×23 mm)	65	70
1074	30c. Hari Raya Aidilfitri (different) (diamond, 36×23 mm)	65	70
1075	30c. Deepavali (different) (diamond, 36×23 mm)	65	70
1076	30c. Christmas (different) (diamond, 36×23 mm)	65	70

(b) Self-adhesive.

1077	(22c.) Type **270**	85	90
1078	(22c.) As No. 1070	85	90
1079	(22c.) As No. 1071	85	90
1080	(22c.) As No. 1072	85	90

Nos. 1069/72 and 1077/80 are inscribed "FOR LOCAL ADDRESSES ONLY".

2000. "Guangzhou 2000" International Stamp and Coin Exhibition, China. Sheet 123×75 mm. Multicoloured.

MS1081	(22c.) As Type **262**; $2 No. 1025	2·50	3·00

271 Snake

2001. Chinese New Year ("Year of the Snake"). Multicoloured.

1082	(22c.) Type **271**	30	20
1083	$2 Two snakes	2·00	2·50

No. 1082 is inscribed "FOR LOCAL ADDRESSES ONLY".

2001. "Hong Kong 2001" Stamp Exhibition. Sheet 123×75 mm. Multicoloured.

MS1084	22c. As Type **271**; $2 No. 1083	3·25	3·50

272 Tan Tock Seng

2001. Famous Citizens of Singapore. Multicoloured.

1085	$1 Type **272**	1·00	1·10
1086	$1 Eunos bin Abdullah	1·00	1·10
1087	$1 P. Govindasamy Pillai	1·00	1·10
1088	$1 Edwin John Tessensohn	1·00	1·10

273 People holding Hands ("Co-operation")

2001. 25th Anniv of Commonwealth Day. Multicoloured.

1089	(22c.) Type **273**	25	20
1090	60c. People using computers ("Education")	60	60
1091	$1 Sporting activities ("Sports")	1·25	1·00
1092	$2 Dancers and musicians ("Arts and Culture")	1·75	2·25

No. 1089 is inscribed "FOR LOCAL ADDRESSES ONLY".

274 Balloons

2001. Self-adhesive Greetings Stamps. "Occasions". Multicoloured.

1093	(22c.) Type **274**	40	55
1094	(22c.) Stars	40	55
1095	(22c.) Tulips	40	55
1096	(22c.) Parcels	40	55
1097	(22c.) Musical instruments	40	55

Nos. 1093/7 are inscribed "FOR LOCAL ADDRESSES ONLY".

275 "Music" ("a")

2001. Arts Festival. Multicoloured.

1098	(22c.) Type **275**	25	40
1099	60c. "Painting" ("r")	55	80
1100	$1 "Dance" ("t")	90	1·25
1101	$2 "Theatre" ("s")	1·75	2·00

No. 1098 is inscribed "For Local Addresses Only".

2001. "BELGICA 2001" International Stamp Exhibtion, Brussels. Sheet 123×75 mm. Multicoloured.

MS1102	(22c) Type **271**; $2 No. 1083	3·50	4·00

276 Cockatiels **277**

2001. "Singpex '01" National Stamp Exhibition. Pets

(a) Multicoloured

1103	(22c.) Type **276**	40	50
1104	(22c.) Fish in tank	40	50
1105	(22c.) Tortoise	40	50
1106	(22c.) Ducklings	40	50
1107	(22c.) Cat looking at mouse (24×34 mm)	40	50
1108	(22c.) Dog looking at fish in bowl (24×34 mm)	40	50
1109	50c. West Highland white terrier and bird (24×41 mm)	65	75
1110	50c. Two cats (24×41 mm)	65	75
1111	$1 Green-winged macaw and Senegal parrot (24×41 mm)	85	90
1112	$1 Cat in basket and rabbit (24×41 mm)	85	90

(b) T **277** and similar multicoloured frame. Self-adhesive.

1113	(22c.) Type **277** (24×24 mm)	30	30
1114	(22c.) As Type **277**, but 24×34 mm	30	30

Nos. 1103/8 and 1113/14 are inscribed "For local addresses only".
Nos. 1103/12 were printed together, *se-tenant*, forming a composite picture of household pets.

2001. "Philanippon '01" International Stamp Exhibition, Tokyo. Sheet 123×75 mm. Multicoloured.

MS1115	(22c.) Type **271**; $2 No. 1083	2·50	3·00

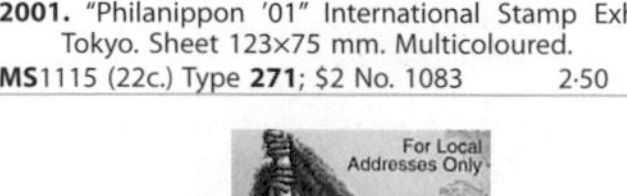

278 Young Ah Meng

2001. Orang Utan Conservation. Designs showing Ah Meng. Multicoloured

(a) Ordinary gum

1116	(22c.) Type **278**	50	55
1117	60c. Ah Meng with mate	80	90
1118	$1 Ah Meng with offspring	1·10	1·25
1119	$1 Three generations of Ah Meng's family	1·10	1·25
MS1120	190×180 mm. Nos. 1116/19 (sold for $3.90)	4·75	5·00

(b) Self-adhesive

1121	(22c.) Type **278**	50	50

Nos. 1116 and 1121 are inscribed "For Local Addresses Only".
No. **MS**1120 is in the shape of a seated orang utan.

279 *Melastoma malabathricum*

2001. Singapore–Switzerland Joint Issue. Flowers. Multicoloured.

1122	(22c.) Type **279**	25	20
1123	60c. *Leontopodium alpinum*	60	60
1124	$1 *Saraca cauliflora*	90	1·10
1125	$2 *Gentiana clusii*	1·75	2·50
MS1126	98×68 mm. Nos. 1122/5	3·25	4·00

No. 1122 is inscribed "FOR LOCAL ADDRESSES ONLY".
Two types of 50c.:
I. Inscribed "xanthometopon" in error.
II. Correctly inscribed "xanthometapon".

280 Moorish Idol

2001. Tropical Marine Fish. Multicoloured. Size 26×19 mm

(a) Ordinary gum

1127	5c. Type **280**	15	30
1128	20c. Thread-finned butterflyfish	45	20
1129	(22c.) Copper-banded butterflyfish	45	20
1130	30c. Pearl-scaled butterflyfish	50	25
1130a	31c. Eight-banded butterflyfish	60	25
1130b	(31c.) Eight-banded butterflyfish	1·25	25
1131	40c. Melon butterflyfish ("Rainbow Butterflyfish")	85	30
1132	50c. Yellow-faced angelfish	1·25	35
1133	60c. Emperor angelfish	1·25	45
1134	70c. Sail-finned tang	1·50	50
1135	80c. Palette surgeonfish ("Palette Tang")	1·60	55
MS1136	149×90 mm. Nos. 1127/35	7·00	8·00

(b) Size 29×24½ mm.

1137	$1 Blue turquoise	2·00	70
1138	$2 Brown discus	3·25	1·40
1139	$5 Red alenguer	6·00	3·50
1140	$10 Red turquoise	11·00	8·00
MS1141	128×75 mm. Nos. 1137/40	22·00	24·00

(c) Self-adhesive.

1142	(22c.) As No. 1129	30	35
1142c	(23c.) As No. 1129	30	35

Nos. 1129 and 1142 are inscribed "FOR LOCAL ADDRESSES ONLY". No. 1130b is inscribed "2nd Local". No. 1142c is inscribed "1st Local".

281 Horse

2002. Chinese New Year ("Year of the Horse"). Multicoloured.

1143	(22c.) Type **281**	25	20
1144	(22c.) As Type 290 but horse embossed in silver	1·25	1·50
1145	$2 Two horses rearing	1·40	1·60
1146	$2 As No. 1145, but horses embossed in gold	3·00	4·00

Nos. 1143/4 are inscribed "FOR LOCAL ADDRESSES ONLY" and were sold for 22c. each.

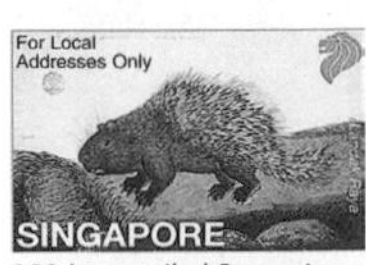

282 Long-tailed Porcupine

2002. Natural History Drawings from The William Farquhar Collection (1st series). Animals, Reptiles, Fruit and Plants. Multicoloured. Ordinary or self-adhesive gum.

1147	(22c.) Type **282**	35	40
1148	(22c.) Tapir	35	40
1149	(22c.) "Landak Kelubu"	35	40
1150	(22c.) Slow loris	35	40
1151	(22c.) "Biawak Tanah" (lizard)	35	40
1152	(22c.) Flying fox	35	40
1153	(22c.) Small-clawed otter	35	40
1154	(22c.) "Biawak Pasir" (lizard)	35	40
1155	(22c.) "Tupai Kerawak" (mouse) (vert)	35	40
1156	(22c.) Mouse deer (vert)	35	40
1157	(22c.) "Buah rumenia"	35	40

1158	(22c.) "Manggis Hutan"	35	40
1159	(22c.) "Cempedak"	35	40
1160	(22c.) "Bunga Dedap"	35	40
1161	(22c.) "Jeringau" (vert)	35	40
1162	(22c.) "Rotang" (vert)	35	40
1163	(22c.) "Tuba" (vert)	35	40
1164	(22c.) "Tebu Gagak" (vert)	35	40
1165	(22c.) "Temu Kunci" (vert)	35	40
1166	(22c.) "Rambutan" (vert)	35	40

Nos. 1147/56 (animals and reptiles), 1157/66 (fruits and plants), and are inscribed "For Local Addresses Only". Each stamp was sold for 22c.

2002. Natural History Drawings from The William Farquhar Collection (2nd series). Birds and Fish. As T **282**. Multicoloured. Ordinary or self-adhesive gum.

1187	(22c.) "Burung Gaji-gaji"	35	40
1188	(22c.) "Kuau Cermin"	35	40
1189	(22c.) "Ayam Kolam"	35	40
1190	(22c.) "Kelengking"	35	40
1191	(22c.) "Burung Kuang"	35	40
1192	(22c.) "Puhung"	35	40
1193	(22c.) "Burung Kunyit" (vert)	35	40
1194	(22c.) "Burung Pacap Sayat Biru" (vert)	35	40
1195	(22c.) "Burung Murai" (vert)	35	40
1196	(22c.) "Burung Berek-Berek" (vert)	35	40
1197	(22c.) "Ikan Tenggiri Papan"	35	40
1198	(22c.) "Ikan Kertang"	35	40
1199	(22c.) "Ikan Kakatua"	35	40
1200	(22c.) "Ikan Bambangan"	35	40
1201	(22c.) "Ikan Parang"	35	40
1202	(22c.) "Ikan Buntal Pisang"	35	40
1203	(22c.) "Ikan Ketang"	35	40
1204	(22c.) "Pari Hitam"	35	40
1205	(22c.) "Telinga Gajah"	35	40
1206	(22c.) "Ikan Babi"	35	40

Nos. 1187/96 (birds), 1197/206 (fish), and are inscribed "For Local Addresses Only". Each stamp was sold for 22c.

283 Lego Town

2002. Toys. Multicoloured.

1227	(22c.) Type **283**	25	20
1228	60c. Cowboy, Indian, soldier and robot	70	55
1229	70c. Dolls	80	70
1230	$1 Racing cars and bike	1·25	1·50

No. 1227 is inscribed "For local addresses only" and was sold for 22c.

284 Red-throated Sunbird

2002. Singapore – Malaysia Joint Issue. Birds. Multicoloured.

1231	(22c.) Type **284**	45	20
1232	40c. Asian fairy bluebird	65	55
1233	$1 Black-naped oriole	1·50	1·10
1234	$2 White-bellied woodpecker	2·50	3·00
MS1235	135×94 mm Nos. 1231/4	4·50	4·50

2002. "Philakorea 2002" International Stamp Exhibition, Seoul.

MS1236	123×75 mm. Nos. 1143 and 1145	2·50	3·00

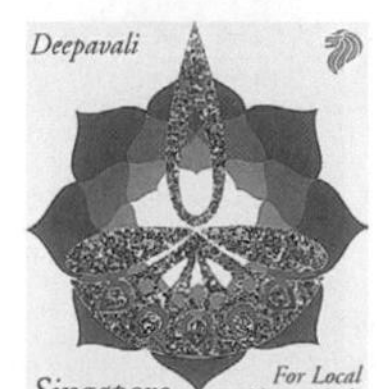

285 Kolam (doorstep decoration), Deepavali

286 Kolam (doorstep decoration), Deepavali

2002. Festivals. Multicoloured. (a) T **285**. Ordinary or self-adhesive gum.

(a) T **285**. PVA gum

1237	(22c.) Type **285**	70	70
1238	(22c.) Ketupat (rice cake) wrapper, Hari Raya Aidilfitri	70	70
1239	(22c.) Snowflake in bauble, Christmas	70	70
1240	(22c.) Fish paper decoration, Chinese New Year	70	70

(b) Self-adhesive

(c) T **286**.

1245	50c. Type **286**	90	1·00
1246	50c. Ketupat (rice cake) wrapper, Hari Raya Aidilfitri	90	1·00
1247	50c. Snowflake in bauble, Christmas	90	1·00
1248	50c. Fish paper decoration, Chinese New Year	90	1·00

Nos. 1237/44 are inscribed "For Local Addresses Only" and each stamp was sold for 22c.

The central designs on Nos. 1237/48 are foil holograms.

287 Flame of the Forest

2002. Heritage Trees Scheme. Multicoloured.

1249	(22c.) Type **287**	35	20
1250	60c. Rain Tree	70	45
1251	$1 Kapok Tree	1·25	1·50
1252	$1 Tembusu	1·25	1·50

No. 1249 also comes self-adhesive.

Nos. 1249 and 1253 are inscribed "FOR LOCAL ADDRESSES ONLY" and were sold for 22c.

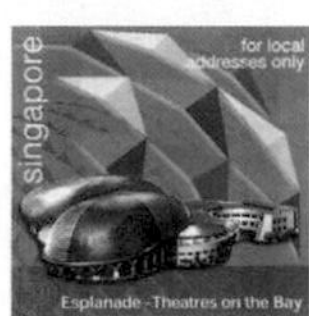

288 Esplanade, Performing Arts Centre, Marina Bay

2002. Esplanade, Theatres on the Bay. Esplanade from different angles. Multicoloured.

1254	(22c.) Type **288**	30	20
1255	60c. With brown background	70	50
1256	$1 Single shell of Esplanade	1·10	1·10
1257	$2 Aerial view of both shells	2·00	2·50
MS1258	104×80 mm. Nos. 1254/7	3·50	4·00

289 Two Yachts

2002. Singapore-A Global City. (1st series). Leisure and Lifestyle. Multicoloured.

1259	$2 Type **289**	2·00	2·25
1260	$2 Conductor's hands and baton	2·00	2·25
MS1261	135×95 mm. Nos. 1259/60	5·00	6·00

See also Nos. 1277/**MS**1279 and 1405/**MS**1407.

290 Goat

2003. Chinese New Year ("Year of the Goat"). Multicoloured.

1262	(22c.) Type **290**	40	20
1263	$2 Goat butting tree	2·00	2·50

No. 1262 is inscribed "FOR LOCAL ADDRESSES ONLY" and was sold for 22c.

291 Empress Place Building as Government Offices

2003. Opening of Asian Civilizations Museum in Empress Place Building. Multicoloured.

1264	(22c.) Type **291**	35	20
1265	60c. Empress Place Building as Registrar's Office	80	50
1266	$1 Empress Place Museum	1·25	1·25
1267	$2 Empress Place Building, as Asian Civilizations Museum	2·50	3·00

No. 1264 is inscribed "For local addresses only" and was sold for 22c.

292 Tarsier

2003. Creatures of the Night. Multicoloured.

1268	(22c.) Type **292**	35	20
1269	40c. Barn owl	85	50
1270	$1 Babirusa	1·25	1·25
1271	$2 Clouded leopard	2·25	2·75
MS1272	136×94 mm. Nos. 1268/71	4·00	4·50

No. 1268 is inscribed "FOR LOCAL ADDRESSES ONLY" and was sold for 22c.

293 Community Policewomen and Block of Flats

2003. Singapore Police Force. Multicoloured

1273	(22c.) Type **293**	50	20
1274	40c. Traffic policeman with motor-cycle	85	40
1275	$1 Maritime policeman and launch	1·75	1·40
1276	$2 Singapore police on U.N. peacekeeping duties	3·00	3·00

No. 1273 is inscribed "For Local Addresses Only" and was sold at 22c.

294 Satellite

2003. Singapore–A Global City (2nd series). Communications and Technology. Multicoloured.

1277	$2 Type **294**	2·25	2·25
1278	$2 Robot	2·25	2·25
MS1279	135×95 mm. Nos. 1277/8	4·50	4·50

295 Cheshire Cat ("Joy!")

2003. Greetings Stamps. "Joy and Caring". Multicoloured. Ordinary or self-adhesive gum.

1280	(22c.) Type **295**	30	40
1281	(22c.) Heart with smiling face ("joy!")	30	40
1282	(22c.) Teddy bear ("joy!")	30	40
1283	(22c.) Woman laughing ("joy")	30	40
1284	(22c.) Ostrich ("joy!")	30	40
1285	(22c.) Apple ("caring")	30	40
1286	(22c.) Hand with painted heart ("Helping Hands")	30	40
1287	(22c.) Multicoloured hearts ("Togetherness")	30	40
1288	(22c.) Daisy ("Beauty of a caring heart")	30	40
1289	(22c.) Night sky ("KEEPING IN TOUCH KEEPS US GOING")	30	40

Nos. 1280/9 are inscribed "For local addresses only", and were sold for 22c. each.

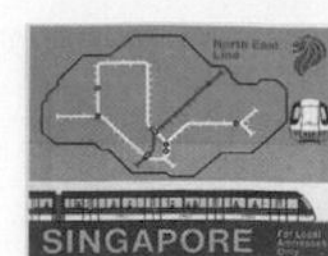

296 Map of Singapore Mass Rapid Transit System

2003. Opening of North East Line of Singapore Mass Rapid Transit System. Multicoloured.

1300	(22c.) Type **296**	40	20
1301	60c. Passengers	1·00	60
1302	$2 Control centre	2·75	3·25
MS1303	135×93 mm. 10c. Type **169**; 60c. As No. 573; $2 As No. 574 and Nos. 1300/2	6·50	7·00

No. 1300 is inscribed "For Local Addresses Only" and were sold at 22c. each.

297 National Flag

2003. National Day. Multicoloured.

1304	(22c.) Type **297**	30	20
1305	60c. *Vanda* "Miss Joaquim"	70	45
1306	$1 "Merlion" statue and Singapore skyline	1·25	1·25
1307	$2 Children	2·25	2·75
MS1308	140×75 mm. Nos. 1304/7	4·00	4·25

No. 1305 is inscribed "For local addresses only" and were sold for 22c. each.

298 Alouette III (helicopter)

2003. Centenary of Powered Flight. Multicoloured. Ordinary or self-adhesive gum.

1309	(22c.) Type **298**	45	45
1310	(22c.) E-2C Hawkeye	45	45
1311	(22c.) Hawker Hunter	45	45
1312	(22c.) Super Puma AS-332M (helicopter)	45	45
1313	(22c.) Hercules C-130H	45	45
1314	(22c.) F-16 C/D Fighting Falcon	45	45
1315	(22c.) AH-64D Apache (helicopter)	45	45
1316	(22c.) KC-135R Stratotanker	45	45
1317	(22c.) Cessna 172	45	45
1318	(22c.) F-5E Tiger II	45	45
1319	(22c.) A340-500	45	45
1320	(22c.) B747-400	45	45
1321	(22c.) B777-200	45	45
1322	(22c.) B747-400 Freighter	45	45
1323	(22c.) A320	45	45
1324	(22c.) Concorde	45	45
1325	(22c.) B737-100	45	45
1326	(22c.) Comet IV	45	45
1327	(22c.) Viscount	45	45
1328	(22c.) Airspeed Consul	45	45
MS1329	282×188 mm. Nos. 1309/28	8·00	8·00

Nos. 1309/28, and are inscribed "For local addresses only" and were sold at 22c. each.

2003. "Bangkok 2003" World Stamp Exhibition, Thailand. Sheet 123×75 mm. Multicoloured.

MS1350	(22c.) Type **290**; $2 No. 1263	2·75	3·50

299 Singapore Botanic Gardens

2003. Parks and Gardens. Multicoloured

(a) Ordinary gum

1351	(22c.) Type **299**	45	20
1352	60c. Fort Canning Park	1·25	45
1353	$1 Marina City Park	1·90	1·75
1354	$1 Stork's nest, Sungei Buloh Wetland Reserve	1·90	1·75

Nos. 1351 and 1355 are inscribed "FOR LOCAL ADDRESSES ONLY" and were sold for 22c.

(b) Self-adhesive gum.

1355	(22c.) Type **299**	40	45

2003. "China 2003" International Stamp Exhibition, Mianyang. Sheet 122×75 mm.

MS1356	(22c.) Type **290**; $2 No. 1263	2·75	3·50

300 Monkey with Heart

2004. Chinese New Year ("Year of the Monkey"). Multicoloured.

1357	(23c.) Type **300**	40	30
1358	$2 Two monkeys	2·75	2·75

No. 1357 is inscribed "FOR LOCAL ADDRESSES ONLY" and was sold for 22c.

2004. Hong Kong 2004 International Stamp Exhibition. Sheet 123×75 mm. Multicoloured.

MS1359 (23c.) Type **300**; $2 No. 1358 3·00 3·50

301 "Farmer's House" (Liu Kang)

2004. Paintings by Liu Kang and Ong Kim Seng. Multicoloured. Ordinary or self-adhesive gum.

1360	(23c.) Type **301**	40	40
1361	(23c.) "Artist and Model" (Liu Kang)	40	40
1362	(23c.) "Lanterns Galore" (Liu Kang)	40	40
1363	(23c.) "Enjoying a Smoke, Kashmir" (Liu Kang)	40	40
1364	(23c.) "Life by the River" (Liu Kang)	40	40
1365	(23c.) "Tenth Trip up to Huang-shan" (Liu Kang)	40	40
1366	(23c.) "My Young Wife" (Liu Kang) (vert)	40	40
1367	(23c.) "Kek Lok Si, Penang" (Liu Kang) (vert)	40	40
1368	(23c.) "Souri" (Liu Kang) (vert)	40	40
1369	(23c.) "Siesta in Bali" (Liu Kang) (vert)	40	40
1370	(23c.) "Kampong Tengah, Singapore" (Ong Kim Seng)	40	40
1371	(23c.) "Gyantse Market" (Ong Kim Seng)	40	40
1372	(23c.) "Sebatu Spring, Bali" (Ong Kim Seng)	40	40
1373	(23c.) "Jetty, Bangkok" (Ong Kim Seng)	40	40
1374	(23c.) "Resort, Bali" (Ong Kim Seng)	40	40
1375	(23c.) "Dance Studio, Bali" (Ong Kim Seng)	40	40
1376	(23c.) "Telok Ayer Market" (Ong Kim Seng)	40	40
1377	(23c.) "Kathmandu, Nepal" (Ong Kim Seng)	40	40
1378	(23c.) "Portofino, Italy" (Ong Kim Seng) (vert)	40	40
1379	(23c.) "Boats at Rest" (Ong Kim Seng) (vert)	40	40

Nos. 1360/79 are inscribed "For local addresses only" and were sold for 23c. each.

302 "Harmony" Sculpture and Suzhou Industrial Park

2004. Tenth Anniv of Suzhou Industrial Park.

1400	302	60c. multicoloured	1·25	1·00

303 Colonial and Modern Buildings

2004. Singapore Skyline. Multicoloured.

1401	(23c.) Type **303**	40	20
1402	60c. Merlion statue and waterfront	1·00	70
1403	70c. Singapore skyline	1·10	1·40

MS1404 Two sheets, each 113×80 mm. (a) $1 Singapore from the Roads, c. 1900 (95×35 mm). (b) $5 Singapore skyline, 2004 (95×35 mm) Set of 2 sheets 7·50 8·50

No. 1401 is inscribed "1st Local" and was sold for 23c.

304 Containers

2004. Singapore—A Global City (3rd series). Trade and Industry. Multicoloured.

1405	$2 Type **304**	2·50	2·75
1406	$2 Oil refinery	2·50	2·75

MS1407 135×95 mm. Nos. 1405/6 and double stamp-size label 5·00 5·50

305 Football Field

2004. Centenary of FIFA (Federation Internationale de Football Association). Multicoloured.

1408	30c. Type **305**	40	25
1409	60c. Football	80	50
1410	$1 Football shirt	1·40	1·40
1411	$2 World map	3·00	3·25

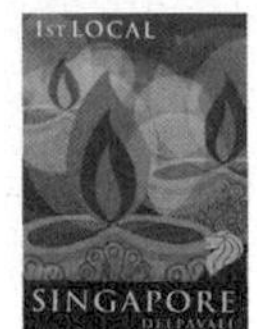
306 Three Candles (Deepavali)

2004. Festivals. Multicoloured

(a) Ordinary gum

1412	(23c.) Type **306**	35	35
1413	(23c.) One candle (Hari Raya Aidilfitri)	35	35
1414	(23c.) Toy Father Christmas and Rudolph (Christmas)	35	35
1415	(23c.) Plum blossom and oranges (Chinese New Year)	35	35
1416	50c. Woman and oil lamp (Deepavali)	65	75
1417	50c. Girl holding sparkler (Hari Raya Aidilfitri)	65	75
1418	50c. Carol singers (Christmas)	65	75
1419	50c. Woman wearing orange kimono	65	75

(b) Self-adhesive

1420	(23c.) Type **306**	35	45
1421	(23c.) One candle (Hari Raya Aidilfitri)	35	45
1422	(23c.) Toy Father Christmas and Rudolph (Christmas)	35	45
1423	(23c.) Plum blossom and oranges (Chinese New Year)	35	45

Nos. 1412/19 are inscribed "1st LOCAL" and were sold at 23c. each.

307 Column, City Hall

2004. National Day. Monuments. Multicoloured.

1424	(23c.) Type **307**	40	50
1425	(23c.) City Hall (41×27 mm)	40	50
1426	30c. Concert Hall bell tower	50	60
1427	30c. Victoria Theatre and Concert Hall (41×27 mm)	50	60
1428	60c. Dome of courthouse	90	1·25
1429	60c. Supreme Court (41×27 mm)	90	1·25
1430	$1 Detail of gate, the Istana	1·40	1·75
1431	$1 The Istana (41×27 mm)	1·40	1·75

MS1432 140×70 mm. Nos. 1425, 1427, 1429 and 1431 2·75 3·50

Nos. 1424/5 are inscribed "1st Local" and were sold for 23c. each.

308 Running

2004. Olympic Games, Athens, Greece. Designs showing Olympic sports depicted on pebbles. Multicoloured.

1433	(23c.) Type **308**	40	20
1434	30c. Swimming	55	25
1435	$1 Weight-lifting	1·40	1·10
1436	$2 Sailing	2·75	3·25

2004. World Stamp Championship, Singapore. Sheet 161×85 mm containing Nos. 1259/60, 1277/8 and 1405/6. Multicoloured.

MS1437 $2 Containers; $2 Oil refinery; $2 Two yachts; $2 Conductor's hands and baton; $2 Satellite; $2 Robot 14·00 16·00

309 Linked Wrists and Singapore Post Centre

2004. 150th Anniv of Introduction of Stamps. Designs showing early Singapore stamps and postmarks. Multicoloured.

1438	(23c.) Type **309**	40	20
1439	60c. King George VI and General Post Office, Fullerton Building	90	55
1440	$1 King Edward VII and General Post Office	1·40	1·10
1441	$2 Queen Victoria and the Post Office, Singapore River	2·25	2·75

MS1442 135×94 mm. Nos. 1438/41 4·50 4·75

No. 1438 is inscribed "1st Local" and was sold for 23c.

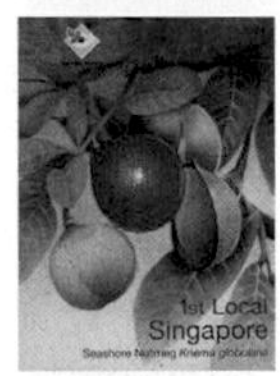
310 Seashore Nutmeg

2004. Wildlife of Chek Jawa. Multicoloured

(a) Ordinary gum

1443	(23c.) Type **310**	65	65
1444	(23c.) Oriental pied hornbill	65	65
1445	$1 Knobbly Sea stars	1·50	1·50
1446	$1 Common seahorses	1·50	1·50

(b) Self-adhesive

1447	(23c.) Type **310**	40	50
1448	(23c.) Oriental pied hornbill	40	50

311 Rooster

2005. Chinese New Year ("Year of the Rooster"). Multicoloured.

1449	(23c.) Type **311**	40	20
1450	$2 Rooster and hen	2·75	3·25

No. 1449 is inscribed "1st Local" and was sold for 23c.

312 Balloon Dog

2005. Greetings. Multicoloured

(a) Ordinary gum

1451	(23c.) Type **312**	40	45
1452	(23c.) Lily	40	45
1453	(23c.) Gift box	40	45
1454	(23c.) Love heart and bears flower arrangement	40	45
1455	(23c.) Candle	40	45

(b) Size 30×25 mm. Self-adhesive

1456	(23c.) Candle	35	45
1457	(23c.) Love heart and bears flower arrangement	35	45
1458	(23c.) Gift box	35	45
1459	(23c.) Lily	35	45
1460	(23c.) Balloon dog	35	45

Nos. 1451/60 were each inscribed "1st Local" and sold for 23c.

313 *Thumbelina*

2005. Birth Bicentenary of Hans Christian Andersen (artist and children's writer). Multicoloured.

1461	(23c.) Type **313**	40	20
1462	60c. *The Ugly Duckling*	70	55
1463	$1 *The Emperor's New Clothes*	1·25	1·25
1464	$2 *The Little Mermaid*	2·25	2·75

MS1465 200×67 mm. Nos. 1461/4 4·25 4·50

No. 1461 was inscribed "1st Local" and initially sold for 23c.

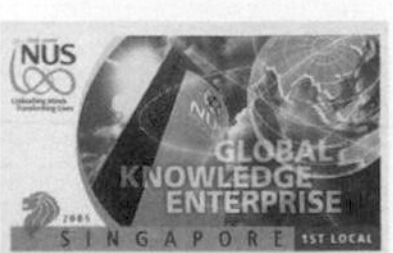
314 National University of Singapore Monument and Globe

2005. Centenary of National University of Singapore. Multicoloured.

1466	(23c.) Type **314**	40	20
1467	60c. Students	70	55
1468	70c. Dancers and sculpture outside building	80	90
1469	$1 Science student and equipment	1·25	1·40

2005. Pacific Explorer 2005 World Stamp Expo, Sydney. Sheet 123×75 mm. Multicoloured.

MS1469a (23c) Type **311**; $2 Rooster and hen 7·00 7·50

315 Istana Kampong Gelam (Malay Heritage Centre)

2005. Malay Heritage Centre. Multicoloured.

1470	(2nd.) Type **315**	40	20
1471	60c. Fountain pen and seal	70	55
1472	$1 Mandolin	1·25	1·25
1473	$2 Sail boat	2·25	2·75

No. 1470 was inscribed "2nd Local" and initially sold for 31c.

316 Admiral Zheng He

2005. 600th Anniv of the Voyages of Admiral Zheng He. Multicoloured.

1474	(23c.) Type **316**	60	60
1475	(23c.) Three sailing ships	60	60
1476	60c. Four sailing ships	1·25	90
1477	$1 Sailing ships near port	1·90	1·75

Nos. 1474/5 were inscribed "1st Local" and initially sold for 23c.

317 Football, Table Tennis and Cycling

2005. 117th International Olympic Committee Session. Each showing the five competing cities and flight paths to Singapore. Multicoloured.

1478	(23c.) Type **317**	75	25
1479	50c. Athletics, tennis and basketball	90	60
1480	60c. Football, tennis and javelin throwing	1·10	80
1481	$1 Gymnastics and athletics	1·75	1·75

No. 1478 was inscribed "1st Local" and initially sold for 23c.

318 Smiling Stickmen (needlework)

2005. National Day. "Fabric of the Nation". Showing needlework by Singaporeans. Multicoloured

(a) PVA gum

1482	(23c.) Type **318**	30	40
1483	(23c.) Hearts on patches	30	40
1484	(23c.) Smiling yellow flower	30	40
1485	(23c.) Round Tower	30	40
1486	(23c.) Red orchid	30	40
1487	(23c.) Sun, rainbow and cloud	30	40
1488	(23c.) "Peace"	30	40
1489	(23c.) Outline of Singapore with red heart inside	30	40
1490	(23c.) White orchid	30	40
1491	(23c.) Red heart with orange flowers inside	30	40
1492	(23c.) "Happy Birthday"	30	40

1493	(23c.) Two hands	30	40
1494	(23c.) Cats and dogs	30	40
1495	(23c.) Stars	30	40
1496	(23c.) Washing on lines	30	40
1497	(23c.) Plane and patchwork clouds	30	40
1498	(23c.) Patchwork quarters	30	40
1499	(23c.) Plate with food	30	40
1500	(23c.) Hearts	30	40
1501	(23c.) Skyline	30	40
1502	(23c.) "1" and flowers	30	40
1503	(23c.) Four children and jigsaw pieces	30	40
1504	(23c.) Four heads around flag	30	40
1505	(23c.) Rainbow and clouds	30	40
1506	(23c.) Face upturned amongst bowed heads	30	40
1507	(23c.) Four butterflies	30	40
1508	(23c.) Cross-stitch	30	40
1509	(23c.) Heart-shaped fruit	30	40
1510	(23c.) Frog	30	40
1511	(23c.) Bird kites	30	40
1512	(23c.) Four hands around yellow heart	30	40
1513	(23c.) Skyline and "Singapore My Home"	30	40
1514	(23c.) Green orchid	30	40
1515	(23c.) Patchwork hearts as tree	30	40
1516	(23c.) "I", heart and outline of Singapore	30	40
1517	(23c.) Hand and buttons	30	40
1518	(23c.) "Singapore", hills and heart	30	40
1519	(23c.) Four hearts in quarters	30	40
1520	(23c.) Hearts, stars and people in quarters	30	40
1521	(23c.) "The Pledge"	30	40
MS1522	62×90 mm. $1 Needlework designs (39×60 mm)	1·40	1·60

2005. TAIPEI 2005 International Stamp Exhibition. Sheet 123×75 mm. Multicoloured.

MS1562a	(23c.) Type **311**; $2 Rooster and hen	7·50	8·50

319 Belgian Centre for Comic Strip Art, Brussels

2005. Architecture. Multicoloured.

1563	(23c.) Type **319**	40	20
1564	60c. Kandahar Street	70	55
1565	$1 Bukit Pasoh Road	1·25	1·25
1566	$2 Museum of Musical Instruments, Belgium	2·25	2·75
MS1567	170×95 mm. Nos. 1563/6	4·25	4·50

No. 1563 was inscribed "1st Local" and initially sold for 23c.

Stamps of the same design were issued by Belgium.

320 Colugo

2005. HSBC Tree Top Walk, Central Catchment Nature Reserve. Multicoloured

(a) Ordinary gum

1568	(23c.) Type **320**	50	50
1569	60c. Fruits of Singapore adenia (climbing vine)	90	90
1570	$1 Red-crowned barbet (bird)	1·50	1·75
1571	$1 Common tree nymph (butterfly)	1·50	1·75

321 Dog chasing ball

2006. Chinese New Year ("Year of the Dog"). Multicoloured.

1573	(23c.) Type **321**	45	20
1574	$2 Two dogs	2·25	2·75

322 "White Cloud"

2006. Art by Tan Swie Hian. Multicoloured.

1575	(23c.) Type **322**	40	45
1576	(23c.) "Ganges"	40	45
1577	(23c.) "Soaring over the Flower Field"	40	45
1578	(23c.) "Kuta is a Song"	40	45
1579	(23c.) "The Winged Steed" (sculpture)	40	45
1580	50c. "Black Panther (pine)" (29×59 mm)	55	65
1581	50c. "Gingko (Male)" (29×59 mm)	55	65
1582	50c. "White Elephant" (29×59 mm)	55	65
1583	50c. "Summer Lotus" (29×59 mm)	55	65
1584	50c. "Water Dhyana" (29×59 mm)	55	65
MS1585	62×90 mm. $2 Calligraphy (40×59 mm)	2·75	3·00

Nos. 1575/9 were inscribed "1st LOCAL" and initially sold for 23c.

323 Indo-Pacific Bottlenose Dolphin

2006. Undersea World. Sea Mammals. Multicoloured

(a) Ordinary gum

1586	(23c.) Type **323**	40	20
1587	(31c.) Indo-Pacific hump-backed dolphin	50	30
1588	$1 Finless porpoise	1·25	1·25
1589	$2 Dugong	2·50	3·00
MS1590	140×74 mm. Nos. 1586/9	4·25	4·50

(b) Self-adhesive

1591	(23c.) As No. 1586	35	35

No. 1586/7 are inscribed "1ST LOCAL" and "2ND LOCAL" and were initially sold for 23c. and 31c. respectively.

324 Chinese New Year

325 Chinese New Year

2006. Festivals. Multicoloured

(a) Ordinary gum. (i) As T **324**.

1592	(23c.) Type **324**	35	35
1593	(23c.) Christmas	35	35
1594	(23c.) Deepavali	35	35
1595	(23c.) Hari Raya Aidilfitri	35	35

(ii) As T **325**

1596	50c. Type **325**	60	70
1597	50c. Christmas	60	70
1598	50c. Deepavali	60	70
1599	50c. Hari Raya Aidilfitri	60	70

(b) Self-adhesive. As T **324**

1600	(23c.) Type **324**	35	40
1601	(23c.) Christmas	35	40
1602	(23c.) Deepavali	35	40
1603	(23c.) Hari Raya Aidilfitri	35	40

326 Clog Maker

2006. Vanishing Trades. Multicoloured

(a) Ordinary gum

1604	(23c.) Type **326**	40	40
1605	(23c.) Wooden bucket maker	40	40
1606	(23c.) Spice grinder	40	40
1607	(23c.) Snake charmer	40	40
1608	(23c.) Satay man	40	40
1609	80c. Mama store	95	1·10
1610	80c. Roti man	95	1·10
1611	80c. Backlane barber	95	1·10
1612	80c. Chinese medicinal tea shop	95	1·10
1613	80c. Tin bucker maker	95	1·10

(b) Self-adhesive

1614	(23c.) Type **326**	30	40
1615	(23c.) As No. 1605	30	40
1616	(23c.) As No. 1606	30	40
1617	(23c.) As No. 1607	30	40
1618	(23c.) As No. 1608	30	40

Nos. 1604/8 and 1614/18 are inscribed "1st Local" and were initially sold for 23c.

2006. Washington 2006 International Stamp Exhibition. Sheet 123×75 mm. Multicoloured.

MS1619	(23c.) Type **321**; $2 No. 1574	3·75	4·00

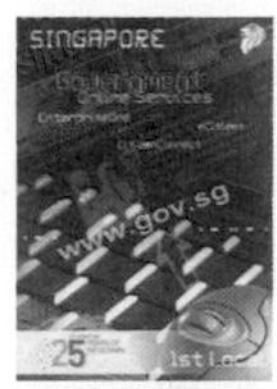

327 Keyboard (Government)

2006. 25th Anniv of Infocomm. Multicoloured.

1620	(23c.) Type **327**	30	30
1621	60c. Trade	75	55
1622	80c. Boy using computer (Education)	1·00	1·25
1623	$1 Satellite dish (Telecommunications)	1·25	1·75

328 SCCCI Building

2006. Centenary of Singapore Chinese Chamber of Commerce and Industry. Multicoloured.

1624	(23c.) Type **328**	40	30
1625	(31c.) *Dendrobium* "Singapore Chinese Chamber of Commerce and Industry"	1·50	80
1626	80c. Logo of World Chinese Entrepreneurs Convention	1·40	1·40
1627	$1 Administration building, Nanyang University	1·40	1·40
1628	$2 War Memorial and Sun Yat Sen Nanyang Memorial Hall	2·25	2·75
MS1629	140×75 mm. Nos. 1624/8	6·00	6·50

No. 1624 is inscribed "1ST LOCAL" and No. 1625 "2ND LOCAL". They were initially sold for 23c. and 31c. respectively.

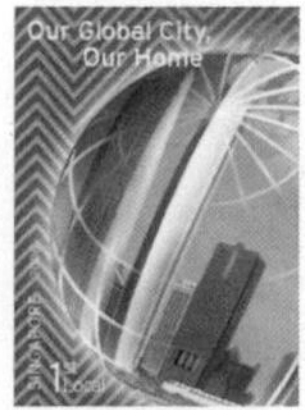

329 City of Singapore

2006. National Day. Multicoloured.

1630	(23c.) Type **329**	40	30
1631	60c. People of Singapore	1·00	65
1632	80c. Containers	1·25	1·25
1633	$1 Entertainers	1·50	1·75
MS1634	113×80 mm. $2 City of Singapore reflected in glass globe (48×48 mm)	2·25	2·50

No. 1630 is inscribed "1st Local" and was initially sold for 23c.

330 Orchids

331 £1 Coin

2006. International Monetary Fund and World Bank Group Boards of Governors Annual Meetings

(a) Horiz designs as T **330**. Multicoloured

1635	50c. Type **330**	70	40
1636	80c. Esplanade–Theatres on the Bay	1·00	80
1637	$1 Singapore skyline	1·25	1·10

(b) Square designs as T **331**. Gold and black ($1) or silver and black ($5).

1638	$1 £1 coin	1·50	1·50
1639	$5 £5 coin	6·50	7·50

332 "singapore biennale 06" (image scaled to 50% of original size)

2006. Singapore Biennale (2006).

1640	**332**	$2 multicoloured	2·25	2·75

333 Vanda "Mimi Palmer"

2006. Flowers. Multicoloured.

1641	(23c.) Type **333**	60	40
1642	(23c.) Renanthera "Singaporeans"	60	40
1643	70c. Vanda "Miss Joaquim"	1·10	1·10
1644	70c. Mokara "Lion's Gold"	1·10	1·10
1645	$1 Heron and hollyhocks (48×35 mm)	1·75	1·50
1646	$2 Moorhen and irises (48×35 mm)	2·50	3·00

Nos. 1641/2 are inscribed "1st Local" and were initially sold for 23c. each.

Nos. 1641/commemorate the 40th Anniversary of Diplomatic Relations between Singapore and Japan. Stamps in similar designs were issued by Japan.

Nos. 1645/6 depict details from two different screen paintings by Houitsu Sakai both with the title "Flowers and Birds of the Four Seasons".

334 Singapore Merlion and St. Peter's Basilica, Rome

2006. 25th Anniv of Diplomatic Relations between Singapore and Vatican City. Multicoloured.

1647	50c. Type **334**	1·25	45
1648	$2 Flags of Singapore and Vatican City	4·25	4·25
MS1649	123×75 mm. Nos. 1648/9	5·50	5·50

335 Common Palm Civet

2006. "Fun with Nature" (children's nature education programme). Multicoloured

(a) Ordinary gum

1650	(23c.) Type **335**	50	50
1651	(23c.) Common flying dragon	50	50
1652	$1 Black-spotted sticky frog	1·75	2·00
1653	$1 Common tiger butterfly	1·75	2·00

(b) Self-adhesive

1654	(23c.) Type **335**	40	40
1655	(23c.) As No. 1652	40	40

Nos. 1650/1 and 1654/5 were inscribed "1st Local" and initially sold for 23c. each. Nos. 1650/3 were printed together, *se-tenant*, forming a composite background design.

2006. Belgica 2006 International Stamp Exhibition, Brussels. Sheet 123×75 mm. Multicoloured.

MS1656	(23c.) Type **321**; $2 Two dogs	2·50	2·75

336 Pig

2007. Chinese New Year ("Year of the Boar"). Multicoloured.

1657	(25c.) Type **336**	25	20
1658	$2 Two pigs	2·25	2·50

No. 1657 is inscribed "1st LOCAL" and was sold for 25c.

337 Family with Bicycle and Children holding Hands

2007. Tenth Anniv of Singapore Kindness Movement. Designs showing winning Singapore entries for ASEAN–Japan children's competition. Multicoloured. Ordinary or Self-adhesive gum.

1659	(25c.) Type **337**	40	40
1660	(25c.) Girl catching falling girl (horiz)	40	40
1661	(25c.) Distribution of Red Cross parcels (horiz)	40	40
1662	(25c.) Four people sharing umbrella (horiz)	40	40
1663	(25c.) Children visiting the elderly (horiz)	40	40
1664	(25c.) Boy opening door for woman	40	40
1665	(25c.) People on bus (horiz)	40	40
1666	(25c.) Woman and boy (horiz)	40	40
1667	(25c.) Sighted person helping blind man (horiz)	40	40
1668	(25c.) Zebra crossing (horiz)	40	40

338 Korean Wedding Costumes

2007. Traditional Wedding Costumes. Multicoloured.

1679	(25c.) Type **338**	45	50
1680	(25c.) Korean (man in dark grey)	45	50
1681	65c. Chinese	80	90
1682	65c. Indian	80	90
1683	65c. Malay	80	90
1684	65c. Eurasian	80	90
1685	$1.10 Korean (man in dark blue)	1·25	1·50
1686	$1.10 Korean (man in white)	1·25	1·50
MS1687	170×95 mm. Nos. 1679/86	5·50	5·75

Stamps in similar designs were issued by Korea.

339 Chinese Dances

2007. Cultural Dances. Multicoloured.

1688	(25c.) Type **339**	40	30
1689	(31c.) Indian classical dancer	50	40
1690	$1.10 Eurasian and Western dances	1·25	1·25
1691	$2 Malay dances	2·25	2·50

No. 1688 is inscribed "1ST LOCAL" and was initially sold for 25c.

No. 1689 is inscribed "2ND LOCAL" and was initially sold for 31c.

340 Crimson Sunbird

2007. Flora and Fauna . Multicoloured.

(a) Ordinary gum

1692	5c. Type **340**	40	50
1693	20c. Yellow-rumped flycatcher	1·00	65
1694	(25c.) Frangipani (30×27 mm)	50	25
1694a	(26c.) Blue pea vine (30x27 mm) (6.5.09)	1·00	40
1694b	(26c.) Pigeon orchid (30x27 mm) (6.5.09)	1·25	40
1694c	(26c.) *Dillenia suffruticosa* (23.6.2010)	60	25
1695	30c. Blue-throated bee-eater	1·25	50
1696	(31c.) Torch ginger (30×27 mm)	1·00	25
1696a	(32c.) Singapore rhododendron	80	25
1697	45c. Yellow wagtail	1·75	70
1698	50c. Stork-billed kingfisher	1·75	70
1699	55c. Blue-crowned hanging parrot	1·75	1·00
1700	65c. Common goldenback (woodpecker)	2·00	1·00
1701	80c. Jambu fruit dove	2·00	1·00
1702	$1.10 Large Indian civet (49×29 mm)	2·00	1·25
1703	$2 Banded leaf monkey (49×29 mm)	3·75	2·75
1704	$5 Malayan pangolin (49×29 mm)	6·00	4·00
1705	$10 Cream-coloured giant squirrel (49×29 mm)	11·00	8·75

(b) Self-adhesive

1706	(25c.) As No. 1694	50	50
1706b	(26c.) As No. 1694a	75	75
1706c	(26c.) As No. 1694*b*	1·00	1·00
1706d	(26c.) As No. 1694*c*	55	55

Nos. 1694/*c* and 1706/*d* were all inscr '1ST LOCAL'. Nos. 1694 and 1706 were initially sold for 25c. and Nos. 1694*a*/*c* and 1706*b*/*d* for 26c.

Nos. 1696/a were both inscr '2ND LOCAL' and originally sold for 31c. (1696) or 32c. (1696a).

341 Singapore Men taking Oath of Allegiance

2007. 40 Years of National Service. Multicoloured.

1707	(26c.) Type **341**	30	20
1708	(32c.) Basic military training exercises	35	25
1709	$1.10 Drill and regimentation	1·40	1·25
1710	$2 Operational training with rifles	2·75	3·00

Nos. 1707 is inscr '1st local' and was initially sold for 26c.

No. 1708 is inscr '2nd local' and was initially sold for 32c.

2007. Bangkok 2007 20th Asian International Stamp Exhibition. Sheet 123×75 mm. Multicoloured.

MS1711	(26c.) Type **336**; $2 Two pigs	2·75	2·75

342 Secretariat Building, Brunei

2007. 40th Anniv of ASEAN (Association of South-east Asian Nations). Ancient and Modern Architecture. Multicoloured.

1712	(26c.) Type **342**	65	65
1713	(26c.) National Museum of Cambodia	65	65
1714	(26c.) Fatahillah Museum, Jakarta, Indonesia	65	65
1715	(26c.) Lao Typical House	65	65
1716	(26c.) Malayan Railway Headquarters Building, Kuala Lumpur, Malaysia	65	65
1717	(26c.) Yangon Post Office, Myanmar	65	65
1718	(26c.) Malacañang Palace, Philippines	65	65
1719	(26c.) National Museum of Singapore	65	65
1720	(26c.) Vimanmek Mansion, Bangkok, Thailand	65	65
1721	(26c.) Presidential Palace, Hanoi, Vietnam	65	65

Nos. 1712/21 are all inscribed '1st Local'. Similar designs were issued on the same day by the ten member countries, Indonesia, Malaysia, Philippines, Thailand, Brunei, Vietnam, Laos, Myanmar and Cambodia.

343 Chinatown

2007. National Day. Tourist Landmarks. Multicoloured.

1722	(26c.) Type **343**	55	25
1723	65c. Kampong glam	1·25	70
1724	80c. Little India	1·40	1·25
1725	$1.10 Orchard Road	2·00	2·25
MS1726	122×80 mm. $5 Merlion statue at Marina Bay (vert)	6·50	7·50

No. 1722 is inscr '1st local' and was sold for 26c.

344 National Cadet Corps

2007. Uniformed Groups in Schools. Multicoloured.

1727	(32c.) Type **344**	60	60
1728	(32c.) The Singapore Scout Association	60	60
1729	(32c.) Girl Guides Singapore	60	60
1730	(32c.) The Girls' Brigade Singapore	60	60
1731	(32c.) The Boys' Brigade in Singapore	60	60
1732	(32c.) St. John Ambulance Brigade Singapore	60	60
1733	(32c.) Red Cross Youth	60	60
1734	(32c.) National Police Cadet Corps	60	60
1735	(32c.) National Civil Defence Cadet Corps	60	60

Nos. 1727/35 were inscr '2nd Local' and sold for 32c. each.

345 False Clown Anemone Fish and Sea Anemone (*Stichodactyla* sp.)

2007. Shores and Reefs. Multicoloured

(a) Ordinary gum

1736	(26c.) Type **345**	1·10	1·10
1737	(26c.) Singapore goby and blind shrimp (*Alpheus* sp.)	1·10	1·10
1738	$1.10 Hawksbill turtle and remora (*Echeneis naucrates*)	2·50	2·50
1739	$1.10 Razorfish (*Aeoliscus strigatus*) and sea urchin (*Diadema* sp.)	2·50	2·50

(b) Self-adhesive

1740	(26c.) As Type **345**	80	80
1741	(26c.) As No. 1737	80	80

Nos. 1736/9 were printed together, *se-tenant*, forming a composite background design.

Nos. 1736/7 and 1740/1 were inscr '1st Local' and initially sold for 26c. each.

346 Profile ('Libraries Spark Imagination')

2007. National Library Board 'L2010' Five Year Plan. Multicoloured.

1742	(26c.) Type **346**	40	30
1743	80c. Couple dancing ('Libraries Bring Knowledge Alive')	1·10	85
1744	$1.10 Students using computer ('Libraries Create Possibility')	1·60	1·25
1745	$2 Montage of profiles ('Libraries for Life Knowledge for Success')	3·00	3·50

No. 1742 is inscribed '1st LOCAL' and was sold for 26c.

347 Roof of Terminal 3 with Skylights and Reflector Panels

2008. Opening of Terminal 3 at Singapore Changi Airport. Multicoloured.

1746	(26c.) Type **347**	55	30
1747	65c. Singapore Airlines Airbus A380	1·40	90
1748	$1.10 Palm trees and 'Green Wall' vertical garden inside Terminal 3	1·70	1·50
1749	$2 Terminal 3 and Control Tower	3·25	4·00

No. 1746 was inscr '1st Local' and sold for 26c.

348 Rat

2008. Chinese New Year ('Year of the Rat'). Multicoloured

(a) Ordinary gum

1750	(26c.) Type **348**	50	30
1751	65c. Rat and orange	1·00	70
1752	$1.10 Two rats (44×34 mm)	1·75	2·00

(b) Self-adhesive.

1753	(26c.) As Type **348**	40	40

Nos. 1750 and 1753 were inscr '1st Local' and sold for 26c. each.

349 Chinese New Year

2008. Festivals. Multicoloured

(a) Ordinary gum

1754	(26c.) Type **349**	40	40
1755	(26c.) Christmas (Mary, shepherds and sheep)	40	40
1756	(26c.) Deepavali (people celebrating, fireworks and elephants)	40	40
1757	(26c.) Hari Raya Aidilfitri (women carrying food and lighted lamp)	40	40
1758	(32c.) Easter	45	45
1759	(32c.) Hari Raya Haji	45	45
1760	(32c.) Chinese Mid-Autumn Festival	45	45
1761	(32c.) Pongal	45	45
1762	55c. Chinese New Year (children carrying hong baos)	65	65
1763	55c. Christmas (flying Santas and reindeer)	65	65
1764	55c. Deepavali (people carrying oil lamps and peacocks)	65	65
1765	55c. Hari Raya Aidilfitri (couple, girl kneeling and boy receiving gift)	65	65

(b) Self-adhesive.

1766	(26c.) As Type **349**	45	50
1767	(26c.) As No. 1755	45	50
1768	(26c.) As No. 1756	45	50
1769	(26c.) As No. 1757	45	50

Nos. 1754/7 and 1766/9 are inscr '1st LOCAL' and sold for 26c. each.

Nos. 1758/61 are inscr '2nd LOCAL' and sold for 32c. each.

2008. Taipei 2008 21st Asian International Stamp Exhibition. Sheet 160×80 mm containing Nos. 1750/2.

MS1770	(26c.) Type **348**; 65c. Rat and orange; $1.10 Two rats (44×24 mm)	2·75	3·00

350 Porcelain Plate

2008. Peranakan Museum Collection. Showing Peranakan embroidery, beadwork and porcelain. Multicoloured.

1771	(26c.) Type **350**	40	40
1772	(26c.) Bird design	40	40
1773	(32c.) Dragon embroidery	50	50
1774	(32c.) Peony embroidery	50	50
1775	65c. Phoenix and flowers design from vase	90	1·00
1776	65c. Flying phoenix design from vase	90	1·00
1777	$1.10 Crane design from plate	1·40	1·75
1778	$1.10 Poppy design porcelain	1·40	1·75

Nos. 1771/2 are inscr '1st Local' and sold for 26c. each.

Nos. 1773/4 are inscr '2nd Local' and sold for 32c. each.

351 Crowd celebrating

2008. Youth Olympic Games, Singapore, 2010. Multicoloured.

1779 (26c.) Type **351** 40 40
1780 $2 Crowd with flag, schoolchildren and Supreme Court building 2·40 2·75

Nos. 1779/80 were printed together, *se-tenant*, forming a composite design showing a crowd celebrating the announcement that Singapore had been selected as host city.

No. 1779 is inscr '1st local' and sold for 26c.

352 Carne de porco à Alentejana (pork and clams)

2008. Local Delights. Multicoloured.

1781 (26c.) Type **352** 45 45
1782 (26c.) Lombo de bacalhau braseado em lascas (grilled codfish slices) 45 45
1783 (26c.) Yangzhou fried rice 45 45
1784 (26c.) Crispy fried chicken 45 45
1785 65c. Roti Prata 80 80
1786 65c. Hainanese chicken rice 80 80
1787 65c. Laksa 80 80
1788 65c. Satay 80 80
MS1789 140×90 mm. $2×2 Clay pot rice (vert); Chilli crab (vert) 5·00 5·00

Nos. 1781/4 and 1785/8 were each printed together, *se-tenant*, as blocks of four stamps forming a composite design of a dish.

Nos. 1781/4 are inscr '1ST LOCAL' and sold for 26c. each.

Stamps in similar designs were issued by Macau.

353 Table Tennis

2008. Olympic Games, Beijing. Multicoloured.

1790 (26c.) Type **253** 40 35
1791 (32c.) Sailing 50 50
1792 $1.10 Shooting 1·60 1·75
1793 $1.10 Badminton 1·60 1·75

No. 1790 is inscr '1ST LOCAL' and sold for 26c.
No. 1791 is inscr '2ND LOCAL' and sold for 32c.

2008. Olympex Olympic Stamp Expo, Beijing. Sheet 160×80 mm containing Nos. 1750/2.

MS1794 (26c.) Type **348**; 65c. Rat and orange; $1.10 Two rats (44×24 mm) 2·75 3·00

354 Parliament House (David Tay Poey Cher)

2008. National Day. 'Singapore Today'. Ddesigns showing photographs by Cultural Medallion winning photographers. Multicoloured.

1795 (26c.) Type **354** 50 50
1796 (26c.) Tampines North Community Centre (Foo Tee Jun) 50 50
1797 (26c.) Metal sculptures and high-rise buildings of financial sector (Chua Soo Bin) 50 50
1798 (26c.) North Bridge and financial sector (Teo Bee Yen) 50 50
1799 (26c.) People in Temple Street (Si Ma Lu Guanyin) (Tan Lip Seng) 50 50
1800 50c. People at Orchard MRT Station (David Tay Poey Cher) 75 75
1801 50c. Train at Orchard MRT Station (Foo Tee Jun) 75 75
1802 50c. Glass-fronted and other high-rise buildings (Chua Soo Bin) 75 75
1803 50c. Temple within Central Business District (Teo Bee Yen) 75 75
1804 50c. Fish stall at Tekka Market (Tan Lip Seng) 75 75
MS1805 75×75 mm. $2 Montage of photographs of Singapore buildings (60×60 mm) 2·75 3·00

Nos. 1795/9 were all inscr '1ST LOCAL' and sold for 26c. each.

355 Pilots, Fighter Plane and Helicopter

2008. 40th Anniv of the Republic of Singapore Air Force (RSAF). Multicoloured.

1806 (26c.) Type **355** 75 35
1807 (32c.) Weapon Systems Officers monitoring aircraft in Singapore airspace 90 60
1808 65c. Unmanned Aerial Vehicle and pilot (on ground) 1·40 85
1809 80c. Senior Technicians and helicopter 1·75 1·50
1810 $1.10 Weapon Systems Officers and Air Defence Artillery 2·00 2·25

No. 1806 is inscr '1st Local' and sold for 26c.
No. 1807 is inscr '2nd Local' and sold for 32c.

356 Racing Car and City of Singapore

2008. First Formula 1 Singapore Grand Prix. Multicoloured.

1811 $2 Type **356** 2·00 2·25
1812 $2 Racing car and chequered flag 2·00 2·25

Nos. 1811/12 were each printed together, se-tenant, forming a composite background design.

2008. Jakarta 2008 International Stamp Exhibition, Jakarta, Indonesia. Sheet 160×80 mm containing Nos. 1750/2.

MS1813 (26c.) Type **348**; 65c. Rat and orange; $1.10 Two rats (44×24 mm) 3·00 3·25

357 Postman, 2008

2008. Postal Services through the Years. Multicoloured.

1814 (26c.) Type **357** 40 25
1815 (32c.) Postman with motor scooter, c. 1980 55 35
1816 50c. Postman with bicycle, c. 1970 1·25 90
1817 80c. Postman and pillar box, c. 1950 1·40 1·40
1818 $1.10 Postman, c. 1910 1·50 2·00

No. 1814 is inscr '1ST LOCAL' and sold for 26c.
No. 1815 is inscr '2ND LOCAL' and sold for 32c.

358 Pepper (*Piper nigrum*)

2008. Cash Crops of Early Singapore. T **358** and similar vert designs. Multicoloured

(a) Ordinary gum

1819 (26c.) Type **358** 55 30
1820 65c. Tapioca (*Manihot esculenta*) 1·25 95
1821 $1.10 Rubber (*Hevea brasiliensis*) 1·75 1·75
1822 $2 Nutmeg (*Myristica fragrans*) 2·75 3·50

(b) Self-adhesive.

1823 (26c.) As Type **358** 40 40

359 Dragon Fruit

2008. Fruit. Multicoloured.

1824 65c. Type **359** 1·25 1·25
1825 $1.10 Durian 1·75 1·75
MS1826 135×94 mm. Nos. 1824/5 3·00 3·25

Stamps in similar designs were issued by Vietnam.

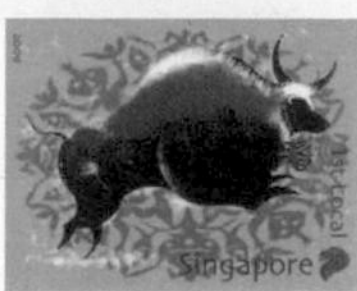

360 Ox

2009. Chinese New Year. Year of the Ox. Multicoloured

(a) Ordinary gum

1827 (26c.) Type **360** 55 35
1828 65c. Ox (facing left) 1·25 1·10
1829 $1.10 Two oxen (34×44 mm) 1·75 2·25

(b) Self-adhesive.

1830 (26c.) Type **360** 45 45

Nos. 1827 and 1830 were inscr '1st Local' and initially sold for 26c. each.

361 Couple's Faces in Champagne Glass

2009. Greetings Stamps. 'Let's Celebrate'. Multicoloured. Ordinary or self-adhesive gum.

1831 (26c.) Type **361** 45 50
1832 (26c.) Girl and birthday candles 45 50
1833 (26c.) Couple 45 50
1834 (26c.) Girl with teddy bear and wrapped presents 45 50
1835 (26c.) Boy holding red balloons 45 50

362 Cathay, 1939

2009. Cinema Theatres of Yesteryear. Multicoloured.

1841 (26c.) Type **362** 45 25
1842 50c. The Majestic, 1928 75 60
1843 80c. Capitol Building, 1933 1·25 85
1844 $1.10 Queens, c.1920 1·75 2·25
1845 $1.10 Rex, 1946 1·75 2·25

No. 1840 was inscribed '1st Local' and originally sold for 26c.

2009. China 2009 World Stamp Exhibition, Luoyang, China. Sheet 120×75 mm containing Nos. 1827/9.

MS1846 (26c.) Type **360**; 65c. Ox (facing left); $1.10 Two oxen (34×44 mm) 3·00 3·25

2009. Hong Kong 2009 International Stamp Exhibition. Sheet 120×75 mm containing Nos. 1827/9.

MS1847 (26c.) Type **360**; 65c. Ox (facing left); $1.10 Two oxen (34×44 mm) 3·00 3·25

363 Map of Circle Line System on Singapore Map

2009. Launch of SMRT Circle Line. Multicoloured.

1848 (26c.) Type **363** 60 30
1849 80c. New Circle Line station 1·40 1·10
1850 $1.10 Circle Line train 1·75 1·60
1851 $2 Circle Line Operation Control Centre 3·50 4·50

364 Visitor Centre

2009. 150th Anniv of Singapore Botanic Gardens. Multicoloured.

1852 (26c.) Type **364** 1·00 1·00
1853 (26c.) Rain tree and Band Stand 1·00 1·00
1854 $1.10 Orchids, girl on a swing (sculpture) and pavilion 2·25 2·25
1855 $1.10 Flying swans and heliconias at Swan Lake 2·25 2·25
MS1856 113×80 mm. $2 Black swans (47×47 mm) 4·25 4·25

Nos. 1852/5 were printed together, se-tenant, forming a composite design.

365 Ice Kacang (shaved ice with red beans)

2009. Local Desserts. Multicoloured.

1857 (26c.) Type **365** 40 35
1858 (32c.) Ondeh-ondeh (dough filled with palm sugar) 50 45
1859 65c. Ang ku kueh (rice flour cake with bean paste or peanut paste filling) 1·00 90
1860 80c. Lapis sagu (tapioca layer cake) 1·25 1·10
1861 $1.10 Mithai (assorted Indian sweets) 1·50 1·75

No. 1857 was inscr '1ST LOCAL' and originally sold for 26c.

No. 1858 was inscr '2ND LOCAL' and originally sold for 32c.

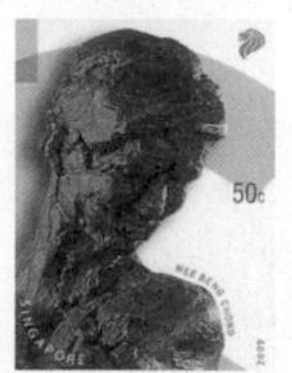

366 *Standing Figure* (Wee Beng Chong)

2009. National Day. Sculptures. Multicoloured.

1862 50c. Type **366** 80 80
1863 50c. *We're Happy. Are You Happy?* (Teo Eng Seng) 80 80
1864 50c. *Art Trees* (Han Sai Por) 80 80
1865 50c. *Aspirations* (Anthony Poon) 80 80
1866 50c. *Nude 2* (Tay Chee Toh) (horiz) 80 80
1867 50c. *Signature* (Brother Joseph McNally) (horiz) 80 80
1868 50c. *Wealth* (Ng Eng Teng) (horiz) 80 80
MS1869 113×80 mm. $2 Sculptures (as shown on Nos. 1862/8) (95×37 mm) 2·75 3·00

367 Gymnast ('Excellence')

2009. Youth Olympic Games, Singapore, 2010 (2nd issue). Multicoloured.

1870 (26c.) Type **367** 45 35
1871 65c. Athlete greeting tennis player ('Hello') 1·00 90
1872 $1.10 Three athletes ('Friendship') 1·60 1·50
1873 $2 Hurdler ('Respect') 3·00 3·25

No. 1870 was inscr '1st Local' and originally sold for 26c.

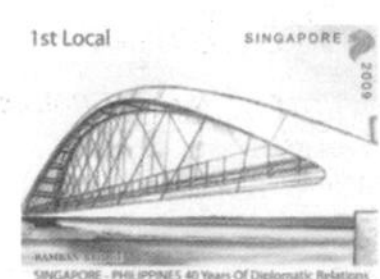

368 Bamban Bridge, Philippines

2009. 40th Anniv of Diplomatic Relations between Singapore and the Philippines. Bridges. Multicoloured.

1874 (26c.) Type **368** 45 35
1875 65c. Cavenagh Bridge, Singapore 1·10 1·00
1876 80c. Henderson Waves and Alexandra Arch, Singapore 1·25 1·25
1877 $1.10 Marcelo B. Fernan Bridge, Cebu, Philippines 1·60 1·75
MS1878 120×75 mm. Nos. 1874/7 4·00 4·00

No. 1874 was inscr '1st Local' and originally sold for 26c.

Stamps in similar designs were issued on the same date by the Phillippines.

369 Singaraja Statue, Bali

2009. Tourist Attractions. Multicoloured.

1879 (26c.) Type **369** 45 35
1880 65c. Merlion and Sentosa Island resort 1·10 1·00
1881 80c. Taman Mini Indonesia Park, Jakarta 1·25 1·25
1882 $1.10 Sentosa Island resort 1·60 1·75
MS1883 120×75 mm. Nos. 1879/82 4·00 4·00

No. 1879 was inscr '1ST LOCAL' and originally sold for 26c.

Stamps in similar designs were issued by Indonesia.

370 Park and City Skyline, Singapore

2009. Asia-Pacific Economic Co-operation (APEC) Meetings, Singapore. Multicoloured.

1884	(26c.) Type **370**	60	60
1885	80c. Singapore at night	1·50	1·50
1886	$1.10 Airliner and cargo	2·25	2·25
1887	$2 Harbour and city skyline, Singapore	3·25	3·25

No. 1884 was inscr '1st LOCAL' and originally sold for 26c.

371 Tiger

2010. Chinese New Year. Year of the Tiger. Multicoloured

(a) Ordinary gum

1888	(26c.) Type **371**	50	35
1889	65c. Pink and black tiger	1·10	1·00
1890	$1.10 Two tigers (35×45 mm)	1·75	2·00

(b) Self-adhesive.

1891	(26c.) Type **371**	45	45

Nos. 1888 and 1891 were inscr '1st Local' and originally sold for 26c.

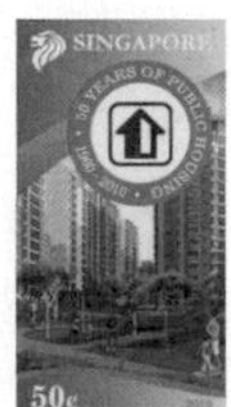

372 Modern Flats

2010. Anniversaries. Multicoloured.

1892	50c. Type **372** (50th anniv of Housing and Development Board)	90	90
1893	50c. Citizens (50th anniv of People's Association)	90	90
1894	$1 Customs Officers (Centenary of Singapore Customs) (horiz)	1·60	1·60
1895	$1 Scouts (Centenary of scouting in Singapore) (horiz)	1·60	1·60

373 Children in Playground

2010. Playgrounds. Multicoloured.

1896	(26c.) Type **373**	45	35
1897	50c. Playground with 'dragon's head' tubular apparatus	90	75
1898	65c. Slide, treetop boardwalk and path with steps through trees	1·10	90
1899	80c. Roundabout, rings and climbing frame	1·40	1·25
1900	$1.10 Tubular apparatus and seesaw	1·75	1·75
1901	$2 Rope climbing frames and slides	3·25	4·00

No. 1896 was inscr '1st Local' and originally sold for 26c.

374 Common Birdwing

2010. Butterflies. Multicoloured.

(a) Phosphorised paper.

1902	(26c.) Type **374**	60	45
1903	80c. Tailed jay	1·40	1·10
1904	$1.10 Common posy	1·90	1·90
1905	$2 Blue glassy tiger	3·50	4·00

(b) Self-adhesive

1906	(26c.) As Type **374**	60	60

2010. London 2010 Festival of Stamps. Sheet 120×75 mm containing Nos. 1888/90

MS1907	(26c.) Type **371**; 65c. Pink and black tiger; $1.10 Two tigers (35×45 mm)	3·25	3·25

375 Saga (*Adenanthera pavonina*)

2010. 'know 10 trees'

(a) Ordinary gum

1908	(26c.) Type **375**	55	55
1909	(26c.) Rain tree (*Samanea saman*)	55	55
1910	(26c.) Yellow flame (*Peltophorum pterocarpum*)	55	55
1911	(26c.) Tembusu (*Fagraea fragrans*)	55	55
1912	(26c.) Angsana (*Pterocarpus indicus*) (vert)	55	55
1913	(26c.) Sea almond (*Terminalia catappa*) (vert)	55	55
1914	(26c.) Broad-leafed mahogany (*Swietenia macrophylla*) (vert)	55	55
1915	(26c.) Sea apple (*Syzygium grande*) (vert)	55	55
1916	(26c.) Senegal mahogany (*Khaya senegalensis*) (vert)	55	55
1917	(26c.) Trumpet tree (*Tabebuia rosea*) (vert)	55	55

(b) Self-adhesive

1918	(26c.) As Type **375**	55	55
1919	(26c.) As No. 1909	55	55
1920	(26c.) As No. 1910	55	55
1921	(26c.) As No. 1911	55	55
1922	(26c.) As No. 1912 (vert)	55	55
1923	(26c.) As No. 1913 (vert)	55	55
1924	(26c.) As No. 1914 (vert)	55	55
1925	(26c.) As No. 1915 (vert)	55	55
1926	(26c.) As No. 1916 (vert)	55	55
1927	(26c.) As No. 1917 (vert)	55	55

Nos. 1908/27 were all inscr '1st Local' and originally sold for 26c. each.

2010. Bangkok 2010 International Stamp Exhibition, Thailand. Sheet 120×75 mm containing Nos. 1888/90

MS1928	(26c.) Type **371**; 65c. Pink and black tiger; $1.10 Two tigers (35×45 mm)	3·50	3·75

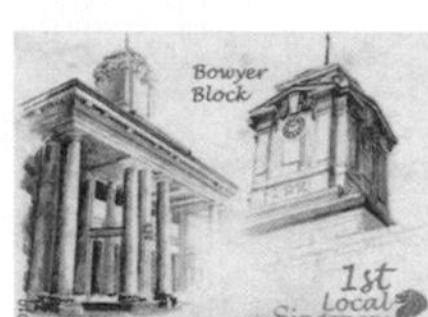

376 Bowyer Block

2010. National Day. Multicoloured.

1929	(26c.) Type **376**	45	35
1930	(32c.) College of Medicine Building	55	45
1931	55c. Command House	90	80
1932	65c. Hwa Chong Institution Clock Tower	1·25	1·10
1933	80c. Former Raffles College	1·50	1·50
1934	$1.10 Tan Teck Guan Building	2·00	2·50
MS1935	113×80 mm. $2 Hwa Chong Institution clock tower, Tan Teck Guan Building entrance, stone carving from College of Medicine Building, grille from Command House, pillar and urn from former Raffles College and Bowyer Block clock tower (100×40 mm). P 14×13½	3·75	4·00

No. 1929 was inscr '1st Local' and originally sold for 26c.

No. 1930 was inscr '2nd Local' and originally sold for 32c.

377 Mascots Lyo and Merly on Globe

2010. Youth Olympic Games, Singapore (3rd issue). Multicoloured.

1936	(26c.) Type **377**	45	35
1937	65c. Lyo and Merly on desert island	1·25	1·10
1938	$1.10 Merly on surfboard	2·00	2·00
1939	$2 Lyo playing basketball	3·50	3·75

No. 1936 was inscr '1st Local' and originally sold for 26c.

378 Second World War Soldiers (Battle for Pasir Panjang)

2010. Kent Ridge Park Heritage Trail. Multicoloured.

1940	(32c.) Type **378**	1·00	1·00
1941	65c. Straw-headed bulbul, white lilies and canopy walk	1·50	1·50
1942	80c. White lilies, eagle and canopy walk	1·60	1·60
1943	$1.10 *Dillenia suffruticosa*, other trees and pavilion	1·75	1·75

Nos. 1940/3 were printed together, *se-tenant*, forming a composite design showing plants and trees.

No. 1940 was inscr '2nd LOCAL' and originally sold for 32c.

379 Lion Dance (Chinese New Year)

2010. Festivals in Singapore. Multicoloured.

(a) Ordinary gum

1944	(26c.) Type **379**	70	70
1945	(26c.) Candles, greenery and star (Christmas)	70	70
1946	(26c.) Candles in holders (Hari Raya Aidilfitri)	70	70
1947	(26c.) Peacocks (Deepavali)	70	70
1948	55c. Fruit and wreath (Chinese New Year)	1·25	1·25
1949	55c. Baubles (Christmas)	1·25	1·25
1950	55c. Mosaic pattern with streamers and star and crescent within star (Hari Raya Aidilfitri)	1·25	1·25
1951	55c. Lamp (Deepavali)	1·25	1·25

(b) Self-adhesive

1952	(26c.) As Type **379**	70	70
1953	(26c.) As No. 1945	70	70
1954	(26c.) As No. 1946	70	70
1955	(26c.) As No. 1947	70	70

Nos. 1944/7 and 1952/5 were all inscr '1st LOCAL' and originally sold for 26c. each.

380 Rabbit

2011. Chinese New Year. Year of the Rabbit. Multicoloured.

(a) Ordinary gum

1956	(26c.) Type **380**	55	40
1957	65c. Rabbit (facing left)	1·40	1·25
1958	$1.10 Two rabbits (35×45 mm)	2·50	2·75

(b) Self-adhesive

1959	(26c.) As Type **380**	1·00	1·00

Nos. 1956 and 1959 were inscr '1st Local' and originally sold for 26c.

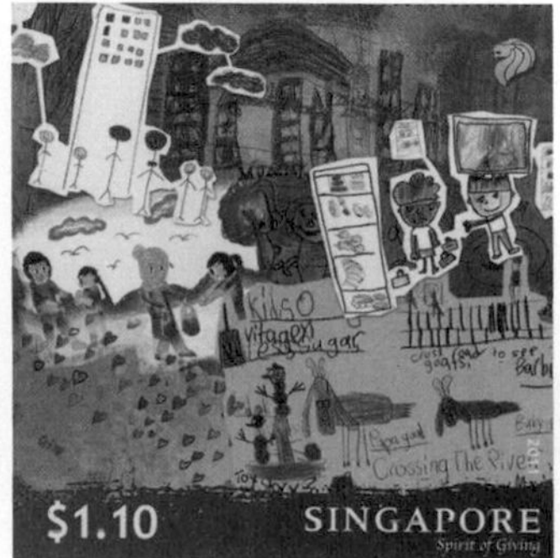

381 Children's Drawings and Paintings

2011. 'Spirit of Giving'. Multicoloured.

1960	$1.10 Type **381**	2·25	1·75
1961	$2 Children's drawings and paintings including helping hands and children packing parcel and giving gift to woman in wheelchair	4·25	4·75

2011. Indipex 2011 International Stamp Exhibition, New Delhi. Sheet 120×75 mm containing Nos. 1956/8

MS1962	(26c.) As Type **380**; 65c. Rabbit (facing left); $1.10 Two rabbits (35×45 mm)	4·00	4·25

382 Common Tilapia (*Oreochromis mossambicus*)

2011. Pond Life. Multicoloured.

(a) Ordinary gum

1963	5c. White-collared Kingfisher (*Todiramphus chloris*) (40×30 mm) (13.4.11)	20	20
1964	20c. Diving Beetle (*Cybister rugosus*) (40×30 mm) (13.4.11)	35	25
1965	(26c.) Water Lily (*Nymphaea odorata*) (30×27 mm) (13.4.11)	65	35
1966	(26c.) Yellow Burhead flower (*Limnocharis flava*) (30×27 mm) (12.3.12)	65	35
1966*a*	(26c.) Geli Geli (*Lasia spinosa*) (aquatic plant) (30×27 mm) (20.3.13)	35	25
1967	30c. Common Redbolt Dragonfly (*Rhodothemis rufa*) (13.4.11)	40	40
1968	(32c.) Water Hyacinth (*Eichhornia crassipes*) (30×27 mm) (13.4.11)	70	40
1969	(32c.) Water Lettuce (*Pistia stratiotes*) (30×27 mm) (12.3.12)	70	40
1969a	(32c.) Water Gentian (*Nymphoides indica*) (30×27 mm) (20.3.13)	40	40
1970	45c. Ornate Coraltail Damselflies (*Ceriagrion cerinorubellum*) (40×30 mm) (13.4.11)	60	50
1971	50c. Black Marsh Terrapin (*Siebenrockiella crassicollis*) (40×30 mm) (13.4.11)	60	50
1972	55c. White-breasted Waterhen (*Amaurornis phoenicurus*) (40×30 mm) (13.4.11)	80	80
1973	65c. Common Greenback Frog (*Rana erythraea*) (40×30 mm) (13.4.11)	1·00	1·00
1974	80c. Common Toad (*Bufo melanostictus*) (40×30 mm) (13.4.11)	1·40	1·40
1975	$1.10 Type **382**	2·25	2·25
1976	$2 Pond Wolf Spider (*Pardosa pseudoannulata*)	5·50	3·75
1977	$5 Water Strider (*Neogerris parvulus*)	9·00	7·50
1978	$10 Water Scorpion (*Laccotrephes simclatus*)	12·00	10·00

(b) Self-adhesive

1979	(26c.) As No. 1965 (13.4.11)	80	80
1979*b*	(26c.) As No. 1966 (12.3.12)	80	80
1979*c*	(26c.) As No. 1966a (20.3.13)	35	35

Nos. 1965/6*a* and 1979/*c* were inscr '1st Local' and were originally valid for 26c.

Nos. 1968/9*a* were inscr '2nd Local' and originally sold for 32c.

383 Bristol Box Kite taking off from Farrer Park, 16 March 1911

2011. Centenary of Aviation in Singapore. Multicoloured.

1980	(26c.) Type **383**	70	40
1981	45c. Fokker F-7A, Seletar Airport, c. 1930	1·25	70
1982	65c. Airspeed Consul, Kallang Airport	1·75	1·25
1983	80c. F-15SG, Paya Lebar Air Base	2·00	2·00
1984	$1.10 Airbus A380, Singapore Changi Airport	2·25	2·50

No. 1980 was inscr '1st LOCAL' and originally sold for 26c

384 Lau Pa Sat

2011. Hawker Centres of Singapore. Multicoloured.

1985	80c. Type **384**	1·75	1·75
1986	80c. East Coast Hawker Centre	1·75	1·75
1987	80c. Maxwell Hawker Centre	1·75	1·75
1988	80c. Newton Hawker Centre	1·75	1·75

385 Otter swimming

2011. Oriental Small-clawed Otter (*Aonyx cinerea*). Multicoloured.

1989	50c. Type **385**	1·75	1·75
1990	50c. Otter on land (tree in background)	1·75	1·75
1991	$1.10 Two otters	2·50	2·50
1992	$1.10 Head of otter	2·50	2·50

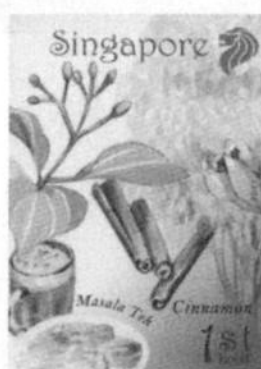

386 Cinnamon and Masala The

2011. Spices. Multicoloured.

1993	(26c.) Type **386**	45	35
1994	(32c.) Coriander and satay	50	40
1995	65c. Star anise and braised duck	1·25	1·00
1996	80c. Tamarind and Assam prawns	1·40	1·40
1997	$1.10 Turmeric and fish head curry	2·40	2·75

No. 1993 was inscr '1st Local' and originally sold for 26c.

No. 1994 was inscr '2nd Local' and originally sold for 32c.

2011. Philanippon 2011 World Stamp Exhibition, Yokohama, Japan. Sheet 120×75 mm containing Nos. 1956/8. Multicoloured.

MS1998	(26c.) Type **380**; 65c. Rabbit (facing left); $1.10 Two rabbits (35×45 mm)	3·75	4·00

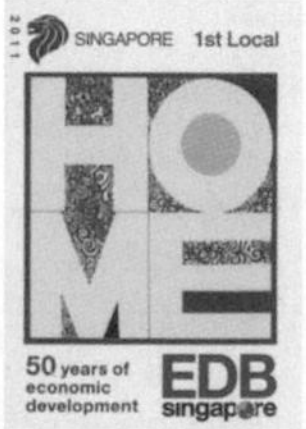

387 'HOME'

2011. 50th Anniv of Singapore Economic Development Board. Multicoloured.

1999	(26c.) Type **387**	45	30
2000	$2 Stylized tree	4·00	4·50

No. 1999 was inscr '1st Local' and originally sold for 26c.

388 Joo Chiat

2011. National Day. Areas of Historical Significance (1st series). Multicoloured.

2001	50c. Type **388**	80	80
2002	50c. Taman Jurong	80	80
2003	$1.10 Old Joo Chiat	2·40	2·40
2004	$1.10 Old Taman Jurong	2·40	2·40
MS2005	102×81 mm. $2 Old and modern Joo Chiat and Taman Jurong (72×51 mm)	5·50	5·50

389 Film

2011. 'Greetings from YourSingapore'. Multicoloured.

(a) Ordinary gum

2006	(26c.) Type **389**	50	50
2007	(26c.) Pattern of blue spheres	50	50
2008	(26c.) Red, blue and purple squares	50	50
2009	(26c.) Plants and flowers	50	50
2010	(26c.) Montage of images including faces and smiling sun	50	50
2011	(26c.) Blue checked and red and blue striped carrier bags	50	50
2012	(26c.) Green bubbles	50	50
2013	(26c.) Food	50	50
2014	(26c.) Grey, purple and dark red squares	50	50
2015	(26c.) Red roses	50	50

(b) Self-adhesive

2016	(26c.) As Type **389**	50	50
2017	(26c.) As No. 2007	50	50
2018	(26c.) As No. 2008	50	50
2019	(26c.) As No. 2009	50	50
2020	(26c.) As No. 2010	50	50
2021	(26c.) As No. 2011	50	50
2022	(26c.) As No. 2012	50	50
2023	(26c.) As No. 2013	50	50
2024	(26c.) As No. 2014	50	50
2025	(26c.) As No. 2015	50	50

Nos. 2006/25 were all inscr '1st LOCAL' and originally sold for 26c.

390 Singapore River (image scaled to 30% of original size)

2011. Significant Rivers. Multicoloured.

2026	$1.10 Type **390**	1·75	1·75
2027	$2 Nile river	3·75	3·75
MS2028	135×90 mm. Nos. 2026/7	5·50	5·50

Similar designs were issued by Egypt.

2011. China 2011 27th Asian International Stamp Exhibition, Wuxi, China. Sheet 120×75 mm containing Nos. 1956/8

MS2029	(26c.) Type **380**; 65c. Rabbit (facing left); $1.10 Two rabbits (35×45 mm)	3·50	3·50

391 *Vanda* Miss Joaquim

2011. 20th World Orchid Conference, Singapore. Multicoloured.

2030	(26c.) Type **391**	45	25
2031	45c. *Renanthera*	60	35
2032	65c. *Dendrobium* World Peace	1·10	85
2033	80c. *Cyrtocidium Goldiana*	1·40	1·25
2034	$2 *Grammatophyllum speciosum*	4·25	5·00

No. 2030 was inscr '1ST LOCAL' and originally sold for 26c.

392 Dragon

2012. Chinese New Year. Year of the Dragon. Multicoloured.

(a) Ordinary gum

2035	(26c.) Type **392**	35	25
2036	65c. Dragon (different)	1·10	1·10
2037	$1.10 Two dragons (35×45 mm)	2·40	2·50

(b) Self-adhesive

2038	(26c.) As Type **392**	35	35

Nos. 2035 and 2038 were inscr '1st Local' and originally sold for 26c.

393 Lapis Sagu (coconut milk, tapioca flour and pandan)

2012. Local Tea Time Snacks. Multicoloured.

(a) Ordinary gum

2039	(26c.) Type **393**	35	25
2040	50c. Kueh dadar (coconut pancake)	65	50
2041	80c. Bao (Chinese bun)	1·60	1·60
2042	$1.10 Kueh tutu	2·50	2·75

(b) Self-adhesive

2043	(26c.) As Type **393**	35	35

Nos. 2039 and 2043 were inscr '1st Local' and originally sold for 26c. each.

394 Punggol Reservoir

2012. Reservoirs of Singapore. Multicoloured.

2044	(26c.) Type **394**	35	35
2045	(26c.) Jurong Lake	35	35
2046	(26c.) Lower Seletar Reservoir	35	35
2047	(26c.) Serangoon Reservoir	35	35
2048	(26c.) Marina Reservoir	35	35
2049	50c. Lower Pierce Reservoir	60	60
2050	50c. MacRitchie Reservoir	60	60
2051	50c. Bedolc Reservoir	60	60
2052	50c. Pandan Reservoir	60	60
2053	50c. Upper Seletar Reservoir	60	60

Nos. 2044/8 were inscr '1st LOCAL' and originally sold for 26c. each

395 Produce Stall

2012. Local Markets. Multicoloured.

2054	80c. Type **395**	1·40	1·40
2055	80c. Fishmonger	1·40	1·40
2056	80c. Two men at produce stall	1·40	1·40
2057	80c. Man and two women at market stall	1·40	1·40

396 Singapore in 2012

2012. United Nations International Year of Co-operatives. Multicoloured.

2058	(26c.) Type **396**	25	25
2059	(26c.) Birth of the Singapore National Co-operative Federation, 1980	25	25
2060	50c. Trade Union Seminar (Birth of the NTUC Co-operatives), 1969	45	45
2061	$1.10 Birth of Singapore's first co-operative, the Singapore Government Staff Credit Co-operative Society, 1925	2·25	2·25
2062	$1.10 Founders of the Co-operative Principles, Rochdale, England, 1844	2·25	2·25

2012. Indonesia 2012 World Stamp Championship and Exhibition, Jakarta. Sheet 120×75 mm containing Nos. 2035/7

MS2063	(26c.) Type **392**; 65c. Dragon (different); $1.10 Two dragons (35×45 mm)	3·50	3·50

397 Biomes and Solar-powered "Supertrees", Bay South (image scaled to 41% of original size)

2012. Gardens by the Bay. Multicoloured.

2064	$1.10 Type **397**	2·75	2·50
2065	$1.10 Kingfisher and dragonfly in gardens	2·75	2·50

398 Mascot Wenlock playing Table Tennis

2012. Olympic Games, London. Official Mascot Wenlock and Sports. Multicoluored.

2066	(26c.) Type **398**	25	25
2067	65c. Wenlock swimming	85	85
2068	$1.10 Wenlock sailing	2·25	2·25
2069	$2 Wenlock playing badminton	4·50	4·50

No. 2066 was inscr '1st Local' and originally sold for 26c.

399 Tiong Bahru (Present)

2012. National Day. Areas of Historical Significance. Multicoloured.

2070	(32c.) Type **399**	40	40
2071	50c. Balestier (Present)	45	45
2072	80c. Tiong Bahru (Past)	1·40	1·40
2073	$1.10 Balestier (Past)	2·25	2·25
MS2074	114×81 mm. $2 Tiong Bahru and Balestier (100×81 mm)	4·50	4·50

No. 2070 was inscr '2nd Local' and originally sold for 32c.

400 White-bellied Sea Eagle (*Haliaeetus leucogaster*)

2012. Singapore 2015 World Stamp Exhibition (1st issue). Multicoloured.

2075	$2 Type **400**	5·00	5·00
2076	$2 Yellow-bellied sunbird (*Leptocoma jugularis*)	5·00	5·00

401 Giant Panda 'Kai Kai'

2012. Giant Pandas. Multicoloured.

(a) Ordinary gum

2077	50c. Type **401**	45	45
2078	65c. Jia Jia in tree	85	85
2079	$2 Kia Kia and Jia Jia (30×56 mm)	4·50	4·50

(b) Self-adhesive

2080	50c. As Type **401**	45	45

402 Chinese New Year

2012. Festivals. Multicoloured.

(a) Ordinary gum

2081	(26c.) Type **402**	25	25
2082	(26c.) Christmas	25	25
2083	(26c.) Deepavali	25	25
2084	(26c.) Hari Raya Aidilfitri	25	25
2085	55c. Chinese New Year (girl wearing lion costume)	50	50
2086	55c. Christmas (children and decorations)	50	50
2087	55c. Deepavali (woman, boy and candles)	50	50
2088	55c. Hari Raya Aidilfitri (family and table of food)	50	50

(b) Self-adhesive

2089	(26c.) As Type **402**	25	25
2090	(26c.) As No. 2082	25	25
2091	(26c.) As No. 2083	25	25
2092	(26c.) As No. 2084	25	25

2012. Beijing International Stamp and Coin Expo 2012. Sheet 120×76 mm containing Nos. 2035/7

MS2093	(26c.) Type **392**; 65c. Dragon (different); $1.10 Two dragons (35×45 mm)	3·50	3·50

403 First President Encik Yusof Bin Ishak (from $100 banknote), *Vanda Rothscildiana* 'Teo Choo Hong' ($50 banknote), Trading Vessel *Palari* ($10 banknote) and Yellow-breasted Sunbird ($20 banknote)

2012. 45th Anniv of Currency Interchangeability Agreement between Singapore and Brunei. Multicoloured.

2094 $1 Type **403** 2·10 2·10
2095 $2 Singapore scene and Omar Ali Saifuddien Mosque, Brunei from back of 40th anniversary commemorative note, 2007 4·50 4·50
MS2096 120×75 mm. Nos. 2094/5 and $1 *Ipomoea pescaprae* (plant) (2007 $20 note), Omar Ali Saifuddien Mosque (1967 banknotes), Rain Forest Floor (1966 $5 Notes) and Vendor in Boat (1989 banknote) (Brunei) 8·50 8·50

Stamps in similar designs were issued by Brunei.

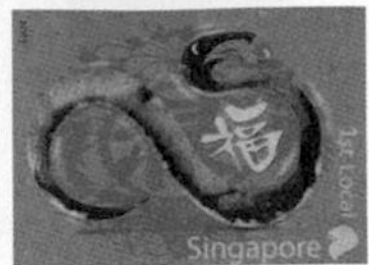

404 Snake

2013. Chinese New Year. Year of the Snake. Multicoloured.

(a) Ordinary gum

2097 (26c.) Type **404** 25 25
2098 65c. Snake (facing left) 85 85
2099 $1.10 Two snakes (35×45 mm) 2·25 2·25

(b) Self-adhesive

2100 (26c.) As Type **404** 25 25

Nos. 2097 and 2100 were inscr '1st Local' and originally sold for 26c.

405 Tanjong Pagar Railway Station

2013. Historical Railway Stations. Multicoloured.

2101 (26c.) Type **405** 40 25
2102 65c. Bukit Timah Railway Station 1·25 85
2103 $1.10 Waiting hall of Tanjong Pagar Railway Station 2·50 2·25
2104 $2 Railway at Bukit Timah 5·00 5·50

No. 2101 was inscr '1ST LOCAL' and originally sold for 26c.

2013. Australia 2013 International Stamp Exhibition, Melbourne. Sheet 120×75 mm containing Nos. 2097/9

MS2105 (26c.) Type **404**; 65c. Snake (facing left); $1.10 Two snakes (35×45 mm) 3·00 3·25

406 The Fullerton Hotel

2013. Marina Bay Skyline. Multicoloured.

2106 (26c.) Type **406** 60 60
2107 (32c.) The Singapore Flyer 80 80
2108 65c. Esplanade - Theatres on the Bay (arts centre with concert hall and theatre) 1·50 1·50
2109 $2 Marina Bay Sands 4·00 4·00

No. 2106 was inscr '1st Local' and originally sold for 26c.

No. 2107 was inscr '2nd Local' and originally sold for 32c.

Nos. 2106/9 were printed together as blocks of four stamps, each block forming a composite design with a circle of Singapore skyline with Marina Bay scenes contained within it. Nos. 2107/8 are inverted within the block of four.

407 'Hi'

2013. Greetings in Sign Language. Multicoloured.

(a) Ordinary gum

2110 (26c.) Type **407** 25 25
2111 (26c.) 'Welcome' 25 25
2112 (26c.) 'I Love You' 25 25
2113 (26c.) 'Thanks' 25 25
2114 (26c.) 'Goodbye' 25 25

(b) Self-adhesive

2115 (26c.) As Type **407** 25 25
2116 (26c.) As No. 2111 25 25
2117 (26c.) As No. 2112 25 25
2118 (26c.) As No. 2113 25 25
2119 (26c.) As No. 2114 25 25

Nos. 2110/19 were each inscr '1ST LOCAL' and were originally sold for 26c.

408 Flowers, Pangolin, Kingfisher, Lizard and Gardens by the Bay

2013. Our City in a Garden. Multicoloured.

(a) Ordinary gum

2120 (26c.) Type **408** 45 25
2121 50c. Hornbill, crab and joggers in park 85 60
2122 80c. Orchids, flowers, magpie robin, butterfly, caterpillar and cyclist in park 1·50 1·50
2123 $1.10 Otter, dragonfly and parks with trees 1·60 1·75

(b) Self-adhesive

MS2124 115×135 mm. As Nos. 2120/1, each ×2 2·50 2·50

No. 2120 was inscr '1st Local' and originally sold for 26c.

2013. Thailand 2013 World Stamp Exhibition, Bangkok. Sheet 120×75 mm containing Nos. 2097/9

MS2125 (26c.) Type **404**; 65c. Snake (facing left); $1.10 Two snakes (35×45 mm) 3·00 3·25

409 Beating SARS Together, 2003

2013. 48th Anniv of Independence. Multicoloured.

2126 (26c.) Type **409** 35 20
2127 50c. Gardens by the Bay and aerial view of Singapore River ('Cleaning and Greening our City') 55 35
2128 65c. NEWater staff and people with pails of water ('Conquering our Water Challenges') 80 65
2129 80c. Modern Singaporeans and soldiers in streets during racial riots of 1964 ('Living Together in Harmony') 1·10 75
2130 $1.10 Modern Singapore and Singapore in 1960s ('Forging a Vibrant Economy') 1·40 1·60
MS2131 113×80 mm. $2 '1965 - 2013 48 Years of Independence' in gold foil on gold background (48×48 mm) 2·75 3·25

410 Sea Shells

2013. Singapore 2015 World Stamp Exhibition (2nd issue). Multicoloured.

2132 $2 Type **410** 5·00 5·00
2133 $2 Veil-tailed Guppies 5·00 5·00

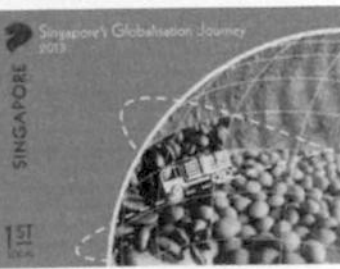

411 Produce and Lorry

2013. Singapore's Globalisation Journey. Multicoloured.

2134 (26c.) Type **411** 25 25
2135 65c. Containers and ship 85 85
2136 80c. City of Singapore and airliner 1·30 1·30
2137 $1.10 Handshake, computer screens and train 2·25 2·25

No. 2134 was inscr '1ST LOCAL' and originally sold for 26c.

Nos. 2134/7 commemorate the 30th anniversary of International Enterprise (IE) Singapore (formerly the Trade Development Board).

412 Grey Peacock Pheasant

2013. 40th Anniv of Diplomatic Relations between Singapore and Vietnam. Multicoloured.

2138 (26c.) Type **412** 25 25
2139 $2 Red Junglefowl 4·50 4·50
MS2140 120×75 mm. Nos. 2138/9 4·75 4·75

No. 2138 was inscr '1ST LOCAL' and originally sold for 26c.

Stamps in similar designs were issued by Vietnam.

413 Kachang Puteh Seller

2013. Vanishing Trades. Multicoloured.

(a) Ordinary gum

2141 5c. Type **413** 10 10
2142 20c. Lantern maker
2143 (26c.) Dairy man 25 25
2144 30c. Songkok (Malay headgear) maker 30 30
2145 (32c.) Beaded slippers maker 40 40
2146 45c. Goldsmith 45 45
2147 50c. Cobbler 45 45
2148 55c. Knife sharpener 50 50
2149 65c. Ice-ball seller 85 85
2150 80c. Parrot astrologer 1·25 1·25

(b) Self-adhesive

2159 (26c.) As No. 2143 25 25
2160 50c. As No. 2147 45 45

Nos. 2143 and 2151 were inscr '1st Local' and originally sold for 26c.

No. 2145 was inscr '2nd Local' and originally sold for 32c.

Nos. 2151/8 and 2161/2 are left for possible additions to these definitive stamps.

414 Models wearing French Fashion

2013. Fashion. Multicoloured.

2163 (26c.) Type **414** 25 25
2164 65c. Mannequins 85 85
2165 $1.10 Models wearing Singapore fashion 2·25 2·25
2166 $2 Mannequins wearing Singapore fashions 4·50 4·50
MS2167 120×75 mm. Nos. 2163/6 7·75 7·75

No. 2163 was inscr '1st Local' and originally sold for 26c.

Similar designs were issued by France.

415 Tablet, Mobile Phone, Remote Control and HD Television

2013. 50th Anniv of First Television Broadcast in Singapore. Multicoloured.

2168 (26c.) Type **415** 25 25
2169 50c. Family looking at on screen TV guide 45 45
2170 65c. Cameraman and performers 85 85
2171 80c. Men watching football match 1·25 1·25
2172 $1.10 Family watching black and white TV Singapura, 1963 2·25 2·25

No. 2168 was inscr '1st Local' and originally sold for 26c.

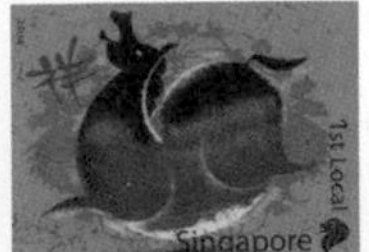

416 Horse

2014. Chinese New Year. Year of the Horse. Multicoloured.

(a) Ordinary gum

2173 (26c.) Type **416** 25 25
2174 65c. Horse (facing right) 85 85
2175 $1.10 Two horses (35×46 mm) 2·25 2·25

(b) Self-adhesive

2176 (26c.) As Type **416** 25 25

Nos. 2173 and 2176 were inscr '1st Local' and originally sold for 26c.

417 *Angiopteris evecta* (elephant fern) (unfurling frond)

2014. Ferns. Multicoloured.

(a) Ordinary gum

2177 (26c.) Type **417** 25 25
2178 50c. *Angiopteris evecta* (frond with spores) 45 45
2179 80c. *Cibotium barometz* (golden chicken fern) (unfurling frond) 1·25 1·25
2180 $1 *Cibotium barometz* (frond with spores) 2·10 2·10

(b) Self-adhesive

2181 $1 As No. 2180 2·10 2·10

No. 2177 was inscr '1ST LOCAL' and originally sold for 26c.

418 'IT'S YOUR SPECIAL OCCASION'

2014. 'Let's Celebrate'. Multicoloured.

(a) Ordinary gum

2182 (26c.) Type **418** 25 25
2183 (26c.) Heart formed from the word 'LOVE' 25 25
2184 (26c.) Wedding rings silhouette and 'MR AND MRS' 25 25
2185 50c. Champagne glasses silhouette and 'LET'S CELEBRATE' 'PARTY' 45 45
2186 $1 'FRIENDS' 2·10 2·10

(b) Self-adhesive

2187 (26c.) As Type **418** 25 25
2188 (26c.) As No. 2183 25 25
2189 (26c.) As No. 2184 25 25
2190 50c. As No. 2185 45 45
2191 $1 As No. 2186 2·10 2·10

Nos. 2182/4 and 2187/9 were inscr '1st Local' and originally sold for 26c.

POSTAGE DUE STAMPS

The postage due stamps of Malayan Postal Union were in use in Singapore from 1948 until replaced by the following issue.

D1

1968

D1 **D1** 1c. green 60 2·00

D2	D1	2c. red	1·60	2·50
D3	D1	4c. orange	2·00	5·50
D4	D1	8c. brown	1·00	2·00
D5	D1	10c. mauve	1·00	90
D6	D1	12c. violet	2·75	3·25
D7	D1	20c. blue	2·00	3·50
D8	D1	50c. green	11·00	5·50

D2

1978

D16a	D2	1c. green	15	4·25
D17a	D2	4c. orange	20	6·00
D18a	D2	10c. blue	50	2·00
D19a	D2	20c. blue	65	2·25
D20a	D2	50c. green	90	2·75

D3

1989

D21	D3	1c. green	25·00	25·00
D22	D3	4c. brown	35·00	35·00
D23	D3	5c. mauve	20	50
D24	D3	10c. red	20	40
D25	D3	20c. blue	30	60
D26	D3	50c. green	60	1·00
D27	D3	$1 brown	3·00	4·00

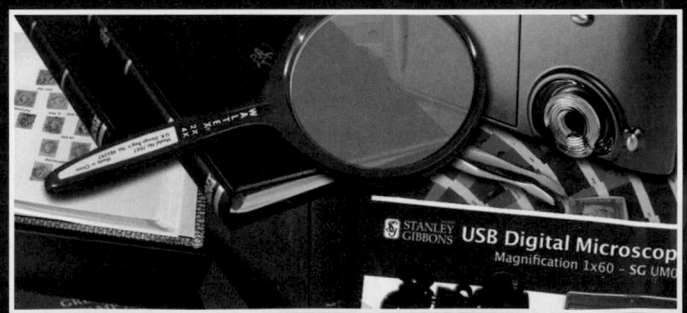

Index